CW00342815

Contents

Sommaire Inhaltsverzeichnis
Sommario Sumario 目次

France 2009

100th Edition

100th Edition

Dear Readers,

2009 marks a historic date: the one hundredth edition of the MICHELIN Guide France. Born in 1900, it celebrates its 100th edition today because the war years interrupted its publication. A significant anniversary for the Michelin Group therefore, for you on your travels, who seek to mix business with pleasure, and for the world of good food and quality hotels.

In 1900 fewer than 3,000 automobiles motored along the roads of France, and a journey was often synonymous with adventure! The Michelin brothers were nonetheless convinced of the future of the automobile, and to further its development, and that of the Manufacture Française des Pneus Michelin which they had founded, they decided to offer motorists a small publication to help them in their travels. Thus in August 1900, nearly 35,000 copies of the first MICHELIN Guide were printed.

In the foreword, André Michelin wrote: "this volume was created at the turn of the century and will last at least as long", a prediction that has proved highly prescient!

The first MICHELIN Guide comprised a great deal of practical information – the opening pages were devoted to recommendations about how to change a tyre and look after ones motor vehicle for example, while the section on Paris only indicated a list of automobile manufacturers and did not feature hotels or restaurants.

A selection of restaurants was added to the Guide in 1921, with a specific classification system, in addition to a list of Parisian hotels for the first time.

In 1926, the good food star was born, joined in 1931 by two- and three-star rankings, first for establishments in provincial France and then in 1933 for Paris. Their definitions (one star "a very good restaurant in its category", two stars "worth a detour" and three stars "worth a special journey") date from 1936 and haven't changed since.

The MICHELIN Guide is a guide for everyone, with restaurants ranging from the thrilling three-star to the value for money Bib Gourmand, and accommodation from luxury hotels to charming guesthouses.

The assistance with mobility philosophy behind the Guide's creation has never wavered over the years and remains at the heart of what has become the worldwide Michelin brand.

The Guide has extended this development outside France, in Europe, the United States Asia: from West to East, the MICHELIN Guide has pursued its quest for the best good food, in search of talents, wherever they may be. The selection criteria have remained unchanged and provide a guarantee of quality, founded on the independence of inspectors, that has forged the Guide's reputation over the years and throughout the world.

This hundredth edition of the MICHELIN Guide France is, of course, no different and we sincerely trust that you will find everything that has contributed to its longstanding popularity. This anniversary also provides us with the opportunity to thank you, our several million loyal readers, who have granted us your confidence for so many decades and to pay tribute to the thousands of hotels and restaurants which have helped make the MICHELIN Guide for 109 years.

Accompanying you in your travels, a simple idea that has definitely come a long way! We wager that the chefs and hoteliers of tomorrow, inspectors of the MICHELIN guides of France, Europe, America and Asia, and you, dear readers, with your precious comments, will continue to bring life to future editions throughout the 21st century.

Michel Rollier

Chief Executive Officer Michelin

100th Edition

Providing "assistance with mobility" to travellers and to motorists, in particular, is the vocation of the Manufacture Française des Pneumatiques Michelin. Indeed, the first edition of the "little red book", free up until 1914, featured a selection of some 1300 establishments right at the start. After the First World War, as early as the spring of 1919 following the armistice, the Guide was again published and available in all Michelin garages and dealers.

The 1920 publication saw the advent of the "paying" era, at which time the guide was sold for 7 French francs, providing the opportunity to delete all advertising from its pages and by so doing, assert its desire for independence.

From good road holding to well-run establishments

At the same time the desire to implement more qualitative selection, founded on criteria that were to become genuine commandments, acquired more weight. The Michelin Guide's new ambition began to emerge.

1926 witnessed the birth of the famous "restaurant star", a small symbol that highlighted the care taken with the cuisine. In 1931, two- and three-star rankings were awarded to establishments in provincial France, before being extended to Parisian establishments three years later. These little flower-shaped stars were to embody the innovative character of the Guide that was no longer intended just for motorists, but also for gourmets! From that moment on, Michelin was clearly on the road to gastronomy.

It was moreover at the same time that the profession of "inspector" took form. The selection of establishments, up until then compiled thanks to the letters and recommendations of discerning readers, was now entrusted to a squadron of professional incorruptible "travellers", entrusted with carrying out anonymous visits and who systematically settled their own bill, thereby guaranteeing the integrity of their evaluations, backed up by objective observations.

Companion of History...

Even though the Second World War once again interrupted the Guide's publication, its popularity was in no way affected. On the contrary, the 1939 edition was considered so useful by the Allied Staff that they decided to reprint it in Washington, because the Guide's hundreds of detailed and updated maps were felt to be an invaluable tool that would help the troops find their bearings in unknown territory and facilitate their progress. It was thus with the Michelin guide in their pocket that the Allied forces disembarked in 1944! Needless to say, the 1939 reprint is one of those most sought after by collectors...

France had hardly been liberated when the 1945 edition was published on 16th May, just one week after the signature of the armistice. Faithful to its guiding precepts, the Guide remained true to its service commitment, but in this era of rationing, star establishments were understandably few and far between and only began to flourish again from 1951 to the immense satisfaction of gourmets.

A witness, sometimes even a participant of History, the Guide has ever sought to remain abreast of the evolution of French society. For example, good food doesn't necessarily have to be costly and the budgets of all gourmets must be satisfied. For which reason the 1954 edition saw the creation of a "well-prepared food at reasonable prices" label, whose success was confirmed with the "Bib Gourmand" and its motto: good food at moderate prices. This value for money criterion was moreover extended to hotels from 2003, with its blue counterpart, the "Bib Hotel".

... and of tomorrow

The years have passed and the realm of the Michelin Guide has never ceased growing, accompanying the expansion of tyres whilst leaving its own hallmark wherever the art of good food flourishes. Beyond the borders of Europe, the Guide crossed the Atlantic to New York, San Francisco, Los Angeles and Las Vegas, before taking a seat at the flavoursome counters of Tokyo and Hong Kong. Now a collection in its own right, the Michelin Guide also features a range of themed works in order to better satisfy its diverse clientele: the Bib Gourmand has its own illustrated guide to France, but also to Spain, Portugal and Benelux. As do the most delightful guesthouses in France and the most charming hotels in Italy.

24 red-bound titles in all, teeming with stars, excellent restaurants and hotels of all sorts, from luxury hotels to delightful guesthouses, so that the journey with Michelin can continue, as ever under the sign of quality, novelty and pleasure.

How to use this guide

TOURIST INFORMATION

Distances from the main towns, tourist offices, local tourist attractions, means of transport, golf courses and leisure activities...

ACCOMMODATION

From 🏨🏨🏨🏨🏨 to 🏠, ⌂:
categories of comfort
In red 🏨🏨🏨🏨🏨... 🏠, ⌂:
the most pleasant

GOOD FOOD AND ACCOMMODATION AT MODERATE PRICES

Bib Gourmand
Bib Hotel

RESTAURANTS

From XXXXX to X:
categories of comfort
In red XXXXX... X:
the most pleasant

STARS

✿✿✿ Worth a special journey
✿✿ Worth a detour
✿ A very good restaurant

ABBAYE DE FONTFROIDE – 03 Aude **344** J4 – see Narbo

ABBAYE DE SAINT-WANDRILLE – 18 Cher – **323** K6 – s

ABBEVILLE – 80 Somme – **301** E7 – pop 24 567 – alt.8 m
Northern France and the Paris Region
Paris 186 – Amiens 51 – Boulogne-sur-Mer 7
Dunkerque, 𝒞 04 90 31 51 12, by N3 et N7 :
Office de tourisme, 1 place de l'Amiral Cou
- office.tourisme.abbeville@wanadoo.fr -
of Abbeville, Route du Val, by rte St-Vale
- 𝒞 03 55 35 96 54 - Fax 03 55 35 96 54
Modern stained-glass windows of St-S
St-Vulfran collégiate church AE**D** - Mu
Vallée de la Somme★ SE - Château d

Les Jardins du Château
rte du Port – 𝒞 04 79 01 36 46 – www.j
hoteljardins.fr – Fax 04 12 23 45 53 – C
1st May and 15 August
15 rm – € 55/75 € 85/170 – 3 s
Rest Les Terrasses – 𝒞 04 79 01
Rest Le Cœur d'Or – Closed Mo
• Built as a private house in 18
contemporary rooms include s
garden and terraces.

La Feme des Lions
45 rue des Lions, D541 : 1 km
– relaisdelaposte@reservat
42 rm – € 45/60 € 55
• Red-brick 18C listed fa
house overlooks meado
bread and preserves. In

Atelier des Sav
10 bd Croisette –
– atelierdessav
Rest – (bookin
Spec. Salad
nuts and pis
des bois an
A count

OTHER MICHELIN PUBLICATIONS

References for the MICHELIN map and Green Guide which cover the area

LOCATING THE TOWN

Locate the town on the map at the end of the guide (map number and coordinates)

LOCATING THE ESTABLISHMENT

Located on the town plan (coordinates and letters giving the location)

DESCRIPTION OF THE ESTABLISHMENT

Atmosphere, style, character and specialities

QUIET HOTELS

quiet hotel
very quiet hotel

FACILITIES AND SERVICES

PRICES

ne
st-Amand-Montrond
36 **A1**
✉ 80100
- Rouen 106
m
et, ✆ 03 22 24 27 92
x 03 25 24 27 96
sur-Somme : 4 km
80132
ulcre church★★ AM**B** - Façade★ of
Boucher de Perthes★ BY**M**
agatelle★ S

50 P AE VISA

insduchateau.com – welcome@ Z **d**
sed 15 December-30 April,
s – € 7,50
46 (dinner only) Menu € 34 – Carte € 25/35
y – Menu € 35/65 bi – Carte € 17/25
now with modern and stylish public areas. The
e of the art facilities. Sleek restaurant overlooks

P AE VISA

AU **c**
✆ 04 79 01 32 25 – www.fermedeslions.com
s.fr – Fax 04 79 01 32 26 – Closed 25 December
) **Rest** – Menu € 19 – Carte € 22/45
house on a working farm... with beautiful blue windows;
Sunny garden room for breakfast, including home-made
aculate rooms.

16 AE VISA

Y **a**
(François Thomas)
79 02 33 18 – *www.atelierdessaveurs.com*
rancoisthomas.fr – Fax 04 79 01 33 17 –Closed July
ntial) Menu € 55/76 (weekdays lunch) – € Carte 48/85
ked eel, pig's trotter and apple purée. Braised turbot with pea-
s and asparagus. Cannelloni of apricot, Strawberry sorbet, fraises

with a wood panelled dining room, with smart first floor bar and
ssful views over the sea.

AE VISA

Y **c**
79 02 33 18 – Fax 04 79 01 33 17 –Closed July
turday) Menu € 35/47 bi – Carte € 22/35
r for this old Abbeville house. Classic
ved at reasonable prices.

Classification & awards

CATEGORIES OF COMFORT

The MICHELIN guide selection lists the best hotels and restaurants in each category of comfort and price. The establishments we choose are classified according to their levels of comfort and, within each category, are listed in order of preference.

🏨🏨🏨🏨🏨	XXXXX	**Luxury in the traditional style**
🏨🏨🏨🏨	XXXX	**Top class comfort**
🏨🏨🏨	XXX	**Very comfortable**
🏨🏨	XX	**Comfortable**
🏨	X	**Quite comfortable**
⌂		**Guesthouse**
without rest		**This hotel has no restaurant**
without rm		**This restaurant also offers accommodation**

THE AWARDS

To help you make the best choice, some exceptional establishments have been given an award in this year's guide.
For those awarded a star or a Bib Gourmand, the mention "**Rest**" appears in red in the description of the establishment.
For those awarded a Bib Hotel, the mention "**rm**" appears in blue in the description of the establishment.

THE STARS: THE BEST CUISINE

MICHELIN stars are awarded to establishments serving cuisine, of whatever style, which is of the highest quality. The cuisine is judged on the quality of ingredients, the flair and skill in their preparation, the combination of flavours, the value for money and the consistency of culinary standards.

✿✿✿ 26	**Exceptional cuisine, worth a special journey** One always eats extremely well here, sometimes superbly.
✿✿ 73	**Excellent cooking, worth a detour**
✿ 449	**A very good restaurant in its category**

THE BIB : GOOD FOOD AND ACCOMMODATION AT MODERATE PRICES

527 **Bib Gourmand**
Establishment offering good quality cuisine at a maximum price of €29 or €35 in the Paris region (price of a meal not including drinks). Outside the Paris region, these establishments generally specialise in regional cooking.

293 **Bib Hotel**
Establishment offering good levels of comfort and service, with most rooms priced at a maximum price of €75 or under €90 in the main cities and popular tourist resorts (price of a room for 2 people not including breakfast).

PLEASANT HOTELS AND RESTAURANTS

Symbols shown in red indicate particularly pleasant or restful establishments: the character of the building, its décor, the setting, the welcome and services offered may all contribute to this special appeal.

to **Pleasant hotels**
Pleasant guesthouses
to **Pleasant restaurants**

OTHER SPECIAL FEATURES

As well as the categories and awards given to the establishment, MICHELIN inspectors also make special note of other criteria which can be important when choosing an establishment.

LOCATION

If you are looking for a particularly restful establishment, or one with a special view, look out for the following symbols:

Quiet hotel
Very quiet hotel
Interesting view
Exceptional view

WINE LIST

If you are looking for an establishment with a particularly interesting wine list, look out for the following symbol:

Particularly interesting wine list
This symbol might cover the list presented by a sommelier in a luxury restaurant or that of a simple inn where the owner has a passion for wine. The two lists will offer something exceptional but very different, so beware of comparing them by each other's standards.

Facilities & services

30 rm	Number of rooms
	Garden – Park
	Meals served in garden or on terrace
	Swimming pool: outdoor or indoor
Spa	An extensive facility for relaxation and well-being
	Exercise room – Tennis court
	Lift – Establishment at least partly accessible to those of restricted mobility
A/C	Air conditioning
	Rooms for non-smokers available
	Wireless/broadband connection in bedrooms
	Private dining rooms
	Equipped conference room
	Restaurant offering valet parking (tipping customary)
P P	Car park / Enclosed car park for customers only
	Garage (additional charge in most cases)
	No dogs allowed
M	Nearest metro station
Open / Closed May-October	Dates when open or closed as indicated by the hotelier.

TABLES D'HÔTES

Tables d'hôtes serve meals – generally dinner – to residents and by reservation only.
Meals are not always available every day of the week, so don't forget to check opening times and to reserve a table if you wish to dine during your stay.

Prices quoted in this guide are for autumn 2008. They are subject to alteration if goods and service costs are revised.
By supplying the information, hotels and restaurants have undertaken to maintain these rates for our readers.
In some towns, when commercial, cultural or sporting events are taking place the hotel rates are likely to be considerably higher.
Out of season, certain establishments offer special rates. Ask when booking.

RESERVATION AND DEPOSITS

Some establishments will ask you to confirm your reservation by giving your credit card number or require a deposit which confirms the commitment of both the customer and the establishment. Ask the hotelier to provide you with all the terms and conditions applicable to your reservation in their written confirmation.

CREDIT CARDS

VISA MC AE DC	Credit cards accepted by the establishment: Visa – MasterCard – American Express – Diners Club

ROOMS

rm – † €50/80	Lowest price / highest price for a single room
rm – †† €60/100	Lowest price / highest price for a double or a twin room
☕ €9	Price of breakfast
rm ☕	Breakfast included

HALF BOARD

½ P €50/70	Lowest and highest prices for half board (room, breakfast and a meal) per person. These prices are valid for a double room occupied by two people for a minimum stay of three nights. If a single person occupies a double room a supplement may apply. Most of the hotels also offer full board terms on request.

RESTAURANT

(€13)	2 course meal, on weekday lunchtimes
(coins symbol)	Menu for less than €19
Menu €15 (lunch)	Set menu served only at lunchtime
Menu €17 (weekdays)	Set menu served only on weekdays
Menu €16/38	Cheapest set meal / Highest set menu
Carte €24/48	**A la carte meal**, drinks not included. The first figure is for a plain meal and includes first course, main dish of the day and dessert. The second price is for a fuller meal (with speciality) including starter, main course, cheese and dessert.
bi	House wine included

Towns

GENERAL INFORMATION

63300	Local postal number *the first two numbers are the same as the département number*
✉ **57130 Ars**	Postal number and the name of the postal area
P SP	Prefecture – Sub-prefecture
337 E5	Number of the appropriate sheet and grid square reference of the Michelin road map in the "DEPARTEMENTS France" MICHELIN series
Jura	See the regional MICHELIN Green Guide
pop. 1057	Population (source: www.insee.fr)
alt. 75	Altitude (in metres)
1200/1900	Altitude of resort and highest point reached by lifts
2	Number of cable-cars
14	Number of ski and chair-lifts
	Cross-country skiing
BY **b**	Letters giving the location of a place on a town plan
9	Golf course and number of holes
	Panoramic view, viewpoint
	Airport – Places with motorail pick-up point. *Further information from phone number listed*
	Shipping line – Passenger transport only
	Tourist information

TOURIST INFORMATION

STAR-RATING

★★★	Highly recommended
★★	Recommended
★	Interesting *Museums and art galleries are generally closed on Tuesday*

LOCATION

	Sights in town
	On the outskirts
N, S, E, W	The sight lies north, south, east or west of the town
② ④	Signs ② or ④ on the town plan show the road leading to a place of interest and correspond to the same signs on MICHELIN road maps.
6 km	Distance in kilometres

Town plans

Hotels
Restaurants

SIGHTS

Place of interest
Interesting place of worship:
- Catholic – Protestant

ROAD

Motorway, dual carriageway
Numbered junctions : complete, limited
Major thoroughfare
One-way street – Unsuitable for traffic or street subject to restrictions
Pedestrian street – Tramway
Car park – Park and Ride
Gateway – Street passing under arch – Tunnel
Station and railway – Motorail
Funicular – Cable-car
Lever bridge – Car ferry

VARIOUS SIGNS

Tourist Information Centre
Mosque – Synagogue
Tower – Ruins – Windmill – Water tower
Garden, park, wood – Cemetery – Cross
Stadium – Golf course – Racecourse – Skating rink
Outdoor or indoor swimming pool
View – Panorama – Viewing table
Monument – Fountain – Factory
Shopping centre – Multiplex Cinema
Pleasure boat harbour – Lighthouse – Communications tower
S.N.C.F. Airport – Underground station – Coach station
Ferry services : passengers and cars, passengers only
(3) Reference number common to town plans
Main post office with poste restante and telephone
Hospital – Covered market – Barracks
Public buildings located by letter :
A C - Chamber of Agriculture – Chamber of Commerce
G H J - Gendarmerie – Town Hall – Law Courts
M P T - Museum – Prefecture or sub-prefecture – Theatre
U - University, College
POL. - Police (in large towns police headquarters)
4.4 18T (18) Low headroom (15 ft. max.) – Load limit (under 19 t)

Please note: the *route nationale* and *route départementale* road numbers are currently being changed in France.

Chers lecteurs,

Le millésime 2009 marque une date historique : la centième édition du guide MICHELIN France. Né en 1900, celui-ci ne fête sa centième édition qu'aujourd'hui, car sa parution fut interrompue pendant les années de guerre. Un anniversaire émouvant, donc, pour le groupe Michelin ; pour vous aussi, qui voyagez et cherchez à joindre l'utile à l'agréable, et enfin pour le monde de la gastronomie et de l'hôtellerie.

En 1900, moins de 3000 automobiles seulement roulent en France. Le voyage tourne alors, bien souvent, à l'aventure ! Malgré tout, les frères Michelin croient dur comme fer à l'avenir de l'automobile. Pour aider à son développement, et par là-même, à celui de la Manufacture Française des Pneumatiques Michelin qu'ils ont créée, ils décident de mettre à la disposition des automobilistes un document facilitant leurs déplacements, un petit carnet pratique pour améliorer la mobilité : le fameux guide MICHELIN, dont la première édition, parue en août 1900, sera tirée à près de 35 000 exemplaires…

Dans la préface, André Michelin écrit : « cet ouvrage paraîtra avec le siècle. Il durera autant que lui ». Une prédiction qui ne s'est pas démentie. Mieux, la réalité l'a dépassée !

Le premier guide MICHELIN comporte beaucoup de renseignements pratiques : dans ses premières pages il indique comment changer son pneumatique, comment entretenir son véhicule, etc. Ainsi, à Paris, seule était mentionnée la liste des constructeurs d'automobiles ; il n'y avait pas encore de sélection d'hôtels et de restaurants. C'est en 1921 que les restaurants font leur entrée dans le guide, avec leur classification propre et, pour la première fois, figure une liste d'hôtels parisiens.

En 1926 naît « l'étoile de bonne table » et, en 1931, c'est au tour des deux et trois étoiles de voir le jour , tout d'abord en province, puis à Paris en 1933. Quant aux définitions (une étoile : « une très bonne table dans sa catégorie » ; deux étoiles : « mérite le détour » et trois étoiles : « mérite le voyage »), elles datent de 1936… et elles sont toujours d'actualité.

Car le guide MICHELIN est un guide pour tous, du restaurant « trois étoiles » au « Bib Gourmand » proposant un très bon rapport qualité-prix, du palace à l'hôtel de charme, et pour toutes les occasions.

La philosophie qui a présidé à la création du guide – l'aide à la mobilité – a persisté à travers les époques et elle est le socle de la Marque Michelin devenue mondiale. Le guide a suivi ce développement hors de l'Hexagone, en Europe, aux États-unis et en Asie : de l'Ouest à l'Est, il poursuit et élargit encore sa quête du meilleur en matière de gastronomie, à la recherche des talents, quels qu'ils soient. Les critères de sélection restent les mêmes, garantie de qualité fondée sur l'indépendance des inspecteurs et qui a forgé la réputation du guide au fil des années, partout dans le monde.

Cette centième édition du guide MICHELIN France ne déroge évidemment pas à la règle et nous espérons bien que vous y retrouverez tout ce qui en a fait sa richesse, d'année en année. Cet anniversaire est aussi l'occasion de vous remercier, chers fidèles lecteurs – vous êtes plusieurs millions ! – qui nous accordez votre confiance depuis des décennies, et de rendre hommage à ces milliers d'hôteliers et de restaurateurs qui, avec nous, font le guide MICHELIN depuis 109 ans.

Vous accompagner dans vos déplacements… L'idée, simple, a fait son bonhomme de chemin autour du monde ! Gageons que les chefs de demain, les futurs hôteliers, les inspecteurs du guide MICHELIN de France, d'Europe, d'Amérique et d'Asie, et vous, chers lecteurs, par vos courriers toujours riches de précieux commentaires, sauront faire vivre les prochaines éditions de ce 21e siècle.

Michel Rollier
Gérant du Groupe Michelin

Mode d'emploi

INFORMATIONS TOURISTIQUES

Distances depuis les villes principales, offices de tourisme, sites touristiques locaux, moyens de transports, golfs et loisirs...

L'HÉBERGEMENT

De ⌂⌂⌂⌂⌂ à ⌂, ⌂ : catégories de confort
En rouge ⌂⌂⌂⌂⌂ ... ⌂, ⌂ : les plus agréables

LES MEILLEURES ADRESSES À PETITS PRIX

- Bib Gourmand
- Bib Hôtel

LES RESTAURANTS

De XXXXX à X : catégories de confort. En rouge XXXXX ... X : les plus agréables

LES TABLES ÉTOILÉES

- ✿✿✿ Vaut le voyage
- ✿✿ Mérite un détour
- ✿ Très bonne cuisine

ABBAYE DE FONTFROIDE – 03 Aude – 344 J4 – se
ABBAYE DE SAINT-WANDRILLE – 18 Cher – 323
ABBEVILLE – 80 Somme – 301 E7 – pop 24 567 –
Northern France and the Paris Region
Paris 186 – Amiens 51 – Boulogne-sur-
Dunkerque, ✆ 04 90 31 51 12, by N3 et
Office de tourisme, 1 place de l'Amira
- office.tourisme.abbeville@wanadoo
of Abbeville, Route du Val, by rte St-
- ✆ 03 55 35 96 54 - Fax 03 55 35 96
Modern stained-glass windows of
St-Vulfran collégiate church AED -
Vallée de la Somme★ SE - Châtea

Les Jardins du Château
rte du Port – ✆ 04 79 01 36 46 – ww
hoteljardins.fr – Fax 04 12 23 45 53
1st May and 15 August
15 rm – € 55/75 € 85/170 – 3
Rest Les Terrasses – ✆ 04 79 01
Rest Le Cœur d'Or – Closed Mo
◆ Built as a private house in 18
contemporary rooms include
garden and terraces.

La Feme des Lions
45 rue des Lions, D541 : 1 km
– relaisdelaposte@reservati
42 rm – € 45/60 € 55/
◆ Red-brick 18C listed farm
house overlooks meadow
bread and preserves. Imn

Atelier des Saveurs
10 bd Croisette – ✆ 04
– atelierdessaveurs@fr
Rest – (booking esse
Spec. Salad of smok
nuts and pistachios
des bois and mint.
◆ A country inn wi
terrace with blissf

AUTRES PUBLICATIONS MICHELIN

Références de la carte MICHELIN
et du Guide Vert
où vous retrouverez la localité

LOCALISER LA VILLE

Repérage de la localité
sur la carte régionale en fin de guide
(n° de la carte et coordonnées)

LOCALISER L'ÉTABLISSEMENT

Localisation sur le plan de ville
(coordonnées et indice)

DESCRIPTION DE L'ÉTABLISSEMENT

Atmosphère, style,
caractère et spécialités

LES HÔTELS TRANQUILLES

hôtel tranquille
hôtel très tranquille

ÉQUIPEMENTS ET SERVICES

PRIX

Amand-Montrond
36 **A1**
80100
uen 106
03 22 24 27 92
25 24 27 96
omme : 4 km
32
church★★ AM**B** - Façade★ of
cher de Perthes★ BY**M**
lle★ S
50 P AE VISA
chateau.com – welcome@
December-30 April,
Z **d**
€ 7,50
er only) Menu € 34 – Carte € 25/35
u € 35/65 bi – Carte € 17/25
th modern and stylish public areas. The
art facilities. Sleek restaurant overlooks
P AE VISA
AU **c**
01 32 25 – www.fermedeslions.com
04 79 01 32 26 – Closed 25 December
Menu € 19 – Carte € 22/45
a working farm... with beautiful blue windows;
rden room for breakfast, including home-made
oms.
16 AE VISA
Y **a**
Thomas)
– www.atelierdessaveurs.com
mas.fr – Fax 04 79 01 33 17 – Closed July
u € 55/76 (weekdays lunch) – € Carte 48/85
's trotter and apple purée. Braised turbot with pea-
agus. Cannelloni of apricot, Strawberry sorbet, fraises
panelled dining room, with smart first floor bar and
ver the sea.
AE VISA
Y **c**
04 79 02 33 18 – Fax 04 79 01 33 17 – Closed July
turday) Menu € 35/47 bi – Carte € 22/35
for this old Abbeville house. Classic
at reasonable prices.

Classement & distinctions

LES CATÉGORIES DE CONFORT

Le guide MICHELIN retient dans sa sélection les meilleures adresses dans chaque catégorie de confort et de prix. Les établissements sélectionnés sont classés selon leur confort et cités par ordre de préférence dans chaque catégorie.

🏨🏨🏨🏨🏨	XXXXX	**Grand luxe et tradition**
🏨🏨🏨🏨	XXXX	**Grand confort**
🏨🏨🏨	XXX	**Très confortable**
🏨🏨	XX	**De bon confort**
🏨	X	**Assez confortable**
⌂		**Maison d'hôtes**
without rest		**L'hôtel n'a pas de restaurant**
with rm		**Le restaurant possède des chambres**

LES DISTINCTIONS

Pour vous aider à faire le meilleur choix, certaines adresses particulièrement remarquables ont reçu cette année une distinction.

Pour les adresses distinguées par une étoile ou un Bib Gourmand, la mention « **Rest** » apparaît en rouge dans le descriptif de l'établissement.

Pour les adresses distinguées par un Bib Hôtel, la mention « **rm** » apparaît en bleu dans le descriptif de l'établissement.

LES ÉTOILES : LES MEILLEURES TABLES

Les étoiles distinguent les établissements, tous styles de cuisine confondus, qui proposent la meilleure qualité de cuisine. Les critères retenus sont : le choix des produits, la personnalité de la cuisine, la maîtrise des cuissons et des saveurs, le rapport qualité-prix ainsi que la régularité.

✿✿✿ 26	**Cuisine remarquable, cette table vaut le voyage** On y mange toujours très bien, parfois merveilleusement.
✿✿ 73	**Cuisine excellente, cette table mérite un détour**
✿ 449	**Une très bonne cuisine dans sa catégorie**

LES BIBS : LES MEILLEURES ADRESSES À PETIT PRIX

☺ 527	**Bib Gourmand** Établissement proposant une cuisine de qualité au prix maximum de 29 € en province et 35 € à Paris (prix d'un repas hors boisson). En province, il s'agit le plus souvent d'une cuisine de type régional.

293 **Bib Hôtel**
Établissement offrant une prestation de qualité avec une majorité de chambres au prix maximum de 75 € en province et 90 € dans les grandes villes et stations touristiques importantes (prix pour 2 personnes, hors petit-déjeuner).

LES ADRESSES LES PLUS AGRÉABLES

Le rouge signale les établissements particulièrement agréables. Cela peut tenir au caractère de l'édifice, à l'originalité du décor, au site, à l'accueil ou aux services proposés.

- à — **Hôtels agréables**
- **Maisons d'hôtes agréables**
- à — **Restaurants agréables**

LES MENTIONS PARTICULIÈRES

En dehors des distinctions décernées aux établissements, les inspecteurs MICHELIN apprécient d'autres critères souvent importants dans le choix d'un établissement.

SITUATION

Vous cherchez un établissement tranquille ou offrant une vue attractive ?
Suivez les symboles suivants :

- **Hôtel tranquille**
- **Hôtel très tranquille**
- **Vue intéressante**
- **Vue exceptionnelle**

CARTE DES VINS

Vous cherchez un restaurant dont la carte des vins offre un choix particulièrement intéressant ?
Suivez le symbole suivant :

Carte des vins particulièrement attractive
Toutefois, ne comparez pas la carte présentée par le sommelier d'un grand restaurant avec celle d'une auberge dont le patron se passionne pour les vins de sa région.

Équipements & services

30 rm	Nombre de chambres
	Jardin de repos – Parc
	Repas servi au jardin ou en terrasse
	Piscine de plein air / couverte
Spa	Bel espace de bien-être et de relaxation
	Salle de remise en forme – Court de tennis
	Ascenseur – Aménagements pour personnes à mobilité réduite
A/C	Air conditionné
	Chambres non-fumeurs disponibles
	Connexion Internet Wifi/ADSL dans les chambres
	Salons pour repas privés
	Salles de conférences
	Restaurant proposant un service voiturier (pourboire d'usage)
P P	Parking / parking clos réservé à la clientèle
	Garage (généralement payant)
	Accès interdit aux chiens
M	Station de métro la plus proche
Open / Closed May-October	Période d'ouverture ou de fermeture communiquée par l'hôtelier

TABLES D'HÔTES

Les tables d'hôtes sont réservées exclusivement aux résidents.
Elles ne sont généralement proposées que le soir, le plus souvent sur réservation et pas forcément tous les jours.
Aussi, pensez à vérifier les jours de fermeture et à réserver votre dîner si vous souhaitez profiter de la table lors de votre séjour.

Prix

Les prix indiqués dans ce guide ont été établis à l'automne 2008. Ils sont susceptibles de modifications, notamment en cas de variation des prix des biens et des services. Ils s'entendent taxes et service compris. Aucune majoration ne doit figurer sur votre note sauf éventuellement la taxe de séjour. Les hôteliers et restaurateurs se sont engagés, sous leur propre responsabilité, à appliquer ces prix aux clients. À l'occasion de certaines manifestations : congrès, foires, salons, festivals, événements sportifs..., les prix demandés par les hôteliers peuvent être sensiblement majorés. Par ailleurs, renseignez-vous pour connaître les éventuelles conditions avantageuses accordées par les hôteliers.

RÉSERVATION ET ARRHES

Pour la confirmation de la réservation certains établissements demandent le numéro de carte de paiement ou un versement d'arrhes. Il s'agit d'un dépôt-garantie qui engage l'établissement comme le client. Bien demander à l'hôtelier de vous fournir dans sa lettre d'accord toutes précisions utiles sur la réservation et les conditions de séjour.

CARTES DE PAIEMENT

	Cartes de paiement acceptées :
VISA MC AE DC	Visa – MasterCard – American Express – Diners Club

CHAMBRES

rm – 1 pers. €50/80	Prix des chambres minimum / maximum pour 1 personne
rm – 2 pers. €60/100	Prix des chambres minimum / maximum pour 2 personnes
€9	Prix du petit-déjeuner
rm	Petit-déjeuner compris

DEMI-PENSION

½ P €50/70	Prix de la demi-pension mini / maxi (chambre, petit-déjeuner et un repas) par personne. Ces prix s'entendent pour une chambre double occupée par deux personnes pour un séjour de trois jours minimum. Une personne seule occupant une chambre double se voit souvent appliquer une majoration. La plupart des hôtels de séjour pratiquent également la pension complète.

RESTAURANT

(€13)	Formule entrée-plat ou plat-dessert au déjeuner en semaine
	Menu à moins de €19
Menu €15 (lunch)	Menu uniquement servi au déjeuner
Menu €17 (weekdays)	Menu uniquement servi en semaine
Menu €16/38	Menu le moins cher / le plus cher
Carte €24/48	**Repas à la carte hors boisson** Le premier prix correspond à un repas simple comprenant une entrée, un plat et un dessert. Le deuxième prix concerne un repas plus complet (avec spécialité) comprenant deux plats, fromage et dessert.
bi	Boisson comprise

Villes

GÉNÉRALITÉS

63300	Numéro de code postal de la localité *les deux premiers chiffres correspondent au numéro de département*
✉ **57130 Ars**	Numéro de code postal et nom de la commune de destination
P SP	Préfecture – Sous-préfecture
337 E5	Numéro de la carte « DEPARTEMENTS France » MICHELIN et coordonnées permettant de se repérer sur la carte
Jura	Voir le Guide Vert MICHELIN de la région
pop. 1057	Nombre d'habitants (source : www.insee.fr)
alt. 75	Altitude de la localité
Spa	Station thermale
1200/1900	Altitude de la station et altitude maximum atteinte par les remontées mécaniques
2	Nombre de téléphériques ou télécabines
14	Nombre de remonte-pentes et télésièges
	Ski de fond
BY **b**	Lettres repérant un emplacement sur le plan de ville
9	Golf et nombre de trous
	Panorama, point de vue
	Aéroport – Localité desservie par train-auto *Renseignements au numéro de téléphone indiqué*
	Transports maritimes
	Transports maritimes pour passagers seulement
i	Information touristique

INFORMATIONS TOURISTIQUES

INTÉRÊT TOURISTIQUE

★★★	Vaut le voyage
★★	Mérite un détour
★	Intéressant

Les musées sont généralement fermés le mardi

SITUATION DU SITE

	A voir dans la ville
	A voir aux environs de la ville
N, S, E, W	La curiosité est située : au Nord, au Sud, à l'Est, à l'Ouest
② ④	On s'y rend par la sortie ② ou ④ repérée par le même signe sur le plan du guide
6 km	Distance en kilomètres

Plans

Hôtels
Restaurants

CURIOSITÉS

Bâtiment intéressant
Édifice religieux intéressant :
- Catholique – Protestant

VOIRIE

Autoroute, double chaussée de type autoroutier
Échangeurs numérotés : complet, partiels
Grande voie de circulation
Sens unique – Rue réglementée ou impraticable
Rue piétonne – Tramway
Parking – Parking Relais
Porte – Passage sous voûte – Tunnel
Gare et voie ferrée – Auto-Train
Funiculaire – Téléphérique, télécabine
Pont mobile – Bac pour autos

SIGNES DIVERS

Information touristique
Mosquée – Synagogue
Tour – Ruines – Moulin à vent – Château d'eau
Jardin, parc, bois – Cimetière – Calvaire
Stade – Golf – Hippodrome – Patinoire
Piscine de plein air, couverte
Vue – Panorama – Table d'orientation
Monument – Fontaine – Usine
Centre commercial – Cinéma Multiplex
Port de plaisance – Phare – Tour de télécommunications
Aéroport – Station de métro – Gare routière
Transport par bateau : passagers et voitures, passagers seulement
Pastille de sortie de ville
Bureau principal de poste restante et Téléphone
Hôpital – Marché couvert – Caserne
Bâtiment public repéré par une lettre :
A C - Chambre d'agriculture – Chambre de commerce
G H J - Gendarmerie – Hôtel de ville – Palais de justice
M P T - Musée – Préfecture, sous-préfecture – Théâtre
U - Université, grande école
POL. - Police (commissariat central)
Passage bas (inf. à 4 m 50) – Charge limitée (inf. à 19 t)

Attention : en France, nouvelle numérotation en cours des routes nationales et départementales.

Cari lettori,

L'edizione 2009 segna una data storica: la centesima edizione della Guida Michelin Francia. Nata nel 1900, la guida festeggia la sua centesima edizione solamente oggi perché la pubblicazione fu sospesa durante le due guerre mondiali. Si tratta quindi di una celebrazione importante per il gruppo Michelin, ma anche per i nostri lettori che viaggiano cercando di unire l'utile al dilettevole e naturalmente per l'universo della gastronomia e dell'ospitalità.

Nel 1900, in Francia, circolano meno di 3000 automobili e un viaggio si trasforma spesso in una grande avventura. Nonostante tutto, però, i fratelli Michelin sono convinti che l'automobile sia il mezzo di trasporto del futuro. Per contribuire al suo sviluppo, e a quello della società per la produzione di pneumatici che hanno appena fondato, decidono di proporre agli automobilisti una piccola guida per facilitare i loro viaggi, rendendo più immediata la mobilità: nasce così la famosa guida MICHELIN. La prima edizione dell'agosto 1900 vanta quasi 35 000 esemplari e nella prefazione André Michelin scrive: "Questa guida è data alle stampe coll'apparire di un nuovo secolo. Vivrà cent'anni come lui". Una previsione che non solo si è avverata, ma che è stata persino superata dalla realtà.

Nella prima guida MICHELIN vengono forniti molti consigli pratici: nelle prime pagine si spiega ai lettori come cambiare una gomma, come prendersi cura dell'automobile, ecc. Per la città di Parigi, per esempio, si indica solo una lista di costruttori automobilistici, ma non si fa alcuna menzione di alberghi o ristoranti.

Solo nel 1921 viene presentata una sezione dedicata unicamente ai ristoranti e nella stessa edizione figura per la prima volta una lista di alberghi parigini.

Nel 1926 viene assegnata la prima stella Michelin e nel 1931 i migliori esercizi delle regioni francesi sono ricompensati anche con due e tre stelle, che arrivano a Parigi solo nel 1933. Le definizioni che accompagnano le tavole stellate (una stella: "Ottima cucina nella sua categoria", due stelle: "Merita una deviazione", tre stelle: "Vale il viaggio") risalgono invece al 1936 e sono ancor'oggi le stesse.

La guida MICHELIN accontenta tutti, da chi ricerca un ristorante con tre stelle a chi preferisce un Bib Gourmand, offrendo al contempo un ottimo rapporto qualità-prezzo per tutte le occasioni, che si tratti di un hotel di lusso o di un alberghetto di charme.

La filosofia su cui, fin dall'inizio, si è basata la guida Michelin, destinata a facilitare la mobilità dei lettori, è rimasta inalterata in tutti questi anni, diventando al contempo il valore portante del marchio Michelin, affermatosi nel mondo intero.
Anche la guida « rossa » ha saputo imporsi oltre le frontiere francesi, prima negli altri paesi d'Europa e in seguito negli Stati Uniti e in Asia: oggi la guida porta ancora più lontano la ricerca del meglio in campo gastronomico, allargando i suoi orizzonti a tre continenti, dove si è lanciata anche alla scoperta di nuovi talenti di ogni tipo. I criteri di selezione sono rimasti inalterati: un'immutata garanzia di qualità, basata sull'indipendenza degli ispettori, su cui si è costruita la reputazione della guida anno dopo anno, in tutto il mondo.

In questa centesima edizione della guida Francia, che non fa eccezione alla regola, speriamo che i lettori ritrovino tutte le caratteristiche che costituiscono la ricchezza della guida Michelin da un secolo a questa parte.
Questo anniversario è anche un'ottima occasione per ringraziare i nostri fedeli lettori, ormai svariati milioni, che ci hanno accordato la loro fiducia da decenni, ma anche per rendere omaggio a quelle migliaia di albergatori e di chef che, insieme a noi, hanno costruito l'identità della guida MICHELIN da 109 anni.
Accompagnare i lettori nei loro spostamenti: un'idea piuttosto semplice che ha avuto un successo considerevole in tutti i paesi del mondo. Siamo sicuri che i futuri chef, gli albergatori di domani e gli ispettori della guida MICHELIN in Francia, Europa, America e Asia, insieme ai nostri lettori che ci inviano preziosi suggerimenti, sapranno rendere ancora più vive le prossime edizioni di questo ventunesimo secolo.

Michel Rollier

Gerente del Gruppo Michelin

Come leggere la guida

INFORMAZIONI TURISTICHE

Distanza dalle città di riferimento, uffici turismo, siti turistici locali, mezzi di trasporto, golfs e tempo libero...

L'ALLOGGIO

Da 🏠🏠🏠🏠🏠 a 🏠, ⌂:
categorie di confort
In rosso 🏠🏠🏠🏠🏠... 🏠, ⌂:
I più ameni

I MIGLIORI ESERCIZI A PREZZI CONTENUTI

Bib Gourmand
Bib Hotel

I RISTORANTI

Da XXXXX a X:
categorie di confort
In rosso XXXXX... X:
i più ameni

LE TAVOLE STELLATE

✿✿✿ Vale il viaggio
✿✿ Merita una deviazione
✿ Ottima cucina

ABBAYE DE FONTFROIDE – 03 Aude – 344 J4 – see Narb
ABBAYE DE SAINT-WANDRILLE – 18 Cher – 323 K6 –
ABBEVILLE – 80 Somme – 301 E7 – pop 24 567 – alt.8 m
Northern France and the Paris Region
Paris 186 – Amiens 51 – Boulogne-sur-Mer
Dunkerque, ☎ 04 90 31 51 12, by N3 et N7
Office de tourisme, 1 place de l'Amiral Co
- office.tourisme.abbeville@wanadoo.fr -
of Abbeville, Route du Val, by rte St-Vale
- ☎ 03 55 35 96 54 - Fax 03 55 35 96 54
Modern stained-glass windows of St-S
St-Vulfran collégiate church AED - Mu
Vallée de la Somme★ SE - Château d

Les Jardins du Château
rte du Port – ☎ 04 79 01 36 46 – www.
hoteljardins.fr – Fax 04 12 23 45 53 –
1st May and 15 August
15 rm – † € 55/75 †† € 85/170 – 3 s
Rest Les Terrasses – ☎ 04 79 01
Rest Le Cœur d'Or – Closed Mo
• Built as a private house in 18
contemporary rooms include
garden and terraces.

La Feme des Lions
45 rue des Lions, D541 : 1 km
– relaisdelaposte@reservat
42 rm – † € 45/60 € 55
• Red-brick 18C listed fa
house overlooks meado
bread and preserves. In

Atelier des Save
10 bd Croisette – ☎
– atelierdessaveurs
Rest – (booking e
Spec. Salad of sn
nuts and pistach
des bois and mi
• A country in
ace with

ALTRE PUBBLICAZIONI MICHELIN

Riferimento alla carta MICHELIN ed alla Guida Verde in cui figura la località

LOCALIZZARE LA CITTÀ

Posizione della località sulla carta regionale alla fine della guida (n° della carta e coordinate)

LOCALIZZARE L'ESERCIZIO

Localizzazione sulla pianta di città (coordinate ed indice)

DESCRIZIONE DELL'ESERCIZIO

Atmosfera, stile, carattere e specialità

GLI ALBERGHI TRANQUILLI

Albergo tranquillo

Albergo molto tranquillo

PREZZI

INSTALLAZIONI E SERVIZI

-Montrond
36 **A1**

)6
2 24 27 92
27 96
e : 4 km
ch★★ AM**B** - Façade★ of
de Perthes★ BY**M**
S
50
Z **d**
eau.com – welcome@
ember-30 April,
50
only) Menu € 34 – Carte € 25/35
€ 35/65 bi – Carte € 17/25
modern and stylish public areas. The
rt facilities. Sleek restaurant overlooks
AU **c**
32 25 – www.fermedeslions.com
04 79 01 32 26 – Closed 25 December
Menu € 19 – Carte € 22/45
a working farm... with beautiful blue windows;
den room for breakfast, including home-made
oms.
16
Y **a**
s Thomas)
3 – www.atelierdessaveurs.com
omas.fr – Fax 04 79 01 33 17 – Closed July
nu € 55/76 (weekdays lunch) – € Carte 48/85
g's trotter and apple purée. Braised turbot with pea-
ragus. Cannelloni of apricot, Strawberry sorbet, fraises
od panelled dining room, with smart first floor bar and
s over the sea.
Y **c**
€ 04 79 02 33 18 – Fax 04 79 01 33 17 – Closed July
day-Saturday) Menu € 35/47 bi – Carte € 22/35
interior for this old Abbeville house. Classic
es, served at reasonable prices.

Categorie & simboli distintivi

LE CATEGORIE DI CONFORT

Nella selezione della guida MICHELIN vengono segnalati i migliori indirizzi per ogni categoria di confort e di prezzo.Gli esercizi selezionati sono classificati in base al confort che offrono e vengono citati in ordine di preferenza per ogni categoria.

🏨🏨🏨🏨🏨	XXXXX	**Gran lusso e tradizione**
🏨🏨🏨🏨	XXXX	**Gran confort**
🏨🏨🏨	XXX	**Molto confortevole**
🏨🏨	XX	**Di buon confort**
🏨	X	**Abbastanza confortevole**
⌂		**Locande, affittacamere**
without rest		**L'albergo non ha ristorante**
with rm		**Il ristorante dispone di camere**

I SIMBOLI DISTINTIVI

Per aiutarvi ad effettuare la scelta migliore, segnaliamo gli esercizi che si distinguono in modo particolare.

Per gli indirizzi che si distinguono con una stella o un Bib Gourmand, la menzione "**Rest**" appare in rosso nella descrizione dell'esercizio

Per gli indirizzi che si distinguono con il Bib Hotel, la menzione "**rm**" appare in blu nella descrizione dell'esercizio.

LE MIGLIORI TAVOLE

Le stelle distinguono gli esercizi che propongono la miglior qualità in campo gastronomico, indipendentemente dagli stili di cucina. I criteri presi in considerazione sono: la scelta dei prodotti, la personalità della cucina, la padronanza delle tecniche di cottura e dei sapori, il rapporto qualità/prezzo, nonché la regolarità.

✿✿✿ 26	**Una delle migliori cucine, questa tavola vale il viaggio** Vi si mangia sempre molto bene, a volte meravigliosamente.
✿✿ 73	**Cucina eccellente, questa tavola merita una deviazione**
✿ 449	**Un'ottima cucina nella sua categoria**

I MIGLIORI ESERCIZI A PREZZI CONTENUTI

☺	**Bib Gourmand**
527	Esercizio che offre una cucina di qualità, spesso a carattere tipicamente regionale, al prezzo massimo di 29 € (35 € nelle città capoluogo e turistiche importanti). Prezzo di un pasto, bevanda esclusa.
	Bib Hotel
293	Esercizio che offre un soggiorno di qualità al prezzo massimo di 75 € (90 € nelle città e località turistiche importanti) per la maggior parte delle camere. Prezzi per 2 persone, prima colazione esclusa.

GLI ESERCIZI AMENI

Il rosso indica gli esercizi particolarmente ameni. Questo per le caratteristiche dell'edificio, le decorazioni non comuni, la sua posizione ed il servizio offerto.

a	**Alberghi ameni**
	Locande e affittacamere ameni
X a XXXXX	**Ristoranti ameni**

LE SEGNALAZIONI PARTICOLARI

Oltre alle distinzioni conferite agli esercizi, gli ispettori MICHELIN apprezzano altri criteri spesso importanti nella scelta di un esericizio.

POSIZIONE

Cercate un esercizio tranquillo o che offre una vista piacevole?
Seguite i simboli seguenti :

Albergo tranquillo

Albergo molto tranquillo

Vista interessante

Vista eccezionale

CARTA DEI VINI

Cercate un ristorante la cui carta dei vini offra una scelta particolarmente interessante?
Seguite il simbolo seguente:

Carta dei vini particolarmente interessante

Attenzione a non confrontare la carta presentata da un sommelier in un grande ristorante con quella di una trattoria dove il proprietario ha una grande passione per i vini della regione.

Installazioni & servizi

30 rm	Numero di camere
	Giardino – Parco
	Pasti serviti in giardino o in terrazza
	Piscina: all'aperto, coperta
Spa	Centro attrezzato per il benessere ed il relax
	Palestra – Campo di tennis
	Ascensore – Esercizio accessibile in parte alle persone con difficoltà motorie
A/C	Aria condizionata
	Camere disponibili per i non fumatori
	Connessione Internet wifi in camera - Connessione Internet ad alta definizione in camera
	Saloni particolari
	Sale per conferenze
	Ristorante con servizio di posteggiatore (è consuetudine lasciare una mancia)
P P	Parcheggio / Parcheggio chiuso riservato alla clientela
	Garage nell'albergo (generalmente a pagamento)
	Accesso vietato ai cani
M	Stazione della metropolitana più vicina
Open/ Closed May-October	Periodo di apertura o chiusura comunicato dal proprietario

TABLES D'HÔTES

Le "tables d'hôtes" (pasti presso la struttura ospitante) sono riservate esclusivamente ai residenti.
Generalmente vengono proposte solo la sera, la maggior parte delle volte su prenotazione e non necessariamente tutti i giorni.
Abbiate quindi cura di controllare i giorni di chiusura e di prenotare la cena se desiderate approfittare di questa opportunità durante il vostro soggiorno.

Prezzi

I prezzi che indichiamo in questa guida sono stati stabiliti nell'autunno 2008. Potranno subire delle variazioni in relazione ai cambiamenti dei prezzi di beni e servizi. Essi s'intendono comprensivi di tasse e servizio. Sul conto da pagare non deve figurare alcuna maggiorazione, ad eccezione dell'eventuale tassa di soggiorno. Gli albergatori e i ristoratori si sono impegnati, sotto la propria responsabilità, a praticare questi prezzi ai clienti. In occasione di alcune manifestazioni (congressi, fiere, saloni, festival, eventi sportivi...) i prezzi richiesti dagli albergatori potrebbero subire un sensibile aumento. Per eventuali promozioni offerte, non esitate a chiederle direttamente all'albergatore.

PRENOTAZIONE E CAPARRA

Come conferma della prenotazione alcuni esercizi chiedono il numero di una carta di credito o il versamento di una caparra. Si tratta di un deposito-garanzia che impegna sia l'albergatore che il cliente. Chiedete una lettera di conferma su ogni dettaglio della prenotazione e sulle condizioni di soggiorno.

CARTE DI CREDITO

	Carte di credito accettate :
VISA MC AE DC	Visa – MasterCard –American Express –Diners Club

CAMERE

rm – † €50/80	Prezzo minimo / massimo per camera singola
rm – †† €60/100	Prezzo minimo / massimo per camera doppia.
☕ €9	Prezzo per la prima colazione.
rm ☕	Prima colazione compresa

MEZZA PENSIONE

½ P €50/70	Prezzo minimo/massimo della mezza pensione (camera, prima colazione ed un pasto) per persona. Questi prezzi sono validi per la camera doppia occupata da due persone, per un soggiorno minimo di tre giorni; la persona singola potrà talvolta vedersi applicata una maggiorazione. La maggior parte degli alberghi pratica anche la pensione completa.

RISTORANTE

(€13)	Pasto composto dal piatto del giorno, da un antipasto o dessert, a mezzogiorno in settimana
⊜	Pasto per meno di €19
Menu €15 (lunch)	Menu servito solo a mezzogiorno
Menu €17 (weekdays)	Menu servito solo nei giorni feriali
Menu €16/38	Menu: il meno caro / il più caro
Carte €24/48	Pasto alla carta bevanda esclusa. Il primo prezzo corrisponde ad un pasto semplice comprendente: antipasto, piatto del giorno e dessert. Il secondo prezzo corrisponde ad un pasto più completo (con specialità) comprendente: due piatti, formaggio e dessert.
bi	Bevanda compresa

Città

GENERALITÀ

63300	Codice di avviamento postale *le prime due cifre corrispondono al numero del dipartimento*
✉ **57130 Ars**	Numero di codice e sede dell'Ufficio Postale
P SP	Prefettura – Sottoprefettura
337 E5	Numero della carta "DEPARTEMENTS France" MICHELIN e coordinate riferite alla quadrettatura
Jura	Vedere la Guida Verde MICHELIN regionale
pop. 1057	Popolazione residente (funte: www.insee.fr)
alt. 75	Altitudine
Spa	Stazione termale
1200/1900	Altitudine della località e altitudine massima raggiungibile con gli impianti di risalita
2	Numero di funivie o cabinovie
14	Numero di sciovie e seggiovie
	Sci di fondo
BY **b**	Lettere indicanti l'ubicazione sulla pianta
9	Golf e numero di buche
	Panorama, vista
	Aeroporto
	Località con servizio auto su treno *Informarsi al numero di telefono indicato*
	Trasporti marittimi
	Trasporti marittimi (solo passeggeri)
	Informazioni turistiche

INFORMAZIONI TURISTICHE

INTERESSE TURISTICO

★★★	Vale il viaggio
★★	Merita una deviazione
★	Interessante

I musei sono generalmente chiusi il martedì

UBICAZIONE

	Nella città
	Nei dintorni della città
N, S, E, W	Il luogo si trova a Nord, a Sud, a Est, a Ovest della località
② ④	Ci si va dalla uscita ② o ④ indicata con lo stesso segno sulla pianta
6 km	Distanza chilometrica

Piante

Alberghi
Ristoranti

CURIOSITÀ

Edificio interessante
Costruzione religiosa interessante:
- Cattolica – Protestante

VIABILITÀ

Autostrada, doppia carreggiata tipo autostrada
Svincoli numerati: completo, parziale
Grande via di circolazione
Senso unico – Via regolamentata o impraticabile
Via pedonale – Tranvia
Parcheggio – Parcheggio Ristoro
Porta – Sottopassaggio – Galleria
Stazione e ferrovia – Auto/Treno
Funicolare – Funivia, Cabinovia
Ponte mobile – Traghetto per auto

SIMBOLI VARI

Ufficio informazioni turistiche
Moschea – Sinagoga
Torre – Ruderi – Mulino a vento – Torre idrica
Giardino, parco, bosco – Cimitero – Via Crucis
Stadio – Golf – Ippodromo – Pista di pattinaggio
Piscina: all'aperto, coperta
Vista – Panorama – Tavola d'orientamento
Monumento – Fontana – Fabbrica
Centro commerciale – Cinema Multisala
Porto turistico – Faro – Torre per telecomunicazioni
S.N.C.F. Aeroporto – Stazione della Metropolitana – Autostazione
Trasporto con traghetto:
- passeggeri ed autovetture, solo passeggeri
(3) Simbolo di riferimento comune alle piante particolareggiate
Ufficio centrale di fermo posta e telefono
Ospedale – Mercato coperto – Caserma
Edificio pubblico indicato con lettera:
A C Camera di Agricoltura – Camera di Commercio
G H J - Gendarmeria – Municipio – Palazzo di Giustizia
M P T - Museo – Prefettura, Sottoprefettura – Teatro
U - Università, grande scuola
POL. - Polizia (Questura, nelle grandi città)
4.4 18T (18) Sottopassaggio (altezza inferiore a m 4,50) – Portata limitata (inf. a 19 t)

Attenzione: in Francia, nuova numerazione per le strade nazionali regionali in corso.

Liebe Leser,

das Jahr 2009 ist ein historisches Jahr, nämlich das der 100. Ausgabe des MICHELIN-Führers Frankreich. Der 1900 entstandene „Rote Führer" feiert seine 100. Ausgabe erst heute, da die Veröffentlichung des Führers während des Krieges mehrere Jahre unterbrochen wurde. Ein bewegender Geburtstag für die Michelingruppe, aber auch für Sie, die gerne reisen und das Angenehme mit dem Nützlichen verbinden, auch in der Welt der Gastronomie und des Hotelfachs.

1900 verkehrten weniger als 3000 Autos auf den Straßen Frankreichs. Und eine Reise war oft ein großes Abenteuer! Trotzdem glaubten die Michelin-Brüder fest an die Zukunft des Automobils. Um die Entwicklung des Autos und damit die Entwicklung ihrer Reifenmanufaktur zu fördern, beschlossen sie, einen kleinen Führer herauszugeben, um die Reisen mit dem Auto zu erleichtern, die Mobilität zu verbessern… Die erste Ausgabe des berühmten MICHELIN-Führers erschien im August 1900 in einer Auflage von ca. 35.000 Exemplaren. Im Vorwort schrieb André Michelin: „Dieses Werk erscheint zu Beginn des neuen Jahrhunderts und wird das gesamte Jahrhundert begleiten." Er sollte Recht behalten. Der Michelin-Führer hat das Jahrhundert sogar überlebt.

Der erste MICHELIN-Führer enthielt viele praktische Hinweise: Auf den ersten Seiten standen eine Anleitung zum Reifenwechsel, Informationen über die Wartung des Autos usw. Unter dem Stichwort Paris fand der Leser eine Liste von Automobilherstellern, aber noch keine Adressen ausgewählter Hotels und Restaurants.

Ab 1921 wurden im MICHELIN-Führer auch Restaurants mit Bewertung aufgenommen und zum ersten Mal eine Liste mit Pariser Hotels aufgeführt.

1926 wurde der Stern als Bewertung für gute Restaurants eingeführt und 1931 kamen der zweite und dritte Stern hinzu, zuerst in der französischen Provinz und ab 1933 in Paris. Das Drei-Sterne-System (ein Stern „gute Küche am Ort" – zwei Sterne „lohnt einen Umweg" und drei Sterne „eine Reise wert") wurde 1936 festgelegt und gilt heute noch.

Der MICHELIN-Führer ist ein Restaurant- und Hotelführer für jedermann und jeden Anlass mit Adressen von Drei-Sterne-Restaurants bis zu Restaurants, die ein sehr gutes Preis-Leistungs-Verhältnis bieten und mit dem „Bib Gourmand" ausgezeichnet sind, vom Luxushotel bis zum Hotel mit besonderen Charme.

„Mobil sein", die Philosophie, die der ersten Auflage des Führers zu Grunde lag, bildet heute noch die Grundlage der internationalen Marke Michelin.
Der « Rote » Führer ist der Entwicklung des Unternehmens über die Grenzen Frankreichs hinaus, nach Amerika und Asien gefolgt. Von Westen nach Osten verfolgt und erweitert der Führer seine Suche nach dem Besten im Bereich der Gastronomie, um immer neue Talente jeder Art aufzuspüren. Die Auswahlkriterien wurden beibehalten, eine Qualitätsgarantie, die auf der Unabhängigkeit der Inspektoren basiert und das Ansehen des Roten Führers über Jahre hinweg weltweit begründet hat.

Auch die 100. Ausgabe des MICHELIN-Führers Frankreich stellt keine Ausnahme von der Regel dar, und wir hoffen, dass jeder hier das wiederfinden wird, was seit jeher jedes Jahr seinen Reichtum ausmacht. Dieses Jubiläum bietet uns auch die Gelegenheit, Ihnen, unseren treuen Lesern – und Sie sind Millionen! –, zu danken, dass Sie uns seit Jahrzehnten Ihr Vertrauen schenken. Nicht unerwähnt bleiben sollen auch die Tausende von Hotel- und Restaurantchefs, die gemeinsam mit Ihnen den MICHELIN-Führer seit 109 Jahren zuwege bringen.

Sie auf Ihren Reisen zu begleiten, diese einfache Idee ist um die ganze Welt gereist. Wir bauen darauf, dass die Hotel- und Restaurantchefs von morgen, die Inspektoren des MICHELIN-Führers Frankreich, Europa, USA und Asien und Sie, liebe Leser, durch Ihre wertvollen Briefe und Kommentare den Roten Führer auch im 21. Jahrhundert weiter leben lassen.

Michel Rollier

Geschäftsleitung der Michelingruppe

Hinweise zur Benutzung

TOURISTISCHE INFORMATIONEN

Entfernungen zu größeren Städten, Informationsstellen, Sehenswürdigkeiten, Verkehrsmittel, Golfplätze und lokale Veranstaltungen...

DIE UNTERBRINGUNG

Von 🏠🏠🏠🏠🏠 bis 🏠, ⌂:
Komfortkategorien
In rot 🏠🏠🏠🏠🏠 ... 🏠, ⌂:
Besonders angenehme Häuser

DIE BESTEN PREISWERTEN ADRESSEN

Bib Gourmand
Bib Hotel

DIE RESTAURANTS

Von XXXXX bis X:
Komfortkategorien
In rot XXXXX ... X: Besonders angenehme Häuser

DIE STERNE-RESTAURANTS

✿✿✿ Eine Reise wert
✿✿ Verdient einen Umweg
✿ Eine sehr gute Küche

ABBAYE DE FONTFROIDE – 03 Aude – **344** J4 – se
ABBAYE DE SAINT-WANDRILLE – 18 Cher – **323**
ABBEVILLE – 80 Somme – **301** E7 – pop 24 567 –
Northern France and the Paris Region
Paris 186 – Amiens 51 – Boulogne-sur
Dunkerque, ✆ 04 90 31 51 12, by N3 e
Office de tourisme, 1 place de l'Amir
- office.tourisme.abbeville@wanado
of Abbeville, Route du Val, by rte S
- ✆ 03 55 35 96 54 - Fax 03 55 35 9
Modern stained-glass windows o
St-Vulfran collégiate church AE**D**
Vallée de la Somme★ SE - Châte

Les Jardins du Château
rte du Port – ✆ 04 79 01 36 46 – w
hoteljardins.fr – Fax 04 12 23 45 5
1st May and 15 August
15 rm – † € 55/75 †† € 85/170 –
Rest Les Terrasses – ✆ 04 79
Rest Le Cœur d'Or – Closed
• Built as a private house in
contemporary rooms includ
garden and terraces.

La Feme des Lions
45 rue des Lions, D541 : 1
– relaisdelaposte@reserv
42 rm – † € 45/60 €
• Red-brick 18C listed
house overlooks mead
bread and preserves.

Atelier des Save
10 bd Croisette – ✆
– atelierdessaveurs
Rest – (booking e
Spec. Salad of sr
nuts and pistach
des bois and mi
• A country in
terrace with b

ANDERE MICHELIN-PUBLIKATIONEN

Angabe der MICHELIN-Karte und des Grünen MICHELIN-Reiseführers, wo der Ort zu finden ist

LAGE DER STADT

Markierung des Ortes auf der Regionalkarte am Ende des Buchs (Nr. der Karte und Koordinaten)

LAGE DES HAUSES

Markierung auf dem Stadtplan (Planquadrat und Koordinate)

BESCHREIBUNG DES HAUSES

Atmosphäre, Stil, Charakter und Spezialitäten

RUHIGE HOTELS

ruhiges Hotel
sehr ruhiges Hotel

EINRICHTUNG UND SERVICE

PREISE

mand-Montrond
36 **A1**
0100
uen 106
03 22 24 27 92
25 24 27 96
omme : 4 km
32
church★★ AM**B** - Façade★ of
cher de Perthes★ BY**M**
lle★ S
50
chateau.com – welcome@
Z **d**
December-30 April,
€ 7,50
ner only) Menu € 34 – Carte € 25/35
nu € 35/65 bi – Carte € 17/25
ith modern and stylish public areas. The
e art facilities. Sleek restaurant overlooks

AU **c**
01 32 25 – www.fermedeslions.com
x 04 79 01 32 26 – Closed 25 December
– Menu € 19 – Carte € 22/45
a working farm... with beautiful blue windows;
arden room for breakfast, including home-made
ooms.

16
Y **a**
is Thomas)
8 – www.atelierdessaveurs.com
omas.fr – Fax 04 79 01 33 17 – Closed July
nu € 55/76 (weekdays lunch) – € Carte 48/85
ig's trotter and apple purée. Braised turbot with pea-
aragus. Cannelloni of apricot, Strawberry sorbet, fraises
od panelled dining room, with smart first floor bar and
s over the sea.

Y **c**
04 79 02 33 18 – Fax 04 79 01 33 17 – Closed July
Saturday) Menu € 35/47 bi – Carte € 22/35
rior for this old Abbeville house. Classic
rved at reasonable prices.

Kategorien & Auszeichnungen

KOMFORTKATEGORIEN

Der MICHELIN-Führer bietet in seiner Auswahl die besten Adressen jeder Komfort- und Preiskategorie. Die ausgewählten Häuser sind nach dem gebotenen Komfort geordnet; die Reihenfolge innerhalb jeder Kategorie drückt eine weitere Rangordnung aus.

🏨🏨🏨🏨🏨	XXXXX	**Großer Luxus und Tradition**
🏨🏨🏨🏨	XXXX	**Großer Komfort**
🏨🏨🏨	XXX	**Sehr komfortabel**
🏨🏨	XX	**Mit gutem Komfort**
🏨	X	**Mit Standard-Komfort**
	🏠	**Privatzimmer**
without rest		**Hotel ohne Restaurant**
with rm		**Restaurant vermietet auch Zimmer**

AUSZEICHNUNGEN

Um ihnen behilflich zu sein, die bestmögliche Wahl zu treffen, haben einige besonders bemerkenswerte Adressen dieses Jahr eine Auszeichnung erhalten. Die Sterne bzw. „Bib Gourmand" sind durch das entsprechende Symbol ✿ bzw. ☺ und **Rest** gekennzeichnet.
Ist ein Haus mit einem Bib Hotel ausgezeichnet, wird die Bezeichnung **„rm"** (für die Angabe der Zimmerzahl) in blau gedruckt.

DIE STERNE: DIE BESTEN RESTAURANTS

Die Häuser, die eine überdurchschnittlich gute Küche bieten, wobei alle Stilrichtungen vertreten sind, wurden mit einem Stern ausgezeichnet. Die Kriterien sind: die Auswahl der Produkte, die persönlichen Akzente der Küche, das Knowhow bei der Zubereitung und im Geschmack, das Preis-Leistungs-Verhältnis und die immer gleich bleibende Qualität.

✿✿✿ **Eine der besten Küchen: eine Reise wert**
26 Man isst hier immer sehr gut, öfters auch exzellent.

✿✿ **Eine hervorragende Küche: verdient einen Umweg**
73

✿ **Ein sehr gutes Restaurant in seiner Kategorie**
449

DIE BIB: DIE BESTEN PREISWERTEN HÄUSER

☺ **Bib Gourmand**
527 Häuser, die eine gute Küche bis 29 € bieten – in Paris : bis 35 € (Preis für eine dreigängige Mahlzeit ohne Getränke).
Außerhalb von Paris handelt es sich meist um eine regional geprägte Küche.

Bib Hotel

293 Häuser, die eine Mehrzahl ihrer komfortablen Zimmer bis 75 € anbieten – bzw. weniger als 90 € in größeren Städten und Urlaubsorten (Preis für 2 Personen ohne Frühstück).

DIE ANGENEHMSTEN ADRESSEN

Die rote Kennzeichnung weist auf besonders angenehme Häuser hin. Dies kann sich auf den besonderen Charakter des Gebäudes, die nicht alltägliche Einrichtung, die Lage, den Empfang oder den gebotenen Service beziehen.

bis **Angenehme Hotels**

Angenehme Privatzimmer

bis **Angenehme Restaurants**

BESONDERE ANGABEN

Neben den Auszeichnungen, die den Häusern verliehen werden, legen die MICHELIN-Inspektoren auch Wert auf andere Kriterien, die bei der Wahl einer Adresse oft von Bedeutung sind.

LAGE

Wenn Sie eine ruhige Adresse oder ein Haus mit einer schönen Aussicht suchen, achten Sie auf diese Symbole:

Ruhiges Hotel

Sehr ruhiges Hotel

Interessante Sicht

Besonders schöne Aussicht

WEINKARTE

Wenn Sie ein Restaurant mit einer besonders interessanten Weinauswahl suchen, achten Sie auf dieses Symbol:

Weinkarte mit besonders attraktivem Angebot
Aber vergleichen Sie bitte nicht die Weinkarte, die Ihnen vom Sommelier eines großen Hauses präsentiert wird, mit der Auswahl eines Gasthauses, dessen Besitzer die Weine der Region mit Sorgfalt zusammenstellt.

Einrichtung & Service

30 rm	Anzahl der Zimmer
	Garten, Liegewiese – Park
	Garten-, Terrassenrestaurant
	Freibad oder Hallenbad
Spa	Wellnessbereich
	Fitnessraum – Tennisplatz
	Fahrstuhl
	Für Körperbehinderte leicht zugängliches Haus
A/C	Klimaanlage
	Nichtraucher Zimmer vorhanden
	Internetzugang mit W-Lan/ADSL in den Zimmern
	Veranstaltungsraum
	Konferenzraum
	Restaurant mit Wagenmeister-Service (Trinkgeld üblich)
P P	Parkplatz / gesicherter Parkplatz für Gäste
	Garage (wird gewöhnlich berechnet)
	Hunde sind unerwünscht
M	Nächstgelegene U-Bahnstation
Open / Closed May-October	Öffnungszeit / Schließungszeit, vom Hotelier mitgeteilt

TABLES D'HÔTES

Mahlzeiten nur für Hausgäste. Sie werden im Allgemeinen nur abends angeboten, meistens auf Anfrage und nicht unbedingt täglich. Möchten Sie während Ihres Aufenthalts im Hause speisen, reservieren Sie das Abendessen und beachten Sie die Öffnungszeiten.

Preise

Die in diesem Führer genannten Preise wurden uns im Herbst 2008 angegeben. Sie können sich mit den Preisen von Waren und Dienstleistungen ändern. Sie enthalten Bedienung und MwSt. Es sind Inklusivpreise, die sich nur noch durch die evtl. zu zahlende Kurtaxe erhöhen können. Die Häuser haben sich verpflichtet, die von den Hoteliers selbst angegebenen Preise den Kunden zu berechnen. Anlässlich größerer Veranstaltungen, Messen und Ausstellungen werden von den Hotels in manchen Städten und deren Umgebung erhöhte Preise verlangt. Erkundigen Sie sich bei den Hoteliers nach eventuellen Sonder- bedingungen.

RESERVATION UND ANZAHLUNG

Einige Häuser verlangen zur Bestätigung der Reservierung eine Anzahlung oder die Kreditkartennummer. Diese ist als Garantie sowohl für die Häuser als auch für den Gast anzusehen. Bitten Sie den Hotelier, dass er Ihnen in seinem Bestätigungsschreiben die genauen Bedingungen mitteilt.

KREDITKARTEN

	Akzeptierte Kreditkarten:
VISA MC AE DC	Visa – MasterCard – American Express – Diners Club

ZIMMER

rm – 👤 €50/80	Mindest- und Höchstpreis für ein Einzelzimmer
rm – 👥 €60/100	Mindest- und Höchstpreis für ein Doppelzimmer
☕ €9	Preis für Frühstück
rm ☕	Zimmerpreis inkl. Frühstück

HALBPENSION

½ P €50/70	Mindest- und Höchstpreis für Halbpension (Zimmerpreis inkl. Frühstück und einer Mahlzeit) pro Person, bei einem von zwei Personen belegten Doppelzimmer für einen Aufenthalt von mindestens 3 Tagen. Falls eine Einzelperson ein Doppelzimmer belegt, kann ein Preisaufschlag verlangt werden. In den meisten Hotels wird auch Vollpension angeboten.

RESTAURANT

(€13)	Preis für ein Menu, bestehend aus Vorspeise/Hauptgericht oder Hauptgericht/Dessert, das unter der Woche mittags serviert wird
🪙	Menu unter €19
Menu €15 (lunch)	Menu wird nur mittags angeboten
Menu €17 (weekdays)	Menu wird nur unter der Woche angeboten
Menu €16/38	Mindest- und Höchstpreis der Menus
Carte €24/48	Der erste Preis entspricht einer einfachen Mahlzeit und umfasst Vorspeise, Hauptgericht, Dessert. Der zweite Preis entspricht einer reichlicheren Mahlzeit (mit Spezialität) bestehend aus Vorspeise, Hauptgang, Käse und Dessert.
bi	Getränke inklusiv

Städte

ALLGEMEINES

63300	Postleitzahl *die beiden ersten Ziffern sind gleichzeitig die Departements-Nummer*
✉ **57130 Ars**	Postleitzahl und Name des Verteilerpostamtes
P ⟨SP⟩	Präfektur – Unterpräfektur
337 E5	Nummer der Michelin-Karte « DEPARTEMENTS France » MICHELIN und Koordinatenangabe
Jura	Siehe den Grünen MICHELIN-Reiseführer der Region
pop. 1057	Einwohnerzahl (Quelle: www.insee.fr)
alt. 75	Höhe
Spa	Thermalbad
1200/1900	Höhe des Wintersportortes und Maximalhöhe, die mit Kabinenbahn oder Lift erreicht werden kann
2	Anzahl der Kabinenbahnen
14	Anzahl der Schlepp- oder Sessellifte
	Langlaufloipen
BY **b**	Markierung auf dem Stadtplan
9	Golfplatz und Anzahl der Löcher
	Rundblick, Aussichtspunkt
	Flughafen
	Ladestelle für Autoreisezüge *Auskunft unter der angegebenen Telefonnummer*
	Autofähre – Personenfähre
i	Informationsstelle

SEHENSWÜRDIGKEITEN

BEWERTUNG

★★★	Eine Reise wert
★★	Verdient einen Umweg
★	Sehenswert

Museen sind im allgemeinen dienstags geschlossen

LAGE

	In der Stadt
	In der Umgebung der Stadt
N, S, E, W	Die Sehenswürdigkeit befindet sich: im Norden, Süden, Osten, Westen der Stadt
② ④	Zu erreichen über die Ausfallstraße ② bzw. ④, die auf dem Stadtplan identisch gekennzeichnet sind.
6 km	Entfernung in Kilometern

Stadtpläne

Hotels
Restaurants

SEHENSWÜRDIGKEITEN

Sehenswertes Gebäude
Sehenswerte katholische bzw. evangelische Kirche

STRAßEN

Autobahn, Schnellstraße
Numerierte Anschlußstelle: Autobahneinfahrt – und/oder -ausfahrt
Hauptverkehrsstraße
Einbahnstraße – Gesperrte Straße oder mit Verkehrsbeschränkungen
Fußgängerzone – Straßenbahn
Parkplatz, Parkhaus – Park-and-Ride-Plätze
Tor – Passage – Tunnel
Bahnhof und Bahnlinie – Autoreisezug
Standseilbahn – Seilschwebebahn
Bewegliche Brücke – Autofähre

SONSTIGE ZEICHEN

Informationsstelle
Moschee – Synagoge
Turm – Ruine – Windmühle – Wasserturm
Garten, Park, Wäldchen – Friedhof – Bildstock
Stadion – Golfplatz – Pferderennbahn – Eisbahn
- Freibad – Hallenbad
Aussicht – Rundblick – Orientierungstafel
Denkmal – Brunnen – Fabrik
Einkaufszentrum – Multiplex-Kino
Jachthafen – Leuchtturm – Funk-, Fernsehturm
Flughafen – U-Bahnstation – Autobusbahnhof
S.N.C.F.
Schiffsverbindungen: Autofähre – Personenfähre
Straßenkennzeichnung (identisch auf Michelin-Stadtplänen und Abschnittskarten)
Hauptpostamt (postlagernde Sendungen) u. Telefon
Krankenhaus – Markthalle – Kaserne
Öffentliches Gebäude, durch einen Buchstaben gekennzeichnet:
A C - Landwirtschaftskammer – Handelskammer
G H J - Gendarmerie – Rathaus – Gerichtsgebäude
M P T - Museum – Präfektur, Unterpräfektur – Theater
U - Universität, Hochschule
POL. - Polizei (in größeren Städten Polizeipräsidium)
4,4 18T 18 Unterführung (Höhe bis 4,50 m) – Höchstbelastung (unter 19 t)

Achtung: Die Nummerierung der National-und der Landstraßen in Frankreich wird z. Zt. Geändert.

Estimados lectores,

El año 2009 marca una fecha histórica: la centésima edición de La Guía Michelin de Francia. ¡Aunque nacida en 1900, la Guía no celebra su 100ª edición hasta este año, ya que su publicación tuvo que interrumpirse durante los años de guerra! Un emotivo aniversario tanto para el Grupo Michelin, como para usted que viaja y que busca combinar lo útil con lo agradable, y finalmente, también para el mundo de la gastronomía y de la hostelería.

En 1900, había menos de 3.000 automóviles circulando por toda Francia. ¡En aquellos tiempos, un viaje acababa casi siempre siendo una aventura! Pero a pesar de todo, los hermanos Michelin creen firmemente en el futuro del automóvil. Para contribuir a su desarrollo, y al mismo tiempo, al de la Manufacture Française des Pneus Michelin que habían creado, deciden poner a disposición de los automovilistas un documento que les ayude en sus viajes, una pequeña guía para mejorar la movilidad…, la famosa Guía MICHELIN, cuya primera edición, publicada en agosto de 1900, tendrá una tirada de casi 35.000 ejemplares… En el prefacio, André Michelin escribe lo siguiente: «Esta obra aparece con el siglo y durará tanto como él». Una predicción que se ha cumplido. Más aún, la realidad ha superado las expectativas más halagüeñas.

La primera Guía MICHELIN incluye una gran cantidad de información práctica: sus primeras páginas facilitan información sobre cómo cambiar un neumático, cómo mantener su vehículo, etc. En París, por ejemplo, se citaba únicamente la lista de los fabricantes de automóviles. No se incluía ninguna selección de hoteles ni de restaurantes. Los restaurantes no hicieron su entrada en La Guía hasta 1921 con una clasificación propia. En esa edición figuraba también, por primera vez, una lista de hoteles parisinos.

En 1926, nace la estrella de la buena mesa y, en 1931, ven el día la segunda y la tercera estrella, primero en provincias, y más adelante, en 1933, en París. En cuanto a las definiciones (una estrella, «una muy buena mesa dentro de su categoría», dos estrellas «merece el desvío» y tres estrellas «merece el viaje») se remontan a 1936... y siguen estando de actualidad.

La Guía MICHELIN es una guía para todo el mundo y para todas las ocasiones que abarca desde el restaurante de tres estrellas hasta el Bib Gourmand -con una excelente relación calidad-precio-, del palacio al hotel con encanto.

La filosofía que ha presidido la creación de La Guía, la ayuda a la movilidad, se ha mantenido a través del tiempo, convirtiéndose en la plataforma mundial de la Marca Michelin.
La Guía « Roja » ha proseguido este desarrollo fuera de Francia, en Europa, en Estados Unidos y en Asia: del oeste al este, La Guía MICHELIN perpetúa y amplía todavía más su búsqueda de lo mejor en materia gastronómica, en busca siempre de los nuevos talentos allá donde surjan. Los criterios de selección siguen siendo los mismos, una garantía de calidad basada en la independencia de los inspectores que ha labrado la reputación de la Guía a lo largo de los años, en todos los rincones del mundo.

Y esta edición número cien de La Guía MICHELIN de Francia no es, por supuesto, una excepción a la regla. Esperamos que encuentre en ella todos los elementos que han forjado su riqueza de año en año.
Este aniversario nos ofrece también la oportunidad de agradecer a nuestros fieles lectores –¡son ustedes varios millones!– la confianza que vienen otorgándonos desde hace décadas, y de rendir un homenaje a esos miles de hoteleros y de restauradores que, junto con ustedes, han hecho realidad la Guía Michelin desde hace 109 años.
Acompañarles en sus desplazamientos... ¡Esta sencilla idea ha recorrido un largo trecho alrededor del mundo! Estamos seguros de que los chefs del mañana, los futuros hoteleros, los inspectores de La Guía MICHELIN de Francia, de Europa, de América y de Asia, y por supuesto ustedes, estimados lectores, con sus correos repletos siempre de valiosos comentarios, sabrán dar vida a las próximas ediciones de este siglo XXI.

Michel Rollier

Gerente del Grupo Michelin

Modo de empleo

INFORMACIÓN TURÍSTICA

Distancias desde las poblaciones principales, oficinas de turismo, puntos de interés turístico locales, medios de transporte, campos de golf y ocio...

EL ALOJAMIENTO

De 🏠🏠🏠🏠 a 🏠, ⌂:
categorías de confort
En rojo 🏠🏠🏠🏠 ... 🏠, ⌂:
los más agradables

LAS MEJORES DIRECCIONES A PRECIOS MODERADOS

☺ Bib Gourmand
☺ Bib Hotel

RESTAURANTES

De XXXXX a X: categorías de confort
En rojo XXXXX ... X: los más agradables

ESTRELLAS

✿✿✿ Justifica el viaje
✿✿ Vale la pena desviarse
✿ Muy buena cocina

ABBAYE DE FONTFROIDE – 03 Aude – **344** J4 – see
ABBAYE DE SAINT-WANDRILLE – 18 Cher – **323**
ABBEVILLE – 80 Somme – **301** E7 – pop 24 567 – a
Northern France and the Paris Region
Paris 186 – Amiens 51 – Boulogne-sur-M
Dunkerque, ✆ 04 90 31 51 12, by N3 et
Office de tourisme, 1 place de l'Amiral
- office.tourisme.abbeville@wanadoo
of Abbeville, Route du Val, by rte St-V
- Fax 03 55 35 96 54 - Fax 03 55 35 96
- ✆ 03 55 35 96 54
Modern stained-glass windows of S
St-Vulfran collégiate church AED -
Vallée de la Somme★ SE - Châteat

Les Jardins du Château
rte du Port – ✆ 04 79 01 36 46 – www
hoteljardins.fr – Fax 04 12 23 45 53 -
1st May and 15 August
15 rm – € 55/75 € 85/170 – 3
Rest Les Terrasses – ✆ 04 79 01
Rest Le Cœur d'Or – Closed Mo
◆ Built as a private house in 18
contemporary rooms include s
garden and terraces.

La Feme des Lions
45 rue des Lions, D541 : 1 km
– relaisdelaposte@reservatic
42 rm – € 45/60 € 55/7
◆ Red-brick 18C listed farm
house overlooks meadow
bread and preserves. Imm

Atelier des Saveurs
10 bd Croisette – ✆ 04 7
– atelierdessaveurs@fr
Rest – (booking esser
Spec. Salad of smoke
nuts and pistachios a
des bois and mint.
◆ A country inn wi
terrace with blissf

OTRAS PUBLICACIONES MICHELIN

Referencia del mapa MICHELIN y de la Guía Verde en los que se encuentra la localidad

LOCALIZAR LA CIUDAD

Emplazamiento de la localidad en el mapa regional situado al final de la guía (nº del mapa y coordenadas)

LOCALIZAR EL ESTABLECIMIENTO

Localización en el plano de la ciudad (coordenadas e índice)

DESCRIPCIÓN DEL ESTABLECIMIENTO

Ambiente, estilo, carácter y especialidades

HOTELES TRANQUILOS

Hotel tranquilo

Hotel muy tranquilo

PRECIOS

INSTALACIONES Y SERVICIOS

Amand-Montrond
36 **A1**
30100
uen 106
03 22 24 27 92
25 24 27 96
omme : 4 km
32
church★★ AM**B** - Façade★ of
cher de Perthes★ BY**M**
le★ S
50 AE VISA
Z **d**
hateau.com – welcome@
December-30 April,
7,50
er only) Menu € 34 – Carte € 25/35
u € 35/65 bi – Carte € 17/25
h modern and stylish public areas. The
art facilities. Sleek restaurant overlooks
AE VISA
AU **c**
www.fermedeslions.com
1 32 25 – www.fermedeslions.com
04 79 01 32 26 – Closed 25 December
Menu € 19 – Carte € 22/45
working farm... with beautiful blue windows;
den room for breakfast, including home-made
ms.
16 AE VISA
Y **a**
Thomas)
– www.atelierdessaveurs.com
as.fr – Fax 04 79 01 33 17 – Closed July
€ 55/76 (weekdays lunch) – € Carte 48/85
s trotter and apple purée. Braised turbot with pea-
gus. Cannelloni of apricot, Strawberry sorbet, fraises
panelled dining room, with smart first floor bar and
ver the sea.
AE VISA
Y **c**
04 79 02 33 18 – Fax 04 79 01 33 17 – Closed July
Saturday) Menu € 35/47 bi – Carte € 22/35
for this old Abbeville house. Classic
d at reasonable prices.

Categorías y distinciones

CATEGORÍAS DE CONFORT

La guía MICHELIN incluye en su selección los mejores establecimientos en cada categoría de confort y de precio. Los establecimientos están clasificados según su confort y se citan por orden de preferencia dentro de cada categoría.

🏨🏨🏨🏨🏨	XXXXX	**Gran lujo y tradición**
🏨🏨🏨🏨	XXXX	**Gran confort**
🏨🏨🏨	XXX	**Muy confortable**
🏨🏨	XX	**Confortable**
🏨	X	**Sencillo pero confortable**
⌂		**Turismo rural**
without rest		**El hotel no dispone de restaurante**
with rm		**El restaurante tiene habitaciones**

DISTINCIONES

Para ayudarle a hacer la mejor selección, algunos establecimientos especialmente interesantes han recibido este año una distinción.

Para los establecimientos distinguidos por una estrella o un Bib Gourmand, la mención "**Rest**" aparece en color rojo en la descripción del establecimiento.

Para los establecimientos ditinguidos por un Bib Hotel, la mención "**rm**" aparece en color azul en la descripción del establecimiento.

LAS ESTRELLAS: LAS MEJORES MESAS

Los criterios que se han seguido son: los productos utilizados, la personalidad de la cocina, el dominio de las cocciones y de los sabores, la relación calidad/precio, así como la regularidad.

✿✿✿ 26	**Cocina de nivel excepcional, esta mesa justifica el viaje** Establecimiento donde siempre se come bien y, en ocasiones, maravillosamente.
✿✿ 73	**Excelente cocina, vale la pena desviarse**
✿ 449	**Muy buena cocina en su categoría**

LOS BIB:
LAS MEJORES DIRECCIONES A PRECIOS MODERADOS

527 **Bib Gourmand**
Establecimiento que ofrece una cocina de calidad, generalmente de tipo regional, a un máximo de 29 € (35 € en París). Precio de una comida sin la bebida.

293 **Bib Hotel**
Establecimiento que ofrece un cierto nivel de calidad con habitaciones a un máximo de 75 € (90 € en grandes ciudades y zonas turisticas). Precio para 2 personas sin el desayuno.

LAS DIRECCIONES MÁS AGRADABLES

El rojo indica los establecimientos especialmente agradables tanto por las características del edificio, la decoración original, el emplazamiento, el trato y los servicios que ofrece.

a **Hoteles agradables**

Turismos rurales agradables

a **Restaurantes agradables**

MENCIONES PARTICULARES

Además de las distinciones concedidas a los establecimientos, los inspectores de MICHELIN también tienen en cuenta otros criterios con frecuencia importantes cuando se elige un establecimiento.

SITUACIÓN

Los establecimientos tranquilos o con vistas aparecen señalados con los símbolos:

Hotel tranquilo

Hotel muy tranquilo

Vista interesante

Vista excepcional

CARTA DE VINOS

Los restaurantes con una carta de vinos especialmente interesante aparecen señalados con el símbolo:

Carta de vinos particularmente atractiva
Pero no compare la carta que presenta el sumiller de un restaurante de lujo y tradición con la de un establecimiento más sencillo cuyo propietario sienta predilección por los vinos de la zona.

Instalaciones y servicios

30 rm	Número de habitaciones
	Jardín – Parque
	Comidas servidas en el jardín o en la terraza
	Piscina al aire libre o cubierta
	Espacio dedicado al bienestar y la relajación
	Gimnasio – Cancha de tenis
	Ascensor – Instalaciones adaptadas para discapacitados
	Aire acondicionado
	Habitaciones disponibles para no fumadores
	Conexión a Internet en la habitación, con sistema de alta velocidad (Wi-Fi/ ADSL)
	Salones privados en los restaurantes
	Salas de reuniones
	Restaurante con servicio de aparcacoches (es costumbre dejar propina)
	Aparcamiento / Aparcamiento cerrado reservado a los clientes
	Garaje (generalmente de pago)
	No se admiten perros
	Estación de metro más próxima
Open / Closed May-October	Período de apertura comunicado por el hotelero

TABLES D'HÔTES

Las "tables d'hôtes" están reservadas exclusivamente a los residentes. Normalmente, sólo se preparan para la cena, y es necesario reservarlas con antelación; tampoco tienen por qué servirse todos los días. Por ello, no olvide comprobar los días de cierre y reservar su cena si desea disfrutar de esta mesa especial durante su estancia.

Precios

Los precios que indicamos en esta guía nos fueron facilitados en el otoño de 2008. Pueden sufrir modificaciones debido a las variaciones de los precios de bienes y servicios. El servicio y los impuestos están incluidos. En la factura no debe figurar ningún recargo excepto una eventual tasa de alojamiento. Los hoteles y restaurantes se han comprometido, bajo su responsabilidad, a aplicar estos precios al cliente. Durante la celebración de determinados eventos (congresos, ferias, salones, festivales, pruebas deportivas...) los precios indicados por los hoteleros pueden sufrir importantes aumentos. Por otra parte, infórmese con antelación porque muchos establecimientos aplican tarifas muy ventajosas.

RESERVAS Y ARRAS

Para confirmar la reserva, algunos establecimientos piden el número de la tarjeta de crédito o el abono de arras. Se trata de un depósito-garantía que compromete tanto al establecimiento como al cliente. Pida al hotelero confirmación escrita de las condiciones de estancia así como de todos los detalles útiles.

TARJETAS DE CRÉDITO

	Tarjetas de crédito aceptadas:
VISA MC AE DC	Visa – MasterCard – American Express – Diners Club

HABITACIONES

rm – 🚹 €50/80	Precio de las habitaciones mínimo/máximo para 1 persona
rm – 🚹🚹 €60/100	Precio de las habitaciones mínimo/máximo para 2 personas
☕ €9	Precio del desayvro
rm ☕	Desayuno incluido

MEDIA PENSIÓN

½ P €50/70	Precio mínimo/máximo de la media pensión (habitación, desayuno y una comida) por persona. Precio de la habitación doble ocupada por dos personas y durante una estancia mínima de tres días. Si una persona sola ocupa una habitación doble se le suele aplicar un suplemento. La mayoría de estos hoteles ofrecen también la pensión completa.

RESTAURANTE

(€13)	Comida compuesta por un plato fuerte del día y una entrada o un postre, servida generalmente a mediodía los días de semana
⚭	Menú a menos de €19
Menu €15 (lunch)	Menú servido sólo a mediodía
Menu €17 (weekdays)	Menú servido sólo los días de semana
Menu €16/38	Menú más económico / más caro
Carte €24/48	**Comida a la carta sin bebida.** El primer precio corresponde a una comida normal que incluye: entrada, plato fuerte del día y postre. El segundo precio se refiere a una comida más completa (con especialidad) que incluye: dos platos, queso y postre.
bi	Bebida incluida

Localidades

GENERALIDADES

63300	Código postal de la localidad *los dos primeros dígitos corresponden al número del departamento o provincia*
✉ **57130 Ars**	Código postal y lugar de destino
P SP	Prefectura – Subprefectura
337 E5	Mapa Michelin "DEPARTEMENTS France" MICHELIN y coordenadas en los mapas
Jura	Ver La Guía Verde Michelin de la region
pop. 1057	Población (según datos: www.insee.fr)
alt. 75	Altitud de la localidad
Spa	Balneario
1200/1900	Altitud de la estación y altitud máxima alcanzada por los remontes mecánicos
2	Número de teleféricos o telecabinas
14	Número de telesquíes o telesillas
	Esquí de fondo
BY **b**	Letras para localizar un emplazamiento en el plano
9	Golf y número de hoyos
	Panorama, vista
	Aeropuerto – Localidad con servicio Auto-Tren *Información en el número indicado*
	Transportes marítimos
	Transportes marítimos sólo para pasajeros
	Información turística

INFORMACIONES TURÍSTICAS

INTERÉS TURÍSTICO

★★★	Justifica el viaje
★★	Vale la pena desviarse
★	Interesante
	Los museos cierran generalmente los martes

SITUACIÓN

	En la población
	En los alrededores de la población
N, S, E, W	El lugar de interés está situado: al norte, al sur, al este, al oeste
② ④	Salga por la salida ② o ④ identificada por el mismo signo en el plano de la Guía y en el mapa Michelin
6 km	Distancia en kilómetros

Planos

Hoteles
Restaurantes

CURIOSIDADES

Edificio interesante
Edificio religioso interesante:
- Católico – Protestante

VÍAS DE CIRCULACIÓN

Autopista, autovía
número del acceso : completo-parcial
Vía importante de circulación
Sentido único – Calle impracticable, de uso restringido
Calle peatonal – Tranvía
P Aparcamiento – Aparcamientos "P + R"
Puerta – Pasaje cubierto – Túnel
Estación y línea férrea – Auto-tren
Funicular – Teleférico, telecabina
B Puente móvil – Barcaza para coches

SIGNOS DIVERSOS

Oficina de Información de Turismo
Mezquita – Sinagoga
Torre – Ruinas – Molino de viento – Depósito de agua
Jardín, parque, bosque – Cementerio – Crucero
Estadio – Golf – Hipódromo – Pista de patinaje
Piscina al aire libre, cubierta
Vista – Panorama – Mesa de Orientación
Monumento – Fuente – Fábrica
Centro comercial – Multicines
Puerto deportivo – Faro – Torreta de telecomunicación
S.N.C.F. Aeropuerto – Boca de metro – Estación de autobuses
Transporte por barco : pasajeros y vehículos, pasajeros solamente
③ Referencia común a los planos y a los mapas detallados Michelin
Oficina central de lista de correos – Teléfonos
Hospital – Mercado cubierto – Cuartel
Edificio público localizado con letra :
A C - Cámara de Agricultura – Cámara de Comercio
G H J -Guardia civil – Ayuntamiento – Palacio de Justicia
M P T -Museo – Gobierno civil –Teatro
U -Universidad, Escuela superior
POL. - Policía (en las grandes ciudades: Jefatura)
4.4 18T ⑱ Pasaje bajo (inf. a 4m 50) – Carga limitada (inf. a 19 t)

¡Cuidado! En Francia, nueva numeración de carreteras naciaonales y regionales en curso.

読者の皆様へ

２００９年度版はひとつの歴史的な日を刻んでいます。フランス「ミシュラン・ガイド」の第百号目にあたるのです。

創刊号は１９００年でしたが、世界大戦をはさんだ数年間休刊したため、第百号の出版記念は今年になってしまいました！

したがって、本年はミシュラン・グループをはじめ、実用性と快適さを探し求める読者の皆様方、そして美食やホテル関係者の方々にとって誠に感慨深い年となりましょう。

１９００年にフランスの道路を走っていた車の数は3千台にも満たない状態でした。その頃の旅は、ほとんど冒険に近かったのです！

それでもミシュラン兄弟は鉄のように固い意志で自動車の未来を信じました。自動車の発展を願うだけでなく、ミシュラン兄弟が創設した仏ミシュランタイヤ社の発展の手助けになるよう、旅を楽にするための資料、つまりモバイリビリティを高めるための小さなガイドブックをドライバーに配布することに決めたのです。有名なミシュラン・ガイドの第1号が3万5千部ほどの発行部数で１９００年8月に刊行されました。創刊号の「まえがき」にアンドレ・ミシュランが「このガイドブックは新しい世紀とともに誕生し、その世紀と共に生き続けるだろう」と述べています。この予言は見事に的中しました。しかも、予想を上回るほどに発展していったのです。

ミシュラン・ガイドの第1号は実用情報が満載していました。冒頭の数ページがタイヤの交換や車の整備の方法などに割かれ、たとえば、パリでは自動車メーカーのリストのみ記載されていました。まだホテルやレストランの部はありませんでした。

1921年になってレストランとその独自の分類法がミシュラン・ガイド入りし、初めてパリのホテル・リストが載りました。

1926年に美味しい料理を提供するレストランを示す星が誕生しました。そして1931年、まずはフランスの地方で、続いて1933年にパリで二つ星と三つ星が生まれました。一つ星が「そのカテゴリーの中で非常に美味しい料理を提供するレストラン」、二つ星が「遠回りしてでも訪れる価値があるレストラン」、三つ星が「わざわざ訪れる価値があるレストラン」という星付けの定義は1936年にさかのぼるものですが、それはなお有効で今日までずっと引き継がれています。

ミシュラン・ガイドは、三ツ星レストランから手頃な値段と質のビブ・グルマン、また最高級のホテルから快適なホテルまで、あらゆる機会に対応する皆様のためのガイドブックです。

ミシュラン・ガイドの創刊時に掲げられた「モバイリビリティへの手助け」の哲学は時代の波にも生き残り、ミシュラン社のモットーとなって世界中に普及しました。

赤表紙のミシュラン・ガイドはフランスを離れて欧米からアジアへと発展したのです。西から東へと絶えず最良の美食を追いかけ、才能があれば、たとえそれがどんなもの、どこであろうとも、貪欲に求め続けています。ミシュラン・ガイドの選択基準は創刊以来まったく変わっていません。調査員の独立性に基づいたこの品質保証のおかげで、年を追うごとにミシュラン・ガイドの評判が高まってゆき、あらゆる読者層の信頼を得ることになったのです。

もちろん、ミシュラン・ガイドの第百号にあたる本版はこれまでの規範を破るものではありません。年々充実してゆくその内容を読み取っていただければ幸いです。この第百号出版記念にあたり、ミシュラン・ガイドに長年にわたって信頼を寄せ、ご愛読いただいている-数百万人もの!-読者の皆様方にお礼を申し上げるとともに、109年前の創刊時より私共とともにミシュラン・ガイドを作り上げてくださったこれら多数のホテルならびにレストラン関係者の方々にも敬意を表したいと存じます。

皆様方の移動のお伴をするという、このさりげないアイデアがこつこつと世界中に根を張っていったのです！明日のシェフ、未来のホテルマン、フランスやヨーロッパ、アメリカ、アジアのミシュラン・ガイドの調査員たち、そして貴重でかつ内容豊かなコメントをレターで伝えてくださった読者の皆様方のおかげで、この21世紀もさらにミシュラン・ガイドの新版を重ねることができるものだと確信しております。

Michel Rollier

ミシュラン*CEO*

本書の使い方

観光情報

主要都市からの距離、観光局、観光名所、交通手段、ゴルフ場、レジャー施設など。

宿泊施設

から、：快適さのカテゴリー

から、：そのカテゴリーで特に快適

手頃な値段でクオリティの高いホテル・レストラン

ビブ・グルマン

ビブ・ホテル

レストラン

XXXXX から X：快適さのカテゴリー

XXXXX から X：そのカテゴリーで特に快適

星付きレストラン

✿✿✿ そのために旅行する価値がある卓越した料理

✿✿ 遠回りしてでも訪れる価値がある素晴らしい料理

✿ そのカテゴリーで特に美味しい料理

ABBAYE DE FONTFROIDE – 03 Aude – 344 J4 – see

ABBAYE DE SAINT-WANDRILLE – 18 Cher – 323

ABBEVILLE – 80 Somme – 301 E7 – pop 24 567 – al

Northern France and the Paris Region

Paris 186 – Amiens 51 – Boulogne-sur-M

Dunkerque, ✆ 04 90 31 51 12, by N3 et

Office de tourisme, 1 place de l'Amiral

- office.tourisme.abbeville@wanadoo

of Abbeville, Route du Val, by rte St-V

- ✆ 03 55 35 96 54 - Fax 03 55 35 96

Modern stained-glass windows of S

St-Vulfran collégiate church AED -

Vallée de la Somme★ SE - Châteaux

Les Jardins du Château

rte du Port – ✆ 04 79 01 36 46 – www

hoteljardins.fr – Fax 04 12 23 45 53 –

1st May and 15 August

15 rm – € 55/75 € 85/170 – 3

Rest Les Terrasses – ✆ 04 79 01

Rest Le Cœur d'Or – Closed Mor

◆ Built as a private house in 18

contemporary rooms include s

garden and terraces.

La Feme des Lions

45 rue des Lions, D541 : 1 km

– relaisdelaposte@reservatio

42 rm – € 45/60 € 55/7

◆ Red-brick 18C listed farm

house overlooks meadow

bread and preserves. Imm

Atelier des Saveurs

10 bd Croisette – ✆ 04 7

– atelierdessaveurs@fr

Rest – (booking esser

Spec. Salad of smoke

nuts and pistachios a

des bois and mint.

◆ A country inn wit

terrace with blissf

Amand-Montrond
36 **A1**
30100
uen 106
03 22 24 27 92
25 24 27 96
omme : 4 km
32
church★★ AM**B** - Façade★ of
cher de Perthes★ BY**M**
lle★ S
50
Z **d**
hateau.com – welcome@
December-30 April,
Carte € 25/35
7,50
er only) Menu € 34 – Carte € 17/25
u € 35/65 bi – Carte € 17/25
h modern and stylish public areas. The
art facilities. Sleek restaurant overlooks
AU **c**
www.fermedeslions.com
1 32 25 – www.fermedeslions.com
04 79 01 32 26 – Closed 25 December
Menu € 19 – Carte € 22/45
working farm... with beautiful blue windows;
den room for breakfast, including home-made
16
oms.
Y **a**
Thomas)
– www.atelierdessaveurs.com
nas.fr – Fax 04 79 01 33 17 –Closed July
€ 55/76 (weekdays lunch) – € Carte 48/85
s trotter and apple purée. Braised turbot with pea-
gus. Cannelloni of apricot, Strawberry sorbet, fraises
panelled dining room, with smart first floor bar and
ver the sea.
Y **c**
04 79 02 33 18 – Fax 04 79 01 33 17 –Closed July
Saturday) Menu € 35/47 bi – Carte € 22/35
for this old Abbeville house. Classic
at reasonable prices.

ミシュランの他の刊行物

ミシュラン地図やミシュラン・グリーンガイドにおける施設の所在地

該当地域を確認

巻末に、フランスの地方別地図を掲載しており、該当地域を確認することができます（図番号、経線・緯線間をアルファベット、数字で表記）

ホテル・レストランの所在地を確認

地域の市街地図でホテル、レストランの所在地を確認することができます（アルファベット表記）

ホテル・レストランの簡単な説明

その雰囲気、スタイル、個性、スペシャリテなどが記載されています

静かなホテル

静かなホテル

非常に静かなホテル

設備とサービス

値段

Awards 2009

Distinctions 2009
Le distinzioni 2009
Auszeichnungen 2009
Distinciones 2009

Starred establishments 2009

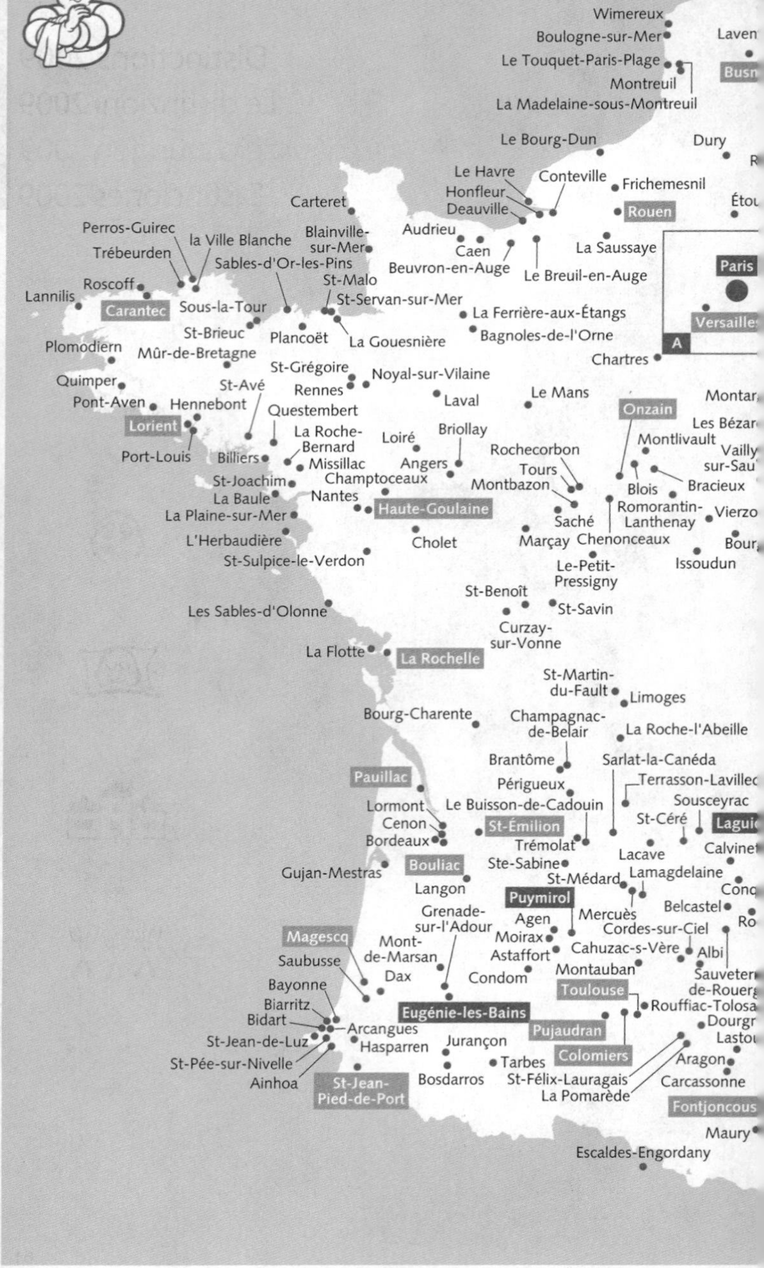

Wimereux
Boulogne-sur-Mer
Laven
Le Touquet-Paris-Plage
Busn
Montreuil
La Madelaine-sous-Montreuil
Le Bourg-Dun
Dury
Le Havre
Conteville
Frichemesnil
Honfleur
Deauville
Rouen
Étou
Carteret
Audrieu
Caen
La Saussaye
Perros-Guirec
la Ville Blanche
Blainville-sur-Mer
Trébeurden
Sables-d'Or-les-Pins
Beuvron-en-Auge
Le Breuil-en-Auge
Paris
Roscoff
St-Malo
Lannilis
Carantec
Sous-la-Tour
St-Servan-sur-Mer
La Ferrière-aux-Étangs
Versailles
St-Brieuc
Plancoët
La Gouesnière
Bagnoles-de-l'Orne
A
Plomodiern
Mûr-de-Bretagne
Chartres
St-Grégoire
Noyal-sur-Vilaine
Quimper
St-Avé
Rennes
Laval
Le Mans
Montar
Pont-Aven
Hennebont
Questembert
Onzain
Lorient
La Roche-Bernard
Loiré
Briollay
Les Bézar
Montlivault
Port-Louis
Billiers
Missillac
Angers
Rochecorbon
Vailly-sur-Sau
St-Joachim
Champtoceaux
Tours
Montbazon
Blois
Bracieux
La Baule
Nantes
Romorantin-Lanthenay
Vierzo
La Plaine-sur-Mer
Haute-Goulaine
Saché
L'Herbaudière
Cholet
Marçay
Chenonceaux
Bour
St-Sulpice-le-Verdon
Issoudun
Le-Petit-Pressigny
St-Benoît
Les Sables-d'Olonne
St-Savin
Curzay-sur-Vonne
La Flotte
La Rochelle
St-Martin-du-Fault
Limoges
Bourg-Charente
Champagnac-de-Belair
La Roche-l'Abeille
Brantôme
Sarlat-la-Canéda
Pauillac
Périgueux
Terrasson-Lavillec
Lormont
Le Buisson-de-Cadouin
Sousceyrac
Cenon
St-Émilion
St-Céré
Lagui
Bordeaux
Trémolat
Calvinet
Lacave
Gujan-Mestras
Bouliac
Ste-Sabine
Lamagdelaine
Langon
St-Médard
Conq
Puymirol
Belcastel
Grenade-sur-l'Adour
Agen
Mercuès
Ro
Magescq
Moirax
Cordes-sur-Ciel
Mont-de-Marsan
Astaffort
Cahuzac-s-Vère
Albi
Saubusse
Montauban
Sauveter-de-Rouerg
Dax
Condom
Bayonne
Toulouse
Biarritz
Eugénie-les-Bains
Rouffiac-Tolosa
Bidart
Arcangues
Pujaudran
Dourgr
St-Jean-de-Luz
Hasparren
Jurançon
Lastou
St-Pée-sur-Nivelle
Tarbes
Colomiers
Aragon
Ainhoa
St-Jean-Pied-de-Port
Bosdarros
St-Félix-Lauragais
Carcassonne
La Pomarède
Fontjoncous
Maury
Escaldes-Engordany

The colour corresponds to the establishment with the most stars in this location.

Paris — This location has at least one 3 star restaurant. ✻✻✻

Rouen — This location has at least one 2 star restaurant. ✻✻

Rennes — This location has at least one 1 star restaurant. ✻

Starred establishments 2009

The colour corresponds to the establishment with the most stars in this location

Ile-de-France

Provence

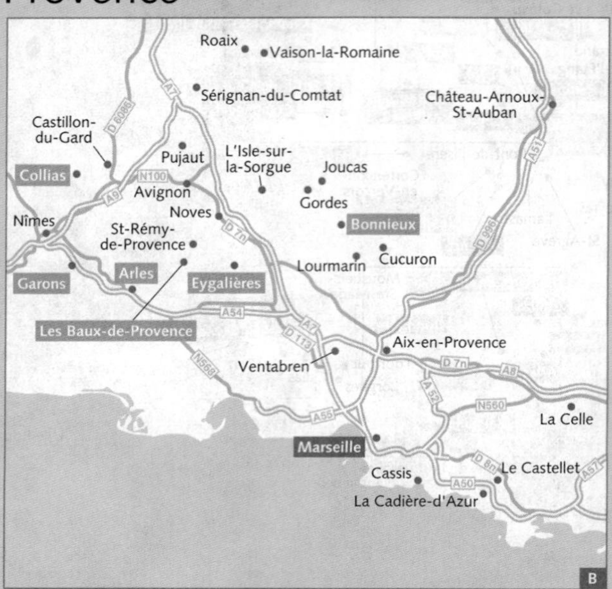

Alsace

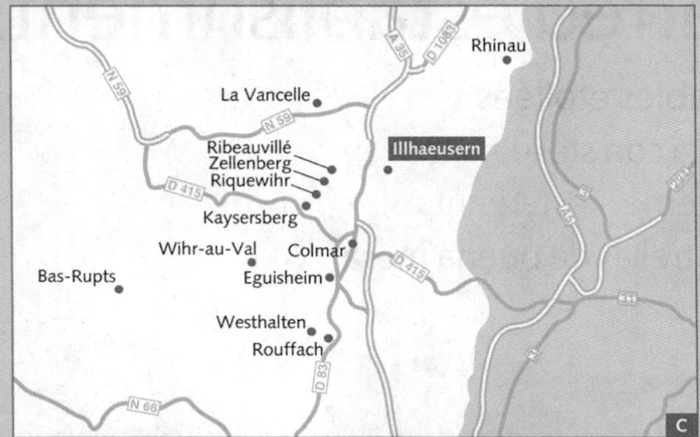
Rhinau
La Vancelle
Illhaeusern
Ribeauvillé
Zellenberg
Riquewihr
Kaysersberg
Wihr-au-Val
Colmar
Bas-Rupts
Eguisheim
Westhalten
Rouffach
N 59
D 415
N 66
D 83
A 35
D 1083
C

Rhône-Alpes

Viré
Montrevel-en-Bresse
Chaintré
Mâcon
Fleurie
La Chapelle-de-Guinchay
Vonnas
Péronnas
Thoiry
Thonon-les-Bains
Douvaine
Bossey
Chasselay
Mionnay
Bagnols
Annecy
Cordon
Chamonix-Mont-Blanc
Veyrier-du-Lac
Talloires
Megève
Charbonnières-les-Bains
Rillieux-la-Pape
Lyon
Jongieux
Le-Bourget-du-Lac
Montrond-les-Bains
Les Catons
Chambéry-le-Vieux
St-Just-St-Rambert
Vienne
La Tania
Val-d'Isère
Courchevel 1850
St-Étienne
Chonas-l'Amballan
Andrezieux-Bouthéon
Val-Thorens
St-Martin-de-Belleville
N79
A40
A6
D 1083
N7
A 42
D 1504
A41
D 1005
D 1090
A43
A47
A48
D 1006
A 41
A7
A5
D

Côte-d'Azur

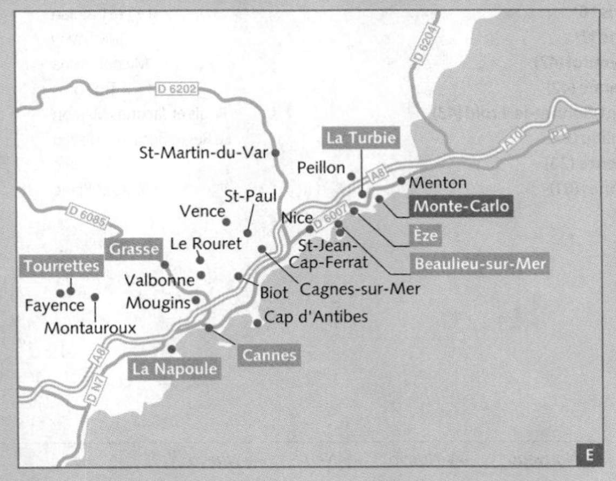
D 6202
D 6204
La Turbie
St-Martin-du-Var
Peillon
Menton
St-Paul
Monte-Carlo
Vence
Nice
Èze
Grasse
Le Rouret
St-Jean-Cap-Ferrat
Beaulieu-sur-Mer
Tourrettes
Valbonne
Biot
Cagnes-sur-Mer
Fayence
Mougins
Montauroux
Cap d'Antibes
Cannes
La Napoule
D 6085
D 6007
A8
A10
D N7
E

Starred establishments

Les Tables étoilées
Esercizi con stelle
Die Sterne-Restaurants
Las estrellas de buena mesa

100th Edition

✿✿✿ 2009

Annecy / Veyrier-du-Lac (74)	La Maison de Marc Veyrat
Baerenthal / Untermuhlthal (57)	L'Arnsbourg
Chagny (71)	Lameloise
Eugénie-les-Bains (40)	Les Prés d'Eugénie
Illhaeusern (68)	Auberge de l'Ill
Joigny (89)	La Côte St-Jacques
Laguiole (12)	Bras
Lyon (69)	Paul Bocuse
Marseille (13)	Le Petit Nice
Monte-Carlo (MC)	Le Louis XV-Alain Ducasse
Paris 1er	le Meurice
Paris 4e	L'Ambroisie
Paris 7e	Arpège
Paris 8e	Alain Ducasse au Plaza Athénée
Paris 8e	Le Bristol **N**
Paris 8e	Ledoyen
Paris 8e	Pierre Gagnaire
Paris 16e	Astrance
Paris 16e	Le Pré Catelan
Paris 17e	Guy Savoy
Puymirol (47)	Michel Trama
Roanne (42)	Troisgros
Saint-Bonnet-le-Froid (43)	Régis et Jacques Marcon
Saulieu (21)	Le Relais Bernard Loiseau
Valence (26)	Pic
Vonnas (01)	Georges Blanc

→ **N** *New* → *Nouveau* → *Nuovo* → *Neu* → *Nuevo*

✿✿ 2009

→ *In red the 2009 Rising Stars for ✿✿✿* → *En rouge les espoirs 2009 pour ✿✿✿*
→ *In rosso le promesse 2009 per ✿✿✿* → *In rote die Hoffnungsträger 2009 fur ✿✿✿*
→ *In rojo las mesas 2009 con posibilidades para ✿✿✿*

Annecy (74) Le Clos des Sens
Arbois (39) Jean-Paul Jeunet
Arles (13) L'Atelier de Jean Luc Rabanel **N**
Les Baux-de-Provence (13) L' Oustaù de Baumanière
Beaulieu-sur-Mer (06) La Réserve de Beaulieu
Béthune / Busnes (62) Le Château de Beaulieu
Bonnieux (84) La Bastide de Capelongue
Bordeaux / Bouliac (33) Le St-James **N**
Le-Bourget-du-Lac (73) Le Bateau Ivre
Calvi (2B) La Villa
Cannes (06) La Palme d'Or
Carantec (29) L'Hôtel de Carantec-Patrick Jeffroy
Chamonix-Mont-Blanc (74) Hameau Albert 1er
Chasselay (69) Guy Lassausaie **N**
Courchevel / Courchevel 1850 (73) Le Bateau Ivre
Courchevel / Courchevel 1850 (73) Le Chabichou
Eygalières (13) Bistrot d'Eygalières "Chez Bru"
Èze (06) Château de la Chèvre d'Or
Fontjoncouse (11) Auberge du Vieux Puits
Grasse (06) La Bastide St-Antoine
Gundershoffen (67) Au Cygne
L'Isle-Jourdain / Pujaudran (32) Le Puits St-Jacques
Lorient (56) L'Amphitryon
Lyon (69) Auberge de l'Île
Lyon (69) Mère Brazier **N**
Lyon (69) Nicolas Le Bec
Lyon / Charbonnières-les-Bains (69) La Rotonde
Magescq (40) Relais de la Poste
Mandelieu / La Napoule (06) L'Oasis
Megève / Leutaz (74) Flocons de Sel
Mionnay (01) Alain Chapel
Monte-Carlo (MC) Joël Robuchon Monte-Carlo
Montpellier (34) Le Jardin des Sens
Nantes / Haute-Goulaine (44) Manoir de la Boulaie
Nîmes / Garons (30) Alexandre
Obernai (67) La Fourchette des Ducs
Onzain (41) Domaine des Hauts de Loire
Paris 1er Carré des Feuillants
Paris 1er L'Espadon **N**
Paris 1er Le Grand Véfour
Paris 6e Hélène Darroze-La Salle à Manger
Paris 6e Relais Louis XIII
Paris 7e L'Atelier de Joël Robuchon
Paris 8e Les Ambassadeurs
Paris 8e Apicius
Paris 8e Le "Cinq"
Paris 8e Lasserre
Paris 8e Senderens
Paris 8e Taillevent
Paris 16e La Table de Joël Robuchon
Paris 17e Michel Rostang
Pauillac (33) Château Cordeillan Bages
Pont-du-Gard / Collias (30) Hostellerie Le Castellas **N**
Porto-Vecchio (2A) Casadelmar **N**
Reims (51) L'Assiette Champenoise
Reims (51) Château les Crayères
La Rochelle (17) Richard et Christopher Coutanceau
Romans-sur-Isère / Granges-les-Beaumont (26) Les Cèdres
Rouen (76) Gill
Saint-Émilion (33) Hostellerie de Plaisance
Saint-Jean-Pied-de-Port (64) Les Pyrénées
Saint-Just-Saint-Rambert (42) Le Neuvième Art
Saint-Martin-de-Belleville (73) La Bouitte
Sens (89) La Madeleine
Strasbourg (67) Au Crocodile
Toulouse (31) Michel Sarran
Toulouse / Colomiers (31) L'Amphitryon
Tourrettes (83) Faventia **N**
La Turbie (06) Hostellerie Jérôme
Uriage-les-Bains (38) Grand Hôtel
Versailles (78) Gordon Ramsay au Trianon **N**
Vézelay / Saint-Père (89) L'Espérance
Vienne (38) La Pyramide

→ **N** *New* → *Nouveau* → *Nuovo* → *Neu* → *Nuevo*

✿ 2009

→ *In red the 2009 Rising Stars for* ✿✿
→ *In rosso le promesse 2009 per* ✿✿
→ *In rojo las mesas 2009 con posibilidades para* ✿✿
→ *En rouge les espoirs 2009 pour* ✿✿
→ *In rote die Hoffnungsträger 2009 fur* ✿✿

Agen (47) Mariottat
Agen / Moirax (47) Auberge le Prieuré
Ainhoa (64) Ithurria
Aix-en-Provence (13) Le Clos de la Violette
Aix-en-Provence (13) Pierre Reboul
Albi (81) L'Esprit du Vin
Alleyras (43) Le Haut-Allier
Ambierle (42) Le Prieuré **N**
Amiens / Dury (80) L'Aubergade
Andrézieux-Bouthéon (42) Les Iris
Anduze / Tornac (30) Les Demeures du Ranquet
Angers (49) Le Favre d'Anne
Annecy (74) Le Belvédère
Annecy (74) La Ciboulette
Antibes / Cap d'Antibes (06) Bacon
Antibes / Cap d'Antibes (06) Les Pêcheurs
Arles (13) La Chassagnette **N**
Arles (13) Le Cilantro
Arpajon (91) Le Saint Clément
Astaffort (47) Le Square "Michel Latrille"
Astaffort (47) Une Auberge en Gascogne
Aulnay-sous-Bois (93) Auberge des Saints Pères
Aumont-Aubrac (48) Chez Camillou
Auxerre (89) Barnabet
Avignon (84) Christian Étienne
Avignon (84) La Mirande
Avignon (84) Le Saule Pleureur **N**
Azay-le-Rideau / Saché (37) Auberge du XIIe Siècle
Bagnoles-de-l'Orne (61) Le Manoir du Lys
Bagnols (69) Château de Bagnols
Barbizon (77) Les Pléiades **N**
Barneville-Carteret / Carteret (50) De la Marine
La Baule (44) Castel Marie-Louise
Les Baux-de-Provence (13) La Cabro d'Or
Bayeux / Audrieu (14) Château d'Audrieu
Bayonne (64) Auberge du Cheval Blanc
Beaune (21) Le Bénaton
Beaune (21) Le Jardin des Remparts
Beaune / Levernois (21) Hostellerie de Levernois
Beaune / Pernand-Vergelesses (21) Le Charlemagne
Belcastel (12) Vieux Pont
Belle-Église (60) La Grange de Belle-Église
Belleville (54) Le Bistroquet
Beuvron-en-Auge (14) Le Pavé d'Auge
Les Bézards (45) Auberge des Templiers
Béziers (34) L'Ambassade
Béziers (34) Octopus
Biarritz (64) Du Palais
Biarritz (64) Les Rosiers **N**
Biarritz / Arcangues (64) Le Moulin d'Alotz
Bidart (64) Table et Hostellerie des Frères Ibarboure
Billiers (56) Domaine de Rochevilaine
Biot (06) Les Terraillers
Bitche (57) Le Strasbourg **N**
Blainville-sur-Mer (50) Le Mascaret **N**
Blois (41) Au Rendez-vous des Pêcheurs
Blois (41) Le Médicis
Blois (41) L'Orangerie du Château
Bonnétage (25) L'Etang du Moulin
Bordeaux (33) Le Chapon Fin
Bordeaux (33) Le Pavillon des Boulevards
Bordeaux / Cenon (33) La Cape
Bordeaux / Lormont (33) Jean-Marie Amat
Bosdarros (64) Auberge Labarthe
Bougival (78) Le Camélia
Boulogne-Billancourt (92) Au Comte de Gascogne
Boulogne-Billancourt (92) Ducoté Cuisine **N**
Boulogne-sur-Mer (62) La Matelote
Le Bourg-Dun (76) Auberge du Dun
Bourg-en-Bresse / Péronnas (01) La Marelle
Bourges (18) L' Abbaye St-Ambroix
Bourges (18) Le d'Antan Sancerrois **N**
Bourges (18) Le Piet à Terre **N**
Le-Bourget-du-Lac (73) Auberge Lamartine
Le-Bourget-du-Lac / Les Catons (73) Atmosphères **N**
Bracieux (41) Bernard Robin - Le Relais de Bracieux
Brantôme (24) Le Moulin de l'Abbaye
Brantôme / Champagnac-de-Belair (24) Le Moulin du Roc
Le Breuil-en-Auge (14) Le Dauphin
Briollay (49) Château de Noirieux
Le Buisson-de-Cadouin (24) Le Manoir de Bellerive
La Bussière-sur-Ouche (21) Abbaye de la Bussière

→ **N** *New* → *Nouveau* → *Nuovo* → *Neu* → *Nuevo*

La Cadière-d'Azur (83) Hostellerie Bérard
Caen (14) Incognito **N**
Cagnes-sur-Mer (06) Josy-Jo
Cahors / Lamagdelaine (46) Claude et Richard Marco
Cahors / Mercuès (46) Château de Mercuès
Cahuzac-sur-Vère (81) Château de Salettes
Cahuzac-sur-Vère (81 La Falaise **N**
Callas (83) Hostellerie Les Gorges de Pennafort
Calvi (2B) Emile's **N**
Calvinet (15) Beauséjour
Carcassonne (11) De La Cité
Carcassonne (11) Domaine d'Auriac
Carcassonne (11) Le Parc Franck Putelat
Carcassonne / Aragon (11) La Bergerie **N**
Cassis (13) La Villa Madie
Le Castellet (83) Du Castellet
La Celle (83) Hostellerie de l'Abbaye de la Celle
Chablis (89) Hostellerie des Clos
Chaintré (71) La Table de Chaintré
Châlons-en-Champagne (51) D'Angleterre
Chalon-sur-Saône / Saint-Rémy (71) Moulin de Martorey
Chambéry / Chambéry-le-Vieux (73) Château de Candie
Chamesol (25) Mon Plaisir
Chamonix-Mont-Blanc (74) Le Bistrot
Champtoceaux (49) Les Jardins de la Forge
Chantilly (60) Dolce Chantilly
La Chapelle-de-Guinchay (71) La Poularde **N**
Chartres (28) Le Grand Monarque **N**
Chassagne-Montrachet (21) Le Chassagne **N**
Château-Arnoux-Saint-Auban (04) La Bonne Étape
Châteaufort (78) La Belle Époque
Chenonceaux (37) Auberge du Bon Laboureur
Chinon / Marçay (37) Château de Marçay
Cholet (49) Au Passé Simple **N**
Clères / Frichemesnil (76) Au Souper Fin
Clermont / Étouy (60) L'Orée de la Forêt
Clermont-Ferrand (63) Emmanuel Hodencq
Clermont-Ferrand (63) Jean-Claude Leclerc
Collioure (66) Relais des Trois Mas **N**
Colmar (68) JY'S
Colmar (68) Rendez-vous de Chasse
Colombey-les-Deux-Églises (52) Hostellerie la Montagne
Compiègne / Rethondes (60) Alain Blot
Condom (32) La Table des Cordeliers
Conques (12) Le Moulin de Cambelong
Conteville (27) Auberge du Vieux Logis **N**
Cordes-sur-Ciel (81) Le Grand Écuyer
Cordon (74) Les Roches Fleuries
Couilly-Pont-aux-Dames (77) Auberge de la Brie
Courcelles-sur-Vesle (02) Château de Courcelles
Courchevel / Courchevel 1850 (73) Le Kilimandjaro **N**
Courchevel / La Tania (73) Le Farçon
Cucuron (84) La Petite Maison **N**
Curzay-sur-Vonne (86) Château de Curzay
Dampierre-en-Yvelines (78) Auberge du Château "Table des Blot"
Dax (40) Une Cuisine en Ville
Deauville (14) Royal-Barrière
Les Deux-Alpes (38) Chalet Mounier **N**
Dijon (21) Hostellerie du Chapeau Rouge
Dijon (21) Le Pré aux Clercs
Dijon (21) Stéphane Derbord
Dijon / Prenois (21) Auberge de la Charme **N**
Dole (39) La Chaumière
Dole / Sampans (39) Château du Mont Joly
Dourgne (81) Les Saveurs de St-Avit **N**
Douvaine (74) Ô Flaveurs
Eguisheim (68) Caveau d'Eguisheim
Épernay (51) Les Berceaux
Épernay / Vinay (51) Hostellerie La Briqueterie
Épinal (88) Ducs de Lorraine
Erbalunga (2B) Le Pirate
Escaldes-Engordany (AN) Aquarius
Èze (06) Château Eza
Fayence (83) Le Castellaras
Flers / La Ferrière-aux-Étangs (61) Auberge de la Mine
Fleurie (69) Le Cep
Forbach / Stiring-Wendel (57) La Bonne Auberge
Gérardmer / Bas-Rupts (88) Les Bas-Rupts
Gignac (34) de Lauzun **N**
Gordes (84) Les Bories et Spa
La Gouesnière (35) Maison Tirel-Guérin
Grasse (06) Lou Fassum "La Tourmaline"
Grenade-sur-l'Adour (40) Pain Adour et Fantaisie
Gujan-Mestras (33) La Guérinière
Hagondange (57) Quai des Saveurs **N**
Hasparren (64) Ferme Hégia
Le Havre (76) Jean-Luc Tartarin **N**
Hennebont (56) Château de Locguénolé
Honfleur (14) Sa. Qua. Na
Honfleur (14) La Terrasse et l'Assiette
Île de Noirmoutier / L'Herbaudière (85) La Marine

→ **N** *New* → *Nouveau* → *Nuovo* → *Neu* → *Nuevo*

Île de Porquerolles (83)	Mas du Langoustier
Île de Ré / La Flotte (17)	Richelieu
L'Île-Rousse (2B)	Pasquale Paoli **N**
L'Isle-sur-la-Sorgue (84)	Le Vivier
Issoudun (36)	Rest. La Cognette
Jarnac / Bourg-Charente (16)	La Ribaudière
Jongieux (73)	Auberge Les Morainières
Joucas (84)	Hostellerie Le Phébus
Joucas (84)	Le Mas des Herbes Blanches
Kaysersberg (68)	Chambard
Lacave (46)	Château de la Treyne
Lacave (46)	Pont de l'Ouysse
Laguiole (12)	Grand Hôtel Auguy
Lamastre (07)	Midi
Langon (33)	Claude Darroze
Languimberg (57)	Chez Michèle **N**
Lannilis (29)	Auberge des Abers **N**
Lannion / la Ville Blanche (22)	La Ville Blanche
Lastours (11)	Le Puits du Trésor
Laval (53)	Bistro de Paris
Le Lavandou / Aiguebelle (83)	Mathias Dandine
Laventie (62)	Le Cerisier
Lembach (67)	Auberge du Cheval Blanc **N**
Lezoux / Bort-l'Étang (63)	Château de Codignat
Lièpvre / La Vancelle (67)	Auberge Frankenbourg
Ligny-en-Cambrésis (59)	Château de Ligny
Lille (59)	A L'Huîtrière
Lille (59)	La Laiterie
Lille (59)	Le Sébastopol
Lille / Bondues (59)	Val d'Auge
Limoges (87)	Amphitryon
Limoges / Saint-Martin-du-Fault (87)	La Chapelle St-Martin
Loiré (49)	Auberge de la Diligence
Lorgues (83)	Bruno
Lorient (56)	Henri et Joseph
Lourmarin (84)	Auberge La Fenière
Lunéville (54)	Château d'Adoménil
Lyon (69)	L' Alexandrin
Lyon (69)	Auberge de Fond Rose
Lyon (69)	Christian Têtedoie
Lyon (69)	Le Gourmet de Sèze
Lyon (69)	Pierre Orsi
Lyon (69)	Les Terrasses de Lyon
Lyon (69)	Les Trois Dômes
Lyon / Rillieux-la-Pape (69)	Larivoire
Mâcon (71)	Pierre
Maisons-Laffitte (78)	Tastevin
Malbuisson (25)	Le Bon Accueil
Le Mans (72)	Le Beaulieu
Marlenheim (67)	Le Cerf
Marseille (13)	L'Épuisette
Marseille (13)	Péron
Marseille (13)	Une Table au Sud
Maury (66)	Pascal Borrell
Melun / Vaux-le-Pénil (77)	La Table St-Just
Menton (06)	Mirazur
Menton (06)	Paris Rome
Metz (57)	Citadelle
Metz (57)	L'Écluse
Meudon (92)	L'Escarbille
Missillac (44)	La Bretesche
Montargis (45)	La Gloire
Montauban (82)	Crowne Plaza
Montauroux (83)	Auberge des Fontaines d'Aragon
Montbazon (37)	Chancelière "Jeu de Cartes"
Montbéliard (25)	Le St-Martin
Montceau-les-Mines (71)	Le France
Mont-de-Marsan (40)	Les Clefs d'Argent **N**
Monte-Carlo (MC)	Bar Boeuf & Co
Monte-Carlo (MC)	Grill de l'Hôtel de Paris
Monte-Carlo (MC)	Mandarine **N**
Montlivault (41)	La Maison d'à Côté **N**
Montreuil (62)	Château de Montreuil
Montreuil / La Madelaine-sous-Montreuil (62)	Auberge de la Grenouillère
Montrevel-en-Bresse (01)	Léa
Montrond-les-Bains (42)	Hostellerie La Poularde
Morteau (25)	Auberge de la Roche
Mougins (06)	Le Mas Candille
Moustiers-Sainte-Marie (04)	Bastide de Moustiers
Mulhouse (68)	Il Cortile
Mulhouse / Landser (68)	Hostellerie Paulus
Mulhouse / Riedisheim (68)	La Poste
Munster / Wihr-au-Val (68)	Nouvelle Auberge **N**
Mûr-de-Bretagne (22)	Auberge Grand'Maison **N**
Nancy (54)	Le Grenier à Sel
Nantes (44)	L'Atlantide
Narbonne (11)	La Table St-Crescent
Neuilly-sur-Seine (92)	La Truffe Noire
Nevers (58)	Jean-Michel Couron
Nice (06)	Chantecler
Nice (06)	Jouni "Atelier du Goût"
Nice (06)	Keisuke Matsushima
Nice (06)	L'Univers-Christian Plumail
Nîmes (30)	Le Lisita
Noves (13)	Auberge de Noves
Obernai (67)	Le Bistro des Saveurs
Orange / Sérignan-du-Comtat (84)	Le Pré du Moulin
Paris 1er	Gérard Besson

→ **N** *New* → *Nouveau* → *Nuovo* → *Neu* → *Nuevo*

Paris 2e	Le Céladon
Paris 2e	Le Pur' Grill
Paris 4e	Benoit
Paris 5e	La Tour d'Argent
Paris 6e	Fogón **N**
Paris 6e	Jacques Cagna
Paris 6e	Paris
Paris 6e	Le Restaurant
Paris 6e	Ze Kitchen Galerie
Paris 7e	Aida
Paris 7e	Auguste
Paris 7e	Les Fables de La Fontaine
Paris 7e	Gaya Rive Gauche par Pierre Gagnaire
Paris 7e	Il Vino d'Enrico Bernardo
Paris 7e	Le Jules Verne **N**
Paris 7e	Le Divellec
Paris 7e	35 ° Ouest **N**
Paris 7e	Vin sur Vin
Paris 7e	Le Violon d'Ingres
Paris 8e	L'Angle du Faubourg
Paris 8e	L'Arôme **N**
Paris 8e	Le Chiberta
Paris 8e	Dominique Bouchet
Paris 8e	Laurent
Paris 8e	Stella Maris
Paris 8e	La Table du Lancaster
Paris 9e	Jean
Paris 12e	Au Trou Gascon
Paris 14e	Montparnasse'25
Paris 16e	etc... **N**
Paris 16e	La Grande Cascade
Paris 16e	Hiramatsu
Paris 16e	Passiflore
Paris 16e	Le Pergolèse
Paris 16e	Relais d'Auteuil
Paris 16e	La Table du Baltimore
Paris 17e	Agapé **N**
Paris 17e	Bath's
Paris 17e	Bigarrade **N**
Paris 17e	La Braisière
Pau / Jurançon (64)	Chez Ruffet
Peillon (06)	Auberge de la Madone
Périgueux (24)	L'Essentiel
Perpignan (66)	La Galinette
Perpignan (66)	Park Hôtel **N**
Le Perreux-sur-Marne (94)	Les Magnolias
Perros-Guirec (22)	La Clarté
Le-Petit-Pressigny (37)	La Promenade
Phalsbourg (57)	Au Soldat de l'An II
La Plaine-sur-Mer (44)	Anne de Bretagne
Plancoët (22)	Maxime et Jean-Pierre Crouzil et Hôtel L'Ecrin
Plomodiern (29)	Auberge des Glazicks
Poitiers / Saint-Benoît (86)	Passions et Gourmandises
La Pomarède (11)	Hostellerie du Château de la Pomarède
Pont-Aven (29)	Moulin de Rosmadec
Pont-Aven (29)	La Taupinière
Pont-du-Gard / Castillon-du-Gard (30)	Le Vieux Castillon
Port-Lesney (39)	Château de Germigney
Port-Louis (56)	Avel Vor
Porto-Vecchio (2A)	Belvédère
Porto-Vecchio (2A)	Grand Hôtel de Cala Rossa
Port-sur-Saône / Vauchoux (70)	Château de Vauchoux
Pujaut (30)	Entre Vigne et Garrigue **N**
Le Puy-en-Velay (43)	François Gagnaire
Questembert (56)	Le Bretagne et sa Résidence
Quimper (29)	La Roseraie de Bel Air
Reims (51)	Le Foch
Reims (51)	Le Millénaire
Reims / Montchenot (51)	Grand Cerf
Rennes (35)	Coq-Gadby
Rennes (35)	La Fontaine aux Perles
Rennes / Noyal-sur-Vilaine (35)	Auberge du Pont d'Acigné
Rennes / Saint-Grégoire (35)	Le Saison
Reuilly-Sauvigny (02)	Auberge Le Relais
Rhinau (67)	Au Vieux Couvent
Ribeauvillé (68)	Au Valet de Cœur et Hostel de la Pépinière
Riquewihr (68)	Table du Gourmet
Riquewihr / Zellenberg (68)	Maximilien
Roanne / Le Coteau (42)	L'Auberge Costelloise
La Roche-Bernard (56)	L'Auberge Bretonne
La Roche-l'Abeille (87)	Le Moulin de la Gorce
Rodez (12)	Goûts et Couleurs
Romorantin-Lanthenay (41)	Grand Hôtel du Lion d'Or
Roscoff (29)	Le Brittany
Roscoff (29)	Le Temps de Vivre
Rosheim (67)	Hostellerie du Rosenmeer
Rouen (76)	Les Nymphéas
Rouffach (68)	Philippe Bohrer
Le Rouret (06)	Le Clos St-Pierre
Roye (80)	La Flamiche
Les Sables-d'Olonne / Anse de Cayola (85)	Cayola
Sables-d'Or-les-Pins (22)	La Voile d'Or - La Lagune
Saint-Agrève (07)	Faurie
Saint-Brieuc (22)	Aux Pesked
Saint-Brieuc (22)	Youpala Bistrot

→ **N** *New* → *Nouveau* → *Nuovo* → *Neu* → *Nuevo*

Saint-Brieuc / Sous-la-Tour (22) La Vieille Tour
Saint-Céré (46) Les Trois Soleils de Montal
Saint-Cyprien (66) L'Île de la Lagune
Saint-Étienne (42) Nouvelle
Saint-Félix-Lauragais (31) Auberge du Poids Public
Saint-Florent (2B) La Roya **N**
Saint-Jean-Cap-Ferrat (06) Le Cap
Saint-Jean-Cap-Ferrat (06) La Table du Cap **N**
Saint-Jean-de-Luz (64) Grand Hôtel
Saint-Joachim (44) La Mare aux Oiseaux **N**
Saint-Julien-en-Genevois / Bossey (74) La Ferme de l'Hospital
Saint-Malo (35) A la Duchesse Anne
Saint-Malo (35) Le Chalut
Saint-Malo / Saint-Servan-sur-Mer (35) Le St-Placide
Saint-Martin-du-Var (06) Jean-François Issautier
Saint-Maur-des-Fossés / La Varenne-Saint-Hilaire (94) La Bretèche
Saint-Médard (46) Gindreau
Saint-Paul (06) Le Saint-Paul
Saint-Pée-sur-Nivelle (64) L' Auberge Basque **N**
Saint-Rémy-de-Provence (13) La Maison de Bournissac
Saint-Rémy-de-Provence (13) La Maison Jaune
Saint-Rémy-de-Provence (13) Marc de Passorio **N**
Saint-Savin (86) Christophe Cadieu
Saint-Sulpice-le-Verdon (85) Thierry Drapeau Logis de la Chabotterie
Saint-Tropez (83) Résidence de la Pinède
Saint-Tropez (83) Villa Belrose
Sainte-Sabine (24) Étincelles-La Gentilhommière **N**
Sarlat-la-Canéda (24) Le Grand Bleu
Sarrebourg (57) Mathis
Sarreguemines (57) Auberge St-Walfrid
Saubusse (40) Villa Stings
La Saussaye (27) Manoir des Saules
Sauveterre-de-Rouergue (12) Le Sénéchal
Sénart / Pouilly-le-Fort (77) Le Pouilly
Sennecey-le-Grand (71) L'Amaryllis
Sierentz (68) Auberge St-Laurent
Sousceyrac (46) Au Déjeuner de Sousceyrac
Strasbourg (67) Buerehiesel
Strasbourg (67) La Casserole
Strasbourg (67) Umami **N**
Talloires (74) L'Auberge du Père Bise
Tarbes (65) L'Ambroisie
Terrasson-Lavilledieu (24) L'Imaginaire
Thoiry (01) Les Cépages
Thonon-les-Bains (74) Le Prieuré
Toulouse (31) En Marge
Toulouse (31) Metropolitan
Toulouse / Rouffiac-Tolosan (31) Ô Saveurs
Le Touquet-Paris-Plage (62) Westminster
Tournus (71) Aux Terrasses
Tournus (71) Rest. Greuze **N**
Tours (37) Charles Barrier
Tours (37) Rive Gauche **N**
Tours (37) La Roche Le Roy
Tours / Rochecorbon (37) Les Hautes Roches
Tourtour (83) Les Chênes Verts
Trébeurden (22) Manoir de Lan-Kerellec
Le Tremblay-sur-Mauldre (78) Laurent Trochain
Trémolat (24) Vieux Logis
Troyes / Pont-Sainte-Marie (10) Hostellerie de Pont-Ste-Marie
Vailly-sur-Sauldre (18) Le Lièvre Gourmand
Vaison-la-Romaine (84) Le Moulin à Huile
Vaison-la-Romaine / Roaix (84) Le Grand Pré
Valbonne (06) Lou Cigalon
Val-d'Isère (73) Les Barmes de l'Ours
Valence (26) La Cachette **N**
Valence (26) Flaveurs **N**
Valence / Pont-de-l'Isère (26) Michel Chabran
Val-Thorens (73) L'Oxalys
Vannes / Saint-Avé (56) Le Pressoir
Vence (06) Les Bacchanales **N**
Vence (06) Château St-Martin & Spa **N**
Ventabren (13) La Table de Ventabren **N**
Versailles (78) L'Angélique **N**
Vichy (03) Maison Decoret
Vienne / Chonas-l'Amballan (38) Domaine de Clairefontaine
Vierzon (18) La Maison de Célestin
Villard-de-Lans / Corrençon-en-Vercors (38) du Golf
Villers-le-Lac (25) Le France
Viré (71) Relais de Montmartre **N**
Westhalten (68) Auberge du Cheval Blanc
Wimereux (62) Epicure
Zoufftgen (57) La Lorraine

→ **N** *New* → *Nouveau* → *Nuovo* → *Neu* → *Nuevo*

THE 2009 RISING STARS FOR ✿

Les espoirs 2009 pour ✿
Le promesse 2009 per ✿
Die Hoffnungsträger 2009 fur ✿
Las mesas 2009
con posibilidades para ✿

Belfort / Danjoutin (90)	Le Pot d'Étain
Bormes-les-Mimosas (83)	La Rastègue
Carcassonne / Pezens (11)	L'Ambrosia
Clermont-Ferrand (63)	Fleur de Sel
Dijon / Marsannay-la-Côte (21)	Les Gourmets
Istres (13)	La Table de Sébastien
Lumio (2B)	Chez Charles
Lyon (69)	La Rémanence
Montpellier (34)	La Réserve Rimbaud
Névez / Raguenès-Plage (29)	Ar Men Du
Nice (06)	L'Aromate
Niederschaeffolsheim (67)	Au Bœuf Rouge
Porto-Vecchio (2A)	Le Troubadour
Saverne (67)	Kasbür

Bib Gourmand

Good food at moderate prices
Repas soignés à prix modérés
Pasti accurati a prezzi contenuti
Sorgfältig zubereitete, preiswerte mahlzeiten
Buenas comidas a precios moderados

Abbeville (80) — La Corne
Agde / Le Grau-d'Agde (34) — L'Adagio
Agen (47) — Le Margoton
Aiguebelette-le-Lac / Novalaise (73) — Novalaise-Plage
Aire-sur-la-Lys / Isbergues (62) — Le Buffet
Aix-en-Provence / Le Canet (13) — L'Auberge Provençale
Aix-les-Bains (73) — Auberge St-Simond **N**
Aizenay (85) — La Sittelle
Ajaccio (2A) — U Licettu
Albi (81) — La Table du Sommelier **N**
Alès / Méjannes-lès-Alès (30) — Auberge des Voutins
Altwiller (67) — L'Écluse 16
Ambert (63) — Les Copains
Ambronay (01) — Auberge de l'Abbaye
Amiens (80) — Au Relais des Orfèvres
Ammerschwihr (68) — Aux Armes de France
Ancenis (44) — La Toile à Beurre
Angers (49) — Le Relais
Angoulême (16) — L'Aromate
Angoulême (16) — Le Terminus
Annecy (74) — Contresens
Annonay (07) — Marc et Christine
Antibes (06) — Oscar's
Antraigues-sur-Volane (07) — La Remise
Argoules (80) — Auberge du Coq-en-Pâte
Asnières-sur-Seine (92) — La Petite Auberge
Aube (61) — Auberge St-James
Aumont-Aubrac (48) — Le Compostelle
Aumont-Aubrac (48) — Le Gabale **N**
Autun (71) — Le Chapitre **N**
Auxerre (89) — Le Bourgogne
Auxerre / Vincelottes (89) — Auberge Les Tilleuls
Avallon / Valloux (89) — Auberge des Chenêts
Avignon (84) — L'Essentiel **N**
Ax-les-Thermes (09) — Le Chalet
Azay-le-Rideau (37) — L'Aigle d'Or
Baden (56) — Le Gavrinis
Bâgé-le-Châtel (01) — La Table Bâgésienne
Bagnères-de-Bigorre (65) — L'Auberge Gourmande **N**
Bagnoles-de-l'Orne (61) — Ô Gayot **N**
Ban-de-Laveline (88) — Auberge Lorraine
Bandol (83) — Le Clocher
Banyuls-sur-Mer (66) — Al Fanal et H. El Llagut
Barr (67) — Aux Saisons Gourmandes
Bar-sur-Aube (10) — La Toque Baralbine
Bastia (2B) — La Corniche
La Bâtie-Divisin (38) — L'Olivier
Bayonne (64) — Bayonnais
Bayonne (64) — François Miura
Beaune (21) — La Ciboulette
Beaune / Ladoix-Serrigny (21) — Les Terrasses de Corton
Beaune / Levernois (21) — La Garaudière
Beaune / Levernois (21) — Le Bistrot du Bord de l'Eau **N**
Beauzac (43) — L'Air du Temps
Beauzac / Bransac (43) — La Table du Barret
Bédarieux / Villemagne-l'Argentière (34) — Auberge de l'Abbaye
Bellême / Nocé (61) — Auberge des 3 J.
Belleville (69) — Le Beaujolais
Bergerac / Moulin de Malfourat (24) — La Tour des Vents
Bergheim (68) — Wistub du Sommelier
La Bernerie-en-Retz (44) — L'Artimon
Le Bessat (42) — La Fondue "Chez l'Père Charles"

→ **N** *New* → *Nouveau* → *Nuovo* → *Neu* → *Nuevo*

Béthune / Busnes (62) Le Jardin d'Alice
Biarritz (64) Le Clos Basque
Blangy-sur-Bresle (76) Les Pieds dans le Plat
Blienschwiller (67) Le Pressoir de Bacchus
Blois / Molineuf (41) Poste **N**
Bois-Colombes (92) Le Chefson
Bonlieu (39) La Poutre
Bonneuil-Matours (86) Le Pavillon Bleu
Bonneville / Vougy (74) Le Capucin Gourmand
Bonny-sur-Loire (45) Des Voyageurs
Bordeaux (33) Auberge ' Inn **N**
Bordeaux (33) Gravelier
Boudes (63) Le Boudes La Vigne
Bourg-en-Bresse (01) Les Quatre Saisons
Bourg-en-Bresse (01) Mets et Vins
Bourg-Saint-Maurice (73) L'Arssiban
Bourth (27) Auberge Chantecler
Bouzel (63) L'Auberge du Ver Luisant
Bozouls (12) A la Route d'Argent
Bracieux (41) Le Rendez vous des Gourmets
La Bresse (88) Le Clos des Hortensias
Bretenoux / Port-de-Gagnac (46) Hostellerie Belle Rive
Brévonnes (10) Au Vieux Logis
Briançon (05) Le Péché Gourmand
Brioude (43) Poste et Champanne
Brive-la-Gaillarde (19) La Toupine
Brou (28) L'Ascalier
Buellas (01) L'Auberge Bressane
Bully (69) Auberge du Château
Buxy (71) Aux Années Vins
Buzançais (36) L'Hermitage
Cabourg / Dives-sur-Mer (14) Chez le Bougnat
Caen (14) Café Mancel
Caen (14) Le Bouchon du Vaugueux **N**
Cahors (46) La Garenne
Cahors (46) L'Ô à la Bouche
Calais (62) Au Côte d'Argent
Cambrai (59) Auberge Fontenoise
Cancale (35) Surcouf
Cannes (06) Comme Chez Soi
Carhaix-Plouguer / Port-de-Carhaix (29) Auberge du Poher
Carignan (08) La Gourmandière
Casteljaloux (47) La Vieille Auberge
Castellane / La Garde (04) Auberge du Teillon
Castéra-Verduzan (32) Le Florida
Castillon-en-Couserans / Audressein (09) L'Auberge d'Audressein
Castres / Burlats (81) Les Mets d'Adélaïde **N**
Caussade / Monteils (82) Le Clos Monteils
Cauterets (65) L' Abri du Benques **N**

Challans / La Garnache (85) Le Petit St-Thomas
Challans / Le Perrier (85) Les Tendelles
Chalon-sur-Saône (71) L'Auberge des Alouettes
Chalon-sur-Saône / Saint-Loup-de-Varennes (71) Le Saint Loup **N**
Chamonix-Mont-Blanc (74) Atmosphère
Chamonix-Mont-Blanc (74) La Maison Carrier
Chamonix-Mont-Blanc / Les Praz-de-Chamonix (74) La Cabane des Praz
Chandolas (07) Auberge les Murets
La Chapelle-d'Abondance (74) L'Ensoleillé
La Chapelle-d'Abondance (74) Les Gentianettes
Charette (38) Auberge du Vernay
Charleville-Mézières (08) La Table d' Arthur "R"
Charroux (03) Ferme Saint-Sébastien
Chartres (28) Le St-Hilaire
Châtelaillon-Plage (17) Les Flots
Châtellerault (86) Bernard Gautier
Chavanoz (38) Aux Berges du Rhône **N**
Chénérailles (23) Coq d'Or
Cherbourg-Octeville (50) Café de Paris
Cherbourg-Octeville (50) Le Pily
Cherbourg-Octeville (50) Le Vauban
Chilleurs-aux-Bois (45) Le Lancelot
Chinon (37) L'Océanic
Chisseaux (37) Auberge du Cheval Rouge
Cholet (49) La Grange
Clères (76) Auberge du Moulin
Clermont-Ferrand (63) Amphitryon Capucine
Clermont-Ferrand / Orcines (63) Auberge de la Baraque
Clermont-Ferrand / Puy de Dôme (63) Mont Fraternité
Clisson / Gétigné (44) La Gétignière
Col de la Schlucht (88) Le Collet
Coligny (01) Au Petit Relais
Colmar (68) Aux Trois Poissons
Colmar (68) Chez Hansi
Colmar / Ingersheim (68) La Taverne Alsacienne
Combeaufontaine (70) Le Balcon
Conilhac-Corbières (11) Auberge Coté Jardin
Conques (12) Auberge St-Jacques
Contamine-sur-Arve (74) Le Tourne Bride
Cordon (74) Le Cordonant
Coullons (45) La Canardière
Coulon (79) Le Central
Le Creusot / Montcenis (71) Le Montcenis
Le Croisic (44) Le Saint-Alys

→ **N** *New* → *Nouveau* → *Nuovo* → *Neu* → *Nuevo*

Crozon (29) Le Mutin Gourmand
Cucugnan (11) Auberge de Cucugnan
Daglan (24) Le Petit Paris
Dax (40) L'Amphitryon
Deauville / Touques (14) L 'Orangeraie **N**
Deauville / Touques (14) Les Landiers **N**
Dijon (21) Du Nord **N**
Dijon / Chenôve (21) Le Clos du Roy
Dinan (22) Au Coin du Feu **N**
Douarnenez (29) Le Clos de Vallombreuse
Doué-la-Fontaine (49) Auberge Bienvenue
Draguignan / Flayosc (83) L'Oustaou
Dreux / Chérisy (28) Le Vallon de Chérisy **N**
Dunes (82) Les Templiers
Dunières (43) La Tour
Dunkerque / Coudekerque-Branche (59) Le Soubise
Épernay (51) La Grillade Gourmande **N**
Espalion (12) Le Méjane
Estaing (12) L' Auberge St-Fleuret
Évreux (27) La Vieille Gabelle **N**
Évron (53) Relais du Gué de Selle
Évron (53) La Toque des Coëvrons
Eygalières (13) Sous Les Micocouliers
Les Eyzies-de-Tayac (24) La Métairie
Faverges (74) Florimont
Favières (80) La Clé des Champs
Fayence (83) La Table d'Yves **N**
Fléré-la-Rivière (36) Le Relais du Berry
Flers (61) Au Bout de la Rue **N**
Florac (48) Des Gorges du Tarn
Florac / Cocurès (48) La Lozerette
Fondamente (12) Baldy
Fontvieille (13) Le Patio
Fontvieille (13) La Table du Meunier
Fouday (67) Julien
Fouesnant / Cap-Coz (29) De la Pointe du Cap Coz
Fougères (35) Haute Sève **N**
Francescas (47) Le Relais de la Hire
Fréjus (83) L'Amandier
Fréjus (83) Les Potiers
Froncles-Buxières (52) Au Château
Gagny (93) Le Vilgacy
Gasny (27) Auberge du Prieuré Normand
Gassin (83) Auberge la Verdoyante
Geneston (44) Le Pélican
Gevrey-Chambertin (21) Chez Guy **N**
Gigondas (84) Les Florets
Gilette / Vescous (06) La Capeline
Gourdon (46) Hostellerie de la Bouriane
Grandcamp-Maisy (14) La Marée
Grandvillers (88) Europe et Commerce
Grenoble (38) Le Coup de Torchon

Gresse-en-Vercors (38) Le Chalet
Le Gua (17) Le Moulin de Châlons **N**
La Guerche-de-Bretagne (35) La Calèche
Guilliers (56) Au Relais du Porhoët
Le Havre (76) La Petite Auberge
Honfleur (14) Le Bréard
Houlgate (14) L'Eden
L'Isle-sur-la-Sorgue (84) L'Oustau de l'Isle **N**
L'Isle-sur-Serein (89) Auberge du Pot d'Étain
Kaysersberg (68) À l'Arbre Vert
Lanarce (07) Le Provence
Langeac / Reilhac (43) Val d'Allier
Langon / Saint-Macaire (33) Abricotier
Lantosque (06) La Source
Largentière / Sanilhac (07) Auberge de la Tour de Brison
Larrau (64) Etchemaïté
Lavelanet / Nalzen (09) Les Sapins
Leutenheim (67) Auberge Au Vieux Couvent
Libourne (33) Chez Servais
Liessies (59) Le Carillon
Lille / Capinghem (59) La Marmite de Pierrot
Limoges (87) Le Vanteaux
Lorris (45) Guillaume de Lorris
Lourdes (65) Alexandra **N**
Le Luc (83) Le Gourmandin
Luché-Pringé (72) Auberge du Port des Roches **N**
Luçon (85) La Mirabelle
Lunel (34) Chodoreille **N**
Lyon (69) Daniel et Denise
Lyon (69) L'Est
Lyon (69) Le Garet
Lyon (69) Léon de Lyon **N**
Lyon (69) M **N**
Lyon (69) Les Oliviers **N**
Lyon (69) L'Ouest **N**
Lyon (69) 33 Cité
Lyon (69) Le Verre et l'Assiette
Lys-Saint-Georges (36) Auberge La Forge **N**
Madiran (65) Le Prieuré **N**
Magalas (34) Ô. Bontemps **N**
Malbuisson / Granges-Sainte-Marie (25) Auberge du Coude
Mancey (71) Auberge du Col des Chèvres
Mansle / Luxé (16) Auberge du Cheval Blanc
Manzac-sur-Vern (24) Le Lion d'Or
Margaux / Arcins (33) Le Lion d'Or
Marseillan (34) Chez Philippe
Mazaye (63) Auberge de Mazayes
Mende (48) Le Mazel
Mende (48) La Safranière
Messery (74) Atelier des Saveurs
Meyronne (46) La Terrasse
Meyrueis (48) Du Mont Aigoual

→ **N** *New* ☺ → *Nouveau* ☺ → *Nuovo* ☺ → *Neu* ☺ → *Nuevo* ☺

Minerve (34)	Relais Chantovent
Mittelbergheim (67)	Am Lindeplatzel
Mittelbergheim (67)	Gilg
Les Molunes (39)	Le Pré Fillet
Monestier-de-Clermont (38)	Au Sans Souci
Montbard / Saint-Rémy (21)	La Mirabelle **N**
Montbrison / Savigneux (42)	Yves Thollot
Montech (82)	La Maison de l'Eclusier
Montmorillon (86)	Hôtel de France et Lucullus
Montpellier (34)	Prouhèze Saveurs
Montpon-Ménestérol / Ménestérol (24)	Auberge de l'Eclade
Montreuil / Inxent (62)	Auberge d'Inxent
Montsalvy (15)	L'Auberge Fleurie
Montsoreau (49)	Diane de Méridor
Mouzon (08)	Les Échevins **N**
Mur-de-Barrez (12)	Auberge du Barrez
Najac (12)	Le Belle Rive
Najac (12)	L' Oustal del Barry
Nancy (54)	V Four
Nantes (44)	La Divate
Nantes / Couëron (44)	François II
Nantes / Saint-Herblain (44)	Les Caudalies
Narbonne / Bages (11)	Le Portanel
Natzwiller (67)	Auberge Metzger
Nestier (65)	Relais du Castéra **N**
Neufchâtel-sur-Aisne (02)	Le Jardin
Neuillé-le-Lierre (37)	Auberge de la Brenne
Nevers (58)	Le Bengy
Nevers / Sauvigny-les-Bois (58)	Moulin de l'Étang
Neyrac-les-Bains (07)	Du Levant
Nice (06)	Au Rendez-vous des Amis
Niedersteinbach (67)	Cheval Blanc
Nîmes (30)	Aux Plaisirs des Halles
Nîmes (30)	Le Bouchon et L'Assiette
Noailhac (81)	Hostellerie d'Oc **N**
Nogent-le-Roi (28)	Relais des Remparts
Nogent-sur-Seine (10)	Beau Rivage
Notre-Dame-de-Bellecombe (73)	La Ferme de Victorine
Noyalo (56)	L'Hortensia
Nuits-Saint-Georges (21)	La Cabotte
Nyons (26)	Le Petit Caveau
Obernai / Ottrott (67)	À l'Ami Fritz
Oisly (41)	St-Vincent **N**
Orange (84)	Le Parvis **N**
Orléans (45)	La Dariole
Orléans (45)	Eugène
Orléans / Olivet (45)	Laurendière
Ornans (25)	Courbet
Oucques (41)	Du Commerce
Pailherols (15)	Auberge des Montagnes
Paimpol (22)	De la Marne
Pamiers (09)	De France
Paris 1er	Au Gourmand
Paris 1er	Willi's Wine Bar **N**
Paris 1er	Zen **N**
Paris 2e	Aux Lyonnais
Paris 3e	Ambassade d'Auvergne
Paris 3e	Café des Musées **N**
Paris 3e	Pramil **N**
Paris 4e	Suan Thaï **N**
Paris 5e	Papilles
Paris 5e	Ribouldingue
Paris 6e	La Maison du Jardin **N**
Paris 6e	Le Timbre **N**
Paris 6e	L'Épi Dupin
Paris 6e	L'Épigramme **N**
Paris 7e	L'Affriolé
Paris 7e	Au Bon Accueil
Paris 7e	Café Constant
Paris 7e	Chez l'Ami Jean
Paris 7e	Chez les Anges
Paris 7e	Le Clos des Gourmets
Paris 7e	Les Cocottes **N**
Paris 9e	La Petite Sirène de Copenhague
Paris 9e	Le Pré Cadet
Paris 9e	Spring
Paris 10e	Café Panique
Paris 10e	Chez Michel
Paris 10e	Urbane
Paris 11e	Auberge Pyrénées Cévennes
Paris 11e	Bistrot Paul Bert **N**
Paris 11e	Mansouria
Paris 12e	L'Auberge Aveyronnaise **N**
Paris 12e	Jean-Pierre Frelet
Paris 13e	Les Cailloux **N**
Paris 13e	Impérial Choisy **N**
Paris 13e	L'Ourcine **N**
Paris 14e	La Cantine du Troquet **N**
Paris 14e	La Cerisaie
Paris 14e	L'Entêtée **N**
Paris 14e	La Régalade
Paris 15e	Afaria
Paris 15e	Le Bélisaire
Paris 15e	Beurre Noisette
Paris 15e	Caroubier
Paris 15e	Le Dirigeable
Paris 15e	Le Grand Pan
Paris 15e	Jadis **N**
Paris 15e	L'Os à Moëlle **N**
Paris 15e	Stéphane Martin
Paris 15e	Le Troquet
Paris 16e	A et M Restaurant
Paris 16e	Chez Géraud
Paris 17e	Chez Mathilde-Paris XVII

→ **N** *New* → *Nouveau* → *Nuovo* → *Neu* → *Nuevo*

Paris 17ᵉ	L'Entredgeu
Paris 17ᵉ	Graindorge
Paris 17ᵉ	Meating **N**
Paris 18ᵉ	La Table d'Eugène **N**
Paris 20ᵉ	Le Baratin **N**
Pau / Lescar (64)	La Terrasse
Pauillac (33)	Café Lavinal **N**
Perpignan (66)	Les Antiquaires
La-Petite-Pierre / Graufthal (67)	Le Cheval Blanc
Plaisians (26)	Auberge de la Clue
Pléneuf-Val-André / Le-Val-André (22)	Au Biniou
Ploemeur / Lomener (56)	Le Vivier
Ploubalay (22)	De la Gare
Polliat (01)	De la Place
Pons (17)	De Bordeaux
Pont-de-Vaux (01)	Les Platanes **N**
Pont-de-Vaux (01)	Le Raisin
Pontlevoy (41)	De l'École
Porto (2A)	Bella Vista
Pouillon (40)	L'Auberge du Pas de Vent
Le Puy-en-Velay (43)	Tournayre
Le Puy-en-Velay / Espaly-Saint-Marcel (43)	L'Ermitage
Puy-Saint-Vincent (05)	La Pendine **N**
Quarré-les-Tombes (89)	Le Morvan
Quédillac (35)	Le Relais de la Rance
Quiberon (56)	La Chaumine
Quimper / Ty-Sanquer (29)	Auberge de Ti-Coz
Réalmont (81)	Les Secrets Gourmands
Rennes (35)	Le Quatre B
La Réole (33)	Aux Fontaines **N**
Reugny (03)	La Table de Reugny
Rians (83)	La Roquette
Riom (63)	Le Flamboyant
Riquewihr (68)	Le Sarment d'Or
Roanne (42)	Le Central
Robion (84)	L 'Escanson **N**
Rodez (12)	Les Jardins de l'Acropolis
Romorantin-Lanthenay (41)	Auberge le Lanthenay
La Roque-Gageac (24)	La Belle Étoile
Rostrenen (22)	L'Eventail des Saveurs
Rouvres-en-Xaintois (88)	Burnel
Les Sables-d'Olonne (85)	La Pilotine
Saint-Alban-les-Eaux (42)	Le Petit Prince
Saint-Amand-Montrond / Bruère-Allichamps (18)	Les Tilleuls
Saint-Amand-Montrond / Abbaye-de-Noirlac (18)	Auberge de l'Abbaye de Noirlac
Saint-Benoît-sur-Loire (45)	Grand St-Benoît
Saint-Bonnet-le-Froid (43)	André Chatelard
Saint-Bonnet-le-Froid (43)	Le Fort du Pré
Saint-Bonnet-le-Froid (43)	Le Clos des Cimes
Saint-Brieuc (22)	Ô Saveurs
Saint-Brieuc / Cesson (22)	La Croix Blanche
Saint-Clément-les-Places (69)	L'Auberge de Saint-Clément
Saint-Disdier (05)	La Neyrette
Saint-Dizier (52)	La Gentilhommière
Saint-Flour (15)	Grand Hôtel de l'Étape
Saint-Georges-des-Sept-Voies (49)	Auberge de la Sansonnière
Saint-Germain-du-Bois (71)	Hostellerie Bressane
Saint-Gervais-les-Bains (74)	Le Sérac **N**
Saint-Hilaire-des-Loges (85)	Le Pantagruelion
Saint-Hippolyte (68)	Le Parc
Saint-Jean-du-Bruel (12)	Du Midi-Papillon
Saint-Julien-Chapteuil (43)	Vidal
St-Julien-du-Sault (89)	Les Bons Enfants **N**
Saint-Julien-en-Champsaur (05)	Les Chenets **N**
Saint-Justin (40)	France
Saint-Malo (35)	La Grassinais
Saint-Malo / Saint-Servan-sur-Mer (35)	La Gourmandise **N**
Saint-Martin-de-Londres (34)	Auberge de Saugras
Saint-Martin-en-Bresse (71)	Au Puits Enchanté
Saint-Michel-en-l'Herm (85)	La Rose Trémière
Saint-Michel-Mont-Mercure (85)	Auberge du Mont Mercure
Saint-Palais-sur-Mer (17)	Les Agapes
Saint-Quirin (57)	Hostellerie du Prieuré
Saint-Romain (21)	Les Roches **N**
Saint-Suliac (35)	La Ferme du Boucanier
Saint-Thégonnec (29)	Auberge St-Thégonnec
Saint-Vaast-la-Hougue (50)	France et Fuchsias
Saint-Valery-en-Caux (76)	Du Port
Saint-Valery-sur-Somme (80)	Du Port et des Bains **N**
Sainte-Cécile-les-Vignes (84)	Campagne, Vignes et Gourmandises
Sainte-Croix-de-Verdon (04)	L'Olivier
Sainte-Euphémie (01)	Au Petit Moulin
Sainte-Menéhould (51)	Le Cheval Rouge **N**
Saintes-Maries-de-la-Mer (13)	Hostellerie du Pont de Gau

→ **N** *New* → *Nouveau* → *Nuovo* → *Neu* → *Nuevo*

Salies-de-Béarn / Castagnède (64) La Belle Auberge
Salignac-Eyvigues (24) La Meynardie
Sancerre (18) La Pomme d'Or
Santenay (21) Le Terroir
Le Sappey-en-Chartreuse (38) Les Skieurs
Sassetot-le-Mauconduit (76) Le Relais des Dalles
Saugues (43) La Terrasse
Saumur (49) Le Gambetta
Sauternes (33) Saprien
Sauxillanges (63) Restaurant de la Mairie
Savonnières (37) La Maison Tourangelle
Seillonnaz (01) La Cigale d'Or
Semblançay (37) La Mère Hamard
Senones (88) Au Bon Gîte
Sérignan (34) L 'Harmonie
Serre-Chevalier / Le Monêtier-les-Bains (05) Le Chazal **N**
Servon (50) Auberge du Terroir
Sète (34) Paris Méditerranée
Sillé-le-Guillaume (72) Le Bretagne
Sochaux / Étupes (25) Au Fil des Saisons
Soissons (02) Chez Raphaël
Sorges (24) Auberge de la Truffe
Sospel (06) Des Étrangers
La Souterraine / Saint-Étienne-de-Fursac (23) Nougier
Steenvoorde (59) Auprès de mon Arbre **N**
Strasbourg (67) Le Clou
Strasbourg / Fegersheim (67) Auberge du Bruchrhein
Tamniès (24) Laborderie
Tarnac (19) Des Voyageurs
Tharon-Plage (44) Le Belem
Thonon-les-Bains / Port-de-Séchex (74) Le Clos du Lac
Toulouse / Castanet-Tolosan (31) La Table des Merville
Tourcoing (59) La Baratte
Tournus / Ozenay (71) Le Relais d'Ozenay **N**
Tournus / Le Villars (71) L 'Auberge des Gourmets
Tours (37) L'Arche de Meslay
Tours (37) La Deuvalière
Tours (37) Le Bistrot de la Tranchée **N**
Tours / Vallières (37) Auberge de Port Vallières
Trémolat (24) Bistrot d'en Face
Troyes / Pont-Sainte-Marie (10) Bistrot DuPont
Tulle (19) La Toque Blanche
La Turballe (44) Le Terminus
La Turbie (06) Café de la Fontaine
Uchaux (84) Côté Sud
Uchaux (84) Le Temps de Vivre
Uzerche / Saint-Ybard (19) Auberge St-Roch
Uzès / à St-Siffret (30) L'Authentic
Vagney (88) Les Lilas **N**
Vaison-la-Romaine (84) Le Bistro du O **N**
Vaison-la-Romaine / Séguret (84) Le Mesclun **N**
Valbonne (06) L'Auberge Fleurie
Le-Val-d'Ajol (88) La Résidence
Valence (26) Le 7
Valence-sur-Baïse (32) La Ferme de Flaran
Valloire (73) Relais du Galibier
Valmont (76) Le Bec au Cauchois
Valréas (84) Au Délice de Provence **N**
Le Valtin (88) Auberge du Val Joli
Vannes (56) Roscanvec
Vannes (56) Le vent d'Est
Varades (44) La Closerie des Roses
Venarey-les-Laumes / Alise-Sainte-Reine (21) Cheval Blanc
Vence (06) Le Vieux Couvent
Vendôme (41) Le Terre à TR
Vernon (27) Les Fleurs
Vichy (03) L'Alambic
Vic-sur-Cère / Col-de-Curebourse (15) Hostellerie St-Clément
Vierzon (18) Le Champêtre
Villard-de-Lans (38) Les Trente Pas
Villars (84) La Table de Pablo **N**
Villedieu-les-Poêles (50) Manoir de l'Acherie
Villefranche-de-Rouergue (12) L'Épicurien
Villefranche-sur-Saône (69) Le Juliénas
Villeneuve-sur-Lot / Pujols (47) Lou Calel
Villié-Morgon (69) Le Morgon
Villiers-sur-Marne (52) La Source Bleue
Viviers (07) Le Relais du Vivarais
Wierre-Effroy (62) La Ferme du Vert
Wissembourg (67) Le Carrousel Bleu

→ **N** *New* → *Nouveau* → *Nuovo* → *Neu* → *Nuevo*

Bib Hotel

Good accommodation at moderate prices outside the Paris region
Bonnes nuits à petits prix en province
Buona sistemazione a prezzi contenuti in provincia
Hier übernachten Sie gut und preiswert in der Provinz
Grato descanso a precios moderados en provincias

Aguessac (12)	Auberge le Rascalat
Aire-sur-l'Adour / Ségos (32)	Minvielle et les Oliviers **N**
Aix-les-Bains (73)	Auberge St-Simond
Ajaccio (2A)	Kallisté
Alençon (61)	Des Ducs **N**
Allevard (38)	Les Alpes
Ampuis (69)	Le Domaine des Vignes **N**
Angers (49)	Du Mail
Angers (49)	Le Progrès
Annecy (74)	Nord
Annot (04)	L'Avenue
Arèches (73)	Auberge du Poncellamont **N**
Argentat (19)	Fouillade
Aubeterre-sur-Dronne (16)	Hostellerie du Périgord
Aubrac (12)	La Dômerie
Aubusson (23)	Villa Adonis
Aulnay (17)	Du Donjon
Auray (56)	Du Loch
Aurec-sur-Loire (43)	Les Cèdres Bleus
Autrans (38)	Les Tilleuls
Autun (71)	La Tête Noire
Auxerre (89)	Normandie
Availles-Limouzine (86)	La Chatellenie
Avignon / Île de la Barthelasse (84)	La Ferme
Ax-les-Thermes (09)	Le Chalet
Azay-le-Rideau (37)	De Biencourt
Azay-le-Rideau (37)	Des Châteaux
Baerenthal (57)	Le Kirchberg
Bagnères-de-Bigorre / Beaudéan (65)	Le Catala
Baix (07)	Les Quatre Vents
Balot (21)	Auberge de la Baume
Ban-de-Laveline (88)	Auberge Lorraine
Baratier (05)	Les Peupliers
Beaugency (45)	De la Sologne
Beaune (21)	Grillon
Beaune / Levernois (21)	Le Parc
Beauzac (43)	L'Air du Temps
Beauzac / Bransac (43)	La Table du Barret
Bénodet (29)	Domaine de Kereven
Berck-sur-Mer / Berck-Plage (62)	L'Impératrice
Béthune (62)	L'Éden
Biarritz (64)	Maïtagaria
Biarritz / Arbonne (64)	Laminak
Bitche (57)	Le Strasbourg **N**
Blienschwiller (67)	Winzenberg
Bollezeele (59)	Hostellerie St-Louis
Bonifacio (2A)	Domaine de Licetto
Bonnétage (25)	L'Etang du Moulin
Bonneval-sur-Arc (73)	À la Pastourelle
La Bouilladisse (13)	La Fenière
Bourges (18)	Le Berry
Bourges (18)	Le Christina
Bourges (18)	Les Tilleuls
Bozouls (12)	A la Route d'Argent
Bracieux (41)	De la Bonnheure
Bretenoux / Port-de-Gagnac (46)	Hostellerie Belle Rive
Brissac-Quincé (49)	Le Castel
Le Bugue / Campagne (24)	Du Château
Buis-les-Baronnies (26)	Les Arcades-Le Lion d'Or
Burnhaupt-le-Haut (68)	Le Coquelicot
Buzançais (36)	L'Hermitage **N**

→ **N** *New* → *Nouveau* → *Nuovo* → *Neu* → *Nuevo*

Caen (14)	Des Quatrans
Calais (62)	Métropol Hôtel
Calais / Blériot-Plage (62)	Les Dunes
Calvinet (15)	Beauséjour
Camaret-sur-Mer (29)	Vauban
Cambo-les-Bains (64)	Ursula
Camiers (62)	Les Cèdres
Cancale (35)	Le Chatellier
Cannes (06)	Florian
Carennac (46)	Hostellerie Fénelon
Carhaix-Plouguer (29)	Noz Vad
Castelnaudary (11)	Du Canal
Céret (66)	Les Arcades
Chagny (71)	De la Poste
Challans (85)	De l'Antiquité
Chamonix-Mont-Blanc / Les Bossons (74)	Aiguille du Midi
Champtoceaux (49)	Le Champalud
Chandolas (07)	Auberge les Murets
Château-Gontier (53)	Parc Hôtel
Château-Gontier / Coudray (53)	L'Amphitryon **N**
Chaudes-Aigues (15)	Beauséjour
Chaumont / Chamarandes (52)	Au Rendez-Vous des Amis
Chauvigny (86)	Lion d'Or
Chépy (80)	L'Auberge Picarde
Cherbourg-Octeville (50)	La Renaissance
Chézery-Forens (01)	Commerce
Chinon (37)	Diderot
Col de la Schlucht (88)	Le Collet
Comps-sur-Artuby (83)	Grand Hôtel Bain
Cordon (74)	Le Cordonant
Coti-Chiavari (2A)	Le Belvédère
Coulon (79)	Le Central **N**
Cour-Cheverny (41)	St-Hubert
La Courtine (23)	Au Petit Breuil
Coutras (33)	Henri IV
Crozon (29)	De la Presqu'île
Cruis (04)	Auberge de l'Abbaye
Dambach-la-Ville (67)	Le Vignoble
Damgan (56)	Albatros
Donzenac (19)	Relais du Bas Limousin
Doué-la-Fontaine (49)	Auberge Bienvenue
Entraygues-sur-Truyère / Le Fel (12)	Auberge du Fel
Épaignes (27)	L'Auberge du Beau Carré
Erquy (22)	Beauséjour
Espalion (12)	De France
Estaing (12)	L' Auberge St-Fleuret
Eymet (24)	Les Vieilles Pierres
Le Falgoux (15)	Des Voyageurs
La Ferté-Saint-Cyr (41)	Saint-Cyr
Florac / Cocurès (48)	La Lozerette
Fouesnant / Cap-Coz (29)	Belle-Vue
Fougères (35)	Les Voyageurs
Gaillac (81)	La Verrerie
Gennes (49)	Les Naulets d'Anjou
Gérardmer (88)	Gérard d'Alsace
Giffaumont-Champaubert (51)	Le Cheval Blanc **N**
Gimel-les-Cascades (19)	Hostellerie de la Vallée
Gordes (84)	Auberge de Carcarille
Goumois (25)	Le Moulin du Plain
Gresse-en-Vercors (38)	Le Chalet
Guebwiller (68)	Domaine du Lac
Guilliers (56)	Au Relais du Porhoët
Hagetmau (40)	Le Jambon
Hesdin (62)	Trois Fontaines
Les Houches (74)	Auberge Le Montagny
Île-de-Sein (29)	Ar Men
Île d'Yeu / Port-Joinville (85)	Atlantic Hôtel
Illhaeusern (68)	Les Hirondelles
L'Isle-d'Abeau (38)	Le Relais du Çatey
L'Isle-sur-Serein (89)	Auberge du Pot d'Étain
Itxassou (64)	Le Chêne
Jonzac / Clam (17)	Le Vieux Logis
Jougne (25)	La Couronne
Juliénas (69)	Chez la Rose
Juvigny-sous-Andaine (61)	Au Bon Accueil
Kaysersberg (68)	Constantin
Kilstett (67)	Oberlé
Labaroche (68)	La Rochette
Lacapelle-Viescamp (15)	Du Lac
Lac Chambon (63)	Le Grillon
Laguiole (12)	Régis **N**
Lanarce (07)	Le Provence
Langeac / Reilhac (43)	Val d'Allier
Largentière / Sanilhac (07)	Auberge de la Tour de Brison
Larrau (64)	Etchemaïte
Lascelle (15)	Du Lac des Graves
Libourne (33)	De France **N**
Lodève (34)	Paix **N**
Lons-le-Saunier (39)	Nouvel Hôtel
Lorient (56)	Astoria
Loudéac (22)	Voyageurs **N**
Luz-Saint-Sauveur / Esquièze-Sère (65)	Terminus
Lyon (69)	Célestins
Mandelieu / La Napoule (06)	Villa Parisiana
Margès (26)	Auberge Le Pont du Chalon
Masseret (19)	De la Tour
Mauriac (15)	Auv'Hôtel
Mazaye (63)	Auberge de Mazayes
Megève (74)	La Chaumine **N**
Melle (79)	Les Glycines **N**
Métabief (25)	Étoile des Neiges

→ **N** *New* → *Nouveau* → *Nuovo* → *Neu* → *Nuevo*

- **Meyrueis (48)** Family Hôtel
- **Meyrueis (48)** Du Mont Aigoual
- **Millau (12)** Château de Creissels
- **Mittelhausen (67)** À l'Étoile
- **Molsheim (67)** Le Bugatti
- **Les Molunes (39)** Le Pré Fillet
- **Monestier-de-Clermont (38)** Au Sans Souci
- **Montargis / Amilly (45)** Le Belvédère
- **Montauban (82)** Du Commerce
- **Montélier (26)** La Martinière
- **Montigny-la-Resle (89)** Le Soleil d'Or
- **Montigny-sur-Avre (28)** Moulin des Planches
- **Montluel (01)** Petit Casset
- **Montmelard (71)** Le St-Cyr
- **Montpellier (34)** Du Parc
- **Montpellier (34)** Ulysse **N**
- **Montsalvy (15)** L'Auberge Fleurie
- **Mortagne-au-Perche (61)** Du Tribunal **N**
- **Morteau / Les Combes (25)** L'Auberge de la Motte
- **Mulhouse / Frœningen (68)** Auberge de Froeningen
- **Nantua (01)** L'Embarcadère
- **Natzwiller (67)** Auberge Metzger
- **Niederschaeffolsheim (67)** Au Bœuf Rouge
- **Niedersteinbach (67)** Cheval Blanc
- **Nogent-le-Rotrou (28)** Brit Hôtel du Perche
- **Nogent-le-Rotrou (28)** Sully
- **Nogent-sur-Seine (10)** Beau Rivage
- **Nontron (24)** Grand Hôtel
- **Le Nouvion-en-Thiérache (02)** Paix
- **Noyalo (56)** L'Hortensia
- **Oberhaslach (67)** Hostellerie St-Florent
- **Obersteinbach (67)** Anthon
- **Orléans (45)** Marguerite
- **Pailherols (15)** Auberge des Montagnes
- **Paimpol / Ploubazlanec (22)** Les Agapanthes
- **Patrimonio (2B)** Du Vignoble **N**
- **Pau (64)** Le Bourbon
- **Pégomas (06)** Le Bosquet
- **Pierre-Buffière (87)** La Providence
- **Pierrefort (15)** Du Midi
- **Pont-Aven (29)** Les Ajoncs d'Or
- **Pont-de-Vaux (01)** Les Platanes **N**
- **Pont-du-Bouchet (63)** La Crémaillère
- **Le Pouldu (29)** Le Panoramique
- **Prats-de-Mollo-la-Preste / La Preste (66)** Ribes
- **Le Puy-en-Velay / Espaly-Saint-Marcel (43)** L'Ermitage
- **Quarré-les-Tombes (89)** Le Morvan
- **Quédillac (35)** Le Relais de la Rance
- **Quintin (22)** Du Commerce **N**
- **Reipertswiller (67)** La Couronne
- **Rennes (35)** Britannia
- **Rennes (35)** Des Lices
- **Réville (50)** Au Moyne de Saire
- **Rieumes (31)** Auberge les Palmiers
- **Riom-Ès-Montagnes (15)** St-Georges
- **Rochefort (17)** Roca Fortis
- **La Rochette (73)** Du Parc
- **Romagnieu (38)** Auberge les Forges de la Massotte
- **Ronchamp / Champagney (70)** Le Pré Serroux
- **Roussillon (84)** Les Sables d'Ocre
- **Rouvres-en-Xaintois (88)** Burnel
- **Les Sables-d'Olonne (85)** Antoine
- **Les Sables-d'Olonne (85)** Les Embruns
- **Saillagouse (66)** Planes (La Vieille Maison Cerdane)
- **Saint-Agnan (58)** La Vieille Auberge
- **Saint-Ambroix / Larnac (30)** Le Clos des Arts
- **Saint-Bonnet-en-Champsaur (05)** La Crémaillère
- **Saint-Chély-d'Apcher / La Garde (48)** Le Rocher Blanc
- **Saint-Disdier (05)** La Neyrette
- **Saint-Flour (15)** Auberge de La Providence
- **Saint-Gervais-d'Auvergne (63)** Le Relais d'Auvergne
- **Saint-Jean-de-Maurienne (73)** St-Georges
- **Saint-Jean-du-Bruel (12)** Du Midi-Papillon
- **Saint-Jean-en-Royans / Col de la Machine (26)** Du Col de la Machine
- **Saint-Lary (09)** Auberge de l'Isard
- **Saint-Malo (35)** San Pedro
- **Saint-Rémy-de-Provence (13)** L'Amandière
- **Saint-Sernin-sur-Rance (12)** Carayon
- **Saint-Valery-en-Caux (76)** Les Remparts
- **Sainte-Menéhould (51)** Le Cheval Rouge
- **Saintes (17)** L'Avenue
- **Saintes-Maries-de-la-Mer (13)** Pont Blanc
- **Salers (15)** Le Bailliage
- **Salies-de-Béarn / Castagnède (64)** La Belle Auberge
- **Sallanches (74)** Auberge de l'Orangerie
- **Sand (67)** Hostellerie la Charrue **N**
- **Sarlat-la-Canéda (24)** Le Mas de Castel
- **Sarlat-la-Canéda (24)** Le Mas del Pechs
- **Sarrebourg (57)** Les Cèdres
- **Sarreguemines (57)** Amadeus
- **Sars-Poteries (59)** Marquais
- **Saugues (43)** La Terrasse
- **Sauveterre-de-Béarn (64)** La Maison de Navarre
- **Saverne (67)** Le Clos de la Garenne

→ **N** *New* → *Nouveau* → *Nuovo* → *Neu* → *Nuevo*

Sées / Macé (61)	Île de Sées
Semblançay (37)	La Mère Hamard
Semur-en-Auxois (21)	Les Cymaises
Senones (88)	Au Bon Gîte
Servon (50)	Auberge du Terroir
Sommières (30)	De l'Estelou
Sondernach (68)	A l'Orée du Bois
Souillac (46)	Le Quercy
Sousceyrac (46)	Au Déjeuner de Sousceyrac
Strasbourg / Blaesheim (67)	Au Bœuf
Strasbourg / Entzheim (67)	Père Benoit
Tain-l'Hermitage (26)	Les 2 Côteaux **N**
Tarnac (19)	Des Voyageurs
Thann (68)	Aux Sapins
Le Thillot / Le Ménil (88)	Les Sapins
Thizy (69)	La Terrasse
Le Touquet-Paris-Plage / Stella-Plage (62)	Des Pelouses
Tournon-sur-Rhône (07)	Les Amandiers
Turckheim (68)	Le Berceau du Vigneron
Uriage-les-Bains (38)	Les Mésanges
Uzès (30)	Le Patio de Violette
Valence-sur-Baïse (32)	La Ferme de Flaran **N**
Valgorge (07)	Le Tanargue
Valleraugue (30)	Auberge Cévenole
Valmont (76)	Le Bec au Cauchois **N**
Vaux-sous-Aubigny (52)	Le Vauxois
Vézelay / Pierre-Perthuis (89)	Les Deux Ponts
Viaduc-de-Garabit (15)	Beau Site
Vic-en-Bigorre (65)	Réverbère **N**
Vichy / Abrest (03)	La Colombière
Villé (67)	La Bonne Franquette
Vittel (88)	Providence
Viviers (07)	Le Relais du Vivarais
Vougeot / Gilly-lès-Cîteaux (21)	L'Orée des Vignes
Wimereux (62)	Du Centre
Wissembourg (67)	Au Moulin de la Walk
Yvetot (76)	Du Havre **N**

→ **N** *New* → *Nouveau* → *Nuovo* → *Neu* → *Nuevo*

Pleasant accommodation

Hébergements agréables

Alloggio ameno

Angenehme Unterbringung

Alojamientos agradables

Antibes / Cap d'Antibes (06) Du Cap
La Baule (44) Hermitage Barrière
Beaulieu-sur-Mer (06) La Réserve de Beaulieu et Spa
Biarritz (64) Du Palais
Cannes (06) Carlton Inter Continental
Cannes (06) Majestic Barrière
Cannes (06) Martinez
Courchevel / Courchevel 1850 (73) Les Airelles
Deauville (14) Normandy-Barrière
Deauville (14) Royal-Barrière
Évian-les-Bains (74) Royal
Monte-Carlo (MC) Paris
Nice (06) Negresco
Paris 1er Le Meurice
Paris 1er Ritz
Paris 8e Le Bristol
Paris 8e Crillon
Paris 8e Four Seasons George V
Paris 8e Plaza Athénée
Paris 9e Intercontinental Le Grand
Paris 16e Raphael
Saint-Jean-Cap-Ferrat (06) Grand Hôtel du Cap Ferrat
Saint-Tropez (83) Byblos
Saint-Tropez (83) Château de la Messardière
Tourrettes (83) Four Seasons Resort Provence at Terre Blanche

Ablis (78) Château d'Esclimont
Aix-en-Provence (13) Villa Gallici
Antibes / Cap d'Antibes (06) Impérial Garoupe
Avallon / Vault-de-Lugny (89) Château de Vault de Lugny
Avignon (84) La Mirande
Bagnols (69) Château de Bagnols
Beaune (21) Le Cep
Beaune / Levernois (21) Hostellerie de Levernois
Belle-Île / Port-Goulphar (56) Castel Clara
Béthune / Busnes (62) Le Château de Beaulieu
Les Bézards (45) Auberge des Templiers
Bidarray (64) Ostapé
Billiers (56) Domaine de Rochevilaine
Bordeaux (33) Burdigala
Bordeaux (33) The Regent Grand Hotel
Bordeaux / Martillac (33) Les Sources de Caudalie
Briollay (49) Château de Noirieux
Brive-la-Gaillarde / Varetz (19) Château de Castel Novel
Cahors / Mercuès (46) Château de Mercuès
Calvi (2B) La Villa
Cannes (06) 3.14 Hôtel
Carcassonne (11) De La Cité
Le Castellet / Le Castellet (83) Du Castellet
Cavalière (83) Le Club de Cavalière et Spa
Chamonix-Mont-Blanc (74) Hameau Albert 1er
Colroy-la-Roche (67) Hostellerie La Cheneaudière
Courcelles-sur-Vesle (02) Château de Courcelles
Courchevel / Courchevel 1850 (73) Amanresorts Le Mélézin
Courchevel / Courchevel 1850 (73) Cheval Blanc
Courchevel / Courchevel 1850 (73) Le Kilimandjaro
Curzay-sur-Vonne (86) Château de Curzay
Divonne-les-Bains (01) Le Grand Hôtel
Eugénie-les-Bains (40) Les Prés d'Eugénie
Évian-les-Bains (74) Ermitage
Èze (06) Château de la Chèvre d'Or

Èze-Bord-de-Mer (06) Cap Estel
Figeac (46) Château du Viguier du Roy
Forcalquier / Mane (04) Couvent des Minimes
Gordes (84) La Bastide de Gordes et Spa
Grasse (06) La Bastide St-Antoine
Honfleur (14) La Ferme St-Siméon
Île de Ré / La Flotte (17) Richelieu
Joigny (89) La Côte St-Jacques
Juan-les-Pins (06) Belles Rives
Juan-les-Pins (06) Juana
Lacave (46) Château de la Treyne
Ligny-en-Cambrésis (59) Château de Ligny
Lille (59) L'Hermitage Gantois
Luynes (37) Domaine de Beauvois
Lyon (69) Cour des Loges
Lyon (69) Villa Florentine
Lyon / Charbonnières-les-Bains (69) Le Pavillon de la Rotonde
Megève (74) Les Fermes de Marie
Megève (74) Lodge Park
Mirambeau (17) Château de Mirambeau
Montbazon (37) Château d'Artigny
Monte-Carlo (MC) Hermitage
Monte-Carlo (MC) Monte Carlo Bay Hôtel and Resort
Monte-Carlo (MC) Métropole
Monte-Carlo / Monte-Carlo-Beach (MC) Monte-Carlo Beach Hôtel
Mougins (06) Le Mas Candille
Onzain (41) Domaine des Hauts de Loire
Paris 1er Costes
Paris 1er De Vendôme
Paris 3e Murano
Paris 3e Pavillon de la Reine
Paris 8e Champs-Élysées Plaza
Paris 8e Napoléon
Paris 16e Renaissance Parc-Trocadéro
Paris 16e St-James Paris
Perros-Guirec (22) L' Agapa
Pont-du-Gard / Castillon-du-Gard (30) Le Vieux Castillon
Porticcio (2A) Le Maquis
Porto-Vecchio (2A) Casadelmar
Porto-Vecchio (2A) Grand Hôtel de Cala Rossa
Pouilly-en-Auxois / Chailly-sur-Armançon (21) Château de Chailly
Puymirol (47) Michel Trama
Reims (51) Château les Crayères
Roanne (42) Troisgros
Roquebrune (06) Vista Palace
Rouffach (68) Château d'Isenbourg
Saint-Émilion (33) Hostellerie de Plaisance
Saint-Jean-Cap-Ferrat (06) La Voile d'Or
Saint-Jean-Cap-Ferrat (06) Royal Riviera
Saint-Tropez (83) La Bastide de St-Tropez
Saint-Tropez (83) Résidence de la Pinède
Saint-Tropez (83) Villa Belrose
Saint-Tropez (83) Villa Marie
Sainte-Foy-la-Grande (33) Château des Vigiers
Sainte-Maxime (83) Le Beauvallon
Saulieu (21) Le Relais Bernard Loiseau
Strasbourg (67) Régent Petite France
Talloires (74) L'Auberge du Père Bise
Valence (26) Pic
Versailles (78) Trianon Palace
Vienne (38) La Pyramide
Villeneuve-lès-Avignon (30) Le Prieuré
Vitrac (24) Domaine de Rochebois
Vonnas (01) Georges Blanc
Vougeot / Gilly-lès-Cîteaux (21) Château de Gilly

Aigues-Mortes (30) Villa Mazarin
Aillant-sur-Tholon (89) Domaine du Roncemay
Aix-en-Provence (13) Le Pigonnet
Aix-en-Provence / Celony (13) Le Mas d'Entremont
Ajaccio (2A) Palazzu U Domu
Albi (81) La Réserve
Alpe-d'Huez (38) Au Chamois d'Or
Amboise (37) Le Choiseul
Amboise (37) Le Manoir Les Minimes
Arles (13) L'Hôtel Particulier
Avignon / Montfavet (84) Hostellerie Les Frênes
Avignon / Le Pontet (84) Auberge de Cassagne
Bagnoles-de-l'Orne (61) Le Manoir du Lys
Bagnols-sur-Cèze (30) Château de Montcaud
Barbizon (77) Hôtellerie du Bas-Bréau
La Baule (44) Castel Marie-Louise
Les Baux-de-Provence (13) La Cabro d'Or
Bayeux (14) Château de Sully
Bayeux / Audrieu (14) Château d'Audrieu
Beaune (21) L'Hôtel
Bénodet / Sainte-Marine (29) Villa Tri Men
Béthune / Gosnay (62) Chartreuse du Val St-Esprit
Biarritz (64) Beaumanoir
Biarritz / Lac de Brindos (64) Château de Brindos
Bordeaux / Bouliac (33) Le St-James
Boulogne-sur-Mer (62) La Matelote
Le-Bourget-du-Lac (73) Ombremont
Boutigny-sur-Essonne (91) Domaine de Bélesbat
Brantôme (24) Le Moulin de l'Abbaye
Brantôme / Champagnac-de-Belair (24) Le Moulin du Roc

Le Buisson-de-Cadouin (24) Le Manoir de Bellerive
La Bussière-sur-Ouche (21) Abbaye de la Bussière
La Cadière-d'Azur (83) Hostellerie Bérard
Cagnes-sur-Mer (06) Le Cagnard
Callas (83) Hostellerie Les Gorges de Pennafort
Calvi (2B) La Signoria
Cancale (35) De Bricourt-Richeux
Carantec (29) L'Hôtel de Carantec-Patrick Jeffroy
Carcassonne (11) Domaine d'Auriac
Carcassonne / Cavanac (11) Château de Cavanac
Carpentras / Mazan (84) Château de Mazan
Les Carroz-d'Arâches (74) Les Servages d'Armelle
Cassel (59) Châtellerie de Schoebeque
La Celle (83) Hostellerie de l'Abbaye de la Celle
Chagny (71) Lameloise
Chambéry / Chambéry-le-Vieux (73) Château de Candie
Chambolle-Musigny (21) Château André Ziltener
Chamonix-Mont-Blanc (74) Grand Hôtel des Alpes
Château-Arnoux-Saint-Auban (04) La Bonne Étape
Chenonceaux (37) Auberge du Bon Laboureur
Chinon / Marçay (37) Château de Marçay
Cognac (16) Château de l'Yeuse
Coise-Saint-Jean-Pied-Gauthier (73) Château de la Tour du Puits
La Colle-sur-Loup (06) Le Clos des Arts
Colmar (68) Les Têtes
Colombey-les-Deux-Églises (52) Hostellerie la Montagne
Condrieu (69) Hôtellerie Beau Rivage
Connelles (27) Le Moulin de Connelles
Cordes-sur-Ciel (81) Le Grand Écuyer
Cordon (74) Le Cerf Amoureux
Cordon (74) Les Roches Fleuries
Courchevel / Courchevel 1850 (73) La Sivolière
Courchevel / Courchevel 1850 (73) Le Chabichou
Crillon-le-Brave (84) Crillon le Brave
Le Croisic (44) Le Fort de l'Océan
La Croix-Valmer / Gigaro (83) Château de Valmer
Crozet (01) Jiva Hill Park Hôtel
Cruseilles (74) Château des Avenières
Deauville (14) Hostellerie de Tourgéville
Dinard (35) Villa Reine Hortense
Enghien-les-Bains (95) Grand Hôtel Barrière
Épernay / Champillon (51) Royal Champagne
Épernay / Vinay (51) Hostellerie La Briqueterie
Èze (06) Château Eza
Fère-en-Tardenois (02) Château de Fère

Gargas (84) Domaine La Coquillade
Gémenos (13) Relais de la Magdeleine
Gérardmer (88) Le Manoir au Lac
Gérardmer / Bas-Rupts (88) Les Bas-Rupts
Gordes (84) Les Bories et Spa
Grasse (06) La Bastide St-Mathieu
Le Grau-du-Roi / Port-Camargue (30) Spinaker
Gressy (77) Le Manoir de Gressy
Grignan (26) Manoir de la Roseraie
Guidel (56) Le Domaine de Kerbastic
Hennebont (56) Château de Locguénolé
Honfleur (14) Le Manoir du Butin
Igé (71) Château d'Igé
Île de Porquerolles (83) Le Mas du Langoustier
Île de Ré / Saint-Martin-de-Ré (17) De Toiras
Île de Ré / Saint-Martin-de-Ré (17) Le Clos St-Martin
Joucas (84) Hostellerie Le Phébus
Lacave (46) Pont de l'Ouysse
Laguiole (12) Bras
Langeais / Saint-Patrice (37) Château de Rochecotte
Le Lavandou / Aiguebelle (83) Les Roches
Lencloître / à Savigny-sous-Faye (86) Château Hôtel de Savigny
Lezoux / Bort-l'Étang (63) Château de Codignat
Lille / Emmerin (59) La Howarderie
Limoges / Saint-Martin-du-Fault (87) Chapelle St-Martin
Locquirec (29) Le Grand Hôtel des Bains
Lorgues (83) Château de Berne
Lourmarin (84) Le Moulin de Lourmarin
Lunéville (54) Château d'Adoménil
Lyon (69) Le Royal Lyon
Magescq (40) Relais de la Poste
La Malène (48) Château de la Caze
Manigod (74) Chalet Hôtel Croix-Fry
Marseille (13) Le Petit Nice
Maussane-les-Alpilles / Paradou (13) Le Hameau des Baux
Megève (74) Chalet du Mont d'Arbois
Megève (74) Chalet St-Georges
Megève (74) Le Fer à Cheval
Megève (74) Mont-Blanc
Méribel (73) Allodis
Méribel (73) Le Grand Cœur et Spa
Méribel (73) Le Yéti
Missillac (44) La Bretesche
Moëlan-sur-Mer (29) Manoir de Kertalg
Moissac (82) Le Manoir St-Jean
Molitg-les-Bains (66) Château de Riell
Monaco (MC) Columbus
Montbazon (37) Domaine de la Tortinière
Montélimar (26) Domaine du Colombier
Montpellier / Castelnau-le-Lez (34) Domaine de Verchant

Montreuil (62) Château de Montreuil
Montrichard / Chissay-en-Touraine (41) Château de Chissay
Mougins (06) De Mougins
Moustiers-Sainte-Marie (04) Bastide de Moustiers
Najac (12) Les Demeures de Longcol
Nans-les-Pins (83) Domaine de Châteauneuf
Nice (06) La Pérouse
Nieuil (16) Château de Nieuil
Nîmes (30) Jardins Secrets
Obernai (67) A la Cour d'Alsace
Obernai (67) Le Parc
Paris 6e D'Aubusson
Paris 6e Esprit Saint-Germain
Paris 6e L'Hôtel
Paris 6e Relais Christine
Paris 6e Relais St-Germain
Paris 7e Duc de St-Simon
Paris 7e Pont Royal
Paris 8e Daniel
Paris 8e De Sers
Paris 8e François 1er
Paris 11e Les Jardins du Marais
Paris 16e Keppler
Paris 16e Sezz
Paris 16e Square
Paris 16e Trocadero Dokhan's
Paris 18e Kube
Pau (64) Villa Navarre
Pauillac (33) Château Cordeillan Bages
Pérouges (01) Ostellerie du Vieux Pérouges
Poligny / Monts-de-Vaux (39) Hostellerie des Monts de Vaux
Pons / Mosnac (17) Moulin du Val de Seugne
Pornichet (44) Sud Bretagne
Port-en-Bessin (14) La Chenevière
Port-Lesney (39) Château de Germigney
Porto-Vecchio (2A) Belvédère
Propriano (2A) Grand Hôtel Miramar
Rayol-Canadel-sur-Mer (83) Le Bailli de Suffren
Reims (51) L'Assiette Champenoise
Ribeauvillé (68) Le Clos St-Vincent
Roscoff (29) Le Brittany
Saint-Arcons-d'Allier (43) Les Deux Abbesses
Saint-Bonnet-le-Froid (43) Le Clos des Cimes
Saint-Émilion (33) Château Grand Barrail
Saint-Florent (2B) Demeure Loredana
Saint-Florent (2B) La Dimora
Saint-Germain-en-Laye (78) La Forestière
Saint-Jean-de-Luz (64) Grand Hôtel
Saint-Jean-de-Luz (64) Parc Victoria
Saint-Jean-de-Luz (64) Zazpi Hôtel
Saint-Jean-Pied-de-Port (64) Les Pyrénées
Saint-Omer / Tilques (62) Château Tilques
Saint-Paul (06) La Colombe d'Or
Saint-Paul (06) Le Mas de Pierre
Saint-Paul (06) Le Saint-Paul
Saint-Paul-Trois-Châteaux (26) Villa Augusta
Saint-Rémy-de-Provence (13) Hostellerie du Vallon de Valrugues
Saint-Rémy-de-Provence (13) Le Château des Alpilles
Saint-Rémy-de-Provence (13) Les Ateliers de l'Image
Saint-Tropez (83) La Tartane Saint-Amour
Saint-Tropez (83) Le Yaca
Saint-Tropez (83) Pan Deï Palais
Sainte-Anne-la-Palud (29) De La Plage
Sainte-Lucie-de-Porto-Vecchio (2A) Le Pinarello
Sainte-Maure-de-Touraine / Noyant-de Touraine (37) Château de Brou
Sainte-Preuve (02) Domaine du Château de Barive
Saintes (17) Relais du Bois St-Georges
Saintes-Maries-de-la-Mer (13) Le Mas de la Fouque
Salon-de-Provence (13) Abbaye de Sainte-Croix
Le Sambuc (13) Le Mas de Peint
Sarlat-la-Canéda (24) Clos La Boëtie
Sault (84) Hostellerie du Val de Sault
Saumur (49) Château de Verrières
Saumur / Chênehutte-les-Tuffeaux (49) Le Prieuré
La Saussaye (27) Manoir des Saules
Strasbourg (67) Régent Contades
Strasbourg / Plobsheim (67) Le Kempferhof
Tarbes (65) Le Rex Hotel
Théoule-sur-Mer / Miramar (06) Miramar Beach
Thuret (63) Château de la Canière
Tignes (73) Les Campanules
Tournus (71) Hôtel de Greuze
Tours / Joué-lès-Tours (37) Château de Beaulieu
Tours / Rochecorbon (37) Les Hautes Roches
Tourtour (83) La Bastide de Tourtour
Trébeurden (22) Manoir de Lan-Kerellec
Trébeurden (22) Ti al Lannec
Trégunc (29) Auberge Les Grandes Roches
Trémolat (24) Le Vieux Logis
Trigance (83) Château de Trigance
Troyes (10) La Maison de Rhodes
Troyes (10) Le Champ des Oiseaux
Uriage-les-Bains (38) Grand Hôtel
Verdun / Les Monthairons (55) Hostellerie du Château des Monthairons
Verneuil-sur-Avre (27) Le Clos
Vervins (02) Tour du Roy
Vézelay / Saint-Père (89) L'Espérance
Ville-d'Avray (92) Les Étangs de Corot
Villeneuve-lès-Avignon (30) La Magnaneraie
Villiers-le-Mahieu (78) Château de Villiers le Mahieu

Agde / Le Cap-d'Agde (34) La Bergerie du Cap
Aisonville-et-Bernoville (02) Le 1748
Aix-en-Provence (13) Bastide du Cours
Ajaccio (2A) Les Mouettes
Alençon / Saint-Paterne (72) Château de St-Paterne
Alleyras (43) Le Haut-Allier
Amboise (37) Château de Pray
Anduze / Tornac (30) Les Demeures du Ranquet
Argelès-sur-Mer (66) Le Cottage
Argenton-sur-Creuse / Bouesse (36) Château de Bouesse
Astaffort (47) Le Square "Michel Latrille"
Auribeau-sur-Siagne (06) Auberge de la Vignette Haute
Aurillac / Vézac (15) Château de Salles
Auxerre (89) Le Parc des Maréchaux
Bagnoles-de-l'Orne (61) Bois Joli
Barneville-Carteret / Carteret (50) Des Ormes
Le Bar-sur-Loup (06) Hostellerie du Château
Les Baux-de-Provence (13) La Riboto de Taven
Les Baux-de-Provence (13) Mas de l'Oulivié
Beaulieu (07) La Santoline
Beaune / Montagny-lès-Beaune (21) Le Clos
Beaune / Savigny-lès-Beaune (21) Le Hameau de Barboron
Bédarieux / Hérépian (34) Le Couvent d'Hérépian
Belle-Île / Bangor (56) La Désirade
Bergerac (24) Château Rauly-Saulieut
Bergerac / Saint-Nexans (24) La Chartreuse du Bignac
Bermicourt (62) La Cour de Rémi
Besançon (25) Charles Quint
Biarritz (64) Le Château du Clair de Lune
Bidart (64) L'Hacienda
Bidart (64) Villa L'Arche
Bize-Minervois (11) La Bastide Cabezac
Bonifacio (2A) Genovese
Bonnat (23) L'Orangerie
Bonnieux (84) Auberge de l'Aiguebrun
Bourges (18) D'Angleterre
Cambremer (14) Château Les Bruyères
Cangey (37) Le Fleuray
Cannes (06) Cavendish
Carpentras / Monteux (84) Domaine de Bournereau
Carsac-Aillac (24) La Villa Romaine
Céret (66) Le Mas Trilles
Chablis (89) Du Vieux Moulin
Chablis (89) Hostellerie des Clos
Châteaudun / Flacey (28) Domaine de Moresville
Le Châtelet / Notre-Dame d'Orsan (18) La Maison d'Orsan
Châtillon-sur-Chalaronne (01) La Tour
Cogolin (83) La Maison du Monde
La Colle-sur-Loup (06) L'Abbaye
Colmar (68) Hostellerie Le Maréchal
Condom (32) Les Trois Lys

Conques (12) Le Moulin de Cambelong
Crépon (14) Ferme de la Rançonnière
Deauville (14) 81 L'Hôtel
Les Deux-Alpes (38) Chalet Mounier
Épernay (51) La Villa Eugène
Épernay (51) Le Clos Raymi
Erbalunga (2B) Castel'Brando
Ermenonville (60) Le Prieuré
Eugénie-les-Bains (40) La Maison Rose
Les Eyzies-de-Tayac (24) Ferme Lamy
Fayence (83) Moulin de la Camandoule
Fontaine-de-Vaucluse (84) Du Poète
Fort-Mahon-Plage (80) Auberge Le Fiacre
Fréjus (83) L'Aréna
Gensac (33) Château de Sanse
Gex / Échenevex (01) Auberge des Chasseurs
Goumois (25) Taillard
Graveson (13) Moulin d'Aure
Grignan (26) Le Clair de la Plume
Guéthary (64) Villa Catarie
Gundershoffen (67) Le Moulin
Hauteluce (73) La Ferme du Chozal
Le Havre (76) Vent d'Ouest
Honfleur (14) L'Absinthe
Honfleur (14) L'Écrin
Honfleur (14) La Chaumière
Honfleur (14) La Maison de Lucie
Honfleur (14) Les Maisons de Léa
Hossegor (40) Les Hortensias du Lac
Île de Noirmoutier / Noirmoutier-en-l'Île (85) Fleur de Sel
Île de Port-Cros (83) Le Manoir
L'Île-Rousse (2B) U Palazzu
L'Isle-sur-la-Sorgue (84) Hostellerie La Grangette
Juan-les-Pins (06) La Villa
Juan-les-Pins (06) Ste-Valérie
Jumièges (76) Le Clos des Fontaines
Jungholtz (68) Les Violettes
Lacabarède (81) Demeure de Flore
Lapoutroie (68) Les Alisiers
Lille (59) Art Déco Romarin
Limoux (11) Grand Hôtel Moderne et Pigeon
Lourmarin (84) La Bastide de Lourmarin
Lumbres (62) Moulin de Mombreux
Lyons-la-Forêt (27) La Licorne
Madières (34) Château de Madières
La Malène (48) Manoir de Montesquiou
Marlenheim (67) Le Cerf
Marsolan (32) Lous Grits
Martel (46) Relais Ste-Anne
Maussane-les-Alpilles / Paradou (13) Du Côté des Olivades
Megève (74) Au Coin du Feu
Ménerbes (84) La Bastide de Marie
Meyronne (46) La Terrasse
Monpazier (24) Edward 1er
Montpellier (34) D'Aragon
Montpellier / Castries (34) Disini

Montsoreau (49) La Marine de Loire
Moudeyres (43) Le Pré Bossu
Mougins (06) Le Manoir de l'Étang
Mougins (06) Les Muscadins
Mussidan / Sourzac (24) Le Chaufourg en Périgord
Nancy (54) D'Haussonville
Neauphle-le-Château (78) Domaine du Verbois
Nice (06) Le Grimaldi
Nîmes (30) La Maison de Sophie
Nitry (89) Auberge la Beursaudière
Nyons (26) La Bastide des Monges
Oradour-sur-Vayres (87) La Bergerie des Chapelles
Orgon (13) Le Mas de la Rose
Osthouse (67) À la Ferme
Paris 2e Noailles
Paris 3e Du Petit Moulin
Paris 4e Bourg Tibourg
Paris 6e Des Académies et des Arts
Paris 7e Le Bellechasse
Paris 8e Le A
Paris 8e Centvingttrois
Paris 8e Chambiges Élysées
Paris 8e De l'Arcade
Paris 16e Bassano
Paris 16e Kléber
Paris 17e Banville
Paris 17e Waldorf Arc de Triomphe
Paris 18e L'Hôtel Particulier
Paris 20e Mama Shelter
Peillon (06) Auberge de la Madone
Perros-Guirec (22) Le Manoir du Sphinx
Petit-Bersac (24) Château Le Mas de Montet
Le Pradet / Les Oursinières (83) L'Escapade
Le Puy-en-Velay (43) Du Parc
Puy-l'Évêque (46) Bellevue
Quimper (29) Manoir-Hôtel des Indes
Rennes (35) Le Coq-Gadby
Rocamadour (46) Domaine de la Rhue
Rodez (12) La Ferme de Bourran
Romans-sur-Isère (26) L'Orée du Parc
La Roque-sur-Pernes (84) Château la Roque
Le Rouret (06) Du Clos
Roussillon (84) Le Clos de la Glycine
Saillagouse / Llo (66) L'Atalaya
Saint-Affrique-les-Montagnes (81) Domaine de Rasigous
Saint-Amour-Bellevue (71) Auberge du Paradis
Saint-Émilion (33) Au Logis des Remparts
Saint-Étienne-de-Baïgorry (64) Arcé
Saint-Flour / Saint-Georges (15) Le Château de Varillettes
Saint-Jean-de-Luz (64) La Devinière
Saint-Laurent-des-Arbres (30) Le Saint-Laurent
Saint-Paul (06) La Grande Bastide
Saint-Paul (06) Le Hameau
Saint-Rémy-de-Provence (13) Gounod
Saint-Rémy-de-Provence (13) La Maison de Bournissac
Saint-Saud-Lacoussière (24) Hostellerie St-Jacques
Saint-Tropez (83) Benkiraï
Saint-Tropez (83) La Maison Blanche
Saint-Tropez (83) La Mistralée
Saint-Tropez (83) Pastis
Saint-Vallier (26) Domaine des Buis
Sainte-Anne-d'Auray (56) L'Auberge
Salers / Le Theil (15) Hostellerie de la Maronne
Sare (64) Arraya
Saulxures (67) La Belle Vue
Sauternes (33) Relais du Château d'Arche
Sauveterre (30) Château de Varenne
Sélestat (67) Auberge de l'Illwald
Sélestat (67) Les Prés d'Ondine
Sézanne / Mondement-Montgivroux (51) Domaine de Montgivroux
Strasbourg (67) Chut - Au Bain aux Plantes
Toulouse (31) Garonne
Tournus / Brancion (71) La Montagne de Brancion
La Trinité-sur-Mer (56) Le Lodge Kerisper
Turquant (49) Demeure de la Vignole
Uchaux (84) Château de Massillan
Uzès (30) Hostellerie Provençale
Valaurie (26) Le Moulin de Valaurie
Vannes (56) Villa Kerasy
Vannes / Arradon (56) Le Logis de Parc er Gréo
Ygrande (03) Château d'Ygrande

Argenton-sur-Creuse (36) Manoir de Boisvillers
Avensan (33) Le Clos de Meyre
Beaune / Puligny-Montrachet (21) La Chouette
Biarritz (64) Maison Garnier
Bormes-les-Mimosas (83) Hostellerie du Cigalou
Boulbon (13) La Bastide de Boulbon
Cancale (35) Auberge de la Motte Jean
Clermont-l'Hérault / Saint-Saturnin-de-Lucian (34) Du Mimosa
Cliousclat (26) La Treille Muscate
Crest-Voland (73) Le Caprice des Neiges
Cuq-Toulza (81) Cuq en Terrasses
Deauville (14) Villa Joséphine
Eygalières (13) Mas dou Pastré
Florac / Cocurès (48) La Lozerette
Forcalquier (04) Auberge Charembeau
La Garde-Guérin (48) Auberge Régordane
Le Grand-Bornand / Le Chinaillon (74) Les Cimes
Graveson (13) Le Cadran Solaire
Île de Ré / Ars-en-Ré (17) Le Sénéchal
Île de Ré / Saint-Martin-de-Ré (17) La Maison Douce
L'Isle-sur-la-Sorgue (84) Le Mas des Grès

Lyons-la-Forêt (27) Les Lions de Beauclerc
Le Mans / Saint-Saturnin (72) Domaine de Chatenay
Maubec (84) La bastide du Bois Bréant
Montauban-sur-l'Ouvèze (26) La Badiane
Montclus (30) La Magnanerie de Bernas
Moustiers-Sainte-Marie (04) La Ferme Rose
Nyons (26) Une Autre Maison
Paris 16e Windsor Home
Propriano (2A) Le Lido
Puycelci (81) L'Ancienne Auberge
Rocamadour (46) Troubadour
Saint-Alban-sur-Limagnole (48) Relais St-Roch
Saint-Céré (46) Villa Ric
Saint-Disdier (05) La Neyrette
Saint-Laurent-du-Verdon (04) Le Moulin du Château
Saint-Malo / Saint-Servan-sur-Mer (35) L'Ascott
Saint-Prix (95) Hostellerie du Prieuré
Salers (15) Saluces
Sancerre / Saint-Thibault (18) De la Loire
Seignosse (40) Villa de l'Étang Blanc
Serre-Chevalier / Le Monêtier-les-Bains (05) Alliey
Le Thor (84) La Bastide Rose
Tréguier (22) Kastell Dinec'h
Vaison-la-Romaine / Crestet (84) Mas d'Hélène
Valberg (06) Blanche Neige
Val-d'Isère (73) La Becca
Wierre-Effroy (62) La Ferme du Vert

Alès / Saint-Hilaire-de-Brethmas (30) Comptoir St-Hilaire
Alleins (13) Domaine de Méjeans
Amboise (37) Vieux Manoir
Apt / Saignon (84) Chambre de Séjour avec Vue
Arbois (39) Closerie les Capucines
Argelès-sur-Mer (66) Château Valmy
Aureille (13) Le Balcon des Alpilles
Autun (71) Le Moulin Renaudiots
Auxerre / Appoigny (89) Le Puits d'Athie
Avignon (84) Lumani
Ay (51) Le Manoir des Charmes
Ayguesvives (31) La Pradasse
Barcelonnette / Saint-Pons (04) Domaine de Lara
Le Barroux (84) L'Aube Safran
Bastia (2B) Château Cagninacci
La Bastide-Clairence (64) Maison Maxana
La Baume (74) La Ferme aux Ours
Bazouges-la-Pérouse (35) Le Château de la Ballue
Beaulieu-sur-Dordogne / Brivezac (19) Château de la Grèze
Beaune (21) La Terre d'Or
Belle-Île / Le Palais (56) Château de Bordenéo
Bessonies (46) Château de Bessonies
Béziers / Villeneuve-lès-Béziers (34) La Chamberte
Biarritz (64) Nere-Chocoa
Biarritz (64) Villa Le Goëland
Biarritz / Arcangues (64) Les Volets Bleus
Bonneuil (16) Le Maine Pertubaud-Jenssen
La Bourboule (63) La Lauzeraie
Bourg-en-Bresse / Lalleyriat (01) Le Nid à Bibi
Bras (83) Une Campagne en Provence
Le Bugue (24) Maison Oléa
Caderousse (84) La Bastide des Princes
Cambrai (59) Le Clos St-Jacques
Cancale (35) Les Rimains
Cancon / Saint-Eutrope-de-Born (47) Domaine du Moulin de Labique
Carcassonne (11) La Maison Coste
Carpentras (84) Château du Martinet
Cascastel-des-Corbières (11) Domaine Grand Guilhem
Cerdon (45) Les Vieux Guays
Cervione (2B) Casa Corsa
Chamonix-Mont-Blanc / Le Lavancher (74) Les Chalets de Philippe
Charolles (71) Le Clos de l'Argolay
Chassagne-Montrachet (21) Château de Chassagne-Montrachet
Clémont (18) Domaine des Givrys
Collonges-la-Rouge (19) Jeanne
Colonzelle (26) La Maison de Soize
Cordes-sur-Ciel / Campes (81) Le Domaine de la Borie Grande
Corvol-d'Embernard (58) Le Colombier de Corvol
Coux-et-Bigaroque (24) Manoir de la Brunie
Crazannes (17) Château de Crazannes
Cucugnan (11) La Tourette
Cult (70) Les Egrignes
Danizy (02) Domaine le Parc
Derchigny (76) Manoir de Graincourt
Drain (49) Le Mésangeau
Eccica-Suarella (2A) Carpe Diem Palazzu
Ennordres (18) Les Chatelains
Escatalens (82) Maison des Chevaliers
Espelette (64) Irazabala
Farges-Allichamps (18) Château de la Commanderie
Fontenay (88) La Grange
Fontenay-le-Comte (85) Le Logis de la Clef de Bois
Fréland (68) La Haute Grange
Fresne-Cauverville (27) Le Clos de l'Ambroisie
Garrigues (34) Château de Roumanières
Gramat (46) Moulin de Fresquet
Le Grand-Bornand / Le Bouchet (74) Le Chalet des Troncs
Grasse (06) Moulin St-François
Grez-en-Bouère (53) Château de Chanay

Grignan (26) La Maison du Moulin
Guebwiller / Murbach (68) Le Schaeferhof
Guéthary (64) Arguibel
Hasparren (64) Ferme Hégia
Honfleur (14) Le Clos Bourdet
Honfleur (14) La Petite Folie
Île de Noirmoutier / Noirmoutier-en-l'Île (85) La Maison de Marine
Île de Ré / Saint-Martin-de-Ré (17) Domaine de la Baronnie
Île de Ré / Saint-Martin-de-Ré (17) La Coursive St-Martin
Île de Ré / Saint-Martin-de-Ré (17) Le Corps de Garde - La Maison du Port
Ivoy-le-Pré (18) Château d'Ivoy
Jarnac (16) Château St-Martial
Jullié (69) Domaine de la Chapelle de Vâtre
Lascabanes (46) Le Domaine de Saint-Géry
Lavannes (51) La Closerie des Sacres
Lestiac-sur-Garonne (33) Les Logis de Lestiac
Libourne / La Rivière (33) Château de La Rivière
Lille (59) La Maison Carrée
Linières-Bouton (49) Château de Boissimon
Lissac-sur-Couze (19) Château de Lissac
Lodève (34) Domaine du Canalet
Lorgues (83) La Bastide du Pin
Lyon / Écully (69) Les Hautes Bruyères
Mâcon / Hurigny (71) Château des Poccards
Martigné-Briand (49) Château des Noyers
Maussane-les-Alpilles / Paradou (13) La Maison du Paradou
Meaux / Trilbardou (77) M. et Mme Cantin
Meauzac (82) Manoir des Chanterelles
Merry-sur-Yonne (89) Le Charme Merry
Monhoudou (72) Château de Monhoudou
Montbenoît / La Longeville (25) Le Crêt l'Agneau
Moustiers-Sainte-Marie (04) La Bouscatière
Muro (2B) Casa Theodora
Mutigny (51) Manoir de Montflambert
Le Muy (83) Château des Demoiselles
Nancy (54) Maison de Myon
Nantes / La Haie-Fouassière (44) Château du Breil
Neauphle-le-Château (78) Le Clos St-Nicolas
Notre-Dame-du-Guildo (22) Château du Val d' Arguenon
Notre-Dame-du-Pé (72) La Reboursière
Oinville-sous-Auneau (28) Caroline Lethuillier
Orange (84) Justin de Provence
Pérignac (16) Château de Lerse
Planguenoual (22) Manoir de la Hazaie
Plazac (24) Béchanou
Pleudihen-sur-Rance (22) Manoir de St-Meleuc
Plougasnou (29) Ar Velin Avel
Pluvigner (56) Domaine de Kerbarh
Poitiers / Lavoux (86) Logis du Château du Bois Dousset
Poligny (05) Le Chalet des Alpages
Portel-des-Corbières (11) Domaine de la Pierre Chaude
Privas / Rochessauve (07) Château de Rochessauve
Quimperlé (29) Château de Kerlarec
Riantec (56) La Chaumière de Kervassal
Riquewihr (68) Le B. Espace Suites
Rochefort (17) Palmier sur Cour
Rodez (12) Château de Labro
Roquebrune (06) Le Roquebrune
Rouen / Martainville-Épreville (76) Sweet Home
Rustrel (84) La Forge
Saint-Adjutory (16) Château du Mesnieux
Saint-André-de-Roquelongue (11) Demeure de Roquelongue
Saint-Bômer-les-Forges (61) Château de la Maigraire
Saint-Calais (72) Château de la Barre
Saint-Étienne-la-Thillaye (14) La Maison de Sophie
Saint-Florent (2B) La Maison Rorqual
Saint-Front (43) La Vidalle d'Eyglet
Saint-Léon (47) Le Hameau des Coquelicots
Saint-Mathurin (85) Le Château de la Millière
Saint-Michel-Escalus (40) La Bergerie-St-Michel
Saint-Michel-Mont-Mercure (85) Château de la Flocellière
Saint-Palais-sur-Mer (17) Ma Maison de Mer
Saint-Pierre-d'Albigny (73) Château des Allues
Saint-Rémy-de-Provence (13) La Maison du Village
Saint-Silvain-Bellegarde (23) Les Trois Ponts
Saint-Sornin (17) La Caussolière
Saint-Valery-en-Caux (76) Château du Mesnil Geoffroy
Sainte-Mère-Église (50) Château de L'Isle Marie
Sainte-Nathalene (24) La Roche d'Esteil
Segonzac (19) Pré Laminon
Soustons (40) Domaine de Bellegarde
Strasbourg (67) La Belle Strasbourgeoise
Terraube (32) Maison Ardure
Le Thoronet (83) Bastide des Hautes Moures
Toulouse (31) Les Loges de St-Sernin
Tournus (71) La Tour du Trésorier
Tourrettes-sur-Loup (06) Histoires de Bastide
Troyes / Moussey (10) Domaine de la Creuse
Tulette (26) K-Za
Uzer (07) Château d'Uzer
Uzès / Montaren-et-Saint-Médiers (30) Clos du Léthé
Valojoulx (24) La Licorne
Vals-les-Bains (07) Château Clément
Vals-les-Bains (07) Villa Aimée
Vauville (14) Manoir de la Haulle
Vence (06) La Colline de Vence
Vergoncey (50) Château de Boucéel
Verteuil-sur-Charente (16) Le Couvent des Cordeliers
Villemontais (42) Domaine de Fontenay
Villiers-sous-Grez (77) La Cerisaie
Vollore-Ville (63) Château de Vollore
Vouvray (37) Domaine des Bidaudières

Pleasant restaurants

Restaurants agréables

Ristoranti ameni

Angenehme Restaurants

Restaurantes agradables

XXXXX

Annecy / Veyrier-du-Lac (74)	La Maison de Marc Veyrat
Antibes / Cap d'Antibes (06)	Eden Roc
Les Baux-de-Provence (13)	L' Oustaù de Baumanière
Illhaeusern (68)	Auberge de l'Ill
Lyon (69)	Paul Bocuse
Monte-Carlo (MC)	Le Louis XV-Alain Ducasse
Paris 1er	L'Espadon
Paris 1er	le Meurice
Paris 5e	La Tour d'Argent
Paris 8e	Alain Ducasse au Plaza Athénée
Paris 8e	Les Ambassadeurs
Paris 8e	Apicius
Paris 8e	Le Bristol
Paris 8e	Le "Cinq"
Paris 8e	Lasserre
Paris 8e	Ledoyen
Paris 8e	Taillevent

XXXX

Baerenthal / Untermuhlthal (57)	L'Arnsbourg
Le-Bourget-du-Lac (73)	Le Bateau Ivre
Cannes (06)	La Palme d'Or
Lille (59)	A L'Huîtrière
Lyon (69)	Pierre Orsi
Lyon / Charbonnières-les-Bains (69)	La Rotonde
Mandelieu / La Napoule (06)	L'Oasis
Mionnay (01)	Alain Chapel
Monte-Carlo (MC)	Grill de l'Hôtel de Paris
Monte-Carlo (MC)	Joël Robuchon Monte-Carlo
Montpellier (34)	Le Jardin des Sens
Nice (06)	Chantecler
Nîmes / Garons (30)	Alexandre
Paris 1er	Le Grand Véfour
Paris 4e	L'Ambroisie
Paris 8e	Laurent
Paris 16e	La Grande Cascade
Paris 16e	Le Pré Catelan
La Rochelle (17)	Richard et Christopher Coutanceau
Romans-sur-Isère / Granges-les-Beaumont (26)	Les Cèdres
Saint-Bonnet-le-Froid (43)	Régis et Jacques Marcon
Tourrettes (83)	Faventia
Versailles (78)	Gordon Ramsay au Trianon

XXX

Agen (47)	Mariottat
Aix-en-Provence (13)	Le Clos de la Violette
Antibes / Cap d'Antibes (06)	Bacon
Antibes / Cap d'Antibes (06)	Les Pêcheurs
Avignon (84)	Christian Étienne
Balleroy (14)	Manoir de la Drôme
Belle-Église (60)	La Grange de Belle-Église
Bidart (64)	Table et Hostellerie des Frères Ibarboure
Biot (06)	Les Terraillers
Bonnieux (84)	La Bastide de Capelongue

Boulogne-sur-Mer (62) La Matelote
Bourges (18) L'Abbaye St-Ambroix
Cassis (13) La Villa Madie
Chalon-sur-Saône / Saint-Rémy (71) Moulin de Martorey
Champtoceaux (49) Les Jardins de la Forge
Chasselay (69) Guy Lassausaie
Clisson (44) La Bonne Auberge
Compiègne / Rethondes (60) Alain Blot
Conteville (27) Auberge du Vieux Logis
Courchevel / Courchevel 1850 (73) Le Bateau Ivre
Dole / Sampans (39) Château du Mont Joly
Dunkerque / Coudekerque-Branche (59) Le Soubise
Fayence (83) Le Castellaras
Fontevraud-l'Abbaye (49) La Licorne
Fontjoncouse (11) Auberge du Vieux Puits
Forbach / Stiring-Wendel (57) La Bonne Auberge
Grenade-sur-l'Adour (40) Pain Adour et Fantaisie
Gundershoffen (67) Au Cygne
Jarnac / Bourg-Charente (16) La Ribaudière
Le Lavandou / Aiguebelle (83) Mathias Dandine
Lourmarin (84) Auberge La Fenière
Lyon (69) Les Terrasses de Lyon
Maisons-Laffitte (78) Tastevin
Malbuisson (25) Le Bon Accueil
Megève / Leutaz (74) Flocons de Sel
Monte-Carlo (MC) Vistamar
Montpellier / Lattes (34) Domaine de Soriech
Moulins (03) Le Clos de Bourgogne

Nantes / Haute-Goulaine (44) Manoir de la Boulaie
Obernai (67) La Fourchette des Ducs
Orléans / Olivet (45) Le Rivage
Ozoir-la-Ferrière (77) La Gueulardière
Pacy-sur-Eure / Cocherel (27) La Ferme de Cocherel
Paris 6e Paris
Paris 7e Le Jules Verne
Pau (64) Au Fin Gourmet
Pont-Aven (29) Moulin de Rosmadec
Port-sur-Saône / Vauchoux (70) Château de Vauchoux
Le Puy-en-Velay (43) François Gagnaire
Questembert (56) Le Bretagne et sa Résidence
Reims / Montchenot (51) Grand Cerf
Riquewihr (68) Table du Gourmet
La Roche-Bernard (56) L'Auberge Bretonne
La Roche-l'Abeille (87) Le Moulin de la Gorce
Saint-Germain-en-Laye (78) Cazaudehore
Saint-Saturnin-lès-Apt (84) Domaine des Andéols
Sénart / Pouilly-le-Fort (77) Le Pouilly
Sierentz (68) Auberge St-Laurent
Strasbourg (67) Buerehiesel
Toulon (83) Les Pins Penchés
Toulouse / Colomiers (31) L'Amphitryon
Tournus (71) Rest. Greuze
Vannes / Saint-Avé (56) Le Pressoir
Villeneuve-le-Comte (77) A la Bonne Marmite
Zoufftgen (57) La Lorraine

Aire-sur-la-Lys / Isbergues (62) Le Buffet
Ajaccio (2A) Palm Beach
Albi (81) L'Esprit du Vin
Alès / Saint-Privat-des-Vieux (30) Le Vertige des Senteurs
Antibes (06) Oscar's
Ay (51) Le Vieux Puits
Azay-le-Rideau / Saché (37) Auberge du XIIe Siècle
Bannegon (18) Moulin de Chaméron
Le Barroux (84) Gajulea
Le Bar-sur-Loup (06) La Jarrerie
Beaune (21) Caveau des Arches
Bédoin (84) Le Mas des Vignes
Belcastel (12) Vieux Pont
Biarritz (64) Campagne et Gourmandise
Blainville-sur-Mer (50) Le Mascaret
Le-Bourget-du-Lac (73) La Grange à Sel
Bray-et-Lû (95) Les Jardins d'Epicure
Le Breuil-en-Auge (14) Le Dauphin
Bully (69) Auberge du Château

Cancale (35) Le Coquillage
Chaintré (71) La Table de Chaintré
Chamonix-Mont-Blanc (74) La Maison Carrier
Chamonix-Mont-Blanc / Les Praz-de-Chamonix (74) La Cabane des Praz
Charroux (03) Ferme Saint-Sébastien
Châtillon-sur-Chalaronne / L'Abergement-Clémenciat (01) St-Lazare
Clermont-l'Hérault / Saint-Guiraud (34) Le Mimosa
Couilly-Pont-aux-Dames (77) Auberge de la Brie
Divonne-les-Bains (01) Le Rectiligne
Eugénie-les-Bains (40) La Ferme aux Grives
Eygalières (13) Bistrot d'Eygalières "Chez Bru"
Falicon (06) Parcours
Ferrières-les-Verreries (34) La Cour-Mas de Baumes
Gordes (84) Le Mas Tourteron
Le Havre (76) Jean-Luc Tartarin
Île de Ré / Saint-Martin-de-Ré (17) Bô
L'Isle-sur-la-Sorgue (84) La Prévôté

L'Isle-sur-Serein (89) Auberge du Pot d'Étain
Kilstett (67) Au Cheval Noir
Labaroche (68) Blanche Neige
Loiré (49) Auberge de la Diligence
Lyon (69) Auberge de l'Île
Lyon (69) La Rémanence
Marseille (13) L'Épuisette
Megève / Leutaz (74) La Sauvageonne
Meudon (92) L'Escarbille
Mollégès (13) Mas du Capoun
Montauroux (83) Auberge des Fontaines d'Aragon
Montbazon (37) Chancelière "Jeu de Cartes"
Monte-Carlo (MC) Maya Bay
Morteau (25) Auberge de la Roche
Nans-les-Pins (83) Château de Nans
Nantes (44) L'Océanide
Nice (06) Jouni "Atelier du Goût"
Nieuil (16) La Grange aux Oies
Orange (84) Le Mas des Aigras - Table du Verger
Paris 6e Le Restaurant
Paris 7e Il Vino d'Enrico Bernardo
Paris 8e 1728
Le Pradet / Les Oursinières (83) La Chanterelle
Le Puy-en-Velay / Espaly-Saint-Marcel (43) L'Ermitage
La Rivière-Thibouville (27) Le Manoir du Soleil d'Or
Le Rouret (06) Le Clos St-Pierre
Saint-Agrève (07) Domaine de Rilhac
Saint-Joachim (44) La Mare aux Oiseaux
Saint-Malo / Saint-Servan-sur-Mer (35) Le St-Placide
Saint-Martin-de-Belleville (73) La Bouitte
Saint-Pée-sur-Nivelle (64) L' Auberge Basque
Sassetot-le-Mauconduit (76) Le Relais des Dalles
Sessenheim (67) Au Bœuf
Strasbourg (67) La Cambuse
La Turbie (06) Hostellerie Jérôme
Uchaux (84) Côté Sud
Vaison-la-Romaine (84) Le Moulin à Huile
Vaison-la-Romaine / Roaix (84) Le Grand Pré
Valbonne (06) Lou Cigalon
Vence (06) Le Vieux Couvent
Verdun-sur-le-Doubs (71) Hostellerie Bourguignonne
Villefranche-sur-Mer (06) L'Oursin Bleu

Aix-en-Provence (13) Pierre Reboul
Ansouis (84) La Closerie
Arles (13) La Chassagnette
Auvers-sur-Oise (95) Auberge Ravoux
Avignon (84) Les 5 Sens
Bairols (06) Auberge du Moulin
Bastia (2B) A Casarella
Beaune / Levernois (21) Le Bistrot du Bord de l'Eau
Bédarieux / Villemagne-l'Argentière (34) Auberge de l'Abbaye
Biarritz (64) Philippe
Blois (41) Au Rendez-vous des Pêcheurs
Bonnieux (84) L'Arôme
Bonnieux (84) Le Fournil
Cancale (35) La Maison de la Marine
Carnac (56) La Calypso
Cernay-la-Ville / à La Celle-les-Bordes (78) L' Auberge de l'Élan
Chalon-sur-Saône (71) Le Bistrot
Cherbourg-Octeville (50) Le Pommier
Clermont-Ferrand (63) Fleur de Sel
Cormeilles (27) Gourmandises
Dax (40) Une Cuisine en Ville
Dinard / Saint-Lunaire (35) Le Décollé
Épaignes (27) L'Auberge du Beau Carré
Erquy / Saint-Aubin (22) Relais St-Aubin
Fontvieille (13) Le Patio
Hendaye (64) Ez Kecha Bar Lieu Dit Vin
Iguerande (71) La Colline du Colombier
Langon (33) Chez Cyril
Lavaur (24) Auberge de Bayle Viel
Lyon (69) Maison Clovis
Magalas (34) Ô. Bontemps
Notre-Dame-de-Bellecombe (73) La Ferme de Victorine
Paris 7e L'Atelier de Joël Robuchon
Pratz (39) Les Louvières
Le Puy-en-Velay (43) Le Poivrier
Roussillon (84) Le Piquebaure-Côté Soleil
Saint-Agrève (07) Faurie
Saint-Alban-sur-Limagnole (48) La Petite Maison
Saint-Marc-à-Loubaud (23) Les Mille Sources
Saint-Paul (06) La Toile Blanche
Saint-Vaast-la-Hougue (50) Le Chasse Marée
Sainte-Cécile-les-Vignes (84) Campagne, Vignes et Gourmandises
Sare (64) Olhabidea
Turenne (19) Maison des Chanoines
Vence (06) Les Bacchanales
Vichy (03) Brasserie du Casino
Yvetot (76) Auberge du Val au Cesne

Further information

Pour en savoir plus

Per saperne di piú

Gut zu wissen

Para saber más

Vineyards & Regional Specialities

Vignobles & Spécialités régionales
Vini e Specialità regionali
Weinberge & regionale Spezialitäten
Viñedos y Especialidades regionales

① NORMANDIE

Demoiselles de Cherbourg à la nage,
Andouille de Vire,
Sole dieppoise,
Poulet Vallée d'Auge,
Tripes à la mode de Caen,
Canard à la rouennaise,
Agneau de pré-salé,
Camembert, Livarot, Pont-l'Évêque,
Neufchâtel,
Tarte aux pommes au calvados,
Crêpes à la normande, Douillons

② BRETAGNE

Fruits de mer, Crustacés, Huîtres de Belon,
Galettes au sarrazin/blé noir, Charcuteries,
Andouille de Guéméné, St-Jacques à la bretonne,
Homard à l'armoricaine,
Poissons : bar, turbot, lieu jaune,
maquereau, etc.,
Cotriade, Kig Ha Farz,
Légumes : artichaut, chou-fleur, etc.,
Crêpes, Gâteau breton, Far, Kouing-aman

③ VAL DE LOIRE

Rillettes de Tours, Andouillette au vouvray,
Poissons de rivière : brochet, sandre, etc.,
Saumon beurre blanc, Gibier de Sologne,
Fromages de chèvre : Ste-Maure, Valençay,
Crémet d'Angers, Macarons, Nougat glacé,
Pithiviers, Tarte tatin

④ SUD-OUEST

Garbure, Ttoro, Jambon de Bayonne,
Foie gras, Omelette aux truffes,
Pipérade, Lamproie à la bordelaise,
Poulet basquaise, Cassoulet,
Confit de canard ou d'oie,
Cèpes à la bordelaise,
Tomme de brebis, Roquefort,
Gâteau basque, Pruneaux à l'armagnac

⑤ CENTRE-AUVERGNE

Cochonnailles, Tripous,
Champignons : cèpes, girolles, etc.,
Pâté bourbonnais, Aligot, Potée auvergnate,
Chou farci, Pounti, Lentilles du Puy,
Cantal, St-Nectaire, Fourme d'Ambert,
Flognarde, Gâteau à la broche

⑬ NORD-PICARDIE

Moules, Ficelle picarde,
Flamiche aux poireaux,
Poissons : sole, turbot, etc.,
Potjevlesch, Waterzoï,
Gibier d'eau,
Lapin à la bière, Hochepot,
Boulette d'Avesnes,
Maroilles, Gaufres

⑫ BOURGOGNE

Jambon persillé,
Gougère,
Escargots de Bourgogne,
Œufs en meurette,
Pochouse, Coq au vin,
Jambon chaud à la crème,
Viande de charolais,
Bœuf bourguignon,
Époisses, Poire dijonnaise,
Desserts au pain d'épice

⑪ ALSACE-LORRAINE

Charcuterie, Presskopf,
Quiche lorraine, Tarte à l'oignon,
Grenouilles, Asperges,
Poissons : sandre, carpe, anguille,
Coq au riesling, Spaetzle,
Choucroute, Baeckeoffe,
Gibiers : biche, chevreuil, sanglier,
Munster, Kougelhopf,
Tarte aux mirabelles ou aux quetsches, Vacherin glacé

⑩ FRANCHE-COMTÉ/JURA

Jésus de Morteau, Saucisse de Montbéliard,
Croûte aux morilles, Soufflé au fromage,
Poissons de lac et rivières : brochet, truite,
Grenouilles, Coq au vin jaune, Comté, vacherin,
Morbier, Cancoillotte, Gaudes au maïs

⑨ LYONNAIS-PAYS BRESSAN

Rosette de Lyon, Grenouilles de la Dombes,
Gâteau de foies blonds, Quenelles de brochet,
Saucisson truffé pistaché, Poularde demi-deuil,
Tablier de sapeur, Cardons à la mœlle,
Volailles de Bresse à la crème,
Cervelle de canut, Bugnes

⑧ SAVOIE-DAUPHINÉ

Gratin de queues d'écrevisses,
Poissons de lac : omble chevalier, perche, féra,
Ravioles du Royans, Fondue, Raclette, Tartiflette,
Diots au vin blanc, Fricassée de caïon, Potée savoyarde,
Farçon, Farcement, Gratin dauphinois,
Beaufort, Reblochon, Tomme de Savoie,
St-Marcellin, Gâteau de Savoie, Gâteau aux noix,
Tarte aux myrtilles

⑦ PROVENCE-MÉDITERRANÉE

Aïoli, Pissaladière, Salade niçoise, Bouillabaisse,
Anchois de Collioure, Loup grillé au fenouil,
Brandade nîmoise, Bourride sétoise,
Pieds paquets à la marseillaise, Petits farcis niçois,
Daube provençale,
Agneau de Sisteron,
Picodon, Crème catalane,
Calissons, Fruits confits

⑥ CORSE

Jambon, Figatelli,
Lonzo, Coppa,
Langouste,
Omelette au brocciu,
Civet de sanglier,
Chevreau,
Fromages de brebis (Niolu),
Flan de châtaignes,
Fiadone

BORDEAUX
Pomerol
Tursan

→Vineyards
→Vignobles
→Vini
→Viñedos
→Weinberge

⑦ CORSE

Jambon

→Spécialités régionales
→Regional specialities
→Vini e Specialità regionali
→Viñedos y Especialidades regionales
→Weinberge und regionale Spezialitäten

Choosing a good wine

Choisir le bon vin
Scegliere un buon vino
Der richtige Wein
Escoger el vino

	1996	1997	1998	1999	2000	2001	2002	2003	2004	2005	2006	2007
Alsace	Good	Great	Good	Good	Great	Great	Good	Good	Good	Great	Good	Great
Bordeaux blanc	Great	Good	Good	Average	Great	Good	Average	Good	Good	Great	Good	Good
Bordeaux rouge	Great	Average	Good	Good	Great	Good	Good	Good	Good	Great	Good	Good
Bourgogne blanc	Great	Great	Good	Good	Good	Average	Great	Good	Good	Great	Good	Average
Bourgogne rouge	Great	Good	Good	Great	Good	Average	Great	Good	Good	Great	Good	Average
Beaujolais	Average	Great	Good	Great	Great	Good	Good	Great	Good	Great	Good	Good
Champagne	Great	Good	Good	Great	Average	Average	Good	Great	Good	Good	Good	Average
Côtes du Rhône Septentrionales	Great	Good	Good	Great	Good	Good	Good	Good	Good	Great	Great	Good
Côtes du Rhône Méridionales	Great	Good	Great	Good	Great	Great	Average	Good	Good	Great	Good	Good
Provence	Good	Good	Average	Good	Good	Great	Average	Good	Good	Good	Good	Good
Languedoc *Roussillon*	Great	Good	Great	Good	Good	Good	Average	Good	Good	Good	Good	Good
Val de Loire *Muscadet*	Great	Good	Good	Good	Good	Good	Good	Great	Good	Great	Good	Average
Val de Loire *Anjou-Touraine*	Great	Good	Good	Good	Good	Good	Good	Great	Good	Great	Good	Average
Val de Loire *Pouilly-Sancerre*	Great	Great	Good	Good	Great	Good	Good	Great	Good	Great	Good	Average

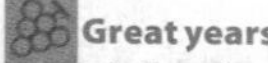
Great years
→ Grandes années
→ Grandi annate
→ Großen Jahrgänge
→ Añadas excelentes

Good years
→ Bonnes années
→ Buone annate
→ Gute Jahrgänge
→ Buenas añadas

Average years
→ Années moyennes
→ Annate corrette
→ Mittlere Jahrgänge
→ Añadas correcias

The greatest vintages since 1970 : 1970 - 1975 - 1979 - 1982 - 1985 - 1989 - 1990 - 1996 - 2005
→ Les grandes années depuis 1970
→ Le grandi annate dal 1970
→ Dis größten Jahrgänge seit 1970
→ Las grandes añadas desde 1970

SUGGESTIONS FOR COMPLEMENTARY DISHES AND WINES

→ **Associer les mets & vins**
→ **Suggerimento per l'abbinamento tra cibo e vini**
→ **Empfehlungen welcher Wein zum welchem Gericht**
→ **Sugerencias para combinar platos y vinos**

→ **SHELLFISH** Dry whites → CRUSTACÉS & COQUILLAGES : Blancs secs → CROSTACEI : Bianchi secchi → SCHALENTIERE : Trockene Weiße → CRUSTÁCEOS : Blancos seccos	Alsace Bordeaux Bourgogne Côtes du Rhône Provence Languedoc-Roussillon Val de Loire	Sylvaner/Riesling Entre-deux-Mers Chablis/Mâcon Villages St Joseph Cassis/Palette Picpoul de Pinet Muscadet/Montlouis
→ **FISH** Dry whites → POISSONS : Blancs secs → PESCI : Bianchi secchi → FISCHE : Trockene Weiße → PESCADOS : Blancos seccos	Alsace Bordeaux Bourgogne Côtes du Rhône Provence Corse Languedoc-Roussillon Val de Loire	Riesling Pessac-Léognan/Graves Meursault/Chassagne-Montrachet Hermitage/Condrieu Bellet/Bandol Patrimonio Coteaux du Languedoc Sancerre/Menetou-Salon
→ **POULTRY** Whites and light reds → VOLAILLES & CHARCUTERIES : Blancs et rouges légers → POLLAME : Bianchi e rossi leggeri → GEFLÜGEL : Weiße und leichte Rote → AVES : Blancos y tintos suaves	Alsace Champagne Bordeaux Bourgogne Beaujolais Côtes du Rhône Provence Corse Languedoc-Roussillon Val de Loire	Tokay-Pinot gris/Pinot noir Coteaux Champenois blanc et rouge Côtes de Bourg/Blaye/Castillon Mâcon/St Romain Beaujolais Villages Tavel (rosé)/Côtes du Ventoux Coteaux d'Aix-en-Provence Coteaux d'Ajaccio/Porto-Vecchio Faugères Anjou/Vouvray
→ **MEATS** Reds → VIANDES : Rouges → CARNI : Rossi → FLEISCH : Rote → CARNES : Tintos	Bordeaux/Sud-Ouest Bourgogne Beaujolais Côtes du Rhône Provence Languedoc-Roussillon Val de Loire	Médoc/St Émilion/Buzet Volnay/Hautes Côtes de Beaune Moulin à Vent/Morgon Vacqueyras/Gigondas Bandol/Côtes de Provence Fitou/Minervois Bourgueil/Saumur
→ **GAME** Hearty reds → GIBIER : Rouges corsés → SELVAGGINA : Rossi di corpo → WILD : Kräftige Rote → CAZAS : Tintos con cuerpo	Bordeaux/Sud-Ouest Bourgogne Côtes du Rhône Languedoc-Roussillon Val de Loire	Pauillac/St Estèphe/Madiran/Cahors Pommard/Gevrey-Chambertin Côte-Rotie/Cornas Corbières/Collioure Chinon
→ **CHEESES** Whites and reds → FROMAGES : Blancs et rouges → FORMAGGI : Bianchi e rossi → KÄSESORTEN : Weiße und Rote → QUESOS : Blancos y tintos	Alsace Bordeaux Bourgogne Beaujolais Côtes du Rhône Languedoc-Roussillon Jura/Savoie Val de Loire	Gewurztraminer St Julien/Pomerol/Margaux Pouilly-Fuissé/Santenay St Amour/Fleurie Hermitage/Châteauneuf-du-Pape St Chinian Vin Jaune/Chignin Pouilly-Fumé/Valençay
→ **DESSERTS** Dessert wines → DESSERTS : Vins de desserts → DESSERT : Vini da dessert → NACHTISCHE : Dessert-Weine → POSTRES : Vinos dulces	Alsace Champagne Bordeaux/Sud-Ouest Bourgogne Jura/Bugey Côtes du Rhône Languedoc-Roussillon Val de Loire	Muscat d'Alsace/Crémant d'Alsace Champagne blanc et rosé Sauternes/Monbazillac/Jurançon Crémant de Bourgogne Vin de Paille/Cerdon Muscat de Beaumes-de-Venise Banyuls/Maury/Muscats/Limoux Coteaux du Layon/Bonnezeaux

→ Region of production → Région vinicole → Regione vinicola → Wein gegend → Regiõn vinicola

→ Appellation → Appellation → Denominazione → Appellation → Denominaciõn

Towns
from A to Z

Villes
de A à Z

Città
da A a Z

Städte
von A bis Z

Ciudades
de A a Z

地名
アルファベット順

ABBEVILLE – 80 Somme – 301 E7 – pop. 24 000 – alt. 8 m – ✉ 80100 Northern France and the Paris Region

36 **A1**

Paris 186 – Amiens 51 – Boulogne-sur-Mer 79 – Rouen 106

d'Abbeville Abbeville Route du Val, 4 km on the St-Valéry-sur-Somme road, ✆ 03 22 24 98 58

Modern stained-glass windows★★ of St-Sépulcre church - Façade★ of St-Vulfran collegiate church - Musée Boucher de Perthes★ BY **M.**

Vallée de la Somme★ SE - Château de Bagatelle★ S.

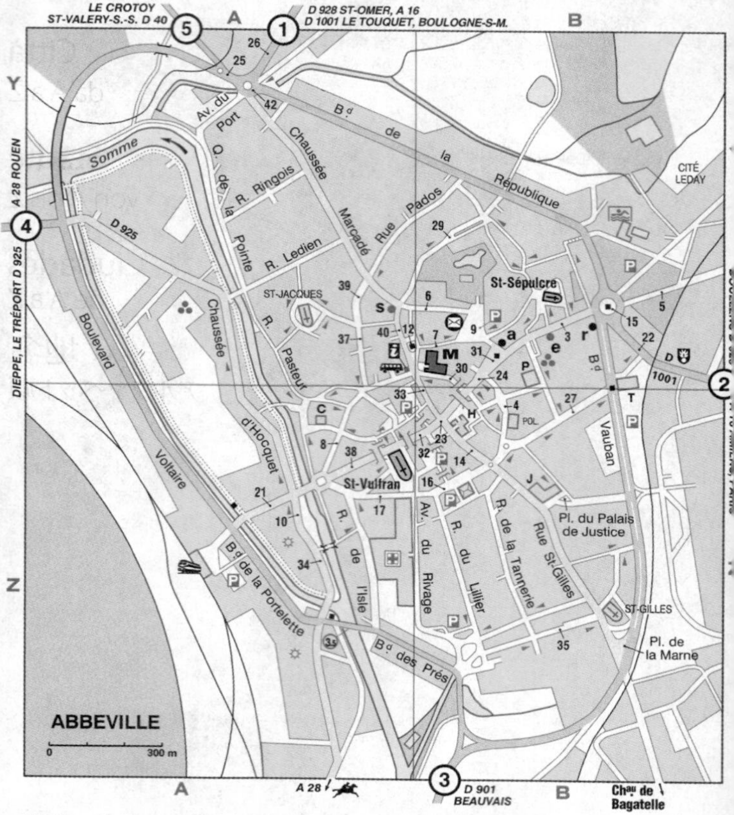

LE CROTOY ST-VALERY-S.-S. D 40 (5)

D 928 ST-OMER, A 16 D 1001 LE TOUQUET, BOULOGNE-S-M. (1)

A 28 ROUEN (4) DIEPPE, LE TRÉPORT D 925

A 28 (3) D 901 BEAUVAIS

Chau de Bagatelle

ABBEVILLE

0 300 m

Street	Grid	No.
Bois (Chaussée du)	BY	3
Boucher-de-Perthes (R.)	BZ	4
Briand (Av. A.)	BY	5
Capucins (R. des)	BY	6
Carmes (R. des)	BY	7
Chevalier-de-la-Barre (R. du)	AZ	8
Clemenceau (Pl.)	BY	9
Cordeliers (R. des)	AZ	10
Courbet (Pl. Amiral)	AY	12
Foch (R. du Mar.)	BZ	14
Gaulle (Pl. Général-de)	BY	15
Grand-Marché (Pl. du)	BZ	16
Hôtel-Dieu (R. de l')	AZ	17
Jean-Jaurès (R.)	AZ	21
Leclerc (Av. du Gén.)	BY	22
Lejeune (Pl. M.)	BZ	23
Lingers (R. des)	BYZ	24
Menchecourt (R. de)	AY	25
Mennesson (R. Jean)	AY	26
Millevoye (R.)	BZ	27
Pareurs (R. aux)	BY	29
Patin (R. Gontier)	BY	30
Pilori (Pl. du)	BY	31
Ponthieu (R. J. de)	ABZ	33
Pont-aux-Brouettes (R.)	ABZ	32
Portelette (R. de la)	AZ	34
Prayel (R. du)	BZ	35
Rapporteurs (R. des)	AY	37
St-Vulfran (R.)	AZ	38
Sauvage (R. P.)	AY	39
Teinturiers (R. des)	AY	40
Verdun (Pl. de)	AY	42

Mercure Hôtel de France
19 pl. du Pilori – ✆ 03 22 24 00 42 – www.mercure.com – h5440@accor.com – Fax 03 22 24 26 15 BY **a**
72 rm – €94/115 €110/135, ☕ €13
Rest – Menu (€17), €21 – Carte €25/44
◆ This large town centre establishment with a brick façade offers fresh, well-equipped rooms, as well as one suite with a 'spa' bath. Refined wine bar. A bright veranda dining room with rotisserie corner; grills and traditional cuisine.

Relais Vauban without rest
4 bd Vauban – ✆ 03 22 25 38 00 – www.relais-vauban.com – contact@relais-vauban.com – Fax 03 22 31 75 97 – Closed 1-9 March and 20 December-4 January BY **r**
22 rm – €52/55 €54/58, ☕ €8,50
◆ Small hotel on a busy street near the town centre, offering bright and functional rooms. Friendly service and extremely well kept.

La Fermette des Prés de Mautort without rest
10 imp. de la Croix, via ⑤ – ✆ 03 22 24 57 62 – http://perso.wanadoo.fr/lespresdemautort – fermettemautort@gmail.com – Fax 03 22 24 57 62
3 rm ☕ – €45/50 €60
◆ Distinctive country farm offering the promise of a good night's sleep in comfortable rooms. Breakfast on the veranda or terrace overlooking the garden (indoor pool).

L'Escale en Picardie
15 r. des Teinturiers – ✆ 03 22 24 21 51 – Closed 20 August-4 September, 24 February-10 March, Thursday dinner, Sunday dinner, Monday and bank holidays AY **s**
Rest – Menu (€23 bi), €25/70 – Carte €50/72
◆ Succulent fish and seafood served in a rustic dining room with beams and a stone fireplace: a charming welcome awaits you in this restaurant.

La Corne
32 chaussée du Bois – ✆ 03 22 24 06 34 – mlematelot@aol.com – Fax 03 22 24 03 65 – Closed 15 July-4 August, 21 December-4 January, Wednesday dinner, Saturday lunch and Sunday BY **e**
Rest – Menu (€17), €26 – Carte €31/56
◆ A blue façade and an attractive retro interior for this old Abbeville house, transformed into a restaurant. Generous, bistro-style cuisine, including calf's sweetbreads and *andouillette*...

in St-Riquier **9 km by ②, D 925 – pop. 1 186 – alt. 29 m – ✉ 80135**

Syndicat d'initiative, le Beffroi ✆ 03 22 28 91 72, Fax 03 22 28 02 73

Jean de Bruges without rest
18 pl. de l'Église – ✆ 03 22 28 30 30 – www.hotel-jean-de-bruges.com – jeandebruges@wanadoo.fr – Fax 03 22 28 00 69
11 rm – €95/100 €110/115, ☕ €14
◆ On the square in front of the Abbey, an elegant 17C house in white stone. Rooms have lots of character and contain antique furniture. Breakfast room under a glass canopy.

in Mareuil-Caubert **4 km South by D 928 (direction hippodrome then Rouen road) – pop. 908 – alt. 12 m – ✉ 80132**

Auberge du Colvert
4 rte de Rouen – ✆ 03 22 31 32 32 – auberge-du-colvert@9business.fr – Fax 03 22 31 32 32 – Closed 29 June-5 July, 24-30 August, Monday dinner from September to June, Sunday dinner, Tuesday dinner and Wednesday
Rest – Menu (€14), €20/32 – Carte approx. €35
◆ A country inn with a wood-panelled dining room, brightened by large bay windows and heated by a hanging fireplace. Traditional seasonal cuisine.

L'ABERGEMENT-CLÉMENCIAT – **01 Ain – 328** C4 – see Châtillon-sur-Chalaronne

ABLIS – 78 Yvelines – 311 G4 – pop. 2 705 – alt. 151 m – ✉ 78660 18 A2

Paris 62 – Chartres 31 – Mantes-la-Jolie 64 – Orléans 79 – Rambouillet 14 – Versailles 49

Syndicat d'initiative, Hôtel de Ville ✆ 01 30 46 06 06, Fax 01 30 46 06 07

West 6 km by D 168 – ✉28700 St-Symphorien-le-Château

Château d'Esclimont

2 r. Château d'Esclimont – ✆ 02 37 31 15 15 – www.esclimont.fr – esclimont@grandesetapes.fr – Fax 02 37 31 57 91

52 rm – †€ 180/890 ††€ 180/890, ☕ € 24 – 5 suites

Rest – Menu € 43 (weekday lunch), € 59/93 – Carte € 88/113

◆ For a taste of château life, visit this 15C and 16C residence, former home of the La Rochefoucauld family. Magnificent park with lake, river and landscaped gardens. Modern cuisine served in an 18C style dining room and another renowned for its exquisite Cordova leather.

ABRESCHVILLER – 57 Moselle – 307 N7 – pop. 1 481 – alt. 340 m – ✉ 57560 Alsace-Lorraine 27 D2

Paris 433 – Baccarat 46 – Lunéville 62 – Phalsbourg 23 – Sarrebourg 17 – Strasbourg 79

Office de tourisme, 78, rue Jordy ✆ 03 87 03 77 26, Fax 03 87 03 77 26

Auberge de la Forêt

276 r. des Verriers, in Lettenbach : 0,5 km – ✆ 03 87 03 71 78 – www.aubergedelaforet57.com – aubergedelaforet2@wanadoo.fr – Fax 03 87 03 79 96 – Closed 1st-21 January, Tuesday dinner and Monday

Rest – Menu (€ 18), € 25/40 – Carte € 33/52

◆ Smart village inn with charming dining rooms, the most recent with splendid contemporary decor. Traditional cuisine and regional specialities.

ABREST – 03 Allier – 326 H6 – see Vichy

ACCOLAY – 89 Yonne – 319 F6 – pop. 462 – alt. 125 m – ✉ 89460 Burgundy-Jura 7 B2

Paris 188 – Avallon 31 – Auxerre 23 – Tonnerre 40

Hostellerie de la Fontaine with rm

16 r. Reigny – ✆ 03 86 81 54 02 – www.coeurdelyonne.com – hostellerie.fontaine@wanadoo.fr – Fax 03 86 81 52 78 – Open 14 February-15 November, and closed Sunday dinner 1st October-31 March, Tuesday lunch and Monday

11 rm – †€ 52/55 ††€ 53/55, ☕ € 10 – ½ P € 62

Rest – *(closed at lunch from Monday to Thursday)* Menu (€ 15), € 26/50 – Carte € 31/48

◆ A Burgundian house located in a sleepy village in the Cure valley. Meals are served in the old wine cellar or, weather permitting, in the pleasant flower garden.

ACQUIGNY – 27 Eure – 304 H6 – pop. 1 614 – alt. 19 m – ✉ 27400 33 D2

Paris 105 – Évreux 22 – Mantes-la-Jolie 54 – Rouen 38

L' Hostellerie

1 r. d'Evreux – ✆ 02 32 50 20 05 – Fax 02 32 50 56 04 – Closed 13 July-4 August, 8-22 February, Monday and Tuesday

Rest – Menu (€ 20), € 30/72 bi – Carte € 46/70

◆ Updated fare and market suggestions served in the plush, cosy ambience of a warm-coloured, discreetly modern dining room.

La Table du Béarnais

40 r. A.-Briand – ✆ 02 32 40 37 73 – jean-claude.lalane@orange.fr – Closed 20-27 September, 22 December-2 January, Thursday dinner, Sunday dinner and Monday

Rest – Menu € 13 (weekday lunch), € 30/49 – Carte € 63/78

◆ This pleasant house welcomes you in two rustic dining rooms (exposed beams, lamps on the tables). The tasty dishes are full of flavours from Béarn and Landes.

LES ADRETS-DE-L'ESTÉREL – 83 Var – 340 P4 – pop. 2 063 – alt. 295 m – ✉ 83600 42 E2

Paris 881 – Cannes 26 – Draguignan 44 – Fréjus 17 – Grasse 30 – Mandelieu-la-Napoule 15

Office de tourisme, place de la Mairie ✆ 04 94 40 93 57, Fax 04.94.19.36.69

Massif de l'Estérel★★★, Côte d'Azur (French Riviera)

La Verrerie without rest
Chemin de la Verrerie – ✆ 04 94 40 93 51 – www.laverrerie.com – reservations@laverrerie.com – Fax 04 94 44 10 35
7 rm – †€ 50/75 ††€ 50/75, ☕ € 8
◆ Mediterranean-style building situated within the village, appreciated for its relaxing surroundings. The simple, neo-rustic rooms are cool and spacious.

Southeast 3 km by D 237 and D N7 – ✉ 83600 Les Adrets-de-l'Esterel

Auberge des Adrets AC rm, P VISA
– ✆ 04 94 82 11 82 – www.auberge-adrets.com – info@auberge-adrets.com – Fax 04 94 82 11 80 – Open 9 April-13 October
10 rm – †€ 150/240 ††€ 166/266, ☕ € 18
Rest – *(Open 9 April-30 September and closed lunch from Monday to Thursday in July and August, Sunday dinner and Monday in low season)* Menu € 38 – Carte € 54/76
◆ Building with character where each room is personalised with lovely furniture. Welcoming lounge, small, pleasant swimming pool and pretty green garden with hammocks. Elegant and cosy restaurant. The terrace offers magnificent views of the Esterel Hills.

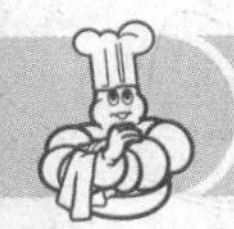

Do not confuse ✕ with ✿!
✕ defines comfort, while stars are awarded for the best cuisine, across all categories of comfort.

AFA – 2A Corse-du-Sud – 345 B8 – see Corse (Ajaccio)

AFFIEUX – 19 Corrèze – 329 L2 – pop. 368 – alt. 480 m – ✉ 19260 25 C2

Paris 472 – Limoges 83 – Tulle 39 – Brive-la-Gaillarde 64 – Ussel 66

Le Cantou P VISA
au bourg – ✆ 05 55 98 13 67 – Fax 05 55 98 13 67 – Closed 1-10 January, Sunday dinner and Wednesday
Rest – Menu (€ 13), € 17/39 – Carte € 17/70
◆ A small romantic dining room for the winter months and a veranda for the summer. Whatever the season, enjoy a delicious mix of traditional and regional cuisine.

AGDE – 34 Hérault – 339 F9 – pop. 19 988 – alt. 5 m – Casino : at Cap d'Agde BY – ✉ 34300 Languedoc-Roussillon-Tarn Gorges 23 C2

Paris 754 – Béziers 24 – Lodève 60 – Millau 118 – Montpellier 56 – Sète 25

Office de tourisme, 1, place Molière ✆ 04 67 94 29 68, Fax 04 67 94 03 50

du Cap-d'Agde Le Cap-d'Agde 4 avenue des Alizés, S : 4 km on D 32, ✆ 04 67 26 54 40

Former St-Étienne cathedral ★.

Athéna without rest AC P VISA
av. F.-Mitterrand, Cap d'Agde road, D 32^{E10} – ✆ 04 67 94 21 90 – www.cap-hotelathena.com – hotel.athena@free.fr – Fax 04 67 94 80 80 – Closed 4-22 February
32 rm – †€ 48/85 ††€ 48/85, ☕ € 7
◆ Modern hotel on the outskirts of the town. Rooms are well-equipped and decorated in sober Provencal style, some with terrace or loggia. Quieter to the rear.

LE CAP D'AGDE

Street	Grid	No.
Acadiens (Allée des)	CX	3
Alfonse (Av. du Chevalier d')	AX	4
Alizés (Av. des)	AXY	
Antilles (Rd-Pt des)	AY	6
Beaupré (Quai du)	CX	7
Belle Isle (Av. de)	ABX	
Bon Accueil (Rd-Pt du)	BX	9
Bouteillou (Rd-Pt du)	CX	10
Cantinières (Av. des)	CX	
Capelet (Quai du)	AX	12
Challiès (Av. du Passeur)	ABY	
Chandelles (R. des)	BX	15
Contrebandiers (Av. des)	BCX	
Corsaires (R. des)	AY	
Courette (R. de la)	CX	17
Dominico (Quai Di)	BX	18
Estacade (R. de l')	BY	19
Falaise (R. de la)	CY	21
Flânerie (Allée de la)	CX	23
Fouquet (Rd-Pt Nicolas)	BX	24
Gabelle (R. de la)	BX	26
Galères (Av. des)	CX	
Gallo-Romains (R. des)	AX	
Garnison (R. de la)	CXY	
Gentilshommes (Cours des)	CXY	
Gouverneur (R. du)	CX	
Grenadiers (R. des)	CX	31
Hallebardes (Av. des)	CX	32
Hune (R. de la)	BX	34
Iles-d'Amérique (Av. des)	AY	36
Ile (Av. de l')	BCY	
Jetée (Av. de la)	CY	
Joutes (Quai des)	BX	39
Labech (R. du)	BX	
Louisiane (Allée de la)	CX	40
Méditerranée (Av. de la)	CX	
Miquel (Quai Jean)	BCX	
Outre-Mer (Av. d')	AY	
Pacifique (R. du)	AY	
Phocéens (Quai des)	CY	42
Radoub (Rd-Pt du)	CY	43
St-Martin-des-Vignes (R.)	AX	
St-Martin (Quai)	BX	48
Sarret-de-Coussergue (R.)	ABX	
Sergents (Av. des)	BCX	
Soldats (Av. des)	CX	
Surintendant (Av. du)	BX	
Tambour (R. du)	BX	51
Tirème (Quai de la)	CXY	56
Tours-de-St-Martin (Rd-Pt des)	AX	53
Trinquette (Quai de la)	CX	54
Vaisseaux (R. des)	CX	
Vent-des-Dames (R. du)	BX	
Vieux Cap (Quai du)	BY	
Volvire-de-Brassac (R.)	AX	
2-Frères (R. des)	CY	
4-Cantons (Allée des)	CX	60

XX **La Table de Stéphane** A/C VISA MC

2 r. des Moulins-à-Huile, (The Sept Fonts area)
– 04 67 26 45 22 – www.latabledestephane.com
– caroline@latabledestephane.com – Fax 04 67 26 45 22
– Closed 20-30 October, 2-9 January,
Sunday dinner except from 12 July to 30 August, Saturday lunch and Monday
Rest – *(pre-book)* Menu (€ 18), € 26/59 – Carte € 22/50

◆ Dishes in keeping with current tastes and good regional wines served in a modern decor enhanced by splashes of pastels or on the shaded terrace. Drinks and coffee served in the lounge.

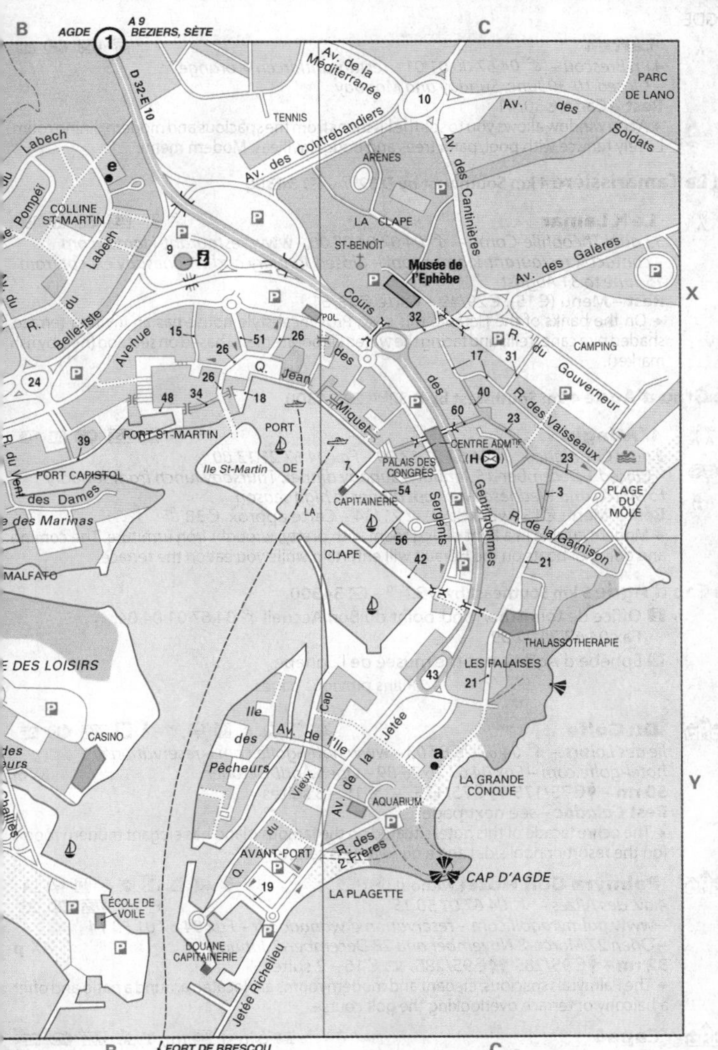

XX **Le Bistrot d'Hervé** AC VISA

47 r. Brescou
– ☎ 04 67 62 30 69
– bistroherve@gmail.com
– Fax 04 67 62 30 72
– Closed Saturday lunch, Sunday lunch and Wednesday

Rest – *(number of covers limited, pre-book)* Menu (€ 16) – Carte € 31/49

◆ Modern cuisine awaits in the simple contemporary dining room of this bistro and, weather-permitting, in the pleasant sunny courtyard.

Larcen
41 r. Brescou – 04 67 00 01 01 – restaurantlarcen@orange.fr – Closed 10-30 June, Sunday and Monday
Rest – Carte € 30/41
◆ A bay window allows you to see the kitchens from the spacious and modern dining room. Lovely terrace with pool, palm trees and bougainvilleas. Modern menu.

in La Tamarissière **4 km Southwest by D 32[E12] – ✉ 34300**

Le K Lamar
33 quai Théophile-Cornu – 04 67 94 05 06 – www.restaurant-klamar.com – contact@restaurant-klamar.com – Closed January and Wednesday except from 15 June to 31 August
Rest – Menu (€ 15), € 29/49 – Carte € 33/51
◆ On the banks of the Hérault, this cosy, Provençal-style house has an inviting terrace, shaded by a cane trellis and facing the water. Elaborate menu based on seafood (nearby fish market).

in Grau d'Agde **4 km Southwest by D 32[E] – ✉ 34300**

L'Adagio
3 quai Cdt-Méric – 04 67 21 13 00 – Fax 04 67 21 13 00 – Closed 1 December-15 January, Sunday dinner, Thursday lunch from January to March and Wednesday except dinner in high season
Rest – Menu € 15 (weekdays), € 21/34 – Carte approx. € 38
◆ Modern cuisine in a light dining room with pretty, wrought iron furniture. The coming and going of boats on the Hérault will entertain while you eat on the terrace.

in Cap d'Agde **5 km Southeast by D 32[E10] – ✉ 34300**

Office de tourisme, rond-point du Bon Accueil 04 67 01 04 04, Fax 04 67 26 22 99

Ephèbe d'Agde★★ at the musée de l'Ephèbe.

Plans previous pages

Du Golfe
Île des Loisirs – 04 67 26 87 03 – www.hotel-golfe.com – reservation@hotel-golfe.com – Fax 04 67 26 26 89 – Open April-October BY **m**
50 rm – € 75/175 € 75/175, € 15 – 3 suites
Rest *Caladoc* – see next page
◆ The ochre façade of this hotel situated on the famous island has elegant modern rooms (on the resort or pool side) and a good fitness centre.

Palmyra Golf Hôtel without rest
4 av. des Alizés – 04 67 01 50 15 – www.palmyragolf.com – reservation@wanadoo.fr – Fax 04 67 01 50 14 – Open 27 March-8 November and 28 December-3 January AX **p**
32 rm – € 95/285 € 95/285, € 16 – 2 suites
◆ The Palmyra's spacious, elegant and modern rooms are located around a patio and offer a balcony or terrace overlooking the golf course.

Capaô rest, rm,
r. des Corsaires – 04 67 26 99 44 – www.capao.com – contact@capao.com – Fax 04 67 26 55 41 – Open 4 April-4 October AY **b**
55 rm – € 75/135 € 82/150, € 13
Rest *Capaô Beach* – *04 67 26 41 25 (open 1st May-30 September) (lunch only)*
Carte € 28/55
◆ This hotel complex, near the Richelieu beach, offers numerous sports facilities. Spacious rooms with balconies. At lunchtime: salads, fish, shellfish and grilled food by the waterside.

La Bergerie du Cap without rest
4 av. Cassiopée – 04 67 01 71 35 – www.labergerieducap.com – labergerieducap@hotmail.fr – Fax 04 67 26 14 11 – Open 10 April-26 September
12 rm – € 89/260 € 89/260, € 16
◆ This 18C sheep farm converted into a hotel houses rooms of varying styles, some duplex and all cosy. Terrace opposite the pleasant swimming pool surrounded by plants, and Jacuzzi.

La Grande Conque without rest
r. Estruque, La Grande Conque – 04 67 26 11 42 – www.hotelgrandeconque.com – informations@hotelgrandeconque.com – Fax 04 67 26 24 15 – Open April-October CY **a**
20 rm – €80/130 €105/130, €13
◆ This hotel perched on basalt cliffs has an attractive location facing the sea and the black sand beach. The functional rooms are spacious and all have loggia.

Hélios without rest
12 r. Labech – 04 67 01 37 68 – www.hotel-helios.com – info@hotel-helios.com – Fax 04 67 01 54 68 – Open 3 April-30 September BX **e**
40 rm – €65/125 €65/125, €10
◆ Elegant Provencal-style abode in a delightful garden. Lounge-bar, pool and sunny terraces. The guestrooms are decorated in a contemporary or exotic decor.

Les Grenadines without rest
6 impasse Marie-Céleste – 04 67 26 27 40 – www.hotelgrenadines.com – hotelgrenadines@hotelgrenadines.com – Fax 04 67 26 10 80 – Open 15 February-4 November AY **k**
20 rm – €58/98 €58/98, €10
◆ A pleasant residence, noted for its family atmosphere and its practical rooms. Its proximity to the beaches, Aqualand and to the "Île des Loisirs" will appeal to children and adults alike.

Azur without rest
18 av. Îles d'Amérique – 04 67 26 98 22 – www.hotelazur.com – contact@hotelazur.com – Fax 04 67 26 48 14 AX **f**
34 rm – €48/95 €48/95, €8
◆ A privileged site in the centre of the resort, well-equipped rooms - some with mezzanine - and a pleasant swimming pool are just some of the advantages of this hotel.

XX **Caladoc** – Hôtel du Golfe
Île des Loisirs – 04 67 26 87 18 – www.hotel-golfe.com – reservation@hotel-golfe.com – Fax 04 67 26 26 89 – Open April-October and closed Sunday and Monday except in July-August BY **m**
Rest – *(dinner only)* Menu €25/35 – Carte €35/45
◆ Designer furnishings and wood panelling (wenge, mangrove): minimalist decor for a cuisine in keeping with current taste. Languedoc wines in the feature cellar.

AGEN P – **47 Lot-et-Garonne** – **336** F4 – **pop. 33 600** – **alt. 50 m** – ✉ **47000** Atlantic Coast 4 **C2**

Paris 662 – Auch 74 – Bordeaux 141 – Pau 159 – Toulouse 116
Agen-la-Garenne: 05 53 77 00 88, Southwest: 3 km.
Office de tourisme, 107, boulevard Carnot 05 53 47 36 09, Fax 05 53 47 29 98
Agen Bon-Encontre Bon-Encontre Route de Saint Ferréol, 7 km on the Toulouse road, 05 53 96 95 78
de Pleneselve Bon-Encontre NE : 8 km on D 656 and minor road, 05 53 67 52 65
Musée des Beaux-Arts★★ AXY **M** - Walibi leisure park★ 4 km by ⑤.

Plan on following page

Château des Jacobins without rest
1 ter pl. des Jacobins – 05 53 47 03 31 – www.chateau-des-jacobins.com – hotel@chateau-des-jacobins.com – Fax 05 53 47 02 80 AY **f**
14 rm – €78 €180, €12
◆ Antique furniture and curios endow this town mansion. Built in 1830 for the Count of Cassigneau, it has the feel of an opulent bourgeois home. Well-proportioned rooms.

Stim'Otel
105 bd Carnot – 05 53 47 31 23 – www.stimotel.com – stimotel@wanadoo.fr – Fax 05 53 47 48 70 BY **a**
58 rm – €50/68 €50/68, €9 – ½ P €52/61
Rest – *(closed 1st-24 August, 24 December-3 January, Saturday and Sunday)* Menu (€13), €17
◆ This hotel is well prepared to cater to a business clientele and groups of tourists: meeting rooms and functional, spruced up bedrooms on the first and second floors. This contemporary restaurant offers a simple slate menu focused on regional produce.

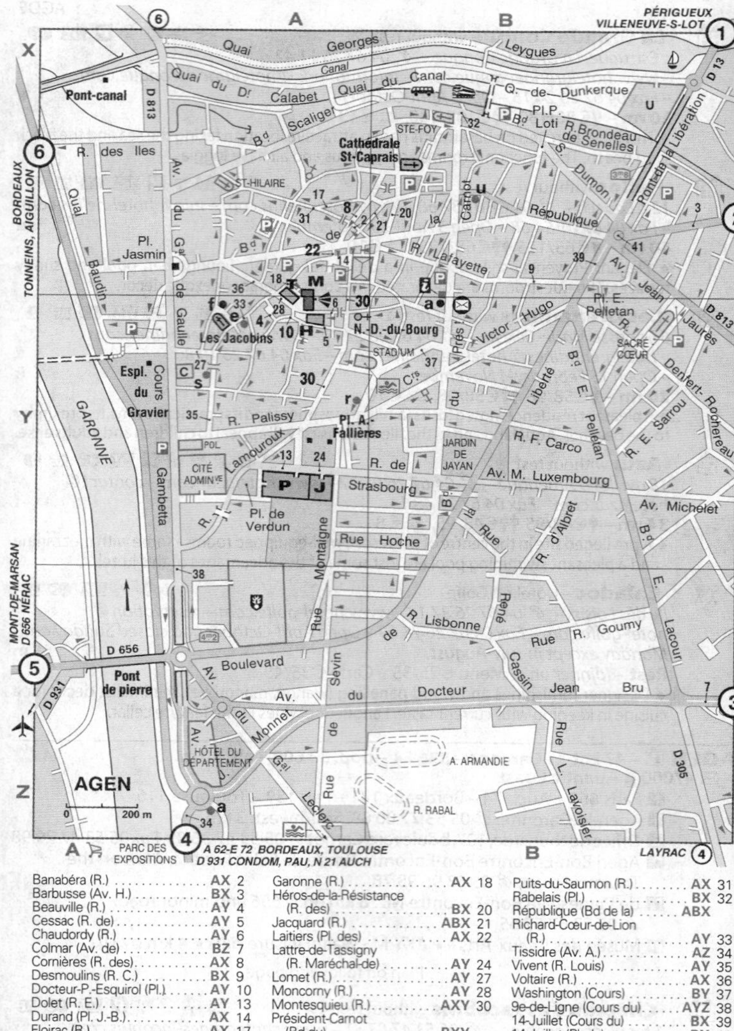

Banabéra (R.) . . . . AX 2
Barbusse (Av. H.) . . . . BX 3
Beauville (R.) . . . . AY 4
Cessac (R. de) . . . . AY 5
Chaudordy (R.) . . . . AY 6
Colmar (Av. de) . . . . BZ 7
Cornières (R. des) . . . . AX 8
Desmoulins (R. C.) . . . . BX 9
Docteur-P.-Esquirol (Pl.) . . . . AY 10
Dolet (R. E.) . . . . AY 13
Durand (Pl. J.-B.) . . . . AX 14
Floirac (R.) . . . . AX 17
Garonne (R.) . . . . AX 18
Héros-de-la-Résistance (R. des) . . . . BX 20
Jacquard (R.) . . . . ABX 21
Laitiers (Pl. des) . . . . AX 22
Lattre-de-Tassigny (R. Maréchal-de) . . . . AY 24
Lomet (R.) . . . . AY 27
Moncorny (R.) . . . . AY 28
Montesquieu (R.) . . . . AXY 30
Président-Carnot (Bd du) . . . . BXY
Puits-du-Saumon (R.) . . . . . . AX 31
Rabelais (Pl.) . . . . BX 32
République (Bd de la) . . . . . ABX
Richard-Cœur-de-Lion (R.) . . . . AY 33
Tissidre (Av. A.) . . . . AZ 34
Vivent (R. Louis) . . . . AY 35
Voltaire (R.) . . . . AX 36
Washington (Cours) . . . . BY 37
9e-de-Ligne (Cours du) . . . . . AYZ 38
14-Juillet (Cours du) . . . . . . BX 39
14-Juillet (Pl. du) . . . . BX 41

XXX ✿ **Mariottat** (Eric Mariottat)
25 r. L.-Vivent – ✆ 05 53 77 99 77 – www.restaurant-mariottat.com – contact@restaurant-mariottat.com – Fax 05 53 77 99 79
– Closed 20-27 April, 1st-4 November, 24-28 December, Wednesday lunch from October to April, Saturday lunch, Sunday dinner and Monday AY **s**
Rest – Menu € 28 (weekday lunch), € 42/72 – Carte € 69/80
Spec. Œuf de poule cassé, purée de ratte aux truffes. Pied de porc noir de Gascogne farci au homard. Le "Vert", fenouil, granny smith, avocat, verveine et huile d'olive. **Wines** Buzet, Côte de Duras.
◆ A plush bourgeois interior, pleasant summer terrace, sophisticated seasonal menu and extensive wine list: this 19C town house is most popular with Agen's gourmets.

Le Washington
7 cours Washington – ✆ 05 53 48 25 50 – www.le-washington.com – contact@le-washington.com – Fax 05 53 48 25 55 – Closed 31 July-23 August, Saturday and Sunday AY r
Rest – Menu (€ 15 bi), € 21 (weekday lunch)/38 – Carte € 32/70
◆ This contemporary restaurant is in a house built by the architect Charles Garnier. It serves a traditional menu and market based dishes, supported by a fine wine list.

La Table d' Armandie
1350 av. du Midi – ✆ 05 53 96 15 15 – latable.darmandie@orange.fr – Closed 9-17 August, Sunday and Monday AZ a
Rest – Menu (€ 16), € 20/46 – Carte € 38/55
◆ A minimalist contemporary style, large communal table, open kitchen and a giant TV screen (sporting events). Market fresh menu and predominantly regional wine list.

Le Margoton
52 r. Richard-Coeur-de-Lion – ✆ 05 53 48 11 55 – perso.orange.fr/lemargoton – contact@lemargoton.com – Fax 05 53 48 11 55 – Closed 18 August-4 August, 22 December-6 January, Saturday lunch, Sunday and Monday AY e
Rest – Menu (€ 17), € 24/35 – Carte € 38/50
◆ A pleasant address in the old town: family atmosphere, décor based on traditional materials, warm colours and contemporary twist. Appetising modern cuisine.

La Part des Anges
14 r. Émile-Sentini – ✆ 05 53 68 31 00 – www.lapartdesanges.eu – Fax 05 53 68 03 21 – Closed 15-31 August, February holidays, Sunday dinner and Monday BX u
Rest – Menu (€ 12), € 19/40 – Carte € 25/40
◆ Cookery books and old crates of wine adorn this small town centre restaurant where you are made to feel at home. Generous regional fare at reasonable prices.

in Pont-du-Casse 6 km by ② and D 656 – pop. 4 415 – alt. 67 m – ✉ 47480

Château de Cambes
– ✆ 05 53 87 46 37 – chateaudecambes@aol.com – Fax 05 53 87 46 37
8 rm – €135/225 €€ 135/225 **Table d'hôte** – Menu € 40
◆ A 14C castle is now home to spacious rooms adorned with period furniture and fireplaces (except one). Immense park, small chapel, library, pool, sauna and Jacuzzi tub. Meals are prepared on request by owner-chef.

at Moirax 9 km by ④, N 21 and D 268 – pop. 1 061 – alt. 154 m – ✉ 47310

Syndicat d'initiative, Le bourg ✆ 05 53 68 30 00, Fax 05 53 68 30 00

Auberge le Prieuré (Benjamin Toursel)
Le Bourg – ✆ 05 53 47 59 55 – Fax 05 53 68 02 01 – Closed autumn half-term holidays, February holidays, Sunday dinner, Monday and Tuesday
Rest – *(number of covers limited, pre-book)* Menu (€ 40 bi), € 60 – Carte approx. € 60
Spec. Langoustines en cappuccino de fenouil. Rouleau de thon au ketchup framboise-poivron (summer). Croustillant de chocolat et sorbet passion. **Wines** Côtes du Marmandais, Côtes de Duras.
◆ Delicious personalised cuisine in this pretty village house that is several hundred years old. The location is extremely charming: country style interior (photos) and a shaded terrace.

Southwest 12 km via ④, Auch road (N 21) then D 268 – ✉ 47310 Laplume

Château de Lassalle
rm,
Brimont – ✆ 05 53 95 10 58 – www.chateaudelassalle.com – info@chateaudelassalle.com – Fax 05 53 95 13 01 – Closed Christmas holidays, February holidays, Saturday and Sunday from 1st November to 30 April
17 rm – € 139/149 € 139/189, € 13 **Rest** – Menu € 32/42
◆ Snug contemporary rooms (wood, stone and light colours) and an enchanting guest-house ambience in this 18C manor house set in 8ha of parkland. Theme stays. One dining room with a glass roof, and the other in the 11C guardroom. Classic cuisine.

in Brax 6 km by ⑤ and D 119 – pop. 1 615 – alt. 49 m – ✉ 47310

Au Colombier du Touron rm, VISA

187 av. des Landes – ✆ 05 53 87 87 91 – www.colombierdutouron.com – contact@colombierdutouron.com – Fax 05 53 87 82 37 – Closed 27 October-3 November and 23 February-2 March

9 rm – †€ 49/57 ††€ 58/69, ☕ € 10 – ½ P € 58/65

Rest – *(Closed Sunday dinner and Monday)* Menu (€ 15), € 29/52 – Carte € 31/48

◆ The sign evokes the 18C dovecote adjoining the hotel. Rooms personalised little by little, in shimmering colours. A comfortable dining room leading into the garden or onto a shaded terrace. Gascony cuisine.

AGNIERES-EN-DEVOLUY – 05 Hautes-Alpes – 334 D4 – pop. 266 – alt. 1 263 m – ✉ 05250 40 B1

Paris 690 – Marseille 204 – Gap 42 – Vizille 73 – Vif 109

Le Refuge de l'Eterlou without rest VISA

La Joue du Loup, 4 km east – ✆ 04 92 23 33 80 – www.hotel-eterlou.com – refuge-eterlou@orange.fr – Fax 04 92 23 19 13 – Open 16 June-15 October and 19 December-20 April

6 rm – †€ 60/75 ††€ 65/80, ☕ € 8

◆ This engaging modern establishment is located in the upper reaches of the resort. Predominantly wood decor in the breakfast room and spacious contemporary style rooms.

AGUESSAC – 12 Aveyron – 338 K6 – pop. 832 – alt. 375 m – ✉ 12520 29 D2

Paris 628 – Florac 76 – Mende 87 – Millau 9 – Rodez 60 – Sévérac-le-Château 25

Auberge le Rascalat VISA

2 km Verrières road on D 809 – ✆ 05 65 59 80 43 – www.auberge-lerascalat.fr – societe.exploitation.rascalat@wanadoo.fr – Fax 05 65 59 73 90 – Open 2 April-2 November

14 rm – †€ 60/80 ††€ 60/80, ☕ € 10

Rest – *(closed Monday lunch, Tuesday lunch, Wednesday lunch and Thursday lunch)* Menu € 24 – Carte € 28/50

◆ This former oil mill is situated in a rural setting between the Causses and the river. Country style bedrooms and an attractive swimming pool in the garden. Breakfast is served in the vaulted cellar. A rustic restaurant where lamb is roasted on a spit over the open fire in spring. Summer terrace.

AHETZE – 64 Pyrénées-Atlantiques – 342 C2 – pop. 1 452 – alt. 28 m – ✉ 64210 3 A3

Paris 767 – Bordeaux 207 – Pau 127 – Donostia-San Sebastián 52 – Irun 32

La Ferme Ostalapia with rm VISA

chemin d' Ostalapia, 3 km south on D 855 – ✆ 05 59 54 73 79 – www.ostalapia.com – ostalapia@wanadoo.fr – Fax 05 59 54 98 85 – Closed 15 December-1st February, Wednesday, Thursday except July-August and lunch in July-August

5 rm – †€ 65/155 ††€ 65/155, ☕ € 10 **Rest** – Menu (€ 15) – Carte € 28/45

◆ An old country farm with an unbeatable local reputation. Local cuisine served in two typically Basque dining rooms or on the terrace opposite the mountains. Bed and breakfast with well-kept, rustic and charming rooms.

L'AIGLE – 61 Orne – 310 M2 – pop. 8 489 – alt. 220 m – ✉ 61300 33 C2

Normandy

Paris 137 – Alençon 68 – Chartres 79 – Dreux 61 – Évreux 56 – Lisieux 59

Office de tourisme, place Fulbert-de-Beina ✆ 02 33 24 12 40, Fax 02 33 34 23 77

Du Dauphin VISA

pl. de la Halle – ✆ 02 33 84 18 00 – www.hoteldudauphin.free.fr – regis.ligot@free.fr – Fax 02 33 34 09 28

30 rm – †€ 62/85 ††€ 62/85, ☕ € 10

Rest – *(closed Sunday dinner)* Menu € 35/40 – Carte € 46/80

Rest *La Renaissance* – brasserie Menu (€ 12) – Carte € 16/37

◆ The older of these two buildings was already a hostelry back in 1618. Rooms with all mod cons, fireside lounge and shop selling regional produce. Modern menu served in a traditionally decorated dining room. A pleasant 1940s-style decor at the Renaissance.

Toque et Vins

35 r. L.-Pasteur, (Argentan road) – ✆ 02 33 24 05 27 – Closed 25 July-15 August, Wednesday dinner, Sunday dinner and Monday

Rest – Menu € 11 (weekdays), € 17/33 – Carte € 20/35

◆ A refreshingly unpretentious and inviting bistro decor serving impeccably prepared traditional dishes, such as the tête de veau poêlé à la sauce ravigote.

Dreux road 3.5 km east on N 26 – ✉ 61300 St-Michel-Tuboeuf

Auberge St-Michel

– ✆ 02 33 24 20 12 – aubergesaintmichel@yahoo.fr – Fax 02 33 34 96 62 – Closed Tuesday dinner, Wednesday dinner and Thursday

Rest – Menu (€ 17 bi), € 25/38 – Carte € 32/51

◆ The original, plush, antique furnished lounge of this stylish country inn sets the scene. A series of rustic, cosy rooms serving regional recipes.

AIGUEBELETTE-LE-LAC – 73 Savoie – 333 H4 – pop. 224 – alt. 410 m – ✉ 73610 French Alps

46 **F2**

Paris 552 – Belley 34 – Chambéry 22 – Grenoble 76 – Voiron 35

Lake★ - Panorama★★ on the col de l'Épine road North.

in la Combe (East bank) 4 km by D 921d – ✉ 73610

La Combe "chez Michelon" with rm

– ✆ 04 79 36 05 02 – www.chez-michelon.fr – chezmichelon@aol.com – Fax 04 79 44 11 93 – Closed mid-November to mid-December, Monday except lunch from May to September and Tuesday

5 rm – †€ 59/71 ††€ 59/80, ☐ € 8,50

Rest – Menu (€ 19), € 24/48 – Carte € 35/56

◆ Perfect stopover for nature lovers: located between lake, mountain and forest. Modern dining room and terrace shaded by chestnut trees. Good selection of Savoyard wines.

in Novalaise-Lac (West bank) 7 km by D 921 – pop. 1 612 – alt. 427 m – ✉ 73470

Novalaise-Plage

Le Neyret – ✆ 04 79 36 02 19 – www.le-chaletdulac.com – reservation@le-chaletdulac.com – Fax 04 79 36 04 22 – Closed 2 January-5 February

13 rm – †€ 57/68 ††€ 75/88, ☐ € 8 – ½ P € 58/75

Rest – *(closed Tuesday dinner and Wednesday from October to March)* Menu € 28/88 – Carte € 60/84

◆ Relax in the middle of the countryside at this chalet on Lake Aiguebelette. Simple rooms with views over the water. Modern, tasty and well-presented food served in an elegant setting lit by bay windows. In summer, dine on the panoramic terrace.

in St-Alban-de-Montbel (West bank) 7 km by D 921 – pop. 447 – alt. 400 m – ✉ 73610

Les Lodges du Lac

La Curiaz, D 921 – ✆ 04 79 36 00 10 – www.leslodgesdulac.com – bienvenue@leslodgesdulac.com – Fax 04 79 44 10 57 – Closed Sunday dinner and Monday from 15 September to 15 June

13 rm – †€ 50/70 ††€ 50/70, ☐ € 8 – 3 suites – ½ P € 51/60

Rest – *(Closed one week in March and one week at Christmas)* Menu (€ 14), € 19/26 – Carte € 28/42

◆ Set back from the lake, the annexe of this hotel has ground-floor rooms opening out onto the garden; the duplex rooms are particularly suitable for families. Boats available. Traditional cuisine is served in the restaurant. Special diets catered for on request.

AIGUEBELLE – 83 Var – 340 N7 – see Le Lavandou

AIGUES-MORTES – 30 Gard – 339 K7 – pop. 6 798 – alt. 3 m – ✉ 30220 Provence

23 **C2**

Paris 745 – Arles 49 – Montpellier 38 – Nîmes 42 – Sète 56

Office de tourisme, place Saint-Louis ✆ 04 66 53 73 00, Fax 04 66 53 65 94

Ramparts★★ and Tour de Constance★★: ✳★★ - Notre-Dame des Sablons church ★.

Villa Mazarin without rest
35 bd Gambetta – ✆ 04 66 73 90 48 – www.villamazarin.com – am@villamazarin.com – Fax 04 66 73 90 49 – Closed 12 January-12 February
20 rm – †€ 95/220 ††€ 120/255, ☕ € 14
◆ This splendid mansion invites guests to enjoy the refinement of its sitting rooms and the shade of its lovely garden. Comfortable rooms, indoor pool and relaxation facilities.

St-Louis
10 r. Am.-Courbet – ✆ 04 66 53 72 68 – www.lesaintlouis.fr – hotel.saint-louis@wanadoo.fr – Fax 04 66 53 75 92 – Open 2 April-4 October
22 rm – †€ 62/94 ††€ 79/112, ☕ € 12 – ½ P € 65/77
Rest – *(closed Saturday lunch, Tuesday and Wednesday)* Menu (€ 15), € 19/32 – Carte € 30/45
◆ Inside the town walls, near the Constance Tower, an elegant 18C building with comfortable, colourful rooms. Those on the 2nd floor are more spacious. Enjoy the Provençal style indoor dining area with fireplace in winter. In summer, pretty, shaded patio.

Canal without rest
440 rte de Nîmes – ✆ 04 66 80 50 04 – www.hotelcanal.fr – contact@hotelcanal.fr – Fax 04 66 80 50 32 – Closed 15 November-15 December and 10 January-20 February
25 rm – †€ 68/152 ††€ 68/152, ☕ € 12
◆ At the entrance to the town, opposite the canal, is this contemporary style hotel. The functional, air-conditioned rooms are well soundproofed. Swimming pool and sun deck.

Les Arcades with rm
23 bd Gambetta – ✆ 04 66 53 81 13 – www.les-arcades.fr – info@les-arcades.fr – Fax 04 66 53 75 46 – Closed 3-25 March, 6-22 October, Tuesday lunch, Thursday lunch and Monday except dinner in July-August
9 rm ☕ – †€ 95/110 ††€ 95/145
Rest – Menu (€ 24), € 36/48 – Carte € 46/62
◆ Beautiful 16C house in a refined Provençal decor of bare stone. Arcaded terrace, regional cuisine and attractive rooms. Peace and quiet guaranteed.

La Salicorne
9 r. Alsace-Lorraine – ✆ 04 66 53 62 67 – www.la-salicorne.com – Closed 3 January-7 February and Tuesday except school holidays
Rest – *(dinner only)* Carte € 52/70
◆ Stonework, exposed beams, a fireplace, wrought iron, a pleasant summer terrace and food with a southern flavour – a little bit of Provence behind the Sablons church.

AILEFROIDE – 05 Hautes-Alpes – 334 G3 – see Pelvoux (District of)

AILLANT-SUR-THOLON – 89 Yonne – 319 D4 – pop. 1 416 – alt. 112 m – ✉ 89110 7 B1

Paris 144 – Auxerre 20 – Briare 70 – Clamecy 61 – Gien 80 – Montargis 59
Office de tourisme, 1, cour de la Halle aux Grains ✆ 03 86 63 54 17, Fax 03 86 63 54 17

Southwest 7 km by D 955, D 57 and secondary road – ✉ 89110 Chassy

Domaine du Roncemay
– ✆ 03 86 73 50 50 – www.roncemay.com – info@roncemay.com – Fax 03 86 73 69 46 – Closed from mid-December to early January
18 rm – †€ 100/220 ††€ 100/220, ☕ € 18 – 3 suites
Rest – *(closed Monday in low season)* Menu (€ 22), € 35 (weekdays)/54 – Carte € 55/68
◆ This beautiful hotel, adjoining a vast golf course, embodies the style of the region. Attractive rustic rooms. Fitness facilities and a superb Turkish bath. Modern food inspired by the traditions of Burgundy, served in a pleasant room overlooking the park.

AIMARGUES – 30 Gard – 339 K6 – pop. 4 090 – alt. 6 m – ✉ 30470 23 C2

Paris 740 – Montpellier 40 – Aigues-Mortes 16 – Alès 62 – Arles 41 – Nîmes 25

XX **Un Mazet sous les platanes**

3 bd St-Louis – ✆ 04 66 51 73 03 – lemazetsouslesplatanes@wanadoo.fr – Fax 04 66 51 73 03 – Closed 20 December-19 January, Saturday lunch, Sunday lunch and Monday

Rest – Menu (€ 16), € 28

◆ Attractive house with an inner courtyard terrace offering a view of the kitchens. Smart dining rooms mixing Provençal and Oriental influences, in line with the menu.

AINCILLE – 64 Pyrénées-Atlantiques – 342 E6 – see St-Jean-Pied-de-Port

AINHOA – 64 Pyrénées-Atlantiques – 342 C5 – pop. 651 – alt. 130 m – ✉ 64250 Atlantic Coast 3 A3

Paris 791 – Bayonne 28 – Biarritz 29 – Cambo-les-Bains 11 – Pau 125 – St-Jean-de-Luz 26

Typical Basque village ★.

Ithurria (Xavier Isabal)

pl. du Fronton – ✆ 05 59 29 92 11 – www.ithurria.com – hotel@ithurria.com – Fax 05 59 29 81 28 – Open 11 April-2 November

28 rm – †€ 95/110 ††€ 135/155, ☐ € 12 – ½ P € 107/120

Rest – *(closed Thursday lunch except July-August and Wednesday) (pre-book on weekend)* Menu € 37/61 – Carte € 50/78

Spec. Rossini de pied de porc. Ventrèche de thon et chipirons sautés en persillade (June-August). Délice à l'Izarra et son coulis de cerises noires. **Wines** Irouléguy, Jurançon sec.

◆ Attractive 17C Basque-style house facing the pelota wall of the village. Elegant lounge and comfortable rooms adorned with antique furniture. Charming restaurant with antique ranges, exposed beams, traditional floor tiles, fireplace and copper ornaments. Delicious regional cuisine with a light touch.

Argi Eder

rte de la Chapelle – ✆ 05 59 93 72 00 – www.argi-eder.com – argi.eder@wanadoo.fr – Fax 05 59 93 72 13 – Open 5 April-1 November

19 rm – †€ 100/125 ††€ 100/125, ☐ € 13 – 7 suites – ½ P € 91/124

Rest – *(closed Wednesday except dinner in July-August, Monday lunch, and Friday lunch)* Menu € 32/50 – Carte € 40/60

◆ On a hillside, a large building typical of the region with a pool in the grounds overlooking the countryside. Vast redecorated rooms and a lounge/bar (fine collection of Armagnacs). Regional food in a Basque-style dining room. Excellent choice of Bordeaux wines.

XX **Oppoca** with rm

r. Principale – ✆ 05 59 29 90 72 – www.oppoca.com – contact@oppoca.com – Fax 05 59 29 81 03 – Closed 15 November-16 December, 5 January-5 February, Sunday dinner and Monday

10 rm **Rest** – Menu (€ 20), € 26/46 – Carte approx. € 53

◆ Country inn with two refurbished rustic dining rooms, one with Basque furniture and dresser and another, brighter room on the garden side. Traditional cuisine; terrace. New, comfortable and well-equipped rooms.

AIRAINES – 80 Somme – 301 E8 – pop. 2 101 – alt. 30 m – ✉ 80270 Northern France and the Paris Region 36 A1

Paris 172 – Abbeville 22 – Amiens 30 – Beauvais 69 – Le Tréport 51

Syndicat d'initiative, place de la Mairie ✆ 03 22 29 34 07, Fax 03 22 29 47 50

in Allery 5 km West by D 936 – pop. 760 – alt. 50 m – ✉ 80270

X **Relais Forestier du Pont d'Hure**

rte du Treport – ✆ 03 22 29 42 10 – www.pontdhure.com – lepontdhure@wanadoo.fr – Fax 03 22 2722 91 – Closed 1-19 August, 2-20 January and dinner except Saturday

Rest – Menu (€ 15), € 18 (weekdays)/37 – Carte € 25/45

◆ Dine here after a walk in the forest: food is prepared and grilled over a wood fire, in the rustic fireplace of a dining room adorned with hunting trophies.

AIRE-SUR-L'ADOUR – 40 Landes – 335 J12 – pop. 6 070 – alt. 80 m 3 B3
– ✉ 40800 Atlantic Coast

Paris 722 – Auch 84 – Condom 68 – Dax 77 – Mont-de-Marsan 33 – Orthez 59 – Pau 51

Office de tourisme, place Général-de-Gaulle ✆ 05 58 71 64 70, Fax 05 58 71 64 70

Sarcophagus of Ste-Quitterie★ in St-Pierre-du-Mas church.

Chez l'Ahumat with rm — P VISA MC AE

2 r. Mendès-France – ✆ 05 58 71 82 61 – Closed 17-31 March, 1-16 September

12 rm – €28/32 €35/42, €5

Rest – *(closed Tuesday dinner and Wednesday)* Menu €12/30 – Carte €21/35

◆ Restaurant run by the same family for three generations. Country-style dining rooms that display a collection of antique plates. Regional cuisine.

Bordeaux road on the N 124 – ✉ 40270 Cazères-sur-l'Adour

Aliotel — rm, AC P VISA MC

– ✆ 05 58 71 72 72 – http://pro.pagesjaunes.fr/aliotel/ – aliotel@free.fr – Fax 05 58 71 81 94

34 rm – €39 €46, €6 **Rest** – Menu €12/15

◆ A functional establishment offering practical, standardised rooms, that are well soundproofed. Well-designed sports facilities in a country setting. A simple restaurant with large dining area in cafeteria style.

in Ségos (32 Gers) 9 km on the N 134 and D 260 – pop. 234 – alt. 111 m – ✉ 32400

Domaine de Bassibé — P VISA MC AE

– ✆ 05 62 09 46 71 – www.bassibe.fr – bassibe@relaischateaux.com – Fax 05 62 08 40 15 – Open 9 April-2 January and closed Tuesday and Wednesday except July-August

9 rm – €140/210 €140/210, €16 – 7 suites – ½ P €134/169

Rest – *(dinner only except Saturday, Sunday and July-August)* Menu €48/60

◆ The cosy guestrooms add to the romantic air of this country property. Rustic living areas. Restaurant located in the estate's old wine press (whitewashed beams, fireplace) with quiet terrace in the shade of the plane trees.

Minvielle et les Oliviers — rm, AC rest, P VISA MC AE

– ✆ 05 62 09 40 90 – lminvielle@wanadoo.fr – Fax 05 62 08 48 62

18 rm – €45/52 €52/59, €7 – ½ P €60/67

Rest – *(closed Sunday dinner October-April and Saturday lunch)* Menu (€13 bi), €15 bi (weekdays)/28 – Carte €30/45

◆ In a small village in Gers, this modern building is in a regional style. The rooms in the annex are more recent and have a smart, Provencal decor and a large balcony. Huge, rustic dining room where traditional food is served.

AIRE-SUR-LA-LYS – 62 Pas-de-Calais – 301 H4 – pop. 9 651 30 B2
– alt. 30 m – ✉ 62120 Northern France and the Paris Region

Paris 236 – Arras 56 – Boulogne-sur-Mer 68 – Calais 60 – Lille 62

Office de tourisme, Grand-Place ✆ 03 21 39 65 66, Fax 03 21 39 65 66

Bailiwick★ - Tower★ of St-Pierre collegiate church ★.

Hostellerie des 3 Mousquetaires — P VISA MC AE

Château de la Redoute, Béthune road (D 943) – ✆ 03 21 39 01 11 – www.hostelleriedes3mousquetaires.com – hotel.mousquetaires@wanadoo.fr – Fax 03 21 39 50 10 – Closed 21 December-10 January

33 rm – €55/110 €110/150, €15 – 2 suites – ½ P €119/130

Rest – Menu (€19), €24 (weekdays)/46 – Carte €55/71

◆ A 19C house with country charm, in a park with a pond and hundred-year-old trees. Rooms with personal touches. Choose what you would like a view of: the open kitchen or the Lys valley from the bay windows.

in Isbergues 6 km Southeast by D 187 – **pop. 9 836 – alt. 25 m** – ✉ **62330**

Le Buffet with rm — AC rest, VISA
22 r. de la Gare – ☎ 03 21 25 82 40 – www.le-buffet.com – lebuffetisbergues@wanadoo.fr – Fax 03 21 27 86 42 – Closed 3-21 August, February holidays, Monday (except bank holidays lunch) and Sunday dinner
5 rm – †€ 62 ††€ 70, ☕ € 10
Rest – Menu (€ 17), € 20 (weekdays), € 25/88 bi – Carte € 45/65
◆ The former station buffet is now particularly attractive with two elegant dining rooms, carefully laid tables and tasty regional seasonal cuisine.

AISONVILLE-ET-BERNOVILLE – 02 Aisne – 306 D3 – pop. 300 – alt. 155 m – ✉ 02110

37 **C1**

▶ Paris 200 – Amiens 115 – Laon 50 – Saint-Quentin 31 – Valenciennes 65

Le 1748 — P VISA
9 r. de Condé – ☎ 03 23 66 85 85 – http://le1748.monsite.orange.fr – le1748@wanadoo.fr – Fax 03 23 66 85 70 – Closed 1-12 January
16 rm – †€ 55/95 ††€ 55/95, ☕ € 8 – ½ P € 58/70
Rest – Menu (€ 20 bi), € 28/45 – Carte € 28/47
◆ This outstanding hotel is housed in the old farm and stables of a château, said to be among the most beautiful in France. Cosy, individually decorated rooms. Regional produce and the local beer, Bernoville, served in a cheerful café setting.

AIX (ÎLE) – 17 Charente-Maritime – 324 C3 – see Île-d'Aix

AIX-EN-PROVENCE – 13 Bouches-du-Rhône – 340 H4 – pop. 141 200 – alt. 206 m – Casino AY – ✉ 13100 Provence

40 **B3**

▶ Paris 752 – Avignon 82 – Marseille 30 – Nice 177 – Sisteron 102 – Toulon 84

Office de tourisme, 2, place du Général-de-Gaulle ☎ 04 42 16 11 61, Fax 04 42 16 11 62

Set Golf 1335 chemin de Granet, W : 6 km on D 17, ☎ 04 42 29 63 69

d'Aix-Marseille Les Milles Domaine de Riquetti, 8 km on the Marignane road and the D 9, ☎ 04 42 24 20 41

Sainte-Victoire Golf Club Fuveau "Lieu dit ""Château l'Arc""", 14 km on the Aubagne road and D 6, ☎ 04 42 29 83 43

Old Aix★★ - Cours Mirabeau★★ - St-Sauveur cathedral ★: triptych of the Burning Bush★★ - Cloister★ BX **B**[8] - Place Albertas★ BY **3** - Place★ de l'hôtel de ville BY **37** - Courtyard ★ of the town hall BY **H** - Mazarin district ★: Quatre-Dauphins fountain ★ BY **D** - Musée Granet★ CY **M**[6] - Musée des Tapisseries★ BX **M**[2] - Vasarely Foundation ★ AV **M**[5].

Plans on following pages

Villa Gallici — rm, AC P VISA AE
18 bis av. de la Violette – ☎ 04 42 23 29 23 – www.villagallici.com – reservation@villagallici.com – Fax 04 42 96 30 45 – Closed 20-26 December and 3 January-6 February — BV **k**
17 rm – †€ 220/780 ††€ 220/780, ☕ € 28 – 5 suites
Rest – *(closed Wednesday from October to May and Tuesday except July) (number of covers limited, pre-book)* Carte € 90/110
◆ This high perched villa is a résumé of the best of Provence, with its plane trees, cypresses, fountain, pool, crickets, tasteful fabrics and wrought iron. Charming 19C-styled rooms. Classic Mediterranean flavoured cuisine. Tempting shaded summer terrace.

Le Pigonnet — AC P VISA AE
5 av. du Pigonnet ✉ 13090 – ☎ 04 42 59 02 90 – www.hotelpigonnet.com – reservation@hotelpigonnet.com – Fax 04 42 59 47 77 — AV **a**
51 rm – †€ 135/175 ††€ 160/320, ☕ € 25
Rest – *(closed 22-30 December, Saturday lunch and Sunday from October to March)* Menu (€ 39), € 59 – Carte € 68/89
◆ Paul Cézanne was inspired by the scents and colours of Provence in this gracious abode, set in a flower-decked park. Cosy, plush and romantic interior. Elegant dining rooms and a terrace overlooking the garden. Up-to-date menu.

AIX-EN-PROVENCE

Berger (Av. G.)	BV	7
Brossolette (Av.)	AV	13
Club Hippique (Av.)	AV	18
Dalmas (Av. J.)	AV	23
Ferrini (Av. F.)	AV	30
Fourane (Av. de la)	AV	32
Galice (Rte de)	AV	33
Isaac (Av. J.)	BV	41
Malacrida (Av. H.)	BV	48
Minimes (Crs des)	AV	52
Moulin (Av. J.)	BV	56
Pigonnet (Av. du)	AV	62
Poilus (Bd des)	BV	67
Prados (Av. E.)	AV	68
Solari (Av. Ph.)	AV	76

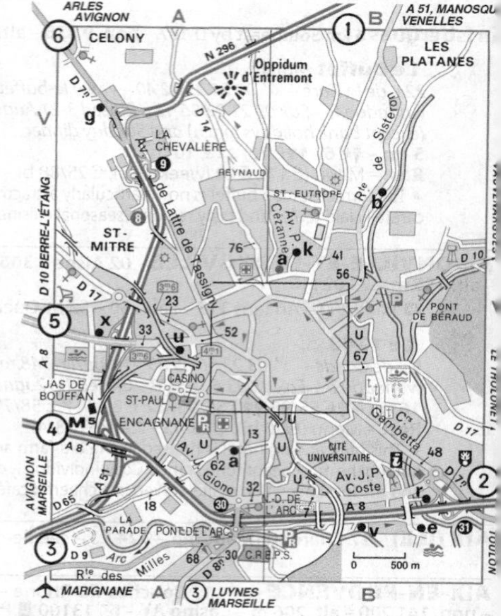

Aquabella
2 r. des Étuves – ✆ 04 42 99 15 00 – www.aquabella.fr – info@aquabella.fr – Fax 04 42 99 15 01 AX **a**
110 rm – €149/169 €169/195, ☕ €18 – ½ P €129
Rest *L'Orangerie* – Menu (€22), €27/51 – Carte €45/71
◆ Adjoining the Sextius thermal baths this hotel has modern rooms in Provençal shades. Those on the upper floors have a terrace and overlook the old town. This contemporary restaurant is housed in a glass and steel structure and has a poolside terrace.

Grand Hôtel Mercure Roi René
24 bd du Roi-René – ✆ 04 42 37 61 00 – www.mercure.com – h1169@accor.com – Fax 04 42 37 61 11 BZ **b**
134 rm – €205/245 €225/265, ☕ €22 – 3 suites
Rest *La Table du Roi* – Menu €38 – Carte approx. €38
◆ Modern hotel whose exterior pays homage to the regional style, while its partially refurbished interior is distinctly contemporary and minimalist. Patio and pool. Classic cuisine at the Table du Roi (undergoing refurbishment).

Des Augustins without rest
3 r. de la Masse – ✆ 04 42 27 28 59 – www.hotel-augustins.com – hotel.augustins@wanadoo.fr – Fax 04 42 26 74 87 BY **x**
29 rm – €99/200 €99/250, ☕ €10
◆ Luther the reformer stayed in this 15C convent in his time. Personalised rooms with modern comforts. Reception in the 12C chapel.

Le Galice
5 rte Galice – ✆ 04 42 52 75 27 – www.bestwestern-legalice.com – hotelgalice@bestwestern-aix.com – Fax 04 42 52 75 28 AV **u**
90 rm – €140/180 €140/180, ☕ €12
Rest – *(closed Saturday lunch and Sunday)* Menu (€19) – Carte €28/36
◆ This modern, glazed hotel has spacious, comfortable and well-soundproofed rooms. Those on the pool side are the most pleasant. Classic menu with Mediterranean influences served in a cosy room or on the terrace.

AIX-EN-PROVENCE

Street	Grid	No.
Agard (Passage)	CY	2
Albertas (Pl.)	BY	3
Aude (R.)	BY	4
Bagniers (R. des)	BY	5
Bellegarde (Pl.)	CX	7
Bon Pasteur (R.)	BX	9
Boulégon (R.)	BX	12
Brossolette (Av.)	AZ	13
Cardeurs (Pl. des)	BY	16
Clemenceau (R.)	BY	18
Cordeliers (R. des)	BY	20
Couronne (R. de la)	BY	21
Curie (R. Pierre-et-Marie)	BX	22
Espariat (R.)	BY	26
Fabrot (R.)	BY	28
Foch (R. du Maréchal)	BY	30
Hôtel de Ville (Pl.)	BY	37
Italie (R. d')	CY	42
Lattre-de-Tassigny (Av. de)	AY	46
De-la-Roque (R. J.)	BX	25
Matheron (R.)	BY	49
Méjanes (R.)	BY	51
Minimes (Crs des)	AY	52
Mirabeau (Cours)	BCY	
Montigny (R. de)	BY	55
Napoléon-Bonaparte (Av.)	AY	57
Nazareth (R.)	BY	58
Opéra (R. de l')	CY	62
Pasteur (Av.)	BX	64
Paul-Bert (R.)	BX	66
Prêcheurs (Pl. des)	CY	70
Richelme (Pl.)	BY	72
Saporta (R. G.-de)	BX	75
Thiers (R.)	CY	80
Verdun (Pl. de)	CY	85
4-Septembre (R.)	BZ	87

Novotel Beaumanoir

r. Marcel-Arnaud, Résidence Beaumanoir, Motorway exit 3, Sautets – ✆ 04 42 91 15 15 – www.novotel.com – h0393@accor.com – Fax 04 42 91 15 05 BV **r**

102 rm – †€ 132/145 ††€ 132/145, ☕ € 14 **Rest** – Carte € 22/46

◆ This establishment with its comfortable rooms (the majority refurbished) offers reasonably peaceful surroundings, including a landscaped garden and small botanical trail. Contemporary dining room extending onto a terrace overlooking the swimming pool.

Kyriad Prestige

42 rte de Galice – ✆ 04 42 95 04 41 – www.kyriadprestige.fr – aixenprovence@kyriadprestige.fr – Fax 04 42 59 47 29 AV **x**

84 rm – †€ 103/120 ††€ 103/120, ☕ € 14

Rest – Menu € 19/26 – Carte € 24/34

◆ A modern, semi-circular building by the ring road. Pleasant, soundproofed rooms, although those on the upper floors are even quieter. Small fitness centre. Buffet menus served in a marine style dining room. Poolside terrace.

Bastide du Cours rm, rm, VISA MC AE

43-47 cours Mirabeau – ✆ 04 42 26 10 06 – www.bastiducours.com – info@bastideducours.com – Fax 04 42 93 07 65 BY **e**

11 rm – †€ 145/330 ††€ 145/400, ☕ € 6,50 – 4 suites

Rest – Menu € 20 (lunch), € 30/40 – Carte € 32/63

◆ This large house offers well equipped, comfortable rooms decorated in an individual, old-fashioned spirit. Four overlook the cours Mirabeau. Up-to-date restaurant brasserie, cosy atmosphere (warm colours, sitting rooms, libraries, cane armchairs).

Cézanne without rest VISA MC AE

40 av. Victor-Hugo – ✆ 04 42 91 11 11 – www.hotelaix.com/cezanne – hotelcezanne@hotelaix.com – Fax 04 42 91 11 10 BZ **h**

55 rm – †€ 155/220 ††€ 175/240, ☕ € 18 – 2 suites

◆ A business centre, Wifi, free mini bar in the rooms, open bar and baskets of fruit: details that make a difference! Contemporary lobby and renovated guestrooms.

St-Christophe rm, VISA MC AE

2 av. Victor-Hugo – ✆ 04 42 26 01 24 – www.hotel-saintchristophe.com – saintchristophe@francemarket.com – Fax 04 42 38 53 17 BY **a**

60 rm – †€ 81/88 ††€ 88/98, ☕ € 12 – 12 suites

Rest *Brasserie Léopold* – Menu (€ 21), € 28 (lunch) – Carte € 29/50

◆ Practical rooms with a 1930s atmosphere or Provençal style charm, with or without terrace. Regional cuisine and brasserie dishes in an attractive Art Deco setting. A pavement terrace for fine weather.

Novotel Pont de l'Arc P VISA MC AE

av. Arc-de-Meyran, Aix Pont de l'Arc motorway exit – ✆ 04 42 16 09 09 – h0394@accor.com – Fax 04 42 26 00 09 BV **v**

80 rm – †€ 115/140 ††€ 115/140, ☕ € 14 **Rest** – Carte € 30/45

◆ A Novotel set between the motorway and Arc. Fully renovated and soundproofed rooms, the nicest face the garden and pool. Riverside fitness track. Comfortable dining room and shaded terraces, one embellished with a fountain.

Le Globe without rest VISA MC AE

74 cours Sextius – ✆ 04 42 26 03 58 – www.hotelduglobe.com – contact@hotelduglobe.com – Fax 04 42 26 13 68 – Closed 20 December-20 January

46 rm – †€ 59/62 ††€ 71/75, ☕ € 9 AY **e**

◆ A yellow building home to plain, well soundproofed, very well kept and not too expensive rooms. The lobby has been treated to a makeover. Rooftop sundeck/terrace.

Le Manoir without rest P VISA MC AE

8 r. Entrecasteaux – ✆ 04 42 26 27 20 – www.hotelmanoir.com – msg@hotelmanoir.com – Fax 04 42 27 17 97 – Closed 8 January-1st February

40 rm – †€ 62 ††€ 75/92, ☕ € 10 AY **d**

◆ Once a monastery, then a millinery and now an unassuming, well-kept hotel, gradually being renovated. Summer terrace in part of the old cloisters. Retro lounge.

Le Clos de la Violette (Jean-Marc Banzo) VISA MC AE

10 av. de la Violette – ✆ 04 42 23 30 71 – www.closdelaviolette.fr – restaurant@closdelaviolette.fr – Fax 04 42 21 93 03 – Closed in August, Sunday and Monday BV **a**

Rest – *(number of covers limited, pre-book)* Menu € 50 (weekday lunch), € 90/130 – Carte € 108/115

Spec. Charlotte de truffe noire à la moelle (December-March). Pigeon fermier en sanguette paysanne. Petits babas bouchons au rhum. **Wines** Coteaux d'Aix-en-Provence.

◆ Located in a garden away from the old town centre, Le Clos de la Violette has a new look: shades of brown for the low-key side, large bay windows and a verdant terrace.

Les 2 Frères P VISA MC AE

4 av. Reine-Astrid – ✆ 04 42 27 90 32 – www.les2freres.com – les-deuxfreres@wanadoo.fr – Fax 04 42 12 47 08 AZ **s**

Rest – Menu (€ 19), € 33 – Carte € 45/65

◆ As the name suggests, this restaurant is run by two brothers: the older one prepares the delicious, modern cuisine (his labours are projected onto a screen in the dining room), while his sibling works front of house. Trendy bistro atmosphere.

Amphitryon
2 r. Paul-Doumer – 04 42 26 54 10 – www.restaurant-anphitryon.fr – amphitryon22@wanadoo.fr – Fax 04 42 38 36 15 – Closed 15 August-1st September, Sunday and Monday BY **s**
Rest – Menu (€ 20), € 23 (lunch), € 28/37 – Carte € 45/55
◆ Near the Cours Mirabeau, with a mix of classical and modern decor. Enjoy regional cuisine in the dining room or at the more informal counter. Enthusiastic service. Quiet patio.

Pierre Reboul
11 Petite-Rue-St-Jean – 04 42 20 58 26 – www.restaurant-pierre-reboul.com – restaurant-pierre-reboul@orange.fr – Fax 04 42 38 79 67 – Closed 20 December-4 January, Sunday and Monday CY **a**
Rest – *(number of covers limited, pre-book)* Menu € 39 (weekdays)/110 – Carte € 80/100
Spec. Escalope de foie gras à la pomme et au fruit de la passion. Truffe melanosporum (winter). Macaron chocolat. **Wines** Vin de Pays des Bouches du Rhône, Cassis.
◆ In the heart of the old town, this elegant, contemporary restaurant specialises in delicious and innovative cuisine which focuses on ingredients' quality.

Le Passage
10 r. Villars – 04 42 37 09 00 – www.le-passage.fr – contact@le-passage.fr – Fax 04 42 37 09 09 BY **b**
Rest – Menu (€ 13 bi), € 25/35 – Carte € 29/58
◆ Metal, walkways and contemporary furniture have rejuvenated this 19C confectionary. Situated on three floors it has a bistro, wine bar, tapas bar, cookery school and tearoom.

Le Formal
32 r. Espariat – 04 42 27 08 31 – Fax 04 42 27 08 31 – Closed 26 April-4 May, 23 August-7 September, 27 December-4 January, Saturday lunch, Sunday and Monday BY **w**
Rest – Menu (€ 20), € 23 bi (weekday lunch), € 34/58
◆ A restaurant occupying 15C vaulted cellars adorned with a collection of contemporary paintings. Inventive, well-presented cuisine.

Chez Féraud
8 r. du Puits-Juif – 04 42 63 07 27 – marcferaud@cegetel.net – Closed August, Sunday and Monday BY **k**
Rest – Menu (€ 22), € 30 – Carte € 40/55
◆ Hidden in a back street of old Aix, this charming family-run establishment boasts a 12C well. Provençal cuisine (pistou, stew, etc.) and grilled meat are prepared in the dining room.

Yamato
21 av. des Belges – 04 42 38 00 20 – www.restaurant-yamato.com – contact@restaurant-yamato.com – Fax 04 42 38 52 65 – Closed Monday except dinner in July and Tuesday lunch AZ **e**
Rest – Menu € 49/98 – Carte € 12/45
◆ Mrs Yuriko, the owner of this small Japanese restaurant, greets guests in traditional costume. The decor is also typically Japanese, and the restaurant has a veranda, terrace and garden. "Discovery" menus.

Yôji
7 av. Victor-Hugo – 04 42 38 48 76 – www.yoji.fr – Fax 04 42 38 47 01 – Closed Monday lunch and Sunday BY **g**
Rest – Menu € 18 (lunch), € 23/30 – Carte € 22/60
◆ Take a trip from the land of sunshine to the Land of the Rising Sun: Japanese food, a Korean barbecue and sushi bar in a Zen decor.

St-Canadet road 9 km by ①, D 96 and D 13 – ✉ 13100 Aix-en-Provence

Domaine De La Brillane without rest
195 rte de Couteron, on D 13 and secondary road – 06 74 77 01 20 – www.labrillane.com – domaine@labrillane.com – Fax 04 42 54 31 25 – Closed 20 December-4 January
5 rm – € 130/160 € 130/160
◆ Named after wines, the snug guestrooms have a view of the vineyards or Ste Victoire Mountain. Tastings of the estate's organic wine.

in Le Canet 8 km via ② on D 7n – ✉ 13590 Meyreuil

L'Auberge Provençale

at Le Canet de Meyreuil – ☎ 04 42 58 68 54 – www.auberge-provencale.fr – aubergiste@aol.com – Fax 04 42 58 68 05 – Closed 15-30 July, Tuesday except lunch September-May and Wednesday

Rest – Menu € 25/49 – Carte approx. € 65

◆ A pretty roadside inn with pleasant Provencal dining rooms. Generous, traditional food and a fine regional wine list.

via ③ 5 km D9 or A 51, Les Milles exit– ✉13546 Aix-en-Provence

Château de la Pioline rm,

260 r. Guillaume-du-Vair – ☎ 04 42 52 27 27 – www.chateaudelapioline.fr – info@chateaudelapioline.fr – Fax 04 42 52 27 28

30 rm – €170/235 €170/235, € 20 – 3 suites

Rest – *(resident only)* Menu (€ 28 bi), € 45/68 – Carte € 50/80

◆ A fine, listed property, housing large, attractively furnished rooms. Those in the recently built wing are smaller but boast a terrace. Formal garden. This Louis XVI style dining room is decorated with charcoal sketches. Concert dinners.

in Celony 3 km on D 7n – ✉ 13090 Aix-en-Provence

Le Mas d'Entremont rm,

315 rte Nationale 7 – ☎ 04 42 17 42 42 – www.masdentremont.com – entremont@wanadoo.fr – Fax 04 42 21 15 83 – Open 15 March-31 October

AV **g**

14 rm – €150/155 €150/190, € 18 – 6 suites – ½ P € 130/184

Rest – *(Closed Sunday dinner and Monday lunch)* Menu € 41 – Carte € 55/65

◆ Handsome ochre-coloured country house tucked away in the upper part of Aix. Park, water features and antique columns. Spacious personalised rooms and suites. Welcoming winter restaurant and delightful shaded terrace for summer dining. Traditional, seasonal cuisine.

AIX-LES-BAINS – 73 Savoie – 333 I3 – pop. 27 500 – alt. 200 m – Spa : mid Jan.-mid Dec. – Casinos : Grand Cercle CZ, New Casino BZ – ✉ 73100

46 **F2**

French Alps

Paris 539 – Annecy 34 – Bourg-en-Bresse 115 – Chambéry 18 – Lyon 107

Chambéry-Savoie: ☎ 04 79 54 49 54, to Viviers-du-Lac by ③: 8 km.

Office de tourisme, place Maurice Mollard ☎ 04 79 88 68 00, Fax 04 79 88 68 01

d'Aix-les-Bains Avenue du Golf, 3 km on the Chambéry road, ☎ 04 79 61 23 35

Esplanade du Lac★ - Town hall★ staircase CZ **H** - Musée Faure★ - Roman remains★ - Casino Grand Cercle★.

Lac du Bourget★★ - Abbaye de Hautecombe★★ - Les Bauges★.

Plan on next page

Radisson SAS rm,

av. Ch.-de-Gaulle – ☎ 04 79 34 19 19 – www.aixlesbains.radissonsas.com – info.aixlesbains@radissonsas.com – Fax 04 79 88 11 49

CZ **x**

92 rm – €150/205 €150/205, € 18 – 10 suites – ½ P € 85/97

Rest – brasserie – Menu (€ 21), € 26 – Carte approx. € 38

◆ In the heart of the casino park with a Japanese garden, this imposing modern hotel has functional and well-equipped rooms. Spa centre; meeting rooms. Small brasserie-inspired menu served in a modern setting or on the pleasant terrace.

Mercure Ariana rm,

111 av. de Marlioz, at Marlioz: 1.5 km – ☎ 04 79 61 79 79 – h2945@accor.com – Fax 04 79 61 79 00 – Closed 5-11 January

AX **a**

60 rm – €98/160 €110/172, € 16 – ½ P € 88/119

Rest – Menu (€ 23), € 28 – Carte € 45/55

◆ Establishment that is part of the Marlioz spa resort. Spacious rooms and a state-of-the-art balneotherapy centre. Nautical style decor. Well-lit dining room and attractive terrace overlooking a park shaded by 100-year-old trees.

AIX-LES-BAINS

Street	Square	No.
Bains (R. des)	CZ	2
Berthollet (Bd)	CZ	3
Boucher (Sq. A.)	CY	5
Carnot (Pl.)	CZ	6
Casino (R. du)	CZ	8
Chambéry (R. de)	CZ	9
Charcot (Bd J.)	AX	10
Clemenceau (Pl.)	BY	12
Dacquin (R.)	CZ	13
Davat (R.)	CZ	15
Fleurs (Av. des)	CZ	16
Garibaldi (Bd)	AX	17
Garrod (R. Sir-A.)	CZ	18
Gaulle (Av. de)	CZ	19
Georges-1er (R.)	CZ	21
Lamartine (R.)	CZ	22
Lattre-de-Tassigny (Bd. Mar.-de)	AX, BY	23
Liège (R. de)	CZ	24
Marlioz (Av. de)	AX	25
Mollard (Pl. M.)	CZ	26
Monard (R. S.)	CZ	27
Petit Port (Av. du)	AX, BYZ	28
Pierpont-Morgan (Bd)	BY	29
Près-Riants (R.)	BY	30
République (R.)	CY	32
Revard (Pl. du)	CZ	33
Roche-du-Roi (Bd de la)	CZ	34
Roosevelt (Av. F.)	AX	35
Rops (Av. D.)	AX	37
Russie (Bd de)	AX	39
Seyssel (R. C.-de)	CZ	40
Temple-de-Diane (Sq.)	CZ	45
Temple (R. du)	CZ	43
Verdun (Av. de)	BZ	46
Victoria (Av.)	CZ	47

Astoria rm, VISA

pl. des Thermes – 04 79 35 12 28 – www.hotelastoria.fr – hotel.astoria-savoie@wanadoo.fr – Fax 04 79 35 11 05 – Open 1st April-30 November CZ **z**

94 rm – €85 €105, €11 – ½ P €69 **Rest** – Menu €24

◆ This former luxury hotel (1906) near the thermal baths is a reminder of the sumptuous past of Aix-les-Bains. Skilfully renovated, Belle Époque decor and modern comfort. The Art Nouveau character of this large, elegant dining room has been preserved.

Le Manoir rest, VISA

37 r. Georges-1er – 04 79 61 44 00 – www.hotel-lemanoir.com – hotel-le-manoir@wanadoo.fr – Fax 04 79 35 67 67 – Closed 21-31 December CZ **r**

73 rm – €89/129 €99/179, €14 – ½ P €89/129

Rest – Menu €29/69 – Carte €32/80

◆ Hotel located in the converted outbuildings of the Splendide and Royal luxury hotels. Rooms in the 1900-style Villa Grimotière are more refined. Peaceful flower-filled garden; wellness centre. Dining room extending out to a veranda that opens onto an expanse of green. Pleasant terrace.

Agora rm, rest, VISA

1 av. de Marlioz – 04 79 34 20 20 – www.hotel-agora.com – reception@hotel-agora.com – Fax 04 79 34 20 30 – Closed 19 December-4 January CZ **u**

61 rm – €67/89 €79/101, €13 – ½ P €72/83

Rest – Menu (€24) – Carte €28/52

◆ The advantages of this hotel include its central location and excellent facilities. Functional rooms, the quieter of which are to the rear. Pool, sauna and steam baths. New contemporary decor in the restaurant and international cuisine (tajines, wok, tartare).

Grand Hôtel du Parc rest, VISA

28 r. de Chambéry – 04 79 61 29 11 – www.grand-hotel-du-parc.com – info@grand-hotel-du-parc.com – Fax 04 79 88 33 49 – Closed 21 December-7 February CZ **n**

38 rm – €49 €59/71, €10 – ½ P €60/75

Rest *La Bonne Fourchette* – *(closed Wednesday lunch off season, Sunday dinner and Monday)* Menu (€23), €30/70 – Carte €55/70

◆ 1817 building near the open-air theatre. Spacious and simple rooms. The lounge retains its attractive period decor. At the Bonne Fourchette there is a pleasantly nostalgic dining room and traditional food.

Auberge St-Simond rm, VISA

130 av. St-Simond – 04 79 88 35 02 – www.saintsimond.com – auberge@saintsimond.com – Fax 04 79 88 38 45 – Closed 1st-10 November, 20 December-25 January, Monday lunch 1st October-30 April and Sunday dinner AX **e**

24 rm – €55/62 €60/75, €11 – ½ P €54/69

Rest – Menu €23 (weekday lunch), €28/37 – Carte €31/44

◆ Smart, well-maintained guestrooms with individual touches in this hotel, renowned for its friendly atmosphere and pleasant garden with a swimming pool. Traditional cuisine. Service on the terrace in good weather.

Revotel without rest VISA

198 r. de Genève – 04 79 35 03 37 – www.revotel.fr – revotel@wanadoo.fr – Fax 04 79 88 82 99 – Closed 1st December-5 February CZ **v**

18 rm – €34/41 €34/41, €6

◆ Pleasant welcome at this low-cost establishment near the livelier districts. Functional rooms with 1970s-style furniture. Quieter rooms towards the back.

Auberge du Pont Rouge VISA

151 av. du Grand-Port – 04 79 63 43 90 – alain.accorsi@orange.fr – Fax 04 79 63 43 90 – Closed Sunday dinner, Tuesday dinner, Wednesday dinner and Monday AX **f**

Rest – Menu (€24), €28/39

◆ Enjoy the warm, modern setting (red toned decor) and terrace in fine weather. Market dishes of the day, specialities from southwest France and fish from the lake.

L'Annexe
205 bord du Lac – ✆ 04 79 35 25 64 – www.restaurant-lannexe.com – Fax 04 79 35 20 45 – Closed 25 October-10 November, 20-27 December, 15 February-3 March, Sunday and Monday AX **b**
Rest – Menu (€ 12), € 16 (weekday lunch), € 27/42 – Carte € 34/64
◆ A modern lakeside building. Minimalist, contemporary dining room, plus an attractive panoramic terrace adorned with teak furniture. Fusion cuisine.

AIZENAY – 85 Vendée – **316** G7 – **pop. 7 147** – **alt. 62 m** – ✉ **85190** 34 **B3**

Paris 435 – Challans 26 – Nantes 60 – La Roche-sur-Yon 18 – Les Sables-d'Olonne 33

Office de tourisme, avenue de la Gare ✆ 02 51 94 62 72, Fax 02 51 94 62 72

La Sittelle
33 r. Mar- Leclerc – ✆ 02 51 34 79 90 – Fax 02 51 94 81 77 – Closed August, 1st-7 January, Monday and dinner except Saturday
Rest – *(number of covers limited, pre-book)* Menu € 24/35
◆ Brick fireplaces, moulded ceilings and old parquet floors: the rooms in this discreet manor are refined. Careful and personalised classic cuisine.

AJACCIO – 2A Corse-du-Sud – **345** B8 – see Corse

ALBAN – 81 Tarn – **338** G7 – **pop. 848** – **alt. 600 m** – ✉ **81250** 29 **C2**

Paris 723 – Albi 29 – Castres 54 – Toulouse 106

Syndicat d'initiative, 21, place des Tilleuls ✆ 05 63 55 93 90, Fax 05 63 55 93 90

Au Bon Accueil with rm
49 av. de Millau – ✆ 05 63 55 81 03 – Bardyj@wanadoo.fr – Fax 05 63 55 82 97 – Closed January
11 rm – € 45/66 € 45/66, € 8 – ½ P € 55/60
Rest – *(Closed Friday dinner, Sunday dinner and Monday)* Menu (€ 17), € 22/34 – Carte € 33/55
◆ Practically located between Albi and Pau, this small family inn offers generous helpings of traditional food. Countrified decor (original wood panelling and beams). Simple, spruced up rooms, quieter to the rear.

ALBERT – 80 Somme – **301** I8 – **pop. 10 065** – **alt. 65 m** – ✉ **80300** 36 **B1**
Northern France and the Paris Region

Paris 156 – Amiens 30 – Arras 50 – St-Quentin 53

Office de tourisme, 9, r. Léon Gambetta ✆ 03 22 75 16 42, Fax 03 22 75 11 72

Royal Picardie
138 av. du Gén. Leclerc, (Amiens road) – ✆ 03 22 75 37 00 – www.royalpicardie.com – reservation@royalpicardie.com – Fax 03 22 75 60 19
23 rm – € 78/153 € 89/173, € 10
Rest – *(dinner only)* Menu € 27/35 – Carte € 32/59
◆ This impressive building on the outskirts of town offers functional guestrooms with added extras such as an electric trouser press and courtesy tray. At the restaurant, traditional cuisine served in a dining room adorned with Louis XIII furniture.

in Authuille 5 km north by D 50 – **pop. 167** – **alt. 85 m** – ✉ **80300**

Auberge de la Vallée d'Ancre
6 r. Moulin – ✆ 03 22 75 15 18 – Closed 17 August-2 September, 8-22 February, Sunday dinner, Wednesday dinner and Monday
Rest – Menu € 23/33 – Carte € 35/55
◆ Lovely country inn beside a river. Charming atmosphere, where the regulars greet the chef who cooks up traditional dishes in his open kitchen.

ALBERTVILLE – 73 Savoie – **333** L3 – **pop. 18 300** – **alt. 344 m** – ✉ **73200** French Alps 46 **F2**

Paris 581 – Annecy 46 – Chambéry 51 – Chamonix-Mont-Blanc 64

Office de tourisme, place de l'Europe ✆ 04 79 32 04 22, Fax 04 79 32 87 09

Bourg de Conflans★, porte de Savoie ≤★, Grande Place★ - Fort du Mont road ★★.

Million rest, VISA

8 pl. de la Liberté – 04 79 32 25 15 – www.hotelmillion.com – hotel.million@wanadoo.fr – Fax 04 79 32 25 36 – Closed 27 April-4 May
26 rm – €93/121 €137/181
Rest – *(closed 3-17 August, 26 October-2 November, Saturday lunch, Sunday dinner and Monday)* Menu €28/80 – Carte €63/77
◆ This proud town centre residence has been a hotel since 1770. The rooms, some of which are air-conditioned, are furnished in varying styles. The restaurant dining room opens onto a pleasant verdant terrace. Modern cuisine.

Albert 1er rest, VISA

38 av. Victor-Hugo – 04 79 37 77 33 – www.alberter.fr – contact@albert1er.fr – Fax 04 79 37 89 01
16 rm – €59/72 €76/83 – ½ P €71/85
Rest – *(Closed Sunday dinner)* Menu €12 (weekdays)/26 – Carte €22/37
◆ The hotel dates from 1880 and is located next to the station. Simple, functional rooms. Those on the first floor are more pleasant and are decorated in an alpine style. Brasserie type restaurant offering some regional specialities.

Le Bistrot Gourmand VISA

8 pl. Charles-Albert – 04 79 32 79 06 – danielandré96@neuf.fr – Fax 04 79 31 77 30 – Closed 27 July-15 August, Christmas holidays, Sunday dinner, Tuesday dinner and Wednesday
Rest – Menu (€16), €24/35 – Carte €41/65
◆ This establishment, whose bistro decor offers a view on the kitchen, serves simple, seasonal dishes. Pleasant, relaxed atmosphere.

at Monthion **7 km south by Chambéry road(exit 26) and D 64 – 73200**

Les 16 Clochers VISA

91 chemin des 16 Clochers – 04 79 31 30 39 – Fax 04 79 31 30 39 – Closed 14-21 April, 1st-8 September, 23 December-15 January, Sunday dinner, Tuesday dinner and Monday
Rest – Menu (€24), €33/49 – Carte €49/65
◆ Warm chalet-style interior and panoramic summer terrace offering a superb view of the valley and mountains. Traditional cuisine with creative flavour combinations.

ALBI – 81 Tarn – 338 E7 – pop. 48 600 – alt. 174 m – 81000 29 C2

Languedoc-Roussillon-Tarn Gorges

Paris 694 – Béziers 150 – Clermont-Ferrand 286 – Toulouse 76
Office de tourisme, place Sainte-Cécile 05 63 49 48 80, Fax 05 63 49 48 98
Albi Lasbordes Château de Lasbordes, W : 4 km on r. de la Berchère, 05 63 54 98 07
de Florentin-Gaillac Marssac-sur-Tarn Al Bosc, 11 km on the Toulouse road, 05 63 55 20 50
Race circuit 05 63 43 23 00, 2 km by ⑤.
Ste-Cécile cathedral ★★★: Rood-screen★★★ - Palais de la Berbie★: musée Toulouse-Lautrec★★ - Le Vieil Albi★★: hôtel Reynès★ Z **C** - Pont Vieux★ - Pharmacie des Pénitents★ - ★ from the moulins albigeois (Albi windmills).

Plan on next page

La Réserve rm, VISA

rte de Cordes, via ⑥: 3 km – 05 63 60 80 80 – www.relaischateaux.fr/reservealbi – reservealbi@relaischateaux.com – Fax 05 63 47 63 60 – Open 1st May-31 October
24 rm – €158/328 €228/468, €20 – 2 suites
Rest – *(closed lunch except Sunday and holidays)* Menu €40/60 – Carte €70/90
◆ This large, welcoming villa is set in gardens bordering the Tarn. It offers rooms furnished in a mixture of old and new, overlooking the pool and the quiet river. Bright, modern dining room with a huge terrace overlooking the river.

Hostellerie St-Antoine without rest VISA

17 r. St-Antoine – 05 63 54 04 04 – www.hotel-saint-antoine-albi.com – courriel@hotel-saint-antoine-albi.com – Fax 05 63 47 10 47 Z **d**
42 rm – €85/165 €95/225, €18 – 2 suites
◆ Founded in 1734, the hotel (one of the oldest in France), garden and antique furniture create a cosy, bygone atmosphere, without forgoing modern comforts.

ALBI

Alsace-Lorraine (Bd) V
Andrieu (Bd Ed.) . . . . X 2
Archevêché (Pl. de l') . . . . . Y 3
Berchère (R. de la) . . . . Z
Bodin (Bd P.) . . . . X 5
Cantepau (R. de) V
Carnot (Bd). X
Castelviel (R. du) . . . . Y 7
Choiseul (Quai) . . . . Y 8
Croix-Blanche (R. de la) . . . Z 9
Croix-Verte (R.) . . . . V, YZ 12
Dembourg (Av.) . . . . V 13
Dr-Camboulives (R. du) . . . . Z 14
Empeyralots (R. d') . . . . Z 15
Foch (Av. Mar.) X
Gambetta (Av.). X
Gaulle (Av. Gén.-de) X
Genève (R. de). . . . . Z 17
Gorsse (Pl. H. de) . . . . Y 18
Grand (R. E.). . . . . Y
Hôtel-de-Ville (R. de l') . . . . Z 19
Jean-Jaurès (Pl.) . . . . Z
Joffre (Av. Mar.). . . . . X 22
Lacombe (Bd) . . . . X 23
Lamothe (R. de) . . . . V, Y
Lapérouse (Pl.) . . . . Z
Lattre-de-Tassigny (Av. Mar.-de). . . . . V 24
Loirat (Av. du). V
Lude (Bd du) X
Malroux (R. A.) . . . . Y 25
Maquis (Pl. du) . . . . X 26
Mariès (R.) . . . . Y
Montebello (Bd) . . . . X 27
Moulin (Lices J.) . . . . Z
Nobles (R. des) . . . . Z 28
Oulmet (R. de l') . . . . Z 29
Palais (Pl. du) . . . . Z 30
Palais (R. du) . . . . Z 31
Partisans (Espl. des) . . . . . . Y
Pénitents (R. des) . . . . Z 33
Peyrolière (R.) . . . . YZ 34
Pompidou (Lices G.) . . . . . YZ
Porta (R.) . . . . Y
Porte-Neuve (R. de la) . . . . Z 35
Puech-Bérenguier (R.) . . . . Z 37
République (R. de la) . . . . V, Y
Rinaldi (R.) . . . . Y
Rivière (R. de la). . . . . Y 40
Roquelaure (R.) . . . . Z 41
Ste-Cécile (Pl.) . . . . Y 46
Ste-Cécile (R.) . . . . Z 47
Ste-Claire (R.) . . . . Y 48
St-Afric (R.) . . . . Y 42
St-Amarand (Pl.) . . . . V 69
St-Antoine (R.) . . . . Z 43
St-Clair (R.) . . . . Z 44
St-Julien (R.). . . . . Y 45
Saunal (R. de) . . . . Z 49
Savary (R. H.) . . . . Z 51
Sel (R. du). . . . . Z 52
Séré-de-Rivière (R.) . . . . . . Z 53
Sibille (Bd Gén.) . . . . Z
Soult (Bd) VX
Strasbourg (Bd de) . . . . . . V, Y 54
Teyssier (Av. Col.). X
Thomas (Av. A.) . . . . V 57
Timbal (R.) . . . . Z 58
Toulouse-Lautrec (R. H.-de) Z 60
Valmy (Bd). VX
Verdier (Av. F.) . . . . X 62
Verdun (Pl. de) . . . . X 63
Verdusse (R. de) . . . . Z 64
Vigan (Pl. du) . . . . Z 65
Visitation (R. de la) . . . . . . Y 67
8-Mai-1945 (Pl. du) X

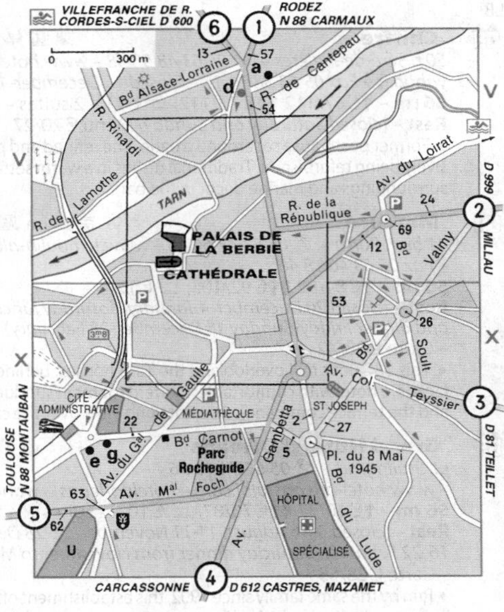

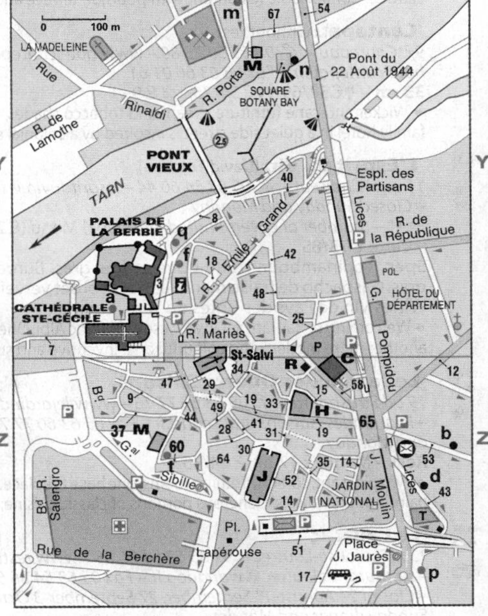

Chiffre
50 r. Séré-de-Rivières – 05 63 48 58 48 – www.hotelchiffre.com – hotel.chiffre@yahoo.fr – Fax 05 63 38 11 15 – Closed 15 December-15 January Z **b**
36 rm – €67/112 €72/112, €11 – 2 suites – ½ P €71/86
Rest – *(closed Saturday and Sunday)* Menu €20/27
◆ Former post house set around a patio. The refined and personalised rooms are progressively being refurbished. Traditional dishes in a warm setting (wood-panelled walls, lavish surroundings and marine decor in the bar).

Mercure
rm, VISA
41 bis r. Porta – 05 63 47 66 66 – www.lemoulin-albi.fr – h1211-gm@accor.com – Fax 05 63 46 18 40 Y **n**
56 rm – €84/92 €92/105, €12
Rest – *(closed 20 December-4 January, Saturday lunch, Sunday lunch and dinner Friday-Sunday 1st December-28 February)* Menu (€17), €20/45 bi – Carte €28/42
◆ This 18C flour mill overlooking the Tarn houses, behind the typical regional pink brick façade, a hotel with comfortable, modern rooms in subdued surroundings. The restaurant and the terrace command a breathtaking view over the cathedral. Updated menu.

Grand Hôtel d'Orléans
rest, VISA
pl. Stalingrad – 05 63 54 16 56 – www.hotel-orleans-albi.com – hoteldorleans@wanadoo.fr – Fax 05 63 54 43 41
56 rm – €60/77 €70/87, €10 – 2 suites – ½ P €70/74 X **e**
Rest – *(closed 3-16 August, 1st-11 November, 22-28 December, 2-18 January, 16-22 February, Saturday dinner from November to March)* Menu (€17), €23 – Carte €38/55
◆ Run by the same family since 1902, this establishment offers functional rooms, which are being gradually refurbished in a contemporary style: ideal for a peaceful stay in the land of Lautrec. Comfortable restaurant with poolside terrace and traditional cuisine.

Cantepau without rest
VISA
9 r. Cantepau – 05 63 60 75 80 – www.hotelcantepau.fr – contact@hotelcantepau.fr – Fax 05 63 60 01 61 V **a**
33 rm – €54/69 €54/75, €9
◆ Wicker and cane furniture, cream and tobacco shades, fans etc.: the decor of this little family hotel in a quiet side street is inspired by a colonial style. Friendly welcome.

L'Esprit du Vin (David Enjalran)
VISA
11 quai Choiseul – 05 63 54 60 44 – lespritduvin@free.fr – Fax 05 63 54 54 79 – Closed Sunday and Monday Y **q**
Rest – *(number of covers limited, pre-book)* Menu (€26), €30 (lunch)/95 – Carte €73/85
Spec. Topinambour, truffe noire et foie gras. Burger de bœuf charolais et foie gras. Gaspacho de fraise mara des bois, sorbet verveine citron (June-September).
Wines Vin de Pays des Côtes du Tarn, Gaillac.
◆ Welcoming restaurant set in a house in historic Albi. One large vaulted dining room and another more modern and colourful one. Inventive and subtle gourmet cuisine.

Le Jardin des Quatre Saisons
VISA
19 bd Strasbourg – 05 63 60 77 76 – www.lejardindes4saisons.fr.st – lejardindes4saisons@aliceadsl.fr – Fax 05 63 60 77 76 – Closed Sunday dinner and Monday V **d**
Rest – Menu (€17 bi), €24/35
◆ Two pleasant, colourful dining rooms: one has a fireplace, while the other is adorned with paintings and plants. Generous portions of classic cuisine; fine wine list.

Le Lautrec
VISA
13 r. Toulouse-Lautrec – 05 63 54 86 55 – www.restaurant-le-lautrec.com – restaurantlelautrec@wanadoo.fr – Fax 05 63 54 86 55 – Closed 24 August-1st September, 27 September-3 October, 18-25 February, Sunday dinner and Monday
Rest – Menu (€16), €18 (weekdays)/50 bi – Carte approx. €32 Z **t**
◆ Unspoilt nature depicts these former stables, in the middle of which stands an old well rich in history. Patio-terrace dining in fine weather, and regionally sourced fresh produce on the menu.

La Table du Sommelier
20 r. Porta – ☎ 05 63 46 20 10 – www.latabledusommelier.com – latabledusommelier@orange.fr – Fax 05 63 36 58 51 – Closed Sunday and Monday
Rest – Menu (€ 13), € 16 (weekdays), € 25/40 – Carte € 24/33 Y **m**
◆ The name and the wooden crates stacked in the entrance set the scene. Tasty bistro-style cuisine in an updated version, served, of course, with a fine selection of wines.

L'Epicurien
42 pl. Jean-Jaurès – ☎ 05 63 53 10 70 – www.restaurantlepicurien.com – l-epicurien@wanadoo.fr – Fax 05 63 43 16 90 – Closed Sunday and Monday
Rest – Menu (€ 17), € 20 (weekday lunch), € 28/65 – Carte € 61/70 Z **p**
◆ This is Albi's fashionable address. Minimalist but nonetheless a welcoming setting with benches, bay windows, and a direct view of the kitchens. Modern menu.

La Fourchette Adroite
7 pl. de l'Archevêché – ☎ 05 63 49 77 81 – lafourchetteadroite81@orange.fr – Fax 05 63 49 77 81 Y **f**
Rest – Menu (€ 13), € 16 (lunch), € 28/42 bi – Carte € 33/45
◆ Modern architecture in a historic setting: this loft-style restaurant is as friendly as it is fashionable. Inventive cuisine fils totally with the trendy atmosphere.

Stéphane Laurens
10 pl. Monseigneur-Mignot – ☎ 05 63 43 62 41 – www.stephanelaurens.com – stephanelaurens.restaurant@orange.fr – Fax 05 63 43 67 79 Y **a**
Rest – Menu € 19/24 – Carte € 28/54
◆ This elegant property offers two impressive high-ceilinged vast rooms whose minimalist decor is Japanese inspired. Reinterpreted classics recipes rich in flavour and aroma.

in Castelnau-de-Lévis 7 km by ⑥, D 600 and D 1 – pop. 1 520 – alt. 221 m – ✉ 81150

La Taverne with rm rest,
r. Aubijoux – ☎ 05 63 60 90 16 – www.tavernebesson.com – contact@tavernebesson.com – Fax 05 63 60 96 73
8 rm – †€ 58/65 ††€ 58/85, ☕ € 9
Rest – *(Closed February holiday, Sunday dinner and Monday in low season)*
Menu € 23/61 – Carte € 44/60
◆ Former bakers' co-operative whose brick ovens adorn one of the two comfortable dining rooms. Refined cuisine inspired by local and traditional recipes.

ALENÇON P – 61 Orne – 310 J4 – pop. 28 400 – alt. 135 m – ✉ 61000 33 C3
Normandy

Paris 190 – Chartres 119 – Évreux 119 – Laval 90 – Le Mans 54 – Rouen 150

Office de tourisme, place de la Magdeleine ☎ 02 33 80 66 33, Fax 02 33 80 66 32

d'Alençon-en-Arçonnay Arçonnay Le Petit Maleffre, 3 km on the Le Mans road, ☎ 02 33 28 56 67

Église Notre-Dame (Notre Dame Church)★ - Musée des Beaux-Arts et de la Dentelle (Museum of Fine Arts and Lacework)★ : lace collection ★ BZ **M²**.

Plan on following page

Mercure without rest
187 av. Gén- Leclerc, 2 km on ④ – ☎ 02 33 28 64 64 – www.mercure.com – H1359@accor.com – Fax 02 33 28 64 72 – Closed 24 December-4 January
53 rm – †€ 66/72 ††€ 68/76, ☕ € 10
◆ Establishment located in a small shopping area. All the practical and well-soundproofed rooms have been renovated (those on the second floor are more contemporary in style). Attractive sitting room-bar.

Des Ducs without rest
50 av. Thomas Wilson – ☎ 02 33 29 03 93 – www.hoteldesducs-alencon.fr – hoteldesducs@orange.fr – Fax 02 33 29 28 59 AY **r**
24 rm – †€ 49/59 ††€ 55/65, ☕ € 8
◆ This hotel opposite the station has enjoyed a full-scale facelift and now offers modern, practical, well-equipped rooms in trendy colours. Bar, garden and terrace.

ALENÇON

Argentan (R. d') . . . . **AY** 2
Basingstoke (Av. de) . . . . **AY** 3
Bercail (R. du) . . . . **BZ** 4
Capucins (R. des) . . . . **CZ** 6
Clemenceau (Cours) . . . . . . **BCZ**
Duchamp (Bd) . . . . **AY** 8
Écusson (R. de l') . . . . **AY** 9
Fresnay (R. de) . . . . **BZ** 13
Grandes-Poteries (R. des) . . **BZ** 14
Grande-Rue . . . . **BZ** 15
Halle-au-Blé (Pl. de la) . . . . . **BZ** 17
Lattre-de-Tassigny
(R. du Mar.-de) . . . . **BCZ** 19
Leclerc (Av. du Gén.) . . . . . . **AY** 20
La Magdeleine (Pl.) . . . . **CZ** 18
Mans (R. du) . . . . **AY** 24
Marguerite-de-Lorraine (Pl.) . **BZ** 25
Porte-de-la-Barre (R.) . . . . . . **BZ** 30
Poterne (R. de la) . . . . **CZ** 33
Quakenbruck (Av. de) . . . . . . **AY** 34
Rhin-et-Danube (Av.) . . . . **AY** 35
Sieurs (R. aux) . . . . **BZ**
Tisons (R. des) . . . . **AY** 39
1er Chasseurs (Bd) . . . . **AY** 40
14e Hussards (R. du) . . . . **AY** 42

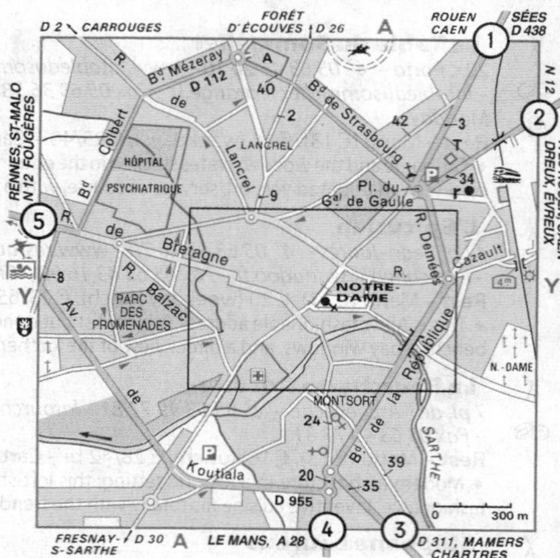

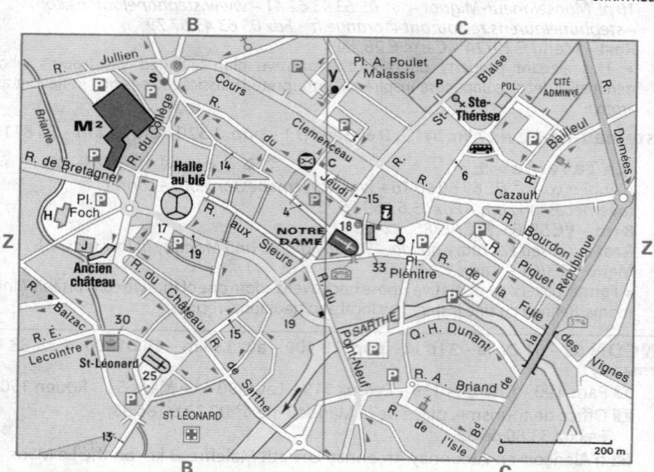

Ibis without rest
13 pl. Poulet-Malassis – ✆ 02 33 80 67 67 – www.ibishotel.com – h0982@accor.com – Fax 02 33 26 02 88 CZ **y**
52 rm – †€ 50/73 ††€ 50/73, ☕ € 8
◆ Two minutes from the town centre, in a quiet residential neighbourhood. Contemporary furnishings in the guestrooms and breakfast room. Muted ambience in the lounge bar.

Au Petit Vatel
72 pl. Cdt-Desmeulles – ✆ 02 33 26 23 78 – aupetitvatel@orange.fr – Fax 02 33 82 64 57 – Closed 22 July-12 August, 18 February-4 March, Sunday dinner, Tuesday dinner and Wednesday BZ **s**
Rest – Menu (€ 17 bi), € 20/70 bi – Carte € 33/63
◆ A rural spirit reigns throughout this house built in local stone. A pastel colour scheme and artwork depict the interior. Faultless choice of regional dishes.

via ① N 138 and secondary road - ✉ 61250 Valframbert

Château de Sarceaux
– ✆ 02 33 28 85 11 – *www.chateau-de-sarceaux.com – chateaudesarceaux@yahoo.fr – Fax 02 33 28 85 11 – Closed 2 February-5 March*
5 rm – €110/150 €110/150 **Table d'hôte** – Menu €49 bi
◆ A 12-ha park with a pond surrounds this 17C and 19C castle with refined rooms decorated with authentic furniture and family paintings, all facing south. Candle-light dinner in the restaurant; traditional menu.

in St-Paterne (72 Sarthe) 4 km via ③ – **pop. 1 635 – alt. 160 m** – ✉ **72610**

Château de St-Paterne
1 r. Perseigne – ✆ *02 33 27 54 71 – www.chateau-saintpaterne.com – contact@chateau-saintpaterne.com – Fax 02 33 29 16 71 – Closed 1st January-15 March*
10 rm – €135/240 €135/240, €13
Rest – *(dinner only) (resident only)* Menu €47
◆ A romantic sojourn awaits you in this château set in vast grounds planted with century-old trees. Period lounge and personal touches in the rooms, whose decor varies from historical to fashionable. A warm decor provides the setting for candle-lit dinners concocted by the lord of the house (set menu).

ALÉRIA – **2B Haute-Corse** – **345** G7 – **see Corse**

ALÈS – **30 Gard** – **339** J4 – **pop. 40 000 – alt. 136 m** – ✉ **30100** 23 **C1**
Languedoc-Roussillon-Tarn Gorges

Paris 706 – Albi 226 – Avignon 72 – Montpellier 70 – Nîmes 46
Office de tourisme, place de la Mairie ✆ 04 66 52 32 15, Fax 04 66 52 57 09
Musée minéralogique de l'Ecole des Mines★ N - Musée-bibliothèque Pierre-André-Benoit★ West: 2 km - Mine-témoin★ West: 3 km.

Plan on following page

Ibis without rest
18 r. E.-Quinet – ✆ *04 66 52 27 07 – www.ibishotel.com – h0338@accor.com – Fax 04 66 52 36 33* B **e**
75 rm – €55/79 €55/79, €8
◆ A 1970s hotel in the heart of Alès. All the spacious and well-soundproofed rooms have been renovated. Lounge bar. Bicycle shed.

Le Riche with rm
42 pl. Sémard – ✆ *04 66 86 00 33 – www.leriche.fr – reception@leriche.fr – Fax 04 66 30 02 63 – Closed August* B **n**
19 rm – €49 €65, €8,50 – ½ P €54
Rest – Menu €21/50 – Carte €30/45
◆ Fine, early-20C building. Art Nouveau dining room with a high ceiling and brightly coloured wood panelling. Classic cuisine. A contemporary spirit reigns in the rooms.

L'Atelier des Saveurs
16 fg de Rochebelle – ✆ *04 66 86 27 77 – www.latelierdessaveurs.net – gouny.henri@wanadoo.fr – Fax 04 66 86 27 77 – Closed 24 August-13 September, Saturday lunch, Sunday dinner and Monday* A **t**
Rest – Menu (€19), €28/62 – Carte €35/53
◆ The scene at this 'workshop of flavours' is a bright, discreetly countrified interior, inviting shaded patio, warm, friendly atmosphere and appealing up-to-date recipes full of southern flavour.

in St-Martin-de-Valgalgues 2 km by ① – **pop. 4 283 – alt. 148 m** – ✉ **30520**

Le Mas de la Filoselle rest,
344 r. du 19 mars 1962 – ✆ *04 66 24 74 60 – http://filoselle.free.fr/ – filoselle@wanadoo.fr*
3 rm – €69 €80 – ½ P €65 **Table d'hôte** – Menu €25 bi
◆ You will soon feel at home in this former silk farm in the upper reaches of the village. Exquisite theme rooms (Lavender, Olive, etc.) and beautiful terraced garden.

ALÈS

- Albert-1er (R.) . . . . B 2
- Audibert (R. Cdt) . . . . A 3
- Avéjan (R. d') . . . . B
- Barbusse (Pl. Henri) . . . . B 4
- Docteur-Serres (R.) . . . . B
- Edgar-Quinet (R.). . . . . B
- Hôtel-de-Ville (Pl. de l') . . . . . . A 5
- Lattre-de-Tassigny (Av. de) . . . B 6
- Leclerc (Pl. Gén.) . . . . B 8
- Louis-Blanc (Bd) . . . . B
- Martyrs-de-la-Résistance (Pl.) . B 9
- Michelet (R.) . . . . B 10
- Paul (R. Marcel) . . . . B 12
- Péri (Pl. Gabriel) . . . . B 13
- Rollin (R.) . . . . A 14
- St-Vincent (R.) . . . . B 15
- Semard (Pl. Pierre) . . . . B 16
- Soleil (R. du Faubourg du) . . . . B 17
- Stalingrad (Av. de) . . . . B 18
- Taisson (R.) . . . . B 19
- Talabot (Bd) . . . . B 20

in St-Hilaire-de-Brethmas 3 km by ② and D 936 – pop. 4 099 – alt. 125 m – ✉ 30560

Comptoir St-Hilaire

Mas de la Rouquette, 2 km east – ✆ 04 66 30 82 65 – www.comptoir-saint-hilaire.com – contact@comptoir-saint-hilaire.com – Fax 04 66 25 64 02

7 rm – †€ 250/390 ††€ 250/390 **Table d'hôte** – Menu € 30/50

◆ Catherine Painvin has entirely remodelled this 17C mas: characterful rooms and suites, discreet luxury throughout, and superb garden with views of the Cevennes as far as the eye can see. Magical moments at the themed table d'hôte dinners.

Auberge de St-Hilaire

5 r. André Schenk – ✆ 04 66 30 11 42 – www.aubergesainthilaire.com – Fax 04 66 86 72 79 – Closed Sunday dinner and Monday

Rest – Menu € 26/75 – Carte € 65/85

◆ Tasty classical cuisine with a modern slant served in the half-contemporary, half-Riviera-inspired dining room of this elegant lodge. Inviting terrace dominated by an olive tree.

in St-Privat-des-Vieux 4 km by ②, Montélimar road, D 216 and secondary road – pop. 4 349 – alt. 180 m – ✉ 30340

Le Vertige des Senteurs

35 chemin de l'Usclade – ✆ 04 66 91 08 84 – www.vertige-des-senteurs.fr – stephane.delsuc@neuf.fr – Fax 04 66 91 08 84 – Closed 1st-10 January, Saturday lunch in July-August, Sunday dinner and Monday

Rest – Menu (€ 19), € 35/70

◆ This attractively restored farmhouse serves carefully prepared inventive cuisine. Sophisticated contemporary dining rooms (one with fireplace) commanding a view of the Cévennes. Shop and wine cellar.

in Méjannes-lès-Alès 7.5 km by ② and D 981 – pop. 975 – alt. 141 m – ✉ 30340

Auberge des Voutins
rte d'Uzès – ✆ 04 66 61 38 03 – Fax 04 66 61 04 19 – Closed Tuesday lunch, Sunday dinner and Monday except bank holidays
Rest – Menu € 28/60 – Carte € 50/60
◆ Building typical of the region, sheltered from the road by a line of trees. Traditional cuisine to be enjoyed in a country style dining room or on the terrace shaded by a lime tree.

ALFORTVILLE – 94 Val-de-Marne – **312** D3 – **101** 27 – see Paris, Area

ALGAJOLA – 2B Haute-Corse – **345** C4 – see Corse

ALISE-STE-REINE – 21 Côte-d'Or – **320** G4 – see Venarey-les-Laumes

ALIX – 69 Rhône – **327** G4 – pop. 690 – alt. 287 m – ✉ 69380 43 **E1**
Paris 442 – L'Arbresle 12 – Lyon 28 – Villefranche-sur-Saône 12

Le Vieux Moulin
chemin du Vieux-Moulin – ✆ 04 78 43 91 66 – www.lemoulindalix.com – lemoulindalix@wanadoo.fr – Fax 04 78 47 98 46 – Closed Monday and Tuesday
Rest – Menu (€ 16), € 26/53 – Carte € 34/56
◆ This Rhone mill, built in stone, has been converted into a village inn. Countrified interior and a peaceful shaded terrace very popular in summer. Classic fare and daily specials.

ALLAIN – 54 Meurthe-et-Moselle – **307** G7 – pop. 459 – alt. 306 m – ✉ 54170 26 **B2**
Paris 305 – Nancy 34 – Neufchâteau 28 – Toul 16 – Vittel 49

La Haie des Vignes without rest
0.5 km at the A 31 interchange, Neufchâteau road – ✆ 03 83 52 81 82 – hotel.haiedesvignes.free.fr – hotel.haiedesvignes@free.fr – Fax 03 83 52 04 27
39 rm – †€ 42/57 ††€ 42/57, ☕ € 6,50
◆ Motel-style modern building located near the motorway, but in the quiet of the Lorraine countryside. Rooms are functional, subdued and well kept, with direct garden access.

ALLAS-LES-MINES – 24 Dordogne – **329** H6 – see St-Cyprien

ALLEINS – 13 Bouches-du-Rhône – **340** F3 – pop. 2 368 – alt. 180 m – ✉ 13980 42 **E1**
Paris 725 – Marseille 63 – Aix-en-Provence 34 – Avignon 47

Domaine de Méjeans rm,
R.D.71B – ✆ 04 90 57 31 74 – www.domainedemejeans.com – info@domainedemejeans.com – Fax 04 90 57 31 74
5 rm ☕ – †€ 160/180 ††€ 160/220
Table d'hôte – Menu € 40/50
◆ A poplar lined drive leads up to this comfortable and luxurious property set in quiet grounds (with pond, garden and swimming pool). Luxurious, well-equipped rooms.

ALLERY – 80 Somme – **301** E8 – see Airaines

ALLEVARD – 38 Isère – **333** J5 – pop. 3 571 – alt. 470 m – Winter sports : at Collet d'Allevard 1 450/2 100 m 13 – Spa : early March-mid Oct. – Casino – ✉ 38580 French Alps 46 **F2**
Paris 593 – Albertville 50 – Chambéry 33 – Grenoble 40
Office de tourisme, place de la Résistance ✆ 04 76 45 10 11, Fax 04 76 97 59 32
le Collet road ★★ by D525A.

ALLEVARD

Baroz (R. Emma) 2
Bir-Hakeim (R. de) 3
Charamil (R.) 5
Chataing (R. Laurent) 6
Chenal (R.) 7
Davallet (Av.) 8
Docteur-Mansord (R.) 9
Gerin (Av. Louis) 15
Grand Pont (R. du) 19
Libération (R. de la) 21
Louaraz (Av.) 22
Niepce (R. Bernard) 23
Ponsard (R.) 24
Rambaud (Pl. P.) 25
Résistance (Pl. de la) 27
Savoie (Av. de) 28
Thermes (R. des) 29
Verdun (Pl. de) 32
8-Mai-1945 (R. du) 34

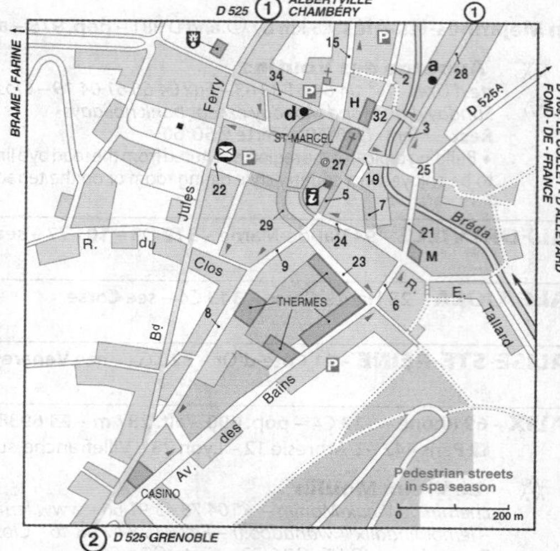

Les Alpes

rest,

pl. du Temple – ✆ 04 76 45 94 10 – www.lesalpesallevard.com
– hotel@lesalpesallevard.com – Fax 04 76 45 80 81
– Closed 10-26 April, 24 October-5 November and Sunday dinner in winter
15 rm – €58 €66 d
Rest – *(closed Friday dinner off season and Sunday dinner)*
Menu €17 (weekday lunch), €30/48 – Carte €25/40

◆ A family hotel, easily recognisable by its yellow and green facade, in the heart of the spa resort. Rather spacious, spotless rooms with personal touches. The recently renovated dining room sports a classic influence in keeping with the traditional menu.

Les Terrasses

29 av. de Savoie – ✆ 04 76 45 84 42 – www.hotellesterrasses.com
– responsable@hotellesterrasses.com – Fax 04 76 13 57 65
– Closed 21 March-6 April and 7-26 November
16 rm – €37/44 €37/51, €6,50 – ½ P €45/52 a
Rest – *(closed Sunday dinner, Monday lunch and Wednesday)* Menu (€11), €14 (weekdays)/25 – Carte €25/32

◆ A friendly welcome awaits guests in this tall 1930s house, situated near the River Bréda. Functional bedrooms; those at the back facing the garden are quieter. Simple Provençal decor in the dining room; traditional dishes.

in Pinsot 7 km South by D 525 A – pop. 175 – alt. 730 m – ✉ 38580

Pic de la Belle Étoile

– ✆ 04 76 45 89 45 – www.pbetoile.com
– hotel@pbetoile.com – Fax 04 76 45 89 46
– Closed 24 April-9 May, 17 July-13 August, 23 October-2 November, Friday dinner, Saturday and Sunday except 6-14 April, 19 December-4 January and 6 February-9 March
40 rm – €67/98 €82/122, €12 – ½ P €78/100
Rest – Menu €24/47

◆ This imposing local style residence, with a recent extension, offers a garden that rolls down to a stream. Choose the rooms in the recently-built wing. Classic dishes with a regional accent are served in a modern dining area or on the terrace.

South 17 km on the D 525A and minor road - ✉ 38580 Allevard

Auberge Nemoz
at village "La Martinette" – ✆ 04 76 45 03 10 – www.auberge-nemoz.com – aubergenemoz@wanadoo.fr – Fax 04 76 45 03 10 – Closed 14-28 April and November
5 rm – €77 €87 **Table d'hôte** – Menu €23/32
◆ In the Haut Bréda valley, this wood and stone chalet houses personalised rooms (antique furniture and family ornaments). Horse riding or snowshoe excursions (winter). Rustic and extremely lively restaurant. The fireplace is used for raclettes. Local dishes.

ALLEX – 26 Drôme – **332** C5 – **pop. 2 413** – **alt. 160 m** – ✉ 26400 44 **B3**

Paris 588 – Lyon 126 – Valence 24 – Romans-sur-Isère 46 – Montélimar 34

Syndicat d'initiative, avenue Henri Seguin ✆ 04 75 62 73 13, Fax 04 75 62 69 20

La Petite Aiguebonne without rest
chemin d'Aiguebonne, 2 km East on D 93 – ✆ 04 75 62 60 68 – www.petite-aiguebonne.com – contact@petite-aiguebonne.com
5 rm – €85/100 €85/120
◆ Tuscan, African, Indian, American...As many decorative themes as there are charming rooms in this old (13C) but well-equipped Drôme farmhouse.

ALLEYRAS – 43 Haute-Loire – **331** E4 – **pop. 183** – **alt. 779 m** – ✉ 43580 6 **C3**

Paris 549 – Brioude 71 – Langogne 43 – Le Puy-en-Velay 32 – St-Chély-d'Apcher 59

Le Haut-Allier (Philippe Brun) rest, rm, VISA AE
2 km at the Pont d'Alleyras, northward along the D 40 – ✆ 04 71 57 57 63 – www.hotel-lehautallier.com – hot.rest.hautallier@wanadoo.fr – Fax 04 71 57 57 99 – Open from mid March-mid November and closed Monday and Tuesday except July-August
12 rm – €95/125 €95/125, €13 – ½ P €98/110
Rest – *(closed Monday and Tuesday except dinner July-August)*
Menu €28 (weekday lunch), €48/95 – Carte €50/88
Spec. Déclinaison autour des champignons. Pièce de boeuf fin gras du Mézenc (spring). Fruits rouges et noirs des monts du Velay (summer). **Wines** Saint-Joseph, Boudes.
◆ Hidden away in the depths of a valley, this hotel along the Gorges de l'Allier worth a visit. Charming guestrooms in traditional or minimalist style, fitness facilities and friendly service. In the restaurant, discreet luxury and delicious inventive cuisine inspired by local produce.

LES ALLUES – 73 Savoie – **333** M5 – **see Méribel**

ALLY – 15 Cantal – **330** B3 – **pop. 700** – **alt. 720 m** – ✉ 15700 5 **A3**

Paris 532 – Clermont-Ferrand 119 – Aurillac 46 – Tulle 71 – Ussel 69

Château de la Vigne without rest
1 km North-East on D 680 – ✆ 04 71 69 00 20 – www.chateaudelavigne.com – la.vigne@wanadoo.fr – Fax 04 71 69 00 20 – Open April-October
3 rm – €110/140 €110/140, €7
◆ In the same family since it was built (15-18C), this château offers rooms with décors that spans the ages: Louis XV, Troubadour, Directoire...

ALOXE-CORTON – 21 Côte-d'Or – **320** J7 – **see Beaune**

ALPE D'HUEZ – 38 Isère – 333 J7 – pop. 1 479 – alt. 1 860 m – Winter sports : 1 250/3 330 m 15 69 – ✉ 38750 French Alps

45 **C2**

Paris 625 – Le Bourg-d'Oisans 12 – Briançon 71 – Grenoble 63

Altiport ✆ 04 76 11 21 73, Southeast.

Office de tourisme, place Paganon ✆ 04 76 11 44 44

Pic du Lac Blanc ✱★★★ by cable car - Villars-Reculas road★ 4 km by D 211[B].

ALPE D'HUEZ

Bergers (Chemin des) ....B 2	Cognet (Pl. du) ....B 4	Pic Bayle (R. du) ....B 8
	Fontbelle (R. de) ....B 5	Poste (Rte de la) ....A 9
	Meije (R. de la) ....B 6	Poutat (R. du).............B 10
	Paganon (Pl. Joseph) .....A 7	Siou Coulet (Rte du) .....A 12

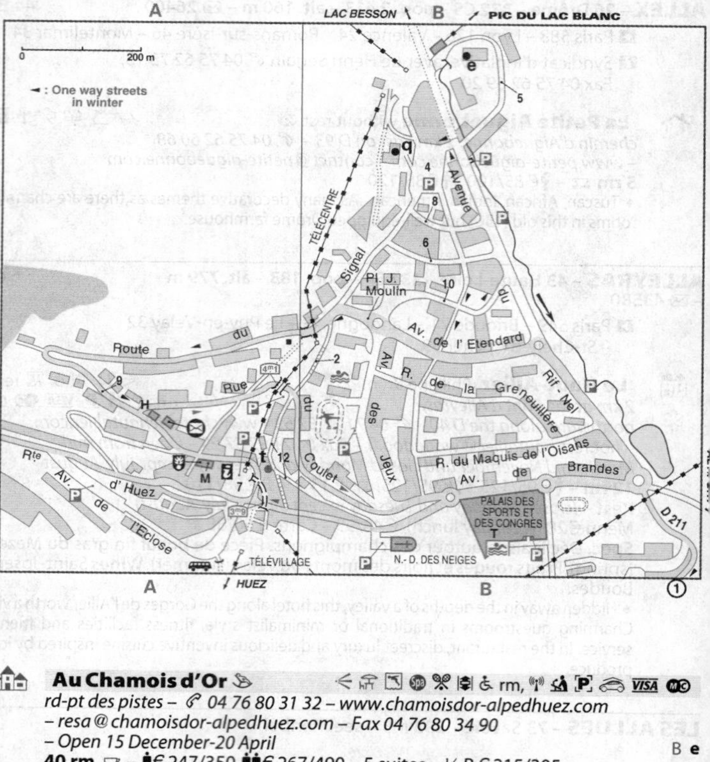

Au Chamois d'Or

rm,

rd-pt des pistes – ✆ *04 76 80 31 32* – *www.chamoisdor-alpedhuez.com* – *resa@chamoisdor-alpedhuez.com* – *Fax 04 76 80 34 90* – *Open 15 December-20 April*

B **e**

40 rm – €247/350 €267/490 – 5 suites – ½ P €215/305

Rest – Menu €32 (lunch), €35/67 – Carte €39/95

◆ Redecorated interior, full spa, children's play area, south-facing terrace and warm rooms (some overlook the Oisans mountain range) in this large chalet at the foot of the slopes. Attractive mountain-chic style restaurant with a classic, well-prepared menu.

Le Pic Blanc

r. Rif-Briant – ✆ *04 76 11 42 42* – *www.hmc-hotels.com* – *hotel.pic.blanc@hmc-hotel.com* – *Fax 04 76 11 42 43* – *Open 1st June-31 August and 1st December-25 April*

94 rm – €141/278 €189/463, €18 – ½ P €105/242

Rest – *(dinner only)* Menu €27

◆ Large, modern, chalet style building set at the top of the resort. Spacious, English style rooms all with a balcony. Sun deck, swimming pool and sauna. Restaurant serving traditional food.

Le Printemps de Juliette without rest
av. des Jeux – ✆ 04 76 11 44 38 – www.leprintempsdejuliette.com – info@leprintempsdejuliette.com – Fax 04 76 11 44 37 – Open July-August and 15 December-15 April B **a**
8 rm – €140/380 €140/380, ☕ €14 – 4 suites
◆ A gem of a hotel in the heart of the resort: individualised rooms and suite decked in pastel shades (balconies). Tea room where a saxophonist plays live some evenings in season.

Le Dôme
pl. du Cognet – ✆ 04 76 80 32 11 – www.dome-alpedhuez.com – info@dome-alpedhuez.com – Fax 04 76 80 66 48 – Open July-August and December- April B **q**
23 rm – €82/179 €96/198, ☕ €13 – ½ P €103/154
Rest – *(open December-April)* Menu (€18), €30 – Carte €28/51
◆ The hotel, founded by the current owner's grandfather, stands on the site of a former refuge of the Touring Club. Rooms recently redone in local style. Shopping arcade. Small dining room with a mountain style atmosphere. Traditional and regional menu.

Au P'tit Creux
chemin des Bergers – ✆ 04 76 80 62 80 – ptit.creux@wanadoo.fr – Fax 04 76 80 39 37 – Closed 8 May-25 June, 11 November-6 December, Monday lunch, Tuesday lunch from 1st January to 8 May, Monday dinner and Tuesday dinner from 1st September to 11 November A **t**
Rest – *(pre-book)* Menu €48 – Carte €28/50
◆ Old wainscoting, red and beige tablecloths and straw chairs depict the new alpine decor of this smart restaurant and veranda extension. Classic cuisine.

in Huez 3.5 km Southwest by D 211 – **pop. 1 327 – alt. 1 495 m** – ✉ **38750**

L' Ancolie
av. de l'Église – ✆ 04 76 11 13 13 – www.ancolie-hotel.com – forestieryves@aol.com – Fax 04 76 11 13 11 – Open 1st June-23 August, 2-30 September and 30 November-26 April
16 rm – €59/106 €68/115, ☕ €11 – ½ P €68/92
Rest – Menu (€13), €15 (weekday lunch), €27/50 – Carte €30/52
◆ Lovely local-style house situated in a preserved old village. Renovated, mountain-style interior (wood and stone decor), smart rooms and a peaceful environment. Traditional food, local specialities and pretty view of Oisans from the restaurant.

ALPUECH – 12 Aveyron – 338 J2 – pop. 80 – alt. 1 082 m – ✉ 12210 29 **D1**

Paris 566 – Toulouse 213 – Rodez 66 – Aurillac 81 – Onet-le-Château 64

Air Aubrac rm,
La Violette, south 5 km on Laguiole road – ✆ 05 65 44 33 64 – www.airaubrac.fr – airaubrac@wanadoo.fr – Fax 05 65 44 33 64 – Open 11 April-4 October
5 rm ☕ – €56 €62 – ½ P €49/51 **Table d'hôte** – Menu €20 bi
◆ This typical old farm surrounded by pastureland in the Aubrac is run by a hot-air balloon pilot (trips available). Charming, comfortable guestrooms. The owner prepares simple dishes using regional ingredients and produce from her own vegetable garden.

ALTENSTADT – 67 Bas-Rhin – 315 L2 – see Wissembourg

ALTHEN-DES-PALUDS – 84 Vaucluse – 332 C9 – pop. 1 988 – alt. 34 m – ✉ 84210 42 **E1**

Paris 676 – Avignon 18 – Carpentras 12 – Cavaillon 24 – Orange 22

Hostellerie du Moulin de la Roque
La Roque road – ✆ 04 90 62 14 62 – www.moulin-de-la-roque.com – hotel@moulin-de-la-roque.com – Fax 04 90 62 18 50
28 rm ☕ – €70/130 €85/160
Rest – *(closed Monday except dinner season, Saturday except dinner off season and Sunday dinner off season)* Menu €27/55 – Carte €45/55
◆ An impressive drive lined in plane trees leads up to this restored 17C mill. Personalised rooms, overlooking the park crossed by the Sorgue (angling). Sample seasonal cuisine in the appealing bourgeois dining room or on the shaded terrace.

ALTKIRCH – 68 Haut-Rhin – 315 H11 – pop. 5 526 – alt. 312 m – ✉ 68130 Alsace-Lorraine — 1 A3

Paris 457 – Basel 33 – Belfort 35 – Montbéliard 52 – Mulhouse 19 – Thann 27

Office de tourisme, 5, place Xavier Jourdain ✆ 03 89 40 02 90, Fax 03 89 40 02 90

de la Largue Seppois-le-Bas Rue du Golf, S : 23 km on D 432, ✆ 03 89 07 67 67

in Wahlbach 10 km East by D 419 and D 19[B] – pop. 323 – alt. 320 m – ✉ 68130

Auberge de la Gloriette with rm

9 r. Principale – ✆ 03 89 07 81 49 – www.lagloriette68.com – la-gloriette2@wanadoo.fr – Fax 03 89 07 40 56 – Closed 26 January-10 February

8 rm – €48 €60, €9

Rest – *(closed Monday and Tuesday)* Menu €15 (weekday lunch), €28/58 – Carte €15/58

◆ This farmstead offers refined classic cuisine in the dining room with a pleasant decor mixing old and new. The rooms are more comfortable (antiques) in the main wing.

ALTWILLER – 67 Bas-Rhin – 315 F3 – pop. 399 – alt. 220 m – ✉ 67260 — 1 A1

Paris 412 – Metz 86 – Nancy 73 – Le Haras 10 – Strasbourg 94

L'Écluse 16

Bonne Fontaine, Southeast: 3.5 km – ✆ 03 88 00 90 42 – www.ecluse16.com – clerouxmugler@aol.com – Fax 03 88 00 91 94 – Closed 1st-6 March, 27 September-7 October, 20 December-1st January, Monday and Tuesday

Rest – Menu €18 (weekdays), €29/42 – Carte approx. €35

◆ Former towpath lodge on the banks of the Houillères de la Sarre canal. Simple decor in the sunny dining room where tasty, modern food is served.

ALVIGNAC – 46 Lot – 337 G3 – pop. 632 – alt. 400 m – ✉ 46500 — 29 C1

Paris 529 – Brive-la-Gaillarde 52 – Cahors 65 – Figeac 43 – Rocamadour 8 – Tulle 65

Syndicat d'initiative, le bourg ✆ 05 65 33 66 42, Fax 05 65 33 60 62

Du Château

Rocamadour Padirac road – ✆ 05 65 33 60 14 – www.hotel-chateau-alvignac.com – hotel-du-chateau@wanadoo.fr – Fax 05 65 33 69 28 – Open 4 April-5 November

20 rm – €39/43 €39/43, €8 – ½ P €44/49

Rest – *(closed Wednesday dinner and Sunday dinner except July-August)* Menu €13 (weekday lunch), €17/27 – Carte €15/34

◆ This ancient building with its stone facade covered in ivy is set against the church. The functional, well-kept rooms are being gradually renovated. Pleasant garden. Simple and welcoming dining room in harmony with the local food.

AMBÉRIEU-EN-BUGEY – 01 Ain – 328 F5 – pop. 12 600 – alt. 300 m – ✉ 01500 Burgundy-Jura — 44 B1

Paris 468 – Bourg-en-Bresse 31 – Lyon 55 – Nantua 44

Ambotel

(Pragnat North business park), North by D1075 towards Bourg-en-Bresse – ✆ 04 74 46 42 22 – www.ambotel.fr – Fax 04 74 46 87 92

35 rm – €56 €64, €6,50 **Rest** – Menu (€12), €20/35 – Carte €25/45

◆ This new construction is characterised by its contemporary architecture and smart ochre facade. Modern rooms practically furnished in lightwood. The attractive colourful dining room offers traditional, unpretentious food.

AMBÉRIEUX-EN-DOMBES – 01 Ain – 328 C5 – pop. 1 442 – alt. 296 m – ✉ 01330 — 43 E1

Paris 437 – Bourg-en-Bresse 40 – Lyon 35 – Mâcon 43 – Villefranche-sur-Saône 18

Syndicat d'initiative, 289, rue Gombette ✆ 04 74 00 84 15, Fax 04 74 00 84 04

Auberge des Bichonnières

545 rte du 3-Septembre-1944 – ✆ 04 74 00 82 07 – www.aubergedesbichonnieres.com – bichonnier@wanadoo.fr – Fax 04 74 00 89 61 – Closed 20 December-25 January, Sunday dinner except hotel in July-August, Monday and Tuesday lunch

9 rm – †€ 50 ††€ 57/67, ☕ € 9 – ½ P € 59/72

Rest – *(number of covers limited, pre-book)* Menu (€ 18 bi), € 25/33 – Carte € 40/48

◆ This typical old Dombes farmhouse offers soberly rustic rooms, adorned with locally inspired murals. Flower-decked terrace located in an attractive courtyard. Traditional cooking with a regional accent served in a rustic decor.

AMBERT – 63 Puy-de-Dôme – 326 J9 – pop. 7 309 – alt. 535 m – ✉ 63600 Auvergne 6 C2

Paris 438 – Brioude 63 – Clermont-Ferrand 77 – Thiers 53

Office de tourisme, 4, place de Hôtel de Ville ✆ 04 73 82 61 90, Fax 04 73 82 48 36

St-Jean church ★ - La Dore valley ★ North and South - Moulin Richard-de-Bas★ 5.5 km East by D 996 - Musée de la Fourme et du fromage - Panoramic train★ (July-August).

Les Copains with rm

42 bd Henri-IV – ✆ 04 73 82 01 02 – www.hotelrestaurantlescopains.com – info@hotelrestaurantlescopains.com – Fax 04 73 82 67 34 – Closed 12-19 April, 6 September-5 October, 20 February-1st March, Sunday dinner, Saturday and dinner bank holidays

10 rm – †€ 46/48 ††€ 48/60, ☕ € 7 – ½ P € 50/70

Rest – Menu € 13 (weekday lunch), € 25/52 – Carte € 33/44

◆ Opposite the picturesque rotunda (town hall) made famous by Jules Romains in his novel, Les Copains. Regional dishes and the renowned Fourme cheese served in a dining room decorated in sunny colours.

AMBIALET – 81 Tarn – 338 G7 – pop. 436 – alt. 220 m – ✉ 81430 29 C2
Languedoc-Roussillon-Tarn Gorges

Paris 718 – Albi 23 – Castres 55 – Lacaune 52 – Rodez 71 – St-Affrique 60

Syndicat d'initiative, le bourg ✆ 05 63 55 39 14, Fax 05 63 55 39 14

Site★.

Du Pont

– ✆ 05 63 55 32 07 – www.hotel-du-pont.com – hotel-restaurant.pont@wanadoo.fr – Fax 05 63 55 37 21 – Closed 2 January-13 February and Sunday dinner

20 rm – †€ 57/59 ††€ 63/65, ☕ € 8 – ½ P € 60/63

Rest – Menu (€ 15), € 23/34 – Carte € 39/57

◆ Traditional house located on the banks of the Tarn with views over Ambialet. Fresh rooms (air-conditioning) overlooking the countryside or the river. The dining room is furnished in a rustic style. On fine days, sample traditional dishes on the panoramic terrace.

AMBIERLE – 42 Loire – 327 C3 – pop. 1 813 – alt. 467 m – ✉ 42820 44 A1
Lyon - Rhone Valley

Paris 379 – Lapalisse 33 – Roanne 18 – Thiers 81 – Vichy 58

Church ★.

Le Prieuré (Thierry Fernandes)

r. de la Mairie – ✆ 04 77 65 63 24 – www.restaurant-le-prieure-ambierle.com – leprieureambierle@wanadoo.fr – Fax 04 77 65 69 90 – Closed Sunday dinner, Tuesday and Wednesday

Rest – Menu € 26/63 – Carte € 55/80

Spec. Pains surprises de foie gras. Quasi de veau fermier en cuisson de douze heures. Trilogie chocolat.

◆ Comfortable restaurant with refined decor, located in the village centre, opposite an old priory. A warm welcome and fine, full-flavoured and characterful cuisine.

L'AMBITION – 28 Eure-et-Loir – 311 B6 – see Nogent-le-Rotrou

AMBOISE – 37 Indre-et-Loire – 317 O4 – pop. 12 400 – alt. 60 m – ✉ 37400 Châteaux of the Loire
11 **A1**

Paris 223 – Blois 36 – Loches 37 – Tours 27 – Vierzon 96

Office de tourisme, quai Général de Gaulle ✆ 02 47 57 09 28, Fax 02 47 57 14 35

Château★★: ≤★★ from the terrace, ≤★★ of the Minimes tower - Clos-Lucé★ - Chanteloup pagoda ★ 3 km by ④.

Lussault-sur-Loire: aquarium de Touraine★ West: 8 km by ⑤.

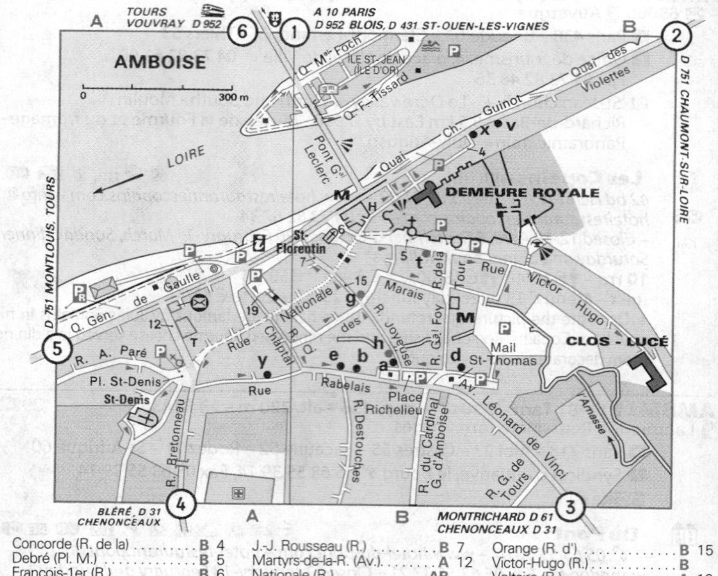

Le Choiseul

36 quai Ch.-Guinot – ✆ 02 47 30 45 45 – www.le-choiseul.com – choiseul@grandesetapes.fr – Fax 02 47 30 46 10
B **v**

32 rm – †€ 112/312 ††€ 124/312 – 4 suites – ½ P € 130/260

Rest – *(closed lunch except Sunday and holidays)* Menu € 60/90 – Carte € 45/82

Rest *Le 36* – *(closed Sunday and holidays) (lunch only)* Menu (€ 25), € 32

◆ Elegant property facing the River Loire with a flower garden and pool. Plush rooms. Updated cuisine served in a panoramic dining room overlooking the island of St Jean. At Le 36, find a conservatory setting and simple dishes.

Le Manoir Les Minimes without rest

34 quai Ch.-Guinot – ✆ 02 47 30 40 40 – www.manoirlesminimes.com – reservation@manoirlesminimes.com – Fax 02 47 30 40 77 – Open 11 March-11 November
B **x**

13 rm – †€ 122/190 ††€ 122/190, ☕ € 13 – 2 suites

◆ A fine 18C abode on the banks of the River Loire. Handsome sitting rooms and refined bedrooms adorned with splendid furniture from a variety of periods.

Le Manoir St Thomas without rest
1 Mail St-Thomas – 02 47 23 21 82 – www.manoir-saint-thomas.com – info@manoir-saint-thomas.com – Fax 02 47 23 24 96 – Closed 12 November-15 December and January B **d**
8 rm – €120/180 €120/180, €17 – 2 suites
◆ Nothing is too much trouble for guests' comfort in this Renaissance manor. Garden with pool, attractive sitting rooms and characterful bedrooms (exposed beams or painted ceilings).

Novotel
17 rue des Sablonnières, 2 km south via ③ Chenonceaux road – 02 47 57 42 07 – www.novotel.com – novotel.amboise@wanadoo.fr – Fax 02 47 30 40 76
121 rm – €118/148 €118/148, €14 **Rest** – Carte €28/40
◆ This building dominates Amboise and the Loire valley. Spacious, modern rooms in keeping with the chain's standards; some overlook the château. Contemporary dining room. A simple menu based on grills, salads and pasta.

Château de Pray
3 km, Chargé road via ② and D 751 – 02 47 57 23 67 – http://praycastel.online.fr – chateau.depray@wanadoo.fr – Fax 02 47 57 32 50 – Closed 16-30 November and 5-26 January
19 rm – €115/190 €115/190, €17 – 1 suite – ½ P €118/155
Rest – *(closed Monday and Tuesday except from 1st April to 30 November)*
Menu €50/90 – Carte €51/84
◆ Set in a vast forested park, this old fortress dates from the Crusades and was extended in the 17C. Rooms with period furniture. Renaissance style dining room. Terrace overlooking the kitchen garden. Up-to-the-minute cuisine.

Clos d'Amboise without rest
27 r. Rabelais – 02 47 30 10 20 – www.leclosamboise.com – le-clos-amboise@wanadoo.fr – Fax 02 47 57 33 43 – Closed 6 December-5 February B **b**
17 rm – €75/135 €75/135, €12
◆ A lovely garden with heated pool and smart personalised rooms characterise this manor house near the château. Fitness facilities in the former stables.

Domaine de l'Arbrelle
Berthellerie, on the D31 – 02 47 57 57 17 – www.arbrelle.com – contact@arbrelle.com – Fax 02 47 57 64 89 – Closed 29 November-15 January
21 rm – €70/140 €70/140, €11
Rest – *(dinner only)* Menu €25/41 – Carte €40/49
◆ In the heart of a park situated on the edge of the forest, this establishment features a stylish lounge and pleasant, contemporary rooms. Small, rustic-bourgeois dining room; pergola and terrace facing the garden.

Le Vinci Loire Valley without rest
12 av. E. Gounin, 1 km South via ④ – 02 47 57 10 90 – www.vinciloirevalley.com – reservation@vinciloirevalley.com – Fax 02 47 57 17 52
26 rm – €75/92 €75/92, €11
◆ In the town suburbs, this hotel has been renovated in a pleasant contemporary style. Comfortable, well-equipped rooms.

Le Blason without rest
11 pl. Richelieu – 02 47 23 22 41 – www.leblason.fr – hotel@leblason.fr – Fax 02 47 57 56 18 – Closed 11 January-11 February B **a**
25 rm – €45 €49/60, €8
◆ A delightful 15C half-timbered façade adds to the charm of this hotel located in a small square a short distance from the town centre. Practical rooms.

Vieux Manoir without rest
13 r. Rabelais – 02 47 30 41 27 – www.le-vieux-manoir.com – info@le-vieux-manoir.com – Fax 02 47 30 41 27 – Open 15 February-15 November A **y**
6 rm – €135/145 €135/150
◆ A French style garden surrounds this 18C manor and the pavilion, home to a lovely apartment. "Vintage" decor in the rooms with antique wardrobes and paintings.

Au Charme Rabelaisien without rest
25 r. Rabelais – ✆ 02 47 57 53 84 – www.au-charme-rabelaisien.com – aucharmerabelaisien@wanadoo.fr – Fax 02 47 57 53 84 – Open 15 February-15 November B e
3 rm – **†**€ 80/90 **††**€ 125/145
◆ This bourgeois mansion was formerly a bank, school and solicitors offices. It now offers tasteful rooms, a friendly welcome, tranquillity and a small garden with pool.

Le Pavillon des Lys with rm
9 r. Orange – ✆ 02 47 30 01 01 – www.pavillondeslys.com – pavillondeslys@wanadoo.fr – Fax 02 47 30 01 90 – Closed 20 November-4 February, Tuesday and lunch except Saturday and Sunday B g
7 rm – **†**€ 95/210 **††**€ 95/210, € 12 **Rest** – Menu € 28/39
◆ This 18C abode houses two small, opulent dining rooms and a lounge. In summer, the terrace is laid in the interior courtyard. Inventive market inspired menu.

L'Alliance
14 r. Joyeuse – ✆ 02 47 30 52 13 – www.lalliance-amboise.fr – restaurant.lalliance@wanadoo.fr – Fax 02 47 30 52 13 – Closed 2 January-13 February, Tuesday and Wednesday except dinner from June to August B h
Rest – Menu (€ 16), € 21/50 – Carte € 36/50
◆ A stone's throw from the town centre, this appealing restaurant is run by a young couple. Modern style dining room, wrought iron on the veranda/terrace. Contemporary cuisine.

L'Épicerie
46 pl. M-Debré – ✆ 02 47 57 08 94 – Fax 02 47 57 08 89 – Closed 15 December-4 February, Monday and Tuesday except from July to September B t
Rest – Menu € 12 (weekday lunch), € 22/34 – Carte € 40/60
◆ This half-timbered 1338 house and its pleasant terrace are admirably located opposite the château. Country-style interior and tightly packed tables. Regional cuisine.

in St-Ouen-les-Vignes 6.5 km by ① and D 431 – pop. 1 020 – alt. 80 m – ✉ 37530

L'Aubinière with rm
rest,
29 r. Jules-Gautier – ✆ 02 47 30 15 29 – www.aubiniere.com – restaurant-laubiniere@wanadoo.fr – Fax 02 47 30 02 44 – Closed February
6 rm – **†**€ 85/110 **††**€ 110/140, € 13 – ½ P € 105/135
Rest – *(closed Sunday dinner from October to May, Wednesday except dinner from June to September and Monday)* Menu (€ 22), € 26 (weekday lunch), € 35/64 – Carte € 50/75
◆ Beautiful dining room, terrace overlooking a pretty garden, up-to-date cuisine, rich regional wine list and cosy rooms: this inn has it all!

in Limeray 7 km by ① and D 952 – pop. 1 030 – alt. 70 m – ✉ 37530

Auberge de Launay with rm
rm,
9 r. de la Rivière – ✆ 02 47 30 16 82 – www.aubergedelaunay.com – info@aubergedelaunay.com – Fax 02 47 30 15 16 – Closed mid-December to mid-January
15 rm – **†**€ 55/73 **††**€ 55/73, € 8 – ½ P € 51/62
Rest – *(closed Sunday dinner from November to February and Saturday lunch)* Menu (€ 19), € 25/35
◆ Old 18C farm housing a rustic dining room, a veranda and a pleasant terrace. Renovated rooms in warm colours. The herbs and vegetables come from the cottage garden.

AMBONNAY – 51 Marne – 306 H8 – pop. 938 – alt. 95 m – ✉ 51150 13 B2

Paris 169 – Châlons-en-Champagne 24 – Épernay 19 – Reims 28 – Vouziers 65

Auberge St-Vincent with rm
rest, rm,
1 r. St. Vincent – ✆ 03 26 57 01 98 – www.auberge-st-vincent.com – info@auberge-st-vincent.com – Fax 03 26 57 81 48 – Closed 18 August-3 September, 10 February-12 March, Tuesday lunch, Sunday dinner and Monday
10 rm – **†**€ 55 **††**€ 58, € 10 **Rest** – Menu (€ 25), € 30/71 – Carte € 66/96
◆ Regional cooking is the order of the day in this spruce Champagne inn. Old kitchen utensils decorate the dining room fireplace. Simple, well-kept guestrooms.

AMBRONAY – 01 Ain – **328** F4 – **pop. 2 219 – alt. 250 m** – ✉ **01500** 44 **B1**
Burgundy-Jura

Paris 463 – Belley 53 – Bourg-en-Bresse 28 – Lyon 59 – Nantua 39

Auberge de l'Abbaye
47 pl. des Anciens-Combattants – ✆ 04 74 46 42 54 – www.aubergedelabbaye-ambronay.com – lavaux.ivan@wanadoo.fr – Fax 04 74 38 82 68 – Closed 6-10 April, 27 July-10 August, 19-26 October, Wednesday dinner, Sunday dinner and Monday
Rest – Menu (€ 22), € 29/36
◆ A delightful inn whose chef 'shouts out' the appetising set menu made with market-fresh produce. Vaulted wine cellar where you can choose your own wine!

Le Comptoir des Moines
45 pl. des Anciens-Combattants – ✆ 04 74 36 56 28 – lecomptoirdesmoines@yahoo.fr – Closed 13-20 April, 3-20 August, Wednesday dinner, Sunday and Monday
Rest – Menu € 26
◆ Discerning bistro with village grocery shop decor (wine and conserves on sale). Blackboard menu of simple, hearty, generous cuisine at reasonable prices.

AMÉLIE-LES-BAINS-PALALDA – **66 Pyrénées-Orientales** 22 **B3**
– **344** H8 – **pop. 3 644 – alt. 230 m – Spa : late Jan.-late Dec. – Casino** – ✉ **66110**
Languedoc-Roussillon-Tarn Gorges

Paris 882 – Céret 9 – Perpignan 41 – Prats-de-Mollo-la-Preste 24

Office de tourisme, 22, avenue du Vallespir ✆ 04 68 39 01 98, Fax 04 68 39 20 20

de Falgos Saint-Laurent-de-Cerdans Domaine de Falgos, S : 4 km on D 3 and D 3A, ✆ 04 68 39 51 42

Medieval town of Palalda★.

Des Bains et des Gorges
6 pl. Arago – ✆ 04 68 39 29 02 – www.hotel-restaurant-bains-gorges.com – hotel-bains-gorges@wanadoo.fr – Fax 04 68 39 82 52 – Closed 15 December-15 February
43 rm – 🛉€ 33/39 🛉🛉€ 37/45, ☕ € 6 – ½ P € 34/38 **Rest** – Menu € 14/16
◆ The main advantage of this hotel is its location near the thermal baths. Simple, clean rooms, some of which have a balcony. Catalan cuisine served in a spacious dining room with rustic furniture and 1970s decor.

L'AMÉLIE-SUR-MER – **33 Gironde** – **335** E2 – **see Soulac-sur-Mer**

AMIENS Ⓟ – **80 Somme** – **301** G8 – **pop. 136 600 – Built-up area 160 815 – alt. 34 m** – ✉ **80000** Northern France and the Paris Region 36 **B2**

Paris 142 – Lille 123 – Reims 173 – Rouen 122 – St-Quentin 81

Office de tourisme, 6 bis, rue Dusevel ✆ 03 22 71 60 50, Fax 03 22 71 60 51

d'Amiens Querrieu D 929, 7 km on the Albert road, ✆ 03 22 93 04 26

de Salouel Salouel Rue Robert Mallet, SW : 5 km, ✆ 03 22 95 40 49

Notre-Dame cathedral ★★★ (stalls ★★★) - Hortillonnages★ - Hôtel de Berny★ CY **M³** - Quartier St-Leu★ - Musée de Picardie★★ - Théatre de marionnettes "ché cabotans d'Amiens" CY **T²**.

Plans on following pages

Carlton rest,
42 r. Noyon – ✆ 03 22 97 72 22 – www.lecarlton.fr – reservation@lecarlton.fr – Fax 03 22 97 72 00 CZ **s**
24 rm – 🛉€ 75 🛉🛉€ 105/130, ☕ € 10 – ½ P € 76
Rest – Menu (€ 13 bi), € 18/25 – Carte € 29/48
◆ A 19C building near the station. Cosy rooms with dark wood furniture and murals. Excellent soundproofing. Friendly atmosphere and brasserie décor (banquettes, booths etc.) in the restaurant.

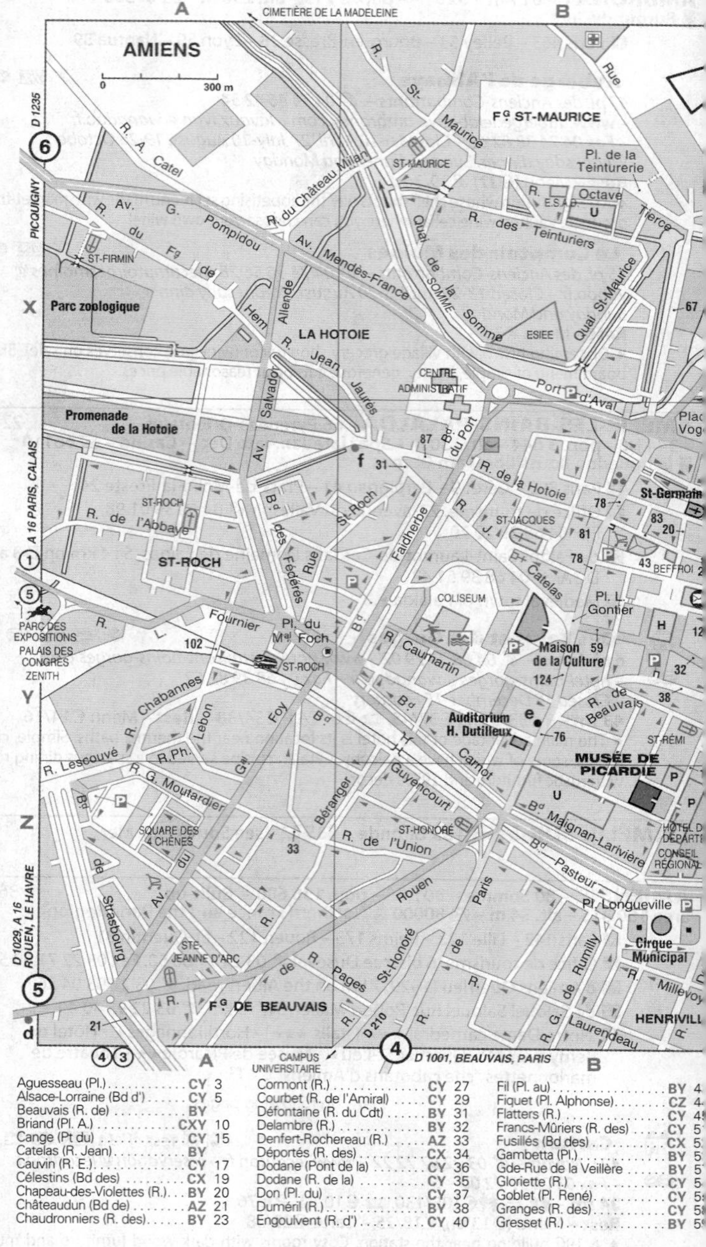

Aguesseau (Pl.) .... CY 3	Cormont (R.) .... CY 27	Fil (Pl. au) .... BY 4
Alsace-Lorraine (Bd d') ...... CY 5	Courbet (R. de l'Amiral) ..... CY 29	Fiquet (Pl. Alphonse) .... CZ 4
Beauvais (R. de) .... BY	Défontaine (R. du Cdt) ...... BY 31	Flatters (R.) .... CY 4
Briand (Pl. A.) .... CXY 10	Delambre (R.) .... BY 32	Francs-Mûriers (R. des) ..... CY 5
Cange (Pt du) .... CY 15	Denfert-Rochereau (R.) ...... AZ 33	Fusillés (Bd des) .... CX 5
Catelas (R. Jean) .... BY	Déportés (R. des) .... CX 34	Gambetta (Pl.) .... BY 5
Cauvin (R. E.) .... CY 17	Dodane (Pont de la) .... CY 36	Gde-Rue de la Veillère .... BY 5
Célestins (Bd des) .... CX 19	Dodane (R. de la) .... CY 35	Gloriette (R.) .... CY 5
Chapeau-des-Violettes (R.) ... BY 20	Don (Pl. du) .... CY 37	Goblet (Pl. René) .... CY 5
Châteaudun (Bd de) .... AZ 21	Duméril (R.) .... BY 38	Granges (R. des) .... CY 5
Chaudronniers (R. des) ...... BY 23	Engoulvent (R. d') .... CY 40	Gresset (R.) .... BY 5

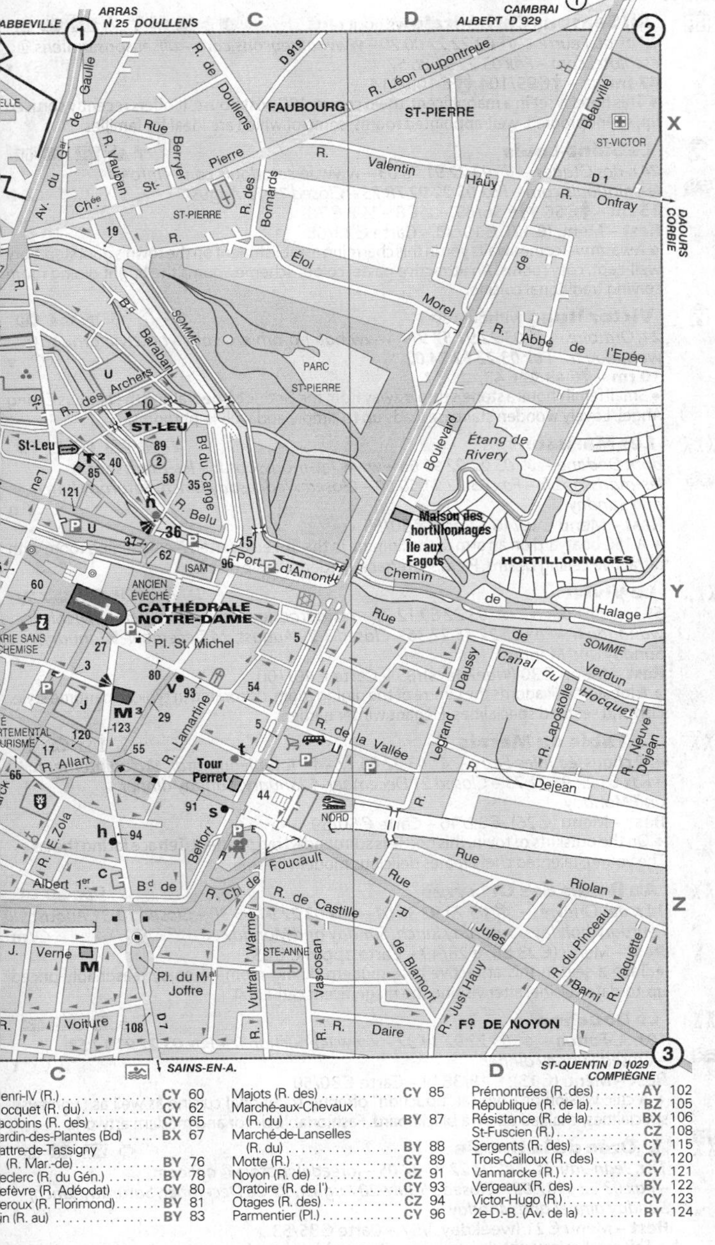

enri-IV (R.)	CY	60
ocquet (R. du)	CY	62
acobins (R. des)	CY	65
erdin-des-Plantes (Bd)	BX	67
attre-de-Tassigny (R. Mar.-de)	BY	76
eclerc (R. du Gén.)	BY	78
efèvre (R. Adéodat)	CY	80
eroux (R. Florimond)	BY	81
in (R. au)	BY	83
Majots (R. des)	CY	85
Marché-aux-Chevaux (R. du)	BY	87
Marché-de-Lanselles (R. du)	BY	88
Motte (R.)	CY	89
Noyon (R. de)	CZ	91
Oratoire (R. de l')	CY	93
Otages (R. des)	CZ	94
Parmentier (Pl.)	CY	96
Prémontrées (R. des)	AY	102
République (R. de la)	BZ	105
Résistance (R. de la)	BX	106
St-Fuscien (R.)	CZ	108
Sergents (R. des)	CY	115
Trois-Cailloux (R. des)	CY	120
Vanmarcke (R.)	CY	121
Vergeaux (R. des)	BY	122
Victor-Hugo (R.)	CY	123
2e-D.-B. (Av. de la)	BY	124

All Seasons Cathédrale without rest
17 pl. au Feurre – ✆ 03 22 22 00 20 – www.allseasons.com – allseasons.amiens@escalotel.com – Fax 03 22 91 86 57 BY **r**
47 rm – €99/104 €109/114
◆ This hotel is set in a magnificent, town centre, 18C post house. It offers recently spruced up, soundproofed, well-appointed rooms, some of which are ideal for families.

Le Saint-Louis
24 r. des Otages – ✆ 03 22 91 76 03 – www.le-saintlouis.com – info@le-saintlouis.com – Fax 03 22 92 78 75 – Closed 1st-15 August CZ **h**
15 rm – €56 €56/69, €8 – ½ P €78
Rest – Menu (€17), €19/33 – Carte €33/68
◆ A warm welcome awaits you in this charming establishment on the town's doorstep. Very well-kept, cosy rooms. An attractive pastel colour scheme adorns the bright dining room serving traditional cuisine.

Victor Hugo without rest
2 r. Oratoire – ✆ 03 22 91 57 91 – www.hotel-a-amiens.com – hotelvictorhugo@wanadoo.fr – Fax 03 22 92 74 02 CY **v**
10 rm – €43 €43, €7
◆ Small family hotel a stone's throw away from the Gothic cathedral and the famous Crying Angel. Lovely wooden staircase leads up to simple and well-kept rooms.

Les Marissons
pont Dodane – ✆ 03 22 92 96 66 – www.les-marissons.fr – les-marissons@les-marissons.fr – Fax 03 22 91 50 50 – Closed Wednesday lunch, Saturday lunch and Sunday CY **n**
Rest – Menu €19/46 – Carte €50/65
◆ A 15C boatyard on an arm of the Somme in the St-Leu quarter. A cosy dining room with attractive ceiling beams. Pleasant terrace-garden. Classic dishes.

Le Vivier
593 rte de Rouen – ✆ 03 22 89 12 21 – restaurantlevivieramiens.com – vivier.le@wanadoo.fr – Fax 03 22 45 27 36 – Closed 3-29 August, 24 December-5 January, Sunday and Monday AZ **d**
Rest – Menu €30 (weekdays)/85 – Carte €40/100
◆ A lobster tank adorns the centre of the dining room, decorated in typical maritime style. Fish and seafood specialities. Elegant winter garden.

La Table du Marais
472 chaussée Jules-Ferry – ✆ 03 22 46 17 44 – latabledumarais@clubinternet.fr – Fax 03 22 95 21 73 – Closed 21 December-4 January, Sunday dinner and Monday
Rest – Menu (€26), €32/46 – Carte €50/59
◆ On the outskirts of town, this house is surrounded by greenery. Terrace facing the lakes. The young, talented chef creates delicious modern cuisine.

Au Relais des Orfèvres
14 r. des Orfèvres – ✆ 03 22 92 36 01 – Fax 03 22 91 83 30 – Closed 10-31 August, February holidays, Saturday lunch, Sunday and Monday CY **m**
Rest – Menu (€23 bi), €28/49 – Carte approx. €55
◆ Take a seat in this attractive blue modern dining room, to enjoy reasonably-priced up-to-date cuisine, after visiting the magnificent cathedral.

Le Bouchon
10 r. A.-Fatton – ✆ 03 22 92 14 32 – www.lebouchon.fr – Fax 03 22 91 12 58 – Closed Sunday dinner CY **t**
Rest – Menu (€13), €18/38 bi – Carte €30/50
◆ A chic version of a typical "bouchon" offering traditional cuisine as well as Lyonnaise specialities, chalked up on a blackboard. Fashionable decor and modern artwork.

L' Orée de la Hotoie
17 r. Jean-Jaurès – ✆ 03 22 91 37 05 – loreedelahotoie@aol.com – Fax 03 22 9137 05 – Closed 25 July-20 August, 22-28 December, Saturday lunch, Sunday dinner and Monday BY **f**
Rest – Menu €21 (weekdays)/57 – Carte €35/53
◆ This small restaurant situated opposite a park is known for its tranquil setting and for the traditional cuisine prepared by its enthusiastic chef. Attractive dining room decorated in muted tones.

Roye road 7 km via ③, N 29 and D 934 – ✉ 80440 Boves

Novotel rm, VISA
bd Michel-Strogoff – ✆ 03 22 50 42 42 – www.novotel.com – H0396@accor.com – Fax 03 22 50 42 49
94 rm – €135 €135, ☕ €14 **Rest** – Menu (€ 19) – Carte approx. € 28
◆ This 1970s hotel has been successfully refurbished: the comfortable rooms are in line with Novotel's latest standards and bathrooms resemble ship's cabins. Modern dining room opens onto the poolside terrace. Traditional menu.

in Dury 6 km by ④ – **pop. 1 248 – alt. 115 m** – ✉ **80480**

Petit Château without rest
2 r. Grimaux – ✆ 03 22 95 29 52 – http://perso.wanadoo.fr/am.saguez – a.saguez@wanadoo.fr – Fax 03 22 95 29 52
5 rm ☕ – €55 €70/78
◆ A charming welcome is waiting for you in this former farmhouse, which used to be an outbuilding of the local castle. If you like vintage cars, the owner will open up the doors of his workshop for you.

L'Aubergade (Eric Boutté) VISA
78 rte Nationale – ✆ 03 22 89 51 41 – www.aubergade-dury.com – aubergade.dury@wanadoo.fr – Fax 03 22 95 44 05 – Closed 19 April-4 May, 9-24 August, 20 December-3 January, Sunday and Monday
Rest – Menu € 39/75 – Carte € 69/96
Spec. Coquilles Saint-Jacques (October-April). Canard sauvage en deux services (October-December). Boule craquante de chocolat noir en forêt noire, crème glacée à la pistache (October-May).
◆ Limed wood furniture, antique-style colonnades and pastel shades make up the dining room decor. French doors open onto the summer terrace. Tasty up-to-date menu.

La Bonne Auberge VISA
63 rte Nationale – ✆ 03 22 95 03 33 – Closed 12 July-11 August, Sunday dinner, Monday and Tuesday
Rest – Menu (€ 20), € 25 (weekdays)/50 – Carte € 45/60
◆ This smart regional façade is covered with flowers in summer. In the recently redecorated dining room you will be offered contemporary cuisine.

AMILLY – 45 Loiret – 318 N4 – see Montargis

AMMERSCHWIHR – 68 Haut-Rhin – 315 H8 – pop. 1 875 – alt. 215 m – ✉ 68770 Alsace-Lorraine 2 C2

Paris 441 – Colmar 9 – Gérardmer 49 – St-Dié 44 – Sélestat 29

A l'Arbre Vert VISA
7 r. des Cigognes – ✆ 03 89 47 12 23 – www.arbre-vert.net – info@arbre-vert.net – Fax 03 89 78 27 21 – Closed 21 February-12 March, Monday from November to April and Tuesday
17 rm – €42 €51/64, ☕ €9 – ½ P €59/65
Rest – *(dinner only)* Menu € 22/49 – Carte € 38/50
◆ Alsatian house in a village at the foot of sloping vineyards offering functional rooms, of which those in the annex are more modern. Restaurant (non-smoking) with fine wood carvings of vineyard scenes serving carefully-prepared regional dishes. Smoking room.

Aux Armes de France with rm VISA
1 Grand'Rue – ✆ 03 89 47 10 12 – www.aux-armes-de-france.com – contact@armesfrance.fr – Fax 03 89 47 38 12 – Closed Wednesday
10 rm – €69/84 €69/94, ☕ €12
Rest – Menu (€ 18), € 27 (weekdays)/48 – Carte € 37/80
◆ Venture over the threshold of this regional style hostelry to discover the flavours of a classical menu with modern touches, served in an updated refined Alsatian décor. Summer terrace.

Aux Trois Merles
5 r. de la 5ème Division Blindée – 03 89 78 24 35 – www.troismerles.com – info@trois-merles.com – Fax 03 89 78 13 06 – Closed Saturday lunch, Sunday dinner and Monday
Rest – Menu (€ 13), € 28/38
◆ A pleasant restaurant situated in one of the villages on the famous Wine Road. Neat, rustic interior, a shady terrace facing the garden and traditional cuisine.

AMNÉVILLE – 57 Moselle – 307 H3 – pop. 10 017 – alt. 162 m – Spa : early March-early Dec. – Casino – ✉ 57360 Alsace-Lorraine — 26 B1

Paris 319 – Briey 17 – Metz 21 – Thionville 16 – Verdun 67
Office de tourisme, 2, rue du casino 03 87 70 10 40, Fax 03 87 71 90 94
d'Amneville BP 99, S : 2 km, 03 87 71 30 13
Parc zoologique du bois de Coulange (zoo) ★★.
Walibi-Schtroumpf Amusement Park ★ 3 km S.

at Parc de Loisirs (leisure park) 2.5 km, Bois de Coulange South – ✉ 57360 Amnéville

Diane without rest
R. de la Source – 03 87 70 16 33 – www.accueil-amneville.com – accueilhotel.diane@wanadoo.fr – Fax 03 87 72 36 72
48 rm – € 69 € 78, € 9 – 3 suites
◆ Hotel in the centre of the leisure park with comfortable rooms, recently renovated in a plain and contemporary style. Breakfast room overlooking the countryside.

Marso
– 03 87 15 15 40 – www.hotel-marso.com – matt.hotel@orange.fr – Fax 03 87 58 39 88
50 rm – € 82/85 € 82/85, € 12 – ½ P € 95/98
Rest – *(Closed Saturday lunch, Monday and Tuesday)* Carte € 23/50
◆ Recently built hotel which enjoys a position near the leisure park (dry ski slope, zoo, cinema). Functional rooms, all with a small terrace. Bar and hair salon. Dishes based on local produce, served in the large restaurant dining room.

La Forêt
1 r. de la Source – 03 87 70 34 34 – www.restaurant-laforet.com – resto.laforet@wanadoo.fr – Fax 03 87 70 34 25 – Closed 26 July-9 August, 21 December-6 January, Sunday dinner, Monday and bank holidays dinner
Rest – Menu € 21 (weekdays)/42 – Carte € 32/50
◆ Traditional dishes on the menu of this family restaurant. Bright, spacious restaurant, recently refurbished, and terrace overlooking the Coulange forest. Good wine list.

AMOU – 40 Landes – 335 G13 – pop. 1 583 – alt. 44 m – ✉ 40330 — 3 B3

Paris 760 – Aire-sur-l'Adour 51 – Dax 31 – Mont-de-Marsan 47 – Orthez 14 – Pau 50
Office de tourisme, 10, place de la poste 05 58 89 02 25, Fax 05 58 89 02 25

Au Feu de Bois
20 av. des Pyrénées – 05 58 89 06 76 – www.hotel-aufeudebois.fr – postmaster@hotel-aufeudebois.fr – Fax 05 58 89 05 95
11 rm – € 45/75 € 45/75, € 7 – ½ P € 53/83
Rest – *(closed Tuesday dinner from September to May)* Menu (€ 12 bi), € 16/35 – Carte € 19/33
◆ This former staging post has been renovated and now offers comfortable, up-to-date accommodation. Cosy bar, lovely lounge and modern, refined rooms. Stone and wood feature in the contemporary restaurant. Traditional cuisine.

Le Commerce
(near the church) – 05 58 89 02 28 – www.hotel-lecommerceamou.com – lecommerceamou@orange.fr – Fax 05 58 89 24 45 – Closed 10 November-1st December, 9-22 February, Sunday dinner and Monday except July-August
15 rm – € 55 € 65, € 7 **Rest** – Menu (€ 15), € 25/45 – Carte € 35/50
◆ Family-run establishment that has kept all the charm of an old village inn. Very well-kept rooms; bar on the ground floor. The house specialities in this restaurant are pâté, terrine and confit, either served in the rustic dining room or under the arbour.

AMPHION-LES-BAINS – 74 Haute-Savoie – 328 M2 – ✉ 74500 46 F1
French Alps

Paris 573 – Annecy 81 – Évian-les-Bains 4 – Genève 40 – Thonon-les-Bains 6

Office de tourisme, 215, rue de la Plage ✆ 04 50 70 00 63, Fax 04 50 70 03 03

Princes
rm, VISA MC AE

21 av. de la Rive – ✆ 04 50 75 02 94 – www.hoteldesprinces.fr – hotel.des.princes@wanadoo.fr – Fax 04 50 75 59 93 – Open from end April to end September

33 rm – €63/100 €70/134, €11 – 2 suites – ½ P €60/118

Rest – *(closed Wednesday except 9 July-20 August)* Menu (€19), €23/38 – Carte €35/65

◆ A 19C building on the banks of the Léman. The rooms with a view of the lake are to be preferred, for the view and the peace and quiet. Charming little private port. Restaurants with panoramic views, one of which is on the waterside. Mainly fish menu.

Le Tilleul with rm
VISA MC AE

252 RN5 – ✆ 04 50 70 00 39 – www.letilleul.com – letilleul@aol.com – Fax 04 50 70 05 57 – Closed 22 December-5 January, 29 June-14 July, Sunday dinner and Monday

19 rm – €61/70 €65/80, €9 – ½ P €68/78

Rest – Menu (€12), €18/45 – Carte €40/61

◆ In the restaurant: beams, regional furniture and copperware. On the table: perch and whitefish from Lake Léman. Garden service in summer.

AMPUIS – 69 Rhône – 327 H7 – pop. 2 538 – alt. 150 m – ✉ 69420 44 B2

Paris 492 – Condrieu 5 – Givors 17 – Lyon 37 – Rive-de-Gier 33 – Vienne 7

Le Domaine des Vignes without rest
VISA MC AE

41 rte Taquière - D 386 – ✆ 04 74 59 21 24 – www.hoteldomainedesvignes.com – contact@hoteldomainedesvignes.com – Fax 04 37 02 20 09

12 rm – €75 €85

◆ Comfort and modernity depict this immense villa in the heart of the renowned Côte Rôtie vineyards. Delightful modern rooms graced with artwork. Good value.

ANCENIS – 44 Loire-Atlantique – 316 I3 – pop. 7 010 – alt. 13 m – ✉ 44150 34 B2
Châteaux of the Loire

Paris 347 – Angers 55 – Châteaubriant 48 – Cholet 49 – Laval 100 – Nantes 41

Office de tourisme, 27, rue du Château ✆ 02 40 83 07 44, Fax 02 40 83 07 44

Akwaba
rest, VISA MC AE

bd Dr-Moutel – ✆ 02 40 83 30 30 – www.hotel-akwaba.com – hotelakwaba@yahoo.fr – Fax 02 40 83 25 10

57 rm – €60/70 €66/76, €8 – 1 suite

Rest – *(closed August and Sunday lunch)* Menu (€12), €18/24 – Carte €21/40

◆ An Ivory Coast welcome in this hotel situated in the heart of a small shopping centre. Functional rooms. Lounge and restaurant renovated in a contemporary style serving spicy Southern style food.

La Charbonnière
VISA MC AE

On the banks of the Loire on Joubert boulevard – ✆ 02 40 83 25 17 – www.restaurant-la-charbonniere.com – cuasante.pierre@wanadoo.fr – Fax 02 40 98 85 00 – Closed Saturday lunch October-March, Sunday dinner, Wednesday dinner and dinners holidays

Rest – Menu €16 (weekdays)/53 – Carte €60/78

◆ Space and tranquillity characterise this place: the veranda and terrace set in the garden offer a pretty view of the Loire and the suspension bridge. Traditional dishes.

Les Terrasses de Bel Air
VISA MC

1 km eastward Angers road – ✆ 02 40 83 02 87 – http://terrassebelair.free.fr – terrassebelair.jpg@wanadoo.fr – Fax 02 40 83 33 46 – Closed 1st-12 July, Sunday dinner and Monday

Rest – Menu €17 (weekday lunch), €29/53

◆ Located on a busy road, but facing the Loire, these two dining rooms have a homely atmosphere with fireplace, parquet and period furniture.

La Toile à Beurre VISA AE

82 r. St-Pierre – 02 40 98 89 64 – latoileabeurre@wanadoo.fr – Fax 02 40 96 01 49 – Closed 17-31 March, 1st-18 September, Sunday dinner, Monday and Tuesday

Rest – Menu (€ 19), € 27/55 – Carte € 33/42

◆ Exposed stonework and beams, terracotta floor tiles and a fine fireplace form an authentic rustic setting in this house built in 1753. Attractive terrace. Traditional dishes and fish from the Loire.

Look out for red symbols, indicating particularly pleasant establishments.

ANCY-LE-FRANC – 89 Yonne – 319 H5 – pop. 1 090 – alt. 180 m — 7 B1

– ✉ 89160 Burgundy-Jura

Paris 215 – Auxerre 54 – Châtillon-sur-Seine 38 – Montbard 27 – Tonnerre 18

Syndicat d'initiative, 59, Grande Rue 03 86 75 03 15, Fax 03 86 75 04 41

Château★★.

Hostellerie du Centre rm, VISA AE

34 Grande-Rue – 03 86 75 15 11 – www.diaphora.com/hostellerieducentre – hostellerieducentre@diaphora.com – Fax 03 86 75 14 13 – Closed 18 January-10 February, Sunday dinner and Monday from 15 November-15 March

22 rm – †€ 44/54 ††€ 49/62, ☐ € 7 – ½ P € 44/54

Rest – Menu (€ 12), € 18/46 – Carte € 23/66

◆ Little old building offering cool, practical rooms with the more spacious ones being in the annex. The covered swimming pool can be enjoyed at any time of year. Simple dining room where you are served a traditional cuisine and some Burgundian specialities.

LES ANDELYS – 27 Eure – 304 I6 – pop. 8 208 – alt. 28 m — 33 D2

– ✉ 27700 Normandy

Paris 93 – Évreux 38 – Gisors 30 – Mantes-la-Jolie 54 – Rouen 40

Syndicat d'initiative, rue Philippe Auguste 02 32 54 41 93, Fax 02 32 54 41 93

Ruins of Château Gaillard★★ ←★★ - Notre-Dame church ★.

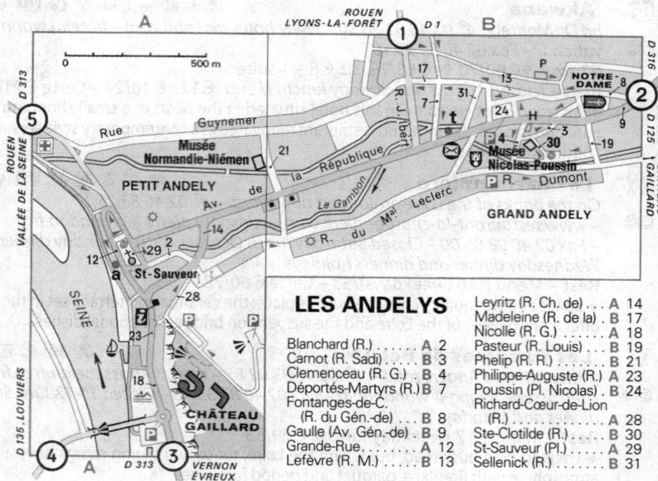

XXX **La Chaîne d'Or** with rm

25 r. Grande – ✆ 02 32 54 00 31 – www.hotel-lachainedor.com – chaineor@wanadoo.fr – Fax 02 32 54 05 68 – Closed All Saint's Day holidays, Christmas holidays, 2-22 January, February holidays, Monday and Tuesday from October to May

12 rm – †€ 80/135 ††€ 80/135, ☕ € 12 A a

Rest – Menu (€ 21), € 29 (weekdays)/88 – Carte € 58/100

◆ This 18C post house was also a tollhouse: a chain used to block the Seine. An elegant dining room facing the river. Contemporary cuisine.

XX **De Paris** with rm

10 av. de la République – ✆ 02 32 54 00 33 – www.hotel-andelys.fr – h.paristhierry@wanadoo.fr – Fax 02 32 54 65 92 B t

11 rm ☕ – †€ 63/72 ††€ 71/80

Rest – *(closed 2-12 January, Sunday dinner, Monday lunch and Wednesday)* Menu (€ 17), € 24/38 – Carte € 25/38

◆ An attractive mansion (1880) is the location for this restaurant, elegantly redesigned in a classical bijou spirit. Traditional cuisine and pleasant courtyard terrace. Simply decorated rooms. The three newest rooms occupy a wing.

ANDLAU – 67 Bas-Rhin – 315 I6 – pop. 1 788 – alt. 215 m – ✉ 67140 2 C1

Alsace-Lorraine

▶ Paris 501 – Erstein 25 – Le Hohwald 8 – Molsheim 25 – Sélestat 18 – Strasbourg 43

ℹ Syndicat d'initiative, 5, rue du Général-de-Gaulle ✆ 03 88 08 22 57, Fax 03 88 08 42 22

◉ St-Pierre and St-Paul church ★: portal ★★, crypt ★.

Zinckhotel without rest

13 r. de la Marne – ✆ 03 88 08 27 30 – www.zinckhotel.com – zinck.hotel@wanadoo.fr – Fax 03 88 08 42 50

18 rm – †€ 59/95 ††€ 59/95, ☕ € 8

◆ An unusually decorated old mill: rooms with personal touches (zen, pop, jazz or Empire styles) and corridors resembling boat decks. The modern wing overlooks the vineyard.

Kastelberg

10 r. Gén.-Koenig – ✆ 03 88 08 97 83 – www.kastelberg.com – kastelberg@wanadoo.fr – Fax 03 88 08 48 34

29 rm – †€ 59 ††€ 62/71, ☕ € 10 – ½ P € 61/66

Rest – *(open 12 March-2 November and 28 November-4 January) (dinner only)* Menu € 19/45 – Carte € 25/56

◆ A smart Alsatian façade surrounded by vineyards. The simple, practical rooms have sloping ceilings or a balcony and rustic furniture. Rustic but smart restaurant with attractively set tables. Wholesome country cooking.

XX **Bœuf Rouge**

6 r. du Dr-Stoltz – ✆ 03 88 08 96 26 – auboeufrouge@wanadoo.fr – Fax 03 88 08 99 29 – Closed 24 June-10 July, 6-22 February, Wednesday and Thursday except from 11 July to 30 September

Rest – Menu (€ 10), € 16/31 – Carte € 15/60

◆ A friendly and typical Alsatian restaurant housed in a former 17C post house. Local specialities served in an elegant wood panelled room.

ANDORRE (PRINCIPALITY) – 343 H9 – see the end of the guide

ANDREZÉ – 49 Maine-et-Loire – 317 D5 – pop. 1 798 – alt. 87 m – ✉ 49600 34 B2

▶ Paris 371 – Nantes 59 – Angers 80 – Cholet 16 – Rezé 71

Le Château de la Morinière

– ✆ 02 41 75 40 30 – www.chateau-de-la-moriniere.com – pringarbe.pascal@wanadoo.fr

5 rm ☕ – †€ 84/89 ††€ 84/89 **Table d'hôte** – Menu € 32 bi

◆ Built on the ruins of a medieval château destroyed during the Vendée wars, this romantic edifice is Napoleon III in style. Personalised, very quiet rooms. Candle lit dining at the table d'hôte. Cookery lessons.

ANDRÉZIEUX-BOUTHÉON – 42 Loire – 327 E6 – pop. 9 153 – alt. 395 m – ✉ 42160 44 A2

Paris 460 – Lyon 76 – Montbrison 20 – Roanne 71 – St-Étienne 19

Office de tourisme, 11, rue Charles-de-Gaulle ✆ 04 77 55 37 03, Fax 04 77 55 88 46

Lac de retenue de Grangent (Grangent barrier lake) ★★ S : 9 km

Auvergne-Rhone Valley

Novotel rest, VISA

1 r. 18-Juin-1827 – ✆ 04 77 36 10 50 – www.accorhotels.com – h0435@accor.com – Fax 04 77 36 10 57

98 rm – €67/125 €67/125, € 14

Rest – Menu (€ 19), € 22 – Carte € 25/50

◆ This chain hotel, built in 1974, is still in good condition. Spacious lobby, lounge and bar, plus a choice of meeting rooms. Ask for the more recently redecorated guestrooms. The restaurant has a simple, gay contemporary setting. A terrace opposite the swimming pool.

XXX **Les Iris** (Lionel Githenay) with rm VISA

32 av. J.-Martouret, (towards the station) – ✆ 04 77 36 09 09 – www.les-iris.com – les-iris42@orange.fr – Fax 04 77 36 09 00 – Closed 20-30 August, 1st-22 January and Sunday dinner

10 rm – €75 €85, € 12 – ½ P € 89

Rest – *(closed Sunday dinner, Monday and Tuesday)* Menu (€ 35), € 48/95 – Carte € 70/90

Spec. Salade de homard bleu (June-August). Pigeon "comme un rôti" (February-April). Moelleux tiède au potimarron (October-December). **Wines** Côtes du Forez.

◆ Tasty creative cuisine served in a pleasant and refurbished environment. Classic decor now with contemporary touches: parquet, mouldings, up-to-date colours and furniture. Small bedrooms in the annexe; few overlooking the garden.

ANDUZE – 30 Gard – 339 I4 – pop. 3 243 – alt. 135 m – ✉ 30140 23 C2

Languedoc-Roussillon-Tarn Gorges

Paris 718 – Montpellier 60 – Alès 15 – Florac 68 – Lodève 84 – Nîmes 46 – Le Vigan 52

Office de tourisme, plan de Brie ✆ 04 66 61 98 17, Fax 04 66 61 79 77

Bambouseraie de Prafrance (bamboo garden) ★★ North: 3 km by D 129.

Grottoes of Trabuc★★ Northwest: 11 km - Le Mas soubeyran: Desert Museum★ (17C-18C Protestant remembrance) Northwest: 7 km.

Northwest by St-Jean-du-Gard road – ✉ 30140 Anduze

La Porte des Cévennes VISA

3 km – ✆ 04 66 61 99 44 – www.porte-cevennes.com – reception@porte-cevennes.com – Fax 04 66 61 73 65 – Open 1st April-15 October

34 rm – €76/83 €76/83, € 10 – ½ P € 68/72

Rest – *(dinner only)* Menu € 24/30 – Carte € 32/45

◆ A peaceful house near the bamboo plantation where the 'Wages of Fear' was filmed. Spacious, practical rooms, half of which overlook the Gardon valley. Classic menu in a countrified decor or on the panoramic terrace.

XX **Le Moulin de Corbès** with rm VISA

4 km away – ✆ 04 66 61 61 83 – www.moulin-corbes.com – contact@moulin-corbes.com – Fax 04 66 61 68 06

6 rm – €80 €80/90, € 12 **Rest** – Menu € 36/90 bi

◆ On the banks of the Gardon this inviting restaurant with three sunny dining rooms is decorated on the theme of wine (wine-tasting courses). Practical, quiet rooms.

in Générargues 5.5 km Northwest by D 129 and D 50 – pop. 639 – alt. 160 m – ✉ 30140

Auberge des Trois Barbus VISA

rte de Mialet – ✆ 04 66 61 72 12 – www.aubergeles3barbus.com – les3barbus@free.fr – Fax 04 66 61 72 74 – Closed 2 January-15 March, Sunday dinner from October to April, Tuesday from November to March, Tuesday lunch from May to September and Monday except dinner from May to September

32 rm – €61/125 €61/125, € 10 – ½ P € 65/96

Rest – Menu (€ 17), € 27/49 – Carte € 43/60

◆ This hillside hotel on the edge of the "Cevennes Desert" offers large rooms with regional furniture and overlooks the Camisards valley. Tasteful restaurant. A classic menu using fresh products. Grilled dishes by the pool.

in Tornac 6 km Southeast by D 982 – pop. 718 – alt. 140 m – ✉ 30140

Les Demeures du Ranquet (Anne Majourel) rm,
St-Hippolyte-du-Fort road : 2 km –
✆ 04 66 77 51 63 – www.ranquet.com – contact@ranquet.com
– Fax 04 66 77 55 62 – Open 19 March-15 November
10 rm – €130/175 €130/175, €16 – ½ P €125/160
Rest – *(closed Tuesday and Wednesday except dinner from 1st June to 15 September and Monday lunch in summer)* Menu €58/80 – Carte €75/108
Spec. Bonbon de brandade de morue, calamar, tagliatelle de courgette et huile d'herbes. Duo d'Agneau, noisette rosée et souris confite. Déclinaison de "4 C son", café, cacao, chicorée, chocolat. **Wines** Vin de Pays du Gard, Costières de Nîmes.
◆ This enticing Cévennes farmhouse and its recent well-equipped outbuildings are tucked away in parkland surrounded by scrub. Peace and quiet, art exhibitions and a golf practice. The inventive regional menu has an emphasis on home-grown vegetables and herbs.

If breakfast is included the symbol appears after the number of rooms.

ANET – **28 Eure-et-Loir** – **311** E2 – **pop. 2 626** – **alt. 73 m** – ✉ **28260** 11 **B1**

Paris 76 – Chartres 51 – Dreux 16 – Évreux 37 – Mantes-la-Jolie 28 – Versailles 58

Syndicat d'initiative, 8, rue Delacroix ✆ 02 37 41 49 09, Fax 02 37 41 49 09

Castle★ **Normandy**

Auberge de la Rose
6 r. Ch.-Lechevrel – ✆ 02 37 41 90 64 – Fax 02 37 41 47 88
– Closed 12 December-3 January, Sunday evening and Monday
Rest – Menu €25 – Carte €47/65
◆ This family-run inn was already in the Michelin Guide in 1900! Classic gastronomy served in three stylish dining rooms, furnished in a Louis XIII-style.

Manoir d'Anet
3 pl. du Château – ✆ 02 37 41 91 05 – www.lemanoirdanet.com
– Fax 02 37 41 91 04 – Closed Tuesday and Wednesday
Rest – Menu €26 (weekdays)/48 – Carte €53/75
◆ A restaurant in an ideal location opposite Diane de Poitiers' castle. The rustic and flower-decked dining room is graced by an imposing stone fireplace. Bar, tearoom.

ANGERS Ⓟ – **49 Maine-et-Loire** – **317** F4 – **pop. 153 000** – **Built-up area 226 843** – **alt. 41 m** – ✉ **49000** **Châteaux of the Loire** 35 **C2**

Paris 294 – Laval 79 – Le Mans 97 – Nantes 88 – Rennes 129 – Tours 108

Aéroport d'Angers-Loire, ✆ 02 41 33 50 20, 20 km on the ①

Office de tourisme, 7, place Kennedy ✆ 02 41 23 50 00, Fax 02 41 23 50 09

d'Avrille Avrillé Château de la Perrière, NW : 5 km on D 175, ✆ 02 41 69 22 50

d'Angers Brissac-Quincé Moulin de Pistrait, 8 km on the Cholet road and D 751, ✆ 02 41 91 96 56

Golf d'Anjou Champigné Route de Cheffes, N : 24 km on D 775 and D 768, ✆ 02 41 42 01 01

Château★★★: hanging of the Apocalypse★★★, hanging of the Passion and Tapisseries mille-fleurs (tapestries of a thousand flowers) ★★, ≤★ from the Moulin tower - Old town★: cathedral★, Romanesque gallery★★ of the prefecture★ BZ **P**, David d'Angers gallery ★ BZ **B**, - Maison d'Adam (Adam's House) ★ BYZ **K** - Hôtel Pincé★ - Choir★★ of St-Serge church★ - Musée Jean Lurçat et de la Tapisserie contemporaine★★ in former St-Jean hospital★ - La Doutre★ AY - Musée régional de l'Air★.

Château de Pignerolle★: European Museum of Communication★★ East: 8 km by D 61.

Plans on following pages

Anjou
1 bd Mar.- Foch – ☎ 02 41 21 12 11 – www.hoteldanjou.fr – info@hoteldanjou.fr – Fax 02 41 87 22 21 CZ **h**
53 rm – €109/162 €119/173, ☕ €16
Rest ***La Salamandre*** – *☎ 02 41 88 99 55 (Closed Sunday except lunch from September to June)* Menu (€22), €28 (weekdays)/75 – Carte €40/65
◆ This building from 1845 boasts a lovely interior decor: lounges adorned with Art Deco mosaics and plush rooms furnished in a variety of periods. Captivating Renaissance-style restaurant: frescoes, French-style ceiling and salamanders.

Hôtel de France
8 pl. de la Gare – ☎ 02 41 88 49 42 – www.hoteldefrance-angers.com – reservation@hoteldefrance-angers.com – Fax 02 41 87 19 50 AZ **t**
55 rm – €80/165 €80/165, ☕ €14 – 1 suite
Rest ***Les Plantagenêts*** – *☎ 02 41 88 02 27 (closed August, Saturday lunch, Sunday dinner and Wednesday)* Menu (€21), €31/45 – Carte €46/57
◆ Plush, well-equipped rooms, small sitting rooms, seminar room and tasty breakfasts (local produce): equally popular with business and leisure guests. Les Plantagenêts provides a low-key atmosphere, serving up-to-date cuisine with a good local wine list.

Mercure Centre rest, rest,
pl. Mendès-France, (Congressional Centre) – ☎ 02 41 60 34 81 – www.mercure.com – h0540@accor.com – Fax 02 41 60 57 84 CY **a**
84 rm – €65/169 €70/179, ☕ €15
Rest ***Le Grand Jardin*** – *(Closed 24 December-2 January)* Menu (€16), €21 (lunch)/29 – Carte €21/38
◆ Situated next to a conference centre, this modern hotel offers functional, well-soundproofed rooms, some of which overlook the Jardin des Plantes. Pleasant wine bar. The restaurant opens onto leafy greenery. Contemporary decor and cuisine; Anjou wines.

Du Mail without rest
8 r. des Ursules – ☎ 02 41 25 05 25 – www.hotel-du-mail.com – hoteldumailangers@yahoo.fr – Fax 02 41 86 91 20 CY **b**
26 rm – €40/90 €65/90, ☕ €15
◆ A hotel with character housed in the discreet walls of a 17C former convent. Most of the personalised rooms are spacious.

Le Progrès without rest
26 av. D.-Papin – ☎ 02 41 88 10 14 – www.hotelleprogres.com – hotel.leprogres@wanadoo.fr – Fax 02 41 87 82 93 – Closed 7-16 August and 24 December-3 January AZ **f**
41 rm – €55/60 €55/66, ☕ €8
◆ A welcoming hotel, opposite the railway station with modern, bright and practical rooms. Breakfast is served in a pleasant room facing a flower-decked courtyard.

Continental without rest
14 r. L.-de-Romain – ☎ 02 41 86 94 94 – www.hotellecontinental.com – reservation@hotellecontinental.com – Fax 02 41 86 96 60 BYZ **n**
25 rm – €60/70 €70/79, ☕ €10
◆ This centrally located hotel in an old building features bright, recently refurbished, well-kept and well-soundproofed rooms.

De l'Europe without rest
3 r. Châteaugontier – ☎ 02 41 88 67 45 – www.hoteldeleurope-angers.com – hoteldeleurope-angers@wanadoo.fr – Fax 02 41 86 17 42 CZ **a**
29 rm – €57 €68, ☕ €8
◆ This hotel with a pleasant family atmosphere is located in a shopping district. Small, brightly coloured rooms. Pleasant breakfast room.

Grand Hôtel de la Gare without rest
5 pl. de la Gare – ☎ 02 41 88 40 69 – www.hotel-angers.fr – info@hotel-angers.fr – Fax 02 41 88 45 41 – Closed 31 July-22 August, and 18 December-3 January BZ **a**
52 rm – €48/80 €58/80, ☕ €8
◆ The corridors and breakfast room are adorned with brightly coloured frescoes. Pretty modern rooms overlooking the fountain in front of the station.

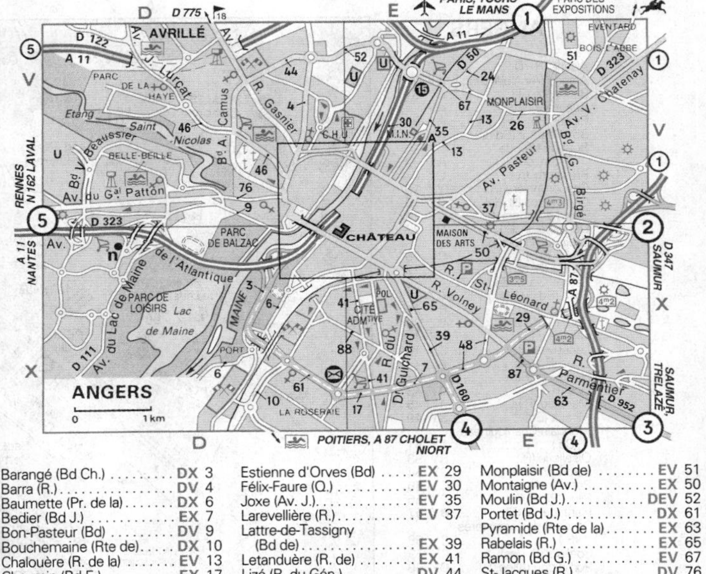

Street	Grid	No.
Barangé (Bd Ch.)	DX	3
Barra (R.)	DV	4
Baumette (Pr. de la)	DX	6
Bedier (Bd J.)	EX	7
Bon-Pasteur (Bd)	DV	9
Bouchemaine (Rte de)	DX	10
Chalouère (R. de la)	EV	13
Chaumin (Bd E.)	EX	17
Doyenné (Bd du)	EV	24
Dunant (Bd H.)	EV	26
Estienne d'Orves (Bd)	EX	29
Félix-Faure (Q.)	EV	30
Joxe (Av. J.)	EV	35
Larevellière (R.)	EV	37
Lattre-de-Tassigny (Bd de)	EX	39
Letanduère (R. de)	EX	41
Lizé (R. du Gén.)	DV	44
Meignanne (R. de la)	DV	46
Millot (Bd J.)	EX	48
Monplaisir (Bd de)	EV	51
Montaigne (Av.)	EX	50
Moulin (Bd J.)	DEV	52
Portet (Bd J.)	DX	61
Pyramide (Rte de la)	EX	63
Rabelais (R.)	EX	65
Ramon (Bd G.)	EV	67
St-Jacques (R.)	DV	76
Saumuroise (R.)	EX	87
Strasbourg (Bd de)	DEX	88

Le Favre d'Anne (Pascal Favre d'Anne)

18 quai des Carmes – 02 41 36 12 12 – www.lefavredanne.fr – contact@lefavredanne.fr – Closed 26 July-13 August, Sunday and Monday AY **t**

Rest – Menu (€ 20), € 40/90

Rest *L' R du Temps* – *(closed Monday in July-August and Sunday) (lunch only)* Menu (€ 20), € 24 (weekdays)/32

Spec. Tarte fine aux langoustines, glace au beurre blanc (summer). Filet de bœuf "Maine Anjou" et sushi de foie gras cru (autumn). Framboises du pays, sorbet au poivron rouge et biscuit à l'huile d'olive (summer). **Wines** Savennières, Saumur-Champigny.

◆ In this private hotel, the chef offers good cuisine that is both modern and creative, and already popular with the clientele. Contemporary décor and a view over the château and the Maine. L'R du Temps wears its name well: contemporary décor and modern dishes.

Le Relais

9 r. de la Gare – 02 41 88 42 51 – www.destination.anjou.com/relais – c.noel10@wanadoo.fr – Fax 02 41 24 75 20 – Closed 1st-4 May, 9 August-2 September, 20 December-4 January, Sunday and Monday BZ **u**

Rest – Menu (€ 19), € 24/43

◆ This establishment's modern, low-key, elegant decoration includes bench seating, mosaic flooring and fine murals depicting wine and the 'good life'. Appetising traditional cuisine.

Provence Caffé

9 pl. Ralliement – 02 41 87 44 15 – www.provence-caffe.com – f_derouet@yahoo.fr – Fax 02 41 87 44 15 – Closed Sunday and Monday

Rest – *(pre-book)* Menu (€ 16), € 20 (weekdays)/32 – Carte approx. € 26 BCY **e**

◆ Designer furniture, soft lighting and music: the Caffé has been treated to a trendy minimalist lounge style, without however forgoing its southern flavour (spices, fish, etc.).

ANGERS

Alsace (R. d') . . . . CZ
Aragon (Av. Yolande d') . AY 2
Baudrière (R.) . . . . BY 5
Beaurepaire (R.) . . . . AY
Bichat (R.) . . . . AY 8
Bon-Pasteur (Bd du) . . . . AY 9
Bout-du-Monde (Prom. du) . . . . AY 12
Bressigny (R.) . . . . CZ
Chaperonnière (R.) . . . . BYZ 15
Commerce (R. du) . . . . . CY 19
David-d'Angers (R.) . . . . CY 21
Denis-Papin (R.) . . . . BZ 22
Droits-de-l'Homme (Av. des) . . . . CY 25
Espine (R. de l') . . . . BY 27
Estoile (Sq. J. de l') . . . . . AY 28
Foch (Bd du Mar.) . . . . . BCZ
Freppel (Pl.) . . . . BY 31
Gare (R. de la) . . . . BZ 32
Laiterie (Pl.) . . . . AY
Lenepveu (R.) . . . . CY 40
Lices (R. des) . . . . BZ
Lionnaise (R.) . . . . AY
Lise (R. P.) . . . . CY 43
Marceau (R.) . . . . AZ 45
Mirault (Bd) . . . . BY 49
Mondain-Chanlouineau (Sq.) . . . . BY 51
Oisellerie (R.) . . . . BY 53
Parcheminerie (R.) . . . . . BY 54
Pasteur (Av.) . . . . CY 55
Pilori (Pl. du) . . . . CY 56
Plantagenêt (R.) . . . . BY 57
Pocquet-de-Livonnières (R.) . . . . CY 58
Poëliers (R. des) . . . . CY 59
Pompidou (Allées) . . . . . . CY 60
Prés.-Kennedy (Place du) AZ 62
Ralliement (Pl. du) . . . . . BY 66
Résistance-et-de-la-Déport. (Bd) . . . . CY 68
Robert (Bd) . . . . BY 69
La Rochefoucauld Liancourt (Pl.) . . . . ABY 38
Roë (R. de la) . . . . BY 70
Ronceray (Bd du) . . . . AY 71
Ste-Croix (Pl.) . . . . BZ 86
St-Aignan (R.) . . . . AY 72
St-Aubin (R.) . . . . BZ 73
St-Étienne (R.) . . . . CY 75
St-Julien (R.) . . . . BCZ
St-Laud (R.) . . . . BY 77
St-Lazare (R.) . . . . AY 79
St-Martin (R.) . . . . BZ 80
St-Maurice (Mtée) . . . . . . BY 82
St-Maurille (R.) . . . . CY 83
St-Michel (Bd) . . . . CY 84
St-Samson (R.) . . . . CY 85
Talot (R.) . . . . BZ 89
Tonneliers (R. des) . . . . . AY 90
Ursules (R. des) . . . . CY 91
Voltaire (R.) . . . . BZ 93
8-Mai-1945 (Av. du) . . . . . CZ 94

Le Petit Comptoir

40 r. David-d'Angers – ✆ 02 41 88 81 57 – lepetitcomptoir@9business.fr – Fax 02 41 88 81 57 – Closed 28 July-18 August, 5-12 May, 19-31 January, Sunday and Monday CZ **d**

Rest – Menu (€ 19), € 30/35

◆ The crimson red façade of this Angers bistro hides a tiny but welcoming dining room. Relaxed atmosphere and generous food with a lot of creativity.

Le Crèmet d'Anjou

21 r. Delaâge – ✆ 02 41 88 38 38 – Fax 02 41 88 38 38 – Closed 18 July-17 August, 24 December-4 January, Saturday and Sunday BZ **e**

Rest – Menu (€ 16), € 23 (weekdays)/27

◆ Named after a famous local dessert, this establishment is renowned for its owner's jovial character and his generous traditional fare, prepared before your very eyes.

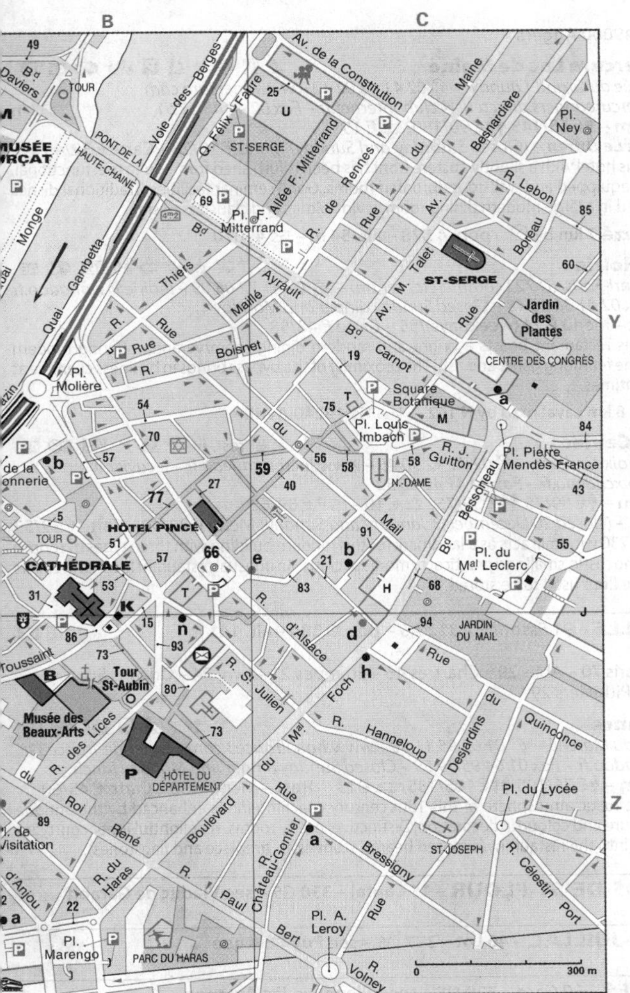

in Trélazé by ③ – pop. 12 200 – alt. 20 m – ✉ 49800

Hôtel de Loire
328 r. Jean-Jaurès
– ✆ 02 41 818 918 – www.hoteldeloire.com
– bateliers@hoteldeloire.com – Fax 02 41 818 920
49 rm – 🛉€ 67/93 🛉🛉€ 74/100, ☕ € 8,50 – ½ P € 69/82
Rest – Menu (€ 12), € 15 (weekday lunch), € 25/32 – Carte € 30/50
◆ This recent hotel on a busy road houses non-smoking rooms decorated with lovely simplicity (minimalist, mahogany-type furniture, chocolate shades...). The restaurant has modern decor with references to the Loire and a brasserie-style menu.

West – ✉ 49000 Angers

Mercure Lac de Maine

2 allée du Grand-Launay – ✆ 02 41 48 02 12 – www.mercure.com – mercureangers.directeur@club-internet.fr – Fax 02 41 48 57 51 DX **n**

77 rm – €55/145 €90/180, ☕ €15

Rest ***Le Diffen*** – *(Closed Saturday and Sunday)* Menu €19/28 – Carte €32/45

◆ This hotel with a slightly austere front has been refurbished from top to toe: functional, well-equipped and well-soundproofed rooms. Good seminar facilities. Traditional dishes served in a large modern dining room: vivid colours and claustras design.

in Beaucouzé 7 km by ⑤ – pop. 4 578 – alt. 54 m – ✉ **49070**

L'Hoirie

r. Henri-Faris, (D 723 commercial centre) – ✆ 02 41 72 06 09 – lhoirie@wanadoo.fr – Fax 02 41 36 35 48 – Closed Sunday dinner and Monday

Rest – Menu €24 (weekdays)/55 – Carte €48/58

◆ This restaurant boasts a bright and modern dining room/veranda offering modern cuisine featuring game and fish. The proximity of the bypass brings in business clientele at lunchtimes.

Northwest 8 km Laval road by N 162 - DV – ✉ **49240 Avrillé**

Le Cavier

rest,

La Croix-Cadeau – ✆ 02 41 42 30 45 – www.lacroixcadeau.fr – lecavier@lacroixcadeau.fr – Fax 02 41 42 40 32

43 rm – €59/75 €59/75, ☕ €10 – ½ P €59/62

Rest – *(closed 20 December-3 January and Sunday)* Menu €22/40 – Carte €32/53

◆ A 1730 windmill acts as a landmark for this modern building with three types of rooms: old and rustic, small and practical or more spacious. An unusual restaurant located in cellars where flour used to be stored.

ANGERVILLE – 91 Essonne – 312 A6 – pop. 3 384 – alt. 141 m – ✉ 91670

18 **B3**

Paris 70 – Ablis 29 – Chartres 46 – Étampes 21 – Évry 54 – Orléans 56 – Pithiviers 29

France

2 pl. du Marché – ✆ 01 69 95 11 30 – www.hotelfrance3.com – hotel-de-france3@wanadoo.fr – Fax 01 64 95 39 59 – Closed Sunday dinner and Monday lunch

20 rm – €75/105 €105/135, ☕ €13 **Rest** – Menu €30 – Carte €45/60

◆ The rustic atmosphere of this 18th century coaching inn is enhanced by the antique furniture and colourful decoration. Distinctive, pretty rooms. A delightful inner courtyard leads into the restaurant (exposed beams, stonework, fireplace and flagstones).

ANGLARDS-DE-ST-FLOUR – 15 Cantal – 330 G5 – see Viaduc de Garabit

---

ANGLARS-JUILLAC – 46 Lot – 337 D5 – see Puy-l'Évêque

LES ANGLES – 30 Gard – 339 N5 – see Villeneuve-lès-Avignon

ANGLES-SUR-L'ANGLIN – 86 Vienne – 322 L4 – pop. 391 – alt. 100 m – ✉ 86260 Atlantic Coast

39 **D1**

Paris 336 – Châteauroux 78 – Châtellerault 34 – Montmorillon 34 – Poitiers 51

Office de tourisme, 1, rue de l'Église ✆ 05 49 48 86 87, Fax 05 49 48 27 55

Site★ - château ruins★.

Le Relais du Lyon d'Or

rm,

4 r. d'Enfer – ✆ 05 49 48 32 53 – www.lyondor.com – contact@lyondor.com – Fax 05 49 84 02 28 – Closed January and February

10 rm – €75/125 €75/135, ☕ €15 – ½ P €78/113

Rest – *(open 21 March-7 November) (dinner only)* Carte approx. €34

◆ This 14C house has pretty rooms furnished with antique furniture and a delicious, relaxing garden. Meals are served around the hearth or in the courtyard during the summer months. Wine list put together by the owner, a former wine merchant.

ANGLET – 64 Pyrénées-Atlantiques – 342 C4 – pop. 37 500 – alt. 20 m 3 A3
– ✉ 64600 Atlantic Coast

Paris 769 – Bayonne 5 – Biarritz 4 – Cambo-les-Bains 18 – Pau 114 – St-Jean-de-Luz 21

Biarritz-Anglet-Bayonne ✆ 05 59 43 83 83, Southwest: 2 km.

Office de tourisme, 1, avenue de la Chambre d'Amour ✆ 05 59 03 77 01, Fax 05 59 03 55 91

de Chiberta 104 boulevard des Plages, N : 5 km on D 5, ✆ 05 59 52 51 10

Plan: see Biarritz-Anglet-Bayonne

De Chiberta et du Golf

rm, rm, rest, VISA MC AE

104 bd des Plages – ✆ 05 59 58 48 48 – www.hmc-hotels.com – hotelchiberta@hmc-hotels.com – Fax 05 59 63 57 84 AB

92 rm – €115/260 €115/260, €14 **Rest** – Menu €27 – Carte €42/50

◆ This 1920s residence situated next to the prestigious Chiberta golf course has comfortable rooms offering a view of the greens and the lake. Dining room-veranda and pretty, shaded terrace; traditional menu.

Atlanthal

rest, VISA MC AE

153 bd des Plages – ✆ 05 59 52 75 75 – www.atlanthal.com – info@atlanthal.com – Fax 05 59 52 75 13 AB

99 rm – €110/266 €160/392, €11 – ½ P €109/225

Rest – Menu €29 – Carte approx. €49

◆ A modern complex with excellent leisure facilities, including well-equipped thalassotherapy and fitness centres. Lovely views of the Atlantic. Spacious guestrooms. Traditional cuisine served in the veranda-restaurant facing the sea. Basque dishes and a tapas bar.

Novotel Biarritz Aéroport

VISA MC AE

68 av. d'Espagne, (D 810) – ✆ 05 59 58 50 50 – www.novotel.com – h0994@accor.com – Fax 05 59 03 33 55 BX **m**

121 rm – €99/143 €103/150, €14

Rest – Menu (€16 bi) – Carte €23/54

◆ A large establishment on the edge of a park. The spacious rooms, most of which have been refurbished, are quieter facing the woods. Leisure facilities. Pleasant dining room incorporating wood, bricks and warm colours.

La Fleur de Sel

VISA MC

5 av. de la Fôret – ✆ 05 59 63 88 66 – jf.fleurdesel@wanadoo.fr – Closed 22 February-8 March, 22 June-2 July, 16 November-1st December, Tuesday lunch in July-August, Sunday dinner in low season, Wednesday lunch and Monday BX **a**

Rest – Menu (€25) – Carte €36/49

◆ This friendly restaurant has a bright, spacious dining room overlooking a summer terrace. Modern decor and traditional, market-inspired cuisine.

ANGOULÊME P – 16 Charente – 324 K6 – pop. 41 700 – Built-up area 103 746 – alt. 98 m – ✉ 16000 Atlantic Coast 39 C3

Paris 447 – Bordeaux 119 – Limoges 105 – Niort 116 – Périgueux 85

Angoulême-Brie Champniers: ✆ 05 45 69 88 09, 15 km Northeast

Office de tourisme, 7 bis, rue du Chat ✆ 05 45 95 16 84, Fax 05 45 95 91 76

de l'Hirondelle Chemin de l'Hirondelle, S : 2 km, ✆ 05 45 61 16 94

Site★ - High town ★★ - St-Pierre cathedral ★: front★★ Y **F** - C.N.B.D.I. (Centre national de la bande dessinée et de l'image – National strip cartoon and picture centre)★ Y.

Plan on following page

Mercure Hôtel de France

rm, VISA MC AE

1 pl. des Halles-Centrales – ✆ 05 45 95 47 95 – h1213@accor.com – Fax 05 45 92 02 70 Y **e**

89 rm – €101/112 €111/122, €14

Rest – *(closed Sunday lunch and Saturday)* Menu €20/40 – Carte €34/43

◆ Occupying the house where Guez de Balzac was born, this hotel is extended by a modern wing. Pleasant, modern rooms; a pretty garden overlooking the Charente. Pleasant contemporary dining room with a quiet summer terrace.

ANGOULÊME

Aguesseau (Rampe d') . . . . . Y 2
Arsenal (R. de l') . . . . Z 4
Basseau (R. de) . . . . X 6
Beaulieu (Rempart de) . . . . . Y 8
Belat (R. de) . . . . Z 10
Bouillaud (Pl.) . . . . Z 12
Briand (Bd A.) . . . . Y 14
Chabasse (Bd R.) . . . . X 17
Churchill (Bd W.) . . . . Z 20
Corderie (R. de la) . . . . Y 24
Desaix (Rempart) . . . . Z 26
Dr-E.-Roux (Bd du) . . . . Z 28
Fontaine-du-Lizier (R.) . . . . . Y 30
Frères-Lumière (R. des) . . . . Y 32
Gambetta (Av.) . . . . Y 34
Gaulle (Av. du Gén.-de) . . . . Y 36
Guérin (R. J.) . . . . Y 37
Guillon (Pl. G.) . . . . Y 38
Iéna (R. d') . . . . Z 40
Lattre-de-Tassigny (Av. du Mar. de) . . . . X, Y 42
Liedot (Bd) . . . . X 44
Louvel (Pl. F.) . . . . Y 46
Marengo (Pl.) . . . . YZ 47
Midi (Rempart du) . . . . Y 48
Monlogis (R.) . . . . X 50
Papin (R. D.) . . . . Y 52
Paris (R. de) . . . . Y
Pasteur (Bd) . . . . Y 53
Périgueux (R. de) . . . . X 55
Postes (R. des) . . . . Y 57
Renoleau (R. A.) . . . . Z 58
République (Bd de la) . . . X, Y 59
La Rochefoucauld (R. de la) . . Y 41
Saintes (R. de) X
St-André (R.) . . . . Y 60
St-Antoine (R.) . . . . X 61
St-Martial (Pl. et R.) . . . . . . Z 65
St-Roch (R.) . . . . X, Y 67
Soleil (R. du) . . . . Y 70
Tharaud (Bd J. et J.) . . . . . . Z 72
Turenne (R. de) . . . . Y 73
3-Fours (R. des) . . . . Y 75
8-Mai-1945 (Bd du) . . . . X 80

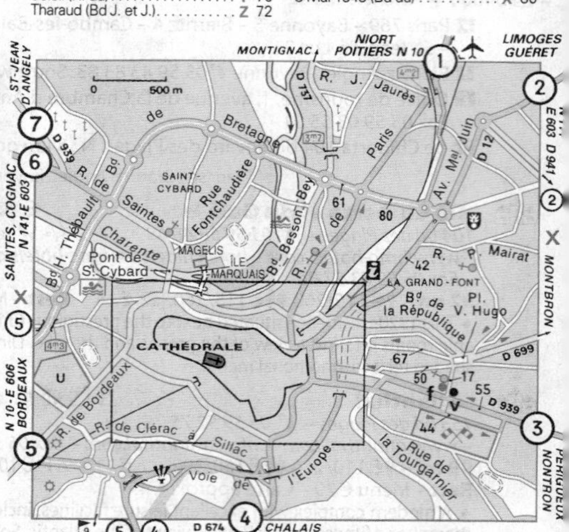

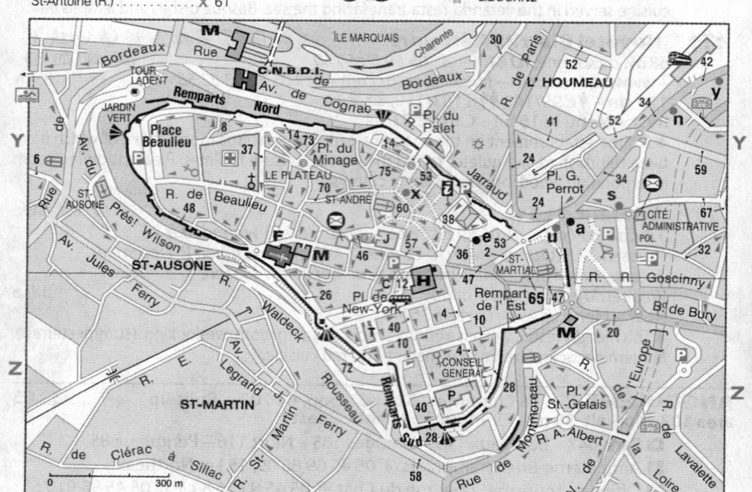

Européen without rest
1 pl. G.-Perot – 05 45 92 06 42 – www.europeenhotel.com – europeenhotel@wanadoo.fr – Fax 05 45 94 88 29 – Closed 19 December-3 January Y a
31 rm – €49/75 €49/75, €9
◆ Within easy walking distance from the city walls, a family establishment in the process of being renovated, with well-soundproofed rooms; those on the 3rd floor have more character.

L'Épi d'Or without rest
66 bd René-Chabasse – 05 45 95 67 64 – www.hotel-epidor.fr – info@hotel-epidor.fr – Fax 05 45 92 97 23 – **33 rm** – €55/75 €60/80, €10 X v
◆ Useful address within a short distance of the place Victor Hugo where a lively market is held. The spacious and practical rooms are quieter to the rear.

Le Palma VISA AE
4 rampe d'Aguesseau – ✆ 05 45 95 22 89 – lepalma@aliceadsl.fr – Fax 05 45 94 26 66 – Closed 19 December-5 January, Saturday lunch and Sunday
9 rm – €62 €66, €8 **Rest** – Menu (€13), €15/34 – Carte €40/50 Y u
◆ Comfortable non-smoking rooms, tastefully decorated and graced with painted or natural wood furniture. The sober and light restaurant (traditional menu) has a room serving dishes of the day and a few Spanish specialities.

Champ Fleuri without rest P
Chemin de l'Hirondelle, (at the golf course), 2 km, south of the map – ✆ 06 85 34 47 68 – www.champ-fleuri.com – xbparlant@free.fr
5 rm – €60/80 €60/80
◆ Lovely old house and walled garden next to the golf course. Pretty personalised rooms, panoramic view of Angoulême, terrace and swimming pool: the best of town and country.

Le Terminus VISA AE
3 pl. de la Gare – ✆ 05 45 95 27 13 – www.le-terminus.com – Fax 05 45 94 04 09 – Closed Sunday Y n
Rest – Menu (€17), €25/31 – Carte €40/55
◆ A chic modern brasserie all in black and white. The up-to-date menu takes Atlantic seafood and enriches it with regional touches. Lovely terrace.

L'Aromate VISA
41 bd René-Chabasse – ✆ 05 45 92 62 18 – Closed 1st-11 May, 25 July-25 August, 21 December-5 January, Tuesday dinner, Wednesday dinner, Sunday dinner and Monday X f
Rest – *(number of covers limited, pre-book)* Menu €16 (weekdays), €29/36 – Carte €33/40
◆ This small neighbourhood bistro offers good traditional cuisine with a modern twist, a friendly welcome and unpretentious rustic decor.

Côté Gourmet VISA
23 pl. de la Gare – ✆ 05 45 95 00 27 – cotegourmet@gmail.com – Fax 05 45 95 00 27 – Closed 2-8 March, 2-24 August, Tuesday dinner, Saturday lunch and Sunday Y y
Rest – Menu (€16 bi), €23/33 – Carte €36/42
◆ Modern-bistro style upstairs and high tables on the ground floor; simple up-to-date cuisine popular with local gourmets.

La Cité VISA AE
28 r. St-Roch – ✆ 05 45 92 42 69 – gicebet@aol.com – Closed 1st-25 August, 15 February-3 March, Sunday and Monday Y s
Rest – Menu €15 (weekday lunch), €19/30 – Carte €22/36
◆ Country-style furniture and fresh, bright decor set the scene for this family-run establishment serving traditional cuisine dominated by fish.

in Soyaux 4 km by ③ – **pop. 10 177 – alt. 133 m – ✉ 16800**

La Cigogne P VISA AE
5 imp. Cabane Bambou, at the Town Hall take Rue A.-Briand and 1.5 km – ✆ 05 45 95 89 23 – www.la-cigogne-angouleme.com – lacigogne16@wanadoo.fr – Closed 14-21 March, 25 October-10 November, 22 December-3 January, Wednesday dinner, Sunday dinner and Monday
Rest – Menu (€20 bi), €38/50 – Carte €59/84
◆ Next to an old mushroom farm, this house welcomes you to its bright dining room and shaded terrace looking out over fields. The menu combines tradition and modernity.

in Roullet 14 km by ⑤ and N 10, dir. Bordeaux – **pop. 3 686 – alt. 50 m – ✉ 16440**

La Vieille Étable rest, P VISA AE
Mouthiers road : 1,5 km – ✆ 05 45 66 31 75 – http://hotel-vieille-etable.com – vieille.etable@wanadoo.fr – Fax 05 45 66 47 45 – Closed Sunday dinner from October to mid May
29 rm – €67/125 €67/140, €13
Rest – Menu (€14), €18 (weekdays)/52 – Carte €45/61
◆ Surrounded by parkland with pond, this restored farm has neo-rustic rooms; the three new rooms are tastefully personalised. Traditional cuisine served by the fireplace or on the shaded terrace; gastronomic menu, children's meals.

ANNECY 🅿 – 74 Haute-Savoie – **328** J5 – **pop. 51 000 – Built-up area 136 815 – alt. 448 m – Casino : the Impérial** – ✉ **74000** French Alps **46 F1**

- Paris 536 – Aix-les-Bains 34 – Genève 42 – Lyon 138 – St-Étienne 187
- Annecy-Haute-Savoie ✆ 04 50 27 30 06, by N 508 BU and D 14: 4 km.
- Office de tourisme, 1, rue Jean Jaurès, Bonlieu ✆ 04 50 45 00 33, Fax 04 50 51 87 20
- du Belvédère Saint-Martin-Bellevue Chef Lieu, 6 km on the La Roche-sur-Foron road, ✆ 04 50 60 31 78
- du Lac d'Annecy Veyrier-du-Lac Route du Golf, 10 km on the Talloires road, ✆ 04 50 60 12 89
- de Giez-Lac-d'Annecy Giez 24 km on the Albertville road, ✆ 04 50 44 48 41
- Old Annecy★★: Deposition★ in St-Maurice church EY **E**, Palais de l'Isle★★ EY M^2, rue Ste-Claire★ - bridge over the Thiou ⩽★ EY **N** - Musée-château d'Annecy★ - Les Jardins de l'Europe (Gardens of Europe) ★ - Lakeside★★ ⩽★*.
- Tour of the lake★★★ - Gorges du Fier★★: 11 km by D 16 BV - Col de la Forclaz★★ - Forêt du crêt du Maure★: ⩽★★ 3 km by D 41 CV.

ANNECY

Aléry (Av. d') . . . . BV 4
Aléry (Gde-R. d') . . . . BV 7
Balmettes (Fg des) . . . . CV 10
Beauregard (Av. de) . . . . . . BV 13
Bel-Air (R. du) . . . . CU 15
Bordeaux (R. Henry) . . . . . . CU 18
Boschetti (Av. Lucien) . . . . BCV 21
Chambéry (Av. de) . . . . BV 23
Chevêne (Av. de) . . . . BV 29
Corniche (Bd de la) . . . . CV 32
Crête (R. de la) . . . . BU 38
Crêt-de-Maure (Av. du) . . . . CV 35
Fins Nord (Ch. des) . . . . . BCU 45
Hirondelles (Av. des) . . . . . . BV 52
Leclerc (R. du Mar.) . . . . . . BU 59
Loverchy (Av. de) . . . . BV 63
Martyrs-de-la-Déportation (R. des) . . . . CU 64
Mendès-France (Av. Pierre) . BV 65
Mermoz (R. Jean) . . . . CU 66
Novel (Av. de) . . . . CU 69
Perréard (Av. Germain) . . . . BU 73
Pont-Neuf (Av. du) . . . . BV 77
Prélevet (Av. de) . . . . BV 79
Prés-Riants (R. des) . . . . . . CU 81
Saint-Exupéry (R. A.-de) . . . CU 86
Stade (Av. du) . . . . BCU 92
Theuriet (R. André) . . . . CV 93
Thônes (Av. de) . . . . CU 94
Trésum (Av. de) . . . . CV 97
Trois-Fontaines (Av. des) . . . . BV 98
Val-Vert (R. du) . . . . BV 99

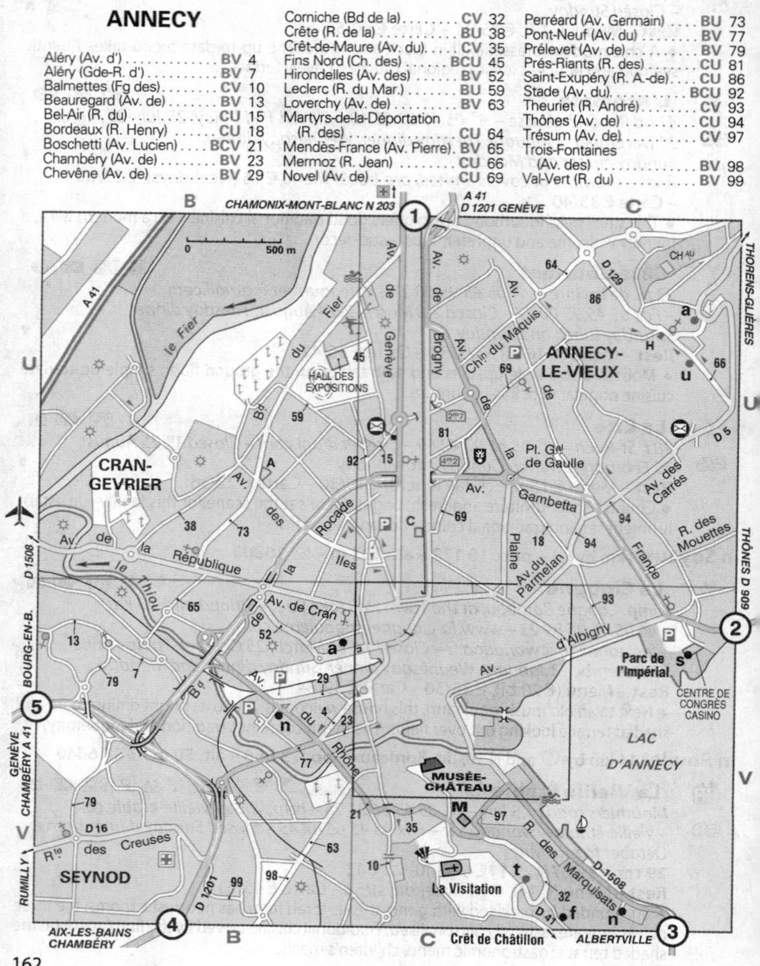

ANNECY

Chambéry (Av. de) . . . . . . DY 23	Hôtel-de-Ville (Pl. de l') . . . . . EY 53	Poste (R. de la) . . . . DY 78
Chappuis (Q. Eustache) . . . . EY 26	Jean-Jacques-Rousseau (R.) DY 55	République (R.) . . . . DY 83
Filaterie (R.) . . . . EY 43	Lac (R. du) . . . . EY 57	Royale (R.) . . . . DY 85
Grenette (R.) . . . . EY 51	Libération (Pl. de la) . . . . . . EY 61	Ste-Claire (Fg et R.) . . . . . . DY 91
	Pâquier (R. du) . . . . EY 71	St-François-de-Sales (Pl.) . . . EY 87
	Perrière (R.) . . . . EY 75	St-François-de-Sales (R.) . . . DY 89
	Pont-Morens (R. du) . . . . . . EY 76	Tour-la-Reine (Ch.) . . . . EY 95

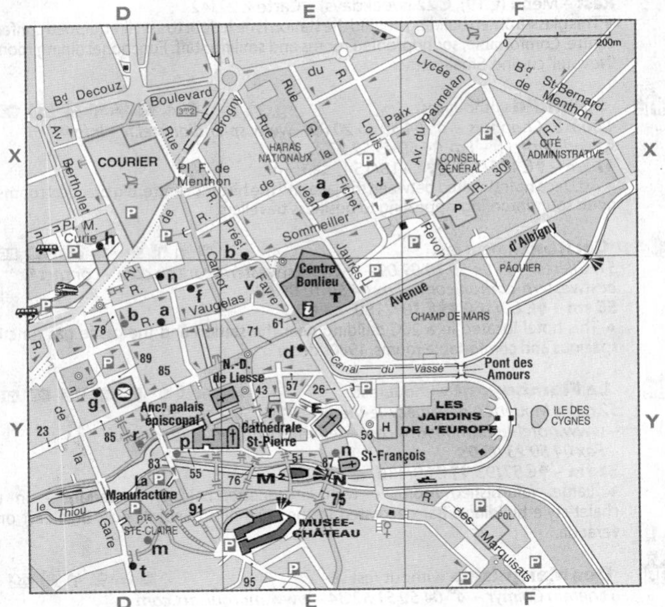

L'Impérial Palace rm, rest,
allée de l'Impérial – ✆ 04 50 09 30 00 – www.hotel-imperial-palace.com – reservation@hotel-imperial-palace.com – Fax 04 50 09 33 33 CV **s**
91 rm – €300/450 €300/450, €25 – 8 suites
Rest *La Voile* – Carte €49/82
◆ Magnificent views of the lake from this 1913 luxury hotel set in a park. Contemporary, well-equipped rooms, conference centre, casino, fitness facilities and beauty parlour. Pleasant dining room with a superb terrace opening onto the gardens and lake.

Les Trésoms
3 bd de la Corniche – ✆ 04 50 51 43 84 – www.lestresoms.com – info@lestresoms.com – Fax 04 50 45 56 49 CV **f**
50 rm – €119/219 €139/279, €16
Rest *La Rotonde* – *(Closed Saturday lunch, Sunday dinner, Monday and lunch from 15 July to 30 August)* Menu (€25), €29 (weekday lunch), €35/89 – Carte €65/85
Rest *La Coupole* – *(closed Tuesday dinner, Wednesday dinner, Thursday dinner and lunch except July-August)* Menu (€28), €35
◆ Situated in a tranquil garden, a restored 1930s residence retaining its Art Deco charm. Around half the warmly decorated rooms have lake views. Spa. La Rotonde serves modern dishes (splendid panoramic terrace). Simple cuisine at La Coupole.

Le Pré Carré without rest
27 r. Sommeiller – ✆ 04 50 52 14 14 – www.hotel-annecy.net – precarre@hotel-annecy.net – Fax 04 50 63 26 19 EX **b**
27 rm – €152/202 €182/232, €14 – 2 suites
◆ Recent hotel near to the old town and the lake. The very modern rooms are decorated in a mixture of soft shades. Breakfast under glass. Jacuzzi, sauna.

Novotel Atria

1 av. Berthollet – ✆ 04 50 33 54 54 – www.novotel.com – h1357@accor.com – Fax 04 50 45 50 68

DX **h**

95 rm – €85/165 €85/165, ☕ €15

Rest – Menu (€19), €22 (weekdays) – Carte €22/42

◆ This glass-fronted building behind the station is next door to a well-equipped conference centre. Comfortable, soundproofed rooms and smiling staff. Functional dining room and 'Novotel' cuisine. Small terrace.

Splendid without rest

4 quai E.-Chappuis – ✆ 04 50 45 20 00 – www.splendidhotel.fr – info@splendidhotel.fr – Fax 04 50 45 52 23

EY **d**

47 rm – €107/139 €118/154, ☕ €14

◆ Art Deco hotel located between the lake and the historic centre. Big practical rooms with good soundproofing; appealing to business travellers.

Carlton without rest

5 r. Glières – ✆ 04 50 10 09 09 – www.bestwestern-carlton.com – contact@bestwestern-carlton.com – Fax 04 50 10 09 60

DY **g**

55 rm – €80/160 €107/180, ☕ €15

◆ This hotel located in a 20C building near the station and the castle has functional, spacious and comfortable rooms. 1980s decor.

Le Flamboyant without rest

52 r. des Mouettes, at Annecy-le-Vieux – ✆ 04 50 23 61 69 – www.hotel-le-flamboyant.com – leflamboyant74@wanadoo.fr – Fax 04 50 23 05 03

CU

31 rm – €57/93 €69/116, ☕ €12

◆ Large, refurbished rooms – with kitchenette, balcony or terrace – in three chalet-style buildings. Bar decorated in the style of an English pub. Breakfast on the veranda.

Des Marquisats without rest

6 chemin Colmyr – ✆ 04 50 51 52 34 – www.marquisats.com – reservations@marquisats.com – Fax 04 50 51 89 42

CV **n**

23 rm – €71/118 €71/118, ☕ €11

◆ On a hillside close to a beach, this progressively renovated stone house has a variety of decorative styles in its comfortable rooms which face the lake or woodland.

International

19 av. du Rhône – ✆ 04 50 52 35 35 – www.bestwestern-hotelinternational.com – reservation@bestwestern-hotelinternational.com – Fax 04 50 52 35 00

BV **n**

134 rm – €95/160 €95/160, ☕ €11

Rest – *(Closed Friday dinner, Saturday and Sunday)* Menu €15/35 – Carte €24/46

◆ Modern, functional rooms, some with a balcony; those facing away from the ring road are preferable. Good seminar facilities and English-style bar. Wood dominates the restaurant. Traditional menu.

Mercure without rest

26 r. Vaugelas – ✆ 04 50 45 59 80 – h2812@accor.com – Fax 04 50 45 21 99

DY **a**

39 rm – €95/140 €105/140, ☕ €14

◆ This establishment is centrally located with practical, calm rooms decorated in blue and yellow (in homage to Provence). Breakfast buffet menu.

Allobroges Park without rest

11 r. Sommeiller – ✆ 04 50 45 03 11 – www.allobroges.com – info@allobroges.com – Fax 04 50 51 88 32

DY **n**

47 rm – €68/88 €78/98, ☕ €8,50 – 3 suites

◆ The sign of this town centre hotel recalls the Celtic tribe that used to inhabit the region. Modern renovated rooms in beige and brown harmonies.

Amiral without rest
61 r. Centrale, at Annecy-le-Vieux on ② ✉ 74940 – ✆ 04 50 23 29 26
– www.amiral-hotel.com – contact@amiral-hotel.com
– Fax 04 50 23 74 18
36 rm – †€ 57/62 ††€ 67/80, ☕ € 8,50 – 1 suite
◆ Situated near the beaches along the lakeshore, this colonial-style hotel has small, renovated guestrooms.

Nord without rest
24 r. Sommeiller – ✆ 04 50 45 08 78 – www.annecy-hotel-du-nord.com
– contact@annecy-hotel-du-nord.com – Fax 04 50 51 22 04 DY **f**
30 rm – †€ 45/68 ††€ 55/68, ☕ € 7
◆ Ideally located in the centre, this small unpretentious hotel is the perfect base from which to explore the town. Cheerful and bright modern decor in the rooms.

de Bonlieu without rest
5 r. Bonlieu – ✆ 04 50 45 17 16 – www.annecybonlieuhotel.fr – info@annecybonlieuhotel.fr – Fax 04 50 45 11 48 – Closed 1st-10 November EX **a**
35 rm – †€ 78/102 ††€ 86/110, ☕ € 11
◆ In a quiet street near the centre of town, a modern little hotel with rooms that are practical, modern and relaxing, if a little cramped.

Kyriad Centre without rest
1 fg Balmettes – ✆ 04 50 45 04 12 – www.annecy-hotel-kyriad.com
– annecy.hotel.kyriad@wanadoo.fr – Fax 04 50 45 90 92 DY **t**
24 rm – †€ 60/80 ††€ 60/80, ☕ € 8
◆ Situated near the old part of Annecy, this 16C building is undergoing a rebirth. Rooms vary in size; simply furnished and enlivened with shades of yellow and blue.

Les Terrasses
15 r. L.-Chaumontel – ✆ 04 50 57 08 98 – www.hotel-les-terrasses-annecy.com
– lesterrasses@wanadoo.fr – Fax 04 50 57 05 28 BV **a**
20 rm – †€ 63/72 ††€ 68/76, ☕ € 8 – ½ P € 55/61
Rest – *(closed 15 December-18 January, Saturday and Sunday except July-August) (dinner only) (residents only)* Menu € 16/23
◆ In a residential area near to the train station, a good hotel with smart rooms furnished in a country style. A warm family welcome. An attractively simple partly panelled restaurant; terracing on the garden side.

XXX ✿✿ **Le Clos des Sens** (Laurent Petit) with rm
13 r J.-Mermoz ✉ 74940 – ✆ 04 50 23 07 90
– www.closdessens.com – artisanculinaire@closdessens.com – Fax 04 50 66 56 54
– Closed 27 April-5 May, 31 August-17 September, Sunday except dinner in July-August, Tuesday lunch and Monday CU **u**
5 rm – †€ 180/230 ††€ 180/230, ☕ € 17
Rest – Menu (€ 33), € 48/100 – Carte € 80/100
Spec. Tarte fine de légumes "sans pâte" (March to October). Féra à l'ail des bois et citron confit (spring). Madeleines tièdes au miel, gelée de myrtilles (spring-autumn). **Wines** Chignin-Bergeron, Vin rouge de Chautagne
◆ Thoughtful and inventive dishes beautifully presented in an elegantly contemporary setting and enhanced by a fine wine list. Terrace overlooking Annecy; unusual and refined rooms.

XXX ✿ **La Ciboulette** (Georges Paccard)
10 r. Vaugelas, (Court of the Pré Carré) – ✆ 04 50 45 74 57
– www.laciboulette-annecy.com – laciboulette74@wanadoo.fr
– Closed 1st-24 July, for the All Saint's Day holidays, for the February holidays, Sunday and Monday EY **v**
Rest – Menu € 30 (weekday lunch), € 45/58 – Carte € 65/85
Spec. Langoustines, joue de cochon confite et cardon. Cœur de ris de veau crousti-moelleux piqué d'un bâton d'enfance. Soufflé chaud de l'Abbaye de la Grande Chartreuse, liqueur secrète et famboises (winter). **Wines** Chignin-Bergeron, Vin de Pays de Savoie
◆ Classic and contemporary styles combine in the thoughtful, tasteful decor of this restaurant serving classical cuisine with a modern twist.

XXX **Le Belvédère** (Vincent Lugrin) with rm
7 chemin Belvédère, 2 km, Semnoz road south-eastward via Rue Marquisat – ✆ 04 50 45 04 90 – www.belvedere-annecy.com – b@belvedere-annecy.com – Fax 04 50 45 67 25 – Closed 1st-14 December, January, Sunday dinner, Tuesday and Wednesday CV **t**
5 rm – €80/105 €80/135, €10 – ½ P €98/113
Rest – Menu €28 (weekday lunch), €39/85 – Carte €75/90
Spec. Foie gras de canard aux perles de vanille bourbon. Omble chevalier cuit sur peau, lait d'amande et eau de rose. Cigare en chocolat noir fourré d'une mousse café. **Wines** Chignin-Bergeron, Mondeuse d'Arbin.
◆ This restaurant offers appetising modern cuisine and a view of Lake Annecy. Inviting summer terrace and quiet bedrooms, which also command a stunning view.

XX **Le Bilboquet**
14 fg Ste-Claire – ✆ 04 50 45 21 68 – www.restaurant-lebilboquet.fr – eric.besson@neuf.fr – Fax 04 50 45 21 68 – Closed 1st-15 July, Sunday except dinner July-August and Monday DY **m**
Rest – Menu (€20), €27/46 – Carte €42/58
◆ Thick old walls guarantee a cool ambiance in this pleasant restaurant by the port of Ste-Claire. Enticing menu mixing tradition and modernity.

XX **Auberge du Lyonnais** with rm
9 r. de la République – ✆ 04 50 51 26 10 – www.auberge-du-lyonnais.com – aubergedulyonnais@wanadoo.fr – Fax 04 50 51 05 04 – Closed All Saint's Day holidays DY **p**
10 rm – €45/70 €50/75, €8
Rest – Menu €25/40 – Carte approx. €55
◆ Old house in the historic centre between two branches of the Thiou canal. Good brasserie-style cuisine served in a nautical setting, or better still on the fine waterside terrace. Simple mountain-style accommodation.

XX **Auberge de Savoie**
1 pl. St-François – ✆ 04 50 45 03 05 – www.aubergedesavoie.fr – aubergedesavoie@laposte.net – Fax 04 50 51 18 28 – Closed 8-25 November, 3-13 January, Tuesday except July-August and Wednesday EY **n**
Rest – Menu (€21), €27/59 – Carte €57/72
◆ Professional welcome and service at this warm, modern restaurant built against the church of St François. The terrace on a small square has views of the Thiou and chateau.

XX **La Brasserie St-Maurice**
7 r. Collège-Chapuisien – ✆ 04 50 51 24 49 – www.stmau.com – stmau@stmau.com – Fax 04 50 51 24 49 – Closed Sunday and Monday
Rest – Menu €18 (weekday lunch), €24/42 – Carte €33/55 EY **r**
◆ A low key restaurant set in a magnificent house built in 1675. The splendid timber pillars in the dining room are original. Summer terrace and traditional cuisine.

X **Contresens**
10 r. de la Poste – ✆ 04 50 51 22 10 – www.closdessens.com – artisanculinaire@closdessens.com – Fax 04 50 51 34 26 – Closed 28 December-10 January, Sunday and Monday DY **b**
Rest – Menu (€22), €27
◆ Shoulder to shoulder dining in this popular restaurant serving deliciously light-hearted contemporary fare in a modern bistro setting.

X **Nature et Saveur**
pl. des Cordeliers – ✆ 04 50 45 82 29 – www.nature-saveur.com – postmaster@nature-saveur.com – Closed mid-July to mid-August, 24 December-4 January, Sunday and Monday DY **r**
Rest – Menu (€19), €39 (lunch), €49/62 bi
◆ Unusual and personal cuisine: this is the concept behind this small restaurant run by a trained naturopath and passionate chef. Organic produce.

Café Brunet
18 pl. Gabriel-Fauré – ✆ 04 50 27 65 65 – www.closdessens.com – artisanculinaire@closdessens.com – Fax 04 50 05 04 67 – Closed 1st-15 January, Sunday except lunch in July-August and Monday
Rest – Menu (€ 21), € 27 CU **a**
◆ Time seems to have stood still in this café from 1875 (terrace, pétanque). Now an annex of the 'Clos des Sens', it has retained its authentic bistro spirit. Traditional style cuisine.

in Chavoires **4,5 km by ② – ✉ 74290 Veyrier-du-Lac**

Demeure de Chavoire without rest
71 rte d'Annecy – ✆ 04 50 60 04 38 – www.demeuredechavoire.com – demeure.chavoire@wanadoo.fr – Fax 04 50 60 05 36 – Closed 10 - 24 November
10 rm – †€ 134/180 ††€ 165/195, € 16 – 3 suites
◆ A discreet façade for a hotel with character. Cosy, romantic rooms, antique furniture, pastel colour scheme and pleasant garden-terrace facing the lake.

in Veyrier-du-Lac **5,5 km by ② – pop. 2 138 – alt. 504 m – ✉ 74290**

Office de tourisme, rue de la Tournette ✆ 04 50 60 22 71, Fax 04 50 60 00 90

La Veyrolaine
30 rte Crêt des Vignes – ✆ 04 50 60 15 87 – http://pagesperso-orange.fr/laveyrolaine.annecy – la.veyrolaine@orange.fr
3 rm – †€ 65/115 ††€ 75/115 **Table d'hôte** – *(dinner)* Menu € 30
◆ There are many reasons to stay at this fine villa where guests are made to feel at home, among them the kind hosts, comfortable, elegant interior and proximity of the lake. Savoury, seasonal cuisine prepared by the owner, once the chef at a luxury hotel. Summer terrace.

La Maison de Marc Veyrat with rm
13 vieille rte des Pensières – ✆ 04 50 60 24 00 – www.marcveyrat.fr – contact@marcveyrat.fr – Fax 04 50 60 23 63 – Open mid February-end October and closed Tuesday except July-August, Monday and lunch except Saturday and Sunday
11 rm – †€ 300/880 ††€ 300/880, € 79 – 2 suites
Rest – Menu € 368 – Carte approx. € 285
Spec. Yaourt virtuel de foie gras et jus d'acha. Filet de bœuf, sirop de cresson. Les trois crèmes brûlées d'ici et d'ailleurs. **Wines** Mondeuse d'Arbin, Roussette de Savoie.
◆ Brilliant food with pastureland herbs and flowers, superb Savoy decor and a divine terrace facing the lake: a gastronomic genie watches over this enchanting blue house.

in Sévrier **6 km South by ③ – pop. 3 905 – alt. 456 m – ✉ 74320**

Office de tourisme, ✆ 04 50 52 40 56, Fax 04 50 52 48 66
Musée de la Cloche★.

Auberge de Létraz
921 rte d'Albertville – ✆ 04 50 52 40 36 – www.auberge-de-letraz.com – accueil@auberge-de-letraz.com – Fax 04 50 52 63 36
23 rm – †€ 59/182 ††€ 59/182, € 17 – 1 suite
Rest – *(closed mid November-mid December, Sunday dinner and Monday October-May)* Menu € 40/75 – Carte € 65/85
◆ The garden of this hotel is perfectly located in front of the lake. The rooms overlooking the lake are quieter, and are refurbished in a modern vein. Traditional menu and theme evenings in this restaurant overlooking the jewel of Annecy.

Beauregard rm, rest,
691 rte d'Albertville – ✆ 04 50 52 40 59 – www.hotel-beauregard.com – info@hotel-beauregard.com – Fax 04 50 52 44 71 – Closed 13 November-11 January
45 rm – †€ 62/81 ††€ 72/118 – ½ P € 57/76
Rest – *(closed Sunday from October to April)* Menu (€ 15), € 21/47 – Carte € 29/43
◆ Large Savoyard style establishment poised between the lake and the road. Practical, well-kept rooms; good seminar facilities. The rotunda restaurant and shaded terraces offer a fine view of the lake. Simple, classic cuisine.

in Pringy 8 km north by ① and secondary road – pop. 2 616 – alt. 483 m – ✉ 74370

XX Le Clos du Château

70 rte Cuvat, towards Promery – Tel. 04 50 66 82 23 – www.le-clos-du-chateau.com – leclosduchateau@wanadoo.fr – Fax 04 50 66 87 18 – Closed 27 July-18 August, 21 December-5 January, Sunday dinner and Monday

Rest – Menu (€ 19), € 22 (weekday lunch), € 31/54 – Carte € 44/58

◆ This restaurant adjoining the château is under new management. Trendy, modern and minimalist decor and table settings. Updated seasonal menu.

ANNEMASSE – 74 Haute-Savoie – 328 K3 – pop. 27 900 – Built-up area 106 673 – alt. 432 m – Casino : Grand Casino – ✉ 74100

46 **F1**

Paris 538 – Annecy 46 – Bonneville 22 – Genève 8 – Thonon-les-Bains 31

Office de tourisme, place de la Gare Tel. 04 50 95 07 10, Fax 04 50 37 11 71

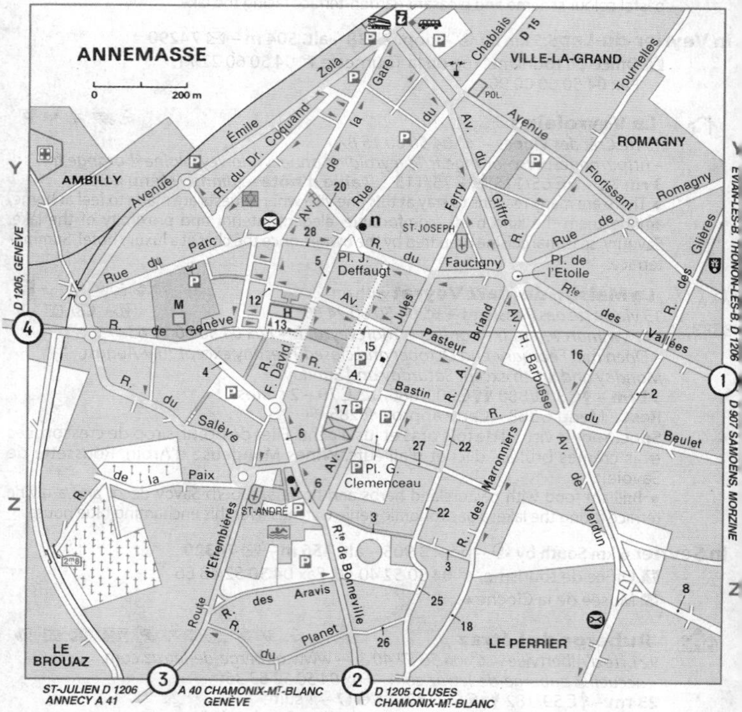

Alsace-Lorraine (Av. d') . . . . **Z** 2
Château Rouge (R. du) . . . . . . **Z** 3
Clos Fleury (R. du) . . . . **Z** 4
Commerce (R. du) . . . . **Y** 5
Courriard (R. M.) . . . . **Z** 6
Dusonchet (R. Cl.-Ph.) . . . . **Z** 8
Gare (R. de la) . . . . **Y** 12
Hôtel de Ville (Pl. de l') . . . . . **Y** 13
Libération (Pl. de la) . . . . **Z** 15
Malbrande (R. de) . . . . **Z** 16
Marché de Gros (Pl. du) . . . . . **Z** 17
Massenet (R.) . . . . **Z** 18
Mont-Blanc (R. du) . . . . **Y** 20
Petit Malbrande (R. du) . . . . **Z** 22
Saget (R. du) . . . . **Z** 25
Vaillat (R. L.) . . . . **Z** 27
Voirons (R. des) . . . . **Y** 28

Mercure

9 r. des Jardins, by ③ and Gaillard road ✉ 74240 – Tel. 04 50 92 05 25 – www.mercure.com – h0343@accor.com – Fax 04 50 87 14 50

78 rm – single €69/179, double €79/189, breakfast € 16 **Rest** – Carte € 22/35

◆ Situated near the motorway and a river, this hotel is surrounded by greenery. Fairly spacious, comfortable and soundproofed rooms. Sober poolside dining room and terrace. Traditional dishes.

La Place without rest
10 pl. J.-Deffaugt – ☎ 04 50 92 06 44 – www.laplacehotel.com – hotel.la.place@wanadoo.fr – Fax 04 50 87 07 45 Y **n**
43 rm – †€ 59/89 ††€ 77/122, ☕ € 8
◆ A central hotel conveniently located on the way to Switzerland. Handsome designer lounge, immaculate rooms with contemporary wooden furniture, pleasant welcome.

St-André without rest
20 r. M.-Courriard – ☎ 04 50 84 07 00 – www.hotel-st-andre.com – resa@hotel-st-andre.com – Fax 04 50 84 36 22 Z **v**
40 rm – †€ 58 ††€ 68, ☕ € 8 – 3 suites
◆ Situated in an office district, this recent establishment offers spacious, light, well-equipped rooms that are ideal for business travellers (practically furnished).

ANNONAY – 07 Ardèche – 331 K2 – pop. 17 300 – alt. 350 m – ✉ 07100 Lyon - Rhone Valley 44 B2

Paris 529 – St-Étienne 44 – Valence 56 – Yssingeaux 57
Office de tourisme, place des Cordeliers ☎ 04 75 33 24 51, Fax 04 75 32 47 79
du Domaine de Saint-Clair Le Pelou, 6 km on the Serrières road and D 820, ☎ 04 75 67 03 84
d'Albon Saint-Rambert-d'Albon Château de Senaud, E : 19 km on D 82, ☎ 04 75 03 03 90

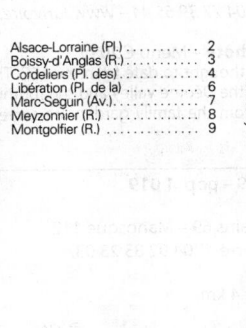

Alsace-Lorraine (Pl.) 2
Boissy-d'Anglas (R.) 3
Cordeliers (Pl. des) 4
Libération (Pl. de la) 6
Marc-Seguin (Av.) 7
Meyzonnier (R.) 8
Montgolfier (R.) 9

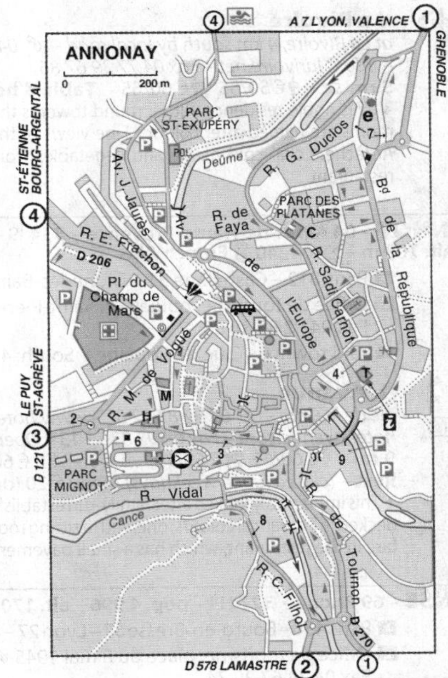

Marc et Christine
29 av. Marc-Seguin – ☎ 04 75 33 46 97 – marc-et-christine@wanadoo.fr – Closed 19-26 April, 16-30 August, 22 February-1st March, Sunday dinner and Monday e
Rest – Menu € 19/48 – Carte € 24/45
◆ This family-run gourmet bistro is a short trek from the town centre. Sample traditional cuisine made with regional produce in a delightfully provincial atmosphere.

in Golf de Gourdan 6.5 km by ① and D 1082 (St-Étienne road) – ✉ 07430 Annonay

Domaine du Golf de Saint Clair rm, rm,
rte du Golf – 04 75 67 01 00 – www.domainestclair.fr – reception@domainestclair.fr – Fax 04 75 67 07 38
54 rm – €98/105 €110/120, €13 – 2 suites **Rest** – Carte €32/45
◆ Renovated hotel, popular with business travellers, set in a quiet location surrounded by a golf course. Contemporary guestrooms, most with a balcony. Spa. Modern restaurant under the beams of a large barn. Traditional cuisine.

in St-Marcel-lès-Annonay 8,5 km by ④, D 206 and D 1082 – pop. 1 223 – alt. 450 m – ✉ 07100

Auberge du Lac
Le Ternay – 04 75 67 12 03 – www.aubergedulac.fr – contact@aubergedulac.fr – Fax 04 75 34 90 20 – Closed January and All Saint's Day holidays
12 rm – €80/145 €80/145, €12 – ½ P €82/115
Rest – *(closed Tuesday lunch except in July-August, Sunday dinner and Monday)* Menu €35/60
◆ Former auberge facing the dam, transformed into a luxurious and cosy hotel. Well-appointed, personalised bedrooms decorated with a floral theme. Roof terrace. Provençal dining room or outdoor tables with views of the lake and Le Pilat.

in St-Julien-Molin-Molette 10.5 km by ④, D 206 and D 1082 – pop. 1 180 – alt. 589 m – ✉ 42220

La Rivoire
at La Rivoire, 4 km south by local road – 04 77 39 65 44 – www.larivoire.net – info@larivoire.net – Fax 04 77 39 67 86
5 rm – €50/55 €60/65 **Table d'hôte** – Menu €20 bi
◆ This noble residence with a round tower is thought to date from the 15C. The bright rooms are named after colours. Fine views of the Déome valley and the foothills of the Ardèche. Local cold meats and vegetables from the family garden are served in this restaurant.

ANNOT – 04 Alpes-de-Haute-Provence – 334 I9 – pop. 1 019 – alt. 708 m – ✉ 04240 French Alps 41 C2

Paris 812 – Castellane 31 – Digne-les-Bains 69 – Manosque 112
Office de tourisme, boulevard Saint-Pierre 04 92 83 23 03, Fax 04 92 83 30 63
Old town ★ - Clue de Rouaine★ South: 4 km.

L'Avenue rm,
av. de la Gare – 04 92 83 22 07 – www.hotel-avenue.com – contact@hotel-avenue.com – Fax 04 92 83 33 13 – Open 1st April-30 October
9 rm – €60/62 €60/75, €9 – ½ P €60/65
Rest – *(closed lunch weekdays)* Menu €20 (dinner)/29
◆ This impeccably looked after family-run establishment is more than inviting. Guestrooms decked in Provençal colours; one, with a sitting room, is more contemporary. Tasty regional fare in the restaurant, which has a small pavement terrace.

ANSE – 69 Rhône – 327 H4 – pop. 4 996 – alt. 170 m – ✉ 69480 43 E1

Paris 436 – Bourg-en-Bresse 57 – Lyon 27 – Mâcon 51 – Villefranche-sur-Saône 7
Office de tourisme, place du 8 mai 1945 04 74 60 26 16, Fax 04 74 67 29 74

St-Romain
rte des Graves – 04 74 60 24 46 – hotel-saint-romain@wanadoo.fr – Fax 04 74 67 12 85 – Closed Sunday dinner from November to April
24 rm – €47 €50/55, €8 – ½ P €52
Rest – Menu €20 (weekdays)/35 – Carte €40/49
◆ An old renovated farm in Beaujolais style whose rustic rooms are extremely well looked after. A country-style dining room where the menu is resolutely traditional. Good choice of local wines.

Au Colombier

126 allée Colombier – ✆ 04 74 67 04 68 – www.aucolombier.com – info@aucolombier.com – Fax 04 74 67 20 30 – Closed Sunday dinner and Monday from October to May

Rest – Menu € 19 (weekday lunch), € 28/46

◆ Sturdy 18C residence on the banks of the River Saône. Meals are served on the terrace in summer and in front of the stone fireplace in winter. Good, innovative cuisine.

ANSOUIS – 84 Vaucluse – 332 F11 – pop. 1 091 – alt. 380 m – ✉ 84240 40 B2

Paris 751 – Marseille 63 – Avignon 79 – Aix-en-Provence 35

Syndicat d'initiative, place du Château ✆ 04 90 09 86 98, Fax 04 90 09 86 98

La Closerie

bd des Platanes – ✆ 04 90 09 90 54 – Fax 04 90 09 90 54 – Closed 1st-15 January and All Saint's Day holidays

Rest – *(number of covers limited, pre-book)* Menu € 21 (weekday lunch)/34 – Carte € 47/57

◆ Booking is essential in order to sample the cuisine, rich with enticing flavours. The inspired chef often renews his set menus. Lovely terrace overlooking the Luberon.

ANTHY-SUR-LÉMAN – 74 Haute-Savoie – 328 L2 – see Thonon-les-Bains

ANTIBES – 06 Alpes-Maritimes – 341 D6 – pop. 75 000 – alt. 2 m – Casino : "la Siesta" seaside by ① – ✉ 06600 French Riviera 42 E2

Paris 909 – Aix-en-Provence 160 – Cannes 11 – Nice 21

Office de tourisme, 11, place du Général-de-Gaulle ✆ 04 92 90 53 00, Fax 04 92 90 53 01

Old town ★: Promenade Amiral-de-Grasse ≤★ DXY - Château Grimaldi (Déposition de Croix★, Musée donation Picasso★) DX - Musée Peynet et de la Caricature★ DX M² - Marineland★ 4 km by ①.

Plans on following pages

Josse without rest

8 bd James-Wyllie – ✆ 04 92 93 38 38 – www.hotel-josse.com – hotel.josse@wanadoo.fr – Fax 04 92 93 38 39 BU **s**

26 rm – €91/183 €102/183, ☕ €11

◆ A boulevard separates this long building from Salis beach. All the rooms have tasteful furnishings and balconies with a sea view.

Mas Djoliba

29 av. de Provence – ✆ 04 93 34 02 48 – www.hotel-djoliba.com – contact@hotel-djoliba.com – Fax 04 93 34 05 81 – Open 10 March-12 November CY **d**

13 rm (½ board only) – €85/100 €90/130 – ½ P €84/114

Rest – *(open 1st May-30 September) (dinner only) (residents only)*

◆ Relax poolside in a garden planted with palm trees and bougainvillea, or in the charming rooms of this 1920s villa; those on the top floor have a terrace overlooking the Cap.

Petit Castel without rest

22 chemin des Sables – ✆ 04 93 61 59 37 – www.hotel-petitcastel.fr – hotel@lepetitcastel.fr – Fax 04 93 67 51 28 BU **b**

16 rm ☕ – €78/168 €88/188

◆ A hospitable, refurbished villa on a main road in a residential district. Soundproofing and air-conditioning in the rooms, rooftop sundeck and Jacuzzi, bicycles.

Modern Hôtel without rest

1 r. Fourmilière – ✆ 04 92 90 59 05 – Fax 04 92 90 59 06 – Closed 15 December-15 January CX **a**

17 rm – €58/68 €66/82, ☕ €6

◆ This hotel located at the beginning of the pedestrian area has been renovated. Soberly decorated rooms, new bedding and functional furniture.

ANTIBES

Châtaignier (Av. du) . . . . . . AU 13
Contrebandiers (Ch. des) . . BV 16
Ferrié (Av. Gén.) . . . . AU 26
Gardiole-Bacon (Bd) . . . . BUV 31
Garoupe (Bd de la) . . . . BV 33
Garoupe (Ch. de la) . . . . BV 34
Grec (Av. Jules) . . . . ABU 38
Malespine (Av.) . . . . BV 50
Phare (Rte du) . . . . BV 62
Raymond (Ch.) . . . . BV 64
Reibaud (Av.) . . . . AU 65
Salis (Av. de la) . . . . BV 77
Sella (Av. André) . . . . BV 78
Tamisier (Ch. du) . . . . BV 79
Tour-Gandolphe (Av. de la) . . . . BV 82
Vautrin (Bd. du Gén.) . . . . . BU 84
11-Novembre (Av. du) . . . . BU 91

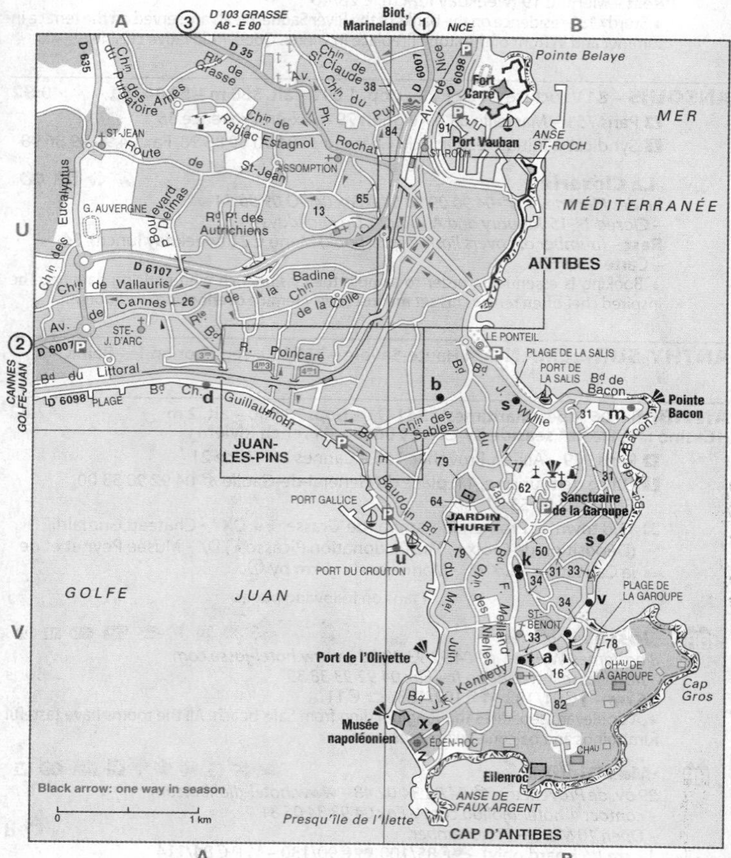

Les Vieux Murs VISA AE

25 promenade Amiral-de-Grasse – ✆ 04 93 34 06 73 – www.lesvieuxmurs.com – lesvieuxmurs@wanadoo.fr – Fax 04 93 34 81 08 – Closed 12 November-3 December, Tuesday lunch, Monday from mid-September to mid-April

Rest – Menu (€ 31), € 36 (lunch), € 41/65 – Carte € 62/83 DY **f**

◆ This house and terrace on the ramparts facing the sea is decorated in warm shades of orange. Tasty contemporary cuisine. Bar-lounge (art exhibitions).

Le Figuier de St-Esprit VISA AE

14 r. St-Esprit – ✆ 04 93 34 50 12 – www.christianmorisset.fr – lefiguier@christianmorisset.fr – Fax 04 93 34 94 25 – Closed Monday lunch, Wednesday lunch and Tuesday DX **a**

Rest – Menu (€ 38 bi), € 55/75 – Carte € 75/95

◆ Good restaurant near the cathedral and city walls. The chef prepares his interpretation of Provencal dishes. Bright, modern dining room; patio under the fig tree.

ANTIBES

Albert 1er (Bd) . . . . CDY
Alger (R. d') . . . . CX 3
Arazy (R.) . . . . DXY 4
Barnaud (Pl. Amiral) . . . . DY 6
Barquier (Av.) . . . . DY 8
Bas-Castelet (R. du) . . . . DY 9
Bateau (R. du) . . . . DX 10
Clemenceau (R. G.) . . . . DX 14
Dames-Blanches (Av. des) . . CY 19
Directeur Chaudon (R.) . . . . CY 20
Docteur Rostan (R. du) . . . . DX 24
Gambetta (Av.) . . . . CX 30
Gaulle (Pl. du Gén.-de) . . . . CXY
Grand-Cavalier (Av. du) . . . . CX 37
Guynemer (Pl.) . . . . CX 40
Haut-Castelet (R. du) . . . . . . DY 42
Horloge (R. de l') . . . . DX 43
Martyrs-de-la-Résistance
(Pl. des) . . . . CDX 51
Masséna (Cours) . . . . DX 52
Meissonnier (Av.) . . . . CDY 54
Nationale (Pl.) . . . . DX 55
Orme (R. de l') . . . . DX 57
République (R. de la) . . . . . CDX 67
Revely (R. du) . . . . DX 68
Revennes (R. des) . . . . DY 69
St-Roch (Av.) . . . . CX 72
Saleurs (Rampe des) . . . . . . DX 75
Tourraque (R. de la) . . . . DY 83
Vautrin (Bd. du Gén.) . . . . . . CX 84
8-Mai 1945
(Square du) . . . . DX 90
24-Août (Av. du) . . . . CY 92

Oscar's

8 r. Rostan – ✆ 04 93 34 90 14 – www.oscars-antibes.com – Fax 04 93 34 90 14 – Closed 1st-15 June, 23 December-10 January, Sunday and Monday DX **s**

Rest – *(number of covers limited, pre-book)* Menu € 29/56 – Carte € 70/90

◆ Enjoy the surprisingly original decor of sculptures set in niches and ancient landscapes. The restaurant owes its success to its tasty Italian Provençal cuisine.

Le Sucrier

6 r. des Bains – ✆ 04 93 34 85 40 – www.lesucrier.com – info@lesucrier.com – Closed 12-23 November, 7-26 January, Tuesday lunch from October to May and Monday DY **a**

Rest – Menu € 20/39 – Carte € 40/65

◆ This restaurant serves Italian specialities, such as fresh pasta and fish dishes, as well as traditional cuisine. Attractive dining rooms (one of which is vaulted) and a terrace.

Nice road by ① and D 6007 – ✉ 06600 Antibes

Baie des Anges-Thalazur rm, rest,
770 chemin Moyennes-Breguières, (near the hospital) – ✆ 04 92 91 82 00 – www.thalazur.fr – antibes@thalazur.fr – Fax 04 93 65 94 14 – Reopening in the spring after refurbishment
164 rm – €69/299 €93/299, €15 **Rest** – Carte €34/55
◆ The hotel and thalassotherapy centre have just been fully renovated. Large, well-equipped rooms (some with a view of the bay); attractive panoramic swimming pools. Traditional or special-diet meals served in the veranda-dining room with a marine decor.

Bleu Marine without rest
chemin des 4 Chemins, (near the hospital) – ✆ 04 93 74 84 84 – www.bleumarineantibes.com – hotel-bleu-marine@wanadoo.fr – Fax 04 93 95 90 26
18 rm – €58/65 €68/82, €7
◆ A modern hotel near the hospital. Practical, well-maintained rooms. The rooms on the top floors have a view of the sea.

Chrys Hôtel without rest
50 chemin de la Parouquine, route nationale 7 – ✆ 04 92 91 70 20 – www.chrys-hotel.com – chrys-hotel@wanadoo.fr – Fax 04 92 91 70 21 – Closed 15 December-7 January
31 rm – €69/95 €82/110, €10
◆ A white, regional-style building with small, functional, soundproofed rooms. A welcoming breakfast room opposite the swimming pool.

CAP D'ANTIBES – 06 Alpes-Maritimes

Paris 922 – Marseille 174 – Nice 35 – Antibes 6 – Cannes 14
Plateau de la Garoupe ★★ - Jardin Thuret★ - ★ Pointe Bacon - ★ de la plate-forme du bastion (musée naval) [of the bastion platform (naval museum)].

Du Cap rest,
bd JF-Kennedy – ✆ 04 93 61 39 01 – www.hotel-du-cap-eden-roc.com – reservation@hdcer.com – Fax 04 93 67 76 04 – Open 10 April-18 October BV **x**
110 rm – €340/1640 €470/1640, €35 – 11 suites
Rest *Eden Roc* – see below
◆ A haunt of the jet set, this 19C luxury hotel is set in a large park with flowers facing the sea. Luxurious, sophisticated, spacious and peaceful - a magical place.

Impérial Garoupe
770 chemin Garoupe – ✆ 04 92 93 31 61 – www.imperial-garoupe.com – cap@imperial-garoupe.com – Fax 04 92 93 31 62 – Open 15 April-25 October BV **r**
30 rm – €295/670 €295/670, €27 – 4 suites
Rest *Le Pavillon* – *✆ 04 92 93 31 64 (open 29 December-25 October and closed Tuesday 1st January-15 April and Wednesday)* Carte €75/100
◆ Beautiful Mediterranean residence surrounded by luxuriant vegetation. The highly sophisticated rooms are personalised and have a balcony, terrace or tiny private garden. Southern cuisine suited to the smart dining room decoration.

Don César rm,
46 bd de la Garoupe – ✆ 04 93 67 15 30 – www.hotel-doncesar.com – hotel.don.cesar@wanadoo.fr – Fax 04 93 67 18 25 – Open 13 March-5 November BV **s**
21 rm – €165/335 €165/495, €20
Rest – *(Open 15 April-30 September and Closed Sunday and Monday) (dinner only) (number of covers limited, pre-book)* Menu €45 – Carte €54/70
◆ Among the pluses of this large Mediterranean villa: a private terrace overlooking the sea for each of the extremely luxurious rooms, and an inviting infinity edge swimming pool. Intimate dining room. Inventive cuisine with an emphasis on regional produce.

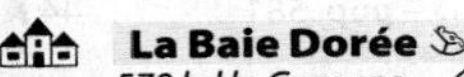

La Baie Dorée
579 bd la Garoupe – 04 93 67 30 67 – www.baiedoree.com – baiedoree@wanadoo.fr – Fax 04 92 93 76 39 BV **v**
18 rm – €240/520 €240/520, €20
Rest – *(open from April to September)* Carte €60/90
◆ This bright Mediterranean villa practically has its "feet in the water". Rooms are welcoming, well cared-for, with a terrace or balcony, all have a view over the bay. Private jetty. In fine weather, the tables are laid facing the sea. Seafood cuisine.

Beau Site without rest
141 bd Kennedy – 04 93 61 53 43 – www.hotelbeausite.net – hbeausit@club-internet.fr – Fax 04 93 67 78 16 – Open 1st March-5 November BV **t**
27 rm – €70/135 €80/200, €13
◆ A neat façade, rooms with furniture painted in 18C Provençal style, a shaded terrace and the swimming pool are the attractions of this friendly hotel on a delicious peninsula.

La Garoupe et Gardiole without rest
60 chemin Garoupe – 04 92 93 33 33 – www.hotel-lagaroupe-gardiole.com – info@hotel-lagaroupe-gardiole.com – Fax 04 93 67 61 87 – Open 27 March-18 October BV **k**
37 rm – €78/130 €98/175, €12
◆ Attractive houses restored in Provençal style enhanced by a pool, garden and splendid pergola-terrace. Fresh-looking rooms in the Garoupe and a more rustic look in the Gardiole.

Castel Garoupe without rest
959 bd la Garoupe – 04 93 61 36 51 – www.castel-garoupe.com – castel-garoupe@wanadoo.fr – Fax 04 93 67 74 88 – Open from March to October
25 rm – €96/145 €128/169, €10 – 3 suites BV **a**
◆ The interior sports a mixture of antique furniture and ornaments and modern decoration. Comfortable rooms with balcony. Swimming pool in a lush garden; new tennis court.

Eden Roc – Hôtel du Cap
bd JF-Kennedy – 04 93 61 39 01 – www.hotel-du-cap-eden-roc.com – reservation@hdcer.com – Fax 04 93 67 76 04 – Open 10 April-18 October
Rest – Carte €106/296 BV **z**
◆ A superb villa, in splendid isolation on a rock by the sea: it would be difficult to find a better location for sampling the luxury of this mythical establishment where lingering at a table on the terrace is a must.

Bacon
bd Bacon – 04 93 61 50 02 – www.restaurantdebacon.com – contact@restaurantdebacon.com – Fax 04 93 61 65 19 – Open 1st March-31 October and closed Tuesday lunch and Monday BU **m**
Rest – Menu €49 (weekday lunch)/79 – Carte €80/230
Spec. Délices de loup truffé. Bouillabaisse. Millefeuille tiède. **Wines** Bellet, Côte de Provence.
◆ This family-run establishment (since 1948) is well-known for its seafood cuisine. Elegant, discreet décor with a touch of the ocean wave.

Les Pêcheurs
10 bd Mar. Juin – 04 92 93 71 55 – www.lespecheurs-lecap.com – information@lespecheurs-lecap.com – Fax 04 92 93 15 04 – Open 1st May-1st November BV **u**
Rest – *(dinner only)* Menu €80/105 – Carte €75/137
Rest *La Plage* – 04 92 93 13 30 *(open April-September and closed dinner except in July-August)* Carte €41/70
Spec. Risotto moelleux de langoustine en parfum de crustacés. Poissons de Méditerranée cuits au plat. Intemporel feuillet des bois, fraîcheur passion et crème légère. **Wines** Les Baux-de-Provence, Côtes de Provence.
◆ Attractive, modern decor, a delightful terrace with a panoramic view and subtle food using produce from the sea offered in this restaurant superbly situated at the water's edge. The Plage restaurant serves simple meals under the seaside pine trees.

ANTONY – 92 Hauts-de-Seine – **311** J3 – **101** 25 – see Paris, Area

ANTRAIGUES-SUR-VOLANE – 07 Ardèche – 331 I5 – pop. 581 – alt. 470 m – ✉ 07530 Lyon - Rhone Valley
44 **A3**

Paris 637 – Aubenas 15 – Lamastre 58 – Langogne 67 – Privas 42 – Le Puy-en-Velay 75

Syndicat d'initiative, le village ✆ 04 75 88 23 06, Fax 04 75 88 23 06

La Remise

at the pont de l'Huile – ✆ 04 75 38 70 74 – Closed 23 June-3 July, 7-15 September, 14 December-5 January, Sunday dinner, Thursday dinner and Friday except July-August

Rest – *(pre-book)* Menu € 22/35

◆ Here, the owner of the house presents orally the choice of regional recipes which depend on the products available at the daily market. Informal service and gingham tablecloths in an old Ardèche barn.

ANZIN-ST-AUBIN – 62 Pas-de-Calais – 301 J6 – see Arras

AOSTE – 38 Isère – 333 G4 – pop. 1 914 – alt. 221 m – ✉ 38490 French Alps
45 **C2**

Paris 512 – Belley 25 – Chambéry 37 – Grenoble 55 – Lyon 71

in la Gare de l'Est 2 km northeast on D 1516 – ✉ 38490 Aoste

Au Coq en Velours with rm

1800 rte de St-Genix – ✆ 04 76 31 60 04 – www.au-coq-en-velours.com – contact@au-coq-en-velours.com – Fax 04 76 31 77 55 – Closed 19-28 August, 31 December-29 January, Thursday dinner (except hotel), Sunday dinner and Monday

7 rm – †€ 68/76 ††€ 68/76, ☕ € 10 **Rest** – Menu € 29/59 – Carte € 35/55

◆ Smart village inn run by the same family since 1900. Warm contemporary dining room decorated on a cockerel theme, flower-decked garden and terrace, tasty regional menu. Large rooms, peaceful opposite the garden.

APPOIGNY – 89 Yonne – 319 E4 – see Auxerre

APREMONT – 73 Savoie – 333 I4 – pop. 934 – alt. 330 m – ✉ 73190
46 **F2**

Paris 569 – Grenoble 50 – Albertville 48 – Chambéry 9 – St-Jean-de-Maurienne 71

du Granier Apremont Chemin de Fontaine Rouge, N : 1 km on D 201, ✆ 04 79 28 21 26

Col de Granier: ≤★★ from chalet-hotel terraces, Southwest: 14 km, French Alps.

Auberge St-Vincent

– ✆ 04 79 28 21 85 – gvandenbussches@yahoo.fr – Fax 04 79 71 62 06 – Closed Sunday dinner, Tuesday and Wednesday

Rest – Menu € 16 (weekday lunch)/30 – Carte approx. € 45

◆ This charming inn, popular with the locals, stands in the heart of a village famous for its wine. Traditional fare in a rustic setting or on the terrace. Booking advised.

APT – 84 Vaucluse – 332 F10 – pop. 11 300 – alt. 250 m – ✉ 84400 Provence
42 **E1**

Paris 728 – Aix-en-Provence 56 – Avignon 54 – Digne-les-Bains 91

Office de tourisme, 20, avenue Ph. de Girard ✆ 04 90 74 03 18, Fax 04 90 04 64 30

Plan on next page

Le Couvent without rest

36 r. Louis-Rousset – ✆ 04 90 04 55 36 – www.loucouvent.com – loucouvent@wanadoo.fr – Fax 08 71 33 50 81
B **d**

5 rm ☕ – †€ 85/95 ††€ 95/140

◆ Inside the walls of this former 17C convent you will forget that you are in the middle of the town centre. Rooms full of character, opening onto a garden. Breakfast under the refectory's vaulted ceiling.

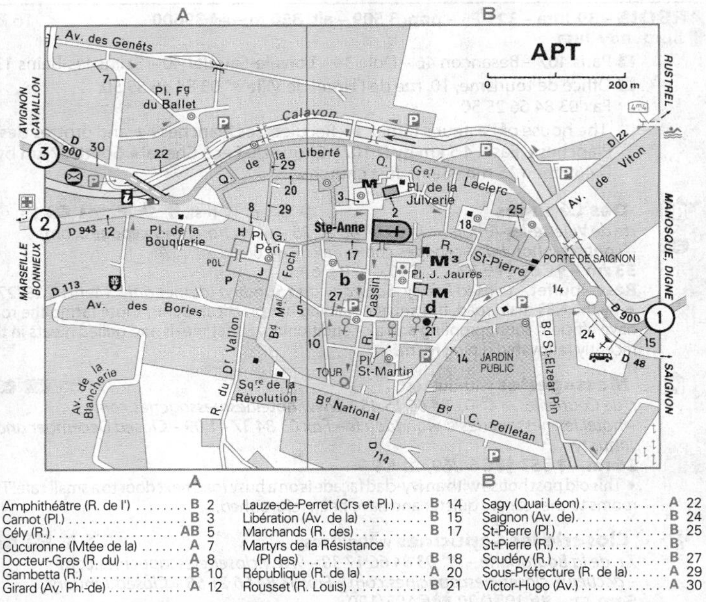

Amphithéâtre (R. de l')	B	2	Lauze-de-Perret (Crs et Pl.)	B	14	Sagy (Quai Léon)	A	22
Carnot (Pl.)	B	3	Libération (Av. de la)	B	15	Saignon (Av. de)	B	24
Cély (R.)	AB	5	Marchands (R. des)	B	17	St-Pierre (Pl.)	B	25
Cucuronne (Mtée de la)	A	7	Martyrs de la Résistance (Pl des)	B	18	St-Pierre (R.)	B	
Docteur-Gros (R. du)	A	8				Scudéry (R.)	B	27
Gambetta (R.)	B	10	République (R. de la)	A	20	Sous-Préfecture (R. de la)	A	29
Girard (Av. Ph.-de)	A	12	Rousset (R. Louis)	B	21	Victor-Hugo (Av.)	A	30

in Saignon 4 km Southeast by D 48 – **pop. 1 005 – alt. 450 m – ✉ 84400**

Auberge du Presbytère

pl. de la fontaine – ✆ 04 90 74 11 50 – www.auberge-presbytere.com – auberge.presbytere@wanadoo.fr – Fax 04 90 04 68 51 – Closed mid-January to end February

16 rm – †€ 50/100 ††€ 50/200, ☕ € 11

Rest – *(closed Wednesday) (pre-book)* Menu € 29/39

◆ Antique furniture, red floor tiles, exposed beams and a fireplace uphold the spirit of this lovely house. Pleasant rooms, two of which have a terrace with a matchless view. Pretty dining room and veranda, patio and terrace set up at lunch time on the village square.

Chambre de séjour avec vue without rest

r. de la Burgade – ✆ 04 90 04 85 01 – www.chambreavecvue.com – info@chambreavecvue.com – Fax 04 90 04 85 01 – Open March to November

5 rm ☕ – †€ 80 ††€ 80/100

◆ A guesthouse that regularly welcomes resident artists. Contemporary artwork throughout and minimalist rooms decorated with the precision of an art collector.

ARAGON – 11 Aude – 344 E3 – see Carcassonne

ARBIGNY – 01 Ain – 328 C2 – pop. 349 – alt. 280 m – ✉ 01190 44 B1

Paris 381 – Lyon 99 – Bourg-en-Bresse 61 – Chalon-sur-Saône 42 – Mâcon 28

Moulin de la Brevette without rest

rte de Cuisery – ✆ 03 85 36 49 27 – www.moulindelabrevette.com – contact@moulindelabrevette.com – Fax 03 85 30 66 91 – Closed one week in February and for the All Saint's Day holidays

17 rm – †€ 48 ††€ 52, ☕ € 8

◆ In the tranquil greenery, this 18C mill beside the river offers simple, fresh rooms. Breakfast is served in a rustic dining room or in the courtyard.

ARBOIS – 39 Jura – 321 E5 – pop. 3 509 – alt. 350 m – ✉ 39600 16 B2

Burgundy-Jura

Paris 407 – Besançon 46 – Dole 34 – Lons-le-Saunier 40 – Salins-les-Bains 13

Office de tourisme, 10, rue de l'Hôtel de Ville ✆ 03 84 66 55 50, Fax 03 84 66 25 50

The house of Pasteur's father ★ - Reculée des Planches★★ and grottes des Planches★ East : 4,5 km by D 107 - Cirque du Fer à Cheval★ South : 7 km by D 469 then 15 mn - Saint-Just church★.

Des Cépages

rm, rest, VISA

rte de Villette-les-Arbois – ✆ 03 84 66 25 25 – www.hotel-des-cepages.com – contact@hotel-des-cepages.com – Fax 03 84 66 08 24

33 rm – €63 €72, €11 – ½ P €62

Rest – buffet – *(closed Friday, Saturday and Sunday) (dinner only)* Menu €19/27

◆ By the N83 main road, this square building has practical rooms; those facing the road have efficient soundproofing and air-conditioning. Buffet meals and grilled meats in the recently renovated dining room.

Messageries without rest

VISA

r. de Courcelles – ✆ 03 84 66 15 45 – www.hoteldesmessageries.com – hotel.lesmessageries@wanadoo.fr – Fax 03 84 37 41 09 – Closed December and January

26 rm – €53 €64/69, €9

◆ This old post house with an ivy-clad façade is on a busy road next door to a small café. The rooms to the rear are quieter and have been refurbished.

Closerie les Capucines without rest

VISA

7 r. de la Bourgogne – ✆ 03 84 66 17 38 – www.closerielescapucines.com – accueil@closerielescapucines.com – Fax 03 84 66 21 58 – Closed January

5 rm – €105/120 €105/120

◆ This former 17C convent tries hard to be quiet, authentic and comfortable... and succeeds, thanks to its modern, personalised guestrooms, delightful patio and smart garden.

Jean-Paul Jeunet with rm

rest, VISA

9 r. de l'Hôtel-de-Ville – ✆ 03 84 66 05 67 – www.jeanpauljeunet.com – jpjeunet@wanadoo.fr – Fax 03 84 66 24 20 – Closed December, January, Tuesday and Wednesday except dinner July-mid September

19 rm – €72/92 €88/140, €17 – ½ P €118/130

Rest – Menu €55/135 – Carte €80/110

Spec. Truffes et pomme de terre ratte. Poularde de Bresse aux morilles. Macaron aux noix (autumn). Wines Arbois, Château-Chalon.

◆ This gourmet restaurant has a winning combination of an elegantly rustic dining room, shaded terrace, inventive local cuisine and a superb wine list.

Le Prieuré

P VISA

– Closed December, January, Tuesday and Wednesday from mid September to June

7 rm – €72/88 €88/130

◆ A comfortable 17C building with a pleasant flowering garden 200m away from the main residence. It offers comfortable rooms with period furnishings.

La Balance Mets et Vins

VISA

47 r. de Courcelles – ✆ 03 84 37 45 00 – www.labalance.fr – contact@labalance.fr – Fax 03 84 66 14 55 – Closed 22-29 June, 22 December-5 March, Tuesday dinner from September to June and Wednesday

Rest – Menu (€19 bi), €23/55 – Carte €37/49

◆ The chef of this restaurant is a wine lover and concocts his dishes using a splash of wine from the Jura region. Minimalist interior décor, pleasant terrace and fine selection of regional wines.

Le Caveau d'Arbois

P VISA

3 rte de Besançon – ✆ 03 84 66 10 70 – www.caveau-arbois.com – contact@caveau-arbois.com – Fax 03 84 37 49 62

Rest – Menu (€14 bi), €19/35 – Carte €30/49

◆ A regional style building on the edge of Arbois. Traditional fare, embellished with local specialities is savoured in a light and soberly decorated dining room.

ARBONNE – 64 Pyrénées-Atlantiques – 342 C4 – see Biarritz

L'ARBRESLE – 69 Rhône – 327 G4 – pop. 6 020 – alt. 230 m – ✉ 69210 43 E1

Paris 453 – Lyon 28 – Mâcon 68 – Roanne 58 – Villefranche-sur-Saône 23

Office de tourisme, 18, place Sapéon ☎ 04 74 01 48 87

Capucin

27 r. P.-Brossolette – ☎ 04 37 58 02 47 – restaucap@msn.com – Closed 4-27 August, 22 December-2 January, Sunday and Monday

Rest – Menu € 14 bi (weekday lunch), € 19/31 – Carte € 28/42

◆ A 17C house bordering a pedestrian street on which it sets up its summer terrace. Exposed stone and rustic chairs indoors. Classic menu.

ARCACHON – 33 Gironde – 335 D7 – pop. 12 200 – alt. 5 m – Casino BZ – ✉ 33120 Atlantic Coast 3 B2

Paris 650 – Agen 196 – Bayonne 181 – Bordeaux 67 – Dax 145 – Royan 192

Office de tourisme, esplanade Georges Pompidou ☎ 05 57 52 97 97, Fax 05 57 52 97 77

d'Arcachon La Teste-de-Buch 35 boulevard d'Arcachon, ☎ 05 56 54 44 00

Seafront★: ≤★ of the pier - Boulevard de la Mer★ - La Ville d'Hiver★ - Musée de la maquette marine: port★ BZ **M.**

Plan on following page

Park Inn without rest

4 r. Prof.-Jolyet – ☎ 05 56 83 99 91 – www.parkinn.fr – info.arcachon@rezidorparkinn.com – Fax 05 56 83 87 92 – Closed 14-29 December BZ **r**

57 rm – †€ 91/197 ††€ 101/208, ☕ € 15

◆ Contemporary hotel facing the sea with modern comforts. Choose rooms with a balcony and view of the Bassin d'Arcachon. Conference rooms in the adjoining congress centre.

Point France without rest

1 r. Grenier – ☎ 05 56 83 46 74 – www.hotel-point-france.com – hotel-point-france@hotel-point-france.com – Fax 05 56 22 53 24 – Open from March to beg. of November BZ **q**

34 rm – †€ 88/116 ††€ 98/188, ☕ € 13

◆ Pleasant 1970s hotel whose rooms have been renovated and decorated in different styles, from modern to more ethnic. Some have seafront terraces.

Les Vagues

9 bd de l'Océan – ☎ 05 56 83 03 75 – www.lesvagues.fr – info@lesvagues.fr – Fax 05 56 83 77 16 AZ **b**

33 rm – †€ 73/189 ††€ 73/189, ☕ € 13 – ½ P € 89/143

Rest – *(open 10 April-end October)* Menu € 30/37 – Carte € 27/51

◆ This hotel offers direct access to the beach. Spruce, well-equipped rooms; those on the top floor are enlarged by a bow-window. Panoramic view from this pleasant dining room with a nautical decor. Fish, seafood and traditional dishes.

Les Mimosas without rest

77bis av. de la République – ☎ 05 56 83 45 86 – www.mimosas-hotel.com – contact.hotel@wanadoo.fr – Fax 05 56 22 53 40 – Open 15 February-15 November BZ **f**

21 rm – †€ 45/60 ††€ 50/85, ☕ € 6,50

◆ Two regional-style buildings in a quiet residential area with modest, rustic, well-kept rooms. Pleasant summer terrace and reasonable prices.

Le Patio

10 bd de la Plage – ☎ 05 56 83 02 72 – www.lepatio-thierryrenou.com – lepatio.sarl@wanadoo.fr – Fax 05 56 54 89 98 – Closed 19-31 October, 16-28 February, Sunday dinner and Wednesday

Rest – Menu (€ 37 bi), € 53/70 – Carte € 56/70 BX **t**

◆ This restaurant sports a trendy new lime green, chocolate and taupe colour scheme. The dining room opens onto a patio terrace. Cuisine focused on fish and seafood.

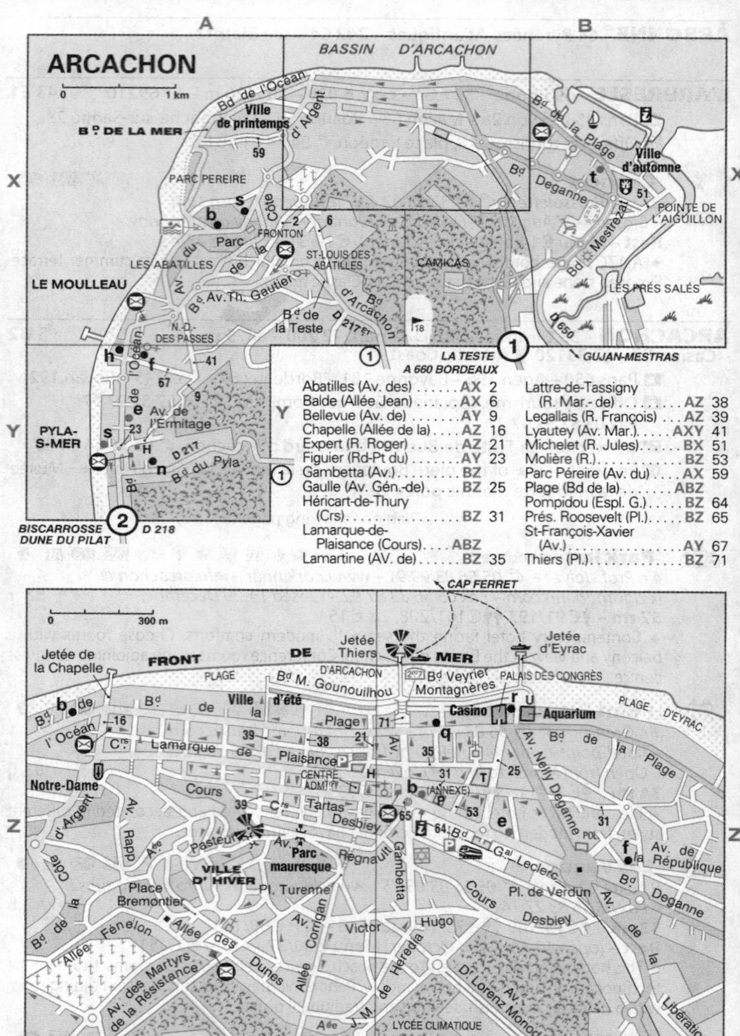

Aux Mille Saveurs

25 bd Gén.-Leclerc – ✆ 05 56 83 40 28
– www.auxmillesaveurs.com – auxmillesaveurs@wanadoo.fr
– Fax 05 56 83 12 14 – Closed 26 October-6 November, 15-24 February, Sunday dinner except July-August, Tuesday dinner except August and Wednesday

Rest – Menu € 20 (weekday lunch), € 30/48 – Carte € 42/63

BZ **e**

◆ A wide array of subtly spiced flavours with contemporary touches. The large dining room has been completely redecorated and extended by a veranda.

Chez Yvette

59 bd Gén.-Leclerc – ☎ 05 56 83 05 11 – restaurant.yvette@orange.fr – Fax 05 56 22 51 62 BZ **b**

Rest – Menu € 21 – Carte € 35/73

◆ This restaurant renowned for its seafood is a local institution. It has been run by a family of oyster-farmers for over 30 years. Nautical setting and a lively atmosphere.

in Abatilles **2 km Southwest– ✉ 33120 Arcachon**

Novotel rest, VISA

av. du Parc – ☎ 05 57 72 06 72 – www.novotel.com – h3382@accor.com – Fax 05 57 72 06 82 – Closed 4-17 January AX **b**

94 rm – €118/185 €149/185, €15

Rest *Côté d'Arguin* – Menu (€ 19 bi), € 29/40 bi – Carte € 42/104

◆ A new Novotel in a pine grove 100m from the beach, combined with a thalassotherapy centre. Modern, comfortable rooms. Solarium. Appealing menu with flavours of the sea, slimmers' menu and a good choice of Côté d'Arguin Bordeaux.

Parc without rest VISA

5 av. du Parc – ☎ 05 56 83 10 58 – www.hotelduparc-arcachon.com – b.dronne@wanadoo.fr – Fax 05 56 54 05 30 – Open 1st May-30 September

30 rm – €70/90 €78/109 AX **s**

◆ Surrounded by pine trees, this family hotel, run by the second generation, is enjoying a new lease of life. Spacious comfortable rooms with balconies.

in Moulleau **5 km Southwest– ✉ 33120 Arcachon**

Yatt without rest VISA

253 bd Côte-d'Argent – ☎ 05 57 72 03 72 – www.yatt-hotel.com. – information@yatt-hotel.com – Fax 05 56 22 51 34 – Open April-October

28 rm – €48/75 €48/75, €8 AY **h**

◆ Hotel with a bright white façade. Simple and well-kept rooms, smaller on the first floor. Buffet breakfast. Terrace.

Les Buissonnets without rest VISA

12 r. L.-Garros – ☎ 05 56 54 00 83 – http://hotelbuissonnets.monsite.wanadoo.fr – hotellesbuissonnets@wanadoo.fr – Fax 05 56 22 55 13 – Closed October and January AY **f**

13 rm – €100 €100, €9

◆ An attractive villa (1895) covered in Virginia creeper. Most of the practical, discreetly personalised rooms overlook a flower garden. Shop selling local produce.

ARCANGUES – **64 Pyrénées-Atlantiques** – **342** C4 – **see Biarritz**

ARC-EN-BARROIS – **52 Haute-Marne** – **313** K6 – **pop. 773** – **alt. 270 m** 14 **C3**
– ✉ **52210** Northern France and the Paris Region

Paris 263 – Bar-sur-Aube 55 – Châtillon-sur-Seine 44 – Chaumont 24 – Langres 30

Office de tourisme, place Moreau ☎ 03 25 02 52 17, Fax 03 25 02 52 17

d'Arc-en-Barrois Club House, S : 1 km on D 6, ☎ 03 25 01 54 54

Du Parc VISA

1 pl. Moreau – ☎ 03 25 02 53 07 – www.relais-sud-champagne.com – parc.arc@orange.fr – Fax 03 25 02 42 84 – Closed 28 February-15 April, Sunday dinner and Monday from 16 April to 15 June, Tuesday dinner and Wednesday from 1st September to 28 February

16 rm – €59 €65, €8 – ½ P €62

Rest – Menu (€ 15), € 19/42 – Carte € 21/52

◆ Former staging post, parts of which date from the 17C, housing small, renovated rooms in warm colours. Classic cuisine served in a dining room with parquet flooring and period furnishings. Contemporary decor in the brasserie.

ARCHAMPS – **74 Haute-Savoie** – **328** J4 – **see St-Julien-en-Genevois**

ARCHINGEAY – **17 Charente-Maritime** – **324** F4 – **pop. 597** – **alt. 22 m** – ✉ 17380 38 **B2**

▶ Paris 462 – La Rochelle 55 – Niort 64 – Poitiers 128

Les Hortensias & rm, P

16 r. des Sablières – ✆ 05 46 97 85 70 – www.chambres-hotes-hortensias.com – jpmt.jacques@wanadoo.fr – Fax 05 46 97 61 89 – Closed 22 December-15 January

3 rm – †€ 53 ††€ 56/62 **Table d'hôte** – Menu € 24 bi

◆ This former wine-producing farm is very peaceful. The rooms and the suite have lovely Charentes, cherry wood furniture. You may have your copious breakfast whilst admiring the flower-decked garden, the vegetable plot and the small orchard. Family food.

ARCINS – **33 Gironde** – **335** G4 – **see Margaux**

ARCIZANS-AVANT – **65 Hautes-Pyrénées** – **342** L7 – **see Argelès-Gazost**

LES ARCS – **73 Savoie** – **333** N4 – **Winter sports : 1 600/3 226 m** 7 54 – ✉ **73700 Bourg St Maurice** French Alps 45 **D2**

▶ Paris 644 – Albertville 64 – Bourg-St-Maurice 11 – Chambéry 113 – Val-d'Isère 41

Office de tourisme, 105, place de la Gare ✆ 04 79 07 12 57, Fax 04 79 07 24 90

Arc 1800 ★ - Arc 1600 ★ - Arc 2000 ★ - Le Transac cable car ★★ - La Cachette chairlift ★.

Grand Hôtel Paradiso & rm, VISA AE

Les Arcs 1800, (Charmettoger village) – ✆ 04 79 07 65 00 – www.grand-hotel-lesarcs.com – reservation@grandhotelparadiso.com – Fax 04 79 07 64 08 – Open July-August and 23 December-18 April

81 rm – †€ 215/255 ††€ 330/380 – 6 suites – ½ P € 145/190

Rest – Menu € 30 (dinner) – Carte € 30/50

◆ A happy marriage of Savoyard decor and modern comfort depict this chalet at the foot of the slopes. Some rooms command a view of Mont Blanc. Sundeck and pool. Sample brasserie dishes and relax on the panoramic terrace overlooking the valley.

LES ARCS – **83 Var** – **340** N5 – **pop. 6 217** – **alt. 80 m** – ✉ **83460** French Riviera 41 **C3**

▶ Paris 848 – Cannes 59 – Draguignan 11 – Fréjus 25 – St-Raphaël 29

Polyptyque★ in the church - Ste-Roseline chapel ★ Northeast: 4 km.

Le Relais des Moines AC P VISA AE

1.5 km eastward along the St. Roseline road – ✆ 04 94 47 40 93 – www.lerelaisdesmoines.com – contact@lerelaisdesmoines.com – Fax 04 94 47 40 93 – Closed 22 November-15 December, Sunday dinner from September to June and Monday

Rest – Menu (€ 28 bi), € 36/70 – Carte € 60/80

◆ This former sheepfold built on the hillside used to house monks. Lovely 16C stone arches and a charming shady terrace enhance the rustic interior. An ideal spot to enjoy contemporary cuisine.

Logis du Guetteur with rm AC rm, P VISA AE

at the village médiéval – ✆ 04 94 99 51 10 – www.logisduguetteur.com – contact@logisduguetteur.com – Fax 04 94 99 51 29 – Closed 15 February-16 March

13 rm – †€ 90/150 ††€ 90/230, € 17

Rest – Menu (€ 29), € 44/95 – Carte € 55/80

◆ Discover the picturesque charm of a medieval 11C abode complete with keep. Dining rooms beneath ancient vaulted ceilings, panoramic terrace and cuisine suited to modern tastes. Rustic-bourgeois is the style of the rooms in this authentic building.

ARC-SUR-TILLE – 21 Côte-d'Or – 320 L5 – pop. 2 450 – alt. 219 m – ✉ 21560 8 D1

▶ Paris 323 – Avallon 119 – Besançon 97 – Dijon 13 – Langres 73

Auberge Les Marronniers

16 r. de Dijon – ✆ 03 80 37 09 62 – les.marronniers.arc@wanadoo.fr – Fax 03 80 37 24 94

18 rm – †€ 60 ††€ 85, ☕ € 9 **Rest** – Menu € 23 (weekdays)/66

◆ Large, prettily decorated rooms (wrought iron, painted wood, coloured fabrics) and with particularly well-designed bathrooms. A rustic style dining room with a shellfish tank. Pretty terrace beneath horse chestnut trees.

ARDENAIS – 18 Cher – 323 K7 – pop. 195 – alt. 233 m – ✉ 18170 12 C3

▶ Paris 299 – Orléans 173 – Bourges 66 – Montluçon 46 – Issoudun 51

Domaine de Vilotte

4 km south on D 38 – ✆ 02 48 96 04 96 – www.domainedevilotte.com – tour.dev@wanadoo.fr – Fax 02 48 96 04 96 – Open from April to October

5 rm ☕ – †€ 80 ††€ 90 **Table d'hôte** – Menu € 25 bi

◆ Discover the bucolic charm of this family-run farm surrounded by a splendid park with a lake, set in the heart of the countryside. Pretty Empire style interior that is patinated with age. Table d'hôte located in an old-fashioned kitchen (copper pans, beams). Local dishes.

ARDENTES – 36 Indre – 323 H6 – pop. 3 616 – alt. 172 m – ✉ 36120 12 C3

Dordogne-Berry-Limousin

▶ Paris 275 – Argenton-sur-Creuse 43 – Bourges 66 – Châteauroux 14 – La Châtre 23

La Gare

2 r. de la Gare – ✆ 02 54 36 20 24 – Fax 02 54 36 92 07 – Closed 21 July-12 August, Sunday dinner, Wednesday dinner, Monday and bank holidays dinner

Rest – Menu € 23 (weekdays)/31

◆ Situated in a quiet area near the old station, a relatively uninteresting façade conceals a rustic and well-laid out restaurant with exposed beams. Traditional cuisine in large portions.

ARDRES – 62 Pas-de-Calais – 301 E2 – pop. 4 171 – alt. 11 m – ✉ 62610 30 A1

Northern France and the Paris Region

▶ Paris 273 – Calais 18 – Arras 93 – Boulogne-sur-Mer 38 – Lille 90

ℹ Office de tourisme, place d'Armes ✆ 03 21 35 28 51, Fax 03 21 35 28 51

Le François 1er

pl. des Armes – ✆ 03 21 85 94 00 – www.lefrancois1er.com – lewandowski@lefrancois1er.com – Fax 03 21 85 87 53 – Closed 1st-13 September, 31 December-12 January, Sunday dinner, Wednesday dinner and Monday

Rest – Menu € 29/49 – Carte € 51/70

◆ Attractive residence on the picturesque Grand Place. The white walls enhance the tastefully elegant dining room's parquet floor and fine beams. Up-to-date cuisine.

ARÊCHES – 73 Savoie – 333 M3 – alt. 1 080 m – Winter sports : 1 050/2 300 m 15 – ✉ 73270 Beaufort sur Doron French Alps 45 D1

▶ Paris 606 – Albertville 26 – Chambéry 77 – Megève 42

ℹ Office de tourisme, route Grand Mont ✆ 04 79 38 37 57, Fax 04 79 38 16 70

◉ Hameau de Boudin★ East: 2 km.

Auberge du Poncellamont

– ✆ 04 79 38 10 23 – http://jean.peretto.free.fr – jean.peretto@free.fr – Fax 04 79 38 13 98 – Open 15 June-15 September and 20 December-15 April and closed Sunday dinner, Monday lunch and Wednesday in low season

14 rm – †€ 55/60 ††€ 70/80, ☕ € 10 – ½ P € 60/65

Rest – Menu (€ 16), € 23/41 – Carte € 30/40

◆ Situated in the village, a Savoy chalet (entirely non-smoking) is decked in flowers in summer. The rooms are simple and practical, some are attic rooms and some have balconies. Simple but pleasant country-style dining room and a terrace where one is gently rocked by the murmur of a fountain.

ARÈS – 33 Gironde – 335 E6 – pop. 5 335 – alt. 6 m – ✉ 33740 3 B1
Atlantic Coast

Paris 627 – Arcachon 47 – Bordeaux 48

Office de tourisme, esplanade G. Dartiquelongue ☎ 05 56 60 91 85, Fax 05 56 60 39 41

des Aiguilles Vertes Lanton Route de Bordeaux, SE : 12 km, ☎ 05 56 82 95 71

St-Éloi with rm VISA MC

11 bd Aérium – ☎ 05 56 60 20 46 – www.le-saint-eloi.com – nlatour2@wanadoo.fr – Closed 5 January-10 February, Wednesday dinner, Sunday dinner and Monday from 15 September to 15 June

8 rm – †€ 55/65 ††€ 60/85, ☐ € 8 – ½ P € 45/55

Rest – Menu (€ 18), € 32 (weekdays)/58

◆ White seaside house near the Bassin D'Arcachon. Pleasant contemporary dining room, terrace, traditional cuisine and ethnic-style rooms.

ARGELÈS-GAZOST – 65 Hautes-Pyrénées – 342 L6 – pop. 3 255 – alt. 462 m – Spa : mid April-late Oct. – Casino Y – ✉ 65400 28 A3
Languedoc-Roussillon-Tarn Gorges

Paris 863 – Lourdes 13 – Pau 58 – Tarbes 32

Office de tourisme, 15, place République ☎ 05 62 97 00 25, Fax 05 62 97 50 60

Plan on next page

Le Miramont rm, rest, VISA MC AE

44 av. des Pyrénées – ☎ 05 62 97 01 26 – www.bestwestern-lemiramont.com – hotel-miramont@sudfr.com – Fax 05 62 97 56 67 – Closed mid-November to mid-December Z **n**

19 rm – †€ 52/135 ††€ 65/165, ☐ € 13

Rest – *(closed Wednesday except dinner in July-August) (pre-book on weekend)* Menu (€ 15), € 22/47 bi – Carte approx. € 38

◆ This lovely white 1930s villa with a cruise liner look is set in the middle of a pretty garden. Comfortable rooms. Bright, veranda-dining room serving fine, modern cuisine.

Les Cimes rest, P VISA MC

pl. Ourout – ☎ 05 62 97 00 10 – www.hotel-lescimes.com – contact@hotel-lescimes.com – Fax 05 62 97 10 19 – Closed 2 November-25 December and 2 January-5 February Z **a**

26 rm – †€ 48/59 ††€ 69/76, ☐ € 10

Rest – Menu (€ 11 bi), € 20/45 – Carte € 20/45

◆ A large building with differently styled rooms, some of which have balconies. Pleasant flowered patio-veranda for breakfast. Indoor pool. Traditional menu in the restaurant overlooking greenery.

Soleil Levant rest, P VISA MC AE

17 av. des Pyrénées – ☎ 05 62 97 08 68 – www.lesoleillevant.com – hsoleillevant@orange.fr – Fax 05 62 97 04 60 – Closed 30 March-6 April and 24 November-23 December Y **t**

32 rm – †€ 43/52 ††€ 43/52, ☐ € 8 – ½ P € 44/49

Rest – Menu € 13 (weekdays)/44

◆ Hotel in the lower part of town with practical, well-kept rooms, some of which have a view of the surrounding mountains. Bar, lounge, terrace and well-kept garden. Two joining dining rooms with a family guesthouse atmosphere. Traditional fare.

in St-Savin 3 km South by D 101 - Z – pop. 381 – alt. 580 m – ✉ 65400

Site★ of the Piétat chapel South: 1 km.

Le Viscos with rm rest, P VISA MC AE

1 r. Lamarque – ☎ 05 62 97 02 28 – www.hotel-leviscos.com – leviscos.jpsaint-martin@wanadoo.fr – Fax 05 62 97 04 95 – Closed three weeks in January, Sunday dinner and Monday dinner from November to February, except school holidays

7 rm – †€ 65/109 ††€ 65/109, ☐ € 10 – ½ P € 78/88

Rest – *(Closed Sunday dinner and Monday dinner except July-August and Monday lunch)* Menu € 28/82 – Carte € 47/80

◆ This family inn has been welcoming guests since 1840. The dining room opens out onto a terrace with views of the mountains. Generous portions of regional cuisine. Cosy guestrooms.

ARGELÈS-GAZOST

Alicot (R. Michel) . . . . Y 3
Bourdette (R. Jean) . . . . Z 18
Bourg Neuf (R. du) . . . . Y 19
Coubertin (Av. P. de) . . . . Z 29
Dambé (Av. Jules) . . . . Y 30
Digoy (R. Capitaine) . . . . . . YZ 33
Edouard-VII (Pl.) . . . . Z 36
Foch (R. du Mar.) . . . . Y 39
Gassan (Av. Emile) . . . . Y 42
Joffre (Pl.) . . . . YZ 53
Nansouty (Av. du Gén.) . . . . . Y 69
Pasteur (R.) . . . . Z 75
Pérus (Pl.) . . . . Y 77
Poilus (R. des) . . . . Y 80
Reine Nathalie (Av.) . . . . Y 84
République (Pl. de la) . . . . Z 85
Sainte-Castere (R.) . . . . Z 91
Saint-Orens (R.) . . . . Z 88
Sassere (Av. Hector) . . . . Y 92
Sorbe (R.) . . . . Y 93
Sylvestre (Av. Armand) . . . . . Z 96
Victoire (Pl. de la) . . . . Y 100
Vieuzac (R. de) . . . . Y 101
8-Mai (R. du) . . . . Y 106

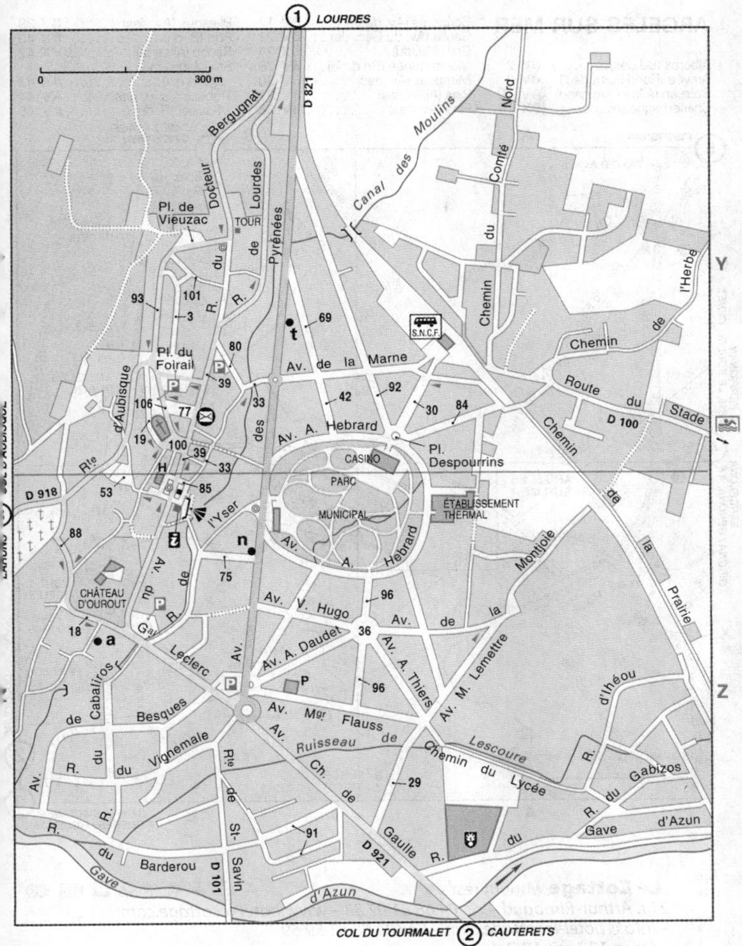

in Arcizans-Avant 4.5 km South by D 101 and D 13 – pop. 352 – alt. 640 m – ✉ 65400

Auberge Le Cabaliros with rm

16 r. de l'Église – ✆ 05 62 97 04 31 – www.auberge-cabaliros.com
– auberge.cabaliros@wanadoo.fr – Fax 05 62 97 91 48
– Closed 3 November-5 February, Tuesday and Wednesday except July-August

8 rm – †€ 59/66 ††€ 59/66, ☕ € 10 – ½ P € 55/58

Rest – Menu € 22/50 – Carte € 30/50

◆ A traditional village inn facing the peaks of the Pyrenees. The view from the terrace at one end of the rustic dining room is splendid, and a soothing log fire crackles in winter. Local dishes; clean and simple rooms.

ARGELÈS-SUR-MER – 66 Pyrénées-Orientales – 344 J7 – pop. 9 869 22 B3

– alt. 19 m – Casino : Argelès-Plage BV – ✉ 66700

Languedoc-Roussillon-Tarn Gorges

Paris 872 – Céret 28 – Perpignan 22 – Port-Vendres 9 – Prades 66

Office de tourisme, place de l'Europe ✆ 04 68 81 15 85, Fax 04 68 81 16 01

ARGELÈS-SUR-MER

Albères (Bd des) . . . . BV 2
Arrivée (Rond-Point de l') . . BV 6
Buisson (Allée Ferdinand) . AV 10
Charlemagne (Av. de). . . . . BX 16
Corbières (Av. des) . . . . BV 17
Gaulle (Av. du Gén.-de) . . . BV 21
Grau (Av. du). . . . . BX 24
Méditerranée (Bd de la) . . . BV 29
Mimosas (Av. des) . . . . BV 30
Pins (Allée des) . . . . BV 37
Pins (Av. des) . . . . BV 38
Platanes (Av. des). . . . . BV 39
Port (R. du) . . . . BX 40
Racou (Allée du) . . . . BVX 42
Ste-Madeleine (Chemin) . . . . AX 43
Trabucaires (R. des) . . . . . . AV 44
14-Juillet (R. du) . . . . AV 49

Le Cottage without rest

21 r. Arthur-Rimbaud – ✆ 04 68 81 07 33 – www.hotel-lecottage.com
– info@hotel-lecottage.com – Fax 04 68 81 59 69
– Open 10 April-17 October DY **a**

33 rm – †€ 74/300 ††€ 74/300, ☕ € 15

◆ Modern building with leisure and relaxation facilities (pool, crazy golf and spa). Nice rooms with the advantages of a garden and the peace of a residential area.

Château Valmy without rest

chemin de Valmy – ✆ 04 68 95 95 25 – www.chateau-valmy.com
– contact@chateau-valmy.com – Fax 04 68 81 15 18
– Open April-November AX **a**

5 rm ☕ – †€ 190/370 ††€ 190/370

◆ Chateau built by a Danish architect in 1900 magnificently set among the vines. Luxurious rooms with splendid sea views and wine tasting sessions.

ARGELÈS-SUR-MER

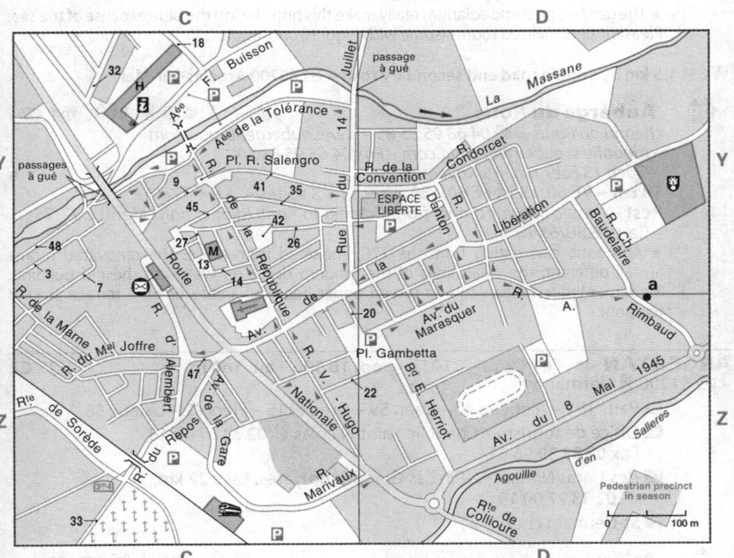

in Argelès-Plage 2,5 km East – ✉ 66700 Argelès-sur-Mer
Languedoc-Roussillon-Tarn Gorges

Southeast: Côte Vermeille★★.

Grand Hôtel du Lido
rm, VISA MC AE

50 bd de la Mer – ☎ 04 68 81 10 32 – www.hotel-le-lido.com – contact@hotel-le-lido.com – Fax 04 68 81 51 89 – Open 10 April-3 October

66 rm – †€ 80/108 ††€ 80/205, ☕ € 11 – ½ P € 75/140 BV **u**

Rest – buffet – Menu (€ 19 bi), € 26 (lunch), € 28/40 – Carte € 36/55

◆ In a pleasant location on the sea front, the Lido has well-equipped rooms with balconies or terraces, most of them with a sea view. Veranda-dining room; some meals (buffets) are also served on the terrace by the pool.

De la Plage des Pins without rest
VISA MC AE

allée des Pins – ☎ 04 68 81 09 05 – www.plage-des-pins.com – contact@plage-des-pins.com – Fax 04 68 55 19 12 – Open from mid-May to end September BV **r**

50 rm – †€ 65/150 ††€ 75/186, ☕ € 11

◆ Bordering on the Mediterranean, the hotel has plain, functional rooms with balconies. Those overlooking the sea are larger. Beautiful pool.

L'Amadeus
VISA MC

av. des Platanes – ☎ 04 68 81 12 38 – www.lamadeus.com – contact@lamadeus.com – Fax 04 68 81 12 38 – Closed 12 November-20 December, 2 January-2 February, Monday and Tuesday except dinner in high season and Wednesday lunch from 16 June to 14 September BV **n**

Rest – Menu € 24, € 29/37 – Carte € 43/61

◆ Regional specialities are served in the modern dining room decorated with house plants and a fireplace or on the pleasant teak deck. Quiet patio to the rear.

Collioure road 4 km – ✉ 66700 Argelès-sur-Mer

Les Mouettes without rest

– ✆ *04 68 81 82 83 – www.hotel-lesmouettes.com – info@hotel-lesmouettes.com – Fax 04 68 81 32 73 – Open 4 April-12 October*

31 rm – †€ 90/200 ††€ 90/200, ☕ € 15

◆ The garden, pool and solarium really make this hotel facing the blue expanse of the sea. Pleasant personalised rooms (some with loggias) and studios.

West 1,5 km by Sorède road and secondary road – ✉ 66700 Argelès-sur-Mer

Auberge du Roua

chemin du Roua – ✆ 04 68 95 85 85 – www.aubergeduroua.com – magalie@aubergeduroua.com – Fax 04 68 95 83 50 – Open 13 February-15 November AX **h**

14 rm – †€ 60/135 ††€ 60/189, ☕ € 11 – 3 suites – ½ P € 77/142

Rest – *(closed Sunday dinner from October to April) (dinner only)* Menu € 27/75 – Carte € 50/65

◆ Authentic mas dating from the 17C, sheltered from noise. The renovated rooms are all different; the clean lines of the modern decor go well with the old building. Modern, Mediterranean cuisine served under beautiful arches or on a terrace around the pool.

ARGENTAN – 61 Orne – 310 I2 – pop. 16 596 – alt. 160 m – ✉ 61200 Normandy 33 **C2**

Paris 191 – Alençon 46 – Caen 59 – Dreux 115 – Flers 42 – Lisieux 58

Office de tourisme, Chapelle Saint-Nicolas ✆ 02 33 67 12 48, Fax 02 33 39 96 61

des Haras Nonant-le-Pin Les Grandes Bruyères, East: 22 km, ✆ 02 33 27 00 19

St-Germain church ★.

Ariès rm,

Z.A. Beurrerie, 1 km via D 916 – ✆ 02 33 39 13 13 – www.arieshotel.fr – accueil@arieshotel.fr – Fax 02 33 39 34 71

43 rm – †€ 46/51 ††€ 51/60, ☕ € 8 – ½ P € 61/70

Rest – *(closed Friday dinner, Saturday and Sunday)* Menu € 10 (lunch), € 16/30 – Carte € 20/40

◆ A very well soundproofed, unpretentious hotel situated by a busy road. All the functional guestrooms are identically decorated. A light, spacious dining room, bistro-style furniture, classic menu, buffets and dishes of the day.

XXX **La Renaissance** with rm rest,

20 av. 2e-Division-Blindée – ✆ 02 33 36 14 20 – www.hotel-larenaissance.com – larenaissance.viel@wanadoo.fr – Fax 02 33 36 65 50 – Closed 13 July-3 August, 21 February-1 March and Sunday dinner

14 rm – †€ 64/86 ††€ 69/90, ☕ € 10 – ½ P € 71/97

Rest – *(closed Saturday lunch from September to June, Tuesday lunch in July-August, Sunday dinner and Monday)* Menu (€ 21), € 26/65 – Carte € 59/94

◆ Large bay windows overlooking the garden light up this elegant, rustic-bourgeois dining room, which has a lovely Renaissance-style fireplace. Tasty, inventive cuisine.

North-East 11 km by N 26 and D 729 – ✉ 61310 Silly-en-Gouffern

Pavillon de Gouffern

l'Orée du bois – ✆ 02 33 36 64 26 – www.pavillondegouffern.com – pavillondegouffern@wanadoo.fr – Fax 02 33 36 53 81

20 rm – †€ 45/130 ††€ 60/200, ☕ € 12 **Rest** – Menu (€ 25), € 38/55 bi

◆ This half-timbered, 19C-hunting lodge is situated in a park surrounded by woods. Generously dimensioned rooms, fitted out in a refreshing contemporary spirit. The two dining rooms renovated in a modern style command a fine view of the estate. Traditional cuisine.

in Fontenai-sur-Orne 4.5 km southwest – **pop. 266** – **alt. 65 m** – ✉ **61200**

XX **Faisan Doré** with rm
– ✆ 02 33 67 18 11 – www.lefaisandore.com – lefaisandore@wanadoo.fr – Fax 02 33 35 82 15 – Closed Saturday lunch and Sunday dinner
16 rm – †€ 60/150 ††€ 60/150, ☕ € 9
Rest – Menu (€ 17), € 23 (weekdays)/79 bi – Carte € 28/56
◆ A Normandy inn situated on a busy road. The dining room, reached through a cosy bar-lounge, sports a bold choice of floral patterns and bright colours. Regional menu. Gradually renovated rooms in contemporary fashionable shades of chocolate.

ARGENTAT – 19 Corrèze – 329 M5 – pop. 3 111 – alt. 183 m – ✉ 19400 25 C3

Dordogne-Berry-Limousin

Paris 503 – Aurillac 54 – Brive-la-Gaillarde 45 – Mauriac 49 – St-Céré 40 – Tulle 29

Office de tourisme, place da Maïa ✆ 05 55 28 16 05, Fax 05 55 28 45 16

Le Sablier du Temps rest, VISA AE
13 r. J.-Vachal – ✆ 05 55 28 94 90 – www.sablier-du-temps.com – lesablierdutemps@wanadoo.fr – Fax 05 55 28 94 99 – Closed 5 January-9 February
24 rm – †€ 48/55 ††€ 50/88, ☕ € 8
Rest – *(closed Friday from October to April)* Menu (€ 12), € 15 (weekday lunch), € 21/43 – Carte € 25/65
◆ This hotel near the town centre has a garden planted with trees and a pool. Functionally equipped rooms with modern decoration. Country cuisine served in a rustic dining room, on the veranda or on a leafy terrace.

Fouillade rest, VISA AE
11 pl. Gambetta – ✆ 05 55 28 10 17 – www.fouillade.com – hotel.fouillade.argentat@wanadoo.fr – Fax 05 55 28 90 52 – Closed 26 November-26 December
15 rm – †€ 48 ††€ 49/73, ☕ € 7 – ½ P € 44/55
Rest – *(closed Sunday dinner and Monday)* Menu (€ 11 bi), € 14 (weekdays)/38 – Carte € 20/50
◆ The rooms of this century-old establishment have been rejuvenated with contemporary decor, ergonomic furniture and new bedding. Traditional dishes with regional touches served under the beams of the rustic dining room; terrace at the front.

XX **Saint-Jacques** VISA
39 av. Foch – ✆ 05 55 28 89 87 – www.saintjacques-ceaux.com – lesaintjacquesceaux@orange.fr – Fax 05 55 28 86 41 – Closed 1-23 March, 28 September-12 October, Sunday dinner from October to April and Monday
Rest – Menu (€ 19 bi), € 32/47 – Carte € 39/58
◆ Monsieur rustles up local dishes in the kitchen while Madame welcomes you into a refurbished, comfortable and elegant dining room. Veranda and shaded terrace.

X **Auberge des Gabariers** VISA
15 quai Lestourgie – ✆ 05 55 28 05 87 – pascal-jacquinot@orange.fr – Fax 05 55 28 69 63 – Open 28 March-10 November and closed Tuesday dinner and Wednesday except July-August
Rest – Menu (€ 16), € 27/36 – Carte € 40/53
◆ A lovely 16C house on the banks of the Dordogne. Rustic atmosphere, spit-roast dishes and a riverside terrace in the shade of a linden tree.

ARGENTEUIL – 95 Val-d'Oise – 305 E7 – 101 14 – see Paris, Area

---

ARGENTIÈRE – 74 Haute-Savoie – 328 O5 – alt. 1 252 m – Winter sports : see Chamonix – ✉ 74400 45 D1

French Alps

Paris 619 – Annecy 106 – Chamonix-Mont-Blanc 10 – Vallorcine 10

Office de tourisme, 24, route du village ✆ 04 50 54 02 14, Fax 04 50 54 06 39

Aiguille des Grands Montets★★★: ✻★★★ - Aiguilles Rouges natural reserve ★★★ North: 3 km - Col de la Balme★★: ✻★★.

Grands Montets without rest
340 Chemin des Arberons, (near the Lognon cable car) VISA AE
– ✆ 04 50 54 06 66 – www.hotel-grands-montets.com
– info@hotel-grands-montets.com – Fax 04 50 54 05 42
– Open 26 June-30 August and 19 December-5 May
45 rm – †€ 110/190 ††€ 120/250 – 3 suites
◆ This hotel has many charming attractions: It is quiet, near the cable car, sports regional decor in the lounge bar, has a pool and rooms (some nicely refurbished) with a view.

Montana rm, VISA AE
24 clos du Montana – ✆ 04 50 54 14 99 – www.hotel-montana.fr
– info@hotel-montana.fr – Fax 04 50 54 03 40
– Open 15 June-30 September and 8 December-11 May
24 rm – †€ 137/181 ††€ 154/198 – ½ P € 176/196
Rest – *(open 15 June-30 September) (dinner only) (residents only)* Menu € 28
◆ Popular for its particularly friendly family ambiance. Plainly furnished rooms with balconies facing the Grands Montets. Restaurant with alpine decor and terrace facing the mountains. Traditional simple dishes.

ARGENTON-SUR-CREUSE – 36 Indre – 323 F7 – pop. 5 180 – alt. 100 m – ✉ 36200 Dordogne-Berry-Limousin 11 B3

Paris 297 – Châteauroux 32 – Limoges 93 – Montluçon 103 – Poitiers 100
Office de tourisme, 13, place de la République ✆ 02 54 24 05 30, Fax 02 54 24 28 13
Old bridge ≤★ - ≤★ from the terrace of N.-D.-des-Bancs chapel.

ARGENTON-SUR-CREUSE

Acacias (Allée des) . . . 2
Barbès (R.) . . . 5
Brillaud (R. Charles) . . . 6
Chapelle-N.-D. (R. de la) . . . 7
Châteauneuf (R.) . . . 8
Chauvigny (R. A. de) . . . 10
Coursière (R. de la) . . . 12
Gare (R. de la) . . . 14
Grande (R.) . . . 15
Merle-Blanc (R. du) . . . 18
Point-du-Jour (R. du) . . . 20
Pont-Neuf (R. du) . . . 23
Raspail (R.) . . . 24
République (Pl. de la) . . . 25
Rochers-St-Jean (R. des) . . . 27
Rosette (R.) . . . 28
Rousseau (R. Jean-J.) . . . 29
Tanneurs (R. des) . . . 31
Victor-Hugo (R.) . . . 33
Villers (Impasse de) . . . 35

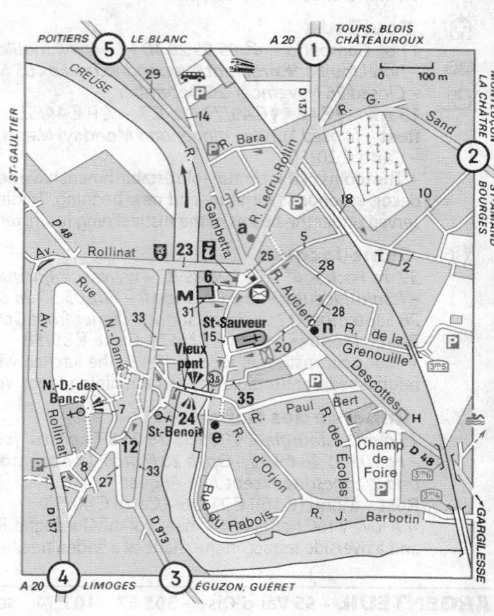

Manoir de Boisvillers without rest VISA
11 r. Moulin-de-Bord – ✆ 02 54 24 13 88 – www.manoir-de-boisvillers.com
– manoir.de.boisvillers@wanadoo.fr – Fax 02 54 24 27 83
– Closed 12 January-8 February e
16 rm – †€ 54/109 ††€ 58/109, € 8
◆ Fine 18C bourgeois residence on the banks of the Creuse. Stylish ethnic or rustic rooms, a contemporary sitting room and a pleasant poolside garden.

Le Cheval Noir rest, VISA

27 r. Auclert-Descottes – ✆ 02 54 24 00 06 – www.le-chevalnoir.fr – chevalnoirhotel@wanadoo.fr – Fax 02 54 24 11 22 – Closed Sunday dinner off season n

20 rm – €46 €60, ☕ €7 – ½ P €57

Rest – Menu (€10), €15 (lunch), €22/30 – Carte €25/38

◆ A former post house owned by the same family for over a century. Plain rooms in various sizes and styles. Modern dining room and flowered courtyard in summer. Traditional cuisine and set menu at lunchtimes.

La Source VISA AE

9 r. Ledru-rollin – ✆ 02 54 24 30 21 – Fax 02 54 24 30 21 – Closed 22-28 October,8-14 February, Tuesday dinner and Wednesday a

Rest – Menu (€15), €24/40 – Carte €38/46

◆ Family restaurant in an old post house. Two dining rooms (one rustic, the other more classic and decorated with frescos).Traditional cuisine.

in Bouësse **11 km by ② – pop. 394 – alt. 185 m – ✉ 36200**

Château de Bouesse VISA AE

– ✆ 02 54 25 12 20 – www.chateaubouesse.com – chateau.bouesse@wanadoo.fr – Fax 02 54 25 12 30 – Open 2 April-1st January and closed Monday and Tuesday except 16 May-30 September

8 rm – €85/150 €85/150, ☕ €12 – 4 suites – ½ P €88/121

Rest – Menu €22 (weekday lunch), €36/47 – Carte €58/68

◆ Joan of Arc is said to have stayed in this 13C castle surrounded by a park. Its interior has a medieval atmosphere and modern comfort. Antiques grace the rooms and there is one lovely room in the keep. An 18C decor and modern dishes in the restaurant.

ARGENT-SUR-SAULDRE – 18 Cher – 323 K1 – pop. 2 502 – alt. 171 m – ✉ 18410 Dordogne-Berry-Limousin

12 **C2**

Paris 171 – Bourges 57 – Cosne-sur-Loire 46 – Gien 22 – Orléans 62 – Salbris 42 – Vierzon 54

Relais du Cor d'Argent with rm VISA

39 r. Nationale – ✆ 02 48 73 63 49 – cordargent@wanadoo.fr – Fax 02 48 73 37 55 – Closed 30 June-10 July, 20-29 October, 16 February-18 March, Tuesday and Wednesday

7 rm – €42/44 €42/56, ☕ €8 – ½ P €45

Rest – Menu €18/58 – Carte €45/65

◆ The building is decked with flowers in summer. Discreet dining rooms serving traditional cuisine based on the market produce available. Simple little rooms.

ARGOULES – 80 Somme – 301 E5 – pop. 335 – alt. 18 m – ✉ 80120 Northern France and the Paris Region

36 **A1**

Paris 217 – Abbeville 34 – Amiens 82 – Calais 93 – Hesdin 17 – Montreuil 21

Abbey★★ and gardens★★ of Valloires Northwest: 2 km.

Auberge du Coq-en-Pâte VISA

37 rte de Valloires – ✆ 03 22 29 92 09 – Fax 03 22 29 92 09 – Closed 31 March-7 April, 1st-15 September, 5-29 January, Sunday dinner, Wednesday dinner and Monday except bank holidays

Rest – *(number of covers limited, pre-book)* Menu €20 – Carte €23/45

◆ A charming little house near Valloires Abbey. The dining room is decorated with prints and paintings of animals. Tasty half-traditional, half-modern cuisine.

Undecided between two equivalent establishments? Within each category, establishments are classified in our order of preference.

ARLEMPDES – 43 Haute-Loire – **331** F4 – **pop. 114** – **alt. 840 m** 6 **C3**
– ✉ **43490** ▮ Lyon - Rhone Valley

Paris 559 – Aubenas 67 – Langogne 27 – Le Puy-en-Velay 29

Site★★.

Le Manoir rm, VISA
– ✆ *04 71 57 17 14 – Fax 04 71 57 19 68 – Open 15 March-25 October and closed Sunday dinner except July-August*
13 rm – €35 €45/60, €8 – ½ P €44 **Rest** – Menu €17 (weekdays)/40
◆ This country house with small rooms is situated in the heart of a picturesque village, dominated by a volcanic peak and a ruined castle. Classic menu of regional inspiration; stonework and a handsome fireplace in the dining room.

ARLES – 13 Bouches-du-Rhône – **340** C3 – **pop. 52 400** – **alt. 13 m** 40 **A3**
– ✉ **13200** ▮ Provence

Paris 719 – Aix-en-Provence 77 – Avignon 37 – Marseille 94 – Nîmes 32

Office de tourisme, boulevard des Lices ✆ 04 90 18 41 20, Fax 04 90 18 41 29

Amphitheatre★★ - Théâtre antique★★ - St-Trophime cloister★★ and church★: portal★★ - Les Alyscamps★ - Palais Constantin★ Y **S** - Town hall: vestibule ★ vault Z **H** - Cryptoportiques★ Z **E** - Musée de l'Arles antique★★ (sarcophagus★★) - Museon Arlaten★ Z **M**[6] - Musée Réattu★ Y **M**[4] - Ruins of Montmajour abbey ★ 5 km by ①.

Plan on next page

Jules César VISA AE
bd des Lices – ✆ *04 90 52 52 52 – www.hotel-julescesar.fr – contact@julescesar.fr – Fax 04 90 52 52 53 – Closed Saturday and Sunday from November to March* Z **b**
50 rm – €130/315 €160/315, €20 – 1 suite
Rest *Lou Marquès* – *(Closed Saturday lunch, Sunday dinner and Monday except bank holidays)* Menu (€21), €28/60 – Carte €54/112
◆ Former Carmelite convent surrounded by a walled garden: the epitome of elegance and serenity. Beautiful antique furnished rooms, vaulted meeting rooms, cloister and chapel with a baroque altarpiece. Attractive terrace and southern flavours at the subtly modern Lou Marquès.

Nord Pinus rm, rm, VISA AE
pl. du Forum – ✆ *04 90 93 44 44 – www.nord-pinus.com – info@nord-pinus.com – Fax 04 90 93 34 00 – Open 15 February-15 November* Z **t**
24 rm – €175 €175/240, €25 – 2 suites
Rest – *(open 15 March-15 November and closed Monday and Tuesday)* Menu (€22), €28 – Carte €37/54
◆ A veritable Arles institution with such illustrious guests as Cocteau, Picasso and Dominguin whose 'traje de luces' illuminates the bar. The decor, which is a combination of baroque and bull fighting, is a treat for the eye. A pleasant restaurant with an Art Deco touch, serving brasserie-style cuisine.

L'Hôtel Particulier rm, rest, VISA AE
4 r. de la Monnaie – ✆ *04 90 52 51 40 – www.hotel-particulier.com – contact@hotel-particulier.com – Fax 04 90 96 16 70* Z **d**
8 rm – €209/289 €209/289, €22 – 5 suites **Rest** – Menu (€35), €55
◆ Superb 18C mansion in the Roquette district. Fine interior combining old and new. Rooms with personal touches. Pretty courtyard garden, sauna, steam bath, etc. Meals based on fresh produce.

D'Arlatan without rest VISA AE
26 r. Sauvage, (near Place du Forum) – ✆ *04 90 93 56 66 – www.hotel-arlatan.fr – hotel-arlatan@wanadoo.fr – Fax 04 90 49 68 45 – Closed 3 January-4 February* Y **f**
41 rm – €55/85 €85/157, €14 – 7 suites
◆ This graceful 15C residence, with 4C foundations, relives its past through exhibitions of archaeological remains. Decor with personal touches and fine antique furniture.

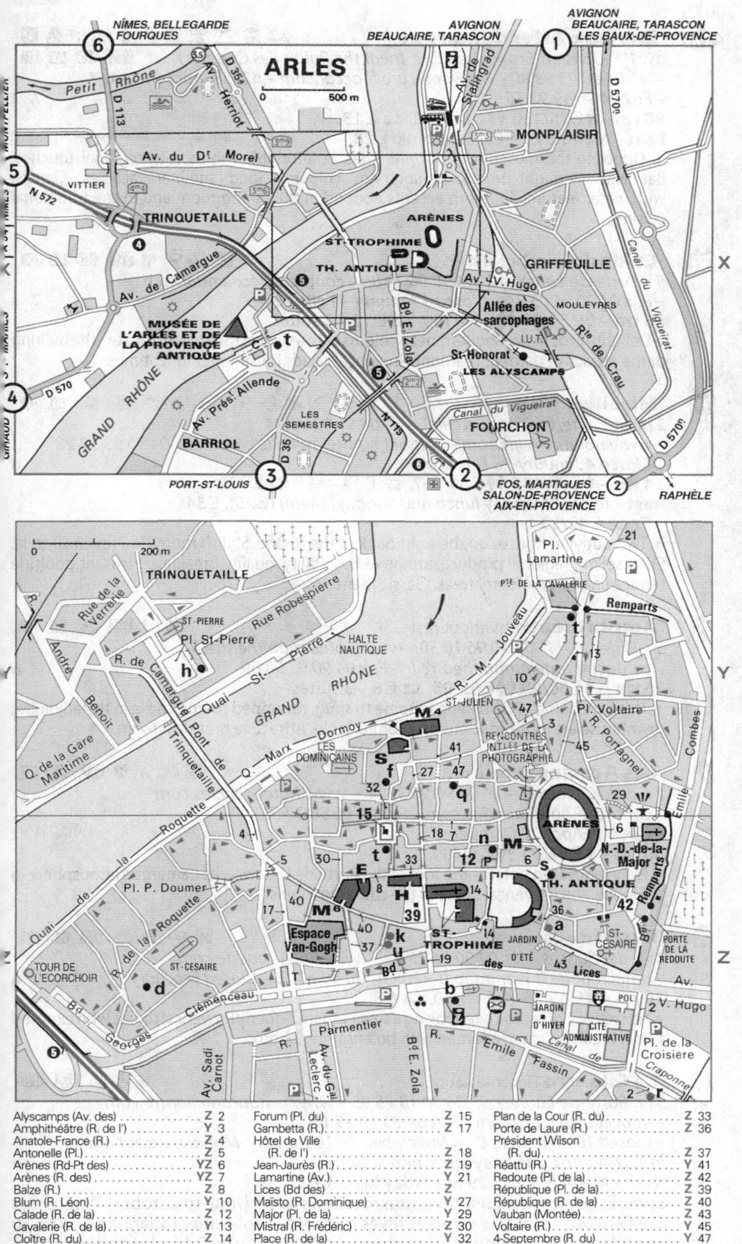

Alyscamps (Av. des) . . . . . Z 2
Amphithéâtre (R. de l') . . . . . Y 3
Anatole-France (R.) . . . . . Z 4
Antonelle (Pl.) . . . . . Z 5
Arènes (Rd-Pt des) . . . . . YZ 6
Arènes (R. des) . . . . . YZ 7
Balze (R.) . . . . . Z 8
Blum (R. Léon) . . . . . Y 10
Calade (R. de la) . . . . . Z 12
Cavalerie (R. de la) . . . . . Y 13
Cloître (R. du) . . . . . Z 14
Forum (Pl. du) . . . . . Z 15
Gambetta (R.) . . . . . Z 17
Hôtel de Ville (R. de l') . . . . . Z 18
Jean-Jaurès (R.) . . . . . Z 19
Lamartine (Av.) . . . . . Y 21
Lices (Bd des) . . . . . Z
Maïsto (R. Dominique) . . . . . Y 27
Major (Pl. de la) . . . . . Y 29
Mistral (R. Frédéric) . . . . . Z 30
Place (R. de la) . . . . . Y 32
Plan de la Cour (R. du) . . . . . Z 33
Porte de Laure (R.) . . . . . Z 36
Président Wilson (R. du) . . . . . Z 37
Réattu (R.) . . . . . Y 41
Redoute (Pl. de la) . . . . . Z 42
République (Pl. de la) . . . . . Z 39
République (R. de la) . . . . . Z 40
Vauban (Montée) . . . . . Z 43
Voltaire (R.) . . . . . Y 45
4-Septembre (R. du) . . . . . Y 47

Mercure Arles Camargue
av. 1ère -Division-Française-Libre, (near the Palais des Congrès) VISA AE
– 04 90 93 98 80 – www.mercure@accor.com – h2738@accor.com
– Fax 04 90 49 92 76 X **t**
80 rm – €75/130 €87/140, €13
Rest – Menu €20 – Carte approx. €28
◆ Opposite the museum of ancient Arles, comfortable rooms with regional touches. Bar with wrought iron and southern colours. Good seminar facilities. Garden with water feature. Southern accents abound in the dining room and in the traditional cuisine.

Calendal without rest VISA AE
5 r. Porte-de-Laure – 04 90 96 11 89 – contact@lecalendal.com
– Fax 04 90 96 05 84 – Closed 4 January-4 February Z **s**
35 rm – €59/99 €99/159, €12 – 3 suites
◆ Delightful rooms in Mediterranean colours with a view of the ancient theatre, the bullring or the attractive garden. Tearoom. Provençal salads for summer lunchtimes.

Mireille rest, VISA AE
2 pl. St-Pierre, (at Trinquetaille) – 04 90 93 70 74
– www.hotel-mireille.com – contact@hotel-mireille.com – Fax 04 90 93 87 28
– Closed 4 January-28 February Y **h**
34 rm – €75/135 €89/157, €14 – ½ P €89/122
Rest – *(closed Monday lunch and Sunday)* Menu (€25), €34
– Carte €42/53
◆ Two outlying houses on the right bank of the Rhône. Stylish rooms in Provencal style. Shop selling regional produce, attentive hospitality, quality breakfast. Pleasant poolside terrace lined by mulberry trees. Classic menu.

Amphithéâtre without rest VISA AE
5 r. Diderot – 04 90 96 10 30 – www.hotelamphitheatre.fr
– contact@hotelamphitheatre.fr – Fax 04 90 93 98 69 Z **n**
25 rm – €50/55 €55/95, €8 – 3 suites
◆ This handsome 17C building is home to snug, revamped rooms, those in the adjoining townhouse are more spacious and comfortable. Attractive breakfast room.

Les Acacias without rest VISA AE
2 r. de la Cavalerie – 04 90 96 37 88 – www.hotel-acacias.com
– contact@hotel-acacias.com – Fax 04 90 96 32 51
– Open 1st April-22 October Y **t**
33 rm – €51/94 €51/94, €6
◆ Fully renovated hotel at the foot of the Porte de la Cavalerie. Camargue atmosphere in the lobby and Provencal decor in the colourful rooms.

Muette without rest VISA AE
15 r. des Suisses – 04 90 96 15 39 – www.hotel-muette.com
– hotel.muette@wanadoo.fr – Fax 04 90 49 73 16 – Closed February Y **q**
18 rm – €45/56 €48/60, €8
◆ Attractive 12C facade overlooking a small square. Soberly Provençal rooms with exposed stone. Breakfast room adorned with bull-fighting photos.

Le Cilantro (Jérôme Laurent) VISA
31 r. Porte-de-Laure – 04 90 18 25 05 – www.restaurantcilantro.com
– infocilantro@aol.com – Fax 04 90 18 25 10
– Closed 10-16 March, 8-16 November, 1st-10 January, Monday except dinner in July-August, Saturday lunch and Sunday Z **a**
Rest – Menu (€25), €29 (weekday lunch), €65/99
Spec. Ecrevisses de Camargue sous rosace de navet (June to October). Pigeon des Costières en croûte de cacao et fèves de tonka (September to January). Tarte au chocolat et glace cacahuète (March to July). **Wines** Vin de Table du Languedoc, Les Baux-de-Provence.
◆ Behind the antique theatre and near the arenas, this unassuming establishment serves inventive cuisine in a modern, elegant setting. Pleasant summer terrace.

L'Atelier de Jean Luc Rabanel

7 r. des Carmes – ✆ 04 90 91 07 69 – www.rabanel.com – contact@rabanel.com – Closed Monday and Tuesday Z **k**

Rest – *(number of covers limited, pre-book)* Menu € 45 (lunch), € 85/140 bi

Spec. No-nem de haricots verts "kilomètre", éclats de noisettes, cumbawa et sorbet tomate (autumn). Turbot sauvage, artichaut bouquet, feuilles de blettes, bouillon citronnelle et gingembre (autumn). Nage de roquette et basilic, glace à l'huile d'olive et poivron rouge (summer). **Wines** Coteaux du Languedoc, Minervois.

◆ In this minimalist modern bistro, the tapas menus change according to the market and the inspiration of the chef, a devotee of organic produce. Highly commendable inventive cuisine.

Le Jardin de Manon

14 av. des Alyscamps – ✆ 04 90 93 38 68 – Fax 04 90 49 62 03 – Closed 23 October-20 November, 5-22 February, Sunday dinner from September to mid-April, Tuesday dinner and Wednesday Z **r**

Rest – *(closed Tues. evening and Wed.)* Menu € 22/46 – Carte € 44/55

◆ The contemporary style dining rooms of this restaurant offer regional, seasonal menus. Pleasant, peaceful and shaded terrace at the back.

Bistrot "A Côté"

21 r. des Carmes – ✆ 04 90 47 61 13 – www.rabanel.com Z **u**

Rest – Menu € 29 (lunch)/37 – Carte € 30/40

◆ This establishment is an extension to Jean-Luc Rabanel's Atelier establishment next door. Find a relaxed, Spanish-style atmosphere with hams, wine on show, a bar, and quality produce by reservation.

Sambuc road 17 km by ④, D 570 and D 36 – ✉ 13200 Arles

La Chassagnette (Armand Arnal)

– ✆ 04 90 97 26 96 – www.chassagnette.fr – chassagnette@heureuse-camargue.com – Fax 04 90 97 26 95 – Closed 1st January-1st March, Tuesday and Wednesday except from 1st July to 31 August

Rest – *(number of covers limited, pre-book)* Menu € 37 (lunch), € 60/90 – Carte approx. € 60

Spec. Ecrevisses sauvages en gelée, pousse de salade. Sole et moules au curcuma, marmelade d'agrumes. Abricot et glace verveine.

◆ The chef at his remote farmhouse prepares refined cuisine. It is based around his philosophy of respecting seasons and the produce from the organic vegetable garden.

ARMBOUTS-CAPPEL – 59 Nord – 302 C2 – see Dunkerque

ARMOY – 74 Haute-Savoie – 328 M2 – see Thonon-les-Bains

ARNAGE – 72 Sarthe – 310 K7 – see le Mans

ARNAS – 69 Rhône – 327 H3 – see Villefranche-sur-Saône

ARNAY-LE-DUC – 21 Côte-d'Or – 320 G7 – pop. 1 829 – alt. 375 m 8 C2

– ✉ 21230 Burgundy-Jura

Paris 285 – Autun 28 – Beaune 36 – Chagny 38 – Dijon 59 – Montbard 74 – Saulieu 29

Office de tourisme, 15, rue Saint-Jacques ✆ 03 80 90 07 55, Fax 03 80 90 07 55

Chez Camille

1 pl. Edouard-Herriot – ✆ 03 80 90 01 38 – www.chez-camille.fr – chez-camille@wanadoo.fr – Fax 03 80 90 04 64

11 rm – †€ 79 ††€ 79, ☕ € 9 – ½ P € 85 **Rest** – Menu € 22/45

◆ Individual and cosy rooms, some with a small lounge, and others - on the second floor - have exposed beams. Dishes with a Burgundy flavour served in a winter garden-style dining room with a glass roof.

ARPAILLARGUES-ET-AUREILLAC – 30 Gard – 339 L4 – see Uzès

ARPAJON – 91 Essonne – 312 C4 – pop. 9 615 – alt. 51 m – ✉ 91290 18 B2

Paris 32 – Chartres 71 – Évry 18 – Fontainebleau 49 – Melun 45 – Orléans 94 – Versailles 39

Office de tourisme, place de l'Hôtel de Ville ✆ 01 60 83 36 51, Fax 01 60 83 80 00

de Marivaux Janvry Bois de Marivaux, NW : 17 km on D 97, ✆ 01 64 90 85 85

Arpège without rest

23 av. J.-Jaurès – ✆ 01 69 17 10 22 – hotel.arpege@wanadoo.fr – Fax 01 60 83 94 20 – Closed 31 July-30 August

48 rm – €73 €83, ☕ €9

◆ This recently built, town centre hotel offers well soundproofed and well equipped, functional rooms. Photos by Doisneau on the walls.

Le Saint Clément (Jean-Michel Delrieu)

16 av. Hoche, (D 152) – ✆ 01 64 90 21 01 – www.lesaintclement.com – le-saint-clement@wanadoo.fr – Fax 01 60 83 32 67 – Closed 17 August-14 September, Saturday lunch, Sunday dinner and Monday

Rest – Menu €47/57 – Carte €90/101

Spec. Millefeuille chaud de foie gras de canard (October to March). Bourride du "Père Brun" au fumet de homard (October to March). Tarte fine aux figues fraîches (September to November).

◆ Neo-Classical building housing a sober and comfortable dining room; shaded summer terrace. Good classic cooking focusing on French produce.

ARPAJON-SUR-CÈRE – 15 Cantal – 330 C5 – see Aurillac

LES ARQUES – 46 Lot – 337 D4 – pop. 181 – alt. 254 m – ✉ 46250 28 B1

Dordogne-Berry-Limousin

Paris 569 – Cahors 28 – Gourdon 27 – Villefranche-du-Périgord 19 – Villeneuve-sur-Lot 58

St-Laurent church ★: Christ★ and Pietà★ - Frescoes★ of St-André-des-Arques church.

La Récréation

le bourg – ✆ 05 65 22 88 08 – Open from March to October and closed Wednesday and Thursday

Rest – Menu €33

◆ Pleasant, somewhat nostalgic restaurant established in an old village school. Classroom-dining room, schoolyard-terrace, and sculpted totem-chestnut tree in the playground. Updated menu.

ARRADON – 56 Morbihan – 308 O9 – see Vannes

ARRAS Ⓟ – 62 Pas-de-Calais – 301 J6 – pop. 41 400 – Built-up area 124 206 – alt. 72 m – ✉ 62000 Northern France and the Paris Region 30 B2

Paris 179 – Amiens 69 – Calais 110 – Charleville-Mézières 159 – Lille 54

Office de tourisme, place des Héros ✆ 03 21 51 26 95, Fax 03 21 71 07 34

d'Arras Anzin-Saint-Aubin Rue Briquet Taillandier, NW : 5 km on D 341, ✆ 03 21 50 24 24

Grand'Place★★★ and Place des Héros★★★ - Town hall and belfry★ BY **H** - Former St-Vaast abbey★★: musée des Beaux-Arts★.

Plans on following pages

De l'Univers
3 pl. de la Croix-Rouge – ✆ 03 21 71 34 01 – www.hotel-univers-arras.com – univers.hotel@najeti.com – Fax 03 21 71 41 42 BZ **v**
38 rm – †€ 85/130 ††€ 99/150, ☕ € 14 **Rest** – Menu (€ 26) – Carte € 43/67
◆ Once a monastery, then a hospital and finally a hotel: this elegant, peaceful 18C property has personalised rooms, some with a Provençal atmosphere. Restaurant with pleasant decor. Contemporary cuisine served.

D'Angleterre without rest
7 pl. Foch – ✆ 03 21 51 51 16 – www.hotelangleterre.info – info@hotelangleterre.info – Fax 03 21 71 38 20 – Closed 20 December-3 January
19 rm – †€ 85 ††€ 99/160, ☕ € 9 CZ **r**
◆ A regional style brick building dating from 1929, near the TGV station. Spacious, well-equipped rooms with period furnishings. Lounge bar with a British atmosphere.

Mercure Atria
58 bd Carnot – ✆ 03 21 23 88 88 – www.mercure.com – h1560@accor.com – Fax 03 21 23 88 89 CZ **b**
80 rm – †€ 59/112 ††€ 62/122, ☕ € 14
Rest – *(Closed Saturday lunch, Sunday lunch and bank holiday lunch)*
Menu (€ 16) – Carte € 29/39
◆ Large brick and glass complex near the business district. Rooms renovated in a contemporary style. Light wood furniture and trendy colours. A simple restaurant with plants and floral decor.

Moderne without rest
1 bd Faidherbe – ✆ 03 21 23 39 57 – www.hotel-moderne-arras.com – contact@hotel-moderne-arras.com – Fax 03 21 71 55 42 – Closed 20 December-3 January
50 rm – †€ 68/126 ††€ 78/126, ☕ € 9 CZ **m**
◆ Lovely building (1920) opposite the station and near the Grand Place. Rooms with simple, functional furniture, brightened with colourful soft furnishings.

Express By Holiday Inn without rest
3 r. du Dr Brassart – ✆ 03 21 60 88 88 – www.holidayinn-arras.com – reservations@hiexpress-arras.com – Fax 03 21 60 89 00 CZ **y**
98 rm ☕ – †€ 90/150 ††€ 90/150
◆ Modern building adjoining the railway station. Modern rooms with facilities well-suited to the needs of a business clientele.

Ibis without rest
11 r. de la Justice – ✆ 03 21 23 61 61 – www.ibishotel.com – h1567@accor.com – Fax 03 21 71 31 31 CZ **n**
63 rm – †€ 57/95 ††€ 57/95, ☕ € 8
◆ Ideally located between two magnificent Arras squares. The rooms are quite small but functional and soundproofed.

3 Luppars without rest
49 Grand'Place – ✆ 03 21 60 02 03 – www.ostel-les-3luppars.com – contact3.luppars@wanadoo.fr – Fax 03 21 24 24 80 CY **r**
42 rm – †€ 60/70 ††€ 75/80, ☕ € 8
◆ The oldest building in Arras (1467, a superb Gothic façade) offers simple rooms. The rooms to the rear are the quietest.

La Corne d'Or without rest
1 pl. Guy-Mollet – ✆ 03 21 58 85 94 – www.lamaisondhotes.com – franck@lamaisondhotes.com – Closed 19 July-9 August CY **a**
5 rm – †€ 68/89 ††€ 78/115, ☕ € 7 – 2 suites
◆ Savour the romantic atmosphere and refined decor of this private mansion remodelled in the 18C. Choice of classic or contemporary bedrooms, plus attic-style loft rooms and superb cellars.

La Faisanderie
45 Grand'Place – ✆ 03 21 48 20 76 – www.restaurant-la-faisanderie.com – la-faisanderie@wanadoo.fr – Fax 03 21 50 89 18 – Closed 3-24 August, Thursday lunch, Sunday dinner, Monday and bank holidays dinner CY **f**
Rest – Menu € 27 (weekdays)/65 – Carte € 73/90
◆ A 17C house, on the sumptuous square, with a fine cellar whose imposing stone columns support an old brick vaulted ceiling. Up-to-date cuisine.

ARRAS

Adam (R. Paul) . . . . AY 2
Agaches (R. des) . . . . BY 3
Albert-Ier-de-Belgique (R.) BY 4
Ancien-Rivage (Pl. de l') . . BY 5
Barbot (R. du Gén.) . . . . . . BY 6
Baudimont (Rd-Pt) . . . . AY 7
Carabiniers-d'Artois
(R. des) . . . . AY 8
Cardinal (R. du) . . . . CZ 9
Delansorne (R. D.) . . . . BZ 10
Doumer (R. P.) . . . . BY 12
Ernestale (R.) . . . . BZ 13
Ferry (R. J.) . . . . AY 15
Foch (R. Maréchal) . . . . . . CZ 16
Gambetta (R.) . . . . BCZ
Gouvernance (R. de la) . . . BY 18
Guy Mollet (Pl.) . . . . CY 19
Kennedy (Av. J.) . . . . AZ 24
Legrelle (R. E.) . . . . BCZ 25
Madeleine (Pl. de la) . . . . . BY 28
Marché-au-Filé (R. du) . . . BY 30
Marseille (Pl. de) . . . . BZ 31
Robespierre (R.) . . . . BZ 34
Ronville (R.) . . . . CZ 35
Ste-Claire (R.) . . . . AZ 37
Ste-Croix (R.) . . . . CY 39
St-Aubert (R.) . . . . BY
Strasbourg (Bd de) . . . . . . CZ 42
Taillerie (R. de la) . . . . CY 43
Teinturiers (R. des) . . . . . . BY 45
Théâtre (Pl. et R.) . . . . BZ 47
Verdun (Cours de) . . . . AZ 49
Victor-Hugo (Pl.) . . . . AZ 51
Wacquez-Glasson (R.) . . . CZ 52
Wetz-d'Amain (Pl. du) . . . . BY 53
29-Juillet (R. du) . . . . BY 54
33e (Pl. du) . . . . BY 55

XX La Coupole d'Arras

26 bd de Strasbourg – ✆ 03 21 71 88 44 – lacoupoledarras@orange.fr – Fax 03 21 71 52 46 CZ **x**

Rest – Menu (€ 29), € 34 (weekdays) – Carte € 33/60

◆ Large restaurant with a 1920s-type brasserie atmosphere: copies of Mucha, stained glass, Art Deco furniture, etc. Traditional dishes and good choice of home-made cakes.

XX La Clef des Sens

60 pl. des Héros – ✆ 03 21 51 00 50 – www.laclefdessens.com – laclefdessens@wanadoo.fr – Fax 03 21 71 25 15 – Closed 24 December-11 January CZ **u**

Rest – Menu (€ 17), € 26/59 – Carte € 31/80

◆ Brasserie in a 17C building on the picturesque Place des Héros. Red wood panelling, benches and a lobster tank. View of the belfry from the first floor and the terrace.

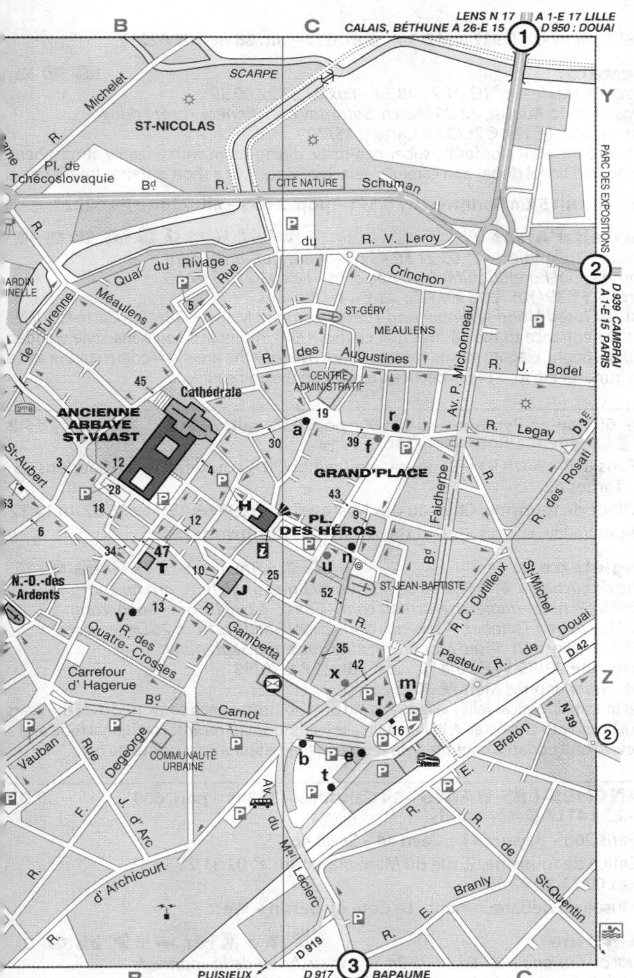

in Rœux 14 km east by ①, N 50, D 33 and D 42 – **pop. 1 410 – alt. 59 m – ✉ 62118**

XX **Le Grand Bleu** ≤ VISA AE

41 r. Henri-Robert – ✆ 03 21 55 41 74
– www.legrandbleu-roeux.fr
– contact@legrandbleu-roeux.fr
– Fax 03 21 55 41 74
– Closed 1st-15 October, Saturday lunch, Sunday dinner, Monday and dinner except Friday and Saturday
Rest – Menu € 27 (lunch)/52
◆ This chalet style house welcomes you in a colourful dining room or, in fine weather, on the pleasant terrace overlooking the lake. Tempting modern cuisine.

in Mercatel 8 km by ③, D 917 and D 34 – pop. 622 – alt. 88 m – ✉ 62217

Mercator

24 r. de la Mairie – ✆ 03 21 73 48 33 – Fax 03 21 22 09 39
– Closed 1st-16 August, 22-29 March, Saturday and dinner except Friday
Rest – Menu (€ 17), € 26/37 – Carte € 35/70
◆ Choose the Mercator for its sober neo-rustic dining room with a family atmosphere, serving traditional dishes and carefully-selected wines, just a short distance from Arras.

in Anzin-St-Aubin 5 km Northwest by D 341 – pop. 2 655 – alt. 71 m – ✉ 62223

Du Golf d'Arras

r. Briquet-Tallandier – ✆ 03 21 50 45 04 – www.golf-arras.com
– commercial.hoteldugolf@fr.oleane.com – Fax 03 21 15 07 00
64 rm – €89/105 €99/115, ☕ € 14 – 8 suites
Rest – *(Closed Monday dinner and Tuesday dinner)* Menu € 28/49 – Carte € 30/38
◆ At the entrance to the 18-hole golf course is this impressive Louisiana style wooden building. Bright, elegant rooms, most of which overlook the greens. Modern cuisine and a light atmosphere for a break between rounds on the golf course.

ARREAU – 65 Hautes-Pyrénées – 342 O7 – pop. 838 – alt. 705 m – ✉ 65240 Languedoc-Roussillon-Tarn Gorges

28 **A3**

Paris 818 – Auch 91 – Bagnères-de-Luchon 34 – Lourdes 81 – St-Gaudens 55 – Tarbes 62

Office de tourisme, Château des Nestes ✆ 05 62 98 63 15, Fax 05 62 40 12 32

Aure Valley ★ S - ✳★★★ of the Aspin Pass Northwest: 13 km.

Angleterre

18 rte de Luchon – ✆ 05 62 98 63 30 – www.hotel-angleterre-arreau.com
– contact@hotel-angleterre-arreau.com – Fax 05 62 98 69 66 – Open from mid-May to mid-October, weekends and school holidays from 26 December to 28 February and closed Monday in May-June and September
17 rm – €70/85 €70/115, ☕ € 10 – ½ P € 70/95
Rest – *(dinner only)* Menu € 20, € 26/40
◆ Set in a small, typical valley village this old post house has been converted over the years into a hotel with character. A lovely staircase leads to smart rooms. Traditional food and a reviewed and updated country-style setting in the restaurant. Cosy lounge bar.

ARROMANCHES-LES-BAINS – 14 Calvados – 303 I3 – pop. 609 – alt. 15 m – ✉ 14117 Normandy

32 **B2**

Paris 266 – Bayeux 11 – Caen 34 – St-Lô 46

Office de tourisme, 2, rue du Maréchal Joffre ✆ 02 31 22 36 45, Fax 02 31 22 92 06

Musée du débarquement - La Côte du Bessin★ West.

La Marine

rest,

1 quai du Canada – ✆ 02 31 22 34 19 – www.hotel-de-la-marine.fr
– hotel.de.la.marine@wanadoo.fr – Fax 02 31 22 98 80
– Open 12 February-11 November
28 rm – €61/86 €61/86, ☕ € 10 – ½ P € 68/90
Rest – Menu € 22/49 – Carte € 36/64
◆ Most of the recently refurbished guestrooms of this house (1837) command a matchless view of the Channel. Wine, gourmet grocers and table decoration shop. Traditional menu in the modern restaurant, whose bay windows overlook the sea.

in Manvieux 2.5 km southwest on the D 516 and D 514 – 303 I3 – pop. 116 – alt. 53 m – ✉ 14117

La Gentilhommière without rest

4 r. du Port, L'Eglise – ✆ 02 31 51 97 91
– www.lagentilhommiere-arromanches.com – lagentilhommiere4@wanadoo.fr
– Fax 02 31 10 03 17
5 rm ☕ – €65 €65
◆ This 18C stone abode is home to a peaceful hotel providing individually styled rooms in varying colours. A fine breakfast is served including homemade yoghurt and brioche.

in La Rosière 3 km Southwest by Bayeux road– ✉14117 Tracy-sur-Mer

La Rosière without rest

14 rte de Bayeux – ☎ 02 31 22 36 17 – www.hotel-larosiere-arromanches.com – hotel.larosiere@wanadoo.fr – Fax 02 31 22 19 33 – Open 13 March-11 November

24 rm – †€ 51/99 ††€ 51/118, ☕ € 8,50

◆ Away from the road, this welcoming hotel has functional and extremely well-kept guestrooms, most of which are at ground level overlooking the garden. Buffet breakfast.

ARS-EN-RÉ – 17 Charente-Maritime – 324 A2 – see Île de Ré

ARTRES – 59 Nord – 302 J6 – see Valenciennes

ARVIEU – 12 Aveyron – 338 H5 – pop. 880 – alt. 730 m – ✉ 12120 29 D2

Paris 663 – Albi 66 – Millau 59 – Rodez 31 – St-Affrique 47 – Villefranche-de-Rouergue 77

Syndicat d'initiative, Le Bourg ☎ 05 65 46 71 06, Fax 05 65 63 19 16

Au Bon Accueil

pl. du Marché – ☎ 05 65 46 72 13 – www.aubon-accueil.com – jean-pierre.pachins@wanadoo.fr – Fax 05 65 74 28 95 – Closed 15 December-20 January

10 rm – †€ 42/48 ††€ 42/48, ☕ € 7

Rest – Menu € 14 bi (weekday lunch), € 19/34

◆ Situated on the main village square, the bar of this delightful inn is popular with the locals. Tastefully redecorated, well-kept and comfortable rooms. Simple traditional cuisine is served in this rustic restaurant as well as some regional dishes.

ARVIEUX – 05 Hautes-Alpes – 334 I4 – pop. 347 – alt. 1 550 m – ✉ 05350 French Alps 41 C1

Paris 782 – Briançon 55 – Gap 80 – Marseille 254

Office de tourisme, la ville ☎ 04 92 46 75 76, Fax 04 92 46 83 03

La Ferme de l'Izoard

La Chalp, Route du Col – ☎ 04 92 46 89 00 – www.laferme.fr – info@laferme.fr – Fax 04 92 46 82 37 – Closed April and 29 September-19 December

23 rm – †€ 60/161 ††€ 60/161, ☕ € 11 – 3 suites – ½ P € 61/111

Rest – *(closed Tuesday lunch and Thursday lunch during term time)*
Menu (€ 15), € 21/51 – Carte € 28/50

◆ Traditional farmhouse-style building. Spacious rooms with a balcony or South-facing terrace on the ground floor. Welcoming lounge decorated with local furniture. The restaurant offers a traditional menu with local specialities and grills.

ARZ (ÎLE) – 56 Morbihan – 308 O9 – see Île-d'Arz

ARZON – 56 Morbihan – 308 N9 – pop. 2 173 – alt. 9 m – Casino – ✉ 56640 Brittany 9 A3

Paris 487 – Auray 52 – Lorient 94 – Quiberon 81 – La Trinité-sur-Mer 66 – Vannes 33

Office de tourisme, rond-point du Crouesty ☎ 02 97 53 69 69, Fax 02 97 53 76 10

Tumulus de Tumiac or butte de César ✳★ East: 2 km then 30 mn.

at Port du Crouesty 2 km Southwest – ✉ 56640 Arzon

Miramar

– ☎ 02 97 53 49 00 – www.miramarcrouesty.com – reservation@miramarcrouesty.com – Fax 02 97 53 49 99 – Closed January

114 rm – †€ 174/340 ††€ 174/340, ☕ € 19 – 6 suites

Rest *Salle à Manger* – Menu (€ 30), € 50/75 – Carte € 53/93

Rest *Ruban Bleu* – Menu (€ 30), € 50 – Carte € 55/75

◆ Anchored off the tip of the Rhuys peninsula, this hotel and thalassotherapy centre resemble an ocean liner from a distance. Spacious standard rooms with balcony. Attractive sea view and ocean liner decor at the Salle à Manger. Diet dishes at the Ruban Bleu.

Le Crouesty without rest
r. du Croisty – ✆ 02 97 53 87 91 – www.hotellecrouesty.com – hotellecrouesty@wanadoo.fr – Fax 02 97 53 66 76 – Open February school holidays-15 November
26 rm – €69/95 €75/95, €10
◆ This hotel near the marina provides small, functional and soberly decorated rooms. Piano lounge adorned with a fireplace.

in Port Navalo 3 km West – ✉ 56640 Arzon

Grand Largue
à l'embarcadère – ✆ 02 97 53 71 58 – www.grand.largue.ifrance.com – largueadam@wanadoo.fr – Fax 02 97 53 92 20 – Closed 12 November-25 December, 5 January-10 February, Tuesday except July-August and Monday
Rest – Menu €35 (weekdays)/78 – Carte €50/80
Rest *Le P'tit Zeph* – by the landing stage, ✆ 02 97 49 40 34 – Menu €28 – Carte €35/52
◆ This villa, proudly facing the entrance to the Morbihan bay, offers inventive seafood cuisine in its attractive dining room with a panoramic sea view. Fish and seafood bistro dishes chalked up on a slate.

ASNIÈRES-SUR-SEINE – 92 Hauts-de-Seine – 311 J2 – 101 15 – see Paris, Area

ASPRES-LES-CORPS – 05 Hautes-Alpes – 334 D4 – see Corps

ASTAFFORT – 47 Lot-et-Garonne – 336 F5 – pop. 1 880 – alt. 65 m – ✉ 47220 4 C2

Paris 674 – Agen 19 – Auvillar 29 – Condom 31 – Lectoure 20
Syndicat d'initiative, 13 place de la Nation ✆ 05 53 67 13 33, Fax 05 53 67 13 33

Le Square "Michel Latrille"
5 pl. Craste – ✆ 05 53 47 20 40 – www.latrille.com – latrille.michel@wanadoo.fr – Fax 05 53 47 10 38 – Closed 1st-26 January and Sunday except July-August
14 rm – €55/140 €65/150, €13
Rest – *(closed 4-11 May, 1st-26 January, Tuesday lunch, Sunday dinner and Monday)*
Menu (€28), €38/58 – Carte €62/95
Spec. Tarte fine croustillante de Saint-Jacques sur caviar d'aubergine (October to April). Suprême de pigeonneau rôti, cuisses confites et légumes de saison. Moelleux au café, sauce arabica et glace vanille. **Wines** Vin de Pays de l'Agenais, Buzet
◆ Contemporary and antique furniture, bright colours and elegant detail. The rooms in these charming houses are full of character; some have been refurbished. Luxurious dining room with arcaded doors onto a cool patio. Panoramic terrace. Traditional cuisine.

Une Auberge en Gascogne (Fabrice Biasiolo)
9 fg. Corné, (opposite the post office) – ✆ 05 53 67 10 27 – www.une-auberge-en-gascogne.com – une-auberge-en-gascogne@wanadoo.fr – Fax 05 53 67 10 22 – Closed 1st-15 January, Sunday dinner and Monday lunch from October to May, Thursday lunch and Wednesday
Rest – Menu (€23), €42/80
Spec. Petit déjeuner gascon. Agneau des Pyrénées. Porc noir gascon. **Wines** Côtes du Marmandais, Cahors.
◆ The contemporary décor is the perfect setting for interesting and inventive cuisine based on local produce. Original sitting room, and quiet summer terrace in the inner courtyard.

ASTEVERGE – 79 Deux-Sèvres – 322 – pop. 1 453 – alt. 65 m – see Thouars – ✉ 79100

ATTICHY – 60 Oise – 305 J4 – pop. 1 852 – alt. 73 m – ✉ 60350 37 C2

▶ Paris 101 – Compiègne 18 – Laon 62 – Noyon 26 – Soissons 24

XX **La Croix d'Or** with rm
13 r. Tondu-de-Metz – ☎ 03 44 42 15 37 – www.croixdor.com – lacroixdor60@aol.com – Fax 03 44 42 15 37
4 rm – €35 €43
Rest – *(closed Sunday dinner, Tuesday dinner and Monday)*
Menu € 18 (weekdays)/45
◆ Two regional-style houses laid out around a courtyard. One offers a fresh, modern dining room serving updated fare, while the other provides simple, practical rooms.

ATTIGNAT – 01 Ain – 328 D3 – pop. 2 567 – alt. 227 m – ✉ 01340 44 B1

▶ Paris 420 – Bourg-en-Bresse 13 – Lons-le-Saunier 76 – Louhans 46 – Mâcon 35 – Tournus 42

XX **Dominique Marcepoil** with rm
481 Grande Rue, (D 975) – ☎ 04 74 30 92 24 – www.marcepoil.com – marcepoil@libertysurf.fr – Fax 04 74 25 93 48 – Closed 10-16 August, 25-31 December, Monday lunch and Sunday
12 rm – €57/65 €63/71, € 10 – ½ P € 72
Rest – Menu € 30 bi/64 bi – Carte € 42/89 dinner only
◆ Frogs' legs and Bresse chicken – the region's best on your plate! The house also offers a fine choice of more modern dishes. Quiet poolside rooms.

AUBAGNE – 13 Bouches-du-Rhône – 340 I6 – pop. 43 500 – alt. 102 m – ✉ 13400 Provence 40 B3

▶ Paris 788 – Aix-en-Provence 39 – Brignoles 48 – Marseille 18 – Toulon 48
ℹ Office de tourisme, 8, cours Barthélémy ☎ 04 42 03 49 98, Fax 04 42 03 83 62

Souléia
4 cours Voltaire – ☎ 04 42 18 64 40 – www.hotel-souleia.com – info@hotel-souleia.com – Fax 04 42 08 13 21
72 rm – €95/110 €95/110, € 10 – ½ P € 108/136
Rest – *(closed Saturday dinner, Sunday lunch and Friday)* Menu € 20 – Carte € 27/41
◆ Situated in the santon (clay figurines) capital, a modern hotel with functional rooms, some of which have a private terrace. Satellite TV. Brasserie overlooking the square on the ground floor; a panoramic restaurant (sun terrace) on the roof serves traditional cuisine.

XX **Les Arômes**
8 r. Moussard – ☎ 04 42 03 72 93 – francoisebesset@neuf.fr – Fax 04 42 03 72 93 – Closed Tuesday dinner, Wednesday dinner, Saturday lunch, Sunday and Monday
Rest – Menu (€ 22), € 30 – Carte € 43/60
◆ Guests are warmly received in this family-run restaurant, beautifully decorated by the lady of the house. Traditional recipes revisited in a modern style. Short, seasonal menu.

in St-Pierre-lès-Aubagne 5 km north by D 96 or D 43 – ✉ 13400

Hostellerie de la Source without rest
– ☎ 04 42 04 09 19 – www.hdelasource.com – hostelleriedelasource@orange.fr – Fax 04 42 04 58 72
26 rm – €73/84 €90/176, € 12
◆ A 17C residence with its own spring, in wooded grounds. Recently built extension. Well looked after rooms and handsome pool with a glass roof.

North 4 km on the D 44 and minor road – ✉ 13400 Aubagne

XX **La Ferme**
La Font de Mai, (Chemin Ruissatel) – ☎ 04 42 03 29 67 – www.aubergelaferme.com – auberge-la-ferme@wanadoo.fr – Closed August, February holidays, Saturday lunch, Monday and dinner except Friday and Saturday
Rest – Menu € 50 – Carte € 47/70
◆ House typical of the region facing Mont Garlaban, much loved by Marcel Pagnol. Here copious market produce is served in the shade of an ancient oak or in a cosy, Provençal dining room.

AUBAZINES – 19 Corrèze – 329 L4 – pop. 798 – alt. 345 m – ✉ 19190 25 C3

Dordogne-Berry-Limousin

Paris 480 – Aurillac 86 – Brive-la-Gaillarde 14 – St-Céré 50 – Tulle 17

Office de tourisme, le bourg ☎ 05 55 25 79 93, Fax 05 55 25 79 93

d'Aubazine Beynat Complexe Touristique Coiroux, E : 4 km, ☎ 05 55 27 26 93

St Etienne Cistercian Abbey★ : clocher (belltower)★, furniture★, tombeau de St-Étienne (Tomb of St Etienne)★★, armoire liturgique (liturgucal cabinet)★.

De la Tour

VISA MC

pl. de l'Église – ☎ 05 55 25 71 17 – www.hoteldelatour19.com – hoteldelatour19@orange.fr – Fax 05 55 84 61 83 – Closed 29 December-19 January, Sunday dinner and Monday lunch except July-August

18 rm – †€ 50/70 ††€ 50/70, ☕ € 7 – ½ P € 60/70

Rest – Menu (€ 18), € 23/30 – Carte € 23/37

◆ Facing the abbey; an old house with character and a tower. Old rooms brightened with colourful wallpaper. Regional food served in rustic rooms decorated with copper and pewter ornaments.

Luxury pad or humble abode?
X and 🏠 denote categories of comfort.

AUBE – 61 Orne – 310 M2 – pop. 1 540 – alt. 230 m – ✉ 61270 33 C3

Normandy

Paris 144 – L'Aigle 7 – Alençon 55 – Argentan 47 – Mortagne-au-Perche 32

Auberge St-James

VISA MC

62 rte de Paris – ☎ 02 33 24 01 40 – Closed Sunday dinner, Tuesday dinner and Wednesday

Rest – Menu € 17/30 – Carte € 35/44

◆ A simple, pleasant address set in the village where the countess of Ségur lived. The menu is made up of tasty little dishes from various regions of France.

AUBENAS – 07 Ardèche – 331 I6 – pop. 11 800 – alt. 330 m – ✉ 07200 44 A3

Lyon - Rhone Valley

Paris 627 – Alès 76 – Montélimar 41 – Privas 32 – Le Puy-en-Velay 91

Office de tourisme, 4, boulevard Gambetta ☎ 04 75 89 02 03, Fax 04 75 89 02 04

Site★ - Façade★ of the château.

Plan on next page

Ibis without rest

VISA MC AE

rte de Montélimar – ☎ 04 75 35 44 45 – www.ibishotel.com – Fax 04 75 93 01 01

63 rm – †€ 69/75 ††€ 69/75, ☕ € 8

◆ Situated on the southern outskirts of the town, this Ibis hotel has rooms in line with the chain's standards. Small restaurant on site, terrace and swimming pool.

Le Coyote

VISA MC

13 bd Mathon – ☎ 04 75 35 01 28 – marc.decker_bretel@aliceadsl.fr – Fax 04 75 35 01 28 – Closed 6-13 July, 25 December-11 January, Sunday and Monday Y e

Rest – *(number of covers limited, pre-book)* Menu (€ 15), € 19/30 – Carte € 32/39

◆ The talented chef of this small unpretentious restaurant is undoubtedly its claim to fame. The regulars adore his market-fresh traditional dishes.

AUBENAS

Béranger de la Tour (R.) . . . . Y 2
Bernardy (R. de) . . . . YZ 3
Bouchet (R. Auguste) . . . . Y 4
Champalbert (R.) . . . . Y 5
Cordeliers (R. des) . . . . Y 6
Couderc (R. G.) . . . . Z 7
Delichères (R.) . . . . Y 8
Gambetta (Bd) . . . . Z
Gaulle (Pl. Gén.-de) . . . . Z 9
Grand'Rue . . . . Y 10
Hoche (R.) . . . . Z 12
Hôtel de Ville (Pl.) . . . . Y 13
Jeanne d'Arc (Pl.) . . . . YZ 16
Jean-Jaurès (R.) . . . . Y 15
Jourdan (R.) . . . . Y 17
Laprade (Bd C.) . . . . Z 18
Lésin-Lacoste (R.) . . . . Y 19
Montlaur (R.) . . . . Y 21
Nationale (R.) . . . . Y 22
Parmentier (Pl.) . . . . Y 24
Radal (R.) . . . . Z 25
République (R. de la) . . . . Y 26
Réservoirs (R. des) . . . . Y 27
Roure (Pl. Jacques) . . . . Y 29
St-Benoît (Rampe) . . . . Y 30
Silhol (R. Henri) . . . . Y 32
Vernon (Bd de) . . . . Z 33
4-Septembre (R.) . . . . Y 35

AUBETERRE-SUR-DRONNE – 16 Charente – 324 L8 – pop. 412 – alt. 72 m – ✉ 16390 Atlantic Coast

39 **C3**

- Paris 494 – Angoulême 48 – Bordeaux 90 – Périgueux 54
- Office de tourisme, place du Château ✆ 05 45 98 57 18, Fax 05 45 98 54 13
- d'Aubeterre Saint-Séverin Le Manoir de Longeveau, NE : 7 km on D 17 and D 78, ✆ 05 45 98 55 13
- Église monolithe★★.

Hostellerie du Périgord

rm, VISA

(Plaisance district) – ✆ *05 45 98 50 46 – www.hostellerie-perigord.com – hpmorel@aol.com – Fax 05 45 98 31 69 – Closed 2 weeks in January*

12 rm – **†**€ 48 **††**€ 56/70, ☕ € 7 – ½ P € 65

Rest – *(closed Sunday dinner and Monday)* Menu € 17 (weekday lunch), € 33/44 – Carte approx. € 38

◆ A successful facelift for this small, family-run hotel at the foot of the famous village. Discreetly contemporary, well-soundproofed and well-maintained rooms. The restaurant offers a menu that is part classic, part modern. Pleasant veranda facing the garden and pool.

AUBIGNY-SUR-NÈRE – 18 Cher – 323 K2 – pop. 5 751 – alt. 180 m – ✉ 18700 Dordogne-Berry-Limousin

12 **C2**

- Paris 180 – Orléans 67 – Bourges 48 – Cosne-sur-Loire 41 – Gien 30 – Salbris 32 – Vierzon 44
- Office de tourisme, 1, rue de l'Église ✆ 02 48 58 40 20, Fax 02 48 58 59 13

La Chaumière A/C rest, VISA MC

2 r. Paul-Lasnier – ✆ 02 48 58 04 01 – www.hotel-restaurant-la-chaumiere.com – lachaumiere.hotel@wanadoo.fr – Fax 02 48 58 10 31 – Closed 9-23 August, 8 February-9 March and Sunday dinner except July-August and bank holidays

19 rm – €55/80 €70/125, ☕ €10 – ½ P €63/91

Rest – *(closed Sunday dinner and Monday except dinner in July-August and public holidays)* Menu €20/55 – Carte €35/50

◆ Painstakingly maintained old building with comfortable bedrooms (wood and stone, personal touches), plus two attractive rustic dining rooms serving traditional cuisine.

Villa Stuart VISA MC

12 av. de Paris – ✆ 02 48 58 93 30 – www.villastuart.com – villastuart@wanadoo.fr

5 rm ☕ – €70 €100 **Table d'hôte** – Menu €27 bi

◆ This elegant residence is the perfect place for a pleasant stay. Four light and spacious guestrooms, each decorated along a particular theme (travel, art, history etc). Food enthusiasts will love this guest house, where the owner makes his own jams and run cookery classes.

Le Bien Aller A/C VISA MC AE

3 r. des Dames – ✆ 02 48 58 03 92 – jeanachard2@aol.com – Closed Tuesday dinner and Wednesday dinner

Rest – Menu €18 (weekdays)/24

◆ Welcoming bistro style interior, wine bar and local dishes. Make up your own menu from daily specials written on a blackboard.

AUBRAC – 12 Aveyron – 338 J3 – alt. 1 300 m – ✉ 12470 29 D1

Languedoc-Roussillon-Tarn Gorges

Paris 581 – Aurillac 97 – Mende 66 – Rodez 56 – St-Flour 62

La Dômerie VISA MC AE

– ✆ 05 65 44 28 42 – www.hoteldomerie.com – david.mc@wanadoo.fr – Fax 05 65 44 21 47 – Open 7 February-12 November

24 rm – €67/93 €67/93, ☕ €12 – ½ P €67/77

Rest – *(closed for lunch from Monday to Friday and Wednesday dinner except mid-July to end August)* Menu €24/43 – Carte €28/49

◆ A lovely old house built out of basalt and granite in the heart of the village. Two generations of comfortable rooms in a rustic or cosy style. Welcoming country dining room serving family cuisine with Aubrac meat a speciality.

AUBUSSON – 23 Creuse – 325 K5 – pop. 4 239 – alt. 440 m – ✉ 23200 25 C2

Dordogne-Berry-Limousin

Paris 387 – Clermont-Ferrand 91 – Guéret 41 – Limoges 89 – Montluçon 64

Office de tourisme, rue Vieille ✆ 05 55 66 32 12, Fax 05 55 83 84 51

Musée départemental de la Tapisserie★ (Jean-Lurçat Cultural Centre).

AUBUSSON

Chapitre (R. du) . . . 2
Chateaufavier (R.) . . . 4
Dayras (Pl. M.) . . . 5
Déportés (R. des) . . . 7
Espagne (Pl. Gén.) . . . 8
Fusillés (R. des) . . . 10
Iles (Quai des) . . . 12
Libération (Pl. de la) . . . 15
Lissiers (Av. des) . . . 16
Lurçat (Pl. J.) . . . 18
Marché (Pl. du) . . . 20
République (Av.) . . . 23
St-Jean (R.) . . . 24
Terrade (Pont de la) . . . 27
Vaveix (R.) . . . 29
Vieille (R.) . . . 30

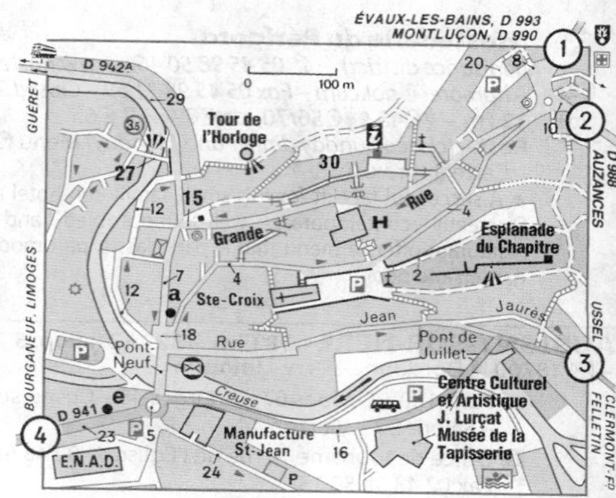

Villa Adonis without rest

14 av. de la République – ✆ 05 55 66 46 00 – www.villa-adonis.com – infos@villa-adonis.com – Fax 05 55 66 17 90 – Closed 30 December-3 January **e**

10 rm – ♦€ 52/62 ♦♦€ 52/62, ☕ € 7

◆ To describe this very pleasant villa in a nutshell: beautiful reception hall, pretty rooms that combine modern comfort, a cosy, contemporary décor, and a superb garden.

Le France

6 r. des Déportés – ✆ 05 55 66 10 22 – www.aubussonlefrance.com – contact@aubussonlefrance.com – Fax 05 55 66 88 64 **a**

21 rm – ♦€ 59/95 ♦♦€ 59/95, ☕ € 12 – Rest – *(closed Sunday dinner from 2 November to 15 March)* Menu (€ 12 bi), € 20/30 – Carte € 31/54

◆ An 18C house between the River Creuse and the old centre with tastefully decorated guestrooms (antique furniture and carefully chosen fabrics) that are gradually being renovated. Elegant dining room and pretty summer terrace in the inside courtyard.

AUCH **P** – **32 Gers** – **336** F8 – **pop. 21 700** – **alt. 169 m** – ✉ **32000** 28 **B2**

Languedoc-Roussillon-Tarn Gorges

▶ Paris 713 – Agen 74 – Bordeaux 205 – Tarbes 74 – Toulouse 79

ℹ Office de tourisme, 1, rue Dessoles ✆ 05 62 05 22 89, Fax 05 62 05 92 04

⛳18 d'Auch-EmbatsW : 5 km on D 924, ✆ 05 62 61 10 11

⛳9 de Gascogne Masseube Les Stournes, S : 25 km, ✆ 05 62 66 03 10

👁 Ste-Marie cathedral ★★: stalls★★★, stained-glass windows★★.

AUCH

Street	Grid	No.
Alsace (Av. d')	BY	2
Caillou (Pl. du)	AZ	4
Caumont (R.)	AZ	5
Convention (R. de la)	AZ	7
Daumesnil (R.)	BY	9
David (Pl. J.)	AY	8
Dessoles (R.)	AY	12
Espagne (R.)	AZ	13
Fabre d'Églantine (R.)	AZ	14
Gambetta (R.)	AY	
Lagarrasic (Allées)	ABZ	17
Lamartine (R.)	AY	15
Lartet (R. Ed.)	AZ	16
Lissagaray (Q.)	BYZ	18
Marceau (R.)	BY	19
Marne (Av. de la)	BY	22
Montebello (R.)	BZ	23
Pasteur (R.)	BZ	25
Pont-National (R. du)	AZ	27
Pouy (R. du)	BY	28
Prieuré (Pt du)	AZ	29
Rabelais (R.)	BZ	31
République (Pl. de la)	AZ	33
Rousseau (R. A.)	AZ	35
Salleneuve (R.)	AY	38
Somme (R. de la)	BY	40

La Table d'Oste

7 r. Lamartine – ☎ 05 62 05 55 62 – www.table-oste-restaurant.com – latabledoste@hotmail.fr – Fax 05 62 05 55 62 – Closed 14-21 June, 20 September-11 October, Saturday dinner in summer, Monday lunch and Sunday AY **b**

Rest – *(number of covers limited, pre-book)* Menu € 16 (weekday lunch), € 24/39 bi – Carte € 25/48

◆ Local specialities to be enjoyed in a small, rustic dining room (exposed beams, antique knick-knacks...) or on the summer terrace overlooking the street.

Agen road 7 km by ① – ✉ 32810 Montaux-les-Créneaux

Le Papillon

N 21 – ☎ 05 62 65 51 29 – www.restaurant-lepapillon.com – lepapillon@wanadoo.fr – Fax 05 62 65 54 33 – Closed 30 June-14 July, 1st-8 September, 22 February-8 March, Sunday dinner and Monday

Rest – Menu € 17 (weekdays)/42 – Carte € 38/49

◆ New building away from the main road. The dining room is bright and decorated with paintings opening onto a pretty shady terrace. Classic food.

AUDERVILLE – 50 Manche – 303 A1 – pop. 283 – alt. 55 m – ✉ 50440 32 A1

Normandie Cotentin

▶ Paris 382 – Caen 149 – Saint-Lô 113 – Cherbourg 29 – Équeurdreville-Hainneville 25

ℹ Office de tourisme, gare Maritime ☎ 02 33 04 50 26

Auberge de Goury

Port de Goury – ☎ 02 33 52 77 01 – www.aubergedegoury.com – Fax 02 33 08 14 37 – Closed January, Sunday dinner except July-August and Monday

Rest – Menu (€ 26), € 60 – Carte € 40/60

◆ This rustic, granite building was once used as a store for goods smuggled between France and the Channel Islands. Fish and seafood on the menu. Terrace.

AUDIERNE – 29 Finistère – 308 D6 – pop. 2 321 – alt. 5 m – ✉ 29770 9 A2

Brittany

▶ Paris 599 – Douarnenez 21 – Pointe du Raz 16 – Pont-l'Abbé 32 – Quimper 37

ℹ Office de tourisme, 8, rue Victor Hugo ☎ 02 98 70 12 20, Fax 02 98 70 20 20

◉ Site★ - Planète Aquarium★★.

Le Goyen

Pl. J. Simon, at the harbour – ☎ 02 98 70 08 88 – www.le-goyen.com – hotel.le.goyen@wanadoo.fr – Fax 02 98 70 18 77 – Open 27 March-15 November and 30 December-4 January

26 rm – †€ 85/177 ††€ 85/177, ☕ € 12 – ½ P € 95/133

Rest – Menu (€ 19), € 25 (weekdays)/89 – Carte € 51/69

◆ Large quayside hotel facing the harbour and the River Goyen's estuary. The charming, snug rooms are furnished traditionally and embellished with colourful and floral fabrics. Modern cuisine and seafood served in this restaurant overlooking the comings and goings of the boats.

Au Roi Gradlon

rest,

on the beach – ☎ 02 98 70 04 51 – www.auroigradlon.com – accueil@auroigradlon.com – Fax 02 98 70 14 73 – Closed 15 December-6 February

19 rm – †€ 48/99 ††€ 48/99, ☕ € 10 – ½ P € 59/79

Rest – *(Closed Wednesday in low season)* Menu € 17 (weekday lunch), € 20/54 – Carte € 30/50

◆ A comfortable hotel with most of the rooms facing the Atlantic. Direct access to the beach invites a healthy stroll along the seafront. Plain dining room overlooking Audierne bay. Predominantly fish and seafood cuisine.

De la Plage

21 bd E. Brusq, on the beach – 02 98 70 01 07 – www.hotel-finistere.com – hotel.laplage@wanadoo.fr – Fax 02 98 75 04 69 – Open 1st April-31 October

22 rm – €52/72 €52/88, €9 – ½ P €60/78

Rest – *(dinner only)* Menu €20, €25/38

◆ Light and colourful rooms (some of which have loggias) and panoramic dining rooms are the main attractions of this waterside hotel.

L'Iroise

8 quai Camille-Pelletan – 02 98 70 15 80 – www.restaurant-liroise.com – restaurant.liroise@wanadoo.fr – Fax 02 98 70 20 82 – Closed 5-31 January, Monday dinner and Tuesday except from 15 July to 31 August

Rest – Menu €25/108

◆ A summer terrace overlooking the quayside and the port lie before this dining room brightened with pastel tones and with exposed-stone walls. Modern dishes and seafood flavours.

AUDINCOURT – **25 Doubs** – **321** L2 – **pop. 15 539** – **alt. 323 m** 17 **C1**
– ✉ **25400** Burgundy-Jura

Paris 476 – Basel 96 – Belfort 21 – Besançon 75 – Montbéliard 6 – Mulhouse 59

Sacré-Coeur church: baptistry ★ AY **B.**

See plan of Montbéliard urban area.

Les Tilleuls without rest

51 r. Foch – 03 81 30 77 00 – http://perso.wanadoo.fr/hotel.tilleuls – hotel.tilleuls@wanadoo.fr – Fax 03 81 30 57 20 Y **s**

47 rm – €51/63 €69/77, €8,50

◆ The hotel is made up of an old restored house and bungalows with wood-panelled rooms. Garden adorned with a pergola. Comfortable and pleasant atmosphere.

in Taillecourt **1.5 km North, Sochaux road** – **pop. 989** – **alt. 330 m** – ✉ **25400**

Auberge La Gogoline

23 r. Croisée – 03 81 94 54 82 – jacquesferrare@orange.fr – Fax 03 81 95 20 42 – Closed 1-23 September, 8-23 February, Saturday lunch, Sunday dinner, Monday and Tuesday Y **k**

Rest – Menu €28/48 – Carte €48/74

◆ Protected from the shops by its garden, this cottage-like house sports a plush, comfortable, countrified interior. Classic cuisine and fine wine list.

AUDRESSEIN – **09 Ariège** – **343** E7 – **see Castillon-en-Couserans**

AUDRIEU – **14 Calvados** – **303** I4 – **see Bayeux**

AUGEROLLES – **63 Puy-de-Dôme** – **326** I8 – **pop. 908** – **alt. 540 m** 6 **C2**
– ✉ **63930**

Paris 411 – Clermont-Ferrand 61 – Montluçon 149 – Roanne 65 – Vichy 55

Les Chênes

rte de Piboulet, 1 km west via D 42 – 04 73 53 50 34 – www.restaurant-les-chenes.com – info@restaurant-les-chenes.com – Fax 04 73 53 52 20 – Closed 30 June-13 July, 24 December-3 January, 15-22 February, Tuesday dinner except July-August, Sunday dinner, Monday dinner and Saturday

Rest – Menu (€12 bi), €19 (weekdays)/47

◆ Family inn housing a smart dining room that mixes rustic and modern styles. The appetising, traditional food focuses on local produce.

AUGERVILLE-LA-RIVIÈRE – 45 Loiret – 318 L2 – pop. 226 – alt. 100 m – ✉ 45330 12 **C1**

Paris 92 – Orléans 76 – Évry 59 – Corbeil-Essonnes 62 – Melun 52

Château d'Augerville rm, VISA AE

pl. du Château – ✆ 02 38 32 12 07 – www.chateau-augerville.com – reservation@chateau.augerville.com – Fax 02 38 32 12 15

38 rm – †€ 135/265 ††€ 175/265, ☕ € 16 – 2 suites

Rest – Menu (€ 20), € 51 – Carte € 50/72

◆ Comfortable rooms designed by architect Patrick Ribes, magnificent 112 ha grounds and an 18-hole golf course – this medieval château is paradise for golfers. Handsome oak panelled dining room and concise modern menu.

AULLÈNE – 2A Corse-du-Sud – 345 D9 – see Corse

AULNAY – 17 Charente-Maritime – 324 H3 – pop. 1 507 – alt. 63 m – ✉ 17470 Atlantic Coast 38 **B2**

Paris 424 – Angoulême 66 – Niort 41 – Poitiers 87 – La Rochelle 72

Office de tourisme, 290, avenue de l'Église ✆ 05 46 33 14 44, Fax 05 46 33 15 46

St-Pierre church ★★.

Du Donjon without rest VISA

4 r. des Hivers – ✆ 05 46 33 67 67 – www.hoteldudonjon.com – hoteldudonjon@wanadoo.fr – Fax 05 46 33 67 64

10 rm – †€ 55/68 ††€ 55/75, ☕ € 7

◆ A charming Saintonge house, not far from the church of St Pierre. Tasteful interior: old beams and stone, rustic furniture and modern comforts. Pretty garden.

AULNAY-SOUS-BOIS – 93 Seine-Saint-Denis – 305 F7 – 101 18 – see Paris, Area

AULON – 65 Hautes-Pyrénées – 342 N7 – pop. 76 – alt. 1 213 m – ✉ 65240 28 **A3**

Paris 830 – Bagnères-de-Luchon 44 – Col d'Aspin 24 – Lannemezan 38 – St-Lary-Soulan 13

Auberge des Aryelets VISA

Pl. du Village – ✆ 05 62 39 95 59 – Fax 05 62 39 95 59 – Closed 1st-8 June, 12 November-17 December, Sunday dinner, Monday and Tuesday except school holidays

Rest – Menu (€ 19), € 23/37 – Carte € 40/55

◆ Dressed stone house that has kept its rustic and authentic character. Generous regional cuisine prepared with fine produce and served in a pleasant atmosphere.

AULUS-LES-BAINS – 09 Ariège – 343 G8 – pop. 189 – alt. 750 m – Spa : late April-late Oct. – ✉ 09140 Languedoc-Roussillon-Tarn Gorges 28 **B3**

Paris 807 – Foix 76 – Oust 17 – St-Girons 34

Office de tourisme, résidence Ars ✆ 05 61 96 01 79

Garbet Valley ★ N.

Hostellerie de la Terrasse VISA

– ✆ 05 61 96 00 98 – ariege.com – jeanfrancois.maurette@wanadoo.fr – Fax 05 61 96 01 42 – Open 2 May-30 October

14 rm – †€ 45/100 ††€ 45/100, ☕ € 8 – ½ P € 55/65

Rest – *(open 2 June-29 September)* Menu € 19/45 – Carte € 25/60

◆ Beyond the river crossed by a footbridge, a family ambiance in this house nearly a century old which offers simple rooms, some with terrace. A semi-rustic, semi-classic restaurant with a shaded terrace lapped by the River Garbet.

Les Oussaillès VISA

– ✆ 05 61 96 03 68 – jcharrue@orange.fr – Closed 15 November-15 December

10 rm (½ board only) – ½ P € 43/50

Rest – *(dinner only) (residents only)* Menu € 15

◆ Old stone house in the Ariège style flanked by an elegant little tower, in the centre of the spa. Some of the rooms overlook the garden. A bright modern dining room and terrace facing the mountain. Home cooking and friendly ambience.

AUMALE – 76 Seine-Maritime – 304 K3 – pop. 2 428 – alt. 130 m – ✉ 76390 Normandy 33 D1

Paris 136 – Amiens 48 – Beauvais 49 – Dieppe 69 – Rouen 74

Syndicat d'initiative, rue Centrale ☎ 02 35 93 41 68, Fax 02 35 93 41 68

Villa des Houx

rm, VISA

6 av. Gén.-de-Gaulle – ☎ 02 35 93 93 30 – www.villa-des-houx.com – contact@villa-des-houx.com – Fax 02 35 93 03 94 – Closed 1st January-10 February and Sunday dinner from 15 September to 15 May except holidays

22 rm – €62/72 €65/100, €9

Rest – *(closed Sunday dinner and Monday 15 September-15 May except holidays)* Menu €24/45 – Carte €34/57

◆ This family establishment has a pretty, half-timbered façade. You will sleep the sleep of the just in these perfectly comfortable rooms. Dining room, veranda and summer terrace give onto the peaceful garden. Classic regionally inspired menu.

AUMONT-AUBRAC – 48 Lozère – 330 H6 – pop. 1 099 – alt. 1 040 m – ✉ 48130 23 C1

Paris 549 – Aurillac 115 – Espalion 57 – Marvejols 25 – Mende 40 – Le Puy-en-Velay 90

Office de tourisme, rue de l'Église ☎ 04 66 42 88 70, Fax 04 66 42 88 70

Grand Hôtel Prouhèze

VISA AE

2 rte du Languedoc – ☎ 04 66 42 80 07 – www.prouheze.com – resa@prouheze.com – Fax 04 66 42 87 78 – Closed 2 November-1st December and 18 January-9 February

23 rm – €50/90 €50/90, €12

Rest *Le Compostelle* – see restaurant below

Rest – *(open 13 March-1st November and closed for lunch except Saturday, Sunday and bank holidays)* Menu €56 – Carte approx. €56

◆ A pleasant mix of colour and simplicity depicts the antique and contemporary lines of this family-run establishment on the station square. Tasty regional cuisine and fine Languedoc wines served in a warm décor.

Chez Camillou (Cyril Attrazic)

VISA AE

10 rte du Languedoc – ☎ 04 66 42 80 22 – www.hotel-camillou.com – chezcamillou@wanadoo.fr – Fax 04 66 42 93 70 – Open 1st April-31 October

38 rm – €65/160 €65/160, €10 – 3 suites – ½ P €57/101

Rest Le Gabale – see restaurant below

Rest *Cyril Attrazic* – ☎ 04 66 42 86 14 *(closed 15 November-15 December, 15 January-21 February, Sunday dinner and Monday except July-August)* Menu €25 (weekdays)/108 bi – Carte €46/70

Spec. Nouilles de céleri, champignons du massif et jus gras. Pièce de bœuf fermier d'Aubrac et bœuf confit. Coupétade revisitée parfumée à l'orange confite. **Wines** Coteaux du Languedoc.

◆ Slightly off the main road, two modern buildings in a wooded area. Spacious rooms, furnished in a rustic style. Bright, contemporary dining room in beige offering updated regional cuisine.

Le Gabale – Hôtel Chez Camillou

VISA AE

10 rte du Languedoc – ☎ 04 66 42 86 14 – www.camillou.com – chezcamillou@wanadoo.fr – Fax 04 66 42 91 78 – Closed 10 January-14 February, Sunday dinner and Monday from November to April

Rest – Menu (€14), €17/22 – Carte €24/37

◆ Comfortable restaurant lit by large bay windows on the ground floor of the Chez Camillou Hotel. Fresco with country scene; summer terrace. Tasty local cuisine.

Le Compostelle – Grand Hôtel Prouhèze

VISA AE

2 rte du Languedoc – ☎ 04 66 42 80 07 – www.prouheze.com – resa@prouheze.com – Fax 04 66 42 87 78 – Closed 2 November-1st December, 18 January-9 February, Monday dinner, Wednesday lunch and Tuesday from December to March

Rest – Menu €18/28

◆ Aligot, stuffed cabbage, tripe specialities... a resume of Aubrac on your plate! Provincial recipes honoured in this bistro with a very countrified charm.

AUNAY-SUR-ODON – 14 Calvados – 303 I5 – pop. 2 902 – alt. 188 m – ✉ 14260 Normandy
32 **B2**

Paris 269 – Caen 36 – Falaise 42 – Flers 37 – St-Lô 53 – Vire 34

Office de tourisme, rue Verdun ✆ 02 31 77 60 32, Fax 02 31 77 65 46

St-Michel with rm

VISA AE

6 r. de Caen – ✆ 02 31 77 63 16 – saint-michel-aunay@wanadoo.fr – Fax 02 31 77 05 83 – Closed in November, in January, Monday except dinner in July-August and Sunday dinner from September to June

6 rm – €45 €45, €8 – ½ P €48

Rest – Menu €15 (weekdays)/45 – Carte €36/50

◆ A discreet little family inn where traditional dishes are prepared with a regional touch. Comfortable, well-lit dining room. Simple, practical rooms.

For a pleasant stay in a charming hotel, look for the red ... symbols.

AUPS – 83 Var – 340 M4 – pop. 1 903 – alt. 496 m – ✉ 83630 French Riviera
41 **C3**

Paris 818 – Aix-en-Provence 90 – Digne-les-Bains 78 – Draguignan 29 – Manosque 59

Syndicat d'initiative, place Frédéric Mistral ✆ 04 94 84 00 69, Fax 04 94 84 00 69

Des Gourmets

VISA

5 r. Voltaire – ✆ 04 94 70 14 97 – lesgourmetsaups@aol.com – Closed 22 June-10 July, 30 November-18 December, Sunday dinner except July-August and Monday

Rest – Menu €17 (weekdays)/36

◆ Family address in the village where Var's largest truffles market is held. Rustic setting with frescos on the walls evoking Provence. Traditional cuisine.

in Moissac-Bellevue 7 km West by D9 – pop. 263 – alt. 599 m – ✉ 83630

Bastide du Calalou

VISA AE

rte de Baudinard – ✆ 04 94 70 17 91 – www.bastide-du-calalou.com – info@bastide-du-calalou.com – Fax 04 94 70 50 11

32 rm – €78/127 €78/210, €16 – ½ P €84/155

Rest – Menu (€23), €29 (weekdays) – Carte approx. €55

◆ Large country house dominating the Var countryside above the village. Bedrooms furnished with care and decorated with old-style paintings, the work of the proprietor. Provencal-style dining room, a flowery and shady terrace and local cuisine.

AURAY – 56 Morbihan – 308 N9 – pop. 12 100 – alt. 35 m – ✉ 56400 Brittany
9 **A3**

Paris 477 – Lorient 41 – Pontivy 54 – Quimper 102 – Vannes 20

✆ 3635 et tapez 42 (0,34 €/mn)

Office de tourisme, 20, rue du Lait ✆ 02 97 24 09 75, Fax 02 97 50 80 75

Quartier St-Goustan★ - Promenade du Loch★ - St-Gildas church ★ - Ste-Avoye: Rood-screen★ and framework★ of the church 4 km by ①.

Plan on next page

Du Loch

rm, VISA AE

2 r. Guhur, (The Forest) – ✆ 02 97 56 48 33 – www.hotel-du-loch.com – contact@hotel-du-loch.com – Fax 02 97 56 63 55 – Closed 15 December-4 January
e

30 rm – €55/74 €60/74, €8 – ½ P €60/67

Rest – *(Closed Sunday dinner and Saturday)* Menu (€17), €22/45 – Carte €28/42

◆ Unusual modern architecture (1970s) surrounded by preserved forestland and on the banks of the Loch. Spacious, functional rooms. Classic dishes (seafood) served in a veranda-style dining room surrounded by greenery.

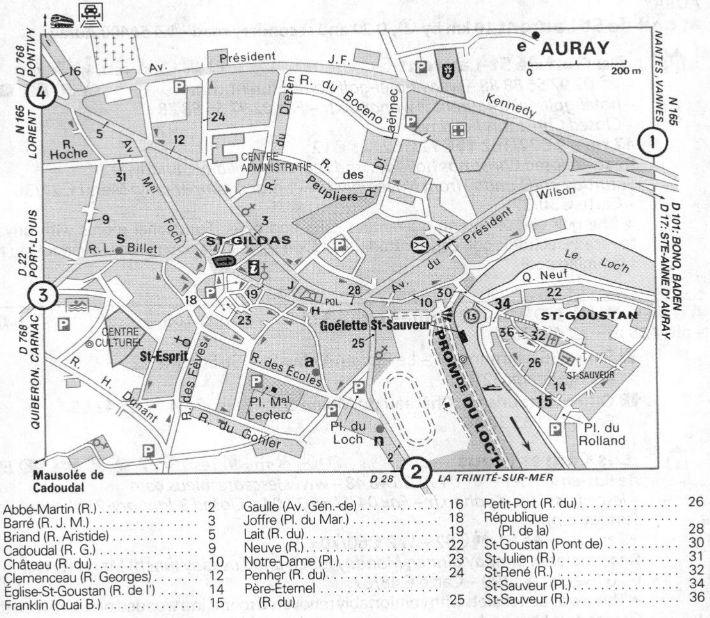

Auditel le Branhoc without rest
at 1.5 km Le Bono road – 02 97 56 41 55 – www.auditel-hotel.fr – auditel@orange.fr – Fax 02 97 56 41 35
4 rm – € 47/69 € 49/79, € 8
◆ A new lease of life for this hospitable hotel with practical and impeccably kept guestrooms (garden view). Snug sitting room.

Closerie de Kerdrain
20 r. L.-Billet – 02 97 56 61 27 – www.lacloseriedekerdrain.com – closerie.kerdrain@wanadoo.fr – Fax 02 97 24 15 79 – Closed 5 January-1st February, Sunday dinner except from Easter to All Saint's Day and Monday s
Rest – Menu (€ 28), € 38/90 – Carte € 64/74
◆ A charming little Breton manor house nestling in a garden. Elegant, wood-panelled dining rooms and a pleasant terrace complement the appetising modern cuisine.

La Table des Marées
16 r. Jeu-de-Paume – 02 97 56 63 60 – www.latabledesmarees.com – info@latabledesmarees.com – Closed 1 week in March, 3 weeks in October, 1 week in December, Saturday lunch, Sunday dinner and Monday a
Rest – Menu (€ 20 bi), € 28/38 – Carte € 55/65
◆ The updated menu evolves depending on the catch of the day. The snug interior sports a blend of modern furniture with old stones and a hearth.

La Chebaudière
6 r. Abbé-J.-Martin – 02 97 24 09 84 – lachebaudiere@orange.fr – Fax 02 97 24 09 84 – Closed 16-27 October, 17-27 February, Tuesday dinner, Sunday dinner and Wednesday n
Rest – Menu € 18 (weekday lunch), € 28/39 – Carte € 32/43
◆ A small, local restaurant serving dishes in keeping with current taste. Discreetly contemporary dining room, a place for painting exhibitions as well.

at golf de St-Laurent 10 km by ③, D 22 and secondary road – ✉ 56400 Auray

Du Golf de St-Laurent

– ✆ *02 97 56 88 88 – www.hotel-golf-saint-laurent.com – hotel-golf-saint-laurent@wanadoo.fr – Fax 02 97 56 88 28 – Closed Christmas holidays*

42 rm – †€ 72/162 ††€ 72/162, ☕ € 12

Rest – *(closed Christmas holidays and February holidays, Friday, Saturday and Sunday from November to February) (dinner only)* Menu € 27/36 – Carte € 30/37

◆ The golf course setting guarantees calm and quiet. Functional rooms with private terraces. Electronic golf course. Traditional food served in a dining room overlooking the swimming pool.

AUREC-SUR-LOIRE – 43 Haute-Loire – 331 H1 – pop. 5 165 – alt. 435 m – ✉ 43110

6 **D2**

Paris 536 – Firminy 11 – Le Puy-en-Velay 56 – St-Étienne 22 – Yssingeaux 32

Office de tourisme, Château du Moine-Sacristain ✆ 04 77 35 42 65, Fax 04 77 35 32 46

Les Cèdres Bleus

rm, rest,

rte Bas-en-Basset – ✆ 04 77 35 48 48 – www.lescedresbleus.com – lescedresbleus@yahoo.fr – Fax 04 77 35 37 04 – Closed 2 January-2 February and Sunday dinner

15 rm ☕ – †€ 51 ††€ 82 – ½ P € 60/70

Rest – *(closed Sunday dinner, Monday lunch and Tuesday lunch)* Menu (€ 17), € 20 (weekdays)/90 – Carte € 48/67

◆ Three wooden chalets with comfortably renovated rooms in a wooded park between the Gorges de la Loire and the Lac de Grangent. Enjoy ambitious traditional cuisine in the leafy surroundings of the panoramic dining room or the flower-decked terrace.

AUREILLE – 13 Bouches-du-Rhône – 340 E3 – pop. 1 463 – alt. 134 m – ✉ 13930

42 **E1**

Paris 719 – Aix-en-Provence 59 – Avignon 38 – Marseille 73

Le Balcon des Alpilles without rest

rte de Mouries, on the D24^A – ✆ 04 90 59 94 24 – http://lebalcondesalpilles.com – contact@lebalcondesalpilles.com – Fax 04 90 59 94 24 – Open 16 March-30 November

5 rm ☕ – †€ 120 ††€ 130

◆ The scent of olive trees, pines and lavender mingle in the garden of this peaceful house. Smart bedrooms with period furniture. Delicious breakfast and a cool terrace. Heated swimming pool.

AURIBEAU-SUR-SIAGNE – 06 Alpes-Maritimes – 341 C6 – pop. 2 694 – alt. 85 m – ✉ 06810 French Riviera

42 **E2**

Paris 900 – Cannes 15 – Draguignan 62 – Grasse 9 – Nice 42 – St-Raphaël 41

Syndicat d'initiative, place en Aïre ✆ 04 93 40 79 56, Fax 04 93 40 79 56

Auberge de la Vignette Haute

rm,

370 rte du Village – ✆ 04 93 42 20 01 – www.vignettehaute.com – info@vignettehaute.com – Fax 04 93 42 31 16

16 rm – †€ 130/170 ††€ 190/340, ☕ € 15 – 1 suite

Rest – *(closed Monday and Tuesday from November to April)* Menu € 49 bi (lunch), € 95 € bi/110 bi – Carte € 80/110 dinner only

◆ The exceptional decor in this hotel on the Côte d'Azur is inspired by the Middle Ages. Comfortable rooms, with some fine pieces of antique furniture. In the restaurant: old stonework, untreated wood, pewter tableware lighting provided by oil lamps and a view of the animal pen

AURILLAC P – 15 Cantal – 330 C5 – pop. 29 700 – alt. 610 m – ✉ 15000 Auvergne

5 **B3**

Paris 557 – Brive-la-Gaillarde 98 – Clermont-Ferrand 158 – Montauban 174

Aurillac ✆ 04 71 64 50 00 3 km on the ③

Office de tourisme, 7 rue des Carmes ✆ 04 71 48 46 58, Fax 04 71 48 99 39

18 de Haute-Auvergne Arpajon-sur-Cère La Bladade, SW : 7 km on N 122 and D 153, ✆ 04 71 47 73 75

9 de Vézac Aurillac Vézac Mairie, SE : 8 km on D 990, ✆ 04 71 62 44 11

Château St-Étienne: muséum des Volcans★.

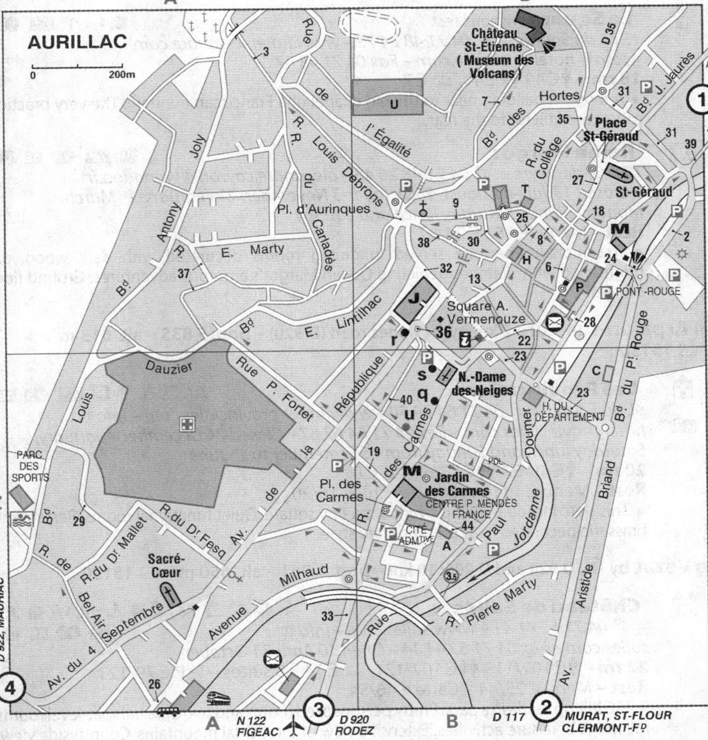

Angoulême (Cours d') ...... BY 2	Gambetta (Av.) .... BZ 23	Pupilles de la Nation (Av. des) .... AZ 33
Arbre Croumaly (R. de l') ...... AY 3	Gerbert (Pl.) .... BY 24	République (Av. de la) .... AZ
Carmes (R. des) .... BZ	Marchande (R.) .... BY 25	St-Géraud (Pl.) .... BY 34
Champeil (R. J.-B.) .... BY 6	Maynard (R. F.) .... AZ 26	St-Jacques (R.) .... BY 35
Château St-Étienne (R. du) .... BY 7	Monastère (R. du) .... BY 27	Square (Pl. du) .... BY 36
Consulat (R. du) .... BY 8	Monthyon (Cours) .... BY 28	Vaissière (R. Robert de la) .... AY 37
Coste (R. de la) .... BY 9	Mont Mouchet (R. du) .... AZ 29	Vermenouze (R. Arsène) ...... BY 38
Duclaux (R. Émile) .... BY 13	Noailles (R. de) .... BY 30	Veyre (Av. J.-B.) .... BY 39
Fargues (R. des) .... BY 18	Pavatou (Bd du) .... BY 31	14-Juillet (R. du) .... BZ 40
Ferry (R. Jules) .... BZ 19	Prés.-Delzons (R. du) .... BY 32	139e-R.-I. (R. du) .... BZ 44
Frères (R. des) .... BY 22		

Grand Hôtel de Bordeaux without rest

2 av. de la République – ✆ 04 71 48 01 84
– www.hotel-de-bordeaux.fr – bestwestern@hotel-de-bordeaux.fr
– Fax 04 71 48 49 93 – Closed 19 December-3 January

VISA MC AE

BY **r**

33 rm – †€ 62/86 ††€ 84/96, ☕ € 11

◆ Most of the rooms of this handsome early-20C building have been refurbished in a pleasant contemporary style; the others are equally attractive (period or cane furniture).

Delcher
20 r. Carmes – ✆ 04 71 48 01 69 – www.hotel-delcher.com – hotel.delcher@wanadoo.fr – Fax 04 71 48 86 66 – Closed 13-19 April, 16 July-2 August and 20 December-3 January BZ **q**
23 rm – €45 €50, €7 – ½ P €47
Rest – *(closed Sunday dinner and bank holidays)* Menu (€14), €17/29 – Carte approx. €30
◆ Unpretentious rooms, some with exposed beams. In one of the rooms and in the lounge there are murals by Danish artist Gorm Hansen, painted to cover his rent! Traditional no-fuss cooking served, in summer, on a courtyard-terrace.

Le Square without rest
15 pl. du Square – ✆ 04 71 48 24 72 – www.hotel-le-square.com – resa@hotel-le-square.com – Fax 04 71 48 47 57 BZ **s**
18 rm – €45 €49, €7
◆ A modern building near to the old chapel of a Franciscan nunnery. The very practical rooms are quieter to the rear.

Reine Margot
19 r. G.-de-Veyre – ✆ 04 71 48 26 46 – alexandre.cayron@wanadoo.fr – Closed 13 July-4 August, 25 October-3 November, 21 February-1st March, Monday dinner, Saturday lunch and Sunday BZ **u**
Rest – Menu (€18), €24/27
◆ Traditional repertoire served in dining rooms decorated with dark woodwork brightened with sketches depicting Queen Margot's amorous adventures. Ground floor brasserie.

in Arpajon-sur-Cère 2 km by ③ Rodez road (D 920) – pop. 5 835 – alt. 613 m – ✉ 15130

Les Provinciales
pl. du Foirail – ✆ 04 71 64 29 50 – www.hotel-provinciales.com – info@hotel-provinciales.com – Fax 04 71 64 67 87 – Closed 24 December-4 January, Saturday lunch and Sunday from 15 September to 1st June
20 rm – €48/57 €57/68, €8
Rest – Menu €13 (weekday lunch), €16/20
◆ This slate façade building overlooks a tiny square. Quiet functional rooms. Restaurant-brasserie decorated in a contemporary style.

in Vézac by ③, D 920 and D 990: 10 km – pop. 1 061 – alt. 650 m – ✉ 15130

Château de Salles
– ✆ 04 71 62 41 41 – www.salles.com – info@salles.com – Fax 04 71 62 44 14 – Open 10 April-31 October
22 rm – €102/113 €102/171, €14 – 8 suites – ½ P €79/123
Rest – Menu €25/44 – Carte €46/54
◆ 15C hilltop castle in a park. Pretty personalized rooms and two unusual split-level rooms; full range of leisure activities. Extensive view of the Cantal mountains. Countryside views from the veranda-dining room, plus a terrace overlooking the Vézac golf course.

AURON – 06 Alpes-Maritimes – 341 C2 – ✉ 06660 St Etienne de Tinee 41 C-D2

French Alps

Paris 914 – Marseille 263 – Nice 93 – Borgo San Dalmazzo 206 – Dronero 228
Office de tourisme, avenue de Malhira ✆ 04 93 23 02 66, Fax 04 93 23 07 39

Le Chalet d'Auron
– ✆ 04 93 23 00 21 – www.chaletdauron.com – mail@chaletdauron.com – Fax 04 93 23 09 19 – Open 7 June-31 August and 14 December-31 March
15 rm – €89/374 €89/374, €15 – 2 suites – ½ P €104/385
Rest – Carte €42/62
◆ This chalet has been completely renovated in typical Alpine style, with a cosy lounge and guestrooms with individual touches. Terrace with views of the mountains. Swimming pool and hammam. Generous portions of fish and seafood are served in this restaurant. Wood decor in the dining room.

AUSSOIS – 73 Savoie – **333** N6 – **pop. 668** – **alt. 1 489 m** – **Winter sports : 1 500/2 750 m** 11 – 73500 French Alps 45 **D2**

Paris 670 – Albertville 97 – Chambéry 110 – Lanslebourg-Mont-Cenis 17 – Modane 7

Office de tourisme, route des Barrages 04 79 20 30 80, Fax 04 79 20 40 23

Monolithe de Sardières ★ Northeast: 3 km - Fortified site of Esseillon ★ South: 4 km.

Du Soleil — rm, VISA MC AE

15 r. de l'Église – 04 79 20 32 42 – www.hotel-du-soleil.com – hotel-du-soleil@wanadoo.fr – Fax 04 79 20 37 78 – Open June to mid-October and mid-December to end April

22 rm – €50/59 €65/106, €10 – ½ P €59/84

Rest – *(dinner only) (pre-book)* Menu €21/38 – Carte €33/57

◆ The hotel's advantages include rooms with mountain views and many places to relax: the sauna, steam room, outdoor hot tub or projection room. For guests only, Savoyard specialities served in a colourful dining room.

Les Mottets — VISA MC AE

6 r. Mottets – 04 79 20 30 86 – www.hotel-lesmottets.com – infos@hotel-lesmottets.com – Fax 04 79 20 34 22 – Closed May and 1st November-14 December

25 rm – €42/49 €60/80, €9 – ½ P €58/67

Rest – Menu (€14), €18/35 – Carte €25/43

◆ 200m from the slopes, a chalet providing a beautiful view of the surrounding summits. Simple and functional rooms. Rustic dining room where regional specialities take pride of place.

The red symbol?
This denotes the very essence of peace –
only the sound of birdsong first thing in the morning...

AUTHUILLE – 80 Somme – **301** J7 – see Albert

AUTRANS – 38 Isère – **333** G6 – **pop. 1 541** – **alt. 1 050 m** – **Winter sports : 1 050/1 710 m** 13 – 38880 French Alps 45 **C2**

Paris 586 – Grenoble 36 – Romans-sur-Isère 58 – St-Marcellin 47 – Villard-de-Lans 16

Office de tourisme, rue du Cinéma 04 76 95 30 70, Fax 04 76 95 38 63

La Poste — rm, VISA MC AE

– 04 76 95 31 03 – www.hotel-barnier.com – contact@hotel-barnier.com – Fax 04 76 95 30 17 – Open 11 May-18 October and 4 December-18 April

29 rm – €60/84 €64/94, €10 – ½ P €63/76

Rest – *(closed Sunday dinner and Monday except July-August and 20 December-14 March)* Menu €22/45 – Carte €32/48

◆ The same family has run this spruce hotel in the village since 1937. Progressively renovated rustic rooms. Oil paintings dotted here and there. Sauna and steam bath. Classic and regional dishes, a wainscoted interior and attractive table settings.

Les Tilleuls — rest, VISA MC AE

la Côte – 04 76 95 32 34 – www.hotel-tilleuls.com – tilleuls.hotel@wanadoo.fr – Fax 04 76 95 31 58 – Closed 14 April-7 May, 26 October-19 November, Tuesday dinner and Wednesday in low season and except school holidays

18 rm – €49/62 €56/76, €9 – 2 suites – ½ P €56/66

Rest – Menu €21/42 – Carte €32/48

◆ Near the centre of the resort in the Vercors nature park, this welcoming building offers practical and well-maintained rooms. Six have been renovated. Classic cuisine, game in season and the house speciality: caillette.

in Méaudre **5.5 km South by D 106^c – pop. 1 171 – alt. 1 012 m – Winter sports : 1000/1600 m 10 – ✉ 38112**

Office de tourisme, le Village ✆ 04 76 95 20 68, Fax 04 76 95 25 93

Auberge du Furon with rm
La Combe – ✆ 04 76 95 21 47 – www.auberge-furon.fr – gaultier.rg@orange.fr – Fax 04 83 07 53 63 – Closed 8-12 June
9 rm – €55/60 €55/60, €8,50
Rest – *(closed Wednesday dinner, Sunday dinner and Monday except school holidays)* Menu (€13), €21/34 – Carte €27/34
◆ This small chalet, at the foot of the ski lifts and decorated in an understated alpine vein, offers a regularly renewed menu. Rooms decorated in a regional style.

AUTREVILLE – **88 Vosges** – **314** D2 – **pop. 157** – **alt. 310 m** – ✉ **88300** 26 **B2**

Paris 313 – Nancy 45 – Neufchâteau 20 – Toul 24

Le Relais Rose
24 r. Neufchâteau – ✆ 03 83 52 04 98 – loeffler.catherine@orange.fr – Fax 03 83 52 06 03
16 rm – €44/70 €49/78, €8,50 – ½ P €51/70
Rest – Menu €13 (weekday lunch), €21/30 – Carte €26/47
◆ A comfortable, cosy family hotel. Each room is a surprising jumble of furniture and styles. Somewhat kitsch but most appealing. Classic, almost country cuisine and specialities of Southwest France. Pretty terrace.

AUTUN – **71 Saône-et-Loire** – **320** F8 – **pop. 15 100** – **alt. 326 m** – ✉ **71400** **Burgundy-Jura** 8 **C2**

Paris 287 – Avallon 78 – Chalon-sur-Saône 51 – Dijon 85 – Mâcon 111

Office de tourisme, 2, avenue Charles de Gaulle ✆ 03 85 86 80 38, Fax 03 85 86 80 49

d'Autun Le Plan d'Eau du Vallon, 3 km on the Chalon-s-Saône, ✆ 03 85 52 09 28

St-Lazare cathedral ★★ (tympanum★★★, capitals★★) - Musée Rolin★ (la Eve's temptation ★★, Cardinal Rolin Nativity ★★, Autun Virgin ★★) BZ **M²** - Porte St-André★ - Gates★ of lycée Bonaparte AZ **B** - Manuscripts★ (Town hall library) BZ **H**.

Plan on next page

La Tête Noire rest,
3 r. Arquebuse – ✆ 03 85 86 59 99 – www.hoteltetenoire.fr – welcome@hoteltetenoire.fr – Fax 03 85 86 33 90 – Closed 20 December-26 January
31 rm – €63/74 €74/80, €10 – ½ P €65/69 BZ **n**
Rest – Menu (€14), €18/50 – Carte €23/55
◆ This town centre establishment offers practical and well-soundproofed guestrooms adorned with rustic, painted wooden furniture. Friendly welcome. Regional and 'terroir' menu.

Ibis rm,
2 km rte Chalon via ③ – ✆ 03 85 52 00 00 – www.ibishotel.com – h3232@accor.com – Fax 03 85 52 20 20
46 rm – €55/64 €55/69, €8
Rest – *(closed Saturday and Sunday in low season) (dinner only)* Menu €17
◆ This Ibis is on the banks of a watersports lake and two minutes from the historic town. It offers functional rooms in keeping with the chain's latest standards. A friendly restaurant serving traditional fare.

Le Moulin Renaudiots
chemin du Vieux-Moulin, 5 km southeast on the N 80 and D 978 – ✆ 03 85 86 97 10 – www.moulinrenaudiots.com – contact@moulinrenaudiots.com – Closed January
5 rm – €100 €125/140
Table d'hôte – *(Closed Monday, Wednesday, Friday and Sunday) (pre-book)* Menu €40
◆ A superb villa clad in Virginia creeper and a French-style garden. Elegant minimalist interior with a comfortable contemporary decor that is most relaxing. A large table d'hôte piled high with local produce at breakfast and dinnertime.

AUTUN

Arbalète (R. de l') . . . . BZ 2
Arquebuse (R. de l') . . . . BZ 3
Cascade (R. de la) . . . . BZ 4
Chauchien (Gde-Rue) . . . . BZ 6
Cocand (R.) . . . . AZ 7
Cordeliers (R. des) . . . . BZ 9
Cordiers (R. aux) . . . . BZ 12
Dijon (R. de) . . . . BY 13
Dr-Renaud (R.) . . . . AZ 15
Eumène (R.) . . . . AY 16
Gaillon (R. de) . . . . BY 18
Gaulle (Av. Ch.-de) . . . . AYZ 19
Grange-Vertu (Rue de la) . . . . . AY 21
Guérin (R.) . . . . BY 23
Jeannin (R.) . . . . BZ 26
Lattre-de-Tassigny (R. de) . . . . BZ 27
Laureau (Bd) . . . . BY 28
Marbres (R. des) . . . . BZ 29
Martin (R. Maître G.) . . . . BY 43
Notre-Dame (R.) . . . . AZ 31
Paris (R. de) . . . . ABY 32
Passage couvert . . . . BZ 33
Pernette (R.) . . . . AZ 35
Raquette (R.) . . . . BZ 37
St-Saulge (R.) . . . . AZ 40
Vieux-Colombier (R. du) . . . . BZ 42

Maison Sainte-Barbe without rest

7 pl. Ste-Barbe – ✆ 03 85 86 24 77 – www.maisonsaintebarbe.com – maisonsaintebarbe@yahoo.fr – Fax 03 85 86 19 28 BZ **t**

3 rm – €60 €65

◆ Former canon's house (15-18C) at the foot of the cathedral. Large, personalised rooms, pretty breakfast room furnished with antiques, walled garden.

Le Chalet Bleu

3 r. Jeannin – ✆ 03 85 86 27 30 – www.lechaletbleu.com – contact@lechaletbleu.com – Fax 03 85 52 74 56 – Closed 1st-5 January, 1st-23 February, Monday dinner, Tuesday and Sunday dinner except July-August BYZ **s**

Rest – Menu € 18 (weekdays)/60 – Carte € 40/70

◆ Behind a glass-front, dining room with walls decorated with murals of imaginary gardens and landscapes. The menu offers a combination of traditional and local dishes; themed set menus on Friday evenings.

Le Chapitre

11 pl. du Terreau – ✆ 03 85 52 04 01 – www.lechapitre71.com – lechapitre.71.autun @ orange.fr – Closed Christmas holidays, 15-28 February, Sunday dinner and Monday BZ **d**

Rest – *(number of covers limited, pre-book)* Menu € 15 (lunch), € 28/35 – Carte € 30/37

◆ At the foot of the cathedral, this small restaurant serves updated tasty fare. Airy dining room graced with wrought iron furniture; romantic candle-lit dinners.

AUVERS – 77 Seine-et-Marne – 312 D5 – see Milly-la-Forêt (Essonne)

AUVERS-SUR-OISE – 95 Val-d'Oise – 305 E6 – 106 6 – 101 3 – see Paris, Area

AUVILLAR – 82 Tarn-et-Garonne – 337 B7 – pop. 994 – alt. 141 m – ✉ 82340 28 **B2**

Paris 652 – Agen 28 – Montauban 42 – Auch 62 – Castelsarrasin 22

Office de tourisme, place de la Halle ✆ 05 63 39 89 82, Fax 05 63 39 89 82

L'Horloge with rm

pl. de l'Horloge – ✆ 05 63 39 91 61 – www.horlogeauvillar.monsite.orange.fr – hoteldelhorloge @ wanadoo.fr – Fax 05 63 39 75 20 – Closed 20 December-4 January, Saturday lunch and Friday from 15 October to 15 April

10 rm – 🚹€ 45 🚹🚹€ 50/75, ☕ € 11

Rest – *(closed Friday except dinner in July-August and Saturday lunch)* Menu (€ 14), € 28/75 – Carte € 62/80

Rest *Le Bouchon* – *(closed Saturday except July-August and Friday) (lunch only)* Menu (€ 14,50), € 18 – Carte approx. € 22

◆ Just next to the graceful Horloge, a delightful place with pretty green shutters and tables under the plane trees. Classy, modern setting. Local cuisine and wines. At lunchtime the Bouchon offers nice little bistro-style dishes with a local flavour.

in Bardigues 4 km South by D 11 – **pop. 240 – alt. 160 m** – ✉ **82340**

Auberge de Bardigues

au bourg – ✆ 05 63 39 05 58 – www.aubergedebardigues.com – info @ aubergedebardigues.com – Closed 1st-7 September, 16-26 October, 15-22 February, Wednesday dinner except July-August, Sunday dinner and Monday

Rest – Menu (€ 12 bi), € 17 bi (weekday lunch), € 29/55 bi

◆ A family establishment run by brothers in the heart of a pretty country village. Panoramic terrace, contemporary decor and gourmet-bistro cuisine.

AUXERRE Ⓟ – 89 Yonne – 319 E5 – pop. 37 100 – alt. 130 m – ✉ 89000 7 **B1**

Burgundy-Jura

Paris 166 – Bourges 144 – Chalon-sur-Saône 176 – Dijon 152 – Sens 59

Office de tourisme, 1-2, quai de la République ✆ 03 86 52 06 19, Fax 03 86 51 23 27

St-Étienne cathedral ★★ (stained-glass windows★★, crypt★, treasure-house★) - Former St-Germain abbey ★★ (crypt★★).

Gy-l'Évêque: Christ aux Orties★ of the chapel 9.5 km by ③.

Plan on next page

Le Parc des Maréchaux without rest

6 av. Foch – ✆ 03 86 51 43 77 – www.hotel-parcmarechaux.com – contact @ hotel-parcmarechaux.com – Fax 03 86 51 31 72 AZ **u**

25 rm – 🚹€ 78/109 🚹🚹€ 89/130, ☕ € 12

◆ This Napoleon III dwelling has pretty, cosy rooms, which are fully renovated and furnished in Empire style; those opening onto the park are quietest. Muted bar decorated in red velvet.

AUXERRE

Street	Grid	No.
Boucheries (R. des)	BZ	3
Bourbotte (Av.)	BY	4
Chesnez (R. M. des)	AZ	5
Coche-d'Eau (Pl. du)	BY	8
Cochois (R.)	BY	9
Diderot (R.)	AZ	10
Dr-Labosse (R. du)	BY	11
Draperie (R. de la)	AZ	12
Eckmühl (R. d')	AZ	14
Fécauderie (R.)	AZ	16
Foch (Av.)	AZ	18
Grand-Caire (R. du)	AY	20
Horloge (R. de l')	AZ	22
Hôtel-de-Ville (Pl. de l')	AZ	23
Jean-Jaurès (Av.)	BY	26
Jean-Jaurès (Pl.)	BZ	27
Leclerc (Pl. du Mar.)	AZ	34
Lepère (Pl. Ch.)	AZ	35
Maison-Fort (R.)	BY	36
Marine (R. de la)	BY	37
Mont-Brenn (R. du)	BY	38
Paris (R. de)	AY	
Puits-des-Dames (R. du)	BZ	40
St-Germain (R.)	ABY	44
St-Nicolas (Pl.)	BY	45
Schaeffer (R. René)	AZ	46
Surugue (Pl. Ch.)	AZ	47
Temple (R. du)	AZ	
Tournelle (Av. de la)	BY	48
Yonne (R. de l')	BY	52
24-Août (R. du)	AZ	54

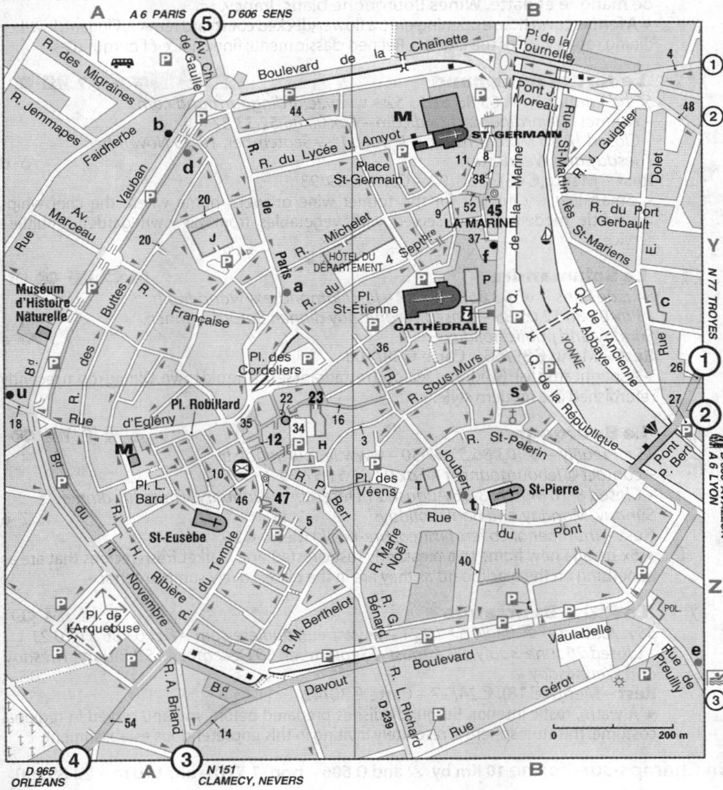

Normandie without rest
41 bd Vauban – ✆ 03 86 52 57 80 – www.hotelnormandie.fr
– reception@hotelnormandie.fr – Fax 03 86 51 54 33
– Closed 19 December-4 January AY **b**
47 rm – €63/69 €69/96, €9
◆ A peaceful courtyard terrace, comfortable rooms (preferable in the main house), an Art Deco furnished lounge bar, billiards and fitness facilities set the scene of this opulent house.

Le Maxime without rest
2 quai de la Marine – ✆ 03 86 52 14 19 – www.lemaxime.com – contact@lemaxime.com – Fax 03 86 52 21 70 BY **f**
26 rm – €72/118 €82/145, €11
◆ On the banks of the Yonne, this former salt warehouse was converted into a hotel in the 19C. Pleasantly renovated rooms (period furniture) overlooking the river or the quieter courtyard.

XXXX **Barnabet** (Jean-Luc Barnabet)
14 quai de la République – 03 86 51 68 88 – Fax 03 86 52 96 85 – Closed 22 December-13 January, Sunday dinner, Tuesday lunch and Monday BYZ **s**
Rest – Menu (€ 31), € 49/77 bi – Carte € 86/107
Spec. Emincé de pied de cochon tiédi sur assiette. Ris de veau doré au four. Pressé de mangue et datte. **Wines** Bourgogne blanc, Irancy.
◆ A former town house opening onto a flower-decked courtyard terrace. Elegant, low-key dining room, view of the kitchen. Refined classic menu; fine choice of burgundies.

XXX **Le Jardin Gourmand**
56 bd Vauban – 03 86 51 53 52 – www.lejardingourmand.com – contact@lejardingourmand.com – Fax 03 86 52 33 82 – Closed 10-18 March, 16 June-1st July, 1st-9 September, 10-25 November, Tuesday and Wednesday AY **d**
Rest – Menu (€ 46), € 58/92 – Carte € 69/93
◆ Smart low-key interior for this former wine grower's home where the chef whips up subtle modern dishes served with vegetables from his own garden. Faultless service.

XX **La Salamandre**
84 r. de Paris – 03 86 52 87 87 – la-salamandre@wanadoo.fr – Fax 03 86 52 05 85 – Closed Wednesday dinner, Saturday lunch, Sunday and public holidays AY **a**
Rest – Menu € 39/66 – Carte € 58/100
◆ A sought after fish (wild) and seafood restaurant set in the old town. Dining room recently refurbished in a modern style.

X **Le Bourgogne**
15 r. Preuilly – 03 86 51 57 50 – www.lebourgogne.fr – contact@lebourgogne.fr – Fax 03 86 51 57 50 – Closed 8-16 March, 3-16 August, 21 December-4 January, Thursday dinner, Sunday, Monday and bank holidays BZ **e**
Rest – *(number of covers limited, pre-book)* Menu € 29
◆ Ex-garage now home to a pleasantly rustic restaurant. Market fresh recipes that are as appetising on the blackboard as they are in the plate. Lovely summer terrace.

X **La P'tite Beursaude**
55 r. Joubert – 03 86 51 10 21 – www.beursaudiere.com – Fax 03 86 51 10 21 – Closed 26 June-3 July, 28 August-4 September, 30 December-15 January, Tuesday and Wednesday BZ **t**
Rest – Menu (€ 18), € 24/27 – Carte € 30/42
◆ A warm, rustic interior, Burgundy dishes prepared before you and served in regional costume: the atmosphere is resolutely inviting in this unpretentious establishment.

in Champs-sur-Yonne **10 Km by ② and D 606 – pop. 1 578 – alt. 110 m – ✉ 89290**

Mas des Lilas without rest
Hameau de la La Cour Barrée – 03 86 53 60 55 – www.lemasdeslilas.com – hotel@lemasdeslilas.com – Fax 03 86 53 30 81 – Closed 28 October-7 November and one week in February
17 rm – †€ 62 ††€ 62, ☕ € 8
◆ Lodges nestling in a pleasant garden dotted with flowers, housing small, well-kept, ground-floor rooms with terraces overlooking greenery.

in Vincelottes **16 km by ② D 606 and D 38 – pop. 310 – alt. 110 m – ✉ 89290**

XX **Auberge Les Tilleuls** with rm
12 quai de l'Yonne – 03 86 42 22 13 – www.auberge-les-tilleuls.com – lestilleulsvincelottes@yahoo.fr – Fax 03 86 42 23 51 – Closed 20 December-24 February, Tuesday and Wednesday
5 rm ☕ – †€ 67/78 ††€ 78/100 – ½ P € 65/76
Rest – Menu € 26/59 – Carte € 46/87
◆ A pastoral stopover on the banks of the Yonne. Pretty rooms with work by local artists and a riverside terrace. Traditional menu and a fine choice of burgundies.

in Chevannes 8 km by ③ and D1 – pop. 1 973 – alt. 170 m – ✉ 89240

XX **La Chamaille** with rm
4 rte Boiloup – ✆ 03 86 41 24 80 – www.lachamaille.fr – contact@lachamaille.fr – Fax 03 86 41 34 80 – Closed 27 October-3 November, 23 February-9 March, Sunday dinner and Monday from March to September
3 rm – †€ 40/50 ††€ 50/60, ☕ € 10 – ½ P € 50/60
Rest – Menu € 39/58 – Carte € 57/73
◆ An old, authentically rural farmstead tucked away in the countryside. A veranda opens onto the flower filled park through which a stream runs. Up-to-date cuisine.

near Auxerre-Nord interchange 7 km by ⑤

Mercure
D 606 – ✆ 03 86 53 25 00 – www.mercure.com – h0348@accor.com – Fax 03 86 53 07 47
77 rm – †€ 85/115 ††€ 95/125, ☕ € 15 **Rest** – Menu € 19/30 – Carte € 20/39
◆ A motel-style construction. Simple rooms laid out around a pool and level with the garden planted with a few grape vines. Bright and pleasant modern restaurant. Traditional and regional cuisine served. Lovely terrace.

in Appoigny 8 km by ⑤ and D 606 – pop. 3 091 – alt. 110 m – ✉ 89380

Syndicat d'initiative, 4, rue du Fer à Cheval ✆ 03 86 53 20 90

Le Puits d'Athie
1 r. de l'Abreuvoir – ✆ 03 86 53 10 59 – www.appoigny.fr – puitsdathie@free.fr – Fax 03 86 53 10 59
4 rm ☕ – †€ 69/160 ††€ 69/160 **Table d'hôte** – *(pre-book)* Menu € 45 bi
◆ The personalised rooms of this Bourguignon house are a feast for the eyes, in particular Mykonos, decorated in blue and white and Porte d'Orient, decorated with an authentic door from Rajasthan. The proprietress rustles up southern and regional dishes.

AVAILLES-LIMOUZINE – 86 Vienne – 322 J8 – pop. 1 312 – alt. 142 m – ✉ 86460 39 C2

Paris 413 – Chauvigny 61 – Poitiers 66 – Saint-Junien 40

Office de tourisme, 6, rue Principale ✆ 05 49 48 63 05, Fax 05 49 48 63 05

La Chatellenie
1 r. du Commerce – ✆ 05 49 84 31 31 – www.chatellenie.fr – contact@chatellenie.fr – Fax 05 49 84 31 32
9 rm – †€ 45/55 ††€ 45/55, ☕ € 6 – ½ P € 60
Rest – *(closed Sunday dinner and Monday)* Menu (€ 10), € 12 (weekday lunch), € 18/49 – Carte approx. € 48
◆ This pleasantly restored 1830 former post house has good-sized rooms with painted wooden furniture and parquet floors. Peaceful family ambiance. Traditional food served in the walled courtyard in summer.

AVALLON – 89 Yonne – 319 G7 – pop. 7 366 – alt. 250 m – ✉ 89200 Burgundy-Jura 7 B2

Paris 222 – Auxerre 51 – Beaune 103 – Chaumont 134 – Nevers 98

Syndicat d'initiative, 6, rue Bocquillot ✆ 03 86 34 14 19, Fax 03 86 34 28 29

Site★ - Fortified town★: Portals★ of St-Lazare church - Miserere★ du musée de l'Avallonnais M[1] - Cousin Valley ★ South by D 427.

Plan on next page

Hostellerie de la Poste
13 pl. Vauban – ✆ 03 86 34 16 16 – www.hostelleriedelaposte.com – info@hostelleriedelaposte.com – Fax 03 86 34 19 19 – Closed January and February
30 rm – †€ 93/113 ††€ 108/190, ☕ € 13 – ½ P € 102/143 **b**
Rest – *(open 16 March-30 November and closed Sunday and Monday) (dinner only)* Menu € 25, € 35/65 – Carte € 37/43
Rest *Bistrot* – *(closed Sunday and Monday) (lunch only)* Menu € 15/20
◆ Handsome former Burgundian post house, from 1707, whose guests have included Napoleon I and John Kennedy! Pretty rooms with personal touches. The restaurant, located in converted stables, serves classic cuisine. Bistro formula at lunchtime.

AVALLON

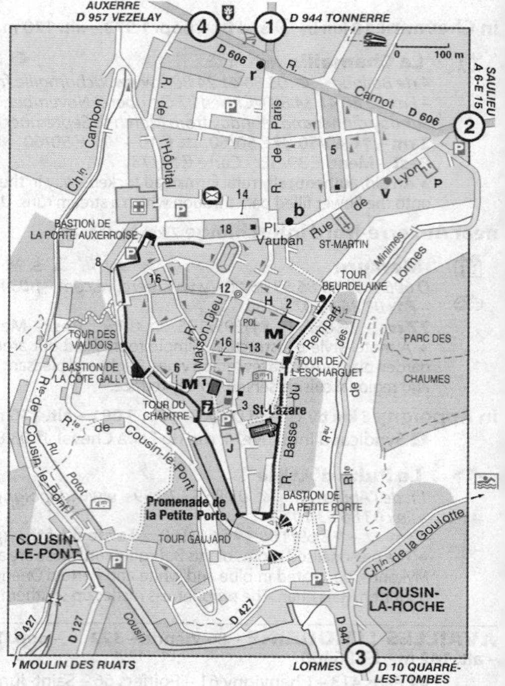

Avallon Vauban without rest

53 r. de Paris – ✆ 03 86 34 36 99 – www.avallonvaubanhotel.com – contact@avallonvaubanhotel.com – Fax 03 86 31 66 31 r

26 rm – †€ 54/60 ††€ 60/75, ☕ € 8,50

◆ By a busy crossroads, this regional style house overlooks a large shaded park around which sculpture by the owner/artist can be seen. Comfortable rooms; the quietest are to the rear.

Dak'Hôtel without rest

119 r. de Lyon, Saulieu road via ② – ✆ 03 86 31 63 20 – www.dak-hotel.com – dakhotel@yahoo.fr – Fax 03 86 34 25 28

26 rm – †€ 56 ††€ 62, ☕ € 8,50

◆ Cube-shaped building near the main road. Functional, well kept and soundproofed rooms. Breakfast room overlooking the garden; swimming pool.

Le Gourmillon

8 r. de Lyon – ✆ 03 86 31 62 01 – www.legourmillon.com – contact@legourmillon.com – Fax 03 86 31 62 01 – Closed 5-18 January, Thursday dinner off season and Sunday dinner v

Rest – Menu (€ 12 bi), € 17/32 – Carte € 25/40

◆ A little downtown address, simple but generous. Airy dining room with tasteful countrified feel. The menus give preference to rustic dishes.

Saulieu road 6 km by ② – ✉ 89200 Avallon

Le Relais Fleuri

La Cerce – ✆ 03 86 34 02 85 – www.relais-fleuri.com – relais-fleuri@lerelais-fleuri.com – Fax 03 86 34 09 98

48 rm – †€ 80/90 ††€ 80/90, ☕ € 13 – ½ P € 82

Rest – Menu € 20/63 bi – Carte € 30/57

◆ This hotel, on the Saulieu road, houses functional, motel-style rooms, level with the 4ha park with tennis courts and a heated pool. Elegant, rustic dining room, reinterpreted traditional menu and a wine cellar rich in Burgundies.

in Pontaubert 5 km by ④ and D 957 – pop. 391 – alt. 160 m – ✉ 89200

Les Fleurs with rm
69 rte de Vézelay – ✆ 03 86 34 13 81 – www.hotel-lesfleurs.com – info@hotel-lesfleurs.com – Fax 03 86 34 23 32 – Closed 21 December-5 February
7 rm – €53/57 €53/57, €8
Rest – *(closed Thursday except from 1st July to 15 September and Wednesday)* Menu €19/44 – Carte €32/50
◆ A gradually refurbished family-run inn: pastel shades prevail indoors, terrace overlooking the garden, and simple rooms. Traditional and regional dishes.

In the Vallée du Cousin 6 km by ④, Pontaubert and D 427 – ✉ 89200 Avallon

Hostellerie du Moulin des Ruats
r. des Îles Labaumes – ✆ 03 86 34 97 00 – www.moulindesruats.com – contact@moulindesruats.com – Fax 03 86 31 65 47 – Open from mid-February to 11 November
24 rm – €82/117 €82/154, €13 – 1 suite – ½ P €99/135
Rest – *(Closed Monday) (dinner only except Sunday)* Menu €30/47 – Carte €50/59
◆ This former 18C mill nestling in the tranquil Cousin valley invites guests to relax: pleasant bar-library with refined atmosphere and rooms with olde worlde charm. The dining room with veranda offers relaxing views over the area. Lovely terrace. Classic cuisine and decor.

in Vault de Lugny 6 km by ④ and D 142 – pop. 328 – alt. 148 m – ✉ 89200

Château de Vault de Lugny rest,
11 r. du Château – ✆ 03 86 34 07 86 – www.lugny.fr – hotel@lugny.fr – Fax 03 86 34 16 36 – Open 9 April-15 November
16 rm – €178/595 €178/595, €24
Rest – *(dinner only)* Menu €65/105 – Carte €55/98
◆ This luxurious 16C chateau encourages the traditional way of life. Superb gardens and vegetable plot, pool set in a vaulted outbuilding, all in an idyllically quiet setting.

in Valloux 6 km by ④ and D 606 – ✉ 89200 Vault-de-Lugny

Auberge des Chenêts
10 rte Nationale 6 – ✆ 03 86 34 23 34 – Fax 03 86 34 21 24 – Closed 22 June-6 July, 12 November-2 December, Tuesday from October to March, Sunday dinner and Monday
Rest – Menu (€18), €26/54 – Carte €48/62
◆ A pleasant country inn on quite a busy road. Settle yourself next to the fireplace and taste the traditional burgundy dishes.

AVÈNE – 34 Hérault – 339 D6 – pop. 289 – alt. 350 m – Spa : early April-late Oct. – ✉ 34260 — 22 **B2**

Paris 705 – Bédarieux 25 – Clermont-l'Hérault 51 – Montpellier 83

Office de tourisme, le Village ✆ 04 67 23 43 38, Fax 04 67 23 16 95

Val d'Orb rm,
Les Bains-d'Avène, at the thermal baths – ✆ 04 67 23 44 45 – www.valdorb.com – val.dorb@pierre.fabre.com – Fax 04 67 23 39 07 – Open April-October
58 rm – €91/96 €96/102, €9 **Rest** – Menu €15/28 – Carte €33/60
◆ Modern establishment, nestled in a verdant little valley and part of a spa centre. Spacious and functional lodging. Modern dining room and terrace off the garden. Traditional menu and diet dishes.

AVENSAN – 33 Gironde – 335 G4 – pop. 1 753 – alt. 25 m – ✉ 33480 — 3 **B1**

Paris 589 – Bordeaux 30 – Mérignac 28 – Pessac 34 – Talence 41

Le Clos de Meyre without rest
16 rte de Castelnau – ✆ 05 56 58 22 84 – www.chateaumeyre.com – closdemeyre@wanadoo.fr – Fax 05 57 71 23 35 – Open 1st March-1st November
7 rm – €90/100 €120/140 – 2 suites
◆ Situated between the Margaux and Haut Médoc vineyards, this château has been a wine estate for three centuries. Traditional and modern rooms full of character. Swimming pool in summer; tennis court.

AVESSAC – 44 Loire-Atlantique – **316** E2 – **pop. 2 387** – **alt. 55 m** – ✉ **44460** 34 **A2**

Paris 406 – Nantes 78 – Rennes 63 – St-Nazaire 54 – Vannes 64

Southeast : **3 km by D 131 (direction Plessé) – ✉ 44460 Avessac**

Restaurant d'Edouard

La Villa en Pierre – ✆ 02 99 91 08 89 – www.edouardset.com – contact@edouardset.com – Fax 02 99 91 02 44 – Closed 29 June-24 September, 10-30 January, 15-28 February, Sunday dinner and Thursday dinner

Rest – Menu € 39/60 – Carte € 63/70

◆ This country restaurant (former farmhouse) sports a well thought out modern interior (fireplace, stonework, designer chairs and modern tableware). Up-to-date market fresh cuisine.

AVIGNON 🅿 – **84 Vaucluse** – **332** B10 – **pop. 90 800** – **Built-up area 253 580** – **alt. 21 m** – ✉ **84000** Provence 42 **E1**

Paris 682 – Aix-en-Provence 82 – Arles 37 – Marseille 98 – Nîmes 46

Avignon: ✆ 04 90 81 51 53, 9 km on the ③ and N 7

✆ 3635 et tapez 42 (0,34 €/mn)

Office de tourisme, 41, cours Jean Jaurès ✆ 04 32 74 32 74, Fax 04 90 82 95 03

de Châteaublanc Morières-lès-Avignon Les Plans, E : 8 km on D 58, ✆ 04 90 33 39 08

du Grand Avignon Vedène Les Chênes Verts, E : 9 km on D 28, ✆ 04 90 31 49 94

Palais des Papes★★★: ≤★★ of the terrasse des Dignitaires - Rocher des Doms ≤★★ - St-Bénézet bridge ★★ - Ramparts★ - Old mansions★ (rue Roi-René) EZ **F²** - Dome★ of Notre-Dame-des-Doms cathedral - Façade★ of the Hôtel des Monnaies (former Mint) EY **K** - Leaves ★ of St-Pierre church EY - Altar-piece★ of St-Didier church EZ - Museums: Petit Palais★★ EY, Calvet★ EZ **M²**, Lapidary ★ EZ **M⁴**, Louis Vouland (earthenware★) DYZ**M⁵** - Angladon-Dubrujeaud Foundation ★★ EZ **M¹**.

Plans on following pages

La Mirande

4 pl. Amirande – ✆ 04 90 85 93 93 – www.la-mirande.fr – mirande@la-mirande.fr – Fax 04 90 86 26 85 EY **g**

20 rm – † € 310/540 †† € 310/540, ☕ € 29 – 1 suite

Rest – *(Closed 5 January-3 February, Tuesday and Wednesday)* Menu (€ 35), € 75/105 – Carte € 82/96 ✿

Spec. Lasagnes végétales de tomates anciennes, chèvre frais et beignets d'anchois (summer). Saint-Pierre rôti, crique Ardéchoise de potimarron, jus mousseux à la muscade (autumn-winter). Soufflé tradition à l'orange, sorbet agrumes (winter). **Wines** Vin de Table blanc de la Drôme, Côtes-du-Rhône.

◆ An 18C Provençal decor, antiques, ornaments and a profusion of refined detail set the simply stunning scene of La Mirande. Inventive menu and appealing terrace-garden. In the evening a set menu is served in the former kitchens.

D'Europe

12 pl. Crillon – ✆ 04 90 14 76 76 – www.heurope.com – reservations@heurope.com – Fax 04 90 14 76 71 EY **d**

41 rm – † € 175/480 †† € 175/480, ☕ € 17 – 3 suites

Rest – *(closed 22 February-9 March, 2-31 August, 22-30 November, 2-9 January, Sunday and Monday)* Menu € 38 (lunch), € 55/120 – Carte € 82/154

◆ Elegant 16C mansion with refined decor in the centre of Avignon. Some suites provide glimpses of the Popes' Palace. Classical dining rooms and pleasant terrace with a fountain.

Cloître St-Louis

20 r. Portail-Boquier – ✆ 04 90 27 55 55 – www.cloitre-saint-louis.com – hotel@cloitre-saint-louis.com – Fax 04 90 82 24 01 EZ **s**

80 rm – † € 175/336 †† € 175/336, ☕ € 16

Rest – *(closed Saturday lunch)* Menu (€ 21), € 34 – Carte € 36/55

◆ The hotel is set in a 16C cloister and modern steel and glass wing. The rooms sport a blend of tasteful modernity and lovely old stonework. Rooftop pool and terrace. Restaurant in the cloisters, overlooking a peaceful courtyard with old plane trees.

Avignon Grand Hôtel rm, AC rm, VISA MC AE
34 bd St-Roch, (at the station) – 04 90 80 98 09 – www.avignon-grand-hotel.com – reservationagh@cloitre-saint-louis.com – Fax 04 90 80 98 10 EZ **t**
122 rm – €175/350 €175/350, €16
Rest – *(closed Saturday and Sunday in winter) (residents only)* Carte €26/32
◆ A decor with medieval and Provençal touches in this hotel at the foot of the ramparts. A choice of rooms, suites and a duplex, plus a small round rooftop pool. The wrought iron furniture and colourful interior match the wines and cuisine.

Mercure Pont d'Avignon without rest AC VISA MC AE
r. Ferruce, quartier Balance – 04 90 80 93 93 – www.mercure.com – h0549@accor.com – Fax 04 90 80 93 94 EY **r**
87 rm – €115/160 €125/190, €14
◆ Provençal furniture and fabrics add a regional note to the practical, airy and peaceful rooms. Attractive breakfast room.

Mercure Cité des Papes AC VISA MC AE
1 r. J.-Vilar – 04 90 80 93 00 – www.mercure.com – h1952@accor.com – Fax 04 90 80 93 01 EY **b**
89 rm – €115/180 €125/190, €13
Rest *Les Domaines* – *04 90 80 93 11* – Carte €31/41
◆ A 1970s building handy for its location in the heart of the Cité des Papes. Rooms have a simple Provençal decor. Modern setting and large terrace for the restaurant that focuses on regional dishes and wines.

Express By Holiday Inn without rest AC P VISA MC AE
2 r. Mère-Térésa, Avenue de la Gare TGV – 04 32 76 88 00 – www.expressbyholidayinn.fr – express.avignon@ihg.com – Fax 04 32 76 89 00
100 rm – €72/141 €72/141 AX **a**
◆ This hotel, near the TGV railway station, offers the advantages of modern constructions: good soundproofing, all mod cons, space and a tasteful, contemporary decor.

Bristol without rest AC VISA MC AE
44 cours Jean-Jaurès – 04 90 16 48 48 – www.bristol-avignon.com – contact@bristol-avignon.com – Fax 04 90 86 22 72 EZ **m**
65 rm – €59/95 €79/116, €11 – 2 suites
◆ This building has an idyllic location between the station and the lively districts, and was already home to a hotel in the 1920s. Practical rooms, spacious for the most part.

De Blauvac without rest VISA MC AE
11 r. de la Bancasse – 04 90 86 34 11 – www.hotel-blauvac.com – blauvac@aol.com – Fax 04 90 86 27 41 EY **m**
16 rm – €62/80 €62/80, €8
◆ The former 17C residence of the Marquis of Blauvac is steeped in the past: the rooms' walls often reveal traces of the original stonework. Rustic-Provençal decor.

Colbert without rest AC VISA MC AE
– 04 90 86 20 20 – www.avignon-hotel-colbert.com – contact@avignon-hotel-colbert.com – Fax 04 90 85 97 00 – Open 2 March-31 October
15 rm – €50/108 €60/108, €10 EZ **a**
◆ Simplicity and family home atmosphere in this discreet hotel. Bedrooms are decorated with Provençal colours, antiques and billboards. Don't miss the charming patio and his palm tree.

La Banasterie without rest AC VISA MC
11 r. de la Banasterie – 04 32 76 30 78 – www.labanasterie.com – labanasterie@labanasterie.com – Fax 04 32 76 30 78 EY **w**
5 rm – €90/115 €100/170
◆ A virgin with child adorns the listed façade of this 16C edifice. A cosy, romantic interior. The rooms are named after chocolate, in tribute to the owner's passion.

Lumani without rest VISA MC
37 Rempart St-Lazare – 04 90 82 94 11 – www.avignon-lumani.com – lux@avignon-lumani.com – Closed 4 November-25 December and 7 January-7 March
5 rm – €90/170 €90/170 FY **a**
◆ The owners of this fine 19C manor house receive guests and artists like old friends. The interior combines old, new and natural materials. Art workshops and an enclosed garden.

AVIGNON

Amandier (Av. de l') . . . CX
Aulnes (Av. des) CX
Avignon (Av. d') CX
Croix Rouge (Av. de la) BX
Docteur-Pons
(Rte Touristique) . . . BV
Eisenhower (Av.) . . . . AX
Europe (Pont de l') . . . AX
Ferry (Bd J.) . . . . AX
Folie (Av. de la) . . . . . BCX 29
Foncouverte (Av. de) BCX 31
Gaulle
(Rocade Ch.-de) . . ABX
Lyon (Rte de) . . . . BV
Marseille (Rte de) . . . BCX 51
Monclar (Av.) . . . . AX
Monod (Bd J.) . . . . AX 58
Montfavet (Rte de) . . BCX 60
Morières (Rte de) . . . BCV
Moulin Notre-Dame
(Av. du) . . . . BX 61
Réalpanier (Carr.) CV
Reine-Jeanne
(Av. de la) . . . . BX 81
Royaume (Pont du) . . . AV 92
St-Chamand (Av.) . . . . BX 95
St-Ruf (Av.) . . . . AX
Semard (Av. P.) . . . . . . BX
Sixte-Isnard (Bd) . . . . . BX 112
Souspirous (Av. de) . . . CX
Tarascon (Av. de) . . . . . AX
1re Division Blindée
(Bd de la) . . . . BX 125

LES ANGLES

Pinède (Ch. de la) . . . . AV

LE PONTET

Avignon (Av. d') CV
Carpentras (Av. de) CV
Delorme (Av. Th.) CV
Goutarel (Av. G.) . . . . . CV 38
Pasteur (Av. L.) CV

VILLENEUVE-LÈS-AVIGNON

Camp de Bataille (R.) . AV 15
Chartreux (Ch. des) . . . AV 16
Ducros (Bd Edmond) . AV
Fort St-André
(Montée du) . . . . AV 32
Gaulle (Av. Ch.-de) . . . . AV 36
Hôpital (R. de l') . . . . . . AV 43
Joffre (Rte) . . . . AV
Leclerc (Av. Gén.) . . . . . AV
Monnaie (R. de la) . . . . AV 57
Pasteur (Av.) . . . . AV
Péri (Av. G.) . . . . AV
Ravoux (Av. Paul) . . . . . AV
République (R. de la) . . AV 87
Tour (Montée de la) . . . AV 115
Verdun (Av. de) . . . . . . AV 117

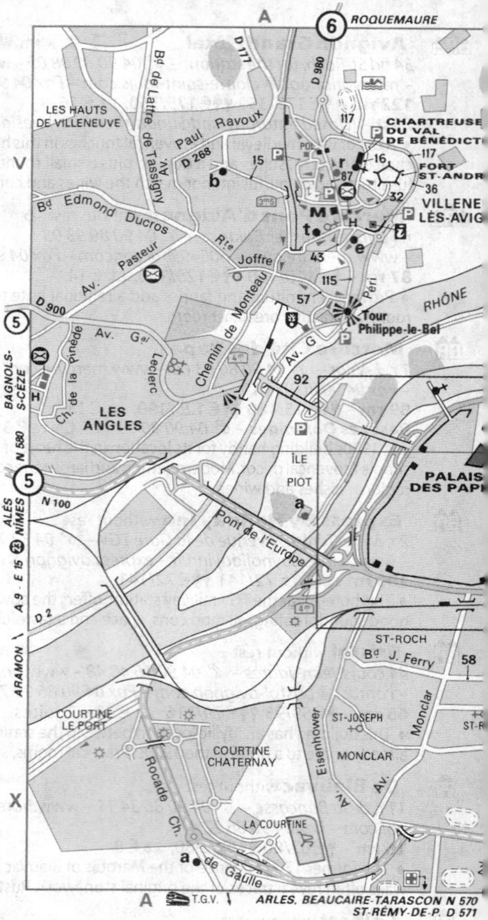

Villa Agapè without rest

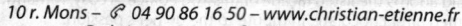

13 r. St-Agricol – ☎ 04 90 85 21 92 – www.villa-agape.com – michele@villa-agape.com – Fax 04 90 82 93 34 – Closed 10-27 April, July and All Saint's Day holidays EY **x**

3 rm – €100/150 €100/150

◆ The Villa Agapè is a cosy little gem of comfort. It is unexpectedly perched on the rooftop of a building in the historic centre of Avignon. It has a pool and flower-decked terrace to boot!

Christian Étienne

10 r. Mons – ☎ 04 90 86 16 50 – www.christian-etienne.fr – contact@christian-etienne.fr – Fax 04 90 86 67 09 – Closed Sunday and Monday except in July EY **h**

Rest – Menu €35 (weekday lunch), €65/120 – Carte €83/95

Spec. Menu "tomate" (June to September). Menu "truffe" (December to February). Menu "homard". **Wines** Viognier, Côtes du Rhône-Villages.

◆ Historically charged setting in 13C and 14C buildings adjoining the Palais des Papes. Here the chef produces fine cuisine that pays tribute to the Provence of his birth.

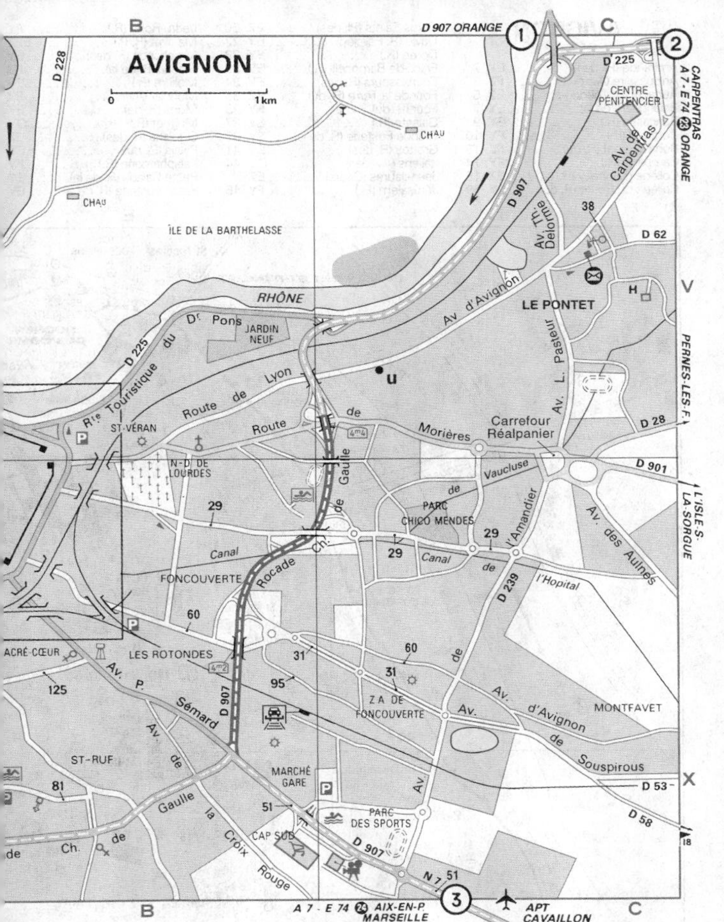

Hiély-Lucullus

5 r. de la République, (1st floor) – ✆ 04 90 86 17 07 – www.hiely-lucullus.com – contact@hiely-lucullus.com – Fax 04 90 86 32 38 – Closed 13-20 January and Saturday lunch EY **n**

Rest – Menu (€ 25), € 35 (weekday lunch), € 70/95 – Carte approx. € 100

◆ A new team and the spruced up Belle Époque decor (stained glass and carved wood panelling) have added a new lease of life to this institution. Reinterpreted classic cuisine.

La Fourchette

17 r. Racine – ✆ 04 90 85 20 93 – restaurant.la.fourchette@wanadoo.fr – Fax 04 90 85 57 60 – Closed 2-23 August, 24 December-4 January, Saturday and Sunday EY **u**

Rest – *(number of covers limited, pre-book)* Menu (€ 26), € 32

◆ Collections of forks, cicadas, photos, ornaments, and greetings cards set the ornate scene in this delightful, often-packed bistro. Cuisine with an authentic southern accent.

AVIGNON

Amirande (Pl. de l') .... EY 2
Arroussaire (Av. de l') .... FZ 3
Aubanel (R. Théodore) .... EZ 5
Balance (R. de la) .... EY 7
Bancasse (R.) .... EY 9
Bertrand (R.) .... FY 10
Bon Martinet (R. du) .... FZ 13
Campane (R.).................. FY 14
Collège d'Annecy (R.) .... EZ 18
Collège du Roure (R. du) .... EY 19
Corps Saints (Pl. des) .... EZ 20
David (R. Félicien) .... EY 22
Dorée (R.) .... EY 23
Folco-de-Baroncelli (R.)...... EY 28
Fourbisseurs (R. des) .... EY 34
Four de la Terre (R. du) ...... FZ 35
Four (R. du) .... FY 33
Galante (R.) .... EY 37
Grande Fusterie (R. de la).... EY 39
Grottes (R. des)............... EY 41
Italiens (Av. des).............. GY 44
Jean-Jaurès (Cours) .... EZ
Jérusalem (Pl.)................. FY 45
Ledru-Rollin (R.)............... FY
Manivet (R. P.)................ EFZ
Marchands (R. des) .... EY
Masse (R. de la)................ FZ
Molière (R.) .... EY
Monclar (Av.) .... EZ
Mons (R. de) .... EY
Muguet (R.) .... GY
Ortolans (R. des) .... EZ
Palais (Pl. du) .... EY
Palapharnerie (R.) .... FY
Petite Calade (R. de la) .... EY
Petite Fusterie (R. de la) ..... EY

te Saunerie (R. de la) .... **FY** 70
'amale (R.) .... **EZ** 72
rollerie (R.) .... **EY** 73
t (R. du) .... **EY** 74
sident-Kennedy (Cours) .. **EZ** 76
vot (R.) .... **EZ** 77
cas (R. de) .... **GY** 79
npart de l'Oulle (R. du) ... **DY** 82
npart du Rhône (R. du) ... **EY** 83
npart St-Michel (R. du) ... **FZ** 84
npart St-Roch (R. du) ... **DEZ** 86
ublique (R. de la) .... **EYZ**
ne (Pte du) .... **EY** 88

Rouge (R.) .... **EY** 90
Ste-Catherine (R.) .... **FY** 109
St-Agricol (R.) .... **EY** 94
St-Christophe (R.) .... **FZ** 97
St-Dominique (Bd) .... **DZ** 98
St-Étienne (R.) .... **EY** 99
St-Jean le Vieux (Pl.) .... **FY** 101
St-Jean le Vieux (R.) .... **FY** 102
St-Joseph (R.) .... **FY** 104
St-Michel (R.) .... **EZ** 105
St-Pierre (Pl.) .... **EY** 106
St-Ruf (Av.) .... **FZ** 108

Saraillerie (R. de la) .... **EYZ** 110
Taulignan (R. de) .... **EY** 113
Tour (R. de la) .... **GY** 116
Vernet (R. Horace) .... **EZ** 118
Vernet (R. Joseph) .... **EYZ**
Viala (R. Jean) .... **EY** 119
Vice-Légat (R.) .... **EY** 120
Vieux Sextier (R. du) .... **EFY** 122
Vilar (R. Jean) .... **EY** 123
Violette (R.) .... **EZ** 124
3 Pilats (R. des) .... **FY** 127
3 Faucons (R. des) .... **EZ** 126

Piedoie
26 r. 3-Faucons – ✆ 04 90 86 51 53 – t.piedoie@gmail.com – Closed in August, 21-30 November, February holidays, Tuesday and Wednesday EZ **d**
Rest – Menu € 19 (weekdays)/65 bi – Carte € 39/54
◆ Beams, parquet floors, white walls and modern art make a simple, pleasant setting. The chef pays attention to the seasons and offers creative cuisine based on market produce.

Le Moutardier du Pape
15 pl. Palais-des-Papes – ✆ 04 90 85 34 76 – www.restaurant-moutardier.fr – info@restaurant-moutardier.fr – Fax 04 90 86 42 18 EY **z**
Rest – Menu (€ 25), € 33/46 – Carte € 38/62
◆ Murals commemorating the 'Moutardier du Pape' adorn the walls of this characterful establishment, but opt for the terrace, as its view of the palace is matchless. Wines by the glass to suit the menu.

Les 5 Sens
18 r. Joseph-Vernet, (Place Plaisance) – ✆ 04 90 85 26 51 – www.restaurantles5sens.com – les5sens2@wanadoo.fr – Closed 2-7 June, 17-31 August, 1st-7 January, Sunday and Monday EY **a**
Rest – Menu (€ 20), € 42 – Carte € 50/70
◆ Fashionable furnishings and warm colours set the elegant scene in this restaurant that focuses on updated mouth-watering cuisine.

L'Essentiel
2 r. Petite-Fusterie – ✆ 04 90 85 87 12 – www.restaurantlessentiel.com – restaurantlessentiel84@live.fr – Closed Sunday EY **v**
Rest – Menu € 26/37 – Carte € 38/58
◆ This restaurant focuses on the 'essential', delighting guests with its generous cuisine, full of sunny French and Italian flavours. Modern decor with clean lines.

Brunel
46 r. Balance – ✆ 04 90 85 24 83 – www.restaurantbrunel.fr – restaurantbrunel@wanadoo.fr – Fax 04 90 86 26 67 – Closed for one week in August, one week in November, Sunday except July and Monday EY **e**
Rest – Menu (€ 20 bi), € 26 (weekday lunch), € 30/33 – Carte € 26/40
◆ Find a minimalist, contemporary decor in this fashionable bistro. It offers a menu with Provençal touches in the evening and, at lunchtime, a shorter set menu (dish of the day).

L'Isle Sonnante
7 r. Racine – ✆ 04 90 82 56 01 – Fax 04 90 82 56 01 – Closed 22 February-1st March, 23 August-2 September, 25 October-5 November, Sunday and Monday EY **v**
Rest – Menu € 25/50 – Carte € 37/47
◆ This wooden fronted restaurant behind the Opera House is a pleasant establishment. A cosy interior combines rustic style with warm tones. Modern dishes with southern flavours.

In île de la Barthelasse 5 km North by D 228 and secondary road – ✉ 84000 Avignon

La Ferme
110 chemin des Bois – ✆ 04 90 82 57 53 – www.hotel-laferme.com – info@hotel-laferme.com – Fax 04 90 27 15 47 – Open 15 March-31 October
20 rm – †€ 66/73 ††€ 76/95, ☕ € 11 – ½ P € 68/79
Rest – *(dinner only)* Menu € 26/41 – Carte € 27/45
◆ This farmhouse is an ideal address for those who are looking for peace not too far from Avignon. Large, simple rooms with Provençal-style painted furniture. Country-style dining room with beams, fireplace and old stone. Shaded terrace.

in Pontet 6 km to ② by Lyon road – pop. 17 100 – alt. 40 m – ✉ 84130

Auberge de Cassagne
450 allée de Cassagne – ✆ 04 90 31 04 18 – www.aubergedecassagne.com – cassagne@wanadoo.fr – Fax 04 90 32 25 09 – Closed 3-29 January
45 rm – †€ 115/459 ††€ 115/459, ☕ € 25 – 3 suites – ½ P € 148/320
Rest – Menu (€ 37), € 59/106 – Carte € 93/116
◆ With a gym, steam room, sauna and pool, everything here is provided for the guests' well being. Provencal-style rooms overlooking the gardens. Menu in keeping with modern tastes and a fine wine list.

 **Les Agassins**

52 av. Ch.-de-Gaulle – ✆ 04 90 32 42 91 – www.agassins.com – avignon@agassins.com – Fax 04 90 32 08 29 – Closed January and February CV **u**

26 rm – †€ 90/200 ††€ 100/300, ☕ € 20 – ½ P € 105/185

Rest – *(Closed Saturday lunch from November to March)* Menu (€ 28 bi), € 22 (lunch), € 36/68 – Carte € 50/70

◆ Large regional building surrounded by a flower garden. Cane furniture and southern colours in the rooms, most of which have a small terrace. Sun-kissed restaurant with summer terrace in the shaded courtyard. Sample Provençal dishes and wines galore.

in Montfavet - CX – ✉ **84140**

 **Hostellerie Les Frênes**

645 av. Vertes-Rives – ✆ 04 90 31 17 93 – www.lesfrenes.com – contact@lesfrenes.com – Fax 04 90 23 95 03

12 rm – †€ 170/750 ††€ 170/750, ☕ € 20 – 6 suites

Rest – Menu (€ 29), € 43/79 – Carte € 65/85

◆ This gracious old mansion (1800) and its more recent outbuildings are hidden in the greenery of its grounds. Period, contemporary, or southern styled rooms. Spruced up dining room in a cosy, trendy style and a pleasant terrace shaded by old plane trees.

to the airport **8 km by ③** – ✉ **84140**

 **Paradou** rm,

– ✆ 04 90 84 18 30 – www.hotel-paradou.fr – contact@hotel-paradou.fr – Fax 04 90 84 19 16

60 rm – †€ 95/140 ††€ 110/170, ☕ € 12

Rest – *(closed Sunday except dinner from April to March)* Menu € 19 (weekdays)/39 – Carte € 24/50

◆ The somewhat humdrum architecture is quickly forgotten in favour of this welcoming picture of comfort. Personalised rooms with balcony or mini terrace. A simple bistro-style decor and regional cuisine and wines.

Carpentras road **12 km on the ② D 942, Althen-des-Paluds exit** – ✉ **84180 Monteux :**

XXX ✿ **Le Saule Pleureur** (Laurent Azoulay)

145 chemin de Beauregard – ✆ 04 90 62 01 35 – www.le-saule-pleureur.com – contact@le-saule-pleureur.fr – Fax 04 90 62 10 90 – Closed 2-8 January, Sunday dinner, Monday except bank holidays and from 3 June to 27 September, Saturday lunch

Rest – Menu € 29 (weekday lunch), € 39/89 – Carte € 65/95

Spec. Cappuccino de châtaigne, royale de foie gras et oeuf mollet en croûte de brioche. Cochon fermier du Ventoux, côte rôtie, boudin noir et légumes anciens. Poire williams au caramel salé, cornet de glace au poivre de Sechuan.

◆ Large villa surrounded by a garden, which makes guests forget about the busy road nearby. Friendly, attentive service. Generous, delicate and cleverly creative cuisine.

See also hotel resources of **Villeneuve-lès-Avignon**

AVIGNON (Airport) – **84 Vaucluse** – **332** C10 – **see Avignon**

AVORIAZ – **74 Haute-Savoie** – **328** N3 – **see Morzine**

AVRANCHES – 50 Manche – 303 D7 – pop. 8 239 – alt. 108 m 32 A3
– ✉ **50300** Normandy

▶ Paris 337 – Caen 105 – Rennes 85 – St-Lô 58 – St-Malo 68

ℹ Office de tourisme, 2, rue Général-de-Gaulle ✆ 02 33 58 00 22, Fax 02 33 68 13 29

◉ Manuscripts ★★ of the Mont-St-Michel (museum) - Jardin des Plantes: ✳★ - The "plate-forme" ✳★.

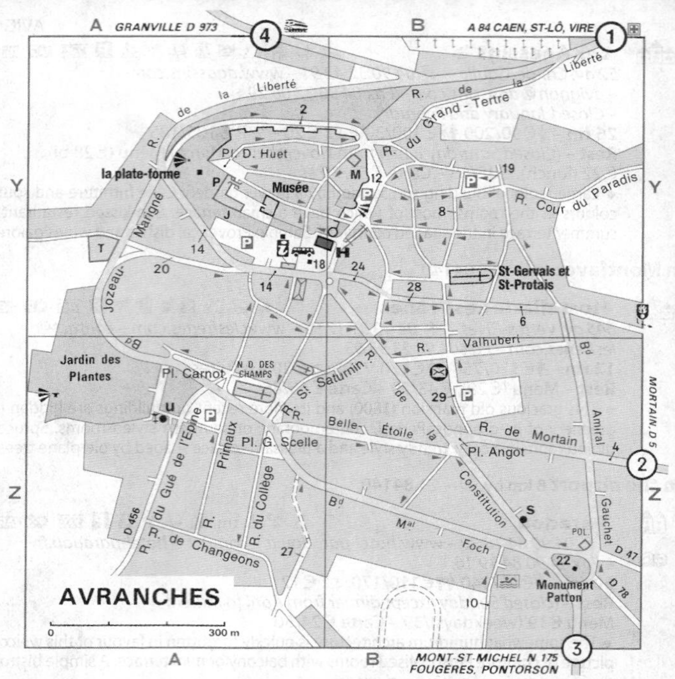

La Croix d'Or
83 r. de la Constitution – ☎ 02 33 58 04 88 – www.hoteldelacroixdor.fr – hotelcroixdor@wanadoo.fr – Fax 02 33 58 06 95 – Closed 1st-25 January and Sunday dinner from 15 October to 1st April
27 rm – †€ 58/65 ††€ 71/102, ☕ € 9 – ½ P € 74/91 BZ **s**
Rest – Menu € 18 (weekday lunch), € 27/54 – Carte € 50/75
◆ A 17C post house with an attractive half-timbered façade and splendid hall-sitting room furnished in a regional style. Most of the attractive rooms look onto the pretty flower garden. An authentic Norman feel to the dining room; a classic and regional menu.

La Ramade without rest
2 r. de la Côte, 1 km via ④ at Marcey les Grèves – ☎ 02 33 58 27 40 – www.laramade.fr – hotel@laramade.fr – Fax 02 33 58 29 30 – Closed 20-30 November and 28 December-4 February
12 rm – †€ 65/99 ††€ 72/185, ☕ € 10
◆ 1950s bourgeois house with cosy personalised rooms on a floral theme. The lounge boasts a hearth. Gazebo in the garden. Non-smoking.

Jardin des Plantes
10 pl. Carnot – ☎ 02 33 58 03 68 – www.le-jardin-des-plantes.fr – contact@le.jardin.des.plantes.fr – Fax 02 33 60 01 72 – Closed 20 December-4 January
25 rm – †€ 50/88 ††€ 50/88, ☕ € 11 – ½ P € 68 AZ **u**
Rest – Menu (€ 15), € 17/42 – Carte € 43/75
◆ A family hotel at the entrance to the jardin des plantes. Reception in the bar popular with locals. Rustic rooms, more spacious in the rear building. A brasserie-style restaurant and covered terrace. Traditional cuisine.

Altos without rest
37 bd Luxembourg, via ③: 0.5 km – ✆ 02 33 58 66 64 – www.hotel-altos.com – hotelaltos@aol.com – Fax 02 33 58 40 11 – Closed 18 December-4 January
29 rm – €55/79 €59/79, €8
◆ A 1980s establishment by the side of a busy road with practical rooms that are gradually being done up in a more modern style.

in St-Quentin-sur-le-Homme **5 km Southeast by D 78** BZ – **pop. 1 090 – alt. 55 m – ✉ 50220**

Le Gué du Holme with rm
14 r. des Estuaires – ✆ 02 33 60 63 76 – www.le-gue-du-holme.com – gue.holme@wanadoo.fr – Fax 02 33 60 06 77
10 rm – €58/70 €65/75, €11
Rest – Menu (€16), €29/65 – Carte €42/70
◆ The modern, wood façade contrasts with the building's stone walls. Dining rooms are elegant, the smallest opening onto a summer terrace. Seasonal menu.

AX-LES-THERMES – 09 Ariège – 343 J8 – pop. 1 498 – alt. 720 m 29 C3

– Winter sports : at Saquet via route du plateau de Bonascre★ (8km) and telecabin 1 400/2 400 m 1 15 – Spa : all year – Casino – ✉ 09110
Languedoc-Roussillon-Tarn Gorges

Paris 803 – Andorra-la-Vella 59 – Carcassonne 106 – Foix 44 – Prades 99 – Quillan 55

Puymorens Tunnel: 2008 toll, one way: cars €5.70, car and caravan €11.60, HGV €18.60 to €30.20, motorcycles €3.50. Special return rates: information ✆ 04 68 04 97 20.

Office de tourisme, 6, avenueThéophile Delcassé ✆ 05 61 64 60 60, Fax 05 61 64 68 18

Orlu Valley ★ Southeast.

Le Chalet
4 av. Turrel – ✆ 05 61 64 24 31 – www.le-chalet.fr – lechalet@club-internet.fr – Fax 05 61 03 55 50 – Closed 10 days in November
19 rm – €55/72 €55/72, €9 – ½ P €57/65
Rest – *(closed Sunday dinner and Monday dinner off school holidays and Monday lunch)* Menu (€22), €26/48 – Carte approx. €47
◆ This chalet-hotel, renovated from top to toe, offers restful, contemporary and well-appointed rooms; some with a balcony. A bright dining room decorated in beige tones, plus a terrace overlooking the river. Delicious modern cuisine.

L'Orry Le Saquet with rm
RN 20, 1 km south on N 20 – ✆ 05 61 64 31 30 – www.auberge-lorry.com – sylvie.heinrich@wanadoo.fr – Fax 05 61 64 00 31 – Closed for the spring holiday, November, Sunday dinner and Wednesday
15 rm – €55/65 €55/65, €8 – ½ P €54/60
Rest – *(dinner only except Saturday and Sunday)* Menu €27 – Carte €27/41
◆ A chalet-type building on the Andorra road. A pleasant restaurant, renovated in the style of a typical country inn. Cookery courses two Saturdays every month.

AY – 51 Marne – 306 F8 – pop. 4 175 – alt. 76 m – ✉ 51160 13 B2

Paris 146 – Reims 29 – Château-Thierry 60 – Épernay 4 – Châlons-en-Champagne 34

Castel Jeanson without rest
24 r. Jeanson – ✆ 03 26 54 21 75 – www.casteljeanson.fr – info@casteljeanson.fr – Fax 03 26 54 32 19 – Closed 22 December-20 January
15 rm – €110/150 €110/150, €12 – 2 suites
◆ The superb poolside Art Nouveau conservatory is the pride and joy of this 19C private mansion. Pleasant rooms, sitting room-cum-library and tastings of the house champagne.

Le Manoir des Charmes without rest
83 bd Charles de Gaulle – ✆ 03 26 54 58 49 – www.lemanoirdescharmes.com – contact@lemanoirdescharmes.fr – Closed 1st January-26 February
5 rm – €110/140 €110/140
◆ Handsome manor built in 1906 overlooking a garden. The lady of the house, a keen bargain hunter, has decorated the personalised rooms. Breakfasts in a lovely conservatory.

Vieux Puits
18 r. Roger-Sondag – ✆ 03 26 56 96 53 – Fax 03 26 56 96 54 – Closed 17-30 August, 23 December-7 January, 8-21 February, Wednesday and Thursday
Rest – Menu (€25), €35/60 – Carte €64/86
◆ This house is home to two immaculate dining rooms, one bourgeois and the other rustic. Interior flower-decked courtyard with an old well. Fine choice of champagnes.

AYGUESVIVES – 31 Haute-Garonne – 343 H4 – pop. 2 143 – alt. 164 m – ✉ 31450 Languedoc-Roussillon-Tarn Gorges 29 C2

Paris 704 – Colomiers 36 – Toulouse 25 – Tournefeuille 38

La Pradasse without rest
39 chemin de Toulouse, D 16 – ✆ 05 61 81 55 96 – www.lapradasse.com – contact@lapradasse.com – Fax 05 61 81 55 96
5 rm – €72/75 €85/92
◆ Designed by the owners, the rooms of this magnificently restored barn sport a delightful mixture of brick, wood and wrought iron. Fine grounds with pond.

AY-SUR-MOSELLE – 57 Moselle – 307 I3 – pop. 1 550 – alt. 160 m – ✉ 57300 26 B1

Paris 327 – Briey 31 – Metz 17 – Saarlouis 56 – Thionville 16

Le Martin Pêcheur
1 rte d'Hagondange – ✆ 03 87 71 42 31 – restaurant-martin-pecheur@wanadoo.fr – Fax 03 87 71 42 31 – Closed 14-20 April, 17 August-2 September, 26 October-2 November, 15-22 February, Wednesday dinner, Saturday lunch, Sunday dinner and Monday
Rest – Menu €40 (weekday lunch), €50 € bi/100 bi – Carte €56/73
◆ Between the canal and Moselle, a former fisherman's house (1928) with a lovely garden where you can eat in summer. Warm welcome, coloured rooms, modern food and well-stocked cellar.

AYTRÉ – 17 Charente-Maritime – 324 D3 – see La Rochelle

AZAY-LE-FERRON – 36 Indre – 323 C5 – pop. 942 – alt. 102 m – ✉ 36290 11 B3

Paris 279 – Orléans 196 – Châteauroux 56 – Châtellerault 46 – Déols 60

Terre de Brenne
rte du Blanc – ✆ 02 54 39 24 43 – www.terredebrenne.com – terredebrenne@wanadoo.fr – Fax 02 54 39 24 43
Rest – Menu (€11 bi), €22/50 – Carte €29/48
◆ This former post house sports an appealing modern decor with period beams. The updated cuisine is both generous and authentic.

AZAY-LE-RIDEAU – 37 Indre-et-Loire – 317 L5 – pop. 3 337 – alt. 51 m – ✉ 37190 Châteaux of the Loire 11 A2

Paris 265 – Châtellerault 61 – Chinon 21 – Loches 58 – Saumur 47 – Tours 26

Office de tourisme, 4, rue du Château ✆ 02 47 45 44 40, Fax 02 47 45 31 46

Château★★★ - Façade★ of St-Symphorien church.

Le Grand Monarque VISA

3 pl. de la République – 02 47 45 40 08 – www.legrandmonarque.com – monarq@club-internet.fr – Fax 02 47 45 46 25 – Closed 29 December-16 January, Sunday dinner, Monday dinner and Tuesday from November to March

24 rm – €70/140 €80/170, €13 – ½ P €78/123

Rest – Menu (€18), €29/44 – Carte €42/64

◆ This Touraine-inspired residence consisting of two buildings separated by a leafy courtyard offers lovely rooms with beams, stonework and old furniture. Elegant, rustic dining room warmed by an imposing fireplace; superb terrace.

Des Châteaux P VISA

2 rte de Villandry – 02 47 45 68 00 – www.hoteldeschateaux.com – info@hoteldeschateaux.com – Fax 02 47 45 68 29 – Open 13 February-8 November

27 rm – €56/79 €61/79, €10 – ½ P €56/65

Rest – *(dinner only)* Menu €21/28 – Carte €24/34

◆ Gradually refurbished hotel on the tourist châteaux route offering delightful, bright and colourful rooms. Traditional home cooking prepared by the lady of the house.

De Biencourt without rest VISA

7 r. Balzac – 02 47 45 20 75 – www.hotelbiencourt.com – biencourt@infonie.fr – Fax 02 47 45 91 73 – Open 28 March-1st October and closed 28 June-4 July

15 rm – €51/56 €51/56, €8

◆ Once occupied by a school (traces of which are still noticeable in the decor), this 18C house is situated near the château. Rustic and Directoire-style furniture. Breakfast served in the refurbished dining room or on the patio.

L'Aigle d'Or AC VISA

10 av. A.-Riché – 02 47 45 24 58 – Fax 02 47 45 90 18 – Closed 2-7 September, 12-28 November, 21 January-4 March, Sunday dinner and Wednesday

Rest – *(pre-book)* Menu (€20), €28/50 – Carte €40/60

◆ Tasty traditional dishes served in a low key dining room with exposed beams and fresh flower arrangements. Pleasant service.

in Saché **6.5 km East by D 17 – pop. 1 150 – alt. 78 m – ✉ 37190**

Auberge du XIIe Siècle (Xavier Aubrun et Thierry Jimenez) VISA

1 r. du Château – 02 47 26 88 77 – Fax 02 47 26 88 21 – Closed 26 May-4 June, 1st-10 September, 17-26 November, 5-21 January, Sunday dinner, Tuesday lunch and Monday

Rest – *(pre-book Saturday - Sunday)* Menu €32/72 – Carte €70/90

Spec. Œufs brouillés à la crème de morilles. Ris de veau braisé à la sauge. Marbré au chocolat fondant. **Wines** Chinon, Touraine Azay-le-Rideau.

◆ A venerable half-timbered inn often visited by Balzac not far from the château where he was often a guest. Well-preserved rustic setting. Classic recipes.

BACCARAT – 54 Meurthe-et-Moselle – 307 L8 – pop. 4 746 – alt. 260 m – ✉ 54120 Alsace-Lorraine 27 C2

Paris 369 – Épinal 43 – Lunéville 27 – Nancy 58 – St-Dié 29 – Sarrebourg 45

Office de tourisme, 2, rue Adrien Michaut 03 83 75 13 37, Fax 03 83 75 36 76

Stained-glass windows★ of St-Rémy church - Musée du cristal.

La Renaissance VISA AE

31 r. des Cristalleries – 03 83 75 11 31 – www.hotel-la-renaissance.com – renaissance.la@wanadoo.fr – Fax 03 83 75 21 09 – Closed 1st-10 January

16 rm – €52 €52, €8 – ½ P €50

Rest – *(closed Saturday dinner off season, Sunday dinner and Friday)* Menu (€12), €17/37 – Carte €29/40

◆ In the home of glassblowing, this handy small hotel near the Crystal Museum has functional and well soundproofed rooms. Traditional unpretentious food served in a rustic dining room or on a small flower-decked terrace.

BADEN – 56 Morbihan – 308 N9 – pop. 3 976 – alt. 28 m – ✉ 56870 9 A3

Paris 473 – Auray 9 – Lorient 52 – Quiberon 40 – Vannes 15

Le Gavrinis rest, P VISA MC AE

1 r. de L'Île Gavrinis, 2 km at Toulbroch via the Vannes road – 02 97 57 00 82 – www.gavrinis.com – gavrinis@wanadoo.fr – Fax 02 97 57 09 47 – Closed 16 November-2 December and 5 January-5 February

18 rm – € 52/120 € 52/120, € 12 – ½ P € 60/85

Rest – *(closed Sunday dinner off season, Monday except dinner in season and Saturday lunch)* Menu (€ 16), € 20 (weekdays), € 23/68 – Carte € 48/69

◆ This recently built Breton style house, surrounded by a fine garden, is pursuing its makeover (6 refurbished rooms, 12 underway) in a restrained, comfortable style. Good modern cuisine inspired by regional recipes. Pleasant interior and stunning terrace.

BAERENTHAL – 57 Moselle – 307 Q5 – pop. 710 – alt. 220 m – ✉ 57230 27 D1

Paris 449 – Bitche 15 – Haguenau 33 – Strasbourg 62 – Wissembourg 45

Office de tourisme, 1, rue du Printemps d'Alsace 03 87 06 50 26, Fax 03 87 06 62 33

Le Kirchberg without rest P VISA MC

8 imp. de la Forêt – 03 87 98 97 70 – www.le-kirchberg.com – resid.hotel.kirchberg@wanadoo.fr – Fax 03 87 98 97 91 – Closed 1st January-5 February

20 rm – € 41/54 € 52/66, € 11

◆ A modern hotel in the heart of the Regional Park. Modern, fresh and neat rooms (ten with a small kitchen), those at the rear have a relaxing view of the Vosges. Fresh air guaranteed!

in Untermuhlthal 4 km Southeast by D 87 – ✉ 57230 Baerenthal

L'Arnsbourg (Jean-Georges Klein) AC P VISA MC AE

– 03 87 06 50 85 – www.arnsbourg.com – l.arnsbourg@wanadoo.fr – Fax 03 87 06 57 67 – Closed 1st-15 September, 29 December-27 January, Tuesday and Wednesday

Rest – *(pre-book Saturday - Sunday)* Menu € 65 (weekday lunch), € 125/160 – Carte € 105/130

Spec. Emulsion de pomme de terre et truffe. Saint-Pierre infusé au laurier en croûte de sel. Tartelette tiède au chocolat, râpée de fève de tonka et crème glacée au grué de cacao. **Wines** Gewurztraminer, Muscat.

◆ This imposing mansion is in the heart of the Vosges countryside. It offers you the pleasure of a deliciously inventive meal in an elegant modern dining room overlooking the Zinsel.

K P VISA MC

– 03 87 27 05 60 – www.arnsbourg.com – hotelk@orange.fr – Fax 03 87 06 88 65 – Closed 1st-15 September, 29 December-27 January, Tuesday and Wednesday

12 rm – € 215/460 € 215/460, € 27 – 6 suites

◆ The modern lines of this almost transparent edifice and its comfortable, minimalist rooms open on to a Japanese garden.

BAFFIE – 63 Puy-de-Dôme – 326 J10 – pop. 114 – alt. 850 m – ✉ 63600 6 C2

Paris 457 – Clermont-Ferrand 90 – Issoire 69 – Montbrison 44 – Thiers 71

Le Relais du Vermont VISA MC

at the Col de Chemintrand – 04 73 95 34 75 – www.relaisduvermont.com – auberge-vermont@wanadoo.fr – Closed 21 December-8 February, Sunday dinner, Tuesday dinner off season and Monday

Rest – Menu € 15/30

◆ Former coach house (1870) built on a pass from where you can enjoy a lovely view. Local dishes and inviting desserts served in a pleasant, rustic setting.

BÂGÉ-LE-CHÂTEL – 01 Ain – 328 C3 – pop. 805 – alt. 209 m – ✉ 01380 44 B1

Paris 396 – Bourg-en-Bresse 35 – Mâcon 11 – Pont-de-Veyle 7 – St-Amour 39 – Tournus 41

Syndicat d'initiative, 2, rue Marsale ✆ 03 85 30 56 66, Fax 03 85 30 56 66

La Table Bâgésienne

Gde-Rue – ✆ 03 85 30 54 22 – latablebagesienne@wanadoo.fr – Fax 03 85 30 58 33 – Closed 25 July-8 August, 22-30 December, 15-26 February, Monday dinner, Tuesday dinner and Wednesday

Rest – Menu € 19 (weekday lunch), € 27/52 – Carte € 53/76

◆ A fireplace, wood panelling, Bresse furniture and country-style décor give a very skilful rustic ambiance. Terrace shaded by a lime tree. Generous portions of updated regional cuisine.

BAGES – 11 Aude – 344 I4 – see Narbonne

BAGNÈRES-DE-BIGORRE – 65 Hautes-Pyrénées – 342 M4 – pop. 8 048 – alt. 551 m – Spa : mid March-late Nov. – Casino – ✉ 65200 28 A3

Languedoc-Roussillon-Tarn Gorges

Paris 829 – Lourdes 24 – Pau 66 – St-Gaudens 65 – Tarbes 23

Office de tourisme, 3, allées Tournefort ✆ 05 62 95 50 71, Fax 05 62 95 33 13

de la Bigorre Pouzac Quartier Serre Devant, NE : 3 km on D 938, ✆ 05 62 91 06 20

Parc thermal de Salut★ via Av. Pierre-Noguès - Grotte de Médous★★ Southeast: 2,5 km by D 935.

La Résidence

rm, VISA

Vallon de Salut – ✆ 05 62 91 19 19 – http://www.residotel.com – residotel@voila.fr – Fax 05 62 95 29 88 – Open 2 May-30 September

26 rm – †€ 85/90 ††€ 85/90, ☕ € 10 – 3 suites – ½ P € 75/80

Rest – *(dinner only) (resident only)* Menu € 25

◆ In the calm pastoral setting of the spa resort park. Large, renovated rooms overlooking the Salut valley. Lounge-cum-video library. Lovely, opulent dining room leading on to a pleasant terrace. Cosy and refined bar.

Hostellerie d'Asté

VISA AE

3.5 km Campan road (D 935) – ✆ 05 62 91 74 27 – www.hotel-aste.com – contacts@hotel-aste.com – Fax 05 62 91 76 74 – Closed 11 November-15 December

21 rm – †€ 53/61 ††€ 53/61, ☕ € 7 – 1 suite – ½ P € 50/56

Rest – *(closed Sunday dinner except school holidays)* Menu € 16/36 – Carte € 26/52

◆ An imposing building between the road and the River Adour. Small simple rooms; the murmur of the river audible in those at the rear. Bright dining room and waterside terrace in the garden. Traditional food focusing on produce from the sea.

Les Petites Vosges without rest

VISA

17 bd Carnot – ✆ 05 62 91 55 30 – www.lespetitesvosges.com – lpv@lespetitesvosges.com – Fax 05 62 91 55 30 – Closed 12-30 November

4 rm ☕ – †€ 65 ††€ 75/90

◆ A tasteful blend of old and new endows this house with a vitality tinged with originality. Cosy guestrooms and stylish tearoom. The lady of the house can be relied on for good advice on hikes in the area.

L'Auberge Gourmande

VISA

1 bd Lyperon – ✆ 05 62 95 52 01 – lauberge.gourmande@orange.fr – Closed 15-30 November, Tuesday except July-August and Monday

Rest – Menu (€ 13), € 26/55 – Carte € 37/64

◆ This attractive country residence houses an elegant dining room where the skilful chef finds inspiration in the flavours of south and southwest France.

in Gerde South 2 km by Campan road – pop. 1 140 – alt. 570 m – ✉ 65200

Le Relais des Pyrénées without rest
1 av. 8-Mai-1945 – ☎ 05 62 44 66 67
– www.relais-des-pyrenees.com – contact@relais-des-pyrenees.com
– Fax 05 62 44 90 14
51 rm – †€ 75/88 ††€ 83/96, ☕ € 10
◆ A former textile factory on the banks of the Adour and at the foot of the Pic du Midi. Modern rooms (light wood furniture and duvets) and a few duplexes. Lovely views of the Pyrenees.

in Beaudéan 4.5 km South by Campan road (D 935) – pop. 378 – alt. 625 m – ✉ 65710

Office de tourisme, place de la Mairie ☎ 05 62 91 79 92
Lesponne Valley ★ Southwest.

Le Catala
12 r. Larrey – ☎ 05 62 91 75 20 – www.le-catala-hotel-pyrenees.com
– le.catala@wanadoo.fr – Fax 05 62 91 79 72 – Closed 1st-8 May, 1st-8 November, Christmas holidays and Sunday except school holidays
24 rm – †€ 50/55 ††€ 52/75, ☕ € 8 – 3 suites – ½ P € 52/65
Rest – *(dinner only) (residents only)* Menu € 18
◆ Behind the discreet façade of this Bigourdan hotel is an original interior: the decor of the rooms matches the painted frescos on the doors (sport, history, etc).

in Lesponne 8 km South by D 935 and D 29 – ✉ 65710 Campan

Domaine de Ramonjuan
– ☎ 05 62 91 75 75 – www.ramonjuan.com – ramonjuan@wanadoo.fr
– Fax 05 62 91 74 54
17 rm – †€ 65/90 ††€ 65/90, ☕ € 10 – ½ P € 60/85
Rest – *(Closed 10-26 November, Sunday and Monday) (dinner only) (resident only)* Carte € 22/40
◆ This old mountain farmstead, converted into a hotel, offers a wide range of leisure facilities. Rustic rooms and modern studios available. A veranda dining area and summer terrace, serving regional dishes.

BAGNÈRES-DE-LUCHON – 31 Haute-Garonne – 343 B8 — 28 B3

– pop. 2 619 – alt. 630 m – Winter sports : at Superbagnères, 1 440/2 260 m 1 14 – Spa : early March-late Oct. – Casino Y – ✉ 31110
Languedoc-Roussillon-Tarn Gorges

Paris 814 – St-Gaudens 48 – Tarbes 98 – Toulouse 141
Office de tourisme, 18, allée d'Étigny ☎ 05 61 79 21 21, Fax 05 61 79 11 23
de Luchon Route de Montauban, ☎ 05 61 79 03 27

Plan on next page

D'Étigny — rest, rest,
opposite thermal baths – ☎ 05 61 79 01 42 – www.hotel-etigny.com
– etigny@aol.com – Fax 05 61 79 80 64 – Open 1st May-24 October — Z **k**
58 rm – †€ 48/115 ††€ 48/125, ☕ € 10 – 5 suites – ½ P € 50/88
Rest – Menu € 18/44 – Carte € 35/60
◆ Opposite the thermal baths, a variety of standard quality rooms . The three renovated ones are the most comfortable. A discreet, bourgeois restaurant and shaded terrace; traditional dishes served.

Corneille
5 av. A.-Dumas – ☎ 05 61 79 36 22 – www.cityblue-luchon.fr
– reservation.luchon@cityblue.fr – Fax 05 61 79 81 11 – Closed 11-31 November
46 rm – †€ 60/130 ††€ 60/130, ☕ € 12 – 4 suites — Y **u**
Rest – Menu € 21/35 – Carte € 30/50
◆ This 19C construction, Luchon's first casino (period stained-glass windows) was fully renovated in 2007 in a modern vein. Minimalist decor in the rooms. View of the Pyrenees. Two dining rooms, one opening onto the garden. Traditional cuisine.

BAGNÈRES-DE-LUCHON

Alexandre-Dumas (Av.) . . . . Y 2
Bains (Allées des) . . . . Z 3
Barrau (Av. J.) . . . . Z 4
Boileau (R. P.) . . . . X 8
Boularan (Av. Jean) . . . . Y 6
Carnot (Av.) . . . . Y 9
Colomic (R.) . . . . X 12
Dardenne (Bd.) . . . . Y 13
Dr-Germès (R. du) . . . . X 14
Étigny (Allées d') . . . . YZ 16
Fontan (Bd A.) . . . . XY 17
Gambetta (R.) . . . . Y 18
Joffre (Pl. Mar.) . . . . X 20
Laity (R.) . . . . X 22
Lamartine (R.) . . . . Y 23
Nadau (R. G.) . . . . X 25
Nérée-Boubée (R.) . . . . X 26
Pyrénées (Av. des) . . . . Z 28
Quinconces (Cours des) . . . . Z 30
Rostand (Bd E.) . . . . Y 32
Thiers (R.) . . . . Y 33
Toulouse (Av. de) . . . . X 34
Victor-Hugo (R.) . . . . Y 36

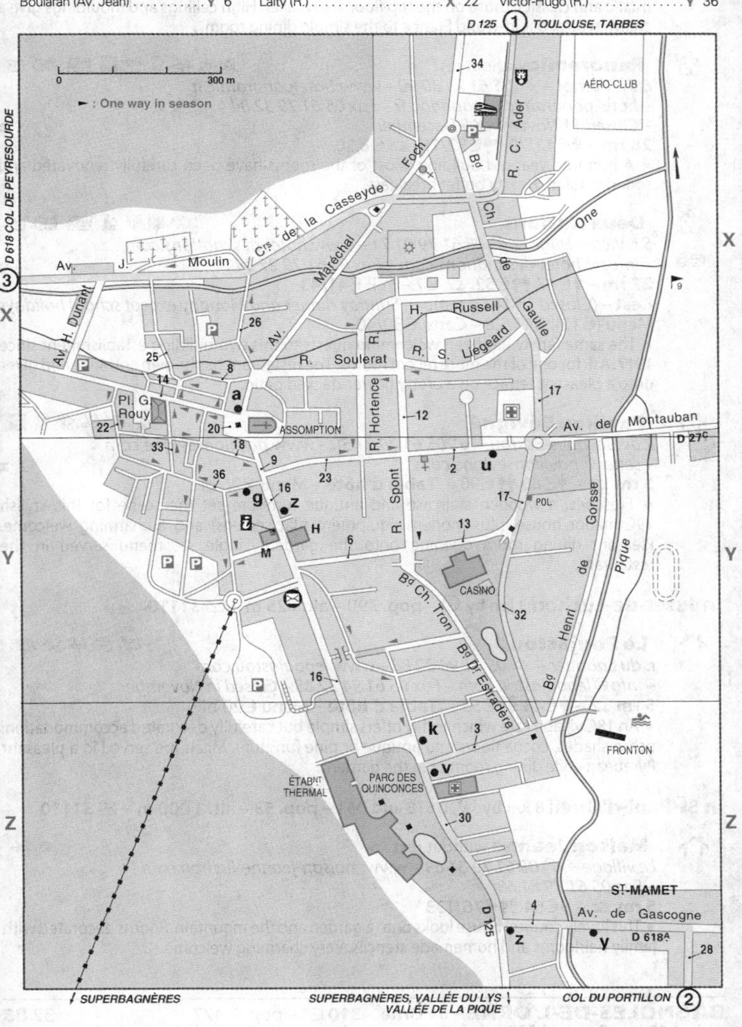

Apsis without rest VISA

19 allées d'Etigny – ✆ 05 61 79 56 97 – www.apsisluchon.com – reception.luchon@apsishotels.com – Fax 05 61 95 43 96 Y **z**

47 rm – €75/99 €95/130, ☕ €15

◆ A business clientele and skiers appreciate this brand new hotel for its central location, attractive, contemporary and well-fitted rooms, and for its "business facilities".

Royal Hôtel rest, VISA
1 cours des Quinconces – 05 61 79 00 62 – Fax 05 61 79 38 35
– Open 25 May-10 October Z **v**
48 rm – €41 €46, €6 – ½ P €43/51 **Rest** – Menu €15 (dinner)/17
◆ Hotel popular with guests taking the spa waters nearby. Rooms with diverse furnishings (rustic and classic); those on the top floor are smaller. High ceilings and mouldings give a charm typical of old-world France to the simple dining room.

Panoramic without rest VISA AE
6 av. Carnot – 05 61 79 30 90 – www.hotelpanoramic.fr
– hotel.panoramic@wanadoo.fr – Fax 05 61 79 32 84
– Closed 11 November-5 December X **a**
28 rm – €42/70 €52/75, €8,50
◆ A hundred-year-old building. Most of the rooms have been carefully renovated and soundproofed. Hearty buffet breakfast.

Deux Nations VISA AE
5 r. Victor-Hugo – 05 61 79 01 71 – www.hotel-des2nations.com
– infos@hotel-des2nations.com – Fax 05 61 79 27 89 Y **g**
27 rm – €47 €52, €7 – ½ P €41/43
Rest – *(Closed 1st-14 December, Sunday dinner and Monday except school holidays)* Menu (€12), €15/28 – Carte €30/40
◆ The same family has been welcoming guests to this two-building establishment since 1917. Ask for one of the more recent rooms. The restaurant has its own entrance and gives onto a pleasant terrace on a pretty flower-decked patio.

Pavillon Sévigné
2 av. Jacques-Barrau – 05 61 79 31 50 – www.pavillonsevigne.com
– seiter@pavillonsevigne.com Z **z**
5 rm – €80 €90 **Table d'hôte** – Menu €25 bi
◆ Frescoes, a wooden staircase and antique furniture set the scene for this stylish 19C manor house, plus modern equipment (flat screens) and a charming welcome. Pleasant dining room opening onto the garden. Single set menu served in the restaurant.

in Juzet-de-Luchon 3 km by ① – **pop. 390 – alt. 625 m – ✉ 31110**

Le Poujastou
r. du Sabotier – 05 61 94 32 88 – www.lepoujastou.com
– info@lepoujastou.com – Fax 05 61 94 32 88 – Closed in November
5 rm – €43 €53 **Table d'hôte** – Menu €20 bi
◆ An 18C village café which today offers simple but carefully decorated accommodation: ochre shades, cocoa floors and antique or pine furniture. Meals are served in a pleasant Pyrenean-style dining room or in the garden.

in St-Paul-d'Oueil 8 km by ③, **D618 and D51 – pop. 53 – alt. 1 000 m – ✉ 31110**

Maison Jeanne without rest
Le village – 05 61 79 81 63 – www.maison-jeanne-luchon.com
– Fax 05 61 79 81 63
5 rm – €64 €76/133
◆ This lovely country house looks onto a garden and the mountain. Rooms decorated with family heirlooms and homemade stencils. Very charming welcome.

BAGNOLES-DE-L'ORNE – 61 Orne – 310 G3 – pop. 2 477 – alt. 140 m – Spa : mid March-late Oct. – Casino A – ✉ 61140 Normandy

32 **B3**

Paris 236 – Alençon 48 – Argentan 39 – Domfront 19 – Falaise 48 – Flers 28

Office de tourisme, place du Marché 02 33 37 85 66, Fax 02 33 30 06 75

de Bagnoles-de-l'Orne Route de Domfront, 02 33 37 81 42

Site★ - Lake★ - Thermal establishment park /I★.

BAGNOLES-DE-L'ORNE

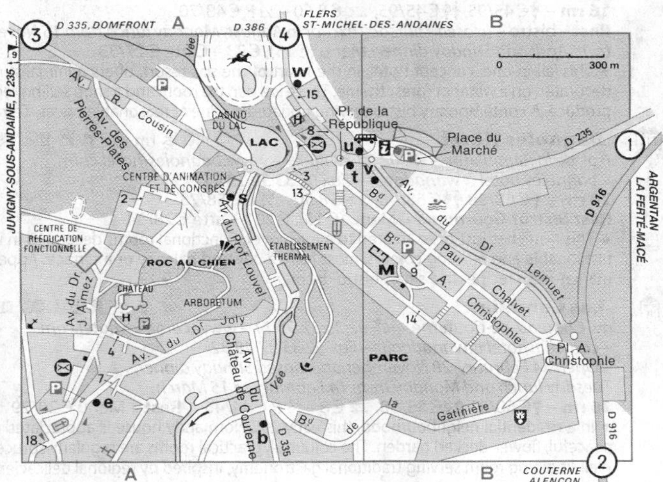

Le Manoir du Lys (Franck Quinton)

2 km rte Juvigny-sous-Andaine via ③ – VISA

02 33 37 80 69 – www.manoir-du-lys.fr – manoir-du-lys@wanadoo.fr – Fax 02 33 30 05 80 – Closed 3 January-12 February, Sunday dinner, Tuesday lunch and Monday from November to April except Easter

23 rm – €80/165 €125/210, €16 – 7 suites – ½ P €110/195

Rest – Menu €40/110 – Carte €60/93

Spec. Andouille de Vire en papillote transparente et foin vert à la crème de camembert. Pigeonneau rôti, jus au cidre et jeunes navets. Macaron à la crème tendre, champignons des bois et sorbet trompette.

◆ In the heart of the woods, a fine Normandy manor surrounded by grounds. Personalised rooms in the manor and, more recent and spacious ones in an unusual pavilion. Regional cuisine served in a superb, modern-style dining room or on an exquisite terrace.

Nouvel Hôtel

rest, VISA

8 av. Dr-P.-Noal – 02 33 30 75 00 – www.nouvel-hotel-bagnoles.fr – contact@nouvel-hotel-bagnoles.fr – Fax 02 33 30 75 13 – Open March-November A **e**

30 rm – €47/78 €59/78, €8 – ½ P €49/62

Rest – Menu €18 (weekdays)/32 – Carte €29/45

◆ This charming early 20C villa has functional, pleasant, well-soundproofed rooms. A lounge with piano and peaceful flower-decked garden. Three rooms, one in a pleasant veranda. Traditional, health food and vegetarian menus are offered.

Bois Joli

rest, VISA

av. Ph.-du-Rozier – 02 33 37 92 77 – www.hotelboisjoli.com – boisjoli@wanadoo.fr – Fax 02 33 37 07 56 A **w**

20 rm – €74/156 €74/156, €11 **Rest** – Menu €21/60 – Carte €39/74

◆ Elegant 19C Anglo-Norman villa set in wooded grounds. Plush interior, antique furniture and pretty, delightfully romantic guestrooms. A welcoming dining room with fine, original wood panelling and a carved fireplace. Concise traditional menu with a regional flavour.

Ô Gayot rest, VISA
2 av. de la Ferté-Macé – ✆ 02 33 38 44 01 – www.ogayot.com – contact@ogayot.com – Fax 02 33 38 47 71 – Closed Sunday dinner from 15 November to 1st April
16 rm – €45/95 €45/95, ☕ €8,50 – ½ P €48/70 A **u**
Rest – bistro – *(closed Thursday except in August, Monday lunch from 15 November to 1st April and Sunday dinner)* Menu (€15), €23 – Carte €27/33
◆ This 'all-in-one' concept hotel, in the heart of the spa resort, offers minimalist rooms decorated on a water or forest theme. There is a bar, tea room and a shop selling regional produce. A contemporary bistro serving updated cuisine at reasonable prices. Terrace.

Bagnoles Hôtel rm, P VISA AE
6 pl. de la République – ✆ 02 33 37 86 79 – www.bagnoles-hotel.com – bagnoles.hotel@wanadoo.fr – Fax 02 33 30 19 74 A **t**
20 rm – €68/88 €68/98, ☕ €8,50 – ½ P €58/73
Rest *Bistrot Gourmand* – Menu (€15), €20 – Carte €28/34
◆ This hotel has just been treated to a makeover. Functional rooms decorated in warm, fashionable and relaxing colours; most have a covered balcony or a terrace. Appetising market-fresh recipes in a smart bistro decor.

Les Camélias P VISA AE
av. Château-de-Couterne – ✆ 02 33 37 93 11 – www.cameliashotel.com – cameliashotel@wanadoo.fr – Fax 02 33 37 48 32 – Open 14 February-28 November and closed Sunday dinner, Tuesday lunch and Monday from 14 February to 15 March A **b**
26 rm – €50/53 €55/58, ☕ €8 – ½ P €44/46 **Rest** – Menu €20/29
◆ In a residential neighbourhood, this early 20C Normandy house is appreciated for its peaceful, flower-decked garden. The colourful, practical rooms are regularly spruced up. Well-lit dining room serving traditional gastronomy, inspired by regional delicacies.

Le Roc au Chien P VISA AE
10 r. Prof.-Louvel – ✆ 02 33 37 97 33 – www.hotelrocauchien.fr – info@hotelrocauchien.fr – Fax 02 33 38 17 76 – Open 7 March-5 November A **s**
39 rm – €52/63 €56/77, ☕ €8
Rest – Menu (€16), €21/30 – Carte €19/40
◆ The Countess of Ségur is said to have stayed in this hotel composed of two small adjoining buildings, one flanked by a brick turret. Rooms in rustic style. The long dining room faces the street; regional dishes and specialities for the health-conscious.

Le Normandie P VISA AE
2 av. du Dr-Lemuet – ✆ 02 33 30 71 30 – www.hotel-le-normandie.com – hotel-le-normandie@wanadoo.fr – Fax 02 33 30 71 31 – Closed January and February B **v**
22 rm – €49/115 €62/115, ☕ €8,50 **Rest** – Menu €18/36 – Carte €39/68
◆ This former post house has lost nothing of its stylish allure. Personalised, comfortable rooms with modern touches: stained wooden furniture and pastel colour scheme. The restaurant focuses on regional recipes and produce that vary according to the season.

BAGNOLET – **93 Seine-Saint-Denis** – **305** F7 – **101** 17 – **see Paris, Area**

BAGNOLS – **69 Rhône** – **327** G4 – **pop. 735** – **alt. 400 m** – ✉ **69620** 43 **E1**
Lyon - Rhone Valley

Paris 444 – Lyon 30 – Tarare 20 – Villefranche-sur-Saône 14

Château de Bagnols rm, rest, P VISA AE
– ✆ 04 74 71 40 00 – www.chateaudebagnols.fr – info@chateaudebagnols.fr – Fax 04 74 71 40 49
16 rm – €460/2575 €460/2575, ☕ €32 – 5 suites
Rest – Menu (€48 bi), €69/125 – Carte €99/170
Spec. Foie gras poêlé aux cocos de Paimpol (automne). Filet de charolais, pomme de terre "dans tous ses états" et jus de betterave. Soufflé aux fruits. **Wines** Mâcon-Villages, Morgon.
◆ Gardens open onto the Beaujolais countryside, access by drawbridge, restored Renaissance frescoes and superb rooms with personal touches - one feels to the manor born! Tempting cuisine served in a majestic guardroom with its splendid Gothic fireplace and ancestral furniture.

BAGNOLS – 63 Puy-de-Dôme – 326 C9 – pop. 503 – alt. 862 m – ✉ 63810 5 B2

Paris 483 – La Bourboule 23 – Clermont-Ferrand 64 – Issoire 63 – Le Mont-Dore 29

Voyageers VISA

au bourg – ☎ 04 73 22 20 12 – www.hotelrestaurantbagnols.com – legouffe.thierry@neuf.fr – Fax 04 73 22 21 18

18 rm – – €30 €45 – ½ P €45/50

Rest – *(closed Sunday dinner, Monday dinner, Tuesday dinner except school holidays)* Menu (€16), €19/58 bi – Carte €35/50

◆ A 1960s building in an Auvergne village built in local style. Simple, practical rooms, gradually being renovated. A modest, yet popular restaurant, which has surely something to do with the contemporary fare!

BAGNOLS-SUR-CÈZE – 30 Gard – 339 M4 – pop. 18 700 – alt. 51 m – ✉ 30200 Provence 23 D1

Paris 653 – Alès 54 – Avignon 34 – Nîmes 56 – Orange 25 – Pont-St-Esprit 12

Office de tourisme, Espace Saint-Gilles ☎ 04 66 89 54 61, Fax 04 66 89 83 38

Musée d'Art moderne Albert-André★.

Site★ of Roques-sur-Cèze.

Château du Val de Cèze rm, VISA AE

69 rue Léon Fontaine, 1 km Avignon road – ☎ 04 66 89 61 26 – www.sud-provence.com – hotelvaldeceze@sud-provence.com – Fax 04 66 89 97 37 – Closed 20 December-4 January

22 rm – €86/120 €96/130, €12 – 1 suite – ½ P €78/99

Rest – *(closed Saturday lunch and Sunday dinner)* Menu (€20), €26/48

◆ Sitting rooms abound in this 17C château. The Provençal style rooms (wrought iron, terracotta tiles, coloured fabrics) are in recent houses dotted around the estate (pool and tennis court). The restaurant serves market-fresh cuisine evolving with the seasons.

Alès road 5 km West by D 6 and D 143 – ✉ 30200 Bagnols-sur-Cèze

Château de Montcaud rm, VISA AE

Hameau de Combe – ☎ 04 66 89 60 60 – www.chateau-de-montcaud.com – montcaud@relaischateaux.com – Fax 04 66 89 45 04 – Open 8 April-24 October

26 rm – €175/360 €185/460, €23 – 2 suites – ½ P €185/345

Rest *Les Jardins de Montcaud* – *(closed lunch except Sunday in season)* Menu €58/88 – Carte €66/74

Rest *Bistrot de Montcaud* – *(closed Saturday and Sunday) (lunch only)* Menu (€23) – Carte €31/37

◆ Noble 19C residence in well-tended parkland. Period furniture and warm colours personalise the attractive rooms in this haven of peace. Smart Provençal restaurant and lovely patio in the Montcaud Gardens. Simple menu in the Bistrot. Jazzy Sunday brunches in summer.

BAIE DES TRÉPASSÉS – 29 Finistère – 308 C6 – see Pointe du Raz

BAILLARGUES – 34 Hérault – 339 J7 – see Montpellier

BAILLEUL – 59 Nord – 302 E3 – pop. 13 500 – alt. 44 m – ✉ 59270 Northern France and the Paris Region 30 B2

Paris 244 – Armentières 13 – Béthune 31 – Dunkerque 44 – Ieper 20 – Lille 30 – St-Omer 37

Office de tourisme, 3, Grand'place ☎ 03 28 43 81 00, Fax 03 28 43 81 01

★ of the belfry.

Belle Hôtel without rest VISA AE

19 r. de Lille – ☎ 03 28 49 19 00 – www.bellehotel.fr – belle.hotel@wanadoo.fr – Fax 03 28 49 22 11 – Closed 10-23 August, 24 December-3 January

31 rm – €85/160 €85/160, €13

◆ Two red-brick Flemish houses. The rooms are spacious and sophisticated (period furniture) in one and more modern in the other, but both are well looked after.

BAIROLS – 06 Alpes-Maritimes – 341 D4 – pop. 109 – alt. 850 m – ✉ 06420 41 **D2**

Paris 836 – Digne-les-Bains 120 – Grasse 74 – Nice 53 – St Martin-Vésubie 40

Auberge du Moulin

4 r. Lou-Coulet – ☎ 04 93 02 92 93 – Closed 15-30 November and Monday
Rest – *(number of covers limited, pre-book)* Menu € 25/35
◆ Former mill at the heart of a medieval hilltop village. Single Italian menu served in a pretty rustic setting and relaxed atmosphere. Bits of old machinery adorn the room.

BAIX – 07 Ardèche – 331 K5 – pop. 1 010 – alt. 80 m – ✉ 07210 44 **B3**

Paris 588 – Crest 30 – Montélimar 22 – Privas 18 – Valence 33

Les Quatre Vents without rest

Chomérac road, 2 km north-westward – ☎ 04 75 85 80 64 – hotel-les-4vents@orange.fr – Fax 04 75 85 05 30 – Closed 21 December-4 January
21 rm – €44/50 €47/53, €7
◆ An ochre façade and blue shutters for these two buildings set back a little from the busy road. Renovated practical rooms. Breakfast served on the terrace in summer, with a country view.

Les Quatre Vents

Chomérac road, 2 km north-westward – ☎ 04 75 85 84 49 – Fax 04 75 85 84 49 – Closed 26 December-15 January, Saturday lunch and Sunday dinner
Rest – Menu (€ 14), € 23 (weekdays)/54 – Carte € 45/60
◆ This restaurant serving modern cuisine offers exposed rafters and redecorated dining rooms with paintings on display.

BALARUC-LES-BAINS – 34 Hérault – 339 H8 – pop. 6 180 – alt. 3 m – Spa : early March-mid Dec. – Casino – ✉ 34540 23 **C2**

Languedoc-Roussillon-Tarn Gorges

Paris 781 – Agde 32 – Béziers 52 – Frontignan 8 – Lodève 54 – Montpellier 33 – Sète 9

Syndicat d'initiative, Pavillon Sévigné ☎ 04 67 46 81 46, Fax 04 67 46 81 54

Le St-Clair

quai du Port – ☎ 04 67 48 48 91 – www.restaurant-saintclair.com – contact@restaurant-saintclair.com – Fax 04 67 18 86 96 – Closed 5 January-6 February
Rest – Menu € 20 (weekday lunch), € 30/60 – Carte € 49/91
◆ Veranda-dining room overlooking the quayside and a terrace, adorned with palm trees, facing the Thau basin. A must for fish and shellfish enthusiasts.

BALDENHEIM – 67 Bas-Rhin – 315 J7 – see Sélestat

BALDERSHEIM – 68 Haut-Rhin – 315 I10 – see Mulhouse

BALLEROY – 14 Calvados – 303 G4 – pop. 754 – alt. 70 m – ✉ 14490 32 **B2**

Normandy

Paris 276 – Bayeux 16 – Caen 42 – St-Lô 23 – Vire 47

Château★.

Manoir de la Drôme

129 r. des Forges – ☎ 02 31 21 60 94 – www.manoir-de-la-drome.com – denisleclerc@wanadoo.fr – Fax 02 31 21 88 67 – Closed 26 October-4 November, 10-28 February, Sunday dinner, Monday and Wednesday
Rest – Menu € 49/70 – Carte € 60/90
◆ This 17C estate with character was owned by a master blacksmith. Classic dishes served in a smart setting. The river Drôme runs through the flower-decked garden.

LA BALME-DE-SILLINGY – 74 Haute-Savoie – 328 J5 – pop. 4 315 – alt. 480 m – ✉ 74330 46 F1

Paris 524 – Annecy 13 – Bellegarde-sur-Valserine 30 – Belley 59 – Frangy 14 – Genève 48

Syndicat d'initiative, 13, route de Choisy ✆ 04 50 68 78 70, Fax 04 50 68 53 29

Les Rochers

rest, VISA AE

D 1508 – ✆ 04 50 68 70 07 – www.hotellesrochers.com – hotel.restaurant.les-rochers@wanadoo.fr – Fax 04 50 68 82 74 – Closed 1st-15 November, January, Sunday dinner and Monday except from 15 June to 15 September

24 rm – €48/55 €52/60, €10 – ½ P €53/61

Rest – Menu €20 (weekdays)/54 – Carte €22/56

◆ Hotel in a small town at the foot of the Mandallaz mountain. All the rooms have been refurbished; those to the rear are quieter. A family guest-house atmosphere dominates the large dining room, furnished in Louis XIII fashion. Traditional fare.

La Chrissandière

VISA AE

at 400 m.

10 rm – €71 €71, €10 – ½ P €70

◆ Thatched cottage in a 3 ha park. Refurbished, nicely decorated rooms. Park and pool: two undeniable strong points for this annexe. Reception is at Les Rochers.

LA BALME-DE-THUY – 74 Haute-Savoie – 328 K5 – see Thônes

BALOT – 21 Côte-d'Or – 320 G3 – pop. 93 – alt. 272 m – ✉ 21330 8 C1

Paris 235 – Auxerre 74 – Chaumont 74 – Dijon 82 – Montbard 28 – Troyes 72

Auberge de la Baume

rm, VISA AE

r. d'en haut – ✆ 03 80 81 40 15 – www.aubergedelabaume.com – la.baume@aliceadsl.fr – Fax 03 80 81 62 87 – Closed 24 December-3 January

10 rm – €48/60 €48/60, €8 – ½ P €62/64

Rest – Menu €16 (weekday lunch), €24/35 – Carte €21/34

◆ Across from the church, this inn offers an attentive welcome and practical and well-maintained guestrooms. A fine collection of antique soup tureens adorns the rustic fireside dining room. Traditional fare.

BAMBECQUE – 59 Nord – 302 D2 – pop. 673 – alt. 8 m – ✉ 59470 30 B1

Paris 271 – Calais 65 – Dunkerque 24 – Hazebrouck 26 – Lille 57 – St-Omer 36

La Vieille Forge

VISA AE

38 r. Principale – ✆ 03 28 27 60 67 – lavieilleforge@voila.fr – Fax 03 28 27 60 67 – Closed Sunday dinner, Monday, Tuesday, Wednesday and Thursday

Rest – Menu €31/65 bi

◆ A magnificent fireplace (remains of the old forge) stands in the lovely rustic dining room. The menu is made up of selections from which guests select.

BANASSAC – 48 Lozère – 330 H8 – pop. 863 – alt. 525 m – ✉ 48500 22 B1

Paris 588 – Florac 55 – Mende 47 – Millau 52

du Sabot La Canourgue Route des Gorges du Tarn, SE : 4 km on D 998, ✆ 04 66 32 84 00

Le Calice du Gévaudan

rest, VISA AE

– ✆ 04 66 32 94 18 – www.hoelcalicegevaudan.com – calice@wanadoo.fr – Fax 04 66 32 98 62 – Closed 22-31 August, autumn half-term holidays, Saturday dinner, Sunday and holidays

28 rm – €52/54 €52/54, €8 **Rest** – Menu (€15), €19 – Carte €24/39

◆ For a place to stop on the way to your holiday, aim for this recent and functional hotel offering rather simply furnished rooms, but which have good soundproofing. A restaurant with a peaceful terrace that gives onto a garden with a children's play area.

BAN-DE-LAVELINE – 88 Vosges – 314 K3 – pop. 1 260 – alt. 427 m – ✉ 88520 27 **D3**

Paris 411 – Colmar 59 – Épinal 67 – St-Dié 14 – Ste-Marie-aux-Mines 15 – Sélestat 39

Auberge Lorraine with rm

5 r. du 8 mai – ✆ 03 29 51 78 17 – www.auberge-lorraine.com – auberge-lorraine.sarl@wanadoo.fr – Fax 03 29 51 71 72 – Closed Sunday dinner and Monday

7 rm – €34/49 €40/65, ☕ €8 – ½ P €47/57

Rest – Menu (€14), €17 (weekday lunch), €24/40 – Carte €27/58

◆ A pleasant stop in the Vosges: hearty helpings of tasty regional fare served in a dolls' house decor. Faultless service. The snug, warmly decorated rooms are spacious and practical. Relaxation area.

Look out for red symbols, indicating particularly pleasant establishments.

BANDOL – 83 Var – 340 J7 – pop. 8 645 – alt. 1 m – Casino Y – ✉ 83150 40 **B3**

French Riviera

Paris 818 – Aix-en-Provence 68 – Marseille 48 – Toulon 18

Access to Île de Bendor by boat (crossing 7mn) ✆ 04 94 29 44 34.

Office de tourisme, allées Vivien ✆ 04 94 29 41 35, Fax 04 94 32 50 39

de Frégate Saint-Cyr-sur-Mer Route de Bandol, 4 km on the Marseille road, ✆ 04 94 29 38 00

Allées Jean-Moulin★.

Plan on next page

Golf Hôtel rm, VISA

on the Renécros beach via bd L. Lumière -Z- ✆ 04 94 29 45 83 – www.golfhotel.fr – golfhotel.surplage@wanadoo.fr – Fax 04 94 32 42 47 – Open mid March-early November

24 rm – €58/120 €58/120, ☕ €10

Rest – beach rest. – *(open April to end September and closed for dinner except from 21 June to 12 September)* Menu €22 – Carte €33/43

◆ This charming villa surrounded by sand dunes has small rooms with varied furnishings, some have loggias or balconies. Meals served on the terrace overlooking the bay, where you can almost put your feet in the water!

Bel Ombra rest, VISA AE

r. de la Fontaine - Y – ✆ 04 94 29 40 90 – www.hotelbelombra.com – hotel.bel.ombra@wanadoo.fr – Fax 04 94 25 01 11 – Open 1 April-15 October

20 rm (½ board only) – €58/88 €58/88 – ½ P €67/75

Rest – *(open 1st July -20 September) (dinner only) (residents only)* Menu €23

◆ Off the beaten track of the holidaymakers, this friendly establishment is located in a quiet neighbourhood. Practical rooms in a modern style, families should ask for those with a mezzanine. Half-board available for residents.

Les Galets rest, VISA AE

49 montée Voisin – ✆ 04 94 29 43 46 – www.lesgalets-bandol.com – info@lesgalets-bandol.com – Fax 04 94 32 44 36 – Open 15 January-5 November

20 rm – €65/85 €80/85, ☕ €8 – ½ P €68/76

Rest – *(open 1st May-30 September)* Menu €18 (weekday lunch), €23/31

◆ A hillside hotel with matchless sea views. Most of the tasteful, light guestrooms boast a balcony overlooking the sea. Rustic restaurant and terrace with panoramic views. Traditional cuisine.

L'Espérance VISA

21 r. L. Marçon – ✆ 04 94 05 85 29 – www.restaurant-lesperance.com – gilles.pradines@orange.fr – Fax 04 94 05 85 29 – Closed 26-31 November, Sunday dinner from mid-September to mid-April and Monday Y x

Rest – Menu (€20 bi), €28/60 – Carte €46/54

◆ Endearing family-run restaurant off the main tourist track. Traditional recipes with a southern tang served in a spruce decor enhanced by Provençal touches.

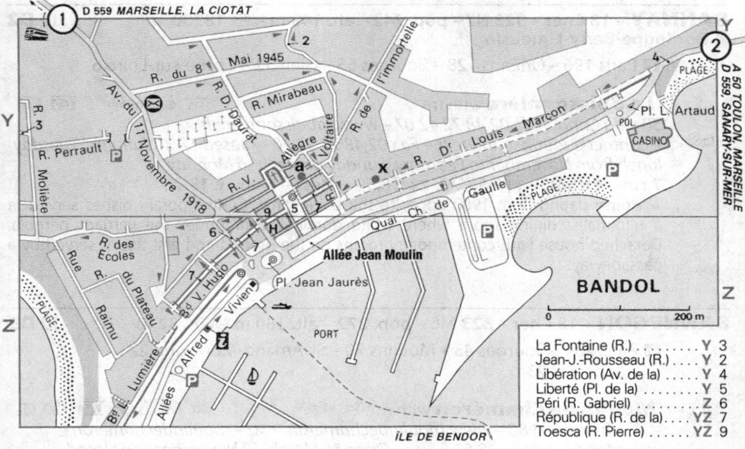

X **Le Clocher**

1 r. de la Paroisse – ✆ 04 94 32 47 65 – le.clocher@wanadoo.fr – Closed Sunday dinner and Wednesday Y **a**

Rest – *(number of covers limited, pre-book)* Menu (€ 13 bi), € 28/35 – Carte € 32/50

◆ A gracious welcome, modern, bistro-style decor, terrace in a side street and lovely, modern food: this small restaurant in old Bandol cannot be faulted.

via ② 1,5 km and Sanary road – ✉ 83110 Sanary-sur-Mer

XX **Le Castel** with rm

925 rte de la Canolle – ✆ 04 94 29 82 98 – Fax 04 94 32 53 32 – Closed 15 January-28 February and Sunday dinner from 15 November to 15 January

9 rm – †€ 62 ††€ 74, ☕ € 8 – ½ P € 71

Rest – *(pre-book)* Menu € 33/42 – Carte € 45/60

◆ Small family inn and engaging rustic dining room, where the chef rustles up authentic, hearty traditional cuisine. Simple guestrooms, for the most part on the ground floor.

BANGOR – 56 Morbihan – 063 11 – see Belle-Île-en-Mer

BANNALEC – 29 Finistère – 308 I7 – pop. 5 016 – alt. 98 m – ✉ 29380 9 **B2**

Paris 535 – Carhaix-Plouguer 51 – Châteaulin 67 – Concarneau 25 – Quimper 33

Office de tourisme, Kerbail ✆ 02 98 39 43 34, Fax 02 98 39 53 44

St-Thurien road 4,5 km Northeast by D 23 and secondary road – ✉ 29380 Bannalec

Le Manoir du Ménec

– ✆ 02 98 39 47 47 – www.manoirdumenec.com – merlinmenec@orange.fr – Fax 02 98 39 46 17

15 rm ☕ – †€ 80/90 ††€ 90/100 – ½ P € 70/75

Rest – *(Closed lunch and Wednesday from mid-November to mid-March)* Menu € 30/50 – Carte € 30/51

◆ Spacious old-style bedrooms in the original manor house, slightly smaller ones in its outbuildings, although often with four-poster beds. Leisure complex. Beams, old stonework and a granite fireplace give character to the dining room. Classic cuisine.

BANNAY – 18 Cher – **323** N2 – **pop. 742** – **alt. 148 m** – ✉ **18300** 12 **D2**
Dordogne-Berry-Limousin

Paris 196 – Orléans 128 – Bourges 55 – Gien 52 – Cosne-sur-Loire 6

La Buissonnière with rm — rm, VISA
58 r. du Canal – ✆ 02 48 72 42 07 – www.labuissonniere.fr – contact@labuissonniere.fr – Fax 02 48 72 35 90 – Closed 17-30 January, Tuesday lunch from November to February, Sunday dinner and Monday
7 rm – €58/79 €58/79, €8,50 **Rest** – Menu €18/28
◆ House dating from 1900 opposite the Loire canal. Contemporary dishes served in a minimalist dining room where white dominates, or under the verdant pergola. Detached house with contemporary rooms on the ground and first floors, served by a passageway.

BANNEGON – 18 Cher – **323** M6 – **pop. 272** – **alt. 180 m** – ✉ **18210** 12 **D3**

Paris 284 – Bourges 43 – Moulins 70 – St-Amand-Montrond 22 – Sancoins 23

Moulin de Chaméron with rm — P VISA AE
– ✆ 02 48 61 83 80 – www.moulindechameron.fr.st/ – moulindechameron@wanadoo.fr – Fax 02 48 61 84 92 – Open 15 March-30 November and closed Tuesday lunch and Monday off season
13 rm – €69 €92, €13 **Rest** – Menu €26/49 – Carte approx. €50
◆ This 18C mill is home to a pleasant restaurant and milling museum in an ideal country setting. The more recent hotel section offers sober rooms.

BANYULS-SUR-MER – 66 Pyrénées-Orientales – **344** J8 – **pop. 4 644** – **alt. 1 m** – ✉ **66650** Languedoc-Roussillon-Tarn Gorges 22 **B3**

Paris 887 – Cerbère 11 – Perpignan 37 – Port-Vendres 7

Office de tourisme, avenue de la République ✆ 04 68 88 31 58, Fax 04 68 88 36 84

★★ du cap Réderis East: 2 km.

Les Elmes — rm, AC P VISA AE
plage des Elmes – ✆ 04 68 88 03 12 – www.hotel.des.elmes.com – contact@hotel-des-elmes.com – Fax 04 68 88 53 03
31 rm – €48/119 €48/119, €10
Rest *Littorine* – *(closed 11 November-10 December and lunch Monday-Wednesday)* Menu €28/48 – Carte €37/51
◆ Welcoming hotel on the beach. The rooms are either traditional, modern or nautical on the second floor (where they have recently been renovated). Fish and shellfish star in this restaurant with views of the Mediterranean from the terrace.

Al Fanal et H. El Llagut with rm — AC VISA AE
av. Fontaulé – ✆ 04 68 88 00 81 – www.al-fanal.com – al.fanal@wanadoo.fr – Fax 04 68 88 13 37 – Closed 1st-20 December
13 rm – €70/80 €70/80, €9 – ½ P €73/78
Rest – *(Closed Wednesday and Thursday except July-August)* Menu (€20), €28/40 – Carte €39/64
◆ Flavourful Catalan cooking centred on seafood. Very good regional wines to be savoured in a pleasant, nautical-style setting or on the seaside terrace. Renovated rooms.

LA BARAQUE – 63 Puy-de-Dôme – **326** F8 – **see Clermont-Ferrand**

BARAQUEVILLE – 12 Aveyron – **338** G5 – **pop. 2 838** – **alt. 792 m** – ✉ **12160** 29 **C1**

Paris 639 – Albi 58 – Millau 75 – Rodez 17 – Villefranche-de-Rouergue 43

Syndicat d'initiative, place du Marché ✆ 05 65 69 10 78, Fax 05 65 71 10 19

Segala Plein Ciel
rte d'Albi – ✆ 05 65 69 03 45 – www.hotel-segala-pleinciel.com – infos@hotel-pleinciel.com – Fax 05 65 70 14 54 – Closed 22 December-8 January, Friday dinner and Sunday dinner except July-August
47 rm – †€ 48 ††€ 75, ☕ € 10 – ½ P € 80
Rest – Menu (€ 15), € 20 (weekdays)/45 – Carte € 30/60
◆ A 1970s building and its grounds overlooking the small market town. The large rooms look out over the valley; most of them have been renovated in a Japanese or Canadian style. Long panoramic dining room, with nautical decor and terrace. Regional cooking.

BARATIER – 05 Hautes-Alpes – **334** G5 – **pop. 519** – **alt. 855 m** – ✉ 05200 — 41 **C1**

Paris 705 – Gap 40 – Grenoble 143 – Marseille 215 – Valence 124

Les Peupliers
chemin de Lesdier – ✆ 04 92 43 03 47 – www.hotel-les-peupliers.com – info@hotel-les-peupliers.com – Fax 04 92 43 41 49 – Closed 13 April-6 May and 27 September-22 October
24 rm – †€ 42 ††€ 50/66, ☕ € 8 – ½ P € 50/58
Rest – *(closed Tuesday lunch, Wednesday lunch, Thursday lunch and Friday lunch except July-August)* Menu € 18/41 – Carte € 22/40
◆ An attractive chalet in the verdant outskirts of a peaceful village. The charming rooms are a blend of mountain and Provencal styles, some with a balcony and lake view. Full spa. Pleasant Alpine dining room warmed by an open fire; shady terrace.

BARBASTE – 47 Lot-et-Garonne – **336** D4 – **pop. 1 467** – **alt. 45 m** – ✉ **47230** Atlantic Coast — 4 **C2**

Paris 703 – Agen 34 – Bordeaux 125 – Villeneuve-sur-Lot 50

Syndicat d'initiative, place de la Mairie ✆ 05 53 65 84 85, Fax 05 53 65 51 38

La Cascade aux Fées
r. Riberotte – ✆ 05 53 97 05 96 – www.cascade-aux-fees.com – gmazurier@aol.com – Open April-December
4 rm – †€ 70/90 ††€ 80/100, ☕ € 9 **Table d'hôte** – Menu € 25 bi/35 bi
◆ Giving onto a magnificent flowery park beside the Gélise river, this 18C residence offers a warm reception. Simple but tasteful decoration (antique furniture). Home cooking at the table d'hôte, set up home-style in the dining room or on the shaded terrace.

BARBAZAN – 31 Haute-Garonne – **343** B6 – **pop. 445** – **alt. 464 m** – ✉ 31510 — 28 **B3**

Paris 779 – Bagnères-de-Luchon 32 – Lannemezan 27 – St-Gaudens 14 – Tarbes 67

Syndicat d'initiative, le village ✆ 05 61 88 35 64, Fax 05 61 88 35 64

Hostellerie de l'Aristou with rm
rte de Sauveterre – ✆ 05 61 88 30 67 – hotel.aristou@orange.fr – Fax 05 61 95 55 66 – Closed 15 November-11 February
6 rm – †€ 65/70 ††€ 65/95, ☕ € 8 – ½ P € 60
Rest – *(closed for lunch from Monday to Thursday from May to end August, Sunday dinner, Monday and Tuesday lunch from September to end April)* Menu € 21 (weekdays)/45 – Carte € 34/52
◆ 19C farm converted into a country inn; two welcoming dining rooms and small covered terrace. Rooms have rustic or period furniture.

LA BARBEN – 13 Bouches-du-Rhône – **340** G4 – see Salon-de-Provence

BARBENTANE – 13 Bouches-du-Rhône – 340 D2 – pop. 3 660 – alt. 40 m – ✉ 13570 Provence
42 **E1**

Paris 692 – Avignon 10 – Arles 33 – Marseille 103 – Nîmes 38 – Tarascon 16

Office de tourisme, 4, le Cours ✆ 04 90 90 85 86, Fax 04 90 95 60 02

Château★★.

Castel Mouisson without rest

– ✆ *04 90 95 51 17 – www.hotel-castelmouisson.com – contact@hotel-castelmouisson.com – Fax 04 90 95 67 63 – Open 15 March-15 October*

17 rm – †€ 49/72 ††€ 49/72, ☐ € 9

◆ This pleasant Provençal house at the foot of the Montagnette offers simple, rustic rooms overlooking an immense, beautiful garden with trees. A warm family welcome.

BARBERAZ – 73 Savoie – 333 I4 – see Chambéry

BARBEZIEUX-ST-HILAIRE – 16 Charente – 324 J7 – pop. 4 693 – alt. 100 m – ✉ 16300 Atlantic Coast
38 **B3**

Paris 480 – Bordeaux 84 – Angoulême 36 – Cognac 36 – Jonzac 24 – Libourne 70

Office de tourisme, Le Château ✆ 05 45 78 91 04, Fax 05 45 78 91 04

La Boule d'Or

9 bd Gambetta – ✆ 05 45 78 64 13 – www.labouledor.net – laboule.dor@wanadoo.fr – Fax 05 45 78 63 83 – Closed 22 December-4 January, Friday dinner and Sunday dinner October-April

18 rm – †€ 55 ††€ 55, ☐ € 6 – ½ P € 48

Rest – Menu (€ 11), € 15 (weekdays)/35 – Carte € 26/48

◆ In the capital of Cognac's Petite Champagne region, this welcoming house dating from 1852 has large functional rooms. Renovated, sober dining room and a peaceful terrace in the shade of an ancient chestnut tree. Traditional cuisine.

BARBIZON – 77 Seine-et-Marne – 312 E5 – pop. 1 569 – alt. 80 m – ✉ 77630 Northern France and the Paris Region
19 **C3**

Paris 56 – Étampes 41 – Fontainebleau 10 – Melun 13 – Pithiviers 45

Office de tourisme, 41, Grande Rue ✆ 01 60 66 41 87, Fax 01 60 66 41 87

Cély Golf Club Cély Route de Saint Germain, W : 9 km on D 64 and D 11, ✆ 01 64 38 03 07

Auberge du Père Ganne★.

Hôtellerie du Bas-Bréau

rm, VISA

22 r. Grande-Rue – ✆ 01 60 66 40 05 – www.bas-breau.com – basbreau@relaischateaux.com – Fax 01 60 69 22 89

16 rm – †€ 260 ††€ 260/380, ☐ € 26 – 4 suites

Rest – Menu (€ 54), € 76 (dinner)/110 – Carte € 90/125

◆ A hotel that owes its reputation to R. L. Stevenson, one of many famous guests. Fine rooms with personal touches looking out on a park with thousands of flowers. Elegant decor in the dining room and shady terrace. Classic cuisine and game in season.

Les Pléiades

21 G. Rue – ✆ 01 60 66 40 25 – www.hotellespleiades.com – hotellespleiades@orange.fr

20 rm – †€ 160 ††€ 190/260, ☐ € 20 – 3 suites

Rest – *(Closed Sunday dinner, Monday, Tuesday and Wednesday)* Menu € 70/95 – Carte € 80/105

Rest *L'Atelier* – *(Closed Sunday dinner)* Carte € 31/48

Spec. Nougat de foie gras. Filet de bar aux ravioles de betterave. Tendresse de pistache aux framboises.

◆ Sample updated recipes, renewed with the seasons, in an elegant setting graced with antiques and a fireplace.

Hostellerie La Clé d'Or

73 Grande-Rue – ✆ 01 60 66 40 96 – www.hotel-restaurant-cledor.com – cle.dor@wanadoo.fr – Fax 01 60 66 42 71

16 rm – €56/60 €75/97, €11 – ½ P €85

Rest – *(closed Sunday dinner from October to March)* Menu €32/42 – Carte €44/70

◆ Each of the rooms of this former 18C post house is different but all are situated around an interior garden. Traditional food depending on the season is to be enjoyed in a cosy dining room or on the pleasant terrace. Wide choice of wines (250 labels).

L'Angélus

31 r. Grande-Rue – ✆ 01 60 66 40 30 – angelusbarbizon.monsite.wanadoo.fr – restaurant.angelus@wanadoo.fr – Fax 01 60 66 42 12 – Closed Monday and Tuesday

Rest – Carte €38/57

◆ This spick and span rustic inn bears a sign in homage to one of Millet's most famous works, painted at Barbizon. Shaded terrace and traditional menu.

BARBOTAN-LES-THERMES – **32 Gers** – **336** B6 – **Spa : late Feb.-late Nov.** – **Casino** – ✉ **32150 Cazaubon** — 28 **A2**

Languedoc-Roussillon-Tarn Gorges

Paris 703 – Aire-sur-l'Adour 37 – Auch 75 – Condom 37 – Mont-de-Marsan 43

Office de tourisme, place Armagnac ✆ 05 62 69 52 13, Fax 05 62 69 57 71

De la Paix — rest,

24 av. des Thermes – ✆ 05 62 69 52 06 – www.hotel-paix.fr – contact@hotel-paix.fr – Fax 05 62 09 55 73 – Open 15 March-15 November

29 rm – €45/50 €50/75, €7 – ½ P €65/81

Rest – Menu (€11), €16/26 – Carte €20/26

◆ Recent building near the church and the spa. The spacious, well-kept guestrooms are equipped with functional furniture. The vast rustic dining room is pleasantly bathed in light. Traditional cuisine.

Les Fleurs de Lees — rm,

24 av. Henri IV, rte d'Agen – ✆ 05 62 08 36 36 – www.fleursdelees.com – contact@fleursdelees.com – Fax 05 62 08 36 37 – Open April-October

11 rm – €90 €90, €9 – 5 suites

Rest – Menu (€20), €39/49 – Carte €52/73

◆ Smart house in the heart of Armagnac. Quiet rooms, some with a terrace, and lovely themed suites (Africa, Asia, India, etc.) Furniture and decorative objects from Dubai in the restaurant; the cuisine blends international and local flavours.

Cante Grit — rest,

51 av. des Thermes – ✆ 05 62 69 52 12 – www.cantegrit.com – post@cantegrit.com – Fax 05 62 69 53 98 – Open 16 March-14 November

20 rm – €55 €65, €9 – ½ P €48

Rest – *(dinner for residents only)* Menu (€18) – Carte €22/36

◆ This pretty villa dating from the 1930s is covered in Virginia creeper; it has rooms that are rather large, airy and practical. The welcoming lounge is reminiscent of a family home. Welcoming dining room with fireplace and exposed beams and pleasant summer terrace.

Beauséjour

6 av. des Thermes – ✆ 05 62 08 30 30 – www.hotelgers.com – bernard.urrutia@wanadoo.fr – Fax 05 62 09 50 78 – Open March to November

25 rm – €34/72 €36/75, €10 – ½ P €60/75

Rest – *(dinner for residents only)* Menu €20 (weekdays)/45

◆ Large house in the regional style with smartly renovated rooms. Pretty leafy garden and a British-style small lounge. A restaurant in sunny shades with a terrace facing the Gers countryside. Diet meals on request.

Aubergade rest, VISA

13 av. des Thermes – ✆ 05 62 69 55 43 – www.hotel-aubergade-barbotan.com – aubergade2@wanadoo.fr – Fax 05 62 69 52 09 – Open 1st March-30 November

18 rm – †€ 42 ††€ 44, ☕ € 8 – ½ P € 43

Rest – Menu € 13 (weekdays)/27 – Carte € 28/43

◆ At the entrance to this spa resort where exotic species of plants flourish, is this smart, regional-style house. It offers functional, well-soundproofed rooms. Pleasant dining room and traditional menu or diet dishes (for guests taking the spa waters).

Do not confuse ✗ with ✿!
✗ defines comfort, while stars are awarded for the best cuisine, across all categories of comfort.

BARCELONNETTE – 04 Alpes-de-Haute-Provence – 334 H6 41 **C2**
– **pop. 2 766 – alt. 1 135 m – Winter sports : Le Sauze/Super Sauze 1 400/2 000 m 23 and Pra-Loup 1 500/2 600 m 3 29 – ✉ 04400 French Alps**

Paris 733 – Briançon 86 – Cannes 161 – Digne-les-Bains 88 – Gap 68 – Nice 145

Office de tourisme, place Frédéric Mistral ✆ 04 92 81 04 71, Fax 04 92 81 22 67

St-Pons church ★ Northwest: 2 km.

Azteca without rest VISA

3 r. François-Arnaud – ✆ 04 92 81 46 36 – www.azteca-hotel.fr – hotelazteca@barcelonnette.fr – Fax 04 92 81 43 92 – Closed 11 November-6 December

27 rm – †€ 59/107 ††€ 59/107, ☕ € 10

◆ An attractive villa with an original decor of Mexican furniture and handicrafts, recalling the "Barcelonnettes" who emigrated to Mexico. Three rooms continue this theme.

Le Passe-Montagne VISA AE

in 3 km, Col de la Cayolle road – ✆ 04 92 81 08 58 – Fax 04 92 81 08 58 – Open 1st July-15 September, 20 December-2 May and closed Tuesday and Wednesday except school holidays

Rest – *(dinner only) (pre-book)* Menu (€ 25), € 30 – Carte € 32/44

◆ A warm, friendly atmosphere and rustic, alpine decor in this small chalet by a pinewood. Unfussy regional cuisine: mountain style in winter and Provençal in summer.

in St-Pons 2 km Northwest by D 900 and D 9 – ✉ 04400

Domaine de Lara without rest

– ✆ 04 92 81 52 81 – www.domainedelara.com – arlette.signoret@wanadoo.fr – Fax 04 92 81 07 76 – Closed 25 June-4 July and 12 November-19 December

5 rm ☕ – †€ 81/90 ††€ 86/95

◆ Set in parkland with a fine view of the peaks, this characterful Provençal farmhouse (beams, tiled floors, old stone, family heirlooms) is inviting and cosy. Fine breakfasts.

in Jausiers 8 km Northeast by D 900 – **pop. 1 002 – alt. 1 240 m** – ✉ 04850

Office de tourisme, Principale ✆ 04 92 81 21 45, Fax 04 92 81 59 35

Villa Morelia with rm VISA AE

– ✆ 04 92 84 67 78 – www.villa-morelia.com – inforesa@villa-morelia.com – Fax 04 92 84 65 47 – Closed 1st March-30 April and 1st November-26 December

11 rm – †€ 150/190 ††€ 150/350

Rest – *(closed Sunday, Monday and Tuesday except June, July and August) (dinner only from September to May) (pre-book)* Menu € 68

◆ Built in 1900, this splendid 'Mexican' villa has lost none of its former character. Stylish rooms, lovely dining room and rear terrace overlooking the garden and pool. Inventive market-fresh menu.

in Pra-Loup 8.5 km Southwest by D 902, D 908 and D 109 – ✉ 04400 Uvernet Fours – Winter sports : 1 500/2 600 m 3 29

Office de tourisme, Maison de Pra-Loup ✆ 04 92 84 10 04, Fax 04 92 84 02 93

Le Prieuré de Molanès rest, VISA

à Molanès – ✆ 04 92 84 11 43 – www.prieure-praloup.com – info@prieure.eu – Fax 04 92 84 01 88 – Open 6 June-30 September and 15 December-25 April

13 rm – €55/68 €68/90, €8,50 – ½ P €57/75

Rest – Menu (€14), €20/26 – Carte €25/44

♦ Near to the chairlift, this former priory has been converted into a non-smoking family hotel. Appreciated for its alpine decor and tastefully rustic guestrooms. Regional meals mostly using local produce, in a rustic, welcoming setting (beams, fireplace, farming tools).

BARCUS – 64 Pyrénées-Atlantiques – 342 H5 – pop. 774 – alt. 230 m – ✉ 64130 3 B3

Paris 813 – Mauléon-Licharre 14 – Oloron-Ste-Marie 18 – Pau 52 – St-Jean-Pied-de-Port 53

XXX **Chilo** with rm VISA

– ✆ 05 59 28 90 79 – www.hotel-chilo.com – martine.chilo@wanadoo.fr – Fax 05 59 28 94 49 – Closed Sunday dinner, Monday and Tuesday lunch from 11 November to 30 April

11 rm – €60/95 €67/110 – ½ P €70/91

Rest – Menu (€22), €32/68 – Carte €48/65

♦ Fine house, typical of the region, in the heart of a quiet village. Regional cuisine served in a welcoming dining room (non-smoking). Pleasant garden and swimming pool with a view of the mountain.

BARDIGUES – 82 Tarn-et-Garonne – 337 B7 – see Auvillar

BARFLEUR – 50 Manche – 303 E1 – pop. 650 – alt. 5 m – ✉ 50760 32 A1

Normandy

Paris 355 – Carentan 48 – Cherbourg 29 – St-Lô 75 – Valognes 26

Office de tourisme, 2, rond-point le Conquérant ✆ 02 33 54 02 48, Fax 02 33 54 02 48

Pointe de Barfleur Lighthouse: ✳★★ North: 4 km - Interior★ of Montfarville church 2 km S.

Le Conquérant VISA

18 r. St-Thomas-Becket – ✆ 02 33 54 00 82 – www.hotel-leconquerant.com – contact@hotel-leconquerant.com – Fax 02 33 54 65 25 – Open 15 March-15 November

10 rm – €70 €70/107, €10

Rest – pancake rest. – *(dinner only) (residents only)* Menu €17/34 – Carte €23/40

♦ Handsome 17C granite-built residence with French-style garden a stone's throw from the port. The six largest rooms have been redecorated and fitted with modern bathrooms. Sweet and savoury pancakes prepared traditionally, to order.

XX **Moderne** VISA

1 pl. Gén.-de-Gaulle – ✆ 02 33 23 12 44 – www.hotel-restaurant-moderne-barfleur.com – cauchemez@wanadoo.fr – Closed Tuesday dinner from 15 September-15 July and Wednesday

Rest – Menu €20 (weekdays)/65 – Carte approx. €56

♦ In summer this restaurant overflows onto a pleasant terrace. Updated traditional menu featuring fine seafood.

LES BARILS – 27 Eure – 304 E9 – see Verneuil-sur-Avre

Red = Pleasant. Look for the red X and symbols.

BARJAC – 30 Gard – **339** L3 – **pop. 1 498 – alt. 171 m** – ✉ **30430** 23 **D1**

Paris 666 – Alès 34 – Aubenas 45 – Mende 114

Office de tourisme, place Charles Guynet ✆ 04 66 24 53 44, Fax 04 66 60 23 08

Le Mas du Terme

rm, rm, VISA

4 km south-eastward by D 901 and secondary road – ✆ 04 66 24 56 31 – www.masduterme.com – info@masduterme.com – Fax 04 66 24 58 54 – Open 15 March-15 November

23 rm – €89/163 €89/163, €13 – ½ P €89/163

Rest – *(closed for lunch except Sunday, July-August and Bank holidays)* Menu €38

◆ This old silkworm farm in the heart of the vineyards is quite close to the magical Orgnac pothole. Provençal rooms, apartments or furnished family holiday accommodation (gîtes). This 18C building is home to a restaurant with a vaulted ceiling and an outdoor terrace. Serves daily set menu.

BAR-LE-DUC Ⓟ – **55 Meuse** – **307** B6 – **pop. 15 800 – alt. 188 m** – ✉ **55000** Alsace-Lorraine 26 **A2**

Paris 255 – Metz 97 – Nancy 84 – Reims 113 – St-Dizier 26 – Verdun 56

Office de tourisme, 7, rue Jeanne-d'Arc ✆ 03 29 79 11 13, Fax 03 29 79 21 95

de Combles-en-Barrois Combles-en-Barrois 38 rue Basse, 5 km on the St-Dizier road, ✆ 03 29 45 16 03

"le Transi" (statue)★★ in St-Étienne church.

Bistro St-Jean

VISA

132 bd de La Rochelle – ✆ 03 29 45 40 40 – http://www.bistrosaintjean.fr – bistrosaintjean@orange.fr – Closed Saturday lunch, Monday dinner and Sunday

Rest – Menu (€21), €30 – Carte €37/45

◆ Located in a converted grocers' shop, this characteristic bistro (bar, benches, vintage posters) serves delicious seasonal recipes (bistro dishes and seafood).

in Trémont-sur-Saulx 9.5 km southwest on the D 3 – **pop. 647 – alt. 166 m** – ✉ **55000**

La Source

rest, VISA

2 r. de Beurey – ✆ 03 29 75 45 22 – www.hotel-restaurant-lasource.fr – contact@hotel-restaurant-lasource.fr – Fax 03 29 75 48 55 – Closed 27 July-18 August, 2-18 January, Sunday dinner and Monday lunch

24 rm – €67/100 €76/120, €11

Rest – Menu (€27), €30/56 – Carte €37/64

◆ This eighties motel overlooking the countryside has functional, well-kept rooms (two are more spacious). Friendly welcome. A restaurant whose traditional roots are visible in the decor and the menu (truffles in season).

BARNEVILLE-CARTERET – **50 Manche** – **303** B3 – **pop. 2 324** – **alt. 47 m** – ✉ **50270** Normandy 32 **A2**

Paris 356 – Carentan 43 – Cherbourg 39 – Coutances 47 – St-Lô 62

Office de tourisme, 10, rue des Ecoles ✆ 02 33 04 90 58, Fax 02 33 04 93 24

de la Côte-des-Isles Saint-Jean-de-la-Rivière Chemin des Mielles, SE : 5 km on D 90, ✆ 02 33 93 44 85

in Barneville-Plage

Des Isles

VISA

9 bd Maritime – ✆ 02 33 04 90 76 – www.hoteldesisles.com – hotel-des-isles@wanadoo.fr – Fax 02 33 94 53 83 – Closed February

30 rm – €75/125 €75/125, €12 – ½ P €72/97

Rest – Menu (€16), €29 – Carte €36/90

◆ Recently renovated hotel looking out to sea. Guestrooms of differing size, all elegantly decorated in a cosy maritime style with varying shades of blue and soft duvets. A relaxed atmosphere in which to enjoy an "all-you-can-eat" buffet of starters and desserts.

in Carteret

Office de tourisme, 10, rue des Ecoles ✆ 02.33.04.90.58, Fax 02.33.04.93.24
Viewpoint indicator ≤★.

De la Marine (Laurent Cesne)
11 r. de Paris – ✆ 02 33 53 83 31 – www.hotelmarine.com – infos@hotelmarine.com – Fax 02 33 53 39 60 – Open 1st March-23 December
26 rm – †€ 90/260 ††€ 90/260, ☐ € 15 – ½ P € 92/130
Rest – *(open 1st March-11 November and closed Sunday dinner, Thursday lunch and Monday in March, October and November, Monday lunch and Thursday lunch in April, May, June and September)* Menu € 36/89 – Carte € 64/86
Spec. Ormeau du Cotentin meunière sur vinaigrette de pomme de terre. Bar en filet sur caviar d'artichaut-poivrade, palourdes farcies. Pomme en beignets à l'orientale, glace à la fleur d'oranger.
◆ This waterfront hotel has been run by the same family since 1876. Most of the recent rooms, spacious and modern, have a terrace with views of the port. Enjoy impressive sea views from the restaurant dining room and terrace. Inventive, tasty dishes using quality ingredients.

Des Ormes
quai Barbey d'Aurevilly – ✆ 02 33 52 23 50 – www.hoteldesormes.fr – hoteldesormes@wanadoo.fr – Fax 02 33 52 91 65 – Closed January
12 rm – †€ 79/175 ††€ 79/175, ☐ € 14 – ½ P € 85/135
Rest – *(closed Sunday dinner, Monday and Tuesday off season, Monday lunch and Tuesday lunch season)* Menu € 35/45 – Carte € 39/58
◆ Overlooking the marina, a tastefully renovated 19C abode. Exquisite rooms, cosy sitting room and a lovely flower-decked garden in season. Elegant, romantic and contemporary dining room serving food from the land and sea.

BARON – 60 Oise – 305 H5 – pop. 780 – alt. 80 m – ✉ 60300 36 B3

Northern France and the Paris Region

Paris 65 – Amiens 110 – Argenteuil 63 – Montreuil 55

Le Domaine de Cyclone without rest
2 r. de la Gonesse – ✆ 06 08 98 05 50 – domainedecyclone@wanadoo.fr – Fax 03 44 54 26 10
5 rm ☐ – †€ 70 ††€ 80/90
◆ Joan of Arc is supposed to have slept in this castle. The guests now occupy very tasteful rooms, nearly all of which overlook the park. Pony trekking.

LE BARP – 33 Gironde – 335 G7 – pop. 4 048 – alt. 72 m – ✉ 33114 3 B2

Paris 604 – Bordeaux 45 – Mérignac 41 – Pessac 32 – Talence 34

Le Résinier with rm
RN 10 – ✆ 05 56 88 60 07 – www.leresinier.com – hotel.le.resinier@wanadoo.fr – Fax 05 56 88 67 37
5 rm – †€ 80/110 ††€ 80/110, ☐ € 10
Rest – Menu (€ 15), € 17 (weekdays)/55 – Carte € 40/98
◆ This friendly country house is reminiscent of an inn from yesteryear. Traditional cuisine focused on local produce and wines to be picked from the cellar. Terrace shaded by a vine. Comfortable, gradually refurbished rooms with a focus on nature.

BARR – 67 Bas-Rhin – 315 I6 – pop. 6 417 – alt. 200 m – ✉ 67140 2 C1

Alsace-Lorraine

Paris 495 – Colmar 43 – Le Hohwald 12 – Saverne 46 – Sélestat 20 – Strasbourg 37
Office de tourisme, place de l'Hôtel de Ville ✆ 03 88 08 66 65, Fax 03 88 08 66 51

Aux Saisons Gourmandes
23 r. Kirneck – ✆ 03 88 08 12 77 – www.saisons-gourmandes.com – legafferot@wanadoo.fr – Fax 03 88 08 12 77 – Closed 6-25 July, 3-14 January, February holidays, Sunday dinner from January to April, Tuesday and Wednesday
Rest – Menu € 19 (weekday lunch), € 25/42 – Carte € 33/46
◆ Pretty half-timbered house in the town centre sporting a tasteful, modern interior. Market fresh cuisine with traditional influences is served.

Mont Ste-Odile road by D 854 – ✉ 67140 Barr

Château d'Andlau

113 r. vallée St Ulrich, at 2 km – ✆ 03 88 08 96 78 – www.hotelduchateau-andlau.fr – hotel.chateau-andlau@wanadoo.fr – Fax 03 88 08 00 93 – Closed 11-26 November and 3-25 January
22 rm – †€ 47/56 ††€ 53/68, ☕ € 9 – ½ P € 61/68
Rest – *(open dinner from Tuesday to Saturday, Sunday lunch and public holidays)* Menu € 27/40
◆ The simple, rustic rooms and pastoral setting of this hotel will ensure a good night's sleep. Plush dining room and classic menu. Excellent choice of international wines, unusually presented along the lines of a wine tasting manual.

LE BARROUX – 84 Vaucluse – 332 D9 – pop. 615 – alt. 325 m – ✉ 84330 Provence 42 E1

Paris 684 – Avignon 38 – Carpentras 12 – Vaison-la-Romaine 16

Les Géraniums

rest,
pl. de la Croix – ✆ 04 90 62 41 08 – www.hotel-lesgeraniums.com – les.geraniums@wanadoo.fr – Fax 04 90 62 41 08 – Open 1st March-10 November and 20 December-3 January
20 rm – †€ 65 ††€ 65, ☕ € 10 – ½ P € 65
Rest *Saveurs et Terroirs* – *(Closed Thursday from March to April and Wednesday)* Menu (€ 20), € 28 (weekday lunch), € 36/40 – Carte € 47/55
◆ Set in village clinging to a rocky outcrop, complete with a 12C castle, this old house offers unpretentious rooms with a rustic spirit. Regional fare takes pride of place in this pleasant restaurant with bare beams and a flower-decked terrace.

L'Aube Safran

chemin du Patifiage – ✆ 04 90 62 66 91 – www.aube-safran.com – contact@aube-safran.com – Fax 04 90 62 66 91 – Open 15 March-15 November
5 rm ☕ – †€ 100 ††€ 120 – 1 suite **Table d'hôte** – Menu € 40 bi
◆ The hosts of this Provencal country house left everything for this isolated idyllic location at the foot of Mont Ventoux, where they are reviving the growth of saffron, abandoned at the end of the 19C. Table d'hôte twice a week: saffron adds colour to the different regional dishes. Quality produce for sale.

Gajulea

cours Louise-Raymond – ✆ 04 90 62 36 94 – www.gajulea.fr – philibert@gajulea.fr – Closed 2-15 March, 2-15 November and lunch except Sunday
Rest – *(number of covers limited, pre-book)* Menu € 35 (dinner)/59
◆ This dreamlike plush restaurant boasts a superb terrace overlooking the countryside and scrubland. The cuisine has Provençal flavours and aromas. Wine chosen from a glazed cellar.

BAR-SUR-AUBE – 10 Aube – 313 I4 – pop. 5 510 – alt. 190 m – ✉ 10200 Northern France and the Paris Region 14 C3

Paris 230 – Châtillon-sur-Seine 60 – Chaumont 41 – Troyes 53 – Vitry-le-François 65

Office de tourisme, Place de l'Hôtel de Ville ✆ 03 25 27 24 25, Fax 03 25 27 40 02

St-Pierre church ★.

Le Saint-Nicolas without rest

2 r. du Gén.-de-Gaulle – ✆ 03 25 27 08 65 – www.lesaintnicolas.com – lesaintnicolas2@wanadoo.fr – Fax 03 25 27 60 31
27 rm – †€ 63 ††€ 66, ☕ € 9
◆ Pretty stone houses provide the setting for this quiet hotel, slightly away from the town centre. Rooms set around the swimming pool.

La Toque Baralbine

18 r. Nationale – ✆ 03 25 27 20 34 – www.toquebaralbine.fr.st – toquebaralbine@wanadoo.fr – Fax 03 25 27 20 34 – Closed Sunday dinner except July-August and Monday
Rest – Menu (€ 20), € 25/60 – Carte € 32/55
◆ Choose to eat in the rustic rear dining room which is warmer, or on the flower-decked terrace. Tasty cuisine with a contemporary touch and the accent on local produce.

LE BAR-SUR-LOUP – 06 Alpes-Maritimes – 341 C5 – pop. 2 543 – alt. 320 m – ✉ 06620 French Riviera 42 E2

Paris 916 – Grasse 10 – Nice 31 – Vence 15

Office de tourisme, place Francis Paulet ✆ 04 93 42 72 21, Fax 04 93 42 92 60

Site★ - Danse macabre★ (paintings on wood) in St-Jacques church - ≤★ from place de l'église.

Hostellerie du Château

6 pl. Francis-Paulet – ✆ 04 93 42 41 10 – www.lhostellerieduchateau.com – info@lhostellerieduchateau.com – Fax 04 93 42 69 32

6 rm – †€ 130/150 ††€ 150/180, ☕ € 15

Rest *bigaradier* – *✆ 493424110 (Closed 15 December-1st February, Tuesday lunch, Sunday dinner and Monday)* Menu (€ 23), € 28/52 – Carte € 42/62

◆ Refined Provençal bedrooms (old furniture, expensive wood, floor tiles) add to the allure of this château once owned by the Counts of Grasse. Some rooms enjoy views of the valley. Attentive service, an elegant contemporary setting and delicious modern cuisine.

La Jarrerie

– ✆ 04 93 42 92 92 – www.restaurant-la-jarrerie.com – lajarrerie@orange.fr – Fax 04 93 42 91 22 – Closed 26 October-4 November, 2-31 January, Wednesday except dinner from May to September and Tuesday

Rest – Menu (€ 19), € 27/49 – Carte € 39/52

◆ Once a monastery, then a canning factory and perfumery, this 17C regional property has a large rustic dining room with a fireplace, exposed stones and beams.

BAR-SUR-SEINE – 10 Aube – 313 G5 – pop. 3 476 – alt. 157 m – ✉ 10110 Northern France and the Paris Region 13 B3

Paris 197 – Bar-sur-Aube 37 – Châtillon-sur-Seine 36 – St-Florentin 57 – Troyes 33

Office de tourisme, 33, rue Gambetta ✆ 03 25 29 94 43, Fax 03 25 29 70 21

Interior★ of St-Étienne church.

Du Commerce with rm

30 r. de la République – ✆ 03 25 29 86 36 – www.hotelrestaurantducommerce.fr – hotelducommerce.bar-sur-seine@wanadoo.fr – Fax 03 25 29 64 87 – Closed 21-28 February, Friday dinner and Sunday

13 rm – †€ 43 ††€ 45, ☕ € 6,50 – ½ P € 44

Rest – Menu (€ 10), € 13 (weekdays)/40 – Carte € 30/50

◆ This very simple establishment is in the centre of the small town. Rustic-style dining room adorned with a fireplace. Traditional, unpretentious cuisine and modest guestrooms.

Near interchange 9 km motorway A5, Northeast by D 443 – ✉ 10110 Magnant

Le Val Moret

– ✆ 03 25 29 85 12 – www.le-val-moret.com – contact@le-val-moret.com – Fax 03 25 29 70 81

42 rm – †€ 57/85 ††€ 57/85, ☕ € 10

Rest – Menu € 18 (weekdays)/48 – Carte € 25/52

◆ Motel type, ground floor establishment with functional and fairly spacious rooms in four buildings. Children's play area. Modern dining rooms, one with a veranda: traditional menu and regional dishes.

BAS-RUPTS – 88 Vosges – 314 J4 – see Gérardmer

BASSAC – 16 Charente – 324 I6 – see Jarnac

BASSE-GOULAINE – 44 Loire-Atlantique – 316 H4 – see Nantes

BASTELICA – 2A Corse-du-Sud – 345 D7 – see Corse

BASTIA – 2B Haute-Corse – 345 F3 – see Corse

LA BASTIDE – 83 Var – 340 O3 – pop. 122 – alt. 1 000 m – ✉ 83840 41 **C2**

Paris 813 – Castellane 25 – Digne-les-Bains 78 – Draguignan 43 – Grasse 48

Du Lachens

Le Bas Village – ✆ 04 94 76 80 01 – hotel.lachens@orange.fr – Fax 0494768054 – Closed February and Tuesday except from June to August

13 rm – €52 €58/64, €8 – ½ P €52/67

Rest – Menu (€15), €24/29 – Carte €25/38

◆ In a hamlet tucked away in the upper Var region, a traditional Provençal house with practical and well-maintained rooms. A menu where meat takes pride of place, served in a country-style dining room or on the terrace.

LA BASTIDE-CLAIRENCE – 64 Pyrénées-Atlantiques – 342 – pop. 990 – alt. 50 m – ✉ 64240 3 **B3**

Paris 771 – Bayonne 27 – Irun 59 – Bordeaux 185

Office de tourisme, Place des Arceaux ✆ 05 59 29 65 05, Fax 05 59 29 65 05

Maison Maxana

r. Notre-Dame – ✆ 05 59 70 10 10 – www.maison-maxana.com – ab@maison-maxana.com

5 rm – €90/110 €100/120 **Table d'hôte** – Menu €35 bi

◆ Daydreams, Romance, Travel....The names of the rooms in this Basque house set the tone. A successful combination of antique furniture and African, Asian and modern touches. Regional cuisine and more exotic dishes at the table d'hôte (reservation required).

LA BASTIDE-DES-JOURDANS – 84 Vaucluse – 332 G11 – pop. 1 241 – alt. 412 m – ✉ 84240 40 **B2**

Paris 762 – Aix-en-Provence 39 – Apt 40 – Digne-les-Bains 77 – Manosque 17

Auberge du Cheval Blanc with rm

– ✆ 04 90 77 81 08 – provence.luberon@wanadoo.fr – Fax 04 90 77 86 51 – Closed February and Thursday

4 rm – €70 €70, €10 – ½ P €70

Rest – Menu (€19 bi), €30 – Carte €45/55

◆ Provençal abode in the village centre. Plush dining room in Mediterranean colours, and dishes with local flavours. Pretty rooms with personal touches.

LA BÂTIE-DIVISIN – 38 Isère – 333 G4 – pop. 802 – alt. 521 m – ✉ 38490 45 **C2**

Paris 539 – Lyon 82 – Grenoble 45 – Chambéry 41 – Saint-Martin-d'Hères 53

L'Olivier

100 rte du Vernay, (Les Etraits) – ✆ 04 76 31 00 60 – www.restaurant-l-olivier.com – Fax 04 76 31 00 60 – Closed 24 October-5 November, Sunday dinner and Monday

Rest – Menu (€13), €17 (weekdays), €21/49 – Carte €23/48

◆ The name evokes one of the favourite ingredients of the chef, who creates dishes that are updated, refined and based mainly on... olive oil. Bright dining room and garden terrace.

LA BÂTIE-NEUVE – 05 Hautes-Alpes – 334 F5 – see Gap

BATZ (ÎLE) – 29 Finistère – 308 G2 – see Île-de-Batz

BATZ-SUR-MER – 44 Loire-Atlantique – 316 B4 – pop. 3 206 – alt. 12 m – ✉ 44740 Brittany 34 **A2**

Paris 457 – La Baule 7 – Nantes 84 – Redon 64 – Vannes 79

Syndicat d'initiative, 25, rue de la Plage ✆ 02 40 23 92 36, Fax 02 40 23 74 10

✻★★ of St-Guenolé church ★ - N.-D. du Mûrier chapel★ - guided excursions ★ in marshlands (musée des Marais salants (museum of salt marshes) - La Côte Sauvage★.

Le Lichen without rest

Baie du Manerick - Côte Sauvage, 2 km south-east on D 45 – 02 40 23 91 92 – www.le-lichen.com – alain.paroux@wanadoo.fr – Fax 02 40 23 84 88

17 rm – € 70/250 € 70/250, € 12

◆ This vast neo-Breton style villa (1956) located on the Wild Coast enjoys a unique sea view. Half the airy, fairly large rooms overlook the sea.

LA BAULE – 44 Loire-Atlantique – 316 B4 – pop. 16 300 – alt. 31 m – Casino : Grand Casino BZ – 44500 Brittany

34 **A2**

Paris 450 – Nantes 76 – Rennes 120 – St-Nazaire 19 – Vannes 74

Office de tourisme, 8, place de la Victoire 02 40 24 34 44, Fax 02 40 11 08 10

de Guérande Guérande Ville Blanche, 6 km on the Nantes road, 02 40 66 43 21

de La Baule Saint-André-des-Eaux Domaine de Saint Denac, NE : 9 km, 02 40 60 46 18

Seafront★ - Parc des Dryades★ DZ.

Plan on following page

Hermitage Barrière rm,

5 espl. Lucien-Barrière – 02 40 11 46 46 – www.hermitage-barriere.com – hermitage@lucienbarriere.com – Fax 02 40 11 46 45 – Open 20 March-1st November and 24 December-4 January BZ **h**

202 rm – € 198/808 € 198/808, € 21 – 5 suites

Rest *La Terrasse* – *(open Easter, All Saint's, Christmas holidays, public holidays and July-August)* Menu (€ 35), € 54 (lunch) – Carte € 51/84

Rest *L' Eden Beach* – beach rest. – *02 40 11 46 16 (open 20 March-11 November, 19 December-4 January and Sunday lunch and Saturday in low season)* Menu € 34 – Carte € 39/84

◆ Imposing 1920s Anglo-Norman-style construction on the seafront. Spacious rooms with personal touches and views of the ocean or the garden. Swimming pool, hammam and fitness facilities. Sumptuous decor and classic cuisine. Fish and shellfish specialities at the Eden Beach.

Royal-Thalasso Barrière

6 av. Pierre Loti – 02 40 11 48 48 – www.lucienbarriere.com – royalthalasso@lucienbarriere.com – Fax 02 40 11 48 45 – Closed 5-20 December BZ **t**

91 rm – € 176/502 € 176/502, € 23 – 6 suites

Rest *La Rotonde* – Menu € 46 – Carte € 47/62

Rest *Le Ponton* – beach rest. – *02 40 60 52 05 (closed dinner from October to March except Saturday and school holidays)* Menu (€ 24 bi) – Carte € 35/63

◆ In a park overlooking the sea, an age-old building linked to a modern thalassotherapy centre. Period furniture and glistening fabrics in the rooms. Traditional and diet food at La Rotonde. Seafront cuisine at the Ponton.

Castel Marie-Louise rest,

1 av. Andrieu – 02 40 11 48 38 – www.castel-marie-louise.com – marielouise@relaischateaux.com – Fax 02 40 11 48 35 – Closed 4 January-5 February BZ **g**

31 rm – € 170/655 € 170/655, € 20 – 2 suites – ½ P € 167/410

Rest – *(closed lunch except Saturday in July-August and except Sunday)* Menu € 45 (lunch), € 65/98 – Carte € 87/120

Spec. Encornet et langoustines en fricassée (spring-summer). Epaule de cochon noir cuite lentement, jus d'épices et fruits rôtis. Soufflé à la marmelade de citron jaune et pulpe de tomate en sorbet (spring-summer). **Wines** Muscadet de Sèvre-et-Maine sur lie, Anjou-Villages.

◆ Charming Belle Époque manor house with a cosy atmosphere, surrounded by a well-kept garden. Tasteful and quiet rooms with antique furniture. A cosy restaurant furnished in the style of an English cottage. Fine contemporary cuisine. Pine-shaded terrace.

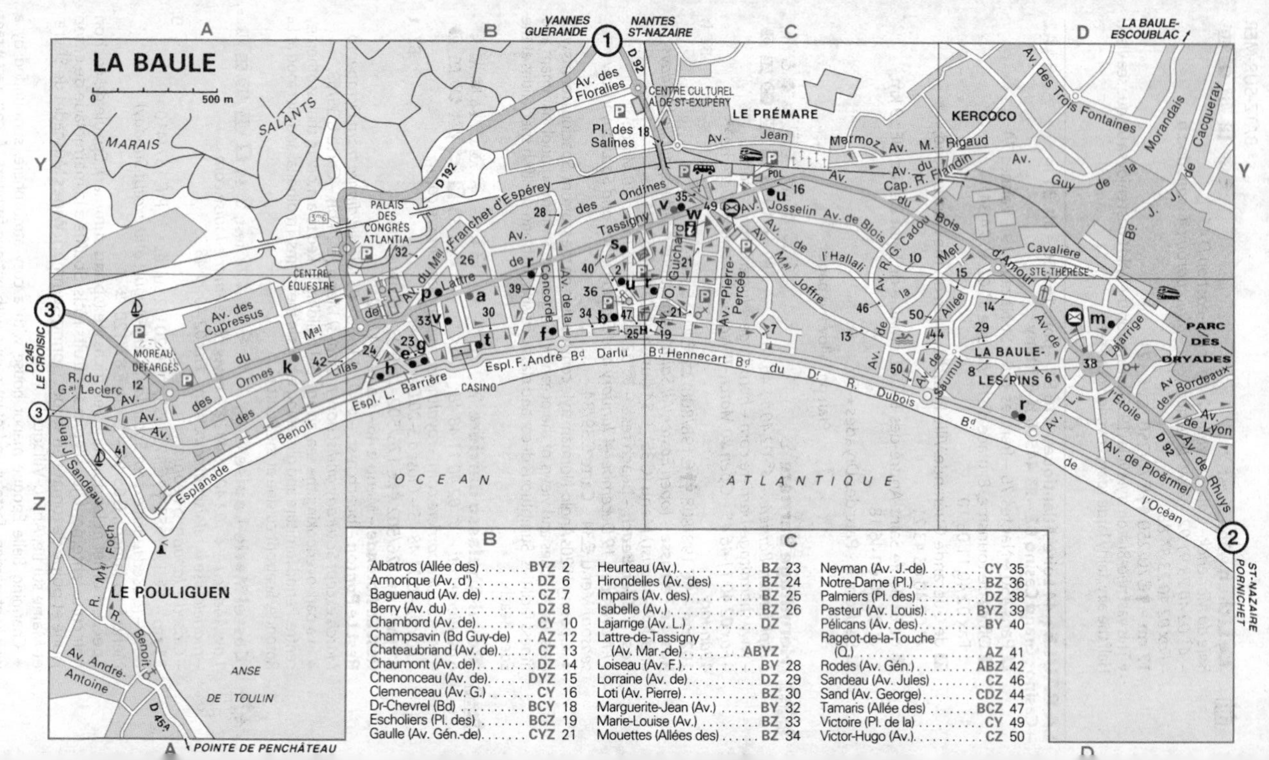

Albatros (Allée des) .... BYZ 2		Heurteau (Av.) .... BZ 23		Neyman (Av. J.-de) .... CY 35			
Armorique (Av. d') .... DZ 6		Hirondelles (Av. des) .... BZ 24		Notre-Dame (Pl.) .... BZ 36			
Baguenaud (Av. de) .... CZ 7		Impairs (Av. des) .... BZ 25		Palmiers (Pl. des) .... DZ 38			
Berry (Av. du) .... DZ 8		Isabelle (Av.) .... BZ 26		Pasteur (Av. Louis) .... BYZ 39			
Chambord (Av. de) .... CY 10		Lajarrige (Av. L.) .... DZ		Pélicans (Av. des) .... BY 40			
Champsavin (Bd Guy-de) ..... AZ 12		Lattre-de-Tassigny (Av. Mar.-de) .... ABYZ		Rageot-de-la-Touche (Q.) .... AZ 41			
Chateaubriand (Av. de) ..... CZ 13		Loiseau (Av. F.) .... BY 28		Rodes (Av. Gén.) .... ABZ 42			
Chaumont (Av. de) .... DZ 14		Lorraine (Av. de) .... DZ 29		Sandeau (Av. Jules) .... CZ 46			
Chenonceau (Av. de) .... DYZ 15		Loti (Av. Pierre) .... BZ 30		Sand (Av. George) .... CDZ 44			
Clemenceau (Av. G.) .... CY 16		Marguerite-Jean (Av.) .... BY 32		Tamaris (Allée des) .... BCZ 47			
Dr-Chevrel (Bd) .... BCY 18		Marie-Louise (Av.) .... BZ 33		Victoire (Pl. de la) .... CY 49			
Escholiers (Pl. des) .... BCZ 19		Mouettes (Allées des) .... BZ 34		Victor-Hugo (Av.) .... CZ 50			
Gaulle (Av. Gén.-de) .... CYZ 21							

Bellevue Plage
27 bd de l'Océan – ✆ 02 40 60 28 55 – www.hotel-bellevue-plage.fr – hotel@hotel-bellevue-plage.fr – Fax 02 40 60 10 18 – Closed 15 December-10 February DZ **r**
35 rm – †€ 95/190 ††€ 95/195, ☕ € 13
Rest *La Véranda* – see restaurant listing
◆ Well-maintained hotel with a modern, designer look. The colourful minimalist rooms overlook either the pine forest or the sea. Rooftop terrace dominating the bay.

Mercure Majestic
espl. Lucien-Barrière – ✆ 02 40 60 24 86 – www.hotelmercure-labaule.com – h5692@accor.com – Fax 02 40 42 03 13 BZ **e**
83 rm – †€ 95/245 ††€ 105/260, ☕ € 16
Rest *Le Ruban Bleu* – Menu (€ 20), € 27/48 – Carte € 43/58
◆ A complete renovation in Art Deco style has breathed new life into this beachfront hotel near the casino. The decor and name of this restaurant evoke the spirit of the famous Blue Riband transatlantic race. Traditional cuisine.

St-Christophe
pl. Notre-Dame – ✆ 02 40 62 40 00 – www.st-christophe.com – reception@st-christophe.com – Fax 02 40 62 40 40 BZ **u**
45 rm – †€ 68/194 ††€ 68/194, ☕ € 11 – ½ P € 69/136
Rest – Menu (€ 20), € 30/40 – Carte € 29/48
◆ Four family seaside villas (three from the early 20C, one more recent) situated in a quiet garden. The rooms vary in style, with traditional and modern furnishings. Classical cuisine served in a colourful dining room or amidst the greenery on the terrace in summer.

Brittany without rest
7 av. des Impairs – ✆ 02 40 60 30 25 – www.hotelbrittany.com – info@hotelbrittany.com – Fax 02 40 24 37 30 BZ **b**
19 rm – †€ 100/140 ††€ 100/190, ☕ € 13
◆ Attractively renovated 1930s villa with well-equipped guestrooms (modern furnishings, flatscreen TV, hydromassage shower). Roof-solarium and cosy lounge with fireplace.

Concorde without rest
1 bis av. Concorde – ✆ 02 40 60 23 09 – www.hotel-la-concorde.com – info@hotel-la-concorde.com – Fax 02 40 42 72 14 – Open 9 April-27 September
47 rm – †€ 77/135 ††€ 77/135, ☕ € 10 BZ **f**
◆ 1900s bathing resort architecture (modified over the years) at this family-run hotel. Rooms with a charming old-fashioned feel, some with balcony or terrace and sea views.

Lutetia et rest. le Rossini rm, rest,
13 av. Olivier-Guichard – ✆ 02 40 60 25 81 – www.lutetia-rossini.com – contact@lutetia-rossini.com – Fax 02 40 42 73 52 CZ **r**
26 rm – †€ 69/110 ††€ 69/185, ☕ € 12 – ½ P € 80/140
Rest – *(closed 9-27 November, 3 January-5 March, Monday dinner from 1st September to 30 June, Sunday dinner from 15 October to 15 April, Monday lunch and Tuesday lunch)* Menu € 26 (weekdays)/50 bi – Carte € 45/52
◆ This establishment comprises the Art Deco-style Le Lutétia, which houses a classic restaurant and rather out-dated rooms (renovation planned), as well as a 1930s villa. The rather traditional menu is dominated by seafood dishes.

La Mascotte rest,
26 av. Marie-Louise – ✆ 02 40 60 26 55 – www.la-mascotte.fr – hotel.la.mascotte@wanadoo.fr – Fax 02 40 60 15 67 BZ **v**
24 rm – †€ 66/108 ††€ 66/108, ☕ € 10 – ½ P € 77/90
Rest – *(open 1st March-5 November) (residents only)* Menu (€ 18), € 26/52
◆ A functional hotel set in a garden with pine and palm trees, 50m from the beach in a residential district. The more spacious rooms are in the recent wing.

Alcyon without rest
19 av. Pétrels – ✆ 02 40 60 19 37 – www.alcyon-hotel.com – info@alcyon-hotel.com – Fax 02 40 42 71 33 – Closed 4-25 January BY **s**
32 rm – †€ 72/128 ††€ 72/128, ☕ € 12
◆ Efficient sound-proofing and balconies in all the guestrooms facing the market (with the exception of the top floor) at this hotel, gradually being renovated. Large bar.

Villa Cap d'Ail without rest
145 av.de Lattre-de-Tassigny – ✆ 02 40 60 29 30 – www.villacapdail.com – villacapdail@wanadoo.fr – Fax 02 40 11 03 96 BZ **p**
22 rm – †€ 60/85 ††€ 69/98, ☕ € 9
◆ Just 100m from the beach, this villa, renovated in a modern spirit (designer details, bright colours) has lost none of its 1920s charm. Friendly atmosphere.

Le Marini without rest
22 av. G.-Clemenceau – ✆ 02 40 60 23 29 – www.residencemvm.fr – interhotelmarini@wanadoo.fr – Fax 02 40 11 16 98 – Closed in January
33 rm – †€ 52/61 ††€ 57/67, ☕ € 8,50 CY **u**
◆ This hotel in a regional-style house offers comfortable, elegant rooms partly furnished with antique furniture. British atmosphere in the bar. Attractive heated indoor swimming pool.

Hostellerie du Bois
65 av Lajarrige – ✆ 02 40 60 24 78 – www.hostellerie-du-bois.com – hostellerie-du-bois@wanadoo.fr – Fax 02 40 42 05 88 – Open 14 March-15 November DZ **m**
15 rm – †€ 60/78 ††€ 60/78, ☕ € 7 – ½ P € 59/68
Rest – *(dinner only) (resident only)*
◆ Charming half-timbered house (1923) with traditionally furnished guestrooms and public areas. Well-maintained and decorated with souvenirs from the owners' travels. Garden. Breakfast served in a quiet, rustic-style room. Evening meals available for residents.

St-Pierre without rest
124 av. du Mar. de Lattre-de-Tassigny – ✆ 02 40 24 05 41 – www.hotel-saint-pierre.com – contact@hotel-saint-pierre.com – Fax 02 40 11 03 41 BYZ **r**
19 rm – †€ 54/72 ††€ 62/92, ☕ € 9
◆ Friendly welcome and reasonable prices at this hotel housed in a typical villa with blue half-timbering. Discreet maritime decor in the rooms. Breakfast served on the veranda.

Les Dunes without rest
277 av. de Lattre-de-Tassigny – ✆ 02 51 75 07 10 – www.hotel-des-dunes.com – info@hotel-des-dunes.com – Fax 02 51 75 07 11 CY **w**
32 rm – †€ 46/70 ††€ 46/70, ☕ € 8
◆ A welcoming and reasonably priced family-run hotel in this busy seaside resort. Well-maintained functional rooms, with those to the rear generally quieter.

La Véranda – Hôtel Bellevue Plage
27 bd de l'Océan – ✆ 02 40 60 57 77 – www.restaurant-laveranda.com – courriel@restaurant-laveranda.com – Fax 02 40 24 00 22 – Closed 15 December-1st February, Wednesday from September to June and Monday except dinner in July-August DZ **r**
Rest – Menu (€ 24 bi), € 39/85 bi – Carte € 55/95
◆ A bright, sober, two-floor modern dining room and veranda, serving tasty, modern cuisine. Most tables overlook the beach.

La Maison Blanche
20 bis av. Pavie – ✆ 02 40 23 00 00 – lamaisonblanchelabaule@orange.fr – Fax 02 40 23 03 60 – Closed Saturday lunch, Sunday dinner and Monday in low season and outside school holidays BZ **a**
Rest – Menu (€ 16), € 24/70 bi – Carte € 35/54
◆ Resolutely contemporary culinary focus at this restaurant occupying an attractive glazed rotunda (with upper floor). Chic lounge ambience and stylish modern decor.

Carpe Diem
29 av. J. Boutroux, 5 km north on Golf de la Baule road – ✆ 02 40 24 13 14 – www.le-carpediem.fr – contact@le-carpediem.fr – Closed 26 January-16 February, Sunday dinner in low season and Monday
Rest – Menu (€ 15), € 20/47 bi
◆ A pleasant rustic-style restaurant (exposed beams, stone fireplace, wood furniture) near the golf course. Carefully prepared contemporary cuisine.

La Ferme du Grand Clos
52 av. de Lattre-de-Tassigny – ☎ 02 40 60 03 30 – www.lafermedugrandclos.com – contact@lafermedugrandclos.com – Fax 02 40 60 03 30 – Closed 16 November-16 December, 15 February-3 March, Tuesday and Wednesday from October to March except school holidays and Monday
Rest – pancake rest. – Carte € 18/35 AZ **k**
◆ This farm, hidden away at the bottom of a garden, is over a hundred years old. Rustic dining room which looks onto the kitchens. Pancakes and other regional specialities.

at the Golf 7 km North by N 171 – ✉ 44117 St-André-des-Eaux

Du Golf International
rte de Brangouré – ☎ 02 40 17 57 57 – www.lucienbarriere.com – hoteldugolflabaule@lucienbarriere.com – Fax 02 40 17 57 58 – Open 3 April-26 October
119 rm – †€ 94/344 ††€ 94/344, ☕ € 19 – 55 suites
Rest ***Le Green*** – *(closed lunch except in July-August)* Menu (€ 21), € 26 – Carte € 31/48
◆ A hotel complex and park at the heart of a huge golf course. Spacious, well-designed guestrooms, plus a few villas available for rent. Children's club. Restaurant with a British feel, with views of the pool or the green. Traditional fare.

LA BAUME – 74 Haute-Savoie – 328 M3 – pop. 250 – alt. 730 m – ✉ 74430 46 F1

Paris 597 – Lyon 214 – Annecy 95 – Genève 52 – Lausanne 138

La Ferme aux Ours
La Voagère – ☎ 04 50 72 19 88 – www.lafermeauxours.com – catherine.coulais@free.fr – Closed November
4 rm ☕ – †€ 90/110 ††€ 95/110 – ½ P € 70/85 **Table d'hôte** – Menu € 28 bi
◆ This secluded handsome Savoyard house dominates the valley. Snug, attractive rooms (teddy bear collection) and a charming welcome from the owner, a keen hiker. Sauna.

BAUME-LES-DAMES – 25 Doubs – 321 I2 – pop. 5 384 – alt. 280 m – ✉ 25110 Burgundy-Jura 17 C2

Paris 440 – Belfort 62 – Besançon 30 – Lure 45 – Montbéliard 45 – Pontarlier 65 – Vesoul 45

Office de tourisme, 8, rue de Provence ☎ 03 81 84 27 98, Fax 03 81 84 15 61

du Château de Bournel CubryN : 20 km on D 50, ☎ 03 81 86 00 10

Hostellerie du Château d'As with rm
24 r. Château-Gaillard – ☎ 03 81 84 00 66 – www.chateau-das.fr – courriel@chateau-das.com – Fax 03 81 84 39 67 – Closed 19 October-11 November, Sunday dinner, Tuesday lunch and Monday
6 rm – †€ 67/79 ††€ 67/79, ☕ € 10 – ½ P € 63/70
Rest – Menu € 21 (weekday lunch), € 31/75 – Carte € 44/77
◆ A large 1930s villa retaining its atmosphere of the past. Bright, elegant dining room (superb mother-of-pearl chandelier) where modern cuisine is served. Spacious rooms.

BAUME-LES-MESSIEURS – 39 Jura – 321 D6 – pop. 196 – alt. 333 m – ✉ 39210 Burgundy-Jura 16 B3

Paris 406 – Champagnole 27 – Dole 54 – Lons-le-Saunier 12 – Poligny 21

Abbey★ (altar-piece with shutter★ in the church) - Belvédère des Roches de Baume (viewpoint)★★★ overlooking cirque★★★ and grottoes★ of Baume South: 3,5 km.

Des Grottes
aux Grottes, 3 km southward – ☎ 03 84 48 23 15 – www.restaurantdesgrottes.com – restaurantdesgrottes@wanadoo.fr – Fax 03 84 48 23 15 – Open 1st April-30 September and closed Monday except July-August
Rest – *(lunch only) (pre-book)* Menu € 15 (weekdays)/35 – Carte € 25/50
◆ Rural house dating from 1900 overlooking a fine waterfall. Non-smoking restaurant with Belle Epoque charm plus a less formal café. Regional fare; fresh trout available.

LES BAUX-DE-PROVENCE – 13 Bouches-du-Rhône – 340 D3 — 42 E1
– pop. 381 – alt. 185 m – ✉ 13520 Provence

Paris 712 – Arles 20 – Avignon 30 – Marseille 86 – Nîmes 44 – St-Rémy-de-Provence 10

Office de tourisme, Maison du Roy ☎ 04 90 54 34 39, Fax 04 90 54 51 15

des Baux-de-Provence Domaine de Manville, S : 2 km, ☎ 04 90 54 40 20

Site★★★ - Village★★★: Square★ and St-Vincent church ★ - Château★: ✻★★ - Monument Charloun Rieu ≤★ - Tour Paravelle ≤★ - Musée Yves-Brayer★ - Cathédrale d'Images★ North: 1 km by D 27 - ✻★★★ on the village North: 2,5 km by D 27.

In the Vallon

La Riboto de Taven rm, rm, VISA MC AE
– ☎ 04 90 54 34 23 – *www.riboto-de-taven.fr – contact@riboto-de-taven.fr*
– Fax 04 90 54 38 88 – Closed 5 January-12 March
5 rm – €170/290 €170/290, €18 – 1 suite – ½ P €161/196
Rest – *(closed Wednesday) (dinner only) (residents only)* Menu €58
◆ This unusual farmhouse is a delight to the eyes and offers a clear view of Les Baux. Flower garden, pleasant pool and tastefully decorated rooms (two of them are troglodyte). Handsome timbered ceiling and large fireplace in the dining room. Market-inspired cuisine.

XXXXX ✿✿ **L' Oustaù de Baumanière** with rm VISA MC AE
– ☎ *04 90 54 33 07 – www.oustaudebaumaniere.com*
– oustau@relaischateaux.com – Fax 04 90 54 40 46
– Closed 4 January-5 March, Monday lunch, Tuesday lunch, Wednesday lunch and Thursday lunch from 5 March to 5 April and from 2 November to 23 December
30 rm – €200/430 €200/430, €22 – ½ P €265/380
Rest – Menu €120 (weekday lunch)/185 – Carte €135/190
Spec. Œuf de poule en gelée de piperade et aïoli en chaud-froid. Rouget barbet, basilic et fleur de thym. Millefeuille à la crème légère vanillée, caramel pistache.
Wines Les Baux-de-Provence, Châteauneuf-du-Pape blanc.
◆ A 16C residence with ancient vaults and a superb terrace with the Alpilles in the background: a magical location for sun-drenched cuisine. Fine wine cellar. Comfortable rooms and stylish suites in the main house and in a small farmhouse (La Guigou).

Le Manoir VISA MC AE
à 1 km rte d'Arles via D 27 – ☎ *04 90 54 33 07 – Closed Wednesday from November to March*
7 rm – €200/430 €200/430, €22 – 7 suites – ½ P €265/380
◆ The rooms in this elegant farmhouse combine the comfort, refinement and charm of Provence in bygone days. A wooded park with a splendid ancient plane tree and a classical garden.

Arles road Southwest by D 27

✿ **La Cabro d'Or** rm, VISA MC AE
1 km – ☎ 04 90 54 33 21 – www.lacabrocor.com – cabro@relaischateaux.com
– Fax 04 90 54 45 98 – Closed Sunday dinner, Tuesday lunch and Monday from November to March
22 rm – €150/315 €150/315, €20 – 8 suites – ½ P €158/240
Rest – Menu €49 bi (weekday lunch), €70/110 – Carte €96/102
Spec. Truffe d'été et artichauts violets, tomates confites au jambon jabugo (June to Sep.). Filet de rouget-barbet rôti, fleurs de courgettes et tartare de légumes (June to Sep.). Volupté croustillante aux olivettes confites, crème légère et sorbet fruits rouges (June to Sep.). **Wines** Vin de Pays des Bouches-du-Rhône, Les-Baux-de-Provence.
◆ Chic country style, with elegant rooms, a beautiful garden and many leisure activities including a riding centre. Cosy, sophisticated dining room, a terrace underneath the lime trees and fine contemporary cuisine. Provence at its best!

Mas de l'Oulivié without rest VISA MC AE
Quartier les Arcoules, 2.5 km – ☎ 04 90 54 35 78 – www.masdeloulivie.com
– contact@masdeloulivie.com – Fax 04 90 54 44 31 – Open 3 April-12 November
27 rm – €110/280 €110/280, €14 – 2 suites
◆ A relaxing break in the heart of olive groves: Provençal decorated rooms, overflow pool in the garden, and massages. Light lunches for residents only.

Auberge de la Benvengudo rm, rest,
Vallon de l'Arcoule, D78F, 2 km – 04 90 54 32 54
– www.benvengudo.fr – reservations@benvengudo.com – Fax 04 90 54 42 58
– Open 20 March-2 November
21 rm – €120/200 €120/200, €15 – 6 suites – ½ P €115/155
Rest – *(closed Sunday) (dinner only)* Menu (€28), €45 – Carte approx. €50
◆ Authentic building with classic Provencal interior in shades of white. Carefully chosen furniture, ornaments and artwork in the bedrooms. Regional menu based on the market produce available, and refurbished dining room with Provencal touches.

BAVAY – 59 Nord – 302 K6 – pop. 3 436 – alt. 148 m – ✉ 59570 31 D2

Northern France and the Paris Region

Paris 229 – Avesnes-sur-Helpe 24 – Lille 79 – Maubeuge 15 – Mons 25

Office de tourisme, rue Saint-Maur 03 27 39 81 65, Fax 03 27 39 81 65

XX **Le Bagacum**
r. Audignies – 03 27 66 87 00 – www.bagacum.com
– contact@bagacum.com – Fax 03 27 66 86 44
– Closed Sunday dinner and Monday except holidays
Rest – Menu €27 bi (weekday lunch), €34/50 bi – Carte €40/60
◆ Red-brick walls, exposed roof beams, ornaments and paintings give character to this restaurant in a converted barn. Flowered terrace. Traditional cuisine.

XX **Le Bourgogne**
porte Gommeries – 03 27 63 12 58 – www.restaurantlebourgogne.fr
– restaurantlebourgogne@orange.fr – Fax 03 27 66 99 74
– Closed 27 July-19 August, 5-21 January, Monday and dinner except Friday and Saturday
Rest – Menu €20 (weekdays)/50 – Carte €32/62
◆ On a busy thoroughfare, this brick building is typical of northern architecture; nice summer terrace. The cuisine is a blend of tradition and invention. Burgundies feature heavily on the wine list.

BAVELLA (COL) – 2A Corse-du-Sud – 345 E9 – see Corse

BAYARD (COL) – 05 Hautes-Alpes – 334 E5 – see Col Bayard

BAYEUX – 14 Calvados – 303 H4 – pop. 14 600 – alt. 50 m – ✉ 14400 32 B2

Normandy

Paris 265 – Caen 31 – Cherbourg 95 – Flers 69 – St-Lô 36 – Vire 60

Office de tourisme, pont Saint-Jean 02 31 51 28 28, Fax 02 31 51 28 29

AS Bayeux Omaha Beach Golf Port-en-Bessin Ferme Saint Sauveur, 11 km on the Port-en-Bessin road and D 514, 02 31 22 12 12

Tapestry of "la reine Mathilde" (Queen Mathilda) ★★★ - Notre-Dame cathedral ★★ - Musée-mémorial de la bataille de Normandie★ Y **M¹** - Half-timbered house★ (rue St-Martin) Z**N.**

Plan on following page

Le Lion d'Or
71 r. St-Jean – 02 31 92 06 90 – www.liondor-bayeux.fr – lion.d-or.bayeux@wanadoo.fr – Fax 02 31 22 15 64 Z **e**
27 rm – €95/185 €95/185, €13 – 1 suite
Rest – *(closed 20 December-15 January, Sunday dinner, Monday dinner from mid-November to mid-March, Monday lunch, Tuesday lunch and Saturday lunch)*
Menu (€20), €25 (lunch), €33/55 – Carte €61/67
◆ This former 18C post house fronted by a lovely paved courtyard is home to quiet guestrooms decorated in different styles. Those in the wing are more recent and modern. Carefully prepared traditional menu. Photos of former famous patrons adorn the plush lounge.

BAYEUX

Aure (Bords de l') . . . . Z 2
Bienvenu (R. du) . . . . Z 3
Bois (Pl. au) . . . . Z 4
Bouchers (R. des) . . . . Z
Bourbesneur (R.) . . . . Z 6
Bretagne (R. de la) . . . . Z
Chanoines (R. des) . . . . Z 7
Chartier (R. A.) . . . . Z 8
Churchill (Bd W.) . . . . Y
Clemenceau (Av. G.) . . . . Z
Conseil (Av.) . . . . Y
Courseulles (R. de) . . . . Y 9
Cuisiniers (R. des) . . . . Z 12
Dais (R. Gén.-de) . . . . Z
Dr-Michel (R.) . . . . Y 13
Eindhoven (Bd) . . . . Y
Eisenhower (Rond-Point) . . . . Y 14
Foch (R. Mar.) . . . . Z 15
Franche (R.) . . . . Z
Gaulle (Pl. Ch.-de) . . . . Z
Laitière (R.) . . . . Z 16
Larcher (R.) . . . . Z
Leclerc (Bd Mar.) . . . . Y 17
Leforestier (R. Lambert) . . . . Z 18
Liberté (Pl. de la) . . . . Z 19
Maîtrise (R. de la) . . . . Z 20
Marché (R. du) . . . . Z 21
Montgomery (Bd Mar.) . . . . . . Y 23
Nesmond (R. de) . . . . Z
Pigache (R. de la) . . . . Y 24
Pont-Trubert (R. du) . . . . Y 25
Poterie (R. de la) . . . . Z 28
Royale (R.) . . . . Z
Sadi-Carnot (Bd) . . . . Y 29
St-Jean (R.) . . . . Y, Z
St-Laurent (R.) . . . . Y, Z
St-Loup (R.) . . . . Y, Z 30
St-Malo (R.) . . . . Z
St-Martin (R.) . . . . Z
St-Patrice (R. et Pl.) . . . . . . Z 31
St-Quentin (R.) . . . . Y 41
Schumann (R. M.) . . . . Z 42
Tardif (R.) . . . . Z
Teinturiers (R. des) . . . . Z 32
Terres (R. des) . . . . Z 33
Vaucelles (Rond-Point de) . . . Y 35
Verdun (R. de) . . . . Y 37
Ware (Bd F.) . . . . Y 38
6-Juin (Bd du) . . . . Y

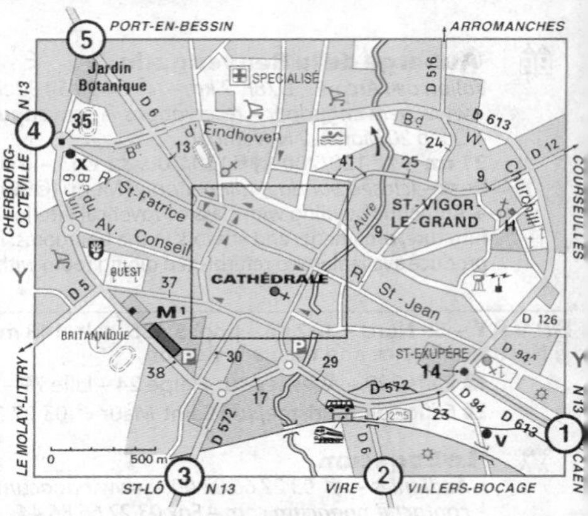

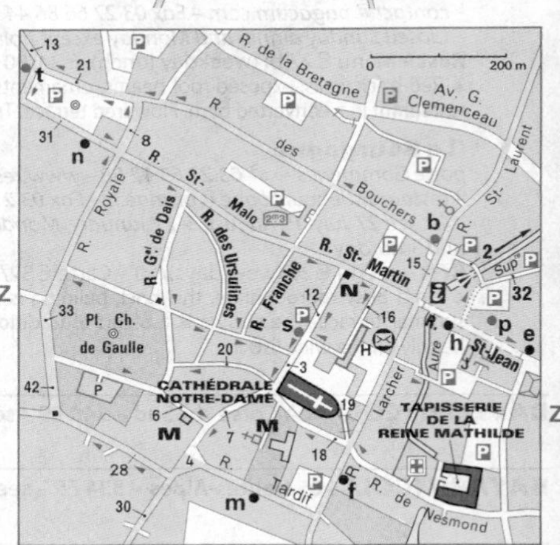

Novotel rm, VISA

117 r. St-Patrice – ☎ 02 31 92 16 11 – www.novotel.com – h0964@accor.com – Fax 02 31 21 88 76 – **77 rm** – 🛉€ 75/92 🛉🛉€ 75/165, ☕ € 14 — Y **x**

Rest – *(closed Sunday lunch and Saturday except 10 July-20 August)*
Menu (€ 17), € 23/49 bi – Carte € 25/40

◆ Smartened up in line with the chain's latest standards: modern bar, lounge and practical guestrooms. The bistro-style restaurant opens onto a terrace opposite the pool. Menu and daily specials on a slate and a fine choice of wines by the glass.

Château de Bellefontaine without rest VISA

49 r. Bellefontaine – ☎ 02 31 22 00 10 – www.hotel-bellefontaine.com – info@hotel-bellefontaine.com – Fax 02 31 22 19 09 – Closed 2 January-2 February — Y **v**

14 rm – 🛉€ 70/115 🛉🛉€ 75/160, ☕ € 12

◆ A wooded park and a pond are the backdrop of this 18C château. Stylish rooms (Louis XIII and Empire furniture). More modern family rooms in the former stables.

Churchill without rest VISA

14 r. St-Jean – ☎ 02 31 21 31 80 – www.hotel-churchill.fr – info@hotel-churchill.fr – Fax 02 31 21 41 66 – Open from March to November — Z **h**

32 rm – 🛉€ 85/105 🛉🛉€ 95/128, ☕ € 10

◆ An appealing hotel offering cosy guestrooms (Louis XVI furniture), as well as an airy sitting room-cum-tearoom, bar, photos of D-Day, a delicatessen and a home decoration shop.

d'Argouges without rest

21 r. St-Patrice – 02 31 92 88 86 – www.hotel-dargouges.com – hotel.dargouges@orange.fr – Fax 02 31 92 69 16 Z n

28 rm – €52/85 €68/118, €9

◆ Two 18C town houses, surrounded by a delightful garden, right in the heart of the town. Handsome refurbished guestrooms with antique furniture, classical lounges.

Le Bayeux without rest

9 r. Tardif – 02 31 92 70 08 – www.lebayeux.net – lebayeux@gmail.com – Fax 02 31 21 15 74 Z m

29 rm – €50/100 €60/100, €8

◆ Friendly, practical family hotel in a quiet street two minutes from the cathedral. Buffet breakfast in a rustic interior.

Tardif Noble Guesthouse without rest

16 r. de Nesmond – 02 31 92 67 72 – www.hoteltardif.com – hoteltardif@orange.fr – Fax 02 31 92 67 72 Z f

5 rm – €50/140 €70/170, €8

◆ This former mansion is tucked away in a garden two minutes from the historical centre. Period furniture, tapestries and paintings lend character to the guestrooms and lounge.

La Rapière

53 r. St-Jean – 02 31 21 05 45 – www.larapiere.net – larapierebayeux@orange.fr – Fax 02 31 21 11 81 – Closed 19 December-19 January, Wednesday and Thursday Z p

Rest – Menu €15 (weekday lunch), €28/34 – Carte €35/51

◆ A 15C house situated in a picturesque street in old Bayeux. A lovely, rustic interior, adorned with old swords and paintings. Tasty menu based on Normandy produce.

La Coline d'Enzo

2 r. des Bouchers – 02 31 92 03 01 – Fax 02 31 92 03 01 – Closed Sunday and Monday Z b

Rest – Menu (€15), €25/35 – Carte approx. €56

◆ This restaurant is named after the owners' two children and offers a modern setting with stonework, beams and chestnut and turquoise colours. Pavement terrace.

Le Bistrot de Paris

pl. St-Patrice – 02 31 92 00 82 – Fax 02 31 92 00 82 – Closed 17-31 August, 16 February-2 March, Monday dinner, Wednesday dinner and Sunday Z t

Rest – Menu (€12), €18 (weekday lunch)/30 – Carte €23/36

◆ Furnishings, mirrors and copperware recreate the decor and ambience of an old Parisian bistro. Traditional menu and daily slate; simpler menu at the neighbouring Annexe.

Le Pommier

40 r. des Cuisiniers – 02 31 21 52 10 – www.restaurantlepommier.com – contact@restaurantlepommier.com – Fax 02 31 21 06 01 – Closed 15 December-15 January and Sunday from 1st November to 31 March

Rest – Menu (€18), €23/37 – Carte €30/46 Z s

◆ The apple green façade tells all: the entire gourmet menu is based on Normandy produce! A relaxed ambience whose rustic decor mingles contemporary touches.

Port-en-Bessin road 3 km by ⑤ – ✉ 14400 Bayeux

Château de Sully rm,

Rte de Port en Bessin, Port en Bessin road – 02 31 22 29 48 – www.chateau-de-sully.com – hotel@chateau-de-sully.com – Fax 02 31 22 64 77 – Open 6 March-6 December

22 rm – €150/190 €150/250, €15 – 1 suite – ½ P €189/250

Rest – *(closed lunch except Sunday) (dinner only) (number of covers limited, pre-book)* Menu €49/85 – Carte €59/77

◆ This 18C castle, with gardens and a chapel at the front, is very attractive. Discreet luxury in the delicately personalised rooms. Pool, jacuzzi and sauna. Choice of a classical or a more modern decor (veranda). Updated cuisine based on excellent, often organic produce.

in Audrieu 13 km by ① and D 158 – **pop. 826** – **alt. 71 m** – ✉ **14250**

Château d'Audrieu

– ✆ 02 31 80 21 52 – www.chateaudaudrieu.com – audrieu@relaischateaux.com
– Fax 02 31 80 24 73 – Closed 6 December-6 February
25 rm – €139/491 €139/491, ☕ €26 – 4 suites – ½ P €156/313
Rest – *(closed Monday and lunch except Saturday, Sunday and public holidays)*
Menu €40 (lunch), €56/99 – Carte €76/103

Spec. Foie gras de canard, "anguille fumée pomme verte". Aloyau de bœuf, pasta "tomate artichaut". "Cacao spirale", potimarron et fruit de la passion.

◆ This listed 18C château lies in the midst of exquisite, secluded grounds. It offers spacious rooms graced with antiques. Stately dining rooms serving inventive cuisine and a good selection of wines – a taste of the good life for discerning palates!

The sun's out – let's eat alfresco!
Look for a terrace:

BAYONNE – 64 Pyrénées-Atlantiques – **342** D2 – **pop. 44 200** – 3 **A3**
Built-up area 178 965 – **alt. 3 m** – ✉ **64100** **Atlantic Coast**

- Paris 765 – Bordeaux 183 – Biarritz 9 – Pamplona 109 – San Sebastián 53
- Biarritz-Anglet-Bayonne: ✆ 05 59 43 83 83, Southwest: 5 km by N 10 AZ.
- Office de tourisme, place des Basques ✆ 08 20 42 64 64, Fax 05 59 59 37 55
- Makila Golf Club Bassussarry Route de Cambo, S : 6 km on D 932, ✆ 05 59 58 42 42
- Ste-Marie cathedral ★ and cloister★ AZ **B** - Fairs★ (start of August) - Musée Bonnat★★ BY - Musée basque★★★.

Access and exits: See Biarritz.

Plan on next page

Auberge du Cheval Blanc (Jean-Claude Tellechea)

68 r. Bourgneuf – ✆ 05 59 59 01 33
– Fax 05 59 59 52 26 – Closed 30 June-9 July, 29 July-2 August, 3-12 November, 15 February-11 March, Saturday lunch, Sunday dinner and Monday BZ **b**
Rest – Menu (€30), €45/90 – Carte €60/90

Spec. Pressé de truite fumée maison, foie gras et poire réduite au porto. Parmentier de xamango au jus de veau truffé. Soufflé chaud au Grand Marnier. **Wines** Irouléguy, Jurançon

◆ This former post house (1715) offers the charm of a dining room in pastel shades, paintings by a Basque artist, flower arrangements, reinvented local cuisine and a fine choice of Irouléguys wine.

François Miura

24 r. Marengo – ✆ 05 59 59 49 89 – Closed in March, 21-31 December, Sunday dinner and Wednesday BZ **r**
Rest – Menu €21/32 – Carte €48/60

◆ In old Bayonne, a vaulted restaurant with paintings and modern furniture. Modern cuisine and local produce.

Bayonnais

38 quai des Corsaires – ✆ 05 59 25 61 19 – Fax 05 59 59 00 64
– Closed 31 May-14 June, 29 July-5 August, 20 December-11 January, Monday except July-August and Sunday BZ **s**
Rest – Menu €17 (weekdays) – Carte €30/45

◆ Near the Basque museum, a good venue offering copious regional dishes. A regional-style dining room completed by a terrace facing the banks of the Nive.

La Grange

26 quai Galuperie – ✆ 05 59 46 17 84 – Closed Sunday BZ **a**
Rest – Menu €20 – Carte €39/49

◆ Décor wise, this former grocer's under the arches has kept its china objects, brick walls and woodwork. A long blackboard list of updated Basque dishes. Wines listed by price.

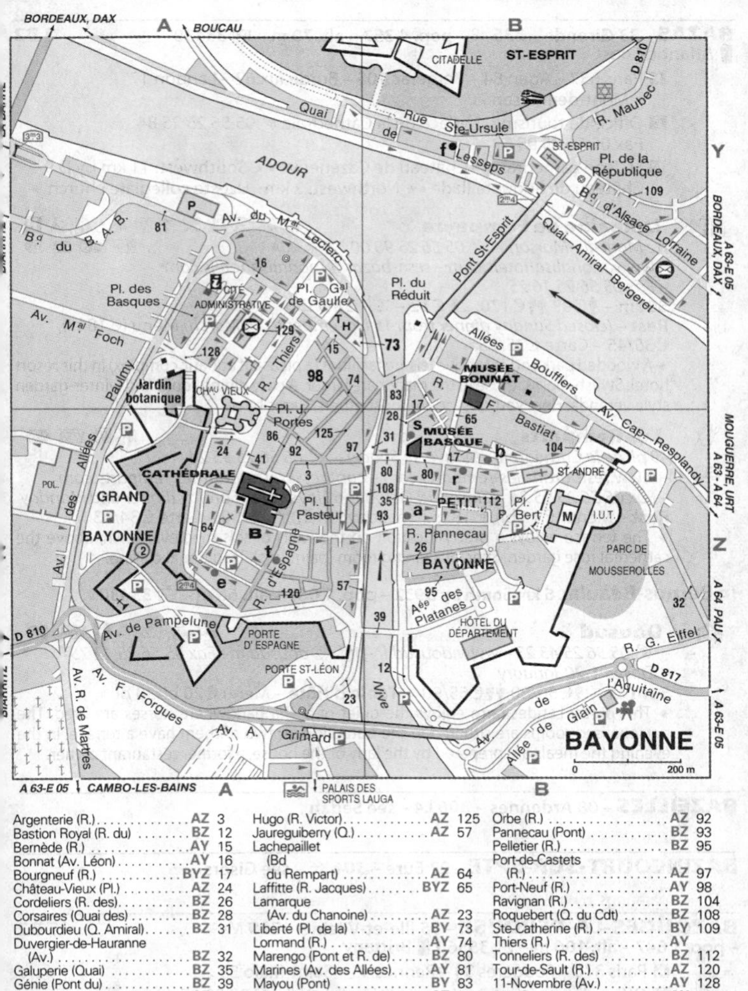

BAY-SUR-AUBE – 52 Haute-Marne – **313** K7 – **pop. 56 – alt. 320 m** – ✉ 52160 14 **C3**

Paris 312 – Châlons-en-Champagne 214 – Chaumont 65 – Langres 33 – Châtillon-sur-Seine 50

La Maison Jaune

r. principale – 03 25 84 99 42 – jwjansen@club-internet.fr – Fax 03 25 87 57 65 – Open from April to October

4 rm – €70 €75 **Table d'hôte** – Menu € 30 bi

◆ Old farmhouse which will enchant lovers of art and culture: superb library, the owner's paintings, antique shop finds. Rooms which are beautiful in their simplicity. Factory lamps from the 1930s bring character to this cosy table d'hôte.

BAZAS – 33 Gironde – **335** J8 – **pop. 4 357 – alt. 70 m** – ✉ **33430** 3 **B2**
Atlantic Coast

Paris 637 – Agen 84 – Bergerac 105 – Bordeaux 62 – Langon 17 – Mont-de-Marsan 70

Office de tourisme, 1, place de la Cathédrale ✆ 05 56 25 25 84, Fax 05 56 25 95 59

St-Jean cathedral ★ - Château de Cazeneuve★★ Southwest: 11 km by D 9 - Château de Roquetaillade★★ Northwest: 2 km - Uzeste collegiate church ★.

Domaine de Fompeyre rest,
rte Mont-de-Marsan – ✆ 05 56 25 98 00 – www.monalisahotels.com – resa-bazas@monalisahotels.com – Fax 05 56 25 16 25 VISA MC AE
50 rm – †€ 99 ††€ 170, ☕ € 12 – ½ P € 89/130
Rest – *(closed Sunday dinner from 16 November to 16 March)* Menu (€ 18 bi), € 35/45 – Carte € 35/75
◆ A wooded park and extensive leisure facilities (a pleasant aquatic complex) in this resort hotel. Stylish rooms, those in the manor are larger. A cosy dining room and winter-garden style veranda. Here you can try, amongst others, Bazas beef.

Les Remparts AC VISA MC
49 pl. de la Cathédrale, (Mauvezin Space) – ✆ 05 56 25 95 24 – www.restaurant-les-remparts.com – contact@restaurant-les-remparts.com – Fax 05 56 25 95 24 – Closed 18 October-6 November, Sunday dinner and Monday
Rest – Menu (€ 16 bi), € 18 bi (weekday lunch), € 25/50 – Carte € 34/63
◆ The terrace enjoys a pretty location on the walls of this medieval town, above the cathedral rose garden. Spacious dining room (paintings). Traditional cuisine.

in Bernos-Beaulac 6 km South by D932 – pop. 1 067 – alt. 66 m – ✉ 33430

Dousud VISA MC
– ✆ 05 56 25 43 23 – www.dousud.fr – info@dousud.fr – Fax 05 56 25 42 75 – Closed 1-20 January
5 rm ☕ – †€ 50/80 ††€ 65/90 **Table d'hôte** – Menu € 20 bi/30 bi
◆ This pretty Landes farm enjoys the quiet of a 9ha park where horses are bred. The personalised rooms are situated in the outbuildings; two of them have a terrace. In the evening the meals are prepared by the lady of the house, a former restaurant owner.

BAZEILLES – 08 Ardennes – **306** L4 – see Sedan

BAZINCOURT-SUR-EPTE – 27 Eure – **304** K6 – see Gisors

BAZOUGES-LA-PÉROUSE – 35 Ille-et-Vilaine – **309** M4 10 **D2**
– **pop. 1 847 – alt. 106 m** – ✉ **35560** Brittany

Paris 376 – Fougères 34 – Rennes 45 – Saint-Malo 53

Office de tourisme, 2, place de l'Hôtel de Ville ✆ 02 99 97 40 94, Fax 02 99 97 40 64

Le Château de la Ballue without rest VISA MC AE
4 km north-east – ✆ 02 99 97 47 86 – www.la-ballue.com – chateau@la-ballue.com – Fax 02 99 97 47 70
5 rm – †€ 160/175 ††€ 180/195, ☕ € 18
◆ Splendid Baroque, French-style gardens surround this 17C château. The elegant, spacious rooms with high ceilings are adorned with lovely period woodwork and antique furniture.

BEAUCAIRE – 30 Gard – **339** M6 – **pop. 14 900 – alt. 18 m** – ✉ **30300** 23 **D2**
Provence

Paris 703 – Arles 18 – Avignon 27 – Nîmes 24

Office de tourisme, 24, cours Gambetta ✆ 04 66 59 26 57, Fax 04 66 59 68 51

Château★.

Les Vignes Blanches
67 av. de Farcinnes, (Nimes road) – ✆ 04 66 59 13 12 – www.lesvignesblanches.com – contact@lesvignesblanches.com – Fax 04 66 58 08 11 – Closed 2 January-8 February
57 rm – †€ 71/99 ††€ 71/99, ☕ € 9 – ½ P € 62/74
Rest – *(closed 2 January-8 February, Tuesday lunch from November to March, Sunday dinner and Monday)* Menu (€ 14 bi), € 20/30 – Carte € 25/45
◆ On a busy street, this well-kept hotel features an unusual lobby, colourful rooms (quieter to the rear), named after their decorative theme. Traditional dishes prepared in a wood-fired oven, served in the bistro or a cosy dining room.

L'Oliveraie
chemin Clapas de Cornut, Nîmes road – ✆ 04 66 59 16 87 – www.oliveraie-hotel.fr – fvalota@club-internet.fr – Fax 04 66 59 08 91
38 rm – †€ 68 ††€ 68, ☕ € 10 – ½ P € 80
Rest – *(closed Sunday dinner except in July-August and Saturday lunch)* Menu € 16 (weekday lunch), € 20/42 – Carte € 36/60
◆ A family atmosphere can be found in this establishment made up of two buildings. Comfortable rooms with a balcony or terrace; those in the recent wing are more modern. Pleasant dining room decorated with numerous knick-knacks; veranda with exposed rafters.

Southwest 6 km (St Gilles road) then left, Nouriguier lock – ✉ 30300 Beaucaire

Mas de Lafont without rest
chemin du Mas d'Aillaud – ✆ 04 66 59 29 59 – www.masdelafont.com – Fax 04 66 59 29 59 – Open 1st May-1st October
80 rm ☕ – †€ 70/80 ††€ 80/90
◆ Amid vines and apricot trees, a 17C country house with spacious rooms furnished with superb Provençal furniture, all overlook the garden. Fully equipped kitchen available.

BEAUCENS – 65 Hautes-Pyrénées – 342 L5 – pop. 416 – alt. 450 m – ✉ 65400 Languedoc-Roussillon-Tarn Gorges 28 **A3**

Paris 866 – Pau 59 – Tarbes 38 – Toulouse 191

Eth Béryè Petit
15 rte Vielle – ✆ 05 62 97 90 02 – www.beryepetit.com – contact@beryepetit.com – Fax 05 62 97 90 02
3 rm ☕ – †€ 56/63 ††€ 56/63
Table d'hôte – *(Open Friday dinner and Saturday dinner from November to April)* Menu € 20 bi
◆ The name of this welcoming Bigourdan house (1790) means little orchard. The quiet guestrooms mix old and new decor and have splendid views of the valley. Dine and breakfast in a pretty sitting room by the fire or on the terrace.

Le Petit Couassert
20 rte de Vielle – ✆ 05 62 97 90 25 – Closed 25 October-25 November and Wednesday except school holidays
Rest – Menu € 18/25 – Carte € 27/41
◆ A mix of contrasting decor at this family inn: stone walls, fireplace, old mirrors and contemporary artwork. Traditional cuisine and fine views from the terrace.

LE BEAUCET – 84 Vaucluse – 332 D10 – see Carpentras

BEAUCOUZÉ – 49 Maine-et-Loire – 317 F4 – see Angers

BEAUDÉAN – 65 Hautes-Pyrénées – 342 M5 – see Bagnères-de-Bigorre

---

BEAUFORT – 73 Savoie – 333 M3 – pop. 2 196 – alt. 750 m – ✉ 73270 French Alps 45 **D1**

Paris 601 – Albertville 21 – Chambéry 72 – Megève 37

Office de tourisme, Grande Rue ✆ 04 79 38 38 62, Fax 04 79 38 31 56

Beaufortain★★.

Le Grand Mont

pl. de l'Église – ✆ *04 79 38 33 36 – www.hotelbeaufort.com – hoteldugrandmont2@wanadoo.fr – Fax 04 79 38 39 07 – Closed 20 April-5 May and 1st October-7 November,*

15 rm – †€ 48/50 ††€ 59/62, ☕ € 9 – ½ P € 51/62

Rest – *(closed Saturday lunch and Sunday dinner except school holidays)*
Menu € 11/32 – Carte € 20/34

◆ This nice village house has belonged to the same family for four generations. Small and family-size (with mezzanine) simple, rustic bedrooms. Beaufort based local cuisine and cheese specialities.

BEAUGENCY – 45 Loiret – 318 G5 – pop. 7 648 – alt. 99 m – ✉ 45190 12 C2

Châteaux of the Loire

Paris 152 – Blois 35 – Châteaudun 42 – Orléans 31 – Vendôme 65

Office de tourisme, 3, place Dr Hyvernaud ✆ 02 38 44 54 42, Fax 02 38 46 45 31

de Ganay Saint-Laurent-Nouan Prieuré de Ganay, S : 7 km on D 925, ✆ 02 54 87 26 24

Les Bordes Golf International Saint-Laurent-Nouan Les Petits Rondis, S : 9 km on D 925, ✆ 02 54 87 72 13

Notre-Dame church ★ - Keep ★ - Hangings ★ in the town hall **H** - Musée régional de l'Orléanais ★ in the château.

BEAUGENCY

Abbaye (R. de l')	2
Bretonnerie (R. de la)	3
Change (R. du)	4
Châteaudun (R. de)	5
Cordonnerie (R. de la)	6
Dr-Hyvernaud (Pl.)	8
Dunois (Pl.)	9
Maille-d'Or (R. de la)	10
Martroi (Pl. du)	
Pellieux (Passage)	12
Pont (R. du)	
Puits-de-l'Ange (R. du)	14
Sirène (R. de la)	15
Traîneau (R. du)	17
Trois-Marchands (R. des)	18

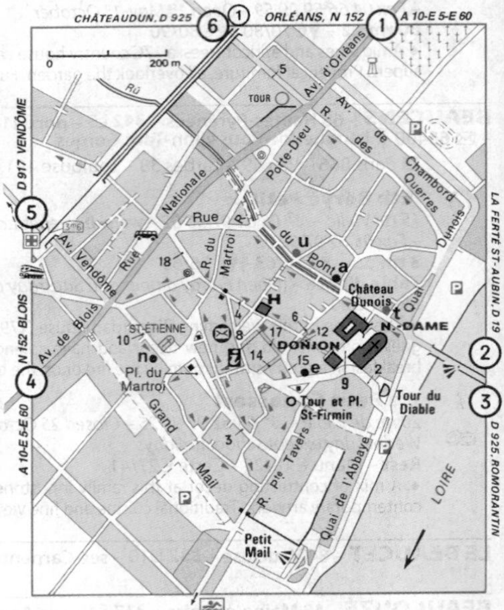

Hostellerie de l'Écu de Bretagne

pl. Martroi – ✆ *02 38 44 67 60 – www.ecu-de-bretagne.fr – ecu-de-bretagne@wanadoo.fr – Fax 02 38 44 68 07* **n**

34 rm – †€ 40/127 ††€ 50/160, ☕ € 12

Rest – Menu (€ 10 bi), € 24/36 – Carte € 51/65

◆ This old coaching inn (1607) and annexe in the heart of town have been given a new lease of life. Pleasant guestrooms with personal touches. A friendly dining room serving traditional cuisine; fine selection of local wines.

De la Sologne without rest
6 pl. St-Firmin – ✆ 02 38 44 50 27 – www.hoteldelasologne.com – hotel-de-la-sologne.beaugency@wanadoo.fr – Fax 02 38 44 90 19 – Closed 20 December-3 January e
16 rm – †€ 54/64 ††€ 54/70, ☕ € 8,50
◆ Pretty, flower-decked steps lead to this Sologne-style building a stone's throw from the Tour St-Firmin. Well-maintained small rooms with individual touches.

Le Relais des Templiers without rest
– ✆ 02 38 44 53 78 – www.hotelrelaistempliers.com – info@hotelrelaistempliers.com – Fax 02 38 46 42 55 – Closed 26 December-12 January
15 rm – †€ 49/52 ††€ 56/62, ☕ € 8 a
◆ This hotel with an attractive stone façade on the edge of the historic centre has fairly spacious rooms decorated in a simple, practical style. Bright breakfast room.

Le Petit Bateau
54 r. du Pont – ✆ 02 38 44 56 38 – www.le-petit-bateau.com – lepetitbateau@wanadoo.fr – Fax 02 38 46 44 37 – Closed 16-30 November and Monday u
Rest – Menu (€ 15), € 21 (weekdays)/45 – Carte € 40/70
◆ Two dining rooms: one has a well-kept rustic decor with exposed beams and fireplace; the other is smaller and opens onto a courtyard terrace. Traditional cuisine.

Le Relais du Château
8 r. du Pont – ✆ 02 38 44 55 10 – carre-philippe45@orange.fr – Closed February, Thursday lunch from July to September, Thursday dinner and Tuesday from October to June and Wednesday t
Rest – Menu € 16/36 – Carte € 33/48
◆ An attractive little restaurant situated in a shopping street near the keep (11C). Exhibitions by regional artists decorate the room. Traditional dishes.

in Tavers **3 km by ④ and secondary road – pop. 1 284 – alt. 100 m – ✉ 45190**

La Tonnellerie without rest
12 r. des Eaux-Bleues, near the church – ✆ 02 38 44 68 15 – www.tonelri.com – tonelri@club-internet.fr – Fax 02 38 44 10 01 – Closed 15 December-15 January
18 rm – †€ 105/180 ††€ 105/180, ☕ € 14 – 2 suites
◆ A Sologne hostelry with a pleasant flower garden and swimming pool. The rooms have period furniture and are decorated as in a private house.

BEAULIEU – 07 Ardèche – 331 H7 – pop. 425 – alt. 130 m – ✉ 07460 44 A3

Paris 668 – Alès 40 – Aubenas 39 – Largentière 29 – Pont-St-Esprit 50 – Privas 71

La Santoline rm, rest,
Lieu-dit Bouchet, 1 km south-east of Beaulieu – ✆ 04 75 39 01 91 – www.lasantoline.com – contacts@lasantoline.com – Fax 04 75 39 38 79 – Open 26 April-14 September
7 rm – †€ 75/145 ††€ 75/145, ☕ € 12 – ½ P € 84/115
Rest – *(closed Thursday) (dinner only) (residents only)* Menu € 31
◆ This 16C building, surrounded by Cévennes garrigue, offers charming service. Pleasant rooms with personal touches adorned with rustic or modern furniture.

BEAULIEU-SUR-DORDOGNE – 19 Corrèze – 329 M6 – pop. 1 288 – alt. 142 m – ✉ 19120 Dordogne-Berry-Limousin 25 C3

Paris 513 – Aurillac 65 – Brive-la-Gaillarde 44 – Figeac 56 – Sarlat-la-Canéda 69 – Tulle 38

Office de tourisme, place Marbot ✆ 05 55 91 09 94, Fax 05 55 91 10 97

St-Pierre church ★★: south portal ★★ - Old town ★.

Manoir de Beaulieu rest,
4 pl. du Champ-de-Mars – ✆ 05 55 91 01 34 – www.manoirdebeaulieu.com – reservation@manoirdebeaulieu.com – Fax 05 55 91 23 57
25 rm – †€ 75/140 ††€ 110/140, ☕ € 12 – 1 suite
Rest – Menu (€ 25), € 38/80 – Carte € 52/90
◆ This distinguished hotel, founded in 1912, has benefited from a recent facelift. Snug rooms embellished with antique furniture and modern bathrooms. Modern cuisine served in a welcoming, rustic restaurant.

Le Relais de Vellinus
17 pl. du Champ-de-Mars – ✆ 05 55 91 11 04 – www.vellinus.com – contact@vellinus.com – Fax 05 55 91 26 16 – Closed 22 December-4 January, Sunday dinner and Saturday lunch
20 rm – †€ 58/95 ††€ 65/130, ☕ € 10 – ½ P € 78
Rest – Menu € 15 (weekday lunch), € 22/37 – Carte € 28/51
◆ Attractively refurbished, this hotel has undergone a major transformation. Contemporary comfort, with each bedroom devoted to a different travel theme (Moorish, zen, the sea, Africa etc). A serene ambience pervades the dining room and terrace. Traditional cuisine.

Les Charmilles with rm
20 bd St-Rodolphe-de-Turenne – ✆ 05 55 91 29 29 – www.auberge-charmilles.com – auberge-charmilles@club-internet.fr – Fax 05 55 91 29 30 – Closed for three weeks in November
8 rm ☕ – †€ 68/110 ††€ 68/110
Rest – *(closed Wednesday October-May)* Menu (€ 12), € 19/45 – Carte € 31/68
◆ A well-renovated regional-style home: pleasant dining room, charming terrace on the banks of the Dordogne, classic menu and smart rooms.

in Brivezac 8 km on the Argentat road via the D 940 and D 12 – **pop. 187 – alt. 140 m – ✉ 19120**

Château de la Grèze
– ✆ 05 55 91 08 68 – www.chateaudelagreze.com – chateaudelagreze@orange.fr – Closed 15 November-15 February
5 rm ☕ – †€ 70/100 ††€ 80/110
Table d'hôte – *(closed Wednesday, Saturday and Sunday in July-August)* Menu € 29 bi
◆ This elegant 18C residence is surrounded by a park. Spacious, personalised bedrooms with wonderful views of the valley. Swimming pool. Horse-trekking possible.

BEAULIEU-SUR-MER – 06 Alpes-Maritimes – 341 F5 – pop. 3 720 — 42 E2
– Casino – ✉ 06310 **French Riviera**

Paris 935 – Menton 20 – Nice 8

Office de tourisme, place Georges Clemenceau ✆ 04 93 01 02 21, Fax 04 93 01 44 04

Site ★ of Villa Kerylos ★ - Baie des Fourmis ★.

Plan on next page

La Réserve de Beaulieu et Spa
5 bd Mar.-Leclerc – ✆ 04 93 01 00 01 – www.reservebeaulieu.com – reservation@reservebeaulieu.com – Fax 04 93 01 28 99 – Closed 26 October-19 December Z **w**
28 rm – †€ 180/1240 ††€ 180/1240, ☕ € 45 – 11 suites
Rest – *(closed lunch from June to October and Monday)* Menu € 75 (lunch), € 150/210 – Carte € 180/250
Spec. Saint Jacques et homard passion, tendre gelée de mandarine berlugane (hiver). Loup de ligne cuit au naturel contisé d'amandes fraîches et zestes de citron (été). Île flottante, gariguettes et "tagada" sans dessus-dessous. **Wines** Côtes de Provence, Bandol.
◆ This seaside luxury hotel, built in 1880 in the style of Florentine Renaissance palaces, has a wealth of modern day comforts. There is a beauty parlour and opulent suites. Refined dining room, terrace with a view over the bay and reinvented Provençal-inspired cuisine.

Carlton without rest
7 av. Edith Cavell – ✆ 04 93 01 44 70 – www.carlton-beaulieu.com – info@carlton-beaulieu.com – Fax 04 93 01 44 30 – Closed 8 January-12 February
33 rm – †€ 79/200 ††€ 79/200, ☕ € 12 Z **s**
◆ 1930s villa in a residential district near the beach and casino with classically furnished bedrooms and a pleasant swimming pool. Attentive staff and professional service.

Frisia without rest
2 bd E- Gauthier – ✆ 04 93 01 01 04 – www.frisia-beaulieu.com – info@frisia-beaulieu.com – Fax 04 93 01 31 92 – Closed 8 November-16 December
33 rm – †€ 52/135 ††€ 59/135, ☕ € 9 – 1 suite Y **r**
◆ Half the rooms and the rooftop sundeck overlook the marina and coast. An annexe in the courtyard-garden is home to one spacious room and a suite with terrace.

BEAULIEU-SUR-MER

Albert-1er (Av.) . . . . Z
Alsace-Lorraine (Bd) . . . . . . Y
Cavell (Av. Edith) . . . . Z 4
Charles II Comte de Provence (Av.) . . . . Z 6
Clemenceau (Pl. et R.) . . . . Y 5
Déroulède (Bd) . . . . Y
Doumer (R. Paul) . . . . Z 7
Dunan (Av. F.) . . . . Z
Edouard-VII (Bd) . . . . Y
Eiffel (R.) . . . . Z
Gaulle (Pl. Charles-de) . . . . . Y
Gauthier (Bd Eugène) . . . . . . Y 13
Hellènes (Av. des) . . . . Z 14
Joffre (Bd Maréchal) . . . . . . Z
Leclerc (Bd Maréchal) . . . . . Z 18
Marinoni (Bd) . . . . Y 19
May (Av. F.) . . . . Z 21
Myrtes (Ch. des) . . . . Y
Orangers (Montée des) . . . . Z 22
Rouvier (Promenade de M.) Z
St-Jean (Pont) . . . . Z
Yougoslavie (R. de) . . . . Z 27

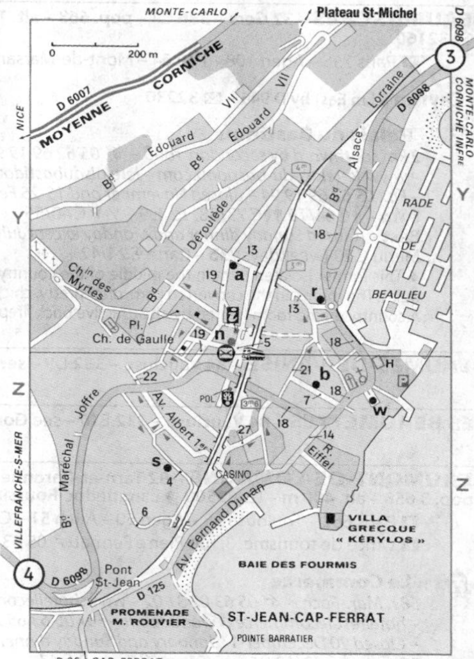

 **Comté de Nice** without rest

bd Marinoni – ✆ 04 93 01 19 70 – www.hotel-comtedenice.com – contact@hotel-comtedenice.com – Fax 04 93 01 23 09 – Closed 22 November-8 December Y **a**

32 rm – †€ 57/108 ††€ 67/118, ☕ € 10

◆ In a discreet building in the town centre find generously proportioned and well-equipped rooms; the seaside rooms are quieter. Comfortable lounges and bar.

Riviera without rest

6 r. Paul-Doumer – ✆ 04 93 01 04 92 – www.hotel-riviera.fr – contact@hotel-riviera.fr – Fax 04 93 01 19 31 – Closed 22 October-27 December Z **b**

12 rm – †€ 55/87 ††€ 55/87, ☕ € 8,50

◆ The engaging owners of this spruce, yellow fronted 1930s villa greet their guests warmly to their entirely non-smoking hotel. Small, practical and well-kept rooms.

XX **Les Agaves**

4 av. Mar.-Foch – ✆ 04 93 01 13 12 – www.lesagaves.com – lelu.jacky@wanadoo.fr – Fax 04 93 01 65 97 – Closed 20 November-14 December Y **n**

Rest – *(dinner only)* Menu € 38 – Carte € 50/60

◆ Wood panelling, original mouldings, parquet floors and a slight Provençal touch in the decor: this discreet Beaulieu restaurant serves cuisine in line with current taste, with a regional flavour.

Other hotel resources see: **St-Jean-Cap-Ferrat**

Your opinions are important to us: please write and let us know about your discoveries and experiences – good and bad!

BEAUMARCHÉS – 32 Gers – 336 C8 – pop. 663 – alt. 175 m – ✉ 32160 28 **A2**

Paris 755 – Agen 108 – Pau 64 – Mont-de-Marsan 65 – Auch 54

in Cayron 5 km East by D 946 – ✉ 32230

Relais du Bastidou VISA MC AE

2 km southward by secondary road – ✆ 05 62 69 19 94 – www.le-relais-du-bastidou.com – lerelaisdubastidou@libertysurf.fr – Fax 05 62 69 19 94 – Closed November and 15-25 February

8 rm – †€ 64/79 ††€ 73/88, ☕ € 9 – ½ P € 40/55

Rest – *(Closed Sunday dinner and Monday except July-August) (pre-book)*
Menu € 20 (weekdays)/36 – Carte € 24/42

◆ This former isolated farm in the middle of the countryside guarantees you maximum quiet. The rooms, in the converted barn, offer pretty, chic, rustic décor. Sauna and jacuzzi. A country dining room heated by an attractive brick fireplace.

BEAUMES-DE-VENISE – 84 Vaucluse – 332 D9 – see Carpentras

LES BEAUMETTES – 84 Vaucluse – 332 E10 – see Gordes

BEAUMONT-DE-LOMAGNE – 82 Tarn-et-Garonne – 337 B8 – pop. 3 658 – alt. 400 m – ✉ 82500 Languedoc-Roussillon-Tarn Gorges 28 **B2**

Paris 662 – Toulouse 58 – Agen 60 – Auch 51 – Condom 64 – Montauban 35

Office de tourisme, 3, rue Pierre Fermat ✆ 05 63 02 42 32, Fax 05 63 65 61 17

Le Commerce AC rest, rm, VISA MC AE

58 r. Mar.-Foch – ✆ 05 63 02 31 02 – www.hotellecommerce.com – hotelrest.lecommerce@wanadoo.fr – Fax 05 63 65 26 22 – Closed 20 December-11 January and Sunday dinner

12 rm – †€ 42/48 ††€ 45/51, ☕ € 7 – ½ P € 47

Rest – *(closed Friday dinner and Saturday in low season and Sunday dinner)*
Menu (€ 12), € 20/27 – Carte € 23/32

◆ Local house by the side of the road running through the village. The renovated and well-kept rooms offer all the desired comforts. The restaurant dining room has retained its country charm. Traditional cuisine.

BEAUMONT-EN-AUGE – 14 Calvados – 303 M4 – pop. 459 – alt. 90 m – ✉ 14950 Normandy 32 **A3**

Paris 199 – Caen 42 – Deauville 12 – Le Havre 49 – Lisieux 21 – Pont-l'Évêque 7

XX **Auberge de l'Abbaye** VISA MC AE

2 r. de la Libération – ✆ 02 31 64 82 31 – www.aubergelabbaye.com – chantalchevrolet@wanadoo.fr – Fax 02 31 64 58 87 – Closed 5-14 October, 4 January-4 February, Monday dinner from November to March, Tuesday except July-August and Wednesday

Rest – Menu € 33/56 – Carte € 50/85

◆ This 18C Norman house has a façade covered with Virginia creeper. Generous portions of traditional dishes served in three small, prettily rustic dining rooms.

BEAUNE – 21 Côte-d'Or – 320 I7 – pop. 21 300 – alt. 220 m – ✉ 21200 Burgundy-Jura 7 **A3**

Paris 308 – Autun 49 – Chalon-sur-Saône 29 – Dijon 45 – Dole 65

Office de tourisme, 6, boulevard Perpeuil ✆ 03 80 26 21 30, Fax 03 80 26 21 39

de Beaune Levernois LevernoisSE : 4 km on D 970, ✆ 03 80 24 10 29

Hôtel-Dieu★★★ : polyptyque du Jugement dernier (polyptych of the Final Judgement)★★★, Grand'salle salle ou chambre des pauvres (Great Hall or Poor Man's Room)★★★ - Collégiale Notre-Dame (Notre Dame Collegiate Church)★ : tapestries★★ - Hôtel de la Rochepot★ AY **B** - ramparts★.

BEAUNE

Alsace (R. d') . . . . AZ 2
Belin (R.) . . . . AZ 4
Bourgelat (R.) . . . . AZ 5
Carnot (Petite-Pl.) . . . . AZ 6
Carnot (Pl.) . . . . AZ 7
Carnot (R.) . . . . AZ 9
Château (R. du) . . . . BY 10
Dames (Rempart des) . . . . . AZ 13
Dr-Jorrot (Pl. du) . . . . BY 15
Enfant (R. de l') . . . . AY 16
Enfert (R. d') . . . . AZ 17
Favart (R.) . . . . AY 18
Fleury (Pl.) . . . . AZ 19
Fraysse (R. E.) . . . . AZ 21
Halle (Pl. de la) . . . . AZ 23
Lorraine (R. de) . . . . AY
Maufoux (R.) . . . . AZ 25
Monge (Pl.) . . . . AY 26
Monge (R.) . . . . AZ 28
Perpreuil (Bd.) . . . . AZ 29
Poterne (R.) . . . . AZ 30
Rolin (R.) . . . . AZ 31
Rousseau-Deslandes (R.) . . . BY 32
Ste-Marguerite (R.) . . . . AY 35
St-Nicolas (R. du Fg) . . . . AY 34
Tonneliers (R. des) . . . . AY 37
Ziem (Pl.) . . . . AZ 40

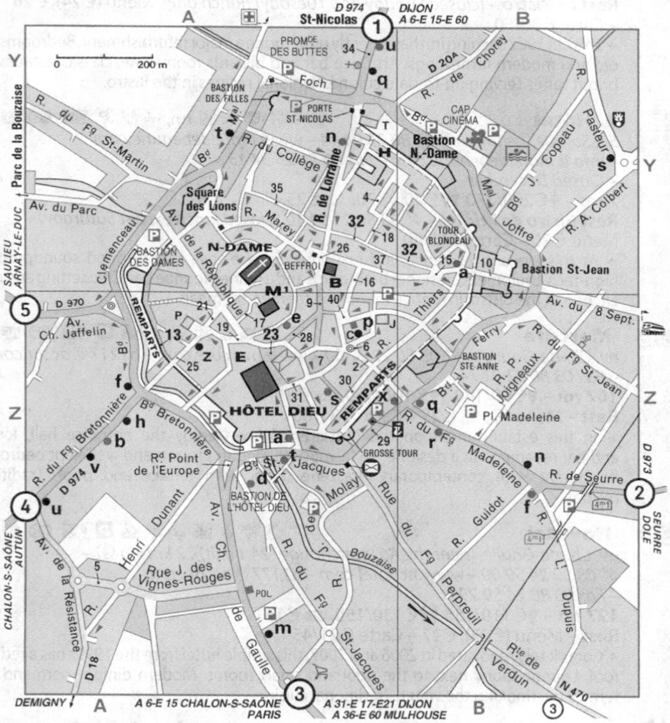

Le Cep without rest

27 r. Maufoux – ☎ 03 80 22 35 48
– www.hotel-cep-beaune.com – resa@hotel-cep-beaune.com
– Fax 03 80 22 76 80 AZ **z**

49 rm – †€ 130/168 ††€ 168/248, ☕ € 22 – 15 suites

◆ Every guestroom in this hotel set in 16C and 18C townhouses is like a veritable museum. Breakfast served in a vaulted cellar or in the Renaissance courtyard in summer.

Hostellerie Le Cèdre

12 bd Mar.-Foch – ☎ 03 80 24 01 01
– www.lecedre-beaune.com – info@lecedre-beaune.com
– Fax 03 80 24 09 90 AY **t**

40 rm – †€ 155/230 ††€ 155/230, ☕ € 18

Rest – *(closed 20-27 December) (dinner only)* Menu € 44, € 50/70 – Carte € 60/95

◆ An attractive early 20C residence and garden with century-old trees. Spacious, elegant rooms and opulent lounge with fireplace. Modern menu in a bourgeois restaurant set in a 19C lodge. Summer terrace in the shade of an old cedar.

De la Poste
5 bd Clemenceau – ✆ 03 80 22 08 11 – www.hoteldelapostebeaune.com – reservation@hoteldelapostebeaune.com – Fax 03 80 24 19 71 AZ **f**
33 rm – 🚹€ 140/300 🚹🚹€ 140/300, ☕ € 18 – 3 suites
Rest – *(closed Tuesday and lunch except Sunday and Bank holidays)*
Menu € 36/60 – Carte € 50/75
Rest *Le Bistro* – *(closed Sunday and Tuesday) (lunch only)* Menu (€ 24), € 26 – Carte € 30/50
◆ This old 19C coaching inn has recently undergone a major refurbishment. Bedrooms with old and modern furnishings. Art Deco bar and billiards room. Fine, classic restaurant in bright tones serving up-to-date cuisine. Regional recipes in the Bistro.

L'Hôtel rm,
5 r. Samuel-Legay – ✆ 03 80 25 94 14 – www.lhoteldebeaune.com – info@lhoteldebeaune.com – Fax 03 80 25 94 13 – Closed December AZ **p**
7 rm – 🚹€ 200/370 🚹🚹€ 200/370, ☕ € 25
Rest *Bistro de l'Hôtel* – *✆ 03 80 25 94 10 (Closed lunch except Saturday)*
Menu € 80 – Carte € 40/80
◆ At this elegant residence find luxurious, Empire-style rooms, good soundproofing, high-tech equipment, designer bathrooms and a refined lounge bar. Chic setting and open kitchen at the Bistro. Inventive menu and themed set meals.

Mercure
av. Ch.-de-Gaulle – ✆ 03 80 22 22 00 – www.mercure.com – h1217@accor.com – Fax 03 80 22 91 74 AZ **m**
107 rm – 🚹€ 90/140 🚹🚹€ 106/160, ☕ € 16
Rest – Menu (€ 19), € 25 – Carte € 31/60
◆ In this establishment on the outskirts of town enjoy the entrance hall, lounge and bar revamped in a designer style, modern meeting rooms and well-kept bedrooms. Restaurant with contemporary brasserie decor with terrace and pool. Traditional recipes.

Novotel
av. Ch.-de-Gaulle, (near the A6 interchange (24.1 exit)), 2 km via ③ – ✆ 03 80 24 59 00 – www.novotel.com – h1177@accor.com – Fax 03 80 24 59 29
127 rm – 🚹€ 119/155 🚹🚹€ 130/155, ☕ € 15
Rest – Menu (€ 23), € 27 – Carte € 21/45
◆ Completely renovated in 2006 and 2007, this simple hotel from the 1990s has a red tiled roof. Lounge-lobby next to the pool and smart rooms. Modern dining room and teak terrace overlooking the water. Traditional cuisine.

Henry II without rest
12 r. fg St-Nicolas – ✆ 03 80 22 83 84 – www.beaune-henry2.com – info@henry2.fr – Fax 03 80 24 15 13 AY **q**
58 rm ☕ – 🚹€ 60/89 🚹🚹€ 60/89
◆ The recent wing of the hotel has been designed to blend in with the part that is listed: a 16C post house. Rooms in various shapes and styles, from Louis XV to Art Deco.

La Closerie without rest
61 rte de Pommard, via ④ – ✆ 03 80 22 15 07 – www.hotel-lacloserie-beaune.com – closeriehotelbeaune@wanadoo.fr – Fax 03 80 24 16 22 – Closed 23 December-15 January
47 rm – 🚹€ 76/98 🚹🚹€ 98/145, ☕ € 13
◆ Between the town centre and the motorways, this hotel stands surrounded by greenery. The well-kept, functional rooms are all identical. Lovely swimming pool.

Belle Époque without rest
15 r. fg Bretonnière – ✆ 03 80 24 66 15 – www.hotel-belleepoque-beaune.com – infos@hotel-belleepoque-beaune.com – Fax 03 80 24 17 49 – Closed 20-25 December AZ **h**
19 rm – 🚹€ 85/93 🚹🚹€ 85/93, ☕ € 9 – 3 suites
◆ An old house with character; a 1900 glass roof, rustic rooms, some with beams or fireplaces, and overlooking the interior courtyard. Stylishly retro bar.

De la Paix without rest
45 r. fg Madeleine – 03 80 24 78 08 – www.hotelpaix.com – contact@hotelpaix.com – Fax 03 80 24 10 18 BZ **n**
22 rm – €56/97 €72/97, €10
◆ Pleasant family stopover on a busy road. Practical, well soundproofed bedrooms; the new rooms are larger and more contemporary. Lounge bar with billiard table.

Grillon without rest
21 rte Seurre, 1 km via ② – 03 80 22 44 25 – www.hotel-grillon.fr – joel.grillon@wanadoo.fr – Fax 03 80 24 94 89 – Closed 2 February-3 March
17 rm – €56 €56/98, €10
◆ A spruce pink building in an enclosed garden. Charming rooms with personal touches (all non-smoking), lounge-bar in the cellar and lower-decked terrace for breakfast in summer.

Hostellerie de Bretonnière without rest
43 r. fg Bretonnière – 03 80 22 15 77 – www.hotelbretonniere.com – infos@hotelbretonniere.com – Fax 03 80 22 72 54 AZ **v**
32 rm – €55/110 €55/110, €8,50
◆ This former post house and outbuildings are laid out around inner courtyards. Most of the rooms are level with the garden. Breakfast served in the conservatory.

La Villa Fleurie without rest
19 pl. Colbert – 03 80 22 66 00 – www.lavillafleurie.fr – la.villa.fleurie@wanadoo.fr – Fax 03 80 22 45 46 – Closed January BY **s**
10 rm – €69/99 €69/99, €8,50
◆ Candy box hotel with a small flower-decked garden at the front. The large rooms are modern or have antique furniture. Elegant lounge and charming breakfast room.

Alésia without rest
4 av. de la Sablière, 1 km rte Dijon via ① – 03 80 22 63 27 – http://perso.wanadoo.fr/hotel.alesia/ – hotel.alesia@wanadoo.fr – Fax 03 80 24 95 28
15 rm – €34/80 €34/80, €8
◆ On the edge of Beaune, a pleasant establishment where the cool, intimate rooms are well kept. A free shuttle bus takes guests to the restaurants of the town centre.

Beaune Hôtel without rest
55 bis r. fg Bretonnière – 03 80 22 11 01 – www.beaunehotel.com – beaunehotel@aol.com – Fax 03 80 22 46 66 – Open 5 March-17 November AZ **u**
21 rm – €71 €74/78, €8
◆ Discreet building situated near to a junction. The rooms are rather small but functional and extremely well kept; nearly all of them overlook the quiet courtyard.

La Terre d'Or without rest
r. Izembart, (at la Montagne), 3 km via ③ and minor road – 03 80 25 90 90 – www.laterredor.com – jlmartin@laterredor.com – Closed February
5 rm – €130/205 €130/205, €15
◆ Attractive rooms at the Terre d'Or (old and modern furniture) with a terraced garden on the hills above Beune. Tasting sessions in the natural cave wine cellar; warm welcome.

Le Jardin des Remparts (Roland Chanliaud)
10 r. Hôtel-Dieu – 03 80 24 79 41 – www.le-jardin-des-remparts.com – info@le-jardin-des-remparts.com – Fax 03 80 24 92 79 – Closed 1st December-13 January, Sunday and Monday except Bank holidays
Rest – Menu €35 (weekday lunch), €70/90 – Carte €73/92 AZ **a**
Spec. Tartare de charolais et huître à l'écume de mer. Sandre rôti aux girolles et jus de torréfaction (autumn). Gâteau tiède au chocolat et ses trois glaces. **Wines** Saint-Aubin, Savigny-lès-Beaune.
◆ Charming 1930s house and delightful garden terrace along the ramparts. Highly inventive cuisine and fine wines. Grand piano and wine-growing utensils in the lounge.

XXX **Loiseau des Vignes**
31 r. Maufoux – ✆ 03 80 24 12 06 – www.bernard-loiseau.com – loiseaudesvignes@bernard-loiseau.com – Fax 03 80 22 06 22 – Closed 1st February-2 March, Sunday and Monday AZ **z**
Rest – Menu (€ 23), € 28 (lunch), € 48/98 bi – Carte € 50/78
◆ A Loiseau Group establishment in the heart of historic Beaune. Smart trendy decor and a menu that features the chef's classics (simpler lunchtime menu). Remarkable choice of wines by the glass.

XXX **L'Écusson**
pl. Malmédy – ✆ 03 80 24 03 82 – www.ecusson.fr – contact@ecusson.fr – Fax 03 80 24 74 02 – Closed 2 February-2 March, Wednesday and Sunday except holidays BZ **f**
Rest – Menu € 28/64 – Carte € 56/77
◆ Up-to-date market inspired menus concocted by the owner-chef, served in a sophisticated classical-rustic setting or on the inviting terrace. Excellent Burgundies.

XX **Le Bénaton** (Bruno Monnoir)
25 r. fg Bretonnière – ✆ 03 80 22 00 26 – www.lebenaton.com – lebenaton@club-internet.fr – Fax 03 80 22 51 95 – Closed 1st-7 July, 5-15 December, February Holidays, Saturday lunch from April to November, Thursday except dinner from April to November and Wednesday AZ **b**
Rest – Menu (€ 23), € 45/78 – Carte € 60/100
Spec. Tête de veau rôtie et grosses langoustines frites. Demi-pigeon désossé, filet rôti, cuisse farcie et jus au melilot. Gâteau au chocolat chaud et cassis. **Wines** Saint-Romain, Nuits-Saint-Georges.
◆ Recipes that play on texture and contrast served on personalised porcelain at this unusual establishment. Dine in the contemporary dining room or on the terrace.

XX **Caveau des Arches**
10 bd Perpreuil – ✆ 03 80 22 10 37 – www.caveau-des-arches.com – info@caveau-des-arches.com – Fax 03 80 22 76 44 – Closed 18 July-19 August, 20 December-19 January, Sunday and Monday ABZ **x**
Rest – Menu (€ 17), € 22/48 – Carte € 30/45
◆ The setting of this restaurant, in an 18C underground stone vault built into the foundations of a 15C bridge, couldn't be more unusual. Traditional meals and a fine selection of Burgundies.

XX **Sushikai**
50 fg St-Nicolas – ✆ 03 80 24 02 87 – www.sushikai.fr – sushi.kai@orange.fr – Fax 03 80 24 79 85 – Closed January, Wednesday and Thursday AY **u**
Rest – Menu (€ 19), € 36/58 – Carte € 37/58
◆ Dark wood, pebbles, bamboo and a Japanese garden with a small bridge: this restaurant with a Zen and minimalist decor offers authentic Japanese food and regional wines.

XX **Auberge du Cheval Noir**
17 bd St-Jacques – ✆ 03 80 22 07 37 – www.restaurant-lechevalnoir.fr – contact@restaurant-lechevalnoir.fr – Fax 03 80 24 06 92 – Closed 1st-15 March, 15-28 February, Sunday dinner from November to April, Tuesday and Wednesday
Rest – Menu € 22 (weekdays)/63 bi – Carte € 29/59 AZ **t**
◆ This friendly inn is popular with the locals for its attractive uncluttered contemporary decor and for the generous portions of market fresh recipes. Attentive service.

X **Via Mokis** with rm
1 r. Eugène Spüller – ✆ 03 80 26 80 80 – www.viamokis.com – bienvenue@viamokis.com – Fax 380268262 – Closed 1 week for Christmas holidays
5 rm – †€ 150/185 ††€ 165/285, ☕ € 18
Rest – *(Closed 1st-15 January)* Menu (€ 18), € 28/59 – Carte € 32/39
◆ Talented and creative cuisine, served in mokis (small dishes) in a trendy bistro setting. Possibility of counter service. Fine choice of wines by the glass. Large, modern, well-soundproofed rooms with personal touches. Basement spa.

X **La Ciboulette**
69 r. de Lorraine – ✆ 03 80 24 70 72 – laurent.male@orange.fr – Fax 03 80 22 79 71 – Closed 3-19 August, 1st-24 February, Monday and Tuesday
Rest – Menu € 20/26 – Carte € 30/50 AY **n**
◆ Two dining rooms brightened by green cane furniture and woodwork. Short but appetising, traditional menu with a Burgundy flavour.

Ma Cuisine
passage Ste-Hélène – ✆ 03 80 22 30 22 – macuisine@wanadoo.fr – Fax 03 80 24 99 79 – Closed August, Wednesday, Saturday and Sunday
Rest – *(number of covers limited, pre-book)* Menu € 24 (weekdays) – Carte € 36/65 AZ **s**
◆ Everything revolves around wine in this small restaurant in Provencal colours. Wine list with some 800 appellations accompanies cuisine based on market produce.

Aux Vignes rouges
4 bd Jules-Ferry – ✆ 03 80 24 71 28 – www.auxvignesrouges.com – contact@auxvignesrouges.com – Fax 03 80 24 68 05 – Closed Tuesday and Wednesday
Rest – Menu € 18/45 – Carte € 30/51 BZ **q**
◆ Two beautiful dining rooms in a vaulted cellar with natural stone decor. Guests enjoy regional cuisine using fresh local produce.

Le P'tit Paradis
25 r. Paradis – ✆ 03 80 24 91 00 – Closed two weeks in August, two weeks in December, two weeks in February, Sunday and Monday AZ **e**
Rest – *(pre-book)* Menu € 27/35 – Carte € 47/58
◆ A little corner of paradise in an old cobbled street in the town centre. A cosy, slightly cramped but charmingly decorated dining room with a seasonal menu. Summer terrace.

Le Comptoir des Tontons
22 r. fg Madeleine – ✆ 03 80 24 19 64 – lestontons@wanadoo.fr – Fax 03 80 22 34 07 – Closed 27 July-25 August, 1st-16 February, Sunday and Monday BZ **r**
Rest – Menu € 25/32
◆ A friendly atmosphere reigns in this small bistro where you can enjoy, in a decor dedicated to a classic film, a market-based set menu that goes well with a good Burgundy.

Bissoh
1a r. du fg St-Jacques – ✆ 03 80 24 99 50 – www.bissoh.com – bis@bissoh.com – Fax 03 80 24 99 50 – Closed 3-25 February, Tuesday and Wednesday AZ **d**
Rest – Menu € 13 (weekday lunch), € 15/62 – Carte € 22/46 dinner only
◆ The Japanese born chef prepares traditional dishes from his country using French sourced produce. Simple restaurant where the wine list complements the cuisine.

in Savigny-lès-Beaune 7 km by ①, D 18 and D 2 – pop. 1 403 – alt. 237 m – ✉ 21420
Syndicat d'initiative, 13, rue Vauchey Very ✆ 03 80 26 12 56, Fax 03 80 26 12 56

Le Hameau de Barboron
rm, rest,
– ✆ 03 80 21 58 35 – www.hameaudebarboron.com – lehameaudebarboron@wanadoo.fr – Fax 03 80 26 10 59
12 rm – † € 100/160 †† € 100/200, ☕ € 15
Rest – *(dinner only) (residents only)* Menu € 35, € 45/62
◆ In the middle of a huge hunting reserve, a series of superbly restored fortified farm buildings (16C) where you will stay in personalised rooms with a preserved country charm. Simple country cooking, served in a small perfectly rustic dining room.

La Cuverie
5 r. Chanoine-Donin – ✆ 03 80 21 50 03 – Fax 03 80 21 50 03 – Closed 20 December-20 January, Tuesday and Wednesday
Rest – Menu € 17/41 – Carte € 31/48
◆ Burgundy furniture exposed stone walls and a fine collection of coffee pots in this former fermenting room (18C). Traditional meals based on local produce.

in Pernand-Vergelesses 7 km North by D18 – pop. 292 – alt. 275 m – ✉ 21420

Le Charlemagne (Laurent Peugeot)
Vergelesses road – ✆ 03 80 21 51 45 – www.lecharlemagne.fr – laurent.peugeot@wanadoo.fr – Fax 03 80 21 58 52 – Closed 29 July-6 August, 29 January-4 March, Tuesday and Wednesday
Rest – Menu € 29 (weekday lunch), € 45/82 – Carte € 72/82
Spec. Bar en paupiettes de tapenade. Pigeon cuisiné selon la saison. Moelleux au chocolat, coeur fondant banane et fraîcheur au poivre de Sichuan. **Wines** Pernand-Vergelesses, Beaune
◆ Inventive food served in a minimalist modern setting, on the terrace overlooking the Charlemagne Corton vineyards, or in the kitchen (two chef's tables have been set up!).

Dijon road 4 km by ① – ✉ 21200 Chorey-lès-Beaune

Ermitage de Corton
– ✆ 03 80 22 05 28 – *www.ermitagecorton.com – ermitage.corton@wanadoo.fr – Fax 03 80 24 64 51 – Closed 25-30 December and 22 February-19 March*
6 rm – †€ 150/230 ††€ 170/250, ☕ € 17 – 6 suites
Rest – *(closed Wednesday)* Menu (€ 28), € 46/75 – Carte € 68/84
◆ This imposing inn is situated between the main road and the vineyard. It offers spacious rooms and suites, most of them redecorated in a trendy style. Spacious classical dining room (coffered ceiling) and beautifully laid tables. Seasonally inspired menu.

in Aloxe-Corton 6 km by ① – pop. 181 – alt. 255 m – ✉ 21420

Villa Louise without rest
9 r. Franche – ✆ 03 80 26 46 70 – www.hotel-villa-louise.fr – hotel-villa-louise@wanadoo.fr – Fax 03 80 26 47 16 – Closed 11 January-15 February
12 rm – †€ 85/190 ††€ 85/190, ☕ € 15
◆ A fine 17C wine producer's house with a garden (old lime tree) in the Corton vineyards. Personalised rooms, which are all non-smoking, and cosy ambience in the lounge.

in Ladoix-Serrigny 7 km by ① and D 974 – pop. 1 710 – alt. 200 m – ✉ 21550

La Buissonnière
2 impasse Villot, rte de Dijon – ✆ 03 80 26 43 58 – www.restaurant-labuissonniere.com – restaurantlabuissonniere@wanadoo.fr – Closed 23 December-7 January, Thursday from December to March, Tuesday and Wednesday
Rest – Carte € 29/53
◆ Informal welcome at this pleasant address. Dine in the plain, modern dining room under the veranda or in the rustic decor of the former cellar, where an old wine press has pride of place. Small terrace.

Les Terrasses de Corton with rm
38-40 rte de Beaune – ✆ 03 80 26 42 37 – www.terrasses-de-corton.com – terrasses-de-corton@orange.com – Fax 03 80 26 42 13 – Closed 1st-8 March, 24-27 December, 10 January-28 February, Sunday dinner from November to March, Thursday lunch and Wednesday
10 rm – †€ 45 ††€ 58, ☕ € 9 – ½ P € 55 **Rest** – Menu € 24/45 – Carte € 27/50
◆ In the heart of this little winegrowing village, find this family-run inn that serves a menu of local dishes and reasonably priced wines. Shaded terrace. Simple, well-kept guestrooms upstairs.

in Challanges 4 km by ② then D 111 – ✉ 21200

Château de Challanges without rest
478 r. des Templiers – ✆ 03 80 26 32 62 – www.chateaudechallanges.com – chateau.challanges@wanadoo.fr – Fax 03 80 26 32 52 – Closed 1st December-31 January
16 rm – †€ 96/140 ††€ 96/140, ☕ € 14 – 4 suites
◆ Fine 1870 gentleman's residence in parkland. Bygone charm blends with modern comfort in the rooms. Regional wine tasting sessions in the cellars and hot air ballooning in summer.

in Levernois 5 km Southeast by Verdun-sur-le-Doubs road, D 970 and D 111L - BZ – pop. 269 – alt. 198 m – ✉ 21200

Hostellerie de Levernois
r. du Golf – ✆ 03 80 24 73 58 – www.levernois.com – levernois@relaischateaux.com – Fax 03 80 22 78 00 – Closed 25 January-13 March
25 rm – †€ 130/265 ††€ 130/265, ☕ € 20 – 1 suite
Rest Le Bistrot du bord de l'Eau – see below
Rest – *(closed Wednesday from November to March and lunch except Sunday)* Menu € 65/98 – Carte € 76/110
Spec. Risotto carnaroli au vert, cuisses de grenouilles et escargots de bourgogne. Pièce de bœuf charolais, confit d'échalote au cassis. Soufflé chaud au marc de bourgogne, glace au pain d'épice. **Wines** Clos de Vougeot blanc, Beaune.
◆ A spruce manor house (19C) and its outbuildings, surrounded by a park with a stream running through it. Lovely guestrooms with character. Elegant, modern restaurant overlooking the landscaped garden. Themed evenings and wine tasting sessions.

Golf Hôtel Colvert without rest

23 r. du Golf – 03 80 24 78 20 – www.colvert-golf-hotel.com – hotelcolvert@wanadoo.fr – Fax 03 80 24 77 70

24 rm – €70/90 €75/120, €12

◆ A modern building opening onto the golf course. Functional rooms with map of the Burgundy vineyard on the wall, and balcony overlooking the greens. Bright lounge with fireplace.

Le Parc without rest

13 r. du Golf – 03 80 24 63 00 – www.hotelleparc.fr – leparc@levernois.com – Fax 03 80 24 21 19 – Closed 24 January-28 February

17 rm – €55/70 €55/70, €8

◆ A flowered courtyard and a pretty park overlooking the countryside make this former farm (18C) a relaxing stop-over. Cosy rooms, classically furnished.

Le Bistrot du Bord de l'Eau – Hostellerie de Levernois

r. du Golf – 03 80 24 89 58 – www.levernois.com – levernois@relaischateaux.com – Fax 03 80 22 78 00 – Closed 24 January-13 March, Tuesday, Wednesday, Thursday and Sunday

Rest – *(lunch only)* Menu (€25), €28/32

◆ Tasty regionally inspired cuisine takes pride of place in this countrified bistro. Waterside terrace.

La Garaudière

10 Grand'Rue – 03 80 22 47 70 – Fax 03 80 22 64 01 – Closed 1st December-15 January, Saturday lunch from April to November, Sunday from mid January to end March and Monday

Rest – Menu €17 (weekdays), €21/32 – Carte €30/55

◆ A former barn converted into a pleasant inn. Regional and charcoal welcoming dishes served in a rustic interior or at the terrace under an arbour.

in Montagny-lès-Beaune 3 km by ③ and D 113 – pop. 660 – alt. 206 m – 21200

Le Clos without rest

22 r. Gravières – 03 80 25 97 98 – www.hotelleclos.com – hotelleclos@wanadoo.fr – Fax 03 80 25 94 70 – Closed 22 November-15 January

24 rm – €80/200 €80/200, €12

◆ This wine-maker's property dating from 1779 houses guests in pretty rooms furnished with antique furniture. Breakfast served in a bakery-style dining room. Fine garden.

Adélie without rest

1 rte de Bligny – 03 80 22 37 74 – www.hoteladelie.com – reservation@hoteladelie.com – Fax 03 80 24 23 18

19 rm – €56 €65, €8

◆ An ideal stopping point near the motorway but away from the noise of the traffic. Small, very well kept rooms with pine furniture.

in Meursault 8 km by ④ – pop. 1 563 – alt. 243 m – 21190

Office de tourisme, place de l'Hôtel de Ville 03 80 21 25 90, Fax 03 80 21 61 62

Les Charmes without rest

10 pl.du Murger – 03 80 21 63 53 – www.hotellescharmes.com – contact@hotellescharmes.com – Fax 03 80 21 62 89

14 rm – €85/100 €95/115, €10

◆ Former winegrower's property from the 18C. Spacious rooms (non-smoking) with antique furniture or rooms that are more modern and colourful. Pretty tree-filled garden.

Le Relais de la Diligence

49 r. de la Gare, 2.5 km southeast on the D 23 – 03 80 21 21 32 – www.relaisdeladiligence.com – diligence.la@orange.fr – Fax 03 80 21 64 69 – Closed 18 December-25 January, Tuesday dinner and Wednesday

Rest – Menu (€12), €18 (weekdays)/42 – Carte €29/45

◆ Former coach house made of local stone near to the station. Two dining rooms, are largely open onto the vineyards, the same goes for the terrace. Traditional menu.

Le Chevreuil with rm — rest, VISA AE
pl. de l'Hôtel-de-Ville – ✆ 03 80 21 23 25 – www.lechevreuil.fr
– reception@lechevreuil.fr – Fax 03 80 21 65 51 – Closed February, Thursday lunch, Sunday dinner and Wednesday
14 rm – €50 €58, €8 **Rest** – Menu €19/58 – Carte €44/55
◆ This renovated inn has lost nothing of its former charm. Among the many tasty recipes, the unavoidable hot terrine is the house speciality. Fine wine list. Unpretentious rustic bedrooms.

Le Bouchon — VISA
1 pl. de l'Hôtel-de-Ville – ✆ 03 80 21 29 56 – www.restaurant-le-bouchon.com
– aubouchon@orange.fr – Fax 03 80 21 29 56
– Closed 22 November-5 January 23 February-9 March, Saturday lunch, Sunday dinner and Monday
Rest – Menu €16 (weekdays)/28 – Carte €30/45
◆ A bouchon (Lyonnais style bistro) near the town hall with its shiny tiles. Traditional menus and country cooking prepared in a kitchen that opens on to the dining room.

in Puligny-Montrachet 12 km by ④ and D 974 – pop. 426 – alt. 227 m – ✉ 21190

Le Montrachet — rest, P VISA AE
10 place des Marronniers – ✆ 03 80 21 30 06 – www.le-montrachet.com
– info@le-montrachet.com – Fax 03 80 21 39 06 – Closed 29 November-8 January
30 rm – €120/140 €120/140, €15 – ½ P €135/138
Rest – Menu €30 (lunch), €58/78 – Carte €63/85
◆ This pretty village house (1824) and converted stables offers comfortable rustic or modern rooms and suites. Modern menu and good selection of Burgundy wines in the fine dining room or on the terrace overlooking the garden.

La Maison d'Olivier Leflaive — VISA
10 pl. du Monument – ✆ 03 80 21 95 27 – www.maison-olivierleflaive.com
– maison@olivier-leflaive.com – Fax 03 80 20 86 16
– Closed 31 December-30 January
13 rm – €150/180 €150/180, €10
Rest – *(closed Sunday)* Menu €25/50 bi
◆ Large house set in the centre of the village. Charming rooms decorated in different styles, including Baroque, rustic, pop, romantic and retro. Light dishes served to accompany the wine tasting (vineyard and cellar tours).

La Chouette without rest — P VISA AE
3 bis r. des Creux de Chagny – ✆ 03 80 21 95 60 – www.la-chouette.fr
– info@la-chouette.fr – Fax 03 80 21 95 61 – Closed 19 December-3 January
6 rm – €125/135 €140/150
◆ A quiet Burgundian house for a pleasant stay in large rooms personalised in a cosy style. Comfortable, classic-modern lounge with fireplace and garden overlooking the vines.

in Volnay by ④ and D 974 – pop. 297 – alt. 290 m – ✉ 21190

Auberge des Vignes — P VISA
D 974 – ✆ 03 80 22 24 48 – www.aubergedesvignes.fr – contact@aubergedesvignes.fr – Fax 03 80 22 24 48 – Closed 1st-8 July, 8-22 February, Wednesday dinner, Sunday dinner and Monday except bank holidays
Rest – Menu €16 (weekday lunch), €19/40 – Carte €29/54
◆ Former farm where traditional dishes and mellow Volnay wines can be enjoyed in a rustic setting. Comforting fire in winter; veranda and terrace facing the vineyard.

in Bouze-lès-Beaune 6.5 km by ⑤ and D 970 – pop. 300 – alt. 400 m – ✉ 21200

La Bouzerotte — VISA AE
– ✆ 03 80 26 01 37 – www.labouzerotte.com – contact@labouzerotte.com
– Fax 03 80 26 09 37 – Closed 22 December-8 January, 22 February-2 March, Monday and Tuesday
Rest – *(pre-book on weekend)* Menu €18 (weekday lunch), €24/60 – Carte €25/45
◆ A nice restaurant on the Beaune mountainside serving seasonal food and a regional set menu. Dine in a neo-rustic setting or on the leafy terrace.

See also hotel resource of **Bouilland**

BEAUREPAIRE-EN-BRESSE – 71 Saône-et-Loire – 320 M9 – pop. 515 – alt. 147 m – ✉ 71580 8 D3

Paris 383 – Châlon-sur-Saône 49 – Bourg-en-Bresse 65 – Lons-le-Saunier 13 – Tournus 45

Auberge de la Croix Blanche

– ✆ 03 85 74 13 22 – www.elphicom.com/lacroixblanche – aubergelacroixblanche@libertysurf.fr – Fax 03 85 74 13 25 – Closed 15-22 June, 16 November-7 December, 5-12 January, Sunday dinner and Monday except July-August

14 rm – †€ 38/43 ††€ 38/49, ☕ € 8 – ½ P € 50/56

Rest – Menu (€ 20 bi), € 15 (weekdays)/42 – Carte € 30/48

◆ Near a busy road, this inn has a roof that's easy to find with a white cross on it and ears of corn drying under the façade lean-to. Very clean rooms overlooking the garden. Bressan décor in the restaurant; regional produce prepared in a modern setting.

BEAUSOLEIL – 06 Alpes-Maritimes – 341 F5 – pop. 13 400 – alt. 89 m – ✉ 06240 42 E2

Paris 947 – Monaco 4 – Menton 11 – Monte-Carlo 2 – Nice 21

Office de tourisme, 32, boulevard de la République ✆ 04 93 78 01 55, Fax 04 93 78 85 85

See plan of Monaco (Principality of).

Olympia without rest

17 bis bd Gén.- Leclerc – ✆ 04 93 78 12 70 – www.olympiahotel.fr – olympiahotel@hotmail.com – Fax 04 93 41 85 04 DX t

31 rm – †€ 85/120 ††€ 85/160, ☕ € 10 – 1 suite

◆ Fine freestone fronted building adorned with balconies and a finely worked cornice located on the French-Monegasque border. Sober, soundproofed and tasteful rooms.

BEAUVAIS Ⓟ – 60 Oise – 305 D4 – pop. 55 100 – Built-up area 100 733 – alt. 67 m – ✉ 60000 Northern France and the Paris Region 36 B2

Paris 87 – Amiens 63 – Boulogne-sur-Mer 182 – Compiègne 60 – Rouen 82

Beauvais-Tillé ✆ 03 44 11 46 70, 3.5 km northeast

Office de tourisme, 1, rue Beauregard ✆ 03 44 15 30 30, Fax 03 44 15 30 31

du Vivier Ons-en-Bray RN 31, 15 km on the Gournay-en-Bray road, ✆ 03 44 84 24 11

St-Pierre cathedral★★★: astronomical clock★ - St-Étienne church★: stained-glass windows★★ and Jesse tree★★★ - Musée départemental de l'Oise★ in the former bishop's palace **M²**.

Plan on following page

Hostellerie St-Vincent

3 km by ③ (Espace St-Germain), 241 Rue de Clermont – ✆ 03 44 05 49 99 – www.stvincent-beauvais.com – h.st.vincent@wanadoo.fr – Fax 03 44 05 52 94

79 rm – †€ 69 ††€ 69, ☕ € 10 – 1 suite – ½ P € 55

Rest – Menu (€ 13), € 18/32 – Carte € 27/44

◆ A recently-built hotel near main roads and the motorway slip road, offering redecorated, functional and soundproofed rooms. Internet access available. Spacious and light dining room; traditional menus completed by blackboard specials.

La Maison Haute

128 r. de Paris, (Voisinlieu district), 1.5 km on ④ – ✆ 03 44 02 61 60 – www.lamaisonhaute.fr – Fax 03 44 02 15 36 – Closed 28 April-2 May, 21 July-17 August, 24 December-4 January, Saturday lunch, Sunday and Monday

Rest – Menu (€ 30), € 35/39

◆ In a residential district, this restaurant with a contemporary setting (light colours and dark woodwork) is in perfect keeping with its modern cuisine. Friendly welcome.

BEAUVAIS

Beauregard (R.)	2
Brière (Bd J.)	3
Carnot (R.)	
Clemenceau (Pl.)	4
Dr-Gérard (R.)	5
Dr-Lamotte (Bd du)	6
Dreux (R. Ph. de)	7
Gambetta	
Grenier-à-Sel (R.)	8
Guéhengnies (R. de)	9
Hachette (Pl. J.)	10
Halles (Pl. des)	12
Leclerc (R. Mar.)	13
Lignières (R. J. de)	15
Loisel (Bd A.)	16
Malherbe (R. de)	18
Nully-d'Hécourt (R.)	19
République (Av. de la)	20
St-André (Bd)	22
St-Laurent (R.)	23
St-Pierre (R.)	24
Scellier (Cours)	27
Taillerie (R. de la)	29
Tapisserie (R. de la)	30
Villiers-de-l'Isle-Adam (R.)	35
Vincent-de-Beauvais (R.)	26
Watrin (R. du Gén.)	36
27-Juin (R. du)	38

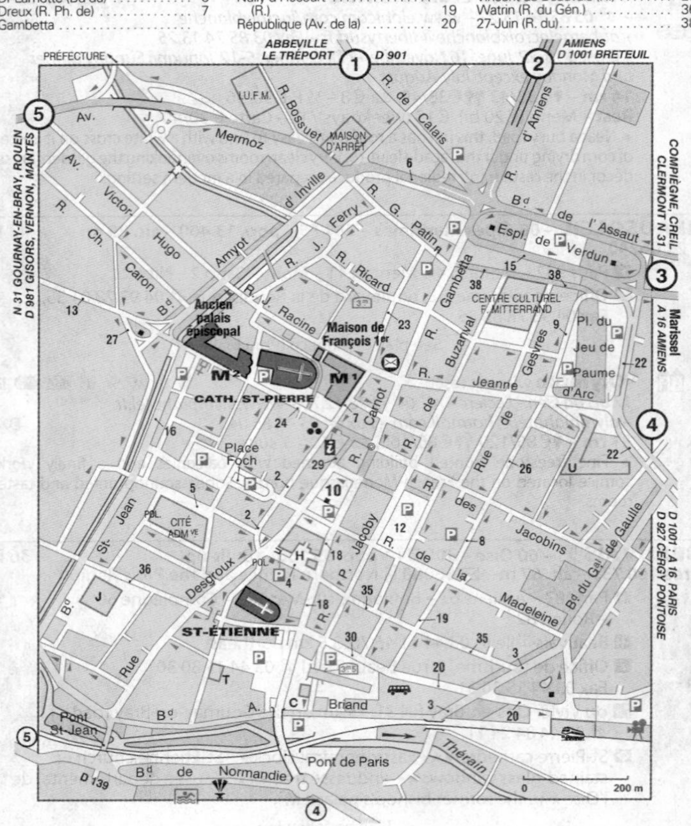

La Baie d'Halong

32 r. de Clermont, 1 km by ③ – ☎ 03 44 45 39 83 – ta.hoang@wanadoo.fr – Closed 20 April-4 May, 14 July-15 August, 21 December-2 January, Wednesday lunch, Saturday, Sunday and Monday

Rest – Menu € 23/31

◆ Exclusively Vietnamese cuisine combining fresh ingredients with a delicate use of spices. Paintings depicting the Bay of Halong adorn the dining room.

via ④ 5 km, D 1001 (towards Paris) – ✉ 60000 Beauvais

Mercure

rm, rest, VISA AE

21 av. Montaigne – ☎ 03 44 02 80 80 – mercure;com – h0350@accor.com – Fax 03 44 02 12 50

60 rm – †€ 105 ††€ 115, ☕ € 14 **Rest** – Menu € 25 – Carte € 25/40

◆ A 1970s building, offering good-sized, renovated and well-soundproofed rooms. Dining room adorned with a fireplace and summer terrace by the pool. Traditional cuisine served.

XX **Le Bellevue**

3 av. Rhin-et-Danube – ✆ 03 44 02 17 11 – www.restaurantlebellevue.com – restaurantlebellevue@wanadoo.fr – Fax 03 44 02 54 44 – Closed 7-24 August, Saturday and Sunday

Rest – Carte € 38/60

◆ This simple modern restaurant, in a shopping area on the outskirts of town, is adorned with paintings and serves classic cuisine with fresh market produce.

"Rest" appears in red for establishments with a ✿ (star) or ☺ (Bib Gourmand).

BEAUVOIR-SUR-MER – 85 Vendée – **316** D6 – **pop. 3 399 – alt. 8 m** – ✉ 85230 ▮ Atlantic Coast 34 **A3**

▶ Paris 443 – Challans 15 – Nantes 59 – Noirmoutier-en-l'Île 22 – La Roche-sur-Yon 59

ℹ Office de tourisme, rue Charles Gallet ✆ 02 51 68 71 13, Fax 02 51 49 05 04

Le Relais des Touristes without rest

rte de Gois – ✆ 02 51 68 70 19 – www.lerelaisdestouristes.com – relaisdestouristes@free.fr – Fax 02 51 49 33 45 – Closed 16 February-4 March

39 rm – †€ 59/68 ††€ 65/75, ☕ € 8

◆ In addition to practical, well-kept rooms, the hotel also boasts a lovely indoor pool and a new breakfast room.

BEAUVOIS-EN-CAMBRÉSIS – 59 Nord – **302** I7 – **pop. 2 093** – alt. 89 m – ✉ 59157 31 **C3**

▶ Paris 190 – St-Quentin 40 – Arras 48 – Cambrai 12 – Valenciennes 37

XX **La Buissonnière**

92 r Victor Watiemez – ✆ 03 27 85 29 97 – www.la-buissonniere.fr.st – labuissonniere@aol.com – Fax 03 27 76 25 74 – Closed August, Sunday dinner, Wednesday dinner and Monday

Rest – Menu (€ 17), € 21 (weekdays)/35 – Carte € 30/50

◆ At the gates to the town, a restaurant serving traditional cuisine made with seasonal market produce. Two dining rooms, one of them is rustic and recently redecorated, overlooking the terrace.

BEAUZAC – 43 Haute-Loire – **331** G2 – **pop. 2 557 – alt. 565 m** – ✉ 43590 ▮ Lyon - Rhone Valley 6 **C3**

▶ Paris 556 – Craponne-sur-Arzon 31 – Le Puy-en-Velay 45 – St-Étienne 44

ℹ Office de tourisme, place de l'Église ✆ 04 71 61 50 74, Fax 04 71 61 50 62

XX **L'Air du Temps** with rm

in Confolent, 4 km eastward along the D 461 – ✆ 04 71 61 49 05 – www.airdutemps.fr.st – airdutemps.hotel@wanadoo.fr – Fax 04 71 61 50 91 – Closed January, Sunday dinner and Monday

8 rm – †€ 47/52 ††€ 47/52, ☕ € 8 – ½ P € 46

Rest – Menu € 16 (weekday lunch), € 21/53 – Carte € 30/65

◆ This country house offers a bright dining room, enlarged by a pretty veranda, a varied and creative regional menu and comfortable, well-equipped rooms.

in Bransac 3 km South by D 42 – ✉ 43590

XX **La Table du Barret** with rm

– ✆ 04 71 61 47 74 – www.latabledubarret.com – info@latabledubarret.com – Fax 04 71 61 52 73 – Closed 3-10 September, 12-19 November, 1st January-5 February, Sunday dinner, Tuesday and Wednesday

8 rm – †€ 55 ††€ 60, ☕ € 10 **Rest** – Menu (€ 19), € 29/90 bi – Carte € 40/65

◆ A peaceful hamlet near the Loire is the site of this understated contemporary restaurant. Its menu is characterised by tasty up-to-date recipes. Comfortable bedrooms.

BEBLENHEIM – 68 Haut-Rhin – 315 H8 – pop. 954 – alt. 212 m 2 C2
– ✉ 68980 Alsace-Lorraine

Paris 444 – Colmar 11 – Gérardmer 55 – Ribeauvillé 5 – St-Dié 48 – Sélestat 19

Auberge Le Bouc Bleu

2 r. 5-Décembre – ✆ 03 89 47 88 21 – Fax 03 89 86 01 04 – Closed Wednesday and Thursday

Rest – *(number of covers limited, pre-book)* Menu (€ 26) – Carte € 33/40

◆ Books, antiques and old menus endow this pleasant countrified restaurant (non-smoking) with a flea market spirit. Paved courtyard terrace and market-fresh cuisine.

LE BEC-HELLOUIN – 27 Eure – 304 E6 – pop. 414 – alt. 101 m 33 C2
– ✉ 27800 Normandy, G. Brittany

Paris 153 – Bernay 22 – Évreux 46 – Lisieux 46 – Pont-Audemer 23 – Rouen 41

Abbey★★.

Auberge de l'Abbaye

rm,

12 pl. Guillaume-le-Conquérant – ✆ 02 32 44 86 02 – www.auberge-abbaye-bec-hellouin.com – catherine-fabrice.c@wanadoo.fr – Fax 02 32 46 32 23 – Closed 30 November-1st February, Wednesday from October to March and Tuesday

8 rm – †€ 70 ††€ 80, ☕ € 10 – 1 suite – ½ P € 78

Rest – Menu € 22/30 – Carte € 29/42

◆ A haven for travellers since the 18C, this smart half-timbered residence houses renovated, prettily personalised rooms. Traditional food enriched with local produce, served in country-style dining rooms.

Le Canterbury

3 r. de Canterbury – ✆ 02 32 44 14 59 – Fax 02 32 44 14 59 – Closed Sunday dinner, Tuesday dinner and Wednesday

Rest – Menu € 19 (weekdays)/44 – Carte € 35/45

◆ Behind a half-timbered façade covered with Virginia creeper is a modern setting in pastel tones. Traditional cuisine. Plant-filled terrace popular on sunny days.

BÉDARIEUX – 34 Hérault – 339 D7 – pop. 6 518 – alt. 196 m 22 B2
– ✉ 34600

Paris 723 – Béziers 34 – Lodève 29 – Montpellier 70

Office de tourisme, 1, rue de la République ✆ 04 67 95 08 79, Fax 04 67 95 39 69

La Forge

22 av. Abbé-Tarroux, (opposite the tourist information centre) – ✆ 04 67 95 13 13 – Fax 04 67 95 10 81 – Closed 16-30 November, 4-25 January, Sunday dinner, Wednesday dinner except July-August and Monday

Rest – Menu € 16/36 – Carte € 43/57

◆ These 17C vaults used to house a forge and stables. Unusual interior architecture, a monumental fireplace and large flower-decked, shady terrace. Traditional food.

in Hérépian 6 km southeast on the D 908 – pop. 1 368 – alt. 191 m – ✉ 34600

Office de tourisme, espace Campanaire Malraux ✆ 04 67 23 23 96

Le Couvent d'Hérépian without rest

2 r. du Couvent – ✆ 04 67 23 36 30 – www.couventherepian.com – contact@couventherepian.com – Fax 04 67 23 36 48

7 rm – †€ 110/200 ††€ 110/200, ☕ € 10 – 6 suites

◆ Refurbished 17C convent, now a luxuriously appointed residence with character. Cosy, uncluttered and well-equipped rooms. Relaxation areas; refined wine bar.

in Villemagne-l'Argentière 8 km West by D 908 and D 922 – pop. 429 – alt. 193 m – ✉ 34600

Auberge de l'Abbaye with rm

rm,

pl. du couvent – ✆ 04 67 95 34 84 – www.aubergeabbaye.fr – auberge.abbaye@free.fr – Fax 04 67 95 34 84 – Closed 15 November-13 February, Wednesday lunch from November to March, Tuesday except dinner in high season and Monday

3 rm ☕ – †€ 100 ††€ 130 **Rest** – Menu (€ 15 bi), € 27/58 – Carte € 20/55

◆ A monastic ambience, but not an austere one in the vaulted dining room of this old convent. Dishes mix local produce, spices and sweet/savoury flavours. New themed bedrooms.

BÉDOIN – 84 Vaucluse – 332 E9 – pop. 2 942 – alt. 295 m – ✉ 84410 42 E1
Provence

Paris 692 – Avignon 43 – Carpentras 16 – Nyons 36 – Sault 35 – Vaison-la-Romaine 21

Office de tourisme, Espace Marie-Louis Gravier ✆ 04 90 65 63 95, Fax 04 90 12 81 55

Le Paty ←★ Northwest: 4,5 km.

Des Pins rm, rest, rest, VISA

ch. des Crans, 1 km eastward by secondary road – ✆ 04 90 65 92 92 – www.hoteldespins.net – hoteldespins@wanadoo.fr – Fax 04 90 65 60 66

25 rm – †€ 60/105 ††€ 60/105, ☕ € 10 – ½ P € 63/85

Rest – *(open mid-March to October and closed at lunch on weekdays)* Menu € 27/40 – Carte € 31/48

◆ A delightful Provençal house in the middle of a pine grove home to a water feature and a pool. Rooms with personal touches, some on the garden level have terraces. In a countrified interior or in the open-air, this establishment serves a market-fresh menu.

in Ste-Colombe 4 km East by Mont-Ventoux road – ✉ 84410

La Garance without rest VISA

Ste-Colombe – ✆ 04 90 12 81 00 – www.lagarance.fr – info@lagarance.fr – Open 3 April-31 October

13 rm – †€ 52/77 ††€ 52/77, ☕ € 8

◆ This old farmstead favoured by hikers is set in a hamlet amid vineyards and orchards, with the Ventoux in the background. The rooms boast a terrace.

Mont-Ventoux road 6 km East – ✉ 84410 Bédoin

XX **Le Mas des Vignes**

au virage de St-Estève – ✆ 04 90 65 63 91 – lemasdesvignes@aol.com – Open April-November and closed Tuesday lunch and Monday except July-August and at lunch in July-August except Sunday and public holidays

Rest – Menu € 35/50 – Carte € 35/45

◆ A flower-decked garden, rockery and small vegetable plot surround this enchanting farmhouse and its panoramic terrace. Regional gastronomy made with impeccable produce. Gracious welcome.

BÈGLES – 33 Gironde – 335 H5 – see Bordeaux

BEG-MEIL – 29 Finistère – 308 H7 – ✉ 29170 Brittany 9 B2

Paris 560 – Concarneau 16 – Pont-l'Abbé 23 – Quimper 20 – Quimperlé 44

Site★.

Thalamot rest, VISA

4-6 Le Chemin Creux – ✆ 02 98 94 97 38 – www.hotel-thalamot.com – resa@hotel-thalamot.com – Fax 02 98 94 49 92 – Open 10 April-30 September

30 rm – †€ 58/75 ††€ 59/77, ☕ € 9 – ½ P € 59/78

Rest – Menu (€ 17), € 24/48 – Carte € 27/75

◆ In a quiet area near the beaches, simple and modern rooms. A collection of early 20C paintings depicting scenes of Brittany. Fish and seafood served in a restaurant giving onto a garden terrace with trees.

LA BÉGUDE-DE-MAZENC – 26 Drôme – 332 C6 – pop. 1 421 – alt. 215 m – ✉ 26160 44 B3

Paris 621 – Lyon 160 – Montélimar 16 – Valence 56

Office de tourisme, avenue du Président Loubet ✆ 04 75 46 24 42, Fax 04 75 46 24 42

Le Jabron VISA

5 av. Mme-de-Sévigné – ✆ 04 75 46 28 85 – www.lejabron.fr – hotel-lejabron@wanadoo.fr – Fax 04 75 46 24 31

12 rm – †€ 58 ††€ 58, ☕ € 7 – ½ P € 58

Rest – Menu € 12 (weekday lunch), € 19/36 – Carte € 25/48

◆ In the village, a small hotel that is always well-kept, following its recent renovations. The bright and colourful rooms have double glazing. Conference room. Traditional food served on the terrace or in the dining room.

BÉHEN – 80 Somme – 301 D7 – pop. 435 – alt. 105 m – ✉ 80870 36 A1

Paris 195 – Amiens 77 – Abbeville 19 – Berck 59 – Eu 30

Chateau de Béhen

8 r. du Château – ✆ 03 22 31 58 30 – www.chateau-de-behen.com – info@cuvelier.com – Fax 03 22 31 58 39

7 rm – †€ 105/147 ††€ 115/157 **Table d'hôte** – Menu € 41 bi/51 bi

◆ Live the castle life while staying in this beautiful 18C building surrounded by a park. Antique or period furniture in the lounge and bedrooms (which have dormer windows on the second floor). Traditional dishes served in the classic dining room with rustic furnishings.

BELCAIRE – 11 Aude – 344 C6 – pop. 405 – alt. 1 002 m – ✉ 11340 22 A3

Paris 810 – Ax-les-Thermes 26 – Carcassonne 81 – Foix 54 – Quillan 29

Office de tourisme, 22, avenue d'Ax les Thermes ✆ 04 68 20 75 89, Fax 04 68 20 79 13

Forests★★ of the Plaine and Comus Northwest.

Belvédère du Pas de l'Ours★★ East: 13 km then 15 mn, **Languedoc-Roussillon-Tarn Gorges**

Bayle with rm

38 av. des Thermes – ✆ 04 68 20 31 05 – hotel-bayle.com – hotel-bayle@wanadoo.fr – Fax 04 68 20 35 24 – Closed 12 November-5 December

12 rm – †€ 25/41 ††€ 25/41, € 6 **Rest** – Carte € 23/41

◆ A family restaurant in a village in the land of the Cathars. Rustic dining room with a terrace overlooking the countryside. Dishes inspired by local cuisine. Well-kept rooms.

BELCASTEL – 12 Aveyron – 338 G4 – pop. 242 – alt. 406 m – ✉ 12390 29 C1

Languedoc-Roussillon-Tarn Gorges

Paris 623 – Decazeville 28 – Rodez 25 – Villefranche-de-Rouergue 36

Syndicat d'initiative, Maison du Patrimoine ✆ 05 65 64 46 11, Fax 05 65 64 46 11

Vieux Pont (Nicole Fagegaltier et Bruno Rouquier) with rm

– ✆ 05 65 64 52 29 – www.hotelbelcastel.com – hotel-du-vieux-pont@wanadoo.fr – Fax 05 65 64 44 32 – Closed 2 January-15 March, 29 June-4 July, Sunday dinner except July-August, Tuesday lunch and Monday

7 rm – †€ 82 ††€ 97, € 13 – ½ P € 100/105

Rest – *(number of covers limited, pre-book)* Menu € 28 (weekday lunch), € 45/85 – Carte € 52/70

Spec. Ris d'agneau "allaiton". Pigeon du Mont Royal croûté de cèpes secs et d'ail. Millefeuille de nougatine. **Wines** Marcillac, Vin d'Entraygues et du Fel.

◆ Two houses on either side of a 15C stone bridge. Fine contemporary, regional cuisine served in an elegant modern setting. Quiet, cosy bedrooms in an old barn on the other side of the river. Breakfast served on the banks of the river in summer.

BELFORT Ⓟ – 90 Territoire de Belfort – 315 F11 – pop. 50 700 – Built-up area 104 962 – alt. 360 m – ✉ 90000 Burgundy-Jura 17 C1

Paris 422 – Basel 78 – Besançon 93 – Épinal 95 – Mulhouse 41

Office de tourisme, 2 bis, rue Clemenceau ✆ 03 84 55 90 90, Fax 03 84 55 90 70

de Rougemont-le-Château Rougemont-le-Château Route de Masevaux, NE : 16 km on D 83 and D 25, ✆ 03 84 23 74 74

Le Lion★★ - Fortified camp ★★: ☀★★ from the fort terrace - Old town★: porte de Brisach★ - Organ★ of St-Christophe cathedral Y **B** - Frescoe★ (car park: rue de l'As-de-Carreau Z 6) - Amateur's study★: Donation Maurice Jardot **M**[1].

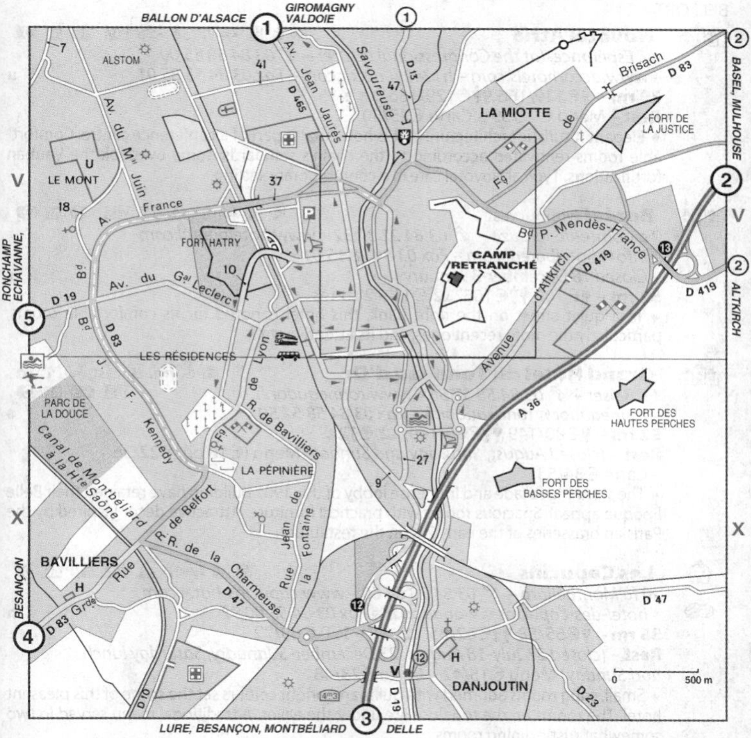

BELFORT

Street	Grid	No.
Ancêtres (Fg des)	Y	3
Armes (Pl. d')	Y	5
As-de-Carreau (R. de l')	Z	6
Auxelles (Via d')	V	7
Besançon (R. de)	X	9
Boulloche (Pt A.)	V	10
Bourgeois (Pl. des)	Y	12
Carnot (Bd)	Z	15
Château-d'Eau (Av. du)	V	18
Clemenceau (R. G.)	Y	20
Denfert-Rochereau (R.)	Z	21
Dr-Corbis (Pl. du)	Z	23
Dr-Fréry (R. du)	Y	24
Dreyfus-Schmidt (R.)	Y	25
Dunant (Bd H.)	X	27
Espérance (Av. de l')	Y	28
Foch (Av. Mar.)	Z	29
France (Fg de)	Z	30
Gaulard (R. du Gén.)	Z	31
Grande-Fontaine (Pl. de la)	Z	32
Grande-Fontaine (R.)	Y	33
Grand'Rue	Y	34
Joffre (Bd du Mar.)	VY	37
Lebleu (R. F.)	Z	40
Lille (R. de)	V	41
Magasin (Q. du)	Y	43
Metz-Juteau (R.)	Y	45
Moulin (Av. J.)	V	47
Mulhouse (R. de)	Y	46
Pompidou (R. G.)	Y	48
République (Pl. de la)	Y	49
République (R. de la)	Z	50
Roussel (R. du Gén.)	Y	51
Sarrail (Av. du Gén.)	Z	52
Vauban (Q.)	Y	60

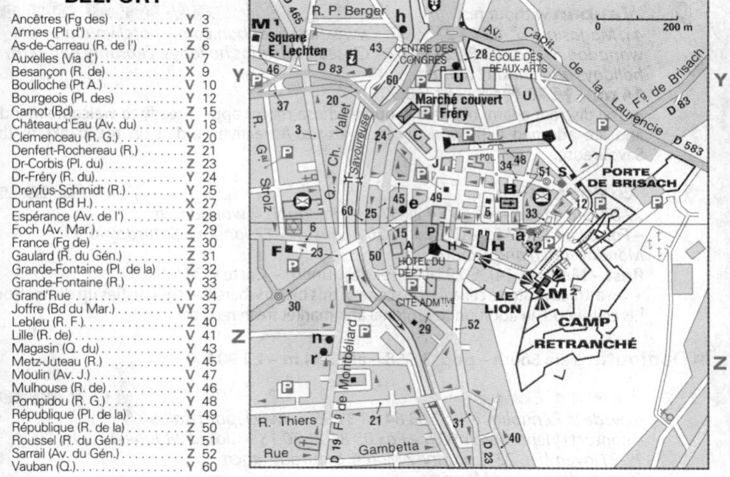

Novotel Atria
av. Espérance, (at the Congressional centre) – 03 84 58 85 00 – www.accorhotels.com – h1742@accor.com – Fax 03 84 58 85 01 Y **u**
79 rm – €129/166 €129/166, €15
Rest – Menu €22/39 – Carte €25/50
◆ Elegant futuristic architecture in this hotel that is part of a conference centre. Comfortable rooms renovated according to the chain's standards; some overlook the Vauban fortifications. Typical Novotel café in a contemporary setting.

Boréal without rest
2 r. Comte-de-la-Suze – 03 84 22 32 32 – www.hotelboreal.com – info@hotelboreal.com – Fax 03 84 28 15 01 – Closed 18 December-3 January Z **r**
52 rm – €100 €105, €11 – 2 suites
◆ In a quiet street on the right bank, this hotel is noted for its comfortable rooms, particularly the more recent ones, and its attentive staff.

Grand Hôtel du Tonneau d'Or rm, rest,
1 r. Reiset – 03 84 58 57 56 – www.tonneaudor.fr – tonneaudor@tonneaudor.fr – Fax 03 84 58 57 50 Y **e**
52 rm – €80/149 €86/149, €12
Rest – *(closed August, Saturday and Sunday)* Menu (€18 bi), €22/36 – Carte €34/53
◆ The stunning façade and immense lobby of this 1907 building have retained their Belle Époque appeal. Spacious rooms with practical furniture. Attractive decor inspired by the Parisian brasseries of the early 20C in the restaurant.

Les Capucins
20 fg Montbéliard – 03 84 28 04 60 – www.capucins-hotel.com – hotel-des-capucins@wanadoo.fr – Fax 03 84 55 00 92 Z **n**
35 rm – €55/58 €62/65, €8 – ½ P €69/72
Rest – *(closed 27 July-18 August, 23 December-5 January, Saturday lunch and Sunday)* Menu €15/42 – Carte €23/48
◆ Small, snug rooms adorned with quilts and bright colours set the scene of this pleasant hotel. The rooms on the top floor are under the eaves. A traditional menu served in two somewhat rustic dining rooms.

Vauban without rest
4 r. Magasin – 03 84 21 59 37 – www.hotel-vauban.com – hotel.vauban@wanadoo.fr – Fax 03 84 21 41 67 – Closed Christmas holidays, February half-term holidays and Sunday dinner Y **h**
14 rm – €70 €81, €8,50
◆ The discreet charm of a family home whose rooms appear ready to welcome friends, and are adorned with work by local artists. Attractive garden on the banks of the Savoureuse.

Le Pot au Feu
27 bis Grand'rue – 03 84 28 57 84 – mf.lunois@wanadoo.fr – Fax 03 84 58 17 65 – Closed 1st-20 August, 1st-12 January, Saturday lunch, Monday lunch and Sunday Y **s**
Rest – Menu (€14), €29 bi (weekday lunch) – Carte €34/60
◆ An attractive stone cellar is the scene of this bistro where the chef rustles up dishes from his childhood, in addition to regional and market fresh recipes.

in Danjoutin 3 km South – pop. 3 558 – alt. 354 m – ✉ 90400

Le Pot d'Étain
4 av. de la République – 03 84 28 31 95 – www.lepotdetain90.fr – contact@lepotdetain90.fr – Fax 03 84 21 70 15 – Closed 28 June-12 July, 1st-9 November, 22 February-2 March, Saturday lunch, Sunday dinner and Monday X **v**
Rest – Menu €30, €49/80 – Carte €55/90
◆ A new team have taken over the house and the new chef creates convincing cuisine. Table d'hôtes in the first dining room, elegant decor in the second.

BELGENTIER – 83 Var – 340 L6 – pop. 2 180 – alt. 152 m – ✉ 83210 41 C3

Paris 826 – Draguignan 71 – Marseille 62 – Toulon 23

XX **Le Moulin du Gapeau**

pl. Granet – ✆ 04 94 48 98 68 – www.moulin-du-gapeau.fr – moulin-du-gapeau@wanadoo.fr – Fax 04 94 28 11 45 – Closed 15-30 March, 15-30 November, Monday lunch in July-August, Sunday dinner, Thursday dinner except July-August and Wednesday

Rest – Menu € 31/85 – Carte € 60/77

◆ Old machinery decorates the dining room of this restaurant set in a 17C oil mill. Mediterranean inspired menu. Modern patio-terrace.

BELLEAU – 54 Meurthe-et-Moselle – 307 I6 – pop. 721 – alt. 172 m – ✉ 54610 26 B2

Paris 340 – Metz 47 – Nancy 25 – Vandœuvre-lès-Nancy 35

Château de Morey

19 r. Saint-Pierre, at Morey on the D 44 A – ✆ 03 83 31 50 98 – www.chateaudemorey.com – chateaudemorey@wanadoo.fr

5 rm – †€ 55/65 ††€ 65/75 – ½ P € 75/85

Table d'hôte – Menu € 20 bi/25 bi

◆ A 16C castle set in a huge park that dominates the valley. Families appreciate the large guestrooms (with lounges). Simple rustic decor. Swimming pool, mountain bikes and games room. Table d'hôte available on reservation.

BELLE-ÉGLISE – 60 Oise – 305 E5 – pop. 568 – alt. 69 m – ✉ 60540 36 B3

Paris 53 – Beauvais 32 – Compiègne 64 – Pontoise 29

XXX **La Grange de Belle-Église** (Marc Duval)

28 bd René-Aimé-Lagabrielle – ✆ 03 44 08 49 00 – www.lagrangedebelleeglise.fr – Fax 03 44 08 45 97 – Closed 4-26 August, 16 February-3 March, Sunday dinner, Tuesday lunch and Monday

Rest – Menu (€ 28), € 60/85 – Carte € 87/132

Spec. Fraîcheur de homard bleu en salade au safran (May-September). Noisettes de chevreuil sauce grand veneur (October-February). Petit beurre à la mangue, glace aux poivres (October-February).

◆ This elegant restaurant offers a dining room with overhead beams, pleasant veranda overlooking a delightful garden and fine silverware in display cabinets. Classic dishes.

BELLEGARDE – 45 Loiret – 318 L4 – pop. 1 676 – alt. 113 m – ✉ 45270 12 C2

Châteaux of the Loire

Paris 110 – Gien 41 – Montargis 24 – Nemours 41 – Orléans 50 – Pithiviers 30

Syndicat d'initiative, 12 bis, place Charles Desvergnes ✆ 02 38 90 25 37, Fax 02 38 90 28 32

Château★.

in Montliard 7 km Northwest by D 44 – pop. 221 – alt. 126 m – ✉ 45340

Château de Montliard

3 rte de Nesploy – ✆ 02 38 33 71 40 – www.chateau-de-montliard.com – a.galizia@infonie.fr – Fax 02 38 33 86 41 – Open from Easter to All Saint's Day

4 rm – †€ 56/80 ††€ 68/90 **Table d'hôte** – Menu € 23 bi/33 bi

◆ In the same family since 1384, this castle surrounded by a moat still has a lovely historic interior (spiral staircase, thick walls and stained glass windows). Rooms with fireplaces. The restaurant serves one set menu in a lovely, rustic setting.

BELLEGARDE-SUR-VALSERINE – 01 Ain – 328 H4 – pop. 11 400 – alt. 350 m – ✉ 01200 Burgundy-Jura 45 C1

Paris 497 – Annecy 43 – Bourg-en-Bresse 73 – Genève 43 – Lyon 113

Office de tourisme, 24, place Victor Bérard ✆ 04 50 48 48 68, Fax 04 50 48 65 08

Banks of the Valserine North: 2 km by N84.

in Lancrans 3 km North by D 1084 and D 991 – pop. 935 – alt. 500 m – ✉ 01200

Le Sorgia

39 Gde-Rue – ✆ 04 50 48 15 81 – mariondo@wanadoo.fr – Fax 04 50 48 44 72 – Closed 31 July-18 August, 19 December-11 January, Sunday and Monday

17 rm – €51/55 €51/55, €8 – ½ P €50

Rest – *(closed Saturday lunch, Sunday dinner and Monday)* Menu (€17), €27/48 – Carte €22/47

◆ The same family has been greeting guests in this inn at the heart of the village since 1890. Simple but neat and regularly spruced up rooms A countrified dining room and flower-decked terrace facing the garden. Regularly renewed regional menu.

in Eloise (74 H.-Savoie) 5 km southeast by D 1508 and secondary road – pop. 872 – alt. 511 m – ✉ 01200

Le Fartoret

130 r. du 14 juin 1944 – ✆ 04 50 48 07 18 – www.fartoret.com – lefartoret@wanadoo.fr – Fax 04 50 48 23 85 – Closed 23 December-3 January and Sunday dinner off season

41 rm – €42 €60/95, €10 – ½ P €68/87

Rest – Menu €20 (weekday lunch), €27/45 – Carte €35/54

◆ A hotel set in the grounds of a century-old farmhouse with pool and tennis court. The rooms, though not very modern, are well kept. Fine collection of cockerels. View of the trees from the large dining rooms and covered terrace. Classic cuisine.

BELLE-ÎLE-EN-MER ★★ – 56 Morbihan – 308 L10 Brittany 9 B3

Access by sea transport for **Le Palais** (in summer **compulsory booking** for taking vehicles).

from **Quiberon** (Port-Maria) - 30 min crossing – Information and prices: S.M.N. ✆ 0 820 056 000 (Le Palais), Fax 02 97 29 50 34, www.smn-navigation.fr

from **Port-Navalo** - **(Apr-Oct)** - 1 hr crossing - Information and prices: Navix S.A. at Port-Navalo ✆ 0 825 132 120 (0.15 €/min)

from **Vannes** - (Apr-Oct) - 2 hr crossing - Information and prices: Navix S.A., Gare Maritime ✆ 0 825 132 (0.15 €/min), Fax 02 97 46 60 29, www.navix.fr

from **Lorient** - Seasonal service - 50 min crossing (passengers only, booking required) - Information and prices S.M.N. ✆ 820 056 000 (0.12 €/min) - For **Le Palais** and for **Sauzon** : from **Quiberon** - Seasonal service - 25 min crossing - Information and prices: S.M.N. ✆ 0 820 056 000 (0.12 €/min) (Quiberon) - Information and prices: Navix S.A.

from **Locmariaquer** - ✆ 0 825 162 130 (0.15 €/min) - **Auray Le Bono** - ✆ 0 825 162 140 (0.15 €/min) - **La Trinité-sur-Mer** crossing 1 hr (14 Jul-22 Aug) - ✆ 0 825 132 150 (0.15 €/min), Fax 02 97 46 60 29.

Office de tourisme, quai Bonnelle, Le Palais ✆ 02 97 31 81 93, Fax 02 97 31 56 17

Côte sauvage★★★ - Pointe des Poulains★★★.

BANGOR – 56 Morbihan – pop. 894 – alt. 45 m – ✉ 56360

Paris 513 – Rennes 162 – Vannes 53 – Auray 34 – Larmor-Plage 12

Le Palais: Vauban citadel ★ Northeast: 3,5 km.

La Désirade

rest,

Le Petit Cosquet – ✆ 02 97 31 70 70 – www.hotel-la-desirade.com – hotel-la-desirade@wanadoo.fr – Fax 02 97 31 89 63 – Open 29 March-3 November and 27 December-3 January

31 rm – €105/154 €125/168, €16 – 1 suite – ½ P €98/127

Rest *La Table* – *(closed for lunch during the week and school holidays)* Menu €30/51 – Carte €40/60

◆ This cluster of modern Breton style houses extends a warm welcome. Cosy interior and predominantly wood rooms with personal touches. Brand new wellness centre. Pleasant establishment serving up-to-the-minute recipes.

LE PALAIS – 56 Morbihan – pop. 2 537 – alt. 7 m – ✉ 56360

Paris 508 – Rennes 157 – Vannes 48 – Lorient 3 – Ploemeur 9

Citadelle Vauban (Vauban Citadel)★.

Citadelle Vauban

– *02 97 31 84 17 – www.citadellevauban.com – reception.vauban@leshotelsparticuliers.com – Fax 02 97 31 89 47 – Open April-5 October*

40 rm – €125/355 €125/355, €15 – 3 suites – ½ P €118/232

Rest *La Table du Gouverneur* – Menu €25 (lunch)/68 – Carte €45/85

◆ This hotel and museum that dominates the port is within the Vauban citadel and gardens. The Indian inspiration in the rooms, almost all of which face the sea, invites you to dream of travelling afar. Seafood cuisine served in an interior which combines 18C-19C paintings with a modern decor.

Le Clos Fleuri rest,

Sauzon road, at Bellevue – 02 97 31 45 45 – www.hotel-leclosfleuri.com – hotel-leclosfleuri@wanadoo.fr – Fax 02 97 31 45 57

20 rm – €77/140 €77/140, €10

Rest – *(dinner only) (residents only)* Menu €30

◆ On the heights of the town, this distinctive regional hotel offers small, smart rooms with country furniture and painted different colours. Set menu on a slate, served in the evenings to guests, changes daily.

Château de Bordenéo without rest

2 km Sauzon Bordenéo road north-westward – 02 97 31 80 77 – www.chateau-bordeneo.fr – chateaudebordeneo@wanadoo.fr – Fax 02 97 31 50 17

5 rm – €122/202 €134/214

◆ This elegant 19C gentleman's house is very restful and makes the most of its park planted with century-old trees. Each of the cosy rooms decorated in pastel shades has its own atmosphere.

L'Annexe

3 quai Yser – 02 97 31 81 53 – Fax 02 97 31 81 53 – Closed March, Monday and Tuesday from November to February and Wednesday

Rest – Carte €25/40

◆ A pleasant atmosphere reigns among the tightly packed tables. The service is fast and informal and the quality of the seafood beyond reproach. Wood fire grilled dishes.

PORT-GOULPHAR – 56 Morbihan – ✉ 56360 Bangor

Paris 517 – Rennes 166 – Vannes 57 – Auray 38 – Larmor-Plage 16

Site★: ≤★.

Castel Clara rest,

– *02 97 31 84 21 – www.castel-clara.com – contact@castel-clara.com – Fax 02 97 31 51 69 – Closed 12 January-13 February*

59 rm – €165/330 €165/330, €25 – 4 suites

Rest – *(dinner only)* Menu €95/160 – Carte €80/91

Rest *Le Buffet* – Menu (€65)

◆ An idyllic spot on the Wild Coast, a thalassotherapy centre, refined rooms with a panoramic view - discreet luxury at the end of the world! Elegant dining room and terrace with a view of the cliffs. Modern cuisine. Theme restaurant offering a buffet.

SAUZON – 56 Morbihan – pop. 860 – alt. 35 m – ✉ 56360

Paris 515 – Rennes 164 – Vannes 55 – Lorient 9 – Lanester 13

Site★ - Pointe des Poulains★★ : ✻★ 3 km northwest then 30 min - Port-Donnant: site★★ 6 km south then 30 min.

Hostellerie La Touline without rest

r. du Port-Vihan – 02 97 31 69 69 – www.hostellerielatouline.com – info@hostellerielatouline.com – Fax 02 97 31 66 00 – Open 15 March-12 November

5 rm – €110 €110, €13

◆ Attractive hamlet of small houses perched above the small harbour. The rooms are decorated according to different themes: Brittany, Zanzibar... Relaxing garden.

XX **Roz Avel**
r. du Lieutenant Riau, (behind the church) – ✆ 02 97 31 61 48
– Closed 11 November-15 December, 1st January-15 March and Wednesday
Rest – *(number of covers limited, pre-book)* Menu € 30/44 – Carte € 52/61
◆ A country house with Breton furniture in the dining room and a terrace with a small garden at one end. Excellent fish and seafood prepared with care.

X **Le Contre Quai**
r. St-Nicolas – ✆ 02 97 31 60 60 – lucien.coquant@wanadoo.fr
– Open 26 June-13 September and closed Sunday except July-August
Rest – *(dinner only)* Menu € 42 – Carte € 60/75
◆ Pleasant restaurant overlooking the picturesque harbour of Sauzon. Appetising 'surf n'turf' cuisine served in an attractive dining room with stylish nautical decor.

X **Café de la Cale**
Quai Guerveur – ✆ 02 97 31 65 74 – Open from April to end September, autumn half-term holidays, Christmas holidays and February holidays
Rest – *(pre-book)* Menu € 19 – Carte € 32/58
◆ An old sardine factory converted into a smart, fashionable bistro. Well known yachtsmen and tourists flock here to enjoy the appetising fish, shellfish and regional cuisine.

X **Les Embruns**
Le Quai – ✆ 02 97 31 64 78 – Fax 02 97 31 63 32 – Open 4 April-4 November
Rest – pancake rest. – Carte € 10/20
◆ One hundred percent organic sweet and savoury pancakes. From the flour and eggs to the fillings (salmon, etc). Built against the cliffs, the house and terrace face the port.

BELLÊME – 61 Orne – 310 M4 – pop. 1 576 – alt. 241 m – ✉ 61130 — 33 C3
Normandy

Paris 168 – Alençon 42 – La Ferté-Bernard 23 – Le Mans 55 – Mortagne-au-Perche 18

Office de tourisme, boulevard Bansard des Bois ✆ 02 33 73 09 69, Fax 02 33 83 95 17

De Bellême Saint-Martin Les Sablons, SW : 2 km, ✆ 02 33 73 12 79

Forest★.

Relais Saint-Louis — rm,
1 bd Bansard des Bois – ✆ 02 33 73 12 21 – www.relais-st-louis.com
– relais.st-louis@wanadoo.fr – Fax 02 33 83 71 19
– Closed 15-22 February and 12-30 November
9 rm – †€ 55/80 ††€ 60/85, ☕ € 7
Rest – Menu (€ 13), € 16 (weekdays)/44 – Carte € 25/38
◆ This well-renovated former post house is pleasingly romantic in style. Charming rooms with canopy- or four-poster beds; they are more modern at the annexe. In the restaurant lovely fireplace, collection of old tools and regionally focused cuisine.

in Nocé 8 km East by D 203 – **pop. 760** – **alt. 120 m** – ✉ **61340**

XX **Auberge des 3 J.**
– ✆ 02 33 73 41 03 – Fax 02 33 83 33 66 – Closed 15-30 September, 1st-15 January, Tuesday from September to June, Sunday dinner and Monday
Rest – Menu € 26/46
◆ Prettily laid tables and paintings in a rustic dining room where stone and wood dominate. Well-prepared food, both traditional and local dishes.

BELLEU – 02 Aisne – 306 C6 – see Soissons

BELLEVAUX – 74 Haute-Savoie – 328 M3 – pop. 1 344 – alt. 913 m — 46 F1
– Winter sports : 1 100/1 800 m 23 – ✉ 74470 French Alps

Paris 572 – Annecy 70 – Bonneville 29 – Genève 44 – Thonon-les-Bains 23

Office de tourisme, les Contamines ✆ 04 50 73 71 53, Fax 04 50 73 78 60

Site★.

La Cascade
– *04 50 73 70 22 – www.hotel-lacascade.com – hotelacascade@wanadoo.fr – Fax 04 50 73 77 46 – Closed 24 March-12 April and October*
11 rm – €38 €, €6 – ½ P €50
Rest – Menu (€12), €20 – Carte €17/29
◆ Modern building in the centre of the small resort. Spacious and bright rooms, all with balconies and views of the surrounding mountains. Very well-kept. Comfortable circular dining room with a rooftop terrace that offers a fine panoramic view.

Les Moineaux
Le Borgel – 04 50 73 71 11 – www.hotel-les-moineaux.com – info@hotel-les-moineaux.com – Fax 04 50 73 75 79 – Open 16 June-10 September and 20 December-10 April
14 rm – €50 €69 – ½ P €49/69 **Rest** – Menu (€19), €23/32
◆ Two chalet-type buildings at the bottom of the village. The functional rooms are equipped with balconies overlooking the mountains. Sober, regional décor, very well-kept. Simple restaurant with a modern setting, family-style cuisine with Savoy touches and a vegetarian set menu.

in Hirmentaz **7 km Southwest by D 26 and D 32 – 74470 Bellevaux**

Le Christania
Hirmentaz – 04 50 73 70 77 – www.hotel-christania.com – info@hotel-christania.com – Fax 04 50 73 76 08 – Open 1st June-15 September and 20 December-1st April
35 rm – €52/56 €56/58, €8 – ½ P €54/65
Rest – Menu (€15), €18/30 – Carte €26/38
◆ 1970s-style family hotel at the foot of the pistes. Rustic rooms, most with balconies; sloped ceilings in those on the top floor. Restaurant facing the pool and terrace. Regional cuisine and snack menu.

BELLEVILLE – 54 Meurthe-et-Moselle – 307 H6 – pop. 1 487 – alt. 190 m – 54940 — 26 B2

Paris 359 – Metz 42 – Nancy 19 – Pont-à-Mousson 14 – Toul 36

Le Bistroquet
97 rte Nationale – 03 83 24 90 12 – le-bistroquet@wanadoo.fr – Fax 03 83 24 04 01
Rest – *(number of covers limited, pre-book)* Menu €35, €54/69 – Carte €72/91
Spec. Foie gras de canard lorrain poêlé. Pigeon braisé en cocotte. Soufflé à la liqueur de mirabelle de Lorraine. **Wines** Gris de Toul, Pinot noir des Côtes de Toul.
◆ 1900-style dining room (mirrors, posters and chandeliers) behind a discreet façade. A flower-decked terrace and skilfully prepared classic food.

La Moselle
1 r. Prosper-Cabirol, (opposite the station) – 03 83 24 91 44 – www.restaurant-lamoselle.fr – lamoselle@wanadoo.fr – Fax 03 83 24 99 38 – Closed 17 August-2 September, 15 February-1st March, Sunday dinner, Tuesday dinner and Wednesday
Rest – Menu (€18 bi), €23 (weekdays)/53 – Carte €45/75
◆ The two dining rooms of this small family restaurant are separated by panels decorated with stained glass windows in the style of the School of Nancy. Lovely shady terrace.

BELLEVILLE – 69 Rhône – 327 H3 – pop. 5 840 – alt. 192 m – 69220 — 43 E1

Lyon - Rhone Valley

Paris 416 – Bourg-en-Bresse 43 – Lyon 45 – Mâcon 31 – Villefranche-sur-Saône 15

Office de tourisme, 27, rue du Moulin 04 74 66 44 67, Fax 04 74 06 43 56

L'Ange Couronné
18 r. de la République – 04 74 66 42 00 – www.angecouronne.com – angecouronne@wanadoo.fr – Fax 04 74 66 49 20 – Closed 24-28 May, 27 September-6 October, 4-26 January, Tuesday lunch, Sunday dinner and Monday
15 rm – €45 €50, €7 **Rest** – Menu (€12), €17/37 – Carte €33/39
◆ A former post house on the main road of Belleville. An atrium designed like a winter garden leads to simple, functional rooms. An attractively modern dining room where the focus is on traditional cuisine.

Le Beaujolais
40 r. Mar.-Foch, (near the station) – 04 74 66 05 31 – restaurant-le-beaujolais.com – postmaster@restaurant-le-beaujolais.com – Fax 04 74 07 90 46 – Closed 14-19 April, 2-26 August, 21-27 December, Sunday dinner, Tuesday dinner and Wednesday
Rest – Menu (€ 13), € 17 (weekday lunch), € 26/42 – Carte € 26/34
◆ A warm family inn near the station, recently refurbished. Friendly welcome and service. Traditional, generous cuisine. Nice local wines.

in Pizay 5 km Northwest by D 18 and D 69 – ✉ 69220 St-Jean-d'Ardières

Château de Pizay
– 04 74 66 51 41 – www.chateau-pizay.com – info@chateau-pizay.com – Fax 04 74 69 65 63 – Closed 18 December-4 January
62 rm – €235 €235, € 19 **Rest** – Menu € 47/71 – Carte € 62/80
◆ A beautiful 15C-17C château standing in the middle of the vineyards. Traditional rooms and more contemporary duplex suites in an outbuilding in the park. Superb spa. Enjoy the dining room that mixes old and new, a terrace in the main courtyard, and a classic menu.

BELLEY – 01 Ain – 328 H6 – pop. 8 466 – alt. 279 m – ✉ 01300 45 **C1**
Burgundy-Jura

Paris 507 – Aix-les-Bains 31 – Bourg-en-Bresse 83 – Chambéry 36 – Lyon 96
Office de tourisme, 34, Grande Rue 04 79 81 29 06, Fax 04 79 81 08 80
Choir★ of St-Jean cathedral - Framework★ of the château des Allymes.

Sweet Home
bd du Mail – 04 79 81 01 20 – www.sweethomehotel.com – info@sweethomehotel.com – Fax 04 79 81 53 83
35 rm – €50/65 €50/65, €8,50
Rest – *(Closed Saturday lunch and Sunday)* Menu € 15 bi (lunch)/18 – Carte approx. € 25
◆ A convenient hotel for an overnight stay in the town centre. Practical, modern rooms. Buffet breakfast. Black and white photos of actors adorn the walls. Concise, classic menu.

Southeast 3 km on Chambéry road – ✉ 01300 Belley

Auberge La Fine Fourchette
N 504 – 04 79 81 59 33 – Fax 04 79 81 55 43 – Closed 18 August-1st September, 23 December-2 January, Sunday dinner and Monday
Rest – Menu (€ 22), € 24/54 – Carte € 42/60
◆ A charming house overlooking the road, and facing the countryside and the Rhône Canal. The redecorated dining room's bay windows open onto a terrace. Classic cuisine.

in Contrevoz 9 km Northwest on D 32 – pop. 464 – alt. 320 m – ✉ 01300

Auberge de Contrevoz
– 04 79 81 82 54 – www.auberge-de-contrevoz.com – lauberge.de.contrevoz@orange.fr – Fax 04 79 81 80 17 – Closed Wednesday dinner, Sunday dinner and Monday
Rest – Menu € 25 (weekdays)/40
◆ A welcoming regional house decorated in a fitting rustic style. Generous portions of updated cuisine with a regional twist (seasonal theme menus, Bugey truffles).

in Pugieu 9 km northwest on D 1504 – pop. 126 – alt. 247 m – ✉ 01510

Le Moulin du Martinet
– 04 79 87 82 03 – www.moulindumartinet.fr – moulindumartinet@gmail.com – Fax 04 79 42 06 38 – Closed 10-20 March, 10-20 October, 2-12 January, Sunday dinner except July-August, Tuesday dinner and Wednesday
Rest – Menu € 13 (weekday lunch), € 17/48 – Carte € 29/47
◆ This appealing old mill (1825) offers a garden facing the mountain, with free-range ducks, a trout pool and pleasant terrace. Modern cuisine, with meals by the fireplace in winter.

BELVES – 24 Dordogne – 329 H7 – pop. 1 483 – alt. 175 m – ✉ 24170

Paris 552 – Bordeaux 197 – Périgueux 66 – Bergerac 56 – Villeneuve-sur-Lot 66

Office de tourisme, 1, rue des Filhols ✆ 05 53 29 10 20, Fax 05 53 29 10 20

Clément V without rest

15 r. J.-Manchotte – ✆ 05 53 28 68 80 – www.clement5.com – contact@clement5.com – Fax 05 53 28 14 21

10 rm – €95/120 €95/200, €12

◆ Situated in an isolated setting above the village, this charming house is well worth the detour for its original guestrooms with individual touches, its 11C vaulted cellars and its beautiful winter garden.

in Sagelat 2 km north by D 53 – pop. 325 – alt. 78 m – ✉ 24170

Auberge de la Nauze with rm rest,

Fongauffier – ✆ 05 53 28 44 81 – www.aubergedelanauze.fr – aubergedelanauze@wanadoo.fr – Fax 05 53 29 99 18 – Closed 20-29 June, 22 November-8 December, February holidays, Monday except dinner in July-August, Tuesday dinner and Saturday lunch from September to June

8 rm – €44/54 €50/60 – ½ P €38/48

Rest – Menu €14 (weekday lunch), €22/52 – Carte €30/64

◆ Appetising, traditional food is served in this stone, local-style house with a dining room offering exposed beams and leading onto a terrace. Pastel-toned rooms.

BENFELD – 67 Bas-Rhin – 315 J6 – pop. 5 315 – alt. 160 m – ✉ 67230

Alsace-Lorraine

Paris 502 – Colmar 41 – Obernai 17 – Sélestat 19 – Strasbourg 36

Office de tourisme, 3, rue de l'Église ✆ 03 88 74 04 02, Fax 03 88 58 10 45

Au Petit Rempart

1 r. du Petit-Rempart – ✆ 03 88 74 42 26 – www.petit-rempart.fr – Fax 03 88 74 18 58 – Closed 15 July-10 August, 8-20 February, 1st-6 March, Monday dinner, Tuesday dinner, Thursday dinner and Wednesday

Rest – Menu €10 (weekday lunch), €14/42 – Carte €30/45

◆ The main dining room offers a refined setting with wood carvings, coffer ceilings and Louis XIII-style chairs while the other houses a wine bar. Traditional menu.

BÉNODET – 29 Finistère – 308 G7 – pop. 3 159 – Casino – ✉ 29950 9 A2

Brittany

Paris 563 – Concarneau 19 – Fouesnant 8 – Pont-l'Abbé 13 – Quimper 17 – Quimperlé 47

Office de tourisme, 29, avenue de la Mer ✆ 02 98 57 00 14, Fax 02 98 57 23 00

18 de l'Odet Clohars Fouesnant, N : 4 km on D 34, ✆ 02 98 54 87 88

Pont de Cornouaille ≤★ - The Odet★★ by boat: 1h30.

Ker Moor

corniche de la Plage – ✆ 02 98 57 04 48 – www.kermoor.com – kermoor.hotel@wanadoo.fr – Fax 02 98 57 17 96 – Closed 18 December-8 January

69 rm – €80/140 €80/140, €10 – 15 suites – ½ P €66/95

Rest – *(open March to October)* Menu €33/77 – Carte €33/69

◆ Large 1930s building and annex (conference rooms and bar) in the middle of a wooded park. Modern rooms of various sizes and long-stay apartments. A dining room adorned with works by the artist Pierre de Belay and Sixties leatherette chairs.

Le Grand Hôtel Abbatiale rm,

4 av. Odet – ✆ 02 98 66 21 66 – www.hotelabbatiale.com – abbatiale.benodet@wanadoo.fr – Fax 02 98 66 21 50 – Closed 14-28 December

50 rm – €67/86 €77/98, €11 – ½ P €70/84

Rest – *(closed Saturday lunch)* Menu (€21), €23/31 – Carte €32/45

◆ This fully refurbished hotel's major advantage is its matchless location opposite the port of this Breton seaside resort. Practical rooms; some overlooking the ocean. Traditional cuisine and seafood.

Domaine de Kereven without rest
2 km Quimper road – 02 98 57 02 46 – www.kereven.com – domaine-de-kereven@wanadoo.fr – Fax 02 98 66 22 61 – Open 11 April-30 September
12 rm – €48/58 €64/75, €9
◆ In a rustic park, a new and regionally inspired, peaceful complex. Cosy rooms and guest cottages (gîtes). Breton furniture in the dining room where hot crêpes are served for breakfast.

Les Bains de Mer rest, VISA AE
11 r. Kerguelen – 02 98 57 03 41 – www.lesbainsdemer.com – accueilbainsdemer@lesbainsdemer.com – Fax 02 98 57 11 07 – Closed January
32 rm – €44/59 €52/74, €8,50 – ½ P €50/68
Rest – *(closed Saturday lunch, Tuesday lunch and Friday 1st October-Easter)*
Menu (€11), €13 (weekday lunch), €21/55 – Carte €27/46
◆ After a dip in the sea, you will enjoy your smart, modern room in this welcoming hotel, in the adopted town of yachtsman Eric Tabarly. A traditional restaurant decorated in contrasting tones, with green walls and plum-coloured curtains and chairs.

in Clohars-Fouesnant 3 km Northeast by D 34 and secondary road – pop. 1 899 – alt. 30 m – ✉ 29950

La Forge d'Antan VISA
31 rte de Nors Vraz – 02 98 54 84 00 – www.laforgedantan.monsite.orange.fr – laforgedantan2@wanadoo.fr – Fax 02 98 54 89 11 – Closed Monday and Tuesday
Rest – Menu €30 (weekday lunch), €39/65 – Carte €45/65
◆ An appealing countryside inn with two dining rooms: one decorated in an inviting rustic style, the other brighter, facing the garden. Classic fare, fish and shellfish.

in Ste-Marine 5 km West by pont de Cornouaille – ✉ 29120 Combrit

Villa Tri Men rm, VISA AE
16 r. du Phare – 02 98 51 94 94 – www.trimen.fr – contact@trimen.fr – Fax 02 98 51 95 50 – Closed 16 November-19 December and 4 January-5 February
20 rm – €115/280 €115/280, €14
Rest – *(closed Sunday and Monday except from 15 June to 15 September) (dinner only)* Menu €35 – Carte €45/70
◆ Lovely 1900 villa, nestling in a leafy, seaside garden. Elegant and understated rooms with modern furniture. Pleasant modern dining room and attractive terrace overlooking the estuary. Up-to-the-minute menu.

BÉNOUVILLE – 14 Calvados – 303 K4 – see Caen

BERCK-SUR-MER – 62 Pas-de-Calais – 301 C5 – pop. 14 800 – alt. 5 m 30 **A2**
– Casino – ✉ 62600 **Northern France and the Paris Region**

Paris 232 – Abbeville 48 – Arras 93 – Boulogne-sur-Mer 40 – Calais 83 – Montreuil 16

Office de tourisme, 5, avenue Francis Tattegrain 03 21 09 50 00, Fax 03 21 09 15 60

de Nampont Saint-Martin Nampont-Saint-Martin Maison Forte, 15 km on D 940 and D 901, 03 22 29 92 90

Parc d'attractions de Bagatelle (amusement park) ★ 5 km by ①.

in Berck-Plage – ✉ 62600

L'Impératrice rest, VISA
43 r. Division-Leclerc – 03 21 09 01 09 – www.limperatrice.com – hotel-imperatrice@wanadoo.fr – Fax 03 21 09 72 80
12 rm – €60/65 €60/77 – ½ P €80/85
Rest – *(dinner only) (residents only)* Menu €22/32
◆ Empress Eugenie inaugurated the first naval hospital here in Berck. Pleasant small and functional rooms. A colourful restaurant with a welcoming atmosphere, serving regional cuisine and seafood dishes.

XX **La Verrière**

pl. 18-Juin – ✆ 03 21 84 27 25 – nvincent@g-partouche.fr – Fax 03 21 84 14 65 – Closed 16-23 March, 16-23 November, Sunday dinner and Monday

Rest – Menu (€ 14 bi), € 21/53 – Carte approx. € 53

◆ Large modern, bright and well-kept restaurant dining room, in a former bus station converted into a casino, serving savoury contemporary cuisine.

BERGERAC – 24 Dordogne – 329 D6 – pop. 27 700 – alt. 37 m – ✉ 24100 Dordogne-Berry-Limousin 4 C1

Paris 534 – Agen 91 – Angoulême 110 – Bordeaux 94 – Périgueux 48

Bergerac-Roumanières: ✆ 05 53 22 25 25, 3 km on the ③

Office de tourisme, 97, rue Neuve d'Argenson ✆ 05 53 57 03 11, Fax 05 53 61 11 04

Château les Merles Mouleydier D 660, 15 km on the Sarlat road, ✆ 05 53 63 13 42

Old Bergerac★★: musée du Tabac★★ (maison Peyrarède★) - Musée du Vin, de la Batellerie et de la Tonnellerie★ M³.

Plan on following page

De France without rest

18 pl. Gambetta – ✆ 05 53 57 11 61 – www.hoteldefrance-bergerac.com – hoteldefrance15@wanadoo.fr – Fax 05 53 61 25 70 – Closed February AY **b**

20 rm – †€ 65/78 ††€ 65/78

◆ Opposite the shaded market square (Wednesdays and Saturdays), the De France has been fully refurbished. Simple rooms, quieter on the pool side.

Europ Hôtel without rest

20 r. Petit-Sol – ✆ 05 53 57 06 54 – http://www.europ-hotel-bergerac.com/ – europ.hotel.bergerac@wanadoo.fr – Fax 05 53 58 67 60 AY **v**

22 rm – †€ 43 ††€ 43/57, € 8

◆ The poolside garden is the best feature of this hotel near the railway station. Renovated, well-kept rooms with air-conditioning and double-glazing on the road side .

XX **L'Imparfait**

8 r. Fontaines – ✆ 05 53 57 47 92 – www.imparfait.com – sarl.lesfontaines@orange.fr – Closed 20 December-20 January, Sunday and Monday AZ **n**

Rest – Menu (€ 21 bi), € 28 (lunch), € 43/56 – Carte € 48/73

◆ This medieval house in the historic centre welcomes you to its large dining room where stones and exposed beams lend it character. Fine, traditional cuisine.

X **Le Repaire de Savinien**

15 r. Mounet-Sully – ✆ 05 53 24 35 46 – Closed 1st-7 September, 21-28 February, Monday from September to May, Sunday and bank holidays AY **e**

Rest – Carte € 31/41

◆ Bistro ambience two minutes from Notre Dame Church: tightly packed tables and a slate menu. Traditional dishes that vary with the seasons and market availability.

in St-Julien-de-Crempse 12 km by ①, N 21, D 107 and secondary road – pop. 182 – alt. 150 m – ✉ 24140

Manoir du Grand Vignoble

– ✆ 05 53 24 23 18 – www.manoirdugrandvignoble.com – grand-vignoble@orange.fr – Fax 05 53 24 20 89 – Open 21 March-11 November

44 rm – †€ 60/84 ††€ 82/112, € 11 – ½ P € 59/82

Rest – Menu € 24/47 – Carte € 30/50

◆ Peace and quiet in this 17C manor set in the heart of the grounds, which is also home to a riding centre. The rooms in the main house are old, with more modern ones in the outbuildings. A rustic restaurant with a veranda and terrace that overlooks the park. Regional cuisine.

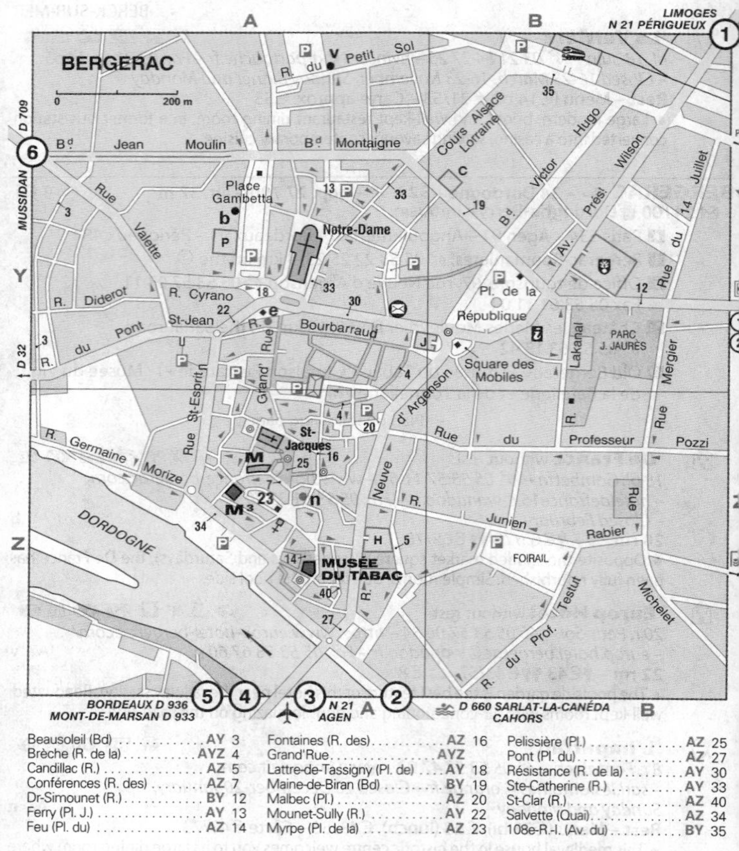

Beausoleil (Bd)	AY	3	Fontaines (R. des)	AZ	16	Pelissière (Pl.)	AZ	25
Brèche (R. de la)	AYZ	4	Grand'Rue	AYZ		Pont (Pl. du)	AZ	27
Candillac (R.)	AZ	5	Lattre-de-Tassigny (Pl. de)	AY	18	Résistance (R. de la)	AY	30
Conférences (R. des)	AZ	7	Maine-de-Biran (Bd)	BY	19	Ste-Catherine (R.)	AY	33
Dr-Simounet (R.)	BY	12	Malbec (Pl.)	AZ	20	St-Clar (R.)	AZ	40
Ferry (Pl. J.)	AY	13	Mounet-Sully (R.)	AY	22	Salvette (Quai)	AZ	34
Feu (Pl. du)	AZ	14	Myrpe (Pl. de la)	AZ	23	108e-R.-I. (Av. du)	BY	35

in St-Nexans 10 km via ③, N 21 and D 19 – pop. 802 – alt. 120 m – ✉ 24520

La Chartreuse du Bignac

Le Bignac – ☎ 05 53 22 12 80 – www.abignac.com – info@abignac.com – Fax 05 53 22 12 81 – Closed January

12 rm – †€ 145/155 ††€ 145/185, ☕ € 17 – 1 suite – ½ P € 130/149

Rest – *(closed Tuesday) (dinner only) (residents only)* Menu € 40 – Carte € 25/45

◆ This charterhouse is located in 12h of parkland with a dovecote, water feature and fishing pond. Its huge, elegant rooms combine old and new details; two of them occupy the former wine store. Family food and wine bar.

at Moulin de Malfourat 8 km by ④, dir. Mont-de-Marsan and secondary road – ✉ 24240 Monbazillac

La Tour des Vents

– ☎ 05 53 58 30 10 – www.tourdesvents.com – moulin.malfourat@wanadoo.fr – Fax 05 53 58 89 55 – Closed one week in October, January, Sunday dinner and Tuesday lunch except July-August and Monday

Rest – Menu € 27 – Carte € 40/62

◆ This restaurant built by the ruins of a 15C windmill, serves inventive cuisine washed down with a fine choice of Bergerac wines. Stunning view of the Monbazillac vineyards and a pleasant terrace.

in Rauly 8 km by ④, dir. Mont-de-Marsan and secondary road – ✉ 24240 Monbazillac

Château Rauly-Saulieut without rest VISA MC
Le Rauly – ✆ 05 53 24 92 55 – www.perigord-residences-privees.eu – normanthies@wanadoo.fr – Fax 05 53 57 80 87 – Open 16 February-1st November
5 rm – †€ 105 ††€ 125/160, ☕ € 13 – 10 suites – ††€ 160/185
◆ Peace and quiet are guaranteed in this 19C château, surrounded by a park and vineyards. Tastefully decorated and well- proportioned apartments and suites. Pool and sauna.

Good food and accommodation at moderate prices?
Look for the Bib symbols: red Bib Gourmand for food, blue Bib Hotel for hotels.

BERGÈRES-LÈS-VERTUS – **51 Marne** – **306** F9 – **see Vertus**

BERGHEIM – 68 Haut-Rhin – 315 I7 – pop. 1 850 – alt. 235 m – ✉ 68750 Alsace-Lorraine

2 **C2**

Paris 449 – Colmar 18 – Ribeauvillé 4 – Sélestat 11

XX **La Bacchante** with rm AC P VISA MC AE
Grand Rue – ✆ 03 89 73 31 15 – www.cheznorbert.com – labacchante@wanadoo.fr – Fax 03 89 73 60 65 – Closed 2-9 July, 12-20 November, 5-21 January
12 rm – †€ 60 ††€ 80/115, ☕ € 15
Rest – *(closed Wednesday lunch, Friday lunch and Thursday)* Menu € 22 (weekday lunch), € 28/49 – Carte € 29/41
◆ This former winery sports a rustic decor full of character. Pretty terrace in an inner courtyard. Cuisine based on local produce with dishes of the day.

X **Wistub du Sommelier** VISA MC
51 grand rue – ✆ 03 89 73 69 99 – www.wistub-du-sommelier.com – info@wistub-du-sommelier.com – Fax 03 89 73 36 58 – Closed 15-31 July, February holidays, Sunday dinner, Tuesday dinner and Wednesday
Rest – Menu € 21 (weekdays), € 28/58 bi – Carte € 29/48
◆ 19C parquet floor and bar, wainscoting and an earthenware stove: a pleasant but modernized Winstub decor lies behind this pretty Alsatian façade. Tasty locally sourced dishes.

BERGUES – 59 Nord – 302 C2 – pop. 3 923 – alt. 4 m – ✉ 59380 Northern France and the Paris Region

30 **B1**

Paris 279 – Calais 52 – Dunkerque 9 – Hazebrouck 34 – Lille 65 – St-Omer 31
Office de tourisme, Place Henri Billiaert ✆ 03 28 68 71 06, Fax 03 28 68 71 06
Hondschoote Crown ★.

Au Tonnelier P VISA MC AE
4 r. Mont-de-Piété, (near the church) – ✆ 03 28 68 70 05 – www.autonnelier.com – contact@autonnelier.com – Fax 03 28 68 21 87 – Closed 20 December-4 January
25 rm – †€ 48 ††€ 58, ☕ € 11
Rest – *(closed Sunday dinner)* Menu (€ 12), € 16 (weekday lunch), € 18/30 – Carte € 27/39
◆ In the town whose fortifications were the work of Vauban, find this small family hotel in a brick house with a profusion of flowers. Practical rooms. An inviting dining room (wood panelling and bistro furniture) serving traditional cuisine.

XXX **Cornet d'Or** VISA MC
26 r. Espagnole – ✆ 03 28 68 66 27 – Closed Sunday dinner and Monday
Rest – Menu € 29/41 – Carte approx. € 55
◆ Restaurant with an appealing Flemish façade and an elegant bourgeois dining room. Good simple produce takes pride of place in the generous menu of traditional fare.

BERMICOURT – 62 Pas-de-Calais – **301** G5 – **pop. 152** – **alt. 118 m** – ✉ 62130 30 **B2**

Paris 234 – Lille 100 – Arras 50 – Lens 61 – Liévin 58

La Cour de Rémi rm, VISA

1 r. Baillet – ✆ 03 21 03 33 33 – www.lacourderemi.com – sebastien@lacourderemi.com – Closed 14 January-3 February

8 rm – †€ 80 ††€ 80/130, ☕ € 10

Rest – *(Closed Saturday lunch, Sunday dinner and Monday)*
Menu € 18 (weekday lunch), € 29/34 – Carte € 33/45

◆ Charming hotel incorporating the outbuildings of a country château. Friendly service and cosy rooms with a personal touch. Enjoy modern cuisine in a bright and uncluttered contemporary style dining room, or outdoors. Daily specials on the board.

BERNAY – 27 Eure – **304** D7 – **pop. 10 600** – **alt. 105 m** – ✉ **27300** 33 **C2**
Normandy

Paris 155 – Argentan 69 – Évreux 49 – Le Havre 72 – Louviers 52 – Rouen 60

Syndicat d'initiative, 29, rue Thiers ✆ 02 32 43 32 08, Fax 02 32 45 82 68

Boulevard des Monts★.

Acropole Hôtel without rest VISA AE

10 rue Grande Malouve, 3 km south-west on Broglie road(D 438) – ✆ 02 32 46 06 06 – www.hotel-acropole.com – acropolehotel@wanadoo.fr – Fax 02 32 44 01 04

51 rm – †€ 56/66 ††€ 56/66, ☕ € 8

◆ Just outside the shopping area, an establishment with above all practical accommodation. Soundproofing and facilities useful for a restful stop or business stay.

Hostellerie du Moulin Fouret VISA

3.5 km southward along the St-Quentin-des-Isles road – ✆ 02 32 43 19 95 – www.moulin-fouret.com – lemoulinfouret@wanadoo.fr – Fax 02 32 45 55 50 – Closed Sunday dinner and Monday except July-August

Rest – Menu (€ 28), € 41/56 – Carte € 65/80

◆ Elegant dining room opening onto the bar which contains the old workings of this converted mill. The peaceful terrace leads into a riverside flower garden. Modern menu.

LA BERNERIE-EN-RETZ – 44 Loire-Atlantique – **316** D5 – **pop. 2 499** – **alt. 24 m** – ✉ **44760** 34 **A2**

Paris 434 – Nantes 46 – Saint-Nazaire 38 – Saint-Herblain 46 – Rezé 43

Office de tourisme, 3, chaussée du Pays de Retz ✆ 02 40 82 70 99, Fax 02 51 74 61 40

L'Artimon A/C VISA

17 r. J. du Plessis – ✆ 02 51 74 61 60 – Closed Sunday dinner, Tuesday and Wednesday from September to June and Monday

Rest – *(number of covers limited, pre-book)* Menu € 18 (weekday lunch), € 26/34

◆ Well located on the market square. The restrained interior of wood and murals by a local artist pays homage to the sea. Unusual menu in a contemporary spirit.

BERNEUIL-SUR-AISNE – 60 Oise – **305** J4 – **pop. 998** – **alt. 45 m** – ✉ 60350 37 **C2**

Paris 107 – Amiens 97 – Compiègne 17 – Creil 55

Le Manoir de Rochefort without rest

– ✆ 03 44 85 81 78 – www.domainederochefort.fr – rochefort1@orange.fr – Fax 03 44 85 81 78 – Closed 1st January-15 March

4 rm ☕ – †€ 75 ††€ 85

◆ The former chapel (17C) of this manor houses understated and elegant rooms, all with a garden terraces. The nearby forest and quiet atmosphere are added attractions.

BERNEX – 74 Haute-Savoie – **328** N2 – **pop. 1 178** – **alt. 955 m** – **Winter sports : 1 000/2 000 m** 13 – ✉ **74500** French Alps 46 **F1**

Paris 590 – Annecy 97 – Évian-les-Bains 10 – Morzine 32 – Thonon-les-Bains 20

Office de tourisme, le Clos du Moulin ✆ 04 50 73 60 72, Fax 04 50 73 16 17

 **Chez Tante Marie** rm, VISA AE

– ✆ 04 50 73 60 35 – *www.chez-tante-marie.com – chez-tante-marie@wanadoo.fr – Fax 04 50 73 61 73 – Closed 23 March-11 April and 15 October-20 December*

27 rm – €65/75 €78/85, € 10 – ½ P € 70/85

Rest – *(closed Sunday dinner off school holidays)* Menu (€ 15), € 21 (weekdays)/39 – Carte € 23/45

◆ Nestled in the Alps, this hotel has a warm family atmosphere. The somewhat faded, rustically furnished rooms command a fine view of the peaks and the meadow-garden. Countrified dining room and panoramic terrace; classic and regional cuisine.

in La Beunaz 1,5 km Northwest by D 52 – ✉74500 Bernex – alt. 1 000 m

Bois Joli VISA AE

Saint Paul – ✆ 04 50 73 60 11 – info@hotel-bois-joli.fr – hboisjoli@wanadoo.fr – Fax 04 50 73 65 28 – Open 11 April-16-October and 18 December-15 March

29 rm – €60/72 €74/90, € 10 – ½ P € 62/72

Rest – *(closed Sunday dinner and Wednesday)* Menu € 26/48 – Carte € 42/59

◆ A smart chalet amid a sea of greenery. Quiet rooms decorated in Alpine style with balconies facing the Dent d'Oche or Mount Billiat. Fully equipped relaxation centre. Dining room with wood-panelling and a summer terrace, both with beautiful views.

BERNIÈRES-SUR-MER – 14 Calvados – 303 J4 – pop. 2 373 — 32 B2

– ✉ 14990 Normandy

Paris 252 – Caen 20 – Hérouville-Saint-Clair 21 – Le Havre 107

Syndicat d'initiative, 159, rue Victor Tesnières ✆ 02 31 96 44 02, Fax 02 31 96 98 96

L'As de Trèfle VISA AE

420 r. L.-Hettier – ✆ 02 31 97 22 60 – asdetrefle3@wanadoo.fr – Fax 02 31 97 22 60 – Closed 6 January-10 February, Tuesday except July-August and Monday

Rest – Menu € 22 (weekdays)/39 – Carte € 35/62

◆ Not far from the coast, this 1934 house has a Moorish influence. Still lives adorn the dining room, which specialises in traditional seafood dishes (locally fished).

BERNOS-BEAULAC – 33 Gironde – 335 J8 – see Bazas

BERRIC – 56 Morbihan – 308 P9 – pop. 1 428 – alt. 65 m – ✉ 56230 — 10 C3

Paris 474 – Rennes 113 – Vannes 24 – Saint-Nazaire 73

Le Moulin du Bois VISA

3 km north-east on D 7 (Questembert road) – ✆ 02 97 67 04 44 – www.moulindubois.com – tgoujon@wanadoo.fr – Fax 02 97 67 06 79

3 rm – €84/104 €90/110 **Table d'hôte** – Menu € 40 bi/50 bi

◆ This old house on the hillside is home to tastefully decorated attractive rooms. Ideal for nature lovers (nearby forest and lake).

BERRWILLER – 68 Haut-Rhin – 315 H9 – pop. 1 058 – alt. 260 m — 1 A3

– ✉ 68500

Paris 467 – Belfort 45 – Colmar 31 – Épinal 99 – Guebwiller 9 – Mulhouse 20

L'Arbre Vert VISA

96 r. Principale – ✆ 03 89 76 73 19 – www.restaurant-koenig.com – rest.koenig.arbrevert@wanadoo.fr – Fax 03 89 76 73 68 – Closed 6-26 July, Sunday dinner and Monday

Rest – Menu (€ 12), € 21 (weekdays)/46 – Carte € 30/59

◆ This charming flower-decked inn serves delicious regional food served in an elegant, contemporary-style dining room. Daily specials also available in the bistro.

BERRY-AU-BAC – **02 Aisne** – **306** F6 – **pop. 521** – **alt. 62 m** – ✉ **02190** 37 **D2**

Paris 161 – Laon 30 – Reims 21 – Rethel 46 – Soissons 48 – Vouziers 66

XX **La Cote 108**

– ✆ 03 23 79 95 04 – www.lacote108.com – lacote108@orange.fr – Closed 26 July-11 August, 20 December-5 January, Sunday dinner, Monday and Tuesday

Rest – *(pre-book on weekend)* Menu (€ 21), € 28/62 – Carte € 49/64

◆ A gourmet break facing Hill 108: this roadside restaurant serves modern cuisine in a refined, contemporary setting. Flower garden.

BERRY-BOUY – **18 Cher** – **323** J4 – **pop. 934** – **alt. 136 m** – ✉ **18500** 12 **C3**

Paris 238 – Orléans 112 – Bourges 9 – Vierzon 27 – Issoudun 41

L'Ermitage without rest

– ✆ 02 48 26 87 46 – www.hotes-ermitage.com – domaine-ermitage@wanadoo.fr – Fax 02 48 26 03 28 – Closed mid November-early January

5 rm – €50/53 €65/68

◆ Set in grounds planted with century-old trees, this wine estate extends a friendly welcome (wine tasting) to guests. Tastefully personalised rooms.

BERZE-LA-VILLE – **71 Saône-et-Loire** – **320** I11 – **pop. 519** – **alt. 350 m** – ✉ **71960** Burgundy-Jura 8 **C3**

Paris 408 – Mâcon 13 – Charolles 47 – Cluny 13 – Roanne 85

in la Croix-Blanche 2 km West – ✉ 71960

XX **Le Relais du Mâconnais**

lieu-dit la Croix Blanche, D 17 – ✆ 03 85 36 60 72 – www.lannuel.com – resa@lannuel.com – Fax 03 85 36 65 47 – Closed January, Sunday dinner and Monday

Rest – Menu € 28/60 bi – Carte € 48/57

◆ Fine, regional style house in the town centre. Contemporary cuisine served in a modern dining room decorated in tones of brown and sea green.

BESANÇON P – **25 Doubs** – **321** G3 – **pop. 116 100** – **Built-up area 134 376** – **alt. 250 m** – **Casino** BY – ✉ **25000** Burgundy-Jura 16 **B2**

Paris 405 – Basel 167 – Bern 180 – Dijon 91 – Lyon 225 – Nancy 204

Office de tourisme, 2, place de la 1ère Armée Française ✆ 03 81 80 92 55, Fax 03 81 80 58 30

de Besançon Mamirolle La Chevillotte, E : 13 km on N 57, D 464 and D 104, ✆ 03 81 55 73 54

Site★★★ - Citadel★★: musée d'Histoire naturelle★ **M³**, musée comtois★ **M²**, musée de la Résistance et de la Déportation★ **M⁴** - Old town★★ ABYZ : Palais Granvelle★, cathedral★ (Virgins with Saints★), astronomical clock★, façades of 17C houses.★ - Prefecture★ AZ **P** - Bibliothèque municipale (Municipal library)★ BZ **B** - Gate★ of St-Jacques hospital AZ - Musée des Beaux-Arts et d'Archéologie★★.

Plans on following pages

Mercure Parc Micaud

3 av. Ed.-Droz – ✆ 03 81 40 34 34 – www.mercure.com – h1220@accor.com – Fax 03 81 40 34 39 BY **d**

91 rm – €85/148 €95/158, € 15

Rest – *(closed Saturday lunch and Sunday lunch)* Carte € 30/50

◆ This hotel benefits from a lovely location facing the Doubs, near the old town where Victor Hugo was born in 1802. Renovated rooms catering for business travellers. This contemporary-style restaurant, decorated on the theme of time, has a view of the casino gardens.

Charles Quint without rest

3 r. Chapitre – ✆ 03 81 82 05 49 – www.hotel-charlesquint.com – hotel-charlesquint@wanadoo.fr – Fax 03 81 82 61 45 – Closed 19-25 April and 22-28 February BZ **f**

9 rm – €89 €145, € 12

◆ Successful renovation has brought a shine back to this noble 18C residence. The rooms decorated with wood panelling and mouldings overlook the cathedral or the garden.

BESANÇON

Allende (Bd S.) . . . . AX 2
Belfort (R. de) . . . . BX
Brulard (R. Gén.) . . . . AX 5
Carnot (Av.) . . . . BX 7
Chaillot (R. de) . . . . BX 12
Clemenceau (Av. Georges) . AX 15
Clerc (R. F.) . . . . BX 16
Fontaine-Argent (Av.) . . . . BX 19
Jouchoux (R. A.) . . . . AX 25
Lagrange (Av. Léo) . . . . AX 27
Montrapon (Av. de) . . . . AX 34
Observatoire (Av. de l') . . . . . AX 35
Ouest (Bd) . . . . AX 37
Paix (Av. de la) . . . . BX 38
Vaite (R. de la) . . . . BX 55
Voirin (R.) . . . . BX 57

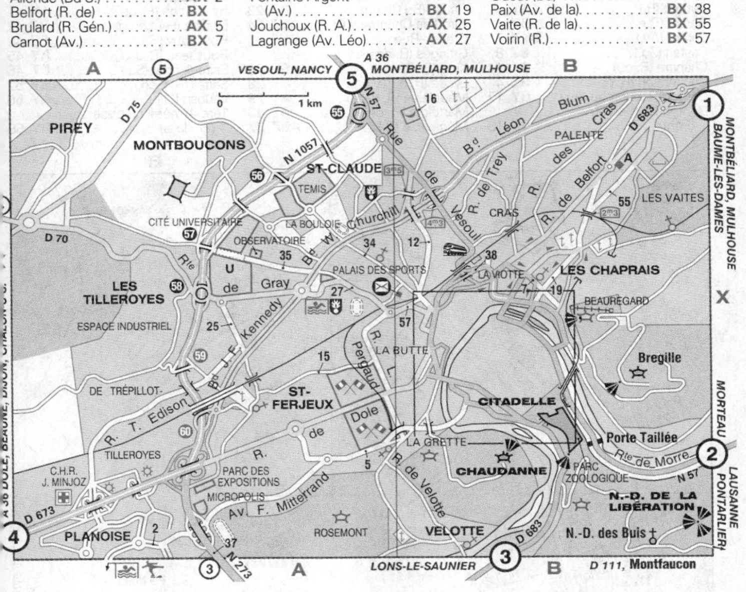

Ibis La City

1 av. Louise-Michel – ✆ 03 81 85 11 70 – www.ibishotel.com – h3297@accor.com – Fax 03 81 85 11 77 AZ **m**

119 rm – €54/76 €54/76, €8

Rest – Menu (€18), €22/34 – Carte €21/60

◆ Unusual, futuristic vessel anchored to a bank of the Doubs river. The rooms, decorated in line with the chain's standards, prove to be more spacious that those of many Ibis hotels. Brasserie food (seafood and sauerkraut specialities) served under a 1900-style glass roof or on the terrace.

Ibis Centre without rest

21 r. Gambetta – ✆ 03 81 81 02 02 – www.ibishotel.com – H1364@accor.com – Fax 03 81 81 89 65 BY **k**

49 rm – €55/78 €55/78, €8

◆ This freestone industrial building is a former 19C watch hand factory. Rooms are in line with Ibis standards and there is a contemporary breakfast room.

Hôtel du Nord without rest

8 r. Moncey – ✆ 03 81 81 34 56 – www.hotel-du-nord-besancon.com – hoteldunord3@wanadoo.fr – Fax 03 81 81 85 96 BY **r**

44 rm – €42/47 €54/62, €7

◆ Leave your car in the garage and discover the old town on foot from this very central 19C building. Practical and soundproofed rooms. Considerate service.

Le Manège

2 fg Rivotte – ✆ 03 81 48 01 48 – www.restaurant-le-manege.fr – restaurant-le-manege@wanadoo.fr – Fax 03 81 82 74 50 – Closed 3-17 August, Saturday lunch, Sunday dinner and Monday BZ **u**

Rest – Menu (€16), €26/51 – Carte €47/71

◆ This former military stables office, situated at the foot of the citadel, has been given a new lease of life with contemporary decor, equestrian photos and engravings plus traditional, well-presented dishes.

BESANÇON

Battant (Pont) . . . . AY 3
Battant (R.) . . . . AY
Bersot (R.) . . . . BY
Carnot (Av.) . . . . BYX 7
Castan (Sq.) . . . . BZ 8
Chapitre (R. du) . . . . BZ 14
Convention (R. de la) . . . . . . BZ 4
Denfert-Rochereau (Av.) . . . . BY 17
Denfert-Rochereau (Pont) . . . . BY 18
Fusillés-de-la-Résistance (R. des) . . . . BZ 20
Gambetta (R.) . . . . ABY 21
Gare-d'eau (Av. de la) . . . . . . AZ 22
Gaulle (Bd Ch.de) . . . . AZ 23
Girod-de-Chantrans (R.) . . . AYZ 24
Grande-Rue . . . . ABYZ
Granges (R. des) . . . . ABY
Krug (R. Ch.) . . . . BY 26
Lycée (R. du) . . . . AY 28
Madeleine (R. de la) . . . . AY 29
Martelots (Pl. des) . . . . BZ 30
Mégevand (R.) . . . . ABZ 32
Moncey (R.) . . . . BY 33
Orme-de-Chamars (R. de l') . AZ 36
Pouillet (R. C.) . . . . AY 39
République (R. de la) . . . . . ABY 40
Révolution (Pl. de la) . . . . . . AY 41
Rivotte (Faubourg) . . . . BZ 42
Ronchaux (R.) . . . . BZ 43
Rousseau (R. J. J.) . . . . AY 45
Saint-Amour (Sq.) . . . . BY 48
Sarrail (R. Gén.) . . . . ABY 52
Vauban (Q.) . . . . AY 56
1ère-Armée-Française (Pl. de la) . . . . BY 58

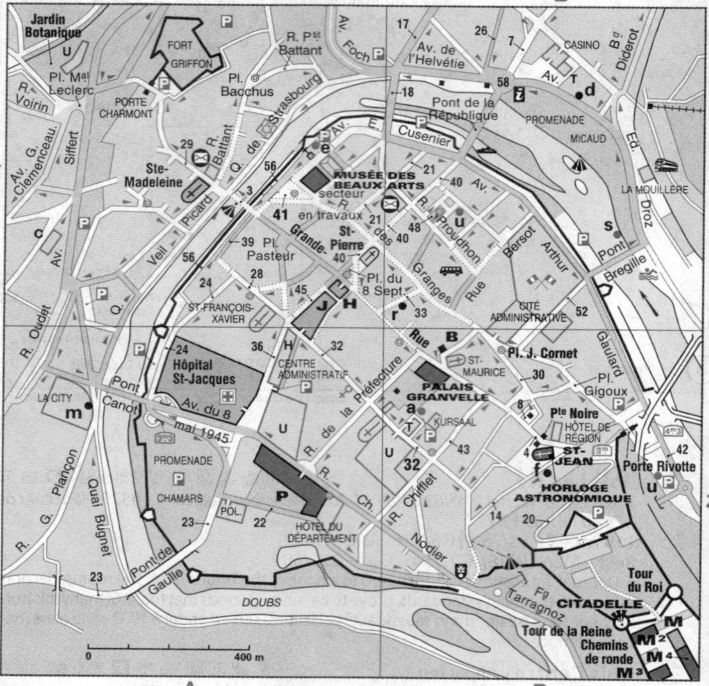

XX Le Poker d'As

AC VISA MC AE

14 square St-Amour – ☎ 03 81 81 42 49 – Fax 03 81 81 05 59 – Closed 12 July-11 August, Christmas holidays, Sunday dinner and Monday BY **u**

Rest – Menu € 19/49 – Carte € 30/60

◆ Completely family run business: the young chef creates traditional and regional dishes, served in a rustic dining room decorated with wood sculptures created by his grandfather.

XX Le Chaland

AC VISA MC AE

promenade Micaud, near Bregille bridge – ☎ 03 81 80 61 61 – www.chaland.com – chaland@chaland.com – Fax 03 81 88 67 42 – Closed Saturday lunch and Sunday dinner BY **s**

Rest – Menu € 17 (lunch)/35

◆ Barge from 1904, converted into a restaurant in the 1960s. The rocking of passing boats makes for a lively meal on the Doubs. Classic and regional cuisine.

XX **Christophe Menozzi** VISA MC AE

11 r. Jean-Petit – ✆ 03 81 81 28 01 – menozzi.christophe@orange.fr – Fax 03 81 83 36 97 – Closed three weeks in August, one week in January, Sunday, Monday and bank holidays AY e

Rest – Menu (€ 17), € 22/52 bi – Carte € 35/48

◆ Housed in an old, regional-style building, this restaurant, run by Christophe Menozzi, serves local cuisine accompanied by a good choice of wines.

in Chalezeule 5,5 km by ① and D 217 – pop. 1 054 – alt. 252 m – ✉ 25220

Les Trois Îles rest, P VISA MC AE

1 r. des Vergers – ✆ 03 81 61 00 66 – www.hoteldes3iles.com – hotel.3iles@wanadoo.fr – Fax 03 81 61 73 09 – Closed 26 December-8 January

17 rm – †€ 56/80 ††€ 56/80, ☕ € 8 – ½ P € 56/70

Rest – *(closed 23 December-10 January) (dinner only)* Menu € 20

◆ Family-run establishment renowned for its calm and green surroundings. Opt for one of the five Club Rooms, which are slightly more spacious and comfortable than the others. Single daily set menu served in a veranda-dining room decorated in southern style colours.

in Montfaucon 9 km by ②, D 464 and D 146 – pop. 1 372 – alt. 491 m – ✉ 25660

XX **La Cheminée** P VISA MC

Belvédère road – ✆ 03 81 81 17 48 – restaurantlacheminee@wanadoo.fr – Fax 03 81 82 86 45 – Closed 15 February-8 March, 27 July-10 August, Sunday dinner, Tuesday lunch and Monday

Rest – Menu € 22 (weekdays)/50 – Carte € 45/80

◆ You will willingly linger in this restaurant, seduced by its pretty rustic dining rooms (one with a view of the pine trees), its classic and regional dishes, and its cosy lounge-fireplace.

in Champvans-les-Moulins 8 km by ④ On D 70 – pop. 319 – alt. 252 m – ✉ 25170

X **La Source** P VISA MC AE

4 r. des Sources – ✆ 03 81 59 90 57 – www.lasource-besancon.com – lasource.ch@wanadoo.fr – Fax 03 81 59 09 39 – Fermé31 August-9 September, 28 December-18 January, Wednesday dinner except from June to August, Sunday dinner and Monday

Rest – Menu € 17 (weekday lunch), € 23/35 – Carte € 36/55

◆ Modern building with a garden and its pond. Traditional and local dishes served in a dining room with overhead exposed beams or on the terrace.

in Geneuille 13 km by ⑤, N 57 and D 1 – pop. 1 225 – alt. 220 m – ✉ 25870

Château de la Dame Blanche P VISA MC AE

1 chemin de la Goulotte – ✆ 03 81 57 64 64 – www.chateau-de-la-dame-blanche.com – contact@chateau-de-la-dame-blanche.fr – Fax 03 81 57 65 70 – Closed Sunday dinner

26 rm – †€ 95/147 ††€ 112/164, ☕ € 12 – 2 suites

Rest – *(closed Sunday dinner and Monday)* Menu (€ 25), € 39/89 – Carte € 64/80

◆ Large mansion with elegant personalised rooms in the heart of an English style park. Simpler and more modern rooms in the annexe. Traditional food to be enjoyed under the moulded ceilings and crystal chandeliers of the pleasant dining rooms.

BESSANS – 73 Savoie – 333 O6 – pop. 311 – alt. 1 730 m – Winter sports : 1 750/2 050 m 4 – ✉ 73480 French Alps 45 D2

Paris 698 – Albertville 125 – Chambéry 138 – Lanslebourg-Mont-Cenis 13 – Val-d'Isère 41

Office de tourisme, rue Maison Morte ✆ 04 79 05 96 52, Fax 04 79 05 83 11

Paintings★ of St-Antoine chapel.

Avérole Valley ★★.

Le Mont-Iseran rest, VISA MC

pl. de la Mairie – ✆ 04 79 05 95 97 – www.montiseran.com – Fax 04 79 05 84 67 – Open 20 June-25 September and 15 December-10 April

19 rm – †€ 32/75 ††€ 32/75, ☕ € 7 – ½ P € 52/75

Rest – Menu (€ 12), € 12/45 – Carte € 24/45

◆ In the centre of the village and near the slopes, a chalet with regularly renovated rooms, often with balcony. Bar-tea salon. Dining room decorated with painted wainscoting and a statuette of the mythical "devil of Bessans"; classic cuisine.

LE BESSAT – 42 Loire – 327 G7 – pop. 439 – alt. 1 170 m – Winter sports : 1 170/1 427 m – ✉ 42660 — 44 B2

Paris 530 – Annonay 29 – St-Chamond 19 – St-Étienne 19 – Yssingeaux 65

Syndicat d'initiative, Maison Communale ☎ 04 77 20 43 76, Fax 04 77 20 46 10

La Fondue "Chez l'Père Charles" with rm

Gde-rue – ☎ 04 77 20 40 09 – Fax 04 77 20 45 20 – Open 16 March-14 November and closed Sunday dinner and Monday lunch except school holidays

8 rm – †€ 45 ††€ 55, ☕ € 8 – ½ P € 65

Rest – Menu € 15 (weekdays), € 23/52 – Carte € 46/68

◆ Countrified dining rooms in this inn situated in the centre of the village. Tasty, traditional cuisine with a regional touch. Simple bedrooms.

BESSE-ET-ST-ANASTAISE – 63 Puy-de-Dôme – 326 E9 – pop. 1 632 – alt. 1 050 m – Winter sports : to Super Besse – ✉ 63610 Auvergne — 5 B2

Paris 462 – Clermont-Ferrand 46 – Condat 28 – Issoire 30 – Le Mont-Dore 25

Office de tourisme, place du Dr Pipet ☎ 04 73 79 52 84, Fax 04 73 79 52 08

St-André church ★ - Rue de la Boucherie★ - Town gate★ - Pavin lake ★★ ≤★ and Puy de Montchal★★ ✳★★ Southwest: 4 km by D 978.

Les Mouflons

VISA MC AE

Berthelage – ☎ 04 73 79 56 93 – www.hotel-mouflons-besse.com – info@hotel-mouflons-besse.com – Fax 04 73 79 51 18 – Closed 15 November-15 December

51 rm – †€ 40/75 ††€ 40/80, ☕ € 8,50 – ½ P € 50/62

Rest – *(closed lunch except weekends)* Menu € 20

◆ Imposing 1970s building with chalet features. Choose one of the renovated rooms. The others are simpler and slightly antiquated. A spacious restaurant partitioned by sections of lava stone. Regional cuisine.

La Gazelle

≤ VISA MC

Compains road – ☎ 04 73 79 50 26 – www.lagazelle.fr – Fax 04 73 79 89 03 – Closed 16 March-24 April and 16 October-17 December

35 rm – †€ 58/69 ††€ 58/69, ☕ € 8,50 – ½ P € 56/63

Rest – *(dinner only)* Menu € 19

◆ From its imposing location, this hotel enjoys a splendid view of medieval Besse. Guestrooms decorated in Alpine style. Breakfast served on the veranda. Traditional cuisine served in a simply furnished dining room with a superb view.

Hostellerie du Beffroy with rm

VISA MC AE

26 r. Abbé-Blot – ☎ 04 73 79 50 08 – www.lebeffroy.com – lebeffroy@orange.fr – Fax 04 73 79 57 87 – Closed 20 December-12 April (except hotel), Tuesday lunch, Monday dinner from September to June and Monday lunch

12 rm – †€ 52/67 ††€ 56/120, ☕ € 12 – ½ P € 66/90

Rest – *(pre-book on weekend)* Menu € 35, € 39/67 – Carte € 50/60

◆ This 15C house was a former belfry keepers' residence. It has two rustic dining rooms with furniture polished by the ages. Contemporary cuisine.

BESSINES-SUR-GARTEMPE – 87 Haute-Vienne – 325 F4 – pop. 2 885 – alt. 335 m – ✉ 87250 — 24 B1

Paris 355 – Argenton-sur-Creuse 58 – Bellac 29 – Guéret 55 – Limoges 38

Office de tourisme, 6, avenue du 11 novembre ☎ 05 55 76 09 28, Fax 05 55 76 68 45

Bellevue

VISA MC AE

2 av. de Limoges – ☎ 05 55 76 01 99 – www.bellevue87.com – hotel.bellevue@netcourrier.com – Fax 05 55 76 68 81 – Closed 9 January-9 February, Saturday lunch and Friday dinner except July-August

12 rm – †€ 52 ††€ 52, ☕ € 8 – ½ P € 67

Rest – Menu (€ 11), € 14 (weekday lunch), € 21/51 – Carte € 31/38

◆ This family-run inn on the main road through the village is a practical stopover. The accommodation here is in simple, functional guestrooms. Traditional establishment whose sole vocation is to satisfy your hunger.

Château Constant

av. 11 novembre-1918 – ✆ 05 55 76 78 42 – www.chateau-constant.com – chateau_constant@yahoo.com

5 rm – €69 €77/79 **Table d'hôte** – Menu €24 bi

◆ This large house surrounded by centuries-old trees is run by a friendly Dutch couple who are well-travelled. Furnishings in a variety of styles: period, antique, ethnic, etc. International cuisine served in a large bright dining room.

in La Croix-du-Breuil 3 km North On D 220 – ✉ 87250 Bessines-sur-Gartempe

Manoir Henri IV

– ✆ 05 55 76 00 56 – http://manoirhenriIV.free.fr – manoirhenriIV@free.fr – Fax 05 55 76 14 14 – Closed Monday from October to May and Sunday dinner

11 rm – €47/61 €47/67, €9

Rest – Menu (€18), €25 (weekday lunch), €28/50 – Carte €48/71

◆ Henry IV allegedly was the guest of this fortified farmhouse from the 16C, now with a recently added new wing. You will stay in rustic rooms. Traditional dishes to savour in the dining rooms of the manor which have retained their country charm.

BESSONIES – 46 Lot – 337 I3 – pop. 112 – alt. 520 m – ✉ 46210 29 C1

Paris 587 – Toulouse 215 – Cahors 95 – Aurillac 34 – Figeac 39

Château de Bessonies

Le Bourg – ✆ 06 03 82 20 18 – www.chateau-bessonies.com – info@chateau-bessonies.com – Open from April to mid-November

5 rm – €139/159 €139/179 **Table d'hôte** – Menu €30

◆ Marshal Ney, hero of the Napoleonic Wars, sought refuge in this 1550 château before he was arrested for treason. Spacious rooms furnished in period style. A communal table serving regional fare takes pride of place in the dining room.

BÉTHUNE – 62 Pas-de-Calais – 301 I4 – pop. 28 400 – Built-up area 259 198 – alt. 34 m – ✉ 62400 Northern France and the Paris Region 30 B2

Paris 214 – Arras 34 – Calais 83 – Boulogne-sur-Mer 90 – Lille 39

Office de tourisme, 42-48 rue St Pry ✆ 03 21 57 25 47, Fax 03 21 57 01 60

18 du Vert-Parc Illies 3 route d'Ecuelles, 18 km on the Lille road, ✆ 03 20 29 37 87

Plan on following page

L'Éden without rest

pl. de la République – ✆ 03 21 68 83 83 – www.hotel-eden.biz – hotel-eden@aliceadsl.fr – Fax 03 21 68 83 84 Y e

34 rm – €58/110 €58/110, €9

◆ A brick house in the town centre. Warm interior (light wood, colourful soft furnishings) with rooms of various sizes, some with massage-jet baths.

Au Départ

1 r. F. Mitterand, opposite SNCF train station – ✆ 03 21 57 18 04 – jfrancois.buche@wanadoo.fr – Fax 03 21 01 18 20 – Closed 3-24 August, 15-21 February, Tuesday lunch, Saturday lunch, Sunday dinner and Monday

Rest – Menu €20 (weekday lunch), €32/62 – Carte €60/85

◆ Opposite the railway station, a regional house that sports a daring colourful façade (black and white walls and a bow window). Warmly welcoming. Carefully prepared modern cuisine.

in Labourse 4 km by ②, D 943 and D 65 – pop. 2 188 – alt. 25 m – ✉ 62113

Terre et Mer

16 r. A.-Larue – ✆ 03 21 64 03 57 – Closed 20-26 April, 3-24 August, Saturday lunch, Sunday dinner and Monday

Rest – Menu (€14), €17 (weekday lunch), €28/40 – Carte €42/55

◆ Family restaurant in the Béthune suburbs. Brick walls, a marble fireplace and striped wallpaper set the scene for the well prepared, traditional food.

BÉTHUNE

Albert-1er (R.) . . . . . . YZ 2
Arras (R. d') . . . . . . Z 3
Bruay (R. de) . . . . . . Z 6
Buridan (R.) . . . . . . Z 7
Clemenceau (Pl. G.) . . . . . . Z
Egalité (R. de l') . . . . . . Y 8
Gambetta (R.) . . . . . . YZ 10
Grand'Place . . . . . . Z
Haynaut (R. Eugène) . . . . . . Z 12
Juin (Av. du Mar.). . . . . . Z 14
Kennedy (Av. du Prés.) . . . . . . Y 15
Lamartine (Pl.) . . . . . . Y 17
Lattre-de-Tassigny (Av. de) . . . Z 18
Pont de Pierre (R. du) . . . . . . Y 20
Quai du Rivage (R. du) . . . . . . Y 21
République (Pl. de la) . . . . . . Y 22
Sadi-Carnot (R.) . . . . . . Y
Treilles (R. des) . . . . . . Z 25
Vauban (Bd) . . . . . . Z 26
Zola (R. Emile) . . . . . . Z 27

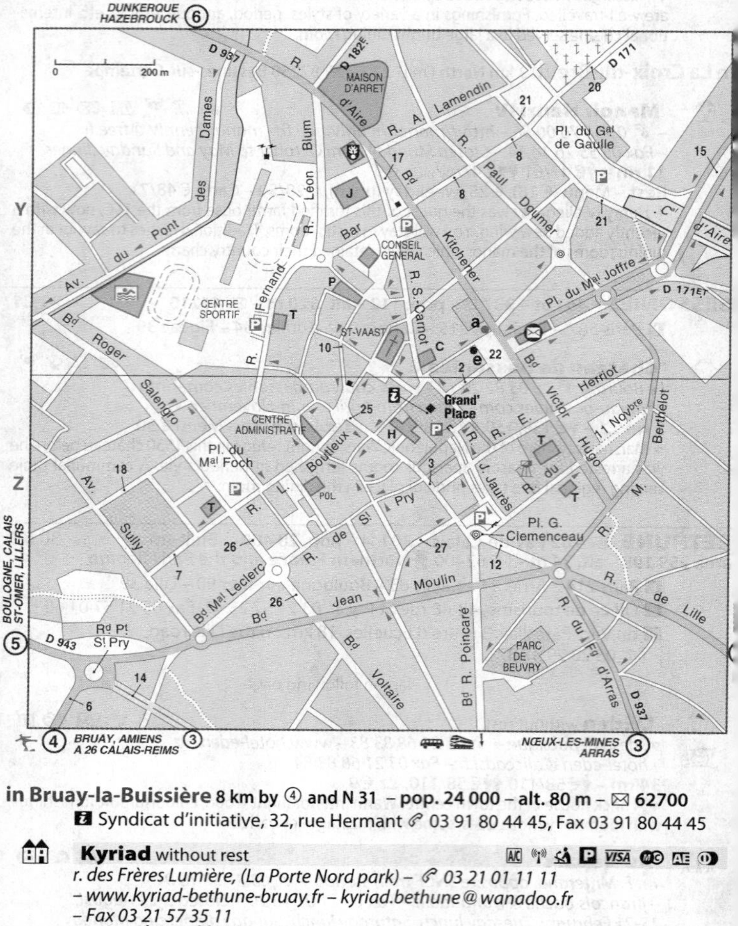

in Bruay-la-Buissière 8 km by ④ and N 31 – pop. 24 000 – alt. 80 m – ✉ 62700

Syndicat d'initiative, 32, rue Hermant ☎ 03 91 80 44 45, Fax 03 91 80 44 45

Kyriad without rest

r. des Frères Lumière, (La Porte Nord park) – ☎ 03 21 01 11 11 – www.kyriad-bethune-bruay.fr – kyriad.bethune@wanadoo.fr – Fax 03 21 57 35 11

69 rm – €69 €69, €8,50

◆ Modern hotel with low-key, contemporary rooms, ideal for business clients. A practical stopover, close to cinemas, bowling alleys, etc.

in Gosnay 5 km by ④, D 941 and D 181 – pop. 1 195 – alt. 29 m – ✉ 62199

Chartreuse du Val St-Esprit rm,

1 r. Fouquières – ☎ 03 21 62 80 00 – www.lachartreuse.com – levalsaintesprit@lachartreuse.com – Fax 03 21 62 42 50

53 rm – €140/380 €140/380, €17 – 1 suite

Rest *Robert II* – Menu €59/76 – Carte €68/138

◆ Built on the ruins of an old Charterhouse, this elegant château (1762) has beautiful, characterful rooms typical of the style of the place. Rooms overlook a wooded park. Modern cuisine and appealing selection of wines, served in a plush Robert II dining room.

in Busnes 14 km by ⑤, D 943 and D 187 – ✉ 62350

Le Château de Beaulieu (Marc Meurin)
VISA
1098 rte de Lillers – ✆ 03 21 68 88 88
– www.lechateaudebeaulieu.fr – contact@lechateaudebeaulieu.fr
– Fax 03 21 68 88 89
16 rm – €160/280 €160/280, € 22 – 4 suites
Rest Le Jardin d'Alice – see below
Rest *Meurin* – *(Closed 3-23 August, 4-17 January, Tuesday lunch, Saturday lunch, Sunday dinner and Monday)* Menu € 90 bi (weekday lunch), € 95/120 – Carte € 120/140
Spec. Collection d'automne, foie gras et champignons (September-October). Le turbot côtier, purée d'artichaut camus, melée d'asperges blanches, girolles et roquette. Les trois petits desserts - Figue, chocolat blanc et poire (September-December).

◆ This elegant castle and park houses an entirely renovated hotel. Some of the rooms, personalised in a modern style, are daringly decorated. Lovely contemporary cuisine served at the Meurin.

Le Jardin d'Alice – Hôtel le Château de Beaulieu
VISA
1098 rte de Lillers – ✆ 03 21 68 88 88 – www.lechateaudebeaulieu.fr – contact@lechateaudebeaulieu.fr – Fax 03 21 68 88 89
Rest – *(closed Sunday dinner 1st November-1st May)* Menu (€ 20), € 28, € 35/62 bi – Carte € 28/58

◆ Le Jardin d'Alice enjoys a pleasant location to the rear of the Château de Beaulieu, with bay windows and terrace. Lounge-style atmosphere and fine traditional cuisine.

LE BETTEX – 74 Haute-Savoie – 328 N5 – see St-Gervais-les-Bains

---

BEUIL – 06 Alpes-Maritimes – 341 C3 – pop. 460 – alt. 1 450 m – Winter sports : 1 470/2 100 m 26 – ✉ 06470 French Alps — 41 D2

Paris 809 – Barcelonnette 80 – Digne-les-Bains 117 – Nice 79 – Puget-Théniers 31

Syndicat d'initiative, quartier du Pissaïre ✆ 04 93 02 32 58, Fax 04 93 02 35 72

Site★ - Church ★ paintings.

L'Escapade
VISA
Le village – ✆ 04 93 02 31 27 – www.monsite.wanadoo.fr/hotelescapade
– hotel-escapade@wanadoo.fr – Fax 04 93 02 20 50
– Closed 30 March-10 April and 1st October-26 December
11 rm – €55/83 €55/83, € 11 – ½ P € 62/76
Rest – Menu € 27/29

◆ Small, but well kept rooms decorated in a mountain style. Some are under the eaves, others have a south facing balcony. The restaurant has a nice country setting decorated with old agricultural objects. Regional cuisine.

LA BEUNAZ – 74 Haute-Savoie – 328 M2 – see Bernex

BEUVRON-EN-AUGE – 14 Calvados – 303 L4 – pop. 213 – alt. 11 m – ✉ 14430 Normandy — 33 C2

Paris 219 – Cabourg 14 – Caen 32 – Lisieux 25 – Pont-l'Évêque 33

Village★ - Clermont-en-Auge★ Northeast: 3 km.

Le Pavé d'Hôtes without rest
VISA
– ✆ 02 31 39 39 10 – www.pavedauge.com – info@pavedhotes.com
– Fax 02 31 39 04 45 – Closed 23 November-26 December and one week in February
4 rm – €73/103 €80/110

◆ Peaceful house set on an old 19C farm. Minimalist rooms combine traditional taste with good comfort. Home-produced apple juice and jam.

XXX **Le Pavé d'Auge** (Jérôme Bansard) VISA

– ✆ 02 31 79 26 71 – www.pavedauge.com – info@pavedauge.com – Fax 02 31 39 04 45 – Closed 24 November-26 December, 16-23 February, Monday and Tuesday except dinner July-August

Rest – Menu € 36, € 52/60

Spec. Homard bleu en royale et jus à l'estragon crémé (May-September). Epaule d'agneau de lait au four, citron confit et coriande (February-June). Papillote d'ananas et baba dans un grog au rhum épicé (October-May). **Wines** Vin de Pays du Calvados.

◆ A convivial and typically Norman atmosphere (beams and stone chimney) at this restaurant set in the former covered markets. Traditional cuisine; professional service.

X **Auberge de la Boule d'Or** VISA

– ✆ 02 31 79 78 78 – Fax 02 31 39 61 50 – Closed mid January-mid February, Tuesday dinner and Wednesday

Rest – Menu € 25/37 – Carte € 37/71

◆ On the square, behind a typical half-timbered façade with two smart, rustic dining rooms. The room on the ground floor is warmed by a fire. Traditional food with a local flavour.

We try to be as accurate as possible when giving room rates. But prices are open to change, so please check rates when booking.

BEUZEVILLE – **27 Eure** – **304** C5 – **pop. 3 568** – **alt. 129 m** – ✉ **27210** 32 **A3**
Normandy

Paris 179 – Bernay 38 – Deauville 26 – Évreux 76 – Honfleur 16 – Le Havre 34

Office de tourisme, 52, rue Constant Fouché ✆ 02 32 57 72 10, Fax 02 32 57 72 10

West 3 km by N 175 – ✉ 14130 Quetteville

Hostellerie de la Hauquerie-Chevotel rm, rest, rest, VISA

At La Hocquerie

– ✆ 02 31 65 62 40 – www.chevotel.com – info@chevotel.com – Fax 02 31 64 24 52 – Open 1st March-30 November

16 rm – € 120/190 € 120/210, € 14 – 2 suites – ½ P € 105/152

Rest – *(dinner only)* Menu € 35/49 – Carte € 48/60

◆ Cottage atmosphere in this hotel-haras dedicated to our pure-blooded friends. The rooms, whose decor evokes the names of famous studs, opens out onto an area of green. Understated elegance distinguishes the small dining room where modern food is served.

BEYNAC ET CAZENAC – **24 Dordogne** – **329** H6 – **pop. 511** 4 **D3**
– **alt. 75 m** – ✉ **24220** **Dordogne-Berry-Limousin**

Paris 537 – Brive-la-Gaillarde 63 – Gourdon 28 – Périgueux 66 – Sarlat-la-Canéda 12

Office de tourisme, La Balme ✆ 05 53 29 43 08, Fax 05 53 29 43 08

Site★★ - Village★ - Calvary ✻★★ - Château★★: ✻★★.

in Vézac 2 km Southeast on the Sarlat road – **pop. 586** – **alt. 90 m** – ✉ **24220**

XX **Le Relais des Cinq Châteaux** with rm rm, rest, VISA

– ✆ 05 53 30 30 72 – www.relaisdes5chateaux.com – 5chateaux@perigord.com – Fax 05 53 30 30 08 – Closed from mid-November to early March except from Friday dinner to Sunday lunch

14 rm – € 52/135 € 52/135, € 8

Rest – Menu (€ 17 bi), € 25 (lunch), € 27/50 – Carte € 40/60

◆ This modern regional house has two rooms, one with a veranda. The terrace commands a fine view of the countryside and three fortified castles. Tasty classic dishes.

LES BÉZARDS – 45 Loiret – 318 N5 – ✉ 45290 12 D2

Paris 136 – Auxerre 79 – Gien 17 – Joigny 58 – Montargis 23 – Orléans 75

Auberge des Templiers rm, VISA AE

4 km from motorway A77, exit 19 – ✆ 02 38 31 80 01 – www.lestempliers.com – templiers@relaischateaux.com – Fax 02 38 31 84 51 – Closed February and Monday lunch

20 rm – €195/285 €195/285, €25 – 10 suites – ½ P €180/225

Rest – Menu €45 (lunch), €78/125 – Carte €78/150

Spec. Araignée de mer et bar à cru en marinade d'artichauts poivrade. Gibier de Sologne (season). Les entremets de l'auberge. **Wines** Pouilly-Fumé, Sancerre.

◆ A unique hotel with personalised and refined decor. Cottages spread throughout the park house luxurious apartments. Hunting trips organised. A very chic ambiance in this restaurant and terrace surrounded by roses; updated classic menu.

BÈZE – 21 Côte-d'Or – 320 L5 – pop. 709 – alt. 217 m – ✉ 21310 8 D2

Paris 337 – Dijon 34 – Dole 86 – Chenôve 47 – Talant 37

Le Bourguignon rm, rest, VISA

8 r. Porte de Bessey – ✆ 03 80 75 34 51 – www.lebourguignon.com – hotel-le-bourguignon@wanadoo.fr – Fax 03 80 75 37 06 – Closed 24 October-22 November

25 rm – €45 €60, €8,50 – ½ P €60/63

Rest – Menu (€13 bi), €21/40 – Carte €30/60

◆ A distinctive friendly atmosphere reigns in this establishment made up of three buildings, one of which is half-timbered. Well-kept rooms (ask for one of the prettier refurbished rooms). Behind a Renaissance façade, the rustic dining room specialises in regional gastronomy.

BÉZIERS – 34 Hérault – 339 E8 – pop. 71 600 – Built-up area 124 967 – alt. 17 m – ✉ 34500 Languedoc-Roussillon-Tarn Gorges 22 B2

Paris 758 – Marseille 234 – Montpellier 71 – Perpignan 93

Béziers-Vias: ✆ 04 67 80 99 09, 10 km on the ③

Office de tourisme, 29, avenue Saint-Saëns ✆ 04 67 76 84 00, Fax 04 67 76 50 80

de Saint-Thomas Route de Pezenas, NE : 12 km, ✆ 04 67 39 03 09

Former St-Nazaire cathedral ★: terrace ≤★ - Musée du Biterois★ BZ M³ - Jardin St Jacques ≤★.

Plans on following pages

Mercure without rest VISA AE

33 av. Camille-St-Saëns – ✆ 04 67 00 19 96 – www.mercure.com – h5639@accor.com – Fax 04 67 00 19 98 CY f

58 rm – €104/144 €120/154, €13

◆ New hotel built between the tourist office and the conference centre. Rooms decorated in boat cabin style: wood panelling, portholes and rounded forms.

Champ de Mars without rest VISA

17 r. de Metz – ✆ 04 67 28 35 53 – www.hotel-champdemars.com – hotel-champdemars@wanadoo.fr – Fax 04 67 28 61 42 – Closed 22 December-4 January CY v

10 rm – €35/53 €39/53, €7

◆ Small family hotel in a quiet street away from the town centre. The rooms are of average size, well-equipped and are being gradually redecorated.

Des Poètes without rest VISA AE

80 Allées Paul-Riquet – ✆ 04 67 76 38 66 – www.hoteldespoetes.net – hoteldespoetes@cegetel.net – Fax 04 67 76 25 88 – Closed 23 December-15 January CZ t

14 rm – €55/70 €60/75, €8

◆ Modern, well-maintained rooms in this small, comfortable hotel in the town centre. The breakfast room with a lit fire in the winter has views of the parc des Poètes.

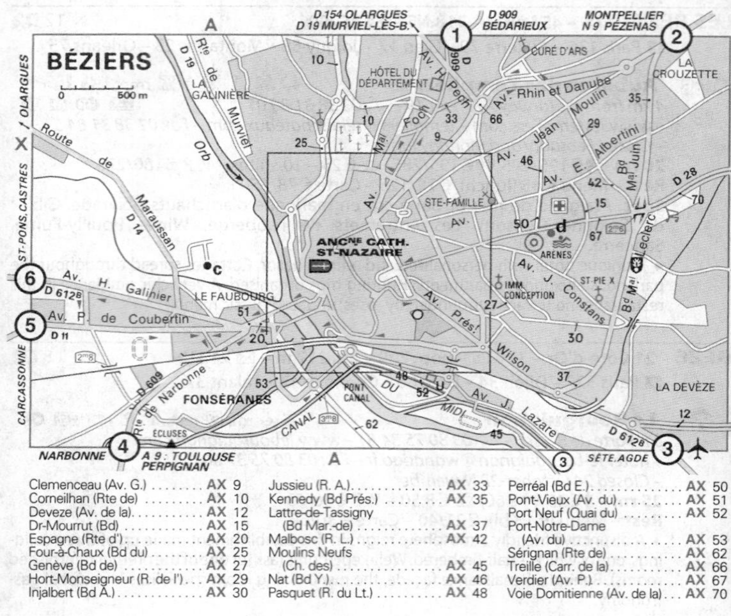

Les Jardins du Rebaut without rest
103 chemin rural, (Maraussan road) – ✆ 04 67 28 68 58
– www.beziers-vacances.com – lesjardinsdurebaut@wanadoo.fr
– Open 1st March-30 October AX **w**
5 rm – €75 €75
◆ This former wine and spirits storehouse benefits from a quiet, verdant setting with personalised rooms and a clear view of the cathedral (the Syrah room is the exception).

L'Ambassade (Patrick Olry)
22 bd de Verdun, (opposite the station) – ✆ 04 67 76 06 24
– http://www.tables-gourmandes.fr/restaurant_lambassade.php
– lambassade-beziers@wanadoo.fr – Fax 04 67 76 74 05
– Closed Sunday and Monday CZ **n**
Rest – Menu € 29 (weekdays)/110 – Carte € 55/100
Spec. Marbré d'aubergines, tomate, poivron et piquillos aux amandes fraîches et chipirons (summer). Saint-Pierre à la peau, cannelloni de couteaux au poireau et crème battue grattinée (summer). Croustillant de mangue à la noix de coco et sorbet pinacolada (summer). **Wines** Saint-Chinian, Coteaux du Languedoc.
◆ Resolutely modern decoration (light wood panelling, frosted glass), appetising dishes and an exceptional wine list. Extremely popular with locals.

Octopus (Fabien Lefebvre)
12 r. Boïeldieu – ✆ 04 67 49 90 00 – www.restaurant-octopus.com
– Fax 04 67 28 06 73 – Closed 17 August-7 September, Christmas holidays, Sunday and Monday CY **t**
Rest – Menu (€ 22 bi), € 30/72 – Carte € 63/92
Spec. Pot-au-feu "croq'n truffe". Loup laqué d'un caramel d'oignon, céleri et champignons sauvages (autumn). Sur sablé breton, glace arabica et chocolat chaud tradition. **Wines** Faugères, Corbières
◆ Enjoy well-presented modern dishes in one of the contemporary dining rooms, or on the terrace set in the interior courtyard.

BÉZIERS

Street	Grid	No.
Abreuvoir (R. de l')	BZ	2
Albert-1er (Av.)	CY	3
Bonsi (R. de)	BZ	4
Brousse (Av. Pierre)	BZ	5
Canterelles (R.)	BZ	6
Capus (R. du)	BZ	7
Citadelle (R. de la)	BZ	9
Drs-Bourguet (R. des)	BZ	13
Estienne-d'Orves (Av. d')	BZ	22
Flourens (R.)	BY	23
Garibaldi (Pl.)	CZ	26
Joffre (Av. Mar.)	CZ	32
Massol (R.)	BZ	43
Moulins (Rampe des)	BY	44
Orb (R. de l')	BZ	47
Péri (Pl. G.)	BYZ	49
Puits-des-Arènes (R. du)	BZ	54
République (R. de la)	BY	55
Révolution (Pl. de la)	BZ	57
Riquet (R. P.)	BY	58
St-Jacques (R.)	BZ	60
Strasbourg (Bd de)	CY	64
Tourventouse (Bd)	BZ	65
Victoire (Pl. de la)	BCY	68
Viennet (R.)	BZ	69
4-Septembre (R. du)	BY	72
11-Novembre (Pl. du)	CY	74

La Maison de Campagne

22 av. Pierre Verdier – ☎ 04 67 30 91 85 – www.aupauvrejacques.fr – aupauvrejacques@wanadoo.fr – Fax 04 67 30 47 32 – Closed 17 August-3 September, 28 October-3 November, Sunday, Monday and dinner Tuesday-Thursday AX **d**

Rest – Menu € 18 (weekdays)/25 bi – Carte € 30/70

◆ Extremely pleasant in the summer, this country house offers a pretty, rustic and chic setting. It has a hacienda style and a large patio-terrace. Modern cuisine and tapas bar.

via ③ 6 km near A9-Béziers-Est interchange – ✉ 34420 Villeneuve-lès-Béziers

Le Pavillon

rm, rest, VISA

Z.A la Montagnette, Valras road 1 km – ☎ 04 67 39 40 00 – hotel.pavillon@orange.fr – Fax 04 67 39 39 61 – Closed 25 December-2 January

78 rm – † € 65/85 †† € 65/85, ☕ € 8

Rest – Menu (€ 14), € 20/35 – Carte € 25/50

◆ Situated on the outskirts of town, this is a useful stopover on the way to Spain. Functional, air-conditioned rooms. Good sports facilities and children's playground. Modern dining rooms serving traditional cuisine and buffet meals.

in Villeneuve-lès-Béziers 7 km by ③, **D 612 and D 37 – pop. 3 573 – alt. 6 m – ✉ 34420**

Office de tourisme, place de la Fontaine ✆ 04 67 39 48 83

La Chamberte rm,

r. de la Source – ✆ 04 67 39 84 83 – www.lachamberte.com – contact@lachamberte.com – Closed 1st-15 March and 1st-21 November

5 rm – €70 €98

Table d'hôte – *(closed Monday dinner) (pre-book)* Menu €35 bi/45

◆ Former wine cellar covered with greenery with a fine patio garden that is a haven of peace. Up-to-date and warm decor (Andalusian and exotic influences). Enjoy dishes made with market-fresh ingredients in a spacious, relaxing setting. .

in Maraussan 6 km West by D 14 – **pop. 3 180 – alt. 38 m – ✉ 34370**

Parfums de Garrigues VISA

37 r. de l'Ancienne-Poste – ✆ 04 67 90 33 76 – www.parfumsdegarrigues.com – Fax 04 67 90 33 76 – Closed 13-20 April, 15-24 June, 25 August-2 September, Sunday dinner from September to June, Thursday lunch from July to September, Tuesday and Wednesday

Rest – Menu €25/60 – Carte €41/58

◆ Comfortable dining room with southern colours and shady terrace in the interior courtyard of this prettily-restored building. Cuisine with the flavours of the garrigue.

Le Vieux Puits VISA

207 av. de Cazouls – ✆ 04 67 90 05 59 – levieuxpuits@9business.fr – Fax 04 67 26 60 45 – Closed 2-14 January, Saturday lunch, Sunday dinner and Monday

Rest – Menu €20/47 bi – Carte €25/45

◆ 'The Old Well' is named after the well at the entrance to the dining room. Bright, colourful interior decorated with murals. Pleasant summer terrace and traditional food.

BIARRITZ – 64 Pyrénées-Atlantiques – **342** C4 – **pop. 30 055 – alt. 19 m – Casino – ✉ 64200** Atlantic Coast 3 **A3**

Paris 772 – Bayonne 9 – Bordeaux 190 – Pau 122 – San Sebastián 47

Biarritz-Anglet-Bayonne: ✆ 05 59 43 83 83, 2 km ABX.

✆ 3635 et tapez 42 (0,34 €/mn)

Office de tourisme, square d'Ixelles - Javalquinto ✆ 05 59 22 37 00, Fax 05 59 24 14 19

de Biarritz 2 avenue Edith Cavell, NE : 1 km, ✆ 05 59 03 71 80

d'Ilbarritz Bidart Avenue du Château, S : 3 km on D 911, ✆ 05 59 43 81 30

d'Arcangues Arcangues Jaureguiborde, SE : 8 km, ✆ 05 59 43 10 56

≤★★ from the Perspective - ≤★ lighthouse and Pointe St-Martin AX - Rocher de la Vierge (Virgin's Rock) ★ - Musée de la mer★.

Plans on following pages

Du Palais VISA

1 av. de l'Impératrice – ✆ 05 59 41 64 00 – www.hotel-du-palais.com – reception@hotel-du-palais.com – Fax 05 59 41 67 99 EY **k**

122 rm – €300/500 €375/575, €42 – 30 suites

Rest *La Villa Eugénie* – *(closed February and for lunch in July-August)* Menu €120 – Carte €112/140

Rest *La Rotonde* – *(closed February)* Menu €65 – Carte €60/85

Rest *L'Hippocampe* – swimming pool rest. *(open from April to mid-October and closed for dinner except July-August)* Menu (€57) – Carte €68/90

Spec. Velouté "Eugénie" (autumn-winter). Blanc de bar, poireau au vin blanc d'Irouléguy et caviar d'Aquitaine (September-May). Ananas rôti aux épices et sa crème légère (winter-spring). **Wines** Irouléguy, Jurançon.

◆ This elegant seaside edifice, a gift from Napoleon III to his Empress, offers the luxury of a palace. Most of the rooms have Empire furniture. Magnificent imperial spa. Villa Eugénie offers an updated regional menu in an elegant setting. La Rotonde commands a fine sea view. Buffets and grills at L'Hippocampe (in season).

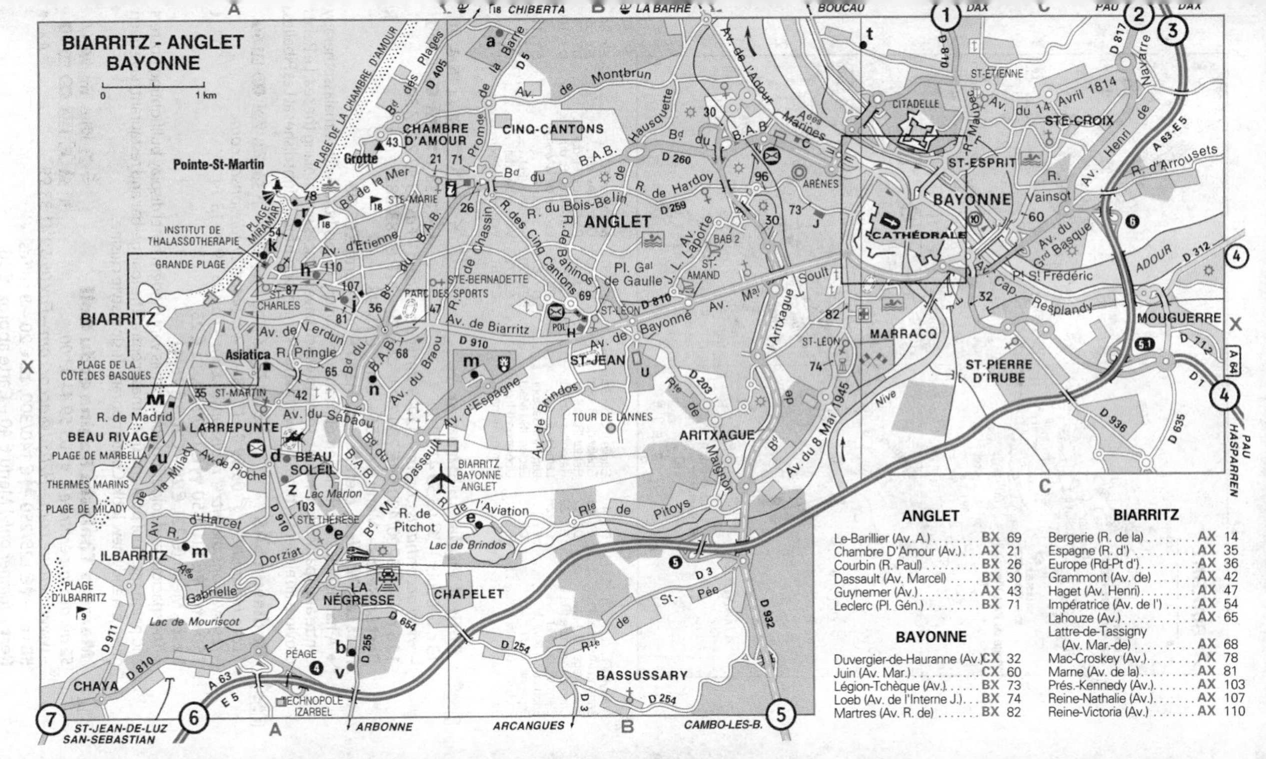
BIARRITZ - ANGLET
BAYONNE
0 1 km
ANGLET
Le-Barillier (Av. A.) BX 69
Chambre D'Amour (Av.) AX 21
Courbin (R. Paul) BX 26
Dassault (Av. Marcel) BX 30
Guynemer (Av.) AX 43
Leclerc (Pl. Gén.) BX 71
BAYONNE
Duvergier-de-Hauranne (Av.) CX 32
Juin (Av. Mar.) CX 60
Légion-Tchèque (Av.) BX 73
Loeb (Av. de l'Interne J.) BX 74
Martres (Av. R. de) BX 82
BIARRITZ
Bergerie (R. de la) AX 14
Espagne (R. d') AX 35
Europe (Rd-Pt d') AX 36
Grammont (Av. de) AX 42
Haget (Av. Henri) AX 47
Impératrice (Av. de l') AX 54
Lahouze (Av.) AX 65
Lattre-de-Tassigny (Av. Mar.-de) AX 68
Mac-Croskey (Av.) AX 78
Marne (Av. de la) AX 81
Prés.-Kennedy (Av.) AX 103
Reine-Nathalie (Av.) AX 107
Reine-Victoria (Av.) AX 110
CHIBERTA
LA BARRE
BOUCAU
DAX
PAU
PAU HASPARREN
CAMBO-LES-B.
ARCANGUES
ARBONNE
ST-JEAN-DE-LUZ SAN-SEBASTIAN
BIARRITZ
ANGLET
BAYONNE
CHAMBRE D'AMOUR
CINQ-CANTONS
ST-ESPRIT
STE-CROIX
CATHÉDRALE
CITADELLE
MARRACQ
ST-PIERRE D'IRUBE
MOUGUERRE
ARITXAGUE
ST-JEAN
BASSUSSARY
CHAPELET
LA NÉGRESSE
ILBARRITZ
CHAYA
LARREPUNTE
BEAU SOLEIL
BEAU RIVAGE
Pointe-St-Martin
GRANDE PLAGE
PLAGE DE LA CÔTE DES BASQUES
PLAGE DE MARBELLA
PLAGE DE MILADY
PLAGE D'ILBARRITZ
BIARRITZ BAYONNE ANGLET
Lac de Brindos
Lac de Mouriscot
Lac Marion

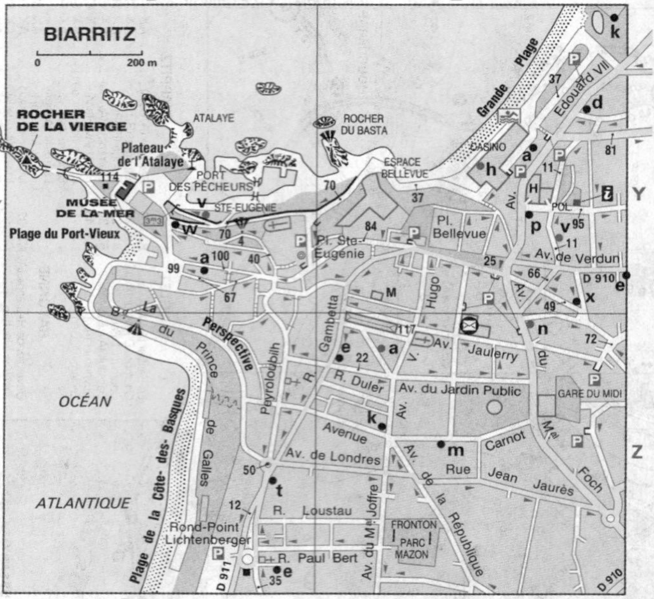

BIARRITZ

Atalaye (Pl.) ... DY 4
Barthou (Av. Louis) ... EY 11
Beaurivage (Av.) ... DZ 12
Champ-Lacombe (R.) ... EZ 22
Clemenceau (Pl.) ... EY 25
Édouard-VII (Av.) ... EY
Espagne (R. d') ... DZ 35
Foch (Av. du Mar.) ... EZ
Gambetta (R.) ... DEZ
Gaulle (Bd du Gén.-de) ... EY 37
Goélands (R. des) ... DY 40
Helder (R. du) ... EY 49
Hélianthe (Rd-Pt) ... DZ 50
Larralde (R.) ... EY 66
Larre (R. Gaston) ... DY 67
Leclerc (Bd Mar.) ... DEY 70
Libération (Pl. de la) ... EZ 72
Marne (Av. de la) ... EY 81
Mazagran (R.) ... EY 84
Osuna (Av. d') ... EY 95
Port-Vieux (Pl. du) ... DY 99
Port-Vieux (R. du) ... DY 100
Rocher de la Vierge (Espl. du) ... DY 114
Sobradiel (Pl.) ... EZ 117
Verdun (Av. de) ... EY
Victor-Hugo (Av.) ... EYZ

Sofitel Thalassa Miramar
13 r. L.-Bobet – 05 59 41 30 00
– www.accorthalassa.com – h2049-am@accor.com – Fax 05 59 24 77 20
126 rm – € 200/480 € 280/600, € 28 – ½ P € 183/383 — AX **k**
Rest *Le Relais* – Menu € 42/56 – Carte € 76/98
Rest *Les Piballes* – dietetic rest. Menu € 56 – Carte € 65/88
◆ A harmonious combination of health and luxury in this hotel with a thalassotherapy centre and spa. Modern rooms, some of which have terraces overlooking the sea. Le Relais provides an elegant setting, a view of the reefs and modern food. Light dishes at Les Piballes.

Radisson SAS — rm, VISA
1 carr. Hélianthe – 05 59 01 13 13 – www.biarritz.radissonsas.com
– reservations.biarritz@radissonsas.com – Fax 05 59 01 13 14 — DZ **t**
150 rm – € 110/550 € 110/550, € 23
Rest – Menu (€ 22), € 28 – Carte € 26/41
◆ The spacious and colourful rooms of this very modern hotel display bullfighting posters and paintings. Roof pool and fine fitness centre. The lounge-bar and restaurant have been given a trendy new look. Contemporary, fusion-style cuisine.

Mercure Thalassa Regina et du Golf — rm,
52 av. de l'Impératrice – 05 59 41 33 00 — VISA
– www.mercure.com – H2050@accor.com – Fax 05 59 41 33 99 — AX **r**
58 rm – € 125/250 € 140/300, € 20 – 8 suites
Rest – *(dinner only)* Menu € 40 – Carte approx. € 56
◆ An elegant Second Empire-style residence. Comfortable rooms facing the golf course or the ocean, reached by gangways that look down on the glass-roofed atrium. The restaurant has attractive maritime decor and a canopied area.

Mercure Plaza Centre without rest
av. Édouard-VII – ✆ 05 59 24 74 00 – www.groupe-segeric.com – h5681@accor.com – Fax 05 59 22 22 01 EY **p**
69 rm – €124/198 €136/218, €16
◆ Sympathetic renovation for this hotel with its attractive Art Deco facade facing the beach and casino. Pleasant rooms. Jazz evenings.

Tonic
58 av. Édouard-VII – ✆ 05 59 24 58 58 – www.tonichotel.com – reservation-biarritz@tonichotel.com – Fax 05 59 24 86 14 EY **d**
63 rm – €135/295 €155/325, €18
Rest *La Maison Blanche* – *(closed Sunday and Monday from November to March)* Carte €40/77
◆ Hotel near the Grande Plage (beach), offering elegant and modern rooms, all equipped with hydromassage baths for an invigorating wake-up! A pleasantly fashionable dining room and updated cuisine to match.

Beaumanoir without rest
av. de Tamames – ✆ 05 59 24 89 29 – www.lebeaumanoir.com – reception@lebeaumanoir.com – Fax 05 59 24 89 46 – Open 3 April-11 November AX **n**
5 rm – €285/385 €285/385, €24 – 3 suites
◆ A luxurious hotel occupying former stables near the centre and beaches. Rooms, suites and apartments adorned with Baroque and designer furniture; lounge with a glass ceiling; swimming pool and park.

Édouard VII without rest
21 av. Carnot – ✆ 05 59 22 39 80 – www.hotel-edouardvii.com – contact@hotel-edouardvii.com – Fax 05 59 22 39 71 EZ **k**
18 rm – €80/145 €80/145, €10
◆ The well-maintained rooms in this attractive 18C Biarritz villa offer a number of pleasant personal touches. Friendly service.

Alcyon without rest
8 r. Maison-Suisse – ✆ 05 59 22 64 60 – www.hotel-alcyon-biarritz.com – contact@hotel-alcyon-biarritz.com – Fax 05 59 22 64 64 – Closed 1st-15 March
15 rm – €75/95 €85/130, €9 EY **x**
◆ This hotel combines the charm of an old building with modern comforts. Contemporary-style lounge, designer breakfast room and elegant, well-renovated rooms.

Windsor
19 Bd du Gén. de Gaulle, (Grande Plage) – ✆ 05 59 24 08 52 – www.hotelwindsorbiarritz.com – hotelwindsor-biarritz@wanadoo.fr – Fax 05 59 24 98 90 EY **a**
48 rm – €70/265 €70/265, €13
Rest *Le Galion* – ✆ *05 59 24 20 32 (closed Sunday dinner from 16 November-29 February, Monday except dinner from 1st July-15 September and Tuesday lunch)* Menu (€18), €20/30 – Carte €42/58
◆ Rooms with a sea view, facing the town or overlooking a courtyard at this hotel near the Grande Plage. Those renovated are simple and modern in style. Panoramic dining room facing the Atlantic; traditional food focusing on seafood.

Biarritz
30 av. de la Milady – ✆ 05 59 23 83 03 – www.hotel-lebiarritz-.com – info@biarritz-thalasso.com – Fax 05 59 23 88 12 AX **u**
49 rm – €74/183 €108/306 – ½ P €76/205
Rest – *(Closed Sunday dinner and Monday lunch from November to end February except school holidays and bank holidays)* Menu €22/31 – Carte €31/37
◆ This hotel not far from the seawater spa (special rates for guests), has been fully refurbished and offers comfortable, contemporary rooms with a seaside atmosphere. Bay windows with ocean views and food served on the terrace in fine weather. Modern menu.

Maïtagaria without rest
34 av. Carnot – ✆ 05 59 24 26 65 – www.hotel-maitagaria.com – hotel.maitagaria@wanadoo.fr – Fax 05 59 24 26 30 – Closed 23 November-15 December EZ **m**
15 rm – €53/63 €60/90, €8,50
◆ A friendly welcome awaits guests in this regional-style hotel offering functional or more comfortable rooms, most with attractive Art Deco furniture.

Maison Garnier without rest
29 r. Gambetta – ☎ 05 59 01 60 70 – www.hotel-biarritz.com – maison-garnier@hotel-biarritz.com – Fax 05 59 01 60 80 – Closed 10-24 December, 5-15 January EZ **e**
7 rm – †€ 95/155 ††€ 95/160, ☕ € 10
◆ This 19C Biarritz mansion is pleasantly decorated in a guest house style. The antique furniture and careful decoration give character to the fairly large rooms.

Marbella rm,
11 r. Port-Vieux – ☎ 05 59 24 04 06 – www.hotel-marbella.fr – infos@hotel-marbella.fr – Fax 05 59 24 63 26 DY **a**
29 rm – †€ 82/160 ††€ 82/160, ☕ € 10
Rest – *(dinner only)* Menu € 18, € 20/35 – Carte € 35/55
◆ A building on a shopping street, near the Rocher de la Vierge and the Musée de la Mer. Somewhat small but pleasant, well-kept rooms. Regional, simple food chalked up on the board every day and served in a rustic setting.

Oxo without rest
38 av. de Verdun – ☎ 05 59 24 26 17 – www.hotel-oxo.com – oxo@biarritz-hotel.com – Fax 05 59 24 66 08 – Closed 23 December-3 January EY **e**
20 rm – †€ 58/85 ††€ 58/90, ☕ € 8
◆ Complete renovation and a new name (the oxygen of the Pyrenees meets the ocean) for this hotel on a busy avenue opposite the media library.

Villa Le Goëland without rest
12 plateau de l'Atalaye – ☎ 05 59 24 25 76 – www.villagoeland.com – info@villagoeland.com – Fax 05 59 22 36 83 DY **w**
4 rm – †€ 130/250 ††€ 130/250, ☕ € 10
◆ This large villa occupying one of the most attractive sites in Biarritz offers breath-taking views extending from Spain to the Landes coast. Some rooms have a terrace.

Nere-Chocoa without rest
28 r. Larreguy – ☎ 06 08 33 84 35 – www.nerechocoa.com – maryse.cadou@wanadoo.fr – Fax 05 59 41 07 95 AX **e**
5 rm – †€ 75/115 ††€ 75/115, ☕ € 9
◆ This house surrounded by oak trees has hosted illustrious guests such as Empress Eugénie. Huge, elegant guestrooms, a collection of paintings and a comfortable lounge for musical evenings.

La Ferme de Biarritz without rest
15 r. Harcet – ☎ 05 59 23 40 27 – www.fermedebiarritz.com – info@fermedebiarritz.com – Closed 6-17 December AX **m**
5 rm – †€ 55/80 ††€ 55/80, ☕ € 8
◆ A well-restored 17C Basque farmhouse near the beach. The smart, attic rooms (non-smoking) are furnished with antiques. Breakfast in the garden or beside the fire.

Sissinou
5 av. Mar.-Foch – ☎ 05 59 22 51 50 – restaurant.sissinou@wanadoo.fr – Fax 05 59 22 50 58 – Closed one week in April, February holidays, Sunday and Monday except August and lunch in August EZ **n**
Rest – Menu € 52
◆ This fashionable restaurant offers relaxed service in a contemporary setting (aubergine bench seats, green walls and designer lighting). Both contemporary and classic dishes available.

Les Rosiers (Andrée et Stéphane Rosier)
32 av. Beausoleil – ☎ 05 59 23 13 68 – www.restaurant-lesrosiers.fr AX **z**
Rest – *(Closed Wednesday lunch in summer, Monday and Tuesday except dinner from mid-July to mid-September)* Menu € 40 bi (weekday lunch)/70 – Carte € 54/66
Spec. Grosses crevettes croustillantes et tartare de tomate. Saint-Pierre à la marinière mousseuse de citron. Moelleux au chocolat et crème glacée caramel.
◆ Welcoming house run by a couple, where the wife is the first woman chef to win the award 'Meilleur Ouvrier de France'. Delightful, unfussy and refined cuisine served in a simple, elegant decor.

XX **Café de la Grande Plage**
1 av. Edouard-VII, (casino) – ☎ 05 59 22 77 88 – www.lucienbarriere.com – casinobiarritz@lucienbarriere.com – Fax 05 59 22 77 99 EY **h**
Rest – Menu (€ 20), € 29 – Carte € 30/45
◆ A little hungry between two games of black-jack? On the ground floor of the casino, Art Deco style brasserie decorated with mosaics. Ideal view over the beach and the surfers.

XX **L'Atelier**
18 r. de la Bergerie – ☎ 05 59 22 09 37 – www.latelierbiarritz.com – mail@latelierbiarritz.com – Fax 05 59 22 21 50 AX **h**
Rest – *(Closed 2 weeks in March and in November, 1 week in June, Sunday dinner and Monday except July-August)* Menu (€ 25), € 45/70 – Carte € 45/51
◆ This 'culinary workshop' has a surprise in store: modern dishes with creative touches served with fine wines. The refined dining area adds elegance to the place.

XX **La Table d'Aranda**
87 av. de la Marne – ☎ 05 59 22 16 04 – www.tabledaranda.fr – contact@tabledaranda.fr – Fax 05 59 22 16 04 – Closed 3-18 January, Monday except dinner July-August and Sunday AX **j**
Rest – Menu (€ 15), € 20 (weekday lunch) – Carte approx. € 42
◆ Word-of-mouth has brought a loyal following to this restaurant with a rustic Basque decor within the walls of a former rotisserie. Personalised, inventive cuisine combining sweet and savoury flavours.

X **Philippe**
30 av. du Lac Marion – ☎ 05 59 23 13 12 – www.restaurantphilippe.fr – philippe@restaurant-biarritz.com – Closed 2 weeks in March, 2 weeks in November, Monday except from July to September and Tuesday except dinner in August AX **d**
Rest – *(dinner only) (number of covers limited, pre-book)* Carte approx. € 55
◆ An open-plan kitchen, a wood-fired oven for suckling pig and lamb, inventive cooking and avant-garde decor at this surprising restaurant. Exhibition and sale of contemporary art.

X **Le Clos Basque**
12 r. L.-Barthou – ☎ 05 59 24 24 96 – leclosbasque@gmail.com – Fax 05 59 22 34 46 – Closed 23 June-3 July, 27 October-17 November, 23 February-12 March, Sunday dinner except July-August and Monday
Rest – *(number of covers limited, pre-book)* Menu € 24 EY **v**
◆ Exposed stone and azulejos give a Spanish air to this little dining room with a friendly atmosphere. Popular summer terrace. Regional specialities.

X **Chez Albert**
au Port-des-Pêcheurs – ☎ 05 59 24 43 84 – www.chezalbert.fr – Fax 05 59 24 20 13 – Closed 22 November-16 December, 4 January-10 February and Wednesday
Rest – Menu € 40 – Carte € 36/60 DY **v**
◆ Seafood and fish are the main focus at this busy but relaxed restaurant with a fine view of the little fishing port. The terrace is often packed in summer.

at Brindos Lake 4 km Southeast – ✉ 64600 Anglet

Château de Brindos rm,
1 allée du Château – ☎ 05 59 23 89 80 – www.chateaudebrindos.com – brindos@relaischateaux.com – Fax 05 59 23 89 81 – Closed 15 February-5 March BX **e**
24 rm – † € 160/270 †† € 210/320, ☐ € 25 – 5 suites
Rest – *(closed Sunday dinner and Monday except from May to October)*
Menu € 35 (lunch)/70 – Carte € 60/80
◆ Elegant building, facing a 10-ha lake and ideal for relaxing, offering very spacious bedrooms with luxury bathrooms and lounges adorned with attractive wood panelling. A rotunda-style dining room and tree-shaded terrace by the lake. Refined modern cuisine.

Arbonne road 4 km South via La Négresse and D 255 – ✉ 64200 Biarritz

Le Château du Clair de Lune without rest
48 av. Alan-Seeger – ☎ 05 59 41 53 20 – www.chateauduclairdelune.com – hotel-clair-de-lune@wanadoo.fr – Fax 05 59 41 53 29 AX **b**
17 rm – † € 80/175 †† € 80/175, ☐ € 10
◆ Charming mansion dating from 1902 surrounded by attractive grounds. Elegant rooms, with a more rural decor in the separate lodge - ideal for gazing at the moonlight in Biarritz!

XX **Campagne et Gourmandise**
52 av. Alan-Seeger, (Arbonne road) – ✆ 05 59 41 10 11 – www.campagneetgourmandise.com – Fax 05 59 43 96 16 – Closed Sunday dinner except from 12 July to 31 August, Monday lunch and Wednesday AX **v**
Rest – Menu € 46/56
◆ This old farmhouse, surrounded by a large garden facing the Pyrenees, specialises in regional cuisine. Smart country-style interior (attractive fireplace), veranda and pretty terrace.

in Arbonne **7 km South via La Négresse and D 255 – pop. 1 460 – alt. 37 m – ✉ 64210**

Laminak without rest
rte de St-Pée – ✆ 05 59 41 95 40 – www.hotel-laminak.com – info@hotel-laminak.com – Fax 05 59 41 87 65 – Closed 22 January-10 February
12 rm – **†**€ 71 **††**€ 71/99, ☕ € 10
◆ 18C farmhouse on the outskirts of this pretty village. Recently decorated rooms with personal touches. Breakfast served in the veranda facing the delightful garden. Swimming pool.

in Arcangues **8 km via La Négresse, D 254 and D 3 – pop. 2 985 – alt. 80 m – ✉ 64200**
Office de tourisme, le bourg ✆ 05 59 43 08 55, Fax 05 59 43 39 16

Les Volets Bleus without rest
chemin Etchegaraya, 2 km South on the old St Pée road – ✆ 06 07 69 03 85 – www.lesvoletsbleus.fr – maisonlesvoletsbleus@wanadoo.fr – Fax 05 59 43 39 25 – Closed January and February
5 rm ☕ – **†**€ 95/150 **††**€ 105/160
◆ Enjoy the peaceful garden and refinement of this Basque villa restored with antique materials. Patina-effect walls, terracotta tiles and traditional quilts in the rooms.

Maison Gastelhur without rest
chemin Gastelhur, 2 km West on secondary road – ✆ 05 59 43 01 46 – www.gastelhur.com – agnes.lagrolet@orange.fr – Fax 05 59 43 12 96 – Closed 20 February-8 March
3 rm – **†**€ 110/130 **††**€ 110/130, ☕ € 8,50
◆ Set in grounds bordering a golf course, this 18C stately home offers peace and quiet. Spacious rooms adorned with family heirlooms and antiques.

XX **Le Moulin d'Alotz** (Benoît Sarthou)
3 km South on the Arbonne road and minor road – ✆ 05 59 43 04 54 – Fax 05 59 43 04 54 – Closed 22-30 June, 4-26 January, Wednesday except dinner in July-August and Tuesday
Rest – *(number of covers limited, pre-book)* Carte € 65/75
Spec. Tarte de Saint Jacques crues et cuites, boudin et céleri caramélisés (15 October-15 February). Pigeonneau caramélisé, foie chaud et purée truffée. Confit de tomate parfumé aux épices, frangipane à la pistache, crème glacée verveine. **Wines** Irouléguy, Jurançon.
◆ Basque mill said to date from 1694. Elegant interior of whitewashed beams and wood panelling. Attractive terrace, flower-filled garden and contemporary cuisine with individual touches.

X **Auberge d'Achtal**
pl. du Fronton, (pedestrian access) – ✆ 05 59 43 05 56 – achtal@wanadoo.fr – Fax 05 59 43 16 98 – Closed 5 January-5 April, Tuesday and Wednesday except from July to mid-September
Rest – Menu € 28 – Carte € 30/45
◆ This picturesque Basque village is the final resting place of Luis Mariano, prince of the operetta. Rustic interior and shaded terrace at the front of the building. Local dishes.

See also resources at **Anglet**

BIDARRAY – 64 Pyrénées-Atlantiques – **342** D3 – **pop. 645** – **alt. 110 m** 3 **A3**
– ✉ **64780** Atlantic Coast

Paris 799 – Biarritz 37 – Cambo-les-Bains 17 – Pau 127 – St-Jean-Pied-de-Port 21

Ostapé rest, VISA

Chahatoa, 4 km North on D 349 – ✆ 05 59 37 91 91 – www.ostape.com – contact@ostape.com – Fax 05 59 37 91 92 – Open March to mid-November

22 suites – ††€ 180/565, ☕ € 22 **Rest** – Menu € 56/100

◆ Splendid Basque-style villas surrounded by a 45 ha park. Spacious, elegant rooms with up-to-date facilities. Swimming pool and fitness room. Regional dishes with a contemporary twist served in an elegant 17C farmhouse.

Barberaenea VISA

pl. de l'Église – ✆ 05 59 37 74 86 – Fax 05 59 37 77 55 – Closed 15 November-15 January

9 rm – †€ 33/60 ††€ 33/60, ☕ € 6,50 **Rest** – Menu € 20/25 – Carte € 22/30

◆ A simple, authentic and friendly Basque hotel near the pelota wall. Rustic rooms with fine views over the surrounding mountains and valleys. This restaurant is decked out with country furniture and typical regional tablecloths; the dishes are made with fresh local produce.

The ✿ award is the crème de la crème.
This is awarded to restaurants which are really worth travelling miles for!

BIDART – 64 Pyrénées-Atlantiques – **342** C4 – **pop. 5 614** – **alt. 40 m** 3 **A3**
– ✉ **64210** Atlantic Coast

Paris 778 – Bayonne 17 – Biarritz 7 – Pau 122 – St-Jean-de-Luz 9

Office de tourisme, rue d'Erretegia ✆ 05 59 54 93 85, Fax 05 59 54 70 51

d'Ilbarritz Avenue du Château, N : 3 km on N 10 and D 911, ✆ 05 59 43 81 30

Ste-Madeleine chapel ✳★.

Villa L'Arche without rest VISA AE

chemin Camboénéa – ✆ 05 59 51 65 95 – www.villalarche.com – contact@villalarche.com – Fax 05 59 51 65 99 – Open 16 February-14 November

8 rm – †€ 115/285 ††€ 115/285, ☕ € 14

◆ Between a quiet residential part of the resort and the ocean shore - a charming villa. The attractive, personalised rooms and pretty garden overlook the waves.

L'Hacienda without rest VISA

50 r. Bassilour, South: 3 km via N10, rte Ahetze and minor road – ✆ 05 59 54 92 82 – www.hacienda-bidart.com – contact@hotel-hacienda.fr – Fax 05 59 26 52 73 – Open April-November

14 rm – †€ 115/180 ††€ 115/180, ☕ € 14

◆ Romanticism and refinement meet in this elegant Spanish-style residence. Themed rooms, deliciously coloured and decorated. Large, flower-filled garden.

Ouessant-Ty without rest VISA

3 r. Erretegia – ✆ 05 59 54 71 89 – www.ouessantty.com – hotel.ouessant.ty@free.fr – Fax 05 59 47 58 70

12 rm – †€ 69/105 ††€ 69/105, ☕ € 8,50

◆ A pleasant, fairly recent hotel which is both centrally located and a stone's throw from the beaches. Large rooms with cane furniture (three family rooms with a small kitchen). Creperie next door.

Irigoian without rest VISA

av. de Biarritz – ✆ 05 59 43 83 00 – www.irigoian.com – irigoian@wanadoo.fr – Fax 05 59 41 19 07

5 rm – †€ 95/125 ††€ 95/125, ☕ € 9

◆ This 17C farmhouse is situated by the sea and next to a golf course. Tastefully decorated rooms with spacious bathrooms.

Table et Hostellerie des Frères Ibarboure
(Jean-Philippe et Xabi Ibarboure) with rm
chemin de Ttalienea, 4 km South via D 810, rte Ahetze and minor road – 05 59 54 81 64 – www.freresibarboure.com – contact@freresibarboure.com – Fax 05 59 54 75 65 – Closed 15 November-7 December and 5-20 January
12 rm – €120/170 €135/230, €14
Rest – *(Closed Wednesday from September to June, Sunday dinner except August and Monday lunch in July-August)* Menu (€39), €49/105 – Carte €66/93
Spec. Sublimation de diverses tomates en saveurs d'automne. (season). Pigeonneau rôti à la goutte de sang, rouelles de figues glacées au curry. (season). Craquant au chocolat et praliné, sorbet poire williams. **Wines** Jurançon
◆ This Basque residence is surrounded by wooded parkland. Cosy dining rooms, garden terrace and cuisine from the southwest. Spacious, personalised and peaceful guestrooms.

BIEF – **25 Doubs** – **321** K3 – **see Villars-sous-Dampjoux**

BIELLE – **64 Pyrénées-Atlantiques** – **342** J6 – **pop. 459** – **alt. 448 m** – 64260 **Atlantic Coast** 3 **B3**

Paris 803 – Laruns 9 – Lourdes 43 – Oloron-Ste-Marie 26 – Pau 31

L'Ayguelade rest,
1 km via Pau road – 05 59 82 60 06 – www.hotel-ayguelade.com – hotel.ayguelade@wanadoo.fr – Fax 05 59 82 61 17 – Closed January, Tuesday and Wednesday except July-August
10 rm – €46 €60, €7 – ½ P €45/49
Rest – Menu €18 (weekdays)/40 – Carte €25/45
◆ A Bearnaise house and annexe along an affluent of the Ossau mountain stream (fishing). Most of the small rooms are modern, colourful and have been renovated. Regional food served under the new veranda in fine weather, or in a rustic dining room.

BIESHEIM – **68 Haut-Rhin** – **315** J8 – **see Neuf-Brisach**

BIGNAN – **56 Morbihan** – **308** O7 – **see Locminé**

BILLIERS – **56 Morbihan** – **308** Q9 – **pop. 910** – **alt. 20 m** – 56190 10 **C3**

Paris 461 – La Baule 42 – Nantes 87 – Redon 39 – La Roche-Bernard 17 – Vannes 28

Domaine de Rochevilaine rest,
à la Pointe de Pen Lan, 2 km by D 5 – 02 97 41 61 61 – www.domainerochevilaine.com – rochevilaine@relaischateaux.com – Fax 02 97 41 44 85
34 rm – €145/416 €145/416, €20 – 4 suites – ½ P €142/415
Rest – Menu €40 (weekday lunch), €72/130 – Carte €85/132
Spec. Huîtres creuses cuisinées en coquille. Homard de casier au beurre demi-sel. Desserts aux grands crus de chocolats noirs.
◆ A hamlet of attractive Breton houses and a balneotherapy centre anchored to the far end of a rocky point facing the ocean. Spacious and personalised bedrooms. Modernised classic menu, served in a setting combining woodwork, mirrors and red fabrics, overlooking the sea.

Les Glycines without rest
17 pl. de l'Église – 06 11 86 07 52 – les-glycines-billiers.com – grimaud.veronique56@wanadoo.fr – Fax 02 97 45 69 68
5 rm – €82/102 €90/110
◆ Blue and white house on the village square. Spruce, colourful interior (piano, knick-knacks, books and paintings). Children's play area.

BIOT – 06 Alpes-Maritimes – **341** D6 – **pop. 8 995** – **alt. 80 m** – ✉ 06410 42 **E2**
French Riviera

Paris 910 – Antibes 6 – Cagnes-sur-Mer 9 – Cannes 17 – Grasse 20 – Nice 21 – Vence 18

Office de tourisme, 46, rue Saint-Sébastien ☎ 04 93 65 78 00, Fax 04 93 65 78 04

de Biot Avenue Michard Pelissier, S : 1 km, ☎ 04 93 65 08 48

Musée national Fernand Léger★★ - Rosaire altar-piece ★ in the church.

Domaine du Jas without rest

625 rte de la Mer, D 4 – ☎ 04 93 65 50 50 – www.domainedujas.com – domaine-du-jas@wanadoo.fr – Fax 04 93 65 02 01 – Open 16 March-4 January

19 rm – €90/120 €100/235, €12

◆ Pretty Provencal-style rooms, including three family rooms and one duplex, with balconies or terraces overlooking the swimming pool, garden or Biot village: live life southern style!

Les Terraillers (Michaël Fulci)

11 rte Chemin-Neuf, below the village – ☎ 04 93 65 01 59 – www.lesterraillers.com – lesterraillers@orange.fr – Fax 04 93 65 13 78 – Closed November, Wednesday and Thursday

Rest – Menu (€39), €55 bi (lunch), €65/110 – Carte €89/105

Spec. Gnocchi à la piémontaise sur purée de truffe. Pigeon désossé, farci de semoule de pignons, citron et raisins secs. Voile de chocolat extra-bitter, glace nesquik, mousseline de mascarpone et macarons. **Wines** Vin de Pays des Alpes Maritimes, Côtes de Provence.

◆ A 16C pottery workshop, the kiln has been transformed into a lounge. Lovely dining room with vaults, stone, exposed beams and fresh flowers. Menu with a Southern touch.

Chez Odile

in the village, chemin des Bachettes – ☎ 04 93 65 15 63 – Closed from 1 December-1 February, lunch in July-August, Wednesday dinner and Thursday in low season

Rest – Menu (€19), €30

◆ This attractive countrified inn is an institution in the neighbourhood. The owner, Odile, is friendly and enthusiastic, announcing the regional menu at your table.

BIOULE – 82 Tarn-et-Garonne – **337** F7 – **pop. 845** – **alt. 84 m** – ✉ 82800 28 **B2**

Paris 613 – Toulouse 75 – Montauban 22 – Cahors 53 – Moissac 60

Les Boissières

708 rte de Caussade – ☎ 05 63 24 50 02 – www.lesboissieres.com – cyril.rosenberg@wanadoo.fr – Fax 05 63 24 60 80 – Closed 10-22 August, autumn school holidays, 2 weeks in January, Saturday lunch, Sunday dinner and Monday

10 rm – €79/119 €79/119, €9

Rest – Menu (€23), €36/55 – Carte approx. €46

◆ Formed from a large house (19C) and its red brick stable (18C), this inn surrounded by a park offers rooms in a rustic or modern style. Dining room complemented by a pergola in good weather. Modern cuisine.

BIRIATOU – 64 Pyrénées-Atlantiques – **342** B4 – see Hendaye

BIRKENWALD – 67 Bas-Rhin – **315** I5 – **pop. 253** – **alt. 295 m** – ✉ 67440 1 **A1**

Paris 461 – Molsheim 23 – Saverne 12 – Strasbourg 34

Au Chasseur

rest,

7 r. de l'Église – ☎ 03 88 70 61 32 – www.chasseurbirkenwald.com – contact@chasseurbirkenwald.com – Fax 03 88 70 66 02 – Closed 21 December-15 January

23 rm – €65/90 €90/100, €13 – 3 suites – ½ P €74/85

Rest – *(closed Wednesday lunch, Monday and Tuesday)* Menu (€12), €15 (weekday lunch), €32/75 – Carte €30/57

◆ The recently renovated rooms in this characterful inn are comfortable and attractively appointed. Some offer views of the Vosges. Elegant, classic regional restaurant adorned with attractive larch and burr wood panelling.

BISCARROSSE – 40 Landes – 335 E8 – pop. 12 031 – alt. 22 m – Casino – ✉ 40600 Atlantic Coast 3 B2

Paris 656 – Arcachon 40 – Bayonne 128 – Bordeaux 74 – Dax 91 – Mont-de-Marsan 84

Office de tourisme, 55, place Georges Dufau ✆ 05 58 78 20 96, Fax 05 58 78 23 65

de Biscarrosse Route d'Ispe, E : 9 km on D 83 and D 305, ✆ 05 58 09 84 93

in Ispe 6 km North by D 652 and D 305 – ✉ 40600 Biscarosse

La Caravelle rm, VISA

5314 rte des lacs – ✆ 05 58 09 82 67 – www.lacaravelle.fr – lacaravelle.40@wanadoo.fr – Fax 05 58 09 82 18 – Open mid February-31 October

15 rm – †€ 48/72 ††€ 72/102, ☕ € 7 – ½ P € 66/81

Rest – *(closed Monday lunch and Tuesday lunch except July-August)* Menu € 16/39 – Carte € 22/56

◆ All the fully refurbished rooms of this hotel command a fine view of the lake. Those on the ground floor wing are surrounded by greenery. "Holiday" atmosphere in the dining room-veranda and a pleasant shady terrace.

at the Golf 7 km Northwest by D 652 and D 305

Le Parcours Gourmand VISA

av. du Golf – ✆ 05 58 09 84 84 – www.biscarrossegolf.com – golfdebiscarrosse@wanadoo.fr – Fax 05 58 09 84 50 – Closed 5 January-12 February and Monday in low season

Rest – Menu (€ 25), € 40 (lunch)/75 bi – Carte € 56/79

◆ Classic menu featuring local produce in this restaurant among pines on the golf course. Elegant interior and terrace overlooking the greens.

BITCHE – 57 Moselle – 307 P4 – pop. 5 674 – alt. 300 m – ✉ 57230 Alsace-Lorraine 27 D1

Paris 438 – Haguenau 43 – Sarrebourg 62 – Sarreguemines 33 – Saverne 51 – Strasbourg 72

Office de tourisme, 4, rue du glacis du Château ✆ 03 87 06 16 16, Fax 03 87 06 16 17

Holigest Golf de Bitche 2 rue des Prés, E : 1 km on D 662, ✆ 03 87 96 15 30

Citadel★ - Ligne Maginot: Heavy work of Simserhof★ West: 4 km.

Le Strasbourg (Lutz Janisch) with rm VISA

24 r. Col-Teyssier – ✆ 03 87 96 00 44 – www.le-strasbourg.fr – le-strasbourg@wanadoo.fr – Fax 03 87 96 11 57 – Closed 13 February-1st March

10 rm – †€ 48/76 ††€ 63/90, ☕ € 10

Rest – *(closed Sunday dinner, Tuesday lunch and Monday)* Menu (€ 23), € 31/54 – Carte € 39/53

Spec. Velouté de potimarron à l'oseille. Cuisse de pintade à la crème de morilles. Tiramisu à nôtre façon.

◆ In a luminous Art Deco inspired dining room, sample the talented chef's generous and moderately priced cooking. Comfortable bedrooms with personalised touches inspired by Africa, Asia and Provence.

La Tour VISA

3 r. de la Gare – ✆ 03 87 96 29 25 – restaurant.la.tour@wanadoo.fr – Fax 03 87 96 02 61 – Closed 12-20 January, Tuesday dinner and Monday

Rest – Menu (€ 13), € 28/58 bi – Carte € 28/50

◆ Between the station and town centre, a large building with a tower. Belle Epoque-style decor for the three attractive dining rooms. Modern menu.

BIZE-MINERVOIS – 11 Aude – 344 I3 – pop. 1 022 – alt. 58 m – ✉ 11120 22 B2

Paris 792 – Béziers 33 – Carcassonne 49 – Narbonne 22 – St-Pons-de-Thomières 33

La Bastide Cabezac

au Hameau de Cabezac, South: 3 km on D 5 – ✆ 04 68 46 66 10 – www.la-bastide-cabezac.com – contact@la-bastide-cabezac.com – Fax 04 68 46 66 29 – Closed 8-30 November, 16-28 February, lunch from Monday to Wednesday in high season, Saturday lunch, Sunday dinner and Monday from 16 September to 14 April

12 rm – €80/130 €80/130, ☕ €10

Rest – Menu (€16), €25/75 – Carte €50/75

◆ An 18C post house in the heart of a hamlet. The refined setting, regional-style furniture and warm colours make this a pleasant place to stay. Elegant restaurant offering local wines and contemporary southern dishes.

BLAESHEIM – **67 Bas-Rhin** – **315** J5 – **see Strasbourg**

BLAGNAC – **31 Haute-Garonne** – **343** G3 – **see Toulouse**

BLAINVILLE-SUR-MER – **50 Manche** – **303** C5 – **pop. 1 483** – **alt. 26 m** – ✉ **50560** 32 **A2**

Paris 347 – Caen 116 – Saint-Lô 41 – Saint Helier 56 – Granville 36

Syndicat d'initiative, 12 bis, route de la mer ✆ 02 33 07 90 89, Fax 02 33 47 97 93

XX ✿ **Le Mascaret** (Philippe Hardy) with rm

1 r. de Bas – ✆ 02 33 45 86 09 – www.restaurant-lemascaret.fr – le.mascaret@wanadoo.fr – Fax 02 33 07 90 01 – Closed 23 November-5 December and 2-28 January

5 rm – €95/185 €95/185, ☕ €17

Rest – *(closed Sunday dinner and Wednesday dinner except 15 July-30 August and Monday)* Menu (€25), €29/69 – Carte €65/85

Spec. Variation autour du coquillage. Raviole de tourteau, coques et cocos, jus de langoustine. Filet de barbue, jus aux herbes, légumes du moment.

◆ This 18C house has a courtyard and herb garden. Inventive cuisine focusing on meat and seafood served in a colourful, luxurious and intimate setting. Bedrooms decorated in an original and Baroque mixture of styles (decorative bathtubs). Wellness spa.

LE BLANC – **36 Indre** – **323** C7 – **pop. 7 015** – **alt. 85 m** – ✉ **36300** 11 **B3**

Dordogne-Berry-Limousin

Paris 326 – Bellac 62 – Châteauroux 61 – Châtellerault 52 – Poitiers 62

Office de tourisme, place de la Libération ✆ 02 54 37 05 13, Fax 02 54 37 31 93

XX **Le Cygne**

8 av. Gambetta – ✆ 02 54 28 71 63 – Closed 22 June-9 July, 20-24 December, 2-19 January, Sunday dinner, Monday and Tuesday

Rest – *(number of covers limited, pre-book)* Menu €19/32 – Carte €38/60

◆ Near the church renowned for its miraculous cures, a pleasant restaurant with well-laid tables. Modern cuisine that varies with the market produce available.

LE BLANC-MESNIL – **93 Seine-Saint-Denis** – **305** F7 – **101** 17 – **see Paris, Environs (Le Bourget)**

BLANGY-SUR-BRESLE – **76 Seine-Maritime** – **304** J2 – **pop. 3 188** – **alt. 70 m** – ✉ **76340** 33 **D1**

Paris 156 – Abbeville 29 – Amiens 56 – Dieppe 55 – Neufchâtel-en-Bray 31 – Le Tréport 26

Syndicat d'initiative, 1, rue Checkroun ✆ 02 35 93 52 48, Fax 02 35 94 06 14

X **Les Pieds dans le Plat**

27 r. St-Denis – ✆ 02 35 93 38 36 – Fax 02 35 93 43 64 – Closed February holidays, Thursday dinner from October to May, Sunday dinner and Monday

Rest – Menu (€14), €16 (weekdays), €25/32 – Carte €30/45

◆ Smart and light dining room brightened with paintings by a local artist and unusual glass flowers. Service with a smile and local, generous, well-made cuisine.

BLANQUEFORT – 33 Gironde – 335 H5 – see Bordeaux

BLAYE – 33 Gironde – 335 H4 – pop. 4 687 – alt. 7 m – ✉ 33390 3 **B1**

Paris 549 – Bordeaux 57 – Mérignac 59 – Pessac 64 – Talence 62

Office de tourisme, allées Marines ✆ 05 57 42 12 09, Fax 05 57 42 91 94

La Citadelle

pl. d'Armes – ✆ 05 57 42 17 10 – www.hotellacitadelle.com – hotelcitadelle.blaye@orange.fr – Fax 05 57 42 10 34

21 rm – †€ 80 ††€ 90/100, ☕ € 12 – ½ P € 90/100

Rest – Menu € 25 (weekday lunch), € 35/45 – Carte € 45/70

◆ Built on the walls of the old town, this establishment dominates the estuary. Bright, wellkept, recently-renovated bedrooms. Pool. Contemporary dining room and fine panoramic terrace.

BLENDECQUES – 62 Pas-de-Calais – 301 G3 – see St-Omer

BLÉNEAU – 89 Yonne – 319 A5 – pop. 1 491 – alt. 200 m – ✉ 89220 7 **A1**

Paris 156 – Auxerre 56 – Clamecy 59 – Gien 30 – Montargis 42

Syndicat d'initiative, 2, rue Aristide Briand ✆ 03 86 74 82 28, Fax 03 86 74 82 28

Château de St Fargeau★★ **Burgundy-Jura**

Blanche de Castille

17 r. d'Orléans – ✆ 03 86 74 92 63 – hotelblanchecastille.facite.com – blanchecastille@orange.fr – Fax 03 86 74 94 43 – Closed Sunday evening

12 rm – †€ 50 ††€ 50, ☕ € 8 – ½ P € 55

Rest – *(closed 7-15 September, 23 December-15 January, Sunday and Thursday)* Menu € 16 (weekdays)/23 – Carte € 22/35

◆ A family-run hotel in a former post house with well-kept rooms; each one has a girl's name. Those on the top floor have sloping roofs. A plush restaurant and a terrace on the inner courtyard, serving updated fare.

Auberge du Point du Jour

pl. de la Mairie – ✆ 03 86 74 94 38 – www.aubergedupointdujour.fr – aubergepointdujour@orange.fr – Fax 03 86 74 85 92 – Closed Sunday dinner, Monday and Tuesday in low season

Rest – Menu € 17 (weekday lunch)/35 – Carte € 40/55

◆ Exposed beams, woodwork and fresh flowers set the welcoming scene in this small establishment. Traditional cuisine with a regional twist.

BLÉNOD-LÈS-PONT-À-MOUSSON – 54 Meurthe-et-Moselle – 307 H5 – see Pont-à-Mousson

BLÉRÉ – 37 Indre-et-Loire – 317 O5 – pop. 5 024 – alt. 59 m – ✉ 37150 11 **A1**

Châteaux of the Loire

Paris 234 – Blois 48 – Château-Renault 36 – Loches 25 – Montrichard 16 – Tours 27

Office de tourisme, 8, rue Jean-Jacques Rousseau ✆ 02 47 57 93 00, Fax 02 47 57 93 00

Cheval Blanc rest,

pl. de l'Église – ✆ 02 47 30 30 14 – www.lechevalblancblere.com – le.cheval.blanc.blere@wanadoo.fr – Fax 02 47 23 52 80 – Closed 16-25 November and 2 January-3 February

12 rm – †€ 64/67 ††€ 64/67, ☕ € 10

Rest – *(Closed Sunday dinner, Friday lunch and Monday except bank holidays) (pre-book)* Menu (€ 22), € 44/61 – Carte € 49/60

◆ A 17C residence whose rooms mostly overlook a peaceful flower-decked courtyard. Pool and garden. Pleasant restaurant with a rustic style dining room to the rear and a brighter area at the front. Classic cooking, Loire valley wines.

BLÉRIOT-PLAGE – 62 Pas-de-Calais – 301 E2 – see Calais

BLESLE – 43 Haute-Loire – 331 B2 – pop. 657 – alt. 520 m – ✉ 43450 5 B3

Auvergne

Paris 484 – Aurillac 92 – Brioude 23 – Issoire 39 – Murat 45 – St-Flour 39

Office de tourisme, place de l'Église ✆ 04 71 76 26 90, Fax 04 71 76 28 17

St-Pierre church ★.

La Bougnate rm, VISA

pl. Vallat – ✆ 04 71 76 29 30 – www.labougnate.com – contact@labougnate.com – Fax 04 71 76 29 39 – Closed December-January and Monday from October to April

8 rm – †€ 55/95 ††€ 55/95, ☕ € 9 **Rest** – Menu € 16/34 – Carte € 24/36

◆ This peaceful attractive inn is located in one of the village's houses. Smart simple rooms; those in the small tower are more picturesque. Craft shop. Pretty, rustic interior, Aubrac beef specialities and a fine wine list.

BLIENSCHWILLER – 67 Bas-Rhin – 315 I6 – pop. 286 – alt. 230 m – ✉ 67650 2 C1

Paris 504 – Barr 51 – Erstein 26 – Obernai 19 – Sélestat 11 – Strasbourg 47

Syndicat d'initiative, 4, rue du Winzenberg ✆ 03 88 92 40 16, Fax 03 88 92 40 16

Winzenberg without rest P VISA AE

58 rte des Vins – ✆ 03 88 92 62 77 – www.winzenberg.fr – winzenberg@orange.fr – Fax 03 88 92 45 22 – Closed 24 December-4 January and 8 February-9 March

13 rm – †€ 42/45 ††€ 45/53, ☕ € 7

◆ This family-run hotel, in a former winegrower's home, has character with its flower-filled, pink facade, pretty inner courtyard and stylish rooms (painted wooden furniture).

Le Pressoir de Bacchus VISA

50 rte des Vins – ✆ 03 88 92 43 01 – lepressoirdebacchus@wanadoo.fr – Fax 03 88 92 43 01 – Closed 29 June-17 July, 23 February-13 March, Wednesday except dinner from April to December and Tuesday

Rest – Menu (€ 18 bi), € 25/46 – Carte € 31/44

◆ Simple and well-kept setting combining Alsatian style and bistro atmosphere. Regional food and wine exclusively from the village. Warm welcome.

BLOIS P – 41 Loir-et-Cher – 318 E6 – pop. 47 900 – Built-up area 116 544 – alt. 73 m – ✉ 41000 11 A1

Châteaux of the Loire

Paris 182 – Le Mans 111 – Orléans 61 – Tours 66

Office de tourisme, 23, place du Château ✆ 02 54 90 41 41, Fax 02 54 90 41 48

du Château de Cheverny Cheverny La Rousselière, 15 km on the Cheverny road, ✆ 02 54 79 24 70

Château★★★: musée des Beaux-Arts★ - Old Blois★: St-Nicolas church ★ - Courtyard with galleries★ of the Hôtel d'Alluye YZ **E** - Jardins de l'Evêché ≤★ - Jardin des simples et des fleurs royales ≤★ Z **L** - Maison de la Magie Robert-Houdin★.

Plan on following page

Mercure Centre VISA AE

28 quai St-Jean – ✆ 02 54 56 66 66 – www.mecure.com – h1621@accor.com – Fax 02 54 56 67 00 Y **f**

96 rm – †€ 115/125 ††€ 135/145, ☕ € 14

Rest – Menu € 19/29 bi – Carte € 32/50

◆ Practical, modern rooms, some of which are reached by a gangway that leads into a lounge bar. View of the Loire from some rooms. The bright dining room overlooks the Loire. Interesting selection of wines by the glass.

BLOIS

Abbé-Grégoire (Quai de l') . Z 2
Anne-de-Bretagne (R.) . . . . Z 3
Augustin Thierry (Sq.) . . . . Z 4
Balzac (R. H. de) . . . . V 5
Beauvoir (R.) . . . . Y 6
Bourg-St-Jean (R. du) . . . . Y 10
Cartier (R. R.) . . . . V 13
Chemonton (R.) . . . . Y 16
Clouseau (Mail) . . . . Y 17
Commerce (R. du) . . . . Z
Cordeliers (R. des) . . . . Y 18
Curie (R. Pierre et Marie) . . X 19
Déportés (Av. des) . . . . X 78
Dion (R. R.) . . . . V 20
Dupuis (Bd D.) . . . . X 21
Fontaine-des-Élus (R.) . . . . Z 22
Fossés-du-Château
(R. des) . . . . Z 23
Gambetta (Av.) . . . . X 25
Gaulle (Pont Ch.-de) . . . . . . X 26
Gentils (Bd R.) . . . . X 27
Industrie (Bd de l') . . . . V 29
Jeanne-d'Arc (R.) . . . . Z 30
Laigret (Av. J.) . . . . Z 32
Leclerc (Av. du Mar.) . . . . . . X 33
Lices (Pl. des) . . . . Z 34
Lion-Ferré (R. du) . . . . Z 35
Maunoury (Av. du Mar.) . . . Y 39
Monsabre (R. du Père) . . . . Z 41

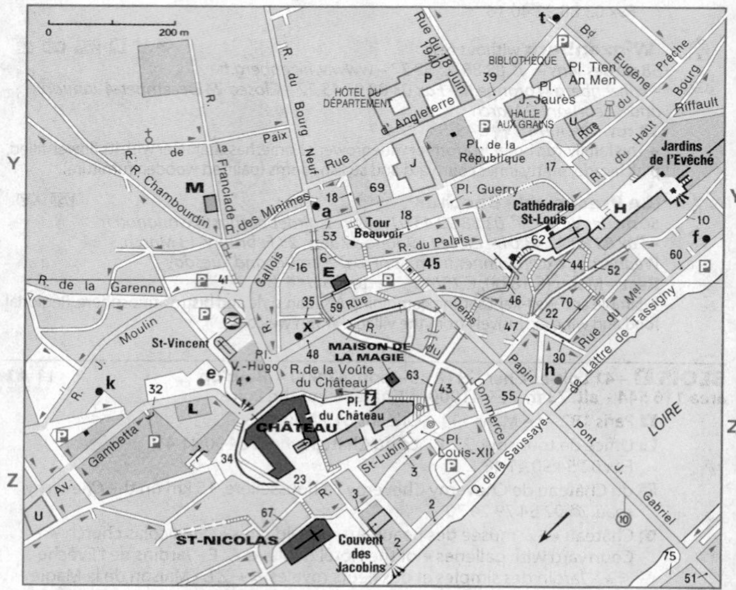

Orfèvres (R. des) . . . . Z 43
Papegaults (R. des) . . . . Y 44
Papin (Escaliers Denis) . . . . . . Y 45
Papin (R. Denis) . . . . Z
Pierre-de-Blois (R.) . . . . Z 46
Poids-du-Roi (R. du) . . . . Z 47
Porte-Côté (R.) . . . . Z 48
Président-Wilson (Av.) . . . . X, Z 51
Puits-Châtel (R. du) . . . . Y 52
Remparts (R. des) . . . . Y 53
Résistance (Carrefour de la) . . Z 55
Ronsard (R. P. de) . . . . X 58
St-Honoré (R.) . . . . YZ 59
St-Jean (Q.) . . . . Y 60
St-Louis (Pl.) . . . . Y 62
St-Martin (R.) . . . . Z 63
Schuman (Av. R.) . . . . V 64
Signeuix (R. de) . . . . V 66
Trois-Marchands (R. des) . . . . Z 67
Trouessard (R.) . . . . Y 69
Vauvert (R.) . . . . Z 70
Verdun (Av. de) . . . . X 72
Vezin (R. A.) . . . . V 74
Villebois-Mareuil (Q.) . . . . X, Z 75

Holiday Inn Garden Court
26 av. Maunoury – 02 54 55 44 88
– www.holiday-inn.fr – holiblois@wanadoo.fr – Fax 02 54 74 57 97 Y **t**
78 rm – €88/110 €88/110, €13
Rest – *(closed Saturday lunch, Sunday lunch and lunch on public holidays)*
Menu (€15), €18 – Carte €30/36
◆ This renovated hotel is slightly outside the town centre but near the corn market (now a concert and exhibition hall). It offers comfortable, welcoming rooms. Contemporary restaurant. Indoor terrace serving grilled meat and salads in summer.

Anne de Bretagne without rest
31 av. J.-Laigret – 02 54 78 05 38 – www.annedebretagne.free.fr
– annedebretagne@free.fr – Fax 02 54 74 37 79
– Closed 15 February-7 March Z **k**
27 rm – €45/51 €54/58, €8
◆ This family establishment on a tree lined square near the château is well worth the stay: cosy sitting room, simple, brightly decorated rooms and summer breakfast terrace.

Monarque
61 r. Porte-Chartraine – 02 54 78 02 35 – http://annedebretagne.free.fr
– lemonarque@free.fr – Fax 02 54 74 82 76
– Closed 21 December-25 January Y **a**
22 rm – €38 €55/59, €6,50 – ½ P €50
Rest – Menu €11 (weekday lunch), €18/28 – Carte approx. €26
◆ This 19C building, home to a welcoming hotel, is a few minutes from the pedestrian streets. All the small, well-kept, tasteful rooms are air-conditioned. A central well of light and a few works of art adorn this restaurant that serves modern cuisine.

Ibis without rest
3 r. Porte-Côté – 02 54 74 01 17 – www.ibishotel.com – H0920@accor.com
– Fax 02 54 74 85 69 Z **x**
56 rm – €59/82 €59/82, €8
◆ A central address combining the style of an old private residence (mosaic in the hall, stucco, mouldings) and the functionality of renovated and well-soundproofed rooms.

Le Plessis without rest
195 r. Albert-1er – 02 54 43 80 08 – www.leplessisblois.com – leplessisblois@wanadoo.fr – Fax 02 54 43 95 24 X **e**
5 rm – €100 €110/130
◆ A stylishly converted winegrowing property: reading room and brunch-style breakfasts in the main 18C house, while elegant bedrooms are in the former wine press.

La Petite Fugue without rest
9 quai du Foix – 02 54 78 42 95 – www.lapetitefugue.com – lapetitefugue@wanadoo.fr X **a**
4 rm – €100/135 €108/145
◆ This stately freestone 18C house stands on the banks of the Loire at the foot of the historic town. Personalised, predominantly grey and white decor, patio and relaxed ambience.

L'Orangerie du Château (Jean-Marc Molveaux)
1 av. J.-Laigret – 02 54 78 05 36
– www.orangerie-du-chateau.fr – contact@orangerie-du-chateau.fr
– Fax 02 54 78 22 78 – Closed 23-30 August, 2-8 November, 16 February-13 March, Monday lunch from May to October, Tuesday dinner from November to April, Sunday dinner and Wednesday Z **e**
Rest – Menu €36 (weekdays)/77 – Carte €73/94
Spec. Huîtres spéciales, chou-fleur, tourteau et foie gras. Pigeonneau du Vendômois rôti aux épices, carotte, miel et citron. Menu autour de l'asperge de Sologne (printemps). **Wines** Cour-Cheverny, Touraine.
◆ A handsome outbuilding of the 15C château and a terrace with a clear view of Francois I's noble abode. Contemporary cuisine. Bright refined dining room.

XXX **Le Médicis** (Damien Garanger) with rm

2 allée François-1er – ☎ 02 54 43 94 04 – www.le-medicis.com – le.medicis@wanadoo.fr – Fax 02 54 42 04 05 – Closed 9-15 November, 5-31 January, Sunday dinner from November to May and Monday from November to March X **p**

10 rm – †€ 87/130 ††€ 87/160, ☕ € 12 – ½ P € 95/114

Rest – Menu (€ 25), € 30/72 – Carte € 52/74

Spec. Pâtes surprise aux escargots et chèvre de Sologne (winter). Pigeon du pays de Racan et foie gras chaud comme un cromesqui (autumn). Finger lavande aux framboises et macaron glacé (summer). **Wines** Vouvray, Bourgueil.

◆ This house dating from 1900 offers good contemporary cuisine in a luxurious dining room/veranda (moulded ceilings, Second Empire furniture). Modernised bedrooms that are well-kept and comfortable.

X **Au Rendez-vous des Pêcheurs** (Christophe Cosme)

27 r. Foix – ☎ 02 54 74 67 48 – www.rendezvousdespecheurs.com – christophe.cosme@wanadoo.fr – Fax 02 54 74 47 67 – Closed 3-17 August, Monday lunch and Sunday X **r**

Rest – *(number of covers limited, pre-book)* Menu € 30 (weekdays)/76 – Carte € 50/80

Spec. Fleur de courgette de la vallée de la Loire farcie aux langoustines. (May-November). Sandre pané au pain d'épice et ratatouille de légumes. Assiette de gourmandises. **Wines** Jasnières, Touraine.

◆ In homage to the former fishermen's haunt it used to be, this friendly bistro-style restaurant offers an inventive menu that happily navigates between land and sea.

X **Côté Loire "Auberge Ligérienne"** with rm

2 pl. de la Gréve – ☎ 02 54 78 07 86 – www.coteloire.com – info@coteloire.com – Fax 02 54 56 87 33 – Closed 4-10 May, 1st-7 September, 16-29 November, 5 January-3 February X **f**

7 rm – †€ 59/69 ††€ 59/79, ☕ € 9 – ½ P € 65/75

Rest – *(closed Saturday lunch in July-August, Sunday and Monday)* Menu (€ 19), € 29

◆ The charm of this country inn derives from the original 16C beams, varnished wooden tables, an antique dresser, and a set blackboard menu prepared from seasonal market produce.

X **Le Bistrot de Léonard**

8 r. Mar.-de Lattre-de-Tassigny – ☎ 02 54 74 83 04 – www.lebistrotdeleonard.com – lebistrotdeleonard@orange.fr – Fax 02 54 74 85 87 – Closed 24 December-1st January, Saturday lunch and Sunday Z **h**

Rest – Carte € 25/45

◆ This bistro with a Parisian ambience is behind an attractive wood façade on the embankment. Specials chalked up on the board, stylish table layout, and references to Leonardo da Vinci throughout.

in St-Denis-sur-Loire 6 km by ② – pop. 867 – alt. 92 m – ✉ 41000

XXX **Le Grand Atelier** with rm

r. 8-Mai-1945 – ☎ 02 54 74 10 64 – www.hotel-restaurant-atelier.com – contact@hotel-restaurant-atelier.com – Fax 02 54 58 86 37 – Closed Sunday dinner and Monday

5 rm – †€ 100/110 ††€ 110/125, ☕ € 12 **Rest** – Menu € 30/59

◆ This attractive house, once the workshop of Bernard Lorjou, has retained its artistic soul. Some of Lorjou's work adorns the elegant dining room, which serves contemporary cuisine. Terrace. Quite cosy rooms.

in Molineuf 9 km by ⑦ – pop. 801 – alt. 115 m – ✉ 41190

XX **Poste**

11 av. de Blois – ☎ 02 54 70 03 25 – www.restaurant-poidras.com – contact@restaurant-poidras.com – Fax 02 54 70 12 46 – Closed 16 November-4 December, 8-19 February, Tuesday from October to April, Sunday dinner from September to June and Wednesday

Rest – Menu € 18/62

◆ Country inn on the edge of Blois forest, housing a colourful modern dining room extended by a bright veranda. Refined contemporary cuisine.

BLONVILLE-SUR-MER – 14 Calvados – **303** M3 – **pop. 1 341** – **alt. 10 m** – ✉ **14910** 32 **A3**

Paris 205 – Caen 46 – Deauville 5 – Le Havre 50 – Lisieux 34 – Pont-l'Évêque 18

Office de tourisme, 32 bis, avenue Michel d'Ornano ✆ 02 31 87 91 14, Fax 02 31 87 11 38

L'Épi d'Or

23 av. Michel-d'Ornano – ✆ 02 31 87 90 48 – www.hotel-normand.com – epidor@hotel-normand.com – Fax 02 31 87 08 98 – Closed 21-30 December and 12 January-19 February

40 rm – †€ 55/70 ††€ 60/110, ☕ € 8 – ½ P € 65/90

Rest – *(closed Wednesday and Thursday except July-August)* Menu € 19/48 – Carte € 36/68

◆ A pleasant, recently renovated, Norman-style house. The rooms are all the same and are above all practical. A tasteful modern dining room and traditional menu: quick meals are served in a rustic setting.

BOIS-COLOMBES – 92 Hauts-de-Seine – **311** J2 – **101** 15 – see Paris, Area

BOIS DE BOULOGNE – 75 Ville-de-Paris – see Paris (Paris 16e)

BOIS DE LA CHAIZE – 85 Vendée – **316** C5 – see Île de Noirmoutier

BOIS-DU-FOUR – 12 Aveyron – **338** J5 – ✉ **12780** 29 **D1**

Paris 627 – Aguessac 16 – Millau 23 – Pont-de-Salars 25 – Rodez 45 – Sévérac-le-Château 18

Relais du Bois du Four

– ✆ 05 65 61 86 17 – www.boisdufour.com – contact@boisdufour.com – Fax 05 65 58 81 37 – Open 20 March-27 June, 3 July-15 November and closed Sunday dinner and Wednesday

26 rm – †€ 51 ††€ 51, ☕ € 8 – ½ P € 53/58

Rest – Menu € 12 (weekday lunch), € 15/31 – Carte € 21/40

◆ Fishing enthusiasts will want to cast a few lines in the pond opposite this former post house. The practical tasteful first floor rooms have been treated to a facelift. Impeccably well-kept. A largey countrified restaurant and cuisine with an Aveyron bias.

BOIS-LE-ROI – 77 Seine-et-Marne – **312** F5 – **pop. 5 452** – **alt. 80 m** – ✉ **77590** 19 **C2**

Paris 58 – Fontainebleau 10 – Melun 10 – Montereau-Fault-Yonne 26

U.C.P.A. Bois-le-Roi Base de loisirs, NW : 2 km, ✆ 01 64 81 33 31

La Marine

52 quai O.-Metra, (near the lock) – ✆ 01 60 69 61 38 – Closed 26 October-5 November, 22 February-6 March, Sunday dinner in winter, Monday and Tuesday except bank holidays

Rest – Menu € 28/45 – Carte € 50/60

◆ This pleasant guesthouse is well placed on the banks of the Seine, opposite a lock. Nice, traditional cuisine in the rustic-style dining room or on the summer terrace.

BOIS-PLAGE-EN-RÉ – 17 Charente-Maritime – **324** B2 – see Île de Ré

BOISSERON – 34 Hérault – **339** J6 – see Sommières

BOISSET – 15 Cantal – **330** B6 – **pop. 637** – **alt. 426 m** – ✉ **15600** 5 **A3**

Paris 559 – Aurillac 31 – Calvinet 18 – Entraygues-sur-Truyère 48 – Figeac 36 – Maurs 14

Auberge de Concasty

Northeast : 3 km via D 64 – ✆ 04 71 62 21 16 – www.auberge-concasty.com – info@auberge-concasty.com – Fax 04 71 62 22 22 – Open 1st April- 30 November

12 rm – †€ 82/92 ††€ 82/92, ☕ € 10 – 1 suite – ½ P € 82/120

Rest – *(dinner only dinner only) (pre-book)* Menu € 32, € 44/60

◆ Fresh air and a restful stay are guaranteed on this estate in the Cantal countryside. Stylish modern rooms, with those in the outbuildings offering more space. Auvergne-style brunch available on request. One set menu marrying tradition and local produce, served in a pleasant, rustic dining room.

BOISSIÈRES – 46 Lot – **337** E4 – **pop. 312** – **alt. 229 m** – ✉ **46150** 28 **B1**

Paris 573 – Toulouse 137 – Cahors 14 – Sarlat-la-Canéda 63 – Caussade 64

Michel & Lydia

at East 1 km on secondary road – ✆ 05 65 21 43 29 – www.micheletlydia.fr – micheletlydia@orange.fr – Fax 05 65 21 43 29 – Closed 3 December-3 January

4 rm ☕ – †€ 60/73 ††€ 65/78 **Table d'hôte** – Menu € 24 bi

◆ The Belgian owners take great care over their delightful modern home. Comfortable, individually decorated rooms (antiques and family heirlooms). The chef, a former baker, prepares traditional cuisine. Home-made bread and pastries.

BOLLENBERG – 68 Haut-Rhin – **315** H9 – **see Rouffach**

BOLLEZEELE – 59 Nord – **302** B2 – **pop. 1 375** – **alt. 40 m** – ✉ **59470** 30 **B1**

Paris 274 – Calais 45 – Dunkerque 24 – Lille 68 – St-Omer 18

Hostellerie St-Louis

47 r. de l'Église – ✆ 03 28 68 81 83 – www.hostelleriesaintlouis.com – contact@hostelleriesaintlouis.com – Fax 03 28 68 01 17 – Closed 20-30 July, 23 December-14 January and Sunday dinner

27 rm – †€ 44 ††€ 58/68, ☕ € 9

Rest – *(closed for lunch except Sunday)* Menu € 25 (dinner), € 34/46 – Carte € 40/64

◆ This lovely early-19C house has a pleasant garden with a water feature. The modern rooms are spacious and practical. Period furniture and pastel shades in a bourgeois setting; classic generous menu served with a smile.

BONDUES – 59 Nord – **302** G3 – **see Lille**

BONIFACIO – 2A Corse-du-Sud – **345** D11 – **see Corse**

BONLIEU – 39 Jura – **321** F7 – **pop. 238** – **alt. 785 m** – ✉ **39130** 16 **B3**

Burgundy-Jura

Paris 439 – Champagnole 23 – Lons-le-Saunier 32 – Morez 24 – St-Claude 42

La Poutre with rm

25 Grde Rue – ✆ 03 84 25 57 77 – Fax 03 84 25 51 61 – Open 7 May-1st November and closed Monday dinner and Tuesday except July-August and Monday lunch

8 rm – †€ 46 ††€ 46/56, ☕ € 8 – ½ P € 60

Rest – Menu € 25/70 – Carte € 48/80

◆ A family farmhouse dating from 1740, located in the town centre. Well-presented, home-cooked and regional dishes are served in the rustic dining room (beams and old stonework).

BONNAT – 23 Creuse – **325** I3 – **pop. 1 301** – **alt. 330 m** – ✉ **23220** 25 **C1**

Paris 329 – Châtre 37 – Guéret 20 – Montluçon 72 – Souterraine 53

L'Orangerie

3 bis r. de la Paix – ✆ 05 55 62 86 86 – www.hotel-lorangerie.fr – reception@hotel-lorangerie.fr – Fax 05 55 62 86 87 – Closed from January to March, lunch in week except July-August, Sunday dinner and Monday from November to April

30 rm – €85 €95 – ½ P €85

Rest – Menu €28/49 – Carte approx. €49

◆ Pleasant lounges and attractive, comfortable bedrooms adorned with Louis XV-style furniture. Breakfasts on the terrace. In summer, traditional gourmet cuisine is served facing the garden (a French-style vegetable garden).

BONNATRAIT – 74 Haute-Savoie – **328** L2 – **see Thonon-les-Bains**

BONNE – 74 Haute-Savoie – **328** K3 – **pop. 2 599** – **alt. 457 m** – ✉ **74380** 46 **F1**

Paris 545 – Annecy 45 – Bonneville 16 – Genève 18 – Morzine 40 – Thonon-les-Bains 31

Baud with rm — rest,

– *✆ 04 50 39 20 15 – www.hotel-baud.com – info@hotel-baud.com – Fax 04 50 36 28 96*

18 rm – €120/220 €120/220, €14

Rest – *(closed Sunday dinner)* Menu (€23), €39/72 – Carte €44/64

◆ Cosy, elegant, contemporary dining rooms, updated bistro menu, tempting wine list, plush sitting rooms and a secret garden on the banks of the Ménoge.

at Pont-de-Fillinges 2,5 km East – ✉ **74250**

Le Pré d'Antoine

rte Boëge – ✆ 04 50 36 45 06 – www.lepredantoine.com – lepredantoine@aol.com – Fax 04 50 31 12 28 – Closed 1st to 8 January, Tuesday dinner and Wednesday

Rest – Menu (€20), €22 (weekdays)/52 – Carte €50/65

◆ A modern building in chalet style with a large wood-panelled dining room and a well-exposed terrace. Classic cuisine with dishes varying between country and tradition.

BONNE-FONTAINE – 57 Moselle – **307** O6 – **see Phalsbourg**

BONNÉTAGE – 25 Doubs – **321** K3 – **pop. 714** – **alt. 960 m** – ✉ **25210** 17 **C2**

Paris 468 – Belfort 69 – Besançon 65 – Biel/Bienne 62 – La Chaux-de-Fonds 29

L'Etang du Moulin (Jacques Barnachon) with rm — rest,

5 chemin de l'étang du Moulin, 1.5 km via D 236 and private road – ✆ 03 81 68 92 78 – www.etang-du-moulin.fr – etang.du.moulin@wanadoo.fr – Fax 03 81 68 94 42 – Closed 21-29 December, 4 January-6 February, Sunday dinner and Monday from 15 November to 15 March, Wednesday lunch and Tuesday

18 rm – €55/65 €65/85, €8,50 – ½ P €55/60

Rest – Menu €24/90 – Carte €36/78

Spec. Ragoût de morilles à la crème fraîche et vin jaune. Ris de veau caramélisés au miel de sapin et vinaigre balsamique. Dessert autour du vin jaune et tuile aux noix. **Wines** Arbois Savagnin, Vin de Pays de Franche-Comté.

◆ A large chalet in the middle of the countryside, near a small lake. Comfortable, modern dining room serving delicious local dishes (selection of foie gras) and fine wine list.

Les Perce-Neige with rm — rest,

D 437 – ✆ 03 81 68 91 51 – www.hotel-les-perce-neige.com – patrick-bole@wanadoo.fr – Fax 03 81 68 95 25 – Closed 20-30 January

12 rm – €43 €50, €7 – ½ P €52

Rest – *(closed Sunday dinner)* Menu (€15), €19/33 – Carte €25/50

◆ Traditional dishes served in a rustic setting; chalet ambiance perfect for sampling the fondue. Functional rooms in a building next to a road that is fairly quiet at night.

BONNEUIL – 16 Charente – 324 J6 – pop. 247 – alt. 100 m – ✉ 16120 39 **B3**

Paris 482 – Poitiers 146 – Angoulême 34 – Saintes 59 – Cognac 25

Le Maine Pertubaud-Jenssen

2 km East on the D 669 – ✆ 05 45 96 99 50 – www.jenssen.fr – reception@jenssen.fr – Fax 05 45 96 99 48 – Closed 9-16 August and 20-27 December

5 rm – †€ 100/120 ††€ 120/140, ☕ € 12 – 1 suite

Table d'hôte – Menu € 35 bi/55 bi

◆ A tiny 18C hamlet in the middle of a 24ha Champagne vineyard. Renovated to a luxurious standard with top of the range comforts in the modern villa. Jenssen cognac distillery on site. Table d'hote with a rustic dining room. Traditional cuisine.

BONNEUIL-MATOURS – 86 Vienne – 322 J4 – pop. 1 887 – alt. 60 m 39 **C1** – ✉ 86210

Paris 322 – Bellac 79 – Le Blanc 51 – Châtellerault 17 – Montmorillon 42 – Poitiers 25

Office de tourisme, Carrefour Maurice Fombeure ✆ 05 49 85 08 62, Fax 05 49 85 08 62

Le Pavillon Bleu

D 749, (opposite the bridge) – ✆ 05 49 85 28 05 – c.ribardiere@wanadoo.fr – Fax 05 49 21 61 94 – Closed 28 September-12 October, Wednesday dinner from October to May, Sunday dinner and Monday

Rest – Menu (€ 13), € 19/39

◆ Take the suspension bridge across the River Vienne to this pretty family inn popular for its relaxing atmosphere and tasty traditional fare.

BONNEVAL – 28 Eure-et-Loir – 311 E6 – pop. 4 218 – alt. 128 m 11 **B1** – ✉ 28800 Châteaux of the Loire

Paris 121 – Chartres 31 – Lucé 34 – Orléans 66

Office de tourisme, 2, square Westerham ✆ 02 37 47 55 89, Fax 02 37 96 28 62

Hostellerie du Bois Guibert

in Guibert, 2 km Southwest – ✆ 02 37 47 22 33 – www.bois-guibert.com – bois-guibert@wanadoo.fr – Fax 02 37 47 50 69 – Closed 15 February-12 March and 26 October to 5 November

20 rm – †€ 69/160 ††€ 69/160, ☕ € 12 – ½ P € 82/126

Rest – *(closed Saturday lunch, Sunday dinner and Monday from November to April)* Menu € 28 (weekdays)/67 – Carte € 46/84

◆ In the heart of delightful grounds, this 18C country house offers guests comfortable rooms embellished with antiques. Those in the recent wing are more spacious and up-to-date. An elegant restaurant and a pleasant terrace looking onto the garden. Classic food and a vegetarian menu.

BONNEVAL-SUR-ARC – 73 Savoie – 333 P5 – pop. 239 – alt. 1 800 m 45 **D2** – Winter sports : 1 800/3 000 m 10 – ✉ 73480 French Alps

Paris 706 – Albertville 133 – Chambéry 146 – Lanslebourg 21 – Val-d'Isère 30

Syndicat d'initiative, la Ciamarella ✆ 04 79 05 95 95, Fax 04 79 05 86 87

Old village★★.

À la Pastourelle

– ✆ 04 79 05 81 56 – www.pastourelle.com – hotel.pastourelle@wanadoo.fr – Fax 04 79 05 85 44 – Closed 1 week in June and autumn school holidays

12 rm – †€ 50/58 ††€ 58/62, ☕ € 7 – ½ P € 55

Rest – *(open 20 December-20 April) (dinner only)* Carte € 15/25

◆ Quiet and cosy comfort in this family establishment typical of the charming old village. Restaurant-creperie with beams, fireplace, stone arch and photos of ancestors. On the menu are raclettes, fondues, crêpes and "diot", the regional speciality.

La Bergerie
– 04 79 05 94 97 – Fax 04 79 05 93 24
– *Open 14 June-26 September and 19 December-20 April*
22 rm – €42/52 €58/64, €10 – ½ P €60/65
Rest – Menu €18/23 – Carte €28/45
◆ Enter the Bergerie and relax in its peace and quiet in bright rooms with fine views of the Évettes massif. The numerous copper pans and country objects on the walls give the dining room a rustic feel.

BONNEVILLE – 74 Haute-Savoie – **328** L4 – **pop. 10 463** – **alt. 450 m** – 74130 **French Alps** 46 **F1**

Paris 556 – Annecy 42 – Chamonix-Mont-Blanc 54 – Nantua 87 – Thonon-les-Bains 45

Office de tourisme, 148, place de l'Hôtel de Ville 04 50 97 38 37, Fax 04 50 97 19 33

Bellevue
in Ayze, 2.5 km East by D 6 – 04 50 97 20 83 – eric.delajoud@wanadoo.fr – Fax 04 50 25 28 38 – Open 14 April-11 October, February holidays and closed Sunday dinner
20 rm – €45/48 €52/58, €8
Rest – *(open 11 June-31 August and closed Sunday dinner and lunch except 1st July-24 August)* Menu €18 (weekdays)/32
◆ Built in the 1960s, this family establishment has simple rooms; some overlook the Ayze vines. At garden level, a panoramic dining room and terrace commanding a view over the Arve plain; traditional food.

in Vougy 5 km East by D 1205 – pop. 958 – alt. 471 m – 74130

Le Capucin Gourmand
1520 rte de Genève, D 1205 – 04 50 34 03 50 – www.lecapucingourmand.com – infos@lecapucingourmand.com – Fax 04 50 34 57 57 – Closed 7-31 August, 1st-11 January, Saturday lunch, Sunday and Monday except bank holidays
Rest – Menu €56 – Carte €52/83
Rest ***Le Bistro du Capucin*** – Menu (€22 bi), €28 – Carte €38/50
◆ Walls decorated with stencilling, stylish furniture and trinkets set the scene in the restaurant where guests can enjoy modern cuisine and a good wine list. At the Bistro, authentic decor, informal ambiance and traditional bistro-type menu.

Do not confuse X with ✿!
X defines comfort, while stars are awarded for the best cuisine, across all categories of comfort.

BONNIEUX – 84 Vaucluse – **332** E11 – **pop. 1 363** – **alt. 400 m** – 84480 **Provence** 42 **E1**

Paris 721 – Aix-en-Provence 49 – Apt 12 – Carpentras 42 – Cavaillon 27

Office de tourisme, 7, place Carnot 04 90 75 91 90, Fax 04 90 75 92 94

Terrace ★.

Le Clos du Buis without rest
– 04 90 75 88 48 – www.leclosdubuis.com – le-clos-du-buis@wanadoo.fr – Fax 04 90 75 88 57 – Closed 5 January-1st March and 15 November-22 December*
8 rm – €84/120 €92/120, €6
◆ This imposing villa with beautiful garden and swimming pool blends tradition with comfort. Attractive bedrooms and cosy sitting-room around the old bread oven.

La Bastide de Capelongue (Edouard Loubet) with rm
Lourmarin road, then D 232 and minor road: 1,5 km – ✆ 04 90 75 89 78 – www.edouardloubet.com – contact@capelongue.com – Fax 04 90 75 93 03 – Open from mid March to mid November
17 rm – †€ 160/380 ††€ 190/380, ☕ € 22
Rest – *(closed Tuesday lunch and Wednesday)* Menu € 70 (weekday lunch), € 140/190 – Carte € 130/205
Spec. Cœur de tournesol à la truffe d'été, salade de girolles et rémoulade de bulbes (July-September). Rouget de roche piqué au lard maigre et vermicelles à la crème de rouget. Pulpe de pruneaux moelleux, mousse "péché mignon". **Wines** Côtes du Luberon.
◆ Large residence with a traditional feel set in the countryside. Elegant dining room (beige shades) and pleasant terrace with wrought iron furnishings. Inventive food. Provençal bedrooms; some enjoy a pretty view of the village.

La Ferme de Capelongue
– www.fermedecapelongue.com
1 rm – †€ 220/420, ☕ € 22 – 9 suites – ††€ 220/420
◆ Opposite the Bastide, in a small renovated hamlet, apartments and studios with minimalist décor making the most of the old stone walls. Huge garden with a swimming pool.

Le Fournil
pl. Carnot – ✆ 04 90 75 83 62 – Fax 04 90 75 96 19 – Closed 20 November-20 December, 6 January-20 February, Saturday lunch and Tuesday except dinner d April-September and Monday
Rest – *(number of covers limited, pre-book)* Menu € 28, € 42/45
◆ House set against the hillside offering you a terrace on the small square or an unusual, naturally cool dining room cut into the cliff, with modern decor.

L'Arôme
2 r. Lucien-Blanc – ✆ 04 90 75 88 62 – www.larome-restaurant.com – larome.restaurant@orange.fr – Fax 04 90 04 06 27 – Closed 16 February-23 March, Thursday except dinner from March to October and Wednesday
Rest – Menu (€ 21), € 29/39 – Carte € 36/55
◆ Lovely stone house whose dining rooms (14C vaulted cellars and an 11C cave) and terrace are a picture of welcoming sophistication. Fish and regional specialties.

Southeast 6 km by D 36 and D 943 – ✉ 84480 Bonnieux

Auberge de l'Aiguebrun
Domaine de la Tour – ✆ 04 90 04 47 00 – www.aubergedelaiguebrun.fr – resa@aubergedelaiguebrun.fr – Fax 04 90 04 47 01 – Closed 2 January-15 March
11 rm ☕ – †€ 155/170 ††€ 155/215 – ½ P € 128/158
Rest – *(closed Tuesday and Wednesday except dinner 1st July-15 September)* Menu € 30/65 – Carte € 56/66
◆ This inn, surrounded by a garden complete with pool and dotted with delightful cabins near a river, is a picture of serenity. Provençal rooms. A romantic country chic dining room opening onto a pleasantly shaded terrace. Regional produce of excellent quality.

Red = Pleasant. Look for the red and symbols.

BONNY-SUR-LOIRE – 45 Loiret – 318 O6 – pop. 2 005 – alt. 190 m – ✉ 45420 12 D2

Paris 167 – Auxerre 64 – Cosne-sur-Loire 25 – Gien 24 – Montargis 57
Office de tourisme, 29, Grande Rue ✆ 02 38 31 57 71, Fax 02 38 31 57 71

Des Voyageurs with rm — rest,
10 Grande-Rue – ✆ 02 38 27 01 45 – hotel-des-voyageurs9@wanadoo.fr – Fax 02 38 27 01 46 – Closed 24 August-8 September, 2-8 January, 15 February-2 March, Sunday dinner, Tuesday lunch and Monday
6 rm – †€ 40 ††€ 50, ☕ € 6 – ½ P € 54
Rest – Menu € 19 (weekdays), € 28/47 – Carte € 28/52
◆ Travellers can enjoy modern cuisine that is both gastronomic and faultless. The dining room has a bourgeois touch (exhibition of paintings). Functional bedrooms.

LE BONO – 56 Morbihan – 308 N9 – pop. 2 148 – alt. 10 m – ✉ 56400 9 A3

Paris 475 – Auray 6 – Lorient 49 – Quiberon 37 – Vannes 17

Alicia

1 r. du Gén.-de-Gaulle – ☎ 02 97 57 88 65 – www.hotel-alicia.com – hotelalicia@orange.fr – Fax 02 97 57 92 76 – Closed 1st January-9 February and 23-29 November

21 rm – †€ 60/95 ††€ 60/95, ☕ € 10 – ½ P € 60/78

Rest – *(dinner only)* Menu € 20, € 28/30 – Carte € 24/36

◆ A friendly establishment near the bridge on the shore of the gulf. The impeccable guestrooms, most of which boast a balcony, sport a modern, minimalist look. Traditional fare served by the lovely riverside terrace in fine weather.

BONS-EN-CHABLAIS – 74 Haute-Savoie – 328 L3 – pop. 3 980 – alt. 565 m – ✉ 74890 46 F1

Paris 552 – Annecy 60 – Bonneville 30 – Genève 25 – Thonon-les-Bains 16

Le Progrès

rm, VISA

r. Annexion – ☎ 04 50 36 11 09 – www.hotel-le-progres.com – hotelleprogres2@wanadoo.fr – Fax 04 50 39 44 16 – Closed 15 June-4 July, 1st-18 January, Sunday dinner and Monday

10 rm – †€ 52 ††€ 61, ☕ € 10 – ½ P € 59

Rest – Menu (€ 15), € 18/50 – Carte € 30/49

◆ Two village houses, one with comfortable modern rooms. An ideal base for walks around the Grand Signal des Voirons. Part rustic, part elegant, this restaurant has been decorated with care. Classic cuisine.

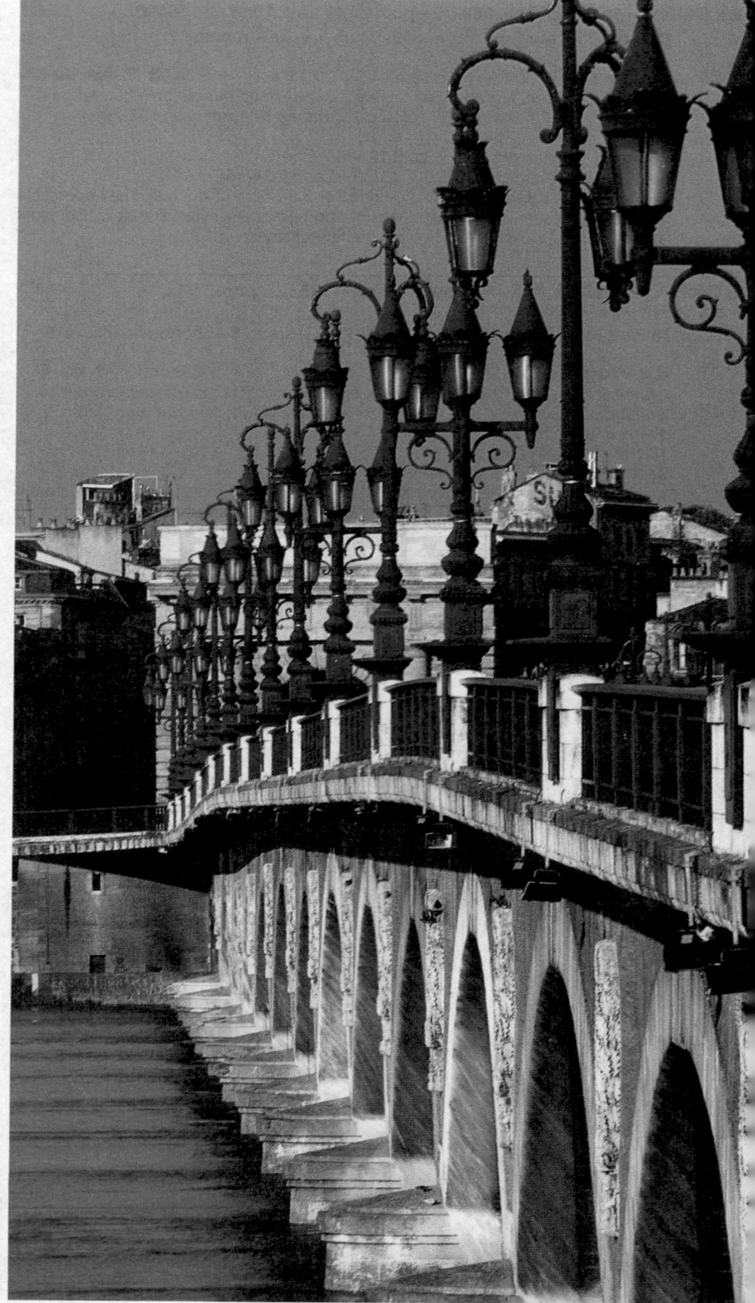

Le pont de Pierre

BORDEAUX

P **Department:** 33 Gironde
Michelin LOCAL map: nº **335** H5
Paris 579 – Lyon 537 – Nantes 323 – Strasbourg 970 – Toulouse 244
Population: 229 500

Pop. built-up area: 753 931
Altitude: 4 m
Postal Code: ✉ 33000
Atlantic Coast
Carte régionale 3 **B1**

USEFUL INFORMATION

TOURIST OFFICE

12, cours du 30 juillet ✆ 05 56 00 66 00, Fax 05 56 00 66 01
Office de tourisme, 12, Cours du 30 Juillet ✆ 05 56 00 66 00, Fax 05 56 00 66 01

MAISON DU VIN DE BORDEAUX

(information, tasting) (closed weekends and public holidays)
1 cours 30 Juillet ✆ 05 56 00 22 66
wine bar open daily from 11:00 to 22:00.

TRANSPORT

Auto-train ✆ 3635 and type 42 (0,34 €/mn)

AIRPORT

Bordeaux-Mérignac: ✆ 05 56 34 50 00, **AU** : 10 km

CASINO

Bordeaux-Lac, r. Cardinal Richaud ✆ 05 56 69 49 00 BT

A FEW GOLF COURSES

- 36 de Bordeaux-Lac Avenue de Pernon, N : 5 km on D 209, ✆ 05 56 50 92 72
- 36 du Médoc Le Pian-Médoc Chemin de Courmateau, 16 km on the Castelnau road, ✆ 05 56 70 11 90
- 27 de Pessac Pessac Rue de la Princesse, SW : 16 km on D 1250, ✆ 05 57 26 03 33

TO BE SEEN

18C BORDEAUX

Grand théâtre★★ - Place de la Comédie - Place Gambetta - Cours de l'intendance - Notre-Dame church ★ **DX** - Place de la Bourse★★ - Place du Parlement★ - St-Michel basilica ★ - Porte de la Grosse Cloche★ **EY** - Fountains★ of the Girondins monument, Esplanade des Quinconces.

QUARTIER DES CHARTRONS

Wine warehouses - Balconies★ of cours Xavier-Arnozan - Entrepôt Lainé★ : musée d'Art contemporain (Modern Art Museum)★ **BU** M^2 - Musée des Chartrons **BU** M^5

QUARTIER PEY BERLAND

St-André Cathedral ★ - Town hall **DY** H - ⋞★★ of the Pey Berland Tower ★ **DY** Q - Museum: Beaux-Arts (fine arts)★ **DY** M^4 - Aquitaine★★ **DY** M^1 - Arts décoratifs★ **DY** M^3

BORDEAUX CONTEMPORAIN

Quartier Mériadeck **CY**: green spaces, glass and concrete building (Caisse d'Épargne (savings bank), Bibliothèque (library), Hôtel de Région (regional authorities building), Hôtel des Impôts (tax office).

The Regent Grand Hotel
2 pl. de la Comédie – ✆ 05 57 30 44 44 – www.theregentbordeaux.com – info.bordeaux@rezidorregent.com – Fax 05 57 30 44 45 p. 6 DX **r**
150 rm – †€ 450 ††€ 450, ☕ € 30 – 22 suites
Rest – ✆ *05 57 30 43 04* – Menu (€ 59), € 70 (lunch), € 120/180 – Carte € 96/145
Rest – ✆ *05 57 30 43 46* – Menu (€ 25) – Carte € 37/67
◆ Prestigious hotel in an 18C building opposite the Grand Theatre. Opulent rooms with neo-classical decor by J Garcia, which combines elegance with high tech facilities. Classic menu at the Pressoir d'Argent. The Brasserie l'Europe enjoys a fine terrace on the place de la Comédie.

Burdigala rm, VISA AE
115 r. G.-Bonnac – ✆ 05 56 90 16 16 – www.burdigala.com – burdigala@burdigala.com – Fax 05 56 93 15 06 p. 6 CX **r**
77 rm – †€ 210/320 ††€ 210/320, ☕ € 21 – 6 suites
Rest *Le Jardin de Burdigala* – Menu (€ 30), € 40 – Carte € 50/75
◆ The elegant and quiet rooms of this luxury hotel have period and modern furniture, fine materials, the latest equipment and are perfectly soundproofed. The Jardin de Burdigala has a refined rotunda dining room, with a central structure and a skylight.

Seeko'o without rest
54 quai de Bacalan – ✆ 05 56 39 07 07 – www.seekoo-hotel.com – contact@seekoo-hotel.com – Fax 05 56 39 07 09 p. 5 BT **h**
45 rm – †€ 189 ††€ 189, ☕ € 16
◆ The hotel's name, Seeko'o, which means iceberg in Inuit, sets the tone: the building's corian façade rises up from the edge of the Gironde river. Designer rooms with a pop look.

Mercure Cité Mondiale rm,

18 parvis des Chartrons – ✆ 05 56 01 79 79 – h2877@accor.com – Fax 05 56 01 79 00 p. 5 BU **k**
96 rm – †€ 95/160 ††€ 110/175, ☕ € 14
Rest *Le 20* – ✆ *05 56 01 78 78 (closed 28 July-18 August, 22 December-2 January, Friday dinner, Saturday and Sunday)* Menu € 19/38 – Carte € 24/37
◆ Contemporary rooms, meeting facilities and a roof-terrace with a view over Bordeaux where breakfast is served in the summer. Situated in the Cité Mondiale complex. At the 20: tasting of wines to accompany the bistro-type meals. Smart brand new decor.

Mercure Mériadeck rm,
5 r. R.-Lateulade – ✆ 05 56 56 43 43 – www.mercure.com – h1281@accor.com – Fax 05 56 96 50 59 p. 6 CY **v**
194 rm – †€ 115/135 ††€ 125/145, ☕ € 15 – 2 suites
Rest – *(closed Saturday and Sunday) (dinner only)* Menu € 16, € 22/29 – Carte € 35/50
◆ Cinematic décor (posters, photos and objects relating to films), comfortable rooms, many of which have been redecorated, and well-equipped conference rooms. Café-lounge offering a seasonal menu in a snug setting.

Bayonne Etche-Ona without rest
4 r. Martignac – ✆ 05 56 48 00 88 – www.bordeaux-hotel.com – bayetche@bordeaux-hotel.com – Fax 05 56 48 41 60 – Closed 19 December-3 January p. 6 DX **f**
58 rm – †€ 143/160 ††€ 166/187, ☕ € 14 – 3 suites
◆ In the "Golden Triangle", this hotel on two floors of an 18C building mingles tradition and elegance in its personalised, well-cared for rooms with modern fixtures and fittings.

Novotel Bordeaux-Centre rm,
45 cours Mar- Juin – ✆ 05 56 51 46 46 – www.novotel.com – h1023@accor.com – Fax 05 56 98 25 56 p. 6 CY **m**
137 rm – †€ 92/145 ††€ 92/145, ☕ € 15 **Rest** – Carte € 23/40
◆ Architecture that blends well into the Meriadeck district; big functional rooms, regularly redecorated and well-soundproofed in this Novotel. A discreet dining room and a terrace overlooking the city. Designer café area.

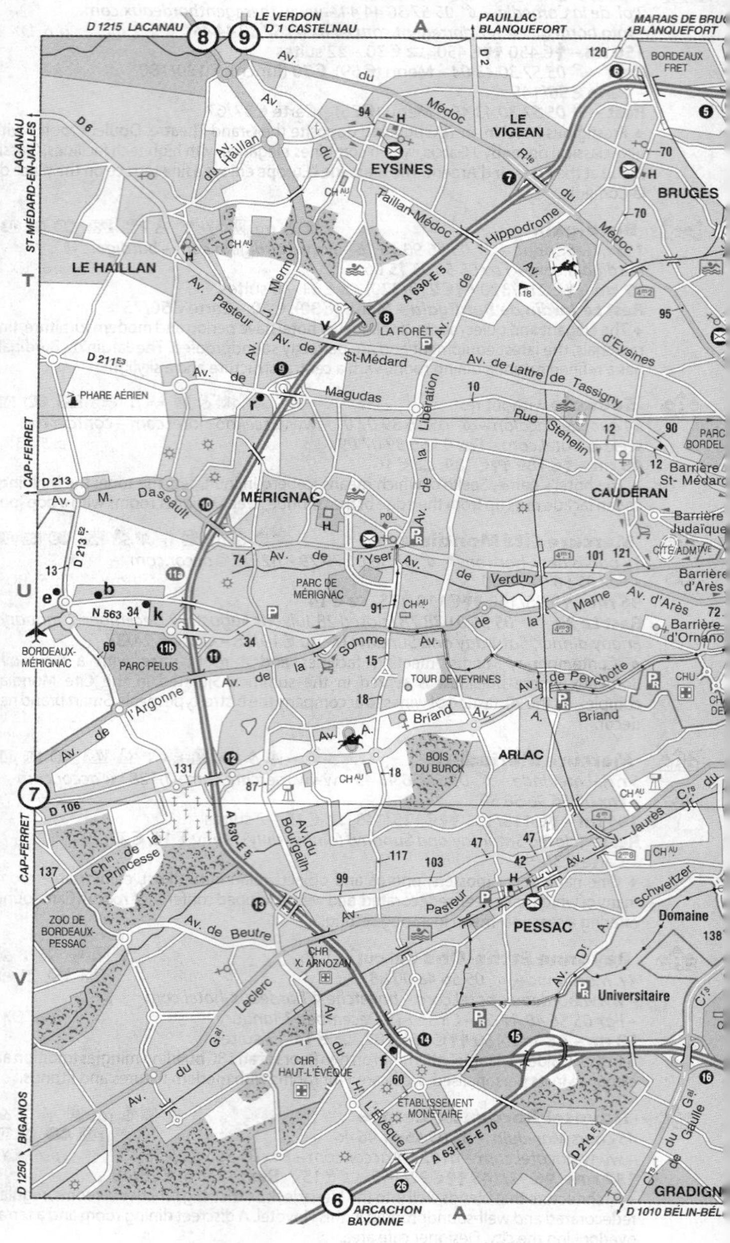
LE VERDON
D 1 CASTELNAU
D 1215 LACANAU
PAUILLAC
BLANQUEFORT
MARAIS DE BRUG
BLANQUEFORT
BORDEAUX FRET
EYSINES
LE VIGEAN
BRUGES
LE HAILLAN
LA FORÊT
PHARE AÉRIEN
MÉRIGNAC
CAUDÉRAN
Barrière St- Médard
Barrière Judaïque
Barrière d'Arès
Barrière d'Ornano
PARC DE MÉRIGNAC
BORDEAUX-MÉRIGNAC
PARC PELUS
TOUR DE VEYRINES
ARLAC
BOIS DU BURCK
ZOO DE BORDEAUX-PESSAC
PESSAC
CHR X. ARNOZAN
CHR HAUT-L'ÉVÊQUE
ÉTABLISSEMENT MONETAIRE
Universitaire
Domaine
GRADIGN
ARCACHON
BAYONNE
D 1010 BÉLIN-BÉL
A 630-E 5
A 63-E 5-E 70
CAP-FERRET
LACANAU
ST-MÉDARD-EN-JALLES
BIGANOS
D 1250

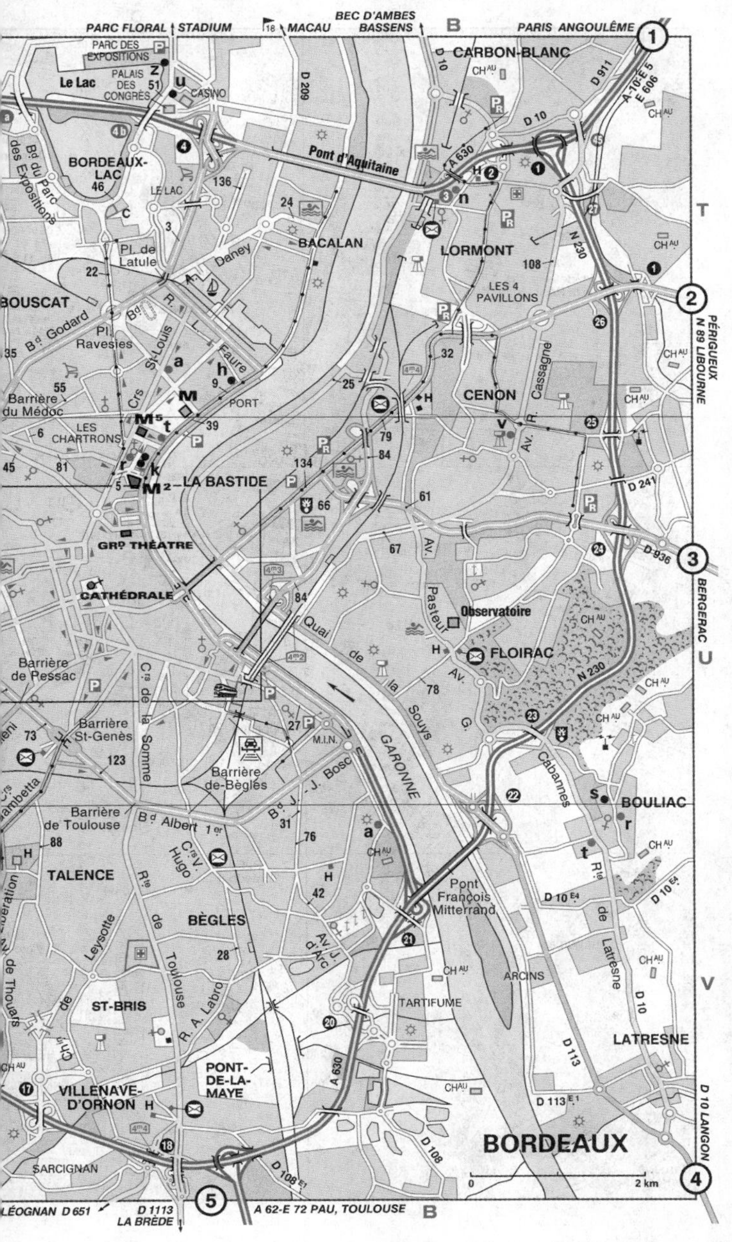
PARC FLORAL
STADIUM
MACAU
BEC D'AMBES
BASSENS
PARIS ANGOULÊME
CARBON-BLANC
PARC DES EXPOSITIONS
PALAIS DES CONGRÈS
CASINO
Le Lac
BORDEAUX-LAC
Bd du Parc des Expositions
Pont d'Aquitaine
LE LAC
BACALAN
LORMONT
Pl. de Latule
BOUSCAT
Bd Godard
Pl. Ravesies
Barrière du Médoc
LES CHARTRONS
PORT
LES 4 PAVILLONS
CENON
LA BASTIDE
GRD THÉATRE
CATHÉDRALE
Observatoire
FLOIRAC
Quai de la Souys
Barrière de Pessac
Barrière St-Genès
Barrière de-Bègles
Barrière de Toulouse
Bd Albert 1er
GARONNE
M.I.N.
BOULIAC
TALENCE
BÈGLES
Pont François Mitterrand
ARCINS
ST-BRIS
TARTIFUME
LATRESNE
PONT-DE-LA-MAYE
VILLENAVE-D'ORNON
SARCIGNAN
BORDEAUX
PÉRIGUEUX N 89 LIBOURNE
BERGERAC
D 10 LANGON
LÉOGNAN D 651
D 1113 LA BRÈDE
A 62-E 72 PAU, TOULOUSE
0
2 km

C
D
X
Y
Z
Turenne
Barraud
Allo
Rue
Turenne
Fondaudège
139
Pl. de Tourny
Espl. d
Quincon
Huguerie
Clemenceau
Aées de Tourny
MAISON DU DE BORDE
St-Seurin
Thiac
POL.
Pl. des Martyrs de la Résistance
Lachassaigne
30
75
Pl. du Chapelet
43
N.-DAME
133
100
GRAN THÉAT
l'Intendance
Judaïque
Pl. Gambetta
21
Pte Dijeaux
40
Bonnac
Pte Dijeaux
48
PEY BERLAND
R. des Remparts
VIEUX
BORDEAUX
Centre Jean Moulin
3 Conils
130
Bonnier
MÉRIADECK
CATH. ST-ANDRÉ
ST-BRUNO
HÔTEL DU DÉPT
Esplanade Ch. de Gaulle
d' Alsace
57
ST-PAUL
PALAIS DES SPORTS
Hôtel de Région
ECOLE NATLE DE LA MAGISTRATURE
Joffre
d'Albret
Juin
63
POL.
Pl. de la République
R. de Cursol
R. J. Burguet
STE-EULALIE
François
Mouneyra
Belleville
de la Libération
Pasteur
Pl. de Pressensé
Briand
Port d'Aqui
R. Ed. Costedoat
R. Villedieu
ST-VICTOR
Sourdis
Tondu
Belfort
Pl. de la Victoire
Pessac
R. de Lamourous
St-Genès
Mazarin
Leberthon
l' Argonne
R. F. Audeguil
R. P. Duhen
R. Cadroin
R. St-Nicolas
ST-NICOLAS
N.-D. DES ANGES
des Treuils
R. A. Bayssselance
R. G. Rioux
Barrière de Pessac

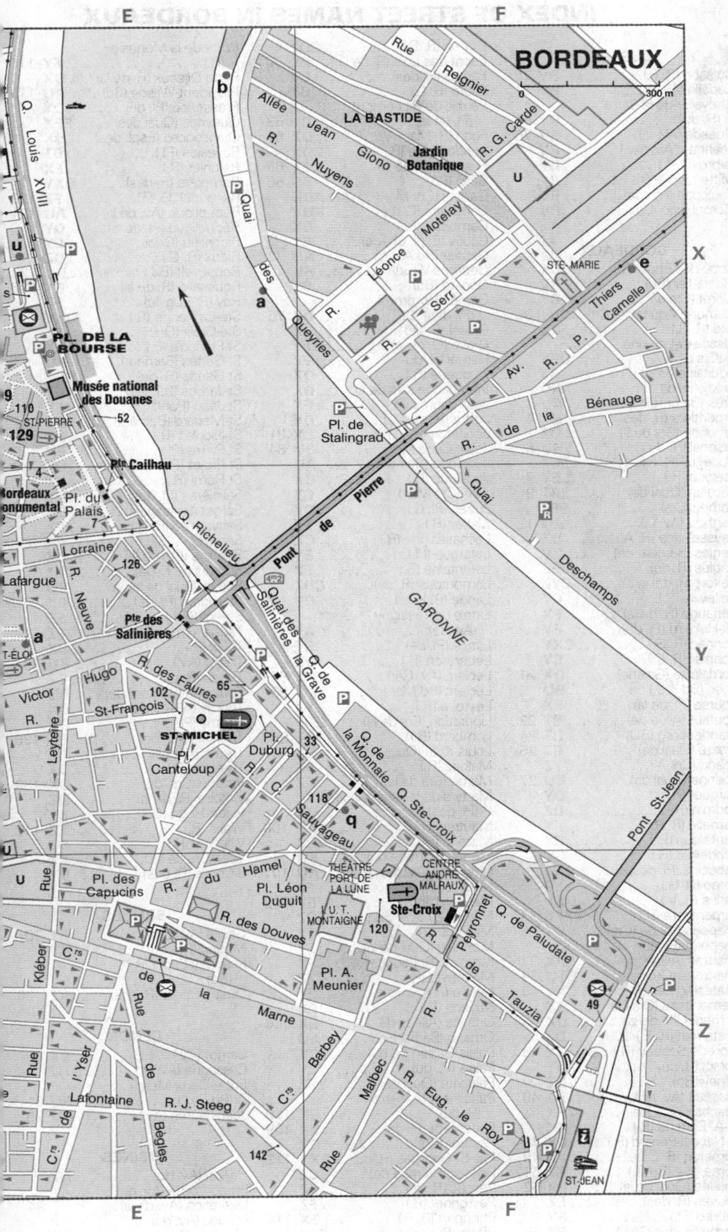
BORDEAUX
0
300 m
E
F
X
Y
Z
LA BASTIDE
Jardin Botanique
Rue Reignier
R. G. Carde
Allée Jean Giono
R. Nuyens
Quai des Queyries
R. Léonce Motelay
R. Serr
STE-MARIE
Av. Thiers
R. Camelle
R. de la Bénauge
Pl. de Stalingrad
Pont de Pierre
Quai Deschamps
GARONNE
Q. Louis XVIII
PL. DE LA BOURSE
Musée national des Douanes
ST-PIERRE
Pte Cailhau
Bordeaux Monumental
Pl. du Palais
Q. Richelieu
Lorraine
R. Neuve
Lafargue
Pte des Salinières
Quai des Salinières
Q. de la Grave
Q. de la Monnaie
Q. Ste-Croix
R. des Faures
Hugo
Victor
R. Leyteire
St-François
ST-MICHEL
Pl. Duburg
Pl. Canteloup
R. C. Sauvageau
Pl. des Capucins
R. du Hamel
Pl. Léon Duguit
THÉATRE PORT DE LA LUNE
CENTRE ANDRÉ MALRAUX
I.U.T. MONTAIGNE
Ste-Croix
R. des Douves
R. Peyronnet
Q. de Paludate
R. de Tauzia
Pont St-Jean
Pl. A. Meunier
Crs de la Marne
Rue Kléber
Rue de Bègles
Rue de l' Yser
Lafontaine
R. J. Steeg
Crs Barbey
Rue Malbec
R. Eug. le Roy
Crs de
ST-JEAN
110
129
52
4
7
126
102
65
33
118
120
49
142
a
b
e
q
u

INDEX OF STREET NAMES IN BORDEAUX

De Normandie without rest
7 cours 30-Juillet – 05 56 52 16 80 – www.hotel-de-normandie-bordeaux.com – info@hotel-de-normandie-bordeaux.com – Fax 05 56 51 68 91 p. 6 DX **z**
100 rm – €62/115 €103/250, €15
◆ An immense elegant hall leads to a variety of functional rooms decorated in pastel shades, those on the top floor have been redone (contemporary, comfortable and with balconies).

Majestic without rest
2 r. Condé – 05 56 52 60 44 – www.hotel-majestic.com – majestic@hotel-majestic.com – Fax 05 56 79 26 70 p. 6 DX **a**
49 rm – €85/230 €85/230, €9
◆ This elegant 18C building typical of the Bordeaux region is home to well-maintained and varied guestrooms, a cosy lounge, and a stylish breakfast room.

Grand Hôtel Français without rest
12 r. du Temple – 05 56 48 10 35 – www.bestwestern-grandhotelfrancais.com – infos@grand-hotel-francais.com – Fax 05 56 81 76 18 p. 6 DX **v**
35 rm – €109/151 €135/184
◆ A fine, 18C house with ironwork balconies on the façade. The lounges and staircase have retained their original character. The comfortable rooms are in a more modern vein.

De la Presse without rest
6 r. Porte-Dijeaux – 05 56 48 53 88 – www.hoteldelapresse.com – info@hoteldelapresse.com – Fax 05 56 01 05 82 – Closed 23 December-5 January
27 rm – €67/85 €76/96, €10 p. 6 DX **k**
◆ In the centre of the pedestrian area, a stone façade fronts a recently renovated and well-kept hotel. Functional rooms. Regulated car access.

Des Quatre Sœurs without rest
6 cours 30-Juillet – 05 57 81 19 20 – www.4soeurs.free.fr – 4soeurs@mailcity.com – Fax 05 56 01 04 28 p. 6 DX **u**
34 rm – €85 €95, €8
◆ This venerable hotel is proud to say that the musician Richard Wagner and the writer John Dos Passos have stayed there. Today it houses well-soundproofed rooms, personalised with pretty painted furniture.

Continental without rest
10 r. Montesquieu – 05 56 52 66 00 – www.hotel-le-continental.com – continental@hotel-le-continental.com – Fax 05 56 52 77 97 p. 6 DX **b**
50 rm – €78/89 €85/104, €8,50 – 1 suite
◆ Former 18C mansion near the Galerie des Grands Hommes. Pleasant refurbished rooms of various sizes. Cosy, well-furnished sitting room.

De l'Opéra without rest VISA AE

35 r. Esprit-des-Lois – 05 56 81 41 27 – www.hotel-de-lopera.com – hotel.opera.bx@wanadoo.fr – Fax 05 56 51 78 80 p. 6 DX **n**

28 rm – €50 €55, €6

◆ Family hotel in an 18C building near the historic district. Well-kept, simple rooms, with sloping ceilings on the top floor; non-smoking.

Notre-Dame without rest VISA AE

36 r. Notre-Dame – 05 56 52 88 24 – www.hotelnotredame33.com – hnd33@free.fr – Fax 05 56 79 12 67 p. 5 BU **k**

22 rm – €45/51 €53/59, €7

◆ Lovers of antiques will enjoy this small hotel in a quarter brimming over with shops selling antique furniture and objects. Practical rooms at a reasonable price.

Une Chambre en Ville without rest VISA AE

35 r. Bouffard – 05 56 81 34 53 – www.bandb-bx.com – ucev@bandb-bx.com – Fax 05 56 81 34 54 p. 6 DXY **t**

5 rm – €89/99 €89/99, €9

◆ In the heart of the historic town centre, impeccable rooms decorated with varied themes and called Bordelais, Nautical, Oriental... Breakfast is served in a modern lounge.

Le Chapon Fin AC VISA AE

5 r. Montesquieu – 05 56 79 10 10 – www.chapon-fin.com – contact@chapon-fin.com – Fax 05 56 79 09 10 – Closed 26 July-25 August, 21-28 February, Sunday, Monday and Bank holidays

Rest – Menu €35 (lunch), €60/90 – Carte €90/110 p. 6 DX **p**

Spec. Langoustines et caviar d'Aquitaine "en boîte". Pigeon contisé a l'ail confit, tête de violon et noix fraîches (autumn-winter). Pressé de pain d'épice façon tatin, tuile au sésame et glace cannelle (winter). **Wines** Côtes de Blaye, Saint-Estèphe.

◆ A genuine institution in Bordeaux popular with gourmets for its updated cuisine, fine wine list and original 1900 decor.

Le Pavillon des Boulevards (Denis Franc) AC VISA AE

120 r. Croix-de-Seguey – 05 56 81 51 02 – pavillon.des.boulevards@orange.fr – Fax 05 56 51 14 58 – Closed 9-31 August, 24 December-3 January, Saturday lunch, Monday lunch and Sunday p. 5 BU **a**

Rest – Menu €40 (lunch), €70/100 – Carte €80/100

Spec. Saint-Jacques fumées à l'anis étoilé (October-mid April). Pigeonneau rôti et civet, arôme de chocolat et parfum de cannelle. Poire pochée au sauternes, purée de coing, émulsion cacao et chataîgnes confites (September-December). **Wines** Médoc, Pessac-Léognan.

◆ Opening onto a verdant terrace, this restaurant is the image of pleasant modernity: sobriety (light colours, parquet flooring), colourful touches (china, flowers), and an inventive, thoughtful menu.

Jean Ramet AC VISA AE

7 pl. J.-Jaurès – 05 56 44 12 51 – Fax 05 56 52 19 80 – Closed 12-20 April, 2-24 August, Sunday and Monday p. 7 EX **u**

Rest – Menu €35 (lunch), €55/65 – Carte €60/82

◆ Local gourmets enjoy the classic, updated cuisine in this restaurant near the Garonne, decorated in sunny shades that match the fittings and furnishings.

Le Vieux Bordeaux AC VISA AE

27 r. Buhan – 05 56 52 94 36 – www.levieuxbordeaux.com – Fax 05 56 44 25 11 – Closed 3-24 August, 23 February-8 March, Sunday, Monday and bank holidays p. 7 EY **a**

Rest – Menu (€21 bi), €30 (weekdays)/52 – Carte €36/65

◆ Two dining rooms tastefully redecorated in shades of grey, period and contemporary furniture. One opens onto a pleasant patio. Generous portions of classic cooking.

L'Alhambra AC VISA

111bis r. Judaïque – 05 56 96 06 91 – Fax 05 56 98 00 52 – Closed 14 July-15 August, Saturday lunch, Monday lunch and Sunday p. 6 CX **e**

Rest – Menu €20 (weekday lunch), €30/42 – Carte €42/60

◆ Attractively laid out in a winter garden style with a green colour scheme and comfortable cane furniture. Flavoursome traditional cuisine.

La Table Calvet
81 cours Médoc – ✆ 05 56 39 62 80 – www.latablecalvet.fr – latablecalvet@latablecalvet.com – Fax 05 56 39 62 80 – Closed 1st-30 August, 24 December-2 January, 23-31 March, Saturday lunch, Sunday and Monday p.5 BT **a**
Rest – Menu € 20 (weekday lunch), € 28/55 – Carte € 46/55
◆ The Calvet wine merchants have opened a gourmet restaurant with creative, seasonal cuisine. Food is served in the attractive setting of a former 19C wine and spirit storehouse.

Le Clos d'Augusta
339 r. Georges-Bonnac – ✆ 05 56 96 32 51 – leclosdaugusta@wanadoo.fr – Fax 05 56 51 80 46 – Closed 26 July-18 August, 20-30 December, Monday dinner, Saturday lunch, Sunday and bank holidays p. 4 AU **a**
Rest – Menu € 22 (weekday lunch), € 43/65 – Carte € 50/68
◆ The restaurant is named after a famous American golf course. The chef has two passions: cooking and golf. Pleasant garden-terrace at the rear. Modern recipes.

L'Oiseau Bleu
127 av. Thiers – ✆ 05 56 81 09 39 – www.loiseaubleu.fr – sophielafon@aol.com – Closed 12-20 April, 26 July-17 August, 20-28 December, Sunday and Monday p. 7 FX **e**
Rest – Menu (€ 23), € 36/80 bi – Carte € 59/67
◆ New establishment in an attractive stone house. Two minimalist, predominantly blue dining rooms overlook a delightful terrace and garden. Up-to-the-minute menu.

La Tupina
6 r. Porte-de-la-Monnaie – ✆ 05 56 91 56 37 – www.latupina.com – latupina@latupina.com – Fax 05 56 31 92 11 p. 7 FY **q**
Rest – Menu (€ 16), € 32 bi (weekday lunch)/55 – Carte € 50/75
◆ Relaxed atmosphere at this country-style house. Dishes from the southwest roast on the fireplace or on the stove as in the olden days. Good wine list.

Gravelier
114 cours Verdun – ✆ 05 56 48 17 15 – restogravelier@yahoo.fr – Fax 05 56 51 96 07 – Closed 26 July-24 August, February holidays, Saturday and Sunday p. 5 BU **r**
Rest – Menu (€ 24), € 28, € 39/60 – Carte € 55/65
◆ Teak and zinc furniture, striking colours and a view of the glazed kitchens. Inventive menu with Asian influences concocted by a creative chef.

L'Estaquade
quai Queyries – ✆ 05 57 54 02 50 – www.lestacade.com – Fax 05 57 54 02 51 – Closed 23 December-2 January p. 7 EX **a**
Rest – *(pre-book)* Menu € 17 (weekday lunch) – Carte approx. € 48
◆ By the Garonne, this unusual construction on piles overlooks old Bordeaux. Deliberately sparse decor, daily specials and a seasonal menu: a popular spot.

Auberge ' Inn
245 r. de Turenne – ✆ 05 56 81 97 86 – http://auberge-inn.cartesurtables.com – auberge-inn@orange.fr – Fax 05 56 81 34 71 – Closed 1st-24 August, 19-27 December, 20-28 February, Saturday, Sunday and bank holidays p. 5 BU **b**
Rest – Menu € 19, € 27/50 – Carte € 40/60
◆ Stone and aubergine coloured walls, minimalist modern decor, a small warm terrace and up-to-date food: a very in inn!

La Petite Gironde
75 quai des Queyries – ✆ 05 57 80 33 33 – www.lapetitegironde.fr – jean-pierre.vergnolle@wanadoo.fr – Fax 05 57 80 33 31 – Closed 24 December-4 January, Saturday lunch and Sunday dinner p. 7 EX **b**
Rest – Menu € 16/33 – Carte € 31/49
◆ This riverside restaurant on the Garonne's right bank has pleasantly trendy decor. The waterside terrace is very popular; traditional menu.

Quaizaco
80 quai des Chartrons – 05 57 87 67 72 – quaizaco@orange.fr – Fax 05 57 87 34 42 – Closed 8-18 August, Saturday lunch and Sunday p. 5 BU **t**
Rest – Menu (€ 11), € 14 (weekday lunch) – Carte € 34/42
◆ Behind the façade of these 18C warehouses is a striking interior adorned with contemporary furnishings and temporary exhibitions of modern art. Up-to-date cuisine.

in Bordeaux-Lac (near the parc des expositions) (exhibition centre) - ✉ 33300 - Bordeaux

Pullman rm, VISA
av. J.-G.-Domergue – 05 56 69 66 66 – www.pullmanhotels.com – h0669@accor.com – Fax 05 56 69 66 00 p. 5 BT **u**
166 rm – †€ 120/350 ††€ 140/370, ☕ € 22 – 19 suites
Rest *l'Aquitania* – Menu (€ 26 bi), € 32 bi – Carte € 48/74
◆ A hotel popular with business clients due to its direct access to the Convention Centre, 2000m² meeting facilities and comfortable designer rooms; all in all a successful renovation. Contemporary decor and a summer terrace overlooking the lake.

Novotel-Bordeaux Lac rm, VISA
av. J.-G.-Domergue – 05 56 43 65 00 – h0403@accor.com – Fax 05 56 43 65 01 p. 5 BT **z**
175 rm – †€ 105/160 ††€ 105/160, ☕ € 15
Rest – Menu € 23 (weekdays) – Carte € 28/46
◆ Near the exhibition centre; the rooms (ask for one on the lake side), have been partly renovated in keeping with the chain's latest standards. Garden with children's area. Dine in the ultra fashionable interior or on the poolside terrace.

via A 630 bypass:

in Blanquefort 3 km North, exit 6 – pop. 15 300 – alt. 17 m – ✉ 33290

Hostellerie des Criquets rm, VISA
130 av. 11-Novembre (D 210) – 05 56 35 09 24 – www.lescriquets.com – hotel@lescriquets.com – Fax 05 56 57 13 83
21 rm – †€ 65/77 ††€ 88/100, ☕ € 12 – ½ P € 84/96
Rest – *(closed Saturday lunch, Sunday dinner and Monday)*
Menu € 20 (weekday lunch), € 40/65 – Carte € 52/76
◆ A pleasant country home feel pervades this old farmstead and its smart modern rooms (wood, wrought iron and bright fabrics). Pleasant dining room, terrace facing the garden and tasty updated menu.

in Lormont Northeast, exit 2 – pop. 21 000 – alt. 60 m – ✉ 33310

Office de tourisme, 4, avenue de la Libération 05 56 74 29 17

Jean-Marie Amat VISA
26 r. Raymond-Lis – 05 56 06 12 52 – www.jm-amat.com – Fax 05 56 74 77 89 – Closed two weeks in August, one week in December, Saturday lunch, Sunday and Monday p. 5 BT **n**
Rest – Menu € 30 (weekday lunch) – Carte € 70/100
Spec. Salade d'huîtres au caviar d'Aquitaine et crépinette grillée. Homard rôti aux pommes de terre et gousses d'ail. Croustade aux pommes et sorbet pomme-gingembre. **Wines** Côtes de Blaye blanc, Bordeaux rouge.
◆ This contemporary restaurant in a renovated château signals the return of the "enfant terrible". Fine modern cuisine, elegant veranda, views of the countryside and the Pont d'Aquitaine.

in Cenon East, exit 25 – pop. 23 100 – alt. 50 m – ✉ 33150

La Cape (Nicolas Magie) VISA
allée Morlette – 05 57 80 24 25 – Fax 05 56 32 37 46 – Closed 1st-21 August, Christmas holidays, Saturday, Sunday and Bank holidays p. 5 BU **v**
Rest – Menu € 40 (weekdays)/80 bi – Carte € 52/80
Spec. Menu du marché.
◆ This establishment is often full thanks to its delicious inventive cuisine, highly original and strikingly colourful decor and its pleasant garden-terrace.

in Bouliac Southeast, exit n° 23 – **pop. 3 087 – alt. 74 m** – ✉ **33270**

Le St-James rm, VISA AE
3 pl. Camille Hostein, near the church – ✆ *05 57 97 06 00*
– www.saintjames-bouliac.com – stjames@relaischateaux.com
– Fax 05 56 20 92 58 p. 5 BU **s**
15 rm – €185/310 €185/310, €25 – 3 suites
Rest – *(closed 12-27 April, 25 October-5 November, 1st-18 January, Sunday and Monday)* Menu (€34), €62 bi/125 – Carte €100/140
Rest *Côté Cour* – ✆ *05 57 97 06 06 (Closed 1st-23 August, 18-31 January, Saturday and Sunday)* Menu (€19), €26 – Carte €31/50
Spec. Homard bleu grillé au beurre de corail, risotto iodé. Saint-Pierre rôti sur la peau, pommes safranées, soupe de crustacés. Chocolat noir guanaja en chaud-froid et groseilles. **Wines** Saint-Estèphe, Premières Côtes de Bordeaux.
◆ The architecture of the local, traditional tobacco drying buildings inspired this house designed by Jean Novel. It has views of the vineyards and sleek designer rooms. The chef is reputed for his delicate and sophisticated blend of subtle flavours and aromas. Seasonal market produce at the Côté Cour.

Café de l'Espérance VISA AE
10 r. de l'Esplanade, (behind the church) – ✆ *05 56 20 52 16*
– www.saintjames-bouliac.com – stjames@relaischateaux.com
– Fax 05 56 20 92 58 p. 5 BV **r**
Rest – Menu €15 (weekday lunch) – Carte €28/40
◆ Fans of the little village café will love this bistro, where you can take your time over a drink under the trellis. Traditional cuisine and grills listed on the blackboard.

in Bègles Southeast, exit 21 – **pop. 24 400 – alt. 6 m** – ✉ **33130**

Chiopot VISA AE
281 r. des Quatre-Castera – ✆ *05 56 85 62 41 – http://chiopot.free.fr*
– chiopot@free.fr – Fax 05 56 85 07 24 – Closed Saturday lunch and Sunday
Rest – Menu (€22 bi), €33 – Carte €22/72 p. 5 BV **a**
◆ With its bistro-brasserie trademark, this restaurant guarantees a lively atmosphere, whether in the dining room or on the shaded terrace. Traditional menu, grilled meats and good wines (on sale in the shop).

in Martillac 9 km south, exit 18, D 1113 and secondary road – **pop. 2 293 – alt. 40 m** – ✉ **33650**

Les Sources de Caudalie rm,
chemin de Smith-Haut-Lafitte – ✆ *05 57 83 83 83* VISA AE
– www.sources-caudalie.com – sources@sources-caudalie.com
– Fax 05 57 83 83 84 – **43 rm** – €200/380 €200/380, €22 – 7 suites
Rest *La Grand'Vigne* – *(Closed Monday and Tuesday except in July-August)* Menu €85 – Carte €82/101
Rest *La Table du Lavoir* – Menu (€26), €35
◆ This estate has a vinotherapy institute and offers luxury, relaxation and health farm facilities in the heart of the vineyards. Up-to-date menu and good choice of wine at the 18C Grand'Vigne. La Table was once the wash house for grape pickers.

Château de Lantic without rest VISA AE
10 rte de Lartigue – ✆ *05 56 72 58 68 – www.chateau-de-lantic.com*
– contact@chateau-de-lantic.com – Fax 05 56 72 58 67
13 rm – €89/159 €89/159
◆ This adorable castle offers rooms with antique furniture often decorated with a romantic feel. Some have a small kitchen. There are exhibitions in an outbuilding.

Southwest Exit 14 - ✉ 33600 Pessac

Holiday Inn Bordeaux Sud VISA AE
10 av. Antoine Becquerel – ✆ *05 56 07 59 59 – www.holidayinn.fr – contact@hi-pessac.com – Fax 05 56 07 59 69* p. 5 AV **f**
90 rm – €80/155 €80/155, €16
Rest – *(Closed Saturday, Sunday and public holidays)* Menu (€19), €23 – Carte €30/45 dinner only
◆ Near a motorway ring road, this hotel was built in 2004 and offers modern, comfortable rooms (king-size beds). State-of-the-art meeting rooms. Welcoming, bistro-style dining room offering traditional food.

in Mérignac West, exit n° 9 – pop. 63 900 – alt. 35 m – ✉ 33700

Kyriad Prestige rm, VISA
116 av. Magudas – ✆ 05 57 92 00 00 – www.bordeaux-hotels.net – kprestige@bordeaux-hotels.net – Fax 05 57 92 00 60 p.4 AT **r**
75 rm – †€ 85/115 ††€ 85/115, ☕ € 13 – 2 suites
Rest – *(closed Sunday)* Menu (€ 21), € 26/50 – Carte € 32/42
◆ Spacious, well-soundproofed rooms of various categories: relatively plain standard rooms, more contemporary executive rooms (teak furnishings) and family rooms with a mezzanine. Cold or hot buffets in a dining room with a fireplace and exposed beams.

in Eysines West, exit n° 9 – pop. 19 000 – alt. 15 m – ✉ 33320

Les Tilleuls VISA
à La Forêt, 205 av. St-Médard – ✆ 05 56 28 04 56 – restotilleuls@wanadoo.fr – Fax 05 56 28 05 41 – Closed 17-23 February, Saturday lunch, Sunday dinner and Monday p.4 AT **v**
Rest – Menu € 19 (weekday lunch)/28 – Carte € 40/55
◆ A pleasant restaurant serving classical dishes and regional specialities. A rustic dining room decorated in warm, bright colours, and a pretty terrace in the summer.

to Bordeaux-Mérignac Airport West, exit 11 from the South, exit 11b from the North – ✉ 33700 Mérignac

Mercure Bordeaux Aéroport rm, VISA
1 av. Ch.-Lindbergh – ✆ 05 56 34 74 74 – www.mercure.com – h1508@accor.com – Fax 05 56 34 30 84 p.4 AU **e**
149 rm – †€ 75/135 ††€ 85/145, ☕ € 16
Rest – Menu € 21 (weekdays) – Carte € 31/46
◆ Hotel designed for a good rest between flights. English-style bar, meeting rooms and well-thought out bedrooms (decor on the theme of the five continents). Traditional cuisine served in an elegant dining room overlooking a terrace.

Novotel Aéroport rm, VISA
80 av. J.F.-Kennedy – ✆ 05 57 53 13 30 – www.accor-hotels.com – h0402@accor.com p.4 AU **k**
137 rm – †€ 115/150 ††€ 115/150, ☕ € 15
Rest – Menu € 16 (weekdays)/20 – Carte € 30/40
◆ This hotel has updated its image with trendier renovated rooms and a café in line with the chain's latest specifications. Pine wood and outside play area for children. Simple cuisine based mainly on grills and a pleasant view of the garden.

L' Iguane VISA
83 av. J.F.-Kennedy – ✆ 05 56 34 07 39 – contact@liguane.fr – Fax 05 56 34 41 37 – Closed 26 July-31 August, Friday dinner, Saturday lunch and Sunday p.4 AU **b**
Rest – Menu (€ 21), € 32/65 – Carte € 39/82
Rest *L'Olive de Mer* – Menu (€ 21), € 32/65 – Carte € 39/82
◆ Bright, contemporary long dining room, with parquet flooring and slatted blinds). Attentive service, white tablecloths and seasonal menu. Sea-inspired menu at the Olive de Mer (designer furniture and fashionable decor).

LES BORDES – 45 Loiret – 318 L5 – see Sully-sur-Loire

BORMES-LES-MIMOSAS – 83 Var – 340 N7 – pop. 6 324 – alt. 180 m – ✉ 83230 French Riviera 41 **C3**

Paris 871 – Fréjus 57 – Hyères 21 – Le Lavandou 4 – St-Tropez 35 – Toulon 39

Office de tourisme, 1, place Gambetta ✆ 04 94 01 38 38, Fax 04 94 01 38 39

de Valcros La Londe-les-MauresNW : 12 km, ✆ 04 94 66 81 02

Site★ - Old streets★ - ≤★ of the château.

Hostellerie du Cigalou rm, VISA AE

pl. Gambetta, In the old village – 04 94 41 51 27 – www.hostellerieducigalou.com – resas@hostellerieducigalou.com – Fax 04 94 46 20 73

17 rm – €108/254 €108/254, €14 – 3 suites

Rest – Menu €17/36 – Carte €31/47

◆ The owner of this pretty house has decorated the rooms with sophistication, mixing Provencal and baroque styles. Some of the rooms have private terraces. Regional recipes served in a relaxed bistro atmosphere.

La Bastide des Vignes

464 chemin du Patelin – 04 94 71 20 29 – www.bastidedesvignes.fr – bastidedesvignes@orange.fr – Fax 04 94 15 12 71

5 rm – €110/132 €110/132 **Table d'hôte** – Menu €40 bi

◆ A charming winegrower's home (1902) surrounded by vineyards. The personalised rooms (no TV) sport Provençal colours and overlook the garden. A haven of peace and quiet. Sample regional wines and dishes at the table d'hôte, reservations necessary.

Les Plumbagos without rest

88 impasse du Pin, Le Pin district, Mont Roses – 06 09 82 42 86 – www.lesplumbagos.com – plumbagos@wanadoo.fr – Open March-October

3 rm – €95/120 €105/130

◆ The attractions of this lovely 1920s building include a splendid, tranquil location overlooking the bay, pretty Provencal-style guestrooms and a delightful garden.

La Rastègue VISA

48 bd Levant, 2 km South, quartier Le Pin – 04 94 15 19 41 – www.larastegue.com – contact@larastegue.com – Closed 4-31 January, lunch except Sunday and Monday

Rest – Menu €39

◆ Pleasant terrace and restaurant with open kitchen and cellar. Delightful, unpretentious cuisine, using local produce.

La Tonnelle de Gil Renard VISA

pl. Gambetta – 04 94 71 34 84 – www.la-tonnelle-bormes.com – restau.la.tonnelle@free.fr – Closed mid-November to mid-December, lunch in July-August, Thursday lunch and Wednesday

Rest – Menu €27/42 – Carte €40/49

◆ A dining room with veranda is the setting for a regionally-inspired meal, with a few exotic touches. Warm-coloured décor and a boutique which appeals to children and adults alike.

Lou Portaou VISA AE

r. Cubert-des-Poètes – 04 94 64 86 37 – www.louportaou.fr – contact@louportaou.fr – Fax 04 94 64 81 43 – Closed 15 November-20 December, Saturday lunch in season, Sunday dinner and Monday off season

Rest – *(pre-book)* Menu (€26 bi), €39 (dinner) – Carte approx. €45 dinner only

◆ This former 12C watch post lacks neither character nor charm. Medieval style and personalised decor in the two small vaulted dining rooms. Traditional dishes.

South 1 km – 83230 Bormes-les-Mimosas

Le Domaine du Mirage rm, VISA AE

38 r. Vue-des-Îles – 04 94 05 32 60 – www.domainedumirage.com – resas@domainedumirage.com – Fax 04 94 64 93 03 – Open 27 March-31 October

35 rm – €127/272 €141/286

Rest – Menu €35 (dinner) – Carte €36/44 lunch only

◆ Pleasant hotel on the heights of Bormes in the midst of lush vegetation. Pretty Provencal-style furnished rooms with a balcony or terrace. Wrought iron, southern shades and murals form the restaurant decor (set lunch menu).

in la Favière 4 km south – ✉ **83230 Bormes-les-Mimosas**

De la Plage

rest, P VISA MC AE

Bd de la Plage – ✆ 04 94 71 02 74 – www.hotelbormes.com
– hoteldelaplage.bormes@wanadoo.fr – Fax 04 94 71 77 22
– Open 1st April-30 September

45 rm – †€ 60/87 ††€ 60/87, ☕ € 8,50 – ½ P € 60/73

Rest – *(dinner only except Sunday)* Menu € 23/30 – Carte € 32/49

◆ A stone's throw from Cap Bénat and the Brégançon Fort, this family-run hotel has rustic-style rooms, well kept and simply furnished. Tradition and Provencal dishes to the fore, served in a bright dining room or in the shade of the plane trees in the summer.

BORNY – **57 Moselle** – **307** I4 – **see Metz**

BORT-L'ÉTANG – **63 Puy-de-Dôme** – **326** H8 – **see Lezoux**

BOSDARROS – **64 Pyrénées-Atlantiques** – **342** J5 – **pop. 998** 3 **B3**
– **alt. 370 m** – ✉ **64290**

Paris 790 – Pau 14 – Lourdes 36 – Oloron-Ste-Marie 29 – Tarbes 50

Auberge Labarthe (Eric Dequin)

AC VISA MC AE

1 r. P.-Bidau – ✆ 05 59 21 50 13 – www.auberge-pau.com – auberge-labarthe@wanadoo.fr – Fax 05 59 21 68 55
– Closed 1st-15 July, 10-31 January, Sunday dinner, Monday and Tuesday

Rest – *(pre-book weekends)* Menu € 27 (weekdays), € 46/69 – Carte approx. € 75

Spec. Foie frais poêlé aux fraises, réduction de banuyls et parfum de basilic (summer). Grande assiette de poissons de mer grillés à la plancha. Fondue au chocolat, mignardises et brochettes de fruits (autumn-winter). **Wines** Jurançon, Béarn rouge.

◆ A smart flower-decked house behind the church. The quietly contemporary dining room provides a discreet setting for generous portions of delicious regional cuisine.

BOSSEY – **74 Haute-Savoie** – **328** J4 – **see St-Julien-en-Genevois**

LES BOSSONS – **74 Haute-Savoie** – **328** O5 – **see Chamonix**

BOUAYE – **44 Loire-Atlantique** – **316** F5 – **see Nantes**

BOUC-BEL-AIR – **13 Bouches-du-Rhône** – **340** H5 – **pop. 13 700** 40 **B3**
– **alt. 259 m** – ✉ **13320**

Paris 758 – Aix-en-Provence 10 – Aubagne 41 – Marseille 22
– Salon-de-Provence 43

L'Étape Lani

rm, AC rm, rm, P VISA MC AE

South on D 6 Gardane-Marseille road – ✆ 04 42 22 61 90 – www.lani.fr
– etapelani@worldonline.fr – Fax 04 42 22 68 67
– Closed Saturday lunch and Sunday dinner

33 rm – †€ 70/78 ††€ 78/88, ☕ € 12

Rest – *(closed 23 December-5 January, Monday lunch, Saturday lunch and Sunday in July-August)* Menu € 18 (weekday lunch), € 27/56 – Carte € 42/56

◆ The warm welcome and well-soundproofed rooms in the main building and the pleasant Provençal decor in the new annexe quickly make guests forget about the busy nearby road. Charming restaurant in sunny tones, serving cuisine with a distinct Southern flavour.

BOUCÉ – **03 Allier** – **326** H5 – **see Varennes-sur-Allier**

LE BOUCHET – **74 Haute-Savoie** – **328** L5 – **see Le Grand-Bornand**

BOUDES – 63 Puy-de-Dôme – 326 G10 – pop. 266 – alt. 466 m 5 B2 – ✉ 63340

▶ Paris 462 – Brioude 29 – Clermont-Fd 52 – Issoire 16 – St-Flour 62

XX **Le Boudes La Vigne** with rm rest, VISA

pl. de la Mairie – ✆ 04 73 96 55 66 – http://perso.wanadoo.fr/leboudeslavigne – Fax 04 73 96 55 55 – Closed 30 June-8 July, 25 August-3 September, 2-22 January, Sunday dinner, Tuesday lunch and Monday

11 rm – †€ 40/55 ††€ 40/90, ☕ € 7 **Rest** – Menu (€ 17), € 22/50

◆ A house built on the old fortifications. Updated cuisine served in a refurbished room decorated in pastel shades with stonewalls. Fine selection of local vintages.

For a pleasant stay in a charming hotel, look for the red ... symbols.

BOUËSSE – 36 Indre – 323 G7 – see Argenton-sur-Creuse

BOUGIVAL – 78 Yvelines – 311 I2 – 101 13 – see Paris, Area

LA BOUILLADISSE – 13 Bouches-du-Rhône – 340 I5 – pop. 4 904 40 B3 – alt. 220 m – ✉ 13720

▶ Paris 776 – Aix-en-Provence 27 – Brignoles 43 – Marseille 31 – Toulon 60

ℹ Syndicat d'initiative, place de la Libération ✆ 04 42 62 97 08, Fax 04 42 62 98 65

La Fenière rm, rest, VISA

8 r. J. Pourchier – ✆ 04 42 72 56 32 – www.hotelfeniere.com – la.feniere@wanadoo.fr – Fax 04 42 62 30 54 – Closed Saturday lunch and Sunday

10 rm – †€ 58/65 ††€ 58/68, ☕ € 7

Rest – Menu (€ 16), € 20/24 – Carte € 20/48

◆ Establishment housed in two buildings. On the garden/swimming pool side you will find small, practical and meticulously well-kept rooms. A Provençal style restaurant (exposed beams and fireplace) leading onto a terrace serving regional cuisine.

BOUILLAND – 21 Côte-d'Or – 320 I7 – pop. 188 – alt. 400 m 8 C2 – ✉ 21420 Burgundy-Jura

▶ Paris 295 – Autun 54 – Beaune 17 – Bligny-sur-Ouche 13 – Dijon 41 – Saulieu 57

Hostellerie du Vieux Moulin rm, rest, VISA

1 r. de la Forge – ✆ 03 80 21 51 16 – www.le-moulin-de-bouilland.com – le-moulin@le-moulin-de-bouilland.com – Fax 03 80 21 59 90 – Open 13 March-29 November and 14 December-2 January

23 rm – †€ 90/165 ††€ 90/165, ☕ € 18 – 3 suites – ½ P € 109/189

Rest – *(closed lunch Monday-Thursday and Wednesday dinner October-May)* Menu € 43/105 – Carte € 88/125

◆ Located two minutes from the A6 motorway and Burgundy's prestigious vineyards. These two buildings, one of which is a former watermill, offers partly renovated rooms, a fitness centre, and a pool. Updated cuisine served in a contemporary dining room. View of the countryside; attentive service.

X **Auberge St-Martin** VISA

17 rte de Beaune – ✆ 03 80 21 53 01 – auberge-saint-martin@orange.fr – Fax 03 80 21 53 01 – Closed 30 June-8 July, Tuesday and Wednesday

Rest – Menu € 20/28 – Carte € 23/37

◆ The small, countrified dining room of this welcoming 18C inn looks onto a small balcony-terrace. Appetising traditional dishes alongside regional specialities.

LA BOUILLE – 76 Seine-Maritime – 304 F5 – pop. 808 – alt. 5 m – ✉ 76530 Normandy 33 **D2**

Paris 132 – Bernay 44 – Elbeuf 12 – Louviers 32 – Pont-Audemer 35 – Rouen 21

Le Bellevue

rest, VISA MO AE

13 quai Hector-Malot – ☎ 02 35 18 05 05 – www.hotel-le-bellevue.com – bellevuehotel@wanadoo.fr – Fax 02 35 18 00 92 – Closed 23-27 December

20 rm – †€ 60/68 ††€ 60/68, ☕ € 9 – ½ P € 104/114

Rest – *(Closed Sunday dinner from 1st October to 15 April)* Menu € 15 (weekdays), € 20/42 – Carte € 42/72

◆ Early 20C edifice on a bank of the Seine. Gradually renovated spruce and colourful rooms; some enjoy fine views of the river. Traditional fare served in the restaurant that has lost none of its Normandy character.

St-Pierre

VISA MO AE

4 pl. du Bateau – ☎ 02 35 68 02 01 – www.restaurantlesaintpierre.com – blanchardlau@wanadoo.fr – Fax 02 35 68 04 26 – Closed 24 August-9 September, Sunday dinner from September to Easter, Monday and Tuesday

Rest – Menu (€ 20), € 27 (weekdays)/65 – Carte € 61/82

◆ A bright, modern dining room and pleasant terrace with the Seine as a backdrop. Contemporary cuisine and friendly, efficient service.

De la Poste

VISA MO

6 pl.du Bateau – ☎ 02 35 18 03 90 – Fax 02 35 18 18 91 – Closed 17 December-9 January, Sunday dinner, Monday dinner and Tuesday

Rest – Menu € 30/44 – Carte approx. € 50

◆ Half-timbered 18C post house on the embankment. Rustic dining room or, upstairs, a more modern and brighter decor with a view of the Seine. Classic menu.

Les Gastronomes

VISA MO

1 pl. du Bateau – ☎ 02 35 18 02 07 – www.lesgastronomes-labouille.com – Fax 02 35 18 14 49 – Closed 24 October-13 November, 20 February-5 March, Wednesday and Thursday except holidays

Rest – Menu € 20 (weekdays)/45 – Carte € 48/56

◆ Next to the church, a family restaurant with two dining rooms; the one on the ground floor is like a Belle Époque bistro; rustic touches and a panormaic view upstairs.

BOUIN – 85 Vendée – 316 E6 – pop. 2 242 – alt. 5 m – ✉ 85230 34 **A3**

Paris 435 – Challans 22 – Nantes 51 – Noirmoutier-en-l'Île 29 – La Roche-sur-Yon 66

Office de tourisme, boulevard Sébastien Luneau ☎ 02 51 68 88 85

Du Martinet

rm, VISA MO AE

pl. du Gén.-Charette – ☎ 02 51 49 08 94 – www.domaine-lemartinet.com – contact@domaine-lemartinet.com – Fax 02 51 49 83 08

30 rm – †€ 49/95 ††€ 56/105, ☕ € 10 – ½ P € 66/115

Rest – *(closed Monday lunch and Tuesday lunch)* Menu € 17/32 – Carte € 25/55

◆ Old house with a family ambiance in a quiet village in the Breton Vendée marshland. The rooms on the garden level are pleasant and cosy. Characterful dining room (furniture and antique objects) and pretty veranda. Local seafood.

BOULBON – 13 Bouches-du-Rhône – 340 D2 – pop. 1 510 – alt. 18 m – ✉ 13150 42 **E1**

Paris 703 – Marseille 113 – Nîmes 34 – Avignon 18 – Arles 25

La Bastide de Boulbon

rm, AC P VISA MO AE

r. de l'Hôtel-de-Ville – ☎ 04 90 93 11 11 – www.labastidedeboulbon.com – contact@labastidedeboulbon.com – Fax 04 90 97 04 01 – Closed 2 November-1st April

10 rm – †€ 85/155 ††€ 85/155, ☕ € 14

Rest – *(dinner only) (residents only)* Menu € 34

◆ This fine bourgeois home, built in 1850, has the feel of a guesthouse. Superb garden planted with two-century-old plane trees. Modern guestrooms. Market fresh cuisine served in a cosy dining room or on a shaded terrace in summer.

BOULIAC – 33 Gironde – 335 H6 – see Bordeaux

BOULIGNEUX – 01 Ain – 328 C4 – see Villars-les-Dombes

BOULOGNE-SUR-MER – 62 Pas-de-Calais – 301 C3 30 A2

– pop. 44 600 – Built-up area 135 116 – alt. 58 m – Casino (private) Z – ✉ 62200

Northern France and the Paris Region

Paris 265 – Amiens 130 – Arras 122 – Calais 35 – Lille 118 – Rouen 185

Office de tourisme, 24, quai Gambetta ☎ 03 21 10 88 10, Fax 03 21 10 88 11

de Wimereux Wimereux Avenue François Mitterrand, 8 km on the Wimereux road, ☎ 03 21 32 43 20

Nausicaa★★★ - Ville haute★★: crypt and treasure-house★ of the basilica ≤★ of the belfry Y H - Views★ from the ramparts - Calvaire des marins ≤★ Y - Château-museum ★: Greek vases★★, Inuit and Aleout masks ★★ - Colonne de la Grande Armée★: ✻★★ 5 km by ① - Côte d'Opale★ by ①.

Plan on following page

La Matelote

70 bd Ste-Beuve – ☎ 03 21 30 33 33 – www.la-matelote.com – tony.lestienne@la-matelote.com – Fax 03 21 30 87 40 Y q

35 rm – †€ 85/115 ††€ 95/175, ☕ € 15

Rest *La Matelote* – see below

◆ An elegant 1930s building on the seafront, opposite Nausicaa. Comfortable rooms, warm atmosphere, attentive service and a new relaxation centre.

Métropole without rest

51 r. Thiers – ☎ 03 21 31 54 30 – www.hotel-metropole-boulogne.com – hotel.metropol@wanadoo.fr – Fax 03 21 30 45 72 – Closed 20 December-12 January Z e

25 rm – †€ 71 ††€ 97, ☕ € 11

◆ Town-centre family hotel. The spacious rooms offer modern facilities (new bedding). Attractive breakfast room overlooking the garden.

Hamiot

1 r. Faidherbe – ☎ 03 21 31 44 20 – www.hotelhamiot.com – hotelrestauranthamiot@wanadoo.fr – Fax 03 21 83 71 56 Z h

12 rm – †€ 65/95 ††€ 80/100, ☕ € 10

Rest *Grand Restaurant* – *(Closed 25 June-12 July, 1st-15 September, 16-29 December, Sunday dinner and Wednesday)* Menu € 22/39 – Carte € 41/52

Rest *Brasserie* – Menu € 14/32 – Carte € 27/46

◆ This post-war building overlooks the port and has renovated rooms (fine wooden furniture) that are comfortable and well soundproofed. The Grand Restaurant offers a low-key atmosphere and overlooks the harbour. Brasserie with a lively atmosphere and summer terrace.

H. de la Plage without rest

168 bd Ste-Beuve – ☎ 03 21 32 15 15 – hotelboulogneplage.com – hoteldelaplage4@wanadoo.fr – Fax 03 21 30 47 97 X u

42 rm – †€ 55 ††€ 75, ☕ € 7

◆ The hotel is right on the seafront, hence the name ("Beach"). Functional rooms; those at the back are quiet and those at the front from the third floor up are best for views.

La Matelote (Tony Lestienne)

80 bd Ste Beuve – ☎ 03 21 30 17 97 – www.la-matelote.com – tony.lestienne@la-matelote.com – Fax 03 21 83 29 24 – Closed 20 December-20 January and Thursday lunch Y q

Rest – Menu € 33/75 – Carte € 65/85

Spec. Salade de homard tiède, velouté de crustacés. Darne de turbot rôtie, beurre de thym. Soufflé frangipane, sorbet cassis et lait d'orgeat.

◆ Hues of red and gold, Louis XVI-style furniture and nautical ornaments form an elegant, refined setting for this restaurant. Seafood prepared to perfection. Summer terrace.

Rest. de la Plage

124 bd Ste-Beuve – ☎ 03 21 99 90 90 – la-plage@wanadoo.fr – Fax 03 21 87 23 14 – Closed Sunday dinner and Monday dinner X v

Rest – Menu € 28 bi (weekdays)/59 – Carte € 39/64

◆ An address that honours the town's maritime role, offering a menu rich in seafood, to be enjoyed in an elegant, modern setting with attractive, pastel shades.

BOULOGNE-SUR-MER

Adam (R. A.)	X	2
Aumont (R. d')	Z	7
Beaucerf (Bd)	Z	8
Beaurepaire (R.)	X	9
Bras-d'Or (R. du)	Z	13
Colonne (R. de la)	X	17
Diderot (Bd)	X	18
Duflos (R. Louis)	X	19
Dutertre (R.)	Y	20
Égalité (R. de)	X	22
Entente-Cordiale (Pont de l')	Z	23
Faidherbe (R.)	Y	
Grande-Rue	Z	
Huguet (R. A.)	X	29
Jean-Jaurès (Bd et Viaduc)	X	30
J.-J. Rousseau (Viaduc)	X	31
Lampe (R. de la)	Z	32
Lattre-de-Tassigny (Av. de)	Y	33
Lavocat (R. Albert)	X	34
Liberté (Bd de la)	X	35
Lille (R. de)	Y	37
Marguet (Pont)	Z	38
Michelet (R. J.)	X	39
Mitterrand (Bd F.)	Z	40
Montesquieu (Bd)	X	42
Mont-Neuf (R. du)	X	44
Orme (R. de l')	X	46
Perrochel (R. de)	Z	48
Porte-Neuve (R.)	Y	49
Puits-d'Amour (R.)	Z	53
Résistance (Pl.)	Y	55
Ste-Beuve (Bd)	XY	59
St-Louis (R.)	Y	56
Thiers (R. A.)	YZ	60
Tour-N.-Dame (R.)	Y	61
Victoires (R. des)	Y	63
Victor-Hugo (R.)	YZ	
Wicardenne (R. de)	X	64

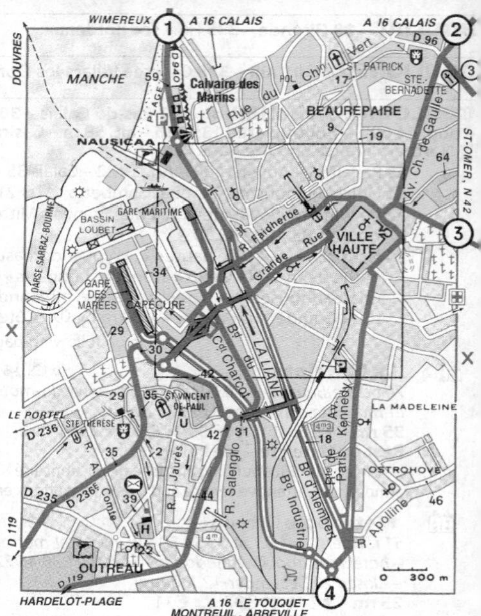

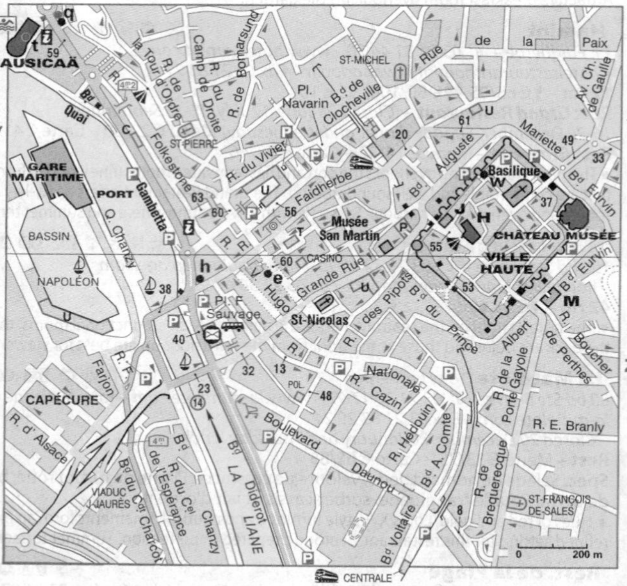

Rest. de Nausicaa
bd Ste-Beuve – 03 21 33 24 24 – sylvie.montuy@orange.fr – Fax 03 21 30 15 63 – Closed Monday off season Y t
Rest – Menu € 22/37 bi – Carte € 31/56
◆ Stop for a meal near the fascinating Centre National de la Mer. A lively atmosphere in two immense, modern brasserie-style dining rooms. A panoramic view over the harbour and beach.

in Pont-de-Briques 5 km by ④ – ✉ 62360

Hostellerie de la Rivière with rm
17 r. de la Gare – 03 21 32 22 81 – www.lhostelleriedelariviere.fr – hostelleriedelariviere@wanadoo.fr – Fax 03 21 87 45 48 – Closed 16 August-3 September, 7-29 January, Sunday dinner, Tuesday lunch and Monday
8 rm – †€ 70/80 ††€ 95/105, ☕ € 10
Rest – Menu (€ 30 bi), € 39/59 – Carte € 65/90
◆ A secluded family-run restaurant in a cul-de-sac with a welcoming dining room plus a garden for outdoor dining on warm summer days. Modern cuisine.

in Hesdin-l'Abbé 9 km by ④ and D 901 – pop. 1 915 – alt. 50 m – ✉ 62360

Cléry
r. du Château, in the village – 03 21 83 19 83 – www.hotelclery-hesdin-labbe.com – chateau-clery.hotel@najeti.com – Fax 03 21 87 52 59
27 rm – †€ 150/395 ††€ 150/395, ☕ € 18
Rest – *(closed Saturday lunch)* Menu € 29 (weekday lunch), € 35/69 – Carte € 50/68
◆ An 18C mansion and cottage offering cosy rooms with personal touches. Pleasant reading room. Park with flower beds, hundred-year-old trees and a vegetable garden. Pleasant dining room and beautiful veranda opening onto the wooded grounds.

LE BOULOU – 66 Pyrénées-Orientales – 344 I7 – pop. 4 858 – alt. 90 m – Spa : mid Feb.-late Nov. – Casino – ✉ 66160 Languedoc-Roussillon-Tarn Gorges 22 B3

Paris 869 – Argelès-sur-Mer 20 – Barcelona 169 – Céret 10 – Perpignan 22
Office de tourisme, 1, rue du Château 04 68 87 50 95, Fax 04 68 87 50 96

at village catalan 7 km North by D 900 – ✉ 66300 Banyuls-dels-Aspres

Village Catalan without rest
access on D 900 and A 9 – 04 68 21 66 66 – www.little-france.com/hcatalan – hotel-catalan@wanadoo.fr – Fax 04 68 21 70 95
77 rm – †€ 65/72 ††€ 85/93, ☕ € 10
◆ On a motorway service area, functional, well-soundproofed rooms, some of which overlook the garden and pool; eight have a private garage.

Southeast 4.5 km by D 900, D 618 and secondary road – ✉ 66160 Le Boulou

Relais des Chartreuses
106 av. d'En-Carbouner – 04 68 83 15 88 – http://www.relais-des-chartreuses.fr – contact@relais-des-chartreuses.fr – Fax 04 68 83 26 62 – Closed 1st January-1st March and 11 November-20 December
11 rm – †€ 60/98 ††€ 60/150, ☕ € 10 – 1 suite – ½ P € 65/170
Rest – *(dinner only)* Menu € 33
◆ Built on a hillside, a stone farmhouse from the 17C that has been entirely restored. Spacious personalised rooms. Sauna, jacuzzi and terrace under the lime trees.

in Vivès 5 km West by D 115 and D 73 – pop. 128 – alt. 228 m – ✉ 66490

L'Hostalet de Vivès with rm
r. de la Mairie – 04 68 83 05 52 – www.hostalet-vives.com – hostalet.de.vives@free.fr – Fax 04 68 83 51 91 – Closed 13 January-5 March, Tuesday off season and Wednesday
3 rm – †€ 60/75 ††€ 60/75, ☕ € 12
Rest – Menu € 22 (weekday lunch)/33 – Carte € 40/60
◆ This fine 12C stone house has preserved all its old charm. Staff wear traditional costumes and serve huge Catalan dishes. A few functional guest rooms.

BOURBACH-LE-BAS – 68 Haut-Rhin – 315 G10 – pop. 618 – alt. 340 m – ✉ 68290 1 A3

Paris 451 – Altkirch 27 – Belfort 26 – Mulhouse 25 – Thann 10

A la Couronne d'Or with rm

9 r. Principale – ☎ 03 89 82 51 77 – famille.muninger@gmail.com – Fax 03 89 82 58 03 – Closed 15-28 February, Tuesday dinner and Monday

7 rm – †€ 42 ††€ 58, ☕ € 8 – ½ P € 52

Rest – Menu (€ 11), € 21 (dinner), € 25/55 – Carte € 29/55

◆ In a little village in the Doller Valley. Long cottage with a sectional rustic dining room and a smaller room with a stove. Simple, well-soundproofed rooms.

BOURBON-LANCY – 71 Saône-et-Loire – 320 C10 – pop. 5 502 – alt. 240 m – Spa : early April-late Oct. – Casino – ✉ 71140 Burgundy-Jura 7 B3

Paris 308 – Autun 62 – Mâcon 110 – Montceau-les-Mines 55 – Moulins 36

Office de tourisme, place d'Aligre ☎ 03 85 89 18 27, Fax 03 85 89 28 38

de Givalois Givallois, E : 3 km, ☎ 03 85 89 05 48

Wooden house and Clock tower ★ B.

BOURBON-LANCY

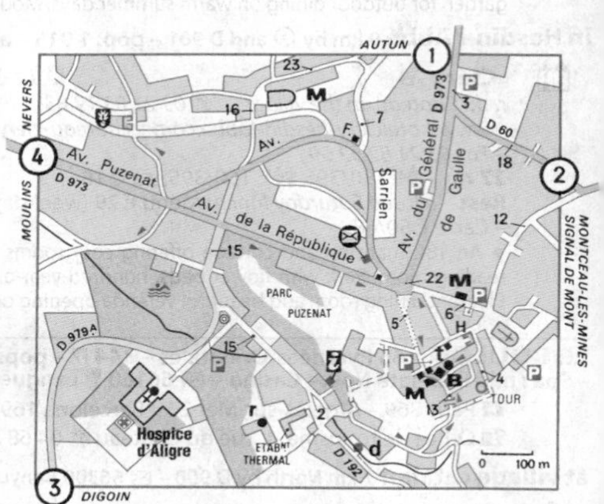

Le Manoir de Sornat

allée Sornat, 2 km Moulins road via ④ – ☎ 03 85 89 17 39 – www.chateauxhotels.com – manoir-de-sornat@wanadoo.fr – Fax 03 85 89 29 47 – Closed 2 January-10 February, Sunday dinner except July-August and Bank holidays, Monday lunch and Tuesday lunch

13 rm – †€ 62/110 ††€ 62/140, ☕ € 12 – ½ P € 80/110

Rest – Menu (€ 28), € 32/90 – Carte € 55/95

◆ Normandy mansion in a pleasant wooded park. Fine woodwork in the hall and sitting room. Spacious rooms furnished in contemporary style. The decoration of the plush dining room pays homage to Monet; updated classic cuisine.

Le Grand Hôtel

1 parc Thermal – ☎ 03 85 89 08 87 – www.grand-hotel-thermal.com – ghthermal@stbl.fr – Fax 03 85 89 25 45 – Closed 20 December-28 February

28 rm, ☕ € 7 – ½ P € 54/66 r

Rest – Menu (€ 14), € 18 (weekday lunch), € 23/35 – Carte € 29/38

◆ Old convent bordering the park of the spa. Spacious rooms, with modern or period furniture. Traditional restaurant and pretty terrace in the former cloister. Low fat meals on request.

La Tourelle du Beffroi without rest

17 pl. de la Mairie – ☎ 03 85 89 39 20 – www.latourelle.fr – hotellatourelle@aol.com – Fax 03 85 89 39 29 t

8 rm – †€ 55 ††€ 73, ☕ € 9

◆ Good spot by the belfry for this lovely 1900 house with a tower and balustraded terrace. Rooms decorated with care. Guesthouse ambiance.

XX **Villa du Vieux Puits** with rm rest, VISA

7 r. Bel-Air – ✆ 03 85 89 04 04 – hubert.perraudin@orange.fr – Fax 03 85 89 13 87 – Closed 1st-15 March, 24 October-2 November, Sunday dinner and Monday **d**

7 rm – †€ 50/55 ††€ 55/65, ☐ € 10 – ½ P € 65/75

Rest – *(dinner only)* Menu € 20/40 – Carte € 40/52

◆ Pretty guesthouse in the walls of a former tannery hidden away in a garden below the road. Country-style restaurant and cosy rooms.

BOURBON-L'ARCHAMBAULT – 03 Allier – 326 F3 – pop. 2 576 – alt. 367 m – Spa : early March-early Nov. – Casino – ✉ 03160 Auvergne

5 **B1**

Paris 292 – Montluçon 53 – Moulins 24 – Nevers 54

Office de tourisme, 1, place de l'Hotel de Ville ✆ 04 70 67 09 79, Fax 04 70 67 15 20

New park ≤★ - Château ≤★.

Grand Hôtel Montespan-Talleyrand rest, rest, VISA

pl. des Thermes – ✆ 04 70 67 00 24 – www.hotel-montespan.com – hotelmontespan@wanadoo.fr – Fax 04 70 67 12 00 – Open 4 April-24 October

42 rm – †€ 59/62 ††€ 64/126, ☐ € 13 – 2 suites – ½ P € 64/85

Rest – Menu (€ 11), € 25/53 – Carte € 37/47

◆ These three old houses were the homes of Mme de Montespan, Mme de Sévigné and Talleyrand. Spacious and personalised rooms. Solarium, classical interior garden. In the restaurant, original beams and stones harmonise with tasteful contemporary decoration.

BOURBONNE-LES-BAINS – 52 Haute-Marne – 313 O6 – pop. 2 276 – alt. 290 m – Spa : early March-late Nov. – Casino – ✉ 52400 Northern France and the Paris Region

14 **D3**

Paris 313 – Chaumont 55 – Dijon 124 – Langres 39 – Neufchâteau 53

Office de tourisme, place des Bains ✆ 03 25 90 01 71, Fax 03 25 90 14 12

BOURBONNE-LES-BAINS

Bains (R. des) 2
Bassigny (R. du) 3
Capucins (R. des) 4
Daprey Blache (R.) 5
Écoles (R. des) 6
Gouby (Av. du Lieutenant) 7
Grande-Rue 9
Hôtel-Dieu (R. de l') 12
Lattre-de-Tassigny (Av. Maréchal-de) 14
Maistre (R. du Gén.) 15
Pierre (R. Amiral) 22
Porte Galon (R.) 23
Verdun (Pl. de) 25
Walferdin (R.) 26

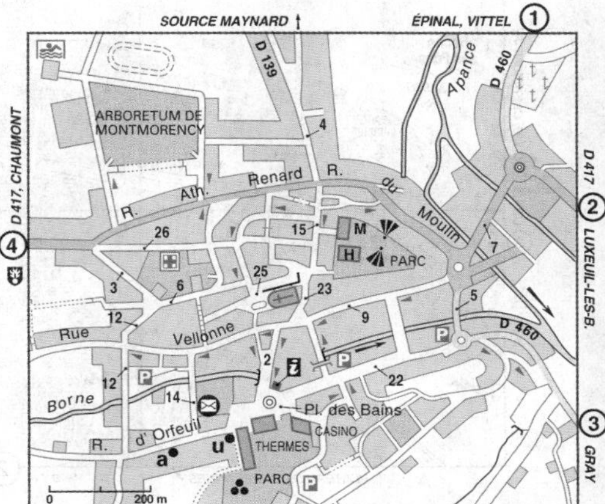

Orfeuil rest, VISA

29 r. Orfeuil – ✆ 03 25 90 05 71 – hotel-orfeuil@wanadoo.fr – Fax 03 25 84 46 25 – Open 5 April-24 October **a**

43 rm – †€ 47/54 ††€ 52/61, ☐ € 9 – ½ P € 40/46

Rest – *(closed Sunday evening and Monday)* Menu € 14/24 – Carte € 19/35

◆ The main building (18C) has an elegant salon and regularly renovated, comfortable rooms. The annexe has spacious studios that are plainer. Sixties furnishings and greenery in a bright dining room and a flower-filled garden in summer.

Des Sources rm, rest, VISA MC
pl. des Bains – ✆ 03 25 87 86 00 – logis-de-france.fr
– hotel-des-sources@wanadoo.fr – Fax 03 25 87 86 33
– Open 5 April-28 November **u**
23 rm – €47/58 €52/68, €9 – ½ P €42/48
Rest – *(closed Wednesday dinner)* Menu €14/30 – Carte €24/40
◆ Family establishment near the baths, with simple, functional and well-kept rooms. The dining room opens up onto a pretty verdant patio with a small pool, where tables are set in good weather.

If breakfast is included the symbol appears after the number of rooms.

LA BOURBOULE – 63 Puy-de-Dôme – **326** D9 – **pop. 2 061** 5 **B2**
– **alt. 880 m** – **Spa : early Feb.-early Oct.** – **Casino** AZ – ✉ **63150** **Auvergne**

Paris 469 – Aubusson 82 – Clermont-Ferrand 50 – Mauriac 71 – Ussel 51
Office de tourisme, place de la République ✆ 04 73 65 57 71, Fax 04 73 65 50 21
Parc Fenêstre★ - Murat-le-Quaire: musée de la Toinette★ North: 2 km.

LA BOURBOULE

Alsace-Lorraine (Av.) . . . . **BY** 2
Clemenceau (Bd G.) . . . . . **ABY**
États-Unis (Av. des) . . . . **BY** 3
Féron (Quai) . . . . **BY**
Foch (Av. Mar.) . . . . **AY** 6
Gambetta (Quai) . . . . **AZ** 7
Guéneau-de-Mussy (Av.) . . . **AY** 8
Hôtel de Ville (Quai) . . . . **AY** 10
Jeanne-d'Arc (Quai) . . . . **BY** 12
Jet-d'eau (Square du) . . . . . . **AY** 13
Joffre (Sq. du Mar.) . . . . **BY** 15
Lacoste (Pl. G.) . . . . **AY** 16
Libération (Q. de la) . . . . **AZ** 17
Mangin (Av. du Général) . . . . **AZ** 19
République (Pl. de la) . . . . **AZ** 21
Souvenir (Pl. du) . . . . **BY** 22
Victoire (Pl. de la) . . . . **AY** 23

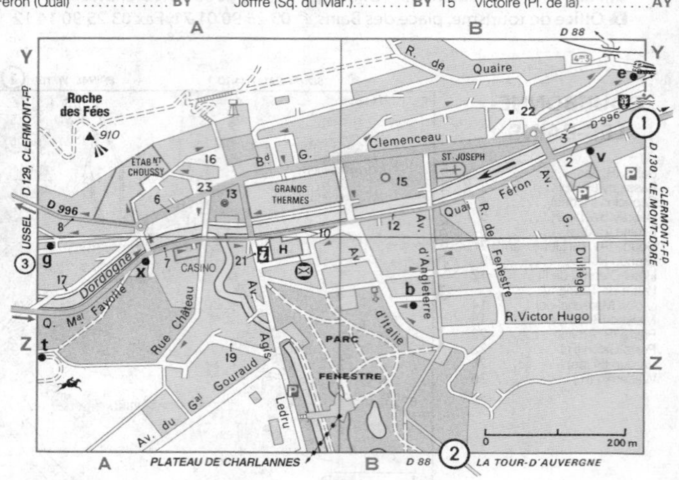

Régina VISA MC AE
av. Alsace-Lorraine – ✆ 04 73 81 09 22 – www.hotelregina-labourboule.com
– reservation@hotelregina-labourboule.com – Fax 04 73 81 08 55
– Closed 1st-20 December and 5 January-5 February BY **v**
20 rm – €58/65 €70/140, €8 **Rest** – Menu €16/29 – Carte €27/42
◆ A 19C residence on the banks of the Dordogne. Rooms are modern and well equipped. Leisure area. Two dining rooms: one Art Deco with moulded ceiling and old parquet flooring; the other is modern. The chef prepares wholesome traditional recipes.

Le Charlet
bd L.-Choussy – ✆ 04 73 81 33 00 – www.lecharlet.fr
– contact@lecharlet.fr – Fax 04 73 65 50 82
– Closed 10 November-20 December AZ **g**
36 rm – †€ 47/72 ††€ 52/77, ☕ € 9 – ½ P € 47/63
Rest – Menu € 16/35 – Carte € 23/38
♦ Hotel in a fairly quiet district, offering small, clean rooms in perfect condition. Full relaxation and sports facilities. A restaurant with bistro style furniture, green plants and screens. Extensive, traditional and regional menu.

Le Parc des Fées
107 quai Mar.-Fayolle – ✆ 04 73 81 01 77 – www.parcdesfees.com
– info@parcdesfees.com – Fax 04 73 81 30 49
– Closed 18 October-18 December AZ **x**
42 rm – †€ 51/59 ††€ 64/69, ☕ € 9 – ½ P € 58/66
Rest – Menu € 14/32 – Carte € 27/32
♦ Half of the rooms in this century-old building overlook the Dordogne. Space, modern decoration and comfort are on the menu. Games room for children. Welcoming restaurant where pastel tones and mirrors abound. Traditional menu.

Aviation
r. de Metz – ✆ 04 73 81 32 32 – www.aviation.fr – aviation@nat.fr
– Fax 04 73 81 02 85 – Closed 1st October-19 December BZ **b**
45 rm – †€ 50/65 ††€ 50/65, ☕ € 7 – ½ P € 47/58
Rest – Menu € 16/20 – Carte € 15/28
♦ Hotel in an early-20C house near the Fenestre park. Home to functional rooms and a wide range of leisure facilities: pool, fitness, games room, billiards, etc. Classic, regional meals served in a spacious dining room with entirely new decor.

Au Val Doré
r. de Belgique – ✆ 04 73 81 06 14 – www.hotel-val-dore.com
– valdore@wanadoo.fr – Fax 04 73 65 58 79
– Closed 5 November-25 December BY **e**
29 rm – †€ 54/71 ††€ 54/71, ☕ € 7 – ½ P € 48/55
Rest – Menu € 14/23 – Carte € 16/29
♦ A family-run hotel near the railway station. The rooms are decorated in a low-key modern fashion. Small indoor pool and fitness facilities. Have a drink before dinner in the lounge (fireplace) followed by simple dishes in the spacious, sunny dining room decorated with flowers.

La Lauzeraie without rest
577 chemin de la Suchère – ✆ 04 73 81 15 70 – www.lalauzeraie.net
– goigoux.martine@wanadoo.fr – Closed 15 October-15 November,
24-26 December and 31 December-8 January AZ **t**
4 rm ☕ – †€ 75/100 ††€ 95/135
♦ Serenity and comfort await you in this recent house built using old materials. Lovely rooms decorated with antiques or period furniture. Indoor pool, fitness facilities and steam bath.

in St-Sauves-d'Auvergne **5 km by ③ – pop. 1 140 – alt. 791 m – ✉ 63950**
Office de tourisme, le bourg ✆ 04 73 65 50 40

De la Poste
pl. du Portique – ✆ 04 73 81 10 33 – www.hotel-poste-auvergne.com
– hoteldelaposte63@aol.com – Fax 04 73 81 02 27
– Closed 5-31 January
15 rm – †€ 38/43 ††€ 43/47, ☕ € 6,50
Rest – Menu (€ 12), € 16/29 – Carte € 24/46
♦ This old post house is also a bar and newsagents. Rustic rooms with a somewhat old feel but well kept. Two country dining rooms with exposed beams. Traditional menu and Auvergne specialities.

BOURDEILLES – **24 Dordogne** – **329** E4 – **see Brantôme**

BOURG-ACHARD – **27 Eure** – **304** E5 – **pop. 2 773** – **alt. 124 m** – ✉ **27310** Normandy 33 **C2**

Paris 141 – Bernay 39 – Évreux 62 – Le Havre 62 – Rouen 30

L'Amandier

581 rte Rouen – ☎ 02 32 57 11 49 – restaurant.amandier@wanadoo.fr – Fax 02 32 57 11 49 – Closed 3-13 August, 18-29 January, Sunday dinner, Monday dinner, Wednesday dinner and Tuesday

Rest – Menu € 19 (weekday lunch), € 28/48 – Carte € 58/72

◆ Pleasant village centre restaurant decorated in a modern, low-key style (bay windows facing the garden). Friendly welcome and generous portions of updated cuisine.

BOURG-CHARENTE – **16 Charente** – **324** I5 – **see Jarnac**

LE BOURG-DUN – **76 Seine-Maritime** – **304** F2 – **pop. 457** – **alt. 17 m** – ✉ **76740** Normandy 33 **C1**

Paris 188 – Dieppe 20 – Fontaine-le-Dun 7 – Rouen 56 – St-Valery-en-Caux 15

Office de tourisme, 6, place du Village ☎ 02 35 97 63 05, Fax 02 35 57 24 51

Church ★ tower.

Auberge du Dun (Pierre Chrétien)

3 rte de Dieppe, (opposite the church) – ☎ 02 35 83 05 84 – Closed 22 September-6 October, 16 February-1st March, Wednesday except lunch from 1st March to 15 September, Sunday dinner and Monday

Rest – *(pre-book weekends)* Menu € 32 (weekdays)/87 – Carte € 75/110

Spec. Foie gras chaud de canard caramélisé aux figues (August-October). Turbotin aux artichauts parfumé au thym-citron. Crêpes soufflées au calvados.

◆ Pretty inn with two rustic dining rooms, separated from the busy kitchens by a bay window. Modern cuisine prepared with care.

BOURG-EN-BRESSE Ⓟ – **01 Ain** – **328** E3 – **pop. 40 300** – **Built-up area 101 016** – **alt. 251 m** – ✉ **01000** Burgundy-Jura 44 **B1**

Paris 424 – Annecy 113 – Genève 112 – Lyon 82 – Mâcon 38

Office de tourisme, 6, avenue Alsace Lorraine ☎ 04 74 22 49 40, Fax 04 74 23 06 28

de Bourg-en-Bresse Parc de Loisirs de Bouvent, 2 km on the Nantua road, ☎ 04 74 24 65 17

Brou church ★★ (tombs★★★, stalls★★, rood-screen★★, stained-glass wwindows★★, chapel and oratories★★★, portal★) X **B** - Stalls★ of Notre-Dame church Y - Musée du monastère★ X **E**.

Plan on next page

Mercure rm, rm, VISA AE

10 av. Bad-Kreuznach – ☎ 04 74 22 44 88 – mercure.com – h1187@accor.com – Fax 04 74 23 43 57 X **e**

60 rm – †€ 80/97 ††€ 85/108, ☐ € 13

Rest – *(closed Sunday lunch and Saturday)* Menu (€ 19), € 29 (dinner) – Carte € 32/45

◆ This Mercure offers several types of comfortable rooms; all are comfortable and well equipped. This restaurant features a contemporary style but has lost none of its refined charm. Covered terrace and view of the garden. Traditional cuisine.

De France without rest VISA AE

19 pl. Bernard – ☎ 04 74 23 30 24 – www.grand-hoteldefrance.com – infos@grand-hoteldefrance.com – Fax 04 74 23 69 90 Y **r**

44 rm – †€ 80 ††€ 89, ☐ € 13 – 1 suite

◆ This hotel near Notre Dame Church sports a stylish mixture of cosy and modern details: spacious, attractive rooms and a lobby restored to its original 1900 glory.

BOURG-EN-BRESSE

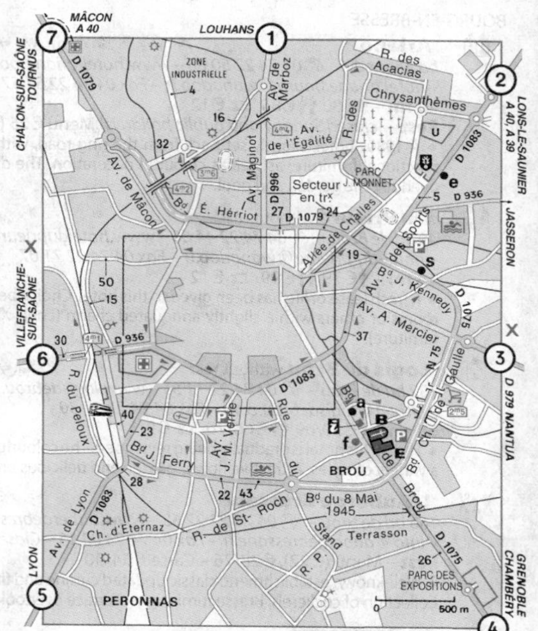

Av. de Mâcon
Av. Maginot
R. G. Vicaire
R. du 23ème R.I.
CHAMP DE FOIRE
Rond-Point G. Pompidou
Allée de Challes
Leclerc
PARC DE LA VISITATION
R. Bourgmayer
Promde du Bastion
Pl. Carriat
N-Dame
R. A. Mas
Ch. Robin
CHAMP DE MARS
R. des Casernes
R. O. H.
Bd de Brou
Groboz
Reyssouze
Av. L. Jourdan
Pl. Joubert
Lorraine
R. Dr Ebrard
R. de la République
Square du Bourgneuf
Bd St-Nicolas
Pl. André Malraux
R. du Lycée
HÔPITAL PSYCHIATRIQUE STE-MADELEINE
Av. Alsace
Bd Paul Bert
Victor Hugo
R. L. Carnot
Bd Voltaire
Pl. Perrier Labalme
Bd de Brou
200m

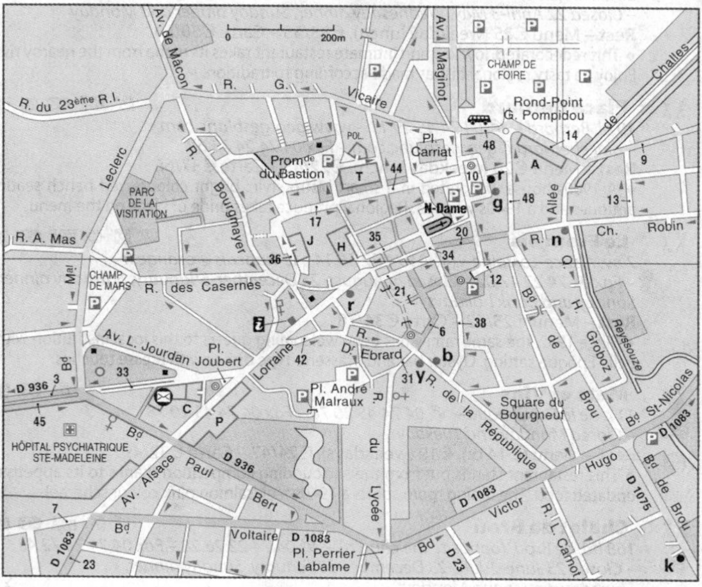

Ariane rm, VISA AE

bd Kennedy – ✆ 04 74 22 50 88 – www.hotel-ariane-bourg.com – hotel.ariane.bourg@wanadoo.fr – Fax 04 74 22 51 57 X **s**

40 rm – €80 €85, €12

Rest – *(closed Sunday and public holidays)* Menu €25 (weekdays)/45

◆ A 1980s hotel, slightly set back from the ring road, with modern rooms and simple, functional furniture, as well as colourful decoration. The dining room and terrace both overlook the garden and pool.

Du Prieuré without rest VISA AE

49 bd de Brou – ✆ 04 74 22 44 60 – www.hoteldupieure.com – hotel-du-prieure@wanadoo.fr – Fax 04 74 22 71 07 X **a**

14 rm – €79 €99, €12

◆ A fresh lease of life has been given to this hotel. Choice between first floor, modernised rooms or others with a slightly antiquated charm (Louis XV, Louis XVI or Bresse period furniture).

Logis de Brou without rest VISA AE

132 bd de Brou – ✆ 04 74 22 11 55 – www.logisdebrou.com – citotel@logisdebrou.com – Fax 04 74 22 37 30 Z **k**

30 rm – €59/69 €66/76, €9

◆ This 1970s hotel is gradually being revamped. The colourful rooms, with balconies, sport a variety of styles. Attractive flower garden and delicious breakfasts.

L'Auberge Bressane VISA AE

166 bd de Brou – ✆ 04 74 22 22 68 – www.aubergebressane.fr – info@aubergebressane.fr – Fax 04 74 23 03 15 – Closed Tuesday X **f**

Rest – Menu (€22), €28/76 – Carte €54/90

◆ Well-known establishment: classic updated cuisine and fine choice of Burgundy wines. Collection of cockerels, Bresse furnishings. Terrace overlooking Brou church.

La Reyssouze VISA AE

20 r. Ch.-Robin – ✆ 04 74 23 11 50 – Fax 04 74 23 94 32 – Closed 22 April-3 May, Wednesday dinner, Sunday dinner and Monday

Rest – Menu €25 (weekday lunch), €35/55 – Carte €50/80 Y **n**

◆ This redecorated, low key and intimate restaurant takes its name from the nearby river. Enjoy its tasty regional dishes made according to tradition.

Place Bernard VISA AE

19 pl. Bernard – ✆ 04 74 45 29 11 – www.georgesblanc.com – placebernard@georgesblanc.com – Fax 04 74 24 73 69 Y **g**

Rest – Menu €20 (weekday lunch), €22/45 – Carte €37/66

◆ A 1900s house, decorated in a smart bistro style: bright colours, red bench seating, antiques and a 1940s veranda. Regional produce takes pride of place on the menu.

Le Français VISA AE

7 av. Alsace-Lorraine – ✆ 04 74 22 55 14 – le-francais@orange.fr – Fax 04 74 22 47 02 – Closed in August, 25 December-5 January, Saturday dinner, Sunday and bank holidays Z **r**

Rest – Menu €25/52 – Carte €34/78

◆ Since 1932, the same family has been welcoming guests to this local institution with a Belle Epoque setting. Oyster bar and brasserie-type dishes with Bresse touches.

Mets et Vins VISA AE

11 r. de la République – ✆ 04 74 45 20 78 – Fax 04 74 45 20 78 – Closed Monday and Tuesday Z **b**

Rest – Menu (€14 bi), €19 (weekdays), €24/47 – Carte €32/49

◆ This restaurant stands out from the surrounding competition thanks to its appetising updated food. The dining room sports a 1940s feel (salmon pink colour scheme).

Chalet de Brou VISA AE

168 bd. de Brou, (opposite the church) – ✆ 04 74 22 26 28 – Fax 04 74 24 72 42 – Closed 25 June-2 July, 23 December-20 January, Sunday dinner, Thursday dinner and Monday X **f**

Rest – Menu €17 (weekdays)/45 – Carte €23/55

◆ An architectural gem opposite Brou church, this family restaurant upholds the local traditional cuisine in a charming old-fashioned setting.

Les Quatre Saisons
6 r. de la République – ✆ 04 74 22 01 86 – turc.phil@wanadoo.fr – Fax 04 74 21 10 35 – Closed 1st-10 May, 15-30 August, 2-10 January, Saturday lunch, Sunday and Monday Z y
Rest – Menu € 20 (weekdays), € 28/55 – Carte € 29/55
◆ The chef, a fan of local wines and produce, will set your taste buds tingling with his generous, cleverly reinterpreted regional recipes. Friendly and informal atmosphere.

Lons-le-Saunier road 6,5 km by ② N 83 – ✉ 01370 St-Étienne-du-Bois

Les Mangettes
– ✆ 04 74 22 70 66 – Fax 04 74 22 70 66 – Closed 18-26 June, 1st-10 October, 7-22 January, Sunday dinner, Monday dinner and Tuesday
Rest – *(number of covers limited, pre-book)* Menu € 19 (weekday lunch), € 24/38 – Carte € 25/36
◆ A country house with a simple rustic interior. Tasty regional cuisine, lovely desserts. Interior of stuffed animals, old postcards and fireplace.

in Péronnas 3 km by ⑤, D 1083 – pop. 6 106 – alt. 281 m – ✉ 01960

La Marelle (Didier Goiffon)
1593 av. de Lyon – ✆ 04 74 21 75 21 – www.lamarelle.fr – contact@lamarelle.fr – Fax 04 74 21 06 81 – Closed 27 April-11 May, 17 August-7 September, 2-16 January, Sunday dinner, Tuesday and Wednesday
Rest – Menu € 28 (weekday lunch), € 40 € bi/80 – Carte € 39/52
Spec. Foie gras. Paleron de bœuf (winter). Poire aux morilles (season). **Wines** Manicle, Mâcon.
◆ La Marelle can be relied upon to rustle up inventive, mouth watering dishes served in a smart, warm interior that mixes country chic with contemporary.

in Lalleyriat 7 km via ⑤, N 83 and D 22 – ✉ 01960

Le Nid à Bibi
Les Grandes Terres – ✆ 04 74 21 11 47 – www.lenidabibi.com – lenidabibi@wanadoo.fr – Fax 04 74 21 02 83
5 rm – **†**€ 90/115 **††**€ 105/135 – ½ P € 70/90
Table d'hôte – Menu € 22 (weekday dinner), € 30/38
◆ This hotel provides quiet, attractive rooms, delicious breakfasts and a host of leisure activities. Faultless welcome. Home from home! Delicious regional produce turned into tasty recipes.

BOURGES P – **18 Cher – 323** K4 – **pop. 70 800 – Built-up area 123 584** 12 **C3** – **alt. 153 m – ✉ 18000** **Dordogne-Berry-Limousin**

Paris 244 – Châteauroux 65 – Dijon 254 – Nevers 69 – Orléans 121

Office de tourisme, 21, rue Victor Hugo ✆ 02 48 23 02 60, Fax 02 48 23 02 69

Bourges Golf Club Route de Lazenay, S : 5 km on D 106, ✆ 02 48 20 11 08

St-Étienne cathedral ★★★: North Tower ≤★★ Z - Jardins de l'Archevêché★ - Palais Jacques-Coeur★★ - Jardins des Prés-Fichaux★ - Half-timbered houses★ - Hôtel des Échevins★: musée Estève★ Y **M²** - Hôtel Lallemant★ Y **M³** - Hôtel Cujas★: Musée du Berry★ Y **M¹** - Muséum d'histoire naturelle★ Z - Marshlands★ V - Ramparts walkway★.

Plan on following page

De Bourbon
bd de la République – ✆ 02 48 70 70 00 – www.hoteldebourbon.fr – contact@hoteldebourbon.fr – Fax 02 48 70 21 22 Y b
58 rm – **†**€ 120/260 **††**€ 135/260, € 16
Rest *L'Abbaye St-Ambroix* – see below
◆ The De Bourbon occupies a former 17C abbey near the town centre. All the hotel's bedrooms have been recently refurbished. Elegant lounge-bar.

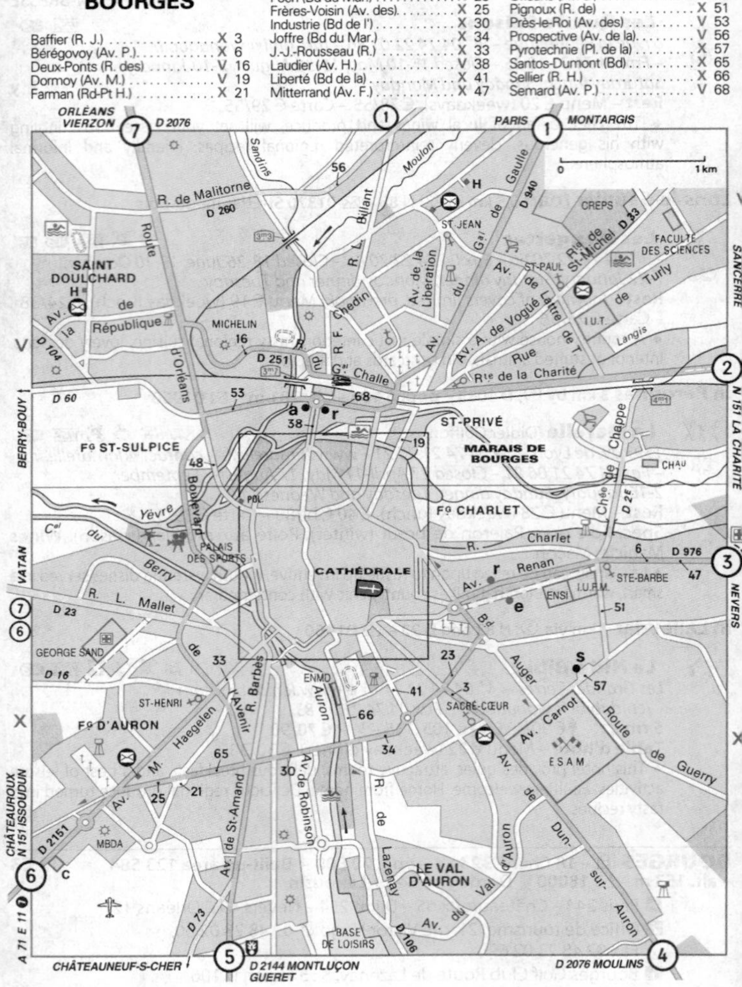

Le Berry V a

3 pl. Gén.-Leclerc – ✆ 02 48 65 99 30
– www.le-berry.com
– leberry.bourges@wanadoo.fr
– Fax 02 48 24 29 17

64 rm – †€ 59/65 ††€ 63/69, ☕ € 8,50

Rest – *(closed 24 December-1st January, Saturday lunch and Sunday)* Menu (€ 17) – Carte € 23/40

◆ A large modern building opposite the station with rooms that are being renovated in stages. Bright colours, painted wood panelling and African artwork. Restaurant with exotic decoration and world cuisine.

BOURGES

Armuriers (R. des) . . . . Z 2
Auron (Bd d') . . . . Z
Barbès (R.) . . . . Z 4
Beaux-Arts (R. des) . . . . Y 5
Bourbonnoux (Prom.) . . . . YZ
Calvin (R.) . . . . Y 7
Cambournac (R.) . . . . Y 8
Champ-de-Foire (R. du) . . . . Z 12
Commerce (R. du) . . . . Y 13
Coursarlon (R.) . . . . Y
Cujas (Pl.) . . . . Y 15
Dr-Témoin (R. du) . . . . Y 17
Dormoy (Av. Marx) . . . . Y 19
Équerre (R. de l') . . . . Z 20
George-Sand (Escalier) . . . . Y 27
Hémerettes (R. des) . . . . Z 29
Jacobins (Cour des) . . . . Z 31
Jacques-Coeur (R.) . . . . Y 32
Jean-Jaurès (Av.) . . . . Y
Joyeuse (R.) . . . . Y 35
Juranville (Pl.) . . . . Z 36
J.-J. Rousseau (R.) . . . . Z 33
Leblanc (R. N.) . . . . YZ 40
Linières (R. de) . . . . Z 42
Louis XI (Av.) . . . . Z 43
Mallet (R. L.) . . . . Z 44
Marceau (Rampe) . . . . Z 45
Mirebeau (R.) . . . . Y
Moyenne (R.) . . . . YZ
Orléans (Av. d') . . . . Y 48
Pelvoysin (R.) . . . . Y 50
Poissonnerie (R. de la) . . . . Y 52
Prinal (R. du) . . . . Y 55
Rimbault (R. J.) . . . . Z 61
Strasbourg (Bd de) . . . . Z 71
Thaumassière (R. de la) . . . . Y 72
Tory (R. G.) . . . . Y 73
Victor-Hugo (R.) . . . . Z 74
3-Maillets (R. des) . . . . Z 75
4-Piliers (Pl. des) . . . . Z 76
95e-de-Ligne (Av. du) . . . . Z 78

D'Angleterre without rest
1 pl. Quatre-Piliers
– ✆ 02 48 24 68 51
– www.bestwestern-angleterre-bourges.com
– hotel@bestwestern-angleterre-bourges.com – Fax 02 48 65 21 41
– Closed 27 December-3 January Y **t**
31 rm – †€ 94/138 ††€ 114/138
◆ This hotel, which has benefited from a recent facelift, enjoys a good location near the Palais Jacques Cœur. A pleasant and comfortable base for your stay.

Le Christina without rest
5 r. de la Halle – ✆ 02 48 70 56 50 – www.le-christina.com – info@le-christina.com – Fax 02 48 70 58 13 Z **m**
71 rm – †€ 50/80 ††€ 50/80, ☕ € 9
◆ A practical location near the centre of town, opposite the impressive 19C corn exchange *halle au blé*. Functional guestrooms decorated with Basque furniture and warm tones.

Les Tilleuls without rest
7 pl. Pyrotechnie – ✆ 02 48 20 49 04 – www.les-tilleuls.com – lestilleuls.bourges@wanadoo.fr – Fax 02 48 50 61 73 – Closed 26 December-3 January X **s**
39 rm – †€ 58 ††€ 66/71, ☕ € 8
◆ Flower-decked hotel with air-conditioned guestrooms, either rustic or more classical in style. Those in the annexe have been renovated. Swimming pool and small fitness room.

Ibis
r. Jankélévitch, Prado district – ✆ 02 48 65 89 99 – www.ibishotel.com – h0819@accor.com – Fax 02 48 65 18 47 Z **v**
86 rm – †€ 56/75 ††€ 56/75, ☕ € 8,50 **Rest** – *(dinner only)* Menu € 15
◆ A practical choice just 10 minutes' walk from the cathedral and palace. Well-maintained guestrooms and friendly staff. Bar, lounge and dining room separated by partitions. Buffet-style menus.

Arcane without rest
2 pl. du Gén.-Leclerc – ✆ 02 48 24 20 87 – www.arcane-hotel.com – arcane.bourges@wanadoo.fr – Fax 02 48 69 00 67 V **r**
30 rm – †€ 47 ††€ 47, ☕ € 7
◆ This completely renovated hotel facing the railway station offers affordably priced, functional guestrooms and a good buffet breakfast.

Le Cèdre Bleu without rest
14 r. Voltaire – ✆ 02 48 25 07 37 – www.lecedrebleu.fr – lecedre-bleu@wanadoo.fr – Closed 1st-8 March and 1st-23 August Y **n**
4 rm ☕ – †€ 54/71 ††€ 59/76
◆ A rare pearl in the centre of the town, this impressive Napoleon III-style residence with its pleasant garden offers beautifully maintained and individually decorated bedrooms.

L' Abbaye St-Ambroix – Hôtel de Bourbon
60 av. J.-Jaurès – ✆ 02 48 70 80 00 – www.abbayesaintambroix.fr – contact@abbayesaintambroix.fr – Fax 02 48 70 21 22 – Closed Sunday dinner from November to March, Monday and Tuesday Y **b**
Rest – Menu (€ 32 bi), € 49/90 – Carte € 81/89
Spec. Queues de grosses langoutines (summer). Noix de ris de veau croustillante aux amandes. Crêpes suzette.
◆ The abbey's former chapel (17C) with its huge vaulted ceiling has been magnificently renovated in contemporary style. A superb setting for fine up-to-date cuisine.

Le Piet à Terre (Thierry Finet)
44 bd Lahitolle – ✆ 02 48 67 95 60 – www.lepietaterre.fr – tfinet@wanadoo.fr – Closed 5-25 August, February holidays, Monday lunch, Saturday lunch and Sunday X **e**
Rest – Menu € 34 (weekday lunch), € 39/96 – Carte € 75/105
Spec. "Artichaut dans l'artichaut". Bar de ligne à la vapeur douce, jus acidulé à la verveine. Texture de chocolat.
◆ This plush bourgeois house in the town's suburbs provides the backdrop for the inspired, creative cuisine of its owner-chef. Friendly service and welcome.

Le Jardin Gourmand
15 bis av. E.-Renan – ✆ 02 48 21 35 91 – www.jardingourmand.fr – Fax 02 48 20 59 75 – Closed 20 December-20 January, 8-28 July, Sunday dinner, Tuesday lunch and Monday X **r**
Rest – Menu € 16 (weekdays)/42 – Carte € 39/50
◆ Tasteful mansion on a boulevard outside the town centre with three small, classically furnished dining rooms. Attractive lounge with wooden fireplace. Traditional cuisine.

XXX **Beauvoir** AC VISA MC

1 av. Marx-Dormoy – ✆ 02 48 65 42 44 – www.restaurantlebeauvoir.com – didier-guyot@club-internet.fr – Fax 02 48 24 80 84 – Closed 2-23 August and Sunday dinner Y e

Rest – Menu € 19 (weekdays)/48 – Carte € 50/65

◆ A contemporary, bright interior decorated in warm tones adds to the charm of this delightful suburban restaurant. Modern cuisine and an impressive wine list.

XX **Le Bourbonnoux** AC VISA MC AE

44 r. Bourbonnoux – ✆ 02 48 24 14 76 – restaurantbourbonnoux@wanadoo.fr – Fax 02 48 24 77 67 – Closed 18-26 April, 15 August-4 September, 13-21 February, Saturday lunch, Sunday dinner and Friday Y a

Rest – Menu € 13 (weekdays)/32 – Carte € 26/40

◆ Bright colours and half-timbered walls make up the pleasant interior of this restaurant, situated in a street lined with craft shops. Friendly service. Updated classic cuisine.

XX **Le d'Antan Sancerrois** (Stéphane Rétif) AC VISA MC AE

50 r. Bourbonnoux – ✆ 02 48 65 96 26 – www.dantansancerrois.com – dantan.sancerrois@wanadoo.fr – Fax 02 48 70 50 82 – Closed 4-25 August, 23 December-4 January, Sunday, Monday and bank holidays Z n

Rest – Menu (€ 32), € 57/85 – Carte € 49/61

Spec. Cœur de filet de thon façon sashimi. Dos de Saint-Pierre rôti. Croustillant au chocolat.

◆ A pedestrian cobbled street leads to this inviting and friendly establishment. An unusual menu with a striking combination of flavours.

Châteauroux road 7 km by ⑥, near A 71 interchange – ✉ 18570 Le Subdray

Novotel AC P VISA MC AE

rte de Chateauroux – ✆ 02 48 26 53 33 – www.novotel.com – h1302@accor.com – Fax 02 48 26 52 22

93 rm – †€ 115/150 ††€ 125/150, ☕ € 14

Rest – Menu (€ 18), € 22/27 bi – Carte approx. € 29

◆ This Novotel near a motorway toll booth has been given a facelift in keeping with the hotel chain's new Novation look. Buffet breakfast. This simple, contemporary dining room opens onto a garden and a terrace by the swimming pool.

in St-Doulchard -V-to ⑦ – **pop. 9 048 – alt. 158 m – ✉ 18230**

Logitel without rest P VISA MC AE

r. de Malitorne – ✆ 02 48 70 07 26 – www.logitel.fr – hotel.logitel@wanadoo.fr – Fax 02 48 24 59 94

30 rm – †€ 50 ††€ 50, ☕ € 6

◆ Basic rooms furnished in the 1980s style, well kept up and at reasonable prices; a simple place to stop at the edge of Bourges. Family-style welcome.

LE BOURGET – 93 Seine-Saint-Denis – 305 F7 – **101** 17 – **see Paris, Area**

BOURG-ET-COMIN – 02 Aisne – 306 D6 – **pop. 738 – alt. 55 m** 37 **D2** – ✉ **02160**

Paris 141 – Reims 40 – Château-Thierry 54 – Laon 25 – Soissons 27

De la Vallée P VISA MC

6 r. d'Oeuilly – ✆ 03 23 25 81 58 – www.auberge-delavallee.com – lavallee02@aol.com – Fax 03 23 25 38 10 – Closed 9-16 April, 18-24 September, January, Tuesday dinner and Wednesday

9 rm – †€ 50 ††€ 50, ☕ € 8 – ½ P € 52

Rest – Menu (€ 13 bi), € 17/38 – Carte € 30/50

◆ A pretty stop-off on the Chemin des Dames circuit. The functional, well-kept rooms have been recently renovated. Warm welcome. Traditional food served in a bright dining room-veranda.

LE BOURGET-DU-LAC – 73 Savoie – 333 I4 – pop. 3 945 – alt. 240 m – ✉ 73370 French Alps

46 **F2**

Paris 531 – Aix-les-Bains 10 – Annecy 44 – Belley 23 – Chambéry 13 – La Tour-du-Pin 52

Office de tourisme, place Général Sevez ✆ 04 79 25 01 99, Fax 04 79 26 10 76

Lake★★ - Church: carved frieze ★ in choir.

Ombremont

2 km North on D 1504 – ✆ 04 79 25 00 23 – www.hotel-ombremont.com – ombremontbateauivre@wanadoo.fr – Fax 04 79 25 25 77 – Closed 15-30 April, November, Monday and Tuesday from December to April

17 rm – €140/260 €140/260, €24 – ½ P €150/210

Rest ***Le Bateau Ivre*** – see below

◆ In a tree-lined, flower-decked park, this vast 1930s property has pretty, personalised rooms. Nearly all of which command a superb view of the lake. Swimming pool.

Le Bateau Ivre (Jean-Pierre Jacob) – Hôtel Ombremont

2 km North on D 1504 – ✆ 04 79 25 00 23 – www.hotel-ombremont.com – ombremontbateauivre@wanadoo.fr – Fax 04 79 25 25 77 – Closed 14-30 April, November, Monday except dinner mid June-mid September, Tuesday except dinner May-October and Thursday lunch May-October

Rest – Menu €59 (weekdays), €85/170 – Carte €97/172

Spec. Quenelles de brochet, émulsion d'écrevisses (May-October). Porc noir de Bigorre, croustillant de béarnaise (May-October). Chocolat mi-amer en mousse soufflée chaude, sorbet (May-October). **Wines** Chignin-Bergeron, Roussette de Monterminod.

◆ Regionally sourced seasonal produce takes pride of place at the Bateau Ivre. Superb panoramic views of the lake and Mount Revard.

Auberge Lamartine (Pierre Marin)

3.5 km North by D 1504 – ✆ 04 79 25 01 03 – www.lamartine-marin.com – info@lamartine-marin.com – Fax 04 79 25 20 66 – Closed 20 December-20 January, Sunday dinner and Monday except bank holidays

Rest – Menu €26 (weekday lunch), €42/82 – Carte €72/91

Spec. Croustillant de ris de veau et foie gras de canard aux griottes acidulées (June-September). Homard breton rôti sur écrasé de pomme de terre (summer). Framboises sur pain perdu à l'émulsion au safran (season). **Wines** Apremont, Mondeuse.

◆ Delicate cuisine, attentive welcome and service (glass-enclosed wine cellar, paintings, fireplace, etc), and terrace looking out onto the Lamartine Lake: O time, suspend thy flight!

La Grange à Sel

– ✆ 04 79 25 02 66 – www.lagrangasel.com – info@lagrangeasel.com – Fax 04 79 25 25 03 – Closed 2 January-12 February, Sunday dinner and Wednesday

Rest – Menu €27 (weekday lunch), €38/80 – Carte €56/80

◆ This converted salt barn has retained its period stonework and open beams. Personalised cuisine, served in the shaded garden in fine weather.

Beaurivage with rm

– ✆ 04 79 25 00 38 – www.beaurivage-bourget-du-lac.com – webmaster@beaurivage-bourget-du-lac.com – Fax 04 79 25 06 49 – Closed 20 October-21 November, 16-23 February, Wednesday dinner except July-August, Sunday dinner and Monday

4 rm – €65/70 €65/70, €5

Rest – Menu (€21), €25 (weekday lunch), €31/65 – Carte €52/61

◆ Substantial and inventive menu making the most of fine regional produce and fish from the lake. Pleasant shaded terrace. Comfortable rooms with nice views.

in Catons 2,5 km Northwest by D 42 – ✉ 73370

Atmosphères (Alain Périllat-Mercerot) with rm

rest,

618 rte des Tournelles – ✆ 04 79 25 01 29 – www.atmospheres-hotel.com – info@atmospheres-hotel.com – Closed 15 October-15 November, Tuesday and Wednesday except hotel from May to September

4 rm – €100/120 €100/120, €13 **Rest** – Menu (€25), €40/65

Spec. Filets de perche, potimarron et citron confit. Demi-pigeon cuit rosé et bois de réglisse. Cent pour cent chocolat.

◆ The superb modern decor and lakeside view provides a fine setting for the chef's cuisine. Without forgoing his classical training, he concocts creative recipes steeped in delicate harmonious flavours. Minimalist decor and hip colour scheme in the delightful rooms.

BOURGOIN-JALLIEU – 38 Isère – 333 E4 – pop. 22 947 – alt. 235 m – ✉ 38300 Lyon - Rhone Valley

Paris 503 – Bourg-en-Bresse 81 – Grenoble 66 – Lyon 43 – La Tour-du-Pin 16

Syndicat d'initiative, 1, place Carnot ✆ 04 74 93 47 50, Fax 04 74 93 76 01

des Trois Vallons L'Isle-d'Abeau Le Rival, 5 km on the Lyon road (D 1006), ✆ 04 74 43 28 84

BOURGOIN-JALLIEU

Street	Square	No.
Alpes (Av. des)	A	2
Belmont (R. Robert)	B	4
Carnot (Pl.)	B	5
Champ de Mars (Pl. du)	B	6
Clemenceau (R. Georges)	A	9
Diéderichs (Pl. Ch.)	B	10
Dos de l'Âne (R. du)	B	12
Gambetta (Av.)	A	13
Génin (Av. Ambroise)	A	15
Halle (Pl. de la)	B	16
Libération (R. de la)	B	
Liberté (R. de la)	B	19
Moulins (R. des)	B	22
Moulin (R. J.)	B	21
Nations-Unies (Av. des)	B	23
Paix (R. de la)	A	25
Pontcottier (R.)	B	
Pouchelon (R. de)	B	26
République (Pl. de la)	A	29
République (R. de la)	AB	31
St-Michel (Pl.)	B	32
Seigner (R. Joseph)	A	35
Victor-Hugo (R.)	B	36
1er Atelier (R. du)	A	37
19-Mars-1962 (R. du)	AB	39
23-Août-1944 (Pl. du)	B	41

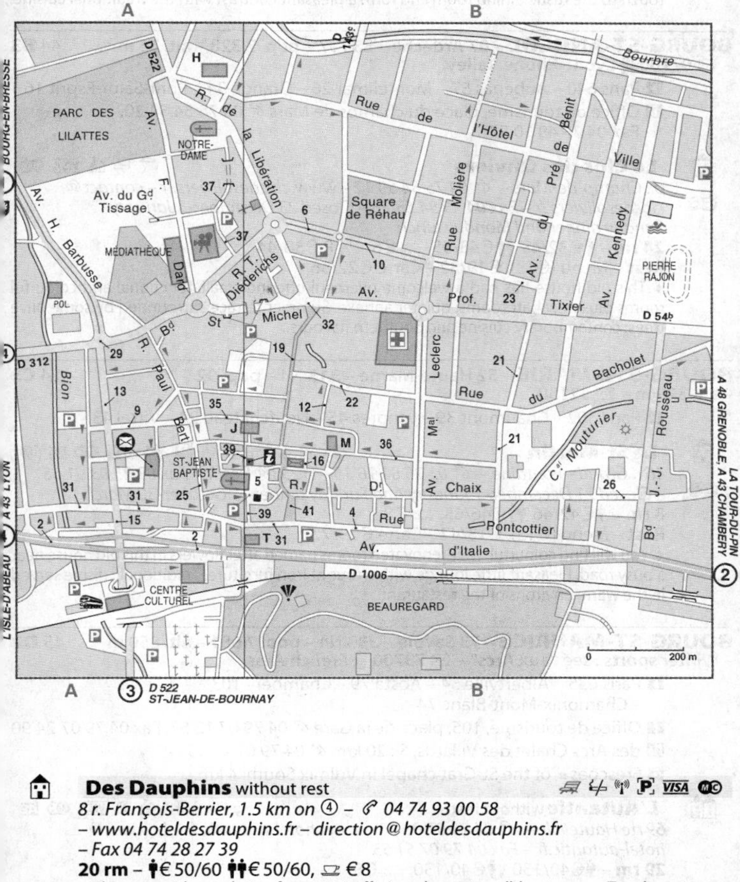

Des Dauphins without rest

8 r. François-Berrier, 1.5 km on ④ – ✆ 04 74 93 00 58
– www.hoteldesdauphins.fr – direction@hoteldesdauphins.fr
– Fax 04 74 28 27 39

20 rm – †€ 50/60 ††€ 50/60, ☕ € 8

◆ Elegant residence dating from 1910 offering pleasant, well-kept rooms. To relax: a terrace overlooking the garden with a fine sequoia tree and a small spa.

via ② 2 km by D 1006 and Boussieu road – ✉ 38300 Bourgoin-Jallieu

Domaine des Séquoias
rest,

54 Vie-de-Boussieu – ☎ 04 74 93 78 00 – www.domaine-sequoias.com – info@domaine-sequoias.com – Fax 04 74 28 60 90

19 rm – †€ 110/130 ††€ 110/200, ☕ € 18

Rest – *(closed in August, 24 December-5 January, Sunday dinner, Tuesday lunch and Monday)* Menu € 30 (weekday lunch), € 38/110 – Carte € 61/97

◆ Tasteful, designer rooms in the wing. An elegant 18C mansion hides a smart contemporary dining room opening into a tree lined garden. Traditional menu and fine choice of Côtes du Rhône wines.

in La Grive 4.5 km by ④ – ✉38300 Bourgoin-Jallieu

Bernard Lantelme

D 312 – ☎ 04 74 28 19 12 – www.restaurantlantelme.com – b.lantelme@free.fr – Fax 04 74 93 78 88 – Closed 26 July-25 August, Saturday and Sunday

Rest – Menu (€ 20), € 24/44 – Carte € 39/51

◆ A 19C farmhouse converted into a restaurant. The modern paintings bring a colourful touch to the rustic dining room and form a pleasant contrast with the traditional cuisine.

BOURG-ST-ANDÉOL – 07 Ardèche – 331 J7 – pop. 7 328 – alt. 36 m – ✉ 07700 Lyon - Rhone Valley
44 **B3**

Paris 640 – Aubenas 57 – Montélimar 26 – Orange 34 – Pont-Saint-Esprit 16

Office de tourisme, place du champs de Mars ☎ 04 75 54 54 20, Fax 04 75 49 10 57

Le Clos des Oliviers

pl. Champ-de-Mars – ☎ 04 75 54 50 12 – www.closdesoliviers.fr – contact@closdesoliviers.fr – Fax 04 75 54 63 26 – Closed 23 December-3 January, Sunday dinner and Monday lunch

24 rm – †€ 32/43 ††€ 48/55, ☕ € 6 – ½ P € 38/44

Rest – Menu (€ 13), € 19/32 – Carte € 22/56

◆ This old house has had a welcome overhaul offering small, functional and colourful rooms plus new bathrooms; quieter annexe. Summer terrace surrounded by some olive trees; contemporary cuisine and Southern flavours.

BOURG-STE-MARIE – 52 Haute-Marne – 313 N4 – pop. 92 – alt. 329 m – ✉ 52150
14 **C3**

Paris 302 – Chaumont 39 – Langres 45 – Neufchâteau 24 – Vittel 43

Le St-Martin
rm,

46 r. Grande-Fontaine – ☎ 03 25 01 10 15 – f1253@free.fr – Fax 03 25 03 91 68 – Closed 21 December-5 January and Sunday dinner 15 October-30 March

8 rm – †€ 42/46 ††€ 46/65, ☕ € 8

Rest – Menu (€ 13), € 18/42 – Carte € 29/77

◆ You will find colourful, well-renovated rooms named after flowers in this old house near a busy road. Pleasant little lounge with wrought iron furniture. Traditional cuisine served in the warm environs of the restaurant.

BOURG-ST-MAURICE – 73 Savoie – 333 N4 – pop. 7 681 – alt. 850 m – Winter sports : see "aux Arcs" – ✉ 73700 French Alps
45 **D2**

Paris 635 – Albertville 54 – Aosta 79 – Chambéry 103 – Chamonix-Mont-Blanc 74

Office de tourisme, 105, place de la Gare ☎ 04 79 07 12 57, Fax 04 79 07 24 90

18 des Arcs Chalet des Villards, S : 20 km, ☎ 04 79 07 43 95

Frescoes★ of the St-Grat chapel in Vulmix South: 4 km.

L'Autantic without rest

69 rte Hauteville – ☎ 04 79 07 01 70 – www.hotel-autantic.fr – bonjour@hotel-autantic.fr – Fax 04 79 07 51 55

29 rm – †€ 40/130 ††€ 40/130, ☕ € 8

◆ This hotel is home to simple rooms graced with wooden or wrought iron furniture; some have a terrace or a balcony. Attractive indoor pool.

L'Arssiban
253 av. Antoine-Borrel – 04 79 07 77 35 – Fax 04 79 07 77 35 – Closed 21 June-11 July, 25 October-5 November, 3-7 January, Wednesday from September to June and Sunday dinner
Rest – Menu € 26/35 – Carte € 33/67
◆ Stone vaults, old tiling, and well-waxed, wooden tables: authentic decor that goes well with the generous, contemporary cuisine.

Le Montagnole
26 av. du Stade – 04 79 07 11 52 – Fax 04 79 07 11 52 – Closed 8-26 June, 17 November-11 December, Monday dinner, Wednesday dinner in low season and Tuesday
Rest – Menu (€ 15), € 18/38 – Carte € 39/50
◆ The artwork and poems displayed in the dining room are the work of the owner-artists. Their cuisine is equally inventive and unusual.

BOURGUEIL – 37 Indre-et-Loire – 317 J5 – pop. 3 923 – alt. 42 m – ✉ 37140 Châteaux of the Loire — 11 A2

Paris 281 – Angers 81 – Chinon 16 – Saumur 23 – Tours 45

Syndicat d'initiative, 16, place de l'église 02 47 97 91 39, Fax 02 47 97 91 39

La Rose de Pindare
4 pl. Hublin – 02 47 97 70 50 – Fax 02 47 97 70 50 – Closed Wednesday
Rest – Menu € 18/38 – Carte € 30/65
◆ Its name is an anagram of Pierre Ronsard. La Rose de Pindare offers a white and flowery simple decor with visible beams. Modern cuisine. Pleasant terrace.

Le Moulin Bleu
7 rte du Moulin-Bleu, 2 km Northward via rte de Courléon – 02 47 97 73 13 – www.lemoulinbleu.com – moulinbleu.bourgueil@wanadoo.fr – Fax 02 47 97 79 66 – Closed from mid-November to end February, Sunday dinner, Monday dinner, Tuesday dinner and Wednesday
Rest – Menu (€ 15), € 19 (weekdays)/48 – Carte € 32/53
◆ A 15C regional style mill. Vaulted dining rooms and a terrace overlooking the vineyards. Traditional dishes and local wines.

BOURNEVILLE – 27 Eure – 304 D5 – pop. 736 – alt. 124 m – ✉ 27500 — 32 B3

Paris 155 – Le Havre 45 – Rouen 43 – Brionne 25 – Caudebec-en-Caux 25

Office de tourisme, le Bourg 02 32 57 32 23, Fax 02 32 57 15 48

Risle Seine
5 pl. de la Mairie – 02 32 42 30 22 – www.risle-seine.com – risle.seine@free.fr – Fax 02 32 42 30 22 – Closed for the November holidays, February holidays, Tuesday dinner and Wednesday
Rest – Menu € 18/32 – Carte € 20/35
◆ This little inn in the centre of the village has a rustic dining room and a veranda overlooking a green setting. Traditional, carefully prepared cuisine.

BOURRON-MARLOTTE – 77 Seine-et-Marne – 312 F5 – pop. 2 850 – alt. 71 m – ✉ 77780 — 19 C3

Paris 72 – Fontainebleau 9 – Melun 26 – Montereau-Fault-Yonne 26 – Nemours 11

Office de tourisme, 37, rue Murger 01 64 45 88 86, Fax 01 64 45 86 80

Les Prémices
Château de Bourron – 01 64 78 33 00 – www.restaurant-les-premices.com – lespremices@aol.com – Fax 01 64 78 36 00 – Closed 1st-15 August, 25 December-1st January, February holidays, Sunday dinner, Monday and Tuesday
Rest – Menu € 38/75 – Carte € 70/110
◆ Modern decoration in the outbuildings of this 16C Bourron castle. Inventive cuisine using many exotic products. Fine wines from Burgundy and Bordeaux.

BOURTH – 27 Eure – **304** E9 – **pop. 1 201** – **alt. 182 m** – ✉ **27580** 33 **C2**

Paris 125 – L'Aigle 16 – Alençon 78 – Évreux 46 – Verneuil-sur-Avre 11

Auberge Chantecler

(opposite the church) – ✆ 02 32 32 61 45 – Fax 02 32 32 61 45 – Closed 20 July-6 August, 8-21 February, Sunday dinner and Monday

Rest – Menu € 16 (weekday lunch), € 27/44 – Carte € 38/55

◆ The limed-brick façade is covered with flowers in summer. A collection of cockerels, regularly added to by regulars, is on display in the two dining rooms. Traditional food.

BOUSSAC – 23 Creuse – **325** K2 – **pop. 1 412** – **alt. 376 m** – ✉ **23600** 25 **C1**

Dordogne-Berry-Limousin

Paris 333 – Aubusson 50 – La Châtre 37 – Guéret 41 – Montluçon 38

Office de tourisme, place de l'Hôtel de Ville ✆ 05 55 65 05 95, Fax 05 55 65 00 94

Site★.

in Nouzerines 10 km Northwest by D97 – **pop. 252** – **alt. 407 m** – ✉ **23600**

La Bonne Auberge with rm

1 r. Lilas – ✆ 05 55 82 01 18 – www.la-bonne-auberge.net – labonneauberge-23@orange.fr – Closed 12-27 October, 1st-10 March, Sunday dinner and Monday

5 rm – †€ 40 ††€ 40, ☕ € 7

Rest – Menu (€ 13), € 16 (weekdays)/50 – Carte € 39/63

◆ A country restaurant in a discreet house serving traditional cuisine with a local flavour. Terrace covered with a pergola in the garden.

BOUTIGNY-SUR-ESSONNE – 91 Essonne – **312** D5 – **pop. 3 002** – **alt. 61 m** – ✉ **91820** 18 **B3**

Paris 58 – Corbeil-Essonnes 29 – Étampes 19 – Fontainebleau 29 – Melun 33

Domaine de Bélesbat rm,

– ✆ 01 69 23 19 00 – www.belesbat.com – reception@belesbat.com – Fax 01 69 23 19 01 – Closed 19 December-4 January

59 rm ☕ – †€ 370 ††€ 370 – 1 suite

Rest *L'Orangerie* – *✆ 01 69 23 19 30* – Menu € 40 (lunch), € 65/100 – Carte € 40/60

◆ Henry IV and Voltaire stayed in this 15 and 18C chateau which now offers luxury contemporary or classic rooms. A branch of the Essonne runs through the fine park; 18-hole golf course. Short traditional menu served in a superb glasshouse.

BOUZEL – 63 Puy-de-Dôme – **326** G8 – **pop. 687** – **alt. 320 m** – ✉ **63910** 6 **C2**

Paris 432 – Ambert 57 – Clermont-Ferrand 23 – Issoire 38 – Thiers 25 – Vichy 47

L'Auberge du Ver Luisant

2 r. Breuil – ✆ 04 73 62 93 83 – Fax 04 73 62 93 83 – Closed 14-20 April, 17 August-7 September, 1st-8 January, Sunday dinner, Wednesday dinner and Monday

Rest – Menu (€ 15), € 25/48 – Carte € 35/50

◆ This delightful country house has managed to retain all of its rustic charm. Thoughtful traditional cuisine and good produce that varies with the seasons.

BOUZE-LÈS-BEAUNE – 21 Côte-d'Or – **320** I7 – **see Beaune**

BOUZIGUES – 34 Hérault – **339** G8 – **see Mèze**

BOUZY – 51 Marne – **306** G8 – **pop. 967** – **alt. 111 m** – ✉ **51150** 13 **B2**

Paris 168 – Châlons-en-Champagne 29 – Épernay 21 – Reims 27

Les Barbotines without rest

1 pl. A. Tritant – ✆ 03 26 57 07 31 – www.lesbarbotines.com – contact@lesbarbotines.com – Fax 03 26 58 26 36 – Closed 1st-12 August and 15 December-1st February

5 rm ☕ – †€ 70 ††€ 90

◆ You can contemplate the prestigious Champagne route from this lovely, 19C wine producer's house. Smart, personalised rooms with antique furniture.

BOYARDVILLE – 17 Charente-Maritime – 324 C4 – see île d'Oléron

BOZOULS – 12 Aveyron – 338 I4 – pop. 2 723 – alt. 530 m – ✉ 12340 29 D1

Languedoc-Roussillon-Tarn Gorges

Paris 603 – Espalion 11 – Mende 94 – Rodez 22 – Sévérac-le-Château 41

Office de tourisme, 2 bis, place de la Mairie ✆ 05 65 48 50 52, Fax 05 65 48 50 52

Trou de Bozouls★.

A la Route d'Argent rm, rest, VISA

rte d' Espalion – ✆ 05 65 44 92 27 – www.larouteargent.com – yves.catusse@wanadoo.fr – Fax 05 65 48 81 40 – Closed 2 January-15 February

21 rm – €45/60 €45/60, €8 – ½ P €50/65

Rest – *(closed Monday except dinner in July-August and Sunday dinner off season)* Menu €20 (weekdays)/45

◆ Modern (late 20C) hotel with rooms overlooking the road or swimming pool and car park. Six new rooms of the same standard in a nearby villa. Traditional cuisine that varies according to market availability, served in a contemporary-style dining room with frosted glass panels, subdued lighting and modern paintings.

Les Brunes without rest VISA

hamlet "Les Brunes", 5 km South along the D 920 and secondary road – ✆ 05 65 48 50 11 – www.lesbrunes.com – lesbrunes@wanadoo.fr

5 rm – €79/122 €86/129

◆ Quiet, cosy accommodation in this attractive, 18C turreted manor house. Elegant interior decor, breakfast served by the fireplace, garden-orchard and open countryside as a backdrop.

Le Belvédère with rm VISA

11 rte du Maquis Jean-Pierre, St Julien road – ✆ 05 65 44 92 66 – www.belvedere-bozouls.com – belvedere.bozouls@wanadoo.fr – Closed 2-20 March, 28 September-23 October, Sunday dinner and Monday

12 rm – €45/63 €45/63, €8 – ½ P €50

Rest – Menu €18 (weekdays)/40 – Carte €33/45

◆ This house overlooking the Gorge du Dourdou is full of rustic character. Modern cuisine inspired by the market. The hotel has old and new guestrooms.

BRACIEUX – 41 Loir-et-Cher – 318 G6 – pop. 1 265 – alt. 70 m 11 B1

– ✉ 41250 Châteaux of the Loire

Paris 185 – Blois 19 – Montrichard 39 – Orléans 64 – Romorantin-Lanthenay 30

Syndicat d'initiative, 10 Les Jardins du Moulin ✆ 02 54 46 09 15, Fax 02 54 46 09 15

De la Bonnheure without rest VISA AE

9 bis r. R. Masson – ✆ 02 54 46 41 57 – www.hoteldelabonnheur.com – Fax 02 54 46 05 90 – Open mid March-early December

14 rm – €55/90 €55/90, €9 – 2 suites

◆ This delightful hotel offers rustic rooms, a garden displaying farm tools, carefully-prepared breakfasts and services for cyclists and hikers. Rise and shine!

Du Cygne without rest VISA AE

5 r. René-Masson – ✆ 02 54 46 41 07 – www.hotelducygne.com – autebert@wanadoo.fr – Fax 02 54 46 04 87 – Closed 20 December-10 February, Sunday and Monday off season

19 rm – €54 €62/69, €8

◆ Simple, functional rooms spread over several typical local buildings in the town centre. Some rooms have been modernised. Quiet pool to the rear.

Bernard Robin - Le Relais de Bracieux

1 av. de Chambord – ✆ 02 54 46 41 22 VISA AE

– www.relaisdebracieux.com – robin@relaischateaux.com – Fax 02 54 46 03 69 – Closed 22 December-31 January, Wednesday except July-August and Tuesday

Rest – *(number of covers limited, pre-book)* Menu (€32), €62/129 – Carte €75/120

Spec. Croustillant de homard de Roscoff aux tomates séchées. Lièvre à la royale (season). Croque-agrumes croustillant à l'orange, crème légère au citron, sorbet passion. **Wines** Cheverny, Gamay de Touraine.

◆ Old paintings and tapestries adorn the elegant dining room overlooking the garden. Classic cuisine and very fine wine list.

Le Rendez vous des Gourmets
20 r. Roger-Brun – ✆ 02 54 46 03 87 – r.d.v.desgourmets@orange.fr – Fax 02 54 56 88 32 – Closed spring and autumn school holidays, 23 December-15 January, Sunday dinner except July-August, Saturday lunch and Wednesday
Rest – Menu € 17 (weekday lunch), € 20/59 – Carte € 38/77
◆ This simple, rustic restaurant has the charm of a family inn. The chef/owner prepares contemporary cuisine. Small courtyard terrace in fine weather

BRANCION – 71 Saône-et-Loire – **320** I10 – see Tournus

LA BRANDE – 36 Indre – **323** H7 – see Montipouret

BRANSAC – 43 Haute-Loire – **331** G2 – see Beauzac

BRANTÔME – 24 Dordogne – **329** E3 – pop. 2 122 – alt. 104 m – ✉ 24310 Dordogne-Berry-Limousin 4 **C1**

Paris 470 – Angoulême 58 – Limoges 83 – Nontron 23 – Périgueux 27 – Thiviers 26

Syndicat d'initiative, boulevard Charlemagne ✆ 05 53 05 80 52, Fax 05 53 05 80 52

Steeple★★ of the abbey church - Banks of the Dronne★★.

Le Moulin de l'Abbaye
1 rte de Bourdeilles – ✆ 05 53 05 80 22 – www.moulinabbaye.com – moulin@relaischateaux.com – Fax 05 53 05 75 27 – Open 15 April-15 November
13 rm – †€ 150/330 ††€ 150/330, ☕ € 21 – ½ P € 170/250
Rest – *(closed lunch except weekends and public holidays)* Menu € 60/80 – Carte € 75/95
Spec. Thon rouge mariné, caviar d'aubergine et fromage frais "des Terres Vieilles". Suprême de pigeonneau à la farce fine de foie gras. Tour au chocolat noir, glace à la crème brûlée et expresso en émulsion. **Wines** Montravel, Pécharmant.
◆ This charming mill and miller's house provide a romantic setting for the individually decorated rooms, bathed in the murmur of a waterfall. Bucolic views of the Dronne from the elegant, freshly redecorated restaurant and riverside terrace. Regional cuisine.

Chabrol
57 r. Gambetta – ✆ 05 53 05 70 15 – www.lesfrerescharbonnel.com – charbonnel.freres@wanadoo.fr – Fax 05 53 05 71 85 – Closed 15 November-15 December, 1st February-10 March, Sunday dinner from October to June and Monday
19 rm – †€ 55/65 ††€ 65/90, ☕ € 14 – ½ P € 70/90
Rest – Menu € 30 (weekdays)/70 – Carte € 48/120
◆ The expression "traditional house" applies perfectly to the Chabrol hotel. The bedrooms, which have been renovated gradually are now more comfortable. A dining room with a provincial setting and panoramic terrace overlooking the River Dronne.

Moulin de Vigonac
– ✆ 05 53 05 87 59 – www.moulin-de-vigonac.com – contact@moulindevigonac.com – Fax 05 53 35 03 92 – Open 15 March-15 November
10 rm – †€ 105/270 ††€ 105/270, ☕ € 15
Rest – *(Closed Tuesday dinner and Wednesday except July-August) (number of covers limited, pre-book)* Menu € 45/65 – Carte € 47/74
◆ Everything is new in this 16C windmill, lapped by the Dronne. The modern decor brings serenity and comfort and doesn't detract from the original charm of the place. Private park; pool. Traditional cuisine.

Au Fil du Temps
1 chemin du Vert Galand – ✆ 05 53 05 24 12 – www.fildutemps.com – fildutemps@filedutemps.fr – Fax 05 53 05 18 01 – Closed Monday dinner and Tuesday except July-August
Rest – Menu (€ 12), € 24/35
◆ One dining room with a rotisserie, a second with an open fire, and a terrace beneath the shade of a lime tree: three delightful settings in which to enjoy local specialities and grilled meats.

Au Fil de l'Eau
21 quai Bertin – 05 53 05 73 65 – www.fildeleau.com – fildeleau@fildeleau.com – Fax 05 53 35 04 81 – Open 15 April-15 October and closed Wednesday and Thursday except in July-August and September
Rest – Menu € 24/31
◆ Attractive café with terrace beneath weeping willows on the banks of the Dronne. Fried fish and *matelote* (fish stew) to a backdrop of fishing-inspired decor.

in Champagnac de Belair **6 km Northeast by D 78 and D 83 – pop. 736 – alt. 135 m – ✉ 24530**

Le Moulin du Roc (Alain Gardillou)
– 05 53 02 86 00 – www.moulinduroc.com – info@moulinduroc.com – Fax 05 53 54 21 31 – Open 8 May-12 October
13 rm – €170/210 €170/210, € 18 – ½ P € 170/215
Rest – *(closed Wednesday lunch and Tuesday)* Menu € 40 bi (weekday lunch)/65
Spec. Fine tarte croustillante à l'artichaut, betterave et foie gras. Truffe du Périgord en trois services. Croustade aux framboises soufflée à la pistache, crème glacée aux pistaches (June to Sept.) **Wines** Bergerac, Pécharmant.
◆ A magical place: an old oil mill on the Dronne surrounded by countryside. The interior has personalised characterful rooms. Waterside garden. Modern, regional cuisine (set menu) served in two rustic-style dining rooms. Terrace overlooking the river.

in Bourdeilles **10 km Southwest by D 78 – pop. 784 – alt. 103 m – ✉ 24310**
Syndicat d'initiative, place des Tilleuls 05 53 03 42 96, Fax 05 53 54 56 27
Château★: furniture★★, dining room★★ fireplace.

Hostellerie Les Griffons rest,
Le Pont – 05 53 45 45 35 – www.griffons.fr – info@griffons.fr – Fax 05 53 45 45 20 – Open 11 April-1st November
10 rm – €85/110 €85/110, € 12 – ½ P € 80/90
Rest – *(dinner only)* Menu € 35/40
◆ At the foot of the castle, a 16C bourgeois house overlooking the Dronne. Rooms have antique furniture, stonework, beams and attractive roof beams on the top floor. Comfortable lounge, bright veranda facing the river, and terrace overlooking the garden. Classical cuisine.

BRAS – **83 Var** – **340** K5 – **pop. 1 784** – **alt. 280 m** – **✉ 83149** 41 **C3**
Paris 814 – Aix-en-Provence 55 – Marseille 62 – Toulon 61
Syndicat d'initiative, place du 14 juillet 04 94 69 98 26

Une Campagne en Provence
Domaine Le Peyrourier, 3 km South-west along the D 28 and secondary road – 04 98 05 10 20 – www.provence4u.com – info@provence4u.com – Fax 04 98 05 10 21 – Closed 7 January-3 March
5 rm – €85/115 €90/120 **Table d'hôte** – Menu € 32 bi
◆ Huge estate surrounded by prairies and vineyards. The peaceful old farmhouse dates back to the Templars (12C). Personalised rooms in local style. Provencal cuisine and estate wines at the table d'hote. Terrace.

BRAX – **47 Lot-et-Garonne** – **336** F4 – **see Agen**

BRAY-ET-LU – **95 Val-d'Oise** – **305** A6 – **106** – **pop. 753** – **alt. 28 m** – **✉ 95710** 18 **A1**
Paris 70 – Rouen 61 – Gisors 26 – Pontoise 36 – Vernon 18

Les Jardins d'Epicure with rm
16 Grande-Rue – 01 34 67 75 87 – www.lesjardinsdepicure.com – info@lesjardinsdepicure.com – Fax 01 34 67 90 22 – Closed 2 January-11 February, Thursday lunch, Tuesday and Wednesday from November to March, Tuesday lunch in April-May and September-October, Sunday dinner and Monday from October to May
15 rm – €110/350 €110/350, € 25 – 3 suites
Rest – Menu € 39/105 – Carte € 63/74
◆ A handsome mansion (1852) nestling in a pretty park with river. Plush dining room opening onto a veranda and a pool. Rooms with character.

BREBIÈRES – 62 Pas-de-Calais – 301 L5 – see Douai

BRÉDANNAZ – 74 Haute-Savoie – 328 K6 – alt. 450 m – ✉ 74210 46 **F1**

Paris 550 – Albertville 31 – Annecy 15 – Megève 46

in Chaparon 1.5 km South by secondary road - ✉ 74210 Doussard

La Châtaigneraie

325 chemin des Fontaines – ✆ 04 50 44 30 67 – www.hotelchataigneraie.com – info@hotelchataigneraie.com – Fax 04 50 44 83 71 – Open 15 April-1st October and closed Sunday dinner and Monday except from May to September

Rest – Menu € 21 (weekdays)/34 – Carte € 29/42

◆ Regional cuisine served in a large, country-style dining room with a fireplace, on a quiet terrace at the back of the restaurant, or in a shaded garden facing the mountains.

BRÉHAT (ÎLE) – 22 Côtes-d'Armor – 309 D1 – see Île-de-Bréhat

BRELES – 29 Finistère – 308 C4 – pop. 779 – alt. 52 m – ✉ 29810 9 **A1**

Paris 616 – Rennes 264 – Quimper 99 – Brest 25 – Landerneau 47

Auberge de Bel Air

Lanildiut road – ✆ 02 98 04 36 01 – www.aumoulindebelair.com – y.mony@orange.fr – Fax 02 98 04 36 01 – Closed 20 September-10 October and 5-31 January

3 rm – €50/60 €64/70 – ½ P €59/62

Table d'hôte – *(closed Tuesday except school holidays, Sunday dinner and Monday)* Menu € 28 bi

◆ This old granite farm in a verdant setting next to the Aber Ildut looks onto a large garden and pond. Cosy, comfortable bedrooms; riverside terrace. Market fresh menus served in a rustic setting. Cooking lessons from the owner.

BRÉLIDY – 22 Côtes-d'Armor – 309 C3 – pop. 335 – alt. 100 m – ✉ 22140 9 **B1**

Paris 503 – Rennes 151 – Saint-Brieuc 55 – Lannion 27 – Morlaix 66

Château de Brélidy rest,

– ✆ 02 96 95 69 38 – www.chateau-brelidy.com – chateau.brelidy@worldonline.fr – Fax 02 96 95 18 03 – 31 March-1st January

15 rm – €82/96 €102/128, € 13 – ½ P € 100/133

Rest – *(dinner only)* Menu € 30/64 bi

◆ A 16C château of irresistible appeal: small rooms decorated with personal touches, cosy sitting rooms, rustic dining room and parkland (angling in the river).

LA BRESSE – 88 Vosges – 314 J4 – pop. 4 700 – alt. 636 m – Winter sports : 650/1 350 m 31 – ✉ 88250 Alsace-Lorraine 27 **C3**

Paris 437 – Colmar 52 – Épinal 52 – Gérardmer 13 – Thann 39 – Le Thillot 20

Office de tourisme, 2a, rue des Proyes ✆ 03 29 25 41 29, Fax 03 29 25 64 61

Les Vallées

31 r. P.-Claudel – ✆ 03 29 25 41 39 – www.labellemontagne.com – hotel.lesvallees@remy-loisirs.com – Fax 03 29 25 64 38

56 rm – €55/69 €73/100, € 12 – ½ P € 66/79

Rest – *(closed November)* Menu € 18 (weekday lunch), € 29/52 – Carte € 23/60

◆ Functional rooms of varying sizes, and extensive conference and leisure facilities, mean that this hotel is fully booked winter come summer. The restaurant consists of a tall, light coloured, timber structure, huge bay windows and regionally sourced dishes.

South 3 km, Cornimont road by D 486 – ✉ 88250 La Bresse

Le Clos des Hortensias

51 rte de Cornimont – ✆ 03 29 25 41 08 – restaurantclosdeshortensias@yahoo.fr – Fax 03 29 25 65 34 – Closed 11-24 November, Sunday dinner and Monday

Rest – *(pre-book)* Menu € 17 (weekdays), € 27/40

◆ A mural representing hydrangeas decorates the façade of this family restaurant. Traditional, carefully prepared cuisine served in a décor that is as pleasant as the service.

BRESSIEUX – 38 Isère – **333** E6 – **pop. 86 – alt. 510 m** – ✉ **38870** 43 **E2**

Paris 533 – Grenoble 50 – Lyon 76 – Valence 73 – Vienne 45 – Voiron 30

Auberge du Château

– ☎ 04 74 20 91 01 – www.aubergedebressieux.fr – Fax 04 74 20 54 69 – Closed 20 October-13 November, 16 February-12 March, Sunday dinner off season, Tuesday and Wednesday

Rest – Menu (€ 23), € 32/69 – Carte € 38/59

◆ In an old mountain village, this friendly establishment has been admirably restored. The shaded terrace offers a beautiful view of the valley and the Lyonnais mountains.

BRESSON – 38 Isère – **333** H7 – **see Grenoble**

BRESSUIRE – 79 Deux-Sèvres – **322** D3 – **pop. 18 200** – **alt. 186 m** – ✉ **79300** Atlantic Coast 38 **B1**

Paris 364 – Angers 84 – Cholet 45 – Niort 64 – Poitiers 82 – La Roche-sur-Yon 87

Office de tourisme, place de l'Hotel de Ville ☎ 05 49 65 10 27, Fax 05 49 80 41 49

Les 3 Marchands

les Sicaudières, (2 km on Nantes road) – ☎ 05 49 65 01 19 – www.hotel-restaurant-bressuire.com – les3marchands@wanadoo.fr – Fax 05 49 65 82 16 – Closed 2-14 August

21 rm – †€ 48 ††€ 58, ☕ € 8 – ½ P € 56

Rest – Menu € 13 (weekday lunch), € 19/39 – Carte € 24/46

◆ On the Nantes road, this dependable family inn is ideal for a stop between the Puy du Fou and the Futuroscope. Practical rooms, some of which are more recent. This neo-rustic restaurant flooded in light, serves traditional fare.

BREST – 29 Finistère – **308** E4 – **pop. 145 100** – **Built-up area 210 055** – **alt. 35 m** – ✉ **29200** Brittany 9 **A2**

Paris 596 – Lorient 133 – Quimper 72 – Rennes 246 – St-Brieuc 145

Brest-Bretagne ☎ 02 98 32 86 00, 10 km northeast

Office de tourisme, Place de la Liberté ☎ 02 98 44 24 96, Fax 02 98 44 53 73

de Brest les Abers Plouarzel Kerhoaden, NE : 24 km on D 5, ☎ 02 98 89 68 33

Océanopolis ★★★ - Cours Dajot ≤★★ - Crossing the harbour★ - Arsenal and naval base ★ DZ - Musée des Beaux-Arts★ EZ **M¹** - Musée de la Marine★ DZ **M²** - Botanic Conservatory of vallon du Stang-Alar★.

Les Abers ★★

Plans on following pages

Le Continental without rest

41 r. E.-Zola – ☎ 02 98 80 50 40 – www.oceaniahotels.com – continental.brest@oceaniahotels.com – Fax 02 98 43 17 47 EY **f**

73 rm – †€ 130 ††€ 130, ☕ € 14

◆ This hotel is popular with Brest's visiting dignitaries. Bernard Buffet reproductions in the hall and spacious and cosy, modern or Art Deco rooms.

L'Amirauté

41 r. Branda – ☎ 02 98 80 84 00 – www.oceaniahotels.com – amirautebrest@oceaniahotels.com – Fax 02 98 80 84 84 BX **t**

84 rm – †€ 108/128 ††€ 108/128, ☕ € 14

Rest – *(closed 13 July-23 August, 24 December-4 January, Saturday, Sunday and bank holidays)* Menu (€ 20), € 30 (weekdays) – Carte € 33/52

◆ Modern architecture with elegant lines. Rooms are well soundproofed and have tasteful modern furniture. A restaurant in a brasserie style. Modern cuisine made with regional produce.

La Paix without rest

32 r. Algésiras – ☎ 02 98 80 12 97 – www.hoteldelapaix-brest.com – hoteldelapaixbrest@wanadoo.fr – Fax 02 98 43 30 95 – Closed 19 December-3 January EY **y**

29 rm – †€ 70/85 ††€ 88/140, ☕ € 11

◆ Small, town centre hotel entirely redecorated in a minimalist, modern style. Brand new, well equipped, soundproofed rooms. Generous buffet breakfast.

BREST

A B
PLOUDALMÉZEAU
BOHARS D 26
ST-RENAN GUILERS
PENFELD
GRAND SPERNOT
LAMBÉZELLEC
D 205
PARC DES EXPOSITIONS DE PENFELD
Av. de Provence
BELLEVUE
R. de Normandie
Av. Victor Le Gorgeu
R. T. Botrel
R. du Cdt Drogou
R. Robespierre
R. A. Kervern
Bd L. Blum
ST-LUC
Pl. Albert 1er
LA CAVALE BLANCHE
Penfeld
Pont de l'Harteloire
R. Dupuy-de-Lôme
STE-THÉRÈSE
LE CONQUET D 789
R. de Guilers
R. St-Exupéry
R. de Maissin
R. A. France
R. P. Loti
RECOUVRANCE
R. de Kerraros
R. Amiral Nicol
Porte Caffarelli
Rte de la Corniche
ARSENAL MARITIME
Porte de la Grde Rivière
PORT DE LANINON
PORT DE COMMERCE
R. de l'E
LES QUATRE POMPES
OUESSANT
V
X

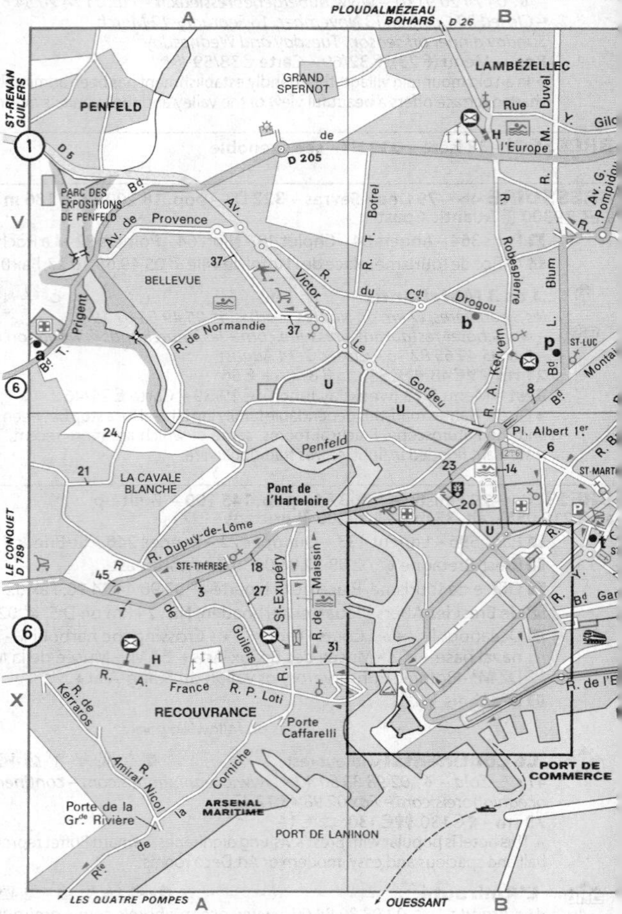

Océania rest, VISA

82 r. Siam – ✆ 02 98 80 66 66
– www.oceaniahotels.com – oceania.brest@oceaniahotels.com
– Fax 02 98 80 65 50 EY **r**

82 rm – 🛉€ 79/155 🛉🛉€ 79/155, ☕ € 14

Rest – Menu (€ 16), € 20 (weekday lunch) – Carte € 27/34

◆ Comfortable hotel in the Rue de Siam, mentioned in a famous poem by J. Prévert (Barbara). The rooms have all been redecorated and fall into two categories. Contemporary menu. Modern dishes, both meat and seafood.

esmoulins (Av. C.) . . . . BX 6
r-Kerrien (R. du) . . . . AX 7
oumer (R. Paul) . . . . BV 8
ourjacq (Rte du) CV
rogou (R. Com.) . . . . BV
upuy-de-Lôme (R.) . . . . AX
uquesne (R.) . . . . EY

Duval (R. Marcellin) . . . . BV
Eau-Blanche (R. de l') CV
Elorn (R. de l') . . . . BX
Europe (Bd de l') . . . . ACV
Ferry (R. J.) . . . . BCX 12
Foch (Av. Mar.) . . . . BX 14
Forestou (Pont du) . . . . CX 15
Français-Libres (Bd des) . . . . DZ 16
Frégate-La-Belle-Poule (R. de la) . . . . EZ 17
Gallieni (R. du Mar.) . . . . AX 18
Gambetta (Bd) . . . . BX
Le Gorgeu (Av. Victor) . . . . AV
Gouesnou (Rte de) CV
Grande-Rivière (Porte de la) . . . . AX
Guilers (R. de) . . . . AX
Harteloire (Pt. de l') . . . . AX
Harteloire (R. de l') . . . . AX 20
Hoche (R.) . . . . BV
Jean-Jaurès (R.) . . . . EY
Kent (R. de) . . . . AX 21
Kérabécam (R. de) . . . . EY 22
Kérraros (R. de) . . . . AX
Kervern (R. Auguste) . . . . BV
Kiel (Av. de) CX
Lamotte-Picquet (R.) . . . . BX 23
Lesven (R. Jules) . . . . BCV
Libération (Av. de la) . . . . AX 24
Liberté (Pl. de la) . . . . EY
Loti (R. Pierre) . . . . AX
Louppe (R. Albert) CV
Lyon (R. de) . . . . DEY
Macé (R. Jean) . . . . EZ
Maissin (R. de) . . . . AX
Marine (Bd de la) . . . . DZ 25
Michelet (R.) . . . . DV
Montaigne (Bd) . . . . BV
Mouchotte (Bd Cdt) . . . . AX 27
Moulin (Bd Jean) . . . . DY
Nicol (R. de l'Amiral) . . . . AX
Normandie (R. de) . . . . AV
Paris (R. de) CV
Pompidou (R. G.) . . . . BV
Porte (R. de la) . . . . AX 31
Prigent (Bd T.) . . . . AV
Provence (Av. de) . . . . AV
Quimper (Rte de) CV
Recouvrance (Pt de) . . . . DZ
Réveillère (Av. Amiral) . . . . EY 33
Richelieu (R.) CX
Robespierre (R.) . . . . BY
Roosevelt (Av. Fr.) . . . . DZ 34
Saint-Exupéry (R.) . . . . AX
St-Marc (R.) CX
Salaün-Penquer (Av.) . . . . EZ
Sébastopol (R.) . . . . CX 35
Semard (R. Pierre) CX
Siam (R. de) . . . . EY
Strasbourg (Pl. de) CV
Tarente (Av. de) . . . . AV 37
Tourbihan (R. de) . . . . CV 38
Tourville (Porte) . . . . DZ
Tritshler (R. du) CX
Troude (R. Amiral) . . . . BX 39
Valmy (R. de) . . . . CX 40
Verdun (R. de) CX
Victor-Hugo (R.) . . . . BX 41
Vieux-St-Marc (R. du) CX
Villeneuve (R. de la) CV
Voltaire (R.) . . . . EZ
Wilson (Pl.) . . . . EZ
Zédé (R. G.) CV
Zola (R. Émile) . . . . EY
2e-R.C.I. (R. du) . . . . DY
8-Mai-1945 (R. du) CV
11-Martyrs (R. des) . . . . EY 42
19-Mars-1962 (R. du) . . . . AX 45

Center rm, AC rest, P, VISA, MC, AE

4 bd. Léon Blum – ☎ 02 98 80 78 07
– www.hotelcenter.com – info@hotelcenter.com
– Fax 02 98 80 78 78 BV **p**

146 rm – †€ 63 ††€ 66, ☕ € 8

Rest – *(closed 22 December-4 January, Saturday and Sunday except July-August)*
Menu (€ 12), € 16 (weekdays)/32 – Carte € 24/37

◆ Well equipped for its business clientele, this new establishment offers practical, generously proportioned rooms, some of which also have a mezzanine (children's bed). Unpretentious, traditional cuisine served in a nautically-inspired dining room.

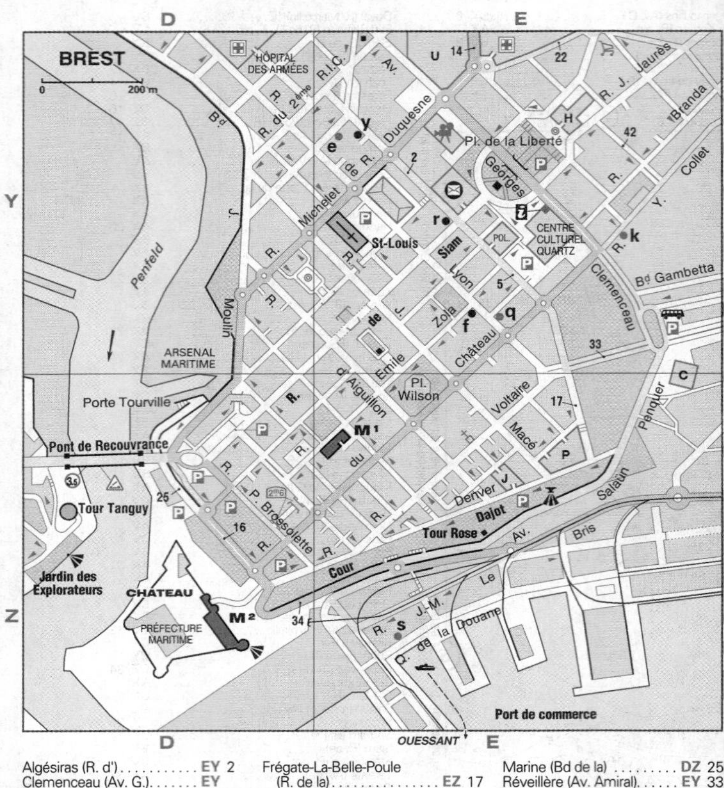

Algésiras (R. d') . . . . EY 2
Clemenceau (Av. G.) . . . . EY
Colbert (R.) . . . . EY 5
Foch (Av. Mar.) . . . . EY 14
Français-Libres (Bd des) . . . . DZ 16
Frégate-La-Belle-Poule (R. de la) . . . . EZ 17
Jean-Jaurès (R.) . . . . EY
Kérabécam (R. de) . . . . EY 22
Liberté (Pl. de la) . . . . EY
Lyon (R. de) . . . . DEY
Marine (Bd de la) . . . . DZ 25
Réveillère (Av. Amiral) . . . . . EY 33
Roosevelt (Av. Fr.) . . . . DZ 34
Siam (R. de) . . . . EY
11-Martyrs (R. des) . . . . EY 42

Du Questel without rest

120 r. F.-Thomas – 02 98 45 99 20 – www.hotel-du-questel.fr – hotel-du-questel@orange.fr – Fax 02 98 45 94 02 AV **a**

36 rm – € 39/49 € 49/55, € 8

◆ A brand new, very handy hotel just off the north ring-road, but very quiet. Practical, well-kept rooms, reasonable prices and, on request, a small range of snacks.

La Fleur de Sel

15 bis r. de Lyon – 02 98 44 38 65 – Fax 02 98 44 38 53 – Closed 1st-22 August, 1st-10 January, Saturday lunch, Monday lunch and Sunday EY **q**

Rest – Menu (€ 22 bi), € 30/42 – Carte approx. € 55

◆ The chef of this establishment prepares inventive, tasty dishes that enhance regional produce, herbs and flavours. Modern, minimalist interior and warm welcome.

Le M

22 r. du Cdt-Drogou – 02 98 47 90 00 – www.le-m.fr – contact@le-m.fr – Fax 02 98 47 90 00 – Closed 17 August-6 September BV **b**

Rest – Menu (€ 32), € 38/52

◆ Fine Breton house under new management, with modernised interior and smoking room. Contemporary cuisine mixing sweet and savoury. Flower garden.

XX **Le Ruffé**

1 bis r. Y.-Collet – ✆ 02 98 46 07 70 – www.leruffe.com – le-ruffe@wanadoo.fr – Fax 02 98 44 31 46 – Closed Sunday dinner and Monday EY **k**

Rest – Menu (€ 14), € 20/36 – Carte € 23/54

◆ In a boat-cum-brasserie inspired decor, this restaurant serves traditional dishes in which regional produce and seafood take pride of place.

XX **L'Imaginaire**

23 r. Fautras – ✆ 02 98 43 30 13 – imaginaire-restaurant@neuf.fr – Fax 02 98 43 30 13 – Closed 10-30 August, 1st-16 January, Wednesday dinner, Sunday dinner and Monday EY **e**

Rest – Menu (€ 17 bi), € 28/56 – Carte € 38/54

◆ This restaurant has acquired a faithful crowd of regulars, as much for its up-to-date 'surf n' turf' menu, enlivened by herbs and spices, as for its spruced up soothing pastel decor.

X **La Maison de l'Océan**

2 quai de la Douane, (commercial port) – ✆ 02 98 80 44 84 – www.maisondelocean.com – Fax 02 98 46 19 83 EZ **s**

Rest – Menu € 17/38 – Carte € 26/104

◆ 'L'Océan' pays homage to the ocean in its decor (scaling bench, furniture and ornaments) and menu (seafood). A popular wharfside establishment.

North 5 km by D 788 CV – ✉ 29200 Brest

Oceania Brest Aéroport rm, rest,

32 av. Baron Lacrosse – ✆ 02 98 02 32 83 – www.oceaniahotels.com – oceania.brestaeroport@oceaniahotels.com – Fax 02 98 41 69 27

82 rm – †€ 59/99 ††€ 59/130, ☕ € 14

Rest – *(closed lunch from 1st to 16 August, Saturday, Sunday and bank holidays)* Menu (€ 18), € 22 (weekday lunch) – Carte € 24/34

◆ A Seventies building in a green setting. Fully renovated, spacious, practical rooms; some look onto the swimming pool. Restaurant with modern decor. Traditional dishes.

at Port du Moulin Blanc 7 km by ⑤ – ✉ 29200 Brest

Plaisance Hôtel rest,

37 r. du Moulin Blanc – ✆ 02 98 42 33 33 – leplaisancehotel@hotmail.fr – Fax 02 98 02 59 34

46 rm – †€ 62/72 ††€ 69/79, ☕ € 8 – ½ P € 82/86

Rest – *(closed Saturday lunch in winter and Sunday dinner)* Menu (€ 14), € 27/38 – Carte € 31/44

◆ Well-located hotel offering functional, colourful and identically decorated rooms. Perfect for an excursion to Oceanopolis. Tasteful contemporary interior in this restaurant serving brasserie style cuisine.

X **Ma Petite Folie**

r. Eugène Bere – ✆ 02 98 42 44 42 – Fax 02 98 41 43 68

Rest – Menu (€ 16), € 22/28 – Carte € 35/50

◆ A new lease of life for this old lobster boat (1952): the upper and lower decks are now dining rooms serving delicious seafood cuisine in a nautical décor. There is a terrace that extends into the water.

BRETENOUX – 46 Lot – **337** H2 – **pop. 1 322** – **alt. 136 m** – ✉ **46130** 29 **C1**

Dordogne-Berry-Limousin

▶ Paris 521 – Brive-la-Gaillarde 44 – Cahors 83 – Figeac 48 – Sarlat-la-Canéda 65 – Tulle 47

ℹ Office de tourisme, avenue de la Libération ✆ 05 65 38 59 53, Fax 05 65 39 72 14

◉ Château of Castelnau-bretenoux★★: ≤★ Southwest: 3,5 km.

at Port de Gagnac **6 km Northeast by D 940 and D 14 – ✉ 46130 Gagnac-sur-Cère**

Hostellerie Belle Rive
Port de Gagnac – ✆ 05 65 38 50 04 – www.bellerive-dordogne-lot.com – hostelleriebellerive@yahoo.fr – Fax 05 65 38 47 72 – Closed 19 December-3 January
12 rm – †€ 50 ††€ 60/75, ☕ € 8 – 1 suite – ½ P € 58/65
Rest – *(closed Friday dinner and Sunday dinner from mid-April to mid-July and from end August to mid-October, Saturday except dinner from mid-October to mid-April)* Menu € 16 (weekday lunch), € 25/40 – Carte € 43/60
◆ This old house in typical regional style, in a hamlet on the banks of the River Cère, offers renovated, warm and well-kept rooms. Attractive dining room in a contemporary style, with the original fireplace and a 19C wooden wine press. Updated traditional cuisine.

BRÉTIGNOLLES-SUR-MER – **85 Vendée** – **316** E8 – **pop. 3 182** – **alt. 14 m** – ✉ **85470** 34 **A3**

Paris 465 – Challans 30 – La Roche-sur-Yon 44 – Nantes 86

Office de tourisme, 1, boulevard du Nord ✆ 02 51 90 12 78, Fax 02 51 22 40 72

J.-M. Pérochon et Hôtellerie des Brisants with rm rest,
63 av. de la Grand'Roche – ✆ 02 51 33 65 53 – www.lesbrisants.com – perochonjeanmarc@wanadoo.fr – Fax 02 51 33 89 10 – Closed 12 November-4 December and 15 February-10 March
15 rm – †€ 53/80 ††€ 58/85, ☕ € 9 – ½ P € 67/81
Rest – *(closed Monday except dinner July-August, Sunday dinner September-June, and Tuesday lunch)* Menu € 33/76 bi – Carte € 56/75
◆ Pretty view of the Atlantic from this large dining room, spruced up in a contemporary minimalist spirit. Updated seafood menu. Redecorated rooms.

BRETTEVILLE-SUR-LAIZE – **14 Calvados** – **303** C2 – **pop. 1 558** – **alt. 54 m** – ✉ **14680** 32 **B2**

Paris 245 – Caen 18 – Hérouville-Saint-Clair 23 – Lisieux 52

Château des Riffets
– ✆ 02 31 23 53 21 – www.chateau-des-riffets.com – chateau.riffets@wanadoo.fr – Fax 02 31 23 75 14
4 rm ☕ – †€ 110 ††€ 170 **Table d'hôte** – Menu € 50 bi
◆ Dominating wooded parkland, this 1850 manor is home to spacious, elegant rooms. Period furniture and modern fixtures and fittings make it faultlessly comfortable. Regionally inspired family cooking served in a dining room with character.

LE BREUIL – **71 Saône-et-Loire** – **320** G9 – **see le Creusot**

LE BREUIL-EN-AUGE – **14 Calvados** – **303** N4 – **pop. 939** – **alt. 38 m** – ✉ **14130** 33 **C2**

Paris 196 – Caen 55 – Deauville 21 – Lisieux 10

Le Dauphin (Régis Lecomte)
2 r. de l'Église – ✆ 02 31 65 08 11 – www.ledauphin-restaurant.com – dauphin.le@wanadoo.fr – Fax 02 31 65 12 08 – Closed 12 November-2 December, February holidays, Sunday dinner and Monday
Rest – Menu € 38/46 – Carte € 80/100
Spec. Pressé de langoustines et andouille blanche de Vire. Homard façon Créances. Soufflé au Grand Marnier.
◆ Normandy restaurant appreciated as much for its personalised cuisine as for its welcoming, country-chic decor, complete with a coat of arms, chrome plated stove and watercolours.

in St-Philbert-des-Champs 2.5 km Northeast by D 264 – pop. 606 – alt. 143 m – ✉ 14130

Le Bonheur est dans le Pré

Le Montmain – ✆ 02 31 64 29 79 – http://lebonheurdanslepre.free.fr – lebonheurdanslepre@wanadoo.fr

3 rm – †€ 80/98 ††€ **Table d'hôte** – Menu € 25 bi/30 bi

◆ Looking for a haven of peace in the middle of the countryside? This well-restored farm dating from 1760 with a more recent extension and outbuildings is perfect. Simple rooms. Generous platefuls of Normandy specialities (local produce) prepared by the owner.

BREUILLET – 17 Charente-Maritime – 324 D5 – pop. 2 178 – alt. 28 m – ✉ 17920 38 **A3**

Paris 509 – Poitiers 176 – La Rochelle 69 – Rochefort 39 – Saintes 38

L'Aquarelle VISA

22 rte du Candé – ✆ 05 46 22 11 38 – Closed 1 week in June, 1 week in October, 1 week in January, Tuesday lunch and Monday

Rest – Menu € 24/66 – Carte € 48/62

◆ Nicely refurbished interior in green tones and up-to-date menu in which the chef lets his – sometimes daring – creativity run wild. Definitely worth a visit.

BREUREY-LES-FAVERNEY – 70 Haute-Saône – 314 E6 – see Faverney

---

BRÉVONNES – 10 Aube – 313 G3 – pop. 584 – alt. 120 m – ✉ 10220 13 **B3**

Paris 198 – Bar-sur-Aube 30 – St-Dizier 59 – Troyes 28 – Vitry-le-François 51

Au Vieux Logis with rm rest, VISA

1 r. Piney – ✆ 03 25 46 30 17 – www.auvieuxlogis.com – logisbrevonnes@wanadoo.fr – Fax 03 25 46 37 20 – Closed Sunday dinner and Monday

5 rm – †€ 46/55 ††€ 46/55, € 8 – ½ P € 56/63 **Rest** – Menu € 17/34

◆ The family atmosphere is jealously guarded in the rustic decor filled with all the charm of the houses of our grandmothers. Tasty traditional menu.

BRIANÇON – 05 Hautes-Alpes – 334 H3 – pop. 12 100 – alt. 1 321 m – Winter sports : 1 200/2 800 m 9 67 – Casino – ✉ 05100 41 **C1**

French Alps

Paris 681 – Digne-les-Bains 145 – Gap 89 – Grenoble 119 – Torino 109

✆ 3635 et tapez 42 (0,34 €/mn)

Office de tourisme, 1, place du Temple ✆ 04 92 21 08 50, Fax 04 92 20 56 45

de Montgenèvre Montgenèvre Route d'Italie, NE : 12 km, ✆ 04 92 21 94 23

High town★★: Grande Gargouille★, Statue "La France"★ - Upper covered way ★, ≤★ of porte de la Durance - Puy St-Pierre ✳★★ of the church Southwest: 3 km via Rte de Puy St-Pierre.

Croix de Toulouse ≤★★ via Av. de Toulouse and D232T : 8,5 km.

Plan on following page

Parc Hôtel without rest VISA AE

Central Parc – ✆ 04 92 20 37 47 – www.monalisahotels.com – resa-serre-che1@monalisahotels.com – Fax 04 92 20 53 74 A **a**

60 rm – †€ 62/114 ††€ 62/114, € 11

◆ This eminently practical town centre hotel offers generously proportioned rooms, all non-smoking.

La Chaussée VISA AE

4 r. Centrale – ✆ 04 92 21 10 37 – hotel-de-la-chaussee.com – hotel-de-la-chaussee@wanadoo.fr – Fax 04 92 20 03 94 – Closed 28 April-24 May, 5-30 October, Monday lunch, Tuesday lunch and Wednesday lunch A **e**

13 rm – †€ 60/70 ††€ 65/85, € 8 – ½ P € 60/70

Rest – Menu € 20/39 – Carte € 21/40

◆ The 'home from home' appeal of this family hotel, converted into a 'mountain refuge', is unequivocal: antiques and heirlooms, spruce inviting rooms and handsome bathrooms. The restaurant's decor and cuisine, both distinctively regional, are in perfect harmony.

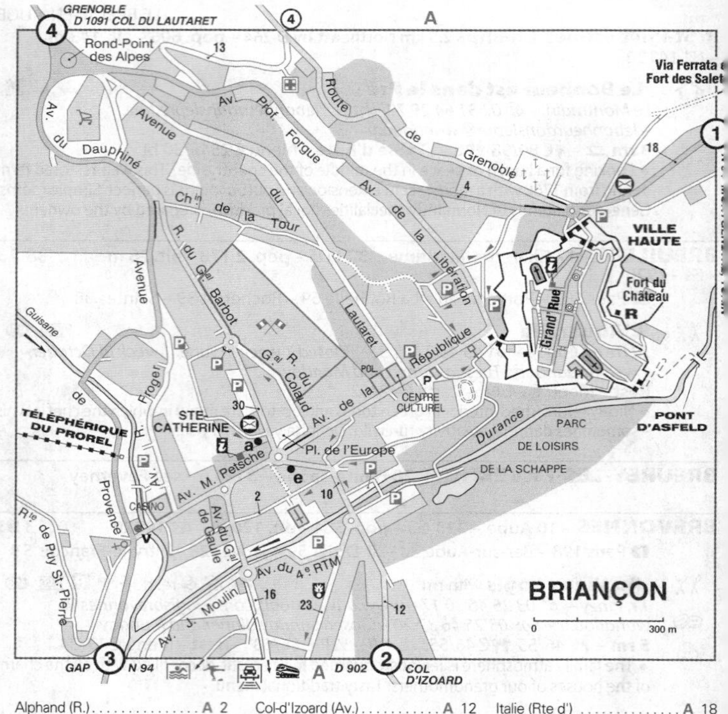

Alphand (R.) . . . . A 2
Baldenberger (Av. P.) . . . . A 4
Centrale (R.) . . . . A 10
Col-d'Izoard (Av.) . . . . A 12
Daurelle (Av. A.) . . . . A 13
Gaulle (Av. Gén.-de) . . . . A 16
Italie (Rte d') . . . . A 18
Pasteur (R.) . . . . A 23
159e-R.-I.-A. (Av.) . . . . A 30

Le Péché Gourmand

2 rte de Gap – ✆ 04 92 21 33 21 – Fax 04 92 21 33 21 – Closed Easter holidays, 14-21 September, Tuesday lunch, Sunday dinner and Monday A **v**

Rest – Menu € 25/50 – Carte € 50/70

◆ Charm and gourmet delight on the banks of the Guisane, in this former mill converted into a restaurant. Countrified interior enlivened with artwork. Inventive cuisine and a fine cheese selection.

in La Vachette 3 km by ① – ✉ 05100

Le Vach' tin

rte d'Italie – ✆ 04 92 46 93 13 – Closed autumn school holidays and Monday except July-August

Rest – *(dinner only) (pre-book)* Carte € 29/49

◆ An old stone house set in a characteristic village. The vaulted dining room is most stylish with its semi-rustic, semi-regional decor. Traditional and regional recipes.

in Puy-St-Pierre 3 km West by D 135 – pop. 496 – ✉ 05100

La Maison de Catherine

chemin des Blés – ✆ 04 92 20 40 89 – www.aubergecatherine.fr – aubergecatherine@orange.fr – Fax 04 92 23 50 46 – Closed 20 April-4 May

11 rm – †€ 52 ††€ 60 – ½ P € 45

Rest – *(closed Sunday dinner, Wednesday lunch and Monday)* Menu € 21/35

◆ An ideal address for mountain sports' lovers. This nice, family house (reserved for non-smokers) has simple and very clean rooms furnished in pine. The traditional dishes are served in a dining room decorated with old farmhouse objects.

BRIARE – 45 Loiret – 318 N6 – pop. 5 660 – alt. 135 m – ✉ 45250 12 D2
Châteaux of the Loire

Paris 155 – Auxerre 76 – Cosne-sur-Loire 31 – Gien 10 – Orléans 80

Office de tourisme, 1, place de Gaulle ✆ 02 38 31 24 51, Fax 02 38 37 15 16

Le Domaine des Roches
2 r. de la Plaine – ✆ 02 38 05 09 00 – www.domainesdesroches.com – contact@domainedesroches.com – Fax 02 38 05 09 05
12 rm – €95 €200, €14 – 1 suite **Rest** – Menu €34/46
◆ Dominating Briare, this handsome, well-restored, 19C abode is home to classical, comfortable rooms. Peaceful park ideal to relax and wind down. Up-to-date, seasonal menu served in a well-cared for, elegant setting.

Luxury pad or humble abode?
and denote categories of comfort.

BRICQUEBEC – 50 Manche – 303 C3 – pop. 4 221 – alt. 145 m – ✉ 50260 32 A1

Paris 348 – Caen 115 – Saint-Lô 76 – Cherbourg 26 – Saint Helier 26

Office de tourisme, 13, place Sainte-Anne ✆ 02 33 52 21 65, Fax 02 33 52 21 65

L'Hostellerie du Château
Cour du Château – ✆ 02 33 52 24 49 – www.lhostellerie-bricquebec.com – lhostellerie.chateau@wanadoo.fr – Fax 02 33 52 62 71 – Closed 15 December-31 January
17 rm – €72 €72/100, €10 – ½ P €73/80
Rest – *(closed Tuesday lunch)* Menu (€16), €21/39 – Carte €30/50
◆ A mixture of styles in this house full of character: gothic façade, medieval hall, rustic breakfast room and personalised rooms (the most pretty of which is the "Reine"). Traditional cuisine served in a setting of beams and huge columns.

BRIDES-LES-BAINS – 73 Savoie – 333 M5 – pop. 575 – alt. 580 m – Winter sports : 1 450/2 950 m 16 45 – Spa : early March-late Oct. – Casino – ✉ 73570 46 F2
French Alps

Paris 612 – Albertville 32 – Annecy 77 – Chambéry 81 – Courchevel 18 – Moûtiers 7

Office de tourisme, place du Centenaire ✆ 04 79 55 20 64, Fax 04 79 55 20 40

Grand Hôtel des Thermes rm, rest,
Parc Thermal – ✆ 04 79 55 38 38 – www.gdhotel-brides.com – info@gdhotel-brides.com – Fax 04 79 55 28 29 – Closed 2 November-28 December
102 rm – €110 €110/170 – 4 suites **Rest** – Menu €26 – Carte €25/35
◆ This 19C building is directly attached to the spas by a walkway. Large, Art Deco style rooms and fitness facilities under the veranda. Huge old-fashioned dining room, (preserved high ceilings and beams). Modern menu and healthy set menus.

Golf-Hôtel rest,
– ✆ 04 79 55 28 12 – www.golfhotel-brides.com – golfhotel-brides@wanadoo.fr – Fax 04 79 55 24 78 – Closed 1st November-25 December
55 rm – €84/142 €84/142, €10 – 1 suite – ½ P €72/155
Rest – *(closed lunch 26 December-9 March)* Menu €26
◆ This elegant 1920s hotel has had a facelift. Superb reception area, spacious and modern rooms, some with a pretty view over the Vanoise mountain. Traditional cuisine served in the elegant and modern restaurant.

Amélie
r. Émile-Machet – ✆ 04 79 55 30 15 – www.hotel-amelie.com – info@hotel-amelie.com – Fax 04 79 55 28 08 – Closed 1st November-19 December
40 rm – €91/166 €102/177 – ½ P €90/181
Rest ***Les Cerisiers*** – Menu €21/27 – Carte €48/58
◆ Modern, practical hotel in the heart of the village. Well-soundproofed rooms with marble bathrooms. Attractive cosy sitting room and bar. Savoyard specialities and diet menus served in a modern dining room.

Altis Val Vert
quartier de l'Olympe – ✆ 04 79 55 22 62 – www.altisvalvert.com – altisvalvert@wanadoo.fr – Fax 04 79 55 29 12 – Closed 31 October-19 December
28 rm – €50/61 €61/75, €10 – ½ P €62/65
Rest – *(closed lunch mid December-early April)* Menu (€17), €21 (weekdays)/26 – Carte approx. €37
◆ Opposite the spa establishment, these two chalets are separated by an exquisite garden. The rooms are comfortable and colourful. An appealing neighbourhood ambience reigns in the restaurant. The lovely terrace in the garden is quite delightful in summer.

Des Sources
av. des Marronniers – ✆ 04 79 55 29 22 – www.hotel-des-sources.com – les.sources.1@wanadoo.fr – Fax 04 79 55 27 06 – Closed 1st November-22 December
70 rm – €54/64 €56/66, €6 – ½ P €71/75 **Rest** – Menu (€16), €19
◆ The imposing façade of this hotel hides a host of appeals: impeccable service, rooms (undergoing renovation) with balconies, sitting rooms and an indoor pool. A fresco of the history of alpinism adds a country note to this restaurant.

Le Belvédère without rest
r. Émile-Machet, Sources district – ✆ 04 79 55 23 41 – www.hotel-73-belvedere.com – hotel.belvedere@wanadoo.fr – Fax 04 79 55 24 96 – Closed end October-mid December
28 rm – €40/55 €74/90
◆ This handsome bourgeois abode faces the Vanoise range. Comfort and charm reign in the rooms, furnished in a chalet style. Jacuzzi tub, hammam and heated summer pool.

BRIE-COMTE-ROBERT – 77 Seine-et-Marne – 312 E3 – 101 39 – see Paris, Area

LA BRIGUE – 06 Alpes-Maritimes – 341 G3 – see Tende

BRINON-SUR-SAULDRE – 18 Cher – 323 J1 – pop. 1 042 – alt. 147 m – ✉ 18410 12 C2

Paris 190 – Bourges 66 – Cosne-sur-Loire 59 – Gien 37 – Orléans 53 – Salbris 25

Les Bouffards
– ✆ 02 48 58 59 88 – www.bouffards.fr – bouffards@wanadoo.fr – Fax 02 48 58 32 11
5 rm – €70/105 €105 – ½ P €88/120 **Table d'hôte** – Menu €18/25 bi
◆ Welcoming family home in attractive parkland complete with pool. Spacious comfortable rooms ensure you will make the most of the peaceful setting.

BRIOLLAY – 49 Maine-et-Loire – 317 F3 – pop. 2 282 – alt. 20 m – ✉ 49125 35 C2

Paris 288 – Angers 15 – Château-Gontier 44 – La Flèche 45

Syndicat d'initiative, 6, rue de la Mairie ✆ 02 41 42 16 84, Fax 02 41 37 92 89

Ceiling★★★ of the Guards' Room of the chateau de Plessis-Bourré Northwest: 10 km **Châteaux of the Loire**

via Soucelles road 3 km (D 109) – ✉ 49125 Briollay

Château de Noirieux
26 rte du Moulin – ✆ 02 41 42 50 05 – www.chateaudenoirieux.com – noirieux@relaischateaux.com – Fax 02 41 37 91 00 – Closed 15 February-15 March, 15 November-2 December, Sunday and Monday from October to May
19 rm – †€ 175/400 ††€ 175/400, ☕ € 22 – ½ P € 163/264
Rest – *(closed Sunday dinner October-May, Tuesday except dinner from October to May and Monday)* Menu € 50 (weekday lunch), € 62/115 – Carte € 100/125
Rest *Côté Véranda* – *(closed Tuesday from October to May, Sunday and Monday) (lunch only)* Carte € 32/49
Spec. Lasagne d'araignée de mer à la truffe. Médaillon de ris de veau de lait légèrement fumé en croûte de thym et citron grillé. Soufflé au Cointreau. **Wines** Saumur, Anjou.
◆ This magnificent estate includes a 17C château, 15C manor and a chapel in a park overlooking the River Loir. Refined rooms. Elegant dining room and shady terrace; lovely, contemporary cuisine. The Côté Véranda is only open for lunch.

BRION – **01 Ain** – **328** G3 – **see Nantua**

BRIONNE – **27 Eure** – **304** E6 – **pop. 4 306** – **alt. 56 m** – ✉ **27800** 33 **C2**
Normandy

- Paris 156 – Bernay 16 – Évreux 40 – Lisieux 40 – Pont-Audemer 27 – Rouen 44
- Office de tourisme, 1, rue du Général-de-Gaulle ✆ 02 32 45 70 51, Fax 02 32 45 70 51
- du Champ de Bataille Le Neubourg Château du Champ de Bataille, W : 18 km on D 137 and D 39, ✆ 02 32 35 03 72
- Bec-Hellouin abbey ★★ North: 6 km - Harcourt: château★ and arboretum★ Southeast: 7 km.

Le Logis with rm
pl. St-Denis – ✆ 02 32 44 81 73 – www.lelogisdebrionne.com – lelogisdebrionne@free.fr – Fax 02 32 45 10 92 – Closed two weeks in August, one week in November, two weeks February-March, Saturday lunch, Sunday dinner and Monday
12 rm – †€ 70 ††€, ☕ € 12 – ½ P € 78/85
Rest – Menu (€ 21), € 29/55 – Carte approx. € 66
◆ A contemporary dining room with numerous green plants, serving food in keeping with current tastes and local specialities. Rooms decorated with old-fashioned furniture.

BRIOUDE – **43 Haute-Loire** – **331** C2 – **pop. 6 695** – **alt. 427 m** 6 **C3**
– ✉ **43100** **Auvergne**

- Paris 479 – Clermont-Ferrand 69 – Le Puy-en-Velay 62 – St-Flour 52
- Office de tourisme, place Lafayette ✆ 04 71 74 97 49, Fax 04 71 74 97 87
- St-Julien basilica★★ (apse★★, capitals★★).
- Lavaudieu: frescoes★ in the church and cloisters★★ of the former abbey 9.5 km by ①.

Plan on following page

La Sapinière rest,
av. P.-Chambriard – ✆ 04 71 50 87 30 – hotel.la.sapiniere@wanadoo.fr – Fax 04 71 50 87 39 – Closed February, November school holidays and Sunday dinner except July-August m
11 rm – †€ 82/90 ††€ 98/107, ☕ € 10
Rest – *(open from Easter to 31 December and closed autumn half-term holidays, Sunday dinner, Monday and lunch except Sunday)* Menu € 22, € 28/48 – Carte € 35/51
◆ An attractive modern building in the heart of the town yet quiet with a pleasant garden, with spacious countrified rooms. Lovely indoor swimming pool; Jacuzzi. Exposed rafters and light-coloured wood in this pleasantly bright restaurant.

BRIOUDE

Assas (R. d') 2
Blum (Av. Léon) 3
Briand (Bd Aristide) 4
Chambriard (Av. P.) 5
Chapitre (R. du) 6
Chèvrerie (R. de la) 7
Commerce (R. du) 8
La-Fayette (Pl.) 12
Gilbert (Pl. Eugène) 9
Grégoire-de-Tours (Pl.) 10
Lamothe (Av. de) 13
Liberté (Pl. de la) 14
Maigne (R. J.) 15
Mendès-France (Av. P.) 16
Michel-de-l'Hospital (R.) 17
Pascal (R.) 18
République (R. de la) 19
Résistance (Pl. de la) 20
St-Jean (Pl.) 21
Sébastopol (R.) 22
Séguret (R.) 23
Talairat (R.) 24
Vercingétorix (Bd) 25
Victor-Hugo (Av.) 26
4-Septembre (R. du) 27
14-Juillet (R. du) 28
21-Juin-1944 (R. du) 29

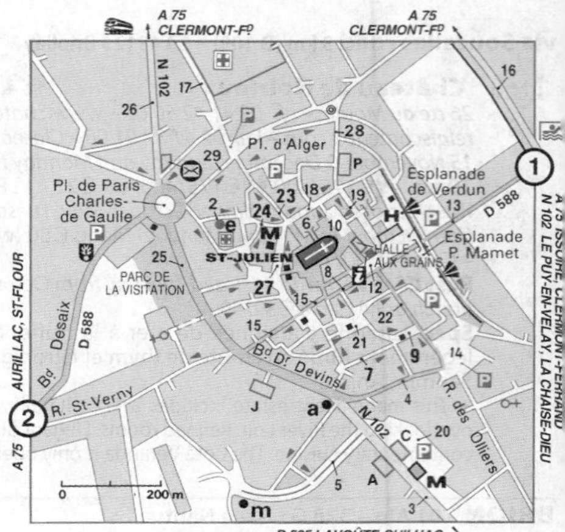

Artemis
rm, VISA

Parc des Conchettes, Rocade N102: 2 km Northwest – 04 71 50 45 04
– www.artemis-hotel.com – info@artemis-hotel.com – Fax 04 71 50 45 05
40 rm – €60/74 €60/74, €8 – ½ P €57/59
Rest – Menu (€14), €17/39 – Carte €27/56
◆ By the main road bypassing Brioude, this hotel offers rooms, garden, swimming pool and seminar room. Contemporary modern fittings and well soundproofed. Modern dining room in shades of cream serving traditional cuisine.

Poste et Champanne
rest, VISA

1 bd Dr-Devins – 04 71 50 14 62 – hpbrioude@wanadoo.fr – Fax 04 71 50 10 55
– Closed autumn school holidays, February, Sunday dinner and Monday lunch a
17 rm – €49 €49/58, €7 – ½ P €49
Rest – Menu €16 (weekdays), €23/45
◆ A town-centre family establishment. Refurbished rooms, functional in the main building and quieter and more comfortable in the annexe. This rustic old-fashioned restaurant is very authentic, as is its generous "one hundred percent" tasty Auvergne cuisine.

BRISSAC – 34 Hérault – 339 H5 – pop. 555 – alt. 145 m – ✉ 34190 23 C2

Paris 732 – Alès 55 – Montpellier 41 – Le Vigan 25

Jardin aux Sources with rm
rm, rm,
VISA

30 av. du Parc – 04 67 73 31 16
– www.lejardinauxsources.com – isaje@club-internet.fr – Fax 04 67 73 31 16
– Closed 20 October-8 November, 2-20 January, Sunday dinner, Monday and Wednesday in low season
3 rm – €85/110 €95/125
Rest – *(number of covers limited, pre-book)* Menu (€19), €29 (weekday lunch), €31/70 – Carte approx. €43
◆ Stone house in a picturesque village. Vaulted restaurant overlooking the kitchen, delightful terrace and inventive cuisine. Charming rooms.

BRISSAC-QUINCÉ – 49 Maine-et-Loire – 317 G4 – pop. 2 588 – alt. 65 m – ✉ 49320 Châteaux of the Loire 35 C2

Paris 307 – Angers 18 – Cholet 62 – Saumur 39

Office de tourisme, 8, place de la République 02 41 91 21 50, Fax 02 41 91 28 12

Château★★.

Le Castel without rest

1 r. L.-Moron, (opposite the château) – ✆ 02 41 91 24 74 – www.hotel-lecastel.com – le.castel.brissac@wanadoo.fr – Fax 02 41 91 71 55

11 rm – 🚹€ 45 🚹🚹€ 77, ☕ € 6,50

◆ A family-run hotel offering comfortable and charming rooms, including one more sumptuous bridal suite, a luxurious lounge, and a breakfast room opening onto the garden.

BRIVE-LA-GAILLARDE – 19 Corrèze – 329 K5 – pop. 49 900 – alt. 142 m – ✉ 19100 Dordogne-Berry-Limousin

24 **B3**

Paris 480 – Albi 218 – Clermont-Ferrand 170 – Limoges 92 – Toulouse 201

✆3635 et tapez 42 (0,34 €/mn)

Office de tourisme, place du 14 Juillet ✆ 05 55 24 08 80, Fax 05 55 24 58 24

de Brive Vallée de Planchetorte, SW : 5 km, ✆ 05 55 87 57 57

Musée de Labenche★.

BRIVE-LA-GAILLARDE

Blum (Av. L.) . . . . AX 4
Clemenceau (Bd) . . . . . . AX 6
Dalton (R. Gén.) . . . . AX 7
Dellessert (R. B.) . . . . . . AX 9
Dr-Marbeau (Bd). . . . . . . AX 10
Dormoy (Bd M.) . . . . AX 13
Dubois (Bd Cardinal). . . . AX 15
Foch (Av. du Mar.) . . . . . AX 17
Germain (Bd Colonel). . . AX 20
Grivel (Bd Amiral) . . . . . AX 22
Hériot (Av. E). . . . . AX 24
Leclerc (Av. Mar.). . . . . . AX 31
Michelet (Bd) . . . . AX 33
Paris (Av. de). . . . . AX 34
Pasteur (Av.). . . . . AX 35
Pompidou (Av. G.) . . . . . AX 37

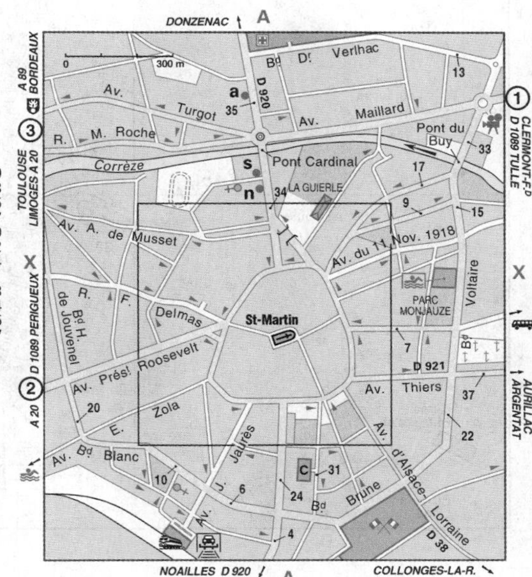

La Truffe Noire

22 bd A.-France – ✆ 05 55 92 45 00 – www.la-truffe-noire.com – contact@la-truffe-noire.com – Fax 05 55 92 45 13

CY **v**

27 rm – 🚹€ 95 🚹🚹€ 115, ☕ € 12 **Rest** – Menu (€ 18), € 28/38 – Carte € 28/50

◆ A new lease of life for this large regional 19C house located on the threshold of the old town. Welcoming lounge with fireplace and smart bedrooms. Truffles and Corrèze specialities served in the modern dining room or outside.

Château de Lacan

r. Jean-Macé, via ① Tulle road – ✆ 05 55 74 79 79 – www.chateaulacan.fr – chateaulacan@orange.fr – Fax 05 55 23 19 83

15 rm – 🚹€ 130/250 🚹🚹€ 130/250, ☕ € 12 – ½ P € 160/290

Rest – *(closed Sunday dinner and Monday)* Menu (€ 19), € 38/68 – Carte € 45/66

◆ Three 11-12C houses successfully revamped in a modern designer spirit. Fashionable colour schemes and antique woodwork in the rooms. Contemporary look for the restaurant, where the counter offers a view of the cooks at work. Additional, more classical dining room.

BRIVE-LA-GAILLARDE

Alsace-Lorraine (Av. d') . . . . . **CZ** 2
Anatole-France (Bd) . . . . **CY** 3
Dalton (R. Gén.) . . . . **CY** 7
Dauzier (Pl. J.-M.) . . . . **CY** 8
Dellessert (R. B.). . . . . **CY** 9
Dr-Massénat (R.). . . . . **CY** 12
Échevins (R. des) . . . . **CZ** 14
Faro (R. du Lt-Colonel) . . . . . **CZ** 16
Gambetta (R.) . . . . **CZ**
Gaulle (Pl. Ch. de) . . . . **CZ** 18
Halle (Pl. de la) . . . . **CY** 23
Herriot (Av. E.). . . . . **CZ** 24
Hôtel-de-Ville (Pl. de l') . . . . . **CY** 26
Hôtel-de-Ville (R. de l') . . . . . **BZ** 27
Latreille (Pl.). . . . . **CZ** 30
Lattre-de-Tassigny (Pl. de) . . . . **CZ** 29
Leclerc (Av. Mar.) . . . . **CZ** 31
Lyautey (Bd Mar.) . . . . **BZ** 32
Majour (R.) . . . . **BYZ** 36
Paris (Av. de). . . . . **BY**
Puyblanc (Bd de). . . . . **CZ** 19
Raynal (R. B.). . . . . **CZ** 40
République (Pl. de la) . . . . . . **BZ** 42
République (R. de la) . . . . **BZ** 43
Salan (R. du). . . . . **CZ** 45
Ségéral-Verninac (R.) . . . . **BY** 46
Teyssier (R.). . . . . **CY** 47
Toulzac (R.). . . . . **CY** 48
14 Juillet (Av. du) . . . . **CY** 21

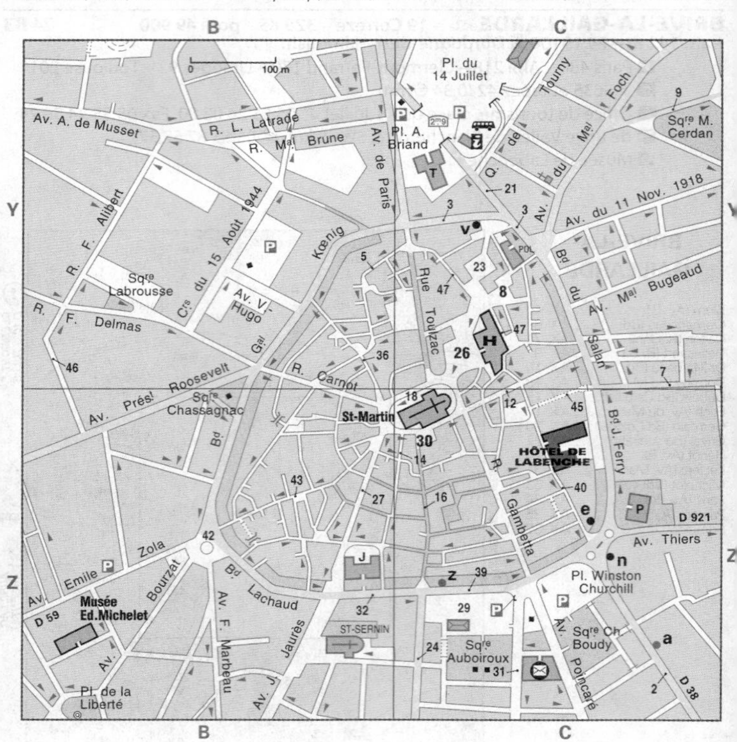

Le Collonges without rest
3 pl. W.-Churchill – ✆ 05 55 74 09 58
– www.hotel-le-collonges.com – lecollonges@wanadoo.fr
– Fax 05 55 74 11 25
CZ **n**
24 rm – †€ 52/57 ††€ 52/62, ☕ € 9
◆ This family-run hotel is located just off the ring road round the town centre. A smart lounge bar and soberly modern rooms assure the well being of travellers.

Le Coq d'Or without rest
16 bd Jules-Ferry – ✆ 05 55 17 12 92
– www.hotel-coqdor.com – marc.belacel@wanadoo.fr
– Fax 05 55 88 39 90
CZ **e**
8 rm – †€ 55 ††€ 60, ☕ € 9
◆ A renovated hotel on the ring road, just a short distance from the centre. Small bedrooms adorned with antique furniture. Bar-tabac and pavement terrace beneath the shade of the plane trees.

XXX **Les Arums**
15 av. Alsace-Lorraine – ✆ 05 55 24 26 55 – www.lesarums.fr – restaurant.lesarums@wanadoo.fr – Fax 05 55 17 13 22 – Closed 24-31 August, Saturday lunch, Sunday dinner and Monday except bank holidays CZ **a**
Rest – Menu (€ 25 bi), € 38/65 – Carte € 47/65
◆ Minimalist, contemporary dining room enhanced by colourful modern art. Creative cuisine. Leafy terrace.

XX **La Toupine**
27 av. Pasteur – ✆ 05 55 23 71 58 – toup.maurin@free.fr – Fax 05 55 23 71 58 – Closed 1st-25 August, February holidays, Sunday and Monday AX **a**
Rest – *(pre-book)* Menu (€ 13), € 26/29 – Carte € 35/43
◆ A quiet restaurant with a tasteful contemporary decor of stainless steel and rosewood. Delicious modern cuisine.

XX **La Crémaillère** with rm
53 av. de Paris – ✆ 05 55 74 32 47 – www.hotel-la-cremaillere.net – hotel.restaurant-la.cremaillere@wanadoo.fr – Fax 05 55 74 00 15 – Closed 21-27 December and Sunday AX **n**
8 rm – † € 49/60 †† € 49/60, ☕ € 7 – ½ P € 59/70 **Rest** – Menu (€ 24), € 28/42
◆ On a busy main street, this place makes for a nice break with modern paintings and sculptures by a local artist. A century-old linden tree shades the terrace.

X **Chez Francis**
61 av. de Paris – ✆ 05 55 74 41 72 – www.chezfrancis.fr – contact@chezfrancis.fr – Fax 05 55 17 20 54 – Closed 31 May-8 June, 31 August-3 September, 24-28 January, Sunday and Monday AX **s**
Rest – *(number of covers limited, pre-book)* Menu € 16 (weekdays)/25 – Carte € 46/68
◆ Retro ads and dedications left by the customers decorate this nice restaurant with Parisian bistro overtones. Updated traditional cooking; Languedoc wines.

X **Auberge de Chanlat**
34 r. G-Buisson, (South of the map), 2 km by Noailles road – ✆ 05 55 24 02 03 – Fax 05 55 74 39 06 – Closed 23 June-1st July, 25 August-9 September, Monday and Tuesday
Rest – Menu (€ 15), € 28/42 – Carte € 38/68
◆ Family-run inn on the edge of the countryside. Enjoy local cuisine and grilled dishes in the contemporary décor of a panoramic dining room opening onto the valley.

Aurillac road Est by D 921 CZ – ✉ 19360 Malemort

Auberge des Vieux Chênes
31 av. Honoré-de-Balzac, at 2.5 km – ✆ 05 55 24 13 55 – www.aubergedesvieuxchenes.fr – aubergedesvieuxchenes@wanadoo.fr – Fax 05 55 24 56 82 – Closed Sunday and public holidays
16 rm – † € 48/58 †† € 50/68, ☕ € 6,50 – ½ P € 50/68
Rest – Menu (€ 14), € 18/36 – Carte € 38/65
◆ Big building at the gates of Brive, housing a café, newsagents and hotel. Practical rooms, including four new, larger, modern rooms. Restaurant with a sober modern setting and classical cuisine with a regional accent.

in Varetz 10 km by ③, D 901 and D 152 – pop. 2 109 – alt. 109 m – ✉ 19240

Château de Castel Novel
in Varetz – ✆ 05 55 85 00 01 – www.castelnovel.com – novel@relaischateaux.com – Fax 05 55 85 09 03 – Closed 2-25 January, Sunday dinner and Monday except July-August
32 rm – † € 88/365 †† € 108/385, ☕ € 20 – 5 suites
Rest – *(closed lunch in July-August except Sunday, Sunday dinner and Monday dinner from September to June, Saturday lunch and Monday lunch)*
Menu (€ 25), € 34 (weekday lunch), € 43/76 – Carte € 74/85
◆ Colette loved the amazing peacefulness of this 13C château built in red sandstone and its surrounding park. Bedrooms of real character in which you can be the lord or lady of the manor for a night. Classic cuisine paying homage to the author of 'Le Blé en Herbe'.

BRIVEZAC – 19 Corrèze – 329 M5 – see Beaulieu-sur-Dordogne

BRON – 69 Rhône – 327 I5 – see Lyon

BROU – 28 Eure-et-Loir – 311 C6 – pop. 3 604 – alt. 150 m – ✉ 28160 11 **B1**

Paris 142 – Chartres 38 – Châteaudun 22 – Le Mans 86 – Nogent-le-Rotrou 33

Office de tourisme, rue de la Chevalerie ✆ 02 37 47 01 12, Fax 02 37 47 01 12

L'Ascalier

9 pl. du Dauphin – ✆ 02 37 96 05 52 – lascalier@wanadoo.fr – Fax 02 37 47 02 41 – Closed Sunday dinner, Monday dinner and Tuesday dinner

Rest – (pre-book) Menu (€ 14), € 19/34

◆ The lovely 16C 'ascalier' (staircase in local parlance) leads to the upstairs dining room of this popular address. Rustic interior, flower-decked terrace and fine classic fare.

BROUCKERQUE – 59 Nord – 302 B2 – pop. 1 276 – alt. 2 m – ✉ 59630 30 **B1**

Paris 283 – Calais 37 – Cassel 26 – Dunkerque 14 – Lille 74 – St-Omer 28

Middel Houck

pl. du Village – ✆ 03 28 27 13 46 – www.mh-receptions.com – middelhouck@wanadoo.fr – Fax 03 28 27 19 19 – Closed 10-19 August, dinner from Sunday to Friday and Saturday

Rest – Menu € 18 (weekday lunch), € 26/55 bi – Carte € 34/48

◆ Brick walls, exposed beams and freshly cut flowers set the scene in this friendly former post house. Traditional menu with regional accents.

BROUILLA – 66 Pyrénées-Orientales – 344 I7 – pop. 918 – alt. 45 m – ✉ 66620 22 **B3**

Paris 873 – Montpellier 176 – Perpignan 20 – Figueres 47 – Roses 66

L'Ancienne Gare without rest

at "Le Millery", 1 km North by D 8 B – ✆ 04 68 89 88 21 – www.anciennegare.net – ancienne-gare@wanadoo.fr – Closed 20 December-6 January

5 rm – €57 €67

◆ Very close to the Spanish border, this former railway station has become a very welcoming guest house. Romantic rooms, old-world charm, terrace and views over the Canigou.

BROUILLAMNON – 18 Cher – 323 I4 – see Charost

BROUSSE-LE-CHÂTEAU – 12 Aveyron – 338 H7 – pop. 177 – alt. 239 m – ✉ 12480 Languedoc-Roussillon-Tarn Gorges 29 **D2**

Paris 696 – Albi 54 – Cassagnes-Bégonhès 35 – Lacaune 50 – Rodez 61 – St-Affrique 29

Perched village★.

Le Relays du Chasteau rest,

– ✆ 05 65 99 40 15 – www.le-relays-du-chasteau.com – lerelaysduchasteau@wanadoo.fr – Fax 05 65 99 21 25 – Closed 20 December-20 February, Friday dinner and Saturday from October to May

12 rm – €37/45 €37/48, €7 – ½ P €42/56

Rest – Menu € 16/33 bi – Carte € 15/30

◆ Pretty Aveyron house with simple functional rooms, all facing the medieval château. A fireplace heats the country-style dining room (copper pots and bare wood). Regionally inspired menu.

LES BROUZILS – 85 Vendée – 316 I6 – pop. 2 260 – alt. 64 m – ✉ 85260 34 **B3**

Paris 427 – Nantes 46 – La Roche-sur-Yon 37 – Cholet 77 – Saint-Herblain 53

Manoir de la Thébline without rest

l'Herbergement road – ✆ 02 51 42 99 98 – www.manoirthebline.com – contact@manoirthebline.com

3 rm – €90 €90

◆ Elegant old furniture adds style to the cosy guestrooms in this attractive 19C residence. Pleasant flower garden, billiard room and library. Very well-maintained.

BRUAY-LA-BUISSIERE – 62 Pas-de-Calais – 301 I5 – see Béthune

BRUÈRE-ALLICHAMPS – 18 Cher – 323 K6 – see St-Amand-Montrond

BRÛLON – 72 Sarthe – 310 H 7 – pop. 1 411 – alt. 102 m – ✉ 72350 35 C1

Paris 239 – Nantes 167 – Le Mans 41 – Laval 55 – La Flèche 43

Office de tourisme, place Albert Liébault ✆ 02 43 95 05 10, Fax 02 43 95 05 10

Château de l'Enclos without rest

2 av. de la Libération – ✆ 02 43 92 17 85 – www.chateau-enclos.com – jean-claude.guillou5@wanadoo.fr

4 rm – †€ 100 ††€ 100/150

◆ This handsome bourgeois abode is a genuine treasure trove. From the unusual cellar lounge and snug rooms in the château to the 'kota' (wooden Lapp tree house) perched in three trees in the park.

BRUMATH – 67 Bas-Rhin – 315 K4 – pop. 9 825 – alt. 145 m – ✉ 67170 1 B1

Paris 472 – Haguenau 14 – Molsheim 45 – Saverne 35 – Strasbourg 19

À L'Écrevisse VISA AE

4 av. de Strasbourg – ✆ 03 88 51 11 08 – www.hostellerie-ecrevisse.com – ecrevisse@wanadoo.fr – Fax 03 88 51 89 02

Rest – Menu € 38/69 – Carte € 47/71

Rest *Krebs'Stuebel* – *(Closed Monday dinner and Tuesday)* Menu € 19/27 – Carte € 29/49

◆ The same family has run this Alsatian establishment for seven generations. Elegant restaurant dining room serving classic cuisine. At the Krebs'Stuebel, the atmosphere and decor is winstub-style; spur-of-the-moment cuisine and tapas.

LE BRUSC – 83 Var – 340 J7 – see Six-Fours-les-Plages

BRY-SUR-MARNE – 94 Val-de-Marne – 312 E2 – 101 18 – see Paris, Area

BUELLAS – 01 Ain – 328 D3 – pop. 1 538 – alt. 225 m – ✉ 01310 43 E1

Paris 424 – Annecy 120 – Bourg-en-Bresse 9 – Lyon 69 – Mâcon 32

L'Auberge Bressane VISA AE

10 rte de Buelle – ✆ 04 74 24 20 20 – www.auberge-buellas.com – aubergebressanedebuellas@orange.fr – Fax 04 74 24 20 20 – Closed 2-8 August, autumn school holidays, 16-28 February, Sunday dinner, Tuesday and Wednesday

Rest – Menu (€ 12 bi), € 21/43 – Carte € 34/47

◆ Tasty regional fare, a zest of southern flavours and a sprinkling of creativity to tempt the palate in this former bakery, now a Provençal-inspired restaurant. Attentive staff.

LE BUGUE – 24 Dordogne – 329 G6 – pop. 2 760 – alt. 62 m – ✉ 24260 4 C3

Dordogne-Berry-Limousin

Paris 522 – Bergerac 47 – Brive-la-Gaillarde 72 – Périgueux 42 – Sarlat-la-Canéda 32

Office de tourisme, porte de la Vézère ✆ 05 53 07 20 48, Fax 05 53 54 92 30

de La Marterie Saint-Félix-de-Reillac-et-Mortemart Domaine de la Marterie, N : 13 km on D 710, ✆ 05 53 05 61 00

Gouffre de Proumeyssac★★ South: 3 km.

Domaine de la Barde rm, VISA AE

rte de Périgueux – ✆ 05 53 07 16 54 – www.domainedelabarde.com – hotel@domainedelabarde.com – Fax 05 53 54 76 19 – Closed 3 January-15 March

18 rm – †€ 95/155 ††€ 95/240, € 15 – ½ P € 128/171

Rest *Le Vélo Rouge* – *(closed lunch Tuesday-Friday and Monday)* Menu € 39 (weekdays) – Carte approx. € 52

◆ Beautiful 18C Périgord mansion overlooking a French style garden. Two converted outhouses, an old mill and forge are home to spacious, tastefully decorated rooms. Traditional dishes take pride of place on the table without forgetting regional specialities.

Sarlat road 3 km East by D 703 and secondary road ✉ 24260

Maison Oléa without rest
La Combe de Leygue – ✆ 05 53 08 48 93 – www.olea-dordogne.com – info@olea-dordogne.com – Fax 05 53 08 48 93 – Closed 21 December-4 January
5 rm – †€ 70/90 ††€ 75/95
◆ The rooms of this guesthouse have south-facing balconies with a view of the Vézère valley. Tasteful interior. Open air summer pool and vegetable garden.

in Campagne 4 km Southeast by D 703 – **pop. 317** – **alt. 60 m** – ✉ **24260**

Du Château rm, VISA
– ✆ 05 53 07 23 50 – www.hotelrestaurantduchateau24.com – hotduchateau@aol.com – Fax 05 53 03 93 69 – Open 1st April-15 October
12 rm – †€ 52/60 ††€ 52/60, € 8 – ½ P € 57/67
Rest – Menu € 20/35 – Carte € 35/55
◆ This inn full of character is located in the heart of the Périgord Noir, opposite the Château de Campagne. It has old rooms that are well-maintained in a rustic style. Rustic style decor in the dining room and veranda; unpretentious menu.

BUIS-LES-BARONNIES – **26 Drôme** – **332** E8 – **pop. 2 283** 44 **B3**
– **alt. 365 m** – ✉ **26170** French Alps

Paris 685 – Carpentras 39 – Nyons 29 – Orange 50 – Sault 38 – Sisteron 72 – Valence 130

Office de tourisme, 14, boulevard Eysserie ✆ 04 75 28 04 59, Fax 04 75 28 13 63

Old town ★.

Les Arcades-Le Lion d'Or without rest VISA
pl. du Marché – ✆ 04 75 28 11 31 – www.hotelarcades.fr – info@hotelarcades.fr – Fax 04 75 28 12 07 – Open from March to November
15 rm – †€ 45/68 ††€ 55/73, € 8,50 – 1 suite
◆ The entrance to the hotel is found beneath the 15C arcades in the central square. Renovated, prettily personalised rooms. The charming interior garden is worth seeing.

LE BUISSON-CORBLIN – **61 Orne** – **310** F2 – **see Flers**

LE BUISSON-DE-CADOUIN – **24 Dordogne** – **329** G6 – **pop. 2 114** 4 **C3**
– **alt. 63 m** – ✉ **24480**

Paris 532 – Bergerac 38 – Brive-la-Gaillarde 81 – Périgueux 52 – Sarlat-la-Canéda 36

Office de tourisme, place André Boissière ✆ 05 53 22 06 09, Fax 05 53 22 06 09

Le Manoir de Bellerive rm, AC rm,
Siorac road: 1.5 km – ✆ 05 53 22 16 16 VISA AE
– www.bellerivehotel.com – manoir.bellerive@wanadoo.fr – Fax 05 53 22 09 05 – Closed 30 November-12 February
21 rm – †€ 135/260 ††€ 135/260, € 18 – ½ P € 123/185
Rest ***Les Délices d'Hortense*** – *(closed Monday except July-August, Tuesday from October to May and lunch Monday to Thursday)* Menu € 48/90 – Carte € 80/92
Rest ***La Table de Louis*** – bistro *(closed Monday lunch)* Menu (€ 22), € 28
Spec. Marbré de volaille et foie gras. Chou farci à l'araignée de mer. Epaule d'agneau du Quercy confite aux épices. **Wines** Pécharmant, Bergerac.
◆ This Napoleon III manor house sports a countrified spirit: large mirrors, floral wallpaper, period furniture and views of the English style park or the Dordogne region. Personalised classic cuisine served in an elegant dining room in ochre and plum tones. Traditional fare at La Table de Louis.

in Paleyrac 4 km Southeast by D 25 and secondary road – ✉ **24480**

Le Clos Lascazes without rest VISA
– ✆ 05 53 74 33 94 – www.clos-lascazes.fr – clos-lascazes@wanadoo.fr – Fax 05 53 74 03 22 – Open March-mid November
5 rm – †€ 68/89 ††€ 68/89, € 8
◆ Three houses built in different centuries extend an invitation to relax and wind down (park, salt water pool). White walls, embroidered bed linen and prints set the scene in the bright rooms.

BULGNEVILLE – 88 Vosges – 314 D3 – pop. 1 284 – alt. 350 m – ✉ 88140 Alsace-Lorraine 26 B3

Paris 342 – Belfort 133 – Épinal 55 – Langres 71 – Vesoul 92

Syndicat d'initiative, 105, rue de l'Hôtel de Ville ✆ 03 29 09 14 67, Fax 03 29 09 14 67

Benoit Breton without rest

74 r. des Récollets – ✆ 03 29 09 21 72 – benoitbreton.chambresdhotes@wanadoo.fr – Fax 03 29 09 21 72

4 rm – €65 €70

◆ An antique dealer by profession, Mr Breton has left his stamp on the spacious rooms furnished stylishly with antiques and ornaments. Chickens, ducks and a goat roam free in the garden.

XX **La Marmite Beaujolaise** VISA AE

34 r. de l'Hôtel-de-Ville – ✆ 03 29 09 16 58 – www.restaurant-lamarmitebeaujolaise.com – Closed 31 December-14 January, Sunday dinner and Monday

Rest – Menu € 14 (weekday lunch), € 21/39 – Carte € 38/50

◆ 17C inn serving tasty, traditional food with a regional slant. Stylish rustic décor of beams, bare stonewalls and fireplace.

BULLY – 69 Rhône – 327 G4 – pop. 2 003 – alt. 313 m – ✉ 69210 43 E1

Paris 471 – Lyon 32 – Saint-Étienne 92 – Villeurbanne 41

XX **Auberge du Château** VISA AE

pl. de l'Église – ✆ 04 74 01 25 36 – www.aubergedu-chateau.com – aubergeduchateau@yahoo.fr – Fax 04 74 72 50 95 – Closed 5-11 May, 1st-15 September, 1st-15 January, Tuesday from November to March, Saturday lunch, Sunday dinner and Monday

Rest – Menu € 20 (weekday lunch), € 28/59 – Carte € 45/70

◆ Opposite the village church, this ancient inn dating from 1749 hides a restaurant with a contemporary interior and terrace. Open kitchen; concise updated menu.

BURLATS – 81 Tarn – 338 F9 – see Castres

BURNHAUPT-LE-HAUT – 68 Haut-Rhin – 315 G10 – pop. 1 550 – alt. 300 m – ✉ 68520 1 A3

Paris 454 – Altkirch 16 – Belfort 32 – Mulhouse 17 – Thann 12

Le Coquelicot rm, rest, VISA AE

at the Pont d'Aspach, 1 km North – ✆ 03 89 83 10 10 – www.le coquelicot.fr – info@aigleor.com – Fax 03 89 83 10 33 – Closed 26 December-4 January

26 rm – €68 €68, € 11 – ½ P € 62/72

Rest – *(closed 25 July-10 August, 26 December-4 January, Saturday lunch and Sunday dinner)* Menu (€ 12), € 24/57 – Carte € 27/49

◆ The village is situated at the edge of the picturesque region of Sundgau. Well located for the road network, this hotel has practical, comfortable bedrooms. Pastel colours and floral prints create a spring atmosphere in the Coquelicot dining room.

BUSNES – 62 Pas-de-Calais – 301 I4 – see Béthune

BUSSEAU-SUR-CREUSE – 23 Creuse – 325 J4 – ✉ 23150 Ahun 25 C1

Paris 368 – Aubusson 27 – Guéret 17

Moutier d'Ahun: panelling★★ of the church Southeast: 5,5 km - Ahun: panelling★ of the church Southeast: 6 km, Dordogne-Berry-Limousin.

XX **Le Viaduc** with rm VISA

9 Busseau Gare – ✆ 05 55 62 57 20 – www.restaurant-leviaduc.com – ch-cl-lemestre@wanadoo.fr – Fax 05 55 62 55 80 – Closed 5-25 January, Sunday dinner and Monday

7 rm – €48 €48, € 7 – ½ P € 65

Rest – Menu (€ 15), € 26/45 – Carte € 14/20

◆ This auberge makes the most of its commanding position. The rustic dining room and terrace offer a beautiful view over the 1863 viaduct straddling the River Creuse. Well-maintained rooms.

LA BUSSIÈRE – 45 Loiret – 318 N5 – pop. 774 – alt. 160 m – ✉ 45230 12 D2
Burgundy-Jura

Paris 142 – Auxerre 74 – Cosne-sur-Loire 46 – Gien 14 – Montargis 29 – Orléans 79

Château des pêcheurs★.

Le Nuage
rm, VISA MC AE

95 bis r. Briare – ✆ 02 38 35 90 73 – www.lenuage.com – contact@lenuage.com – Fax 02 38 35 90 62 – Closed 2-20 January

16 rm – †€ 48 ††€ 52, ☕ € 7 – 1 suite – ½ P € 43

Rest – *(dinner only except weekends) (residents only weekdays)* Menu € 12 (dinner) – Carte € 20/40

◆ New motel-type establishment located at the entrance to the town. Practical, well laid-out bedrooms. Relaxing setting with a gym. Classic recipes and grilled food served in an all-pink dining room topped with a mezzanine lounge.

LA BUSSIÈRE-SUR-OUCHE – 21 Côte-d'Or – 320 I6 – pop. 159 – alt. 320 m – ✉ 21360 Burgundy-Jura 8 C2

Paris 297 – Dijon 34 – Chalon-sur-Saône 63 – Beaune 34 – Autun 59

Abbaye de la Bussière
VISA MC AE

R.D. 33 – ✆ 03 80 49 02 29 – www.abbayedelabussiere.fr – info@abbayedelabussiere.fr – Fax 03 80 49 05 23

16 rm – †€ 175/450 ††€ 175/450, ☕ € 29 – ½ P € 190/366

Rest – *(closed Monday, Tuesday and lunch except Sunday)* Menu € 60 (dinner), € 80/110 – Carte € 97/141

Rest *Le Bistrot* – *(closed Monday and Tuesday) (lunch only)* Menu € 29/33

Spec. Les couteaux "XL" au crabe royal acidulé et crémeux iodé. Cochon cul noir et jus au poivre noir de Tasmanie. Soufflé chaud au cassis frais. **Wines** Morey Saint-Denis, Beaune blanc.

◆ A tastefully restored 12C Cistercian abbey surrounded by superb grounds. Cosy sitting rooms and lavishly appointed guestrooms with all modern comforts. Gourmet fare based on good quality, seasonal produce takes pride of place in the restaurant (former cloisters). The bistro offers a concise lunchtime menu and a rustic decor.

BUSSY-ST-GEORGES – 77 Seine-et-Marne – 312 F2 – 101 20 – see Paris, Area (Marne-la-Vallée)

BUXEUIL – 86 Vienne – 317 N7 – see Descartes

BUXY – 71 Saône-et-Loire – 320 I9 – pop. 2 164 – alt. 263 m – ✉ 71390 8 C3

Paris 351 – Chagny 25 – Chalon-sur-Saône 17 – Montceau-les-Mines 33

Office de tourisme, place de la gare ✆ 03 85 92 00 16, Fax 03 85 92 00 57

Relais du Montagny without rest
VISA MC AE

12 rte de Chalon – ✆ 03 85 94 94 94 – www.lerelaisdumontagny.fr – le.relais.du.montagny@wanadoo.fr – Fax 03 85 92 07 19 – Closed 19-27 December, 3-24 January, Friday dinner and Sunday dinner from November to March

30 rm – †€ 52/60 ††€ 54/64, ☕ € 10

◆ This establishment houses identical functional bedrooms, a bar and billiards. The Voie Verte, an old railway line converted into a path, makes for a great excursion.

Aux Années Vins
VISA MC AE

2 Grande-Rue – ✆ 03 85 92 15 76 – www.aux-annees-vins.com – aux.annees.vins@wanadoo.fr – Fax 03 85 92 12 20 – Closed 24 August-2 September, 25 January-24 February, Wednesday except dinner from 1st April to 11 November, Monday dinner from 11 November to 31 March and Tuesday

Rest – Menu (€ 17), € 21/59 – Carte € 35/53

◆ Well-situated right in the centre of the village, large dining room decorated with a stone fireplace. Interior terrace underneath the arches. Traditional cuisine made with care.

BUZANÇAIS – 36 Indre – 323 E5 – pop. 4 581 – alt. 111 m – ✉ 36500 11 B3

Paris 286 – Le Blanc 47 – Châteauroux 25 – Chatellerault 78 – Tours 91

Syndicat d'initiative, 11, passage du Marché ✆ 02 54 84 22 00, Fax 02 54 02 13 45

L'Hermitage

rest, rm, VISA

1 chemin de Vilaine – ✆ 02 54 84 03 90 – www.lhermitagehotel.com – logis-hermitage@wanadoo.fr – Fax 02 54 02 13 19 – Closed 2-25 January, Sunday dinner and Monday except July-August, Monday lunch in July-August

12 rm – €59 €71, €8 – ½ P €68/85

Rest – *(pre-book Sat - Sun)* Menu €16 (weekday lunch), €26/52 – Carte €40/60

◆ Welcoming property with a leafy garden where the River Indre runs. The rooms are well equipped and rustic in style and nearly all command a view of the peaceful landscape. In fine weather, contemporary cuisine is served under a pergola facing the terrace.

CABANAC-SÉGUENVILLE – 31 Haute-Garonne – 343 E2 – pop. 128 – alt. 200 m – ✉ 31480 28 B2

Paris 668 – Colomiers 39 – Montauban 46 – Toulouse 51

Château de Séguenville

via D 1 and D 89A – ✆ 05 62 13 42 67 – www.chateau-de-seguenville.com – info@chateau-de-seguenville.com – Closed 15 December-15 January

5 rm – €105 €120

Table d'hôte – *(closed Saturday in July-August and Sunday)* Menu €25/50

◆ This pretty 19C Gascon castle is surrounded by century-old trees. It houses vast, tastefully furnished rooms, one of which boasts an enormous terrace with sweeping views of the countryside. Regional food.

CABESTANY – 66 Pyrénées-Orientales – 344 I6 – see Perpignan

CABOURG – 14 Calvados – 303 L4 – pop. 4 027 – alt. 3 m – Casino – ✉ 14390 Normandy 32 B2

Paris 220 – Caen 24 – Deauville 23 – Lisieux 35 – Pont-l'Évêque 34

Office de tourisme, jardins de l'Hotel deVille ✆ 02 31 06 20 00, Fax 02 31 06 20 10

Public de Cabourg Avenue de l'Hippodrome, 1 km on the av. de l'Hippodrome, ✆ 02 31 91 70 53

de Cabourg Le Home Varaville 38 avenue du Pdt René Coty, 3 km on the Caen road, ✆ 02 31 91 25 56

Plan on following page

Grand Hôtel

rest, VISA

prom. M.-Proust – ✆ 02 31 91 01 79 – www.mercure.com – h1282@accor.com – Fax 02 31 24 03 20 A s

68 rm – €165/370 €165/370, €20 – 2 suites

Rest – *(closed January, Monday and Tuesday except July-August)* Menu (€33), €45 – Carte €56/74

◆ Palace on the sea front haunted by the memory of Marcel Proust: his room has been entirely reconstituted. The others remain personalised and comfortable. Traditional food and refined atmosphere in the elegant dining room opening onto the beach.

Mercure Hippodrome

rm, rest, VISA

av. M.-d'Ornano, on av. Hippodrome A – ✆ 02 31 24 04 04 – www.mercure.com – mercurecabourghippodrome@wanadoo.fr – Fax 02 31 91 03 99

75 rm – €105/149 €105/149, €13

Rest – *(Open 1st April-15 November) (dinner only)* Carte €20/30

◆ These two new Norman-style buildings are near the racecourse. The rooms are decorated in a modern and practical style. A welcoming, comfortable dining room with an excellent view of the racecourse.

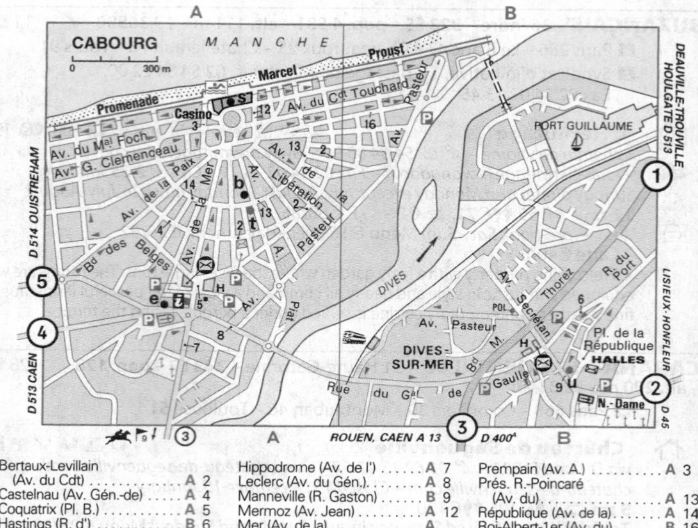

Bertaux-Levillain (Av. du Cdt) . . . . A 2	Hippodrome (Av. de l') . . . . . . A 7	Prempain (Av. A.) . . . . A 3
Castelnau (Av. Gén.-de) . . . . . A 4	Leclerc (Av. du Gén.). . . . . A 8	Prés. R.-Poincaré (Av. du) . . . . A 13
Coquatrix (Pl. B.) . . . . A 5	Manneville (R. Gaston) . . . . . . B 9	République (Av. de la). . . . . . A 14
Hastings (R. d') . . . . B 6	Mermoz (Av. Jean) . . . . A 12	Roi-Albert-1er (Av. du). . . . . . B 16
	Mer (Av. de la). . . . . A	

Du Golf

av. M.-d'Ornano, via av. Racecourse A – ✆ 02 31 24 12 34
– www.hotel-du-golf-cabourg.com – contact@hotel-du-golf-cabourg.com
– Fax 02 31 24 18 51 – Open 16 March-15 November
39 rm – 🚹€ 60/78 🚹🚹€ 60/78, ☕ € 8 – ½ P € 57/66
Rest – *(closed for lunch from 30 September to 15 November, Friday and Sunday)*
Menu € 18 (lunch), € 25/37 – Carte € 20/45

◆ A motel-type establishment, on the edge of the golf course, offering simple, functional ground-floor rooms overlooking the garden or terrace. A comfortable, discreetly contemporary dining room overlooking the greens.

Castel Fleuri without rest

4 av. Alfred-Piat – ✆ 02 31 91 27 57
– www.castel-fleuri.com – info@castel-fleuri.com
– Fax 02 31 24 03 48 – Closed 5-24 January A **b**
22 rm ☕ – 🚹€ 74 🚹🚹€ 79

◆ Townhouse from 1920 with a pretty garden where breakfast is served when the weather permits. Smart, fresh rooms; pleasant, smiley welcome.

Le Cottage without rest

24 av. Gén.-Leclerc – ✆ 02 31 91 65 61
– info@hotel-cottage-cabourg.com A **e**
14 rm – 🚹€ 49/58 🚹🚹€ 54/68, ☕ € 7

◆ A guesthouse atmosphere in this 1900s cottage with a small garden at the front. Rooms are simple but regularly renovated, all have different décor.

Le Baligan

8 av. Alfred-Piat – ✆ 02 31 24 10 92
– www.lebaligan.fr – info@lebaligan.fr – Fax 02 31 28 99 09
– Closed 21 December-10 January and Wednesday except bank holidays A **t**
Rest – Menu € 17 (weekday lunch), € 27/55 – Carte € 29/48

◆ Marine inspired bistro (fishing rods, lithographs, frescos) serving produce fresh from the local fish market. Summer street terrace.

in Dives-sur-Mer South of map – pop. 5 881 – alt. 3 m – ✉ 14160

Office de tourisme, rue du Général-de-Gaulle ✆ 02 31 91 24 66, Fax 02 31 24 42 28

Covered market★.

Chez le Bougnat

27 r. G.-Manneville – ✆ 02 31 91 06 13 – www.chezlebougnat.fr – chezlebougnat@orange.fr – Fax 02 31 91 09 87 – Closed 6-12 October, 22 December-10 January and dinner from Sunday to Wednesday except school holidays B u

Rest – Menu € 17 (weekday lunch), € 23/27 – Carte € 21/48

◆ A former ironmongery transformed into a friendly bistro. Walls covered with old posters and a surprising bric-a-brac of antique objects. Dishes of the day.

in Hôme 2 km by ⑤ – ✉ 14390

Syndicat d'initiative, Mairie ✆ 02 31 24 73 83, Fax 02 31 24 72 41

Manoir de la Marjolaine without rest

5 av. du Prés.-Coty – ✆ 02 31 91 70 25 – http://manoirdelamarjolaine.free.fr – eric.faye@orange.fr – Fax 02 31 91 77 10

5 rm – †€ 70/80 ††€ 80/120

◆ After having fallen under the charm of the small leafy park, you will discover the manor (1850) and its spacious rooms decorated with original paintings. Pleasant welcome.

Au Pied des Marais

26 av. du Prés.-Coty – ✆ 02 31 91 27 55 – Fax 02 31 91 86 13 – Closed 16-24 June, 15-27 December, 26 January-11 February, Tuesday and Wednesday except dinner in July-August

Rest – Menu € 21 bi (weekday lunch), € 31/51 – Carte € 44/72

◆ Traditional cooking, specialities (including the famous pigs' trotters) and wood-fired grilled meats, all of which in a rustic decor enhanced with modern details.

CABRERETS – 46 Lot – 337 F4 – pop. 231 – alt. 130 m – ✉ 46330 29 C1

Dordogne-Berry-Limousin

Paris 565 – Cahors 26 – Figeac 44 – Gourdon 42 – St-Céré 58 – Villefranche-de-Rouergue 44

Office de tourisme, place du Sombral ✆ 05 65 31 29 06, Fax 05 65 31 29 06

Château de Gontaut-Biron★ - ≤★ of the left bank of the Célé.

Grotte du Pech Merle★★★ Northwest: 3 km.

Auberge de la Sagne

grotte de Pech-Merle road – ✆ 05 65 31 26 62 – www.hotel-auberge-cabrerets.com – contact@hotel-auberge-cabrerets.com – Fax 05 65 30 27 43 – Open 15 May-15 September

8 rm – †€ 50/54 ††€ 50/54, ☕ € 7

Rest – *(dinner only) (number of covers limited, pre-book)* Carte € 26/33

◆ Building inspired by regional design with simple but cosy bedrooms, in a country style. The bedrooms on the top floor have sloping roofs. Attractive shaded garden. Lot specialities in this discreetly rustic restaurant warmed by an open fireplace.

CABRIÈRES – 30 Gard – 339 L5 – pop. 1 309 – alt. 120 m – ✉ 30210 23 D2

Paris 695 – Avignon 33 – Alès 64 – Arles 40 – Nîmes 15 – Orange 45 – Pont-St-Esprit 52

L'Enclos des Lauriers Roses rm,

71 r. du 14-Juillet – ✆ 04 66 75 25 42 – www.hotel-lauriersroses.com – reception@hotel-lauriersroses.com – Fax 04 66 75 25 21 – Open 14 March-7 November

20 rm – †€ 80/110 ††€ 80/110, ☕ € 12 – 2 suites – ½ P € 70/95

Rest – Menu € 24/43 – Carte € 33/50

◆ Buildings typical of the Gard region in the village overlooking an attractive garden with five varieties of oleander. Stylish, Provençal rooms, most of which have a terrace. A restaurant decorated in Provençal style serving classic and regional cuisine.

CABRIÈRES-D'AVIGNON – 84 Vaucluse – 332 D10 – pop. 1 744 – alt. 167 m – ✉ 84220 Provence 42 E1

Paris 715 – Aix-en-Provence 74 – Avignon 34 – Marseille 88

La Bastide de Voulonne rest, VISA MC

D 148 – ✆ 04 90 76 77 55 – www.bastide-voulonne.com – contact@bastide-voulonne.com – Fax 04 90 76 77 56 – Open from mid February to mid November

13 rm – †€ 90/149 ††€ 90/149, ☕ € 12 – ½ P € 86/113

Rest – *(closed Sunday except from June to September) (dinner only) (residents only)* Menu € 32

◆ In open country, this 1764 farmhouse among vines and fruit trees has been well restored. Smart, well-presented rooms, friendly welcome and themed itineraries. Evenings only set menu (regional fare) served at communal tables; shady terrace.

Le Vieux Bistrot with rm rm, VISA MC

Grande-Rue – ✆ 04 90 76 82 08 – www.vieuxbistrot.com – resa@vieuxbistrot.com – Fax 04 90 76 98 98 – Closed 1st-15 December and 1st-20 January, lunch from June to September, Saturday lunch, Sunday and Monday

5 rm ☕ – †€ 65/100 ††€ 65/100 **Rest** – Menu (€ 15), € 28/37 – Carte € 28/47

◆ This authentic bistro occupies a charming village house. Well-preserved, stylish decor with mirrors, old posters and original bar. Friendly atmosphere and updated regional menu. Smart, personalised rooms, with terraces on the top floor.

CABRIS – 06 Alpes-Maritimes – 341 C6 – see Grasse

CADEROUSSE – 84 Vaucluse – 332 B9 – pop. 2 712 – alt. 40 m – ✉ 84860 42 E1

Paris 667 – Marseille 124 – Avignon 28 – Nîmes 65 – Arles 92

La Bastide des Princes VISA MC

chemin de Bigonnet – ✆ 04 90 51 04 59 – www.bastide-princes.com – paumel.pierre@orange.fr – Fax 04 90 51 04 59 – Open 8 April to 15 November

5 rm ☕ – †€ 109/120 ††€ 109/135 **Table d'hôte** – Menu € 45 bi/110 bi

◆ A blissful sojourn awaits you at Pierre Paumel, Master Chef of France, in a stylish 17C abode set in parkland. Tastefully stylish rooms, pool and relaxation area. The chef concocts delicious seasonal recipes, the secrets of which he shares during cookery lessons.

LA CADIÈRE-D'AZUR – 83 Var – 340 J6 – pop. 4 239 – alt. 144 m – ✉ 83740 French Riviera 40 B3

Paris 815 – Aix-en-Provence 66 – Brignoles 53 – Marseille 45 – Toulon 22

Office de tourisme, place Général-de-Gaulle ✆ 04 94 90 12 56, Fax 04 94 98 30 13

≤★ - Le Castelet: Village★ Northeast: 4 km.

Hostellerie Bérard (René et Jean-François Bérard) VISA MC AE

av. Gabriel-Péri – ✆ 04 94 90 11 43 – www.hotel-berard.com – berard@hotel-berard.com – Fax 04 94 90 01 94 – Closed 4 January-13 February

35 rm – †€ 93/174 ††€ 93/174, ☕ € 20 – 2 suites – ½ P € 133/173

Rest – *(closed Tuesday except dinner from 15 May to 1st October and Monday)* Menu € 49/146 – Carte € 86/130

Rest *Le Petit Jardin* – *(closed Thursday except for dinner from 10 July to 1st September and Wednesday)* Carte € 31/52

Spec. Salade de homard version contemporaine. Poulette de Bresse rôtie à la broche, fourrée sous la peau à la brousse d'herbes. Figues gratinées au miel de romarin (autumn-winter). **Wines** Bandol, Côtes de Provence.

◆ This family hostelry, comprised of characterful houses, including an 11C convent, provides the backdrop for beautifully decorated Provençal rooms. Magnificent Gallo-Roman inspired spa. Restaurant overlooking Bandol's vineyards. Lovely terrace and updated cuisine. Le Petit Jardin is ideal for a quick snack.

CADILLAC – 33 Gironde – 335 J7 – pop. 2 435 – alt. 16 m – ✉ 33410 3 **B2**
Atlantic Coast

Paris 607 – Bordeaux 41 – Langon 12 – Libourne 40

Office de tourisme, 9, place de la Libération ✆ 05 56 62 12 92, Fax 05 56 76 99 72

Du Château de la Tour rm, VISA AE
av. de la libération, (D 10) – ✆ 05 56 76 92 00 – www.hotel-restaurant-chateaudelatour.com – contact@hotel-restaurant-chateaudelatour.com – Fax 05 56 62 11 59
32 rm – €75/105 €90/145, ☕ €11
Rest – *(closed Sunday dinner from November to February)* Menu (€15), €28/55 – Carte €36/53
◆ This gradually updated hotel built in the old kitchen garden of the Dukes of Épernon offers modern rooms, sauna and jacuzzi. Riverside park. A restaurant with roof beams, summer terrace, traditional menu and regional specialities.

CAEN Ⓟ – 14 Calvados – 303 J4 – pop. 108 900 – Built-up area 199 490 – alt. 25 m – ✉ 14000 Normandy 32 **B2**

Paris 236 – Alençon 105 – Cherbourg 125 – Le Havre 91 – Rennes 189

Caen-Carpiquet: ✆ 02 31 71 20 10, by D 9: 7 km.

Office de tourisme, 12, place Saint-Pierre ✆ 02 31 27 14 14, Fax 02 31 27 14 13

de Caen Biéville-Beuville Le Vallon, N : 5 km on D 60, ✆ 02 31 94 72 09

de Garcelles Garcelles-Secqueville Route de Lorguichon, 15 km on the Falaise road, ✆ 02 31 39 09 09

Abbaye aux Hommes★★: St-Etienne church ★★ - Abbaye aux Dames★: La Trinité church ★★ - Apse★★, frieze★★ and vaults★★ of St-Pierre church ★ - St-Nicolas church and cemetery ★ - Lantern tower★ St-Jean church EZ - Hôtel d'Escoville★ DY **B** - Old houses★ (n° 52 and 54 rue St-Pierre) DY **K** - Musée des Beaux-Arts★★ in the château★ DX **M¹** - Memorial★★★ AV - Musée de Normandie★ DX **M²**.

Plans on following pages

Le Dauphin rm, VISA AE
29 r. Gemare – ✆ 02 31 86 22 26 – www.le-dauphin-normandie.com – dauphin.caen@wanadoo.fr – Fax 02 31 86 35 14 DY **a**
37 rm – €80/185 €90/190, ☕ €14 – ½ P €85/130
Rest – *(closed 23 July-10 August, 26 October-4 November, 15-21 February, Saturday lunch and Sunday)* Menu (€19), €23 (weekdays)/56 – Carte €40/80
◆ An old priory near the château walls. Personalised rooms, some with age-old beams and period furniture. A pleasant stylish dining room and classic cuisine with a regional touch. A Norman setting in the adjoining lounge bar.

Moderne without rest VISA AE
116 bd Mar.-Leclerc – ✆ 02 31 86 04 23 – www.hotel-caen.com – info@hotel-caen.com – Fax 02 31 85 37 93 DY **d**
40 rm – €85/120 €100/260, ☕ €14
◆ Discreet post war building with regularly spruced up rooms. A view over the town rooftops from the 5th floor breakfast room.

Mercure Port de Plaisance without rest VISA AE
1 r. Courtonne – ✆ 02 31 47 24 24 – www.mercure.com – h0869@accor.com – Fax 02 31 47 43 88 EY **b**
126 rm – €89/160 €89/180, ☕ €15 – 3 suites
◆ This chain hotel faces the marina. Artwork adorns the lobby. Cosy guestrooms, gradually being refurbished in a tasteful manner.

Des Quatrans without rest VISA
17 r. Gemare – ✆ 02 31 86 25 57 – www.hotel-des-quatrans.com – contact@hotel-des-quatrans.com – Fax 02 31 85 27 80 DY **p**
47 rm – €57 €66, ☕ €8
◆ Ideally located in the heart of the town centre near the castle. Lobby, sitting room and cosy bar. Regularly refurbished rooms (quieter to the rear) in warm colours.

Du Château without rest
5 av. du 6-Juin – ✆ 02 31 86 15 37 – www.hotel-chateau-caen.com – hotel-chateau-caen@wanadoo.fr – Fax 02 31 86 58 08 EY **n**
24 rm – €50 €60, €8
◆ A well situated hotel between the marina and the castle. Small but pleasantly decorated rooms in pastel colours. Friendly and welcoming.

Du Havre without rest
11 r. du Havre – ✆ 02 31 86 19 80 – www.hotelduhavre.com – resa@hotelduhavre.com – Fax 02 31 38 87 67 – Closed 17 December-3 January
19 rm – €48 €55/60, €8 EZ **v**
◆ Extremely well kept and reasonably priced, this regularly refurbished family hotel has practical if not luxurious rooms. Those at the rear are quieter. Friendly welcome.

Bristol without rest
31 r. 11-Novembre – ✆ 02 31 84 59 76 – www.hotelbristolcaen.com – hotelbristol@wanadoo.fr – Fax 02 31 52 29 28 EZ **s**
24 rm – €55/70 €70/90, €8
◆ Located near the racetrack and station, this hotel built in 1955 offers small, well-kept rooms, which are quieter to the rear. Buffet breakfast.

De France without rest
10 r. de la Gare – ✆ 02 31 52 16 99 – www.hoteldefrance-caen.com – contact@hoteldefrance-caen.com – Fax 02 31 83 23 16 EZ **e**
47 rm – €64/93 €64/93, €9
◆ This renovated establishment is two minutes from the station. It has clean and simple medium sized rooms with excellent bedding, wood veneer furniture and double-glazing.

Le Pressoir
3 av. H.-Chéron – ✆ 02 31 73 32 71 – www.restaurant-le-pressoir.com – info@restaurant-le-pressoir.com – Fax 02 31 26 76 64 – Closed 8-15 August, Sunday dinner, Saturday lunch and Monday AV **v**
Rest – Menu €33 (weekday lunch), €49/75 – Carte €60/75
◆ This prettily restored old house – once the post house – has a contemporary feel and is located in the suburbs of the town. Conservatory. Up-to-date cuisine.

Incognito (Stéphane Carbone)
14 r. de la Courtonne – ✆ 02 31 28 36 60 – www.restaurant-incognito.fr – reservation@restaurant-incognito.fr – Fax 02 31 53 75 58 – Closed August, Saturday lunch and Sunday EY **u**
Rest – Menu (€26), €29 (lunch), €39/95 – Carte €45/85
Spec. Foie gras de canard poêlé, réduction de vinaigre balsamique. Saint-Pierre à l'étuvée, infusion pomme-citronnelle. L'intemporel baba au rhum et ananas Victoria.
◆ Contemporary restaurant near the St-Pierre basin. The chef concocts tasty dishes inspired by the local catch and the seasons. Pleasant terrace-smoking room.

La Normande
41 bd du Mar.-Leclerc – ✆ 02 31 30 10 40 – brasserielanormande@hotmail.fr – Fax 02 31 30 10 41 DY **j**
Rest – Menu €18 bi/28 – Carte €35/55
◆ Smart brasserie in the heart of Caen very close to the theatre. Popular with a business clientele for its tasty cuisine and light surroundings (veranda, 1900-inspired fresco).

ArchiDona
9 r. Gémare – ✆ 02 31 85 30 30 – www.archidona.fr – contact@archidona.fr – Fax 02 31 85 27 80 – Closed 1st-15 August, Sunday and Monday DY **h**
Rest – Menu (€14), €18 (weekday lunch), €25/46 – Carte €30/42
◆ This restaurant takes its name from an Andalusian town and is located near the château. Sleek, simple setting, dimmed lighting and modern cuisine.

Villa Eugène
75 bd André-Detolle – ✆ 02 31 75 12 12 – info@villa-eugene.fr – Fax 02 31 74 43 04 – Closed Saturday lunch, Sunday and bank holidays
Rest – Menu (€16), €21 (lunch) – Carte €28/40 AV **q**
◆ This new restaurant sports an attractive, trendy plum coloured decor and pleasant terrace. Up-to-date menu, interesting wine list.

CAEN

Baladas (Bd des) . . . . AV 6	Côte-de-Nacre (Av. de la) . . . AV 24	Pasteur (R. L.) . . . . BV 63
Chemin-vert (R. du) . . . . AV 19	Courseulles (Av. de) . . . . AV 25	Père-Ch.-de-Foucault (Av.) . . AV 64
Chéron (Av. Henri) . . . . AV 20	Délivrande (R. de la) . . . . AV 29	Poincaré (Bd R.) . . . . BV 66
Clemenceau (Av. G.) . . . . . . BV 22	Demi-Lune (Pl. de la) . . . . . . BV 30	Pompidou (Bd G.) . . . . AV 67
Copernic (Av. N.) . . . . ABV 23	Lyautey (Bd Mar.) . . . . AV 53	Rethel (Bd de) . . . . BV 70
	Montalivet (Cours) . . . . BV 59	Richemond (Bd) . . . . AV 71
	Montgomery (Av. Mar.) . . . . AV 60	Rouen (Av. de) . . . . BV 95
	Mountbatten (Av. Am.) . . . . AV 62	Trouville (Rte de) . . . . BV 84

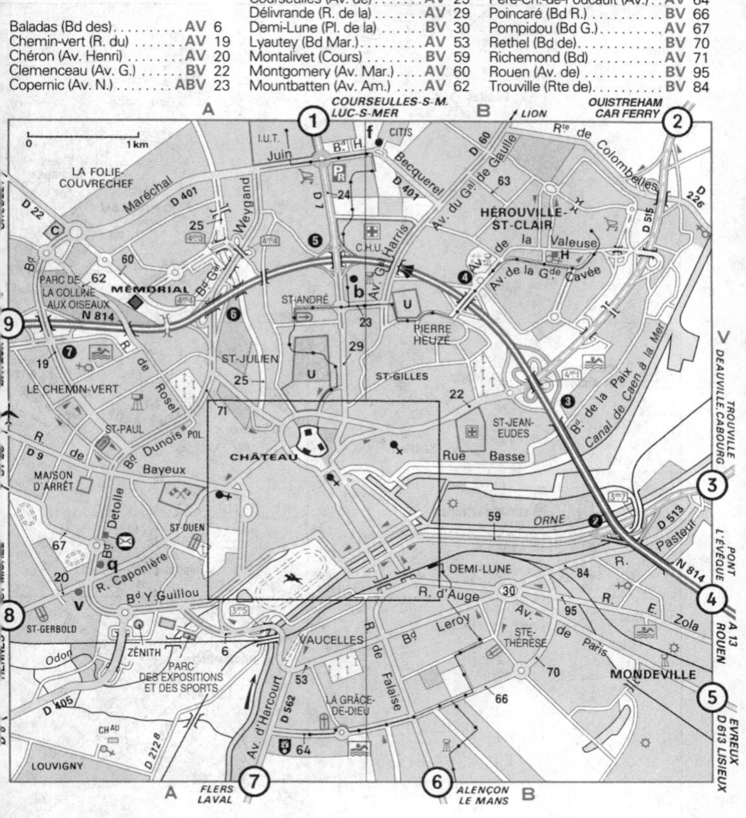

XX Le Carlotta

16 quai Vendeuvre – ✆ 02 31 86 68 99 – www.lecarlotta.fr – Fax 02 31 38 92 31 – Closed Sunday EY **m**

Rest – Menu € 23 (weekdays)/37 – Carte € 42/48

◆ Large Art Deco inspired brasserie, popular for its lively atmosphere and brasserie style menu, enriched with fish dishes. Summer veranda overlooking the harbour.

X Café Mancel

at the Château – ✆ 02 31 86 63 64 – www.cafemancel.com – cafe.mancel@wanadoo.fr – Fax 02 31 86 63 40 – Closed February school holidays, Sunday dinner and Monday DX **t**

Rest – Menu (€ 17), € 23/34 – Carte € 26/39

◆ The café of the musée des Beaux-Arts, situated within the Château, is certainly worth a visit: sober, modern setting, terrace, musical evenings and above all appetising, contemporary dishes.

X Pub William's

13 r. Prairies-St-Gilles – ✆ 02 31 93 45 52 – pubwilliams@aol.com – Fax 02 31 93 45 52 – Closed 3-23 August and Sunday EY **t**

Rest – Menu (€ 18), € 23/33 – Carte € 26/50

◆ This welcoming pub is close to Saint Pierre marina. Wooden bar, beams, fireplace and reproductions of the Bayeux tapestry set the scene. Traditional seasonal slate menu.

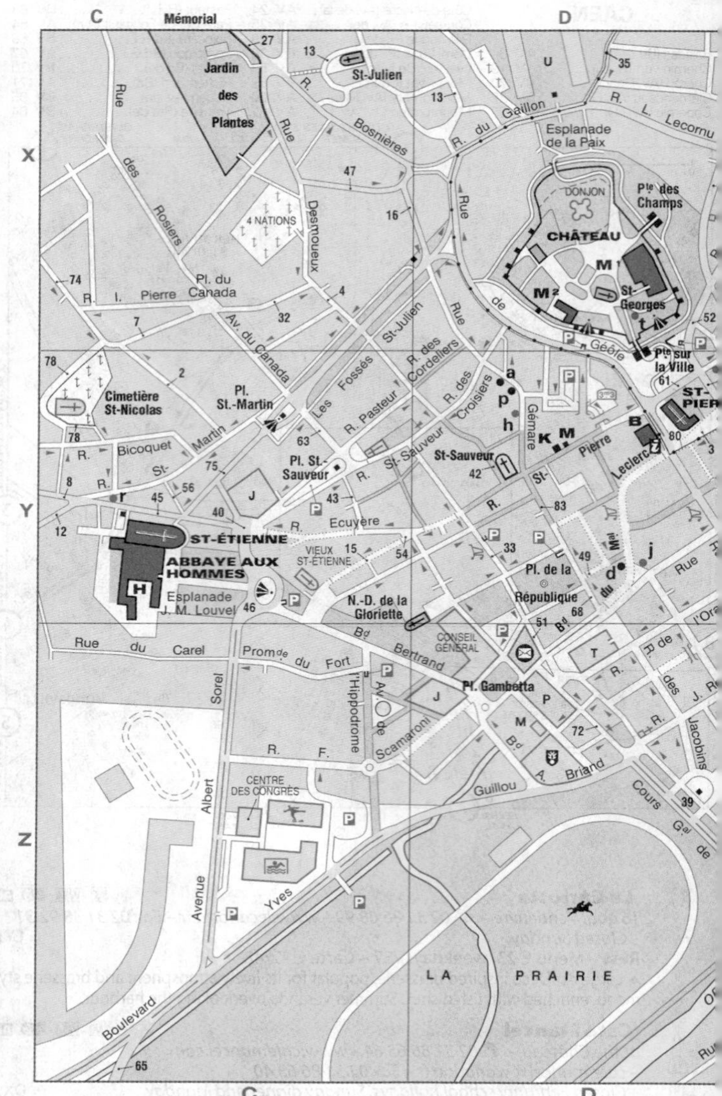

Pain et Beurre AC VISA

46 r. Guillaume-le-Conquérant – ✆ 02 31 86 04 57
– Closed 1st-20 August, Saturday lunch, Sunday dinner and Monday CY **r**
Rest – Menu (€ 22), € 28

◆ Near Saint Etienne church and the Abbaye aux Hommes, this three-storey house has been refurbished in a minimalist style. Fusion menu using seasonal produce.

CAEN

Street	Grid	No.
Académie (R. de l')	CY	2
Alliés (Bd des)	DY	3
Bagatelle (Av. de)	CX	4
Barbey-d'Aurevilly (R.)	CX	7
Bayeux (R. de)	CX	8
Bir-Hakeim (Pont de)	EZ	9
Brunet (R. H.)	EYZ	10
Caponière (R.)	CY	12
Carrières-St-Julien (R. des)	CDX	13
Caumont (R. A. de)	CY	15
Chanoine X. de St-Paul (R.)	CDX	16
Chaussée-Ferrée (R. de la)	EZ	18
Churchill (Pont)	EZ	21
Courtonne (Pl.)	EY	26
Creully (Av. de)	CX	27
Decaen (R. Gén.)	EZ	28
Délivrande (R. de la)	DX	29
Docteur-Rayer (R.)	CX	32
Doumer (R. Paul)	DY	33
Écuyère (R.)	CY	
Édimbourg (Av. d')	DX	35
Falaise (R. de)	EZ	38
Foch (Pl. Mar.)	DZ	39
Fontette (Pl.)	CY	40
Froide (R.)	DY	42
Fromages (R. aux)	CY	43
Guillaume-le-Conquérant (R.)	CY	45
Guillouard (Pl. L.)	CY	46
Juifs (R. aux)	CX	47
Lair (R. P.-A.)	DY	49
Lebisey (R. de)	EX	50
Lebret (R. G.)	DYZ	51
Leclerc (Bd Mar.)	DYZ	
Libération (Av. de la)	DXY	52
Malherbe (Pl.)	CDY	54
Manissier (R.)	EX	55
Marot (R. J.)	CY	56
Meslin (Q. E.)	EZ	57
Miséricorde (R. de la)	EYZ	58
Montalivet (Cours)	EZ	59
Montoir-Poissonnerie (R.)	DY	61
Pémagnie (R.)	CX	63
Petit-Vallerent (Bd du)	CZ	65
Pont-St-Jacques (R. du)	DY	68
Reine-Mathilde (Pl.)	EX	69
Sadi-Carnot (R.)	DZ	72
St-Gabriel (R.)	CX	74
St-Jean (R.)	DEYZ	
St-Manvieu (R.)	CY	75
St-Michel (R.)	EZ	77
St-Nicolas (R.)	CY	78
St-Pierre (Pl.)	DY	80
St-Pierre (R.)	DY	
Sévigné (Prom. de)	EZ	81
Strasbourg (R. de)	DY	83
Vaucelles (R. de)	EZ	85
Vaugueux (R. du)	DX	86
6-Juin (Av. du)	DEYZ	
11-Novembre (R. du)	DEZ	90

Le Bouchon du Vaugueux

VISA MC

12 r. Graindorge – ✆ 02 31 44 26 26
– Closed 9-24 August, Sunday and Monday DY **g**

Rest – bistro – *(pre-book)* Menu € 18 (weekdays)/26 – Carte approx. € 30

◆ This pleasant, deceptively simple Lyon-style bistro serves up-to-date dishes with a seasonal slant. Selection of small vineyard wines chalked on a slate.

to Caen-Université interchange (ring road slip road, exit n° 5) – ✉ 14000 Caen

Novotel Côte de Nacre VISA AE
av. de la Côte-de-Nacre – ☎ 02 31 43 42 00 – www.novotel.com – h0405@accor.com – Fax 02 31 44 07 28 AV **b**
126 rm – €75/139 €75/139, ☕ €14 **Rest** – Menu (€20) – Carte €24/40
◆ Near the main thoroughfares, a modern hotel where most of the rooms have been renovated in line with the hotel chain's standards. Restaurant serving the Novotel Café set menu. Minimalist setting overlooking the pool. Nice lounge bar.

in Hérouville St-Clair 3 km Northeast – pop. 23 000 – alt. 20 m – ✉ 14200

Mercure Côte de Nacre rest, VISA AE
2 pl. Boston-Citis – ☎ 02 31 44 05 05 – www.mercure.com – h5712@accor.com – Fax 02 31 44 95 94 BV **f**
88 rm – €90 €110, ☕ €14
Rest – *(closed 24 December-3 January, Saturday lunch and Sunday lunch)*
Menu (€16), €20 (weekdays)/23 – Carte €30/44
◆ Near the Caen Memorial in the heart of the office district. Find well-kept, functional rooms and a pleasant, cosy lounge-bar. English-style decor in the restaurant where maroon tones dominate. Traditional menu.

in Bénouville 10 km by ② – pop. 1 924 – alt. 8 m – ✉ 14970
Château★: main staircase★★ - Pegasus Bridge★.

La Glycine AC rest, VISA AE
11 pl. Commando-n° 4, (opposite church) – ☎ 02 31 44 61 94 – www.la-glycine.com – la-glycine@wanadoo.fr – Fax 02 31 43 67 30 – Closed 20 Dec.-10 Jan.
35 rm – €58 €68, ☕ €8,50 – ½ P €68
Rest – *(closed Sunday dinner October-April)* Menu €20 (weekdays)/58 – Carte €38/60
◆ The famous Pegasus Bridge disputed during D Day is near these two houses linked by a flowered patio. The recent guestrooms in the wing are more modern and minimalist. A contemporary dining room. Traditional dishes.

Le Manoir d'Hastings et la Pommeraie with rm VISA
18 av. Côte-de-Nacre, (near the church) – ☎ 02 31 44 62 43 – www.manoirhastings.com – contact@manoirhastings.com – Fax 02 31 44 76 18
15 rm – €75/80 €90/95, ☕ €12 – ½ P €80/90
Rest – Menu (€22), €28 (weekday lunch), €35/65 – Carte €64/85
◆ A rustic dining room, veranda and charming rooms on the priory side (17C), more functional facilities in the more recent building. Traditional cuisine. Tree-lined garden.

in Fleury-sur-Orne 4 km by ⑦ – pop. 4 014 – alt. 33 m – ✉ 14123

Auberge de l'Île Enchantée VISA
1 r. St-André, (beside the Orne) – ☎ 02 31 52 15 52 – www.aubergelileenchantee.com – auberge-ile-enchantee@wanadoo.fr – Fax 02 31 72 67 17 – Closed 4-10 August, Wednesday dinner, Sunday dinner and Monday
Rest – Menu (€15), €19 (weekdays)/42 – Carte €40/56
◆ Old fishermens' bar dating from the 1930s, now a half-timbered inn, partly covered in Virginia creeper. The country-style dining rooms overlook the Orne river. Modern dishes.

CAGNES-SUR-MER – 06 Alpes-Maritimes – **341** D6 – pop. 48 800 – alt. 20 m – Casino – ✉ 06800 French Riviera 42 **E2**
Paris 915 – Antibes 11 – Cannes 21 – Grasse 25 – Nice 13 – Vence 9
Office de tourisme, 6, boulevard Maréchal Juin ☎ 04 93 20 61 64, Fax 04 93 20 52 63
Haut-de-Cagnes★ - Château-museum★: patio★★, ✳★ of the tower - Musée Renoir.

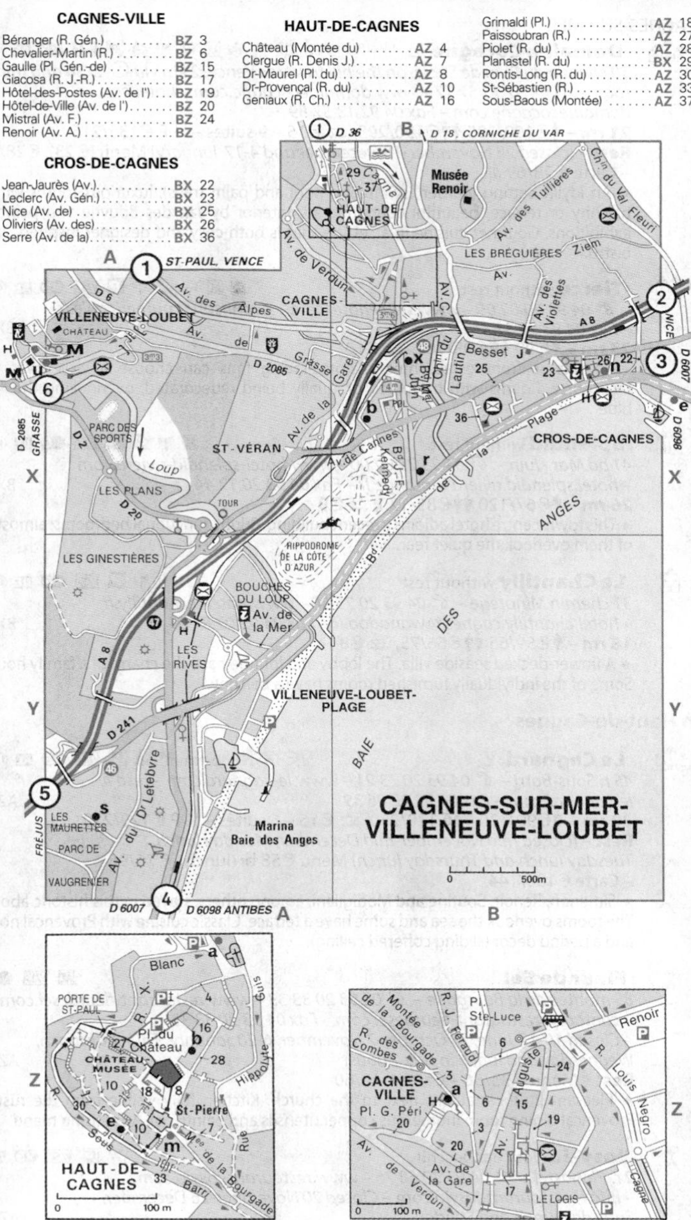
CAGNES-VILLE
Béranger (R. Gén.) . . . . BZ 3
Chevalier-Martin (R.) . . . . BZ 6
Gaulle (Pl. Gén.-de) . . . . BZ 15
Giacosa (R. J.-R.) . . . . BZ 17
Hôtel-des-Postes (Av. de l') . . . BZ 19
Hôtel-de-Ville (Av. de l') . . . . BZ 20
Mistral (Av. F.) . . . . BZ 24
Renoir (Av. A.) . . . . BZ
CROS-DE-CAGNES
Jean-Jaurès (Av.) . . . . BX 22
Leclerc (Av. Gén.) . . . . BX 23
Nice (Av. de) . . . . BX 25
Oliviers (Av. des) . . . . BX 26
Serre (Av. de la) . . . . BX 36
HAUT-DE-CAGNES
Château (Montée du) . . . . AZ 4
Clergue (R. Denis J.) . . . . AZ 7
Dr-Maurel (Pl. du) . . . . AZ 8
Dr-Provençal (R. du) . . . . AZ 10
Geniaux (R. Ch.) . . . . AZ 16
Grimaldi (Pl.) . . . . AZ 18
Paissoubran (R.) . . . . AZ 27
Piolet (R. du) . . . . AZ 28
Planastel (R. du) . . . . BX 29
Pontis-Long (R. du) . . . . AZ 30
St-Sébastien (R.) . . . . AZ 33
Sous-Baous (Montée) . . . . AZ 37
D 36
D 18, CORNICHE DU VAR
ST-PAUL, VENCE
Musée Renoir
HAUT-DE-CAGNES
CAGNES-VILLE
VILLENEUVE-LOUBET
CHÂTEAU
LES BRÉGUIÈRES
Av. des Tuillières
Ch^in du Val Fleuri
Av. des Alpes
Av. de Verdun
Av. de Grasse
D 2085
Av. de la Gare
Av. des Violettes
Lautin
Besset
A 8
NICE
D 6007
D 6098
CROS-DE-CAGNES
PARC DES SPORTS
Loup
ST-VÉRAN
LES PLANS
TOUR
Av. de Cannes
Bd J.-F. Kennedy
Bd de la Plage
ANGES
RIPPODROME DE LA CÔTE D'AZUR
LES GINESTIÈRES
BOUCHES DU LOUP
Av. de la Mer
LES RIVES
DES
VILLENEUVE-LOUBET-PLAGE
BAIE
D 241
FRÉJUS
GRASSE
LES MAURETTES
PARC DE VAUGRENIER
Av. du Dr Lefebvre
Marina Baie des Anges
CAGNES-SUR-MER-VILLENEUVE-LOUBET
0 500m
D 6007
D 6098 ANTIBES
Blanc
PORTE DE ST-PAUL
Pl. du Château
CHÂTEAU-MUSÉE
St-Pierre
Rue Hippolyte Guis
M^ée de la Bourgade
Sous Barri
HAUT-DE-CAGNES
0 100 m
Montée de la Bourgade
R. J. Féraud
Pl. Ste-Luce
R. des Combes
Renoir
R. Louis Négro
CAGNES-VILLE
Pl. G. Péri
Av. Auguste
Av. de Verdun
Av. de la Gare
LE LOGIS
Cagne
0 100 m

Domaine Cocagne

30 chemin du Pain de Sucre, on the hill towards Vence, 2 km via ①, D 36 and minor road – ☎ 04 92 13 57 77 – www.domainecocagne.com – hotel@domainecocagne.com – Fax 04 92 13 57 89

21 rm – €190/295 €190/295, ☕ €15 – 9 suites – ½ P €135/215

Rest – *(closed 28 November-18 December and 4-17 January)* Menu (€23), €28/92 – Carte €28/69

◆ An idyllic setting (garden, swimming pool and palm trees), luxurious rooms with a balcony or terrace, beautiful contemporary interior by Jan des Bouvrie and painting exhibitions. Gourmet cuisine in a setting that is both cosy and designer inspired. New bistro.

Tiercé without rest

– ☎ 04 93 20 02 09 – www.tiercehotel.com – dvannson@numericable.fr – Fax 04 93 29 31 44 BX **r**

23 rm – €90 €98/161, ☕ €10

◆ In this seafront establishment, horse-racing fans can choose a view over the racecourse. Rooms with balconies, gradually being redecorated, overlooking the "big blue".

Splendid without rest

41 bd Mar.-Juin – ☎ 04 93 22 02 00 – www.hotel-splendid-riviera.com – hotel.splendid.riviera@orange.fr – Fax 04 93 20 12 44 BX **x**

26 rm – €67/120 €83/120, ☕ €9

◆ This town-centre hotel adjoins a recent building. Bright, functional bedrooms; almost all of them overlook the quiet rear.

Le Chantilly without rest

31 chemin Minoterie – ☎ 04 93 20 25 50 – www.hotel-lechantilly.fr – hotel.chantilly.cagnes@wanadoo.fr – Fax 04 92 02 82 63 BX **b**

18 rm – €59/65 €66/75, ☕ €8

◆ A flower-decked seaside villa. The lobby and lounge have the charm of a family house. Some of the individually furnished rooms have a balcony.

in Haut-de-Cagnes

Le Cagnard

rm,

45 r. Sous-Barri – ☎ 04 93 20 73 21 – www.le-cagnard.com – resa@le-cagnard.com – Fax 04 93 22 06 39 AZ **e**

20 rm – €90/130 €120/250, ☕ €16 – 6 suites – ½ P €120/210

Rest – *(closed mid November-mid December, Monday lunch, Tuesday lunch and Thursday lunch)* Menu €58 bi (lunch), €76/96 – Carte €106/144

◆ Simenon, Renoir, Soutine and Modigliani, among others, stayed in this historic abode. The rooms overlook the sea and some have a terrace. Classic cuisine with Provençal notes and a period decor (sliding coffered ceiling).

Fleur de Sel

85 montée de la Bourgade – ☎ 04 93 20 33 33 – www.restaurant-fleurdesel.com – contact@restaurant-fleurdesel.com – Fax 04 93 20 33 33 – Closed 10-17 June, 25 October-7 November, 6-20 January, Thursday lunch, Wednesday and lunch in July-August AZ **m**

Rest – Menu €33/56 – Carte €45/60

◆ Pleasant little restaurant next to the church. Kitchen fully visible from the rustic/Provençal dining room (numerous copper utensils and paintings). Appetising menu.

Josy-Jo (Josy Bandecchi)

2 r. Planastel – ☎ 04 93 20 68 76 – www.restaurant-josyjo.com – info@restaurant-josyjo.com – Closed 20 November-26 December, Saturday lunch and Sunday AZ **a**

Rest – Menu €29 bi (lunch)/40 – Carte €45/80

Spec. Farcis grand' mère. Grillades au charbon de bois. Mousse aux citrons du pays. **Wines** Côtes de Provence, Vin de Pays des Alpes Maritimes.

◆ A simple yet friendly setting with old stone walls, paintings, ironware and a view of the kitchen. No fuss service, fine grills and good Provençal dishes.

in Cros-de-Cagnes 2 km southeast – ✉ 06800 Cagnes-sur-Mer

XXX **La Bourride**
(Cros port) – ☎ 04 93 31 07 75 – Fax 04 93 31 89 11 – Closed February holidays, Tuesday dinner and Wednesday BX **e**
Rest – Menu € 39 – Carte € 64/84
◆ A dining room decorated with a mural depicting the sea, a patio with umbrella pines and a terrace opposite the harbour: three delightful spaces to taste fish and seafood.

XX **Réserve "Loulou"**
91 bd de la Plage – ☎ 04 93 31 00 17 – louloulareserve@wanadoo.fr – Fax 04 93 22 09 26 – Closed 10-25 May, lunch 15 July-6 September, Saturday lunch and Sunday BX **n**
Rest – Menu 42 – Carte € 48/80
◆ A pretty regional setting, paintings and lithographs as decoration, fish and grills prepared in front of you: an enticingly relaxed establishment.

CAHORS P – **46 Lot** – **337** E5 – **pop. 20 300** – **alt. 135 m** – ✉ **46000** 28 **B1**
Dordogne-Berry-Limousin

Paris 575 – Agen 85 – Albi 110 – Brive-la-Gaillarde 98 – Montauban 64

Office de tourisme, place François Mitterrand ☎ 05 65 53 20 65, Fax 05 65 53 20 74

Pont Valentré★★ - North portal ★★ and cloister★ of St-Etienne cathedral ★BY **E** - ≤★ of Cabessut bridge - Croix de Magne ≤★ West: 5 km by D 27 - Barbican and tour St-Jean★ - ≤★ from north of town.

Plan on following page

Terminus
5 av. Ch.-de-Freycinet – ☎ 05 65 53 32 00 – www.balandre.com – terminus.balandre@wanadoo.fr – Fax 05 65 53 32 26 – Closed 15-30 November AY **s**
22 rm – †€ 55/100 ††€ 65/160, ☐ € 12
Rest ***Le Balandre*** – see restaurant listing
◆ In theory, everyone should end up at The Terminus! An impressive 1910 house home to large, clean and soundproofed rooms. Art Deco lounge bar.

Jean XXII without rest
2 r. E. Albe – ☎ 05 65 35 07 66 – www.hotel-jeanxxii.com – Fax 05 65 53 92 38 – Closed in November, in February and Sunday from October to May BY **v**
9 rm – †€ 45/55 ††€ 55/61, ☐ € 7,50
◆ Practically located and quiet hotel near the John XXII tower. The walls of this palace, built by the Pope's family, are home to gradually refurbished rooms.

De la Paix without rest
30 pl. St-Maurice – ☎ 05 65 35 03 40 – www.hoteldelapaix-cahors.com – hoteldelapaix-cahors@wanadoo.fr – Fax 05 65 35 40 88 BZ **t**
21 rm – †€ 48/54 ††€ 54/75, ☐ € 6
◆ In the wake of a full makeover, this small central hotel is once again proud to offer quiet, simple and practical rooms. The most cheerful overlook the market.

XXX **Le Balandre** – Hôtel Terminus
5 av. Ch.-de-Freycinet – ☎ 05 65 53 32 00 – www.balandre.com – terminus.balandre@wanadoo.fr – Fax 05 65 53 32 26 – Closed 15-30 November, Sunday except bank holidays and Monday AY **s**
Rest – Menu € 31 (lunch)/60 – Carte € 60/72
◆ The chef enthusiastically prepares up-to-date dishes, served in an elegant room adorned with stained glass. Magnificent wine list and a simpler lunchtime menu.

XX **L'Ô à la Bouche**
134 r. Ste-Urcisse – ☎ 05 65 35 65 69 – dive264@orange.fr – Closed Easter holidays, autumn half-term holidays, Sunday and Monday BZ **a**
Rest – Menu (€ 19 bi), € 26/37 – Carte € 29/35
◆ Up-to-date menu to the delight of gourmets! Old stone, brickwork, beams and a fireplace lend undeniable character to this restaurant, renowned for its mouth-watering fare.

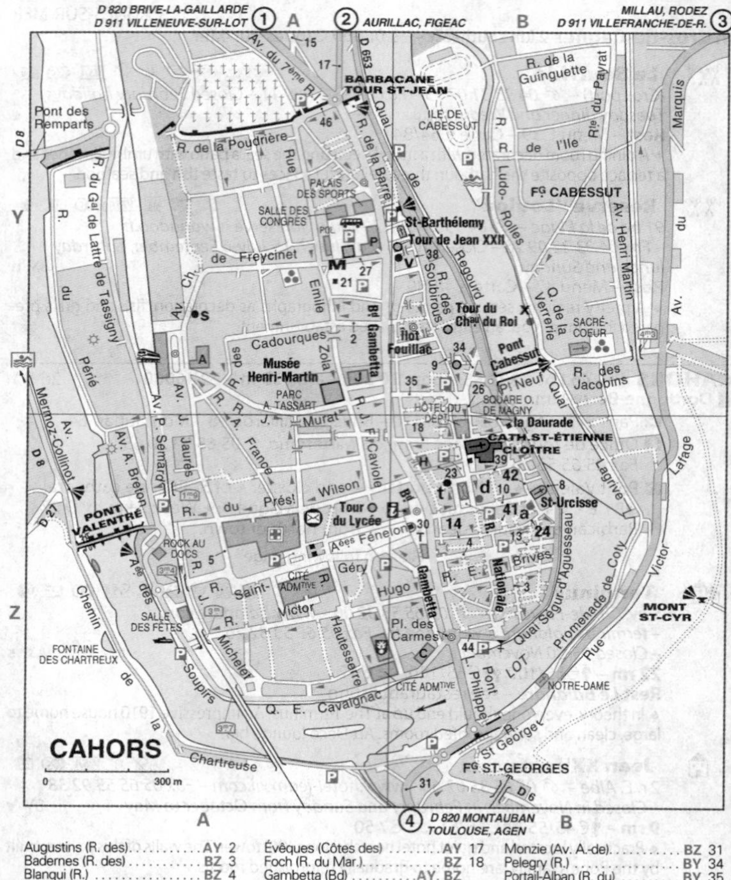

Le Marché

27 pl. Chapou – ☏ 05 65 35 27 27 – www.restaurantlemarche.com – restaurant.le.marche@cegetel.net – Fax 05 65 21 09 98 – Closed 11-20 April, 25 October-11 November, Monday except August and Sunday BZ **d**

Rest – Menu (€ 16), € 19 (lunch), € 30/45

◆ An in vogue establishment, as much for its elongated room with beige and plum bench seating, a wall of light and one of slate, as for its fashionable and inspired cuisine.

Au Fil des Douceurs

90 quai de la Verrerie – ☏ 05 65 22 13 04 – Fax 05 65 35 61 09 – Closed 15 June-3 July, 2-25 January, Sunday and Monday BY **x**

Rest – Menu € 14 (weekday lunch), € 24/55 – Carte € 35/92

◆ Climb on board this boat and enjoy the stunning view of the Lot and old Cahors. Traditional fare served in two dining rooms, one above the other.

in Caillac 13 km by ①, Villeneuve-sur-Lot road and D145 – pop. 533 – alt. 161 m – ✉ 46140

XX **Le Vinois** with rm
Le bourg – ☎ 05 65 30 53 60 – www.levinois.com – contact@levinois.com – Fax 05 65 21 67 27 – Closed 5-19 October, 12 January-12 February
10 rm – €81/145 €88/145, ☕ €15 – ½ P €83/112
Rest – *(Closed Monday except dinner in July-August, Sunday dinner and Tuesday lunch)* Menu (€19), €35/58 – Carte €44/55
◆ In the heart of the Cahors vineyards, don't miss this stunning inn that sports a minimalist contemporary style in keeping with the cuisine. Jazz in the background. The hotel's rooms display a smart sobriety: personalised detail and a designer spirit.

in Mercuès 10 km by ① and D 811 – pop. 1 056 – alt. 133 m – ✉ 46090

Château de Mercuès
– ☎ 05 65 20 00 01 – www.chateaudemercues.com – mercues@relaischateaux.com – Fax 05 65 20 05 72 – Open from end March to early November
24 rm – €180 €190/380, ☕ €24 – 6 suites – ½ P €184/279
Rest – *(closed Tuesday lunch, Wednesday lunch, Thursday lunch and Monday)* Menu €65/120 – Carte €86/120
Spec. Foie gras de canard en terrine, marbré aux morilles et cuisses confites. Risotto de truffes au jus de céleri et croustille parmesane. Croustillant de fraises, crème brûlée à la vanille et sorbet litchi. **Wines** Cahors.
◆ Designer François Champsaur is behind the contemporary style of this historic 13C castle. Majestic bedrooms and a stunning view of the Lot Valley. The chef rustles up inventive meals in keeping with the designer decor.

Le Mas Azemar
r. du Mas-de-Vinssou – ☎ 05 65 30 96 85 – www.masazemar.com – masazemar@aol.com – Fax 05 65 30 53 82
5 rm ☕ – €97/107 €97/107 **Table d'hôte** – Menu €34 bi/42 bi
◆ This 18C residence, which was an outbuilding of the Château de Mercuès, today houses comfortable rooms with period furnishings. Wholesome home cooking served in a spacious, countrified and welcoming setting (beams, stonewalls, fireplace and large communal table).

Brive road by ① and D 820 – ✉ 46000 Cahors

XX **La Garenne**
St-Henri, 7 km – ☎ 05 65 35 40 67 – michel.carrendier@wanadoo.fr – Fax 05 65 35 40 67 – Closed 1st February-15 March, Monday dinner, Tuesday dinner and Wednesday
Rest – Menu €20 (weekday lunch), €28/50 – Carte €35/69
◆ You could almost believe you're in the stables of an old farmhouse! The cuisine is in keeping with this old-fashioned spirit, mixing classic recipes with regional influences.

in Lamagdelaine 7 km by ② – pop. 762 – alt. 122 m – ✉ 46090

XXX **Claude et Richard Marco** with rm
chemin des Ecoles – ☎ 05 65 35 30 64 – www.restaurantmarco.com – info@restaurantmarco.com – Fax 05 65 30 31 40 – Closed 11-21 October, 3 January-4 March, Sunday dinner from 15 September to 15 June, Monday except dinner from 15 June to 15 September and Tuesday lunch
5 rm – €110/145 €110/145, ☕ €12
Rest – Menu €30 (weekdays)/85 – Carte €54/84
Spec. Foie gras de canard à la braise sur fond d'artichaut et cèpes, jus de truffe crémé. Poêlée de sole, Saint-Jacques et langoustines aux cèpes, émulsion de safran (October to April). Déclinaison de fraises "mara des bois" (June to Sept.). **Wines** Cahors.
◆ Duck and regional produce take pride of place in the updated cuisine served in a handsome vaulted room (formerly the wine cellar) or on the terrace. Attractive bedrooms.

If breakfast is included the ☕ symbol appears after the number of rooms.

CAHUZAC-SUR-VÈRE – 81 Tarn – 338 D7 – pop. 1 022 – alt. 240 m – ✉ 81140 29 C2

Paris 655 – Albi 28 – Gaillac 11 – Montauban 60 – Rodez 86 – Toulouse 69

Syndicat d'initiative, Mairie ✆ 05 63 33 68 91, Fax 05 63 33 68 92

Château de Salettes

3 km south on the D 922 – ✆ 05 63 33 60 60 – www.chateaudesalettes.com – salettes@chateaudesalettes.com – Fax 05 63 33 60 61 – Closed 4-January-4 February

18 rm – €131/300 €145/330, €18 – ½ P €126/330

Rest – *(closed Sunday dinner, Wednesday lunch, Monday and Tuesday from October to April, Tuesday lunch and Monday in May-June and September, Monday lunch, Tuesday lunch, Wednesday lunch and Thursday lunch in July-August)* Menu €37 (weekdays)/80 – Carte €72/94

Spec. Anneau de biscuit café et Saint-Jacques. Canard aux dragées. Palet chocolat et nougatine au piment. **Wines** Gaillac.

◆ This 13C château in the heart of the vineyards has been entirely rebuilt. Beautiful modern decoration and designer furniture. Spacious rooms. The sleek decor provides an attractive backdrop for the chef's interesting cuisine. Tasting of the estate wines.

La Falaise (Guillaume Salvan)

rte de Cordes – ✆ 05 63 33 96 31 – www.lafalaiserestaurant.com – guillaume.salvan@orange.fr – Closed Sunday evening, Tuesday lunch and Monday

Rest – Menu (€17), €20 (weekday lunch), €31/57 – Carte €47/64

Spec. Rouget grillé à la flamme, cerfeuil tubéreux et carottes fondantes. Confit de canard maison doré au four et frites à l'ail rose du Tarn. Fruits d'automne poêlés au miel de forêt, sorbet butternut et crumble (autumn).

◆ Small house on the outskirts of the village where the chef prepares delightful, flavourful cuisine. Fine selection of wines from the nearby Gaillac vineyard. Dine under the willows on the terrace in summer.

in Donnazac 5 km Northeast on the D 922 and minor road – pop. 92 – alt. 291 m – ✉ 81170

Les Vents Bleus without rest

Caussade road – ✆ 05 63 56 86 11 – www.lesventsbleus.com – lesventsbleus@orange.fr – Fax 05 63 56 86 11 – Open 1st April-24 October

5 rm – €80 €80/150

◆ This fine (1844) white stone edifice, flanked by a dovecote, stands in the heart of the Gaillac vineyard. Individually and tastefully decorated rooms in the former wine warehouse. Patio-terrace.

CAILLAC – 46 Lot – 337 E5 – see Cahors

CAIRANNE – 84 Vaucluse – 332 C8 – pop. 847 – alt. 136 m – ✉ 84290 40 A2

Paris 650 – Avignon 43 – Bollène 47 – Montélimar 51 – Nyons 25 – Orange 18

Office de tourisme, Avenue du Général de Gaulle ✆ 04 90 30 76 53

Auberge Castel Miréïo rm,

Carpentras road by D 8 – ✆ 04 90 30 82 20 – www.castelmireio.fr – info@castelmireio.fr – Fax 04 90 30 78 39 – Closed 31 December-14 February

8 rm – €60/65 €62/70, €8 – 1 suite – ½ P €57/63

Rest – *(closed Thursday lunch in July-August and Monday)*

Menu €19 (weekday lunch), €23/28 – Carte €26/38

◆ This 19C family home has been extended with a wing where the rooms are located. They are simple, brightened by Provençal fabrics and named after vines. Rustic dining room proud of its 100-year-old tiling. Wholesome regional cuisine. Terrace.

Le Tourne au Verre

Ste-Cécile road – ✆ 04 90 30 72 18 – letourneauverre@wanadoo.fr – Fax 04 90 12 71 75 – Closed Sunday dinner and Tuesday from October to April and Wednesday

Rest – Menu (€14), €23

◆ Traditional house (1800) and a lovely terrace shaded by old plane trees. Bar, contemporary dining room (huge glazed wine cellar) and regional recipes chalked up on a slate.

CAJARC – 46 Lot – 337 H5 – pop. 1 096 – alt. 160 m – ✉ 46160 29 C1

Dordogne-Berry-Limousin

Paris 586 – Cahors 52 – Figeac 25 – Rocamadour 59 – Villefranche-de-Rouergue 27

Office de tourisme, La Chapelle ✆ 05 65 40 72 89, Fax 05 65 40 39 05

La Ségalière

380 av. François Mitterrand, (rte de Capdenac) – ✆ 05 65 40 65 35 – www.lasegaliere.com – hotel@lasegaliere.com – Fax 05 65 40 74 92 – Open 15 March-31 October

25 rm – €50/82 €65/97, €10 – ½ P €66/81

Rest – *(closed for lunch except weekends and bank holidays)* Menu €23/38

◆ Françoise Sagan was born in this village. This modern hotel offers very pleasant rooms with balconies. The large pool and garden are greatly appreciated. The menu features traditional fare with a creative twist. Summer terrace.

CALACUCCIA – 2B Haute-Corse – 345 D5 – see Corse

CALAIS – 62 Pas-de-Calais – 301 E2 – pop. 74 200 – Built-up area 104 852 – alt. 5 m – Casino CX – ✉ 62100 30 A1

Northern France and the Paris Region

Paris 290 – Boulogne-sur-Mer 35 – Dunkerque 46 – St-Omer 43

Channel Tunnel : Coquelles Terminal AU, info **"Shuttle"** ✆ 03 21 00 61 00.

✆ 3635 et tapez 42 (0,34 €/mn)

Office de tourisme, 12, boulevard Clemenceau ✆ 03 21 96 62 40, Fax 03 21 96 01 92

Monument of the Bourgeois de Calais (Rodin)★★ - Lighthouse ★★ DX - Musée des Beaux-Arts et de la Dentelle★ CX M².

Cap Blanc Nez★★: 13 km by ④.

Plans on following pages

Meurice

5 r. E.-Roche – ✆ 03 21 34 57 03 – www.hotel-meurice.fr – meurice@wanadoo.fr – Fax 03 21 96 28 12 CX **v**

41 rm – €85/150 €85/150, €14

Rest – *(closed Saturday lunch)* Menu (€15), €18/50 – Carte €35/43

◆ Traditional hotel with a huge lobby steeped in the atmosphere of 'Old France'. Delightfully antiquated large rooms; modern decor in the more recent wing. Beams, carved wood and period furniture form the cosy setting for this restaurant.

Holiday Inn rm, rest,

bd des Alliés – ✆ 03 21 34 69 69 – www.holidayinn.fr/calais-nord – holidayinn@holidayinn-calais.com – Fax 03 21 97 09 15 CX **a**

63 rm – €136 €151, €14

Rest – *(closed Saturday lunch, Sunday lunch and holidays lunch)* Menu (€9), €18 bi/24 bi – Carte €28/36

◆ This imposing hotel is pleasantly located opposite the marina. It has spacious, comfortable rooms, half of which have sea views. The bay windows of the restaurant overlook the masts of the yachts. Traditional cuisine is served in a contemporary decor.

Métropol Hôtel without rest

43 quai du Rhin – ✆ 03 21 97 54 00 – www.metropolhotel.com – metropol@metropolhotel.com – Fax 03 21 96 69 70 – Closed 21 December-11 January CY **h**

40 rm – €46 €68, €10 – 1 suite

◆ An old, red-brick façade. Practical, soundproofed rooms, some with an English decorative note, like the bar which has a distinctly British design.

Mercure Centre without rest

36 r. Royale – ✆ 03 21 97 68 00 – www.georgev-calais.com – h6739@accor.com – Fax 03 21 97 34 73 CX **d**

41 rm – €85/100 €105/125, €13

◆ This hotel on a main shopping street near the casino embraces the chain's new concept: contemporary rooms, monochromes of grey-brown and brushed aluminium furniture.

CALAIS

Bossuet (R.) .... BT 9
Cambronne (R.) .... AU 12
Chateaubriand (R.) .... BT 15
Égalité (Bd de l') .... BT 18
Einstein (Bd) .... AU 19
La-Fayette (Bd) .... AT 39
Fontinettes (R. des) .... ATU 25
Four-à-Chaux (R. du) .... AU 27
Gambetta (Bd Léon) .... AT 28
Gaulle (Bd du Gén.-de) .... AT 30
Hoche (R.) .... ATU 33
Jacquard (Bd) .... AT 34
Lattre-de-Tassigny (R. Mar.-de) .... AT 40
Lheureux (Quai L.) .... BU 41
Maubeuge (R. de) .... BT 43
Phalsbourg (R. de) .... BT 51
Prairies (R. des) .... AU 52
Ragueneau (R. de) .... BTU 57
Valenciennes (R. de) .... AU 69
Verdun (R. de) .... AT 73

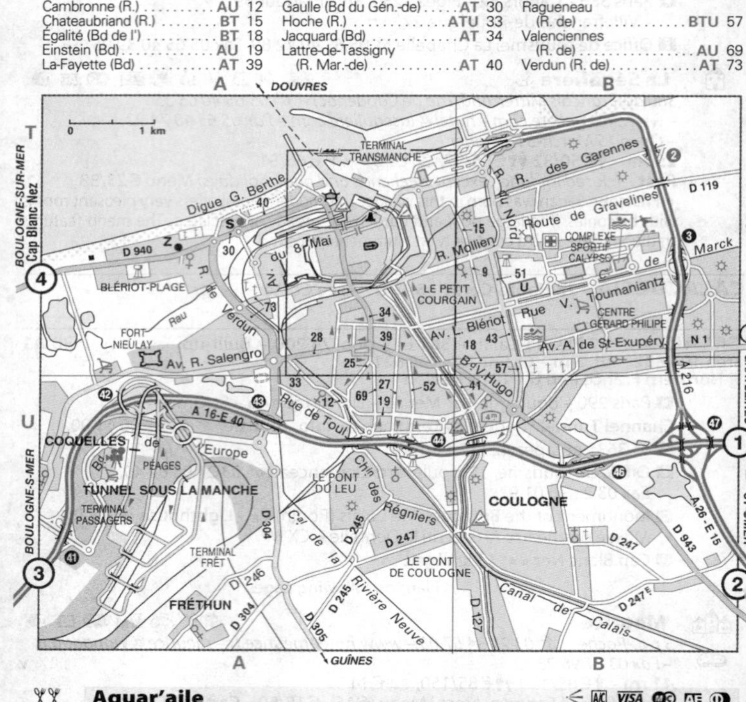

XX **Aquar'aile**
255 r. J.-Moulin, (4th Floor) – 03 21 34 00 00 – www.aquaraile.com – f.leroy@aquaraile.com – Fax 03 21 34 15 00 – Closed Sunday evening
Rest – Menu € 30/45 – Carte € 42/76 AT **s**
◆ A unique view of the English Channel, the North Sea, and the English coastline on the horizon from this pleasant fish restaurant on the fouth floor of a building.

XX **Au Côte d'Argent**
1 digue G.-Berthe – 03 21 34 68 07 – www.cotedargent.com – lefebvre@cotedargent.com – Fax 03 21 96 42 10 – Closed 17 August-7 September, Wednesday dinner from September to March, Sunday dinner and Monday CX **f**
Rest – Menu € 18 (weekdays), € 25/40 – Carte € 32/56
◆ All on board for a gourmet voyage with a fish and seafood flavour. A ship's cabin decor with a view of the busy ferry traffic in the background.

XX **Channel**
3 bd de la Résistance – 03 21 34 42 30 – www.restaurant-lechannel.com – contact@restaurant-lechannel.com – Fax 03 21 97 42 43 – Closed 26 July-9 August, 22 December-20 January, Sunday dinner and Tuesday
Rest – Menu € 22/58 – Carte € 50/90 CX **e**
◆ Elegant, modern décor, first-rate fish and seafood and an appealing wine list (cellar opening on to the room): a pleasant stop-off before crossing the channel.

X **Histoire Ancienne**
20 r. Royale – 03 21 34 11 20 – www.histoire-ancienne.com – p.comte@histoire-ancienne.com – Fax 03 21 96 19 58 – Closed 1st-15 August, Monday dinner and Sunday CX **x**
Rest – Menu (€ 12), € 19/36 – Carte € 25/38
◆ This charming dining room has carefully preserved its bistro style: bench seating, wooden chairs and old zinc. Grilled food, traditional dishes and local produce.

CALAIS

DOUVRES
C
D
CAPITAINERIE
POSTE 5
POSTE 6
BASSIN A MARÉE
POSTE 7
POSTE 8
PÉAGE (FRET)
TERMINAL TRANSMANCHE
PÉAGE (TOURISME)
Plage
POSTE 1
POSTE 2
POSTE 3
POSTE 4
TERMINAL TRANSMANCHE
BASE DE VOILE
AVANT PORT
Fort Risban
Colonne Louis XVIII
Av. R. Poincaré
Bd du Gal de Gaulle
Pt H. Hénon
COURGAIN
BASSIN DES CHASSES
BASSIN DU PARADIS
Bd des Alliés
Phare
Pl. de Suède
X
BASSIN OUEST
Bd de la Résistance
Av. du 8 Mai 45
Rue de Moscou
BASSIN CARNOT
Quai de la Loire
Place d'Armes
R. J. Quehen
SQUARE VAUBAN
Espl.
CASINO
N.-Dame
STADE DU SOUVENIR
Pl. des Fusillés
Pl. de Norvège
CITADELLE
PARC RICHELIEU
BASSIN DE LA BATTELLERIE
Vendroux
Mollien
R. Diderot
Av. de Coubertin
Chin du Cimetière Nord
CENTRALE
Q. de la Gendarmerie
Rue R. Descartes
Anatole France
R. Condorcet
MONT DES BOURGEOIS DE CALAIS
PARC ST-PIERRE
R. A. Briand
Quai
Rue de Vic
Av. Louis Blériot
Y
R. des Soupirants
R. A. Delcluze
R. du 11 Novembre
Jacquard
R. de la Tannerie
R. du Temple
Quai du Commerce
Canal de l'Yser
R. Neuve
Bd Léon Gambetta
Bd Pasteur
Bd
R. Verte
R. du 29 Juillet
Rue Auber
Place Crevecœur
R. du Four à Chaux
Lafayette
R. Van Grutten
R. Colbert
ST-PIERRE
0
200 m

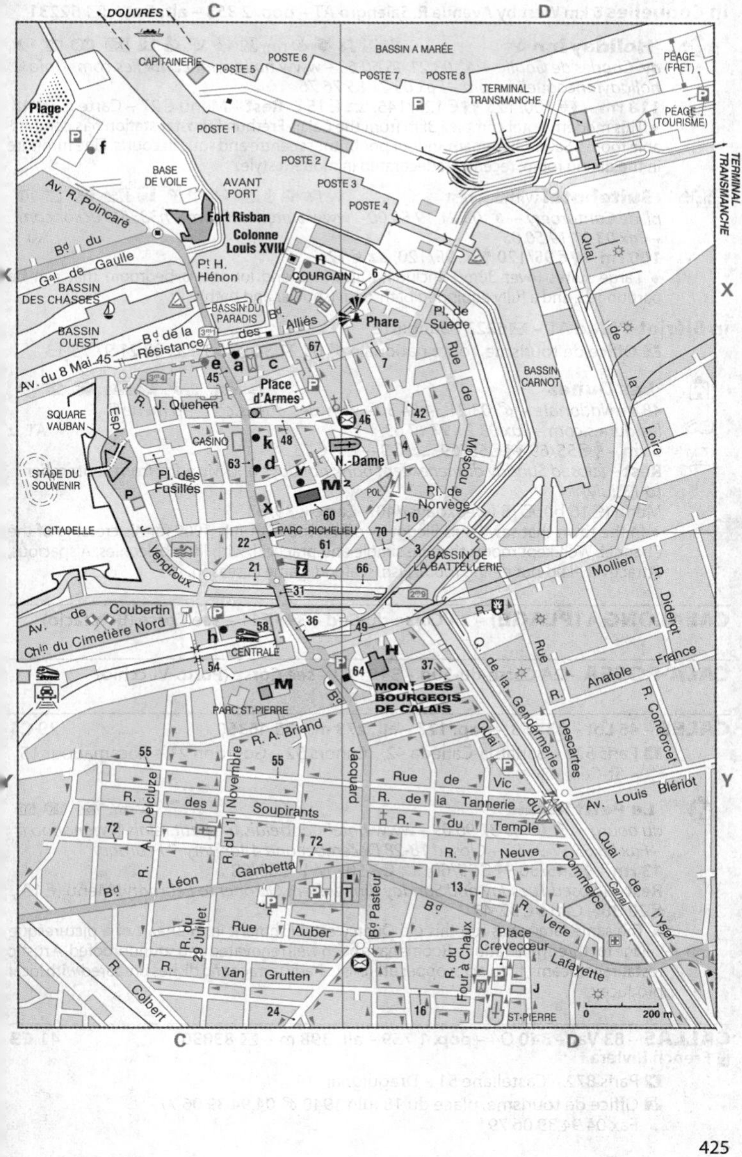

Le Grand Bleu

quai de la Colonne – ☎ 03 21 97 97 98 – www.legrandbleu-calais.com – Fax 03 21 82 53 03 – Closed 26 August-10 September, 17-26 February, Tuesday dinner and Wednesday CX n

Rest – Menu (€ 16), € 19 (weekdays)/45 – Carte € 37/47

◆ The name says it all: this restaurant celebrates all aspects of the sea, both in its decor and its predominantly seafood menu.

in Coquelles **6 km West by Avenue R. Salengro** AT – **pop. 2 353** – **alt. 5 m** – ✉ **62231**

Holiday Inn rm, VISA MC AE

av. Charles de Gaulle – ☎ 03 21 46 60 60 – www.holidayinncoquelles.com – info@holidayinncoquelles.com – Fax 03 21 85 76 76

118 rm – €100/125 €125/145, ☕ €15 **Rest** – Menu € 27 – Carte € 35/48

◆ This modern hotel complex 3km from the Calais Fréthun Eurostar station has comfortable rooms. Sauna, hammam, indoor pool, fitness centre and squash courts. Fine furniture in the dining room, recently redecorated in modern style.

Suitehotel without rest VISA MC AE

pl. de Cantorbery – ☎ 03 21 19 50 00 – www.suitehotel.com – h3335@accor.com – Fax 03 21 19 50 05 AU

100 rm – €95/120 €95/120, ☕ €12

◆ Large suites (over 30m²), including an office and lounge, a bedroom that can be partitioned, and a fully equipped bathroom (shower and bath).

in Blériot-Plage AT – ✉**62231 Sangatte**

Office de tourisme, route nationale ☎ 03 21 34 97 98, Fax 03 21 97 75 13

Les Dunes rest, VISA MC AE

48 rte Nationale – ☎ 03 21 34 54 30 – www.les-dunes.com – p.mene@les-dunes.com – Fax 03 21 97 17 63 AT z

9 rm – €55/69 €55/69, ☕ €9 – ½ P €73

Rest – *(closed Sunday dinner except bank holidays and Monday from September to 13 July)*

Menu (€ 16 bi), € 18 (weekdays)/40 – Carte € 39/63

◆ In the town that saw Louis Blériot fly off on the 25th July 1909 for his crossing of the Channel. Well-kept rooms that are simple and practical, with little balconies. A spacious, attractively-laid-out dining room. Fish, seafood, game in season.

CALALONGA (PLAGE) – 2A Corse-du-Sud – 345 E11 – see Corse (Bonifacio)

CALA-ROSSA – 2A Corse-du-Sud – 345 F10 – see Corse (Porto-Vecchio)

CALÈS – 46 Lot – 337 F3 – pop. 127 – alt. 273 m – ✉ 46350 29 C1

Paris 528 – Sarlat-la-Canéda 42 – Cahors 52 – Gourdon 21 – Rocamadour 15 – St-Céré 43

Le Petit Relais rm, VISA MC AE

au bourg – ☎ 05 65 37 96 09 – www.hotel-petitrelais.fr – petit.relais@wanadoo.fr – Fax 05 65 37 95 93 – Closed 18-28 December and 4 January-7 February

13 rm – €45/50 €55/60, ☕ €8,50 – ½ P €58/68

Rest – *(closed Tuesday and Sunday dinner from October to February)* Menu (€ 13), € 20/38 – Carte € 32/42

◆ The same family has run this old Quercy establishment in the heart of a picturesque village for three generations. Rooms have been well renovated and soundproofed. A rustic restaurant (beams, fireplace, copper utensils), shady terrace and dishes prepared with local produce.

CALLAS – 83 Var – 340 O4 – pop. 1 759 – alt. 398 m – ✉ 83830 41 C3

French Riviera

Paris 872 – Castellane 51 – Draguignan 14

Office de tourisme, place du 18 juin 1940 ☎ 04 94 39 06 77, Fax 04 94 39 06 79

Muy road 7 km Southeast by D 25 – ✉ 83830 Callas

Hostellerie Les Gorges de Pennafort
D 25 – ✆ 04 94 76 66 51
– www.hostellerie-pennafort.com – info@hostellerie-pennafort.com
– Fax 04 94 76 67 23 – Closed from mid January to mid March
16 rm – †€ 135/150 ††€ 185/220, ☕ € 19 – 4 suites – ½ P € 165/195
Rest – *(closed Sunday dinner except July-August, Monday except dinner in July-August and Wednesday lunch)* Menu (€ 47), € 58/140 – Carte € 120/160
Spec. Ravioli de foie gras et parmesan. Carré d'agneau rôti au jus truffé. Bâtonnet de chocolat noir amer, pain de Gênes et parfait glacé au fruit de la passion. **Wines** Coteaux Varois, Côtes de Provence.
◆ The colour scheme and building materials blend harmoniously, creating a refined ambience. In the evening, the gorges' red walls are dramatically lit. Contemporary, Art Deco – inspired dining room. Tasty food and a well-stocked cellar.

CALVI – 2B Haute-Corse – 345 B4 – see Corse

CALVINET – 15 Cantal – 330 C6 – pop. 432 – alt. 600 m – ✉ 15340 — 5 A3

Paris 576 – Aurillac 34 – Entraygues-sur-Truyère 32 – Figeac 40 – Maurs 19 – Rodez 56

Beauséjour (Louis-Bernard Puech) with rm
– ✆ 04 71 49 91 68 – www.cantal-restaurant-puech.com – beausejour.puech@wanadoo.fr – Fax 04 71 49 98 63 – Closed 15-20 June, 23 November-5 December, 4 January-12 February, Sunday dinner from October to May, Monday except dinner in July-August, Tuesday except dinner from March to September and Wednesday except dinner from June to September
8 rm – †€ 60/75 ††€ 60/100, ☕ € 15 – ½ P € 68/90
Rest – *(number of covers limited, pre-book)* Menu (€ 20 bi), € 27/62
Spec. Gaufre de foie de canard, caramel à la gentiane. Poulet de ferme. Sablé à la châtaigne et poêlée de pommes reinettes. **Wines** Côtes d'Auvergne, Marcillac.
◆ A country property that seeks to combine inventive recipes with locally sourced produce. Reasonably priced regional wines. Modern guestrooms. Non-smoking.

CAMARET-SUR-MER – 29 Finistère – 308 D5 – pop. 2 618 – alt. 4 m – ✉ 29570 Brittany — 9 A2

Paris 597 – Brest 4 – Châteaulin 45 – Crozon 11 – Morlaix 91 – Quimper 60
Office de tourisme, 15, quai Kleber ✆ 02 98 27 93 60, Fax 02 98 27 87 22
Pointe de Penhir★★★ Southwest: 3,5 km.

De France — rest,
quai G.-Toudouze – ✆ 02 98 27 93 06 – www.hotel-thalassa.com
– hotel-france-camaret@wanadoo.fr – Fax 02 98 27 88 14
– Open Easter-1st November
20 rm – †€ 43/93 ††€ 52/93, ☕ € 9 – ½ P € 52/72
Rest – *(open 4 April-1 November)* Menu (€ 15), € 20/45 – Carte € 30/120
◆ Decorated with a seafaring theme, the rooms are well kept and soundproofed. Half enjoy a view of the sea; the others are smaller but quieter. This restaurant spread over two floors offers seafood specialities with the harbour as a backdrop.

Bellevue
– ✆ 02 98 17 12 50 – hotel-france-camaret@wanadoo.fr – Fax 02 98 27 88 14
– Closed 15 January-15 February
15 rm – †€ 65/85 ††€ 65/140 – ½ P € 60/85
◆ The annexe to this hotel enjoys panoramic views of the port. Quiet, functional guestrooms, all of which are equipped with kitchenettes.

Vauban without rest
4 quai du Styvel – ✆ 02 98 27 91 36 – Fax 02 98 27 96 34
– Closed December and January
16 rm – †€ 40/50 ††€ 40/50, ☕ € 6,50
◆ Travellers can't go wrong if they make a stop here: the hotel is rather modest but its reasonable prices and warm welcome justify making a detour!

LA CAMBE – 14 Calvados – 303 F3 – pop. 609 – alt. 25 m – ✉ 14230 32 B2

Paris 289 – Bayeux 26 – Caen 56 – Saint-Lô 31

Ferme Savigny without rest
2.5 km on D 613 and D113 – ✆ 02 31 21 12 33
– http://perso.wanadoo.fr/ferme-savigny/ – re.ledevin@libertysurf.fr
4 rm – †€ 40 ††€ 48
◆ This 16-17C farmstead has a lovely stone staircase leading up to rustically decorated simple guestrooms. Homemade breakfast served in a delightful garden in summertime.

CAMBO-LES-BAINS – 64 Pyrénées-Atlantiques – 342 D4 3 A3
– pop. 5 849 – alt. 67 m – Spa : early March-mid Dec. – ✉ 64250
Atlantic Coast

Paris 783 – Biarritz 21 – Pau 115

Syndicat d'initiative, avenue de la Mairie ✆ 05 59 29 70 25, Fax 05 59 29 90 77

Epherra Souraïde Urloko Bidea, W : 13 km on D 918, ✆ 05 59 93 84 06

Villa Arnaga★★.

Ursula without rest
Bas-Cambo district, 2 km north – ✆ 05 59 29 88 88
– www.hotel-ursula.fr – infos@hotel-ursula.fr – Fax 05 59 29 22 15
– Closed 20 December-10 January
15 rm – †€ 46/51 ††€ 51/56, € 10
◆ This small, lively hotel situated in the picturesque quarter of Bas-Cambo offers you large, well-kept and personalised rooms.

Le Trinquet without rest
r. Trinquet – ✆ 05 59 29 73 38 – www.hotel-trinquet-cambo.com
– sarl.du.trinquet@wanadoo.fr – Fax 05 59 29 25 61
– Closed 2 November-8 December and Tuesday except from 1 July to 14 September
13 rm – †€ 29/48 ††€ 29/48, € 6,50
◆ This large house takes its name from a variant of Basque pelota. The simple and well-kept rooms lie above a café. Family atmosphere.

Le Bellevue with rm rest,
r. des Terrasses – ✆ 05 59 93 75 75 – www.hotel-bellevue64.fr
– contact@hotel-bellevue64.fr – Fax 05 59 93 75 85
– Closed 8 January-12 February
1 rm – †€ 70/80 ††€ 80/95, € 7 – 6 suites – ††€ 90/110
Rest – *(Closed Thursday dinner except July-August, Sunday dinner and Monday)*
Menu (€ 13), € 20 (weekday lunch), € 36/40
◆ Contemporary furniture and immaculate walls hung with modern paintings provide the decor in this restaurant serving modern cuisine. This charming, well-renovated 19C house has attractive, contemporary-style family suites.

Auberge "Chez Tante Ursule" with rm
fronton du Bas-Cambo, 2 km north – ✆ 05 59 29 78 23 – www.tante-ursule.com
– chez.tante.ursule@wanadoo.fr – Fax 05 59 29 28 57
– Closed 15-28 February and Tuesday
7 rm – †€ 30 ††€ 45, € 8 – ½ P € 55
Rest – Menu € 16 (weekday lunch), € 20/35 – Carte € 23/41
◆ This establishment situated near to the Bas Cambo fronton has a smart dining room with a pretty dresser. Food focuses on the Basque region. Rustic, well-kept rooms (antique furniture).

Do not confuse X with ✪!
X defines comfort, while stars are awarded for the best cuisine, across all categories of comfort.

CAMBRAI – 59 Nord – 302 H6 – pop. 32 800 – alt. 53 m – ✉ 59400 31 C3

Northern France and the Paris Region

Paris 179 – Amiens 98 – Arras 36 – Lille 77 – St-Quentin 51

Office de tourisme, 48, rue du Noyon ✆ 03 27 78 36 15, Fax 03 27 74 82 82

Burial ★★ by Rubens in St-Géry church AY - Musée Beaux-Arts: choir railings★, procession float★ AZ **M.**

CAMBRAI

Albert-1er (Av.) . . . . **BY** 2
Alsace-Lorraine (R. d') . . . . **BYZ** 4
Berlaimont (Bd de) . . . . **BZ** 5
Briand (Pl. A.) . . . . **AYZ** 6
Cantimpré (R. de) . . . . **AY** 7
Capucins (R. des) . . . . **AY** 8
Château-de-Selles (R. du) . . . **AY** 10
Clefs (R. des) . . . . **AY** 12
Épée (R. de l') . . . . **AZ** 13
Fénelon (Gde-R.) . . . . **AY** 15
Fénelon (Pl.) . . . . **AY** 16
Feutriers (R. des) . . . . **AY** 17
Gaulle (R. Gén.-de) . . . . **BZ** 18
Grand-Séminaire (R. du) . . . . **AZ** 19
Lattre-de-Tassigny (R. Mar.-de) . . . . **BZ** 21
Leclerc (Pl. du Mar.) . . . . **BZ** 22
Lille (R. de) . . . . **BY** 23
Liniers (R. des) . . . . **AZ** 24
Moulin (Pl. J.) . . . . **AZ** 25
Nice (R. de) . . . . **AY** 27
Pasteur (R.) . . . . **AY** 29
Porte-de-Paris (Pl. de la) . . . . **AZ** 32
Porte-Notre-Dame (R.) . . . . . **BY** 31
Râtelots (R. des) . . . . **AZ** 33
Sadi-Carnot (R.) . . . . **AY** 35
St-Aubert (R.) . . . . **AY** 36
St-Géry (R.) . . . . **AY** 37
St-Ladre (R.) . . . . **BZ** 39
St-Martin (Mail) . . . . **AZ** 40
St-Sépulcre (Pl.) . . . . **AZ** 41
Selles (R. de) . . . . **AY** 43
Vaucelette (R.) . . . . **AZ** 45
Victoire (Av. de la) . . . . **AZ** 46
Watteau (R.) . . . . **BZ** 47
9-Octobre (Pl. du) . . . . **AY** 48

Château de la Motte Fénelon
square du Château, via allée St Roch - north of the map BY – ✆ 03 27 83 61 38 – www.cambrai-chateau-motte-fenelon.com – contact@cambrai-chateau-motte-fenelon.com – Fax 03 27 83 71 61
10 rm – €90/260 €90/260, ☕ €10
Rest – Menu €26/39 – Carte €27/40
◆ This château, built by Hittorff in 1850, has green surroundings and houses rooms with character, adorned by period or limed furniture. Century-old brick vaults, tasteful decor and traditional menu are the characteristics of this restaurant.

Orangerie Parc
30 rm – €59/85 €59/85, ☕ €10
◆ The orangery offers comfortable accommodation just a few steps from the castle. Simpler service in the bungalows set in an 8-ha park.

Beatus
718 av. de Paris, 1.5 km via ⑤ – ✆ 03 27 81 45 70 – www.hotel.beatus.fr – hotel.beatus@wanadoo.fr – Fax 03 27 78 00 83
32 rm – €69/81 €74/87, ☕ €10
Rest – *(Closed August, 24 December-4 January and weekends) (dinner only) (resident only)* Menu €22 – Carte €27/60
◆ Shaded by tall trees, a white building whose superb staircase leads up to spacious modern or classical style bedrooms, all of which are different. Snug lounge-bar.

Le Clos St-Jacques without rest
9 r. St-Jacques – ✆ 03 27 74 37 61 – www.leclosstjacques.com – rquero@wanadoo.fr – Fax 03 27 74 37 61 – Closed 12-23 August and 21 December-4 January BY **e**
5 rm – €74/110 €74/110, ☕ €10
◆ Monsieur happily relates the history of this lovely mansion that Madame has superbly redecorated whilst respecting its original character. Delicious breakfasts, charming welcome.

L'Escargot
10 r. Gén.-de-Gaulle – ✆ 03 27 81 24 54 – restaurantlescargot@wanadoo.fr – Fax 03 27 83 95 21 – Closed 15-31 July, 21-26 December, Friday dinner and merc BZ **n**
Rest – Menu (€19 bi), €25/40 – Carte €25/48
◆ A discreet restaurant in the centre of this town famous for its sweets. Rustic dining rooms, including a mezzanine, serving traditional cuisine in an informal atmosphere.

Au Fil de l'Eau
1 bd Dupleix – ✆ 03 27 74 65 31 – Fax 03 27 74 65 31 – Closed 14 July-14 August, 23 February-9 March, Sunday dinner, Wednesday dinner and Monday AY **f**
Rest – Menu (€19), €23/47 – Carte €27/41
◆ Pleasant little restaurant near a lock on the St Quentin Canal. Fresh and colourful dining room with tasty traditional cuisine and seafood.

Bapaume road **4 km by ⑥ – ✉ 59400 Fontaine-Notre-Dame**

Auberge Fontenoise
543 rte de Bapaume – ✆ 03 27 37 71 24 – www.auberge-fontenoise.com – auberge.fontenoise@wanadoo.fr – Fax 03 27 70 34 91 – Closed Monday except lunch from September to June and Sunday dinner
Rest – Menu €26/46 – Carte approx. €48
◆ This discreet family inn has a rustic dining room where diners savour appetising regional food masterfully prepared with quality produce.

CAMBREMER – 14 Calvados – 303 M5 – pop. 1 096 – alt. 100 m – ✉ 14340 33 C2

Paris 211 – Caen 38 – Deauville 28 – Falaise 38 – Lisieux 15 – Saint-Lô 110

Syndicat d'initiative, rue Pasteur ✆ 02 31 63 08 87, Fax 02 31 63 08 21

Château Les Bruyères
rte du Cadran (D 85) – ☎ 02 31 32 22 45 – www.chateaulesbruyeres.com – reception@chateaulesbruyeres.com – Fax 02 31 32 22 58 – Closed 6 January-5 February
13 rm – €95/180 €95/220, ☕ €15 – 1 suite – ½ P €140/225
Rest – *(closed Monday and Tuesday in low season) (dinner only)* Menu €42/75 – Carte €55/95
◆ This noble establishment is set in a wooded park. An elegant bourgeois dining room and attractive personalised guestrooms for a peaceful stay. Seasonal market surf and turf dishes with savoury herbs and vegetable garden produce.

CAMIERS – 62 Pas-de-Calais – 301 C4 – pop. 2 252 – alt. 23 m – ✉ 62176 30 A2

Paris 244 – Arras 101 – Boulogne-sur-Mer 21 – Calais 58 – Le Touquet 10
Office de tourisme, esplanade Ste-Cécile-Plage ☎ 03 21 84 72 18, Fax 03 21 84 72 18

Les Cèdres
64 r. Vieux-Moulin – ☎ 03 21 84 94 54 – www.hotel-cedres.com – hotel-cedres@wanadoo.fr – Closed December and January
27 rm – €50/66 €50/66, ☕ €8
Rest *L'Orangeraie* – *(dinner only)* Menu €25/32
◆ Two town centre houses separated by a pleasant terrace-courtyard. Modest but well-kept rooms, livened up by bright colours. Comfortable bar and British style lounge. A veranda-dining room opening onto a summer terrace. Traditional and regional cuisine.

CAMON – 09 Ariège – 343 J6 – pop. 157 – alt. 349 m – ✉ 09500 29 C3
Languedoc-Roussillon-Tarn Gorges

Paris 780 – Carcassonne 63 – Pamiers 37 – Toulouse 103
Office de tourisme, 10, rue Georges d'Armagnac ☎ 05 61 68 88 26, Fax 05 61 68 88 26

L'Abbaye-Château de Camon
– ☎ 05 61 60 31 23 – www.chateaudecamon.com – katie@chateaudecamon.com – Fax 05 61 60 31 23 – Open 16 March-31 October
6 rm – €100/150 €130/180, ☕ €18
Table d'hôte – *(closed Wednesday)* Menu €38/40
◆ Time seems to have stopped in this enchanting location where the garden offers many secluded spots. The personalised rooms are in former monks' cells. In the evening you can return to the cloister where nice, regional dishes await you.

CAMPAGNE – 24 Dordogne – 329 G6 – see le Bugue

CAMPES – 81 Tarn – 338 D6 – see Cordes-sur-Ciel

CAMPIGNY – 27 Eure – 304 D6 – see Pont-Audemer

CANAPVILLE – 14 Calvados – 303 M4 – see Deauville

CANCALE – 35 Ille-et-Vilaine – 309 K2 – pop. 5 293 – alt. 50 m – ✉ 35260 Brittany 10 D1

Paris 398 – Avranches 61 – Dinan 35 – Fougères 73 – St-Malo 16
Office de tourisme, 44, rue du Port ☎ 02 99 89 63 72, Fax 02 99 89 75 08
Site★ - Port de la Houle★ - ❋★ from St-Méen church tower - Pointe du Hock and sentier des Douaniers ≤★.
Pointe du Grouin★★.

Plan on following page

De Bricourt-Richeux
Mont-St-Michel road: 6.5 km via D76, D155 and minor road – ☎ 02 99 89 64 76 www.maisons-de-bricourt.com – bricourt@relaischateaux.com – Fax 02 99 89 88 47
11 rm – €165/310 €165/310, ☕ €21 – 2 suites
Rest *Le Coquillage* – see restaurant listing
◆ This superb 1922 villa, where Léon Blum once stayed, is in a park (aromatic plants and livestock) overlooking the Bay of Mont St Michel. Extremely refined rooms. Faultless welcome.

CANCALE

- Bricourt (Pl.) . . . . Y 3
- Calvaire (Pl. du) . . . . Z 4
- Duguay-Trouin (Quai) . . . . Z 9
- Duquesne (R.) . . . . Y 10
- Du-Guesclin (R.) . . . . Y 8
- Fenêtre (Jetée de la) . . . . Z 12
- Gallais (R.) . . . . Y 13
- Gambetta (Quai) . . . . Z 14
- Hock (R. du) . . . . Z 16
- Jacques-Cartier (Quai) . . . . Z 17
- Juin (R. du Mar.) . . . . Z 18
- Kennedy (Quai) . . . . Z 19
- Leclerc (R. Gén.) . . . . YZ 20
- Mennais (R. de la) . . . . Y 22
- Port (R. du) . . . . Z
- République (Pl. de la) . . . . Z 23
- Rimains (R. des) . . . . Y 24
- Roulette (R. de la) . . . . Z 25
- Stade (R. du) . . . . Y 27
- Surcouf (R.) . . . . Y 28
- Thomas (Quai) . . . . Z 30

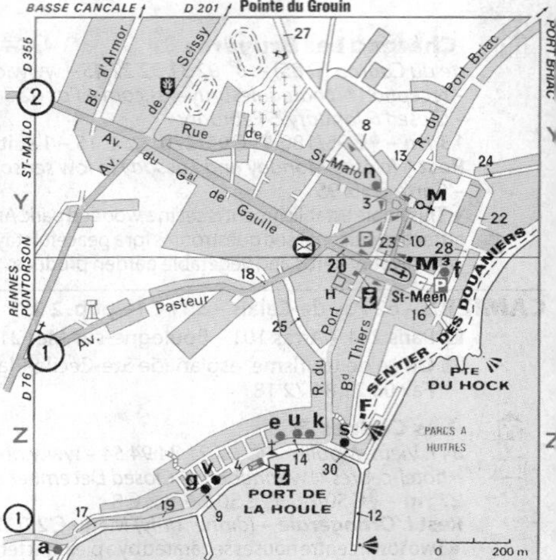

Le Continental

VISA MC AE

quai Thomas – ✆ 02 99 89 60 16 – www.hotel-cancale.com – hotel-conti@wanadoo.fr – Fax 02 99 89 69 58 – Closed 12 January-9 February

16 rm – †€ 70/130 ††€ 70/155, ☕ € 13 — Z **s**

Rest – *(closed Wednesday except dinner June-September and Tuesday)* Menu € 19 (weekday lunch), € 24/45 – Carte € 31/49

◆ An exceptional location opposite the port. Find a warm welcome, comfortable and well-kept rooms and home-made jams for breakfast: a delightful little establishment. Beautiful wainscoting hung with mirrors in the dining room with a view of the fishing fleet.

Le Querrien

rest, VISA MC AE

7 quai Duguay-Trouin – ✆ 02 99 89 64 56 – www.le-querrien.com – le-querrien@wanadoo.fr – Fax 02 99 89 79 35 — Z **v**

15 rm – †€ 59/79 ††€ 85/138, ☕ € 9

Rest – Menu € 17 (weekdays)/28 – Carte € 25/65

◆ Breton House with a wooden veranda on the quayside. The spacious rooms, all named after ships, are decorated in the colours of the sea. Nine overlook the waves. A restaurant that pays homage to the ocean in its menu and decor (fish tank, wainscoting and fresco).

Auberge de la Motte Jean without rest

P VISA MC

2 km via ② via D 355 – ✆ 02 99 89 41 99 – www.hotelpointedugrouin.com – hotel-pointe-du-grouin@wanadoo.fr – Fax 02 99 89 92 22 – Closed 1 December-31 January

13 rm – †€ 65/78 ††€ 65/78, ☕ € 8

◆ The main building of a former farm set in the Cancale countryside. Very quiet, well-cared-for garden with a pond. Guestrooms with personal touches and antique furniture. Personalised service.

Duguay Trouin without rest

VISA MC AE

11 quai Duguay-Trouin – ✆ 02 23 15 12 07 – www.hotelduguaytrouin.com – leduguaytrouin1@aol.com – Fax 02 99 89 75 20 — Z **g**

7 rm – †€ 70/85 ††€ 85/105, ☕ € 8

◆ Guests are received simply and cordially in this fully renovated hotel in a fishing port. A low-key nautical theme in the rooms (sea chests) overlooking the bay or the cliffs.

Le Chatellier without rest

P VISA MC AE

Quatrevais, 1 km via ② via D 355 – ✆ 02 99 89 81 84 – www.hotellechatellier.com – contact@hotellechatellier.com – Fax 02 99 89 61 69 – Closed December and January

13 rm – †€ 52/57 ††€ 67/85, ☕ € 8,50

◆ Lovely traditional Breton house whose homely charm continues to prevail. Country chic guestrooms under the eaves upstairs. Some overlook the garden.

Les Rimains without rest
r. Rimains – 02 99 89 64 76 – www.maisons-de-bricourt.com – Fax 02 99 89 88 47 – Open from mid-March to mid-December
4 rm – €170/290 €170/290, €21
◆ Delightful 1930s cottage nestling in a garden overlooking the sea. Olivier Rœllinger offers tastefully decorated rooms with furniture from antique markets. Guesthouse ambience.

Le Manoir des Douets Fleuris without rest
1.5 km via ② via D 365 – 02 23 15 13 81 – www.manoirdesdouetsfleuris.com – contact@manoirdesdouetsfleuris.com – Fax 02 99 89 98 19 – Closed January
10 rm – €79/160 €79/160, €12
◆ A 17C manor with pond and garden. The bedrooms are individually decorated, and one sports a canopied bed and granite fireplace. Monumental hearth in the lounge.

Le Coquillage – Hôtel de Bricourt-Richeux
Mt-St-Michel road : 6.5 km on D 76, D 155 and minor road – 02 99 89 25 25 – www.maisons-de-bricourt.com – bricourt@relaischateaux.com – Fax 299891849
Rest – *(closed mid-January to mid-February)* Menu €29/60
◆ Tasty seafood served in a panoramic dining room decorated in a low-key, classical spirit. Summer terrace shaded by pine trees.

Côté Mer
4 r. E. Larmort, (rte de la corniche) – 02 99 89 66 08 – www.restaurant-cotemer.fr – restaurant.cotemer@orange.fr – Fax 02 99 89 89 20 – Closed 2 weeks in November, February holiday, Tuesday dinner and Sunday dinner in low season and Wednesday Z **a**
Rest – Menu (€24), €29/65 – Carte €44/75
◆ Well-presented, modern cuisine awaits at this contemporary, elegant and nautical-style restaurant overlooking the harbour. Pleasant veranda; summer terrace.

Le Cancalais with rm
12 quai Gambetta – 02 99 89 61 93 – Fax 02 99 89 89 24 – Closed January, Sunday dinner and Monday Z **u**
10 rm – €65/75 €80/90, €8
Rest – Menu €18 (weekdays)/65 – Carte €40/54
◆ This Cancale institution serves a half-classic and half-seafood menu. It has a rustic interior of Breton inspiration and a panoramic veranda. Attractive rooms.

Surcouf
7 quai Gambetta – 02 99 89 61 75 – Closed December, January, Tuesday and Wednesday Z **k**
Rest – Menu €17 (weekdays), €27/44 – Carte €45/65
◆ This spruce nautical bistro stands out from the others lining the port of Cancale. View of the jetty (even better upstairs) and delicious seafood cuisine.

Le Troquet
19 quai Gambetta – 02 99 89 99 42 – Closed 15 November-31 January, Thursday and Friday except in August Z **e**
Rest – Menu €20 (weekdays)/44 – Carte €39/65
◆ A pleasant little bistro, well worth tracking down amidst all the others along the quayside. Fish and seafood take pride of place, including the renowned Cancale oysters.

La Maison de la Marine with rm
23 r. Marine – 02 99 89 88 53 – www.maisondelamarine.com – info@maisondelamarine.com – Fax 02 99 89 83 27 Z **f**
5 rm – €80/90 €90/140, €12
Rest – *(closed Sunday dinner and Monday off season)* Menu €24 (weekday lunch), €32/44 – Carte €38/54
◆ A superbly converted former shipping office: intimate buccaneering-inspired decor, terrace facing the garden, sitting room with British accents. The menu mixes Breton and Mediterranean cuisine. Well-worn antiques and luxurious fixtures and fittings make the bedrooms irresistible.

at Pointe du Grouin ★★ 4.5 km north by D 201 – ✉ 35260 Cancale

La Pointe du Grouin
– ✆ 02 99 89 60 55 – *www.hotelpointedugrouin.com*
– hotel-pointe-du-grouin@wanadoo.fr – Fax 02 99 89 60 55
– Open 1 April-15 November
16 rm – †€ 85/90 ††€ 85/120, ☕ € 9 – ½ P € 85/100
Rest – *(Closed Thursday lunch except from 14 July to 31 August and Tuesday)*
Menu € 24/77 – Carte € 50/64
◆ A marvellous windswept location for this cliff top Breton house with a magnificent view of the islands and Mont St Michel. Countrified, well-equipped rooms. Reserve a table by the windows and enjoy an exceptional view of the open sea.

CANCON – **47 Lot-et-Garonne** – **336** F2 – **pop. 1 287** – **alt. 199 m** – ✉ **47290** 4 **C2**

Paris 581 – Agen 51 – Bergerac 40 – Bordeaux 134
Syndicat d'initiative, place de la Halle ✆ 05 53 01 09 89, Fax 05 53 01 64 70

in St-Eutrope-de-Born **9 km Northeast by D 124 and D 153 – pop. 609 – alt. 95 m – ✉ 47210**

Domaine du Moulin de Labique
Villeréal road – ✆ *05 53 01 63 90*
– www.moulin-de-labique.fr – moulin-de-labique@wanadoo.fr
– Fax 05 53 01 73 17 – Closed 17-23 November
6 rm – †€ 75/100 ††€ 90/115, ☕ € 10 – ½ P € 83/95
Table d'hôte – Menu € 25/31
◆ A brook runs alongside this large estate with pool, vegetable garden and fishing. The rooms, set in the former stables, the barn or the main house, are tastefully decorated. Local cuisine served in a rustic dining room.

CANDES-ST-MARTIN – **37 Indre-et-Loire** – **317** J5 – **pop. 227** – **alt. 35 m** – ✉ **37500** Châteaux of the Loire 11 **A2**

Paris 290 – Angers 76 – Chinon 16 – Saumur 13 – Tours 54
Collegiate church ★.

Auberge de la Route d'Or
2 pl. de l'Église – ✆ *02 47 95 81 10 – routedor@club-internet.fr*
– Fax 02 47 95 81 10 – Open 25 March-11 November,
Tuesday except lunch in July-August and Wednesday
Rest – *(number of covers limited, pre-book)* Menu (€ 17), € 23/35 – Carte € 35/46
◆ A rustic inn located in two old houses, one of which dates from the 17C. Cosy dining room with a fireplace. Regionally inspired, classic cuisine.

CANDÉ-SUR-BEUVRON – **41 Loir-et-Cher** – **318** E7 – **pop. 1 437** – **alt. 70 m** – ✉ **41120** 11 **A1**

Paris 199 – Blois 15 – Chaumont-sur-Loire 7 – Montrichard 21 – Orléans 78 – Tours 51
Syndicat d'initiative, 10, route de Blois ✆ 02 54 44 00 44, Fax 02 54 44 00 44

La Caillère
36 rte de Montils – ✆ *02 54 44 03 08 – www.lacaillere.com*
– lacaillere2@wanadoo.fr – Fax 02 54 44 00 95 – Closed January and February
18 rm – †€ 50 ††€ 63/66, ☕ € 11 – ½ P € 58/65
Rest – *(Closed Monday lunch, Thursday lunch and Wednesday)*
Menu € 20 (weekdays)/46 – Carte € 40/53
◆ Old farmhouse, extended by a modern wing and separated from the road by a curtain of greenery. Plain, well kept rooms. A pleasant dining room which has kept its country atmosphere. Modern, seasonal cuisine and tables decorated with old soup tureens.

LE CANET – **13 Bouches-du-Rhône** – **340** I5 – **see Aix-en-Provence**

CANET-EN-ROUSSILLON – 66 Pyrénées-Orientales – 344 J6 22 B3 – pop. 10 182 – alt. 11 m – Casino BZ – ✉ 66140

Paris 849 – Argelès-sur-Mer 21 – Narbonne 66 – Perpignan 11

Office de tourisme, espace Méditerranée ✆ 04 68 86 72 00, Fax 04 68 86 72 12

Plan on following page

in Canet-Plage – ✉ 66140

Les Flamants Roses
1 voie des Flamants-Roses – ✆ 04 68 51 60 60 – www.hotel-flamants-roses.com – contact@hotel-flamants-roses.com – Fax 04 68 51 60 61
59 rm – €140/230 €170/275, €18 – 4 suites – ½ P €118/180
Rest *L'Horizon* – dietetic rest. *(closed Monday lunch and Tuesday lunch)* Menu €29 bi (weekday lunch), €44/62 – Carte approx. €46
Rest *Le Canotier* – buffet *(lunch only)* Menu €29 bi
◆ A modern establishment joined to a thalassotherapy centre situated next to the beach. The rooms, mostly opening on to the sea, are warm and welcoming. Modern and "light" food is served at this restaurant overlooking the sea. Brasserie-type food is served at Le Canotier.

Le Mas de la Plage rm, VISA
34 av. Roussillon – ✆ 04 68 80 32 63 – www.lemasdelaplageetdespins.com – contact@lemasdelaplageetdespins.com – Fax 04 68 80 49 19 – Open 2 April-30 October AY **a**
16 rm (½ board only) – ½ P €90/110
Rest – *(dinner only) (resident only)* Menu €30/40
◆ In the shade of the pine trees in ancient parkland, this charming 19C Catalan villa offers comfortable rooms painted in southern shades. Fireplace decorated with pottery shards from the restaurant.

Mercure without rest VISA
120 prom. de la Côte-Vermeille – ✆ 04 68 80 28 59 – www.mercure.com – h3590@accor.com – Fax 04 68 80 80 60 BZ **b**
48 rm – €95/125 €105/135, €11
◆ This hotel is right on the seashore. It offers fully renovated, contemporary rooms (king size beds), half of which face the sea and have balconies.

Le Galion VISA
20 bis av. Grand-large – ✆ 04 68 80 28 23 – www.hotel-le-galion.com – contact@hotel-le-galion.com – Fax 04 68 80 20 46 – Closed Sun. evening and Mon. lunch from 20 Oct. - 15 Mar. BZ **r**
28 rm – €64/99 €64/99, €11 – ½ P €64/99
Rest – *(closed Sun. evening and Mon. lunch from 20 Oct. - 15 Mar.)* Menu (€18), €26/30 – Carte approx. €36
◆ This galleon is situated some 150m from the waves. Family-run establishment; most of the progressively refurbished rooms have a balcony. The restaurant opens onto the swimming pool and terrace (barbecues in summertime). Regional specialities.

Du Port rm, VISA
21 bd de la Jetée – ✆ 04 68 80 62 44 – www.hotel-du-port.net – info@hotel-du-port.net – Fax 04 68 73 28 83 – Hotel: open May-October; rest: open June-September BY **e**
35 rm – €60/90 €60/90, €8 – ½ P €55/75
Rest – *(dinner only) (resident only)* Menu €15
◆ A 1980s building, half-way between the harbour and beach. Enjoy the calm and comfort of its simple bedrooms, all with balconies. The dining room has been refurbished in a nautical style. Traditional unpretentious cuisine.

La Frégate without rest VISA
12 r. Cerdagne – ✆ 04 68 80 22 87 – www.hotel-lafregate.fr – contact@hotel-lafregate.fr – Fax 04 68 73 82 72 BY **f**
27 rm – €58/95 €63/103, €8
◆ Situated 100m from the beach, this hotel has small bedrooms, all with pleasant regional-style rustic furniture. Excellent soundproofing and faultless upkeep.

CANET-PLAGE

Aigues Marines (R. des) . . . . **BZ** 2
Albères (R. des) . . . . **BY** 5
Amandiers (R. des) . . . . **BY** 6
Anémones (Bd des) . . . . **AYZ** 7
Balcons du Front de Mer (Av. des) **BZ** 8
Bourgogne-Morvan (R.) . . . . **BZ** 9
Capcir (Galerie du) . . . . **BY** 12
Cassanyes (Galerie) . . . . **BY** 14
Catalogne (Av. de la) . . . . **BY** 15
Cerdagne (R. de) . . . . **BY** 18
Cerisiers (R. des) . . . . **BY** 20
Champagne (R. de) . . . . **BZ** 22
Coquillages (R. des) . . . . **BZ** 25
Corbières (R. des) . . . . **BY** 28
Grande-Bretagne (R. de) . . . . **BYZ** 29
Gratia (Av. Edmond) . . . . **BZ** 30
Île-de-France (R.) . . . . **BZ** 32
Jouy d'Arnaud (R.) . . . . **BY** 33
Pountarrou (Av. du) . . . . **AY** 34
Pyrénées (R. des) . . . . **BY** 35
Sardane (R. de la) . . . . **ABY** 36

Le Don Quichotte

22 av. de Catalogne – ✆ 04 68 80 35 17 – www.ledonquichotte.com – ledonquichotte@wanadoo.fr – Closed mid January-mid February, Monday and Tuesday except holidays BY **r**

Rest – Menu € 18 (weekday lunch)/45 – Carte € 29/64

◆ The proprietor of this friendly restaurant supports the local wine growers by offering a fine choice of their production to accompany his semi-traditional, semi-regional menu.

CANGEY – **37 Indre-et-Loire** – **317** P4 – **pop. 985** – **alt. 85 m** – ✉ **37530** 11 **A1**

Paris 210 – Amboise 12 – Blois 28 – Montrichard 26 – Tours 35

de Fleuray Route de Dame-Marie-les-Bois, N : 8 km on D 74, ✆ 02 47 56 07 07

Le Fleuray

7 km north, on D 74 Dame-Marie-les-Bois road – ✆ 02 47 56 09 25 – www.lefleurayhotel.com – lefleurayhotel@wanadoo.fr – Fax 02 47 56 93 97 – Closed 21 December-4 January

23 rm – € 78/96 € 78/130, € 13 – ½ P € 81/117

Rest – *(closed Monday from November to February) (dinner only) (number of covers limited, pre-book)* Menu € 29/49 – Carte € 50/80

◆ This old restored farm is all the more charming with its orchard garden and swimming pool. Nice reception and cosy guestrooms named after flowers. Updated traditional cuisine served in a well-lit country chic dining room or on a pretty summer terrace.

CANNES – **06 Alpes-Maritimes** – **341** D6 – **pop. 70 400** – **alt. 2 m** 42 **E2**
– **Casinos : Palm Beach** X, **Croisette** BZ – ✉ **06400** **French Riviera**

Paris 898 – Aix-en-Provence 149 – Marseille 160 – Nice 33 – Toulon 120

Office de tourisme, 1, boulevard de La Croisette ✆ 04 92 99 84 22, Fax 04 92 99 84 23

Riviera Golf Club Mandelieu Avenue des Amazones, 8 km on the Napoule road, ✆ 04 92 97 49 49

de Cannes Mougins Mougins 175 avenue du Golf, NW : 9 km, ✆ 04 93 75 79 13

Royal Mougins Golf Club Mougins 424 avenue du Roi, 10 km on the Grasse road, ✆ 04 92 92 49 69

Site★★ - Seafront★★: boulevard★★ and pointe★ de la croisette - ≤★ from the tour du Mont-Chevalier AZ - Musée de la Castre★★ AZ - Chemin des Collines★ Northeast: 4 km V - La Croix des Gardes X ≤★ West: 5 km then 15 mn.

Plans on following pages

Carlton Inter Continental

58 bd de la Croisette – ✆ 04 93 06 40 06 – www.ichotelsgroup.com – cannes@ichotelsgroup.com – Fax 04 93 06 40 25 CZ **e**

342 rm – € 315/1100 € 315/1100, € 39 – 39 suites

Rest *Brasserie Carlton* – Menu € 46 – Carte € 68/130

Rest *La Plage* – beach rest. – *✆ 04 93 06 44 94 (Open April-October) (lunch only)* Menu (€ 43) – Carte € 67/134

◆ Hitchcock filmed scenes from the film To Catch a Thief in this famous hotel with its twin cupolas. Luxurious Belle Epoque interior, superb suites and an interesting history. Elegant decor, seasonal cuisine and a view of the Croisette at the Brasserie Carlton.

Martinez

73 bd de la Croisette – ✆ 04 92 98 73 00 – www.hotel-martinez.com – martinez@concorde-hotels.com – Fax 04 93 39 67 82 DZ **n**

396 rm – € 570/2900 € 570/2900, € 35 – 16 suites

Rest *La Palme d'Or* – see restaurant listing

Rest *Relais Martinez* – *✆ 04 92 98 74 12* – Menu € 38 – Carte € 60/95

Rest *Z. Plage* – beach rest. – *✆ 04 92 98 74 22 (open May-September) (lunch only)* Menu (€ 37) – Carte € 45/75

◆ Popular with the stars at festival time; Art Deco or contemporary style rooms, sumptuous suites, modern facilities, Givenchy spa and superb fitness centre. A smart, relaxed atmosphere, gourmet cuisine and summer terrace at the Relais Martinez.

CANNES

Street	Grid	No.
Albert-Édouard (Jetée)	BZ	
Alexandre-III (Bd)	X	2
Alsace (Bd)	BDY	
Anc.-Combattants-d'Afrique-du-Nord (Av.)	AYZ	4
André (R. du Cdt)	CZ	
Antibes (R. d')	BCY	
Bachaga-Saïd-Boualam (Av.)	AY	5
Beauséjour (Av.)	DYZ	
Beau-Soleil (Bd)	X	10
Belges (R. des)	BZ	12
Blanc (R. Louis)	AYZ	
Broussailles (Av. des)	V	16
Buttura (R.)	BZ	17
Canada (R. du)	DZ	
Carnot (Bd)	X	
Carnot (Square)	V	20
Castre (Pl. de la)	AZ	21
Chabaud (R.)	CY	22
Clemenceau (R. G.)	AZ	
Coteaux (Av. des)	V	
Croisette (Bd de la)	BDZ	
Croix-des-Gardes (Bd)	VX	29
Delaup (Bd)	AY	30
Dr-Pierre Gazagnaire (R.)	AZ	32
Dr-R. Picaud (Av.)	X	
Dollfus (R. Jean)	AZ	33
États-Unis (R. des)	CZ	35
Favorite (Av. de la)	X	38
Félix-Faure (R.)	ABZ	
Ferrage (Bd de la)	ABY	40
Fiesole (Av.)	X	43
Foch (R. du Mar.)	BY	44
Gallieni (R. du Mar.)	BY	48
Gaulle (Pl. Gén.-de)	BZ	51
Gazagnaire (Bd Eugène)	X	
Grasse (Av. de)	VX	53
Guynemer (Bd)	AY	
Hespérides (Av. des)	X	55
Hibert (Bd Jean)	AZ	
Hibert (R.)	AZ	
Isola-Bella (Av. d')	X	
Jean-Jaurès (R.)	BCY	
Joffre (R. du Mar.)	BY	60
Juin (Av. Mar.)	DZ	
Koening (Av. Gén.)	DY	
Lacour (Bd Alexandre)	X	62
Latour-Maubourg (R.)	DZ	
Lattre-de-Tassigny (Av. de)	AY	63
Laubeuf (Quai Max)	AZ	
Lérins (Av. de)	X	65
Liberté-Charles de Gaulle (A. de la)	AZ	70
Lorraine (Bd de)	CDY	
Macé (R.)	CZ	66
Madrid (Av. de)	DZ	
Meynadier (R.)	ABY	
Midi (Bd du)	X	
Mimont (R. de)	BY	
Montfleury (Bd)	CDY	74
Monti (R. Marius)	AY	75
Mont-Chevalier (R. du)	AZ	72
Noailles (Av. J.-de)	X	
Observatoire (Bd de l')	X	84
Oxford (Bd d')	V	87
Paillassou (Av. R. et I.)	V	64
Pantiero (La)	ABZ	
Paradis-Terrestre (Corniches du)	V	88
Pasteur (R.)	DZ	
Pastour (R. Louis)	AY	90
Perier (Bd du)	V	91
Perrissol (R. Louis)	AZ	92
Petit-Juas (Av. du)	VX	
Pins (Bd des)	X	95
Pompidou (Espl. G.)	BZ	
Prince-de-Galles (Av. du)	X	97
République (Bd de la)	X	
Riouffe (R. Jean de)	BY	98
Riou (Bd du)	VX	
Roi-Albert 1er (Av.)	X	
Rouguière (R.)	BY	100
St-Antoine (R.)	AZ	102
St-Nicolas (Av.)	BY	105
St-Pierre (Quai)	AZ	
Sardou (R. Léandre)	X	108
Serbes (R. des)	BZ	110
Source (Bd de la)	X	112
Stanislas (Pl.)	AY	
Strasbourg (Bd de)	CDY	
Teisseire (R.)	CY	114
Tuby (Bd Victor)	AYZ	115
Vallauris (Av. de)	VX	116
Vallombrosa (Bd)	AY	1
Vautrin (Bd Gén.)	DZ	
Vidal (R. du Cdt)	CY	1
Wemyss (Av. Amiral Wester)	X	1
1ère Division-Française (Bd de la)	BCY	1

LE CANNET

Street	Grid	No.
Aubarède (Ch. de l')	V	8
Bellevue (Pl.)	V	1
Bréguières (Rte des)	V	1
Cannes (R. de)	V	1
Carnot (Bd)	V	
Cheval (Av. Maurice)	V	2
Collines (Ch. des)	V	
Doumer (Bd Paul)	V	3
Écoles (Av. des)	V	3
Four-à-Chaux (Bd du)	V	4
Gambetta (Bd)	V	5
Gaulle (Av. Gén.-de)	V	
Jeanpierre (Av. Maurice)	V	5
Mermoz (Av. Jean)	V	6
Monod (Bd Jacques)	V	6
Mont-Joli (Av. du)	V	7
N.-D.-des-Anges (Av.)	V	7
Olivetum (Bd d')	V	8
Olivet (Ch. de l')	V	8
Paris (R. de)	V	8
Pinède (Av. de la)	V	9
Pompidou (Av. Georges)	V	9
République (Bd de la)	V	
Roosevelt (Av. Franklin)	V	9
St-Sauveur (R.)	V	1
Victoria (Av.)	V	
Victor-Hugo (R.)	V	1

VALLAURIS

Street	Grid	No.
Cannes (Av. de)	V	1
Clemenceau (Av. G.)	V	2
Golfe (Av. du)	V	5
Isnard (Pl. Paul)	V	5
Picasso (Av. Pablo)	V	9
Rouvier (Bd Maurice)	V	1
Tapis-Vert (Av. du)	V	1

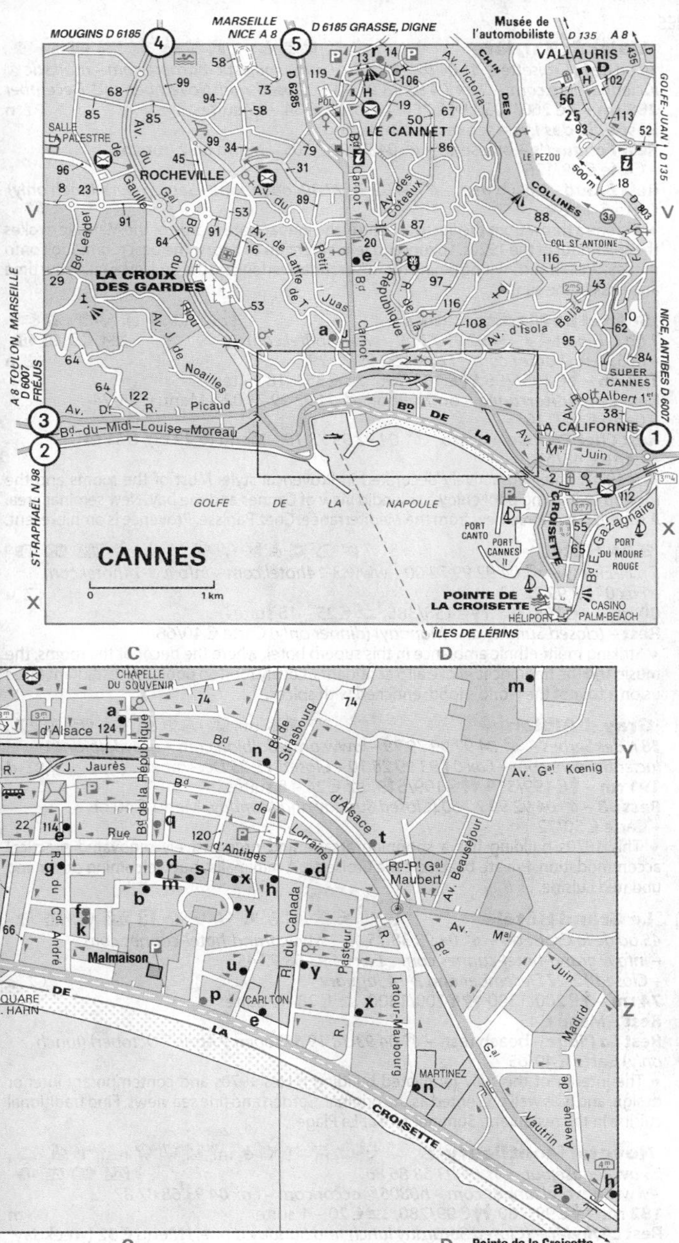
MOUGINS D 6185
MARSEILLE NICE A 8
D 6185 GRASSE, DIGNE
Musée de l'automobiliste
D 135
A 8
VALLAURIS
GOLFE-JUAN D 135
SALLE LA PALESTRE
ROCHEVILLE
LE CANNET
LE PEZOU
COLLINES
CH^IN DES
Av. Victoria
Av. de Gaulle
Bd Carnot
Av. des Coteaux
Av. du Petit Juas
Av. de Lattre de T.
R. de la République
COL ST-ANTOINE
LA CROIX DES GARDES
Bd Leader
Av. J. de Noailles
Riou
Av. d'Isola Bella
SUPER CANNES
Av. Roi Albert 1er
LA CALIFORNIE
A 8 TOULON, MARSEILLE D 6007 FRÉJUS
NICE, ANTIBES D 6007
Av. Dr R. Picaud
Bd-du-Midi-Louise-Moreau
BD DE LA
Av. Mal Juin
CROISETTE
GOLFE DE LA NAPOULE
PORT CANTO
PORT CANNES II
PORT DU MOURE ROUGE
Bd E. Gazagnaire
ST-RAPHAËL N 98
CANNES
0 1 km
POINTE DE LA CROISETTE
HÉLIPORT
CASINO PALM-BEACH
ÎLES DE LÉRINS
CHAPELLE DU SOUVENIR
d'Alsace
R. J. Jaurès
Bd de Strasbourg
Bd d'Alsace
Av. Gal Kœnig
Bd de Lorraine
Rue d'Antibes
Bd de la République
R. du Cdt André
Rd-Pt Gal Maubert
Av. Beauséjour
R. du Canada
R. Pasteur
Malmaison
CARLTON
R. Latour-Maubourg
Av. Mal Juin
Bd Gal Vautrin
Avenue de Madrid
MARTINEZ
SQUARE R. HAHN
DE LA CROISETTE
Pointe de la Croisette

Majestic Barrière
10 bd de la Croisette – ✆ 04 92 98 77 00 – www.majestic-barriere.com – majestic@lucienbarriere.com – Fax 04 93 38 97 90 – Closed mid November-end December
288 rm – †€ 260/1050 ††€ 260/1050, ☕ € 34 – 17 suites BZ **n**
Rest *Villa des Lys* – see restaurant listing
Rest *Fouquet's* – brasserie – ✆ *04 92 98 77 05* – Menu € 52 (lunch) – Carte € 49/126
Rest *B. Sud* – beach rest. – ✆ *04 92 98 77 30 (open June - September) (lunch only)* Carte € 48/84
◆ A stone's throw from the Festival Centre, the immaculate façade of the Majestic evokes the splendour of the 1920s. Luxury and refinement on all floors. The best rooms look onto the sea. Well-lit and inviting dining room/veranda overlooking the Croisette: take your time and bask in the sun!

Sofitel Le Méditerranée
1 bd J.-Hibert – ✆ 04 92 99 73 00 – www.sofitel.com – h0591-re@accor.com – Fax 04 92 99 73 29 AZ **n**
108 rm – †€ 195/796 ††€ 195/796, ☕ € 35 – 18 suites
Rest *Le Méditerranée* – on 7rd floor, ✆ *04 92 99 73 02* – Menu € 44/74 – Carte € 92/110
Rest *Chez Panisse* – bistro – ✆ *04 92 99 73 10* – Menu (€ 22 bi), € 31 bi – Carte € 48/63
◆ A 1930s hotel, attractively decorated in Provençal style. Most of the rooms and the rooftop swimming pool enjoy a splendid view of Cannes and the bay. New seminar area. A superb panoramic view from the Méditerranée. Chez Panisse, Provence is omnipresent.

3.14 Hôtel
5 r. F.-Einesy – ✆ 04 92 99 72 00 – www.3-14hotel.com – info@3-14hotel.com – Fax 04 92 99 72 12 CZ **u**
80 rm – †€ 155/385 ††€ 155/385, ☕ € 25 – 15 suites
Rest – *(closed Sunday and Monday) (dinner only)* Carte € 40/68
◆ Striking multi-ethnic ambiance in this superb hotel, where the decor of the rooms, the music and the fragrances evoke all 5 continents. Lovely rooftop pool. The restaurant takes us on a tour of the world's food; enriched with spices.

Gray d'Albion
38 r. des Serbes – ✆ 04 92 99 79 79 – www.gray-dalbion.com – graydalbion@lucienbarriere.com – Fax 04 93 99 26 10 – Closed 12-25 December BZ **d**
191 rm – †€ 199/519 ††€ 199/519, ☕ € 24 – 8 suites
Rest *38* – ✆ *04 92 99 79 60 (Closed Sunday and Monday)* Menu € 40 bi – Carte € 50/72
◆ This 1970s building has a shopping arcade and progressively renovated practical accommodation. Private beach on the Croisette. A minimalist but welcoming decor and updated cuisine.

Le Grand Hôtel
45 bd de la Croisette – ✆ 04 93 38 15 45 – www.grand-hotel-cannes.com – info@grand-hotel-cannes.com – Fax 04 93 68 97 45 – Closed 12-27 December and 2-14 January CZ **s**
74 rm – †€ 200/1300 ††€ 200/1300, ☕ € 28 – 2 suites
Rest – Menu € 45
Rest *La Plage* – beach rest. – ✆ *04 93 38 19 57 (open 9 April-7 October) (lunch only)* Carte € 49/65
◆ The interior of this fully renovated building mixes 1970s and contemporary interior design, and is as well presented as the original. Garden and fine sea views. Find traditional cuisine in the restaurant. Summer fare at La Plage.

Novotel Montfleury
25 av. Beauséjour – ✆ 04 93 68 86 86 – www.novotelcannes.com – h0806@accor.com – Fax 04 93 68 87 87
182 rm – †€ 99/280 ††€ 99/280, ☕ € 20 – 1 suite DY **m**
Rest *L'Olivier* – *(Closed Saturday lunch and Sunday dinner)* Menu € 32 (weekday lunch)/43 – Carte € 48/59
◆ On the edge of the Californie district with its luxurious villas, this hotel has comfortable rooms in nautical or Provençal style. An attractive swimming pool and terrace in the shade of palm trees. Pleasant sunny decor, view of the kitchens and Mediterranean style menu at the Olivier.

Croisette Beach without rest
13 r. du Canada – ✆ 04 92 18 88 00 – www.croisettebeach.com – H1284@accor.com – Fax 04 93 68 35 38 – Closed 8-28 December DZ **y**
94 rm – €95/335 €95/335, ☕ €20
◆ Generally spacious and fully renovated rooms with modern comforts. Most have a terrace. Private beach on the Croisette.

Sun Riviera without rest
138 r. d'Antibes – ✆ 04 93 06 77 77 – www.sun-riviera.com – info@sun-riviera.com – Fax 04 93 38 31 10 – Closed 14-26 December
42 rm – €132/265 €132/265, ☕ €16 CZ **h**
◆ On a street lined with luxury boutiques, this hotel boasts large, stylish and well-equipped rooms; those overlooking the garden are quieter and have a balcony.

Eden Hôtel
133 r. d'Antibes – ✆ 04 93 68 78 00 – www.eden-hotel-cannes.com – reception@eden-hotel-cannes.com – Fax 04 93 68 78 01 DZ **d**
116 rm – €125/280 €125/280, ☕ €20
Rest – *(closed Sunday and Monday) (dinner only) (resident only)* Carte €28/40
◆ Ideal for shoppers: the hotel is in the prestigious Rue d'Antibes. The renovated rooms have parquet floors and contemporary furnishings. Traditional restaurant where the modern cuisine adopts a fusion style.

Belle Plage without rest
2 r. Brougham – ✆ 04 93 06 25 50 – www.cannes-hotel-belle-plage.com – belleplage@wanadoo.fr – Fax 04 93 99 61 06 – Open 15 March-15 November
48 rm – €120/310 €120/310, ☕ €16 AZ **u**
◆ At the foot of the old town; film star photos hang in the rooms with balconies, around half of which overlook the sea. Roof terrace with small pool.

Amarante
78 bd Carnot – ✆ 04 93 39 22 23 – www.jjwhotels.com – amarante-cannes@jjwhotels.com – Fax 04 93 39 40 22 V **e**
71 rm – €130/200 €130/200, ☕ €20 – ½ P €90/125
Rest – *(closed 29 November-29 December, Saturday and Sunday)* Menu (€19 bi), €28/37 – Carte €33/57
◆ On a busy boulevard with colourful, well-equipped rooms. Handy underground parking; inner courtyard with swimming pool. Pleasant dining room with terrace, where decor and menu are both Provençal.

Splendid without rest
4 r. F.-Faure – ✆ 04 97 06 22 22 – www.splendid-hotel-cannes.fr – accueil@splendid-hotel-cannes.fr – Fax 04 93 99 55 02 BZ **a**
62 rm – €103/240 €104/240, ☕ €12
◆ The exclusively female staff of this 19C hotel are faultlessly hospitable. Most of the progressively renovated rooms overlook the port and the Suquet.

Cavendish without rest
11 bd Carnot – ✆ 04 97 06 26 00 – 04 97 06 26 01 – reservation@cavendish-cannes.com – Fax 04 97 06 26 01 BY **t**
34 rm ☕ – €120/280 €140/330
◆ Charming establishment with pretty soundproofed rooms, extensive facilities, home-made breakfasts, guests' bar in the evenings and warm welcome.

Victoria without rest
rd-pt Duboys-d'Angers – ✆ 04 92 59 40 00 – www.cannes-hotel-victoria.com – reservation@cannes-hotel-victoria.com – Fax 04 93 38 03 91 – Closed 30 January-20 February CZ **x**
25 rm – €110/435 €110/435, ☕ €17
◆ Renovated hotel occupying two floors of a residential building. Light, contemporary accommodation (beige and blue hues); terrace with small pool opposite the bar.

America without rest
13 r. St-Honoré – ✆ 04 93 06 75 75 – www.hotel-america.com – info@hotel-america.com – Fax 04 93 68 04 58 – Closed 15 December-15 January
28 rm – €90/115 €110/130, ☕ €15 BZ **r**
◆ In a quiet street near the Croisette. The impeccably-kept rooms are fresh and modern, generally spacious and are well soundproofed.

Château de la Tour
10 av. Font-de-Veyre, via ③ – 04 93 90 52 52 – www.hotelchateaudelatour.com – reservation@hotelduchateaudelatour.com – Fax 04 93 47 86 61 – Closed 26 January-19 February
34 rm – €125/375 €125/375, €17
Rest – *(closed Sunday and Monday) (dinner only)* Menu €37/49 – Carte €51/72
◆ This former nobleman's house has a walled garden offering delicious tranquillity. Very comfortable, entirely renovated rooms in a neo-baroque style. The restaurant offers Provençal dishes in a subdued yet pleasant dining room.

Fouquet's without rest
2 rd-pt Duboys-d'Angers – 04 92 59 25 00 – www.le-fouquets.com – info@le-fouquets.com – Fax 04 92 98 03 39 – Open April-8 November
13 rm – €120/210 €140/250, €14 CZ **y**
◆ On a fairly quiet roundabout, a hotel with large and cheerful rooms revamped in Provençal style. Very well kept; courteous welcome.

California without rest
8 traverse Alexandre-III – 04 93 94 12 21 – www.hotel-californias.com – resa@californias-hotel.com – Fax 04 93 43 55 17 DZ **h**
33 rm – €101/168 €101/300, €14
◆ Attractive houses around a pretty garden with pool. Non-smoking rooms in southern shades, some of which have a terrace.

Le Mondial without rest
1 r. Teisseire – 04 93 68 70 00 – www.hotellemondial.com – reservation@hotellemondial.com – Fax 04 93 99 39 11 CY **e**
49 rm – €80/175 €110/410, €14
◆ Elagant Art Deco façade, behind which are chocolate-coloured rooms that are ethnic in style; some have balcony with sea view (upper floors).

Cannes Riviera without rest
16 bd d'Alsace – 04 97 06 20 40 – www.cannesriviera.com – reservation@cannesriviera.com – Fax 04 93 39 20 75 BY **r**
58 rm – €85/125 €105/140, €15 – 5 suites
◆ An eye-catching façade decorated with a giant portrait of Marilyn Monroe hides a distinctly Provencal-style interior. Renovated rooms; rooftop pool with fine views.

De Paris without rest
34 bd d'Alsace – 04 97 06 98 81 – www.hoteldeparis.fr – reservation@hoteldeparis.fr – Fax 04 93 39 04 61 – Closed 8-25 December and 7-21 January
47 rm – €80/145 €95/165, €18 – 3 suites CY **a**
◆ A 19C town house near a busy road but with first-rate soundproofing. Elegant and well-kept rooms (non-smoking). Pool surrounded by palm trees.

Régina without rest
31 r. Pasteur – 04 93 94 05 43 – www.hotel-regina-cannes.com – reception@hotel-regina-cannes.com – Fax 04 93 43 20 54 – Closed 11-29 December, 25 January-20 February DZ **x**
19 rm – €100/200 €100/200, €16
◆ Close to the Croisette, well-kept rooms (new linen and carpets) decorated in local style, most with balcony. Wi-fi.

Renoir without rest
7 r. Edith-Cavell – 04 92 99 62 62 – www.hotel-renoir-cannes.com – contact@hotel-renoir-cannes.com – Fax 04 92 99 62 82 BY **x**
26 rm – €139/209 €159/229, €15
◆ Everything behind the characterful 1913 façade is brand new. A Hollywood look in the rooms, but the modern suites sport a baroque style.

Cézanne without rest
40 bd d'Alsace – 04 92 59 41 00 – www.hotel-cezanne.com – contact@hotel-cezanne.com – Fax 04 92 99 20 99 CY **n**
28 rm – €139/259 €139/259, €17
◆ Stylish contemporary rooms, each of which matches grey with another livlier colour (yellow, turquoise). Fitness facilties, hammam and breakfast under the palm trees. Enchanting!

Villa de l'Olivier without rest
5 r. Tambourinaires – ✆ 04 93 39 53 28 – www.hotelolivier.com – reception@hotelolivier.com – Fax 04 93 39 55 85 – Closed 21 November-26 December, 7-17 January and 23 January-22 February AZ **e**
23 rm – €100/120 €110/155, €12
◆ Near the town centre and the Suquet, this family villa has smart, well-soundproofed rooms. Buffet breakfast on the veranda or on the terrace in summer.

Festival without rest
3 r. Molière – ✆ 04 97 06 64 40 – www.hotel-festival.com – infos@hotel-festival.com – Fax 04 97 06 64 45 – Closed 4-14 January CZ **m**
14 rm – €59/129 €69/169, €10
◆ Breakfast served in the rooms at this recently revamped hotel; lively colours and good soundproofing. Sauna, Jacuzzi.

La Villa Tosca without rest
11 r. Hoche – ✆ 04 93 38 34 40 – www.villa-tosca.com – contact@villa-tosca.com – Fax 04 93 38 73 34 – Closed 13-28 December BY **e**
22 rm – €61/98 €82/220, €13
◆ Fine Italianate façade behind which is a lemon yellow contemporary interior mixing old and new furnishings. Prettily renovated little rooms.

L'Estérel without rest
15 r. du 24-Août – ✆ 04 93 38 82 82 – www.hotellesterel.com – reservation@hotellesterel.com – Fax 04 93 99 04 18 BY **d**
55 rm – €50/80 €63/90, €8
◆ Brand new hotel near the station offering compact but well-equipped rooms. Breakfast on the veranda with views of l'Estérel, the rooftops and the sea.

Le Mistral without rest
13 r. des Belges – ✆ 04 93 39 91 46 – www.mistral-hotel.com – contact@mistral-hotel.com – Fax 04 93 38 35 17 – Closed 13-26 December BZ **b**
10 rm – €79/119 €79/119, €10
◆ Brand new small hotel behind the Palais des Festivals with pretty little rooms named after the winds. Attentive family welcome.

De Provence without rest
9 r. Molière – ✆ 04 93 38 44 35 – www.hotel-de-provence.com – contact@hotel-de-provence.com – Fax 04 93 39 63 14 – Closed 1st-27 December
30 rm – €65/82 €82/122, €10 CZ **s**
◆ A charming garden with palm trees fronts this hotel that is ideally located near the Croisette. Small yet smart rooms in Provençal style (some with balcony).

Florian without rest
8 r. Cdt-André – ✆ 04 93 39 24 82 – www.hotel-leflorian.com – contact@hotel-leflorian.com – Fax 04 92 99 18 30 – Closed 1st December-10 January
20 rm – €50/70 €65/85, €6 CZ **g**
◆ A smiling welcome at this family hotel offering simple yet well-kept rooms.Some with balcony where a good breakfast can be enjoyed.

La Palme d'Or – Hôtel Martinez
73 bd de la Croisette – ✆ 04 92 98 74 14 – www.hotel-martinez.com – lapalmedor@concorde-hotels.com – Fax 04 93 39 03 38 – Closed 3 January-1st March, Sunday and Monday DZ **n**
Rest – Menu €64 bi (lunch), €83/189 – Carte €140/185
Spec. "Éclosion lumineuse" d'escargot (autumn-winter). "Authentique" sardine grillée comme un stockfish. Soufflé "tout pomme" (autumn-winter). **Wines** Côtes du Luberon, Côtes de Provence.
◆ An Art Deco interior featuring photos of stars and fine woods, with views of the Croisette. Fine panoramic terrace; excellent sunny cuisine.

Le Mesclun
16 r. St-Antoine – ✆ 04 93 99 45 19 – www.lemesclun-restaurant.com – mesclun.cannes@wanadoo.fr – Fax 04 93 49 29 11 – Closed 28 June-8 July, 31 January-2 March and Sunday AZ **t**
Rest – *(dinner only)* Menu €39 – Carte €75/115
◆ Subtle lighting, woodwork, paintings and warm tones comprise the ideal setting in which to enjoy well-prepared tasty Mediterranean cuisine. Competent and friendly service.

XX **Le Festival**
52 bd de la Croisette – ✆ 04 93 38 04 81 – www.lefestival.fr – contact@lefestival.fr – Fax 04 93 38 13 82 – Closed 17 November-26 December CZ **p**
Rest – Menu € 28 (lunch), € 35/43 – Carte € 39/60
Rest *Grill* – Carte € 35/50
◆ Drawings of ships brighten the pale-wainscoting in this large retro brasserie. Terrace opposite the Croisette with an awe-inspiring view that must be seen! At the Grill, the ambience is friendly, the setting discreet. Salads, daily specials, diet dishes etc.

XX **Mantel**
22 r. St-Antoine – ✆ 04 93 39 13 10 – www.restaurantmantel.fr – noel.mantel@wanadoo.fr – Fax 04 93 38 77 29 – Closed 1st-15 July, 23-29 December, Thursday lunch, Wednesday and lunch July-August AZ **c**
Rest – Menu € 27 (lunch), € 39/60 – Carte € 50/90
◆ One of many restaurants in a picturesque street on the Suquet. This one stands out for its carefully prepared Provençal dishes and intimate decor.

XX **Il Rigoletto**
60 bd d'Alsace – ✆ 04 93 43 32 19 – Fax 04 93 43 32 19 – Closed 23 November-15 December, Tuesday dinner except in July-August and Sunday DY **t**
Rest – Menu (€ 13), € 26/52 – Carte € 55/82
◆ Retro dining room serving reasonably priced fine Italian cuisine made with fresh produce; a charming family establishment off the beaten track.

XX **Comme Chez Soi**
4 r. Batéguier – ✆ 04 93 39 62 68 – www.restaurantcommechezsoi.net – info@commechezsoi.net – Fax 04 93 46 41 60 – Closed 22-27 December and Monday
Rest – *(dinner only)* Menu € 27/80 – Carte € 58/90 CZ **k**
◆ A homely atmosphere with knick-knacks from around the world and eclectic furnishings. Tasty, well prepared regional fare and a choice of traditional recipes.

XX **Rest. Arménien**
82 bd de la Croisette – ✆ 04 93 94 00 58 – www.lerestaurantarmenien.com – infos@lerestaurantarmenien.com – Fax 04 93 94 56 12 – Closed 11 December-3 January DZ **a**
Rest – *(dinner only)* Menu € 45
◆ No choice but copious servings; a slice of Armenia's culinary heritage. Slightly kitsch setting, light with stained glass, open until late and plenty of regulars.

XX **Relais des Semailles**
9 r. St-Antoine – ✆ 04 93 39 22 32 – cannessemailles@orange.fr – Fax 04 93 39 84 73 – Closed Monday lunch AZ **z**
Rest – Menu € 22 (lunch)/34 – Carte € 53/83
◆ Paintings, antique furniture and ornaments create a cosy atmosphere in this restaurant in an old-town alleyway. Regional dishes.

XX **Côté Jardin**
12 av. St-Louis – ✆ 04 93 38 60 28 – www.restaurant-cotejardin.com – cotejardin.com@wanadoo.fr – Fax 04 93 38 60 28 – Closed 27 October-5 November, Sunday and Monday X **a**
Rest – Menu € 24/38
◆ Restaurant located in a residential area. Dining room/veranda and small garden with shaded terrace. Family, market sourced cooking, chalked up on a blackboard.

X **L'Affable**
5 r. la Fontaine – ✆ 04 93 68 02 09 – www.restaurant-laffable.fr – laffable@wanadoo.fr – Fax 04 93 68 19 09 – Closed August, Saturday lunch and Sunday
Rest – Menu (€ 20), € 24 (lunch)/38 – Carte € 60/90 CZ **d**
◆ Minimalist decor, tribal art and an open kitchen in this contemporary bistro with a brief yet thoughtful and appetising menu.

X **Caveau 30**
45 r. F.-Faure – ✆ 04 93 39 06 33 – www.lecaveau30.com – lecaveau30@wanadoo.fr – Fax 04 92 98 05 38 AZ **f**
Rest – brasserie – Menu (€ 17), € 24/36 – Carte € 40/70
◆ 1930s brasserie style in the two large dining rooms. Terrace opening onto a large shaded square. Seafood and traditional fare.

Rendez-Vous
35 r. F.-Faure – ✆ 04 93 68 55 10 – restaurantrdv@orange.fr – Fax 04 93 38 96 21 – Closed 26 January-12 February AZ **g**
Rest – Menu (€ 17), € 22/30 – Carte € 38/55
◆ Meet up in this smart restaurant with a new Art Deco inspired modern decor. Sample seafood, shellfish and traditional fare with a Mediterranean twist.

La Cave
9 bd de la République – ✆ 04 93 99 79 87 – www.restaurant-lacave.com – info@restaurantlacave.com – Fax 04 93 68 91 19 – Closed Saturday lunch and Sunday CY **q**
Rest – bistro – Menu € 31 – Carte € 42/70
◆ An authentic bistro with a modern, lively ambiance, dishes of the day on the blackboard and a well-compiled wine list. Non-smoking.

Aux Bons Enfants
80 r. Meynadier – Closed 22 November-4 January, Sunday and Monday AZ **r**
Rest – *(number of covers limited)* Menu € 24
◆ This old-fashioned looking, family establishment has perfected the art of hospitality. Tasty regional cuisine and house specialities. The restaurant does not have a phone and only takes cash.

at Cannet 3 km North - V – **pop. 42 800 – alt. 80 m** – ✉ **06110**

Office de tourisme, avenue du Campon ✆ 04 93 45 34 27, Fax 04 93 45 28 06

Pézou
346 r. St-Sauveur – ✆ 04 93 69 32 50 – Fax 04 93 43 69 14 – Closed 22-30 June, November, Monday lunch in July-August, Sunday dinner from September to June and Wednesday V **r**
Rest – Menu (€ 13), € 18 (lunch), € 26/32 – Carte € 32/39
◆ For a break from the Croisette, a pleasant restaurant by a pretty little square with a summer terrace. Provençal-inspired fare.

LE CANNET – 06 Alpes-Maritimes – 341 D6 – see Cannes

CAPBRETON – 40 Landes – 335 C13 – pop. 7 546 – alt. 6 m – Casino – ✉ 40130 Atlantic Coast 3 **A3**

Paris 749 – Bayonne 22 – Biarritz 29 – Mont-de-Marsan 90 – St-Vincent-de-Tyrosse 12

Office de tourisme, avenue Georges Pompidou ✆ 05 58 72 12 11, Fax 05 58 41 00 29

de Seignosse Seignosse Avenue du Belvédère, N : 8 km on D 152, ✆ 05 58 41 68 30

quartier de la plage (beach area)

Cap Club Hôtel
85 av. Mar.-de-Lattre-de-Tassigny – ✆ 05 58 41 80 00 – www.capclubhotel.com – contact@capclubhotel.com – Fax 05 58 41 80 41
75 rm – †€ 70/276 ††€ 70/276, ☕ € 12 **Rest** – Menu (€ 18) – Carte € 30/60
◆ Sport, fitness or relaxation: you can choose the theme of your stay in this hotel opposite the beach. Modern rooms and many sports facilities. This restaurant has a contemporary setting, lovely view of the ocean and traditional food.

L'Océan
rest,
85 av. G.-Pompidou – ✆ 05 58 72 10 22 – www.hotel-capbreton.com – hotel-capbreton@wanadoo.fr – Fax 05 58 72 08 43 – Closed 30 November-20 December and 4-30 January
25 rm – †€ 55/90 ††€ 65/109, ☕ € 8,50 **Rest** – Menu € 17/25 – Carte € 30/55
◆ On the banks of the channel, an immaculate façade housing rooms with balconies. Opt for the quieter ones at the back. The Atlantic has place of honour here, in terms of both decor and food. Pizzeria for snacks.

quartier la Pêcherie

XXX **Le Regalty**

port de plaisance – ✆ 05 58 72 22 80 – leregalty@cegetel.net – Fax 05 58 72 22 80 – Closed 1-8 December, 15-31 January, Wednesday dinner, Sunday dinner and Monday

Rest – Menu (€ 20), € 28 – Carte € 45/65

◆ Restaurant on the ground floor of a modern building. Appreciate a short market menu and seafood in the redecorated dining room and new terrace.

X **Le Pavé du Port**

port de plaisance – ✆ 05 58 72 29 28 – www.le-pave-du-port.com – le-pave@hotmail.fr – Fax 05 58 72 29 28 – Closed Christmas holidays to mid-January, Monday lunch in July-August, Tuesday from October to April and Wednesday except dinner in July-August

Rest – Menu € 18 (weekdays)/27 – Carte € 30/40

◆ Very freshly caught fish is on the menu at this restaurant overlooking the harbour. Dining rooms with discreet nautical touches and terrace-veranda.

CAP COZ – 29 Finistère – 308 H7 – see Fouesnant

CAP-d'AGDE – 34 Hérault – 339 G9 – see Agde

CAP d'AIL – 06 Alpes-Maritimes – 341 F5 – pop. 4 532 – alt. 51 m – ✉ 06320 42 E2

Paris 945 – Monaco 3 – Menton 14 – Monte-Carlo 4 – Nice 18

Office de tourisme, 87, avenue du 3 Septembre ✆ 04 93 78 02 33, Fax 04 92 10 74 36

See plan of Monaco (Principality of)

Marriott Riviera la Porte de Monaco rm,

au port – ✆ 04 92 10 67 67 – www.mariott.com/mcmcd – thierry.derrien@marriotthotels.com – Fax 04 92 10 67 00 AV **n**

186 rm – € 179/499 € 179/499, € 21 – 15 suites

Rest – Menu € 20 (weekday lunch), € 35/39 – Carte € 36/54

◆ Modern building facing the Cap d'Ail marina. Very comfortable rooms in compliance with its chain standards. Most of them have loggias overlooking the sea. Elegant brasserie-style restaurant. Traditional cuisine.

CAP d'ANTIBES – 06 Alpes-Maritimes – 341 D6 – see Antibes

CAPDENAC-GARE – 12 Aveyron – 338 E3 – pop. 4 601 – alt. 175 m – ✉ 12700 29 C1

Paris 587 – Aurillac 65 – Rodez 59 – Villefranche-de-Rouergue 31

Office de tourisme, place du 14 juillet ✆ 05 65 64 74 87, Fax 05 65 80 88 15

in St-Julien-d'Empare **2 km South by D 86 and D 558 – ✉ 12700 Capdenac - railway station**

Auberge La Diège rm,

– ✆ 05 65 64 70 54 – www.diege.com – hotel@diege.com – Fax 05 65 80 81 58 – Closed 16 December-7 January

28 rm – € 45/60 € 52/65, € 8 – 2 suites – ½ P € 50/65

Rest – *(closed Friday dinner, Sunday dinner and Saturday from 1st October to 1st April)* Menu (€ 15), € 18/35 – Carte € 28/55

◆ A bold marriage between a resolutely contemporary building (home to functional, stylish and well-kept rooms) and an old sandstone farmhouse where the restaurant is located. Beams, stonework and a fireplace make for a rustic ambiance; regional cuisine.

CAPDENAC-LE-HAUT – 46 Lot – 337 I4 – see Figeac

CAP FERRET – 33 Gironde – 335 D7 – alt. 11 m – ✉ 33970 3 B2
Atlantic Coast

Paris 650 – Arcachon 66 – Bordeaux 71 – Lacanau-Océan 55 – Lesparre-Médoc 88

✻★ of the lighthouse.

La Frégate without rest
34 av. de l'Océan – ✆ 05 56 60 41 62 – www.hotel-la-fregate.net – resa@hotel-la-fregate.net – Fax 05 56 03 76 18 – Closed December and January
29 rm – †€ 48/155 ††€ 48/155, ☕ € 11
◆ Seaside houses set around the swimming pool. The rooms are gradually being updated and are simple, modern and chic.

Le Pinasse Café
2 bis av. de l'Océan – ✆ 05 56 03 77 87 – www.pinassecafe.com – pinassecafe@wanadoo.fr – Fax 05 56 60 63 47 – Open 2 March-11 November
Rest – Menu (€ 23 bi), € 39 – Carte € 33/130
◆ This pleasant bistro favours the sea in its decor (works with a nautical theme) and in its cooking (fish and shellfish). Terrace view of the water and Pilat Dune.

CAP FRÉHEL – 22 Côtes-d'Armor – 309 I2 – Casino Brittany 10 C1

Paris 438 – Dinan 43 – Dinard 36 – Lamballe 36 – Rennes 96 – St-Brieuc 48 – St-Malo 42

Site★★★ - ✻★★★ - Fort La Latte: site★★, ✻★★ Southeast: 5 km.

La Fauconnière
à la Pointe – ✆ 02 96 41 54 20 – Open 1st April-5 November and closed Wednesday from September to October
Rest – *(lunch only)* Menu € 20/28 – Carte € 26/46
◆ This restaurant situated in a protected site accessible on foot, is solidly anchored on the purplish red rocks of La Fauconnière. Very simple decor, but a fantastic view.

CAP GRIS-NEZ ★★ – 62 Pas-de-Calais – 301 C2 – ✉ 62179 30 A1
Audinghen Northern France and the Paris Region

Paris 288 – Arras 139 – Boulogne-sur-Mer 21 – Calais 32 – Marquise 13 – St-Omer 61

La Sirène
– ✆ 03 21 32 95 97 – Fax 03 21 32 74 75 – Closed 15 December-25 January, dinner except from May to August and Saturday from September to April, Sunday dinner and Monday
Rest – Menu € 24/43 – Carte € 36/57
◆ No mermaids in sight but lobsters and fish to charm your palate in this waterside restaurant, facing the English coastline which is visible in fine weather.

CAPINGHEM – 59 Nord – 302 F4 – see Lille

CAPPELLE-LA-GRANDE – 59 Nord – 302 C2 – see Dunkerque

CARANTEC – 29 Finistère – 308 H2 – pop. 3 088 – alt. 37 m – ✉ 29660 9 B1
Brittany

Paris 552 – Brest 71 – Lannion 53 – Morlaix 14 – Quimper 90 – St-Pol-de-Léon 10

Office de tourisme, 4, rue Pasteur ✆ 02 98 67 00 43, Fax 02 98 67 90 51

de Carantec Rue de Kergrist, S : 1 km on D 73, ✆ 02 98 67 09 14

Procession cross ★ in the church - "Chaise du Curé" (platform) ⋞★.

Pointe de Pen-al-Lann ⋞★★ East: 1.5 km then 15 mn.

L'Hôtel de Carantec-Patrick Jeffroy

r. du Kelenn – ✆ 02 98 67 00 47 – www.hoteldecarantec.com – patrick.jeffroy@wanadoo.fr – Fax 02 98 67 08 25 – Closed 16 November-9 December, 18 January-3 February, Sunday evening, Monday and Tuesday except bank holidays and except school holidays from 14 September to 16 June, Monday lunch, Tuesday lunch and Thursday lunch from 17 June to 13 September

12 rm – € 120/190 € 158/232, € 19 – ½ P € 165/203

Rest – *(pre-book)* Menu (€ 29), € 39/138 – Carte € 85/170

Spec. Saint-Jacques de la baie de Morlaix (Nov. to April). Homard bleu et tête de veau rôtie (May to Nov.). Macaron aux framboises de Taulé (June to Oct.).

◆ This charming hotel, built in 1936, overlooks the marvellous Morlaix Bay. The contemporary welcoming rooms (with terrace on the first floor) all overlook the English Channel. A panoramic restaurant where you can enjoy creative 'surf and turf' dishes.

Le Manoir de Kervézec without rest

Chemin L. Le Guennec – ✆ 02 98 67 00 26 – Fax 02 98 67 00 52 – Open April to September

5 rm – € 40/60 € 48/68, € 6

◆ Fine 19C manor house in the centre of a huge garden overlooking the sea. Family heirlooms, century-old trees, delicious breakfasts (organic products) and utter peace and quiet.

Le Cabestan

au port – ✆ 02 98 67 01 87 – www.lecabestan.fr – godec.michel@wanadoo.fr – Fax 02 98 67 90 49 – Closed 5 January-6 February, Tuesday except dinner in July-August and Monday

Rest – Menu € 19/36 – Carte € 26/45

◆ A rustic-style dining room with fine views of Callot island from the first floor. Brasserie cuisine, with the emphasis on seafood.

CARCASSONNE – 11 Aude – 344 F3 – pop. 45 500 – alt. 110 m 22 B2

– ✉ 11000 Languedoc-Roussillon-Tarn Gorges

Paris 768 – Albi 110 – Narbonne 61 – Perpignan 114 – Toulouse 92

Carcassonne-Salvaza: ✆ 04 68 71 96 46, by ④: 3 km.

Office de tourisme, 28, rue de Verdun ✆ 04 68 10 24 30, Fax 04 68 10 24 38

de Carcassonne Route de Saint Hilaire, S : 4 km on D 118 and D 104, ✆ 06 13 20 85 43

La Cité★★★ - St-Nazaire basilica★: stained glass windows★★, statues★★ - Musée du château Comtal: calvary★ de Villanière - Montolieu★ (book village) - Châteaux de Latours★.

Plan on next page

La Maison Coste rest,

40 r. Coste-Reboulh – ✆ 04 68 77 12 15 – www.maison-coste.com – contact@maison-coste.com – Fax 04 68 77 59 91 – Closed 30 January-8 February BZ **n**

5 rm – € 70/145 € 85/160 **Table d'hôte** – Menu € 25

◆ Every effort has been made to ensure that guests enjoy this tasteful, welcoming, contemporary-style establishment. Garden-terrace, Jacuzzi and sun deck. Single set menu changed nightly at the table d'hôte; aperitif and coffee on the house.

Le Parc Franck Putelat

80 chemin des Anglais, South of the Cité – ✆ 04 68 71 80 80 – www.leparcfranckputelat.com – fr.putelat@wanadoo.fr – Fax 04 68 71 80 79 – Closed January, Sunday and Monday except public holidays

Rest – Menu (€ 29 bi), € 48/95 – Carte € 70/120

Spec. Pomme de terre du pays de Sault, brousse de brebis et truffe d'été (summer). Filet de bœuf "Bocuse d'Or 2003". Guimauve à la violette de Toulouse et sablé spéculoos (summer). **Wines** Corbières, Côtes du Roussillon.

◆ The restaurant below Carcassonne is as sophisticated as its inventive modern cuisine. Bright minimalist dining room overlooking the countryside.

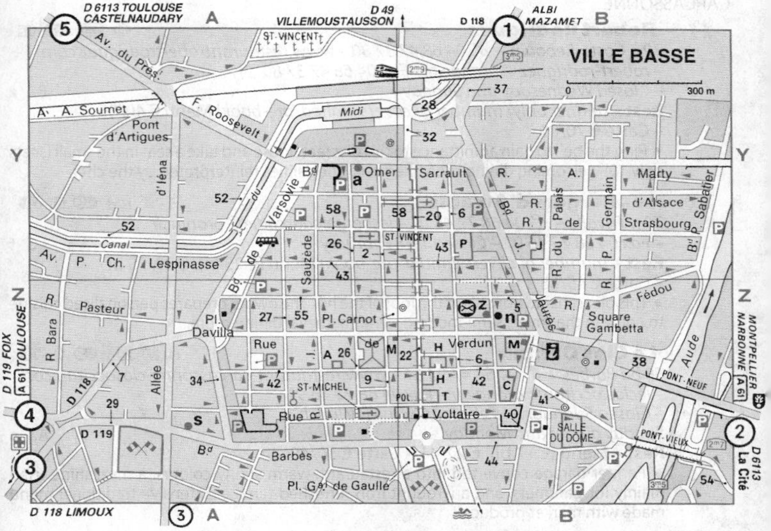

D 6113 TOULOUSE CASTELNAUDARY
VILLEMOUSTAUSSON D 49
D 118 ALBI MAZAMET

VILLE BASSE

0 300 m

ST-VINCENT · Midi · Av. du Prést F. Roosevelt · A. A. Soumet · Pont d'Artigues · Bd Omer Sarrault · R. A. Marty · R. d'Alsace · Strasbourg · Bd P. Sabatier · R. de Palais · R. Germain · Bd du Varsovie · d'Iéna · Canal · Av. P. Ch. Lespinasse · R. Pasteur · R. Bara · Pl. Davilla · Allée · Rue de Verdun · Pl. Carnot · Sauzède · Bd Jaurès · Square Gambetta · R. Fédou · Aude · PONT-NEUF · PONT-VIEUX · SALLE DU DÔME · ST-MICHEL · Rue Voltaire · Bd Barbès · Pl. Gal de Gaulle · D 119 · D 118

D 119 FOIX TOULOUSE A 61 · D 118 LIMOUX · MONTPELLIER NARBONNE A 61 · D 6113 La Cité

CARCASSONNE

Street	Grid	No.
Armagnac (R. A.)	AY	2
Barbès (R.)	BZ	5
Bringer (R. Jean)	BYZ	6
Bunau-Varilla (Av.)	AZ	7
Chartran (R.)	AZ	9
Clemenceau (R. G.)	BY	20
Combéléran (Mtée G.)	D	21
Courtejaire (R.)	BZ	22
Cros-Mayrevieille (R.)	D	24
Dr-A.-Tomey (R.)	AYZ	26
Études (R. des)	AZ	27
Foch (Av. du Mar.)	BY	28
Gout (Av. Henri)	AZ	29
Grand-Puits (R. du)	CD	30
Joffre (Av. du Mar.)	BY	32
Marcou (Bd)	AZ	34
Médiévale (Voie)	D	36
Minervoise (Rte)	BY	37
Mullot (Av. Arthur)	BZ	38
Pelletan (Bd C.)	BZ	40
Pont-Vieux (R. du)	BZ	41
Ramon (R. A.)	ABZ	42
République (R. de la)	ABY	43
Roumens (Bd du Cdt)	BZ	44
St-Jean (R.)	C	46
St-Saëns (R. C.)	D	48
St-Sernin (R.)	D	49
Semard (Av. Pierre)	AY	52
Trivalle (R.)	BZ	54
Verdun (R. de)	ABZ	
Victor-Hugo (R.)	AZ	55
Viollet-le-Duc (R.)	C	56
4-Septembre (R. du)	ABY	58

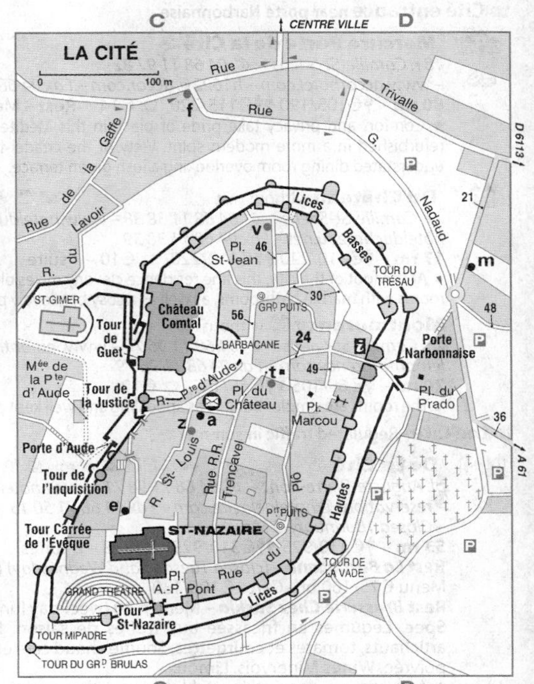

Robert Rodriguez
39 r. Coste-Reboulh – ✆ 04 68 47 37 80 – www.restaurantrobertrodriguez.com – robert-rodriguez@orange.fr – Fax 04 68 47 37 80 – Closed Wednesday and Sunday BZ **z**
Rest – *(dinner only) (number of covers limited, pre-book)* Menu € 40/85 – Carte € 70/80
◆ Ring the bell to gain admittance to this discreet house and take a seat in the small (seats only 10) welcoming dining room. Regional specialities reinterpreted by the chef.

Les Bergers d'Arcadie
70 r. Trivalle – ✆ 04 68 72 46 01 – lesbergersdarcadie@orange.fr – Fax 04 68 72 46 01 – Closed 1-28 February C **f**
Rest – *(number of covers limited, pre-book)* Menu (€ 25 bi), € 39/75 bi – Carte € 45/85
◆ This pleasant old house is at the foot of the hill. The owner prepares personalised cuisine to enjoy in the smart, semi-modern, semi-medieval dining room.

Le Clos Occitan
68 bd Barbès – ✆ 04 68 47 93 64 – www.restaurant-carcassonne-closoccitan.com – leclos.occitan@orange.fr – Fax 04 68 72 46 91 – Closed 5 January-1 February, Saturday lunch, Sunday dinner and Monday AZ **s**
Rest – Menu (€ 17 bi), € 22/41 – Carte € 30/48
◆ Former garage converted into a restaurant: warm sunny colours, a mezzanine used mainly for banquets, and a wrought iron furnished terrace. Extensive traditional menu made with market produce.

to Cité entrance near porte Narbonnaise

Mercure Porte de la Cité rm, rest,
18 r. Camille-St-Saens – ✆ 04 68 11 92 82 – www.accorhotel.com – h1622@accor.com – Fax 04 68 71 11 45
80 rm – †€ 105/190 ††€ 115/220, ☕ € 14 **Rest** – Menu € 18 – Carte € 22/50
◆ Comfort and privacy take pride of place in this Mediterranean decor that is being refurbished in a more modern spirit. View of the citadel from some rooms. Elegantly understated dining room overlooking a lush green terrace.

Du Château without rest
2 r. Camille-St-Saens – ✆ 04 68 11 38 38 – www.hotelduchateau.net – contact@hotelduchateau.net – Fax 04 68 11 38 39 D**m**
17 rm – †€ 110/220 ††€ 110/220, ☕ € 10 – 1 suite
◆ At the foot of the city, this fine residence cleverly mixes old and new. Find very refined rooms with marble bathrooms, as well as a cosy bar, lovely pool and terrace.

Montmorency without rest
2 r. Camille-St-Saens – ✆ 04 68 11 96 70 – www.lemontmorency.com – contact@lemontmorency.com – Fax 04 68 11 96 79
20 rm – †€ 65/105 ††€ 65/105, ☕ € 10
◆ The rooms are simpler but just as appealing and well kept as those in the main building.

In the Cité - Regulated traffic in summer

De La Cité rm,
pl. Auguste-Pierre-Pont – ✆ 04 68 71 98 71 – www.hoteldelacite.com – reservations@hoteldelacite.com – Fax 04 68 71 50 15 – Closed 18 January-5 March C **e**
53 rm – †€ 310/925 ††€ 310/925, ☕ € 28 – 8 suites
Rest *La Barbacane* – *(closed Tuesday and Wednesday) (dinner only)* Menu € 75/160 bi – Carte € 100/130
Rest *Brasserie Chez Saskia* – Menu € 30 (weekday lunch)/45 – Carte € 35/50
Spec. Légumes en fricassée aux truffes de saison. Pavé de loup braisé aux artichauts, tomates et courgettes. Soufflé chaud café et chocolat, sorbet menthe poivrée. **Wines** Minervois, Limoux.
◆ A prestigious, neo-Gothic establishment with a garden and swimming pool on the ramparts side. Luxuriously appointed individually decorated rooms, a few balconies and terraces overlooking the city. Modern cuisine and a refined medieval setting at the Barbacane. Chez Saskia – a brasserie with a relaxed atmosphere.

Le Donjon rm,
2 r. Comte-Roger – 04 68 11 23 00 – www.hotel-donjon.fr – info@bestwestern-donjon.com – Fax 04 68 25 06 60 C **a**
62 rm – €105/158 €105/158, €11 – 2 suites
Rest – *(closed Sunday evening from November to March)* Menu (€17), €20/29 – Carte €31/46
◆ An orphanage in the 15C, this medieval house with two villas in the garden is now a fully renovated hotel. Personalised rooms, some of which have a tiny terrace. Traditional cuisine in a bright, contemporary brasserie setting. Wine shop.

Comte Roger
14 r. St-Louis – 04 68 11 93 40 – www.comteroger.com – restaurant@comteroger.com – Fax 04 68 11 93 41 – Closed 8 February-3 March, Sunday and Monday except in high season and bank holidays C **z**
Rest – Menu (€20), €35 (dinner)/45 – Carte €50/60
◆ You may come across this shady terrace on a lively street as you walk around the historic town. Modern minimalist interior and market-fresh menu.

La Marquière
13 r. St-Jean – 04 68 71 52 00 – http://perso.orange.fr/lamarquiere – lamarquiere@wanadoo.fr – Fax 04 68 71 30 81 – Closed 10 January-10 February, Thursday except July-August and Wednesday
Rest – Menu €20 bi/60 – Carte €40/78 C **v**
◆ Located near the northern ramparts, this house has a restrained provincial interior and a pretty little courtyard terrace. Simple, tasty traditional cooking.

Auberge de Dame Carcas
3 pl. du Château – 04 68 71 23 23 – www.damecarcas.com – contact@damecarcas.com – Fax 04 68 72 46 17 – Closed 23-27 December and Wednesday C **t**
Rest – Menu €15/26
◆ The sign outside depicts Dame Carcas, who according to legend ended the siege of the town, carrying a pig. So you will not be surprised to learn that the menu has a strong pork bias.

in Aragon **10 km by ① D 118 and D 935 – pop. 445 – alt. 195 m – ✉ 11600**

La Bergerie (Fabien Galibert) rm, rm,
allée Pech-Marie – 04 68 26 10 65 – www.labergeriearagon.com – info@labergeriearagon.com – Fax 04 68 77 02 23 – Closed 5-21 October and 1st-22 January
8 rm – €70/90 €90/120, €10 – ½ P €80/105
Rest – *(closed Tuesday and Wednesday except dinner from June to September)* Menu €25 bi (weekday lunch), €37/85 bi – Carte €64/74
Spec. Filet de bar aux spaghetti de courgette. Pièce de veau à la purée de maïs. Figues rôties.
◆ This recent construction built in the local style is situated in a picturesque high-perched village. The pleasant and colourful guestrooms offer a pretty view of the Cabardès vineyard. Smart dining room in sunny colours; inventive menu using high quality regional produce.

at Montredon hamlet **4 km Northeast by A. Marty road** BY – ✉ **11000 Carcassonne**

Hostellerie St-Martin
– 04 68 47 44 41 – www.chateausaintmartin.net – hostellerie@chateausaintmartin.net – Fax 04 68 47 74 70 – Open 15 March-15 November
15 rm – €65/75 €80/100, €10
Rest *Château St-Martin* – see restaurant listing
◆ This recent regional-style building is set in a peaceful park in the heart of the countryside. Pleasant rooms with a Provençal-cum-rustic decor

Château St-Martin "Trencavel"
– 04 68 71 09 53 – www.chateausaintmartin.net – restaurant@chateausaintmartin.net – Fax 04 68 25 46 55 – Closed 21-27 February, Sunday evening and Wednesday
Rest – Menu €33/57 – Carte €46/60
◆ An attractive 14C/17C building in parkland, flanked by a 12C tower. Discreet interior decorated with a mural and pleasant summer terrace. Classic cuisine.

in Floure 11 km by ② and D 6113 – **pop. 338 – alt. 77 m –** ✉ **11800**

Château de Floure rest, rm,

1 allée Gaston-Bonheur – ✆ 04 68 79 11 29
– www.chateau-de-floure.com – contact@chateau-de-floure.com
– Fax 04 68 79 04 61 – Closed 15 November-14 February
21 rm – †€ 110/190 ††€ 110/190, ☕ € 16 – 4 suites – ½ P € 116/156
Rest – *(dinner only)* Menu € 49/79 – Carte € 72/87
◆ Formerly a Roman villa, then a monastery, this 12C castle sports a plush decor of gilding and tapestries. The characterful rooms overlook the formal French gardens. A recent makeover has introduced a contemporary flavour alongside the 17C beams and statues. View of Mont Alaric.

South via ③ **3 km and by D104 –** ✉ **11000 Carcassonne**

Domaine d'Auriac

– ✆ 04 68 25 72 22 – www.domaine-d-auriac.com
– auriac@relaischateaux.com – Fax 04 68 47 35 54
– Closed 8-16 November, 3 January-8 February, Sunday dinner and Monday from 4 October to 6 April
24 rm – †€ 100/200 ††€ 100/450, ☕ € 22 – ½ P € 150/325
Rest – *(closed Sunday dinner and Monday from October to March, Monday lunch, Tuesday lunch and Wednesday lunch from April to September except bank holidays)* Menu € 70/110 – Carte € 78/106
Rest *Bistrot d'Auriac* – *✆ 04 68 25 37 19 (closed 24 November-1st December, Monday and dinner Tuesday to Thursday from October-April and Sunday dinner except public holidays)* Menu € 17 (lunch), € 24/45 – Carte € 26/30
Spec. Assiette de dégustation d'anchois de Collioure. Cassoulet. Gibier (Oct. to Jan.). **Wines** Cabardès, Corbières.
◆ A stylish 19C abode in parkland complete with an 18-hole golf course. Personalised rooms in the chateau, larger and more Provençal in spirit in the outhouses. Tasty local dishes served in a plush dining room that leads onto a terrace. Bistro-style clubhouse.

in Cavanac 7 km by ③ and St-Hilaire road – **pop. 773 – alt. 138 m –** ✉ **11570**

Château de Cavanac rm, rm, rm,

– ✆ 04 68 79 61 04 – www.chateau-de-cavanac.fr
– infos@chateau-de-cavanac.fr – Fax 04 68 79 79 67
– Closed 3 weeks in November, January and February
24 rm – †€ 68/150 ††€ 78/155, ☕ € 12 – 4 suites
Rest – *(closed Monday and Sunday) (dinner only)* Menu € 42 bi
◆ This 17C château is set on a winegrowing estate in the heart of the countryside. The attractive rooms are named after flowers. Breakfast is served on the veranda-terrace. Rustic-style restaurant set in the former stables. Traditional dishes and grills; wines from the estate.

in Pezens 10 km northeast via ⑤ and D 6113 – **pop. 1 114 – alt. 117 m –** ✉ **11170**

L'Ambrosia with rm rest,

carrefour la Madeleine, D 6113 – ✆ 04 68 24 92 53 – Fax 04 68 24 84 01
– Restaurant: Closed 2-18 November, 4-26 January, Tuesday from mid-September to end June, Sunday from July to mid-September and Monday;
Hotel: Open from April to October
6 rm – †€ 60/65 ††€ 60/65, ☕ € 10 **Rest** – Menu € 27/77 – Carte € 58/72
◆ A simple hotel restaurant next to the D 6113 road, with veranda. The young chef shows surprising maturity in his creativity and his recipes hit the spot. Small, functional guestrooms.

CARENNAC – 46 Lot – 337 G2 – **pop. 386 – alt. 123 m –** ✉ **46110** 29 **C1**
Dordogne-Berry-Limousin

Paris 520 – Brive-la-Gaillarde 39 – Cahors 79 – Martel 16 – St-Céré 17 – Tulle 51

Office de tourisme, le bourg ✆ 05 65 10 97 01, Fax 05 65 10 51 22

Portal★ of St Pierre church - Burial★ in the cloister chapter house.

Hostellerie Fénelon
Le Bourg – ✆ 05 65 10 96 46 – www.hotel-fenelon.com – contact@hotel-fenelon.com – Fax 05 65 10 94 86 – Closed 16 November-19 December, 5 January-14 March and Friday from 1st October-30 April
15 rm – €50/57 €54/69, ☕ €10 – ½ P €60/69
Rest – *(closed Monday lunch, Friday lunch and Saturday lunch except July-August and Friday from 1st October to 30 April)* Menu (€18), €24/51 – Carte €25/57
◆ A large Quercy house with a family atmosphere where you may prefer the bedrooms with a view of the Dordogne. Beams and stonework, a fireplace and country ornaments give character to the dining room with views of the surrounding countryside.

CARGÈSE – **2A Corse-du-Sud** – **345** A7 – **see Corse**

CARHAIX-PLOUGUER – **29 Finistère** – **308** J5 – **pop. 7 667** – **alt. 138 m** – ✉ **29270** ▮ **Brittany** 9 **B2**

Paris 506 – Brest 86 – Guingamp 49 – Lorient 74 – Morlaix 51 – Pontivy 59 – Quimper 61

Office de tourisme, rue Brizeux ✆ 02 98 93 04 42, Fax 02 98 93 23 83

Noz Vad without rest
12 bd de la République – ✆ 02 98 99 12 12 – www.nozvad.com – aemcs@nozvad.com – Fax 02 98 99 44 32 – Closed 21 December-11 January
44 rm – €44/89 €51/95, ☕ €10
◆ Local artists took part in the renovation of this hotel which now has an attractive Breton decor: paintings, photos, fresco. Practical, modern guestrooms.

in Port de Carhaix **6 km southwest by Lorient road** – ✉ **29270 Carhaix-Plouguer**

Auberge du Poher
– ✆ 0298995118 – www.auberge-du-poher.com – aubergedupoher@orange.fr – Fax 0298995118 – Closed 26 December-5 January and Wednesday
Rest – Menu (€13), €24/48 – Carte €24/50
◆ Appealing inn with a pleasant rustic dining room facing the garden. Copious portions of traditional fare; very reasonably priced.

CARIGNAN – **08 Ardennes** – **306** N5 – **pop. 3 178** – **alt. 174 m** – ✉ **08110** 14 **C1**

Paris 264 – Charleville-Mézières 43 – Mouzon 8 – Montmédy 24 – Sedan 20 – Verdun 70

La Gourmandière
19 av. Blagny – ✆ 03 24 22 20 99 – www.la-gourmandiere.com – la-gourmandiere2@wanadoo.fr – Fax 03 24 22 20 99 – Closed Monday except public holidays
Rest – Menu (€20), €29/55
◆ An elegant bourgeois house from 1890 offering guests generous, tasty food using vegetable garden produce, interesting wine list, refined interior and garden terrace.

CARNAC – **56 Morbihan** – **308** M9 – **pop. 4 445** – **alt. 16 m** – **Casino** Z – ✉ **56340** ▮ **Brittany** 9 **B3**

Paris 490 – Auray 13 – Lorient 49 – Quiberon 19 – Vannes 33

Office de tourisme, 74, avenue des Druides ✆ 02 97 52 13 52, Fax 02 97 52 86 10

de Villarceaux Auray Ploemel, N : 8 km on D 196, ✆ 02 97 56 85 18

Musée de préhistoire★★ **M** - St-Cornély church ★ **E** - St-Michel tumulus ★: ≤★ - Le Ménec alignments ★★ by D 196: 1.5 km - Kermario alignments ★★ y ②: 2 km - Kerlescan alignments ★ by ②: 4.5 km.

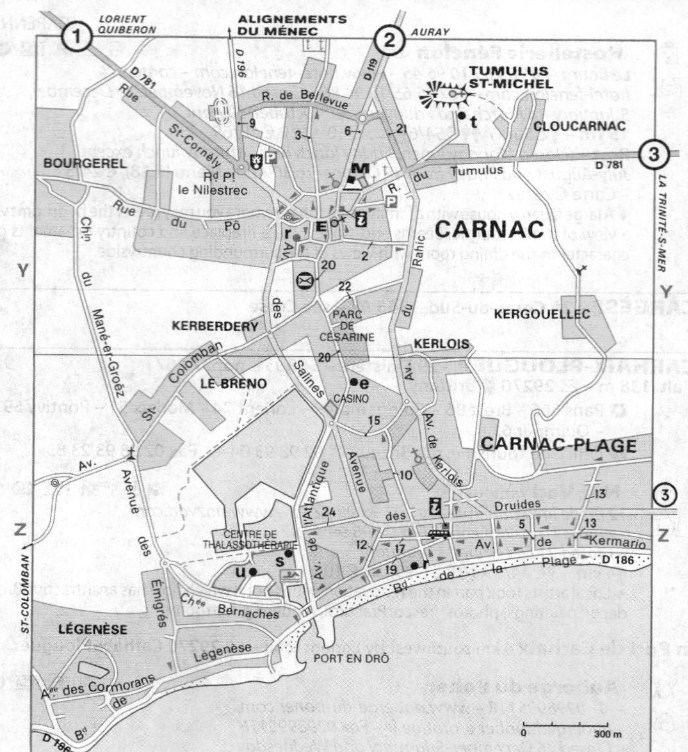

Colary (R.) . . . . Y 2
Courdiec (R. de) . . . . Y 3
Cromlech (Allée du) . . . . Z 5
Korrigans (R. des) . . . . Y 6
Ménec (R. du) . . . . Y 9
Menhirs (Av. des) . . . . Z 10
Miln (Av.) . . . . Z 12
Montagne (Allée de la) . . . . Z 13
Palud (Av. du) . . . . Z 15
Parc (Allée du) . . . . Z 17
Port en Dro (Av. de) . . . . Z 19
Poste (Av. de la) . . . . Y 20
Poul Person (R. de) . . . . Y 21
Roer (Av. du) . . . . Y 22
Talleyrand (R. de) . . . . Z 24

Le Diana

21 bd de la Plage – ✆ 02 97 52 05 38 – www.lediana.com – contact@lediana.com – Fax 02 97 52 87 91 – Open 10 April-4 November Z r

38 rm – €105/250 €120/250, ☕ €21 – 3 suites – ½ P €115/180

Rest – *(open 2 May-4 October and closed Wednesday in low season) (dinner only except Sunday and bank holidays)* Menu €39/69 – Carte €50/69

◆ Large building with an elegant atmosphere, housing rather spacious rooms with a sea view. Those overlooking the mini golf course are quieter. Wellness centre. A veranda and terrace facing the beach. Regionally inspired cuisine with extensive wine and rum list.

Novotel

av. de l'Atlantique – ✆ *02 97 52 53 00* – *www.thalasso-carnac.com* – *h0406@accor.com* – *Fax 02 97 52 53 55* – *Closed 4-18 January* Z s

109 rm – €103/198 €119/198, ☕ €15 – 1 suite

Rest *Le Clipper* – Menu (€23), €30 – Carte €35/55

Rest *Diététique* – Menu €30 bi

◆ Direct access to the thalassotherapy centre, seawater swimming pool, fitness centre and tennis court. The rooms have been renovated in the usual dynamic Novotel spirit! The Clipper offers traditional dishes and a nautical setting. The Diététique offers set menus for those taking a cure, based on the advice of a dietician.

Celtique rest,

82 av. des Druides – 02 97 52 14 15 – www.hotel-celtique.com – reservation@hotelceltique.com – Fax 02 97 52 71 10 Z **h**

58 rm – €70/150 €70/150, €13 – 6 suites

Rest – *(dinner only)* Menu €29 bi/35 – Carte €33/45

◆ A recent building in the midst of old pine trees houses modern and light rooms decorated in a Breton fashion. Near the beach, pool with a sliding roof, Jacuzzi and fitness centre. A classic menu enriched by fish and seafood dishes to the delight of its regulars.

Tumulus

chemin du Tumulus – 02 97 52 08 21 – www.hotel-tumulus.com – info@hotel-tumulus.com – Fax 02 97 52 81 88 – Closed 5 November-12 February Y **t**

23 rm – €90/285 €90/295, €16

Rest – *(Closed lunch from Monday to Friday)* Menu €27/56 – Carte €30/60

◆ 1920s hillside hotel, renovated in 2006, with a great view of the coast. Rooms upstairs, bungalows with terrace, pool and Jacuzzi in the garden. Unpretentious classic menu in this restaurant facing the bay of Quiberon.

Ibis rest,

av. de l'Atlantique – 02 97 52 54 00 – www.thalasso-carnac.com – h1054@accor.com – Fax 02 97 52 53 66 – Closed 4-18 January Z **u**

121 rm – €64/101 €72/141, €11 – ½ P €65/100

Rest – Menu €22 – Carte €27/45

◆ This hotel at the foot of the former saltworks is directly connected to the spa centre. Bedrooms with a full range of facilities and balconies. Attractive indoor pool. Large buffet laid in a stylish blue and white dining room, leading into a small garden.

La Côte

3 impasse er Forn (Alignements de Kermario), via ②: 2 km – 02 97 52 02 80 – www.restaurant-la-cote.com – restaurant.lacote@orange.fr – Closed 28 September-2 October, 23-27 November, 3 January-10 February, Saturday lunch, Sunday dinner from September to June, Tuesday lunch in July-August and Monday

Rest – Menu (€24), €35/85 – Carte €55/90

◆ A restaurant in a converted farmhouse not far from the famous Kermario megaliths. Pretty rustic dining room, veranda, terrace in the garden. Inventive repertory.

La Calypso

158 r. du Pô, (le Pô oyster beds) – 02 97 52 06 14 – www.calypso-carnac.com – Fax 02 97 52 20 39 – Closed 16 November-4 February, Sunday dinner except July-August and Monday

Rest – Carte €32/108

◆ Regulars enjoy coming to this charming nautical bistro for its remarkably fresh and simply prepared fish, shellfish and seafood.

Auberge le Râtelier with rm

4 chemin du Douet – 02 97 52 05 04 – www.le.ratelier.com – contact@le.ratelier.com – Fax 02 97 52 76 11 – Closed 17 November-10 December and 5 January-4 February Y **r**

8 rm – €43/62 €43/62, €8 – ½ P €49/62

Rest – *(closed Tuesday and Wednesday from October to Easter, Tuesday lunch and Wednesday lunch in June and September)* Menu €20/45 – Carte €37/77

◆ A 19C farmhouse with a granite façade covered in Virginia creeper. A welcoming dining room serving regional cuisine with fish in pride of place. Simple bedrooms.

Good food without spending a fortune?
Look out for the Bib Gourmand

CARNON-PLAGE – 34 Hérault – 339 I7 – ✉ 34280 — 23 C2

Paris 758 – Aigues-Mortes 20 – Montpellier 20 – Nîmes 56 – Sète 37

Office de tourisme, rue du Levant ✆ 04 67 50 51 15, Fax 04 67 50 54 04

Neptune

au port – ✆ 04 67 50 88 00 – www.hotel-neptune.fr – hotel-neptune@wanadoo.fr – Fax 04 67 50 96 72 – Closed 19 December-11 January

53 rm – †€ 55/90 ††€ 65/105, ☕ € 10 – ½ P € 61/81

Rest – *(closed 20 December-11 January, Saturday lunch and Sunday dinner except July-August)* Menu (€ 17), € 25/35

◆ Opposite the marina, this modern building is home to airy, comfortable guestrooms, gradually being refurbished in a contemporary style. Friendly welcome. Modern menu in the restaurant opening onto a summer poolside terrace.

CARPENTRAS – 84 Vaucluse – 332 D9 – pop. 27 000 – alt. 102 m – ✉ 84200 Provence — 42 E1

Paris 679 – Avignon 30 – Digne-les-Bains 139 – Gap 146 – Marseille 105

Office de tourisme, place Aristide Briand ✆ 04 90 63 00 78, Fax 04 90 60 41 02

Provence Country Club Saumane-de-Vaucluse Route de Fontaine de Vaucluse, 18 km on the Cavaillon road, ✆ 04 90 20 20 65

Former St-Siffrein cathedral ★: Synagogue★.

Plan on next page

Le Comtadin without rest

65 bd Albin-Durand – ✆ 04 90 67 75 00 – www.le-comtadin.com – Fax 04 90 67 75 01 – Closed 19 December-4 January, and Sunday from October to February Z u

19 rm – †€ 55/95 ††€ 75/115, ☕ € 12

◆ Handsome late-18C mansion. The majority of the rooms, which are light and well soundproofed, overlook the patio where breakfast is served in summer. Inviting lounge.

Du Fiacre without rest

153 r. de la Vigne – ✆ 04 90 63 03 15 – www.hotel-du-fiacre.com – contact@hotel-du-fiacre.com – Fax 04 90 60 49 73 Z f

18 rm – †€ 63 ††€ 68, ☕ € 11

◆ This 18C mansion in the old town has retained its period bourgeois atmosphere. The warm and comfortable rooms are graced with personal touches. Lovely patio-terrace.

Château du Martinet without rest

rte de Mazan, 5 km via ① – ✆ 04 90 63 03 03 – www.chateau-du-martinet.fr – contact@chateau-du-martinet.fr – Fax 04 90 30 78 96 – Open from April to December

5 rm ☕ – †€ 179/284 ††€ 190/295

◆ This superb 18C château steeped in history is now a listed monument. The rooms sport a delightful mixture of old and new. Fitness trail in the park.

Chez Serge

90 r. Cottier – ✆ 04 90 63 21 24 – www.chez-serge.com – restaurant@chez-serge.com – Fax 04 90 60 30 71 – Closed Sunday from September to May Z a

Rest – Menu (€ 19), € 29/39 – Carte € 33/45

◆ In a warm decor mixing rustic, fashionable, chic and industrial details, this restaurant stands out for its generous cuisine and magnificent wine list.

in Beaumes-de-Venise 10 km by ① D 7 then D 21 – ✉ 84190

Office de tourisme, place du Marché ✆ 04 90 62 94 39, Fax 04 90 62 93 25

Dolium

pl. Balma-Vénitia, cave des vignerons – ✆ 04 90 12 80 00 – www.dolium-restaurant.com – dolium@orange.fr – Closed 15 December-15 January, Thursday lunch in summer and Wednesday

Rest – Menu (€ 18), € 28/55

◆ Restaurant located in the cellar of the winegrowers of Beaumes de Venise. Regional cuisine focused on quality produce and wines from near and far are served in a bold, fashionable decor.

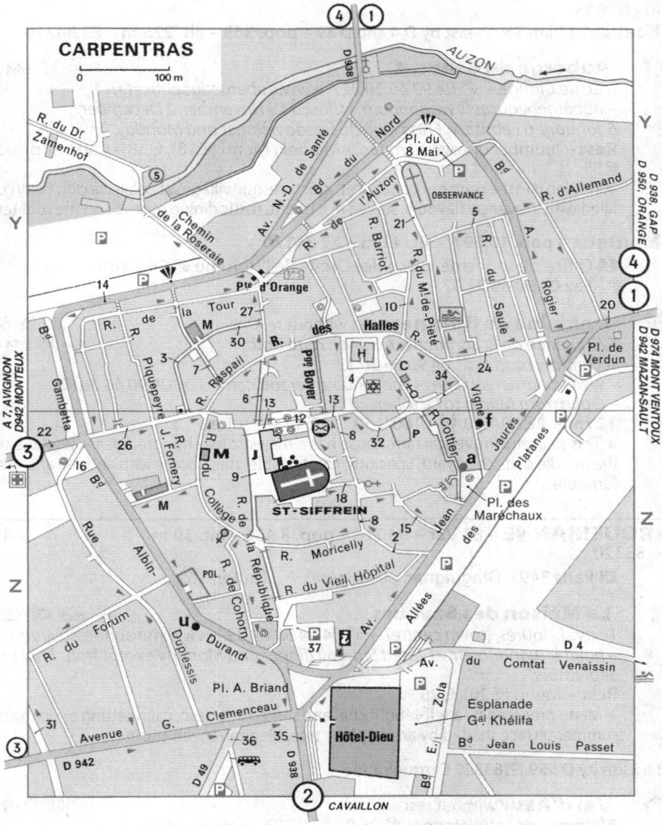

CARPENTRAS

Street	Zone	No.
Barjavel (R.)	Z	2
Briand (Pl. A.)	Z	
Carmel (R. du)	Y	3
Charretier (Pl. M.)	Y	4
Clapiès (R. de)	Y	5
Évêché (R. de l')	Y	6
Frères-Laurens (R. des)	Y	7
Gaudibert-Barret (R.)	Z	8
Gaulle (Pl. du Gén.-de)	Z	9
Guillabert (R. D.)	Y	10
Halles (R. des)	Y	
Inguimbert (Pl. d')	Z	12
Inguimbert (R. d')	YZ	13
Khélifa (Espl. Gén.)	Z	
Leclerc (Bd Mar.)	Y	14
Marins (R. des)	Z	15
Marotte (Pl. de la)	Z	16
Mercière (R.)	Z	18
Mont Ventoux (Av. du)	Y	20
Observance (R. de l')	Y	21
Pétrarque (Av.)	Z	22
Pte de Mazan (R.)	Y	24
Pte de Monteux (R.)	Z	26
Pte Orange (R.)	Y	27
République (R. de la)	Z	
Stes-Maries (R. des)	Y	30
St-Jean (R.)	Y	34
Sémard (Av. Pierre)	Z	31
Sous-Préfecture (R.)	Z	32
Victor-Hugo (Av.)	Z	35
Wilson (Av.)	Z	36
25-Août-1944 (Pl. du)	Z	37

in Mazan **7 km East by D 942 – pop. 4 943 – alt. 100 m – ✉ 84380**

Office de tourisme, 83, place du 8 Mai ✆ 04 90 69 74 27

Cemetery ⩽★.

Château de Mazan ♿ rm, AC rm, P VISA MC AE

pl. Napoléon – ✆ 04 90 69 62 61 – www.chateaudemazan.fr
– chateaudemazan@wanadoo.fr – Fax 04 90 69 76 62
– Closed 3 January-5 March

28 rm – †€ 98/275 ††€ 98/275, ☕ € 17 – 2 suites

Rest – *(closed lunch weekdays, Monday from November-April and Tuesday)*
Menu € 42/48 – Carte € 50/60

◆ The 18C residence of the Marquis de Sade has a delightful decor with a harmony of period mouldings, elegant furniture and modern touches. Attractive swimming pool and garden. Charming sitting rooms and a superb shady terrace set the scene for creative cuisine.

in Beaucet 11 km Southeast by D 4 and D 39 – pop. 363 – alt. 275 m – ✉ 84210

XX **Auberge du Beaucet** VISA

r. Coste Claude – ✆ 04 90 66 10 82 – www.aubergedubeaucet.fr – aubergebeaucet@wanadoo.fr – Closed 15 November-2 December, 6 January-6 February, Friday lunch, Sunday dinner and Monday

Rest – *(number of covers limited, pre-book)* Menu (€ 18), € 38 – Carte approx. € 55

◆ This inn is in the centre of Le Beaucet, a picturesque village set against a cliff. Tasty cuisine filled with Provençal flavours, served in a bright, rustic dining room or on the roof terrace.

in Monteux – pop. 10 597 – alt. 42 m – ✉ 84170

Office de tourisme, place des Droits de l'Homme ✆ 04 90 66 97 52, Fax 04 90 66 32 97

Domaine de Bournereau without rest VISA

579 chemin de la Sorguette, Avignon road and secondary road – ✆ 04 90 66 36 13 – www.bournereau.com – mail@bournereau.com – Fax 04 90 66 36 93 – Open from March to October

12 rm – €90/110 €100/160, € 13 – 1 suite

◆ This peaceful Provençal farmhouse has a majestic two-hundred-year-old plane tree in the middle of its courtyard. Spacious, comfortable guestrooms with antique and modern furniture.

CARQUEIRANNE – 83 Var – 340 L7 – pop. 8 436 – alt. 30 m – ✉ 83320 — 41 C3

Paris 849 – Draguignan 80 – Hyères 7 – Toulon 16

X **La Maison des Saveurs** VISA AE

18 av. J.-Jaurès, (town centre) – ✆ 04 94 58 62 33 – www.maisondessaveurs.com – hollit@wanadoo.fr – Closed Sunday dinner and Monday except from May to September

Rest – Menu (€ 20), € 26

◆ Menu prepared by a self-taught chef and served in a fresh, calm setting or on the pretty summer terrace shaded by an old plane tree. Mediterranean cuisine.

East 2 km by D 559 ✉83320 Carqueiranne

Val d'Azur without rest A/C P

3 impasse de la Valérane – ✆ 06.09.07.23.87 – www.valdazur.com – valdazur@hotmail.fr – Fax 04 94 48 07 16

5 rm – €90/130 €90/130

◆ Near the sea, on the hill above Carqueiranne, this fine modern villa offers comfortable personalised rooms, which are exotic and well presented (choice of steam or spa bath).

CARRIÈRES-SUR-SEINE – 78 Yvelines – 311 J2 – 101 14 – see Paris, Area

---

LES CARROZ-D'ARÂCHES – 74 Haute-Savoie – 328 M4 – alt. 1 140 m – Winter sports : 1 140/2 500 m 5 70 – ✉ 74300 French Alps — 46 F1

Paris 580 – Annecy 67 – Bonneville 25 – Chamonix-Mont-Blanc 47 – Thonon-les-Bains 70

Office de tourisme, 9, place Ambiance ✆ 04 50 90 00 04, Fax 04 50 90 07 00

18 de Pierre Carrée Flaine E : 12 km on D 106, ✆ 04 50 90 85 44

Les Servages d'Armelle rm, P VISA AE

841 rte des Servages – ✆ 04 50 90 01 62 – www.servages.com – servages@wanadoo.fr – Fax 04 50 90 39 41 – Closed May and November

8 rm – €190/350 €190/350, € 25 – 3 suites

Rest – *(closed Tuesday and Wednesday off season and Monday)* Carte € 30/75

◆ Venerable woodwork, hi-tech facilities and designer interior combined; refined accommodation at this superb, sensitively restored chalet. Stylish mountain restaurant with a view of hyper-modern kitchens. Regional cuisine.

Les Airelles
346 rte Moulins – ✆ 04 50 90 01 02 – www.chalet-lesairelles.com – lesairelles@free.fr – Fax 04 50 90 03 75 – Open 22 June-30 September and 15 December-22 April
12 rm – €48/54 €66/96, ☕ €10 – 3 suites – ½ P €69/87
Rest – *(Closed Saturday and Sunday in September) (dinner only in winter)*
Menu (€19), €25/40 – Carte €30/50
◆ The rooms in the first chalet are small but truly delightful (wood, warm colour scheme); the brand new second chalet offers comfortable apartments. Distinctive alpine restaurant in terms of decor and cuisine (house speciality: mountain sausages with cabbage).

La Croix de Savoie
768 rte du Pernand – ✆ 04 50 90 00 26 – www.lacroixdesavoie.fr – info@lacroixdesavoie.fr – Fax 04 50 90 00 63
Rest – Menu €21/48 – Carte €37/48
◆ Rustic, mountain-style dining room, appetising regional dishes reinterpreted by the owner, family welcome, summer terrace and a superb view of the mountains and the valley.

CARRY-LE-ROUET – 13 Bouches-du-Rhône – 340 F6 – pop. 6 355 – alt. 5 m – Casino – ✉ 13620 Provence 40 B3

Paris 765 – Aix-en-Provence 39 – Marseille 34 – Martigues 20 – Salon-de-Provence 45

Office de tourisme, avenue Aristide Briand ✆ 04 42 13 20 36, Fax 04 42 44 52 03

Le Madrigal
4 av. Dr G. Montus – ✆ 04 42 44 58 63 – www.restaurant-lemadrigal.com – info@restaurant-lemadrigal.com – Fax 04 42 44 58 63 – Closed from mid-November to early December, Sunday dinner and Monday from September to April
Rest – Menu €32/55 – Carte €41/70
◆ In the upper section of Carry, overlooking the harbour, this pink house has a pleasant terrace offering picture postcard views. Traditional cuisine and fish dishes.

CARSAC-AILLAC – 24 Dordogne – 329 I6 – pop. 1 410 – alt. 80 m – ✉ 24200 Dordogne-Berry-Limousin 4 D3

Paris 536 – Brive-la-Gaillarde 59 – Gourdon 18 – Sarlat-la-Canéda 9

La Villa Romaine
St-Rome, 3 km on Gourdon road – ✆ 05 53 28 52 07 – www.lavillaromaine.com – contact@lavillaromaine.com – Fax 05 53 28 58 10 – Closed 15 November-6 December and 15 February-15 March
17 rm – €110/160 €110/160, ☕ €15 – 2 suites – ½ P €95/122
Rest – *(open 30 April-30 September and closed Wednesday except July-August) (dinner only)* Carte €36/55
◆ Attractively restored old farmhouse built on a Gallo-Roman site near the Dordogne. Spacious, well-kept rooms. Pleasant terraces, garden and pool. At the restaurant, rustic setting, wrought iron furniture and contemporary cuisine.

CARTERET – 50 Manche – 303 B3 – see Barneville-Carteret

CARVIN – 62 Pas-de-Calais – 301 K5 – pop. 17 800 – alt. 31 m – ✉ 62220 31 C2

Paris 204 – Arras 35 – Béthune 28 – Douai 23 – Lille 24

Parc Hôtel
Z.I. du Château – ✆ 03 21 79 65 65 – www.parc-hotel.com – customer@parc-hotel.com – Fax 03 21 79 80 00
46 rm – €50/75 €60/85, ☕ €10,50
Rest – *(closed Sunday dinner and holiday dinner)* Menu €18/35 bi – Carte €28/36
◆ Near the motorway, a modern establishment offering functional, well-soundproofed rooms decorated in pastel colours; those overlooking the countryside are quieter. A light, spacious dining room where meals can be served buffet style.

XX **Le Charolais**

Domaine de la Gloriette, 143 bis r. Mar.-Foch – ✆ 03 21 40 12 98 – www.le-charolais.fr – lecharolais@wanadoo.fr – Fax 03 21 40 41 15 – Closed 5-25 August, Tuesday dinner, Sunday dinner and Monday
Rest – Menu (€ 17 bi), € 37/47 – Carte € 40/60
◆ This house is very much in the regional style with its white painted brick façade. Classic dishes and Charolais beef specialities are served in the simple dining room.

CASAMOZZA – 2B Haute-Corse – **345** F4 – **see Corse**

CASCASTEL-DES-CORBIÈRES – 11 Aude – **344** H5 – **pop. 208** – **alt. 140 m** – ✉ **11360** 22 **B3**

Paris 835 – Perpignan 52 – Carcassonne 70 – Narbonne 48

Domaine Grand Guilhem without rest

chemin du Col-de-la-Serre – ✆ 04 68 45 86 67 – www.grandguilhem.com – gguilhem@aol.com – Fax 04 68 45 29 58
4 rm – €80 €90
◆ This renovated, 19C, stone residence has kept all its authenticity. Charming guestrooms; wine tasting in the cellar.

X **Le Clos de Cascastel**

quai de la Berre – ✆ 04 68 45 06 22 – leclosdecascastel@orange.fr – Fax 04 68 45 06 22 – Closed mid November-mid December, mid January-beg. February and Tuesday
Rest – Menu (€ 17), € 27/39 bi
◆ Regional dishes and a selection of Corbière wines. Enjoy them in a warm, modernised dining room or under the rushes of the terrace with its teak furniture, beside the plane and olive trees.

CASSEL – 59 Nord – **302** C3 – **pop. 2 290** – **alt. 175 m** – ✉ **59670** 30 **B2**
Northern France and the Paris Region

Paris 250 – Calais 58 – Dunkerque 30 – Hazebrouck 11 – Lille 52 – St-Omer 21
Syndicat d'initiative, 20, Grand'Place ✆ 03 28 40 52 55, Fax 03 28 40 59 17
Site★.

Châtellerie de Schoebeque without rest

32 r. du Maréchal Foch – ✆ 03 28 42 42 67 – www.schoebeque.com – contact@schoebeque.com – Fax 03 28 42 21 86
14 rm – €95/159 € 105/239, € 15
◆ Luxury, charm, peace and quiet in this historic 18C abode. Fine rooms, spa (beauty centre) and a matchless view of Flanders from the breakfast veranda.

XXX **Au Petit Bruxelles**

1656 rte Nationale, at the Petit-Bruxelles, south-east: 3.5 km on D 916 – ✆ 03 28 42 44 64 – www.aupetitbruxelles.com – aupetitbruxelles@wanadoo.fr – Fax 03 28 40 58 13 – Closed Sunday dinner, Monday dinner, Tuesday and Wednesday
Rest – Menu € 30/62 – Carte € 41/59
◆ An old coaching inn with a spruce, red-brick façade typical of the region. Warm rustic dining room, informal ambience and sophisticated updated cuisine.

in St-Sylvestre-Cappel 6 km Northeast by D 916 – **pop. 1 093** – **alt. 55 m** – ✉ **59114**

XX **Le St Sylvestre**

57 rte Nationale – ✆ 03 28 42 82 13 – www.le-saint-sylvestre.com – restaurantlesaintsylvestre@wanadoo.fr – Closed 2-26 August, February holiday, Monday dinner, Saturday lunch, Sunday dinner and Wednesday
Rest – Menu € 19/49 – Carte € 42/51
◆ The black façade hides a designer decor, bright colours and Chaplin films on plasma screens. A setting in keeping with the refined cuisine, which is constantly updated.

CASSIS – 13 Bouches-du-Rhône – **340** I6 – **pop. 7 766** – **alt. 10 m** 40 **B3**
– **Casino** – ✉ **13260** Provence

Paris 800 – Aix-en-Provence 51 – La Ciotat 10 – Marseille 30 – Toulon 42

Office de tourisme, Quai des Moulins ✆ 08 92 25 98 92, Fax 04 42 01 28 31

Site★ - Les Calanques★★ (1h by boat) - Mt de la Saoupe ✻★★: 2 km by D 41A.

Cap Canaille, Europe's highest sea cliff, ≤★★★ 5 km by D41A - Semaphore ✻★★★ - Corniche des Crêtes★★ de Cassis à la Ciotat.

CASSIS

Abbé-Mouton (R.) 2
Arène (R. de l') 4
Autheman (R. V.) 5
Baragnon (Pl.) 6
Barthélemy (Bd) 7
Barthélemy (Quai Jean-Jacques) . . . 8
Baux (Quai des) 9
Ciotat (R. de la) 10
Clemenceau (Pl.) 12
Ganteaume (Av. de l'Amiral) . 14
Jean-Jaurès (Av.) 16
Leriche (Av. Professeur) 17
Mirabeau (Pl.) 22
Moulins (Quai des) 23
République (Pl.) 25
Revestel (Av. du) 26
St-Michel (Pl.) 27
Thiers (R. Adolphe) 29
Victor-Hugo (Av.) 32

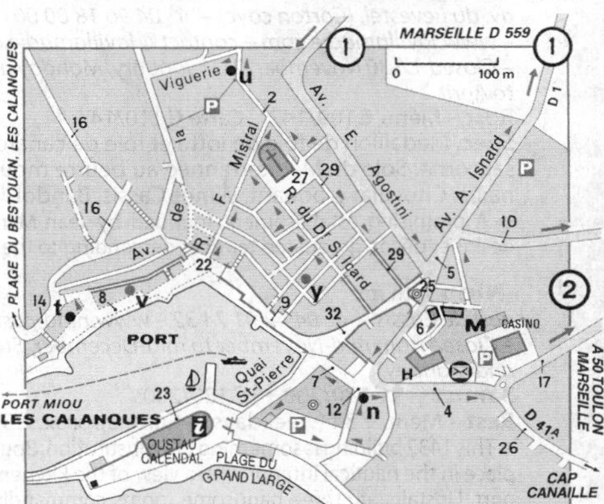

Royal Cottage without rest
6 av. 11 Novembre, via ① – ✆ 04 42 01 33 34
– www.royal-cottage.com – info@royal-cottage.com – Fax 04 42 01 06 90
– Closed 11-28 December
25 rm – €95/227 €107/239
◆ A small Provençal paradise flourishing amid lush exotic vegetation. A contemporary interior. The terraces of some rooms command a fine view of the harbour.

Les Jardins de Cassis without rest
r. A. Favier, 1 km via ① – ✆ 04 42 01 84 85
– www.lesjardinsdecassis.com – contact@lesjardinsdecassis.com
– Fax 04 42 01 32 38 – Open mid-March to mid-November
36 rm – €62/127 €62/127, €12
◆ A series of ochre coloured buildings dominating Cassis. Smart rooms, often with private terraces. Attractive Mediterranean garden and pool. Jacuzzi tub.

Le Golfe without rest
3 pl. Grand Carnot – ✆ 04 42 01 00 21 – www.legolfe-cassis.fr – contact@legolfe-cassis.fr – Fax 04 42 01 92 08 – Open 28 March-8 November t
30 rm – €70/95 €70/95, €11
◆ This appealing, unpretentious hotel has small, practical, air-conditioned rooms, some with a sea view and a terrace shaded by plane trees overlooking the harbour.

Le Clos des Arômes
10 r. Abbé Paul Mouton – ✆ 04 42 01 71 84 – www.le-clos-des-aromes.com
– closdesaromes@orange.fr – Fax 04 42 01 31 76
– Closed 3 January-25 February u
14 rm – €55 €75, €9
Rest – *(Closed Tuesday lunch, Wednesday lunch and Monday)* Menu €27/43
– Carte €33/50
◆ The doors of this charming house open onto a flower-decked garden. Rooms, both discreet and contemporary, are gaily and tastefully decorated. A tiny dining room and delightful terrace, Southern cuisine: fish stews such as bourride or bouillabaisse.

Cassitel without rest
pl. Clemenceau – 04 42 01 83 44 – www.hotel-cassis.com – cassitel@hotel-cassis.com – Fax 04 42 01 96 31 n
32 rm – €60/63 €71/90, €8
◆ A hotel near the beach but also in the centre of the lively part of Cassis and its nightlife (discotheques and bars). Practical rooms, renovated on the harbour side. Provençal breakfast room.

XXX **La Villa Madie** (Jean-Marc Banzo)
av. du Revestel, (Corton cove) – 04 96 18 00 00 – www.lavillamadie.com – contact@lavillamadie.com – Fax 04 96 18 00 01 – Closed 17-30 November, 2-31 January, Monday and Tuesday from October to April
Rest – Menu €109/147 – Carte €110/144
Spec. Médaillon de foie de lotte et foie de canard, cœur d'artichaut et salade de salicorne. Sole de Méditerrannée au beurre mousseux et pommes de terre grenaille. Chocolat croquant. **Wines** Cassis, Bandol.
◆ A promising establishment founded by Jean-Marc Banzo: modern cuisine, refined designer décor, graduated terraces descending to the sea and stunning view.

X **Nino** with rm
port de Cassis – 04 42 01 74 32 – www.nino-cassis.com – Fax 04 42 42 01 34 51 – Closed from mid-November to mid-December, Sunday dinner in low season and Monday v
3 rm – €180/200 €180/200
Rest – Menu €34 (weekdays) – Carte approx. €53
◆ This 1432 building is something of an institution. Bouillabaisse and seafood take pride of place in the nautical interior with a view of the kitchen. Flower-decked terrace facing the port. Upstairs are three handsome rooms commanding a fine view. They are designed along the lines of boat cabins.

CASTAGNÈDE – 64 Pyrénées-Atlantiques – 342 G4 – see Salies-de-Béarn

CASTANET-TOLOSAN – 31 Haute-Garonne – 343 H3 – see Toulouse

CASTELJALOUX – 47 Lot-et-Garonne – 336 C4 – pop. 4 755 – alt. 52 m – ✉ 47700 Atlantic Coast 4 C2

- Paris 674 – Agen 55 – Langon 55 – Marmande 23 – Mont-de-Marsan 73 – Nérac 30
- Office de tourisme, Maison du Roy 05 53 93 00 00, Fax 05 53 20 74 32
- de Casteljaloux Route de Mont de Marsan, S: 4 km on D 933, 05 53 93 51 60

Les Cordeliers rest,
r. Cordeliers – 05 53 93 02 19 – www.hotel-cordeliers.fr – hotel.lescordeliers@wanadoo.fr – Fax 05 53 93 55 48 – Closed 23 December-13 January
24 rm – €44 €47/68, €8
Rest – *(closed Sunday dinner)* Menu (€12), €16/29 – Carte €28/43
◆ A warm welcome awaits at this establishment situated in an alley off the main square. The functional, well-kept rooms have been recently renovated. The restaurant is decorated in a modern, sober style, the tables are laid with care and the food is traditional.

XXX **La Vieille Auberge**
11 r. Posterne – 05 53 93 01 36 – www.restaurant-la-vieille-auberge.fr – la.vieille.auberge.47@wanadoo.fr – Fax 05 53 93 18 89 – Closed 22 June-5 July, 23 November-6 December, 23 February-1st March, Sunday dinner, Tuesday dinner and Wednesday
Rest – Menu (€20), €27/65 – Carte €38/48
◆ A charming stone house in a tiny street in the old town. Bright, colourful dining room with lots of flowers. Fine, classical cuisine.

CASTELLANE – 04 Alpes-de-Haute-Provence – 334 H9 41 C2
– pop. 1 592 – alt. 730 m – ✉ 04120 French Alps

Paris 797 – Digne-les-Bains 54 – Draguignan 59 – Grasse 64 – Manosque 92

Office de tourisme, rue Nationale ✆ 04 92 83 61 14, Fax 04 92 83 76 89

de Taulane La Martre Le Logis du Pin, E : 17 km on D 4085, ✆ 04 93 60 31 30

Site★ - Chaudanne lake ★ 4 km by ①.

Grand canyon du Verdon★★★.

in la Garde 6 km on the D 559 and D 4085 – pop. 84 – alt. 928 m – ✉ 04120

Auberge du Teillon with rm
rte Napoléon – ✆ 04 92 83 60 88 – www.auberge-teillon.com – contact@auberge-teillon.com – Fax 04 92 83 74 08 – Open 15 March-15 November and closed Sunday evening and Monday except July-August and public holidays, Tuesday lunch in July-August
8 rm – †€ 55/60 ††€ 55/60, ☕ € 8 – ½ P € 57/60
Rest – Menu € 22/49 – Carte € 38/54
◆ A warm welcome and friendly atmosphere in this rustic roadside inn. Tasty, traditional cuisine with a modern touch; selection of Provençal dishes. Small refurbished rooms upstairs, ideal for an overnight stop.

A good night's sleep without spending a fortune?
Look for a Bib Hotel.

LE CASTELLET – 83 Var – 340 J6 – pop. 4 154 – alt. 252 m – ✉ 83330 40 B3

Paris 816 – Marseille 46 – Toulon 23 – Aubagne 30 – Bandol 11

Paul Ricard race circuit ✆ 04 94 98 36 66

in Ste-Anne-du-Castellet 4,5 km North by D 226 and D 26 – ✉ 83330

Castel Ste-Anne without rest
81 chemin Chapelle – ✆ 04 94 32 60 08 – hotelcastelstanne@wanadoo.fr – Fax 04 94 32 68 16
17 rm – †€ 55/65 ††€ 60/70, ☕ € 8
◆ Peace and quiet, a flower garden and an attractive swimming pool form the setting for this family hotel. Tasteful rooms; those in the more recent wing have terraces.

at Circuit Paul Ricard 11 km North by D 226, D 26 and D N8 – ✉ 83330 Le Beausset

Du Castellet
3001 rte Hauts du Camp – ✆ 04 94 98 37 77 – www.hotelducastellet.com – welcome@hotelducastellet.com – Fax 04 94 98 37 78
34 rm – †€ 320/530 ††€ 320/530, ☕ € 32 – 13 suites
Rest ***Monte Cristo*** – Menu € 50 (weekday lunch)/100 – Carte € 100/200
Spec. Raviole de langoustine à l'écorce de citron vert. Carré d'agneau de Provence "garam masala" aux zestes de citron confit. Arlette croustillante et poire pochée au cœur des vignes, accord épicé (autumn-winter). **Wines** Bandol.
◆ By the racetrack, this luxurious and stylishly decorated property mingles Provençal and Tuscan architectural influences. Inviting, plush and cosy guestrooms. An elegant restaurant where the chef adds a personal Mediterranean note to the menu. Italian cuisine by the pool house in summertime.

Résidence des Équipages without rest
3100 rte des Hauts du Camp – ✆ 04 94 98 37 77 – welcome@hotelducastellet.com – Fax 04 94 98 37 78
19 rm – †€ 120/160 ††€ 120/160, ☕ € 15
◆ Extremely popular with airline crews and transit passengers. This modern hotel, built next to the airport, is faultlessly soundproofed and offers an extensive range of modern amenities.

CASTELNAUDARY – 11 Aude – **344** C3 – **pop. 10 851 – alt. 175 m** 22 **A2**
– ✉ 11400 Languedoc-Roussillon-Tarn Gorges

Paris 735 – Carcassonne 42 – Foix 70 – Pamiers 49 – Toulouse 60

Office de tourisme, place de Verdun ✆ 04 68 23 05 73, Fax 04 68 23 61 40

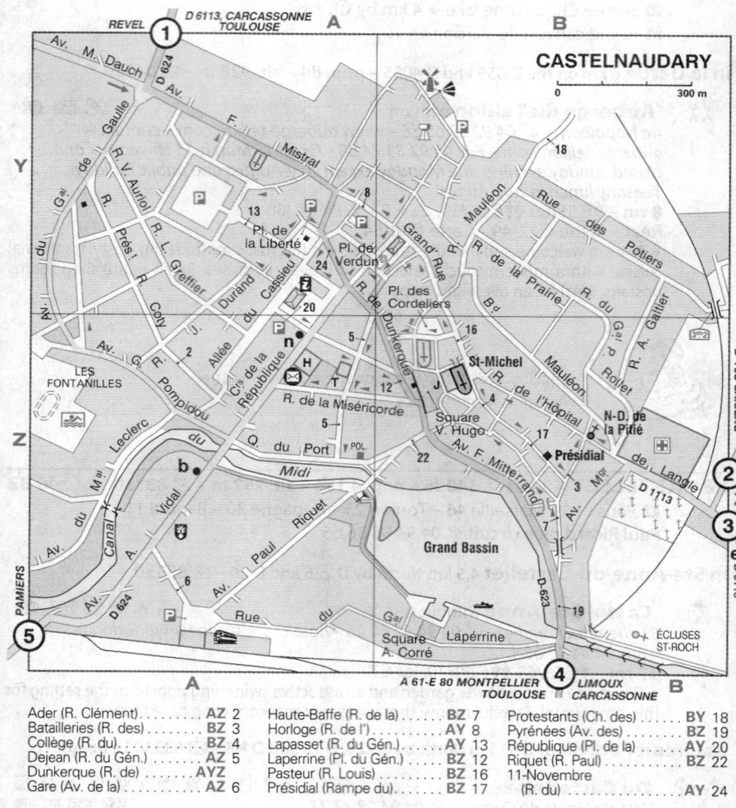

Ader (R. Clément) .... **AZ** 2
Batailleries (R. des) .... **BZ** 3
Collège (R. du) .... **BZ** 4
Dejean (R. du Gén.) .... **AZ** 5
Dunkerque (R. de) .... **AYZ**
Gare (Av. de la) .... **AZ** 6
Haute-Baffe (R. de la) .... **BZ** 7
Horloge (R. de l') .... **AY** 8
Lapasset (R. du Gén.) .... **AY** 13
Laperrine (Pl. du Gén.) .... **BZ** 12
Pasteur (R. Louis) .... **BZ** 16
Présidial (Rampe du) .... **BZ** 17
Protestants (Ch. des) .... **BY** 18
Pyrénées (Av. des) .... **BZ** 19
République (Pl. de la) .... **AY** 20
Riquet (R. Paul) .... **BZ** 22
11-Novembre (R. du) .... **AY** 24

Du Canal without rest VISA

2 ter av. A. Vidal – ✆ 04 68 94 05 05 – www.hotelducanal.com – hotelducanal@wanadoo.fr – Fax 04 68 94 05 06 AZ **b**

38 rm – †€ 50/59 ††€ 58/68, ☕ € 8

◆ A beautiful ochre building, once a lime kiln, by the Canal du Midi. Practical, well soundproofed rooms. Breakfast served at the water's edge. Pretty garden.

Du Centre et du Lauragais VISA

31 cours République – ✆ 04 68 23 25 95
– www.hotel-centre-lauragais.com – hcl11@live.fr – Fax 04 68 94 01 66
– Closed 5-27 January and Sunday dinner AZ **n**

16 rm – †€ 50 ††€ 70, ☕ € 8 – ½ P € 70

Rest – Menu € 19 (weekday lunch), € 25/53 – Carte € 34/64

◆ Attractive town house on Castelnaudary's main street. Practical rooms with cane furnishings. Fully refurbished neo-bistro style décor. Serving traditional fare plus local specialities including the renowned cassoulet.

Le Clos Fleuri St-Siméon rm, VISA

134 av. Mgr. de Langle, via ③ – 04 68 94 01 20 – www.leclosfleuri.fr – leclos@hotmail.fr – Fax 04 68 94 05 47
31 rm – €57 €57, €6 – ½ P €48
Rest – *(closed 1-9 March, 23 December-5 January, Saturday and Sunday)* Menu (€14) – Carte €23/39
◆ Isolated from the commercial buildings by its walled garden, this hotel has well-kept rooms in pastel colours and double-glazing. The restaurant has a terrace giving onto a small garden and the swimming pool. Simple meals and home-made cassoulet.

Le Tirou VISA

90 av. Mgr de Langle – 04 68 94 15 95 – www.letirou.com – letirou@wanadoo.fr – Fax 04 68 94 15 96 – Closed 23-30 June, 20 December-20 January and Monday
Rest – *(lunch only)* Menu €21 (weekdays)/39 – Carte €36/60 BZ e
◆ The chef uses only farm-reared pork in his cassoulet. Fine choice of local wines and pleasant dining room facing the garden given over to donkeys and goats.

CASTELNAU-DE-LÉVIS – 81 Tarn – 338 E7 – see Albi

CASTELNAU-DE-MONTMIRAL – 81 Tarn – 338 C7 – pop. 895 – alt. 287 m – ✉ 81140 29 C2

Paris 645 – Toulouse 69 – Cordes-sur-Ciel 22 – Gaillac 12
Office de tourisme, place des Arcades 05 63 33 15 11, Fax 05 63 33 17 60

Des Consuls without rest VISA

pl.des Arcades – 05 63 33 17 44 – www.hoteldesconsuls.com – hoteldesconsuls@orange.fr – Fax 05 63 33 78 52
15 rm – €48/78 €48/78, €9
◆ The old houses on the main square of this picturesque 13C fortified town offer rooms that are rustically decorated, simple or refurbished.

CASTELNAU-LE-LEZ – 34 Hérault – 339 I7 – see Montpellier

CASTÉRA-VERDUZAN – 32 Gers – 336 E7 – pop. 901 – alt. 114 m – Spa : early March-mid Dec. – Casino – ✉ 32410 28 A2

Paris 720 – Agen 61 – Auch 26 – Condom 20
Syndicat d'initiative, avenue des Thermes 05 62 68 10 66, Fax 05 62 68 14 58

Le Florida VISA

2 r. du Lac – 05 62 68 13 22 – restaurant.florida@orange.fr – Fax 05 62 68 10 44 – Closed February school holidays, Sunday dinner and Monday except public holidays
Rest – Menu (€15), €25 bi (weekdays)/52 – Carte €43/61
◆ Specialities from the Gers to savour, in winter, in the refurbished warm dining room by the fireside and, in summer, on the shaded terrace decked with flowers.

CASTILLON-DU-GARD – 30 Gard – 339 M5 – see Pont-du-Gard

CASTILLON-EN-COUSERANS – 09 Ariège – 343 E7 – pop. 399 – alt. 543 m – ✉ 09800 Languedoc-Roussillon-Tarn Gorges 28 B3

Paris 787 – Bagnères-de-Luchon 61 – Foix 58 – St-Girons 14
Office de tourisme, rue Noël Peyrevidal 05 61 96 72 64, Fax 05 34 14 06 82

in Audressein 1 km on the Bagnères-de-Luchon road – pop. 119 – alt. 509 m – ✉ 09800

L'Auberge d'Audressein with rm rest, VISA

– 05 61 96 11 80 – www.auberge-audressein.com – aubergeaudressein@club-internet.fr – Fax 05 61 96 82 96 – Closed 15 October-15 December, 10 January-15 March, Sunday dinner and Monday
7 rm – €55/65 €55/65, €9 – ½ P €45/65
Rest – Menu €16/85 – Carte €35/60
◆ These old stonewalls once sheltered a 19C forge. A warm-toned dining room, pleasant veranda overhanging the river and appetising food inspired by the region.

CASTRES – 81 Tarn – 338 F9 – pop. 42 900 – alt. 170 m – ✉ 81100 29 **C2**

Languedoc-Roussillon-Tarn Gorges

Paris 718 – Albi 43 – Béziers 107 – Carcassonne 70 – Toulouse 79

Castres-Mazamet: ✆ 05 63 70 34 77 by ③: 8 km.

Office de tourisme, 2, place de la Republique ✆ 05 63 62 63 62, Fax 05 63 62 63 60

de Castres Gourjade Domaine de Gourjade, N : 3 km on the Roquecourbe road, ✆ 05 63 72 27 06

Musée Goya★ - Hôtel de Nayrac★ AY - Centre national et musée Jean-Jaurès (Jean-Jaurès National Centre and Museum) AY.

Le Sidobre★ 9 km by ① - Musée du Protestantisme at Ferrières.

Plan on next page

Occitan

201 av. Ch. de Gaulle, via ③ – ✆ 05 63 35 34 20 – www.hotel-restaurant-l-occitan.fr – hotel-occitan@wanadoo.fr – Fax 05 63 35 70 32 – Closed 19 December-3 January

62 rm – €60/86 €66/95, €11 – ½ P €58/75

Rest – *(closed Sunday lunch in August and Saturday lunch)*

Menu €15 (weekdays)/40 – Carte €30/50

◆ Practical location for a stopover on the outskirts of town. All the rooms have air-conditioning and have been renovated; some occupy a new wing. Sauna and jacuzzi. Traditional food served in a contemporary setting or on the terrace opposite the swimming pool.

Miredames

1 pl. R. Salengro – ✆ 05 63 71 38 18 – www.hotel-miredames.com – bienvenue@hotel-miredames.com – Fax 05 63 71 38 19 BY **f**

14 rm – €53/55 €58/63, €8 – ½ P €49

Rest ***Relais du Pont Vieux*** – ✆ *05 63 35 56 14* – Menu (€13 bi), €17/33 – Carte €24/45

◆ The sign of this house in historic Castres shows a horse drawn barge going up the River Agout. Functional, well kept rooms. The Relais du Pont Vieux overlooks a square with a fountain but the terrace is on the riverside. Traditional menu.

Le Victoria

24 pl. 8-Mai-1945 – ✆ 05 63 59 14 68 – Fax 05 63 59 14 68 – Closed Saturday lunch and Sunday BZ **s**

Rest – Menu (€13), €24/45 – Carte €28/53

◆ Three quite cosy dining rooms in a vaulted basement. The nicest of the three has a view of the wine cellars protected by a pane of glass. Traditional food made with care.

Mandragore

1 r. Malpas – ✆ 05 63 59 51 27 – Fax 05 63 59 51 27 – Closed 15-30 March, 15-30 September, Sunday and Monday BY **e**

Rest – Menu €13 bi (weekday lunch), €16/25 – Carte €30/45

◆ This house in old Castres has been completely renovated in a modern style, featuring light wood and frosted glass. Traditional cuisine.

La Table du Sommelier

6 pl. Pélisson – ✆ 05 63 82 20 10 – contact@lechaisdusommelier.fr – Fax 05 63 82 20 10 – Closed Sunday and Monday AY **t**

Rest – Menu (€14 bi), €18/37 bi

◆ Wine bar located opposite the Musée Jean Jaurès sporting a decor of wine crates and bottles. Selected vintages and generous, market fresh menu.

in Burlats **9 km by ①, D 89 and D 58 – pop. 1 844 – alt. 191 m – ✉ 81100**

Le Castel de Burlats

8 pl. du 8-Mai-1945 – ✆ 05 63 35 29 20 – www.lecasteldeburlats.fr.st – le.castel.de-burlats@wanadoo.fr – Fax 05 63 51 14 69 – Closed 13 February-1 March

10 rm – €70/110 €70/110, €10

Rest Les Mets d'Adélaïde – see restaurant listing

◆ This 14C and 16C castel has a beautiful Renaissance-style sitting room. Its guestrooms are spacious, individually decorated and overlook a park and French-style garden. Guesthouse ambience.

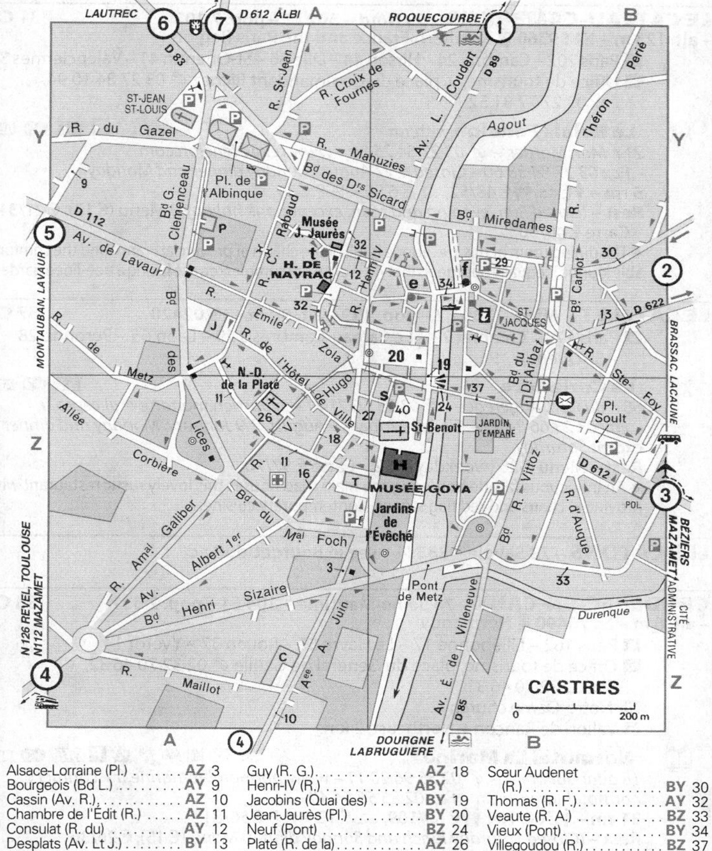

XX **Les Mets d'Adélaïde** – Hôtel Le Castel de Burlats VISA MC
8 pl.du 8-Mai-1945 – ✆ 05 63 35 78 42 – Fax 05 63 35 78 42
Rest – *(closed Sunday dinner in low season, Tuesday except dinner in winter and Monday) (number of covers limited, pre-book)* Menu (€ 19), € 25/56 – Carte € 45/60
◆ A plush bourgeois decor and a pleasantly shaded terrace. Concise seasonal and very well-prepared menu. Fine choice of regional wines.

in Lagarrigue 4 km by ③ – **pop. 1 641 – alt. 200 m** – ✉ **81090**

Montagne Noire without rest VISA MC AE
29 av. Castres, on RN 112 – ✆ 05 63 35 52 00 – www.lamontagnenoire.com – contact@lamontagnenoire.com – Fax 05 63 35 25 59
30 rm – †€ 88/106 ††€ 99/117, ☕ € 12
◆ By a busy road, a hotel with well-soundproofed practical rooms. Generous breakfasts served in a Provençal inspired room.

CASTRIES – **34 Hérault** – **339** I6 – **see Montpellier**

LE CATEAU-CAMBRÉSIS – 59 Nord – 302 J7 – pop. 7 102 31 C3
– alt. 123 m – ✉ 59360 Northern France and the Paris Region

Paris 202 – Cambrai 24 – Hirson 44 – Lille 86 – St-Quentin 41 – Valenciennes 33

Office de tourisme, 9, place du Commandant Richez ✆ 03 27 84 10 94, Fax 03 27 77 81 52

XX Le Relais Fénelon with rm

21 r. Mar. Mortier – ✆ 03 27 84 25 80 – www.relais-fenelon.com – Fax 03 27 84 38 60 – Closed 4-27 August, Sunday dinner and Monday

5 rm – €45 €45/52, €6,50 – ½ P €39

Rest – *(closed Sun. evening and Mon. except bank holidays)* Menu (€17), €21/31 – Carte €40/50

◆ The dining room of this 19C abode is full of the charm of provincial France and the comfortable lounge is equally bourgeois in style. A pleasant summer terrace facing a tree-lined garden.

LE CATELET – Aisne – 306 B2 – pop. 199 – alt. 90 m – ✉ 02420 37 C1

Paris 170 – Cambrai 22 – Le Cateau-Cambrésis 29 – Laon 66 – Péronne 28 – St-Quentin 19

XX La Coriandre

68 r. du Gén. Augereau – ✆ 03 23 66 21 71 – sebastien.monatte@alicepro.fr – Fax 03 23 66 84 23 – Closed 27 July-19 August, 2-9 January, Monday and dinner except Saturday

Rest – Menu €25 (weekdays)/52 – Carte €57/70

◆ An innocuous façade bordering the main road houses this lovely rustic restaurant with provincial chairs and red flag stones. Contemporary cuisine.

LES CATONS – 73 Savoie – 333 I4 – see le Bourget-du-Lac

CAUDEBEC-EN-CAUX – 76 Seine-Maritime – 304 E4 – pop. 2 331 33 C1
– alt. 6 m – ✉ 76490 Normandy

Paris 162 – Lillebonne 17 – Le Havre 53 – Rouen 37 – Yvetot 14

Office de tourisme, place du General de Gaulle ✆ 02 32 70 46 32, Fax 02 32 70 46 31

Notre-Dame church★.

Vallon de Rançon★ Northeast: 2 km.

Normotel La Marine

18 quai Guilbaud – ✆ 02 35 96 20 11 – www.normotel-lamarine.fr – contact@normotel-lamarine.fr – Fax 02 35 56 54 40

31 rm – €60/109 €60/109, €12 – ½ P €56/81

Rest – *(Closed Saturday lunch and Sunday dinner)* Menu (€15), €26/36 – Carte €41/61

◆ On the banks of the Seine, where boats come and go, the best rooms in this large hotel building have a balcony overlooking the river. Panoramic dining room where traditional fare is served. Riverside summer terrace.

Le Normandie

19 quai Guilbaud – ✆ 02 35 96 25 11 – www.le-normandie.fr – info@le-normandie.fr – Fax 02 35 96 68 15 – Closed 20 December-4 January

16 rm – €58 €60, €8

Rest – *(closed Monday lunch, Wednesday lunch and Sunday dinner)* Menu (€15), €20/42 – Carte €32/55

◆ On the banks of the Seine, functional rooms, some furnished in a rustic style. The largest, at the front, have a small balcony and offer a view of the river. A captivating view from the restaurant bay windows; traditional and Norman dishes.

Le Cheval Blanc

4 pl. R. Coty – ✆ 02 35 96 21 66 – www.le-cheval-blanc.fr – le-cheval-blanc-info@wanadoo.fr – Fax 02 35 95 35 40

14 rm – €56 €58, €6,50 – ½ P €53

Rest – *(closed 21 December-1st January, Saturday lunch, Sunday dinner and Friday)* Menu (€13), €15 (weekdays)/37 – Carte €35/50

◆ All the spruce, bright rooms of this town centre establishment have been well soundproofed. The rooms on the second floor have an attic roof. The owner-chef specialises in regional cuisine. Flower-decked summer terrace.

CAUREL – 22 Côtes-d'Armor – **309** D5 – pop. 384 – alt. 188 m – ✉ 22530 10 **C2**

Paris 461 – Carhaix-Plouguer 45 – Guingamp 48 – Loudéac 24 – Pontivy 22 – St-Brieuc 48

Beau Rivage with rm VISA

au Lac de Guerlédan, 2 km on D 111 – ☎ 02 96 28 52 15 – www.le-beau-rivage.net – stefetcie@orange.fr – Fax 02 96 26 01 16 – Closed 15-30 March, Monday off season and Sunday dinner

3 rm – †€ 60 ††€ 60, ☕ € 9 **Rest** – Menu (€ 21 bi), € 30/47 – Carte € 40/70

◆ Popular with the locals and tourists alike, this house makes the most of its waterside location by Lake Guerlédan. Panoramic restaurant and pleasantly classic menu. Simple rooms overlooking the lake.

CAURO – 2A Corse-du-Sud – **345** C8 – see Corse

CAUSSADE – 82 Tarn-et-Garonne – **337** F7 – pop. 6 268 – alt. 109 m – ✉ 82300 29 **C2**

Paris 606 – Cahors 38 – Gaillac 51 – Montauban 28 – Villefranche-de-Rouergue 52

Office de tourisme, 11, rue de la République ☎ 05 63 26 04 04, Fax 05 63 26 04 04

Dupont rm, VISA

r. Récollets – ☎ 05 63 65 05 00 – www.hotel-restaurant-dupont.com – hotel-resto-dupont@cegetel.net – Fax 05 63 65 12 62

30 rm – †€ 45/62 ††€ 45/62, ☕ € 9 – ½ P € 55/65

Rest – *(Closed Friday from October to May, Saturday and Sunday) (dinner only)* Menu € 17/29 – Carte € 21/35

◆ This former 18C post house lies in this town known as "the capital of straw hats"! Choose the more modern rooms at the back. Pleasant rustic dining room and regional cuisine.

in Monteils 3 km Northeast by D 17 – pop. 1 163 – alt. 120 m – ✉ 82300

Le Clos Monteils VISA

7 chemin du Moulin – ☎ 05 63 93 03 51 – Fax 05 63 93 03 51 – Closed from mid-January to mid-February, Tuesday except July-August, Saturday lunch, Sunday dinner and Monday

Rest – *(number of covers limited, pre-book)* Menu € 17 (weekday lunch), € 28/54

◆ The former presbytery (1771) of this Quercy village, converted into a restaurant, is decorated in the style of a private house. Pleasant terrace. Regional cooking with a contemporary touch.

CAUTERETS – 65 Hautes-Pyrénées – **342** L7 – pop. 1 107 – alt. 932 m – Winter sports : 1 000/2 350 m 3 18 – Spa : early Feb.-late Nov. – Casino – ✉ 65110 Languedoc-Roussillon-Tarn Gorges 28 **A3**

Paris 880 – Argelès-Gazost 17 – Lourdes 30 – Pau 75 – Tarbes 49

Office de tourisme, place Foch ☎ 05 62 92 50 50, Fax 05 62 92 11 70

La station★ - Pont d'Espagne road and site ★★★ (chutes du Gave (waterfall) South by D 920 - Cascade★★ and Lutour valley★ South: 2.5 km by D 920.

Cirque du Lys★★.

Plan on following page

Astérides-Sacca rest, rest, VISA

bd Latapie-Flurin – ☎ 05 62 92 50 02 – hotel.le.sacca@wanadoo.fr – Fax 05 62 92 64 63 – Closed 15 October-15 December **a**

56 rm – †€ 45/75 ††€ 45/75, ☕ € 8 – ½ P € 41/58

Rest – Menu € 19/45 – Carte € 30/55

◆ Rooms with balconies furnished in a functional, contemporary style. Hall decorated with pale wood. Welcoming dining room where well-prepared, traditional recipes are served.

Le Bois Joli without rest VISA

1 pl. Mar. Foch – ☎ 05 62 92 53 85 – www.hotel-leboisjoli.com – skibar@wanadoo.fr – Fax 05 62 92 02 23 – Closed 26 April-20 May and 11 October-5 December

12 rm – †€ 85/90 ††€ 90/102, ☕ € 9 **e**

◆ In the centre of the spa, a well-preserved hotel built in 1905, where guests stay in rooms with fine wood furnishings. Pleasant bar and sunny terrace.

CAUTERETS

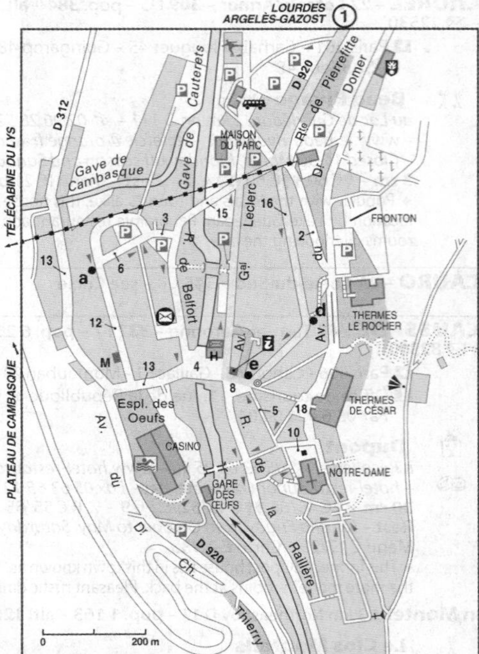

Du Lion d'Or

12 r. Richelieu – ✆ 05 62 92 52 87 – www.liondor.eu – hotel.lion.dor@wanadoo.fr – Fax 05 62 92 03 67 – Closed 26 April-16 May and 11 October-18 December **d**

19 rm – †€ 65/105 ††€ 70/110, ☐ € 10 – ½ P € 64/84

Rest – *(dinner only) (resident only)* Menu € 21/28 – Carte € 22/28

◆ Pleasant hotel run by the same family for four generations and recognisable by its lovely (19C) façade (glass doors open onto wrought iron balconies). Cosy rooms personalised with objects from antique shops. Small flower-decked patio in summer.

La Balaguère without rest

– ✆ 05 62 92 91 85 – http://labalaguere.monsite.wanadoo.fr – gitelabalagure@wanadoo.fr

4 rm ☐ – †€ 45/50 ††€ 50/60

◆ This new house nestled in a hamlet has fine rooms with rustic furnishings, slightly Spanish in style. Wonderful view of the nearby mountains.

L' Abri du Benques

2 km north on the D 920 la Raillère – ✆ 05 62 92 50 15 – Closed 12 November-20 December, Monday dinner, Tuesday dinner and Wednesday except school holidays

Rest – Menu € 13 (weekday lunch), € 19/42 – Carte € 32/48

◆ This restaurant is in a magical location on the Pont d'Espagne road, surrounded by countryside and mountain streams. Enjoy the warm ambience with mountain decor and the generous modern cuisine.

CAVAILLON – 84 Vaucluse – 332 D10 – pop. 26 200 – alt. 75 m 42 E1
– ✉ 84300 Provence

Paris 702 – Aix-en-Provence 60 – Arles 44 – Avignon 25 – Manosque 70

Office de tourisme, place Francois Tourel ✆ 04 90 71 32 01, Fax 04 90 71 42 99

Musée de l'Hôtel-Dieu: archeological collection ★ - ≤★ from St-Jacques hill.

Mercure

VISA

601 av. Boscodomini, at South by D 99 – ✆ 04 90 71 07 79 – www.mercure.com – h1951@accor.com – Fax 04 90 78 27 94

46 rm – €106/160 €116/170, €14

Rest – *(closed Saturday lunch and Sunday lunch from October to March)* Menu (€15), €20/23 – Carte €24/35

◆ Five minutes from the motorway, this regional-style modern hotel was renovated in 2007. Practical bedrooms with balconies, those facing south are quieter. Spacious, contemporary-style restaurant, tree-lined terrace and regional specialities.

Prévôt

VISA

353 av. Verdun – ✆ 04 90 71 32 43 – www.restaurant-prevot.com – contact@restaurant-prevot.com – Closed Sunday and Monday except July-August and bank holidays

Rest – Menu €25 (lunch), €35/110 – Carte €60/79

◆ The paintings, ornaments, crockery and cuisine all pay tribute to melons (including an entire menu). Truffles and regional vegetables also take pride of place on the menu.

in Cheval-Blanc 5 km east on the D 973 – pop. 4 048 – alt. 83 m – ✉ 84460

L' Auberge de Cheval Blanc

VISA

481 av. de la Canebière – ✆ 04 32 50 18 55 – www.auberge-de-chevalblanc.com – contact@auberge-de-chevalblanc.com – Fax 04 32 50 18 52 – Closed Toussaint holiday, lunch in July-August except Sunday, Saturday lunch, Sunday dinner and Monday from September to June

Rest – *(number of covers limited, pre-book)* Menu (€23 bi), €38, €28/68 – Carte €48/60

◆ This unassuming roadside inn is a pleasant stopover. Idyllic terrace with fountain. Elegant decor of mirrors and pale colours. Modern, seasonal cuisine.

CAVALAIRE-SUR-MER – 83 Var – 340 O6 – pop. 5 237 – alt. 2 m 41 C3
– Casino – ✉ 83240 French Riviera

Paris 880 – Draguignan 55 – Fréjus 41 – Le Lavandou 21 – St-Tropez 20 – Toulon 61

Office de tourisme, Maison de la Mer ✆ 04 94 01 92 10, Fax 04 94 05 49 89

Massif des Maures★★★.

La Calanque

≤ rest, VISA

r. de la Calanque – ✆ 04 94 01 95 00 – www.residences-du-soleil.com/lacalanque – lacalanque@residences-du-soleil.com – Fax 04 94 64 66 20 – Open 4 April-14 November

25 rm – €178/463 €178/463, €20 – 3 suites

Rest – Menu €30/55 – Carte €40/80

◆ Set in a residential neighbourhood, close to a rocky inlet of the Maures Massif. Spacious rooms decorated in a low-key, modern style, overlooking the Mediterranean. Admire the sea view from the panoramic restaurant and terrace as you sample traditional specialities.

LA CAVALERIE – 12 Aveyron – 338 K6 – pop. 984 – alt. 800 m 29 D2
– ✉ 12230

Paris 655 – Montpellier 96 – Millau 20 – Rodez 87

De la Poste

rest, rm, VISA

54 rte du Grand Chemin, D 809 – ✆ 05 65 62 70 66 – www.hotel-larzac.com – contact@hotel-larzac.com – Fax 05 65 62 78 24 – Closed Sunday dinner from 1st November to Easter, Friday dinner and Saturday from November to March

31 rm – €50 €50, €7 – ½ P €60/65

Rest – Menu (€14), €18 (weekdays)/55 – Carte €19/55

◆ Convenient hotel for a stopover on the way to your holiday destination, in the heart of the Grands Causses regional nature reserve. Functional, colourful and relatively spacious rooms. Minimalist dining room and air-conditioned patio; traditional and regional dishes. Very hospitable welcome.

CAVALIÈRE – 83 Var – **340** N7 – **alt. 4 m** – ✉ **83980 Le Lavandou** 41 **C3**
French Riviera

Paris 880 – Draguignan 68 – Fréjus 55 – Le Lavandou 7 – St-Tropez 33 – Toulon 48

Massif des Maures★★★.

Le Club de Cavalière & Spa rm,
30 av. Cap Nègre – 04 98 04 34 34 – www.clubdecavaliere.com – cavaliere@relaischateaux.com – Fax 04 94 05 73 16 – Open 8 May-27 September
32 rm – €285/400 €385/755, €25 – 5 suites
Rest – Menu €80 (dinner), €85/95 – Carte €95/155
◆ Opposite the sea, an elegant residence with magnificent, modern rooms and superb leisure facilities: pool, private beach, spa, sauna, Jacuzzi, fitness centre, hammam, etc. Provençal-inspired restaurant with a sliding glass roof and shaded terraces overlooking the beach.

CAVANAC – 11 Aude – **344** E3 – **see Carcassonne**

CEILLAC – 05 Hautes-Alpes – **334** I4 – **pop. 297** – **alt. 1 640 m** – **Winter sports : 1 700/2 500 m** 6 – ✉ **05600** French Alps 41 **C1**

Paris 729 – Briançon 50 – Gap 75 – Guillestre 14

Office de tourisme, le village 04 92 45 05 74, Fax 04 92 45 47 05

Site★ - St-Sébastien church ★.

Vallon du Mélezet★ - Lac Ste-Anne★★.

La Cascade
at the foot of Mélezet, 2 km South East – 04 92 45 05 92 – www.hotel-la-cascade.com – info@hotel-la-cascade.com – Fax 04 92 45 22 09 – Open 29-13 September and 19 December-31 March
22 rm – €44/62 €52/74, €9 – ½ P €55/66
Rest – Menu €16/29 – Carte €28/37
◆ Located on a remote, beautiful alpine site, the hotel will appeal to nature lovers. Rooms have pine furniture with carvings, typical of the Queyras region. The dining room and terrace offer an attractive view of the mountains. Regional cuisine.

CEILLOUX – 63 Puy-de-Dôme – **326** I9 – **pop. 156** – **alt. 615 m** – ✉ **63520** 6 **C2**

Paris 464 – Clermont-Ferrand 50 – Cournon-d'Auvergne 36 – Riom 62

Domaine de Gaudon without rest
4 km north on the D 304 – 04 73 70 76 25 – www.domainedegaudon.fr – domainedegaudon@wanadoo.fr
5 rm – €90 €110
◆ This 19C house bordered by a park and a fishing pond is a rare find. The rooms and the dining room, where breakfast is served, are superb.

LA CELLE – 83 Var – **340** L5 – **pop. 1 239** – **alt. 260 m** – ✉ **83170** 41 **C3**

Paris 812 – Aix-en-Provence 63 – Draguignan 62 – Marseille 65 – Toulon 48

Office de tourisme, place des Ormeaux 04 94 59 19 05

Hostellerie de l'Abbaye de la Celle rm, rm,
10 pl. du Gén. de Gaulle – 04 98 05 14 14 – www.abbaye-celle.com – contact@abbaye-celle.com – Fax 04 98 05 14 15 – Closed 11 January-7 February, Tuesday and Wednesday from mid-October to mid-April
10 rm – €250/330 €250/450, €20
Rest – Menu €45 (weekday lunch), €62/82 – Carte €66/90
Spec. Légumes de printemps en vinaigrette tiède et herbes d'ici. (spring). Encornet de Méditerranée farci puis braisé. Crêpes suzette. **Wines** Coteaux Varois en Provence
◆ This delightful 18C Provencal house next to the abbey was once a priory and a silkworm farm, and played host to de Gaulle. Spacious, comfortable guestrooms with old furniture. Dining rooms full of character and a fine shaded terrace. Delightful mediterranean cooking.

LA CELLE-LES-BORDES – 78 Yvelines – 311 H4 – 106 28 – 101 31 – see Paris, Area (Cernay-la-Ville)

CELLES-SUR-BELLE – 79 Deux-Sèvres – 322 E7 – pop. 3 591 – alt. 117 m – ✉ 79370 ▌Atlantic Coast 38 B2

Paris 400 – Couhé 37 – Niort 22 – Poitiers 69 – St-Jean-d'Angély 52

Office de tourisme, 14, rue des Halles ✆ 05 49 32 92 28

Portal★ of Notre-Dame church.

Hostellerie de l'Abbaye

1 pl. Epoux-Laurant – ✆ 05 49 32 93 32 – www.hotel-restaurant-abbaye.com – hostellerie.abbaye@wanadoo.fr – Fax 05 49 79 72 65

20 rm – †€ 50/78 ††€ 50/78, ☕ € 8

Rest – Menu (€ 12), € 33/60 – Carte € 45/98

◆ A young couple have breathed new life into this fine local hotel. Simple rustic and colourful rooms, being renovated in stages. A semi-bourgeois, semi-rustic dining room and a terrace facing the courtyard; traditional food inspired from the Charente region. Fine selection of Armagnac.

CELLETTES – 41 Loir-et-Cher – 318 F6 – pop. 2 186 – alt. 78 m – ✉ 41120 11 A1

Paris 189 – Blois 9 – Orléans 68 – Romorantin-Lanthenay 36 – Tours 73

Syndicat d'initiative, 2, rue de la Rozelle ✆ 02 54 70 30 46, Fax 02 54 70 30 46

La Vieille Tour

7 r. Nationale – ✆ 02 54 70 46 31 – www.lavieilletour.fr – lavieilletour@yahoo.fr – Closed 23-29 June, 23-29 December, 10-31 January, Wednesday from September to June and Tuesday

Rest – Menu (€ 20 bi), € 25/50 – Carte € 33/57

◆ An attractive 15C building recognisable by its old tower. Muted atmosphere and updated rustic decor in the dining room, where the emphasis is on refined traditional cuisine.

CELONY – 13 Bouches-du-Rhône – 340 H4 – see Aix-en-Provence

CÉLY – 77 Seine-et-Marne – 312 E5 – pop. 1 071 – alt. 62 m – ✉ 77930 19 C2

Paris 56 – Melun 15 – Boulogne-Billancourt 56 – Montreuil 57 – Créteil 47

Chateau de Cély

rte de St Germain – ✆ 01 64 38 03 07 – www.club-albatros.com – cely@club-albatros.com – Fax 01 64 38 08 78 – Closed 25 December-1 January

4 rm – †€ 275/325 ††€ 275/325, ☕ € 25 – 10 suites – ††€ 275/325

Rest – *(lunch only)* Menu € 21 bi/25 bi – Carte € 30/40

◆ A 14C château surrounded by parkland. The contemporary, well-equipped bedrooms enjoy splendid views of the golf course surrounded by landscaped gardens. An ideal seminar venue. Housed in a large conservatory with views of the gardens, this restaurant serves traditional cuisine.

CÉNAC-ET-ST-JULIEN – 24 Dordogne – 329 I7 – pop. 1 193 – alt. 70 m – ✉ 24250 4 D1

Paris 547 – Bordeaux 205 – Périgueux 73 – Cahors 71 – Sarlat-la-Canéda 12

La Guérinière

on D 46 – ✆ 05 53 29 91 97 – www.la-gueriniere-dordogne.com – contact@la-gueriniere-dordogne.com – Fax 05 53 29 91 97 – Open 1 April-2 November

5 rm (½ board only) – ½ P € 58/71

Table d'hôte – *(closed Wednesday and Sunday)* Menu € 25

◆ A driveway lined by plane trees leads to this Périgord Carthusian monastery, which offers carefully decorated, charming rooms, a small swimming pool and a tennis court. In the evening, the owner, a former restaurateur, serves local dishes in a spacious rustic dining hall.

Le Moulin Rouge without rest
– *05 53 28 23 66 – www.lemoulinrouge.org – lemoulinrouge@perigord.com*
4 rm – €42/65 €45/70, €8
◆ Pastoral setting for this mill beside a small lake (bathing possible). The charming owners are only too pleased to tell you its history. Cosy rooms.

CENON – 33 Gironde – 335 H5 – see Bordeaux

CERDON – 01 Ain – 328 F4 – pop. 758 – alt. 300 m – 01450 44 B1

Paris 460 – Ambérieu-en-Bugey 25 – Bourg-en-Bresse 32 – Nantua 20 – Oyonnax 32

Syndicat d'initiative, place F. Allombert 04 74 39 93 02, Fax 04 74 39 93 02

Vieille Côte
pl. Mairie – 04 74 39 96 86 – www.lavieillecote.com – c.b.france@wanadoo.fr – Fax 04 74 39 93 42 – Closed 2-27 February, Tuesday and Wednesday off season
Rest – Menu €18/39 – Carte €21/44
◆ Madame rustles up regional dishes using home-grown herbs, while Monsieur jovially welcomes guests into two countrified dining rooms. Bugey wines.

CERDON – 45 Loiret – 318 L6 – pop. 1 056 – alt. 145 m – 45620 12 C2

Paris 185 – Orléans 73 – Fleury-les-Aubrais 63 – Olivet 59 – Saint-Jean-de-Braye 60

Les Vieux Guays without rest
rte des Hauteraults – 02 38 36 03 76 – www.lesvieuxguays.com – lvg45@orange.fr – Fax 02 38 36 03 76 – Closed 21 February-9 March
5 rm – €60/75 €60/75
◆ Superb unspoilt property complete with lake, pool and tennis court. This former hunting lodge offers comfortable rooms whose tasteful decoration upholds local traditions.

CÉRET – 66 Pyrénées-Orientales – 344 H8 – pop. 7 568 – alt. 153 m – 66400 Languedoc-Roussillon-Tarn Gorges 22 B3

Paris 875 – Gerona 81 – Perpignan 34 – Port-Vendres 37 – Prades 72

Office de tourisme, 1, avenue Georges Clemenceau 04 68 87 00 53, Fax 04 68 87 00 56

Old bridge★ - Musée d'Art Moderne★★.

La Terrasse au Soleil rm, rm,
West : 1.5 km along rte Fontfrède – 04 68 87 01 94 – www.terrasse-au-soleil.com – terrasse-au-soleil.hotel@wanadoo.fr – Fax 04 68 87 39 24 – Closed 16 December-12 February
34 rm – €87/217 €112/242, €15 – 2 suites – ½ P €106/171
Rest – Menu €35/68 – Carte €50/71
◆ Charles Trenet lived in this isolated Catalan house on the green hills of Céret. Functional rooms to the back of the hotel. Swimming pool, jacuzzi and spa. Bright dining room adorned with earthenware and regional furniture. Terrace overlooking the Pic du Canigou.

Le Mas Trilles without rest
at Pont de Reynès: 3 km after Céret, towards Amélie-les-Bains – 04 68 87 38 37 – www.le-mas-trilles.com – mastrilles@free.fr – Fax 04 68 87 42 62 – Open 30 April-8 October
8 rm – €90/110 €110/230 – 2 suites
◆ A 17C house hidden in a small valley. Delightful rooms in Mediterranean colours, many with a terrace or private garden. Swimming pool overlooking the River Tech.

Les Arcades without rest
1 pl. Picasso – 04 68 87 12 30 – www.hotel-arcades-ceret.com – hotelarcades.ceret@wanadoo.fr – Fax 04 68 87 49 44
30 rm – €44/60 €44/60, €7
◆ Pleasant hotel adorned with works of art by the Céret School. Bright rooms with Catalan-style furnishings. Good breakfast including local produce.

X **Le Chat qui Rit**
at la Cabanasse: 1.5 km on Amélie road – ✆ 04 68 87 02 22 – lechatquirit@wanadoo.fr – Fax 04 68 87 43 40 – Closed 16-24 November, 4-31 January, Tuesday except July-August, Sunday dinner and Monday
Rest – buffet – Menu (€ 15 bi), € 24/38 – Carte € 36/55
◆ As the name of this restaurant suggests, cats play an integral part in its modern decor. Large, central buffet table laid out with Catalan specialities.

X **Del Bisbe** with rm
4 pl. Soutine – ✆ 04 68 87 00 85 – www.hotelvidalceret.com – bisbe@club-internet.fr – Fax 04 68 87 62 33 – Closed June, November, February, Tuesday and Wednesday
9 rm – †€ 40 ††€ 40, ☕ € 6
Rest – Menu (€ 10), € 20 (weekdays)/32 – Carte € 25/40
◆ This 18C residence, whose Catalan name translates as "Bishop's House", is decorated in an authentic, rustic style. Attractive vine-covered terrace. Regional cuisine and tapas bar. The reasonably priced rooms on the first floor have been refurbished. New bedding.

LE CERGNE – 42 Loire – 327 E3 – pop. 708 – alt. 640 m – ✉ 42460 44 A1

▶ Paris 414 – Charlieu 17 – Chauffailles 15 – Lyon 78 – Mâcon 72 – Roanne 27 – St-Étienne 107

XX **Bel'Vue** with rm
– ✆ 04 74 89 87 73 – lebelvue.com – lebelvue@wanadoo.fr – Fax 04 74 89 78 61 – Closed 8-23 August, 7-13 February, Friday dinner, Sunday dinner and Monday lunch
15 rm – †€ 50 ††€ 55/95, ☕ € 8,50
Rest – Menu € 19 (weekday lunch), € 24 € bi/60 – Carte € 32/55
◆ A spruce inn with, as its name indicates, a fine view of the valley from the panoramic dining room. Traditional cuisine. Well-kept guestrooms upstairs.

CERGY – 95 Val-d'Oise – 305 D6 – 106 5 – 101 2 – see Paris, Area (Cergy-Pontoise)

CÉRILLY – 03 Allier – 326 D3 – pop. 1 384 – alt. 340 m – ✉ 03350 5 B1
Auvergne

▶ Paris 298 – Bourges 66 – Montluçon 41 – Moulins 47 – St-Amand-Montrond 33
ℹ Office de tourisme, place du Champ de Foire ✆ 04 70 67 55 89, Fax 04 70 67 31 73

Chez Chaumat
pl. Péron – ✆ 04 70 67 52 21 – www.chezchaumat.com – chezchaumat@alicepro.fr – Fax 04 70 67 35 28 – Closed 30 June-10 July, 1-13 September, 20 December-5 January, Sunday dinner and Monday
8 rm – †€ 43 ††€ 49, ☕ € 7 – ½ P € 50
Rest – Menu € 12 (weekday lunch), € 18/35 – Carte € 15/35
◆ A family hotel a few metres from the superb Tronçais forest. Rooms are simple but have been refurbished and soundproofed. Two dining rooms: one a country-style bistro, the other wood-panelled and furnished in Louis XIII style.

CERNAY – 68 Haut-Rhin – 315 H10 – pop. 11 000 – alt. 275 m – ✉ 68700 1 A3
Alsace-Lorraine

▶ Paris 461 – Altkirch 26 – Belfort 39 – Colmar 37 – Guebwiller 15 – Mulhouse 18 – Thann 6
ℹ Office de tourisme, 1, rue Latouche ✆ 03 89 75 50 35, Fax 03 89 75 49 24

XX **Hostellerie d'Alsace** with rm
61 r. Poincaré – ✆ 03 89 75 59 81 – www.hostellerie-alsace.fr – hostellerie.alsace@wanadoo.fr – Fax 03 89 75 70 22 – Closed 27 July-16 August, 26 December-10 January, Saturday and Sunday
10 rm – †€ 49 ††€ 60, ☕ € 8
Rest – Menu € 21 (weekdays)/58 – Carte € 41/62
◆ Large half-timbered hoouse in the Alsatian tradition. By contrast, the dining room and renovated accommodation are contemporary and functional.

CERNAY-LA-VILLE – 78 Yvelines – **311** H3 – **106** 29 – **101** 31 – see Paris, Area

CERVIONE – 2B Haute-Corse – **345** F6 – see Corse

CESSON – 22 Côtes-d'Armor – **309** F3 – see St-Brieuc

CESSON-SÉVIGNÉ – 35 Ille-et-Vilaine – **309** M6 – see Rennes

CESTAYROLS – 81 Tarn – **338** D7 – **pop. 500** – **alt. 233 m** – ✉ **81150** 29 **C2**

Paris 660 – Albi 19 – Castres 59 – Toulouse 71

Lou Cantoun

Le village – ✆ 05 63 53 28 39 – www.loucantoun.fr – lou.cantoun@orange.fr – Closed January, Tuesday dinner and Wednesday

Rest – Menu (€ 14 bi), € 23/38 – Carte € 28/42

◆ In this restaurant that also sells bread, a shaded terrace leads off two modern, countrified dining rooms. Traditional and regional menu.

CETTE-EYGUN – 64 Pyrénées-Atlantiques – **342** I7 – **pop. 86** – **alt. 700 m** – ✉ **64490** 3 **B3**

Paris 844 – Pau 68 – Lescun 10 – Lurbe-St-Christau 25 – Urdos 10

Au Château d'Arance

r. Centrale – ✆ 05 59 34 75 50 – www.hotel-auchateaudarance.com – didier.ziane@orange.fr – Fax 05 59 34 57 62 – Closed 12 November-11 December, 3 January-14 February

8 rm – † € 60/66 †† € 60/66, ☕ € 8,50 – ½ P € 58/61

Rest – *(closed Monday dinner and Tuesday)* Menu € 13/30 – Carte € 32/40

◆ This 13C "castel" overlooking the Aspe Valley offers a successful combination of old and new. Rooms have simple decor of parquet flooring, white walls and contemporary furniture. The old château stables house a modern dining room. Panoramic terrace.

CEVINS – 73 Savoie – **333** L4 – **pop. 657** – **alt. 400 m** – ✉ **73730** 46 **F2**

Paris 629 – Lyon 172 – Chambéry 63 – Annecy 57 – Aix-les-Bains 79

La Fleur de Sel

Les Marais – ✆ 04 79 37 49 98 – www.restaurant-fleurdesel.fr – restaufleurdesel@aol.com – Fax 04 79 37 40 44 – Closed 1st-12 July, Monday and Tuesday

Rest – Menu € 29/65 – Carte € 50/70

◆ A welcoming halt along the Albertville-Moûtiers expressway, this establishment offers tasty regional cuisine served in front of the fireplace. Summer terrace.

CHABLIS – 89 Yonne – **319** F5 – **pop. 2 476** – **alt. 135 m** – ✉ **89800** 7 **B1**
Burgundy-Jura

Paris 181 – Auxerre 21 – Avallon 39 – Tonnerre 18 – Troyes 76

Office de tourisme, 1, rue du Maréchal de Lattre ✆ 03 86 42 80 80, Fax 03 86 42 49 71

Du Vieux Moulin

18 r. des Moulins – ✆ 03 86 42 47 30 – www.larochehotel.fr – vieuxmoulin@larochewines.com – Fax 03 86 42 84 44 – Closed 22 December-4 February and Sunday evening in low season

7 rm ☕ – † € 125/130 †† € 125/130 – 2 suites

Rest *Laroche Wine Bar* – *(closed dinner from Tuesday to Saturday except in high season and Monday)* Menu € 16 bi (weekday lunch)/30 – Carte approx. € 38

◆ A subtle blend of tradition (bare beams and stonework) and modernity (hi-tech bathrooms and wifi): understated luxury at its best! Authentic country dishes that are well suited to the wines of the estate. Wine tasting courses run in the shop.

Hostellerie des Clos (Michel Vignaud)

18 r. Jules Rathier – ✆ 03 86 42 10 63
– www.hostellerie-des-clos.fr – host.clos@wanadoo.fr – Fax 03 86 42 17 11
– Closed 21 December-16 January
32 rm – €60/100 €80/130, ☕ €15 – 4 suites – ½ P €105/135
Rest – Menu €42/79 – Carte €65/110
Spec. Fricassée d'escargots de Bourgogne. Dos de sandre saisi sur peau au beurre de légumes au chablis. Fondue de fruits à l'estragon (June to Oct.). **Wines** Chablis, Irancy.
◆ Elegant hostelry partially housed in a former hospice, offering well-kept guestrooms (larger at the Résidence), plush sitting rooms and a wine tasting cellar. The restaurant opens onto a garden. Classic and regional fare; good choice of local wines.

CHAGNY – 71 Saône-et-Loire – 320 I8 – pop. 5 391 – alt. 215 m – ✉ 71150

7 **A3**

Paris 327 – Autun 44 – Beaune 15 – Chalon-sur-Saône 20 – Mâcon 77

Office de tourisme, 2, place des Halles ✆ 03 85 87 25 95, Fax 03 85 87 14 44

Lameloise (Jacques Lameloise)
36 pl. d'Armes – ✆ 03 85 87 65 65 – www.lameloise.fr – lameloise@relaischateaux.com – Fax 03 85 87 03 57 – Closed 8-15 July, 16 December-21 January and Wednesday from October to June
16 rm – €145/300 €145/300, ☕ €23
Rest – *(closed Wednesday except dinner from July to September, Tuesday lunch and Thursday lunch) (pre-book)* Menu €75 bi (weekday lunch), €100/165 – Carte €90/150
Spec. Pommes de terre ratte grillées aux escargots de Bourgogne. Millefeuille de filet de bœuf et foie gras poêlé, pommes de terre soufflées. Grande assiette du chocolatier. **Wines** Rully blanc, Chassagne-Montrachet rouge
◆ This large Burgundy house has a stylish interior, home to spacious, classical guestrooms. Rustic elegance, cuisine in the grand tradition and a perfect welcome: a food lover's institution.

De la Poste without rest
17 r. Poste – ✆ 03 85 87 64 40 – www.hoteldelaposte-chagny71.com
– info@hoteldelaposte-chagny71.com – Fax 03 85 87 64 41
– Closed 24-31 August, 19 December-4 January
11 rm – €42/50 €45/60, ☕ €7
◆ This establishment is in the centre of the village in a quiet cul-de-sac. All the renovated and well-kept rooms are at garden level.

La Ferté without rest
11 bd Liberté – ✆ 03 85 87 07 47 – www.hotelferte.com
– reservation@hotelferte.com – Fax 03 85 87 37 64
– Closed 29 November-17 December
13 rm – €39/60 €41/68, ☕ €8
◆ The owners, who are also artists, of this small establishment welcome guests with open arms. Art exhibition, flower-decked garden. Located a stone's throw from Lameloise.

Chalon road 2 km Southeast by N 6 and secondary road – ✉ 71150 Chagny

Hostellerie du Château de Bellecroix
– ✆ 03 85 87 13 86 – www.chateau-bellecroix.com
– info@chateau-bellecroix.com – Fax 03 85 91 28 62
– Closed 15 December-13 February and Wednesday except from June to September
19 rm – €87/220 €87/220, ☕ €15 – 1 suite – ½ P €107/190
Rest – *(closed Mon. lunch, Thurs. lunch and Wed.)* Menu (€25), €50/64 – Carte €52/97
◆ Thos former home of the Knights of Malta is set in a park. The rooms, with an individual touch, are very large in the 12C commander's residence and smaller in the 18C château. This restaurant has a stylish look: Chimney, woodwork and period-style furniture.

in Chassey-le-Camp 6 km Southwest by D 974 and D 109 – pop. 302 – alt. 300 m – ✉ 71150

Auberge du Camp Romain rm, rest,
au bourg – ✆ 03 85 87 09 91
– www.auberge-du-camp-romain.com – contact@auberge-du-camp-romain.com
– Fax 03 85 87 11 51
41 rm – €74/95 €74/95 – 1 suite – ½ P €72/82
Rest – Menu €26/46 – Carte €30/48
◆ Amid vines and woods, close to a Neolithic camp. The main building has simple rooms; those in the annexe are larger and more modern. Copious traditional cuisine served in a rustic dining room or on the veranda.

CHAILLES – 73 Savoie – **333** H5 – see les Échelles

CHAILLY-SUR-ARMANÇON – 21 Côte-d'Or – **320** G6 – see Pouilly-en-Auxois

---

CHAINTRÉ – 71 Saône-et-Loire – **320** I12 – pop. 519 – alt. 284 m 8 **C3**
– ✉ 71570

Paris 397 – Bourg-en-Bresse 45 – Lyon 70 – Mâcon 10

La Table de Chaintré (Sébastien Grospellier)
– ✆ 03 85 32 90 95 – www.latabledechaintre.com
– info@latabledechaintre.com – Fax 03 85 32 91 04
– Closed 28 July-10 August, Monday and Tuesday except public holidays
Rest – *(number of covers limited, pre-book)* Menu (€38), €52
Spec. Ecrevisses du lac Léman sur un fin sablé au gingembre et vinaigrette à l'orange. Lièvre à la royale (Oct. to Jan.). Figue "Paradis" rôtie en clafoutis et glace au porto (season). **Wines** Mâcon-Chaintré, Morgon.
◆ Warm welcome in the heart of the Pouilly-Fuissé vineyards. Small, elegant dining room and delicious, seasonal tasting menu. Wine from the best French vineyards.

LA CHAISE-DIEU – 43 Haute-Loire – **331** E2 – pop. 814 – alt. 1 080 m 6 **C3**
– ✉ 43160 Auvergne

Paris 503 – Ambert 29 – Brioude 35 – Issoire 59 – Le Puy-en-Velay 42 – St-Étienne 81
Office de tourisme, place de la Mairie ✆ 04 71 00 01 16, Fax 04 71 00 03 45
St-Robert abbey church ★★: tapestries ★★★.

Casadeï
pl. Abbaye – ✆ 04 71 00 00 58 – www.hotel-la-casadei.com
– lacasadei@msn.com – Fax 04 71 00 01 67 – Open 2 May-end October
9 rm – €39/49 €49/69, €9 – ½ P €60/72
Rest – *(open 14 July-30 August)* Menu €14/17
◆ At the foot of the abbey, a family hotel with sober practical rooms. A local craft and regional produce shop; art gallery with works by local and other artists. Delightful antique-shop ambiance in this restaurant which serves authentic country recipes.

L'Écho et l'Abbaye with rm
pl. Écho – ✆ 04 71 00 00 45 – hoteldelecho@orange.fr – Fax 04 71 00 00 22
– Open 3 April-8 November and closed Wednesday except July-August
10 rm – €49 €55/72, €8,50 – ½ P €59
Rest – *(number of covers limited, pre-book)* Menu (€17), €27/39 – Carte €27/48
◆ Attractive dining room, traditional cuisine, large wine list and V.I.P. guests during the music festival. Some rooms overlook the cloister.

CHALAIS – 16 Charente – **324** K8 – pop. 1 991 – alt. 70 m – ✉ 16210 39 **C3**
Atlantic Coast

Paris 494 – Angoulême 47 – Bordeaux 83 – Périgueux 66
Office de tourisme, 8, rue de Barbezieux ✆ 05 45 98 02 71, Fax 05 45 78 54 17

Relais du Château

au château – ✆ 05 45 98 23 58
– relaisduchateautalleyrand@wanadoo.fr – Fax 05 45 98 00 53
– Closed 2-30 November, Sunday dinner, Tuesday lunch and Monday
Rest – Menu € 18 (weekdays)/31 – Carte € 30/40
◆ Guests cross a footbridge to reach this restaurant with a digniified vaulted room in a château built on the heights of Chalais. Medieval setting, pleasant courtyard-terrace.

CHALEZEULE – 25 Doubs – 321 G3 – see Besançon

CHALLANGES – 21 Côte-d'Or – 320 J7 – see Beaune

CHALLANS – 85 Vendée – 316 E6 – pop. 17 500 – alt. 8 m – ✉ 85300 34 A3

Atlantic Coast

Paris 436 – Cholet 84 – Nantes 58 – La Roche-sur-Yon 42
Office de tourisme, place de l'Europe ✆ 02 51 93 19 75, Fax 02 51 49 76 04

CHALLANS

Baudry (R. P.) . . . . A
Bazin (Bd R.) . . . . A
Biochaud (Av.) . . . . B
Bois de Céné (R. de) . . . A 2
Bonne Fontaine (R.) . . . . B
Briand (Pl. A.) . . . . A 3
Calmette (R.) . . . . B
Carnot (R.) . . . . A
Champ de Foire (Pl. du) . B 4
Cholet (R. de) . . . . B 5
Clemenceau (Bd) . . . . . . A
Dodin (Bd L.) . . . . B
F.F.I. (Bd des) . . . . A 6
Gambetta (R.) . . . . B
Gare (Bd de la) . . . . B
Gaulle (Pl. du Gén.-de) . A 7
Guérin (Bd) . . . . B
Leclerc (R. du Général) . A 8
Lézardière (R. P. de) . . . A 10
Lorraine (R. de) . . . . A 12
Marzelles (R. des) . . . . . B 13
Monnier (R. P.) . . . . A 15
Nantes (R. de) . . . . AB
Roche-sur-Yon (R. de la) B 16
Sables (R. des) . . . . B 17
Strasbourg (Bd de) . . . . A
Viaud Grand Marais (Bd) B
Yole (Bd J.) . . . . AB

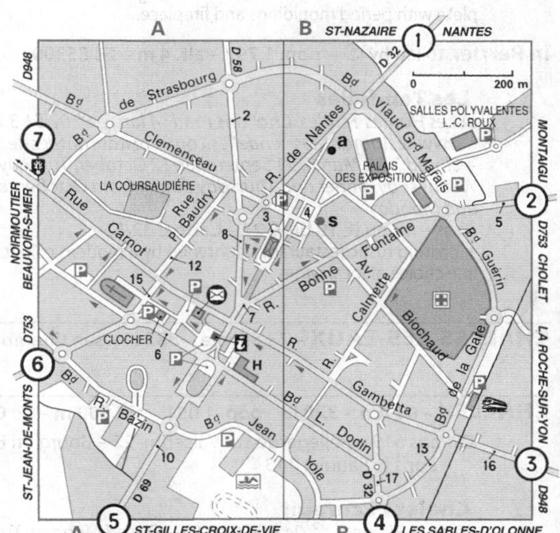

De l'Antiquité without rest

14 r. Galliéni – ✆ 02 51 68 02 84 – www.hotelantiquite.com
– hotelantiquite@wanadoo.fr – Fax 02 51 35 55 74 B **a**
20 rm – †€ 53/85 ††€ 58/90, ☕ € 7
◆ A Vendée-style modern house. Antique furniture personalises the rooms, all of which face the courtyard; the ones in the annexe are very well kept.

Chez Charles

8 pl. Champ de Foire – ✆ 02 51 93 36 65 – www.restaurantchezcharles.com
– chezcharles85@aol.com – Fax 02 51 49 31 88 – Closed 23 December-24 January, Sunday dinner and Monday B **s**
Rest – Menu € 18 (weekdays)/54 – Carte € 35/49
◆ A nice little family restaurant in a bistro style. Classic cuisine inspired by market availability and regional produce.

in la Garnache 6,5 km by ① – pop. 4 202 – alt. 28 m – ✉ 85710

XX **Le Petit St-Thomas**

25 r. de Lattre-de-Tassigny – ✆ 02 51 49 05 99 – www.restaurant-petit-st-thomas.com – bienvenue@restaurant-petit-st-thomas.com – Closed 11-29 April, 22 June-9 July, 2-16 January, Sunday dinner, Wednesday dinner and Monday

Rest – Menu (€ 17), € 24 (weekdays)/50 – Carte € 44/63

◆ A typical auberge from the region serving traditional, well-prepared dishes based on market produce. The veranda overlooks a small courtyard.

St-Gilles-Croix-de-Vie road by ⑤ – ✉ 85300 Challans

Château de la Vérie

rte de Soullans, 2.5 km on D 69 – ✆ 02 51 35 33 44 – www.chateau-de-la-verie.com – info@chateau-de-la-verie.com – Fax 02 51 35 14 84

21 rm – €75/168 €75/168, € 13 – ½ P € 84/130

Rest – *(closed Sunday dinner, Tuesday lunch and Monday off season)* Menu (€ 17), € 26/49 – Carte € 35/49

◆ This 16C house offers guests spacious rooms with antique furniture. Country walks in the grounds, by the river and marshes. Dining room redecorated in Provence colours, complete with period mouldings and fireplace.

in Perrier 10 km by ⑥ – pop. 1 797 – alt. 4 m – ✉ 85300

XX **Les Tendelles**

at Les Hautes Tendes, Challans road : 4 km – ✆ 02 51 35 36 94 – www.restaurant-les-tendelles.com – restaurant-les-tendelles@wanadoo.fr – Closed 2-22 March, 21 September-12 October, Tuesday dinner, Wednesday dinner and Thursday dinner from October to March, Sunday dinner and Monday

Rest – Menu (€ 19 bi), € 27 – Carte € 32/55

◆ Inviting rustic restaurant brightened by a modern colour scheme. Seasonal menu and fine choice of local wines.

CHALLES-LES-EAUX – 73 Savoie – 333 I4 – see Chambéry

CHALLEX – 01 Ain – 328 I3 – pop. 1 051 – alt. 500 m – ✉ 01630 45 C1

Paris 519 – Bellegarde sur Valserine 22 – Bourg en Bresse 94 – Gex 20 – Lons le Saunier 113

X **Chalet l'Ecureuil**

rte de la Plaine – ✆ 04 50 56 40 82 – Closed Monday, Tuesday, Wednesday and lunch except Sunday

Rest – Menu € 28/39 – Carte € 50/63

◆ Pleasant chalet restaurant located away from the village. Rustic dining room decorated with old utensils, veranda, and traditional cuisine with inventive touches.

CHÂLONS-EN-CHAMPAGNE P – 51 Marne – 306 I9 – pop. 46 300 – alt. 83 m – ✉ 51000 Northern France and the Paris Region 13 B2

Paris 188 – Dijon 259 – Metz 157 – Nancy 162 – Reims 47 – Troyes 82

Office de tourisme, 3, quai des Arts ✆ 03 26 65 17 89, Fax 03 26 65 35 65

de la Grande-Romanie Courtisols Route Départementale 994, 15 km on the Verdun road, ✆ 03 26 66 65 97

St-Étienne cathedral ★★ - N.-D.-en-Vaux church ★: interior★★ **F** - Statues-columns★★ of the musée du cloître in N.-D.-en-Vaux★ AY **M**[1].

Basilica of N.-D.-de-l'Épine★★.

CHÂLONS-EN-CHAMPAGNE

Arche-de-Mauvillain (Pt de l') . BZ 2
Bourgeois (R. Léon) . . . . ABY
Brossolette (Av. Pierre) . . . . X 4
Chastillon (R. de) . . . . ABZ 6
Croix-des-Teinturiers (R.) . . . . AZ 9
Dr-Pellier (R. du) . . . . X 11
Flocmagny (R. du) . . . . BY 12
Foch (Pl. du Maréchal) . . . . . . AY 13
Gantelet (Rue du) . . . . AY 14
Gaulle (Av. du Gén. Charles-de) . . BZ 15
Godart (Pl.) . . . . AY 17
Jacquiert (R. Clovis) . . . . X 18
Jeanne-d'Arc (Av.) . . . . X 21
Jean-Jaurès (R.) . . . . AZ 20
Jessaint (R. de) . . . . BZ 22
Libération (Pl. de la) . . . . AZ 24
Mariniers (Pt des) . . . . AY 26
Marne (R. de la) . . . . AY
Martyrs-de-la-Résistance (R. des) . . . . BY 29
Orfeuil (R. d') . . . . AZ 31
Ormesson (Cours d') . . . . AZ 32
Prieur-de-la-Marne (R.) . . . . . . BY 36
Récamier (R. Juliette) . . . . AZ 38
République (Pl. de la) . . . . AZ 39
Roosevelt (Av. du Prés.) . . . . . . X 41
Simon (Av. Jacques) . . . . X 45
Vaux (R. de) . . . . AY 47
Vieilles-Postes (R. des) . . . . X 48
Vinetz (R. de) . . . . BZ 49
Viviers (Pt des) . . . . AY 50

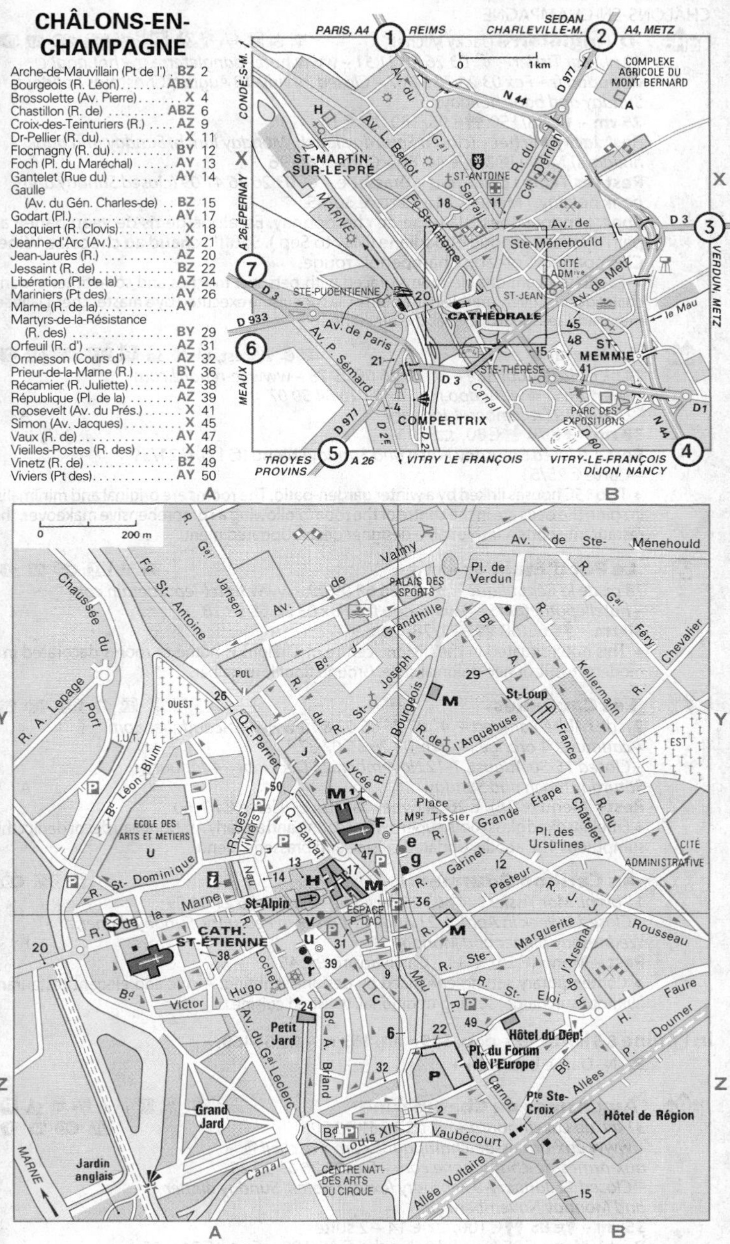

D'Angleterre (Jacky Michel)
19 pl. Mgr Tissier – 03 26 68 21 51 – www.hotel-dangleterre.fr – hot.angl@wanadoo.fr – Fax 03 26 70 51 67 – Closed 26 July-18 August, Christmas holidays, Sunday and bank holidays BY **g**
25 rm – €85/150 €95/180, €16
Rest ***Jacky Michel*** – *(closed Saturday lunch, Monday lunch, Sunday and bank holidays)* Menu (€36), €40/89 – Carte €60/96
Rest ***Les Temps changent*** – brasserie – *03 26 66 41 09 (closed Sunday and bank holidays)* Menu €24 – Carte €30/45
Spec. Langoustines à la nage de chardonnay. Escalope de ris de veau panée au pain d'épices, fenouil et badiane (May to Sep.). Soufflé chaud au chocolat. **Wines** Champagne, Coteaux Champenois rouge.
◆ Faultlessly comfortable rooms graced with personal touches and sometimes a warm chalet decor. Lovely marble bathrooms. Classic cuisine executed by a master chef. Daily set menu and seasonal dishes at the brasserie.

Le Renard rest,
24 pl. de la République – 03 26 68 03 78 – www.le-renard.com – lerenard51@wanadoo.fr – Fax 03 26 64 50 07 – Closed 19 December-4 January AZ **r**
38 rm – €70 €80, €11
Rest – *(closed Saturday lunch and Sunday)* Menu (€17), €21/39 – Carte €25/51
◆ Two 15C houses linked by a winter garden-patio. The rooms are original and minimalist in spirit: the beds are in the centre of the room. Following a comprehensive makeover, this restaurant sports a fashionable designer decor. Updated menu.

Le Pot d'Étain without rest
18 pl. de la République – 03 26 68 09 09 – www.hotel-lepotdetain.com – hotellepotdetain51@wanadoo.fr – Fax 03 26 68 58 18 AZ **u**
30 rm – €66/68 €71/78, €9
◆ This hotel situated in the historic centre of Châlons is home to rooms decorated in a modern, rustic or neo-colonial style. Ground floor lounge bar.

Les Caudalies
2 r. de l'Abbé-Lambert – 03 26 65 07 87 – www.les-caudalies.com – caudalies@orange.fr – Fax 03 26 65 07 87 – Closed 15-30 August, 1-12 November, 23 December-4 January, Saturday lunch and Sunday AY **v**
Rest – Menu (€16), €26 bi (weekdays)/41 – Carte €37/60
◆ Eiffel-inspired glass roofs, superb wainscoting and an early Art Nouveau decor depict this sumptuous 19C abode. Updated cuisine and brasserie menu.

Au Carillon Gourmand
15 bis pl. Mgr Tissier – 03 26 64 45 07 – Fax 03 26 21 06 09 – Closed 1 week in April, 1-21 August, 1 week in February, Sunday dinner, Wednesday dinner and Monday BY **e**
Rest – Menu (€25), €33 – Carte approx. €45
◆ Contemporary setting enhanced by designer lighting. A chic and elegant restaurant (without surcharge) serving traditional, revisited cuisine.

in l'Épine 8,5 km by ③ – pop. 645 – alt. 153 m – ✉ 51460
N.-Dame basilica ★★.

Aux Armes de Champagne rest,
31 av. du Luxembourg – 03 26 69 30 30 – www.aux-armes-de-champagne.com – accueil@aux-armes-de-champagne.com – Fax 03 26 69 30 26 – Closed 12 January-9 February (except hotel), Sunday dinner and Monday November-April
35 rm – €85 €100, €14 – 2 suites
Rest – Menu €25 (weekday lunch), €45/100 – Carte €76/105
◆ Smart Champagne inn coupled to a comfortable, refined hotel. Cosy rooms with a personal touch. Snug sitting room-bar. The rustic-bourgeois dining room commands views of the basilica. Classic repertory.

in Matougues 11 km via ⑦ – **pop. 640 – alt. 82 m** – ✉ **51510**

Auberge des Moissons

8 rte Nationale – ✆ 03 26 70 99 17 – www.des-moissons.com – desmoissons@orange.fr – Fax 03 26 66 56 94 – Closed 28 July-12 August and 22 December-13 January

27 rm – †€ 71 ††€ 82, ☕ € 8,50 – ½ P € 72

Rest – *(closed for lunch during the week and Sunday dinner)* Menu € 25/42 – Carte € 36/48

◆ This inn-farm has been perfecting the art of hospitality for generations. Comfortable, modern rooms partly overlooking an inner patio. A pleasantly countrified decor depicts this converted stable. Recipes made with local truffles in season.

CHALON-SUR-SAÔNE – 71 Saône-et-Loire – **320** J9 — 8 **C3**

– **pop. 46 200** – **Built-up area 130 825 – alt. 180 m** – ✉ **71100** Burgundy-Jura

Paris 335 – Besançon 132 – Dijon 68 – Lyon 125 – Mâcon 59

Office de tourisme, 4, place du Port de Villiers ✆ 03 85 48 37 97, Fax 03 85 48 63 55

de Chalon-sur-Saône Châtenoy-en-Bresse Parc de Loisirs Saint Nicolas, ✆ 03 85 93 49 65

Museums: Denon★ BZ **M**[1], Nicéphore Niepce★★ BZ **M**[2] - Roseraie St-Nicolas (rose garden) ★ Southeast: 4 km X.

Plan on following page

St-Régis

22 bd République – ✆ 03 85 90 95 60 – www.saint-regis-chalon.com – saint-regis@saint-regis-chalon.fr – Fax 03 85 90 95 70 BZ **v**

36 rm – †€ 84/105 ††€ 106/179, ☕ € 15

Rest – *(closed Saturday lunch and Sunday dinner)* Menu (€ 23), € 35 (weekdays)/48 – Carte € 51/76

◆ An early 20C building with provincial charm on a busy avenue. Some rooms have been renovated in a modern style; most retain a bourgeois air. Pleasant lounge. Traditional cuisine served in an elegant dining room (panelling).

St-Georges

32 av. J. Jaurès – ✆ 03 85 90 80 50 – www.le-saintgeorges.fr – reservation@le-saintgeorges.fr – Fax 03 85 90 80 55 AZ **s**

50 rm – †€ 77 ††€ 90, ☕ € 11 – ½ P € 87

Rest – *(Closed 21 July-23 August, Saturday lunch and Sunday dinner)* Menu € 26/60 – Carte € 45/63

Rest *Le Petit Comptoir d'à Côté* – *✆ 03 85 90 80 52 (closed Saturday lunch, Sunday and public holidays)* Menu (€ 15), € 17/25 – Carte € 22/30

◆ Large, family-run hotel near the station. Welcoming and well-soundproofed rooms with 1970s decor, although the junior suites are ultra-modern. Restaurant with simple, Art Deco inspired decor. Traditional cuisine. Elegant brasserie decor combining leather and wood.

XX **Le Bourgogne**

28 r. Strasbourg – ✆ 03 85 48 89 18 – www.restau-lebourgogne-chalon.fr – restaurant.lebourgogne@orange.fr – Fax 03 85 93 39 10 – Closed 26 April-4 May, 4-20 July, 8-16 November, 25-30 December, Saturday lunch, Sunday dinner and Monday CZ **t**

Rest – Menu (€ 16), € 19/48 – Carte € 53/76

◆ The high open beam ceiling and Louis XIII-style furniture in the dining room are part of the setting in this rustic, Burgundy-style restaurant. Traditional cuisine.

XX **La Réale**

8 pl. Gén. de Gaulle – ✆ 03 85 48 07 21 – Fax 03 85 48 57 77 – Closed 1-15 May, 14 July-14 August, Sunday dinner and Monday BZ **m**

Rest – Menu € 20/40 – Carte € 37/58

◆ You are in the business district, in the heart of the town, where this brasserie-style restaurant offers regional dishes and seafood.

CHALON-SUR-SAÔNE

Street	Grid	No.
Arnal (R. R.)	X	2
Banque (R. de la)	BZ	3
Blum (Av. L.)	X	4
Châtelet (Pl. du)	BZ	5
Châtelet (R. du)	CZ	6
Citadelle (R. de la)	BY	7
Coubertin (R. P. de)	X	8
Couturier (R. Ph.-L.)	BZ	9
Duhesme (R. du Gén.)	AY	12
Europe (Av. de l')	X	14
Evêché (R. de l')	CZ	15
Fèvres (R. aux)	CZ	16
Gaulle (Pl. Gén.-de)	BZ	17
Grande-R.	BCZ	18
Hôtel-de-Ville (Pl. de l')	BZ	19
Lardy (Av. P.)	X	20
Leclerc (R. Gén.)	BZ	
Lyon (R. de)	BZ	21
Mac-Orlan (R. P.)	X	22
Messiaen (R. O.)	AZ	24
Nugues (Av. P.)	X	25
Obélisque (Pl. de l')	BY	27
Pasteur (R.)	BZ	28
Poilus-d'Orient (R.)	X	29
Poissonnerie (R. de la)	CZ	31
Pompidou (Av. G.)	AZ	32
Pont (R. du)	CZ	35
Porte-de-Lyon (R.)	BZ	36
Port-Villiers (R. du)	BZ	37
Poterne (Q. de la)	CZ	38
Pretet (R. René)	AZ	40
République (Bd)	ABZ	42
Ste-Marie (Prom.)	CZ	47
St-Georges (R.)	BZ	45
St-Vincent (Pl. et R.)	CZ	46
Strasbourg (R. de)	CZ	48
Thénard (R. L.-J.)	X	49
Trémouille (R. de la)	BCY	51
8-Mai-1945 (Av.)	X	52
56e-R.I. (R. du)	X	54
134e-R.I. (R. du)	X	58

Le Bistrot

31 r. Strasbourg – ✆ 03 85 93 22 01 – Fax 03 85 93 27 05 – Closed 8-30 August, February school holidays, Saturday and Sunday CZ **f**

Rest – Menu € 26 (weekday lunch), € 32/37 – Carte approx. € 53

◆ Pleasant all red decorated bistro (woodwork, banquettes, lampshades). Vaulted lounge with glass-walled cellar. Modern cuisine with vegetables from the garden and fine Burgundies.

L'Air du Temps

7 r. de Strasbourg, Île St Laurent – ✆ 03 85 93 39 01 – lair.du.temps.71@orange.fr – Closed 7-20 September, 20 December-4 January and Sunday CZ **f**

Rest – bistro – *(lunch only except Saturday)* Menu € 21/34

◆ A very modern bistro, both in terms of the decor of its two small dining rooms and the food, offering market recipes at reasonable prices.

Chez Jules

11 r. de Strasbourg – ✆ 03 85 48 08 34 – Fax 03 85 48 55 48 – Closed 31 July-24 August, 8 to 22 February, Saturday lunch and Sunday

Rest – Menu € 19/36 – Carte € 28/45 CZ **f**

◆ On the Île St Laurent, a narrow glass façade allows you to see into a rustic, simple dining room. Traditional cuisine, dishes of the day and a wide selection of desserts.

La Table de Fanny

21 r. de Strasbourg – ✆ 03 85 48 23 11 – Fax 03 85 48 23 11 – Closed 24 August-7 September, 21 December-4 January, Monday lunch, Saturday lunch and Sunday

Rest – Menu € 22/32 CZ **f**

◆ An address in the country and the inventive cuisine: these are the secrets behind this trendy restaurant with a nice decor (wicker chairs, brick walls and half-timbering).

in St-Loup-de-Varennes 7 km by ③ – pop. 1 128 – alt. 186 m – ✉ 71240

Le Saint Loup

13 rte Nationale 6 – ✆ 03 85 44 21 58 – www.lesaintloup.com – lesaintloup@orange.fr – Closed 2-8 March, 29 June-13 July, Wednesday and dinner from Sunday to Tuesday

Rest – Menu (€ 16), € 19 (weekday lunch), € 26/46 – Carte € 30/56

◆ A practical stopover option near the photography museum, this Burgundian inn stands alongside the Route Nationale. Honest regional cuisine in a country setting.

in St-Rémy 4 km (Le Creusot road) N 6, N 80 and secondary road – pop. 5 805 – alt. 187 m – ✉ 71100

Moulin de Martorey (Jean-Pierre Gillot)

– ✆ 03 85 48 12 98 – www.moulindemartorey.net – moulindemartorey@wanadoo.fr – Fax 03 85 48 73 67 – Closed 17-31 August, 4-20 January, Sunday dinner, Tuesday lunch and Monday except bank holidays X **k**

Rest – Menu € 30 (weekdays)/84

Spec. Trois préparations d'escargots. Lièvre à la royale (Oct. to Jan.). Fondant au chocolat guanaja et pralin feuilleté. **Wines** Givry, Montagny.

◆ A tranquil 19C flour mill overlooking the mill race. Rustic interior set around the old machinery. Personalised cuisine and a fine wine list. Veranda and terrace.

Givry road 4 km west on the D 69 – ✉ 71880 Châtenoy-le-Royal :

L'Auberge des Alouettes

1 rte de Givry – ✆ 03 85 48 32 15 – aubergedesalouettes@orange.fr – Fax 03 85 93 12 96 – Closed 15 July-5 August, 6-20 January, Sunday dinner, Tuesday dinner and Wednesday X **e**

Rest – Menu € 20/46 – Carte € 30/55

◆ Inn with a warm atmosphere on a busy main road. Take a table near the elegant stone fireplace to sample the daily specials.

in Dracy-le-Fort 6 km by ⑥ and D 978 – pop. 1 227 – alt. 180 m – ✉ 71640

Le Dracy

4 r. du Pressoir – ✆ 03 85 87 81 81 – www.ledracy.com – info@ledracy.com – Fax 03 85 87 77 49 – **47 rm** *– †€ 70/130 ††€ 70/130, ☕ € 11 – ½ P € 72/105*

Rest *La Garenne* – Menu € 20 (weekday lunch), € 28/50 – Carte € 40/50

◆ Ideal for a relaxing break away from it all in the countryside. Cosy, refurbished rooms; those overlooking the garden have a private terrace. Fine pool. Traditional cuisine served in a contemporary dining room or on the terrace.

near A6 Chalon-Nord interchange – ✉ 71100 Chalon-sur-Saône

Mercure rm, AC, P, VISA, MC, AE

av. Europe – ✆ 03 85 46 51 89 – www.mercure.com – h0368@accor.com – Fax 03 85 46 08 96

X a

85 rm – €86/120 €105/157, ☕ €15

Rest – *(Closed Saturday, Sunday lunch)* Menu €17/25 – Carte €30/50

◆ Well placed for access to the motorway, an impersonal 1970s building with functiona rooms. Wine bar and a contemporary style in the restaurant, which overlooks the pool Modern menu.

in Sassenay 9 km Northeast by D 5 – pop. 1 453 – alt. 178 m – ✉ 71530

Le Magny AC VISA MC

29 Grande rue – ✆ 03 85 91 61 58 – www.lemagny.com – salognon.pierre@wanadoo.fr – Fax 03 85 91 77 28 – Closed 4-11 May, 27 July-13 August, 4-11 January, Sunday dinner, Tuesday dinner and Monday

Rest – Menu (€15), €22/35 – Carte €26/61

◆ With its yellow façade with green shutters and its provincial interior (Bressan wardrobes, parquet, fireplace), this village inn provides a welcoming setting. Regional food.

CHAMAGNE – 88 Vosges – 314 F2 – see Charmes

CHAMALIÈRES – 63 Puy-de-Dôme – 326 F8 – see Clermont-Ferrand

CHAMARANDES – 52 Haute-Marne – 313 K5 – see Chaumont

CHAMBERET – 19 Corrèze – 329 L2 – pop. 1 319 – alt. 450 m – ✉ 19370 25 **C2**

Paris 453 – Guéret 84 – Limoges 66 – Tulle 45 – Ussel 64

Syndicat d'initiative, 5, place du Marché ✆ 05 55 98 30 14, Fax 05 55 98 79 34

Mont Gargan ✳★★ Northwest: 9 km, **Dordogne-Berry-Limousin**

De France AC rest, P VISA MC AE

– ✆ 05 55 98 30 14 – hotelfrancechamberet.fr – hotel-france.chamberet@orange.fr – Fax 05 55 73 47 15 – Closed 23 December-25 January, Friday dinner from November to May and Sunday dinner from September to June

15 rm – €40/50 €40/52, ☕ €8

Rest – Menu €13 (weekday lunch), €21/35 – Carte €22/45

◆ Family atmosphere in a smart stone house with renovated rooms. Bar with a local clientele. A stylish restaurant with its old furniture, beams and murals representing Corrèze chateaux and villages. Traditional cuisine and dishes based on local produce.

CHAMBÉRY P – 73 Savoie – 333 I4 – pop. 57 800 – Built-up area 113 457 – alt. 270 m – Casino : at Challes-les-Eaux – ✉ 73000 **French Alps** 46 **F2**

Paris 562 – Annecy 50 – Grenoble 55 – Lyon 101 – Torino 205

Chambéry-Aix-les-Bains: ✆ 04 79 54 49 54, Viviers-du-Lac by ④: 8 km.

Office de tourisme, 24, boulevard de la Colonne ✆ 04 79 33 42 47, Fax 04 79 85 71 39

du Granier Apremont Apremont Chemin de Fontaine Rouge, SE : 8 km on D 201, ✆ 04 79 28 21 26

Old Town★★ : Château (Castle)★, place St-Léger★, railings ★ of the Hôtel de Châteauneuf (18 Rue de la Croix-d'Or) - Crypt ★ of the Eglise St-Pierre-de-Lémenc (St Pierre de Lémenc church) - Rue Basse-du-Château★ - Cathédrale métropolitaine St-François-de-Sales (St François de Sales cathedral)★ - Musée Savoisien (Savoy Museum)★ M[1] - Musée des Beaux-Arts (Fine Arts Museum)★ M[2].

CHAMBÉRY

Allobroges (Q. des) . . . . A 2
Banque (R. de la) . . . . B 3
Basse-du-Château (R.) . . . . . . A 4
Bernardines (Av. des) . . . . A 6
Boigne (R. de) . . . . B
Borrel (Q. du Sénateur A.) . . . B 7
Charvet (R. F.) . . . . B 9
Château (Pl. du) . . . . A 10
Colonne (Bd de la) . . . . B 12
Ducis (R.) . . . . B 13
Ducs-de-Savoie (Av. des) . . . . B 14
Europe (Espl. de l') . . . . B 16
Freizier (R.) . . . . AB 17
Gaulle (Av. Gén.-de) . . . . B 18
Italie (R. d') . . . . B 20
Jean-Jaurès (Av.) . . . . A 21
Jeu-de-Paume (Q. du) . . . . A 23
Juiverie (R.) . . . . A
Lans (R. de) . . . . A 24
Libération (Pl. de la) . . . . B 25
Maché (Pl.) . . . . A 27
Maché (R. du Fg) . . . . A 28
Martin (R. Cl.) . . . . B 30
Métropole (Pl.) . . . . B 31
Michaud (R.) . . . . B 32
Mitterrand (Pl. F.) . . . . B 33
Musée (Bd. du) . . . . AB 34
Ravet (Q. Ch.) . . . . B 35
St-François (R.) . . . . B 38
St-Léger (Pl.) . . . . B
St-Antoine (R.) . . . . A 36
Théâtre (Bd du) . . . . B 39
Vert (Av. du Comte) . . . . A 40

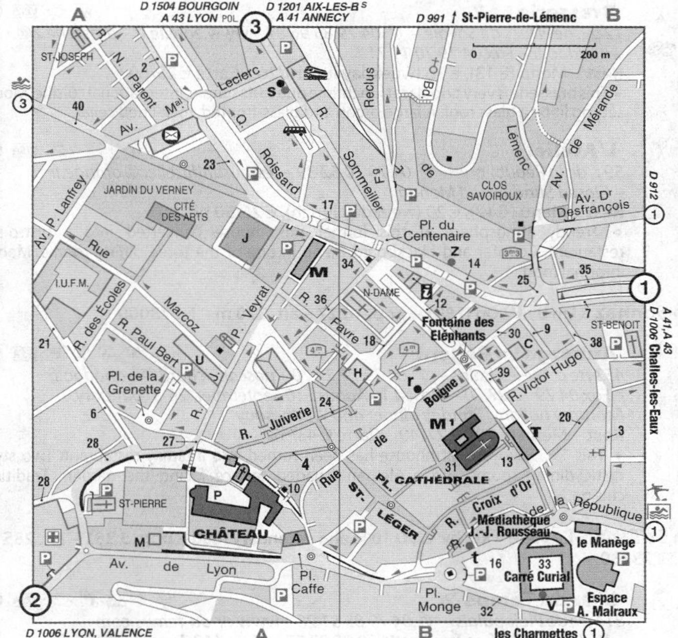

Mercure without rest

183 pl. de la Gare – ✆ 04 79 62 10 11 – www.accorhotels.com – h1541@accor.com – Fax 04 79 62 10 23 A **s**

81 rm – †€ 69/239 ††€ 79/249, ☕ € 16

◆ Across from the station, determinedly modern architecture, alternating between concrete and glass. Pleasant lobby, modern lounge-bar, spacious, soundproofed rooms.

Des Princes without rest

4 r. Boigne – ✆ 04 79 33 45 36 – www.hoteldesprinces.eu – hoteldesprinces@wanadoo.fr – Fax 04 79 70 31 47 B **r**

45 rm – †€ 72/80 ††€ 85/93, ☕ € 9

◆ This charming hotel, near the Elephant Fountain, has an impressive decor: corridors lined with portraits of members of the House of Savoie, and themed decor in the rooms (music, poetry, etc).

L'Hypoténuse

141 Carré Curial – ✆ 04 79 85 80 15 – www.restaurant-hypotenuse.com – resto.hypo@wanadoo.fr – Fax 04 79 85 80 18 – Closed for the spring holiday, 19 July-18 August, Sunday and Monday B **v**

Rest – Menu (€ 18), € 22 (weekdays)/44 – Carte € 33/44

◆ The contemporary decor of the 'Hypotenuse in the Carré (square)' is set off by period furniture and paintings. Traditional cuisine.

Les Comptoirs
183 pl. de la Gare – 04 79 96 97 27 – www.homtel.fr – restaurantlescomptoirs@orange.fr – Fax 04 79 96 17 78 – Closed Saturday lunch and Sunday
A
Rest – Menu € 19/29 – Carte approx. € 32
◆ Contemporary dining room set in a glass pyramid structure, decorated in chocolate shades. Fusion cuisine with an Asian slant. Relaxed atmosphere and service.

Brasserie Le Z
12 av. des Ducs de Savoie – 04 79 85 96 87 – www.zorelle.fr – brasserie.z@wanadoo.fr – Fax 04 79 70 11 71
B
Rest – Menu (€ 13), € 16 (weekday lunch)/26 – Carte € 25/60
◆ This brasserie is very popular at lunchtime due to its simple, international cuisine. Modern setting lit by a glass roof. A large organ and glass-fronted, rock-lined cellar.

L'Atelier
59 r. de la République – 04 79 70 62 39 – restaurantlatelier@orange.fr – Closed Sunday and Monday
B
Rest – Menu (€ 17), € 20 (weekday lunch), € 26/50 bi
◆ Trendy atmosphere at this former post house converted into a bistro-style restaurant. Counter and blackboard menu in one of the three dining rooms. Modern, informal food.

in Sonnaz 8 km by ① On D 991 – pop. 1 227 – alt. 370 m – ✉ 73000

Auberge Le Régent
453 rte d'Aix-les-Bains – 04 79 72 27 70 – pascal.vichard@wanadoo.fr – Fax 04 79 72 27 70 – Closed 16 August-10 September, 26-31 January, February holiday, Sunday dinner and Wednesday
Rest – Menu (€ 20), € 27/49 – Carte € 43/55
◆ This 19C Savoyard farmhouse has been turned into a family restaurant. Two stylish rustic dining rooms and a pleasant shaded terrace facing the garden. Traditional cuisine.

in St-Alban-Leysse 4 km by ①, D 1006 and secondary road – pop. 5 381 – alt. 285 m – ✉ 73230

L'Or du Temps
814 rte de Plainpalais – 04 79 85 51 28 – www.or-du-temps.com – or.du.temps@free.fr – Fax 04 79 85 83 87 – Closed 13 August-2 September and 2-10 January
18 rm – €55 €60, € 6,50
Rest – *(closed Saturday lunchtime, Sunday evening and Monday)* Menu (€ 15), € 24/50 – Carte € 42/55
◆ Nicely restored regional building with a splendid view of the Bauges massif. Modern rooms brightened up with colourful furniture. Modern inspired cuisine served in a cosy room or on a shaded terrace.

in Barberaz 3 3 km via ①, N 201 (exit 19: La Ravoire) – pop. 4 605 – alt. 315 m – ✉ 73000

Altédia Lodge
61 r. de la République – 04 79 60 05 00 – www.hotel-altedia.com – info@hotel-altedia.com – Fax 04 79 60 43 63
34 rm – €80/130 €80/130, € 13 – 2 suites
Rest – *04 79 60 07 00 (Closed 1-15 August)* Menu (€ 16), € 20 (weekday lunch), € 32/39 – Carte approx. € 40
◆ Contemporary hotel complex (Starck furniture), designed with functionality in mind: good soundproofing, DVDs on request, health and beauty areas. Modern setting and cuisine at the Maison Rouge.

Annex
41 rm – €60 €60, € 8
◆ The annexe has family rooms. Buffet breakfast.

in Challes-les-Eaux **7 km by ② by D 1006 and secondary road – pop. 4 829 – alt. 310 m – ✉ 73190**

Office de tourisme, avenue de Chambéry ✆ 04 79 72 86 19, Fax 04 79 71 38 51

Château des Comtes de Challes
247 montée du Château – ✆ 04 79 72 72 72 – www.chateaudescomtesdechalles.com – info@chateaudescomtesdechalles.com – Fax 04 79 72 83 83 – Closed 25 October-12 November
50 rm – †€ 65 ††€ 89, ☕ € 12 – 4 suites – ½ P € 76
Rest – Menu € 28 (weekdays)/58 – Carte € 61/70
◆ A pretty 15C castle and chapel surrounded by a park with very old trees. The rooms have period and more modern furniture, and have nearly all been renovated. A fireplace built in 1650 reigns over the fine, rustic dining room. Inventive cuisine.

in Chambéry-le-Vieux **5 km by ③ by N 201 and secondary road (Chambéry-le-Haut exit) – ✉ 73000**

Château de Candie
r. Bois de Candie – ✆ 04 79 96 63 00 – www.chateaudecandie.com – info@chateaudecandie.com – Fax 04 79 96 63 10 – Closed 14-27 April and 26 October-5 November
23 rm – †€ 160/260 ††€ 160/260, ☕ € 18 – 5 suites – ½ P € 140/190
Rest – *(closed Saturday lunch, Sunday dinner and Monday)* Menu € 32 (weekday lunch), € 52/110 – Carte € 95/140
Spec. Bar de ligne comme un sashimi, vinaigrette pamplemousse, pomelos confits, sorbet agrumes (summer). Turbot côtier cuit vapeur, condiment câpres et citron, tarte tiède de cèpes pickles (autumn). Palet or crousti fondant chocolat noisettes, sorbet passion, jus tiède passion citron vert (autumn). **Wines** Chignin Bergeron, Chautagne.
◆ This 14C fortified house, built by the Crusaders, overlooks the valley. Cosy bedrooms (including eight new rooms) uniting old and modern styles; superb suite in the tower with Jacuzzi bath. Fine, rather inventive market cuisine.

CHAMBOLLE-MUSIGNY – 21 Côte-d'Or – 320 J6 – pop. 308 – alt. 280 m – ✉ 21220 8 D1

Paris 326 – Beaune 28 – Dijon 17

Château André Ziltener without rest
r. de la Fontaine – ✆ 03 80 62 41 62 – www.chateau-ziltener.com – chateau.ziltener@wanadoo.fr – Fax 03 80 62 83 75 – Closed 15 December-28 February
8 rm – †€ 180/220 ††€ 190/285, ☕ € 18 – 2 suites
◆ This 18C residence invites you to share in the discreet luxury of its spacious Louis XV-style rooms, a successful blend of old and new. Small wine museum.

Le Chambolle
28 r. Basse – ✆ 03 80 62 86 26 – www.restaurant-lechambolle.com – lechambolle@orange.fr – Fax 03 80 62 86 26 – Closed 1-16 July, 20 December-22 January, Sunday dinner from December to March, Wednesday and Thursday
Rest – *(number of covers limited, pre-book)* Menu € 26/45 – Carte € 23/54
◆ A smiling welcome awaits you in this warm rustic restaurant (impressive fireplace) that serves local dishes made with good quality regional produce.

CHAMBON-LA-FORÊT – 45 Loiret – 318 K3 – pop. 709 – alt. 117 m – ✉ 45340 12 C2

Paris 96 – Châteauneuf-sur-Loire 26 – Montargis 43 – Orléans 43 – Pithiviers 15

Auberge de la Rive du Bois
11 r. de la Rive du Bois, 1 km north by Pithiviers road – ✆ 02 38 32 28 44 – www.auberge-rivedubois.com – aubergedelarivedubois@wanadoo.fr – Fax 02 38 32 02 61 – Closed 6-25 August, 24 December-5 January, Monday dinner, Tuesday dinner and Wednesday
Rest – Menu € 16 (weekdays)/48 – Carte € 30/52
◆ This peaceful hamlet's welcoming inn is ideal for family and business get-togethers: countrified dining rooms, flower-decked terrace and veranda. Classic menu.

LE CHAMBON-SUR-LIGNON – 43 Haute-Loire – 331 H3 – pop. 2 642 – alt. 967 m – ✉ 43400 Lyon - Rhone Valley 6 D3

Paris 573 – Annonay 48 – Lamastre 32 – Privas 75 – Le Puy-en-Velay 45 – St-Étienne 60

Office de tourisme, 2, route de Tence ✆ 04 71 59 71 56, Fax 04 71 65 88 78

du Chambon-sur-Lignon La Pierre de la Lune, SE : 5 km on D 103, ✆ 04 71 59 28 10

Bel Horizon

rm, rest,

chemin de Molle – ✆ 04 71 59 74 39 – www.belhorizon.fr – info@belhorizon.fr – Fax 04 71 59 79 81 – Closed 2-24 January, Monday (except hotel) and Sunday dinner 1st October-30 April

30 rm – €60/100 €70/100, €10 – ½ P €71/85

Rest – Menu (€15), €18 (weekdays)/43 – Carte €30/60

◆ A relaxed atmosphere in this hotel that focuses on relaxation and leisure (well-being centre). Well kept, light, practical rooms. Restaurant in sunny tones and terrace overlooking the garden. Classic menu.

South 3 km by D 151, La Suchère road and secondary road – ✉ 43400 Chambon-sur-Lignon

Le Bois Vialotte

rest,

rte de la Suchere, La Suchère road – ✆ 04 71 59 74 03 – www.leboisvialotte.com – crosde@wanadoo.fr – Fax 04 71 65 86 32 – Open 28 May-1 October

17 rm – €56/69 €56/69, €10 – ½ P €57/65

Rest – *(resident only)* Menu (€15), €18 (lunch), €22/26

◆ Those seeking quiet will enjoy this family-run hotel located on the edge of a wood. The rooms look out over open countryside and are very well kept. Guesthouse-type, somewhat antiquated, dining room and traditional home cooking.

East 3,5 km by D 157 and D 185 – ✉ 43400 Chambon-sur-Lignon

Clair Matin

rm, rest,

Les Barandons – ✆ 04 71 59 73 03 – www.hotelclairmatin.com – clairmatin@hotelclairmatin.com – Fax 04 71 65 87 66 – Closed 30 November-30 January, Monday and Tuesday in low season

25 rm – €55/105 €55/105, €11 – 2 suites – ½ P €59/93

Rest – Menu (€15), €20 (weekdays)/37 – Carte €30/55

◆ 'On a clear day' you will enjoy a wide view of the Cévennes from this welcoming chalet. Practical rooms, many leisure activities in the park and fresh air guaranteed! The restaurant and terrace have a beautiful panoramic view of the Mézenc and Gerbier-de-Jonc peaks.

CHAMBORD – 41 Loir-et-Cher – 318 G6 – pop. 150 – alt. 71 m – ✉ 41250 11 B1

Paris 176 – Blois 18 – Châteauroux 101 – Orléans 56 – Romorantin-Lanthenay 38 – Salbris 55

Château★★★, Châteaux of the Loire

Du Grand St-Michel

pl. St-Louis – ✆ 02 54 20 31 31 – www.saintmichel-chambord.com – hotelsaintmichel@wanadoo.fr – Fax 02 54 20 36 40 – Closed 12 Nov. - 20 Dec. and Wed. from Dec. to Mar.

40 rm – €53/99 €53/99, €8,50

Rest – *(closed 1 Jan - 1 Apr, Tues lunchtime, Sun evening and Mon)* Menu €23/33 – Carte €41/58

◆ On the marvellous Chambord estate overlooking the castle. Ask for one of the modern, renovated rooms. Vast restaurant decorated with trophies and paintings devoted to hunting. The terrace faces the royal hunting lodge, lit up during sound and light shows.

CHAMBRAY-LÈS-TOURS – 37 Indre-et-Loire – 317 N4 – see Tours

CHAMBRETAUD – 85 Vendée – 316 K6 – pop. 1 275 – alt. 214 m – ✉ 85500 — 34 B3

▶ Paris 373 – Angers 85 – Bressuire 50 – Cholet 21 – Nantes 76 – La Roche-sur-Yon 55

Château du Boisniard — rm, rm,
– ✆ 02 51 67 50 01 – *www.chateau-boisniard.com*
– *contact@chateau-boisniard.com* – *Fax 02 51 67 53 81*
17 rm – €138/240 €138/410, ☕ €18
Rest – *(closed Sunday dinner 30 September-31 March)* Menu (€29), €38/59
– Carte €46/57
◆ A beautiful 15C manor (entirely non-smoking) with attractive rooms redone in a medieval style; those in the outbuildings are new and comfortable. Vast wooded estate and spa. Elegant restaurant with a view of the park. Cuisine based on fresh market produce.

CHAMESOL – 25 Doubs – 321 K2 – pop. 361 – alt. 730 m – ✉ 25190 — 17 C2

▶ Paris 453 – Besançon 91 – Belfort 43 – Montbéliard 30 – Morteau 50

Mon Plaisir (Christian Pilloud)
22 r. Journal – ✆ *03 81 92 56 17* – *mon-plaisir@wanadoo.fr* – *Fax 03 81 92 52 67*
– *Closed 31 August-15 September, 21-29 December, Sunday dinner, Monday and Tuesday except lunch on bank holidays*
Rest – Menu €39/75
Spec. Foie gras dans toutes ses formes. Escargots en capuccino. Farandole de desserts. **Wines** Arbois.
◆ A mixture of styles, numerous knick-knacks, paintings and floral arrangements make up the decor of this family restaurant with old-fashioned charm. Tempting modern cuisine.

CHAMONIX-MONT-BLANC – 74 Haute-Savoie – 328 O5 – pop. 9 086 – alt. 1 040 m – Winter sports : 1 035/3 840 m 14 36 – Casino AY – ✉ 74400 French Alps — 45 D1

▶ Paris 610 – Albertville 65 – Annecy 97 – Aosta 57 – Genève 82

Mont-Blanc Tunnel: 2008 toll, one way: cars €33.20, car and caravan €44, lorries €120.40 to €256, motorbikes €22. Information ATMB ✆ 04 50 55 55 00 and ✆ 04 50 55 39 36.

Office de tourisme, 85, place du Triangle de l'Amitié ✆ 04 50 53 00 24, Fax 04 50 53 58 90

de Chamonix Les Praz-de-Chamonix 35 route du Golf, N : 3 km, ✆ 04 50 53 06 28

East: Mer de glace★★★ and Le Montenvers★★★ by rack railway - Southeast: Aiguille du midi ❋★★★ by cable car (intermediate station: plan de l'Aiguille★★) - Northwest: Le Brévent ❋★★★ by cable car (intermediate station: Planpraz★★) - North: Col de Balme (Balme Pass)★★(Alpages de Charamillon [Charamillon Pastures]).

Plan on following page

Hameau Albert 1er (Pierre Carrier et Pierre Maillet)
rm, rm,
38 rte du Bouchet – ✆ *04 50 53 05 09* – *www.hameaualbert.fr* – *infos@hameaualbert.fr* – *Fax 04 50 55 95 48* – *Closed 11 November-3 December*
21 rm – €140/540 €140/540, ☕ €21 — AX f
Rest – *(closed 12 May-3 June, 5 November-3 December, Tuesday lunch, Thursday lunch and Wednesday)* Menu €56 (lunch), €79/160
– Carte €120/190
Spec. Risotto à la truffe blanche d'Alba (Sep. to Jan.). Omble chevalier du lac Léman. Chocolat-Chartreuse en deux préparations. **Wines** Chignin-Bergeron, Mondeuse.
◆ Centuries-old hotel where tradition and modernity happily coexist. Superb rooms with fine panelling, quality materials and the latest facilities. Smart garden. Elegant restaurant, brilliant classic cuisine with a subtle modern touch, and an extensive wine list.

La Ferme
11 rm – €270/540 €270/540, ☕ €21 – 2 suites — AX f
Rest ***Le Hameau Albert 1er*** and the restaurant ***La Maison Carrier***
– see restaurant listing
◆ Magnificent chalet built with old wood taken from mountain farmhouses. Well-executed interior, resolutely designer in style. Gym and spa.

CHAMONIX-MONT-BLANC

Aiguille-du-Midi (Av.)	AY	2
Angeville (Rte H. d')	AX	3
Balmat (Pl. Jacques)	AY	5
Blanche (Rte)	AY	
Bois-du-Bouchet (Av. du)	AX	6
Cachat-le-Géant (Av.)	AX	7
Courmayeur (Av. de)	AY	9
Cour (Pont de)	AY	8
Cristalliers (Ch. des)	AX	10
Croix-des-Moussoux (Montée)	AZ	12
Croz (Av. Michel)	AY	13
Devouassoux (Ch. F.)	AY	14
Gaillands (Rte des)	AZ	18
Gare (Pl. de la)	AY	20
Helbronner (R.)	AY	
Lyret (R.)	AY	
Majestic (Allée du)	AY	21
Mollard (Ch. de la)	AX	23
Mont-Blanc (Av. et Pl.)	AX	24
Moussoux (Rte des)	AZ	26
Mummery (R.)	AX	27
Nants (Rte des)	AZ	
Paccard (R. du Dr)	AY	28
Pècles (Rte des)	AZ	29
Pèlerins (Rte des)	AZ	
Plage (Av. de la)	AX	
Ravanel-le-Rouge (Av.)	AY	31
Recteur-Payot (Allée)	AXY	32
Roumnaz (Rte de la)	AZ	33
Triangle-de-l'Amitié (Pl. du)	AX	34
Tunnel (Rte du)	AZ	
Vallot (R. J.)	AX	
Whymper (R.)	AX	37

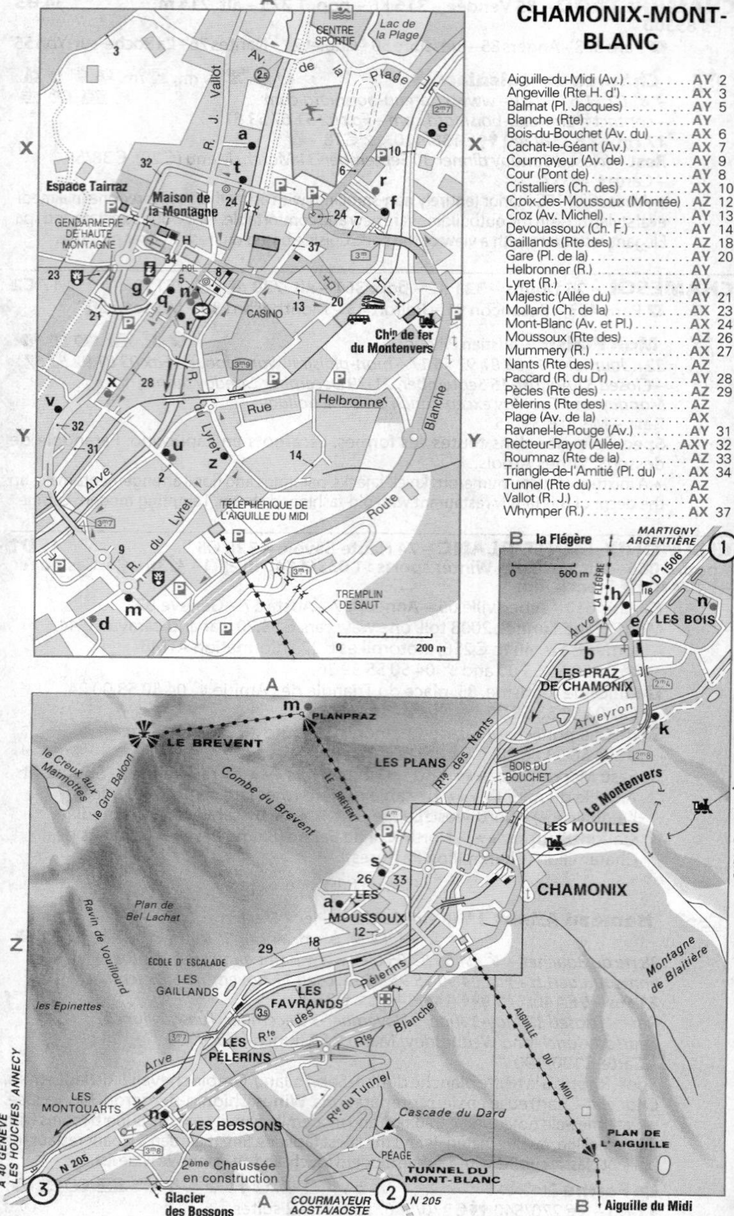

Grand Hôtel des Alpes without rest
75 r. du Dr Paccard – ✆ 04 50 55 37 80 – www.grandhoteldesalpes.com – info@grandhoteldesalpes.com – Fax 04 50 55 88 50 – Open 12 June-30 September and 16 December-10 April AY **r**
27 rm – †€ 150/600 ††€ 150/600, ☕ € 20 – 3 suites
◆ This large hotel built in 1840 was successfully restored in 2004. Opulent hall, quiet bar, elegant lounges and rooms that are as spacious as they are comfortable. Pleasant relaxation area.

Auberge du Bois Prin
69 Chemin de l' Hermine, aux Moussoux, (in Les Moussoux) – ✆ 04 50 53 33 51 – www.boisprin.com – info@boisprin.com – Fax 04 50 53 48 75 – Closed 11-28 May, 27 October-4 December AZ **a**
8 rm – †€ 180/284 ††€ 203/297, ☕ € 14 – 2 suites – ½ P € 147/215
Rest – *(closed Monday lunch, Tuesday lunch and Wednesday lunch)* Menu € 19/49 bi
◆ Pretty Savoy chalet on the heights above the resort. Designer decor, high-tech fittings and panelling are tastefully combined in the luxuriously renovated rooms. Panoramic view of Mont Blanc from the dining room and terrace. Market produce and home-grown vegetables.

Le Morgane
145 av. Aiguille du Midi – ✆ 04 50 53 57 15 – www.morgane-hotel-chamonix.com – reservation@hotelmorganechamonix.com – Fax 04 50 53 28 07 AY **u**
56 rm – †€ 105/220 ††€ 120/350, ☕ € 15 – 16 suites
Rest *Le Bistrot* – see restaurant listing
◆ A new hotel combining local stone and wood with modern comfort. Well-appointed rooms, some with views of Mont Blanc. Small spa.

Alpina rm, rest,
79 av. Mt-Blanc – ✆ 04 50 53 47 77 – www.chamonixhotels.com – alpina@chamonixhotels.com – Fax 04 50 55 98 99 – Closed 11 October-12 December AX **t**
129 rm – †€ 72/107 ††€ 80/164, ☕ € 14 – 9 suites – ½ P € 79/121
Rest – *(Closed lunch in winter)* Menu € 25 – Carte € 40/48
◆ Building with recently renovated façade, well-equipped for seminars. Functional, panelled rooms. Restaurant with a somewhat plain, contemporary decor, offset by a panoramic view of the snow-capped peaks.

Les Aiglons
270 av. Courmayeur – ✆ 04 50 55 90 93 – www.aiglons.com – reservation@hotelaiglonschamonix.com – Fax 04 50 53 51 08 AY **m**
107 rm – †€ 90/210 ††€ 110/230, ☕ € 12 – ½ P € 97/157
Rest – Menu € 17 (lunch)/30 – Carte € 35/60
◆ This hotel near the station and cable car has been renovated and extended. Suitable for sporty guests with families (club atmosphere). Modern, functional rooms. Spa, pool. Traditional cuisine in the modern restaurant.

Chalet Hôtel Hermitage
63 chemin du Cé – ✆ 04 50 53 13 87 – www.hermitage-paccard.com – info@hermitage-paccard.com – Fax 04 50 55 98 14 – Open 19 June-20 September and 19 December-20 April AX **e**
23 rm – †€ 92/124 ††€ 100/180, ☕ € 14 – 5 suites
Rest – *(closed Wednesday in summer) (dinner only) (resident only)* Menu € 24
◆ Large, spacious panelled rooms perfect for family stays. The apartments in the annexe could come in handy. Family cuisine served in a dining room where wood prevails.

L'Oustalet without rest
330 r. Lyret – ✆ 04 50 55 54 99 – www.hotel-oustalet.com – infos@hotel-oustalet.com – Fax 04 50 55 54 98 – Closed 26 May-8 June, 4 November-16 December AY **z**
15 rm – †€ 100/135 ††€ 106/175, ☕ € 14
◆ Recently-built chalet at the foot of the Aiguille du Midi with a warm decor. Spacious, smart rooms overlooking Mont Blanc. Cosy lounge where you can relax by the fire. Hammam, sauna and jacuzzi.

Park Hotel Suisse
75 allée du Majestic – ✆ 04 50 53 07 58 – www.chamonix-park-hotel.com – reservation@chamonix-park-hotel.com – Fax 04 50 55 99 32 – Open 12 June-30 September and 19 December-13 April AY **q**
64 rm – €77/126 €101/177, ☕ €12 – 2 suites – ½ P €70/123
Rest – *(open 12 June-12 September)* Menu €19 (lunch), €23/28 – Carte €48/64
◆ Completely renovated, this hotel blends a very warm mountain-style character with modern comforts. Pretty terrace-solarium on the roof, from where you can admire the Mont Blanc mountain range. Traditional cuisine and specialities from Savoy. Lively décor, the very image of a modern chalet.

De l'Arve
60 impasse Anémones – ✆ 04 50 53 02 31 – www.hotelarve-chamonix.com – contact@hotelarve-chamonix.com – Fax 04 50 53 56 92 – Closed from mid October-mid December AX **a**
37 rm – €51/88 €61/118, ☕ €10 – 1 suite – ½ P €54/82
Rest – *(open 20 June-5 September and closed Tuesday and Wednesday) (dinner only) (resident only)* Menu €18
◆ A large, local style building with rooms renovated in a Savoy style. Small garden facing the Mont Blanc range. Fitness facilities including a climbing wall. Discreet modern dining room, with bay windows facing the Arve.

Arveyron
1650 rte du Bouchet, 2 km – ✆ 04 50 53 18 29 – www.hotel-arveyron.com – hotelarveyron@wanadoo.fr – Fax 04 50 53 06 43 – Open 13 June-22 September and 20 December-mid April BZ **k**
30 rm – €45 €72/79, ☕ €9 – ½ P €58/79
Rest – *(closed Monday and Wednesday)* Menu €23/26 – Carte approx. €27
◆ This pleasant family hotel houses mountain style rooms, quieter on the forest side. Bar-lounge, billiards and a garden...under the Chamonix icicles! Dining room which has been newly refurbished with lots of wood. Pleasant terrace. Traditional, locally inspired cuisine.

La Savoyarde
28 rte Moussoux – ✆ 04 50 53 00 77 – www.lasavoyarde.com – lasavoyarde@wanadoo.fr – Fax 04 50 55 86 82 – Closed May and November AZ **s**
14 rm ☕ – €61/84 €112/158 – ½ P €86/110
Rest – *(Closed Tuesday and Thursday) (dinner only)* Menu (€25), €30 – Carte €35/68
◆ A stylish 19C Chamonix house, 50 m from the Brévent cable car. Simple, panelled rooms, some with sloping roofs or with a mezzanine. The dining rooms enjoy a fine view of the mountains. Traditional fare with regional touches.

Les Jardins du Mont Blanc
62 allée du Majestic – ✆ 04 50 53 05 64 – www.bestmontblanc.com – mont-blanc@chamonixhotels.com – Fax 04 50 55 89 44 – Closed 4 October-11 December
Rest – *(pre-book)* Menu €23/79 – Carte €56/98 dinner only AY **g**
◆ A talented chef brings this town centre establishment to life: gastronomic meals in the evening in the plush, retro-style dining room, and simpler offerings at lunchtime in the garden or bar.

La Maison Carrier – Hôtel Hameau Albert 1er
44 rte du Bouchet – ✆ 04 50 53 00 03 – www.hameaualbert.fr – infos@hameaualbert.fr – Fax 04 50 55 95 48 – Closed 8-25 June, 16 November-15 December, Monday except July-August and bank holidays
Rest – Menu €24 (weekday lunch), €28/39 – Carte €42/65 AX **r**
◆ Room for the guides; towering fireplace where home-made hams and sausages are smoked. A pretty farmhouse rebuilt with old wood from alpine chalets. Good local cuisine.

Atmosphère
123 pl. Balmat – ✆ 04 50 55 97 97 – www.restaurant-atmosphere.com – info@restaurant-atmos.fr – Fax 04 50 53 38 96 AY **n**
Rest – Menu (€20), €23/30 – Carte €32/55
◆ This restaurant has atmosphere! New mountain style decor, uncluttered and cosy, and a veranda overlooking the Arve. Enjoy the extensive wine list, traditional food and regional specialities.

XX **L'Impossible**

9 chemin du Cry – ✆ 04 50 53 20 36 – www.restaurant-impossible.com – contact@restaurant-impossible.com – Fax 04 50 53 58 91 – Open 15 June-15 October and 7 December-15 April AY **d**

Rest – Menu (€ 19), € 28 – Carte € 32/65

◆ In this old 18C farm the chef prepares lovely traditional dishes with regional touches. Cosy dining room with eclectic decoration.

XX **Le Bistrot** (Mickael Bourdillat) – Hôtel Le Morgane

151 av. Aiguille du Midi – ✆ 04 50 53 57 64 – wwww.lebistrotchamonix.com – info@lebistrotchamonix.com – Fax 04 50 53 28 07 AY **u**

Rest – Menu (€ 17), € 42/80 – Carte € 42/80

Spec. Sushi de tartare de bœuf, salade de betterave rouge. Filet mignon de porc, gambas et minute de carotte. Tasse croustillante comme un cappuccino. **Wines** Roussette de Savoie, Chignin-Bergeron

◆ An uncluttered modern look at this pleasant bistro. The menu, based on high quality produce, is accompanied by an enticing choice of wines (glass-fronted wine cellar).

X **Le Panier des Quatre Saisons**

24 galerie Blanc-Neige, (Rue Dr Paccard) – ✆ 04 50 53 98 77 – Fax 04 50 53 98 77 AY **x**

Rest – Menu (€ 12,50), € 29/39 – Carte € 40/50

◆ This restaurant, hidden away in a narrow street, is a delightful house with a country decor. Seasonal dishes and good choice of wines by the glass (40 to choose from).

X **Le National**

3 r. Dr-Paccard – ✆ 04 50 53 02 23 – Fax 04 50 53 71 94 – Closed 15 November-15 December and Monday in October-November

Rest – Menu € 21/30 – Carte € 15/60 AY **n**

◆ Wood panelling, exposed stones and old photos of the resort make up the setting for traditional cuisine including Savoyard specialities. Large, busy terrace.

in Praz-de-Chamonix 2.5 km north – ✉ 74400 Chamonix-Mont-Blanc – alt. 1 060 m

La Flégère ≤★★ by cable car BZ.

Le Labrador without rest

au golf – ✆ 04 50 55 90 09 – www.hotel-labrador.com – info@hotel-labrador.com – Fax 04 50 53 15 85 – Closed 20-30 April and 18 October-4 December BZ **h**

33 rm – †€ 75/200 ††€ 88/250, ☕ € 10 – 2 suites

◆ A chalet of Scandinavian inspiration. All the rooms command a splendid view of the Mont Blanc and Chamonix Valley. Snug sitting rooms.

Eden

35 rte des Gaudenays – ✆ 04 50 53 18 43 – www.hoteleden-chamonix.com – relax@hoteleden-chamonix.com – Fax 04 50 53 51 50 – Closed 5 November-5 December BZ **e**

31 rm – †€ 68/125 ††€ 75/135, ☕ € 11 – ½ P € 73/108

Rest – *(closed 15 October-13 December and Tuesday) (dinner only)* Menu € 29/45 – Carte € 35/52

◆ The Scandinavian-born owners have redecorated this two-hundred-year-old house in a Nordic style: unusual and appealing throughout, from lounge to rooms. The restaurant is graced by a fine exhibition of photos and serves Franco-Swedish fusion cuisine.

Les Lanchers rest,

1459 rte des Praz – ✆ 04 50 53 47 19 – www.hotel-lanchers-chamonix.com – vacances@hotel-lanchers-chamonix.com – Fax 04 50 53 66 14 – Closed 16 November-18 December BZ **b**

11 rm – †€ 58/98 ††€ 58/98, ☕ € 9 – ½ P € 56/78

Rest – Menu (€ 14), € 19/24 – Carte € 24/30

◆ Behind this façade enlivened by colourful frescoes are cool and simple rooms, and a bar frequented by the locals. Dining room-veranda offering a bistro-type setting; traditional fare, Savoyard and Italian specialities.

La Cabane des Praz

23 rte du Golf – ✆ 04 50 53 23 27 – www.restaurant-cabane.com – restaurantlacabane@orange.fr – Fax 04 50 91 15 28

Rest – Menu (€ 19), € 28 – Carte € 32/62

◆ This elegant log cabin has been superbly refurbished to offer a smart, relaxed ambience with a cosy lounge-bar, terrace with views of the golf-course and traditional cuisine.

in Tines **4 km by ①, D 1506 and secondary road – ✉ 74400 Chamonix-Mont-Blanc**

Excelsior

251 chemin de St-Roch – ✆ 04 50 53 18 36 – www.hotelchamonix.info – excelsior@hotelchamonix.info – Fax 04 50 53 56 16 – Closed 11-25 May and 5 November-15 December

36 rm – †€ 40/62 ††€ 65/92, ☕ € 9 – ½ P € 58/87

Rest – *(closed Wednesday lunch 15 December-11 May)* Menu (€ 16), € 28/41 – Carte € 36/49

◆ Run by the same family since 1910, this pleasant establishment is at the foot of the Verte et du Dru peak. Good renovated rooms with light-wood wainscoting. Garden and pool. The windows of the restaurant command views of the peaks. Updated and alpine menu.

in Bois **3,5 km North – ✉ 74400 Chamonix-Mont-Blanc**

Sarpé

83 passage des Mottets – ✆ 04 50 53 29 31 – couttety@hotmail.fr – Closed 12 May-11 June, 5 November-5 December, Monday except school holidays

BZ n

Rest – *(dinner only except school holidays)* Menu € 23/44 – Carte € 29/55

◆ A former carpenter's workshop converted into a restaurant with a rustic setting, typically Savoyard atmosphere and two small terraces. Traditional and Alpine dishes.

in Lavancher **6 km by ①, D 1506 and secondary road – ✉ 74400 Chamonix-Mont-Blanc – Winter sports : see Chamonix**

⊙ ≤★★.

Le Jeu de Paume

705 rte Chapeau – ✆ 04 50 54 03 76 – www.jeudepaumechamonix.com – jeudepaumechamonix@wanadoo.fr – Fax 04 50 54 10 75 – Open 16 June-24 September and 6 December-14 May

24 rm – †€ 155/255 ††€ 155/255, ☕ € 15 – ½ P € 128/178

Rest – *(closed Tuesday lunch and Wednesday lunch)* Menu € 35/58 – Carte € 40/60

◆ Wood and antique furniture throughout make for a refined setting in this traditional chalet at the foot of the Aiguille Verte. A pleasant place to relax. Somewhat baroque alpine decor and world cuisine.

Beausoleil

60 allée des peupliers – ✆ 04 50 54 00 78 – www.hotelbeausoleilchamonix.com – info@hotelbeausoleilchamonix.com – Fax 04 50 54 17 34 – Closed 31 May-12 June and 20 September-20 December

17 rm – †€ 47/56 ††€ 72/108, ☕ € 10 – ½ P € 62/88

Rest – *(dinner only except July-August)* Menu € 15/30 – Carte € 27/43

◆ This (non-smoking) family chalet with an inviting façade has simple wainscoted rooms; some have been refurbished. Flower-decked garden in summer. A rustic alpine restaurant and lovely terrace; regional and cheese specialities.

Les Chalets de Philippe without rest

700-718 rte Chapeau – ✆ 06 07 23 17 26 – www.chaletsphilippe.com – contact@chaletsphilippe.com – Fax 04 50 54 08 28

8 rm – †€ 91/260 ††€ 190/540, ☕ € 15

◆ Old wood, antiques, rare objects and state-of-the-art fixtures and fittings make up the unusual and very personal decor of these hillside chalets among the fir trees.

in Bossons 3.5 km south – ✉ 74400 Chamonix-Mont-Blanc – alt. 1 005 m

Aiguille du Midi rest, rest, VISA AE
479 chemin Napoléon – ✆ 04 50 53 00 65 – www.hotel-aiguilledumidi.com – info@hotel-aiguilledumidi.com – Fax 04 50 55 93 69 – Open 16 May-19 September and 19 December-13 April
40 rm – €72/98 €88/98, ☕ €14 – ½ P €82/85 AZ **n**
Rest – Menu €24/50 – Carte €23/51
◆ Tyrolean-style frescoes adorn the exterior of this hotel built in 1908. Diversely furnished rooms, park facing the Bossons Glacier and well-equipped leisure facilities. Rotunda restaurant, pleasant terrace overlooking the garden. Traditional and Savoyard cuisine.

in Planpraz by cable car – ✉ 74400 Chamonix-Mont-Blanc

La Bergerie de Planpraz VISA AE
– ✆ 04 50 53 05 42 – www.restaurants-altitude.com – contact@serac.biz – Fax 04 50 53 93 40 – Open early June to mid-September and mid-December to end April AZ **m**
Rest – *(lunch only)* Menu €19/27 – Carte €35/55
◆ Breathtaking view of the Mont Blanc range from the terrace of this mountain chalet. Rustic stone and wood interior, tasty generous dishes made with local produce.

CHAMOUILLE – 02 Aisne – 306 D6 – see Laon

CHAMOUSSET – 73 Savoie – 333 K4 – pop. 502 – alt. 215 m – ✉ 73390 46 **F2**

Paris 588 – Albertville 26 – Allevard 25 – Chambéry 28 – Grenoble 61

Christin with rm rest, VISA
– ✆ 04 79 36 42 06 – hotel.christin@wanadoo.fr – Fax 04 79 36 45 43 – Closed Saturday
16 rm – €43 €58, ☕ €7 – ½ P €58
Rest – *(closed Sunday dinner, Monday dinner and Saturday)* Menu €14/23 – Carte €22/45
◆ This restaurant has a family atmosphere and rustic setting. Enjoy authentic cuisine made up of produce from the kitchen garden, washed down with a selection of Savoie wines.

CHAMPAGNAC-DE-BELAIR – 24 Dordogne – 329 F3 – see Brantôme

CHAMPAGNÉ – 72 Sarthe – 310 L6 – pop. 3 565 – alt. 53 m – ✉ 72470 35 **D1**

Paris 205 – Alençon 67 – Le Mans 14 – Nantes 204
Office de tourisme, place de l'Église ✆ 02 43 89 89 89, Fax 02 43 89 58 58

Le Cochon d'Or VISA AE
49 rte de Paris, D 323 – ✆ 02 43 89 50 08 – www.lecochondor.fr – lecochon.dor@wanadoo.fr – Fax 02 43 89 79 34 – Closed 27 July-10 August, Monday and dinner except Saturday
Rest – Menu (€16), €20 (weekday lunch), €30/51 – Carte €44/53
◆ After a makeover, the dining room of this house on a busy street sports bright, fashionable colours. The bay window opens onto the garden. Traditional menu.

CHAMPAGNEUX – 73 Savoie – 333 G4 – see St-Genix-sur-Guiers

CHAMPAGNEY – 70 Haute-Saône – 314 I6 – see Ronchamp

CHAMPAGNOLE – 39 Jura – 321 F6 – pop. 8 296 – alt. 541 m – ✉ 39300 Burgundy-Jura 16 **B3**

Paris 420 – Besançon 66 – Dole 68 – Genève 86 – Lons-le-Saunier 34
Office de tourisme, rue Baronne Delort ✆ 03 84 52 43 67, Fax 03 84 52 54 57
Musée archéologique: buckle plates★.

Le Bois Dormant rm, VISA
rte de Pontarlier, 1.5 km – ✆ 03 84 52 66 66 – www.bois-dormant.com – hotel@bois-dormant.com – Fax 03 84 52 66 67 – Closed 20-27 December
40 rm – €65 €73, €10 – ½ P €63
Rest – Menu (€18), €25/45 – Carte €30/55
◆ Situated in the heart of wooded grounds, this hotel has a warm, modern decor. Functional bedrooms adorned with light wood and shades of pink. Fitness centre and swimming pool in the garden. A large veranda-dining room and quiet terrace. Traditional menu accompanied by wines from the Jura.

Genève road **8 km South – ✉39300 Champagnole**

Auberge des Gourmets with rm VISA
1 la Billaude du haut, on N 5 – ✆ 03 84 51 60 60 – aubergedesgourmets@wanadoo.fr – Fax 03 84 51 62 83 – Closed 1 December-5 February, Sunday dinner and Monday except school holidays
7 rm – €70 €75/88, €9 – ½ P €78
Rest – Menu €18 (weekdays)/48 – Carte €45/80
◆ Tasty, home cooking served in several smart, rustic dining rooms (one of which is a veranda). The hotel rooms on the terrace side are quieter.

CHAMPAGNY-EN-VANOISE – 73 Savoie – 333 N5 – pop. 585 – alt. 1 240 m – ✉ 73350 French Alps 45 D2

Paris 625 – Albertville 44 – Chambéry 94 – Moûtiers 19
Office de tourisme, Le Centre ✆ 04 79 55 06 55, Fax 04 79 55 04 66
Altar-piece★ in the church - Champagny cable car ★: ≤★ - Champagny-le-Haut★★.

L'Ancolie rm, rest, VISA
Les Hauts du Crey – ✆ 04 79 55 05 00 – www.hotel-ancolie.com – contact@hotel-ancolie.com – Fax 04 79 55 04 42 – Open 21 June-6 September and 20 December-19 April
31 rm – €63/97 €63/144, €10 – ½ P €51/92
Rest – Menu €19/21 – Carte €25/49
◆ Hotel dominating an authentic village resort, which is named after a wild flower. Small practical rooms, many of which boast a south-facing balcony. Alpine-style dining room and simple regional fare.

Les Glières rest, VISA
– ✆ 04 79 55 05 52 – www.hotel-glieres.com – accueil@hotel-glieres.com – Fax 04 79 55 04 84 – Open 4 July-24 August and 19 December-18 April
20 rm – €82/112 €82/112 – ½ P €64/79
Rest – *(closed Tuesday in summer)* Menu (€15), €18 – Carte €21/32
◆ This family-run establishment nestles in a quiet hamlet. Progressively spruced up rooms, in a chalet spirit. Sauna and fireside sitting room overlooking a lush green terrace. Characteristic Savoyard dishes and decor.

CHAMPCEVINEL – 24 Dordogne – 329 F4 – see Périgueux

CHAMPEAUX – 50 Manche – 303 C7 – pop. 368 – alt. 80 m – ✉ 50530 32 A2

Paris 353 – Avranches 19 – Granville 17 – St-Lô 69 – St-Malo 85

Au Marquis de Tombelaine et H. les Hermelles with rm VISA
D 911 – ✆ 02 33 61 85 94 – www.aumarquisdetombelaine.com www.hotel-leshermelles.com – claude.giard@wanadoo.fr – Fax 02 33 61 21 52
6 rm – €55/62 €55/62, €8 – ½ P €64/87
Rest – *(Closed 19 December-1 April, Tuesday dinner and Wednesday)* Menu (€12), €25/68 – Carte €46/80
◆ Fish, seafood and local produce come together in the food served in this restaurant perched on a cliff opposite the Mont St. Michel. Rooms with a view over the famous bay.

CHAMPEIX – 63 Puy-de-Dôme – 326 F9 – pop. 1 231 – alt. 456 m 5 B2
– ✉ 63320 Auvergne

Paris 440 – Clermont-Ferrand 30 – Condat 49 – Issoire 14 – Le Mont-Dore 35 – Thiers 63

Syndicat d'initiative, place du Pré ☎ 04 73 96 26 73, Fax 04 73 96 21 77

Église de St-Saturnin★★ North: 10 km.

La Promenade
3 r. Halle – ☎ 04 73 96 70 24 – h.r.lapromenade@wanadoo.fr – Fax 04 73 96 71 76 – Closed October, Wednesday except dinner in July-August, Tuesday dinner and Thursday dinner
Rest – Menu € 15/29 – Carte € 23/34
◆ Small village inn in a time-worn rustic setting. Local atmosphere in harmony with cuisine featuring Auvergne flavours.

in Montaigut-le-Blanc 3 km west by D 996 – pop. 717 – alt. 500 m – ✉ 63320

Le Chastel Montaigu without rest
au château – ☎ 04 73 96 28 49 – www.lechastelmontaigu.com – virginie.sauvadet@laposte.net – Fax 04 73 96 21 60 – Open 1st May-30 September
4 rm – †€ 133 ††€ 145
◆ The appeal of this high-perched guesthouse lies in its superb rooms (four-poster beds) located in the crenelated keep. All enjoy a view of the Dore and Forz mountains.

CHAMPIGNÉ – 49 Maine-et-Loire – 317 F3 – pop. 1 869 – alt. 25 m 35 C2
– ✉ 49330

Paris 287 – Angers 24 – Château-Gontier 24 – La Flèche 41

Anjou Golf & Country Club Route de Cheffes, S : 3 km on D 190, ☎ 02 41 42 01 01

Northwest 3 km by D 768 and D 190 - ✉ 49330 Champigné

Château des Briottières rest,
rte de Marigné – ☎ 02 41 42 00 02 – www.briottieres.com – briottieres@wanadoo.fr – Fax 02 41 42 01 55 – Closed from Monday to Thursday from 1 to 15 March and from 5 November to 13 February
14 rm – †€ 160/180 ††€ 160/380, € 16
Rest – *(closed from Sunday to Friday in winter) (dinner only) (resident only)* Menu € 50
◆ 18C style refinement can be found in this family castle surrounded by a park. Spacious rooms furnished with antique furniture and objects. Lounges and a library. 18C style and refinement can be found in this family château surrounded by a park. Spacious rooms furnished with antique objects. Lounges and a library.

CHAMPILLON – 51 Marne – 306 F8 – see Épernay

CHAMPSANGLARD – 23 Creuse – pop. 228 – alt. 360 m – ✉ 23220 25 C1

Paris 406 – Limoges 104 – Guéret 16 – La Souterraine 51 – Argenton-sur-Creuse 104

Office de tourisme, le bourg ☎ 05 55 51 21 18, Fax 05.55.51.23.76

La Villa des Cagnes without rest
à 600 m, le Villard Ouest – ☎ 05 55 51 98 95 – www.lavilladescagnes.com – corinne.leroy2@wanadoo.fr
4 rm – †€ 80 ††€ 85
◆ Late 19C hunting and fishing lodge set in a quiet garden with pool. The rooms sport a classic influence and are decorated in pastel shades with antique and period furniture.

CHAMPS-SUR-TARENTAINE – 15 Cantal – 330 D2 – pop. 1 037 – alt. 450 m – ✉ 15270 5 B2

Paris 500 – Aurillac 90 – Clermont-Ferrand 82 – Condat 24 – Mauriac 38 – Ussel 36

Syndicat d'initiative, Mairie ✆ 04 71 78 72 75, Fax 04 71 78 75 09

Gorges de la Rhue★★ Southeast: 9 km, Auvergne-Rhone Valley

Auberge du Vieux Chêne without rest
34 rte des Lacs – ✆ 04 71 78 71 64 – http.//advc.free.fr – danielle.moins@wanadoo.fr – Open 1 May-30 September
15 rm – €60/62 €62/90, ☕ €10
◆ A delightful country stopover in an authentic 19C farmhouse. Simple, warm rooms, suitable for a peaceful stay.

CHAMPS-SUR-YONNE – 89 Yonne – 319 E5 – see Auxerre

CHAMPTOCEAUX – 49 Maine-et-Loire – 317 B4 – pop. 1 748 – alt. 68 m – ✉ 49270 Châteaux of the Loire 34 B2

Paris 357 – Ancenis 9 – Angers 65 – Beaupréau 30 – Cholet 50 – Clisson 35 – Nantes 32

Office de tourisme, Le Champalud ✆ 02 40 83 57 49, Fax 02 40 83 54 73

de l'Île d'Or La VarenneW : 5 km on D 751, ✆ 02 40 98 58 00

Site★ - Promenade de Champalud★★.

Le Champalud rm, VISA AE
1 pl. du Chanoine Bricard – ✆ 02 40 83 50 09 – www.lechampalud.com – le-champalud@wanadoo.fr – Fax 02 40 83 53 81
13 rm – €60/76 €60/76, ☕ €8,50 – ½ P €59/80
Rest – *(closed Sunday dinner from October to March)* Menu (€13), €15 (weekdays)/41 – Carte €29/37
◆ Exposed beams and stone walls blend in well with the modern décor of this establishment, situated opposite the church. Completely renovated, well-equipped rooms. A restaurant with rural character; traditional cuisine based on local produce. Pub bar.

Les Jardins de la Forge (Paul Pauvert) with rm rm, rm, VISA AE
1 pl. des Piliers – ✆ 02 40 83 56 23 – www.jardins-de-la-forge.com – jardins.de.la.forge@wanadoo.fr – Fax 02 40 83 59 80 – Closed 7-15 July, 27 October-12 November and 16 February-4 March
7 rm – €80/95 €110/165, ☕ €15
Rest – *(closed Wed from Oct to Mar, Sun evening, Mon and Tues) (pre-book Sat - Sun)* Menu €30 (weekdays)/95 – Carte €68/108
Spec. Homard et Saint-Jacques poêlées, risotto en coquille (Oct. to April). Duo de sandre et alose de Loire poêlés au beurre d'oseille (March to June). Mi-cuit au chocolat, glace au lait d'amande et banane caramélisée. **Wines** Muscadet Coteaux de la Loire sur lie, Anjou-Villages Brissac.
◆ This restaurant, set inside the walls of the family forge, enjoys a view over the château ruins. Classic cuisine. Fine modern guestrooms. Garden and pool.

CHAMPVANS-LES-MOULINS – 25 Doubs – 321 F3 – see Besançon

CHANAS – 38 Isère – 333 B6 – pop. 2 255 – alt. 150 m – ✉ 38150 43 E2

Paris 512 – Grenoble 89 – Lyon 57 – St-Étienne 75 – Valence 51

Mercure VISA AE
à l'échangeur A 7 – ✆ 04 74 84 27 50 – www.mercure.com – h6148@accor.com – Fax 04 74 84 36 61
42 rm – €70/86 €78/94, ☕ €14
Rest – *(closed Saturday lunch and Sunday)* Menu (€12), €17 (weekday lunch) – Carte €21/40
◆ For a stopover on a holiday journey, a hotel with recently renovated, practical rooms, with good soundproofing. Bright restaurant divided up by partitions and green plants. Traditional cuisine.

CHANCEAUX-SUR-CHOISILLE – 37 Indre-et-Loire – 317 N4 – pop. 3 573 – alt. 104 m – ✉ 37390 11 **B2**

Paris 237 – Orléans 113 – Tours 11 – Joué-lès-Tours 25 – Vendôme 50

XX **Le Relais du Moulin de la Planche**

à Langennerie, 2 km north – ☎ 02 47 55 11 96 – www.moulindelaplanche.com – contact@moulindelaplanche.com – Fax 02 47 55 24 34 – Closed 10-25 January, Sunday dinner, Monday dinner and Tuesday dinner

Rest – Menu € 34/76 bi – Carte € 46/57

◆ This 15C mill with outbuildings housing an art gallery is in a calm, pastoral location (garden, small lake). Rustic restaurant and meticulous modern cuisine.

Red = Pleasant. Look for the red X and 🏠 symbols.

CHANCELADE – 24 Dordogne – 329 E4 – see Périgueux

CHANDAI – 61 Orne – 310 N2 – pop. 532 – alt. 200 m – ✉ 61300 33 **C3**

Paris 129 – L'Aigle 10 – Alençon 72 – Chartres 71 – Dreux 53 – Évreux 57 – Lisieux 66

XX **L'Écuyer Normand**

23 rte de Paris, D 626 – ☎ 02 33 24 08 54 – ecuyer-normand@wanadoo.fr – Fax 02 33 34 75 67 – Closed Wednesday dinner, Sunday dinner and Monday

Rest – Menu (€ 14), € 26/39 – Carte € 50/74

◆ This pretty redbrick house offers an elegant decor, adorned with works by a local artist. Traditional fare with a regional slant.

CHANDOLAS – 07 Ardèche – 331 H7 – pop. 342 – alt. 115 m – ✉ 07230 44 **A3**

Paris 662 – Alès 43 – Aubenas 34 – Privas 66

🏠 **Auberge Les Murets**

rm,

D 104, quartier Langarnayre – ☎ 04 75 39 08 32 – www.aubergelesmurets.com – dominique.rignanese@wanadoo.fr – Fax 04 75 39 39 90 – Closed 23 November-5 December, 4 January-6 February

10 rm – †€ 60 ††€ 60, ☕ € 9 – ½ P € 55

Rest – *(closed Monday and Tuesday from 16 November to 31 March and Monday lunch from April to 15 November)* Menu € 16 (weekdays)/31 – Carte € 24/31

◆ An 18C Cévennes farmhouse surrounded by a park in the countryside and among vineyards. Spruce and pleasant rooms with cane furniture. A restaurant in two vaulted cellars. A mulberry tree over a hundred years old provides shade for the attractive terrace.

CHANTELLE – 03 Allier – 326 F5 – pop. 1 040 – alt. 324 m – ✉ 03140 5 **B1**

Auvergne

Paris 339 – Gannat 17 – Montluçon 61 – Moulins 47 – St-Pourçain-sur-Sioule 15

X **Poste** with rm

5 r. de la République – ☎ 04 70 56 62 12 – Fax 04 70 56 62 12 – Closed 20 September-15 October, 17 February-7 March, Tuesday dinner except July-August and Wednesday

12 rm – †€ 33/40 ††€ 33/46, ☕ € 6

Rest – Menu (€ 10), € 18 (weekdays)/37 – Carte € 30/40

◆ This old inn offers you a family welcome. Simple rustic interior, charming shaded summer terrace and traditional meals. Simple rooms. This old coaching inn has simple but well-maintained rooms, with predominantly rustic, eclectic furnishings.

CHANTEMERLE – 05 Hautes-Alpes – 334 H3 – see Serre-Chevalier

CHANTILLY – 60 Oise – 305 F5 – pop. 11 000 – alt. 59 m – ✉ 60500 36 B3

Northern France and the Paris Region

- Paris 51 – Beauvais 55 – Compiègne 44 – Meaux 53 – Pontoise 41
- Office de tourisme, 60, avenue du Maréchal Joffre ✆ 03 44 67 37 37, Fax 03 44 67 37 38
- 18 Dolce Chantilly Vineuil-Saint-Firmin Route d'Apremont, 3 km on the Apremont road, ✆ 03 44 58 47 74
- 18 d'Apremont Apremont CD 606, N : 7 km on D 606, ✆ 03 44 25 61 11
- 27 Les Golfs de Mont-Griffon Luzarches Route Départementale 909, S : 11 km on N 16, ✆ 01 34 68 10 10
- Château★★★ - Park★★ - Grandes Écuries★★: musée vivant du Cheval★★ - L'Aérophile★ (captive balloon flight): ≤★.
- Site★ du château de la Reine-Blanche South: 5,5 km.

CHANTILLY

Berteux (Av. de) . . . . . . A 2
Canardière (Quai de la) . . . . . . A 3
Cascades (R. des) . . . . . . A 4
Chantilly (R. de) . . . . . . B 5
Condé (Av. de) . . . . . . B 6
Connétable (R. du) . . . . . . AB
Embarcadère (R. de l') . . . . . . A 8
Faisanderie (R. de la) . . . . . . B 9
Gaulle (Av. du Gén.-de) . . . . . . A 10
Joffre (Av. du Mar.) . . . . . . A
Leclerc (Av. du Gén.) . . . . . . A 12
Libération Maurice Schumann (Bd de la) . . . . . . A 18
Orgemont (R. d') . . . . . . A 15
Paris (R. de) . . . . . . A 16
Vallon (Pl. Omer) . . . . . . A 21
Victor-Hugo (R.) . . . . . . A 22

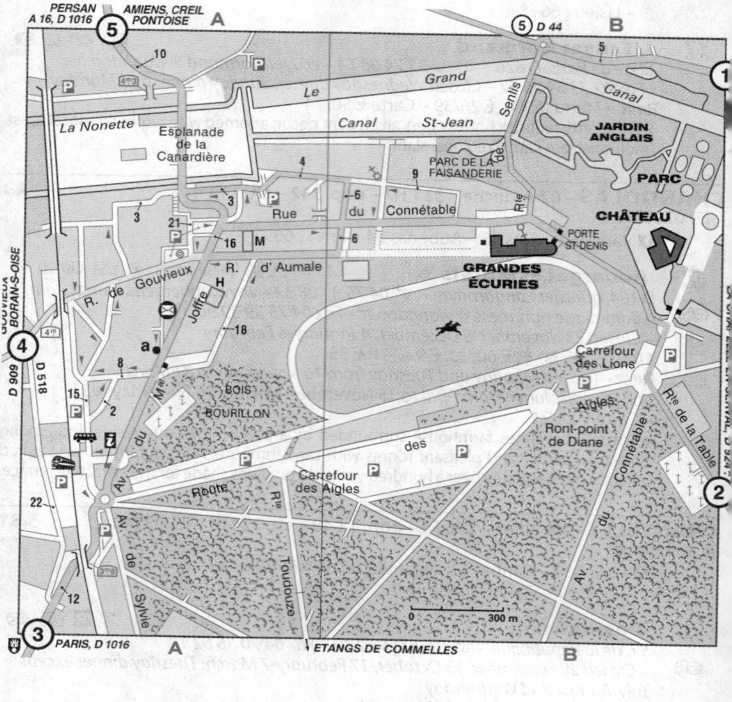

Hotel du Parc without rest
36 av. Mar. Joffre – ✆ 03 44 58 20 00 – www.hotel-parc-chantilly.com – bwhotelduparc@wanadoo.fr – Fax 03 44 57 31 10
57 rm – †€ 100 ††€ 130/150, ☕ € 12 A a

◆ A new hotel with quite spacious, bright and functional rooms, some of which have a terrace. The quietest overlook the garden. English bar.

Apremont road by ① and D 606

Dolce Chantilly
rm,
3 km ✉ 60500 Vineuil-St-Firmin – *03 44 58 47 77*
– www.dolce-chantilly-hotel.com – info_chantilly@dolce.com
– Fax 03 44 58 50 11 – Closed 23 December-1st January
194 rm – € 150/300 € 150/300, € 20 – 6 suites
Rest *Carmontelle* – *03 44 58 47 57 (Closed 2-31 August, Saturday lunch, Sunday, Monday and bank holidays) (number of covers limited, pre-book)*
Menu € 47 bi, € 68 € bi/120 bi – Carte € 104/118
Rest *L'Étoile* – *(dinner only except Sunday)* Menu € 42 bi/55 bi – Carte € 43/63
Spec. Saint-Jacques rôties au beurre de roquette. Homard au beurre d'estragon et carotte jaune au caviar d'Aquitaine. Chocolat en trois textures et trois saveurs.
◆ Large Île de France style hotel on a golf course, offering spacious, practical rooms. Good fitness centre and high quality conference facilities. Inventive gourmet food served in a plush modern setting; attentive staff. At L'Étoile, traditional menu in an attractive circular room.

Auberge La Grange aux Loups with rm
8 rue du 11 novembre, in Apremont, 6 km ✉ 60300 – 03 44 25 33 79
– www.lagrangeauxloups.com – lagrangeauxloups@wanadoo.fr
– Fax 03 44 24 22 22 – Closed 15 September-5 October and Sunday
4 rm – € 85 € 85, € 12
Rest – *(closed Monday)* Menu € 29 (weekdays)/62 bi – Carte € 70/90
◆ Village inn with a rustic dining room and peaceful summer terrace. Classic cuisine. Four quiet rooms in an outbuilding. Well-kept rooms that are calm and spacious, located in an outhouse.

in Montgrésin 5 km by ② – ✉ **60560 Orry-la-Ville**

Relais d'Aumale
rm,
– 03 44 54 61 31 – www.relais-aumale.fr – relaisd.aumale@wanadoo.fr
– Fax 03 44 54 69 15 – Closed 22 December-4 January
22 rm – € 122/152 € 140/182, € 13 – 2 suites
Rest – *(closed Sunday dinner in Winter)* Menu (€ 28), € 44/46 – Carte € 60/80
◆ The Duke of Aumale's former hunting lodge nestles in a garden at the edge of the forest. Comfortable, tastefully appointed rooms. Two dining rooms: one modern, the other more château-like, with panelling, a French style ceiling and paintings. Traditional fare.

in Gouvieux 4 km by ④ – **pop. 9 498 – alt. 26 m** – ✉ **60270**

Château de Montvillargenne
rm,
6 av. F. Mathet – 03 44 62 37 37
– www.montvillargenne.com – info@chmvt.com – Fax 03 44 57 28 97
120 rm – € 185/350 € 185/350, € 18
Rest – Menu € 43/85 – Carte € 48/130
◆ This 19C château, nestling in a large park, offers four categories of comfortable rooms with pleasant personal touches. Large dining room, complemented by a mezzanine and several small wainscoted sitting rooms. Pleasant terrace.

Château de la Tour
rm,
chemin de la Chaussée – 03 44 62 38 38
– www.lechateaudelatour.fr – reception@lechateaudelatour.fr
– Fax 03 44 57 31 97
41 rm – € 150/230 € 150/230 – ½ P € 100/120
Rest – Menu € 39 (weekday lunch), € 45/95 bi – Carte € 52/66
◆ Fine early-20C residence and contemporary extension overlooking a pretty 5 ha park. Elegant, refined interior. Old parquet flooring and fireplaces provide a setting for the restaurant; superb terrace. Classic menu.

Le Pavillon St-Hubert
à Toutevoie – 03 44 57 07 04 – www.pavillon-saint-hubert.com
– pavillon.sthubert@wanadoo.fr – Fax 03 44 57 75 42 – Closed 2-20 January
18 rm – € 60/85 € 60/85, € 9 – ½ P € 75/80
Rest – *(closed 2 January-8 February, Sunday dinner and Monday)*
Menu € 25 (weekdays)/45 – Carte € 35/50
◆ Characterful house and its pretty garden on the banks of the River Oise. Small, comfortable rooms. This restaurant furnished in Louis XIII style serves traditional cuisine. In summer it offers a pleasant terrace shaded by lime trees, overlooking the canal.

La Renardière
2 r. Frères Segard, (La Chaussée) – ☎ 03 44 57 08 23 – www.restaurantlarenardiere.fr – larenardiere@voila.fr – Fax 03 44 57 30 37 – Closed 20-27 April, 3-17 August, Sunday dinner and Monday
Rest – Menu € 16 (weekday lunch), € 28/48 – Carte € 52/91
◆ An attractive inn sporting a pleasant rustic decor. Traditional cooking and an impressive wine list selected by the wine-expert owner.

Ô Relais de la Côte
9 r. de Chantilly – ☎ 03.44.57.01.19 – www.relaisdelacote.fr – lerelaisdelacote@hotmail.fr – Closed 26 July-9 August, Sunday dinner, Monday dinner and Tuesday
Rest – *(number of covers limited, pre-book)* Menu (€ 14), € 28/48 bi – Carte € 35/60
◆ On the way out of town, this entirely redesigned hotel sports a modern style (white walls modern art and furnishings). Lovely tree-lined terrace and modern menu.

Creil road **4 km by ⑤ – ✉ 60740 St-Maximin**

Le Verbois
6 r. L. Dubois, (D 1016) – ☎ 03 44 24 06 22 – www.leverbois.com – Fax 03 44 25 76 63 – Closed 15-31 August, 3-14 January, Sunday dinner and Monday
Rest – Menu € 35/65 – Carte € 49/68
◆ Former coaching inn fronted by a pretty garden, on the edge of the forest. Plush dining rooms. Updated cuisine with a classic base; game in season.

CHANTONNAY – 85 Vendée – 316 J7 – pop. 7 794 – alt. 58 m – ✉ 85110 — 34 B3

Paris 410 – Nantes 79 – La Roche-sur-Yon 34 – Cholet 53 – Bressuire 53
Office de tourisme, place de la Liberté ☎ 02 51 09 45 77, Fax 02 51 09 45 78

Manoir de Ponsay
5 km east along the Pouzauges road and secondary road – ☎ 02 51 46 96 71 – www.manoirdeponsay.com – manoir.de.ponsay@orange.fr – Fax 02 51 46 80 07
5 rm – €62/115 €62/115, € 9 – ½ P € 66/93
Table d'hôte – Menu € 32 bi/40 bi
◆ The perfect place in which to experience château life, this manor house has been in the same family since 1644. Spacious guestrooms decorated with objects collected over the centuries. Park and swimming pool. Attractive dining room, and evening meals on request.

CHAOURCE – 10 Aube – 313 E5 – pop. 1 100 – alt. 150 m – ✉ 10210 — 13 B3

Northern France and the Paris Region

Paris 196 – Auxerre 66 – Bar-sur-Aube 58 – Châtillon-sur-Seine 52 – Troyes 33
Office de tourisme, 2, Place de l'Échiquier ☎ 03 25 40 97 22, Fax 03 25 40 97 22
St-Jean-Baptiste church ★: sepulchre★★.

in Maisons-lès-Chaource **6 km southeast by D 34 – pop. 174 – alt. 235 m – ✉ 10210**

Aux Maisons 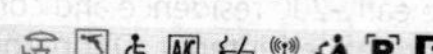
11 r. des AFN – ☎ 03 25 70 07 19 – www.logis-aux-maisons.com – accueil@logis-aux-maisons.com – Fax 03 25 70 07 75
23 rm – €68 €72, € 10 – ½ P € 72
Rest – *(closed Sunday dinner from 15 October to 15 March)* Menu (€ 16), € 31/74 bi – Carte € 42/63
◆ A restored Champagne farmhouse makes up part of this hotel for non-smokers only. Spa showers in the best rooms. Good sound-proofing. Countrified dining room; summer terrace by the swimming pool.

CHAPARON – 74 Haute-Savoie – 328 K6 – see Bredannaz

LA CHAPELLE-AUX-CHASSES – 03 Allier – 326 I2 – pop. 227 – alt. 225 m – ✉ 03230 6 C1

▶ Paris 294 – Moulins 21 – Bourbon-Lancy 22 – Decize 25 – Digoin 50

XX **Auberge de la Chapelle aux Chasses**
– *☎ 04 70 43 44 71 – aubergechapelle@aol.com – Closed 20-31 July, 26 October-6 November, 16-28 February, Tuesday and Wednesday*
Rest – *(pre-book)* Menu (€ 16), € 22/68 – Carte € 41/64
◆ Appetising seasonal up-to-date cuisine served in a sober half-rustic, half-modern setting. Carefully-laid tables and friendly hospitality.

Hotels and restaurants change every year, so change your Michelin guide every year!

LA CHAPELLE-D'ABONDANCE – 74 Haute-Savoie – 328 N3 – pop. 781 – alt. 1 020 m – Winter sports : 1 000/1 850 m 1 11 – ✉ 74360 46 F1

French Alps

▶ Paris 600 – Annecy 108 – Châtel 6 – Évian-les-Bains 29 – Morzine 32 – Thonon-les-Bains 34

ℹ Syndicat d'initiative, Chef-lieu ☎ 04 50 73 51 41, Fax 04 50 73 56 04

Les Cornettes rest, VISA
– *☎ 04 50 73 50 24 – www.lescornettes.com – lescornettes@valdabondance.com – Fax 04 50 73 54 16 – Closed from mid-April to early May and from mid-October to mid-December*
42 rm – €70/100 €125/150, ☕ €12
Rest – Menu € 23 (weekdays)/60 – Carte € 23/90
◆ Run by the same family since 1894, these buildings, linked by an underground passage, have comfortable panelled rooms. Leisure facilities and a small Savoy museum. Immense mountain-style dining room decorated with bric-a-brac. Local cuisine.

Les Gentianettes rm, rest, VISA
rte de Chevenne – ☎ 04 50 73 56 46 – www.gentianettes.fr – bienvenue@gentianettes.fr – Fax 04 50 73 56 39 – Open 20 May-13 September and 19 December to Easter
36 rm – €95/150 €95/150, ☕ €12 – ½ P €72/119
Rest – Menu € 19/58 – Carte € 34/62
◆ Chalet with pleasant balcony rooms, warmly decorated. Sauna, hammam, jacuzzi. Tasty regional cuisine and a cosy atmosphere in the restaurant with wood panelling, coppers, farming objects and thoughtful décor.

L'Ensoleillé VISA
– *☎ 04 50 73 50 42 – www.hotel-ensoleille.com – info@hotel-ensoleille.com – Fax 04 50 73 52 96 – Open from June to mid September and from mid December to end March*
35 rm – €60/80 €70/120, ☕ €10 – ½ P €60/95
Rest – *(closed Tuesday in low season)* Menu (€ 15), € 20 (weekdays)/55 – Carte € 28/60
◆ These two neighbouring chalets provide rooms with balconies and a fully-equipped fitness centre. Hearty Savoyard cuisine served in a dining area with wooden decor, paintings of the village and furniture and decorative objects from the region.

Le Vieux Moulin rm, VISA
rte de Chevenne – ☎ 04 50 73 52 52 – www.hotel-vieuxmoulin.com – maxit-levieuxmoulin@wanadoo.fr – Fax 04 50 73 55 62 – Open 1st June-30 September, 20 December-15 April and closed Wednesday
15 rm – €45/50 €50/70, ☕ €9 – ½ P €57/60
Rest – Menu € 22 (weekdays)/45 – Carte € 26/45
◆ Hotel surrounded by a garden outside the town centre. Functional rooms with wooden panelling and sloping ceiling on the top floor. Regionally and traditionally influenced menu and beautiful vista over the valley from this restaurant.

LA CHAPELLE-DE-GUINCHAY – 71 Saône-et-Loire – 320 I12 – pop. 3 336 – alt. 200 m – ✉ 71570 8 C3

Paris 412 – Bourg-en-Bresse 50 – Caluire-et-Cuire 64 – Dijon 142

La Poularde (Olivier Muguet)
pl. de la Gare – ☎ 03 85 36 72 41 – http://lapoularde.free.fr – Fax 03 85 33 83 25 – Closed 27 July-13 August, 15 February-1st March, Sunday dinner, Tuesday dinner and Wednesday
Rest – Menu € 20 (weekday lunch), € 30/45 – Carte € 49/57
Spec. Pressé de crabe à la coriandre fraîche. Filet de canette aux noisettes. Soufflé glacé à la vanille, caramel frais salé.
◆ Skilful cooking, flavourful and executed with precision and a friendly welcome: reasons to visit this attractive house with a modern decor, located next to the station.

LA CHAPELLE-EN-VERCORS – 26 Drôme – 332 F4 – pop. 656 – alt. 945 m – Winter sports : to Col de Rousset 1 255/1 700 m 8 – ✉ 26420 43 E2

French Alps

Paris 604 – Die 41 – Grenoble 60 – Romans-sur-Isère 47 – St-Marcellin 35 – Valence 63

Office de tourisme, place Piétri ☎ 04 75 48 22 54, Fax 04 75 48 13 81

Chapelle-en-VercorsS : 2 km, ☎ 04 75 48 19 86

Grotte de la Draye blanche★, 5 km South by D 178.

Bellier
– ☎ 04 75 48 20 03 – www.hotel-bellier.com – hotel-bellier@orange.fr – Fax 04 75 48 25 31 – Open from April to mid-October and closed Wednesday evening and Thursday in low season
13 rm – €29/32 €55/65, € 7 – ½ P € 45/60
Rest – Menu € 17/32 – Carte € 18/30
◆ For five generations, the same family has been running this chalet built on an outcrop overlooking the road. Half the rooms have a balcony. Rustic styled dining room with Savoyard furniture. Tree lined terrace.

Des Sports rm,
av. des Grands Goulets – ☎ 04 75 48 20 39 – www.hotel-des-sports.com – hotel.des.sports@wanadoo.fr – Fax 04 75 48 10 52 – Closed 12 November-26 December, 4 January-1st February, Sunday dinner Monday
11 rm – €56/60 €56/60, € 8,50 **Rest** – Menu (€ 14), € 20/32
◆ In a shopping street on the way into the village, a real pied-à-terre for cyclists and hikers visiting the Vercours area. Colourful, very well-renovated rooms. The rustic decor of the restaurant has been treated to a facelift. Traditional and regional dishes.

LA CHAPELLE-ST-MESMIN – 45 Loiret – 318 H4 – see Orléans

CHARBONNIÈRES-LES-BAINS – 69 Rhône – 327 H5 – see Lyon

CHARENTON-LE-PONT – 94 Val-de-Marne – 312 D3 – 101 26 – see Paris, Area

CHARETTE – 38 Isère – 333 F3 – pop. 343 – alt. 250 m – ✉ 38390 44 B1

Paris 479 – Aix-les-Bains 68 – Belley 39 – Grenoble 100 – Lyon 63

Auberge du Vernay
rte Optevoz, (D 52) – ☎ 04 74 88 57 57 – www.auberge-du-vernay.fr – reservation@auberge-du-vernay.fr – Fax 04 74 88 58 57 – Closed 29 June-7 July, 1st-7 September, 3-20 January, Saturday lunch, Sunday dinner and Monday
7 rm – €55 €80, € 10 – ½ P € 85
Rest – *(number of covers limited, pre-book)* Menu € 28/91 – Carte € 39/80
◆ Charming rooms with a personal touch and the quiet of the surrounding countryside are the strengths of this nicely refurbished, attractive 18C farm. The half-rustic, half-contemporary restaurant sports a fine fireplace and serves modern, flavoursome food.

LA CHARITÉ-SUR-LOIRE – 58 Nièvre – 319 B8 – pop. 5 405 – alt. 170 m – ✉ 58400 Burgundy-Jura

7 **A2**

Paris 212 – Auxerre 109 – Bourges 51 – Montargis 102 – Nevers 25

Syndicat d'initiative, 5, place Sainte-Croix ✆ 03 86 70 15 06, Fax 03 86 70 21 55

N.-Dame church ★★: ≤★★ on the apse - Esplanade rue du Clos ≤★.

Auberge de Seyr

4 Grande Rue – ✆ 03 86 70 03 51 – Fax 03 86 70 03 51 – Closed 23-30 March, 17 August-4 September, Sunday dinner and Monday

Rest – Menu € 12 (weekdays)/34 – Carte € 30/40

◆ Take time for a relaxing meal in this unpretentions restaurant made up of two dining rooms with painted beams. Traditional cuisine prepared by the chef.

CHARLEVILLE-MÉZIÈRES Ⓟ – 08 Ardennes – 306 K4 – pop. 51 300 – Built-up area 107 777 – alt. 145 m – ✉ 08000 Northern France and the Paris Region

13 **B1**

Paris 230 – Luxembourg 168 – Reims 85 – Sedan 26

Office de tourisme, 4, place Ducale ✆ 03 24 55 69 90, Fax 03 24 55 69 89

des Sept-Fontaines Fagnon Abbaye de Sept Fontaines, SW : 10 km on D 139, ✆ 03 24 37 38 24

des Ardennes Villers-le-Tilleul Base de Loisirs des Poursaudes, S : 21 km on D 764 and D 33, ✆ 03 24 35 64 65

Place Ducale★★ - Musée de l'Ardenne★ BX **M¹** - Musée Rimbaud BX **M²** - N.-D.-d'Espérance basilica : stained-glass windows ★★ BZ.

Plan on following page

Le Pélican without rest

42 av. du Maréchal Leclerc – ✆ 03 24 56 42 73 – www.hotel-pelican-charleville.com – hotelpelican@wanadoo.fr – Fax 03 24 59 26 16 – Closed 27 December-2 January BY **d**

20 rm – †€ 43/53 ††€ 45/56, ☕ € 8

◆ Set between the station and pedestrianised areas, this hotel offers well-equipped, personalised rooms with a warm decor. Well sound-proofed. Attractive breakfast room.

De Paris without rest

24 av. G. Corneau – ✆ 03 24 33 34 38 – www.hoteldeparis08.fr – hotel.de.paris.08@wanadoo.fr – Fax 03 24 59 11 21 BY **n**

29 rm – †€ 50 ††€ 59, ☕ € 7

◆ Friendly welcome guaranteed in this hotel dating from the early 20C. Three buildings, of which two overlook the courtyard, accommodate respectable rooms.

La Clef des Champs

33 r. du Moulin – ✆ 03 24 56 17 50 – www.laclefdeschamps.fr – courrier@laclefdeschamps.fr – Fax 03 24 59 94 07 – Closed Sunday dinner BX **e**

Rest – Menu (€ 19), € 23/70 – Carte € 52/69

◆ Two pretty dining rooms (one with a brick and wood fireplace) and a summer courtyard terrace in a 17C residence. Updated cuisine with some Asian touches.

La Côte à l'Os

11 cours A. Briand – ✆ 03 24 59 20 16 – www.restaurant-charleville-lacotealos.fr – la.cote.a.l.os@orange.fr – Fax 03 24 22 04 99 BY **e**

Rest – Menu (€ 13), € 20/28 – Carte € 25/40

◆ Meat (game can be enjoyed in season) and impressive seafood platters served in a lively area or the cosier setting of the first floor. Neo-classical, brasserie-style decor.

Le Diapason

25 quai Arthur-Rimbaud – ✆ 03 24 59 94 11 – restaurantlediapason@hotmail.fr – Closed 2-8 March, 20 July-21 August, Saturday lunch, Sunday dinner and Monday BX **f**

Rest – Menu (€ 30), € 35/110 – Carte € 62/70

◆ Country house next to the Arthur Rimbaud museum. Sample creative cooking that favours regional produce in the refined ambiance and rustic decor of the dining room.

CHARLEVILLE-MÉZIÈRES

Arches (Av. d') . . . . **BYZ**
Arquebuse (R. de l') . . . . **BX** 2
Bérégovoy (R. P.) . . . . **BX** 3
Bourbon (R.) . . . . **BX** 4
Carré (R. Irénée) . . . . **BX** 5
Corneau (Av. G.) . . . . **BY** 6
Droits-de-l'Homme (Pl. des) **BX** 7
Fg de Pierre (R. du) . . . . **BZ** 8
Flandre (R. de) . . . . **BX** 9
Hôtel de Ville (Pl. de l') . . . . **BZ** 10
Jean-Jaurès (Av.) . . . . **BY**
Leclerc (Av. Mar.) . . . . **BY** 19
Manchester (Av. de) . . . . **AY** 20
Mantoue (R. de) . . . . **BX** 21
Mitterrand (Av. F.) . . . . **AX** 22
Monge (R.) . . . . **BZ** 23
Montjoly (R. de) . . . . **AX** 24
Moulin (R. du) . . . . **BX** 25
Nevers (Pl. de) . . . . **BX** 27
Petit-Bois (Av. du) . . . . **BX** 28
République (R. de la) . . . . . . **BX** 30
Résistance (Pl. de la) . . . . . . **BZ** 31
St-Julien (Av. de) . . . . **AY** 32
Sévigné (R. Mme de) . . . . . . **BY** 33
Théâtre (R. du) . . . . **BX** 34
91e-Régt-d'Infanterie (Av. du) . . . . **BZ** 36

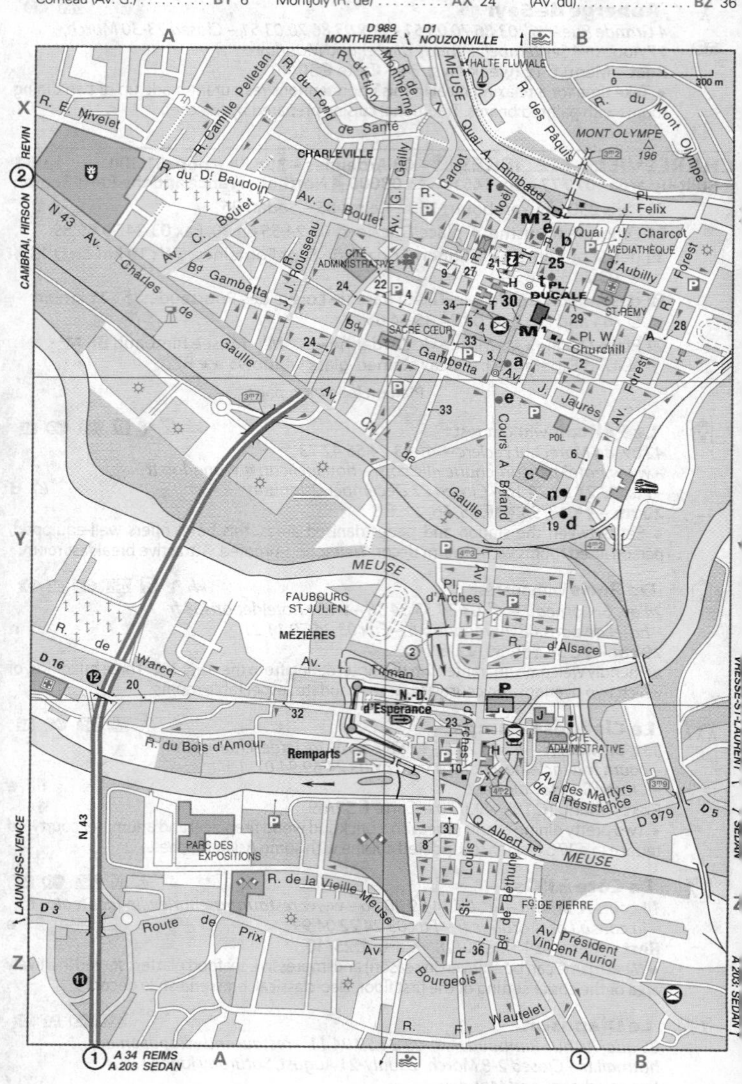

La Papillote
7 bis r. d'Aubilly – 03 24 37 41 34 – Closed August, Saturday lunch, Sunday dinner and Monday BX **b**
Rest – Menu € 28 (weekdays)/45
◆ House dating from the 17C with a warm interior: panelling, exposed beams, fireplace and attractively set tables. Set menu of traditional offerings.

La Table d' Arthur "R"
9 r. Bérégovoy – 03 24 57 05 64 – Fax 03 24 27 65 60 – Closed 20 April-3 May, 9-31 August, Monday dinner, Wednesday dinner, Sunday and bank holidays BX **a**
Rest – Menu (€ 20), € 26/39
◆ At the end of an alley, a world dedicated to wine and good food. After discovering the numerous bottles, you descend into the cellar... to enjoy honest and sincere cuisine.

Amorini
46 pl. Ducale – 03 24 37 48 80 – Closed 1-25 August, Sunday and Monday BX **t**
Rest – *(lunch only)* Carte € 25/32
◆ Sample the 'dolce vita' in the typically Italian setting of this trattoria with cherub frescoes. Italian dishes and wine served in the dining room.

in Montcy-Notre-Dame 4 km north on the D 1 BX – pop. 1 482 – alt. 144 m – ✉ 08090

L'Auberge du Laminak
rte de Nouzonville – 03 24 33 37 55 – www.auberge-ardennes.com – vaqueflo@hotmail.com – Fax 03 24 52 76 58 – Closed 15-30 August, Sunday dinner, Wednesday dinner and Monday
Rest – Menu € 25 (weekday lunch)/38 – Carte € 38/44
◆ The Basque country is very much to the fore at this charming inn on the edge of the forest: warm colours on the walls and tasty, perfectly mastered cooking on the plates.

in Fagnon 8 km by D 3 AZ and D 39 – pop. 345 – alt. 171 m – ✉ 08090

Abbaye de Sept Fontaines rest,
– 03 24 37 38 24 – www.abbayeseptfontaines.fr – abbaye-7-fontaines@wanadoo.fr – Fax 03 24 37 58 75
23 rm – € 89/195 € 98/199, € 14 – ½ P € 92/109
Rest – Menu (€ 19), € 27 (weekday lunch), € 36/68 – Carte € 52/65
◆ A former 17C abbey and estate, now transformed into a hotel. The first floor rooms are more spacious and have lovely views. Eighteen-hole golf course. Magnificent Louis XVI dining room serving classic cuisine. Summer terrace.

CHARLIEU – 42 Loire – 327 E3 – pop. 3 727 – alt. 265 m – ✉ 42190 44 A1

Burgundy-Jura

Paris 398 – Mâcon 77 – Roanne 18 – St-Étienne 102

Office de tourisme, place Saint-Philibert, 04 77 60 12 42, Fax 04 77 60 16 91

Former Benedictine abbey★: façade★★ - Couvent des Cordeliers★.

Plan on following page

Relais de l'Abbaye rest,
415 rte du Beaujolais – 04 77 60 00 88 – www.relais-abbaye.com – relais.de.abbaye@wanadoo.fr – Fax 04 77 60 14 60 – Closed 20 December-10 January **a**
27 rm – € 68/82 € 68/86, € 9 – ½ P € 54
Rest – Menu (€ 14), € 20/49 – Carte € 40/65
◆ A renovated establishment, offering functional, colourful and well-kept rooms. Huge lawn with a children's play area. Neo-rustic dining room and peaceful terrace. Traditional dishes with a local emphasis.

CHARLIEU

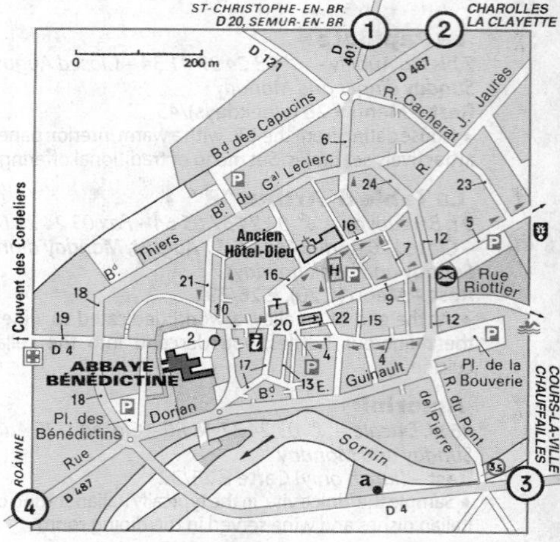

Pouilly road 2.5 km by ④ and secondary road

XX **Le Moulin de Rongefer**
300 chemin de Rongefer ✉ 42190 St-Nizier-sous-Charlieu – ✆ 04 77 60 01 57 – lemoulinderongefer@club-internet.fr – Fax 04 77 60 33 28 – Closed 16 August-10 September, 15 January-5 February, Sunday dinner, Tuesday dinner and Wednesday
Rest – Menu (€ 15), € 25/51 – Carte € 39/59
◆ An old mill on the banks of the Sornin with a country-style dining room and pleasant flower-decked terrace. Modern cuisine accompanied by an excellent wine list focusing on Burgundy.

in St-Pierre-la-Noaille 5.5 km Northwest by secondary road – pop. 357 – alt. 287 m – ✉ 42190

Domaine du Château de Marchangy without rest
– *✆ 04 77 69 96 76 – www.marchangy.com – contact@marchangy.com – Fax 04 77 60 70 37*
3 rm – €80/100 €90/110
◆ A splendid, 18th century chateau stands next door to an attractive wine grower's residence where tastefully decorated rooms offfer views of the Forez mountains and surrounding countryside.

CHARMES – 88 Vosges – **314** F2 – pop. 4 561 – alt. 282 m – ✉ 88130 27 **C3**
Alsace-Lorraine

Paris 381 – Épinal 31 – Lunéville 40 – Nancy 43 – St-Dié 59 – Toul 62 – Vittel 40

Office de tourisme, 2, place Henri Breton ✆ 03 29 38 17 09, Fax 03 29 38 17 09

XX **Dancourt** with rm
6 pl. Henri Breton – ✆ 03 29 38 80 80 – www.hotel-dancourt.com – contact@hotel-dancourt.com – Fax 03 29 38 09 15 – Closed 18 December-18 January, Sunday dinner October-May, Saturday lunch and Friday
16 rm – €42/52 €47/59, € 8,50 – ½ P € 46/53
Rest – Menu (€ 16), € 19 (weekdays)/41 – Carte € 31/63
◆ Hotel near the house where M Barrès was born. Antiquated charm, combining Greek columns and busts, sober modern furniture and plants. Simple, practical rooms.

in Chamagne 4 km North by D 9 – pop. 462 – alt. 265 m – ✉ 88130

Le Chamagnon

236 r. du Patis – ☎ 03 29 38 14 74 – charles.vincent038@orange.fr – Fax 03 29 38 14 74 – Closed 1-24 July, 27 October-5 November, Sunday dinner, Tuesday dinner, Wednesday dinner and Monday

Rest – Menu (€ 11 bi), € 19/53 – Carte € 33/55

◆ Birthplace of artist Claude Gellée (known as Le Lorrain). Hospitable restaurant with a decorative cellar. Menu influenced by flavours from Corsica, Provence and Asia.

in Vincey 4 km Southeast by N 57 – pop. 2 250 – alt. 297 m – ✉ 88450

Relais de Vincey

33 r. de Lorraine – ☎ 03 29 67 40 11 – www.relaisdevincey.fr – relais.de.vincey@wanadoo.fr – Fax 03 29 67 36 66 – Closed 15-31 August and 24 December-4 January

34 rm – †€ 60/72 ††€ 78/87, ☕ € 10 – ½ P € 63/75

Rest – *(closed Saturday lunchtime and Sunday evening)* Menu (€ 22), € 25/35 – Carte € 32/72

◆ The functional rooms of this hotel are in the annexe and overlook the garden. Tennis courts, fitness centre and indoor pool. The main building houses a restaurant with pleasant modern decor where a traditional menu is served. Quick meals served in the bar.

CHARNY-SUR-MEUSE – 55 Meuse – 307 D3 – see Verdun

CHAROLLES – 71 Saône-et-Loire – 320 F11 – pop. 2 864 – alt. 279 m – ✉ 71120 Burgundy-Jura 8 C3

Paris 374 – Autun 80 – Chalon-sur-Saône 67 – Mâcon 55 – Moulins 81 – Roanne 61

Office de tourisme, 24, rue Baudinot ☎ 03 85 24 05 95, Fax 03 85 24 28 12

Le Téméraire without rest

3 av. J. Furtin – ☎ 03 85 24 06 66 – guinet.suzane.@wanadoo.fr – Fax 03 85 24 05 54 – Closed 29 June-12 July

10 rm – †€ 44/52 ††€ 49/59, ☕ € 7

◆ This hotel, named after Charles le Téméraire, is home to well-soundproofed rooms. Small lobby embellished with Charolles faience.

Le Clos de l'Argolay without rest

21 quai de la Poterne – ☎ 03 85 24 10 23 – www.closdelargolay.fr – closdelargolay@orange.fr

3 rm ☕ – †€ 95/105 ††€ 105/115 – 2 suites

◆ This 18C house in the little Venice of Charolais is surrounded by a well-tended enclosed garden. Beautiful suites (period furniture) and modern duplex in the annexe. Quality homemade produce.

De la Poste with rm

av. Libération, (near the church) – ☎ 03 85 24 11 32 – www.la-poste-hotel.com – hotel-de-la-liberation-doucet@wanadoo.fr – Fax 03 85 24 05 74 – Closed 23-30 June, 17-30 November, 23 February-9 March, Sunday dinner, Thursday dinner and Monday in low season

14 rm – †€ 70/130 ††€ 70/130, ☕ € 11

Rest – Menu € 25 (weekdays)/70 – Carte € 54/78

◆ Sample modern cuisine in the refined decor of this regional style house or amid the greenery of the terrace. Comfortable rooms, some located in the recently opened annex.

Southwest 11 km by D 985 and D 270 – ✉ 71120 Changy

Le Chidhouarn

– ☎ 03 85 88 32 07 – Fax 03 85 88 01 23 – Closed 31 August-10 September, 11 January-4 February, Sunday dinner from November to April, Monday and Tuesday

Rest – Menu (€ 14), € 22/51 bi – Carte € 27/45

◆ A collection of sea shells enlivens this rustic building tucked away in the Charolais countryside. Fireplace to warm the lounge. Specialties based around Breton produce.

CHAROST – 18 Cher – 323 I5 – pop. 1 023 – alt. 137 m – ✉ 18290 12 C3
Dordogne-Berry-Limousin

Paris 239 – Châteauroux 39 – Bourges 26 – Dun-sur-Auron 42 – Issoudun 11 – Vierzon 31

in Brouillamnon 3 km northeast by N 151 and D 16E – ✉ 18290 Plou

L'Orée du Bois

– ✆ 02 48 26 21 40 – www.loree-du-bois.fr – loreeduboisplou@orange.fr – Fax 02 48 26 27 81 – Closed 29 July-13 August, 12 January-13 February, Sunday dinner and Monday

Rest – Menu € 15 (weekdays)/36 – Carte € 31/44

◆ This country inn and pleasant garden are in a quiet hamlet. Local dishes served in a bright dining room or on the terrace in summer.

CHARQUEMONT – 25 Doubs – 321 K3 – pop. 2 209 – alt. 864 m – ✉ 25140 17 C2

Paris 478 – Basel 98 – Belfort 66 – Besançon 75 – Montbéliard 49 – Pontarlier 59

Au Bois de la Biche with rm

4.5 km southeast by D 10E and secondary road – ✆ 03 81 44 01 82 – www.boisdelabiche.com – thierry.marcelpoix@wanadoo.fr – Fax 03 81 68 65 09 – Closed 2 January-3 February and Monday

3 rm – €47 €47, € 7 – ½ P € 51 **Rest** – Menu € 19/41 – Carte € 20/70

◆ This former farmhouse, surrounded by woods, is a meeting point for hikers and overlooks the Doubs gorges. Family restaurant with views; regional cuisine. Simple bedrooms.

CHARRECEY – 71 Saône-et-Loire – 320 H8 – pop. 313 – alt. 350 m – ✉ 71510 8 C3

Paris 341 – Autun 36 – Beaune 29 – Chalon-sur-Saône 18 – Mâcon 77

Le Petit Blanc

Le Pont Pïlley, 2 km east by D 978, Chalon-sur-Saône road – ✆ 03 85 45 15 43 – lepetitblanc@orange.fr – Fax 03 85 45 19 80 – Closed 19-26 April, 16-30 August, 24 December-10 January, Sunday dinner and Thursday dinner from 7 October to 22 June, Sunday from 23 June to 6 October and Monday

Rest – Menu € 16 (weekday lunch), € 23/33 – Carte € 33/39

◆ This roadside inn may not appear alluring, but its local renown is deserved: a pleasant country bistro interior and very generous traditional cuisine.

CHARROUX – 03 Allier – 326 F5 – pop. 357 – alt. 420 m – ✉ 03140 5 B1
Auvergne

Paris 344 – Clermont-Ferrand 61 – Montluçon 68 – Moulins 52 – Vichy 30

Office de tourisme, rue de l'Horloge ✆ 04 70 56 87 71

La Maison du Prince de Condé without rest

8 pl. d'Armes – ✆ 04 70 56 81 36 – www.maison-conde.com – jspeer@club-internet.fr

5 rm – €60 €66/91

◆ This guesthouse offers personalised rooms. The duplex, called Porte d'Orient, is situated in the tower. Breakfast is served in a pretty, vaulted, 13C room.

Ferme Saint-Sébastien

chemin de Bourion – ✆ 04 70 56 88 83 – www.fermesaintsebastien.fr – contact@fermesaintsebastien.fr – Fax 04 70 56 86 66 – Closed 29 June-8 July, 28 September-6 October, 20 December-2 February, Tuesday except July-August and Monday

Rest – *(pre-book)* Menu € 26/54 – Carte € 41/73

◆ This authentic Bourbon farmhouse has been renovated and houses an attractive dining room with painted rafters and herbariums. Regionally inspired contemporary cuisine.

in Valignat 8 km West On D 183 – **pop. 69 – alt. 420 m –** ✉ **03330**

Château de l'Ormet without rest
L'Ormet – ✆ 04 70 58 57 23 – www.chateaudelormet.com – lormet@wanadoo.fr – Fax 04 70 58 57 19 – Open April-mid November
4 rm – €64/79 €72/95
◆ Rustic, "gothic" or romantic: the rooms of this 18C Bourbonnais manor each have their own character. All overlook the park where a miniature train is set up – it's the owner's hobby.

CHARTRES – 28 Eure-et-Loir – 311 E5 – pop. 40 000 – Built-up area 130 681 – alt. 142 m – Great Student Pilgrimage (end April-early May) – ✉ 28000 Northern France and the Paris Region

11 **B1**

Paris 89 – Évreux 78 – Le Mans 120 – Orléans 80 – Tours 138
Office de tourisme, place de la Cathédrale ✆ 02 37 18 26 26, Fax 02 37 21 51 91
du Bois d'Ô Saint-Maixme-Hauterive Ferme de Gland, 26 km on the Verneuil-sur-Avre road, ✆ 02 37 51 04 61
Notre-Dame cathedral ★★★: Royal portal ★★★, stained-glass windows★★★ - Old Chartres★: St-Pierre church ★, ≤★ on St-André church, banks of the Eure - Musée des Beaux-Arts: enamels★ Y **M²** - COMPA★ (Conservatoire du Machinisme agricole et des Pratiques Agricoles(Conservatory of farming mechanisation and practices) 2 km by D24.

Plan on following page

Le Grand Monarque rest, VISA AE
22 pl. des Épars – ✆ 02 37 18 15 15 – www.bw-grand-monarque.com – info@bw-grand-monarque.com – Fax 02 37 36 34 18 Z **e**
50 rm – €103 €123, €14 – 5 suites
Rest *Georges* – *(closed Saturday lunch in July-August, Sunday dinner and Monday)* Menu €48/78 – Carte €52/74
Rest *La Cour du Monarque* – Carte €18/35
Spec. Pâté de Chartres. Bar cuit à la plancha, supions et chorizo. Soufflé chaud au Grand Marnier.
◆ This 16C coaching inn, featured in the Michelin Guide since 1900, offers rooms with a personal touch. Friendly atmosphere in the Madrigal bar. Georges offers a classic menu and a very fine wine list. Playful creations served under the glass roof of La Cour du Monarque.

Châtelet without rest VISA AE
6 av. Jehan-de-Beauce – ✆ 02 37 21 78 00 – www.hotelchatelet.com – reservation@hotelchatelet.com – Fax 02 37 36 23 01 – Closed 20 December-3 January Y **d**
48 rm – €92/118 €104/139, €13
◆ Well located near the station and cathedral, the calm, refurbished rooms are graced with contemporary artwork: all of which explains the hotel's appeal.

Ibis Centre VISA AE
14 pl. Drouaise – ✆ 02 37 36 06 36 – www.ibishotel.com – h0917@accor.com – Fax 02 37 36 17 20 X **b**
82 rm – €55/89 €55/89, €8,50
Rest – *(dinner only)* Menu (€15), €19 – Carte €15/25
◆ This hotel near the historic district and cathedral is gradually being renovated. It offers functional and well-kept rooms. The restaurant terrace, on the banks of the Eure, is very pleasant in fine weather.

La Vieille Maison VISA
5 r. au Lait – ✆ 02 37 34 10 67 – www.lavieillemaison.fr. – Fax 02 37 91 12 41 – Closed Sunday dinner and Monday Y **s**
Rest – Menu €28 (weekdays), €41/52 – Carte €65/75
◆ Exposed stonework and beams, rustic furniture and a fireplace lend style to this venerable residence, which is several hundred years old. Traditional cooking.

St-Hilaire VISA
11 r. du Pont St-Hilaire – ✆ 02 37 30 97 57 – Fax 02 37 30 97 57 – Closed 26 July-17 August, autumn and spring school holidays, Sunday and Monday
Rest – *(number of covers limited, pre-book)* Menu (€21 bi), €26/42 – Carte €39/50 YZ **t**
◆ Red floor tiles, beams, painted furniture and paintings by a local artist: this 16C house has style. Classical cuisine with clever touches.

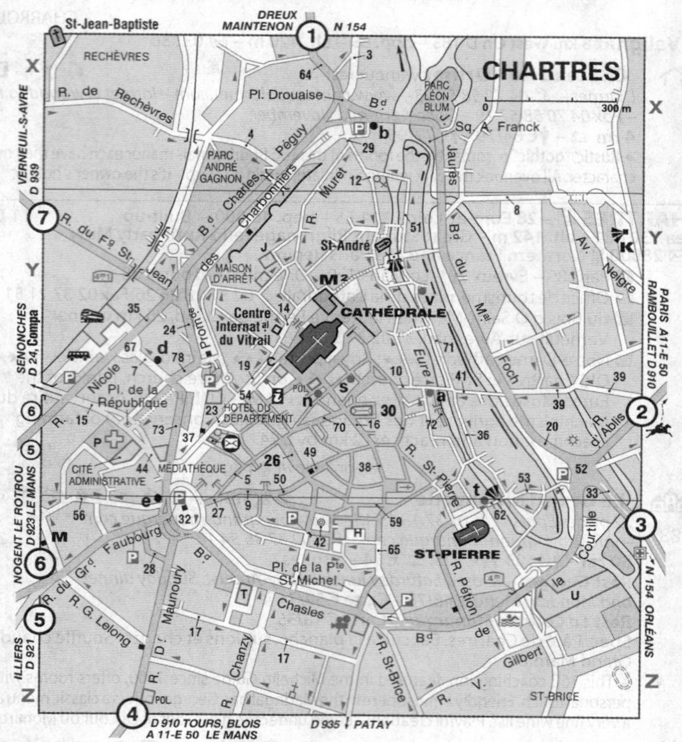

Aligre (Av. d') . . . . X 3
Alsace-Lorraine (Av. d') . . . . X 4
Ballay (R. Noël) . . . . Y 5
Beauce (Av. Jehan-de) . . . . Y 7
Bethouard (Av.) . . . . Y 8
Bois-Merrain (R. du) . . . . Y 9
Bourg (R. du) . . . . Y 10
Brèche (R. de la) . . . . X 12
Cardinal-Pie (R. du) . . . . Y 14
Casanova (R. Danièle) . . . . Y 15
Changes (R. des) . . . . Y 16
Châteaudun (R. de) . . . . Z 17
Châtelet (Pl.) . . . . Y 18
Cheval-Blanc (R. du) . . . . Y 19
Clemenceau (Bd) . . . . Y 20
Collin-d'Harleville (R.) . . . . Y 23
Couronne (R. de la) . . . . Y 24
Cygne (Pl. du) . . . . Y 26
Delacroix (R. Jacques) . . . . Y 27
Dr-Gibert (R. du) . . . . Z 28
Drouaise (R. Porte) . . . . X 29
Écuyers (R. des) . . . . Y 30
Épars (Pl. des) . . . . Z 32
Faubourg La Grappe (R. du) . . . . Y 33
Félibien (R.) . . . . Y 35
Fessard (R. G.) . . . . Y 78
Foulerie (R. de la) . . . . Y 36
Gaulle (Pl. Gén.-de) . . . . Y 37
Grenets (R. des) . . . . Y 38
Guillaume (R. du Fg) . . . . Y 39
Guillaume (R. Porte) . . . . Y 41
Halles (Pl. des) . . . . Z 42
Koenig (R. du Gén.) . . . . Y 44
Marceau (Pl.) . . . . Y 49
Marceau (R.) . . . . Y 50
Massacre (R. du) . . . . Y 51
Morard (Pl.) . . . . Y 52
Morard (R. de la Porte) . . . . Y 53
Moulin (Pl. Jean) . . . . Y 54
Péri (R. Gabriel) . . . . Z 56
Poêle-Percée (R. de la) . . . . Z 59
St-Hilaire (R. du Pont) . . . . Z 62
St-Maurice (R.) . . . . X 64
St-Michel (R.) . . . . Z 65
Semard (Pl. Pierre) . . . . Y 67
Soleil-d'Or (R. du) . . . . Y 70
Tannerie (R. de la) . . . . Y 71
Teinturiers (Q. des) . . . . Y 72
Violette (Bd Maurice) . . . . Y 73

Le Moulin de Ponceau

21 r. de la Tannerie – 02 37 35 30 05 – www.lemoulindeponceau.fr – dominique.latu@orange.fr – Fax 02 37 36 78 94 – Closed 29 December-6 January, Sunday dinner and Monday Y **v**

Rest – Menu € 39 (weekdays)/53 – Carte € 45/67

◆ A tranquil ambience reigns in this listed 16C mill, whose dining room mingles rustic and contemporary details. Pleasant terrace in the converted washhouse. Up-to-the-minute cuisine.

Les Feuillantines

4 r. du Bourg – 02 37 30 22 21 – Fax 02 37 30 22 21 – Closed 28 April-4 May, 11 August-2 September, Christmas holidays, Sunday and Monday Y **a**

Rest – Menu (€ 18), € 25 – Carte € 38/52

◆ The chef of this attractive little restaurant in the historic quarter of town is careful to use the season's specialties in the preparation of an authentically traditional cuisine; the décor is colourful and there is a lovely terrace for summer dining.

Le Bistrot de la Cathédrale
1 Cloître Notre Dame – ✆ 02 37 36 59 60 – jalleratbertrand@wanadoo.fr – Closed Wednesday
Rest – Menu € 22 – Carte € 26/41
◆ This friendly bistro, opposite the cathedral that you can admire from the terrace, is cosy and tasteful. Large choice of dishes chalked up on a slate, including the house speciality: poule au pot.

Northwest **8 km by ① and D121 [9] - ✉28300 Bailleau-l'Évêque**

Ferme du Château
à Levesville – ✆ 02 37 22 97 02 – www.ferme-levesville.com – bnvasseur@orange.fr – Fax 02 37 22 97 02 – Closed 25 December-1st January
3 rm – **€ 45/50 €** 60/65 **Table d'hôte** – Menu € 20 bi
◆ Those who seek the tranquillity of unspoilt nature will find it here in this fine 19C Beauce farmhouse with a garden to the rear. Rustically furnished, spacious guestrooms. Regional produce takes pride of place on the table d'hôte (reservations).

via ② 4 km by D 910 – ✉ 28000 Chartres

Novotel
av. Marcel Proust – ✆ 02 37 88 13 50 – www.novotel.com – h0413@accor.com – Fax 02 37 30 29 56
112 rm – € 92/115 € 102/130, € 15
Rest – Menu (€ 22), € 27 – Carte € 32/47
◆ A 1970s building located between a business estate and express roads. Choose one of the practical and bright renovated rooms. Pleasant patio-garden and children's play area. A contemporary restaurant and Novotel Café menu.

Z. A. de Barjouville 4 km by ④ – ✉ 28630 Barjouville

Mercure
4 km, via ④ – ✆ 02 37 35 35 55 – www.hotelsmercure.com – h3481@accor.com – Fax 02 37 34 72 12
73 rm – € 76/95 € 86/135, € 10 – 1 suite
Rest – *(closed Saturday lunch and Sunday)* Menu € 28/60 bi – Carte approx. € 36
◆ A chain hotel, located in a business park. It offers comfortable rooms, some of which have air-conditioning. Traditional cuisine and smart bistro decor.

in Chazay 12 km west on the D 24 and D 121 - ✉ 28300 St-Aubin-des-Bois

L' Erablais without rest
38 r. Jean Moulin – ✆ 02 37 32 80 53 – www.erablais.com – jmguinard@aol.com – Fax 02 37 32 80 53 – Closed 20 December-4 January
3 rm – € 38/43 € 49/54
◆ The former stables of this 19C farmhouse have been converted into stylish rooms decorated with floral motifs. The peaceful garden looks onto fields sown with rapeseed.

in St-Luperce 13 km west via ⑥ then D 121 and D 114 – pop. 885 – alt. 152 m – ✉ 28190

La Ferme de Mousseau without rest
Lieu-dit "Mousseau" – ✆ 02 37 26 85 01 – www.lafermedemousseau.com – gillesperrin2@wanadoo.fr – Open 1 March-15 November
3 rm – € 45 € 55
◆ An ideal chance to stay in a 'real' working farm: countrified, comfortable decor, tasty breakfast (homemade jams and bread) served in converted stables.

LA CHARTRE-SUR-LE-LOIR – 72 Sarthe – 310 M8 – pop. 1 484 – alt. 55 m – ✉ 72340 Châteaux of the Loire

35 **D2**

Paris 217 – La Flèche 57 – Le Mans 49 – St-Calais 30 – Tours 42 – Vendôme 42

Office de tourisme, 13, place de la République ✆ 02 43 44 40 04, Fax 02 43 44 40 04

De France

20 pl. de la République – ✆ 02 43 44 40 16 – hoteldefrance@worldonline.fr – Fax 02 43 79 62 20 – Closed Christmas holidays, February, Sunday dinner and Monday except dinner July-August

24 rm – †€ 45 ††€ 59, ☕ € 8,50 – ½ P € 48

Rest – *(pre-book Sat - Sun)* Menu (€ 12), € 16 (weekdays)/40 – Carte € 30/55

◆ This 100-year-old post house offers gradually renovated rooms. Small garden on the bank of the Loir and pool. An atmosphere reminiscent of Old France reigns in this restaurant serving traditional cuisine. Wine list with a focus on regional production.

CHARTRETTES – **77 Seine-et-Marne** – **312** F5 – **pop. 2 391** – **alt. 75 m** – ✉ **77590** 19 **C2**

Paris 66 – Créteil 44 – Montreuil 60 – Vitry-sur-Seine 48

Château de Rouillon without rest

41 av. Charles de Gaulle – ✆ 01 60 69 64 40 – www.chateauderouillon.net – chateau.de.rouillon@club.fr – Fax 01 60 69 64 55

5 rm ☕ – †€ 90 ††€ 98/118

◆ This 17C château and its splendid landscaped park border the Seine. Stylish furniture and antiques make up the refined decor both in the lounges and the bedrooms.

CHASSAGNE-MONTRACHET – **21 Côte-d'Or** – **320** I8 – **pop. 396** – **alt. 200 m** – ✉ **21190** 7 **A3**

Paris 327 – Amboise 343 – Beaune 16 – Blois 69 – Chalon-sur-Saône 23

Château de Chassagne-Montrachet without rest

5 r. du Château – ✆ 03 80 21 98 57 – www.michelpicard.com – contact@michelpicard.com – Fax 03 80 21 98 56

5 rm ☕ – †€ 250 ††€ 250

◆ The late 18C château and cellars of this prestigious vineyard estate open its doors to guests. Fine, very contemporary bedrooms and bathrooms designed by the sculptor Argueyrolles.

Le Chassagne (Stéphane Léger)

4 imp. Chenevottes – ✆ 03 80 21 94 94 – www.restaurant-lechassagne.com – lechassagne@wanadoo.fr – Fax 03 80 21 97 77 – Closed 3-24 August, Sunday dinner, Wednesday dinner and Monday

Rest – Menu (€ 23), € 39/75 – Carte € 75/105

Spec. Crème brûlée au foie gras de canard. Burger de pigeonneau du Louhannais. Biscuit praliné-manjari aux fruits exotiques.

◆ A pleasant gourmet stop at this charming house with wine shop on the ground floor. Bright, simple restaurant upstairs. Accomplished modern cuisine.

CHASSELAY – **69 Rhône** – **327** H4 – **pop. 2 590** – **alt. 220 m** – ✉ **69380** 43 **E1**

Paris 443 – L'Arbresle 15 – Lyon 21 – Villefranche-sur-Saône 18

Guy Lassausaie

r. de Belle Sise – ✆ 04 78 47 62 59 – www.guy-lassausaie.com – guy.lassausaie@wanadoo.fr – Fax 04 78 47 06 19 – Closed 3-27 August, 15-25 February, Tuesday and Wednesday

Rest – Menu € 48/95 – Carte € 75/90

Spec. Gâteau de tourteau et avocat au caviar. Suprême de caille et foie gras en coque d'épices. Cône glacé aux épices et poire williams de Chasselay rôtie au miel (autumn-winter). **Wines** Saint-Véran, Fleurie.

◆ This solid family establishment in the heart of the village is fully in tune with its era, illustrated by the enticing classical cuisine served in immense, contemporary dining rooms.

CHASSENEUIL-DU-POITOU – **86 Vienne** – **322** I5 – **see Poitiers**

CHASSE-SUR-RHÔNE – **38 Isère** – **333** B4 – **see Vienne**

CHASSEY-LE-CAMP – **71 Saône-et-Loire** – **320** I8 – **see Chagny**

LA CHÂTAIGNERAIE – 85 Vendée – 316 L8 – pop. 2 663 – alt. 155 m – ✉ 85120 35 C3

Paris 408 – Bressuire 32 – Fontenay-le-Comte 23 – Parthenay 43 – La Roche-sur-Yon 59

Office de tourisme, rond-point des Sources ✆ 02 51 52 62 37, Fax 02 51 52 69 20

Auberge de la Terrasse

7 r. Beauregard – ✆ 02 51 69 68 68 – www.aubergedelaterrasse.com – contact@aubergedelaterrasse.com – Fax 02 51 52 67 96 – Closed 26 April-4 May, 25 October-2 November

14 rm – €55 €70

Rest – *(closed Sunday dinner, Friday dinner, and Saturday lunch 15 September-31 May and Sunday lunch July-August)* Menu (€ 13), € 19/37 – Carte approx. € 41

◆ In a rather quiet district far from the town centre. The hotel has well-maintained, simple and above all practical rooms. Friendly welcome. Small rustic restaurant area decorated with paintings and prints offering a traditional à la carte and fixed-price menus.

Your opinions are important to us: please write and let us know about your discoveries and experiences – good and bad!

CHÂTEAU-ARNOUX-ST-AUBAN – 04 Alpes-de-Haute-Provence – 334 E8 – pop. 5 148 – alt. 440 m – ✉ 04160 French Alps 41 C2

Paris 719 – Digne-les-Bains 26 – Forcalquier 30 – Manosque 42 – Sault 71 – Sisteron 15

Syndicat d'initiative, 4, place de la carrière ✆ 02 96 73 49 57, Fax 02.96.73.53.78
Office de tourisme, Font Robert ✆ 04 92 64 02 64, Fax 04 92 64 54 55

Église St-Donat★ - St-Jean chapel viewpoint★ - Site★ of Montfort.

La Bonne Étape (Jany Gleize)

chemin du lac – ✆ 04 92 64 00 09 – www.bonneetape.com – bonneetape@relaischateaux.com – Fax 04 92 64 37 36 – Closed 4 January-10 February

18 rm – €159/179 €159/386, € 19 – ½ P € 171/285

Rest – *(closed 16 November-1st December, 4 January-10 February, Monday and Tuesday in low season except bank holidays)* Menu (€ 29), € 42/100 – Carte € 71/133

Spec. Suprême de perdreau rôti, jus à la lavande (season). Agneau de Sisteron. Crème glacée au miel de lavande. **Wines** Coteaux de Pierrevert, Palette.

◆ It's difficult not to succumb to the charm of this 18C villa with a Provencal flavour. Spacious guestrooms with antique furniture. Pretty flower-filled garden and superb vegetable plot. Restaurant with attractively rustic decor. Classic cuisine served with a very fine choice of wines.

La Magnanerie with rm

North : 2 km on N 85 – ✆ 04 92 62 60 11 – www.la-magnanerie.net – stefanparoche@aol.com – Fax 04 92 62 63 05 – Closed 20-28 December

8 rm – €49/75 €49/75, € 9 – ½ P € 47/60

Rest – *(closed Sunday dinner and Monday)* Menu € 17 (weekdays)/65 – Carte € 40/85

◆ Completely refurbished silkworm farm with modern decor in keeping with the inventive cuisine (local organic produce). Bar and terrace-garden. Provencal-style guestrooms.

Au Goût du Jour

14 av. Gén. de Gaulle – ✆ 04 92 64 48 48 – goutdujour@bonneetape.com – Fax 04 92 64 37 36 – Closed 4 January-10 February

Rest – Menu (€ 19), € 25

◆ This smart dining room, decorated in Provencal colours, is the place to sample a range of tasty local dishes, chalked up on the blackboard bistro-style.

CHÂTEAUBOURG – 35 Ille-et-Vilaine – 309 N6 – pop. 5 629 – alt. 50 m – ✉ 35220

10 **D2**

Paris 329 – Angers 114 – Châteaubriant 52 – Fougères 44 – Laval 57 – Rennes 24

Ar Milin'

30 r. de Paris – ✆ 02 99 00 30 91 – www.armilin.com – resa.armilin@wanadoo.fr – Fax 02 99 00 37 56 – Closed 20 December-5 January and Sunday dinner from 1 November to 28 February

32 rm – €72/126 €82/148, ☕ €12

Rest – *(Closed Tuesday lunch, Saturday lunch and Monday in July-August)* Menu €29/47 – Carte €41/53

Rest *Bistrot du Moulin* – *(closed Sunday and public holidays) (resident only)* Menu €21/35 – Carte €41/54

◆ This former 19C flour mill stands in a park adorned with immense contemporary works of art. Welcoming rooms (those in the wing are smaller). Light dining room (white colour scheme) and view of the river; traditional cuisine. Elegant decor and relaxed ambience at the Bistrot.

in St-Didier 6 km East by D 33 – pop. 1 558 – alt. 49 m – ✉ 35220

Pen'Roc

rm,

à La Peinière, (D 105) – ✆ 02 99 00 33 02 – www.penroc.fr – hotellerie@penroc.fr – Fax 02 99 62 30 89 – Closed 20 December-20 January

28 rm – €86/102 €98/126, ☕ €13

Rest – *(Closed Sunday dinner in low season)* Menu (€17), €23 (weekdays)/85 – Carte €59/140

◆ Dreaming of peace and quiet? That is one of the pluses of this hotel with rooms decorated in a contemporary or Asian style. Special breakfasts (home-made jams, custard tarts with prunes and yoghurts). Small, stylish dining rooms serving an up-to-date menu.

CHÂTEAUBRIANT – 44 Loire-Atlantique – 316 H1 – pop. 12 500 – alt. 70 m – ✉ 44110 Brittany

34 **B2**

Paris 354 – Angers 72 – Laval 65 – Nantes 62 – Rennes 61

Office de tourisme, 22, rue de Couëré ✆ 02 40 28 20 90, Fax 02 40 28 06 02

Château★.

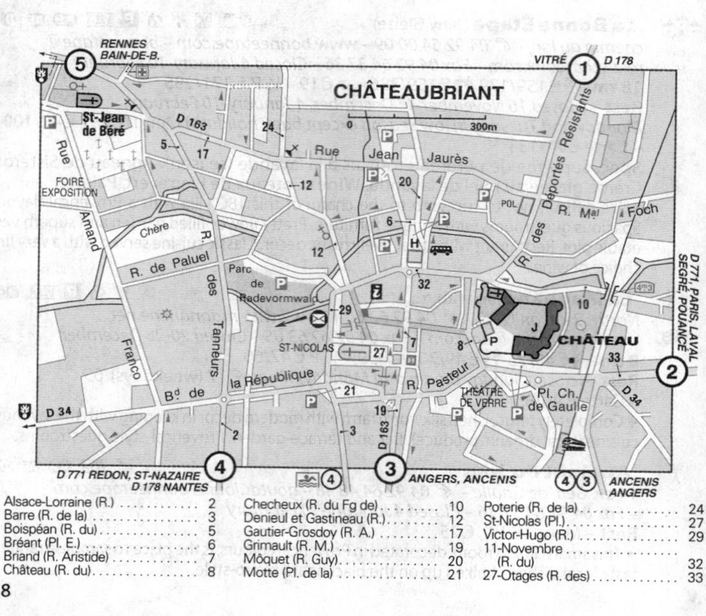

Alsace-Lorraine (R.) . . . 2
Barre (R. de la) . . . 3
Boispéan (R. du) . . . 5
Bréant (Pl. E.) . . . 6
Briand (R. Aristide) . . . 7
Château (R. du) . . . 8
Checheux (R. du Fg de) . . . 10
Denieul et Gastineau (R.) . . . 12
Gautier-Grosdoy (R. A.) . . . 17
Grimault (R. M.) . . . 19
Môquet (R. Guy) . . . 20
Motte (Pl. de la) . . . 21
Poterie (R. de la) . . . 24
St-Nicolas (Pl.) . . . 27
Victor-Hugo (R.) . . . 29
11-Novembre (R. du) . . . 32
27-Otages (R. des) . . . 33

La Ferrière rest, VISA

r. Winston Churchill, Moisdon-la-Rivière road, D 178 by ④ – 02 40 28 00 28 – www.hotelleferriere.fr – hotellaferriere@orange-business.fr – Fax 02 40 28 29 21
19 rm – €71 €71, €11 – ½ P €64/78
Rest – *(closed Sunday dinner)* Menu (€15), €20 (weekdays)/42 – Carte €39/60
◆ Lovely 1840 home surrounded by parkland. Comfortable, upstairs rooms in the main house, not as spacious in the adjacent pavilion. Classic culinary repertory served in characterful dining rooms or in the conservatory.

CHÂTEAU-CHALON – **39 Jura** – **321** D6 – **pop. 167** – **alt. 420 m** – ✉ **39210** Burgundy-Jura 16 **B3**

Paris 409 – Besançon 73 – Dole 51 – Lons-le-Saunier 14

Le Relais des Abbesses

r. de la Roche – 03 84 44 98 56 – www.chambres-hotes-jura.com – relaisdesabbesses@wanadoo.fr – Fax 03 84 44 98 56 – Open February-mid November
5 rm – €63 €65/70
Table d'hôte – *(closed Thursday, Friday and Saturday)* Menu €24 bi/34 bi
◆ It is easy to see why the owners fell in love with this village residence at first sight! Rooms, christened Agnès, Marguerite and Eugénie, have a splendid view of la Bresse, while Violette faces Château-Chalon. Home-made regional cuisine.

CHÂTEAU D'IF – **13 Bouches-du-Rhône** – **340** G6 Provence 40 **B3**

from **Marseille** for Château d'If★★ (✳★★★) 20 mn.

LE CHÂTEAU D'OLÉRON – **17 Charente-Maritime** – **324** C4 – **see Île d'Oléron**

CHÂTEAU-DU-LOIR – **72 Sarthe** – **310** L8 – **pop. 4 730** – **alt. 50 m** – ✉ **72500** 35 **D2**

Paris 235 – La Flèche 41 – Langeais 47 – Le Mans 43 – Tours 42 – Vendôme 59

Office de tourisme, 2, avenue Jean Jaurès 02 43 44 56 68, Fax 02 43 44 56 95

Le Grand Hôtel VISA

pl. Hôtel de Ville – 02 43 44 00 17 – www.grand-hotel-chateau-du-loir.com – avel5@wanadoo.fr – Fax 02 43 44 37 58 – Closed 1st-11 November, Friday dinner and Saturday from November to February
18 rm – €52 €61, €7,50 – ½ P €55
Rest – Menu (€11,50), €22, €26/30 – Carte €28/49
◆ This 19C former coaching inn today offers well-equipped, rustic or modern style rooms; the more restful areas are in the annexe (former stables). Charming old-fashioned dining room and terrace draped in wisteria. Traditional cuisine.

CHÂTEAUDUN – **28 Eure-et-Loir** – **311** D7 – **pop. 13 900** – **alt. 140 m** – ✉ **28200** Châteaux of the Loire 11 **B2**

Paris 131 – Blois 57 – Chartres 45 – Orléans 53 – Tours 94

Office de tourisme, 1, rue de Luynes 02 37 45 22 46, Fax 02 37 66 00 16

Château★★ - Old town★: La Madeleine church ★ - Promenade du Mail ≤★ - Musée des Beaux-Arts et d'Histoire naturelle: Bird collection ★ **M.**

Plan on following page

Aux Trois Pastoureaux VISA

31 r. A. Gillet – 02 37 45 74 40 – www.aux-trois-pastoureaux.fr – j-f.lucchese@wanadoo.fr – Closed 5-21 July, 27 December-4 January, 15-23 February, Sunday and Monday A **s**
Rest – Menu (€19), €24/40 – Carte €33/55
◆ Woodwork, Provençal touches and work by a local artist paint the picture of this restaurant. Traditional fare, a medieval-inspired menu and a fine choice of wines by the glass.

CHÂTEAUDUN

Cap-de-la-Madeleine (Pl.) . . . . A 3
Château (R. du) . . . . A 4
Cuirasserie (R. de la) . . . . A 5
Dunois (Pl. J.-de) . . . . A 6
Gambetta (R.) . . . . AB
Guichet (R. du) . . . . A 7
Huileries (R. des) . . . . A 8
Luynes (R. de) . . . . A 10
Lyautey (R. du Mar.) . . . . A 12
Porte d'Abas (R. de la) . . . . A 14
République (R.) . . . . AB
St-Lubin (R.) . . . . A 18
St-Médard (R.) . . . . A 19
18-Octobre (Pl. du) . . . . A 21

in Flacey 8 km North by ① – ✉ 28800 – **pop. 210 – alt. 157 m** – ✉ **28800**

Domaine de Moresville without rest
rte de Brou, Northwest by D 110 – ☎ 02 37 47 33 94
– www.domaine-moresville.com – resa@domaine-moresville.com
– Fax 02 37 47 56 40
16 rm – †€ 70/160 ††€ 80/200, ☕ € 12 – 1 suite
◆ Set in grounds with a pond, this 18C château boasts attractive lounges and personalised, faultlessly comfortable rooms (five of which are more recent and in the orangerie). Sauna and Jacuzzi tub.

Good food and accommodation at moderate prices?
Look for the Bib symbols: red Bib Gourmand for food,
blue Bib Hotel for hotels.

CHÂTEAUFORT – 78 Yvelines – **311** I3 – **101** 22 – **see Paris, Area**

CHÂTEAU-GONTIER – 53 Mayenne – **310** E8 – **pop. 10 900** – **alt. 33 m** – ✉ **53200** Châteaux of the Loire 35 **C1**

Paris 288 – Angers 50 – Châteaubriant 56 – Laval 30 – Le Mans 95
Office de tourisme, place André Counord ☎ 02 43 70 42 74, Fax 02 43 70 95 52
Romanesque interior ★ of St-Jean-Baptiste church.

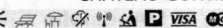

Le Jardin des Arts

5 r. A. Cahour – ✆ 02 43 70 12 12 – www.art8.com – jardin@art8.com – Fax 02 43 70 12 07 – Closed 25 July-17 August, 21 December-4 January and bank holidays A **e**

20 rm – †€ 62/74 ††€ 71/90, ☕ € 9 – ½ P € 57/73

Rest – *(closed Friday dinner, Saturday and Sunday)* Menu € 19 (weekdays)/27 – Carte € 25/35

◆ A former local government building, with a garden overlooking the Mayenne. Spacious rooms, lounges with unusual billiard tables, audio-visual equipment and an auditorium. Parquet flooring, a fireplace, original wood panelling and modern decoration in the restaurant.

Parc Hôtel without rest

46 av. Joffre, via ③ – ✆ 02 43 07 28 41 – www.parchotel.fr – contact@parchotel.fr – Fax 02 43 07 63 79 – Closed 12 February-1st March

21 rm – †€ 59/73 ††€ 67/80, ☕ € 12

◆ A 19C mansion and outhouses set in parkland, complete with swimming pool. Attractive, individually decorated rooms, more spacious in the main house. Warm hospitality.

CHÂTEAU-GONTIER

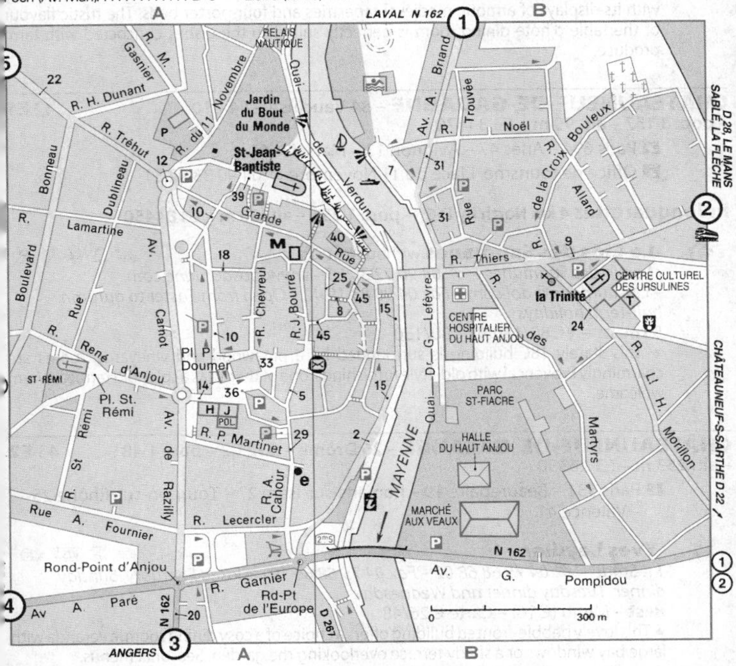

L'Aquarelle

2 r. Félix Marchand, (in Saint-Fort), 1 km south on D 267 (Ménil road)B – 02 43 70 15 44 – www.restaurant-laquarelle.com – emery.bruno@wanadoo.fr – Closed 5-16 October, 5-10 January, Tuesday dinner and Sunday dinner from September to May, Monday lunch in summer and Wednesday except dinner from June to August

Rest – Menu (€ 12), € 15 (weekday lunch), € 20/60 bi – Carte € 31/54

◆ This relaxing restaurant, on the banks of the Mayenne, serves modern cuisine. The bright panoramic dining room is decorated in orange tones. Pleasant summer terrace.

in Coudray **7 km Southeast by D 22 – pop. 784 – alt. 68 m – ✉ 53200**

L'Amphitryon with rm

2 rte de Daon – 02 43 70 46 46 – http://perso.orange.fr/lamphitryon53/ – lamphitryon@wanadoo.fr – Fax 02 43 70 42 93 – Closed 25 October-3 November, 21-28 December, 11-20 April, Tuesday lunch, Sunday dinner and Monday

6 rm – †€ 58/74 ††€ 58/74, ☐ € 8

Rest – Menu € 18 (weekdays)/37 – Carte € 36/59

◆ A pleasantly elegant atmosphere reigns in this 19C house opposite the village church. Nicely dressed tables, modern cuisine and local produce. Attractive, contemporary guestrooms.

in Ruillé-Froid-Fonds **12,5 km by ① and D605 – pop. 496 – alt. 87 m – ✉ 53170**

Logis Villeprouvée

rte du Bignon-du-Maine – 02 43 07 71 62 – http://pagesperso-orange.fr/villeprouve/bb – christ.davenel@orange.fr – Fax 02 43 07 71 62

4 rm ☐ – †€ 36 ††€ 47 – ½ P € 38 **Table d'hôte** – Menu € 15

◆ The refined decor of this former 14C-17C priory takes you back to the days of chivalry with its displays of armour, medieval tapestries and four-poster beds. The rustic flavour of the table d'hôte dining room is perfectly suited to the dishes concocted with farm produce.

CHÂTEAUNEUF-DE-GADAGNE – 84 Vaucluse – 84 C10 – pop. 3 157 – alt. 90 m – ✉ 84470 — 42 E1

Paris 694 – Arles 47 – Avignon 13 – Marseille 95

Office de tourisme, Place du 11 Novembre 04 90 33 92 31

in Jonquerettes **4 km North by D 6 – pop. 1 251 – alt. 60 m – ✉ 84450**

Le Clos des Saumanes without rest

chemin des Saumanes – 04 90 22 30 86 – www.closaumane.com – closaumane@aol.com – Fax 04 90 83 19 42 – Open from Easter to autumn half-term holidays

5 rm ☐ – †€ 80/130 ††€ 80/130

◆ This stately 18C building is surrounded by a pinewood and vineyards; rooms are charmingly Provençal with old-style furnishings; one of them has a splendid terrace. Warm welcome.

CHÂTEAUNEUF-DE-GALAURE – 26 Drôme – 332 C2 – pop. 1 481 – alt. 253 m – ✉ 26330 — 43 E2

Paris 531 – Beaurepaire 19 – Romans-sur-Isère 27 – Tournon-sur-Rhône 25 – Valence 41

Yves Leydier

1 r. Stade – 04 75 68 68 02 – Fax 04 75 68 66 19 – Closed February, Sunday dinner, Tuesday dinner and Wednesday

Rest – Menu (€ 16) – Carte € 26/48

◆ This lovely pebble-fronted building offers a choice of a cosy dining room, a veranda with large bay windows or a shady terrace overlooking the garden. Seasonal menus.

CHÂTEAUNEUF-DU-FAOU – 29 Finistère – 308 I5 – pop. 3 599 – alt. 130 m – ✉ 29520 Brittany 9 B2

Paris 526 – Brest 65 – Carhaix-Plouguer 23 – Châteaulin 24 – Morlaix 51 – Quimper 38

Syndicat d'initiative, 17, rue de la Mairie ✆ 02 98 81 83 90, Fax 02 98 81 79 30

Domaine de Trévarez★ South: 6 km.

Le Relais de Cornouaille

9 r. Paul-Sérusier, Carhaix road – ✆ 02 98 81 75 36 – www.lerelaisdecornouaille.com – relaisdecornouaille@wanadoo.fr – Fax 02 98 81 81 32 – Closed October, Sunday dinner and Saturday off season

30 rm – €43/46 €51/54, €7

Rest – Menu (€12), €16 (weekdays)/38 – Carte €19/48

◆ A family atmosphere in this hotel, whose bar is popular with locals. The bedrooms are a touch on the small side, but are functional and well-maintained. Rustic dining area, friendly service and traditional cuisine with numerous seafood specialities.

CHÂTEAUNEUF-DU-PAPE – 84 Vaucluse – 332 B9 – pop. 2 078 – alt. 87 m – ✉ 84230 Provence 42 E1

Paris 667 – Alès 82 – Avignon 19 – Carpentras 22 – Orange 10 – Roquemaure 10

Syndicat d'initiative, place du Portail ✆ 04 90 83 71 08, Fax 04 90 83 50 34

≤★★ of the château des Papes.

Hostellerie Château des Fines Roches

Sorgues road and private road – ✆ 04 90 83 70 23 – www.chateaufinesroches.com – reservation@chateaufinesroches.com – Fax 04 90 83 78 42 – Closed November and Sunday dinner to Tuesday lunch from December to April

11 rm – €109/309 €109/309, €21

Rest – Menu (€25 bi), €35 bi (weekday lunch), €38/85 – Carte €55/95

◆ The crenellated towers of this amazing 19C castle dominate the vineyards. Sophisticated, Provençal inspired interior decoration in the personalised spacious guestrooms. Updated menu served in plush surroundings or on the terrace facing the vineyards.

Le Verger des Papes

at the château – ✆ 04 90 83 50 40 – www.vergerdespapes.com – estevenin@vergerdespapes.com – Fax 04 90 83 50 49 – Closed 20 December-3 March, Sunday dinner, Monday dinner, Tuesday dinner and Wednesday dinner from October to March

Rest – Menu €20 (weekday lunch)/29 – Carte €36/45

◆ A pleasant restaurant on the ramparts of the château. A shaded terrace commands a splendid panoramic view. Gallo-Roman cellars carved from the rock. Provençal cuisine.

West 4 km by D 17 – ✉ 84230 Châteauneuf-du-Pape

La Sommellerie

rte de Roquemaure – ✆ 04 90 83 50 00 – www.la-sommellerie.fr – la-sommellerie@wanadoo.fr – Fax 04 90 83 51 85 – Closed 2 January-2 February

16 rm – €74/119 €74/119, €13 – 2 suites

Rest – *(closed Saturday lunch and Monday lunch)* Menu €30/62 – Carte €47/65

◆ This well-restored 17C sheepfold is in the heart of the Châteauneuf vineyard. Spruce rooms decked in Provençal colours. Wooded garden. Inviting dining rooms and a pergola terrace overlooking the pool. Regional cuisine according to the seasons.

CHÂTEAURENARD – 13 Bouches-du-Rhône – 340 E2 – pop. 14 200 – alt. 37 m – ✉ 13160 Provence 42 E1

Paris 692 – Avignon 10 – Carpentras 37 – Cavaillon 23 – Marseille 95 – Nîmes 44 – Orange 40

Syndicat d'initiative, 11, cours Carnot ✆ 04 90 24 25 50, Fax 04 90 24 25 52

Château féodal: ✻★ of the Griffon tower.

X **Les Glycines** with rm rm, VISA

14 av. V. Hugo – ✆ 04 90 94 10 66
– www.resthotelesglycines.com
– lesglycines3@wanadoo.fr – Fax 04 90 94 78 10
– *Closed 2 weeks in March, 16-24 August, Sunday dinner and Monday*
10 rm – †€ 49 ††€ 49, ☕ € 6 – ½ P € 48
Rest – Menu (€ 13), € 18/28 – Carte € 31/50
◆ Three dining rooms, one adjacent to the other, a covered patio and a small, attractive terrace for summer dining; regional specialities and bouillabaisse (prepared to order).

CHÂTEAUROUX [P] – 36 Indre – 323 G6 – pop. 47 500 – alt. 155 m 12 C3
– ✉ 36000 ▌Dordogne-Berry-Limousin

Paris 265 – Blois 101 – Bourges 65 – Limoges 125 – Tours 115

Office de tourisme, 1, place de la Gare ✆ 02 54 34 10 74, Fax 02 54 27 57 97

du Val de l'Indre Villedieu-sur-Indre Parc du Château, 13 km on the Loches road, ✆ 02 54 26 59 44

Déols: steeple★ of the former abbey, sarcophagus★ in St-Etienne church.

Plan on next page

Colbert AC VISA AE

4 r. Colbert – ✆ 02 54 35 70 00 – www.hotel-colbert.fr – contact@hotel-colbert.fr – Fax 02 54 27 45 88 BZ **a**
44 rm – †€ 100/110 ††€ 115/125, ☕ € 12 – 6 suites
Rest ***La Manufacture*** – Menu € 20/30 – Carte € 30/50
◆ The former tobacco factory is today home to this modern hotel with designer touches. Duplex rooms also available. 'Bread, wine and rotisserie is the theme at the modern, brasserie-style restaurant.

Ibis rm, AC VISA AE

16 r. V. Hugo – ✆ 02 54 34 61 61 – www.ibishotel.com – h1080@accor.com – Fax 02 54 27 69 51 BY **v**
60 rm – †€ 77 ††€ 77/82, ☕ € 8
Rest – *(closed Saturday and Sunday except July-August)*
Menu (€ 17) – Carte € 25/32
◆ Central and functional hotel, renovated in a contemporary style. Bright, spacious rooms with good soundproofing. Cuisine above average for the chain, served in a comfortable, modern dining room.

Boischaut without rest [P] VISA

135 av. de la Châtre, via ④ – ✆ 02 54 22 22 34 – www.hotel-chateauroux.com – boischaut@hotel-chateauroux.com – Fax 02 54 22 64 89 – Closed 27 December-4 January X **v**
27 rm – †€ 44/46 ††€ 48/52, ☕ € 8
◆ This establishment a few minutes from the town centre has functional rooms, furnished in rustic style or with wrought iron. The breakfast room, on two levels, is bright and modern.

XX **Le Lavoir de la Fonds Charles** VISA

26 r. Château-Raoul – ✆ 02 54 27 11 16 – Fax 02 54 60 02 22 – Closed 17-30 August, 2-15 January, Saturday lunch, Sunday dinner and Monday
Rest – Menu € 20 (weekdays)/48 – Carte € 54/70 AY **n**
◆ Find a piece of the countryside in the town at this old house. Terrace and veranda overlooking the river and its verdant surroundings. Traditional cuisine.

X **Le Sommelier** AC VISA AE

5 pl. Gambetta – ✆ 02 54 07 45 52 – Fax 02 54 08 68 46 – Closed 26 April-11 May, 2-17 August, 1st-5 January, Monday dinner and Sunday BY **t**
Rest – Menu (€ 13), € 16 (lunch) – Carte € 32/44
◆ The sommelier-owner offers a fine wine list that enhances updated seasonal cuisine. A yellow colour scheme dominates in the airy dining room.

CHÂTEAUROUX

Street	Grid	No.
Albert 1er (R.)	BY	2
Argenton (Av. d')	X	4
Augras (R. E.)	X	5
Auvergne (R. d')	X	7
Bourdillon (R.)	BZ	8
Bryas (Bd de)	X	9
Cantrelle (R.)	ABZ	10
Château-Raoul (R. du)	AY	13
Châtre (Av. de la)	X, BZ	14
Croix-Normand (Bd)	BZ	17
Duchâteau (Av. G.)	X	18
États-Unis (R. des)	X, BY	20
Fontaine-St-Germain (R.)	X	22
Fournier (R. A.)	BY	23
Gallieni (R.)	BZ	24
Gambetta (Pl.)	BY	25
Gare (R. de la)	BY	
Gaulle (Av. du Gén.-de)	X	26
Grande (R.)	BY	27
Jeux-Marins (Av. des)	AY	29
J.-J.-Rousseau (R.)	AY	28
Kennedy (Av. J.-F.)	X, AZ	30
Ledru-Rollin (R.)	BY	31
Lemoine (Av. Marcel)	X, BY	32
Marins (Av. des)	X, AY	33
Marins (Bd des)	X	34
Mitterrand (Av. F.)	X, AY	35
Moulin-Neuf (Bd du)	X	36
Palais-de-Justice (R. du)	ABZ	37
Pont-Neuf (Av. du)	X, AY	40
République (Pl. de la)	AY	44
Ste-Hélène (Pl.)	BY	48
St-Denis (Bd)	X	45
St-Luc (R.)	BY	46
Tours (Av. de)	X	50
Valle (Bd de la)	X	51
Verdun (Av. de)	X	52
Victoire et des Alliés (Pl. de la)	AY	53
Victor-Hugo (R.)	ABY	54
3e-Rég.-Aviation-de-Chasse (R. du)	X	55
6-Juin 1944 Débarquement Allié (Av. du)	AY	58

P'tit Bouchon
64 r. Grande – ☎ 02 54 61 50 40 – www.leptitbouchon.fr – leptitbouchon@free.fr – Closed 3 weeks in August, Sunday, Monday and bank holidays BY **e**
Rest – Menu (€ 13,50), € 17 (lunch)/22 – Carte € 29/40
◆ A friendly family atmosphere reigns in this bistro in the historic town. Interesting wines selected by the owner. Local produce on sale next door.

Le Bistrot Gourmand
10 r. du Marché – ☎ 02 54 07 86 98 – www.lebistrotgourmand36.com – bistrotgourmand@mac.com – Closed in March and 17 August-6 September AY **a**
Rest – Menu (€ 13), € 17 (lunch), € 22/32 – Carte € 22/35
◆ Small neighbourhood bistro style restaurant, flanked by a flower-decked patio-terrace in summer. Traditional, reasonably priced menu prepared by the owner chef.

Paris road 6 km near Céré via ① – ✉ 36130 Déols

Relais St-Jacques rest,
D 920 – ☎ 02 54 60 44 44 – www.relais-st-jacques.com – saint-jacques@wanadoo.fr – Fax 02 54 60 44 00
46 rm – €65 €71, ☕ €10
Rest – *(closed Sunday dinner)* Menu € 23 (weekdays)/53 – Carte € 30/75
◆ This 1980s building near the Déols aerodrome is to the north of the bustling Berry town. It offers well-kept, functional rooms. Tasteful decor and traditional cuisine with regional accents at the restaurant.

Le Poinçonnet 6 km by ⑤ – pop. 5 021 – alt. 160 m – ✉ 36330

Le Fin Gourmet
73 av. de la Forêt – ☎ 02 54 35 40 17 – www.lefingourmet.36.com – franck.gatefin@wanadoo.fr – Fax 02 54 35 47 20 – Closed Sunday dinner, Monday and Tuesday
Rest – Menu € 18 (weekday lunch), € 25/52 – Carte € 59/99
◆ The small rooms of this country house sport an elegant contemporary interior with modern artwork and a grey colour scheme. Updated cuisine and seasonal menus.

CHÂTEAU-THÉBAUD – 44 Loire-Atlantique – 316 H5 – see Nantes

CHÂTEAU-THIERRY – 02 Aisne – 306 C8 – pop. 14 967 – alt. 63 m – ✉ 02400 Northern France and the Paris Region 37 C3

Paris 95 – Épernay 56 – Meaux 48 – Reims 58 – Soissons 41 – Troyes 113
Syndicat d'initiative, 9, rue Vallée ☎ 03 23 83 51 14, Fax 03 23 83 14 74
du Val Secret Le Val Secret, N : 5 km, ☎ 03 23 83 07 25
Native house of La Fontaine - Marne Valley ★.

Île de France rest,
60 r. L. Lhermitte, (rte de Soissons) – ☎ 03 23 69 10 12 – www.hotel-iledefrance.com – hotel.ile.de.france@wanadoo.fr – Fax 03 23 83 49 70 – Closed 23-31 December
34 rm – €80 €90, ☕ €10
Rest – *(closed Sunday dinner)* Menu € 27 (weekdays)/55 – Carte € 65/80
◆ Overlooking the Marne valley, this hotel has been reborn. The revamped rooms are relaxing and comfortable. Modern fitness centre and spa. Restaurant with seasonally varying menu; pleasant panoramic terrace.

Ibis rm,
60 av. du Gén. de Gaulle, in Essômes-sur-Marne, 2 km south on D 969 – ☎ 03 23 83 10 10 – www.hotel-ibis-champagne.com – ibis@groupebachelet.com – Fax 03 23 83 45 23
55 rm – €59/69 €69, ☕ €8,50 **Rest** – Menu (€ 23) – Carte € 23/33
◆ Rooms conform to the latest standards of the chain; the quietest are at the rear while others give a view of the American Côte 204 monument commemorating the battles of 1918. The restaurant and the terrace overlook a pool: traditional menu.

CHÂTEL – 74 Haute-Savoie – 328 O3 – pop. 1 254 – alt. 1 180 m – Winter sports : 1 200/2 100 m 2 52 – ✉ 74390 French Alps 46 F1

Paris 578 – Annecy 113 – Évian-les-Bains 34 – Morzine 38 – Thonon-les-Bains 39

Office de tourisme, Chef-Lieu ✆ 04 50 73 22 44, Fax 04 50 73 22 87

Site★ - Pas de Morgins lake★ South: 3 km.

Macchi
rest, rest, VISA MC

94 chemin de l'Etringa – ✆ 04 50 73 24 12 – www.hotelmacchi.com – contact@hotelmacchi.com – Fax 04 50 73 27 25 – Open 20 June-20 September and 20 December-20 April

32 rm – €98/175 €170/310, €14 – ½ P €91/187

Rest – *(dinner only) (resident only)* Menu (€20 bi), €26/50 – Carte €37/57

Rest *Le Cerf* – *(dinner only)* Menu (€27) – Carte €37/57

◆ Pleasant chalet whose finely carved balconies look over the Abondance valley. Tastefully refurbished rooms, adorned with a local artist's fresco. Raclettes and fondues in a Savoyard setting. Varied traditional menu at Le Cerf.

Fleur de Neige without rest
VISA MC AE

564 rte Vonnes – ✆ 04 50 73 20 10 – www.hotel-fleurdeneige.fr – information@hotel-fleurdeneige.fr – Fax 04 50 73 24 55 – Open 21 December-4 April and 29 June-30 August

34 rm – €65/90 €93/145, €12

◆ Mountainside chalet. The rooms are of various sizes and have diverse furnishings. Bar with fireplace; spa.

Le Kandahar
VISA MC

1.5 km South-West via rte Béchigne – ✆ 04 50 73 30 60 – www.lekandahar.com – lekandahar@wanadoo.fr – Fax 04 50 73 25 17 – Closed from 26 April to mid-May, 27 June-10 July, 1 November-18 December and Wednesday in low season

8 rm – €40/50 €60/80, €8 – ½ P €52/65

Rest – *(closed Sunday dinner)* Menu (€14), €20/35 – Carte €21/49

◆ Welcoming, family-run, recently renovated, rustic chalet-hotel. Small, functional guestrooms with wood panelling. Shuttle buses to Le Linga. Regional cuisine served in a welcoming decor. Rustic furniture, grandfather clock, copperware and fireplace.

Belalp
VISA MC

382 rte de Vonnes – ✆ 04 50 73 24 39 – www.hotelbelalp.com – belalpchatel@aol.com – Fax 04 50 73 38 55 – Open 1 July-30 August and 20 December-30 March

26 rm – €49/75 €60/95, €9 – ½ P €53/74

Rest – *(closed Tuesday)* Menu (€14), €20/30 – Carte €27/48

◆ This chalet has a smart façade in light wood brightened with green shutters. The attractive bedrooms have been renovated in Alpine style; ask for one of the rooms overlooking the valley. Savoy specialities are served in front of the fireplace or in the panoramic dining room (for hotel guests).

Le Choucas without rest
VISA MC

303 rte Vonnes – ✆ 04 50 73 22 57 – www.hotel-lechoucas.com – info@hotel-lechoucas.com – Fax 04 50 81 36 70

12 rm – €47/63 €47/63, €8

◆ Completely renovated chalet-type construction with a flower-decked façade. Soberly decorated, alpine-style bedrooms, most with balcony.

XX Les Triolets with rm
rest, VISA MC AE

608 rte Petit Châtel – ✆ 04 50 73 20 28 – www.lestriolets.com – info@lestriolets.com – Fax 04 50 73 24 10 – Open 28 June-4 September and 20 December-31 March

20 rm – €60/87 €85/124, €11 – ½ P €72/92

Rest – *(dinner only in winter)* Menu €21/36

◆ Overlooking the resort in a quiet location, this attractive chalet has a south-facing, panoramic dining room. Typical dishes of the region.

Le Vieux Four
55 rte du Boude – ☎ 04 50 73 30 56 – Fax 04 50 73 38 12 – Open 5 December-17 April, 6 June-5 September and closed Monday
Rest – Menu € 15/42 – Carte € 34/58
◆ The rustic decor of this farm (1852) is embellished by objects and figurines placed in the feeding troughs of the cowshed. Traditional and Savoyard cuisine. Large terrace.

CHÂTELAILLON-PLAGE – 17 Charente-Maritime – 324 D3 – pop. 5 959 – alt. 3 m – Casino – ✉ 17340 Atlantic Coast — 38 A2

Paris 482 – Niort 74 – Rochefort 22 – La Rochelle 19 – Surgères 29

Office de tourisme, 5, avenue de Strasbourg ☎ 05 46 56 26 97, Fax 05 46 56 58 50

Ibis
à la Falaise, 1.5 km – ☎ 05 46 56 35 35 – h1121@accor.com – Fax 05 46 56 33 44
70 rm – €75/115 €90/115, ☕ €10 **Rest** – Menu € 19 – Carte € 18/31
◆ Away from the tourist bustle, this modern building overlooking the sea contains a thalassotherapy centre. Largish functional rooms. The restaurant and terrace face towards the Atlantic. Diet and traditional cuisine.

Majestic Hôtel
bd République – ☎ 05 46 56 20 53 – www.majestic-chatelaillon.com – majestic.chatelaillon@wanadoo.fr – Fax 05 46 56 29 24
34 rm – €48/95 €48/165, ☕ €8,50
Rest – *(closed 2-20 January, Monday lunch and Sunday dinner from October to May, Saturday lunch and Friday)* Menu (€ 14), € 19/35 – Carte € 33/53
◆ In the heart of the resort, an attractive 1920s façade behind which are simply furnished, very well kept rooms of varying sizes. Rattan furniture and a retro look in the dining room. Menu based on seafood.

Le Relais de la Bernache
1 r. Félix Faure – ☎ 05 46 56 20 19 – Closed Sunday dinner, Monday and Tuesday from October to May
Rest – Menu € 26/72 – Carte € 58/76
◆ Regional-style house two minutes from the beach. Classic chic interior, enhanced by exotic features (mahogany chairs and ethnic masks), terrace and traditional menu.

L'Acadie St-Victor with rm
35 bd de la Mer – ☎ 05 46 56 25 13 – www.hotelacadiestvictor.com – stvictor@wanadoo.fr – Fax 05 46 56 25 12 – Closed 1-13 March, 18 October-13 November, 19-28 February, Friday dinner from May to October, Sunday dinner and Monday except from 15 June to 15 September
13 rm – €46/60 €46/68, ☕ €8 – ½ P €56/67
Rest – Menu (€ 16), € 21 (weekdays)/28 – Carte € 28/50
◆ A beautiful view of the ocean from this seaside restaurant. Contemporary and bright with the emphasis on seafood. Also has basic, practical accommodation.

Les Flots with rm
52 bd de la Mer – ☎ 05 46 56 23 42 – www.les-flots.fr – contact@les-flots.fr – Fax 05 46 56 99 37 – Closed 5 December-31 January
11 rm – €56/72 €56/72, ☕ €9 – ½ P €66/80
Rest – *(closed Tuesday from October to March)* Menu € 26 – Carte € 37/59
◆ Nautical decor in this pleasant bistro-style restaurant overlooking the huge beach. Simple, tasty dishes made with market fresh produce announced on a blackboard. Modern guestrooms.

CHÂTELAIS – 49 Maine-et-Loire – 317 D2 – pop. 576 – alt. 65 m – ✉ 49520 — 34 B2

Paris 326 – Nantes 93 – Angers 53 – Laval 43 – Vitré 68

Le Frêne
22 r. St-Sauveur – ☎ 02 41 61 16 45 – http://lefrene.online.fr – lefrene@free.fr – Fax 02 41 61 16 45
4 rm ☕ – €55 €55 **Table d'hôte** – Menu € 19
◆ A pleasant garden ensures the tranquillity of this 17C and 19C mansion. Paintings adorn the rooms. Watercolour courses and gallery. Meals are served in a plush dining room.

LE CHÂTELET – 18 Cher – 323 J7 – pop. 1 139 – alt. 200 m – ✉ 18170 12 C3

▶ Paris 301 – Argenton-sur-Creuse 66 – Bourges 54 – Châteauroux 55

in Notre-Dame d'Orsan 7 km northwest by D 951 and D 65, Lignères road – ✉ 18170 Rezay

La Maison d'Orsan

– ✆ 02 48 56 27 50 – www.prieuredorsan.com – prieuredorsan@wanadoo.fr – Fax 02 48 56 39 64 – Open April-October

6 rm (½ board only) – ½ P € 190/260

Rest – *(closed lunch weekdays in low season) (set menu only)* Menu € 40 (lunch)/64

◆ This 17C priory makes for a delightful stop. The refectory and dormitory have been turned into wonderful contemporary guestrooms. There is an exquisite arbour and recreated monastic gardens. Dishes made with produce from the vegetable garden and the market. Shop and tea room.

CHÂTELGUYON – 63 Puy-de-Dôme – 326 F7 – pop. 6 121 – alt. 430 m – Spa : early May-late Sept. – Casino B – ✉ 63140 ▌Auvergne 5 B2

▶ Paris 411 – Clermont-Ferrand 21 – Gannat 31 – Vichy 43 – Volvic 11

ℹ Office de tourisme, 1, avenue de l'Europe ✆ 04 73 86 01 17, Fax 04 73 86 27 03

Street	Grid	No.
Baraduc (Av.)	B	2
Brocqueville (Av.)	A	3
Brosson (Pl.)	B	4
Chalusset (R. du)	A	6
Château (R. du)	B	7
Commerce (R. du)	C	8
Coulon (R. Roger)	B	10
Dr-Gübler (R.)	B	12
Dr-Levadoux (R.)	B	13
Europe (Av. de l')	C	14
Fénelon (R.)	B	15
Groslier (R. J.)	B	16
Hôtel de Ville (R. de l')	B	17
Lacroix (R.)	B	18
Marché (Pl. du)	B	21
Maupassant (R. Guy-de)	B	22
Mont Oriol (R.)	AB	23
Ormeau (R. de l')	B	26
Orme (Pl. de l')	B	25
Punett (R. A.)	B	27
Remparts (R. des)	B	29
Russie (Av. de)	A	30
Thermal (Bd)	C	32

Splendid

5-7 r. Angleterre – ✆ 04 73 86 04 80 – www.splendid-resort.com – contact@splendid-resort.com – Fax 04 73 86 17 56 – Closed 21 December-3 January, Saturday and Sunday from mid-November to end January A b

90 rm – †€ 60/120 ††€ 60/120, ☕ € 11 – 1 suite – ½ P € 65/95

Rest – Menu (€ 14), € 19 (weekdays)/38 – Carte € 44/72

◆ Guy de Maupassant regularly stayed in this luxury hotel, built in 1872, and a sitting room is named after him. Rooms gradually refurbished in a nostalgic style. A majestic 19C dining area with columns and a beautiful carved wood fireplace.

Le Bellevue

4 r. A. Punett – ☎ 04 73 86 07 62 – www.bellevue63.fr – bellevue63@wanadoo.fr – Fax 04 73 86 02 56 – Open 1st April-15 October B **d**

38 rm – †€ 60/80 ††€ 60/80, ☐ € 10 – ½ P € 66/76

Rest – *(open 1st June-20 September) (dinner only) (resident only)*
Menu € 25/32 – Carte approx. € 37

◆ This 1930s hotel looks down on the small spa resort in the Brayaud countryside. The rooms, functional and fresh, are bigger to the front. A pleasant view over Châtelguyon from the restaurant. Traditional cuisine.

De Paris rest, VISA MC AE

1 r. Dr Levadoux – ☎ 04 73 86 00 12 – www.hoteldeparis-chatelguyon.com – hotel.de.paris@orange.fr – Fax 04 73 86 43 55 – Closed 10-31 October

59 rm – †€ 38/49 ††€ 48/63, ☐ € 8 – ½ P € 65/75 B **s**

Rest – *(closed lunch from Monday to Thursday from 15 October to 15 April and Sunday dinner)* Menu (€ 16), € 21/44 – Carte € 32/43

◆ The well dimensioned rooms are located in the main building of the establishment and in a former chapel at the rear. Sauna available. Dining area with a mixture of old and new decor. Serves traditional and regional cooking.

Régence without rest VISA MC AE

31 av. États-Unis – ☎ 04 73 86 02 60 – www.hotel-regence-central.com – hotel-regence3@wanadoo.fr – Fax 04 73 86 12 49 – Open 20 March-25 October

24 rm – †€ 50 ††€ 59, ☐ € 8,50 C **a**

◆ Built in 1903, this traditional hotel on the high street has preserved its original charm (antique or period furniture, beautiful fireplace). Well-maintained rooms. Cosy lounges.

Chante-Grelet rest, VISA MC

av. Gén. de Gaulle – ☎ 04 73 86 02 05 – www.chante-grelet.com – chante-grelet@wanadoo.fr – Fax 04 73 86 48 58 – Open 2 May-30 September B **r**

35 rm – †€ 49/53 ††€ 50/58, ☐ € 8 – ½ P € 44/53

Rest – Menu € 14 (dinner), € 17/28

◆ A 1960s family-run establishment, slightly out of the centre, and in good condition. Simple, well-kept rooms; half of which overlook the shaded garden. Semi-traditional, semi-regional cuisine served in a rustically furnished restaurant or on the terrace.

La Papillote VISA MC

11 rte de Volvic, (at St-Hippolyte), via ② – ☎ 04 73 67 00 64 – Fax 04 73 86 20 60 – Closed August, February holidays, Sunday dinner, Monday, Tuesday and Wednesday

Rest – Menu (€ 16), € 21/38

◆ Small welcoming establishment in the village of St Hippolyte. The chef's traditional cooking, and the simple rustic interior with modern details are most popular.

CHÂTELLERAULT – 86 Vienne – 322 J4 – pop. 34 100 – alt. 52 m 39 C1

– ✉ 86100 ▌Atlantic Coast

Paris 304 – Châteauroux 98 – Cholet 134 – Poitiers 36 – Tours 71

Office de tourisme, 2, avenue Treuille ☎ 05 49 21 05 47, Fax 05 49 02 03 26

Plan on next page

Villa Richelieu without rest VISA MC

61 av. Richelieu – ☎ 06 70 15 30 90 – www.villarichelieu.com – info@villarichelieu.com – Fax 05 49 20 28 02 AY **e**

9 rm ☐ – †€ 72/115 ††€ 90/115

◆ Guest accommodation in a quiet, courtyard-facing building made of tufa, separate from the owner's house. Cosy bedrooms with lots of individual touches.

La Gourmandine with rm rm, rm, VISA MC

22 av. Président Wilson – ☎ 05 49 21 05 85 – www.la-gourmandine.com – la-gourmandine@wanadoo.fr – Fax 05 49 21 05 85 – Closed 2-14 January, Sunday dinner and Monday lunch AZ **x**

12 rm – †€ 75/85 ††€ 90/180, ☐ € 14 – ½ P € 88/134

Rest – Menu (€ 18), € 24 (weekdays)/60 – Carte € 56/77

◆ Pleasant home whose high ceilings, mouldings and original fireplace are mingled with contemporary touches and bright colours. Garden-terrace and modern menu. Newly created rooms with elegant, personalised decor.

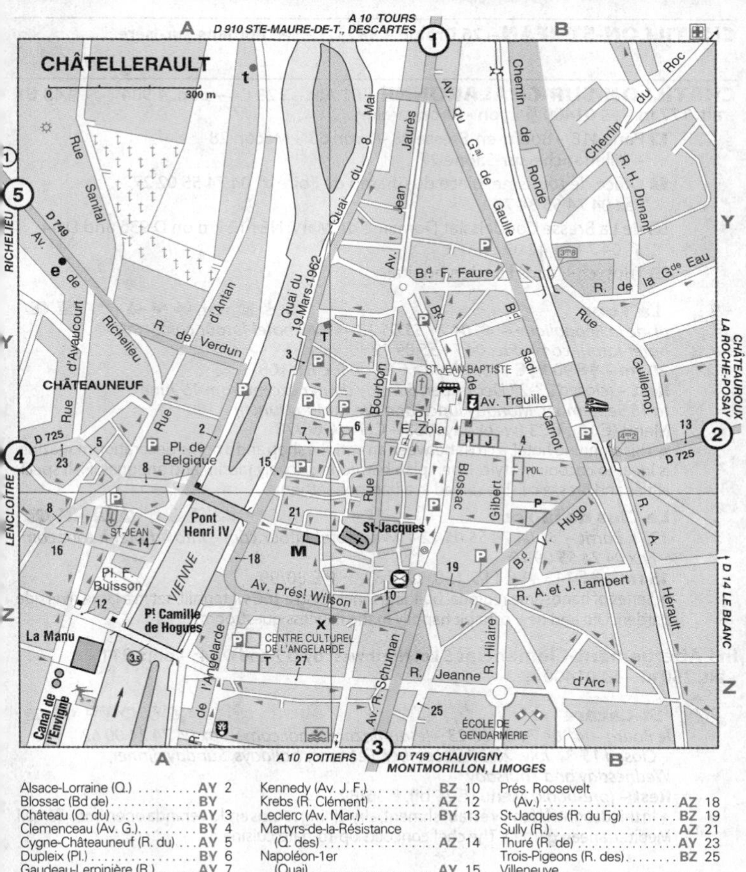

- Alsace-Lorraine (Q.) .... AY 2
- Blossac (Bd de) .... BY
- Château (Q. du) .... AY 3
- Clemenceau (Av. G.) .... BY 4
- Cygne-Châteauneuf (R. du) .... AY 5
- Dupleix (Pl.) .... BY 6
- Gaudeau-Lerpinière (R.) .... AY 7
- Grande-Rue de Châteauneuf .... AZ 8
- Kennedy (Av. J. F.) .... BZ 10
- Krebs (R. Clément) .... AZ 12
- Leclerc (Av. Mar.) .... BY 13
- Martyrs-de-la-Résistance (Q. des) .... AZ 14
- Napoléon-1er (Quai) .... AY 15
- Nouveau-Brunswick (R. du) .... AZ 16
- Prés. Roosevelt (Av.) .... AZ 18
- St-Jacques (R. du Fg) .... BZ 19
- Sully (R.) .... AZ 21
- Thuré (R. de) .... AY 23
- Trois-Pigeons (R. des) .... BZ 25
- Villeneuve (R. Chanoine-de) .... AZ 27

XX **Bernard Gautier** VISA MC

189 r. d'Antran – ✆ 05 49 90 24 74 – Fax 05 49 90 27 85 – Closed 24 August-7 September, 2-9 March, Saturday, Sunday and Monday AY **t**

Rest – Menu (€ 18 bi), € 25/35 – Carte € 45/80

◆ The smart-rustic decor of this restaurant is reminiscent of a family inn, as is the chef's traditional hearty cuisine.

in Usseau 7 km by ⑤, D 749 and D 75 – **pop. 643** – **alt. 82 m** – ✉ **86230**

Château de la Motte VISA MC

– ✆ 05 49 85 88 25 – www.chateau-de-la-motte.net – chateau.delamotte@wanadoo.fr – Open mid-March to mid-November

5 rm – †€ 80/125 ††€ 80/125 **Table d'hôte** – Menu € 30 bi

◆ Run by a couple of history enthusiasts, this 15C castle dominating the valley. Comfort and authenticity galore, from the four-poster beds to the high ceilings. "Forgotten" vegetables from the cottage garden and produce from the orchard on the table.

CHÂTILLON-ST-JEAN – 26 Drôme – 332 D3 – see Romans-sur-Isère

CHÂTILLON-SUR-CHALARONNE – 01 Ain – 328 C4 – pop. 4 904 43 E1
– alt. 177 m – ✉ 01400 Lyon - Rhone Valley

Paris 418 – Bourg-en-Bresse 28 – Lyon 55 – Mâcon 28 – Villefranche-sur-Saône 27

Office de tourisme, place du Champ de Foire ☎ 04 74 55 02 27, Fax 04 74 55 34 78

de La Bresse Condeissiat Domaine de Mary, NE : 12 km on D 936 and D 64, ☎ 04 74 51 42 09

Triptych★ dans l'ancien hôpital.

La Tour rest, VISA

pl. de la République – ☎ 04 74 55 05 12 – www.hotel-latour.com – info@hotel-latour.com – Fax 04 74 55 09 19

20 rm – €90 €115/170, €8 – ½ P €81/108

Rest – *(closed 23-27 December, Sunday dinner except from 15 June to 15 September, Monday lunch and Wednesday lunch)*
Menu (€18), €23 (weekdays)/65 – Carte €66/78

◆ This stunning hotel, a cross between an antique shop and a home decoration magazine, is ideal to cocoon in style. Open plan bathrooms, lovely fabrics and antiques. Fish specialities and Bresse cuisine served in a baroque setting.

Le Clos de la Tour P VISA

135 r. Barrit – ☎ 04 74 55 05 12 – www.hotel-latour.com – info@hotel-latour.com – Fax 04 74 55 09 19

15 rm – €115 €115/150, €8 – ½ P €80/99

◆ Series of handsome regional buildings, including a 16C watermill, set in a large riverside garden. Old and new cohabit happily in the flawless guestrooms.

in l'Abergement-Clémenciat 5 km Northwest by D 7 and D 64C – pop. 811 – alt. 250 m – ✉ 01400

St-Lazare VISA AE

le Bourg – ☎ 04 74 24 00 23 – lesaintlazare@aol.com – Fax 04 74 24 00 62 – Closed 15-31 July, 20-27 December, February holidays, Sunday dinner, Wednesday and Thursday

Rest – *(pre-book)* Menu (€25 bi), €36/82

◆ In this delightful family establishment, airy dining rooms and a veranda open onto a small Mediterranean garden. The chef concocts up-to-date cuisine.

CHÂTILLON-SUR-CLUSES – 74 Haute-Savoie – 328 M4 46 F1
– pop. 1 096 – alt. 730 m – ✉ 74300

Paris 576 – Annecy 63 – Chamonix-Mont-Blanc 47 – Thonon-les-Bains 49

Le Bois du Seigneur P VISA AE

rte Taninges – ☎ 04 50 34 27 40 – www.leboisduseigneur.com – leboisduseigneur@wanadoo.fr – Fax 04 50 34 80 20 – Closed 4-18 October and Sunday dinner

12 rm – €55 €55/72, €7 – ½ P €51/58

Rest – *(closed 5-10 January, Tuesday lunch and Monday)*
Menu (€16), €21/40 – Carte €36/58 dinner only

◆ Savoy building overlooking a through road in a village located above Cluses. Very well kept, simple rustic style rooms. Warm welcome. Traditional fare served by the fireplace in the dining room or out on the veranda.

CHÂTILLON-SUR-INDRE – 36 Indre – 323 D5 – pop. 2 909 11 B3
– alt. 115 m – ✉ 36700

Paris 261 – Orléans 175 – Châteauroux 47 – Déols 51 – Le Blanc 43

Office de tourisme, boulevard du Général Leclerc ☎ 02 54 38 74 19, Fax 02.54.38.74.19

 **La Poignardière**

4 km north-east on D 975 and D 28 direction Le Tranger – ✆ 02 54 38 78 14 – www.lapoignardiere.fr – maryse_lheureux@yahoo.fr – Fax 02 54 38 95 34 – Open from March to November

5 rm – **†**€ 75/80 **††**€ 80/90 **Table d'hôte** – Menu 25 bi

◆ Small castle built in the 1900s, surrounded by a 12-hectare park with trees that are 300-years-old. Swimming pool, boat rides on the lake, tennis court. Bright rooms in a classical or modern style. Traditional cuisine, a pretty wooden fireplace and winter garden beneath a glass roof.

CHÂTILLON-SUR-SEINE – 21 Côte-d'Or – 320 H2 – pop. 5 837 – alt. 219 m – ✉ 21400 Burgundy-Jura 8 C1

Paris 233 – Auxerre 85 – Chaumont 60 – Dijon 83 – Langres 74 – Saulieu 79 – Troyes 69

Office de tourisme, place Marmont ✆ 03 80 91 13 19, Fax 03 80 91 21 46

Source de la Douix★ - Musée★ du Châtillonnais: treasure-house of Vix★★.

 **La Côte d'Or**

2 r. Charles-Ronot – ✆ 03 80 91 13 29 – Fax 03 80 91 29 15 – Closed 2 January-1st March, Monday and Tuesday

9 rm – **†**€ 65/75 **††**€ 65/75, € 10 **Rest** – Menu € 20/45 – Carte € 41/60

◆ A former post house, this traditional hostelry offers refurbished stylish rooms, furnished with antique and period furniture. Traditional and regional Burgundy recipes served in an elegant countrified dining room by the fireside, or beneath the parasols in the garden.

in Montliot-et-Courcelles 4 km northwest by D 971 – pop. 291 – alt. 224 m – ✉ 21400

Le Magiot without rest

r. de Magiot – ✆ 03 80 91 20 51 – http://lemagiot-21.com – lemagiot@wanadoo.fr – Fax 03 80 91 30 20

22 rm – **†**€ 42/44 **††**€ 50/52, € 6,50

◆ A motel-style establishment whose simple, practical rooms are located in the two wings enclosing the terrace-solarium. Veranda fitted out like a sitting room.

For a pleasant stay in a charming hotel, look for the red ... symbols.

LA CHÂTRE – 36 Indre – 323 H7 – pop. 4 547 – alt. 210 m – ✉ 36400 Dordogne-Berry-Limousin 12 C3

Paris 298 – Bourges 69 – Châteauroux 37 – Guéret 53 – Montluçon 65

Office de tourisme, 134, rue Nationale ✆ 02 54 48 22 64, Fax 02 54 06 09 15

les Dryades Pouligny-Notre-Dame Hôtel des Dryades, S : 9 km on D 940, ✆ 02 54 06 60 67

in St-Chartier 9 km North by D 943 and D 918 – pop. 598 – alt. 195 m – ✉ 36400

Vic: frescoes★ of the church Southwest: 2 km.

 **Château de la Vallée Bleue**

rte Verneuil – ✆ 02 54 31 01 91 – www.chateauvalleebleue.com – valleebleu@aol.com – Fax 02 54 31 04 48 – Open from mid-March to mid-November and closed Sunday dinner and Monday from October to May

15 rm – **†**€ 95/145 **††**€ 100/145, € 13 – 2 suites

Rest – *(closed for lunch except weekends and bank holidays)*

Menu (€ 19), € 24 (lunch), € 34/44 – Carte € 40/70

◆ This beautiful 19C mansion, surrounded by 4ha of English-style parkland, was once the home of George Sand's doctor. Tasteful rustic rooms and a lovely duplex in the dovecote. A bourgeois style restaurant, serving traditional recipes and a fine wine list.

CHÂTRES – 77 Seine-et-Marne – 312 F3 – pop. 555 – alt. 116 m – ✉ 77610 19 **C2**

Paris 49 – Boulogne-Billancourt 57 – Montreuil 44 – Saint-Denis 62

Le Portail Bleu

2 rte de Fontenay – ✆ 01 64 25 84 94 – www.leportailbleu.com – leportailbleu@voila.fr – Fax 01 64 25 84 94

4 rm – €45 €62/70 **Table d'hôte** – Menu €23 bi/30 bi

◆ This old farmhouse has benefited from some fine restoration work. The mansard rooms are cosy and furnished with antiques and junk shop finds. Table d'hôtes.

CHAUBLANC – 71 Saône-et-Loire – 320 J8 – see St-Gervais-en-Vallière

CHAUDES-AIGUES – 15 Cantal – 330 G5 – pop. 970 – alt. 750 m – Spa : early April-late Nov. – Casino – ✉ 15110 Auvergne 5 **B3**

Paris 538 – Aurillac 94 – Espalion 54 – St-Chély-d'Apcher 30 – St-Flour 27

Syndicat d'initiative, 1, avenue Georges Pompidou ✆ 04 71 23 52 75, Fax 04 71 23 51 98

Beauséjour

9 av. G. Pompidou – ✆ 04 71 23 52 37 – www.hotel-beausejour-chaudes-aigues.com – beausejour@wanadoo.fr – Fax 04 71 23 56 89 – Open 1st April-25 November

39 rm – €46/53 €58/65, €7 – ½ P €50/54

Rest – Menu €15/35 – Carte €27/43

◆ A stone's throw from the thermal baths, behind the white façade of this 1960s building you will find functional well-kept rooms with double-glazing. Pleasant dining areas and terrace overlooking the heated swimming pool. Regional cuisine.

in Maisonneuve 10 km southwest by D 921 – ✉ 15110 Jabrun

Moulin des Templiers with rm

– ✆ 04 71 73 81 80 – www.lemoulindestempliers.com – info@lemoulindestempliers.com – Fax 04 71 73 81 80 – Closed 10-25 October, Sunday dinner and Monday except hotel July-August

5 rm – €39 €40 – ½ P €40 **Rest** – Menu (€12), €20/34

◆ Friendly inn by the roadside serving traditional Aubrac cooking. Pleasantly rustic dining room and a few functional rooms.

CHAUFFAYER – 05 Hautes-Alpes – 334 E4 – pop. 383 – alt. 910 m – ✉ 05800 40 **B1**

Paris 639 – Gap 27 – Grenoble 77 – St-Bonnet-en-Champsaur 13

Château des Herbeys

2 km north by N 85 and secondary road – ✆ 04 92 55 26 83 – www.hotel-restaurant-delas.com – delas-hotel-restaurant@wanadoo.fr – Fax 04 92 55 29 66 – Open 1st April-15 November and closed Tuesday except school holidays

12 rm – €65 €75/130, €11 – ½ P €65/95

Rest – Menu €23/38 – Carte €35/50

◆ Deer and llamas graze in the pleasant grounds of this 13C residence. The spacious rooms have high ceilings and are enhanced by antique furnishings. The establishment lends itself ideally to banquets and open air activities. The decor here is eclectic but full of character (period furniture and bric-a-brac ornamentation).

CHAULGNES – 58 Nièvre – 319 B9 – pop. 1 326 – alt. 240 m – ✉ 58400 Burgundy-Jura 7 **A2**

Paris 227 – Cosne-sur-Loire 40 – Dijon 201 – Nevers 21

Beaumonde

Le Margat – ✆ 03 86 37 86 16 – www.gites-de-france-nievre.com/beaumonde/ – cheryl.jj.trinquard@wanadoo.fr – Fax 03 86 37 86 16 – Open March-mid November

4 rm – €60 €65/80 **Table d'hôte** – Menu 24 bi

◆ Extensive grounds surround this pink house that offers comfortable, well-furnished rooms. The most luxurious room, called Cristal, has a large corner bath and a terrace of its own. The owner hails from Australia and excels in the preparation of her own country's culinary delights.

CHAUMONT Ⓟ – 52 Haute-Marne – 313 K5 – pop. 24 200 – alt. 318 m – ✉ 52000 Northern France and the Paris Region 14 C3

Paris 264 – Épinal 128 – Langres 35 – St-Dizier 74 – Troyes 101

Office de tourisme, place du Général-de-Gaulle ☎ 03 25 03 80 80, Fax 03 25 32 00 99

Viaduct ★ - St-Jean-Baptiste basilica ★.

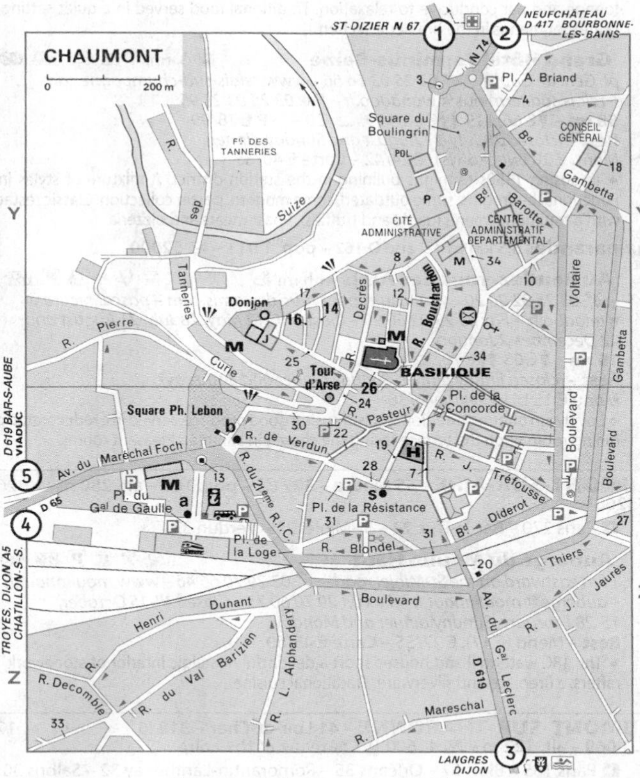

Carnot (Av.)	Y 3	Hautefeuille (R.)	Y 17	Souvenir Français (Av. du)	Z 27
Champ-de-Mars (R. du)	Y 4	Hugueny (R. du Cdt)	Y 18	Toupot-de-Béveaux (R.)	Z 28
Clemenceau (R. G.)	Z 7	Laloy (R.)	Z 19	Tour Charton (R. de la)	Z 30
Dutailly (R. G.)	Y 8	Langres (Pt de)	Z 20	Tour Mongeard (Bd de la)	Z 31
Fourcaut (R. V.)	Y 10	Mariotte (R. V.)	Z 22	Val Anne-Marie (R. du)	Z 33
Girardon (R.)	Y 12	Mgr Desprez (R.)	YZ 24	Verdun (R. de)	Z
Goguenheim (Pl. E.)	Z 13	Palais (R. du)	Y 25	Victoire-de-la-Marne (R.)	Y 34
Gouthière (R.)	Y 14	St-Jean (R.)	YZ 26		
Guyard (R.)	Y 16				

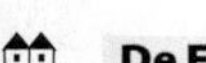

De France

25 r. Toupot de Béveaux – ☎ 03 25 03 01 11 – www.hotel-france-chaumont.com – contact@hotel-france-chaumont.com – Fax 03 25 32 35 80 Z s

20 rm – €73/98 €79/104, ☕ €10 – 7 suites

Rest – *(closed 3-22 August, Sunday and bank holidays) (dinner only)*

Menu €18, €22/38 – Carte €29/42

◆ An inn since the 16C, this hotel offers personalised rooms with individual exotic touches. Good soundproofing and new bedding. A contemporary, welcoming makeover in the restaurant. Traditional dishes.

Les Remparts rm, VISA

72 r. Verdun – ✆ 03 25 32 64 40 – www.hotel-les-remparts.fr – hotel.rest.des.remparts@wanadoo.fr – Fax 03 25 32 51 70 – Closed Sunday dinner Z **b**

17 rm – †€ 75 ††€ 85, ☕ € 12

Rest – Menu (€ 18), € 22 (weekdays)/49 – Carte € 37/70

◆ Family hotel near the train station offering fully renovated rooms of varying sizes. Small lounge and bar conducive to relaxation. Traditional food served in a quiet setting, and buffet set menus in the brasserie section.

Grand Hôtel Terminus-Reine rm, VISA

pl. Gén. de Gaulle – ✆ 03 25 03 66 66 – www.relais-sud-champagne.com – relais.sud.terminus@wanadoo.fr – Fax 03 25 03 28 95 Z **a**

58 rm – †€ 66/119 ††€ 66/119, ☕ € 9 – ½ P € 78/99

Rest – *(closed 28 July-27 August and Sunday dinner)*

Menu € 20 (weekdays), € 24/42 – Carte € 40/65

◆ Imposing 1950s terminus building in the station district. A mixture of styles inside. Functional bedrooms, some outdated, some modern; poster collection. Classic restaurant with a traditional menu (game and truffles). Roast meats and pizzeria.

in Chamarandes 3,5 km by ③ and D 162 – **pop. 1 011** – ✉ **52000**

Au Rendez-vous des Amis with rm VISA

– ✆ 03 25 32 20 20 – www.au-rendezvous-des-amis.com – pascal.nicard@wanadoo.fr – Fax 03 25 02 60 90 – Closed 1st-12 May, 28 July-21 August and 22 December-2 January

19 rm – †€ 63 ††€ 70, ☕ € 11

Rest – *(closed Friday dinner, Sunday dinner and Saturday)*

Menu € 15 bi (weekdays)/36

◆ Lovely inn offering traditional cuisine using good produce, served in a redecorated rustic dining room or on the terrace facing the church in summer. Pleasant rooms.

CHAUMONT-SUR-AIRE – 55 Meuse – 307 C5 – pop. 165 – alt. 250 m – ✉ 55260 26 A2

Paris 270 – Bar-le-Duc 24 – St-Mihiel 25 – Verdun 33

Auberge du Moulin Haut VISA

1 km eastward on the St-Mihiel road – ✆ 03 29 70 66 46 – www.moulinhaut.fr – auberge@moulinhaut.fr – Fax 03 29 70 60 75 – Closed 1st-15 October, 15-28 February, Sunday dinner and Monday

Rest – Menu (€ 17), € 27/55 – Carte € 45/60

◆ The 18C watermill and houses sport a delightful nostalgic interior of stonework, bare rafters, a fireplace and silverware. Traditional cuisine.

CHAUMONT-SUR-THARONNE – 41 Loir-et-Cher – 318 I6 – pop. 1 069 – alt. 122 m – ✉ 41600 Châteaux of the Loire 12 C2

Paris 165 – Blois 52 – Orléans 35 – Romorantin-Lanthenay 32 – Salbris 30

Office de tourisme, 3, place Robert Mottu ✆ 02 54 88 64 00, Fax 02 54 88 60 40

La Grenouillère VISA

rte d'Orléans – ✆ 02 54 88 50 71 – lagrenouillere-sologne@orange.fr – Fax 02 54 88 53 49 – Closed Monday and Tuesday

Rest – Menu (€ 30 bi), € 38/60 – Carte € 58/72

◆ Typical Sologne brick built house on the edge of the forest, extended by a veranda. Snug, rustic interior. Cuisine with a contemporary twist.

CHAUMOUSEY – 88 Vosges – 314 G3 – see Épinal

CHAUNY – 02 Aisne – 306 B5 – pop. 12 600 – alt. 50 m – ✉ 02300 37 C2

Paris 124 – Compiègne 46 – Laon 35 – Noyon 18 – St-Quentin 31 – Soissons 32

Syndicat d'initiative, place du Marché Couvert ✆ 03 23 52 10 79, Fax 03 23 39 38 77

XXX **Toque Blanche** with rm rest,

24 av. V. Hugo – ✆ 03 23 39 98 98 – www.toque-blanche.fr – info@toque-blanche.fr – Fax 03 23 52 32 79 – Closed 4-23 August, 2-4 January, 16-21 February, Saturday lunch, Sunday dinner and Monday
7 rm – †€ 62/88 ††€ 73/88, ☕ € 12
Rest – Menu € 20 (weekday lunch), € 33/73 – Carte € 65/73
◆ Charming 1920s house surrounded by parkland. Sample tasty contemporary cooking in a recently spruced up romantic interior.

in Ognes **2 km West by Noyon road – pop. 1 110 – alt. 55 m – ✉ 02300**

X **L'Ardoise**

26 av. Liberté – ✆ 03 23 52 15 77 – www.lardoise.biz – lardoise@yahoo.fr – Fax 03 23 39 91 52 – Closed 24-31 August, 1st-8 February, Sunday dinner, Monday dinner and Thursday
Rest – Menu (€ 14 bi) – Carte € 22/39
◆ This family-run inn serves bistro style cuisine chalked up on a slate. Contemporary monochrome decor, open kitchen. Terrace facing the garden.

in Rond-d'Orléans **8 km southeast by D 937 and D 1750 – ✉ 02300 Sinceny**

Auberge du Rond d'Orléans

– ✆ 03 23 40 20 10 – www.aubergeduronddorleans-02.com – aubergeduronddorleans@orange.fr – Fax 03 23 52 36 80
21 rm – †€ 48 ††€ 55, ☕ € 10
Rest – *(Closed Sunday dinner)* Menu (€ 15 bi), € 19/60 – Carte € 38/68
◆ In the heart of the state-owned Coucy-Basse forest, a motel-style establishment with functional, well-kept rooms. Breakfast is served in a separate building. Spacious dining rooms with rustic decor, and traditional meals with regional touches.

CHAUSEY (ÎLES) – 50 Manche – 303 B6 – see Îles Chausey

LA CHAUSSÉE D'IVRY – 28 Eure-et-Loir – 311 E2 – pop. 924 – alt. 57 m – ✉ 28260 11 B1

Paris 75 – Orléans 141 – Chartres 60 – Cergy 59 – Évreux 35

Le Gingko without rest

505 r. des Moulins, (near the Parc de Nantilly Golf Course) – ✆ 02 37 64 01 11 – www.hotel-gingko.com – contact@hotel-gingko.com – Fax 02 37 64 32 85
20 rm – †€ 76/160 ††€ 76/160, ☕ € 8
◆ Within easy reach of the golf course, this former 19C mansion and its outbuildings have been renovated from top to toe. Generously proportioned, comfortable contemporary rooms.

CHAUSSIN – 39 Jura – 321 C5 – pop. 1 579 – alt. 191 m – ✉ 39120 16 A2

Paris 354 – Beaune 52 – Besançon 76 – Chalon-sur-Saône 56 – Dijon 62 – Dole 21

Chez Bach

pl. Ancienne Gare – ✆ 03 84 81 80 38 – www.hotel-bach.com – hotel-bach@wanadoo.fr – Fax 03 84 81 83 80 – Closed 22 December-6 January, Friday dinner except 14 July-31 August, Sunday dinner and Monday lunch except holidays
22 rm – †€ 65/85 ††€ 65/85, ☕ € 11 – ½ P € 70/85
Rest – *(pre-book Sat - Sun)* Menu (€ 18), € 26/63 – Carte € 49/68
◆ This partly renovated, family-run hotel is opposite the old station in this village. It is located on the Bresse, Burgundy and Jura borders. Traditional cuisine and fine choice of regional wines.

Val d'Orain

34 r. S.-M. Lévy – ✆ 03 84 81 82 15 – www.aubergevaldorain.fr – aubergevaldorain@wanadoo.fr – Fax 03 84 81 75 24
10 rm – †€ 38 ††€ 50, ☕ € 6 – ½ P € 43
Rest – Menu (€ 13 bi), € 17/28 – Carte € 25/35
◆ An inn by the side of the main road through the village, which is on the River Orain, a tributary of the Doubs. Simple, extremely well kept rooms. Rustic dining room with a veranda, and a terrace in the courtyard. Local cuisine and Jura wines.

CHAUVIGNY – 86 Vienne – 322 J5 – pop. 7 025 – alt. 65 m – ✉ 86300 39 C1
Atlantic Coast

Paris 333 – Bellac 64 – Le Blanc 36 – Châtellerault 30 – Montmorillon 27 – Poitiers 26

Office de tourisme, Mairie ✆ 05 49 45 99 10, Fax 05 49 45 99 10

High town ★ - St-Pierre church ★: choir capitals ★★ - Donjon de Gouzon ★.

St-Savin: abbey ★★ (wall paintings ★★★).

Lion d'Or rm, rest, VISA

8 r. du Marché, (near the church) – ✆ 05 49 46 30 28 – Fax 05 49 47 74 28 – Closed 24 December-15 January

26 rm – †€ 46 ††€ 46, ☕ € 7 – ½ P € 44

Rest – Menu (€ 13), € 19/40 – Carte € 28/56

◆ In the lower part of town, this establishment sports a bright interior and individually decorated, comfortable and well-kept rooms. Decorative wrought iron and Art Nouveau-style chairs set the scene in the restaurant. Tasty traditional cuisine.

CHAUX-NEUVE – 25 Doubs – 321 G6 – pop. 223 – alt. 992 m – ✉ 25240 16 B3

Paris 450 – Besançon 94 – Genève 78 – Lons-le-Saunier 68 – Pontarlier 35 – St-Claude 53

Auberge du Grand Gît rm, VISA

8 r. des Chaumelles – ✆ 03 81 69 25 75 – www.aubergedugrandgit.com – nicod@aubergedugrandgit.com – Fax 03 81 69 15 44 – Open 5 May-14 October, 22 December-24 March and closed Sunday except lunch and Monday

8 rm – †€ 40/45 ††€ 49/52, ☕ € 9 – ½ P € 50/53

Rest – *(dinner only)* Menu € 20/25 – Carte € 28/38

◆ Find a family atmosphere and peaceful, wood panelled rooms in this recently built chalet near the ski jump area. The owner prepares appetising regional cuisine served in a pleasant country dining room.

CHAVANOZ – 38 Isère – 333 E3 – pop. 4 068 – alt. 234 m – ✉ 38230 44 B1

Paris 494 – Lyon 49 – Grenoble 101 – Villeurbanne 38

Aux Berges du Rhône with rm VISA

Grange Rouge hamlet, 2 km southeast on the D 55 rte de Loyettes – ✆ 04 72 02 02 50 – www.aux-berges-du-rhone.com – contact@antonin-restaurant.com – Fax 04 72 02 02 51

7 rm ☕ – †€ 95 ††€ 115 **Rest** – *(closed Sunday dinner and Wednesday)* Menu € 22 (weekday lunch), € 29/59 – Carte € 37/52

◆ Near the Rhone, there is a refined, contemporary style at this recently built establishment surrounded by parkland. Vast restaurant offering mouthwatering modern cuisine. The pleasant, well-soundproofed guestrooms have a minimalist decor.

CHAVIGNOL – 18 Cher – 323 M2 – see Sancerre

CHAVOIRES – 74 Haute-Savoie – 328 K5 – see Annecy

CHAZAY – 28 Eure-et-Loir – 311 E5 – see Chartres

CHAZEY-SUR-AIN – 01 Ain – 328 E5 – pop. 1 329 – alt. 235 m – ✉ 01150 44 B1

Paris 469 – Bourg-en-Bresse 45 – Chambéry 87 – Lyon 43 – Nantua 57

La Louizarde VISA

3 km south by D 62 and secondary road – ✆ 04 74 61 53 23 – Fax 04 74 61 58 47 – Closed 11-19 July, 1-8 September, Tuesday dinner, Wednesday dinner and Thursday dinner from October to March, Saturday lunch, Sunday dinner and Monday

Rest – Menu € 18 bi (weekday lunch), € 29/42 – Carte € 35/56

◆ The outline of this house recalls the architecture of Louisiana. Subtle colonial-style interior decor and attractive terrace opening onto the garden.

CHECY – 45 Loiret – 318 J4 – pop. 7 221 – alt. 112 m – ✉ 45430 12 C2

Paris 142 – Orléans 10 – Fleury-les-Aubrais 13 – Olivet 28 – Saint-Jean-de-Braye 6

XXX **Le Week End**

1 pl. du Cloître – ✆ 02 38 86 84 93 – www.restaurant-leweekend.com – info@restaurant-leweekend.com – Fax 02 38 86 81 30 – Closed Sunday dinner and Monday

Rest – Menu € 28 (weekdays)/65 – Carte € 55/61

◆ In the main square, this pretty house has a bright, comfortable interior. Thoughtful seasonal menu and a good choice of wines from the Loire Valley (cellar adapted for wine-tasting).

CHELLES – 60 Oise – 305 J4 – see Pierrefonds

CHÉNAS – 69 Rhône – 327 H2 – pop. 458 – alt. 253 m – ✉ 69840 43 E1

Paris 407 – Mâcon 18 – Bourg-en-Bresse 45 – Lyon 59 – Villefranche-sur-Saône 28

XX **Les Platanes de Chénas**

in Deschamps, 2 km north by D 68 – ✆ 03 85 36 79 80 – chgerber@wanadoo.fr – Fax 03 85 36 78 33 – Closed 21-28 December, 10 February-10 March, Tuesday and Wednesday

Rest – Menu (€ 17), € 25/68 – Carte € 35/55

◆ Regional dishes and local wines offered in a warm, colourful setting. Alternatively, dine under the plane trees on the terrace with wrought iron furniture and a view of Beaujolais.

CHÊNEHUTTE-LES-TUFFEAUX – 49 Maine-et-Loire – 317 I5 – see Saumur

CHÉNÉRAILLES – 23 Creuse – 325 K4 – pop. 737 – alt. 537 m – ✉ 23130 Dordogne-Berry-Limousin 25 C1

Paris 369 – Aubusson 19 – La Châtre 63 – Guéret 32 – Montluçon 46

Syndicat d'initiative, 32, route de gouzon ✆ 05 55 62 91 22

High relief★ in the church.

XX **Coq d'Or**

7 pl. du Champ de Foire – ✆ 05 55 62 30 83 – p.rulliere-coqdor@wanadoo.fr – Fax 05 55 62 95 18 – Closed 21 June-2 July, 20 September-2 October, 1st-20 January, Sunday dinner, Wednesday dinner and Monday

Rest – Menu (€ 15), € 21/46 – Carte € 31/46

◆ The window at the entrance to this restaurant displays cockerels brought back from around the world by customers. Tasty contemporary cuisine.

CHENONCEAUX – 37 Indre-et-Loire – 317 P5 – pop. 339 – alt. 62 m – ✉ 37150 Châteaux of the Loire 11 A1

Paris 234 – Amboise 12 – Château-Renault 36 – Loches 31 – Montrichard 8 – Tours 33

Syndicat d'initiative, 1, rue Bretonneau ✆ 02 47 23 94 45, Fax 02 47 23 82 41

Château of Chenonceau★★★.

Auberge du Bon Laboureur (Antoine Jeudi) rm,

6 r. Dr Bretonneau – ✆ 02 47 23 90 02 – www.bonlaboureur.com – laboureur@wanadoo.fr – Fax 02 47 23 82 01 – Closed 11 November-19 December, 4 January-14 February and Tuesday lunch

23 rm – †€ 95/155 ††€ 120/230, ☕ € 15 – 3 suites

Rest – Menu € 31 (weekday lunch), € 48/86 – Carte € 65/95

Spec. Crème onctueuse d'écrevisses et concassé de tomate (June to Sep.). Conjugaison de ris et tête de veau sauce gribiche. Tarte au chocolat guanaja, mousse Caraïbes et glace au caramel salé. **Wines** Montlouis, Bourgueil.

◆ A group of charming houses, near the famous Château des Dames offering attractive, peaceful, renovated guestrooms which are all different. Park with a vegetable garden. Elegant, comfortable dining rooms and attractive, shady terrace on the edge of the garden. Classical cuisine.

La Roseraie rm, rm, VISA
7 r. Dr Bretonneau – ✆ 02 47 23 90 09 – www.charmingroseraie.com – sfiorito@wanadoo.fr – Fax 02 47 23 91 59 – Open 3 April-4 November
18 rm – €53/125 €65/125, €10
Rest – *(closed Monday and lunch except Sunday)* Menu €27/44 – Carte €35/50
◆ A long building covered in Virginia creeper with spacious, air-conditioned guestrooms. Rustic decor and a welcoming feel. Garden and swimming pool. A country restaurant with a lounge with open fire and an emphasis on traditional cuisine.

CHENÔVE – 21 Côte-d'Or – 320 K6 – see Dijon

CHÉPY – 80 Somme – 301 C7 – pop. 1 277 – alt. 96 m – ✉ 80210 36 A1

Paris 207 – Abbeville 17 – Amiens 72 – Le Tréport 23

L'Auberge Picarde rm, VISA
pl. de la Gare – ✆ 03 22 26 20 78 – auberge-picarde@wanadoo.fr – Fax 03 22 26 33 34 – Closed 2 weeks in August and 1st-10 January
25 rm – €47/63 €52/69, €6,50
Rest – *(closed Saturday lunch and Sunday dinner)*
Menu (€14), €16 (weekdays)/31 – Carte €22/34
◆ The comfortable rooms in old or modern style are located opposite a disused station, in a rural environment. Billiards. A covered gallery converted into a winter garden leads to the rustic style restaurant. "Tradition et terroir" offerings on the menu.

CHÉRAC – 17 Charente-Maritime – 324 H5 – pop. 1 006 – alt. 54 m – ✉ 17610 38 B3

Paris 495 – Angoulême 59 – Poitiers 162 – Saintes 19

La Pantoufle
5 imp. des Dîmiers – ✆ 05 46 95 37 10 – http://lapantoufle.free.fr – lapantoufle@free.fr
3 rm – €50 €55 **Table d'hôte** – Menu €23 bi
◆ This typical Charente guesthouse with its comfortable rooms and pleasant lounge area with sofas and deckchairs in the enclosed garden constitutes a standing invitation to restful indolence. In the restaurant, the owner, an authentic cordon bleu cook, invariably delights her guests with culinary pleasures based on garden-fresh vegetables and local products.

CHERBOURG-OCTEVILLE – 50 Manche – 303 C2 – pop. 40 500 – Built-up area 117 855 – alt. 10 m – Casino BY – ✉ 50100 Normandy 32 A1

Paris 359 – Brest 399 – Caen 125 – Laval 224 – Le Mans 284 – Rennes 210
Cherbourg-Maupertus: ✆ 02 33 88 57 60, 11 km on the ①
Office de tourisme, 2 quai Alexandre III ✆ 02 33 93 52 02, Fax 02 33 53 66 97
de Cherbourg La Glacerie Domaine des Roches, by Valognes road and D 122: 7 km, ✆ 02 33 44 45 48
Fort du Roule ≤★ - Château de Tourlaville: park★ 5 km by ①.

Plan on next page

Le Louvre without rest VISA
2 r. H. Dunant – ✆ 02 33 53 02 28 – www.hotel-le-louvre.fr – inter.hotel.le.louvre@wanadoo.fr – Fax 02 33 53 43 88 – Closed 24 December-4 January AX **e**
40 rm – €56/62 €62/68, €8,50
◆ A central location, comfortable rooms, good soundproofing and a buffet breakfast are among the attractions of this family hotel.

La Renaissance without rest VISA
4 r. de l'Église – ✆ 02 33 43 23 90 – www.hotel-renaissance-cherbourg.com – contact@hotel-renaissance-cherbourg.com – Fax 02 33 43 96 10 ABX **a**
11 rm – €48/62 €54/74, €9 – 1 suite
◆ Cheerful, faultlessly kept rooms, smiling service, delicious breakfasts and reasonable prices.

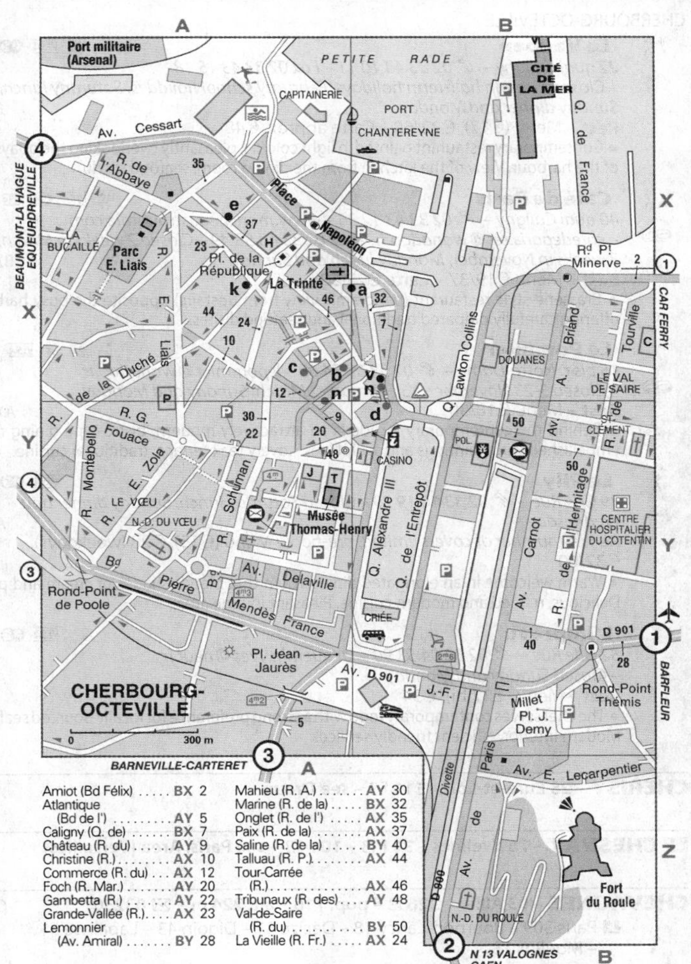

Amiot (Bd Félix)	BX	2
Atlantique (Bd de l')	AY	5
Caligny (Q. de)	BX	7
Château (R. du)	AY	9
Christine (R.)	AX	10
Commerce (R. du)	AX	12
Foch (R. Mar.)	AY	20
Gambetta (R.)	AY	22
Grande-Vallée (R.)	AX	23
Lemonnier (Av. Amiral)	BY	28
Mahieu (R. A.)	AY	30
Marine (R. de la)	BX	32
Onglet (R. de l')	AX	35
Paix (R. de la)	AX	37
Saline (R. de la)	BY	40
Talluau (R. P.)	AX	44
Tour-Carrée (R.)	AX	46
Tribunaux (R. des)	AY	48
Val-de-Saire (R. du)	BY	50
La Vieille (R. Fr.)	AX	24

Ambassadeur without rest
22 quai Caligny – ✆ 02 33 43 10 00 – www.ambassadeurhotel.com – ambassadeur.hotel@wanadoo.fr – Fax 02 33 43 10 01 – Closed 18 December-10 January BX **v**

40 rm – †€ 38/57 ††€ 49/68, ☕ € 6,50

◆ This quayside hotel provides well-equipped rooms. Those at the front overlook the port.

Angleterre without rest
8 r. P. Talluau – ✆ 02 33 53 70 06 – www.hotelangleterre-fr.com – contact@hotelangleterre-fr.com – Fax 33(0) 2 33 53 74 36 AX **k**

23 rm – †€ 37/47 ††€ 42/52, ☕ € 8 – ½ P € 42/47

◆ Near the town centre, a pleasant hotel with a family atmosphere and practical, neat little rooms. Entirely non-smoking.

Le Vauban

22 quai Caligny – ✆ 02 33 43 10 11 – Fax 02 33 43 15 18 – Closed autumn half-term holidays, February school holidays, Saturday lunch, Sunday dinner and Monday BX **n**

Rest – Menu (€ 17), € 22/60 – Carte approx. € 48

◆ Contemporary restaurant painted in light colours, pleasantly overlooking the quaysides of the harbour. View of the kitchen from the dining room; seafood menu.

Café de Paris

40 quai Caligny – ✆ 02 33 43 12 36 – www.manchegastronomie.com – cafedeparis.res@wanadoo.fr – Fax 02 33 43 98 49 – Closed 2 weeks in March, 3 weeks in November, Monday lunch and Sunday BXY **d**

Rest – Menu € 19/37 – Carte € 25/53

◆ Brasserie-style restaurant (panoramic view from upstairs) opposite the busy harbour, offering carefully prepared traditional and seafood dishes.

Le Pommier

15 bis r. Notre-Dame – ✆ 02 33 53 54 60 – lepommier@wanadoo.fr – Closed 3-23 November, 15 February-2 March, Sunday and Monday

Rest – Menu € 18/30 AXY **n**

◆ Behind the contemporary façade is an attractively modern, bistro-type dining room embellished with paintings and sculptures. Lovely teak terrace; traditional cuisine.

Le Pily

39 Gde Rue – ✆ 02 33 10 19 29 – Closed Saturday lunch, Sunday dinner and Wednesday AX **b**

Rest – *(number of covers limited, pre-book)* Menu (€ 15), € 28 (weekdays), € 32/60

◆ Warm welcome in an elongated dining room that blends shades of cream and plum. Delicious, refined and modern cuisine. Pleasant lounge area.

L'Imprévu

32 Gde Rue – ✆ 02 33 04 53 90 – jacquemin.yves@neuf.fr – Closed Sunday and Monday AX **c**

Rest – Menu (€ 17 bi), € 34

◆ The chef serves contemporary food with a strong preference for locally-sourced seafood. Modern interior, efficient friendly service.

CHERISY – **28 Eure-et-Loir** – **311** E3 – **see Dreux**

LE CHESNAY – **78 Yvelines** – **311** I3 – **101** 23 – **see Paris, Area (Versailles)**

CHEVAGNES – **03 Allier** – **326** I3 – **pop. 716** – **alt. 224 m** – ✉ **03230** 6 **C1**

Paris 309 – Bourbon-Lancy 18 – Decize 31 – Digoin 43 – Lapalisse 51 – Moulins 18

Le Goût des Choses

12 rte Nationale – ✆ 04 70 43 11 12 – Closed 26-30 October, Sunday dinner, Tuesday dinner and Monday

Rest – Menu (€ 17 bi), € 24/52 bi – Carte € 42/60

◆ Here, good taste is shown both by the food, prepared with seasonal market produce, and the dining room with its attractive decor and well-laid tables. Small inner courtyard terrace.

CHEVAL-BLANC – **84 Vaucluse** – **332** D11 – **see Cavaillon**

CHEVANNES – **89 Yonne** – **319** D5 – **see Auxerre**

CHEVERNY – **41 Loir-et-Cher** – **318** F7 – **see Cour-Cheverny**

CHEVIGNY – **21 Côte-d'Or** – **320** K6 – **see Dijon**

LE CHEYLARD – 07 Ardèche – 331 I4 – pop. 3 514 – alt. 450 m – ✉ 07160 44 A3

Paris 598 – Aubenas 50 – Lamastre 21 – Privas 47 – Le Puy-en-Velay 62 – Valence 59

Office de tourisme, rue du 5 Juillet 44 ☎ 04 75 29 18 71, Fax 04 75 29 46 75

Le Provençal rest, rm, VISA MC

17 av. de la Gare – ☎ 04 75 29 02 08 – www.hotelrestaurantleprovencal.com – contact@hotelrestaurantleprovencal.com – Fax 04 75 29 35 63 – Closed 13-29 April, 25 September-14 October, 26 December-12 January, Friday dinner, Sunday dinner and Monday

10 rm – €52 €62/80, €9 – ½ P €55/70

Rest – *(resident only)* Menu (€17), €23/55 bi – Carte €32/48

◆ A stone building housing small, simple, well-kept rooms. The bicycle shed is popular with cyclists biking along the corniche road above the Eyrieux. Sober, rustic dining rooms, traditional cuisine inspired by local produce and a selection of local wines.

CHÉZERY-FORENS – 01 Ain – 328 I3 – pop. 399 – alt. 585 m – ✉ 01200 45 C1

Paris 506 – Bellegarde-sur-Valserine 17 – Bourg-en-Bresse 82 – Gex 39 – Nantua 30

Commerce with rm VISA MC

– ☎ 04 50 56 90 67 – www.hotelducommerce-blanc.fr – Fax 04 50 56 92 54 – Open 1 March-30 September and closed 8-30 June, Tuesday dinner and Wednesday except school holidays

8 rm – €55/65 €55/65, €8 – ½ P €50/60

Rest – Menu €15 bi (weekdays)/50 – Carte €30/40

◆ An endearing establishment serving generous regional cuisine (frogs legs in season) in a countrified decor or on the terrace overlooking the fast-flowing Valserine. Small, well-kept rooms and warm hospitality.

CHILLE – 39 Jura – 321 D6 – see Lons-le-Saunier

CHILLEURS-AUX-BOIS – 45 Loiret – 318 J3 – pop. 1 866 – alt. 125 m – ✉ 45170 12 C2

Paris 96 – Orléans 30 – Chartres 71 – Étampes 47 – Pithiviers 14

Le Lancelot VISA MC AE

12 r. des Déportés – ☎ 02 38 32 91 15 – www.restaurant-le-lancelot.com – info@restaurant-le-lancelot.com – Fax 02 38 32 92 11 – Closed 3-24 August, 15-22 February, Wednesday dinner, Sunday dinner and Monday

Rest – *(pre-book Sat - Sun)* Menu (€16), €21 (weekdays)/68 – Carte €59/92

◆ Welcoming flower-decked, countrified restaurant situated in the centre of the village. Generous updated cuisine often inspired by old family recipes.

CHINAILLON – 74 Haute-Savoie – 328 L5 – see le Grand-Bornand

CHINDRIEUX – 73 Savoie – 333 I3 – pop. 1 198 – alt. 300 m – ✉ 73310 45 C1

Paris 520 – Aix-les-Bains 16 – Annecy 48 – Bellegarde-sur-Valserine 39 – Chambéry 33

Abbaye de Hautecombe★★ Southwest: 10 km, French Alps.

Relais de Chautagne rm, VISA MC

7 rte d'Aix – ☎ 04 79 54 20 27 – Fax 04 79 54 51 63 – Closed 24 Dec. - 10 Feb., Sun. evening and Mon.

25 rm – €45/48 €48/55, €9

Rest – Menu €15 (weekdays)/35 – Carte €30/58

◆ La Chautagne is the name of this small part of Savoy and also of a wine from the Mondeuse grape growing region. Family hotel with modest rooms. Traditional cuisine served in a large rustic dining room.

CHINON – 37 Indre-et-Loire – **317** K6 – **pop. 8 169 – alt. 40 m** 11 **A3**
– ✉ **37500** Châteaux of the Loire

▶ Paris 285 – Châtellerault 51 – Poitiers 80 – Saumur 29 – Tours 46

ℹ Office de tourisme, place Hofheim ✆ 02 47 93 17 85, Fax 02 47 93 93 05

Old Chinon★★: Grand Carroi★★ A E - Château★★: ⋞★★.

Château d'Ussé★★ 14 km by ①.

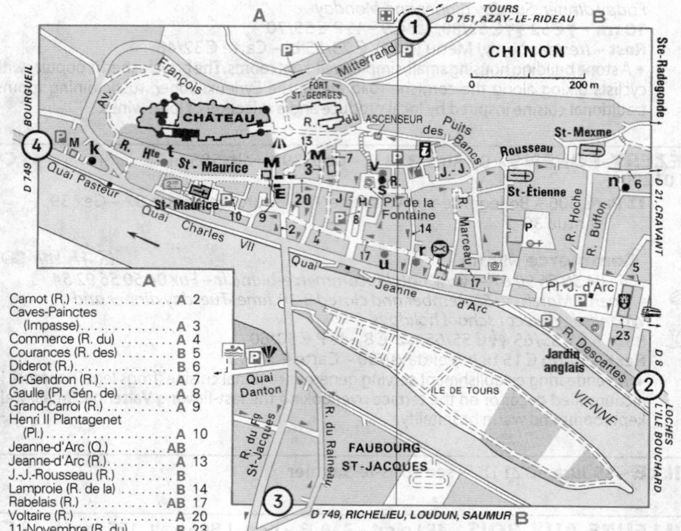

De France without rest
47 pl. Gén. de Gaulle – ✆ 02 47 93 33 91
– www.bestwestern-hoteldefrance-chinon.com – elmachinon@aol.com
– Fax 02 47 98 37 03 – Closed in February, in November and Sunday from November to March A **s**
30 rm – †€ 75/120 ††€ 75/125, ☕ € 10 – 3 suites
◆ Two semi-detached 16C houses with comfortable, well soundproofed, period furnished rooms. Some overlook the square and the castle. Pretty inner courtyard.

Diderot without rest
4 r. de Buffon – ✆ 02 47 93 18 87 – www.hoteldiderot.com
– hoteldiderot@wanadoo.fr – Fax 02 47 93 37 10
– Closed 18 January-5 February B **n**
25 rm – †€ 44 ††€ 55/77, ☕ € 8,50
◆ A fine 18C abode providing regularly spruced up guestrooms furnished in an old-fashioned manner. Table d'hôte style breakfast: farm produce and home-made jam.

Agnès Sorel without rest
4 quai Pasteur – ✆ 02 47 93 04 37
– www.agnes-sorel.com – pierre.catin@orange.fr – Fax 02 47 93 06 37 – Closed 10-31 January A **k**
10 rm – †€ 49/99 ††€ 49/99, ☕ € 8,50
◆ Set in the shadow of the medieval castle, this charming hotel bordering the Vienne has individually decorated rooms. The ones in the wing are larger and quieter. Courtyard garden. Bicycle shed.

XX **Au Chapeau Rouge**

49 pl. du Gén. de Gaulle – ✆ 02 47 98 08 08 – www.chapeaurouge.fr – chapeau.rouge@club-internet.fr – Fax 02 47 98 08 08 – Closed 26 October-17 November, 16 February-17 March, Sunday dinner and Monday A v

Rest – *(closed Sun. evening and Mon.)* Menu € 22 (weekday lunch), € 33/56 – Carte € 39/68

◆ In a shaded square, Le Chapeau Rouge boasts a tasteful décor. Its chef offers an interesting up-to-date menu that varies with the seasons (truffle menu in winter).

XX **L'Océanic**

13 r. Rabelais – ✆ 02 47 93 44 55 – oceanic.restaurant@club-internet.fr – Fax 02 47 93 38 08 – Closed 20-26 April, 27 August-3 September, 31 December-3 January, Sunday dinner and Monday A u

Rest – Menu (€ 16 bi), € 24/68 – Carte € 38/70

◆ Friendly seafood restaurant in a pedestrian street in the town centre. A lobster tank sits imposingly in the middle of the comfortable modern dining room.

X **Les Années Trente**

78 r. Voltaire – ✆ 02 47 93 37 18 – www.lesannées30.com – lebeaucharles@wanadoo.fr – Fax 02 47 93 33 72 – Closed 20-30 June, 16-28 November, 2-12 January, Tuesday except dinner from May to September and Wednesday

Rest – Menu € 27/45 – Carte € 38/54 A t

◆ In this restaurant in old Chinon, knick-knacks, small paintings and photos from the 1930s decorate the dining rooms. Contemporary repertory using fresh produce.

in Marçay 9 km by ③ **and D 116 – pop. 467 – alt. 65 m – ✉ 37500**

Château de Marçay

– ✆ 02 47 93 03 47 – www.chateaudemarcay.com – marcay@relaischateaux.com – Fax 02 47 93 45 33 – Closed 15-27 November and 18 January-13 March

29 rm – €135/335 €215/335, € 22 – 4 suites

Rest – *(closed Sunday dinner in low season, Thursday lunch and Monday except dinner in high season and Tuesday lunch)*

Menu € 63/98 – Carte € 70/95

Spec. Salade de légumes crus-cuits, pistou aux herbes et crevettes bouquet (May to Sep.). Agneau du Poitou aux aubergines en trois façons. Soufflé chaud à la pomme verte. **Wines** Chinon, Saumur-Champigny.

◆ This chateau remodelled in the 15C is all that remains of the original 12C military fortress. Wooded parkland with views over the vineyards (wine tasting) creates a charming setting. Elegant decor, fine cuisine with a contemporary touch, and a selection of Loire wines.

CHIROUBLES – 69 Rhône – pop. 354 – alt. 430 m – ✉ 69115 43 E1

Paris 422 – Lyon 59 – Villeurbanne 67 – Bourg-en-Bresse 60 – Caluire-et-Cuire 63

La Tour

1 km away, Bridge (Fleurie road) – ✆ 04 74 04 20 26 – www.mfjp.bernard.free.fr – mfjp.bernard@free.fr – Open from March to November

4 rm – €75 €85 **Table d'hôte** – Menu € 30 bi

◆ House full of character boasting pretty themed rooms: Romantic and Floral (in the tower), Retro and Pastoral. Pleasant view of the vineyards. Regional cuisine.

CHISSAY-EN-TOURAINE – 41 Loir-et-Cher – 318 D7 – see Montrichard

CHISSEAUX – 37 Indre-et-Loire – 317 P5 – pop. 575 – alt. 58 m – ✉ 37150 11 A1

Paris 235 – Tours 37 – Amboise 14 – Loches 33 – Romorantin-Lanthenay 63

XX **Auberge du Cheval Rouge**

30 r. Nationale – ✆ 02 47 23 86 67 – www.auberge-duchevalrouge.com – cheval-rouge@wanadoo.fr – Fax 02 47 23 92 22 – Closed 7 December-7 January, Monday and Tuesday

Rest – Menu € 25/55 – Carte € 40/58

◆ The former village café now houses a stylish restaurant whose modernised setting has gained a rustic simplicity (light shades). Charming leafy terrace.

CHITENAY – 41 Loir-et-Cher – **318** F7 – **pop. 989** – **alt. 90 m** – ✉ **41120** 11 **A1**

Paris 196 – Orléans 72 – Blois 15 – Romorantin-Lanthenay 39 – Vendôme 47

Auberge du Centre
pl. de l'Église – ✆ 02 54 70 42 11 – www.auberge-du-centre.com – contact@auberge-du-centre.com – Fax 02 54 70 35 03 – Closed 31 January-3 March
26 rm – €59/65 €65/72, €10 – ½ P €77/83
Rest – *(closed Sunday dinner off season, Tuesday lunch and Monday)*
Menu €24 (weekdays)/49 – Carte €37/50
◆ Village inn covered in Virginia creeper near the châteaux of the Loire. Modern, prettily decorated bedrooms. Tree and flower-filled garden. Bright, southern style restaurant offering a traditional menu.

CHOISY-AU-BAC – 60 Oise – **305** I4 – **see Compiègne**

Your opinions are important to us:
please write and let us know about your discoveries
and experiences – good and bad!

CHOLET – 49 Maine-et-Loire – **317** D6 – **pop. 54 200** – **alt. 91 m** 34 **B2**
– ✉ **49300** Châteaux of the Loire

Paris 353 – Ancenis 49 – Angers 64 – Nantes 60 – La Roche-sur-Yon 70

Office de tourisme, 14, avenue Maudet ✆ 02 41 49 80 00, Fax 02 41 49 80 09

de Cholet Allée du Chêne Landry, ✆ 02 41 71 05 01

Musée d'Art et d'Histoire★ Z **M.**

Plan on next page

Grand Hôtel de la Poste without rest
26 bd G.-Richard – ✆ 02 41 62 07 20 – www.sanbenedetto-hotel.com – contact@sanbenedetto-hotel.com – Fax 02 41 58 54 10 Z **e**
50 rm – €85/120 €100/160, €10
◆ This spanking new establishment is also the town's oldest hotel. A distinctive modern decor prevails in the lobby, bar, designer sitting rooms and spacious, pastel rooms.

All Seasons
45 av. d'Angers – ✆ 02 41 71 08 08 – www.all-seasons-hotels.com – h6924@accor.com – Fax 02 41 71 96 96 BX **t**
57 rm – €108/118 €118/128
Rest – *(closed Saturday and Sunday)* Menu €24 – Carte €32/47
◆ Once inside, you will forget the business zone next door. Find a warm interior in which old wood (from Canadian cabins) features prominently; modern, comfortable, well sound-proofed rooms. Pleasant room topped with a glass roof, contemporary interior and classic menu.

Du Parc without rest
4 av. A. Manceau – ✆ 02 41 62 65 45 – hotel.parc.cholet@wanadoo.fr – Fax 02 41 58 64 08 – Closed 21 December-6 January AY **x**
46 rm – €57/65 €57/65, €7
◆ This practical hotel is near Cholet Ice Rink. Pleasant, functional and well-soundproofed rooms. Large conference rooms. Buffet breakfast.

Demeure l'Impériale without rest
28 r. Nationale – ✆ 02 41 58 84 84 – www.demeure-imperiale.com – demeure.imperiale@wanadoo.fr – Fax 02 41 63 17 03 Z **t**
4 rm – €69 €76
◆ This 1860 mansion extends a warm welcome. Bright rooms adorned with flowers, luxurious linen and parquet floors. Breakfasts beneath a glass roof: homemade jams and cakes.

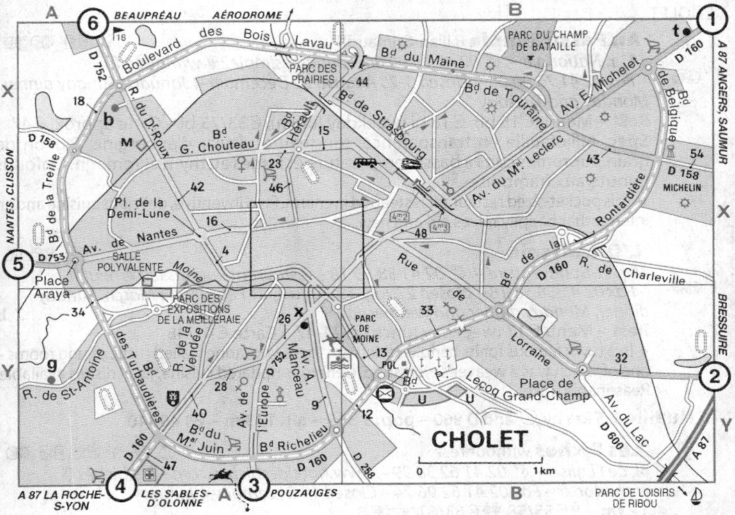

CHOLET

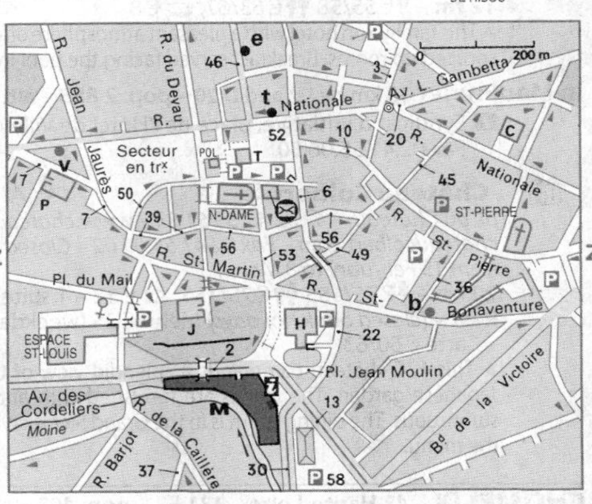

Street	Grid	No.
Abreuvoir (Av. de l')	Z	2
Bons Enfants (R. des)	Z	3
Bouet (Av. F.)	AX	4
Bourg Baudry (R. du)	Z	6
Bretonnaise (R.)	Z	7
Champagny (Av. du Cdt-de)	AY	9
Clemenceau (R. G.)	Z	10
Coubertin (Bd P.-de)	BY	12
Delhumeau-Plessis (Bd)	BY	13
Faidherbe (Bd du Gén.)	AY	15
Foch (Av. du Mar.)	AX	16
Godinière (Bd de la)	AX	18
Guérineau (Pl. A.)	Z	20
Hôtel de Ville (R. de l')	Z	22
Joffre (Bd du Mar.)	AX	23
libération (Av. de la)	AY	26
Marne (Av. de la)	AY	28
Maudet (Av.)	Z	30
Maulévrier (R. de)	BY	32
Minée (Bd de la)	BY	33
Moine (R. de la)	Z	36
Moinie (Bd de la)	AY	34
Montfort (R. G.-de)	Z	37
Nantaise (R.)	Z	39
Napoléon-Bonaparte (Av.)	AY	40
Nationale (R.)	Z	
Pasteur (R. L.)	AX	42
Poitou (Bd du)	BX	43
Pont de Pierre (Bd du)	AB	44
Puits de l'Aire (R. du)	Z	45
Richard (Bd G.)	Z	46
Sablerie (R.)	Z	49
Sables (Av. des)	AY	47
Sadi-Carnot (R.)	BX	48
Sardinerie (R. de la)	Z	50
Toutlemonde (R. de)	BX	54
Travot (Pl.)	Z	52
Travot (R.)	Z	53
Vieux Greniers (R. des)	Z	56
8-Mai-1945 (Pl. du)	Z	58

XX La Grange

64 r. de St-Antoine – ✆ 02 41 62 09 83 – Fax 02 41 62 32 89 – Closed 3-25 August, 15 February-2 March, Wednesday dinner, Sunday dinner and Monday

Rest – Menu € 18 (weekday lunch), € 26/39 bi – Carte approx. € 48,50 AY **g**

◆ Rural objects, exposed beams and a fireplace testify to the past history of the farmhouse where you can now enjoy carefully-prepared food with a contemporary touch at a reasonable price.

XX La Touchetière

41 bd Roux – ✆ 02 41 62 55 03 – www.restaurant-cholet.fr – latouchetiere@orange.fr – Fax 02 41 58 82 10 – Closed 2-21 August, Saturday lunch, Sunday dinner and Monday dinner AX **b**

Rest – Menu (€ 20), € 22/40 – Carte € 38/46

◆ Old inn that has been renovated while preserving its rustic character. Bright dining room with exposed beams, traditional menu. Open fireplace in the winter, flower-decked terrace in the summer.

Au Passé Simple (Lilian Grimaud)
181 r. Nationale – 02 41 75 90 06 – aupassesimple2@wanadoo.fr – Fax 02 41 75 90 06 – Closed 3-25 August, 22 December-4 January, Sunday dinner, Monday and Tuesday Z v
Rest – Menu (€ 15 bi), € 18 bi (weekday lunch), € 33/75 bi – Carte approx. € 47
Spec. Millefeuille en transparence, tourteau et caviar d'aubergine. Pigeon de grain, suprêmes cuits à basse température et fumés au thym et romarin. Clafoutis minute aux framboises.
◆ This pocket-sized restaurant is steeped in charm. Find inventive, delicious cuisine and an interior that happily mixes old and new.

L'Ourdissoir
40 r. St-Bonaventure – 02 41 58 55 18 – restaurant.l.ourdissoir@neuf.fr – Fax 02 41 58 55 18 – Closed 27 July-17 August, 21 February-3 March, Sunday dinner, Monday dinner and Wednesday Z b
Rest – Menu € 17 (weekday lunch), € 24/47 – Carte € 41/48
◆ In a town famous for its handkerchiefs are these two stone walled rustic dining rooms – one of which was a weaver's workshop. Generous updated cuisine, local dishes available. Reasonable prices.

in Nuaillé **7,5 km by ① and D 960 – pop. 1 317 – alt. 133 m – ✉ 49340**

Les Biches without rest
pl. de l'Eglise – 02 41 62 38 99 – www.hoteldesbiches.com – les-biches@wanadoo.fr – Fax 02 41 62 96 24 – Closed 19 December-4 January
12 rm – €55/58 €63/67, €8
◆ This family-run hotel with a pleasant atmosphere offers cheerful, well kept, and regularly spruced up rooms. Breakfast served facing the pool in summer.

in Maulévrier **13 km by ② and D 20 – pop. 2 855 – alt. 130 m – ✉ 49360**

Syndicat d'initiative, place de l'Hôtel de Ville 02 41 55 06 50, Fax 02.41.55.06.50

Château Colbert
pl. du Château – 02 41 55 51 33 – www.chateaucolbert.com – reception@chateaucolbert.com – Fax 02 41 55 09 02 – Closed 18-30 December, Sunday dinner from 15 February to 8 March
20 rm – €75/155 €75/155, € 12 – 1 suite – ½ P € 79/119
Rest – *(closed bank holidays)* Menu € 25 (weekday lunch), € 29/65 – Carte € 50/63
◆ This 17C château commands a splendid view of the oriental park and its gorgeous Japanese garden. The rooms are furnished with antiques; those on the first floor are sumptuous. The dining room is in the Grand Siècle style (17C); try the local specialities on the menu.

CHOMELIX – 43 Haute-Loire – 331 E2 – pop. 493 – alt. 910 m – ✉ 43500 6 C3

Paris 519 – Ambert 36 – Brioude 52 – Le Puy-en-Velay 30 – St-Étienne 77

Auberge de l'Arzon with rm — rm, rest
pl. Fontaine – 04 71 03 62 35 – Fax 04 71 03 61 62 – Open from May to September and closed Thursday lunch and Wednesday in July-August, Sunday dinner, Monday and Tuesday
9 rm – €55 €60/80, € 7 – ½ P € 56/70
Rest – Menu € 20 (weekdays)/47 – Carte € 24/40
◆ In the heart of the village, a stone building in a modern-rustic style serving classic cuisine. Uncluttered table settings; oak and mahogany furniture. Quiet, functional rooms in an outbuilding to the rear.

CHONAS-L'AMBALLAN – 38 Isère – 333 B5 – see Vienne

CHORANCHE – 38 Isère – 333 F7 – pop. 134 – alt. 280 m – ✉ 38680 43 E2

French Alps

Paris 588 – Grenoble 52 – Valence 48 – Villard-de-Lans 20
Grotte de Coufin★★.

Le Jorjane
Le village – 04 76 36 09 50 – www.lejorjane.com – info@lejorjane.com – Fax 04 76 36 00 80 – Closed 15-30 November, Sunday dinner off season and Monday
7 rm – €38/51 €38/51, €8 **Rest** – Menu €17/30 – Carte €18/35
◆ This small family-run inn in the famous village with seven caves has practical, well-kept rooms. Motor cyclists are made very welcome here. A rustic restaurant decorated with antiques. Covered roadside terrace. Traditional dishes, grills, salads, and pizzas.

CIBOURE – **64 Pyrénées-Atlantiques** – **342** C4 – **see St-Jean-de-Luz**

CINQ-CHEMINS – **74 Haute-Savoie** – **328** L2 – **see Thonon-les-Bains**

LA CIOTAT – **13 Bouches-du-Rhône** – **340** I6 – **pop. 31 900** – **Casino** 40 **B3**
– **13600** Provence

Paris 802 – Aix-en-Provence 53 – Brignoles 62 – Marseille 32 – Toulon 36

Office de tourisme, boulevard Anatole France 04 42 08 61 32, Fax 04 42 08 17 88

Calanque de Figuerolles★ Southwest: 1.5 km then 15 mn by D141 - N.-D. de la Garde chapel ★★ West: 2.5 km then 15 mn.

- to Île Verte ★ by boat 30 mn .

in Liouquet 6 km east by D 559 (Bandol road) – **13600 La Ciotat**

Auberge Le Revestel with rm
– 04 42 83 11 06 – www.revestel.com – revestel@wanadoo.fr – Fax 04 42 83 29 50 – Closed 2-17 December and 5 January-11 February
6 rm – €65 €65, €9 – ½ P €76
Rest – *(closed Sunday dinner and Wednesday)*
Menu (€26 bi), €40 – Carte €52/63
◆ This small colourful restaurant is well located on the coast road. The dining room's wide bay windows offer a clear view of the sea. Regional cuisine with a contemporary touch.

CIRES-LÈS-MELLO – **60 Oise** – **305** F5 – **pop. 3 548** – **alt. 39 m** 36 **B3**
– **60660**

Paris 65 – Beauvais 32 – Chantilly 17 – Compiègne 47 – Clermont 16 – Creil 12

Relais du Jeu d'Arc
pl. Jeu-d'Arc, 1 km east – 03 44 56 85 00 – www.relais-jeu-arc.com – jeudarc@cdno.org – Fax 03 44 56 85 19 – Closed August and 21 December-1st January
14 rm – €65/125 €65/125, €10 – ½ P €80
Rest – *(closed Sunday and Monday)*
Menu €18 (weekday lunch), €24/39 – Carte €40/48
◆ Former post house dating back to the 17C. The rooms are modern and comfortable, some with sloping ceilings. Traditional dishes served by the fireside in a pleasant dining room set up in the former stables. Terrace with a view of the castle.

CLAIRAC – **47 Lot-et-Garonne** – **336** E3 – **pop. 2 506** – **alt. 52 m** 4 **C2**
– **47320**

Paris 690 – Agen 42 – Marmande 24 – Nérac 35

Office de tourisme, 16, place Viçoze 05 53 88 71 59, Fax 05 53 88 71 59

L'Auberge de Clairac
12 rte Tonneins – 05 53 79 22 52 – www.aubergedeclairac.fr – aubergedeclairac@orange.fr – Closed for the Toussaint holiday and the February holiday, Sunday dinner, Tuesday dinner and Wednesday
Rest – Menu (€20 bi), €28 – Carte €29/41
◆ This 19C regional house is next to a former tobacco-curing barn. Local dishes with a contemporary touch are served in a pleasant dining room and on a pretty flower-filled terrace.

CLAM – 17 Charente-Maritime – 324 H7 – see Jonzac

CLAMART – 92 Hauts-de-Seine – 311 J3 – 101 25 – see Paris, Area

CLAMECY – 58 Nièvre – 319 E7 – pop. 4 570 – alt. 144 m – ✉ 58500 7 **B2**
Burgundy-Jura

Paris 208 – Auxerre 42 – Avallon 38 – Cosne-sur-Loire 52 – Dijon 145 – Nevers 69

Office de tourisme, 24, rue du Grand Marché ✆ 03 86 27 02 51, Fax 03 86 27 20 65

St-Martin church ★.

Hostellerie de la Poste rm, VISA
9 pl. E. Zola – ✆ 03 86 27 01 55 – www.hostelleriedelaposte.fr – hotelposteclamecy@wanadoo.fr – Fax 03 86 27 05 99
17 rm – €56/76 €56/76, €10 – ½ P €59/67
Rest – Menu €25 (weekdays)/37 – Carte approx. €42
◆ A former coaching inn in a small town where logs used to be spectacularly floated down the river. Smart, small bedrooms (new bathrooms), quieter to the rear. Comfortable dining room in part-classical, part-modern style. Dishes with a contemporary touch.

LES CLAUX – 05 Hautes-Alpes – 334 I5 – see Vars

CLÉMONT – 18 Cher – 323 J1 – pop. 640 – alt. 141 m – ✉ 18410 12 **C2**

Paris 187 – Orléans 72 – Bourges 62 – Vierzon 71 – Olivet 59

Domaine des Givrys
– ✆ 02 48 58 80 74 – www.domainedesgivrys.com – givrys@wanadoo.fr – Fax 02 48 58 80 74
5 rm – €62 €70 **Table d'hôte** – Menu €35 bi
◆ For nature lovers, this old farm in the heart of a vast estate is beside a lake and river. Romantic guestrooms. The region and conviviality take centre stage at the large oak table d'hôte.

CLÈRES – 76 Seine-Maritime – 304 G4 – pop. 1 266 – alt. 113 m – ✉ 76690 Normandy 33 **D1**

Paris 155 – Dieppe 45 – Forges-les-Eaux 35 – Neufchâtel-en-Bray 36 – Rouen 25 – Yvetot 39

Syndicat d'initiative, 59, avenue du Parc ✆ 02 35 33 38 64, Fax 02 35 33 38 64

Parc zoologique (zoo) ★.

in Frichemesnil 4 km Northeast by D 6 and D 100 – pop. 396 – alt. 150 m – ✉ 76690

Au Souper Fin (Eric Buisset) with rm rm, VISA
1 rte de Clères – ✆ 02 35 33 33 88 – www.souperfin.com – buisset.eric@wanadoo.fr – Fax 02 35 33 50 42 – Closed 3-27 August, Sunday dinner, Wednesday and Thursday
3 rm – €55 €65, €10
Rest – Menu €32 (weekdays)/54 – Carte €55/75
Spec. Saint-Jacques poêlées au beurre d'algues (Oct. to Feb.). Carré d'agneau rôti au four et jus réduit au confit d'ail. Millefeuille à la vanille.
◆ A pleasant restaurant with an elegant, modern decor. Well-prepared, up-to-date cuisine and a fine choice of wines. Terrace-pergola facing the garden side. Small, attractive guestrooms.

South 2 km on D 155 – ✉ 76690 Clères

Auberge du Moulin VISA
36 r. des Moulins du Tot – ✆ 02 35 33 62 76 – www.aubergedumoulin.org – marc.halbourg@orange.fr – Fax 02 35 33 62 76 – Closed 17 August-3 September, Tuesday except dinner from February to October, Sunday dinner and Monday
Rest – Menu (€17), €27/49 – Carte €37/53
◆ This friendly inn faces an old mill on the banks of a little river interspersed with watercress beds. The cuisine has a modern touch with local specialities. Terrace.

CLERMONT ⓢⓟ – 60 Oise – 305 F4 – pop. 10 797 – alt. 125 m – ✉ 60600 ▮ Northern France and the Paris Region 36 **B2**

▶ Paris 79 – Amiens 83 – Beauvais 27 – Compiègne 34 – Mantes-la-Jolie 101 – Pontoise 62

ℹ Syndicat d'initiative, 19, place de l'Hôtel de Ville ✆ 03 44 50 40 25, Fax 03 44 50 40 25

in Gicourt-Agnetz 2 km west by old Beauvais road – ✉ 60600 Agnetz

XX **Auberge de Gicourt**

466 av. Philippe Courtial – ✆ 03 44 50 00 31 – www.aubergedegicourt.com – aubergedegicourt@wanadoo.fr – Fax 03 44 50 42 29 – Closed 29 July-19 August, Sunday dinner, Tuesday dinner and Wednesday

Rest – Menu € 20/55 – Carte € 45/65

◆ Close to a forest, spruce rural inn serving traditional cuisine. Recently revamped country-style dining room. Inviting flower-decked summer terrace.

in Étouy 7 km Northwest by D 151 – pop. 772 – alt. 85 m – ✉ 60600

XXX ✿ **L'Orée de la Forêt** (Nicolas Leclercq)

255 r. Forêt – ✆ 03 44 51 65 18 – www.loreedelaforet.fr – info@loreedelaforet.fr – Fax 03 44 78 92 11 – Closed 1st August-3 September, 3-14 January, Saturday lunch, Sunday dinner, Friday and bank holiday evenings

Rest – Menu € 30 (weekday lunch), € 46/80 – Carte € 70/84

Spec. Foie gras poêlé au sirop de betterave. Pigeonneau rôti à la badiane, légumes du potager. Millefeuille vanillé.

◆ Imposing early-20C mansion, with attractive, elegant dining rooms and a peaceful park planted with trees. Charming service and fine cuisine with a contemporary touch.

CLERMONT-FERRAND Ⓟ – 63 Puy-de-Dôme – 326 F8 – pop. 139 300 – Built-up area 258 541 – alt. 401 m – ✉ 63000 ▮ Auvergne 5 **B2**

▶ Paris 420 – Lyon 172 – Moulins 106 – St-Étienne 147

✈ Clermont-Ferrand-Auvergne: ✆ 04 73 62 71 00 by D 766 CY : 6 km.

ℹ Office de tourisme, place de la Victoire ✆ 04 73 98 65 00, Fax 04 73 90 04 11

9 Nouveau Golf de Charade RoyatW : 8 km on D 5, ✆ 04 73 35 73 09

18 des Volcans Orcines La Bruyère des Moines, NW : 9 km, ✆ 04 73 62 15 51

Charade race circuit, St Genès-Champanelle ✆ 04 73 29 52 95 AZ.

◉ Old Clermont ★ EFVX : N.-D.-du-Port basilica ★★ (choir ★★★), Cathedral ★★ (stained-glass windows ★★), Amboise fountain ★, cour★ of the maison de Savaron EV - Courtyard ★ in the Hôtel de Fonfreyde EV **M**1, musée d'archéologie Bargoin★ FX - Old Montferrand★★ : hôtel de Lignat★, hôtel de Fontenilhes★, maison de l'Éléphant★, Courtyard ★ of hôtel Regin, door ★ of hôtel d'Albiat, - Bas-relief★ of Adam and Eve's house - Musée d'art Roger-Quilliot - Viewpoint of the D 941A ⋞★★ AY.

◎ Puy de Dôme ✵★★★ 15 km by ⑥ - Vulcania (Centre Européen du Vulcanisme). Parc Naturel régional des volcans d'Auvergne (Auvergne volcano nature park)★★★.

Plans on following pages

Novotel

Z.I. du Brézet, r. G. Besse ✉ 63100 – ✆ 04 73 41 14 14 – www.novotel.com – h1175@accor.com – Fax 04 73 41 14 00 CY **a**

131 rm – †€ 99/160 ††€ 99/160, ☕ € 15

Rest ***Le Jardin des Puys*** – Menu (€ 20), € 26 (weekdays) – Carte € 27/40

◆ The establishment is spacious, pleasantly decorated and well soundproofed. Book a renovated room if possible. Modern decor in the lobby and bar. The Jardin des Puys has a warm, trendy interior and a view of the pool and park.

Suitehotel without rest

52 av. de la République – ✆ 0 473 423 473 – www.suitehotel.com – H6306@accor.com – Fax 04 73 42 34 77 BY **c**

91 rm – †€ 109/142 ††€ 109/142, ☕ € 16

◆ New hotel with rooms offering a successful modern setting, designed to have a modular office area. Restaurant and business areas on the ground floor.

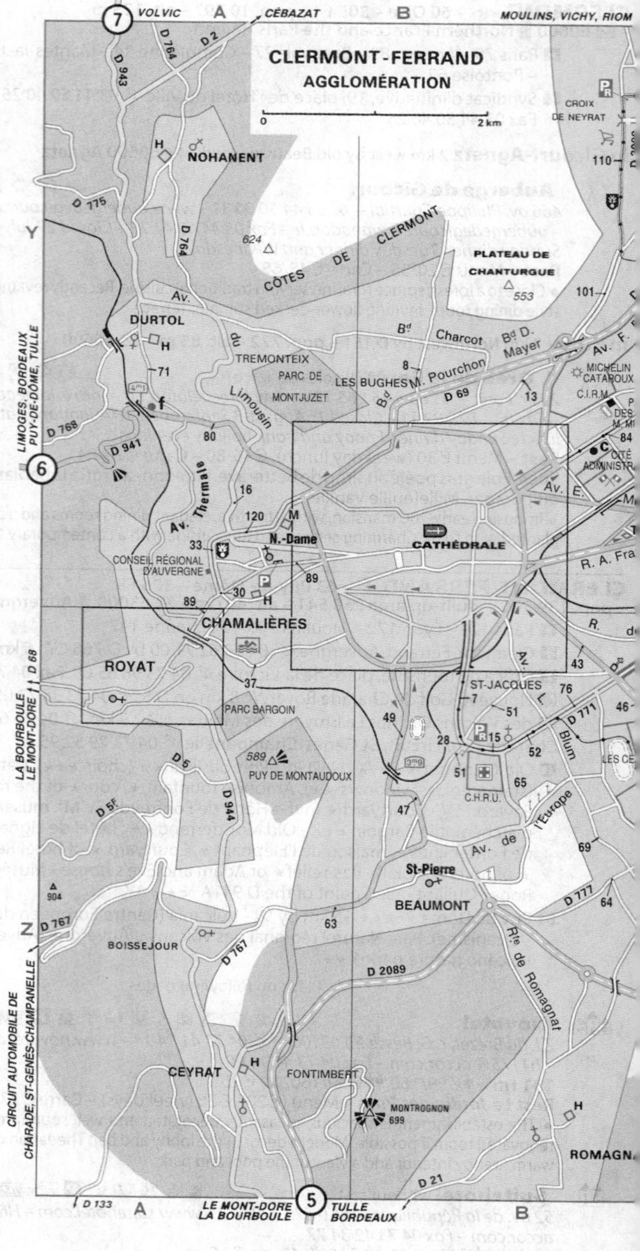

CLERMONT-FERRAND
AGGLOMÉRATION
0
2 km
VOLVIC
CÉBAZAT
MOULINS, VICHY, RIOM
A
B
Y
Z
NOHANENT
DURTOL
CÔTES DE CLERMONT
PLATEAU DE CHANTURGUE
553
624
CROIX DE NEYRAT
TREMONTEIX
PARC DE MONTJUZET
LES BUGHES
MICHELIN CATAROUX
C.I.R.M.
CITÉ ADMINISTR.
N.-Dame
CATHÉDRALE
CONSEIL RÉGIONAL D'AUVERGNE
CHAMALIÈRES
ROYAT
PARC BARGOIN
ST-JACQUES
C.H.R.U.
589
PUY DE MONTAUDOUX
St-Pierre
BEAUMONT
BOISSEJOUR
904
CEYRAT
FONTIMBERT
MONTROGNON
699
ROMAGN.
Av. du Limousin
Av. Thermale
Bd Charcot
Bd D. Mayer
Bd M. Pourchon
Av. de l'Europe
Av. L. Blum
Rte de Romagnat
R. A. Fra
LIMOGES, BORDEAUX PUY-DE-DÔME, TULLE
LA BOURBOULE LE MONT-DORE
CIRCUIT AUTOMOBILE DE CHARADE, ST-GENÈS-CHAMPANELLE
LE MONT-DORE LA BOURBOULE
TULLE BORDEAUX
D 943
D 764
D 2
D 775
D 768
D 941
D 68
D 5
D 5F
D 944
D 767
D 2089
D 69
D 771
D 777
D 21
D 133

AUBIÈRE

Cournon (Av. de). . . . . **CZ**
Maerte (Av. R.) . . . . **CZ** 55
Mont Mouchet (Av. du) . . **BZ** 64
Moulin (Av. Jean) . . . . . . **CZ**
Noellet (Av. J.). . . . . **BZ** 69
Roussillon (Av. du). . . . . . **CZ**

BEAUMONT

Europe (Av. de l'). . . . . . . **BZ**
Leclerc (Av. du Mar.). . . . . **BZ** 47
Mont Dore (Av. du) . . . . **ABZ** 63
Romagnat (Rte de) . . . . . **BZ**

CHAMALIÈRES

Claussat (Av. J.). . . . . **AY** 16
Europe (Carrefour de l') . . **AY** 30
Fontmaure (Av. de) . . . . . **AY** 33
Gambetta (Bd) . . . . **AZ** 37
Royat (Av. de) . . . . **AY** 89
Thermale (Av.). . . . . **AY**
Voltaire (R.) . . . . **AY** 120

CLERMONT-FERRAND

Agriculture (Av. de l'). . . . . **CY** 3
Anatole-France (R.) . . . . . . **BY**
Bernard (Bd Cl.). . . . . **BZ** 7
Bingen (Bd J.) . . . . **BCYZ**
Blanzat (R. de). . . . . **BY** 8
Blériot (R. L.) . . . . **CY** 10
Blum (Av. L.) . . . . **BZ**
Brezet (Av. du). . . . . **CY**
Champfleuri (R. de) . . . . . **BY** 13
Charcot (Bd) . . . . **BY**
Churchill (Bd Winston) . . . **BZ** 15
Clementel (Bd E.) . . . . **BY**
Cugnot (R. N.-J.) . . . . **CY** 22
Dunant (Pl. H.). . . . . **BZ** 28
La-Fayette (Bd). . . . . **BZ** 43
Flaubert (Bd G.) . . . . **CZ** 32
Forest (Av. F.). . . . . **BY**
Jean-Moulin (Bd) . . . . **CY** 39
Jouhaux (Bd L.). . . . . **CY** 40
Kennedy (Bd J.-F.). . . . . **CY** 41
Kennedy (Carrefour) . . . . . **CY** 42
Landais (Av. des) . . . . . . **BCZ** 46
Libération (Av. de la) . . . . . **BZ** 49
Limousin (Av. du) . . . . **AY**
Liondards (Av. des) . . . . . . **BZ** 51
Loucheur (Bd Louis) . . . . . **BZ** 52
Mabrut (R. A.) . . . . **CY** 53
Margeride (Av. de la). . . . . . **CZ** 58
Mayer (Bd D.) . . . . **BY**
Mermoz (Av. J.). . . . . **CY**
Michelin (Av. Édouard) . . . **BY**
Montalembert (R.) . . . . **BZ** 64
Oradour (R. de l') . . . . . . **BCZ**
Pochet-Lagaye (Bd P.). . . . **BZ** 76
Pompidou (Bd G.) . . . . **CY**
Pourchon (Bd M.) . . . . **BY**
Puy de Dôme (Av. du). . . . . **AY** 80
Quinet (Bd Edgar) . . . . **CY**
République (Av. de la). . . . . **BY** 84
St-Jean (Bd). . . . . **CY** 96
Sous les Vignes (R.) . . . . . . **BY** 101
Torpilleur Sirocco (R. du). . **BY** 110
Verne (R. Jules). . . . . **CY** 117
Viviani (R.) . . . . **CY**

DURTOL

Paix (Av. de la). . . . . **AY** 71

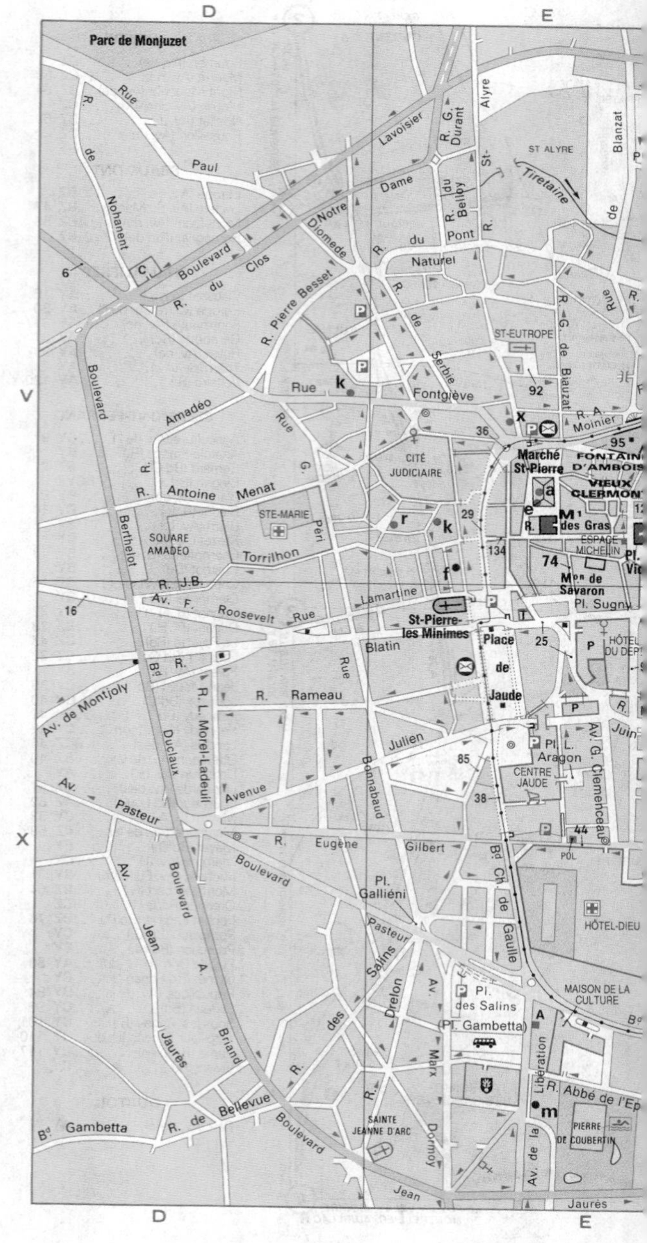
D
E
Parc de Monjuzet
Rue Paul
R. de Nohanent
Boulevard Lavoisier
R. G. Durant
Alyre
St-
ST ALYRE
Tiretaine
Blanzat
Dame
Notre
R. du Belloy
R. du Pont
Diomede
Naturel
R. du Clos
R. Pierre Besset
Boulevard
6
C
ST-EUTROPE
R. G. de Biauzat
R. de Serbie
Rue Fontgiève
Rue Amadéo
Rue G. Péri
92
R. A. Moinier
36
Marché St-Pierre
FONTAINE D'AMBOISE
VIEUX CLERMONT
CITÉ JUDICIAIRE
R. Antoine Menat
STE-MARIE
SQUARE AMADEO
Berthelot
Torrilhon
29
134
R. des Gras
ESPACE MICHELIN
74
Mon de Savaron
Pl. Sugny
R. J.B.
Av. F. Roosevelt
Lamartine
Rue Blatin
St-Pierre-les Minimes
16
Place de Jaude
25
HÔTEL DU DEPT
Bd R.
Av. de Montjoly
R. L. Morel-Ladeuil
R. Rameau
Julien
Duclaux
Pl. L. Aragon
CENTRE JAUDE
85
38
Av. G. Clemenceau
Av. Pasteur
Avenue
Bonnabaud
R. Eugène Gilbert
44
POL
Boulevard
Pl. Galliéni
Bd Ch. de Gaulle
HÔTEL-DIEU
Av. Jean Jaurès
Boulevard A. Briand
Pasteur
Salins
Drelon
Av. Marx
Pl. des Salins
(Pl. Gambetta)
MAISON DE LA CULTURE
R. des
Libération
R. Abbé de l'Ep
m
Bd Gambetta
R. de Bellevue
Boulevard
SAINTE JEANNE D'ARC
Dormoy
PIERRE DE COUBERTIN
Av. de la
Jean
Jaurès
V
X

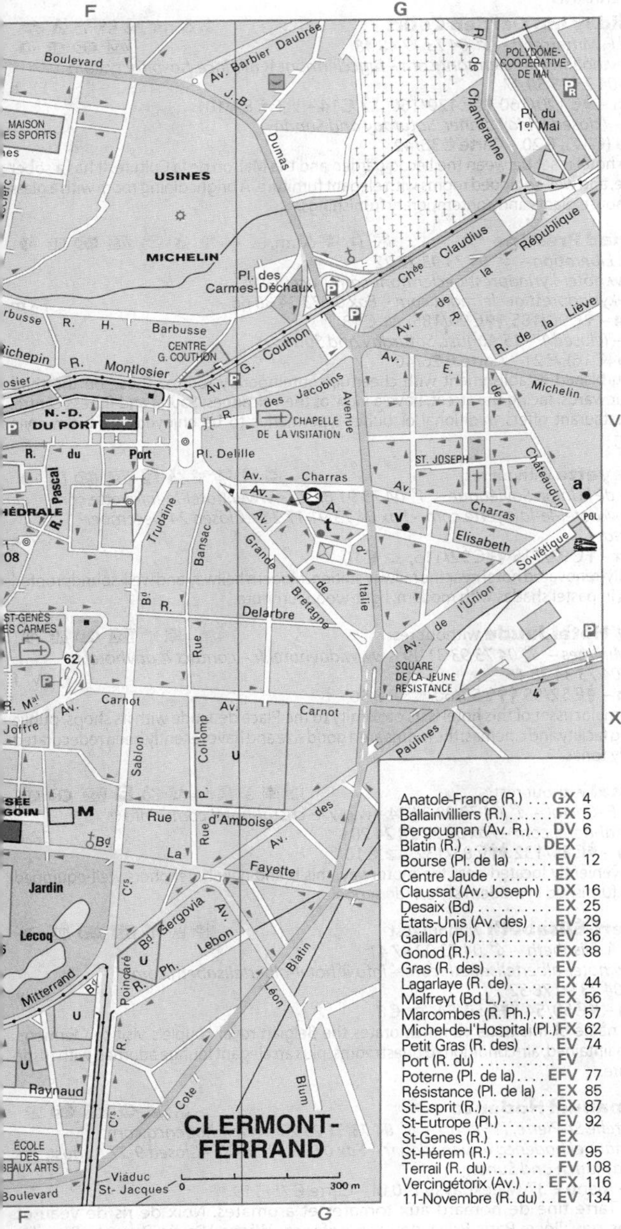
CLERMONT-FERRAND
F
G
V
X
Boulevard
Av. Barbier Daubrée
J.-B. Dumas
R. de Chanteranne
POLYDÔME-COOPÉRATIVE DE MAI
Pl. du 1er Mai
MAISON DES SPORTS
USINES
MICHELIN
Pl. des Carmes-Déchaux
Chée Claudius
Av. de la République
R. de la Lieve
R. H. Barbusse
CENTRE G. COUTHON
Av. G. Couthon
R. Montlosier
N.-D. DU PORT
R. des Jacobins
CHAPELLE DE LA VISITATION
Avenue d'Italie
Av. E. Michelin
Pl. Delille
R. du Port
R. Pascal
Av. Charras
ST. JOSEPH
Châteaudun
Av. Trudaine
Rue Bansac
Av. Grande Bretagne
Av. Elisabeth
Av. de l'Union Soviétique
R. Delarbre
ST-GENÈS DES CARMES
SQUARE DE LA JEUNE RÉSISTANCE
Av. Carnot
R. Mal Joffre
Rue P. Collomp
Sablon
Paulines
Rue d'Amboise
Av. des Fayette
Av. Gergovia
Av. Lebon
Blatin
Léon Blum
Jardin Lecoq
Bd Mitterrand
R. Ph. Marcombes
Poincaré
Raynaud
Cote
ÉCOLE DES BEAUX ARTS
Viaduc St-Jacques
Boulevard
300 m
Anatole-France (R.) . . . GX 4
Ballainvilliers (R.). . . . . FX 5
Bergougnan (Av. R.). . . DV 6
Blatin (R.) . . . . DEX
Bourse (Pl. de la) . . . . . EV 12
Centre Jaude . . . . EX
Claussat (Av. Joseph) . DX 16
Desaix (Bd) . . . . EX 25
États-Unis (Av. des) . . . EV 29
Gaillard (Pl.) . . . . EV 36
Gonod (R.). . . . . EX 38
Gras (R. des). . . . . EV
Lagarlaye (R. de). . . . . EX 44
Malfreyt (Bd L.). . . . . . EX 56
Marcombes (R. Ph.) . . . EV 57
Michel-de-l'Hospital (Pl.) FX 62
Petit Gras (R. des) . . . . EV 74
Port (R. du) . . . . FV
Poterne (Pl. de la). . . . EFV 77
Résistance (Pl. de la) . . EX 85
St-Esprit (R.). . . . . EX 87
St-Eutrope (Pl.) . . . . . . EV 92
St-Genes (R.) . . . . EX
St-Hérem (R.) . . . . EV 95
Terrail (R. du). . . . . FV 108
Vercingétorix (Av.) . . . EFX 116
11-Novembre (R. du) . . EV 134

Holiday Inn Garden Court

59 bd F. Mitterrand – 04 73 17 48 48 – www.holidayinn-clermont.com – higcclermont@alliance-hospitality.com – Fax 04 73 35 58 47

EX **a**

94 rm – €120/160 €120/160, €14 – ½ P €87/101

Rest – *(closed Friday dinner, Saturday and Sunday)*

Menu (€17), €20 – Carte €30/42

◆ The hotel is set between the Lecoq garden and the Maison de la Culture. It has a sober facade, and well equipped rooms with elegant furniture. A bright dining room with a glass roof, house plants and contemporary furnishings.

Kyriad Prestige

25 av. Libération – 04 73 93 22 22 – www.hotel-kyriadprestigeclermont.com – accueil@hotel-kyriadprestigeclermont.com – Fax 04 73 34 88 66

EX **m**

81 rm – €90/185 €90/185, €13

Rest – *(closed 1st- 15 August, Saturday and Sunday)*

Menu (€16), €21 – Carte €26/40

◆ Refurbished establishment with cheerful, contemporary rooms. Those on the third floor upwards, facing the street, have a view of the volcanoes. Sauna and fitness centre. The restaurant offers traditional or buffet-type menus to be enjoyed in a bistro-style setting.

Lafayette without rest

53 av. de l'Union Soviétique – 04 73 91 82 27 – www.hotel-le-lafayette.com – info@hotel-le-lafayette.com – Fax 04 73 91 17 26 – Closed 24 December-4 January

GV **a**

48 rm – €92/115 €92/115, €10

◆ A fully-renovated hotel near the railway station. Modern hallway and well-soundproofed rooms in pastel shades with modern, light-wood furniture.

Dav'Hôtel Jaude without rest

10 r. Minimes – 04 73 93 31 49 – www.davhotel.fr – contact@davhotel.fr – Fax 04 73 34 38 16

EV **f**

28 rm – €52/55 €55/60, €8,50

◆ The major asset of this hotel is its proximity to the Place de Jaude with its shops, public parking facility and cinemas; the rooms are a good size and have recently been redecorated in lively tones.

Cristal without rest

37 av. E.-Cristal – 04 73 28 24 24 – www.le-cristal-hotel.com – info@le-cristal-hotel.com – Fax 04 73 28 24 20

CZ **b**

79 rm – €85/132 €85/132, €10

◆ Conveniently located near the motorway, this brand new hotel offers well-equipped rooms furnished in modern style. Indoor pool.

Albert-Élisabeth without rest

37 av. A. Élisabeth – 04 73 92 47 41 – www.hotel-albertelisabeth.com – info@hotel-albertelisabeth.com – Fax 04 73 90 78 32

GV **v**

38 rm – €50/54 €50/54, €8

◆ The name of this hotel commemorates the Belgian royal couple's visit to Clermont. Well-maintained, air-conditioned guestrooms, plus an elegant lounge adorned with rustic furniture.

Emmanuel Hodencq

pl. Marché St-Pierre, (1st floor) – 04 73 31 23 23 – www.hodencq.com – emmanuel.hodencq@wanadoo.fr – Fax 04 73 31 36 00 – Closed 9-27 August, Monday lunch and Sunday

EV **a**

Rest – Menu €37 (weekdays)/140 bi – Carte €75/119

Spec. Tarte fine de homard aux tomates et aromates. Noix de ris de veau et girolles persillées. Paris-Brest de mon enfance. **Wines** Vin de Pays du Puy-de-Dôme.

◆ This inviting modern restaurant, set above the covered market, opens onto a fine leafy terrace. Tasty cuisine with a contemporary touch.

Jean-Claude Leclerc
12 r. St-Adjutor – ✆ 04 73 36 46 30 – www.restaurant-leclerc.com – jclaude.leclerc@wanadoo.fr – Fax 04 73 31 30 74 – Closed 18-25 May, 10 August-2 September, 2-9 January, Sunday and Monday EV **k**
Rest – Menu € 28 (weekday lunch), € 38/85 – Carte € 70/94
Spec. Tourteau en salade de mangue et avocat, langoustines rôties et pain basquais (summer). Faux-filet de Salers et pommes de terre fondantes au cantal, sauce périgueux. Poire rôtie, cigarettes parfumées et glace au lait d'amande (autumn). **Wines** Châteaugay, Saint-Pourçain.
◆ Take a seat in this elegant modern dining room, close to the law courts, and sample unusual, up-to-date dishes. Pleasant shaded terrace.

Amphitryon Capucine
50 r. Fontgiève – ✆ 04 73 31 38 39 – www.amphitryoncapucine.com – amphitryon63@hotmail.fr – Fax 04 73 31 38 44 – Closed 3-23 August, Sunday except bank holidays and Monday DV **k**
Rest – Menu (€ 22), € 28/75 – Carte € 55/65
◆ This small restaurant with a wooden façade has a renovated dining area with beams and a fireplace. Menus reflect current taste and change with the seasons.

Goûts et Couleurs
6 pl. du Changil – ✆ 04 73 19 37 82 – www.restaurantgoutsetcouleurs.com – Fax 04 73 19 37 83 – Closed 21-28 May, 9 August-31 August and Sunday EV **r**
Rest – Menu (€ 19), € 28/68 – Carte € 47/76
◆ Contemporary cuisine served in an attractive restaurant on a small square. Simple white and mauve decor, with paintings on the walls and a vaulted ceiling.

Brasserie Danièle Bath
pl. Marché St-Pierre – ✆ 04 73 31 23 22 – brasseriebath@orange.fr – Closed 9 February-2 March, 15-31 August, Sunday, Monday and bank holidays
Rest – Menu (€ 18), € 27/36 – Carte € 42/58 EV **e**
◆ This fine-looking dining room with its bistro-style decor is embellished with contemporary artworks. In summer, one can enjoy the terrace facing onto the square. The cuisine is traditional and wines may be ordered by the glass.

Fleur de Sel
8 r. Abbé Girard – ✆ 04 73 90 30 59 – http://perso.orange.fr/restaurantfleurdesel – fleurdesel63@wanadoo.fr – Fax 04 73 90 37 49 – Closed August, Christmas holidays, Sunday, Monday and public holidays FX **a**
Rest – *(number of covers limited, pre-book)* Menu € 30 (weekdays)/70 – Carte € 65/72
◆ Seafood and the day's specials served in a sunny dining room with contemporary furniture: this place has the wind in its sails.

Le Moulin Blanc
48 r. Chandiots – ✆ 04 73 23 06 81 – restaurant.lemoulinblanc@wanadoo.fr – Fax 04 73 23 29 76 – Closed 3-21 August, 2-4 January, dinner during the week, Saturday lunch and Sunday dinner CY **e**
Rest – Menu (€ 13), € 17 (weekdays)/42 – Carte € 31/42
◆ Comfortable, colourful dining room where modern decor and Louis XIII style chairs come together joyfully. Traditional food with a contemporary twist.

Le Comptoir des Saveurs
5 r. Ste-Claire – ✆ 04 73 37 10 31 – www.le-comptoir-des-saveurs.fr – lecomptoirdessaveurs63@neuf.fr – Fax 04 73 37 10 31 – Closed August, 3-12 January, 14-23 February, Tuesday dinner, Wednesday dinner, Thursday dinner, Sunday and Monday EV **x**
Rest – Menu € 25 (lunch), € 30/45
◆ Savour a daily-changing and varied menu, served in mini portions. An interesting dining concept in a contemporary setting.

L'Annexe
1 r. de Coupière – ✆ 04 73 92 50 00 – croixmama@wanadoo.fr – Fax 04 73 92 92 03 – Closed Saturday lunch, Sunday, Monday and holidays
Rest – Menu € 16 (lunch), € 25/40 – Carte € 32/50 GV **t**
◆ Industrial setting and modern, seasonal recipes sum up the spirit of this restaurant in an old printworks. Contemporary furniture and open kitchens.

in Chamalières – pop. 17 800 – alt. 450 m – ✉ 63400

Radio rest, VISA AE
43 av. P. et M.-Curie – ☎ 04 73 30 87 83 – www.hotel-radio.fr – resa@hotel-radio.fr – Fax 04 73 36 42 44 – Closed 1-11 November *Map of Royat* B **w**
26 rm – †€ 86/132 ††€ 96/142, ☕ € 13 – ½ P € 103/130
Rest – *(closed Monday lunch, Saturday lunch and Sunday)*
Menu (€ 39 bi), € 47/90 – Carte € 60/75
◆ Elegant 1930s Art Deco establishment. The large comfortable rooms are more contemporary. Original cuisine, a fine wine list and smart renovated decor that remains full of character.

in Pérignat-lès-Sarliève 8 km – pop. 2 553 – alt. 364 m – ✉ 63170
Plateau de Gergovie★: ★★ South: 8 km.

Hostellerie St-Martin VISA AE
– ☎ 04 73 79 81 00 – www.hostelleriestmartin.com – reception@hostelleriestmartin.com – Fax 04 73 79 81 01 CZ **s**
32 rm – †€ 90/205 ††€ 90/205, ☕ € 13 – 1 suite – ½ P € 85/143
Rest – *(closed Sunday dinner from October to March)*
Menu (€ 21 bi), € 28/44 – Carte € 37/64
◆ This fine residence in a 7ha park houses comfortable rooms with personal touches. Those in the annexe are more basic. A modern restaurant (the new chef has won the title 'Toque d'Auvergne') with an elegant decor and terrace.

Gergovie rm, VISA AE
25 allée du Petit Puy – ☎ 04 73 79 09 95 – www.bestwestern.fr – hotelgergovie@bestwestern.fr – Fax 04 73 79 08 76 CZ **b**
59 rm – †€ 85/150 ††€ 85/150, ☕ € 12 – 3 suites
Rest – *(closed Saturday and Sunday)* Menu (€ 18), € 25 (dinner) – Carte € 27/56
◆ Large modern hotel, recently built on the outskirts of town. Well-appointed, sober, designer-style rooms with air conditioning. Contemporary restaurant serving traditional cuisine. Attractive teak terrace for summer dining.

in La Baraque 6 km by ⑥ - ✉ 63870 Orcines

Le Relais des Puys rm, VISA AE
59 rte de la Baraque – ☎ 04 73 62 10 51 – www.relaisdespuys.com – info@relaisdespuys.com – Fax 04 73 62 22 09 – Closed 11 December-1 February, Sunday dinner in low season and Monday
36 rm – †€ 62/74 ††€ 62/74, ☕ € 9 – ½ P € 61/67
Rest – Menu (€ 16), € 19/46 – Carte € 29/56
◆ For seven generations, the same family has run this former stage-coach inn. The successfully renovated rooms offer every modern comfort. A large Volvic-stone fireplace helps to create an ideal environment in which to enjoy traditional fare and recipes from Auvergne.

in Orcines 8 km by ⑥ – pop. 3 254 – alt. 810 m – ✉ 63870
Office de tourisme, place de la Liberté ☎ 04 73 62 20 08, Fax 04 73 62 73 00

Les Hirondelles VISA AE
34 rte de Limoges – ☎ 04 73 62 22 43 – www.hotel-leshirondelles.com – info@hotel-leshirondelles.com – Fax 04 73 62 19 12 – Open 12 February-11 November and closed Sunday dinner, Tuesday lunch and Monday from February to March
30 rm – †€ 54/75 ††€ 54/75, ☕ € 9 – ½ P € 55/67
Rest – *(closed Monday lunch from October to November)*
Menu € 21 (weekdays)/46 – Carte € 27/40
◆ Former farmhouse, with a pretty name, on the edge of the Volcano Natural Park. Small, discreetly-decorated and well-soundproofed rooms. Dining room laid out in a converted stable with a vaulted ceiling. Auvergne cuisine.

Domaine de Ternant without rest
Ternant, 5.5 km north – ☎ 04 73 62 11 20 – http://domaine.ternant.free.fr – domaine.ternant@free.fr – Fax 04 73 62 29 96 – Open from mid March-mid November
5 rm ☕ – †€ 74/86 ††€ 82/94
◆ This 19C residence, at the foot of the Dôme mountains, stands in a park with more than 200 rose bushes. The rooms have family-type furnishings and colourful patchwork quilts. Tennis and billiards.

XX **Auberge de la Baraque**

2 rte de Bordeaux – ✆ 04 73 62 26 24 – www.laubrieres.com – geraldine@laubrieres.com – Fax 04 73 62 26 26 – Closed 5-22 October, 4-20 January, Monday, Tuesday, Wednesday and bank holidays

Rest – Menu € 26/51 – Carte € 33/60

◆ The cuisine created by the young owner of this former 1800s coaching inn is modern, simple, often reworked, and worth the detour. Served in a classic-style interior.

at the top of Puy-de-Dôme **13 km by ⑥ – ✉ 63870 Orcines – alt. 1 465 m**

XX **Mont Fraternité**

– ✆ 04 73 62 23 00 – Fax 04 73 62 10 30 – Open from early April to end October and closed Monday

Rest – Menu € 28/50 – Carte € 50/60

◆ This modern restaurant, brightened by large picture windows, is in a building also home to a museum, souvenir shop and bar. Tasty cuisine with a contemporary touch.

at col de Ceyssat **12 km by ⑥ and Puy-de-Dôme road– ✉ 63210 Ceyssat – pop. 467 – alt. 800 m**

X **Auberge des Muletiers**

– ✆ 04 73 62 25 95 – Fax 04 73 62 28 03 – Closed December, January, February, Tuesday, Wednesday from March to May, Friday lunch from July to September and Monday

Rest – Menu € 20/33 – Carte € 37/48

◆ A chalet-type building at the foot of the Puy de Dôme. Warm, rustic decor with a dresser and fireplace. Panoramic terrace. Regional dishes.

Look out for red symbols, indicating particularly pleasant establishments.

CLERMONT-L'HÉRAULT – 34 Hérault – 339 F7 – pop. 6 532 – alt. 92 m – ✉ 34800 Languedoc-Roussillon-Tarn Gorges

23 **C2**

Paris 718 – Béziers 46 – Lodève 24 – Montpellier 42 – Pézenas 22 – Sète 55

Office de tourisme, 9, rue Doyen René Gosse ✆ 04 67 96 23 86, Fax 04 67 96 98 58

St-Paul church ★.

XX **Le Tournesol**

2 r. Roger Salengro – ✆ 04 67 96 99 22 – www.letournesol.fr – azemard.christophe@wanadoo.fr – Fax 04 67 88 12 53

Rest – Menu € 16 (weekday lunch), € 22/36 – Carte € 29/76

◆ Town centre establishment offering a traditional repertoire drawing on local influences. Lovely veranda with teak furniture and terrace surrounded by tropical vegetation.

XX **Le Fontenay**

1 r. Georges-Brasssens, Lac du Salagou road – ✆ 04 67 88 04 06 – www.restaurant-fontenay.com – david.galtier@wanadoo.fr – Fax 04 67 88 04 06 – Closed 1-5 July, Sunday dinner Tuesday dinner and Wednesday

Rest – Menu € 16, € 26/55 – Carte € 50/60

◆ Building in a residential area with modern, colourful dining room and a pleasant inner terrace. Cuisine in keeping with current tastes and regional wines.

in St-Guiraud **7.5 km north by D 609, D 908, D 141 and D 130E – pop. 216 – alt. 120 m – ✉ 34725**

XX **Le Mimosa**

– ✆ 04 67 96 67 96 – www.lemimosa.blogspot.com – le.mimosa@free.fr – Open 6 April-4 November and closed lunch except Sunday, Sunday dinner except July-August and Monday

Rest – Menu € 56/84 bi – Carte € 68/96

◆ Set in the heart of the village in a house once owned by a wine-grower. Agreeably modern interior where one can enjoy dishes based on market-fresh, Mediterranean produce. Fine choice of Languedoc wines.

in St-Saturnin-de-Lucian 10 km north by D 609, D 908, D 141 and D 130 – pop. 288 – alt. 150 m – ✉ 34725

Grotte de Clamouse★★ Northeast: 12 km - St-Guilhem-le-Désert: site★★, abbey church★ Northeast: 17 km.

Du Mimosa without rest

10 pl. de la Fontaine – ✆ 04 67 88 62 62 – www.hoteldumimosa.blogspot.com – ostalaria.cardabela@wanadoo.fr – Fax 04 67 88 62 82 – Open from early April to early November

7 rm – †€ 68/95 ††€ 68/95, ☕ € 10

◆ Delightful hundred-year-old house on the village square. Spacious rooms with a blend of ultramodern furniture, old stonework and original fireplaces. Reception open from 5 pm on.

in Brignac 3 km east by D 4 – pop. 345 – alt. 60 m – ✉ 34800

La Missare without rest

9 rte de Clermont – ✆ 04 67 96 07 67 – http://la.missare.free.fr – la.missare@free.fr

4 rm ☕ – †€ 70 ††€ 70

◆ La Missare (which means dormouse in Languedoc) blends charm and tranquillity: spacious rooms, mottled furnishings, antique objects, pretty flower-decked garden, swimming pool and home-made breakfasts.

CLICHY – 92 Hauts-de-Seine – **311** J2 – **101** 15 – see Paris, Area

---

CLIOUSCLAT – 26 Drôme – **332** C5 – pop. 617 – alt. 235 m – ✉ 26270 44 **B3**

Paris 586 – Valence 31 – Montélimar 24

La Treille Muscate

in the village – ✆ 04 75 63 13 10 – www.latreillemuscate.com – latreillemuscate@wanadoo.fr – Fax 04 75 63 10 79 – Closed December and January

11 rm – †€ 65/150 ††€ 65/150, ☕ € 11 – 1 suite

Rest – *(closed Monday)* Menu € 21 (weekday lunch)/28 – Carte € 33/46

◆ This smart inn has plenty of charm: Provençal atmosphere, prettily individualised guestrooms and large orchards as a backdrop. Cliouscat pottery and furnishings from antique markets: the decor of the vaulted dining room is delightful. Cuisine with a southern flavour.

CLISSON – 44 Loire-Atlantique – **316** I5 – pop. 6 691 – alt. 34 m – ✉ 44190 Atlantic Coast 34 **B2**

Paris 396 – Nantes 31 – Niort 130 – Poitiers 151 – La Roche-sur-Yon 54

Office de tourisme, place du Minage ✆ 02 40 54 02 95, Fax 02 40 54 07 77

Site★ - Domaine de la Garenne-Lemot★.

La Bonne Auberge

1 r. O. de Clisson – ✆ 02 40 54 01 90 – labonneauberge2@wanadoo.fr – Fax 02 40 54 08 48 – Closed 11 August-3 September, 1st-20 January, Tuesday lunch, Sunday dinner, Wednesday dinner and Monday

Rest – Menu (€ 25), € 42/62 – Carte € 61/80

◆ Comfortable house with three pleasant, well kept dining rooms (light wood), one of which is a veranda giving onto the small garden. Classical menu.

in Gétigné 3 km southeast by D 149 and secondary road – pop. 3 279 – alt. 26 m – ✉ 44190

La Gétignière

3 r. Navette – ✆ 02 40 36 05 37 – Fax 02 40 54 24 76 – Closed 31 July-10 August, 25 December-1st January, Sunday dinner, Tuesday dinner and Monday

Rest – Menu € 22 (weekday lunch), € 28/45 – Carte € 55/71

◆ Wooden panelling, white boat style awnings and a profusion of plants and flowers. Enjoy modern cuisine in a contemporary dining room.

CLOHARS-FOUESNANT – 29 Finistère – **308** G7 – see Bénodet

CLOYES-SUR-LE-LOIR – 28 Eure-et-Loir – 311 D8 – pop. 2 641 – alt. 97 m – ✉ 28220 Châteaux of the Loire 11 **B2**

Paris 146 – Blois 54 – Orléans 64 – Vendôme 30

Office de tourisme, 11, place Gambetta, Fax 02 37 98 55 27

Le St-Jacques

pl. du Marché aux Oeufs – 02 37 98 40 08 – www.lesaintjacques.fr – info@lesaintjacques.fr – Fax 02 37 98 32 63 – Closed 15-22 November, 23 December-25 January, Sunday and Monday from November to Easter

18 rm – €65/145 €65/170, €13 – ½ P €75/95

Rest – *(Closed Sunday dinner, Tuesday lunch, Wednesday lunch and Monday)* Menu (€20), 28

◆ Tucked away in a garden on the banks of the Loire, this former post house dating from the 16C offers restful rooms that are gradually being renovated. Traditional menu offered in the classic dining room and on the shaded terrace on fine days.

CLUNY – 71 Saône-et-Loire – 320 H11 – pop. 4 543 – alt. 248 m – ✉ 71250 Burgundy-Jura 8 **C3**

Paris 384 – Mâcon 25 – Chalon-sur-Saône 49 – Montceau-les-Mines 44 – Tournus 33

Office de tourisme, 6, rue Mercière 03 85 59 05 34, Fax 03 85 59 06 95

Former abbey★★ : clocher de l'Eau Bénite (Eau Bénite belltower)★★ - Musée Ochier (Ochier Museum)★ **M** - Clocher (Belltower)★ of the église St-Marcel (St Marcel's Church).

Château de Cormatin★★ (St-Cécile study ★★★) North: 13 KM - Taizé Community North: 10 km.

Avril (R. d')	2
Conant (Espace K. J.)	3
Filaterie (R.)	4
Gaulle (Av. Ch.-de)	5
Lamartine (R.)	6
Levée (R. de la)	8
Marché (Pl. du)	9
Mercière (R.)	12
Prud'hon (R.)	14
Pte des Prés (R.)	13
République (R.)	15

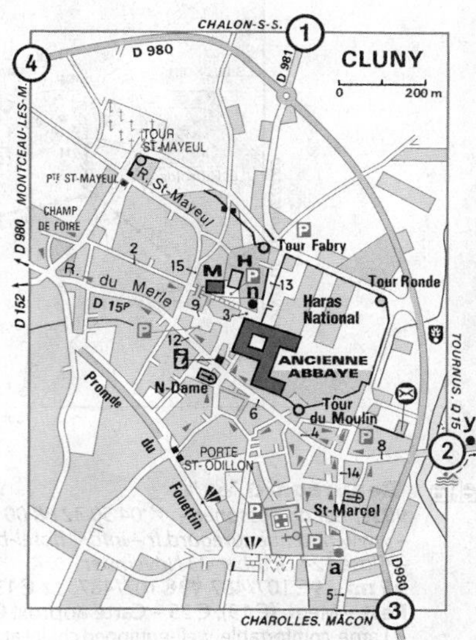

De Bourgogne

pl. l'Abbaye – 03 85 59 00 58 – www.hotel-cluny.com – contact@hotel-cluny.com – Fax 03 85 59 03 73 – Closed 1st December-31 January **n**

14 rm – €87 €97/127, €11 – 2 suites

Rest – *(closed Tuesday and Wednesday)* Menu €25/45 – Carte €40/55

◆ Lamartine stopped over in this interesting town house facing the Benedictine abbey. There is a pleasant lounge and a choice of diversely furnished rooms. Chequered flooring, light coloured walls, Louis XVI chairs and a stone fireplace make up the decor of the restaurant. The cuisine is traditional.

St-Odilon without rest

rte d'Azé – ✆ 03 85 59 25 00 – www.hotelsaintodilon.com – contact@hotelsaintodilon.com – Fax 03 85 59 06 18 y

36 rm – €53 €53, ☕ €7

◆ You will appreciate the country atmosphere in this motel near the Grosne bridge. Small, discreet bedrooms decorated with functional furniture.

Auberge du Cheval Blanc

1 r. Porte de Mâcon – ✆ 03 85 59 01 13 – chevalblanc.auberge@orange.fr – Fax 03 85 59 13 32 – Open from mid-March to November and closed 1-13 July, dinner in March and November, Friday dinner and Saturday a

Rest – Menu €18/41 – Carte €28/39

◆ This inn designed in the local style stands at the entrance to the town. Traditional dishes are served in the restaurant, which features rafters and a high, turquoise-tinted ceiling; the walls are enlivened by festive countryside murals.

LA CLUSAZ – 74 Haute-Savoie – 328 L5 – pop. 2 023 – alt. 1 040 m 46 F1

– Winter sports : 1 100/2 600 m 6 49 – ✉ 74220 French Alps

Paris 564 – Albertville 40 – Annecy 32 – Chamonix-Mont-Blanc 60

Office de tourisme, 161, place de l'église ✆ 04 50 32 65 00, Fax 04 50 32 65 01

East: Vallon des Confins★ - Manigod Valley ★ S - Col des Aravis ≤★★ by ②: 7.5 km.

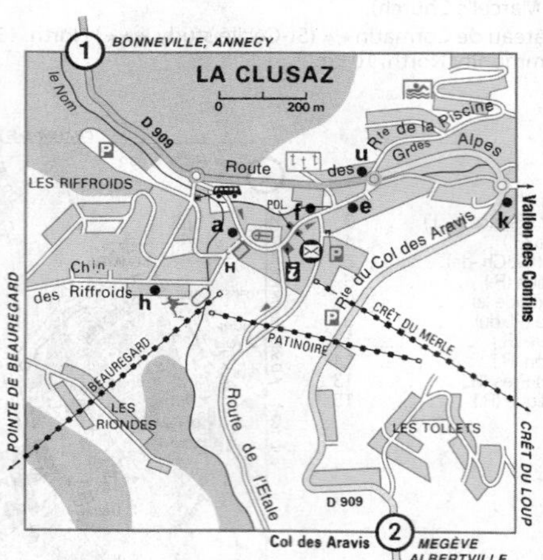

Beauregard rm, rest,

90 sentier du Bossonet – ✆ 04 50 32 68 00 – www.hotel-beauregard.fr – info@hotel-beauregard.fr – Fax 04 50 02 59 00 – Closed 24 October-23 November k

95 rm – €107/487 €107/487, ☕ €13 – ½ P €90/280

Rest – Menu (€19), €25 – Carte approx. €28 lunch only

◆ Large, comfortable, well-equipped chalet at the foot of the ski runs; spacious lounge-bar (billiards), indoor pool and fitness facilities. Light-coloured wood interior, rooms with balcony. Simple, traditional dishes served on the south-facing terrace, weather permitting.

Les Sapins

– ✆ 04 50 63 33 33 – www.clusaz.com – sapins@clusaz.com – Fax 04 50 63 33 34 – Open 16 June-9 September and 19 December-14 April h

24 rm – €55/80 €65/115, ☕ €10 – ½ P €57/122 **Rest** – Menu €22/26

◆ Facing the Aravis mountains, this chalet's alpine-style rooms feature light-coloured woodwork and lively colours; many have a balcony. Direct access to the slopes. Dig into tartiflettes and fondues served against a backdrop of snow-capped peaks.

Alp'Hôtel
192 rte col des Aravis – ✆ 04 50 02 40 06 – www.clusaz.com – alphotel@clusaz.com – Fax 04 50 02 60 16 – Open 1st June-29 September and 2 December-24 April e
15 rm – €70/210 €80/250, €12 **Rest** – Menu €25/64 – Carte €45/60
◆ Situated in the centre of La Clusaz, this chalet has rooms furnished in typical Savoy style, each with its own balcony. Lounge with an open fireplace. Regional cuisine with personal touches, served on the south-facing terrace in summer.

La Montagne
– ✆ 04 50 63 38 38 – www.clusaz.com – montagne@clusaz.com – Fax 04 50 63 38 39 u
27 rm – €60/160 €70/180, €10
Rest – *(Closed Sunday dinner in low season)* Menu (€29) – Carte €34/50
◆ Standard winter-sports resort architecture. All-wood interior with cosy, generously proportioned rooms, nice vaulted bar with fireplace and lounge with billiards table. Restaurant with a panoramic view and terrace. Traditional and regional cooking.

Christiania
– ✆ 04 50 02 60 60 – www.hotelchristiania.fr – contact@hotelchristiania.fr – Fax 04 50 32 66 98 – Open 4 July-14 September and 20 December-15 April f
28 rm – €48/88 €58/130, €10 – ½ P €54/100
Rest – *(closed Tuesday in Winter)* Menu €20/28 – Carte €28/35
◆ A well-maintained family-run country hotel. Practical, renovated, panelled rooms, some with a terrace. Traditional food and cheese recipes served in a simple rustic dining room.

Les Airelles
33 pl. de l'Église – ✆ 04 50 02 40 51 – www.clusaz.com – airelles@clusaz.com – Fax 04 50 32 35 33 – Closed end-April to mid-May and 1-15 December a
14 rm – €60/100 €60/100, €10 – ½ P €60/115
Rest – *(closed 15 November-15 December)* Menu (€15), €22/27 – Carte €28/45
◆ A well located unpretentious hotel near the church and at the foot of the slopes. Small rooms, most have balconies with flowers in the summer. Sauna, Jacuzzi. Restaurant popular for its rustic interior, friendly atmosphere and delicious Savoy cooking.

in Crêt du Loup by chairlifts Crêt du Merle and Crêt du Loup

Le Relais de l'Aiguille
– ✆ 06 19 50 60 68 – aiguille@orange.fr – Open 15 December-30 April
Rest – *(lunch only) (pre-book)* Carte €45/75
◆ Robust wooden furniture, plates hewn from slate: the rustic informality of its setting and the good home cooking make this high-altitude chalet very popular.

Col des Aravis road 4 km by ② – ✉ 74220 La Clusaz

Les Chalets de la Serraz rest,
3862 rte du Col des Aravis – ✆ 04 50 02 48 29 – www.laserraz.com – contact@laserraz.com – Fax 04 50 02 64 12 – Closed 19 April-20 May and 27 September-7 November
10 rm – €100/165 €125/220, €17 – ½ P €95/175
Rest – *(closed lunch except Sunday)* Menu €32/43 – Carte approx. €44
◆ An old farmhouse with stylish rooms all with mountain views. Cosy lounge-bar, hammam and Jacuzzi. Small chalets in the garden providing duplex accommodation. Traditional cuisine and selected wines in a typically Savoyard decor.

LA CLUSE – 01 Ain – **328** G3 – see Nantua

CLUSES – 74 Haute-Savoie – **328** M4 – pop. 18 100 – alt. 486 m 46 **F1**
– ✉ 74300 French Alps

Paris 570 – Annecy 56 – Chamonix-Mont-Blanc 41 – Thonon-les-Bains 59
Office de tourisme, 100, place du 11 Novembre ✆ 04 50 98 31 79, Fax 04 50 96 46 99
Church★ font.

CLUSES

Bargy (R. du) . . . . AZ 3
Berthelot (R. M.) . . . . BZ 4
Chautemps (R. E.) . . . . BZ 7
Colomby (Av. de) . . . . AY 9
Deuxième Div. Blindée
(R. de la) . . . . BY 12
Europe (Carrefour de l') . . . . . BY 13
Ferrié (R. du Gén.) . . . . BZ 15
Gaillard (Av. A.) . . . . AY 18
Gare (Av. de la) . . . . BZ 19
Gaulle (Pl. Ch.-de) . . . . BZ 20
Grande Rue . . . . BZ 22
Grands Champs (R. des) . . . . BY 24
Grand Massif (Av. du) . . . . . . BY 21
Hugard (R. Cl.) . . . . BZ 25
Lattre-de-Tassigny
(R. du Mar.-de) . . . . AY 27
Leclerc (R. du Mar.) . . . . BZ 28
Libération (Av. de la) . . . . . . BZ 30
Louis Armand (R.) . . . . AY 31
Luther King (R. M.) . . . . AY 33
Lycée (R. du) . . . . BZ 34
Mont-Blanc (Rd-Pt du) . . . . . . BZ 37
Pasteur (R.) . . . . BZ 39
Pointe de la Cupoire (R. de la) BY 43
Pointe de la Lanche (R. de la) BY 40
Pointe du Criou (R. de la) . . . BY 42
Pont (R. du) . . . . AY 51
Prairie (R. de la) . . . . BY 48
Pré Benevix (R. du) . . . . BZ 49
Tête de Colonney (R. de la) . BY 52
Trappier (R. P.) . . . . AY 57
8-Mai-1945 (R. du) . . . . BZ 59

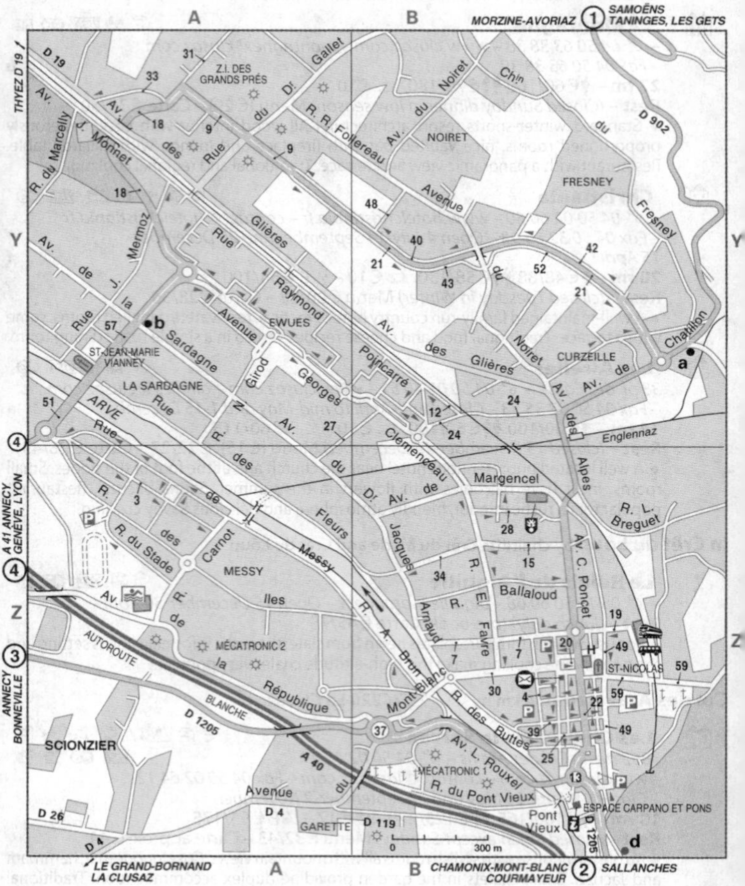

4 C rm, VISA

301 bd Chevran – ✆ 04 50 98 01 00 – www.hotel-4c.com – hotel.4c@orange.fr – Fax 04 50 98 32 20 BY **a**

38 rm – †€ 73/84 ††€ 80/94, ☕ € 10

Rest – *(closed 29 July-1 September, Saturday and Sunday)*

Menu (€ 13), € 16 (lunch)/32 – Carte € 22/51

◆ Slightly away from the centre, this hotel has functional rooms with small balconies (except three) overlooking the countryside. Outdoor Jacuzzi. A large restaurant with sober modern decoration and a fine terrace serving pizzas, pasta and traditional dishes.

Le Bargy
28 av. Sardagne – ✆ 04 50 98 01 96 – www.le-bargy.com – le.bargy@wanadoo.fr – Fax 04 50 98 23 24 AY **b**
30 rm – €64/68 €64/68, ☕ €8,50 – ½ P €84/87
Rest ***Le Cercle des Songes*** – *(Closed 18-24 May, 3-23 August, 24 December-3 January, Sunday from 18 January to 31 March and Saturday)* Menu (€13), €16 (weekdays)/33 – Carte €31/42
◆ Near the town centre, this family establishment has spacious, well-soundproofed rooms, all with a sofa to sit and unwind. Full range of traditional dishes served in a comfortable and subdued setting. Brasserie-bar for quick meals.

Saint-Vincent
14 r. Fg St Vincent, 200 m via ② – ✆ 04 50 96 17 47 – www.le-saint-vincent.com – restaurant@le-saint-vincent.com – Fax 04 50 96 83 75 – Closed 9-23 August, Saturday lunch and Sunday BZ **d**
Rest – Menu (€17), €21 (lunch)/55 – Carte €38/52
◆ Old regional-style inn with a warm interior, semi-rustic, semi-modern. Serves seasonal cuisine based on local produce.

COCHEREL – **27 Eure** – **304** I7 – **see Pacy-sur-Eure**

COCURÈS – **48 Lozère** – **330** J8 – **see Florac**

COGNAC – **16 Charente** – **324** I5 – **pop. 19 400** – **alt. 25 m** – ✉ **16100** **Atlantic Coast** 38 **B3**

Paris 478 – Angoulême 45 – Bordeaux 120 – Niort 83 – Saintes 27
Office de tourisme, 16, rue du 14 juillet ✆ 05 45 82 10 71, Fax 05 45 82 34 47
Du Cognac Saint-Brice La Maurie, E : 8 km on the Bourg-de-Charente road, ✆ 05 45 32 18 17

Plan on following page

Le Valois without rest
35 r. du 14-Juillet – ✆ 05 45 36 83 00 – hotel.le.valois@wanadoo.fr – Fax 05 45 36 83 01 – Closed 24 December-3 January Z **a**
45 rm – €68 €75, ☕ €8,50
◆ A recent building situated near famous wine and cognac estates. Spacious bedrooms decorated with functional furniture. Modern sitting room-bar in the lobby.

Héritage
25 r. d'Angoulême – ✆ 05 45 82 01 26 – www.hheritage.com – hotel.heritage@wanadoo.fr – Fax 05 45 82 20 33 – Closed 31 December-2 January Y **z**
19 rm – €65 €70, ☕ €8
Rest – *(Closed Monday from 15 September to 31 March and Sunday)* Carte €25/50
◆ A mixture of styles, antique furniture and striking colours liven up the Second Empire architecture of this small mansion. Extremely well-designed theme rooms. Both the food and the decor are an original sparkling blend of countless influences.

Les Pigeons Blancs with rm
110 r. J.-Brisson – ✆ 05 45 82 16 36 – www.pigeons-blancs.com – pigeonsblancs@wanadoo.fr – Fax 05 45 82 29 29 – Closed 15-30 November and Sunday dinner from October to April Y **d**
6 rm – €60/85 €70/100, ☕ €12 – ½ P €65/95
Rest – *(closed Sunday dinner and Monday lunch)*
Menu (€25), €36/59 – Carte €50/75
◆ 17C post house which benefits from the quiet of a residential area. Comfortable dining room, bedrooms with a personal touch and a pergola-terrace that looks onto the garden.

La Courtine
allée Fichon, parc François 1er – ✆ 05 45 82 34 78 – www.restaurant-la-courtine.fr – lacourtinecognac@wanadoo.fr – Fax 05 45 82 05 50 – Closed 24 December-14 January Y **t**
Rest – Menu (€20), €27 bi – Carte €27/40
◆ This former open-air dance hall in a park on the banks of the Charente has a warm, wood decor. It serves traditional dishes and grills. There is a sheltered terrace, musical evenings and riverside walks.

COGNAC

Street	Zone	No.
Angoulême (R. d')	Y	
Armes (Pl. d')	Y	
Bazoin (R. Abel)	Y	6
Boucher (R. Cl.)	Y	7
Briand (R. A.)	Y	
Canton (R. du)	Y	8
Champ de Mars (Allées du)	Z	9
Château (Quai du)	Y	10
Cordeliers (R. des)	Y	11
Corderie (Allées de la)	Z	12
François-1er (R.)	Y	13
Germain (R. H.)	Y	14
Grande Rue	Y	15
Isle d'Or (R. de l')	Y	16
Lusignan (R. de)	Y	20
Magdeleine (R.)	Y	21
Martell (Pl. Ed.)	Z	22
Monnet (Pl. Jean)	Z	23
Palais (R. du)	Y	24
Victor-Hugo (Av.)	Z	
14-Juillet (R. du)	Z	26

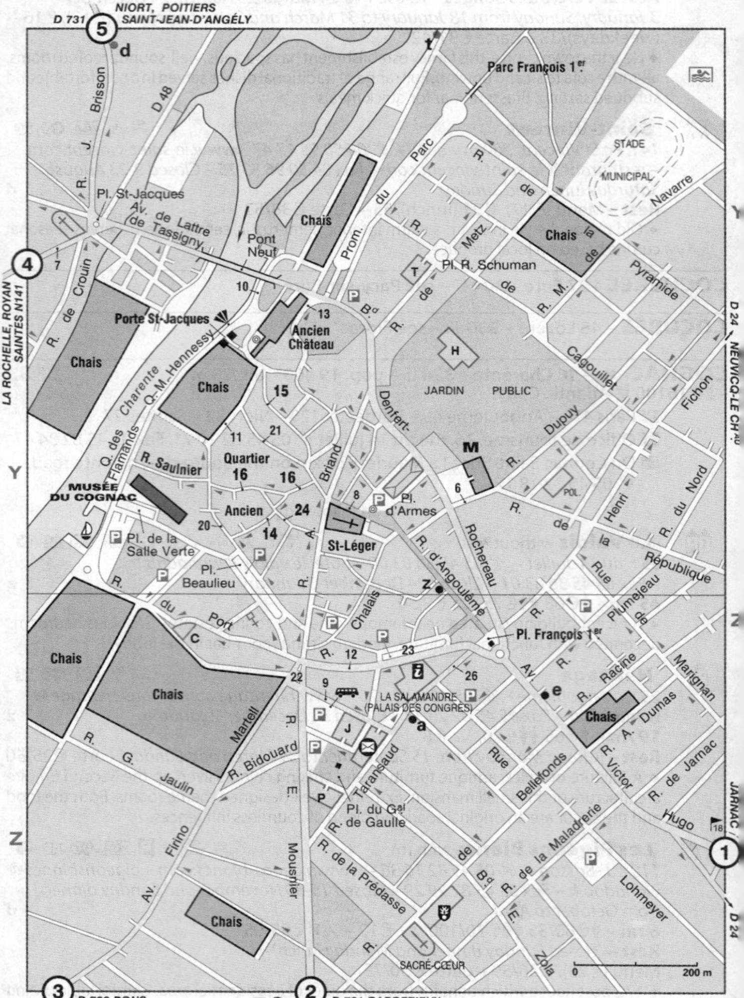

D 731 NIORT, POITIERS SAINT-JEAN-D'ANGÉLY

LA ROCHELLE, ROYAN SAINTES N141

D 24 NEUVICQ-LE CHÂTEAU

JARNAC

D 732 PONS A 10 BORDEAUX

D 731 BARBEZIEUX BORDEAUX

**Good food and accommodation at moderate prices?
Look for the Bib symbols: red Bib Gourmand for food,
blue Bib Hotel for hotels.**

via ① 3 km Angoulême road and Rouillac road (D 15) – ✉ 16100 Châteaubernard

Château de l'Yeuse
quartier l'Échassier, r. Bellevue – ☏ 05 45 36 82 60
– www.yeuse.fr – reservations.yeuse@wanadoo.fr – Fax 05 45 35 06 32
– Closed 20 December-2 February
21 rm – €103/175 €103/175, ☕ €18 – 3 suites – ½ P €110/142
Rest *Château de l'Yeuse* – *(closed Monday lunch, Friday lunch and Saturday lunch)* Menu €48/80 – Carte €65/100
Rest *Le P'tit Yeuse* – *(lunch only)* Menu (€18)
◆ A small, romantic 19C manor house with a new modern wing. Antique furniture and refined decor in the bedrooms. "Cognac and cigar" sitting room. Elegant restaurant and terrace dominating the Charente valley. Excellent creative cuisine. Simpler meals at the P'tit Yeuse.

Domaine de l'Échassier
quartier l'Échassier, 72 r. Bellevue – ☏ 05 45 35 01 09
– www.echassier.com – echassier@wanadoo.fr – Fax 05 45 32 22 43 – Closed 21-29 December and Sunday off season
22 rm – €78 €95, ☕ €12
Rest – *(closed 24 October-5 November and 6-13 February) (dinner only)*
Menu €36/40 – Carte €29/50
◆ This recent establishment, located in a delightful garden, has snug, contemporary style rooms whose decor evokes wine producing activities. A few terraces and balconies. A stylish inviting dining room in a restaurant meets table d'hôte ambiance.

COGOLIN – 83 Var – 340 O6 – pop. 10 984 – alt. 20 m – ✉ 83310 41 C3

Paris 864 – Fréjus 33 – Ste-Maxime 13 – Toulon 60
Office de tourisme, place de la République ☏ 04 94 55 01 10, Fax 04 94 55 01 11

La Maison du Monde without rest
63 r. Carnot – ☏ 04 94 54 77 54 – www.lamaisondumonde.fr
– info@lamaisondumonde.fr – Fax 04 94 54 77 55
– Closed 1st-14 March and 16 November-31 December
12 rm – €75/185 €75/185, ☕ €13
◆ A 19C townhouse set in a garden with palm and plane trees. Rooms with character with furniture from all over the world. Pleasant welcome.

La Grange des Agapes
7 r. du 11-Novembre, (pl. de la Mairie) – ☏ 04 94 54 60 97
– www.grangeagapes.com – grangeagapes@orange.fr – Fax 04 94 54 60 97
– Closed 22 December-5 January, Sunday and Monday
Rest – Menu €20 (weekday lunch), €29/49 – Carte €40/60
◆ Rustic establishment that has been given a modern makeover: lounge bar, open kitchen and green wall. The chef prepares traditional dishes and gives cookery courses.

Grain de Sel
6 r. 11-Novembre, (behind the town hall) – ☏ 04 94 54 46 86
– www.restaurant-cagolin.com – phianne2@orange.fr – Closed 25-31 August, 24-31 December, February holiday, Saturday lunch, Monday from September to June and Sunday
Rest – Menu €31 – Carte €38/45
◆ A tiny Provençal bistro that doesn't lack spice. In the warm dining room the chef prepares the dishes before your very eyes, using market-fresh ingredients chalked up on a slate.

Southeast 5 km on D 98, towards Toulon – ✉ 83310

La Ferme du Magnan
– ☏ 04 94 49 57 54 – www.alpazurhotels.com – sales@alpazurhotels.com
– Fax 04 94 49 57 54 – Open from February to November
Rest – Menu €35/100 – Carte €41/75
◆ A country house in the 16C, a silkworm nursery in the 19C, and now a quaint country restaurant. Copious cuisine based on farm produce. Panoramic terrace adorned with earthenware jars.

COIGNIÈRES – 78 Yvelines – 311 H3 – pop. 4 402 – alt. 160 m – ✉ 78310 18 A2

Paris 39 – Rambouillet 15 – St-Quentin-en-Yvelines 7 – Versailles 21

Le Capucin Gourmand

170 N 10 – ✆ 01 34 61 46 06 – www.capucingourmand.com – capucingourmand@wanadoo.fr – Fax 01 30 49 89 37 – Closed Sunday dinner and Monday dinner

Rest – Menu € 30/60 – Carte € 52/75

◆ An old post house in a business park with charm intact. Dining room both rustic and stylish, heated by an open fire in winter. Quiet flowery terrace.

Le Vivier

296 RN 10 – ✆ 01 34 61 64 39 – www.levivier.net – k-vivier@wanadoo.fr – Fax 01 34 61 94 30 – Closed Sunday evening and Monday

Rest – Menu (€ 35), € 39 – Carte € 45/61

◆ As the sign indicates, the cuisine served is fish and seafood-based. Two beautiful rustic dining rooms, brightened with some nautical touches.

COISE-ST-JEAN-PIED-GAUTHIER – 73 Savoie – 333 J4 – pop. 1 101 – alt. 292 m – ✉ 73800 46 F2

Paris 582 – Albertville 32 – Chambéry 23 – Grenoble 55

Château de la Tour du Puits

1 km via Puits road – ✆ 04 79 28 88 00 – www.chateaupuit.fr – info@chapeaupuit.fr – Fax 04 79 28 88 01 – Closed 20 April-3 May and 2-29 November

7 rm – †€ 170/330 ††€ 170/330, ☕ € 20 – ½ P € 150/230

Rest – *(closed Sunday dinner, Tuesday lunch and Monday)* Menu (€ 25), € 38 (weekday lunch), € 48/65 – Carte € 70/89

◆ This graceful château rebuilt in the 18C has a pepper-pot tower and stands in the middle of a wooded park. Exquisitely decorated guestrooms. Heliport. A modern menu served in the warm, intimate dining room or on a fine shaded terrace.

COL BAYARD – 05 Hautes-Alpes – 334 E5 – alt. 1 248 m – ✉ 05000 Gap ▌French Alps 41 C1

Paris 658 – Gap 7 – La Mure 56 – Sisteron 60

in Laye 2,5 km North by N 85 – pop. 228 – alt. 1 170 m – ✉ 05500

La Laiterie du Col Bayard

– ✆ 04 92 50 50 06 – www.laiterie-col-bayard.com – laiterieducolbayard@orange.fr – Fax 04 92 43 07 42 – Closed 12 November-18 December and Monday except school holidays

Rest – Menu (€ 13 bi), € 17/38 bi – Carte € 14/47

◆ Adjoining a dairy farm and cheese-makers, this original restaurant has a shop selling local produce. Terrace with mountain views. Local dishes and cheeses in pride of place.

COL DE BAVELLA – 2A Corse-du-Sud – 345 E9 – see Corse

COL DE CEYSSAT – 63 Puy-de-Dôme – 326 E8 – see Clermont-Ferrand

COL DE CUREBOURSE – 15 Cantal – 330 D5 – see Vic-sur-Cère

COL DE LA CROIX-FRY – 74 Haute-Savoie – 328 L5 – see Manigod

COL DE LA CROIX-PERRIN – 38 Isère – 333 G7 – see Lans-en-Vercors

COL DE LA FAUCILLE ★★ – 01 Ain – 328 J2 – alt. 1 320 m – Winter sports : (Mijoux-Lelex-la Faucille) 900/1 680 m 3 29 – ✉ 01170 Gex 46 F1

Burgundy-Jura

Paris 480 – Bourg-en-Bresse 108 – Genève 29 – Gex 11 – Morez 28 – Nantua 58

Downhill to Gex★★ (N 5) ※★★ Southeast: 2 km - Mont-Rond★★ (access by cable car – railway station at 500 m Southwest of the pass).

La Mainaz

rest, VISA AE

col de la Faucille, 1 km south on D 1005 – 04 50 41 31 10 – www.la-mainaz.com – mainaz@club-internet.fr – Fax 04 50 41 31 77 – Closed 14 June-2 July, 25 October-9 December, Sunday dinner and Monday except school holidays

21 rm – €79 €79/119, €13 – ½ P €89/119

Rest – Menu (€18), €33/69 – Carte €40/75

◆ This large wooden chalet's undisputed asset is the exceptional view of Lake Léman and the Alps. Spacious rooms, some with a balcony. Some have been renovated. Magnificent panoramic terrace overlooking the region; classic dishes.

La Petite Chaumière

VISA

col de la Faucille – 04 50 41 30 22 – www.petitechaumiere.com – info@petitechaumiere.com – Fax 04 50 41 33 22 – Closed 29 March-26 April and 11 October-20 December

54 rm – €50/57 €58/69, €11 – ½ P €65/73

Rest – Menu (€16), €20 (weekdays)/33 – Carte €31/45

◆ A 1960s Jura chalet at the foot of the ski slopes. Small, simple, wainscoted rooms, some with a balcony. Family flats in the new wing. Look out for the owner's collection of old bellows on your way into this warm, rustic restaurant.

La Couronne

VISA

– 04 50 41 32 65 – www.hotel-de-la-couronne.com – hotel-de-la-couronne@wanadoo.fr – Fax 04 50 41 32 47 – Open 15 May-30 September and 15 December-31 March

15 rm – €65/75 €70/80, €10 – ½ P €67/73

Rest – *(closed Wednesday in June)* Menu €22 bi (lunch), €28/42 – Carte €34/57

◆ A breath of fresh air! Most of the 1970s-style rooms boast a balcony. Some have been refurbished with light wood panelling. Classic menu in the restaurant adorned with beams, knick-knacks and a mural. Open-air terrace.

COL DE LA MACHINE – 26 Drôme – 332 F4 – see St-Jean-en-Royans

COL DE LA SCHLUCHT – 88 Vosges – 314 K4 – alt. 1 258 m – Winter sports : 1 150/1 250 m 27 D3

Alsace-Lorraine

Paris 441 – Colmar 37 – Épinal 56 – Gérardmer 16 – Guebwiller 46 – St-Dié 37 – Thann 43

Route des Crêtes★★★ North and South - Le Hohneck ※★★★ South: 5 km.

Le Collet

rest, VISA AE

at Collet, 2 km on Gérardmer road – 03 29 60 09 57 – www.chalethotel-lecollet.com – hotcollet@aol.com – Fax 03 29 60 08 77 – Closed 2 November-3 December

25 rm – €68 €78, €12 – 6 suites – ½ P €77

Rest – *(closed Thursday lunch and Wednesday except school holidays)* Menu (€18), €26/52 – Carte €38/49

◆ Large, friendly chalet, surrounded by fir trees. Attractive interior decor, cosy rooms and stylish details (embroidered linen and prevalence of wood). Tasty, local food served in a welcoming dining room.

COL DU DONON – 67 Bas-Rhin – 315 G5 – alt. 718 m – ✉ 67130 Grandfontaine 1 A2

Alsace-Lorraine

Paris 402 – Lunéville 61 – St-Dié 41 – Sarrebourg 39 – Sélestat 67 – Strasbourg 61

※★★ on the chain of the Vosges.

Du Donon
– ✆ 03 88 97 20 69 – www.ledonon.com
– hotelrestdudonon@wanadoo.fr – Fax 03 88 97 20 17 – Closed 17-23 March and 12 November-3 December
22 rm – €50 €64, €10 – 1 suite – ½ P €68
Rest – *(lunch only)* Menu (€8,50), €18/37 – Carte €15/37
◆ Family welcome in this inn in the forest. Redecorated rooms and studios (dormer windows). Pretty swimming pool, sauna and Jacuzzi. Regional meals offered in a rustic setting or on the flower-decked terrace in summer.

COL DU LAUTARET – 05 Hautes-Alpes – 334 G2 – alt. 2 058 m – 05480 Villar d Arene 41 C1

Paris 653 – Briançon 27 – Les Deux-Alpes 38 – Valloire 25

Des Glaciers
Col du Lautaret – ✆ 04 92 24 42 21 – www.hotel-bonnabel.com
– bonnabel@hotel-bonnabel.com – Fax 04 92 24 44 81
– Closed 15 September-15 December
23 rm – €165/352 €165/352, €20 – 2 suites – ½ P €133/226
Rest – Menu (€25), €35 – Carte €55/75
◆ An exceptional view over mountains and glaciers from this hotel at the top of a pass (2058 m). Large, chalet-style rooms, attractive fitness room. Traditional cuisine is served in the evening, and midday luncheons are of the brasserie-type. There is also a bar-games room.

COL DU PAVILLON – 69 Rhône – 327 F3 – see Cours

COLIGNY – 01 Ain – 328 F2 – pop. 1 147 – alt. 298 m – 01270 44 B1

Paris 407 – Bourg-en-Bresse 24 – Lons-le-Saunier 39 – Mâcon 57 – Tournus 48

Au Petit Relais
Grande Rue – ✆ 04 74 30 10 07 – au.petit.relais.coligny@orange.fr
– Fax 04 74 30 10 07 – Closed 23 March-2 April, 28 September-8 October, 7-10 December, Wednesday dinner and Thursday
Rest – *(number of covers limited, pre-book)* Menu €17 (weekday lunch), €27/56 bi – Carte €37/78
◆ Tasty cuisine, specialities from Bresse and selected wines to be enjoyed in a smart dining room. Summer terrace in the inner courtyard.

COLLÉGIEN – 77 Seine-et-Marne – 312 F2 – 101 19 – see Paris, Area (Marne-la-Vallée)

LA COLLE-SUR-LOUP – 06 Alpes-Maritimes – 341 D5 – pop. 7 546 – alt. 90 m – 06480 French Riviera 42 E2

Paris 919 – Antibes 15 – Cagnes-sur-Mer 7 – Cannes 26 – Grasse 19 – Nice 18 – Vence 7

Syndicat d'initiative, 28, rue Maréchal Foch ✆ 04 93 32 68 36, Fax 04 93 32 05 07

Le Clos des Arts
350 rte de St Paul – ✆ 04 93 32 40 00 – www.closdesarts.fr
– info@closdesarts.fr – Fax 04 93 32 69 98
– Closed 8 January-10 February
9 rm – €190/430 €190/430, €26
Rest – *(closed Sunday dinner and Monday in low season) (dinner only except weekends)* Menu €45/89 – Carte €51/101
◆ A magnificent hotel comprising two Provençal villas with elegant and personalised junior suites, some with their own terrace. Contemporary cuisine served outdoors or beneath a painted ceiling. Seafood tank, rotisserie and grill.

Marc Hély without rest
535 rte de Cagnes, 800 m south-east on D 6 – ✆ 04 93 22 64 10 – www.hotel-marc-hely.com – contact@hotel-marc-hely.com – Fax 04 93 22 93 84 – Closed 8-20 November and 1-13 February
12 rm – €69/120 €75/120, €10
◆ Most of the bedrooms in this large house enjoy fine views over Saint-Paul-de-Vence. Functional comfort, with breakfast taken on the veranda. Swimming pool. Peace and quiet guaranteed.

L'Abbaye rm,
541 bd Teisseire, (Grasse road) – ✆ 04 93 32 68 34 – www.hotelabbaye.com – contact@hotelabbaye.com – Fax 04 93 32 85 06
17 rm – €85/205 €135/350, €15
Rest – *(closed Monday from mid September to mid June)* Menu (€16), €21 (weekday lunch) – Carte €34/59
◆ Attractive guestrooms with personal touches now stand within the noble walls of this old abbey once occupied by the monks of the Île St-Honorat. 10C chapel. The vaulted restaurant has a new trendy designer decor. Shaded terrace in the old cloister.

Le Blanc Manger
1260 rte de Cagnes – ✆ 04 93 22 51 20 – leblancmanger.fr – leblancmanger@wanadoo.fr – Fax 04 92 02 00 46 – Closed Monday except dinner from 1 June to 15 September, Wednesday lunch from 1 June to 15 September and Tuesday
Rest – *(number of covers limited, pre-book)* Menu €28 (weekday lunch), €32/47
◆ Delicate cuisine with a southern accent is on offer in Le Blanc Manger's bijou, rustic-influenced dining room, or on the attractive, wood-furnished terrace.

COLLEVILLE-SUR-MER – 14 Calvados – 303 G3 – pop. 167 – alt. 42 m – ✉ 14710 Normandy

32 **B2**

Paris 281 – Cherbourg 84 – Caen 49 – Saint-Lô 39

Domaine de L'Hostréière without rest
rte du Cimetière Américain – ✆ 02 31 51 64 64 – www.domainedelhostreiere.com – hotelhostreiere@wanadoo.fr – Fax 02 31 51 64 65 – Open 1 April-31 October
19 rm – €75/112 €75/132, €11
◆ Estate near St Laurent sur Mer American war cemetery. Accommodation in the farm outbuildings or recent wings. Lounge and terrace, swimming pool.

COLLIAS – 30 Gard – 339 L5 – see Pont-du-Gard

COLLIOURE – 66 Pyrénées-Orientales – 344 J7 – pop. 2 944 – alt. 2 m – Casino – ✉ 66190 Languedoc-Roussillon-Tarn Gorges

22 **B3**

Paris 879 – Argelès-sur-Mer 7 – Céret 36 – Perpignan 30 – Port-Vendres 3
Office de tourisme, place du 18 Juin ✆ 04 68 82 15 47, Fax 04 68 82 46 29
Site★★ - Altar-pieces★ in Notre-Dame-des-Anges church.

Plan on following page

Relais des Trois Mas
Port-Vendres road – ✆ 04 68 82 05 07 – www.relaisdestroismas.com – contact@relaisdes3mas.com – Fax 04 68 82 38 08 – Open from early February to end November
B **n**
23 rm – €195/465 €195/465, €18 – ½ P €125/308
Rest *La Balette* – *(closed Tuesday lunch, Wednesday lunch and Monday)* Menu €37/85 – Carte €61/115
Spec. Déclinaison d'anchois de Collioure au vinaigre de Banyuls. Filet de Saint Pierre aux petits farcis et sauce perlée au maury. Biscuit coulant au chocolat noir.
◆ Three renovated mas with wonderful views of the town and harbour. The individually decorated guestrooms are named after painters. Garden, pool and Jacuzzi. Updated regional cuisine served in summer on the pleasant panoramic terrace.

COLLIOURE

Street	Square	No.
Aire (R. de l')	B	2
Amirauté (Q. de l')	B	3
Arago (R. François)	B	4
Argelès (Rte d')	A	
Dagobert (R.)	B	7
Démocratie (R. de la)	B	8
Égalité (R. de l')	B	9
Ferry (R. Jules)	AB	13
Galère (R. de la)	A	
Gaulle (Av. du Gén.)	B	
Jean-Jaurès (Pl.)	B	14
Lamartine (R.)	B	15
Leclerc (Pl. Gén.)	AB	17
Maillol (Av. Aristide)	A	
Mailly (R.)	B	19
Michelet (R. Jules)	A	20
Miradou (Av. du)	A	23
Pasteur (R.)	B	
Pla de Las Fourques (R. du)	A	
République (R. de la)	AB	
Rolland (R. Romain)	A	
Rousseau (R. J.-J.)	AB	29
St-Vincent (R.)	B	30
Soleil (R. du)	B	33
La Tour d'Auvergne (R. de)	B	16
Vauban (R.)	B	34
8 Mai 1945 (Pl. du)	B	35
18-Juin (Pl. du)	B	40

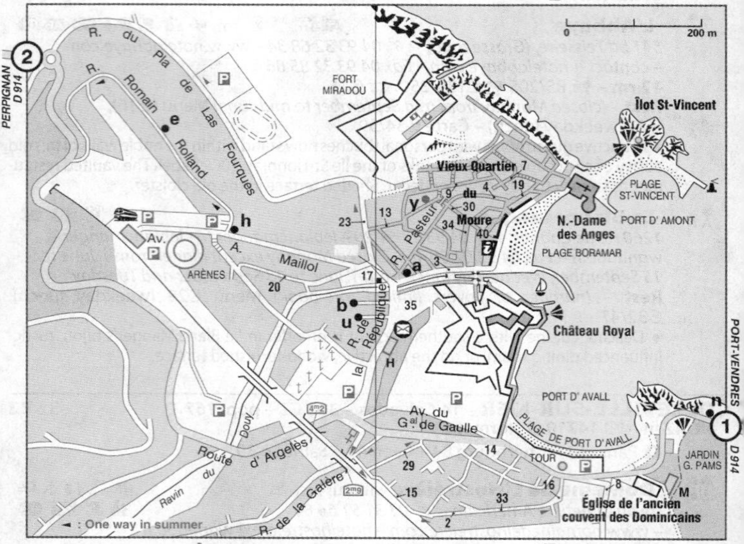

Casa Païral without rest

imp. Palmiers – ✆ 04 68 82 05 81 – www.hotel-casa-pairal.com – contact@hotel-casa-pairal.com – Fax 04 68 82 52 10 – Open 3 April-10 November

A **b**

27 rm – €89/225 €89/225, ☕ €12

◆ A 19C home set around a luxuriant Mediterranean garden with a bubbling fountain. Characterful bedrooms in the main building; those in the other building are quieter.

L'Arapède rm,

rte Port-Vendres – ✆ 04 68 98 09 59 – www.arapede.com – hotelarapede@yahoo.fr – Fax 04 68 98 30 90 – Closed 30 November-5 February

20 rm – €55/80 €65/110, ☕ €11 – ½ P €61/87

Rest – *(dinner only except weekends and bank holidays)* Menu €27/36 – Carte €40/46

◆ Modern hotel on the side of a hill. Attractive Catalan style furniture in the large bedrooms which face the sea and overflow pool. Restaurant decorated with old photos of Collioure, terrace overlooking the sea, and local dishes.

Madeloc without rest

r. R. Rolland – ✆ 04 68 82 07 56 – www.madeloc.com – hotel@madeloc.com – Fax 04 68 82 55 09 – Open 28 March-1 November

A **e**

22 rm – €65/114 €65/114, ☕ €11

◆ A hotel on the heights of the town, with rooms furnished in rattan, many with terraces. Roof pool and hillside garden. Painting and sculpture exhibitions.

La Frégate rm, VISA MC

24 quai de l'Amirauté – ✆ 04 68 82 06 05 – www.fregate-collioure.com – contact@fregate-collioure.com – Fax 04 68 82 55 00 – Closed end November to early February B **a**

26 rm – †€ 50/70 ††€ 70/115, ☕ € 8 – 1 suite – ½ P € 55/105

Rest – *(closed Thursday from October to March)* Menu € 24/40 – Carte € 30/53

◆ A refurbished hotel in an ideal position opposite the chateau. Small Catalan-inspired rooms which are well-kept and have been gradually updated. Two dining rooms with earthenware decoration serving good, simple local dishes.

Méditerranée without rest VISA MC

av. A. Maillol – ✆ 04 68 82 08 60 – www.mediterranee-hotel.com – mediterraneehotel@free.fr – Fax 04 68 82 28 07 – Open April-November A **h**

23 rm – †€ 65/99 ††€ 65/99, ☕ € 10

◆ This 1970s building has functional rooms, all with balconies, which are gradually being updated in local colours. Terraced garden. Solarium.

Le 5ème Péché VISA MC

– ✆ 04 68 98 09 76 – www.le5peche.com – contact@le5peche.com – Fax 04 68 89 33 86 B **y**

Rest – *(number of covers limited, pre-book)* Menu € 23 (lunch), € 34/55 – Carte € 48/59

◆A small restaurant in old-town Collioure that symbolyses the meeting of Japan and Catalonia. The Tokyo-born chef cooks up fine fusion cuisine with a focus on ultra-fresh fish.

COLLONGES-AU-MONT-D'OR – 69 Rhône – 327 I5 – see Lyon

COLLONGES-LA-ROUGE – 19 Corrèze – 329 K5 – pop. 413 – alt. 230 m – ✉ 19500 Dordogne-Berry-Limousin 25 C3

Paris 505 – Brive-la-Gaillarde 21 – Cahors 105 – Figeac 75 – Tulle 35

Office de tourisme, le Bourg ✆ 05 55 25 47 57

Village★★: tympanum★ and steeple★ of the church, castel de Vassinhac★ - Saillac: tympanum★ of the church South: 4 km.

Le Relais de St-Jacques de Compostelle P VISA MC AE

– ✆ 05 55 25 41 02 – sarlmanalese@orange.fr – Fax 05 55 84 08 51 – Closed January, February, Tuesday, Wednesday and Thursday from October to November

11 rm (½ board only) – ½ P € 59/72 **Rest** – Menu € 17/45 – Carte € 30/80

◆ An ideal spot to enjoy the bright village built of red sandstone. The rooms are not very large but are well kept and look out over the manor houses or the countryside. The dining room decor is rural and there is a pleasant terrace. Cuisine from the South-West.

Jeanne P VISA MC

in the village – ✆ 05 55 25 42 31 – www.jeannemaisondhotes.com – info@jeannemaisondhotes.com – Fax 05 55 25 47 80

5 rm ☕ – †€ 90 ††€ 90 **Table d'hôte** – Menu € 35 bi

◆ A noble red-brick residence flanked by a 15C tower. Neo-rustic bedrooms tastefully furnished with a personal touch. Lounge with fireplace. Terrace and enclosed garden. Evening menus include a choice of typical family dishes.

COLMAR P – 68 Haut-Rhin – 315 I8 – pop. 65 300 – Built-up area 116 268 – alt. 194 m – ✉ 68000 Alsace-Lorraine 2 C2

Paris 450 – Basel 68 – Freiburg-im-Breisgau 51 – Nancy 140 – Strasbourg 78

Office de tourisme, 4, rue d'Unterlinden ✆ 03 89 20 68 92, Fax 03 89 20 69 14

18 d'Ammerschwihr Ammerschwihr Allée du Golf, NW : 9 km on D 415 then D 11, ✆ 03 89 47 17 30

Musée d'Unterlinden★★★ (Issenheim altar-piece ★★★) - Old town★★: Maison Pfister★★ BZ **W**, St-Martin collegiate church ★ BY, Maison des Arcades★ CZ**K**, Maison des Têtes★ BY **Y** - Ancienne Douane★ BZ **D**, Ancien Corps de Garde★ BZ **B** - Virgin with rose bush★★ and stained-glass windows★ of the Dominicains church BY - Window of the Great Crucifixion★ of St-Matthieu temple CY - " Little Venice "★: ≤★ of St-Pierre bridge BZ , quartier de la Krutenau★, rue de la Poissonnerie★, façade of the civil court ★ BZ **J** - Maison des vins d'Alsace by ①.

COLMAR

Agen (R. d') .... BY
Alsace (Av. d') .... CYZ
Ancienne Douane (Pl. de l') .... CZ 2
Augustins (R. des) .... BZ 3
Bagatelle (R. de la) .... AY
Bains (R. des) .... BY 5
Bâle (Route de) .... CZ
Bartholdi (R.) .... BCZ
Blés (R. des) .... BZ 9
Boulangers (R. des) .... BY 12
Brasseries (R. des) .... CY 13
Bruat (R.) .... BZ 14
Cathédrale (Pl. de la) .... BY 17
Cavalerie (R. de la) .... BCY
Champ-de-Mars (Bd du) .... BYZ 18
Chauffour (R.) .... BZ 20
Clefs (R. des) .... BCY
Clemenceau (Av. Georges) .... BCZ
Écoles (R. des) .... BZ 22
Est (R. de l') .... CYZ
Fleischhauer (R.) .... BCY
Fleurent (R. J.-B.) .... BY 24
Fleurs (R. des) .... CZ
Florimont (R. du) .... AY 25
Foch (Av.) .... BZ
Fribourg (Av. de) .... CZ
Gare (Pl. et R. de la) .... AZ
Gaulle (Av. Gén.-de) .... ABYZ
Golbéry (R.) .... BY
Grad (R. Charles) .... AY
Grand'Rue .... BCZ 31
Grenouillère (R. de la) .... CYZ 32
Herse (R. de la) .... BZ 33
Ingersheim (Rte d') .... ABY
Jeanne d'Arc (Pl.) .... CY
Joffre (Av.) .... BZ
Kléber (R.) .... BY 35
Ladhof (R. du) .... CY 36
Lasch (R. Georges) .... AZ 37
Lattre-de-Tassigny (Av. J. de) .... ABY 43
Leclerc (Bd du Gén.) .... BZ 45
Liberté (Av. de la) .... AZ
Logelbach (R. du) .... AY
Manège (R. du) .... BZ 49
Marchands (R. des) .... BYZ 50
Marché-aux-Fruits (Pl. du) .... BZ 51
Marne (Av. de la) .... BZ
Messimy (R.) .... ABZ 52
Molly (R. Berthe) .... BYZ 54
Mouton (R. du) .... CY 57
Mulhouse (R. de) .... AZ
Neuf-Brisach (Rte de) .... CY
Nord (R. du) .... BCY
Poincaré (Av. Raymond) .... ABZ
Poissonnerie (R. et Q. de la) .... BCZ 62
Preiss (R. Jacques) .... ABZ 63
Rapp (Pl.) .... BZ
Rapp (R.) .... BCY
Reims (R. de) .... BZ 65
République (Av. de la) .... ABZ
Ribeauvillé (R. de) .... BY 67
Roesselman (R.) .... BY 69
Rouffach (Rte de) .... AZ
St-Jean (R.) .... BZ 71
St-Joseph (Pl. et R.) .... AY
St-Josse (R.) .... CZ
St-Léon (R.) .... AY
St-Nicolas (R.) .... BY 73
St-Pierre (Bd et Pont) .... BCZ
Schlumberger (R. Camille) .... ABZ
Schwendi (R.) .... CZ
Sélestat (Rte de) .... CY
Semm (R. de la) .... CZ
Serruriers (R. des) .... BY 75
Sinn (Quai de la) .... BY 77
Six-Montagnes-Noires (Pl. des) .... BZ 79
Stanislas (R.) .... BY
Tanneurs (R. des) .... CZ 82
Têtes (R. des) .... BY 83
Thann (R. de) .... CY
Tir (R. du) .... AZ
Turckheim (R. de) .... AY
Turenne (R.) .... BCZ
Unterlinden (Pl. d') .... BY 85
Val St-Grégoire (R. du) .... AY
Vauban (R.) .... CY
Voltaire (R.) .... ABZ
Weinemer (R.) .... BZ 86
1ère Armée Française (R. de la) .... BY
2 Février (Pl. du) .... CY 87
5e Division-Blindée (R. de la) .... BY 95
18 Novembre (Pl. du) .... BY 97

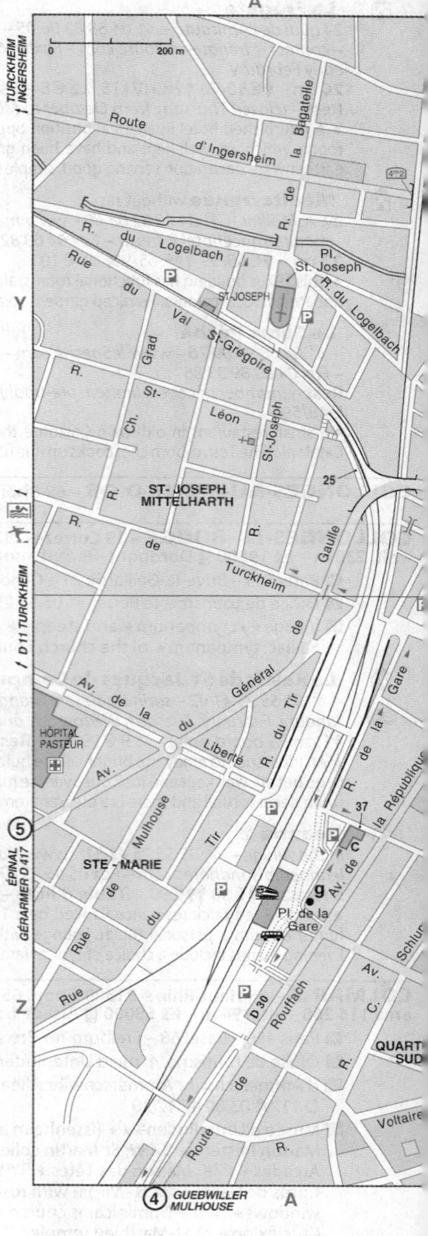

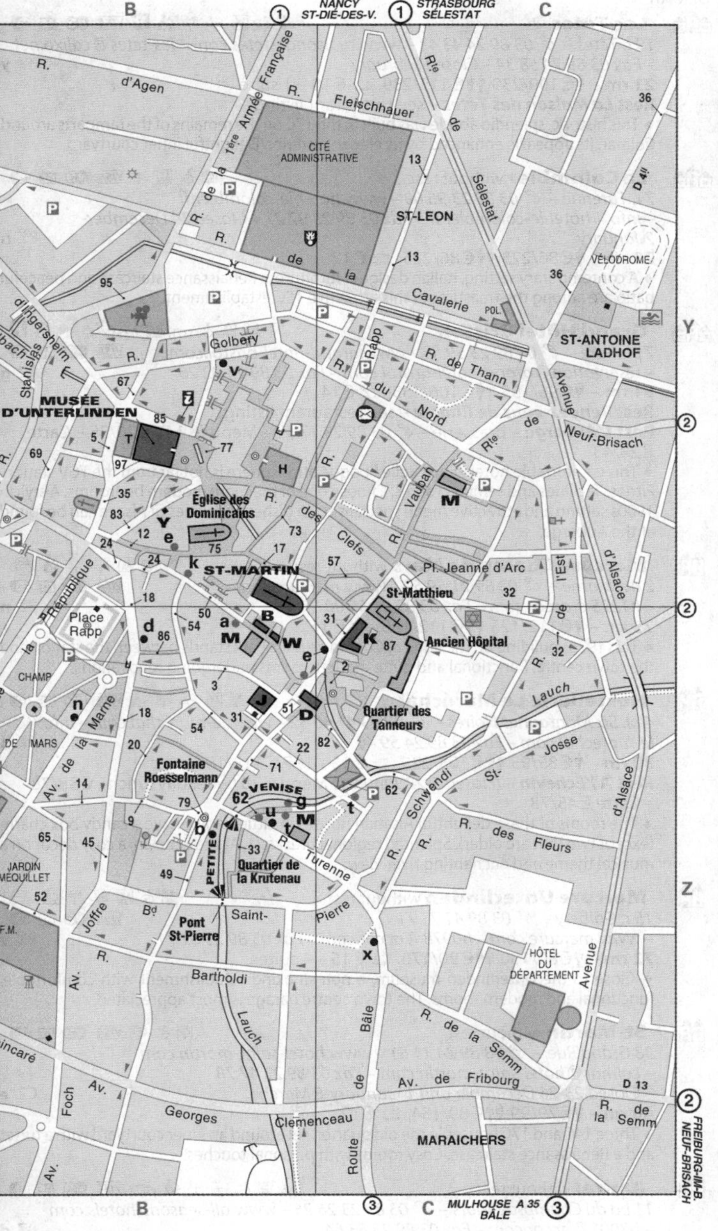

NANCY ST-DIÉ-DES-V.
STRASBOURG SÉLESTAT
CITÉ ADMINISTRATIVE
ST-LEON
VÉLODROME
ST-ANTOINE LADHOF
MUSÉE D'UNTERLINDEN
Église des Dominicains
ST-MARTIN
Pl. Jeanne d'Arc
St-Matthieu
Place Rapp
Ancien Hôpital
CHAMP DE MARS
Quartier des Tanneurs
Fontaine Roesselmann
VENISE
PETITE
Quartier de la Krutenau
Pont St-Pierre
JARDIN MEQUILLET
HÔTEL DU DÉPARTEMENT
MARAICHERS
MULHOUSE A 35 BÂLE
FREIBURG-IM-B. NEUF-BRISACH
R. Fleischhauer
R. de la 1ère Armée Française
Rte de Sélestat
R. de la Cavalerie
R. Golbery
R. Rapp
R. de Thann
R. du Nord
Rte de Neuf-Brisach
Avenue
R. Vauban
R. des Clefs
R. de l'Est
Av. d'Alsace
Lauch
St-Josse
R. Schwendi
R. des Fleurs
R. Turenne
Bd Saint-Pierre
R. Bartholdi
R. de Bâle
R. de la Semm
Av. de Fribourg
Av. Georges Clemenceau
Route de Bâle
Av. Foch
Av. Joffre
Av. de la Marne
Av. de la République
Stanislas
D 13

Les Têtes
19 r. Têtes – 03 89 24 43 43 – www.maisondestetes.com – les-tetes@calixo.net – Fax 03 89 24 58 34 – Closed February BY **y**
21 rm – €109/239 €115/239, €15 – 1 suite
Rest *La Maison des Têtes* – see restaurant listing
◆ This historic, splendid abode was built in the 17C on the remains of the ramparts around Colmar. Its appeal is enhanced by its elegant interior. Delightful inner courtyard.

Le Colombier without rest
7 r. Turenne – 03 89 23 96 00 – www.hotel-le-colombier.fr – info@hotel-le-colombier.fr – Fax 03 89 23 97 27 – Closed 24 December-2 January BZ **u**
28 rm – €86/225 €86/225, €12
◆ A contemporary setting, Italian designer furniture, a Renaissance staircase and peaceful patio are among the treasures of this attractive 15C establishment.

Grand Hôtel Bristol rm, rest,
7 pl. Gare – 03 89 23 59 59 – www.grand-hotel-bristol.com – reservation@grand-hotel-bristol.com – Fax 03 89 23 92 26 AZ **g**
91 rm – €96/155 €106/155, €14
Rest *Rendez-vous de Chasse* – see restaurant listing
Rest *L'Auberge* – brasserie – *03 89 23 17 57* – Menu (€14), €20/35 – Carte €28/43
◆ This comfortable hotel with a Belle Époque atmosphere is not far from the TGV station. Fitness facilities and seminar rooms. Choose one of the more modern bedrooms. A stylish 1900s setting and attractive menu specialising in dishes and wines of Alsace can be found at the Auberge.

Mercure Champ de Mars without rest
2 av. Marne – 03 89 21 59 59 – www.mercure.com – h1225@accor.com – Fax 03 89 21 59 00 BZ **n**
75 rm – €112/125 €112/135, €16
◆ This 1970s building on the edge of Champ de Mars Park stands between the station and the town centre. Functional and quite modern rooms undergoing renovation.

Hostellerie Le Maréchal
4 pl. Six Montagnes Noires – 03 89 41 60 32 – www.le-marechal.com – info@le-marechal.com – Fax 03 89 24 59 40 BZ **b**
30 rm – €85/95 €105/225, €15 – ½ P €113/188
Rest *A l'Échevin* – *(closed 5-22 January)* Menu €28 (weekday lunch), €38/78 – Carte €45/78
◆ The rooms of these delightful Alsatian houses in Little Venice have a candy box charm (except two that are older). Splendid regional breakfast. At the Échevin, a cosy decor on a musical theme and enchanting river view.

Mercure Unterlinden without rest
15 r. Golbery – 03 89 41 71 71 – www.mercure.com – h0978@accor.com – Fax 03 89 23 82 71 BY **v**
72 rm – €80/160 €90/170, €15 – 4 suites
◆ Close to the Unterlinden museum, a non-smoking establishment with comfortable, functional and modern rooms. The town centre garage is most appreciated.

St-Martin without rest
38 Grand'Rue – 03 89 24 11 51 – www.hotel-saint-martin.com – colmar@hotel-saint-martin.com – Fax 03 89 23 47 78 – Closed 23-26 December and 1st January-8 March CZ **e**
40 rm – €79/99 €89/154, €12
◆ Three 14C and 17C houses in the old quarter, set around an inner courtyard with a turret and a Renaissance staircase. Cosy rooms with personal touches.

Amiral without rest
11 bd du Champ-de-Mars – 03 89 23 26 25 – www.all-seasons-hotels.com – h7005@accor.com – Fax 03 89 23 83 64 BZ **d**
47 rm – €66/120 €76/130
◆ This old malthouse is home to pleasant contemporary rooms (larger on the ground floor). Hospitable sitting room with fireplace and cane furniture.

Turenne without rest
10 rte Bâle – ✆ 03 89 21 58 58 – www.turenne.com – infos@turenne.com – Fax 03 89 41 27 64 CZ **x**
82 rm – †€ 49/75 ††€ 65/75, ☕ € 8,50 – 1 suite
◆ Architecture and furniture with a regional flavour in this hotel near Little Venice. Practical rooms, generous breakfasts and reasonable prices.

La Maison des Têtes – Hôtel Les Têtes
19 r. Têtes – ✆ 03 89 24 43 43 – les-tetes@calixo.net – Fax 03 89 24 58 34 – Closed February, Sunday dinner, Tuesday lunch and Monday BY **Y**
Rest – Menu € 30/62 – Carte € 36/61
◆ This fine Renaissance house is one of the gems of Colmar's architectural heritage. Dining room (19C) lined with light wood, traditional cuisine and fine selection of local wines.

Rendez-vous de Chasse – Grand Hôtel Bristol
7 pl. de la Gare – ✆ 03 89 23 15 86 – www.grand-hotel-bristol.com – reservation@grand-hotel-bristol.com – Fax 03 89 23 92 26 AZ **g**
Rest – Menu (€ 29), € 48/80 – Carte € 75/86
Spec. Terrine de foie gras d'oie à la cuillère. Dos de chevreuil d'Alsace, nems aux fruits, sauce épicée (15 Jan.-15 May). Soufflé au Grand Marnier, sorbet aux fruits du soleil. **Wines** Riesling, Pinot noir.
◆ A plush restaurant with a fireplace, stonework and ceiling beams. Original Daumier drawings on display. Up-to-date, gourmet meals and a fine wine list.

JY'S (Jean-Yves Schillinger)
17 r. Poissonnerie – ✆ 03 89 21 53 60 – www.jean-yves-schillinger.com – Fax 03 89 21 53 65 – Closed February holidays, Sunday and Monday BZ **g**
Rest – Menu € 32, € 54/72 – Carte approx. € 60
Spec. Cocktail de chair de tourteau. Pavé de cabillaud rôti, tomates confites et olives noires. Mignon de veau en croûte d'herbes sur risotto sauvage. **Wines** Riesling, Pinot gris.
◆ Highly inventive menu and ultra-modern décor by Olivier Gagnère: this pretty house from 1750 on the banks of the Lauch is Colmar's trendiest spot.

Aux Trois Poissons
15 quai de la Poissonnerie – ✆ 03 89 41 25 21 – auxtroispoissons@calixo.net – Fax 03 89 41 25 21 – Closed 15-31 July, 3-9 November, Sunday dinner, Tuesday dinner and Wednesday CZ **t**
Rest – Menu € 22/45 – Carte € 30/60
◆ Warm atmosphere, stylish dining room and a combination of traditional cuisine and inventive dishes. Predominantly fish on the menu.

L'Arpège
24 r. Marchands – ✆ 03 89 23 37 89 – restaurant.arpege@wanadoo.fr – Fax 03 89 23 39 22 – Closed Saturday and Sunday BZ **a**
Rest – *(number of covers limited, pre-book)* Menu € 23 (weekday lunch), € 27/52 – Carte € 42/110
◆ This house dating from 1463, at the end of a cul-de-sac, used to belong to the Bartholdi family. Up-to-date dining room, terrace in a pretty floral garden, up-to-date cuisine.

Bartholdi
2 r. Boulangers – ✆ 03 89 41 07 74 – http://restaurant-bartholdi.monsite.wanadoo.fr/ – restaurant.bartholdi@wanadoo.fr – Fax 03 89 41 14 65 – Closed 30 June-7 July, February holidays, Sunday dinner and Monday BY **e**
Rest – Menu € 22/53 – Carte € 25/55
◆ Lovers of Alsatian wines cannot fail but be delighted by the vast choice of local vintages offered by this spacious restaurant the appearance of a Winstub. Traditional repertoire.

Chez Hansi
23 r. des Marchands – ✆ 03 89 41 37 84 – Fax 03 89 41 37 84 – Closed 1 week in June, January, Wednesday and Thursday BZ **e**
Rest – Menu € 18/44 – Carte € 30/55
◆ A tavern in typical old Colmar style with a half-timbered façade. Staff serve traditional cuisine in traditional costume.

Wistub Brenner
1 r. Turenne – 03 89 41 42 33 – www.wistub-brenner.fr – Fax 03 89 41 37 99 – Closed 23 June-1 July, 10-18 November, 5-20 January, Tuesday and Wednesday BZ **u**
Rest – Menu € 21/27 – Carte € 34/50
◆ An informal, lively atmosphere in this authentic Winstub with terrace. Regional meals (calf's head and pork trotters) and daily specials marked on a slate.

La Petite Venise
4 r. de la Poissonnerie – 03 89 41 72 59 – www.restaurantpetitevenise.com – Closed 23 December-5 January, Wednesday dinner and Thursday except December BZ **t**
Rest – Carte € 25/42
◆ This restaurant housed in a 17C building has a nostalgic feel, with the menu chalked on a board. The cuisine is regional, based on old family recipes passed down through the generations.

in Horbourg **4 km east by Neuf-Brisach road – 68180 Horbourg Wihr – pop. 5 060 – alt. 188 m**

L'Europe rm, rm,
15 rte Neuf-Brisach – 03 89 20 54 00 – www.hotel-europe-colmar.com – reservation@hotel-europe-colmar.fr – Fax 03 89 41 27 50
128 rm – € 103/125 € 120/164, € 14,50 – 2 suites – ½ P € 107/118
Rest *Eden des Gourmets* – *(closed July, January, Sunday dinner, Monday, Tuesday, Wednesday and lunch except Sunday)* Menu € 47/64 – Carte € 42/63
Rest *Plaisir du Terroir* – Menu (€ 20), € 27 (weekdays)/64 – Carte € 33/49
◆ Imposing neo-Alsatian hotel. Pleasant rooms, some veritably luxurious. Outstanding facilities for seminars and leisure activities. Organic produce takes pride of place on the Eden des Gourmets menu. Alsatian dishes (grilled meat in summer on the terrace).

Cerf without rest
9 Grand'Rue – 03 89 41 20 35 – www.hotelrestaurant-cerf.com – cerf-hotel@orange.fr – Fax 03 89 24 24 98 – Closed 1 January-25 March and Monday except from 15 May to 15 September
25 rm – € 68/73 € 73/83, € 11
◆ A spruce, pink, half-timbered building. The comfortable, if not huge rooms are more peaceful on the garden side. Bar and sitting room in Belle Epoque style.

in Logelheim **9 km Southeast by D 13 and D 45 - CZ – pop. 762 – alt. 195 m – 68280**

A la Vigne rm,
5 Grand'Rue – 03 89 20 99 60 – www.repere.com/la-vigne – restaurant.alavigne@calixo.net – Fax 03 89 20 99 69 – Closed 27 June-12 July and 24 December-10 January
9 rm – € 52/54 € 55/72, € 6,50
Rest – *(closed Saturday lunch, Monday dinner and Sunday except public holidays)* Menu (€ 10), € 22/28 – Carte € 21/39
◆ A simple, welcoming building in the regional style situated at the heart of a peaceful village. Rooms are modern, quiet and well equipped. Countrified dining room; regional fare (tartes flambées, sauerkrauts and spaetezele) and a slate of daily specials.

in Ste-Croix-en-Plaine **10 km by ③ – pop. 2 362 – alt. 192 m – 68127**

Au Moulin
rte d'Herrlisheim, on D 1 – 03 89 49 31 20 – www.aumoulin.net – hotelaumoulin@wanadoo.fr – Fax 03 89 49 23 11 – Open 1 April-20 December and closed Sunday dinner
16 rm – € 48/73 € 61/80, € 9
Rest – *(open 1 April-15 October) (dinner only) (resident only)* Carte € 23/40
◆ The comfortable and completely refurbished rooms of this mill have a view of the Vosges. Small museum of antique Alsatian objects. Snacks available (local dishes).

in Wettolsheim 4,5 km by ⑤ and D 1bis II – alt. 220 m – ✉ 68920

XX **La Palette** with rm

9 r. Herzog – ✆ 03 89 80 79 14 – www.lapalette.fr – lapalette@lapalette.fr – Fax 03 89 79 77 00 – Closed 17-24 August, 1-5 January, 16-23 February
16 rm – †€ 64/70 ††€ 74/110, ☕ € 9
Rest – *(closed Sunday dinner, Tuesday lunch and Monday)* Menu € 14 (weekday lunch), € 25/64 – Carte € 37/56
◆ The dining rooms in this hotel are embellished by a rich palette of styles and colours. Cuisine with a contemporary touch. Attractive, renovated rooms.

in Ingersheim 4 km Northwest – pop. 4 583 – alt. 220 m – ✉ 68040

XX **La Taverne Alsacienne**

99 r. de la République – ✆ 03 89 27 08 41 – tavernealsacienne68@orange.fr – Fax 03 89 80 89 75 – Closed 21 July-7 August, 1st-10 January, Thursday dinner except December, Sunday dinner and Monday
Rest – Menu (€ 16), € 20/55 – Carte € 29/57
◆ On the banks of the Fecht, choose from a large, contemporary and bright dining room, a bar serving daily specials and a redecorated lounge. Classic and regional cuisine and a good selection of Alsatian wines.

COLOMBES – 92 Hauts-de-Seine – 312 C2 – see Paris, Environs

COLOMBEY-LES-DEUX-ÉGLISES – 52 Haute-Marne – 313 J4 14 C3

– pop. 678 – alt. 353 m – ✉ 52330 Northern France and the Paris Region

Paris 248 – Bar-sur-Aube 16 – Châtillon-sur-Seine 63 – Chaumont 26 – Neufchâteau 71

Syndicat d'initiative, 68, rue du Général-de-Gaulle ✆ 03 25 01 52 33, Fax 03 25 01 98 61

Mémorial du Général-de-Gaulle and la Boisserie (museum).

Hostellerie la Montagne (Jean-Baptiste Natali)

r. Pisseloup – ✆ 03 25 01 51 69 – www.hostellerielamontagne.com – contact@hostellerielamontagne.com – Fax 03 25 01 53 20 – Closed 1st-15 October, 22-30 December, 15-31 January, Monday and Tuesday
9 rm – †€ 120/170 ††€ 120/170, ☕ € 14 – 1 suite
Rest – Menu € 28 (weekday lunch), € 52/85 – Carte € 82/97
Spec. Grosse langoustine et foie gras poêlé. Filet de chevreuil d'été pané aux amandes et pignons de pin. Tarte au citron glacée, biscuit aux agrumes (Oct. to Dec.). **Wines** Vin de Pays des Coteaux de Coiffy, Coteaux Champenois.
◆ Set in lovely gardens, this stone-built mansion offers charming guestrooms in rustic style. Fine, inventive cuisine in a contemporary decor. Ask for the 'chef's table' with view over the kitchens.

COLOMBIERS – 34 Hérault – 339 D9 – pop. 2 296 – alt. 25 m 22 B2

– ✉ 34440 Languedoc-Roussillon-Tarn Gorges

Paris 779 – Béziers 10 – Montpellier 78 – Narbonne 23

XX **Château de Colombiers**

1 r. du Château – ✆ 04 67 37 06 93 – www.chateau-colombiers.com – chateaudecolombiers@yahoo.fr – Fax 04 67 37 63 11 – Closed 1st-10 January and Sunday dinner
Rest – Menu (€ 15), € 25/55 – Carte € 35/59
◆ This 18C château has a number of comfortable, modern dining rooms. There is also a huge terrace dotted with chestnut trees. The cuisine has a contemporary touch.

COLOMIERS – 31 Haute-Garonne – 343 F3 – see Toulouse

If breakfast is included the ☕ symbol appears after the number of rooms.

COLONZELLE – **26 Drôme** – **332** C7 – **pop. 474** – **alt. 179 m** – ✉ **26230** 44 **B3**

Paris 642 – Lyon 180 – Montélimar 33 – Orange 37

La Maison de Soize

pl. de l'Église – ✆ 04 75 46 58 58 – Fax 04 75 46 58 58 – Open Easter-30 September

5 rm – €80 €90 **Table d'hôte** – Menu €30 bi

◆ The rooms of this old house are named after flowers. Attractive, fresh, colourful decor, modern bathrooms and excellent bedding. Home-grown vegetables feature in dishes served in the shaded garden or in a dining room decorated with family mementoes.

COLROY-LA-ROCHE – **67 Bas-Rhin** – **315** H6 – **pop. 455** – **alt. 475 m** 1 **A2** – ✉ **67420**

Paris 412 – Lunéville 70 – St-Dié 33 – Sélestat 31 – Strasbourg 66

Hostellerie La Cheneaudière rest,

3 r. Vieux Moulin – ✆ 03 88 97 61 64 – www.cheneaudiere.com – cheneaudiere@relaischateaux.com – Fax 03 88 47 21 73

32 rm – €125/260 €125/260, €25 – 7 suites

Rest – *(closed for lunch from Monday to Thursday except bank holidays)* Menu €52 (lunch), €73/110 – Carte €59/115

◆ A luxury establishment set in a forest of fir trees. The spacious rooms have been refurbished in a soothing, light colour scheme. Indoor pool, massages and sauna. Gourmet menu and regional recipes to be enjoyed in two stylish dining rooms.

COLY – **24 Dordogne** – **329** I5 – **see le Lardin-St-Lazare**

LA COMBE – **73 Savoie** – **333** H4 – **see Aiguebelette-le-Lac**

COMBEAUFONTAINE – **70 Haute-Saône** – **314** D6 – **pop. 496** 16 **B1** – **alt. 259 m** – ✉ **70120**

Paris 336 – Besançon 72 – Épinal 83 – Gray 40 – Langres 52 – Vesoul 24

Syndicat d'initiative, Mairie ✆ 03 84 92 11 80, Fax 03 84 92 15 23

Le Balcon with rm

– ✆ 03 84 92 11 13 – Closed 23 June-2 July, 28 September-3 October, 26 December-15 January, Sunday dinner, Tuesday lunch and Monday

15 rm – €48/68 €58/68, €9 – ½ P €55

Rest – Menu €25/62 – Carte €50/73

◆ This Virginia creeper clad inn sports a stylish dining room (white tablecloths, copperware and polished antique furniture). Tasty, traditional fare. Book a quiet guestroom at the rear.

LES COMBES – **25 Doubs** – **321** J4 – **see Morteau**

COMBES – **34 Hérault** – **339** D7 – **see Lamalou-les-Bains**

COMBLOUX – **74 Haute-Savoie** – **328** M5 – **pop. 2 047** – **alt. 980 m** 46 **F1** – **Winter sports : 1 000/1 850 m** **1** **24** – ✉ **74920** **French Alps**

Paris 593 – Annecy 80 – Bonneville 37 – Chamonix-Mont-Blanc 31 – Megève 6 – Morzine 50

Office de tourisme, 49, chemin des Passerands ✆ 04 50 58 60 49, Fax 04 50 93 33 55

✳★★★ - Viewpoint indicator★ of the Cry.

Aux Ducs de Savoie

au Bouchet – ✆ 04 50 58 61 43 – www.ducs-de-savoie.com – info@ducs-de-savoie.com – Fax 04 50 58 67 43 – Open 1st June-6 October and 15 December-25 April

50 rm – €140/220 €140/220, €18 – ½ P €120/150

Rest – Menu €35/45 – Carte €42/55

◆ This huge wooden chalet offers you a warm welcome and a splendid alpine panorama. Identical rooms, lounge with fireplace and swimming pool opposite Mont-Blanc. Home cooking and Savoy specialities in the "all-wood" panoramic dining room.

Au Coeur des Prés

152 chemin du Champet – ✆ 04 50 93 36 55 – www.hotelaucoeurdespres.com – hotelaucoeurdespres@wanadoo.fr – Fax 04 50 58 69 14 – Open end May-end September and mid December-beg. April

33 rm – €80/100 €120/145, €12 **Rest** – Menu €30

◆ On the heights overlooking Combloux, simple accommodation but bright, wood panelled and fairly spacious with views of the peaks. Pleasant sitting room with fireplace. Extensive view, tasteful decor (wooden ceiling) and classic menu in the restaurant.

Joly Site

81 rte de Sallanches – ✆ 04 50 58 60 07 – www.joly-site.com – joly-site@joly-site.com

10 rm – €75/95 €150/190, €9

Rest – *(closed Monday dinner and Tuesday dinner in low season)* Menu (€12), €19, €26/35 – Carte €22/41

◆ Recently renovated, the hotel offers rooms that are both traditional and modern; many of which have direct access to the garden. Alpine and southern recipes take pride of place in the restaurant, served around the central fireplace.

Coin Savoyard

300 rte Cry, Cuchet – ✆ 04 50 58 60 27 – www.coin-savoyard.com – info@coin-savoyard.com – Fax 04 50 58 64 44 – Open 6 June-20 September and 12 December-11 April

14 rm – €95 €115, €10 – ½ P €82/92

Rest – *(closed Monday lunch in winter except school holidays and Monday in June and September)* Carte €21/45

◆ Friendly 19C farmhouse next to the church. Despite its traditional alpine inn appearance it offers comfortably renovated rooms with views of the peaks. Regional specialities served by the poolside in fine weather.

COMBOURG – 35 Ille-et-Vilaine – 309 L4 – pop. 5 223 – alt. 45 m – ✉ 35270 Brittany — 10 D2

Paris 387 – Avranches 58 – Dinan 25 – Fougères 49 – Rennes 41 – St-Malo 36 – Vitré 56

Office de tourisme, 23, place Albert Parent ✆ 02 99 73 13 93, Fax 02 99 73 52 39

des Ormes Dol-de-Bretagne Epiniac, N : 13 km on D 795, ✆ 02 99 73 54 44

Château★.

Du Château

1 pl. Chateaubriand – ✆ 02 99 73 00 38 – www.hotelduchateau.com – hotelduchateau@wanadoo.fr – Fax 02 99 73 25 79 – Closed 19 December-27 January, Sunday dinner except July-August, Monday lunch and Saturday lunch

33 rm – €57/149 €57/149, €11 – 1 suite – ½ P €89/179

Rest – Menu €21 (weekdays)/55 – Carte €35/70

◆ At the foot of the château and lake made famous by Chateaubriand, is this attractive old house and outbuildings. Personalised, partly refurbished rooms. Menu combining traditional and regional dishes with Chateaubriand steak in pride of place. Summer garden-terrace.

COMBREUX – 45 Loiret – 318 K4 – pop. 202 – alt. 130 m – ✉ 45530 — 12 C2

Paris 113 – Bellegarde 12 – Châteauneuf-sur-Loire 14 – Orléans 41 – Pithiviers 31

Auberge de Combreux

33 rte du Gatinais – ✆ 02 38 46 89 89 – www.auberge-de-combreux.fr – contact@auberge-de-combreux.fr – Fax 02 38 59 36 19 – Closed from mid-December to 24 January and Sunday dinner from November to April

19 rm – €60 €60/79, €9 – ½ P €66/78

Rest – *(closed Friday lunch from May to October, Sunday dinner from November to April and Monday lunch)* Menu (€19), €29/36 – Carte €35/56

◆ Near the forest, an ivy-clad former post house and its annexe consisting of three small houses set in a garden. Rustic-style rooms, two with Jacuzzis. A welcoming dining room with countrified decor, leafy terrace and cuisine with a contemporary touch.

COMMELLE-VERNAY – 42 Loire – 327 D4 – see Roanne

COMMERCY – 55 Meuse – 307 E6 – pop. 6 324 – alt. 240 m – ✉ 55200 26 B2

Paris 269 – Bar-le-Duc 40 – Metz 73 – Nancy 53 – Toul 31 – Verdun 56

Office de tourisme, Château Stanislas ✆ 03 29 91 33 16

Côté Jardin without rest rest, P VISA MC
40 r. St-Mihiel – ✆ 03 29 92 09 09 – www.hotelcommercy.com
– bernard.bou794@orange.fr – Fax 03 29 92 09 10
13 rm – †€ 55/70 ††€ 66/90, ☕ € 8
◆ An immense French-style garden surrounds this inviting house. Spacious rooms decorated in a lovely warm blue and yellow colour scheme.

De la Madeleine P VISA MC
La Louvière, (Nancy road) – ✆ 03 29 91 51 25
– www.commerce-hoteldelamadeleine.com – hotelmadeleine@free.fr
– Fax 03 29 91 09 59
26 rm – †€ 44/62 ††€ 58/70, ☕ € 6
Rest – *(closed Friday dinner and Sunday dinner)* Menu € 12 (weekdays)/32 – Carte € 16/36
◆ A modern hotel in the land of the famous madeleine cake. It offers airy, practical and well-soundproofed rooms, furnished in wood and wrought iron. Quick, simple, traditional dishes served in a dining room lit by wide bay windows.

COMPIÈGNE – 60 Oise – 305 H4 – pop. 41 700 – Built-up area 108 234 – alt. 41 m – ✉ 60200 36 B2

Northern France and the Paris Region

Paris 81 – Amiens 80 – Beauvais 61 – St-Quentin 74 – Soissons 39

Office de tourisme, place de l'Hôtel de Ville ✆ 03 44 40 01 00, Fax 03 44 40 23 28

de Compiègne Avenue Royale, E : on the avenue Royale, ✆ 03 44 38 48 00

du Château d'Humières Monchy Humières Rue de Gournay, NW : 9 km on D 202, ✆ 03 44 86 48 22

Palace★★★: musée de la voiture★★, musée du Second Empire★★ - Town hall★ BZ **H** - Musée de la Figurine historique★ BZ **M** - Musée Vivenel: Greek vases ★★ AZ **M**[1].

Forêt★★ (les Beaux Monts) - Rethondes: Clairière de l'Armistice (Armistice Clearing)★★ (statue of Marshal Foch, memorial stone, Marshal Foch carriage).

Plan on next page

De Flandre without rest VISA MC
16 quai République – ✆ 03 44 83 24 40 – www.hoteldeflandre.com
– hoteldeflandre@wanadoo.fr – Fax 03 44 90 02 75
– Closed 18 December-3 January AY **u**
42 rm – †€ 32/57 ††€ 37/70, ☕ € 8,50
◆ Near the station on the right bank of the Oise. Rustic-style rooms, gradually being modernised. Efficient soundproofing counters the noise from the crossroad traffic.

L'Hostellerie du Royal Lieu with rm rm,
9 r. de Senlis, 2 km to the southwest on the r. de Paris P VISA MC AE
– ✆ 03 44 20 10 24 – www.host-royallieu.com
– hostellerieduroyallieu@hotmail.com – Fax 03 44 86 82 27
15 rm – †€ 110/130 ††€ 110/140, ☕ € 14
Rest – Menu € 30/75 – Carte € 50/125
◆ This classical establishment by the forest is eminently peaceful. Traditional dining room and more up-to-date veranda facing the countryside. Seasonal, updated cuisine. The generously dimensioned rooms are elegant, stylish and comfortable.

COMPIÈGNE

Austerlitz (R. d') . . . . AZ 2
Boucheries (R. des) . . . . AZ 3
Capucins (R. des) . . . . AZ 4
Change (Pl. du) . . . . AZ 5
Clemenceau (Av. G.) . . . . BY 6
Harlay (R. de) . . . . AY 8
Hôtel-de-Ville (Pl. de l') . . . . . . AZ 10
Legendre (R. J.) . . . . BZ 12
Lombards (R. des) . . . . BZ 13
Magenta (R.) . . . . BZ 14
Notre-Dame-de-Bon-Secours (R.) . . . . AZ 15
Noyon (R. de) . . . . AY 16
Paris (R. de) . . . . AZ 17
Pierrefonds (R. de) . . . . BZ 18
St-Antoine (R.) . . . . AZ 19
St-Corneille (R.) . . . . AZ 20
St-Jacques (Pl.) . . . . BZ 22
Soissons (R. de) . . . . BY 24
Solferino (R.) . . . . AYZ 25
Sorel (R. du Prés.) . . . . AZ 26
Sous-Préfecture (R. de la) . . . BZ 27
54e-Rgt.-d'Infanterie (Pl.) . . . . AY 30

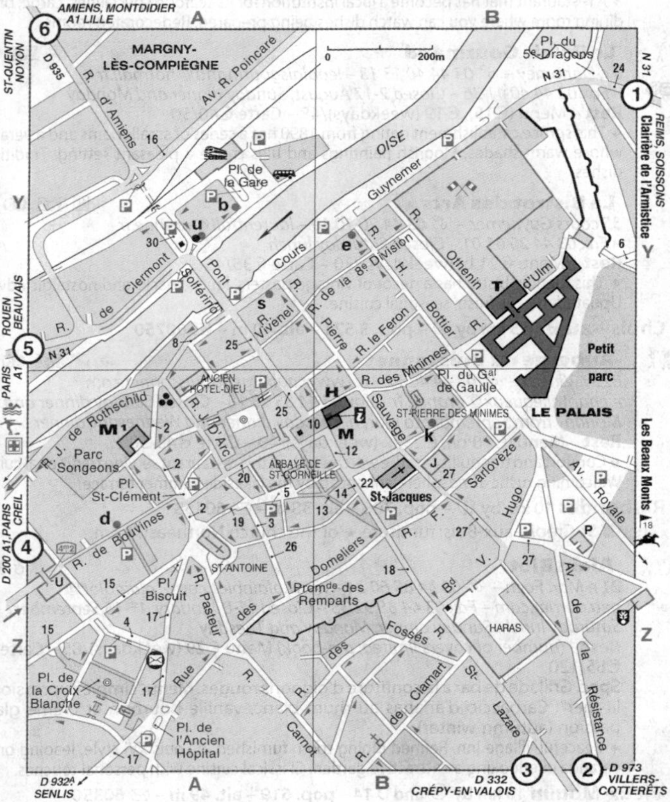

XXX **Rive Gauche** AC VISA MC

13 cours Guynemer – ☎ 03 44 40 29 99 – http://perso.orange.fr/rivegauche – rivegauche@orange.fr – Fax 03 44 40 38 00 – Closed Monday and Tuesday

Rest – Menu € 38/48 – Carte € 65/90 BY **e**

◆ A sober but elegant modern dining room, enlivened by paintings, on the left bank of the Oise. Cuisine with a contemporary touch, and select wines.

XXX **La Part des Anges** AC P VISA MC AE

18 r. Bouvines – ☎ 03 44 86 00 00 – www.lapartdesanges60.com – lapartdesanges60@wanadoo.fr – Fax 03 44 86 09 00 – Closed 27 July-24 August, 21-28 December, Saturday lunch, Sunday dinner and Monday AZ **d**

Rest – Menu (€ 33 bi), € 36/56 – Carte € 42/60

◆ A dining room in two parts (one modern, the other more intimate), adorned with a fresco depicting the 'Angels' share' and cherubs. Carefully prepared cuisine with a contemporary touch.

XX **Du Nord** with rm

pl. de la Gare – 03 44 83 22 30 – hoteldunord@9business.fr – Fax 03 44 90 11 87 – Closed 1st-15 August, Saturday lunch and Sunday dinner AY **b**

20 rm – †€ 49 ††€ 55, ☐ € 7 – ½ P € 71

Rest – Menu € 25 (weekdays)/50 bi – Carte € 43/120

♦ A restaurant that has become a local institution for its seafood specialities. Large, bright dining room where you can watch dishes being prepared. Redecorated rooms.

X **Le Palais Gourmand**

8 r. Dahomey – 03 44 40 13 13 – lepalaisgourmand@hotmail.fr – Fax 03 44 40 41 36 – Closed 2-17 August, Sunday dinner and Monday

Rest – Menu (€ 15), € 19 (weekdays)/48 – Carte € 40/50 BZ **k**

♦ This spruce establishment dating from 1890 has a series of small rooms and a veranda, whose warm shades, Moorish paintings and tiles create a pleasant setting. Traditional dishes.

X **Le Bistrot des Arts**

35 cours Guynemer – 03 44 20 10 10 – laurentfull@orange.fr – Fax 03 44 20 61 01 – Closed Saturday lunch AY **s**

Rest – Menu € 21 bi (weekdays)/30 – Carte € 35/45

♦ This friendly bistro has a decor of vintage posters, knick-knacks and nostalgic adverts. Updated market-fresh, seasonal cuisine.

in Choisy-au-Bac 5 km by ② – pop. 3 571 – alt. 40 m – ✉ 60750

XX **Auberge du Buissonnet**

825 r. Vineux – 03 44 40 17 41 – www.aubergedubuissonnet.com – chantallequeux@orange.fr – Fax 03 44 85 28 18 – Closed Sunday dinner and Monday from September to March, Tuesday dinner and Wednesday dinner

Rest – Menu (€ 18 bi), € 23 bi (weekdays)/40 – Carte € 40/50

♦ Comfort and tranquility are the watchwords at this restaurant serving traditional cuisine. Welcoming rustic atmosphere enhanced by the lakeside summer terrace.

in Rethondes 10 km by ② – pop. 706 – alt. 38 m – ✉ 60153

St-Crépin-aux-Bois: furniture ★ of the church Northeast: 4 km.

XXX **Alain Blot**

21 r. Mar. Foch – 03 44 85 60 24 – www.alainblot.com – alainblot@netcourrier.com – Fax 03 44 85 92 35 – Closed 1st-8 January, 1st-15 September, Saturday lunch, Sunday dinner, Monday and Tuesday

Rest – *(number of covers limited, pre-book)* Menu € 29 (weekdays)/85 – Carte € 85/120

Spec. Grillade de bar à la confiture d'oignons rouges. Menu "simple expression de la mer". Carpaccio d'ananas au rhum blanc, vanille bourbon et crème glacée passion (autumn-winter).

♦ Peaceful village inn. Refined dining room furnished in Louis XVI style, leading onto a veranda overlooking an attractive garden. Classical cuisine with personal touches.

in Vieux-Moulin 10 km by ③ and D 14 – pop. 619 – alt. 49 m – ✉ 60350

Mont St-Marc★ North: 2 km - Les Beaux-Monts★★: ≤★ NorthwestWest: 7 km.

XXX **Auberge du Daguet**

25 r. Saint Jean, (opposite the church) – 03 44 85 60 72 – http://auberge.du.daguet.free.fr – auberge.du.daguet@free.fr – Fax 03 44 85 60 72 – Closed 13-24 July and 4-29 January

Rest – Menu (€ 29), € 36/50 – Carte € 52/83

♦ This welcoming country inn faces the church and its coolie-hat shaped belfry. Stained glass windows, stonework and exposed beams form a medieval setting. Game served in season.

XX **Auberge du Mont St-Pierre**

28 rte des Étangs – 03 44 85 60 00 – www.aubergedumontsaintpierre.fr – contact@aubergedumontsaintpierre.fr – Fax 03 44 85 23 03 – Closed 7-24 August, February holiday, Sunday dinner, Thursday dinner and Monday except bank holidays

Rest – Menu (€ 20), € 28/40 – Carte € 46/67

♦ This local-style inn, on the edge of the forest, has a veranda dining room with hunting decor and a peaceful summer terrace. Seasonal produce and game.

Z.A.C. de Mercières 6 km by ⑤ and D 200 – ✉ 60472 Compiègne

Mercure rm, VISA MC AE

carrefour J. Monnet – ✆ 03 44 30 30 30 – www.mercure.com – H1623@accor.com – Fax 03 44 30 30 44

92 rm – €110 €118, ☕ €15

Rest – *(closed Sunday lunch and Saturday)* Menu (€16), €22 (weekdays) – Carte €32/45

◆ This hotel between the town and the motorway has been designed for the wellbeing of the traveller: comfort, space, good soundproofing and a convivial bar, perfect for relaxation. Large, discreet modern dining room with a summer terrace. "Mercure" menu and grills.

in Meux 11 km by ⑤, D 200 and D 98 – pop. 2 027 – alt. 50 m – ✉ 60880

Auberge de la Vieille Ferme rest, VISA MC AE

58 r. de la République – ✆ 03 44 41 58 54 – auberge.vieille.ferme@wanadoo.fr – Fax 03 44 41 23 50 – Closed 3 weeks in August and 28 December-3 January

14 rm – €62 €70, ☕ €8 – ½ P €90

Rest – *(closed Saturday lunch, Sunday dinner and Monday)* Menu (€20), €27/38 – Carte €30/53

◆ Old farmhouse in red brick from the Oise Valley. Simple, functional and well-kept rooms on either side of two inner courtyards. A restaurant with a country atmosphere serving traditional food based on local products.

XX **L'Annexe** VISA MC

1 r. République – ✆ 03 44 91 10 10 – restaurantlannexe@orange.fr – Fax 03 44 40 38 00 – Closed Sunday dinner, Monday dinner and Tuesday dinner

Rest – Menu (€18), €24/34

◆ Restaurant with interior refurbished in the style of a contemporary bistro using warm shades. Tranquil summer terrace under a wisteria. Contemporary cuisine.

COMPS-SUR-ARTUBY – 83 Var – 340 O3 – pop. 320 – alt. 898 m — 41 C2
– ✉ 83840 French Alps

Paris 892 – Castellane 29 – Digne-les-Bains 82 – Draguignan 31 – Grasse 60 – Manosque 97

Balcons de la Mescla★★★ Northwest: 14,5 km - Tunnels de Fayet ←★★★ West: 20 km.

Grand Hôtel Bain VISA MC AE

Av. de Fayet – ✆ 04 94 76 90 06 – www.grand-hotel-bain.fr – reservation@grand-hotel-bain.fr – Fax 04 94 76 92 24 – Closed 11 November-26 December

17 rm – €58/65 €58/65, ☕ €8,50 – ½ P €56/60

Rest – Menu €18/39 – Carte €34/65

◆ Hotel mentioned in the Book of Records. It has been run by the same family since 1737. Functional rooms in Provencal rustic style. Traditional cuisine with regional accents served in a dining room overlooking the valley.

CONCARNEAU – 29 Finistère – 308 H7 – pop. 19 700 – alt. 4 m — 9 B2
– ✉ 29900 Brittany

Paris 546 – Brest 96 – Lorient 49 – Quimper 22 – Vannes 102

for **Beg Meil** - (July-August) Crossing 25 mn - Information and prices: Vedettes Glenn, opposite yachting harbour at Concarneau ✆ 02 98 97 10 31, Fax 02 98 60 49 70

for Îles Glénan - (April to Sept.) Crossing 1 h 10 mn - Information and prices: Vedettes de l'Odet ✆ for Glénan isles and Rivière de l'Odet - Vieux Port Bénodet

for **La Rivière de l'Odet** - (April to Sept.) Crossing 4 h return - Information and prices: see above (Vedettes Glenn), at Port de pêche of Bénodet.

Office de tourisme, quai d'Aiguillon ✆ 02 98 97 01 44, Fax 02 98 50 88 81

Enclosed town★★ C - Musée de la Pêche★ **M**[1] - Pont du Moros ←★ B - Fête des Filets bleus (Blue nets fair)★ (end of August).

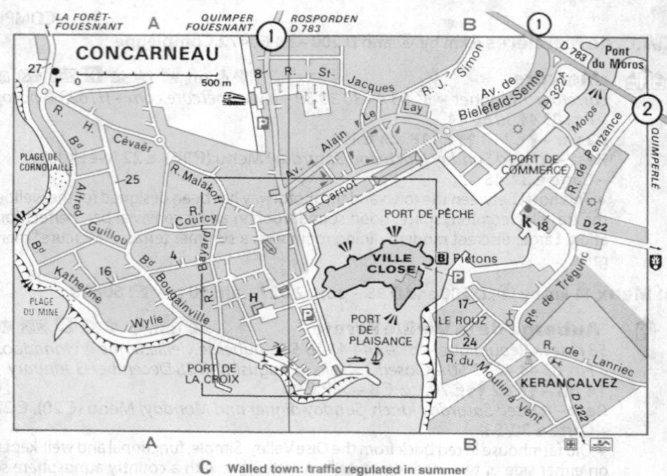

C Walled town: traffic regulated in summer

Bougainville (Bd)	C	3
Courbet (R. Amiral)	A	4
Croix (Quai de la)	C	5
Dr-P.-Nicolas (Av. du)	C	6
Dumont-d'Urville (R.)	C	7
Gare (Av. de la)	AC	8
Gaulle (Pl. Gén.-de)	C	9
Guéguin (Av. Pierre)	C	10
Jean-Jaurès (Pl.)	C	12
Le Lay (Av. Alain)	B	
Libération (R. de la)	A	16
Mauduit-Duplessis (R.)	B	17
Moros (R. du)	B	18
Morvan (R. Gén.)	C	20
Pasteur (R.)	B	24
Renan (R. Ernest)	A	25
Sables-Blancs (R. des)	A	27
Vauban (R.)	C	29

L'Océan rest,

plage des Sables Blancs – ✆ 02 98 50 53 50 – www.hotel-ocean.com – hotel-ocean@wanadoo.fr – Fax 02 98 50 84 16 A **r**

70 rm – †€ 79/125 ††€ 89/145, ☕ € 12 – ½ P € 79/99

Rest – *(Closed December, January, Sunday from October to March, Saturday lunch and Monday lunch)* Menu € 28, € 35/45 – Carte € 30/50

◆ Impressive modern building overlooking the sea. Spacious practical rooms: those at the front have large balconies and an attractive sea view. Large restaurant opposite the bay of Concarneau. Contemporary setting and traditional cuisine.

Les Sables Blancs

plage des Sables Blancs – ✆ 02 98 50 10 12 – www.hotel-les-sables-blancs.com – contact@hotel-les-sables-blancs.com – Fax 02 98 97 20 92 A

20 rm – †€ 95/160 ††€ 105/370, ☕ € 14

Rest – *(closed 11 November-11 December)* Menu (€ 25), € 30/85 – Carte € 50/100

◆ Beautiful hotel on the water's edge with direct access to the beach. Refurbished in a chic, contemporary style. Low key decor in the bedrooms endowed with terraces. Seafood served in the lounge restaurant with ocean views as far as the eye can see.

Des Halles without rest
pl. de l'Hôtel de Ville – ✆ 02 98 97 11 41 – www.hoteldeshalles.com – contact@hoteldeshalles.com – Fax 02 98 50 58 54 C s
25 rm – †€ 43/84 ††€ 54/84, ☕ € 10
◆ A family quality characterises this hotel (non-smokers only); personalised rooms of varying sizes, most of which sport a bright and colourful marine style.

France et Europe without rest
9 av. de la Gare – ✆ 02 98 97 00 64 – www.hotel-france-europe.com – hotel.france-europe@wanadoo.fr – Fax 02 98 50 76 66 – Closed 11 December-11 January and Saturday from mid-November to mid-March C b
25 rm – †€ 54/100 ††€ 54/100, ☕ € 10
◆ The location of the building on a main road does not affect the tranquillity of its functional rooms fitted with double-glazing. Nautical-inspired breakfast room.

La Coquille
1 quai du Moros – ✆ 02 98 97 08 52 – www.lacoquille-concarneau.com – sicallac@wanadoo.fr – Fax 02 98 50 69 13 – Closed Sunday dinner and Monday in low season B k
Rest – Menu € 29/60 – Carte € 40/80
Rest *Le Bistrot* – *(lunch only)* Menu € 15
◆ Facing the port, this rustic restaurant is decorated with light colours and a collection of maritime photos and lithographs. Fish and seafood specialities. This bistro has an attractive, maritime atmosphere. Limited menu at lunchtime.

Chez Armande
15 bis av. Dr Nicolas – ✆ 02 98 97 00 76 – Fax 02 98 60 69 17 – Closed 6-26 November, Tuesday except July-August and Wednesday C d
Rest – Menu (€ 14 bi), € 18/43 – Carte € 40/70
◆ Generous portions of traditional cuisine in which seafood takes pride of place await you in this house opposite the walled city. Attractive, typically Breton dining room.

L'Amiral
1 av. P. Guéguin – ✆ 02 98 60 55 23 – www.restaurant-amiral.com – info@restaurant-amiral.com – Closed 28 September-12 October, February holiday, Sunday dinner and Monday except July-August C t
Rest – Menu (€ 15), € 18 (weekdays)/39 – Carte € 31/51
◆ Handy location between the tourist office and walled town. Pleasant wood and nautical-inspired decoration and traditional menu.

Le Buccin
1 r. Duguay-Trouin – ✆ 02 98 50 54 22 – www.le-buccin.com – Fax 02 98 50 70 37 – Closed 3 weeks in November, Tuesday from October to June and Monday C v
Rest – Menu (€ 14), € 21 (weekdays)/40 – Carte € 38/50
◆ Off the tourist track, this very popular restaurant serves traditional meals with an emphasis on fish in a warm atmosphere (orange and yellow colour scheme and works of art).

CONCHES-EN-OUCHE – 27 Eure – 304 F8 – pop. 4 982 – alt. 123 m – ✉ 27190 Normandy 33 D2

Paris 118 – Bernay 34 – Dreux 49 – Évreux 18 – Rouen 61

Syndicat d'initiative, place A. Briand ✆ 02 32 30 76 42, Fax 02 32 60 22 35

Ste-Foy church ★.

La Grand'Mare
13 av. Croix-de-Fer – ✆ 02 32 30 23 30 – Closed Sunday evening, Tuesday evening and Monday
Rest – Menu (€ 11), € 13/27 – Carte € 21/32
◆ This inn with its elegant wood panelled dining room blends a half-timbered house with a more simple interior (fireplace). Traditional fare and dishes of the day on the blackboard.

CONCHY-LES-POTS – 60 Oise – 305 H3 – pop. 595 – alt. 106 m – ✉ 60490 36 **B2**

Paris 100 – Compiègne 28 – Amiens 55 – Beauvais 68 – Montdidier 14 – Roye 13

Le Relais

D 1017 – ✆ 03 44 85 01 17 – Closed 27 July-11 August, 15-24 February, Sunday dinner, Wednesday dinner, Monday and Tuesday

Rest – Menu € 28/84 – Carte € 60/90

◆ You should have no hesitation in entering this former transport café with its facade painted yellow. The dining room is bright and stylish and you can enjoy generous, traditional cuisine.

CONCREMIERS – 36 Indre – 323 C7 – pop. 630 – alt. 82 m – ✉ 36300 11 **B3**

Paris 337 – Orléans 212 – Châteauroux 66 – Châtellerault 65 – Chauvigny 32

Château de Forges without rest

1 km west on the D 53 – ✆ 02 54 37 40 03 – www.chateaudeforges.fr – chateaudeforges@orange.fr

3 rm – †€ 139 ††€ 148

◆ This medieval fortress on a riverbank has lost none of its character. The lovely rooms mingle old and new details. Regional produce on the breakfast table.

CONDÉ-NORTHEN – 57 Moselle – 307 J4 – pop. 563 – alt. 208 m – ✉ 57220 27 **C1**

Paris 350 – Metz 21 – Pont-à-Mousson 52 – Saarlouis 38 – Saarbrücken 52 – Thionville 49

La Grange de Condé

rm,

41 r. Deux-Nieds – ✆ 03 87 79 30 50 – www.lagrangedeconde.com – lagrangedeconde@wanadoo.fr – Fax 03 87 79 30 51

17 rm – †€ 105 ††€ 105, € 12 – 3 suites – ½ P € 88

Rest – Menu (€ 10), € 16/48 – Carte € 43/60

◆ Additional hotel accommodation has been added to this family farmhouse dating back to 1682. The rooms are comfortable and there is a sauna, Jacuzzi and Turkish bath. Spit-roasts and garden-fresh vegetables are served in the pleasant rustic Lorraine-style dining room.

CONDOM – 32 Gers – 336 E6 – pop. 7 158 – alt. 81 m – ✉ 32100 28 **A2**

Languedoc-Roussillon-Tarn Gorges

Paris 729 – Agen 41 – Mont-de-Marsan 80 – Toulouse 121 – Auch 46

Office de tourisme, place Bossuet ✆ 05 62 28 00 80, Fax 05 62 28 45 46

St-Pierre cathedral ★: Cloister★ Y

Plan on next page

Les Trois Lys

38 r. Gambetta – ✆ 05 62 28 33 33 – www.lestroislys.com – hoteltroislys@wanadoo.fr – Fax 05 62 28 41 85 Y **a**

10 rm – †€ 50/170 ††€ 80/170, € 9

Rest – *(closed Monday lunch, Thursday lunch and Sunday except July-August)* Menu (€ 22 bi), € 35 – Carte approx. € 35

◆ An elegant 18C residence with individually decorated rooms. Many have fine antique furniture and some have a fireplace. Attractive swimming-pool at the rear. Refurbished dining room, teak courtyard terrace, plus a cosy bar.

Continental

rm, rm,

20 r. Mar. Foch – ✆ 05 62 68 37 00 – www.lecontinental.net – lecontinental@lecontinental.net – Fax 05 62 68 23 71 – Closed 20-27 December Y **d**

25 rm – †€ 43/68 ††€ 43/68, € 8

Rest – *(closed Saturday lunchtime, Sunday evening and Monday)* Menu € 14 (weekday lunch), € 21/33 – Carte € 29/35

◆ The River Baïse flows at the foot of this fully refurbished hotel. Comfortable rooms, decorated with old engravings, most of which overlook a small garden. Traditional and regional dishes served in a bright, sunlit dining room. Summer terrace in the courtyard.

CONDOM

Aquitaine (Av. d') . . . . Y 2
Armuriers (R. des) . . . . Y 5
Barlet (Pont) . . . . Y 7
Bonnamy (R.) . . . . YZ 8
Buzon (R. et Quai) . . . . Z 12
Carmes (Pont des) . . . . Z 14
Cazaubon (R. H.) . . . . Z 16
Charron (R.) . . . . Y 19
Cordeliers (R. des) . . . . Z 21
Foch (R. Mar.) . . . . Y 22
Gaichies (R.) . . . . Y 24
Gambetta (R. L.) . . . . Y 26
Jean-Jaurès (R.) . . . . Z 28
Lannelongue (Pl.) . . . . Y 31
Lion-d'Or (Pl. du) . . . . Y 35
Monnaie (R. de la) . . . . YZ 38
Paix (R. de la) . . . . Z 40
Roquepine (R. de) . . . . Z 44
Roques (R.) . . . . Y 47
Saint-Exupéry (R.) . . . . Z 50
St-Pierre (Pl.) . . . . Y 53

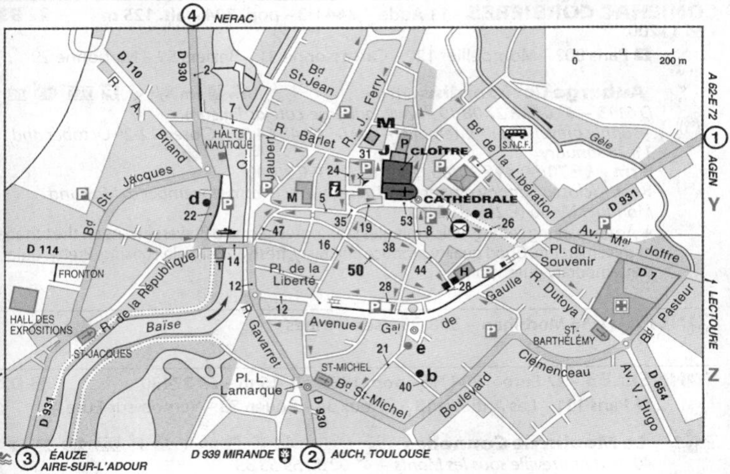

Logis des Cordeliers without rest

r. de la Paix – ✆ 05 62 28 03 68 – www.logisdescordeliers.com – info@logisdescordeliers.com – Fax 05 62 68 29 03 – Closed 2 January-3 February

21 rm – €48/66 €48/70, ☕ €8 Z **b**

◆ New building located in a peaceful district. Functional rooms: opt for those on the swimming pool side, which have small flower-filled balconies. Friendly welcome.

La Table des Cordeliers (Eric Sampietro)

1 r. des Cordeliers – ✆ 05 62 68 43 82 – www.latabledescordeliers.fr – info@latabledescordeliers.fr – Fax 05 62 28 15 92 – Closed 3-19 January, 7-23 February, Sunday dinner, Wednesday dinner in low season, Tuesday lunch and Wednesday lunch in high season and Monday Z **e**

Rest – Menu €25 (weekdays)/95 bi – Carte €50/70

Spec. Saint Jacques à la plancha, racines en salade. Ris de veau poêlé, purée de chou-fleur, noisettes grillées. Figues rôties, massepain aux amandes fraîches (Sep.-Oct.). **Wines** Vin de Pays du Gers.

◆ Housed in the cloisters and chapel of a 13C convent, this modern-style restaurant serves contemporary cuisine centred on locally sourced produce.

CONDRIEU – 69 Rhône – 327 H7 – pop. 3 579 – alt. 150 m – ✉ 69420 44 **B2**

Lyon - Rhone Valley

Paris 497 – Annonay 34 – Lyon 41 – Rive-de-Gier 21 – Tournon-sur-Rhône 55 – Vienne 12

Office de tourisme, place du Séquoïa ✆ 04 74 56 62 83, Fax 04 74 56 65 85

Calvary ≤★.

Hôtellerie Beau Rivage

r. Beau Rivage – ✆ 04 74 56 82 82 – www.hotel-beaurivage.com – infos@hotel-beaurivage.com – Fax 04 74 59 59 36

18 rm – €115/160 €115/160, ☕ €19 – 10 suites

Rest – Menu (€38 bi), €43 (lunch), €60/82 – Carte €68/125

◆ This sturdy bourgeois riverside home stands in one of the Côtes du Rhône's most prestigious vineyards. Elegant rooms. Classic cuisine in a southern French style. Terrace.

CONFLANS-STE-HONORINE – 78 Yvelines – 311 I2 – 101 3 – see Paris, Area

CONFLANS-SUR-LOING – see MONTARGIS

CONILHAC CORBIERES – 11 Aude – 344 H3 – pop. 704 – alt. 125 m – ✉ 11200 22 B3

Paris 802 – Montpellier 120 – Carcassonne 31 – Béziers 59 – Narbonne 29

Auberge Coté Jardin with rm

D 6113 – ✆ 04 68 27 08 19 – www.auberge-cotejardin.com – sophie.prevel@club-internet.fr – Fax 04 68 48 64 60 – Closed 12-29 October and 11-28 January

8 rm – € 70/80 € 70/80, € 10 – ½ P € 70/90

Rest – *(closed Sunday dinner and Tuesday lunch from November to May and Monday)* Menu (€ 20), € 28/50

◆ An enchanting setting which mingles stone, greenery and flowers awaits on the terrace of this smart inn. Good quality produce and tasty, fresh and simple cooking. Pretty, quiet, contemporary guestrooms.

CONLEAU – 56 Morbihan – 308 O9 – see Vannes

CONNELLES – 27 Eure – 304 H6 – pop. 188 – alt. 15 m – ✉ 27430 33 D2

Paris 111 – Les Andelys 13 – Évreux 34 – Rouen 33 – Vernon-sur-Eure 40

Le Moulin de Connelles

40 rte d'Amfreville sous les Monts – ✆ 02 32 59 53 33 – www.moulin-de-connelles.fr – moulindeconnelles@wanadoo.fr – Fax 02 32 59 21 83

8 rm – € 130 € 140/150, € 15 – 6 suites

Rest – *(closed for lunch in July-August, Sunday and Monday from October to April)* Menu € 33/58 – Carte € 46/60

◆ This ravishing Anglo-Norman mansion-mill is nestled in the heart of a park on an island in the Seine. It is poised between romanticism and impressionism and is a haven of peace and quiet. Classical cuisine in a modern setting, as well as a veranda overlooking the river.

CONQUES – 12 Aveyron – 338 G3 – pop. 302 – alt. 350 m – ✉ 12320 29 C1

Languedoc-Roussillon-Tarn Gorges

Paris 601 – Aurillac 53 – Espalion 42 – Figeac 43 – Rodez 37

Office de tourisme, Le Bourg ✆ 08 20 82 08 03, Fax 05 65 72 87 03

Site★★ - Village★ - Ste-Foy abbey church ★★: tympanum of the west portal ★★★ and Conques treasure-house ★★★ - Le Cendié★ West: 2 km by D 232 - Site du Bancarel★ South: 3 km by D 901.

Ste-Foy

r. Principale – ✆ 05 65 69 84 03 – www.hotelsaintefoy.com – hotelsaintefoy@hotelsaintefoy.fr – Fax 05 65 72 81 04 – Open 1 May-25 October

17 rm – € 100/130 € 130/170, € 14

Rest – Menu (€ 18), € 25 (lunch), € 30/53 – Carte € 40/60

◆ 17C house typical of Rouergue, with view of the magnificent abbey. Old stone, beams and rustic or period furniture add character to the rooms. Dining rooms with character and two rustic terraces. Contemporary menu.

Auberge St-Jacques with rm

r. Gonzague Florent – ✆ 05 65 72 86 36 – www.aubergestjacques.fr – info@aubergestjacques.fr – Fax 05 65 72 82 47 – Closed 3 January-3 February

13 rm – € 42/62 € 42/62, € 8,50 – ½ P € 49

Rest – *(closed Sunday dinner and Monday from November to April)* Menu € 18/38 – Carte € 22/40

◆ The chef of this rustic restaurant prepares generous dishes of regional inspiration with creative touches. Simply decorated, calm guestrooms.

South 3 km on D 901 – ✉ 12320 Conques

Le Moulin de Cambelong (Hervé Busset)
– ✆ 05 65 72 84 77 – *www.moulindecambelong.com*
– *domaine-de-cambelong@wanadoo.fr – Fax 05 65 72 83 91*
– *Open 16 March-1st November and closed Monday off season*
10 rm (½ board only) – ½ P € 130/170 **Rest** – Menu € 55/85
Spec. Oeuf "Louisette" au foie de canard fumé. Agneau allaiton d'Aveyron à l'origan. Profiterole au mélilot sauvage. **Wines** Marcillac, Vin de Pays de l'Aveyron.
◆ In one of the last remaining 18C watermills on the Dourdou. Pretty rooms with personal touches, fabric hangings on the walls and period furniture. A creative menu mixing flowers and local produce, with a waterfall in the background.

CONQUES-SUR-ORBIEL – 11 Aude – 344 F3 – pop. 2 269 – alt. 127 m – ✉ 11600

22 **B2**

Paris 777 – Montpellier 155 – Carcassonne 12 – Castres 62 – Castelnaudary 43

La Maison Pujol without rest
17 r. F.-Mistral – ✆ *04 68 26 98 18 – www.lamaisonpujol.com – postmaster@lamaisonpujol.com – Closed January and February*
4 rm – €80 €90
◆ Stylish interior architecture: raw materials, spotless white colour scheme, designer objects, artwork, etc. The same spirit depicts the rooms. Pool. Breakfast beneath a pergola.

LE CONQUET – 29 Finistère – 308 C4 – pop. 2 534 – alt. 30 m – ✉ 29217 Brittany

9 **A2**

Paris 619 – Brest 24 – Brignogan-Plages 59 – St-Pol-de-Léon 85
Office de tourisme, parc de Beauséjour ✆ 02 98 89 11 31, Fax 02 98 89 08 20
Site★.
Île d'Ouessant★★ - Les Abers★★.

in la Pointe de St-Mathieu 4 km south – ✉ 29217 Plougonvelin

Lighthouse ✻★★ – Ruins of the abbey church★.

Hostellerie de la Pointe St-Mathieu
– ✆ *02 98 89 00 19 – www.pointe-saint-mathieu.com*
– *saintmathieu.hotel@wanadoo.fr – Fax 02 98 89 15 68 – Closed February*
27 rm – €90/150 €100/170, € 12 – ½ P € 92/110
Rest – *(closed Sunday dinner)* Menu (€ 18), € 25 (weekday lunch), € 33/78 – Carte € 46/112
◆ An unbeatable end-of-the-world location between the lighthouses and the remains of an abbey. Two generations of guestrooms (ultra-modern or traditional), some with a balcony. Modern cuisine specialising in seafood, served in two contemporary dining rooms.

LES CONTAMINES-MONTJOIE – 74 Haute-Savoie – 328 N6 – pop. 1 125 – alt. 1 164 m – Winter sports : 1 165/2 500 m 4 22 – ✉ 74170 French Alps

46 **F1**

Paris 606 – Annecy 93 – Bonneville 50 – Chamonix-Mont-Blanc 33 – Megève 20
Office de tourisme, 18, route de Notre-Dame de la Gorge ✆ 04 50 47 01 58, Fax 04 50 47 09 54
Le Signal★ (by cable car).

Chalet Hôtel la Chemenaz
30 allée du Nant Rouge, (near the Le Lay ski-lift) – ✆ *04 50 47 02 44*
– *www.chemenaz.com – info@chemenaz.com – Fax 04 50 47 12 73*
– *Open 15 June-15 September and 15 December-15 April*
38 rm – €67/88 €100/132, € 11 – ½ P € 77/90
Rest *La Trabla* – *(dinner only)* Menu € 21/46 – Carte € 29/44
◆ Modern chalet with large glass windows, located in the Lay hamlet opposite the cable car. Bright, well-equipped alpine style rooms (drying room). The Trabla means a shelf for cheese in Savoy dialect. Large central fireplace and home-made smoked dishes.

Chalet Hôtel Gai Soleil rest, VISA

288 chemin des Loyers – ✆ 04 50 47 02 94 – www.gaisoleil.com – gaisoleil2@wanadoo.fr – Fax 04 50 47 18 43 – Open 14 June-15 September and 19 December-17 April

19 rm – †€ 55/65 ††€ 68/78, ☐ € 10 – ½ P € 58/78

Rest – *(open for lunch in winter from 17 January to 7 February and from 7 to 14 March)* Menu (€ 15), € 19/28 – Carte € 24/38 lunch only

◆ Here they look after all the needs of the clientele. Overlooking the resort, this old farm with its roof covered in shingle board, is filled with beautiful flowers in season. Personalised rooms. Pleasant, rustic dining room with a family guesthouse atmosphere. Fondue evening on Tuesdays.

L'Ô à la Bouche VISA

510 rte Notre-Dame de la Gorge – ✆ 04 50 47 81 67 – www.lo-contamines.com – Open 21 June-29 September and 16 December-14 May

Rest – *(pre-book)* Menu (€ 18), € 32/46 – Carte € 33/45

◆ Considered the best in the valley, this restaurant owes its success to its simple, elegant and contemporary mountain decor, and its traditional cuisine (meat specialities). Gastronomic dinners available.

CONTAMINE-SUR-ARVE – 74 Haute-Savoie – 328 L4 – pop. 1 512 – alt. 450 m – ✉ 74130 46 F1

Paris 547 – Annecy 46 – Chamonix-Mont-Blanc 63 – Genève 20 – Thonon-les-Bains 36

Le Tourne Bride with rm AC rest, VISA

94 rte d'Annemasse – ✆ 04 50 03 62 18 – www.letounebride.com – hotel-tourne-bride@wanadoo.fr – Fax 04 50 03 91 99 – Closed 13 July-2 August, 4-25 January, Sunday dinner and Monday

7 rm – †€ 47/49 ††€ 58/65, ☐ € 8 – ½ P € 57/60

Rest – Menu (€ 14), € 23/39 – Carte € 31/48

◆ The spruce facade of this old post house is eye catching. The stables now house a stylish country dining room serving well-prepared traditional cuisine.

CONTES – 06 Alpes-Maritimes – 341 E5 – pop. 6 551 – alt. 250 m – ✉ 06390 41 D2

Paris 954 – Marseille 206 – Nice 21 – Antibes 43 – Cannes 55

Syndicat d'initiative, 13, place Jean Allardi ✆ 04 93 79 13 99, Fax 04.93.79.26.30

La Fleur de Thym AC VISA

3 bd Charles Alunni – ✆ 04 93 79 47 33 – restaurantlafleurdethym@wanadoo.fr – Fax 04 93 79 47 33 – Closed 14-26 August, 24-10 January, Tuesday dinner and Wednesday

Rest – Menu (€ 18), € 29/46 – Carte € 34/48

◆ This small, rustic restaurant has a real feel of Provence, with its orange and yellow tones, fresh flowers, and large, open fireplace. Hearty, traditional cuisine and friendly service.

CONTEVILLE – 27 Eure – 304 C5 – pop. 797 – alt. 33 m – ✉ 27210 32 A3

Paris 181 – Évreux 102 – Le Havre 34 – Honfleur 15 – Pont-Audemer 14 – Pont-l'Évêque 28

Auberge du Vieux Logis (Eric Boilay) VISA

– ✆ 02 32 57 60 16 – Fax 02 32 57 45 84 – Closed 2 weeks in November, Tuesday except July-August, Sunday dinner and Monday

Rest – Menu € 45 (weekdays)/85 – Carte € 65/105

Spec. Foies gras de canard au torchon et poêlé. Filet de bar en écailles de tomate et olive, Saint-Jacques et risotto aux champignons. Tours de nougat glacé.

◆ A young couple is now at the helm of this pleasant Norman restaurant in the heart of the village. Meticulously prepared classic dishes full of flavour.

in Marais Vernier 8 km East by D 312 and D 90 – **pop. 492 – alt. 10 m** – ✉ **27680**

Auberge de l'Etampage with rm — rest, rm, VISA
– ✆ *02 32 57 61 51 – etampage.blaize@wanadoo.fr – Fax 02 32 57 23 47 – Closed 23 December-1st February, Sunday dinner and Wednesday*
3 rm – €39 €39, ☕ €8 **Rest** – Menu €18/29 – Carte €30/45
◆ This half-timbered village residence offers local specialities prepared with fresh, local produce. Interiors are in bistro-style and the three rooms are attractively furnished and well-kept.

CONTRES – 41 Loir-et-Cher – 318 F7 – pop. 3 417 – alt. 98 m – ✉ 41700 — 11 A1

▶ Paris 203 – Blois 22 – Châteauroux 79 – Montrichard 23 – Tours 66

De France — rm, rest, VISA
rte de Blois – ✆ 02 54 79 50 14 – www.hoteldefrance-contres.com – metivier@mond.net – Fax 02 54 79 02 95 – Closed 24 January-11 March, Sunday dinner, Tuesday lunch and Monday in low season
35 rm – €59/85 €66/85, ☕ €11 – 2 suites – ½ P €65/85
Rest – *(closed Monday lunch, Tuesday lunch, Wednesday lunch and Thursday lunch in high season)* Menu €26 (weekdays)/51 – Carte €55/65
◆ A good, family address located in the centre of Contres. Comfortable rooms, mostly facing the pool and garden, which are regularly renovate. Cane furniture in the annexe. Restaurant with an elegant, comfortable setting serving traditional cuisine.

La Botte d'Asperges — VISA
52 r.P. H. Mauger – ✆ 02 54 79 50 49 – www.labotte-dasperges.com – Fax 02 54 79 08 74 – Closed 17-31 August, 2-16 January, Sunday dinner and Monday
Rest – Menu €23/50 – Carte €37/51
◆ Behind the half-timbered facade, this bistro style restaurant has two bright dining rooms decorated with frescos of food and wine. Modern menu.

CONTREVOZ – 01 Ain – 328 G6 – see Belley

CONTREXÉVILLE – 88 Vosges – 314 D3 – pop. 3 507 – alt. 342 m – Spa : early April-early Oct. – Casino – ✉ 88140 Alsace-Lorraine — 26 B3

▶ Paris 337 – Épinal 47 – Langres 75 – Nancy 83 – Neufchâteau 28
Office de tourisme, 116, rue du Shah de Perse ✆ 03 29 08 08 68, Fax 03 29 08 25 40
36 de Vittel Ermittage Vittel HOTEL ERMITAGE, N : 7 km, ✆ 03 29 08 81 53
9 du Bois de Hazeau Centre Préparation Olympique, 4 km on D 429, ✆ 03 29 08 20 85

Cosmos — rm, rest, VISA
13 r. Metz – ✆ 03 29 07 61 61 – www.cosmos-hotel.com – contact@cosmos-hotel.com – Fax 03 29 08 68 67 – Closed 20-28 December
77 rm ☕ – €98 €118 – 6 suites – ½ P €111 **Rest** – Menu €35
◆ The old France atmosphere of this hotel with comfortable rooms transports you to the Belle Epoque. An ideal location for fitness and balneotherapy fans. Large dining room with charming 1940s decor. Traditional menus and diet meals.

COQUELLES – 62 Pas-de-Calais – 301 D2 – see Calais

CORBEIL-ESSONNES – 91 Essonne – 312 D4 – 101 37 – see Paris, Area

Luxury pad or humble abode?
and denote categories of comfort.

CORBIGNY – 58 Nièvre – 319 F8 – pop. 1 681 – alt. 203 m – ✉ 58800 7 B2
Burgundy-Jura

Paris 236 – Autun 76 – Avallon 38 – Clamecy 28 – Nevers 58

Office de tourisme, 8, rue de l'Abbaye ✆ 03 86 20 02 53

Hôtel de L'Europe rm, VISA AE

7 Grande Rue – ✆ 03 86 20 09 87 – hoteleuropelecepage@talicepro.fr – Fax 03 86 20 06 40 – Closed 24 December-4 January and 21 February-9 March

18 rm – €51 €58, €8,50 – ½ P €66

Rest *Le Cépage* – *(closed Sunday dinner, Wednesday dinner and Thursday)*
Menu €28/58 – Carte €26/59

Rest *Le Bistrot* – *(closed Sunday dinner, Wednesday dinner and Thursday)*
Menu €11 (weekday lunch), €18/22 – Carte approx. €24

◆ This friendly, family-run hotel has colourful, well-equipped rooms with lovely bathrooms. The Cépage has a rustic style dining room, traditional cuisine and a very reasonably priced wine list. Le Bistrot offers a Burgundy menu and local dishes.

"Rest" appears in red for establishments with a (star) or (Bib Gourmand).

CORBON – 14 Calvados – 303 L5 – pop. 70 – alt. 8 m – ✉ 14340 33 C2

Paris 215 – Caen 31 – Hérouville-Saint-Clair 30 – Le Havre 70

La Ferme aux Étangs VISA

Chemin de l'Épée – ✆ 02 31 63 99 16 – www.lafermeauxetangs.com – contact@lafermeauxetangs.com – Fax 02 31 63 99 16

5 rm – €68 €78/98 **Table d'hôte** – Menu €30

◆ A quiet break away from it all in this Normandy estate overlooking a pond and parkland. Cosy rustic guestrooms and welcoming sitting room (home cinema facilities). The table d'hôte serves traditional fare and wood oven specialities.

CORDES-SUR-CIEL – 81 Tarn – 338 D6 – pop. 996 – alt. 279 m – ✉ 81170 Languedoc-Roussillon-Tarn Gorges 29 C2

Paris 655 – Albi 25 – Rodez 78 – Toulouse 82 – Villefranche-de-Rouergue 47

Office de tourisme, place Jeanne Ramel-Cals ✆ 05 63 56 00 52, Fax 05 63 56 19 52

Site★★ - High town★★: Gothic houses★★ - musée d'Art et d'Histoire Charles-Portal★.

Le Grand Écuyer (Damien Thuriès) VISA AE

– ✆ 05 63 53 79 50 – www.thuries.fr – grand.ecuyer@thuries.fr – Fax 05 63 53 79 51 – Open 14 March-11 October

12 rm – €135/265 €135/265, €16 – 1 suite – ½ P €135

Rest – *(closed Monday and weekday lunch except July-August)*
Menu €49/84 – Carte €84/92

Spec. Foie gras chaud au fil du temps. Pigeonneau du Mont Royal en cuisson moelleuse. Gratin de fraises des bois au citron et coulis d'abricot. **Wines** Gaillac.

◆ This listed Gothic abode is located in a picturesque street in the high-perched village. Guestrooms combine old-fashioned charm (four-poster beds) with modern comforts. Enjoy the sight of the chef rustling up flavoursome modern dishes in the open kitchen. Fine wine cellar.

Hostellerie du Vieux Cordes VISA AE

21 r. St-Michel – ✆ 05 63 53 79 20 – www.thuries.fr – vieux.cordes@thuries.fr – Fax 05 63 56 02 47 – Closed 2 January-10 February

19 rm – €52/110 €52/110, €12 – ½ P €81

Rest – *(Closed Tuesday lunch and Monday)* Menu €25/46 – Carte approx. €45

◆ The walls of a 13C monastery are home to an attractive spiral staircase. This leads to personalised guestrooms, which have been partly refurbished and modernised. Traditional fare served in a dining room-terrace overlooking the valley or on the wisteria scented patio.

Albi road

L'Envolée sauvage
La Borie – 05 63 56 88 52 – www.lenvolee-sauvage.com – info@lenvolee-sauvage.com – Closed 5 January-28 February
4 rm – €88/115 €90/115 **Table d'hôte** – Menu €35
◆ There is a truly authentic local flavour to this stylish 18C farmhouse still engaged in raising geese. The rooms are individually decorated and there is a large lounge-reading room. Farm produce garnishes the simple but flavoursome cuisine. Cooking lessons are available and visitors are guaranteed a warm welcome.

in Campes **3 km northeast on the D 922, D 98 and minor road – ✉ 81170**

Le Domaine de la Borie Grande
St-Marcel-Campes – 05 63 56 58 24 – www.laboriegrande.com – laboriegrande@wanadoo.fr – Fax 05 63 56 58 24
4 rm – €100/120 €100/150 **Table d'hôte** – Menu €38 bi
◆ This 17-18C abode set in peaceful parkland welcomes guests with open arms. The individually appointed guestrooms have beautiful furniture, tasteful decor and sweeping views. Loft style suite in the former barn. Regional seasonal fare served in an inner courtyard or a countrified dining room.

CORDON – 74 Haute-Savoie – 328 M5 – pop. 983 – alt. 871 m – ✉ 74700 French Alps 46 F1

Paris 589 – Annecy 76 – Bonneville 33 – Chamonix-Mont-Blanc 32 – Megève 10

Office de tourisme, route de Cordon 04 50 58 01 57, Fax 04 50 91 25 36

Site★.

Les Roches Fleuries
rte de la Scie – 04 50 58 06 71 – www.rochesfleuries.com – info@rochesfleuries.com – Fax 04 50 47 82 30 – Open 8 May-20 September and 18 December-4 April
20 rm – €150/240 €150/240, €18 – 5 suites – ½ P €125/185
Rest – *(closed Tuesday lunch, Sunday dinner and Monday except school holidays)* Menu (€35), €52/78 – Carte €65/90
Rest ***La Boîte à Fromages*** – *(open 10 July-25 August, 22 December-20 March and closed Sunday and Monday) (dinner only) (pre-book)* Menu €47 bi
Spec. Foie gras pané aux zestes d'agrumes. Poularde de Bresse aux escargots de Magland, crème d'étrille à la badiane. Soufflé au jus de passion et parfum d'orange. **Wines** Roussette de Marestel, Mondeuse d'Arbin
◆ Stunning floral chalet perched on the heights of the "Balcon du Mont Blanc". A warm, wooden interior and elegant old Savoyard furniture. Restaurant with a subdued alpine setting and creative flavoursome cuisine. Regional recipes at the Boîte à Fromages.

Le Cerf Amoureux
at Nant-Cruy, 2km south (Combloux road) ✉ 74700 Sallanches – 04 50 47 49 24 – www.lecerfamoureux.com – contact@lecerfamoureux.com – Fax 04 50 47 49 25 – Closed 22 September-5 October
11 rm – €130/295 €130/295, €17 – 2 suites
Rest – *(closed Sunday and Monday except school holidays) (dinner only) (residents only)* Menu €36
◆ Wood and stone feature in this chalet's cosy interior. Attractive rooms with balconies facing the Aravis massif or Mont Blanc. The delightful dining room is the backdrop for good quality home cooking.

Le Chamois d'Or
– 04 50 58 05 16 – www.hotel-chamoisdor.com – info@hotel-chamoisdor.com – Fax 04 50 93 72 96 – Open end May to mid-September and 18 December to end March
26 rm – €85/125 €120/185, €16 – 2 suites – ½ P €85/120
Rest – *(closed Wednesday lunch and Thursday lunch)* Menu (€24), €28/45 – Carte €35/60
◆ Large chalet, decked with flowers in the summer and with leisure facilities. Cosy rooms and suites, renovated in an alpine style. Comfy lounge with a fireplace. A rubble wall, regional furniture, all-weather terrace and panoramic view.

Le Cordonant
rest, VISA

120 rte des Miaz – ✆ 04 50 58 34 56 – www.lecordonant.free.fr – lecordonant@wanadoo.fr – Fax 04 50 47 95 57 – Open mid May-end September and mid December-mid April

16 rm – †€ 65/75 ††€ 85/105, ☕ € 10 – ½ P € 70/85

Rest – Menu (€ 20), € 25/32 – Carte € 34/44

◆ A large chalet with a warm, friendly atmosphere. Lovely wooden furnishings in well-kept rooms; some with balcony on the valley side. Delicious traditional cuisine and a splendid view of the mountain tops from the rustic dining room.

CORENC – 38 Isère – 333 H6 – see Grenoble

CORMEILLES – 27 Eure – 304 C6 – pop. 1 203 – alt. 80 m – ✉ 27260 32 A3

▶ Paris 181 – Bernay 441 – Lisieux 19 – Pont-Audemer 17 – Pont-l'Évêque 17

ℹ Office de tourisme, 14, place du Mont Mirel ✆ 02 32 56 02 39, Fax 02 32 42 32 66

L'Auberge du Président
♿ rest, VISA AE

70 r. de l'Abbaye – ✆ 02 32 57 80 37 – www.hotel-cormeilles.com – aubergedupresident@wanadoo.fr – Fax 02 32 57 88 31

14 rm – †€ 50/80 ††€ 55/90, ☕ € 12 – ½ P € 58/75

Rest – *(closed Tuesday lunch, Wednesday lunch, Thursday lunch from October-March, Monday lunch and Sunday dinner)* Menu (€ 15), € 19 (weekdays)/38 – Carte € 25/40

◆ The name pays tribute to René Coty, former President of France, who stayed here. Personalised, well-kept rooms. This pleasant, and ever popular restaurant serves traditional, regionally focused cuisine. It has a Normandy decor with beams and fireplace.

Gourmandises
VISA

29 r. de l'Abbaye – ✆ 02 32 42 10 96 – Closed 29 June-1st July, January, February, Monday, Tuesday and Wednesday except bank holidays

Rest – Carte € 40/53

◆ This former dairy has been successfully converted into a strikingly friendly bistro. Its subtle, trendy decor is ideal to sample the tasty bistro fare.

CORMEILLES-EN-VEXIN – 95 Val-d'Oise – 305 D6 – 106 5 – see Paris, Area (Cergy-Pontoise)

CORMERY – 37 Indre-et-Loire – 317 N5 – pop. 1 542 – alt. 59 m 11 B2
– ✉ 37320 Châteaux of the Loire

▶ Paris 254 – Blois 63 – Château-Renault 48 – Loches 22 – Montrichard 33 – Tours 21

ℹ Syndicat d'initiative, 13, rue Nationale ✆ 02 47 43 30 84, Fax 02 47 43 18 73

Auberge du Mail
VISA AE

pl. Mail – ✆ 02 47 43 40 32 – aubergedumail-cormery.com – aubergedumail@wanadoo.fr – Fax 02 47 43 08 72 – Closed 12-20 April, 26-31 December, dinner mid October-end March, Saturday lunch and Thursday

Rest – Menu (€ 17), € 20 (weekdays)/50 – Carte € 27/54

◆ Local-style inn near the abbey famous for its macaroons. The dining room has a comfortable rustic-style setting, and the terrace is relaxing with its lime trees and wisteria.

Auberge des 2 Cèdres
VISA

av. de la Gare – ✆ 02 47 43 03 09 – Fax 02 47 43 03 09 – Closed 6-22 July, 29 January-9 February, dinner from Sunday to Thursday and Monday

Rest – Menu € 14 (weekdays)/28 – Carte € 25/32

◆ This regional-style building near the railway station provides an open air café atmosphere. Very simple setting and terrace in a tiny garden. Friendly welcome and family cooking.

CORNILLON – 30 Gard – 339 L3 – pop. 847 – alt. 168 m – ✉ 30630 23 D1
Provence

Paris 666 – Avignon 50 – Alès 47 – Bagnols-sur-Cèze 17 – Pont-St-Esprit 25

La Vieille Fontaine with rm
Rue du Château – ✆ 04 66 82 20 56 – www.lavieillefontaine.net – lavieillefontaine400@orange.fr – Fax 04 66 82 33 64 – Open April-October and closed Monday, Tuesday and Wednesday in April and October

8 rm – €105/155 €105/155, €10

Rest – *(closed Mon., Tues. and Wed. from Oct. to Apr.) (dinner only)* Menu €40, €45/60

◆ A house with character built against the medieval walls. Smart rooms, vaulted dining room, traditional cuisine, terraced garden and pool overlooking the valley.

CORPS – 38 Isère – 333 I9 – pop. 456 – alt. 939 m – ✉ 38970 45 C3
French Alps

Paris 626 – Gap 39 – Grenoble 64 – La Mure 24

Office de tourisme, Route Napoléon ✆ 04 76 30 03 85, Fax 04.76.81.12.28

Dam★★ and bridge★ of Le Sautet West: 4 km.

Du Tilleul
r. des Fosses – ✆ 04 76 30 00 43 – www.hotel-restaurant-du-tilleul.com – jourdan@hotel-restaurant-du-tilleul.com – Fax 04 76 30 06 12 – Closed 1st November-20 December

18 rm – €40/46 €46/58, €8 – ½ P €51

Rest – Menu €15/37 – Carte approx. €23

◆ On the imperial Napoleonic road and in the heart of the old village which is very lively in the summer. Cool well-kept rooms, more peaceful in the annexe. Friendly welcome. The dining room is a little dark but has a pleasant country atmosphere. Traditional cuisine.

in Aspres-les-Corps 5 km Southeast by N 85 and D 58 – pop. 126 – alt. 930 m – ✉ 05800

Château d'Aspres
– ✆ 04 92 55 28 90 – www.chateau-d-aspres.com – snc.charpentier@wanadoo.fr – Fax 04 92 55 48 48 – Open 1stMarch-15 November, 30 December-2 January and closed Sunday dinner

7 rm – €88/118 €88/140, €12 – 3 suites – ½ P €78/90

Rest – Menu €24/40 – Carte €29/58

◆ This stately12C-17C residence overlooks the Champsaur valley. The rooms are full of character with splendid antique furnishings. You dine in the company of old portraits in this stylishly furnished dining room. The cuisine is traditional.

CORRENÇON-EN-VERCORS – 38 Isère – 333 G7 – see Villard-de-Lans

CORRÈZE – 19 Corrèze – 329 M3 – pop. 1 175 – alt. 455 m – ✉ 19800 25 C3
Dordogne-Berry-Limousin

Paris 480 – Aubusson 96 – Brive-la-Gaillarde 45 – Tulle 19 – Uzerche 35

Office de tourisme, place de la Mairie ✆ 05 55 21 32 82, Fax 05 55 21 63 56

Mercure Seniorie
rest,

Le Bourg – ✆ 05 55 21 22 88 – www.mercure.com – h5711@accor.com – Fax 05 55 21 24 00 – Closed 18 December-5 January

29 rm – €53/125 €60/135, €12 – ½ P €60/75

Rest – Menu €17/28 – Carte €23/33

◆ This majestic 19C building, formerly a boarding establishment for young women looks over the medieval town. Very spacious rooms, most of which have been renovated. Comfortable dining rooms extended by a large terrace. Short menu of traditional dishes.

Le Parc des 4 Saisons
av. de la Gare – ✆ 05 55 21 44 59 – www.leparc.info – annick.peter@wanadoo.fr – Open 1 April-30 November

5 rm – €58/68 €65/90 **Table d'hôte** – Menu €30 bi

◆ Owned by a young Belgian couple, this house and its grounds once belonged to a notary public. Smart, comfortable rooms, an attractive lounge, summer pool, sauna and massages. Table d'hôte (by reservation) offered three nights a week.

H. Le Gac/MICHELIN

La Balagne : village de Lama

CORSE

🅿 **Department:** Corse
Michelin LOCAL map: n° **345**

Population: 249 729
Corse
Carte régionale 15 **B2**

USEFUL INFORMATION

SEA TRANSPORT

Crossings from mainland France to Corsica leave from Marseilles, Nice and Toulon.
from Marseilles: SNCM - 61 bd des Dames (2e) ✆ 0 825 888 088 (0.15 €/min) and 3260 quoting "SNCM", Fax 04 91 56 36 36. CMN - 4 quai d'Arenc (2e) ✆ 0 810 201 320, Fax 04 91 99 45 95.
from Nice: SNCM - Ferryterranée quai du Commerce ✆ 0 825 888 088 (0.15 €/min). CORSICA FERRIES - Port de Commerce ✆ 0 825 095 095 (0.15 €/min), Fax 04 92 00 42 94.
from Toulon: SNCM - 49 av. Infanterie de Marine (15 Mar.-15 Sep.) ✆ 0 825 888 088 (0.15 €/min). CORSICA FERRIES - Gare Maritime ✆ 0 825 095 095 (0.15 €/min).

AIRPORTS

Corsica has four airports serving Continental France, Italy and part of Europe: Ajaccio ✆ 04 95 23 56 56, Calvi ✆ 04 95 65 88 88, Bastia ✆ 04 95 54 54 54, and Figari-Sud-Corse ✆ 04 95 71 10 10 (Bonifacio and Porto-Vecchio).
See also text for these towns.

A FEW GOLF COURSES

9 Bastia(see the locality), ✆ 04 95 38 33 99
18 de Sperone à Bonifacio(see the locality), ✆ 04 95 73 17 13

AJACCIO 🅿 – **2A Corse-du-Sud – 345** B8 – **pop. 52 880 – Casino** Z – ✉ **20000**

- Bastia 147 – Bonifacio 131 – Calvi 166 – Corte 80 – L'Île-Rousse 141
- Ajaccio-Campo dell'Oro: ✆ 04 95 23 56 56, by ①: 7 km.
- Office de tourisme, 3, boulevard du Roi Jérôme ✆ 04 95 51 53 03, Fax 04 95 51 53 01
- Old town ★ - Musée Fesch★★: Italian paintings★★★ - Bonaparte House ★ - Napoleonic room★ (1st floor of the town hall) - Jetée de la Citadelle ≤★ - Place Gén.-de-Gaulle ou Place du Diamant ≤★.
- Golfe d'Ajaccio★★. . to Îles sanguinaires★★

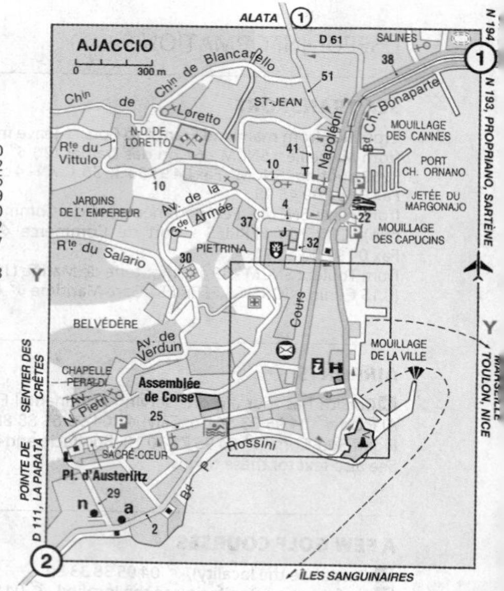

Palazzu U Domu without rest

17 r. Bonaparte – ✆ 04 95 50 00 20 – www.palazzu-domu.com – reservation@palazzu-domu.com – Fax 04 95 50 02 10 Z **e**

45 rm – †€ 130/190 ††€ 130/420, ☕ € 19

◆ Fully restored 18C palace, once home to Count Pozzo di Borgo. Luxurious feel combining modernity and tradition. Chic rooms decorated in a soft contemporary style.

Les Mouettes without rest

9 cours Lucien-Bonaparte – ✆ 04 95 50 40 40 – www.hotellesmouettes.fr – info@hotellesmouettes.fr – Fax 04 95 21 71 80 – Closed 16 November-3 March

28 rm – †€ 100/380 ††€ 100/380, ☕ € 14

◆ Charming residence dating from 1880 with views over the bay, Mediterranean garden and private beach. Spacious, well-decorated rooms, most of them with small balconies.

Napoléon without rest

4 r. Lorenzo Vero – ✆ 04 95 51 54 00 – www.hotelnapoleonajaccio.com – info@hotel-napoleon-ajaccio.com – Fax 04 95 21 80 40 Z **s**

62 rm – †€ 67/95 ††€ 80/110, ☕ € 9

◆ Warm welcome at this hotel in a street perpendicular to Cours Napoléon. The rooms have recently been redecorated in a modern style.

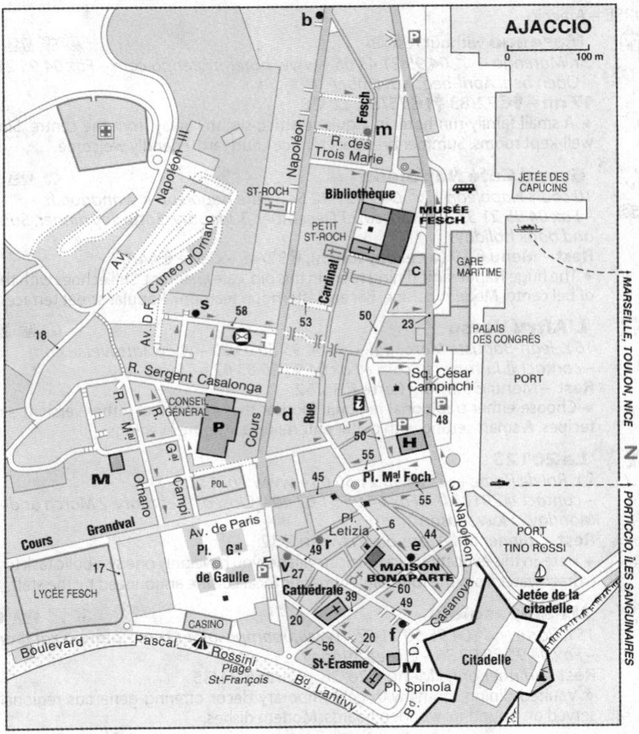

Bonaparte (R.) . . . . Z 6
Dr-Ramaroni (Av. du) . . . . Z 17
Eugénie (Av. Impératrice) . . . . . Z 18
Fesch (R. Cardinal) . . . . Z
Forcioli-Conti (R.) . . . . Z 20
Grandval (Cours) . . . . Z
Herminier (Quai l') . . . . Z 23
Macchini (Av. E.) . . . . Z 27
Napoléon-III (Av.) . . . . Z
Napoléon (Cours) . . . . Z
Notre-Dame (R.) . . . . Z 39
Pozzo-di-Borgo (R.) . . . . Z 44
Premier-Consul (Av.) . . . . Z 45
République (Q. de la) . . . . Z 48
Roi-de-Rome (R.) . . . . Z 49
Roi-Jérôme (Bd) . . . . Z 50
Sebastiani (R. Gén.) . . . . Z 53
Sérafini (Av. A.) . . . . Z 55
Soeur-Alphonse (R.) . . . . Z 56
Vero (R. Lorenzo) . . . . Z 58
Zévaco-Maire (R.) . . . . Z 60

San Carlu without rest

8 bd Casanova – ✆ 04 95 21 13 84 – www.hotel-sancarlu.com – hotel-san-carlu@wanadoo.fr – Fax 04 95 21 09 99 – Closed 22 December-1 February Z **f**

40 rm – €69/120 €89/149, €9

◆ In the heart of old Ajaccio and a stone's throw from St François beach, this hotel boasts practical, well-kept rooms, some with views of the citadel and sea.

Impérial without rest

6 bd Albert 1er – ✆ 04 95 21 50 62 – www.hotelimperial-ajaccio.fr – info@hotelimperial-ajaccio.fr – Fax 04 95 21 15 20 – Open from mid-March to mid-November and from 10 December to 10 January Y **a**

44 rm – €70/130 €70/130, €9

◆ A small building on the edge of the town separated from the sea by a small square. The hotel's huge lobby is completely devoted to Napoleon. Bright, functional rooms.

Kallisté without rest

51 cours Napoléon – ✆ 04 95 51 34 45 – www.hotel-kalliste-ajaccio.com – info@hotel-kalliste-ajaccio.com – Fax 04 95 21 79 00 Z **b**

45 rm – €56/69 €64/79, €8

◆ This 19C construction was built during the reign of Napoleon and has been refurbished with its original vaults cleverly retained. Small, comfortable rooms.

Marengo without rest

2 r. Marengo – ✆ 04 95 21 43 66 – www.hotel-marengo.com – Fax 04 95 21 51 26 – Open beg. April-beg. November Y **n**

17 rm – †€ 72/83 ††€ 75/83, ☕ € 8

◆ A small family-run hotel in a quiet district, slightly away from the centre. Simple but well-kept rooms. Summer breakfast terrace courtyard. Friendly welcome.

Grand Café Napoléon

10 cours Napoléon – ✆ 04 95 21 42 54 – cafe.napoleon@wanadoo.fr – Fax 04 95 21 53 32 – Closed 23 December-3 January, Saturday dinner, Sunday and bank holidays Z **d**

Rest – Menu € 19 (weekday lunch), € 32/45 – Carte € 44/97

◆ The huge Napoleonic dining room in this old 'café chantant' still echoes with the strains of bel canto. Modern cuisine. Bar and afternoon tearoom. Popular street terrace.

L'Altru Versu

16 r. Jean-Baptiste Marcaggi – ✆ 04 95 50 05 22 – www.latruversu.com – contact@laltruversu.com – Fax 04 95 20 83 62 – Closed July Z **m**

Rest – Menu € 32/40 – Carte € 36/52

◆ Choose either traditional regional food or the 'altru versu' (other version) – revisited recipes. A smart setting with guitar entertainment some evenings.

Le 20123

2 r. Roi de Rome – ✆ 04 95 21 50 05 – www.20213.fr – contact@20123.fr – Fax 04 95 51 02 40 – Closed 1 February-2 March and Monday in low season Z **v**

Rest – *(dinner only) (pre-book)* Menu € 32

◆ Here, in this evocation of a Corsican village, you have only one symbolic task to perform – draw water from the fountain! Authentic local cuisine announced by the staff.

U Pampasgiolu

15 r. Porta – ✆ 04 95 50 71 52 – www.upampasgiolu.com – pampa.zdt@orange.fr – Fax 04 95 20 99 36 – Closed Sunday Z **r**

Rest – *(dinner only)* Menu € 26/28 – Carte € 24/35

◆ Vaulted dining rooms with contemporary decor offering generous regional cuisine served on 'spuntinu' wooden boards. Modern dishes.

in Afa by ①: 15 km by Bastia road and D 161 – pop. 2 513 – alt. 150 m – ✉ 20167

Auberge d'Afa

– ✆ 04 95 22 92 27 – Fax 04 95 22 92 27 – Closed 9-16 March and Monday

Rest – *(number of covers limited, pre-book)* Menu (€ 14), € 20 (weekday lunch)/27 – Carte € 49/69

◆ A welcoming inn set in a flower garden, nestling on the edge of the village. Spacious, colourful dining room decorated with Corsican landscapes. South-facing terrace. Traditional cuisine.

Plaine de Cuttoli 15 km by ① by Bastia road, Cuttoli road (D 1) then Bastelicaccia road – ✉ 20167 Mezzavia

U Licettu with rm

– ✆ 04 95 25 61 57 – Fax 04 95 53 71 00 – Closed 1st January-15 February, Sunday dinner and Monday in low season

4 rm ☕ – †€ 80/90 ††€ 90/100 **Rest** – *(pre-book)* Menu € 40 bi

◆ Flower-decked villa overlooking the bay. Warm welcome, and copious, tasty Corsican dishes with home-cured meats: worth lingering for! Recently created, bright and spacious rooms overlooking the garden.

in Pisciatello 12 km by ① and N 196 – ✉ 20117 Cauro

Auberge du Prunelli

– ✆ 04 95 20 02 75 – Closed January and Tuesday

Rest – Menu € 20 (lunch)/31 – Carte € 34/44

◆ 19C Corsican inn by the old bridge which crosses the Prunelli. Cuisine based on local dishes using produce fresh from the orchard and vegetable garden, served in a pleasant rustic setting.

îles Sanguinaires road via ② – ✉ **20000 Ajaccio :**

Dolce Vita rm, VISA AE
9 km – ✆ 04 95 52 42 42 – www.hotel-dolcevita.com – reservation@hotel-dolcevita.com – Fax 04 95 52 07 15 – Open end March-beg. November
30 rm (½ board only) – ½ P € 179/494
Rest *La Mer* – Menu (€ 29), € 41 – Carte € 75/88
◆ La Dolce Vita... and what if Anita Ekberg should rise out of the pool? An understandably popular holiday establishment, offering attractive rooms with sea views. Original food can be enjoyed in the huge dining room or on the lovely terrace facing the bay.

Cala di Sole VISA AE
6 km – ✆ 04 95 52 01 36 – www.caladisole.fr – caladisole@annuaire-corse.com – Fax 04 95 52 00 20 – Open 1 April-15 October
31 rm – †€ 120/210 ††€ 170/210, ☕ € 12
Rest – *(open 15 June-15 September) (dinner only)* Menu € 30/40
◆ An energetic stay in a 1960s hotel at the water's edge: private beach, pool, gym, diving, jet-ski and windsurfing available. Rooms with terrace. Simple, traditional cuisine with an emphasis on fish, served overlooking the sea.

Palm Beach with rm rest, VISA AE
rte des Îles Sanguinaires, at 5 km – ✆ 04 95 52 01 03 – www.palm-beach.fr – hotel@palm-beach.fr – Closed 23 November-20 December, Sunday dinner, Monday from October to March and lunch in July-August
10 rm – †€ 84/110 ††€ 90/110, ☕ € 17
Rest – Menu (€ 22), € 37 (lunch), € 55/89 – Carte € 64/89
◆ Predominantly seafood menu in this smart, refined Mediterranean-style restaurant. Superb terrace overlooking the beach (lit up in the evenings). Simple, elegant furnishings in bedrooms inspired by the fresh sea air. State of the art facilities.

ALÉRIA – **2B Haute-Corse** – **345** G7 – **pop. 2 007** – **alt. 20 m** – ✉ **20270**

Bastia 71 – Corte 50 – Porto Vecchio 72

Office de tourisme, Casa Luciani ✆ 04 95 57 01 51, Fax 04 95 57 03 79

Fort de Matra (Matra Fort) ★ - Musée Jérôme-Carcopino (Jérôme Carcopino Museum) collection of Attican ceramics ★★ - Old Town★.

L'Atrachjata without rest VISA AE
– ✆ 04 95 57 03 93 – www.hotel-atrachjata.net – info@hotel-atrachjata.net – Fax 04 95 57 08 03
30 rm – †€ 49/89 ††€ 59/154, ☕ € 11 – 2 suites
◆ This family-run hotel in the heart of Aléria is located by the road. Large modern rooms with nice bathrooms; choose one to the rear of the building.

L'Empereur VISA AE
lieu-dit Cateraggio, (N 198) – ✆ 04 95 57 02 13 – www.hotel-empereur.com – hotel.empereur@aliceadsl.fr – Fax 04 95 57 02 33
22 rm ☕ – †€ 51/79 ††€ 64/93 – ½ P € 46/60
Rest – *(closed Sunday October-April)* Menu € 15 (weekdays)/25 – Carte € 24/38
◆ Motel type accommodation in this establishment only three minutes from the beach. The rooms are spacious, functional and face the pool; some have a mezzanine. Tasty, traditional Corsican dishes served in a bright dining room.

ALGAJOLA – **2B Haute-Corse** – **345** C4 – **pop. 268** – **alt. 2 m** – ✉ **20220**

Bastia 76 – Calvi 16 – L'Île-Rousse 10

Office de tourisme, rue Droite ✆ 04 95 62 78 32

Citadel★.

Stellamare without rest VISA
chemin Santa Lucia – ✆ 04 95 60 71 18 – www.stellamarehotel.com – info@stellamarehotel.com – Fax 04 95 60 69 39 – Open 1 May-4 October
16 rm – †€ 75/120 ††€ 75/120, ☕ € 10
◆ This hotel and lovely garden stand back from the sea and in the upper part of the resort. Pleasant, regularly spruced up rooms. Moroccan style terrace.

Serenada
– ✆ 04 95 36 43 64 – *www.hotel-serenada.com* – *martelli.paul@wanadoo.fr* – Fax 04 95 36 86 83 – Open April-October
8 rm – €69/123 €75/142, €7 **Rest** – Menu (€23) – Carte €36/47
◆ Near the beach, two modern buildings separated by a quiet lane. The ochre-orange fronted hotel offers contemporary, well-soundproofed rooms. Panoramic restaurant and lovely terrace overlooking the sea. Updated cuisine.

AULLÈNE – **2A Corse-du-Sud** – **345** D9 – **pop. 183** – **alt. 825 m** – ✉ **20116**
Ajaccio 73 – Bonifacio 84 – Corte 103 – Porto-Vecchio 59 – Propriano 37 – Sartène 35

San Larenzu without rest
Pasta di Grano – ✆ 04 95 78 63 12 – *http://san-larenzu.spaces.live.com* – *sanlaurenzu@hotmail.fr* – Fax 04 95 74 24 83
6 rm – €55 €60
◆ Heading for the GR 20? Laurent offers modern, well-kept rooms. The delicious breakfast (including Corsican honey and jams) is served on the terrace in good weather.

BASTELICA – **2A Corse-du-Sud** – **345** D7 – **pop. 460** – **alt. 800 m** – ✉ **20119**
Ajaccio 43 – Corte 69 – Propriano 70 – Sartène 82
Panoramic road ★ of the plateau d'Ese.
400 m from col de Mercujo: belvédère ≤★★ and Southwest: 13,5 km.

Chez Paul with rm
– ✆ 04 95 28 71 59 – Fax 04 95 28 73 13
10 rm (½ board only) – ½ P €45 **Rest** – Menu €12/26
◆ Views of the village and Prunelli Valley from the dining room, which is separated from the kitchens by the road! Corsican cuisine; cold meat platters. Spacious apartments.

BASTIA – **2B Haute-Corse** – **345** F3 – **pop. 42 900** – ✉ **20200**
Ajaccio 148 – Bonifacio 171 – Calvi 92 – Corte 69 – Porto 136
Bastia-Poretta ✆ 04 95 54 54 54, by ②: 20 km.
Office de tourisme, place Saint-Nicolas ✆ 04 95 54 20 40, Fax 04 95 54 20 41
Golf Club Borgo Borgo Castellarese, S : 20 km on the airport road, ✆ 04 95 38 33 99
Terra-Vecchia★: Old harbour★★, Immaculate Conception oratory★ - Terra-Nova★: Assumption of the Virgin★★ in Ste-Marie church, Rococo decor★★ in Ste-Croix chapel .
Ste-Lucie church ≤★★ 6 km Northwest by D 31 X - ✻★★★ of Serra di Pigno 14 km by ③ - ≤★★ of col de Teghime 10 km by ③.

Plan on next page

Les Voyageurs without rest
9 av. Mar. Sébastiani – ✆ 04 95 34 90 80 – *www.hotel-lesvoyageurs.com* – *hotellesvoyageurs@wanadoo.fr* – Fax 04 95 34 00 65 X **r**
24 rm – €75/85 €95/120, €10
◆ This hotel near the station has welcomed travellers for over a century. It has been recently renovated with yellow and blue colours in the rooms, and has good soundproofing.

Corsica Hôtels Bastia Centre without rest
av. J. Zuccarelli, via ③ – ✆ 04 95 55 10 00 – *www.corsica-hotels.fr* – *contact@corsica-hotels.fr* – Fax 04 95 55 05 11
71 rm – €66/96 €78/112, €8,50
◆ A well-equipped building with contemporary architecture. Quiet, comfortable rooms that are undergoing renovation. Small lounge and snack bar.

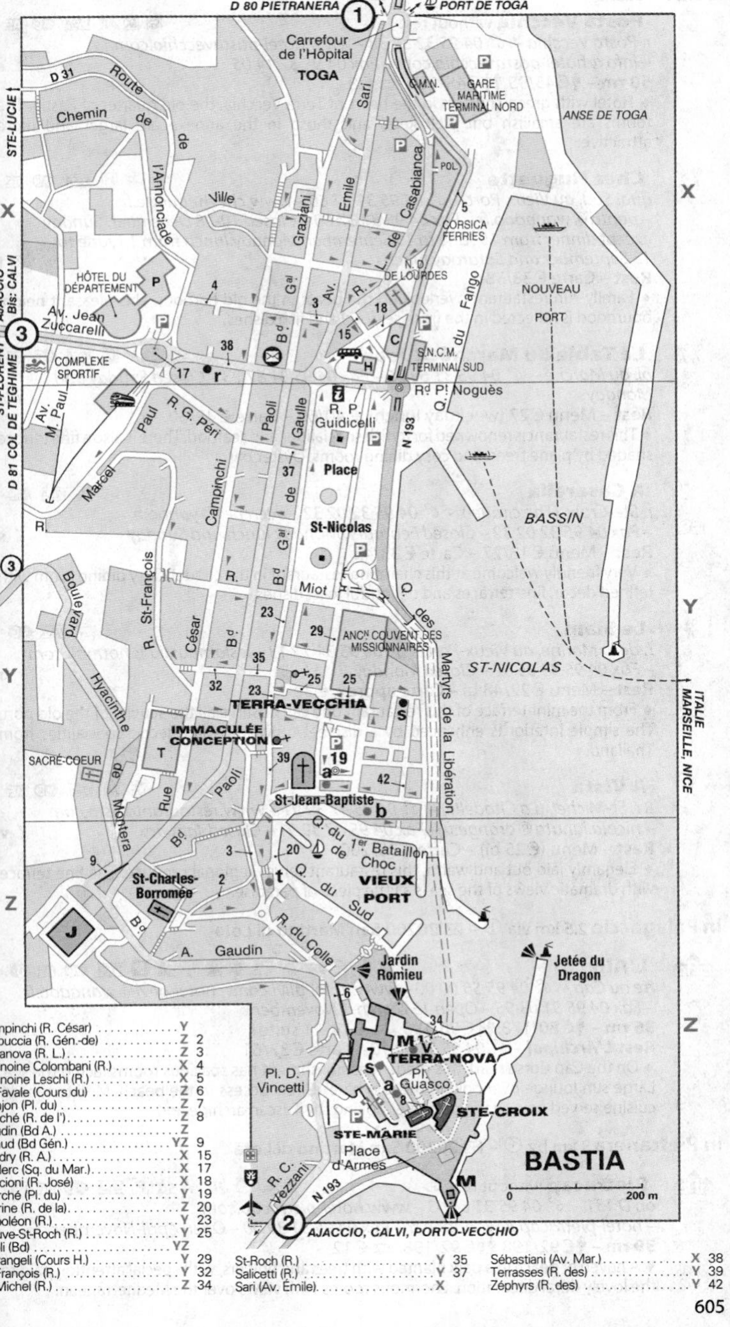

CAP CORSE
D 80 PIETRANERA
PORT DE TOGA
Carrefour de l'Hôpital
TOGA
GARE MARITIME TERMINAL NORD
ANSE DE TOGA
STE-LUCIE
D 31
Route de Ville
Chemin de l'Annonciade
Sari
Emile
Graziani
Casabianca
CORSICA FERRIES
N. D. DE LOURDES
NOUVEAU PORT
HÔTEL DU DÉPARTEMENT
Av. Jean Zuccarelli
AJACCIO Bis: CALVI
ST-FLORENT D 81 COL DE TEGHIME
COMPLEXE SPORTIF
S.N.C.M. TERMINAL SUD
Rd Pt Noguès
R. P. Guidicelli
Fango
N 193
Av. M. Paul
R. G. Péri
Marcel Paul
Campinchi
Paoli
Gaulle
Place St-Nicolas
BASSIN
Miot
Q. des Martyrs de la Libération
ANCN COUVENT DES MISSIONNAIRES
ST-NICOLAS
ITALIE MARSEILLE, NICE
Boulevard Hyacinthe de Montera
R. St-François
César
TERRA-VECCHIA
IMMACULÉE CONCEPTION
SACRÉ-COEUR
St-Jean-Baptiste
Q. du 1er Bataillon de Choc
VIEUX PORT
Q. du Sud
St-Charles-Borromée
A. Gaudin
R. du Colle
Jardin Romieu
Jetée du Dragon
TERRA-NOVA
Pl. Guasco
Pl. D. Vincetti
STE-CROIX
STE-MARIE
Place d'Armes
R. C. Vezzani
BASTIA
0
200 m
AJACCIO, CALVI, PORTO-VECCHIO

Posta Vecchia without rest

r. Posta Vecchia – 04 95 32 32 38 – www.hotel-postavecchia.com – info@hotel-postavecchia.com – Fax 04 95 32 14 05 Y **s**

50 rm – €45/95 €45/100, €8

◆ Hotel with green shutters in the heart of Terra Vecchia, the old quarter of Bastia. The rooms are smallish but well kept, and those in the annexe are larger and more attractive.

Chez Huguette

quai Sud, au Vieux-Port – 04 95 31 37 60 – www.chezhuguette.fr – panta@wanadoo.fr – Fax 04 95 31 37 60 – Closed 10-28 December, Sunday except dinner from 15 June to 15 September, Monday lunch from 15 June to 15 September and Saturday lunch Z **t**

Rest – Carte €38/58

◆ Family-run restaurant overlooking the boats in the old harbour. This pleasant neighbourhood is reflected in the fresh seafood and fish dishes.

La Table du Marché St Jean

pl. du Marché – 04 95 31 64 25 – Fax 04 95 31 87 23 – Closed Sunday and Monday Y **a**

Rest – Menu €27 (weekday lunch), €40/60 – Carte €45/60

◆ This restaurant is renowned for its fish specialities and seafood. There is also a fine terrace shaded by plane trees, and cosy dining rooms. Oyster bar.

A Casarella

r. Ste-Croix, (The citadel) – 04 95 32 02 32 – acerchef@yahoo.fr – Fax 04 95 32 02 32 – Closed February, Monday lunch and Sunday Z **s**

Rest – Menu €18/27 – Carte €33/45

◆ Very friendly welcome at this charming restaurant in the citadel. Cosy dining room with refined decor, fine terraces and delightful local dishes.

Le Siam

r. de la Marine, au Vieux-Port – 04 95 31 72 13 – lesiambastia@hotmail.com – Fax 04 95 34 05 62 – Closed Monday Y **b**

Rest – Menu €22/48 bi – Carte approx. €30

◆ From the mini-terrace of this restaurant one can observe all the activity of the old port. The simple interior is enhanced by a discreet touch of Asian decor. Specialities from Thailand.

A Vista

8 r. St-Michel, (La Citadelle) – 04 95 47 39 91 – www.restaurantavista.com – nicola.lanuto@orange.fr – Fax 04 95 47 39 91 – Closed January Z **v**

Rest – Menu (€25 bi) – Carte €35/200

◆ Elegantly laid out and warm, this restaurant serves regional produce. The fine terrace with dramatic views of the sea is a little piece of paradise.

in Palagaccio 2.5 km via ① – 20200 San Martino di Lota

L'Alivi

rte du Cap – 04 95 55 00 00 – www.hotel-alivi.com – hotel-alivi@wanadoo.fr – Fax 04 95 31 03 95 – Open 15 March-1 November

36 rm – €80/178 €90/195, €14 – 1 suite

Rest *L'Archipel* – *04 95 55 00 10* – Carte €37/61

◆ On the Cap Corse road, this modern establishment has spacious rooms facing the sea. Large sun lounge overlooking the 'big blue'. Direct access to the beach. Mediterranean cuisine served next to the pool overlooking the Tuscan archipelago.

in Pietranera 3 km by ① – 20200 San Martino di Lota

Pietracap without rest

on D 131 – 04 95 31 64 63 – www.hotel-pietracap.com – hotel-pietracap@wanadoo.fr – Fax 04 95 31 39 00 – Open April-November

39 rm – €92/198 €92/198, €12

◆ A haven of peace in a park planted with trees and flowers, with special attention paid to the lovely floral decoration. Enormous rooms with views over the Mediterranean.

Cyrnea without rest
– *04 95 31 41 71 – http://hotelcyrnea.monsite.wanadoo.fr – hotelcyrnea@wanadoo.fr – Fax 04 95 31 72 65 – Closed 15 December-15 January*
19 rm – €50/70 €60/86, €6
◆ Small hotel just beside the church on the main street. It has simple, well-kept rooms; the more attractive face the seafront. The terraced garden gives onto the beach.

in Miomo 5,5 km by ① – ✉ 20200 Santa Maria di Lota

Torremare
rm, rm, VISA
2 rte Bord de Mer – 04 95 33 47 20 – www.hotel-torremare-corse.com – info@hotel-torremare-corse.com – Fax 04 95 33 93 96 – Open beg. May-end September
7 rm – €75/120 €80/150, €15 – ½ P €80/115
Rest – Menu (€15), €17 bi – Carte €35/50
◆ This small hotel, ideally situated beside the beach, offers a lovely view of the Mediterranean and a picturesque Genoese tower. Fresh, bright rooms with minimalist decor. Spotless dining room and panoramic terrace overlooking the sea. Regional cuisine.

in San Martino di Lota 13 km by ① and D 131 – pop. 2 530 – alt. 350 m – ✉ 20200

La Corniche
VISA
hamlet of Castagneto – 04 95 31 40 98 – www.hotel-lacorniche.com – info@hotel-lacorniche.com – Fax 04 95 32 37 69 – Closed January
20 rm – €50/93 €65/123 – ½ P €59/88
Rest – *(closed Sunday dinner off season, Tuesday lunch and Monday)* Menu (€18), €28 – Carte €38/52
◆ This establishment perched on a hillside gives an unforgettable view over the valley and coast. Spacious, colourful and well-soundproofed guestrooms. Authentic, traditional, generous menu served in a warm dining room or under the plane trees.

Château Cagninacci without rest
– *06 78 29 03 94 – www.chateaucagninacci.com – info@chateaucagninacci.com – Open 15 May-1st October*
4 rm – €91/112 €95/116
◆ Peaceful 17C convent remodelled as a château and full of character. Superb bedrooms with traditional furnishings, all overlooking the sea and the island of Elba. Terrace.

Ajaccio road 4 km on the ② – ✉ 20600 Bastia :

Ostella
rm, rm, VISA
av. San Piero – 04 95 30 97 70 – www.hotel-ostella.com – hotel.ostella@wanadoo.fr – Fax 04 95 33 11 70
52 rm – €62/150 €82/150, €12 – 2 suites
Rest – *(closed Saturday lunch and Sunday)* Menu €25/35 – Carte €27/55
◆ Hotel with functional rooms that are gradually being upgraded in a modern style. Some have a small balcony with sea view. Original garden with waterfall. Fine gym. A dining room with marble columns, a terrace and traditional cuisine.

Bastia-Poretta Airport road 18 km via ②, N 193 and D 507 ✉ 20290 Lucciana

Poretta without rest
VISA
rte de l'aéroport – 04 95 36 09 54 – www.hotel-poretta.com – hotel-poretta@wanadoo.fr – Fax 04 95 36 15 32
45 rm – €60/75 €65/80, €8
◆ This modern building stands back from the road and is flanked by palm trees. The rooms vary in size but are fresh and functional. Duplex suites available for families.

BOCOGNANO – 2A Corse-du-Sud – 345 D7 – pop. 343 – alt. 600 m – ✉ 20136
Ajaccio 39 – Bonifacio 155 – Corte 43
Cascade du Voile de la Mariée ★ 3.5 km South.

Beau Séjour with rm
VISA
– *04 95 27 40 26 – www.hotelbocognano.com – ferri-pisani@wanadoo.fr – Fax 04 95 27 40 95 – Open 15 April-7 October*
18 rm – €49 €59, €6,50 **Rest** – Menu €17/23 – Carte €20/36
◆ This building dating from 1890 stands among chestnut trees and is a favourite haunt of walkers and nature lovers. Hearty island specialities are served in a restful flower-filled setting. The rooms here are simply furnished and some offer a fine view of Monte d'Oro.

BONIFACIO – 2A Corse-du-Sud – **345** D11 – **pop. 2 658** – **alt. 55 m** – ✉ **20169**

Ajaccio 132 – Corte 150 – Sartène 50

Figari-Sud-Corse: ✆ 04 95 71 10 10, North: 21 km.

Office de tourisme, 2, rue Fred Scamaroni ✆ 04 95 73 11 88, Fax 04 95 73 14 97

de Sperone Domaine de Sperone, E : 6 km, ✆ 04 95 73 17 13

Site★★★ - High town★★: Place du marché ≤★★ - Treasure-houses r★ of Bonifacio churches (Palazzu Publicu) - St-Dominique church★ - Esplanade St-Francois ≤★★ - Marine cemetery n★.

Sea grottoes and the coast★★.

Genovese rm, rm, VISA AE

Haute Ville – ✆ 04 95 73 12 34 – www.hotelgenovese.com – info@hotel-genovese.com – Fax 04 95 73 09 03 – Closed 16 November-27 December

15 rm – €135/410 €135/410, €20 – 3 suites

Rest – *(open from May to October)* Menu €32/68 – Carte €45/76

◆ The chic and modern minimalist architecture of this place make it conducive to relaxation. Stunning rooms set around a courtyard facing the citadel or harbour. Local produce cooked in keeping with the restaurant's modish setting, overlooking the pool.

Santa Teresa without rest VISA

quartier St-François, (upper town) – ✆ 04 95 73 11 32 – www.hotel-santateresa.com – hotel.santateresa@wanadoo.fr – Fax 04 95 73 15 99 – Open 10 April-12 October

44 rm – €105/250 €105/250, €15

◆ An imposing building overhanging the cliffs. Well-kept, contemporary rooms, some with a dramatic view of the sea and Sardinia.

La Caravelle VISA AE

35 quai Comparetti – ✆ 04 95 73 00 03 – www.hotel-caravelle-corse.com – restaurant.la.caravelle@wanadoo.fr – Fax 04 95 73 00 41 – Open Easter to mid-October

28 rm – €97/300 €97/300, €16 **Rest** – Carte €69/94

◆ Sunny harbour side hotel with intimate atmosphere (shabby chic furniture). Large, comfortable and simple rooms. Menu bursting with very fresh, good quality fish. Pleasant terrace. There are two bars: one in the former chapel, the other outside.

A Trama rm, rest, VISA

2 km east by Santa Manza road – ✆ 04 95 73 17 17 – www.a-trama.com – hotelatrama@aol.com – Fax 04 95 73 17 79 – Closed 5 January-2 February

31 rm – €92/190 €92/190, €15

Rest – *(open 1st April-31 October) (dinner only)* Menu €36 – Carte €28/38

◆ Rooms in five bungalows in attractive grounds with olive and palm trees; they are all well decorated (mosaics) and have a private terrace. Fish of the day is on the menu, served on the veranda overlooking the pool.

A Cheda rm, VISA

rte Porto Vecchio, 2 km northeast on N198 – ✆ 04 95 73 03 82 – www.acheda-hotel.com – acheda@acheda-hotel.com – Fax 04 95 73 17 72

16 rm – €99/759 €99/759, €25 – 5 suites

Rest – *(closed 2 January-15 February, lunch and Tuesday except 1st June-15 September)* Menu (€35), €48 (dinner), €60/70 – Carte €57/68

◆ A garden filled with perfumed plants surrounds the delightful, ground floor rooms and suites (private terrace, sauna). Decor of wood, stone, mosaic and warm colours. Intimate restaurant and terrace overlooking the pool. Modern cuisine using local produce.

Roy d'Aragon without rest VISA AE

13 quai Comparetti – ✆ 04 95 73 03 99 – www.royaragon.com – info@royaragon.com – Fax 04 95 73 07 94 – Closed January and February

31 rm – €54/197 €54/197, €9

◆ This 18C edifice offers practical, colourful rooms, some overlooking the harbour. Fourth floor rooms on the front have a balcony. Breakfast terrace.

Le Voilier
quai Comparetti – 04 95 73 07 06 – lautrerestaurant@wanadoo.fr – Fax 04 95 73 14 27 – Closed 7 January-24 February, Sunday evening and Wednesday in low season
Rest – Menu (€ 24), € 29 – Carte € 55/80
◆ Terrace directly overlooking the quayside. Dining room decorated in cream tones, dark wood furniture, pictures of sailboats and appetising modern seafood cuisine.

Stella d'Oro
7 r. Doria, (upper town) – 04 95 73 03 63 – stella.oro@bonifacio.com – Fax 04 95 73 03 12 – Open April-September
Rest – Menu € 25 – Carte € 39/70
◆ A very pleasant and attractively decorated restaurant (exposed beams, olive press and millstone). Tasty cuisine with fish to the fore. Warm matriarchal welcome.

Domaine de Licetto with rm — rest,
rte Pertusato – 04 95 73 19 48 – www.licetto.com – denisefaby@aol.com – Fax 04 95 72 11 92 – Open 1st April-30 October and closed Sunday
7 rm – € 45/85 € 45/85, € 8
Rest – *(number of covers limited, pre-book)* Menu € 35 bi
◆ Rustic style dining room and flower-decked terrace serving Corsican family dishes made with home-grown vegetables. Spacious rooms. Superb view of the region.

in Gurgazu **6 km Northeast by Santa-Manza road – ✉ 20169 Bonifacio**

Du Golfe — rm, VISA
Golfe Santa Manza – 04 95 73 05 91 – golfe.hotel@wanadoo.fr – Fax 04 95 73 17 18 – Open from mid March-mid October
12 rm (½ board only) – ½ P € 58/80
Rest – Menu (€ 15), € 23/28 – Carte € 26/44
◆ Family-run establishment nestling on a wild stretch of land in Santa Manza Bay, 50m from the sea. An ideal spot for peace, quiet and simplicity. Convivial dining room and terrace with views of the coast. Appetising, unpretentious regional food.

Northeast **10 km on the Porto-Vecchio road (N 198) and minor road – ✉ 20169 Bonifacio :**

U Capu Biancu — rm, rest, VISA
Domaine de Pozzoniello – 04 95 73 05 58 – www.ucapubiancu.com – info@ucapubiancu.com – Fax 04 95 73 18 66 – Open 11 April-1 November and 28 December-5 January
42 rm (½ board only) – 4 suites – ½ P € 173/270 **Rest** – Carte € 43/143
◆ Remotely located in the countryside, facing Santa Manza Gulf. Delightfully personalised rooms, overlooking the sea or the heath. Pool and garden leading to the beach; recreational activities. The chef originally hails from Senegal and skilfully combines Corsican and African flavours.

in la plage de Calalonga **6 km East by D 258 and secondary road – ✉ 20169 Bonifacio**

Marina di Cavu — rm, VISA
– 04 95 73 14 13 – www.hotel-marinadicavu.com – info@marinadicavu.com – Fax 04 95 73 04 82 – Open end April to end October
11 rm – € 130/350 € 130/440, € 22 – 9 suites
Rest – *(Open end April to end October) (number of covers limited, pre-book)* Menu € 68/96 – Carte € 52/89
◆ Set in the Corsican scrub, this hotel looks out towards the islands of Lavezzi and Cavallo. Huge granite boulders feature in the large rooms (mosaics and North African furniture). Access the restaurant via the pool for a superb view. Fine modern menu.

CALACUCCIA – **2B Haute-Corse** – **345** D5 – **pop. 340** – **alt. 830 m** – ✉ **20224**

Bastia 78 – Calvi 97 – Corte 35 – Piana 68 – Porto 58

Office de tourisme, avenue Valdoniello 04 95 47 12 62, Fax 04 95 47 12 62

Calacuccia Lake ★ - Tour of the dam lake ★★ - Defile of la Scala di Santa Regina★★ Northeast: 5 km.

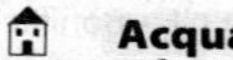

Acqua Viva without rest

– ✆ *04 95 48 06 90 – www.acquaviva-fr.com – stella.acquaviva@wanadoo.fr – Fax 04 95 48 08 82*

14 rm – 🚹€ 58/73 🚹🚹€ 62/77, ☕ € 9

◆ This small family hotel at the mouth of the Scala di Santa Regina gorge, which, legend has it, was hewn by the Holy Virgin herself, has modern and well-kept rooms.

Auberge Casa Balduina without rest

lieu-dit Le Couvent – ✆ 04 95 48 08 57 – www.casabalduina.com – jeannequilichini@aol.com – Closed December and January

7 rm – 🚹€ 57/71 🚹🚹€ 57/71, ☕ € 8

◆ This recently built hotel set in a garden offers smart little bedrooms that have been well renovated. Breakfast is served under a pretty pergola.

CALVI – **2B Haute-Corse** – **345** B4 – **pop. 5 420** – ✉ **20260**

Bastia 92 – Corte 88 – L'Île-Rousse 25 – Porto 73

Calvi-Ste-Catherine: ✆ 04 95 65 88 88, by ①.

Office de tourisme, Port de Plaisance ✆ 04 95 65 16 67, Fax 04 95 65 14 09

Citadel★★: fortifications★ - La Marine★.

Interior★ of St John the Baptist church - La Balagne★★★.. La Balagne★★★.

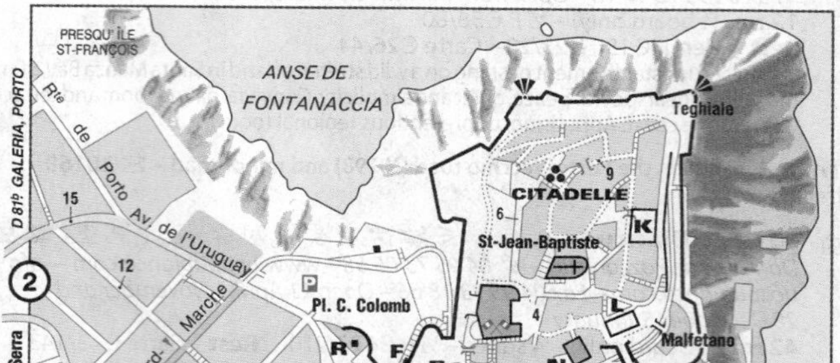

CALVI

In season: traffic flow modified

Alsace-Lorraine (R.) 2
Anges (R. des) 3
Armes (Pl. d') 4
Clemenceau (R. G.)
Colombo (R.) 6
Crudelli (Pl.) 7
Dr-Marchal (Pl. du) 8
Fil (R. du) 9
Joffre (R.) 10
Montée des Écoles (Chemin de) 12
Napoléon (Av.) 15
République (Av. de la) 16
Wilson (Bd)

La Villa – rm,
chemin de Notre Dame de la Serra, 1 km via ① –
☎ 04 95 65 10 10 – www.hotel-lavilla.com – la-villa.reservation@wanadoo.fr
– Fax 04 95 65 10 50 – Open 1st April-31 October
37 rm – €310/950 €310/950, €35 – 13 suites – ½ P €245/565
Rest ***L'Alivu*** – *(closed Monday and Tuesday) (dinner only)* Menu €110/195 – Carte €110/200
Rest ***Le Bistrot*** – Carte €60/90
Spec. Langoustines de nos côtes aux trois saveurs (May to mid-Sep.). Veau Corse et sa garniture de saison (April to Oct.). Soufflé au Grand-Marnier (April to Oct.).
Wines Ajaccio, Calvi.
◆ This contemporary palace between a convent and a Roman villa sits on the hillside, as if bowing to the sea. Wrought iron, mosaics, cane furnishings, terra cotta... It's a hidden jewel! Gourmet Mediterranean dinners by an award winning chef.

Regina without rest
av. Santa Maria, via ① – ☎ 04 95 65 24 23 – www.reginahotelcalvi.com – infos@reginahotelcalvi.com – Fax 04 95 61 00 09
44 rm – €65/320 €65/320, €12
◆ Recent hotel dominating the harbour and Bay of Calvi. Spacious modern rooms facing the sea or the attractive pool.

Balanea without rest
6 r. Clemenceau – ☎ 04 95 65 94 94 – www.hotel-balanea.com
– info@hotel-balanea.com – Fax 04 95 65 29 71
– Open 2 March-30 November **n**
37 rm – €80/220 €80/220, €12 – 1 suite
◆ Access via a pedestrian street. The unusual rooms sport lively colours and neo-rustic or designer furniture; some command a fine view of the harbour.

Mariana without rest
av. Santa Maria, par ① – ☎ 04 95 65 31 38
– www.hotel-mariana-calvi.com – mariana-hotel-calvi@orange.fr
– Fax 04 95 65 32 72
55 rm – €72/180 €72/180, €10 – 5 suites
◆ Modern hotel dominating the Bay of Calvi. Most of the rooms boast a private loggia and sea view. New extension with suites and a rooftop terrace-pool-sundeck.

Hostellerie de l'Abbaye without rest
rte de Santore – ☎ 04 95 65 04 27
– www.hostellerie-abbaye.com – abbaye.hotel@wanadoo.fr – Fax 04 95 65 30 23
– Open 1 April-31 October
43 rm – €99/194 €113/208
◆ The façade of this hotel, built in the walls of a 16C Franciscan abbey, is decked in flowers and greenery, as are the shaded terrace and lovely garden. Cosy rooms.

L'Onda without rest
av. Christophe Colomb, 1 km on ① – ☎ 04 95 65 35 00
– www.hotel-londa.com – hotelonda@yahoo.fr – Fax 04 95 65 16 26
– Open 25 April-2 November
24 rm – €55/94 €60/135, €8
◆ This engaging small building stands near the beach and a pine wood planted in the late 19C. The functional rooms all have a private loggia. Refurbished lobby and sitting room.

Emile's
quai Landry – ☎ 04 95 65 09 60 – www.restaurant-emiles.com
– info@restaurant-emiles.com – Fax 04 95 60 56 40
– Open 15 March-15 October **k**
Rest – Menu €50/120 – Carte €90/110
Spec. Filets de rougets "trémail" juste saisis. Denti de ligne poêlé, risotto de légumes primeurs. Mascarpone à la vanille sur sablé demi-sel aux épices et gariguettes.
◆ The first floor of this characteristic house serves tasty gourmet cuisine in keeping with modern tastes. Terrace overlooking the port and Art Deco style veranda.

E.A.T.
r. Clemenceau, Port ascent – ✆ 04 95 38 21 87 – remi.robert636@orange.fr – Closed 1st-15 November, 1st-15 February, Monday, Tuesday and Wednesday from November to March
Rest – Menu € 28 – Carte € 28/50
◆ Unusual concept at this lounge style restaurant: diners choose either large or extra large portions of the refined modern dishes. Terrace at the foot of the citadel.

Aux Bons Amis
r. Clemenceau – ✆ 04 95 65 05 01 – bons.amis@wanadoo.fr – Fax 04 95 65 32 41 – Open 1 March-15 October and closed Wednesday in low season, Saturday lunch in high season and Wednesday lunch
Rest – Menu € 21/35 – Carte € 40/65
◆ This friendly little restaurant in a pedestrian street has a fishing theme as decoration, with nets and ornaments. Crayfish and lobster tank. Fish and seafood specialities.

via ① 5 km airport road on private lane – ✉ 20260 Calvi :

La Signoria
rte de la forêt de Bonifato – ✆ 04 95 65 93 00 – www.hotel-la-signoria.com – info@hotel-la-signoria.com – Fax 04 95 65 38 77 – Open end March to 31 October
24 rm – € 290/510 € 290/510, € 26 – 2 suites
Rest – *(dinner only)* Menu (€ 35), € 85/120 – Carte € 86/103
◆ A Mediterranean pulse throbs in this 18C building nestling in a pine wood: walls coloured in blue and ochre, Corsican period furniture, country garden and wonderful scents! Fine modern fare, served on the dining room-veranda or on the pretty terrace.

CARGÈSE – 2A Corse-du-Sud – 345 A7 – pop. 1 137 – alt. 75 m – ✉ 20130
Ajaccio 51 – Calvi 106 – Corte 119 – Piana 21 – Porto 33
Office de tourisme, rue du Dr Dragacci ✆ 04 95 26 41 31, Fax 04 95 26 48 80
Greek church ★ - Site★★ from the belvédère de la pointe Molendino (viewpoint) East: 3 km.

Thalassa
plage du Pero, 1.5 km north – ✆ 04 95 26 40 08 – www.thalassalura.com – Fax 04 95 26 41 66 – Open 1st May-30 September
25 rm – € 85/90 € 90/110, € 6 – ½ P € 70/75
Rest – *(open 1st June-18 September) (dinner only) (resident only)*
◆ Pleasant family guesthouse atmosphere at this beachside hotel. The rather small but bright and well-kept rooms mostly face the sea. Pleasant dining room and leafy terrace. Traditional food.

CASAMOZZA – 2B Haute-Corse – 345 F4 – ✉ 20290 Lucciana
Bastia 20 – Corte 49 – Vescovato 6

Chez Walter
N 193 – ✆ 04 95 36 00 09 – www.hotel-chez-walter.com – chez.walter@wanadoo.fr – Fax 04 95 36 18 92
64 rm – € 70/100 € 85/120, € 8 – 2 suites
Rest – *(closed 15 December-6 January and Sunday except dinner in August)* Menu € 21 – Carte € 40/60
◆ A modern hotel complex set in a Mediterranean garden near to Bastia Poretta airport. It has well-equipped rooms of varying size and comfort. Huge dining room with neo-rustic decor. Traditional cuisine, buffets and pizzas.

CAURO – 2A Corse-du-Sud – 345 C8 – pop. 1 060 – alt. 450 m – ✉ 20117
Ajaccio 22 – Sartène 63

Auberge Napoléon
Rte de Sartène – ✆ 04 95 28 40 78 – ghjulia2@free.fr – Open 15 July-15 September and week-ends off season
Rest – *(pre-book)* Menu € 32 – Carte € 30/45
◆ Pleasant inn standing on the main street in the village. A rustic dining room serving dishes with a regional flavour. A relaxed family welcome.

CERVIONE – 2B Haute-Corse – **345** F6 – **pop. 1 628** – **alt. 350 m** – ✉ **20221**

Paris 999 – Ajaccio 140 – Bastia 52 – Corte 78 – Biguglia 45

in Prunete 5,5 km East by D 71 – ✉ **20221**

Casa Corsa without rest
Acqua Nera – ☎ 04 95 38 01 40 – www.casa-corsa.net – casa-corsa1@oronge.fr – Fax 04 95 33 39 27
6 rm – €59 €66
◆ You will be anything but disappointed by the warm welcome at this comfortable guesthouse. Cosy rooms with spacious bathrooms. Lovely garden.

COL DE BAVELLA – 2A Corse-du-Sud – **345** E9 – **alt. 1 218 m** – ✉ **20124 Zonza**

Ajaccio 102 – Bonifacio 76 – Porto-Vecchio 49 – Propriano 49 – Sartène 47

Col and aiguilles de Bavella (pass and peaks)★★★ - Bavella forest ★★.

Auberge du Col de Bavella
– ☎ 04 95 72 09 87 – www.auberge-bavella.com – auberge-bavella@wanadoo.fr – Fax 04 95 72 16 48 – Open April-October
Rest – Menu € 22 – Carte € 20/45
◆ A handy inn close to the GR 20 amid Laricio pines, near the majestic Bavella peaks. Large rustic dining room (fireplace). Corsican specialities and home-made cooked pork products.

CORTE – 2B Haute-Corse – **345** D6 – **pop. 6 747** – **alt. 396 m** – ✉ **20250** **Corse**

Bastia 69 – Bonifacio 150 – Calvi 88 – L'Île-Rousse 63 – Porto 93 – Sartène 149

Office de tourisme, la Citadelle ☎ 04 95 46 26 70, Fax 04 95 46 34 05

High town★: Ste-Croix chapel ★, citadel★ ★, Viewpoint ★ - Musée de la Corse★★.

★★ du Monte Cecu North: 7 km - Southwest: gorges de la Restonica★★.

Le 24
24 cours Paoli – ☎ 04 95 46 02 90 – le24restaurant@yahoo.fr – Fax 04 95 46 21 90 – Closed Saturday lunch and Sunday lunch
Rest – Menu (€ 16), € 25 – Carte € 35/62
◆ A nice little establishment in a pleasantly contemporary setting. Fine blackboard menu mixing traditional Corsican cooking with international dishes. Good local wines.

In the Gorges de La Restonica Southwest on D 623 – ✉ **20250 Corte**

Dominique Colonna without rest
2 km – ☎ 04 95 45 25 65 – www.dominique-colonna.com – info@dominique-colonna.com – Fax 04 95 61 03 91 – Open 23 March-15 November
28 rm – €65/190 €65/190, € 12 – 1 suite
◆ A group of modern, ivy-clad buildings stands at the entrance to the gorges and pinewoods of Corte. The rooms are modern and comfortable and there is a heated swimming-pool.

COTI-CHIAVARI – 2A Corse-du-Sud – **345** B9 – **pop. 490** – **alt. 625 m** – ✉ **20138**

Ajaccio 42 – Propriano 38 – Sartène 50

Le Belvédère

– ☎ 04 95 27 10 32 – www.lebelvederedecoti.com – le.belvedere@wanadoo.fr – Fax 04 95 27 12 99 – Open 1st March to mid-November
13 rm (½ board only) – ½ P € 50/58
Rest – *(closed lunch except Sunday 1st March-31 May) (pre-book)* Menu € 20 (dinner), € 26/30
◆ Perched like an eagle's nest with an astounding view of the Gulf of Ajaccio. The rooms are spacious and functional. The glazed dining room and terrace afford a fantastic vista. Regional cuisine (superb produce).

ECCICA-SUARELLA – 2A Corse-du-Sud – **345** C8 – **pop. 828** – **alt. 300 m** – ✉ **20117**
Paris 964 – Ajaccio 19 – Corte 87 – Ghisonaccia 129 – Propriano 52

Carpe Diem Palazzu rm, VISA
– *☎ 04 95 10 96 10 – www.carpediem-palazzu.com – info@carpediem-palazzu.com – Fax 04 95 23 80 83 – Closed 24 December-25 February*
6 rm – †€ 200/400 ††€ 200/400, ☕ € 19
Table d'hôte – *(closed Monday except school holidays)* Menu € 40/65
◆ Bare stone and wood, period and second hand furniture, well-equipped bathrooms – sophisticated suites whose every detail conveys the desire for wellbeing. Turkish bath. Regional cuisine (top quality produce) served on the terrace or in the garden facing the pool.

ERBALUNGA – 2B Haute-Corse – **345** F3 – ✉ **20222**
Bastia 11 – Rogliano 30
N.-D. des Neiges chapel ★ 3 km West.

Castel'Brando without rest VISA
Rte du Cap – ☎ 04 95 30 10 30 – www.castelbrando.com – info@castelbrando.com – Fax 04 95 33 98 18 – Closed January and February
39 rm – †€ 105/145 ††€ 105/145, ☕ € 13 – 6 suites
◆ This manor house owes its origin to a doctor serving with the Napoleonic armies. Personalised guestrooms, some located in the more modern villas. Fine garden with pools.

Le Pirate VISA AE
au port – ☎ 04 95 33 24 20 – www.restaurantlepirate.com – jeanpierrericci@aol.com – Fax 04 95 33 18 97 – Closed 7 January-28 February, Monday and Tuesday except from June to September
Rest – Menu (€ 29), € 35 (lunch), € 65/90 – Carte € 75/83
Spec. Risotto crémeux de poulpe à l'encre de seiche. Déclinaison du veau "bio" corse. Tour de chocolat ivoire, coeur coulant passion et sorbet pabana. **Wines** Patrimonio, Vin de Corse-Figari
◆ This old stone building has a pleasant terrace facing the little harbour and a veranda-dining room overlooking the sea. Tasty, delicate and precise cuisine.

Ersa – 2B Haute-Corse – **345** F2 – ✉ **20275** 15 **B1**

Le Saint-Jean without rest VISA AE
Botticella – ☎ 04 95 47 71 71 – www.lesaintjean.net – lesaintjeanersa@orange.fr – Fax 04 95 35 24 42 – Closed January and February
9 rm – †€ 50/115 ††€ 55/120, ☕ € 6,50
◆ Former mansion house at the end of the Cap Corse that has been tastefully refurbished. Personalised rooms on a travel theme. Fine terrace looking out to Giraglia.

ÉVISA – 2A Corse-du-Sud – **345** B6 – **pop. 182** – **alt. 850 m** – ✉ **20126**
Ajaccio 71 – Calvi 96 – Corte 70 – Piana 33 – Porto 23
Aïtone forest★★ - Cascades of Aïtone★ Northeast: 3 km then 30 mn.
Col de Vergio ★★ Northeast: 10 km.

Scopa Rossa VISA
– *☎ 04 95 26 20 22 – www.hotelscoparossa.com – scopa-rossa@wanadoo.fr – Fax 04 95 26 24 17 – Open 16 March-29 November*
28 rm – †€ 46/65 ††€ 50/80, ☕ € 8 – ½ P € 52/65
Rest – Menu (€ 22), € 25/30 – Carte € 40/60
◆ The ideal hotel for a family holiday in the centre of this resort. The simple, well-kept bedrooms are divided between the main building and an annexe. The rifles decorating the rustic dining room are no longer used. Dishes based on local produce.

FAVONE – 2A Corse-du-Sud – **345** F9 – ✉ **20135 Conca**
Ajaccio 128 – Bonifacio 58

U Dragulinu
– ✆ 04 95 73 20 30 – www.hoteludragulinu.com – hoteludragulinu@wanadoo.fr
– Fax 04 95 73 22 06 – Open 11 April-30 October
34 rm – €85/220 €95/230
Rest – *(open 15 June-15 September) (lunch only)* Menu €25
◆ This hotel run by two sisters enjoys an idyllic location opposite the beach, ideal for a seaside holiday. Well kept, practical bedrooms, mostly located on the ground floor. Simple family cooking using fresh produce in the restaurant. Pretty terrace.

FELICETO – 2B Haute-Corse – **345** C4 – **pop. 197** – **alt. 350 m** – ✉ **20225**
Bastia 76 – Calvi 26 – Corte 72 – L'Île-Rousse 15

Mare E Monti
– ✆ 04 95 63 02 00 – www.hotel-maremonti.com – mare-e-monti@wanadoo.fr
– Fax 04 95 63 02 01 – Open 1 April-31 October
16 rm – €70/138 €70/138, €9
Rest ***Sol E Luna*** – *(Open 1 April-15 October)* Carte €22/35
◆ Their fortune made in sugar-cane, the ancestors of this family returned from Porto Rico and built this "American Palace" between the sea and the mountain in the 19C. Market fresh cuisine served in the white dining room or on the handsome poolside terrace.

GALÉRIA – 2B Haute-Corse – **345** A5 – **pop. 325** – **alt. 30 m** – ✉ **20245**
Bastia 118 – Calvi 34 – Porto 48
Syndicat d'initiative, Carrefour ✆ 04 95 62 02 27, Fax 04 95 62 02 27
Bay of Galéria★.

in Ferayola 13 km North by D 351 and D 81B – ✉ **20245 Galeria**

Auberge Ferayola rm,
– ✆ 04 95 65 25 25 – www.ferayola.com – ferayola@wanadoo.fr
– Fax 04 95 65 20 78 – Open 8 May-30 September
14 rm – €50/95 €55/114, €8 – ½ P €55/85 **Rest** – Carte €25/45
◆ The hotel stands alone in the maquis overlooking sea – thus assuring peace and restfulness. The rooms are simple but pleasant. Chalets. Unobstructed view of the mountains and beautiful panoramic sunset from the rustic dining room and terrace.

L'ÎLE-ROUSSE – 2B Haute-Corse – **345** C4 – **pop. 2 795** – ✉ **20220**
Bastia 67 – Calvi 25 – Corte 63
Syndicat d'initiative, 7, place Paoli ✆ 04 95 60 04 35, Fax 04 95 60 24 74
Covered market★ - Pietra island ★.
La Balagne★★★.

Perla Rossa without rest
30 r. Notre-Dame – ✆ 04 95 48 45 30 – www.hotelperlarossa.com – info@hotelperlarossa.com – Fax 04 95 48 45 31 – Open early April to end October
10 rm – €190/590 €190/590, €20 – 2 suites
◆ Fine 19C mansion, fully restored in a modern, designer style. Large, bright rooms that are rather minimalist. Magnificent shady terrace facing the sea.

Santa Maria without rest
rte du Port – ✆ 04 95 63 05 05 – www.hotelsantamaria.com – infos@hotelsantamaria.com – Fax 04 95 60 32 48
56 rm – €82/197 €94/209
◆ The hotel is located before the bridge leading to the island of Pietra. Pleasant rooms, some with apocalyptic views of the sea during stormy weather. Nice outdoor hot tub.

Funtana Marina without rest
1 km on Monticello road and secondary road – 04 95 60 16 12 – www.hotel-funtana.com – hotel-funtana-marina@wanadoo.fr – Fax 04 95 60 35 44
29 rm – €55/105 €60/105, €9
◆ Building on a hillside surrounded by rich vegetation. The comfortable rooms overlook the lovely pool, beyond which are the sea and town.

Cala di l'Oru without rest
bd Pierre Pasquini – 04 95 60 14 75 – www.hotel-caladiloru.com – hotelcaladiloru@wanadoo.fr – Fax 04 95 60 36 40 – Open from March to October
26 rm – €60/111 €63/130, €8
◆ The sons of the owner display photos and works of modern art in this well renovated hotel with views of the sea or the mountains. Attractive Mediterranean garden.

L'Amiral without rest
bd Ch.-Marie Savelli – 04 95 60 28 05 – www.hotel-amiral.com – info@hotel-amiral.com – Fax 04 95 60 31 21 – Open April-September
19 rm – €65/110 €65/110, €10
◆ Embark aboard this hotel with a nautical ambiance. Communal areas resemble the inside of a boat. Functional bedrooms.

Le Grillon
av. P. Doumer – 04 95 60 00 49 – www.hotel-grillon.net – hr-le-grillon@wanadoo.fr – Fax 04 95 60 43 69 – Open 1st March-31 October
16 rm – €37/58 €38/60, €6 – ½ P €39/50
Rest – Menu €14/17 – Carte approx. €22,50
◆ Friendly welcome in this simple little hotel where the freshly redecorated and soundproofed rooms have a more modern decor (painted wood furniture). Simple dining room and family cooking with regional touches.

La Pietra
chemin du Phare – 04 95 63 02 30 – www.hotel-lapietra.com – hotellapietra@wanadoo.fr – Fax 04 95 60 15 92 – Open April-October
42 rm – €65/110 €110/112, €10 – ½ P €64/87
Rest – *(dinner only)* Menu €30 – Carte €40/48
◆ This 1970s hotel has a waterfront location next to the harbour. All rooms have balconies overlooking either the sea or the 15C Genoese tower. Piano lounge bar. Local cuisine and dishes of the day against the broad backdrop of the sea.

Pasquale Paoli (Ange Cananzi)
2 pl. Paoli – 04 95 47 67 70 – catherine.cananzi@wanadoo.fr – Fax 04 95 47 67 62 – Closed lunch in July-August and Sunday and Wednesday from September to June
Rest – *(number of covers limited, pre-book)* Menu (€25), €40 (dinner) – Carte €50/70
Spec. Fricassée de poulpes en salade. Lotte de pays aux amandes fraîches. Millefeuille au citron corse.
◆ An exuberant hymn to Corsica sung by two enthusiasts, one in the dining room, (decor devoted to P Paoli) the other in the kitchen. Delicious cuisine using local produce.

in Monticello **4,5 km Southeast by D 63 – pop. 1 565 – alt. 220 m – 20220**

A Pasturella with rm
pl. du Village – 04 95 60 05 65 – www.a-pasturella.com – a.pasturella@wanadoo.fr – Fax 04 95 60 21 78 – Closed 1-8 March, 5 November-18 December, February holiday and Sunday dinner from 18 December to 31 March
12 rm – €65/92 €75/102, €11 – ½ P €81/95
Rest – Menu €40/75 – Carte €33/73
◆ Restaurant located in a picturesque village on the Paoli corniche. Fish of the day and traditional meals served in the renovated dining area or on the lovely terrace.

in Pigna **8 km southwest on the N 197 and D 151 – pop. 97 – alt. 400 m – ✉ 20220**

U Palazzu
– *☎ 04 95 47 32 78 – hotel-corse-palazzu.com – palazzupigna@wanadoo.fr – Fax 04 95 46 08 68 – Open April to October*
3 rm – €150/300 €150/300, ☕ €20 – 2 suites
Rest – *(number of covers limited, pre-book)* Menu (€25), €55
◆ 18C mansion in the village centre with superb views over the plain and the sea. Large guestrooms, some with fireplace or terrace.

LEVIE – **2A Corse-du-Sud** – **345** D9 – **pop. 696** – **alt. 645 m** – ✉ **20170**

Ajaccio 101 – Bonifacio 57 – Porto-Vecchio 39 – Sartène 28
Office de tourisme, rue Sorba ☎ 04 95 78 41 95, Fax 04 95 78 46 74
Musée de l'Alta Rocca★: Christ in ivory★.
Sites★★ of Cucuruzzu and Capula West: 7 km.

La Pergola
r. Sorba – ☎ 04 95 78 41 62 – Open April-October
Rest – *(number of covers limited, pre-book)* Menu (€13), €18
◆ After visiting the Alta Rocca Museum, return to the present under a welcoming bower where they serve Corsican specialities for a reasonable price.

LUMIO – **2B Haute-Corse** – **345** B4 – **pop. 1 012** – **alt. 150 m** – ✉ **20260**

Bastia 82 – Calvi 10 – L'Île-Rousse 16

Chez Charles with rm
– *☎ 04 95 60 61 71 – www.hotel-chezcharles.com – contact@hotel-chezcharles.com – Fax 04 95 60 62 51 – Open 2 April-7 November*
16 rm – €70/125 €70/125, ☕ €15
Rest – *(closed Monday lunch)* Menu €40/70 – Carte €58/70
◆ This pink house by the roadside is home to a light dining room and well-shaded panoramic terrace. Up-to-date menu. Guestrooms of mediterranean inspiration; infinity pool.

MACINAGGIO – **2B Haute-Corse** – **345** F2 – ✉ **20248**

Bastia 37
Syndicat d'initiative, port de plaisnce ☎ 04 95 35 40 34, Fax 04 95 35 40 34

U Libecciu
rte de la Plage – ☎ 04 95 35 43 22 – www.u-libecciu.com – info@u-libecciu.com – Fax 04 95 35 46 08 – Open 1st April-15 October
30 rm – €60/94 €70/125, ☕ €7 – 10 suites
Rest – *(dinner only)* Menu €20/35 – Carte €26/42
◆ The Macinaggio mooring ground has been well known since antiquity. This restaurant near the harbour has spacious rooms with terraces; suites equipped for extended stays. Regional specialities on the menu in the first floor veranda-dining room.

U Ricordu
– *☎ 04 95 35 40 20 – www.hotel-uricordu.com – uricordu@wanadoo.fr – Fax 04 95 35 41 88 – Open 30 March-3 November* – **54 rm** ☕ – €85/175 €90/180 **Rest** – *(open 15 April-15 October)* Menu €18/20 – Carte €30/40
◆ Fresh modern rooms (overlooking either the roadside or the mountains) await you after an invigorating trek along the coastguard path. The heated pool is open in summer. African touches in the decor of the bright dining room. Traditional cuisine.

MURO – **2B Haute-Corse** – **345** C4 – **pop. 263** – **alt. 350 m** – ✉ **20225**

Ajaccio 161 - Bastia 106

Casa Theodora without rest
Piazza a u Duttore – ☎ 04 95 61 78 32 – www.a-casatheodora.com – info@a-casatheodora.com – Fax 04 95 61 78 32 – Open April to end October
5 rm ☕ – €140/270 €140/270
◆ This 16C palazzo, converted into a luxury hotel, is named after the short-lived King of Corsica who stayed here in 1736. Genovese architecture, trompe l'oeil and Baroque frescoes. Small indoor pool.

NONZA – 2B Haute-Corse – 345 F3 – pop. 68 – alt. 100 m – ✉ 20217
Bastia 33 – Rogliano 49 – Saint-Florent 20

Casa Maria without rest
at the foot of the génoise tower – ✆ 04 95 37 80 95 – www.casamaria.fr – casamaria@wanadoo.fr – Fax 04 95 37 80 95 – Open April-October
5 rm – †€ 70/90 ††€ 70/90
◆ This old mansion with fresh and pleasant rooms stands at the foot of a Genoese tower. Warm welcome, family furniture and a splendid view of the sea.

OLETTA – 2B Haute-Corse – 345 F4 – pop. 1 245 – alt. 250 m – ✉ 20232
Bastia 18 – Calvi 78 – Corte 72 – L'Île-Rousse 53

Auberge A Magina VISA
– ✆ 04 95 39 01 01 – Open April to mid-October and closed Monday except July-August
Rest – *(closed Mon.)* Menu € 27 – Carte € 45/60
◆ A breathtaking view and Corsican cuisine, prepared and served in family style in a pleasant dining room. Don't miss the magnificent sunset from the terrace.

OLMETO – 2A Corse-du-Sud – 345 C9 – pop. 1 199 – alt. 320 m – ✉ 20113
Ajaccio 64 – Propriano 8 – Sartène 20
Syndicat d'initiative, Village ✆ 04 95 74 65 87, Fax 04 95 74 62 86

Santa Maria rm, VISA
pl. de l'Église – ✆ 04 95 74 65 59 – www.hotel-restaurant-santa-maria.com – ettorinathalie@aol.com – Fax 04 95 74 60 33 – Closed November and December
12 rm – †€ 45/58 ††€ 45/58, € 6 – ½ P € 44/56
Rest – *(dinner only)* Menu € 23 – Carte € 32/44
◆ A former oil mill with a family atmosphere, near the church. A flight of stairs leading to the functional rooms gives the building character. The restaurant has a lovely, century-old vaulted ceiling and a pretty flower-filled terrace facing the gulf. Corsican dishes.

in Olmeto-Plage 9 km Southwest by D 157 – ✉ 20113

Ruesco P VISA
Capicciolo – ✆ 04 95 76 70 50 – www.hotel-ruesco.com – info@hotel-ruesco.com – Fax 04 95 76 70 51 – Open 25 April-10 October
25 rm – †€ 70/115 ††€ 115/160, € 13
Rest – *(open 15 May-30 September)* Menu € 25 (lunch) – Carte € 35/50
◆ Modern buildings housing spacious rooms. All the rooms, apart from two, have balconies overlooking the water. A garden leads up to the restaurant which specialises in grilled food and pizzas cooked over a wood fire. The terrace looks onto the beach.

South 5 km on the N 196 and minor road – ✉ 20113 Olmeto

Marinca rm, P VISA
Lieu dit Vintricella – ✆ 04 95 70 09 00 – www.hotel-marinca.com – info@hotel-marinca.com – Fax 04 95 76 19 09 – Open April-October
56 rm (½ board only) – 4 suites – ½ P € 110/345
Rest – *(dinner only)* Menu (€ 35), € 45 – Carte € 25/35
◆ Hotel with views of the gulf and surrounded by gardens. Three tiered infinity pools flow towards the private beach. Large rooms with individual touches; balconies on the beach side. Spa. Lovely, Moorish style terrace; traditional cuisine. The Diamant Noir serves more elaborate meals at dinner.

PATRIMONIO – 2B Haute-Corse – 345 F3 – pop. 667 – alt. 100 m – ✉ 20253
Bastia 16 – St-Florent 6 – San-Michele-de-Murato 22
St-Martin church ★.

Du Vignoble without rest P VISA
Santa Maria – ✆ 04 95 37 18 48 – www.hotel-du-vignoble.com – hotel-du-vignoble@wanadoo.fr – Fax 04 95 56 13 10 – Open from April to end October
12 rm – †€ 60/90 ††€ 60/90, € 5
◆ New hotel in the village centre set in a fine house dating from 1846. Warm colours, patinated walls and wrought iron furnishings in the bedrooms. Family wine cellar.

Osteria di San Martinu

Santa Maria – ✆ 04 95 37 11 93 – Open 1st May-30 September and closed Wednesday in September

Rest – Menu € 25 – Carte € 23/35

◆ In summer, it's all systems go on the terrace under the pergola. Corsican dishes and grills are served with Patrimonio wine, produced by the owner's brother.

PERI – 2A Corse-du-Sud – 345 C7 – pop. 1 516 – alt. 450 m – ✉ 20167

Ajaccio 26 – Corte 71 – Propriano 82 – Sartène 94

Chez Séraphin

– ✆ 04 95 25 68 94 – Open early April to 15 October and closed Monday

Rest – Menu € 42 bi

◆ Typical Corsican building in a charming village clinging to the mountainside. Terrace overlooking the valley. Warm welcome and good hearty meals.

PETRETO-BICCHISANO – 2A Corse-du-Sud – 345 C9 – pop. 559 – alt. 600 m – ✉ 20140

Ajaccio 52 – Sartène 35

De France

à Bicchisano – ✆ 04 95 24 30 55 – Fax 04 95 24 30 55 – Open from March to November

Rest – *(pre-book)* Menu € 17 (weekday lunch), € 27/60 – Carte € 40/75

◆ Corsican specialities and home-made products such as cooked meats, jams and liqueurs are served in this well-kept rural style dining room or under the cool arbour.

PIANA – 2A Corse-du-Sud – 345 A6 – pop. 443 – alt. 420 m – ✉ 20115

Ajaccio 72 – Calvi 85 – Évisa 33 – Porto 13

Syndicat d'initiative, ✆ 04 95 27 84 42, Fax 04 95 27 82 72

Bay of Porto★★★.

Capo Rosso

rte des Calanches – ✆ 04 95 27 82 40 – www.caporosso.com – info@caporosso.com – Fax 04 95 27 80 00 – Open 1st April-20 October

46 rm (½ board only in season) – †€ 100/165 ††€ 120/250 – ½ P € 92/218

Rest – Menu € 30 – Carte € 40/70

◆ Unrestricted views of Porto Bay and the Calanche from the swimming pool and the huge rooms (with balconies). Mostly contemporary decor. Restaurant with views, serving family seafood cuisine using the local catch.

Le Scandola

rte Cargèse – ✆ 04 95 27 80 07 – www.hotelscandola.com – infos@hotelscandola.com – Fax 04 95 27 83 88 – Closed 17 November-1st February

12 rm – †€ 40/104 ††€ 52/104, € 10

Rest – *(dinner only)* Menu € 18 – Carte € 29/54

◆ With views of the Scandola peninsula and the Piana gulf, this hotel enjoys an exceptional location. Warm, colourful rooms and balconies facing the sea. Cuisine from around the world served in the lounge restaurant with views.

POGGIO-MEZZANA – 2B Haute-Corse – 345 F5 – pop. 648 – alt. 350 m – ✉ 20230

Levolle Marine

Levolle Sottan, (on the beach) – ✆ 04 95 58 41 50 – www.levollemarine.com – levolle.marine-corse@wanadoo.fr – Fax 04 95 58 41 64 – Open April-October

9 rm – †€ 75/85 ††€ 95/115, € 8,50 – 7 suites **Rest** – Carte € 35/60

◆ This house in the middle of a flower-decked park is prettily decorated with objets d'art, old oil lamps and cafetieres. Comfortable rooms. Traditional dishes in the dining room or on the terrace overlooking the fine sand.

PORTICCIO – 2A Corse-du-Sud – **345** B8 – ✉ **20166**

Ajaccio 19 – Sartène 68

Office de tourisme, les Marines ✆ 04 95 25 01 01, Fax 04 95 25 11 12

Le Maquis rm, rest,

– ✆ *04 95 25 05 55 – www.lemaquis.com – info@lemaquis.com – Fax 04 95 25 11 70 – Closed January and February*

20 rm – €160/720 €180/720, €26 – 5 suites

Rest – Menu €73 (dinner) – Carte €81/133

◆ A pretty Genoese-style building nestling in a luxuriant seaside garden. Spacious guest-rooms with attractive antique furniture. Splendid swimming pools. Inventive cuisine, selected wines and a fine view from the dining room and superb terrace.

Sofitel Thalassa

– ✆ *04 95 29 40 40 – www.sofitel.com – h0587@accor.com – Fax 04 95 25 00 63 – Closed 4-24 January*

96 rm – €211/653 €211/653, €25 – 2 suites

Rest – Menu €49 – Carte €64/90

◆ A hotel complex devoted to Neptune: an isolated location on the tip of Cape Porticcio, a thalassotherapy centre, watersports facilities and rooms facing the sea. Dishes with a contemporary touch and light meals served in a naval decor or outside with a view of the waves.

in Agosta-Plage 2 km South – ✉ ***20166 Porticcio***

Kallisté without rest

rte du Vieux Molini – ✆ 04 95 25 54 19 – www.hotels-kalliste.com – info@hotels-kalliste.com – Fax 04 95 25 59 25 – Open 1 April-1 November

7 rm – €69/109 €69/149, €10 – 1 suite

◆ A walled garden protects the tranquillity of this spruce villa in a residential area. Simply decorated rooms of various sizes overlooking the sea or the garden.

PORTO – 2A Corse-du-Sud – **345** B6 – ✉ **20150 Ota**

Ajaccio 84 – Calvi 73 – Corte 93 – Évisa 23

Office de tourisme, place de La Marine ✆ 04 95 26 10 55, Fax 04 95 26 14 25

Tour génoise★.

Bay of Porto★★★: les Calanche★★★ - Northwest: Scandola reserve★★★, Bay★★ of Girolata.

Capo d'Orto without rest

rte de Calvi – ✆ 04 95 26 11 14 – www.hotel-capo-dorto.com – hotel.capo.d.orto@wanadoo.fr – Fax 04 95 26 13 49 – Open 10 April-20 October

39 rm – €75/155 €75/155

◆ This hotel has three room types, all well sized with balconies facing the sea. Choose one in the recently built extension with a more modern decor.

Le Subrini without rest

at la Marine – ✆ 04 95 26 14 94 – www.hotels-porto.com – subrini@hotels-porto.com – Fax 04 95 26 11 57 – Open from March to October

23 rm – €65/95 €80/130, €10

◆ A freestone building on the main square on the seafront. The large rooms, all recently renovated, are functional and bright. View over the bay.

Le Belvédère without rest

à la Marine – ✆ 04 95 26 12 01 – www.hotel-le-belvedere.com – info@hotel-le-belvedere.com – Fax 04 95 26 11 97 – Open 2 April-1 November

20 rm – €50/120 €50/120, €8

◆ At the foot of the famous Genoese tower stalwartly resisting poundings by the sea. This modern red stone building offers well-equipped rooms; choose one facing the harbour.

Bella Vista
– ✆ *04 95 26 11 08 – www.hotel-corse.com – info@hotel-bellavista.net – Fax 04 95 26 15 18 – Open April-October*
14 rm (½ board only in season) – €55/93 €65/138, €11 – 3 suites
Rest – *(open 15 April-30 September) (dinner only)* Menu €26 – Carte €35/90
◆ A hotel with a family atmosphere and carefully decorated rooms. Unforgettable views of the Capo d'Orto at sunset and good breakfast. Modern dishes with Corsican touches served in a panoramic dining room and terrace.

Romantique without rest
at la Marine – ✆ 04 95 26 10 85 – www.hotel-romantique-porto.com – info@hotel-romantique-porto.com – Fax 04 95 26 14 04 – Open April to mid-October
8 rm – €68/92 €68/92, €8
◆ Spacious rooms with roughcast walls, tiles and handcrafted furniture. All the balconies look onto a little marina and eucalyptus wood.

La Mer
at la Marine – ✆ 04 95 26 11 27 – laora5@wanadoo.fr – Fax 04 95 96 11 27 – Open mid March-beg. November
Rest – Menu €19 (lunch)/29 – Carte €34/58
◆ At the end of the marina, the terrace of this blue-shuttered house is ideal for viewing the mountain as it plunges into the sea. Fish specialities and wood-fire grills.

PORTO-POLLO – 2A Corse-du-Sud – 345 B9 – alt. 140 m – ✉ 20140

Ajaccio 52 – Sartène 31

Les Eucalyptus without rest
– ✆ *04 95 74 01 52 – www.hoteleucalyptus.com – portopollo@hotmail.com – Fax 04 95 74 06 56 – Open 5 April-14 October*
32 rm – €49/112 €49/112, €8
◆ A 1960s hotel overlooking the Gulf of Valinco. Most of the functional rooms have balconies (five have been opened only recently and are more comfortable) with gulf views.

Le Kallisté
– ✆ *04 95 74 02 38 – www.lekalliste.fr – lekalliste@orange.fr – Fax 04 95 74 06 26 – Open April-October*
19 rm – €58/110 €58/110, €8,50 – ½ P €55/70
Rest – *(dinner only)* Menu (€15), €19/24 – Carte €30/40
◆ The rooms here are modern with functional fittings and furniture. Some have a terrace giving a view of the sea. Seasonal family cooking served in a fresh, colourful dining room or out on the terrace.

PORTO-VECCHIO – 2A Corse-du-Sud – 345 E10 – pop. 10 326 – alt. 40 m – ✉ 20137

Ajaccio 141 – Bonifacio 28 – Corte 121 – Sartène 59
Figari-Sud-Corse: ✆ 04 95 71 10 10, Southwest: 23 km.
Office de tourisme, rue du Docteur Camille de Rocca Serra ✆ 04 95 70 09 58, Fax 04 95 70 03 72
The Citadel ★.
Bay of Porto-Vecchio★★ - Castellu d'Arraghju★ ≤★★ North: 7.5 km.

Casadelmar
7 km on Palombaggia road – ✆ 04 95 72 34 34 – www.casadelmar.fr – info@casadelmar.fr – Fax 04 95 72 34 35 – Open 4 April-31 October
14 rm – €360/900 €360/900 – 20 suites – €500/4000
Rest – *(dinner only)* Menu €73/180 – Carte €120/145
Spec. Baccala gambas rouge en sashimi, tapenade liquide d'olive taggiasche. Cannette Miéral à l'eucalyptus, macaron chaud de pois chiche. Cassata à la pâte d'amande. **Wines** Patrimonio.
◆ Set up in the hills, this luxurious, ultra-modern hotel blends into the countryside, and benefits from a view over the gulf. Designer rooms, infinity pool and superb spa. At the restaurant, a blend of Corsican and Italian gourmet cuisine served in an exceptional setting.

Belvédère
rm, rm, rm,

5 km on the Palombaggia beach road – 04 95 70 54 13 – www.hbcorsica.com – info@hbcorsica.com – Fax 04 95 70 42 63 – Closed 4 January-12 March
19 rm – €100/410 €100/410, €20 – ½ P €360/570
Rest – *(Closed Monday and Tuesday from 12 October to 12 April)* Menu (€60), €70/110 – Carte €90/120
Rest *Mari e Tarra* – restaurant-terrace *(open mid-April to early October)* Carte €50/80
Spec. Nougat froid d'huître de Diana et caviar (Oct. to April). Pomme de ris de veau glacée à la myrte. Tarte fine aux figues gratinée à l'amande douce, crème glacée à la vanille bourbon (Oct. to April). **Wines** Ajaccio, Figari.
◆ Fine group of buildings with a pool and panoramic terrace set in an oasis of greenery at the water's edge. Private beach and (partly refurbished) rooms in quiet bungalows. Warm restaurant overlooking the sea; refined cuisine. Simplified summer menu.

Alta Rocca without rest

rte de Palombaggia – 04 95 70 22 01 – www.hotelaltarocca.com – hotelaltarocca@wanadoo.fr – Fax 04 95 70 44 05
16 rm – €235/289 €235/289, €16 – 2 suites
◆ Handsome modern hotel built on the hillside. The rooms (all with balcony or terrace) and the infinity pool command a fantastic view of Porto Vecchio.

Le Goéland
rm,

à la Marine – 04 95 70 14 15 – www.hotelgoeland.com – contact@hotelgoeland.com – Fax 04 95 72 05 18 – Open end March-beg. November
28 rm – €95/195 €110/210 – ½ P €80/180
Rest – Menu (€18 bi), €28/45 – Carte €34/55
◆ This pleasant hotel has been completely refurbished and offers rooms in a maritime style with storm lamps, painted furniture, etc. Large restaurant with views of the golf course and garden. Corsican and Mediterranean dishes on the daily specials board.

Le Syracuse without rest

6 km on Palombaggia road – 04 95 70 53 63 – www.corse-hotelsyracuse.com – contact@corse-hotelsyracuse.com – Fax 04 95 70 28 97 – Open 1st April-1st October
18 rm – €110/271 €116/285, €9
◆ Several modern buildings separated from the sea by lush vegetation. Ground floor garden rooms and others with loggias. Beach and swimming-pool.

Golfe Hôtel
rm,

r. du 9 Septembre 1943 – 04 95 70 48 20 – www.golfehotel.com – info@golfehotel-corse.com – Fax 04 95 70 92 00
42 rm – €78/270 €95/330
Rest – *(closed Saturday and Sunday in low season) (dinner only) (resident only)* Carte €25/40
◆ Hotel set on the road leading to the harbour. Bedrooms with contemporary decor are arranged around a pool. Those in the main building are more basic. Bright, simple dining room offering a buffet.

Alcyon without rest

9 r. Mar. Leclerc, (opposite the post office) – 04 95 70 50 50 – www.hotel-alcyon.com – info@hotel-alcyon.com – Fax 04 95 70 25 84
40 rm – €55/180 €70/280, €10
◆ Modern building in the town centre. Plain, functional rooms, all of which have been renovated. Those at the front have sea views, the others are quieter.

San Giovanni
rest, rm,

rte Arca, 3 km south-west on D 659 – 04 95 70 22 25 – www.hotel-san-giovanni.com – info@hotel-san-giovanni.com – Fax 04 95 70 20 11 – Open 3 March-3 November
30 rm – €65/110 €70/127, €11 – ½ P €64/83
Rest – *(dinner only) (resident only)*
◆ Guesthouse in a fine park planted with trees and flowerbeds and adorned with a pond. Rooms on the ground floor lead onto a small private garden. Pool and jacuzzi. Breakfasts and simple family meals served under the pagoda.

L'Orée du Maquis
à la Trinité, 5 km north by Chemin de la Lézardière – 04 95 70 22 21 – daniellec201@orange.fr – Fax 04 95 70 22 21 – Open 15 June-15 September and closed Monday
Rest – *(dinner only) (number of covers limited, pre-book)* Menu € 70
◆ You reach this isolated villa by a steep road. Open air restaurant with tables shaded by a canopy and views of the coast. Fish, seafood and foie gras feature on the menu.

Le Troubadour
13 r. Gén. Leclerc (1st floor), (near the post office) – 04 95 70 08 62 – bertrandtilloux@orange.fr – Closed 1st-19 January, Sunday from September to June and lunch in July-August
Rest – Menu (€ 30), € 39/89 – Carte € 59/80
◆ The upstairs panelled dining room is home to a collection of copper pans and leads onto a pleasant flower-decked terrace. Up-to-date gourmet cuisine.

at Santa Giulia bay 8 km South by N 198 and secondary road – 20137 Porto-Vecchio

Moby Dick
– 04 95 70 70 00 – www.sud-corse.com – mobydick@sud-corse.com – Fax 04 95 70 70 01 – Open end April to mid-October
44 rm – € 133/191 € 148/206, € 15 **Rest** – Menu € 42 – Carte € 65/75
◆ Idyllic location on the lagoon, isolated from the Polynesian coloured gulf by a sandy beach. Spacious rooms on the sea and garden sides. Mediterranean cuisine and local produce to the fore in the restaurant.

Castell' Verde
– 04 95 70 71 00 – www.sud-corse.com – castellverde@sud-corse.com – Fax 04 95 70 71 01 – Open 26 April-15 October
30 rm (½ board only in season) – ½ P € 95/155
Rest *Le Costa Rica* – see restaurant listing
◆ Spacious bungalows within reach of the sea, set in a protected 5h site. Colourful linen and wooden furniture in the bedrooms. Pool and direct access to the beach.

Alivi without rest
Marina di Santa Giulia – 04 95 52 01 68 – www.marinadisantagiulia.fr – hotel-alvidisantagiulia@orange.fr – Fax 04 95 22 49 08
10 rm – € 118/343 € 133/358, € 16
◆ Relax at this contemporary hotel set between the sea and the Corsican scrub. Rooms decorated in a soothing modern style. Pleasant pool overlooking Santa Giulia bay.

U Santa Marina
Marina Di Santa Giulia – 04 95 70 45 00 – www.usantamarina.com – santamarina@orange.fr – Fax 04 95 70 45 00 – Open 16 March-31 October
Rest – *(dinner only)* Menu € 35, € 65/115 – Carte € 75/102
◆ In this house, enjoy the southern atmosphere and fine modern cuisine using local fish. It has several terraces with fine views of the sea. There is also a grill menu and beach salads.

Le Costa Rica – H. Castell' Verde
– 04 95 72 24 51 – castellverde@sud-corse.com – Fax 04 95 70 05 66 – Open 1st May-15 October
Rest – Menu € 38 (dinner) – Carte € 45/72
◆ The pleasant terrace has a unique view overlooking the bay. Simple decor in the restaurant; contemporary menu focused on the sea.

in Cala Rossa 10 km Northeast by N 198 and D 468 – 20137 Lecci

Grand Hôtel de Cala Rossa
– 04 95 71 61 51 – www.cala-rossa.com – calarossa@relaischateaux.fr – Fax 04 95 71 60 11
30 rm – € 385/655 € 430/1165 – 10 suites – ½ P € 265/635
Rest – *(dinner only)* Menu € 120/170 – Carte € 180/220
Spec. Crevettes rouges snackées au citron confit. Chapon de Méditerranée en filet à la plancha. Chocolat pour amateur de cacao moelleux tiède. **Wines** Vin de Corse-Figari, Patrimonio
◆ Beneath the pine trees, a luxurious garden facing the beach and a private landing stage. An exceptional hotel in a splendid setting. Wonderful spa. Elegant and subtly rustic dining room with luxurious shaded terrace, serving creative dishes.

in la presqu'île du Benedettu 10 km Northeast by N 198 and D 468 – ✉ ***20137 Porto-Vecchio***

U Benedettu rm, VISA

– ☎ 04 95 71 62 81 – www.rent-corsica.com – benedettu@wanadoo.fr – Fax 04 95 71 66 37 – Open end March-end October

20 rm – €80/195 €95/210 – 3 suites **Rest** – Carte €29/50

◆ Idyllically located cluster of villas on an unspoilt headland of white sandy beaches. Rooms and terraces overlooking the Gulf of Porto Vecchio. Concise regional menu in this waterside dining room-veranda.

PROPRIANO – 2A Corse-du-Sud – **345** C9 – **pop. 3 166** – **alt. 5 m** – ✉ 20110

Ajaccio 74 – Bonifacio 62 – Corte 139 – Sartène 13

Office de tourisme, Port de Plaisance ☎ 04 95 76 01 49, Fax 04 95 76 00 65

Grand Hôtel Miramar rm, rm, VISA AE

rte Corniche – ☎ 04 95 76 06 13 – www.grandhotelmiramar.com – miramar@wanadoo.fr – Fax 04 95 76 13 14 – Open May-September

23 rm – €210/505 €210/505, €27 – 3 suites **Rest** – Carte €60/80

◆ Villa with whitewashed walls set in lush gardens overlooking the Gulf of Valinco. Lounge decorated with antique shop finds; smart, spacious bedrooms (with balcony). Refined menu and local produce offered in a smart setting or in the shade of mulberry trees.

Loft Hôtel without rest VISA

3 r. Pandolfi – ☎ 04 95 76 17 48 – loft-hotel@wanadoo.fr – Fax 04 95 76 22 04 – Open 16 March-29 October

25 rm – €47/75 €47/75, €6

◆ Harbourside hotel with large rooms (sloping ceilings on the upper floor). Personalised welcome from the owner; breakfast served on the terrace in fine weather.

Le Lido rm, rm, VISA AE

42 av. Napoléon III – ☎ 04 95 76 06 37 – www.le-lido.com – le.lido@wanadoo.fr – Fax 04 95 76 31 18 – Open 15 April-30 October

11 rm – €150/500 €150/500, €15

Rest – *(open 15 April-30 September, and closed Tuesday lunch and Monday except August)* Menu (€30) – Carte €70/90

◆ Hotel on a peninsula at the water's edge: well-decorated rooms (exotic woods, antiques, Portuguese mosaics), some with beachside terraces. Seafood to the fore in the restaurant, with waterside terrace on a promontory.

Le Tout va Bien "Chez Parenti" VISA AE

13 av. Napoléon – ☎ 04 95 76 12 14 – www.chezparenti.fr – mathieu.andrei@wanadoo.fr – Fax 04 95 76 27 11 – Closed 1st-15 December, 2 January-28 February, Sunday dinner and Monday except dinner in season

Rest – Menu (€23), €32/55 – Carte €55/85

◆ This friendly restaurant, run by the Parenti family since 1935, has a pleasant terrace facing the port. Mixture of traditional and updated recipes.

QUENZA – 2A Corse-du-Sud – **345** D9 – **pop. 243** – **alt. 840 m** – ✉ 20122

Ajaccio 85 – Bonifacio 75 – Porto-Vecchio 47 – Sartène 38

Frescoes★ of Santa-Maria-Assunta chapel.

Sole e Monti without rest VISA AE

– ☎ 04 95 78 62 53 – www.solemonti.com – sole.e.monti@wanadoo.fr – Fax 04 95 78 63 88 – Open 15 April-30 September

19 rm – €80/135 €100/210

◆ Rustic rooms in this village dominated by the majestic Bavella peaks (two of them recently renovated exactly as they were). Choose the ones to the front overlooking the valley.

ST-FLORENT – 2B Haute-Corse – **345** E3 – **pop. 1 597** – ✉ **20217**

Bastia 22 – Calvi 70 – Corte 75 – L'Île-Rousse 45

Office de tourisme, centre Administratif ✆ 04 95 37 06 04, Fax 04 95 35 30 74

Santa Maria Assunta church ★★ - Old town★.

Les Agriates★.

Demeure Loredana without rest

Cisterninu Suttanu – ✆ 04 95 37 22 22 – www.demeureloredana.com – info@demeureloredana.com – Fax 04 95 37 41 91 – Open 31 March-4 November

18 rm – €190/440 €190/440, €23 – 4 suites

◆ An exceptional break awaits guests in this hotel. Lavish attention to detail and a personalised decor that mingles various styles. Sea view and pool.

La Roya rm, VISA AE

La Roya Beach, 1 km on the Calvi road and minor road – ✆ 04 95 37 00 40 – www.hotelroya.com – michel@hotelroya.com – Fax 04 95 37 09 85 – Open 1st April-11 November

33 rm – €140/390 €140/390, €15 – 4 suites

Rest – *(open 1st April-31 October)* Menu €45 – Carte €49/73

Spec. Millefeuille de rouget. Chapon de pêche locale. Chaud-froid aux deux chocolats.

◆ A modern building facing Roya Beach (direct access). The guestrooms, many with balconies overlooking the sea, are decorated with Mediterranean or Asian-style furniture. Modern dining room, superb terrace and a gourmet menu focusing on fine regional produce.

La Dimora without rest

4.5 km on the D 82 Oletta road – ✆ 495352251 – www.ladimora.fr – info@ladimora.fr – Fax 495382531 – Open 2 April-12 November

15 rm – €145/330 €145/330, €18 – 2 suites

◆ Prime regional materials, authenticity and discreet, contemporary luxury characterise this 18C villa where guests are welcomed as friends. Relaxing pool and garden.

Dolce Notte without rest

rte de Bastia – ✆ 04 95 37 06 65 – www.hotel-dolce-notte.com – info@hotel-dolce-notte.com – Fax 04 95 37 10 70 – Open April-October

20 rm – €70/166 €70/166, €8

◆ A long low building on the coast. Rooms with terrace or loggia facing the sea. Some have been refurbished and are more unusual (pebbles, vaults, indirect lighting).

Tettola without rest

1 km north on D 81 – ✆ 04 95 37 08 53 – www.tettola.com – info@tettola.com – Fax 04 95 37 09 19 – Open April-October

30 rm – €50/130 €70/170, €8

◆ A well-renovated hotel and handsome terrace on a pebble beach. Rooms facing the mountain; quieter and brighter rooms facing the sea. Warm welcome.

Les Galets without rest

rte du Front de Mer – ✆ 04 95 37 09 09 – www.hotel-lesgalets.com – info@hotel-lesgalets.com – Fax 04 95 37 48 88 – Open April-October

16 rm – €47/128 €49/128, €7

◆ Next to a residence but independent, this recent hotel has large, functional rooms with a sea view and balcony. A pleasant garden and friendly welcome.

La Florentine without rest

1 km north on the D 81 – ✆ 04 95 37 00 99 – www.hotellaflorentine.com – contact@hotellaflorentine.com – Fax 04 95 31 72 45 – Open 11 April-2 October

20 rm – €80/240 €80/240, €10

◆ A flower-decked garden, shaded terrace, delightful pool, the sparkling coloured decor, fresh and comfortable rooms... so many reasons to visit this brand new hotel on the sea.

Maxime without rest

St Florent – ✆ 04 95 37 05 30 – Closed end November to early February

19 rm – €52/78 €52/78, €9

◆ A white building with blue shutters standing on the banks of a small canal (mooring is possible); most of the rooms have a loggia or balcony.

La Maison Rorqual without rest
rte de la Roya – ✆ 04 95 37 05 37 – www.maison-rorqual.com – info@ maison-rorqual.com – Fax 495370537 – **5 rm** – †€ 250/450 ††€ 250/450, ☕ € 15
◆ This residence was designed to be a tribute to Corsican authenticity by the owner. Every room evokes a different universe, from the romantic to the unusual. Infinity pool.

La Rascasse
promenade des Quais – ✆ 04 95 37 06 09 – atrium-saintflorent@wanadoo.fr – Fax 04 95 37 06 99 – Open April-September and closed Monday except from June to August
Rest – Menu € 38 – Carte € 52/77
◆ This is just the place to enjoy some modern cuisine prepared with fresh produce and quality fish. There are two attractive terraces, one of which overlooks the port.

STE-LUCIE-DE-PORTO-VECCHIO – 2A Corse-du-Sud – 345 F9 – ✉ **20144** Corse
Paris 942 – Ajaccio 157 – Porto-Vecchio 16 – Sartène 76 – Ghisonaccia 42
Syndicat d'initiative, Mairie annexe ✆ 04 95 71 48 99, Fax 04 95 71 48 99

Le Pinarello without rest
Pinarello – ✆ 04 95 71 44 39 – www.lepinarello.com – contact@lepinarello.com – Fax 04 95 70 66 87 – Open mid April-mid October
31 rm – †€ 229/400 ††€ 246/590, ☕ € 22 – 14 suites
◆ This discreetly luxurious hotel stands on a matchless site. Contemporary rooms and suites, fantastic view of the bay, spa. Lunchtime snacks at the plush terrace-bar.

La Fleur de Sel
Pinarello – ✆ 04 95 71 06 49 – crechous@wanadoo.fr – Open 15 March-1 October
Rest – *(dinner only) (number of covers limited, pre-book)* Menu € 32, € 55/80 – Carte € 40/60
◆ Overlooking the sea, this restaurant proposes a menu with a regional slant. Spruce all-white interior and shaded terrace (olive and palm trees, vine and jasmine).

STE-LUCIE-DE-TALLANO – 2A Corse-du-Sud – 345 D9 – **pop. 325 – alt. 450 m** – ✉ **20112**
Ajaccio 92 – Bonifacio 68 – Porto-Vecchio 48 – Sartène 19

Santa Lucia
– ✆ 04 95 78 81 28 – santalucia@alicepro.fr – Fax 04 95 78 81 28 – Closed January and Sunday off season
Rest – Menu € 18/24 – Carte € 25/31
◆ Soothed by the murmer of the fountain, come linger on the shady terrace under the lime and acacia trees, opposite the main square in this picturesque village. Corsican home cooking.

STE-MARIE-SICCHÉ – 2A Corse-du-Sud – 345 C8 – **pop. 361 – alt. 420 m** – ✉ **20190**
Ajaccio 36 – Sartène 51

Santa Maria
– ✆ 04 95 25 72 65 – www.santa-maria-hotel.com – info@ santa-maria-hotel.com – Fax 04 95 25 71 34
22 rm ☕ – †€ 58/67 ††€ 73/90 **Rest** – *(closed 15 Dec. - 15 Feb.)* Menu € 18/25
◆ A family guesthouse atmosphere pervades this 1970s building. Simple but well-kept rooms; some have balconies. A rustic dining area where home-cured cold meats and Corsican dishes are served. Regularly changing menu.

SANT'ANTONINO – 2B Haute-Corse – 345 C4 – **pop. 77 – alt. 500 m** – ✉ **20220**
Paris 959 – Ajaccio 155 – Bastia 99 – Corte 74 – Calvi 21

I Scalini
top of the village – ✆ 04 95 47 12 92 – Open end April to October
Rest – *(number of covers limited, pre-book)* Carte € 39/55
◆ A narrow stone stairway leads to this restaurant perched in the upper part of the village. The interior is highly original (especially the washrooms!) and there are four small, superbly panoramic terraces; one can enjoy delicious specialities in a zen atmosphere.

SARTÈNE – **2A Corse-du-Sud** – **345** C10 – **pop. 3 096** – **alt. 310 m** – ✉ **20100**

Ajaccio 84 – Bonifacio 50 – Corte 149

Office de tourisme, 6, rue Borgo ☎ 04 95 77 15 40, Fax 04 95 77 15 40

Old town ★★ - Musée de Préhistoire corse★.

La Villa Piana without rest
Propriano road – ☎ 04 95 77 07 04 – www.lavillapiana.com – info@lavillapiana.com – Fax 04 95 73 45 65 – Open 6 April-10 October
32 rm – €69/114 €69/118, €9
◆ The hotel grounds command a fine panoramic view of "the most typical of Corsican towns", as Mérimée put it. Overflow swimming pool overlooking the Rizzanèse valley. Pleasant rooms.

SOLENZARA – **2A Corse-du-Sud** – **345** F8 – **pop. 1 169** – **alt. 310 m** – ✉ **20145**

Ajaccio 118 – Bonifacio 68 – Sartène 77

Office de tourisme, Anciennes ecoles ☎ 04 95 57 43 75, Fax 04 95 57 43 59

La Solenzara without rest
quartier du Palais – ☎ 04 95 57 42 18 – www.lasolenzara.com – info@lasolenzara.com – Fax 04 95 57 46 84 – Open mid-March-end October
28 rm – €75/110 €75/110
◆ Impressive Genoese-style 18C abode, surrounded by a garden. Airy, spacious and simple rooms; those to the rear enjoy sea views. Well-being centre, lovely infinity pool.

Francine et Sébastien without rest
Scaffa Rossa, 1.5 km north – ☎ 04 95 57 44 41 – sebastien.roccaserradeperetti@orange.fr – Fax 04 95 57 46 73
4 rm – €100 €100
◆ Pretty house beside the sea, with a meticulously maintained garden with access to three small coves. The interior has family knick-knacks and furniture, rooms with terraces. Breakfasts on the veranda.

A Mandria
1 km north – ☎ 04 95 57 41 95 – marcantoine.roccaserra@orange.fr – Fax 04 95 57 45 96 – Closed January and February, Sunday dinner and Monday in low season
Rest – Menu (€ 16), € 25/30 – Carte € 25/46
◆ Pleasantly rustic restaurant (exposed stone and beams, old tools which remind us that this was once a sheepfold) serving Corsican dishes. Pergola near a small vegetable plot.

ZONZA – **2A Corse-du-Sud** – **345** E9 – **pop. 1 802** – **alt. 780 m** – ✉ **20124**

Ajaccio 93 – Bonifacio 67 – Porto-Vecchio 40 – Sartène 38

Col and aiguilles de Bavella (Bavella pass and peaks) ★★★ Northeast: 9 km.

Le Tourisme without rest
rte de Quenza – ☎ 04 95 78 67 72 – www.hoteldutourisme.fr – letourisme@wanadoo.fr – Fax 04 95 78 73 23 – Open April-October
16 rm – €80/140 €95/155
◆ This old coaching inn dating from 1875 retains its original fountain. It has bright rooms with balconies. There is also a garden and attractive heated pool with views of the Zonza forest.

CORTE – **2B Haute-Corse** – **345** D6 – **see Corse**

Good food without spending a fortune?
Look out for the Bib Gourmand

CORVOL-D'EMBERNARD – 58 Nièvre – 319 D8 – pop. 109 – alt. 260 m – ✉ 58210 7 **B2**

Paris 236 – Cosne-sur-Loire 48 – Dijon 168 – Nevers 45

Le Colombier de Corvol

– *03 86 29 79 60 – www.lecolombierdecorvol.com – robert.collet1@wanadoo.fr – Fax 03 86 29 79 33*

5 rm – €105 €105 **Table d'hôte** – Menu €45 bi/65 bi

◆ This farmhouse dating from 1812 is home to charming bed & breakfast accommodation as well as an art gallery displaying works by contemporary artists from April to September. Lovely swimming pool in the courtyard. Seasonal, traditional recipes.

COSNE-COURS-SUR-LOIRE – 58 Nièvre – 319 A7 – pop. 11 300 – alt. 150 m – ✉ 58200 Burgundy-Jura 7 **A2**

Paris 186 – Auxerre 83 – Bourges 61 – Montargis 76 – Nevers 54

Office de tourisme, place de l'Hôtel de Ville 03 86 28 11 85, Fax 03 86 28 11 85

du Sancerrois SancerreNorth: 10 km by D 955, 02 48 54 11 22

Museum ★ fireplace.

Le Vieux Relais VISA AE

11 r. St-Agnan – 03 86 28 20 21 – le-vieux-relais.fr – contacts@le-vieux-relais.fr – Fax 03 86 26 71 12 – Closed 23 December-13 January, Friday dinner and Sunday dinner 15 September-30 April and Saturday lunch

10 rm – €83 €97, €11 **Rest** – Menu €22/40 – Carte €41/67

◆ This centuries-old post house is between the Loire and the Nohain. The pleasant rooms lead off from a flower-decked courtyard and are named after birds. Old beams and bright colours adorn the refurbished dining room. Traditional repertory.

Les Forges with rm AC rest, rest, VISA AE

21 r. St-Agnan – 03 86 28 23 50 – www.lesforges58.com – denis.cathye@wanadoo.fr – Fax 03 86 28 91 60 – Closed 1 - 6 Jul, 22 - 29 Dec

7 rm – €55/61 €61/70, €10

Rest – *(closed Sunday dinner and Monday)* Menu (€19), €26/39 – Carte €41/51

◆ This welcoming establishment has a warm comfortable dining room serving a concise, regional menu. Attractively decorated and well-kept rooms.

COSQUEVILLE – 50 Manche – 303 D1 – pop. 570 – alt. 22 m – ✉ 50330 32 **A1**

Paris 358 – Caen 124 – Carentan 51 – Cherbourg 21 – St-Lô 79 – Valognes 27

Au Bouquet de Cosqueville with rm P VISA

38 hameau Remond – 02 33 54 32 81 – www.bouquetdecosqueville.com – aubouquet.decosqueville@orange.fr – Fax 02 33 54 63 38 – Closed Monday

7 rm – €30/52 €30/52, €7 – ½ P €58

Rest – Menu €20/58 – Carte €37/54

◆ An old village house covered with Virginia creeper serving seafood and local dishes in an intimate, discreetly rustic setting.

LE COTEAU – 42 Loire – 327 D3 – see Roanne

LA CÔTE-ST-ANDRÉ – 38 Isère – 333 E5 – pop. 4 496 – alt. 370 m – ✉ 38260 Lyon - Rhone Valley 44 **B2**

Paris 525 – Grenoble 50 – Lyon 67 – La Tour-du-Pin 33 – Valence 75 – Vienne 36 – Voiron 32

Office de tourisme, place Hector Berlioz 04 74 20 61 43, Fax 04 74 20 56 25

France with rm AC VISA

16 pl. de l'Église – 04 74 20 25 99 – www.hoteldefrance.info – Fax 04 74 20 35 30

14 rm – €58 €62/75, €11

Rest – *(closed Sunday dinner and Monday except holidays)* Menu (€28), €30 (weekdays)/82 – Carte €44/96

◆ In the heart of Berlioz's hometown, this ancient residence offers cuisine steeped in tradition. Small, simple, refurbished rooms.

COTI-CHIAVARI – 2A Corse-du-Sud – 345 B9 – see Corse

COTINIÈRE – 17 Charente-Maritime – 324 C4 – see île d'Oléron

LA COUARDE-SUR-MER – 17 Charente-Maritime – 324 B2 – see Île de Ré

COUDEKERQUE-BRANCHE – 59 Nord – 302 C1 – see Dunkerque

COUDRAY – 53 Mayenne – 310 F8 – see Château-Gontier

LE COUDRAY-MONTCEAUX – 91 Essonne – 312 D4 – 106 44 – see Paris, Area (Corbeil-Essonnes)

COUERON – 44 Loire-Atlantique – 316 F4 – see Nantes

COUILLY-PONT-AUX-DAMES – 77 Seine-et-Marne – 312 G2 19 **C2**
– pop. 2 007 – alt. 50 m – ✉ 77860 Northern France and the Paris Region

Paris 45 – Coulommiers 20 – Lagny-sur-Marne 12 – Meaux 9 – Melun 45

Auberge de la Brie (Alain Pavard)
14 av. Alphonse Boulingre , (D 436) – ✆ 01 64 63 51 80
– www.aubergedelabrie.com – Fax 01 60 04 69 82
– Closed 12-20 April, 1st-25 August, 20 December-5 January, Sunday and Monday
Rest – *(number of covers limited, pre-book)* Menu (€ 38), € 45/65 – Carte € 69/95
Spec. Foie gras poêlé aux noisettes, tatin de rhubarbe. Saint-Jacques au citron vert, zestes confits et pousses d'épinard (Oct. to April). Profiteroles "minute" à la vanille bourbon, sauce chocolat légèrement fumante.
◆ Among the attractions of this charming Brie house are a refined contemporary décor, delicious modern cuisine with personal touches and a friendly welcome.

COUIZA – 11 Aude – 344 E5 – pop. 1 198 – alt. 228 m – ✉ 11190 22 **B3**
Languedoc-Roussillon-Tarn Gorges

Paris 785 – Carcassonne 41 – Foix 75 – Perpignan 88 – Toulouse 110

Château des Ducs de Joyeuse rest,
allée du Château – ✆ 04 68 74 23 50
– www.chateau-des-ducs.com – reception@chateau-des-ducs.com
– Fax 04 68 74 23 36 – Open 6 March-10 November
35 rm – € 110/140 € 110/230
Rest – *(closed Sunday and Monday except from June to September and lunch from October to May)* Menu (€ 26 bi), € 37 (dinner), € 44/60 – Carte € 53/71
◆ The towers of this splendid 16C fortified château is home to medieval-inspired rooms (stonework, beams, canopied beds); the others are more rustic in style. Elegant vaulted dining room; the menu varies with the seasons and availability of local produce.

COULANDON – 03 Allier – 326 G3 – see Moulins

COULLONS – 45 Loiret – 318 L6 – pop. 2 274 – alt. 166 m – ✉ 45720 12 **C2**

Paris 165 – Aubigny-sur-Nère 18 – Gien 16 – Orléans 60 – Sully-sur-Loire 22

La Canardière
1 r. de la Mairie – ✆ 02 38 29 23 47 – www.restaurantlacanardiere.fr
– la.canardiere@wanadoo.fr – Fax 02 38 29 27 33 – Closed 10 August-1st September, 21 December-5 January, Sunday dinner, Wednesday dinner, Monday and Tuesday
Rest – Menu (€ 20), € 26 (weekday lunch), € 28/69 – Carte € 54/85
Rest *Le Bistro* – Menu € 11 bi (weekday lunch)/18 – Carte € 21/50
◆ Elegant and rustic decor with exposed beams, a fine copper fireplace, hunting trophies and stuffed animals. Traditional cuisine (game in season). The Bistro has a traditional and daily blackboard menu, a welcoming ambience and a simple but pleasant setting.

COULOMBIERS – 86 Vienne – 322 H6 – pop. 1 049 – alt. 141 m – ✉ 86600 39 **C2**

Paris 352 – Couhé 25 – Lusignan 8 – Parthenay 44 – Poitiers 19 – Vivonne 10

Auberge le Centre Poitou rm, VISA

39 r. Nationale – ✆ 05 49 60 90 15 – www.centre-poitou.com – hotelcentre-poitou@wanadoo.fr – Fax 05 49 60 53 70 – Closed 20 October-3 November, 23 February-2 March, Sunday dinner and Monday 15 September-June

13 rm – †€ 48/74 ††€ 54/80, ☕ € 9 – ½ P € 60/85

Rest – Menu (€ 15 bi), € 27/50 – Carte € 65/88

◆ Hotel on the Compostelle road, this regional house has pleasantly furnished rooms in the style of Louis-Philippe. Piano-lounge, luxuriant garden. Welcoming inn-style restaurant, terrace arbour and well-planned up-to-date menu.

COULOMMIERS – 77 Seine-et-Marne – 312 H3 – pop. 13 700 – alt. 85 m – ✉ 77120 Northern France and the Paris Region 19 **D2**

Paris 62 – Châlons-en-Champagne 111 – Meaux 26 – Melun 46 – Provins 39

Office de tourisme, 7, rue du Général-de-Gaulle ✆ 01 64 03 88 09, Fax 01 64 03 88 09

XX **Les Échevins** AC VISA AE

quai de l'Hôtel-de-Ville – ✆ 01 64 20 75 85 – www.lesechevins.com – les.echevins@wanadoo.fr – Fax 01 64 20 03 32 – Closed August, January, Sunday and Monday

Rest – Menu (€ 14), € 18 (weekdays) – Carte € 25/55

◆ House on the banks of the canal in the centre of town. Inside, pastel decor and covered summer terrace. Set menus inspired by the seasons.

in Pommeuse West: 6.5 km – pop. 2 693 – alt. 67 m – ✉ 77515

Le Moulin de Pommeuse without rest VISA

32 av. Gén. Herne – ✆ 01 64 75 29 45 – www.le-moulin-de-pommeuse.com – info@le-moulin-de-pommeuse.com – Fax 01 64 75 29 45

5 rm ☕ – †€ 56 ††€ 80

◆ This 14C watermill has stylish rooms with evocative names: Semailles (sowing), Moisson (harvesting) and Batteuse (thresher). The former machine room is now a lounge.

COULON – 79 Deux-Sèvres – 322 C7 – pop. 2 180 – alt. 6 m – ✉ 79510 Atlantic Coast 38 **B2**

Paris 418 – Fontenay-le-Comte 25 – Niort 11 – La Rochelle 63 – St-Jean-d'Angély 58

Office de tourisme, 31, rue Gabriel Auchier ✆ 05 49 35 99 29, Fax 05 49 35 84 31

Marais poitevin★★.

Au Marais without rest VISA AE

quai L. Tardy – ✆ 05 49 35 90 43 – www.hotel-aumarais.com – information@hotel-aumarais.com – Fax 05 49 35 81 98 – Closed 15 December-1st February

18 rm – †€ 70 ††€ 80, ☕ € 12

◆ Two renovated, former ferrymen's homes opposite the embarkation point to the marshes. Pleasant rooms mixing contemporary and classical details with some overlooking the Sèvre.

XX **Le Central** with rm rm, AC P VISA AE

4 r. d'Autrement – ✆ 05 49 35 90 20 – www.hotel-lecentral-coulon.com – le-central-coulon@wanadoo.fr – Fax 05 49 35 81 07 – Closed 9 February-4 March

13 rm ☕ – †€ 51/55 ††€ 58/72 – ½ P € 58/65

Rest – *(closed 9 February-4 March, 5-21 October, Sunday dinner and Monday)* Menu € 20 (weekdays), € 27/41 – Carte € 36/50

◆ Inn with a trendy dining room serving fine traditional cuisine. Cosy and warm guest-rooms, refurbished in a chic, country style with personal touches.

COUPELLE-VIEILLE – 62 Pas-de-Calais – 301 F4 – pop. 510 – alt. 147 m – ✉ 62310 30 A2

Paris 232 – Abbeville 58 – Arras 64 – Boulogne-sur-Mer 48 – Calais 68 – Lille 90

Le Fournil
r. St- Omer – ✆ 03 21 04 47 13 – www.fournil.new.fr – glefournil@wanadoo.fr – Fax 03 21 47 16 06 – Closed Tuesday dinner, Sunday dinner, dinners holidays and Monday
Rest – Menu (€ 15), € 18 (weekdays)/44 – Carte € 35/58
◆ A restaurant near the Moulin de la Tour amusement park. Warm dining room with carefully-chosen decor, serving cuisine with a contemporary touch. Good wine selection.

COURBAN – 21 Côte-d'Or – 320 I2 – pop. 160 – alt. 262 m – ✉ 21520 8 C1

Paris 252 – Dijon 101 – Chaumont 43 – Langres 58 – Châtillon-sur-Seine 17

Château de Courban
7 r. du Lavoir – ✆ 03 80 93 78 69 – www.chateaudecourban.com – contact@chateaudecourban.com – Fax 03 80 93 79 23
16 rm – †€ 95 ††€ 95, ☕ € 14 – ½ P € 95
Rest – *(dinner only)* Menu € 29/49 – Carte € 39/53
◆ Charm, authenticity and modernity characterise this plush bourgeois home surrounded by lovely gardens. Snug guestrooms, comfortable lounges and a pool. 'Orangerie' style dining room, terrace overlooking the countryside and traditional culinary repertory. Evenings only.

COURBEVOIE – 92 Hauts-de-Seine – 311 J2 – 101 15 – see Paris, Area

COURCELLES-DE-TOURAINE – 37 Indre-et-Loire – 317 K4 – pop. 393 – alt. 85 m – ✉ 37330 11 A2

Paris 267 – Angers 74 – Chinon 46 – Saumur 46 – Tours 35

du Château des Sept-ToursE : 7 km, ✆ 02 47 24 69 75

at the Golf 7 km east towards Ambillou then Château La Vallière – ✉ 37330 Courcelles-de-Touraine :

Château des Sept Tours rm,
Le vivier des Landes - D34 – ✆ 02 47 24 69 75 – www.7tours.com – info@7tours.com – Fax 02 47 24 23 74 – Closed mid-December to mid-February
46 rm – †€ 140/325 ††€ 140/325, ☕ € 18
Rest *Notaboo* – *(closed Sunday dinner and Monday from 1er November to 31 January and lunch from Monday to Thursday)* Menu € 65/130 bi – Carte € 70/86
Rest *Club House* – ✆ *02 47 24 59 67* – Menu (€ 15) – Carte approx. € 24
◆ A 15C chateau surrounded by an 18-hole golf course. Large, simply decorated bedrooms; the Orangerie has a functional decor. The chef concocts inventive cuisine served in a tasteful dining room with a veranda terrace looking out over gardens. Modern menu in the Club House, set in an old chapel.

COURCELLES-SUR-VESLE – 02 Aisne – 306 D6 – pop. 324 – alt. 75 m – ✉ 02220 37 C2

Paris 122 – Fère-en-Tardenois 20 – Laon 35 – Reims 39 – Soissons 21

Château de Courcelles rm, rest,
– ✆ 03 23 74 13 53 – www.chateau-de-courcelles.fr – reservation@chateau-de-courcelles.fr – Fax 03 23 74 06 41
15 rm – †€ 185/360 ††€ 185/360, ☕ € 21 – 3 suites – ½ P € 178/315
Rest – Menu € 50/90 – Carte € 95/125
Spec. Langoustines de petite pêche saisies à l'huile d'olive (summer). Lièvre à la royale (Oct. to Dec.). Chocophile. **Wines** Champagne.
◆ A 17C chateau in a 20-hectare park with a small lake. Crébillon, Rousseau and Cocteau all stayed here, thus confirming the status of this prestigious hotel. Individually decorated guestrooms. Elegant dining room and fine veranda, furnished in the Napoleon III style. Up-to-date cuisine.

COURCHEVEL – 73 Savoie – 333 M5 – Winter sports : 1 100/2 750 m 45 D2

11 54 – ✉ 73120 **French Alps**

▶ Paris 660 – Albertville 52 – Chambéry 99 – Moûtiers 25

Altiport ✆ 04 79 08 31 23, South : 4 km

ℹ Office de tourisme, le Cœur de Courchevel ✆ 04 79 08 00 29, Fax 04 79 08 15 63

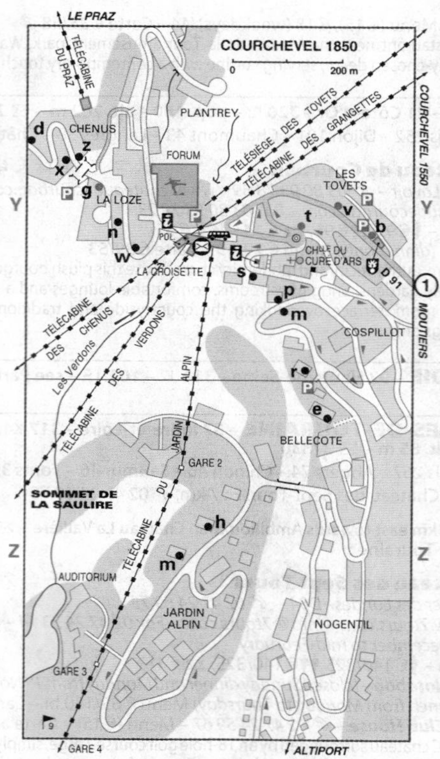

in Courchevel 1850 – alt. 1 850 m – ✉ 73120

[viewpoint] ✻★ - Belvédère la Saulire (viewpoint)★★★ (cable car).

Les Airelles [quiet hotel]

[view] [terrace] [terrace] [terrace] [park] [spa] [gym] [lift] ♿ rm, [AC] rest, [no smoking] [no dogs] [wifi] [garage]

at the Jardin Alpin – ✆ 04 79 00 38 38 – www.airelles.fr VISA MC AE D

– info@airelles.fr – Fax 04 79 00 38 39 – Open 12 December-12 April Z **h**

37 rm (½ board only) – 15 suites – ½ P € 450/1175

Rest *Pierre Gagnaire pour les Airelles* – *(dinner only)* Menu € 280/400 – Carte € 330/565 [wine]

Rest *La Table du Jardin* – Carte € 120/200

Rest *Le Coin Savoyard* – *(dinner only)* Menu € 100/130 – Carte € 110/165

◆ A sumptuous mountain hotel in the heart of the Jardin Alpin. A luxury style Tyrolean setting with huge spa and boutiques. Enjoy the inventive cuisine by Pierre Gagnaire and the elegant decor honouring Elisabeth of Bavaria. Delightful terrace at the Table du Jardin. Carnotzet and cheese menu at the Coin Savoyard.

Cheval Blanc
at the Jardin Alpin – 04 79 00 50 50 – www.chevalblanc.com – info@chevalblanc.com – Fax 04 79 00 50 51 – Open 6 December-13 April Z **m**
32 rm (½ board only) – 2 suites – ½ P € 1150/2360
Rest ***Le 1947*** – Menu € 115 (dinner) – Carte € 160/220
◆ This is a 'haute couture' version of a mountain chalet. Sumptuous designer rooms, a 650 m² apartment, photos by Karl Lagerfeld, a Givenchy spa and luxury boutiques. Brilliant cuisine and selection of Cheval Blanc (a famous Bordeaux).

Le Kilimandjaro
Altiport road – 04 79 01 46 46 – www.hotelkilimandjaro.com – welcome@hotelkilimandjaro.com – Fax 04 79 01 46 40 – Open mid-July to mid-August (except hotel) and mid-December to mid-April
32 rm (½ board only) – 3 suites – ½ P € 450/800
Rest ***La Table du Kilimandjaro*** – Carte € 100/225
Spec. Ravioles au bleu de Bonneval à l'émulsion de pomme verte et noix de Grenoble. Saint-Pierre des côtes bretonnes à l'huile d'olive aglandau et citron. Baba au génépi.
◆ Very comfortable chalets forming a small mountain village, built with stone, wood and traditional roof tiles. High-tech facilities. Enjoy playful and inventive cuisine using fine produce at the Table du Kilimandjaro.

Amanresorts Le Mélézin
r. Bellecôte – 04 79 08 01 33 – www.amanresorts.com – lemelezin@amanresorts.com – Fax 04 79 08 08 96 – Open 19 December-13 April Y **r**
23 rm – †€ 730/1700 ††€ 730/1700, ☕ € 32 – 8 suites **Rest** – Carte € 70/100
◆ Large chalet ideally situated at the bottom of the slopes. Very minimalist ambience in the rooms, the most spacious of which have a 'day bed' area. Thai specialities in addition to a traditional menu.

Annapurna
Altiport road – 04 79 08 04 60 – www.annapurna-courchevel.com – info@annapurna-courchevel.com – Fax 04 79 08 15 31 – Open mid-December to mid-April
66 rm ☕ – †€ 300/800 ††€ 535/1260 – 8 suites
Rest – Menu € 68 (lunch), € 76/175 – Carte € 40/155
◆ This is the highest hotel of Courchevel. A low-key mineral decor and simple, light wood architecture. Most of the rooms face south. Large dining room and terrace facing the ski slopes and the Saulire. Traditional fare.

Le Lana
Bellecote road – 04 79 08 01 10 – www.lelana.com – info@lelana.com – Fax 04 79 08 36 70 – Open 15 December-15 April Y **p**
55 rm (½ board only) – 30 suites – ½ P € 195/685
Rest ***La Table du Lana*** – Menu € 45/90 – Carte € 45/150
◆ One of the first hotels in the resort. The rooms are undergoing renovation but retain their tasteful mountain style. Gym and Clarins beauty salon. On the menu: traditional and regional cuisine and daily specials.

Saint Roch
– 04 79 08 02 66 – www.lesaintroch.com – reservation@lesaintroch.com – Fax 04 79 08 37 94 – Open 13 December-13 April Y **m**
5 rm (½ board only) – 10 suites – ½ P € 330/1010
Rest – *(dinner only)* Menu € 70 – Carte € 90/160
◆ The Saint Roch is the latest in luxury hotels. It boasts resolutely contemporary decor using quality materials and fine furniture. Every guestroom has its own steam room. The restaurant, clothed entirely in black, offers a modern menu and grills.

Des Neiges
r. Bellecôte – 04 79 08 03 77 – www.hoteldesneiges.com – welcome@hoteldesneiges.com – Fax 04 79 08 18 70 – Open 13 December-18 April
42 rm (½ board only) – 6 suites – ½ P € 200/400 Z **e**
Rest – Menu € 70 (dinner) – Carte € 40/75
◆ The spacious and comfortable rooms sport an elegant and refined decor or are modern and trendy in feel (with neutral colour scheme). Gym and piano bar. From the dining room adorned with paintings are views over the pistes and a forest.

La Sivolière rm, VISA AE
r. Chenus – 04 79 08 08 33 – www.hotel-la-sivoliere.com – lasivoliere@ sivoliere.fr – Fax 04 79 08 15 73 – Open 5 December-27 April Y **d**
27 rm – †€ 306/360 ††€ 510/600, □ € 30 – 12 suites
Rest – Menu € 75 – Carte € 94/141
◆ A snug, warm ambience in the delightfully intimate alpine guestrooms. Children's playroom and a superb swimming pool overlooking the forest to boot. Traditional cuisine served in an all-wood decor with a welcoming log fire.

Le Chabichou (Michel Rochedy) rm,
r. Chenus – 04 79 08 00 55 VISA AE
– www.chabichou-courchevel.com – info@lechabichou.com – Fax 04 79 08 33 58 – Open beg. July to beg. September and beg. December to end April Y **z**
33 rm □ – †€ 360/970 ††€ 360/970 – 8 suites
Rest – Menu (€ 50), € 90/200 – Carte € 165/220
Spec. Foie gras de canard et lavaret fumé, gelée au sarrasin, sorbet herbes sauvages. Langoustines à l'huile de Zan, tarte à l'oignon caramélisé. Tout chocolat "Michel Rochedy". **Wines** Chignin-Bergeron, Mondeuse
◆ Two attractive twin chalets all in white. Refined interior and characterful rooms in alpine style. Dining room and terrace overlooking the slopes. Inventive cuisine using fine produce. Smoking lounge (cigars on sale).

Les Grandes Alpes VISA AE
r. de l'Église – 04 79 00 00 00 – www.lesgrandesalpes.com – welcome@ lesgrandesalpes.com – Fax 04 79 08 12 52 – Open from beg. December to end April
43 rm (½ board only) – 5 suites – ½ P € 205/1950 Y **s**
Rest – Menu € 44 (lunch), € 65/85 – Carte € 42/84
◆ Chalet situated opposite the tourist office, above a luxurious shopping mall. Smart spacious rooms, the nicer ones are on the south side (quiet and view of the slopes). At midday, fast food menus. In the evening, traditional menu and Savoyard dishes.

De la Loze without rest VISA AE
r. Park City – 04 79 08 28 25 – www.la-loze.com – info@la-loze.com – Fax 04 79 08 39 29 – Open 12 December-17 April Y **w**
28 rm □ – †€ 250/520 ††€ 250/520 – 1 suite
◆ Austrian inspired hotel overlooking the slopes. Find a warm wooden decor, cosy rooms with mural decoration and staff dressed in Tyrolean dress. Sauna and steam room.

La Pomme de Pin rm, VISA AE
r. Chenus – 04 79 08 36 88 – www.pommedepin.com – info@ pommedepin.com – Fax 04 79 08 38 72 – Open 20 December-14 April Y **x**
49 rm □ – †€ 355/479 ††€ 365/490 – 1 suite – ½ P € 223/360
Rest ***Le Bateau Ivre*** – see restaurant listing
Rest – Menu (€ 28), € 46 (dinner) – Carte € 46/55
◆ The contemporary design of the building in wood and glass is far removed from the chalet style. Large rooms, both modern and alpine in style.

Courcheneige VISA AE
r. de Nogentil – 04 79 08 02 59 – www.courcheneige.com – info@ courcheneige.com – Fax 04 79 08 11 79 – Open 20 December-18 April
85 rm (½ board only) – ½ P € 132/300 **Rest** – Carte € 25/50
◆ A youthful, energetic and pleasant ambience depicts this chalet in the midst of the ski slopes. The regionally decorated rooms are small but well kept (duvets). The restaurant's terrace commands a matchless view of the mountains. Traditional menu.

Le Bateau Ivre (Jean-Pierre Jacob) – Hôtel La Pomme de Pin –
r. Chenus – 04 79 00 11 71 VISA AE
– www.pommedepin.com – pommedepin.courchevel@wanadoo.fr – Fax 04 79 08 38 72 – Open mid December-mid April and closed lunch Monday-Friday Y **x**
Rest – Menu € 95/190 – Carte € 102/202
Spec. Flan moelleux d'oursins, nuage de coquillages. Ris de veau braisé, truffes et asperges. Agrumes montés en mille feuille, crème glacée au caramel. **Wines** Roussette de Savoie, Chignin-Bergeron.
◆ With Courchevel and the Vanoise as the backdrop (the view is spectacular), enjoy creative cuisine that makes the most of Savoyard produce. Good selection of regional wines.

XX **Il Vino d'Enrico Bernardo** VISA MC AE

La Porte de Courchevel – ✆ 04 79 08 29 62 – www.ilvinobyenricobernardo.com – info@ilvinobyenricobernardo.com – Fax 04 79 08 31 91 – Open 12 December-30 April v

Rest – *(dinner only)* Menu € 100 bi/1000 bi – Carte € 95/145

◆ Enrico Bernardo has brought his Parisian concept to Courchevel. Here too, dishes are cooked to match the wine and not the other way round, to stunning effect. Chic, modern decor.

XX **Le Genépi** VISA MC AE

r. Park City – ✆ 04 79 08 08 63 – www.legenepi-courchevel.com – le-genepi@wanadoo.fr – Fax 04 79 06 51 43 – Open September to April and closed Saturday and Sunday from September to November g

Rest – Menu (€ 27), € 49/95 – Carte € 40/80

◆ Behind the chalet-style frontage is a warm, rustic, alpine-style dining room. Regional cuisine served at lunchtime; a more extensive menu is available in the evening.

XX **La Saulire** VISA MC AE

pl. Rocher – ✆ 04 79 08 07 52 – www.lasaulire.fr – info@lasaulire.com – Fax 04 79 08 02 63 – Open 1st December-30 April t

Rest – Menu (€ 30), € 40 (lunch) – Carte € 65/100

◆ This restaurant does not lack charm with its all-wood decor and old mountain tools. Lunchtime daily specials and evening menu enhanced with Perigord truffle recipes.

X **La Fromagerie** VISA MC

La Porte de Courchevel – ✆ 04 79 08 27 47 – Fax 04 79 08 20 91 – Open beg. December-end April b

Rest – *(dinner only)* Menu € 27/38 – Carte € 44/83

◆ Cheese specialities are to the fore but various traditional dishes are also prepared by the chef. Objects from the flea market decorate the room.

in Courchevel 1650 by ①: 4 km – ✉ 73120

Manali VISA MC AE

r. Rosière – ✆ 04 79 08 07 07 – www.hotelmanali.com – info@hotelmanali.com – Fax 04 79 08 07 08 – Open July-August and December-April

29 rm (½ board only) – 7 suites – ½ P € 390/1400

Rest – Menu € 70 (dinner) – Carte € 35/80

◆ Take an invitation to travel in the superb guestrooms of this luxury hotel. The mountain wood combines with decorative elements inspired by India, Switzerland and Canada. Modern menu and recipes using exotic flavours and spices.

Le Seizena VISA MC AE

– ✆ 04 79 08 26 36 – www.hotelseizena.com – jab@hotelkilimandjaro.com – Fax 04 79 08 38 83 – Open mid December-mid April

20 rm – †€ 180/290 ††€ 180/290 **Rest** – *(dinner only)* Carte € 30/50

◆ The name and setting honours the Cessna and flying. Modern rooms just like an aircraft cabin with cockpit-style bathrooms and aeroplane models on display. Savoie specialities and international dishes available.

in Praz (Courchevel 1300) by ①: 8 km – ✉ 73120 St Bon Tarentaise

Les Peupliers VISA MC AE

– ✆ 04 79 08 41 47 – www.lespeupliers.com – infos@lespeupliers.com – Fax 04 79 08 45 05 – Closed May to June and 1 October-20 November

35 rm – †€ 160/205 ††€ 220/305, € 12 – ½ P € 140/190

Rest *La Table de mon Grand-Père* – Menu € 25/30 – Carte € 33/58

◆ This welcoming hotel is next to a small lake. It offers refurbished alpine inspired guestrooms lined in wood; those facing south have balconies. Affable welcome. 'My grandfather's table' offers traditional dishes in a characteristic Savoyard setting.

X **Azimut** VISA MC

Immeuble l'or blanc – ✆ 04 79 06 25 90 – Fax 04 79 06 29 44 – Open 7 December-30 April

Rest – Menu (€ 23), € 28/80 – Carte € 46/96

◆ Simple, wood panelled, modern dining room and friendly ambience. Updated cuisine with a zest of creativity and a pasta lunchtime menu. Fine choice of Jura wines.

in la Tania – ✉ 73120

Paris 661 – Lyon 195 – Chambéry 95 – Albertville 46 – Saint-Jean-de-Maurienne 104

Office de tourisme, Maison de la Tania ✆ 04 79 08 40 40, Fax 04 79 08 45 71

Le Farçon (Julien Machet)

La Kalinka building – ✆ 04 79 08 80 34 – www.lefarcon.fr – info@lefarcon.fr – Fax 04 79 06 92 31 – Open mid June-mid September, beg. December-mid April and closed Sunday dinner and Monday in summer

Rest – Menu € 30 (lunch), € 52/95 – Carte € 60/140

Spec. Soupe de petit pois rafraîchi, framboise et parmesan. (mid June to mid Sep.) L'œuf boule de neige, champignons du moment et écrevisse. Sorbet au foin, pamplemousse rôti et croustillant de noix (mid Dec. to mid April). **Wines** Savoie blanc, Mondeuse.

◆ Although the outdoor sign and chalet decor pay tribute to Savoie, the highly inventive and delicious cuisine takes its inspiration from further afield.

COUR-CHEVERNY – 41 Loir-et-Cher – 318 F6 – pop. 2 606 – alt. 86 m – ✉ 41700 11 AB1

Paris 194 – Blois 14 – Châteauroux 88 – Orléans 73 – Romorantin-Lanthenay 28

Office de tourisme, 12, rue du Chêne des Dames ✆ 02 54 79 95 63, Fax 02 54 79 23 90

Château de Cheverny★★★ South: 1 km - Porte★ from the château de Troussay chapel Southwest: 3,5 km - Château de Beauregard★, **Châteaux of the Loire.**

St-Hubert

122 rte Nationale – ✆ 02 54 79 96 60 – www.hotel-sthubert.com – hotel-sthubert@wanadoo.fr – Fax 02 54 79 21 17

21 rm – †€ 40/54 ††€ 54/70, ☕ € 8,50 – ½ P € 55

Rest – *(closed Sunday dinner from November to March)* Menu € 17 (weekday lunch), € 24/39 – Carte € 34/45

◆ A small hotel owned by the head of the local hunting association in this town with a great hunting tradition. Pleasant provincial ambiance, hearthside lounge and modern guestrooms. Bright, colourful dining room. Traditional menu and game in season.

in Cheverny 1 km South – pop. 986 – alt. 110 m – ✉ 41700

Office de tourisme, 12, rue du Chêne des Dames ✆ 02 54 79 95 63, Fax 02 54 79 23 90

Château du Breuil

23 rte de Fougères, West : 3 km on the D 52 and private road – ✆ 02 54 44 20 20 – www.chateau-du-breuil.fr – info@chateau-du-breuil.fr – Fax 02 54 44 30 40

22 rm ☕ – †€ 120/140 ††€ 140/185 – 4 suites

Rest – *(dinner only) (resident only)* Menu € 40

◆ Visit Cheverny and stay at the 18C Breuil, shielded from the outside world by a 30ha park. Comfortable new rooms in keeping with their surroundings in the orchard.

COURCOURONNES – 91 Essonne – 312 D4 – 101 36 – see Paris, Area (Évry)

COURNIOU – 34 Hérault – 339 B8 – see St-Pons-de-Thomières

We try to be as accurate as possible when giving room rates.
But prices are open to change,
so please check rates when booking.

COURS – 69 Rhône – **327** E3 – **pop. 4 241** – **alt. 543 m** – ✉ **69470** 44 **A1**

Paris 416 – Chauffailles 17 – Lyon 75 – Mâcon 70 – Roanne 28 – Villefranche-sur-Saône 50

at col du Pavillon 4 km East by D 64 – **alt. 755 m** – ✉ **69470 Cours la Ville**

Le Pavillon rm, VISA AE

– *04 74 89 83 55 – www.hotel-pavillon.com – hotel-pavillon@wanadoo.fr – Fax 04 74 64 70 26*

21 rm – €46 €56, €8,50 – ½ P €53

Rest – *(Closed Sunday dinner)* Menu (€15), €19 (weekday lunch)/35 – Carte €30/40

◆ At the top of the pass on the edge of the forest, the peaceful environment, Scandinavian inspired architecture and comfortable rooms are most appreciated. Classic fare in a contemporary dining room with a pleasant veranda.

COUR-ST-MAURICE – 25 Doubs – **321** K3 – **pop. 177** – **alt. 500 m** – ✉ **25380** 17 **C2**

Paris 481 – Baume-les-Dames 50 – Besançon 68 – Montbéliard 44 – Maiche 12 – Morteau 37

Le Moulin VISA

Le Moulin du Milieu, East: 3 km on D 39 – 03 81 44 35 18 – hotel.lemoulin@yahoo.fr – Open March-September and closed Wednesday in low season

6 rm – €45 €60/76, €6,50 – ½ P €58/63

Rest – *(number of covers limited, pre-book)* Menu €21/33 – Carte €29/53

◆ This unusual 1930s villa was built for a miller from the valley. Retro rooms and modern lounge. Pleasant shady garden and fishing stretch reserved for guests. Traditional menu served in a smart dining room facing the river.

COURSAN – 11 Aude – **344** J3 – see Narbonne

COURSEULLES-SUR-MER – 14 Calvados – **303** J4 – **pop. 3 886** – ✉ **14470** Normandy 32 **B2**

Paris 252 – Arromanches-les-Bains 14 – Bayeux 24 – Cabourg 41 – Caen 20

Office de tourisme, 5, rue du 11 novembre 02 31 37 46 80, Fax 02 31 37 29 25

Steeple★ of Bernières-sur-Mer church East: 2.5 km - Tower ★ of Ver-sur-Mer church West: 5 km by D 514.

Château★★ de Fontaine-Henry South: 6.5 km.

XX **La Pêcherie** with rm rm, VISA AE

pl. 6-Juin – 02 31 37 45 84 – www.la-pecherie.fr – pecherie@wanadoo.fr – Fax 02 31 37 90 40

6 rm – €60/90 €60/90, €9 – ½ P €74/84

Rest – Menu €20/38 – Carte €35/65

◆ Behind the half-timbered façade is a nostalgic interior with clocks and portraits. One room has exposed stone, another has a glass ceiling. Seafood menu. Boat cabin styled rooms.

COURTENAY – 45 Loiret – **318** P3 – **pop. 3 601** – **alt. 146 m** – ✉ **45320** 12 **D2**

Paris 118 – Auxerre 56 – Nemours 44 – Orléans 101 – Sens 25

Syndicat d'initiative, 5, rue du Mail 02 38 97 00 60, Fax 02 38 97 39 12

de Clairis Savigny-sur-Clairis Domaine de Clairis, N : 7 km, 03 86 86 33 90

XXX **Auberge La Clé des Champs** with rm VISA AE

rte de Joigny, 1 km – 02 38 97 42 68 – www.hotel-lacledeschamps.fr – info@hotel-lacledeschamps.fr – Fax 02 38 97 38 10 – Closed 13-30 October, 12-29 January, Tuesday and Wednesday

7 rm – €73 €73/131, €10

Rest – *(number of covers limited, pre-book)* Menu €26/46 – Carte €35/58

◆ 17C farmhouse and flower-filled garden. Country-style rooms and an elegant rustic dining area. Private heliport.

in Ervauville 9 km Northwest by N 60, D 32 and D 34 – **pop. 516 – alt. 152 m** – ✉ 45320

Le Gamin

– ✆ 02 38 87 22 02 – Fax 02 38 87 25 40
– *Closed 22 June-3 July, 9-24 November, 25 January-5 February, Sunday dinner, Monday and Tuesday*
Rest – *(number of covers limited, pre-book)* Menu € 48/57 – Carte € 80/120
◆ This former grocery store-cum-bar has become a stylish inn (non-smokers only). The decor is original with large mirrors, fired bricks and curios. The terrace opens onto an attractive garden. Appetising cuisine with a contemporary touch.

LA COURTINE – 23 Creuse – 325 K6 – pop. 890 – alt. 789 m – ✉ 23100 25 D2

Paris 424 – Aubusson 38 – La Bourboule 53 – Guéret 80 – Ussel 21

Syndicat d'initiative, Mairie ✆ 05 55 66 76 58, Fax 05 55 66 70 69

Au Petit Breuil

rm, VISA

rte Felletin – ✆ 05 55 66 76 67 – lepetitbreuil@clubinternet.fr – Fax 05 55 66 71 84 – Closed 19 December-12 January, Friday evening from 15 September to 15 April and Sunday evening
11 rm – †€ 48 ††€ 54, ☐ € 7 – ½ P € 61
Rest – Menu (€ 14), € 18/44 – Carte € 30/56
◆ A family residence over a century old with simply furnished but adequately appointed bedrooms; those to the rear are generally quieter. The decor of stonework, straw-bottomed chairs, antique furniture and copperware brings a rustic feel to the restaurant. Terrace overlooking the swimming pool.

COUSSEY – 88 Vosges – 314 C2 – pop. 707 – alt. 280 m – ✉ 88630 26 B3

Paris 290 – Metz 116 – Toul 48 – Vandœuvre-lès-Nancy 56

La Demeure du Gardien du Temps qui Passe

47 Grand Rue – ✆ 03 29 06 99 83 – www.lademeure88.com – lademeure88@hotmail.fr – Fax 03 29 06 99 83
5 rm ☐ – †€ 45/55 ††€ 65/75 **Table d'hôte** – Menu € 15/20
◆ An authentic charm floats about this former post house dating back to the 18C. The spacious rooms and the lounge-library are dotted with antiques. The island-inspired cuisine is a tropical holiday for the palate.

COUTANCES – 50 Manche – 303 D5 – pop. 9 628 – alt. 91 m – ✉ 50200 Normandy 32 A2

Paris 335 – Avranches 52 – Cherbourg 76 – St-Lô 28 – Vire 66

Office de tourisme, place Georges Leclerc ✆ 02 33 19 08 10, Fax 02 33 19 08 19

Cathedral★★★: lantern tower★★★, high sections★★ - Jardin des Plantes★.

Plan on next page

Cositel

rm, VISA AE

r. de St-Malo – ✆ 02 33 19 15 00 – www.cositel.fr – accueil@cositel.fr – Fax 02 33 19 15 02
55 rm – †€ 59/88 ††€ 59/116, ☐ € 9 – ½ P € 53/60
Rest *Pommeau* – *(closed Saturday lunch and Sunday lunch)* Menu € 21/33 – Carte € 32/47
◆ Modern building on a hillside overlooking the town. Rooms are light and have functional furnishings. Traditional cuisine and summer terrace overlooking small ponds.

Manoir de L'Ecoulanderie without rest

r. de la Broche – ✆ 02 33 45 05 05 – www.l-b-c.com – contact@l-b-c.com Y **b**
4 rm ☐ – †€ 100 ††€ 120/130
◆ Wooded parkland, an indoor pool, Coutances and its cathedral in the distance: all of this adds to the charm of this fine 18C manor and its outbuildings. Personalised rooms.

COUTANCES

Albert-1er (Av.) . . . . Z 2
Croûte (R. de la) . . . . YZ 3
Daniel (R.) . . . . Y 5
Duhamel (R.) . . . . Z 6
Écluse-Chette (R. de l') . . . . . . Y 8
Encoignard (Bd) . . . . Z 9
Foch (R. Mar.) . . . . Z 10
Gambetta (R.) . . . . Y 12
Herbert (R. G.) . . . . Z 13
Leclerc (Av. Division) . . . . Y 15
Legentil-de-la-Galaisière (Bd) . Z 16
Lycée (R. du) . . . . Z 17
Marest (R. Thomas-du) . . . . . . Y 18
Milon (R.) . . . . Y 19
Montbray (R. G.-de) . . . . Z 20
Normandie (R. de) . . . . Y 21
Palais-de-Justice (R. du) . . . . . Y 23
Paynel (Bd J.) . . . . Y 24
Quesnel-Morinière (R.) . . . . . . Z 26
République (Av. de la) . . . . Y 27
St-Dominique (R.) . . . . Y 29
St-Nicolas (R.) . . . . Y 30
Tancrède (R.) . . . . Y 32
Tourville (R.) . . . . Y 33

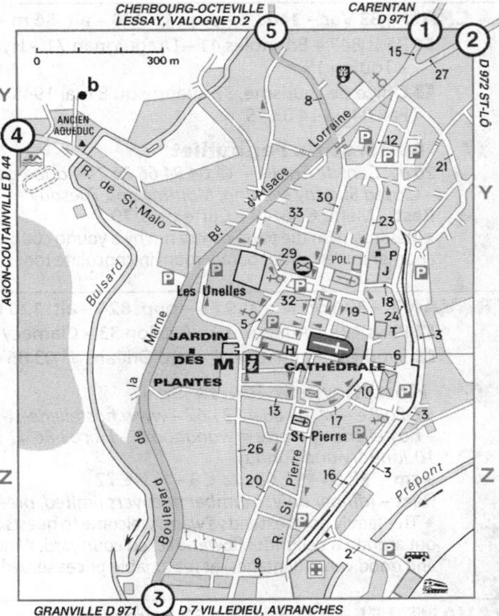

in Gratot 4 km by ④ and D 244 – pop. 612 – alt. 83 m – ✉ 50200

Le Tourne-Bride

85 r. d'Argouges – ☎ 02 33 45 11 00 – Fax 02 33 45 11 00 – Closed February holidays, Sunday dinner and Monday

Rest – Menu (€ 15), € 20/52 – Carte € 34/60

◆ Traditional fare holds sway in this smart 19C post house near Château de Gratot and the Fairy-tale Tower. Warm and rustic ambiance.

COUTRAS – 33 Gironde – 335 K4 – pop. 7 441 – alt. 15 m – ✉ 33230 4 C1

Paris 527 – Bergerac 67 – Blaye 50 – Bordeaux 51 – Jonzac 58 – Libourne 18 – Périgueux 87

Office de tourisme, 17, rue Sully ☎ 05 57 69 36 53, Fax 05 57 69 36 43

Henri IV without rest

pl. du 8 Mai 1945, (opposite the station) – ☎ 05 57 49 34 34 – www.hotelcoutras.com – contact@hotelcoutras.com – Fax 05 57 49 20 72

16 rm – † € 53/56 †† € 59/64, ☕ € 8

◆ Henri of Navarre waged here a battle that gave Coutras a place in history. This 19C manor has comfortable, attractively renovated rooms, some directly under the eaves.

COUX-ET-BIGAROQUE – 24 Dordogne – 329 G7 – pop. 944 – alt. 85 m – ✉ 24220 Dordogne-Berry-Limousin 4 C3

Paris 557 – Bergerac 46 – Bordeaux 180 – Périgueux 55

Manoir de la Brunie

– ☎ 05 53 31 95 62 – www.manoirdelabrunie.com – manoirdelabrunie@wanadoo.fr – Closed December-January

5 rm – † € 63/98 †† € 63/98, ☕ € 8 **Table d'hôte** – Menu € 29 bi

◆ The scent of magnolias perfumes the garden of this fine mansion whose interior has been carefully restored. The guestrooms, that sport antique furniture, are each named after a local château. Périgord recipes take pride of place at the table d'hôte.

LA CRAU – 83 Var – 340 L7 – pop. 15 400 – alt. 36 m – ✉ 83260 41 C3

Paris 847 – Brignoles 41 – Draguignan 71 – Hyères 9 – Marseille 77 – Toulon 15

Office de tourisme, 37 avenue du 8 mai 1945 ✆ 04 94 66 14 48, Fax 04 94 14 03 15

Auberge du Fenouillet

20 av. Gén. de Gaulle – ✆ 04 94 66 76 74 – aubergedu-fenouillet@orange.fr – Closed Sunday evening, Monday and Tuesday

Rest – Menu € 36/48 – Carte € 45/70

◆ Restaurant in the town centre run by a young couple. One neo-rustic dining room, and another more contemporary room in chocolate tones. Patio-terrace. Modern cuisine.

CRAVANT – 89 Yonne – 319 F5 – pop. 824 – alt. 120 m – ✉ 89460 7 B1

Paris 185 – Auxerre 19 – Avallon 33 – Clamecy 35 – Montbard 65

Syndicat d'initiative, 4, rue d'Orléans ✆ 03 86 42 25 71, Fax 03.86.42.25.71

Hostellerie St-Pierre

5 r. Église – ✆ 03 86 42 31 67 – www.hostellerie-st-pierre.com – hostellerie-st-pierre@wanadoo.fr – Fax 03 86 42 37 43 – Closed 20 December-10 January and Sunday

9 rm – €64 €68, € 9 – ½ P € 72

Rest – *(dinner only) (number of covers limited, pre-book)* Menu € 34

◆ This family hotel extends a warm welcome to guests and offers small spruce rooms, laid out around a delightful flower-decked courtyard. Wine tasting cellar. Up-to-date cuisine and good wines (vintages) at reasonable prices served in a light dining room/veranda.

RAVANT-LES-CÔTEAUX – 37 Indre-et-Loire – 317 L6 – pop. 725 – alt. 50 m – ✉ 37500 11 A3

Paris 284 – Orléans 160 – Tours 45 – Joué-lès-Tours 37 – Châtellerault 57

Manoir des Berthaisières

– ✆ 02 47 98 35 07 – www.lesberthaisieres.com – lesberthaisieres@wanadoo.fr – Fax 02 47 98 35 07

3 rm – €55/110 €65/125 – ½ P € 55/80 **Table d'hôte** – Menu € 30 bi

◆ In the heart of a vast estate with vineyards, this manor offers three rooms (two in the detached house, one of which welcomes dogs). Swimming pool, fitness room and Jacuzzi. Traditional cuisine. Cookery lessons given to guests.

CRAZANNES – 17 Charente-Maritime – 324 F4 – pop. 432 – alt. 25 m – ✉ 17350 Atlantic Coast 38 B2

Paris 468 – Poitiers 134 – Rochefort 37 – Saintes 18

Château de Crazannes

– ✆ 06 80 65 40 96 – www.crazannes.com – crazannes@worldonline.fr – Fax 05 46 91 34 46

5 rm – €100/120 €100/120 **Table d'hôte** – Menu € 35 bi

◆ This 15C château surrounded by 8 hectares of parkland is classified as an historic monument. Luxurious rooms in the keep; others are decorated with fine antique furnishings.

CRÈCHES-SUR-SAÔNE – 71 Saône-et-Loire – 320 I12 – see Mâcon

CRÉDIN – 56 Morbihan – 308 O6 – pop. 1 421 – alt. 124 m – ✉ 56580 10 C2

Paris 451 – Rennes 100 – Vannes 49 – Pontivy 19 – Hennebont 64

La Maison Blanche aux Volets Bleus

à Blézouan, 2.5 km east on D11 and secondary road – ✆ 02 97 38 58 61 – www.lamaisonblancheauxvoletsbleus.com – info@lamaisonblancheauxvoletsbleus.com – Closed 5 January-12 February

4 rm – €125 €125/200 **Table d'hôte** – Menu € 50 bi

◆ This engaging house stands on the edge of a hamlet lost in the countryside. The spruce rooms are decorated on the theme of Brittany. Bicycles for rent and cookery courses. Tasty home cooking served on a large teak table.

CREIL – 60 Oise – **305** F5 – pop. 31 200 – alt. 30 m – ✉ 60100 36 **B3**

Northern France and the Paris Region

Paris 63 – Beauvais 45 – Chantilly 9 – Clermont 17 – Compiègne 37

Syndicat d'initiative, 41, place du Général-de-Gaulle ✆ 03 44 55 16 07, Fax 03 44 55 05 27

d'Apremont Apremont CD 606, SE : 6 km on D 1330, ✆ 03 44 25 61 11

La Ferme de Vaux

à Vaux, (on D 120 direction Verneuil) – ✆ 03 44 64 77 00 – www.la-ferme-de-vaux.com – joly.eveline@wanadoo.fr – Fax 03 44 26 81 50

28 rm – €66 €74, €8

Rest – *(closed Saturday lunch and Sunday dinner)* Menu (€18), €26/37 – Carte €42/56

◆ An old Île-de-France-style farmhouse set around an inner courtyard. Modern comfort in the rooms; those on the ground floor are more spacious. Exposed-stone walls and modernised furnishings make up the decor of the dining room. Traditional menu and attentive service.

CRÉMIEU – 38 Isère – **333** E3 – pop. 3 330 – alt. 200 m – ✉ 38460 44 **B2**

Lyon - Rhone Valley

Paris 488 – Belley 49 – Bourg-en-Bresse 64 – Grenoble 86 – Lyon 36 – La Tour-du-Pin 28

Office de tourisme, 9, place de la Nation ✆ 04 74 90 45 13, Fax 04 74 90 02 25

Covered market★.

Auberge de la Chaite with rm

pl. des Tilleuls – ✆ 04 74 90 76 63 – aubergedelachaite@wanadoo.fr – Fax 04 74 90 88 08 – Closed 4-21 April, 24-31 August, 23 December-13 January, Sunday dinner, Wednesday lunch and Monday

10 rm – €52 €56/65, €8

Rest – Menu €18 (weekdays)/38 – Carte €30/51

◆ This country house opposite the Porte de la Loi serves traditional dishes in a rustic-style dining room or on the shaded terrace. Unpretentious rooms.

CREON – 33 Gironde – **335** I6 – pop. 3 774 – alt. 110 m – ✉ 33670 3 **B1**

Atlantic Coast

Paris 597 – Bordeaux 25 – Arcachon 88 – Langon 32 – Libourne 22

Office de tourisme, 62, boulevardd Victor Hugo ✆ 05 56 23 23 00, Fax 05.56.23.23.44

Hostellerie Château Camiac

rm, rest,

rte de Branne, (D 121) – ✆ 05 56 23 20 85 – www.chateaucamiac.com – info@chateaucamiac.com – Fax 05 56 23 38 84 – Open 1st May-30 September

12 rm – €160/280 €160/280, €20 – 2 suites

Rest – *(closed Tues.) (dinner only)* Menu €38 – Carte €60/100

◆ A charming stopover in this Bordelaise vineyard estate built in the 18C. Some of the rooms, decorated with antiques, have unusual windowed bathrooms. Swimming pool, tennis court. The plush cosy atmosphere of this restaurant is enhanced by paintings; the cuisine is modern in style.

CRÉON-D'ARMAGNAC – 40 Landes – **335** K11 – pop. 295 – alt. 130 m – ✉ 40240 4 **C2**

Paris 700 – Bordeaux 122 – Condom 47 – Mont-de-Marsan 36

Le Poutic

Rte de Cazaubon – ✆ 05 58 44 66 97 – www.lepoutic.com – lepoutic@wanadoo.fr

3 rm – €53/60 €58/65

Table d'hôte – *(closed Saturday and Sunday)* Menu €22 bi/40 bi

◆ Oaks and lime trees shade the park that surrounds this beautiful farmhouse in the Landes. The well-kept bedrooms have an independent entrance. Themed stays are available. Traditional and regional dishes.

CREPON – 14 Calvados – 303 I4 – pop. 209 – alt. 52 m – ✉ 14480 32 **B2**
Normandy

Paris 257 – Bayeux 13 – Caen 23 – Deauville 66

Ferme de la Rançonnière
rte d'Arromanches-les-Bains – ☎ 02 31 22 21 73 – www.ranconniere.fr – ranconniere@wanadoo.fr – Fax 02 31 22 98 39
35 rm – €55/160 €55/175, ☕ €12 – 1 suite – ½ P €63/156
Rest – *(closed 5-28 January)* Menu (€24), €30/50 – Carte €38/55
◆ Medieval fortified farm with pretty rooms that are full of character. Ancient beams, 15C furniture and old curios. The fireplace, walls and fine stone vaulting have been carefully preserved at the restaurant.

Ferme de Mathan
800 m. further on
22 rm – €95/260 €95/260, ☕ €12
◆ Guests enjoy peaceful nights in the large rooms of this former 18C smallholding.

CRESSERONS – 14 Calvados – 303 J4 – see Douvres-la-Délivrande

CREST – 26 Drôme – 332 D5 – pop. 7 739 – alt. 196 m – ✉ 26400 44 **B3**
Lyon - Rhone Valley

Paris 585 – Die 37 – Gap 129 – Grenoble 114 – Montélimar 37 – Valence 28

Office de tourisme, place du Docteur Rozier ☎ 04 75 25 11 38, Fax 04 75 76 79 65

du Domaine de Sagnol Gigors-et-Lozeron Domaine de Sagnol, NE : 19 km on D 731, ☎ 04 75 40 98 00

Keep★: ❋★.

Kléber
6 r. A. Dumont – ☎ 04 75 25 11 69 – www.le-kleber.com – Fax 04 75 76 82 82 – Closed 2-11 January, Sunday dinner in low season, Saturday and Monday
Rest – Menu €25 bi (weekday lunch), €35/79 – Carte €64/88
◆ This lends a transalpine touch to the little walled town with its keep: attractive sponge-work on the walls, and red Italian leather seats. Traditional cuisine.

in La Répara-Auriples 8 km south by D 538 and D 166 Autichamp road – pop. 222 – alt. 350 m – ✉ 26400

Le Prieuré Des Sources
lieu dit Bouchassagne – ☎ 04 75 25 03 46 – www.prieuredessources.com – leprieuredessources@wanadoo.fr – Fax 04 75 25 53 07
10 rm – €120/215 €120/215, ☕ €14 **Table d'hôte** – Menu €22/48
◆ Venture through the well-kept garden to this former priory. Admire the vaulted sitting and dining rooms, as well as the spacious guestrooms decorated in an African or Asian style. Modern cuisine using produce (usually organic) from the market and kitchen garden.

LE CRESTET – 84 Vaucluse – 332 D8 – see Vaison-la-Romaine

CREST-VOLAND – 73 Savoie – 333 M3 – pop. 401 – alt. 1 230 m 46 **F1**
– Winter sports : 1 230/2 000 m 17 – ✉ 73590 French Alps

Paris 588 – Albertville 24 – Annecy 53 – Chamonix-Mont-Blanc 47 – Megève 15

Office de tourisme, Maison de Crest-Voland ☎ 04 79 31 62 57, Fax 04 79 31 85 36

Le Caprice des Neiges
Col des Saisies road: 1 km – ☎ 04 79 31 62 95 – www.hotel-capricedesneiges.com – info@hotel-capricedesneiges.com – Fax 04 79 31 79 30 – Closed mid-April to mid-June and mid-September to mid-December
16 rm – €90/110 €90/110, ☕ €11 – ½ P €88/105
Rest – Menu (€15), €20/35 – Carte €28/45
◆ A family-run establishment steeped in charm. Warm chalet-style guestrooms and an attractive bar decked in knick-knacks. Children's play area. Wood and stone abound in the dining room that offers a concise regional menu.

Les Campanules
chemin de la Grange – 04 79 31 81 43 – www.lescampanules.com – chanteline@wanadoo.fr
3 rm – €59/65 €65/72
Table d'hôte – *(open from December to March)* Menu €23 bi
◆ This chalet facing the Aravis chain and Mont Charvin is a hit with nature lovers. Well-kept, simple rooms, a fireside sitting room and hearty breakfasts. Savoyard recipes at the table d'hôte in the evenings (school holidays only).

CRÉTEIL – **94 Val-de-Marne** – **312** D3 – **101** 27 – **see Paris, Area**

CREULLY – **14 Calvados** – **303** I4 – **pop. 1 524** – **alt. 27 m** – ✉ **14480** 32 **B2**

Paris 253 – Bayeux 14 – Caen 20 – Deauville 62

Hostellerie St-Martin with rm
6 pl. Edmond Paillaud – 02 31 80 10 11 – www.hostelleriesaintmartin.com – hostellerie.st.martin@wanadoo.fr – Fax 02 31 08 17 64 – Closed 22 December-12 January
12 rm – €50 €50, €6 – ½ P €50
Rest – Menu €15 (weekdays)/43 – Carte €21/46
◆ These fine 16C vaulted dining rooms with sculptures by a regional artist were once the village market. Traditional dishes. Rooms available.

LE CREUSOT – **71 Saône-et-Loire** – **320** G9 – **pop. 23 600** – **Built-up area 92 000** – **alt. 348 m** – ✉ **71200** **Burgundy-Jura** 8 **C3**

Paris 316 – Autun 30 – Beaune 46 – Chalon-sur-Saône 38 – Mâcon 89
Office de tourisme, château de la Verrerie 03 85 55 02 46, Fax 03 85 80 11 03
Château de la Verrerie★.
Mont St-Vincent★ ✻★★.

La Petite Verrerie
4 r. J. Guesde – 03 85 73 97 97 – www.hotelfp-lecreusot.com – contact@hotelfp-lecreusot.com – Fax 03 85 73 97 90 – Closed 23 December-4 January
43 rm – €88/98 €108/118, €13 – 6 suites
Rest – *(Closed Saturday lunch, Sunday and bank holidays)* Menu (€22), €29/31 – Carte €34/43
◆ From factory pharmacy to employees' association, then a VIP guesthouse and now a comfortable hotel – all steeped in the town's history. Gradually refurbished rooms. A plush dining room with paintings on the theme of metallurgy.

in Breuil **5,5 km East by rue principale and direction Centre équestre** – **pop. 3 547** – **alt. 337 m** – ✉ **71670**

Le Domaine de Montvaltin without rest
– 03 85 55 87 12 – www.domainedemontvaltin.com – domainedemontvaltin@hotmail.com – Fax 03 85 55 54 72 – Closed in January and in September
4 rm – €75/85 €80/90
◆ Only five minutes from Le Creusot, this former property of the Schneider firm has been converted into a guesthouse. Personalised rooms. Indoor pool, well-tended garden and a goldfish pond.

in Montcenis **3 km West by D 784** – **pop. 2 221** – **alt. 400 m** – ✉ **71710**

Le Montcenis
2 pl. du Champ-de-Foire – 03 85 55 44 36 – restaurant.le-montcenis@wanadoo.fr – Fax 03 85 55 89 52 – Closed in July, 2 weeks in February, Sunday dinner, Tuesday dinner and Monday
Rest – *(number of covers limited, pre-book)* Menu (€15), €20 (weekday lunch), €27/45 – Carte €40/53
◆ An inviting decor of a plush sitting room, a vaulted cellar for aperitifs and a neo-Burgundian dining room with exposed beams. Up-to-date cuisine.

in St-Sernin-du-Bois 2 km northeast on the D 138 – **pop. 1 720** – **alt. 447 m** – ✉ 71200

Le Restaurant du Château

le bourg – ✆ 03 85 78 28 42 – lerestaurantduchateau@orange.fr – Fax 03 85 78 28 42 – Closed Christmas holidays, Tuesday and Wednesday

Rest – *(number of covers limited, pre-book)* Menu € 19/29 – Carte € 30/40

◆ An 11C castle in the heart of the village, overlooking the lake. The rustic dining room (beams, stone, wooden furniture) is well suited to the updated traditional fare.

in Torcy 4 km South by D 28 – **pop. 3 136** – **alt. 310 m** – ✉ 71210

Le Vieux Saule

le Vieux Saule – ✆ 03 85 55 09 53 – www.restaurantvieuxsaule.com – restaurant.levieuxsaule@orange.fr – Fax 03 85 80 39 99 – Closed Sunday dinner and Monday

Rest – Menu € 17 (weekdays)/48 – Carte € 47/69

◆ Traditional dishes, some with a contemporary touch, served in the stylish purple walled dining room. The chairs are adorned with Burgundy wine motifs.

CREUTZWALD – 57 Moselle – 307 L3 – pop. 13 600 – alt. 210 m – ✉ 57150 27 C1

Paris 376 – Metz 53 – Neunkirchen 61 – Saarbrücken 37

Syndicat d'initiative, Hôtel de Ville ✆ 03 87 81 89 89, Fax 03 87 82 08 15

Auberge Richebourg

17 r. de la Houve – ✆ 03 87 90 17 54 – www.aubergerichebourg.com – richebourg@wanadoo.fr – Fax 03 87 90 28 56 – Closed 1st-21 August, Saturday lunch, Sunday dinner and Monday

Rest – Menu € 21 (weekdays)/55 – Carte € 39/53

◆ New modern decor at this family restaurant that offers cuisine in keeping with current tastes. Pleasant terrace overlooking an enclosed garden.

La Forge des Grands Aigles

43 r. de la Houve – ✆ 03 87 93 04 08 – forge-des-grands-aigles@orange.fr – Closed 2 weeks in July, 1 week in February, Saturday lunch, Sunday dinner and Monday

Rest – Menu € 21 (weekdays)/75 – Carte € 41/76

◆ A chic restaurant, led by a young and dynamic team, serving Provencal-inspired cuisine. Attentive service and pretty terrace.

CRICQUEBOEUF – 14 Calvados – 303 M3 – see Honfleur

CRILLON – 60 Oise – 305 C3 – pop. 439 – alt. 110 m – ✉ 60112 36 A2

Paris 103 – Aumale 33 – Beauvais 16 – Breteuil 33 – Compiègne 75 – Gournay-en-Bray 18

La Petite France

7 r. Moulin – ✆ 03 44 81 01 13 – lapetitefrance@wanadoo.fr – Fax 03 44 81 01 13 – Closed Sunday dinner, Monday and Tuesday

Rest – Menu (€ 15), € 23 bi (weekdays)/41 – Carte € 35/57

◆ This welcoming inn in a little Beauvaisis village has two rustic dining rooms. Traditional menu, including the house speciality of "tête de veau ravigote" (calf's head).

CRILLON-LE-BRAVE – 84 Vaucluse – 332 D9 – pop. 434 – alt. 340 m – ✉ 84410 42 E1

Paris 687 – Avignon 41 – Carpentras 14 – Nyons 37 – Vaison-la-Romaine 22

Crillon le Brave

rm, rm, P

pl. de l'Église – ✆ 04 90 65 61 61 – www.crillonlebrave.com – crillonbrave@relaischateaux.com – Fax 04 90 65 62 86 – Open 7 March-30 November

28 rm – € 240/740 € 240/740, € 19 – 6 suites **Rest** – Carte € 40/75

◆ Hotel made up of seven typical old houses in a hilltop village facing Mont Ventoux. The Italian garden slopes down to the pool. Charming Provencal bedrooms. Up-to-the-minute cuisine drenched in southern flavours. Lunch snack menu.

CRIQUETOT-L'ESNEVAL – **76 Seine-Maritime** – **304** B4 – **pop. 2 202** – **alt. 127 m** – ✉ **76280** 33 **C1**

▶ Paris 197 – Fécamp 19 – Le Havre 28 – Rouen 81

Le Manoir

5 pl. des Anciens Élèves, (near the church) – ✆ 02 35 29 31 90 – http://monsite.orange.fr/bnbmanoir – serge.quevilly@wanadoo.fr – Fax 02 35 29 31 90

6 rm – €45/50 €62/68 – ½ P €50/55

Table d'hôte – *(pre-book)* Menu €17 bi

◆ Splendid Normandy wardrobes embellish the spacious rooms in this manor house with its stylish facade in stone and brick. Large flower-filled grounds planted with trees.

CRISENOY – **77 Seine-et-Marne** – **312** F4 – **see Melun**

LE CROISIC – **44 Loire-Atlantique** – **316** A4 – **pop. 4 278** – **alt. 6 m** – ✉ **44490** **Brittany** 34 **A2**

▶ Paris 459 – La Baule 9 – Nantes 86 – Redon 66 – Vannes 81

Office de tourisme, place du 18 Juin 1940 ✆ 02 40 23 00 70, Fax 02 40 23 23 70

du Croisic Golf de la Pointe, W : 3 km, ✆ 02 40 23 14 60

Océarium★ - ≤★ of Mont-Lénigo.

Plan on following page

Le Fort de l'Océan

pointe du Croisic – ✆ 02 40 15 77 77 – www.hotelfortocean.com – fortocean@relaischateaux.com – Fax 02 40 15 77 80

9 rm – €190 €280/310, €18 – ½ P €168/228

Rest – *(closed 14 November-20 December, 4 January-6 February, Wednesday lunch and Thursday lunch from 14 July to 31 August, Monday and Tuesday)* Menu €34 (weekday lunch), €45/80 – Carte €78/125

◆ A small, Vauban-style, 17C fort overlooking the ocean. Wonderful view of the Côte Sauvage from all the individually decorated guestrooms. Bikes available. Carefully prepared fish dishes to be enjoyed in an elegant veranda-dining room.

Les Vikings without rest

à Port-Lin – ✆ 02 40 62 90 03 – www.hotel-les-vikings.com – vikings@fr.oleane.com – Fax 02 40 23 28 03 AZ **e**

24 rm – €71/120 €71/120, €13

◆ A holiday spirit pervades this hotel offering spacious rooms, individually decorated with traditional modern furniture. Some have a bow window with a view of the Côte Sauvage.

Les Nids without rest

15 r. Pasteur à Port-Lin – ✆ 02 40 23 00 63 – www.hotellesnids.com – hotellesnids@worldonline.fr – Fax 02 40 23 09 79 – Open 3 April-3 November

24 rm – €64/79 €64/93, €9 AZ **f**

◆ Small, well-kept hotel offering colourful rooms with painted furniture. Breakfast is served beside the covered pool. Children's playground in the garden.

Castel Moor

Baie Castouillet, 1.5 km northwest by D 45 – ✆ 02 40 23 24 18 – www.castel-moor.com – castel@castel-moor.com – Fax 02 40 62 98 90

18 rm – €58/77 €58/82, €10 – ½ P €64/70

Rest – *(closed Sunday dinner October- February)* Menu €24/41 – Carte €33/55

◆ Imposing modern villa on the coast road running along the Côte Sauvage. Most of the spruced up rooms boast a balcony or a terrace. A semi-circular dining room and veranda directly overlooking the sea. The menu favours fish and seafood.

L'Océan

in Port-Lin – ✆ 02 40 62 90 03 – www.restaurantlocean.com – vikings@fr.oleane.com – Fax 02 40 23 28 03 AZ **v**

Rest – Carte €51/110

Rest *Le Bistrot de l'Océan* – Carte €25/35

◆ The main asset of this restaurant clinging to the rocks is its panoramic sea view. Freshly caught fish and seafood. Beside the beach, you submerse yourself in the modern atmosphere of the Bistrot de l'Océan. Seafood dishes and a choice of crêpes and griddle cakes.

LE CROISIC

Aiguillon (Quai d') . . . . AY 2
Cordiers (R. des) . . . . BY 6
Europe (R. de l') . . . . AY 7
Gaulle (Pl. du Gén.-de) . . . . . AZ 9
Grande-Rue . . . . AY 12
Lénigo (Quai du) . . . . AY 13
Lepré (Pl. Donatien) . . . . AY 16
Mail de Broc (R. du) . . . . AY 17
Petite Chambre (Q. de la) . . BY 20
Pilori (R. du) . . . . BY 22
Poilus (R. des) . . . . BZ 23
Port Charly (Quai) . . . . AY 26
Port Ciguet (Quai du) . . . . . . AY 27
Port Lin (Av. de) . . . . AZ 28
Rielle (Quai Hervé) . . . . BY 32
Saint-Christophe (R.) . . . . BY 33
Saint-Goustan (Av. de) . . . . . AY 35
18-Juin-1940 (Pl. du) . . . . BZ 36

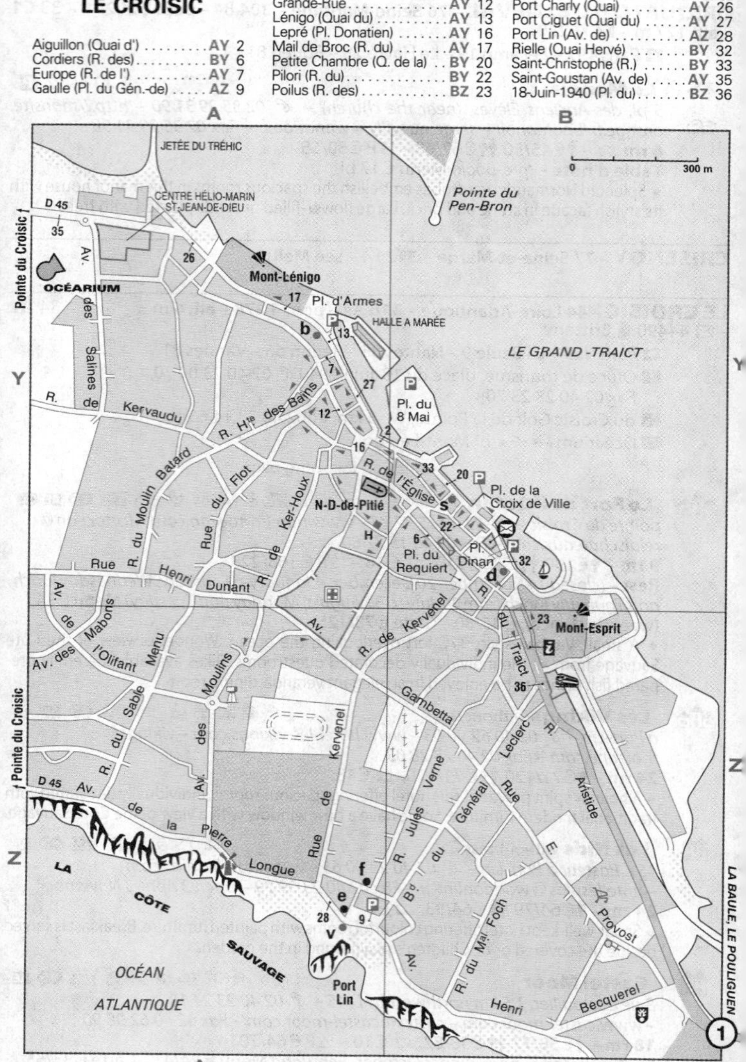

La Bouillabaisse Bretonne

VISA MC

12 quai de la Petite Chambre, (at the harbour) – ✆ 02 40 23 06 74 – labouillabaisse2@wanadoo.fr – Fax 02 40 15 71 43 – Closed 4 January-20 March, Sunday dinner and Tuesday except July-August and Monday BY **s**

Rest – Menu € 20 (weekdays)/33 – Carte € 35/85

◆ The name of the place may surprise visitors from Marseille, but the view over the sea will reconcile Bretons and Provençaux. Lobsters and crayfish welcome you with open pincers.

XX **Le Lénigo**

11 quai Lénigo – ✆ 02 40 23 00 31 – www.le-lenigo.fr – le.lenigo@wanadoo.fr – Fax 02 40 23 01 01 – Open 15 February-15 November and closed Monday and Tuesday except August AY **b**

Rest – Menu € 23/36 – Carte € 28/65

◆ Opposite the fish market, this restaurant is decorated in nautical style (varnished wood, portholes, ropes, etc). Simple but tasty menu with an emphasis on fish and seafood.

X **Le Saint-Alys**

3 quai Hervé-Rielle – ✆ 02 40 23 58 40 – Fax 02 40 23 58 40 – Closed 1-9 July, 16-20 November, 23-26 December, 15 February-3 March, Sunday dinner, Tuesday dinner and Wednesday BY **d**

Rest – Menu (€ 17), € 23/36 – Carte € 34/48

◆ A faultless welcome awaits you in this small well-located establishment opposite the marina. Restrained, tasteful interior in which to sample a modern, predominantly seafood menu.

LA CROIX-BLANCHE – 71 Saône-et-Loire – 320 I11 – see Berzé-la-Ville

---

LA CROIX-DU-BREUIL – 87 Haute-Vienne – 325 F4 – see Bessines-sur-Gartempe

---

LA CROIX-FRY (COL) – 74 Haute-Savoie – 328 L5 – see Manigod

LA CROIX-ST-LEUFROY – 27 Eure – 304 H7 – pop. 1 035 – alt. 24 m – ✉ 27490 33 D2

Paris 98 – Rouen 46 – Évreux 18 – Mantes-la-Jolie 47 – Dreux 62

XX **Le Cheval Blanc**

27 r. de Louviers – ✆ 02 32 34 82 86 – Fax 02 32 34 78 99 – Closed 23 December-9 January, Sunday dinner, Tuesday dinner and Wednesday

Rest – Menu (€ 18), € 26/33 – Carte € 36/54

◆ This 19C house by the main road of the village welcomes diners into a long, half-classical, half-rustic (fireplace) dining room. Updated traditional menu.

LA CROIX-VALMER – 83 Var – 340 O6 – pop. 3 139 – alt. 120 m – ✉ 83420 French Riviera 41 C3

Paris 873 – Draguignan 48 – Fréjus 35 – Le Lavandou 27 – Ste-Maxime 15 – Toulon 68

Office de tourisme, esplanade de la Gare ✆ 04 94 55 12 12, Fax 04 94 55 12 10

Gassin Golf Country Club Gassin Route de Ramatuelle, N : 8 km, ✆ 04 94 55 13 44

L'Orangeraie Parc Hotel without rest

rte de Ramatuelle – ✆ 04 94 55 27 27 – www.hotel-lorangeraie.com – info@hotel-lorangeraie.com – Fax 04 94 54 38 91 – Open 10 April-17 October

32 rm – †€ 130/195 ††€ 130/320

◆ The impressive Belle Époque façade of this former convent hides a vast lobby and immense romantic rooms, most of which overlook the palm grove and sea. Snacks in season.

Southwest 3.5 km on the D 559 then minor road off the Débarquement roundabout – ✉ 83420 La Croix-Valmer

X **La Petite Auberge de Barbigoua**

1 av. des Gabiers, (Barbigoua district) – ✆ 04 94 54 21 82 – Open Easter-30 September and closed Sunday and Monday

Rest – *(dinner only)* Carte € 40/60

◆ An unassuming small restaurant with a pleasant terrace-garden. Friendly atmosphere, rustic interior and a regional menu dominated by fish.

in Gigaro 5 km southeast on the minor road – ✉ 83420 La Croix-Valmer

Château de Valmer rm,
plage de Gigaro – ✆ 04 94 55 15 15 VISA AE
– www.chateauvalmer.com – info@chateauvalmer.com – Fax 04 94 55 15 10
– Open mid-April to mid-October
41 rm – †€ 200/298 ††€ 345/520, ☕ € 27 – 1 suite
Rest – *(closed Tuesday dinner)* Carte € 72/86
◆ This 19C manor house in the heart of a wine growing estate is home to vast, regional style guestrooms and an unusual 'tree cabin'. Pool with palm trees, very well-equipped spa. In the restaurant the colours of Provence feature in the decor and on your plate!

La Pinède-Plage rm, VISA AE
plage de Gigaro – ✆ 04 94 55 16 16 – www.pinedeplage.com – info@pinedeplage.com – Fax 04 94 55 16 10 – Open from May to the beg. October
33 rm – †€ 200/295 ††€ 345/510, ☕ € 27 **Rest** – Carte € 65/90
◆ New fresh and bright decor for this building by the water's edge, shaded by umbrella pine trees. Pleasant rooms, all overlooking the sea. Lovely panoramic terrace overlooking the Îles d'Or. Southern seafood-inspired cuisine is served.

CROS-DE-CAGNES – **06 Alpes-Maritimes** – **341** D6 – **see Cagnes-sur-Mer**

CROZANT – **23 Creuse** – **325** G2 – **pop. 581** – **alt. 263 m** – ✉ **23160** 25 **C1**
Dordogne-Berry-Limousin

Paris 329 – Argenton-sur-Creuse 31 – La Châtre 46 – Guéret 41 – Montmorillon 68

Ruins★.

Auberge de la Vallée VISA
– ✆ 05 55 89 80 03 – Closed 2 January-1 February, Monday dinner and Tuesday
Rest – Menu € 19/45 – Carte € 34/40
◆ This small country guesthouse offers traditional cuisine based on carefully selected local produce; the dining room is quietly rustic in style.

CROZET – **01 Ain** – **328** J3 – **pop. 1 349** – **alt. 540 m** – ✉ **01170** 46 **F1**

Paris 537 – Lyon 153 – Bourg-en-Bresse 105 – Genève 16 – Annecy 57

Jiva Hill Park Hôtel
rte d'Harée – ✆ 04 50 28 48 48 – www.jivahill.com VISA AE
– welcome@jivahill.com – Fax 04 50 28 48 49
33 rm – †€ 280/380 ††€ 320/420, ☕ € 20 – 6 suites
Rest *Shamwari* – *(closed 1st-17 January and Sunday dinner)* Menu (€ 30), € 45/75 – Carte € 45/60
◆ Sophisticated, contemporary luxury only 10 min from Geneva airport. Designed along the lines of a South African hunting lodge, this hotel is the ultimate in chic elegance. Cosy restaurant whose terrace faces Mont Blanc. Up-to-date cuisine.

CROZON – **29 Finistère** – **308** E5 – **pop. 7 535** – **alt. 85 m** – ✉ **29160** 9 **A2**
Brittany

Paris 587 – Brest 60 – Châteaulin 35 – Douarnenez 40 – Morlaix 81 – Quimper 49

Office de tourisme, boulevard de Pralognan ✆ 02 98 27 07 92, Fax 02 98 27 24 89

Church★ altar-piece.

Circuit des Pointes★★★.

La Presqu'île rest, VISA AE
pl. de l'Église – ✆ 02 98 27 29 29 – www.mutingourmand.fr – mutin.gourmand1@wanadoo.fr – Fax 02 98 26 11 97 – Closed 8-31 March, 27 September-20 October, Sunday evening and Monday in low season
13 rm – †€ 50/79 ††€ 50/79, ☕ € 10
Rest *Le Mutin Gourmand* – see restaurant listing
◆ The old Crozon town hall has recently been turned into a hotel with soundproofed rooms decorated in a modern, Breton style. Shop selling wine and regional products.

XX **Le Mutin Gourmand** – Hôtel La Presqu'île
pl. de l'Église – ✆ 02 98 27 06 51 – www.mutingourmand.fr – mutin.gourmand1@wanadoo.fr – Fax 02 98 26 11 97 – Closed 8-31 March, 27 September-20 October, Sunday dinner and Tuesday lunch in low season, Monday except dinner in high season
Rest – Menu € 26/73
◆ Friendly service in this Breton restaurant with modern decor, exposed stone, watercolour paintings and lobster tank. Fine, regional cuisine, with wines from the Languedoc and the Loire.

at Fret 5.5 km north by D 155 and D 55 – ✉ 29160 Crozon

Hostellerie de la Mer
11 quai du Fret – ✆ 02 98 27 61 90 – www.hostelleriedelamer.com – hostellerie.de.la.mer@wanadoo.fr – Fax 02 98 27 65 89 – Closed Saturday and Sunday in January
25 rm – †€ 47/72 ††€ 47/110, ☕ € 10 – ½ P € 57/85
Rest – *(Closed 4 January-4 February)* Menu (€ 19), € 26/75 – Carte € 40/85
◆ An attractive, family-run hotel overlooking the harbour in Brest, with small, simple and well-maintained rooms, some of which have a view. Breton furniture and sea views go hand in hand with a cuisine which has a distinctly maritime flavour.

CRUGNY – 51 Marne – 306 E7 – pop. 603 – alt. 100 m – ✉ 51170 — 13 B2

Northern France and the Paris Region

▶ Paris 135 – Châlons-en-Champagne 71 – Reims 28 – Soissons 39

La Maison Bleue
46 r. Haute – ✆ 03 26 50 84 63 – www.la-maison-bleue.com – maisonbleue@aol.com – Fax 03 26 97 43 92 – Closed 22 December-31 January
6 rm – †€ 88 ††€ 96/161, ☕ € 8 **Table d'hôte** – Menu € 29 bi/50 bi
◆ A welcoming house set in grounds dotted with ponds. Individually decorated rooms. The most spacious, on the top floor, affords a fine view of the village and the Ardre valley. Traditional cuisine with regional accents.

CRUIS – 04 Alpes-de-Haute-Provence – 334 D8 – pop. 590 – alt. 728 m – ✉ 04230 — 40 B2

▶ Paris 732 – Digne-les-Bains 42 – Forcalquier 22 – Manosque 42 – Sisteron 26

X **Auberge de l'Abbaye** with rm
– ✆ 04 92 77 01 93 – http://monsite.wanadoo.fr/auberge-abbaye-cruis – auberge-abbaye-cruis@wanadoo.fr – Fax 04 92 77 01 92 – Closed autumn, Christmas and February school holidays, Sunday dinner and Wednesday from September to June, Tuesday from November to March and lunch from Monday to Thursday in July-August
8 rm – †€ 55/75 ††€ 55/75, ☕ € 10 – ½ P € 63/73
Rest – *(number of covers limited, pre-book)* Menu (€ 24), € 30/55
◆ This inviting family inn with its shaded terrace is located on the town square. Distinctly regional inspired cuisine made with local produce. Simply furnished but well-kept guestrooms. Homemade bread for breakfast.

CRUSEILLES – 74 Haute-Savoie – 328 J4 – pop. 3 186 – alt. 781 m – ✉ 74350 — 46 F1

▶ Paris 537 – Annecy 19 – Bellegarde-sur-Valserine 44 – Bonneville 37 – Genève 27

ℹ Syndicat d'initiative, 46, place de la Mairie ✆ 04 50 44 20 92

XXX **L'Ancolie** with rm — rest,
au parc des Dronières, Northeast : 1 km via D 15 – ✆ 04 50 44 28 98 – www.lancolie.com – info@lancolie.com – Fax 04 50 44 09 73 – Closed autumn half-term holidays
10 rm – †€ 87/123 ††€ 87/123, ☕ € 14 – ½ P € 90/105
Rest – *(closed Sunday dinner except July-August and Monday)* Menu € 29, € 45/72 – Carte € 58/81
◆ Well-equipped modern chalet (quintessentially Savoyard) overlooking a lake. Wood-panelled rooms with balcony (bar one). Classic cuisine, panoramic terrace.

in Avenières 6 km North by D 41 and secondary road – ✉ 74350 Cruseilles

Château des Avenières
– ✆ 04 50 44 02 23 – *www.chateau-des-avenieres.com*
– *reservation@chateau-des-avenieres.com – Fax 04 50 44 29 09 – Closed autumn half-term holidays, Christmas and February holidays*
12 rm – €160/310 €160/310, €18
Rest – *(closed Monday and Tuesday)* Menu €58
◆ A 1907 manor house with a mysterious history. Personalised guestrooms, a charming butterfly-shaped park and a marvellous view of the Aravis mountain range. Superb classic-baroque dining room with woodwork incorporating antique cameos.

CUBRY – 25 Doubs – **321** I2 – **pop. 75** – **alt. 340 m** – ✉ **25680** 17 **C1**

Paris 389 – Belfort 49 – Besançon 53 – Lure 27 – Montbéliard 42 – Vesoul 31

Château de Bournel
– ✆ 03 81 86 00 10 – *www.golf-bournel.com – info@bournel.com*
– *Fax 03 81 86 01 06*
16 rm – €100/120 €150/180, €14 – 2 suites – ½ P €150/165
Rest ***Le Maugré*** – ✆ *03 81 86 06 60 (Closed Sunday dinner, Monday and Tuesday in low season) (dinner only)* Menu €30/55
◆ Hotel in the 18C outbuildings of the château of the Marquis de Moustier, in the heart of an 80h park. Spacious rooms. Formal gardens and 18-hole golf course. Modern cuisine served in a vaulted dining room at Le Maugré. Fast food in the brasserie.

CUCUGNAN – 11 Aude – **344** G5 – **pop. 133** – **alt. 310 m** – ✉ **11350** 22 **B3**
Languedoc-Roussillon-Tarn Gorges

Paris 847 – Carcassonne 77 – Limoux 79 – Perpignan 42 – Quillan 51
Circuit of Corbières cathares★★.

La Tourette without rest
4 passage de la Vierge – ✆ 04 68 45 07 39 – www.latourette.eu – coco@latourette.eu
3 rm – €90/100 €100/120, €10
◆ The lady of the house cannot be faulted for her taste: the Prune, Turquoise and Indigo rooms are not only unusual, they are exquisite. Jacuzzi on the patio under an olive tree.

Auberge du Vigneron with rm
– ✆ *04 68 45 03 00 – www.auberge.vigneron.com – auberge.vigneron@ataraxie.fr – Fax 04 68 45 03 08 – Open 16 March-10 November*
7 rm – €51 €51/65, €8 – ½ P €53/63
Rest – *(closed Sunday dinner off season, Saturday lunch July-August and Monday)* Menu €22 (weekdays)/40 – Carte €33/47
◆ The chef takes great pride in using the finest produce to prepare regional dishes to which he adds his own creative touches. Dining room in the old wine cellar and pretty terrace facing the vineyards.

Auberge de Cucugnan with rm
2 pl. Fontaine – ✆ 04 68 45 40 84 – www.auberge-de-cucugnan.com – contact@auberge-cucugnan.com – Fax 04 68 45 01 52 – Closed 1st January-1st March
9 rm – €50 €50, €6,50 – ½ P €49
Rest – *(closed Thursday)* Menu €18/46 – Carte €23/39
◆ A country atmosphere pervades this converted barn that lies at the end of a maze of alleys. Generous cuisine with a rural flavour. Perfectly maintained rooms.

CUCURON – 84 Vaucluse – **332** F11 – **pop. 1 816** – **alt. 350 m** 42 **E1**
– ✉ **84160** Provence

Paris 739 – Apt 25 – Cavaillon 39 – Digne-les-Bains 109 – Manosque 35
Office de tourisme, rue Léonce Brieugne ✆ 04 90 77 28 37

Le Pavillon de Galon without rest
chemin de Galon – ✆ 04 90 77 24 15 – www.pavillondegalon.com – bibi@pavillondegalon.com – Fax 04 90 77 12 55
3 rm – €135/185 €150/200
◆ Magnificent parkland (French-style garden, vineyards, orchard, maze of yew hedges) surrounds this 18C hunting lodge. The rooms have a refined simplicity and majestic comfort.

XX ✿ **La Petite Maison** (Eric Sapet)
pl. de l'Étang – ☎ 04 90 68 21 99 – www.lapetitemaisondecucuron.com – info@lapetitemaisondecucuron.com – Closed Monday and Tuesday
Rest – *(number of covers limited, pre-book)* Menu € 40/60
Spec. Pressé de bœuf aux olives et carottes fondantes. Sole farcie à la mousseline de Saint-Jacques. Tarte aux pommes caramélisées et son sorbet.
◆ This small house with a shaded terrace is in the village centre near the lake. Fine cuisine that varies with the season, the market, and the chef's inspiration.

X **L'Horloge**
55 r. L. Brieugne – ☎ 04 90 77 12 74 – www.horloge.netfirms.com – horlog@wanadoo.fr – Fax 04 90 77 29 90 – Closed 26-30 June, 18-27 December, 11 February-15 March, Monday from 1 September to 6 April, Tuesday dinner and Wednesday
Rest – Menu (€ 15 bi), € 19/42 – Carte € 35/51
◆ This 14C edifice in a Luberon village was once used as an oil press. It has been converted into a rustic restaurant decorated in bright colours and serves regional dishes.

CUERS – 83 Var – **340** L6 – **pop. 8 174 – alt. 140 m** – ✉ **83390** 41 **C3**

Paris 834 – Brignoles 25 – Draguignan 59 – Marseille 84 – Toulon 22
Office de tourisme, 18, Place de la Convention ☎ 04 94 48 56 27, Fax 04 94 28 03 56

XX **Le Verger des Kouros**
quartier des Cauvets, 2 km on Solliès-Pont road D 97 – ☎ 04 94 28 50 17 – www.le-verger-des-kouros.com – kourosalain@orange.fr – Fax 04 94 48 69 77 – Closed 25 October-10 November, 15-28 February, Tuesday except dinner from June to August and Wednesday
Rest – Menu (€ 20), € 34/45
◆ Despite the restaurant's name, you won't see any statues of ephebes but the three brothers running the place are Greek. Cool dining room and Mediterranean dishes.

X **Terre de Vignes**
36 av. Mar.-Joffre – ☎ 04 94 58 29 70 – terredevignes@voila.fr
Rest – Menu (€ 16), € 32 – Carte € 38/54
◆ Market cuisine blackboard menu served at this small, family establishment. Simple rustic setting and tables prettily set in a contemporary style.

CUISEAUX – 71 Saône-et-Loire – **320** M11 – **pop. 1 766 – alt. 280 m** – ✉ **71480** Burgundy-Jura 8 **D3**

Paris 395 – Chalon-sur-Saône 60 – Lons-le-Saunier 26 – Mâcon 74 – Tournus 52
Syndicat d'initiative, cours des Princes d'Orange ☎ 03 85 72 76 09

Vuillot rest,
36 r. Vuillard – ☎ 03 85 72 71 79 – hotel.vuillot@wanadoo.fr – Fax 03 85 72 54 22 – Closed 8-20 June, 4-25 January, Sunday dinner and Monday
15 rm – †€ 40/42 ††€ 53/55, ☕ € 8 – ½ P € 43/50
Rest – Menu € 14 (weekdays)/46 – Carte € 24/47
◆ A Burgundy building in lovely local stone, with neat and tidy little rooms. The small town still has vestiges of its old fortifications. A veranda extends the pastel coloured restaurant. Specialities from the Bresse and Dombes.

CUISERY – 71 Saône-et-Loire – **320** J10 – **pop. 1 604 – alt. 211 m** – ✉ **71290** Burgundy-Jura 8 **C3**

Paris 367 – Chalon-sur-Saône 35 – Lons-le-Saunier 50 – Mâcon 38 – Tournus 8
Syndicat d'initiative, 32, place d'Armes ☎ 03 85 40 11 70, Fax 03.85.40.11.70

Hostellerie Bressane
56 rte de Tournus – ☎ 03 85 32 30 66 – www.hostellerie-bressane.fr – hostellerie.bressane@wanadoo.fr – Fax 03 85 40 14 96 – Closed 8-18 June, 28 December-4 February, Wednesday and Thursday
15 rm – †€ 60/90 ††€ 70/120, ☕ € 11 – ½ P € 76/85
Rest – Menu (€ 28), € 35/58
◆ This family hostelry from 1870 offers carefully renovated, spacious rooms and a delightful garden. Entirely non-smoking. Traditional local dishes are cheerfully served in a stylish modern setting. Fine plane tree on the terrace.

CULT – 70 Haute-Saône – **321** E3 – **pop. 188** – **alt. 270 m** – ✉ **70150** 16 **B2**

Paris 367 – Besançon 35 – Dole 44 – Vesoul 56

Les Egrignes

rte d'Hugier – ☎ 03 84 31 92 06 – www.les-egrignes.com – lesegrignes@wanadoo.fr – Fax 03 84 31 92 06 – Closed 17 November-6 January

3 rm – †€ 75 ††€ 85

Table d'hôte – *(closed Sunday and Thursday)* Menu € 28 bi

◆ Parkland with century-old trees surrounds this fine abode dating back to 1849. The guestrooms are large and tastefully furnished. Elegant sitting room. The table d'hôte invites guests to discover the region's culinary specialities and wines.

CUQ-TOULZA – 81 Tarn – **338** D9 – **pop. 547** – **alt. 203 m** – ✉ **81470** 29 **C2**

Paris 713 – Toulouse 47 – Albi 72 – Castelnaudary 35 – Castres 33 – Gaillac 54

Cuq en Terrasses rm, rm, VISA MC AE

South-east: 2.5 km on the D 45 – ☎ 05 63 82 54 00 – www.cuqenterrasses.com – info@cuqenterrasses.com – Fax 05 63 82 54 11 – Open 2 April-30 October

6 rm – †€ 95/150 ††€ 100/150, € 14 – 1 suite

Rest – *(closed Wednesday) (dinner only) (residents only)* Menu € 35

◆ This charming 18C house is a little gem: unusual terraced garden, guesthouse ambience and tasteful, individually decorated rooms. Up-to-date dishes of Mediterranean influence, served outdoors in summer.

CUREBOURSE (COL) – 15 Cantal – **330** D5 – **see Vic-sur-Cère**

CURTIL-VERGY – 21 Côte-d'Or – **320** J6 – **see Nuits-St-Georges**

CURZAY-SUR-VONNE – 86 Vienne – **322** G6 – **pop. 458** – **alt. 125 m** – ✉ **86600** 39 **C1**

Paris 364 – Lusignan 11 – Niort 54 – Parthenay 34 – Poitiers 29 – St-Maixent-l'École 28

Château de Curzay rm, rm, P VISA MC AE

rte Jazeneuil – ☎ 05 49 36 17 00 – www.chateau-curzay.com – info@chateau-curzay.com – Fax 05 49 53 57 69 – Open 8 April-11 November

20 rm – †€ 175/190 ††€ 175/380, € 25 – 2 suites – ½ P € 175/225

Rest ***La Cédraie*** – Menu € 38 (lunch), € 75/110 – Carte € 80/120

Spec. Déclinaison gourmande autour de l'huître de Marenne-Oléron (spring-autumn). L'agneau du poitou en quatre façons. Macarons glacés. **Wines** Vin de Pays de la Vienne.

◆ Superb castle (1710) at the heart of a 120 ha-estate crossed by a river and housing a stud farm. Aristocratic guestrooms. At La Cedraie, creative cuisine made from the vegetable and herb gardens.

CUSSAY – 37 Indre-et-Loire – **317** N6 – **pop. 562** – **alt. 105 m** – ✉ **37240** 11 **B3**

Paris 303 – Orléans 179 – Tours 67 – Joué-lès-Tours 62 – Châtellerault 36

La Ferme Blanche

La Chaume-Brangerie – ☎ 02 47 91 94 43 – www.la-ferme-blanche.com – contact@la-ferme-blanche.com – Closed mid-November to end February

5 rm – †€ 120/130 ††€ 120/130 **Table d'hôte** – Menu € 32 bi

◆ This 18C stone farmhouse stands in a pleasant garden overlooking peaceful countryside. The carefully chosen antiques add character to the individually decorated rooms. Sample traditional dishes inspired by the Tours region at the table d'hôte.

Do not confuse X with ✿!
X defines comfort, while stars are awarded for the best cuisine, across all categories of comfort.

CUSSEY-SUR-L'OGNON – 25 Doubs – 321 F2 – pop. 790 – alt. 227 m – ✉ 25870 — 16 B2

Paris 412 – Besançon 14 – Gray 37 – Vesoul 45

Château de Moncley★, Burgundy-Jura.

X **La Vieille Auberge**

1 grande rue – ☎ 03 81 48 51 70 – www.la-vieille-auberge.fr – lavieilleauberge@wanadoo.fr – Fax 03 81 57 62 30 – Closed 24 August-8 September, 28 December-12 January, Friday dinner from November to January, Sunday dinner and Monday

Rest – Menu (€ 18 bi), € 23/48 – Carte € 50/60

◆ Old stone house covered with ivy. Traditional cuisine and regional dishes served in the discreetly rustic dining room.

CUTS – 60 Oise – 305 J3 – pop. 945 – alt. 79 m – ✉ 60400 — 37 C2

Paris 115 – Chauny 16 – Compiègne 26 – Noyon 10 – Soissons 30 – St-Quentin 45

XX **Auberge Le Bois Doré** with rm

5 r. Ramée, D 934 – ☎ 03 44 09 77 66 – www.leboisdore.fr – sarl-le-bois-dore@wanadoo.fr – Fax 03 44 09 79 27 – Closed 15 February-1 March, Tuesday dinner, Sunday dinner and Monday

3 rm – †€ 46 ††€ 50, ☐ € 8 **Rest** – Menu (€ 16), € 20/36 – Carte € 28/42

◆ Building with renovated stone frontage that is over a century old. Traditional cuisine served in a light, simply decorated dining room. Huge banqueting hall upstairs. Some non-smoking rooms for extending the stay.

CUTXAN – 32 Gers – 336 B6 – see Barbotan-les-Thermes

CUVES – 50 Manche – 303 F7 – pop. 360 – alt. 78 m – ✉ 50670 — 32 A2

Paris 334 – Avranches 23 – Domfront 42 – Fougères 47 – St-Lô 54 – Vire 25

XX **Le Moulin de Jean**

north-east: 2 km on the D 48 – ☎ 02 33 48 39 29 – www.lemoulindejean.com – reservations@lemoulindejean.com – Fax 02 33 48 35 32

Rest – Menu (€ 26), € 32/54 – Carte € 32/54

◆ Situated in a bucolic location, this old mill is a harmonious mix of restored stone, parquet flooring and simple, modern decor. Contemporary-style menu. Non-smoking restaurant.

CUVILLY – 60 Oise – 305 H3 – pop. 604 – alt. 78 m – ✉ 60490 — 36 B2

Paris 93 – Compiègne 21 – Amiens 54 – Beauvais 61 – Montdidier 15 – Noyon 32 – Roye 20

XX **L'Auberge Fleurie**

64 rte Flandres, D 1017 – ☎ 03 44 85 06 55 – Fax 03 44 85 06 55 – Closed 17-31 August, 26-31 December, Sunday dinner and Monday

Rest – Menu € 15 (weekdays)/38 – Carte € 40/75

◆ Formerly a post house and then a farmhouse, this creeper-covered restaurant has a rustic dining area set in the old sheepfold and serves traditional meals.

DABISSE – 04 Alpes-de-Haute-Provence – 334 D9 – ✉ 04190 Les Mees — 40 B2

Paris 734 – Digne-les-Bains 34 – Forcalquier 20 – Manosque 27 – Sisteron 30

XXX **Le Vieux Colombier**

rte d'Oraison, 2 km south on D 4 – ☎ 04 92 34 32 32 – www.levieuxcolombier.over-blog.fr – snowak@wanadoo.fr – Fax 04 92 34 34 26 – Closed 1st-15 January, Tuesday dinner October-March, Sunday dinner and Wednesday

Rest – Menu (€ 20 bi), € 30/60 – Carte € 50/65

◆ Dining room in an old farmhouse with exposed beams. Pleasant terrace shaded by two, centuries-old chestnut trees. Traditional cuisine.

DACHSTEIN – 67 Bas-Rhin – **315** J5 – **pop. 1 439 – alt. 160 m** – ✉ **67120** 1 **A1**

Paris 477 – Molsheim 6 – Saverne 28 – Sélestat 40 – Strasbourg 23

Auberge de la Bruche VISA MC AE
– ✆ 03 88 38 14 90 – www.auberge-bruche.com – info@auberge-bruche.com – Fax 03 88 48 81 12 – Closed 2-19 August, 27 December-6 January, Saturday lunch, Sunday dinner and Wednesday
Rest – Menu € 28/70 bi – Carte € 40/56
◆ Head straight for the old watchtower; at its feet flows the Bruche, and beside it, forming a pretty picture, stands this flower-filled and elegantly furnished hotel.

DAGLAN – 24 Dordogne – **337** D3 – **pop. 541 – alt. 101 m** – ✉ **24250** 4 **D2**

Paris 558 – Bordeaux 203 – Cahors 51 – Sarlat-la-Canéda 23

Syndicat d'initiative, le Bourg ✆ 05 53 29 88 84, Fax 05 53 29 88 84

Le Petit Paris VISA MC
in the village – ✆ 05 53 28 41 10 – Fax 05 53 28 41 10 – Open 1st March-14 December and closed Sunday dinner in low season, Saturday lunch and Monday
Rest – *(number of covers limited, pre-book)* Menu (€ 22), € 27/39 – Carte € 45/55
◆ Two rustic style dining rooms - the more comfortable of the two is on the upper floor. Terrace for summer dining. Carefully prepared modern cuisine based on regional produce.

LA DAILLE – 73 Savoie – **333** O5 – **see Val-d'Isère**

DAMBACH-LA-VILLE – 67 Bas-Rhin – **315** I7 – **pop. 1 924** – **alt. 210 m** – ✉ **67650** Alsace-Lorraine 2 **C1**

Paris 443 – Obernai 24 – Saverne 61 – Sélestat 8 – Strasbourg 52

Office de tourisme, 11, place du Marché ✆ 03 88 92 61 00, Fax 03 88 92 47 11

Le Vignoble without rest P VISA MC AE
1 r. de l'Église – ✆ 03 88 92 43 75 – www.hotel-vignoble-alsace.fr – info@hotel-vignoble-alsace.fr – Fax 03 88 92 62 21 – Closed January
7 rm – †€ 58/60 ††€ 60/65, ☕ € 8
◆ Beside the village church, this former barn dating from 1765 offers charming rooms (well sound-proofed) and a warm welcome. Courtyard and small garden.

DAMGAN – 56 Morbihan – **308** P9 – **pop. 1 443** – ✉ **56750** 9 **B3**

Paris 469 – Muzillac 10 – Redon 46 – La Roche-Bernard 25 – Vannes 29

Office de tourisme, Place Alexandre Tiffoche ✆ 02 97 41 11 32, Fax 02.97.41.13.22

De la Plage without rest P VISA MC
38 bd de l'Océan – ✆ 02 97 41 10 07 – www.hotel-morbihan.com – contact@hotel-morbihan.com – Fax 02 97 41 12 82 – Closed 11 November-6 February
17 rm – †€ 65/100 ††€ 65/100, ☕ € 11 – 1 suite
◆ The smiling welcome extended by the owners is irresistible. Most of the rooms command a fine view of the Atlantic. Snacks and a wide choice of salads.

Albatros rest, P VISA MC
1 bd de l'Océan – ✆ 02 97 41 16 85 – www.hotel-albatros-damgan.com – albatros56@wanadoo.fr – Fax 02 97 41 21 34 – Open 15 March-3 November
27 rm – †€ 46/55 ††€ 52/68, ☕ € 8 – ½ P € 53/61
Rest – Menu (€ 12), € 19/42 – Carte € 26/50
◆ This seafront house in a residential neighbourhood is friendly and lively. Most of the rooms enjoy a sea view; all are very well kept. Restaurant with attractive colourful decor and a pleasant view of the sea. Fish menu.

DAMPIERRE-EN-YVELINES – 78 Yvelines – **311** H3 – **101** 31 – **see Paris, Area**

DAMPRICHARD – 25 Doubs – 321 L3 – pop. 1 788 – alt. 825 m – ✉ 25450 17 C2

Paris 505 – Basel 94 – Belfort 64 – Besançon 82 – Montbéliard 47 – Pontarlier 67

Le Lion d'Or

7 pl. du 3ème RTA – ☎ 03 81 44 22 84 – www.hotel-le-lion-dor.com – hotel.damprichard@wanadoo.fr – Fax 03 81 44 23 10 – Closed 24 October-6 November, 15-21 February, Sunday dinner and Monday

Rest – Menu (€ 11), € 14 (weekday lunch), € 22/54 – Carte € 30/61

◆ In the centre of a village bordering Switzerland, a pleasant restaurant (beams and fireplace) serving classic cuisine made with fresh produce. Good choice of wines by the glass.

DANIZY – 02 Aisne – 306 C5 – pop. 553 – alt. 54 m – ✉ 02800 37 C2

Paris 148 – Amiens 111 – Laon 32 – Saint-Quentin 28 – Soissons 53

Domaine le Parc

r. du Quesny – ☎ 03 23 56 55 23 – www.domaineleparc.fr – contact@domaineleparc.fr – Closed 21 December-8 January

5 rm – 🚹€ 65/85 🚹🚹€ 65/85 **Table d'hôte** – Menu € 35 bi

◆ Handsome 18C abode of character standing in magnificent wooded grounds. The rooms are softly lit and classically decorated; some enjoy a view of the Oise valley. The lady of the house's tasty home cooking is greatly appreciated.

DANJOUTIN – 90 Territoire de Belfort – 315 F11 – see Belfort

DANNEMARIE – 68 Haut-Rhin – 315 G11 – pop. 2 259 – alt. 320 m – ✉ 68210 1 A3

Paris 447 – Basel 43 – Belfort 25 – Colmar 58 – Mulhouse 25 – Thann 25

Ritter

(opposite the station) – ☎ 03 89 25 04 30 – restaurant.ritter@wanadoo.fr – Fax 03 89 08 02 34 – Closed 10-24 July, 19-31 December, 16 February-5 March, Monday dinner, Thursday dinner and Tuesday

Rest – Menu € 11 (weekday lunch), € 23/58 bi – Carte € 40/58

◆ The interior of this pretty 1900 house - once the village theatre - is typically Alsatian: a collection of beer mugs and farming implements. Fried carp speciality.

Wach

13 pl. Hôtel-de-Ville – ☎ 03 89 25 00 01 – http://restaurant.wach.free.fr – Fax 03 89 25 00 01 – Closed 3-17 August, 21 December-5 January and Monday

Rest – *(lunch only)* Menu € 13, € 16/35 – Carte € 30/45

◆ The modest façade of this family restaurant is covered in flowers in the summer. The appetising cuisine based on local produce is served with reasonably priced good quality wines.

DAVAYAT – 63 Puy-de-Dôme – 323 F7 – pop. 565 – alt. 369 m – ✉ 63200 Auvergne 5 B2

Paris 402 – Clermont-Ferrand 28 – Cournon-d'Auvergne 29 – Vichy 46

La Maison de la Treille without rest

25 r. de l'Église – ☎ 04 73 63 58 20 – http://honnorat.la.treille.free.fr – honnorat.la.treille@wanadoo.fr

4 rm – 🚹€ 67/83 🚹🚹€ 73/90

◆ The architectural style of this 1810 building draws on Italian neo-classicism. The stylish rooms are in the Orangerie, surrounded by an attractive garden. Tapestry courses available.

Red = Pleasant. Look for the red and symbols.

DAX – 40 Landes – 335 E12 – pop. 20 500 – alt. 12 m – Spa : at St-Paul-lès-Dax : all year – Casinos : La Potinière, and St-Paul-lès-Dax – ✉ 40100 3 **B3**

Atlantic Coast

Paris 727 – Biarritz 61 – Bordeaux 144 – Mont-de-Marsan 54 – Pau 85

Office de tourisme, 11, cours Foch ✆ 05 58 56 86 86, Fax 05 58 56 86 80

DAX

Street	Grid	No.
Aspremont (R. d')	A	2
Augusta (Cours J.)	B	3
Baignots (Allée des)	B	4
Bouvet (Pl. C.)	B	5
Carmes (R. des)	B	6
Carnot (Bd)	A	10
Cazade (R.)	B	12
Chanoine-Bordes (Pl.)	B	13
Chaulet (Av. G.)	AB	14
Clemenceau (Av. G.)	AB	15
Doumer (Av. P.)	A	16
Ducos (Pl. R.)	B	18
Foch (Cours Mar.)	B	19
Francis Plante (Av.)	A	35
Fusillés (R. des)	B	22
Gaulle (Espl. Gén.-de)	B	23
Lorrin (Bd C.)	A	26
Manoir (Bd Y.-du)	AB	28
Milliés-Lacroix (Av. E.)	AB	30
Neuve (R.)	B	31
Pasteur (Cours)	B	34
Sablar (Av. du)	B	37
St-Pierre (Pl.)	B	38
St-Pierre (R.)	B	39
St-Vincent-de-Paul (Av.)	AB	44
St-Vincent (R.)	B	40
Sully (R.)	B	47
Thiers (Pl.)	B	49
Toro (R. du)	B	50
Tuilleries (Av. des)	AB	51
Verdun (Cours de)	B	52
Victor-Hugo (Av.)	AB	54

ST-PAUL-LÈS-DAX

Street	Grid	No.
Foch (R. Mar.)	A	20
Lahillade (R. G.)	A	24
Liberté (Av. de la)	A	25
Loustalot (R. René)	A	27
Résistance (Av. de la)	A	36
St-Vincent-de-Paul (Av.)	A	45
Tambour (R. du)	B	47

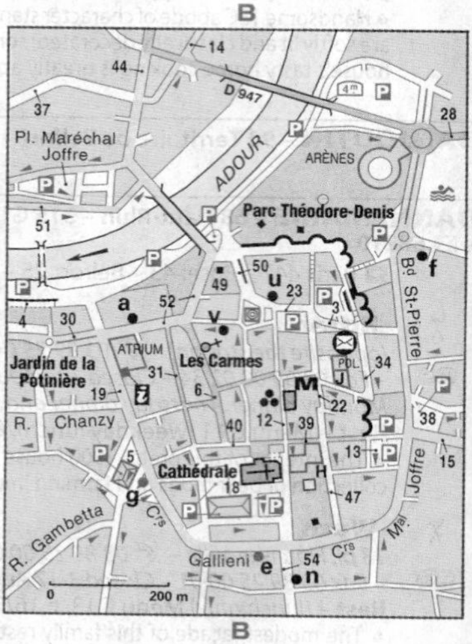

Grand Hôtel Mercure Splendid

cours Verdun – ✆ 05 58 56 70 70 – www.mercure.com – h2148@accor-hotels.com – Fax 05 58 74 76 33 – Closed January and February

100 rm – €82/117 €104/122, ☕ €12 – 6 suites B **a**

Rest – Menu €15 (weekday lunch) – Carte €33/43

◆ The original Art Deco setting has been preciously preserved in the entrance hall, the bar and in the spacious rooms with old-world charm. Renovated spa centre. A magnificent dining hall that some say is reminiscent of the transatlantic liner, Normandie.

Le Grand Hôtel

r. Source – ✆ 05 58 90 53 00 – www.thermes-dax.com – grandhotel@thermesadour.com – Fax 05 58 90 52 88 – Closed 20 December-11 January

128 rm – €71/97 €79/109, ☕ €8 – 8 suites B **f**

Rest – Menu €17/32 – Carte €32/41

◆ This hotel in the heart of town has modern, well-soundproofed rooms that are well equipped. Integrated thermal baths and numerous special events (tea dances). A very spacious dining room mainly used by people taking the waters.

Le Richelieu rm, VISA AE
13 av. V. Hugo – ✆ 05 58 90 49 49 – www.le-richelieu.fr – hotellerichelieu@wanadoo.fr – Fax 05 58 90 80 86 – Closed 25 December-10 January B **n**
30 rm – †€ 60 ††€ 65, ☕ € 8 – ½ P € 90/98
Rest – *(closed Saturday lunch, Sunday dinner and Monday)* Menu € 25 – Carte € 25/45
◆ Set on a busy road, this establishment has a pleasant patio and cosy rooms. The rooms in the annexe are beautifully modern in style. A modern dining room with grey pastel tones and traditional cooking.

La Néhé without rest VISA AE
18 r. de la Fontaine D'eau – ✆ 05 58 90 16 46 – www.hotel-nehe-dax.com – hoteldelanehe@orange.fr – Fax 05 58 90 01 18 – Closed January B **g**
20 rm – †€ 43/46 ††€ 55/63, ☕ € 7
◆ This fully-renovated hotel is in a shopping street very close to the hot water fountain. Spacious and functional rooms fitted out with light-wood furniture.

L'Amphitryon VISA
38 cours Galliéni – ✆ 05 58 74 58 05 – Closed 22 August-3 September, 1st-30 January, Saturday lunch, Sunday dinner and Monday B **e**
Rest – *(number of covers limited, pre-book)* Menu € 22 (weekdays), € 28/40 – Carte € 38/45
◆ The restaurant has been done up from top to toe: immaculate facade and a pleasant dining room with naval decor. Updated regionally sourced cuisine.

Une Cuisine en Ville (Philippe Lagraula) VISA
11 av. G. Clemenceau – ✆ 05 58 90 26 89 – philippe_lagraula@hotmail.com – Fax 05 58 90 26 89 – Closed 15 August-7 September, 2-14 January, Sunday dinner, Monday and Tuesday A **p**
Rest – Menu € 36/60 – Carte approx. € 63
Spec. Foie gras en croque-sandwich. Saint Jacques, potimarron et chanterelles (Oct. to Jan.). Le "Russe" de Dax. **Wines** Jurançon.
◆ Ingenuity reigns in this lovely restaurant, where the refined atmosphere (old stone walls, modern furniture) combines with tasty, personalised cuisine.

La Tête de l'Art VISA AE
pl. Camille-Bouvet – ✆ 05 58 74 00 13 – Closed 23-31 August, Sunday and Monday B **v**
Rest – Menu (€ 19) – Carte € 34/48
◆ Everything contributes to the convivial atmosphere here: the welcoming reception, eclectic rural decor with open kitchen, revisited bistro dishes and terrine specialities.

in St-Paul-lès-Dax – **pop. 12 400** – **alt. 21 m** – ✉ **40990**

Office de tourisme, 68, avenue de la Résistance ✆ 05 58 91 60 01, Fax 05 58 91 97 44

Calicéo rm, rest, VISA AE
355 r. du Centre Aéré, at Lake Christus – ✆ 05 58 90 66 00 – www.hotelcaliceo.com – caliceo@thermesadour.com – Fax 05 58 90 66 64 A **n**
47 rm – †€ 79/92 ††€ 92/104, ☕ € 9,50 – 148 suites – ††€ 111/122
Rest – Menu € 19/28 – Carte € 28/49
◆ Modern hotel with a new spa and treatment area. Most of the bedrooms are suites with elegant and timeless furnishings. The restaurant serves traditional cuisine and health food. Terrace facing Christus lake.

Du Lac rest, VISA AE
allée de Christus – ✆ 05 58 90 60 00 – www.hotel-du-lac-dax.com – hoteldulac@thermesadour.com – Fax 05 58 91 34 88 – Open 1st March-22 November A **t**
209 rm – †€ 65/71 ††€ 73/80, ☕ € 9
Rest *L'Arc-en-Ciel* – ✆ 05 58 90 63 00 – Menu (€ 15), € 18/25 – Carte € 24/38
◆ A well-located imposing hotel and spa complex near the Lac de Christus. Functional rooms, half of which have a loggia. A contemporary decor, waterside setting and classic menu.

XXX **Le Moulin de Poustagnacq**

– ✆ *05 58 91 31 03 – www.moulindepoustagnacq.com – moulindepoustagnacq@orange.fr – Fax 05 58 91 37 97 – Closed autumn half-term holidays, 20-30 December, February holidays, Tuesday lunch, Sunday dinner and Monday* A **r**

Rest – Menu € 29/69 – Carte € 50/65

◆ Former mill on the edge of a wood. Original decoration in the dining room and a terrace beside a pond. Modern cuisine with regional accent.

DEAUVILLE – **14 Calvados** – **303** M3 – **pop. 3 973** – **alt. 2 m** – **Casino** AZ 32 **A3**
– ✉ **14800** Normandy

Paris 202 – Caen 50 – Évreux 101 – Le Havre 44 – Lisieux 30 – Rouen 90

Deauville-St-Gatien: ✆ 02 31 65 65 65, 5 km on the ② BY.

Office de tourisme, place de la Mairie ✆ 02 31 14 40 00, Fax 02 31 88 78 88

New Golf de DeauvilleS : 3 km on D 278, ✆ 02 31 14 24 24

de l'Amirauté Tourgéville Route Départementale 278, S : 4 km on D 278, ✆ 02 31 14 42 00

de Saint-Gatien Saint-Gatien-des-Bois Le Mont Saint Jean, E : 10 km on D 74, ✆ 02 31 65 19 99

Mont Canisy★ 5 km by ④ then 20 mn.

- La corniche normande★★ - La côte fleurie★★

Plan on next page

Normandy-Barrière

38 r. J. Mermoz – ✆ 02 31 98 66 22 – www.lucienbarriere.com – normandy@lucienbarriere.com – Fax 02 31 98 66 23

259 rm – €246/875 €246/875, € 30 – 31 suites AZ **h**

Rest ***La Belle Époque*** – Menu € 55 – Carte € 62/94

◆ The silhouette of the Anglo-Norman manor of this luxury hotel (built in 1912) has become a symbol of the resort. Spacious, stylish and cosy rooms. Fitness facilities. A luxurious Belle Époque style restaurant. Tables laid out in the Norman courtyard in summer.

Royal-Barrière

bd E. Cornuché – ✆ 02 31 98 66 33 – www.lucienbarriere.com – royal@lucienbarriere.com – Fax 02 31 98 66 34 – Open 12 March-1st November

236 rm – €252/748 €252/748, € 30 – 16 suites AZ **y**

Rest ***L'Etrier*** – *(closed at lunch except Saturday and Sunday)* Menu € 67/107 – Carte € 87/135

Rest ***Côté Royal*** – *(dinner only except Saturday, Sunday and public holidays)* Menu € 55 – Carte € 60/92

Spec. Panais, topinambours et carottes jaunes cuisinés à la truffe noire. Matelote au citron et soja, crème basmati et homard au corail. Tuile croustillante, lait aux éclats caramélisés, café corsé, crème glacée aux cacahuètes.

◆ Impressive 1900 hotel popular with the jet set and film stars. Luxuriously appointed rooms, some overlooking the English Channel. The Étrier provides a classical cosy decor (panelling, old photos) and delicious modern cuisine. Luxury hotel atmosphere and traditional menu at the Côté Royal.

L'Augeval without rest

15 av. Hocquart de Turtot – ✆ 02 31 81 13 18 – www.augeval.com – info@augeval.com – Fax 02 31 81 00 40 AZ **d**

40 rm – €68/168 €95/242, € 13 – 2 suites

◆ This attractive Norman manor is near the racecourse and stud farms. It is home to two plush abodes: l'Augeval, nostalgic, and Le Trait d'Union, more modern. Pool and fitness facilities.

81 L'Hôtel rm,

81 av. de la République – ✆ 02 31 14 01 50 – www.81lhotel.com – contact@81lhotel.com – Fax 02 31 87 51 77 AZ **p**

21 rm – €139/190 €190/370, € 14 **Rest** – Menu € 55

◆ Imposing Anglo-Norman manor house (1906). The unusual plush, modern decor mingles period parquet floors and mouldings with silver lacquered furniture, cut glass and reproductions of Lichtenstein. Designer details, chandeliers and grey-plum colour scheme. Up-to-date menu.

DEAUVILLE

Blanc (R. E.) . . . . AZ 4
Colas (R. E.) . . . . AZ 5
Fossorier (R. R.) . . . . ABZ 8
Fracasse (R. A.) . . . . AZ
Gambetta (R.) . . . . BY 9
Gaulle (Av. Gén.-de) . . . . AZ 10
Gontaut-Biron (R.) . . . . AYZ 13
Hoche (R.) . . . . AYZ 20
Le-Hoc (R. D.) . . . . BZ 24
Laplace (R.) . . . . AZ 23
Le Marois (R.) . . . . AZ 25
Mirabeau (R.) . . . . BY 26
Morny (Pl. de) . . . . BZ 28
République (Av. de la) . . . . ABZ

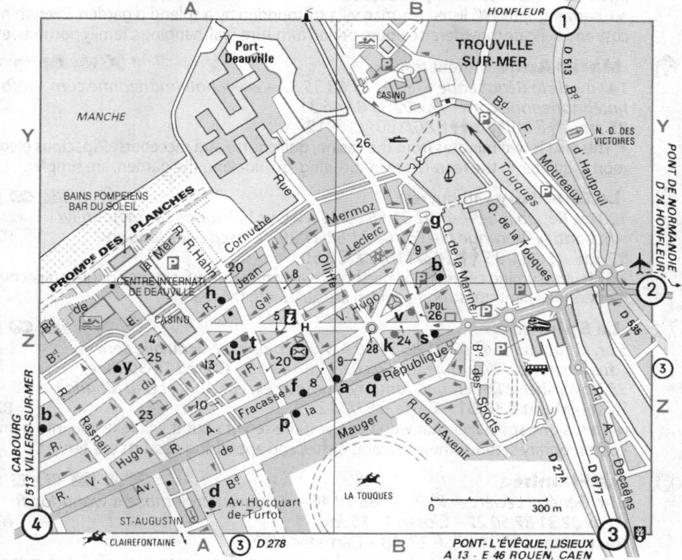

Almoria without rest
37 av. de la République – ✆ 02 31 14 32 32 – www.almoria-deauville.com – info@almoria-deauville.com – Fax 02 31 89 46 99 BZ **q**
60 rm – †€ 71/231 ††€ 72/232, ☕ € 13
♦ Modern comfort and minimalist decor depict this brand new hotel built in a Normandy style. Several guestrooms have direct access to a patio with a summer terrace.

Le Trophée without rest
81 r. Gén. Leclerc – ✆ 02 31 88 45 86 – www.letrophee.com – information@letrophee.com – Fax 02 31 88 07 94 AZ **u**
35 rm – †€ 59/87 ††€ 65/219, ☕ € 13
♦ Stylish modern establishment near the beaches and town centre. The rooms overlook the street or the pool; some have a spa bathtub, most have balconies. Sauna and hammam.

Continental without rest
1 r. Désiré Le Hoc – ✆ 02 31 88 21 06 – www.hotel-continental-deauville.com – info@hotel-continental-deauville.com – Fax 02 31 98 93 67 – Closed 11 November-19 December BZ **s**
42 rm – †€ 61/96 ††€ 61/96, ☕ € 8,50
♦ A busy avenue is the location of this well-kept hotel that pays tribute to Deauville. Regional produce for sale and posters of the American Film Festival in the breakfast room.

Mercure Deauville Hôtel du Yacht Club without rest
2 r. Breney – ✆ 02 31 87 30 00 – www.accor-hotels.com – h2876@accor.com – Fax 02 31 87 05 80 BY **b**
53 rm – †€ 99/183 ††€ 119/203, ☕ € 16
♦ A recently built regional hotel near the marina. Practical rooms (some duplex) decorated on a yachting theme and mainly overlooking the street. Garden-terrace.

Villa Joséphine without rest

23 r. des Villas – 02 31 14 18 00 – www.villajosephine.fr – villajosephine@wanadoo.fr – Fax 02 31 14 18 10 – Closed 5-15 January AZ **b**

9 rm – €110/165 €130/380

◆ Charming, late 19C listed Norman villa surrounded by a splendid garden. Everything is cosy and delicate (powdered colours, period furniture, wall hangings, family portraits, etc.).

Marie-Anne without rest

142 av. de la République – 02 31 88 35 32 – www.hotelmarieanne.com – info@hotelmarieanne.com – Fax 02 31 81 46 31 AZ **f**

25 rm – €80/180 €80/180, €12

◆ This villa is two minutes from the casino, golf course and racecourse. Spacious elegant rooms, quieter to the rear. Those in the wing, overlooking the garden, are simpler.

Le Chantilly without rest

120 av. République – 02 31 88 79 75 – www.123france.com/chantilly/ – hchantilly@orange.fr – Fax 02 31 88 41 29 – Closed 3-20 January BZ **a**

17 rm – €64/95 €83/115, €8,50

◆ This unassuming centrally located hotel is a stone's throw from the Touques racecourse. It offers well-kept guestrooms, which are quieter to the rear.

Le Spinnaker

52 r. Mirabeau – 02 31 88 24 40 – www.spinnaker-deauville.com – fredericlesieur@orange.fr – Fax 02 31 88 43 58 – Closed 15-30 June, 23 November-2 December, January, Tuesday except August and Monday

Rest – Menu €36/51 – Carte €57/112 BZ **v**

◆ This is one spinnaker that won't win you the regatta but it will take you into a pretty contemporary setting where seafood dishes and appetising desserts are served.

La Flambée

81 r. Général Leclerc – 02 31 88 28 46 – restaurant.laflambee@wanadoo.fr – Fax 02 31 87 50 27 – Closed 1 - 15 Jan. AZ **t**

Rest – Menu (€20 bi), €27/48 – Carte €44/69

◆ A cheerful fire burns in the large fireplace where grills are prepared in front of your eyes. Other choices include traditional dishes and lobster from the tank. Brasserie decor.

Augusto Chez Laurent

27 r. Désiré Le Hoc – 02 31 88 34 49 – www.restaurant-augusto.com – augustochezlaurent@orange.fr – Fax 02 31 88 38 88 BZ **k**

Rest – Menu (€17), €35/58 – Carte €38/158

◆ This establishment, known for its lobster and seafood specialities for over 35 years, is forging ahead under the impetus of its new owner. Chic marine decor.

Le Comptoir et la Table

1 quai de la Marine – 02 31 88 92 51 – Fax 02 31 87 34 95 – Closed November, January and Wednesday BY **g**

Rest – Menu (€17) – Carte €40/50

◆ A fine, convivial atmosphere reigns at this marina restaurant with wooden bar and Trouville fresco (1947) on the ceiling. Bistro dishes and vintage wines.

in Touques 2,5 km by ③ – **pop. 3 898 – alt. 10 m – ✉ 14800**

Office de tourisme, place Lemercier 02 31 88 70 93, Fax 02.31.98.06.60

Les Landiers

90 r. Louvel et Brière – 02 31 87 41 08 – www.restaurant-deauville.com – nycgerard@hotmail.com – Fax 02 31 81 90 31 – Closed 22 June-5 July, 1st-7 January, Sunday dinner, Tuesday and Wednesday except school holidays

Rest – Menu (€22), €29/50

◆ A warm welcome, spruce rustic dining rooms, tasty traditional fare and specialities from Eastern Europe: this small restaurant is steeped in charm.

L'Orangeraie

12 quai Monrival – 02 31 81 47 81 – www.lorangeraie-touques.com – isabelle.camillieri@wanadoo.fr – Closed 17-30 November, 6-15 February, Thursday during term time and Wednesday

Rest – Menu €27/45 – Carte €39/86

◆ Generous cuisine that varies with the seasons is served in the minimalist rustic decor of this 15C house. No dessert menu as such, but a tray of tasty delicacies. Pleasant terrace.

in Canapville **6 km by ③ – pop. 237 – alt. 10 m – ✉ 14800**

Le Mont d'Auge without rest

by D 279 and secondary road, St-Gatien road – ✆ 02 31 64 95 17 – www.bedsandbreakfast-france.com – zeniewski@hotmail.com

3 rm – €70/80 €85/95

◆ This half-timbered house is set in quiet countryside. Rustic style spacious rooms. In fine weather, breakfast is served on the terrace leading into the garden.

Auberge du Vieux Tour

on D 677 – ✆ 02 31 65 21 80 – www.levieuxtour.com – le.vieux.tour@free.fr – Fax 02 31 65 03 75 – Closed 30 June-8 July, Christmas holidays, February holiday, Tuesday and Wednesday except from 14 July to 31 August

Rest – Menu € 23 (weekdays)/55 – Carte € 32/66

◆ Thatched roof inn by the main road. The stylish dining room (beams, salmon tinted walls, paintings, red floor tiles) and the terrace on the garden side are peaceful.

in New Golf **3 km South by D 278** - BAZ – **✉ 14800 Deauville**

Du Golf-Barrière

– ✆ 02 31 14 24 00 – www.lucienbarriere.com – hoteldugolfdeauville@lucienbarriere.com – Fax 02 31 14 24 01 – Closed from mid November-end December

178 rm – €185/590 €185/590, € 25 – 9 suites

Rest *Le Lassay* – *(dinner only)* Menu € 42/58 – Carte € 51/72

Rest *Le Club House* – *✆ 02 31 14 24 23 (open 8 March-15 November) (lunch only)* Menu (€ 21), € 26 – Carte € 34/47

◆ Luxury Art Deco hotel on Mount Canisy surrounded by a golf course overlooking the sea and countryside. Spacious rooms with all mod cons. Classic cuisine served in a smart interior, extended by a veranda. Traditional dishes served at midday. Golf pro shop.

South **6 km by D 278 and chemin de l'Orgueil – ✉ 14800 Deauville**

Hostellerie de Tourgéville

– ✆ 02 31 14 48 68 – www.hostellerie-de-tourgeville.fr – info@hostellerie-de-tourgeville.fr – Fax 02 31 14 48 69

19 rm – €130/250 €130/250, € 16 – 6 suites

Rest – *(closed lunch during week except school holidays and bank holidays)* Menu € 39/56 – Carte € 50/75

◆ A delightful Norman manor house in the heart of the Auge woodland. The split or triple-level rooms are named after film stars and each has its own decoration theme (golf, horses, etc.). The delightful country-style dining room gives onto an attractive patio.

at golf de l'Amirauté **7 km South by D 278 – ✉ 14800 Deauville**

Les Chaumes

CD 278 – ✆ 02 31 14 42 00 – www.amiraute.com – golf@amiraute.com – Fax 02 31 88 32 00

Rest – *(closed evenings from Oct. to June) (lunch only)* Menu (€ 23), € 29 – Carte € 41/64

◆ Once a stud farm, now a clubhouse with a panoramic restaurant overlooking the 27-hole golf course adorned with modern sculptures. Simpler bar or terrace formula.

DECAZEVILLE – 12 Aveyron – 338 F3 – pop. 6 294 – alt. 230 m – ✉ 12300 Languedoc-Roussillon-Tarn Gorges

29 **C1**

Paris 605 – Aurillac 64 – Figeac 27 – Rodez 39 – Villefranche-de-Rouergue 39

Office de tourisme, square Jean Segalat ✆ 05 65 43 18 36, Fax 05 65 43 19 89

Moderne et Malpel

16 av. A. Bos, (behind the church) – ✆ 05 65 43 04 33 – Fax 05 65 43 17 17

24 rm – €43 €57, € 7 – ½ P € 50/56

Rest – *(closed Saturday, Sunday and public holidays)* Menu € 16 (weekdays)/29 – Carte € 29/45

◆ Opposite the post office, practical for an overnight stay along the pilgrim trail. Family atmosphere and plainly decorated rooms. Light, half-modern, half-rustic dining room serving robust, regional cuisine.

DECIZE – 58 Nièvre – 319 D11 – pop. 6 456 – alt. 197 m – ✉ 58300 7 B3
Burgundy-Jura

Paris 270 – Châtillon-en-Bazois 34 – Luzy 44 – Moulins 35 – Nevers 34

Office de tourisme, place du Champ de Foire ✆ 03 86 25 27 23, Fax 03 86 77 16 58

Le Charolais
33 bis rte Moulins – ✆ 03 86 25 22 27 – rapiau.franck@neuf.fr – Fax 03 86 25 52 52 – Closed 1-9 January, February holiday, Tuesday from 10 October to 15 June, Sunday dinner and Monday

Rest – Menu € 18/55 – Carte € 45/65

◆ The chef of this contemporary-styled restaurant rustles up dishes in keeping with modern tastes. In fine weather, grilled and plancha dishes are served on the terrace.

LA DÉFENSE – 92 Hauts-de-Seine – 311 J2 – 101 14 – see Paris, Area

DELLE – 90 Territoire de Belfort – 315 G11 – pop. 6 246 – alt. 364 m – ✉ 90100 17 D1

Paris 448 – Besançon 108 – Belfort 25 – Bâle 97 – Mulhouse 62

Office de tourisme, Rue Joachim ✆ 03 84 36 03 06, Fax 03 84 36 68 57

Hostellerie des Remparts
1 pl. de la République – ✆ 03 84 56 32 61 – www.hostellerie-des-remparts.fr – hostelleriedesremparts@wanadoo.fr – Closed in August and in February

Rest – Menu (€ 14), € 27/47 – Carte € 25/35

◆ This former barn built in 1576 against the ramparts, sports a rustic decor enlivened by art exhibitions. Pleasant riverside terrace. Traditional fare.

Undecided between two equivalent establishments?
Within each category,
establishments are classified in our order of preference.

DELME – 57 Moselle – 307 J5 – pop. 859 – alt. 220 m – ✉ 57590 27 C2

Paris 364 – Château-Salins 12 – Metz 33 – Nancy 36 – Pont-à-Mousson 27 – St-Avold 43

Syndicat d'initiative, 33, rue Raymond Poincaré ✆ 03 87 01 37 19, Fax 03 87 01 43 14

A la XIIe Borne
rest, VISA

6 pl. République – ✆ 03 87 01 30 18 – www.12eme-borne.com – info@12eme-borne.com – Fax 03 87 01 38 39 – Closed Sunday dinner and Monday

15 rm – †€ 55/70 ††€ 55/70, ☕ € 8 – ½ P € 60

Rest – Menu (€ 9), € 23/48 – Carte € 52/68

◆ This long building with its pastel-tinted facade and white shutters overlooking the main square is run by four brothers. The rooms are functional and very effectively soundproofed. Traditional cuisine served in a modern setting with restrained decor; calf's head is one of the specialities.

DERCHIGNY – 76 Seine-Maritime – 304 H2 – pop. 476 – alt. 100 m – ✉ 76370 33 D1

Paris 206 – Barentin 64 – Dieppe 10 – Rouen 74

Manoir de Graincourt
10 pl. Ludovic Panel – ✆ 02 35 84 12 88 – www.manoir-de-graincourt.fr – contact@manoir-de-graincourt.fr – Fax 02 35 84 12 88

5 rm ☕ – †€ 82 ††€ 90 **Table d'hôte** – Menu € 37 bi

◆ Renoir stayed in this typically Norman 19C manor house. Themed rooms (family heirlooms and flea market find furniture, fine fabrics, etc) open onto a pretty enclosed garden. Table d'hôte dinner in the lovely rustic kitchen (reservation required).

DESCARTES – 37 Indre-et-Loire – 317 N7 – pop. 3 908 – alt. 50 m – 11 B3
– ✉ 37160 Châteaux of the Loire

Paris 292 – Châteauroux 94 – Châtellerault 24 – Chinon 51 – Loches 32 – Tours 59

Office de tourisme, place Blaise Pascal ✆ 02 47 92 42 20, Fax 02 47 59 72 20

Moderne with rm

15 r. Descartes – ✆ 02 47 59 72 11 – hotel.moderne.fr@wanadoo.fr – Fax 02 47 92 44 90 – Closed 18-26 April, 1-18 January, Monday lunch from mid-April to mid-September, Saturday lunch and Friday from mid-September to mid-April and Sunday dinner

11 rm – †€ 40 ††€ 46, ☕ € 8 – ½ P € 43 **Rest** – Menu € 15/40 – Carte € 35/51

◆ A rustic style restaurant near the house where René Descartes was born, which is now a museum. In summer, tables are laid out on the terrace in the small garden. Traditional dishes. Some simple and practical rooms.

in Buxeuil 3 km west on the D 58 and D 5 - ✉ 37160 Buxeuil

Auberge de Lilette

21 r. Robert-Lecomte, Lilette (86 Vienne) – ✆ 02 47 59 72 22 – www.auberge-lilette.com – auberge.lilette@wanadoo.fr – Fax 02 47 92 93 93 – Closed Sunday dinner in winter and Friday dinner in low season

Rest – Menu (€ 12 bi), € 16/36 – Carte € 27/39

◆ A simple dining area accessible from the village bar-tobacconist. Serves mostly regional dishes at well spaced out tables.

DESVRES – 62 Pas-de-Calais – 301 E3 – pop. 5 118 – alt. 98 m – 30 A2
– ✉ 62240

Paris 263 – Calais 40 – Arras 98 – Boulogne 19

Syndicat d'initiative, 41 bis, rue des Potiers ✆ 03 21 92 09 09, Fax 03 21 92 22 09

Ferme du Moulin aux Draps

rte Crémarest, 1.5 km by D 254E – ✆ 03 21 10 69 59 – hotel-moulinauxdraps.com – moulinauxdraps@orange.fr – Fax 03 21 87 14 56 – Closed 29 December-19 January

20 rm – †€ 85 ††€ 85/115, ☕ € 14 **Rest** – *(dinner only)* Menu € 24/34

◆ This appealing hotel, nestling between peaceful forest and meadows, is steeped in the charm of an ancient family farmhouse. Pleasant rooms.

LES DEUX-ALPES (Alpes de Mont-de-Lans et de Vénosc) – 45 C2
– 38 Isère – 333 J7 – Winter sports : 1 650/3 600 m 7 49 – ✉ 38860
French Alps

Paris 640 – Le Bourg-d'Oisans 26 – Grenoble 78

Office de tourisme, 4, place Deux-Alpes ✆ 04 76 79 22 00, Fax 04 76 79 01 38

des Deux-Alpes Rue des Vikings, E : 2 km, ✆ 04 76 80 52 89

Viewpoints: de la Croix★, des Cîmes★ - Croisière Blanche★★★.

Plan on following page

Chalet Mounier

2 r. de la Chapelle – ✆ 04 76 80 56 90 – www.chalet-mounier.com – doc@chalet-mounier.com – Fax 04 76 79 56 51 – Open 16 June-30 August and 16 December-24 April **n**

42 rm – †€ 154/198 ††€ 180/270, ☕ € 13 – 4 suites – ½ P € 106/180

Rest – *(dinner only) (residents only)*

Rest ***Le P'tit Polyte*** – *(dinner only except Sunday and public holidays)*
Menu (€ 38), € 49/61

Spec. Consommé de queue de bœuf et ravioles. Féra du Léman en croûte de pied de porc et fricassée de cuisses de grenouilles. Pain perdu brioché, crème glacée williamette.

◆ This alpine chalet from 1879 sports a contemporary look: super cosy interior dominated by wood and warm colours in the lounge and (gradually renovated) rooms. Spa. At the P'tit Polyte, inventive food is served in the attractive dining room overlooking the mountain.

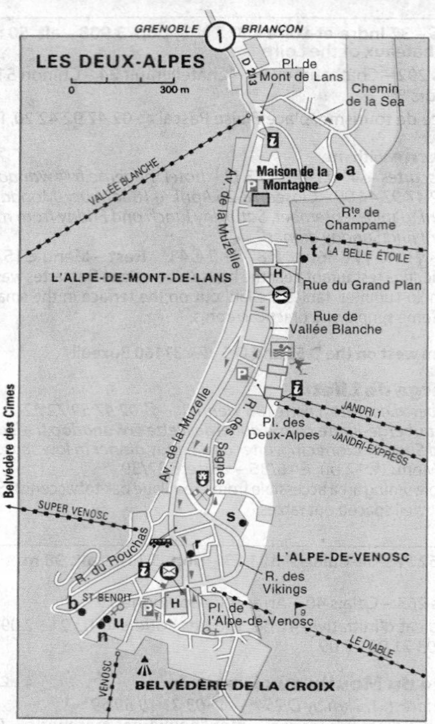

Souleil'Or

10 r. Grand Plan – ✆ 04 76 79 24 69 – www.le-souleil-or.fr
– hotel.le.souleil.or@wanadoo.fr – Fax 04 76 79 20 64 – Open 17 June-31 August and 2 December-20 April **t**

42 rm ☕ – 🚹€ 110/129 🚹🚹€ 139/182 **Rest** – *(dinner only)* Menu € 36

◆ Chalet style hotel with a wooden façade. Gradually renovated rooms with balconies. Comfortable and impeccably looked after establishment. Sauna and steam bath. A restaurant with a terrace by the pool. Traditional dishes and Dauphinois specialities.

Les Mélèzes

– ✆ 04 76 80 50 50 – www.hotelmelezes.com
– reservation@hotelmelezes.com – Fax 04 76 79 20 70
– Open 15 December-26 April **s**

34 rm – 🚹€ 64/73 🚹🚹€ 100/130, ☕ € 11 – 3 suites – ½ P € 83/126
Rest – *(open 20 December-26 April)* Menu € 33/75

◆ At the foot of the ski slopes, this hotel is gradually being redone in a cosy chalet style. Delightful service. Most rooms are south facing. Inviting lounges. Fitness centre, sauna and Jacuzzi. Quite simple food at lunchtime and a set menu in the evening (mountain menu on Tuesdays).

Serre-Palas without rest

13 pl. de l'Alpe de Venosc – ✆ 04 76 80 56 33 – www.hotelserre-palas.fr
– limounier@wanadoo.fr – Fax 04 76 79 04 36 – Open 13 June-30 August, 23 October-2 November and 29 November-30 April **u**

24 rm ☕ – 🚹€ 28/68 🚹🚹€ 40/136

◆ Fifty metres from the Venosc ski lift. Unpretentious rooms (except one, prettily redone in a chalet style), some of which have balconies with views over the Écrins national park.

Le Diable au Coeur
at the top of the Diable cable car – 04 76 79 99 50 – www.lediableaucoeur.com – contact@lediableaucoeur.com – Fax 04 76 80 23 09 – Open 28 June-30 August and 15 December-26 April
Rest – *(pre-book)* Menu € 28 – Carte € 30/45
◆ At the terminus of the Diable cable car (2400m), you'll find this charming mountain restaurant. Find a completely wooden décor, regional specialities and attentive service.

DHUIZON – 41 Loir-et-Cher – 318 G6 – pop. 1 254 – alt. 93 m – ✉ 41220 12 C2

Paris 174 – Beaugency 23 – Blois 29 – Orléans 46 – Romorantin-Lanthenay 27

Auberge du Grand Dauphin with rm
17 pl. St.-Pierre – 02 54 98 31 12 – auberge-grand-dauphin@wanadoo.fr – Fax 02 54 98 37 64 – Closed 1st-20 March, Tuesday from November to March, Sunday dinner and Monday
9 rm – €48 €48, €7 – ½ P €47
Rest – Menu € 16 (weekdays)/38 – Carte € 32/52
◆ This brick faced building in the local style stands near the church. Rustic dining room, traditional cuisine (game in season). Simple rooms overlooking the courtyard.

DIE – 26 Drôme – 332 F5 – pop. 4 376 – alt. 415 m – ✉ 26150 44 B3

French Alps

Paris 623 – Gap 92 – Grenoble 110 – Montélimar 73 – Nyons 77 – Sisteron 103 – Valence 66

Office de tourisme, rue des Jardins 04 75 22 03 03, Fax 04 75 22 40 46

Mosaic★ in the town hall.

Paysages du Diois★★.

Des Alpes without rest
87 r. C. Buffardel – 04 75 22 15 83 – www.hotel-die.com – info@hotel-die.com – Fax 04 69 96 15 83 – Closed January
24 rm – €45/48 €48, €8
◆ This 14C coaching inn has been rebuilt many times and now houses spacious, well-kept rooms that are gradually being renovated.

DIEBOLSHEIM – 67 Bas-Rhin – 315 J7 – pop. 520 – alt. 163 m – ✉ 67230 1 B2

Paris 529 – Strasbourg 44 – Freiburg im Breisgau 59 – Colmar 55 – Offenburg 51

Ambiance Jardin without rest
12 r. de L'Abbé-Wendling – 03 88 74 84 85 – www.ambiance-jardin.com – contact@ambiance-jardin.com
4 rm – €65/75 €75/85
◆ This inviting Alsace abode pays tribute to flowers, roses and gardens. Spacious yet cosy rooms decorated in pastel tones by the proprietress. A little gem!

DIEFFENBACH-AU-VAL – 67 Bas-Rhin – 315 H7 – pop. 630 – alt. 350 m – ✉ 67220 2 C1

Paris 538 – Colmar 33 – Lahr 65 – Strasbourg 53

La Romance without rest
17 r. de Neuve-Église – 03 88 85 67 09 – www.la-romance.net – corinne@la-romance.net – Fax 03 88 57 61 58
5 rm – €83/93 €88/108
◆ This regional-style residence in the upper part of the town offers quiet, colourfully furnished rooms. Two of the rooms have a terrace with views of the valley.

DIEFFENTHAL – 67 Bas-Rhin – 315 I7 – pop. 234 – alt. 185 m – ✉ 67650

2 **C1**

Paris 441 – Lunéville 100 – St-Dié 45 – Sélestat 7 – Strasbourg 54

Le Verger des Châteaux rm, VISA

2 rte Romaine – ☎ 03 88 92 49 13 – www.verger-des-chateau.fr – verger-des-chateaux@villes-et-vignoble.com – Fax 03 88 92 40 99

32 rm – €60/72 €60/120, €9 – ½ P €65

Rest – *(closed Monday lunch)* Menu (€10), €15/30 – Carte €30/58

◆ This imposing building stands by the edge of the famous Alsace vineyards. The somewhat bare rooms are large, with modern furniture. Spacious dining room with restrained decor and a pleasant view overlooking the countryside; traditional food. Winstub with colourful decor.

DIEFMATTEN – 68 Haut-Rhin – 315 G10 – pop. 251 – alt. 300 m – ✉ 68780

1 **A3**

Paris 450 – Belfort 25 – Colmar 48 – Mulhouse 21 – Thann 15

XXX **Auberge du Cheval Blanc** with rm rest, VISA

17 r. Hecken – ☎ 03 89 26 91 08 – www.auchevalblanc.fr – patrick@auchevalblanc.fr – Fax 03 89 26 92 28 – Closed 13-30 July and 11-19 January

8 rm – €54 €54/120, €12

Rest – *(closed Monday and Tuesday except bank holidays)*

Menu (€23 bi), €28/72 – Carte €47/70

◆ This 19C Alsatian house has been redone in a contemporary spirit but without losing its authentic country soul. Splendid view of the park from the rear terrace. Five brand new pleasant apartments; the rooms are older.

DIEPPE – 76 Seine-Maritime – 304 G2 – pop. 33 500 – alt. 6 m – Casino Municipal AY – ✉ 76200 Normandy

33 **D1**

Paris 197 – Abbeville 68 – Caen 176 – Le Havre 111 – Rouen 66

Syndicat d'initiative, pont Jehan Ango ☎ 02 32 14 40 60, Fax 02 32 14 40 61

de Dieppe-Pourville Route de Pourville, W : 2 km om the D 74, ☎ 02 35 84 25 05

St-Jacques church ★ - N.-D.-de-Bon-Secours chapel ≤★ - Château ★ museum (Dieppe ivory★).

Plan on next page

Aguado without rest VISA AE

30 bd Verdun – ☎ 02 35 84 27 00 – www.hoteldieppe.com – chris.bert@aliceadsl.fr – Fax 02 35 06 17 61 BY **s**

56 rm – €55/125 €60/125, €10

◆ The building is on a street leading to the seafront. The well-soundproofed, modern or classic style rooms overlook the beach or the town and harbour.

De l'Europe without rest VISA

63 bd Verdun – ☎ 02 32 90 19 19 – www.hoteldieppe.com – chris.bert@aliceadsl.fr – Fax 02 32 90 19 00 BY **t**

60 rm – €55/110 €70/110, €9

◆ The hotel facade is in wood and concrete. Bright, spacious rooms furnished in wickerwork and facing towards the English Channel. Quiet atmosphere in the bar popular with the locals.

La Villa Florida without rest

24 chemin du Golf, via D 75 – ☎ 02 35 84 40 37 – www.lavillaflorida.com – adn@lavillaflorida.com

4 rm – €68/78 €70/78

◆ This Bed & Breakfast with an oriental atmosphere is a successful conversion of a fine modern architect's house in the residential area. Pleasant garden giving onto the golf course.

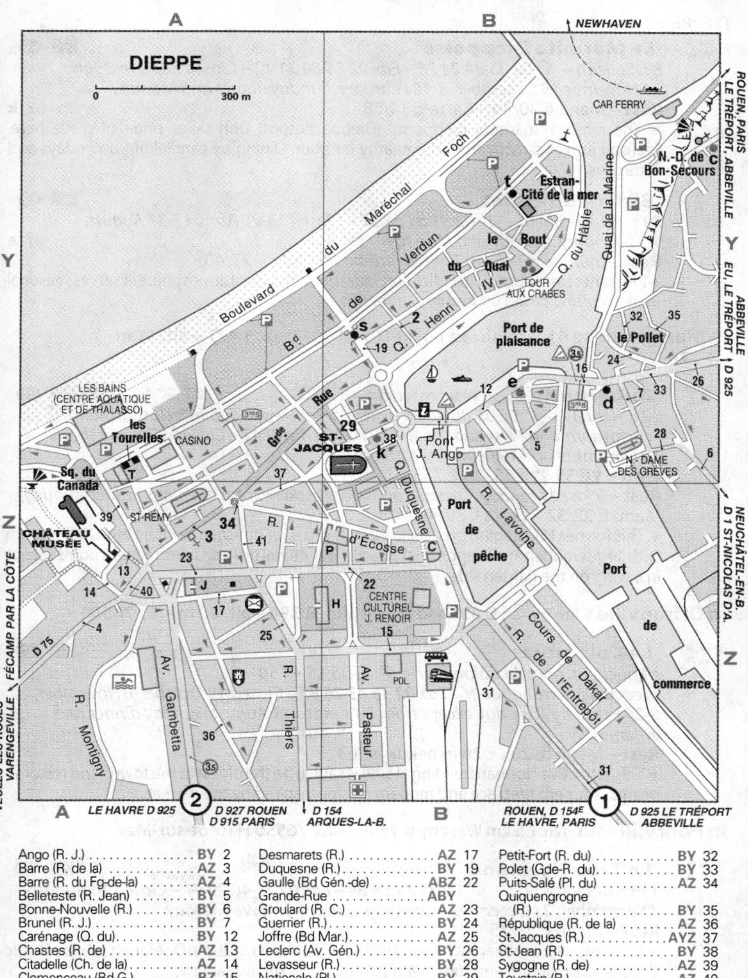

Ango (R. J.)	BY	2	Desmarets (R.)	AZ	17	Petit-Fort (R. du)	BY	32
Barre (R. de la)	AZ	3	Duquesne (R.)	BY	19	Polet (Gde-R. du)	BY	33
Barre (R. du Fg-de-la)	AZ	4	Gaulle (Bd Gén.-de)	ABZ	22	Puits-Salé (Pl. du)	AZ	34
Belleteste (R. Jean)	BY	5	Grande-Rue	ABY		Quiquengrogne (R.)	BY	35
Bonne-Nouvelle (R.)	BY	6	Groulard (R. C.)	AZ	23	République (R. de la)	AZ	36
Brunel (R. J.)	BY	7	Guerrier (R.)	BY	24	St-Jacques (R.)	AYZ	37
Carénage (Q. du)	BY	12	Joffre (Bd Mar.)	AZ	25	St-Jean (R.)	BY	38
Chastes (R. de)	AZ	13	Leclerc (Av. Gén.)	BY	26	Sygogne (R. de)	AZ	39
Citadelle (Ch. de la)	AZ	14	Levasseur (R.)	BY	28	Toustain (R.)	AZ	40
Clemenceau (Bd G.)	BZ	15	Nationale (Pl.)	BY	29	Victor-Hugo (R.)	AZ	41
Colbert (Pont)	BY	16	Normandie-Sussex (Av.)	BZ	31			

Villa des Capucins without rest — VISA MC

11 r. des Capucins – ✆ 02 35 82 16 52 – www.villa-des-capucins.fr – villa.des.capucins@wanadoo.fr – Fax 02 32 90 97 52 BY **d**

5 rm – 🛉€ 60 🛉🛉€ 75

◆ This stylish guesthouse in the Pollet district makes good use of the old priory's outbuildings. Attractive rooms overlooking an enclosed garden. Dining room-kitchen in the old style.

XX **Les Voiles d'Or** — VISA MC AE

2 chemin de la Falaise, near the N.-D.-de-Bon-Secours chapel – ✆ 02 35 84 16 84 – www.lesvoilesdor.fr – Closed 16 November-3 December, Sunday dinner, Monday and Tuesday BY **c**

Rest – *(number of covers limited, pre-book)* Menu € 35 bi (weekday lunch)/52 – Carte € 62/68

◆ Modern restaurant perched on the Pollet cliff, not far from the signal station and chapel of Notre Dame de Bon Secours. Warm, colourful interior with designer furniture.

XX **La Marmite Dieppoise** VISA MC

8 r. St-Jean – ✆ 02 35 84 24 26 – Fax 02 35 84 31 12 – Closed 20 June-3 July, 21 November-9 December, 8-16 February, Sunday dinner and Monday

Rest – Menu € 30/44 – Carte € 34/58 BY **k**

◆ The famous 'marmite dieppoise' (Dieppe hotpot) dish takes pride of place here. Seafood arrives directly from the nearby harbour. Dining by candlelight on Fridays and Saturdays.

X **Bistrot du Pollet** VISA MC

23 r. Tête de Boeuf – ✆ 02 35 84 68 57 – Closed 13-28 April, 17-31 August, 1-11 January, Sunday and Monday BY **e**

Rest – *(number of covers limited, pre-book)* Carte € 25/40

◆ Pleasant seaside bistro on Pollet port island with convivial atmosphere. It serves seasonal market cuisine based on freshly caught fish.

in Martin-Église 6 km southeast on the D 1 - BY 2 – **pop. 1 477 – alt. 11 m – ✉ 76370**

XX **Auberge du Clos Normand** with rm VISA MC

22 r. Henri IV – ✆ 02 35 40 40 40 – http://perso-wanadoo.fr/leclosnormand – leclosnormand2@wanadoo.fr – Fax 02 35 40 40 42 – Closed 19 November-10 December and 19 February-5 March

8 rm – †€ 55 ††€ 65, ☕ € 7

Rest – *(closed Monday, Tuesday and Wednesday except evenings in July-August)* Menu € 22/32 – Carte € 39/46

◆ This former 15C staging post on the banks of a river houses a Norman inn. Dining room with large wooden and Dieppe brick hearth. Traditional dishes. Quiet, refined rooms set out in a wing on the garden side.

in Offranville 6 km by ②, D 927 and D 54 – pop. 3 394 – alt. 80 m – ✉ 76550

XX **Le Colombier** VISA MC

r. Loucheur, parc du Colombier – ✆ 02 35 85 48 50 – lecourski@wanadoo.fr – Fax 02 35 83 76 87 – Closed 19 October-6 November, 8-26 February, Tuesday except from 30 June to 31 August, Sunday dinner and Wednesday

Rest – Menu (€ 20), € 26 (weekdays)/63

◆ This attractive Norman building (1509) is said to be the oldest in the town. Find restored beams, a superb fireplace and modern cuisine inspired by the market.

in Pourville-sur-Mer 5 km West by D 75 AZ – **✉ 76550 Hautot-sur-Mer**

XX **Le Trou Normand** VISA MC

128 r. des Verts Bois – ✆ 02 35 84 59 84 – Fax 02 35 40 29 41 – Closed 16 August-4 September, 23 December-4 January, Sunday and Wednesday

Rest – Menu € 23/35

◆ The inn is near the beach where in 1942 the Canadians landed in Operation Jubilee. Rustic decor and small 'surf and turf' menu based on market availability.

DIEULEFIT – 26 Drôme – 332 D6 – pop. 3 191 – alt. 366 m – ✉ 26220 44 **B3**

Lyon - Rhone Valley

Paris 614 – Crest 30 – Montélimar 29 – Nyons 30 – Orange 58 – Valence 57

Office de tourisme, 1, place Abbé Magnet ✆ 04 75 46 42 49, Fax 04 75 46 36 48

XX **Le Relais du Serre** with rm VISA MC AE

rte de Nyons, 3 km on D 538 – ✆ 04 75 46 43 45 – www.relaisduserre.com – le-relais-du-serre@orange.fr – Fax 04 75 46 40 98 – Closed 5-20 January, Sunday dinner and Monday from September to May

7 rm – †€ 42/48 ††€ 52/70, ☕ € 8 – ½ P € 55/65

Rest – Menu € 13 (weekday lunch), € 22/37 – Carte € 30/80

◆ Pleasant building with a renovated facade on the road to the Lez valley. Colourful dining room embellished by flowers and paintings. Traditional cuisine and game in season.

in Poët-Laval 5 km West by D 540 – pop. 809 – alt. 311 m – ✉ 26160

Site★.

Les Hospitaliers

– ✆ *04 75 46 22 32 – www.hotel-les-hospitaliers.com – contact@hotel-les-hospitaliers.com – Fax 04 75 46 49 99 – Open 21 March-8 November*

20 rm – €78/160 €78/160, €15

Rest – *(closed Monday and Tuesday out of season)*

Menu (€30), €42/55 – Carte €60/76

◆ Rooms in drystone buildings in the old village, and a swimming pool overlooking the valley. Difficult for these Hospitallers to set out on a crusade again! Cuisine with a contemporary touch served in a dining room full of character or on the terrace commanding a panoramic view.

North 9 km by D 538, D 110 and D 245 - ✉ 26460 Truinas

La Bergerie de Féline

Les Charles – ✆ 04 75 49 12 78 – www.labergeriedefeline.com – welcome@labergeriedefeline.com – Closed 20-28 December

5 rm – €130/210 €130/210 **Table d'hôte** – Menu €35 bi/38 bi

◆ This delightful 18C former sheepfold is now home to contemporary rooms. The perfect spot to enjoy the lovely Vercors countryside. Splendid pool, cabin and hammock in the garden. Regional dishes at the table d'hôte in setting which blends authenticity and designer-style.

DIGNE-LES-BAINS 🅿 – 04 Alpes-de-Haute-Provence – 334 F8 41 C2
– pop. 17 600 – alt. 608 m – Spa : early March-early Dec. – ✉ 04000 French Alps

Paris 744 – Aix-en-Provence 109 – Avignon 167 – Cannes 135 – Gap 89

Office de tourisme, place du Tampinet ✆ 04 92 36 62 62, Fax 04 92 32 27 24

de Digne-les-Bains 57 route du Chaffaut, 7 km on the Nice road and D 12, ✆ 04 92 30 58 00

Musée départemental★ B **M²** - N.D.-du-Bourg cathedral ★ - Giant ammonite slabs★ North: 1 km by D 900^A^.

⩤★ of the television relay station.

Plan on next page

Le Grand Paris

19 bd Thiers – ✆ 04 92 31 11 15 – www.hotel-grand-paris.com – info@hotel-grand-paris.com – Fax 04 92 32 32 82 – Open 1st March-30 November A **a**

16 rm – €79/110 €92/144, €17 – 4 suites – ½ P €89/124

Rest – *(closed Monday lunch, Tuesday lunch and Wednesday lunch in low season)* Menu (€26), €33/67 – Carte €58/81

◆ The atmosphere of old France prevails in this former 17C convent. Some rooms have been renovated (modern bathrooms). Birdsong accompanies the traditional cuisine at this restaurant with caged birds at the entrance to the dining room. Shaded terrace.

Central without rest

26 bd Gassendi – ✆ 04 92 31 31 91 – www.lhotel-central.com – webmaster@lhotel-central.com – Fax 04 92 31 49 78 A **t**

20 rm – €33/51 €51, €7

◆ The reception of this little hotel in the capital of the 'Lavender Alps' is to be found on the first floor. Well-kept rooms in rustic Provençal style.

Nice road 2 km by ② and N 85 – ✉ 04000 Digne-les-Bains

Villa Gaïa

rm,

24 rte de Nice – ✆ 04 92 31 21 60 – www.hotel-villagaia-digne.com – hotel.gaia@wanadoo.fr – Fax 04 92 31 20 12 – Open 15 April-30 June and 6 July-21 October

10 rm – €65/102 €72/110, €10

Rest – *(closed 1-11 July and Wednesday) (dinner only) (resident only)* Menu €26

◆ A family atmosphere pervades this welcoming mansion house. Lounges, library, personalised rooms (no TV) and original 'Roman bath' in the tree-filled parkland. Fruit and vegetables play a starring role in the traditional cuisine (dinner).

DIGNE-LES-BAINS

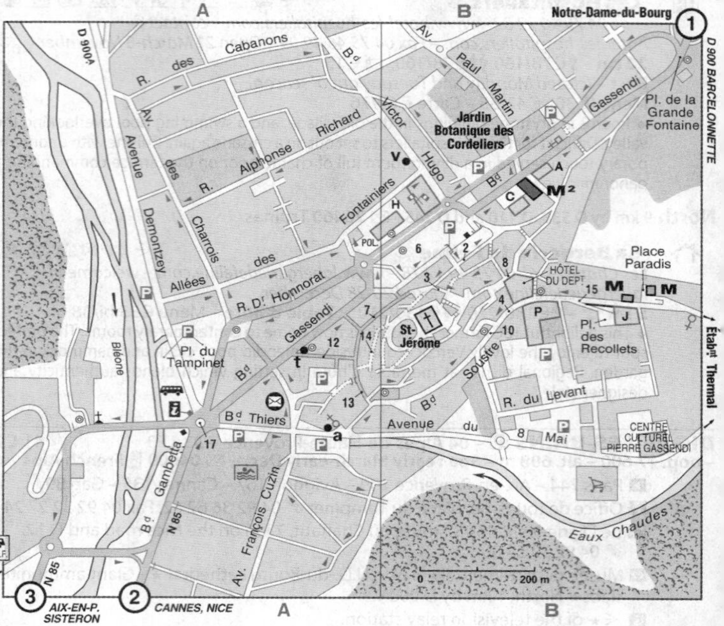

Look out for red symbols, indicating particularly pleasant establishments.

DIGOIN – 71 Saône-et-Loire – **320** D11 – **pop. 8 527** – **alt. 232 m** – ✉ 71160 **Burgundy-Jura** 7 **B3**

Paris 337 – Autun 69 – Charolles 26 – Moulins 57 – Roanne 57 – Vichy 69

Office de tourisme, 8, rue Guilleminot ✆ 03 85 53 00 81, Fax 03 85 53 27 54

De la Gare with rm AC rest, P VISA

79 av. Gén. de Gaulle – ✆ 03 85 53 03 04 – www.hoteldelagare.fr – jean-pierre.mathieu@worldonline.fr – Fax 03 85 53 14 70 – Closed 4 January-5 February, Sunday dinner and Wednesday except July-August

12 rm – †€ 48/50 ††€ 50, ☕ € 8

Rest – Menu € 18 (weekdays)/60 – Carte € 40/75

◆ Traditional type menus with a touch of classicism. The decor is a blend of the Louis XIII style and that of the 1970s. Orange coloured armchairs in the lobby, and rooms with an original combination of antique furnishings.

in Neuzy 4 km Northeast by D 994 – ✉ 71160 Digoin

Le Merle Blanc P VISA

36 rte Gueugnon – ✆ 03 85 53 17 13 – www.lemerleblanc.com – lemerleblanc@wanadoo.fr – Fax 03 85 88 91 71 – Closed Sunday dinner and Monday lunch

15 rm – †€ 37/44 ††€ 44/51, ☕ € 7

Rest – Menu (€ 12), € 16 (weekdays)/42 – Carte € 25/44

◆ This family-run establishment in the centre of Neuzy looks a little like a motel; the facade is framed in a gallery-type colonnade. Rooms with standard furniture. Vast dining room divided up by partitions. A wide choice of traditional dishes on the menu.

in Vigny-les-Paray 9 km northeast by D 994 and D 52 – ✉ 71160

Auberge de Vigny
– ✆ 03 85 81 10 13 – aubergedevigny213@wanadoo.fr – Fax 03 85 81 10 13
– Closed 9-30 October, 2-20 January, Sunday dinner from November to March, Monday and Tuesday
Rest – Menu (€ 18), € 24/34 – Carte € 29/37
◆ New establishment and challenge for the young couple who have taken over this house from 1850 that was formerly a school and town hall. Modern-antique interior, modern menu and south facing terrace-garden.

DIJON Ⓟ – 21 Côte-d'Or – 320 K6 – **pop. 150 800 – Built-up area 236 953 – alt. 245 m** – ✉ **21000** Burgundy-Jura — 8 **D1**

Paris 311 – Auxerre 152 – Besançon 94 – Genève 192 – Lyon 191

Dijon-Bourgogne ✆ 03 80 67 67 67 6 km on the ⑤

Office de tourisme, 34, rue des Forges ✆ 08 92 70 05 58, Fax 03 80 30 90 02

de Dijon Bourgogne Norges-la-Ville Bois de Norges, 15 km on the Langres road, ✆ 03 80 35 71 10

de Quetigny Quetigny Rue du Golf, E : 5 km on D 107, ✆ 03 80 48 95 20

Dijon-Prenois race circuit ✆ 03 80 35 32 22, 16 km by ⑧

Palace of the Burgundian Dukes and States★★ : Musée des Beaux-Arts (Fine Arts Museum)★★ (tombeaux des Ducs de Bourgogne [Tombs of the Dukes of Burgundy]★★★) - Rue des Forges★ - Eglise Notre-Dame (Church of Our Lady)★ - Ceilings★ of the Palais de Justice (Law Courts) DY **J** - Chartreuse de Champmol★ : Puits de Moïse★★★, Portail de la Chapelle★ A - Église St-Michel (St Michael's Church)★ - Jardin de l'Arquebuse★ CY - Rotonda★★ in the Cathédrale St-Bénigne (St Bénigne's Cathedral) - Musée de la Vie bourguignonne (Museum of Burgundian Life)★ DZ **M**[7] - Musée Archéologique (Museum of Archaeology)★ CY **M**[2] - Musée Magnin (Magnin Museum)★ DY **M**[5] - Jardin des Sciences (Science Garden)★ CY **M**[8].

Plans on following pages

Sofitel La Cloche
14 pl. Darcy – ✆ 03 80 30 12 32 – www.hotel-lacloche.com – h1202@accor.com
– Fax 03 80 30 04 15 — CY **f**
64 rm – †€ 175/315 ††€ 210/315, ☕ € 18 – 4 suites
Rest ***Les Jardins de la Cloche*** – Menu (€ 28 bi), € 33/42 – Carte € 63/87
◆ The current building only dates back to the 19C but La Cloche first opened its doors in 1424. Modern, fully refurbished rooms. Cuisine with a contemporary note at the Jardins de la Cloche beneath a glass roof. Attractive terrace.

Hostellerie du Chapeau Rouge (William Frachot)
5 r. Michelet – ✆ 03 80 50 88 88
– www.chapeau-rouge.fr – chapeaurouge@bourgogne.net
– Fax 03 80 50 88 89 — CY **a**
30 rm – †€ 136/155 ††€ 147/164, ☕ € 17 – 2 suites
Rest – (closed 2-17 January) Menu € 42 (lunch), € 48/100 – Carte € 72/86
Spec. Le saumon (Sep. to Dec.). Saint-Pierre cuit à basse température. Le chocolat.
Wines Saint-Aubin, Beaune.
◆ Elegant hostelry opened in 1863. Pleasant, individually decorated rooms – some very contemporary – and a conservatory-style lounge bar with a glass roof. Restaurant renovated in a slightly Japanese style serving delicious, creative cuisine. Good wine list.

Mercure-Centre Clemenceau
22 bd Marne – ✆ 03 80 72 31 13
– www.hotel-mercure-dijon.com – h1227@accor.com
– Fax 03 80 73 61 45 — EX **z**
123 rm – †€ 119/205 ††€ 139/205, ☕ € 15
Rest ***Le Château Bourgogne*** – Menu (€ 28), € 33/52 – Carte € 42/81
◆ Modern building close to the auditorium and the conference and exhibition centres. All the identical rooms are undergoing renovation. Traditional fare, a designer interior and regional wines depict the Château Bourgogne. Poolside terrace.

Philippe Le Bon
18 r. Ste-Anne – ☎ 03 80 30 73 52 – www.hotelphilippelebon.com – hotel-philippe-le-bon@wanadoo.fr – Fax 03 80 30 95 51 DY **p**
32 rm – †€ 83/116 ††€ 97/163, ☕ € 14
Rest *Les Œnophiles* – see restaurant listing
◆ An attractive group of three abodes dating from the 15C, 16C and 17C. Soundproofed non-smoking rooms with functional furniture; some command a fine view of the surrounding Dijon roofs.

Du Nord
pl. Darcy – ☎ 03 80 50 80 50 – www.hotel-nord.fr – contact@hotel-nord.fr – Fax 03 80 50 80 51 – Closed 18 December-4 January CY **w**
27 rm – †€ 82/92 ††€ 92/142, ☕ € 11
Rest *Porte Guillaume* – Menu € 25/40 – Carte € 35/58
◆ This hotel is on the central square, in the lively shopping district of Dijon. The rooms (all non-smoking) are well sound-proofed. Traditional cuisine served in a modernised rustic-style dining room. Wine cellar-bar with a fine stone vaulted ceiling.

Wilson without rest
1 r. de Longvic – ☎ 03 80 66 82 50 – www.wilson-hotel.com – hotelwilson@wanadoo.fr – Fax 03 80 36 41 54 DZ **k**
27 rm – †€ 78/103 ††€ 78/103, ☕ € 12
◆ The rooms in this lovely 17C post house are arranged around an inner courtyard. They are simply decorated with exposed beams. Pleasant fireside breakfast room.

Le Jura without rest
14 av. Mar. Foch – ☎ 03 80 41 61 12 – www.oceaniahotels.com – jura.dijon@oceaniahotels.com – Fax 03 80 41 51 13 CY **r**
76 rm – †€ 132/144 ††€ 132/144, ☕ € 13
◆ This entirely non-smoking 19C hotel is close to the station. It is laid out around a central courtyard, overlooked by half of the rooms. Rustic interior decoration.

Ibis Central
3 pl. Grangier – ☎ 03 80 30 44 00 – www.ibishotel.com – h0654@accor-hotels.com – Fax 03 80 30 77 12 CY **v**
90 rm – †€ 70/78 ††€ 78/90, ☕ € 8,50
Rest *La Rôtisserie* – Menu € 27 – Carte approx. € 45
Rest *Central Place* – Menu (€ 24), € 30 – Carte € 28/75
◆ A convenient hotel to explore the Cité des Grands Ducs, as all the main monuments are close at hand. Spacious, well-soundproofed rooms. The modern Rôtisserie serves spit-roasted meats and regional wines. Simple brasserie fare at the Central Place.

Ibis-Centre Clemenceau without rest
2 av. de Marbotte – ☎ 03 80 74 67 30 – www.ibishotel.com – h5640@accor.com – Fax 03 80 74 67 31 EX **a**
96 rm – †€ 62/82 ††€ 62/82, ☕ € 8
◆ Recent construction near the congress and exhibition centre. Immense lobby-lounge and bar, bright breakfast room and practical, identical rooms.

Victor Hugo without rest
23 r. Fleurs – ☎ 03 80 43 63 45 – www.hotelvictorhugo-dijon.com – hotel.victor.hugo@wanadoo.fr – Fax 03 80 42 13 01 CX **b**
23 rm – †€ 32/40 ††€ 38/50, ☕ € 6
◆ A friendly establishment with tastefully decorated, well-kept and airy rooms. The more spacious rooms overlook the courtyard. There are also two small sitting rooms and a large rustic dining room.

Montigny without rest
8 r. Montigny – ☎ 03 80 30 96 86 – www.hotelmontigny.com – hotel.montigny@wanadoo.fr – Fax 03 80 49 90 36 – Closed 19 December-3 January CY **e**
28 rm – †€ 52/54 ††€ 57/59, ☕ € 8
◆ Hotel conveniently located near the town centre with a private car park. Functional, well soundproofed and faultlessly kept rooms. Courtesy is a hallmark of the service.

DIJON

Street	Grid	No.
Aiguillottes (Bd des)	A	2
Albert-1er (Av.)	A	
Allobroges (Bd des)	A	3
Auxonne (R. d')	B	
Bachelard (Bd Gaston)	A	4
Bellevue (R. de)	A	5
Bertin (Av. J.B.)	B	6
Bourroches (Bd des)	A	
Briand (Av. A.)	B	8
Camus (Av. Albert)	B	12
Castel (Bd du)	A	13
Champollion (Av.)	B	15
Chanoine-Bardy (Imp.)	B	16
Chanoine-Kir (Bd)	A	17
Chateaubriand (R. de)	B	19
Chevreul (R.)	AB	
Chèvre-Morte (Bd de)	A	20
Chicago (Bd de)	B	
Churchill (Bd W.)	B	24
Clomiers (Bd des)	A	26
Concorde (Av. de la)	B	28
Cracovie (R. de)	B	
Dijon (R. de)	A	
Dr-Petitjean (Bd du)	B	
Doumer (Bd Paul)	B	
Drapeau (Av. du)	B	
Dumont (R. Ch.)	AB	
Eiffel (Av. G.)	A	
Einstein (Av. Albert)	A	36
Europe (Bd de l')	B	38
Europe (Rd-Pt de l')	B	40
Faubourg-St-Martin (R. du)	A	
Fauconnet (R. Gén.)	AB	42
Fontaine-des-Suisses (Bd)	B	44
Fontaine-lès-Dijon (R.)	A	43
France-Libre (Pl. de la)	AB	45
Gabriel (Bd)	B	46
Gallieni (Bd Mar.)	AB	48
Gaulle (Crs Gén.-de)	B	50
Gorgets (Bd des)	A	52
Gray (R. de)	B	
Jeanne-d'Arc (Bd)	B	55
Jean-Jaurès (Av.)	A	
Joffre (Bd Mar.)	B	
Jouvence (R. de)	A	
Kennedy (Bd J.)	A	56
Langres (Av. de)	B	
Longvic (R. de)	B	
Magenta (R.)	B	58
Maillard (Bd)	A	60
Malines (R. de)	B	
Mansard (Bd)	B	62
Mayence (R. de)	B	
Mirande (R. de)	B	
Mont-Blanc (Av. du)	B	65
Moulins (R. des)	A	
Moulin (R. Jean)	B	63
Nation (Rd-Pt de la)	B	66
Orfèvres (R. des)	A	68
Ouest (Bd de l')	A	69
Parc (Cours du)	B	70
Pascal (Bd)	B	
Poincaré (Av. R.)	B	71
Pompidou (Rd-Pt Georges)	B	72
Pompidou (Voie Georges)	B	
Pompon (Bd F.)	A	73
Prat (Av. du Colonel)	B	75
Rembrandt (Bd)	B	78
Rolin (Q. Nicolas)	A	79
Roosevelt (Av. F. D.)	B	80
Saint-Exupéry (Pl.)	B	85
Salengro (Pl. R.)	B	
Schuman (Bd Robert)	B	88
Stalingrad (Av. de)	B	
Stearinerie (R. de la)	A	
Strasbourg (Bd de)	B	90
Sully (R.)	B	
Talant (R. de)	A	
Trimolet (Bd)	B	91
Troyes (Bd de)	A	
Université (Bd de l')	B	
Valendons (Bd des)	A	
Valendons (R. des)	A	
Victor-Hugo (Av.)	A	
1er-Consul (Av. du)	A	
8-Mai-1945 (Rd-Pt du)	B	96
26e-Dragons (R. du)	B	98

DIJON

Rue	Carroyage	N°
Adler (Pl. E.)	EZ	
Albert-1er (Av.)	CY	
Arquebuse (R. de l')	CY	
Audra (R.)	CY	
Auxonne (R. d')	EZ	
Barabant (Pl. Henri)	DZ	
Baudin (R. J.-B.)	EYZ	
Berbisey (R.)	CYZ	
Berlier (R.)	DEY	
Bordot (R.)	DZ	
Bossuet (R. et Pl.)	CDY	
Bouhey (Pl. J.)	EX	
Bourg (R. du)	DY	
Briand (Av. A.)	EX	8
Brosses (Bd de)	CY	9
Buffon (R.)	DY	
Cabet (R. P.)	EY	
Carnot (Bd)	DEY	
Castell (Bd du)	CZ	
Cellerier (R. J.)	CX	
Chabot-Charny (R.)	DYZ	
Champagne (Bd de)	EX	14
Charrue (R.)	DY	18
Chouette (R. de la)	DY	21
Clemenceau (Bd G.)	EX	
Colmar (R. de)	EX	
Comte (R. A.)	DY	27
Condorcet (R.)	CY	
Cordeliers (Pl. des)	DY	
Courtépée (R.)	DX	
Darcy (Pl.)	CY	
Daubenton (R.)	CZ	
Davout (R.)	EY	
Devosge (R.)	CDXY	
Diderot (R.)	EY	
Dr-Chaussier (R.)	CY	32
Dubois (Pl. A.)	CY	33
Dumont (R. Ch.)	DZ	
École-de-Droit (R.)	DY	35
Égalité (R. de l')	CX	
Févret (R.)	DZ	
Foch (Av. Mar.)	CY	43
Fontaine-lès-Dijon (R.)	CX	
Forges (R. des)	DY	
Fremiet (R. A.)	DX	
Gagnereaux (R.)	DX	
Garibaldi (Av.)	DX	
Gaulle (Crs Général-de)	DZ	
Godrans (R. des)	DY	51
Grangier (Pl.)	DY	54
Gray (R. de)	EY	
Guillaume-Tell (R.)	CY	
Hôpital (R. de l')	CZ	
Ille (R. de l')	CZ	
Jeannin (R.)	DEY	
Jean-Jaurès (Av.)	CZ	
Jouvence (R. de)	DX	
J.-J.-Rousseau (R.)	DY	
Ledru-Rollin (R.)	EXY	
Libération (Pl. de la)	DY	57
Liberté (R. de la)	CY	
Longvic (R. de)	DEZ	
Magenta (R.)	EZ	58
Manutention (R. de la)	CZ	
Marceau (R.)	DX	
Mariotte (R.)	CY	
Marne (Bd de la)	EX	
Metz (R. de)	EY	
Michelet (R.)	CY	64
Mirande (R. de)	EY	
Monge (R.)	CY	
Montchapet (R. de)	CX	
Mulhouse (R. de)	EXY	
Musette (R.)	DY	
Parmentier (R.)	EX	
Pasteur (R.)	DYZ	
Perrières (R. des)	CY	
Perspective (Pl. de la)	CZ	
Petit-Citeaux (R. du)	CZ	
Petit-Potet (R. du)	DY	71
Piron (R.)	DY	
Préfecture (R. de la)	DY	
Prés.-Wilson (Pl.)	DZ	
Prévert (Pl. J.)	CZ	
Raines (R. du Fg)	CYZ	
Rameau (R.)	DY	77
République (Pl. de la)	DX	
Rolin (Quai N.)	CZ	
Roses (R. des)	CX	
Roussin (R. Amiral)	DY	
Rude (Pl. F.)	DY	
Rude (R. F.)	DY	81
Ste-Anne (R.)	DYZ	
St-Bénigne (Pl.)	CY	82
St-Bernard (Pl.)	DY	83
St-Michel (Pl.)	DY	
Sambin (R.)	DX	
Sévigné (Bd de)	CY	
Suquet (Pl.)	CZ	
Tanneries (Rd-Pt des)	CZ	
Théâtre (Pl. du)	DY	

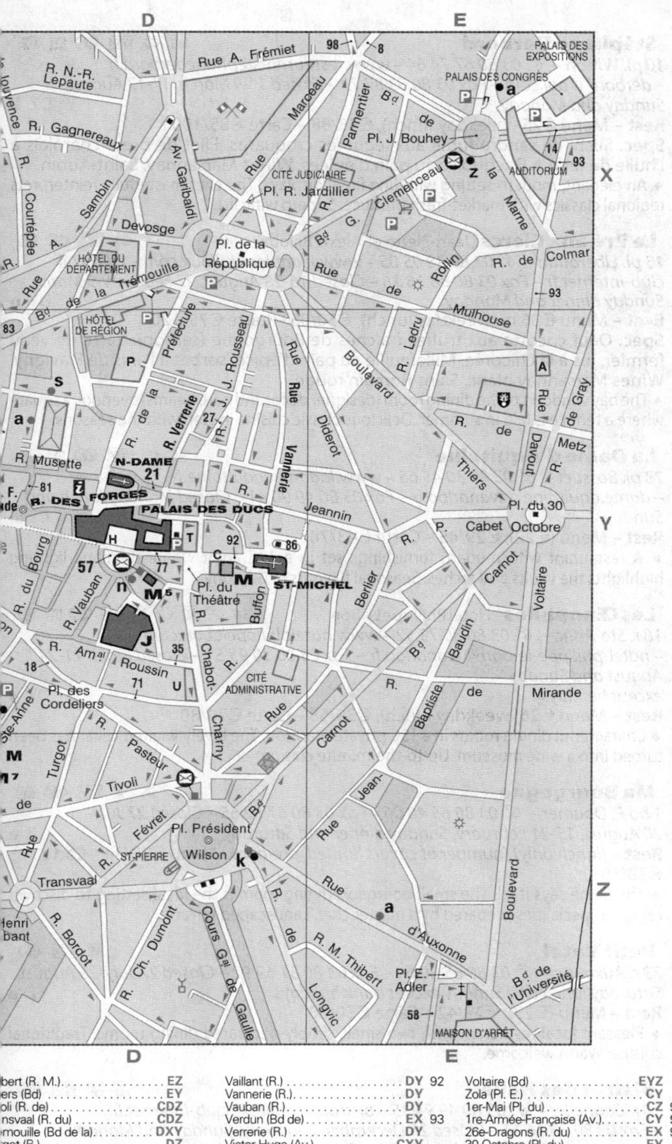
D
E
X
Y
Z
Rue A. Frémiet
98
8
PALAIS DES EXPOSITIONS
PALAIS DES CONGRÈS
a
R. N.-R. Lepaute
Jouvence
R. Gagnereaux
Av. Garibaldi
Rue Marceau
Parmentier
Bd de
Pl. J. Bouhey
14
93
AUDITORIUM
Z
R. Courtépée
Sambin
A.
Rue
CITÉ JUDICIAIRE
Pl. R. Jardillier
Clemenceau
la Marne
Devosge
Bd G.
R.
HÔTEL DU DÉPARTEMENT
Pl. de la République
Rollin
R. de Colmar
Rue de
Rue
Bd de la Trémouille
Mulhouse
93
83
HÔTEL DE RÉGION
Préfecture
J. J. Rousseau
Rue
R. Ledru
Boulevard
P
S
A
R. de la
R. Verrerie
27
J.
Rue Diderot
Rue Vannerie
Rue de Davout
de Gray
a
R. de Thiers
Metz
R. Musette
N-DAME
21
81
F.
R. DES FORGES
PALAIS DES DUCS
R. Jeannin
Pl. du 30 Octobre
P. Cabet
H
T
92
86
C
R. du Bourg
57
77
M
ST-MICHEL
R.
n
M5
Pl. du Théâtre
Buffon
Berlier
Carnot
Voltaire
R. Vauban
R.
J
R. Amal Roussin
35
R. Chabot-Charny
Bd Baudin
18
71
U
CITÉ ADMINISTRATIVE
R.
R. Baptiste de Mirande
Pl. des Cordeliers
Rue
Rue Carnot
Ste-Anne
M
Turgot
Pasteur
Tivoli
de
Fèvret
Bd Jean-
Pl. Président Wilson
ST-PIERRE
Rue
k
Rue
Boulevard
Transvaal
Henri
bant
R. Bordot
R. Ch. Dumont
Cours Gal de Gaulle
R. de Longvic
R. M. Thibert
a
Rue d'Auxonne
Pl. E. Adler
Bd de l'Université
58
MAISON D'ARRÊT

Stéphane Derbord

10 pl. Wilson – 03 80 67 74 64 – www.restaurantstephanederbord.fr – derbord@aol.com – Fax 03 80 63 87 72 – Closed 1st-9 March, 1st-17 August, Sunday and Monday DZ **k**

Rest – Menu € 25 (weekday lunch), € 48/88 – Carte € 85/100

Spec. Sushi de sandre fumé aux légumes croquants. Filet de bœuf charolais à l'huile de raifort. Dacquoise au pain d'épices. **Wines** Marsannay, Saint-Aubin.

◆ An elegant, modern setting with fine floral displays. The chef masterfully reinterprets regional classics with market-fresh produce. Superb wine list.

Le Pré aux Clercs (Jean-Pierre et Alexis Billoux)

13 pl. Libération – 03 80 38 05 05 – www.jeanpierrebilloux.com – billoux@club-internet.fr – Fax 03 80 38 16 16 – Closed 16-28 August, 27 February-9 March, Sunday dinner and Monday DY **n**

Rest – Menu € 36 bi (weekday lunch), € 50/95 – Carte € 75/120

Spec. Oeuf cocotte aux truffes fraîches de Bourgogne (season). Carré de veau fermier, jus à la chicorée. Millefeuille au pain d'épice, sorbet à l'anis de Flavigny. **Wines** Marsannay blanc, Saint-Romain rouge.

◆ The bay windows of the dining room (designer decor and bare beams) overlook a square where a terrace is laid in summer. Delicious classic cuisine in step with the seasons.

La Dame d'Aquitaine

23 pl. Bossuet – 03 80 30 45 65 – www.ladamedaquitaine.fr – dame.aquitaine@wanadoo.fr – Fax 03 80 49 90 41 – Closed Monday lunch and Sunday CY **m**

Rest – Menu (€ 22), € 29/45 – Carte € 43/78

◆ A restaurant with modern furnishings set in a 13C crypt where dramatic lighting highlights the vaults and arches. Seasonal flavours of Gascony.

Les Œnophiles – Hôtel Philippe Le Bon

18 r. Ste-Anne – 03 80 30 73 52 – www.hotelphilippelebon.com – hotel-philippe-le-bon@wanadoo.fr – Fax 03 80 30 95 51 – Closed lunch 11-24 August and Sunday except holidays DY **p**

Rest – Menu € 26 (weekday lunch), € 39/58 – Carte € 70/80

◆ Characterful dining rooms in a 15C private mansion. The lovely vaulted cellar has been turned into a wine museum. Up-to-the-minute cuisine.

Ma Bourgogne

1 bd P. Doumer – 03 80 65 48 06 – Fax 03 80 67 82 65 – Closed 27 July-20 August, 15-21 February, Sunday dinner and Saturday B **e**

Rest – *(lunch only) (number of covers limited, pre-book)* Menu € 22/34 – Carte € 38/58

◆ The name says it all! The small bourgeois dining room is the ideal setting to discover regional specialities prepared by a master chef. Landscaped terrace.

Petit Vatel

73 r. Auxonne – 03 80 65 80 64 – Fax 03 80 31 69 92 – Closed 27 July-20 August, Saturday lunch and Sunday except bank holidays EZ **a**

Rest – Menu (€ 23), € 29/42 – Carte € 50/60

◆ Pleasant local restaurant with two small, simply-decorated dining rooms. Traditional cuisine. Warm welcome.

Bistrot des Halles

10 r. Bannelier – 03 80 49 94 15 – bistrotdeshalles@club-internet.fr – Fax 03 80 38 16 16 – Closed 25 December-2 January, Sunday and Monday

Rest – Menu € 18 (weekday lunch) – Carte € 29/38 DY **s**

◆ Restaurant facing the well-restored covered market. Its popular dishes, rotisserie and slightly theatrical 1900s bistro decor make this a convivial local haunt.

DZ'envies

12 r. Odebert – 03 80 50 09 26 – www.dzenvies.com – Closed Sunday

Rest – Menu (€ 15), € 20/35 – Carte € 35/45 DX **a**

◆ This new restaurant on the market square has a trendy look with a minimalist canteen-style decor (light wood and white tones). Modern, well-priced cuisine.

Chez Septime
11 av. Junot – ✆ 03 80 66 72 98 – goldorak_stef@hotmail.com – Fax 03 80 66 72 98 – Closed 9-20 August, Sunday and Monday B **n**
Rest – Menu (€ 13), € 18 (lunch) – Carte € 30/40
◆ The striking mauve and orange façade is fully in keeping with the contemporary bistro-style interior. Updated repertory and a fine choice of wines by the glass.

at Toison d'Or Park 5 km north by D 974 – ✉ 21000 Dijon

Holiday Inn
1 pl. Marie de Bourgogne – ✆ 03 80 60 46 00 – www.holiday-inn.fr – holiday-inn.dijonfrance@wanadoo.fr – Fax 03 80 72 32 72 B **r**
100 rm – €120/135 €130/140, € 15
Rest – *(closed Saturday lunch, Sunday lunch and lunch on bank holidays)*
Menu (€ 22), € 28/48 – Carte € 36/58
◆ Modern building in the Toison d'Or technology park. Colourful and contemporary interior decor. Fully renovated rooms with designer furniture. Traditional dishes are served in the spacious, modern dining hall.

in Chevigny 9 km via ⑤ and by D 996 – ✉ 21600 Fenay

Le Relais de la Sans Fond
33 rte Dijon, (on the D 996) – ✆ 03 80 36 61 35 – sansfond@aol.com – Fax 03 80 36 94 89 – Closed 20 December-5 January
17 rm – €55/60 €65/70, € 8 – ½ P € 66/71
Rest – *(closed Sunday dinner and Bank Holidays dinner)*
Menu € 16 (weekday lunch), € 26/50 – Carte € 56/63
◆ This is a small, simple, well-kept family-run hotel. The rooms are airy, practical and impeccably looked after. The modern dining rooms and pleasant terrace overlooking the garden serve traditional cuisine.

in Chenôve 6 km by ⑥ – pop. 15 100 – alt. 263 m – ✉ 21300

Quality Hôtel l'Escargotière
120 av. Roland-Carraz – ✆ 03 80 54 04 04 – www.hotel-escargotiere.fr – contact@hotel-escargotiere.fr – Fax 03 80 54 04 05 – Closed 18 December-3 January
41 rm – €62/66 €66/84, € 8,50 – 3 suites
Rest ***La Véranda*** – Menu (€ 21) – Carte € 25/33
◆ The hotel is set along a busy road but all the identical, refurbished rooms are efficiently soundproofed. At La Véranda there is a winter garden atmosphere and a menu of spit-roast dishes, grilled meats and snails.

Le Clos du Roy
35 av. 14-Juillet – ✆ 03 80 51 33 66 – www.restaurant-closduroy.com – clos.du.roy@wanadoo.fr – Fax 03 80 51 36 66 – Closed 3 weeks in August, Wednesday dinner, Sunday dinner and Monday
Rest – Menu (€ 18), € 25/60 – Carte € 51/67
◆ This restaurant with its modern decor is an ideal stopover on the way to the vineyards. Up-to-date cuisine with regional touches, and a fine choice of Burgundy wines.

in Marsannay-la-Côte 8 km by ⑥ – pop. 5 178 – alt. 275 m – ✉ 21160

Office de tourisme, 41, rue de Mazy ✆ 03 80 52 27 73, Fax 03 80 52 30 23

Les Gourmets
8 r. Puits de Têt, (near the church) – ✆ 03 80 52 16 32 – www.les-gourmets.com – detot-lesgourmets@orange.fr – Fax 03 80 52 03 01 – Closed 27 July-11 August, Monday and Tuesday
Rest – Menu (€ 17), € 25/95 – Carte € 58/90
◆ Modern cuisine, faithful to its Burgundy roots. Enjoy the superb regional wine list and the elegant dining room opening onto a terrace in summer. Gourmets are in their element here!

in Talant 4 km – pop. 11 700 – alt. 354 m – ✉ 21240

Viewpoint indicator ≤★.

La Bonbonnière without rest

24 r. Orfèvres, (In the old village) – ✆ 03 80 57 31 95 – www.labonbonnierehotel.fr – labonbonniere@wanadoo.fr – Fax 03 80 57 23 92 – Closed 28 July-15 August and 22 December-4 January

A s

20 rm – †€ 70/80 ††€ 70/95, ☕ € 10

◆ Overlooking the town, this small, family-run hotel commands a fine view of Dijon and Lake Kir. Spacious well-kept rooms and a lovely garden.

in Velars-sur-Ouche 11 km on the ⑦ and A 38 – pop. 1 594 – alt. 280 m – ✉ 21370

L'Auberge Gourmande

17 allée de la Cude – ✆ 03 80 33 62 51 – www.auberge-velars.com – Fax 03 80 33 65 83 – Closed 24 August-17 September, 2-14 January, Sunday dinner, Tuesday and Wednesday

Rest – Menu € 21 (weekdays)/50 – Carte € 30/60

◆ A country inn that lives up to our expectations: warm cosy interior, regional cuisine in keeping with the seasons, and a garden-terrace.

in Prenois 12 km by ⑧ by D 971 and D 104 – pop. 310 – alt. 485 m – ✉ 21370

Auberge de la Charme (David Le Comte et Nicolas Isnard)

12 r. de la Charme – ✆ 03 80 35 32 84 – www.aubergedelacharme.com – contact@aubergedelacharme.com – Fax 03 80 35 34 48 – Closed 21-27 December, Monday and Tuesday

Rest – *(pre-book)* Menu (€ 20 bi), € 27 bi (weekday lunch), € 45/85 – Carte € 75/95

Spec. Oeuf cuit à basse température à la crème de champignons. Paleron de boeuf braisé à la purée d'artichaut. Chocolat cigare au cacao.

◆ In a village with a gourmet reputation, former forge with a contemporary interior. The new owners, tow young couples, combine their talents to produce interesting, inventive cuisine.

Troyes road 4 km by ⑧ – ✉ 21121 Daix

Les Trois Ducs

5 rte de Troyes – ✆ 03 80 56 59 75 – www.eric-briones.com – lestroisducs@gmail.com – Fax 03 80 56 00 16 – Closed 2-23 August, 24 December-5 January, Wednesday dinner from 1 November to 15 March, Saturday lunch, Sunday dinner and Monday

Rest – Menu (€ 22), € 32/115 bi – Carte € 55/70

◆ Comfortable restaurant with a spruce, modern decor enhanced by modern paintings. Cuisine with a contemporary touch. Terrace dining in fine weather.

in Hauteville-lès-Dijon 6 km by ⑧ and D 107^F – pop. 1 076 – alt. 402 m – ✉ 21121

La Musarde with rm

7 r. des Riottes – ✆ 03 80 56 22 82 – www.lamusarde.fr – hotel.rest.lamusarde@wanadoo.fr – Fax 03 80 56 64 40 – Closed 21 December-13 January

11 rm – †€ 51/63 ††€ 57/71, ☕ € 10

Rest – *(closed Tuesday lunch, Sunday dinner and Monday)*
Menu (€ 21 bi), € 28 bi (weekday lunch), € 33/63 – Carte € 47/61

◆ The peaceful green setting of this 19C farmhouse is ideal to while away the hours. The dining room opens onto a lovely summer terrace. Updated cuisine. Simple, well-kept rooms.

We try to be as accurate as possible when giving room rates.
But prices are open to change,
so please check rates when booking.

DINAN ⦅SP⦆ – **22 Côtes-d'Armor** – **309** J4 – **pop. 11 200** – **alt. 92 m** – ✉ **22100** **Brittany** 10 **C2**

- Paris 400 – Rennes 54 – St-Brieuc 61 – St-Malo 32 – Vannes 120
- Office de tourisme, 9, rue du Château ✆ 02 96 87 69 76, Fax 02 96 87 69 77
- La Corbinais Golf Club Saint-Michel-de-Plélan La Corbinais, W : 15 km, ✆ 02 96 27 64 81
- de Saint-Malo Le Tronchet19 km on the Dol-de-Bretagne road, ✆ 02 99 58 96 69
- de Trémereuc Trémereuc 14 rue de Dinan, 11 km on the Dinard road, ✆ 02 96 27 10 40
- Old town ★★: Tour de l'Horloge ✻★★ R, English garden ⩽★★, place des Merciers★ BZ , rue du Jerzual★ BY, - Promenade de la Duchesse-Anne ⩽★, Tour du Gouverneur ⩽★★, Tour Ste-Catherine ⩽★★ - Château★: ✻★.

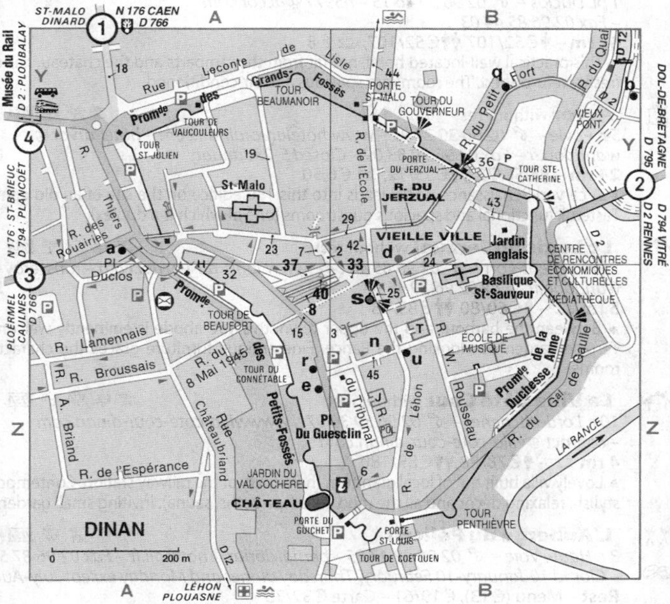

Apport (R. de l')	ABY	2	Garaye (R. Comte de la)	AY	19	Michel (R.)	BY	36
Champ Clos (Pl. du)	ABZ	3	Grande-R.	AY	23	Mittrie (R. de la)	AZ	37
Château (R. du)	BZ	6	Haute-Voie (R.)	BY	24	Petit-Pain (R. du)	AZ	40
Cordeliers (Pl. des)	AY	7	Horloge (R. de l')	BZ	25	Poissonnerie (R. de la)	BY	42
Cordonnerie (R. de la)	AZ	8	Lainerie (R. de la)	BY	29	Rempart (R. du)	BY	43
Ferronerie (R. de la)	AZ	15	Marchix (R. du)	AYZ	32	Ste-Claire (R.)	BZ	45
Gambetta (R.)	AY	18	Merciers (Pl. des)	BYZ	33	St-Malo (R.)	BY	44

Jerzual

26 quai Talards, (at the harbour) – ✆ *02 96 87 02 02*
– *www.bestwesterndinan.fr* – *reservation@bestwesterndinan.fr*
– *Fax 02 96 87 02 03* BY **b**

54 rm – †€ 83/118 ††€ 90/140, ☕ € 14
Rest – Menu (€ 15), € 19/31 – Carte € 27/38

◆ This new hotel, reminiscent of Breton-style cloisters, blends in admirably with the harbour district. The rooms are spacious and modern. Attractive patio with pool. Traditional cuisine served in the all-wood restaurant or on the terrace overlooking the Rance.

Le d'Avaugour without rest
1 pl. du Champ Clos – ✆ 02 96 39 07 49 – www.avaugourhotel.com – contact@avaugourhotel.com – Fax 02 96 85 43 04 – Open 27 February-31 October
24 rm – †€ 80/170 ††€ 80/170, ☕ € 14 AZ **r**
◆ This fine building in local stone is built against the ramparts and its flower-decked garden boasts a tower. Small rooms decorated with personal touches, overlooking the square or greenery.

Le Challonge without rest
29 pl. Duguesclin – ✆ 02 96 87 16 30 – www.hotel-dinan.fr – lechallonge@wanadoo.fr – Fax 02 96 87 16 31 AZ **e**
18 rm – †€ 58/65 ††€ 67/75, ☕ € 8
◆ This town centre building with its long classical façade is warmly welcoming. Comfortable, well-soundproofed rooms with a faintly 'British' atmosphere.

Ibis without rest
1 pl. Duclos – ✆ 02 96 39 46 15 – h5977@accor.com – Fax 02 96 85 44 03 AY **a**
62 rm – †€ 52/107 ††€ 52/107, ☕ € 8
◆ This practical well-located hotel, not far from the ramparts and the château, has been freshly refurbished. The rooms are spacious and air-conditioned.

Arvor without rest
5 r. Pavie – ✆ 02 96 39 21 22 – www.hotelarvordinan.com – hotel-arvor@wanadoo.fr – Fax 02 96 39 83 09 – Closed 5-25 January BZ **u**
24 rm – †€ 50/72 ††€ 53/72, ☕ € 6,50
◆ A carved Renaissance portal leads into this 18C edifice on the site of an old convent. Tasteful, functional and spacious guestrooms (one of which is a duplex).

Le Logis du Jerzual without rest
25 r. du Petit-Fort – ✆ 02 96 85 46 54 – www.logis-du-jerzual.com – ronsseray@wanadoo.fr – Fax 02 96 39 46 94 BY **q**
5 rm ☕ – †€ 60/80 ††€ 85/95
◆ Between the harbour and the upper town, this 15C abode is eminently welcoming. Terrace garden overlooking the Rance. Fine antique furniture graces the characterful rooms.

La Villa Côté Cour without rest
10 r. Lord-Kitchener – ✆ 02 96 39 30 07 – www.villa-cote-cour-dinan.com – contact@villa-cote-cour-dinan.com AY **m**
4 rm ☕ – †€ 78/88 ††€ 85/180
◆ Lovely villa built out of local granite in the vicinity of the railway station. Contemporary, stylish, relaxing décor and all the mod cons (spa baths, sauna). Inviting small garden.

L'Auberge du Pélican
3 r. Haute Voie – ✆ 02 96 39 47 05 – bernardbriat@hotmail.fr – Fax 02 96 87 53 30 – Closed 10 January-10 February, Thursday dinner and Monday except July-August
Rest – Menu (€ 13), € 19/61 – Carte € 32/75 BY **d**
◆ Pleasant restaurant in historic Dinan. The decor of the dining room sports a relaxing blue colour scheme, in tribute to water. Lovely terrace for summer dining. Traditional cuisine and seafood.

Au Coin du Feu
66 r. de Brest, via ③ – ✆ 02 96 85 02 90 – www.coin-du-feu.com – jeanluc.danjou@orange.fr – Fax 02 96 85 03 85 – Closed Sunday dinner and Monday
Rest – Menu € 13 (weekdays), € 23/44 – Carte € 21/51
◆ Traditional, generous and carefully prepared cuisine served in a contemporary style, half-brasserie, half-bistro dining room with open kitchens and wood-fired oven.

Le Cantorbery
6 r. Ste-Claire – ✆ 02 96 39 02 52 – Closed 2 weeks in November, 2 weeks in February and Sunday from October to March BZ **n**
Rest – Menu (€ 13), € 25/38 – Carte € 39/57
◆ In a 17C townhouse, the restaurant specialises in grilled meat cooked in the stone fireplace on the ground floor. Old wood panelling adorns the first floor dining room. Traditional menu.

DINARD – 35 Ille-et-Vilaine – 309 J3 – pop. 10 700 – alt. 25 m – Casino 10 C1
BY – ✉ 35800 Brittany

- Paris 408 – Dinan 22 – Dol-de-Bretagne 31 – Rennes 73 – St-Malo 10
- Dinard-Pleurtuit-St-Malo ✆ 02 99 46 18 46, by ①: 5 km.
- Office de tourisme, 2, boulevard Féart ✆ 02 99 46 94 12, Fax 02 99 88 21 07
- Dinard Golf Saint-Briac-sur-Mer Boulevard de la Houle, W : 7 km, ✆ 02 99 88 32 07
- de Tréméreuc Tréméreuc 14 rue de Dinan, 6 km on the Dinan road, ✆ 02 96 27 10 40
- Pointe du Moulinet ≤★★ - Grande Plage or Plage de l'Écluse★ - Promenade du Clair de Lune★ - Pointe de la Vicomté★★ - La Rance★★ by boat - St-Lunaire: pointe du Décollé ≤★★ and grotte des Sirènes★ 4,5 km by ② - Usine marémotrice de la Rance (wave-powered plant): dike ≤★ Southeast: 4 km.
- Pointe de la Garde Guérin★: ✻★★ by ②: 6 km then 15 mn.

Plan on next page

Grand Hôtel Barrière de Dinard ≤ rm, VISA MC AE
46 av. George V – ✆ 02 99 88 26 26 – www.lucienbarriere.com – grandhoteldinard@lucienbarriere.com – Fax 02 99 88 26 27 – Open 13 March-30 November BY **v**
90 rm – €115/460 €115/460, ☕ €22
Rest *Le Blue B* – *(dinner only)* Menu €39, €54/65 bi – Carte €38/63
Rest *333 Café* – *(lunch only)* Menu (€21 bi) – Carte €32/42
◆ This 19C luxury hotel, on the Clair de Lune seaside promenade, welcomes movie stars during the British Film Festival. Restrained, sophisticated rooms. A lovely sea view from the Blue B. In summertime, the 333 Café serves light snacks on the terrace.

Novotel Thalassa ≤ rm, VISA MC AE
1 av. Château Hébert – ✆ 02 99 16 78 10 – www.accorthalassa.com – H1114@accor.com – Fax 02 99 16 78 29 – Closed 2-25 December AY **r**
106 rm – €160/195 €160/195, ☕ €17
Rest – Menu (€19), €30 – Carte €35/58
◆ A modern complex in a unique setting on St-Énogat's Point. A thalassotherapy centre, beauty parlour and modern rooms with a sea view. Panoramic view over the English Channel, modern decor and diet dishes.

Villa Reine Hortense without rest ≤ VISA MC AE
19 r. Malouine – ✆ 02 99 46 54 31 – www.villa-reine-hortense.com – resa@villa-reine-hortense.com – Fax 02 99 88 15 88 – Open from end March to early October BY **e**
7 rm – €150/245 €150/245, ☕ €16 – 1 suite
◆ The Belle Époque is revived in the decor of this characteristic villa of the Emerald Coast. Luxurious, individually decorated guestrooms, all but one of which overlook the beach.

Mercure Emeraude Plage without rest VISA MC AE
1 bd Albert 1er – ✆ 02 99 46 19 19 – www.hotelemeraudeplage.com – h6956@accor.com – Fax 02 99 46 21 22 BY **a**
47 rm – €85/395 €100/395, ☕ €15
◆ Renovated sea-side hotel near the beach and casino. Practical guestrooms with a travel-themed decor. Cosy lounge and piano-bar.

Crystal without rest ≤ VISA MC AE
15 r. Malouine – ✆ 02 99 46 66 71 – www.crystal-hotel.com – hcrystal@club-internet.fr – Fax 02 99 88 17 73 BY **n**
24 rm – €82/138 €82/138, ☕ €12 – 2 suites
◆ This hotel dating back to the 1970s has spacious, well-kept rooms; those on the street side have been renovated while the others command a view of the beach and the Malouine headland.

La Vallée

6 av. George-V – ✆ 02 99 46 94 00
– www.hoteldelavallee.com – hdlv@wanadoo.fr
– Fax 02 99 88 22 47 – Closed January — BY **g**

24 rm – †€ 70/140 ††€ 70/140, ☕ € 10

Rest – *(closed Sunday dinner and Monday)* Carte € 39/47

◆ Seashore construction built on a former landing stage. Handsome contemporary rooms, decorated in a different colour (rust, turquoise and bright green) depending on the floor. Two modern rooms, one in a loft style overlooking the bay. Fish and seafood menu.

DINARD

Abbé-Langevin (R.) . . . . **AY** 2
Albert-1er (Bd) . . . . **BY** 3
Anciens Combattants (R. des) . . . . **AZ** 5
Barbine (R. de) . . . . **AZ** 7
Boutin (Pl. J.) . . . . **BY** 9
Clemenceau (R. G.) . . . . **BY** 10
Coppinger (R.) . . . . **BY** 12
Corbinais (R. de la) . . . . **AZ** 13
Croix-Guillaume (R.) . . . . **AZ** 15
Douet-Fourche (R. du) . . . . . **AZ** 17
Dunant (R. H.) . . . . **AY** 19
Féart (Bd) . . . . **BYZ**
Français-Libres (R.) . . . . **ABZ** 22
Gaulle (Pl. du Gén.-de) . . . . . **BZ** 25
Giraud (Av. du Gén.) . . . . **BZ** 26
Leclerc (R. Mar.) . . . . **BYZ** 28
Levasseur (R.) . . . . **BY** 29
Lhotelier (Bd) . . . . **AY** 31
Libération (Bd de la) . . . . **AZ** 32
Malouine (R. de la) . . . . **BY** 34
Mettrie (R. de la) . . . . **BZ** 35
Pionnière (R. de la) . . . . **ABY** 38
Prés.-Wilson (Bd) . . . . **BY** 40
Renan (R. E.) . . . . **AY** 43
République (Pl. de la) . . . . . . **BY** 44
St-Lunaire (R. de) . . . . **AY** 48
Vallée (R. de la) . . . . **BYZ** 50
Verney (R. Y.) . . . . **BY** 52

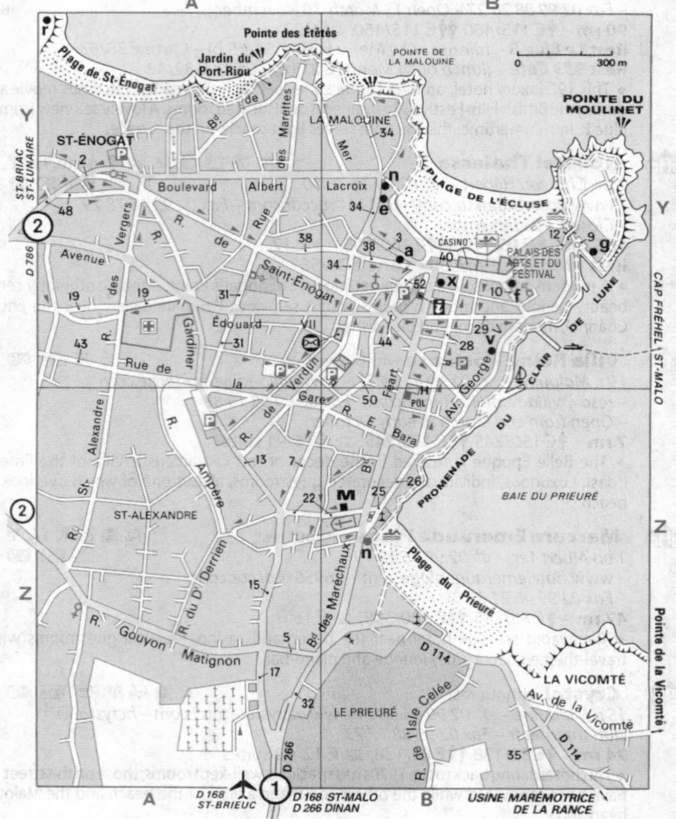

Roche Corneille
4 r. G. Clemenceau – ✆ 02 99 46 14 47 – www.dinard-hotel-roche-corneille.com – roche.corneille@wanadoo.fr – Fax 02 99 46 40 80 BY f
28 rm – €60/165 €60/165, ☕ €13
Rest – *(closed 15 November-31 March except bank holidays, lunch and Monday)* Menu €27/35 – Carte €35/60
◆ Late 19C seaside resort type villa. The interior combines charm and comfort with high quality fixtures and fittings plus wifi access. Seasonal market "surf and turf" cuisine.

La Plage without rest
3 bd Féart – ✆ 02 99 46 14 87 – www.hoteldelaplage-dinard.com – hotel-de-la-plage@wanadoo.fr – Fax 02 99 46 55 52 BY x
18 rm – €65/119 €70/125, ☕ €10
◆ This pleasant hotel promises breakfast on the terrace overlooking Écluse beach and a peaceful night in an attractively-renovated room.

Didier Méril with rm
1 pl. Gén. de Gaulle – ✆ 02 99 46 95 74 – www.restaurant-didier-meril.com – didiermeril@wanadoo.fr – Fax 02 99 16 07 75 – Closed 17 November-2 December BZ n
6 rm – €65/120 €65/160, ☕ €10
Rest – Menu (€22), €29 (weekdays)/75 – Carte €50/65
◆ Oranges and greys, a glazed cellar, designer furniture and, above all, a splendid view of the Prieuré bay: a splendid combination of a modern interior with traditional fare. Small, tastefully decorated rooms.

in St-Lunaire 5 km by ② by D786 – pop. 2 250 – alt. 20 m – ✉ 35800

Office de tourisme, 72, boulevard du Général-de-Gaulle ✆ 02 99 46 31 09, Fax 02 99 46 31 09

Le Décollé
1 Pointe du Décollé – ✆ 02 99 46 01 70 – www.escales-gourmandes.com – Fax 02 99 46 01 70 – Closed 12 November-1st February, Wednesday, Thursday in March, Tuesday except July-August and Monday
Rest – *(pre-book)* Menu (€19), €29/39 – Carte €49/80
◆ The menu here has a steadfast focus on fish and seafood. The restrained decor enhances the magnificent view of the Emerald Coast. Idyllic summer terrace.

DIOU – **36 Indre** – **323** I4 – **see Issoudun**

DISNEYLAND RESORT PARIS – **77 Seine-et-Marne** – **312** F2 – **106** 22 – **see Paris, Area (Marne-la-Vallée)**

DISSAY – **86 Vienne** – **322** I4 – **pop. 2 912** – **alt. 69 m** – ✉ **86130** 39 **C1**
Atlantic Coast

Paris 320 – Châtellerault 19 – Poitiers 16
Office de tourisme, place du 8 Mai 1945 ✆ 05 49 52 34 56, Fax 05 49 62 58 72
Wall paintings★ in the château's chapel.

Le Binjamin
D 910 – ✆ 05 49 52 42 37 – www.binjamin.com – binjamin1@aol.com – Fax 05 49 62 59 06 – Closed Sunday dinner and Monday
Rest – Menu (€17), €25/54
◆ This pleasant family address has undergone a facelift and has a new, contemporary feel. Modern cuisine and brasserie-style set menus.

DIVES-SUR-MER – **14 Calvados** – **303** L4 – **see Cabourg**

A good night's sleep without spending a fortune?
Look for a Bib Hotel.

DIVONNE-LES-BAINS – 01 Ain – 328 J2 – pop. 7 572 – alt. 486 m – Spa : mid March-mid Nov. – Casino – ✉ 01220 Burgundy-Jura

Paris 488 – Bourg-en-Bresse 129 – Genève 18 – Gex 9 – Nyon 9 – Thonon-les-Bains 51

Office de tourisme, rue des Bains ☎ 04 50 20 01 22, Fax 04 50 20 00 40

de Divonne-les-Bains Route de Gex, W : 2 km, ☎ 04 50 40 34 11

de Maison-Blanche ÉchenevexSW : 11 km, ☎ 04 50 42 44 42

Le Grand Hôtel
av. des Thermes – ☎ 04 50 40 34 34 – www.domaine-de-divonne.com – info@domaine-de-divonne.com – Fax 04 50 40 34 24
130 rm – €235/385 €265/385, ☕ €19 – 4 suites
Rest ***La Terrasse*** – *☎ 04 50 40 35 39* – Menu (€35 bi), €39/65 – Carte €46/60
◆ Built in 1931, this luxury hotel stands in a well-tended park. Elegant, spacious guestrooms in three styles: bourgeois, Art Deco or contemporary. Casino and golf course. Summer restaurant in the garden and a conservatory-style dining room.

Château de Divonne rest,
115 r. des Bains – ☎ 04 50 20 00 32 – www.chateau-divonne.com – divonne@grandesetapes.fr – Fax 04 50 20 03 73
26 rm – €135/420 €165/420, ☕ €23 – 6 suites
Rest – Menu (€29), €57, €72/96 – Carte €75/92
◆ A 19C building, constructed on the ruins of an 11C fortified house, surrounded by a splendid park planted with trees. Rooms with personal touches reached via a monumental staircase. Elegant dining room, a panoramic terrace, and cuisine in keeping with current tastes.

La Villa du Lac rm, rm,
93 chemin du Chatelard – ☎ 04 50 20 90 00 – www.lavilladulac.com – info@lavilladulac.com – Fax 04 50 99 40 00
90 rm – €139/185 €139/185, ☕ €14
Rest – Menu (€24) – Carte €31/40
◆ A brand new complex in a quiet location between lake and town. Contemporary style bedrooms with balconies. Hi-tech meeting rooms and a fully equipped spa. Traditional cuisine served in a contemporary-style dining room or on the terrace overlooking the lake.

Le Jura without rest
54 r. d'Arbère – ☎ 04 50 20 05 95 – www.hotel-divonne.com – reservation@hotellejura.com – Fax 04 50 20 21 21
29 rm – €64/122 €71/129, ☕ €10
◆ Family-run hotel with well-kept rooms. Those in the wing are new (modern furniture) and have terraces. Breakfast served on a veranda overlooking the garden.

Le Rectiligne
2981 rte du Lac – ☎ 04 50 20 06 13 – www.lerectiligne.fr – lerectiligne@residencedulac.fr – Fax 04 50 20 53 81 – Closed Sunday and Monday from September to mid-May
Rest – Menu (€23), €39/63 – Carte €53/67
◆ Modern, white establishment with restaurant and terrace overlooking the lake. The look is decidedly minimalist (pastel colours, water wall). Tasty, modern cuisine.

Le Pavillon du Golf
av. des Thermes – ☎ 04 50 40 34 13 – www.domaine-de-divonne.com – Fax 04 50 40 34 24 – Closed 20 December-6 February, Monday and Tuesday off season
Rest – Menu €24 (weekday lunch), €40/55 – Carte €40/52
◆ An old farmhouse next to a golf course. The refurbished dining room is bright and quiet (large fireplace). Charming terrace. Appetising, traditional menu.

DIZY – 51 Marne – 306 F8 – see Épernay

DOLANCOURT – 10 Aube – 313 H4 – pop. 145 – alt. 112 m – ✉ 10200 13 B3

Paris 229 – Châlons-en-Champagne 92 – Saint-Dizier 63 – Troyes 45

Moulin du Landion

5 r. St-Léger – ✆ 03 25 27 92 17 – www.moulindulandion.com – contact@moulindulandion.com – Fax 03 25 27 94 44 – Closed 4-24 January

16 rm – €82/90 €82/90, €11 – ½ P €76/80

Rest – Menu €28/39 – Carte €40/60

◆ Here, an entire family will bend over backwards to please you! The rooms have been renovated, with new bathrooms, and have balconies facing either the Landion river or the park. The restaurant has been set up in the old mill dating back to 1872. Traditional menus.

Your opinions are important to us:
please write and let us know about your discoveries
and experiences – good and bad!

DOLE – 39 Jura – 321 C4 – pop. 23 900 – alt. 220 m – ✉ 39100 16 B2

Burgundy-Jura

Paris 363 – Beaune 65 – Besançon 55 – Dijon 50 – Lons-le-Saunier 57

Office de tourisme, 6, place Grévy ✆ 03 84 72 11 22, Fax 03 84 82 49 27

Public du Val d'Amour Parcey Chemin du Camping, S : 9 km on D 405 and N 5, ✆ 03 84 71 04 23

Old Dole★★ BZ : Notre-Dame collegiate church ★ - Wrought-iron★ railings of St-Jean-l'Evangéliste church AZ - Le musée des Beaux-Arts★.

Fôret de Chaux★.

Plan on following page

La Cloche without rest

1 pl. Grévy – ✆ 03 84 82 06 06 – www.la-cloche.fr – lacloche.hotel@wanadoo.fr – Fax 03 84 72 73 82 – Closed 24 December-2 January BY **v**

28 rm – €60 €70, €8,50

◆ Stendhal is said to have stayed in this old house near the Cours St-Mauris. The rooms are spacious and are gradually being redecorated. Sauna.

La Chaumière (Joël Césari) with rm

346 av. Mar. Juin, 3 km via ③ – ✆ 03 84 70 72 40 – www.la-chaumiere.info.com – lachaumiere.dole@wanadoo.fr – Fax 03 84 79 25 60 – Closed 20 December-5 January, Sunday (except hotel in July-August), Monday lunch and Saturday lunch

19 rm – €70/120 €80/120, €15

Rest – Menu (€20 bi), €33 (weekdays)/78 – Carte €60/70

Spec. Moules de bouchot, carottes reconstituées et pistaches caramélisées au curry (June to Oct.). Ris de veau crevette-crevette et lait caillé à l'hysope. Crème brûlée au cumin, framboises au sucre et sorbet carotte-gingembre (July to Oct.).

Wines Côtes du Jura, Arbois.

◆ This establishment is decorated with a skilled balance of modernity and local tradition. Inventive recipes made with regional sourced produce and a fine selection of regional wines.

La Romanée

13 r. Vieilles Boucheries – ✆ 03 84 79 19 05 – la-romanee.franchini@wanadoo.fr – Fax 03 84 79 26 97 – Closed Sunday dinner and Wednesday BZ **n**

Rest – Menu (€14), €19/50 – Carte €30/54

◆ The meat hooks from this former butcher's shop dating back to 1717 adorn the vaulted dining room. Terrace surrounded by shrubs and flowers. Traditional cuisine.

Le Grévy

2 av. Eisenhower – ✆ 03 84 82 44 42 – Fax 03 84 82 44 42 – Closed 1-21 August, 24 December-1 January, Saturday and Sunday BY **v**

Rest – Menu €15 (weekday lunch) – Carte €30/50

◆ Minimal decor, leather wall seats and checked tablecloths confirm the bistro feel in this little establishment serving Lyonnais style dishes.

DOLE

Arènes (R. des) . . . . ABZ
Besançon (R. de) . . . . BYZ
Béthouart (R. du Gén.) . . . . . BZ 2
Boyvin (R.) . . . . BZ 4
Chifflot (R. L.) . . . . AZ 5
Duhamel (Av. J) . . . . AZ 6
Gouvernement (R. du) . . . . . BY 9
Grande-Rue . . . . BZ 10
Jean-Jaurès (Av.) . . . . BY 13
Juin (Av. du Mar.) . . . . BZ 14
Lattre de Tassigny (Av. du Mar.de) . . . . BY 15
Messageries (R. des) . . . . . AY 16
Nationale, Charles-de-Gaulle (Pl.) . . . . BZ 17
Parlement (R. du) . . . . BZ 18
Rockefeller (R. J.) . . . . BY 21
Sous-Préfecture (R. de la) . . . . BY 22

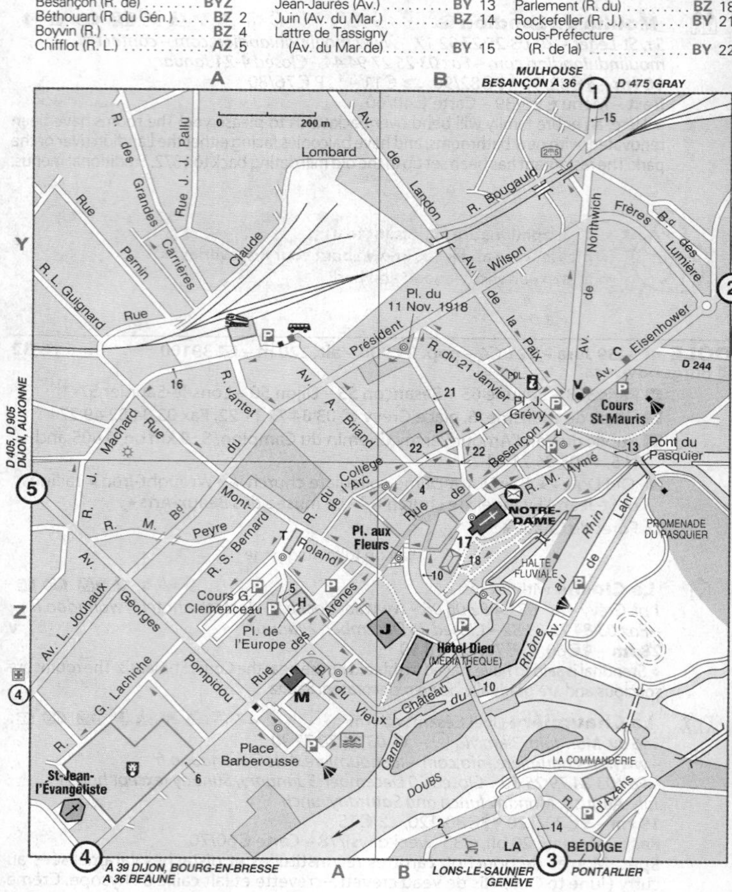

in Rochefort-sur-Nenon 7 km by ② by D 673 – pop. 580 – alt. 210 m – ✉ 39700

Fernoux-Coutenet
r. Barbière – ✆ 03 84 70 60 45
– hotelfernouxcoutenet@wanadoo.fr
– Fax 03 84 70 50 89
– Closed 18 December-10 January and Sunday dinner from October to April
20 rm – †€ 55/57 ††€ 58/60, ☕ € 8,50
Rest – *(closed Saturday lunch and Sunday dinner from October to June)*
Menu (€ 13), € 16 (weekday lunch), € 20/37 – Carte € 23/47
◆ Revamped yet in keeping with its heritage, this family hotel also has a café. Simple accommodation and buffet breakfast. Three rustic dining rooms, one vaulted, serving unpretentious traditional cuisine.

in Parcey 8 km by ③ Lons-le-Saunier road – pop. 918 – alt. 197 m – ✉ 39100

XX **Les Jardins Fleuris**
35 Route Nationale 5 – ✆ 03 84 71 04 84 – lesjardinsfleuris39@orange.fr – Fax 03 84 71 09 43 – Closed 8-20 July, 11 November-2 December, Sunday dinner and Tuesday
Rest – Menu € 17/45 – Carte € 28/49
◆ A simple yet elegant dining room in this stone built village house with pleasant flowered terrace to the rear. Traditional menu with personal touches.

in Sampans 6.5 km north by ① – pop. 777 – alt. 222 m – ✉ 39100

XXX **Château du Mont Joly** (Romuald Fassenet) with rm
6 r. du Mont-Joly – ✆ 03 84 82 43 43 — rest, AC rest,
– www.chateaumontjoly.com – reservation@chateaumontjoly.com – Fax 03 84 79 28 07 – Closed 20-30 April, 1st-15 January, Tuesday and Wednesday except dinner in July-August
7 rm – †€ 90/140 ††€ 90/200, ☕ € 14
Rest – Menu € 30 (weekday lunch), € 35 € bi/100 bi – Carte € 65/85
Spec. Escargots du Jura poêlés aux chanterelles, émulsion au lait d'absinthe. Volaille de Bresse façon "percée du vin jaune". Soufflé aux châtaignes (autumn-winter). **Wines** Côtes du Jura.
◆ This attractive 18C residence in extensive grounds with a swimming pool has a pleasant contemporary dining room with large windows overlooking the garden. Up-to-date cuisine. Comfortable guestrooms in modern style.

DOLUS-D'OLERON – 17 Charente-Maritime – 324 C4 – see île d'Oléron

DOMFRONT – 61 Orne – 310 F3 – pop. 3 995 – alt. 185 m – ✉ 61700 32 B3

Normandy

Paris 250 – Alençon 62 – Argentan 55 – Avranches 65 – Fougères 55 – Mayenne 34 – Vire 41

Office de tourisme, 12, place de la Roirie ✆ 02 33 38 53 97, Fax 02 33 37 40 27

Site★ - Old town ★ - N.-D-sur-l'Eau church ★ - Jardin du donjon ❋★ - Croix du Faubourg ❋★.

XX **L'Auberge du Grandgousier**
1 pl. de la Liberté, (near the post office) – ✆ 02 33 38 97 17 – poupart.sebastien@9business.fr – Closed 5-20 October, Monday dinner, Wednesday dinner except July-August and Thursday
Rest – Menu € 19/57 – Carte € 35/70
◆ This elegant house nestles in the heart of the medieval city. Stonewalls and a superb Rabelais-period fireplace depict the warm interior. Regional cuisine.

DOMFRONT-EN-CHAMPAGNE – 72 Sarthe – 310 J6 – pop. 936 – alt. 131 m – ✉ 72240 35 C1

Paris 216 – Alençon 54 – Laval 77 – Le Mans 20 – Mayenne 55

XX **Midi**
33 r. du Mans, D 304 – ✆ 02 43 20 52 04 – www.restaurantdumidi.com – jeanluc-haudry@orange.fr – Fax 02 43 20 56 03 – Closed 15-31 August, 15 February-15 March, Monday, Tuesday and dinner except Friday and Saturday
Rest – Menu € 13 (weekday lunch), € 19/35 – Carte approx. € 31
◆ Small village inn with a colourful dining room furnished in a modern style. The well-spaced out tables bring the promise of intimacy. Cuisine in keeping with current tastes.

DOMMARTEMONT – 54 Meurthe-et-Moselle – 307 I6 – see Nancy

DOMME – 24 Dordogne – 329 I7 – pop. 1 008 – alt. 250 m – ✉ 24250 4 D1

Dordogne-Berry-Limousin

Paris 538 – Sarlat-la-Canéda 12 – Cahors 51 – Fumel 50 – Gourdon 20 – Périgueux 76

Office de tourisme, place de la Halle ✆ 05 53 31 71 00, Fax 05 53 31 71 09

La bastide★: ❋★★★.

L'Esplanade

2 r. Pontcarral – ✆ 05 53 28 31 41 – www.esplanade-perigord.com – esplanade.domme@wanadoo.fr – Fax 05 53 28 49 92 – Open 14 March-2 November
15 rm – †€ 72/83 ††€ 83/150, ☕ € 13
Rest – *(closed Saturday lunch March-April, Monday except dinner May-September and Wednesday lunch)* Menu € 40/95 – Carte € 50/70
◆ Périgord-style dwelling next to the walled town, overlooking the Dordogne Valley. Elegant rooms, some of which have lovely views. An elegant dining room offering a lovely panoramic view and hearty traditional dishes.

DOMPAIRE – 88 Vosges – 314 F3 – pop. 967 – alt. 300 m – ✉ 88270 26 B3

Paris 366 – Épinal 21 – Luxeuil-les-Bains 61 – Nancy 64 – Neufchâteau 56 – Vittel 24

Le Commerce with rm

pl. Gén. Leclerc – ✆ 03 29 36 50 28 – le-commerce190@orange.fr – Fax 03 29 36 66 12 – Closed 22 December-12 January, Sunday dinner except hotel and Monday
7 rm – †€ 39 ††€ 41/44, ☕ € 6,50 – ½ P € 34/38
Rest – Menu € 13 (weekdays)/33 – Carte € 30/40
◆ Modern dining room, whose large bay window overlooks the garden. Traditional cuisine with a regional twist. Simple, spacious rooms.

DOMPIERRE-SUR-BESBRE – 03 Allier – 326 J3 – pop. 3 307 – alt. 234 m – ✉ 03290 6 C1

Paris 324 – Bourbon-Lancy 19 – Decize 46 – Digoin 27 – Lapalisse 36 – Moulins 31

Office de tourisme, 145, Grande Rue ✆ 04 70 34 61 31, Fax 04 70 34 27 16

Auberge de l'Olive with rm

av. de la Gare – ✆ 04 70 34 51 87 – www.auberge-olive.fr – contact@auberge-olive.fr – Fax 04 70 34 61 68 – Closed 25 September-9 October, Sunday dinner from November to March and Friday except July-August
17 rm – †€ 50/56 ††€ 50/56, ☕ € 7
Rest – Menu € 20 (weekdays)/48 – Carte € 33/50
◆ Two dining areas, one country-style, the other modern with a veranda. Traditional recipes with a contemporary touch. Just two turns of the Ferris wheel away from the Pal amusement park, this inn offers refurbished, rustic-style rooms; those in the annexe are more modern.

DOMPIERRE-SUR-VEYLE – 01 Ain – 328 E4 – pop. 968 – alt. 285 m – ✉ 01240 44 B1

Paris 439 – Belley 70 – Bourg-en-Bresse 18 – Lyon 58 – Mâcon 54 – Nantua 47

L'Auberge de Dompierre

7 r. des Ecoles – ✆ 04 74 30 31 19 – aubergededompierre.com – aubergededompierresurveyle@orange.fr – Closed 31 August-16 September, 22-30 December, February holidays, dinner from Monday to Friday and Wednesday
Rest – *(pre-book)* Menu (€ 12 bi), € 24/38
◆ Village restaurant on the church square. Tastefully refurbished dining room serving Dombes specialities. The daily special is available in the bar.

DONNAZAC – 81 Tarn – 338 D7 – see Cahuzac-sur-Vère

DONON (COL) – 67 Bas-Rhin – 315 G5 – see Col du Donon

DONZENAC – 19 Corrèze – 329 K4 – pop. 2 310 – alt. 204 m – ✉ 19270 24 B3

Dordogne-Berry-Limousin

Paris 469 – Brive-la-Gaillarde 11 – Limoges 81 – Tulle 27 – Uzerche 26

Office de tourisme, 2, rue des Pénitents ✆ 05 55 85 65 35, Fax 05 55 85 72 30

Les Pans de Travassac ★.

Northeast **On D 920, near exit 47 A20, dir. Sadroc**

Relais du Bas Limousin

VISA MC AE

at 6 km – ✆ 05 55 84 52 06 – www.relaisbaslimousin.fr – contact@relaisbaslimousin.fr – Fax 05 55 84 51 41 – Closed 25 October-8 November, 3-11 January, Sunday evening except in July-August and Monday lunch

22 rm – †€ 54/64 ††€ 64/76, ☕ € 9 – ½ P € 59/69

Rest – Menu (€ 15), € 27/42 – Carte € 40/55

◆ This regional style inn is set back from the main road. Individually styled guestrooms. Truly charming welcome. A rustic dining area and veranda, overlooking the garden and pool. Traditional fare.

DONZY – 58 Nièvre – 319 B7 – pop. 1 637 – alt. 188 m – ✉ 58220 7 A2

Burgundy-Jura

Paris 203 – Auxerre 66 – Bourges 73 – Clamecy 39 – Cosne-sur-Loire 19 – Nevers 50

Office de tourisme, 18, rue du Général Leclerc ✆ 03 86 39 45 29

Le Grand Monarque

VISA MC

10 r. de l'Etape, (near the church) – ✆ 03 86 39 35 44 – www.legrandmonarque-donzy.fr – contact@legrandmonarque-donzy.fr – Fax 03 86 39 37 09 – Closed 2 January-15 February, Sunday evening and Monday from 15 October to Easter

11 rm – †€ 49/74 ††€ 58/74, ☕ € 10

Rest – *(closed Sunday dinner and Monday)* Menu (€ 13), € 19/30 – Carte € 25/34

◆ Small family-run hotel in a peaceful village. A fine 16C spiral staircase leads to the guestrooms, some of which are delightful (king size beds). An attractive, original 19C kitchen. Unpretentious, traditional menu.

LE DORAT – 87 Haute-Vienne – 325 D3 – pop. 1 899 – alt. 209 m – ✉ 87210 24 B1

Dordogne-Berry-Limousin

Paris 369 – Bellac 13 – Le Blanc 49 – Guéret 68 – Limoges 58 – Poitiers 77

Office de tourisme, 17, place de la Collégiale ✆ 05 55 60 76 81, Fax 05 55 60 76 81

St-Pierre collegiate church ★★.

La Marmite

VISA MC

29 av. de la Gare – ✆ 05 55 60 66 94 – www.restaurantlamarmite.com – Fax 05 55 60 66 94 – Closed 19-28 June, 8-16 September, 23 February-2 March, Tuesday and Wednesday

Rest – Menu € 12/36 – Carte € 27/35

◆ The chef prepares hearty traditional meals, while the landlady runs the show in the wood panelled dining room. Children's play area in the garden.

DORMANS – 51 Marne – 306 D8 – pop. 3 004 – alt. 70 m – ✉ 51700 13 B2

Champagne

Paris 118 – Château-Thierry 24 – Épernay 25 – Meaux 71 – Reims 41 – Soissons 46

Office de tourisme, parc du Château ✆ 03 26 53 35 86, Fax 03 26 53 35 87

La Table Sourdet

VISA MC AE

6 r. Dr Moret – ✆ 03 26 58 20 57 – Fax 03 26 58 88 82 – Closed Monday

Rest – Menu € 38 (lunch)/65 – Carte € 40/75

Rest *La Petite Table* – *(lunch only)* Menu (€ 12), € 16/34

◆ At the Table Sourdet, culinary art has been handed down from father to son for six generations! This large establishment has a comfortable dining room serving traditional fare. La Petite Table offers veranda dining; simple menus at reasonable prices.

DORRES – 66 Pyrénées-Orientales – 344 C8 – pop. 179 – alt. 1 458 m – ✉ 66760 Languedoc-Roussillon-Tarn Gorges 22 A3

Paris 849 – Ax-les-Thermes 47 – Font-Romeu-Odeillo-Via 15 – Perpignan 104

Marty

3 carrer Major – 04 68 30 07 52 – www.hotelmarty.com – info@hotelmarty.com – Fax 04 68 30 08 12 – Closed 15 October-20 December

21 rm – €47 €54, €7 – ½ P €50 **Rest** – Menu €16/30 – Carte €15/51

◆ Family guesthouse in the Cerdagne hills close to a sulphurous spring and its small lake. Slightly faded rooms, some with loggias. Panoramic restaurant decorated with farm tools and hunting trophies. Generous portions of Catalan cuisine.

DOUAI – 59 Nord – 302 G5 – pop. 43 000 – Built-up area 518 727 – alt. 31 m – ✉ 59500 Northern France and the Paris Region 31 C2

Paris 194 – Arras 26 – Lille 42 – Tournai 39 – Valenciennes 47

Office de tourisme, 70, place d'Armes 03 27 88 26 79, Fax 03 27 99 38 78

de Thumeries Thumeries N : 15 km on D 8, 03 20 86 58 98

Belfry★ BY D - Musée de la Chartreuse★★.

Historical centre of the Lewarde mining area★★ Southeast: 8 km by ②.

Plan on next page

La Terrasse rest,

36 terrasse St-Pierre – 03 27 88 70 04 – www.laterrasse.fr – contact@laterrasse.fr – Fax 03 27 88 36 05 BY a

24 rm – €55/98 €90/115, €11 – ½ P €76/92

Rest – Menu (€18), €27 bi/79 – Carte €56/78

◆ A welcoming hotel tucked away in a small street next to the collegiate Church of St. Peter. The rooms are modest in size and decorated in a 1980s style. Generous classic cuisine, prepared simply but skilfully and an especially good wine list (900 appellations).

Ibis without rest

pl. St-Amé – 03 27 87 27 27 – www.ibishotel.com – h0956@accor.com – Fax 03 27 98 31 64 AY e

42 rm – €57/85 €57/85, €8,50

◆ An Ibis hotel standards in an historic setting. These 16C and 18C houses have practical rooms of various sizes; exposed beams in the 3rd floor attic rooms.

Au Turbotin

9 r. Massue – 03 27 87 04 16 – www.au-turbotin.com – g.coussement@wanadoo.fr – Closed 1-21 August, Christmas holidays, Saturday lunch, Sunday dinner and Monday AY s

Rest – Menu €24 (weekdays)/75 bi – Carte €58/68

◆ The lobster tank is displayed as if it were a work of art in this restaurant, revamped in a pleasantly contemporary spirit. Updated recipes that continue to uphold regional traditions.

Le P'tit Gouverneur

76 r. St-Jean – 03 27 88 90 04 – Fax 03 27 88 90 04 – Closed 23 April-5 May, 1-15 August, Sunday dinner, Monday and Wednesday BY e

Rest – Menu €17, €24/38 – Carte €40/60

◆ This smart bistro on a street corner is adorned with statues of animals, adding a touch of fantasy to the neighbourhood. Choice of five up-to-the-minute menus.

in Roost-Warendin 10 km by ①, D 917 and D 8 – pop. 6 105 – alt. 22 m – ✉ 59286

Syndicat d'initiative, 270, rue Brossolette 03 27 95 90 00, Fax 03 27 95 90 01

Le Chat Botté

Château de Bernicourt – 03 27 80 24 44 – www.restaurantlechatbotte.com – contact@restaurantlechatbotte.com – Fax 03 27 80 35 81 – Closed 1st-15 August, Sunday dinner and Monday

Rest – *(lunch only)* Menu €20/65 – Carte €64/79

◆ This restaurant in an outbuilding of an enchanting 18C château has a new, cosy, modern look with classical cuisine and an impressive wine list. Park, eco-museum and temporary exhibitions.

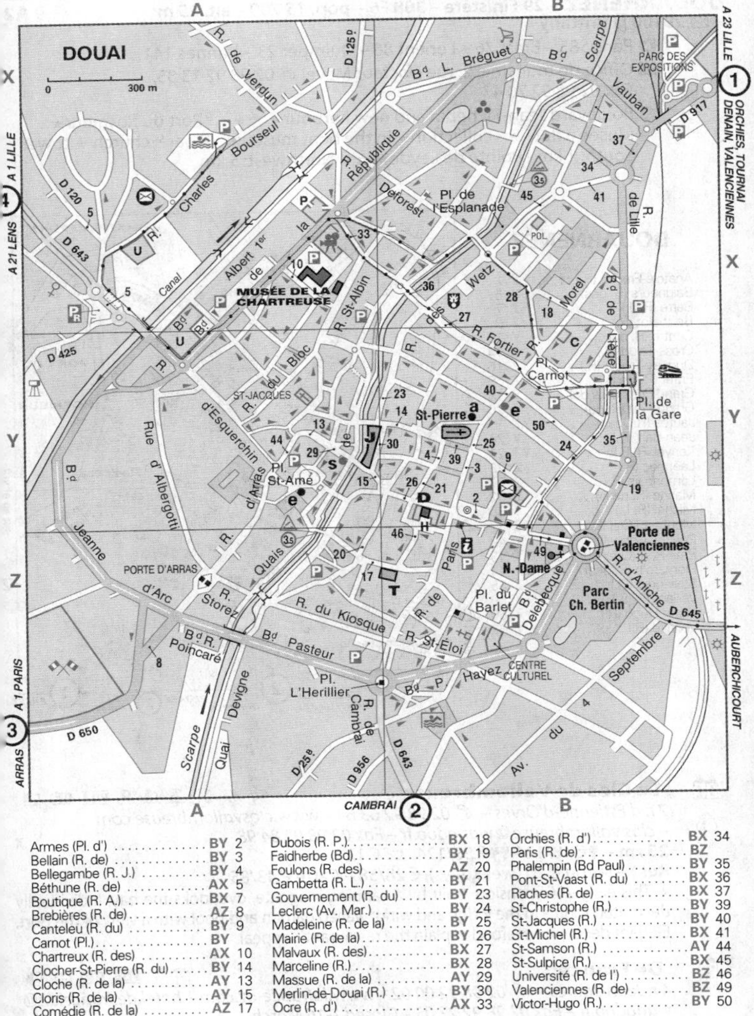

Armes (Pl. d')	BY	2	Dubois (R. P.)	BX	18	Orchies (R. d')	BX	34
Bellain (R. de)	BY	3	Faidherbe (Bd)	BY	19	Paris (R. de)	BZ	
Bellegambe (R. J.)	BY	4	Foulons (R. des)	AZ	20	Phalempin (Bd Paul)	BY	35
Béthune (R. de)	AX	5	Gambetta (R. L.)	BY	21	Pont-St-Vaast (R. du)	BX	36
Boutique (R. A.)	BX	7	Gouvernement (R. du)	BY	23	Raches (R. de)	BX	37
Brebières (R. de)	AZ	8	Leclerc (Av. Mar.)	BY	24	St-Christophe (R.)	BY	39
Canteleu (R. du)	BY	9	Madeleine (R. de la)	BY	25	St-Jacques (R.)	BY	40
Carnot (Pl.)	BY		Mairie (R. de la)	BY	26	St-Michel (R.)	BX	41
Chartreux (R. des)	AX	10	Malvaux (R. des)	BX	27	St-Samson (R.)	AY	44
Clocher-St-Pierre (R. du)	BY	14	Marceline (R.)	BX	28	St-Sulpice (R.)	BX	45
Cloche (R. de la)	AY	13	Massue (R. de la)	AY	29	Université (R. de l')	BZ	46
Cloris (R. de la)	AY	15	Merlin-de-Douai (R.)	BY	30	Valenciennes (R. de)	BZ	49
Comédie (R. de la)	AZ	17	Ocre (R. d')	AX	33	Victor-Hugo (R.)	BY	50

in Brebières 7 km by ③ – **pop. 4 878 – alt. 48 m** – ✉ **62117**

XXX **Air Accueil**

D 950 – ☎ 03 21 50 01 02 – Fax 03 21 50 84 17 – Closed 18 August-8 September, Sunday dinner, Monday and bank holidays

Rest – Menu € 32/42 – Carte € 40/80

◆ A long brick building near an aerodrome. A Louis XIII-style dining room with bright floral fabrics and a luxuriant terrace. Wine-tasting in one of the lounges.

DOUAINS – 27 Eure – **304** I7 – see Vernon

DOUARNENEZ – **29 Finistère** – **308** F6 – **pop. 15 700** – **alt. 25 m** – ✉ **29100** Brittany 9 **A2**

- Paris 585 – Brest 76 – Lorient 88 – Quimper 23 – Vannes 141
- Office de tourisme, 2, rue Docteur Mével ✆ 02 98 92 13 35, Fax 02 98 92 70 47
- Boulevard Jean-Richepin and new harbour★ ≤★ Y - Port du Rosmeur★ - Musée à flot★★ - collection★ in the boat museum - Ploaré: church ★ tower South: 1 km - Pointe de Leydé★ ≤★ Northwest: 5 km.

DOUARNENEZ

Street	Square	No.
Anatole-France (R.)	Y	2
Baigneurs (R. des)	Y	5
Barré (R. J.)	YZ	7
Berthelot (R.)	Z	8
Centre (R. du)	Y	10
Croas-Talud (R.)	Z	14
Duguay-Trouin (R.)	YZ	15
Enfer (Pl. de l')	YZ	16
Grand-Port (Quai du)	Y	19
Grand-Port (R. du)	Y	20
Jaurès (R. Jean)	YZ	
Jean-Bart (R.)	Y	24
Kerivel (R. E.)	YZ	21
Laënnec (R.)	Z	25
Lamennais (R.)	Z	27
Marine (R. de la)	Y	32
Michel (R. L.)	Y	36
Monte-au-Ciel (R.)	Z	37
Péri (Pl. Gabriel)	Z	42
Petit-Port (Quai du)	Y	43
Plomarc'h (R. des)	YZ	44
Stalingrad (Pl.)	Z	65
Vaillant (Pl. E.)	Y	59
Victor-Hugo (R.)	Z	60
Voltaire (R.)	Y	62

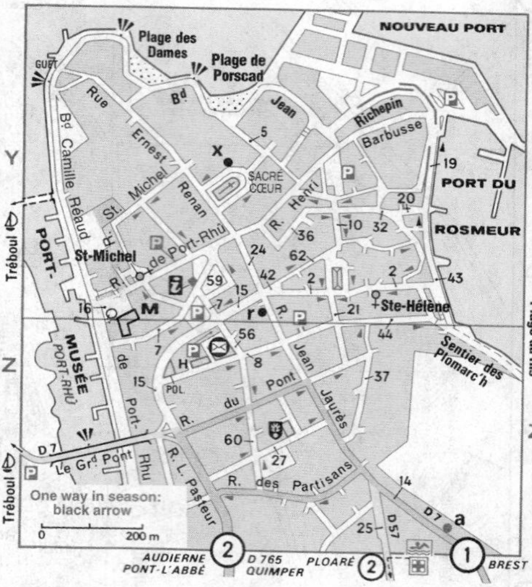

One way in season: black arrow

Le Clos de Vallombreuse

7 r. d'Estienne-d'Orves – ✆ 02 98 92 63 64 – www.closvallombreuse.com – clos.vallombreuse@wanadoo.fr – Fax 02 98 92 84 98 Y **x**

25 rm – €48/124 €58/124, ☕ €12

Rest – Menu €20 (weekdays), €28/58 – Carte €43/85

◆ This early-20C mansion, built by a canning magnate, overlooks the bay. Individually decorated rooms in the lodge and wing; walled garden and pool with a view of the port. Elegant decor and seafood explain the restaurant's appeal.

De France

4 r. Jean-Jaurès – ✆ 02 98 92 00 02 – www.lafrance-dz.com – hotel.de.france.dz@wanadoo.fr – Fax 02 98 92 27 05 – Closed 1-16 March Y **r**

23 rm – €57/67 €57/67, ☕ €8

Rest – Menu (€14), €25/45 – Carte €25/45

◆ Fully renovated town centre hotel with bright, functional and well-kept rooms. Regional cuisine and spices to the fore at the Insolite. Contemporary dining room which retains its old panelling. Terrace.

Le Kériolet with rm

29 r. Croas-Talud – ✆ 02 98 92 16 89 – www.hotel-keriolet.com – keriolet2@wanadoo.fr – Fax 02 98 92 62 94 – Closed 9-22 February and Monday lunch off season Z **a**

8 rm – €54/60 €54/60, ☕ €6,50 – ½ P €58

Rest – Menu €14 (weekday lunch), €20/38 – Carte €26/52

◆ Traditional dishes that do full justice to local country and seafood produce. Tasteful unobtrusive nautical style and views of a small garden. Simple, recent bedrooms.

Quimper road 4 km – ✉ 29100 Douarnenez

Auberge de Kerveoc'h rest, P VISA MC

42, rte de Kerveoc'h, via D 765 – ✆ 02 98 92 07 58 – www.auberge-kerveoch.com – contact@auberge-kerveoch.com – Fax 02 98 92 03 58

14 rm – †€ 47/56 ††€ 47/75, ☕ € 8 – ½ P € 54/68

Rest – *(Closed 2 weeks in November and Sunday dinner from October to May) (dinner only)* Menu € 24/45

◆ The rooms in the farmhouse have been tastefully refurbished; those in the small manor house are older but remain pleasant and attractive. Enjoy the peace and quiet in the pretty garden. Short set menu devised depending on the season and a distinctly countrified decoration.

in Tréboul 3 km Northwest – ✉29100 Douarnenez

Thalasstonic rm, P VISA MC AE

r. des Professeurs Curie – ✆ 02 98 74 45 45 – www.hotel-douarnenez.com – info-hotel-dz@thalasso.com – Fax 02 98 74 36 07 – Closed 22 November-5 December

44 rm – †€ 59/74 ††€ 82/112, ☕ € 12 – 6 suites – ½ P € 79/112

Rest – Menu (€ 20), € 26/35 bi – Carte € 33/50

◆ This non-smoking hotel by the sea is ideal to recharge your batteries (nearby beach and spa centre). Spacious, modern guestrooms. Huge contemporary restaurant with a summer terrace. Choose between traditional cuisine and lighter dishes.

Ty Mad P VISA MC

plage St Jean, near St. Jean's chapel – ✆ 02 98 74 00 53 – www.hoteltymad.com – info@hoteltymad.fr – Fax 02 98 74 15 16 – Open 16 March-9 November

14 rm – †€ 55/177 ††€ 55/177, ☕ € 12 – 1 suite

Rest – *(open 1 June-27 September, school holidays, Friday and Saturday in low season) (dinner only)* Menu (€ 24) – Carte approx. € 28

◆ The Quimper painter Max Jacob is said to have been a frequent visitor to this ty mad (reputable house) overlooking the St-Jean beach. Rooms are personalised and embellished with contemporary or antique furnishings. A dinner menu based on seasonal market produce is served on the bright and stylish veranda overlooking the garden.

DOUBS – 25 Doubs – **321** I5 – see Pontarlier

DOUCIER – 39 Jura – 321 E7 – pop. 306 – alt. 526 m – ✉ 39130 16 B3

Paris 427 – Champagnole 21 – Lons-le-Saunier 25

Chalain Lake ★★ North: 4 km **Burgundy-Jura**

Le Comtois with rm VISA MC AE

– ✆ 03 84 25 71 21 – lecomtoisdoucier – restaurant.comtois@wanadoo.fr – Fax 03 84 25 71 21 – Closed 11 November-10 December, Sunday dinner, Monday from 16 September to 15 June, Saturday lunch and Monday lunch from 16 June to 15 September

7 rm (½ board only) – ½ P € 50 **Rest** – Menu (€ 17), € 55 – Carte € 25/40

◆ Attractive, country-style decor, hearty local cuisine, attentive service and a friendly welcome – all this and a fine selection of Jura wines in this stylish inn!

DOUÉ-LA-FONTAINE – 49 Maine-et-Loire – 317 H5 – pop. 7 428 – alt. 75 m – ✉ 49700 Châteaux of the Loire 35 C2

Paris 322 – Angers 40 – Châtellerault 86 – Cholet 50 – Saumur 19 – Thouars 30

Office de tourisme, 30, place des Fontaines ✆ 02 41 59 20 49, Fax 02 41 59 93 85

Zoo de Doué★★.

La Saulaie without rest P VISA MC AE

2 km on Montreuil-Bellay road – ✆ 02 41 59 96 10 – www.hoteldelasaulaie.com – hoteldelasaulaie@wanadoo.fr – Fax 02 41 59 96 11 – Closed 18 December-3 January

44 rm – †€ 42/54 ††€ 50/62, ☕ € 8

◆ After a visit to the "cave dwellings" in the vicinity, return to natural light in this recently built establishment with modern, colourful and fairly spacious rooms.

Auberge Bienvenue with rm — rm, VISA AE

104 rte de Cholet, (opposite the zoo) – ✆ 02 41 59 22 44 – www.aubergebienvenue.com – info@aubergebienvenue.com – Fax 02 41 59 93 49 – Closed 22 December-14 January

10 rm – †€ 48 ††€ 48/65, ☕ € 9 – ½ P € 65

Rest – *(closed Sunday dinner and Monday)* Menu (€ 16), € 24/52 – Carte € 47/54

◆ This inn serves tasty, traditional dishes in a warm, welcoming atmosphere. Flower-decked terrace. Spacious modern guestrooms.

De France with rm — VISA

17 pl. Champ de Foire – ✆ 02 41 59 12 27 – www.hoteldefrance-doue.com – jarnot@hoteldefrance-doue.com – Fax 02 41 59 76 00 – Closed 20 December-15 January and Monday

17 rm – †€ 42 ††€ 45, ☕ € 7 – ½ P € 48/55

Rest – Menu € 18/37 – Carte € 30/42

◆ A restaurant in the city of the rose with mellow decor: Louis XVI chairs and walls and ceilings hung with drapes. Simple rooms, being progressively renovated.

DOURDAN – 91 Essonne – 312 B4 – pop. 9 590 – alt. 100 m – ✉ 91410 — 18 B2

Northern France and the Paris Region

- Paris 54 – Chartres 48 – Étampes 18 – Évry 44 – Orléans 81 – Rambouillet 22 – Versailles 51
- Office de tourisme, place du Général-de-Gaulle ✆ 01 64 59 86 97, Fax 01 60 81 05 69
- Rochefort Chisan Country Club Rochefort-en-Yvelines Château de Rochefort/Yvelines, N : 8 km on D 836 and D 149, ✆ 01 30 41 31 81
- de Forges-les-Bains Forges-les-Bains Route du Général Leclerc, N : 14 km on D 838, ✆ 01 64 91 48 18
- Place du Marché aux grains★ - Virgin with parrot★ in the museum.

Host. Blanche de Castille — VISA AE

pl. Marché aux Herbes – ✆ 01 60 81 19 10 – www.revalisever.com – info@residourdan.fr – Fax 01 60 81 19 11

32 rm – †€ 94 ††€ 94, ☕ € 8 – 9 suites

Rest – *(closed 1st-15 August, Saturday lunch and Sunday dinner)*
Menu (€ 15), € 27 (weekday lunch), € 35/45 – Carte € 35/55 dinner only

◆ In the heart of old Dourdan, an old house opposite the place des Halles. Comfortable rooms (12 for families). Half of them have views over the church with its three steeples. The dining room is both elegant and rustic (hearth, chandeliers and beams). Traditional menu.

Auberge de l'Angélus — VISA

4 pl. Chariot – ✆ 01 64 59 83 72 – Fax 01 64 59 83 72 – Closed 15 July-13 August, 22 February-3 March, Monday dinner, Tuesday dinner and Wednesday

Rest – Menu € 22 (weekdays)/45 – Carte € 80/90

◆ Just off the picturesque historical centre, 18C posthouse with three recently renovated dining rooms. Pretty courtyard terrace.

DOURGNE – 81 Tarn – 338 E10 – pop. 1 186 – alt. 250 m – ✉ 81110 — 29 C2

- Paris 742 – Toulouse 67 – Carcassonne 52 – Castelnaudary 35 – Castres 19 – Gaillac 64
- Office de tourisme, 1, avenue du maquis ✆ 05 63 74 27 19, Fax 05 63 74 27 19

Hostellerie de la Montagne Noire with rm — rest, VISA AE

15 pl. Promenades – ✆ 05 63 50 31 12 – www.montagnenoire.net – hotel.restaurant.montagne.noire@wanadoo.fr – Fax 05 63 50 13 55 – Closed 31 August-7 September and 16-23 February

9 rm – †€ 49 ††€ 52, ☕ € 8 – ½ P € 42

Rest – *(closed Sunday evening and Monday)* Menu (€ 16), € 22/36 – Carte € 30/43

◆ Traditional, generous cuisine is served in this stone house with two dining rooms – one elegant and one countrified. Terrace shaded by plane trees. Small, simple guestrooms upstairs.

North 4 km by D 85 and D 14 – ✉ 81110 St-Avit

XX **Les Saveurs de St-Avit** (Simon Scott)
✿ *La Baraque – ✆ 05 63 50 11 45 – www.les-saveurs-tarn.com – simonscott6@aol.com – Fax 05 63 50 11 45 – Closed 15-30 November, 1st-15 January, Tuesday lunch, Wednesday lunch and Thursday lunch from mid October to mid April, Saturday lunch, Sunday dinner and Monday*
Rest – *(number of covers limited, pre-book)* Menu € 28/90 bi – Carte € 70/90
Spec. Petit pot de foie gras aux gambas. Rouget barbet cuit à la plancha. Petites prunes du pays et crème glacée à la reine-des-prés.
◆ Restaurant with modern decor set within the rustic walls of an old farmhouse. Skilful contemporary cooking, inventive, but without going over the top.

DOURLERS – 59 Nord – 302 L6 – pop. 568 – alt. 171 m – ✉ 59440 — 31 D3

▶ Paris 245 – Avesnes-sur-Helpe 10 – Lille 94 – Maubeuge 13 – Le Quesnoy 27 – St-Quentin 75

XX **Auberge du Châtelet**
rte d'Avesnes-sur-Helpe, on the N 2 : 1 km – ✆ 03 27 61 06 70 – www.aubergeduchatelet.com – carlierchatelet@aol.com – Fax 03 27 61 20 02 – Closed Sunday dinner and dinner on public holidays
Rest – Menu € 30 bi/60 bi – Carte € 38/66
◆ The same family has been running this pretty long cottage since 1971. A rustic interior, quiet terrace, traditional menu and magnificent wine list (excellent vintages).

DOUSSARD – 74 Haute-Savoie – 328 K6 – pop. 2 781 – alt. 456 m – ✉ 74210 — 46 F1

▶ Paris 555 – Albertville 27 – Annecy 20 – Megève 42

Arcalod rm,
– ✆ 04 50 44 30 22 – www.hotelarcalod.fr – info@hotelarcalod.fr – Fax 04 50 44 85 03 – Open 16 May-30 September
33 rm – †€ 60/85 ††€ 65/95, ☕ € 10 – ½ P € 60/77
Rest – Menu € 19 (weekdays)/32 – Carte approx. € 27
◆ The numerous free leisure activities (bicycling, hiking, archery, etc.) are the great bonus of this family chalet. Small, well kept rooms and large tree lined garden. Spacious, modern dining room serving Savoyard inspired guesthouse cuisine.

DOUVAINE – 74 Haute-Savoie – 328 K3 – pop. 4 494 – alt. 428 m – ✉ 74140 — 46 F1

▶ Paris 555 – Annecy 63 – Chamonix-Mont-Blanc 87 – Genève 18 – Thonon-les-Bains 16

ℹ Office de tourisme, place de l'Hôtel de Ville ✆ 04 50 94 10 55, Fax 04 50 94 36 13

XXX **Ô Flaveurs** (Jérôme Mamet)
✿ *Château de Chilly, 2 km south-east via rte de Crépy – ✆ 04 50 35 46 55 – www.oflaveurs.com – restaurantoflaveurs@wanadoo.fr – Fax 04 50 35 41 31 – Closed Tuesday and Wednesday*
Rest – Menu € 35 (weekday lunch), € 50/80 – Carte € 72/99
Spec. Coeur de saumon frais de l'Adour, fumé minute. Dos de bar rôti, ravioles de tourteau à l'émulsion de coriandre (Oct. to Jan.). Framboises de Ballaison. **Wines** Crépy, Chautagne.
◆ Modern inventive cuisine is to the fore in this refined restaurant occupying a small 15C château which has retained its authentic feel (stone, exposed beams, fireplace).

XX **La Couronne**
1 r. du Centre – ✆ 04 50 85 10 20 – www.hotel-restaurant-lacouronne.com – la.couronne2@freesbee.fr – Fax 04 50 85 10 40 – Closed 26 July-17 August, 22 December-7 January, Sunday dinner and Monday
Rest – Menu € 14 bi (weekday lunch), € 16 € bi/36 – Carte € 38/56
◆ Dating from 1780, this inn has a warm dining room (exposed beams, sunny shades) opening onto a small shaded courtyard. Up-to-date cuisine.

Le 111

111 r. du Centre – ✆ 04 50 85 06 25 – www.le111.fr – le111@orange.fr – Closed 15 July-15 August, Tuesday and Wednesday

Rest – Menu € 15 (weekday lunch), € 22/34 – Carte approx. € 27

◆ Wine bar and traditional cuisine at this establishment run by a wine lover. Light wood-panelled dining room with glass cellar. Lunch served on the veranda.

DOUVRES-LA-DÉLIVRANDE – 14 Calvados – 303 J4 – pop. 4 809 – alt. 19 m – ✉ 14440 Normandy 32 **B2**

Paris 246 – Bayeux 26 – Caen 15 – Deauville 48

Syndicat d'initiative, 41, rue Général-de-Gaulle ✆ 02 31 37 93 10, Fax 02 31 37 93 10

in Cresserons 2 km East by D 35 – pop. 1 217 – alt. 9 m – ✉ 14440

La Valise Gourmande

7 rte de Lion sur Mer – ✆ 02 31 37 39 10 – wwww.lavalisegourmande-caen.com – contact@lavalisegourmande-caen.com – Fax 02 31 37 59 13 – Closed Sunday dinner, Tuesday lunch and Monday

Rest – Menu € 29/54 – Carte € 40/68

◆ This 18C priory has a pretty walled garden. Find three small, elegant countrified dining rooms, one with a fireplace. Classic cuisine with a touch of modernity.

DRACY-LE-FORT – 71 Saône-et-Loire – 320 I9 – see Chalon-sur-Saône

---

DRAGUIGNAN – 83 Var – 340 N4 – pop. 35 900 – alt. 178 m – ✉ 83300 French Riviera 41 **C3**

Paris 862 – Fréjus 30 – Marseille 124 – Nice 89 – Toulon 79

Office de tourisme, 2, avenue Lazard Carnot ✆ 04 98 10 51 05, Fax 04 98 10 51 10

de Saint Endréol La Motte Route de Bagnols en Forêt, 15 km on the Muy road and D 47, ✆ 04 94 51 89 89

Musée des Arts et Traditions populaires de moyenne Provence ★ M².

Site ★ of Trans-en-Provence South: 5 km.

Plan on next page

Mercure without rest

11 bd G. Clemenceau – ✆ 04 94 50 95 09 – h2969@accor.com – Fax 04 94 68 23 49 Z n

38 rm – €94/130 €104/140

◆ Fully renovated and under new management, this town centre hotel is close to the museums. Spacious, well-appointed and soundproofed rooms.

Lou Galoubet

23 bd J. Jaurès – ✆ 04 94 68 08 50 – www.lougaloubet.com – lougaloubet@orange.fr – Fax 04 94 68 08 50 – Closed three weeks in summer, one week in February, Sunday dinner, Tuesday dinner and Wednesday Z e

Rest – Menu (€ 23), € 29/51 – Carte € 40/58

◆ Warm setting at this small restaurant with a bistro feel. Tasty dishes (traditional, regional-style cooking) concocted in the open kitchen visible from the doorway.

Flayosc road 4 km by ③ and D 557 – ✉ 83300 Draguignan

Les Oliviers without rest

rte de Flayosc - D557 – ✆ 04 94 68 25 74 – www.hotel-les-oliviers.com – hotel-les-oliviers@club-internet.fr – Fax 04 94 68 57 54 – Closed 10-20 January

12 rm – €50/59 €52/59, € 8

◆ This welcoming family hotel has perfectly kept rooms all on the ground floor. The flower garden has a pool where one can breakfast in summertime.

DRAGUIGNAN

Cisson (R.) . . . . YZ 3
Clemenceau (Bd) . . . . Z
Clément (R. P.) . . . . Z 4
Droits-de-l'Homme (Parvis des) . . . . Z 5
Gay (Pl. C.) . . . . Y 6
Grasse (Av. de) . . . . Y 8
Joffre (Bd. Mar.) . . . . Z 9
Juiverie (R. de la) . . . . Y 12
Kennedy (Bd J.) . . . . Z 13
Leclerc (Bd Gén.) . . . . Z 14
Marchands (R. des) . . . . Y 15
Marché (Pl. du) . . . . Y 16
Martyrs-de-la-Résistance (Bd des) . . . . Z 17
Marx-Dormoy (Bd) . . . . Z 18
Mireur (R. F.) . . . . Y 19
Observance (R. de l') . . . . Y 20
République (R. de la) . . . . Z 23
Rosso (Av. P.) . . . . Z 24

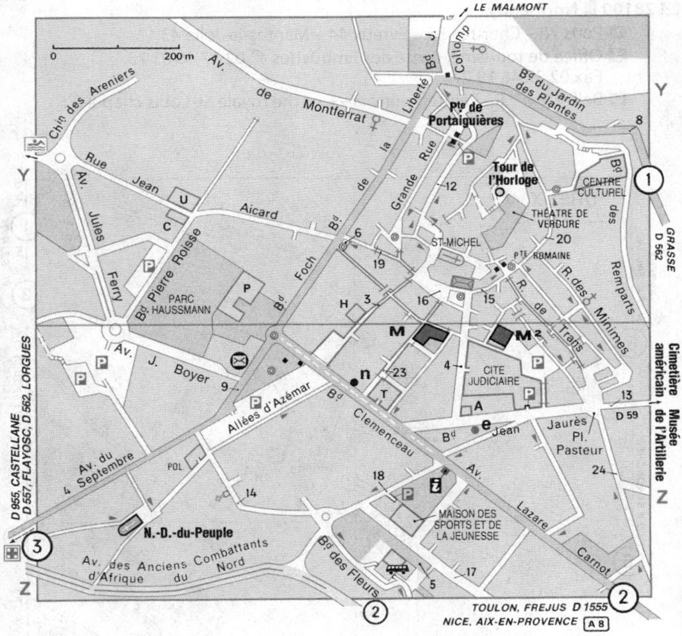

in Flayosc 7 km by ③ and D 557 – pop. 4 341 – alt. 310 m – ✉ 83780

Office de tourisme, place Pied Bari ✆ 04 94 70 41 31, Fax 04 94 70 47 91

XX L'Oustaou

in the village – ✆ 04 94 70 42 69 – Fax 04 94 84 64 92 – Closed 25 October-13 November, Sunday dinner, Monday and Wednesday in low season, Tuesday lunch, Wednesday lunch and Friday lunch in July-August

Rest – Menu (€ 20), € 28/45 – Carte € 40/65

◆ The name of this former post house means small farmhouse. Updated interior decoration in keeping with the modern cuisine, enhanced by regional flavours.

DRAIN – 49 Maine-et-Loire – 317 B4 – pop. 1 690 – alt. 53 m – ✉ 49530 34 B2

Paris 359 – Cholet 60 – Nantes 41 – Saint-Herblain 48

Le Mésangeau

5 km South on the D 154 – ✆ 02 40 98 21 57 – www.loire-mesangeau.com – le.mesangeau@orange.fr – Fax 02 40 98 28 62 – Open from March to November

5 rm – €80/100 €90/110 **Table d'hôte** – Menu € 35 bi

◆ This spacious 1830 residence has a relaxing atmosphere, with extensive gardens, a small lake, golf course and collection of early 20C motor cars. Renovated guestrooms decorated in the style of the region. Rustic table d'hôte with a pretty stone fireplace, offering local dishes.

LE DRAMONT – 83 Var – 340 Q5 – see St-Raphaël

DRAVEIL – 91 Essonne – 312 D3 – 101 36 – see Paris, Area

DREUX – 28 Eure-et-Loir – 311 E3 – pop. 32 300 – alt. 82 m – ✉ 28100 Normandy

11 **B1**

Paris 78 – Chartres 36 – Évreux 44 – Mantes-la-Jolie 43

Office de tourisme, 6, rue des Embûches ✆ 02 37 46 01 73, Fax 02 37 46 19 27

Belfry ★ AY **B** - Painted mirrors★★ of the royale St-Louis chapel AY.

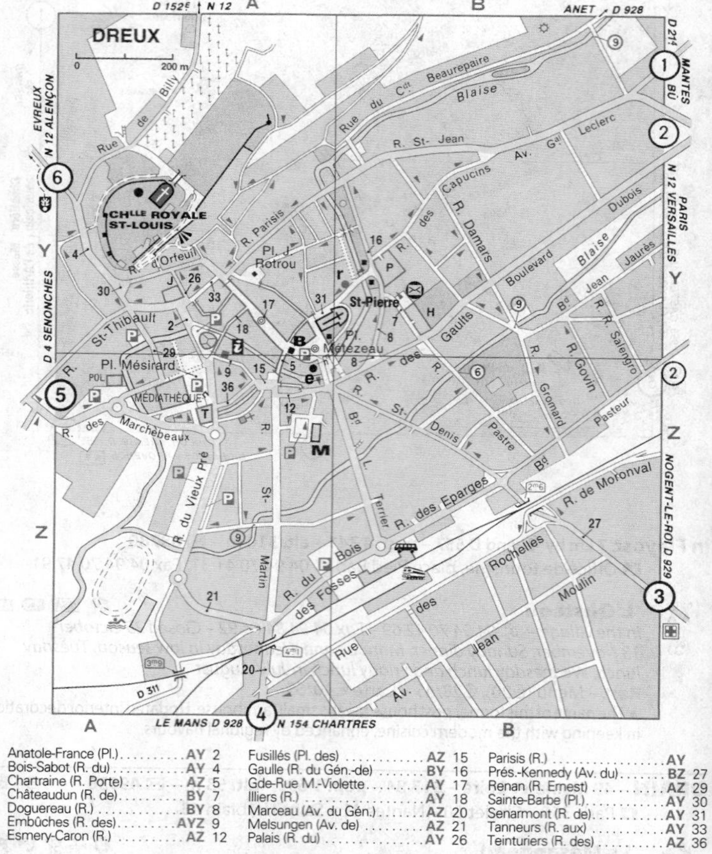

Anatole-France (Pl.) .... **AY** 2	Fusillés (Pl. des) .... **AZ** 15	Parisis (R.) .... **AY**
Bois-Sabot (R. du) .... **AY** 4	Gaulle (R. du Gén.-de) .... **BY** 16	Prés.-Kennedy (Av. du) .... **BZ** 27
Chartraine (R. Porte) .... **AZ** 5	Gde-Rue M.-Violette .... **AY** 17	Renan (R. Ernest) .... **AZ** 29
Châteaudun (R. de) .... **BY** 7	Illiers (R.) .... **AY** 18	Sainte-Barbe (Pl.) .... **AY** 30
Doguereau (R.) .... **BY** 8	Marceau (Av. du Gén.) .... **AZ** 20	Senarmont (R. de) .... **AY** 31
Embûches (R. des) .... **AYZ** 9	Melsungen (Av. de) .... **AZ** 21	Tanneurs (R. aux) .... **AY** 33
Esmery-Caron (R.) .... **AZ** 12	Palais (R. du) .... **AY** 26	Teinturiers (R. des) .... **AZ** 36

Le Beffroi without rest

12 pl. Métézeau – ✆ 02 37 50 02 03 – hotel.beffroi@club-internet.fr – Fax 02 37 42 07 69 – Closed 20 July-17 August

VISA MC AE

15 rm – †€ 69 ††€ 69, ☕ € 8

AZ **e**

◆ All the well-kept rooms of this hotel command a view of the River Blaise or St Pierre Church. Each room is adorned with objects picked up by the owner, a former international reporter.

Le St-Pierre VISA MC

19 r. Sénarmont – ✆ 02 37 46 47 00 – www.lesaint-pierre.com – contact@lesaint-pierre.com – Fax 02 37 64 26 37 – Closed 14-31 July, 6-13 March, Thursday dinner, Sunday dinner and Monday BY r

Rest – Menu (€ 15), € 18 (weekdays)/33 – Carte € 32/50

◆ Not far from the church, this attractive restaurant features three small rooms, prettily redecorated in a classic vein. Tasty traditional fare concocted by the chef.

in Chérisy 4,5 km by ② – pop. 1 797 – alt. 88 m – ✉ 28500

Le Vallon de Chérisy P VISA MC AE

12 rte de Paris – ✆ 02 37 43 70 08 – www.le-vallon-de-cherisy.fr – deshayes.franck@wanadoo.fr – Fax 02 37 43 86 00 – Closed 19 July-5 August, Sunday dinner, Tuesday dinner and Wednesday

Rest – Menu (€ 28 bi), € 28/40 – Carte € 55/66

◆ Half-timbered house well worth the stop for its rustic dining room and sunlit veranda-terrace, and above all for its tasty, seasonally inspired menu.

in Ste-Gemme-Moronval 6 km by ②, N 12, D 912 and D 308[1] – pop. 732 – alt. 79 m – ✉ 28500

L'Escapade P VISA MC AE

– ✆ 02 37 43 72 05 – Fax 02 37 43 86 96 – Closed 17 August-10 September, 16-25 February, Sunday dinner, Monday dinner and Tuesday

Rest – Menu € 39 – Carte € 69/100

◆ Enjoy a culinary treat in this welcoming countrified inn overlooking a quiet terrace. Fresh, traditionally prepared produce takes pride of place on the menu.

in Vernouillet-centre 2 km South by D 311 AZ – pop. 11 800 – alt. 97 m – ✉ 28500

Auberge de la Vallée Verte with rm rm, P VISA MC AE

6 r. Lucien Dupuis, (near church) – ✆ 02 37 46 04 04 – www.aubergevalleeverte.fr – aubergevallee@wanadoo.fr – Fax 02 37 42 91 17 – Closed 2-25 August, 24 December-12 January, Monday except hotel and Sunday

16 rm – €70/80 €70/91, € 10 **Rest** – Menu € 30/60 bi – Carte € 45/60

◆ Exposed beams, a fireplace and attractive paintings depict the serene atmosphere of this restaurant, which serves traditional fare.

DRUSENHEIM – 67 Bas-Rhin – 315 L4 – pop. 4 921 – alt. 122 m – ✉ 67410 1 B1

Paris 499 – Haguenau 17 – Saverne 61 – Strasbourg 33 – Wissembourg 48

Auberge du Gourmet with rm P VISA MC AE

rte Strasbourg, Southwest : 1 km – ✆ 03 88 53 30 60 – www.auberge-gourmet.com – info@auberge-gourmet.com – Fax 03 88 53 31 39 – Closed 25 July-15 August and 18 February-8 March

10 rm – €40/46 €45/57, € 7 – ½ P € 49/55

Rest – *(closed Saturday lunch, Tuesday dinner and Wednesday)*
Menu € 24/39 – Carte € 31/60

◆ The hotel at the entrance to this pleasant village has a welcoming dining room with a coffered ceiling. Alsace cuisine and dishes based on fresh market produce. Stylish rooms.

DRUYES-LES-BELLES-FONTAINES – 89 Yonne – 319 D6 – pop. 290 – alt. 168 m – ✉ 89560 7 B2

Paris 183 – Auxerre 34 – Clamecy 17 – Gien 75 – Montargis 98

L'Auberge des Sources P VISA MC

4 pl. J. Bertin – ✆ 03 86 41 55 14 – www.auberge-dessources.com – aubergedessources@wanadoo.fr – Closed 3 November-25 February

8 rm – €59/69 €59/69, € 7 – ½ P € 70

Rest – *(closed Monday and Tuesday from September to May)*
Menu (€ 20), € 29 – Carte € 29/48

◆ The rooms in this former post house in a quiet Burgundy village were refurbished in 2007. Annexes with guest cottages and a meeting area. Get an overview of regional specialities in the countrified dining room or on the patio terrace.

DUCEY – 50 Manche – **303** E8 – **pop. 2 253 – alt. 15 m** – ✉ **50220** 32 **A3**
Normandy

Paris 348 – Avranches 11 – Fougères 41 – Rennes 80 – St-Hilaire-du-Harcouët 16 – St-Lô 68

Office de tourisme, 4, rue du Génie ✆ 02 33 60 21 53, Fax 02 33 60 54 07

Moulin de Ducey without rest
1 Grande Rue – ✆ 02 33 60 25 25 – www.moulindeducey.com – info@moulindeducey.com – Fax 02 33 60 26 76 – Closed 18 December-3 January and 6-22 February
28 rm – €54/105 €65/105, €11
◆ Between the watercourse and the Sélune, the old mill seems to be sitting on a green islet. English-style rooms and breakfast room overlooking the river (salmon fishing).

Auberge de la Sélune
2 r. St-Germain – ✆ 02 33 48 53 62 – www.selune.com – info@selune.com – Fax 02 33 48 90 30 – Closed 22 November-14 December, 17 January-15 February and Monday from March to September
20 rm – €60 €62/66, €9
Rest – Menu €18 (weekdays)/43 – Carte €23/39
◆ This handsome stone house is home to progressively renovated rooms, some of which enjoy a view of the pretty garden with a picturesque shelter on the banks of the Sélune. Pleasant dining rooms, including one overlooking the greenery.

The ✿ award is the crème de la crème.
This is awarded to restaurants which are really worth travelling miles for!

DUHORT-BACHEN – 40 Landes – **335** J12 – **pop. 619 – alt. 72 m** – ✉ 40800 3 **B3**

Paris 710 – Bordeaux 150 – Mont-de-Marsan 30 – Pau 57 – Billère 57

Les Arcades
232 pl. de la Mairie – ✆ 05 58 71 85 59 – lesarcades40@orange.fr – Fax 05 58 71 85 59 – Closed 25-30 December, Tuesday dinner, Sunday dinner and Monday
Rest – Menu (€11 bi), €16 bi/46 – Carte €26/46
◆ Regional-style house nestled among ivy and flowers. Country-style interior, pleasant arcaded terrace, and light, seasonal dishes.

DUINGT – 74 Haute-Savoie – **328** K6 – **pop. 870 – alt. 450 m** – ✉ **74410** 46 **F1**
French Alps

Paris 548 – Albertville 34 – Annecy 12 – Megève 48 – St-Jorioz 3

Office de tourisme, rue du Vieux Village ✆ 04 50 77 64 75

Le Clos Marcel
410 allée de la Plage – ✆ 04 50 68 67 47 – www.clos-marcel.com – lionel@clos-marcel.com – Fax 04 50 68 61 11 – Open 11 April-27 September
15 rm – €45/89 €45/89, €9
Rest – *(closed Tuesday except July-August)* Menu (€21), €28 – Carte €35/49
◆ All rooms overlook the lake and the peaks on the opposite bank; pleasant lakeside garden and private jetty. Panoramic restaurant and enchanting tree-lined terrace.

Auberge du Roselet with rm
– ✆ 04 50 68 67 19 – www.hotel-restaurant-leroselet.com – info@hotel-restaurant-leroselet.com – Fax 04 50 68 64 80 – Closed 15 November-31 December
14 rm – €84/94 €84/118, €11 – ½ P €82
Rest – Menu €23 (weekdays)/55 – Carte €43/63
◆ Fish fresh from the lake (caught by the owner's cousin) served on the waterside terrace or in one of two dining rooms (one classical, the other more nautical). Rooms that are slightly retro and a small private beach.

DUNES – 82 Tarn-et-Garonne – **337** A7 – **pop. 1 106** – **alt. 120 m** – ✉ **82340** 28 **B2**

Paris 655 – Agen 21 – Auvillar 13 – Miradoux 12 – Moissac 32

Les Templiers
1 pl. des Martyrs – ☎ 05 63 39 86 21 – lestempliers4@wanadoo.fr – Closed autumn school holidays, Tuesday dinner, Saturday lunch, Sunday dinner and Monday
Rest – Menu € 23 (weekdays)/48 – Carte approx. € 50
◆ This 16C building makes the most of its rustic charm. Bright decor (yellow tones, stonework, bricks and flowers) and a terrace under the arches. Contemporary cuisine.

DUNIÈRES – 43 Haute-Loire – **331** I2 – **pop. 3 002** – **alt. 760 m** – ✉ **43220** 6 **D3**

Paris 549 – Le Puy-en-Velay 52 – St-Agrève 30 – St-Étienne 37

La Tour with rm
7 ter r. Fraisse, (D 61) – ☎ 04 71 66 86 66 – www.hotelrestaurantlatour.com – contact@hotelrestaurantlatour.com – Fax 04 71 66 82 32 – Closed 22 August-4 September, 1st-3 January, 15 February-14 March
11 rm – €54/60 €54/60, € 9 – ½ P € 59/65
Rest – *(closed Friday dinner from October to May, Sunday dinner and Monday)* Menu (€ 16), € 23/70 – Carte € 45/66
◆ A modern building overlooking the village of Dunières. Tasteful, modern dining room, flower-decked terrace and well prepared traditional dishes. Practical guestrooms.

DUNKERQUE – 59 Nord – **302** C1 – **pop. 69 400** – **Built-up area 191 173** – **alt. 4 m** – **Casino : Malo-les-Bains** – ✉ **59140** 30 **B1**

Northern France and the Paris Region

Paris 288 – Amiens 205 – Calais 47 – Ieper 56 – Lille 73 – Oostende 57

Office de tourisme, rue de l'Amiral Ronarc'h ☎ 03 28 66 79 21, Fax 03 28 63 38 34

de Dunkerque Coudekerque Fort Vallières, SE : 1 km on D 72, ☎ 03 28 61 07 43

Harbour★★ - Musée d'Art contemporain★: jardin des sculptures (sculpture garden) ★ CDY - Musée des Beaux-Arts★ CDZ **M²** - Musée portuaire★ CZ **M³**.

Plans on following pages

Borel without rest
6 r. L'Hermite – ☎ 03 28 66 51 80 – www.hotelborel.fr – borel@hotelborel.fr – Fax 03 28 59 33 82 CY **u**
48 rm – € 74 € 82, € 10
◆ Brick building near the marina. Well-equipped, well-kept rooms. Agreeable muted sitting room. Buffet breakfast.

Ibis without rest
13 r. Leughenaer – ☎ 03 28 66 29 07 – www.ibishotel.com – h6546@accor.com – Fax 03 28 63 67 87 CY **s**
110 rm – € 69/72 € 69/72, € 8
◆ This fully renovated 1970s hotel offers comfortable rooms, a shopping arcade, contemporary-style bar and a breakfast buffet presented in a fishing boat.

Welcome
37 r. R. Poincaré – ☎ 03 28 59 20 70 – www.hotel-welcome.fr – contact@hotel-welcome.fr – Fax 03 28 21 03 49 CZ **e**
41 rm – € 68 € 78, € 10 – ½ P € 80/85
Rest ***L'Écume Bleue*** – brasserie Menu € 16/24 – Carte € 30/43
◆ Functional rooms in bright cheerful colours and a modern bar with a billiard table. The penthouse suite boasts a hi-tech bathroom. A modern, colourful setting in the dining room, serving traditional fare.

Au Bon Coin with rm
49 av. Kléber – ☎ 03 28 69 12 63 – www.restaurantauboncoin.com – restaurantauboncoin@wanadoo.fr – Fax 03 28 69 64 03
4 rm – € 58,50/63 € 63/73,50
Rest – *(closed Sunday dinner and Monday)* Menu € 28/50 – Carte € 36/70
◆ Proximity to the shore dictates that the menu emphasises seafood. Low-key dining room hung with autographed photos of celebrities. Elegant rooms.

DUNKERQUE

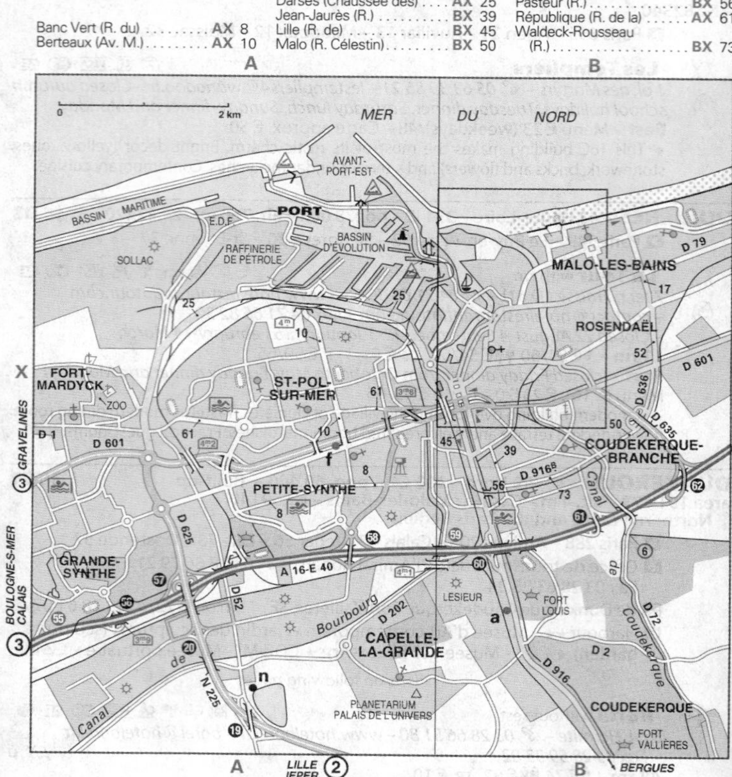

Le Vent d'Ange

VISA MC AE

1449 av. de Petite Synthe – ✆ 03 28 25 28 98 – www.leventdange.com – leventdange@wanadoo.fr – Fax 03 28 58 12 88 – Closed 24 August-6 September, 3-14 January, Tuesday dinner, Sunday dinner and Monday AX **f**

Rest – Menu (€ 18), € 26/55 – Carte € 43/58

◆ A delightful welcome and generous traditional cuisine awaits guests. Modernised decor in an Italian Baroque style, dedicated to angels.

Le Corsaire

AC VISA MC AE

6 quai Citadelle – ✆ 03 28 59 03 61 – tetart.virginie@neuf.fr – Fax 03 28 59 03 61 – Closed 24-31 December, Sunday dinner and Wednesday CZ **a**

Rest – Menu € 26/42 – Carte € 37/56

◆ This restaurant near the harbour museum offers a view of the three-mast ship "Duchesse Anne". Modern, colourful setting and seasonal cuisine.

L'Auberge de Jules

VISA MC

9 r. de la Poudrière – ✆ 03 28 63 68 80 – laubergedejules@orange.fr – Closed Saturday lunch and Sunday CY **a**

Rest – Menu € 20/25 – Carte € 30/50

◆ Suffice it to say that this hotel is a family affair: Monsieur makes the desserts and Madame cooks the fish supplied daily her father and brother, both of whom are trawler skippers.

DUNKERQUE

Street	Grid	No.
Albert-1er (R.)	CZ	2
Alexandre-III (Bd)	CZ	3
Arbres (R. des)	CDY	6
Asseman (Pl. P.)	DY	8
Bergues (R. du Canal de)	CZ	9
Bollaert (Pl. Émile)	CZ	12
Calonne (Pl.)	DZ	16
Carnot (Bd)	DY	18
Carton-Lurat (Av.)	DZ	19
Clemenceau (R.)	CZ	21
Écluse-de-Bergues (R.)	CZ	26
Faidherbe (Av.)	DY	
Fusillés-Marins (R.)	CZ	30
Gare (Pl. de la)	CZ	32
Gaulle (Pl. du Gén.-de)	CZ	33
Geeraert (Av. Adolphe)	DY	
Hermitte (R. l')	CY	35
Hollandais (Quai des)	CZ	36
Hôtel-de-Ville (R. de l')	DY	37
Jardins (Quai des)	CZ	38
Jean-Bart (Pl.)	CZ	41
Jean-Jaurès (R.)	CZ	40
Jeu-de-Paume (R. du)	CZ	42
Leclerc (R. du Mar.)	CY	43
Leughenaer (R. du)	CY	44
Lille (R. de)	CZ	45
Magasin-Général (R.)	CZ	48
Malo (Av. Gaspard)	DY	49
Mar.-de-France (Av. des)	DY	51
Mer (Digue de)	DY	
Minck (Pl. du)	CY	53
Paris (R. de)	CZ	54
Prés.-Poincaré (R. du)	CZ	57
Prés.-Wilson (R. du)	CZ	58
Quatre-Écluses (Quai)	CZ	59
Thiers (R.)	CZ	65
Turenne (Pl.)	DY	67
Valentin (Pl. C.)	CZ	68
Verley (Bd Paul)	DY	69
Victoire (Pl. et R. de la)	CDY	70
Victor-Hugo (Bd)	CZ	72

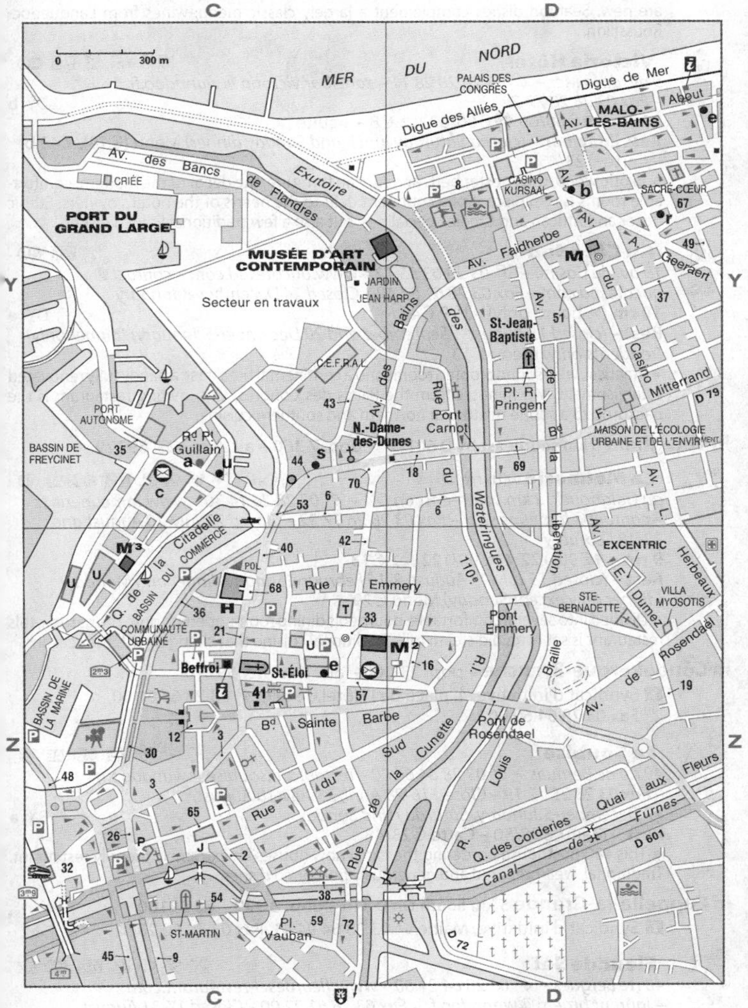

in Malo-les-Bains – ✉ 59240

L'Hirondelle
46 av. Faidherbe – ✆ 03 28 63 17 65 – www.hotelhirondelle.com – info@hotelhirondelle.com – Fax 03 28 66 15 43 DY **r**
50 rm – †€ 57/75 ††€ 68/92, ☕ € 8
Rest – *(closed 1-15 March, 8-30 August, Sunday dinner and Monday lunch)* Menu (€ 15), € 19 (weekdays)/58 – Carte € 30/60
◆ This friendly family hotel is in the heart of a little seaside resort; the rooms are gradually being made over in a pleasant understated contemporary spirit; those in the annexe are new. Seafood dishes complement a largely classic menu; wines from Languedoc-Roussillon.

Victoria Hôtel
5 av. de la Mer – ✆ 03 28 28 28 11 – zanzibar.victoria@wanadoo.fr – Fax 03 28 28 77 29 DY **b**
11 rm – †€ 66/69 ††€ 66/69, ☕ € 8 – 1 suite
Rest *Zanzibar* – *(closed Saturday lunch and Sunday dinner)* Menu (€ 18), € 48 bi – Carte € 23/45
◆ Exotic wood, four-poster beds and African furniture: the decor of the modern, comfortable rooms is reminiscent of a continent dear to the hearts of the hotel's owners. Ethnic decor and African and Creole specialities, but also a few traditional French dishes.

Au Côté Sud
19 av. du Casino – ✆ 03 28 63 55 12 – www.aucotesud.com – contact@aucotesud.com – Fax 03 28 61 54 49 – Closed 24 December-8 January
10 rm (½ board only) – ½ P € 49 DY **e**
Rest – *(closed 15 August-1 September and 20 December-5 January) (dinner only) (residents only)* Menu € 13
◆ Practical, well-soundproofed rooms and a continental breakfast: a handy fully renovated establishment two minutes from the Palais des Congrès. This inviting restaurant is the backdrop to a subtle mixture of northern and southern cuisine.

in Téteghem 6 km southeast by D 601 BX – pop. 7 360 – alt. 1 m – ✉ 59229

La Meunerie with rm
au Galghouck, 2 km south-east on D 4 – ✆ 03 28 26 14 30 – www.lameunerie.fr – contact@lameunerie.fr – Fax 03 28 26 17 32 – Closed 20 July-10 August and 12-18 February
9 rm – †€ 90/122 ††€ 90/122, ☕ € 13
Rest – *(closed 15 July-1st August, 8-16 February, Sunday dinner and Monday) (dinner only except Sunday)* Menu € 29
◆ Divided into several comfortable, bourgeois dining rooms opening onto the garden, this restaurant is set in an old steam mill. Traditional cuisine that changes with the seasons.

in Coudekerque-Branche – pop. 23 000 – alt. 1 m – ✉ 59210

Syndicat d'initiative, 4, place de l'Hôtel de Ville ✆ 03 28 64 60 00, Fax 03 28 64 60 00

Le Soubise
49 rte de Bergues – ✆ 03 28 64 66 00 – restaurant.soubise@wanadoo.fr – Fax 03 28 25 12 19 – Closed 16-28 April, 23 July-18 August, 17 December-5 January, Saturday and Sunday BX **a**
Rest – Menu € 28/50 – Carte € 23/48
◆ This 18C posthouse bordering the canal now houses an extremely friendly restaurant. Traditional, well-prepared and generously portioned dishes.

in Cappelle-la-Grande 5 km South On D 916 – pop. 8 329 – ✉ 59180

Syndicat d'initiative, Mairie ✆ 03 28 64 94 41, Fax 03 28 60 25 31

Fleur de Sel
48 rte Bergues – ✆ 03 28 64 21 80 – www.fleurdesel-restaurant.com – laurent.braem@wanadoo.fr – Fax 03 28 61 22 00 – Closed 17-31 August, 26 December-4 January, Sunday dinner and Monday BX **a**
Rest – Menu € 27/45 – Carte € 30/45
◆ Find a faultless welcome and tasty traditional cuisine in a cosy, modern interior of bare stonework, shades of grey and contemporary art and furniture.

in Armbouts-Cappel by ② N 225 exit 19a – pop. 2 500 – ✉ 59380

Du Lac
2 bordure du Lac – ✆ 03 28 60 70 60 – www.hoteldulacdk.com – contact@ hoteldulacdk.com – Fax 03 28 61 06 39 AX **n**
66 rm – €57/75 €83, €9,50
Rest – *(closed Saturday lunch)* Menu (€13), €16 (weekdays)/24 – Carte €26/41
◆ The hotel is located in a verdant setting on the shores of Lake Armbouts. Comfortable rooms; choose one overlooking the lake for the view, or the car park for more space. This contemporary dining room opens onto a terrace, garden, lake and the Flemish countryside.

DUN-LE-PALESTEL – 23 Creuse – **325** G3 – pop. 1 121 – alt. 370 m – ✉ 23800 25 **C1**

Paris 349 – Limoges 83 – Guéret 29 – La Souterraine 18 – Argenton-sur-Creuse 47

Office de tourisme, 81, Grande Rue ✆ 05 55 89 24 61, Fax 05 55 89 95 11

Joly
3 r. Bazenerye – ✆ 05 55 89 00 23 – www.hoteljoly-limousin.com – hoteljoly@ wanadoo.fr – Fax 05 55 89 15 89 – Closed 3-8 March, 29 September-6 October, Sunday dinner and Monday lunch except holidays
26 rm – €42 €45, €9
Rest – Menu €13 (weekdays)/36 – Carte €30/45
◆ In the centre of the village. The individually furnished rooms in the main building have been completely renovated; those in the annexe are simpler in style. Fresh produce is key to the carefully prepared, traditional dishes served in this rustic restaurant.

DURAS – 47 Lot-et-Garonne – **336** D1 – pop. 1 197 – alt. 122 m – ✉ 47120 Atlantic Coast 4 **C2**

Paris 577 – Agen 90 – Marmande 23 – Périgueux 88 – Ste-Foy-la-Grande 22

Office de tourisme, 14, boulevard Jean Brisseau ✆ 05 53 83 63 06, Fax 05 53 76 04 36

Hostellerie des Ducs with rm
bd. J. Brisseau – ✆ 05 53 83 74 58 – www.hostellerieducs-duras.com – hostellerie.des.ducs@wanadoo.fr – Fax 05 53 83 75 03 – Closed Monday except dinner from July to September, Sunday dinner from October to June and Saturday lunch
rest,
18 rm – €57 €70/150, €10 **Rest** – Menu €15/44 – Carte €60/90
◆ This former presbytery adjacent to the château offers traditional cuisine, served in the Louis XIII-style dining hall or on the veranda. Modern rooms, newer ones in a 13C building.

DURY – 80 Somme – **301** G8 – see Amiens

EAUX-PUISEAUX – 10 Aube – **313** D5 – pop. 234 – alt. 220 m – ✉ 10130 13 **B3**

Paris 161 – Auxerre 53 – Sens 63 – Troyes 32

L'Étape du P'tit Sim without rest
6 Gde-Rue – ✆ 03 25 42 02 21 – www.letapeduptitsim.com – etapeduptitsim@ wanadoo.fr – Fax 03 25 42 03 30 – Closed Sunday
14 rm – €49 €49, €7
◆ Hotel offering modern rooms. Buffet type breakfast. Private car park.

For a pleasant stay in a charming hotel, look for the red ... symbols.

EAUZE – 32 Gers – **336** C6 – **pop. 3 881 – alt. 164 m** – ✉ **32800** 28 **A2**

Paris 719 – Toulouse 131 – Auch 58 – Mont-de-Marsan 64 – Condom 29

Office de tourisme, 2, rue Felix Soules ✆ 05 62 09 85 62, Fax 05 62 08 11 22

La Vie en Rose AC VISA MC

– ✆ 05 62 09 83 29 – Fax 05 62 09 83 29 – Closed spring and autumn school holidays, Tuesday dinner and Wednesday

Rest – Menu (€ 14 bi), € 26/41 – Carte € 37/48

◆ The charming and hushed interior of this restaurant invites the diner to sample regional cuisine. Gascony wines and a friendly welcome.

EBERSMUNSTER – 67 Bas-Rhin – **315** J7 – **pop. 470 – alt. 165 m** – ✉ **67600** 2 **C1**

Paris 508 – Strasbourg 40 – Obernai 23 – Saint-Dié-des-Vosges 55 – Sélestat 9

Des Deux Clefs VISA MC

72 r. Gén. Leclerc – ✆ 03 88 85 71 55 – www.auxdeuxclefs.ifrance.com – Fax 03 88 85 71 55 – Closed 27 July-8 August, 24 December-17 January, Monday and Thursday except bank holidays

Rest – Menu (€ 18 bi), € 30/33 – Carte € 30/46

◆ Restaurant opposite an abbey church well-known for its baroque interior. The restaurant decor is more restrained but just as stylish. Specialities include matelote fish stew, fried fish and eel.

ECCICA-SUARELLA – 2A Corse-du-Sud – **345** C8 – **see Corse**

LES ÉCHELLES – 73 Savoie – **333** H5 – **pop. 1 248 – alt. 386 m** – ✉ **73360 Les Echelles** French Alps 45 **C2**

Paris 552 – Chambéry 24 – Grenoble 40 – Lyon 92 – Valence 106

Office de tourisme, rue Stendhal ✆ 04 79 36 56 24, Fax 04 79 36 53 12

in Chailles 5 km North – ✉ **73360 St Franc**

Auberge du Morge with rm P VISA MC AE

D 1006, Gorges de Chailles – ✆ 04 79 36 62 76 – www.aubergedumorge.com – contact@aubergedumorge.com – Fax 04 79 36 51 65 – Closed 30 November-31 January, Thursday lunch and Wednesday

8 rm – †€ 48/54 ††€ 48/54, ☕ € 9 **Rest** – Carte € 26/42

◆ Located at the entrance to the Chailles gorges, near a river that is popular with fishermen, this inn serves traditional cuisine in a countrified decor. Spruce guestrooms.

ECHENEVEX – 01 Ain – **328** J3 – **see Gex**

LES ÉCHETS – 01 Ain – **328** C5 – **alt. 276 m** – ✉ **01700 Miribel** 43 **E1**

Paris 454 – L'Arbresle 28 – Bourg-en-Bresse 47 – Lyon 20 – Villefranche-sur-Saône 30

Christophe Marguin with rm AC rest, P VISA MC AE

916 rte de Strasbourg – ✆ 04 78 91 80 04 – www.christophe-marguin.com – contact@christophe-marguin.com – Fax 04 78 91 06 83 – Closed 3-23 August, 23 December-5 January, Saturday lunch, Sunday dinner and Monday

7 rm – †€ 65 ††€ 90, ☕ € 14

Rest – Menu € 25 (weekdays)/75 – Carte € 50/95

◆ Photographs of 'ancestors', woodcarvings, library... a pleasant home from home. Semi-classic, semi-regional cuisine and fine list of Bordeaux and Burgundy wines.

ÉCHIROLLES – 38 Isère – **333** H7 – **see Grenoble**

ÉCULLY – 69 Rhône – **327** H5 – **see Lyon**

EFFIAT – 63 Puy-de-Dôme – 326 G6 – pop. 939 – alt. 350 m – ✉ 63260 5 B2
Auvergne

Paris 392 – Clermont-Ferrand 38 – Gannat 11 – Riom 22 – Thiers 39 – Vichy 18

Château★.

Cinq Mars
16 r. Cinq-Mars, (D 984) – ✆ 04 73 63 64 16 – Fax 04 73 64 23 73 – Closed 8-30 August, 13-23 February and dinner during the week

Rest – Menu € 12 bi/18

◆ An 1876 village café near the castle of the Marquis de Cinq Mars. The owner-chef prepares traditional dishes served in a welcoming, countrified dining room.

ÉGLETONS – 19 Corrèze – 329 N3 – pop. 4 424 – alt. 650 m – ✉ 19300 25 C3

Paris 499 – Aubusson 75 – Aurillac 97 – Limoges 112 – Mauriac 46 – Tulle 31 – Ussel 29

Office de tourisme, rue Joseph Vialaneix ✆ 05 55 93 04 34, Fax 05 55 93 00 09

Ibis
rte Ussel via D 1089: 1.5 km – ✆ 05 55 93 25 16 – www.ibishotel.com – h0816@accor.com – Fax 05 55 93 37 54

41 rm – €47/75 €47/75, ☕ €8 **Rest** – Menu (€14), €17

◆ The slightly larger than usual rooms and contemporary furnishings make this Ibis an attractive choice, close to a lake in the rural setting of the upper Correze. The dining area includes a lounge with open fireplace. Traditional menu.

EGUISHEIM – 68 Haut-Rhin – 315 H8 – pop. 1 541 – alt. 210 m – ✉ 68420 Alsace-Lorraine 2 C2

Paris 452 – Belfort 68 – Colmar 7 – Gérardmer 52 – Guebwiller 21 – Mulhouse 42

Office de tourisme, 22a, Grand'Rue ✆ 03 89 23 40 33, Fax 03 89 41 86 20

Ramparts circuit★ - Cinq Châteaux (five castles) road ★ Southwest: 3 km.

Hostellerie du Château without rest
2 r. Château – ✆ 03 89 23 72 00 – www.hostellerieduchateau.com – info@hostellerieduchateau.com – Fax 03 89 41 63 93

11 rm – €68/98 €70/125, ☕ €11

◆ A hotel full of character standing on a pretty square in this small town. Behind the half-timbered façade, guests can enjoy bright, contemporary rooms furnished with a personal touch. Good breakfast.

Hostellerie du Pape
10 Grand'Rue – ✆ 03 89 41 41 21 – www.hostellerie-pape.com – info@hostellerie-pape.com – Fax 03 89 41 41 31 – Closed 4 January-10 February

33 rm – €68 €80/98, ☕ €10

Rest – *(closed Monday and Tuesday)* Menu (€14), €19/33 – Carte €32/51

◆ The name of this former winery refers to Pope Leo IX, whose château is close by. Functional guestrooms which have been modernised in traditional style. Regional dishes are served in the welcoming dining room.

St-Hubert without rest
6 r. Trois Pierres – ✆ 03 89 41 40 50 – www.hotel-st-hubert.com – hotel.st.hubert@wanadoo.fr – Fax 03 89 41 46 88 – Closed end-June, 16-22 November and 10 January-28 February

13 rm – €75/85 €99/109, ☕ €11 – 2 suites

◆ This hotel on the outskirts of the village has a pleasant bed & breakfast ambience. Functional bedrooms basking in the tranquillity of the vineyards. Small terraces and an indoor swimming pool.

Hostellerie des Comtes

2 r. des Trois Châteaux – 03 89 41 16 99 – www.hostellerie-des-comtes.com – aubergedescomtes@wanadoo.fr – Fax 03 89 24 97 10 – Closed 4-26 January
14 rm – €50/59 €59/69, €8 – ½ P €56/63
Rest – *(closed Friday lunch and Thursday)* Menu (€13), €20/39 – Carte €33/42
◆ A family-run auberge with well-maintained, unpretentious bedrooms, some with a small terrace. Traditional cuisine is the order of the day in this rustic restaurant. Outdoor dining on warm, summer days.

Auberge des Trois Châteaux

rm,

26 Grand'Rue – 03 89 23 11 22 – www.auberge-3-chateaux.com – contact@auberge-3-chateaux.com – Fax 03 89 23 72 88 – Closed 4-20 January
12 rm – €50 €55/67, €8 – ½ P €58/64
Rest – *(closed 1-8 July, 28 October-4 November, Tuesday dinner and Wednesday)* Menu €18/35 – Carte €26/42
◆ The three 17C houses that make up this auberge offer typical Alsatian rustic charm with flowers galore on display in spring and summer. The clean, functional guestrooms have all been recently renovated. The menu in this bright and attractive restaurant is centred on local dishes.

Caveau d'Eguisheim (Jean-Christophe Perrin)

3 pl. Château St-Léon – 03 89 41 08 89 – Fax 03 89 23 79 99 – Closed 23-27 December, end January to mid March, Monday and Tuesday
Rest – Menu (€20), €29 (weekday lunch), €38/63 – Carte €57/77
Spec. Pâté en croûte de cochon fermier au foie gras. Pigeonneau de nid cuit façon bécasse. Forêt noire déclinée à notre façon. **Wines** Riesling, Pinot noir.
◆ Authentic winegrower's home with wooden dining room, tasty traditional cuisine, pork specialities and very reasonably priced lunchtime menu.

Au Vieux Porche

16 r. des Trois Châteaux – 03 89 24 01 90 – vieux.porche@wanadoo.fr – Fax 03 89 23 91 25 – Closed 7-14 July, 12-18 November, February holidays, Tuesday and Wednesday
Rest – Menu €24/60 bi – Carte €30/60
◆ Exposed beams, stained glass and wood panelling provide a refined backdrop in this wine-grower's property dating from 1707. Good traditional cuisine and an impressive selection of wines from the estate and beyond.

La Grangelière

59 r. Rempart Sud – 03 89 23 00 30 – www.lagrangeliere.com – lagrangeliere@wanadoo.fr – Fax 03 89 23 61 62 – Closed mid January-mid February, Sunday dinner November-April and Thursday
Rest – Menu €18/67 bi – Carte €24/57
◆ Behind the lovely, half-timbered façade of this typical Alsace property is a friendly ground-floor brasserie and a more refined gastronomic restaurant on the first floor.

Le Pavillon Gourmand

101 r. Rempart Sud – 03 89 24 36 88 – http://perso.orange.fr/pavillon.schubnel/ – pavillon.schubnel@wanadoo.fr – Fax 03 89 23 93 94 – Closed 10 days late June to early July, mid-January to mid-February, Tuesday and Wednesday
Rest – Menu €17/60 bi – Carte €24/60
◆ This family-run restaurant in a picturesque street serves appetising Alsace dishes based on the freshest of produce. Rustic decor with views of the kitchens.

EICHHOFFEN – 67 Bas-Rhin – 315 I6 – pop. 511 – alt. 200 m – ✉ 67140

2 **C1**

Paris 497 – Strasbourg 38 – Colmar 43 – Offenburg 50 – Lahr 65

Les Feuilles d'Or without rest

52 r. du Vignoble – 03 88 08 49 80 – www.lesfeuillesdor.fr.st – kuss.francis@gmail.com – Fax 03 88 08 49 80
5 rm – €75 €80
◆ Between the vineyards and the village, this modern yet traditional looking house offers a cosy half-modern, half-rustic interior (exposed beams, pottery stove). Spacious rooms.

ÉLOISE – 74 Haute-Savoie – 328 I4 – see Bellegarde-sur-Valserine

EMBRUN – 05 Hautes-Alpes – 334 G5 – pop. 6 188 – alt. 871 m – ✉ 05200 French Alps 41 **C1**

Paris 706 – Barcelonnette 55 – Briançon 48 – Digne-les-Bains 97 – Gap 41 – Guillestre 21

Office de tourisme, place Général-Dosse ☎ 04 92 43 72 72, Fax 04 92 43 54 06

N.-D. du Réal cathedral ★: treasure-house★, portal★ - Wall paintings★ in the Cordeliers chapel - Rue de la Liberté and Rue Clovis-Huques★.

Mairie rest, VISA MC AE

pl. Barthelon – ☎ 04 92 43 20 65 – www.hoteldelamairie.com – courrier@hoteldelamairie.com – Fax 04 92 43 47 02 – Closed 15 November-20 December

27 rm – †€ 52/62 ††€ 52/62, ☕ € 8 – ½ P € 50/55

Rest – *(closed Monday except dinner from May to September)*

Menu € 20/27 – Carte € 26/42

◆ A lovely old residence in the heart of the old town, on a picturesque square redolent of Provence. Pre-1940s style bar. Simple rooms with pinewood furnishings. A traditional restaurant with terrace where one dines to the accompaniment of a softly splashing fountain.

Gap road 3 km Southwest by N 94 – ✉ 05200 Embrun

Les Bartavelles rest, VISA MC AE

Clos des Pommiers – ☎ 04 92 43 20 69 – www.bartavelles.com – info@bartavelles.com – Fax 04 92 43 11 92 – Closed 4-17 January

42 rm – †€ 68/98 ††€ 68/98, ☕ € 10 – 1 suite – ½ P € 67/92

Rest – *(closed Sunday dinner and Monday lunch from October to April)*

Menu (€ 18), € 22/48 – Carte € 31/61

◆ Distinctively decorated (larchwood decor of rosettes) rooms and duplex apartments in the main house and three bungalows. Garden and well-equipped spa. Classical dishes served in a rotunda-type room supported by a Guillestre column. In summer, grilled specialities are served on the terrace overlooking the swimming pool.

ÉMERINGES – 69 Rhône – 327 H2 – pop. 215 – alt. 353 m – ✉ 69840 43 **E1**

Paris 408 – Bourg-en-Bresse 56 – Lyon 65 – Mâcon 20 – Villefranche-sur-Saône 33

L'Auberge des Vignerons-La Tassée VISA MC

Les Chavannes – ☎ 04 74 04 45 72 – Fax 04 74 04 45 72 – Closed 22-30 December, February, Sunday dinner, Monday dinner and Tuesday

Rest – Menu € 12 bi (weekdays)/38 – Carte € 41/54

◆ This restaurant, run by a Franco-Japanese couple, has a lovely view of the Beaujolais vineyards. The interior is decorated with wood panelling, check tablecloths and rustic furniture. Traditional cuisine.

EMMERIN – 59 Nord – 302 F4 – see Lille

ENGHIEN-LES-BAINS – 95 Val-d'Oise – 305 E7 – 101 5 – see Paris, Area

ENNORDRES – 18 Cher – 323 K2 – pop. 249 – alt. 166 m – ✉ 18380 12 **C2**

Paris 191 – Orléans 102 – Bourges 44 – Vierzon 38 – Gien 37

Les Chatelains VISA MC

– ☎ 02 48 58 40 37 – www.leschatelains.com – contact@leschatelains.com – Fax 02 48 58 40 37

5 rm ☕ – †€ 69 ††€ 75/105 **Table d'hôte** – Menu € 28 bi

◆ The individual charm of this restored Sologne farm and its outbuildings comes from its cosy setting (antique and old furniture) and the kindness of the hosts. The other plus of the location: the delightfully rustic table d'hôte. Traditional cuisine.

ENSISHEIM – 68 Haut-Rhin – 315 I9 – pop. 6 967 – alt. 217 m – ✉ 68190 1 A3

Paris 487 – Strasbourg 100 – Colmar 27 – Freiburg im Breisgau 68 – Basel 44

Le Domaine du Moulin

44 r. 1ère Armée – ☎ 03 89 83 42 39 – www.hotel-domainedumoulin-alsace.com – reservation@domainedumoulin.com – Fax 03 89 66 21 40

65 rm – €80/110 €86/120, €12 – ½ P €72/90

Rest ***La Villa du Meunier*** – *☎ 03 89 81 15 10 (closed Saturday lunch)*

Menu €20/54 – Carte €34/60

◆ Large modern building with Alsatian charm, opening onto garden with pond. Spacious, practical rooms. Good swimming pool, sauna, hammam and Jacuzzi. Occupying a former mill and dedicated to the local culinary tradition.

ENTRAIGUES-SUR-LA-SORGUE – 84 Vaucluse – 332 C9 – pop. 7 095 – alt. 30 m – ✉ 84320 42 E1

Paris 687 – Marseille 100 – Avignon 13 – Arles 48 – Salon-de-Provence 50

Mas de la Dragonette with rm

rm,

rte de Sorgues – ☎ 04 90 39 20 77 – www.masdeladragonette.com – info@masdeladragonette.com – Fax 04 90 39 08 35 – Closed Saturday lunch, Sunday dinner and Monday

5 rm – €85/120 €85/120, €8

Rest – Menu (€19), €25 (weekday lunch)/35 – Carte €30/45

◆ This 18C Provençal farmhouse, set in remote countryside, is steeped in charm. Find spacious personalised and comfortable rooms, a luxurious romantic terrace, and a vegetable garden and pool. The chef, who also runs cookery courses, concocts gourmet fare using fresh vegetables from the garden.

ENTRAYGUES-SUR-TRUYÈRE – 12 Aveyron – 338 H3 – pop. 1 182 – alt. 236 m – ✉ 12140 Languedoc-Roussillon-Tarn Gorges 29 C1

Paris 600 – Aurillac 45 – Figeac 58 – Rodez 43 – St-Flour 83

Syndicat d'initiative, place de la République ☎ 05 65 44 56 10, Fax 05 65 44 50 85

Old Quarter: Rue Basse★ - Gothic bridge★.

Vallée du Lot★★.

La Rivière

60 av. du Pont-de-Truyère – ☎ 05 65 66 16 83 – www.hotellariviere.com – info@hotellariviere.com – Fax 05 65 66 24 98 – Closed 7-28 December and 16 February-2 March

31 rm – €65/75 €85/105, €11 – ½ P €75/85

Rest – Menu €29/35 – Carte €33/57

◆ This hotel on the banks of the Truyère has enjoyed a recent facelift. The result: a full range of modern comforts and a contemporary decor (harmonious tones, quality materials). Contemporary cuisine in a bright and airy dining room overlooking the river.

Les Deux Vallées

av. du Pont-de-Truyère – ☎ 05 65 44 52 15 – hotel.2vallees@wanadoo.fr – Fax 05 65 44 54 47 – Closed February, November, Christmas holidays, Sunday dinner, Friday dinner and Saturday October-April

20 rm – €45 €45, €7 – ½ P €48

Rest – *(closed 5 - 22 Nov. and 24 - 31 Dec.)* Menu (€12), €16/23 – Carte €26/42

◆ The Lot and Truyère river valleys meet in Entraygues. The well-soundproofed rooms have all been renovated with an eye to practicality rather than aesthetics. Country inn-style restaurant opening onto a small courtyard-terrace.

Le Clos St Georges

rest,

19 côteaux St Georges – ☎ 05 65 48 68 22 – www.leclosstgeorges.com – catherine.rethore@hotmail.fr – Open 2 March-14 November

4 rm – €47 €57 – ½ P €47

Table d'hôte – *(closed Sunday15 June-15 September)* Menu €18 bi

◆ In the upper part of the village, this former wine-grower's house (1637) has pretty rooms, an attractive lounge, paved courtyard and flower garden overlooking a meadow. Meals and breakfasts are served in a former kitchen graced by a fine fireplace.

in Fel 10 km West by D 107 and D 573 – pop. 171 – alt. 530 m – ✉ 12140

Auberge du Fel
Le Fel – ☎ 05 65 44 52 30 – www.auberge-du-fel.com – info@auberge-du-fel.com – Fax 05 65 48 64 96 – Open 5 April-4 November
10 rm – †€ 55/66 ††€ 55/66, ☕ € 8,50 – ½ P € 50/60
Rest – *(Closed lunch in low season except Saturday and Sunday)*
Menu € 20 (weekdays)/41 – Carte € 26/44
◆ A vine-covered shingle-roofed house in a picturesque hamlet overlooking the Lot River. The personalised contemporary rooms are simple and faultlessly kept. Pounti, truffade and cabécou washed down with Fel wine in the restaurant.

ENTRECHAUX – 84 Vaucluse – **332** D8 – see Vaison-la-Romaine

ENTZHEIM – 67 Bas-Rhin – **315** J5 – see Strasbourg

ÉPAIGNES – 27 Eure – **304** C6 – pop. 1 223 – alt. 159 m – ✉ 27260 32 **A3**

Paris 175 – Le Grand-Quevilly 63 – Le Havre 50 – Rouen 69

L'Auberge du Beau Carré with rm
1 rte des Anglais – ☎ 02 32 41 52 42 – http://aubergedubeaucarre.monsite.wanadoo.fr – aubergedubeaucarre@wanadoo.fr – Fax 02 32 41 48 60 – Closed Sunday evening and Monday
7 rm – †€ 45 ††€ 60, ☕ € 6 – ½ P € 45 **Rest** – Menu (€ 18), € 28/55
◆ This well-kept, family-run restaurant is in a smart, redbrick house. Appetising updated repertory using quality produce. Comfortable guestrooms.

Luxury pad or humble abode?
X and 🏠 denote categories of comfort.

ÉPENOUX – 70 Haute-Saône – **314** E7 – see Vesoul

ÉPERNAY – 51 Marne – **306** F8 – pop. 24 500 – alt. 75 m – ✉ 51200 13 **B2**

Northern France and the Paris Region

Paris 143 – Châlons-en-Champagne 35 – Château-Thierry 57 – Reims 28

Office de tourisme, 7, avenue de Champagne ☎ 03 26 53 33 00, Fax 03 26 51 95 22

Caves de Champagne (cellars) ★★ - Archeological collection ★ at the municipal museum.

Plan on following page

La Villa Eugène without rest
82 av. de Champagne, 1 km via ② – ☎ 03 26 32 44 76 – www.villa-eugene.com – info@villa-eugene.com – Fax 03 26 32 44 98
15 rm – †€ 100/300 ††€ 100/300, ☕ € 14
◆ Imposing house, once the home of a famous Champagne producer. Colonial or Louis XVI style bedrooms, a bar devoted to bubbly and breakfast in the conservatory.

Le Clos Raymi without rest
3 r. Joseph de Venoge – ☎ 03 26 51 00 58 – www.closraymi-hotel.com – closraymi@wanadoo.fr – Fax 03 26 51 18 98 – Closed 24 December-2 January BZ **a**
7 rm – †€ 100/160 ††€ 100/160, ☕ € 14
◆ This pretty redbrick family mansion was owned by the Chandon family. Refined, individually decorated guestrooms. Pleasant breakfast room overlooking the garden.

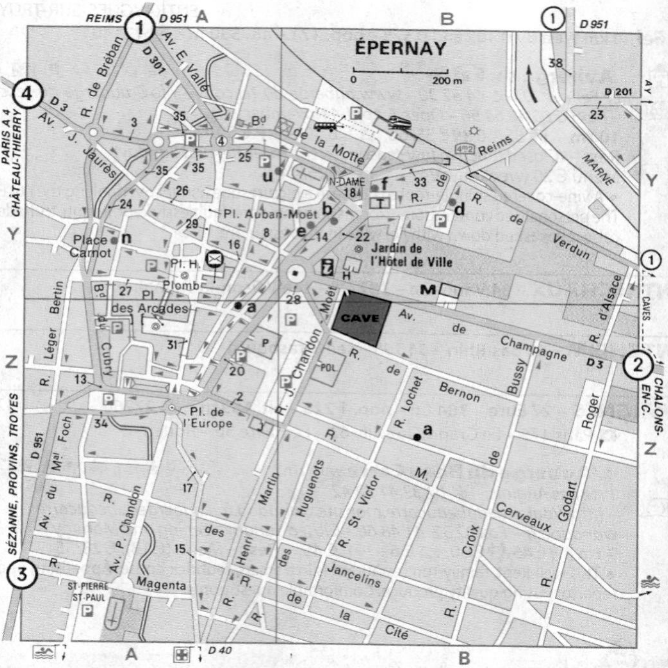

ÉPERNAY

Archers (R. des) . . . . AZ 2
Basse St-Laurent (R.) . . . . AY 3
Bourgeois (Pl. Léon) . . . . AY 4
Flodoard (R.) . . . . AY 8
Gallice (R.) . . . . AZ 13
Gambetta (R.) . . . . BY 14
Hôpital Auban-Moët (R.) . . . . . . AZ 15
Leclerc (R. Gén.) . . . . AY 16
Louis (R. Charles) . . . . AZ 17
Mendès-France (Pl.) . . . . BY 18
Mercier (R. E.) . . . . AZ 20
Moët (R. Jean) . . . . BY 22
Moulin Brûlé (R. du) . . . . AY 24
Moulin (R. Jean) . . . . BY 23
Perrier (Rempart) . . . . AY 25
Plomb (Pl. Hugues) . . . . AY
Porte Lucas (R.) . . . . AY 26
Prof. Langevin (R.) . . . . AY 27
République (Pl.) . . . . BYZ 28
St-Martin (R.) . . . . AY 29
St-Thibault (R.) . . . . AZ 31
Semard (R. Pierre) . . . . BY 33
Sézanne (R. de) . . . . AZ 34
Tanneurs (R. des) . . . . AY 35
Thévenet (Av.) . . . . BY 38

Les Berceaux (Patrick Michelon) rest, VISA

13 r. Berceaux – ✆ 03 26 55 28 84 – www.lesberceaux.com – les.berceaux@wanadoo.fr – Fax 03 26 55 10 36 AZ **a**

28 rm – €95/115 €95/115, €11

Rest – *(closed 15-31 August, February school holidays, Monday and Tuesday)* Menu (€26), €33/69 – Carte €81/98

Rest *Bistrot le 7* – *(closed Wednesday and Thursday)* Menu (€17,50), €24 – Carte €44/56

Spec. Turbot sauvage au vin de Champagne. Lièvre à la royale (season). Grande assiette tout chocolat. **Wines** Champagne.

◆ Set in the bustling heart of the town, an inn with comfortable rooms, all renovated in the same style (yellow tones, dark parquet flooring). Elegant gastronomic restaurant serving an authentically classic menu. Good cellar. Chic, modern atmosphere at the Bistrot le 7; traditional menu.

XX **Théatre** VISA

8 pl. P. Mendès-France – ✆ 03 26 58 88 19 – www.epernay-rest-letheatre.com – Fax 03 26 58 88 38 – Closed 22-28 December, 6-22 February, Sunday dinner, Tuesday dinner and Wednesday BY **f**

Rest – Menu (€18), €25 bi/48 – Carte €51/65

◆ A stone's throw from the theatre, this is one of Epernay's oldest brasseries (early 20C). Carvings, high ceilings and warm colours set the scene. Traditional recipes.

La Table Kobus
3 r. Dr Rousseau – ✆ 03 26 51 53 53
– www.latablekobus.com
– serge.herscher@wanadoo.fr – Fax 03 26 58 42 68
– Closed 12-27 April, 2-16 August, 28 December-11 January, Thursday dinner, Sunday dinner and Monday ABY **u**
Rest – Menu (€ 21), € 28/48 – Carte € 50/65
◆ Pleasant 1900 bistro where you can sip your own champagne without paying corkage! Popular with the locals.

La Cave à Champagne
16 r. Gambetta – ✆ 03 26 55 50 70
– www.la-cave-a-champagne.com
– cave.champagne@wanadoo.fr – Fax 03 26 51 07 24 – Closed Tuesday and Wednesday BY **b**
Rest – *(number of covers limited, pre-book)*
Menu € 17/45 bi – Carte € 30/40
◆ A small cellar with regional wines on display. Reasonably-priced Champagne meals. Traditional cuisine.

La Grillade Gourmande
16 r. de Reims – ✆ 03 26 55 44 22
– www.lagrilladegourmande.com – grilla2gourmande@aol.com
– Fax 03 26 54 01 74 – Closed 25 August-7 September, 22-28 December, 9-22 February, Sunday and Monday BY **d**
Rest – Menu € 19/55 – Carte € 29/65
◆ This tiny, family-run, countrified restaurant serves traditional fare. Champagne specialities and grilled meat prepared before your eyes by the fireside.

in Dizy **3 km by ① – pop. 1 714 – alt. 77 m – ✉ 51530**

Les Grains d'Argent rest, VISA AE
1 allée du Petit Bois – ✆ 03 26 55 76 28
– www.lesgrainsdargent.com – hotel.lesgrainsdargent@wanadoo.fr
– Fax 03 26 55 75 96 – Closed 22 December-4 January
20 rm – †€ 90 ††€ 100, ☕ € 13 – ½ P € 90
Rest – *(closed Saturday lunch, Sunday dinner and Monday)*
Menu (€ 30), € 47/87 – Carte € 75/95
◆ A pleasant welcome, pleasing personalised rooms and a champagne bar set the scene in this contemporary hotel overlooking the vineyards. The restaurant, treated to a modern new decor, serves updated dishes that reflect the changing seasons.

in Champillon **6 km by ① – pop. 516 – alt. 210 m – ✉ 51160**

Royal Champagne rm, rest, VISA AE
D 201 – ✆ 03 26 52 87 11 – www.royalchampagne.com
– reservation@royalchampagne.com – Fax 03 26 52 89 69
– Closed 1st December-1st February
22 rm – †€ 240/375 ††€ 240/375, ☕ € 29 – 3 suites
Rest – *(closed Monday lunch and Tuesday lunch)*
Menu € 38 (weekday lunch), € 65/110 – Carte € 78/97
◆ Overlooking Épernay, this old coaching inn has well-appointed, luxurious guestrooms. The elegant dining room boasts fine views of the Champagne vineyards and the Marne Valley.

Reims road **8 km by ① – ✉ 51160 St-Imoges**

Maison du Vigneron VISA
D 951 – ✆ 03 26 52 88 00 – www.lamaisonduvigneron.com
– Fax 03 26 52 86 03 – Closed 16-24 August, Sunday dinner, Monday dinner and Wednesday
Rest – Menu € 23 (weekdays)/50 – Carte € 62/69
◆ Allow yourself a stopover in the pleasant atmosphere of a forest inn. Beams, wrought iron lamps, fireplace and a beautiful setting for traditional cuisine.

in Vinay 6 km by ③ – **pop. 496 – alt. 102 m** – ✉ **51530**

Hostellerie La Briqueterie
4 rte de Sézanne – ☎ 03 26 59 99 99 – www.labriqueterie.fr – briqueterie@relaischateaux.com – Fax 03 26 59 92 10 – Closed 14 December-15 January and Saturday lunch
rm, rest,
40 rm – €190/490 €220/490, €25 – ½ P €190/320
Rest – Menu €40 (weekday lunch), €65/100 – Carte €82/102
Spec. Légumes rafraîchis en fine gelée au bouzy et joue de bœuf braisée. Carré d'agneau rôti à la sarriette et moutarde de Reims, petites tomates farcies. Fraises et framboises de notre région (season). **Wines** Champagne.
◆ In the midst of the vineyards, this attractive establishment offers personalised guestrooms. Cosy lounge bar with a fine choice of champagnes. Spa and pool. Stylishly decorated restaurant overlooking a landscaped garden. No less than 850 wines accompany the chef's updated recipes.

ÉPINAL P – **88 Vosges** – **314** G3 – **pop. 34 700** – **alt. 324 m** – ✉ **88000** 27 **C3**
Alsace-Lorraine

Paris 385 – Belfort 96 – Colmar 88 – Mulhouse 106 – Nancy 72 – Vesoul 90
Office de tourisme, 6, place Saint-Goëry ☎ 03 29 82 53 32, Fax 03 29 82 88 22
des Images d'Épinal 3 km on the St-Dié-des-Vosges road, ☎ 03 29 31 37 52
Old town★: Basilica★ - Château park★ - Musée départemental d'art ancien et contemporain★ - Imagerie d'Épinal.

Plan on next page

Le Manoir
5 av. Provence – ☎ 03 29 29 55 55 – www.manoir-hotel.com – manoir-hotel@wanadoo.fr – Fax 03 29 29 55 56 BZ **n**
12 rm – €100 €100/149, €14
Rest ***Ducs de Lorraine*** – see below
◆ An attractive large residence dating from 1876. The rooms here are spacious and well-equipped (high-speed Internet access, video game console and fax) with personal touches. Fitness centre.

Mercure
rm,
13 pl. E. Stein – ☎ 03 29 29 12 91 – www.mercure.com – h0831@accor.com – Fax 03 29 29 12 92 AZ **e**
60 rm – €70/160 €80/170, €16
Rest – *(dinner only)* Menu €20/25 – Carte €30/36
◆ A 19C hotel near the Classic and Modern Art Museum. Most of the rooms have been renovated and equipped with a wifi system. The rooms at the back are quieter. A pleasant, modern restaurant with a terrace facing the canal. 'Mercure' menu of traditional inspiration.

Ducs de Lorraine (Claudy Obriot et Stéphane Ringer)
– Hôtel Le Manoir
5 av. Provence – ☎ 03 29 29 56 00 – www.ducsdelorraine.fr – Fax 03 29 29 56 01 – Closed 9-24 August, 2-6 January and Sunday except bank holidays BZ **n**
Rest – Menu €36 (weekday lunch), €44/76 – Carte €70/100
Spec. Crème mousseuse de cèpes aux escargots de Cleurie. Tournedos de pigeon au foie blond. Soufflé mirabelle, coulis et sorbet. **Wines** Côtes de Toul gris, Pinot noir d'Alsace.
◆ Fine-looking late-19C villa. Elegant dining room with mouldings and Louis XV-style furniture. Tasty cuisine with a contemporary touch, and select wines.

La Voûte
7 pl. de l'Atre – ☎ 03 29 35 47 25 – thomas.hd88@neuf.fr – Closed 14-21 March, 25-31 January, Wednesday dinner and Sunday BZ **t**
Rest – *(number of covers limited, pre-book)* Carte €28/49
◆ A friendly welcome awaits you at this small, very simple and refined establishment. Under the vaults that give it its name, you are served fuss free, market based cuisine.

Le Petit Robinson

24 r. R. Poincaré – ✆ 03 29 34 23 51
– www.lepetitrobinson.fr
– lepetitrobinson@free.fr – Fax 03 29 31 27 17
– Closed 1-4 May, 18 July-16 August, 1-4 January, Saturday lunch, Monday lunch and Sunday BZ **a**

Rest – Menu € 20/40 – Carte € 40/57

◆ Family-run restaurant with a colourful facade, between the old town and the River Moselle. Slightly antiquated dining room. Traditional dishes.

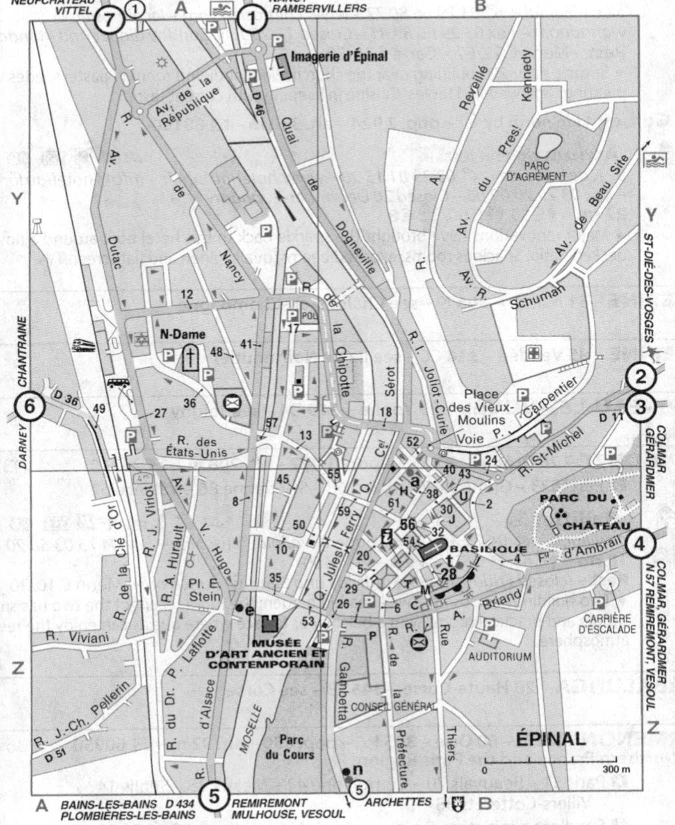

Abbé-Friesenhauser (R.) . . . . . . BZ 2
Ambrail (R. d') . . . . BZ 4
Bassot (Pl. Cl.) . . . . BZ 5
Blaudez (R. F.) . . . . BZ 6
Boegner (R. du Pasteur) . . . . . BZ 7
Bons-Enfants (Quai des) . . . . . AZ 8
Boudiou (Pt et R. du) . . . . AZ 10
Boulay-de-la-Meurthe (R.) . . . . AY 12
Bourg (R. L.) . . . . AY 13
Clemenceau (Pl.) . . . . AY 17
Clemenceau (Pont) . . . . BY 18
Comédie (R. de la) . . . . BZ 20
Entre-les-Deux-Portes (R.) . . . BYZ 24
États-Unis (R. des) . . . . AY
Foch (Pl.) . . . . BZ 26
Gaulle (Av. du Gén.-de) . . . . . . AY 27
Gelée (R. Cl.) . . . . BZ 28
Georgin (R.) . . . . BZ 29
Halles (R. des) . . . . BZ 30
Henri (Pl. E.) . . . . BZ 32
Lattre (Av. Mar.-de) . . . . AY 36
Leclerc (R. Gén.) . . . . BZ 38
Lormont (R.) . . . . BZ 40
Lyautey (R. Mar.) . . . . AY 41
Maix (R. de la) . . . . BZ 43
Minimes (R. des) . . . . AZ 45
Neufchâteau (R. F. de) . . . . . . AY 48
N.-D.-de-Lorette (R.) . . . . AY 49
Pinau (Pl.) . . . . AZ 50
Poincaré (R. Raymond) . . . . . . BY 52
Sadi-Carnot (Pont) . . . . AZ 53
St-Goery (R.) . . . . BZ 54
Schwabisch Hall (Pl. de) . . . . . BZ 55
La Tour (R. G. de la) . . . . AZ 35
Vosges (Pl. des) . . . . BZ 56
4-Nations (Pl. des) . . . . AY 57
170e Régt-d'Inf. (Pont du) . . . . BZ 59
170e-Régt-d'Inf. (R. du) . . . . . BZ 61

via ① 3 km – ✉ 88000 Épinal

La Fayette

3 r. Bazaine (Le-saut-le-Cerf) – ✆ 03 29 81 15 15 – www.bestwestern-lafayette-epinal.com – hotel.lafayette.epinal@wanadoo.fr – Fax 03 29 31 07 08

58 rm – ♦€ 89/220 ♦♦€ 89/220, ☕ € 12 – 1 suite

Rest – Menu € 19/43 – Carte € 40/50

◆ Hotel complex on the doorstep of Épinal. Spacious, functional rooms; ask for one of the new, modern ones. Wellness centre: counter current pool, sauna, Jacuzzi tub. Unpretentious classic and regional cuisine served in a glazed dining room.

in Chaumousey 10 km by ⑥ and D 460 – pop. 868 – alt. 360 m – ✉ 88390

Calmosien

37 r. d'Epinal – ✆ 03 29 66 80 77 – www.calmosien.com – lecalmosien@wanadoo.fr – Fax 03 29 66 89 41 – Closed 11-25 July, Sunday dinner and Monday

Rest – Menu € 22/62 – Carte € 38/50

◆ Spruce, early-20C building near the church. Elegant dining room in pastel shades with paintings and well-laid tables. Cuisine in keeping with current taste.

in Golbey 4 km north by ⑦ – pop. 7 924 – alt. 320 m – ✉ 88190

Atrium without rest

89 r. de Lorraine – ✆ 03 29 81 15 20 – www.hotel-atrium.fr – info@hotel-atrium.fr – Fax 03 29 29 09 06 – Closed 20 December-2 January

22 rm – ♦€ 55 ♦♦€ 60, ☕ € 8

◆ Major renovations have brought the sparkle back to this hotel built around a flower-decked patio. Spacious rooms: exposed beams, quality linen and flat screen TVs.

L'ÉPINE – 51 Marne – 306 I9 – see Châlons-en-Champagne

L'ÉPINE – 85 Vendée – 316 C6 – see Île de Noirmoutier

ÉPINEAU-LES-VOVES – 89 Yonne – 319 D4 – see Joigny

ÉPINOUZE – 26 Drôme – 332 C2 – pop. 1 272 – alt. 208 m – ✉ 26210 43 E2

Paris 523 – Grenoble 79 – Lyon 68 – St-Étienne 86 – Valence 62

Galliffet

au village – ✆ 04 75 31 72 98 – aubergevalloire@tiscali.fr – Fax 04 75 03 58 20

18 rm – ♦€ 45 ♦♦€ 50, ☕ € 5 – ½ P € 50

Rest – *(closed Friday dinner, Saturday and Sunday) (lunch only)* Menu € 10/30

◆ Two buildings enclosing a well-shaded garden; the more recent of the two has small, simple and practical rooms with a balcony or terrace where guests can enjoy the restful atmosphere.

ERBALUNGA – 2B Haute-Corse – 345 F3 – see Corse

ERMENONVILLE – 60 Oise – 305 H6 – pop. 830 – alt. 92 m – ✉ 60950 36 B3

Northern France and the Paris Region

Paris 51 – Beauvais 70 – Compiègne 42 – Meaux 25 – Senlis 14 – Villers-Cotterêts 38

Syndicat d'initiative, 2 bis, rue René de Girardin ✆ 03 44 54 01 58, Fax 03 44 54 04 96

Mer de Sable★ - Ermenonville forest ★ - Chaalis abbey★★ North: 3 km.

Le Prieuré without rest

6 pl. de l'Église – ✆ 03 44 63 66 70 – www.hotel-leprieure.com – reception@hotel-leprieure.com – Fax 03 44 63 95 01 – Closed Christmas holidays and Sunday

9 rm – ♦€ 85/165 ♦♦€ 85/165, ☕ € 12

◆ A B&B atmosphere is to be found in this wonderful 18C residence surrounded by a pretty English garden next to a church. Elegant rooms with hand-picked furniture.

XX **Le Relais de la Croix d'Or** with rm rest, P VISA MC AE
2 r. Prince Radziwill – ✆ 03 44 54 00 04 – www.lacroixdor.net – relaisor@wanadoo.fr – Fax 03 44 54 99 16 – Closed 15-31 August, Sunday dinner and Monday
8 rm – †€ 67/82 ††€ 76/95
Rest – Menu € 20 bi (weekday lunch), € 33/65 – Carte € 46/74
◆ Enjoy traditional cuisine in the wooden-beamed dining room with exposed stone walls, in a vaulted cellar or, in summer, on the terrace overlooking the water and gardens. Functional rooms.

ERMITAGE-DU-FRÈRE-JOSEPH – 88 Vosges – 314 J5 – see Ventron

ERNÉE – 53 Mayenne – 310 D5 – pop. 5 793 – alt. 120 m – ✉ 53500 34 B1
Normandy

Paris 304 – Domfront 47 – Fougères 22 – Laval 31 – Mayenne 25 – Vitré 30
Syndicat d'initiative, place de l'Hôtel de Ville ✆ 02 43 08 71 10

XX **Le Grand Cerf** VISA MC AE
19 r. A.-Briand – ✆ 02 43 05 13 09 – www.legrandcerf.net – infos@legrandcerf.net – Fax 02 43 05 02 90 – Closed 15-31 January, Sunday dinner and Monday
Rest – Menu € 17 (weekday lunch), € 24/34 – Carte € 45/55
◆ The dining room is embellished with sculptures and its decor combines bare stone with modern features. A spruce setting for well-prepared cuisine based on local dishes.

in La Coutancière 9 km East on N 12 – ✉ 53500 Vautorte

X **La Coutancière** P VISA MC
– ✆ 02 43 00 56 27 – Fax 02 43 00 66 09 – Closed Tuesday dinner and Wednesday
Rest – Menu (€ 12), € 15/42 – Carte € 28/44
◆ A welcoming hotel on the edge of the Mayenne forest in the heart of the region described by Balzac in his novel Les Chouans. Traditional cuisine and attentive service.

ERQUY – 22 Côtes-d'Armor – 309 H3 – pop. 3 725 – alt. 12 m – ✉ 22430 10 C1
Brittany

Paris 451 – Dinan 46 – Dinard 39 – Lamballe 21 – Rennes 102 – St-Brieuc 33
Office de tourisme, 3, rue du 19 Mars 1962 ✆ 02 96 72 30 12, Fax 02 96 72 02 88
Cap d'Erquy ★ Northwest: 3.5 km puis 30 mn.

Beauséjour P VISA MC
21 r. Corniche – ✆ 02 96 72 30 39 – www.beausejour-erquy.com – hotel.beausejour@wanadoo.fr – Fax 02 96 72 16 30 – Open 30 March-15 November and closed Monday in low season
15 rm – †€ 54/56 ††€ 58/70, € 9 – ½ P € 59/70
Rest – Menu (€ 15), € 21/36 – Carte € 24/41
◆ Family-run hotel-restaurant, only 100 m from the beach, with well-kept guestrooms enlivened by colourful floral fabrics; half have a view of the fishing port. Seafood dishes and views of the sea from the large dining room windows.

XX **L'Escurial** VISA MC AE
bd de la Mer – ✆ 02 96 72 31 56 – www.restaurantlescurial.com – contact@restaurantlescurial.com – Fax 02 96 63 57 92 – Closed 5 January-3 February, Sunday dinner except July-August, Thursday dinner off season and Monday
Rest – Menu (€ 22), € 33/62 – Carte € 45/70
◆ Elegant contemporary restaurant overlooking the seafront. Updated culinary specialties, fish dishes and, in season, the famous Saint-Jacques scallops.

in St-Aubin 3 km southeast by secondary road – ✉ 22430 Erquy

X **Relais St-Aubin** P VISA MC AE
D 68 – ✆ 02 96 72 13 22 – www.relais-saint-aubin.fr – gilbert.josset@wanadoo.fr – Fax 02 96 63 54 31 – Closed 15 November-15 December, 1st-28 February, Wednesday from 15 November to 18 March, Tuesday in low season and Monday
Rest – Menu € 17 (weekday lunch), € 23 € bi/30 bi – Carte € 30/56
◆ This 17C country residence built in local stone has a lovely rustic-style dining room. In fine weather one can enjoy the terrace and the delightful flower-filled garden.

ERSA – 2B Haute-Corse – **345** F2 – **see Corse**

ERSTEIN – 67 Bas-Rhin – **315** J6 – **pop. 9 632** – **alt. 150 m** – ✉ **67150** 1 **B2**

Paris 514 – Colmar 49 – Molsheim 24 – St-Dié 69 – Sélestat 27 – Strasbourg 28

Office de tourisme, 16, rue du Général-de-Gaulle ✆ 03 88 98 14 33, Fax 03 88 98 12 32

Crystal rest, VISA AE

41-43 av. de la Gare – ✆ 03 88 64 81 00 – www.hotelcrystal.info – baumert@hotelcrystal.info – Fax 03 88 98 11 29 – Closed 1st-10 August

71 rm – †€ 62/75 ††€ 71/108, ☕ € 14 – 3 suites

Rest – *(closed 1-23 August, Friday dinner, Saturday lunch and Sunday)*

Menu € 13 (lunch)/38 – Carte € 30/55

◆ A modern hotel near the main road, with functional, well-arranged rooms. The largest are on the third floor and have sloping ceilings. Bright dining room with contemporary décor, complemented by paintings.

Jean-Victor Kalt VISA

41 av. de la Gare – ✆ 03 88 98 09 54 – jean-victor.kalt@wanadoo.fr – Fax 03 88 98 83 01 – Closed 27 July-15 August, 1-8 January, Sunday dinner, Wednesday dinner, Saturday lunch and Monday

Rest – Menu € 22, € 30/62 – Carte € 45/73

◆ Appealing wood-panelled dining room with Weisbuch paintings and well-spaced out tables. Traditional fare and a fine choice of Asace and Rhône Valley wines.

ERVAUVILLE – 45 Loiret – **318** O3 – **see Courtenay**

ESCATALENS – 82 Tarn-et-Garonne – **337** D8 – **pop. 689** – **alt. 60 m** – ✉ **82700** 28 **B2**

Paris 649 – Colomiers 58 – Montauban 16 – Toulouse 53

Maison des Chevaliers

pl. de la Mairie – ✆ 05 63 68 71 23 – www.maisondeschevaliers.com – claude.choux@wanadoo.fr – Fax 05 63 30 25 90

5 rm ☕ – †€ 70/75 ††€ 90 **Table d'hôte** – Menu € 25 bi

◆ This brick-built residence has very large rooms, richly and carefully furnished with antiques, travel souvenirs, and washbasins and faience from Portugal. Kitchenette and games room for the use of guests. Regional cuisine.

ESCOIRE – 24 Dordogne – **329** G4 – **pop. 429** – **alt. 100 m** – ✉ **24420** 4 **C1**

Paris 485 – Bordeaux 147 – Périgueux 13 – Sarlat-la-Canéda 72 – Coulounieix-Chamiers 18

Château d' Escoire without rest

– ✆ 05 53 05 99 80 – www.escoire-lechateau.com – sylvie.kordalov@wanadoo.fr – Fax 05 53 05 99 80 – Open 1 May-30 October

4 rm ☕ – †€ 65 ††€ 85

◆ This romantic 18C abode dominating the village is surrounded by parkland and a formal French style garden. Majestic breakfast room and spacious bedrooms.

ESPALION – 12 Aveyron – **338** I3 – **pop. 4 457** – **alt. 342 m** – ✉ **12500** 29 **D1**

Languedoc-Roussillon-Tarn Gorges

Paris 592 – Aurillac 72 – Figeac 93 – Mende 101 – Millau 81 – Rodez 31 – St-Flour 80

Office de tourisme, 23, place du Plô ✆ 05 65 44 10 63, Fax 05 65 44 10 39

Perse church ★ Southeast: 1 km.

De France without rest VISA

36 bd J. Poulenc – ✆ 05 65 44 06 13 – Fax 05 65 44 76 26

9 rm – †€ 42 ††€ 46, ☕ € 7

◆ This small, centrally located hotel is close to several museums. Clean bright rooms with light wooden furniture, soundproofing, good service and reasonable prices.

Moderne et rest. l'Eau Vive rest, VISA
27 bd Guizard – ✆ 05 65 44 05 11 – www.hotelmoderne12.com – hotelmoderne12@aol.com – Fax 05 65 48 06 94 – Closed 4 November-10 December and 4-17 January
28 rm – †€ 45/60 ††€ 45/60, ☕ € 7 – ½ P € 43/50
Rest – *(closed Sunday dinner and Monday)* Menu (€ 12), € 24/46 – Carte € 45/64
◆ Half-timbered house that maintains the tradition of welcoming pilgrims. Two generations of ageing rooms; the oldest have the advantage of the courtyard. The angler/chef offers freshwater fish specialities in a bright setting.

Le Méjane VISA
r. Méjane – ✆ 05 65 48 22 37 – lemejane@wanadoo.fr – Fax 05 65 48 13 00 – Closed 2-25 March, 24-30 June, Monday except dinner from September to June, Wednesday except July-August and Sunday dinner
Rest – Menu (€ 18), € 25/58 – Carte € 40/51
◆ The presence of mirrors gives an impression of space in this small dining room. The modern decor is as well thought out as the contemporary cuisine.

ESPALY-ST-MARCEL – 43 Haute-Loire – 331 F3 – alt. 650 m – see le Puy-en-Velay

ESPELETTE – 64 Pyrénées-Atlantiques – 342 D2 – pop. 1 879 – alt. 77 m – ✉ 64250 3 A3

Paris 775 – Bordeaux 215 – Pau 134 – Donostia-San Sebastián 78 – Irun 59
Office de tourisme, 145, route Karrika Nagusia ✆ 05 59 93 95 02

Euzkadi rest, rm, VISA
285 Karrika Nagusia – ✆ 05 59 93 91 88 – www.hotel-restaurant-euzkadi.com – hotel.euzkadi@wanadoo.fr – Fax 05 59 93 90 19 – Closed 1st November-24 December, Tuesday in low season and Monday
27 rm – †€ 44/58 ††€ 54/72, ☕ € 8 – ½ P € 54/63
Rest – Menu € 19/34 – Carte € 27/45
◆ Hotel with a typically Basque-style façade, in the centre of the chilli pepper capital. The completely refurbished first floor rooms are more comfortable than those in the annexe. Swimming pool. Copious and authentic traditional cuisine served in a rustic-style dining room.

Irazabala without rest
155 Mendiko Bidéa – ✆ 05 59 93 93 02 – www.irazabala.com – irazabala@wanadoo.fr
4 rm ☕ – †€ 60/70 ††€ 75/95
◆ A charming residence built in the style of the region using traditional materials. Elegant guestrooms, rustic lounge, peaceful surroundings and the mountains as a backdrop.

ESQUIULE – 64 Pyrénées-Atlantiques – 342 H3 – pop. 541 – alt. 277 m – ✉ 64400 3 B3

Paris 813 – Pau 43 – Lourdes 69 – Orthez 44 – Saint-Jean-Pied-de-Port 62

Chez Château VISA
place du Fronton – ✆ 05 59 39 23 03 – jb.hourcourigaray@wanadoo.fr – Fax 05 59 39 81 97 – Closed 15 February-15 March, Sunday dinner, Monday and Tuesday
Rest – Menu € 20/60 – Carte € 35/58
◆ A bar and restaurant live happily together in this old farmhouse. Pleasant, rustic dining rooms and regional cuisine.

ESTAING – 12 Aveyron – 338 I3 – pop. 610 – alt. 313 m – ✉ 12190 29 D1
Languedoc-Roussillon-Tarn Gorges

Paris 602 – Aurillac 63 – Conques 33 – Espalion 10 – Figeac 74 – Rodez 35
Syndicat d'initiative, 24, rue François d'Estaing ✆ 05 65 44 03 22, Fax 05 65 66 37 81

L' Auberge St-Fleuret

19 r. Francois d'Estaing, opposite the town hall – ✆ 05 65 44 01 44 – www.auberge-st-fleuret.com – info@auberge-st-fleuret.com – Fax 05 65 44 72 19 – Open mid March-mid November and closed Sunday evening and Monday off season, Monday lunch July-August

14 rm – †€ 46/56 ††€ 46/56, ☕ € 8 – ½ P € 48/55

Rest – Menu € 18 (weekdays)/32 – Carte € 42/55

◆ This 19C coaching inn offers modern rooms, either overlooking the garden or the old village dominated by its château. Two dining rooms: one rustic, the other neat and bright. Regional specialities including the famous aligot (potato and cheese dish – served à la carte). Poolside terrace.

Aux Armes d'Estaing

1 quai Lot – ✆ 05 65 44 70 02 – www.estaing.net – remi.catusse@estaing.net – Fax 05 65 44 74 54 – Open 16 March-2 November and closed Sunday dinner and Monday

30 rm – †€ 53/65 ††€ 53/65, ☕ € 8,50 – ½ P € 46/55

Rest – Menu (€ 13), € 18 (weekdays)/43

◆ This establishment is opposite the Gothic bridge spanning the River Lot at the foot of the castle (cradle of the d'Estaing family). Plain, bright rooms. Warm welcome. This restaurant, decorated in a classic style, offers updated, regional specialities.

Le Manoir de la Fabrègues

rte d'Espalion : 3 km – ✆ 05 65 66 37 78 – www.manoirattitude.com – info.lemanoir@ orange.fr – Fax 05 65 66 37 76 – Closed 12 November-11 December

10 rm – †€ 70/85 ††€ 70/85, ☕ € 9 – 1 suite – ½ P € 60/70

Rest – *(Closed Sunday dinner, Tuesday lunch and Monday)* Menu (€ 19), € 25/34

◆ This beautifully renovated 15C manor is steeped in the rustic nostalgia of stately homes. Immense fireplaces, stonework and bare beams. Practical rooms. Terrace dominating the valley. Traditional and regional cuisine.

ESTAING – 65 Hautes-Pyrénées – 342 K7 – pop. 67 – alt. 970 m – ✉ 65400 Atlantic Coast 28 A3

Paris 874 – Argelès-Gazost 12 – Arrens 7 – Laruns 43 – Lourdes 24 – Pau 69 – Tarbes 43

d'Estaing Lake ★ South: 4 km.

Lac d'Estaing with rm

au lac, South : 4 km – ✆ 05 62 97 06 25 – Fax 05 62 97 06 25 – Open 15 May-15 October

7 rm – †€ 50 ††€ 50, ☕ € 8 – ½ P € 53 **Rest** – Menu € 19/40 – Carte € 39/63

◆ Appealing though modest hotel standing on a superb site between the lake and the mountains. Appetising traditional cuisine. Large shady terrace. Small, well-renovated rooms.

ESTÉRENÇUBY – 64 Pyrénées-Atlantiques – 342 E6 – see St-Jean-Pied-de-Port

ESTISSAC – 10 Aube – 313 C4 – pop. 1 724 – alt. 133 m – ✉ 10190 13 B3

Paris 158 – Châlons-en-Champagne 105 – Sens 44 – Troyes 23

Syndicat d'initiative, Mairie ✆ 03 25 40 42 42

Moulin d'Eguebaude

36 r. Pierre Brossolette – ✆ 03 25 40 42 18 – eguebaude@aol.com

8 rm ☕ – †€ 44/52 ††€ 60/73 **Table d'hôte** – Menu € 23 bi

◆ 1789 mill overlooking a vast fish farming estate; the best of the fresh simple rooms are in the annexe. Boutique selling local Aube products. Trout has pride of place on this restaurant's menu, which varies according to market availability.

Domaine du Voirloup

3 pl. Betty Dié – ✆ 03 25 43 14 27 – www.vrlp.com – le.voirloup@free.fr

3 rm ☕ – †€ 60 ††€ 65/85 **Table d'hôte** – Menu € 25/30 bi

◆ This large, elegant 1904 residence is in an extensive park complete with a stream, waterfall and canals; the tastefully colourful rooms are called Orient, Occident and Midi. The menus change according to market availability; home-made cakes and jams at breakfast time.

ESTIVAREILLES – 03 Allier – 326 C4 – pop. 1 019 – alt. 200 m – ✉ 03190 5 B1

▶ Paris 317 – Bourbon-l'Archambault 45 – Montluçon 12 – Montmarault 36 – Moulins 80

Le Lion d'Or with rm

D 2144 – ✆ 04 70 06 00 35 – www.hotel-leliondor.net – rmliondor@orange.fr – Fax 04 70 06 09 78 – Closed 21 July-11 August, 16 February-2 March, Sunday dinner and Monday

9 rm – †€ 47 ††€ 47, ☕ € 7 – ½ P € 47

Rest – Menu (€ 16), € 19 (weekdays)/50 – Carte € 42/53

◆ Age-old building by the side of the main road. Fine beams give the dining room a certain charm. The terrace overlooks a wooded park with a lake. Comfortable, recently refurbished guestrooms, some with a view of the lake.

ESTRABLIN – 38 Isère – 333 C4 – see Vienne

ESTRÉES-ST-DENIS – 60 Oise – 305 G4 – pop. 3 543 – alt. 70 m – ✉ 60190 36 B2

▶ Paris 81 – Beauvais 46 – Clermont 21 – Compiègne 17 – Senlis 34

du Château d'Humières Monchy Humières Rue de Gournay, NE : 11 km, ✆ 03 44 86 48 22

Moulin Brûlé

70 r. Flandres – ✆ 03 44 41 97 10 – lemoulinbrule@wanadoo.fr – Fax 03 44 51 87 96 – Closed 6-10 May, 5 August-3 September, 1-7 January, Sunday dinner, Monday and Tuesday

Rest – *(pre-book)* Menu (€ 17), € 22/50 – Carte € 39/59

◆ Dressed-stone building on the main road through the village. Country-style interior with old beams, pastel shades and a fireplace. Small, peaceful terrace. Cuisine with a contemporary touch.

ÉTAIN – 55 Meuse – 307 E3 – pop. 3 706 – alt. 210 m – ✉ 55400 26 B1

Alsace-Lorraine

▶ Paris 285 – Briey 26 – Longwy 43 – Metz 66

Office de tourisme, 31, rue Raymond Poincaré ✆ 03 29 87 20 80, Fax 03 29 87 20 80

La Sirène

23 r. Prud'homme-Havette, (rte de Metz) – ✆ 03 29 87 10 32 – hotel.sirene@free.fr – Fax 03 29 87 17 65 – Closed 22 December-31 January and Sunday dinner

21 rm – †€ 47/60 ††€ 47/70, ☕ € 7 – ½ P € 43/65

Rest – *(closed Monday)* Menu (€ 13), € 14 (weekdays)/55 – Carte € 31/55

◆ The attractive, white, flower-decked façade hides tastefully decorated practical guestrooms. Traditional cuisine served in two dining rooms (one modern, one classical). On an anecdotal note, Napoleon III is said to have come here after the battle of Gravelotte.

ÉTAMPES – 91 Essonne – 312 B5 – pop. 22 400 – alt. 80 m – ✉ 91150 18 B3

Northern France and the Paris Region

▶ Paris 51 – Chartres 59 – Évry 35 – Fontainebleau 45 – Melun 49 – Orléans 76 – Versailles 58

Office de tourisme, 2, place de l'Hôtel de Ville ✆ 01 69 92 69 00

de Belesbat Boutigny-sur-Essonne Domaine de Belesbat, E : 17 km on D 837 and D 153, ✆ 01 69 23 19 10

Notre-Dame collegiate church ★.

Auberge de la Tour St-Martin

97 r. St-Martin – ✆ 01 69 78 26 19 – toursaintmartin@free.fr – Fax 01 69 78 26 07 – Closed 10-25 August, Sunday dinner and Monday

Rest – Menu (€ 28) – Carte approx. € 47

◆ With ceiling beams, stonework and fireplace, this dining area has a very rustic feel. Traditional meals prepared with choice produce.

in Ormoy-la-Rivière 5 km South by D 49 and secondary road – **pop. 941 – alt. 81 m** – ✉ **91150**

Le Vieux Chaudron

45 Grande Rue – ✆ 01 64 94 39 46 – www.levieuxchaudron.com – guillaume.giblin@wanadoo.fr – Fax 01 64 94 39 46 – Closed 3-24 August, 21 December-4 January, Thursday dinner, Sunday dinner and Monday

Rest – Menu (€ 27), € 34/50 – Carte € 34/50

◆ A small, centrally located inn opposite the church. A country-style interior warmed by its fireplace in winter. Summer dining outdoors. Contemporary dishes.

ÉTANG-DE-HANAU – 57 Moselle – 307 Q4 – see Philippsbourg

LES ÉTANGS-DES-MOINES – 59 Nord – 302 M7 – see Fourmies

ÉTAPLES – 62 Pas-de-Calais – 301 C4 – pop. 11 700 – alt. 10 m 30 A2

– ✉ **62630** **Northern France and the Paris Region**

Paris 228 – Calais 67 – Abbeville 55 – Arras 101 – Boulogne-sur-Mer 28 – Le Touquet-Paris-Plage 6

Office de tourisme, boulevard Bigot Descelers ✆ 03 21 09 56 94, Fax 03 21 09 76 96

Aux Pêcheurs d'Étaples

quai Canche – ✆ 03 21 94 06 90 – www.auxpecheursdetaples.fr – rptetaples@cmeop.com – Fax 03 21 89 74 54 – Closed 1st au 23 January and Sunday dinner October-March

Rest – Menu (€ 16), € 19/36 – Carte € 29/55

◆ Bright restaurant on the first floor of a large fishmonger's on the banks of the Canche. Extremely fresh seafood dishes. View of Le Touquet aerodrome.

ÉTEL – 56 Morbihan – 308 L9 – pop. 2 081 – alt. 20 m – ✉ 56410 9 B2

Brittany

Paris 494 – Lorient 26 – Quiberon 24 – Vannes 37

Syndicat d'initiative, place des Thoniers ✆ 02 97 55 23 80, Fax 02 97 55 44 42

Trianon

rest, VISA AE

14 r. Gén. Leclerc – ✆ 02 97 55 32 41 – www.hotel-le-trianon.com – hotel.letrianon@wanadoo.fr – Fax 02 97 55 44 71

24 rm – € 55/68 € 60/70, € 10

Rest – *(Closed December and January)* Menu (€ 12), € 19/42 – Carte € 27/60

◆ Near the fishing port are faultlessly kept, candy box-style rooms in a 1960s style; choose one in the wing. A lounge with fireplace and peaceful little garden. Well-kept rustic-style dining room serving traditional cuisine.

ÉTOUY – 60 Oise – 305 F4 – see Clermont

ÉTRÉAUPONT – 02 Aisne – 306 F3 – pop. 868 – alt. 127 m – ✉ 02580 37 D1

Paris 184 – Avesnes-sur-Helpe 24 – Hirson 16 – Laon 44 – St-Quentin 51

Clos du Montvinage

VISA AE

8 r. Albert Ledant – ✆ 03 23 97 91 10 – www.clos-du-montvinage.fr – contact@clos-du-montvinage.fr – Fax 03 23 97 48 92 – Closed 9-18 August, 21 December-8 January, Sunday dinner and Monday lunch

20 rm – € 58/93 € 69/104, € 10

Rest *Auberge du Val de l'Oise* – Menu (€ 20), € 22/41 bi – Carte € 35/50

◆ A welcoming 19C family mansion with individually decorated (mountain, bourgeois, etc.) rooms. The leisure facilities include billiards, tennis courts, bicycles and croquet in the park. Don't miss the chance to sample the local delicacy: tourte au maroilles (cheese pie).

ÉTRETAT – 76 Seine-Maritime – 304 B3 – pop. 1 615 – alt. 8 m – Casino – 33 C1
A – ✉ 76790 Normandy

Paris 206 – Bolbec 30 – Fécamp 16 – Le Havre 29 – Rouen 90
Office de tourisme, place Maurice Guillard ✆ 02 35 27 05 21, Fax 03 35 28 87 20
d'Étretat Route du Havre, ✆ 02 35 27 04 89
Le Clos Lupin★ - Falaise d'Aval★★★ - Falaise d'Amont★★.

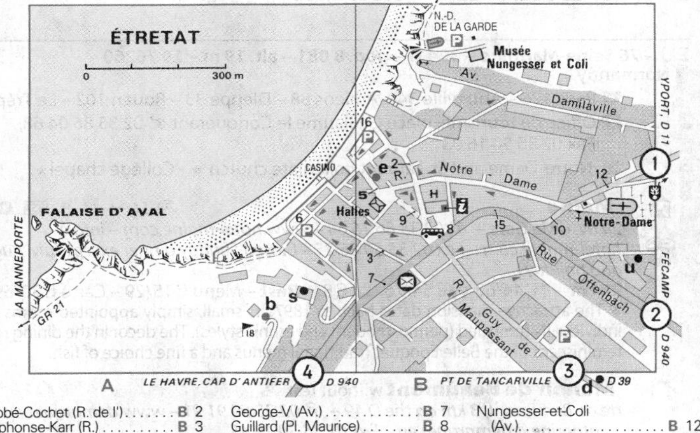

Abbé-Cochet (R. de l') . . . . . . B 2	George-V (Av.) . . . . B 7	Nungesser-et-Coli (Av.) . . . . B 12
Alphonse-Karr (R.) . . . . B 3	Guillard (Pl. Maurice) . . . . . B 8	Verdun (Av. de) . . . . B 15
Coty (Bd R.) . . . . B 5	Monge (R.) . . . . B 9	Victor-Hugo (Pl.) . . . . B 16
Gaulle (Pl. Gén.-de) . . . . . . A 6	Mottet (R. Charles) . . . . . . B 10	

Dormy House
rm, VISA AE

rte du Havre – ✆ 02 35 27 07 88 – www.dormy-house.com – dormy.house@wanadoo.fr – Fax 02 35 29 86 19 A s

60 rm – †€ 65/190 ††€ 65/190, ☕ € 16 – 1 suite

Rest – Menu € 28 (weekday lunch), € 35/72 – Carte approx. € 55

◆ This peaceful 1870 manor house stands in a park near the golf course, overlooking the resort and facing the Amont cliffs. The rooms are in various styles, from classic to cosy to more simple. The restaurant, bar and terrace offer a fine view of the coastline.

Domaine Saint-Clair
VISA AE

chemin de St-Clair – ✆ 02 35 27 08 23 – www.hoteletretat.com – info@hoteletretat.com – Fax 0235 29 92 24 B u

21 rm – †€ 62/192 ††€ 62/352, ☕ € 14

Rest – *(closed Monday and lunch during the week)*
Menu € 39 (weekdays)/85 – Carte € 92/111

◆ Ideal for a relaxing break, this 19C Anglo-Norman château and fine Belle Époque villa are set on the heights of Étretat. The cosy sitting rooms and bedrooms are adorned with choice fabrics. Contemporary cuisine made with garden produce served in a cosy setting.

Villa sans Souci without rest

27 ter r. Guy de Maupassant – ✆ 02 35 28 60 14 – www.villa-sans-souci.fr – villa-sans-souci@orange.fr – Fax 02 35 28 60 14 B d

4 rm ☕ – †€ 55/90 ††€ 95/145

◆ A 1903 villa with a restful atmosphere and individually decorated rooms. The breakfast room decor focuses on cinema and automobiles. Pretty reading room and shady garden.

XX Le Galion
VISA

bd R. Coty – ✆ 02 35 29 48 74 – Fax 02 35 29 74 48 – Closed 17 December-20 January, Tuesday and Wednesday except school holidays B e

Rest – Menu € 25/39 – Carte € 30/45

◆ The treasure of this galleon is not found at the bottom of the hold but on the ceiling: the forest of carved beams dates back to the 14C and comes from a house in Lisieux.

Du Golf
rte du Havre – 02 35 27 04 56 – www.golfetretat.com – Fax 02 35 10 89 12 – Closed Tuesday 1st October-1st April A **b**
Rest – Menu € 22/28 – Carte € 28/42
◆ Superb coastal views from the bay windows of this golf course clubhouse perched above the Aval cliffs. The contemporary menu is highlighted on a slate board.

ÉTUPES – 25 Doubs – 321 L1 – see Sochaux

EU – 76 Seine-Maritime – 304 I1 – pop. 8 081 – alt. 19 m – ✉ 76260 33 D1
Normandy

Paris 176 – Abbeville 34 – Amiens 88 – Dieppe 33 – Rouen 102 – Le Tréport 5

Office de tourisme, place Guillaume le Conquérant 02 35 86 04 68, Fax 02 35 50 16 03

Notre-Dame and St-Laurent collegiate church ★ - Collège chapel★.

Maine
20 av. de la Gare – 02 35 86 16 64 – www.hotel-maine.com – info@hotel-maine.com – Fax 02 35 50 86 25 – Closed Sunday dinner except July-August and holidays
28 rm – €44/62 €54/76, € 8 **Rest** – Menu € 15/29 – Carte € 30/69
◆ The attractive mansion dates back to 1897. Its small, simply appointed rooms are all individually furnished (period, modern and ethnic styles). The decor in the dining room is reminiscent of the Belle Époque. Traditional menus and a fine choice of fish.

Manoir de Beaumont without rest
rte de Beaumont, 3 km on the D 49 – 02 35 50 91 91 – www.demarquet.eu – catherine@demarquet.eu – Fax 02 35 50 19 45
3 rm – €38 €50/59
◆ Former hunting lodge, a stone's throw from Eu forest and five minutes from the beaches. Quiet, personalised rooms, Louis XVI breakfast room and lovely park.

EUGÉNIE-LES-BAINS – 40 Landes – 335 I12 – pop. 476 – alt. 65 m 3 B3
– Spa : mid Feb.-early Dec. – ✉ 40320 Atlantic Coast

Paris 731 – Aire-sur-l'Adour 12 – Dax 71 – Mont-de-Marsan 26 – Orthez 52 – Pau 56

Office de tourisme, 147, rue René Vielle 05 58 51 13 16, Fax 05 58 51 12 02

Les Greens d'Eugénie Bahus-Soubiran Golf du Tursan, S : 4 km on D 11 and D 62, 05 58 51 11 63

Les Prés d'Eugénie (Michel Guérard)
pl. de l'Impératrice – 05 58 05 06 07 – www.michelguerard.com – guerard@relaischateaux.com – Fax 05 58 51 10 10 – Closed 1st-19 March and 4 January-11 February
25 rm – €270/340 €300/360, € 30 – 11 suites
Rest – *(slimmer's menu for residents only)* Menu € 55
Rest *Michel Guérard* – *(closed lunch weekdays except bank holidays and from 7 July to 24 August and Monday dinner) (number of covers limited, pre-book)* Menu € 150/190 – Carte € 131/150
Spec. Oreiller moelleux de mousserons et morilles aux pointes d'asperges. Caneton rosé du Mandarin Jardinier, peau laquée à la ventrèche. Millefeuille tout en dentelle. **Wines** Tursan blanc, Vin de Pays des Terroirs Landais.
◆ Truly splendid, elegantly decorated 19C mansion with a park and spa "farm". A pleasant combination of townhouse and country house, luxury living and healthy living. At Michel Guérard's garden-village, the food is inspired by Mother Nature.

Le Couvent des Herbes
– Closed 1st-19 March and 4 January-11 February
4 rm – €340/500 €340/500, € 30 – 4 suites
◆ Napoleon III had this pretty 18C convent with its pinnacle turret lovingly restored for Empress Eugénie. The delightful guestrooms are surrounded by a heavenly garden.

La Maison Rose rm, rest,
– ✆ 05 58 05 06 07 – www.michelguerard.com
– reservation@michelguerard.com – Fax 05 58 51 10 10
– *Closed 7 December-5 February*
22 rm – € 120/150 € 140/180, € 20 – 9 suites
Rest – *(residents only)*
◆ A highly refined 'guesthouse' ambience depicted by soothing pastel colours, white cane furniture, fresh flowers and a cosy sitting room decked in striped fabric.

La Ferme aux Grives with rm
– ✆ *05 58 05 05 06 – www.michelguerard.com – guerard@relaischateaux.com*
– *Fax 05 58 51 10 10 – Closed 4 January-5 February*
4 suites – € 420/540, € 25
Rest – *(closed Tuesday dinner and Wednesday except from 9 July to 25 August and except bank holidays)* Menu € 46
◆ Old village inn that has had new life breathed into it. Vegetable garden, old beams and floor tiles serve to enhance the reinvigorated country cuisine. Exquisite suites and rooms for a quiet night's rest.

Red = Pleasant. Look for the red and symbols.

ÉVIAN-LES-BAINS – 74 Haute-Savoie – 328 M2 – pop. 7 787 – alt. 370 m – Spa : Feb.-early Nov. – Casino B – ✉ 74500 French Alps

46 **F1**

Paris 577 – Genève 44 – Montreux 40 – Thonon-les-Bains 10

Office de tourisme, place d'Allinges ✆ 04 50 75 04 26, Fax 04 50 75 61 08

Évian Masters Golf Club Rive Sud du Lac de Genève, 1 km on the Thonon road, ✆ 04 50 75 46 66

Lake Geneva ★★★ - Boat trip★★★ - Main staircase ★ of the town hall.

Falaises★★.

Plan on following page

Royal rest,
– ✆ *04 50 26 85 00 – www.evianroyalresort.com*
– *royalpalace@evianroyalresort.com – Fax 04 50 75 38 40* C z
140 rm – € 200/770 € 280/870, € 25 – 12 suites – ½ P € 165/460
Rest *Fresques Royales* – *(closed Sunday) (dinner only)* Menu € 70/110 – Carte € 105/142
Rest *La Véranda* – grill room *(lunch only)* Menu € 60 – Carte approx. € 97
Rest *Le Jardin des Lys* – dietetic rest. *(lunch only)* Menu € 60/110
Rest *Café Sud* – *(dinner only)* Carte € 65/80
◆ Beautiful Art Deco architecture in this luxurious hotel built in 1907. Majestic gardens, superb fitness centre and spacious rooms with period furnishings. At the Fresques Royales, the paintings embellishing the splendid Belle Époque-style decor are the work of Gustave Jaulmes. Terrace with superb lake views. Well-balanced gastronomic cuisine. Buffet and grills at the Véranda. Slimmers' cuisine at the Jardin des Lys. Mediterranean cuisine in the laidback atmosphere of Café Sud.

Ermitage rest,
av. du Léman – ✆ *04 50 26 85 00*
– *www.evianroyalresort.com – ermitage@evianroyalresort.com*
– *Fax 04 50 75 29 37* C a
91 rm – € 120/770 € 180/770, € 25 – 3 suites – ½ P € 170/820
Rest *Le Gourmandin* – ✆ *04 50 26 85 54 (dinner only)*
Menu € 60/80 – Carte € 70/95
Rest *La Toscane* – *(lunch only)* Carte € 35/55
◆ Early-20C luxury hotel in a magnificent park, perfect for a relaxing stay. 16C-style vegetable garden, lovely spa and children's play area. Le Gourmandin has refined decor, a superb terrace and serves regional dishes. La Toscane serves Italian cuisine and salads.

ÉVIAN-LES-BAINS

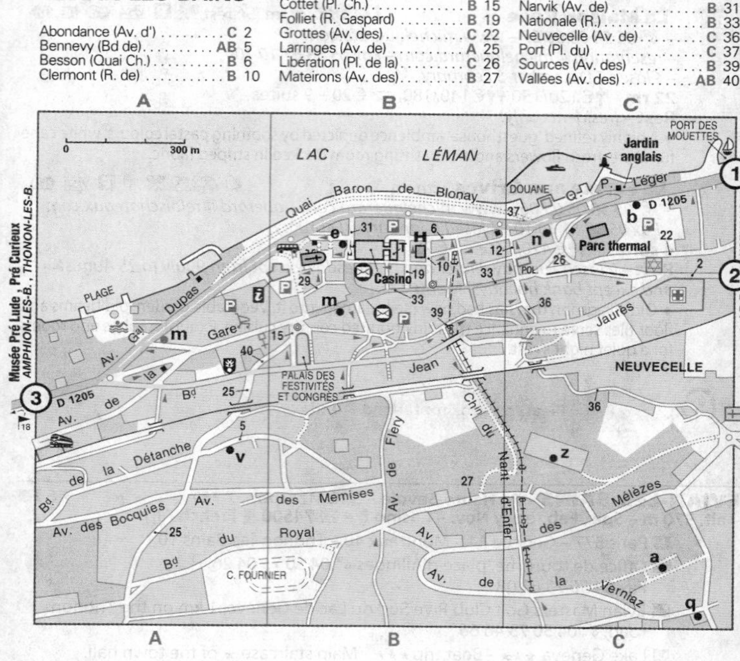

Hilton

53 quai Paul Léger – ✆ 04 50 84 60 00
– www.evianlesbains.hilton.fr – info.hiltonevianlesbains@hilton.com
– Fax 04 50 84 60 50 — C **b**

173 rm – €159/470 €184/495 – 3 suites
Rest ***Cannelle*** – *(dinner only)* Carte €35/52

◆ A modern, uncluttered hotel. Most of the bedrooms (with their own balcony), command a view of the lake. Relax by the pool or in the wellness centre. A modern restaurant where the cuisine mirrors the contemporary decor. Large terrace facing the garden.

La Verniaz et ses Chalets

rte d'Abondance – ✆ 04 50 75 04 90
– www.verniaz.com – verniaz@relaischateaux.com
– Fax 04 50 70 78 92 – Open 6 February-11 November — C **q**

32 rm – €110/230 €130/285, €16 – 6 suites
Rest – Menu (€29), €40/78 – Carte €51/72

◆ A lovely complex of buildings and chalets in a superb park filled with flowers in season. Large, slightly outdated rooms. View over the lake. Classic cuisine, specialities of grills and fish from Lake Leman served in the rustic restaurant.

Alizé — rm,

2 av. J. Léger – ✆ 04 50 75 49 49 – www.hotel-alize-evian.com
– alize.hotel@wanadoo.fr – Fax 04 50 75 50 40
– Closed 15 November-31 January — C **n**

22 rm – €69/96 €77/110, €8,50 **Rest** – Menu €20/32 – Carte €20/39

◆ A well situated hotel opposite the landing stage and near the thermal baths. The rooms are tasteful, practical and clean: most overlook the lake. The restaurant proposes traditional dishes and specialities from Savoie.

Littoral without rest

av. de Narvik – ✆ 04 50 75 64 00 – www.hotel-evian-littoral.com – hotel-littoral-evian@wanadoo.fr – Fax 04 50 75 30 04 – Closed 24 October-11 November B **e**

30 rm – †€ 69/84 ††€ 77/102, ☕ € 9

◆ A modern building near the casino with functional facilities, popular with an international clientele. All the rooms (except two) have a balcony facing the lake.

L' Oasis without rest

11 bd Bennevy – ✆ 04 50 75 13 38 – www.oasis-hotel.com – stephane.berthier3@wanadoo.fr – Fax 04 50 74 90 30 – Open 10 March-10 October A **v**

17 rm – †€ 65/85 ††€ 100/150, ☕ € 10

◆ Situated in the upper section of Évian, a charming hotel with bright, modern rooms; some face the lake, others are housed in two maisonettes nestled within the pretty garden.

Continental without rest

65 r. Nationale – ✆ 04 50 75 37 54 – www.hotel-continental-evian.com – info@hotel-continental-evian.com – Fax 04 50 75 31 11 B **m**

32 rm – †€ 40/57 ††€ 50/67, ☕ € 8

◆ Built in 1868, this hotel is home to large, well-soundproofed rooms and two new suites; those on the fourth floor on the street side enjoy lake views. Refurbished interior and fine antique furniture.

Histoire de Goût

1 av. gén. Dupas – ✆ 04 50 70 09 98 – froissart.dominique@wanadoo.fr – Fax 04 50 70 10 69 – Closed 4-15 January and Monday A **m**

Rest – Menu (€ 18 bi), € 26/40 – Carte € 42/52

◆ With wine racks lining the walls and an attractive pine bar in one dining room, and an arched ceiling and wrought-iron chandelier in the other, this restaurant focuses on contemporary cuisine.

ÉVISA – 2A Corse-du-Sud – 345 B6 – see Corse

ÉVOSGES – 01 Ain – 328 F5 – pop. 127 – alt. 750 m – ✉ 01230 45 **C1**

Paris 481 – Aix-les-Bains 69 – Belley 37 – Bourg-en-Bresse 57 – Lyon 79 – Nantua 32

L'Auberge Campagnarde

le village – ✆ 04 74 38 55 55 – contact@auberge-campagnarde.com – Fax 04 74 38 55 62 – Closed 1-8 September, 16-30 November, January, Tuesday dinner and Wednesday in low season

15 rm – †€ 44/85 ††€ 44/85, ☕ € 10

Rest – Menu € 22 (weekday lunch), € 27/55 – Carte € 41/58

◆ The same family has run this inn, popular with nature lovers, for five generations. Welcoming staff, simple but faultless rooms, crazy golf and pool. Countrified dining room (old utensils) and flower-decked terrace; cuisine with regional touches.

ÉVREUX Ⓟ – 27 Eure – 304 G7 – pop. 50 300 – alt. 64 m – ✉ 27000 33 **D2**

Normandy

Paris 100 – Alençon 119 – Caen 135 – Chartres 78 – Rouen 56

Office de tourisme, 1 ter, place de Gaulle ✆ 02 32 24 04 43, Fax 02 32 31 28 45

d'Évreux Chemin du Valème, 3 km on the Lisieux road, ✆ 02 32 39 66 22

Notre-Dame cathedral★★ - Shrine★★ in St-Taurin church - Museum ★★ M.

Plan on following page

Mercure

rm,

bd Normandie – ✆ 02 32 38 77 77 – www.mercure.com – h1575@accor.com – Fax 02 32 39 04 53 AZ **s**

60 rm – †€ 76/120 ††€ 81/130, ☕ € 11

Rest – Menu (€ 16), € 22/29 – Carte € 22/29

◆ Well located at the edge of the town centre, this modern, practical building houses the chain's usual offering. Functional rooms. Figured wood, warm colours and good lighting create a pleasant ambience in the dining room, where traditional cuisine is served.

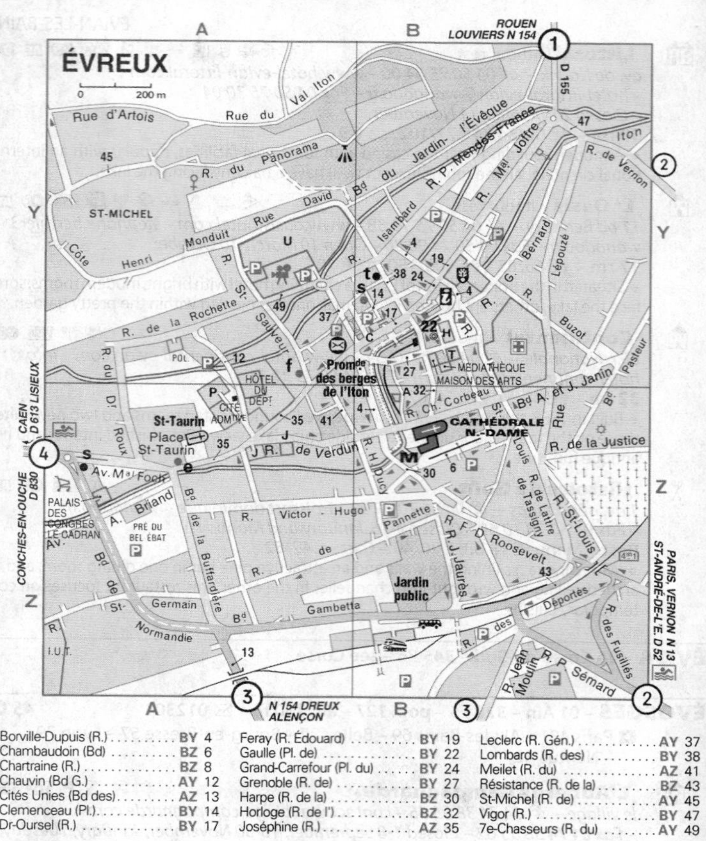

Borville-Dupuis (R.) . . . . BY 4
Chambaudoin (Bd) . . . . BZ 6
Chartraine (R.) . . . . BZ 8
Chauvin (Bd G.) . . . . AY 12
Cités Unies (Bd des) . . . . AZ 13
Clemenceau (Pl.) . . . . BY 14
Dr-Oursel (R.) . . . . BY 17
Feray (R. Édouard) . . . . BY 19
Gaulle (Pl. de) . . . . BY 22
Grand-Carrefour (Pl. du) . . . . . . BY 24
Grenoble (R. de) . . . . BY 27
Harpe (R. de la) . . . . BZ 30
Horloge (R. de l') . . . . BZ 32
Joséphine (R.) . . . . AZ 35
Leclerc (R. Gén.) . . . . AY 37
Lombards (R. des) . . . . BY 38
Meilet (R. du) . . . . AZ 41
Résistance (R. de la) . . . . BZ 43
St-Michel (R. de) . . . . AY 45
Vigor (R.) . . . . BY 47
7e-Chasseurs (R. du) . . . . AY 49

L'Orme without rest

VISA AE

13 r. Lombards – ✆ 02 32 39 34 12 – www.hotel-de-lorme.fr – hote-de-lorme@orange.fr – Fax 02 32 33 62 48 BY **t**

39 rm – †€ 60/65 ††€ 65/72, ☐ € 8

◆ This town centre hotel is convenient for visitors passing through. Most of the plain rooms have been refurbished (flat screen TVs, Wifi).

La Gazette

AC VISA AE

7 r. St-Sauveur – ✆ 02 32 33 43 40 – www.restaurant-lagazette.fr – xavier.buzieux@wanadoo.fr – Fax 02 32 31 38 87 – Closed 2-24 August, Saturday lunch and Sunday AY **f**

Rest – Menu (€ 20), € 23 (weekdays)/47 – Carte € 39/55

◆ Restaurant easily discernable due to its painted wood façade. Inside, modern furniture, coated beams, grey walls and reproductions of old newspapers create a trendy setting.

La Vieille Gabelle

VISA AE

3 r. Vieille-Gabelle – ✆ 02 32 39 77 13 – Fax 02 32 39 77 13 – Closed 1st-24 August, 21 December-4 January, Saturday lunch, Sunday dinner and Monday BY **s**

Rest – Menu € 18 (weekday lunch)/29 – Carte € 40/50

◆ Behind the typically Norman half-timbered façade are two pretty country style dining rooms. Tasty dishes professionally executed.

La Croix d'Or
3 r. Joséphine – ✆ 02 32 33 06 07 – www.la-croix-dor.fr – la.croixdor@orange.fr – Fax 02 32 31 14 27 AZ **e**
Rest – Menu € 13 (weekday lunch), € 17/33 – Carte € 26/44
◆ An oyster bar and lobster tank set the scene: the extensive menu has a distinct fish and shellfish bias. Restrained, rustic-style decor and veranda-terrace.

in Parville 4 km by ④ – **pop. 296 – alt. 130 m** – ✉ **27180**

Côté Jardin
rte de Lisieux – ✆ 02 32 39 19 19 – www.restaurant-cotejardinparville.com – Fax 02 32 31 21 85 – Closed Sunday dinner and Monday
Rest – Menu (€ 16), € 39 bi/59 bi – Carte € 41/50
◆ Pretty half-timbered house by the road. The stylish dining room is just as attractive as the exterior, with its Norman decor repainted in pastel tones. Modern menu.

ÉVRON – 53 Mayenne – 310 G6 – pop. 7 283 – alt. 114 m – ✉ 53600 35 C1
Normandy

Paris 250 – Alençon 58 – La Ferté-Bernard 98 – Laval 32 – Le Mans 55 – Mayenne 25

Office de tourisme, place de la Basilique ✆ 02 43 01 63 75, Fax 02 43 01 63 75

Notre-Dame bassilica★: N.-D.-de l'Épine chapel★★.

La Toque des Coëvrons
4 r. des Prés – ✆ 02 43 01 62 16 – marcmenard@wanadoo.fr – Fax 02 43 37 20 01 – Closed 3-17 August, 7-23 February, Sunday dinner, Wednesday dinner and Monday
Rest – Menu € 18 (weekdays)/33 – Carte € 27/45
◆ The chef of this friendly restaurant is wild about traditional recipes and lovingly prepares tasty dishes. The pretty, rustic-style dining room has recently been refurbished.

Mayenne road 6 km by D 7 – ✉ **53600 Mézangers**

Au Relais du Gué de Selle
rte de Mayenne, (D 7) – ✆ 02 43 91 20 00 – www.relais-du-gue-de-selle.com – relaisduguedeselle@wanadoo.fr – Fax 02 43 91 20 10 – Closed 19 December-12 January, 7-23 February, Friday dinner, Sunday dinner and Monday from October to May
30 rm – †€ 61/158 ††€ 77/178, ☕ € 11
Rest – *(closed Monday lunch from June to September)*
Menu (€ 17 bi), € 25 (weekdays)/70 – Carte € 50/59
◆ An old restored farmhouse and garden on the shore of a lake. Some of the pleasant guestrooms have a lake view. A waterside promenade has been laid out, and there are bikes, fishing etc. Stylish, welcoming dining room decor complete with fireplace.

ÉVRY – 91 Essonne – 312 D4 – 101 37 – see Paris, Area

EYBENS – 38 Isère – 333 H7 – see Grenoble

EYGALIÈRES – 13 Bouches-du-Rhône – 340 E3 – pop. 1 900 – alt. 134 m – ✉ 13810 42 E1
Provence

Paris 701 – Avignon 28 – Cavaillon 14 – Marseille 83 – St-Rémy-de-Provence 12

La Bastide d'Eygalières
Route Orgon (D24[B]) – ✆ 04 90 95 90 06 – www.labastide.com.fr – contact@labastide.com.fr – Fax 04 90 95 99 77
14 rm – †€ 68/88 ††€ 84/135, ☕ € 11
Rest – *(closed lunch October-March)* Menu (€ 16), € 25 (dinner)/36 – Carte € 28/49 dinner only
◆ Charming Provençal farmhouse with blue shutters. The delicate interior sports off white walls, well-worn furniture and old floor tiles. Spacious, refurbished rooms. Organic produce use in the lunchtime salads and the evening traditional menu.

Mas dou Pastré
quartier St Sixte, 1.5 km on Orgon road (D 24B) – ✆ 04 90 95 92 61 – www.masdupastre.com – contact@masdupastre.com – Fax 04 90 90 61 75 – Closed 15 November-15 December
15 rm – †€ 125 ††€ 125, ☕ € 14 – 2 suites
Rest – *(closed Sunday) (lunch only)* Carte € 30/38
◆ This family-run sheep farm has a charm of its own: guesthouse atmosphere, Provence décor with antiques and ornaments, and a garden with three authentic Romany caravans. Seasonal cuisine served in an attractive setting.

Maison Roumanille
in the village – ✆ 04 90 95 92 61 – www.maisonroumanille.com – Fax 04 90 90 61 75 – Closed 15 November-15 December
4 rm – †€ 105/120 ††€ 105/120 – 2 suites
◆ Attractive farmhouse in the centre of the village, decorated in the same style as the main residence. All but one of the individually decorated, cheerful rooms have a terrace. Breakfast veranda.

L'Oliviera
chemin des Jaisses, 1 km on the D 74a – ✆ 04 90 90 65 28 – www.loliviera.fr – contact@loliviera.fr – Open 1 April-1 November
4 rm ☕ – †€ 115/125 ††€ 115/145 **Table d'hôte** – Menu € 35 bi
◆ Nestling amid olive groves, this welcoming Provençal farmhouse is a haven of peace and quiet. Spruce, prettily decorated rooms. Splendid view of the Alpilles from the terrace. The chef lavishly employs local produce and the house olive oil in his menus.

Bistrot d'Eygalières "Chez Bru" (Wout Bru) with rm
r. de la République – ✆ 04 90 90 60 34 – www.chezbru.com – sbru@club-internet.fr – Fax 04 90 90 60 37 – Open 1st May-3 November and closed 2-7 August, Sunday dinner in October, Tuesday lunch from May to September and Monday
7 rm – †€ 130/200 ††€ 130/200, ☕ € 20
Rest – *(number of covers limited, pre-book)* Menu € 95/120 – Carte € 100/145
Spec. Ris de veau aux truffes sur un lit de tomates et glace au parmesan. Croustillant de cochon de lait au porto et champignons. Trilogie à la mousse pralinée.
Wines Vin de Pays des Bouches du Rhône, Les Baux de Provence.
◆ Delicious updated Provençal cuisine served in a stylish bistro. Dine in the room decorated in creams and browns with paintings and sculpture or on an attractive patio terrace.

Sous Les Micocouliers
Traverse de Montfort – ✆ 04 90 95 94 53 – www.souslesmicocouliers.com – contact@souslesmicocouliers.com – Fax 04 32 62 87 73 – Closed Sunday dinner, Monday and Tuesday from October to March, Monday lunch from April to September and Wednesday
Rest – Menu (€ 18), € 28/58 – Carte € 48/75
◆ This colourful dining room with a handsome fireplace and terrace shaded by lime trees pays homage to a modern gourmet menu, which has not forgotten its Provençal roots.

EYGUIÈRES – 13 Bouches-du-Rhône – 340 F3 – pop. 6 278 – alt. 75 m 42 E1
– ✉ 13430 Provence

Paris 715 – Aix-en-Provence 49 – Arles 45 – Avignon 40 – Istres 27 – Marseille 66

Office de tourisme, place de l'ancien Hôtel de Ville ✆ 04 90 59 82 44, Fax 04 90 59 89 07

Le Relais du Coche
pl. Monier – ✆ 04 90 59 86 70 – www.lerelaisducoche.com – Fax 04 90 45 09 78 – Closed 29 June-15 July, 2-19 January, Saturday lunch, Sunday dinner and Monday
Rest – Menu € 16 (weekday lunch) – Carte € 37/47
◆ This restaurant is located in the converted stables of an old 18C coaching inn. A pleasant patio terrace covered with Virginia creeper. Regional menu.

EYMET – 24 Dordogne – 329 D8 – pop. 2 552 – alt. 54 m – ✉ 24500 4 C2

Dordogne-Berry-Limousin

Paris 560 – Arcachon 72 – Bayonne 239 – Bordeaux 101 – Dax 188 – Périgueux 74

Office de tourisme, place de la Bastide ✆ 05 53 23 74 95, Fax 05 53 23 74 95

Les Vieilles Pierres

La Gillette – ✆ 05 53 23 75 99 – www.lesvieillespierres.fr – les.vieilles.pierres@wanadoo.fr – Fax 05 53 27 87 14 – Closed 27 October-17 November and 16 February-9 March

11 rm – †€ 42 ††€ 49/59, ☕ € 7

Rest – *(closed Sunday dinner except July-August)*

Menu (€ 12), € 20 (weekdays)/35 – Carte € 21/40

◆ Simple guestrooms housed in three buildings arranged around a walnut-shaded patio. The converted barn is now a fittingly rustic dining room serving classic cuisine. A glazed summer restaurant overlooks the children's play area.

La Cour d'Eymet with rm

rest, VISA

32 bd National – ✆ 05 53 22 72 83 – Closed 1-8 July, 1-15 March, Thursday lunch, Saturday lunch from April to October, Sunday dinner, Monday, Tuesday from November to March and Wednesday

3 rm ☕ – †€ 80 ††€ 105 **Rest** – *(number of covers limited, pre-book)*

Menu € 28 (weekday lunch), € 39/50 – Carte € 55/70

◆ Restaurant in a fine comfortable building. Discreet, elegant interior and pretty courtyard-terrace. Traditional cuisine and short wine list, rich in local wines. Large, comfortable rooms.

EYRAGUES – 13 Bouches-du-Rhône – 340 D2 – pop. 4 179 – alt. 23 m – ✉ 13630 42 E1

Paris 705 – Marseille 98 – Nîmes 64 – Avignon 14 – Arles 31

Le Pré Gourmand

VISA

175 av. Marx-Dormoy – ✆ 04 90 94 52 63 – www.restaurant-lepregourmand.com – lepregourmand@orange.fr – Closed for the Toussaint holiday and February holiday

Rest – Menu € 26 (weekdays)/68 – Carte € 53/70

◆ Contemporary restaurant with a pleasant countrified decor. Terrace overlooking a meadow of wild flowers. Tasty updated cuisine.

EYSINES – 33 Gironde – 335 H5 – see Bordeaux

LES EYZIES-DE-TAYAC – 24 Dordogne – 329 H6 – pop. 839 – alt. 70 m – ✉ 24620 Dordogne-Berry-Limousin 4 C3

Paris 536 – Brive-la-Gaillarde 62 – Fumel 62 – Périgueux 47 – Sarlat-la-Canéda 21

Office de tourisme, 19, av. de la Préhistoire ✆ 05 53 06 97 05, Fax 05 53 06 90 79

Musée national de Préhistoire★★ - Grotte du Grand Roc★★: ≤★ - Grotte de Font-de-Gaume★★.

Du Centenaire

rm, VISA

2 av. du Cingle – ✆ 05 53 06 68 68 – www.hotelducentenaire.fr – hotel.centenaire@wanadoo.fr – Fax 05 53 06 92 41 – Open February-December

14 rm – †€ 105/305 ††€ 105/305, ☕ € 17 – 5 suites

Rest – Menu € 29/70 – Carte € 50/75

◆ Located at the entrance to this tourist village, this rustic house has cosy bedrooms and an enclosed garden with a pool. Breakfast served under a glass roof. Classic cuisine.

Les Glycines

VISA

4 av. de Laugerie, rte Périgueux – ✆ 05 53 06 97 07 – www.les-glycines-dordogne.com – glycines.dordogne@wanadoo.fr – Fax 05 53 06 92 19 – Open Easter to 1st November

24 rm – †€ 92/232 ††€ 92/232, ☕ € 14

Rest – *(closed Wednesday lunch, Monday and Tuesday except July-August)*

Menu (€ 19), € 49/95

◆ Former post house (1862) in a verdant setting near the Vézère. Impressive grounds and wisteria-clad arbour. Renovated guestrooms, with four at garden level. Restaurant with views of the hotel grounds, a pleasant, tranquil terrace and up-to-date cuisine.

Hostellerie du Passeur

pl. de la Mairie – ✆ 05 53 06 97 13 – www.hostellerie-du-passeur.com – contact@hostellerie-du-passeur.com – Fax 05 53 06 91 63 – Open Easter to 1st November

19 rm – €92/110 €92/110, ☕ €11 – ½ P €85/95

Rest – *(closed Tuesday lunch, Friday lunch and Saturday lunch except July-August)* Menu (€18), €23 (weekday lunch)/35

◆ Beside a small square in the town centre, this old residence of character has charming rooms that have been completely refurbished. Carefully laid tables in the two elegant dining rooms and shaded terrace. Traditional offerings in the evening, with bistro menus at lunchtime.

Moulin de la Beune

2 r. du Moulin Bas – ✆ 05 53 06 94 33 – www.moulindelabeune.com – contact@moulindelabeune.com – Fax 05 53 06 98 06 – Open 10 April-31 October

20 rm – €52 €61, ☕ €7 – ½ P €72

Rest *Au Vieux Moulin* – *(closed Tuesday lunch, Wednesday lunch and Saturday lunch)* Menu €30/42 bi – Carte €42/63

◆ Spacious rooms, antique furniture and tasteful decoration in these two old mills in a peaceful garden with the Beune running through it. Pleasant lounge with an attractive fireplace. A rustic restaurant with views of the mill's paddle wheel. Riverside terrace. Cuisine with a regional flavour.

Des Roches without rest

rte de Sarlat – ✆ 05 53 06 96 59 – www.roches-les-eyzies.com – hotel@roches-les-eyzies.com – Fax 05 53 06 95 54 – Open 11 April-31 October

41 rm – €65/75 €70/90, ☕ €10

◆ Local-style construction at the foot of cliffs crowned by oak trees. Classic decor in the guestrooms. Restful garden by the river; swimming pool.

Le Cro Magnon

54 av. Préhistoire – ✆ 05 53 06 97 06 – www.hostellerie-cro-magnon.com – hotel.cro.magnon.les-eyzies@wanadoo.fr – Fax 05 53 06 95 45 – Open 16 March-22 November

15 rm – €65/75 €75/90, ☕ €10 – ½ P €71/78

Rest – Menu (€17), €23/46 – Carte €32/47

◆ This welcoming hotel built against the cliff-face offers large, individually furnished rooms. Pleasant lounge warmed by an open fire. Swimming pool. Enjoy traditional cuisine either on the veranda or the courtyard terrace. Breakfast is served in the cosy winter dining room.

East 7 km by Sarlat road – ✉ 24620 Les Eyzies-de-Tayac

La Métairie

at Beyssac, on D 47 – ✆ 05 53 29 65 32 – www.toques-perigord.com/metairie – bourgeade@wanadoo.fr – Fax 05 53 29 65 30 – Open from March to November and closed Sunday dinner except July-August, Tuesday lunch and Monday

Rest – Menu (€16), €28

◆ The former farm of the Château de Beyssac stands at the foot of the cliff. The feeding troughs in the rustic dining room testify to the building's initial vocation. Regional cuisine.

East 8 km on the Sarlat road, C 3 towards Meyrals and minor road – ✉ 24220 Meyrals

Ferme Lamy without rest

– ✆ 05 53 29 62 46 – www.ferme-lamy.com – ferme-lamy@wanadoo.fr – Fax 05 53 59 61 41

12 rm – €115/185 €115/185, ☕ €10

◆ A farm with a cosy feel and lovely garden. Quiet guestrooms attractively decorated with antique furniture. Truffle evenings in season and hot-air ballooning.

Good food without spending a fortune?
Look out for the Bib Gourmand

ÈZE – 06 Alpes-Maritimes – 341 F5 – pop. 2 932 – alt. 390 m – ✉ 06360 42 E2

French Riviera

Paris 938 – Cap d'Ail 6 – Menton 17 – Monaco 8 – Monte-Carlo 8 – Nice 12

Office de tourisme, place du Général-de-Gaulle ✆ 04 93 41 26 00, Fax 04 93 41 04 80

Site★★ - Sentier Frédéric Nietzsche★ - Old village★ - Exotic garden ★★★.

"Belvédère" d'Èze (Viewpoint) West : 4 km.

Château de la Chèvre d'Or

r. Barri, (pedestrian access) – ✆ 04 92 10 66 66 – www.chevredor.com – reservation@chevredor.com – Fax 04 93 41 06 72 – Open 14 March-1st December

30 rm – €280/295 €280/295, €45 – 5 suites

Rest – *(closed Wednesday in March, Monday and Tuesday in November) (pre-book)* Menu €65 (weekday lunch), €95/350 – Carte €190/300

Spec. Vieilles variétés de tomates en deux services (summer). Sole de Méditerranée (spring). Poire williams. (autumn) **Wines** Bellet

◆ Picturesque building overlooking the sea, a real eagle's nest with hanging gardens clinging to the rock. This enchanting residence promises an unforgettable stay. This restaurant serves delicious food and commands splendid views.

Château Eza

r. Pise, (pedestrian access) – ✆ 04 93 41 12 24 – www.chateaueza.com – info@chateaueza.com – Fax 04 93 41 16 64 – Closed 1st November-15 December

9 rm – €180/815 €180/815, €35 – 1 suite

Rest – *(closed Monday and Tuesday in January-February)*
Menu €45 (lunch), €55/110 – Carte €113/126

Spec. Artichauts poivrade comme une barigoule. Filet d'agneau mariné et rôti, craquant de sauge à l'anchoïade. Douceur de chocolat blanc à l'olive verte et citron confit de Menton. **Wines** Bellet.

◆ This opulent 14C abode perched between sky and sea commands a breathtaking view of the coast. Elegant, personalised rooms with terrace, balcony or private Jacuzzi tub. Medieval-inspired decor, sliding roof, magnificent view and subtle, up-to-date menu.

Les Terrasses d'Eze

rest,

1138 rte de la Turbie, 1.5 km on the D 6007 and D 45 – ✆ 04 92 41 55 55 – www.hotel-eze.com – info@hotel-eze.com – Fax 04 92 41 55 10 – Closed 9-17 April and 21-27 December

81 rm – €160/210 €160/210, €20 – 6 suites – ½ P €140/165

Rest – Menu €25 (weekday lunch) – Carte €65/90

◆ Contemporary architecture perched on the hillside. Spacious rooms (with a terrace), some of which have been refurbished. The lovely overflow swimming pool enjoys a sea view. Regionally inspired cuisine, and a snack menu in summertime.

Troubadour

r. du Brec, (pedestrian access) – ✆ 04 93 41 19 03 – troubadoureze@wanadoo.fr – Closed 29 June-12 July, 14 November-20 December, Sunday and Monday

Rest – *(pre-book)* Menu €39/52 – Carte €50/60

◆ In the heart of the old village are these three small, fresh and intimate dining areas serving traditional cuisine prepared with market produce. Some Provençal specialities.

at Col d'Èze 3 km Northwest – ✉ 06360 Eze – pop. 2 509 – alt. 390 m

La Bastide aux Camélias without rest

23c rte de l'Adret – ✆ 04 93 41 13 68 – www.bastideauxcamelias.com – sylviane.mathieu@libertysurf.fr – Fax 04 93 41 13 68

4 rm – €110/150 €110/150

◆ The rooms in this splendid villa surrounded by greenery are personalised and stylishly furnished (antique and ethnic furniture); there is a swimming-pool and fitness centre.

ÈZE-BORD-DE-MER – 06 Alpes-Maritimes – 341 F5 – ✉ 06360 Eze 42 **E2**
French Riviera

Paris 959 – Monaco 8 – Nice 14 – Menton 22

Cap Estel

1312 av. Raymond Poincaré – ✆ 04 93 76 29 29
– www.capestel.com – contact@capestel.com – Fax 04 93 01 55 20
– Closed 3 January-26 February
10 rm – €350/1350 €350/1350, €28 – 10 suites
Rest – Menu (€58), €78/98 – Carte €84/124
◆ This haven of peace and tranquillity, built on the peninsula by a Russian prince at the end of the 19C, has regained all its former splendour. Luxurious bedrooms, sumptuous suites, plus a private beach. The elegant restaurant facing the sea serves contemporary cuisine.

FAGNON – 08 Ardennes – 306 J4 – see Charleville-Mézières

FALAISE – 14 Calvados – 303 K6 – pop. 8 438 – alt. 132 m – ✉ 14700 32 **B2**
Normandy

Paris 264 – Argentan 23 – Caen 36 – Flers 37 – Lisieux 45 – St-Lô 107
Office de tourisme, boulevard de la Libération ✆ 02 31 90 17 26, Fax 02 31 90 98 70
Château Guillaume-Le-Conquérant (William the Conqueror's castle) ★ - la Trinité church ★.

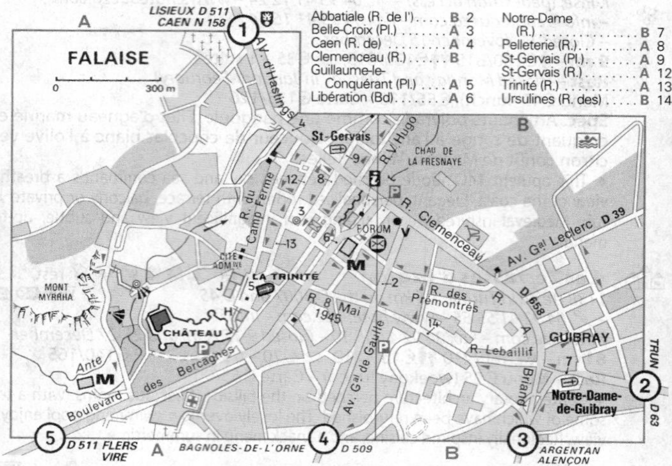

De la Poste

38 r. G. Clemenceau – ✆ 02 31 90 13 14 – hotel.delaposte@wanadoo.fr
– Fax 02 31 90 01 81 – Closed 1st-23 January, Sunday dinner, Friday dinner and Monday October-April B **v**
17 rm – €54/98 €54/98, €8
Rest – Menu €16 (weekdays)/52 – Carte €48/62
◆ The rooms in this post-war building are discreet and well kept; those at the rear are quieter. A dining room in pastel colours serving traditional dishes.

L'Attache

rte de Caen, by ①: 1.5 km – ✆ 02 31 90 05 38 – sarlhastain@orange.fr
– Fax 02 31 90 57 19 – Closed 22 September-9 October, Tuesday and Wednesday
Rest – *(number of covers limited, pre-book)* Menu €20/60 – Carte €41/65
◆ A former coaching inn with a spruce façade and attractive, classic interior. Focus on traditional cuisine with the occasional addition of unjustly forgotten herbs and vegetables.

in St-Pierre-Canivet 4 km via ① and by D 6 – **pop. 350 – alt. 150 m – ✉ 14700**

Domaine de la Tour without rest
– ✆ 02 31 20 53 07 – www.domainedelatour.fr – info@domainedelatour.fr
– Fax 02 31 20 56 63
5 rm – †€ 55/100 ††€ 60/100
◆ This 18C estate is made up of a former hunting lodge and the stables of the Château de la Tour. A country break ideal for families: Normandy inspired guestrooms, children's playroom and park.

LE FALGOUX – 15 Cantal – **330** D4 – **pop. 193 – alt. 930 m – Winter sports : 1 050 m** 1 – ✉ **15380** 5 **B3**

Paris 533 – Aurillac 57 – Mauriac 29 – Murat 34 – Salers 15

Falgoux Valley ★.

Cirque du Falgoux★★ Southeast: 6 km - Puy Mary ❋★★★: 1 h return journey from Pas de Peyrol★★ Southeast: 12 km,
Auvergne-Rhone Valley

Des Voyageurs
– ✆ 04 71 69 51 59 – Fax 04 71 69 48 05 – Closed 2 November-25 January and Wednesday dinner in low season
14 rm – †€ 45 ††€ 45, € 7 – ½ P € 43
Rest – Menu € 17 bi/27 – Carte € 24/38
◆ A typical Auvergne style inn with a large fireplace in the bar. Friendly service, redecorated well-kept guestrooms with rustic furniture. The restaurant commands a fine view of the Cantal mountain landscape. Regional menu.

FALICON – 06 Alpes-Maritimes – **341** E5 – **pop. 1 789 – alt. 396 m – ✉ 06950** 42 **E2**

Paris 935 – Cannes 42 – Nice 12 – Sospel 41 – Vence 32

Parcours
1 pl. Marcel Eusebi – ✆ 04 93 84 94 57
– www.restaurant-parcours.com
– parcourslive@orange.fr
– Fax 04 93 98 66 90 – Closed Sunday dinner, Tuesday lunch and Monday
Rest – Menu (€ 24), € 39/65 – Carte approx. € 40
◆ Restaurant in a modern setting with plasma screens showing the cooks at work, a panoramic terrace and menus that vary according to market availability.

LE FAOU – 29 Finistère – **308** F5 – **pop. 1 669 – alt. 10 m – ✉ 29590** 9 **A2**
Brittany

Paris 560 – Brest 30 – Châteaulin 20 – Landerneau 23 – Morlaix 52 – Quimper 43

Office de tourisme, 10, rue du Gal-de-Gaulle ✆ 02 98 81 06 85, Fax 02 98 73 03 14

Site★.

De Beauvoir
11 pl. Mairie – ✆ 02 98 81 90 31 – www.hotel-beauvoir.com
– la-vieille-renommee@wanadoo.fr – Fax 02 98 81 92 93 – Closed 5-29 December, Sunday dinner and Monday lunch
32 rm – †€ 55/70 ††€ 76/90, € 10
Rest *La Vieille Renommée* – *(closed Sunday dinner October-May, Monday except dinner June-September and Tuesday lunch)* Menu (€ 19), € 27 (weekdays)/60 – Carte € 55/70
◆ Large building in the centre of an typically Breton village nestling at the end of the Faou Estuary. Ask for one of the recently refurbished rooms. The Vieille Renommée dining room has neat table settings and serves traditional cuisine. Good wine list.

FARGES-ALLICHAMPS – 18 Cher – **323** K6 – **pop. 216 – alt. 194 m** 12 **C3**
– ✉ 18200

Paris 290 – Orléans 164 – Bourges 38 – Montluçon 67 – Issoudun 47

Château de la Commanderie VISA

– ✆ *02 48 61 04 19 – www.chateaudelacommanderie.com*
– chateaudelacommanderie@gmail.com – Fax 02 48 61 01 84
5 rm – €110/150 €150/250 **Table d'hôte** – Menu €85 bi

◆ The owners of this old Templar commandery, with its well preserved original interior, are charming. Refined rooms in the very calm setting of a 10-hectare park. Romantic dinner (on reservation) in a splendid dining room.

FARROU – 12 Aveyron – **338** E4 – **see Villefranche-de-Rouergue**

LA FAUCILLE (COL) – 01 Ain – **328** J2 – **see Col de la Faucille**

FAVERGES – 74 Haute-Savoie – **328** K6 – **pop. 6 524 – alt. 507 m** 45 **C1**
– ✉ 74210 **French Alps**

Paris 562 – Albertville 20 – Annecy 27 – Megève 35

Office de tourisme, place Marcel Piquand ✆ 04 50 44 60 24, Fax 04 50 44 45 96

Florimont VISA

rte d'Albertville, 2,5 km – ✆ *04 50 44 50 05 – www.hotelflorimont.com – info@hotelflorimont.com – Fax 04 50 44 43 20 – Closed 18 December-7 January*
27 rm – €67/85 €77/120, €11 – ½ P €75/100
Rest – *(closed 18 December-7 January, Sunday dinner and Saturday)*
Menu €27/65 – Carte €55/80

◆ The Florimont (combination of flora and mountain) is ideally located near a golf course, overlooking Mont Blanc. Brightly decorated, impeccably kept rooms. Two dining rooms, one classic and the other Savoyard in style, together with a garden terrace.

De Genève without rest VISA

34 r. République – ✆ *04 50 32 46 90 – www.hotellegeneve.com – info@hotellegeneve.com – Fax 04 50 44 48 09 – Closed 18 April-4 May, 19 December-4 January*
30 rm – €46/73 €55/80, €8,50

◆ Easily recognisable by its painted façade, this centrally located hotel is very handy. Practical rooms, well soundproofed on the road side. Exhibitions in the bar (snacks).

in Tertenoz 4 km Southeast by D 12 and secondary road – ✉ **74210 Seythenex**

Au Gay Séjour with rm VISA

– ✆ *04 50 44 52 52 – www.hotel-gay-sejour.com – hotel-gay-sejour@wanadoo.fr – Fax 04 50 44 49 52 – Closed Sunday dinner and Monday except bank holidays and July-August*
11 rm – €72/80 €85/105, €13 – ½ P €90/100
Rest – Menu (€25), €35 (weekdays)/82 – Carte €50/60

◆ An imposing 17C farmhouse tucked away in a mountain hamlet with a view of the valley. Traditional cuisine and brightly coloured modern dining room. Simple bedrooms.

FAVERNEY – 70 Haute-Saône – **314** E6 – **pop. 1 052 – alt. 235 m** 16 **B1**
– ✉ 70160

Paris 364 – Besançon 70 – Vesoul 21 – Lure 48 – Remiremont 59

Syndicat d'initiative, place de la Mairie ✆ 03 84 91 30 71, Fax 03 84 91 38 58

in Breurey-lès-Faverney 3 km southeast on the D 434 and D 6 – **pop. 521**
– **alt. 233 m** – ✉ 70160

Château de la Presle VISA

3 r. Louis-Pergaud – ✆ *03 84 91 41 70 – www.chateaudelapresle.com*
– resa@chateaudelapresle.com
5 rm – €90/130 €100/140 **Table d'hôte** – Menu €40 bi

◆ This small 19C château, surrounded by six hectares of parkland, is in the heart of a small village. Lovely personalised, well-equipped rooms. Sitting room with a grand piano and a billiards table under the eaves. Classic bourgeois cuisine served in an elegant room with a fireplace.

LA FAVIÈRE – 83 Var – 340 N7 – see Bormes-les-Mimosas

FAVIÈRES – 80 Somme – 301 C6 – pop. 444 – alt. 1 m – ✉ 80120 36 A1

Paris 212 – Abbeville 22 – Amiens 77 – Berck-Plage 27 – Le Crotoy 5

Le Crotoy: Butte du Moulin ≤★ Southwest: 5 km,

Northern France and the Paris Region

Les Saules without rest

1075 r. Forges – ✆ 03 22 27 04 20 – www.hotel-les-saules – hotellessaules@orange.fr – Fax 03 22 27 00 38 – Closed 5-21 January

13 rm – †€ 64/77 ††€ 70/82, ☕ € 11

◆ Tranquillity is ensured in this modern house near the Marquenterre Bird Park. Functional rooms overlooking a garden or the surrounding countryside.

La Clé des Champs

Place des Frères Caudron – ✆ 03 22 27 88 00 – Fax 03 22 27 79 36 – Closed 25 August-2 September, 5-16 January, 8-21 February, Monday and Tuesday except bank holidays

Rest – Menu € 16/42

◆ This old Picardy farmhouse has been sympathetically restored. The decor remains classic and simple, embellished with paintings by local artists. Market-inspired seasonal menu.

FAVONE – 2A Corse-du-Sud – 345 F9 – see Corse

FAYENCE – 83 Var – 340 P4 – pop. 4 867 – alt. 350 m – ✉ 83440 41 C3

French Riviera

Paris 884 – Castellane 55 – Draguignan 30 – Fréjus 36 – Grasse 26 – St-Raphaël 37

Office du tourisme, place Léon Roux ✆ 04 94 76 20 08, Fax 04 94 39 15 96

≤★ from the church terrace.

Les Oliviers without rest

18 av. St-Christophe, (quartier La Ferrage), Grasse road – ✆ 04 94 76 13 12 – www.lesoliviersfayence.fr – hotel.oliviers.fayen@free.fr – Fax 04 94 76 08 05

22 rm ☕ – †€ 75/80 ††€ 88/98

◆ Small building overlooking the Plaine du Gué and its large gliding centre. Sports enthusiasts and lazybones alike will enjoy the practical rooms at the Oliviers.

La Bégude du Pascouren without rest

74 chemin de la Bane, 7.5 km south on the D 562 (Draguignan road) – ✆ 04 94 68 63 03 – www.chambres-hotes-labegudedupascouren.fr – labegudedupascouren@orange.fr – Fax 04 88 67 60 18

5 rm ☕ – †€ 85/142 ††€ 89/146 – 1 suite

◆ Charming and isolated Provencal villa with a fine garden and pool. Bright contemporary rooms with southern French touches. Bowling green.

La Farigoulette

pl. du Château – ✆ 04 94 84 10 49 – la-farigoulette@wanadoo.fr – Closed 1st-12 March, 6-21 February, Tuesday except from 15 July to 16 August and Wednesday

Rest – Menu (€ 20 bi), € 28/38 – Carte € 39/73

◆ An old stable provides a pleasant rustic setting where open stonework and traditional furnishings combine perfectly with the judiciously updated traditional cuisine.

Le Temps des Cerises

pl. République – ✆ 04 94 76 01 19 – www.descerises.com – louis.schroder@aliceadsl.fr – Fax 04 94 76 92 50 – Closed 1st-27 December and Tuesday

Rest – *(dinner only except Sunday)* Menu € 43 – Carte € 42/51

◆ Charming dining room decorated with artwork by the father of the Dutch chef-owner. Traditional little dishes which have been updated in the chef's own style. Terrace under an arbour.

La Table d'Yves

1357 rte de Fréjus, 2 km on the D563 – ✆ 04 94 76 08 44 – www.latabledyves.com – contact@latabledyves.com – Fax 04 94 76 19 32 – Closed autumn school holidays, the February holiday, Thursday except dinner in high season and Wednesday

Rest – Menu € 28/52 – Carte € 25/55

◆ The terrace with splendid views of the village perched on a hillside, spruce dining rooms enhanced by a sunny decor, market-fresh cuisine – all good reasons to dine at Yves'!

West by Seillans road (D 19) and secondary road – ✉ **83440 Fayence**

Moulin de la Camandoule

at 2 km – ✆ 04 94 76 00 84 – www.moulindelacamandoule.com – moulin.camandoule@wanadoo.fr – Fax 04 94 76 10 40

12 rm – €72/118 €72/195, ☕ €12

Rest – *(closed Thursday except for dinner in July-August and Wednesday from September to June)* Menu € 30/45 – Carte € 40/57

◆ At the centre of a park traversed by a Roman aqueduct, this 17C oil mill today houses pleasant Provençal country style guestrooms. Regional cuisine using local produce in the restaurant. Fine terrace giving onto a charming orchard garden.

Le Castellaras (Alain Carro)

461 chemin Peymeyan, 4 km away – ✆ 04 94 76 13 80 – www.restaurant-castellaras.com – contact@restaurant-castellaras.com – Fax 04 94 84 17 50 – Closed January, Tuesday except dinner in July-August and Monday

Rest – Menu € 45/62 – Carte € 68/75

Spec. Carpaccio de langoustine, vinaigrette à la moutarde à l'ancienne et estragon (summer). Norvégienne de carré d'agneau rôti, petits légumes farcis de Provence (summer). Mazarin praliné au croquant de nougatine. **Wines** Côtes de Provence.

◆ An eminently appealing establishment from the personalised welcome and tasteful decor to the superb terrace overlooking the valley and gourmet Provençal menu.

LE FAYET – 74 Haute-Savoie – 074 08 – see St-Gervais-les-Bains

FÉCAMP – 76 Seine-Maritime – 304 C3 – pop. 19 500 – alt. 15 m – Casino AZ – ✉ 76400 Normandy

33 **C1**

Paris 201 – Amiens 165 – Caen 113 – Dieppe 66 – Le Havre 43 – Rouen 74

Office de tourisme, 113, rue Alexandre le Grand ✆ 02 35 28 51 01, Fax 02 35 27 07 77

La Trinité abbey church ★ - Palais Bénédictine★★ - Musée des Terres-Neuvas et de la Pêche★ M³ - N.-D.-du-Salut chapel ✻★★ North: 2 km by D 79 BY.

Plan on next page

Le Grand Pavois without rest

15 quai Vicomté – ✆ 02 35 10 01 01 – www.hotel-grand-pavois.com – le.grandpavois@wanadoo.fr – Fax 02 35 29 31 67

AY **r**

35 rm – €88/230 €88/230, ☕ €14

◆ Built on the site of a canning factory on the wharf. The lobby sports a nautical decor and the large rooms are furnished with contemporary furniture; some overlook the harbour.

La Ferme de la Chapelle

2 km by ①, rte du Phare and D 79 – ✆ 02 35 10 12 12 – fermedelachapelle@wanadoo.fr – Fax 02 35 10 12 13 – Closed in January

AY **d**

22 rm – €85/95 €85/95, ☕ €10

Rest – *(closed Monday lunch)* Menu (€ 18), € 27/34 – Carte € 28/36

◆ On a cliff, this former 16C seigniorial farmhouse adjoins a seamen's chapel. Neatly furnished rooms around a square courtyard. The restaurant is both simple and welcoming, serving traditional meals.

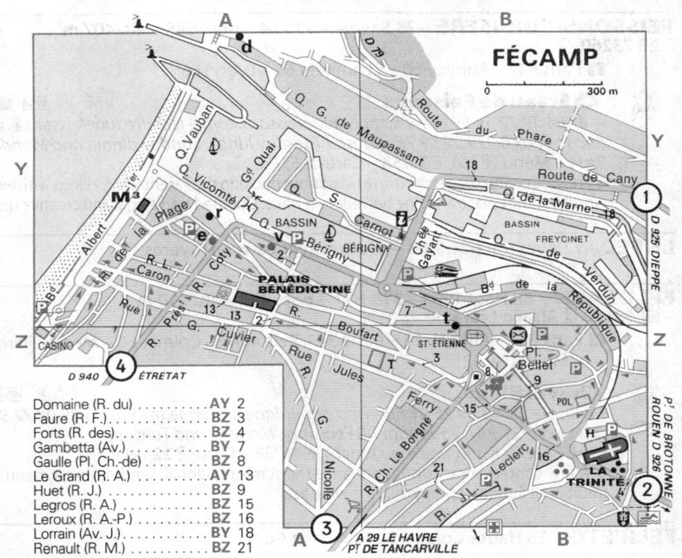

Vent d'Ouest without rest — VISA MC AE

3 av. Gambetta – ☎ 02 35 28 04 04 – www.hotelventdouest.tm.fr – hotel@hotelventdouest.tm.fr – Fax 02 35 28 75 96 — BY **t**

15 rm – 🚹€ 34/40 🚹🚹€ 40/48, ☕ € 5

◆ This unpretentious family hotel, entirely renovated, is suitable for tight budgets. The rooms are painted in yellow and well equipped. A charming breakfast room.

Auberge de la Rouge with rm — P VISA MC AE

rte du Havre, 2 km via ③ – ☎ 02 35 28 07 59 – www.auberge-rouge.com – auberge.rouge@wanadoo.fr – Fax 02 35 28 70 55

8 rm – 🚹€ 65 🚹🚹€ 65, ☕ € 8

Rest – *(closed Saturday lunch, Sunday dinner and Monday)*
Menu (€ 15), € 20/36 – Carte € 70/90

◆ This former post house serves traditional fare in a countrified decor. Flower-decked garden terrace in summer. Rustic rooms.

La Marée — VISA MC AE

77 quai Bérigny, (1st floor) – ☎ 02 35 29 39 15 – fecamp-restaurant-la-maree.com – restaurant-la-maree@wanadoo.fr – Fax 02 35 29 73 27 – Closed Thursday dinner, Sunday dinner and Monday off season — AY **v**

Rest – Menu (€ 17), € 26/36 – Carte € 30/48

◆ Fish recipes predominate on this restaurant's menus; the décor is soberly modern and certain tables give a view of the seaport. The small terrace faces due south.

Le Vicomté — VISA MC

4 r. Prés. R. Coty – ☎ 02 35 28 47 63 – Closed 26 April-3 May, 15 August-3 September, 23 December-3 January, Sunday, Wednesday and bank holidays — AY **e**

Rest – *(number of covers limited, pre-book)* Menu € 18

◆ This charming little bistro (non-smoking) is adjacent to the splendid Benedictine foundation that has given its name to the famous liqueur. The cuisine is based on fresh market produce, and daily menus are chalked up on the slate.

FEGERSHEIM – 67 Bas-Rhin – **315** K6 – see Strasbourg

FEISSONS-SUR-ISÈRE – 73 Savoie – **333** L4 – **pop. 548** – **alt. 407 m** 46 **F2**
– ✉ 73260

Paris 632 – Annecy 60 – Chambéry 66 – Lyon 166

XX **Château de Feissons**

– ✆ *04 79 22 59 59 – www.chateaudefeissons.com – lechateaudefeissons@wanadoo.fr – Fax 04 79 22 59 76 – Closed Tuesday lunch, Sunday dinner and Monday*
Rest – Menu (€ 19), € 29/58 – Carte € 55/78
◆ This 12C château is perched on a hillside overlooking the Tarentaise. Ceilings with exposed woodwork, fireplace and fine belvedere terrace. Updated traditional and creative dishes.

LE FEL – 12 Aveyron – **338** H3 – see Entraygues-sur-Truyères

FELDBACH – 68 Haut-Rhin – **315** H11 – **pop. 433** – **alt. 410 m** 1 **A3**
– ✉ 68640 Alsace-Lorraine

Paris 461 – Altkirch 14 – Basel 34 – Belfort 46 – Colmar 80 – Montbéliard 41 – Mulhouse 32

XX **Cheval Blanc**

1 r. Bisel – ✆ *03 89 25 81 86 – ispa.dominique@orange.fr – Fax 03 89 07 72 88 – Closed 6-21 July, 25 January-9 February, Monday and Tuesday*
Rest – Menu € 11 (weekday lunch), € 16/37 – Carte € 22/49
◆ A few contemporary dishes enhance the semi-traditional, semi-regional menu of this traditional Sundgau property. Fine wine list.

FELICETO – 2B Haute-Corse – **345** C4 – see Corse

FENEYROLS – 82 Tarn-et-Garonne – **337** G7 – **pop. 175** – **alt. 124 m** 29 **C2**
– ✉ 82140

Paris 632 – Cahors 63 – Limoges 245 – Lyon 424 – Montpellier 251 – Toulouse 642

XX **Hostellerie Les Jardins des Thermes** with rm

Le bourg – ✆ *05 63 30 65 49* rm,
– www.jardinsdesthermes.eu – hostellerie@jardinsdesthermes.eu – Fax 05 63 30 60 17 – Open 1st March-15 November
5 rm – €43/51 €43/67, € 8
Rest – *(closed Wednesday and Thursday except July-August)*
Menu (€ 16), € 20 (weekday lunch), € 27/51 bi – Carte € 45/53
◆ On the banks of the Aveyron, this old spa hotel is in a park near the remains of Roman baths. Modern rooms and nicely decorated restaurant.

FERAYOLA – 2B Haute-Corse – **345** B5 – see Corse (Galéria)

FÈRE-EN-TARDENOIS – 02 Aisne – **306** D7 – **pop. 3 306** – **alt. 180 m** 37 **C3**
– ✉ 02130 Northern France and the Paris Region

Paris 111 – Château-Thierry 23 – Laon 55 – Reims 50 – Soissons 27

Office de tourisme, 18, rue Etienne-Moreau-Nelaton ✆ 03 23 82 31 57, Fax 03 23 82 28 19

de Champagne Villers-Agron-Aiguizy Moulin de Neuville, E : 17 km on D 2, ✆ 03 23 71 62 08

Château de Fère★: Bridge-gallery★★ North: 3 km.

Château de Fère rm,

rte de Fismes, 3 km north on D 967 – ✆ *03 23 82 21 13 – www.chateaudefere.com – chateau.fere@wanadoo.fr – Fax 03 23 82 37 81 – Closed 4 January-10 February*
19 rm – € 150/370 € 150/370, € 22 – 7 suites
Rest – *(closed Monday dinner, Tuesday lunch except bank holidays from November to March and Monday lunch)* Menu (€ 36), € 52/90 – Carte € 69/123
◆ With the ruins of the castle of Anne de Montmorency and its famous bridge in the background, this lovely 16C house has sumptuous decor. Vast grounds. The two dining rooms in the restaurant exude elegance (with a fresco depicting the fables of La Fontaine and lovely wood panelling).

FERNEY-VOLTAIRE – 01 Ain – 328 J3 – pop. 7 083 – alt. 430 m – ✉ 01210 Burgundy-Jura 46 F1

Paris 499 – Bellegarde-sur-Valserine 37 – Genève 10 – Gex 10 – Thonon-les-Bains 43

Genève-Cointrin ✆ (00 41 22) 717 71 11, South: 4 km.

Office de tourisme, 26, Grand'Rue ✆ 04 50 28 09 16, Fax 04 50 40 78 99

de Gonville Saint-Jean-de-GonvilleSW : 14 km on D 35 and D 984, ✆ 04 50 56 40 92

Château★.

Genève★★★.

Novotel rm, VISA AE
rte de Meyrin, via D 35 – ✆ 04 50 40 85 23 – www.novotel.com – h0422@accor.com – Fax 04 50 40 76 33
80 rm – †€ 88/250 ††€ 88/250, ☕ € 15 **Rest** – Menu (€ 20) – Carte € 24/37
◆ This Novotel, conveniently located near the Swiss border, has been treated to a make-over. Contemporary rooms in keeping with the chain's latest design: light wood and Japanese influence. Elegant dining room and terrace. Traditional dishes and regional specialities.

XX **De France** with rm VISA AE
1 r. de Genève – ✆ 04 50 40 63 87 – www.hotelfranceferney.com – hotelfranceferney@wanadoo.fr – Fax 04 50 40 47 27 – Closed 26 July-10 August, 25 October-2 November, 20 December-5 January
14 rm – †€ 68/100 ††€ 88/115, ☕ € 9
Rest – *(closed Saturday lunch, Sunday and Monday)*
Menu (€ 21), € 25 (weekday lunch), € 38 € bi/68 – Carte € 32/61
◆ This house built in 1742 has been masterfully taken over: modernised dining room, cosy bar, veranda extended by a terrace lined by lime trees, and an updated menu.

XX **Le Pirate** VISA AE
1 chemin de la Brunette – ✆ 04 50 40 63 52 – www.lepirate.fr – contact@lepirate.fr – Fax 04 50 40 64 50
Rest – Menu (€ 28), € 32 (lunch), € 36/61 – Carte € 50/70
◆ An establishment devoted to seafood. Elegant dining rooms decorated in warm colours and dotted with plants. A veranda enlivened by a fountain in warm weather.

X **Le Chanteclair** VISA
13 r. Versoix – ✆ 04 50 40 79 55 – Fax 04 50 40 93 04 – Closed 3-11 May, 16-31 August, Sunday and Monday
Rest – Menu (€ 24), € 28 (lunch), € 38/62 – Carte € 53/62
◆ The cuisine is in tune with the seasons in this pleasant, predominantly blue and yellow, contemporary style restaurant. Unusual façade covered in 'graffiti'.

FERRETTE – 68 Haut-Rhin – 315 H12 – pop. 1 041 – alt. 470 m – ✉ 68480 Alsace-Lorraine 1 A3

Paris 467 – Altkirch 20 – Basel 28 – Belfort 52 – Colmar 85 – Montbéliard 48 – Mulhouse 38

Office de tourisme, route de Lucelle ✆ 03 89 08 23 88, Fax 03 89 40 33 84

de la Largue Seppois-le-Bas Rue du Golf, W : 10 km on D 473 and D 24, ✆ 03 89 07 67 67

Site★ - Château ruins ≤★.

in Ligsdorf 4 km South by D 432 – pop. 334 – alt. 520 m – ✉ 68480

XX **Le Moulin Bas et rest. La Mezzanine** with rm VISA
1 r. Raedersdorf – ✆ 03 89 40 31 25 – www.le-moulin-bas.fr – info@le-moulin-bas.fr
8 rm – †€ 65/75 ††€ 85/95, ☕ € 10 – ½ P € 69/98
Rest – *(Closed Tuesday)* Menu € 13 (weekday lunch), € 32/57 – Carte € 25/45
Rest *Stuba* – *(Closed Tuesday)* Carte € 25/45
◆ This 1796 mill on the banks of the Ill is home to an elegant dining room, serving regional dishes and grilled meats in season. The winstub-style Stuba displays old machinery; regional cuisine and tartes flambées. Peaceful and practical rooms.

in Moernach 5 km West by D 473 – pop. 542 – alt. 470 m – ✉ 68480

XX **Aux Deux Clefs** with rm
218 r. Hennin Blenner – ✆ 03 89 40 80 56 – auxdeuxclefs@wanadoo.fr – Fax 03 89 08 10 47 – Closed 20 July-5 August, autumn half-term holidays and February holidays
7 rm – 🛉€ 38 🛉🛉€ 48, ☕ € 8 – ½ P € 57
Rest – *(closed Wednesday dinner and Thursday)*
Menu (€ 11), € 20/47 – Carte € 30/43
◆ Pretty half-timbered house typical of the Sundgau. An opulent dining room with paintings; traditional cuisine. Welcoming rooms with parquet floors in a neighbouring annexe.

in Lutter 8 km Southeast by D 23 – pop. 302 – alt. 428 m – ✉ 68480

XX **L'Auberge Paysanne** with rm
1 r. de Wolschwiller – ✆ 03 89 40 71 67 – www.auberge-hostellerie-paysanne.com – aubergepaysanne2@wanadoo.fr – Fax 03 89 07 33 38 – Closed 29 June-14 July, 21 December-11 January, Tuesday lunch and Monday
7 rm – 🛉€ 52/62 🛉🛉€ 52/62, ☕ € 8,50 – ½ P € 51/56
Rest – Menu (€ 10), € 12 (lunch)/40 – Carte € 25/50
◆ Family run establishment near the Swiss border. Among the several dining rooms, the winstub has the most charm. Regional and Mediterranean cuisine. Modern bedrooms.

Hostellerie Paysanne
8 r. de Wolschwiller – ✆ 03 89 40 71 67 – aubergepaysanne2@wanadoo.fr – Fax 03 89 07 33 38
9 rm – 🛉€ 52 🛉🛉€ 62/72, ☕ € 8 – ½ P € 55/59
◆ This Alsatian farm dating from 1618 was dismantled and rebuilt in this village. Rooms with period furniture. A warm welcome at the Auberge Paysanne.

LA FERRIÈRE-AUX-ÉTANGS – 61 Orne – 310 F3 – see Flers

FERRIÈRES-EN-GÂTINAIS – 45 Loiret – 318 N3 – pop. 3 330 – alt. 96 m – ✉ 45210 Burgundy-Jura 12 D2

Paris 99 – Auxerre 81 – Fontainebleau 40 – Montargis 12 – Nemours 26 – Orléans 86

Office de tourisme, place des Églises ✆ 02 38 96 58 86, Fax 02 38 96 60 39

Transept crossing★ of St-Pierre and St-Paul church.

L'Abbaye
– ✆ 02 38 96 53 12 – www.hotel-abbaye.fr – info@hotel-abbaye.fr – Fax 02 38 96 57 63
30 rm – 🛉€ 66 🛉🛉€ 66, ☕ € 9 – ½ P € 61
Rest – Menu (€ 15), € 25 (weekdays)/58 – Carte € 25/48
◆ The name refers to the former abbey of St Peter and St Paul around which the village was built. Choose one of the new, spacious, well-equipped rooms. Large restaurant serving traditional cuisine; terrace popular in summer.

FERRIÈRES-LES-VERRERIES – 34 Hérault – 339 H5 – pop. 55 – alt. 320 m – ✉ 34190 23 C2

Paris 747 – Montpellier 41 – Alès 47 – Florac 86 – Millau 102

XX **La Cour-Mas de Baumes** with rm
4 km east on the D 107E4 – ✆ 04 66 80 88 80 – www.oustaldebaumes.com – info@oustaldebaumes.com – Fax 04 66 80 88 82 – Closed 24 October-5 November, 2-15 January, 13-20 February, Sunday dinner, Monday and Tuesday from 1st November to 15 March
7 rm ☕ – 🛉€ 58/88 🛉🛉€ 70/107
Rest – Menu (€ 18), € 29/68 – Carte € 50/60
◆ Ex-smallholding and glass works isolated in the middle of the countryside. Original food in an elegant setting combining old and new. Pretty, contemporary guestrooms.

FERTE-BEAUHARNAIS – 41 Loir-et-Cher – 318 I6 – pop. 510 – alt. 101 m – ✉ 41210 Châteaux of the Loire
12 C2

Paris 183 – Orléans 45 – Blois 46 – Vierzon 56 – Fleury-les-Aubrais 63

Château de la Ferté Beauharnais without rest

172 r. du Prince-Eugène – ✆ 02 54 83 72 18 – www.chateaudebeauharnais.com – Fax 02 54 83 72 18

3 rm – €140/145 €140/145

◆ This château was once the home of the Beauharnais family, notably Josephine, first wife of Napoleon. Stylish rooms with parquet floors, decorative mouldings and fireplace.

LA FERTÉ-BERNARD – 72 Sarthe – 310 M5 – pop. 9 251 – alt. 90 m – ✉ 72400 Châteaux of the Loire
35 D1

Paris 164 – Alençon 56 – Chartres 79 – Châteaudun 65 – Le Mans 54

Office de tourisme, 15, place de la Lice ✆ 02 43 71 21 21, Fax 02 43 93 25 85

du Perche Souancé-au-Perche La Vallée des Aulnes, NE : 21 km on D 923 and D137, ✆ 02 37 29 17 33

N.-D.-des Marais church ★★.

La Perdrix

A/C VISA MC

2 r. de Paris – ✆ 02 43 93 00 44 – http//monsite.orange.fr/laperdrix – restaurantlaperdrix@hotmail.com – Fax 02 43 93 74 95 – Closed mid-January to mid-February, Monday dinner and Tuesday

Rest – Menu € 18 (weekdays)/39 – Carte € 39/45

◆ A town centre restaurant by a busy road. Traditional cuisine served in the blue room beneath a glass roof or in the predominantly red and beige room.

Le Dauphin

VISA MC

3 r. d'Huisne, (pedestrian access) – ✆ 02 43 93 00 39 – Fax 02 43 71 26 65 – Closed 13-20 April, 3-24 August, Sunday dinner, Thursday dinner and Monday

Rest – Menu € 16 (weekdays)/41 – Carte € 45/60

◆ This 16C house in the old town has lost nothing of its original charm (stonework, beams and fireplace) enhanced by a modern, vibrant colour scheme. Menu in keeping with modern tastes.

LA FERTÉ-IMBAULT – 41 Loir-et-Cher – 318 I7 – pop. 1 035 – alt. 99 m – ✉ 41300
12 C2

Paris 191 – Bourges 66 – Orléans 68 – Romorantin-Lanthenay 19 – Vierzon 23

Syndicat d'initiative, 31, route Nationale ✆ 02 54 96 34 83, Fax 02 54 96 34 83

Auberge À la Tête de Lard

A/C rest, P VISA MC AE

13 pl. des Tilleuls – ✆ 02 54 96 22 32 – www.aubergealatetedelard.com – tetedelard0233@orange.fr – Fax 02 54 96 06 22 – Closed 11 January-9 February, Sunday dinner, Tuesday lunch and Monday

11 rm – €51 €56, €9 – ½ P €53

Rest – Menu (€ 19), € 33/50 – Carte € 36/67

◆ Modern, tasteful rooms in this pleasant little Sologne inn, a former post house. Wide choice of leisure activities: rambling and mountain biking. Rustic dining room in a pretty countrified spirit. Regional cuisine and game in season.

LA FERTÉ-MACÉ – 61 Orne – 310 G3 – pop. 6 102 – alt. 250 m – ✉ 61600 Normandy
32 B3

Paris 227 – Alençon 46 – Argentan 33 – Domfront 23 – Falaise 41 – Flers 26

Syndicat d'initiative, 11, rue de la Victoire ✆ 02 33 37 10 97, Fax 02 33 37 10 97

LA FERTÉ-MACÉ

Armand-Macé (R.) . . . . B 2
Barre (R. de la) . . . . B 4
Chauvière (R.) . . . . B 7
Clouet (R. du) . . . . A 8
De-Contades (Bd Gérard) . . . . A 10
Fossés Nicole (R. des) . . . . B 12
Hautvie (R. d') . . . . B
Leclerc (Pl. du Gén.) . . . . B 15
Le-Meunier-de-la-Raillère (Av.) . . . . B 13
République (Pl. de la) . . . . . . B 16
Teinture (R. de la) . . . . B 18
Val Vert (R. du) . . . . A 19
4-Roues (R. des) . . . . B 21

Auberge d'Andaines

rte Bagnoles-de-l'Orne, via ③: 2 km – ✆ 02 33 37 20 28 – www.aubergeandaines.com – resa@aubergeandaines.com – Fax 02 33 37 25 05 – Closed Friday from 15 October to 1 April

15 rm – †€ 42/65 ††€ 42/65, ☕ € 8 – ½ P € 45/55

Rest – Menu (€ 12), € 16/40

◆ Roadside family inn on the edge of the Andaines Forest. Simple, well kept rooms; choose those facing the garden. A delightful, welcoming restaurant in a slightly retro style. Traditional cuisine.

Auberge de Clouet

Le Clouet – ✆ 02 33 37 18 22 – Fax 02 33 38 28 52 – Closed 1st-17 November, Sunday dinner and Monday October-Easter A **a**

Rest – Menu (€ 18), € 23/75 – Carte € 30/50

◆ Regional produce takes pride of place in this inn. It specialises in generous portions of tasty locally sourced fare, served in a rustic interior or on the flower-decked terrace in summer.

LA FERTÉ-ST-AUBIN – 45 Loiret – 318 I5 – pop. 7 083 – alt. 114 m 12 C2

– ✉ 45240 ▮ Châteaux of the Loire

▶ Paris 153 – Blois 62 – Orléans 23 – Romorantin-Lanthenay 45 – Salbris 34

ℹ Office de tourisme, rue des Jardins ✆ 02 38 64 67 93, Fax 02 38 64 61 39

⛳ des Aisses Domaine des Aisses, SE : 3 km on N 20, ✆ 02 38 64 80 87

⛳ de Sologne Route de Jouy-le-Potier, NW : 5 km, ✆ 02 38 76 57 33

◉ Château★.

XXX **La Ferme de la Lande**
Northeast : 3 km via rte Marcilly – ✆ 02 38 76 64 37 – www.fermedelalande.com – solognote@fermedelalande.com – Fax 02 38 64 68 87 – Closed 21 September-5 October, 19 January-9 February, Sunday dinner and Monday
Rest – Menu € 32/69 – Carte € 53/72
◆ A restaurant in a converted farmhouse whose authenticity has been skilfully preserved (brick and timber-frame walls). Cooking suited to current tastes. A park for a walk before dinner.

XX **Auberge de l'Écu de France**
6 r. Gén.-Leclerc, (N 20) – ✆ 02 38 64 69 22 – Fax 02 38 64 09 54 – Closed Sunday dinner, Wednesday dinner and Monday
Rest – Menu (€ 12), € 17/45 – Carte € 43/58
◆ Small, 17C regional-style house, a stone's throw from the majestic château. Charming country-style interior with half-timbering. Traditional cuisine.

in Menestreau en Villette **7 km East by D 17 – pop. 1 465 – alt. 122 m – ✉ 45240**

XX **Le Relais de Sologne**
63 pl. 8 Mai 1945 – ✆ 02 38 76 97 40 – www.lerelaisdesologne.com – relaisdesologne@gmail.com – Fax 02 38 49 60 43 – Closed 22-28 December, 23 February- 11 March, Sunday dinner, Monday dinner Tuesday dinner and Wednesday
Rest – Menu (€ 18 bi), € 29 (dinner), € 37/55 – Carte € 35/63
◆ Traditional restaurant in the heart of the village with a rustic decor and terrace. Don't miss visiting the Ciran estate wild animal reserve, only 2km away.

Good food and accommodation at moderate prices?
Look for the Bib symbols: red Bib Gourmand for food,
blue Bib Hotel for hotels.

LA FERTÉ-ST-CYR – 41 Loir-et-Cher – 318 H6 – pop. 894 – alt. 82 m – ✉ 41220 — 12 C2

Paris 170 – Orléans 37 – Blois 32 – Romorantin-Lanthenay 35

Saint-Cyr without rest
15 r. de Bretagne – ✆ 02 54 87 90 51 – www.hotel-st-cyr.com – hotelsaintcyr@wanadoo.fr – Fax 02 54 87 94 64 – Closed 20 December-2 January and 25 January-16 March
20 rm – †€ 47 ††€ 52/75, ☕ € 9
◆ Small, colourful rooms decorated with wrought iron furniture and woven banana leaves. Guesthouse atmosphere, shop selling regional produce, cycle hire.

LA FERTÉ-SOUS-JOUARRE – 77 Seine-et-Marne – 312 H2 – pop. 8 584 – alt. 58 m – ✉ 77260 — 19 D1

Paris 67 – Melun 70 – Reims 83 – Troyes 116
Office de tourisme, 34, rue des Pelletiers ✆ 01 60 01 87 99, Fax 01 60 22 99 82

Château des Bondons
47 r. des Bondons, 2 km east on D 70, Montménard road – ✆ 01 60 22 00 98 – www.chateaudesbondons.com – castel@chateaudesbondons.com – Fax 01 60 22 97 01
11 rm – †€ 120/140 ††€ 120/140, ☕ € 15 – 3 suites
Rest – *(closed 2-30 January, Monday and Tuesday)*
Menu € 20 (weekdays)/100 – Carte € 72/112
◆ This 18C residence was once owned by the novelist G. Ohnet and used as headquarters by the French army during the phoney war. Rooms are personalised and vary in size. Modern cuisine in the wood-panelled dining room, decorated with a fresco of Marseille.

in Jouarre 3 km South by D 402 – pop. 4 085 – alt. 141 m – ✉ 77640

Office de tourisme, rue de la Tour ✆ 01 60 22 64 54, Fax 01 60 22 65 15

Crypt★ of the abbey, **Northern France and the Paris Region**

Le Plat d'Étain VISA

6 pl. A. Tinchant – ✆ 01 60 22 06 07 – www.le-plat-d-etain.com – infos@le-plat-d-etain.com – Fax 01 60 22 35 63

18 rm – €62/68 €68, €8

Rest – *(closed Friday dinner, Sunday dinner and Bank Holidays dinner)*
Menu €20 (weekdays)/51 – Carte €45/65

◆ Guesthouse built in 1840 by the abbey and its Carolingian crypts. Smart bedrooms with leaded wood furniture. A pewter plate, evoking the name of the place, decorates a wall of the dining room. Traditional menu.

FEURS – 42 Loire – 327 E5 – pop. 7 408 – alt. 343 m – ✉ 42110 44 A2

Lyon - Rhone Valley

Paris 433 – Lyon 69 – Montbrison 24 – Roanne 38 – St-Étienne 47 – Thiers 68 – Vienne 93

Office de tourisme, place du Forum ✆ 04 77 26 05 27, Fax 04 77 26 00 55

Etésia without rest VISA AE

4 chemin des monts, rte de Roanne – ✆ 04 77 27 07 77 – www.hotel-etesia.fr – contact@hotel-etesia.fr – Fax 04 77 27 03 33 – Closed 25 December-1st January

15 rm – €51/59 €51/59, €8,50

◆ This completely renovated hotel offers attractively furnished garden-floor rooms enlivened by bright colours. There is a pleasant wooded garden; buffet-style breakfasting is an original feature.

La Boule d'Or VISA

42 r. R. Cassin, (Lyon road) – ✆ 04 77 26 20 68 – www.chaletlabouledor.com – labouledorfeurs@wanadoo.fr – Fax 04 77 26 56 84 – Closed 27 July-17 August, Sunday dinner, Monday dinner and Wednesday dinner

Rest – Menu (€18), €29/55 – Carte €33/62

◆ In summertime meals are served beneath a lovely chestnut tree. Inside, the huge rustic dining room is made up of three areas. Traditional, well-prepared cuisine.

in Salt-en-Donzy 5 km Lyon road – pop. 420 – alt. 337 m – ✉ 42110

l'Assiette Saltoise VISA

au bourg – ✆ 04 77 26 04 29 – www.assiette-saltoise.com – info-et-reservation@assiette-saltoise.com – Fax 04 77 28 52 58 – Closed 1-7 January, Tuesday dinner and Wednesday

Rest – Menu €13 (weekday lunch)/22

◆ Wholesome traditional fare such as saucisson lyonnais and bavette d'aloyau set the scene for this friendly, unpretentious inn. Terrace shaded by lime trees in fine weather.

in Naconne 3 km Northwest by N 89 and D 112 – ✉ 42110

Brin de Laurier VISA

– ✆ 04 77 26 07 50 – www.brindelaurier.com – info@brindelaurier.com – Fax 04 77 26 07 50 – Closed 1-10 May, 1-11 September, 21 December-5 January, Saturday lunch, Sunday dinner and Monday

Rest – Menu €15 bi (weekday lunch), €20/39 – Carte approx. €48

◆ A pleasant, non-smoking restaurant situated in the hamlet. The chef takes inspiration from his many travels to create a fusion-style cuisine using regional produce. Attractive summer terrace.

FEYTIAT – 87 Haute-Vienne – 325 E6 – pop. 5 634 – alt. 365 m – ✉ 87220 24 B2

Paris 398 – Limoges 9 – Saint-Junien 41 – Panazol 5 – Isle 13

Prieuré du Puy Marot rest,

allée du Puy-Marot, 2 km north-east on St-Just-le-Martel road (D 98) – ✆ 05 55 48 33 97 – gerardchastagner@wanadoo.fr – Fax 05 55 30 31 86

3 rm – €60 €72 **Table d'hôte** – Menu €30 bi

◆ Peace is guaranteed in this 16-17C priory surrounded by a beautiful enclosed garden and overlooking the Valoisse valley. Comfortable rooms that are personalised by antique furniture. The owner offers you traditional cuisine.

FIGEAC – 46 Lot – 337 I4 – pop. 9 963 – alt. 214 m – ✉ 46100 29 C1

Dordogne-Berry-Limousin

Paris 578 – Aurillac 64 – Rodez 66 – Villefranche-de-Rouergue 36

Office de tourisme, place Vival ✆ 05 65 34 06 25, Fax 05 65 50 04 58

Old Figeac★★: hôtel de la Monnaie★ M¹, musée Champollion★★ M² near place aux Ecritures★ - N.D.-de-Pitié chapel★ in St-Sauveur church.

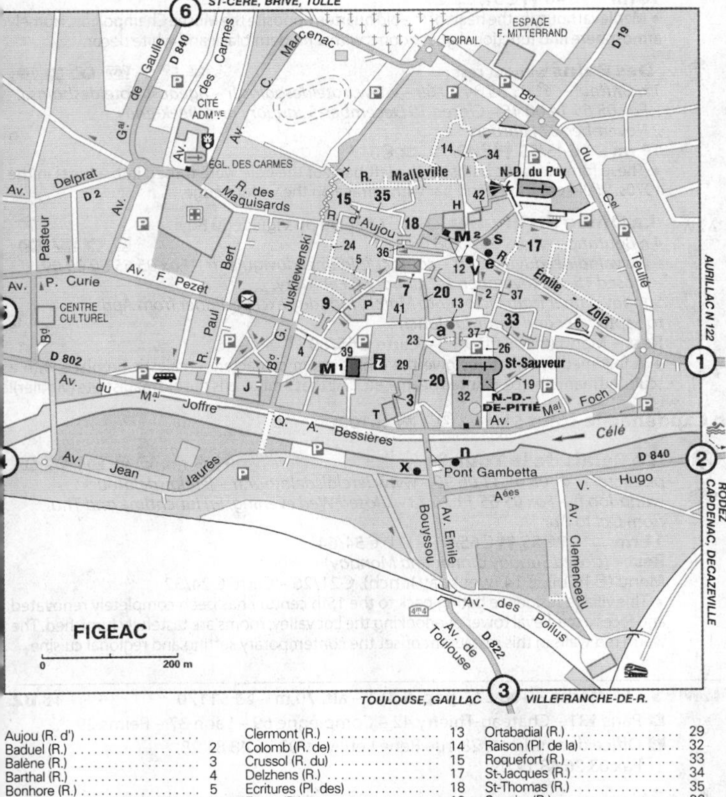

Château du Viguier du Roy

52 r. É. Zola – ✆ 05 65 50 05 05
– www.chateau-viguier-figeac.com – hotel@chateau-viguier-figeac.com
– Fax 05 65 50 06 06
– Open 1st March-15 November

21 rm – †€ 149/459 ††€ 149/459, ☕ € 19

Rest ***La Dînée du Viguier*** – see restaurant listing

e

◆ These appealing, luxuriously restored abodes (12C, 14C and 18C) are set around a delightful terraced garden. Cloisters, chapel, panelling and period furniture.

Le Pont d'Or rm, rm, VISA
2 av. J. Jaurès – 05 65 50 95 00 – www.hotelpontdor.com – contact@hotelpontdor.com – Fax 05 65 50 95 39 **x**
35 rm – €67/122 €67/122, €13 **Rest** – Menu (€12), €15 (lunch)/31
◆ A functional hotel on the banks of the Célé, opposite the old town. Elegant, well-equipped bedrooms; ask for one facing the river.

Le Champollion without rest VISA
3 pl. Champollion – 05 65 34 04 37 – Fax 05 65 34 61 69 **v**
10 rm – €46 €51, €7
◆ Medieval house in the heart of the old quarter, opposite the Musée Champollion. Homely atmosphere and functional guestrooms with a modern black and white decor.

Des Bains without rest VISA
1 r. Griffoul – 05 65 34 10 89 – www.hoteldesbains.fr – figeac@hoteldesbains.fr – Fax 05 65 14 00 45 – Closed 19 December-5 January and week-end 2 November-27 February **n**
19 rm – €45/55 €49/70, €8
◆ These former public baths on the left bank of the Célé were turned into a hotel in the 1970s. Well-kept rooms and bar with terrace on the water's edge.

La Dînée du Viguier – Hôtel Château du Viguier du Roy
4 r. Boutaric – 05 65 50 08 08 VISA
– www.ladineeduviguier.fr – contact@ladineeduviguier.fr – Fax 05 65 50 09 09 – Closed 15-23 November, 17 January-8 February, Sunday dinner from October to March, Monday except dinner from April to September and Saturday lunch **s**
Rest – Menu (€20), €30/75 – Carte €65/80
◆ A few medieval features give the dining room character: a majestic fireplace with a sculpted mantelpiece, painted beams, etc... All that's missing is the old magistrate (viguier)!

in Capdenac-le-Haut 5 km by ② – ✉ 46100

Le Relais de la Tour rm, VISA
pl. Lucter – 05 65 11 06 99 – www.lerelaisdelatour.fr – lerelaisdelatour@wanadoo.fr – Fax 05 65 11 20 73 – Closed Wed evening, Fri lunchtime and Thu from Oct to Apr
11 rm – €55 €65/91 – ½ P €54/64
Rest – *(closed Sunday dinner and Monday)*
Menu (€10 bi), €14 (weekday lunch), €21/26 – Carte €24/32
◆ This village residence dating back to the 15th century has been completely renovated and faces a medieval tower overlooking the Lot valley; rooms are tastefully furnished. The warm red walls in this restaurant offset the contemporary setting and regional cuisine.

FISMES – 51 Marne – 306 E7 – pop. 5 351 – alt. 70 m – ✉ 51170 13 B2

Paris 131 – Château-Thierry 42 – Compiègne 69 – Laon 37 – Reims 29
Office de tourisme, 28, rue René Letilly 03 26 48 81 28, Fax 03 26 48 12 09

La Boule d'Or rest, VISA
11 r. Lefèvre – 03 26 48 11 24 – www.boule-or.com – boule.or@wanadoo.fr – Fax 03 26 48 17 08 – Closed 24 January-11 February, Tuesday lunch, Sunday dinner and Monday
8 rm – €59 €59, €9
Rest – Menu (€16), €19 (weekdays)/52 – Carte €39/58
◆ Long ago, kings of France stopped here en route to their coronation. Today's travelers will find spruce, well-kept rooms. The two adjacent dining rooms are simple but stylish. The cuisine is traditional and includes local specialties.

FITOU – 11 Aude – 344 I5 – pop. 808 – alt. 38 m – ✉ 11510 22 B3

Paris 823 – Carcassonne 90 – Narbonne 40 – Perpignan 29
Fort de Salses★★ Southwest: 11 km,
Languedoc-Roussillon-Tarn Gorges

La Cave d'Agnès
29 r. Gilbert-Salamo – ✆ 04 68 45 75 91 – restocavedagnes@orange.fr – Fax 04 68 45 75 91 – Open 1st April-12 November and closed Wednesday
Rest – *(number of covers limited, pre-book)* Menu € 17 (weekday lunch), € 24/39 – Carte € 30/54
◆ This former barn in the upper part of the village has lost none of its rustic character: fireplace, beams, stonework, bare wood and exhibition s of work by local artists. Tasty regional cuisine.

FLACEY – **28 Eure-et-Loir** – **311** E7 – **see Châteaudun**

FLAGEY-ÉCHEZEAUX – **21 Côte-d'Or** – **320** J7 – **see Vougeot**

FLAMANVILLE – **50 Manche** – **303** A2 – **pop. 1 687** – **alt. 74 m** – ✉ **50340** 32 **A1**

Paris 371 – Barneville-Carteret 23 – Cherbourg 27 – Valognes 36

Syndicat d'initiative, ✆ 02 33 52 61 23

Bel Air without rest
2 r. du Château – ✆ 02 33 04 48 00 – www.hotelbelair-normandie.com – hotelbelair@aol.com – Fax 02 33 04 49 56 – Closed 15 December-30 January
11 rm – €65/99 €65/99, ☕ €10
◆ Once the house occupied by the château's farm manager, this establishment has a peaceful atmosphere. Predominantly rustic-style rooms, each with a different decor.

Le Sémaphore
Chasse de la Houe – ✆ 02 33 52 18 98 – www.restaurantlesemaphore.com – lesemaphore2@wanadoo.fr – Fax 02 33 52 36 39 – Closed 7 December-7 February, Sunday dinner, Tuesday except July-August and Monday
Rest – Menu (€ 13), € 21/38 – Carte € 30/50
◆ Old clifftop signal station commanding a panoramic view of the Channel and the Channel Islands. Traditional cuisine and dishes with a southwest flavour.

FLAVIGNY-SUR-MOSELLE – **54 Meurthe-et-Moselle** – **307** I7 – **see Nancy**

FLAYOSC – **83 Var** – **340** N4 – **see Draguignan**

LA FLÈCHE – **72 Sarthe** – **310** I8 – **pop. 15 500** – **alt. 33 m** – ✉ **72200** Châteaux of the Loire 35 **C2**

Paris 244 – Angers 52 – Laval 70 – Le Mans 44 – Tours 71

Office de tourisme, boulevard de Montréal ✆ 02 43 94 02 53, Fax 02 43 94 43 15

Military academy★ - Panelling★ of N.-D.-des-Vertus chapel - Parc zoologique du Tertre Rouge (zoo)★ 5 km by ② then D 104.

Bazouges-sur-le-Loir: bridge ≤★, 7 km by ④.

Plan on following page

Le Relais Cicero without rest
18 bd Alger – ✆ 02 43 94 14 14 – www.cicero.fr – hotel.cicero@wanadoo.fr – Fax 02 43 45 98 96 – Closed 1st-15 August and 23 December-6 January
21 rm – €79/129 €79/129, ☕ €12 Y **a**
◆ This 17C convent and garden, a genuine haven of peace and quiet, are ideal for a break away from it all. Rustic lounge-bar, well-polished furniture and rooms graced with personal touches.

Le Vert Galant without rest
70 Grande Rue – ✆ 02 43 94 00 51 – www.vghotel.com – contact@vghotel.com – Fax 02 43 45 11 24 Y **r**
21 rm – €77/84 €92/96, ☕ €12
◆ Not far from the Prytanée in the town centre, this former 18C post house sports traditional, sometimes contemporary furniture in the rooms. Breakfast served on the veranda.

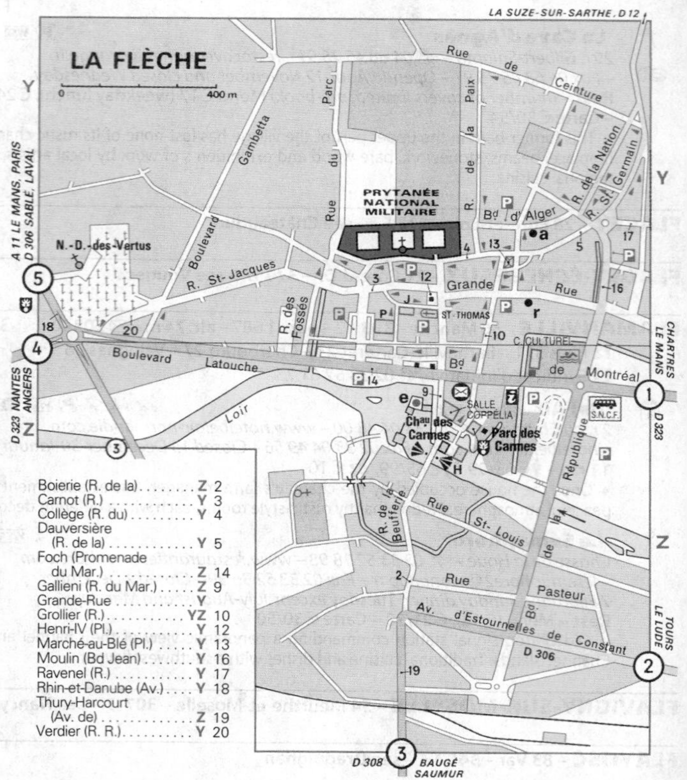

XX **Le Moulin des Quatre Saisons** VISA MC AE

r. Gallieni – ✆ 02 43 45 12 12 – www.moulindesquatresaisons.com – contacts@moulindesquatresaisons.com – Fax 02 43 45 10 31 – Closed autumn half-term holidays, February holidays, Sunday dinner, Wednesday dinner and Monday except July-August Z **e**

Rest – Menu (€ 20), € 26 (weekdays)/38 – Carte € 52/72

◆ A 17C mill on a little island of the Loir. Updated cuisine matched by a handsome wine list, including a few Austrian and Hungarian vintages, all served in a Tyrolean decor.

FLÉCHIN – **62 Pas-de-Calais** – **301** G4 – **pop. 512** – **alt. 96 m** – ✉ **62960** 30 **B2**

Paris 246 – Lille 72 – Arras 63 – Lens 55 – Liévin 50

X **La Maison** VISA MC AE

20 r. Haute – ✆ 03 21 12 69 33 – www.lamaisonrestaurant.com – berthelemy.laurent@wanadoo.fr – Closed 1-8 August, 21-24 December, 23-27 February, Saturday lunch, Wednesday and Monday

Rest – *(number of covers limited, pre-book)* Menu € 17 (weekday lunch), € 25/47 – Carte € 41/68

◆ 1900s building with an attractive dining room (original parquet flooring, antiques). The cuisine here is regional with an emphasis on organic ingredients and heirloom vegetable varieties.

FLÉRÉ-LA-RIVIÈRE – 36 Indre – 323 C4 – pop. 566 – alt. 95 m – ✉ 36700 11 **B3**

Paris 277 – Le Blanc 50 – Châtellerault 60 – Châtillon-sur-Indre 7 – Loches 17 – Tours 61

Le Relais du Berry VISA MC

2 rte de Tours – ✆ 02 54 39 32 57 – Closed January, Sunday dinner, Monday and Tuesday

Rest – *(number of covers limited, pre-book)*

Menu € 15 (weekdays), € 24/40 – Carte € 40/50

◆ Inside this former post house, sample generous traditional cuisine, using garden produce and game in season. Rustic interior.

FLERS – 61 Orne – 310 F2 – pop. 16 947 – alt. 270 m – ✉ 61100 32 **B2**

Normandy

Paris 234 – Alençon 73 – Argentan 42 – Caen 60 – Laval 86 – Vire 31

Office de tourisme, place du Docteur Vayssières ✆ 02 33 65 06 75, Fax 02 33 65 09 84

du Houlme La Selle-la-Forge Le Bourg, 4 km on the Bagnoles-de-l'Orne road, ✆ 02 33 64 42 83

FLERS

Boule (R. de la) . . . . **AY**
Charleston (Pl.) . . . . **AYZ** 3
Delaunay (R.) . . . . **AY** 4
Dr-Vayssières (Pl. du) . . . . . . **AY** 6
Domfront (R. de) . . . . **AZ**
Duhalde (Pl. P.) . . . . **AZ**
Gaulle (Pl. Ch.-de) . . . . **AY** 9
Géroudière (R. de la) . . . . **BZ** 10
Gévelot (R. J.) . . . . **AY** 12
Messei (R. de) . . . . **AZ**
Moulin (R. du) . . . . **ABY** 14
Paris (R. de) . . . . **BY**
Pont Feron (R. du) . . . . **BZ** 15
République (R. de la) . . . . . . **AYZ** 16
St-Gilles (R.) . . . . **BYZ** 18
Salles (R. J.) . . . . **AY** 19
Schnetz (R.) . . . . **AYZ**
6-Juin (R. du) . . . . **AY**

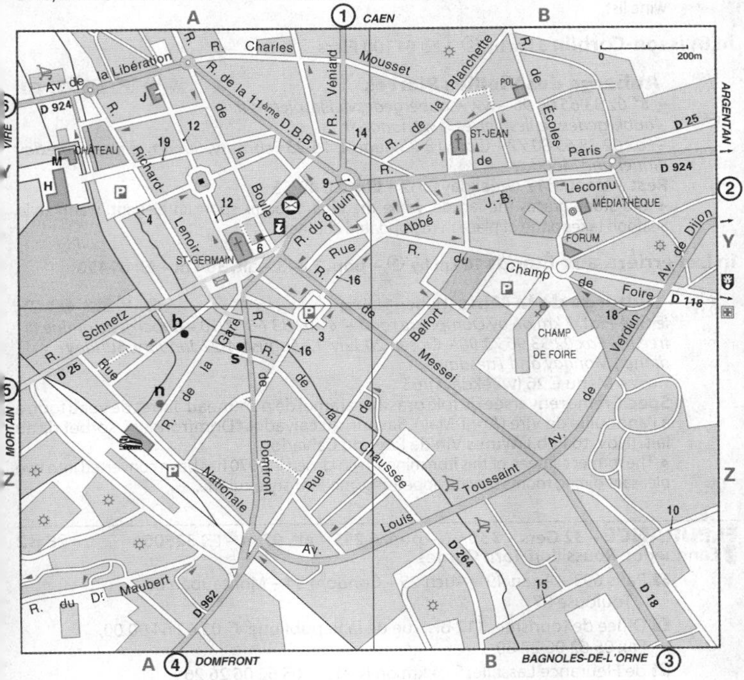

A ① CAEN B
R. Charles Mousset
Av. de la Libération
R. de la 11ème D.B.B.
R. Véniard
R. de la Planchette
R. de Écoles
POL
ST-JEAN
D 924
D 25
ARGENTAN
VIRE
CHÂTEAU
M
H
J
R. Richard-Lenoir
R. de la Boule
ST-GERMAIN
R. du 6 Juin
Rue
R. de Paris
R. J.-B. Lecornu
MÉDIATHÈQUE
FORUM
R. Abbé
R. du Champ de Foire
Av. de Dijon
D 118
CHAMP DE FOIRE
R. Schnetz
D 25
Rue
R. de la Gare
R. de Domfront
R. de la Chaussée
R. de Belfort
R. de Messei
Av. de Verdun
Av. Toussaint
Louis
Av.
Nationale
MORTAIN
R. du Dr Maubert
D 962
D 264
D 18
0 200m
A ④ DOMFRONT
B BAGNOLES-DE-L'ORNE ③
Y
Z

Le Galion without rest

5 r. V. Hugo – ✆ 02 33 64 47 47 – www.hotellegalion.fr – le.galion.hotel@wanadoo.fr – Fax 02 33 65 10 10 AZ **b**

30 rm – €50 €52/57, €9

◆ A quiet hotel in the town centre with good soundproofing. The spacious guestrooms have been treated to a makeover (pastel shades or fabric).

Beverl'inn

9 r. Chaussée – ✆ 02 33 96 79 79 – www.beverlinn.com – beverlinn@beverlinn.com – Fax 02 33 65 94 89 – Closed 22 December-5 January AZ **s**

16 rm – €43/46 €49, €5 – ½ P €45

Rest – grill – *(closed Saturday lunch and Sunday)*

Menu (€10), €14/28 – Carte €18/34

◆ This hotel is located close to the château museum. Rooms with pine furniture that are gradually being redecorated in a somewhat sober style. A cosy restaurant decorated in tones of red and yellow serving traditional recipes and wood-fired meat.

Au Bout de la Rue

60 r. de la Gare – ✆ 02 33 65 31 53 – www.auboutdelarue.com – restaurant@auboutdelarue.com – Fax 02 33 65 46 81 – Closed 1st-10 May, 9-31 August, Wednesday dinner, Saturday lunch, Sunday and bank holidays AZ **n**

Rest – Menu (€17), €22/32 – Carte €26/42

◆ Nothing is hidden from view in this smart bistro-style restaurant. See the chef prepare your choice from the creative and up-to-date menu right in front of your eyes.

Auberge du Relais Fleuri

115 r. Schnetz – ✆ 02 33 65 23 89 – aubergelerelaisfleuri@orange.fr – Closed Friday dinner, Sunday dinner and Monday AYZ

Rest – Menu (€16), €24/48 – Carte €40/60

◆ The first room has a rustic setting enhanced by bare stonework and beams, while the second boasts Norman wood panelling. Inventive, seasonally inspired cuisine and fine wine list.

in Buisson-Corblin 3 km by ② – ✉ 61100 Flers

Auberge des Vieilles Pierres

– ✆ 02 33 65 06 96 – www.aubergedesvieillespierres.fr – aubergedesvieillespierres@wanadoo.fr – Fax 02 33 65 80 72 – Closed 3-25 August, 16-23 February, Sunday dinner, Tuesday dinner and Monday

Rest – Menu €17 (weekdays)/62 – Carte €40/55

◆ Old stone graces the façade, while the dining rooms sport an elegant, warm style. Seafood takes pride of place in the updated cuisine.

in La Ferrière-aux-Étangs 10 km by ③ – pop. 1 643 – alt. 304 m – ✉ 61450

Auberge de la Mine (Hubert Nobis)

le Gué-Plat, 2 km on by Dompierre road – ✆ 02 33 66 91 10 – aubergedelamine@free.fr – Fax 02 33 96 73 90 – Closed 20 July-12 August, 4-27 January, Sunday dinner, Monday and Tuesday

Rest – Menu €26 (weekdays)/65

Spec. Crème renversée de foie gras au caramel de pommeau. Jarret de veau fourré à l'andouille de Vire (April-May). Savarin au calvados "Domfrontais", sorbet riz au lait. (Nov. to Feb.). **Wines** Vin de Pays du Calvados.

◆ The former canteen of this iron mine which closed in 1970 has been converted into two pleasant dining rooms serving appetising, modern-style cuisine.

FLEURANCE – 32 Gers – 336 G6 – pop. 6 255 – alt. 97 m – ✉ 32500 28 **B2**

Languedoc-Roussillon-Tarn Gorges

Paris 693 – Agen 49 – Auch 25 – Condom 34 – Montauban 66 – Toulouse 87

Office de tourisme, 112 bis, rue de la République ✆ 05 62 64 00 00, Fax 05 62 06 27 80

de Fleurance Lassalle, S : 4 km on N 21, ✆ 05 62 06 26 26

Le Fleurance rest, VISA AE

rte d'Agen – ☎ 05 62 06 14 85 – www.hotel-gers.com – lefleurance@gmail.com – Fax 05 62 06 05 15 – Closed 20 December-2 january

23 rm – †€ 47/73 ††€ 59/88, ☐ € 9 – ½ P € 53/77

Rest – *(closed Sunday and Saturday from November to March)*

Menu € 13 (weekday lunch), € 21/41 – Carte € 37/50

◆ Convenient base in the heart of the Lomagne area. Practical rooms, some opening onto the garden or with balcony. Shades of yellow and orange, rattan furniture, and huge bay windows in the dining room extended by a poolside terrace.

Le Relais without rest VISA AE

32 av. Charles de Gaulle, rte d'Auch – ☎ 05 62 06 05 08 – hotel-le-relais@wanadoo.fr – Fax 05 62 06 03 84

20 rm – †€ 43/54 ††€ 49/60, ☐ € 7 – ½ P € 58/67

◆ Small hotel at the gates of the magnificent 13C walled town with its geometric layout and covered market. Good soundproofing; air-conditioned rooms. Pleasant service.

FLEURIE – 69 Rhône – 327 H2 – pop. 1 190 – alt. 320 m – ✉ 69820 43 E1

Lyon - Rhone Valley

Paris 410 – Bourg-en-Bresse 46 – Lyon 58 – Mâcon 22 – Villefranche-sur-Saône 27

Des Grands Vins without rest VISA

r. Grappe Fleurie, 1 km south on the D 119E – ☎ 04 74 69 81 43 – www.hoteldesgrandsvins.com – despres@hoteldesgrandsvins.com – Fax 04 74 69 86 10 – Closed 22 November-7 February

20 rm – †€ 71/85 ††€ 80/85, ☐ € 10

◆ A family establishment with a garden on the edge of a vineyard. Simple, well-kept rooms; a vast dining room. Wines produced in the village are on display and can be purchased.

Domaine du Clos des Garands without rest VISA

1 km east on the D 32 – ☎ 04 74 69 80 01 – www.closdesgarands.fr – contact@closdesgarands.fr – Fax 04 74 69 82 05 – Closed January

4 rm ☐ – †€ 88/108 ††€ 88/108

◆ This wine-producing estate proposes rooms all opening onto Fleurie and the hills of the Beaujolais. Elegant decor. Tastings of the estate wines.

Le Cep (Chantal Chagny) VISA AE

pl. de l'Église – ☎ 04 74 04 10 77 – Fax 04 74 04 10 28 – Closed 29 June-7 July, December, January, Sunday and Monday

Rest – *(pre-book)* Menu € 45/95 – Carte € 72/94

Spec. Cuisses de grenouilles sautées, salades en vinaigrette. Pigeonneau élevé au grain, jus simple au poivre concassé. Cassis de Lancié en sorbet, pulpe acidulée et glace vanille. **Wines** Beaujolais blanc, Fleurie.

◆ This worthy Beaujolais restaurant has renounced luxury, serving authentic tasty regional cuisine in a simple atmosphere.

FLEURVILLE – 71 Saône-et-Loire – 320 J11 – pop. 473 – alt. 174 m – ✉ 71260 8 C3

Paris 375 – Cluny 26 – Mâcon 18 – Pont-de-Vaux 8 – St-Amour 43 – Tournus 16

Château de Fleurville VISA AE

r. du Glamont – ☎ 03 85 27 91 30 – www.chateau-de-fleurville.com – chateaufleurville@free.fr – Fax 03 85 27 91 29

15 rm – †€ 90/120 ††€ 135/175, ☐ € 14 – 1 suite – ½ P € 135/150

Rest – *(closed lunch except Sunday)* Menu € 38, € 58/78 – Carte € 69/87

◆ Set in centuries-old parkland, this small 17C castle built in Burgundian stone has a lovely tower. Renovated rooms with antique furniture and wall hangings. Pool and tennis courts. Rustic dining room with a fireplace and beams. Pleasant terrace. Traditional cuisine.

in Mirande 3 km Northwest – ✉ 71260 Montbellet

La Marande with rm — rest, VISA, MC, AE
Lugny road – ☎ 03 85 33 10 24 – www.hotel-restaurant-la-marande.com
– restaurant-la-marande@wanadoo.fr – Fax 03 85 33 95 06
– Closed 16-26 November, 4 January-4 February, Monday and Tuesday
5 rm – €70 €70, ☕ €8 **Rest** – Menu € 27/65 – Carte € 44/59
◆ This stone house is peacefully located in the Maconnais countryside. New, quality decor. Plant-decked terrace. Modern menu. Rooms for a stopover. Coffee and croissants at breakfast. Garden.

FLEURY-LA-FORÊT – 27 Eure – 304 J5 – pop. 269 – alt. 161 m – ✉ 27480 — 33 D2

Paris 108 – Rouen 42 – Évreux 99 – Beauvais 49 – Mantes-la-Jolie 69

Château de Fleury la Forêt without rest — P
4 rte de Lyons, 1.5 km south-west on D 14 – ☎ 02 32 49 63 91
– www.chateau-fleury-la-foret.com – info@chateau-fleury-la-foret.com
– Fax 02 32 49 71 67
3 rm ☕ – €70 €76
◆ The rooms of this splendid 16C and 18C château are furnished with genuine period pieces. Breakfast is served in the characteristic Normandy kitchen. Collection of antique dolls and objects.

FLEURY-SUR-ORNE – 14 Calvados – 303 J5 – see Caen

FLORAC – 48 Lozère – 330 J9 – pop. 1 908 – alt. 542 m – ✉ 48400 — 23 C1

Languedoc-Roussillon-Tarn Gorges

Paris 622 – Alès 65 – Mende 38 – Millau 84 – Rodez 123 – Le Vigan 72

Office de tourisme, 33, avenue J. Monestier ☎ 04 66 45 01 14, Fax 04 66 45 25 80

Corniche des Cévennes★.

Des Gorges du Tarn — P, VISA, MC
48 r. Pêcher – ☎ 04 66 45 00 63 – www.hotel-gorgesdutarn.com
– gorges-du-tarn.adonis@wanadoo.fr – Fax 04 66 45 10 56 – Open from Easter to 1st November and closed Wednesday except July-August
26 rm – €46/80 €46/80, ☕ €8,50
Rest *L'Adonis* – Menu € 17 (weekdays)/55 – Carte € 37/46
◆ At the entrance (or exit) to the Tarn Gorges. Ask for one of the recently renovated rooms in a modern style; those in the wing are more spacious. The restaurant proposes regional Cévennes dishes in a modern wood panelled decor.

in Cocurès 5.5 km northeast by D 806 and D 998 – pop. 195 – alt. 600 m – ✉ 48400

La Lozerette — rm, P, VISA, MC, AE
– ☎ 04 66 45 06 04 – www.lalozerette.com – lalozerette@wanadoo.fr
– Fax 04 66 45 12 93 – Open from 16 March to autumn half-term holidays
20 rm – €58/78 €58/86, ☕ €9 – ½ P € 57/74
Rest – *(closed Tuesday dinner off season except residents, Tuesday lunch and Wednesday lunch)* Menu € 19 (weekdays), € 26/50 – Carte € 32/50
◆ In a hamlet on the edge of the Cévennes National Park, this old house has spruce, individually decorated rooms. Smart restaurant with exposed beams. Traditional cuisine and a good regional wine list.

FLOURE – 11 Aude – 344 F3 – see Carcassonne

FLUMET – 73 Savoie – 333 M3 – pop. 877 – alt. 920 m – Winter sports : 1 000/2 030 m 11 – ✉ 73590 — 46 F1

French Alps

Paris 582 – Albertville 22 – Annecy 51 – Chamonix-Mont-Blanc 43 – Megève 10

Syndicat d'initiative, avenue de Savoie ☎ 04 79 31 61 08, Fax 04 79 31 84 67

Cœur de Marie

on the D909, at "Les Glières", 5 km north on the rte de la Giettaz – ✆ 04 79 31 38 84 – www.chalet-marie.com – contact@chalet-marie.com – Fax 04 79 31 38 84

4 rm – **†**€ 59 **††**€ 65/73 **Table d'hôte** – Menu € 24 bi

◆ Chalet dating from 1810 with wooden interior. Cosy rooms with embroidered curtains, traditional local fabrics and old books. Fireside dining on the first floor. Savoyard family food and breakfast with homemade jams.

FOIX – 09 Ariège – 343 H7 – pop. 9 109 – alt. 375 m – ✉ 09000 29 C3

Languedoc-Roussillon-Tarn Gorges

- Paris 762 – Andorra-la-Vella 102 – Carcassonne 89 – St-Girons 45
- Office de tourisme, 29, rue Delcassé ✆ 05 61 65 12 12, Fax 05 61 65 64 63
- de l'Ariège La Bastide-de-Sérou Unjat, 15 km on the St-Girons road, ✆ 05 61 64 56 78
- Site★ - ❋★ of the château tower - Route Verte★★ West by D17 A.
- Underground river of Labouiche★ Northwest: 6,5 km by D1.

FOIX

Alsace-Lorraine (Bd) . . . . B 2
Bayle (R.) . . . . B
Chapeliers (R. des) . . . . A 3
Delcassé (R. Th.) . . . . B 4
Delpech (R. Lt P.) . . . . A 5
Duthil (Pl.) . . . . B 6
Fauré (Cours G.) . . . . AB 7
Labistour (R. de) . . . . B 8
Lazéma (R.) . . . . A 9
Lérida (Av. de) . . . . A 10
Lespinet (R. de) . . . . A 13
Marchands (R. des) . . . . B 12
Préfecture (R. de la) . . . . A 14
Rocher (R. du) . . . . A 20
St-Jammes (R.) . . . . A 22
St-Volusien (Pl.) . . . . A 23
Salenques (R. des) . . . . A 24

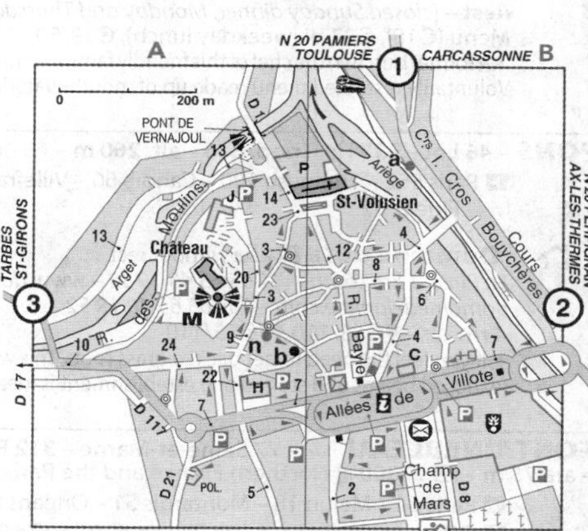

Du Lac

rm, rm, rest,

rte de Toulouse, 3 km via ① – ✆ 05 61 65 17 17 – www.hoteldulac-foix.fr – hotel.du.lac.foix@free.fr – Fax 05 61 02 94 24

35 rm – **†**€ 63/75 **††**€ 63/75, € 9 – ½ P € 65/75

Rest – *(Closed 24 December-1 January and Sunday dinner from October to June)* Menu € 29/38

◆ The new, comfortable guestrooms in this old sheep barn (1599) benefit from the peace and quiet of the park and lake. Numerous water sports on offer, as well as air-conditioned bungalows for rent. The decor in the restaurant is resolutely rustic (exposed beams and stonework, fireplace etc).

Eychenne without rest

11 r. N. Peyrevidal – ✆ 05 61 65 00 04 – www.hotel-eychenne.com – hotel.eychenne@orange.fr – Fax 05 61 65 56 63 A **b**

16 rm – **†**€ 53 **††**€ 55, € 6

◆ Easily recognisable because of its wooden tower and English pub-style bar, this simple but modernised hotel is a practical and well-located choice for visiting Foix.

Le Ste-Marthe

21 r. N. Peyrevidal – ✆ 05 61 02 87 87 – www.le-saintemarthe.fr – restaurant@le-saintemarthe.fr – Fax 05 61 02 87 87 – Closed Tuesday and Wednesday except July-August A **n**

Rest – Menu € 23/42 – Carte € 35/55

◆ This rustic-style restaurant is perfect for those keen on trying local specialities (cassoulet, foie gras etc). Attractive table settings with white tablecloths.

Phoebus
3 cours Irénée Cros – ✆ 05 61 65 10 42 – www.ariege.com/le-phoebus – Fax 05 61 65 10 42 – Closed 19 July-19 August, Saturday lunch, Sunday dinner and Monday B **a**
Rest – Menu (€ 19), € 29/66 – Carte € 45/55
◆ Traditional cuisine served in a dining room overlooking the Ariège with an attractive view of Gaston Phoebus' château. Braille menu for the visually impaired. Attentive service.

FONDAMENTE – 12 Aveyron – 338 K7 – pop. 294 – alt. 430 m – ✉ 12540 29 D2

Paris 679 – Albi 109 – Millau 43 – Montpellier 98 – Rodez 111 – St-Affrique 28

Baldy with rm rm, VISA
Vallée de Sorgues – ✆ 05 65 99 37 38 – www.hotel-sorgues.com – Fax 05 65 99 92 84 – Hotel: Open from Easter to October and closed Sunday dinner and Monday dinner
9 rm – €46/50 €46/50, ☕ € 11 – ½ P € 55/58
Rest – *(closed Sunday dinner, Monday and Thursday) (pre-book)*
Menu (€ 18), € 27 bi (weekday lunch), € 29/50
◆ A former butcher, the chef of this friendly family-run inn, works with only quality produce. Voluntarily restricted menu made up of mouth-watering regional delicacies.

FONS – 46 Lot – 337 H4 – pop. 386 – alt. 260 m – ✉ 46100 29 C1

Paris 562 – Toulouse 190 – Cahors 66 – Villefranche-de-Rouergue 47 – Figeac 12

Domaine de la Piale without rest
La Piale, 1 km south – ✆ 05 65 40 19 52 – www.domainedelapiale.com – accueil@domainedelapiale.com – Fax 05 65 40 19 52
4 rm ☕ – €55/110 €55/110
◆ If you feel the need to get back to grass roots, this welcoming, pleasantly country-style (exposed beams and stonework) establishment is ideal. Rooms in a converted barn.

FONTAINEBLEAU – 77 Seine-et-Marne – 312 F5 – pop. 15 900 – alt. 75 m – ✉ 77300 Northern France and the Paris Region 19 C3

Paris 64 – Melun 18 – Montargis 51 – Orléans 89 – Sens 54

Office de tourisme, 4, rue Royale ✆ 01 60 74 99 99, Fax 01 60 74 80 22

U.C.P.A. Bois-le-Roi Bois-le-Roi Base de loisirs, 10 km on the Melun road, ✆ 01 64 81 33 31

Palace★★★: Grand apartments★★★ (Galerie François 1er★★★, Salle de Bal★★★) - Gardens★ - Musée napoléonien d'Art et d'Histoire militaire: collection of sabres and swords★ M¹ - Forest★★★ - Gorges de Franchard★★ 5 km by ⑥.

Plan on next page

Grand Hôtel de l'Aigle Noir without rest
27 pl. Napoléon Bonaparte – ✆ 01 60 74 60 00 – www.hotelaiglenoir.fr – hotel.aigle.noir@wanadoo.fr – Fax 01 60 74 60 01 – Closed 3 weeks in August and Christmas holidays AZ **a**
15 rm – €100/160 €110/170, ☕ € 15 – 3 suites
◆ Old private mansion built in the 15C next to the castle. Refined atmosphere and rooms with personal touches and fine Empire and period furnishings.

Mercure rm, VISA
41 r. Royale – ✆ 01 64 69 34 34 – www.mercure.com – h1627@accor.com – Fax 01 64 69 34 39 AZ **d**
97 rm – €155 €165, ☕ € 17
Rest – *(closed 31 July-24 August and 21 December-2 January)*
Menu (€ 21) – Carte € 29/36
◆ A comfortable, high quality establishment offering functional rooms. In the evening, relax in front of the fireplace in the lounge or enjoy the snug bar. Traditional cuisine in the contemporary dining room with terrace overlooking the park.

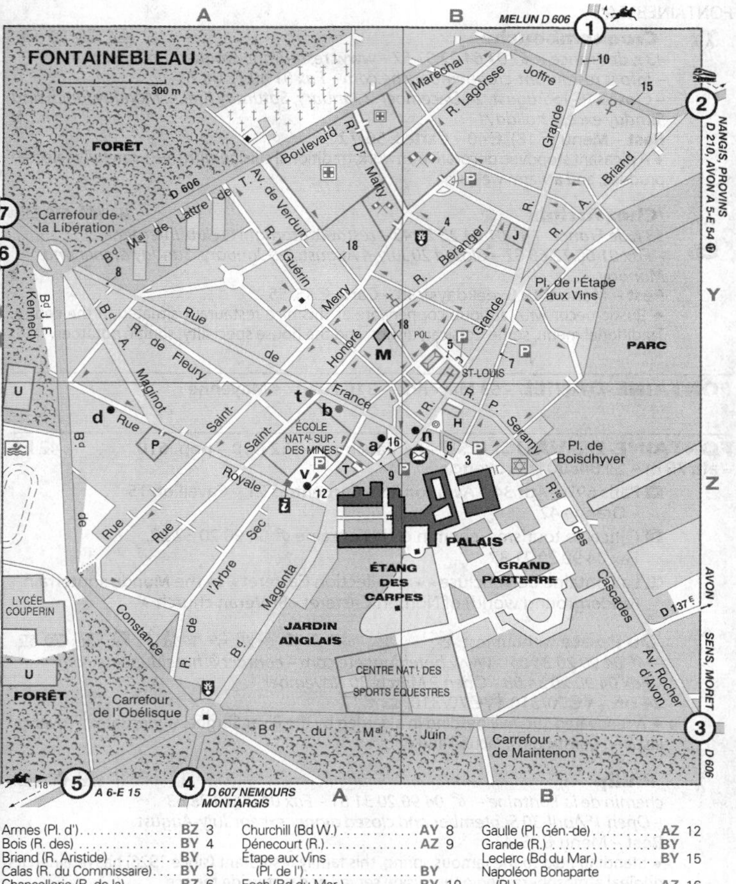

Armes (Pl. d') . . . . **BZ** 3
Bois (R. des) . . . . **BY** 4
Briand (R. Aristide) . . . . **BY**
Calas (R. du Commissaire) . . . . **BY** 5
Chancellerie (R. de la) . . . . **BZ** 6
Château (R. du) . . . . **BY** 7
Churchill (Bd W.) . . . . **AY** 8
Dénecourt (R.) . . . . **AZ** 9
Étape aux Vins (Pl. de l') . . . . **BY**
Foch (Bd du Mar.) . . . . **BY** 10
France (R. de) . . . . **AYZ**
Gaulle (Pl. Gén.-de) . . . . **AZ** 12
Grande (R.) . . . . **BY**
Leclerc (Bd du Mar.) . . . . **BY** 15
Napoléon Bonaparte (Pl.) . . . . **AZ** 16
Paroisse (R. de la) . . . . **AY** 18

Napoléon

9 r. Grande – ℰ 01 60 39 50 50 – www.naposite.com – resa@naposite.com – Fax 01 64 22 20 87 BZ **n**

57 rm – †€ 165 ††€ 165, ☕ € 16

Rest *La Table des Maréchaux* – Menu (€ 35), € 40/55 – Carte € 45/65

◆ Just 100m from the castle where Napoleon made his final appearance in front of the Imperial Guard in 1814. Former post house with Empire-style rooms opening onto an inner courtyard. The elegant Table des Maréchaux, a reference to Malmaison, borders a pleasant patio-terrace.

De Londres without rest

1 pl. Gén. de Gaulle – ℰ 01 64 22 20 21 – www.hoteldelondres.com – hdelondres1850@aol.com – Fax 01 60 72 39 16 – Closed 10-17 August and 23 December-6 January AZ **v**

16 rm – †€ 100/150 ††€ 125/165, ☕ € 11

◆ Facing the castle, this 16C building has large and soundproofed rooms. They are elegantly decorated with fine fabrics, rustic and period furniture and hunting prints.

Croquembouche
43 r. de France – 01 64 22 01 57 – www.restaurant-croquembouche.com – info@restaurant-croquembouche.com – Fax 01 60 72 08 73 – Closed 1st-15 August, 24 December-2 January, Saturday lunch, Monday lunch and Sunday except holidays AZ **b**
Rest – Menu (€ 18), € 40 – Carte € 56/72
◆ A pleasant stopover: decorative artwork, traditional cuisine with fresh, carefully selected produce, and a warm welcome.

Chez Arrighi
53 r. de France – 01 64 22 29 43 – restaurantarrighi@club-internet.fr – Fax 01 60 72 68 02 – Closed 20 July-4 August, 2-9 January, Sunday dinner and Monday AZ **t**
Rest – Menu € 19 (weekdays)/38 – Carte € 35/55
◆ Rustic decor with antique copperware at this nice restaurant situated in the centre. Traditional menu, some Corsican dishes, and the house speciality: soufflé potatoes.

FONTAINE-DANIEL – 53 Mayenne – 310 E5 – see Mayenne

FONTAINE-DE-VAUCLUSE – 84 Vaucluse – 332 D10 – pop. 610 – alt. 75 m – ✉ 84800 Provence

42 **E1**

Paris 697 – Apt 34 – Avignon 33 – Carpentras 21 – Cavaillon 15 – Orange 42

Office de tourisme, chemin de la Fontaine 04 90 20 32 22, Fax 04 90 20 21 37

La Fontaine de Vaucluse★★ - Collection Casteret★ in the Monde souterrain (underground world) of Norbert Casteret - St-Véran church ★.

Du Poète without rest
– 04 90 20 34 05 – www.hoteldupoete.com – contact@hoteldupoete.com – Fax 04 90 20 34 08 – Open 2 March-30 November
24 rm – €70/310 €70/310, € 17
◆ A renovated 19C mill nestling in a garden by the River Sorgue. Understated Provençal inspired guestrooms. Jacuzzi and pool.

Philip
chemin de la Fontaine – 04 90 20 31 81 – Fax 04 90 20 28 63 – Open 1st April-30 September and closed dinner except July-August
Rest – Menu € 25/41
◆ Standing next to the famous spring, this family restaurant (since 1926) has retained its original atmosphere. Regional cuisine served and waterside terrace.

FONTANGES – 15 Cantal – 330 D4 – see Salers

LE FONTANIL – 38 Isère – 333 H6 – see Grenoble

FONTENAI-SUR-ORNE – 61 Orne – 310 I2 – see Argentan

FONTENAY – 88 Vosges – 314 H3 – pop. 474 – alt. 390 m – ✉ 88600

27 **C3**

Paris 410 – Metz 136 – Épinal 13 – Saint-Dié-des-Vosges 38 – Lunéville 96

La Grange
chemin de Framont – 03 29 43 20 55 – www.la-grange-aux-arts.com – caroline.orefice@la-grange-aux-arts.com – Fax 03 29 43 20 56
5 rm – €95 € 105 **Table d'hôte** – Menu € 18/25 bi
◆ Modern villa run by a gallery owner. The personalised rooms reflect a passion for art, decorated on the theme of the five continents. Spa, indoor pool. Traditional table d'hote and candlelit dinners (by reservation).

FONTENAY-LE-COMTE – 85 Vendée – 316 L9 – pop. 14 200 – alt. 21 m – ✉ 85200 Atlantic Coast

Paris 442 – Cholet 103 – La Rochelle 51 – La Roche-sur-Yon 64

Office de tourisme, 8, rue de Grimouard ✆ 02 51 69 44 99, Fax 02 51 50 00 90

Steeple ★ of N.-Dame church **B** - Interior ★ of château de Terre-Neuve.

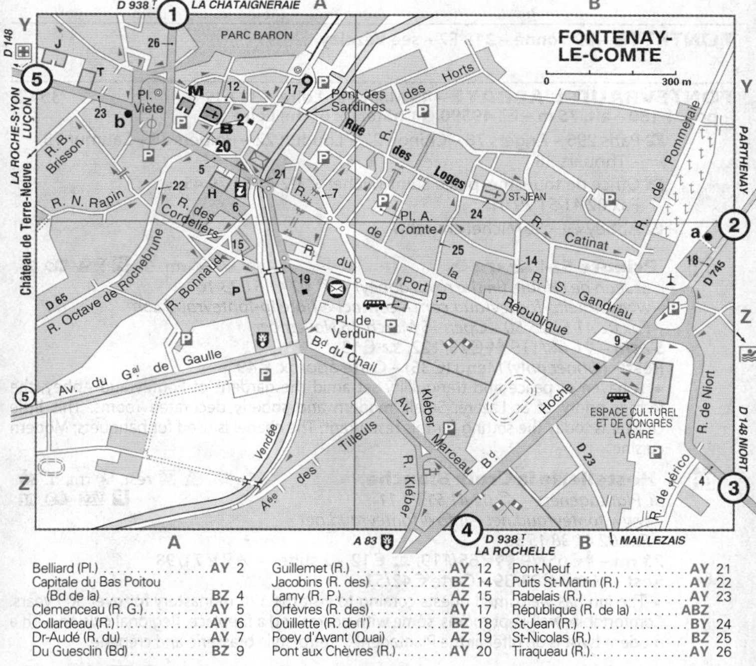

Belliard (Pl.)	AY 2	Guillemet (R.)	AY 12	Pont-Neuf	AY 21
Capitale du Bas Poitou (Bd de la)	BZ 4	Jacobins (R. des)	BZ 14	Puits St-Martin (R.)	AY 22
Clemenceau (R. G.)	AY 5	Lamy (R. P.)	AZ 15	Rabelais (R.)	AY 23
Collardeau (R.)	AY 6	Orfèvres (R. des)	AY 17	République (R. de la)	ABZ
Dr-Audé (R. du)	AY 7	Ouillette (R. de l')	BZ 18	St-Jean (R.)	BY 24
Du Guesclin (Bd)	BZ 9	Poey d'Avant (Quai)	AZ 19	St-Nicolas (R.)	BZ 25
		Pont aux Chèvres (R.)	AY 20	Tiraqueau (R.)	AY 26

Le Rabelais

rm, VISA MC AE

19 r. Ouillette – ✆ 02 51 69 86 20 – www.hotel-lerabelais.com – hotel-lerabelais@wanadoo.fr – Fax 02 51 69 80 45 BZ **a**

54 rm – ✝€ 69/98 ✝✝€ 69/98, ☕ € 10

Rest – Menu (€ 14), € 18/30 – Carte € 26/32

◆ The name refers to the writer who stayed for three years in the town. Most of the functional but pleasantly renovated rooms overlook a flower-decked garden. This restaurant has a terrace by the pool and a large buffet of starters and desserts.

Le Logis de la Clef de Bois without rest

5 r. du Département – ✆ 02 51 69 03 49 – www.clef-de-bois.com – clef_de_bois@hotmail.com – Fax 02 51 69 03 49 AY **b**

4 rm ☕ – ✝€ 90/105 ✝✝€ 120/135

◆ This mansion offers beautifully coloured rooms, each named after a famous writer. The Rabelais suite, with a decor evoking the commedia dell'arte, is the most outstanding.

in Velluire 11 km by ④, D 938 ter and D 68 – **pop. 508 – alt. 9 m –** ✉ **85770**

XXX **Auberge de la Rivière** with rm
r. du Port de la Fouarne – ✆ 02 51 52 32 15 – www.hotel-riviere-vendee.com – auberge.delariviere@wanadoo.fr – Fax 02 51 52 37 42 – Closed 11 January-28 February, Sunday dinner except July-August and Monday
11 rm – †€ 50/85 ††€ 65/94, ☕ € 11 – ½ P € 70/84
Rest – Menu € 26/50 – Carte € 46/67
◆ Stylish inn on the banks of the Vendée serving regional cuisine with a contemporary touch. Rustic dining room. Spacious, well-kept rooms.

FONTETTE – **89 Yonne** – **319** F7 – **see Vézelay**

FONTEVRAUD-L'ABBAYE – 49 Maine-et-Loire – 317 J5 35 C2

– pop. 1 189 – alt. 75 m – ✉ **49590** Châteaux of the Loire

Paris 296 – Angers 78 – Chinon 21 – Loudun 22 – Poitiers 78 – Saumur 15 – Thouars 38

Office de tourisme, place Saint-Michel ✆ 02 41 51 79 45, Fax 02 41 51 79 01

Abbey★★ - St-Michel church ★.

Prieuré St-Lazare rm, VISA AE
r. St Jean de l'Habit, (In the royal abbey) – ✆ 02 41 51 73 16 – www.hotelfp-fontevraud.com – contact@hotelfp-fontevraud.com – Fax 02 41 51 75 50 – Open 15 March-15 November
52 rm – †€ 68/115 ††€ 73/122, ☕ € 13
Rest – *(dinner only)* Menu (€ 35) – Carte approx. € 49
◆ A haven of peace and tranquillity set amid the gardens of Fontevraud Abbey, the former priory of St Lazare. Small, modern and soberly decorated rooms. This little cloister is today the setting for this restaurant. The chapel is used for banquets; Modern cuisine.

Hostellerie la Croix Blanche rest, rm, VISA AE
pl. Plantagenets – ✆ 02 41 51 71 11 – www.fontevraud.net – info@fontevraud.net – Fax 02 41 38 15 38
23 rm – †€ 65/79 ††€ 65/119, ☕ € 12 – 2 suites – ½ P € 71/98
Rest – Menu € 23/39 – Carte € 42/51
◆ The inn has welcomed guests coming to visit the 12C monastery for over 300 years. Comfortable, well-kept rooms, some with beams and a fireplace. Regional cuisine with a modern twist is on offer at the Plantagenêt. Retro-style brasserie and crêperie.

XXX **La Licorne** VISA AE
allée Ste-Catherine – ✆ 02 41 51 72 49 – www.la.licorne.restaurant.com – licorne.fontevraud@free.fr – Fax 02 41 51 70 40 – Closed 21-27 December, Sunday dinner and Monday from 5 October to 11 April
Rest – *(number of covers limited, pre-book)*
Menu € 27/55 – Carte € 50/86
◆ An elegant 18C building fronted by a kitchen garden used as a terrace. Interior decor of tufa rock and tapestry reproductions. Classic cuisine and superb Loire wine list.

X **L'Abbaye "Le Délice"** VISA
8 av. Roches – ✆ 02 41 51 71 04 – Fax 02 41 51 43 10 – Closed 25 October-5 November, 2 February-5 March, Tuesday dinner and Wednesday
Rest – Menu (€ 12), € 14 (weekdays)/28 – Carte € 21/34
◆ Traditional cuisine served in a setting that is pleasantly antiquated, where the house speciality is a delicious cheese croquette. Access is via an attractive café.

The sun's out – let's eat alfresco!
Look for a terrace:

FONTJONCOUSE – 11 Aude – 344 H4 – pop. 133 – alt. 298 m – ✉ 11360 22 B3

▶ Paris 822 – Carcassonne 56 – Narbonne 32 – Perpignan 65

XXX ✿✿ **Auberge du Vieux Puits** (Gilles Goujon) with rm
av. St Victor – ✆ 04 68 44 07 37 – www.aubergeduvieuxpuits.fr – aubergeduvieuxpuits@wanadoo.fr – Fax 04 68 44 08 31 – Closed 2 January-5 March, Monday lunch from 21 June to 14 September, Sunday dinner, Monday and Tuesday from 15 September to 20 June
14 rm – €125/260 €125/260, ☕ €19 – ½ P €190/275
Rest – Menu €58 (weekday lunch), €105/125 – Carte €120/150
Spec. Oeuf de poule aux truffes sur purée de champignons, briochine tiède. Filet de rouget barbet, pomme bonne bouche fourrée d'une brandade à la cèbe en "bullinada". Sablé feuille à feuille de chocolat, surprise de framboise et mousseux tanéa. **Wines** Corbières blanc et rouge
◆ Elegant contemporary dining room, excellent wine list and fine, creative cuisine with regional touches. Modern minimalist rooms.

La Maison des Chefs
(at 300 m in the village) – ✆ 04 68 44 07 37 – www.aubergeduvieuxpuits.fr – aubergeduvieuxpuits@wanadoo.fr – Fax 04 68 44 08 31
6 rm – €105/115 €105/115
◆ The décor of the rooms pays tribute to great chefs with culinary utensils and jackets signed by Bocuse, Troisgros, etc.

FONT-ROMEU – 66 Pyrénées-Orientales – 344 D7 – pop. 2 003 – alt. 1 800 m – Winter sports : 1 900/2 250 m 1 28 – Casino – ✉ 66120 22 A3

Languedoc-Roussillon-Tarn Gorges

▶ Paris 858 – Andorra la Vella 73 – Ax-les-Thermes 56 – Bourg-Madame 18

ℹ Office de tourisme, 38, avenue Emmanuel Brousse ✆ 04 68 30 68 30, Fax 04 68 30 29 70

de Font-Romeu Espace Sportif Colette Besson, N : 1 km, ✆ 04 68 30 10 78

Camaril★★★, altar-piece★ and chapelle★ de l'Ermitage - ✳★★ Calvary.

Plan on next page

Le Grand Tétras without rest
av. E. Brousse – ✆ 04 68 30 01 20 – www.hotelgrandtetras.fr – infos@hotelgrandtetras.fr – Fax 04 68 30 35 67 AX r
36 rm – €69/100 €69/100, ☕ €10
◆ Mountain-style renovated decor. Balcony and panoramic view of the Pyrenees from rooms on the south side. Spa and covered pool on the roof. Wi-fi.

Sun Valley
3 av. Espagne – ✆ 04 68 30 21 21 – www.hotelsunvalley.fr – pierre.mitjaville@wanadoo.fr – Fax 04 68 30 30 38 – Closed 31 October-4 December AX f
41 rm – €83/109 €92/119, ☕ €11 **Rest** – *(resident only)* Menu €22
◆ The rooms, in the process of an alpine-inspired renovation, all have sunny south-facing balconies. Splendid fitness facilities on the top floor. Simple, generous meals.

Clair Soleil
29 av. François Arago, Odeillo road: 1 km – ✆ 04 68 30 13 65 – www.hotel-clair-soleil.com – clairsoleil3@wanadoo.fr – Fax 04 68 30 08 27 – Closed 13 April-16 May and 2 November-18 December AY b
29 rm ☕ – €59/69 €67/76
Rest – *(closed lunch Monday-Thursday off season, Tuesday lunch and Wednesday lunch)* Menu €22/38 – Carte approx. €38
◆ This pleasant well-located family guesthouse (non-smoking) faces the Odeillo solar furnace. Modest rooms with balcony or terrace. A dining room and veranda offering regional cuisine and attentive service.

FONT-ROMEU

Allard (R. Henri) . . . . **BX** 2
Brousse (Av. Emmanuel) . . . **BX** 3
Calvet (R.) . . . . **BX** 5
Capelle (R. du Docteur) . . . . **AX** 6
Cytises (R. des) . . . . **AX** 8
Ecureuils (R. des) . . . . **AX** 9
Espagne (Av. d') . . . . **AX**
Genêts d'Or
(R. des) . . . . **BY** 12
Liberté (R. de la) . . . . **AY** 13
Maillol (R.) . . . . **BX** 15
République
(R. de la) . . . . **AY** 16
Saules (R. des) . . . . **AY** 18
Trombe (R. Professeur) . . . . **AY** 19

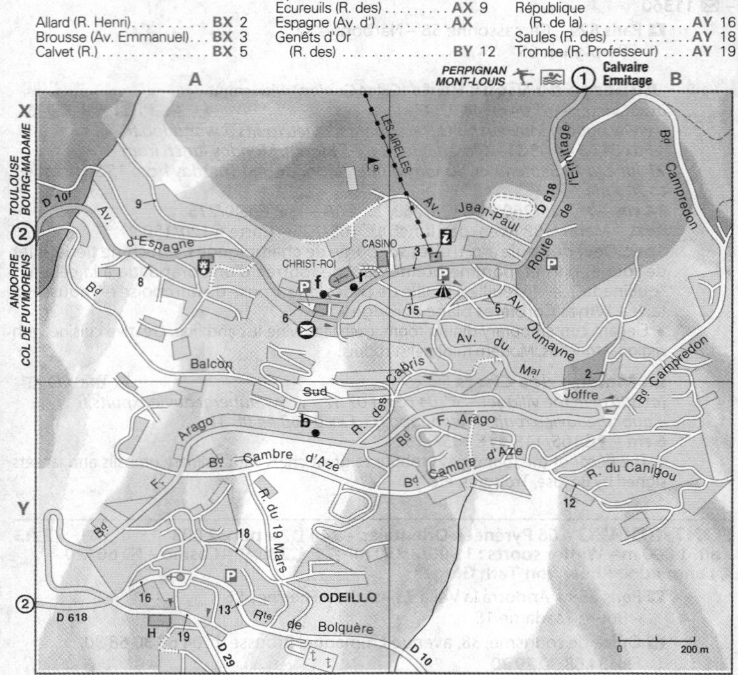

in Via 5 km South by D 29 AY – ✉ **66210 Font Romeu Odeillo Via**

L'Oustalet

av. du Mar. Leclerc – ✆ 04 68 30 11 32 – www.hoteloustalet.com – hoteloustalet@wanadoo.fr – Fax 04 68 30 31 89 – Closed 15 April-8 May and 15 October-15 November

25 rm – †€ 45/60 ††€ 45/60, ☕ € 7 – ½ P € 44/51

Rest – snack – *(dinner only) (resident only)* Menu € 14

◆ This establishment is popular with CNRS research staff. A few rooms furnished in Catalan style; most of the rooms have balconies. Country-style dining room.

FONTVIEILLE – 13 Bouches-du-Rhône – 340 D3 – pop. 3 362 – alt. 20 m – ✉ 13990 Provence

42 **E1**

Paris 712 – Arles 12 – Avignon 30 – Marseille 92 – St-Rémy-de-Provence 18

Office de tourisme, avenue des Moulins ✆ 04 90 54 67 49, Fax 04 90 54 69 82

Moulin de Daudet ≤★.

Chapelle St-Gabriel★ North: 5 km.

La Regalido

r. F. Mistral – ✆ 04 90 54 60 22 – www.laregalido.com – la-regalido@wanadoo.fr – Fax 04 90 54 64 29 – Open mid March-mid November

15 rm – †€ 85/150 ††€ 95/270, ☕ € 15

Rest – *(closed Monday)* Menu (€ 15), € 40 (dinner)

◆ A former oil mill, nestled in the heart of a luxuriant garden, which may have inspired Daudet for some of his 'Letters' celebrating the Provençal-style setting. Pleasant rooms. Vaulted dining room and lush green terrace. Classic and southern French cuisine.

La Peiriero rm,

36 av. des Baux – 04 90 54 76 10 – www.hotel-peiriero.com – info@hotel-peiriero.com – Fax 04 90 54 62 60 – Open from Easter to 1 November

42 rm – €89/135 €89/210, €12 **Rest** – *(dinner only)* Menu €28

◆ Pleasant hotel built on a former stone quarry ("peiriero" in Provençal dialect). Regional style rooms. Crazy golf, giant chess and a sauna. Traditional recipes served in the dining room or on the superb terrace opening onto a leafy garden.

Hostellerie St-Victor without rest

chemin des Fourques, via Arles road – 04 90 54 66 00 – www.hotel-saint-victor.com – aps@hotel-saint-victor.com – Fax 04 90 54 67 88 – Closed 20 February-9 March

11 rm – €80/180 €80/180, €11

◆ This regional-style house lies in a peaceful district. Attractive pool, bedrooms being gradually renovated and striking bathrooms.

Le Val Majour without rest

22 rte d'Arles – 04 90 54 62 33 – www.valmajour.com – contact@valmajour.com – Fax 04 90 54 61 67

32 rm – €55/160 €55/160, €10

◆ Guests staying in this 1970s hotel will sleep peacefully in its spacious and colourful rooms. Some have balconies overlooking the lovely grounds. Pleasant sitting room and pool.

Hostellerie de la Tour

3 r. Plumelets, Arles road – 04 90 54 72 21 – www.hotel-delatour.com – bounoir@wanadoo.fr – Fax 04 90 54 86 26 – Open 30 March-20 October

10 rm – €52 €, €10 – ½ P €55/63

Rest – *(closed Tuesday dinner) (dinner only)* Menu €27

◆ Warm, attentive service in this small inn, popular with regulars for its high standards; small, simple rooms and pleasant garden-pool. Good home cooking served in a room that mingles old stonework with contemporary features.

Le Patio

117 rte du Nord – 04 90 54 73 10 – www.lepatio-alpilles.com – Closed February and autumn school holidays, Tuesday dinner in low season and Wednesday

Rest – *(number of covers limited, pre-book)* Menu (€19 bi), €28/34 – Carte €49/57

◆ This 18C sheepfold features a country-chic interior and an attractive patio shaded by acacias, palm and magnolia trees. Updated Provençal menu.

La Table du Meunier

42 cours Hyacinthe Bellon – 04 90 54 61 05 – Fax 04 90 54 77 24 – Closed February and autumn school holidays, 20-29 December, Tuesday except July-August and Wednesday

Rest – *(number of covers limited, pre-book)* Menu (€21), €26/34 – Carte approx. €35

◆ While Madame prepares tasty regional cuisine, Monsieur is very attentive to your comfort in the rustic dining room or on the terrace, adorned with a henhouse dating from 1765.

Tarascon road **5 km Northwest by D 33 – ✉ 13150 Tarascon**

Les Mazets des Roches

rte de Fonvieille – 04 90 91 34 89 – www.mazetsdesroches.com – mazets-roches@wanadoo.fr – Fax 04 90 43 53 29 – Open from Easter-mid October

37 rm – €60/137 €69/153, €12 – 1 suite

Rest – *(Closed Thursday lunch and Saturday lunch except July-August)* Menu (€23), €25 (weekdays)/39 – Carte €43/64

◆ Ideal establishment for a quiet country break with 13ha of wooded parkland and a 25m pool. Functional, comfortable rooms adorned with bright fabrics. Welcoming dining room-veranda with worn teak furniture, houseplants and floral designs.

FORBACH – 57 Moselle – 307 M3 – pop. 22 300 – Built-up area 104 074 – alt. 222 m – ✉ 57600 Alsace-Lorraine 27 C1

▶ Paris 385 – Metz 59 – St-Avold 23 – Sarreguemines 21 – Saarbrücken 13

ℹ Office de tourisme, 174 c, rue nationale ✆ 03 87 85 02 43, Fax 03 87 85 17 15

FORBACH

Street	Grid	No.
Alliés (R. des)	B	2
Arras (R. d')	A	3
Briand (Pl. A.)	A	6
Chapelle (R. de la)	A	7
Couturier (R.)	B	9
Église (R. de l')	B	10
Gare (R. de la)	B	12
Jardins (R. des)	A	13
Moulins (R. des)	A	15
Nationale (R.)	AB	
Ney (R. P.)	A	17
Parc (R. du)	B	18
Remsing (R. de)	A	20
République (Pl. de la)	B	21
St-Remy (Av.)	AB	
Schlossberg (R. du)	A	23
Schuman (Pl. R.)	B	24
Tuilerie (R. de la)	A	26
22-Novembre (R. du)	B	27

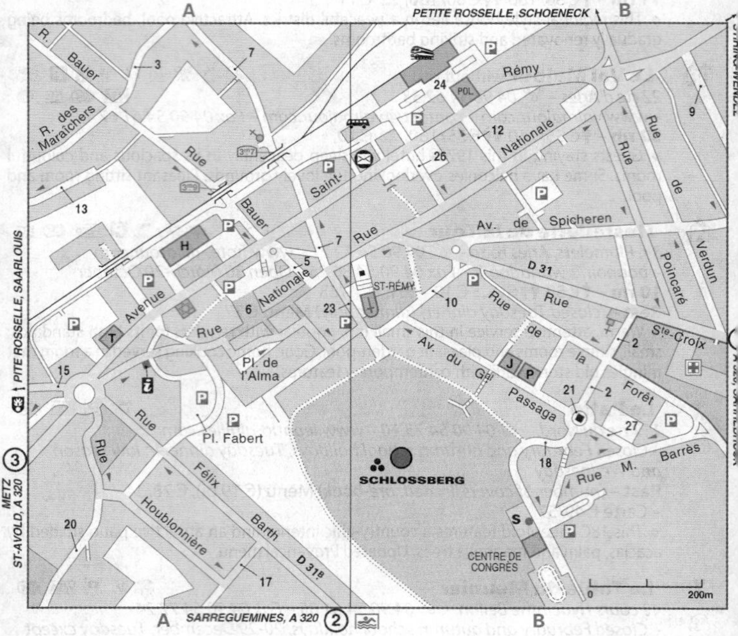

Mercure rm, P VISA MC AE

70 r. F. Barth, via ②, near swimming pool and Forbach-Sud Centre de Loisirs interchange – ✆ 03 87 87 06 06 – www.mercure.com – h1976@accor.com – Fax 03 87 84 04 23

67 rm – 🛉€ 65/95 🛉🛉€ 75/115, ☕ € 14 – ½ P € 85/115

Rest – Menu € 15 (weekdays)/38 bi – Carte € 10/33

◆ Located between the highway and a sport complex, the Mercure provides rooms in two categories ("standard" and "comfortable"). Facilities for conferences. A modern dining room with a veranda.

XX **Le Schlossberg** VISA MC

13 r. Parc – ✆ 03 87 87 88 26 – Fax 03 87 87 83 86 – Closed 20 July-7 August, 27 December-13 January, Sunday dinner, Tuesday dinner and Wednesday B s

Rest – Menu € 20 (weekdays)/49 – Carte € 45/59

◆ Built of local stone, this restaurant stands by the Schlossberg park. Dining room with beautiful inlaid ceiling and bright painted panelling. Terrace under the lime trees.

in Stiring-Wendel 3 km northeast by D 603 – pop. 12 600 – alt. 240 m – ✉ 57350

Syndicat d'initiative, 1, place de Wendel ✆ 03 87 87 07 65, Fax 03 87 87 69 98

XXX ✿ **La Bonne Auberge** (Lydia Egloff)

15 r. Nationale – ✆ 03 87 87 52 78 – Fax 03 87 87 18 19 – Closed 9-31 August, 26 December-4 January, Saturday lunch, Sunday dinner and Monday except bank holidays

Rest – Menu € 40 (weekday lunch), € 55/95 – Carte approx. € 76

Spec. Chaud-froid d'aubergine confite, crème glacée plombières. Sole "filée" à la bergamotte. Chocolat jivaro à l'olive noire.

◆ Elegant dining room set around a winter garden. Inventive cuisine, great wine list: La Bonne Auberge lives up to its name!

in Rosbrück 6 km by ③ – pop. 912 – alt. 200 m – ✉ 57800

XXX **Auberge Albert Marie**

1 r. Nationale – ✆ 03 87 04 70 76 – Fax 03 87 90 52 55 – Closed 20 July-10 August, Saturday lunch, Sunday dinner and Monday

Rest – Menu € 28 bi (weekday lunch), € 38/52 – Carte € 50/65

◆ Tradition is present in the décor as in the menu here, with itds fine setting, coffered ceiling, dark wood carvings and discreet cockerel theme.

The red symbol?
This denotes the very essence of peace –
only the sound of birdsong first thing in the morning…

FORCALQUIER – 04 Alpes-de-Haute-Provence – 334 C9 40 **B2**
– pop. 4 650 – alt. 550 m – ✉ 04300 **French Alps**

Paris 747 – Aix-en-Provence 80 – Apt 42 – Digne-les-Bains 50 – Manosque 23 – Sisteron 43

Office de tourisme, 13, place du Bourguet ✆ 04 92 75 10 02, Fax 04 92 75 26 76

Site★ - Listed cemetery★ - ※★ from the terrace N.-D. de Provence.

Mane★ - St-Michel-l'Observatoire★ - Haute-Provence Obervatory ★.

La Bastide Saint Georges without rest

rte de Banon, 2 km on D 950 – ✆ 04 92 75 72 80 – www.bastidesaintgeorges.com – bastidesaintgeorges@wanadoo.fr – Fax 04 92 75 72 81 – Closed 22 November-25 December and 3 January-1 March

22 rm – †€ 65/110 ††€ 90/225, ☕ € 15 – 1 suite

◆ Provence-style hotel with harmonious, modern, natural decor (wood, rattan, stonework, linen). All rooms except one have a terrace with garden views. Breakfast under the arbour.

X **Les Terrasses de la Bastide**

Rte de Banon – ✆ 04 92 73 32 35 – www.lesterrassesdelabastide.com – lesterrassesdelabastide@yahoo.fr – Closed 15 January-15 March, Sunday dinner, Tuesday lunch and Monday in low season

Rest – Menu (€ 16), € 26 – Carte € 25/38

◆ Mediterranean restaurant decorated with photos on an olive theme. Traditional market cuisine with pieds-paquets (lamb dish) as a speciality. Terrace facing the garden.

East 4 km by D 4100 and secondary road – ✉ 04300 Forcalquier

Auberge Charembeau without rest

rte de Niozelles – ✆ 04 92 70 91 70 – www.charembeau.com – contact@charembeau.com – Fax 04 92 70 91 83 – Open 1st March-15 November

24 rm – †€ 60/85 ††€ 60/128, ☕ € 9

◆ An 18C farmhouse in charming grounds. Visitors enjoy peace and quiet in the lovely surroundings. Provencal-style decoration in the vast guestrooms.

in Mane 4 km south by D 4100 – pop. 1 350 – alt. 500 m – ✉ 04300

Couvent des Minimes
chemin des Jeux de Maï – ✆ 04 92 74 77 77 – www.couventdesminimes-hotelspa.com – info@couventdesminimes-hotelspa.com – Fax 04 92 74 77 78
42 rm – †€ 160/195 ††€ 205/415, ☕ € 25 – 4 suites
Rest *Le Cloître* – *(closed Monday)* Menu € 50/90 – Carte € 60/90
Rest *Le Bancaou* – swimming pool rest. Menu (€ 32) – Carte € 45/66
◆ Convent dating from 1862, superbly refurbished as a luxury hotel. Simple, refined decor and modern facilities in the rooms. Park, perfumed garden. L'Occitane products in the spa. Personalised Mediterranean cuisine at the Cloître. Shaded terrace. Summer buffet menus at the Bancaou.

Mas du Pont Roman without rest
chemin de Châteauneuf, (Apt road) – ✆ 04 92 75 49 46 – www.pontroman.com – info@pontroman.com – Fax 04 92 75 36 73
9 rm – †€ 65 ††€ 80, ☕ € 8
◆ Warm welcome in this traditional farmhouse near an old medieval bridge. Charming lounge and regional style guestrooms. Offering two pools: a spa bath and a counter-current swimming pool.

LA FORÊT-FOUESNANT – 29 Finistère – 308 H7 – pop. 2 809 – alt. 19 m – ✉ 29940 Brittany — 9 B2

Paris 552 – Concarneau 8 – Pont-l'Abbé 22 – Quimper 16 – Quimperlé 36

Office de tourisme, 2, rue du Port ✆ 02 98 51 42 07, Fax 02 98 51 44 52

Beauséjour
pl. de la Baie – ✆ 02 98 56 97 18 – www.h-beausejour.com – beausejourhotel@wanadoo.fr – Fax 02 98 51 40 77 – Open 1st April-15 October
17 rm – †€ 46/60 ††€ 48/64, ☕ € 8
Rest – *(open 1st April-30 September and closed Sunday dinner and Monday)*
Menu (€ 14), € 16/38 – Carte € 30/48
◆ At the end of a cove in the bay of La Forêt, this simple family hotel is well kept. The rooms are bright and spacious for the most part; some are redecorated. Rustic dining room with fireplace and covered terrace just a few metres from the waterside.

Auberge St-Laurent
6 rte de Beg Menez, 2 km Concarneau road along the coast – ✆ 02 98 56 98 07 – auberge.saint-laurent@wanadoo.fr – Closed autumn half-term holidays, February holidays, Monday dinner, Tuesday dinner off season and Wednesday
Rest – Menu (€ 15), € 22/40 – Carte € 25/45
◆ Pleasant guesthouse on the Concarneau coastal road. One of the two rustic dining rooms, with a fireplace and beams, overlooks the garden and the summer terrace.

FORGES-LES-EAUX – 76 Seine-Maritime – 304 J4 – pop. 3 542 – alt. 161 m – Casino – ✉ 76440 Normandy — 33 D1

Paris 117 – Rouen 44 – Abbeville 73 – Amiens 72 – Beauvais 52 – Le Havre 123

Office de tourisme, rue Albert Bochet ✆ 02 35 90 52 10, Fax 02 35 90 34 80

Le Continental without rest
av. des Sources, (Dieppe road) – ✆ 02 32 89 50 50 – www.domainedeforges.com – hotel-lecontinental@g-partouche.fr – Fax 02 35 90 39 52
44 rm – †€ 59/75 ††€ 69/75, ☕ € 10
◆ A small, regional style house featuring spacious rooms sporting a modern touch. Pleasant sitting room and delightful breakfast room.

Auberge du Beau Lieu with rm
rte de Gournay, 2 km via D 915 – ✆ 02 35 90 50 36 – www.aubergedubeaulieu.fr – aubeaulieu@aol.com – Closed 4 January-5 February, Monday except lunch from Easter to 11 November and Tuesday
3 rm – †€ 45/60 ††€ 45/60, ☕ € 13 **Rest** – Menu € 28/58 – Carte € 40/73
◆ Country-style guesthouse in the Bray country. In winter, it is a pleasure to relax near the hearth in the cosy restaurant. Summer terrace. Ground-floor rooms.

FORT-MAHON-PLAGE – **80 Somme** – **301** C5 – **pop. 1 140** – **alt. 2 m** – **Casino** – ✉ **80120** ▮ **Northern France and the Paris Region** 36 **A1**

▶ Paris 225 – Abbeville 41 – Amiens 90 – Berck-sur-Mer 19 – Calais 94 – Étaples 30

ℹ Office de tourisme, 1000, avenue de la Plage ✆ 03 22 23 36 00, Fax 03 22 23 93 40

⛳18 de Belle-Dune Promenade du Marquenterre, (near the Aquaclub), ✆ 03 22 23 45 50

◎ Marquenterre Ornithological Park ★★ South: 15 km.

Auberge Le Fiacre rm, rm, P VISA

at Routhiauville, 2 km south-east on Rue road – ✆ 03 22 23 47 30 – www.aufiacre.fr – lefiacre@wanadoo.fr – Fax 03 22 27 19 80 – Closed 20-28 December, 4 January-1st February

11 rm – †€ 80/102 ††€ 80/102, ☕ € 12 – 3 suites – ½ P € 84/95

Rest – *(closed Monday from December to mid-April)* Menu (€ 28 bi), € 32/45 – Carte € 50/58

◆ The perfect spot for a relaxing country break, this old Marquenterre farm enjoys an attractive rural setting. Cosy atmosphere in the guestrooms, enlivened with individual touches. Classical cuisine served in an elegant dining room or on the terrace overlooking the garden.

La Terrasse rest, AC rest, rm, P VISA

1461 av de la Plage – ✆ 03 22 23 37 77 – www.hotellaterrasse.com – info@hotellaterrasse.com – Fax 03 22 23 36 74 – Closed 4-25 January

56 rm – †€ 41/99 ††€ 41/99, ☕ € 10

Rest – Menu € 15/60 bi – Carte € 30/50

◆ Family-run seafront hotel with comfortable rooms, some with a sea view, the quietest overlooking the courtyard. Panoramic view and nautical decor; seafood menu and terrace on the restaurant side; brasserie section.

LA FOSSETTE (PLAGE) – **83 Var** – **340** N7 – **see le Lavandou**

FOS-SUR-MER – **13 Bouches-du-Rhône** – **340** E5 – **pop. 15 700** – **alt. 11 m** – ✉ **13270** ▮ **Provence** 40 **A3**

▶ Paris 750 – Aix-en-Provence 55 – Arles 42 – Marseille 51 – Martigues 12

ℹ Syndicat d'initiative, avenue René Cassin ✆ 04 42 47 71 96, Fax 04 42 05 27 55

◎ Village ★.

Ariane Fos AC rm, P VISA AE

Istres road: 3 km – ✆ 04 42 05 00 57 – www.arianefoshotel.com – contact@arianefoshotel.com – Fax 04 42 05 51 00

72 rm – †€ 86/141 ††€ 91/146, ☕ € 11

Rest – Menu € 14 (weekday lunch), € 30/36 – Carte € 33/47

◆ Near the Estomac lagoon, a hotel with spacious, soundproofed, modern rooms (a third with balconies). Good leisure and conference facilities. Recently renovated restaurant serving traditional cuisine.

FOUCHÈRES – **10 Aube** – **313** F5 – **pop. 469** – **alt. 138 m** – ✉ **10260** 13 **B3**

▶ Paris 189 – Troyes 25 – Bar-sur-Aube 42 – Bar-sur-Seine 11

Auberge de la Seine AC VISA AE

1 fg de Bourgogne – ✆ 03 25 40 71 11 – www.aubergedelaseine.com – contact@aubergedelaseine.com – Fax 03 25 40 84 09 – Closed 21 February-9 March, Sunday dinner, Monday and Wednesday

Rest – Menu € 19 (weekdays)/65 bi – Carte € 41/59

◆ 18C post house extended by a lovely terrace overlooking the river Seine. Traditional cuisine served in the modern, simple and cosy dining room.

FOUDAY – 67 Bas-Rhin – 315 H6 – pop. 303 – ✉ 67130 1 A2
Alsace-Lorraine

Paris 412 – St-Dié 34 – Saverne 55 – Sélestat 37 – Strasbourg 61

Julien
rm, rest, VISA MC AE

D 1420 – ✆ 03 88 97 30 09 – www.hoteljulien.com – hoteljulien@wanadoo.fr – Fax 03 88 97 36 73 – Closed 5-25 January

37 rm – †€ 102/160 ††€ 102/160, ☕ € 16 – 10 suites – ½ P € 88/110

Rest – *(closed Tuesday)* Menu (€ 15), € 19 (weekday lunch), € 30/55 – Carte € 25/45

◆ This country house offers attractive, elegant rooms in an elegant combination of wood and reds. Extensive wellness centre and theme stays. Generous portions of simple, classic cuisine served in stylish dining rooms.

FOUESNANT – 29 Finistère – 308 G7 – pop. 9 403 – alt. 30 m 9 B2
– ✉ 29170 Brittany

Paris 555 – Carhaix-Plouguer 69 – Concarneau 11 – Quimper 16 – Quimperlé 39

Office de tourisme, Espace Kernevelech ✆ 02 98 51 18 88, Fax 02 98 56 64 02

de Cornouaille La Forêt-Fouesnant Manoir du Mesmeur, E : 4 km on D 44, ✆ 02 98 56 97 09

L'Orée du Bois without rest
VISA MC

4 r. Kergoadig – ✆ 02 98 56 00 06 – www.hotel-oreedubois.com – hotel.loreedubois@wanadoo.fr – Fax 02 98 56 14 17

15 rm – †€ 36/50 ††€ 36/65, ☕ € 8

◆ A new team now manages this house offering small, simple rooms. Depending on the season, breakfast is served in the garden or in a nautically inspired room.

in Cap Coz 2,5 km Southeast by secondary road – ✉ 29170 Fouesnant

Mona Lisa
P VISA MC AE

plage du Cap Coz – ✆ 02 98 51 18 10 – www.monalisahotels.com – resa-capcoz@monalisahotels.com – Fax 02 98 56 03 40 – Open mid March-October

49 rm – †€ 79/130 ††€ 79/130, ☕ € 11

Rest – Menu € 20 – Carte approx. € 25

◆ Renovated building by the beach with cheerful rooms, some providing balconies with a panoramic view (2nd floor). The communal areas are modern and bright. A dining room with a veranda opening onto the foreshore.

De la Pointe du Cap Coz
rest, VISA MC AE

153 av. de la Pointe – ✆ 02 98 56 01 63 – www.hotel-capcoz.com – bienvenue@hotel-capcoz.com – Fax 02 98 56 53 20 – Closed 24-29 November, 1st January-12 February and Sunday evening from 1st October to 15 March

16 rm – †€ 57/60 ††€ 66/96, ☕ € 10 – ½ P € 72/87

Rest – *(closed Sunday dinner and Monday lunch from 15 September to 15 June and Wednesday)* Menu € 25/48 – Carte € 45/81

◆ This hotel sits on the sandy coast of Cap Coz. The functional guestrooms enjoy views over the harbour or the sea. Bright dining room with an attractive view of the coast. Good quality seafood with a contemporary twist.

Belle-Vue
P VISA MC

30 descente Belle-Vue – ✆ 02 98 56 00 33 – hotel-belle-vue.com – hotel-belle-vue@wanadoo.fr – Fax 02 98 51 60 85 – Open 1st March-31 October

16 rm – †€ 54/65 ††€ 62/77, ☕ € 8,50 – ½ P € 59/68

Rest – *(open 15 March-31 October and closed Monday)* Menu € 23/38 – Carte € 26/48

◆ Family guesthouse overlooking the bay of La Forêt. Practical rooms, most with views of the ocean. Simple decor and unpretentious local cuisine in the restaurant. In summer, pleasant panoramic terrace.

in la Pointe de Mousterlin 6 km Southwest by D 145 and D 134 – ✉ 29170 Fouesnant

De la Pointe de Mousterlin

rest, rest, VISA AE

108 rte de la Pointe – ✆ 02 98 56 04 12 – www.mousterlinhotel.com – hoteldelapointe@wanadoo.fr – Fax 02 98 56 61 02 – Closed 6 February-3 March, Tuesday lunch, Sunday dinner and Monday from 15 October to 15 April

42 rm – 🚹€ 55/76 🚹🚹€ 78/152, ☕ € 12 – ½ P € 86/105

Rest – Menu € 26/45 – Carte € 52/68

◆ A seaside complex at the end of the headland. Practical, spacious rooms in three buildings facing the garden. Good leisure facilities. Two dining rooms, one a veranda. Regional and seafood cuisine.

FOUGÈRES – 35 Ille-et-Vilaine – 309 O4 – pop. 20 900 – alt. 115 m – ✉ 35300 Brittany

10 **D2**

Paris 326 – Avranches 44 – Laval 53 – Le Mans 132 – Rennes 52 – St-Malo 80

Office de tourisme, 2, rue Nationale ✆ 02 99 94 12 20, Fax 02 99 94 77 30

Château★★ - St-Sulpice church ★ - Public garden★: ≤★ - Stained-glass windows ★ of St-Léonard church - Rue Nationale★.

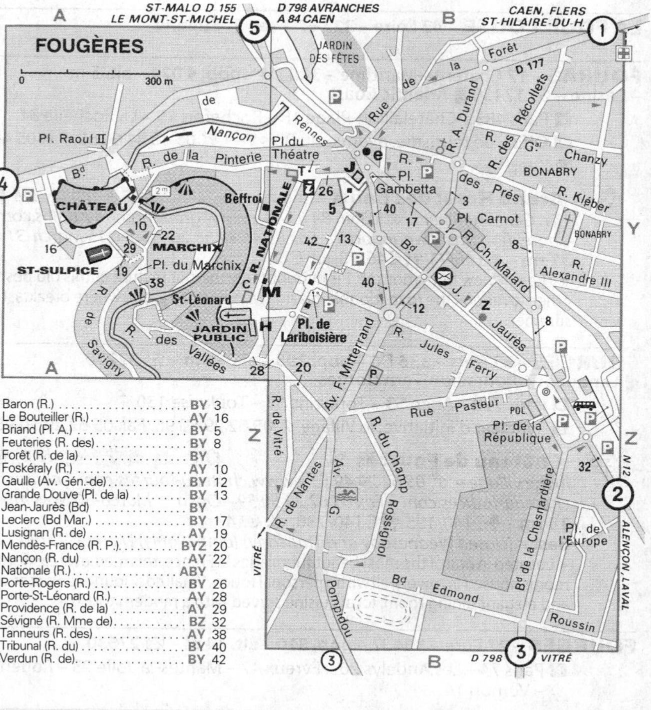

Baron (R.) .... BY 3
Le Bouteiller (R.) .... AY 16
Briand (Pl. A.) .... BY 5
Feuteries (R. des) .... BY 8
Forêt (R. de la) .... BY
Foskéraly (R.) .... AY 10
Gaulle (Av. Gén.-de) .... BY 12
Grande Douve (Pl. de la) .... BY 13
Jean-Jaurès (Bd) .... BY
Leclerc (Bd Mar.) .... BY 17
Lusignan (R. de) .... AY 19
Mendès-France (R. P.) .... BYZ 20
Nançon (R. du) .... AY 22
Nationale (R.) .... ABY
Porte-Rogers (R.) .... BY 26
Porte-St-Léonard (R.) .... AY 28
Providence (R. de la) .... AY 29
Sévigné (R. Mme de) .... BZ 32
Tanneurs (R. des) .... AY 38
Tribunal (R. du) .... BY 40
Verdun (R. de) .... BY 42

Les Voyageurs without rest

VISA AE

10 pl. Gambetta – ✆ 02 99 99 08 20 – www.hotel-fougeres.fr – hotel-voyageurs-fougeres@wanadoo.fr – Fax 02 99 99 99 04 – Closed 23 December-3 January and Saturday in January

BY **e**

37 rm – 🚹€ 52/56 🚹🚹€ 58/72, ☕ € 8

◆ A century-old hotel in the heart of the upper town. Most of the refurbished guestrooms sport a bright, colourful and personal touch.

XX **Haute Sève** VISA MC AE

37 bd J. Jaurès – ✆ 02 99 94 23 39 – Closed 22 July-22 August, 1st-20 January, Sunday dinner and Monday BY **z**

Rest – Menu € 20 (weekdays), € 25/43 – Carte € 35/50

◆ The attractive, half-timbered façade hides a dining room recently refurbished in a contemporary spirit. Updated regional cuisine with market produce.

FOUGEROLLES – **70 Haute-Saône** – **314** G5 – **pop. 3 852** – **alt. 311 m** – ✉ **70220** Burgundy-Jura 17 **C1**

Paris 374 – Épinal 49 – Luxeuil-les-Bains 10 – Remiremont 25 – Vesoul 43

Office de tourisme, 1, rue de la Gare ✆ 03 84 49 12 91, Fax 03 84 49 12 91

Ecomusée du Pays de la Cerise et de la Distillation (Cherry and distillation museum of man and the environment)★.

XX **Au Père Rota** P VISA MC AE

8 Grande Rue – ✆ 03 84 49 12 11 – jean-pierre-kuentz@wanadoo.fr – Fax 03 84 49 14 51 – Closed 31 August-4 September, 4-29 January, Sunday dinner, Tuesday dinner and Monday

Rest – Menu (€ 20), € 26 (weekdays)/70 – Carte € 55/68

◆ Set up in the capital of kirsch, this elegant, understated restaurant offers delicious traditional cuisine. A fine wine list with numerous vintage wines.

LA FOUILLOUSE – **42 Loire** – **327** E7 – **see St-Étienne**

FOURAS – **17 Charente-Maritime** – **324** D4 – **pop. 4 024** – **alt. 5 m** – **Casino** – ✉ **17450** Atlantic Coast 38 **A2**

Paris 485 – Châtelaillon-Plage 18 – Rochefort 15 – La Rochelle 34

Office de tourisme, avenue du Bois Vert ✆ 05 46 84 60 69, Fax 05 46 84 28 04

Keep ✳★.

Grand Hôtel des Bains without rest VISA MC AE

15 r. Gén. Bruncher – ✆ 05 46 84 03 44 – www.grandhotel-desbains.com – hoteldesbains@wanadoo.fr – Fax 05 46 84 58 26 – Open 15 March-31 October

31 rm – €46/71 €46/78, ☕ €8

◆ The sea view from room N° 1 is undoubtedly the star feature of this old post house. The others overlook the road (double-glazing) or flowered patio, where breakfast is served in summer.

FOURCÈS – **32 Gers** – **336** D6 – **pop. 295** – **alt. 76 m** – ✉ **32250** Languedoc-Roussillon-Tarn Gorges 28 **A2**

Paris 728 – Agen 53 – Tonneins 57 – Toulouse 130

Syndicat d'initiative, le Village ✆ 05 62 29 50 96, Fax 05 62 29 50 96

Château de Fourcès rest, P VISA MC AE

in the village – ✆ 05 62 29 49 53 – www.chateau-fources.com – contact@chateau-fources.com – Fax 05 62 29 50 59 – Open 1st March-30 November

18 rm – €140/195 €140/230, ☕ €14

Rest – *(closed Wednesday and Thursday) (dinner only)* Menu € 29/50

◆ Located in one of the most beautiful villages in France, this medieval castle has attractive rooms housed in towers, all with a personal touch. Small cosy lounges. Park and river. Warm and elegant dining room, local cuisine served with a modern touch.

FOURGES – **27 Eure** – **304** J7 – **pop. 810** – **alt. 14 m** – ✉ **27630** 33 **D2**

Paris 74 – Les Andelys 26 – Évreux 47 – Mantes-la-Jolie 23 – Rouen 75 – Vernon 14

XX **Le Moulin de Fourges** VISA MC

38 r. du Moulin – ✆ 02 32 52 12 12 – www.moulindefourges.com – info@moulin-de-fourges.com – Fax 02 32 52 92 56 – Open 1st April-31 October and closed Sunday dinner and Monday

Rest – Menu (€ 21), € 35

◆ The countryside setting of this old mill by the Epte is a favourite with painters and nature lovers. Countrified dining rooms and updated cuisine.

FOURMIES – 59 Nord – **302** M7 – **pop. 13 400** – **alt. 200 m** – ✉ **59610** 31 **D3**
Northern France and the Paris Region

Paris 214 – Avesnes-sur-Helpe 16 – Charleroi 60 – Hirson 14 – Lille 115 – St-Quentin 65

Office de tourisme, 20, rue Jean Jaurès ✆ 03 27 59 69 97, Fax 03 27 57 30 44

Musée du textile et de la vie sociale★.

in Étangs-des-Moines 2 km East by D 964 and secondary road – ✉ **59610 Fourmies**

Ibis without rest VISA MC
r. des Etangs des Moines – ✆ 03 27 60 21 54 – hotelibisfourmies@orange.fr – Fax 03 27 57 40 44
31 rm – €54/62 €54/62, €8
◆ Modern hotel on the edge of a beautiful forest of oaks, perfect for making the most of the quiet, bucolic watery setting. Practical well-kept rooms.

Auberge des Étangs des Moines VISA MC
97 r. des Etangs – ✆ 03 27 60 02 62 – www.restaurant-les-etangs-des-moines.com – Fax 03 27 60 10 25 – Closed 1st-21 August, February holidays, Saturday lunch, Sunday dinner and Monday except holidays
Rest – Menu (€ 15), € 19/39 – Carte € 30/51
◆ This inn has kept its convivial open-air café feel with its warm atmosphere. Veranda overlooking the lakes. Traditional dishes.

LA FOUX D'ALLOS – 04 Alpes-de-Haute-Provence – **334** H7 – see Allos

---

FRANCESCAS – 47 Lot-et-Garonne – **336** E5 – **pop. 732** – **alt. 109 m** – ✉ **47600** 4 **C2**

Paris 720 – Agen 28 – Condom 18 – Nérac 14 – Toulouse 134

Le Relais de la Hire P VISA MC AE
11 r. Porte-Neuve – ✆ 05 53 65 41 59 – www.la-hire.com – contact@la-hire.com – Closed 27 October-4 November, February school holidays, Sunday dinner, Tuesday dinner, Wednesday dinner and Monday
Rest – *(pre-book)* Menu (€ 15 bi), € 22/56 – Carte € 12/56
◆ A comfortable classical decor (sky blue ceiling), summer terrace and intelligently personalised regional fare are what set this attractive 18C abode apart.

FRANQUEVILLE-ST-PIERRE – 76 Seine-Maritime – **304** H5 – see Rouen

---

FRÉHEL – 22 Côtes-d'Armor – **309** H3 – **pop. 2 166** – **alt. 72 m** – **Casino** – ✉ **22240** 10 **C1**

Paris 433 – Dinan 38 – Lamballe 28 – St-Brieuc 40 – St-Cast-le-Guildo 15 – St-Malo 36

Office de tourisme, place de Chambly ✆ 02 96 41 53 81, Fax 02 96 41 59 46

✳★★★.

Fort La Latte★★: site★★, ✳★★ Southeast: 5 km.

Le Victorine VISA MC
3 pl. Chambly – ✆ 02 96 41 55 55 – www.levictorine.net – Fax 02 96 41 55 55 – Closed 19 October-9 November, 15-28 February, Sunday dinner and Monday except from 7 July to 30 August
Rest – Menu € 14 (weekday lunch), € 21/29 – Carte € 29/47
◆ A family restaurant located on the village square. Traditional cuisine using fresh market produce is served in the simply decorated dining area or on the terrace.

LA FREISSINOUSE – 05 Hautes-Alpes – **334** E5 – see Gap

FRÉJUS – 83 Var – 340 P5 – pop. 48 800 – alt. 20 m – ✉ 83600 41 C3

French Riviera

Paris 868 – Cannes 40 – Draguignan 31 – Hyères 90 – Nice 66

3635 et tapez 42 (0,34 €/mn)

Office de tourisme, 325, rue Jean Jaurès 04 94 51 83 83, Fax 04 94 51 00 26

de Roquebrune Roquebrune-sur-Argens Quartier des Planes, 6 km W : on D 8, 04 94 19 60 35

de Valescure Saint-Raphaël Route des golfs, 8 km NE :, 04 94 82 40 46

Groupe épiscopal★★ : baptistry★★, cloister★, cathedral★ - Roman town★ A : amphitheatre★ - Parc zoologique (zoo)★ North: 5 km by ③.

FRÉJUS

- Agachon (Av. de l') A 2
- Alger (Bd) B 5
- Brosset (Av. du Gén.) AB 13
- Carrara (R. Jean) A 16
- Decuers (Bd S.) A 23
- Donnadieu (R.) B 24
- Einaudi (R. Albert) A 25
- Europe (Av. de l') A 26
- Fabre (Av. Hippolyte) B 27
- Garros (R. Roland) B 32
- Libération (Bd de la) B 40
- Papin (R. Denis) B 46
- Triberg (R. de) A 53
- Verdun (Av. de) A 56
- Victor-Hugo (Av.) B 60
- XVe-Corps (Av. du) A 62

ST-RAPHAËL

- Coty (Promenade René) B 20
- Gaulle (Av. du Gén.-de) B 33
- Leclerc (Av. Mar.) B 39
- Mimosas (Bd des) B 43
- Myrtes (Av. des) B 45
- Poincaré (Av. Raymond) B 47
- Rivière (Av. Théodore) B 51
- Valescure (Av. de) B 54

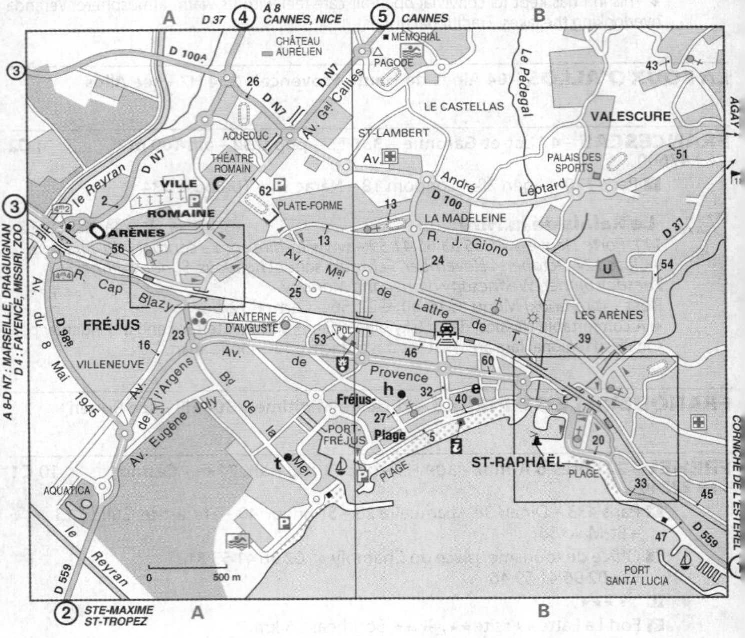

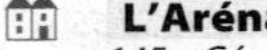

L'Aréna

rm,

145 r. Gén. de Gaulle – 04 94 17 09 40 – www.hotels-ocre-azur.com – hotel.arena@hotels-ocre-azur.com – Fax 04 94 52 01 52 – Closed November

36 rm – ♦€ 85/120 ♦♦€ 85/120, ☕ € 13 – ½ P € 81/98

Rest – Menu (€ 26), € 46/58 – Carte € 53/72 C r

◆ This delightful hotel near the amphitheatre is the epitome of Provence. Enjoy the cosy rooms with regional fabrics and painted furniture, a scented patio and turquoise pool. The restaurant serves sun-drenched cuisine.

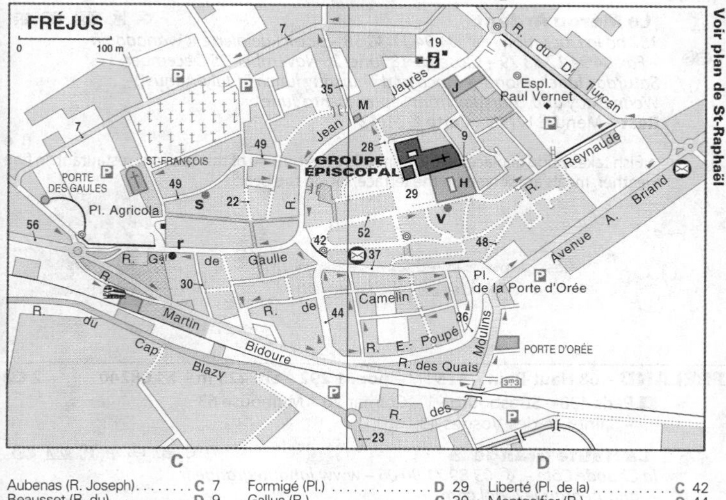

Aubenas (R. Joseph) . . . . C 7
Beausset (R. du) . . . . D 9
Clemenceau (Pl. G.) . . . . D 19
Craponne (R.) . . . . C 22
Decuers (Bd S.) . . . . D 23
Fleury (R. de) . . . . D 28
Formigé (Pl.) . . . . D 29
Gallus (R.) . . . . C 30
Girardin (R.) . . . . C 35
Glacière (Pl. de la) . . . . D 36
Grisolle (R.) . . . . D 37
Jean-Jaurès (R.) C
Liberté (Pl. de la) . . . . C 42
Montgolfier (R.) . . . . C 44
Portalet (Passage du) . . . . D 48
Potiers (R. des) . . . . C 49
Sieyès (R.) . . . . D 52
Verdun (Av. de) . . . . C 56

L'Amandier

19 r. Marc-Antoine Desaugiers – ✆ 04 94 53 48 77 – Closed Monday lunch, Wednesday lunch and Sunday D **v**

Rest – *(number of covers limited, pre-book)* Menu (€ 19), € 23/36 – Carte € 34/46

◆ Pleasant restaurant situated near the town hall. Two simple rustic dining rooms, one with a vaulted ceiling. Tasty southern cuisine and a fine wine list.

Les Potiers

135 r. des Potiers – ✆ 04 94 51 33 74 – www.les-potiers.fr – contact@les-potiers.fr – Closed 5-20 January, lunch in July-August, Wednesday lunch and Tuesday from September to June C **s**

Rest – *(number of covers limited, pre-book)* Menu € 25/36 – Carte € 36/56

◆ Tucked away in a side street, this small restaurant is often fully booked. Friendly atmosphere and tasty, well-prepared cuisine steeped in the flavour of southern France.

in Fréjus-Plage AB – ✉ 83600 Fréjus

L'Oasis without rest

imp. Charcot – ✆ 04 94 51 50 44 – www.hotel-oasis.net – info@hotel-oasis.net – Fax 04 94 53 01 04 – Open 1st February-12 November B **h**

27 rm – †€ 38/69 ††€ 38/69, ☕ € 7

◆ Built in the 1950s, a friendly family atmosphere reigns throughout this hotel in a quiet neighbourhood. Practical neo-rustic rooms. Breakfast beneath the pergola in summertime.

Atoll without rest

923 bd de la Mer – ✆ 04 94 51 53 77 – www.atollhotel.fr – atollhotel@wanadoo.fr – Fax 04 94 51 58 33 A **t**

30 rm – †€ 44/66 ††€ 44/66, ☕ € 6

◆ A stone's throw from the beaches and marina, this small, unpretentious family establishment offers well-kept, practical and simply decorated rooms.

Le Mérou Ardent

157 bd la Libération – 04 94 17 30 58 – patrickdelpierre@wanadoo.fr – Fax 04 94 17 33 79 – Closed 8-18 June, 25 November-25 December, Saturday lunch, Monday lunch and Thursday lunch in July-August, Wednesday and Thursday from September to June
Rest – Menu € 17/36 – Carte € 24/42

B **e**

◆ Fish takes pride of place on the primarily classic menu of this seafront restaurant. In fine weather, meals are served on the terrace, facing the beach.

"Rest" appears in red for establishments with a (star) or (Bib Gourmand).

FRÉLAND – 68 Haut-Rhin – **315** H7 – **pop. 1 292** – **alt. 425 m** – ✉ **68240** 2 **C2**

Paris 438 – Strasbourg 91 – Colmar 20 – Mulhouse 63 – Saint-Dié-des-Vosges 43

La Haute Grange

la Chaude Côte – 03 89 71 90 06 – www.lahautegrange.fr – lahautegrange@aol.com
4 rm – †€ 60/90 ††€ 80/110 **Table d'hôte** – Menu € 45 bi
◆ Peace and quiet are guaranteed at this old house, set in isolated countryside. Cosy rooms, rustic lounge areas (fireplace, library). Personalised cuisine from Madame, with food and wine pairings.

LE FRENEY-D'OISANS – 38 Isère – **333** J7 – **pop. 277** – **alt. 926 m** – ✉ **38142** 45 **C2**

Paris 626 – Bourg-d'Oisans 12 – La Grave 16 – Grenoble 64
Syndicat d'initiative, Le Village 04 76 80 05 82, Fax 04 76 80 05 82
Barrage du Chambon★★ Southeast: 2 km - Gorges de l'Infernet★ Southwest: 2 km, **French Alps.**

in Mizoën Northeast: 4 km by N 91 and D 1091 – pop. 172 – alt. 1 100 m – ✉ 38142

Panoramique

rte des Aymes – 04 76 80 06 25 – www.hotel-panoramique.com – info@hotel-panoramique.com – Fax 04 76 80 25 12 – Open 2 May-21 September and 20 December-31 March
9 rm – †€ 67/85 ††€ 95/105
Rest – *(dinner only except weekend and holidays)* Menu (€ 23), € 27 – Carte approx. € 29
◆ Apart from its lovely surroundings, this flower-decked chalet (for non-smokers only) offers a charming welcome, is extremely well kept and has amenities such as a south-facing solarium and sauna. Panoramic dining room and pleasant summer terrace facing the peaks.

LE FRENZ – 68 Haut-Rhin – **315** F9 – **see Kruth**

FRESNAY-EN-RETZ – 44 Loire-Atlantique – **316** E5 – **pop. 1 017** – **alt. 15 m** – ✉ **44580** 34 **A2**

Paris 425 – Nantes 40 – La Roche-sur-Yon 64 – Saint-Nazaire 51

Le Colvert

14 rte de Pornic – 02 40 21 46 79 – www.lecolvert.fr – Fax 02 40 21 95 99 – Closed 17 August-5 September, Sunday dinner, Tuesday dinner, Wednesday dinner and Monday
Rest – Menu € 18 (weekday lunch), € 28/52 – Carte € 44/60
◆ Roadside house in the heart of the village. The dining room has been fully revamped and is now more contemporary in style, a fitting backdrop for the modern cuisine.

FRESNE-CAUVERVILLE – 27 Eure – 304 C6 – pop. 195 – alt. 160 m – ✉ 27260 33 **C2**

▶ Paris 155 – Rouen 81 – Évreux 59 – Le Havre 62 – Lisieux 26

Le Clos de l'Ambroisie

La Forge Subtile, 500 m to the southeast – ✆ 02 32 42 76 40 – www.closdelambroisie.fr – d.serpat@orange.fr

4 rm – €55 €65 **Table d'hôte** – Menu €25 bi

◆ This 18C, former Norman eider press and its garden invite guests to relax. Rooms decorated on a theme of stones (ruby, citrine, m'bigou, amethyst). Traditional fare with an exotic accent at the table d'hôte (by reservation).

LE FRET – 29 Finistère – 308 D5 – see Crozon

FRICHEMESNIL – 76 Seine-Maritime – 304 G4 – see Clères

FROENINGEN – 68 Haut-Rhin – 315 H10 – see Mulhouse

FROIDETERRE – 70 Haute-Saône – 314 H6 – see Lure

FRONCLES-BUXIERES – 52 Haute-Marne – 313 K4 – pop. 1 680 – alt. 226 m – ✉ 52320 14 **C3**

▶ Paris 282 – Bar-sur-Aube 41 – Chaumont 28 – Neufchâteau 52 – Saint-Dizier 52

Au Château

Parc d'Activités – ✆ 03 25 02 93 84 – http://restaurant.auchateau.monsite.wanadoo.fr – didier.pougeoise@wanadoo.fr – Closed Christmas holidays, Saturday lunch and Sunday dinner

Rest – Menu (€13), €27/50 – Carte €38/54

◆ Large, elegant house with small lounges used as dining rooms and a vast covered terrace overlooking the park. Modern, well-presented food.

FRONTIGNAN – 34 Hérault – 339 H8 – pop. 22 800 – alt. 2 m – ✉ 34110 **Languedoc-Roussillon-Tarn Gorges** 23 **C2**

▶ Paris 775 – Lodève 59 – Montpellier 26 – Sète 10

Montpellier road 4 km northeast on D 612– ✉ 34110 Frontignan

Hôtellerie de Balajan VISA

41 rte de Montpellier – ✆ 04 67 48 13 99 – www.hotel-balajan.com – hotel.balajan@wanadoo.fr – Fax 04 67 43 06 62 – Closed 24 December-4 January, February and Sunday dinner from November to March

18 rm – €73 €73/105, €11

Rest – *(closed Sunday dinner in low season, Saturday lunch, Monday lunch and Tuesday lunch)* Menu (€19), €28/55 – Carte €29/57

◆ Welcoming roadside hotel with practical rooms. Some enjoy a view of the vineyards and the Gardiole mountains. Flower-decked tables add a friendly feel to this restaurant. Mediterranean inspired cuisine; cosy sitting room.

FRONTIGNAN-DE-COMMINGES – 31 Haute-Garonne – pop. 73 – alt. 450 m – ✉ 31510 28 **B3**

▶ Paris 796 – Toulouse 120 – Saint-Gaudens 31 – Bagnères-de-Bigorre 70 – Saint-Girons 77

Le Relais des Frontignes

au village, via D 33^A – ✆ 05 61 79 61 67 – www.relaisdesfrontignes.com – yann.debruycker@wanadoo.fr – Fax 05 61 79 61 67

5 rm – €50 €60 **Table d'hôte** – Menu €20 bi

◆ The owner of this 19C house is more than happy to take guests up into the mountains. Attractive themed bedrooms (Asia, Europe, Africa) and large park with mountain stream.

FRONTONAS – 38 Isère – 333 E4 – pop. 1 829 – alt. 260 m – ✉ 38290 44 B2

Paris 495 – Ambérieu-en-Bugey 44 – Lyon 34 – La Tour-du-Pin 26 – Vienne 35

Auberge du Ru

Le Bergeron-Les-Quatre-Vies – ✆ 04 74 94 25 71 – www.aubergeduru.fr – info@aubergeduru.fr – Fax 04 74 94 25 71 – Closed 16 February-3 March, 14 July-5 August, Sunday dinner, Monday and Tuesday

Rest – Menu € 29 bi/37

◆ Country guesthouse in the heart of a hamlet. Smart dining room decorated with farm implements. Modern cuisine, menu according to daily market produce.

FUISSÉ – 71 Saône-et-Loire – 320 I12 – pop. 326 – alt. 290 m – ✉ 71960 8 C3

Burgundy-Jura

Paris 401 – Charolles 54 – Chauffailles 52 – Mâcon 9 – Villefranche-sur-Saône 48

Au Pouilly Fuissé

le bourg – ✆ 03 85 35 60 68 – www.restaurant.aupouillyfuisse.fr – hotmail@restaurant.com – Fax 03 85 35 60 68 – Closed Sunday dinner, Tuesday dinner and Wednesday

Rest – Menu (€ 20), € 27/47 – Carte € 42/60

◆ Family guesthouse named after the local wine, served to accompany the traditional cuisine. Veranda/dining room and shaded terrace.

FUTEAU – 55 Meuse – 307 B4 – see Ste-Menehould (51 Marne)

FUVEAU – 13 Bouches-du-Rhône – 340 I5 – pop. 8 558 – alt. 283 m – ✉ 13710 40 B3

Paris 765 – Marseille 36 – Brignoles 53 – Manosque 73

Office de tourisme, cours Victor Leydet ✆ 04 42 50 49 77

Mona Lisa

rm,

D 6, (opposite the Château de l'Arc golf course) – ✆ 04 42 68 19 19 – www.monalisahotels.com – dir-ste-victoire@monalisahotels.com – Fax 04 42 68 19 18

81 rm – †€ 125/140 ††€ 125/140, ☕ € 12

Rest – *(closed Saturday lunch and Sunday lunch)* Menu (€ 20), € 24/28 – Carte approx. € 29

◆ A modern style building next to a golf course. Beige monochromes and painted wood furniture in the relaxing and well-designed rooms. High speed internet connection. Sauna and gym. Bright restaurant with bay windows opening onto a terrace and swimming pool.

GABRIAC – 12 Aveyron – 338 I4 – pop. 444 – alt. 580 m – ✉ 12340 29 D1

Paris 605 – Espalion 13 – Mende 88 – Rodez 27 – Sévérac-le-Château 35

Bouloc with rm

La Remise – ✆ 05 65 44 92 89 – franck.bouloc@orange.fr – Fax 05 65 48 86 74 – Closed 5-19 March, 25 June-2 July, 1st-22 October, Wednesday except dinner in July-August and Tuesday dinner from September to June

11 rm – †€ 42/49 ††€ 42/49, ☕ € 7 – ½ P € 48/51

Rest – Menu € 12 bi (weekday lunch), € 17/38

◆ This regional house has been in the same family for six generations. Serves many Rouergue specialities. New dining room/veranda. Rooms have yet to be renovated.

GACÉ – 61 Orne – 310 K2 – pop. 2 140 – alt. 210 m – ✉ 61230 33 C2

Normandy

Paris 172 – Alençon 49 – Caen 78 – Lisieux 48

Office de tourisme, Mairie ✆ 02 33 35 50 24, Fax 02 33 35 92 82

Le Manoir des Camélias

rte d'Alençon – ✆ 02 33 35 67 43 – www.manoirdescamelias.com – delisletraiteur@aol.com – Fax 02 33 67 10 89

10 rm – †€ 50/92 ††€ 50/92, ☕ € 10

Rest – *(closed Wednesday)* Menu (€ 19), € 25/40 – Carte € 40/64

◆ Calm and peaceful atmosphere at this 19C manor house surrounded by a park. Elegant lounge bar with wood panelling, cosy rooms with refined minimalist decor.

GAGNY – 93 Seine-Saint-Denis – **305** G7 – **101** 18 – **see Paris, Area**

GAILLAC – 81 Tarn – **338** D7 – **pop. 12 100 – alt. 143 m** – ✉ **81600** 29 **C2**
Languedoc-Roussillon-Tarn Gorges

Paris 672 – Albi 26 – Cahors 89 – Castres 52 – Montauban 50 – Toulouse 58
Syndicat d'initiative, Abbaye Saint-Michel ✆ 05 63 57 14 65, Fax 05 63 57 61 37

La Verrerie rm, rest, VISA MC AE
r. Égalité – ✆ 05 63 57 32 77 – www.la-verrerie.com – contact@la-verrerie.com – Fax 05 63 57 32 27 – Closed 23-30 December 17 February-2 March
14 rm – €55/85 €55/85, €11
Rest – *(closed Saturday lunch, Sunday dinner and Friday)* Menu (€15 bi), €25 (weekdays)/44 – Carte €41/51
◆ This 200-year-old house built in the style of a Provençal farm was once a glassmaker's. Modern, practical rooms; choose one overlooking the park (bamboo grove). Up-to-the-minute cuisine served in a bright dining room or on the terrace.

Les Sarments VISA MC
27 r. Cabrol, behind St. Michel abbey – ✆ 05 63 57 62 61 – www.restaurantslessarments.com – sarments.les2@orange.fr – Fax 05 63 57 62 61 – Closed 21 December-18 January, 1-7 March, Tuesday dinner from October to February, Wednesday except lunch from March to September, Sunday dinner and Monday
Rest – *(number of covers limited, pre-book)* Menu (€25), €30/48 – Carte approx. €47
◆ Explore Gaillac wines at this medieval wine and spirits house next to the Maison des Vins. Vaulted restaurant adorned with work by the owner-artists. Traditional menu.

La Table du Sommelier VISA MC
34 pl. du Griffoul – ✆ 05 63 81 20 10 – www.latabledusommelier.com – latabledusommelier@orange.fr – Fax 05 63 81 20 10 – Closed Sunday and Monday
Rest – *(dinner only)* Menu €13, €16/34 bi – Carte approx. €24
◆ With such a name, there is no doubt that Bacchus is the guest star of this bistro-shop. Great wine list served by the glass or bottle. Market cuisine served.

GAILLAN-EN-MÉDOC – 33 Gironde – **335** F3 – **see Lesparre-Médoc**

GAILLON – 27 Eure – **304** I7 – **pop. 6 813 – alt. 15 m** – ✉ **27600** 33 **D2**
Normandy

Paris 94 – Les Andelys 13 – Rouen 48 – Évreux 25 – Vernon 15
Office de tourisme, 4, place Aristide Briand ✆ 02 32 53 08 25, Fax 02 32 53 08 25
 de Gaillon Les Artaignes, E : 1 km on D 515, ✆ 02 32 53 89 40

in Vieux-Villez West: 4 km by D 6015 – **pop. 160 – alt. 125 m** – ✉ **27600**

Château Corneille VISA MC
17 r. de l'Eglise – ✆ 02 32 77 44 77 – www.chateau-corneille.fr – chateau-corneille@orange.fr – Fax 02 32 77 48 79
18 rm – €89 €106, €11 – 2 suites
Rest *Closerie* – *✆ 02 32 77 42 97 (Closed 15-31 August and Saturday lunch)* Menu (€17), €23/35 – Carte €30/55
◆ This 18C manor house, surrounded by 100-year-old trees, combines comfort and modernity. The mahogany and pastel decorated rooms overlook the countryside. Traditional menu served in a converted sheepfold with brick walls, fireplace and beams.

GALÉRIA – 2B Haute-Corse – **345** A5 – **see Corse**

GALLARGUES-LE-MONTUEUX – 30 Gard – 339 J6 – pop. 2 957 – alt. 55 m – ✉ 30660 23 C2

▶ Paris 735 – Montpellier 36 – Nîmes 26 – Arles 51 – Alès 68

X Orchidéa

9 pl. Coudoulié – ✆ 04 66 73 34 07 – orchidea30@orange.fr – Closed Sunday

Rest – Menu (€ 18 bi), € 26/36

◆ Restaurant with the spirit of a table d'hôte, lively and relaxed, with cuisine that has accents from the Basque Country, the Camargue and Réunion. Rustic interior that has been modernised with an original touch.

GAMBAIS – 78 Yvelines – 311 G3 – pop. 2 064 – alt. 119 m – ✉ 78950 18 A2

▶ Paris 55 – Dreux 27 – Mantes-la-Jolie 32 – Rambouillet 22 – Versailles 38

XX Auberge du Clos St-Pierre

2 bis r. Goupigny – ✆ 01 34 87 10 55 – www.restaurant-clossaintpierre-78.com – clossaintpierre@wanadoo.fr – Fax 01 34 87 03 88 – Closed 1-24 August, Sunday dinner, Tuesday dinner and Monday

Rest – Menu € 55 – Carte € 32/65

◆ A guesthouse with a red façade serving traditional cuisine in a modern dining area or on the terrace, shaded by a linden tree.

GAN – 64 Pyrénées-Atlantiques – 342 J5 – pop. 5 225 – alt. 210 m – ✉ 64290 3 B3

▶ Paris 786 – Pau 10 – Arudy 17 – Lourdes 39 – Oloron-Ste-Marie 26

XX Hostellerie L'Horizon with rm

chemin Mesplet – ✆ 05 59 21 58 93 – www.hostellerie-horizon.com – eytpierre-hotelresto@wanadoo.fr – Fax 05 59 21 71 80 – Closed 2 January-13 February

10 rm – †€ 60/80 ††€ 65/85, ☕ € 8

Rest – *(Closed Sunday dinner, Tuesday lunch and Monday)* Menu (€ 16), € 28/68 bi – Carte € 50/60

◆ The veranda-dining room and fine terrace overlook a pleasant garden with palm trees; view of the Pyrenees in the distance in fine weather. Stylish rooms.

GANNAT – Allier – 326 G6 – pop. 5 881 – alt. 345 m – ✉ 03800 5 B1

Auvergne

▶ Paris 383 – Clermont-Ferrand 49 – Montluçon 78 – Moulins 58 – Vichy 20

ℹ Office de tourisme, 11, place Hennequin ✆ 04 70 90 17 78, Fax 04 70 90 19 45

◉ Gospel book★ au musée municipal (château) [at the town museum (castle)].

XX Le Frégénie

4 r. des Frères-Bruneau – ✆ 04 70 90 04 65 – www.le-fregenie.com – Fax 04 70 90 04 65 – Closed 24-31 August, 26 December-4 January, Sunday dinner and Monday dinner

Rest – Menu € 15 (lunch), € 24/43 – Carte € 30/45

◆ Situated in a quiet road, this impressive restaurant has two dining rooms decorated in crisp, classical style. Friendly service and contemporary cuisine.

GAP Ⓟ – 05 Hautes-Alpes – 334 E5 – pop. 37 200 – alt. 735 m – ✉ 05000 41 C1

French Alps

▶ Paris 665 – Avignon 209 – Grenoble 103 – Sisteron 52 – Valence 158

ℹ Office de tourisme, 2a, cours Frédéric Mistral ✆ 04 92 52 56 56, Fax 04 92 52 56 57

⛳ Alpes Provence Gap Bayard Station Gap Bayard, 7 km on the Grenoble road, ✆ 04 92 50 16 83

◉ Old town ★ - Musée départemental★.

GAP

Balmens (R.) . . . . Z 3
Carnot (R.) . . . . Z 4
Curie (Bd P. et M.). . . . . Y 5
Dumont (Av. du Cdt) . . . . Y 6
Euzières (Pl. Frédéric) . . . . . . Z 7
Eymar (R. Jean) . . . . Y 8
Faure-du-Serre (R.) . . . . Y 9
France (R. de) . . . . Y 10
Jean-Jaurès (Av.) . . . . Z 12
Ladoucette (Cours) . . . . Y 13
Libération (Bd de) . . . . Y 14
Mazel (R. du) . . . . Z 15
Moreau (R. E.) . . . . Z 16
Révelly (Pl. du) . . . . Y 17
Roux (R. Colonel) . . . . Z 19
St-Arnoux (Pl.) . . . . Z 20
Valserres (R. de). . . . . Z 23

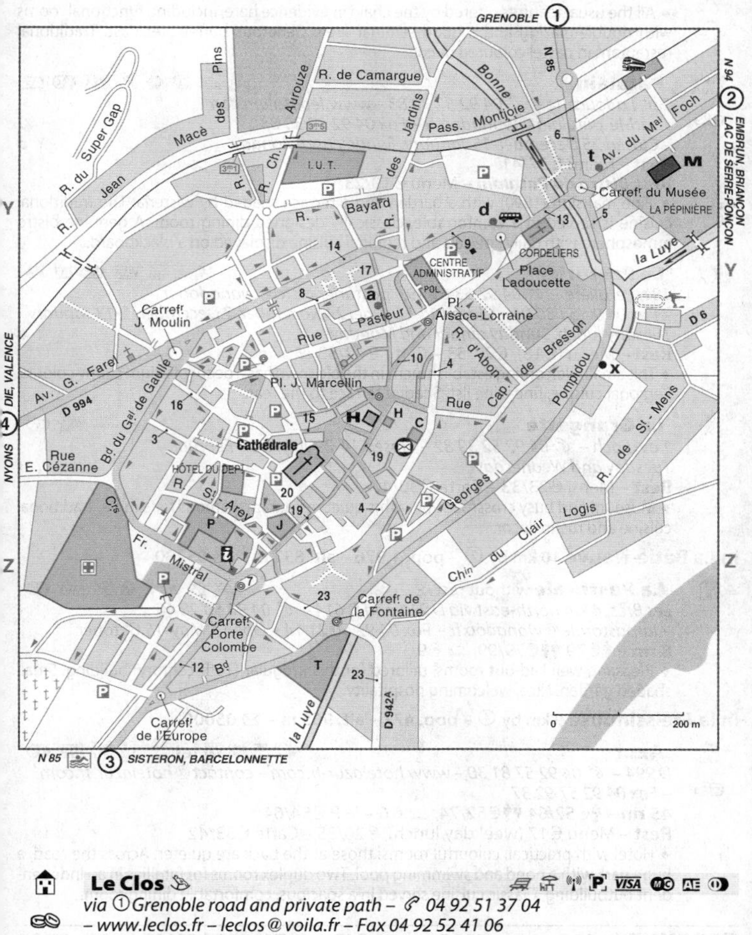

GRENOBLE ①
N 94 ② EMBRUN, BRIANÇON LAC DE SERRE-PONÇON
NYONS ④ DIE, VALENCE
N 85 ③ SISTERON, BARCELONNETTE

R. de Camargue
Pass. Montjoie
Av. du Mal Foch
Carreft du Musée
LA PÉPINIÈRE
CENTRE ADMINISTRATIF
CORDELIERS
Place Ladoucette
Carreft J. Moulin
Pl. Alsace-Lorraine
Pl. J. Marcellin
Cathédrale
HÔTEL DU DEPT
Carreft de la Fontaine
Carreft Porte Colombe
Carreft de l'Europe
Rue E. Cézanne
Av. G. Farel
D 994
D 942A
la Luye

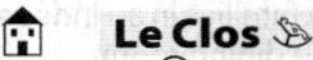

Le Clos 🐎
via ① Grenoble road and private path – ✆ 04 92 51 37 04
– www.leclos.fr – leclos@voila.fr – Fax 04 92 52 41 06
– Closed 20 October-24 November, Monday (except hotel) and Sunday dinner except July-August
28 rm – †€ 48/57 ††€ 52/60, ☕ € 9 **Rest** – Menu € 18/32
◆ This hotel on the outskirts of Gap has well-designed rooms (Wifi, flat-screen TVs), half with balconies. Trees in the garden and games for children. Large, rustic dining room with a veranda and a summer terrace.

Kyriad without rest
5 chemin des Matins Calmes, via ③: 2.5 km (near the swimming pool), rte Sisteron
– ✆ 04 92 51 57 82 – www.kyriad.fr – kyriad.gap@wanadoo.fr
– Fax 04 92 51 56 52
26 rm – †€ 59/75 ††€ 59/75, ☕ € 8
◆ At the entrance to Gap, on the Route Napoléon, a hotel with fresh, spacious rooms laid out around a garden where breakfast is served in fine weather.

Ibis rm, VISA

5 bd G. Pompidou – ✆ 04 92 53 57 57 – www.ibishotel.com – ibisgap@wanadoo.fr – Fax 04 92 53 38 15 Y **x**

61 rm – €54/73 €54/73, €8 **Rest** – Menu (€14), €17

◆ All the usual features offered by the chain in evidence here, including functional rooms with double-glazing and a good seminar area. Generous buffet breakfast. Traditional restaurant in pastel coloured decor.

Patalain VISA

2 pl. Ladoucette – ✆ 04 92 52 30 83 – www.lepatalain.com – sarl-le-patalain@wanadoo.fr – Fax 04 92 52 30 83 – Closed 25 December-15 January, Sunday and Monday Y **d**

Rest – Menu €37/41

Rest ***Bistro du Patalain*** – Menu €19/23

◆ Fine mansion (1890) with a garden and a terrace shaded by wisteria. The traditional cuisine is served in a comfortable, classically designed dining room. A genuine bistro atmosphere with daily specials and regional cuisine displayed on a blackboard.

Le Pasturier VISA

18 r. Pérolière – ✆ 04 92 53 69 29 – pasturier.resto@wanadoo.fr – Fax 04 92 53 30 91 – Closed 1st-16 June, 24 November-2 December, 5-13 January, Tuesday lunch, Sunday dinner and Monday Y **a**

Rest – Menu (€18), €27/53 – Carte €43/53

◆ This small, welcoming establishment in the old town has a decor of bright sunny colours. Regional cuisine, fine wine list. Shaded terrace to the rear.

La Grangette VISA

1 av. Foch – ✆ 04 92 52 39 82 – Closed 14-29 July, 8-20 February, Tuesday and Wednesday Y **t**

Rest – Menu €23/33 – Carte €30/40

◆ Museum and busy crossroads near this quiet restaurant. Famous for simple, traditional cuisine and rustic decor.

in La Bâtie-Neuve 10 km by ② – pop. 1 976 – alt. 852 m – ✉ 05230

La Pastorale without rest VISA

Les Brès, 4 km north-east via D 214 and D 614 – ✆ 04 92 50 28 40 – la-pastorale@wanadoo.fr – Fax 04 92 50 21 14 – Open 1 May-15 October

8 rm – €79 €79/99, €9

◆ Pleasant, well laid-out rooms, tailored for this irregular (16th century) building. Small shaded garden. Nice, welcoming hospitality.

in la Freissinouse 9 km by ④ – pop. 477 – alt. 965 m – ✉ 05000

Azur rest, VISA

D 994 – ✆ 04 92 57 81 30 – www.hotelazur-fr.com – contact@hotelazur-fr.com – Fax 04 92 57 92 37

45 rm – €52/64 €52/74, €6 – ½ P €54/64

Rest – Menu €17 (weekday lunch), €20/35 – Carte €33/42

◆ Hotel with practical, colourful rooms; those at the back are quieter. Across the road, a huge park with a pond and swimming pool. Two duplex rooms for families in an independent outbuilding. Classic cuisine served in a spacious, comfortable dining room.

GAPENNES – 80 Somme – 301 E6 – pop. 247 – alt. 76 m – ✉ 80150 36 A1

Paris 178 – Amiens 50 – Abbeville 17 – Berck 62 – Étaples 70

La Nicoulette without rest

7 r. de St-Riquier – ✆ 03 22 28 92 77 – http://nicoulette.com – nicoulette@wanadoo.fr – Fax 06 07 32 86 75 – Closed 11 November-28 February

5 rm – €76 €78

◆ Old Picardy farmhouse on the outskirts of the village offering well proportioned, ground floor rooms facing a pretty garden. Jacuzzi tub.

GARABIT (VIADUC) – 15 Cantal – 330 H5 – see Viaduc de Garabit

LA GARDE – 04 Alpes-de-Haute-Provence – 334 H10 – see Castellane

LA GARDE – 48 Lozère – 330 H5 – see St-Chély-d'Apcher

LA GARDE-ADHÉMAR – 26 Drôme – 332 B7 – pop. 1 128 44 B3
– alt. 178 m – ✉ 26700 Lyon - Rhone Valley

Paris 624 – Montélimar 24 – Nyons 42 – Pierrelatte 7
Syndicat d'initiative, le village ✆ 04 75 04 40 10
Church ★ - ≤★ from the terrace.

Le Logis de l'Escalin rm, rm, rm, VISA
1 km north on the D 572 – ✆ 04 75 04 41 32 – www.lescalin.com – info@lescalin.com – Fax 04 75 04 40 05 – Closed autumn school holidays and February holidays
14 rm – †€ 65/68 ††€ 68/80, ☕ € 12 – ½ P € 73/78
Rest – *(closed Sunday dinner and Monday)* Menu (€ 21 bi), € 27 (weekdays)/63 – Carte € 51/71
◆ Escalin, Baron de la Garde, Ambassador of Francis 1 might have been born in this farm. Rooms have every comfort and a pleasant, colourful decor. A Provençal dining room, warmed by an open fireplace, with a pleasant terrace in the shade of the plane trees.

LA GARDE-GUÉRIN – 48 Lozère – 330 L8 – ✉ 48800 23 C1
Languedoc-Roussillon-Tarn Gorges

Paris 610 – Alès 59 – Aubenas 69 – Florac 71 – Langogne 37 – Mende 55
Keep ✳★ - Belvédère du Chassezac (viewpoint)★★.

Auberge Régordane VISA
Prévenchères – ✆ 04 66 46 82 88 – www.regordane.com – aubergeregordane@orange.fr – Fax 04 66 46 90 29 – Open 11 April-11 October
16 rm – †€ 57 ††€ 57/68, ☕ € 9 – ½ P € 56/64
Rest – Menu € 20/39 – Carte € 37/50
◆ Nice interior with great character in this 16th century house, located in the heart of a fortified medieval village on the ancient Voie Regordane running between Auvergne and Languedoc. Granite vaults, spruce rustic decor and a pretty terrace lend the restaurant charm.

LA GARENNE-COLOMBES – 92 Hauts-de-Seine – 311 J2 – 101 – see Paris, Area

GARGAS – 84 Vaucluse – 332 F10 – pop. 2 980 – alt. 275 m – ✉ 84400 42 E1

Paris 735 – Marseille 107 – Avignon 53 – Aix-en-Provence 91 – Salon-de-Provence 58

Domaine La Coquillade ≤ VISA
– ✆ 04 90 74 71 71 – www.coquillade.fr – info@coquillade.fr – Fax 04 90 74 71 72 – Closed 11 January-26 March
13 rm – †€ 220/1190 ††€ 240/1210, ☕ € 15 – 15 suites – ††€ 350/1210
Rest – table d'hôte – Menu € 29 (lunch), € 46/72 – Carte € 54/65
◆ Situated on the wine estate, charming Provencal hamlet combining luxury with ecology. Refined guestrooms and suites, piano bar, works by well-known artists, pool... Superb table d'hôtes. Tasting and sale of regional wines in the cellar.

GARIDECH – 31 Haute-Garonne – 343 H2 – pop. 1 498 – alt. 180 m 29 C2
– ✉ 31380

Paris 687 – Toulouse 21 – Albi 58 – Auch 96

Le Club VISA
rte d'Albi – ✆ 05 61 84 20 23 – www.leclubchampetre.com – rest-leclub@wanadoo.fr – Fax 05 61 84 43 21 – Closed 18 August-1st September, 16-22 February, Saturday lunch, Sunday dinner and Monday
Rest – Menu (€ 17), € 27/42 – Carte € 43/55
◆ Family house in a garden set back from the main road. Charming rustic dining room. Terrace and veranda overlooking the countryside. Traditional menu.

GARNACHE – 85 Vendée – 316 F6 – see Challans

GARONS – 30 Gard – 339 L6 – see Nîmes

GARREVAQUES – 81 Tarn – 338 D10 – pop. 271 – alt. 192 m – ✉ 81700 29 C2

Paris 727 – Carcassonne 53 – Castres 31 – Toulouse 52

Le Pavillon du Château
Château de Garrevaques – ☎ 05 63 75 04 54
– www.garrevaques.com – m.c.combes@wanadoo.fr – Fax 05 63 70 26 44
15 rm – €150/220 €180/220, €15 – ½ P €110/130
Rest – *(closed Tuesday and Wednesday) (number of covers limited, pre-book)*
Menu (€17) – Carte €25/60
◆ This hotel is located in the outbuildings of a chateau, and is home to fine rooms with period or old-style furnishings. Superb spa with modern facilities. Modern cuisine served in a vaulted cellar.

Le Château de Garrevaques
– ☎ 05 63 75 04 54 – www.garrevaques.com
– m.c.combes@wanadoo.fr – Fax 05 63 70 26 44
15 rm – €170/200 €180/220, €15 – ½ P €110/130
◆ Refined, plush rooms available in this 16th century chateau, renovated in the 19th century. Pleasant, lovely park.

GARRIGUES – 34 Hérault – 339 J6 – pop. 153 – alt. 62 m – ✉ 34160 23 C2

Paris 756 – Montpellier 37 – Nîmes 46 – Alès 51 – Lunel 21

Château de Roumanières without rest
pl. de la Mairie – ☎ 04 67 86 49 70 – www.chateauroumanieres.com
– gravegeal.amelie@wanadoo.fr
5 rm – €75/98 €80/98
◆ This family property, a fortified farmhouse adjoining a wine estate, boasted two towers in the 13C, hence its château status. The guestrooms have an admirable blend of old and new.

GASNY – 27 Eure – 304 J7 – pop. 2 860 – alt. 36 m – ✉ 27620 33 D2

Paris 77 – Évreux 43 – Mantes-la-Jolie 20 – Rouen 71 – Vernon 10 – Versailles 67

de Villarceaux Chaussy Château du Couvent, N : 11 km on D 37, ☎ 01 34 67 73 83

Auberge du Prieuré Normand
1 pl. de la République – ☎ 02 32 52 10 01 – www.aubergeduprieurenormand.com
– prieure.normand@wanadoo.fr – Closed Tuesday dinner and Wednesday
Rest – Menu (€19), €26/45 – Carte approx. €48
◆ From Roche-Guyon, the road winds through rocky chalkland to this pleasant village inn serving well-prepared, traditional cuisine.

GASSIN – 83 Var – 340 O6 – pop. 2 800 – alt. 200 m – ✉ 83580 41 C3

French Riviera

Paris 872 – Fréjus 34 – Le Lavandou 31 – St-Tropez 9 – Ste-Maxime 14 – Toulon 69

Gassin Golf Country Club Route de Ramatuelle, ☎ 04 94 55 13 44

Terrasse des Barri ★.

Moulins de Paillas ★★ Southeast: 3,5 km.

Auberge la Verdoyante
866 chemin vicinal Coste Brigade – ☎ 04 94 56 16 23
– la.verdoyante@wanadoo.fr – Fax 04 94 56 43 10 – Open mid February-mid November and closed Monday-Thursday in February and March, Monday lunch and Wednesday from April to mid November
Rest – Menu €28/50 – Carte approx. €52
◆ Inn nestling in greenery. Appetizing regional cuisine served on the terrace overlooking the bay of St Tropez or in a charming Provençal decor with fireplace.

GAURIAC – 33 Gironde – 335 H4 – pop. 826 – alt. 50 m – ✉ 33710 3 B1

Paris 551 – Blaye 11 – Bordeaux 42 – Jonzac 57 – Libourne 38

La Filadière

rte de la Corniche, 2 km west on the D 669[E1] – ☎ 05 57 64 94 05 – www.lafiladiere.com – la-filadiere@wanadoo.fr – Fax 05 57 64 94 06 – Closed Sunday dinner, Tuesday and Wednesday

Rest – Menu € 31/34 – Carte € 30/65

◆ The panoramic terrace on the banks of the Gironde estuary is a major plus point for this restaurant located in what was once an oil storage complex.

GAVARNIE – 65 Hautes-Pyrénées – 342 L8 – pop. 154 – alt. 1 350 m – Winter sports : 1 350/2 400 m ⛷ 11 ⛷ – ✉ 65120 28 A3

Languedoc-Roussillon-Tarn Gorges

Paris 901 – Lourdes 52 – Luz-St-Sauveur 20 – Pau 96 – Tarbes 71

Office de tourisme, le village ☎ 05 62 92 48 05, Fax 05 62 92 42 47

Village★ - Cirque de Gavarnie★★★ South: 3 h 30.

Vignemale without rest

chemin du Cirque – ☎ 05 62 92 40 00 – www.hotel-vignemale.com – hotel.vignemale@orange.fr – Fax 05 62 92 40 08 – Open 15 May-30 September

24 rm – †€ 150 ††€ 150/350, ☕ € 15

◆ Massive stone building (1902) overlooking the cirque of Gavarnie. Functional bedrooms. Pine trees and horses on the estate.

GAZERAN – 78 Yvelines – 311 G4 – see Rambouillet

GÉMENOS – 13 Bouches-du-Rhône – 340 I6 – pop. 5 485 – alt. 150 m – ✉ 13420 Provence 40 B3

Paris 788 – Aix-en-Provence 39 – Brignoles 48 – Marseille 25 – Toulon 50

Syndicat d'initiative, cours Pasteur ☎ 04 42 32 18 44, Fax 04 42 32 15 49

Parc de St-Pons★ East: 3 km.

Relais de la Magdeleine

rd-pt de la Madeleine, N 396 – ☎ 04 42 32 20 16 – www.relais-magdeleine.com – contact@relais-magdeleine.com – Fax 04 42 32 02 26 – Open 15 March-15 November

28 rm – †€ 100/150 ††€ 110/220, ☕ € 15

Rest – *(closed Monday lunch and Wednesday lunch)* Menu € 35 (weekday lunch), € 45/55 – Carte € 55/80

◆ Provence can be felt throughout this stylish 18C house with its antique furniture, floor tiles, paintings, drapes... right down to the cicadas chirping in the garden! Classic food and refined decor characterise this restaurant.

Bed & Suites without rest

au parc d'activités de Gémenos, Sud : 2 km, (250 av. Château de Jouques) – ☎ 04 42 32 72 73 – www.bestwestern-gemenos.com – bedandsuites@voila.fr – Fax 04 42 32 72 74

29 rm – †€ 85/125 ††€ 85/125, ☕ € 12

◆ New hotel with an ochre façade. Modern and simple Provençal and nautical inspired rooms; some have balconies and terraces. Front rooms quieter.

Du Parc

Vallée St-Pons, 1 km via D 2 – ☎ 04 42 32 20 38 – www.hotel-parc-gemenos.com – hotel.parc.gemenos@wanadoo.fr – Fax 04 42 32 10 26

13 rm – †€ 51/57 ††€ 58/63, ☕ € 8,50 – ½ P € 58/73

Rest – Menu (€ 13), € 17 (weekday lunch), € 27/37 – Carte € 40/64

◆ Not far from St Pons park, in a garden set back from the road, this pleasant, lively establishment has colourful rooms. Regional specialities served in a spacious restaurant or on the shaded terrace.

GENAS – 69 Rhône – 327 J5 – pop. 11 700 – alt. 218 m – see Lyon

GÉNÉRARGUES – 30 Gard – 339 I4 – see Anduze

GENESTON – 44 Loire-Atlantique – 316 G5 – pop. 3 380 – alt. 28 m 34 B2
– ✉ 44140

Paris 398 – Cholet 60 – Nantes 20 – La Roche-sur-Yon 47

Le Pélican

13 pl. G. Gaudet – ✆ 02 40 04 77 88 – Fax 02 40 04 77 88 – Closed 31 July-28 August, 15-26 February, Sunday dinner, Monday and Tuesday

Rest – Menu € 20/30

◆ Behind this smart painted wood façade are two small dining rooms, renovated in shades of blue and yellow. Updated cuisine with regional inspiration.

GENEUILLE – 25 Doubs – 321 F3 – see Besançon

GENILLÉ – 37 Indre-et-Loire – 317 P5 – pop. 1 509 – alt. 88 m 11 B3
– ✉ 37460 Châteaux of the Loire

Paris 239 – Tours 48 – Blois 57 – Châtellerault 67 – Loches 12

Syndicat d'initiative, 17, place Agnès Sorel ✆ 02 47 59 57 85, Fax 02 47 59 57 85

Agnès Sorel with rm

6 pl. Agnès Sorel – ✆ 02 47 59 50 17 – www.agnessorel.com – agnessorel@wanadoo.fr – Fax 02 47 59 59 50 – Closed 4-13 October, 2 January-1 February, Tuesday from September to June, Sunday dinner and Monday except August

3 rm – †€ 45/59 ††€ 45/59, ☕ € 8

Rest – Menu (€ 21), € 26/57 – Carte € 43/57

◆ A local-style house with two pleasant dining rooms, serving tasty up-to-date cuisine.

GÉNIN (LAC) – 01 Ain – 328 H3 – see Oyonnax

GENNES – 49 Maine-et-Loire – 317 H4 – pop. 1 952 – alt. 28 m 35 C2
– ✉ 49350 Châteaux of the Loire

Paris 305 – Angers 33 – Bressuire 65 – Cholet 68 – La Flèche 46 – Saumur 20

Office de tourisme, square de l'Europe ✆ 02 41 51 84 14

Church ★★ of Cunault Southeast: 2.5 km - Church ★ of Trèves-Cunault Southeast: 3 km.

Les Naulets d'Anjou

18 r. Croix de Mission – ✆ 02 41 51 81 88 – www.hotel-lesnauletsdanjou.com – lesnauletsdanjou@wanadoo.fr – Fax 02 41 38 00 78 – Closed 23 December-31 January

19 rm – †€ 50/56 ††€ 50/56, ☕ € 8,50 – ½ P € 47/51

Rest – *(closed Wednesday from 15 October to 15 April) (dinner only)* Menu € 17, € 21/38 – Carte € 25/31

◆ A 1970s building in the upper part of the village, an ideal stopover between Anjou and Saumurois. Bright modern restaurant with a balcony-terrace overlooking the pool and garden. Simple, traditional cuisine.

L'Aubergade

7 av. des Cadets – ✆ 02 41 51 81 07 – www.restaurant-laubergade.com – bodinjeanfrancois@wanadoo.fr – Closed Toussaint holiday and winter holiday

Rest – Menu (€ 18), € 27/68 – Carte € 50/75

◆ Back to his roots after living in South America, the establishment's owner-chef concocts up-to-the-minute dishes, skilfully mingling local produce and world flavours.

GENNEVILLE – 14 Calvados – 303 M4 – pop. 718 – alt. 90 m 32 A3
– ✉ 14600

Paris 189 – Caen 61 – Le Havre 28 – Lisieux 30 – Fécamp 51

Le Grand Clos de St-Martin without rest

Hameau St-Martin – ✆ 02 31 87 80 44 – www.legrandclosdesaintmartin.com – legrandclosdesaintmartin@wanadoo.fr – Fax 02 31 87 80 44

3 rm ☕ – †€ 75 ††€ 85

◆ Gardens, a lake, apple trees and horses all make up the authentic Norman countryside that surrounds this lovely, peaceful half-timbered house. Cosy rooms, home-made breakfast.

GENSAC – 33 Gironde – **335** L6 – **pop. 844** – **alt. 78 m** – ✉ **33890** 4 **C1**

Paris 554 – Bergerac 39 – Bordeaux 63 – Libourne 33 – La Réole 34

Office de tourisme, 5, place de la Mairie ✆ 05 57 47 46 67, Fax 05 57 47 46 63

XX **Remparts** with rm rm, VISA AE

16 r. Château – ✆ 05 57 47 43 46 – www.lesremparts.net – info@lesremparts.net – Fax 05 57 47 46 76 – Closed 1st January-4 March – ½ P € 64/76

Rest – *(closed Sunday dinner, Monday and lunch except Sunday)* Menu € 25, € 27/32 – Carte € 20/32

◆ An English chef runs this characteristic restaurant near the church. Traditional fare in a pleasant understated dining room, furnished with rustic chairs. Great view of the valley. Pleasant rooms housed in a medieval presbytery in the shadow of a bell tower. Well-tended garden.

North 2 km by D16 and D130 (Juillac road) – ✉ **33890 Juillac**

XX **Le Belvédère** VISA AE

– ✆ 05 57 47 40 33 – www.restaurantlebelvedere.fr – le-belvedere@wanadoo.fr – Fax 05 57 47 48 07 – Closed October, Tuesday except at lunch in July-August and Wednesday

Rest – Menu € 19 bi (weekdays)/58 – Carte € 31/61

◆ This immense chalet overlooks a meander in the Dordogne. Welcoming restaurant with a distinctly rustic feel and pleasant viewpoint terrace. Regional-inspired fare.

Southwest 2 km by D18 and D15[E1] – ✉ **33350 Ste-Radegonde**

Château de Sanse rest, VISA AE

– ✆ 05 57 56 41 10 – www.chateaudesanse.com – contact@chateaudesanse.com – Fax 05 57 56 41 29 – Closed 1st January-28 February

12 rm – € 100/135 € 100/135, € 12 – 4 suites – ½ P € 87/130

Rest – *(closed November and December except Saturday dinner and Sunday lunch and Wednesday and Thursday except from May to September)* Menu (€ 19), € 27 (weekday lunch)/35 – Carte € 37/50 dinner only

◆ This noble 18C building built of white stone enjoys views of the surrounding countryside and vineyards. Attractive grounds and swimming pool. Modern, spacious and quiet bedrooms full of character. Up-to-date cuisine served in a pleasant modern veranda or on a high-perched terrace.

GÉRARDMER – **88 Vosges** – **314** J4 – **pop. 8 845** – **alt. 669 m** – **Winter sports : 660/1 350 m** 31 – **Casino** AZ – ✉ **88400** 27 **C3**

Alsace-Lorraine

Paris 425 – Belfort 78 – Colmar 52 – Épinal 40 – St-Dié 27 – Thann 50

Office de tourisme, 4, place des Déportés ✆ 03 29 27 27 27, Fax 03 29 27 23 25

Gerardmer lake ★ - Longemer lake ★ - Saut des Cuves★ East: 3 km by ①.

Plan on following page

Le Grand Hôtel VISA AE

pl. du Tilleul – ✆ 03 29 63 06 31 – www.grandhotel-gerardmer.com – contact@grandhotel-gerardmer.com – Fax 03 29 63 46 81 AZ **f**

61 rm – € 78/130 € 98/195, € 16 – 14 suites

Rest *Le Pavillon Pétrus* – *(dinner only except Sunday and holidays)* Menu € 45, € 60/90 – Carte € 46/88

Rest *L'Assiette du Coq à l'Âne* – Menu (€ 15 bi), € 18 (weekdays)/28 – Carte € 29/42

Rest *Le Grand Cerf* – *(dinner only except Sunday and holidays)* Menu € 26

◆ An impressive19C edifice set in a tree-lined garden provides the backdrop to snug, stylish rooms. Lovely suites that mix contemporary and mountain influences in a chalet. An elegant setting and modern dishes at Le Pavillon Pétrus. Pretty, regional decor and local specialities on offer at l'Assiette du Coq à l'Âne. Classic food on offer at the Grand Cerf.

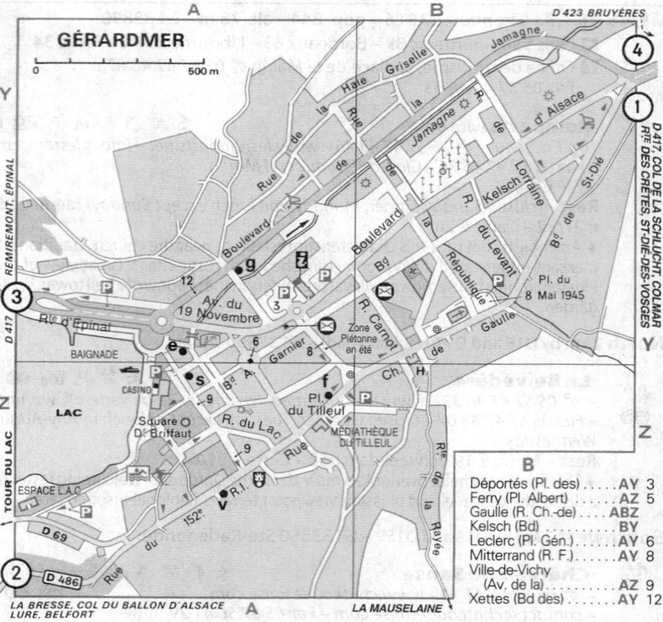

GÉRARDMER

A B
D 423 BRUYÈRES
D 417, COL DE LA SCHLUCHT, COLMAR
RTE DES CRÊTES, ST-DIÉ-DES-VOSGES
REMIREMONT, ÉPINAL
TOUR DU LAC
LA BRESSE, COL DU BALLON D'ALSACE
LURE, BELFORT
LA MAUSELAINE

Déportés (Pl. des) . . . . AY 3
Ferry (Pl. Albert) . . . . AZ 5
Gaulle (R. Ch.-de) . . . . ABZ
Kelsch (Bd) . . . . BY
Leclerc (Pl. Gén.) . . . . AY 6
Mitterrand (R. F.) . . . . . AY 8
Ville-de-Vichy (Av. de la) . . . . AZ 9
Xettes (Bd des) . . . . . AY 12

Le Manoir au Lac ⊗ rm, AC rest,

chemin de la Droite du Lac, 1 km Épinal road via ③
– ✆ 03 29 27 10 20 – www.manoir-au-lac.com
– contact@manoir-au-lac.com – Fax 03 29 27 10 27
VISA MC AE

12 rm – †€ 150/200 ††€ 150/300, ☕ € 20 – ½ P € 130/250

Rest – *(closed Sunday and Monday) (dinner only) (residents only)* Menu € 30

◆ Typical Vosges chalet from 1830 in a park where Maupassant used to stay. Guesthouse atmosphere, piano, fine furniture, stylish guestrooms and superb view of the lake. Tearoom.

Beau Rivage VISA MC AE

esplanade du Lac – ✆ 03 29 63 22 28 – www.hotel-beaurivage.fr
– hotel-beau-rivage@wanadoo.fr – Fax 03 29 63 29 83 AY **e**

51 rm – †€ 67/159 ††€ 85/189, ☕ € 12 – 1 suite

Rest *Côté Lac* – *(closed Saturday lunch and Friday off season, school holidays and holidays)* Menu (€ 25), € 41 (lunch), € 48/75 – Carte € 56/105

Rest *Le Toit du Lac* – *(closed Wednesday off season, school holidays and holidays)* Carte € 36/50

◆ From comfortable standard rooms to lavish suites overlooking the lake, a contemporary spirit reigns throughout this tasteful establishment. Luxurious spa. Modern cuisine served in a smart setting with an elegant fashionable design. Lounge bar and grilled plancha cooking.

Jamagne AC VISA MC AE

2 bd Jamagne – ✆ 03 29 63 36 86 – www.jamagne.com
– hotel@jamagne.com – Fax 03 29 60 05 87
– Closed 15 November-18 December AY **g**

48 rm – †€ 55/75 ††€ 65/110, ☕ € 10

Rest – *(closed Friday lunch except school holidays)* Menu € 16/45 – Carte € 26/53

◆ From the fully refurbished rooms to the brand new wellness centre, this hotel, run by the same family since 1905, is clearly devoted to relaxation. Enjoy traditional cuisine and local specialities and wines in a large room decorated in sunny colours.

Gérard d'Alsace without rest
14 r. du 152ᵉ R.I. – ✆ 03 29 63 02 38 – www.hotel-gerard-dalsace.com – contact@hotel-gerard-dalsace.com – Fax 03 29 60 85 21 – Closed 3-9 April and 27 June-10 July AZ **v**
13 rm – †€ 55/70 ††€ 55/70, ☕ € 8
◆ The recent renovation has borne fruit: you will find an attentive welcome, snug, charming and modern rooms, all of which are perfectly soundproofed.

Paix rest, VISA
6 av. Ville-de-Vichy – ✆ 03 29 63 38 78 – www.hoteldelapaix.fr – hotel.delapaix@wanadoo.fr – Fax 03 29 63 18 53 AZ **s**
24 rm – †€ 53/88 ††€ 60/95, ☕ € 8,50 – ½ P € 59/81
Rest *Bistrot des Bateliers* – *(closed Sunday dinner and Monday except school holidays and public holidays)* Menu (€ 12), € 21/32 – Carte € 22/40
◆ Family hotel opposite the lake and casino offers refurbished rooms for stopovers. Access to the indoor pool, spa and massage facilities of the Beau Rivage next door. Appetising specials, a view of the lake, and a bistro atmosphere.

Les Reflets du Lac without rest VISA
201 chemin du Tour du Lac, at the end of the lake, 2.5 km via ③ – ✆ 03 29 60 31 50 – www.lesrefletsdulac.com – contact@lesrefletsdulac.com – Fax 03 29 60 31 51 – Closed 15 November-15 December
14 rm – †€ 49/57 ††€ 49/57, ☕ € 6,50
◆ The restful view of the lake from most of the rooms is undoubtedly the highpoint of the establishment. The rooms are decorated simply, faultlessly kept and quite comfortable.

in Xonrupt-Longemer 4 km by ① – pop. 1 557 – alt. 714 m – ✉ 88400

Les Jardins de Sophie - Domaine de la Moineaudière
rte du Valtin, 4 km north-west on D23 and secondary road – ✆ 03 29 63 37 11 – www.hotel-lesjardinsdesophie.com – jardinsdesophie@compagnie-dhdl.com – Fax 03 29 63 17 63 VISA
32 rm – †€ 100/220 ††€ 150/250, ☕ € 17 – ½ P € 129/182
Rest – *(closed Tuesday dinner and Wednesday in low season and outwith school holidays)* Menu € 30 (weekday lunch), € 45/75 – Carte € 65/85
◆ Nestling amongst spruce trees, this fully revamped luxury hotel is both sophisticated and cosy. Tasteful blend of Alpine and designer-inspired decor. A warm wood interior highlights the minimalist elegance of the restaurant's tables. Updated cuisine.

La Devinière without rest
318 montée des Broches – ✆ 03 29 63 23 89 – www.chambredhote-deviniere.com – feltzsylvie@hotmail.com
5 rm ☕ – †€ 63/83 ††€ 68/88
◆ This restored farm is known for its peacefulness, the view of the forest, and its wellness centre (Finnish sauna). Five large rooms, including one for families.

in Bas-Rupts 4 km by ② – ✉ 88400 Gérardmer

Les Bas-Rupts (Michel Philippe) rest, A/C rest, VISA
181 rte de la Bresse – ✆ 03 29 63 09 25 – www.bas-rupts.com – basrupts@relaischateaux.com – Fax 03 29 63 00 40
21 rm – †€ 150/180 ††€ 150/220, ☕ € 22 – 4 suites – ½ P € 150/255
Rest – *(pre-book Sat - Sun)* Menu € 35 (weekday lunch), € 52/98 – Carte € 60/100
Spec. Tripes au riesling à la crème et moutarde. Fricassée de poulet de Bresse au vin jaune et morilles. Moelleux chocolat, crème glacée à la cannelle. **Wines** Muscat d'Alsace, Pinot noir d'Alsace.
◆ A wood façade, fine Austrian-style rustic décor, pleasant rooms with personal touches, indoor pool, sauna and steam bath: this chalet is both cosy and comfortable. Smart country restaurant that features regional dishes with an inventive twist.

Cap Sud VISA
144 rte de la Bresse – ✆ 03 29 63 06 83 – www.capsud-bellemaree.fr – olivier.colonna@club.fr – Fax 03 29 63 20 76 – Closed Monday except bank holidays
Rest – Menu (€ 16), € 28/52 – Carte € 30/48
◆ A port of call in the Vosges: portholes and mahogany liner fittings in the dining room, view of the mountains from the veranda, and Mediterranean inspired cuisine.

GERBEROY – 60 Oise – 305 C3 – pop. 102 – alt. 180 m – ✉ 60380 36 A2

Paris 110 – Aumale 30 – Beauvais 22 – Breteuil 37 – Compiègne 82 – Rouen 62

Hostellerie du Vieux Logis

25 r. Logis du Roy – ✆ 03 44 82 71 66 – www.hostellerieduvieuxlogis.com – vieux.logis@worldonline.fr – Fax 03 44 82 61 65 – Closed Christmas and February school holidays, dinner except Saturday from November to March, Tuesday dinner, Sunday dinner and Wednesday

Rest – Menu (€ 25), € 25/48 – Carte € 47/60

◆ House at the entrance to the old fortified village now invaded by flowers, painters and tourists. Fireplace and exposed beams brighten the restaurant.

GERMIGNY-L'ÉVÊQUE – 77 Seine-et-Marne – 312 G2 – see Meaux

GESTEL – 56 Morbihan – 308 K8 – pop. 2 472 – alt. 47 m – ✉ 56530 9 B2

Paris 510 – Rennes 158 – Vannes 65 – Lorient 13 – Lanester 13

Piscine et Golf without rest

6 allée Kerguestenen, 3 km south-east on D 163 and secondary road – ✆ 02 97 05 15 03 – kerguestenen.pagesperso-orange.fr – ng.gwen@tiscali.fr – Fax 02 97 05 15 03 – Closed 9-18 January

4 rm – †€ 59/74 ††€ 59/74

◆ This peaceful house in a residential estate is home to pleasant, theme-decorated rooms (Roses, Angels) overlooking the golf course. Small heated pool (30°C) with counter current.

GÉTIGNÉ – 44 Loire-Atlantique – 316 I5 – see Clisson

LES GETS – 74 Haute-Savoie – 328 N4 – pop. 1 332 – alt. 1 170 m – Winter sports : 1 170/2 000 m 5 47 – ✉ 74260 French Alps 46 F1

Paris 579 – Annecy 77 – Bonneville 33 – Cluses 19 – Morzine 7 – Thonon-les-Bains 36

Office de tourisme, place de la Mairie ✆ 04 50 75 80 80, Fax 04 50 79 76 90

des Gets Les Chavannes, E : 3 km, ✆ 04 50 75 87 63

Mont Chéry ✱★★.

Le Labrador

rte de La Turche – ✆ 04 50 75 80 00 – www.labrador-hotel.com – info@labrador-hotel.com – Fax 04 50 79 87 03 – Open 21 June-7 September and 20 December-13 April

23 rm – †€ 130/230 ††€ 190/290

Rest *Le St-Laurent* – *(dinner only except summer)* Menu € 28, € 38/80 – Carte € 36/62

◆ This chalet with a pretty garden offers numerous services and leisure opportunities. Richly decorated lounge and rooms with balconies, often with a mountain view. Modern cuisine and grills prepared before your very eyes in the Savoy-style dining room.

La Marmotte

61 r. du Chêne – ✆ 04 50 75 80 33 – www.hotel-marmotte.com – info@hotel-marmotte.com – Fax 04 50 75 83 26 – Open 27 June-30 August and 20 December-19 April

48 rm – †€ 170/279 ††€ 255/372, € 12

Rest – *(dinner only) (resident only)* Menu € 30, € 50/70

◆ After a day's skiing relax near the fireplace before treating yourself to the superb spa (750sq.m). Recently refurbished and cosy rooms featuring woodwork. Restaurant looking out onto the ski slopes.

Mont Chéry without rest

421 r. du Centre – ✆ 04 50 75 80 75 – www.hotelmontchery.com – hotelmontchery@orange.fr – Fax 04 50 79 70 13 – Open 21 December-29 March

27 rm – †€ 120/200 ††€ 170/280

◆ At the foot of the ski lifts, spruce rooms with chic Alpine decor. Those in the chalet category look out over the ski slopes. Panoramic jacuzzi and pool, sauna.

Alpina rest, VISA

55 imp. de la Grange-Neuve – ✆ 04 50 75 80 22 – www.hotelalpina.fr – resa@hotelalpina.fr – Fax 04 50 75 83 48 – Open 25 May-25 September and 15 December-15 April

32 rm – €67/87 €93/156, €9 – 1 suite – ½ P €78/128

Rest – Menu €21 (weekday lunch), €26/38 – Carte €32/52

◆ This chalet-hotel which dominates the town offers mainly large rooms, redecorated in a gay, modern Savoy style. A pleasant garden in the summer. A welcoming decor in warm colours awaits you in the two dining rooms. Cuisine with a local flavour.

Crychar VISA AE

136 impasse de la Grange-Neuve, via rte La Turche – ✆ 04 50 75 80 50 – www.crychar.com – info@crychar.com – Fax 04 50 79 83 12 – Open 1 July-5 September and 19 December-19 April

14 rm – €95/168 €126/225, €12 – 1 suite – ½ P €105/160

Rest – *(dinner only) (resident only)* Menu €38

◆ With the snow in winter and green Alps in the summer, this little building has simple rooms with balconies in surroundings that are popular with sporty types. Restaurant with pretty neo-Savoy style décor: exposed beams, pale wood and hand-woven fabrics.

Régina rest, VISA AE

534 r. du Centre – ✆ 04 50 75 80 44 – www.hotelregina74.com – hotelpla@wanadoo.fr – Fax 04 50 79 87 29 – Open 29 June-5 September and 21 December-12 April

21 rm – €58/82 €67/110, €10 – ½ P €63/93

Rest – *(closed Tuesday lunch and Wednesday lunch)* Menu €18 (weekday lunch), €22/38 – Carte €30/44

◆ One of the first hotels opened in the resort and run by the same family since 1937; the current owner is also an alpine guide. Simple rooms and a warm friendly ambience. An all wood decor and fireplace in the restaurant; classic dishes and local specialities.

GEVREY-CHAMBERTIN – 21 Côte-d'Or – 320 J6 – pop. 3 120 – alt. 275 m – ✉ 21220 Burgundy-Jura   8 D1

Paris 315 – Beaune 33 – Dijon 13 – Dole 61

Office de tourisme, 1, rue Gaston Roupnel ✆ 03 80 34 38 40, Fax 03 80 34 15 49

Plan on following page

Arts et Terroirs without rest VISA AE

28 rte de Dijon – ✆ 03 80 34 30 76 – www.arts-et-terroirs.com – arts-et-terroirs@wanadoo.fr – Fax 03 80 34 11 79 B **e**

20 rm – €69/89 €69/89, €11

◆ Most of the appealing, renovated rooms overlook a peaceful garden. Three face the road but are well soundproofed. Chesterfield sitting room with piano.

Grands Crus without rest AC VISA AE

r. de Lavaux – ✆ 03 80 34 34 15 – www.hoteldesgrandscrus.com – hotel.lesgrandscrus@nerim.net – Fax 03 80 51 89 07 – Open from March to November A **c**

24 rm – €80/90 €80/90, €12

◆ The vineyards of the great vintages are just next to this warm village house surrounded by a pretty flower garden. Comfortable rooms and a salon with plenty of character.

Chez Guy AC VISA

3 pl. de la Mairie – ✆ 03 80 58 51 51 – www.hotel-bourgogne.com – chez-guy@hotel-bourgogne.com – Fax 03 80 58 50 39 A **z**

Rest – Menu (€26), €29/50

◆ Fine choice of Burgundies available to accompany the updated regional cuisine at this modern restaurant. The decor includes colourful paintings on a culinary theme and a decorative fireplace.

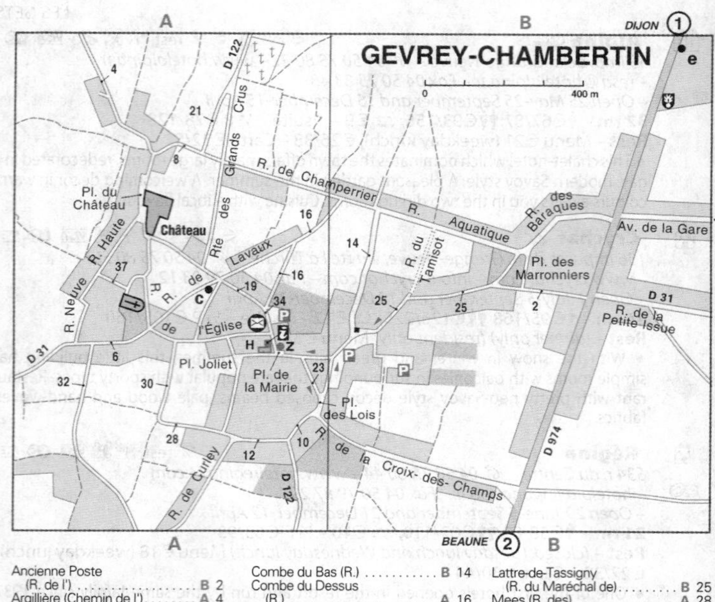

Ancienne Poste (R. de l') . . . . B 2
Argillière (Chemin de l') . . . . A 4
Aumonerie (R. de l') . . . . A 6
Caron (R. du) . . . . A 8
Chambertin (R. du) . . . . A 10
Chêne (R. du) . . . . A 12
Combe du Bas (R.) . . . . B 14
Combe du Dessus (R.) . . . . A 16
Docteur-Magnon-Pujo (R. du) . . . . A 19
En Songe (R. d') . . . . A 21
Gaizot (R. du) . . . . A 23
Lattre-de-Tassigny (R. du Maréchal de) . . . . B 25
Mees (R. des) . . . . A 28
Meixvelle (R. de) . . . . A 30
Planteligone (R. de) . . . . A 32
Roupnel (R. Gaston) . . . . A 34
Tison (R. du) . . . . A 37

GEX – 01 Ain – **328** J3 – pop. 8 913 – alt. 626 m – ✉ 01170 46 **F1**

Burgundy-Jura

Paris 490 – Genève 19 – Lons-le-Saunier 93 – Pontarlier 110 – St-Claude 42

Office de tourisme, square Jean Clerc ✆ 04 50 41 53 85, Fax 04 50 41 81 00

de Maison-Blanche ÉchenevexS : 3 km on D 984, ✆ 04 50 42 44 42

in Echenevex 4 km south on the D 984ᶜ and minor road – pop. 1 197 – alt. 580 m – ✉ 01170

Auberge des Chasseurs

Naz Dessus – ✆ 04 50 41 54 07 – www.aubergedeschasseurs.com – aubergedeschasseurs@wanadoo.fr – Fax 04 50 41 90 61 – Open 1st March-16 November and closed Sunday dinner and Monday except July - August

15 rm – €80 €100/160, €12 – ½ P €105/130

Rest – *(closed Sunday dinner except July-August, Tuesday lunch, Wednesday lunch and Monday) (pre-book)* Menu (€15), €33/45 – Carte €45/75

◆ A charming ivy clad country house whose fine interior features painted ceilings, photos by Cartier Bresson, and other works of art. Individually decorated rooms. Friendly rustic restaurant and attractive terrace with views of Mont Blanc.

GICOURT – 60 Oise – **305** F4 – see Clermont

see Clermont

GIEN – 45 Loiret – **318** M5 – pop. 15 300 – alt. 162 m – ✉ 45500 12 **C2**

Châteaux of the Loire

Paris 149 – Auxerre 85 – Bourges 77 – Cosne-sur-Loire 46 – Orléans 70

Office de tourisme, place Jean Jaurès ✆ 02 38 67 25 28, Fax 02 38 38 23 16

Château★: musée de la Chasse★★, château terrace ≤★ M - Bridge ≤★.

Pont-canal★★ de Briare: 10 km by ②.

GIEN

Anne-de-Beaujeu (R.) . . . . Z 2
Bildstein (R. du Lt.) . . . . Y 3
Briqueteries (R. des) . . . . Y
Château (Pl. du) . . . . Z
Clemenceau (R. G.) . . . . Z 5
Curie (Pl.) . . . . Y
Gambetta (R.) . . . . Z 6
Hôtel-de-Ville (R. de l') . . . . . Z 7
Jeanne-d'Arc (R.) . . . . YZ
Jean-Jaurès (Pl.) . . . . Z 9
Joffre (Q. du Mar.) . . . . Z
Leclerc (Av. du Mar.) . . . . Z 12
Lenoir (Quai) . . . . Z
Louis-Blanc (R.) . . . . Z 13
Marienne (R. de l'Adj.-Chef) . . Z 15
Montbricon (R. de) . . . . YZ
Noé (R. de) . . . . Y
Paris (R. de) . . . . YZ
Paul-Bert (R.) . . . . Z 16
Président-Wilson (Av.) . . . . . . Y 17
République (Av. de la) . . . . . . Y 19
Thiers (R.) . . . . Z 23
Verdun (R. de) . . . . Y
Victor-Hugo (R.) . . . . Z 24
Vieille Boucherie (R.) . . . . . . Z 25
Villejean (R. J.) . . . . Y

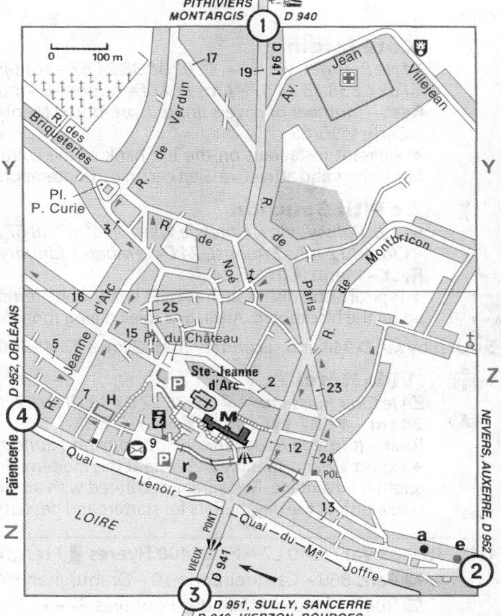

Rivage without rest — VISA AE
1 quai de Nice – ✆ 02 38 37 79 00 – hoteldurivage@orange.fr – Fax 02 38 38 10 21 – Closed Christmas holidays Z **a**
16 rm – €59/95 €95/115, €9
◆ Some of the rooms in this hotel overlook the Loire and its picturesque old bridge; nearly half of them have been recently decorated. Comfortable bar and lounge.

Axotel without rest — VISA AE
14 r. de la Bosserie, 3 km on ① – ✆ 02 38 67 11 99 – www.axotelgien.com – axotelgien.com@wanadoo.fr – Fax 02 38 38 16 61
48 rm – €57/62 €62/72, €7
◆ Modern hotel at the northern entrance to the town. Comfortable, cheerfully-decorated lounges and spacious rooms, adorned with limed wood furniture and colourful drapes.

Anne de Beaujeu without rest — VISA AE
10 rte de Bourges, via ③ – ✆ 02 38 29 39 39 – www.hotel-anne-de-beaujeu.com – hotel.a.beaujeu@wanadoo.fr – Fax 02 38 38 27 29
30 rm – €43/46 €49/56, €7
◆ This left-bank establishment is named after the famous Countess of Gien. Functional rooms. Choose one at the back.

Sanotel without rest — VISA AE
21 quai Sully, 0.5 km via ③ – ✆ 02 38 67 61 46 – www.sanotel.fr – sanotel-gien@wanadoo.fr – Fax 02 38 67 13 01
60 rm – €38/48 €38/48, €7
◆ This modern building set on the banks of the Loire offers practical rooms, many with a view of the chateau and the river.

La Poularde with rm — AC rest, VISA AE
13 quai Nice – ✆ 02 38 67 36 05 – www.lapoularde.fr – contact@lapoularde.fr – Fax 02 38 38 18 78 – Closed Monday except hotel and Sunday dinner Z **e**
9 rm – €53 €60, €8,50
Rest – Menu (€20 bi), €29/75 – Carte approx. €70
◆ Traditional cuisine served in an elegant riverside dining room embellished with paintings, antique tapestries, Gien crockery and silverware. Well-maintained guestrooms.

XX **Côté Jardin** AC VISA MC

14 rte Bourges, via ③ – ✆ 02 38 38 24 67 – cote-jardin45@orange.fr – Fax 02 38 38 24 67 – Closed 21 December-8 January, Tuesday and Wednesday

Rest – *(number of covers limited, pre-book)* Menu € 28 (weekdays)/65 – Carte € 50/65

◆ Pleasant restaurant on the left bank of the Loire with a revitalised decor of classic furnishings and attractive Gien ceramics. Contemporary cuisine.

X **Le P'tit Bouchon** VISA MC

66 r. B. Palissy, via r. Hôtel de Ville Z – ✆ 02 38 67 84 40 – Fax 02 38 67 84 40 – Closed 12 July-2 August, 24 December-3 January, Thursday dinner and Sunday

Rest – Menu (€ 16), € 24

◆ Typical bistro dishes such as calf's head, rabbit terrine and Morteau sausage are chalked up on the blackboard. Attractive small dining room furnished with bentwood chairs.

South by ③, D 940 and secondary road: 3 km – ✉ *45500 Poilly-lez-Gien*

Villa Hôtel ♨ & rm, ✆ P VISA MC

ZA le Clair Ruisseau – ✆ 02 38 27 03 30 – Fax 02 38 27 03 43

24 rm – †€ 37 ††€ 37, ☕ € 6 – ½ P € 38

Rest – *(Closed Friday dinner, Saturday and Sunday) (dinner only)* Menu € 13/16

◆ Expect a warm, friendly welcome at this modern, simple hotel. The well-kept rooms are another advantage. Restaurant decorated with attractive pieces of Gien earthenware. A single dish of the day; buffets for starters and desserts.

GIENS – 83 Var – 340 L7 – ✉ 83400 Hyeres ▮ French Riviera 41 C3

▶ Paris 860 – Carqueiranne 10 – Draguignan 87 – Hyères 9 – Toulon 27

◉ Ruins of the château des Pontevès ✻★★.

See plan of Giens to Hyères.

Le Provençal P VISA MC AE

pl. St-Pierre – ✆ 04 98 04 54 54 – www.provencalhotel.com – leprovencal@wanadoo.fr – Fax 04 98 04 54 50 – Open 4 April-18 October X s

41 rm – †€ 86/142 ††€ 107/168, ☕ € 15 – ½ P € 95/133

Rest – Menu € 28/55 – Carte € 49/90

◆ The hotel is set on a hillside and has a shaded flower garden that descends in terraces to the sea. Provence-style rooms. Private parking 500m away. The view this restaurant commands perhaps inspired the poet Saint-John Perse, a famous resident of this peninsula.

GIFFAUMONT-CHAMPAUBERT – 51 Marne – 306 K11 – pop. 254 – alt. 130 m – ✉ 51290 ▮ Northern France and the Paris Region 14 C2

▶ Paris 208 – Bar-le-Duc 53 – Chaumont 75 – St-Dizier 25 – Vitry-le-François 28

ℹ Office de tourisme, Maison du Lac ✆ 03 26 72 62 80, Fax 03 26 72 64 69

◉ Der-chantecoq Lake ★★.

Le Cheval Blanc & rest, rm, P VISA MC AE

21 r. du Lac – ✆ 03 26 72 62 65 – www.lechevalblanc.net – lechevalblanc7@aol.com – Fax 03 26 73 96 97 – Closed 30 August-17 September, 1st-21 January, Tuesday lunch, Sunday evening and Monday

14 rm – †€ 60 ††€ 65, ☕ € 8 – ½ P € 65 **Rest** – Menu € 25/55 – Carte € 43/63

◆ An inviting hotel 1.2 km from the largest man-made lake in Europe, Lac du Der. Comfortable sitting room-veranda and bright, faultlessly kept rooms. A classic decor, well-laid tables and a traditional menu at the restaurant.

GIF-SUR-YVETTE – 91 Essonne – 312 B3 – pop. 21 900 – alt. 61 m – ✉ 91190 20 A3

▶ Paris 34 – Évry 37 – Boulogne-Billancourt 23 – Montreuil 41 – Argenteuil 42

X **Les Saveurs Sauvages** & AC VISA MC

4 r. Croix Grignon – ✆ 01 69 07 01 16 – les-saveurs-sauvages@wanadoo.fr – Fax 01 69 07 20 84 – Closed 5-25 August, 25 December-2 January, Sunday and Monday

Rest – Menu € 19/39 – Carte € 42/49

◆ A concise seasonal menu which changes daily. Bright dining room-veranda in this non-smoking restaurant opposite the RER train station.

GIGARO – 83 Var – 340 O6 – see La Croix-Valmer

GIGNAC – 34 Hérault – 339 G7 – pop. 4 827 – alt. 53 m – ✉ 34150 23 C2

Paris 719 – Béziers 58 – Lodève 25 – Montpellier 30 – Sète 57

Office de tourisme, 3, Parc d'activités ✆ 04 67 57 58 83, Fax 04 67 57 67 95

XX ✿ **de Lauzun** (Matthieu de Lauzun) AC VISA MC

3 bd de l'Esplanade – ✆ 04 67 57 50 83 – www.restaurant-delauzun.com – contact@restaurant-delauzun.com – Closed March, Sunday dinner and Monday

Rest – Menu (€ 21), € 39/56 – Carte € 42/70

Spec. Mosaïque de petits légumes confits et gaspacho andalou (summer). Tarte fine de thon "façon pissaladière". Millefeuille renversé et biscuit aux amandes.

◆ A talented young chef has relaunched this restaurant with his friendly wife assisting in the dining room. Simple, well-presented decor, just like the delightful cuisine.

GIGONDAS – 84 Vaucluse – 332 D9 – pop. 590 – alt. 313 m – ✉ 84190 42 E1
Provence

Paris 662 – Avignon 40 – Nyons 31 – Orange 20 – Vaison-la-Romaine 16

Office de tourisme, rue du Portail ✆ 04 90 65 85 46, Fax 04 90 65 88 42

Les Florets VISA MC AE

2 km east on minor road – ✆ 04 90 65 85 01 – www.hotel-lesflorets.com – accueil@hotel-lesflorets.com – Fax 04 90 65 83 80 – Closed January and February school holidays

15 rm – †€ 74/105 ††€ 74/105, ☕ € 14 – ½ P € 85/100

Rest – *(closed Wednesday) (number of covers limited, pre-book)* Menu (€ 24), € 29/44 – Carte € 52/65

◆ Hotel surrounded by vineyards at the foot of the Montmirail Dentelles. Attractive colourful rooms (those in the annexe have a terrace). Decor and tasty cuisine inspired by the region. Local wines; pretty summer terrace.

XX **L'Oustalet** VISA MC AE

pl. Gabrielle Andéol – ✆ 04 90 65 85 30 – www.restaurant-oustalet.fr – cyril-glemot@restaurant-oustalet.fr – Fax 04 90 12 30 03 – Closed 22 December-20 January, Monday dinner, Wednesday dinner, Sunday dinner, Thursday dinner from November to March and Tuesday except from mid-June to August

Rest – Menu (€ 21), € 29/75 – Carte € 48/76

◆ The unmistakable feel of the south of France at this smart restaurant: terrace shaded by lime trees, modern cuisine with Provencal flavours and regional wines.

GILETTE – 06 Alpes-Maritimes – 341 D4 – pop. 1 449 – alt. 420 m 41 D2
– ✉ 06830 French Riviera

Paris 946 – Antibes 43 – Nice 36 – St-Martin-Vésubie 45

Syndicat d'initiative, place du Dr Morani ✆ 04 92 08 98 08, Fax 04 93 08 55 24

☼ ★★ of the château ruins.

in Vescous by Rosquesteron road (D 17): 9 km – ✉ 06830 Toudon

X **La Capeline** P VISA MC

rte de Roquesteron – ✆ 04 93 08 58 06 – Fax 04 93 08 58 06 – Open March-October, weekends from November to March and closed Wednesday

Rest – *(closed dinner except Friday and Saturday in season) (pre-book)* Menu (€ 20), € 24/28 – Carte approx. € 29

◆ A small and remote roadside restaurant in the Esteron valley. The tasty menu, based on local produce, is announced at each table. Pleasant shaded terrace.

GILLY-LÈS-CÎTEAUX – 21 Côte-d'Or – 320 J6 – see Vougeot

GIMBELHOF – 67 Bas-Rhin – 315 K2 – see Lembach

GIMEL-LES-CASCADES – 19 Corrèze – **329** M4 – **pop. 670** – **alt. 375 m** – ✉ **19800** 25 **C3**

Paris 493 – Limoges 104 – Tulle 13 – Brive-la-Gaillarde 40 – Ussel 56
Office de tourisme, le Bourg ✆ 05 55 21 44 32, Fax 05 55 21 44 32

Hostellerie de la Vallée VISA

in the village – ✆ 05 55 21 40 60 – hostellerie_de_la_vallee@hotmail.com – Fax 05 55 21 38 74 – Closed 20 December-5 January, Sunday evening, Monday lunch, Friday and Saturday from 1st October to 31 March
9 rm – **†**€ 56/60 **††**€ 56/60, € 10 – ½ P € 71/74
Rest – Menu (€ 17), € 26/40 – Carte € 40/50
◆ At the heart of a village renowned for its waterfalls, this renovated country house offers guests comfortable bedrooms, three of which face the valley. Panoramic dining room where the traditional cuisine is prepared by a mother and daughter team.

LA GIMOND – 42 Loire – **327** F6 – **pop. 240** – **alt. 625 m** – ✉ **42140** 44 **A2**

Paris 485 – Saint-Étienne 18 – Annonay 67 – Lyon 58 – Montbrison 37 – Vienne 64

XX **Le Vallon du Moulin** P VISA

– ✆ 04 77 30 97 06 – Fax 04 77 30 97 06 – Closed 30 July-14 August, 1-10 January, 15-23 February, Sunday dinner and Monday
Rest – Menu € 28 (weekdays)/47
◆ Refurbished in a contemporary style, this restaurant in the heart of a small village, offers an up-to-date menu that varies with the seasons.

GIMONT – 32 Gers – **336** H8 – **pop. 2 825** – **alt. 180 m** – ✉ **32200** 28 **B2**
Languedoc-Roussillon-Tarn Gorges

Paris 701 – Colomiers 40 – Toulouse 51 – Tournefeuille 40
Office de tourisme, 83, rue Nationale ✆ 05 62 67 77 87, Fax 05 62 67 93 61

Château de Larroque rest, P VISA AE

rte de Toulouse – ✆ 05 62 67 77 44 – www.chateaularroque.fr – chateaularroque@free.fr – Fax 05 62 67 88 90 – Closed 5-21 January, 9-18 November, Sunday dinner, Tuesday lunch and Monday from October to April
16 rm – **†**€ 90/103 **††**€ 115/176, € 14 – 1 suite – ½ P € 106/134
Rest – Menu € 25, € 38/57 – Carte € 37/69
◆ This chateau built in 1805 is set in a peaceful park, with comfortable and refined interiors, pleasant personalised rooms and fine lounges. Traditional cuisine served in an elegant dining area or on the shaded terrace.

GINASSERVIS – 83 Var – **340** K3 – **pop. 1 382** – **alt. 407 m** – ✉ **83560** 40 **B3**

Paris 781 – Aix-en-Provence 53 – Avignon 111 – Manosque 23 – Marseille 82 – Toulon 91

X **Chez Marceau** with rm VISA AE

pl. Jean Jaurès – ✆ 04 94 80 11 21 – chezmarceau@wanadoo.fr – Fax 04 94 80 16 82 – Closed 22-26 December, 12-30 January, Tuesday dinner except July-August and merc
7 rm – **†**€ 45/50 **††**€ 50/55, € 6 – ½ P € 50/55
Rest – Menu € 17 bi (weekdays)/40 – Carte € 31/49
◆ Poised between the Durance and Verdon rivers, this pleasant inn is the epitome of the Mediterranean. Terrace on the village square. Regional cuisine and overnight rooms available.

GINCLA – 11 Aude – **344** E6 – **pop. 45** – **alt. 570 m** – ✉ **11140** 22 **B3**

Paris 821 – Carcassonne 77 – Foix 88 – Perpignan 67 – Quillan 25

Hostellerie du Grand Duc P VISA

2 rte de Boucheville – ✆ 04 68 20 55 02 – www.host-du-grand-duc.com – hotelgranduc@wanadoo.fr – Fax 04 68 20 61 22 – Open 1st April-1st November
12 rm – **†**€ 60/65 **††**€ 73/80, € 12 – ½ P € 78/82
Rest – *(closed Wednesday lunch)* Menu € 33/70 – Carte € 40/65
◆ Exposed stonework, wood panelling and antique furniture give character to the rooms of this 18C country house in the land of the Cathars. Walled wooded garden. Smart, rustic dining room, terrace and giant helpings of traditional fare.

GIRMONT-VAL-D'AJOL – 88 Vosges – 314 H5 – see Remiremont

GIROUSSENS – 81 Tarn – 338 C8 – see Lavaur

GISORS – 27 Eure – 304 K6 – pop. 11 400 – alt. 60 m – ✉ 27140 33 D2

Normandy

Paris 73 – Beauvais 33 – Évreux 66 – Mantes-la-Jolie 40 – Pontoise 38 – Rouen 59

Office de tourisme, 4, rue du Général-de-Gaulle ✆ 02 32 27 60 63, Fax 02 32 27 60 75

de Chaumont-en-Vexin Chaumont-en-Vexin Château de Bertichères, E : 8 km on D 982, ✆ 03 44 49 00 81

de Rebetz Chaumont-en-Vexin Route de Noailles, E : 12 km on D 981, ✆ 03 44 49 15 54

Fortified castle ★★ - St-Gervais and St-Protais church ★.

Moderne

1 pl. de la Gare – ✆ 02 32 55 23 51 – www.hotel-moderne-gisors.fr – hotel.moderne@orange.fr – Fax 02 32 55 08 75 – Closed 15 August-2 September

31 rm – €55 €55/90, €7

Rest – *(Closed 1August-1September, Friday dinner, Sunday dinner and Saturday)* Menu € 14 (weekdays)/27 – Carte € 25/39

◆ This family hotel opposite the station is suitable for an overnight stay. The discreetly-decorated rooms are well kept. A rustic dining area, serving traditional cuisine and a cheery "table d'hôte" menu.

Le Cappeville

17 r. Cappeville, (transfer arranged) – ✆ 02 32 55 11 08 – www.lecappeville.com – sppotel@orange.fr – Fax 02 32 55 93 92 – Closed in August, in February, Wednesday and Thursday

Rest – Menu € 28/50 – Carte € 45/55

◆ This restaurant, in the capital of the Normandy Vexin region, is decorated with bright colours but has kept its well-worn beams and fireplace. Regional cuisine.

in Bazincourt-sur-Epte 6 km north on the D 14 – pop. 633 – alt. 55 m – ✉ 27140

Château de la Rapée

2 km west on secondary road – ✆ 02 32 55 11 61 – www.hotel-la-rapee.com – infos@hotel-la-rapee.com – Fax 02 32 55 95 65 – Closed 17 August-1 September and 2 February-4 March

13 rm – €92/125 €92/150, € 12 – ½ P € 85/107

Rest – *(closed Wednesday)* Menu € 36/54 – Carte € 60/80

◆ This Anglo-Norman château is surrounded by unspoilt countryside (stud farms nearby). Spacious rooms with antique furniture overlooking the parkland. Classical cuisine served in a comfortable and welcoming decor with attractive wood panelling.

in St-Denis-le-Ferment 7 km north east on the minor road and D 17 – pop. 451 – alt. 70 m – ✉ 27140

Auberge de l'Atelier

55 r. Guérard – ✆ 02 32 55 24 00 – Fax 02 32 55 10 20 – Closed 15-30 September, Sunday dinner, Tuesday dinner and Monday

Rest – Menu € 28/55 – Carte € 53/66

◆ Savour traditional cuisine in this spacious, pastel coloured dining room graced with flower arrangements and period furniture.

GIVET – 08 Ardennes – 306 K2 – pop. 6 949 – alt. 103 m – ✉ 08600 14 C1

Northern France and the Paris Region

Paris 287 – Charleville-Mézières 58 – Fumay 23 – Rocroi 41

Office de tourisme, 10, quai des Fours ✆ 08 10 81 09 75, Fax 03 24 42 92 41

≤★ from Charlemont fort ★.

Les Reflets Jaunes without rest
2 r. du Gén. de Gaulle – ✆ 03 24 42 85 85 – www.les-reflets-jaunes.com – reflets.jaunes@wanadoo.fr – Fax 03 24 42 85 86
17 rm – †€ 51/92 ††€ 57/118, ☕ € 9,50
◆ Set near the historic town centre, this red-brick hotel from 1685 has spacious and comfortable rooms (some with Jacuzzi bath). Generous breakfast.

Le Val St-Hilaire without rest
7 quai des Fours – ✆ 03 24 42 38 50 – www.hotel-val-st-hilaire.com – hotel.val.saint.hilaire@wanadoo.fr – Fax 03 24 42 07 36
20 rm – †€ 65 ††€ 75, ☕ € 10
◆ This mansion (1719) set on the banks of the Meuse has practical, well-kept rooms with good soundproofing. Fine views of the river from the rooms at the front. Friendly welcome.

Le Roosevelt without rest
14 quai des Remparts – ✆ 03 24 42 14 14 – www.hotel-leroosevelt.com – Fax 03 24 42 15 15 – Closed 26 December-3 January
8 rm – †€ 50/60 ††€ 50/60, ☕ € 8
◆ This old stone house on the banks of the Meuse has small, well-kept guestrooms that are regularly redecorated. The breakfast room is also a tea room and creperie.

Auberge de la Tour
6 quai des Fours – ✆ 03 24 40 41 71 – www.auberge-de-la-tour.net – info@auberge-de-la-tour.net – Fax 03 24 56 90 78 – Closed 14 December-13 January and Monday from October to March
Rest – Menu € 17 (weekday lunch), € 26/42 – Carte € 26/51
◆ The chef of this spruce rustic inn overlooking the Meuse specialises in classic traditional cuisine. A few dishes are based on lobster from the house tank. Summer terrace.

GLAINE-MONTAIGUT – 63 Puy-de-Dôme – 326 H8 – pop. 536 – alt. 350 m – ✉ 63160 6 C2

Paris 440 – Clermont-Ferrand 31 – Issoire 37 – Thiers 21

Auberge de la Forge with rm
– ✆ 04 73 73 41 80 – ericguemon@neuf.fr – Fax 04 73 73 33 83 – Closed Sunday dinner and Wednesday
4 rm – †€ 30/39 ††€ 42/48, ☕ € 6 – ½ P € 38/46
Rest – Menu (€ 13), € 16/35 – Carte € 18/43
◆ Opposite the beautiful Romanesque church, a pleasant inn refitted in the old style (adobe walls) with a reconstruction of the village forge (fire, bellows, anvil).

GLUIRAS – 07 Ardèche – 331 J4 – pop. 349 – alt. 800 m – ✉ 07190 44 B3

Paris 606 – Le Cheylard 20 – Lamastre 40 – Privas 33 – Valence 48

Le Relais de Sully with rm
pl. centrale – ✆ 04 75 66 63 41 – www.lerelaisdesully.com – lerelaisdesully@orange.fr – Fax 04 75 64 69 88 – Closed 20-27 December, 1st February-15 March, Sunday dinner, Wednesday dinner and Monday except July-August
4 rm – †€ 34 ††€ 34, ☕ € 6 **Rest** – Menu (€ 14 bi), € 18 (weekdays)/37
◆ This stone building in the centre of a mountain village is thought to have been a monastery. Local country cuisine served in a smart dining room veranda and on the terrace.

GOLBEY – 88 Vosges – 314 G3 – see Épinal

GOLFE DE SANTA-GIULIA – 2A Corse-du-Sud – 345 E10 – see Corse (Porto-Vecchio)

LE GOLFE-JUAN – 06 Alpes-Maritimes – 341 D6 – ✉ 06220 Vallauris 42 E2

French Riviera

Paris 905 – Antibes 5 – Cannes 6 – Grasse 23 – Nice 29

Office de tourisme, boulevard des Frères Roustan ✆ 04 93 63 73 12, Fax 04 93 63 21 07

for Vallauris see plan of Cannes

 **Beau Soleil** without rest

6 impasse Beau-Soleil, via D6007 (towards Antibes) – 04 93 63 63 63 – www.hotel-beau-soleil.com – contact@hotel-beau-soleil.com – Fax 04 93 63 02 89 – Open 6 March-17 October

30 rm – €56/78 €70/136, €10

◆ This modern hotel, located in a cul-de-sac 500m from the Midi beach and Théâtre de la Mer, has colourful, well-kept rooms, some with balconies.

XX **Tétou**

10 bd des Frères Roustan, on the beach – 04 93 63 71 16 – Fax 04 93 63 16 77 – Open April-15 October and closed Wednesday

Rest – Carte €120/200

◆ This local institution, founded in 1920 and recently renovated, has lost none of its seaside resort ambience. Bouillabaisse, seafood and regional dishes on the menu.

XX **Nounou**

à la plage – 04 93 63 71 73 – www.nounou.fr – Fax 04 93 63 46 91 – Closed 12 November-25 December, Sunday dinner and Monday except July-August

Rest – Menu €42/65 – Carte €83/110

◆ A beach restaurant with bay windows overlooking the coast. Fish and seafood dishes together with a few Provençal specialities complete the seaside atmosphere.

in Vallauris **Northwest: 2,5 km by D 135 – pop. 30 500 – alt. 120 m – 06220**

Office de tourisme, 84, avenue de la Liberté 04 93 63 18 38, Fax 04 93 63 95 01

Musée national la Guerre et la Paix (château) - Musée de l'Automobile★ Northwest: 4 km.

Le Mas Samarcande without rest

138 Grand-Boulevard de Super-Cannes – 04 93 63 97 73 – www.mas-samarcande.com – mireille.diot@wanadoo.fr – Fax 04 93 63 97 73 – Closed 18-28 December

5 rm – €120/130 €120/130

◆ This charming villa provides refined, distinctive rooms combining Provençal and exotic styles, with a terrace affording a superb view.

X **Café Llorca**

pl. Paul Isnard, (pl. de l'Église) – 04 93 64 30 42 – www.cafellorca.com – reservation@cafellorca.com – Fax 04 93 64 97 35

Rest – Carte €30/40

◆ On the church square, opposite Picasso's 'L'homme au mouton' statue. Market cuisine, daily specials and pastries at this spacious, modern restaurant with pleasant terrace.

GORDES – 84 Vaucluse – 332 E10 – pop. 2 092 – alt. 372 m – 84220 42 E1

Provence

Paris 712 – Apt 19 – Avignon 38 – Carpentras 26 – Cavaillon 18 – Sault 35

Office de tourisme, le Château 04 90 72 02 75, Fax 04 90 72 02 26

Site★ - Village★ - Château: fireplace★ - Village des Bories★★ Southwest: 2 km by D 15 then 15 mn - Sénanque abbey ★★ Northwest: 4 km - Press★ in the musée des Moulins de Bouillons South: 5 km.

La Bastide de Gordes & Spa rm,

in the village – 04 90 72 12 12 – www.bastide-de-gordes.com – mail@bastide-de-gordes.com – Fax 04 90 72 05 20 – Closed 2 January-7 February

40 rm – €247/455 €247/455, €27 – 5 suites – ½ P €207/516

Rest – Menu €39 (lunch), €64/94 – Carte €94/110

◆ This 16C residence boasts Provençal style elegance, with rooms overlooking the valley or the village. Excellent spa. Mediterranean-style food and a fine selection of regional wines served in an elegant setting. Veranda facing a hanging garden and a panoramic terrace with magnificent views of the Lubéron and the Alpilles.

Les Bories et Spa rest,
rte de l'Abbaye de Sénanque, 2 km –
VISA AE
04 90 72 00 51 – www.hotellesbories.com – lesbories@wanadoo.fr – Fax 04 90 72 01 22 – Closed 4 January-13 February
27 rm – †€ 200/430 ††€ 200/430, ☐ € 23 – 2 suites – ½ P € 185/300
Rest – *(closed Sunday dinner and Monday from 3 November to 30 April and lunch Monday-Thursday in July-August) (pre-book)* Menu € 57/92 – Carte € 84/98
Spec. Courgettes fleurs soufflées au basilic (April to Sep.). Carré d'agneau laqué au citron (June to Aug.). Pêche jaune, crumble, sorbet verveine et jus framboise (June to Aug.). **Wines** Côtes du Luberon blanc et rouge
◆ These luxurious "bories" (shepherds' shelters) seem lost in the garrigue, amidst the lavender and olive trees. Stylish rooms. Superb pool and spa. Restaurant occupying an old sheepfold with an attractive shaded terrace and herb garden. Mediterranean cooking and local wines.

Le Gordos without rest
VISA AE
1.5 km via rte de Cavaillon – 04 90 72 00 75 – www.hotel-le-gordos.com – mail@hotel-le-gordos.com – Fax 04 90 72 07 00 – Open 27 March-1 November
19 rm – †€ 119/160 ††€ 119/216, ☐ € 16
◆ This dry stone farmstead at the entrance to the village remains refreshingly cool even at the height of summer. Each room has its own flower-decked fragrant terrace.

Le Mas des Romarins without rest
VISA
rte de Sénanque – 04 90 72 12 13 – www.masromarins.com – info@masromarins.com – Fax 04 90 72 13 13 – Closed 15 November-19 December, 6 January-7 March
13 rm ☐ – †€ 87/180 ††€ 99/192
◆ Breakfast with the sunrise on the terrace of this 100-year-old farm overlooking Gordes. Neat and tidy rooms with individualised furnishings. Non-smoking.

Mas de la Beaume without rest
VISA
rte de Cavaillon – 04 90 72 02 96 – www.labeaume.com – la.beaume@wanadoo.fr – Fax 04 90 72 06 89
5 rm ☐ – †€ 110/175 ††€ 110/175
◆ A former barn in a garden of olive trees and perfumed plants is now a roadside hotel. The rooms are decorated in pretty, Provençal style. Terrace, pool and Jacuzzi.

Apt road 2 km east on the D 2 – ✉ 84220 Gordes

Auberge de Carcarille rm,
VISA AE
Apt road, on the D2: 4 km – 04 90 72 02 63 – www.auberge-carcarille.com – carcaril@club-internet.fr – Fax 04 90 72 05 74 – Closed 11 November-26 January
20 rm – †€ 70/110 ††€ 70/110, ☐ € 12 – ½ P € 82/102
Rest – *(closed Friday except dinner from April to September)* Menu € 20 (lunch), € 31/50 – Carte € 25/60
◆ This pleasant dry-stone building is located just below the village. It has rooms decorated in a Provençal style with a balcony or terrace. Pristine white walls in the restaurant set off by colourful chairs and floral curtains. Tasty regional fare.

des Imberts road Southwest: 4 km by D 2 – ✉ 84220 Gordes

Mas de la Senancole
VISA AE
– 04 90 76 76 55 – www.mas-de-la-senancole.com – gordes@mas-de-la-senancole.com – Fax 04 90 76 70 44 – Closed 21 December-17 January
21 rm – †€ 98/229 ††€ 98/229, ☐ € 13
Rest L'Estellan – see below
◆ The Sénancole runs near the soundproofed rooms with painted furniture. Some have a private terrace. Breakfast room beside the pool.

Le Moulin des Sources
Hameau des Gros – 04 90 72 11 69 – www.le-moulin-des-sources.com – contact@le-moulin-des-sources.com – Closed 30 November-15 February
5 rm ☐ – †€ 95/180 ††€ 95/180 – 1 suite **Table d'hôte** – Menu € 35 bi
◆ A peaceful stay guaranteed in this establishment as you wander from the lounge-library to the garden and swimming pool. Cosy guestrooms. A vaulted, partly troglodyte dining room is the setting for cuisine based on fresh, local produce.

XX **Le Mas Tourteron**

chemin de St-Blaise – ✆ 04 90 72 00 16 – www.contact.mastourteron.com – elisabeth.bourgeois1@wanadoo.fr – Fax 04 90 72 09 81 – Open 4 March-8 November, weekends in November and December and closed Sunday dinner in October and March, Monday and Tuesday

Rest – *(dinner only except Sunday)* Menu € 62 – Carte € 66/75

◆ A 'cook in her house' is how the proprietress of this farmhouse sums up her culinary know-how and friendly nature. Rustic Provençal decor and lovely garden.

XX **L'Estellan** – Hôtel Mas de la Senancole

– ✆ 04 90 72 04 90 – www.restaurant-estellan.com – gordes@mas-de-la-senancole.com – Fax 04 90 76 70 44 – Closed 6-29 December, Sunday dinner and Monday from November to March

Rest – Menu (€ 20), € 26 (lunch), € 36/75 – Carte € 55/75

◆ Delightful restaurant occupying an old stone farmhouse. Sale of regional produce and home decoration items. Shaded terrace. Regional cuisine.

in Beaumettes 5.5 km south on the D 15 and D 103 – pop. 193 – alt. 127 m – ✉ 84220

Le Domaine du Moulin Blanc

D 900, chemin du moulin – ✆ 04 90 72 10 10 – www.revalisever.com – info@reveluberon.fr – Fax 04 32 50 10 12

18 rm – †€ 99/119 ††€ 99/119, ☕ € 10 **Rest** – Menu € 17/47 – Carte € 38/56

◆ 15C-16C farmhouse in a garden full of trees. Swimming pool. The comfortable and spacious rooms have beams and modern facilities.

GORGES DE LA RESTONICA – 2B Haute-Corse – 345 D6 – see Corse (Corte)

GORZE – 57 Moselle – 307 H4 – pop. 1 392 – alt. 300 m – ✉ 57680 26 B1

Alsace-Lorraine

Paris 324 – Jarny 17 – Metz 20 – Pont-à-Mousson 22 – St-Mihiel 43 – Verdun 54

Office de tourisme, 22, rue de l'Église ✆ 03 87 52 04 57, Fax 03 87 52 04 57

XX **Hostellerie du Lion d'Or** with rm

105 r. Commerce – ✆ 03 87 52 00 90 – h.r.liondor@wanadoo.fr – Fax 03 87 52 09 62 – Closed Tuesday lunch, Sunday dinner and Monday

17 rm – †€ 51 ††€ 60/63, ☕ € 8 – ½ P € 60

Rest – Menu € 24 (weekday lunch), € 32/42 – Carte € 37/50

◆ This 19C post house has kept its original beams, stonework and fireplace. Regional cuisine served, accompanied by a good wine list. Functional rooms.

GOSNAY – 62 Pas-de-Calais – 301 I4 – see Béthune

LA GOUESNIÈRE – 35 Ille-et-Vilaine – 309 K3 – pop. 1 575 – alt. 22 m – ✉ 35350 10 D1

Paris 390 – Dinan 25 – Dol-de-Bretagne 13 – Lamballe 65 – Rennes 64 – St-Malo 13

Maison Tirel-Guérin (Jean-Luc Guérin)

at the station (Cancale road): 1.5 km on the D 76 – ✆ 02 99 89 10 46 – www.tirelguerin.com – info@tirel-guerin.com – Fax 02 99 89 12 62 – Closed 22 December-1st February

54 rm – †€ 65/138 ††€ 82/153, ☕ € 13 – 2 suites – ½ P € 75/119

Rest – *(closed Sunday dinner October-March and Monday lunch except public holidays) (pre-book Sat - Sun)* Menu € 27 (weekdays)/108 – Carte € 53/105

Spec. Saint-Jacques marinées, caviar d'Aquitaine et salade d'herbes maraîchères (Oct. to March). Homard bleu braisé "Jean-Luc" en 2 services. Soufflé au Grand Marnier.

◆ A family house, opposite a country station, with many assets: flower garden, spacious and well-kept guestrooms, jacuzzi and faultless service. Delicious personalised cuisine served in a dining room infused with a pleasant, bucolic atmosphere.

Château de Bonaban

r. Alfred de Folliny – 02 99 58 24 50 – www.hotel-chateau-bonaban.com – chateau.bonaban@wanadoo.fr – Fax 02 99 58 28 41

34 rm – €120/300 €120/300, €16

Rest – *(Closed lunch in week except bank holidays and Wednesday from November to February)* Menu €30 (weekdays)/55 – Carte €47/56

◆ This 18th century chateau has retained its original marble staircase and wood panelling. A range of rooms available, with a view of the park. Simpler accommodation in the second wing. Slightly aristocratic atmosphere in the dining rooms.

GOULT – 84 Vaucluse – **332** E10 – **pop. 1 207** – **alt. 258 m** – 84220 — 42 **E1**

Paris 714 – Apt 14 – Avignon 41 – Bonnieux 8 – Carpentras 35 – Cavaillon 19 – Sault 38

La Bartavelle

r. Cheval Blanc – 04 90 72 33 72 – labartavelle.free.fr – Fax 04 90 72 33 72 – Open from beg. March-mid November and closed Tuesday and Wednesday

Rest – *(dinner only)* Menu €40

◆ 'Petit Marcel' and his hunter father would have appreciated this vaulted dining room with its floor tiles as red as a rock partridge! Small restaurant serving regional dishes.

Le Garage à Lumières

Hameau de Lumières – 04 32 50 29 32 – legarage@hotmail.fr

Rest – Carte €26/39

◆ A former garage turned into a trendy high-design restaurant, walls decored with toy cars, contemporary paintings and films. Fine, up-to-date cuisine.

GOUMOIS – 25 Doubs – **321** L3 – **pop. 196** – **alt. 490 m** – 25470 — 17 **C2**

Paris 513 – Besançon 92 – Bienne 486 – Montbéliard 55 – Morteau 47

Corniche de Goumois★★, Burgundy-Jura

Taillard

3 rte de la Corniche – 03 81 44 20 75 – www.hoteltaillard.com – hotel.taillard@wanadoo.fr – Fax 03 81 44 26 15 – Open 16 March-14 November

20 rm – €80/104 €80/180, €13 – ½ P €84/115

Rest – *(closed Wednesday dinner October-March, Monday lunch and Wednesday lunch)* Menu €24 (lunch), €36/95 bi – Carte €45/70

◆ Family hotel (1875) set in gardens in the Corniche de Gourmois offering pleasant guestrooms with individual touches. Plainer rooms in the annexe. Classic cuisine and fine list of local wines in the restaurant with views of the valley.

Le Moulin du Plain

at Le Moulin du Plain – 03 81 44 41 99 – www.moulinduplain.com – moulinduplain@orange.fr – Fax 03 81 44 45 70 – Open 25 February-31 October

22 rm – €51 €74 – ½ P €105 **Rest** – Menu €21/35 – Carte €24/38

◆ This hotel on the banks of the Doubs is surrounded by woodland. Some rooms have a view of the river. Paradise for anglers. Trout, morel mushrooms and other local produce take pride of place on the table.

GOUPILLIÈRES – 14 Calvados – **303** J5 – **pop. 151** – **alt. 162 m** – 14210 — 32 **B2**

Paris 255 – Caen 24 – Condé-sur-Noireau 27 – Falaise 34 – Saint-Lô 63

Auberge du Pont de Brie

Halte de Grimbosq, east: 1.5 km – 02 31 79 37 84 – www.pontdebrie.com – contact@pontdebrie.com – Closed 29 June-8 July, 21 December-21 January, 15-25 February, November and December except weekends, Sunday dinner from October to Easter, Tuesday except July-August and Monday

Rest – Menu €22/44 – Carte €29/52

◆ Small family inn tucked away in the Orne valley. Entirely refurbished bright veranda dining room and a summer terrace. Traditional fare.

GOURDON – 46 Lot – 337 E3 – pop. 4 882 – alt. 250 m – ✉ 46300 28 B1
Dordogne-Berry-Limousin

Paris 543 – Sarlat-la-Canéda 26 – Bergerac 91 – Brive-la-Gaillarde 66 – Cahors 44 – Figeac 63

Office de tourisme, 24, rue du Majou ✆ 05 65 27 52 50, Fax 05 65 27 52 52

Rue du Majou★ - Font★ in the Cordeliers church - Esplanade ✻★.

Grottes de Cougnac★ Northwest: 3 km.

Hostellerie de la Bouriane rest, VISA MC
pl. du Foirail – ✆ 05 65 41 16 37 – www.hotellabouriane.fr – hostellerie-la-bouriane@wanadoo.fr – Fax 05 65 41 04 92 – Closed 11-20 October, 22 January-9 March, Sunday evening and Monday from 11 October to 30 April
20 rm – †€ 74/112 ††€ 74/112, ☐ € 13 – ½ P € 77/91
Rest – *(closed for lunch except Sunday)* Menu € 26/42 – Carte € 45/85
◆ This century-old hotel has retained its tradition of hospitality. Rustic, elegant rooms, with attic ceilings on the top floor. Pleasant garden. Aubusson tapestries and paintings adorn the dining room. Tasty traditional cuisine.

in Vigan 5 km East by D 801 – pop. 1 324 – alt. 224 m – ✉ 46300

Auberge Chez Louise VISA MC
au village – ✆ 05 65 32 64 88 – Closed January, February, March, Sunday dinner and Monday except July-August
Rest – Menu € 23 bi
◆ This village restaurant has retained its original rustic charm, with its old bar counter, beams and stone work. Traditional cuisine in a very friendly atmosphere.

GOURDON – 06 Alpes-Maritimes – 341 C5 – pop. 437 – alt. 800 m 42 E2
– ✉ 06620 French Riviera

Paris 921 – Cannes 27 – Castellane 62 – Grasse 15 – Nice 39 – Vence 25

Office de tourisme, place Victoria ✆ 04 93 09 68 25, Fax 04 93 09 68 25

Site★★ - ≤★★ of the church apse - Château : musée des Arts décoratifs et de la modernité.

Au Vieux Four VISA MC
r. Basse – ✆ 04 93 09 68 60 – www.auvieuxfour.fr – Fax 04 93 36 05 79 – Closed 15 November-15 December, 10 January-10 February, dinner from 15 September to 1 July except Thursday, Friday and Saturday
Rest – *(number of covers limited, pre-book)* Menu € 22 (weekday lunch), € 35/50 – Carte € 20/30
◆ An charming old house tucked away in the village. Warm welcome; the menu of the day, which reveals a marked southern accent and perfume, is marked up on a blackboard.

GOURETTE – 64 Pyrénées-Atlantiques – 342 K7 – alt. 1 400 m – Winter sports : 1 400/2 400 m 1 18 – ✉ 64440 Eaux Bonnes Atlantic Coast 3 B3

Paris 829 – Argelès-Gazost 35 – Eaux-Bonnes 9 – Laruns 14 – Lourdes 47 – Pau 52

Office de tourisme, place Sarrière ✆ 05 59 05 12 17, Fax 05 59 05 12 56

Col d'Aubisque ✻★★ North: 4 km.

Boule de Neige ≤ rm, VISA MC
– ✆ 05 59 05 10 05 – www.hotel-bouledeneige.com – bouledeneige@wanadoo.fr – Fax 05 59 05 11 81 – Open from early July to end August and from end November to 15 April
22 rm – †€ 55/100 ††€ 65/110, ☐ € 9 – ½ P € 65/74
Rest – Menu € 20/35 – Carte € 28/49 dinner only
◆ The pluses of this hotel: its location at the foot of the ski slopes, opposite the peaks, its small, chalet-style rooms (half with a mezzanine) and its panoramic fitness room. Family restaurant and busy terrace. Traditional cuisine; snacks at lunchtime.

L'Amoulat with rm
– *05 59 05 12 06 – chalet.hotel.amoulat@wanadoo.fr – Fax 05 59 05 13 45 – Open 15 June-11 September and 19 December-28 March*
12 rm (½ board only) – ½ P € 62/66
Rest – *(closed for lunch except in July-August)* Menu € 20/26 – Carte € 20/50
◆ A chalet situated on the Aubisque Pass, a famous stretch in the Tour de France cycle race. Rustic dining room and veranda. Regional dishes and up-to-date cuisine. Simple rooms.

GOURNAY-EN-BRAY – **76 Seine-Maritime** – **304** K5 – **pop. 6 174** – **alt. 94 m** – ✉ **76220** Normandy 33 **D2**

Paris 97 – Amiens 78 – Les Andelys 38 – Beauvais 31 – Dieppe 76 – Gisors 25 – Rouen 50

Office de tourisme, 9, place d'Armes ☎ 02 35 90 28 34, Fax 02 35 09 62 07

Le Saint Aubin
Dieppe road 3 km on D 915 – ☎ 02 35 097 097 – www.hotel-saint-aubin.fr – hotel.le.saint.aubin@wanadoo.fr – Fax 02 35 093 093
60 rm – †€ 55/120 ††€ 55/120, ☐ € 8
Rest – *(closed Sunday and Saturday)* Carte approx. € 27
◆ This modern building, slightly set back from the road, has functional rooms, suitable for an overnight stay. The restaurant in the hotel basement serves unpretentious, traditional cuisine. Simple decor.

Le Cygne without rest
20 r. Notre Dame – ☎ 02 35 90 27 80 – www.lecygne.c.la – hotel.le.cygne@orange.fr – Fax 02 35 90 59 00
29 rm – †€ 52 ††€ 57, ☐ € 6,50
◆ This welcoming, homely hotel is located in the centre of this small town in the Bray region. Simple, refurbished and well-kept rooms; those facing the rear are quieter.

GOUVIEUX – **60 Oise** – **305** F5 – **see Chantilly**

GOUY-ST-ANDRÉ – **62 Pas-de-Calais** – **301** E5 – **see Hesdin**

GRAMAT – **46 Lot** – **337** G3 – **pop. 3 545** – **alt. 305 m** – ✉ **46500** Dordogne-Berry-Limousin 29 **C1**

Paris 534 – Brive-la-Gaillarde 57 – Cahors 58 – Figeac 36 – Gourdon 38 – St-Céré 22

Office de tourisme, place de la République ☎ 05 65 38 73 60, Fax 05 65 33 46 38

Lion d'Or rm,
8 pl. de la République – ☎ 05 65 10 46 10 – liondor46@orange.fr – Fax 05 65 34 37 85
15 rm – †€ 50/70 ††€ 60/95, ☐ € 10 – ½ P € 68/88
Rest – *(closed Friday lunch and Saturday lunch from 11 November to end - March)* Menu (€ 12), € 18 (weekdays)/75 bi – Carte € 45/60
◆ This local house with character in the town centre offers refurbished, tastefully decorated rooms. The restaurant offers regional and classic dishes in the chic dining room. Pleasant bar-lounge. Shaded and flower-decked terrace.

Le Relais des Gourmands rm,
2 av. de la Gare, (at the station) – ☎ 05 65 38 83 92 – www.relais-des-gourmands.fr – relais-des-gourmands@orange.fr – Fax 05 65 38 70 99 – Closed one week in October, 15 February-8 March, Sunday dinner and Monday except July-August
16 rm – †€ 56/77 ††€ 56/77, ☐ € 9 – ½ P € 60/75
Rest – *(closed Sunday dinner and Monday)* Menu (€ 17), € 19 (weekdays)/42 – Carte € 29/45
◆ Attentive service in this establishment with modern rooms opposite the station. Lovely swimming pool surrounded by a garden. Bright modern restaurant with yellow colours. Regional menu.

Hostellerie du Causse
2 km on Cahors road – ✆ 05 65 10 60 60 – www.hostellerieducausse.com – contact@hostellerieducausse.com – Fax 05 65 10 60 61 – Closed 2-31 January
28 rm – †€ 48/58 ††€ 60/75, ☕ € 9 – ½ P € 57/60
Rest – Menu (€ 14 bi), € 17 (weekdays)/59 – Carte € 34/62
◆ Located outside the town centre, this modern, local-style building offers spacious and well-kept rooms. Swimming pool. Generous traditional cuisine, enriched by local specialities, served in an attractive dining room or on the summer terrace.

Du Centre rm, rest,
pl. de la République – ✆ 05 65 38 73 37 – wwww.lecentre.fr – le.centre@wanadoo.fr – Fax 05 65 38 73 66
18 rm – †€ 46/55 ††€ 46/65, ☕ € 8 – ½ P € 55
Rest – Menu (€ 11), € 16 (weekdays)/39 – Carte € 22/60
◆ Functional guestrooms in the centre of a town hosting regular agricultural shows. Traditional, Breton-influenced cuisine served in a bright dining room or on the terrace in fine weather.

Moulin de Fresquet
1 km via Figeac road – ✆ 05 65 38 70 60 – www.moulindefresquet.com – info@moulindefresquet.com – Fax 05 65 33 60 13 – Open April-October
5 rm ☕ – †€ 64/87 ††€ 64/110 **Table d'hôte** – *(closed Thurs.)*
Menu € 25 bi
◆ This mill, with elements from the 14C to 19C, is set in a garden with a mill race and an amazing assortment of ducks. The rooms are decorated with antique furniture and paintings; some also come with a terrace. The restaurant serves appetising regional cuisine.

in Lavergne **Northeast: 4 km by D 677 – pop. 417 – alt. 320 m – ✉ 46500**

Le Limargue with rm
– ✆ 05 65 38 76 02 – www.hotelrestaurantlelimargue.com – lelimargue@wanadoo.fr – Fax 05 65 38 76 02 – Open 4 April-10 November and closed 12-23 October, Tuesday and Wednesday except July-August
3 rm – †€ 45 ††€ 45/50, ☕ € 6 – ½ P € 47
Rest – Menu € 15/26 – Carte € 23/40
◆ Stop at this pleasant freestone building, while crossing the Gramat plateau, to savour the Quercy cuisine. Rooms with attractive personal touches.

LE GRAND-BORNAND – 74 Haute-Savoie – 328 L5 – pop. 2 202 – alt. 934 m – Winter sports : 1 000/2 100 m 2 37 – ✉ 74450

46 **F1**

French Alps

Paris 564 – Albertville 47 – Annecy 31 – Bonneville 23 – Chamonix-Mont-Blanc 76

Office de tourisme, place de l'Église ✆ 04 50 02 78 00, Fax 04 50 02 78 01

Vermont without rest
rte du Bouchet – ✆ 04 50 02 36 22 – www.hotelvermont.com – hotel.vermont@wanadoo.fr – Fax 04 50 02 39 36 – Open mid June-mid September and mid December-mid April
23 rm ☕ – †€ 55/105 ††€ 85/130
◆ Close to the La Joyère cable car, a regional construction with plenty of space for relaxation and revitalisation (jacuzzi and sauna). Panelled rooms, often with balconies.

Delta without rest
L'Envers de Villeneuve – ✆ 04 50 02 26 25 – www.hotel-delta74.com – info@hotel-delta74.com – Fax 04 50 02 32 71 – Open mid June-mid September and mid December-mid April
15 rm – †€ 57/76 ††€ 57/76, ☕ € 7
◆ A small recently built chalet on the outskirts of the village, containing a sports shop (ski hire) and a hotel with reasonably-sized, wood-panelled rooms. Library, billiard table and games for children.

Croix St-Maurice rest,
(opposite the church) – 04 50 02 20 05 – www.hotel-lacroixstmaurice.com – info@hotel-lacroixstmaurice.com – Fax 04 50 02 35 37 – Closed 26 September-25 October
21 rm – €49/85 €49/85, €7 – ½ P €47/74
Rest – Menu €19/29 – Carte €30/45
◆ Traditional chalet in the heart of the town famous for its Reblochon cheese. The rooms, many of which have balconies, have been renovated in regional style. Traditional cuisine and Savoyard specialities. Lovely view of the church and Aravis mountain range from the dining room.

L'Hysope
Le Pont de Suize, (Bouchet road) – 04 50 02 29 87 – Fax 04 50 02 29 87 – Closed 6-26 October, Wednesday and Thursday off season
Rest – Menu €29/69 – Carte €58/95
◆ This bright, convivial dining room is very different from a typical mountain restaurant. Comprehensive wine list (about 40 wines) and contemporary, personalised cuisine. Meals served on the terrace in summer.

in Chinaillon North: 5,5 km by D 4 – ✉ **74450 Le Grand Bornand**

Les Cimes without rest
– 04 50 27 00 38 – www.hotel-les-cimes.com – info@hotel-les-cimes.com – Fax 04 50 27 08 46 – Open 21 June-4 September, 26 October-6 November and 6 December-24 April
10 rm – €70/110 €80/159, €11
◆ A little chalet with pretty rooms in the centre of the Grand Bo sporting hamlet; contemporary mountain-style décor, antique furniture, trinkets, etc. A real find!

Crémaillère
Le Chinaillon – 04 50 27 02 33 – www.hotel-la-cremaillere.fr – cremaill@wanadoo.fr – Fax 04 50 27 07 91 – Open 15 June-15 September and 20 December-20 April
15 rm – €62/97 €62/97, €8 – ½ P €57/75
Rest – *(closed Tuesday lunch and Monday)* Menu €18 (lunch), €24/34 – Carte €24/48
◆ All rooms in this small family-run hotel have balconies and face south towards the ski slopes. Very well-maintained. Cosy lounge with a fireplace. Savoyard cuisine served in the rustic, light wood decor of the dining room.

in la Vallée du Bouchet – ✉ **74450**

Le Chalet des Troncs
3.5 km east – 04 50 02 28 50 – www.chaletdestroncs.com – contact@chaletdestroncs.com – Fax 04 50 63 25 28
4 rm – €132/228 €148/228, €15
Table d'hôte – *(open 22 December-23 April and July-August)* Menu €40/55
◆ The rooms of this old farmhouse deep in the countryside are little alpine gems. Panoramic hammam and magnificent indoor pool fed by spring water. Family cooking made with home-grown produce served by the fireside.

GRANDCAMP-MAISY – 14 Calvados – 303 F3 – pop. 1 757 – alt. 5 m 32 B2
– ✉ 14450 **Normandy**

Paris 297 – Caen 63 – Cherbourg 73 – St-Lô 40
Office de tourisme, 118, rue Aristide-Briand 02 31 22 62 44, Fax 02 31 22 62 44

La Faisanderie without rest
av. du Col.-Courson – 02 31 22 70 06
3 rm – €45 €50
◆ A welcoming house covered in Virginia creeper, located on an estate with a stud farm. Guestrooms graced with rustic family heirlooms. Peace and quiet guaranteed.

La Marée
5 quai Henri Cheron – 02 31 21 41 00 – www.restolamaree.com – restolamaree@wanadoo.fr – Fax 02 31 21 44 55 – Closed 30 December-10 February
Rest – Menu €15/25 – Carte €45/70
◆ Maritime ambience and decor opposite the fish market. The dining room has a veranda and serves fresh seafood caught in the Channel or the ocean.

GRAND'COMBE-CHÂTELEU – 25 Doubs – 321 J4 – see Morteau

LA GRANDE-MOTTE – 34 Hérault – 339 J7 – pop. 8 202 – alt. 1 m 23 C2
– Casino – ✉ 34280 Languedoc-Roussillon-Tarn Gorges

Paris 747 – Aigues-Mortes 12 – Lunel 16 – Montpellier 28 – Nîmes 45 – Sète 47

Office de tourisme, allée des Parcs ✆ 04 67 56 42 00, Fax 04 67 29 91 42

de La Grande-Motte Avenue du Golf, 2 km N :, ✆ 04 67 56 05 00

Les Corallines rest, rest,
615 allée de la Plage, (Le Point Zéro) – ✆ 04 67 29 13 13
– www.thalasso-grandemotte.com – info@thalasso-grandemotte.com
– Fax 04 67 29 14 74 – Closed 26 December-29 January
39 rm – €120/178 €120/178, €14 – 3 suites
Rest – Menu (€25), €31 – Carte €45/60
◆ This recent seaside hotel complex boasts its own spa facilities. Guestrooms with a balcony. Fine pool and panoramic terrace. A modern decor and Mediterranean inspired cuisine at this restaurant.

Mercure rm,
140 r. du port – ✆ 04 67 56 90 81 – www.mercure.com – h1230@accor.com
– Fax 04 67 56 92 29
117 rm – €130/180 €140/200, €13 – 18 suites
Rest – Menu (€24) – Carte €40/60
◆ Located in the heart of this busy seaside resort, this impressive hotel dominates the marina. The spacious guestrooms all have balconies. Classic cuisine served in a contemporary dining room or terrace shaded by plane trees.

Novotel
1641 av. du Golf – ✆ 04 67 29 88 88 – www.novotel.com – h2190@accor.com
– Fax 04 67 29 17 01
81 rm – €95/180 €95/180, €14 **Rest** – Carte €23/43
◆ At the entrance of this hotel is a glass atrium. The spacious, practical guestrooms are in keeping with the chain's standards. Located at the golf course entrance. Brasserie-style fare in a contemporary dining room with a terrace.

Golf Hôtel without rest
1920 av. du Golf – ✆ 04 67 29 72 00 – www.golfhotel34.com
– golfhotel34@wanadoo.fr – Fax 04 67 56 12 44
44 rm – €86/134 €90/147, €13 – 1 suite
◆ Delightful hotel tucked away in a quiet district. Gradually refurbished rooms, all with loggias overlooking the golf course or Ponant lake. Pleasant garden and pool.

Azur Bord de Mer without rest
pl. Justin – ✆ 04 67 56 56 00 – www.hotelazur.net
– hotelazur34@aol.com – Fax 04 67 29 81 26
20 rm – €95/130 €95/140, €13
◆ Located on the jetty on the south side of the port, this establishment has a matchless sea view. Snug guestrooms decorated in a classic or modern vein. Verdant surroundings.

Europe without rest
allée des Parcs – ✆ 04 67 56 62 60 – www.hoteleurope34.com
– hoteleurope@wanadoo.fr – Fax 04 67 56 93 07 – Open from March to October
34 rm – €67/118 €67/118, €11
◆ A cheerful family hotel located behind the conference centre. Practical, well-kept guestrooms, currently being refurbished. Pool and sundeck terrace.

De la Plage rm, rest,
allée du Levant, (towards Grau-du-Roi) – ✆ 04 67 29 93 00
– www.hp-lagrandemotte.fr – contact@hp-lagrandemotte.fr – Fax 04 67 56 00 07
– Open 2 March-5 November and 7 December-1 January
39 rm – €70/130 €70/130, €14 – ½ P €63/93
Rest – *(open 1 April-10 October and closed Sunday and Monday in low season) (dinner only)* Carte €28/49
◆ Idyllically located seaside hotel, gradually refurbished in a modern spirit. Smart new lobby, large guestrooms with loggia for those overlooking the sea. The restaurant serves traditional fare with a seafood slant. Evenings only.

Alexandre
esplanade Maurice Justin – 04 67 56 63 63 – www.alexandre-restaurant.com – michel@alexandre-restaurant.com – Fax 04 67 29 74 69 – Closed 29 October-4 November, Sunday dinner except July-August, Monday and Tuesday from October to March
Rest – Menu (€ 32), € 50/80 – Carte € 65/85
Rest ***Bistrot d'Alexandre*** – *(open 23 June-2 September)* Menu € 20
◆ This restaurant provides a view of the port and the sea. Modern décor and elegant presentation. Classic meals and seafood dishes with a good selection of wines from the Languedoc region. The Bistrot offers a relaxed atmosphere and a menu featuring grilled meat and fish dishes.

GRAND-FOUGERAY – 35 Ille-et-Vilaine – 309 L8 – pop. 1 970 – alt. 40 m – ✉ 35390 — 10 D2

Paris 392 – Rennes 49 – Cesson-Sévigné 52 – Bruz 41 – Châteaubriant 34

Les Palis
15 pl. de l'Église – 02 99 08 30 80 – www.restaurant-les-palis.fr – contact@restaurantlespalis.fr – Fax 02 99 08 45 20
13 rm – €75 €75, ☕ € 11 – ½ P € 70
Rest – *(Closed Sunday dinner)* Menu € 21 (weekdays)/38 – Carte € 45/52
◆ Totally renovated hotel located in the main village square. The rooms have been decorated in a Zen style, in grey and white, with pale wood furniture. Traditional cuisine to be enjoyed beneath a fresco of Bacchus and visible timberwork.

LE GRAND VILLAGE PLAGE – 17 Charente-Maritime – 324 C4 – see Île d'Oléron

GRANDVILLERS – 88 Vosges – 314 I3 – pop. 712 – alt. 365 m – ✉ 88600 — 27 C3

Paris 404 – Épinal 22 – Lunéville 48 – Gérardmer 29 – Remiremont 38 – St-Dié 28

Europe et Commerce
3 et 4 rte de Bruyères – 03 29 65 71 17 – www.hotel-europe-commerce.fr – hotel.bastien.europe@wanadoo.fr – Fax 03 29 65 85 23
21 rm – € 46/56 € 56/66, ☕ € 7 – ½ P € 46/56
Rest – *(closed Friday dinner and Sunday dinner)* Menu (€ 13), € 16 (weekdays), € 25/38 – Carte € 20/40
◆ A charming house, the old part of the hotel, houses several simple rooms. Those in the annexe are more spacious, quieter and overlook the garden. Bright, stylish dining room where you can enjoy tasty, classic cuisine.

GRANE – 26 Drôme – 332 C5 – pop. 1 694 – alt. 175 m – ✉ 26400 — 44 B3

Paris 599 – Lyon 136 – Valence 32 – Montélimar 35 – Romans-sur-Isère 52

Syndicat d'initiative, route de La Roche-sur-Grâne 04 75 62 66 08, Fax 04 75 62 73 26

Giffon "La Demeure de Grâne" with rm
8 pl. de l'Église – 04 75 62 60 64 – www.hotelrestaurant-giffon.com – contact@hotelrestaurant-giffon.com – Fax 04 75 62 70 11
8 rm – € 55 € 55, ☕ € 10 – ½ P € 80/115
Rest – *(Closed Sunday dinner, Monday and Tuesday except from mid-June to mid-September, Wednesday lunch and Thursday lunch)*
Menu € 23 (weekdays)/55
◆ This pleasant inn on the church square has a traditional feel. Terrace shaded by old trees. New, functional rooms.

GRANGES-LÈS-BEAUMONT – 26 Drôme – 332 C3 – see Romans-sur-Isère

LES GRANGES-STE-MARIE – 25 Doubs – 321 H6 – see Malbuisson

GRANS – 13 Bouches-du-Rhône – 340 F4 – pop. 4 078 – alt. 52 m – ✉ 13450 40 **B3**

Paris 729 – Arles 43 – Marseille 50 – Martigues 29 – Salon-de-Provence 7

Syndicat d'initiative, boulevard Victor Jauffret ✆ 04 90 55 88 92, Fax 04 90 55 86 27

Le Planet VISA

pl. J. Jaurès – ✆ 04 90 55 83 66 – Fax 04 90 55 83 66 – Closed 20 September-6 October, for the Toussaint holiday, for the February holiday, Sunday dinner from November to February, Monday and Tuesday

Rest – Menu (€ 18), € 25/40 – Carte € 34/55

◆ This old oil mill now houses a little vaulted restaurant with roughcast walls. Pleasant terrace under the plane trees. Friendly service, regional cuisine.

We try to be as accurate as possible when giving room rates.
But prices are open to change,
so please check rates when booking.

GRANVILLE – 50 Manche – 303 C6 – pop. 12 900 – alt. 10 m – Casino Z, and St-Pair-sur-Mer – ✉ 50400 Normandy 32 **A2**

Paris 342 – Avranches 27 – Cherbourg 105 – St-Lô 57 – St-Malo 93

Office de tourisme, 4, cours Jonville ✆ 02 33 91 30 03, Fax 02 33 91 30 19

de Granville Bréville-sur-Mer Pavillon du Golf, 5 km on the Coutances road, ✆ 02 33 50 23 06

Tour of the ramparts★: place de l'Isthme ≤★ Z - Pointe du Roc: site★.

Plan on following page

Mercure le Grand Large without rest VISA AE

5 r. Falaise – ✆ 02 33 91 19 19 – www.mercure-granville.com – infos@mercure-granville.com – Fax 02 33 91 19 00 Z **r**

51 rm – €73/159 €73/159, € 12

◆ Looking down over the beach from the clifftop, this hotel associated with a thalassotherapy centre offers duplex or studio accommodation, mostly with sea views.

Michelet without rest P VISA

5 r. J. Michelet – ✆ 02 33 50 06 55 – www.hotel-michelet-granville.com – contact@hotel-michelet-granville.com – Fax 02 33 50 12 25 Z **u**

19 rm – €30/57 €30/57, € 7

◆ This hotel was named for one of the resort's famous visitors. Simple, quiet rooms; some with a glimpse of the Channel. Choose one that has been renovated. Warm hospitality.

La Citadelle A/C VISA

34 r. Port – ✆ 02 33 50 34 10 – www.restaurant-la-citabelle.com – citadell@club-internet.fr – Fax 02 33 50 15 36 – Closed 17 March-1 April, 8 December-13 January, Tuesday from October to March and Wednesday

Rest – Menu € 20/35 – Carte € 28/46 Y **d**

◆ Taste the Chausey lobster and other seafood in a marine decor or on the sheltered terrace overlooking the harbour. It was from here that privateers and Newfoundland fishermen used to set sail.

in St-Pair-sur-Mer 4 km by ④ – pop. 3 719 – alt. 30 m – ✉ 50380

Office de tourisme, 3, rue Charles Mathurin ✆ 02 33 50 52 77

Au Pied de Cheval A/C VISA

2 r. de la Plage – ✆ 02 33 91 34 01 – restauration.stpair@joa-casino.com – Fax 02 33 50 26 27 – Closed 1-21 October, 1-17 January, Monday and Tuesday except July-August

Rest – Menu € 19 (weekdays)/26 – Carte € 30/40

◆ Restaurant near the casino and beach overlooking Granville. A large brasserie style low-key dining room serving French and Italian cuisine.

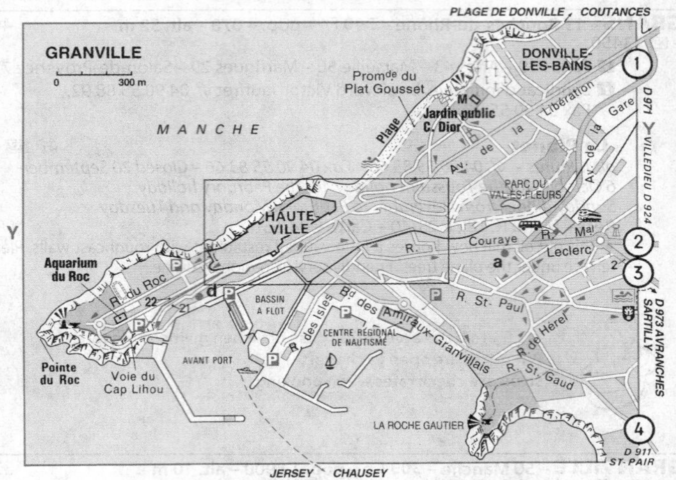

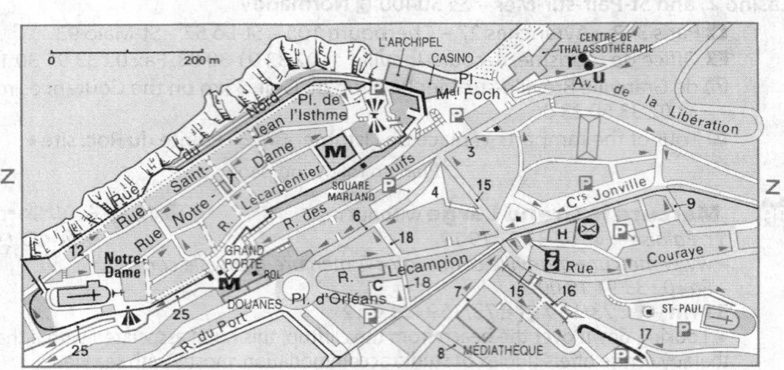

Briand (Av. A.) . . . . Y 2
Clemenceau (R. G.) . . . . Z 3
Corsaires (Pl. des) . . . . Z 4
Corsaires (R. des) . . . . Z 6
Couraye (R.) . . . . Z
Desmaisons (R. C.) . . . . Z 7
Granvillais (Bd des Amiraux) . . . . Z 8
Hauteserve (Bd d') . . . . Z 9
Juifs (R. des) . . . . Z
Lecampion (R.) . . . . Z
Leclerc (Av. Gén.) . . . . Y
Parvis-Notre-Dame (Montée du) . . . . Z 12
Poirier (R. Paul) . . . . Z 15
Ste-Geneviève (R.) . . . . Z 17
Saintonge (R.) . . . . Z 18
St-Sauveur (R.) . . . . Z 16
Terreneuviers (Bd des) . . . . . . Y 21
Vaufleury (Bd) . . . . Y 22
2e-et-202e-de-Ligne (Bd du) . . . . Z 25

GRASSE – **06 Alpes-Maritimes** – **341** C6 – **pop. 49 100** – **alt. 250 m** – **Casino** – ✉ **06130** **French Riviera** — 42 **E2**

Paris 905 – Cannes 17 – Digne-les-Bains 118 – Draguignan 53 – Nice 40

Office de tourisme, 22, cours Honoré Cresp ✆ 04 93 36 66 66, Fax 04 93 36 03 56

de St-Donat Le Plan-de-Grasse 270 route de Cannes, 5 km on the Cannes road, ✆ 04 93 09 76 60

Grasse Country Club 1 route des 3 Ponts, W : 5 km on D 11, ✆ 04 93 60 55 44

de la Grande Bastide Châteauneuf-Grasse 761 Chemin des Picholines, E : 6 km on D 7, ✆ 04 93 77 70 08

Opio Valbonne Opio Château de la Bégude, E : 11 km on D 4, ✆ 04 93 12 00 08

Saint-Philippe Golf Academy Sophia-Antipolis Avenue Roumanille, E : 12 km, ✆ 04 93 00 00 57

Old town★: Place du Cours★ ≤★ Z - Paintings★ by Rubens in Notre-Dame-du-Puy cathedral Z **B** - Parc de la Corniche ☼★★ 30 mn Z - Jardin de la Princesse Pauline ≤★ X **K** - Musée international de la Parfumerie★ Z **M³**.

Climbing up to col du Pilon ≤★★ 9 km by ④.

GRASSE

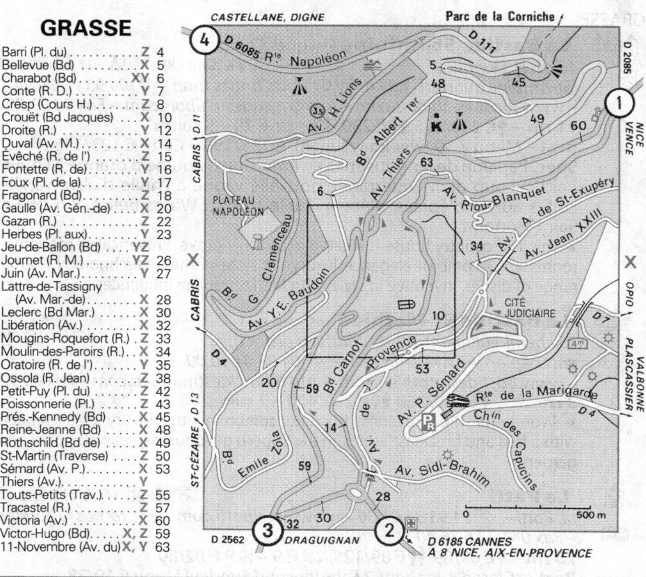

Barri (Pl. du)	Z	4
Bellevue (Bd)	X	5
Charabot (Bd)	XY	6
Conte (R. D.)	Y	7
Cresp (Cours H.)	Z	8
Crouët (Bd Jacques)	X	10
Droite (R.)	Y	12
Duval (Av. M.)	X	14
Évêché (R. de l')	Z	15
Fontette (R. de)	Y	16
Foux (Pl. de la)	Y	17
Fragonard (Bd)	Z	18
Gaulle (Av. Gén.-de)	X	20
Gazan (R.)	Z	22
Herbes (Pl. aux)	Y	23
Jeu-de-Ballon (Bd)	YZ	25
Journet (R. M.)	YZ	26
Juin (Av. Mar.)	Y	27
Lattre-de-Tassigny (Av. Mar.-de)	X	28
Leclerc (Bd Mar.)	X	30
Libération (Av.)	X	32
Mougins-Roquefort (R.)	Z	33
Moulin-des-Paroirs (R.)	X	34
Oratoire (R. de l')	Y	35
Ossola (R. Jean)	Z	38
Petit-Puy (Pl. du)	Z	42
Poissonnerie (Pl.)	Z	43
Prés.-Kennedy (Bd)	X	45
Reine-Jeanne (Bd)	X	48
Rothschild (Bd de)	X	49
St-Martin (Traverse)	Z	50
Sémard (Av. P.)	X	53
Thiers (Av.)	Y	
Touts-Petits (Trav.)	Z	55
Tracastel (R.)	Z	57
Victoria (Av.)	X	60
Victor-Hugo (Bd)	X, Z	59
11-Novembre (Av. du)	X, Y	63

CASTELLANE, DIGNE
Parc de la Corniche
D 6085 Rte Napoléon
D 111
D 2085
NICE
VENCE
Av. H. Lions
Bd Albert 1er
Av. Thiers
Av. Riou-Blanquet
Av. A. de St-Exupéry
Av. Jean XXIII
PLATEAU NAPOLÉON
Bd G. Clemenceau
Av. Y. E. Baudoin
CABRIS D 11
CABRIS
D 4
ST-CÉZAIRE D 13
CITÉ JUDICIAIRE
D 7
OPIO
VALBONNE
PLASCASSIER
Rte de la Marigarde
Chin des Capucins
Av. P. Sémard
Bd Carnot
Av. de Provence
Bd Emile Zola
Av. Sidi-Brahim
D 4
500 m
D 2562
DRAGUIGNAN
D 6185 CANNES
A 8 NICE, AIX-EN-PROVENCE

100 m
Av. Thiers
Pl. Martelly
Riou-
Blanquet
THÉATRE DE GRASSE
R. Paul Goby
Bd Gambetta
Place de la Roque
R. des Carrières
Pl. Morel
Pl. aux Aires
Bd du Jeu-de-Ballon
Av. Yves E. Baudoin
R. Amiral de Grasse
VIEILLE VILLE
Pl. de l'Évêché
PORTE NEUVE
Pl. C. Ossola
Av. Chiris
Pl. du 24 Août
CASINO
PALAIS DES CONGRÈS
PL. DU COURS
R. Mirabeau
Bd Carnot
Bd Jacques Crouët
Av. de Provence
Av. P. Sémard

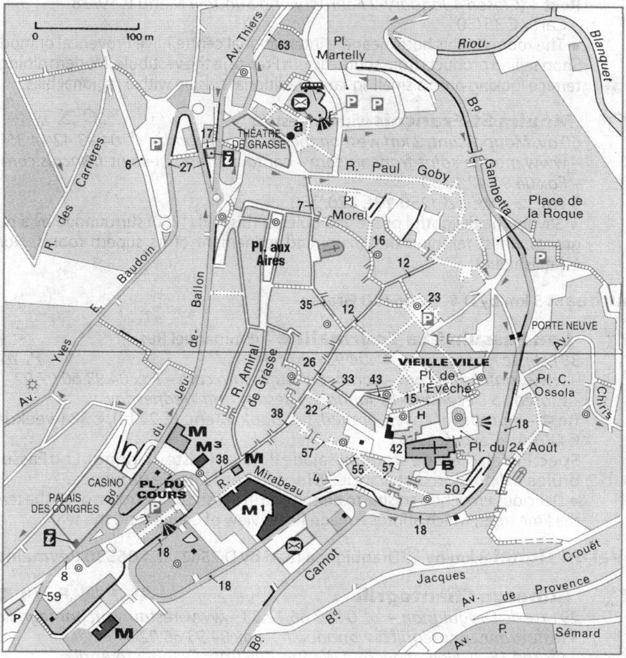

La Bastide St-Antoine (Jacques Chibois)
48 av. H. Dunant,
(St-Antoine quarter), 1,5 km by ② and Cannes road – ✆ 04 93 70 94 94
– www.jacques-chibois.com – info@jacques-chibois.com – Fax 04 93 70 94 95
11 rm – €230/395 €230/395, €29 – 5 suites
Rest – Menu €59 (weekday lunch), €155/190 – Carte €103/196
Spec. Papillon de langoustines en émulsion de pulpe d'orange à l'huile d'olive et basilic. Loup de Méditerranée nouvelle vague à l'huile d'olive vanillée. Fraises cuites au vin d'épices, glace à l'huile d'olive. **Wines** Bellet, Vin de Pays de l'Île Saint-Honorat.
◆ This 18C country house is located in an olive grove. Provençal or modern-style guestrooms which combine elegance, luxury and state-of-the-art technology. A subtle and tasty range of dishes, inventive in style, with Mediterranean influences.

La Bastide St-Mathieu without rest
35 chemin Blumenthal, (St-Mathieu district),
east of plan via Ave Jean XXIII – ✆ 04 97 01 10 00
– www.bastidestmathieu.com – info@bastidestmathieu.com – Fax 04 97 01 10 09
3 rm – €250/360 €270/400 – 2 suites
◆ Wonderful 18C Provençal building combining the luxury of a characterful hotel with a bed and breakfast atmosphere. Superb guestrooms, seawater pool and delightful garden.

Le Patti
pl. Patti – ✆ 04 93 36 01 00 – www.hotelpatti.com – eric.ramos@hotelpatti.com
– Fax 04 93 36 36 40 Y **a**
73 rm – €69/89 €89/125, €9 – ½ P €62/80
Rest – *(Closed 4 January-2 February and Sunday)* Menu €19/38
– Carte €35/50
◆ The rooms in this hotel near the international centre have Provencal or modern decor. Shop selling products from southeastern France in the vestibule. Modern dining room and terrace looking onto a small square. Traditional cuisine with a regional bias.

Moulin St-François without rest
60 av. Maupassant, 2 km west on the St-Cézaire road – ✆ 04 93 42 14 35
– www.moulin-saint-francois.com – contact@moulin-saint-francois.com
– Fax 04 93 42 13 53
3 rm – €220/250 €220/250
◆ Savour the delightful peace and quiet of this mill (1760) surrounded by a park of olive groves whilst relishing the luxury and refinement of its superb rooms. Non-smoking establishment.

Southeast 5 km by D 4- ✉ 06130 Grasse

Lou Fassum "La Tourmaline" (Emmanuel Ruz)
381 rte de Plascassier – ✆ 04 93 60 14 44
– www.loufassum.com – contact@loufassum.com – Fax 04 93 60 07 92
– Closed 15 December-15 January, Tuesday and Wednesday
Rest – *(number of covers limited, pre-book)* Menu (€22 bi), €38 (weekday lunch), €48/64 – Carte €63/92
Spec. Pissaladière de scampis, salade florale et pistou (spring). Lou Fassum. Créme brûlée à l'infusion de lavande. **Wines** Bellet, Côte de Provence.
◆ Delicious Provencal cuisine to be enjoyed in a rustic dining room or on the terrace under the lime trees, which affords a magnificent view of Cannes and the sea.

in Val du Tignet 8 km by ③ Draguignan road by D 2562 – ✉ 06530 Peymeinade

Auberge Chantegrill
291 rte de Draguignan – ✆ 04 93 66 12 33 – www.restaurantchantegrill.com
– restaurant.chantegrill@wanadoo.fr – Fax 04 93 66 02 31
– Closed 15-30 November and Wednesday from October to April
Rest – Menu (€17), €22 (weekdays)/49 – Carte €50/62
◆ Whether you dine by the fireside or overlooking the flowered garden-terrace, you will be treated to generous portions of traditional fare. Friendly welcome and attentive service.

in Cabris 5 km West by D 4 X – **pop. 1 534 – alt. 550 m** – ✉ **06530**

Syndicat d'initiative, 4, rue de la Porte Haute ✆ 04 93 60 55 63, Fax 04 93 60 55 94

Site★ - ⩤★★ of the château ruins.

Horizon without rest

100 Promenade St-Jean – ✆ 04 93 60 51 69 – hotel-horizon.cabris@wanadoo.fr – Fax 04 93 60 56 29 – Open 15April-15 October

22 rm – †€ 85/120 ††€ 85/140, ☕ € 11

◆ A charming hillside village where the writer Saint-Exupéry lived for a while. The view from the terrace, pool and rooms is stupendous. Local history museum.

Auberge du Vieux Château with rm

pl. Panorama – ✆ 04 93 60 50 12 – www.aubergeduvieuxchateau.com – aubergeduvieuxchateau@wanadoo.fr – Fax 04 93 60 58 47 – Closed 1-15 December

5 rm – †€ 71/116 ††€ 71/116, ☕ € 12

Rest – *(closed Tuesday except dinner in July-August and Monday)* Menu (€ 29), € 39 (weekday lunch)/45

◆ An old building near the ruined château. Provençal-style dining room and attractive terrace overlooking the countryside. Charming rooms.

Le Petit Prince

15 r. F. Mistral – ✆ 04 93 60 63 14 – www.lepetitprince-cabris.com – knoettler@wanadoo.fr – Fax 04 93 60 62 87

Rest – Menu (€ 15), € 23/33 – Carte € 31/52

◆ "Draw me a ... kid goat!" St-Exupéry's mother lived in this village. Rustic-styled restaurant decorated with engravings and objects recalling the Little Prince. Lovely shaded terrace.

GRATENTOUR – 31 Haute-Garonne – 343 G2 – see Toulouse

GRATOT – 50 Manche – 303 D5 – see Coutances

LE GRAU-D'AGDE – 34 Hérault – 339 F9 – see Agde

LE GRAU-DU-ROI – 30 Gard – 339 J7 – pop. 8 173 – alt. 2 m – Casino 23 C2

– ✉ 30240 Provence

Paris 751 – Aigues-Mortes 7 – Arles 55 – Lunel 22 – Montpellier 34 – Nîmes 49 – Sète 52

Office de tourisme, 30, rue Michel Rédarès ✆ 04 66 51 67 70, Fax 04 66 51 06 80

Les Acacias without rest

21 r. Egalité – ✆ 04 66 51 40 86 – www.hotellesacacias.free.fr – hotellesacacias@free.fr – Fax 04 66 51 17 66 – Closed 10 December-10 February

29 rm – †€ 55/83 ††€ 55/83, ☕ € 9

◆ Renovated 1940s style family hotel two steps from the beach. A small terrace with flowering acacias flanked by two houses. Provençal style rooms and smaller, simply decorated ones.

in Port Camargue South: 3 km by D 62B – ✉ **30240 Le Grau du Roi**

Spinaker

pointe de la Presqu'île – ✆ 04 66 53 36 37 – www.spinaker.com – spinaker@wanadoo.fr – Fax 04 66 53 17 47 – Closed 21-27 December

16 rm – †€ 88/169 ††€ 88/169, ☕ € 12 – 5 suites

Rest *Carré des Gourmets* – *(closed Monday and Tuesday except July-August)* Carte € 61/113

◆ Hotel by the marina quayside at the end of the peninsula. Attractive, personalised, ground floor guestrooms (Provence, Africa and Morocco) opening onto the garden and pool, lined with palm trees. Contemporary restaurant and terrace overlooking the marina.

Mercure rest,
rte Marines – ✆ 04 66 73 60 60 – www.thalassa.com
– h1947@accor.com – Fax 04 66 73 60 50 – Closed 7-27 December
89 rm – €110/180 €110/180, €12 – ½ P €97/132
Rest – Menu €27/30 – Carte €27/40
◆ Opposite the dunes and the sea, the hotel complex houses a thalassotherapy centre. Comfortable rooms refurbished in a modern style with balconies. This restaurant situated on the sixth floor, offers a choice between traditional and diet dishes.

L'Oustau Camarguen rm, rest,
3 rte Marines – ✆ 04 66 51 51 65
– www.oustaucamarguen.com – oustaucamarguen@wanadoo.fr
– Fax 04 66 53 06 65 – Open 20 March-11 November and weekends from February to mid-March
39 rm – €81/105 €81/105, €12 – 8 suites – ½ P €78/90
Rest – *(open 1st May-end September and closed Wednesday dinner except July-August) (dinner only except weekend from May to September)* Menu €28/31 – Carte €32/44
◆ Small Camargue farmhouse decorated in the Provence style (wrought iron, terracotta, polished wood). Spacious rooms with private gardens or terraces. Pleasant wellness centre. Classic cuisine served in a rustic dining area or outside by the pool.

L'Amarette
centre commercial Camargue 2000 – ✆ 04 66 51 47 63
– www.l-amarette.com – lamarette2@wanadoo.fr – Fax 04 66 51 47 63
– Closed end November-mid January
Rest – Menu (€23), €37/60 – Carte €40/60
◆ A well-kept interior and pleasant terrace on the first floor of a shopping centre, near the North beach. Fresh fish and seafood cuisine.

GRAUFTHAL – 67 Bas-Rhin – **315** H4 – see La Petite-Pierre

GRAULHET – 81 Tarn – **338** D8 – pop. 12 000 – alt. 166 m – ✉ 81300 29 **C2**

Paris 694 – Albi 39 – Castres 31 – Toulouse 63
Office de tourisme, square Maréchal Foch ✆ 05 63 34 75 09, Fax 05 63 34 75 09

La Rigaudié
rte de St-Julien-du-Puy – ✆ 05 63 34 49 54 – www.larigaudie-restaurant.com
– genevieve@larigaudie-restaurant.com
– Closed 1-12 May, 27 August-14 September, 2-5 January, Saturday lunch, Sunday dinner and Monday
Rest – Menu (€12), €15 bi (weekday lunch), €18/64 – Carte €35/70
◆ A fine 19C manor house, whose plush welcoming dining room overlooks the park. Terrace shaded by plane trees. Modern cuisine.

LA GRAVE – 05 Hautes-Alpes – **334** F2 – pop. 491 – alt. 1 526 m 41 **C1**
– Winter sports : 1 450/3 250 m 2 2 – ✉ 05320 French Alps

Paris 642 – Briançon 38 – Gap 126 – Grenoble 80 – Col du Lautaret 11
Office de tourisme, route nationale 91 ✆ 04 76 79 90 05, Fax 04 76 79 91 65
Glacier de la Meije★★★ (by cable car) - ★★★.
Oratoire du Chazelet★★★ Northwest: 6 km.

Les Chalets de la Meije without rest
– ✆ 04 76 79 97 97 – www.hotel-la-grave.fr
– contact@chalet-meije.com – Fax 04 76 79 97 98
– Closed 3-29 May and 11 October-19 December
18 rm – €77/88 €93/102 – 9 suites
◆ A hotel and residential complex on a superb site facing Écrins park. Pretty rooms (wood panels, wrought iron, exotic furniture) located in several different chalets.

 **La Meijette** rest, VISA

– ✆ 04 76 79 90 34 – *hotel.lameijette.juge@wanadoo.fr* – *Fax 04 76 79 94 76* – *Open 31 May-30 September*

18 rm – †€ 60/90 ††€ 60/90, ☕ € 9 – ½ P € 65/85

Rest – Menu (€ 16), € 20 – Carte € 27/46

◆ Two buildings opposite the grandiose Meije mountain range, separated by a road. Rooms are furnished in pine, well kept and often spacious. Superb view of the glaciers from the restaurant, particularly from the ideally situated panoramic terrace.

GRAVELINES – 59 Nord – 302 A2 – pop. 11 800 – ✉ 59820 — 30 A1

Northern France and the Paris Region

Paris 287 – Calais 26 – Cassel 38 – Dunkerque 21 – Lille 89 – St-Omer 36

Office de tourisme, 11, rue de la République ✆ 03 28 51 94 00, Fax 03 28 65 58 19

Hostellerie du Beffroi rm, VISA

2 pl. Ch. Valentin – ✆ *03 28 23 24 25* – *www.hoteldubeffroi.com* – *contact.hoteldubeffroi@wanadoo.fr* – *Fax 03 28 65 59 71*

40 rm – †€ 70 ††€ 78, ☕ € 9,50

Rest – *(closed Saturday lunch and Sunday dinner)* Menu (€ 15 bi), € 16/25 – Carte € 28/40

◆ A modern brick-built building at the foot of the belfry inside the Vauban town wall. Functional, well-kept rooms available. Modern dining room with a terrace facing the square. Traditional unpretentious cuisine.

GRAVESON – 13 Bouches-du-Rhône – 340 D2 – pop. 3 570 – alt. 14 m – ✉ 13690 — 42 E1

Provence

Paris 696 – Avignon 14 – Carpentras 40 – Cavaillon 30 – Marseille 102 – Nîmes 38

Office de tourisme, cours National ✆ 04 90 95 88 44, Fax 04 90 95 81 75

Musée Auguste-chabaud★.

Moulin d'Aure rest, VISA

St-Rémy-de-Provence road, 1 km via D 5 – ✆ *04 90 95 84 05* – *www.hotel-moulindaure.com* – *reception@hotel-moulindaure.com* – *Fax 04 90 95 73 84* – *Closed 5-30 January*

19 rm – †€ 72/200 ††€ 72/200, ☕ € 16

Rest – *(open March-15 November and closed Monday lunch except in July-August)* Menu (€ 25), € 45 – Carte € 45/100

◆ This recent villa set in a large olive grove has attractive Provençal-style rooms (wrought iron, terracotta tile floors), some with a terrace. Bright, welcoming dining room with exposed rafters, overlooking the pool.

Le Cadran Solaire without rest VISA

5 r. du Cabaret-Neuf – ✆ *04 90 95 71 79* – *www.hotel-en-provence.com* – *cadransolaire@wanadoo.fr* – *Fax 04 90 90 55 04* – *Open 21 March-19 November*

12 rm – †€ 65 ††€ 65, ☕ € 8

◆ The façade of this charming 16C coaching inn, tucked away in a pretty garden, is decorated with a sundial. Delightfully cosy rooms (no TV) and a delicious terrace.

Le Mas des Amandiers rm, rest, VISA

rte d'Avignon, 1.5 km – ✆ *04 90 95 81 76* – *www.hotel-des-amandiers.com* – *contact@hotel-des-amandiers.com* – *Fax 04 90 95 85 18* – *Open 15 March-15 October*

28 rm – †€ 58 ††€ 63, ☕ € 9 – ½ P € 60

Rest – Menu (€ 14 bi), € 20 (weekday lunch), € 27/45 – Carte € 18/26

◆ Plain but spruced up rooms, graced with rustic furniture and grouped around a pool. Botanical trail. Bicycles and scooters for hire. Modern dining room decorated with a hint of Provence; classic, regional menu.

Le Clos des Cyprès VISA

rte de Châteaurenard – ✆ *04 90 90 53 44* – *Closed one week in January, dinner during the week in low season, Wednesday dinner, Sunday dinner and Monday in high season*

Rest – *(pre-book)* Menu € 27/34

◆ Set in parkland, a Provençal villa with plush dining room (ochre tones) and canopied terrace. Attentive staff and up-to-date gourmet menu chalked up on the blackboard.

GRAY – 70 Haute-Saône – 314 B8 – pop. 6 773 – alt. 220 m – ✉ 70100 16 B2

Burgundy-Jura

Paris 336 – Besançon 45 – Dijon 50 – Dole 46 – Langres 56 – Vesoul 58

Office de tourisme, Île Sauzay ☎ 03 84 65 14 24, Fax 03 84 65 46 26

Town hall ★ - Collection of pastels and drawings ★ by Prud'hon at the musée Baron-Martin ★ M[1].

in Rigny by ① D 70 and D 2: 5 km – pop. 604 – alt. 196 m – ✉ 70100

Château de Rigny rm,

– ☎ *03 84 65 25 01 – www.chateau-de-rigny.com*
– info@chateau-de-rigny.com – Fax 03 84 65 44 45
28 rm – €75/130 €95/230, €12 – ½ P €99/169
Rest – Menu €36/48 – Carte €41/56

◆ The paths through the park attached to this 17th century hotel wind down to the Saône. The rooms include old-style furnishings. Choose one in the silk farm. Comfortable dining room or pleasant terrace. Classic, seasonal cuisine.

in Nantilly by ① and D 2: 5 km – pop. 511 – alt. 200 m – ✉ 70100

Château de Nantilly rm,

r. Millerand – ☎ *03 84 67 78 00*
– www.chateau-de-nantilly.com – contact@chateau-de-nantilly.fr
– Fax 03 84 67 78 01 – Closed 2 January-28 February
41 rm – €70/110 €110/190, €10 – ½ P €120/160
Rest – *(closed Sunday dinner, Monday and Tuesday) (dinner only)* Menu €37, €49/63 – Carte €56/64

◆ Pretty vine-clad 1830 chateau set in a park crossed by a river. The rooms in the main wing have more charm than those in the outbuilding. Elegant, light and spacious restaurant. Regional cuisine.

GRENADE-SUR-L'ADOUR – 40 Landes – 335 I12 – pop. 2 265 – alt. 55 m – ✉ 40270 3 B2

Paris 720 – Aire-sur-l'Adour 18 – Mont-de-Marsan 15 – Orthez 53 – St-Sever 14 – Tartas 33

Office de tourisme, 1, place des Déportés ☎ 05 58 45 45 98, Fax 05 58 45 45 55

Pain Adour et Fantaisie (Philippe Garret) with rm rm,

14 pl. des Tilleuls – ☎ *05 58 45 18 80*
– pain.adour.fantaisie@wanadoo.fr – Fax 05 58 45 16 57
– Closed Sunday and Monday from mid December to Easter
11 rm – €70/164 €70/164, €15
Rest – *(closed Monday except dinner from 14 July to 31 August, Sunday dinner from September to mid July and Wednesday lunch)* Menu (€18), €40/72 – Carte €58/78

Spec. Foie gras de canard confit au genièvre et Jurançon. Rouget grillé aux cébettes et réduction de safran (season). Cube de chocolat Caraïbe et gelée de menthe. **Wines** Vin de Pays de Côtes de Gascogne, Madiran.

◆ The name of this 17C hotel evokes the neo-Realist cinema of Italy. Luxurious interior, terrace on the banks of the Adour, contemporary cuisine and a selection of regional wines.

Southeast 7,5 km by Larrivière and D 352 - ✉ 40270 Renung

Domaine de Benauge without rest

29 chemin de Benauge – ☎ *05 58 71 77 30 – www.benauge.com*
– ppancel@orange.fr
5 rm – €35 €60

◆ This commander's residence dating from the 15C has retained traces of its original fortifications. Attractive contemporary-style guestrooms, plus a garden overlooking the surrounding countryside.

If breakfast is included the symbol appears after the number of rooms.

GRENOBLE Ⓟ – 38 Isère – **333** H6 – **pop. 155 100** – **Built-up area 419 334** – **alt. 213 m** – ✉ **38000** French Alps 45 **C2**

Paris 566 – Chambéry 55 – Genève 143 – Lyon 105 – Torino 235

Grenoble-Isère ☎ 04 76 65 48 48, 39km on the ⑥

Office de tourisme, 14, rue de la République ☎ 04 76 42 41 41, Fax 04 76 00 18 98

de Seyssins Seyssins 29 rue du Plâtre, ☎ 04 76 70 12 63

de Grenoble Bresson Route de Montavie, S : 6 km on D 269, ☎ 04 76 73 65 00

Site★★★ - St Laurent's Church-museum★★ : crypte St-Oyand (St Oyrand's crypt)★★ FY - Fort de la Bastille (Bastille Fort) ❋★★ by cable car EY - Vieille ville (Old Town)★ EY : Palais de Justice (Law Courts)★ (panelling★) - staircase★ of the hôtel d'Ornacieux EY **J** - Museums: de Grenoble★★★ FY, de la Résistance et de la Déportation (Resistance and Deportation)★ F , de l'ancien Evêché-Patrimoines de l'Isère(Former Bishop's Palace – Heritage of Isère)★★ - Musée dauphinois (Museum of the Dauphin)★ : chapel★★, themed exhibition★★ EY.

Plans on following pages

Park Hôtel VISA MC AE

10 pl. Paul Mistral – ☎ 04 76 85 81 23 – www.park-hotel-grenoble.fr – resa@park-hotel-grenoble.fr – Fax 04 76 46 49 88 – Closed 25 July-23 August and 24 December-3 January FZ **w**

50 rm – †€ 150/195 ††€ 180/225, ☕ € 16 – 10 suites

Rest ***louis 10*** – *(closed Sunday lunch, Saturday and lunch holidays)* Menu € 29/54 – Carte € 35/66

◆ The spacious guestrooms exude a certain antiquated charm in this cosy hotel which brings to mind the atmosphere of an English gentlemen's club. Very chic, contemporary setting. Fusion cooking with sushi, sashimi and maki menu.

Novotel Centre rm, VISA MC AE

à Europole, pl. R. Schuman – ☎ 04 76 70 84 84 – www.novotel.com – jacques.poyade@accor.com – Fax 04 76 70 24 93 AV **r**

116 rm – †€ 95/155 ††€ 95/155, ☕ € 15 – 2 suites

Rest – Menu (€ 19 bi), € 23 (weekdays)/45 bi – Carte € 20/47

◆ Opposite the station, contemporary style hotel adjoining the WTC and a conference centre. Spacious rooms with Japanese-inspired décor; impressive modern fitness centre. Traditional recipes and grilled dishes feature on the menu of this contemporary restaurant.

Grand Hôtel Mercure Président rm, VISA MC AE

11 r. Gén. Mangin ✉ 38100 – ☎ 04 76 56 26 56 – www.mercure.com – h2947@accor.com – Fax 04 76 56 26 82 AX **y**

105 rm – †€ 125/259 ††€ 137/271, ☕ € 17

Rest – *(closed 10-23 August, 19 December-3 January)* Carte € 22/37

◆ Successful renovation for this pleasant Mercure. Facilities include comfortable guestrooms, an exotic bar and lobby, meeting and fitness facilities, sauna, Jacuzzi and terrace-garden. Wide choice of traditional recipes.

Mercure Centre Alpotel rm, VISA MC AE

12 bd Mar. Joffre – ☎ 04 76 87 88 41 – www.mercure.com – h0652@accor.com – Fax 04 76 47 58 52 EZ **d**

88 rm – †€ 89/189 ††€ 99/199, ☕ € 17

Rest – *(closed 2-24 August, 20 December-1st January, Saturday, Sunday and holidays)* Menu € 17 (weekday lunch) – Carte € 26/37

◆ Built for the 1968 Olympics and a symbol of the 'concrete' trend of the time, this hotel is now a listed building (non-smoking). Modern and well-appointed rooms. The Café Pourpre's designer decor is the backdrop for a menu of traditional and straightforward cuisine.

Lesdiguières rm, VISA MC

122 cours de la Libération – ☎ 04 38 70 19 50 – www.hotellesdiguieres.com – hotellesdiguieres@gastronomie.com – Fax 04 38 70 19 69 – Closed school holidays, Friday, Saturday and Sunday AX **b**

23 rm – †€ 64 ††€ 72, ☕ € 8 – 1 suite – ½ P € 84

Rest – Menu (€ 16), € 22 (weekday dinner), € 28/51

◆ A veritable Grenoble institution, home to a renowned hotel school since 1917. Comfortable guestrooms with those facing the park generally quieter. Attractive menus focusing on Dauphiné regional produce.

CORENC

Eygala (Av. de l') .... BCV
Grésivaudan (Av. du) .... BCV

EYBENS

Innsbruck (Av. d') .... BX 38
Jean-Jaurès (Av.) .... BX
Mendès-France (R.) .... BX
Poisat (Av. de) .... BX 47

ÉCHIROLLES

Etats-Généraux (Av. des) .... AX 30
Grugliasco (Av. de) .... AX
Jean-Jaurès (Crs) .... AX
Kimberley (Av. de) .... ABX

FONTAINE

Briand (Av. A.) .... AV
Joliot-Curie (Bd) .... AV
Vercors (Av. du) .... AV

GRENOBLE

Alliés (R. des) .... AX
Alsace-Lorraine (Av.) .... DYZ 3
Ampère (R.) .... AV
Augereau (R.) .... DZ
Barnavel (R.) .... EFY 5
Bayard (R.) .... FY 6
Belgique (Av. Albert-1er de) .... EFZ 7
Belgrade (R. de) .... EY 9
Bernard (Q. Cl.) .... DY
Berriat (Crs) .... AV, DZ
Berthelot (Av. M.) .... BX
Bistesi (R.) .... FZ 10
Bizanet (R.) .... FGY
Blanchard (R. P.) .... EYZ
Blum (Av. Léon) .... AX
Boissieux (R. B.-de) .... EZ
Bonne (R. de) .... EZ 12
Brenier (R. C.) .... DY 13
Briand (Pl. A.) .... DY
Brocherie (R.) .... EY 15
Casimir-Périer (R.) .... EZ 16
Champollion (R.) .... FZ 17
Champon (Av. Gén.) .... FZ
Chanrion (R. J.) .... FYZ
Chenoise (R.) .... EFY 18
Claudel (R. P.) .... BX 20
Clemenceau (Bd) .... FGZ
Clot-Bey (R.) .... EYZ 21
Condillac (R.) .... EZ
Condorcet (R.) .... DZ
Créqui (Q.) .... DEY
Diables-Bleus (Bd des) .... FZ 24
Diderot (R.) .... AV 25
Dr-Girard (Pl.) .... FY 26
Driant (Bd Col.) .... FZ 27
Dubedout (Pl. H.) .... DY 28
Esclangon (R. F.) .... AV 29
Esmonin (Av. E.) .... AX
l'Europe (Av. de) .... BX 31
Fantin-Latour (R.) .... FZ 32
Faure (R. E.) .... FZ
La Fayette (R.) .... EY 39
Flandrin (R. J.) .... GZ 33
Foch (Bd Mar.) .... DEZ
La Fontaine (Crs) .... EZ
Fourier (R.) .... FZ 34
France (Q. de) .... DEY
Gambetta (Bd) .... DEZ
Graille (Q. de la) .... DY
Grande-Rue .... EY 37
Grenette (Pl.) .... EY
Gueymard (R. E.) .... DY
Haxo (R.) .... FZ
Hébert (R.) .... FYZ
L'Herminier (R. Cdt) .... FY 41
Hoche (R.) .... EZ
Jay (Q. S.) .... EY
Jeanne-d'Arc (Av.) .... GZ
Jean-Jaurès (Crs) .... DYZ
Joffre (Bd Mar.) .... DEZ
Jongking (Q.) .... FY
Jouhaux (R. L.) .... BX, GZ
Jouvin (Q. X.) .... FY
Lakanal (R.) .... EZ
Lavalette (Pl.) .... FY 40
Leclerc (Av. Mar.) .... FY
Lesdiguières (R.) .... EZ
Libération et du Gén.-de Gaulle (Crs de la) .... AX
Lyautey (Bd Mar.) .... EZ 42
Lyon (Rte de) .... DY
Malakoff (R.) .... FGZ
Mallifaud (R.) .... EFZ
Martyrs (R. des) .... AV
Mistral (Pl. P.) .... FZ
Montorge (R.) .... EY 43
Mortillet (R. de) .... FGY
Moyrand (R.) .... FGZ
Notre-Dame (Pl.) .... FY
Pain (Bd J.) .... FZ
Palanka (R.) .... EY 44
Pasteur (Pl.) .... FZ 45
Perrière (Q.) .... EY 46
Perrot (Av. J.) .... BX, FZ
Poulat (R. F.) .... EY 48
Prévost (R. J.) .... DZ
Randon (Av. Mar.) .... FY
Reynier (R. A.) .... AX 49
Reynoard (Av. M.) .... BX 5
Rey (Bd Ed.) .... EY
Rhin-et-Danube (Av.) .... AX
Rivet (Pl. G.) .... EZ 5
Rousseau (R. J.-J.) .... EY 5
Sablon (Pont du) .... GY
Ste-Claire (Pl.) .... EY 5
St-André (Pl.) .... EY 5
Sembat (Bd A.) .... EZ
Servan (R.) .... FY 5
Stalingrad (R. de) .... AX 6
Strasbourg (R. de) .... EFZ 6
Thiers (R.) .... DZ
Très-Cloîtres (R.) .... FY
Turenne (R.) .... DZ

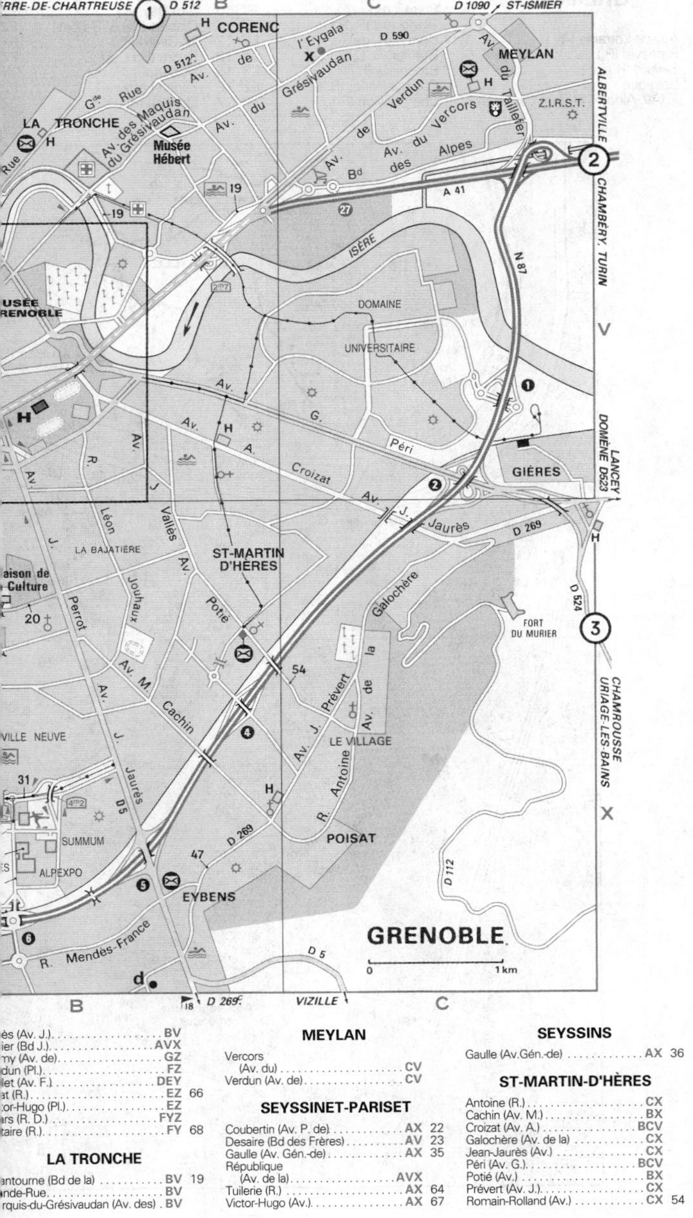

RRE-DE-CHARTREUSE
1
D 512
B
C
D 1090
ST-ISMIER
CORENC
H
l'Eygala
D 590
D 512A
Av. de Grésivaudan
MEYLAN
Av. du Taillefer
Gde Rue
LA TRONCHE
Av. des Maquis du Grésivaudan
Av. du Verdun
Av. de Verdun
Av. du Vercors
Z.I.R.S.T.
ALBERTVILLE
Musée Hébert
Bd des Alpes
Av.
2
CHAMBÉRY, TURIN
A 41
19
27
ISÈRE
N 87
USÉE
RENOBLE
DOMAINE
UNIVERSITAIRE
V
Av. G. Péri
Av. A. Croizat
GIÈRES
LANCEY
DOMÈNE D523
Av. J. Jaurès
D 269
R. Léon Jouhaux
LA BAJATIÈRE
Av. Vallès
ST-MARTIN D'HÈRES
aison de
Culture
Av. J. Perrot
Av. Potié
Galochère
D 524
FORT DU MURIER
3
20
54
Av. M. Cachin
Av. J. Prévert
Av. de la
CHAMROUSSE
URIAGE-LES-BAINS
VILLE NEUVE
LE VILLAGE
R. Antoine
Av. J. Jaurès
31
D5
X
SUMMUM
POISAT
ALPEXPO
47
D 269
D 112
EYBENS
GRENOBLE
R. Mendès-France
D 5
0
1 km
d
B
D 269c
VIZILLE
C

GRENOBLE

Alsace-Lorraine (Av.) . . . . **DYZ** 3
Barnavel (R.) . . . . **EFY** 5
Bayard (R.) . . . . **FY** 6
Belgique
(Av. Albert-1er-de) . . . . . **EFZ** 7
Belgrade (R. de) . . . . **EY** 9
Bistesi (R.) . . . . **FZ** 10
Blanchard (R. P.) . . . . **EYZ**
Bonne (R. de) . . . . **EZ** 12
Brenier (R. C.) . . . . **DY** 13
Brocherie (R.) . . . . **EY** 15
Casimir-Périer (R.) . . . . **EZ** 16
Champollion (R.) . . . . **FZ** 17
Chenoise (R.) . . . . **EFY**
Clot-Bey (R.) . . . . **EYZ**
Diables-Bleus (Bd des) . . . . **FZ**
Dr-Girard (Pl.) . . . . **FY**
Driant (Bd Col.) . . . . **FZ**
Dubedout (Pl. H.) . . . . **DY**
Fantin-Latour (R.) . . . . **FZ**
Flandrin (R. J.) . . . . **GZ**

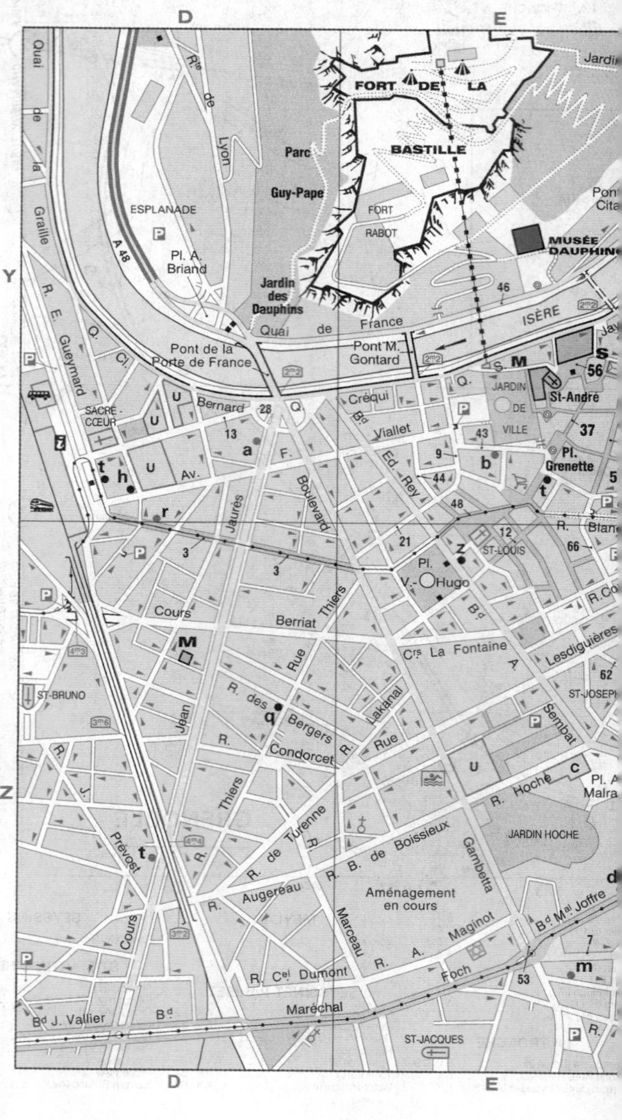

h (Bd Mar.) . . . . **DEZ**	Montorge (R.) . . . . **EY** 43	St-André (Pl.) . . . . **EY** 56
rier (R.) . . . . **FZ** 34	Palanka (R.) . . . . **EY** 44	Servan (R.) . . . . **FY** 59
nde-Rue . . . . **EY** 37	Pasteur (Pl.) . . . . **FZ** 45	Strasbourg (R. de) . . . . . . **EFZ** 62
nette (Pl.) . . . . **EY**	Perrière (Q.) . . . . **EY** 46	Très-Cloître (R.) . . . . **FY** 63
alette (Pl.) . . . . **FY** 40	Poulat (R. F.) . . . . **EY** 48	Vicat (R.) . . . . **EZ** 66
Fayette (R.) . . . . **EY** 39	Rivet (Pl. G.) . . . . **EZ** 53	Victor-Hugo (Pl.) . . . . **EZ**
erminier (R. Cdt) . . . . . . **FY** 41	Rousseau (R. J.-J.) . . . . **EY** 55	Voltaire (R.) . . . . **FY** 68
utey (Bd Mar.) . . . . **EZ** 42	Ste-Claire (Pl.) . . . . **EY** 57	

Terminus without rest
10 pl. de la Gare – 04 76 87 24 33 – www.terminus-hotel-grenoble.fr – Fax 04 76 50 38 28 DY **t**
39 rm – €68/99 €84/149, €12
◆ As its name suggests, this family-run hotel is located opposite the railway station. Views of the Moucherotte and Vercors range from the upper floors, breakfast served beneath a glass roof.

Patrick Hotel without rest
116 cours de la Libération – 04 76 21 26 63 – www.patrickhotel-grenoble.com – contact@patrickhotel-grenoble.com – Fax 04 76 48 01 07 AX **n**
56 rm – €87 €97, €12
◆ Tile-covered façade for this hotel located on a major road. Well-maintained, modern rooms with good sound-proofing. Small bar-lounge refurbished in chocolate tones.

Angleterre without rest
5 pl. Victor-Hugo – 04 76 87 37 21 – www.hotel-angleterre-grenoble.com – reservations@hotel-angleterre-grenoble.com – Fax 04 76 50 94 10 EZ **z**
62 rm – €110/185 €110/185, €13
◆ Well-located in front of a park, this hotel offers functional rooms adorned with cane and wood furniture, some with sloping ceilings, others with Jacuzzis.

Splendid without rest
22 r. Thiers – 04 76 46 33 12 – www.splendid-hotel.com – info@splendid-hotel.com – Fax 04 76 46 35 24 DZ **q**
45 rm – €59/89 €75/95, €8
◆ The guestrooms (some adorned with original frescoes) in this hotel close to the Musée des Rêves Mécaniques are gradually being renovated. Buffet breakfast.

Europe without rest
22 pl. Grenette – 04 76 46 16 94 – www.hoteleurope.fr – hotel.europe.gre@wanadoo.fr – Fax 04 76 43 13 65 EY **t**
45 rm – €31/72 €40/80, €8
◆ Located in the heart of historic Grenoble, the Europe (the town's first hotel) offers rooms refurbished in a tasteful, modern style. Attractive, fashionable breakfast room.

Gallia without rest
7 bd Mar. Joffre – 04 76 87 39 21 – www.hotel-gallia.com – gallia-hotel@wanadoo.fr – Fax 04 76 87 65 76 – Closed 25 July-24 August
35 rm – €54/61 €58/65, €8 EZ **s**
◆ Most of the guestrooms in this family-run hotel have been brightly refurbished in Provençal tones. Pleasant lobby-lounge.

Institut without rest
10 r. L. Barbillon – 04 76 46 36 44 – www.institut-hotel.fr – contact@institut-hotel.fr – Fax 04 76 47 73 09 DY **h**
48 rm – €58/61 €61, €8
◆ The main selling-points of this functional hotel are its friendly welcome, well-maintained facilities and reasonable prices. Brightly decorated, well-appointed guestrooms.

XXX **Le Fantin Latour**
1 r. Gén. Beylié – 04 76 01 00 97 – www.fantin-latour.net – reservation@fantin-latour.net – Fax 04 76 01 02 41 FZ **a**
Rest – *(closed Sunday and Monday) (dinner only except Saturday)* Menu €49/96 – Carte €78/110
Rest *Le 18.36* – 5 r. Abbé de la Salle, *04.76.01.00.97 (closed Saturday and Sunday) (lunch only)* Menu €20 bi/26 bi – Carte €42/57
◆ The new chef concocts an inventive cuisine based on alpine plants in this lovely 19C mansion. It was once home to a museum devoted to the artist Fantin Latour. Named after the year in which the artist was born. Concise brasserie *carte* and daily set menu.

XXX **Auberge Napoléon**
7 r. Montorge – 04 76 87 53 64 – www.auberge-napoleon.fr – fcaby@wanadoo.fr – Closed 1-10 May, 10-25 August, 5-12 January and Sunday
Rest – *(dinner only) (number of covers limited, pre-book)* Menu €47, €78/89 – Carte €59/81 EY **b**
◆ Restaurant dedicated to the memory of Napoleon Bonaparte, its most famous guest. Personalised, inventive cuisine served in the Empire-style dining room.

XX **A Ma Table** A/C VISA MC

92 cours J. Jaurès – ✆ 04 76 96 77 04 – Fax 04 76 96 77 04
– Closed August, Saturday lunch, Sunday and Monday DZ **t**

Rest – *(number of covers limited, pre-book)* Carte € 50/67

◆ A tiny, welcoming restaurant which makes you feel very much at home. Generous and flavoursome classical cuisine.

XX **Marie Margaux** A/C VISA MC AE ①

12 r. Marcel Porte ✉ 38100 – ✆ 04 76 46 46 46 – www.lemariemargaux.com
– lemariemargaux@orange.fr – Fax 04 76 46 46 46
– Closed 28 June-13 July, Sunday dinner and Monday dinner EZ **m**

Rest – Menu (€ 11), € 19 (weekday lunch), € 32/51 – Carte € 36/60

◆ A welcoming family establishment (named after the two grandmothers) with a Provençal decor and a straightforward repertoire of traditionally-cooked fish.

XX **Chasse-Spleen** VISA MC AE ①

6 pl. Lavalette – ✆ 04 38 37 03 52 – escalier@wanadoo.fr – Fax 04 76 63 01 58
– Closed Saturday and Sunday FY **e**

Rest – Menu (€ 21), € 26 (weekdays)/34 – Carte € 30/54

◆ Hommage to Charles Baudelaire who named this wine during a stay at Moulis-en-Médoc. Poems by the author on the walls, as food for thought. Dauphiné dishes.

X **Grill Parisien** VISA MC AE

34 bd Alsace-Lorraine – ✆ 04 76 46 10 16 – Closed 30 July-30 August,
Saturday, Sunday and bank holidays DYZ **r**

Rest – Menu (€ 21), € 39 (dinner) – Carte € 45/61

◆ Regulars to this bistro enjoy traditional Mediterranean cuisine either sitting at the kitchen table or beneath the wooden beams in the dining room.

X **Le Coup de Torchon** VISA MC ①

8 r. Dominique Villars – ✆ 04 76 63 20 58 – Closed Wednesday dinner,
Sunday and Monday FY **a**

Rest – Menu (€ 10), € 16 (lunch)/22 – Carte € 29/37

◆ Close to the city's antique shops, this restaurant serves well-prepared, reasonably priced modern cuisine based around seasonal market produce. Attractive setting.

X **La Glycine** VISA MC

168 cours Berriat – ✆ 04 76 21 95 33 – Fax 04 76 96 58 65
– Closed 3-17 August and Sunday AV **n**

Rest – *(pre-book)* Menu (€ 17), € 33 (weekdays)/39

◆ Rustic dining rooms, decorated with old plates and posters. In summer, a meal beneath the superb wisteria (glycine), a listed monument, is a must. Mediterranean-inspired cuisine.

X **L'Exception** A/C VISA MC AE

4 cours Jean-Jaurès – ✆ 04 76 47 03 12 – www.lexception.com
– contact@lexception.com – Fax 04 76 47 03 12 – Closed 19 July-3 August,
3-11 January, Saturday and Sunday DY **a**

Rest – Menu (€ 13), € 25/52 – Carte € 47/69

◆ This small unpretentious restaurant is always busy. Abundant creative cuisine drawing inspiration from the local area, and reasonable prices.

X **Le Village** A/C VISA MC AE

20 r. de Strasbourg – ✆ 04 76 87 88 44 – gavet.michel@orange.fr
– Closed 4-27 July, 19 December-4 January, Sunday and Monday FZ **b**

Rest – Menu (€ 14), € 26/40 – Carte € 32/45

◆ This simply furnished restaurant in a village-like district in the centre of town is often full, testimony to the friendly atmosphere and fine modern cuisine.

in Corenc – pop. 3 773 – alt. 450 m – ✉ 38700

XX **Corne d' Or** P VISA MC AE

159 rte de Chartreuse, par ① : 3,5 km sur D 512 – ✆ 04 38 86 62 36
– www.cornedor.fr – info@cornedor.fr – Fax 04 38 86 62 37
– Closed 16 August-6 September, Sunday dinner, Tuesday and Wednesday

Rest – Menu (€ 18), € 26, € 40/78 – Carte € 63/89

◆ The window tables and the terrace allow pleasant views of Grenoble and the Belledonne mountains. Contemporary menu inspired by some of the country's leading chefs.

Le Provence
28 av. du Grésivaudan – ✆ 04 76 90 03 38 – www.leprovence.fr – contact@leprovence.fr – Fax 04 76 90 46 13 – Closed 27 July-25 August, Monday lunch, Saturday lunch and Sunday dinner CV **x**
Rest – Menu (€ 21), € 26 (weekday lunch), € 30/64 – Carte € 37/65
◆ Fish, simply grilled with olive oil in Provençal style is the speciality here. Sunlit dining room and terrace for the summer months.

in Eybens : **5 km – pop. 9 454 – alt. 230 m – ✉ 38320**

Château de la Commanderie
17 av. d'Échirolles – ✆ 04 76 25 34 58 – www.commanderie.fr – resa@commanderie.fr – Fax 04 76 24 07 31 – Closed 20 December-3 January BX **d**
43 rm – €119/150 €145/168, € 15
Rest – *(closed for the Toussaint and Christmas holidays, Saturday lunch, Sunday and Monday)* Menu (€ 28 bi), € 43/75 – Carte € 69/97
◆ A little castle - former command post of the Templar Knights - in a tree-lined garden. Ancestral furniture, family portraits and Aubusson tapestries. A place steeped in history. Modernised classic cuisine in a plush setting or on the summer terrace.

in Bresson South via Avenue J. Jaurès: 8 km by D 269c – pop. 705 – alt. 300 m – ✉ 38320

Chavant with rm
2 r. Emile Chavant – ✆ 04 76 25 25 38 – www.chavanthotel.com – chavant@wanadoo.fr – Fax 04 76 62 06 55 – Closed 9-17 August and 20-28 December, Saturday lunch, Sunday dinner and Monday
5 rm – €120/140 €120/140, € 15 – 2 suites
Rest – *(closed Saturday lunch, Sunday dinner and Monday)* Menu € 35 (lunch), € 52/120 – Carte € 68/100
◆ A country inn with a wood-panelled dining room and a terrace overlooking the garden. Cellar offering tastings and wines for purchase. Spacious, somewhat old-fashioned guestrooms.

in Échirolles : **4 km – pop. 35 700 – alt. 237 m – ✉ 38130**

Dauphitel
16 av. Kimberley – ✆ 04 76 33 60 60 – www.dauphitel.fr – info@dauphitel.fr – Fax 04 76 33 60 00 AX **e**
68 rm – €68/115 €68/115, € 10
Rest – *(closed 1-23 August, 24 December-3 January, Saturday, Sunday and bank holidays)* Menu (€ 22), € 29 (weekdays)/35 – Carte € 29/45
◆ A modern hotel offering guests comfortable, functional and sound-proofed rooms, a full range of conference facilities, and a swimming pool adjoining the garden. Large, bright dining room, summer terrace and traditional cuisine.

via exit ⑥ :

in Fontanil : **8 km by A 48, exit 14 and D 1075 – pop. 2 614 – alt. 210 m – ✉ 38120**

La Queue de Cochon
rte de Lyon – ✆ 04 76 75 65 54 – www.laqueuedecochon.fr – qcochon@wanadoo.fr – Fax 04 76 75 76 85 – Closed Saturday lunch, Sunday dinner and Monday
Rest – buffet – Menu € 28/59 – Carte € 35/75
◆ This establishment is as popular for its buffets and grills as for its immense terrace surrounded by greenery. Modern decor with lobster tank; pig theme on the tableware.

near A 48 interchange exit n° 12/13: 12 km – ✉ 38340 Voreppe

Novotel
1625 rte de Veurey – ✆ 04 76 50 55 55 – www.novotel.com – h0423@accor.com – Fax 04 76 56 76 26
114 rm – €69/135 €69/135, € 15
Rest – Menu (€ 20), € 24 – Carte € 28/40
◆ Near the motorway yet surrounded by fields, this hotel offers spacious, comfortable rooms, some refurbished in line with the chain's latest standards. Novotel Café. Summer terrace overlooking the garden, traditional menu and plancha dishes.

GRÉOUX-LES-BAINS – 04 Alpes-de-Haute-Provence – 334 D10 40 B2
– pop. 2 455 – alt. 386 m – Spa : early March-mid Dec. – Casino – ✉ 04800
French Alps

Paris 783 – Aix-en-Provence 55 – Brignoles 52 – Digne-les-Bains 69 – Manosque 14

Office de tourisme, 5, avenue des Marronniers ✆ 04 92 78 01 08, Fax 04 92 78 13 00

La Crémaillère rm, rm, VISA MC AE
rte de Riez – ✆ 04 92 70 40 04 – www.chainethermale.fr – lacremaillere@chainethermale.fr – Fax 04 92 78 19 80 – Open 22 March-11 December
51 rm – €90/115 €90/140, €17 – ½ P €75/105
Rest – Menu €26/41 – Carte approx. €41
◆ The rooms with balcony or loggia feature a bright and colourful contemporary décor for a pleasant stay, not far from the troglodyte thermal baths. Provençal-style cuisine and decor in this restaurant. Health food menu for those taking the waters.

Villa Borghèse VISA MC AE
av. des Thermes – ✆ 04 92 78 00 91 – www.villa-borghese.com – villa.borghese@wanadoo.fr – Fax 04 92 78 09 55 – Open 16 March-7 December
67 rm – €59/154 €79/154, €13 – ½ P €78/117
Rest – Menu (€21), €32 – Carte €42/48
◆ No art collections in this Villa Borghese clad in ampelopsis vines, but spacious classical guestrooms with balconies. Sauna, beauty salon and bridge club (lessons). A restaurant with warm, contemporary décor serving tasty classic cuisine.

La Chêneraie VISA MC AE
Les Hautes Plaines, via av. Thermes – ✆ 04 92 78 03 23 – www.la-cheneraie.com – contact@la-cheneraie.com – Fax 04 92 78 11 72 – Open 1 March to mid-November
20 rm – €60/82 €68/90, €11 – ½ P €55/76
Rest – Menu (€16), €20/29 – Carte €29/52
◆ Modern building on a hill in this resort, in a quiet residential area. Functional rooms of a good size. The dining room's bay windows overlook the pool, historic village and castle. Generous helpings of Provençal fare.

Le Verdon rest, rest, VISA MC AE
rte de Riez – ✆ 0 826 46 81 83 – www.chainethermale.fr – leverdon@chainethermale.fr – Fax 04 92 70 43 99 – Open 2 March-28 November
64 rm – €65/80 €65/80, €14 – ½ P €67/95
Rest – Menu (€18), €24/45
◆ This hotel is home to spruce, practical rooms with balconies overlooking the village or the garrigue (scrubland). Pleasant garden with a pétanque ground. Spacious, modern dining room and lush terrace.

Les Alpes VISA MC AE
av. des Alpes – ✆ 04 92 74 24 24 – www.hoteldesalpes.fr – hoteldesalpes.greoux@wanadoo.fr – Fax 04 92 74 24 26 – Closed January
26 rm – €60/130 €80/135 – ½ P €56/81
Rest – Menu €23/28 – Carte €28/43
◆ This small family hotel, in a renovated building at the foot of the Knights Templars' castle, is gradually being smartened up. Neat practical (wireless internet) rooms, five with a terrace. Despite its name, this restaurant is well and truly Provençal. Pleasantly shaded terrace.

GRESSE-EN-VERCORS – 38 Isère – 333 G8 – pop. 360 – alt. 1 205 m 45 C2
– Winter sports : 1 300/1 700 m 16 – ✉ 38650 French Alps

Paris 610 – Clelles 22 – Grenoble 48 – Monestier-de-Clermont 14 – Vizille 43

Office de tourisme, le Faubourg ✆ 04 76 34 33 40, Fax 04 76 34 31 26

Col de l'Allimas ★ South: 2 km.

Le Chalet
– ✆ 04 76 34 32 08 – http://lechalet.free.fr – hotel.lechalet38@orange.fr – Fax 04 76 34 31 06 – Closed 9 March-3 May, 12 October-20 December and Wednesday lunch except school holidays
25 rm – €48/57 €83, €11 – ½ P €65/85
Rest – Menu €21 (weekdays)/53 – Carte €31/48
◆ This is a Dauphinois-style house, rather than a chalet, which looks after its guests well. Large guestrooms, which are being gradually renovated. Some have a loggia. Generous, traditional cuisine served in an elegant dining room or on a pleasant summer terrace.

GRESSY – 77 Seine-et-Marne – 312 F2 – 101 10 – see Paris, Area

---

GRÉSY-SUR-ISÈRE – 73 Savoie – 333 K4 – pop. 1 200 – alt. 350 m – ✉ 73460 — 46 **F2**

Paris 595 – Aiguebelle 12 – Albertville 18 – Chambéry 35 – St-Jean-de-Maurienne 48

Site★★ - Château de Miolans ≤★: Tour St-Pierre ≤★★, underground defence network★ Alpes du Nord

La Tour de Pacoret with rm — rest, VISA
North-east: 1.5 km on D 201 – ✆ 04 79 37 91 59 – www.hotel-pacoret-savoie.com – info@hotel-pacoret-savoie.com – Fax 04 79 37 93 84 – Open 1 May-20 October
10 rm – €65/180 €65/180, €12 – ½ P €70/115
Rest – *(Closed Wednesday lunch except July-August, Monday in October and Tuesday)* Menu (€15), €19/62 – Carte €40/60
◆ This watchtower built in 1283 still guards the Savoy Combe. A bright dining area with pleasant terrace affording views of the mountains. Traditional cuisine.

GREZ-EN-BOUÈRE – 53 Mayenne – 310 F7 – pop. 981 – alt. 85 m – ✉ 53290 — 35 **C1**

Paris 276 – Nantes 143 – Laval 35 – Angers 66 – La Flèche 43

Château de Chanay
4 km west on D 28 – ✆ 02 43 70 98 81 – www.chateau-de-chanay.com – info@chateau-de-chanay.com
3 rm – €75/105 €85/115 **Table d'hôte** – Menu €29 bi
◆ Set in wooded parkland in the heart of the countryside, this abode has lost none of its original style. Personalised, comfortable guestrooms, stylish sitting room-library. The table d'hôte serves home cooking in a classic dining room.

GRÈZES – 46 Lot – 337 G4 – pop. 157 – alt. 312 m – ✉ 46320 — 29 **C1**

Paris 562 – Aurillac 84 – Cahors 50 – Figeac 21 – Rocamadour 37

Le Grézalide — VISA
– ✆ 05 65 11 20 40 – www.grezalide.com – chateaugrezes@wanadoo.fr – Fax 05 65 11 20 41 – Open 1 April-30 September
19 rm – €77/97 €77/97, €10 – ½ P €70/80
Rest – *(dinner only)* Menu €28
◆ This establishment, in the heart of a Quercy village, takes you on a journey of art through its rooms devoted to artists (Dali, Rodin, etc.) and its exhibition centre. Regionally inspired cuisine served in an attractive, vaulted dining room.

LA GRIÈRE – 85 Vendée – 316 H9 – see La Tranche-sur-Mer

GRIGNAN – 26 Drôme – 332 C7 – pop. 1 452 – alt. 198 m – ✉ 26230 — 44 **B3**
Provence

Paris 629 – Crest 46 – Montélimar 25 – Nyons 25 – Orange 52 – Pont-St-Esprit 38

Office de tourisme, place du jeu de Ballon ✆ 04 75 46 56 75, Fax 04 75 46 55 89

Château★★ - St-Sauveur church ❋★.

 **Manoir de la Roseraie** ⛰ ≤ ♫ ⛱ ⛲ ♿ rm, AC ⇸ ✗ rest, ⛰ P
chemin des Grands Prés, (Valréas road) – VISA MC AE ⓓ
✆ 04 75 46 58 15 – www.manoirdelaroseraie.com – roseraie.hotel@wanadoo.fr – Fax 04 75 46 91 55 – Closed weekdays from 13 February to 31 May and from 14 September to 3 November
21 rm – †€ 152/380 ††€ 152/380, ☕ € 20
Rest – *(closed for lunch from June to September except Saturday and Sunday) (pre-book)* Menu (€ 23), € 35/58 – Carte € 54/69
◆ "Exquisite," may well have been how the Marchioness would have described this elegant 19C manor at the foot of the castle. Spacious rooms, a rose garden and attractive swimming pool. The elegant rotunda dining room has a conservatory overlooking parkland. Up-to-date menu.

Le Clair de la Plume without rest ⛰ AC ⇸ VISA MC AE ⓓ
pl. du Mail – ✆ 04 75 91 81 30 – www.clairplume.com – plume2@wanadoo.fr – Fax 04 75 91 81 31
15 rm – †€ 98/170 ††€ 98/170, ☕ € 14
◆ This attractive 18C edifice offers Provençal style guestrooms set around a cottage garden. Other equally charming rooms available in a second house. Tea room.

La Bastide de Grignan without rest ⛰ ⛲ ♿ AC ⇸
1 km on D 541 Montélimar road – ✆ 04 75 90 67 09 P VISA MC AE
– www.lerelaisdegrignan.com – info@labastidedegrignan.com – Fax 04 75 46 10 62
16 rm – †€ 68/110 ††€ 68/110, ☕ € 12
◆ This brand new establishment, built on former truffle producing land, offers charming rooms with modern Provencal décor.

XXX **La Table des Délices** ⛱ P VISA MC
1 km on D 541 Montélimar road – ✆ 04 75 46 57 22 – www.latabledesdelices.com – contact@latabledesdelices.fr – Fax 04 75 46 92 96 – Closed Tuesday dinner off season, Sunday dinner and Monday
Rest – Menu (€ 25), € 35/90 – Carte € 50/70
◆ On the road to the grotto of Madame de Sévigné. Enjoy updated cuisine served in a warm, modern interior or beneath a shaded cane trellis. Fine choice of Côtes du Rhône wines.

X **Le Poème de Grignan** AC ✗ VISA MC
r. St-Louis – ✆ 04 75 91 10 90 – www.lepoemedegrignan.com – hervepoeme@aol.com – Fax 04 75 91 10 90 – Closed 1 week in March, 17-30 November and Wednesday
Rest – Menu € 25 (lunch), € 28/48 – Carte € 52/66
◆ Tiny restaurant with Provençal decor in a pedestrian street in historic Grignan. Market-fresh, seasonal cuisine with a southern accent.

Montélimar road 4 km on the D 541 and minor road - ✉ 26230 Grignan

La Maison du Moulin ⛰ ⛱ ⛲ ⇸ P
– ✆ 04 75 46 56 94 – www.maisondumoulin.com – maisondumoulin@wanadoo.fr – Closed 24 October-5 November and 19 December-5 January
5 rm ☕ – †€ 65/140 ††€ 75/150 – ½ P € 65/92
Table d'hôte – Menu € 30/50 bi
◆ An 18C mill on the banks of a peaceful river. Charming guestrooms with antique furnishings, bright dining room, flower-decked garden and pool. Regional cuisine and cookery
classes.

GRIMAUD – **83 Var** – **340** O6 – **pop. 4 233** – **alt. 105 m** – ✉ **83310** 41 **C3**
French Riviera

Paris 861 – Fréjus 32 – Le Lavandou 32 – St-Tropez 12 – Ste-Maxime 12 – Toulon 64

Office de tourisme, 1, boulevard des Aliziers ✆ 04 94 55 43 83, Fax 04 94 55 72 20

Château ≤★.

Port Grimaud★: ≤★ 5 km.

La Boulangerie without rest

2 km west via rte de Collobrières D14 – 04 94 43 23 16 – www.hotel-laboulangerie.com – hotelboulangerie@orange.fr – Fax 04 94 43 38 27 – Open Easter-9 October

10 rm – €115/119 €119/139, €11 – 2 suites

◆ Relaxation and well being in this little farmhouse hidden away in a park dominating the village. Provençal spirit in the rooms; friendly atmosphere.

Le Verger Maelvi without rest

2 km west on the D 14 rte de Collobrières – 04 94 55 57 80 – www.hotel-grimaud.com – levergergrimaud@aol.com – Fax 04 94 43 33 92 – Open 28 March-9 November

12 rm – €160/200 €160/350, €16

◆ This peaceful farmstead offers comfortable contemporary or more traditional rooms. In summer, generous breakfasts are served beneath a pretty pergola opposite the pool.

Athénopolis

rm, rest,

3.5 km north-west on D 558, La Garde-Freinet road – 04 98 12 66 44 – www.athenopolis.com – hotel@athenopolis.com – Fax 04 98 12 66 40 – Open 2 April-31 October

11 rm – €87/95 €99/130, €10 – ½ P €82/90

Rest – *(closed Wednesday except July-August)* Menu (€19), €24 – Carte €32/50

◆ In the Mediterranean, almost Greek countryside of the Maures mountain range stands a house with blue shutters and colourful rooms with a loggia or private terrace. Traditional cuisine in the restaurant.

Hostellerie du Coteau Fleuri

pl. des Pénitents – 04 94 43 20 17 – www.coteaufleuri.fr – coteaufleuri@wanadoo.fr – Fax 04 94 43 33 42 – Closed 1st November-20 December

14 rm – €46/115 €46/115, €12

Rest – *(closed lunch in July-August, Monday lunch, Friday lunch and Tuesday)* Menu (€30 bi), €45/125 bi – Carte €58/75

◆ Former silk farm overlooking the picturesque square of the historic village. The uncluttered rooms are tasteful and well kept. Pleasant rustic dining room with large fireplace and a terrace-balcony overlooking the Maures mountain range. Classic culinary repertory.

Les Santons

rte Nationale – 04 94 43 21 02 – lessantons@wanadoo.fr – Fax 04 94 43 24 92 – Closed 12 November-15 December, Thursday lunch in season, Wednesday except dinner in winter, Monday and Tuesday off season

Rest – Menu (€35 bi), €56 – Carte €80/150

◆ Characterful inn on the main road through the village. Classic cuisine served in a rustic decor graced with painted clay figurines (santons), copperware and fresh flowers.

La Bretonnière

pl. des Pénitents – 04 94 43 25 26 – Fax 04 94 43 25 26 – Closed 15 November-29 December, Wednesday dinner and Sunday in low season

Rest – Menu (€22), €32/45 – Carte €60/74

◆ In the heart of the medieval town, the appeal of this restaurant lies in its traditional cuisine and stylish atmosphere. The decor combines dark wood Louis Philippe furniture with a blue colour scheme.

LA GRIVE – 38 Isère – 333 E4 – see Bourgoin-Jallieu

GROISY – 74 Haute-Savoie – 328 K4 – pop. 2 937 – alt. 690 m – 74570

46 **F1**

Paris 534 – Annecy 17 – Bellegarde-sur-Valserine 40 – Bonneville 29 – Genève 37

Auberge de Groisy

34 rte du Chef-Lieu – 04 50 68 09 54 – www.auberge-groisy.com – Fax 04 50 68 09 54 – Closed 1-15 September, Sunday dinner, Monday and Tuesday

Rest – *(number of covers limited, pre-book)* Menu (€20), €30/67 – Carte €41/88

◆ Next to the church, this 19C farm is well restored (exposed beams and stonework); a pleasantly rustic spot offering thoughful modern cuisine.

GROIX (ÎLE) – 56 Morbihan – **308** K9 – see Île de Groix

GRUFFY – 74 Haute-Savoie – **328** J6 – pop. 1 327 – alt. 570 m 46 **F1**
– ✉ 74540

Paris 545 – Aix-les-Bains 19 – Annecy 17 – Chambéry 36 – Genève 62

Aux Gorges du Chéran rm, VISA
au Pont de l'Abîme – ✆ 04 50 52 51 13 – www.gorgesducheran.com
– savary.marc@wanadoo.fr – Fax 04 50 52 57 33 – Open 1 April-30 October
8 rm (½ board only) – ½ P € 65/74
Rest – *(dinner only) (residents only)* Menu € 22
◆ Quiet rooms with wood panelling in an establishment with a remarkable backdrop: the spectacular metallic bridge (1887) spanning the gorges. Generous traditional cuisine drawing on local inspiration plus snack menu. Fine panoramic terrace.

GRUISSAN – 11 Aude – **344** J4 – pop. 4 267 – alt. 2 m – Casino 22 **B3**
– ✉ 11430 **Languedoc-Roussillon-Tarn Gorges**

Paris 796 – Carcassonne 73 – Narbonne 15 – Perpignan 76

Office de tourisme, 1, boulevard du Pech-Maynaud ✆ 04 68 49 09 00, Fax 04 68 49 33 12

Le Phoebus rm, VISA
bd Sagne, (at the casino) – ✆ 04 68 49 03 05 – www.phoebus-sa.com
– hotel.lephoebus@casinos-sfc.com – Fax 04 68 49 07 67
50 rm – € 79/105 € 92/118, € 10
Rest – Menu (€ 14), € 20/45 – Carte € 25/40
◆ Motel-style comfortable rooms in the casino complex, decorated according to themes, such as The South, The Sea, Fishermen or Customs and Traditions. Small gardens on the ground floor. A restaurant in a modern setting with a grill menu in the summer by the swimming pool.

Accueil de la Plage without rest VISA
13 r. Bernard l'Hermite, At Chalands beach – ✆ 04 68 49 00 75
– www.hotel-de-la-plage.com – accueildelaplage@hotmail.fr – Fax 04 68 49 00 75
– Open 1 April-1 November
17 rm – € 53/61 € 62/66
◆ In a quiet alley, two minutes from the stilt houses immortalised in the film "Betty Blue" are these bright well-kept rooms, some with a balcony. Pleasant welcome.

L'Estagnol VISA
12 av. Narbonne – ✆ 04 68 49 01 27 – Open April to end September and closed Sunday dinner except July-August, Tuesday lunch from September to June and Monday
Rest – Menu € 16 (weekday lunch), € 25/31 – Carte € 28/42
◆ An authentic former fisherman's house: Provençal decor, small terrace overlooking the lake and good simple regional cuisine with the emphasis on fish.

LE GUA – 17 Charente-Maritime – **324** E5 – pop. 1 920 – alt. 3 m 38 **B3**
– ✉ 17600

Paris 493 – Bordeaux 126 – Rochefort 26 – La Rochelle 63 – Royan 16

Syndicat d'initiative, 28, rue Saint-Laurent ✆ 05 46 23 17 28, Fax 05 46 23 17 28

Le Moulin de Châlons with rm rm, VISA
at Châlons, 1 km west on the Royan road – ✆ 05 46 22 82 72
– www.moulin-de-chalons.com – moulin-de-chalons@wanadoo.fr
– Fax 05 46 22 91 07
10 rm – € 100/160 € 100/160, € 13
Rest – Menu € 28/48 – Carte € 40/80
◆ An appetising up-to-date menu and welcoming rustic-bourgeois decor (exposed stonework and beams) distinguish this authentic 18C tide mill. The rooms, all of which have been attractively renovated, overlook the pastoral parkland.

GUEBERSCHWIHR – 68 Haut-Rhin – 315 H8 – pop. 836 – alt. 260 m 1 A2
– ✉ 68420 Alsace-Lorraine

Paris 487 – Colmar 12 – Guebwiller 18 – Mulhouse 36 – Strasbourg 92

Relais du Vignoble
33 r. Forgerons – ✆ 03 89 49 22 22 – www.relaisduvignoble.com – relaisduvignoble@wanadoo.fr – Fax 03 89 49 27 82 – Closed 1st February-1st March
30 rm – €60/65 €64/68 – ½ P €65/68
Rest *Belle Vue* – *✆ 03 89 49 31 09 (closed Thursday lunch and Wednesday)*
Menu €16/38 – Carte €31/44
◆ A "spiritual" stop on la Route des Vins: the new building is next to the family cellar and most of the old fashioned but well-kept rooms are facing the vineyards. Seminary facilities. Traditional dishes and local wines to be sampled on the panoramic terrace in fine weather.

GUEBWILLER – 68 Haut-Rhin – 315 H9 – pop. 11 500 – alt. 300 m 1 A3
– ✉ 68500 Alsace-Lorraine

Paris 474 – Belfort 52 – Colmar 27 – Épinal 96 – Mulhouse 24 – Strasbourg 107

Office de tourisme, 73, rue de la République ✆ 03 89 76 10 63, Fax 03 89 76 52 72

St-Léger church ★: west front ★★ - Interior ★★ of N.-Dame church ★: High altar ★★ - Town hall ★ - Musée du Florival ★.

Guebwiller Valley ★★ Northwest.

Domaine du Lac
244 r. de la République, towards Buhl – ✆ 03 89 76 15 00 – www.domainedulac-alsace.com – contact@domainedulac-alsace.com – Fax 03 89 74 14 63
68 rm – €41/75 €41/75, €9
Rest *Les Terrasses* – *✆ 03 89 76 15 76 (closed Saturday lunch)* Menu (€17), €20 (weekday lunch), €28/45 – Carte €33/43
◆ Within the estate, a first hotel with a minimalist decor, joined more recently by a second establishement in cosy, contemporary style. Views of the lake or stream to the rear. Designer inspired restaurant and panoramic terrace. Regional specialities take pride of place on the contemporary menu.

L'Ange
4 r. de la Gare – ✆ 03 89 76 22 11 – www.hotel-ange.com – hoteldelange@wanadoo.fr – Fax 03 89 76 50 08
36 rm – €45/58 €65/78, €9 – ½ P €62/70
Rest – *(closed Saturday lunch)* Menu (€10), €23/36 – Carte €28/45
◆ The name – unless it's a coincidence – and an elevator used as a lift show that the hotel was indeed once a maternity hospital. Functional rooms set around a well of light. Italian and Alsatian cuisine influences the menu here; pretty shaded terrace.

in Murbach 5 km Northwest by D 40ll – pop. 136 – alt. 420 m – ✉ 68530

Church ★★.

Hostellerie St-Barnabé without rest
53 r. de Murbach – ✆ 03 89 62 14 14 – www.hostellerie-st-barnabe.com – hostellerie.st.barnabe@wanadoo.fr – Fax 03 89 62 14 15 – Closed 24-26 December and 6 January-6 February
26 rm – €68/195 €80/207
◆ An old Alsatian house and garden sitting brightly in the scenic Murbach Valley. Some rooms renovated in a modern and colourful style. Comfortable lounge.

Le Schaeferhof
6 r. de Guebwiller – ✆ 03 89 74 98 98 – www.schaeferhof.fr – maisondhotes@schaeferhof.fr – Fax 03 89 74 98 99 – Closed 10-30 January
4 rm – €110/125 €130/145
Table d'hôte – Menu €40 (weekdays)/130
◆ This former tenanted 18C farm is now a hotel with well-designed guestrooms (sitting rooms, flat screens and power showers): no detail has been forgotten. Modern Alsatian cuisine, and a fine choice of wines. Home-made breakfasts.

in Rimbach-près-Guebwiller 11 km West by D 5[1] – pop. 243 – alt. 550 m – ✉ 68500

X **L'Aigle d'Or** with rm

5 r. Principale – ✆ 03 89 76 89 90 – www.hotelaigledor.com – hotelmarck@aol.com – Fax 03 89 74 32 41 – Closed 23 February-23 March
15 rm – †€ 28/35 ††€ 35/53, ☕ € 8 – ½ P € 38/52
Rest – *(closed Monday from mid-July to mid-September)* Menu (€ 10), € 17/35 – Carte € 27/52
◆ A simple family inn, ideal for a peaceful meal in an authentic environment, serving regional style cuisine around the fireplace. Simple well-kept rooms.

GUÉCÉLARD – 72 Sarthe – **310** J7 – pop. 2 689 – alt. 45 m – ✉ 72230 35 **C1**

Paris 219 – Château-du-Loir 38 – La Flèche 26 – Le Grand-Lucé 38 – Le Mans 19

XX **La Botte d'Asperges**

49 r. Nationale – ✆ 02 43 87 29 61 – Fax 02 43 87 29 61 – Closed 9-23 March, 3-24 August, Sunday dinner and Monday except bank holidays
Rest – Menu € 18/52 – Carte € 45/70
◆ Former post house in the heart of the village. Frescoes and paintings with floral motifs adorn the dining room. Traditional menu including the famous local asparagus (in season).

GUENROUËT – 44 Loire-Atlantique – **316** E2 – pop. 2 833 – alt. 30 m 34 **A2** – ✉ 44530

Paris 430 – Nantes 56 – Redon 21 – St-Nazaire 41 – Vannes 72

XXX **Relais St-Clair**

31 r. de l'Isac, (Nozay road) – ✆ 02 40 87 66 11 – www.relais-saint-clair.com – contact@relais-saint-clair.com – Fax 02 40 87 71 01 – Closed 1-8 December, 4-11 January, Tuesday dinner, Wednesday dinner and Monday
Rest – Menu (€ 25 bi), € 32/68 – Carte € 45/66
Rest *Le Jardin de l'Isac* – buffet Menu (€ 10), € 13 (weekday lunch)/20 – Carte € 23/31
◆ A flower-decked building near the Nantes-Brest canal and a small outdoor leisure complex. Traditional cuisine and fine Loire wine list. A buffet of starters, grilled dishes and desserts are served at the Jardin d'Isaac.

XX **Le Paradis des Pêcheurs**

au Cougou, 5 km northwest by D 102 – ✆ 02 40 87 64 10 – leparadisdespecheurs@wanadoo.fr – Fax 02 40 87 64 10 – Closed autumn half-term holidays, from February, Monday dinner, Tuesday dinner, Thursday dinner and Wednesday
Rest – Menu (€ 12), € 22 (weekdays)/35 – Carte € 37/44
◆ A 1930s house, surrounded by pine and chestnut trees, in a peaceful Argoat hamlet. Old wood panelling in the bar and dining room. Traditional dishes.

GUÉRANDE – 44 Loire-Atlantique – **316** B4 – pop. 15 300 – alt. 54 m 34 **A2** – ✉ 44350 Brittany

Paris 450 – La Baule 6 – Nantes 77 – St-Nazaire 20 – Vannes 69

Office de tourisme, 1, place du Marché au Bois ✆ 02 40 24 96 71, Fax 02 40 62 04 24

St-Aubin collegiate church ★.

Les Voyageurs

12 bd de l'Abreuvoir – ✆ 02 40 24 90 13 – contact@hotel-voyageurs.fr – Fax 02 40 62 06 64 – Closed 22 December-19 January
12 rm – †€ 51/57 ††€ 51/57, ☕ € 7 – ½ P € 56
Rest – *(Closed Sunday dinner and Monday)* Menu (€ 10), € 14 (weekdays)/35 – Carte € 34/52
◆ This old house was built outside the town walls facing the ramparts. Charming 1940s style interior. Well-maintained rooms with recent bedding. Find four countrified dining rooms and simple, classic dishes here.

La Guérandière without rest
5 r. Vannetaise – ✆ 02 40 62 17 15 – www.guerandiere.com – contact@guerandiere.com
7 rm – €59/79 €59/89, ☕ €10
◆ This charming 19C hotel at the foot of the battlements provides cosy rooms with colourful decor, all with a fireplace. Breakfasts are served in the garden or in the conservatory in summer.

Les Remparts with rm
bd Nord – ✆ 02 40 24 90 69 – Fax 02 40 62 17 99 – Hotel: Open 15 March-15 November and closed Sunday and Monday except August; Restaurant: Closed 15 December-15 January, 15-20 February and dinner from 15 November to 15 March, Sunday dinner and Monday except August
8 rm – €48 €48, ☕ €6,50 – ½ P €52
Rest – Menu (€14), €17 (weekdays)/41
◆ This restaurant faces the ramparts. Traditional and fish dishes, sprinkled with Guérande salt, naturally. Small, very simple, somewhat antiquated but quiet rooms.

Le Balzac
2 pl. du Vieux Marché – ✆ 02 40 42 97 46 – Fax 02 51 76 92 71 – Closed 9-20 March, 6-21 November, Sunday dinner, Wednesday dinner except July-August and Thursday
Rest – Menu (€14), €17/35 – Carte €30/52
◆ On a small square behind the collegiate church, this traditional Breton house with red shutters is a restaurant with an attractive décor; modern cuisine with traditional touches.

LA GUERCHE-DE-BRETAGNE – **35 Ille-et-Vilaine** – **309** O7 – **pop. 4 163** – **alt. 77 m** – ✉ **35130** Brittany — 10 **D2**

Paris 324 – Châteaubriant 30 – Laval 53 – Redon 84 – Rennes 55 – Vitré 22
Office du tourisme, 30, rue Du Guesclin ✆ 02 99 96 30 78, Fax 02 99 96 41 43

La Calèche with rm
16 av. Gén. Leclerc – ✆ 02 99 96 21 63 – www.restaurant-la-caleche.com – contact@lacaleche.com – Fax 02 99 96 49 52 – Closed 2-25 August, 25-31 December, Monday except hotel, Friday dinner and Sunday dinner
12 rm – €49 €60, ☕ €11 – ½ P €67
Rest – Menu (€13), €15 (weekdays), €26/35 – Carte €31/69
◆ Tasteful dining room, extended by a veranda and small bistro area, serving generous local cuisine. Practical guestrooms.

GUÉRET Ⓟ – **23 Creuse** – **325** I3 – **pop. 13 900** – **alt. 457 m** – ✉ **23000** Dordogne-Berry-Limousin — 25 **C1**

Paris 351 – Châteauroux 90 – Limoges 93 – Montluçon 66
Office de tourisme, 1, rue Eugène France ✆ 05 55 52 14 29, Fax 05 55 41 19 38
Champlevé enamels★ of the musée d'art et d'archéologie de la Sénatorerie (art and archeology museum).

Le Coq en Pâte
2 r. de Pommeil – ✆ 05 55 41 43 43 – Fax 05 55 41 43 42 – Closed 1-15 June, 22 October-5 November, Sunday dinner in low season and Monday dinner
Rest – Menu €17 (weekdays)/56 – Carte €50/100
◆ A sympathetically restored 19C house with a terrace overlooking a pleasant wooded garden. Generous and refined modern cuisine.

in Ste-Feyre 7 km east – **pop. 2 250** – **alt. 450 m** – ✉ **23000**

Les Touristes-Michel Roux
1 pl. de la mairie – ✆ 05 55 80 00 07 – Fax 05 55 81 11 04 – Closed Wednesday dinner, Sunday dinner and Monday
Rest – Menu (€15), €17 (weekdays)/28 – Carte €40/60
◆ A regional building in the heart of the village, featuring a dining area with colourful and floral décor and a nice herb cupboard. Market cuisine served.

GUÉRY (LAC) – **63 Puy-de-Dôme** – **326** D9 – **see le Mont-Dore**

GUÉTHARY – 64 Pyrénées-Atlantiques – **342** C4 – **pop. 1 284** 3 **A3**
– **alt. 15 m** – ✉ **64210** **Atlantic Coast**

Paris 780 – Bayonne 19 – Biarritz 9 – Pau 125 – St-Jean-de-Luz 7

Office de tourisme, 74, rue du Comte de Swiecinski ☎ 05 59 26 56 60, Fax 05 59 54 92 67

Villa Catarie without rest

415 av. Gén. de Gaulle – ☎ 05 59 47 59 00 – www.villa-catarie.com – hotel@villa-catarie.com – Fax 05 59 47 59 02 – Closed 6 November-18 December and 4 January-12 February

14 rm – †€ 125/185 ††€ 125/185, ☕ € 12 – 2 suites

◆ Delightful Basque house built in 1830 with elegant, cosy guestrooms in pastel shades and handsome antique furniture. Charming breakfast room.

Brikéténia rest, VISA MC AE

r. de l'Eglise – ☎ 05 59 26 51 34 – www.briketenia.com – briketenia@orange.fr – Fax 05 59 54 71 55

16 rm – †€ 65/95 ††€ 70/95, ☕ € 10

Rest – Menu € 33 (weekday lunch), € 52/78 – Carte € 35/57

◆ Two handsome and characteristic 17C houses. The one with the red shutters is home to guestrooms partly furnished with antiques. Inviting sitting room. An opulent bourgeois ambience reigns in this comfortable restaurant, set in the second, totally refurbished house. Updated cuisine.

Arguibel without rest

1146 chemin de Laharraga – ☎ 05 59 41 90 46 – www.arguibel.fr – contact@arguibel.fr – Fax 05 59 41 98 87

5 rm – †€ 100/250 ††€ 110/270, ☕ € 15

◆ A superb neo-Basque villa. The refined interior blends designer details, traditional furniture and work by local artists. Each guestroom is individually and distinctively appointed.

LE GUÉTIN – 18 Cher – **323** O5 – ✉ **18150** 12 **D3**

Paris 252 – Bourges 58 – La Guerche-sur-l'Aubois 11 – Nevers 13 – St-Pierre-le-Moutier 29

Auberge du Pont-Canal VISA MC

37 r.des Ecluses – ☎ 02 48 80 40 76 – Fax 02 48 80 45 11 – Closed 2-10 January, Sunday dinner from 30 October-30 April and Monday

Rest – Menu € 13 (weekday lunch), € 20/36 – Carte € 31/45

◆ Family inn beside the Allier bridge. Renovated main dining room and veranda opening onto the countryside. Traditional cuisine and fish fried in an old-fashioned style.

GUEUGNON – 71 Saône-et-Loire – **320** E10 – **pop. 7 910** – **alt. 243 m** 7 **B3**
– ✉ **71130**

Paris 335 – Bourbon-Lancy 27 – Mâcon 87 – Montceau-les-Mines 29 – Moulins 63

Du Centre rest, VISA MC

34 r. de la Liberté – ☎ 03 85 85 21 01 – www.hotel-centre.com – Fax 03 85 85 02 67

18 rm – †€ 40 ††€ 50, ☕ € 6 – ½ P € 45

Rest – *(Closed Sunday dinner)* Menu € 16/30 – Carte € 30/48

◆ This family hotel on the main road through the village of Forgerons offers practical rooms, gradually being restored. Plush rustic-style dining areas, serving classic cuisine in a pleasing 'Old France' atmosphere.

GUEWENHEIM – 68 Haut-Rhin – **315** G10 – **pop. 1 205** – **alt. 323 m** 1 **A3**
– ✉ **68116**

Paris 458 – Altkirch 23 – Belfort 36 – Mulhouse 21 – Thann 9

De la Gare VISA MC

2 r. Soppe – ☎ 03 89 82 51 29 – Fax 03 89 82 84 62 – Closed 22 July-13 August, 16 February-5 March, Tuesday dinner and Wednesday

Rest – Menu (€ 10), € 28/45 – Carte € 30/55

◆ Once a village café, this pleasant restaurant has been run by the same family for four generations; traditional and local dishes. The superb wine list is worth the trip alone!

GUIDEL – 56 Morbihan – **308** K8 – **pop. 9 682** – **alt. 38 m** – ✉ **56520** 9 **B2**

Paris 511 – Quimper 60 – Lorient 14 – Pont-Aven 26 – Quimperlé 12

Office de tourisme, 9, rue Saint-Maurice ✆ 02 97 65 01 74, Fax 02 97 65 09 36

Le Domaine de Kerbastic

rte de Locmaria – ✆ 02 97 65 98 01 – www.domaine-de-kerbastic.com – info@domaine-de-kerbastic.com – Fax 02 97 65 01 30 – Closed 30 November-14 February

15 rm – €160/385 €160/385, €17 **Rest** – Menu €37/52

◆ This magnificent stately home is entirely devoted to art. The souvenirs of illustrious guests (Cocteau, Stravinsky, etc.) adorn the personalised guestrooms. Traditional fare served in a plush elegant dining room.

GUIGNIÈRE – 37 Indre-et-Loire – **317** M4 – see Tours

GUILHERAND-GRANGES – 07 Ardèche – **331** L4 – see Valence (26 Drôme)

GUILLESTRE – 05 Hautes-Alpes – **334** H5 – **pop. 2 276** – **alt. 1 000 m** – ✉ **05600** French Alps 41 **C1**

Paris 715 – Barcelonnette 51 – Briançon 36 – Digne-les-Bains 114 – Gap 61

Office de tourisme, place Salva ✆ 04 92 45 04 37, Fax 04 95 45 19 09

Porch★ of the church - Pied-la-Viste ≤★ East: 2 km - Peyre-Haute ≤★ South: 4 km then 15 mn.

Combe du Queyras★★ Northeast: 5,5 km.

Dedans Dehors

ruelle Sani – ✆ 04 92 44 29 07 – albandedansdehors@yahoo.fr – Open mid-May to end September

Rest – Carte €28/38

◆ This vaulted cellar is located in a medieval street, serving salads, regional plancha dishes and toasted meals to satisfy your appetite in an eclectic and charming bistro-style atmosphere.

in Mont-Dauphin gare 4 km Northwest by D 902A and N 94 – **pop. 87** – **alt. 1 050 m** – ✉ **05600**

Office de tourisme, rue Rouget de Lisle ✆ 04 92 45 17 80

Framework★ of Rochambeau barracks.

Lacour et rest. Gare

– ✆ 04 92 45 03 08 – www.hotel-lacour.com – renseignement@hotel-lacour.com – Fax 04 92 45 40 09 – Closed Saturday from 20 April to 30 June and from 1st September to 26 December

46 rm – €35/65 €35/65, €7,50 – ½ P €39/55

Rest – Menu (€12), €16/31 – Carte €16/45

◆ Just below the fortifications of Mont-Dauphin, this entirely restored family hotel offers simple rooms, quieter on the garden side. A modern-style restaurant located in a separate building with a sundial on the façade.

GUILLIERS – 56 Morbihan – **308** Q6 – **pop. 1 288** – **alt. 86 m** – ✉ **56490** 10 **C2**

Paris 418 – Dinan 66 – Lorient 91 – Ploërmel 13 – Rennes 69 – Vannes 59

Au Relais du Porhoët rm,

11 pl. de l'Église – ✆ 02 97 74 40 17 – www.aurelaisduporhoet.com – aurelaisduporhoet@wanadoo.fr – Fax 02 97 74 45 65 – Closed 4-18 January

12 rm – €39/50 €44/58, €8

Rest – *(closed Monday except dinner in July-August and Sunday dinner)* Menu (€11), €14 (weekdays), €20/43 – Carte €28/42

◆ This hotel has an attractive seasonal floral façade. Pleasant, soundproofed guestrooms for non-smokers only. A grand fireplace warms one of the dining rooms in the restaurant where tasty, regional cuisine is served.

Paris 484 – Carhaix-Plouguer 49 – Lannion 32 – Morlaix 53 – St-Brieuc 32

Office de tourisme, place Champ au Roy ✆ 02 96 43 73 89, Fax 02 96 40 01 95

de Bégard Bégard Krec'h An Onn, 13 km on the Lannion road, ✆ 02 96 45 32 64

N.D.-de-Bon-Secours basilica ★ B.

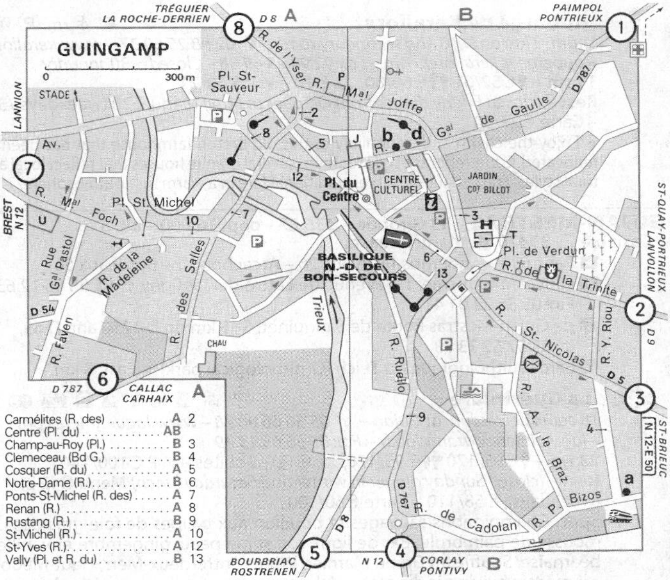

GUINGAMP

Street	Square	No.
Carmélites (R. des)	A	2
Centre (Pl. du)	AB	
Champ-au-Roy (Pl.)	B	3
Clemeceau (Bd G.)	B	4
Cosquer (R. du)	A	5
Notre-Dame (R.)	B	6
Ponts-St-Michel (R. des)	A	7
Renan (R.)	A	8
Rustang (R.)	B	9
St-Michel (R.)	A	10
St-Yves (R.)	A	12
Vally (Pl. et R. du)	B	13

La Demeure without rest

5 r. Gén.de Gaulle – ✆ 02 96 44 28 53 – www.demeure-vb.com – contact-demeure@wanadoo.fr – Fax 02 96 44 45 54 – Closed 22-27 June, 31 August-5 September and 1-15 January B **b**

10 rm – €66/119 €85/169, €9

◆ In the town centre, this 18th century mansion provides large rooms with period furnishings. Breakfast is served on the veranda overlooking the garden.

De l'Arrivée without rest

19 bd Clemenceau, (opposite the station) – ✆ 02 96 40 04 57 – www.hotel-arrivee.com – hoteldelarrivee.guingamp@wanadoo.fr B **a**

28 rm – €42/80 €56/95, €8

◆ The sign evokes the nearby railway station. This is a handy hotel for travellers to and from Guingamp, with small but well-renovated rooms.

La Boissière

90 r. Yser, 1 km via ⑧ – ✆ 02 96 21 06 35 – www.restaurant-la-boissiere.com – Fax 02 96 21 13 38 – Closed 1-14 March, 17 August-6 September, Saturday lunch, Sunday dinner and Monday

Rest – Menu (€13), €16 (weekday lunch), €23/60 – Carte €42/63

◆ A large century-old house nestling in a park. Traditional cuisine, changing according to the season, is served in two pleasant and comfortable dining rooms.

Le Clos de la Fontaine

9 r. Gén. de Gaulle – ✆ 02 96 21 33 63 – Fax 02 96 21 29 78 – Closed 10-25 July, 15-28 February, Sunday dinner and Monday

B d

Rest – Menu (€ 13), € 28/46 – Carte € 40/67

◆ This restaurant serves updated traditional cuisine in one of two classically decorated dining areas with parquet and exposed stone work, or on the patio terrace.

GUISSENY – 29 Finistère – 308 E3 – pop. 1 811 – alt. 18 m – ✉ 29880 9 A1

Paris 591 – Brest 35 – Landerneau 27 – Morlaix 56 – Quimper 91

Office de tourisme, place Saint Sezny ✆ 02 98 25 67 99, Fax 02 98 25 69 69

Auberge de Keralloret

rm, VISA

South: 3 km on D 10 and secondary road – ✆ 02 98 25 60 37 – www.keralloret.com – auberge@keralloret.com – Fax 02 98 25 69 88 – Closed 5-30 January

11 rm – €52/61 €60/80, € 10 – ½ P € 60/71

Rest – *(closed Friday dinner from October to May)* Menu € 20 (weekdays)/35 – Carte € 27/50

◆ Enjoy the charm and tranquillity of this old Breton farmhouse that has been prettily renovated. Contemporary-style rooms in several granite houses that reflect local architectural styles. The restaurant serves traditional fare in a warm rustic atmosphere.

GUJAN-MESTRAS – 33 Gironde – 335 E7 – pop. 16 600 – alt. 5 m – Casino – ✉ 33470 Atlantic Coast 3 B2

Paris 638 – Andernos-les-Bains 26 – Arcachon 10 – Bordeaux 56

Office de tourisme, 19, avenue de Lattre-de-Tassigny ✆ 05 56 66 12 65, Fax 05 56 22 01 41

de Gujan-Mestras Route de Sanguinet, S : 5 km on D 1250 and D 65, ✆ 05 57 52 73 73

Parc ornithologique du Teich (Ornithological park) ★ East: 5 km.

La Guérinière

VISA AE

18 cours de Verdun, at Gujan – ✆ 05 56 66 08 78 – www.laguerinere.com – laguerinere@wanadoo.fr – Fax 05 56 66 13 39

23 rm – €95/170 €95/170, € 12 – 2 suites – ½ P € 100/140

Rest – *(closed Sunday dinner in winter and Saturday lunch)* Menu € 42 bi (weekdays), € 58/110 – Carte € 60/100

Spec. Champignons sauvages et bouillon aux galipes de foie gras des Landes, mousse de pain brulé. Bar de ligne rôti sur la peau, gingembre et vanille façon béarnaise. Soufflé au Grand Marnier. **Wines** Entre-deux-Mers, Haut-Médoc.

◆ A modern building in the centre of the main oyster farming area of the Arcachon Basin. Spacious guestrooms with tasteful, minimalist decor. Contemporary, fragrant cuisine served in an elegant, modern setting or overlooking the swimming pool.

GUNDERSHOFFEN – 67 Bas-Rhin – 315 J3 – pop. 3 490 – alt. 180 m – ✉ 67110 1 B1

Paris 466 – Haguenau 16 – Sarreguemines 61 – Strasbourg 45 – Wissembourg 33

Le Moulin without rest

VISA AE

r. Moulin – ✆ 03 88 07 33 30 – www.hotellemoulin.com – hotel.le.moulin@wanadoo.fr – Fax 03 88 72 83 97 – Closed 4-24 August, 5-12 January and 16 February-3 March

12 rm – €70/90 €95/220, € 19

◆ This former mill is surrounded by a parkland and stream. The guestrooms have a personal touch, in modern or country-chic styles. Charming, peaceful and sophisticated.

Au Cygne (François Paul)

VISA AE

35 Gd'Rue – ✆ 03 88 72 96 43 – www.aucygne.fr – contact@aucygne.fr – Fax 03 88 72 86 47 – Closed 3-24 August, 4-11 January, 16 February-2 March, Sunday dinner, Tuesday lunch and Monday

Rest – Menu € 47 (weekdays)/99 – Carte € 81/103

Spec. Tartare de langoustines aux pois gourmands, tapenade à l'olive et noisettes. Filet et selle de chevreuil aux spaetzele. Beignets de quetsches et sabayon au kirsch d'Alsace, glace streussel (summer-early autumn). **Wines** Pinot blanc, Muscat.

◆ This fine half-timbered building houses an elegant, recently refurbished dining room offering creative and sophisticated cuisine.

XX **Le Soufflet**

13 r. de la Gare – ✆ 03 88 72 91 20 – www.lesoufflet.fr – lesoufflet@free.fr – Fax 03 88 72 91 20 – Closed Saturday lunch, Monday dinner and Wednesday dinner

Rest – Menu (€ 13), € 26/66 bi – Carte € 30/53

Rest *Bahnstub* – Menu (€ 13) – Carte € 22/47

◆ Flower-decked restaurant opposite the railway station serving classic fare in an interior that sports stuffed animals. Pleasant pergola-terrace. Informal atmosphere: dishes of the day and a small menu of Alsatian specialities.

GY – **70 Haute-Saône** – **314** C8 – **pop. 1 018** – **alt. 237 m** – ✉ **70700** 16 **B2**

Burgundy-Jura

Paris 356 – Besançon 32 – Dijon 69 – Dôle 50 – Gray 20 – Langres 75 – Vesoul 39

Office de tourisme, 15, grande rue ✆ 03 84 32 93 93, Fax 03 84 32 86 87

Château★.

Pinocchio without rest

r. Beauregard – ✆ 03 84 32 95 95 – Fax 03 84 32 95 75 – Closed 25 December-1st January

14 rm – €51 €66, €7

◆ This attractive house, typical of the region, has been decorated along the theme of the famous puppet after which it is named. Practical guestrooms, some of which sleep families.

GYE-SUR-SEINE – **10 Aube** – **313** G5 – **pop. 520** – **alt. 172 m** – ✉ **10250** 13 **B3**

Paris 209 – Troyes 45 – Châtillon-sur-Seine 26 – Tonnerre 45

Des Voyageurs

6 r. de la Nation – ✆ 03 25 38 20 09 – Fax 03 25 38 25 37 – Closed 17-23 August, February holidays, Sunday dinner and Wednesday

7 rm – €48 €48, €6 – ½ P €58/60

Rest – Menu €15, €22/45 – Carte €30/45

◆ This late-19C coaching inn, with an attractive stone façade, offers spruce and colourful rooms. Restaurant with modern decor, cane furniture and a traditional menu.

HABÈRE-POCHE – **74 Haute-Savoie** – **328** L3 – **pop. 1 193** – **alt. 945 m** – **Winter sports** – ✉ **74420** 46 **F1**

Paris 564 – Annecy 63 – Bonneville 33 – Genève 37 – Thonon-les-Bains 19

Office de tourisme, Chef-Lieu ✆ 04 50 39 54 46, Fax 04 50 39 56 62

Col de Cou★ Northwest: 4 km, **French Alps**

X **Tiennolet**

– ✆ 04 50 39 51 01 – pierre.bonnet008@orange.fr – Fax 04 50 39 58 15 – Closed 2-28 June, 13 October-14 November, Sunday dinner, Tuesday dinner and Wednesday except school holidays

Rest – Menu (€ 15), € 26/37 – Carte € 35/45

◆ In the centre of the village, above the family-run pastry shop, a restaurant with a cosy Alpine atmosphere. Classic and regional cuisine. South-facing terrace.

L'HABITARELLE – **48 Lozère** – **330** K7 – ✉ **48170 Chateauneuf de Randon** 23 **C1**

Paris 587 – Langogne 19 – Mende 27 – Le Puy-en-Velay 62

Poste rm,

– ✆ 04 66 47 90 05 – www.hoteldelaposte48.com – contact@hoteldelaposte48.com – Fax 04 66 47 91 41 – Closed 28 June-3 July, 1-12 November, 20 December-10 February, Sunday dinner and Monday except July-August

16 rm – €46 €46/53, €8 – ½ P €47

Rest – *(closed Friday dinner, Saturday lunch and Sunday dinner except July Aug.)* Menu (€ 12), € 16/37 – Carte € 23/32

◆ This quaint 18C post-house is situated near the temple erected in honour of Bertrand Du Guesclin, who died from drinking water that was too icy. A restaurant in a converted hay-barn with stone walls and pinewood beams. Regional dishes.

HAGETMAU – 40 Landes – 335 H13 – pop. 4 480 – alt. 96 m – ✉ 40700 3 B3
Atlantic Coast

Paris 737 – Aire-sur-l'Adour 34 – Dax 45 – Mont-de-Marsan 29 – Orthez 25 – Pau 56

Office de tourisme, place de la République ✆ 05 58 79 38 26, Fax 05 58 79 47 27

Capitals★ in the St-Girons crypt.

Les Lacs d'Halco
3 km southwest on the rte de Cazalis – ✆ 05 58 79 30 79 – www.hotel-des-lacs-dhalco.fr – contact@hotel-des-lacs-dhalco.fr – Fax 05 58 79 36 15

24 rm – †€ 75/130 ††€ 75/130, ☕ € 15 – ½ P € 80/125

Rest – Menu € 30/60 – Carte € 39/58

◆ Steel, glass, wood and stone create the minimalist look of this amazing example of modern design overlooking lakes and forest. Attractive rooms. Boating, crazy golf. The dining room is in a pleasant waterside rotunda overlooking the countryside.

Le Jambon
rest, VISA AE

245 av. Carnot – ✆ 05 58 79 32 02 – www.hotellejambon.fr – hotellejambon@wanadoo.fr – Fax 05 58 79 34 78 – Closed January, Sunday evening and Monday

9 rm – †€ 60 ††€ 70, ☕ € 8 **Rest** – Menu € 16 (weekdays)/45 – Carte € 35/60

◆ This large hotel in the centre of town has modern, spacious rooms all overlooking the courtyard/swimming pool area. Good soundproofing and maintenance. The plush, stylish restaurant serves generous portions of traditional and regional cuisine.

HAGONDANGE – 57 Moselle – 307 I3 – pop. 9 053 – alt. 160 m – ✉ 57300 Alsace Lorraine Champagne 26 B1

Paris 324 – Metz 21 – Luxembourg 49 – Thionville 17 – Saarlouis 78

Syndicat d'initiative, place Jean Burger ✆ 03 87 70 35 27, Fax 03 87 73 92 20

Quai des Saveurs (Frédéric Sandrini)
VISA

69 r. de la Gare – ✆ 03 87 71 24 98 – www.quaidessaveurs.com – info@quaidessaveurs.com – Fax 03 87 71 53 21 – Closed Sunday dinner and Monday

Rest – Menu € 26 (weekdays)/42 – Carte € 53/66

Spec. Compressé de poireaux, foie gras de canard et pot-au-feu. Filet de grosse sole, salade de légumes cuits-crus, écume de basilic. Entremets chocolat intense, glace vanille, sauce caramel au beurre salé.

◆ An engaging restaurant opposite the station. Modern decor, giant aquarium and up-to-the-minute recipes, as inventive as they are delicious.

HAGUENAU – 67 Bas-Rhin – 315 K4 – pop. 35 100 – alt. 150 m – ✉ 67500 Alsace-Lorraine 1 B1

Paris 478 – Baden-Baden 41 – Sarreguemines 93 – Strasbourg 33

Office de tourisme, place de la Gare ✆ 03 88 93 70 00, Fax 03 88 93 69 89

Soufflenheim Baden-Baden Soufflenheim Allée du Golf, E : 14 km on D 1063, ✆ 03 88 05 77 00

Musée historique★ BZ M² - Altar-piece★ in St-Georges church - Panelling★ in St-Nicolas church.

Plan on next page

Le Jardin
VISA

16 r. Redoute – ✆ 03 88 93 29 39 – Fax 03 88 93 29 39 – Closed 1-6 March, 3-14 August, 26 October-4 November, 16-24 February, Tuesday and Wednesday BZ **n**

Rest – Menu € 17 (lunch), € 37/42 – Carte € 37/49

◆ Attractive Hagenau façade revamped in a Renaissance style, and a fine interior decor with a simple, minimalist feel (taupe and brown tones). Classic revisited cuisine.

Southeast 3 km by D 329 and secondary road – ✉ 67500 Haguenau

Champ'Alsace rm, rest, P, VISA, AE
12 r. St-Exupéry – ✆ 03 88 93 30 13 – www.champ-alsace.com – champalsace@aol.com – Fax 03 88 73 90 04
40 rm – €62/72 €62/72, €8 – ½ P €54/64
Rest – *(closed August, Friday, Saturday and Sunday) (dinner only)* Menu €18 – Carte approx. €22
◆ Modern hotel complex in an industrial zone. Spacious rooms, furnished with uniform furniture. Two simple dining rooms, brightened with frescos representing regional landscapes and a distillery.

LA HAIE-FOUASSIÈRE – 44 Loire-Atlantique – 316 H5 – see Nantes

LA HAIE-TONDUE – 14 Calvados – 303 M4 – ✉ 14950 32 A3

Paris 198 – Caen 41 – Deauville 15 – Le Havre 53 – Lisieux 20 – Pont-l'Évêque 8

La Haie Tondue AC P VISA AE
– ✆ 02 31 64 85 00 – www.restaurants.honfleur.com – la-haie-tondue@wanadoo.fr – Fax 02 31 64 78 35 – Closed for one week in June, 11-17 November, 5-15 January, Monday dinner except August and Tuesday from 1 April to 30 September
Rest – Menu €26/48 – Carte €28/38
◆ Warm hospitality in this regional-style restaurant with a vine covered façade. Renovated rustic dining areas with beams and a fireplace. Generous, traditional cuisine.

HAMBACH – 57 Moselle – 307 N4 – pop. 2 501 – alt. 230 m – ✉ 57910 27 C1

Paris 396 – Metz 70 – Saarbrücken 23 – Sarreguemines 8 – Strasbourg 98

Hostellerie St-Hubert
La Verte Forêt – ☎ 03 87 98 39 55 – www.hostellerie-saint-hubert.com – contact@hotelsaint-hubert.com – Fax 03 87 98 39 57 – Closed 22-30 December
53 rm – †€ 59/62 ††€ 79/82, ☕ € 9 – 3 suites – ½ P € 79
Rest – Menu € 29/69 – Carte € 45/55
◆ A modern hotel on the banks of the small lake within a sports centre. Spacious rooms, some with painted wood furniture, also occasional loggias. Two dining areas, a tavern and waterside terrace serving traditional cuisine.

HAMBYE – 50 Manche – 303 E6 – pop. 1 155 – alt. 111 m – ✉ 50450 32 A2
Normandy

Paris 316 – Coutances 20 – Granville 30 – St-Lô 25 – Villedieu-les-Poêles 17
Abbey church ★★.

to the Abbey 3,5 km South by D 51 – ✉ 50450 Hambye

Auberge de l'Abbaye with rm
5 rte de l'Abbaye – ☎ 02 33 61 42 19 – aubergedelabbaye@wanadoo.fr – Fax 02 33 61 00 85 – Closed 1st-15 October, 15-28 February, Sunday dinner and Monday
7 rm – †€ 44 ††€ 55, ☕ € 9 – ½ P € 60
Rest – Menu (€ 23 bi), € 26/67 – Carte € 34/55
◆ A large freestone house near the ruins of the abbey. Summer terrace in a small garden. Smart-rustic dining room; traditional cuisine.

HANVEC – 29 Finistère – 308 G5 – pop. 1 867 – alt. 103 m – ✉ 29460 9 A-B2

Paris 568 – Rennes 216 – Quimper 48 – Brest 35 – Morlaix 47

Les Chaumières de Kerguan without rest
Kerguan, 2 km on Sizun road – ☎ 06 01 96 87 53 – www.kerguan.neuf.fr – kerguan@neuf.fr
4 rm ☕ – †€ 35 ††€ 50/54
◆ A typical, thatch-roofed longère in a quiet hamlet of restored agricultural buildings. Charming, reasonably priced rooms.

HARDELOT-PLAGE – 62 Pas-de-Calais – 301 C4 – ✉ 62152 30 A2
Neufchatel Hardelot **Northern France and the Paris Region**

Paris 254 – Arras 114 – Boulogne-sur-Mer 15 – Calais 51 – Le Touquet-Paris-Plage 23
Office de tourisme, 476, avenue Francois-1er ☎ 03 21 83 51 02, Fax 03 21 91 84 60
d'Hardelot Neufchâtel-Hardelot 3 avenue du Golf, E : 1 km, ☎ 03 21 83 73 10

Du Parc
111 av. Francois 1er – ☎ 03 21 33 22 11 – www.hotelduparc-hardelot.com – parc.hotel@najeti.com – Fax 03 21 83 29 71
106 rm – †€ 115/165 ††€ 115/165, ☕ € 14 – 1 suite – ½ P € 88/115
Rest – Menu (€ 22 bi), € 28/41 – Carte € 45/60
◆ A recent hotel and sports complex in a woodland environment. Spacious, cosy rooms (painted furniture) looking onto the park. Seafood aromas and tastes abound in this bright restaurant, whose walls are covered in wainscoting and woodwork.

Régina
185 av. François 1er – ☎ 03 21 83 81 88 – www.lereginahotel.fr – leregina.hotel@wanadoo.fr – Fax 03 21 87 44 01 – Closed 29 November-28 February
42 rm – †€ 67/75 ††€ 67/75, ☕ € 11 – ½ P € 59/63
Rest – *(closed Sunday dinner except July to September, Tuesday lunch from July to September and Monday)* Menu (€ 20), € 23/37 – Carte € 26/45
◆ A modern building on the edge of the pine forest, which stretches to the entrance of this elegant Côte d'Opale resort. First and second floor rooms are refurbished. Fish and seafood are served in the restaurant with a warm, modern decor. Pleasant terrace.

HARRICOURT – 08 Ardennes – pop. 52 – alt. 180 m – ✉ 08240 14 C1

Paris 236 – Châlons-en-Champagne 86 – Charleville-Mézières 61 – Sedan 42 – Verdun 58

La Montgomière
1 r. St-Georges – ✆ 03 24 71 66 50 – www.lamontgoniere.net – regnault.montgon@wanadoo.fr – Fax 03 24 71 66 50 – Closed January
3 rm – €80/90 €90/110 **Table d'hôte** – Menu €25
◆ In the heart of the village, peaceful parkland and a pond surround this 17C country house. Wainscoted sitting rooms, antique furnished rooms and library with games. Table d'hôte (by reservation) serving wholesome family cooking in a period decor.

HASPARREN – 64 Pyrénées-Atlantiques – 342 E4 – pop. 5 742 – alt. 50 m – ✉ 64240 Atlantic Coast 3 AB3

Paris 783 – Bayonne 24 – Biarritz 34 – Cambo-les-Bains 9 – Pau 106
Office de tourisme, 2, place Saint-Jean ✆ 05 59 29 62 02, Fax 05 59 29 13 80
Grottoes of Oxocelhaya and Isturits ★★ Southeast: 11 km.

Les Tilleuls
pl. Verdun – ✆ 05 59 29 62 20 – hotel.lestilleuls@wanadoo.fr – Fax 05 59 29 13 58 – Closed 2-9 November, 20 February-8 March, Sunday dinner and Saturday from 26 September to 4 July except bank holidays
25 rm – €46/52 €55/60, €7 – ½ P €47/51
Rest – Menu €15/30 – Carte €23/42
◆ The former home of writer Francis Jammes is a stone's throw from this Basque-style construction with well-renovated rooms. Delightful rustic restaurant serving regional dishes.

South 6km by D152 and secondary road - ✉64240 Hasparren

Ferme Hégia (Arnaud Daguin)
chemin Curutxeta, (Zelai district) – ✆ 05 59 29 67 86 – www.hegia.com – info@hegia.com
5 rm (½ board only) – ½ P €325
Table d'hôte – *(set menu only, guests only)*
Spec. Menu du marché
◆ An old farmhouse built in 1746 surrounded by mountains. The interior, superbly renovated in contemporary style, is embellished with high-quality fabrics and materials. The chef prepares his dishes under the eyes of his guests. Cuisine inspired by the daily market.

HASPRES – 59 Nord – 302 I6 – pop. 2 692 – alt. 44 m – ✉ 59198 31 C3

Paris 197 – Avesnes-sur-Helpe 49 – Cambrai 18 – Lille 66 – Valenciennes 16

Auberge St-Hubert
62 r. A. Brunet, rte Denain 1km D 955 – ✆ 03 27 25 70 97 – www.lestoquesblanchesduhainaut.com – auberge.st.hubert.haspres@wanadoo.fr – Fax 03 27 25 76 21 – Closed August, 3-12 January, Tuesday dinner and Monday except bank holidays
Rest – Menu €22 (weekdays)/50 bi – Carte €36/49
◆ This spruce inn, situated in the Selle valley, is popular for its small garden, rustic-style dining rooms and traditional cuisine (game in season).

HAUTEFORT – 24 Dordogne – 329 H4 – pop. 1 135 – alt. 160 m – ✉ 24390 Dordogne-Berry-Limousin 4 D1

Paris 466 – Bordeaux 189 – Périgueux 59 – Brive-la-Gaillarde 57 – Tulle 92
Office de tourisme, place du Marquis J. F. de Hautefort ✆ 05 53 50 40 27, Fax 05 53 51 99 73

Au Périgord Noir without rest
La Genèbre – ✆ 05 53 50 40 30 – www.hotel.auperigordnoir.com – hotel@auperigordnoir.com – Fax 05 53 51 86 70
29 rm – €45/50 €45/50, €7
◆ Contemporary and impersonal building opposite the Château de Hautefort offering quiet, well-kept, functional rooms. Panoramic breakfast room.

HAUTE-GOULAINE – 44 Loire-Atlantique – 316 H4 – see Nantes

HAUTE-INDRE – 44 Loire-Atlantique – 316 F4 – see Nantes

HAUTELUCE – 73 Savoie – 333 M3 – pop. 875 – alt. 1 150 m 45 D1
– ✉ 73620 French Alps

Paris 606 – Albertville 24 – Annecy 62 – Chambéry 77 – Megève 31

Office de tourisme, 316, Avenue des Jeux Olympiques ✆ 04 79 38 90 30, Fax 04 79 38 96 29

La Ferme du Chozal ← rm, rest,
– ✆ 04 79 38 18 18 – www.lafermeduchozal.com
– informations@lafermeduchozal.com – Fax 04 79 38 87 20
– Open early June to mid-October and mid-December to mid-April
11 rm – †€ 100/225 ††€ 100/225, ☕ € 15 – ½ P € 95/158
Rest – *(closed Monday lunch, Tuesday lunch and Wednesday lunch in July-August, Monday dinner and Sunday dinner in June and in September-October)*
Menu € 28/100 bi – Carte € 43/66

◆ Modern comfort and Savoyard charm go hand in hand at this pretty chalet-farm: cosy rooms, a library-lounge and spa (sauna, steam room, Jacuzzi, massages). Modern dinner menu, simpler fare at lunch, and fine Alpine-European wine list.

HAUTERIVES – 26 Drôme – 332 D2 – pop. 1 333 – alt. 299 m 43 E2
– ✉ 26390 Lyon - Rhone Valley

Paris 540 – Grenoble 77 – Lyon 85 – Valence 46 – Vienne 42

Office de tourisme, rue du Palais Idéal ✆ 04 75 68 86 82, Fax 04 75 68 92 96

Le Palais Idéal★★.

Le Relais
1 pl. Gén.-de-Miribel – ✆ 04 75 68 81 12 – www.hotel-relais-drome.com
– contact@hotel-relais-drome.com – Fax 04 75 68 92 42
– Closed 15 January-28 February, Sunday dinner except July-August and Monday
16 rm – †€ 55 ††€ 61, ☕ € 8,50 – ½ P € 54
Rest – Menu € 17/37 – Carte € 32/40

◆ Visitors to the Ideal Palace built by Cheval will appreciate this hotel with a façade featuring rolled pebble ornaments. Simple, well-kept rooms. Small, traditional dishes served in the rustic dining area or on the terrace.

LES HAUTES-RIVIÈRES – 08 Ardennes – 306 L3 – pop. 1 781 14 C1
– alt. 175 m – ✉ 08800 Northern France and the Paris Region

Paris 254 – Châlons-en-Champagne 150 – Charleville-Mézières 22 – Sedan 29 – Dinant 56

Croix d'Enfer (Hell's Cross) ←★ South: 1.5 km by D 13 then 30 mn - Vallon de Linchamps★ North: 4 km.

Auberge en Ardenne
15 r. Hôtel de Ville – ✆ 03 24 53 41 93 – www.aubergeenardenne.fr
– auberge.ardenne@orange.fr – Fax 03 24 53 60 10
– Closed 20 December-10 January
14 rm – †€ 53 ††€ 53, ☕ € 7 – ½ P € 54
Rest – *(closed Saturday lunch and Sunday dinner off season)* Menu (€ 13), € 16/28 – Carte € 15/37

◆ The rooms of this inn located on both sides of the road and are well kept, functional and simple. Two dining rooms: one rustic set in the former cow-shed, the other more modern, looking out over the river.

Les Saisons
5 Grande Rue – ✆ 03 24 53 40 94 – www.restaurant-lessaisons.com
– Fax 03 24 54 57 51 – Closed 16-31 August, 14-22 February, Sunday dinner, Wednesday dinner and Monday except bank holidays
Rest – Menu € 22/39 – Carte € 30/45

◆ Traditional cooking making use of local produce: wild boar, game and mushrooms in season. Several dining rooms, including one reserved for daily specials.

HAUTEVILLE-LÈS-DIJON – 21 Côte-d'Or – 320 J5 – see Dijon

LE HAVRE – 76 Seine-Maritime – 304 A5 – pop. 183 600 – Built-up area 248 547 – alt. 4 m – Casino HZ – ✉ 76600 Normandy 33 C2

Paris 198 – Amiens 184 – Caen 90 – Lille 318 – Nantes 382 – Rouen 87

Havre-Octeville: ✆ 02 35 54 65 00 A.

Office de tourisme, 186, boulevard Clemenceau ✆ 02 32 74 04 04, Fax 02 35 42 38 39

du Havre Octeville-sur-Mer Hameau Saint Supplix, 10 km on the Etretat road, ✆ 02 35 46 36 50

Harbour★★ EZ - Modern quarter ★ EFYZ : interior★★ of St-Joseph church ★ EZ, pl. de l'Hôtel-de-Ville★ FY47, Av. Foch★ EFY - Musée des Beaux-Arts André-Malraux★ EZ.

Ste-Adresse★: circuit★.

Plans on following pages

Pasino rm, VISA MC AE

pl. Jules Ferry, (At the Casino) – ✆ 02 35 26 00 00 – www.pasino-lehavre.fr – reservation-lehavre@g-partouche.fr – Fax 02 35 25 62 18 FZ **b**

45 rm – †€ 130/360 ††€ 130/360, ☕ € 18

Rest *Le Havre des Sens* – *(Closed Sunday and Monday)* Menu (€ 30), € 38/60 – Carte € 46/77

Rest *La Brasserie* – Menu (€ 14), € 18 (weekdays)/29 bi – Carte € 22/53

◆ Rooms, junior suites and a spa in this ultra trendy hotel-casino. Modern decor and cuisine at Le Havre des Sens. Modern brasserie with a waterfront terrace.

Novotel VISA MC AE

20 cours Lafayette – ✆ 02 35 19 23 23 – www.novotel.com – h5650@accor.com – Fax 02 35 19 23 25 HZ **a**

134 rm – †€ 95/170 ††€ 95/170, ☕ € 15 – 6 suites

Rest – Menu (€ 24), € 30 – Carte € 25/46

◆ A modern-style hotel on the banks of Vauban docks, not far from the station. Comfortable rooms characteristic of the Novotel chain. This restaurant has a designer decor and bay windows opening onto the inner garden. Traditional cuisine.

Vent d'Ouest without rest VISA MC AE

4 r. Caligny – ✆ 02 35 42 50 69 – www.ventdouest.fr – contact@ventdouest.fr – Fax 02 35 42 58 00 EZ **a**

35 rm – †€ 100 ††€ 130, ☕ € 12 – 4 suites

◆ This Le Havre hotel on the edge of the town has many advantages: rooms with attractive decor on themes such as Seaside, Captain and Mountain, a pleasant lounge and library with billiard table.

Les Voiles without rest VISA MC AE

3 pl. Clemenceau, at Ste-Adresse ✉ 76310 – ✆ 02 35 54 68 90 – www.hotel-lesvoiles.com – reservation@hotel-lesvoiles.com – Fax 02 35 54 68 91

16 rm – †€ 85/170 ††€ 85/170, ☕ € 11 A **e**

◆ An ideal location facing the sea for this hotel with a warm, contemporary decor. All but four of the rooms have a sea view.

Art Hôtel without rest VISA MC AE

147 r. L. Brindeau – ✆ 02 35 22 69 44 – www.art-hotel.fr – arthotel@free.fr – Fax 02 35 42 09 27 FZ **g**

31 rm – †€ 89/130 ††€ 110/150, ☕ € 12

◆ Facing the Espace Oscar Niemeyer, this building from the 1950s (with listed façade), honours architecture and modern art. Bright, simple rooms; exhibitions.

Terminus VISA MC AE

23 cours République – ✆ 02 35 25 42 48 – www.grand-hotel-terminus.fr – inter@terminus-lehavre.com – Fax 02 35 24 46 55 – Closed 24-27 December and 31 December-3 January HZ **e**

44 rm – †€ 57/97 ††€ 69/97, ☕ € 8 – 1 suite

Rest – *(Closed 17 July-23 August, 24 December-3 January, Friday, Saturday and Sunday) (dinner only) (resident only)* Menu € 18 bi

◆ In the centre of Le Havre, opposite the station this hotel has renovated rooms that are fresh and functional. Low-key lounge bar in red tones; billiard table.

HARFLEUR

Doumer (R. Paul) . . . . D 30
Verdun (Av. de) . . . . D 90
104 (R. des) . . . . D 98

LE HAVRE

Abbaye (R. de l') . . . . C 2
Aplemont (Av. d') . . . . C 7
Churchill (Bd W.) . . . . B 24
Hermann-du-Pasquier (Quai) . B 44
Joannès-Couvert (Quai) . . . . . B
Mouchez (Bd Amiral) . . . . B
Octeville (Rte d') . . . . A
Picasso (Av. Pablo) C
Rouelles (R. de) C
Sakharov (R. Andréï) C

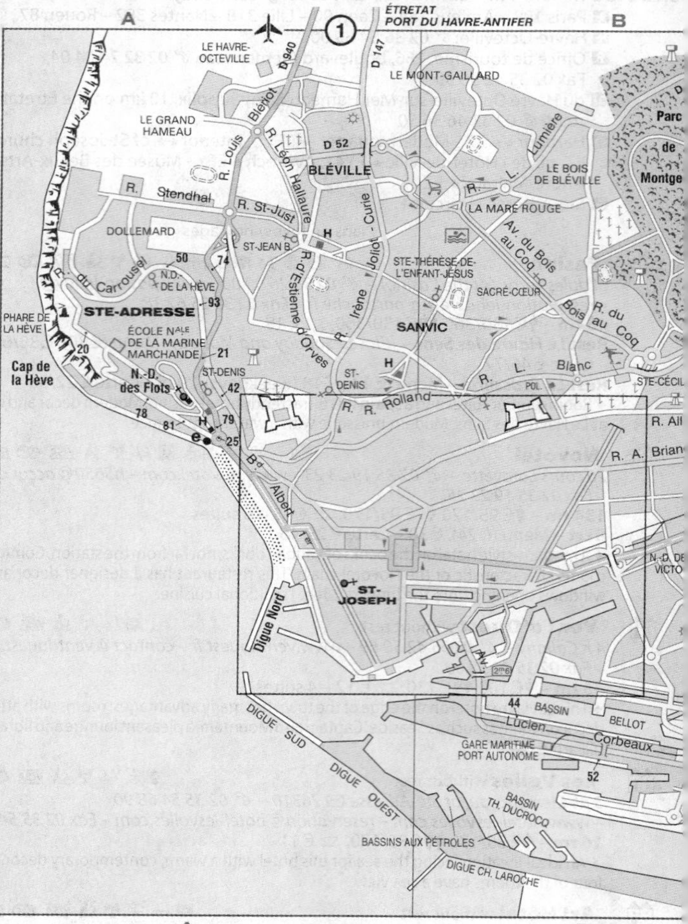

 **Le Richelieu** without rest — VISA MC AE D
132 r. Paris – ☏ 02 35 42 38 71
– www.hotel-lerichelieu-76.com
– hotel.lerichelieu@wanadoo.fr
– Fax 02 35 21 07 28 — FZ **f**
19 rm – †€ 48 ††€ 50, ☕ € 8
◆ A simple hotel in a busy street bordered by many shops. Lounge-lobby done in sea tones. Rooms fully renovated and variously furnished.

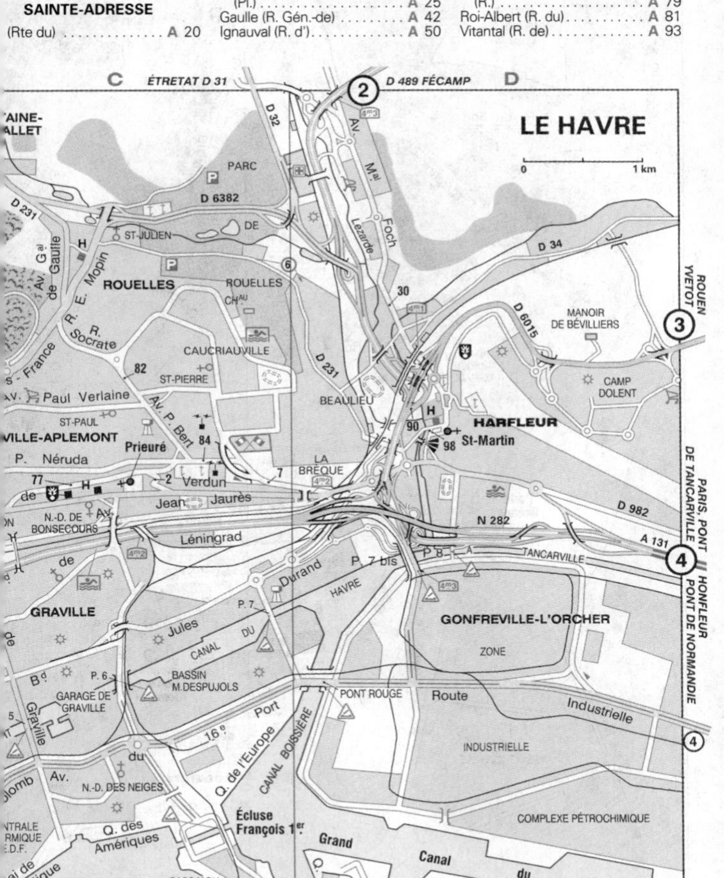

Jean-Luc Tartarin

73 av. Foch – 02 35 45 46 20 – www.jeanluc-tartarin.com – info@jeanluc-tartarin.com – Fax 02 35 45 46 22 – Closed Sunday and Monday FY **t**

Rest – Menu (€ 29), € 40/145 – Carte € 80/95

Spec. Homard poudré d'orange caramélisée dans un bouillon de cocos de Paimpol. Pigeonneau cuit en vessie au cacao, jus de citron salé. Bonbons de chocolat blanc fourrés au jus de fruit de la passion.

◆ Contemporary decor in taupe and chocolate colours with bay windows and artwork. The regularly renewed modern menu is a mouth-watering prospect.

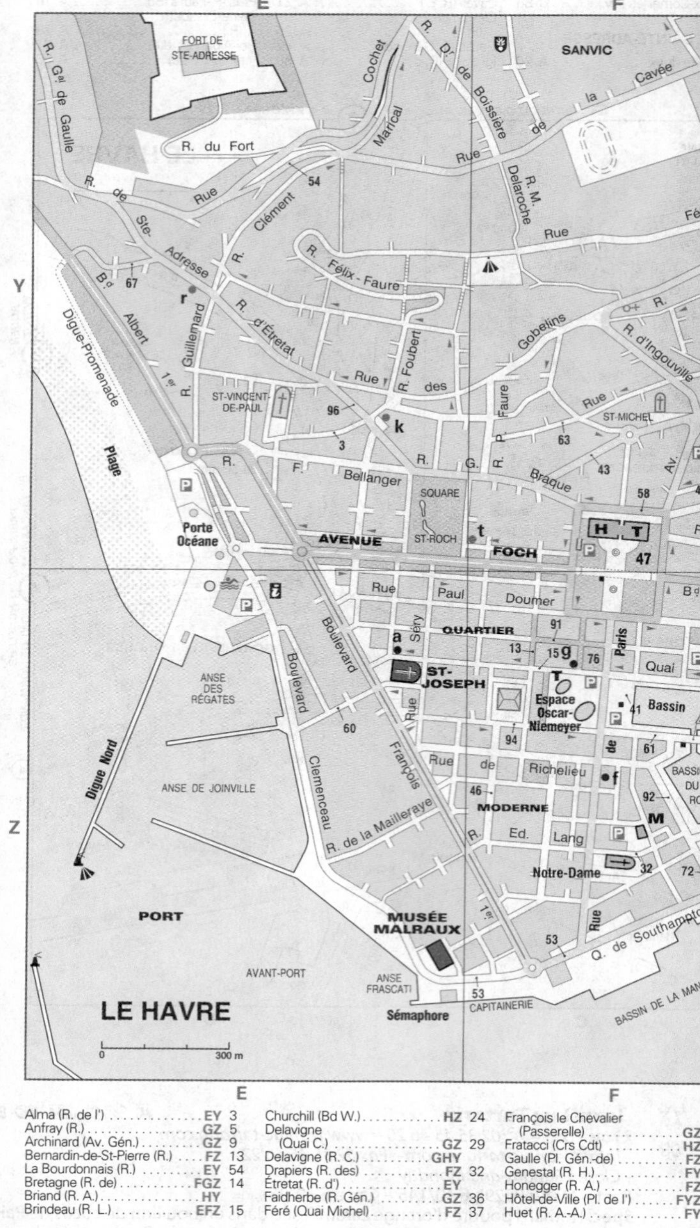

Alma (R. de l') . . . . **EY** 3
Anfray (R.) . . . . **GZ** 5
Archinard (Av. Gén.) . . . . **GZ** 9
Bernardin-de-St-Pierre (R.) . . . . **FZ** 13
La Bourdonnais (R.) . . . . **EY** 54
Bretagne (R. de) . . . . **FGZ** 14
Briand (R. A.) . . . . **HY**
Brindeau (R. L.) . . . . **EFZ** 15
Churchill (Bd W.) . . . . **HZ** 24
Delavigne (Quai C.) . . . . **GZ** 29
Delavigne (R. C.) . . . . **GHY**
Drapiers (R. des) . . . . **FZ** 32
Étretat (R. d') . . . . **EY**
Faidherbe (R. Gén.) . . . . **GZ** 36
Féré (Quai Michel) . . . . **FZ** 37
François le Chevalier (Passerelle) . . . . **GZ**
Fratacci (Crs Cdt) . . . . **HZ**
Gaulle (Pl. Gén.-de) . . . . **FZ**
Genestal (R. H.) . . . . **FY**
Honegger (R. A.) . . . . **FZ**
Hôtel-de-Ville (Pl. de l') . . . . . . **FYZ**
Huet (R. A.-A.) . . . . **FY**

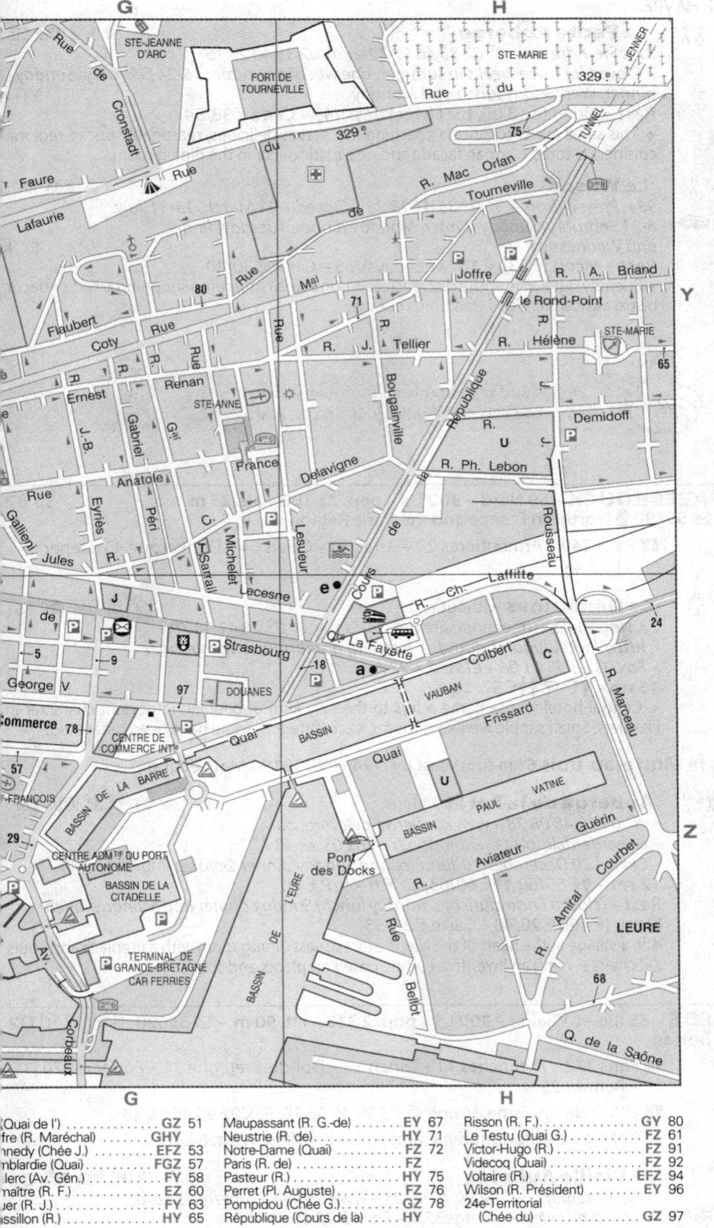

G
H
STE-JEANNE D'ARC
FORT DE TOURNEVILLE
STE-MARIE
JENNER
329 e
Rue du
Rue de Cronstadt
TUNNEL
75
R. Mac Orlan
Tourneville
Rue Faure
Lafaurie
de
Joffre
R. A. Briand
Y
80
Rue Mal
71
le Rond-Point
Flaubert
Coty Rue
R. J. Tellier
R. Hélène
STE-MARIE
65
Renan
STE-ANNE
Ernest
Bougainville
République
Demidoff
U
J.-B.
Gabriel
Gal
France
Delavigne
R. Ph. Lebon
Anatole
Rue Gallieni
Eyriès
Péri
Michelet
Lesueur
Cours de la
Rousseau
Jules
Sarrail
Laffitte
R. Ch.
Lecesne
e
J
de
24
Strasbourg
Qre La Fayette
Colbert
C
5
9
18
a
George V
97
DOUANES
VAUBAN
R. Marceau
Commerce
78
CENTRE DE COMMERCE INTle
Quai
BASSIN
Frissard
57
BASSIN DE LA BARRE
Quai
U
VATINE
F.-FRANÇOIS
PAUL
BASSIN
Guérin
Z
29
CENTRE ADMTIF DU PORT AUTONOME
Pont des Docks
R. Aviateur
Courbet
BASSIN DE LA CITADELLE
BASSIN DE L'EURE
Rue
R. Amiral
LEURE
Av.
TERMINAL DE GRANDE-BRETAGNE CAR FERRIES
Bellot
68
Corbeaux
Q. de la Saône
G
H

XX La Petite Auberge

32 r. Ste-Adresse – ✆ 02 35 46 27 32 – Fax 02 35 48 26 15 – Closed for three weeks in summer, one week in autumn, 15-24 February, Sunday dinner, Wednesday lunch and Monday EY **r**

Rest – Menu (€ 18 bi), € 23 (weekdays)/43 – Carte € 38/54

◆ This small auberge, once a coaching inn, serves delicious, reasonably priced regional cuisine. Restored Norman façade and neo-rustic decor in the dining room.

X Le Wilson

98 r. Prés. Wilson – ✆ 02 35 41 18 28 – Closed 1-11 March, 13-31 July, 8-21 February, Sunday dinner, Monday dinner, Tuesday dinner and Wednesday EY **k**

Rest – Menu (€ 13), € 18 (weekdays)/35 – Carte € 30/40

◆ Friendly restaurant with a discreet facade, on a small square in a shopping area. Sea decor, bistro atmosphere and traditional cuisine.

Hotels and restaurants change every year, so change your Michelin guide every year!

HAZEBROUCK – 59 Nord – 302 D3 – pop. 21 100 – alt. 25 m – ✉ 59190 Northern France and the Paris Region 30 **B2**

Paris 240 – Armentières 28 – Arras 60 – Calais 64 – Dunkerque 43 – Ieper 37 – Lille 43

Le Gambrinus without rest

2 r. Nationale, (street opposite the station) – ✆ 03 28 41 98 79 – http://hoteldugambrinus.fr – hotel.du.gambrinus@wanadoo.fr – Fax 03 28 43 11 06 – Closed 3-23 August

16 rm – †€ 47 ††€ 52, ☕ € 6

◆ Central hotel whose name refers to the jolly king of beer, an important character in Flanders. Small simple well-kept rooms, each different; some have been renovated.

in la Motte-au-Bois 6 km southeast by D 946 – ✉ 59190 Morbecque

XXX Auberge de la Forêt with rm

– ✆ 03 28 48 08 78 – www.auberge-delaforet.com – auberge-delaforet@wanadoo.fr – Fax 03 28 40 77 76 – Closed 20 December-10 January and Sunday dinner October-March

12 rm – †€ 55/60 ††€ 60/63, ☕ € 8 – ½ P € 60

Rest – *(closed Friday lunch, Saturday lunch, Sunday dinner and Monday lunch)* Menu (€ 16), € 20/40 – Carte € 39/53

◆ In a village at the heart of the Nieppe forest; vast dining room with a fireplace and Louis XIII chairs serving an inventive cuisine based on plants and spices.

HÉDÉ – 35 Ille-et-Vilaine – 309 L5 – pop. 2 318 – alt. 90 m – ✉ 35630 Brittany 10 **D2**

Paris 372 – Avranches 71 – Dinan 33 – Dol-de-Bretagne 31 – Fougères 70 – Rennes 25

Office de tourisme, Mairie ✆ 02 99 45 46 18, Fax 02 99 45 50 48

Château de Montmuran★ and église des Iffs★ West: 8 km.

XX La Vieille Auberge

rte de Tinténiac – ✆ 02 99 45 46 25 – www.lavieilleauberge35.com – contact@lavieilleauberge35.fr – Fax 02 99 45 51 35 – Closed 17 August-1 September, 15 February-2 March, Sunday dinner and Monday

Rest – Menu € 18 (weekday lunch), € 26/80 – Carte € 44/120

◆ A 17C mill of pastoral charm with a delightful, leafy pondside terrace and a pretty little flower-decked garden. Informal ambience and delicious classic cuisine.

HENDAYE – 64 Pyrénées-Atlantiques – **342** B4 – **pop. 13 000** 3 **A3**
– **alt. 30 m** – **Casino** – ✉ **64700** **Atlantic Coast**

Paris 799 – Biarritz 31 – Pau 143 – St-Jean-de-Luz 12 – San Sebastián 21

Office de tourisme, 67, boulevard de la Mer ✆ 05 59 20 00 34, Fax 05 59 20 79 17

Large crucifix★ in St-Vincent church - Château of Antoine-Abbadie★★ (lounge★) 3 km.

Ez Kecha Bar Lieu Dit Vin

3 rte de Béhobie – ✆ 05 59 20 67 09 – www.eguiazabal.com – contact@eguiazabal.com – Fax 05 59 48 20 12 – Closed February school holidays, Sunday, Monday and bank holidays

Rest – *(number of covers limited, pre-book)* Menu € 35/65 bi – Carte € 35/58

◆ Restaurant set in a wine shop with over 500 wines to accompany the seasonal cuisine. Tasting sessions at the bar, in the cosy dining areas or on the terrace. Expert service. Deli.

in Hendaye Plage

Serge Blanco rm, rest,

bd de la Mer – ✆ 05 59 51 35 35 – www.thalassoblanco.com – info@thalassoblanco.com – Fax 05 59 51 36 00 – Closed in December

90 rm – †€ 87/260 ††€ 132/342, ☕ € 14 – ½ P € 108/213

Rest – ✆ 0 825 00 00 15 – Carte € 39/51

◆ The famous rugby player is the owner of this hotel and its thalassotherapy centre, between the beach and marina. Contemporary-style rooms. Some have been renovated. A choice of three types of meals: diet dishes, gastronomic cuisine and grilled food in summer.

in Biriatou 4 km southeast by D 811 – pop. 831 – alt. 60 m – ✉ 64700

Les Jardins de Bakéa

r. Herri Alde – ✆ 05 59 20 02 01 – www.bakea.fr – contact@bakea.fr – Fax 05 59 20 58 21 – Closed 16 November-3 December and 17 January-3 February

25 rm – †€ 45/125 ††€ 55/125, ☕ € 10 – ½ P € 74/109

Rest – *(Closed Monday and Tuesday except dinner from April to November)* Menu (€ 28), € 47/67 – Carte € 48/85

◆ This early-20C residence built in regional architectural style is currently being renovated. Once it is finished, it will offer eight comfortable rooms, four of which will be in the attic. New restaurant (exposed beams) and pleasant summer terrace beneath the plane trees.

HÉNIN-BEAUMONT – 62 Pas-de-Calais – **301** K5 – **pop. 26 100** 31 **C2**
– **alt. 30 m** – ✉ **62110** **Northern France and the Paris Region**

Paris 194 – Arras 25 – Béthune 30 – Douai 13 – Lens 11 – Lille 34

Novotel rm, rm,

av. de la République, near junction of A1 motorway, via D943 ✉ 62950 – ✆ 03 21 08 58 08 – www.novotel.com – h0426@accor.com – Fax 03 21 08 58 00

81 rm – †€ 79/145 ††€ 79/145, ☕ € 15 **Rest** – Carte approx. € 30

◆ In a shopping centre near a motorway interchange in an oasis of greenery. Rooms being refurbished in stages; choose one facing the patio-terrace. Modern dining room and tables by the swimming pool, weather permitting.

HENNEBONT – 56 Morbihan – **308** L8 – **pop. 14 300** – **alt. 15 m** 9 **B2**
– ✉ **56700** **Brittany**

Paris 492 – Concarneau 57 – Lorient 13 – Pontivy 51 – Quimperlé 26 – Vannes 50

Office de tourisme, 9, place Maréchal-Foch ✆ 02 97 36 24 52, Fax 02 97 36 21 91

Clock tower★ of N.-D.-de-Paradis basilica.

Port-Louis: citadel★★ (musée de la Compagnie des Indes★★, musée de l'Arsenal★) South: 13 km.

Port-Louis road 4 km South by D 781 – ✉ 56700 Hennebont

Château de Locguénolé rest, VISA MC AE
– ☎ 02 97 76 76 76
– *www.chateau-de-locguenole.com – locguenole@relaischateaux.com*
– Fax 02 97 76 82 35 – Closed 4 January-13 February
18 rm – †€ 112/289 ††€ 112/289, ☕ € 23 – 4 suites – ½ P € 143/234
Rest – *(closed Monday except August and lunch except Sunday)* Menu € 49/96 – Carte € 72/119
Spec. Galette de sarrasin farcie de tourteau (July-Aug.). Langoustines grillées minute en coque (May to Oct.). Riz arborio fondant aux fruits rouges, dentelle riz soufflé et glace à l'huile d'olive (May to Oct.).
◆ Two historical houses in a 120-ha park sloping down to the Blavet ria. Spacious, elegant guestrooms with personal touches. Pleasant dining room serving a mixture of seafood and vegetable dishes; good wine selection.

Chaumières de Kerniaven VISA MC AE
3 km – ☎ 02 97 76 91 90 – www.chaumieres-de-kerniaven.com
– locguenole@relaischateaux.com – Fax 02 97 76 82 35
– Open 1st May-27 September
9 rm – †€ 68/112 ††€ 78/112, ☕ € 17
◆ After checking in at the reception of Château de Locguénolé, you will be taken to these two 17C cottages, deep in the countryside and ideal for relaxing and recuperating.

L'HERBAUDIÈRE – 85 Vendée – 316 C5 – see Île de Noirmoutier

HERBAULT – 41 Loir-et-Cher – 318 D6 – pop. 1 208 – alt. 138 m – ✉ 41190 11 A1

▶ Paris 196 – Blois 17 – Château-Renault 18 – Montrichard 38 – Tours 47 – Vendôme 26

Auberge des Trois Marchands VISA MC AE
34 pl. de l'Hôtel-de-Ville – ☎ 02 54 46 12 18 – www.restaurant-herbault.com
Rest – Menu (€ 13 bi), € 18/45 – Carte € 28/49
◆ Situated on the main square in the village, this simple auberge serves traditional cuisine in a bright, country style dining room.

LES HERBIERS – 85 Vendée – 316 J6 – pop. 14 900 – alt. 110 m – ✉ 85500 ▌Atlantic Coast 34 B3

▶ Paris 381 – Bressuire 48 – Chantonnay 25 – Cholet 26 – Clisson 35 – La Roche-sur-Yon 40

ℹ Office de tourisme, 2, grande rue Saint-Blaise ☎ 02 51 92 92 92, Fax 02 51 92 93 70

◎ Mont des Alouettes★: windmill ≤★★ North: 2 km - Chemin de fer de la Vendée (railway) ★.

◎ Route des Moulins★.

Chez Camille rest, VISA MC AE
2 r. Mgr Massé – ☎ 02 51 91 07 57 – www.chez-camille.com – chez.camille@online.fr – Fax 02 51 67 19 28
13 rm – †€ 47/60 ††€ 51/69, ☕ € 8 – ½ P € 47/56
Rest – *(closed Sunday dinner, Friday dinner and Saturday off season)* Menu (€ 16), € 19/30 – Carte € 21/41
◆ Near the old Ardelay keep, an establishment with a pleasantly provincial atmosphere (the bar is the HQ of the local football club). Standard rooms. The restaurant's friendly, easy-going ambience can be traced to its unpretentious cuisine.

HERBIGNAC – 44 Loire-Atlantique – 316 C3 – pop. 5 117 – alt. 18 m – ✉ 44410 34 A2

▶ Paris 446 – Nantes 72 – La Baule 24 – Redon 37 – St Nazaire 28

ℹ Syndicat d'initiative, 2, rue Pasteur ☎ 02 40 19 90 01

South 6 km Guérande road by D774 – ✉ 44410 Herbignac

XX **La Chaumière des Marais**
– ✆ 02 40 91 32 36 – lachaumieredesmarais@orange.fr – Fax 02 40 91 33 87
– Closed mid-October to mid-November, February holidays, Monday and Tuesday except July-August
Rest – Menu € 18 (weekday lunch), € 28/62 bi – Carte approx. € 48
◆ Pretty flower-decked cottage with terrace and vegetable garden. Charming countrified dining room with a huge fireplace and modern cuisine enriched with herbs and spices.

HÉRÉPIAN – 34 Hérault – **339** D7 – **see Bédarieux**

LES HERMAUX – 48 Lozère – **330** G7 – **pop. 117** – **alt. 1 045 m** – ✉ 48340 22 **B1**

Paris 594 – Espalion 56 – Florac 73 – Mende 50 – Millau 67 – Rodez 75 – St-Flour 90

Vergnet
– ✆ 04 66 32 60 78 – www.hotel-vergnet.com – vergnet.christophe@wanadoo.fr
– Closed Sunday dinner off season
12 rm – †€ 40 ††€ 40, ☕ € 6 – ½ P € 40
Rest – *(closed Sun. evening)* Menu € 14/23
◆ Family hotel set in a picturesque Aubrac hamlet. Some of the rustic-style rooms could do with a fresh coat of paint. The somewhat outmoded dining room, decorated with stuffed animals, serves unfussy cuisine such as aligot and sausages.

HÉROUVILLE – 95 Val-d'Oise – **305** D6 – **106** 6 – **see Paris, Area (Cergy-Pontoise)**

HÉROUVILLE-ST-CLAIR – 14 Calvados – **303** J4 – **see Caen**

HESDIN – 62 Pas-de-Calais – **301** F5 – **pop. 2 420** – **alt. 27 m** – ✉ 62140 30 **A2**
Northern France and the Paris Region

Paris 210 – Abbeville 36 – Arras 58 – Boulogne-sur-Mer 65 – Calais 89 – Lille 89

Office de tourisme, place d' Armes ✆ 03 21 86 19 19, Fax 03 21 86 04 05

Trois Fontaines
16 rte d'Abbeville – ✆ 03 21 86 81 65 – www.hotel-les3fontaines.com
– hotel.3fontaines@wanadoo.fr – Fax 03 21 86 33 34
– Closed 22 December-5 January, Monday lunch and Saturday lunch
16 rm – †€ 53/63 ††€ 59/72, ☕ € 7 **Rest** – Menu (€ 16), € 19 (weekdays)/35
◆ The hotel is made up of two buildings, with small, redecorated, ground floor guestrooms opening onto the garden. Choose one in the recent Scandinavian style extension. Reasonably-priced food served in a pleasant dining room with a fireplace.

XX **L'Écurie**
17 r. Jacquemont – ✆ 03 21 86 86 86 – lecurie846@orange.fr – Fax 03 21 86 86 86
– Closed Sunday dinner, Tuesday dinner and Monday
Rest – Menu € 15 (weekday lunch), € 24/26 – Carte € 25/35
◆ Pleasant restaurant with equine theme (sculptures, signage) situated a short walk from the beautiful town hall. Bright dining area decorated with pottery. Traditional cooking.

in Gouy-St-André 14 km west by N 39 and D 137 – **pop. 613** – **alt. 100 m** – ✉ 62870

XX **Le Clos de la Prairie**
17 r. de St-Rémy – ✆ 03 21 90 39 58 – leclosdelaprairie@orange.fr
– Closed 1-10 October, 23-30 December, Thursday lunch and Wednesday
Rest – Menu € 30/100 bi – Carte € 30/100
◆ Warm restaurant set in an old farmhouse in a pleasant little village. Its terrace looks out over the countryside. Tasty, modern cuisine using market produce.

HESDIN-L'ABBÉ – 62 Pas-de-Calais – **301** D3 – **see Boulogne-sur-Mer**

HÉSINGUE – 68 Haut-Rhin – **315** J11 – **see St-Louis**

HEUDICOURT-SOUS-LES-CÔTES – 55 Meuse – **307** F5 – **see St-Mihiel**

HEYRIEUX – 38 Isère – **333** D4 – **pop. 4 163** – **alt. 220 m** – ✉ **38540** 44 **B2**

Paris 487 – Lyon 30 – Pont-de-Chéruy 22 – La Tour-du-Pin 35 – Vienne 25

XXX **L'Alouette** VISA AE

rte de St-Jean-de-Bournay, at 3 km ✉ 38090 – ☎ 04 78 40 06 08
– www.jcmarlhins.com – alouette@jcmarlhins.com – Fax 04 78 40 54 74
– Closed 14-20 April, 26 July-13 August, 21 December-4 January, Saturday lunch, Sunday dinner and Monday
Rest – Menu € 21 (weekday lunch), € 31/51 – Carte € 35/60
◆ Restaurant in three parts with exposed beams, decorated with paintings and sculptures by a regional artist. Pleasant table settings and traditional cuisine.

HIERES-SUR-AMBY – 38 Isère – **333** E3 – **pop. 998** – **alt. 216 m** 44 **B1**
– ✉ 38118

Paris 489 – Lyon 61 – Grenoble 107 – Bourg-en-Bresse 57
– Villeurbanne 48

X **Le Val d'Amby** with rm rest, VISA

pl. de la République – ☎ 04 74 82 42 67 – www.hotel-levaldamby.com
– carlona527@wanadoo.fr – Fax 04 74 82 42 68
– Closed 13-17 April, 11-24 August, 23-26 December, 15-21 February, Sunday dinner and Wednesday
13 rm – †€ 42 ††€ 49/60, ☕ € 8
Rest – Menu (€ 13 bi), € 25 (weekday lunch), € 30/59 – Carte € 33/55
◆ Pretty stone country house in the village square. Menu of the day served in the cafeteria and traditional cuisine in the more comfortable dining room. Terrace. Simple and well-kept rooms.

HINSINGEN – 67 Bas-Rhin – **315** F3 – **pop. 84** – **alt. 220 m** – ✉ **67260** 1 **A1**

Paris 405 – St-Avold 35 – Sarrebourg 37 – Sarreguemines 22
– Strasbourg 92

X **Grange du Paysan** VISA

r. Principale – ☎ 03 88 00 91 83 – Fax 03 88 00 93 23 – Closed Mon.
Rest – Menu € 10 (weekdays)/52 – Carte € 18/52
◆ Old rafters, halters and other farming objects endow this restaurant with a rustic feel. Serves good, local cuisine using produce from the family farm.

HIRMENTAZ – 74 Haute-Savoie – **328** M3 – **see Bellevaux**

HIRTZBACH – 68 Haut-Rhin – **315** H11 – **pop. 1 259** – **alt. 308 m** 1 **A3**
– ✉ 68118

Paris 462 – Mulhouse 24 – Altkirch 5 – Belfort 31 – Colmar 71

XX **Hostellerie de l'Illberg** VISA AE

17 r. Mar. de Lattre de Tassigny – ☎ 03 89 40 93 22 – www.hostelillberg.fr
– hostelillberg@orange.fr – Fax 03 89 08 85 19 – Closed for the spring holidays, in August, Monday and Tuesday
Rest – *(Closed Monday and Tuesday)* Menu € 25 (weekdays)/95 bi
– Carte € 49/58
Rest *Bistrot d'Arthur* – *(Closed Sunday lunch)* Menu (€ 12), € 21/26
– Carte € 26/46
◆ Works by local artists adorn the dining room of this attractive house. Classic cuisine with an innovative twist and an emphasis on regional produce. This extremely friendly bistro features a choice of appetising dishes or daily specials.

HOERDT – 67 Bas-Rhin – 315 K4 – pop. 4 337 – alt. 135 m – ✉ 67720 1 B1

Paris 483 – Haguenau 21 – Molsheim 44 – Saverne 46 – Strasbourg 18

A la Charrue

30 r. République – ✆ 03 88 51 31 11 – www.lacharrue.fr – lacharrue@wanadoo.fr – Fax 03 88 51 32 55 – Closed 24 December-5 January, dinner except Friday and Saturday and Monday except bank holidays

Rest – Menu (€ 10), € 15 (weekday lunch), € 27/36 – Carte € 25/44

◆ The main speciality is asparagus (in season). And so the whole region - including members of the Council of Europe - come here to celebrate.

HOHRODBERG – 68 Haut-Rhin – 315 G8 – alt. 750 m – ✉ 68140 1 A2

Alsace-Lorraine

Paris 462 – Colmar 26 – Gérardmer 37 – Guebwiller 47 – Munster 8 – Le Thillot 57

≤★★.

Panorama

3 rte de Linge – ✆ 03 89 77 36 53 – www.hotel-panorama-alsace.com – info@hotel-panorama-alsace.com – Fax 03 89 77 03 93 – Closed 2-26 November and 4 January-5 February

30 rm – †€ 46/73 ††€ 46/73, ☕ € 11 – ½ P € 50/69

Rest – Menu € 17 (weekdays)/39 – Carte € 25/53

◆ An old building and modern wing facing the Munster valley. Comfortable rooms, some with a view of the Vosges, decorated with frescoes with a regional theme. Magnificent panoramic view from the restaurant, which serves specialities such as the sea Presskopf.

LE HOHWALD – 67 Bas-Rhin – 315 H6 – pop. 386 – alt. 570 m – Winter sports : 600/1 100 m ⛷1 ⛷ – ✉ 67140 Alsace-Lorraine 2 C1

Paris 430 – Lunéville 89 – Molsheim 33 – St-Dié 46 – Sélestat 26 – Strasbourg 51

Office de tourisme, square Kuntz ✆ 03 88 08 33 92, Fax 03 88 08 30 14

Le Neuntelstein★★ ≤★★ North: 6 km then 30 mn.

La Forestière

10 A chemin du Eck – ✆ 03 88 08 31 08 – http://laforestiere.fr.monsite.orange.fr – catherine.marchal15@orange.fr – Fax 03 88 08 32 96 – Closed 1-8 March, 22-29 April and 4-10 July

5 rm ☕ – †€ 71/81 ††€ 86/96 – ½ P € 71 **Table d'hôte** – Menu € 26 bi/36 bi

◆ In the upper reaches of the village, close to the forest, this newly built and quiet establishment offers spacious rooms furnished in pale wood, Alsace style. Table d'hôte (evenings) offering regional specialities and game in a family atmosphere.

HOLNON – 02 Aisne – 306 B3 – see St-Quentin

LE HÔME – 14 Calvados – 303 L4 – see Cabourg

HONDSCHOOTE – 59 Nord – 302 D2 – pop. 3 749 – alt. 5 m – ✉ 59122 30 B1

Paris 286 – Lille 63 – Dunkerque 22 – Oostende 52 – Roeselare 51

Office de tourisme, 2, rue des Moeresd ✆ 03 28 62 53 00, Fax 03 28 68 30 99

Les Jardins de l'Haezepoël

1151 r. de Looweg – ✆ 03 28 62 50 50 – www.hzpl.com – Fax 03 28 68 31 01 – Closed Monday dinner and Tuesday

Rest – grill – Menu (€ 15) – Carte € 25/35

◆ A handsome brick house that is also home to a cabaret. In a countrified setting, you will be served meat grilled in front of you and regional specialities (potjevleech).

HONFLEUR – 14 Calvados – **303** N3 – **pop. 8 139 – alt. 5 m** – ✉ **14600** 32 **A3**

Normandy

Paris 195 – Caen 69 – Le Havre 27 – Lisieux 38 – Rouen 83

Office de tourisme, quai Lepaulmier ☎ 02 31 89 23 30, Fax 02 31 89 31 82

Old Honfleur★★: Old basin★★ AZ, Ste-Catherine church ★★ AY and steeple ★ AY **B** - Côte de Grâce★★AY: calvary★★.

Pont de Normandie★★ by ①: 4 km (toll).

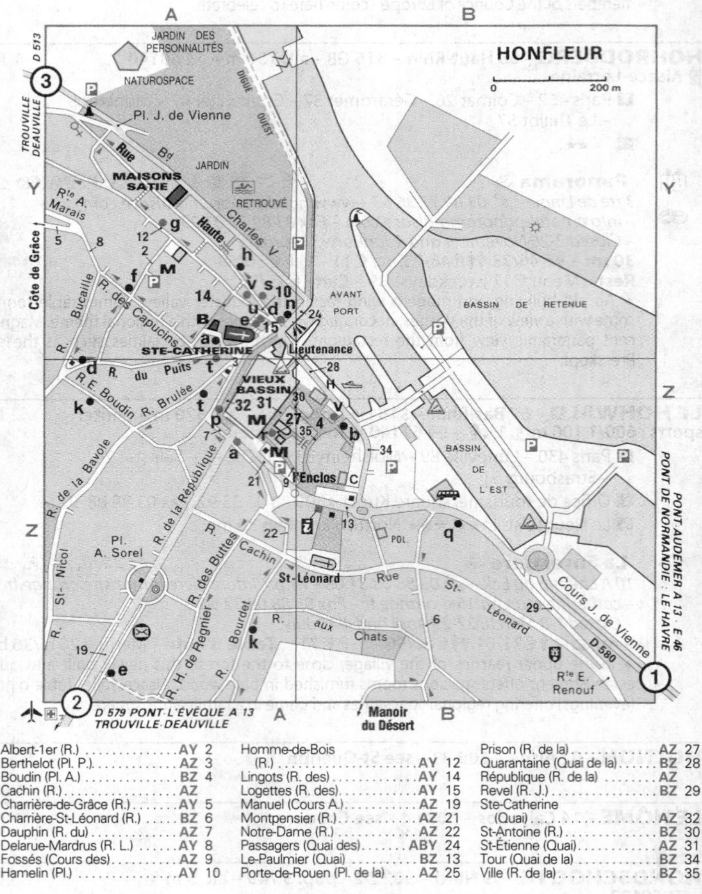

Street		No.
Albert-1er (R.)	AY	2
Berthelot (Pl. P.)	AZ	3
Boudin (Pl. A.)	BZ	4
Cachin (R.)	AZ	
Charrière-de-Grâce (R.)	AY	5
Charrière-St-Léonard (R.)	BZ	6
Dauphin (R. du)	AZ	7
Delarue-Mardrus (R. L.)	AY	8
Fossés (Cours des)	AZ	9
Hamelin (Pl.)	AY	10
Homme-de-Bois (R.)	AY	12
Lingots (R. des)	AY	14
Logettes (R. des)	AY	15
Manuel (Cours A.)	AZ	19
Montpensier (R.)	AZ	21
Notre-Dame (R.)	AZ	22
Passagers (Quai des)	ABY	24
Le-Paulmier (Quai)	BZ	13
Porte-de-Rouen (Pl. de la)	AZ	25
Prison (R. de la)	AZ	27
Quarantaine (Quai de la)	BZ	28
République (R. de la)	AZ	
Revel (R. J.)	BZ	29
Ste-Catherine (Quai)	AZ	32
St-Antoine (R.)	BZ	30
St-Étienne (Quai)	AZ	31
Tour (Quai de la)	BZ	34
Ville (R. de la)	BZ	35

La Ferme St-Siméon & rm, rest,

r. A. Marais, via ③ – ☎ 02 31 81 78 00 P VISA MC AE

– www.fermesaintsimeon.fr – accueil@fermesaintsimeon.fr – Fax 02 31 89 48 48

30 rm – †€ 150/850 ††€ 150/850, ☕ € 27 – 4 suites – ½ P € 304/576

Rest – Menu € 55/129 – Carte € 96/148

◆ A major site in the history of painting, this inn was frequented by Impressionist artists. It is now a magnificent hotel complex with a park overlooking the estuary. Relaxation and fitness facilities. Refined restaurant with a terrace looking out onto the sea, fine selection of calvados and classic cuisine.

Le Manoir du Butin
r. A. Marais, via ③ – 02 31 81 63 00 – www.hotel-lemanoir.fr – accueil@hotel-lemanoir.fr – Fax 02 31 89 59 23
10 rm – €120/350 €120/350, €17 – ½ P €140/240
Rest – *(dinner only except Sunday)* Menu €35/48 – Carte €49/83
◆ Painted timbers, latticed windows, an asymetric roof and a park: an 18C manor steeped in charm. Cosy guestrooms. A discreet elegance reigns in the well-lit dining room; modern menu.

Les Maisons de Léa without rest
pl. Ste-Catherine – 02 31 14 49 49 – www.lesmaisonsdelea.com – contact@lesmaisonsdelea.com – Fax 02 31 89 28 61 AY **a**
27 rm – €125/205 €125/205, €15 – 7 suites
◆ Three old 16C fishing houses and a former salt granary make up this charming hotel near the wooden bell tower of St Catherine. Thematic decor throughout the hotel. Exquisite rooms and cosy lounges.

L'Écrin without rest
19 r. E. Boudin – 02 31 14 43 45 – www.honfleur.com – hotel.ecrin@honfleur.com – Fax 02 31 89 24 41 AZ **k**
27 rm – €100/180 €100/180, €16 – 3 suites
◆ A museum-like hotel providing guestrooms and lounges with objets d'art and antique ornaments spread over five different period buildings. The main building from the 18th century is the most sumptuous. Breakfast served in a veranda overlooking the garden.

La Maison de Lucie without rest
44 r. Capucins – 02 31 14 40 40 – www.lamaisondelucie.com – info@lamaisondelucie.com – Fax 02 31 14 40 41 – Closed 30 November-19 December and 4-23 January AY **f**
11 rm – €150/220 €150/220, €18 – 2 suites
◆ Charm and sophistication await guests in the smart bedrooms of this 18C house. Breakfast served in the beamed and panelled lounges or on the paved interior courtyard.

L'Absinthe without rest
1 r. de la Ville – 02 31 89 23 23 – www.absinthe.fr – reservation@absinthe.fr – Fax 02 31 89 53 60 – Closed 13 November-13 December BZ **v**
10 rm – €115/250 €115/250, €12 – 2 suites
◆ This 16C presbytery is home to a quiet, out of the ordinary hotel. Soothing colour scheme and a blend of rustic and modern details. Some guestrooms are in another wharfside house.

des Loges without rest
18 r. Brûlée – 02 31 89 38 26 – www.hoteldesloges.com – info@hoteldesloges.com – Fax 02 31 89 42 79 – Closed 5-29 January AZ **t**
14 rm – €110/135 €110/135, €12
◆ Three 17C houses nicely renovated to provide an unusual boutique hotel. Contemporary setting with minimalist feel in the bedrooms.

Castel Albertine without rest
19 cours A. Manuel – 02 31 98 85 56 – www.residencemvm.fr – info@honfleurhotels.com – Fax 02 31 98 83 18 – Closed January AZ **e**
27 rm – €75/150 €75/150, €10
◆ This lovely 19C family mansion belonged to the diplomat historian, Albert Sorel, a native of Honfleur. Personalised rooms, a charming lounge and veranda, plus a small, shady park.

Mercure without rest
r. Vases – 02 31 89 50 50 – www.accor-hotels.com – h0986@accor.com – Fax 02 31 89 58 77 BZ **q**
56 rm – €85/130 €85/130, €12
◆ Near the centre, this chain hotel is fronted by a vaguely Normandy-style façade. Functional guestrooms, with those at the back generally quieter.

Le Cheval Blanc without rest
2 quai des Passagers – 02 31 81 65 00 – www.hotel-honfleur.com – lecheval.blanc@wanadoo.fr – Fax 02 31 89 52 80 – Closed January AY **n**
34 rm – €70/160 €80/200, €10 – 1 suite
◆ A former 15C post house that has been well renovated, with modern rooms (larger on the first floor) with views over the outer harbour. Buffet breakfast. Friendly reception.

Kyriad rest, VISA MC AE
62 cours A. Manuel, via ② – 02 31 89 41 77 – www.kyriad.fr – kyriad.honfleur@free.fr – Fax 02 31 89 48 09
50 rm – †€ 65/78 ††€ 65/78, □ € 8
Rest – Menu (€ 17), € 24 – Carte approx. € 26
◆ Renovated hotel situated away from the town centre. The functional rooms are small but well soundproofed; those at the rear overlook a small garden. Traditional cuisine, buffet menu and Sunday brunch.

La Petite Folie without rest VISA MC
44 r. Haute – 02 31 88 71 55 – www.lapetitefolie-honfleur.com – info@lapetitefolie-honfleur.com – Fax 02 31 88 71 55 – Closed January
5 rm □ – †€ 135 ††€ 135 AY **h**
◆ Antiques, traditional floor tiles, luxurious bedlinen - all the little touches you'd expect of an elegant guesthouse are to be found here. Breakfast served in the garden in summer.

Le Clos Bourdet without rest P VISA MC
50 r. Bourdet – 02 31 89 49 11 – www.leclosbourdet.com – leclosbourdet@orange.fr – Closed January AZ **k**
5 rm □ – †€ 130/180 ††€ 140/190
◆ Set on a hillside in a large enclosed garden, it's fair to say that this beautifully elegant 18C house enjoys a peaceful location! Personalised guestrooms.

La Cour Ste-Catherine without rest
74 r. du Puits – 02 31 89 42 40 – www.coursaintecatherine.com – coursaintecatherine@orange.fr AYZ **d**
5 rm □ – †€ 70/90 ††€ 75/95
◆ Hotel in the old upper town centre of Honfleur, built as a convent in the 17C and also occupying a former cider works. It provides quiet rooms that combine old and new. Breakfast served in the old press room.

L'Absinthe AC rm, VISA MC AE
10 quai Quarantaine – 02 31 89 39 00 – www.absinthe.fr – reservation@absinthe.fr – Fax 02 31 89 53 60 – Closed 15 November-15 December BZ **b**
Rest – Menu € 33/70 – Carte € 66/84
◆ Located in front of the fishing harbour, this restaurant – a former fishermen's bar – serves modern cuisine in two houses from the 15C and 17C or on the front terrace.

La Terrasse et l'Assiette (Gérard Bonnefoy) VISA MC AE
8 pl. Ste-Catherine – 02 31 89 31 33 – Fax 02 31 89 90 17 – Closed 5 January-5 February, Tuesday except July-August and Monday
Rest – Menu € 32/53 – Carte € 78/88 AY **e**
Spec. Gaspacho d'huîtres au piment d'Espelette. Poitrine de pigeon rôti au jus d'abats. Petit gâteau chaud au chocolat et coulant pistache.
◆ Half-timbering and brickwork give this restaurant a distinctive atmosphere. With pleasant terrace opposite the church built out of wood. Fine traditional cuisine.

Sa. Qua. Na (Alexandre Bourdas) VISA MC
22 pl. Hamelin – 02 31 89 40 80 – www.alexandre-bourdas.com – saquana@alexandre-bourdas.com – Closed from mid January to end February, Wednesday, Thursday and weekday lunch AY **u**
Rest – *(number of covers limited, pre-book)* Menu € 50/80
Spec. Homard poché au citron vert. Pastilla de pigeonneau. Feuille de nougatine cacao et truffe.
◆ Flavour, quality, nature and fish (sakana in Japanese) are all key ingredients here. Inventive cuisine in a modern, minimalist setting close to the old port.

Entre Terre et Mer with rm VISA MC AE
12 pl. Hamelin – 02 31 89 70 60 – www.entreterreetmer-honfleur.com – info@entreterreetmer-honfleur.com – Fax 02 31 89 40 55 – Closed 15 January-5 February AY **d**
14 rm □ – †€ 98 ††€ 120 **Rest** – Menu (€ 23), € 28/54 – Carte € 52/78
◆ On a square near the old port. Two contemporary dining rooms, one adorned with photos of Normandy and the other with regional landscapes. 'Surf n' turf' updated menu. Snug comfortable guestrooms in the wing opposite.

Le Bréard
7 r. du Puits – ✆ 02 31 89 53 40 – www.restaurant-lebreard.com – lebreard@wanadoo.fr – Fax 02 31 88 60 37 – Closed 1st-26 December, 4-12 February, Tuesday lunch, Thursday lunch and Wednesday AY **t**
Rest – Menu (€ 20), € 28/38 – Carte € 60/67
◆ Located in a cobbled lane near St Catherine's church, the plain façade hides two small, bright dining rooms separated by a pretty inner terrace, heated in winter. Modern cuisine.

La Fleur de Sel
17 r. Haute – ✆ 02 31 89 01 92 – lafleurdesel-honfleur.com – info@lafleurdesel-honfleur.com – Fax 02 31 89 01 92 – Closed January, Tuesday and Wednesday AY **v**
Rest – Menu € 28/48
◆ This pleasant restaurant serves modern cuisine in two small dining areas with a modern rustic decor, including culinary photos and a collection of Michelin guides.

Au Vieux Honfleur
13 quai St-Étienne – ✆ 02 31 89 15 31 – www.auvieuxhonfleur.com – contact@auvieuxhonfleur.com – Fax 02 31 89 92 04 AZ **r**
Rest – Menu € 33/55 – Carte € 41/87
◆ This 12C half-timbered house with a terrace and the Vieux Bassin as a backdrop, specialises in seafood and Normandy specialities.

Au P'tit Mareyeur
4 r. Haute – ✆ 02 31 98 84 23 – www.auptitmareyeur.com – auptitmareyeur@free.fr – Fax 02 31 89 99 32 – Closed 4 January-2 February, Monday and Tuesday AY **s**
Rest – *(number of covers limited, pre-book)* Carte € 42/51
◆ Half-timbered walls, paintings with a nautical theme and nicely set tables lend this restaurant an intimate character. Seafood dominates the menu: Honfleur bouillabaisse is a speciality.

L'Ecailleur
1 r. de la République – ✆ 02 31 89 93 34 – www.lecailleur.fr – lecailleur@wanadoo.fr – Fax 02 31 89 53 73 – Closed in March, 17 June-4 July, 12-21 November, 8-25 December, Wednesday and Thursday in low season AZ **a**
Rest – Menu € 26/37 – Carte € 34/53
◆ Modern cuisine served in a warm decor inspired by the old steam liners, with wooden panelling, ropes and porthole windows. A large bay window offers a fine view of the port.

La Tortue
36 r. de l'Homme de Bois – ✆ 02 31 81 24 60 – www.restaurantlatortue.fr – lesterressafran@orange.fr – Fax 02 31 81 24 60 AY **g**
Rest – Menu (€ 14), € 19/36 – Carte € 25/42
◆ In a little backstreet in old Honfleur, this regional-style restaurant changes its menu every day according to what arrives in the daily catch. Small delicatessen.

in la Rivière-St-Sauveur **2 km by ① – pop. 1 685 – alt. 1 m – ✉ 14600**

Antarès without rest
– ✆ 02 31 89 10 10 – www.antares-honfleur.com – info@antares-honfleur.com – Fax 02 31 89 58 57
78 rm – €65/122 €75/165, ☕ € 13
◆ This 1990s hotel complex has practical facilities and provides small rooms. Half the rooms overlook the Normandy bridge. Well-designed family duplexes. Pool.

Les Bleuets without rest
11 r. Desseaux – ✆ 02 31 81 63 90 – www.motel-les-bleuets.com – contact@motel-les-bleuets.com – Fax 02 31 89 92 12 – Closed 5-22 January
18 rm – €59/86 €59/86, ☕ € 6,50
◆ A motel-style hotel with a holiday village feel. Blue and white walls and a relaxation area. Well-kept rooms with small terrace or balcony.

via ③ 3 km Trouville road – ✉ 14600 Vasouy

La Chaumière

rte du Littoral, Vasouy – ✆ 02 31 81 63 20 – www.hotel-chaumiere.fr – accueil@hotel-chaumiere.fr – Fax 02 31 89 59 23 – Closed 24 November-11 December and 5-22 January
9 rm – †€ 150/450 ††€ 150/450, ☕ € 15 – ½ P € 150/300
Rest – *(closed Wednesday lunch, Thursday lunch and Tuesday) (number of covers limited, pre-book)* Menu € 40/60 – Carte € 40/55
◆ This pretty Norman farm (17C) stands opposite the Seine estuary in a park that reaches down to the sea. Cosy guestrooms with fine antique furniture. Beams worn smooth and an attractive fireplace add to the cosy atmosphere of the restaurant.

via ③ 8 km Trouville road and secondary road – ✉ 14600 Honfleur

Le Romantica

chemin Petit Paris – ✆ 02 31 81 14 00 – www.romantica-honfleur.com – hotelromantica@free.fr – Fax 02 31 81 54 78
34 rm – †€ 60/68 ††€ 70/138, ☕ € 9 – ½ P € 69/97
Rest – *(closed Thursday lunch and Wednesday except high season)*
Menu (€ 17), € 28/39 – Carte € 29/52
◆ Set above the village, this regional-style building provides warm, quiet and comfortable rooms in a rustic style. Pleasant indoor pool. Glimpse the countryside and English Channel from the restaurant's bay windows.

in Cricqueboeuf 9 km by ③ and **Trouville road – pop. 208 – alt. 25 m – ✉ 14113**

Manoir de la Poterie

chemin P. Ruel – ✆ 02 31 88 10 40 – www.honfleur-hotel.com – info@honfleur-hotel.com – Fax 02 31 88 10 90
23 rm – †€ 147/285 ††€ 147/285, ☕ € 18 – 1 suite
Rest – *(closed lunch week)* Menu € 33 (weekdays)/75 – Carte € 44/78
◆ This Norman-style modern manor overlooks the sea. Louis XVI, Directoire, marine and contemporary-style rooms with a view of the sea or the countryside. Spa centre. Cosy atmosphere and contemporary cuisine in a more intimate dining room.

in Villerville 10 km by ③, **Trouville road – pop. 676 – alt. 10 m – ✉ 14113**
Office de tourisme, rue Général Leclerc ✆ 02 31 87 21 49, Fax 02 31 98 30 65

Le Bellevue

rte d'Honfleur – ✆ 02 31 87 20 22 – www.bellevue-hotel.fr – resa@bellevue-hotel.fr – Fax 02 31 87 20 56 – Closed 23 November-17 December and 5 January-12 February
26 rm – †€ 75/115 ††€ 95/115, ☕ € 14 – 2 suites – ½ P € 85/120
Rest – *(closed Tuesday lunch, Wednesday lunch and Thursday lunch)*
Menu € 25/46 – Carte € 37/53
◆ This house overlooking the sea was the summer residence of a Paris Opera director in the late 19C. Comfortable rooms, either rustic or contemporary. The charming veranda-dining area offers a pretty view of the garden and coastline.

HORBOURG – 68 Haut-Rhin – 315 I8 – see Colmar

HOSSEGOR – 40 Landes – 335 C13 – alt. 4 m – Casino – ✉ 40150 — 3 A3

Atlantic Coast

Paris 752 – Bayonne 25 – Biarritz 32 – Bordeaux 170 – Dax 40 – Mont-de-Marsan 93
Office de tourisme, place des Halles ✆ 05 58 41 79 00, Fax 05 58 41 79 09
d'Hossegor 333 avenue du Golf, SE : 0.5 km, ✆ 05 58 43 56 99
de Seignosse Seignosse Avenue du Belvédère, N : 5 km on D 152, ✆ 05 58 41 68 30
de Pinsolle Soustons Port d'Albret Sud, N : 10 km on D 4, ✆ 05 58 48 03 92
The lake ★ - Basque-Landes style villas★.

Les Hortensias du Lac without rest
1578 av. du Tour du Lac – 05 58 43 99 00 – www.hortensias-du-lac.com – reception@hortensias-du-lac.com – Fax 05 58 43 42 81 – Open from mid-March to mid-November
20 rm – €130/210 €130/210, €20 – 4 suites
◆ Three lovely 1930s houses surrounded by a pine forest on the lakeside make up this hotel providing tastefully decorated guestrooms with balcony or terrace. Lounge with great views.

Pavillon Bleu
av. Touring Club de France – 05 58 41 99 50 – www.pavillonbleu.fr – pavillon.bleu@wanadoo.fr – Fax 05 58 41 99 59
21 rm – €70/166 €70/166, €10 – ½ P €75/123
Rest – *(closed 26 December-20 January and Monday 15 September-15 April)* Menu (€21 bi), €31/68 – Carte €50/80
◆ A brand new establishment where, if you book a room with a balcony overlooking the lake, you can watch the sailing dinghies and wind-surfers. The restaurant has a contemporary interior, an attractive waterside terrace and modern cuisine.

Mercédès without rest
63 av. du Tour du Lac – 05 58 41 98 00 – www.hotel.mercedes@wanadoo.fr – hotel.mercedes@wanadoo.fr – Fax 05 58 41 98 10 – Open 1 April-1 November
40 rm – €70/90 €85/145, €10
◆ A seaside building near a marine lake is home to rooms both simple in style and pleasant, all with balcony. Breakfast served around the pool in summer.

HOUAT (ÎLE) – **56 Morbihan** – **308** N10 – **see Île d'Houat**

LA HOUBE – **57 Moselle** – **307** O7 – **57850 Dabo** 27 **D2**

Paris 453 – Lunéville 86 – Phalsbourg 18 – Sarrebourg 27 – Saverne 17 – Strasbourg 45

Des Vosges rm,

41 r. de la Forêt Brulée 57850 La Hoube Dabo – 03 87 08 80 44 – www.hotel-restaurant-vosges.com – info@hotel-restaurant-vosges.com – Fax 03 87 08 85 96 – Closed 28 September-11 October, 8 February-8 March, Tuesday evening and Wednesday
9 rm – €33 €48, €8 – ½ P €44
Rest – Menu €11 (weekday lunch), €20/30 – Carte €22/35
◆ Small, family-run inn located on the edge of the village. Simple, well-kept rooms and relaxing garden. Dining area overlooking the Vosges forest, serving tasty regional cuisine.

LES HOUCHES – **74 Haute-Savoie** – **328** N5 – **pop. 3 037** – **alt. 1 004 m** – **Winter sports : 1 010/1 900 m** **2** **16** – **74310** **French Alps** 46 **F1**

Paris 602 – Annecy 89 – Bonneville 47 – Chamonix-Mont-Blanc 9 – Megève 26

Office de tourisme, place de la Mairie 04 50 55 50 62, Fax 04 50 55 53 16

Le Prarion★★.

Du Bois
La Griaz – 04 50 54 50 35 – www.hotel-du-bois.com – reception@hotel-du-bois.com – Fax 04 50 55 50 87 – Closed 3 November-3 December
43 rm – €50/162 €50/182, €9
Rest – *(closed 14 April-11 May and 6 October-8 December) (dinner only)* Menu €24 – Carte €20/40
◆ Distinctive building with Mont Blanc on the horizon. Practical rooms or modern apartments in the new wing. Pretty indoor swimming pool, sauna and exterior pool. Attractive Savoy-style dining room decorated with farming implements. Updated cuisine.

Auberge Beau Site
(near the church) – ✆ 04 50 55 51 16 – www.hotel-beausite.com – reservation@hotel-beausite.com – Fax 04 50 54 53 11 – Open 1 June-29 September and 21 December-20 April
18 rm – †€ 69/92 ††€ 82/115, ☕ € 10
Rest ***Le Pèle*** – *(closed 1-15 June, 15-29 September and lunch in winter)* Menu € 25/35
◆ Pretty family house at the foot of the bell tower in the little resort made famous by Lord Kandahar. Practical rooms of a good size with bright red and green fabrics. Warm restaurant; wooden blocks standing near the fireplace with its copper utensils.

Auberge Le Montagny without rest
490 rte du Pont – ✆ 04 50 54 57 37 – www.chamonix-hotel.com – hotel.montagny@wanadoo.fr – Fax 04 50 54 52 97 – Open 21 June-19 September and 21 December-13 April
8 rm – †€ 80 ††€ 80, ☕ € 9
◆ Wood predominates throughout in this charming little chalet which incorporates the door and some beams of an 1876 farmhouse; stylish mountain style guestrooms.

Chris-Tal
242 av. des Alpages – ✆ 04 50 54 50 55 – www.chris-tal.com – info@chris-tal.com – Fax 04 50 54 45 77 – Open 16 June-14 September and 16 December-14 April
23 rm – †€ 75/125 ††€ 85/125, ☕ € 10 – ½ P € 75/92
Rest – *(dinner only)* Menu € 20/30 – Carte € 30/42
◆ In the centre of the little resort are cosy guestrooms that focus on space and practicality. Most overlook the famous Kandahar 'Green' ski slope. A mixture of traditional and local cuisine is on offer in the warm and welcoming dining room.

in Prarion by télécabine – ✉ **74310 Les Houches**
✳★★ 30 mn.

Le Prarion
alt.1 860 – ✆ 04 50 54 40 07 – www.prarion.com – yves@prarion.com – Fax 04 50 54 40 03 – Open 20 June-13 September and 19 December to end March
12 rm (½ board only) – ½ P € 75/110
Rest – self – Menu € 29 (dinner) – Carte € 16/32
◆ This hotel enjoys superb vistas of the snow-capped peaks of the Mont-Blanc and Aravis ranges and the Chamonix and Sallanches valleys. Small, simply furnished bedrooms. Traditional meals at lunch (buffet style in winter), set menu in the evening.

HOUDAN – 78 Yvelines – 311 F3 – pop. 3 140 – alt. 104 m – ✉ 78550 18 A2

Northern France and the Paris Region

Paris 60 – Chartres 55 – Dreux 20 – Évreux 52 – Mantes-la-Jolie 28 – Versailles 42

Office de tourisme, 4, place de la Tour ✆ 01 30 59 53 86, Fax 01 30 59 66 84

36 de la Vaucouleurs Civry-la-Forêt Rue de l'Eglise, N : 11 km on D 983, ✆ 01 34 87 62 29

27 des Yvelines La Queue-les-Yvelines Château de la Couharde, E : 12 km on N 12, ✆ 01 34 86 48 89

La Poularde
24 av. République, (rte Maulette D 912) – ✆ 01 30 59 60 50 – www.alapoularde.com – contact@alapoularde.com – Fax 01 30 59 79 71 – Closed 3-11 August, Sunday dinner, Monday and Tuesday
Rest – Menu (€ 22), € 35/65 – Carte € 56/70
◆ In the garden of this lovely house, the famous Houdan chickens cluck - soon to be placed in your plate! Elegant comfortable room, traditional menu.

Donjon
14 r. Epernon, (near the church) – ✆ 01 30 59 79 14 – www.restaurant-ledonjon.fr – deserville.eric@wanadoo.fr – Closed 9-30 August, 1 week in March, Sunday dinner, Thursday dinner and Monday
Rest – Menu (€ 24 bi), € 30/45 – Carte € 48/55
◆ All that remains of the medieval castle is its keep, close to this restaurant named after it. Classic cuisine served in a pretty and colourful contemporary setting.

HOUDEMONT – 54 Meurthe-et-Moselle – **307** H7 – see Nancy

HOULGATE – 14 Calvados – **303** L4 – pop. 1 908 – alt. 11 m – Casino 32 **B2**
– ✉ 14510 Normandy

Paris 214 – Caen 29 – Deauville 14 – Lisieux 33 – Pont-l'Évêque 25

Office de tourisme, 10, boulevard des Belges ✆ 02 31 24 34 79, Fax 02 31 24 42 27

d'Houlgate Gonneville-sur-MerE : 3 km on D 513, ✆ 02 31 24 80 49

Vaches Noires cliff ★ Northeast.

L'Eden

7 r. Henri Fouchard – ✆ 02 31 24 84 37 – www.restaurant-leden.com – nicolas.tougard@wanadoo.fr – Fax 02 31 28 32 34 – Closed 5-13 October, 4 January-10 February, Monday and Tuesday except 10 July to 30 August

Rest – Menu (€ 20), € 26/43 – Carte € 40/55

◆ Appetising traditional dishes with a focus on seafood, served in a contemporary decor or in the winter garden-style veranda with a view of the kitchen.

HUEZ – 38 Isère – **333** J7 – see Alpe d'Huez

HUNINGUE – 68 Haut-Rhin – **315** J11 – see St-Louis

HURIGNY – 71 Saône-et-Loire – **320** I12 – see Mâcon

HUSSEREN-LES-CHÂTEAUX – 68 Haut-Rhin – **315** H8 – pop. 488 2 **C2**
– alt. 380 m – ✉ 68420 Alsace-Lorraine

Paris 455 – Belfort 69 – Colmar 10 – Gérardmer 55 – Guebwiller 22 – Mulhouse 40

Husseren-les-Châteaux rm,

r. Schlossberg – ✆ 03 89 49 22 93 – www.hotel-husseren-les-chateaux.com – mail@hotel-husseren-les-chateaux.com – Fax 03 89 49 24 84

36 rm – €88/103 €115/138, € 13 – 2 suites

Rest – Menu (€ 12), € 21/49 – Carte € 23/48

◆ Standing in the foothills of the Vosges mountains, this modern building has large functional bedrooms, some of which are split-level. Indoor swimming pool and a tennis court. Enjoy fine views over the Rhine valley from this bright restaurant serving traditional cuisine.

HYÈRES – 83 Var – **340** L7 – pop. 53 700 – alt. 40 m – Casino : 41 **C3**
des Palmiers Z – ✉ 83400 French Riviera

Paris 851 – Aix-en-Provence 102 – Cannes 123 – Draguignan 78 – Toulon 19

Toulon-Hyères: ✆ 0 825 01 83 87, Southeast: 4 km V.

Syndicat d'initiative, 3, avenue Ambroise Thomas ✆ 04 94 01 84 50, Fax 04 94 01 84 51

★ from place St-Paul Y **49** - ★ from St-Bernard park Y - ★ from the N.-D. de Consolation chapel esplanande V **B** - ★ from the Château des aires ruins - Presqu'île de Giens (peninsula) ★★.

Plan on following page

Mercure rm, rm,

19 av. A. Thomas – ✆ 04 94 65 03 04 – www.mercure.com – h1055@accor.com – Fax 04 94 35 58 20 V **x**

84 rm – €109/165 €122/199, € 15 **Rest** – Menu (€ 25) – Carte € 28/40

◆ Modern hotel which forms part of a business centre situated alongside the Olbia highway. Comfortable, contemporary rooms renovated in the Mercure style. Restaurant decorated with a seaside theme, opening onto the terrace and swimming pool; regionally-inspired recipes.

HYÈRES-GIENS

Almanarre (Rte de l') . . . . X 2
Barbacane (R.) . . . . Y 3
Barruc (R.) . . . . Y 4
Belgique (Av. de) . . . . Y 5
Bourgneuf (R.) . . . . Y 6
Chateaubriand (Bd) . . . . Y 7
Clemenceau (Pl.) . . . . Y 9
Clotis (Av. J.) . . . . V 10
Costebelle (Montée) . . . . V 12
Degioanni (R. R.) . . . . X 13
Denis (Av. A.) . . . . Y
Dr-Perron (Av.) . . . . Z 14
Foch (Av. Mar.) . . . . Z 15
Gambetta (Av.) . . . . Z
Gaulle (Av. de) . . . . Y 16
Geoffroy-St-Hilaire (Av.) . . . . V 17
Godillot (Av. A.) . . . . V 18
Herriot (Bd E.) . . . . X 20
Iles d'Or (Av. des) . . . . Z
Lattre-de-Tassigny (Av. de) . . . V 22
Lefebvre (Pl. Th.) . . . . Z 23
Macri (Ch. Soldat) . . . . V 25
Madrague (Rte de la) . . . . X 26
Mangin (Av. Gén.) . . . . Y 28
Massillon (Pl. et R.) . . . . Y 29
Millet (Av. E.) . . . . Z 32
Moulin-Premier (Chemin du) . V 33
Noailles (Montée de) . . . . Y 34
Nocart (Bd) . . . . Y 35
Palyvestre (Chemin du) . . . . . V 36
Paradis (R. de) . . . . Y 37
Plaine-de-Bouisson (Chemin) . X 38
Provence (R. de) . . . . V 40
Rabaton (R.) . . . . Y 41
République (Pl. et R.) . . . . . . Y 42
Riondet (Av.) . . . . YZ 43
Riquier (Av. O.) . . . . V 44
Roubaud (Ch.) . . . . V 45
Ste-Catherine (R.) . . . . Y 50
Ste-Claire (R.) . . . . Y 51
St-Bernard (R.) . . . . Y 46
St-Esprit (R.) . . . . Y 47
St-Paul (Pl. et R.) . . . . Y 49
Strasbourg (Cours) . . . . Y 52
Versin (Pl. L.) . . . . Z 53
Victoria (Av.) . . . . Z 54
11-Novembre (Pl.) . . . . V 56
15e-Corps-d'Armée (Av. du) . . V 57

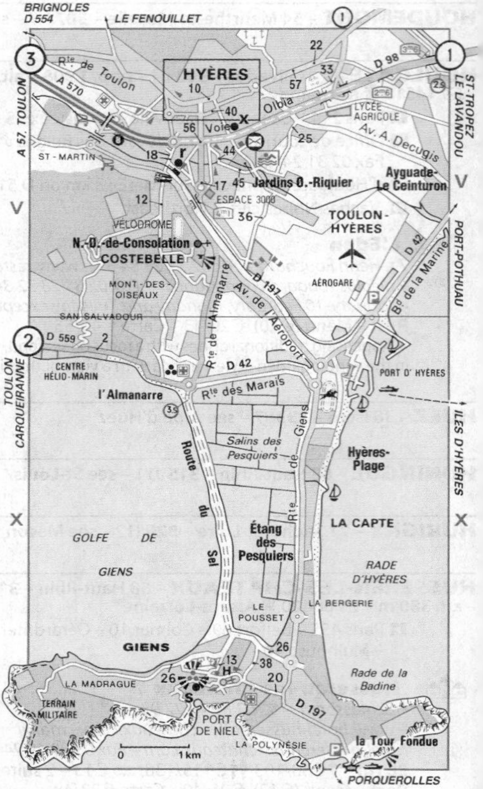

BRIGNOLES
D 554
LE FENOUILLET
HYÈRES
Rte. de Toulon
A 570
A 57. TOULON
D 98
Olbia
LYCÉE AGRICOLE
Av. A. Decugis
ST-TROPEZ LE LAVANDOU
ST - MARTIN
Voie
Jardins O.-Riquier
Ayguade-Le Ceinturon
ESPACE 3000
VÉLODROME
TOULON-HYÈRES
N.-D.-de-Consolation
COSTEBELLE
MONT - DES - OISEAUX
SAN SALVADOUR
D 197
Av. de l'Aéroport
Rte de l'Almanarre
AÉROGARE
D 42
Bd de la Marine
PORT-POTHUAU
D 559
CENTRE HÉLIO-MARIN
TOULON CARQUEIRANNE
l'Almanarre
Rte des Marais
PORT D' HYÈRES
ILES D'HYÈRES
Salins des Pesquiers
Route du Sel
Rte. de Giens
Hyères-Plage
LA CAPTE
GOLFE DE GIENS
Étang des Pesquiers
RADE D'HYÈRES
LE POUSSET
LA BERGERIE
GIENS
LA MADRAGUE
Rade de la Badine
TERRAIN MILITAIRE
PORT DE NIEL
D 197
LA POLYNÉSIE
la Tour Fondue
0 1 km
PORQUEROLLES

HYÈRES
0 200 m
Château des Aires
Parc St-Bernard
Chin de la Porte St-Jean
Av. Paul Long
Bd Matignon
Bd d' Orient
Parc du Château Ste-Claire
Porte des Princes
VIEILLE VILLE
JARDIN DENIS
St-Louis
R. Victor
Av. Edith Wharton
Basch
Collégiale St-Paul
Av. A. Denis
Av. Nocart
Av. des Iles d'Or
Musée municipal
Bd Pasteur
Av. J.-Jaurès
Bd Soldat
CASINO DES PALMIERS
FORUM CASINO
R. Galliéni
Av. A. Godillot
ÉGLISE ANGLICANE
Av. de D. Beauregard
Av. J. Aicard
Av. Gambetta
R. Paul Gensollen
Thomas
Ferrari
Av. de la Paix
Av. F. Arène

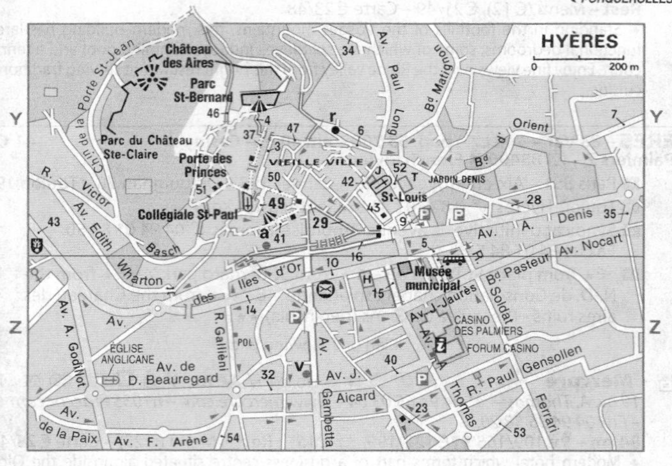

L'Europe without rest
45 av. E. Cavell – ✆ 04 94 00 67 77 – www.hotel-europe-hyeres.com – contact@hotel-europe-hyeres.com – Fax 04 94 00 68 48 V r
25 rm – †€ 55/92 ††€ 60/92, ☕ € 8
◆ Progressively renovated, 19C, family-run hotel opposite the station. Practical, well refurbished rooms boasting brand new bathrooms.

Le Soleil without rest
r. du Rempart – ✆ 04 94 65 16 26 – www.hoteldusoleil.fr – soleil@hotel-du-soleil.fr – Fax 04 94 35 46 00 Y r
20 rm ☕ – †€ 64/94 ††€ 71/104
◆ Old house with lots of character in the upper part of the old town, near the Noailles villa-museum. Small but clean rooms; Provence-style breakfast room.

Les Jardins de Bacchus
32 av. Gambetta – ✆ 04 94 65 77 63 – santionijeanclaude@wanadoo.fr – Fax 04 94 65 71 19 – Closed 2-8 January, Saturday lunch, Sunday dinner and Monday Z v
Rest – Menu € 27/55 – Carte € 58/80
◆ A pleasant stop in the town centre, serving regional wines and local style meals in a renovated and modern-style dining area or on the summer terrace.

Joy
24 r. de Limans – ✆ 04 94 20 84 98 – restaurant.joy@orange.fr – Fax 04 94 20 84 98 – Closed two weeks in November and January, Sunday dinner, Monday in low season, Wednesday lunch and Tuesday Y a
Rest – *(pre-book)* Menu (€ 23), € 29 (dinner), € 36/60 – Carte € 32/53 dinner only
◆ Contemporary restaurant run by a Dutch couple. Mini-terrace on a pedestrianised street. Daily specials, lunch menu read out loud, and more substantial evening menu.

in La Bayorre 2,5 km West by Toulon road – ✉ ***83400 Hyères***

La Colombe
663 Rte de Toulon – ✆ 04 94 35 35 16 – www.restaurantlacolombe.com – restauranlacolombe@orange.fr – Fax 04 94 35 37 68 – Closed Sunday dinner from September to June, Tuesday lunch in July-August, Saturday lunch and Monday
Rest – Menu € 29/37 – Carte € 55/67
◆ At the foot of the Maurettes, this restaurant is decorated in colours of the South in perfect harmony with the pleasant and copious local cuisine. Fine summer terrace at the back.

HYÈVRE-PAROISSE – 25 Doubs – 321 I2 – pop. 192 – alt. 288 m – ✉ 25110 17 C2

▶ Paris 445 – Belfort 61 – Besançon 37 – Lure 51 – Montbéliard 44 – Pontarlier 72 – Vesoul 50

Le Relais de la Vallée rest,
r. Principale, D 683 – ✆ 03 81 84 46 46 – http://perso.wanadoo.fr/relaisdelavallee/ – pierrecossu@wanadoo.fr – Fax 03 81 84 37 52
21 rm – †€ 55/59 ††€ 55/59, ☕ € 8,50
Rest – Menu € 15 (weekdays)/38 – Carte € 30/60
◆ This 1970s building has functional guestrooms with balconies overlooking the main road and the Vallée du Doubs. White wood panelling, red wall hangings and jazzy statues adorn the restaurant. Terrace beneath an awning. Franche-Comté specialities.

IFFENDIC – 35 Ille-et-Vilaine – 309 J6 – pop. 3 778 – alt. 48 m – ✉ 35750 10 C2

▶ Paris 393 – Rennes 40 – Cesson-Sévigné 50 – Bruz 36 – Dinan 46

Château du Pin without rest
6 km north-east on D 31 and D 125 – ✆ 02 99 09 34 05 – www.chateaudupin-bretagne.com – luc.ruan@wanadoo.fr – Fax 02 99 09 03 76
5 rm – †€ 85/140 ††€ 95/160, ☕ € 12
◆ This small country house dating from 1793 is a refuge for lovers of literature and art. Large library-lounge, rooms named after writers (Hugo, Proust, etc.) and views over the park.

IGÉ – 71 Saône-et-Loire – **320** I11 – **pop. 866** – **alt. 265 m** – ✉ **71960** 8 **C3**

Paris 396 – Cluny 13 – Mâcon 14 – Tournus 34

Château d'Igé

r. du Château – ✆ 03 85 33 33 99 – www.chateaudige.com – chateau.ige@wanadoo.fr – Fax 03 85 33 41 41 – Open 27 February-29 November and closed Sunday evening, Monday and Tuesday except from 18 March to 11 November

12 rm – €95/190 €95/190, □ €16 – 4 suites – ½ P €108/156

Rest – *(dinner only except Saturday, Sunday and public holidays)* Menu €32/78 – Carte €55/72

◆ Situated in the Mâcon region, this castle built in 1235 offers a choice of elegant guestrooms with individual touches (tapestries, four-poster beds, vaulted ceilings etc). Apartments available in the towers. Regionally sourced gourmet fare served in a medieval-inspired decor or on the terrace facing the superb garden.

IGUERANDE – 71 Saône-et-Loire – **320** E12 – **pop. 988** – **alt. 280 m** – ✉ **71340** 7 **B3**

Paris 399 – Dijon 184 – Mâcon 105 – Roanne 21 – Tarare 60

La Colline du Colombier with rm

3.5 km southwest on the D 9 and minor road – ✆ 03 85 84 07 24 – www.troisgros.com – la-colline-du-colombier@troisgros.com – Fax 03 85 84 17 43 – Closed 21 December-4 March, Thursday lunch from October to December and Wednesday

5 rm – €250/350 €250/350 **Rest** – Menu (€23), €35/40 – Carte €50/60

◆ Overlooking the Loire, this remote farmhouse has been converted into a country-chic restaurant (bare beams and stonework). Tasty, regional inspired menu. A peaceful stay guaranteed in the 'cadoles' – ecological houses on stilts.

ILAY – 39 Jura – **321** F7 – ✉ **39150 Chaux du Dombief** **Burgundy-Jura** 16 **B3**

Paris 439 – Champagnole 19 – Lons-le-Saunier 36 – Morez 22 – St-Claude 39

Cascades du Hérisson★★★.

Auberge du Hérisson

5 rte des Lacs, (carrefour D 75-D 39) – ✆ 03 84 25 58 18 – www.herisson.com – auberge@herisson.com – Fax 03 84 25 51 11 – Open February-October

16 rm – €35 €40/60, □ €8 – ½ P €45/50

Rest – Menu €18/43 – Carte €25/50

◆ This family inn is perched above the picturesque waterfalls of the Hérisson, near Ilay Lake. All the hotel's guestrooms have been renovated. Franche-Comté cuisine, frogs' legs in season and local wines.

ÎLE-AUX-MOINES – 56 Morbihan – **308** N9 – **pop. 527** – **alt. 16 m** – ✉ **56780** **Brittany** 9 **A3**

Paris 474 – Auray 15 – Quiberon 46 – Vannes 15

Les Embruns

r. Commerce – ✆ 02 97 26 30 86 – www.restaurantlesembruns.com – restaurant.lesembruns@orange.fr – Fax 02 97 26 31 94 – Closed 1st-15 October, January, February and Wednesday except July-August

Rest – Menu €19/26 – Carte €24/34

◆ This friendly, unpretentious bar-restaurant, serves simple cuisine influenced by market availability. Splendid shellfish platter.

L'ÎLE BOUCHARD – 37 Indre-et-Loire – **317** L6 – **pop. 1 740** – **alt. 41 m** – ✉ **37220** **Châteaux of the Loire** 11 **A3**

Paris 284 – Châteauroux 118 – Chinon 16 – Châtellerault 49 – Saumur 42 – Tours 45

Office de tourisme, 16, place Bouchard ✆ 02 47 58 67 75, Fax 02 47 58 67 75

Capitals/I★ and throne chair ★ in St-Léonard priory.

Champigny-sur-Veude: stained-glass windows★★ of the Ste-Chapelle★ Southwest: 10.5 km.

XXX **Auberge de l'Île**

3 pl. Bouchard – ✆ 02 47 58 51 07 – www.aubergedelile.fr – aubergedelile@wanadoo.fr – Fax 02 47 58 51 07 – Closed 1st-15 December, 19 February-12 March, Tuesday and Wednesday except holidays
Rest – Menu € 24/39 – Carte € 33/44
◆ On an island that once belonged to Richelieu, this inn is much appreciated by lovers of fine produce. Up-to-date cuisine served in a modern decor (art and table settings).

in Sazilly **7 km west by D 760 – 317** L6 – ✉ **37220**

X **Auberge du Val de Vienne**

30 rte de Chinon – ✆ 02 47 95 26 49 – www.aubergeduvaldevienne.com – valdevienne@wanadoo.fr – Fax 02 47 95 25 97 – Closed 2-23 January, Sunday dinner and Monday
Rest – Menu € 17 (weekday lunch), € 35/46
◆ Make a gastronomic stop in this former post house (1870) in the heart of the Chinon vineyards. Warm décor blends perfectly with quality contemporary cuisine.

The award is the crème de la crème.
This is awarded to restaurants which are really worth travelling miles for!

ÎLE-D'AIX ★ – **17 Charente-Maritime – 324** C3 – **pop. 186 – alt. 10 m** – ✉ **17123** Atlantic Coast — 38 **A2**

Access by sea transport
- from **Pointe de la Fumée** (2.5 km northwest of Fouras) - 25 min crossing - Information and prices from Société Fouras-Aix ✆ 0 820 160 017 (0.12 €/min), Fax 05 46 37 56 82.
- from **La Rochelle** - Seasonal service (April-Oct.) - 1h15 mn crossing - Information: Croisières Inter Îles, ✆ 0 825 135 500 (0,15 €/mn) (La Rochelle)
- from **Boyardville** (Île d'Oléron) - Seasonal service - 30 mn crossing- Information Inter Îles ✆ 0 825 135 500 (0,15 €/mn),(Boyardville)
- from **Sablanceaux** (Île de Ré) - Seasonal service - Inter Îles agencies in Sablonceaux - Information and prices ✆ 0 825 135 500
- from **Fouras** 20 mn crossing - Service Maritime-Sté Fouras-Aix) - 0 820 16 00 17 (0,12 €/min) ; Permanent service - 30 mn crossing- Information and prices ✆ 0 820 160 017 (0,12 €/mn), Fax 05 46 41 16 96.

ÎLE-D'ARZ – **56 Morbihan – 308** O9 – **pop. 231 – alt. 25 m** – ✉ **56840** Brittany — 9 **A3**

Access by sea transport.
- from **Barrarach and Conleau** - 20 min crossing - Information: Compagnie du Golfe ✆ 02 97 01 22 80, Fax 02 97 47 01 60, www.lactm.com
- from **Vannes** Apr-late Sep - 30 min crossing - Information: Navix S.A. Gare Maritime (Vannes) ✆ 0825 132 100.

ÎLE-DE-BATZ – **29 Finistère – 308** G2 – **pop. 594 – alt. 30 m** – ✉ **29253** Brittany — 9 **B1**

Access by sea transport.
- from **Roscoff** - Crossing 15 mn - Information and prices: CFTM BP 10 - 29253 Île de Batz ✆ 02 98 61 78 87 - Armein ✆ 02 98 61 77 75 - Armor Excursion ✆ 02 98 61 79 66.
- Syndicat d'initiative, lieu-dit le Débarcadère ✆ 02 98 61 75 70
  Syndicat d'initiative, Mairie ✆ 02 98 61 75 70, Fax 02 98 61 75 85

Ti Va Zadou without rest

au bourg – ✆ 02 98 61 76 91 – Open 7 February-10 November
4 rm – 🚹€ 50 🚹🚹€ 60/65
◆ Smart, nautical rooms, including a family room, await you in this typical regional-style house whose blue shutters are immediately noticeable on reaching the island. Bike hire.

ÎLE-DE-BRÉHAT ★ – 22 Côtes-d'Armor – 309 D1 – pop. 421 – alt. 7 m – ✉ 22870 Brittany 10 C1

Access by sea transport, for **Port-Clos.**

- from **Pointe de l'Arcouest** - Crossing 10 mn - Information and prices: Vedettes de Bréhat ✆ 02 96 55 79 50, Fax 02 96 55 79 55
- from **St-Quay-Portrieux** - Seasonal service - Crossing 1 h 15 mn - Information and prices: Vedettes de Bréhat (see above)
- from **Binic** - Seasonal service - Crossing 1 h 30 mn - Information and prices: Vedettes de Bréhat (see above).
- from **Erquy** - Seasonal service - Crossing 1 h 15 mn - Information and prices: Vedettes de Bréhat (see above).
- Syndicat d'initiative, le Bourg ✆ 02 96 20 04 15, Fax 02 96 20 06 94
- Tour of the island★★ - Phare du Paon (lighthouse) ★ - Maudez Cross ★ - St-Michel chapel ★★ - Bois de la citadelle ★.

Bellevue

VISA

Port-Clos – ✆ 02 96 20 00 05 – www.hotel-bellevue-brehat.com – hotelbellevue.brehat@wanadoo.fr – Fax 02 96 20 06 06 – Closed 11 November-19 December and 4 January-13 February

17 rm – €87 €128, €11 – ½ P €84/105

Rest – Menu €25/40 – Carte €28/70

◆ This regional house was built in 1904. It faces the jetty and the Arcouest headland, a view that can be enjoyed from the guestrooms at the front. Garden. Bikes for hire. Restaurant whose maritime style decor suits its seafood menu. Bay windows and terrace.

La Vieille Auberge

VISA

au bourg – ✆ 02 96 20 00 24 – www.brehat-vieilleauberge.eu – vieille-auberge.brehat@wanadoo.fr – Fax 02 96 20 05 12 – Open 11 April-2 November

14 rm – €76/92 €76/92, €10 – ½ P €70

Rest – Menu €18 (lunch) – Carte approx. €32

◆ Access to this old privateer's house in the town is on foot; the island's exceptional ecological heritage is worth leaving your car behind for! Functional bedrooms. Traditional fare served in a dining room decorated with fishing nets or in the flower-decked courtyard.

ÎLE DE GROIX ★ – 56 Morbihan – 308 K9 – ✉ 56590 Brittany 9 B2

Access by sea transport for **Port-Tudy** (in summer **booking recommended** for vehicles).

- from **Lorient** - 35 min crossing - Information about prices: S.M.N., rue G. Gahinet ✆ 0 820 056 000, Fax 02 97 29 50 34, www.smn-navigation.fr.
- Site★ of Port-Lay - Trou de l'Enfer (Hell's Hole) ★.

De la Marine

VISA

7 r. Gén. de Gaulle, in the town – ✆ 02 97 86 80 05 – www.hoteldelamarine.com – hotel.dela.marine@wanadoo.fr – Fax 02 97 86 56 37 – Closed 23 November-8 December, 4 January-5 February, Sunday dinner and Monday October-March except school holidays

22 rm – €34/39 €39/96, €9 – ½ P €50/78

Rest – Menu (€12), €18/35 – Carte €35/50

◆ A warm welcome in this house offering various room categories. The bar with a nautical atmosphere is popular with the islanders. Attractive rustic dining room (lovely old dresser) and marine menu, including the famous sardines à la groisillonne.

La Jetée without rest

VISA

1 quai Port-Tudy – ✆ 02 97 86 80 82 – laurence.tonnerre@wanadoo.fr – Fax 02 97 86 56 11 – Closed 5 January-15 March

8 rm – €53/64 €64/84, €8

◆ This modest white house makes the most of its splendid location and eight of its pretty rooms overlook the wharf or the Gripp coast, as do the breakfast terraces.

ÎLE DE JERSEY ★★ – JSY Jersey – 309 J1 – pop. 85 150 Normandy

Access by sea transport for **St-Helier (compulsory booking).**

from **St-Malo** (compulsory booking). by **Hydroglisseur** (Condor Ferries) - Crossing 1 h 15 mn - Information and prices : gare maritime de la bourse (St-Malo) Terminal Ferry du Naye ✆ 0 825 135 135 (0.15 €/mn).
from **Carteret :** Catamaran – seasonal service (crossing 50 mn -Gorey) by Manche Îles Express ✆ 0 825 133 050 (0.15 €/mn).

from **Granville** - Fast catamaran - crossing 60 mn (St-Helier) by Manche Îles Express: ✆ 0 825 133 050 (0.15 €/mn) - from**Carteret** - Catamaran - seasonal service - crossing 50 mn (Gorey) by Manche Îles Express: ✆ 0 825 133 050 (0.15 €/mn).

Hotels see Michelin Guide : **Great Britain and Ireland**

For a pleasant stay in a charming hotel, look for the red ... symbols.

ÎLE DE NOIRMOUTIER – 85 Vendée – 316 C6 – alt. 8 m
Atlantic Coast

Access - by road bridge from Fromentine: free passage.
- via Gois**: 4.5 km.
- during the first or last moon quarter in fine weather (high winds) an hour-and-a-half before low tide, to about an hour-and-a-half after low tide.
- during full or new moon in normal weather: two hours before low tide, to two hours after low tide.
- in all seasons during bad weather (low winds) do not stray from low tide time. See on-site display boards, before access to Gois.

L'ÉPINE – 85 Vendée – pop. 1 685 – alt. 2 m – ✉ 85740

Paris 463 – Cholet 134 – Nantes 79 – Noirmoutier-en-l'Île 4 – La Roche-sur-Yon 85

Punta Lara
rest, VISA MC AE

2 km south by D 95 and secondary road ✉ 85680 – ✆ 02 51 39 11 58 – www.hotelpuntalara.com – puntalara@leshotelsparticuliers.com – Fax 02 51 39 69 12 – Open May-September

61 rm – †€ 112/225 ††€ 112/225, ☕ € 15 – 2 suites – ½ P € 101/158

Rest – Menu € 30/45 – Carte € 40/60

◆ Vendée-style bungalows, in a pine forest between the ocean and salt marshes. Well looked after bedrooms, all of which have a balcony or terrace facing the Atlantic. Vast dining room with timber ceiling, opening onto the circular swimming pool.

L'HERBAUDIÈRE – 85 Vendée – ✉ 85330 Noirmoutier en l Île

Paris 469 – Cholet 140 – Nantes 85 – La Roche-sur-Yon 91

La Marine (Alexandre Couillon)
P VISA MC AE

3 r. Marie Lemonnier, (at the port) – ✆ 02 51 39 23 09 – Closed 6-21 October, 22 November-9 December, 4-20 January, Sunday dinner, Tuesday and Wednesday

Rest – Menu € 46/96 bi

Rest *La Table d'Elise* – ✆ *02 28 10 68 35* – Menu € 19 (weekdays) – Carte approx. € 26

Spec. "Crackers" de sardine marinée (spring-summer). Bar de ligne de l'Herbaudière cuisiné à basse température (spring-summer). Coque de chocolat et framboise (spring-summer). **Wines** Fiefs Vendéens, Vin de Pays de Vendée.

◆ Refurbished country house opposite the fishing port. Inventive personalised cuisine with a seafood focus served in a new water themed decor. La Table d'Elise occupies the original living room of this residence, refurbished as a convivial bistro.

NOIRMOUTIER-EN-L'ÎLE – 85 Vendée – pop. 4 847 – alt. 8 m – ✉ 85330

Paris 464 – Cholet 135 – Nantes 80 – La Roche-sur-Yon 86

Office de tourisme, Route du Pont ✆ 02.51.39.80.71, Fax 02.51.39.53.16

Collection of English earthenware★ in the château.

Fleur de Sel rest, VISA AE

r. des Saulniers – ✆ 02 51 39 09 07 – www.fleurdesel.fr – contact@fleurdesel.fr – Fax 02 51 39 09 76 – Open 1st April-2 November

35 rm – €90/185 €90/185, €13 – ½ P €82/134

Rest – *(closed Monday lunch and Tuesday lunch except July-August and public holidays)* Menu (€21), €29/39 – Carte €38/58

◆ A peaceful green setting, golf practice range, terrace, pretty sitting rooms and attractive bedrooms (cosily decorated or in nautical style): above all, calm, comfortable and relaxing. Sea-inspired decorative theme in the restaurant and a menu suited to current tastes.

Général d'Elbée without rest VISA AE

pl. Château – ✆ 02 51 39 10 29 – www.generaldelbee.com – elbee@leshotelsparticuliers.com – Fax 02 51 39 08 23 – Open May-September

27 rm – €98/270 €98/270, €15

◆ A historical 18C property full of bygone charm (period furniture and beams). Some of the rooms overlook the château that is lit up at night.

La Maison de Marine without rest VISA

3 r. Parmentier – ✆ 02 28 10 27 21 – www.lamaisondemarine.com – lamaisondemarine@hotmail.fr

5 rm – €90 €110/130

◆ Lovely personalised bedrooms, flower-decked terraces overlooking the patio-pool, sitting room with fireplace, spa, aromatic garden: a heavenly property devoted to guests' wellbeing.

Le Grand Four VISA AE

1 r. Cure, (behind the château) – ✆ 02 51 39 61 97 – www.legrandfour.com – legrandfour@orange.fr – Fax 02 51 39 61 97 – Closed 1st December-31 January, Sunday dinner and Monday except July-August

Rest – Menu €19 (weekday lunch), €26/85 – Carte €47/85

◆ A Virginia creeper-clad building. Two dining rooms, one of which is embellished by paintings and trinkets; the other has a less exuberant maritime theme. Seafood dishes.

L'Étier VISA AE

rte de L'Épine, 1 km southwest – ✆ 02 51 39 10 28 – www.restaurant-letier.fr – restaurant.etier@wanadoo.fr – Fax 02 51 39 23 00 – Closed December-January, Tuesday except July-August and Monday

Rest – Menu €18/38 – Carte €35/54 dinner only

◆ This low-built old cottage is typical of the island's architecture. Rustic interior, plus a terrace-veranda overlooking the Arceau. Fish from the local catch.

Côté Jardin VISA

1 bis r. du Grand Four, (behind the castle) – ✆ 02 51 39 03 02 – restaurantcotejardin@orange.fr – Closed 15 November-6 February, Sunday dinner, Wednesday dinner, Thursday except July-August and Monday

Rest – Menu (€14), €18/26 – Carte €32/50

◆ This restaurant owes its popularity to its traditional cuisine with local produce taking pride of place. Patio-terrace next-door to an old chapel; exhibition of work by local artist.

at Bois de la Chaize 2 km East – ✉ *85330 Noirmoutier-en-l'Île*

Wood★.

Les Prateaux rm, rm, VISA

allée du Tambourin – ✆ 02 51 39 12 52 – www.lesprateaux.com – contact@lesprateaux.com – Fax 02 51 39 46 28 – Open 14 February-30 October

18 rm – €98/165 €98/165, €14 – 1 suite – ½ P €91/130

Rest – *(closed Wednesday lunch and Tuesday)* Menu (€22), €28/62 – Carte €37/65

◆ Among this hotel's features are its proximity to Dames beach, the calm of a pinewood setting and a flower-decked garden. Spacious, mainly ground-floor, rooms with period furnishings. Bright blue and white dining room; sea produce takes pride of place on the menu.

St-Paul

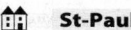

15 av. Mar.-Foch – ☎ 02 51 39 05 63 – www.hotel-saint-paul.net – contact@hotel-saint-paul.net – Fax 02 51 39 73 98 – Open 1 March-30 October

34 rm – †€ 84/151 ††€ 84/151, ☕ € 11 – ½ P € 82/120

Rest – *(closed Sunday dinner and Monday off season)* Menu (€ 22 bi), € 30/70 – Carte € 49/65

◆ This property stands in a handsome flowered park surrounded by woodland. Cosy bedrooms (rustic or period furniture) and welcoming sitting room-bar. Traditional dishes, fish and seafood served in an elegant dining room.

Château du Pélavé

9 allée de Chaillot – ☎ 02 51 39 01 94 – www.chateau-du-pelave.fr – chateau-du-pelave@wanadoo.fr – Fax 02 51 39 70 42

16 rm – †€ 69/119 ††€ 89/255, ☕ € 13 – ½ P € 78/170

Rest – *(Closed 1-25 December, 10 January-10 February, Sunday dinner, Monday, Tuesday and Wednesday from October to March except school holidays and bank holidays)* Menu € 28/56 bi – Carte € 32/49

◆ This late-19C château nestled in delighted wooded grounds with abundant floral displays is the perfect base for a quiet, relaxing stay. Personalised guestrooms in a range of styles. Local produce and an impressive choice of domain-bottled wines take pride of place here. Terrace.

Les Capucines without rest

38 av. de la Victoire – ☎ 02 51 39 06 82 – capucineshotel@aol.com – Fax 02 51 39 33 10 – Open 1 April-1 September

21 rm – †€ 41/78 ††€ 41/101, ☕ € 8

◆ Two buildings set on either side of the pool. Simple but practical rooms; larger in the annexe and quieter overlooking the garden. Friendly welcome.

ÎLE DE PORQUEROLLES – 83 Var – 340 M7 – ✉ 83400 — 41 C3

Access by sea transport.

from **La Tour Fondue** (Giens peninsula) - 20 mn crossing - Information and prices: T.L.V. and T.V.M. ☎ 04 94 58 21 81, www.tlv-tvm.com (La Tour Fondue) - from **Cavalaire** - Seasonal service - 1 h 40 mn crossing or **Le Lavandou** - seasonal service - 50 mn crossing. Information and prices: Vedettes Îles d'Or 15 quai Gabriel-Péri ☎ 04 94 71 01 02 (Le Lavandou), Fax 04 94 01 06 13

from **Toulon** - seasonal service - 1 h crossing - Information and services: Toulon Tourist Office ☎ 04 94 18 53 00.

Le Mas du Langoustier

3.5 km west of the port – ☎ 04 94 58 30 09 – www.langoustier.com – langoustier@wanadoo.fr – Fax 04 94 58 36 02 – Open from end April to early October

45 rm (½ board only) – 4 suites – ½ P € 180/315

Rest – Menu € 58/110 – Carte € 70/130

Spec. Filets de rougets poêlés, sablé au parmesan. Filet de Saint-Pierre rôti au beurre de gingembre et coriandre. Arlettes caramélisées aux graines de cumin.

Wines Vin de Pays de l'Île de Porquerolles.

◆ Fine, Provencal-style residence with elegant decor housing large, well-kept guestrooms. Regular shuttle from the harbour. Sun-kissed cuisine with a bright modern touch and an endless blue ocean view.

Villa Sainte Anne — rm, rm

pl. d'Armes – ☎ 04 98 04 63 00 – www.sainteanne.com – courrier@sainteanne.com – Fax 04 94 58 32 26 – Closed 2 November-21 February

25 rm (½ board only) – ½ P € 148/258

Rest – Menu (€ 18), € 25 – Carte € 34/48

◆ Rustic rooms with a Provencal feel in the main house (1930) on the village square. Larger and more modern rooms in the wing. Traditional cuisine served in a bistro-style dining room or on the shaded terrace.

Auberge des Glycines AC rm, rm, VISA MC

pl. d'Armes – 04 94 58 30 36 – www.auberge-glycines.com – auberge.glycines@orange.fr – Fax 04 94 58 35 22

11 rm – €119/269 €119/269, €8 – ½ P €99/169

Rest – Menu (€20), €25 – Carte €46/57

◆ Family inn set on the place d'Armes offering a very pleasant welcome. Warm, colourful, regional decor in the rooms. Southern dishes served on the patio.

ÎLE DE PORT-CROS ★★★ – 83 Var – 340 N7 – ✉ 83400 41 C3

French Riviera

Access by sea transport

From **Hyères** - information and prices: T.L.V. and T.V.M. 04 94 57 44 07 - from **Le Lavandou** - 35 mn crossing- Information and prices: Vedettes Îles d'Or 15 quai Gabriel-Péri 04 94 71 01 02 (Le Lavandou), Fax 04 94 01 06 13

from **Cavalaire** - 45 mn crossing - Information and prices: see above

from **La Tour Fondue** - 1 h crossing- Information and prices: T.L.V. - T.V.M. 04 94 58 21 81.

Le Manoir VISA MC

– 04 94 05 90 52 – http://monsite.wanadoo.fr/hotelmanoirportcros – lemanoir.portcros@wanadoo.fr – Fax 04 94 05 90 89 – Open 30 April-5 October

22 rm (½ board only) – ½ P €155/245

Rest – Menu €45 (dinner)/55 – Carte approx. €58

◆ This attractive 19C house surrounded by a park enjoys an idyllic location on an unspoilt island. Perfect for nature-lovers. The restaurant and terrace command a view of the yachts anchored in the Rade de Port-Cros. Regional cuisine.

ÎLE DE RÉ ★ – 17 Charente-Maritime – 324 B2 Atlantic Coast 38 A2

Access by road bridge (see La Rochelle).

ARS-EN-RÉ – 17 Charente-Maritime – pop. 1 294 – alt. 4 m – ✉ 17590

Paris 506 – Fontenay-le-Comte 85 – Luçon 75 – La Rochelle 34

Office de tourisme, 26, place Carnot 05 46 29 46 09, Fax 05 46 29 68 30

Le Sénéchal without rest VISA MC

6 r. Gambetta – 05 46 29 40 42 – www.hotel-le-senechal.com – hotel.le.senechal@wanadoo.fr – Fax 05 46 29 21 25

22 rm – €50/230 €50/230, €12 – 4 suites

◆ A guesthouse feel, with tasteful interiors combining old stonework and stylish decoration. Breakfast served on a flower-decked patio. Plenty of charm and character.

Le Parasol AC rest, rm, P VISA MC

1 km northwest by Le phare des Baleines road – 05 46 29 46 17 – www.leparasol.com – contact@leparasol.com – Fax 05 46 29 05 09 – Closed 1st January-12 February

30 rm – €67/99 €67/99, €10 – ½ P €63/94

Rest – Menu (€12), €20/35 – Carte €27/46

◆ Five small buildings in a green setting; neo-rustic rooms and studios. Faultless upkeep and welcome. Outdoor Jacuzzi and play area. Five small buildings in a green setting; neo-rustic rooms and studios. Faultless upkeep and welcome. Outdoor Jacuzzi and play area.

Le Bistrot de Bernard VISA MC

1 quai Criée – 05 46 29 40 26 – www.bistrotdebernard.com – bistrot.de.bernard@wanadoo.fr – Fax 05 46 29 28 99 – Closed 15 November-15 February, Monday and Tuesday in low season

Rest – Menu (€23), €27 – Carte €50/70

◆ The flowered courtyard lends a colonial air to this restaurant occupying one of the island's old houses. Bronze sculptures and mosaic frames decorate the dining room.

La Cabane du Fier P VISA MC

Le Martray, 3 km east by D 735 – 05 46 29 64 84 – cabanedufier@free.fr – Fax 05 46 29 64 84 – Open 16 March-14 November and closed Tuesday dinner and Wednesday except July-August

Rest – Menu (€19) – Carte €30/45

◆ A wooden building adjoining an oyster farmer's cabin. A delightful nautical bistro and terrace facing the Fier d'Ars. Daily seafood specials chalked up on a blackboard.

LE BOIS-PLAGE-EN-RÉ – 17 Charente-Maritime – pop. 2 303 – alt. 5 m – ✉ 17580

Paris 494 – Fontenay-le-Comte 74 – Luçon 64 – La Rochelle 23

Office de tourisme, 87, rue des Barjottes ✆ 05 46 09 23 26, Fax 05 46 09 13 15

Les Bois Flottais without rest

chemin des Mouettes – ✆ 05 46 09 27 00 – www.lesboisflottais.com – lesboisflottais@wanadoo.fr – Fax 05 46 09 28 00 – Open 2 March-12 November and Christmas holidays

19 rm – €75/110 €81/125, ☕ €12

◆ A beige and chocolate colour scheme, tiled floors, stained wood and nautical trinkets create the delightful decor of the comfortable rooms. All the rooms are level with the patio-pool.

L'Océan

172 r. St-Martin – ✆ 05 46 09 23 07 – www.re-hotel-ocean.com – info@re-hotel-ocean.com – Fax 05 46 09 05 40 – Closed 4 January-4 February

29 rm – €72/120 €72/180, ☕ €10

Rest – *(closed Wednesday except dinner from April to September)* Menu (€19), €24/32 – Carte €39/57

◆ Houses with whitewashed walls, whose light wood, counterpanes and embroidered fabrics recreate the charm of Isle of Ré homes. Stylish rooms, seven of which are more modern. Pretty Île de Ré style dining room opening onto a courtyard-terrace. Bar lounge.

Les Gollandières

av. des Gollandières – ✆ 05 46 09 23 99 – www.lesgollandieres.com – hotel-les-gollandieres@wanadoo.fr – Fax 05 46 09 09 84 – Open 14 March-7 November

34 rm – €98/118 €98/118, ☕ €12 – ½ P €93/148 **Rest** – Menu €42

◆ Behind the dunes, this hotel has small, simple rooms laid out around two patios. Pleasant swimming pool. This restaurant serves traditional cuisine made with high-quality local produce. Pleasant summer terrace.

La Villa Passagère without rest

25 av. du Pas des Bœufs – ✆ 05 46 00 26 70 – www.lavillapassagere.net – reception@lavillapassagere.net – Fax 05 46 00 26 84 – Open 2 February-15 November

13 rm – €60/120 €60/130, ☕ €8

◆ A new hotel made up of small regional style houses laid out around a herb garden and swimming pool. Simple, light ground floor rooms.

LA COUARDE-SUR-MER – 17 Charente-Maritime – pop. 1 213 – alt. 1 m – ✉ 17670

Paris 497 – Fontenay-le-Comte 76 – Luçon 66 – La Rochelle 26

Syndicat d'initiative, rue Pasteur ✆ 05 46 29 82 93, Fax 05 46 29 63 02

Le Vieux Gréement without rest

13 pl. Carnot – ✆ 05 46 29 82 18 – www.levieuxgreement.com – hotelvieuxgreement@wanadoo.fr – Fax 05 46 29 50 79 – Open 27 March-15 November

19 rm – €60/80 €70/120, ☕ €12 – 2 suites

◆ On the village square, a family establishment of character. Spruce rooms, pretty patio, terrace shaded by a linden tree and a wine bar serving tapas and salads.

LA FLOTTE – 17 Charente-Maritime – pop. 2 907 – alt. 4 m – ✉ 17630

Paris 489 – Fontenay-le-Comte 68 – Luçon 58 – La Rochelle 17

Office de tourisme, quai de Sénac ✆ 05 46 09 60 38, Fax 05 46 09 64 88

Richelieu

44 av. de la Plage – ✆ 05 46 09 60 70 – www.hotel-le-richelieu.com – info@hotel-le-richelieu.com – Fax 05 46 09 50 59 – Closed 4 January-5 February

37 rm – €140/625 €140/625, ☕ €30 – 3 suites – ½ P €125/375

Rest – Menu €50 (weekday lunch), €55/65 – Carte €66/80

Spec. "Maki-sushi" aux huîtres de l'Île de Ré. Marinière de sole de nos côtes aux moules de Charron. Coque macaronée, chocolat guanaja, banane caramélisée et palet caramel. **Wines** Vin de Pays de la Vienne, Fiefs Vendéens.

◆ Luxurious, personalised guestrooms with period furniture. The most pleasant have a vast terrace overlooking the sea. Thalassotherapy centre. The restaurant affords views of the garden and the Atlantic. Refined original cuisine.

L'Écailler
3 quai Sénac – 05 46 09 56 40 – flosenac@orange.fr – Fax 09 77 92 18 03 – Open 1 March-11 November and closed Monday and Tuesday from 21 September to 31 March

Rest – Menu € 36 (lunch)/54 – Carte € 55/90

◆ Terrace overlooking the harbour, tasteful interior (wainscoting, fireplace and old parquet floors) and recipes that focus on the local catch: this 1652 shipowner's house is full of charm.

Chai nous comme Chai vous
1 r. de la Garde – 05 46 09 49 85 – Closed 9-23 March, 5-19 October, Friday lunch and Saturday lunch in school holidays, Wednesday and Thursday except school holidays

Rest – *(number of covers limited, pre-book)* Menu € 39/54

◆ You feel a little like you're at home in this very simple restaurant run by a married couple. The menu boasts seafood, inventiveness and attention to detail. Careful choice of wines.

RIVEDOUX-PLAGE – 17 Charente-Maritime – pop. 2 260 – alt. 2 m – ✉ 17940

Paris 483 – Fontenay-le-Comte 63 – Luçon 53 – La Rochelle 12

Syndicat d'initiative, place de la République 05 46 09 80 62, Fax 05 46 09 80 62

De la Marée
321 av. A. Sarrault, rte de St-Martin – 05 46 09 80 02 – www.hoteldelamaree.com – contact@hoteldelamaree.com – Fax 05 46 09 88 25

26 rm – †€ 58/168 ††€ 58/168, € 12 – 2 suites – ½ P € 69/151

Rest – Menu € 20/48 – Carte € 32/68

◆ Painted furniture adorn the rooms; the most pleasant have terraces giving onto the rose garden and swimming pool; countless sitting rooms, nooks and crannies. Charming welcome. Blackboard menu in the restaurant (panoramic dining room and lounge), depending on what is available from the port and market.

Le Grand Large
154 av. des Dunes – 05 46 09 89 51 – www.hoteldugrandlarge.com – hotel-legrandlarge@orange.fr – Open from mid-March to end September

32 rm – †€ 55/350 ††€ 55/350 – ½ P € 64/200

Rest – Menu (€ 16) – Carte € 29/40

◆ Refurbished hotel facing the beach and sea is set around a fine heated pool. Bright and functional rooms with terraces or balconies. A relaxed seaside ambience to savour regional cuisine, pasta and pizzas.

ST-CLÉMENT-DES-BALEINES – 17 Charente-Maritime – pop. 716 – alt. 2 m – ✉ 17590

Paris 509 – Fontenay-le-Comte 89 – Luçon 79 – La Rochelle 38

Office de tourisme, 200, rue du Centre 05 46 29 24 19, Fax 05 46 29 08 14

L'Arche de Noé (amusement park): Naturama★ (collection of stuffed animals) - Phare des Baleines (lighthouse) ❋★ North: 2.5 km.

Le Chat Botté without rest
2 pl. de l'Église – 05 46 29 21 93 – www.hotelchatbotte.com – hotelchatbotte@wanadoo.fr – Fax 05 46 29 29 97 – Closed late November to early December and early January to mid-February

20 rm – †€ 55/58 ††€ 61/152, € 11 – 3 suites

◆ A cosy interior (pastel shades, wood and antique furniture), adorable garden where breakfasts are served and a beauty centre: ideal to relax and be pampered!

Le Chat Botté
r. de la Mairie – 05 46 29 42 09 – www.restaurant-lechatbotte.com – restaurant-lechatbotte@wanadoo.fr – Fax 05 46 29 29 77 – Closed December-January, Sunday dinner October-March and Monday

Rest – Menu € 25 (weekdays)/75 – Carte € 55/65

◆ The restaurant's name is derived from Chabot, one of the village's five hamlets. A comfortable dining room with nautical decor, overlooking a pleasant garden.

ST-MARTIN-DE-RÉ – 17 Charente-Maritime – pop. 2 588 – alt. 14 m – ✉ 17410

Paris 493 – Fontenay-le-Comte 72 – Luçon 62 – La Rochelle 22

Syndicat d'initiative, 2, quai Nicolas Baudin ✆ 05 46 09 20 06, Fax 05 46 09 06 18

Fortifications★.

De Toiras

rm, VISA

1 quai Job Foran – ✆ 05 46 35 40 32 – www.hotel-de-toiras.com – contact@hotel-de-toiras.com – Fax 05 46 35 64 59

17 rm – †€ 135/1500 ††€ 165/1500, ☕ € 26 – 3 suites – ½ P € 135/175

Rest – *(closed Tuesday from October to March, Sunday from April to September and Monday) (dinner only)* Carte € 60/100

◆ A tasteful interior decoration, both luxurious and simple, charming rooms and a delightfully attentive welcome: this 17C shipowner's home is a rare gem. Meals are served in an attractive dining room or on the terrace in fine weather.

Le Clos St-Martin without rest

VISA

8 cours Pasteur – ✆ 05 46 01 10 62 – www.le-clos-saint-martin.com – reservation@le-clos-saint-martin.com – Fax 05 46 01 99 89

32 rm – †€ 120/400 ††€ 120/400, ☕ € 19

◆ This recent house and pretty walled park are only a short distance from the harbour. Simple but pleasant rooms, some on the same level with the patio-pool.

La Jetée without rest

VISA

quai G. Clemenceau – ✆ 05 46 09 36 36 – www.hotel-lajetee.com – info@hotel-lajetee.com – Fax 05 46 09 36 06

24 rm – †€ 96/125 ††€ 96/125, ☕ € 12 – 7 suites

◆ A harbour hotel renovated in a warm contemporary style: trendy colour scheme and minimalist furnishings in the rooms, arranged round a patio (where breakfast is served in summer).

Le Galion without rest

VISA

allée Guyane – ✆ 05 46 09 03 19 – www.hotel-legalion.com – hotel.le.galion@wanadoo.fr – Fax 05 46 09 13 26

29 rm – †€ 70/110 ††€ 75/115, ☕ € 9

◆ Vauban's ramparts protect the hotel from the pounding of the ocean. Modern, well-kept rooms, almost all of them facing the sea or the patio. Asian-inspired sitting room.

La Maison Douce without rest

VISA

25 r. Mérindot – ✆ 05 46 09 20 20 – www.lamaisondouce.com – lamaisondouce@wanadoo.fr – Fax 05 46 09 09 90 – Closed 15 November-25 December and 7 January-15 February

11 rm – †€ 120/210 ††€ 120/210, ☕ € 15

◆ A 19C establishment typical of Ré. Low-key interior, delightful rooms with 1940s bathrooms; courtyard garden where breakfast is served in summer.

Du Port without rest

VISA

29 quai Poitheviniѐre – ✆ 05 46 09 21 21 – www.iledere-hot-port.com – iledere-hot.port@wanadoo.fr – Fax 05 46 09 06 85 – Closed 4-29 January

35 rm – †€ 65/95 ††€ 75/105, ☕ € 8,50

◆ This is the lively district of St-Martin-de-Ré. A hotel with simply-furnished, colourful rooms, some with a harbour view.

Les Colonnes

VISA

19 quai Job-Foran – ✆ 05 46 09 21 58 – www.hotellescolonnes.com – info@hotellescolonnes.com – Fax 05 46 09 21 49 – Closed 15 December-1st February

30 rm – †€ 75/99 ††€ 95/99, ☕ € 9

Rest – *(Closed Wednesday)* Menu (€ 24), € 29

◆ This regional-style house is fronted by a vast terrace popular with fishermen and locals: friendly and informal! Neat, well-kept rooms, overlooking the harbour or the courtyard. Dining room-veranda with extensive view of the waterfront; traditional cuisine.

Domaine de la Baronnie without rest
21 r. Baron de Chantal – 05 46 09 21 29 – www.domainedelabaronnie.com – info@domainedelabaronnie.com – Fax 05 46 09 95 29 – Open 4 April-1st November
5 rm – €175/225 €190/240
◆ This 18C mansion has been restored in the fashion of a country home, with individually furnished rooms. Those in the tower overlook the garden and the rooftops of the town.

Le Corps de Garde – La Maison du Port without rest
3 quai Clemenceau – 05 46 09 10 50 – www.lecorpsdegarde.com – info@lecorpsdegarde.com – Fax 08 11 38 17 50
5 rm – €120/225 €120/225, €12
◆ Antique furniture and ornaments, splendid old-fashioned bathrooms and guestrooms overlooking the lock or the sea; this 17C former guardroom oozes with charm.

La Coursive St-Martin without rest
13 cours Déchézeaux – 05 46 09 22 87 – www.lacoursive.com – mail@lacoursive.com – Fax 05 46 09 22 87 – Closed December and January
3 rm – €90/155 €90/160, €10
◆ A charming stopover can be had at this extensive 18C Rhétaise residence, steeped in history, surrounded by high walls and complemented by a beautiful flower filled garden. Personalised rooms.

Bô
20 cours Vauban – 05 46 07 04 04 – www.bo-restaurant.com – le-bo@wanadoo.fr – Fax 05 46 29 08 20 – Closed 3 January-4 February and Wednesday except July-August
Rest – Menu €29 (lunch)/39 – Carte €38/50
◆ A stone's throw from the port, Bô will seduce you with its gentle contemporary atmosphere (candles, plants, cosy sofas) and its luxurious terrace. Modern seafood cuisine.

La Baleine Bleue
sur L'Îlot – 05 46 09 03 30 – www.baleinebleue.com – info@baleinebleue.com – Fax 05 46 09 30 86 – Closed 12 November-19 December, 5 January-5 February, Tuesday October-March and Monday except July-August
Rest – Menu (€24), €32 (lunch)/39
◆ A cheerful restaurant and vast terrace facing the port. A warm interior with a 1930s zinc counter, serving updated cuisine featuring many seafood dishes.

STE-MARIE-DE-RÉ – 17 Charente-Maritime – pop. 3 082 – alt. 9 m – 17740

Paris 486 – Fontenay-le-Comte 66 – Luçon 55 – La Rochelle 15

Office de tourisme, place d'Antioche 05 46 30 22 92, Fax 05 46 30 01 68

Atalante rest,
r. Port Notre-Dame – 05 46 30 22 44 – www.relaisthalasso.com – restauration-iledere@relaisthalasso.com – Fax 05 46 30 13 49 – Closed 4-18 January
108 rm – €86/257 €119/388, €15
Rest – Menu (€25), €29/35 – Carte €60/80
◆ This hotel facing the sea has modern rooms in acid shades. Those in the modern wing are larger and more comfortable. Direct access to the thalassotherapy centre The veranda-dining room is a veritable window onto the Atlantic.

Les Vignes de la Chapelle without rest
5 r. de la Manne – 05 46 30 20 30 – www.lesvignesdelachapelle.com – hotel@lesvignesdelachapelle.com – Open 1st April-11 November
2 rm – €85/190 €85/190, €12 – 17 suites – €100/230
◆ Opposite the vineyards and sea, this brand new hotel was built along ecological lines (materials, heating). Contemporary ground floor suites with terrace.

The sun's out – let's eat alfresco!
Look for a terrace:

ÎLE-DE-SEIN – 29 Finistère – 308 B6 – pop. 239 – alt. 14 m – ✉ 29990 9 A2
Brittany

Pedestrians only

from **Brest** (Sun in July and Aug) - 1 h 30 mn crossing - Information and prices: Cie Maritime Penn Ar Bed (Brest) ✆ 02 98 70 70 70
- from **Audierne** (all year) 1 h crossing - Information and prices: see above.

from **Camaret** (Sun in July-Aug) 1 h crossing - Information and prices: Cie Maritime Penn Ar Bed (Brest) 02 98 70 70 70

Ar Men

rte Phare – ✆ 02 98 70 90 77 – www.hotel-armen.net – hotel.armen@wanadoo.fr – Fax 02 98 70 93 25 – Closed 5 November-16 December and 4 January-6 February

10 rm – †€ 45 ††€ 55/70, ☕ € 7 – ½ P € 53/70

Rest – *(closed Wednesday from April to November and Sunday dinner)* Menu € 20

◆ A charming family-run island hotel, easy to spot from its pink exterior by the road to the lighthouse near the church. Ocean colours in the rooms that overlook the sea. The local catch takes pride of place in the tasteful dining room. Lobster stew by reservation.

ÎLE-D'HOUAT – 56 Morbihan – 308 N10 – pop. 318 – alt. 31 m – ✉ 56170 Brittany 10 C3

Access by sea transport

from **Quiberon** - 45 mn crossing - Information and prices: Compagnie Océane Le Palais SMN ✆ 0 820 056 000 (0,12 €/mn)(Quiberon) www.smn-navigation.fr

depuis **La Trinité-sur-Mer** (Jul-Aug) 1 h crossing - Navix: cours des quais ✆ 0 825 162 100 - from Vannes, Port Navalo, Locmariaquer, la Turballe and le Croisic - information and prices: Compagnie des Îles 0825 164 100 www.compagniedesiles.com

Le Bourg ⋞★.

La Sirène

rte du Port – ✆ 02 97 30 66 73 – la-sirene-houat@wanadoo.fr – Fax 02 97 30 66 94 – Open from Easter to end September

20 rm – †€ 110/130 ††€ 110/150, ☕ € 12 – ½ P € 80/100

Rest – Menu (€ 16), € 22 (weekdays)/33 – Carte € 38/180

◆ Family run hotel in the heart of a small town. Friendly service. The practical and soundproofed rooms, including nine new ones, promise a pleasant stay. Restaurant with nautical decor leading onto a terrace serving traditional and seafood dishes.

ÎLE D'OLÉRON ★ – 17 Charente-Maritime – 324 C4 Atlantic Coast 38 A2

Access by viaduct bridge: no toll.

BOYARDVILLE – 17 Charente-Maritime – ✉ 17190 St-Georges-d'Oléron

Paris 517 – Marennes 24 – Rochefort 45 – La Rochelle 82 – Saintes 65

Office de tourisme, 14, avenue de l'Océan ✆ 05 46 47 04 76

d'Oléron Saint-Pierre-d'Oléron La Vieille Perrotine, S : 2 km on D 126, ✆ 05 46 47 11 59

Des Bains

1 r. des Quais, (at the port) – ✆ 05 46 47 01 02 – info@hoteldesbains-oleron.com – Fax 05 46 47 16 90 – Open 30 May-20 September and closed Wednesday except dinner from 8 July to 20 September

Rest – Menu € 22/39 – Carte € 33/71

◆ Beams, stonework, copperware and rustic furniture endow this canalside family restaurant with the feel of an old inn. Traditional culinary repertoire.

LE CHÂTEAU-D'OLÉRON – 17 Charente-Maritime – pop. 3 876 – alt. 9 m – ✉ 17480

Paris 524 – Poitiers 190 – La Rochelle 72 – Saintes 54 – Rochefort 35

XX Les Jardins d'Aliénor with rm

11 r. Mar. Foch – ✆ 05 46 76 48 30 – www.lesjardinsdalienor.com – lesjardinsdalienor@wanadoo.fr – Fax 05 46 76 58 47 – Closed lunch in July-August and Monday

4 rm – €77/117 €77/117 **Rest** – Menu €25 (lunch)/40 – Carte €43/50

◆ An interior that mixes old and new and a patio-terrace with a wall of plants: the decor is baroque and full of character, as is the chef's cuisine. Attractive rooms, one of which has a private terrace.

LA COTINIÈRE – 17 Charente-Maritime – ✉ 17310 St-Pierre-d'Oléron

Paris 522 – Marennes 22 – Rochefort 44 – La Rochelle 80 – Royan 54 – Saintes 63

Face aux Flots without rest

24 r. du Four – ✆ 05 46 47 10 05 – www.hotel-faceauxflots-oleron.com – face.aux.flots@wanadoo.fr – Fax 05 46 47 45 95 – Open 10 February-11 November and Christmas holidays

21 rm – €49/102 €52/110, €8

◆ The rooms of this appealing family hotel have been refurbished; they are now modern, colourful and nearly all overlook the sea (four have a small balcony).

Île de Lumière without rest

av. des Pins – ✆ 05 46 47 10 80 – www.moteliledelumiere.com – ile.de.lumiere@wanadoo.fr – Fax 05 46 47 30 87 – Open 4 April-26 September

45 rm – €74/96 €74/134

◆ In an unspoilt site, subudued ground floor rooms, many of which have terraces with a view of the ocean, dunes or swimming pool. Some are more modern in style.

in la Ménounière 2 km North by secondary road ✉ 17310 St-Pierre-d'Oléron

XX Saveurs des Îles

18 r. de la Plage – ✆ 05 46 75 86 68 – www.saveursdesiles.fr – osaveursdesiles@wanadoo.fr – Fax 05 46 75 86 68 – Closed 8 November-28 December, 3 January-31 March, Monday except dinner in July-August, Wednesday lunch in July-August and Tuesday in low season

Rest – Menu €25/40 – Carte €45/60

◆ The owners built this Asian-inspired restaurant themselves, decorating it with Indonesian furniture. Garden-terrace. Creative menu enhanced by exotic spices and flavours.

LE GRAND VILLAGE PLAGE – 17 Charente-Maritime – pop. 981 – alt. 6 m – ✉ 17370

Paris 525 – Poitiers 191 – La Rochelle 73 – Rochefort 36 – Royan 44

X Le Relais des Salines

Port des Salines – ✆ 05 46 75 82 42 – james.robert@hotmail.fr – Fax 05 46 75 16 70 – Open from beg. March to end November and closed Monday except school holidays

Rest – Menu €17 (weekday lunch) – Carte approx. €35

◆ Relaxed atmosphere, trendy nautical-inspired bistro decor, terrace overlooking the salt marshes and an impressive choice of seafood on the slate menu: this old oyster farmer's cabin is a gem!

ST-PIERRE-D'OLÉRON – 17 Charente-Maritime – pop. 6 239 – alt. 8 m – ✉ 17310

Paris 522 – Marennes 22 – Rochefort 44 – La Rochelle 80 – Royan 54 – Saintes 63

Office de tourisme, place Gambetta ✆ 05 46 47 11 39, Fax 05 46 47 10 41

Church ⁂★.

X Les Alizés

4 r. Dubois-Aubry – ✆ 05 46 47 20 20 – marilyn.philippe.oleron@orange.fr – Fax 05 46 47 20 20 – Open from beg. March to beg. December and closed Tuesday and Wednesday except mid July-mid September and public holidays

Rest – Menu €19/34 – Carte €23/46

◆ This restaurant has a dining area with wooden panelling and a marine décor theme. In fine weather, enjoy a meal outside on the pleasant patio. Seafood served.

ST-TROJAN-LES-BAINS – 17 Charente-Maritime – pop. 1 495 – alt. 5 m – ✉ 17370

Paris 509 – Marennes 16 – Rochefort 38 – La Rochelle 74 – Royan 47 – Saintes 57

Office de tourisme, carrefour du Port ☎ 05 46 76 00 86, Fax 05 46 76 17 64

Novotel – rm, rm, rest,
beach of Gatseau, 2.5 km south – ☎ 05 46 76 02 46 – www.accorthalassa.com – h0417@accor.com – Fax 05 46 76 09 33 – Closed 29 November-19 December
109 rm – †€ 105/220 ††€ 140/250, ☕ € 17 – ½ P € 105/165
Rest – Menu (€ 25), € 32 – Carte € 35/55
◆ Relax in this hotel opposite the beach which boasts its own thalassotherapy centre. Ask for one of the renovated or recently created more contemporary rooms. Enjoy the sea view while watching your figure (partially "diet" conscious menu).

Hostellerie Les Cleunes
25 bd Plage – ☎ 05 46 76 03 08 – www.hotel-les-cleunes.com – hotellescleunes@aol.com – Fax 05 46 76 08 95 – Open early February to mid-November
40 rm – †€ 83/235 ††€ 83/235, ☕ € 12
Rest – *(closed Monday lunch outwith school holidays and bank holidays)* Menu (€ 28), € 40/58 – Carte € 50/160
◆ A seashore family establishment that has been renovated from top to toe: comfortable, welcoming rooms, cosy sitting room with billiards table, and a lovely patio-swimming pool. A menu that features a modern repertoire with input from the ocean beyond.

Mer et Forêt – rest,
16 bd P. Wiehn – ☎ 05 46 76 00 15 – www.hotel-ile-oleron.com – laforet.oleron@wanadoo.fr – Fax 05 46 76 14 67 – Open 10 April-1 November
43 rm – †€ 52/83 ††€ 52/118, ☕ € 9 – ½ P € 54/92
Rest – Menu (€ 14 bi), € 18/36 – Carte € 31/44
◆ Hotel in a quiet residential neighbourhood. Practical, modern rooms with a view over the pine forest or the ocean; pleasant pool. Panoramic views of the viaduct-bridge and the mainland from the restaurant and terrace.

L'Albatros – rm, rest,
11 bd Dr Pineau – ☎ 05 46 76 00 08 – www.albatros-hotel-oleron.com – allooleron@free.fr – Fax 05 46 76 03 58 – Open 7 February-2 November
12 rm – †€ 70/110 ††€ 70/110, ☕ € 10 – ½ P € 73/93
Rest – Menu € 20/56 – Carte € 33/68
◆ To make the most of this fantastic waterfront location, book one of the rooms that have been treated to a pleasant contemporary-style makeover. Local seafood features prominently on the menu; brasserie decor and panoramic sea view terrace.

ÎLE D'OUESSANT – 29 Finistère – **308** A4 – ✉ **29242** Brittany 9 **A1**

Pedestrians only - from **Brest** - Crossing 2 h 15 mn - Information and prices: Cie Maritime Penn Ar Bed (Brest) ☎ 02 98 80 80 80 -

from **Le Conquet** - Crossing 1 h - Information and prices: see above -

from **Camaret** (mid-July to mid-August only) - Crossing 1 h 15 mn - Information and prices: see above.

Ti Jan Ar C' Hafé without rest
Kernigou – ☎ 02 98 48 82 64 – hoteltijan@wanadoo.fr – Fax 02 98 48 88 15 – Closed 11 November-20 December and 4 January-15 March
8 rm – †€ 68/118 ††€ 68/118, ☕ € 12
◆ This charming small hotel between the port and town extends a warm welcome to its guests. Smart lounge, bright breakfast room and pleasant bedrooms.

Le Roc'h Ar Mor – rm,
in Lampaul – ☎ 02 98 48 80 19 – www.rocharmor.com – roch.armor@wanadoo.fr – Fax 02 98 48 87 51 – Closed 15 November-15 December and 3 January-10 February
15 rm – †€ 55/87 ††€ 55/87, ☕ € 10 – ½ P € 52/67
Rest – *(Closed Sunday dinner and Monday)* Menu (€ 15), € 22/30 – Carte € 30/65
◆ This hotel sits on France's westernmost point. Plain rooms, some with a view of Lampaul Bay. Unpretentious ambience. A bar/brasserie with a panoramic terrace and low-key dining room. Single menu for residents only.

Ty Korn VISA

in Lampaul – ✆ 02 98 48 87 33 – Fax 02 98 48 87 33 – Closed 8-14 June, 16-30 November, 4-25 January, Sunday dinner and Monday except bank holidays

Rest – *(number of covers limited, pre-book)* Menu (€ 15), € 29 – Carte € 35/70

◆ A popular pub-restaurant near the church. Fish and seafood are on offer in the small dining room with the Atlantic as a backdrop.

ÎLE D'YEU ★★ – 85 Vendée – 361 BC7 – pop. 4 941 Atlantic Coast 34 A3

Access by sea transport for **Port-Joinville.**

from Fromentine : Crossing from 30 to 70 mn - Information to Cie Yeu Continent BP 16-85550 La Barre-de-Monts ✆ 0 825 853 000 (0,15 €/mn), www.compagnie-yeu-continent.fr.

from Fromentine (all year) - Crossing from 30 to 45 mn - Information and prices : Cie Yeu Continent (to Fromentine) ✆ 0 825 853 000 (0,15 €/mn), www.compagnie-yeu-continent.fr - from Barbâtre : Cie V.I.I.V. ✆ 02 51 39 00 00 - from St-Gilles-Croix-de-Vie and from Les Sables d'Olonne (Quai Bénatier) (April to Sept.) : Cie Vendéenne ✆ 0 825 139 085 (0,15 €/mn), www.compagnievendeenne.com Seasonal service (April to Sept.).

Office de tourisme, 1, place du Marché ✆ 02 51 58 32 58, Fax 02 51 58 40 48

PORT-DE-LA-MEULE – 85 Vendée – ✉ 85350 L'Île d'Yeu

Paris 460 – Nantes 72 – La Roche-sur-Yon 73 – Challans 29 – Saint-Hilaire-de-Riez 36

Côte Sauvage★★: ≤★★ East and West - Pointe de la Tranche★ Southeast.

PORT-JOINVILLE – 85 Vendée – pop. 4 807 – ✉ 85350 L'Île d'Yeu

Paris 457 – Nantes 69 – La Roche-sur-Yon 70 – Challans 26 – Pornic 43

Old château ★: ≤★★ Southwest: 3,5 km - Grand Phare ≤★ Southwest: 3 km.

Atlantic Hôtel without rest ≤ AC VISA AE

quai Carnot – ✆ 02 51 58 38 80 – www.hotel-yeu.com – atlantic-hotel-yeu@club-internet.fr – Fax 02 51 58 35 92 – Closed 5 January-1st February

18 rm – †€ 43/95 ††€ 43/95, ☕ € 8

◆ Opposite the wharf, with light rooms from where you can hear the chinking of the masts, as you can from the breakfast room. Tranquil fishing village with tiny gardens.

L'Escale without rest VISA

r. de La Croix de Port – ✆ 02 51 58 50 28 – www.yeu-escale.fr – yeu.escale@voila.fr – Fax 02 51 59 33 55 – Closed 15 November-15 December

29 rm – †€ 52/73 ††€ 52/73, ☕ € 8

◆ Set just behind the port, this hotel has a white exterior with coloured shutters. Simple, well-kept rooms, some of which have air-conditioning. Breakfast room with marine decor.

Port Baron VISA

9 r. Georgette – ✆ 02 51 26 01 61 – baron-michel@hotmail.com – Fax 02 51 26 01 61 – Closed 2 weeks in October, Tuesday lunch and Monday

Rest – Menu (€ 18), € 33/39

◆ A retro-style bistro decorated with old posters, banquettes, photos, old records and other mementoes. The menu is based around seasonal produce and the day's catch.

L'ILE-ROUSSE – 2B Haute-Corse – 345 C4 – see Corse

ÎLE STE-MARGUERITE ★★ – 06 Alpes-Maritimes – 341 D6 – ✉ 06400 Cannes French Riviera 42 E2

Access by sea transport.

from **Cannes** Crossing 15 mn by Cie Esterel Chanteclair-Gare Maritime des Îles ✆ 04 93 38 66 33, Fax 04 92 98 80 32.

Forest★★ - ≤★ of the Fort-Royal terrace.

ÎLES CHAUSEY – **50 Manche** – **303** B6 – ✉ **50400** **Normandy** 32 **A2**

Access by sea transport.

from **Granville** - Crossing 50 mn - Information: Vedette "Jolie France II" Gare Maritime ✆ 02 33 50 31 81 (Granville), Fax 02 33 50 39 90, Compagnie Corsaire : ✆ 0 825 138 050 (0,15 €/mn), Fax 02 33 50 87 80, www.compagniecorsaire.com –

from **St-Malo** - Crossing 1 h 10 mn - Compagnie Corsaire : ✆ 0 825 138 035 (0.15 €/mn), Fax 02 23 18 02 97.

Grande Île★.

Fort et des Îles with rm rm, VISA MC

– *✆ 02 33 50 25 02 – hoteldufortetdesiles@orange.fr – Fax 02 33 50 25 02 – Open 11 April-27 September and closed Monday except bank holidays*

8 rm (½ board only) – ½ P € 70

Rest – *(pre-book in high season)* Menu € 22/80 – Carte € 28/90

◆ Lobster, crab, oysters and fish: seafood cuisine based on the day's catch and superb view over the archipelago. A great place to revitalise far from the turbulence of the mainland. Very basic rooms without television to better enjoy the island's tranquillity.

LAS ILLAS – **66 Pyrénées-Orientales** – **344** H8 – **see Maureillas-las-Illas**

ILLHAEUSERN – **68 Haut-Rhin** – **315** I7 – **pop. 711** – **alt. 173 m** – ✉ **68970** 2 **C2**

Paris 452 – Artzenheim 15 – Colmar 19 – St-Dié 55 – Sélestat 15 – Strasbourg 69

La Clairière without rest P VISA MC AE

rte de Guémar – ✆ 03 89 71 80 80 – www.hotel-la-clairiere.com – hotel.la.clairiere@orange.fr – Fax 03 89 71 86 22 – Closed January and February

25 rm – †€ 77 ††€ 98/210, ☕ € 12

◆ On the edge of the Ill forest, a vast building with Alsatian-style architecture. Quiet, spacious, personalised rooms, some of which overlook the Vosges mountains.

Les Hirondelles without rest AC P VISA MC

au village – ✆ 03 89 71 83 76 – www.hotelleshirondelles.com – hotelleshirondelles@orange.fr – Fax 03 89 71 86 40 – Closed 1st-27 March and 12-24 November

19 rm ☕ – †€ 66/72 ††€ 76/82

◆ A warm welcome awaits you in the rustic decor of this old farmstead. Well-equipped rooms, laid out around a pretty courtyard and splendid heated swimming pool.

Auberge de l'Ill (Marc Haeberlin) AC P VISA MC AE

✿✿✿ *2 r. de Collonges – ✆ 03 89 71 89 00 – www.auberge-de-l-ill.com – aubergedelill@aubergedelill.com – Fax 03 89 71 82 83 – Closed 1st-8 January, February, Monday and Tuesday*

Rest – *(pre-book)* Menu € 96 (weekday lunch), € 117/149 – Carte € 121/248

Spec. Mousseline de grenouilles Paul Haeberlin. Côtelette de perdreau romanov (September to November). Pêche Haeberlin. **Wines** Pinot blanc, Klevner.

◆ Designer decor by P. Jouin, excellent service, magical views of the Ill, superb Alsatian-inspired classical cuisine and splendid choice of wines: a truly luxurious dining experience.

Hôtel des Berges AC VISA MC AE

– *✆ 03 89 71 87 87 – www.hoteldesberges.com – hotel-des-berges@wanadoo.fr – Fax 03 89 71 87 88 – Closed 1st-8 January, 4 February-5 March, Monday and Tuesday*

13 rm – †€ 300 ††€ 520

◆ An original reconstruction of a tobacco drier from the Ried marshlands, at the bottom of the Auberge de l'Ill's garden. Extremely refined rooms, an outside jacuzzi and breakfast served on a wooden boat!

ILLKIRCH-GRAFFENSTADEN – **67 Bas-Rhin** – **315** K5 – **see Strasbourg**

INGERSHEIM – **68 Haut-Rhin** – **315** H8 – **see Colmar**

INNENHEIM – 67 Bas-Rhin – **315** J6 – **pop. 1 027** – **alt. 150 m** 1 **B2**
– ✉ **67880**

▶ Paris 487 – Molsheim 12 – Obernai 10 – Sélestat 34 – Strasbourg 23

Au Cep de Vigne
5 r. Barr – ☎ 03 88 95 75 45 – www.aucepdevigne.com – resa@aucepdevigne.com – Fax 03 88 95 79 73 – Closed 15 February-3 March, Sunday dinner and Monday
37 rm – 🚹€ 58 🚹🚹€ 63, ☕ € 8,50 – ½ P € 65
Rest – Menu € 15 (weekdays)/42 – Carte € 20/75
◆ A typical Alsatian inn, with a half-timbered facade, housing comfortable rooms. Those overlooking the garden are quieter. The regional food served in this restaurant goes well with the local wines (vineyards just a step away).

INXENT – 62 Pas-de-Calais – **301** D4 – **see Montreuil**

ISBERGUES – 62 Pas-de-Calais – **301** H4 – **see Aire-sur-la-Lys**

ISIGNY-SUR-MER – 14 Calvados – **303** F4 – **pop. 2 763** – **alt. 4 m** 32 **A2**
– ✉ **14230** **Normandy**

▶ Paris 298 – Bayeux 35 – Caen 64 – Carentan 14 – Cherbourg 63 – St-Lô 29

ℹ Office de tourisme, 16, rue Émile Demagny ☎ 02 31 21 46 00, Fax 02 31 22 90 21

De France
13 r. E. Demagny – ☎ 02 31 22 00 33 – www.hotel-france-isigny.com – hotels.france.isigny@wanadoo.fr – Fax 02 31 22 79 19 – Closed 21 December-3 January, Friday dinner, Saturday lunch and Sunday dinner from October to March
18 rm – 🚹€ 50/58 🚹🚹€ 59, ☕ € 8
Rest – Menu (€ 12), € 15 bi (weekday lunch), € 20/30 – Carte € 20/32
◆ On the main street of this small town specialising in dairy produce, is this old hotel built around a courtyard. Spruced up, simple and well-kept guestrooms. Traditional dishes, fish and seafood (including local oysters) served in two neat dining rooms.

L'ISLE-ADAM – 95 Val-d'Oise – **305** E6 – **pop. 11 200** – **alt. 28 m** 18 **B1**
– ✉ **95290** **Northern France and the Paris Region**

▶ Paris 41 – Beauvais 49 – Chantilly 24 – Compiègne 66 – Pontoise 13 – Taverny 16

ℹ Office de tourisme, 46, Grande Rue ☎ 01 34 69 41 99, Fax 01 34 08 09 79

18 de l'Isle-Adam 1 chemin des Vanneaux, NE : 5 km, ☎ 01 34 08 11 11

27 Les Golfs de Mont Griffon Luzarches Route Départementale 909, NE : 5 km, ☎ 01 34 68 10 10

18 Paris International Golf Club Baillet-en-France 18 route du Golf, SE : 15 km on D 301, ☎ 01 34 69 90 00

👁 Pulpit★ of St-Martin church.

Maison Delaleu without rest
131 av. Foch, in Parmain, 2 km west – ☎ 01 34 73 02 92 – chambresdhotes.parmain@wanadoo.fr – Fax 01 34 08 80 76
4 rm ☕ – 🚹€ 44 🚹🚹€ 57
◆ Ideally situated to discover the Vexin region, this hotel is part of a farm estate still in operation. Spacious, low-key rooms and a lively breakfast around a large table.

Le Gai Rivage
11 r. de Conti – ☎ 01 34 69 01 09 – www.legairivage.com – contact@legairivage.com – Closed 24 August-9 September, 26 December-7 January, 16 February-4 March, Sunday dinner, Tuesday dinner and Monday
Rest – Menu € 36 (weekdays)/40 – Carte € 50/70
◆ The restaurant is located on an island. Its bay windows and charming terrace offer a view of the passing boats on the Oise. Traditional cuisine.

X **Le Relais Fleuri**

61 bis r. St-Lazare – ✆ 01 34 69 01 85 – Closed 3-28 August, Sunday dinner, Monday dinner, Wednesday dinner and Tuesday
Rest – Menu € 24/31
◆ This family inn sports three styles: rustic dining room, Regency sitting room and a veranda in a more modern style. Classic repertoire served under lime trees in fine weather.

L'ISLE-D'ABEAU – 38 Isère – 333 E4 – pop. 15 000 – alt. 265 m – ✉ 38080 44 B2

Paris 499 – Bourgoin-Jallieu 6 – Grenoble 72 – Lyon 38 – La Tour du Pin 21

XX **Le Relais du Çatey** with rm

10 r. Didier, (in the village) – ✆ 04 74 18 26 50 – www.le-relais-du-catey.com – relais.du.catey@orange.fr – Fax 04 74 18 26 59 – Closed 1st-25 August, 27 December-4 January
7 rm – €59/70 €59/70, € 8 – ½ P € 52/57
Rest – *(closed Sunday and Monday)*
Menu € 22 (weekday lunch), € 32/55 – Carte € 37/52
◆ The contemporary decor and lighting emphasise the preserved character of this Dauphinois house built in 1774. Lush green terrace. Modern cuisine. Pretty rooms.

in l'Isle-d'Abeau-Ville-Nouvelle West: 4 km by N 6 – ✉ 38080 L'Isle-d'Abeau – pop. 38 769

Mercure rm,

20 r. Condorcet – ✆ 04 74 96 80 00 – H1132@accor.com – Fax 04 74 96 80 99
189 rm – € 103/145 € 129/160, € 12 – 40 suites
Rest *La Belle Époque* – *(closed 19 July-25 August, Saturday and Sunday from May to August)* Menu (€ 20), € 25 – Carte € 29/46
Rest *New Sunset* – brasserie *(Closed Friday dinner, Saturday and Sunday from October to March)* Menu (€ 12,50), € 17 – Carte € 25/35
◆ This Mercure hotel was built according to Feng Shui principles to ensure the well being and tranquillity of its guests. It has a fitness centre and a full range of sports facilities. Refurbished rooms. Traditional cuisine is to be found at La Belle Époque. Brasserie menu at the New Sunset piano bar.

L'ISLE-JOURDAIN – 32 Gers – 336 I8 – pop. 6 148 – alt. 116 m – ✉ 32600 Languedoc-Roussillon-Tarn Gorges 28 B2

Paris 682 – Toulouse 37 – Auch 45 – Montauban 58
Office de tourisme, route de Mauvezin ✆ 05 62 07 25 57, Fax 05 62 07 24 81
Las Martines Route de Saint Livrade, N : 4 km, ✆ 05 62 07 27 12
du Château de Barbet Lombez Route de Boulogne, SW : 25 km on D 634, ✆ 05 62 62 08 54
Centre-musée européen d'art campanaire (European Bell-making Museum and Centre)-★.

in Pujaudran East: 8 km by N 124 – pop. 1 167 – alt. 302 m – ✉ 32600

XXX **Le Puits St-Jacques** (Bernard Bach)

av. Victor Capoul – ✆ 05 62 07 41 11 – www.lepuitssaintjacques.com – lepuitsstjacques@free.fr – Fax 05 62 07 44 09 – Closed 30 August-16 September, 1st-20 January, Tuesday except dinner in November, Sunday dinner and Monday
Rest – *(pre-book Sat - Sun)* Menu € 27 (weekday lunch), € 58/95 – Carte € 82/95
Spec. Tronçon de lobe de foie gras pané au pain d'épice. Pigeonneau en deux cuissons et jus réglissé. Véritable chocolat liégeois servi devant vous. **Wines** Vin de Pays des Côtes de Gascogne, Pacherenc du Vic-Bihl.
◆ This typical Gers-style house, a former staging-post on the road to Compostelle, is now home to an elegant restaurant and a patio with a Mediterranean feel. Delicate modern cuisine, inspired by the region.

L'ISLE-JOURDAIN – 86 Vienne – 322 K7 – pop. 1 287 – alt. 142 m – ✉ 86150 Atlantic Coast 39 C2

Paris 375 – Confolens 29 – Niort 104 – Poitiers 53

Syndicat d'initiative, place de l'Ancienne Gare ✆ 05 49 48 80 36, Fax 05 49 48 80 36

in Port de Salles South: 7 km by D 8 and secondary road – ✉ 86150

Val de Vienne without rest

– ✆ 05 49 48 27 27 – www.hotel-valdevienne.com – info@hotel-valdevienne.com – Fax 05 49 48 47 47

20 rm – †€ 65/88 ††€ 65/88, ☕ € 12 – 1 suite

◆ Deep in the countryside, on the banks of the Vienne, this hotel provides quiet and functional rooms with terraces. Pleasant lounge bar on the veranda overlooking the pool.

L'ISLE-SUR-LA-SORGUE – 84 Vaucluse – 332 D10 – pop. 16 900 – alt. 57 m – ✉ 84800 Provence 42 E1

Paris 693 – Apt 34 – Avignon 23 – Carpentras 18 – Cavaillon 11 – Orange 35

Office de tourisme, place de la Liberté ✆ 04 90 38 04 78, Fax 04 90 38 35 43

Decoration ★ of Notre-Dame des Anges collegiate church.

★ du Thor church West: 5 km.

Les Névons without rest

chemin des Névons, (behind the mail) – ✆ 04 90 20 72 00 – www.hotel-les-nevons.com – info@hotel-les-nevons.com – Fax 04 90 20 56 20 – Closed 13 December-25 January

44 rm – †€ 51/92 ††€ 51/92, ☕ € 8,50

◆ Town centre hotel with functional rooms. Those in the second building are more spacious and modern; some have a balcony. Rooftop sundeck and pool.

XX **La Prévôté** with rm rest,

4 bis r. J.-J.-Rousseau, (behind the church) – ✆ 04 90 38 57 29 – www.la-prevote.fr – contact@la-prevote.fr – Fax 04 90 38 57 29 – Closed 1st-13 March, 17 November-5 December, Wednesday except July-August and Tuesday

5 rm ☕ – †€ 110/130 ††€ 110/200

Rest – *(number of covers limited, pre-book)*

Menu (€ 20), € 26 (weekday lunch), € 39/68 – Carte approx. € 60

◆ Set in a 17C convent on a branch of the River Sorgue, this restaurant, home to an old public washhouse, is a picture of rustic calm overlooking the river. Individualised rooms.

XX **L'Oustau de l'Isle**

147 Chemin du Bosquet, 1 km via Apt road – ✆ 04 90 20 81 36 – www.restaurant-oustau.com – contact@restaurant-oustau.com – Fax 04 90 38 50 07 – Closed 12 November-4 December, 18 January-5 February, Wednesday except dinner from mid-June to mid-September and Tuesday

Rest – Menu (€ 18), € 29/50 – Carte € 35/89

◆ This farmhouse surrounded by greenery boasts an attractive shaded terrace. It has two uncluttered dining areas with large scale Modigliani reproductions. Tasty regional cuisine.

XX **Le Vivier** (Patrick Fischnaller)

800 cours F. Peyre (Carpentras road) – ✆ 04 90 38 52 80 – www.levivier-restaurant.com – info.levivier@wanadoo.fr – Closed 28 August-4 September, 2-6 January, 24 February-17 March, Thursday lunch in July-August, Sunday dinner from September to June, Friday lunch, Saturday lunch and Monday

Rest – Menu € 28 (weekday lunch), € 43/70 – Carte € 48/68

Spec. Assiette façon "tapas". Pithiviers de pigeon des Costières, cèpes et foie gras. Dessert "tout chocolat". **Wines** Côtes du Luberon, Vin de table des Bouches du Rhône.

◆ Very modern, delicate cuisine is the order of the day in this designer-style restaurant with bright colour scheme and windows overlooking the Sorgue. Charming service.

Café Fleurs
9 r. T.-Aubanel – ✆ 04 90 20 66 94 – www.cafefleurs.com – contact@cafefleurs.com – Fax 04 90 21 14 87 – Closed 3 weeks in December, 2 weeks in February, Tuesday dinner and Wednesday
Rest – Menu (€ 25), € 39/55 – Carte € 48/68
◆ Two cosy dining rooms with refined Provencal décor (exhibition of local works of art), and a pleasant shaded terrace at the water's edge: this contemporary restaurant is charming.

Le Jardin du Quai
91 av. J. Guigue, (near the station) – ✆ 04 90 20 14 98 – Fax 04 90 20 31 92 – Closed Tuesday and Wednesday except from mid-June to mid-September
Rest – Menu € 35 (weekday lunch)/43
◆ With its garden-terrace, this bistrot recalls the charm of the Provence of a bygone era. Set menu based on market produce, simply prepared.

North by D 938 and secondary road – ✉ 84740 Velleron

Hostellerie La Grangette rest,
807 chemin Cambuisson, 6 km – ✆ 04 90 20 00 77 – www.la-grangette-provence.com – hostellerie-la-grangette@club-internet.fr – Fax 04 90 20 07 06 – Open 13 February-10 November
16 rm – €95/228 €95/228 – ½ P € 98/164
Rest – *(closed Monday except from June to September) (dinner only) (number of covers limited, pre-book)* Menu € 55 – Carte € 30/60
◆ A Provencal farmhouse with a lively but refined atmosphere. Rooms with a stylish decor and fine bed linen: everything you need for a peaceful stay. Non-smokers only. Sun drenched regional cuisine served in a cosy dining room or outdoors in summer.

Apt road Southeast: 6 km by D 900 – ✉ 84800 L'Isle-sur-la-Sorgue

Le Mas des Grès rm,
D 901 – ✆ 04 90 20 32 85 – www.masdesgres.com – info@masdesgres.com – Fax 04 90 20 21 45 – Open 20 March-11 November
14 rm – €80/150 €120/230, € 12 – ½ P € 90/145
Rest – *(dinner only except July-August) (pre-book)* Menu € 22 (lunch)/38
◆ This tastefully restored Provençal farmhouse is a picture of relaxation and rest, with garden, shaded terrace, children's play area, gym and spa. Spruce personalised rooms. The tables are laid under the arbour or plane trees. Market fresh cuisine.

Southwest 4 km by D 938 (Cavaillon road) and secondary road – ✉ 84800 L'Isle-sur-la-Sorgue

Mas de Cure Bourse
120 chemin de serre – ✆ 04 90 38 16 58 – www.masdecurebourse.com – masdecurebourse@wanadoo.fr – Fax 04 90 38 52 31
13 rm – €44/63 €87/125, € 10 – ½ P € 75/112
Rest – *(closed 1st-15 January, Monday from November to February)* Menu (€ 27), € 48/51 – Carte € 43/51
◆ Peace and quiet reign in this authentic 18C farmhouse hidden among the orchards. Rustic interior, impeccable rooms, pool and a shaded garden. Southern cuisine in the Provençal dining room or under the ancient trees on the terrace.

L'ISLE-SUR-SEREIN – 89 Yonne – 319 H6 – pop. 758 – alt. 190 m – ✉ 89440 7 B2

Paris 209 – Auxerre 50 – Avallon 17 – Montbard 36 – Tonnerre 36

Auberge du Pot d'Étain with rm
24 r. Bouchardat – ✆ 03 86 33 88 10 – potdetain@ipoint.fr – Fax 03 86 33 90 93 – Closed 12-27 October, February, Sunday dinner and Tuesday lunch except July-August and Monday
9 rm – €60/80 €60/80, € 8,50 – ½ P € 65
Rest – Menu € 26/52 – Carte € 45/60
◆ Regional cuisine, wide choice of Burgundy wines and charming colourful rooms. A delightful inn in the peaceful Serein valley, easily accessible from the A6 motorway!

ISPE – 40 Landes – **335** D8 – see Biscarrosse

LES ISSAMBRES – 83 Var – **340** P5 – ✉ 83380 ▮ French Riviera 41 **C3**

▶ Paris 877 – Draguignan 40 – Fréjus 11 – St-Raphaël 14 – Ste-Maxime 9 – Toulon 99

ℹ Office de tourisme, place San-Peire ☎ 04 94 49 66 55

in San-Peire-sur-Mer – ✉ 83520

Le Provençal rm, P VISA MC AE

D 559 – ☎ 04 94 55 32 33 – www.hotel-leprovencal.com – hotel-le-provencal@wanadoo.fr – Fax 04 94 55 32 34 – Open 15 February-15 October

27 rm – †€ 79/108 ††€ 97/134, ☕ € 12 – ½ P € 73/98

Rest ***Les Mûriers*** – *(closed Tuesday lunch in July-August)* Menu € 29/65 – Carte € 50/100

◆ In the Gulf of St Tropez, this family-run hotel is now managed by the fourth generation. Practical rooms, some with sea views (and some with balconies); quieter to the rear. Mediterranean cuisine served in a Provençal dining room or in the shade of the terrace's mulberry trees.

at parc des Issambres – ✉ 83380 Les Issambres

La Quiétude rm, P VISA MC

D 559 – ☎ 0494969434 – www.hotel-laquietude.com – laquietude@hotmail.com – Fax 04 94 49 67 82 – Open 15 March-15 November

20 rm – †€ 50/75 ††€ 62/99, ☕ € 10 – ½ P € 62/80

Rest – *(dinner only except Sunday)* Menu € 28/38 – Carte € 36/46

◆ This 1960s house is set in a small garden by a busy road. Functional and colourful guestrooms; a few have views of the open sea. Enjoy a quiet meal overlooking the sea from the restaurant terrace. The simple menu is focused on tradition and southern flavours.

in la calanque des Issambres – ✉ 83380 Les Issambres

XX **Chante-Mer** VISA MC

au village – ☎ 04 94 96 93 23 – Fax 04 94 96 88 49 – Closed 15 December-31 January, Sunday dinner from October to Easter, Tuesday lunch and Monday in low season

Rest – Menu € 24/45 – Carte € 46/72

◆ Far from the tourist bustle, this friendly establishment serves traditional fare. Small, inviting dining room with light wooden wainscoting and summer terrace at the front.

ISSOIRE – 63 Puy-de-Dôme – **326** G9 – **pop. 14 200 – alt. 400 m** – ✉ 63500 ▮ Auvergne 5 **B2**

▶ Paris 446 – Clermont-Ferrand 36 – Le Puy-en-Velay 94 – Thiers 56

ℹ Office de tourisme, place Charles de Gaulle ☎ 04 73 89 15 90, Fax 04 73 89 96 13

◎ Former St-Austremoine abbey church ★★ Z.

Plan on next page

Le Pariou P VISA MC AE

18 av. Kennedy, 1 km via ① – ☎ 04 73 55 90 37 – www.hotel-pariou.com – info@hotel-pariou.com – Fax 04 73 55 96 16 – Closed 19 December-4 January

54 rm – †€ 65/85 ††€ 70/85, ☕ € 10

Rest ***Le Jardin*** – *(closed Sunday and Monday)* Menu (€ 16), € 21 (weekdays)/40 – Carte € 34/43

◆ 1950s building with guestrooms that that are gradually being renovated. Modern furniture, with rooms in the new wing offering more space. Two dining rooms, one painted in southern colours and overlooking the garden. Modern food.

X **Le Relais** with rm VISA MC

1 av. de la Gare – ☎ 04 73 89 16 61 – www.hotel-relais-issoire.com – lerelais-issoire@laposte.net – Fax 04 73 89 55 62 – Closed 25-30 June, 25 October-5 November, 15-28 February, Sunday dinner from November to June and Monday

6 rm – †€ 36/48 ††€ 36/58, ☕ € 6,50 – ½ P € 40/50 YZ **a**

Rest – Menu € 13 (weekdays)/31 – Carte € 23/39

◆ Former post house, a stone's throw from St. Austremoine abbey church. Spacious and colourful dining room. Traditional cuisine and regional specialities. Small rooms.

ISSOIRE

Street	Zone	No.
Altaroche (Pl.)	Z	2
Ambert (R. d')	Y	
Ancienne Caserne (R. de l')	Z	3
Berbiziale (R. de la)	Y	
Buisson (Bd A.)	Y	
Cerf Volant (R. du)	Y	4
Châteaudun (R. de)	Z	5
Cibrand (Bd J.)	Y	
Dr-Sauvat (R.)	Z	
Duprat (Pl. Ch.)	Y	
Espagnon (R. d')	Z	
Foirail (Pl. du)	Y	
Fours (R. des)	Z	
Gambetta (R.)	Z	6
Gare (Av. de la)	Z	9
Gaulle (Pl. du Gén.-de)	Y	
Gauttier (R. Eugène)	Y	
Haïnl (Bd G.)	Z	
Hauterive (R. E. d')	Z	
Libération (Av. de la)	Z	10
Manlière (Bd de la)	Z	
Mas (R. du)	Y	
Montagne (Pl. de la)	Y	
Notre-Dame des Filles (R.)	Z	12
Palais (R. du)	Y	
Pomel (Pl. N.)	Z	13
Ponteil (R. du)	Y	16
Pont (R. du)	Z	14
Postillon (R. du)	Z	
République (Pl. de la)	Z	
St-Avit (Pl.)	Y	22
Sous-Préfecture (Bd de la)	Z	
Terraille (R. de la)	Z	24
Triozon-Bayle (Bd)	YZ	25
Verdun (Pl. de)	Z	26
8 Mai (Av. du)	Y	30

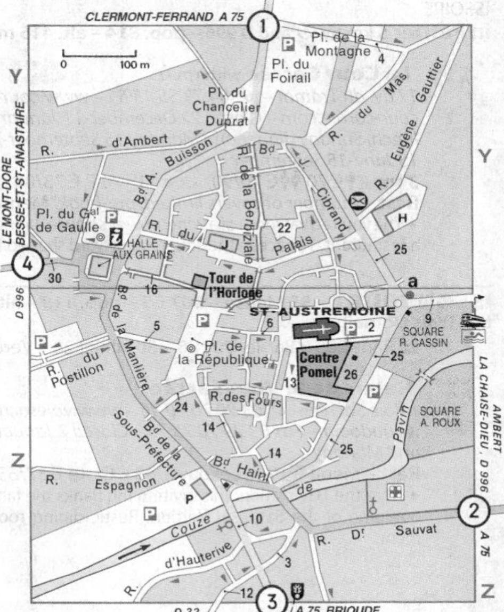

in Varennes-sur-Usson 5 km by ② and D 996 – pop. 155 – alt. 315 m – ✉ 63500

Les Baudarts without rest
17 chemin des Baudarts – ✆ 04 73 89 05 51 – Open 1st May-30 September
4 rm – €65/70 €80/85
♦ This impressive manor set in a park proudly displays artwork throughout the house. Rooms in three themes – Africa, Teddy Bear and Lace, and Loft.

in St-Rémy-de-Chargnat 7 km by ② and D 999 – pop. 550 – alt. 400 m – ✉ 63500

Château de la Vernède without rest
– ✆ 04 73 71 07 03 – www.chateauvernedeauvergne.com – chateauvernede@aol.com
5 rm – €68 €68/100
♦ This former hunting lodge (1850) once owned by Queen Margot is now home to guestrooms adorned with antique furnishings and fresh flowers. Leisure activities include billiards and trout fishing.

in Sarpoil 10 km by ② and D 999 – ✉ 63490 St-Jean-en-Val

XX **La Bergerie** VISA
– ✆ 04 73 71 02 54 – www.labergeriedesarpoil.com – cyrille.zen@wanadoo.fr – Fax 04 73 71 01 99 – Closed 8-14 June, 14-21 September, 2 January-1st February, Wednesday from 15 October to 30 March, Sunday dinner and Monday
Rest – *(number of covers limited, pre-book)* Menu € 16 (weekday lunch), € 22/68 – Carte € 43/71
♦ Catch an enticing glimpse of the kitchens and rotisserie as you enter this restaurant. Classic dining room with an open fire in winter and a menu focusing on contemporary dishes.

in Perrier 5 km by ④ and D 996 – **pop. 814** – **alt. 415 m** – ✉ **63500**

XX **La Cour Carrée** with rm — rm, VISA AE
17 av. du Tramot – ✆ 04 73 55 15 55 – www.cour-carree.com – contact@cour-carree.com – Closed 22 December-11 January, Wednesday lunch, Saturday lunch, Sunday dinner and Monday 15 September-15 June and lunch except Sunday 15 June-15 September
3 rm – €70 €70/90, €11 – ½ P €73/83
Rest – *(number of covers limited, pre-book)* Menu €28/40
◆ The vaulted vat room of a winegrower's house dating from 1830 has been converted into a restaurant. Terrace in the square courtyard shaded by a horse chestnut tree.

ISSONCOURT – 55 Meuse – 307 C5 – pop. 119 – alt. 260 m – ✉ 55220 — 26 A2
Les Trois Domaines

Paris 265 – Bar-le-Duc 28 – St-Mihiel 28 – Verdun 28

XX **Relais de la Voie Sacrée** — VISA AE
1 Voie Sacrée – ✆ 03 29 70 70 46 – www.voiesacree.com – christian-caillet@wanadoo.fr – Fax 03 29 70 75 75 – Closed 2 January-13 February, Sunday dinner and Monday
Rest – Menu €19 (weekdays)/48 – Carte €37/65
◆ Near the TGV station, this inviting inn flanks the famous Holy Way, which changed the outcome of the Battle of Verdun. Rustic dining room, shaded terrace and traditional menu.

Good food and accommodation at moderate prices?
Look for the Bib symbols: red Bib Gourmand for food,
blue Bib Hotel for hotels.

ISSOUDUN – 36 Indre – 323 H5 – pop. 14 100 – alt. 130 m – ✉ 36100 Dordogne-Berry-Limousin — 12 C3

Paris 244 – Bourges 37 – Châteauroux 29 – Tours 127 – Vierzon 35
Syndicat d'initiative, place Saint-Cyr ✆ 02 54 21 74 02, Fax 02 54 03 03 36
des Sarrays Les Sarrays, SW : 12 km on D 151 and minor road, ✆ 02 54 49 54 49
Musée de l'hospice St-Roch★ : Jesse tree ★ in the chapel and apothecary's ★ AB.

Plan on next page

Hôtel La Cognette — VISA AE
r. des Minimes – ✆ 02 54 03 59 59 – www.la-cognette.com – lacognettehotel@wanadoo.fr – Fax 02 54 03 13 03 — A e
13 rm – €85 €85, €13 – 3 suites
Rest *La Cognette* – see below
◆ Comfortable rooms with period furniture, named after famous people. Most of them are on the level of the small garden, where breakfast is served in summer.

XXX **Rest. La Cognette** (Alain Nonnet et Jean-Jacques Daumy) — VISA AE
bd Stalingrad – ✆ 02 54 03 59 59 – www.la-cognette.com – lacognette@wanadoo.fr – Fax 02 54 03 13 03 – Closed January, Sunday dinner, Tuesday lunch and Monday from October to May — A z
Rest – *(pre-book)* Menu (€27), €35/72 – Carte €45/75
Spec. Crème de lentilles vertes du Berry aux truffes. Cannelloni d'huîtres, jus de cresson et gingembre. Massepain d'Issoudun à la fleur d'oranger. **Wines** Reuilly, Quincy.
◆ This inn was the inspiration for Balzac's "La Rabouilleuse". It boasts a rich, refined decor, typical of the 19C, and perfectly in tune with the elegant cuisine.

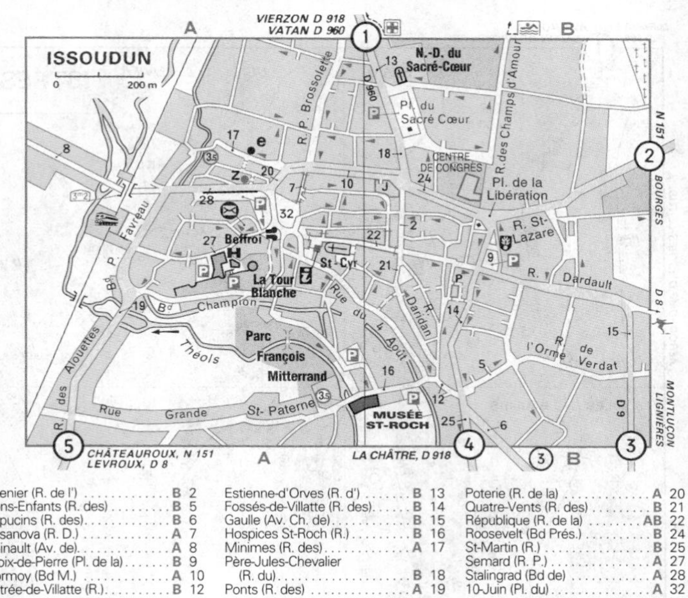

in Diou by ①: 12 km on D 918 – pop. 235 – alt. 130 m – ✉ 36260

XX **L'Aubergeade**
rte d'Issoudun – ✆ *02 54 49 22 28 – jacky.patron@wanadoo.fr*
– Fax 02 54 49 27 48 – Closed Sunday dinner and Wednesday dinner
Rest – Menu € 20 (weekday lunch), € 30/40 – Carte € 42/51
◆ The wine list at the Aubergeade offers a delicious little tour around the world of wine. Cuisine in keeping with modern tastes and terrace overlooking the garden.

IS-SUR-TILLE – 21 Côte-d'Or – 320 K4 – pop. 3 824 – alt. 284 m – ✉ 21120 — 8 C2

▶ Paris 332 – Dijon 30 – Chenôve 43 – Talant 32 – Chevigny-Saint-Sauveur 45

ℹ Office de tourisme, rue du Général Charbonnel ✆ 03 80 95 24 03, Fax 03 80 95 28 08

Auberge Côté Rivière
3 r. des Capucins – ✆ *03 80 95 65 40 – www.auberge-cote-riviere.com*
– cote.riviere@wanadoo.fr – Fax 03 80 95 65 41
– Closed 1 week in August and 1 week in January
9 rm – †€ 75 ††€ 75, ☕ € 8,50
Rest – *(closed Sunday and Monday)* Menu € 19 (weekday lunch), € 29/60 – Carte approx. € 42
◆ Two buildings surrounded by a riverside garden. The fully refurbished bourgeois house is home to contemporary guestrooms. The restaurant, in a farmhouse, has lost nothing of its former charm despite its modern decor. Traditional dishes.

ISSY-LES-MOULINEAUX – 92 Hauts-de-Seine – 311 J3 – 101 25 – see Paris, Area

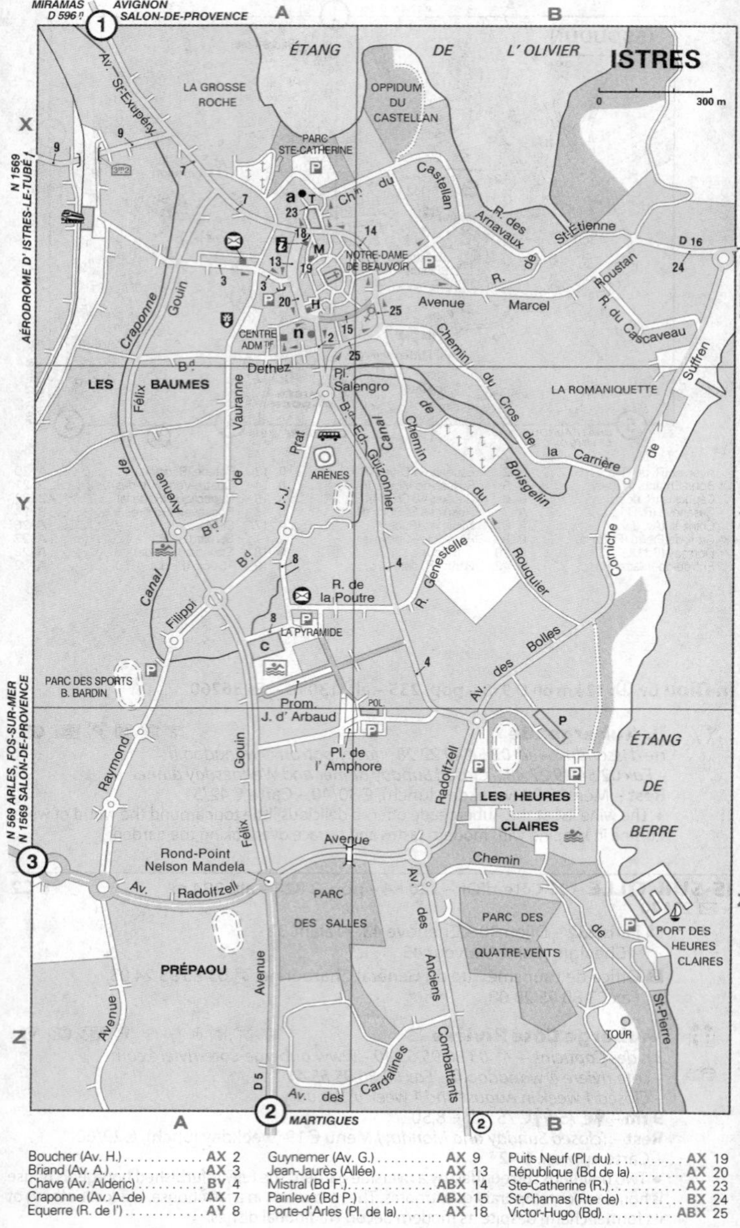

Boucher (Av. H.) . . . . **AX** 2	Guynemer (Av. G.) . . . . **AX** 9	Puits Neuf (Pl. du) . . . . **AX** 19
Briand (Av. A.) . . . . **AX** 3	Jean-Jaurès (Allée) . . . . **AX** 13	République (Bd de la) . . . . . . **AX** 20
Chave (Av. Alderic) . . . . **BY** 4	Mistral (Bd F.) . . . . **ABX** 14	Ste-Catherine (R.) . . . . **AX** 23
Craponne (Av. A.-de) . . . . **AX** 7	Painlevé (Bd P.) . . . . **ABX** 15	St-Chamas (Rte de) . . . . **BX** 24
Equerre (R. de l') . . . . **AY** 8	Porte-d'Arles (Pl. de la) . . . . . . **AX** 18	Victor-Hugo (Bd) . . . . **ABX** 25

ISTRES – 13 Bouches-du-Rhône – **340** E5 – **pop. 41 200 – alt. 32 m** 40 **A3**
– ✉ **13800** Provence

Paris 745 – Arles 46 – Marseille 55 – Martigues 14 – Salon-de-Provence 25

Office de tourisme, 30, allées Jean Jaurés ☎ 04 42 81 76 00, Fax 04 42 81 76 15

Plan on previous page

Le Castellan without rest
15 bd L. Blum – ☎ 04 42 55 13 09 – www.hotel-lecastellan.com – renseignements@hotel-lecastellan.com – Fax 04 42 56 91 36 AX **a**
17 rm – €49/52 €58/62, €6,50
◆ Close to the Greco-Ligurian Place du Castellan. Rooms are spacious and airy, some decorated in Provençal style. A friendly welcome at this impeccably well-kept hotel.

La Table de Sébastien
7 av. H.-Boucher – ☎ 04 42 55 16 01 – www.latabledesebastien.fr – contact@latabledesebastien.fr – Fax 04 42 55 95 02 – Closed 6-13 April, 18-31 August, 22 December-3 January, Sunday dinner and Monday AX **n**
Rest – Menu €28/103 bi – Carte €55/65
◆ Deliciously inventive cuisine prepared by a young chef and complemented by a fine selection of regional wines. Choose between the renovated dining room or the shaded courtyard terrace.

North 4 km by ③, N 569 and secondary road – ✉ **13800 Istres**

Ariane without rest
12 av. de Flore – ☎ 04 42 11 13 13 – www.arianehotel-istres.com – contact@arianehotel.com – Fax 04 42 11 13 00
73 rm – €78/93 €83/98, €11
◆ This modern hotel provides comfortable rooms, some with kitchenette or a terrace overlooking the pool. Also providing simple accommodation in the second building.

ITTERSWILLER – 67 Bas-Rhin – **315** I6 – **pop. 275 – alt. 235 m** 2 **C1**
– ✉ **67140** Alsace-Lorraine

Paris 502 – Erstein 25 – Mittelbergheim 5 – Molsheim 26 – Sélestat 16 – Strasbourg 45

Syndicat d'initiative, Mairie ☎ 03 88 85 50 12, Fax 03 88 85 56 09

Arnold
98 rte des vins – ☎ 03 88 85 50 58 – www.hotel-arnold.com – arnold-hotel@wanadoo.fr – Fax 03 88 85 55 54
28 rm – €80/114 €80/114, €12 – 1 suite – ½ P €79/98
Rest *Winstub Arnold* – *(closed Sunday dinner from November to May and Monday)* Menu €25 (weekdays)/60 – Carte €38/66
◆ Two fine half-timbered houses in a village on the Route des Vins (Wine Route). Smart, pine furnished rooms, most of which overlook the vineyard. The decor of the Winstub Arnold is deeply rooted in the local area. Alsatian specialities take pride of place.

ITXASSOU – 64 Pyrénées-Atlantiques – **342** D5 – **pop. 1 770 – alt. 39 m** 3 **A3**
– ✉ **64250** Atlantic Coast

Paris 787 – Bayonne 24 – Biarritz 25 – Cambo-les-Bains 5 – Pau 119 – St-Jean-de-Luz 34

Church ★.

Txistulari
– ☎ 05 59 29 75 09 – www.txistulari.fr – hotel.txistulari@wanadoo.fr – Fax 05 59 29 80 07
20 rm – €42/47 €44/54, €7
Rest – *(closed Sunday dinner and Saturday lunch off season)*
Menu €13 (weekday lunch), €17/31 – Carte €20/30
◆ The hotel is just beyond the narrow road leading to Pas de Roland. Simple, well-kept rooms; peaceful green surroundings. If the weather is fine, eat your meals under a covered terrace; otherwise opt for the large, colourful dining room.

Le Chêne

near the church – ✆ 05 59 29 75 01 – hotel.chene.itxassou@wanadoo.fr – Fax 05 59 29 27 39 – Closed 14 December-27 February, Tuesday except from July to September and Monday

16 rm – €36/42 €48/54, €7 – ½ P €49/55

Rest – Menu €18/35 – Carte €29/50

◆ This pretty inn opposite the village church has been welcoming travellers since 1696. Old, but well-kept rooms. Brick tiles, coloured beams and regional-style tablecloths decorate this restaurant. Cuisine dedicated to Basque Country. Lovely terrace.

Du Fronton rm, rest,

– ✆ 05 59 29 75 10 – www.hotelrestaurantfronton.com – reservation@hotelrestaurantfronton.com – Fax 05 59 29 23 50 – Closed 17-22 November, 1st January-15 February and Wednesday

23 rm – €48/68 €48/68 – ½ P €50/60

Rest – Menu €21/35 – Carte €37/55

◆ A Basque-style house backing onto the village pelota wall. The old rooms have been redecorated, while those in the new wing are larger. Country-style dining room looking out over the Itxassou hills where you can try the famous black cherry jam.

IVOY-LE-PRÉ – 18 Cher – pop. 873 – alt. 276 m – ✉ 18380 12 C2

Paris 202 – Orléans 105 – Bourges 38 – Vierzon 41 – Gien 47

Château d'Ivoy without rest

rte d'Henrichemont – ✆ 02 48 58 85 01 – www.chateaudivoy.com – chateau.divoy@wanadoo.fr – Fax 02 48 58 85 02

5 rm – €150 €195

◆ This 16-17C château in the heart of a preserved estate comes with a history: Henri IV stayed here and Le Grand Meaulnes was filmed here. English manor house feel.

IVRY-LA-BATAILLE – 27 Eure – 304 I8 – pop. 2 653 – alt. 54 m – ✉ 27540 Normandy 33 D2

Paris 75 – Anet 6 – Dreux 21 – Évreux 36 – Mantes-la-Jolie 25 – Pacy-sur-Eure 17

de La Chaussée d'Ivry La Chaussée-d'Ivry, N : 2 km, ✆ 02 37 63 06 30

Moulin d'Ivry

10 r. Henri IV – ✆ 02 32 36 40 51 – Fax 02 32 26 05 15 – Closed 7-20 October, 10 February-2 March, Monday and Tuesday except bank holidays

Rest – Menu €30 (weekdays)/50 – Carte €65/90

◆ An old mill with several small country-style rooms, with a deliberately antiquated charm. A garden and terrace pleasantly situated on the banks of the River Eure. Classic dishes.

JANVRY – 91 Essonne – 101 33 – see Paris, Area

JARNAC – 16 Charente – 324 I5 – pop. 4 508 – alt. 26 m – ✉ 16200 Atlantic Coast 38 B3

Paris 475 – Angoulême 31 – Barbezieux 30 – Bordeaux 113 – Cognac 15 – Jonzac 41

Office de tourisme, place du Château ✆ 05 45 81 09 30, Fax 05 45 36 52 45

Donation François-Mitterrand - Courvoisier House - Louis-Royer House

Château St-Martial without rest

56 r. des Chabannes – ✆ 05 45 83 38 64 – http://chateau.st.martial.free.fr – brigitte.cariou@wanadoo.fr – Fax 05 45 83 38 38 – Closed 1st-9 March, 23 October-1st November, 18-27 December and 6-22 February

5 rm – €75/115 €90/135

◆ The Bisquit family, famous for its cognac, lived in this splendid 19C chateau. Paintings, period furniture, spacious comfortable rooms and pleasant wooded park.

Du Château

15 pl. du Château – 05 45 81 07 17 – www.restaurant-du-chateau.com – contact@restaurant-du-chateau.com – Fax 05 45 35 35 71 – Closed Sunday dinner and Monday

Rest – Menu (€ 25), € 29 (lunch), € 44/73 bi – Carte € 58/64

◆ Friendly restaurant next-door to the storehouse of the Maison Courvoisier. The local-born chef selects excellent regional produce for his high-quality cuisine.

in Bourg-Charente **West: 6 km by N 141 and secondary road – pop. 710 – alt. 14 m – ✉ 16200**

La Ribaudière (Thierry Verrat)

2 pl. du port – 05 45 81 30 54 – www.laribaudiere.com – la.ribaudiere@wanadoo.fr – Fax 05 45 81 28 05 – Closed 20 October-7 November, February school holidays, Sunday dinner, Tuesday lunch and Monday

Rest – Menu € 42/78 – Carte € 75/90

Spec. Escalope de foie gras poêlé, créme de cèpes et lard "noir de Bigorre" séché (September to December). Pavé de bar fumé aux aiguilles de pin, risotto de petites pâtes aux truffes. Sablé charentais abricot givré, mousse romarin (summer). **Wines** Vin de Pays Charentais, Fiefs Vendéens.

◆ Refined contemporary décor, designer furniture, cognathèque (cognac shop), fine modern cuisine, split level terraces overlooking the water: come and eat on the left bank... of the Charente!

in Bassac **Southeast: 7 km by N 141 and D 22 – pop. 461 – alt. 20 m – ✉ 16120**

L'Essille

r. de Condé – 05 45 81 94 13 – hotel-restaurant-essille.com – l.essille@wanadoo.fr – Fax 05 45 81 97 26 – Closed 1st-8 January

14 rm – € 52/70 € 52/70, € 9 – ½ P € 61/70

Rest – *(closed Saturday lunch and Sunday dinner)*

Menu € 16 (weekday lunch), € 26/45 – Carte € 43/49

◆ Family run hotel with a charming welcome, a stone's throw from the abbey. Spacious revamped rooms with period furniture. Dining room-veranda overlooking the park; traditional cuisine and fine cognac list (over 100 choices).

JARVILLE-LA-MALGRANGE – 54 Meurthe-et-Moselle – 307 I6 – see Nancy

---

JAUJAC – 07 Ardèche – 331 H6 – pop. 1 181 – alt. 450 m – ✉ 07380 44 A3

Lyon - Rhone Valley

Paris 616 – Lyon 185 – Montélimar 59 – Pierrelatte 71

Syndicat d'initiative, La Calade 04 75 93 28 54, Fax 04 75 93 28 54

Le Rucher des Roudils without rest

Les Roudils, 4 km north-west – 04 75 93 21 11 – www.lesroudils.com – le-rucher-des-roudils@wanadoo.fr – Open 2 April-14 November

3 rm – € 58 € 60

◆ This hotel overlooks the Tanargue mountains, with charming rooms and a lounge with a Cevennes-style fireplace.

JAUSIERS – 04 Alpes-de-Haute-Provence – 334 I6 – see Barcelonnette

---

JERSEY (ÎLE) – JSY Jersey – 309 J1 – see Île de Jersey

JOIGNY – 89 Yonne – 319 D4 – pop. 10 100 – alt. 79 m – ✉ 89300 7 B1

Burgundy-Jura

Paris 144 – Auxerre 28 – Gien 74 – Montargis 59 – Sens 33 – Troyes 76

Office de tourisme, 4, quai Ragobert 03 86 62 11 05, Fax 03 86 91 76 38

du Roncemay Chassy Château du Roncemay, 18 km on the Montargis road, 03 86 73 50 50

Smiling Virgin ★ in St-Thibault church A E - Côte St-Jacques ★ ★ 1,5 km by D 20 A.

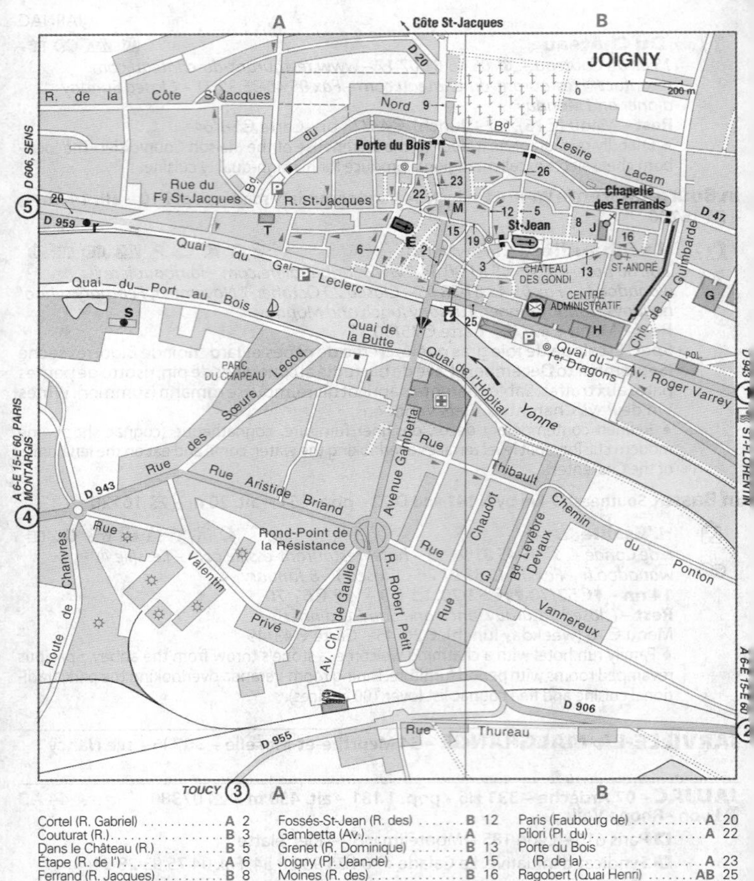

Cortel (R. Gabriel)	A	2
Couturat (R.)	B	3
Dans le Château (R.)	B	5
Étape (R. de l')	A	6
Ferrand (R. Jacques)	B	8
Forêt d'Othe (Av. de la)	A	9
Fossés-St-Jean (R. des)	B	12
Gambetta (Av.)	A	
Grenet (R. Dominique)	B	13
Joigny (Pl. Jean-de)	A	15
Moines (R. des)	B	16
Montant au Palais (R.)	B	19
Paris (Faubourg de)	A	20
Pilori (Pl. du)	A	22
Porte du Bois (R. de la)	A	23
Ragobert (Quai Henri)	AB	25
Tour Carrée (R. de la)	B	26

La Côte St-Jacques (Jean-Michel Lorain)

14 fg de Paris
– *03 86 62 09 70 – www.cotesaintjacques.com – lorain@relaischateaux.com*
– *Fax 03 86 91 49 70*
– *Closed 4-28 January, Monday lunch and Tuesday lunch* A r

31 rm – € 150/600 € 150/600, € 33 – 1 suite – ½ P € 235/310

Rest – *(pre-book Sat - Sun)* Menu € 100 bi (weekday lunch), € 140/170 – Carte € 120/190

Spec. Genèse d'un plat sur le thème de l'huître. Homard servi dans un bouillon parfumé à la réglisse, mini-fenouils et perles du Japon. Glace à la rose en tulipe croustillante et pétales de rose cristallisés. **Wines** Bourgogne-Chardonnay, Irancy.

◆ A luxury hotel facing the Yonne with stylish rooms. Pool, spa, private boat (river trips) and shop. The prestigious restaurant is renowned for its creative cuisine made with only the finest produce. Sumptuous wine list. Surrounded by gardens.

Rive Gauche — rm, rest, VISA AE
r. Port-au-Bois – ✆ 03 86 91 46 66 – www.hotel-le-rive-gauche.fr – contact@hotel-le-rive-gauche.fr – Fax 03 86 91 46 93 A s
42 rm – €70/80 €70/80, ☕ €10 – ½ P €72
Rest – *(closed Sunday dinner from November to Easter)*
Menu (€17 bi), €20 (weekday lunch), €30/38 – Carte €40/50
◆ Well located on the left bank of the Yonne. Spacious, practical and light rooms. Pleasant park with ornamental lake and helicopter landing pad. The veranda/dining room and terrace both overlook the river.

JOINVILLE – 52 Haute-Marne – 313 K3 – pop. 3 809 – alt. 195 m – ✉ 52300 Northern France and the Paris Region 14 C2

Paris 244 – Bar-le-Duc 54 – Bar-sur-Aube 47 – Chaumont 44 – St-Dizier 32
Syndicat d'initiative, place Saunoise ✆ 03 25 94 17 90, Fax 03 25 94 68 93
Château du Grand Jardin★.

Le Soleil d'Or — rest, VISA
9 r. des Capucins – ✆ 03 25 94 15 66 – www.hotellesoleildor.fr – hotellesoleildor@wanadoo.fr – Fax 03 25 94 39 02
26 rm – €65/100 €75/130, ☕ €10
Rest – *(closed 16-31 August, 14-28 February, Sunday and Monday)*
Menu (€15 bi), €22 (weekdays)/45 – Carte €63/74
◆ Warm house dating back to the 17C, in the birthplace of the De Guise family. Rooms undergoing renovation in stages; plain decor that is tasteful in the most recent rooms. Neo-gothic restaurant with medieval sculpture and contemporary paintings.

JOINVILLE-LE-PONT – 94 Val-de-Marne – 312 D3 – 101 27 – see Paris, Area

---

JONGIEUX – 73 Savoie – 333 H3 – pop. 233 – alt. 300 m – ✉ 73170 45 C1

Paris 528 – Annecy 58 – Chambéry 25 – Lyon 103

Auberge Les Morainières (Michaël Arnoult) — VISA
rte de Marétel – ✆ 04 79 44 09 39 – www.les-morainieres.com – lesmorainieres@wanadoo.fr – Fax 04 79 44 09 46 – Closed 30 March-6 April, 21 September-5 October, 4-25 January, Tuesday except dinner in July-August and Monday
Rest – Menu €28 (weekday lunch), €38/68 – Carte €62/75
Spec. Foie gras chaud, rhubarbe et fleur de sureau (May to July). Dos de bar de ligne confit en écaille de truffe de Jongieux et sabayon (December to March). Tube croustillant de pêche de vigne rôtie, amande et lait battu à la verveine (July to September). **Wines** Roussette de Marestel, Chignin-Bergeron.
◆ This gourmet inn is set in an old storeroom on a vine-covered hillside overlooking the Rhone. Fine modern creative cuisine.

JONQUERETTES – 84 Vaucluse – 332 C10 – see Châteauneuf-de-Gadagne

---

JONS – 69 Rhône – 327 J5 – pop. 1 210 – alt. 205 m – ✉ 69330 43 E1

Paris 476 – Lyon 28 – Meyzieu 10 – Montluel 8 – Pont-de-Chéruy 12

Auberge de Jons without rest — VISA AE
rte du Pont – ✆ 04 78 31 29 85 – www.auberge-de-jons.fr – hotel.de.jons@wanadoo.fr – Fax 04 72 02 48 24
33 rm – €75/160 €85/180, ☕ €12 – 3 suites
◆ A modern hotel complex on the banks of the Rhône. Colourful, well-equipped rooms, two duplexes and eight personalised bungalows (small kitchens). Pleasant swimming pool.

JONZAC – 17 Charente-Maritime – 324 H7 – pop. 3 511 – alt. 40 m – Spa : Early March-early Dec. – Casino – ✉ 17500 Atlantic Coast 38 B3

Paris 512 – Bordeaux 84 – Angoulême 59 – Cognac 36 – Royan 60 – Saintes 44
Office de tourisme, 22, place du Château ✆ 05 46 48 49 29, Fax 05 46 48 51 07

Hostellerie du Coq d'Or with rm
18 pl. du Château – ✆ 05 46 48 00 06 – www.lecoqdor.fr – a.medvedeff@wanadoo.fr – Closed in January
5 rm – €85/95 €85/95, ☕ €10
Rest – Menu (€13), €29 – Carte €25/52
◆ Magnificent old residence on the château square. Bistro service at the 1900-style bar and a more elaborate menu in the very trendy dining room with exposed stone. Comfortable rooms brilliantly mixing old with new.

in Clam **6 km north on the D 142 – pop. 322 – alt. 67 m – ✉ 17500**

Le Vieux Logis rm, rest, rm, VISA
r. du 8 mai 1945 – ✆ 05 46 70 20 13 – www.vieuxlogis.com – info@vieuxlogis.com – Fax 05 46 70 20 64
10 rm – €58/70 €58/70, ☕ €10 – ½ P €50/56
Rest – Menu €17 (weekdays)/38 – Carte €30/50
◆ Hotel in the heart of the Jonzac region. Photographs by the owner on display. Contemporary, well kept, ground floor rooms with terrace. The chef's regional cuisine is served in one of three neo-rustic dining rooms.

JOUARRE – **77 Seine-et-Marne – 312** H2 – **see La Ferté-sous-Jouarre**

JOUCAS – **84 Vaucluse – 332** E10 – **pop. 317 – alt. 263 m – ✉ 84220** 42 **E1**

Paris 716 – Apt 14 – Avignon 42 – Carpentras 32 – Cavaillon 22

Hostellerie Le Phébus (Xavier Mathieu) rm, rm, VISA
rte de Murs – ✆ 04 90 05 78 83 – www.lephebus.com – phebus@relaischateaux.com – Fax 04 90 05 73 61 – Open 2 April-2 November
14 rm – €245/300 €245/300, ☕ €20 – 10 suites
Rest ***Xavier Mathieu*** – *(closed Tuesday lunch, Wednesday lunch and Thursday lunch)* Menu €60/110 – Carte €86/125
Rest ***Le Café de la Fontaine*** – *(open April to October) (lunch only)* Menu €45/65 – Carte €49/76
Spec. Brouillade aux truffes et marinière de légumes ravigotés. (spring-autumn). Agneau confit à l'os (summer). Citron vert, gingembre, framboise et sorbet basilic (summer). **Wines** Les Baux de Provence rouge, Côtes du Luberon blanc.
◆ Stone farmhouse standing alone in the scrubland. Lovely rooms and suites, some with private pool. Inventive dishes served in a chic dining room or outside, with the Luberon in the background. Charming terrace and southern bistro atmosphere at the Café de la Fontaine.

Le Mas des Herbes Blanches VISA
rte Murs: 2.5 km – ✆ 04 90 05 79 79 – www.herbesblanches.com – reservation@herbesblanches.com – Fax 04 90 05 71 96 – Closed 2 January-6 March
19 rm – €158/371 €158/371, ☕ €23 – 2 suites – ½ P €199/406
Rest – *(closed Tuesday and Wednesday from 15 October to 16 April)*
Menu €55 (weekdays)/115 – Carte €70/129
Spec. Pressé de foie gras de canard, fine gelée à l'arabica et feuilles craquantes de cacao. Déclinaison de cochon du Ventoux. Tartelette au cacao et fèves de tonka. **Wines** Côtes du Luberon, Côteaux d'Aix-en-Provence.
◆ This superb establishment, set against the Vaucluse plateau and overlooking the Apt plain, houses individually decorated rooms which have either a balcony or private garden. Chic restaurant and terrace offering an unforgettable view over Mount Luberon. Excellent modern cuisine.

Le Mas du Loriot rm, VISA
rte de Murs, 4 km – ✆ 04 90 72 62 62 – www.masduloriot.com – mas.du.loriot@wanadoo.fr – Fax 04 90 72 62 54 – Open 27 March-11 November
7 rm – €55/135 €55/135, ☕ €12 – ½ P €67/104
Rest – *(closed Tuesday, Thursday, Saturday and Sunday) (dinner only) (residents only)* Menu €30
◆ Family house hidden away in the countryside with the Luberon as a backdrop. Small, up-to-the-minute rooms on the garden level. Pleasant pool among the pine trees and lavender.

JOUGNE – 25 Doubs – 321 I6 – pop. 1 328 – alt. 1 001 m – Winter sports : to Métabief 880/1 450 m 22 – ✉ 25370 Burgundy-Jura — 17 C3

Paris 464 – Besançon 79 – Champagnole 50 – Lausanne 48 – Morez 49 – Pontarlier 20

La Couronne

6 r. de l'Église – 03 81 49 10 50 – www.hotel-couronne-jougne.com – lacouronnejougne@wanadoo.fr – Fax 03 81 49 19 77 – Closed November, Sunday dinner and Monday dinner except high season and school holidays

11 rm – €52 €52/95, €8 – ½ P €59/80

Rest – Menu €19 (weekdays)/47 – Carte €35/54

◆ Near the church, this beautiful 18C house has been almost entirely renovated. Comfortable rooms, including some with views of the Monts du Jura. Warm setting in the restaurant and generous regional cuisine.

JOUILLAT – 23 Creuse – pop. 402 – alt. 396 m – ✉ 23220 — 25 C1

Paris 345 – Limoges 102 – Guéret 15 – Domérat 74 – La Souterraine 47

La Maison Verte

2 Lombarteix, 2 km north on D 940 and secondary road – 05 55 51 93 34 – www.lamaisonvertecreuse.com – info@lamaisonvertecreuse.com

4 rm – €70 €90 **Table d'hôte** – Menu €22

◆ Located in the heart of the countryside, this perfectly preserved 19C farm has a kitchen garden and a summer pool. The large rooms are carefully decorated with taste. The owner prepares traditional cuisine for his guests, and serves it in a modernised rustic dining room.

JOUX – 69 Rhône – 327 F4 – pop. 653 – alt. 520 m – ✉ 69170 — 44 A1

Paris 437 – Lyon 51 – Saint-Étienne 102 – Villeurbanne 60

Le Tilia

pl. du Plaisir – 04 74 05 19 46 – www.letilia.com – m.tilia@orange.fr – Fax 04 74 05 17 90 – Closed 17-31 August, 8-15 February, Sunday dinner, Monday and Tuesday

Rest – Menu €15 (weekday lunch), €26/55 – Carte €43/62

◆ Near the château, this regional cosy house and its four-century-old linden tree has light wood fixtures and beautifully laid tables. Generous traditional menu. Lovely summer terrace.

JOYEUSE – 07 Ardèche – 331 H7 – pop. 1 545 – alt. 180 m – ✉ 07260 — 44 A3
Lyon - Rhone Valley

Paris 650 – Alès 54 – Mende 97 – Privas 55

Office de tourisme, montée de la Chastellane 04 75 89 80 92, Fax 04 75 89 80 95

Corniche du Vivarais Cévenol★★ West.

Les Cèdres — rm, rm,

la Glacière district – 04 75 39 40 60 – www.hotelcedres.com – hotel.cedres@orange.fr – Fax 04 75 39 90 16 – Open 11 April-15 October

43 rm – €53/56 €62/65, €8 – ½ P €59/62

Rest – Menu €17/31 – Carte €35/50

◆ This hotel is in a former textile factory overlooking the Beaume. Small, well-kept rooms. Archery, canoeing, heated pool and theme evenings. Traditional cuisine served in a refurbished dining room with terrace.

JUAN-LES-PINS – 06 Alpes-Maritimes – 341 D6 – alt. 2 m – Casino : Eden Beach FZ – ✉ 06160 French Riviera — 42 E2

Paris 910 – Aix-en-Provence 161 – Cannes 10 – Nice 22

Office de tourisme, 51, boulevard Guillaumont 04 92 90 53 05, Fax 04 93 61 55 13

Massif de l'Esterel★★★ - Massif de Tanneron★.

JUAN-LES-PINS

Ardisson (Bd B.)	FZ	5
Courbet (Av. Amiral)	EZ	18
Docteur-Dautheville (Av.)	FZ	22
Docteur-Hochet (Av. du)	FZ	23
Gallet (Av. Louis)	EZ	27
Gallice (Av. G.)	FZ	29
Hôtel-des-Postes (R. de l')	FZ	44
Iles (R. des)	EZ	46
Joffre (Av. du Maréchal)	EFZ	47
Lauriers (Av. des)	FZ	48
Maupassant (Av. Guy-de)	EFZ	53
Oratoire (R. de l')	FZ	56
Palmiers (Av. des)	FZ	59
Paul (R. M.)	EZ	60
Printemps (R. du)	FZ	63
Ste-Marguerite (R.)	EZ	74
St-Honorat (R.)	EZ	71
Vilmorin (Av.)	EZ	88

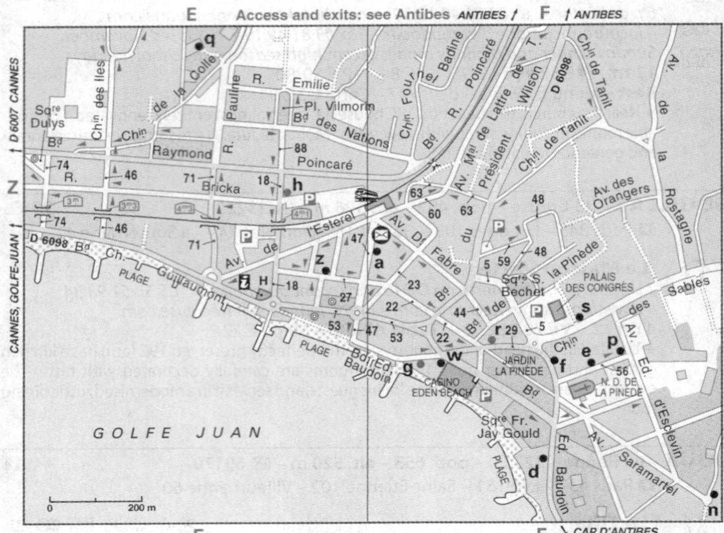

Juana — la Pinède, av. G. Gallice – ✆ 04 93 61 08 70 – www.hotel-juana.com – reservation@hotel-juana.com – Fax 04 93 61 76 60 – Closed 26 October-29 December — FZ **f**

37 rm – †€ 160/665 ††€ 160/665, ☕ € 25 – 3 suites

Rest – Menu € 45/59 – Carte € 55/87

◆ A luxurious 1930s hotel, with a real tradition of hospitality. Elegant, renovated Art Deco-style rooms with high-quality facilities. Attractive swimming pool. Veranda restaurant and lounge full of natural light. Pleasant terrace facing the pine forest.

Belles Rives — 33 bd E. Baudoin – ✆ 04 93 61 02 79 – www.bellesrives.com – info@brj-hotels.com – Fax 04 93 67 43 51 – Closed 3 January-10 March — FZ **d**

38 rm – †€ 150/750 ††€ 150/750, ☕ € 25 – 5 suites

Rest *La Passagère* – *(closed Monday and Tuesday off season)* Menu (€ 30), € 45 (weekdays)/95 – Carte € 75/105

Rest *Plage Belles Rives* – *(Open April-October)* Carte € 45/75

◆ This little Art Deco gem right on the edge of the sea seems to await the return of F. Scott Fitzgerald. Private beach and pontoon. The 'Passenger' serves fine modern cuisine in a dining area with a 1930s steam liner décor. Tables with sea views at the Plage Belle Rives.

Méridien Garden Beach — rm, — 15 bd E. Baudoin – ✆ 04 92 93 57 57 – www.garden-beach-hotel.com – contactgardenbeach@g-partouche.fr – Fax 04 92 93 57 71 – Closed 29 November-27 December — FZ **w**

175 rm – †€ 127/431 ††€ 127/431, ☕ € 23 – 17 suites

Rest *La Plage* – *(Open March-October)* Menu (€ 29 bi) – Carte € 55/80

◆ A glass and concrete building next to the casino with views over the sea. Spacious, comfortable rooms; choose one overlooking the bay. Sports facilities. Mediterranean cuisine, salads and grilled dishes served at the brasserie de la Plage.

Ambassadeur
50 chemin des Sables – ✆ 04 92 93 74 10 – www.hotel-ambassadeur.com – manager@hotel-ambassadeur.com – Fax 04 93 67 79 85 – Closed December FZ **s**
225 rm – €120/320 €120/320, €25
Rest *Grill Les Palmiers* – *(Open July-August) (lunch only)* Carte €42/54
Rest *Le Cézanne* – *(Closed lunch in July-August)* Carte €50/63
◆ This vast hotel complex behind the convention centre caters to seminars and holiday-makers. It offers a central patio bathed in light, sunny coloured rooms and a lovely tree-lined pool. Simple summertime menu at the Grill les Palmiers. Provençal decor and regional cuisine.

Ste-Valérie without rest
r. Oratoire – ✆ 04 93 61 07 15 – www.juanlespins.net – saintevalerie@juanlespins.net – Fax 04 93 61 47 52 – Open 29 April-14 October FZ **p**
24 rm – €200/265 €200/400, €23 – 6 suites
◆ A peaceful hotel set against a swathe of greenery and flowers. Well-presented rooms decorated in Mediterranean style, overlooking the garden and pool. Charming welcome.

La Villa without rest
av. Saramartel – ✆ 04 92 93 48 00 – www.hotel-la-villa.fr – resa@hotel-la-villa.fr – Fax 04 93 61 86 78 – Open from March to end November FZ **n**
26 rm – €169/339 €169/339, €18
◆ The garden and swimming pool add charm to this peaceful, recently refurbished villa. Colonial-style lounge-bar, and modern, simply furnished rooms with wenge wood. Delicious welcome.

Astoria without rest
15 av. Mar. Joffre – ✆ 04 93 61 23 65 – www.hotellastoria.com – reservation@hotellastoria.com – Fax 04 93 67 10 40 FZ **a**
49 rm – €88/155 €88/155, €10
◆ A small, entirely refurbished building close to the station and two minutes from the beach. The rooms at the back are quieter. Attractive breakfast room.

Des Mimosas without rest
r. Pauline – ✆ 04 93 61 04 16 – www.hotelmimosas.com – hotel.mimosas@wanadoo.fr – Fax 04 92 93 06 46 – Open 1st May-30 September EZ **q**
34 rm – €95/135 €95/145, €10
◆ The immaculate façade of this hotel rises in the centre of a park with palm trees. Renovated rooms; garden and swimming pool.

Juan Beach without rest
5 r. Oratoire – ✆ 04 93 61 02 89 – www.hoteljuanbeach.com – info@hoteljuanbeach.com – Fax 04 93 61 16 63 – Open from April to October FZ **e**
24 rm – €80/145 €95/170, €10 – 3 suites
◆ A warm atmosphere can be enjoyed in this all-renovated white and blue villa providing Provençal-style rooms, also featuring a bar & lounge with marine-style décor looking onto the pool.

Eden Hôtel without rest
16 av. L. Gallet – ✆ 04 93 61 05 20 – www.edenhoteljuan.com – edenhoteljuan@wanadoo.fr – Fax 04 92 93 05 31 – Open from March to October EZ **z**
17 rm – €55/86 €70/92, €6,50
◆ The plus points of this 1930s hotel: breakfast on the terrace, the beach close by and a friendly atmosphere. Simple rooms, some with a glimpse of the sea.

Bijou Plage
bd du Littoral – ✆ 04 93 61 39 07 – www.bijouplage.com – bijou.plage@free.fr – Fax 04 93 67 81 78 *see map of Antibes* AU **d**
Rest – Menu €23/52 – Carte €43/80
◆ A beach restaurant redecorated in a pleasant low-key lounge style (beiges and a large fish tank) and extended by a veranda. Lovely sandy terrace; Mediterranean sourced produce.

L'Amiral
7 av. Amiral Courbet – ✆ 04 93 67 34 61 – restaurant.amiral@wanadoo.fr – Fax 04 93 67 34 61 – Closed 4-14 April, 30 June-15 July, December, Tuesday except dinner May-September, Sunday dinner October-April and Monday EZ **h**
Rest – Menu € 25/35 – Carte € 34/54
◆ This pleasant family restaurant serves traditional and fish/seafood dishes in an intimate dining room adorned with paintings.

Le Perroquet
La Pinède, av. G. Gallice – ✆ 04 93 61 02 20 – Closed 3 November-26 December and lunch in July-August FZ **r**
Rest – Menu € 29/36 – Carte € 29/60
◆ Opposite the pinewoods where regular festivals are held. Ornaments, coffee grinders and flowers adorn the pretty Provençal dining room. Traditional cuisine.

Le Paradis
13 bd Beaudouin – ✆ 04 93 61 22 30 – www.restaurant-le-paradis.com – resto.paradis@orange.fr – Fax 04 93 67 46 60 – Closed November, Sunday dinner and Monday from December to February FZ **g**
Rest – Menu (€ 28), € 42/85 bi – Carte € 45/93
◆ A designer-influenced dining room with ethnic touches, splendid sea views and an appetising up-to-date menu. Accessible via a passageway beneath a building near the casino.

JULIÉNAS – 69 Rhône – 327 H2 – pop. 812 – alt. 276 m – ✉ 69840 43 E1
Lyon - Rhone Valley

Paris 403 – Bourg-en-Bresse 51 – Lyon 63 – Mâcon 15 – Villefranche-sur-Saône 32

Les Vignes without rest
0.5 km from St-Amour road – ✆ 04 74 04 43 70 – www.hoteldesvignes.com – contact@hoteldesvignes.com – Fax 04 74 04 41 95 – Closed 20 December-3 January
22 rm – †€ 54/64 ††€ 64/78, ☕ € 10
◆ On a hillside surrounded by vineyards, a hotel with bedrooms that are neat, tidy and well-soundproofed. Choice of cold meats from the Beaujolais for breakfast.

Chez la Rose with rm
pl. du Marché – ✆ 04 74 04 41 20 – www.chez-la-rose.fr – info@chez-la-rose.fr – Fax 04 74 04 49 29 – Closed 8 December-2 March, Tuesday lunch, Thursday lunch, Friday lunch and Monday
8 rm – †€ 50/67 ††€ 50/67, ☕ € 10
Rest – Menu (€ 19), € 29/55 – Carte € 38/80
◆ Good local cuisine served in a rustic decor or on the floral terrace outside. Rooms of varying sizes fitted with antique or rustic furniture. Modern breakfast room.

Le Coq à Juliénas
pl. du Marché – ✆ 04 74 04 41 98 – www.coq-julienas.com – bistrotsdecuisiniers@leondelyon.com – Fax 04 74 04 41 44 – Closed 13 December-14 January, Tuesday dinner and Wednesday
Rest – Menu (€ 20), € 23
◆ Lavender-blue shutters, a distinct retro interior with cockerel ornaments, Bacchic frescoes and popular summer terrace: a stylish chef's bistro.

JULLIÉ – 69 Rhône – 327 H2 – pop. 403 – alt. 370 m – ✉ 69840 43 E1

Paris 415 – Bourg-en-Bresse 55 – Lyon 67 – Mâcon 20

Domaine de la Chapelle de Vâtre without rest
Le Bourbon, 2 km south on the D 68 – ✆ 04 74 04 43 57 – www.vatre.com – vatre@wanadoo.fr – Fax 04 74 04 40 27
3 rm ☕ – †€ 50/80 ††€ 70/95
◆ This wine-growing estate set on the top of a hill boasts an exceptional view of the Saone plain and rooms with superb, contemporary décor.

JUMIÈGES – 76 Seine-Maritime – 304 E5 – pop. 1 715 – alt. 25 m – 33 C2
– ✉ 76480 Normandy

Paris 160 – Caudebec-en-Caux 16 – Rouen 28

Office de tourisme, rue Guillaume le Conquérant ✆ 02 35 37 28 97, Fax 02 35 37 07 07

Abbey ruins★★★.

Le Clos des Fontaines without rest
191 r. des Fontaines – ✆ 02 35 33 96 96
– www.leclosdesfontaines.com – hotel@leclosdesfontaines.com
– Fax 02 35 33 96 97 – Closed 19 December-12 January
19 rm – €90/220 €90/230, €15
◆ New hotel built in regional style and located close to the ruins of the abbey. Cosy rooms with the look and feel of far-away places.

L'Auberge des Ruines
17 pl. de la Mairie – ✆ 02 35 37 24 05 – www.auberge-des-ruines.fr
– loic.henry9@wanadoo.fr – Closed 19 August-2 September, 23 December-14 January, 19-27 February, Monday dinner and Thursday dinner from November to February, Sunday dinner, Tuesday and Wednesday
Rest – Menu €35/72 – Carte €74/80
◆ Enjoyable stop opposite the ruins of the Benedictine abbey. A terrace and veranda serve as extensions of the main room. Modern decor that preserves some older fittings.

JUNGHOLTZ – 68 Haut-Rhin – 315 H9 – pop. 889 – alt. 332 m – 1 A3
– ✉ 68500

Paris 475 – Mulhouse 23 – Belfort 62 – Colmar 32 – Guebwiller 6

Les Violettes
rm, rest,
rte de Thierenbach, westward : 1 km –
✆ 03 89 76 91 19 – www.les-violettes.com – reservation@lesviolettes.com
– Fax 03 89 74 29 12 – Closed 5-19 January
22 rm – €160/380 €160/430, €23 – 1 suite
Rest – *(Closed 5-28 January)* Menu (€48), €52 (weekdays)/68 – Carte €52/75
◆ This former hunting lodge, surrounded by greenery, is home to superb Alsace-style rooms and suites (comfortable but less plush at the country house). Lavish spa and fitness centre. Stylish restaurant and huge terrace serving a seasonal menu.

JURANÇON – 64 Pyrénées-Atlantiques – 342 J5 – see Pau

JUVIGNAC – 34 Hérault – 339 H7 – see Montpellier

JUVIGNY-SOUS-ANDAINE – 61 Orne – 310 F3 – pop. 1 058 – 32 B3
– alt. 200 m – ✉ 61140

Paris 239 – Alençon 51 – Argentan 47 – Domfront 12 – Mayenne 33

Au Bon Accueil with rm
rest,
23 pl. St Michel – ✆ 02 33 38 10 04
– www.bonaccueil-normand.com – hotel.bonaccueil@wanadoo.fr
– Fax 02 33 37 44 92
– Closed 15 February-15 March, Sunday evening and Monday
8 rm – €53 €67, €10 – ½ P €58
Rest – Menu (€13), €15 (weekday lunch), €27/43 – Carte €45/55
◆ This elegant fronted establishment lives up to its name. Generous portions of tasty regional cuisine served in two dining rooms, one of which has a glass roof and a small winter garden.

JUZET-DE-LUCHON – 31 Haute-Garonne – 343 B8 – see Bagnères-de-Luchon

KATZENTHAL – 68 Haut-Rhin – 315 H8 – pop. 544 – alt. 280 m 2 C2
– ✉ 68230

Paris 445 – Colmar 8 – Gérardmer 53 – Munster 18 – St-Dié 48

A l'Agneau with rm
16 Grand'Rue – ☎ 03 89 80 90 25 – www.agneau-katzenthal.com – contact@agneau-katzenthal.com – Fax 03 89 27 59 58 – Closed 29 June-8 July, 12-19 November, Christmas holidays, 11 January-11 February
12 rm – †€ 45/60 ††€ 45/60, ☕ € 10
Rest – *(closed Thursday except dinner from July to mid-October and Wednesday)* Menu € 18 bi (weekday lunch), € 22/46 – Carte € 25/40
◆ Regional-style house, adjacent to the family-run winery, with two smart, typically Alsatian dining rooms. Cuisine based on local and market produce, wines from the estate.

KAYSERSBERG – 68 Haut-Rhin – 315 H8 – pop. 2 676 – alt. 242 m 2 C2
– ✉ 68240 Alsace-Lorraine

Paris 438 – Colmar 12 – Gérardmer 46 – Guebwiller 35 – Munster 22 – St-Dié 41 – Sélestat 24

Office de tourisme, 39, rue du Gal-de-Gaulle ☎ 03 89 78 22 78, Fax 03 89 78 27 44

Ste-Croix church ★: altar-piece★★ - Town hall★ - Old houses★ - Fortified bridge★ - Maison Brief★.

Chambard (Olivier Nasti) rm, VISA MC AE
r. Gén.-de-Gaulle – ☎ 03 89 47 10 17 – www.lechambard.fr – info@lechambard.fr – Fax 03 89 47 35 03
27 rm – †€ 140 ††€ 140, ☕ € 18 – 5 suites – ½ P € 114/163
Rest – *(Closed Tuesday lunch, Wednesday lunch and Monday)* Menu € 34 (weekday lunch), € 54/75 – Carte € 65/85
Rest *Winstub* – Menu € 19/45 – Carte € 25/35
Spec. Escargots de la Weiss à l'Alsacienne. Baeckeoffa de foie gras d'oie entier au lard paysan. Goutte de café dans l'esprit d'un cappuccino (winter). **Wines** Riesling, Pinot gris.
◆ A large hotel at the entrance to the town. Comfortable rooms and three magnificent modern suites. Elegant restaurant, attractive terrace, fine wine list and tasty, inventive dishes. Alsatian setting at the Winstub.

Les Remparts without rest VISA MC AE
4 r. Flieh – ☎ 03 89 47 12 12 – www.lesremparts.com – hotel@lesremparts.com – Fax 03 89 47 37 24
28 rm – †€ 54/69 ††€ 69/83, ☕ € 8,50
◆ Hotel in a quiet residential area on the town's outskirts. Practical rooms with large terraces that are decked with flowers in summer.

Les Terrasses without rest VISA MC AE
– ☎ 389471212 – www.lesremparts.com – hotel@lesremparts.com – Fax 389473724
15 rm – †€ 54/69 ††€ 69/88, ☕ € 8,50
◆ Neo-Alsatian architecture, a quiet environment and comfortable rooms characterise the annexe of the hotel where you can find the reception, shared by both establishments.

Constantin without rest VISA MC AE
10 r. Père Kohlman – ☎ 03 89 47 19 90 – www.hotel-constantin.com – reservation@hotel-constantin.com – Fax 03 89 47 37 82
20 rm – †€ 50/55 ††€ 64/74, ☕ € 8
◆ This old wine-grower's house now provides comfortable rooms, some on two levels. Breakfast room with glass ceiling and attractive earthenware stove.

À l'Arbre Vert VISA MC AE
1 r. Haute du Rempart – ☎ 03 89 47 11 51 – Fax 03 89 78 13 40 – Closed 6 January-3 February
19 rm – †€ 55/59 ††€ 65/76, ☕ € 10 – ½ P € 69/75
Rest – *(closed Tuesday lunch and Monday)* Menu (€ 19), € 24/32 – Carte € 35/55
◆ Regional-style house, facing the Docteur Schweitzer Museum, with an appealing floral façade. Rustic guestrooms. Dining room with warm wood panelling, serving traditional Alsatian cuisine.

XX **Le Moreote**

12 r. du Gén.-Rieder – ✆ 03 89 47 39 08 – www.moreote.com – moreote@wanadoo.fr – Closed 20 July-16 August, Friday lunch and Thursday
Rest – *(number of covers limited, pre-book)*
Menu € 34/59 – Carte € 60/72
◆ The fine wine list and updated local dishes pay tribute to the region. Warm, rustic decor and a pavement terrace.

X **La Vieille Forge**

1 r. des Écoles – ✆ 03 89 47 17 51 – Fax 03 89 78 13 53 – Closed 2-15 June, 31 December-18 January, Wednesday and Thursday
Rest – Menu (€ 10), € 20/33 – Carte € 30/50
◆ A family restaurant hidden behind a charming half-timbered 16C façade. Regional menu supplemented by seasonal suggestions.

X **Au Lion d'Or**

66 r. Gén. de Gaulle – ✆ 03 89 47 11 16 – www.auliondor.fr – auliond.or@wanadoo.fr – Fax 03 89 47 19 02 – Closed 1-8 July, 24 January-4 March, Tuesday except lunch from May to October and Wednesday
Rest – Menu € 15/35 – Carte € 20/38
◆ A house built in 1521 and run by the same family since 1764! Period dining rooms, one with an authentic fireplace, that can seat up to 180 guests!

in Kientzheim East: 3 km by D 28 – **pop. 779** – **alt. 225 m** – ✉ **68240**

Tombstones★ in the church.

L'Abbaye d'Alspach without rest

2 r. Foch – ✆ 03 89 47 16 00 – www.abbayealspach.com – hotel@abbayealspach.com – Fax 03 89 78 29 73 – Closed 7 January-15 March
34 rm – †€ 67/84 ††€ 74/113, ☕ € 11 – 5 suites
◆ A hotel located in the outhouses of a 13C convent. Five superb suites; attractive courtyard; delicious breakfasts (kougelhopf and home-made jams).

Hostellerie Schwendi

2 pl. Schwendi – ✆ 03 89 47 30 50 – www.schwendi.fr – hotel@schwendi.fr – Fax 03 89 49 04 49
29 rm – †€ 66 ††€ 79/105, ☕ € 10 – ½ P € 80/93
Rest – *(closed 24 December-10 March, Thursday lunch and Wednesday)*
Menu € 23/62 – Carte € 27/55
◆ This house with a beautiful half-timbered façade stands on a small cobbled square. Partly rustic, partly stylish interior. Pretty personalised rooms, even more comfortable in the annexe. Regional menu and wines from the estate served on the terrace overlooking a fountain in summer.

KEMBS-LOÉCHLÉ – 68 Haut-Rhin – 315 J11 – alt. 245 m – ✉ 68680 1 B3

Paris 493 – Altkirch 26 – Basel 16 – Belfort 70 – Colmar 60 – Mulhouse 25

X **Les Écluses**

8 r. Rosenau – ✆ 03 89 48 37 77 – restaurantlesecluses@orange.fr – Fax 03 89 48 49 31 – Closed 31 August-13 September, 5-17 January, Wednesday dinner from October to April, Sunday dinner and Monday
Rest – Menu (€ 11), € 16/40 – Carte € 27/52
◆ Near the Huningue Canal and the Alsatian Petite Camargue, this friendly establishment offers fish specialities in a contemporary-style dining room.

KIENTZHEIM – 68 Haut-Rhin – 315 H8 – see Kaysersberg

KILSTETT – 67 Bas-Rhin – 315 L4 – pop. 1 923 – alt. 130 m – ✉ 67840 1 B1

Paris 489 – Haguenau 23 – Saverne 51 – Strasbourg 14 – Wissembourg 60

Oberlé

11 rte Nationale – 03 88 96 21 17 – www.hotel-restaurant-oberle.fr – hotel.oberle@orange.fr – Fax 03 88 96 62 29 – Closed 17 August-1st September and 8-22 February

30 rm – €45 €60, €6,50

Rest – *(closed Friday lunch and Thursday)* Menu €10 (weekday lunch), €22/37 – Carte €26/52

◆ This family-run establishment offers several types of room (recently renovated), all of which are fairly comfortable, modern and very well soundproofed. Décor in a rustic spirit, a lively atmosphere and regionally inspired cuisine in the restaurant.

Au Cheval Noir

1 r. du Sous-Lieutenant-Maussire – 03 88 96 22 01 – www.restaurant-cheval-noir.fr – Fax 03 88 96 61 30 – Closed 16 July-10 August, 10-25 January, Monday and Tuesday

Rest – Menu €13 (weekday lunch), €16/42 – Carte €36/42

◆ The same family has run the restaurant for five generations in this fine, 18C, half-timbered house. A welcoming interior with a hunting scene mural and traditional menu.

KOENIGSMACKER – 57 Moselle – 307 I2 – pop. 2 010 – alt. 150 m – ✉ 57970 26 B1

Paris 349 – Luxembourg 50 – Metz 39 – Völklingen 69

Syndicat d'initiative, 1, square du Père Scheil 03 82 83 75 54, Fax 03 82 83 75 54

Moulin de Méwinckel without rest

– 03 82 55 03 28

5 rm – €47/52 €55/70

◆ Peaceful, comfortable rooms located in an old 18C barn. Authentic farm atmosphere, warm hospitality and a country setting, where the wheel of the mill still turns.

LE KREMLIN-BICÊTRE – 94 Val-de-Marne – 312 D3 – 101 26 – see Paris, Area

---

KRUTH – 68 Haut-Rhin – 315 F9 – pop. 1 019 – alt. 498 m – ✉ 68820 1 A3

Alsace Lorraine

Paris 453 – Colmar 63 – Épinal 68 – Gérardmer 31 – Mulhouse 40 – Thann 20 – Le Thillot 29

Cascade St-Nicolas★ Southwest: 3 km by D 13b[1] - Musée du textile et des costumes de Haute-Alsace à Husseren-Wesserling Southeast: 6 km.

in Frenz West: 5 km by D 13bis – ✉ 68820 Kruth – pop. 1 019 – alt. 498 m

Les Quatre Saisons

r. Frentz – 03 89 82 28 61 – www.hotel4saisons.com – hotel4saisons@wanadoo.fr – Fax 03 89 82 21 42 – Closed 1 week in March

9 rm – €50/60 €50/85, €9 – ½ P €46/55

Rest – *(closed Tuesday and Wednesday)* Menu €18/37 – Carte €30/37

◆ Retaining its mountain roots yet prettily modernised, this family chalet has pleasant accommodation, cosy reading room and home-made breakfasts. Updated regional dishes and good selection of wines. Attractive dining room with view of the Vosges.

LABAROCHE – 68 Haut-Rhin – 315 H8 – pop. 1 985 – alt. 750 m – ✉ 68910 2 C2

Paris 441 – Colmar 17 – Gérardmer 49 – Munster 25 – St-Dié 44

Office de tourisme, 2, impasse Prés. Poincaré 03 89 49 80 56, Fax 03 89 49 80 68

La Rochette

at La Rochette – 03 89 49 80 40 – www.larochette-hotel.fr – hotel.la.rochette@wanadoo.fr – Fax 03 89 78 94 82 – Closed 12-23 November and 20 February-15 March

7 rm – €52/55 €55/60, €10 – ½ P €63/67

Rest – *(closed Monday dinner from November to March and Tuesday)* Menu (€15), €20/45 – Carte €24/42

◆ Enjoy a drink before dinner in the lush garden that surrounds this family home. Stylish, brigth guestrooms that are well soundproofed. Attractive predominantly yellow and green dining room; regionally focused menu.

Blanche Neige
692 Les Evaux, 6 km south-east along the D 11 and secondary road – ✆ 03 89 78 94 71 – www.auberge-blanche-neige.com – info@auberge-blanche-neige.com – Closed Thursday lunch, Tuesday and Wednesday
Rest – Menu € 25 (weekday lunch), € 40/100 bi – Carte € 55/65
◆ At an altitude of 700m, a delightful inn overlooking the Vosges. The tasteful blend of old and new inside is extremely effective. Splendid terrace and creative menu.

LABARTHE-SUR-LÈZE – 31 Haute-Garonne – 343 G4 – pop. 4 758 – alt. 162 m – ✉ 31860 28 B2

Paris 694 – Auch 91 – Pamiers 45 – St-Gaudens 81 – Toulouse 21

de Toulouse VieillevigneN : 10 km on D 4, ✆ 05 61 73 45 48

Le Poêlon
19 pl. V. Auriol – ✆ 05 61 08 68 49 – pascal.mouls@wanadoo.fr – Fax 05 61 08 78 48 – Closed 4-24 August, 22 December-4 January, Sunday and Monday
Rest – Menu € 22 (weekdays)/43 – Carte € 40/55
◆ A plush bourgeois home that is popular with the regulars for its traditional cuisine and a fine wine list (over 600 choices). Exhibition-sale of art, shaded terrace.

La Rose des Vents
2292 rte du Plantaurel, crossroads D 19-D 4 – ✆ 05 61 08 67 01 – www.larosedesvents-31.com – sarl.rosedesvents@orange.fr – Fax 05 61 08 85 84 – Closed 2 weeks in August, Sunday dinner, Monday and Tuesday
Rest – Menu (€ 15), € 27/37 – Carte € 30/52
◆ A comfortable regional-style house shielded from the noise of the road by its surrounding greenery. Take a seat by the fireside or on the veranda covered by a Virginia creeper.

LABASTIDE-BEAUVOIR – 31 Haute-Garonne – 343 I4 – pop. 952 – alt. 260 m – ✉ 31450 29 C2

Paris 701 – Toulouse 25 – Albi 97 – Castelnaudary 35 – Foix 76

L'Oustal du Lauragais
rte de Mauremont – ✆ 05 34 66 16 16 – www.oustal-lauragais.fr – contact@oustal-lauragais.fr – Fax 05 34 66 16 26 – Closed 23 December-3 January
14 rm – †€ 65 ††€ 65, ☕ € 7 – ½ P € 80
Rest – *(closed 3-29 August)* Menu € 16 (weekdays)/25 – Carte approx. € 25
◆ This former farmhouse has been restored and converted into a peaceful hotel providing simply furnished rooms with fine bathroom facilities. Traditional food served in the modern-style dining room.

LABASTIDE DE VIRAC – 07 Ardèche – pop. 210 – alt. 207 m – ✉ 07150 44 A3

Paris 675 – Lyon 213 – Privas 73 – Alès 42 – Montélimar 67

Le Mas Rêvé
3 km east on D 217 and secondary road – ✆ 04 75 38 69 13 – www.lemasreve.com – info@lemasreve.com – Open 15 April-30 September
5 rm ☕ – †€ 95/105 ††€ 95/145 **Table d'hôte** – Menu € 32 bi
◆ Admire the pretty rooms of this old Ardèche farmhouse, tastefully restored by Marie Rose and Guido Goossens. Lovely garden and pool. At the table d'hôte: dishes made from local produce.

LABASTIDE-MURAT – 46 Lot – 337 F4 – pop. 660 – alt. 447 m – ✉ 46240 Dordogne-Berry-Limousin 29 C1

Paris 543 – Brive-la-Gaillarde 66 – Cahors 32 – Figeac 45 – Gourdon 26 – Sarlat-la-Canéda 50

Office de tourisme, Grand'Rue ✆ 05 65 21 11 39, Fax 05 65 24 57 66

La Garissade rm, VISA AE

20 pl. de la Mairie – ✆ 05 65 21 18 80 – www.garissade.com – garissade@wanadoo.fr – Fax 05 65 21 10 97 – Open April-October

19 rm – †€ 61/67 ††€ 67/73, ☕ € 8 – ½ P € 65/70

Rest – *(closed Monday lunch)* Menu € 13 (weekday lunch), € 27/32

◆ An informal atmosphere depicts this 13C village house. Low-key rooms with painted wood furniture, made by a local craftsman. The restaurant has adopted a more contemporary decor, in harmony with the modern menu.

LABATUT – 40 Landes – 335 F13 – pop. 1 187 – alt. 45 m – ✉ 40300 3 B3

Paris 759 – Anglet 58 – Bayonne 53 – Bordeaux 173

Le Bousquet P VISA

37 bd de l'Océan – ✆ 05 58 98 11 01 – aubergedubousquet@yahoo.fr – Fax 05 58 98 11 63 – Closed Sunday dinner, Monday dinner and Wednesday

Rest – Menu (€ 15 bi), € 25/55 – Carte € 40/53

◆ This charming 18C house is home to a restaurant in a country setting, with wooden beams and rustic furniture. Serving modern cuisine. Herb garden.

LABÈGE – 31 Haute-Garonne – 343 H3 – see Toulouse

LABOURSE – 62 Pas-de-Calais – 301 J5 – see Béthune

LACABARÈDE – 81 Tarn – 338 H10 – pop. 307 – alt. 325 m – ✉ 81240 29 C2

Paris 754 – Béziers 71 – Carcassonne 53 – Castres 36 – Mazamet 19 – Narbonne 62

Demeure de Flore rm, P VISA

106 Grand'rue – ✆ 05 63 98 32 32 – www.demeuredeflore.com – contact@demeuredeflore.com – Fax 05 63 98 47 56 – Closed 2-30 January and Monday off season

11 rm – †€ 75 ††€ 100/110, ☕ € 10 – ½ P € 93/98

Rest – Menu € 27 (lunch)/35

◆ The Roman goddess gave this 19C family house a beautiful green setting facing the Montagne Noire (Black Mountain). Stylish interior, antique furnishings and an attentive welcome. Market cuisine with a Provençal touch or Italian influences, served in a modern, refined atmosphere.

LACAPELLE-MARIVAL – 46 Lot – 337 H3 – pop. 1 317 – alt. 375 m – ✉ 46120 Dordogne-Berry-Limousin 29 C1

Paris 555 – Aurillac 66 – Cahors 64 – Figeac 21 – Gramat 22 – Rocamadour 32 – Tulle 75

Office de tourisme, place de la Halle ✆ 05 65 40 81 11, Fax 05 65 40 81 11

La Terrasse with rm rest, VISA AE

(near the chateau) – ✆ 05 65 40 80 07 – www.hotel-restaurant-la-terrasse-lot.fr – hotel-restaurant-la-terrasse@wanadoo.fr – Fax 05 65 40 99 45 – Closed January-February, 22-27 December and Sunday dinner in low season

4 rm – †€ 47/63 ††€ 54/70, ☕ € 78

Rest – *(closed Sunday dinner, Monday dinner and Tuesday lunch October-June and Monday lunch)* Menu (€ 17), € 23 (weekday lunch), € 26/58 – Carte € 58/85

◆ Appetising modern food to be enjoyed in a light, renovated dining room. Hotel near the château's huge square keep. Functional, well-kept rooms. Some have been renovated. Pleasant garden bordered by a stream.

Your opinions are important to us:
please write and let us know about your discoveries
and experiences – good and bad!

LACAPELLE-VIESCAMP – 15 Cantal – 330 B5 – pop. 448 – alt. 550 m – ✉ 15150 5 A3

Paris 547 – Aurillac 19 – Figeac 57 – Laroquebrou 12 – St-Céré 48

Du Lac rm, VISA

– ✆ 04 71 46 31 57 – www.hoteldulac-cantal.com – info@hoteldulac-cantal.com – Fax 04 71 46 31 64 – Closed 20 December-1st March, Friday evening, Sunday evening and Monday evening from 1st November to Easter

23 rm – €50/55 €55/70, €10 – ½ P €59/68

Rest – Menu (€14), €21 (weekday lunch), €25/41 – Carte €27/43

◆ This 1950s establishment is full of appeal: peace and quiet, close to St Etienne Cantalès Lake, which is good for fishing, perfectly kept rooms and a convivial welcome. The restaurant, overlooking the surrounding countryside, serves traditional fare and regional wines.

LACAUNE – 81 Tarn – 338 I8 – pop. 2 844 – alt. 793 m – Casino – ✉ 81230 Languedoc-Roussillon-Tarn Gorges 29 D2

Paris 708 – Albi 67 – Béziers 89 – Castres 48 – Lodève 73 – Millau 69 – Montpellier 131

Office de tourisme, place Général-de-Gaulle ✆ 05 63 37 04 98, Fax 05 63 37 03 01

Le Relais de Fusies VISA

– ✆ 05 63 37 02 03 – www.hotelfusies.fr – contact@hotelfusies.fr – Fax 05 63 37 10 98

30 rm – €58/70 €64/85, €9 – ½ P €60/65

Rest – *(closed Monday except dinner in July-August)*
Menu (€13), €16/60 bi – Carte €34/55

◆ This hotel near the church welcomes guests in its pleasantly retro hall, bar and lounge (antiques, panelling). Modern bathrooms in the rooms, which are being gradually updated. Traditional cuisine served in a large, partly arcaded dining room.

Calas with rm rest, VISA

pl. Vierge – ✆ 05 63 37 03 28 – www.hotel-calas.fr – hotelcalas@wanadoo.fr – Fax 05 63 37 09 19 – Closed 15 December-15 January

16 rm – €37/45 €40/55, €7 – ½ P €40/45

Rest – *(closed Friday dinner and Saturday lunch from October to April)*
Menu (€13 bi), €16 (weekdays)/36 – Carte €30/50

◆ In the same family for four generations, this restaurant serves wholesome regional fare. Works by local artists adorn the restaurant. Colourful guestrooms.

LACAVE – 46 Lot – 337 F2 – pop. 289 – alt. 130 m – ✉ 46200 Dordogne-Berry-Limousin 29 C1

Paris 528 – Brive-La-Gaillarde 51 – Cahors 58 – Gourdon 26 – Sarlat-La-Canéda 41

Grottoes★★.

Château de la Treyne VISA

3 km west on the D 23, D 43 and private road – ✆ 05 65 27 60 60 – www.chateaudelatreyne.com – treyne@relaischateaux.com – Fax 05 65 27 60 70 – Open 28 March-15 November and 23 December-3 January

14 rm – €180/420 €180/420, €24 – 2 suites – ½ P €300/540

Rest – *(closed lunch from Tuesday to Friday)* Menu €48 (lunch), €96/138 – Carte €107/137

Spec. Déclinaison de foie gras de canard. Dos de bar de ligne rôti (May to October). Verrine de fruits frais marinés au safran. **Wines** Cahors, Bergerac

◆ A 17C château overlooking the Dordogne in a park with a formal garden and Romanesque chapel (exhibitions, concerts). An idyllic setting and sumptuous guest rooms. Fine wood panelling and coffered ceiling in the restaurant serving modern cuisine.

Pont de l'Ouysse (Daniel Chambon) rm, P VISA MC AE
– ✆ 05 65 37 87 04 – www.lepontdelouysse.fr
– pont.ouysse@wanadoo.fr – Fax 05 65 32 77 41 – Open mid-March to mid-November and closed Monday except dinner in high season and Tuesday lunch
14 rm – †€ 140/150 ††€ 140/150, ☕ € 16 – ½ P € 150/160
Rest – Menu € 50/140 – Carte € 60/119
Spec. Foie de canard "Bonne Maman". Pommes de terre charlotte en habit noir de truffe. Millefeuille caramélisé au chocolat et crème légère à la vanille. **Wines** Cahors, Vin de Pays du Lot.
◆ This delightful 19C house built into the cliff boasts an attractive dining room, shaded terrace, and a pathway along the banks of the Ouysse. Inventive cuisine inspired by the south-west.

LAC CHAMBON ★★ – 63 Puy-de-Dôme – 326 E9 – alt. 877 m – Winter sports : 1 150/1 760 m 9 – ✉ 63790 Chambon sur Lac Auvergne 5 B2

Paris 456 – Clermont-Ferrand 37 – Condat 39 – Issoire 32 – Le Mont-Dore 18

Le Grillon P VISA MC
– ✆ 04 73 88 60 66 – www.hotel-grillon.com – info@hotel-grillon.com
– Fax 04 73 88 65 55 – Open 1st February-1st November
22 rm – †€ 40/45 ††€ 40/55, ☕ € 8 – ½ P € 45/55
Rest – *(closed Monday lunch except from 22 June to 7 September)*
Menu (€ 15), € 19 (weekdays)/40 – Carte € 32/50
◆ A well-run family establishment. The stylish, colourful rooms all bear witness to the lady of the house's decorative talents. Traditional and regional dishes served in the dining room or on the terrace overlooking the lake.

Beau Site P VISA MC AE
– ✆ 04 73 88 61 29 – www.beau-site.com – info@beau-site.com
– Fax 04 73 88 66 73 – Open 1st February-30 October
17 rm – †€ 45/50 ††€ 50/55, ☕ € 8 – ½ P € 45/55
Rest – *(open February holidays-30 October and closed lunch March and October except weekends)* Menu (€ 15), € 18/30 – Carte € 25/36
◆ A hillside hotel overlooking the lake. Rooms of varying sizes facing the water and beach. Terrace and modern dining rooms whose bay windows overlook the lake. Regional food.

LAC DE GUÉRY – 63 Puy-de-Dôme – 326 D9 – see le Mont-Dore

LAC DE LA LIEZ – 52 Haute-Marne – 313 M6 – see Langres

LAC DE PONT – 21 Côte-d'Or – 320 G5 – see Semur-en-Auxois

LAC DE VASSIVIÈRE – 23 Creuse – 325 I6 – see Peyrat-le-Château (87 H.-Vienne)

LAC GÉNIN – 01 Ain – 328 H3 – see Oyonnax

LACHASSAGNE – 69 Rhône – 327 H4 – pop. 846 – alt. 368 m – ✉ 69480 43 E1

Paris 445 – Lyon 30 – Villeurbanne 39 – Vénissieux 43 – Caluire-et-Cuire 34

Au Goutillon Beaujolais P VISA MC
850 rte de la colline – ✆ 04 74 67 14 99 – www.au-goutillon-beaujolais.com – au-goutillon-beaujolais@wanadoo.fr – Fax 04 74 67 14 99 – Closed dinner from 15 September to 30 June, Sunday dinner, Saturday lunch and Wednesday
Rest – Menu (€ 20), € 24/46 – Carte € 31/49
◆ Modern cuisine with exotic touches served in this establishment located among vineyards. The terrace overlooking the Saône valley is especially charming.

LACROIX-FALGARDE – 31 Haute-Garonne – 343 G3 – see Toulouse

LADOIX-SERRIGNY – 21 Côte-d'Or – 320 J7 – see Beaune

LAFARE – 84 Vaucluse – 332 D9 – pop. 102 – alt. 220 m – ✉ 84190 42 **E1**

Paris 670 – Avignon 37 – Carpentras 13 – Nyons 34 – Orange 26

Le Grand Jardin rm, VISA MC AE

– *04 90 62 97 93 – www.legrandjardin.biz – bonnin-noel@wanadoo.fr – Fax 04 90 65 03 74 – Open 4 March-2 November and closed Tuesday lunch and Monday*

5 rm – €75/80 €80/98, €12 – ½ P €73/83

Rest – Menu (€19), €27/43 – Carte approx. €52

◆ A new building surrounded by Côtes-du-Rhône vines. Rooms decorated in Provençal style. Warm welcome. Contemplate the Dentelles de Montmirail from the flower-decked terrace by the shade of bamboo canes. Classic menu.

LAGARDE-ENVAL – 19 Corrèze – 329 L4 – pop. 744 – alt. 480 m – ✉ 19150 25 **C3**

Paris 488 – Aurillac 71 – Brive-la-Gaillarde 35 – Mauriac 66 – St-Céré 48 – Tulle 14

Auberge du Pays with rm VISA MC

rte de l' étang – 05 55 27 16 12 – www.aubergedupays.fr – hotelmestre19@orange.fr – Fax 05 55 27 48 00 – Closed September

7 rm – €45 €45, €6

Rest – *(closed Saturday and Sunday)* Menu €13 (lunch), €22/30 – Carte €45/65

◆ Friendly family-run hotel also home to the village bar. Rustic dining room serving typical Corrèze meals. Modest guest rooms.

LAGARRIGUE – 81 Tarn – 338 F9 – see Castres

LAGRASSE – 11 Aude – 344 G4 – pop. 615 – alt. 108 m – ✉ 11220 22 **B3**

Languedoc-Roussillon-Tarn Gorges

Paris 819 – Montpellier 133 – Carcassonne 51 – Perpignan 97 – Narbonne 43

Syndicat d'initiative, 6, boulevard de la Promenade 04 68 43 11 56, Fax 04 68 43 16 34

Hostellerie des Corbières VISA MC

9 bd de la Promenade – 04 68 43 15 22 – www.hostelleriecorbieres.com – hostelleriecorbieres@free.fr – Fax 04 68 43 16 56 – Closed 15-30 November and 2 January-10 February

6 rm – €70 €70/90, €9 – ½ P €68/78

Rest – *(Closed Wednesday from 16 October to 14 March and Thursday)* Menu (€17), €20/37 – Carte €45/55

◆ The character of this small, renovated mansion on the outskirts of the village has been carefully preserved. Louis Philippe style furniture in the rooms (some with a small lounge). The shaded terrace of the restaurant commands a view of the Corbières vineyards.

LAGUÉPIE – 82 Tarn-et-Garonne – 337 H7 – pop. 727 – alt. 149 m – ✉ 82250 29 **C2**

Paris 649 – Albi 38 – Montauban 71 – Rodez 70 – Villefranche-de-Rouergue 34

Office de tourisme, place de Foirail 05 63 30 20 34, Fax 05 63 30 20 34

Les Deux Rivières rm, VISA MC AE

av. Puech-Mignon – 05 63 31 41 41 – les2rivieres.laguepie@wanadoo.fr – Fax 05 63 30 20 91 – Closed February half-term holidays, Saturday lunch, Sunday dinner and Friday

8 rm (½ board only) – ½ P €38/58

Rest – Menu €12 (lunch), €20/33 – Carte €24/35

◆ At the confluence of the Aveyron and the Viaur, a small welcoming hotel with modest but well-maintained rooms. Lunchtime service in the bar. Evening meals are served in a functional dining room.

LAGUIOLE – 12 Aveyron – **338** J2 – **pop. 1 261 – alt. 1 004 m – Winter sports : 1 100/1 400 m** ⛷ **12** – ✉ **12210** Languedoc-Roussillon-Tarn Gorges 29 **D1**

Paris 571 – Aurillac 79 – Espalion 22 – Mende 83 – Rodez 52 – St-Flour 59

Office de tourisme, place de la Mairie ✆ 05 65 44 35 94, Fax 05 65 44 35 76

de Mezeyrac Soulages, W : 12 km on D 541, ✆ 05 65 44 41 41

Grand Hôtel Auguy (Isabelle Muylaert-Auguy)
2 allée de l'Amicale – ✆ 05 65 44 31 11 – www.hotel-auguy.fr – contact@hotel-auguy.fr – Fax 05 65 51 50 81 – Open 2 April-4 November and closed Monday except July-August
19 rm – †€ 60/110 ††€ 60/110, ☕ € 12 – ½ P € 85/125
Rest – *(closed Monday except dinner in July-August, Tuesday lunch and Thursday lunch except July-August, Friday lunch in July-August and Wednesday lunch) (number of covers limited, pre-book)*
Menu € 32 (weekday lunch)/59 – Carte € 65/78
Spec. Filet de truite fario, farçous aux blettes et gaspacho de roquette au laguiole glacé. Côte de veau des Lucs, consommé au gomasio et nems de légumes. Cigares au caramel sur poire rôtie, glace au gingembre et transparent passion. **Wines** Marcillac, Coteaux du Languedoc
◆ This fine hotel perpetuates its tradition of hospitality, offering colourful, well-maintained guestrooms and a peaceful garden. Comfortable restaurant where you can taste the fine specialities from the Aubrac.

Le Relais de Laguiole
espace Les Cayres – ✆ 05 65 54 19 66 – www.relais-laguiole.com – relais.de.laguiole@wanadoo.fr – Fax 05 65 54 19 49 – Open 11 April-1st November
33 rm – †€ 76/173 ††€ 76/173, ☕ € 11 – ½ P € 66/99
Rest – *(dinner only)* Menu € 21/26 – Carte € 34/54
◆ A modern building with a slate roof, large functional rooms and a beautiful indoor swimming pool. Copious breakfast buffet. Ideal for groups. This bright restaurant is decorated with modern chandeliers and white curtains and furniture.

Régis without rest
3 pl. de la patte d'oie – ✆ 05 65 44 30 05 – www.hotel-regis-laguiole.com – hotel.regis@wanadoo.fr – Fax 05 65 48 46 44 – Open 10 February-5 November
20 rm – †€ 38/47 ††€ 40/98, ☕ € 10
◆ A 19C coaching inn, tucked away in the centre of this small Aveyron town. The largest, particularly comfortable rooms are on the second floor. Pleasant swimming pool to the rear.

La Ferme de Moulhac without rest
2.5 km north-eastward by secondary road – ✆ 05 65 44 33 25 – Fax 05 65 44 33 25 – Closed 26-29 May and 14-17 September
5 rm ☕ – †€ 58/60 ††€ 65/100
◆ A peaceful, relaxing atmosphere and fresh air are guaranteed at this family farm. Attractive rooms, simply furnished in a mix of old and modern styles. Generous home-made breakfast, and a small kitchen available for guests.

East 6 km by L'Aubrac road (D 15) – ✉ **12210 Laguiole**

Bras (Michel et Sébastien Bras)
rm, rest, rest,
– ✆ 05 65 51 18 20 – www.michel-bras.fr – info@michel-bras.fr – Fax 05 65 48 47 02 – Open from beg. of April to end of October and closed Monday except July-August
13 rm – †€ 260/580 ††€ 260/580, ☕ € 28
Rest – *(closed Tuesday lunch and Wednesday lunch except July-August and Monday) (number of covers limited, pre-book)*
Menu € 113/180 – Carte € 130/165
Spec. Gargouillou de jeunes légumes relevé d'herbes champêtres et de fleurs. Selle d'agneau allaiton rôtie sur l'os. Biscuit tiède de chocolat coulant. **Wines** Gaillac, Marcillac
◆ This futuristic construction seems lost among the harsh landscapes of the Aubrac. Large guestrooms with a refined contemporary decor overlooking the countryside and superb botanical gardens. Cuisine based on local produce served in an ultra-modern, panoramic restaurant.

at the Golf 12 km West by D541, D213 and secondary road

Domaine de Mezeyrac rm, rm, rm, VISA
– *05 65 44 41 41*
– *www.hotel-golfdemezeyrac.com – golfhotel-mezeyrac@wanadoo.fr*
– *Fax 05 65 44 46 90 – Open 4 April-2 November*
15 rm – €60/90 €60/90, €9
Rest – *(lunch only)* Menu (€17), €19/21 – Carte approx. €43
◆ An old farm converted into hostelry and complex devoted to golf. Peace and quiet guaranteed, comfortable rooms and a view of the golf course. Restaurant in a converted barn.

in Soulages-Bonneval 5 km west on the D 541 – **pop. 235** – **alt. 830 m** – ✉ **12210**

LAILLY-EN-VAL – **45 Loiret** – **318** H5 – **pop. 2 367** – **alt. 86 m** – ✉ **45740** 12 **C2**

Paris 158 – Orléans 31 – Blois 42 – Fleury-les-Aubrais 37 – Olivet 33

Domaine de Montizeau VISA
– *02 38 45 34 74 – www.domaine-montizeau.com*
– *abeille@domaine-montizeau.com*
4 rm – €70 €75/95 **Table d'hôte** – Menu €28 bi
◆ Set in parkland, a flower-bedecked longère (long house) ideal for completely relaxing. Detailed cosy decoration in the rooms, with touches from hunting, Italy, etc. Modern cuisine.

LAJOUX – **39 Jura** – **321** F8 – **see Lamoura**

LALACELLE – **61 Orne** – **310** I4 – **pop. 264** – **alt. 300 m** – ✉ **61320** 32 **B3**

Paris 208 – Alençon 20 – Argentan 34 – Domfront 42 – Falaise 57 – Mayenne 41

Château de Carrouges★★ North: 11 km, **Normandy**

La Lentillère rest, VISA
rte d'Alençon: 1.5 km by N 12 – 02 33 27 38 48 – www.lalentillere.fr
– *lalentillere@wanadoo.fr – Fax 02 33 27 38 30*
8 rm – €45/76 €45/76, €8,50 – ½ P €49/59
Rest – Menu (€15), €18/41 – Carte €22/40
◆ By the side of a main road, this former post house offers refurbished guestrooms in a resolutely modern style and spa showers in the bathrooms. Seasonal menus and regional produce await you in the countrified restaurant and pleasant summer garden.

LALINDE – **24 Dordogne** – **329** F6 – **pop. 2 938** – **alt. 46 m** – ✉ **24150** 4 **C1**

Paris 537 – Bergerac 23 – Brive-La-Gaillarde 103 – Périgueux 49 – Villeneuve-sur-Lot 61

Office de tourisme, Jardin Public 05 53 61 08 55, Fax 05 53 61 00 64

in St-Capraise-de-Lalinde West, Bergerac road: 7 km – **pop. 554** – **alt. 42 m** – ✉ **24150**

Relais St-Jacques with rm rest, VISA
pl. de l'Église – 05 53 63 47 54 – patrick.rossignol12@wanadoo.fr
– *Fax 05 53 73 33 52 – Closed Wednesday*
7 rm – €50 €54, €8 – ½ P €45/55
Rest – Menu €19 (weekdays)/46 – Carte €38/57
◆ This former post house near a church on the pilgrim route to Compostela is believed to date back to the 13C. Rustic decor, warm hospitality and regional dishes.

LALLEYRIAT – **01 Ain** – **328** E4 – **see Bourg-en-Bresse**

LAMAGDELAINE – **46 Lot** – **337** E5 – **see Cahors**

LAMALOU-LES-BAINS – 34 Hérault – 339 D7 – pop. 2 256 – alt. 200 m – Spa : mid Feb.-mid Dec. – Casino – ✉ 34240 22 B2

Languedoc-Roussillon-Tarn Gorges

Paris 732 – Béziers 39 – Lodève 38 – Montpellier 79 – St-Pons-de-Thomières 38

Office de tourisme, 1, avenue Capus ✆ 04 67 95 70 91, Fax 04 67 95 64 52

de Lamalou-les-Bains Route de Saint-Pons, SE : 2 km on D 908, ✆ 04 67 95 08 47

St-Pierre-de-Rhèdes church ★ Southwest: 1,5 km.

St-Pierre-de-Rhèdes★ Southwest: 1,5 km.

L'Arbousier

18 r. Alphonse Daudet – ✆ 04 67 95 63 11 – www.arbousierhotel.com – arbousier.hotel@wanadoo.fr – Fax 04 67 95 67 64 – Closed from 19 January-6 February

31 rm – €50/62 €50/85, €8,50 – ½ P €56/65

Rest – Menu (€13), €24/41 – Carte €29/54

◆ A charming hotel near the baths and casino, undergoing gradual redecoration in a pleasant modern style. Choose a recently redecorated room. Southern ambiance and a terrace shaded by plane trees. Traditional food.

Du Square without rest

11 av. Mal.-Foch – ✆ 04 67 23 09 93 – www.hoteldusquare.com – contact@hoteldusquare.com – Fax 04 67 23 04 27 – Closed 21 December-31 January

14 rm – €42/50 €44/52, €7

◆ Motel type building offering ground floor rooms that are simply decorated, but practical. Those at the rear are quieter. Some have a small terrace.

Les Marronniers

8 av. Capus, (D 22) – ✆ 04 67 95 76 00 – restolesmarronniers@free.fr – Fax 04 67 95 29 75 – Closed 19 January-9 February, Wednesday dinner in low season, Sunday dinner and Monday

Rest – Menu €14/62 bi – Carte approx. €32

◆ A friendly welcome awaits at this house away from the town centre. Enjoy traditional cuisine in a warm setting decorated with artwork.

in Combes 10 km west on the D 908 and D 180 – pop. 308 – alt. 480 m – ✉ 34240

Auberge de Combes

– ✆ 04 67 95 66 55 – Fax 04 67 95 03 24 – Closed January, Tuesday from September to February, Sunday dinner and Monday

Rest – Menu €28 (lunch), €45/60

◆ An authentic inn with contemporary setting overlooking the superb Parc du Haut-Languedoc. Father and son prepare the cuisine, marrying traditional with modern flavours.

LAMASTRE – 07 Ardèche – 331 J4 – pop. 2 520 – alt. 375 m – ✉ 07270 44 B2

Lyon - Rhone Valley

Paris 577 – Privas 55 – Le Puy-en-Velay 72 – St-Étienne 90 – Valence 38 – Vienne 92

Office de tourisme, place Montgolfier ✆ 04 75 06 48 99, Fax 04 75 06 37 53

Château d'Urbilhac

rte de Vernoux, 2 km southeast on the rte Vernoux-en-Vivarais – ✆ 04 75 06 42 11 – www.chateaudurbilhac.fr – info@chateaudurbilhac.fr – Fax 04 75 06 52 75

6 rm – €100/130 €160/180 – ½ P €110 **Table d'hôte** – Menu 38

◆ A small, neo-Renaissance château (built in the 16C and restored in the 19C) prized for its park overlooking the Doux valley. Fine panoramic swimming pool. Refurbished lodge.

Midi (Bernard Perrier)

pl. Seignobos – ✆ 04 75 06 41 50 – Fax 04 75 06 49 75 – Closed 23-29 June, end December to end January, Friday dinner, Sunday dinner and Monday

Rest – Menu €39/88

Spec. Salade tiède de foie gras de canard et champignons des bois. Poularde de Bresse en vessie. Soufflé glacé aux marrons de l'Ardèche. **Wines** Saint-Joseph, Saint-Péray.

◆ This restaurant in the heart of the village has retained its original charm, with a comfortable dining area, and well-prepared classic cuisine.

LAMBALLE – 22 Côtes-d'Armor – **309** G4 – **pop. 11 000 – alt. 55 m** 10 **C2**
– ✉ 22400 Brittany

Paris 431 – Dinan 42 – Rennes 81 – St-Brieuc 21 – St-Malo 50 – Vannes 130
Office de tourisme, place du Champ de Foire ✆ 02 96 31 05 38, Fax 02 96 50 88 54
Haras national★.

LAMBALLE

Augustins (R. des) . . . . A 2
Bario (R.) . . . . A 3
Blois (R. Ch. de) . . . . B 5
Boucouets (R. des) . . . . B 7
Cartel (R. Ch.) . . . . A 8
Charpentier (R. Y.) . . . . B 14
Dr-A.-Calmette (R. du) . . . . A 15
Dr-Lavergne (R. du) . . . . A 16
Foch (R. Mar.) . . . . B 19
Gesle (Ch. de la) . . . . A 23
Grand Bd (R. du) . . . . A 24
Hurel (R. du Bg) . . . . B 25
Jeu-de-Paume (R. du) . . . . A 26
Leclerc (R. Gén.) . . . . B 29
Marché (Pl. du) . . . . A 30
Martray (Pl. du) . . . . A
Mouëxigné (R.) . . . . B 31
Poincaré (R.) . . . . B 34
Préville (R.) . . . . B 35
St-Jean (R.) . . . . A 37
St-Lazare (R.) . . . . A 38
Tery (R. G.) . . . . A 39
Tour-aux-Chouettes (R.) . . . . B 42
Val (R. du) . . . . AB
Villedeneu (R.) . . . . A 45

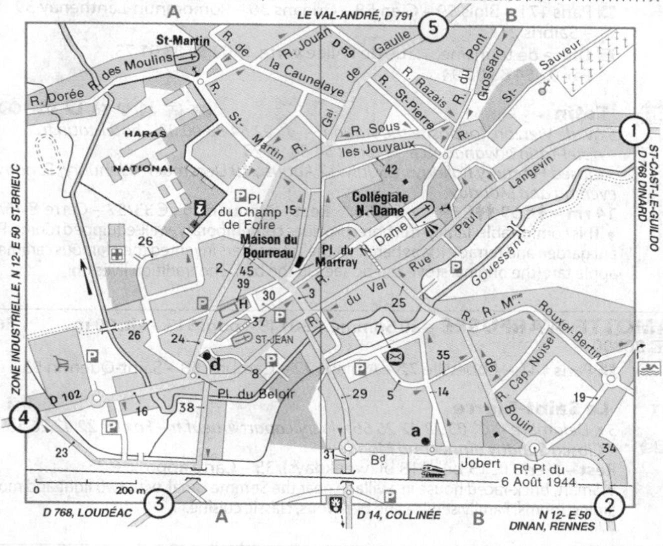

Kyriad without rest

29 bd Jobert – ✆ 02 96 31 00 16 – www.hotel-lamballe.com – kyriad.lamballe@wanadoo.fr – Fax 02 96 31 91 54 B **a**

27 rm – †€ 58/98 ††€ 58/98, ☕ € 10

◆ This hotel just opposite the station offers practical, identically decorated and well-soundproofed rooms. Buffet breakfast served in a bright room.

Lion d'Or without rest

3 r. du Lion d'Or – ✆ 02 96 31 20 36 – www.leliondor-lamballe.com – leliondorhotel@wanadoo.fr – Fax 02 96 31 93 79 – Closed 23 December-6 January A **d**

17 rm – †€ 49/56 ††€ 51/59, ☕ € 8

◆ This family-run establishment has been treated to a new lease of life. The small, well-kept rooms have been repainted in white for more luminosity. Buffet breakfast.

Au Clos du Lit

in St-Aaron, r. de la Ville-D'Ys, 6 km north via ⑤ and D 14 – ✆ 02 96 31 17 48 – www.auclosdulit.com – auclosdulit@auclosdulit.com

4 rm ☕ – †€ 40/50 ††€ 49/59 **Table d'hôte** – Menu € 18 bi

◆ Keen adepts of country tourism, the owners of this small manor have adopted a decor that pays tribute to authentic Brittany. Personalised, quiet rooms, library and garden. In this welcoming table d'hôte, find copious portions and a rustic setting packed with family heirlooms.

in la Poterie East: 3,5 km – ✉ 22400 Lamballe

Manoir des Portes
– ✆ 02 96 31 13 62 – www.manoirdesportes.com – contact@manoirdesportes.com – Fax 02 96 31 20 53 – Closed 22 December-5 January
15 rm – †€ 48/55 ††€ 57/100, ☕ € 8 **Rest** – Menu (€ 18), € 24
◆ A 16C manor, close to a horse riding centre, set in flower-decked grounds with a vegetable garden and an orchard. Peaceful, cosy guestrooms. Rustic dining room, with beams and a fireplace, offering a set, traditional menu.

LAMOTTE-BEUVRON – 41 Loir-et-Cher – **318** J6 – **pop. 4 529** – alt. 114 m – ✉ 41600 12 **C2**

Paris 171 – Blois 59 – Gien 58 – Orléans 36 – Romorantin-Lanthenay 39 – Salbris 21

Office de tourisme, 1, rue de l'Allée verte ✆ 02 54 83 01 73, Fax 02 54 83 00 94

Tatin
5 av. de Vierzon, (opposite the station) – ✆ 02 54 88 00 03 – hotel-tatin.fr – hotel-tatin@wanadoo.fr – Fax 02 54 88 96 73 – Closed February holidays, 25 July-12 August, 19 December-4 January, Sunday evening and Monday
14 rm – †€ 59 ††€ 59, ☕ € 8,50 **Rest** – Menu (€ 26), € 33/57 – Carte € 46/62
◆ This comfortable, family-run hotel provides contemporary, well-equipped rooms. Pleasant garden and terrace. It was here that the Tatin sisters invented their famous caramelised apple tart (the original stove can be seen in the bar). The tradition lives on!

LAMOTTE-WARFUSEE – 80 Somme – **301** I8 – **pop. 513** – **alt. 90 m** – ✉ 80800 36 **B2**

Paris 141 – Abbeville 72 – Amiens 22 – Cambrai 68 – Saint-Quentin 53

Le Saint-Pierre
3 r. Delambre – ✆ 03 22 42 26 66 – lacry.capart@neuf.fr – Fax 03 22 42 26 16 – Closed Sunday dinner and Monday
Rest – Menu (€ 15 bi), € 18 bi (weekdays)/35 – Carte approx. € 35
◆ Smart, brick-faced house in a village near the Somme canal, with two light and modern dining rooms. Family service and generous, classic cuisine.

LAMOURA – 39 Jura – **321** F8 – **pop. 524** – **alt. 1 156 m** – **Winter sports : see "aux Rousses"** – ✉ 39310 16 **B3**

Paris 477 – Genève 47 – Gex 29 – Lons-le-Saunier 74 – St-Claude 16

Office de tourisme, Grande Rue ✆ 03 84 41 27 01, Fax 03 84 41 25 59

La Spatule
Grande'rue – ✆ 03 84 41 20 23 – www.hotellaspatule.com – la-spatule2@wanadoo.fr – Fax 03 84 41 24 16 – Closed 19 April-5 May, 20 October-15 December and Monday off season
26 rm – †€ 40/44 ††€ 55/63, ☕ € 9 – ½ P € 53/59
Rest – Menu (€ 13), € 17/35 – Carte € 26/40
◆ At the foot of the slopes, a non-smoking chalet offering functional rooms with firwood furnishings (choose rooms with mountain view). Regional fare and interesting cheeses. Dish of the day available in adjoining café.

in Lajoux 6 km south by D 292 – ✉ 39310 – **pop. 256** – **alt. 1 180 m**

De la Haute Montagne without rest
– ✆ 03 84 41 20 47 – www.hotel-de-la-montagne.com – hotel-haute-montagne@wanadoo.fr – Fax 03 84 41 24 20 – Closed 13 April-2 May and 3 October-15 December
20 rm – †€ 38 ††€ 54, ☕ € 8 – ½ P € 49/54
◆ A family-run hotel founded by a former cross country skiing champion in the heart of the Haut Jura nature park. Modest, well-kept rooms. Garden.

LAMPAUL- PLOUARZEL – 29 Finistère – 308 C4 – pop. 1 967 – alt. 34 m – ✉ 29810 9 A1

Paris 615 – Rennes 263 – Quimper 98 – Brest 24 – Landerneau 46

Office de tourisme, 7, rue de la Mairie ✆ 02 98 84 04 74, Fax 02 98 84 04 34

Auberge du Vieux Puits VISA MC

pl. de l'Église – ✆ 02 98 84 09 13 – j.pierre.stephan@wanadoo.fr – Fax 02 98 84 09 13 – Closed 9-28 March, 21 September-10 October, Sunday dinner and Monday

Rest – Menu € 22 (weekday lunch), € 34/49 – Carte € 40/60

◆ Typical old granite building in the village centre. Traditional cuisine served in a rustic dining room or on the south-facing terrace, where the old well that gives its name to the restaurant can be seen.

LAMURE-SUR-AZERGUES – 69 Rhône – 327 F3 – pop. 1 055 – alt. 383 m – ✉ 69870 44 B1

Paris 446 – Lyon 50 – Mâcon 51 – Roanne 49 – Tarare 36 – Villefranche-sur-Saône 29

Office de tourisme, rue du Vieux Pont ✆ 04 74 03 13 26, Fax 04 74 03 13 26

Château de Pramenoux P

2 km to the west – ✆ 04 74 03 16 43 – www.pramenoux.com – emmanuel@pramenoux.com

4 rm – †€ 120 ††€ 125 **Table d'hôte** – Menu € 35 bi

◆ This château features a large entrance hall with a magnificent staircase and quiet rooms furnished with antiques. The Royal room also features a four-poster bed. Candlelit dinner accompanied by fine music.

LANARCE – 07 Ardèche – 331 G5 – pop. 172 – alt. 1 180 m – ✉ 07660 44 A3

Paris 579 – Aubenas 44 – Langogne 18 – Privas 72 – Le Puy-en-Velay 48

Le Provence rm, P VISA MC

N 102 – ✆ 04 66 69 46 06 – www.hotel-le-provence.com – reservation@hotel-le-provence.com – Fax 04 66 69 41 56 – Open 15 March-12 November

19 rm – †€ 44/57 ††€ 44/57, € 8 – ½ P € 46/57

Rest – Menu (€ 14), € 19/35 – Carte € 21/33

◆ All the rooms in this modern building, on a busy thoroughfare, are soundproofed and overlook the rear. Choose those that have just been renovated. Appetising local cuisine served in the dining room or on the peaceful terrace.

LANCIÉ – 69 Rhône – 327 H2 – pop. 719 – alt. 210 m – ✉ 69220 43 E1

Paris 418 – Lyon 56 – Villeurbanne 65 – Saint-Étienne 115

Le Petit Nid de Pierres AC rm, P VISA MC

Le Chatelard – ✆ 04 74 04 10 39 – www.pariaud.com – marcel.pariaud@wanadoo.fr – Fax 04 74 69 82 10

5 rm – †€ 70/75 ††€ 80 **Table d'hôte** – Menu € 25 bi/27 bi

◆ Hidden by thick stonewalls, this well-restored old farmhouse is ideal for a relaxed stay in the country. Well-equipped rooms with personal touches. Flower-decked balconies, fountain and pool. Regional dishes are served in a country chic decor. Tasting evenings in the cellar.

LANCIEUX – 22 Côtes-d'Armor – 309 J3 – pop. 1 298 – alt. 24 m – ✉ 22770 10 C1

Paris 413 – Rennes 80 – Saint-Brieuc 85 – Saint-Malo 18 – Plérin 87

Office de tourisme, square Jean Conan ✆ 02 96 86 25 37, Fax 02 96 86 29 81

Des Bains without rest P VISA MC AE

20 r. Poncel – ✆ 02 96 86 31 33 – http://pagesperso-orange.fr/bertrand.mehouas – bertrand.mehouas@wanadoo.fr – Fax 02 96 86 22 85 – Closed Sunday from December to March

12 rm – †€ 60/100 ††€ 65/100, € 8

◆ Near the shore, this family-run hotel was founded in 1894. Functional rooms, some with kitchenettes. Breakfast served on the veranda. Creperie in high season.

LANCRANS – 01 Ain – **328** I4 – see Bellegarde-sur-Valserine

LANDES-LE-GAULOIS – 41 Loir-et-Cher – **318** E6 – pop. 657 – alt. 105 m – ✉ 41190 11 **B2**

Paris 195 – Blois 17 – Château-Renault 25 – Tours 54 – Vendôme 21

Château de Moulins without rest
north-east: 2 km on the D 26 – ✆ 02 54 20 17 93 – Fax 02 54 20 17 99
23 rm – †€ 105/205 ††€ 153/205, ☕ € 11 – 3 suites
◆ In the heart of a wooded estate with a lake, this elegant château, built between the 12C and 17C has large rooms, many of which are furnished with antiques. Heliport.

LANDSER – 68 Haut-Rhin – **315** I10 – see Mulhouse

LANGEAC – 43 Haute-Loire – **331** C3 – pop. 4 004 – alt. 505 m – ✉ 43300 Auvergne 6 **C3**

Paris 508 – Brioude 31 – Mende 92 – Le Puy-en-Velay 45 – St-Flour 54
Office de tourisme, place Aristide Briand ✆ 04 71 77 05 41, Fax 04 71 77 19 93

in Reilhac North: 3 km by D 585 – ✉ 43300 Mazeyrat-d'Allier

Val d'Allier rest, rest, VISA
– ✆ 04 71 77 02 11 – hotel.val-allier@wanadoo.fr – Fax 04 71 77 19 20
– Open 1st April-31 October and closed Sunday evening and Monday off season
22 rm – †€ 46/51 ††€ 57/62, ☕ € 9 – ½ P € 52/58
Rest – *(dinner only) (pre-book)* Menu (€ 20), € 25, € 30/38
◆ This comfortable hotel in a typical village in the Gorges de l'Allier is particularly popular with hikers and sports' enthusiasts. Traditional, regional cuisine served in a renovated modern dining room.

LANGEAIS – 37 Indre-et-Loire – **317** L5 – pop. 3 848 – alt. 41 m – ✉ 37130 Châteaux of the Loire 11 **A2**

Paris 259 – Angers 101 – Château-la-Vallière 28 – Chinon 26 – Saumur 41 – Tours 24
Office de tourisme, place du 14 Juillet ✆ 02 47 96 58 22, Fax 02 47 96 83 41
Château★★: apartments★★★.
Park ★ du château de Cinq-Mars-la-Pile Northeast: 5 km by N 152.

Errard VISA AE
2 r. Gambetta – ✆ 02 47 96 82 12 – www.errard.com – info@errard.com
– Fax 02 47 96 56 72 – Closed 15 December-6 February, Sunday dinner and Monday from 1st October to 14 May
Rest – Menu € 29/53 bi – Carte € 52/68
◆ Former post house (1653) in a tasteful rustic setting near the château. Classic family cooking featuring Touraine flavours.

Au Coin des Halles VISA AE
9 r. Gambetta – ✆ 02 47 96 37 25 – aucoindeshalles@hotmail.fr
– Fax 02 47 96 37 25 – Closed Thursday lunch and Wednesday except July-August
Rest – Menu (€ 15), € 29/49 – Carte € 39/49
◆ Traditional house typical of the local area, near the château. Elegant decor in the dining room where seasonal dishes are served. Friendly welcome. Terrace dining in fine weather.

in St-Patrice West: 10 km by Bourgueil road – pop. 681 – alt. 39 m – ✉ 37130

Château de Rochecotte rest, VISA AE
43 r. Dorothée de Dino – ✆ 02 47 96 16 16
– www.chateau-de-rochecotte.fr – chateau.rochecotte@wanadoo.fr
– Fax 02 47 96 90 59 – Closed 16 January-8 March
32 rm – †€ 135/242 ††€ 135/242, ☕ € 18 – 3 suites – ½ P € 124/174
Rest – Menu (€ 38), € 43 – Carte € 68/85
◆ Aristocratic residence frequented by the Prince de Talleyrand. Period furnishings in the bedrooms and pleasant terrace with pergola overlooking the gardens. The dining rooms sport an elegant 18C style. Up-to-date cuisine.

LANGON – 33 Gironde – 335 J7 – pop. 6 168 – alt. 10 m – ✉ 33210 3 B2
Atlantic Coast

Paris 624 – Bergerac 83 – Bordeaux 49 – Libourne 54 – Marmande 47 – Mont-de-Marsan 86

Office de tourisme, 11, allées Jean-Jaurès ✆ 05 56 63 68 00, Fax 05 56 63 68 09

des Graves et Sauternais Lac de Seguin, E : 5 km on D 116, ✆ 05 56 62 25 43

Château de Roquetaillade★★ South: 7 km.

Claude Darroze with rm

95 cours Gén. Leclerc – ✆ 05 56 63 00 48 – www.darroze.com – restaurant.darroze@wanadoo.fr – Fax 05 56 63 41 15 – Closed 14 October-7 November, 5-22 January, Sunday dinner and Monday lunch

15 rm – €60 €75/105, €13 – ½ P €95/115

Rest – Menu €42/80 – Carte €70/105

Spec. Lamproie à la bordelaise aux blancs de poireaux (Jan. to April). Noix de ris de veau braisée au jus, saveur andalouse. Soufflé léger au Grand Marnier. **Wines** Cotes de Bordeaux-Saint-Macaire, Graves.

◆ Delicious classic cuisine and a sumptuous Bordeaux wine list (600 appellations): this traditional establishment is an invitation to pleasure. Terrace under the plane trees.

Chez Cyril

62 cours Fossés – ✆ 05 56 76 25 66 – www.restaurant-chez-cyril.com – sarlles3c@orange.fr – Fax 05 56 63 25 21 – Closed Sunday

Rest – Menu €12 (weekday lunch), €22/29 – Carte €28/55

◆ Pleasant welcome in a warm contemporary dining room (teak furnishings) or on the courtyard terrace with fountain. Traditional cuisine.

in St-Macaire North: 2 km – pop. 1 670 – alt. 15 m – ✉ 33490

Verdelais: calvary ≤★ North: 3 km - Château de Malromé★ North: 6 km - Ste-Croix-du-Mont: ≤★, grottoes★ Northwest: 5 km.

Abricotier with rm

RN 113 – ✆ 05 56 76 83 63 – restaurant.abricotier@wanadoo.fr – Fax 05 56 76 28 51 – Closed 23-30 March, 29 June-3 July, 31 August-4 September, 12 November-9 December, Tuesday dinner and Monday

3 rm – €55 €60, €7 **Rest** – Menu €20/40 – Carte €40/50

◆ A regional building near the medieval city. Welcoming modern decor, shaded terrace garden and appetising traditional cuisine.

Do not confuse X with ✿!
X defines comfort, while stars are awarded for the best cuisine, across all categories of comfort.

LANGRES – 52 Haute-Marne – 313 L6 – pop. 8 761 – alt. 466 m – ✉ 52200 14 C3
Northern France and the Paris Region

Paris 285 – Chaumont 35 – Dijon 79 – Nancy 142 – Vesoul 76

Office de tourisme, square Olivier Lahalle ✆ 03 25 87 67 67, Fax 03 25 87 73 33

Site★★ - Ramparts walkway★★ - St-Mammès cathedral★ Y - Gallo-Roman Section ★ in the musée d'art et d'histoire Y **M**[1].

Plan on following page

Le Cheval Blanc

4 r. de l'Estres – ✆ 03 25 87 07 00 – www.hotel-langres.com – info@hotel-langres.com – Fax 03 25 87 23 13 – Closed 2-30 November Z a

23 rm – €69 €69/95, €10 – ½ P €80/110

Rest – *(closed Wednesday lunch)* Menu (€21), €34 – Carte €55/70

◆ Bishop Bossuet received the sub-deacons at this historic church which became an inn during the Revolution. Characterful rooms, more functional in the annexe. Dining room decorated with work by local artists. Quiet terrace. Modern menu.

LANGRES

- Aubert (R.) . . . . Y
- Barbier-d'Aucourt (R.) . . . . Y 3
- Beligné (R. Ch.) . . . . Y 4
- Belle-Allée (La) . . . . Y 5
- Boillot (R.) . . . . Y 6
- Boulière (Porte) . . . . Y
- Boulière (R.) . . . . Y 7
- Canon (R.) . . . . Y 8
- Centenaire (Pl. du) . . . . Y 10
- Chambrûlard (R.) . . . . X 12
- Chavannes (R. des) . . . . Z 13
- Crémaillière (R. de la) . . . . . . Y 14
- Croc (R. du) . . . . Y 15
- Denfert-Rochereau (R.) . . . . . . Z 16
- Diderot (Pl.) . . . . Y
- Diderot (R.) . . . . YZ
- Durand (R. Pierre) . . . . Y 17
- Duvet (Pl. J.) . . . . Y
- États-Unis (Pl. des) . . . . Z
- Gambetta (R.) . . . . Y 18
- Grand-Bie (R. du) . . . . Y 19
- Grand-Cloître (R. du) . . . . . . Y 20
- Grouchy (Pl. Col.-de) . . . . . . Z 21
- Hôtel-de-Ville (Porte de l') . . . . Y
- Jenson (Pl.) . . . . Z
- Lambert-Payen (R.) . . . . Y 24
- Lattre-de-Tassigny (Bd Mar.-de) . . . . YZ
- Leclerc (R. Général) . . . . Y 25
- Lescornel (R.) . . . . Y 26
- Longe-Porte (Porte de) X
- Longe-Porte (R. de) . . . . X 27
- Mance (Square J.) . . . . Y 28
- Minot (R.) . . . . Z 31
- Morlot (R. Card.) . . . . Y 32
- Roger (R.) . . . . Y 33
- Roussat (R. Jean) . . . . Y 35
- St-Didier (R.) . . . . Y 36
- Tassel (R.) X
- Terreaux (R. des) . . . . Y 37
- Tournelle (R. de la) . . . . Y 39
- Turenne (R. de) . . . . Y 41
- Ursulines (R. des) . . . . Y 43
- Verdun (Pl. de) X
- Walferdin (R.) . . . . Y 44
- Ziegler (Pl.) . . . . Y 45

Grand Hôtel de L'Europe

23 r. Diderot – ☎ 03 25 87 10 88 – hotel-europe.langres@wanadoo.fr – Fax 03 25 87 60 65 – Closed Sunday dinner from 1st November to 31 May — Z e

26 rm – €75 €99, €9 **Rest** – Menu (€18), €27/46 – Carte €28/52

◆ Inside the ramparts, a former posthouse along a main road in the old town. Spacious rooms, quieter at the back. Light wood, parquet flooring and country furniture in this dining room adjoining the hotel bar.

at Lac de la Liez by ②, N 19 and D 284: 6 km – ✉ 52200 Langres

Auberge des Voiliers with rm

au bord du Lac – ☎ 03 25 87 05 74 – www.hotel-voiliers.com – auberge.voiliers@wanadoo.fr – Fax 03 25 87 24 22 – Open 18 March-1 November and closed Sunday dinner, Tuesday lunch and Monday

10 rm – €50/90 €50/110, €8

Rest – Menu €20 (weekday lunch), €22/34 – Carte €26/49

◆ An inn ideally situated next to the lake. Restaurant dining room decorated with frescos; views from the veranda. Small, air-conditioned rooms on a nautical theme.

The red symbol?
This denotes the very essence of peace – only the sound of birdsong first thing in the morning…

LANGUIMBERG – 57 Moselle – 307 M6 – pop. 208 – alt. 290 m – ✉ 57810 27 C2

Paris 411 – Lunéville 43 – Metz 79 – Nancy 65 – Sarrebourg 21 – Saverne 48

Chez Michèle (Bruno Poiré)
– ✆ 03 87 03 92 25 – www.chezmichele.fr – contact@chezmichele.fr – Fax 03 87 03 93 47 – Closed 23 December-10 January, Tuesday except lunch from May to August and Wednesday
Rest – Menu (€ 18), € 27 – Carte € 30/70
Spec. Fine tarte de légumes en tempura. Moelleux de brochet de nos étangs. Café liégeois.
◆ The old village café is now a gourmet inn. Family atmosphere where the young chef produces precise, generous and judiciously inventive cuisine.

LANNILIS – Finistère – 308 D3 – pop. 4 473 – alt. 48 m – ✉ 29870 9 A1

Paris 599 – Brest 23 – Landerneau 29 – Morlaix 63 – Quimper 89

Office de tourisme, 1, place de l'Église ✆ 02 98 04 05 43, Fax 02.98.04.05.43

Auberge des Abers (Jean-Luc L'Hourre)
5 pl. Gén. Leclerc, (near the church) – ✆ 02 98 04 00 29 – anne-laure.brouzet@wanadoo.fr – Closed 15-30 September and 15-30 January
Rest – *(open evenings Wednesday to Saturday and Sunday lunchtime) (number of covers limited, pre-book)* Menu € 48/125 bi
Rest *Côté Bistrot* – *(open for lunch from Tuesday to Saturday)* Menu € 22/27 – Carte € 20/40
Spec. Tourteau aux petits légumes. Lotte au citron et aux asperges. Millefeuille aux pommes, glace au sarrasin.
◆ Fine and light gastronomic cuisine with the focus on fish and seafood. Elegant decor (display of menus from prestigious restaurants where the chef has eaten). Cookery class on Tuesday evenings. Home cooking served at Côté Bistrot.

LANNION – 22 Côtes-d'Armor – 309 B2 – pop. 19 400 – alt. 12 m – ✉ 22300 Brittany 9 B1

Paris 516 – Brest 96 – Morlaix 42 – St-Brieuc 65

Lannion: ✆ 02 96 05 82 00, 4 km north

Office de tourisme, 2, quai d'Aiguillon ✆ 02 96 46 41 00, Fax 02 96 37 19 64

Old houses★ (pl.Général Leclerc) - Brélévenez church ★: burial★.

Manoir du Launay without rest
chemin de Ker Ar Faout, in Servel, 3 km northwest on the D 21 – ✆ 02 96 47 21 24 – www.manoirdulaunay.com – manoirdulaunay@orange.fr – Fax 02 96 47 21 24
5 rm – †€ 78/108 ††€ 85/115
◆ Plush sitting room, antiques and personal touches in the spacious and stylish guestrooms. This 17C manor reconciles the charm of yesteryear with modern comforts. Park.

Perros-Guirec road 5 km on the D 788 – ✉ 22300 Lannion

Arcadia

Crec'h-Quillé – ✆ 02 96 48 45 65 – www.hotel-arcadia.com – hotel-arcadia@wanadoo.fr – Fax 02 96 48 15 68 – Closed 19 December-4 January
29 rm – †€ 49/65 ††€ 50/65, € 7
Rest – Menu (€ 12), € 16 (weekdays)/20 – Carte € 25/35
◆ Not far from the Telecom centre, this modern-looking hotel provides spruced up rooms (quieter to the rear); some duplexes. Billiards bar and pool in a veranda. Simple dishes and grilled meats served in the contemporary restaurant next to the hotel.

in La Ville-Blanche on the Tréguier road: 5 km on the D 786 – ✉ 22300 Rospez

XXX **La Ville Blanche** (Jean-Yves Jaguin)
– ✆ 02 96 37 04 28 – www.la-ville-blanche.com – jaguin@la-ville-blanche.com – Fax 02 96 46 57 82 – Closed 29 June-8 July, 20 December-29 January, Sunday dinner and Wednesday except July-August and Monday
Rest – *(pre-book Sat - Sun)* Menu € 36 (weekdays)/80 – Carte € 68/85
Spec. Saint-Jacques des Côtes d'Armor (Oct. to Mar.). Homard rôti au beurre salé, ses pinces en ragoût (April to Oct.). Parfait glacé à la menthe et au chocolat.
◆ A delightful family home decorated in an uncluttered classical style. Fresh herbs from the cottage garden subtly enhance the chef's flavoursome cuisine.

LANS-EN-VERCORS – 38 Isère – 333 G7 – pop. 2 303 – alt. 1 120 m – Winter sports : 1 020/1 980 m 16 – ✉ 38250 45 **C2**

Paris 576 – Grenoble 27 – Villard-de-Lans 8 – Voiron 37
Office de tourisme, 246, avenue Léopold Fabre ✆ 08 11 46 00 38, Fax 04 76 95 47 99

Le Val Fleuri rest,
730 av. L. Fabre – ✆ 04 76 95 41 09 – www.le-val-fleuri.com – hotel.levalfleuri@orange.fr – Fax 04 76 94 34 69 – Open 2 May-17 October, 19 December-21 March and closed Sunday dinner and Monday in May, September and October
14 rm – €40 €40, € 9,50 – ½ P € 54/68 **Rest** – Menu (€ 17), € 26/35
◆ Time seems to have stood still in this attractive residence from 1928, with a perfectly preserved pre-1940s character. Extremely well-kept rooms, sometimes adorned with Art Deco furniture and lamps. Lovely 1930s dining room, terrace under the lime trees and traditional recipes.

at col de la Croix-Perrin Southwest: 4 km by D 106 – ✉ 38250 Lans-en-Vercors

X **Auberge de la Croix Perrin** with rm
Croix-Perrin pass – ✆ 04 76 95 40 02 – www.aubergedelacroixperrin.com – frederic.joly10@wanadoo.fr – Fax 04 76 94 33 10 – Closed 10 April-15 May and 23 October-18 December
9 rm – €41/45 €46/60, € 8 – ½ P € 45/53
Rest – *(closed Wednesday and weekday dinner except school holidays)*
Menu € 16 (weekday lunch), € 23/28 – Carte € 22/38 lunch only
◆ The dining room of this old forest house, surrounded by fir trees, offers a clear view. Local lunchtime dishes and more inventive cuisine in the evening. Charming rooms.

Undecided between two equivalent establishments?
Within each category,
establishments are classified in our order of preference.

LANSLEBOURG-MONT-CENIS – 73 Savoie – 333 O6 – pop. 604 – alt. 1 399 m – Winter sports : 1 400/2 800 m 1 21 – ✉ 73480 French Alps 45 **D2**

Paris 685 – Albertville 112 – Chambéry 125 – St-Jean-de-Maurienne 53 – Torino 94
Office de tourisme, Grande Rue ✆ 04 79 05 23 66, Fax 04 79 05 82 17

La Vieille Poste
87 r. du Mont Cenis – ✆ 04 79 05 93 47 – www.lavieilleposte.com – info@lavieilleposte.com – Fax 04 79 05 86 85 – Closed 20 April-11 May and 18 October-23 November
17 rm – €55/65 €65/70, € 8,50 – ½ P € 65/73
Rest – Menu € 15 (weekday lunch), € 22/39 – Carte approx. € 39 dinner only
◆ A friendly, recently renovated family pension in the centre of this resort in the Haute Maurienne. Small, up-to-the-minute, impeccably maintained rooms. Rustic Savoyard decor in the dining room.

LANTOSQUE – 06 Alpes-Maritimes – 341 E4 – pop. 1 207 – alt. 550 m – ✉ 06450 — 41 D2

▶ Paris 883 – Nice 51 – Puget-Théniers 53 – St-Martin-Vésubie 16 – Sospel 42

ℹ Syndicat d'initiative, Mairie ✆ 04 93 03 00 02, Fax 04 93 03 03 12

La Source

Montée des casernes, D 373 – ✆ 04 93 03 05 44 – lasource11@wanadoo.fr – Closed 1st-18 January, Sunday dinner and Monday

Rest – *(number of covers limited, pre-book)* Menu (€ 18), € 25

◆ A small Provençal inn with rustic charm and a lively atmosphere. The owner, who is passionate about cooking, offers a simply prepared but delicious set menu.

LAON Ⓟ – 02 Aisne – 306 D5 – pop. 26 500 – alt. 181 m – ✉ 02000 — 37 D2

Northern France and the Paris Region

▶ Paris 141 – Reims 62 – St-Quentin 48 – Soissons 38

ℹ Office de tourisme, place du Parvis Gautier de Mortagne ✆ 03 23 20 28 62, Fax 03 23 20 68 11

⛳ de l'Ailette Cerny-en-LaonnoisS : 16 km on D 967, ✆ 03 23 24 83 99

👁 Site★★ - Notre-Dame cathedral ★★: nave★★★ - Rempart du Midi and porte d'Ardon★ CZ - St-Martin abbey ★ BZ - Porte de Soissons★ ABZ - Rue Thibesard ≤★ BZ - Museum ★ and Templiers church ★ CZ.

Plans on following pages

La Bannière de France

11 r. F. Roosevelt – ✆ 03 23 23 21 44 – www.hoteldelabannieredefrance.com – hotel.banniere.de.france@wanadoo.fr – Fax 03 23 23 31 56 – Closed 22 December-3 January BCZ **t**

18 rm – 🛉€ 55 🛉🛉€ 68, ☕ € 9 – ½ P € 64/69

Rest – Menu (€ 23), € 29 – Carte € 25/36

◆ This post house in the upper part of town was built in 1685, but in the 1920s it was home to the town's first cinema. Simple rooms. The classicism of the long narrow dining room is full of old French charm.

Hostellerie St-Vincent

111 av. Ch. de Gaulle, via ② – ✆ 03 23 23 42 43 – www.stvincent-laon.com – hotel.st.vincent@wanadoo.fr – Fax 03 23 79 22 55

47 rm – 🛉€ 60/68 🛉🛉€ 60/68, ☕ € 8

Rest – *(closed Sunday)* Menu (€ 13), € 18 – Carte € 17/35

◆ A modern motel-style establishment built below the old Carolingian capital perched on its rock. Functional rooms. Spacious dining room in a restaurant where Alsatian gastronomy is given pride of place.

Zorn- La Petite Auberge

45 bd Brossolette – ✆ 03 23 23 02 38 – palaon@orange.fr – Fax 03 23 23 31 01 – Closed 27 April-3 May, 9-23 August, February holiday, Saturday lunch, Monday dinner and Sunday except bank holidays CY **a**

Rest – Menu (€ 20), € 27/50 – Carte € 49/70

Rest *Bistrot St-Amour* – Menu (€ 12), € 15/17 – Carte approx. € 30

◆ In the lower part of town, this restaurant has been completely renovated in a contemporary style: clean lines, simple colours, modern lighting. Inventive modern menu and speedy service in a simple bistro.

in Samoussy by ② and D 977: 13 km – pop. 379 – alt. 84 m – ✉ 02840

Le Relais Charlemagne

4 rte de Laon – ✆ 03 23 22 21 50 – www.lerelaischarlemagne.fr – relais.charlemagne@wanadoo.fr – Fax 03 23 22 18 75 – Closed 1st-16 August, February holidays, Wednesday dinner, Sunday dinner and Monday

Rest – Menu (€ 25), € 45/58 – Carte € 53/62

◆ Berthe, the mother of Charlemagne, was originally from this village. The restaurant has two elegant dining areas, one overlooking the garden. Classic cuisine.

LAON

- Arquebuse (R. de l') . . . . CZ 2
- Aubry (Pl.) . . . . CZ 3
- Berthelot (R. Marcelin) . . . . . AZ 5
- Bossus (R. de l'Abbé) . . . . . DY 6
- Bourg (R. du) . . . . BCZ 8
- Carnot (Av.) . . . . CY
- Change (R. du) . . . . CZ 9
- Charles de Gaulle (Av.) . . . . DY 12
- Châtelaine (R.) . . . . CZ 13
- Cloître (R. du) . . . . CZ
- Combattants d'Afrique du Nord (Pl. des) . . . . DZ
- Cordeliers (R. des) . . . . CZ
- Doumer (R. Paul) . . . . CZ
- Ermant (R. Georges) . . . . CZ

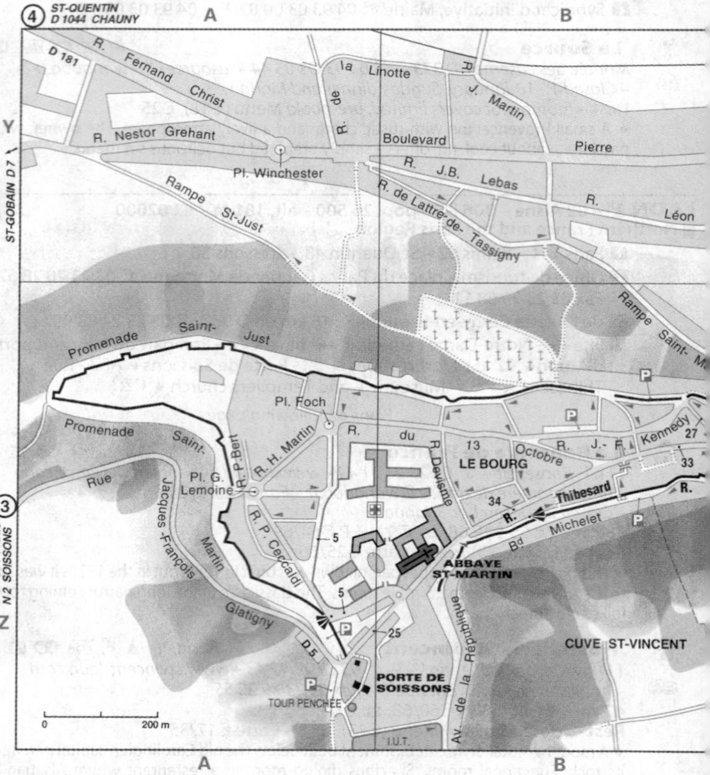

in Chamouille by D 967 DZ : **13 km – pop. 243 – alt. 112 m – ✉ 02860**

Mercure — rm, rest, rest,

parc nautique de l'Ailette, 0.5 km south by D 967 –
☎ 03 23 24 84 85 – www.ailette.net
– hotel-mercure@ailette.fr
– Fax 03 23 24 81 20
VISA MC AE

58 rm – 🚹€ 95 🚹🚹€ 105, ☕ € 13
Rest – Menu (€ 21), € 26/50 – Carte € 22/45

◆ A modern building standing alone on the banks of a huge stretch of water with water sports facilities. Spacious rooms with loggias. Golf. A modern dining room and terrace by the swimming pool, on the banks of the Ailette water park.

"Rest" appears in red for establishments with a ✿ (star) or ☺ (Bib Gourmand).

…urée (R. de la) . . . . **DY** 23
…r (Prom. Barthélémy de) . . **CZ** 24
…educ (R. Eugène) . . . . **DY**
…bération (R. de la) . . . . . . **ABZ** 25
…arquette (R. Père) . . . . **BZ** 27
Martinot (Allée Jean) . . . . . . **DZ** 28
Mortagne (Pl. Gautier de) . . . **CZ** 29
Rabin (Promenade Yitzhak) . **CZ** 30
Roosevelt (R. Franklin) . . . . . **CZ** 31
St-Jean (R.) . . . . **BZ** 33
St-Martin (R.) . . . . **BZ** 34
Signier (R. de) . . . . **CZ** 36
Thuillart (R. Fernand) . . . . . . **DY** 37
Victor-Hugo (Pl.) . . . . **DY** 39
Vinchon (R.) . . . . **CZ** 40

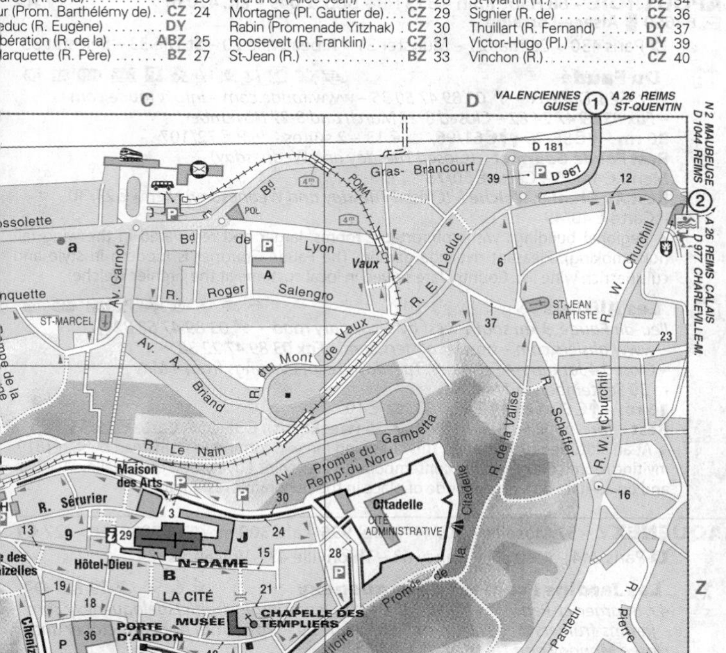

LAPALISSE – 03 Allier – 326 I5 – pop. 3 332 – alt. 280 m – ✉ 03120 6 **C1**

Auvergne

Paris 346 – Digoin 45 – Mâcon 122 – Moulins 50 – Roanne 49 – St-Pourçain-sur-Sioule 30

Office de tourisme, 26, rue Winston Churchill ✆ 04 70 99 08 39, Fax 04 70 99 28 09

Château ★★.

Galland with rm

20 pl. de la République – ✆ 04 70 99 07 21 – www.hotelgalland.fr – contact@hotelgalland.fr – Fax 04 43 23 41 15 – Closed 24 November-9 December, 26 January-9 February, Sunday dinner except July-August and Monday

8 rm – †€ 50/75 ††€ 50/75, ☕ € 8 – ½ P € 50/68

Rest – *(pre-book Sat - Sun)* Menu € 26/57 – Carte € 39/55

◆ Elegant, contemporary dining room in pastel shades serving modern dishes; comfortable, well-kept rooms.

LAPOUTROIE – 68 Haut-Rhin – 315 H8 – pop. 2 049 – alt. 420 m – ✉ 68650 Alsace-Lorraine 1 A2

Paris 430 – Colmar 21 – Munster 31 – Ribeauvillé 20 – St-Dié 33 – Sélestat 33

Du Faudé

28 r. Gén. Dufieux – ☎ 03 89 47 50 35 – www.faude.com – info@faude.com – Fax 03 89 47 24 82 – Closed 8-27 March and 8-27 November

30 rm – †€ 55/75 ††€ 61/96, ☕ € 13 – 2 suites – ½ P € 72/107

Rest *Faudé Gourmet* – *(Closed Tuesday and Wednesday)*
Menu € 44/76 – Carte € 50/75

Rest *Au Grenier Welche* – *(Closed Tuesday and Wednesday)* Menu € 23/30 – Carte € 40/49

◆ Regional buildings with comfortable rooms, larger and renovated in the wing (all non-smoking). Pleasant riverside garden. The Faudé Gourmet is modern in style and cuisine; rich wine list. Country fare served in local costume at the Grenier Welche.

Les Alisiers

lieu-dit Faudé, 3 km south-west by secondary road – ☎ 03 89 47 52 82 – www.alisiers.com – hotel@alisiers.com – Fax 03 89 47 22 38 – Closed 4 January-4 February, Tuesday except evenings from 4 May to 30 September and Monday

16 rm – †€ 50/125 ††€ 50/180, ☕ € 10

Rest – *(pre-book Sat - Sun)* Menu € 25 (weekdays), € 35/55 – Carte € 35/55

◆ At an altitude of 700 metres, this charming inn was formerly a farmstead built in 1819. Inviting rooms, decorated in a contemporary chalet spirit. Lovely view of the valley. Alsatian and up-to-date dishes take pride of place in the panoramic restaurant.

LAQUENEXY – 57 Moselle – 307 I4 – pop. 995 – alt. 300 m – ✉ 57530 27 C1

Paris 344 – Metz 17 – Nancy 63 – Thionville 43 – Völklingen 84

Les Jardins Fruitiers de Laquenexy

4 r. Bourger-et-Perrin – ☎ 03 87 35 01 00 – www.jardinsfruitiersdelaquenexy.com – jardins-fruitiers@cg57.fr – Fax 03 87 35 01 09 – Open from April to October and closed Monday and Tuesday

Rest – *(lunch only) (number of covers limited, pre-book)* Menu (€ 15), € 20 – Carte approx. € 24

◆ Delightful terrace overlooking a wonderful garden with over a thousand varieties of fruit trees. Modern cuisine using fruit and veg from the kitchen plot. Fine food store.

LAQUEUILLE – 63 Puy-de-Dôme – 326 D9 – pop. 397 – alt. 1 000 m – ✉ 63820 5 B2

Paris 455 – Aubusson 74 – Clermont-Ferrand 40 – Mauriac 73 – Le Mont-Dore 15 – Ussel 43

Northeast : **2 km by D 922 and secondary road – ✉ 63820 Laqueuille**

Auberge de Fondain

Fondain – ☎ 04 73 22 01 35 – www.auberge-fondain.com – auberge.de.fondain@wanadoo.fr – Fax 04 73 22 06 13 – Closed 24 October-early December

6 rm – †€ 36/60 ††€ 48/80, ☕ € 8 – ½ P € 40/85

Rest – *(pre-book)* Menu € 17/25

◆ A large old house lost in the countryside, individual rooms with flower themes, mountain biking, a fitness centre, etc. A lovely green setting! Rustic interior serving classic fare: Auvergne specialities chalked up on a slate.

LARAGNE-MONTÉGLIN – 05 Hautes-Alpes – 334 C7 – pop. 3 296 – alt. 571 m – ✉ 05300 40 B2

Paris 687 – Digne-les-Bains 58 – Gap 40 – Sault 60 – Serres 17 – Sisteron 18

Office de tourisme, place des Aires ☎ 04 92 65 09 38, Fax 04 92 65 28 41

Chrisma without rest

rte de Grenoble – ☎ 04 92 65 09 36 – Fax 04 92 65 08 12 – Open 1st March-30 November

13 rm – †€ 45/50 ††€ 45/50, ☕ € 6

◆ The pleasant garden and terrace are the main assets of this hotel at the foot of the Chabre mountain, famous for hang-gliding. The rooms are spacious and well-renovated.

Les Terrasses
av. de Provence, (D 1075) – ✆ 04 92 65 08 54 – hotellesterrasses@wanadoo.fr – Fax 04 92 65 21 08 – Open 1st April-1st November
15 rm – †€ 29/53 ††€ 45/53, ☕ € 7 – ½ P € 51
Rest – *(open 1er May-1st October) (dinner only)* Menu (€ 17), € 22 – Carte € 23/33
◆ A small family guesthouse with simple, very well-kept rooms; those on the garden side are quieter and have a terrace with views of the village and Chabre mountain. Traditional meals served in a sunny dining area or under the vine-covered pergola.

L'Araignée Gourmande
8 r. de la Paix – ✆ 04 92 65 13 39 – Closed 16-30 November, February holiday, Sunday dinner except from April to October, Tuesday dinner and Wednesday
Rest – Menu (€ 11), € 14 (weekday lunch), € 24/45 – Carte € 40/55
◆ This family-run eatery with fairly modest decor has all the qualities of a successful restaurant - simple, delicious traditional cuisine, friendly service and reasonable prices.

LARÇAY – 37 Indre-et-Loire – 317 N4 – pop. 2 037 – alt. 82 m – ✉ 37270 — 11 B2

Paris 243 – Angers 134 – Blois 55 – Poitiers 103 – Tours 10 – Vierzon 113

Manoir de Clairbois without rest
2 imp. du Cher – ✆ 02 47 50 59 75 – www.manoirdeclairbois.com – info@manoirdeclairbois.com – Fax 02 47 50 59 76
3 rm ☕ – †€ 115 ††€ 115
◆ This 19C manor stands in a park along the Cher river. Offering large, bright rooms with fine decor and bed linen. The communal areas are furnished with period pieces.

Les Chandelles Gourmandes
44 r. Nationale – ✆ 02 47 50 50 02 – www.chandelles-gourmandes.fr – charret@chandelles-gourmandes.fr – Fax 02 47 50 55 94 – Closed 25 July-5 August, 25 August-5 September, 21-26 December, Sunday dinner and Monday
Rest – Menu € 31/70 – Carte € 42/54
◆ Beams, fireplace and antiques embellish the dining room of this restaurant on the banks of the Cher. Personalised, regional cuisine with fish and other specialities from the Loire.

LE LARDIN-ST-LAZARE – 24 Dordogne – 329 I5 – pop. 1 978 – alt. 86 m – ✉ 24570 — 4 D1

Paris 503 – Brive-la-Gaillarde 28 – Lanouaille 38 – Périgueux 47 – Sarlat-la-Canéda 31

South : 4 km on the D 704, D 62 and minor road – ✉ 24570 Condat-sur-Vézère :

Château de la Fleunie
– ✆ 05 53 51 32 74 – www.lafleunie.com – lafleunie@free.fr – Fax 05 53 50 58 98 – Closed 30 November-1st March
33 rm – †€ 70/90 ††€ 70/180, ☕ € 14 – ½ P € 75/130 **Rest** – Menu 45
◆ This medieval castle, surrounded by a 100-ha park with an animal enclosure, houses rooms with character, sometimes adorned with beams. Other rooms available in a more recent building. Classic food to enjoy in a "château" dining room with a noble air.

in Coly Southeast: 6 km by D 74 and D 62 – **pop. 219** – **alt. 113 m** – ✉ **24120**

Church ★★ of St-Amand-de-Coly Southwest: 3 km, **Dordogne-Berry-Limousin.**

Manoir d'Hautegente
– ✆ 05 53 51 68 03 – www.manoir-hautegente.com – hotel@manoir-hautegente.com – Fax 05 53 50 38 52 – Open 2 April-31 October
17 rm – †€ 95/250 ††€ 95/250, ☕ € 14 – ½ P € 113/185
Rest – Menu € 35 (weekdays)/100 bi – Carte approx. € 70
◆ In a riverside park, this 14C Virginia creeper-clad mill is now an elegant hotel. Cosy interior with antique furniture. Succession of charming vaulted dining rooms and pretty riverside terrace.

LARDY – 91 Essonne – **312** C4 – **pop. 5 638** – **alt. 70 m** – ✉ **91510** 18 **B2**

Paris 46 – Évry 29 – Boulogne-Billancourt 49 – Montreuil 47 – Argenteuil 63

Auberge de l'Espérance

80 Grande-Rue – ✆ 01 69 27 40 82 – Closed 7-31 August, February school holidays, Wednesday dinner, Sunday dinner and Monday

Rest – Menu (€ 19), € 31 – Carte approx. € 46

◆ Smart tables, Lois XVI-style chairs and large central buffet. The fine contemporary cuisine is served in a gayly floral country-style room.

LARGENTIÈRE – **07 Ardèche** – **331** H6 – **pop. 1 942** – **alt. 240 m** – ✉ **07110** **Lyon - Rhone Valley** 44 **A3**

Paris 645 – Alès 66 – Aubenas 18 – Privas 49

Office de tourisme, 8, rue Camille Vielfaure ✆ 04 75 39 14 28, Fax 04 75 39 23 66

Old Largentière★.

in Rocher **North: 4 km by D 5 – pop. 275 – alt. 353 m** – ✉ **07110**

Le Chêne Vert rm, rm, VISA

– ✆ 04 75 88 34 02 – www.hotellechenevert.com – contact@hotellechenevert.com – Fax 04 75 88 33 85 – Open 1 April-31 October and closed Monday and Tuesday in October

25 rm – €59/80 €59/80, €10 – ½ P €53/70

Rest – *(closed Monday lunch)* Menu €20/45 – Carte €35/50

◆ On the border between Vivarais and Cévennes, a convivial place with practical guest rooms, some of which have a balcony and a view over the attractive swimming pool. Traditional dishes and regional recipes served in a discreet, modern setting.

in Sanilhac **South: 7 km by D 312 – pop. 346 – alt. 420 m** – ✉ **07110**

Auberge de la Tour de Brison rm, rm, VISA

at la Chapelette

– ✆ 04 75 39 29 00 – www.belinbrison.com

– belin.c@wanadoo.fr – Fax 04 75 39 19 56

– Open 1st April-31 October and closed Wednesday except from June to August

14 rm – €60/85 €60/85, €10 – ½ P €62/75

Rest – *(pre-book)* Menu €29 – Carte €27/37

◆ This friendly inn is built on a hillside, and commands a view of the valley and the Coiron plateau. Modern rooms, garden and overflow pool. Warm and welcoming, panoramic terrace and tasty regional cuisine.

LARMOR-BADEN – **56 Morbihan** – **308** N9 – **pop. 954** – **alt. 10 m** – ✉ **56870** 9 **A3**

Paris 474 – Auray 15 – Lorient 59 – Pontivy 66 – Vannes 15

Office de tourisme, 24, rue Pen Lannic ✆ 02 97 58 01 26

Cairn ★★ of Gavrinis island: 15 mn by boat.

Aub. du Parc Fétan rest, VISA

17 r. Berder – ✆ 02 97 57 04 38 – www.hotel-parcfetan.com – contact@hotel-parcfetan.com – Fax 02 97 57 21 55 – Open 1 March-12 November

25 rm – €45/52 €45/52, €8 – ½ P €58/62

Rest – *(closed Tuesday dinner except July-August)*

Menu (€17), €25 (dinner), €31/40 – Carte €35/47

◆ This friendly, beautifully kept hotel, a stone's throw from a small beach, offers small but bright guestrooms, most of which overlook Morbihan Bay.

LARMOR-PLAGE – **56 Morbihan** – **308** K8 – **pop. 8 415** – **alt. 4 m** – ✉ **56260** **Brittany** 9 **B2**

Paris 510 – Lorient 7 – Quimper 74 – Vannes 66

≤★ of St-Maurice bridge.

Les Rives du Ter
bd Jean-Monnet – 02 97 35 33 50 – www.lesrivesduter.com – info@lesrivesduter.com – Fax 02 97 35 39 02
58 rm – €94/122 €102/122, €14 – ½ P €85/93
Rest – Menu €23/43 – Carte approx. €30
◆ Quietly located near a bridge, this large, modern hotel provides refined and warm rooms with balconies overlooking the Ter lake. Restaurant with a concise, modern menu, contemporary decor and a lake view.

Les Mouettes
Anse de Kerguélen, 1.5 km west – 02 97 65 50 30 – www.lesmouettes.com – info@lesmouettes.com – Fax 02 97 33 65 33
21 rm – €78 €85, €11 – ½ P €86
Rest – Menu €26 (weekdays)/76 – Carte €48/82
◆ Peace and quiet (out of season), barely interrupted by the cries of the seagulls, in this modern seaside hotel in Kerguelen cove. Gradually renovated rooms. Stunning view of the sea and the isle of Groix from the terrace or dining room.

LARNAC – 30 Gard – 339 K3 – see St-Ambroix

LAROQUE-DES-ALBERES – 66 Pyrénées-Orientales – 344 I7 – pop. 1 941 – alt. 100 m – ✉ 66740 22 B3

Paris 883 – Montpellier 187 – Perpignan 39 – Figueres 50 – Banyoles 90

Office de tourisme, 20, rue Carbonneil 04 68 95 49 97, Fax 04 68 95 42 58

Les Palmiers
33 av. Louis et Michel Soler – 04 68 89 73 61 – www.lespalmiers.eu – contact@lespalmiers.eu – Fax 04 68 81 08 76 – Closed 9-20 March, November, Sunday dinner and Tuesday from mid-September to June, Saturday lunch and Monday
Rest – Menu €22 (weekday lunch), €38/95 – Carte €55/95
◆ Les Palmiers is known for its friendly staff and carefully prepared modern cuisine. Mediterranean fish and seafood washed down with a good choice of Roussillon wines.

LARRAU – 64 Pyrénées-Atlantiques – 342 G6 – pop. 214 – alt. 636 m – ✉ 64560 3 B3

Paris 832 – Oloron-Ste-Marie 42 – Pau 75 – St-Jean-Pied-de-Port 64

Etchemaïté
rm,
in the village – 05 59 28 61 45 – www.hotel-etchemaite.fr – hotel.etchemaite@wanadoo.fr – Fax 05 59 28 72 71 – Closed 8 January-11 February, Sunday evening and Monday from November to April
16 rm – €42/64 €42/64, €8 – ½ P €44/56
Rest – *(closed Sunday dinner and Monday 11 November-31 May)*
Menu €18 (weekdays), €24/45 – Carte €32/45
◆ Simplicity and a family atmosphere in this mountain inn situated in a hamlet in picturesque High Soule. Cosy rooms. Welcoming dining room with exposed stonework and beams, Basque tablecloths, fireplace and view over the valley. Local dishes.

LASCABANES – 46 Lot – 337 D5 – pop. 167 – alt. 180 m – ✉ 46800 28 B1

Paris 598 – Montauban 69 – Toulouse 120 – Villeneuve-sur-Lot 61

Le Domaine de Saint-Géry
– 05 65 31 82 51 – www.saint-gery.com – info@saint-gery.com – Fax 05 65 22 92 89 – Open 16 May-30 September
5 rm – €226/285 €226/611, €28 **Table d'hôte** – Menu €116
◆ This estate includes a truffle and general agricultural farm, with pleasant walking paths and five rooms in different buildings. The décor combines a mixture of old and modern styles. Regional cuisine and roast meat dishes at the table d'hôte.

LASCELLE – 15 Cantal – 330 D4 – pop. 316 – alt. 760 m – ✉ 15590 5 B3

Paris 555 – Aurillac 16 – Bort-les-Orgues 84 – Brioude 94 – Murat 36

Lac des Graves rm, rest, VISA

Jaulhac – ✆ 04 71 47 94 06 – www.lacdesgraves.com – hotel.lac.graves@wanadoo.fr – Fax 04 71 47 96 55 – Closed 5-25 November and 3-18 January

23 rm – †€ 55/80 ††€ 65/85, ☕ € 7

Rest – *(Closed Saturday lunch and Monday lunch)* Menu € 15/28 – Carte € 30/40

◆ In extensive grounds near a popular fishing lake, unusual lakeside wooden chalets; a few family rooms. The large dining room and panoramic terrace overlook beautiful countryside.

LASSEUBE – 64 Pyrénées-Atlantiques – 342 J3 – pop. 1 600 – alt. 188 m – ✉ 64290 3 B3

Paris 797 – Bordeaux 219 – Pau 19 – Tarbes 60

La Ferme Dagué without rest

chemin Croix de Dagué – ✆ 05 59 04 27 11 – www.ferme-dague.com – famille.maumus@wanadoo.fr – Fax 05 59 04 27 11 – Open 28 April-30 October

5 rm ☕ – †€ 43/62 ††€ 52/62

◆ This 18C regional-style farm has retained its superb courtyard with outdoor gallery. Providing charming rooms located in the old loft. Copious breakfast served.

LASTOURS – 11 Aude – 344 F3 – ✉ 11600 22 B2

Paris 782 – Toulouse 107 – Carcassonne 19 – Castres 52 – Narbonne 18

Le Puits du Trésor (Jean-Marc Boyer) VISA

21 rte Quatre Châteaux – ✆ 04 68 77 50 24 – www.lepuitsdutresor.com – contact@lepuitsdutresor.com – Closed 5-20 January, 15 February-10 March, Sunday dinner, Monday and Tuesday

Rest – *(number of covers limited, pre-book)* Menu € 39/75 – Carte € 50/75

Spec. Terrine de foie gras de canard à l'anguille fumée (June to Sep.). Dragée de pigeon du mont royal au suc de raisin muscat (Sep. to Nov.). Soufflé de pomme au mendiant, glace au rhum (Sep. to Dec.). **Wines** Vin de Pays de l'Aude, Vin de Pays des Pyrénées Orientales.

◆ In a village at the foot of the ruined Lastours Castle, modern restaurant serving creative dishes. Simpler bistro area for lunchtime specials only.

LATOUR-DE-CAROL – 66 Pyrénées-Orientales – 344 C8 – pop. 386 – alt. 1 260 m – ✉ 66760 22 A3

Paris 839 – Ax-les-Thermes 37 – Font-Romeu-Odeillo-Via 21 – Perpignan 110

Auberge Catalane VISA

10 av. Puymorens – ✆ 04 68 04 80 66 – www.auberge-catalane.fr – auberge-catalane@orange.fr – Fax 04 68 04 95 25 – Closed 19-27 April, 8 November-7 December, Sunday dinner and Monday

10 rm – †€ 41/45 ††€ 51/55, ☕ € 8 – ½ P € 53/59

Rest – Menu (€ 16), € 26 – Carte approx. € 42 dinner only

◆ At the heart of the Cerdagne plateau, a 100% Catalan inn, taken over recently by a new team. Stylish, well-renovated rooms. Dine in the spruce, rustic dining room, veranda or terrace.

LATTES – 34 Hérault – 339 I7 – see Montpellier

LAUTARET (COL) – 05 Hautes-Alpes – 334 G2 – see Col du Lautaret

LAUTERBOURG – 67 Bas-Rhin – 315 N3 – pop. 2 247 – alt. 115 m – ✉ 67630 1 B1

Paris 519 – Haguenau 40 – Karlsruhe 22 – Strasbourg 63 – Wissembourg 20

Office de tourisme, 21, rue de la 1ère Armée ✆ 03 88 94 66 10, Fax 03 88 54 61 33

XXX **La Poêle d'Or**

35 r. Gén. Mittelhauser – ✆ 03 88 94 84 16 – www.poeledor.com – info@poeledor.com – Fax 03 88 54 62 30 – Closed 25 July-10 August, 5-26 January, Wednesday and Thursday

Rest – Menu € 27 (weekday lunch), € 45/74 – Carte € 40/65

◆ A half-timbered house with an elegant dining room (Louis XIII-style furniture), veranda and terrace. Classical cuisine and a tempting dessert trolley for those with a sweet tooth.

LAUZERTE – 82 Tarn-et-Garonne – 337 C6 – pop. 1 487 – alt. 224 m – ✉ 82110

28 **B1**

- Paris 614 – Agen 53 – Auch 98 – Cahors 39 – Montauban 38
- Office de tourisme, place des Cornières ✆ 05 63 94 61 94, Fax 05 63 94 61 93
- des Roucous SauveterreE : 16 km on D 34, ✆ 05 63 95 83 70

X **Du Quercy** with rm

rest, P VISA MC

fg d'Auriac – ✆ 05 63 94 66 36 – hotel.du.quercy@wanadoo.fr – Fax 05 63 39 06 56 – Closed Toussaint holiday and February holiday, Sunday dinner except July-August and Monday

11 rm – †€ 36/40 ††€ 40/50, ☕ € 7 **Rest** – Menu (€ 12), € 25/35

◆ In the heart of the town known as the "Toledo of Quercy," this 19C country-style house is home to a charming restaurant featuring a light bistro-style dining area with views of the surrounding hills and valleys. Regional cuisine served. Some rooms affording views of the valley.

LAVAL P – 53 Mayenne – 310 E6 – pop. 51 000 – alt. 65 m – ✉ 53000

Normandy

35 **C1**

- Paris 280 – Angers 79 – Le Mans 86 – Rennes 76 – St-Nazaire 153
- Office de tourisme, 1, allée du Vieux Saint-Louis ✆ 02 43 49 46 46, Fax 02 43 49 46 21
- de Laval Changé Le Jariel, N : 8 km on D 104, ✆ 02 43 53 16 03
- Old château★ Z : framework★★ of the keep, musée d'Art naïf★, <★ from the ramparts - Old town★ YZ: - Embankments★ <★ - Jardin de la Perrine★ Z - Apse★ of N.-D. d'Avesnières basilica X - N.-D. des Cordeliers church ★: altar-pieces★★ X - Lactopôle★★.

Plan on following page

De Paris without rest

VISA MC AE

22 r. de la Paix – ✆ 02 43 53 76 20 – www.hotel-de-paris-laval.fr – hoteldeparislaval@wanadoo.fr – Fax 02 43 56 91 83 – Closed 24 December-4 January

Y **a**

50 rm – †€ 65/155 ††€ 70/165, ☕ € 9

◆ Fully renovated building, constructed in 1954, in the heart of a shopping area. Modern, functional rooms, well looked after and quieter at the rear.

Marin'Hôtel without rest

VISA MC

102 av. R. Buron – ✆ 02 43 53 09 68 – www.marin-hotel.fr – contact@marin-hotel.fr – Fax 02 43 56 95 35

X **d**

25 rm – †€ 50 ††€ 58, ☕ € 7

◆ The grotesque figures on the façade reflect the age of the building but the rooms are modern and practical. Those to the rear are quieter. Continental breakfasts.

XXX ✿ **Bistro de Paris** (Guy Lemercier)

VISA MC AE

67 r. Val de Mayenne – ✆ 02 43 56 98 29 – www.lebistro-de-paris.com – bistro.de.paris@wanadoo.fr – Fax 02 43 56 52 85 – Closed 2-25 August, Saturday lunch, Sunday dinner and Monday

Y **k**

Rest – Menu € 28/48 – Carte approx. € 46

Spec. Poêlée de foie gras et ris de veau. Turbot aux herbes. Craquant de banane poêlée au chocolat, glace au poivre. **Wines** Savennières, Anjou-Villages.

◆ In an old house, this elegant bistro is decorated in a very welcoming Art Nouveau style. Delicious contemporary cuisine.

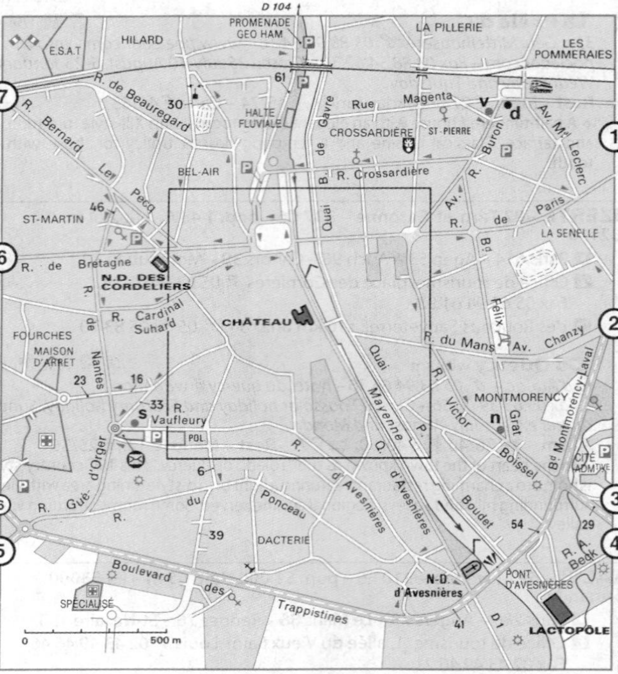

D 104
PROMENADE GEO HAM
LA PILLERIE
LES POMMERAIES
HILARD
E.S.A.T
A 81-E 50
7
R. de Beauregard
R. Bernard Le Pecq
30
61
HALTE FLUVIALE
Rue Magenta
v
d
Av. Mal Leclerc
1
MAYENNE N 162
ST-MALO FOUGÈRES D 30
B. de Gavre
CROSSARDIÈRE
ST-PIERRE
R. Buron
BEL-AIR
R. Crossardière
Quai
Av. R.
R. de Paris
LA SENELLE
46
ST-MARTIN
6
R. de Bretagne
N.D. DES CORDELIERS
Bd Félix
LE MANS D 57
R. Cardinal Suhard
CHÂTEAU
R. de Nantes
2
R. du Mans
Av. Chanzy
X
FOURCHES
MAISON D'ARRET
Quai Mayenne
Bd Montmorency-Laval
RENNES, VITRÉ D 57
23
16
33
R. Vaufleury
S
MONTMORENCY
n
R. Victor Boissel
P. Grat
TOURS LA FLÈCHE D 21
X
POL
CITÉ ADMTIVE
R. Gué d'Orger
6
R. d'Avesnières
Q. d'Avesnières
R. du Ponceau
R. Boudet
3
6
54
29
39
DACTERIE
R. A. Beck
4
5
Boulevard des Trappistines
N-D. d'Avesnières
PONT D'AVESNIÈRES
N 162 CHÂ-GONTIER ANGERS
SPÉCIALISÉ
ST-NAZAIRE D 771
0
500 m
41
D1
LACTOPÔLE

LAVAL

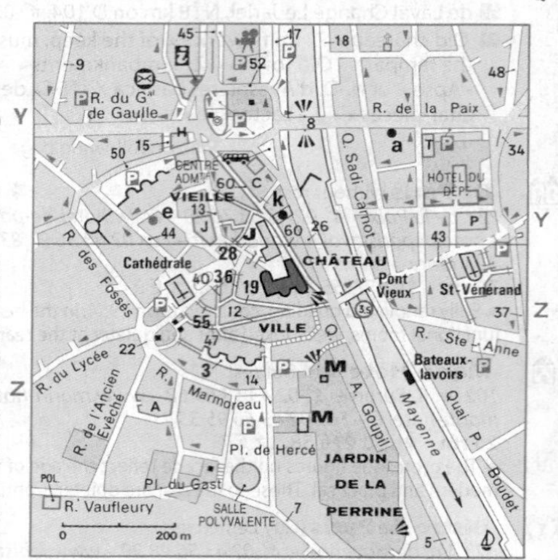

XXX **Le Capucin Gourmand**

66 r. Vaufleury – ✆ 02 43 66 02 02 – http://capucingourmand.free.fr – capucingourmand@free.fr – Fax 02 43 66 13 50 – Closed 3-24 August, Sunday dinner, Tuesday lunch and Monday X s

Rest – Menu (€ 18 bi), € 22 (weekdays)/47 – Carte € 42/48

◆ Behind a Virginia clad façade, this restaurant is home to smart, welcoming dining rooms. Contemporary cuisine served on the quiet terrace in fine weather.

XX **La Gerbe de Blé** with rm

83 r. V.-Boissel – ✆ 02 43 53 14 10 – www.gerbedeble.com – gerbedeble@wanadoo.fr – Fax 02 43 49 02 84 – Closed 1-10 May, 26 July-18 August, 15-21 February, Saturday lunch and Sunday X n

8 rm – €78/98 €95/135, € 11 **Rest** – Menu (€ 19), € 28/52

◆ Traditional cuisine made with seasonal, local produce served in an up-to-date, welcoming dining room (cream tones, carefully lit). Functional rooms.

XX **Hostellerie à la Bonne Auberge** with rm

170 r. de Bretagne par ⑥ – ✆ 02 43 69 07 81 – www.alabonneauberge.com – contact@alabonneauberge.com – Fax 02 43 91 15 02 – Closed August, 24 December-3 January, Friday dinner, Sunday dinner, Saturday and bank holidays dinner

12 rm – €68/78 €78/88, € 10

Rest – Menu € 18 (weekdays)/45 – Carte € 31/52

◆ Away from the town centre, a regional-style building, covered with Virginia creeper. The dining room, enlarged by a veranda, is bright and modern. Tasty traditional cuisine.

XX **L'Antiquaire**

5 r. Béliers – ✆ 02 43 53 66 76 – Fax 02 43 56 92 18 – Closed 1st-22 July, 6-27 January, Saturday lunch, Sunday dinner and Monday Y e

Rest – Menu (€ 16), € 22/47 – Carte € 27/52

◆ This restaurant located in the heart of the old town centre has a pleasant dining area serving generous classic cuisine with modern touches.

X **Edelweiss**

99 av. R. Buron – ✆ 02 43 53 11 00 – restau.edelweiss@wanadoo.fr – Closed 10-26 April, 15 July-12 August, Sunday and Monday X v

Rest – Menu € 19/34 – Carte approx. € 30

◆ Restaurant, next to the railway station, with a dining room redecorated in a modern style (pastel shades). Enjoy traditional dishes here in a friendly atmosphere without ceremony.

LAVALADE – 24 Dordogne – 329 G7 – pop. 97 – alt. 190 m – ✉ 24540 4 C2

Paris 580 – Bordeaux 144 – Périgueux 94 – Bergerac 46 – Villeneuve-sur-Lot 48

Le Grand Cèdre without rest

Le Bourg – ✆ 05 53 22 57 70 – www.legrandcedre.com – legrandcedre.j@wanadoo.fr – Open Easter-11 November

5 rm – €55 €65

◆ This house has been renovated to preserve its original character. Well kept and soundproofed rooms, all large (except one) and personalised with antique furniture.

LE LAVANCHER – 74 Haute-Savoie – 328 O5 – see Chamonix

LE LAVANDOU – 83 Var – 340 N7 – pop. 5 825 – alt. 1 m – ✉ 83980 41 C3

French Riviera

Paris 873 – Cannes 102 – Draguignan 75 – Fréjus 61 – Toulon 41

Office de tourisme, quai Gabriel-Péri, ✆ 04 94 00 40 50, Fax 04 94 00 40 59

Île d'Hyères★★★.

LE LAVANDOU

Bois-Notre-Dame (R. du) . . . . . . A 2
Bouvet (Bd Gén.-G) . . . . A 3
Cazin (R. Charles) . . . . A 4
Gaulle (Av. Gén.-de) . . . . AB
Lattre-de-Tassigny (Bd de) . . . . A 7
Martyrs-de-la-Résistance (Av. des) . . . . A 8
Patron Ravello (R.) . . . . B 10
Péri (Quai Gabriel) . . . . B 12
Port Cros (R.) . . . . A 15
Port (R. du) . . . . B 13
Vincent-Auriol (Av. Prés.) . . . . A 16

Le Rabelais without rest
face au vieux port – ✆ 04 94 71 00 56 – www.le-rabelais.fr – hotel.lerabelais@wanadoo.fr – Fax 04 94 71 82 55 – Closed 11 November-1st January B **a**
21 rm – 🚹€ 50/105 🚹🚹€ 50/105, ☕ € 6
◆ Well-located on the seafront, this hotel has small yet cool and colourful rooms. In summer, breakfast is served on the terrace facing the harbour.

La Petite Bohème
av. F.-Roosevelt – ✆ 04 94 71 10 30 – www.hotel-petiteboheme.com – hotelpetiteboheme@wanadoo.fr – Fax 04 94 64 73 92 B **f**
17 rm – 🚹€ 43/72 🚹🚹€ 72/112, ☕ € 9 – ½ P € 59/83
Rest – *(closed 6 November-15 February, lunch from Monday to Thursday from 28 June to 15 September, Tuesday and Wednesday in low season)*
Menu € 25/31 – Carte € 35/45
◆ Have a lie-in in a simple Provencal-style room, then a siesta on a sun lounger under the arbour: a real Bohemian lifestyle! Mediterranean-style dining room and shaded terrace beside the garden. Blackboard daily specials.

in St-Clair by ①: 2 km – ✉ 83980 Le Lavandou

Roc Hôtel without rest
r. des Dryades – ✆ 04 94 01 33 66 – www.roc-hotel.com – roc-hotel@wanadoo.fr – Fax 04 94 01 33 67 – Open from end March to mid-October
29 rm – 🚹€ 75/160 🚹🚹€ 75/160, ☕ € 10
◆ A modern hotel built on rocks washed by the waves. Bright rooms with terrace. Choose one overlooking the sea. A refreshing break guaranteed.

Méditerranée
– ✆ 04 94 01 47 70 – http://perso.wanadoo.fr/hotel-mediterranee – hotel.med@wanadoo.fr – Fax 04 94 01 47 71 – Open 17 March-20 October
20 rm – 🚹€ 80/88 🚹🚹€ 80/124, ☕ € 8,50 – ½ P € 70/92
Rest – *(closed Wednesday) (dinner only) (resident only)*
◆ Sun and the pleasures of the Mediterranean at this hotel built near a fine sandy beach. Contemporary and functional rooms; choose one overlooking the sea. Family atmosphere. A pleasant shaded terrace. Serving traditional cuisine.

Belle Vue
– 04 94 00 45 00 – www.bellevue.fr – belle-vue@wanadoo.fr
– Fax 04 94 00 45 25 – Open April-October
19 rm – €80/90 €90/230, €15
Rest – *(open June-September and closed Sunday) (dinner only)*
Menu €34/36 – Carte €41/54
◆ Away from the busy seaside, a pleasant villa on the flower-decked outskirts overlooking the bay of St Clair. Rustic rooms, some of which enjoy a lovely view. Stunning views of sunsets over the coast from the restaurant.

La Bastide without rest
pl. des Pins Penchés – 04 94 01 57 00 – www.hotel-la-bastide.fr – contact@hotel-la-bastide.fr – Fax 04 94 01 57 13 – Open 1st April-10 November
18 rm – €60/118 €60/118, €9
◆ Family house in southern style near the St Clair beach. Immaculate walls, colourful shutters and Roman tiles. Fresh rooms with terrace or balcony.

Les Tamaris "Chez Raymond"
– 04 94 71 07 22 – Fax 04 94 71 88 64 – Closed 11 Nov.-14 Feb., lunch from 15 June to 20 Sep., Tuesday dinner and dinner in low season
Rest – Carte €45/80
◆ Former café serving fish from the local catch in a rustic setting. Freshness and direct flavours assured!

in la Plage de La Fossette by ①: 3 km – ✉ 83980 Le Lavandou

83 Hôtel
– 04 94 71 20 15 – www.83hotel.com – hotel83@wanadoo.fr
– Fax 04 94 71 63 42 – Open from Easter to end September
30 rm – €120/295 €120/295, €15 – ½ P €110/145
Rest – *(dinner only)* Menu €39 – Carte €45/55
◆ The Var coast takes on the appearance of a Pacific island here. Save yourself travelling thousands of kilometres by staying in this hotel designed purely for pleasure. Spacious rooms. Restaurant with a veranda dining area and pleasant terrace with fine views. Traditional cuisine served.

in Aiguebelle by ①: 4,5 km – ✉ 83980 Le Lavandou

Les Roches
1 av. des Trois-Dauphins – 04 94 71 05 07 – www.hotellesroches.com – resa@hotellesroches.com – Fax 04 94 71 08 40
33 rm – €160/320 €160/550, €28 – 6 suites
Rest Mathias Dandine – see restaurant listing
◆ The opulent rooms with terraces rising up the slope by the creek make this hotel a little seaside paradise.

Les Alcyons without rest
av. des Trois-Dauphins – 04 94 05 84 18 – www.beausoleil-alcyons.com – hotellesalcyons@free.fr – Fax 04 94 05 70 89 – Open April-mid October
24 rm – €62/108 €62/108, €7
◆ The meeting of the Halcyons is a sign of peace and tranquillity. The attentive welcome and good housekeeping in this establishment tend to support the legend.

Hydra without rest
av. du Levant – 04 94 71 65 46 – www.hotel-hydra.fr – hydra.hotel@wanadoo.fr – Fax 04 94 15 08 07
30 rm – €78/98 €90/115, €14 – 3 suites
◆ This hotel has inherited the brightness of the Greek island that gave it its name. Comfortable rooms and huge family suites. An underground passage leads directly to the sea.

Beau Soleil
av. des Trois Dauphins – 04 94 05 84 55 – www.hotel-lavandou.com – beausoleil@hotel-lavandou.com – Fax 04 94 22 27 05 – Open beg. April-beg. October
15 rm – €52 €52/92, €7 – ½ P €58/79
Rest – snack – *(open beg. May-beg. October)* Menu €27/37
◆ The 'beautiful sunshine' is the perfect place to spend your holidays, with comfortable rooms featuring balconies. A modern dining room, plus a terrace under plane trees. Light lunches; set menus and local specialities in the evening.

XXX **Mathias Dandine** – Hôtel Les Roches
1 av. des Trois-Dauphins – ✆ 04 94 71 15 53 – www.mathiasdandine.com – restaurant@mathiasdandine.com – Fax 04 94 71 66 66
Rest – Menu € 60/125 – Carte € 105/130
Spec. Bouillabaisse d'œuf de ferme (Sep.-Oct.). Langoustines aux parfums de Siam (Mar.-April and Sep.-Oct.). Carré de chocolat craquant et verrine café (Dec.-Jan.).
Wines Côtes de Provence.
◆ Creative cuisine served in this panoramic restaurant which rules the waves. Jazz evenings on Sundays.

LAVANNES – 51 Marne – 306 H7 – pop. 446 – alt. 100 m – ✉ 51110 13 B2

Paris 161 – Châlons-en-Champagne 56 – Épernay 43 – Reims 14

La Closerie des Sacres without rest
7 r. Chefossez – ✆ 03 26 02 05 05 – www.closerie-des-sacres.com – closerie-des-sacres@wanadoo.fr – Fax 03 26 08 06 73
3 rm – €74 €88
◆ The stables of this old farm have been tastefully converted into a guesthouse providing rooms with wrought-iron furnishings and fine fabrics. Breakfast is served around a stone fireplace.

LAVARDIN – 41 Loir-et-Cher – 318 C5 – see Montoire-sur-le-Loir

---

LAVAUDIEU – 43 Haute-Loire – 331 C2 – pop. 225 – alt. 465 m – ✉ 43100 Auvergne 6 C3

Paris 488 – Brioude 11 – Clermont-Ferrand 78 – Le Puy-en-Velay 56 – St-Flour 63

Frescoes★ of the abbey church - Cloister★ - Carrefour du vitrail (stained-glass window centre)★.

Le Colombier without rest
rte des Fontannes – ✆ 04 71 76 09 86 – www.lecolombier-lavaudieu.com – colombier.chambredhote@wanadoo.fr – Open 15 April-15 October
4 rm – €60 €70
◆ A modern stone house in which the bedrooms are individually themed – Velay, Africa (bamboo four-poster bed), Morocco (wrought-iron bed). Old dovecote, plus attractive views of the surrounding countryside.

X **Auberge de l'Abbaye**
– ✆ 04 71 76 44 44 – http://lavaudieu.free.fr – auberge.de.labbaye@wanadoo.fr – Fax 04 71 76 41 08 – Closed 15 November-1 February, Sunday dinner and Thursday except school holidays
Rest – Menu € 19/27
◆ This inn beside the abbey exudes rustic style with a modern touch. Here, conviviality blends with regional, market based cuisine.

X **Court La Vigne**
– ✆ 04 71 76 45 79 – Fax 04 71 76 45 79 – Closed December, January, Tuesday and Wednesday
Rest – *(number of covers limited, pre-book)* Menu € 18/28
◆ Charming 15C sheepfold next door to medieval cloisters. Tastefully furnished, bar with open fire, art gallery and a pleasant courtyard. Good regional cooking made with fresh produce.

LES LAVAULTS – 89 Yonne – 319 H8 – see Quarré-les-Tombes

LAVAUR – 81 Tarn – 338 C8 – pop. 10 036 – alt. 140 m – ✉ 81500 Languedoc-Roussillon-Tarn Gorges 29 C2

Paris 682 – Albi 51 – Castelnaudary 56 – Castres 40 – Montauban 58 – Toulouse 44

Office de tourisme, Tour des Rondes ✆ 05 63 58 02 00, Fax 05 63 41 42 89

des Étangs de Fiac Fiac Brazis, E : 11 km on D 112, ✆ 05 63 70 64 70

St-Alain cathedral ★.

Ibis without rest
1 av. G. Pompidou – ✆ 05 63 83 08 08 – www.ibishotel.com – loic.borie@accor.com – Fax 05 63 83 01 05
58 rm – †€ 52/71 ††€ 52/71, ☕ € 8
◆ This hotel in a residential area provides large, bright and functional rooms with air conditioning. Pleasant small garden and floral terrace with fountain.

in Giroussens **10 km northwest on the D 87 and D 38 – pop. 1 040 – alt. 204 m – ✉ 81500**

L'Échauguette
pl. de la Mairie – ✆ 05 63 41 63 65 – www.lechauguette.net – echauguette81@hotmail.fr – Fax 05 63 41 63 13 – Closed 27 September-11 October, 27 December-17 January, Thursday dinner, Sunday dinner and Monday except from June to August
Rest – Menu (€ 20), € 30/70 – Carte € 45/85
◆ A handsome 13C and 19C abode, whose glass roofed dining room commands a splendid view of the Agout Valley. Arts and crafts by local artists. Updated cuisine by an English chef.

LAVAUR – **24 Dordogne** – **329** H8 – **pop. 81** – **alt. 250 m** – **✉ 24550** 4 **D2**
Paris 622 – Bordeaux 213 – Périgueux 87 – Villeneuve-sur-Lot 45 – Cahors 49

Auberge de Bayle Viel with rm rest,
– ✆ 05 53 28 16 89 – aubergebayle@wanadoo.fr – Fax 05 53 28 16 89
5 rm – †€ 45/86 ††€ 45/86, ☕ € 8,50
Rest – *(number of covers limited, pre-book)*
Menu € 24 (weekday lunch), € 29/46 – Carte € 17/32
◆ The interior of this old barn (timber frame, exposed stones, oak and chestnut furniture) blends well with the regional cuisine based on produce from the kitchen garden. Bright and welcoming rooms in timber framed cottages, three with terrace.

Red = Pleasant. Look for the red and symbols.

LAVELANET – **09 Ariège** – **343** J7 – **pop. 6 769** – **alt. 512 m** – **✉ 09300** 29 **C3**
Paris 784 – Carcassonne 71 – Castelnaudary 53 – Foix 28 – Limoux 47 – Pamiers 42
Office de tourisme, place Henri-Dunant ✆ 05 61 01 22 20, Fax 05 61 03 06 39

in Nalzen **West: 6 km on D 117 – pop. 136 – alt. 632 m – ✉ 09300**

Les Sapins
Conte – ✆ 05 61 03 03 85 – www.restaurantlessapins.com – restaurantlessapins@yahoo.fr – Fax 05 61 65 58 45 – Closed Wednesday dinner, Sunday dinner and Monday except public holidays
Rest – Menu € 15 bi (weekday lunch), € 22/48 – Carte € 35/55
◆ Traditional chalet nestling at the foot of a forest of fir trees. Good wholesome cooking served in a simple countrified interior.

in Montségur **South: 13 km by D 109 and D 9 – pop. 108 – alt. 900 m – ✉ 09300**
Syndicat d'initiative, Village ✆ 05 61 03 03 03, Fax 05 61 03 11 27

Costes with rm
– ✆ 05 61 01 10 24 – www.chez-costes.com – info@chez-costes.com – Fax 05 61 03 06 28
13 rm – †€ 29/120 ††€ 29/120, ☕ € 8 – ½ P € 103/194
Rest – Menu € 15/32 – Carte € 20/40
◆ A friendly inn with a decor dominated by stone and wood. Seasonal local cuisine (stews, confits, magret etc) prepared using organic produce from mountain farms. Comfortable rooms equipped with bathrooms with Jacuzzi spa baths.

LAVENTIE – 62 Pas-de-Calais – **301** J4 – **pop. 4 383** – **alt. 18 m** – ✉ 62840 30 **B2**

Paris 229 – Armentières 13 – Arras 45 – Béthune 18 – Lille 29 – Dunkerque 63 – Ieper 30

Le Cerisier (Eric Delerue) VISA AE

3 r. de la Gare – ✆ 03 21 27 60 59 – www.lecerisier.com – contact@lecerisier.com – Fax 03 21 27 60 87 – Closed August, 23 February-4 March, Sunday dinner, Saturday lunch and Monday

Rest – Menu € 29/70 – Carte € 70/94

Spec. Pain perdu de foie gras et caramel de betterave rouge. Côte de veau "sous la mère" aux cèpes (automne). Rouleau de mangue tiède, gelée à la menthe et glace mangue-wasabi.

◆ An elegant red-brick building which has been recently refurbished. Delicious modern cuisine served in two dining rooms with a contemporary decor.

LAVERGNE – 46 Lot – **337** G3 – **see Gramat**

LAVOUX – 86 Vienne – **322** J5 – **see Poitiers**

LAYE – 05 Hautes-Alpes – **334** E5 – **see Col Bayard**

LA LÉCHÈRE – 73 Savoie – **333** L4 – **pop. 1 936** – **alt. 461 m** – **Spa : early April-late Oct.** – ✉ 73260 **French Alps** 46 **F2**

Paris 602 – Albertville 21 – Celliers 16 – Chambéry 70 – Moûtiers 6

Office de tourisme, les Eaux-Claires ✆ 04 79 22 51 60, Fax 04 79 22 57 10

Radiana rm, rest, VISA AE

– ✆ 04 79 22 61 61 – www.radiana.net – hotels@radiana.net – Fax 04 79 22 65 25 – Closed 26 October-26 December

86 rm – †€ 57/113 ††€ 72/128, ☕ € 10 – ½ P € 63/129

Rest – dietetic rest. – *(closed 22-29 March and 25 October-1 February)* Menu € 20/26

◆ This 1930s hotel has kept its original Art Deco façade. Direct access to the spa, and functional rooms that overlook the spa and park. Traditional dishes and a low calorie menu (in high season only).

LES LECQUES – 83 Var – **340** J6 – **see St-Cyr-sur-Mer**

LECTOURE – 32 Gers – **336** F6 – **pop. 3 933** – **alt. 155 m** – ✉ 32700 **Languedoc-Roussillon-Tarn Gorges** 28 **B2**

Paris 708 – Agen 39 – Auch 35 – Condom 26 – Montauban 84 – Toulouse 114

Syndicat d'initiative, place du Général-de-Gaulle ✆ 05 62 68 76 98, Fax 05 62 68 79 30

Site★ - Promenade du bastion ≤★ - Musée municipal★.

De Bastard VISA

r. Lagrange – ✆ 05 62 68 82 44 – www.hotel-de-bastard.com – hoteldebastard@wanadoo.fr – Fax 05 62 68 76 81 – Closed 21 December-1st February

28 rm – †€ 50/80 ††€ 50/80, ☕ € 11 – 2 suites – ½ P € 55/75

Rest – *(closed Sunday dinner, Tuesday lunch and Monday)*

Menu € 17 (weekday lunch), € 28/50 – Carte € 49/60

◆ In the heart of Gers, this fine 18C hotel has stylishly renovated rooms. Those on the second floor have attic ceilings. Cosy bar. Three fine lounges with Louis 16th furnishings, and a pleasant summer terrace. Serving tasty regional cuisine.

L'Auberge des Bouviers VISA

8 r. Montebello – ✆ 05 62 68 95 13 – www.auberge-des-bouviers.com – auberge.bouvier@wanadoo.fr – Fax 05 62 68 75 33 – Closed 24 November-1st December, 5 January-2 February, Saturday lunch, Sunday dinner and Monday

Rest – Menu (€ 15), € 24/30 – Carte € 38/64

◆ Warm restaurant set in an 18C residence with original stonework and exposed beams. Tasty, updated traditional cooking, prepared using fresh produce.

LEMBACH – 67 Bas-Rhin – 315 K2 – pop. 1 728 – alt. 190 m – ✉ 67510 1 B1
Alsace-Lorraine

Paris 470 – Bitche 32 – Haguenau 25 – Strasbourg 58 – Wissembourg 15

Syndicat d'initiative, 23, route de Bitche ✆ 03 88 94 43 16, Fax 03 88 94 20 04

Château de Fleckenstein ★ Northwest: 7 km.

Au Heimbach without rest

15 rte de Wissembourg – ✆ 03 88 94 43 46 – www.hotel-au-heimbach.fr – contact@hotel-au-heimbach.fr – Fax 03 88 94 20 85

18 rm – €45/55 €57/110, €10

◆ A regional-style, half-timbered building with rustic rooms, in the heart of a small, typically Alsatian town. Generous breakfasts.

Auberge du Cheval Blanc (Pascal Bastian) with rm

4 rte Wissembourg – ✆ 03 88 94 41 86 – www.au-cheval-blanc.fr – info@au-cheval-blanc.fr – Fax 03 88 94 20 74 – Closed 22 June-10 July and 12 January-6 February

12 rm – €105/250 €105/250, €15

Rest – *(closed Monday and Tuesday)* Menu €46/95 – Carte €70/93

Rest *D'Rössel Stub* – Menu (€16), €26 – Carte €25/43

Spec. Foie gras de canard aux fraises (April to Oct.). Pigeon rôti aux petits pois (April to Jan.). Grand dessert. **Wines** Pinot gris, Riesling.

◆ The new owners of this elegant 18C post house want to make their mark on the place. The decor has been updated and there is a menu of classic and revisited, inventive dishes. The D'Rössel Stub is located in the rustic setting of a former farm. Regional dishes; country style rooms.

in Gimbelhof North: 10 km by D 3, D 925 and forest road – ✉ 67510 Lembach

Gimbelhof with rm

– ✆ 03 88 94 43 58 – gimbelhof.com – info@gimbelhof.com – Fax 03 88 94 23 30 – Closed 17 November-26 December

8 rm – €39/54 €46/63, €7 – ½ P €48/55

Rest – *(closed Mon. and Tues.)* Menu €13 (weekdays)/30 bi – Carte €16/40

◆ This forest inn isolated in the Vosges massif in "three frontiers country" will charm nature lovers. Very simple guest rooms and dining room.

LEMPDES – 63 Puy-de-Dôme – 326 G8 – pop. 8 579 – alt. 330 m – ✉ 63370 5 B2

Paris 420 – Clermont-Ferrand 11 – Issoire 36 – Thiers 36 – Vichy 51

Sébastien Perrier

6 r. Caire – ✆ 04 73 61 74 71 – www.sebastienperrier.fr – Fax 04 73 61 74 71 – Closed August, 2-5 January, Sunday dinner and Monday

Rest – Menu €18 (weekday lunch), €27/46 – Carte €38/54

◆ The town scales were once situated on the village square opposite this friendly restaurant specialising in Mediterranean-influenced cuisine. Traditional decor and a contemporary-style mezzanine.

LENCLOITRE – 86 Vienne – 322 H4 – pop. 2 322 – alt. 71 m – ✉ 86140 39 C1
Atlantic Coast

Paris 319 – Châtellerault 18 – Mirebeau 12 – Poitiers 30 – Richelieu 24

Office de tourisme, place du Champ de Foire ✆ 05 49 19 70 75, Fax 05 49 19 70 76

in Savigny-sous-Faye 10 km North by D 757, D 14 and D 72 – pop. 327 – alt. 120 m – ✉ 86140

Château Hôtel de Savigny rest,

6 r. du Château – ✆ 05 49 20 41 14 – www.chsfrance.com – chateau-hotel-savigny@chsfrance.com – Fax 05 49 86 76 38 – Closed January and February

10 rm – €130/290 €130/290, €20

Rest – *(closed Monday and Tuesday and lunch except weekends and bank holidays)* Menu €39 (dinner), €65/85 – Carte €66/94

◆ This elegant Renaissance-inspired chateau looks like something out of a fairytale. Refined and personalised rooms affording views of the park. Modern cuisine served in the restaurant with two elegant dining areas, one featuring a grand fireplace.

LENS – 62 Pas-de-Calais – 301 J5 – pop. 35 300 – Built-up area 323 174 – alt. 38 m – ✉ 62300 Northern France and the Paris Region 30 B2

▶ Paris 199 – Arras 18 – Béthune 19 – Douai 24 – Lille 37 – St-Omer 69

ℹ Office de tourisme, 26, rue de la Paix ✆ 03 21 67 66 66, Fax 03 21 67 65 66

LENS

Street	Grid	No.
Anatole-France (R.)	BXY	2
Basly (Bd Émile)	ABY	
Berthelot (R. Marcelin)	BY	3
Combes (R. Émile)	CX	4
Decrombecque (R. Guilsain)	BXY	6
Diderot (R. Denis)	CY	7
Faidherbe (R. Louis)	BY	8
Flament (R. Étienne)	BX	10
Freycinet (R. Louis-de)	CX	12
Gare (R. de la)	BCY	
Gauthier (R. François)	BY	13
Havre (R. du)	BY	14
Hospice (R. de l')	CY	15
Huleux (R. François)	BXY	16
Jean-Jaurès (Pl.)	BY	18
Jean-Moulin (R.)	BX	19
Lamendin (R. Arthur)	CXY	20
Lanoy (R. René)	BXY	21
Leclerc (R. du Mar.)	BY	22
Paix (R. de la)	BY	23
Paris (R. de)	BY	24
Pasteur (R. Louis)	BX	25
Pourquoi Pas (R. du)	ABX	26
Pressense (R. Francis-de)	CX	27
République (Pl. de la)	BY	28
Reumaux (Av. Elie)	ABX	29
Sorriaux (R. Uriane)	BCX	30
Varsovie (Av. de)	CY	31
Wetz (R. du)	BX	32
8-Mai-1945 (R.)	CY	33
11-Novembre (R. du)	ABX	36

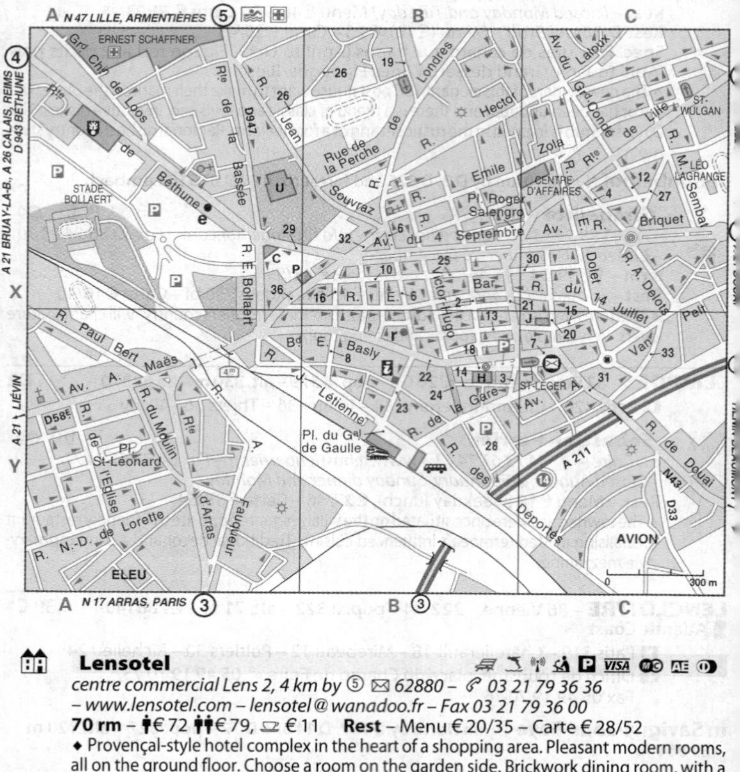

A N 47 LILLE, ARMENTIÈRES (5) — B — C

(4) A 21 BRUAY-LA-B., A 26 CALAIS, REIMS D 943 BÉTHUNE

A 21 LIÉVIN

A N 17 ARRAS, PARIS (3) — B (3) — C

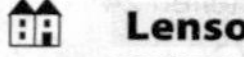

Lensotel

centre commercial Lens 2, 4 km by ⑤ ✉ 62880 – ✆ 03 21 79 36 36 – www.lensotel.com – lensotel@wanadoo.fr – Fax 03 21 79 36 00

70 rm – €72 €79, ☕ €11 **Rest** – Menu €20/35 – Carte €28/52

◆ Provençal-style hotel complex in the heart of a shopping area. Pleasant modern rooms, all on the ground floor. Choose a room on the garden side. Brickwork dining room, with a fireplace and veranda facing the swimming pool.

XX L'Arcadie II

13 r. Decrombecque – ✆ 03 21 70 32 22 – www.restaurant-arcadie2.fr – arcadie.2@wanadoo.fr – Fax 03 21 70 32 22 – Closed Saturday lunch and dinner from Sunday to Wednesday BY **r**

Rest – Menu (€17), €24 (weekdays)/38 – Carte €35/49

◆ Elegant restaurant in the town centre (colourful pictures and large silver chandeliers) welcomes gourmets who enjoy well-prepared, modern cuisine.

LÉON – 40 Landes – **335** D11 – **pop. 1 695** – **alt. 9 m** – ✉ **40550** 3 **B2**

Paris 724 – Castets 14 – Dax 30 – Mont-de-Marsan 75

Syndicat d'initiative, 65, place Jean Baptiste Courtiau ✆ 05 58 48 76 03, Fax 05 58 48 70 38

de Moliets Moliets-et-Maa Côte d'Argent - Club House, SW : 8 km on D 652 then D 117, ✆ 05 58 48 54 65

Courant d'Huchet★ by barge Northwest: 1.5 km, **Atlantic Coast.**

Hôtel du Lac without rest VISA

2 r. des Berges du Lac – ✆ 05 58 48 73 11 – www.hoteldulac-leon.com – contact@hoteldulac-leon.com – Fax 05 58 49 27 79 – Open from end April to end September

14 rm – €47/50 €50/60, €7

◆ Hotel providing simple but well-kept rooms, most overlooking the lake. Breakfast served on the veranda or summer terrace on the waterside.

LÉRAN – 09 Ariège – **343** J7 – **pop. 518** – **alt. 395 m** – ✉ **09600** 29 **C3**

Paris 781 – Carcassonne 67 – Pamiers 38 – Toulouse 104

Office de tourisme, rue de la Mairie ✆ 05 61 01 34 93, Fax 05 61 01 11 73

L'Impasse du Temple VISA

1 imp. du Temple – ✆ 05 61 01 50 02 – www.chezfurness.com – john.furness@wanadoo.fr – Fax 05 61 01 50 02

5 rm – €63 €75 **Table d'hôte** – Menu €25

◆ An old house with spacious guestrooms with a blue and white colour scheme, antique furniture and top-of-the-range bedding. This restaurant serves cuisine from Australia, the owners' country of origin.

LESCAR – 64 Pyrénées-Atlantiques – **342** J5 – see Pau

LESPARRE-MÉDOC – 33 Gironde – **335** F3 – **pop. 5 195** – **alt. 12 m** – ✉ **33340** 3 **B1**

Paris 541 – Bordeaux 68 – Soulac-sur-Mer 31

Office de tourisme, 37, cours du Maréchal de Tassigny ✆ 05 56 41 21 96, Fax 05 56 41 21 96

in Gaillan-en-Médoc Northwest: 2 km by D 1215 – pop. 1 991 – alt. 9 m – ✉ 33340

Château Beau Jardin rest, VISA

50 rte de Soulac, 3 km on the rte de Verdon – ✆ 05 56 41 26 83 – www.chateaubeaujardin.com – book@chateaubeaujardin.com – Fax 05 56 41 19 52 – Closed February

7 rm – €90/120 €100/140, €15

Rest – Menu €25 (weekday lunch), €40/55 – Carte €40/62

◆ This elegant 19C château with a garden is in the heart of the Médoc vineyards. Classic cuisine and wines from the region. Comfortable guestrooms.

La Table d'Olivier VISA

La Mare aux Grenouilles, 53 rte Lesparre – ✆ 05 56 41 13 32 – www.restaurantlatabledolivier.com – Fax 05 56 41 17 57 – Closed 16-23 February, Saturday lunch, Sunday dinner and Monday except July-August

Rest – Menu (€17 bi), €26 bi (weekday lunch), €35/49 – Carte €60/73

◆ A pleasant restaurant by a small lake with frogs. Sober modern interior with wooden tables, wrought-iron chairs and paintings. Seasonal cuisine.

LESPIGNAN – 34 Hérault – **339** E9 – **pop. 2 996** – **alt. 61 m** – ✉ **34710** 22 **B2**

Paris 769 – Béziers 11 – Capestang 20 – Montpellier 78 – Narbonne 20

Hostellerie du Château VISA

4 r. Figuiers – ✆ 04 67 37 67 71 – hostellerie-du-chateau-lespignan@wanadoo.fr – Closed Monday in high season, Tuesday and Wednesday in low season

Rest – Menu €28/42 – Carte €32/40

◆ Spurred on by the new owner, this château has undergone some changes, with a less cluttered setting and modern menu. The terrace keeps its uninterrupted view of the nearby villages.

LESPONNE – 65 Hautes-Pyrénées – 342 M4 – see Bagnères-de-Bigorre

LESTELLE-BÉTHARRAM – 64 Pyrénées-Atlantiques – 342 K6 – pop. 801 – alt. 299 m – ✉ 64800 Atlantic Coast 3 B3

Paris 801 – Laruns 35 – Lourdes 17 – Nay 8 – Oloron-Ste-Marie 42 – Pau 28

Office de tourisme, Mairie ✆ 05.59.61.93.59, Fax 05.59.61.99.19

Grottoes★ of Bétharram South: 5 km.

Le Vieux Logis

rm, VISA MC AE

2 km Grottes de Bétharram road – ✆ 05 59 71 94 87 – www.hotel-levieuxlogis.com – contact@hotel-levieuxlogis.com – Fax 05 59 71 96 75 – Closed 31 October-6 November, 22 December-4 January, 16 February-1st March, Sunday dinner and Monday off season

34 rm – †€ 55/79 ††€ 55/79, ☕ € 11 – ½ P € 62/74

Rest – *(closed Monday lunch)* Menu (€ 18 bi), € 25/40 – Carte € 35/58

◆ In the middle of a park near the Bétharram caves with five bungalows and a swimming pool. The restaurant is in the former farmhouse. The new wing has functional rooms. Warm, rustic dining rooms, regional food and attentive service.

LESTIAC-SUR-GARONNE – 33 Gironde – 335 I6 – pop. 609 – alt. 80 m – ✉ 33550 3 B2

Paris 604 – Bordeaux 28 – Mérignac 40 – Pessac 34

Les Logis de Lestiac

71 rte de Bordeaux – ✆ 05 56 72 17 90 – www.logisdelestiac.com – philippe@logisdelestiac.com

5 rm ☕ – †€ 80/95 ††€ 80/95 **Table d'hôte** – Menu € 25 bi/30 bi

◆ The owner's passion for redecoration is evident in this superbly restored 18C mansion, featuring rooms on the first floor decorated with a seasonal theme and a duplex on the ground floor. The restaurant serves tasty sweet and savoury dishes.

LEUCATE – 11 Aude – 344 J5 – pop. 3 392 – alt. 21 m – ✉ 11370 22 B3

Languedoc-Roussillon-Tarn Gorges

Paris 821 – Carcassonne 88 – Narbonne 38 – Perpignan 35 – Port-la-Nouvelle 18

Office de tourisme, Espace Culturel ✆ 04 68 40 91 31, Fax 04 68 40 24 76

≤★ from the the Cap semaphore East: 2 km.

Jardin des Filoche

VISA MC

64 av. J.-Jaurès – ✆ 04 68 40 01 12 – Fax 04 68 40 74 80 – Closed January, February, lunch except Sunday, Tuesday from 1st October to 31 March and Monday

Rest – Menu € 27

◆ Pleasant restaurant surrounded by a walled garden and shaded terrace that isolates it from the urban hustle and bustle. Classic cuisine and view of the kitchen.

Le Village

AC VISA MC

129 av. J.-Jaurès – ✆ 04 68 40 06 91 – Closed Monday dinner, Tuesday dinner and Wednesday except school holidays

Rest – Menu € 17/22 – Carte € 30/38

◆ The walls are covered with posters, photos and nautical paraphernalia while the blue tablecloths reinforce the marine character of this old farm building. Traditional fare.

in Port-Leucate South: 7 km by D 627 – ✉ 11370 Leucate

Syndicat d'initiative, rue Dour ✆ 04 68 40 91 31

Des Deux Golfs without rest

VISA MC

on the harbour – ✆ 04 68 40 99 42 – www.hoteldes2golfs.com – contact@hoteldes2golfs.com – Fax 04 68 40 79 79 – Open May-15 November

30 rm – †€ 36/48 ††€ 48/64, ☕ € 6

◆ In the marina built between the lake and the sea is this new building with small, functional rooms. Most have private loggias looking out over the yachts.

LEUTENHEIM – 67 Bas-Rhin – **315** M3 – **pop. 845** – **alt. 119 m** 1 **B1**
– ✉ 67480

Paris 501 – Haguenau 22 – Karlsruhe 46 – Strasbourg 45

Auberge Au Vieux Couvent
at Koenigsbruck – ✆ 03 88 86 39 86 – hirschel.vieux-couvent@wanadoo.fr – Fax 03 88 05 28 78 – Closed 21 August-5 September, 22-28 February, Monday and Tuesday
Rest – Menu (€ 8,50), € 28/37 – Carte € 27/50
◆ Proverbs in gothic script adorning the walls, wood panelling, and china frogs: this half-timbered house (dating from the end of the 17C) blends rustic charm and refinement. Modern cuisine.

LEVALLOIS-PERRET – 92 Hauts-de-Seine – **311** J2 – **101** 15 – **see Paris, Area**

LEVENS – 06 Alpes-Maritimes – **341** E4 – **pop. 4 427** – **alt. 600 m** 41 **D2**
– ✉ 06670 French Riviera

Paris 946 – Antibes 43 – Cannes 53 – Nice 25 – Puget-Théniers 50 – St-Martin-Vésubie 39

Office de tourisme, 3, placette Paul Olivier ✆ 04 93 79 71 00, Fax 04 93 79 75 64

≤★ - Saut des Français★★ North: 8 km.

La Vigneraie
1.5 km St-Blaise road – ✆ 04 93 79 77 60 – Fax 04 93 79 82 35 – Open 15 February-11 October
18 rm – †€ 40 ††€ 47/54, ☕ € 6 – ½ P € 46/56
Rest – Menu € 17 (weekdays)/26
◆ A family atmosphere and generous cuisine in this house in a green setting. Rustic guest rooms, some with balconies. Wide bay windows in the dining room.

LEVERNOIS – 21 Côte-d'Or – **320** J8 – **see Beaune**

LEVIE – 2A Corse-du-Sud – **345** D9 – **see Corse**

LEYNES – 71 Saône-et-Loire – **320** I12 – **pop. 503** – **alt. 340 m** 8 **C3**
– ✉ 71570

Paris 402 – Mâcon 15 – Bourg-en-Bresse 51 – Charolles 58 – Villefranche-sur-Saône 36

Le Fin Bec
pl. de la Mairie – ✆ 03 85 35 11 77 – www.lefinbec.com – perard.frederik@orange.fr – Closed 10-20 November, 1-15 January, Thursday dinner, Sunday dinner and Monday
Rest – Menu € 18 (weekdays)/42 – Carte € 34/57
◆ This restaurant provides a warm welcome in a pleasant rustic dining area featuring ceramic paintings depicting Beaujolais wine themes. Copious regional cuisine served.

LÉZIGNAN-CORBIÈRES – 11 Aude – **344** H3 – **pop. 8 906** – **alt. 51 m** 22 **B3**
– ✉ 11200

Paris 804 – Carcassonne 39 – Narbonne 22 – Perpignan 85 – Prades 129

Office de tourisme, 9, cours de la République ✆ 04 68 27 05 42, Fax 04 68 27 05 42

Le Mas de Gaujac
r. Gustave Eiffel, Gaujac Industrial Estate towards A61 access – ✆ 04 68 58 16 90 – www.masdegaujac.fr – masdegaujac@free.fr – Fax 04 68 58 16 91 – Closed 11-26 April, 20 December-4 January, Saturday and Sunday from October to May
21 rm – †€ 75 ††€ 75, ☕ € 10 **Rest** – Menu € 16/35 – Carte € 26/54
◆ Recent red-ochre coloured building situated near a shopping area. The rooms are simple, fresh and above all practical and handy for a stopover. Contemporary dining room in warm tones; traditional, unpretentious food.

Rest. Le Tournedos et H. Le Tassigny with rm
rd-pt de Lattre-de-Tassigny – 04 68 27 11 51 – tournedos@wanadoo.fr – Fax 04 68 27 67 31 – Closed Sunday dinner and Monday
19 rm – €42 €46/48, €8
Rest – *(closed 30 June-3 July, Sunday dinner and Monday)*
Menu (€14 bi), €17 bi (weekdays)/46 – Carte €32/65
◆ Grills and tournedos - the house specialities - are served in a well-lit pale yellow dining room. The rooms, in the same style, have been partially made over.

LEZOUX – 63 Puy-de-Dôme – 326 H8 – pop. 5 358 – alt. 340 m 6 **C2**
– ✉ 63190 **Auvergne**

Paris 434 – Clermont-Ferrand 33 – Issoire 43 – Riom 38 – Thiers 16 – Vichy 43

Syndicat d'initiative, rue Pasteur 04 73 73 01 00, Fax 04 73 73 04 48

Les Voyageurs with rm
2 pl. de la Mairie – 04 73 73 10 49 – hotelvoyageurs.lezoux@orange.fr – Fax 04 73 73 92 60 – Closed 17 August-6 September, 26 December-3 January, Friday dinner, Sunday dinner and Saturday
10 rm – €42 €50, €7
Rest – Menu €14 (weekday lunch), €18/42 – Carte €28/40
◆ This 1960s building opposite the town hall serves traditional cuisine in a spacious dining room, adorned with an old rubber plant. Well-kept rooms.

in Bort-l'Étang 8 km Southeast by D 223 and D 309 – pop. 513 – alt. 420 m – ✉ 63190

✲★ from the château terrace ★ to Ravel West: 5 km.

Château de Codignat rm,
west: 1 km – 04 73 68 43 03 – www.codignat.com – codignat@relaischateaux.com – Fax 04 73 68 93 54 – Open 20 March-2 November
15 rm (½ board only) – 5 suites – ½ P €185/360
Rest – *(closed lunch from Monday to Friday except public holidays) (number of covers limited, pre-book)*
Menu €56/100 – Carte €94/116
Spec. Emietté de chair de tourteau. Homard bleu rôti au melon caramélisé (July-August). Grosse madeleine, mousseline vanille, fraises des bois et framboises (season). **Wines** Saint-Pourçain, Côtes d'Auvergne.
◆ A charming 15C chateau in a superb park, with refined rooms, most named after and decorated on the theme of a famous person, including many kings of France. Fine, personalised cuisine served in the medieval keep, around the impressive fireplace.

West 5 km by N 89 ✉63190 Seychalles

Chante Bise
at Courcourt – 04 73 62 91 41 – restaurant.chantebise@wanadoo.fr – Fax 04 73 68 29 53 – Closed 16 August-6 September, 15 February-6 March, Sunday dinner, Wednesday dinner and Monday except holidays
Rest – Menu (€13 bi), €20/37 – Carte €21/43
◆ A friendly atmosphere in this family restaurant featuring exposed stone and wood work. Traditional cuisine changing over the seasons. Shaded terrace area.

LIBOURNE – 33 Gironde – 335 J5 – pop. 22 600 – alt. 7 m 3 **B1**
– ✉ 33500 **Atlantic Coast**

Paris 576 – Agen 129 – Bergerac 64 – Bordeaux 30 – Périgueux 100

Office de tourisme, 45, allée Robert Boulin 05 57 51 15 04, Fax 05 57 25 00 58

de Teynac Beychac-et-Caillau Domaine de Teynac, 15 km on the Bordeaux road and D 1089, 05 56 72 85 62

de Bordeaux Cameyrac Saint-Sulpice-et-Cameyrac16 km on the Bordeaux road and D1089, 05 56 72 96 79

LIBOURNE

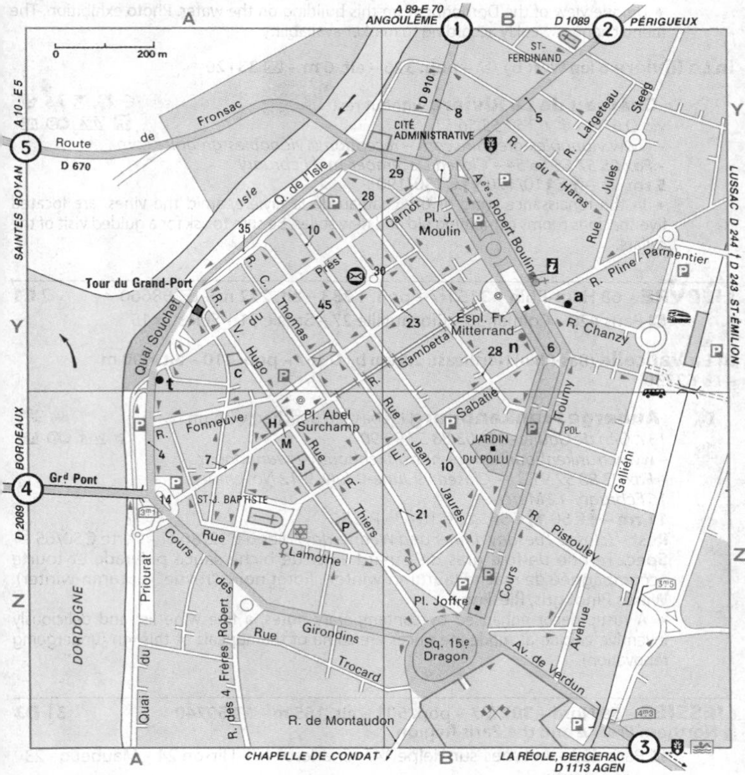

Mercure without rest — rest, VISA, AE

3 quai Souchet – ☎ 05 57 25 64 18 – www.mercure.com – H6238@accor.com – Fax 05 57 25 64 19 AY **t**

81 rm – †€ 70/115 ††€ 80/125, ☕ € 14 – 3 suites

◆ On the banks of the Dordogne, this new building is decorated in a contemporary style and is uniform across the rooms. There are also three suites and a seminar room.

De France without rest — VISA, AE

7 r. Chanzy – ☎ 05 57 51 01 66 – www.hoteldefrancelibourne.com – hotelde france33@aliceadsl.fr – Fax 05 57 25 34 04 BY **a**

19 rm – †€ 55/145 ††€ 60/145, ☕ € 11

◆ The décor of this fully renovated post house is a mix of traditional and modern: warm tones, modern, oriental and reproduction furnishings. Comfortable rooms.

Chez Servais — VISA, AE

14 pl. Decazes – ☎ 05 57 51 83 97 – Fax 05 57 51 83 97 – Closed 1st-10 May, 16-30 August, Sunday dinner and Monday BY **n**

Rest – Menu (€ 19), € 26/49

◆ Warm hospitality, a relaxed atmosphere, contemporary cuisine and light interior at this restaurant in the heart of the fortified town.

XX **Bord d'Eau**

via ⑤: 1,5 km – ✆ 05 57 51 99 91 – Fax 05 57 25 11 56 – Closed one week in September, 16-30 November, 15 February-2 March, Wednesday dinner, Sunday dinner and Monday

Rest – Menu € 20 (weekdays)/48 – Carte approx. € 46

◆ Unique view of the Dordogne from this building on the water. Photo exhibition. The menu changes weekly according to market availability.

in La Rivière 6 km West by ⑤ – **pop. 326 – alt. 6 m** – ✉ **33126**

Château de La Rivière without rest

via D 670 – ✆ 05 57 55 56 51 – www.vignobles-gregoire.com – reception@vignobles-gregoire.com – Fax 05 57 55 56 54 – Closed December-mid February

5 rm – €110/170 €130/190

◆ In the renaissance wing of the chateau de la Rivière, amid the vines, are located five spacious rooms combining old and new styles. Be sure to ask for a guided visit of the cellars.

LIÈPVRE – 68 Haut-Rhin – **315** H7 – **pop. 1 733 – alt. 272 m** – ✉ **68660** 2 **C1**

Paris 428 – Colmar 35 – Ribeauvillé 27 – St-Dié 31 – Sélestat 15

in La Vancelle (Bas-Rhin) **Northeast: 2,5 km by D 167 – pop. 410 – alt. 400 m** – ✉ **67730**

XX **Auberge Frankenbourg** (Sébastien Buecher) with rm

13 r. Gén.de Gaulle – ✆ 03 88 57 93 90 – www.frankenbourg.com – hr.frankenbourg@wanadoo.fr – Fax 03 88 57 91 31 – Closed 29 June-9 July, 9-12 November, 16 February-12 March

11 rm – €50 €56, € 10 – ½ P € 56

Rest – *(closed Tuesday dinner and Wednesday)* Menu € 32/86 bi – Carte € 50/65

Spec. Terrine de foie gras de canard. Filet de biche sauce poivrade et tourte accompagnée de mâche (autumn-winter). Forêt noire "revue" (autumn-winter).

Wines Pinot gris, Riesling.

◆ A rustic decor enhanced by contemporary notes, a fine wine list and deliciously inventive cuisine at moderate prices are some of the appeals of this inn (undergoing renovation).

LIESSIES – 59 Nord – **302** M7 – **pop. 501 – alt. 165 m** – ✉ **59740** 31 **D3**

Northern France and the Paris Region

Paris 223 – Avesnes-sur-Helpe 14 – Charleroi 48 – Hirson 24 – Maubeuge 23 – St-Quentin 74

Syndicat d'initiative, 20, rue du Maréchal Foch ✆ 03 27 57 91 11, Fax 03 27 57 91 11

Parc départemental du Val Joly★ East: 5 km.

Château de la Motte

14 r. de la Motte, South: 1 km by secondary road – ✆ 03 27 61 81 94 – www.chateaudelamotte.fr – contact@chateaudelamotte.fr – Fax 03 27 61 83 57 – Closed 19 December-9 February, Sunday dinner and Monday lunch off season

9 rm – €58 €69, € 9 – ½ P € 69

Rest – Menu (€ 19), € 23 (weekdays)/65 – Carte € 35/59

◆ Once a retreat for the monks from the neighbouring abbey, this brick building surrounded by fine parkland provides well-equipped accommodation. A dining room of character, terrace overlooking the countryside and traditional and regional dishes.

La Forge de l'Abbaye without rest

13 r. de la Forge – ✆ 03 27 60 74 27 – www.laforgedelabbaye.com – Fax 03 27 60 74 27 – Closed 2 January-9 February

4 rm – €53 €61

◆ A delightful country ambience reigns in this old forge full of character. Attractive rooms, kitchen available for the use of guests and a view of the country and a pond. Non-smoking.

Le Carillon VISA MC

opposite the church – ☎ 03 27 61 80 21 – www.le-carillon.com – contact@le-carillon.com – Fax 03 27 61 82 34 – Closed 15 April-6 May, 19-26 August, 17 November-2 December, Monday dinner, Tuesday dinner, Thursday dinner, Sunday dinner and Wednesday

Rest – *(number of covers limited, pre-book)* Menu € 18 (weekdays), € 27/43

◆ A house of some charm; terrace shaded by plane trees and a dining room featuring beams and bricks. Traditional recipes based on local market produce. Gourmet shop.

LA LIEZ (LAC) – **52 Haute-Marne** – **313** M6 – **see Langres**

LIGNY-EN-CAMBRÉSIS – **59 Nord** – **302** I7 – **pop. 1 691** – **alt. 127 m** – ✉ **59191** 31 **C3**

Paris 193 – Arras 51 – Cambrai 17 – Valenciennes 42 – St-Quentin 35

Château de Ligny rm, P VISA MC AE

2 r. Curie – ☎ 03 27 85 25 84 – www.chateau-de-ligny.fr – contact@chateau-de-ligny.fr – Fax 03 27 85 79 79 – Closed 3-16 August, 2 February-3 March, Sunday evening, Monday and Tuesday

21 rm – †€ 120 ††€ 120/200, ☕ € 15 – 5 suites – ½ P € 128/317

Rest – Menu € 48/110 – Carte € 73/105

Spec. Tarte friande de rouget barbet au romarin. Sole et petits crustacés mijotés dans bisque de crevettes grises. Soufflé chaud à la chicorée et son coulis.

◆ This lovely medieval manor has personalised rooms; those in the new "Résidence" are larger. Superb modern wellness facilities. The former armoury room and library-lounge give the restaurant an aristocratic touch.

LIGSDORF – **68 Haut-Rhin** – **315** H12 – **see Ferrette**

P. Cheuva/PHOTONONSTOP

Chamber of commerce: belfry

LILLE

🅿 **Department:** 59 Nord
Michelin LOCAL map: nº **302** G4
▶ Paris 223 – Bruxelles 114 – Gent 75 – Luxembourg 310 – Strasbourg 530
Population: 224 900

Pop. built-up area: 1 000 900
Altitude: 10 m
Postal Code: ✉ 59000
Northern France and the Paris Region
Carte régionale 31 **C2**

USEFUL INFORMATION

TOURIST OFFICE

place Rihour ✆ 08 91 56 20 04, Fax 03 59 57 94 14

TRANSPORT

Auto-train ✆ 3635 et tapez 42 (0,34 €/mn)

AIRPORT

✈ Lille-Lesquin: ✆ 0 891 67 32 10 (0.23 €/min), 7 km on the A1 HT

A FEW GOLF COURSES

- 18 Lille Métropole Ronchin Rond Point des Acacias, ✆ 03 20 47 42 42
- 36 du Sart Villeneuve-d'Ascq 5 rue Jean Jaurès, 7 km on D 656, ✆ 03 20 72 02 51
- 9 de Bondues Bondues Château de la Vigne, N : 10 km, ✆ 03 20 23 20 62
- 18 des Flandres Marcq-en-Baroeul 159 boulevard Clémenceau, 4.5 km on D 670, ✆ 03 20 72 20 74
- 36 de Brigode Villeneuve-d'Ascq 36 avenue du Golf, 9 km on D 146, ✆ 03 20 91 17 86

TO BE SEEN

AROUND CITY HALL BELFRY

Quartier St-Sauveur FZ : porte de Paris★, ⋞★ du beffroi - Palais des Beaux-Arts ★★★ EZ

AROUND CHAMBER OF COMMERCE BELFRY

Le Vieux Lille★★ EY: Vieille Bourse★★, House of Gilles de la Boé★ (29 place Louise-de-Bettignies) - rue de la Monnaie★ - Hospice Comtesse★ - House where General de Gaulle was born EY - St-Maurice church ★ EFY, The Citadel ★ BV

LIVELY DISTRICTS

Place du Général de Gaulle (Grand'Place)★ EY - Place Rihour EY - Rue de Béthune (cinemas) EYZ - Euralille (Crédit Lyonnais Tower★)

- and around Lille-Flandres railway station FY

... AND SURROUNDING AREA

Villeneuve d'Ascq: musée d'Art moderne (Modern Art Museum)★★ HS M

- Bondues: château du Vert-Bois★ HR
- Bouvines: church stained-glass windows and evocation of the battle JT

L'Hermitage Gantois
224 r. de Paris – 03 20 85 30 30 – www.hotelhermitagegantois.com – reservation@hotelhermitagegantois.com – Fax 03 20 42 31 31
p. 8 EZ **b**
72 rm – €210/265 €210/265, €19
Rest – Menu (€35) – Carte €45/75
Rest *L'Estaminet* – brasserie *(closed Sat. lunch and Sun.)* Menu (€16), €19/26 – Carte €19/26
◆ Delightful personalized rooms, beautiful modern bathrooms, massage salon: luxury, history, comfort and modern design are tastefully combined in this 14C hospice. Restaurant with red and gold vaults offering a seasonal menu. The Estaminet has a brasserie atmosphere and serves generous portions of Flemish dishes.

Crowne Plaza
rm, VISA AE
335 bd Leeds – 03 20 42 46 46 – www.lille-crowneplaza.com – contact@lille-crowneplaza.com – Fax 03 20 40 13 14
p. 8 FY **n**
121 rm – €195/265 €195/265, €19 – 1 suite
Rest – Menu €21 (weekdays)/28 – Carte €37/55
◆ A modern hotel opposite the TGV railway station. Large, modern, well-equipped rooms with a 'Zen' influence; some with a splendid view of Lille and its belfry. A designer restaurant (furniture by Starck), up-to-date menu and buffets.

Alliance
rm, rm, P VISA AE
17 quai du Wault 59800 – 03 20 30 62 62 – www.alliance-lille.com – alliancelille@alliance-couventdesminimes.com – Fax 03 20 42 94 25
p. 6 BV **d**
83 rm – €215/250 €215/250, €19 – 8 suites
Rest – *(closed Monday 15 July-20 August)* Menu (€18 bi), €42 bi (weekdays)/52 bi – Carte €48/60
◆ A 17C red brick convent located between old Lille and the Citadel. Contemporary decor in the bedrooms, set around an interior garden. A huge, pyramid-shaped glass roof covers the cloister where this restaurant is situated. Piano bar.

Novotel Centre Grand Place
rm, rm, VISA AE
116 r. de L'Hôpital-Militaire – 03 28 38 53 53 – www.novotel.com – h0918@accor.com – Fax 03 28 38 53 54
p. 8 EY **k**
104 rm – €70/179 €70/179, €15 **Rest** – Carte €23/42
◆ Completely refurbished hotel in line with Novotel's latest concept: large contemporary bedrooms, designed for both work and leisure (modular furniture) and modern bathrooms. Traditional dishes with the emphasis on healthy eating in the restaurant. Service all day long.

Grand Hôtel Bellevue without rest
VISA AE
5 r. J. Roisin – 03 20 57 45 64 – www.grandhotelbellevue.com – contact@grandhotelbellevue.com – Fax 03 20 40 07 93
p. 8 EY **a**
60 rm – €99/155 €99/155, €12
◆ The rooms, graced with Directoire-style furniture and marble bathrooms, are unabashedly elegant; the most sought-after overlook the Grand'Place.

Novotel Lille Gares
rm, VISA AE
49 r. Tournai 59800 – 03 28 38 67 00 – www.novotel.com – h3165@accor.com – Fax 03 28 38 67 10
p. 8 FZ **u**
96 rm – €99/210 €99/210, €16 – 5 suites **Rest** – Carte €32/49
◆ The hotel, next to the Lille-Flandres station, is gradually renovating its rooms to meet the chain's latest standards: space, comfort, modern fittings and a minimalist decor. Meals served at the bar or in the trendy dining room (simple menu and daily suggestions).

Mercure Opéra without rest
VISA AE
2 bd Carnot 59800 – 03 20 14 71 47 – www.mercure.com – h0802@accor.com – Fax 03 20 14 71 48
p. 8 EY **h**
101 rm – €95/200 €105/210, €15
◆ Beams and bricks in the reception area and the lounges reflect the charm of this century-old, freestone building. Modern, carefully renovated rooms.

HAUBOURDIN

Carnot (R. Sadi) .... GT 22
Vanderhaghen (R. A.) .... GT 157

HELLEMMES-LILLE

Salengro (R. Roger) .... HS 142

HEM

Clemenceau (Bd G.) .... JS 28
Croix (R. de) .... JS 40
Gaulle (Av. Ch.-de) .... JS 64

LAMBERSART

Hippodrome (Av. de l') .... GS 76

LANNOY

Leclerc (R. du Gén.) .... JS 97
Tournai (R. de) .... JS 153

LA MADELEINE

Gambetta (R.) .... GS 63
Gaulle (R. du Gén.-de) .... HS 69
Lalau (R.) .... HS 87

LILLE

Arras (R. du Fg d') .... GT 4
Postes (R. du Fg des) .... GST 129

LOMME

Dunkerque (Av. de) .... GS 52

LOOS

Doumer (R. Paul) .... GT 49
Foch (R. du Mar.) .... GST 58
Potié (R. Georges) .... GT 130

LYS-LEZ-LANNOY

Guesde (R. Jules) .... JS 75
Lebas (R. J.-B.) .... JS 94

MARCQ-EN-BARŒUL

Clemenceau (Bd) .... HS 30
Couture (R. de la) .... HS 39
Foch (Av. Mar.) .... HS 57
Nationale (R.) .... HS 122

MARQUETTE-LEZ-LILLE

Lille (R. de) .... GS 103
Menin (R. de) .... HS 117

MONS-EN-BARŒUL

Gaulle (R. du Gén.-de) .... HS 70

MOUVAUX

Carnot (Bd) .... HR 21

ST-ANDRÉ-LEZ-LILLE

Lattre-de-Tassigny (Av. du Mar.-de) GS 91
Leclerc (R. du Gén.) .... GS 99

TOUFFLERS

Déportés (R. des) .... JS 48

TOURCOING

Yser (R. de l') .... JR 165
3-Pierres (R. des) .... JR 166

VILLENEUVE-D'ASCQ

Ouest (Bd de l') .... HS 124
Ronsse (R. Ch.) .... JT 136
Tournai (Bd de) .... JT 151

WAMBRECHIES

Marquette (R. de) .... GZ 108

WATTIGNIES

Clemenceau (R.) .... GT 31
Gaulle (R. du Gén.-de) .... GT 72
Victor-Hugo (R.) .... GT 160

WATTRELOS

Carnot (R.) .... JRS 24
Jean-Jaurès (R.) .... JR 82
Lebas (R. J.-B.) .... JR 96
Mont-à-Leux (R. du) .... JR 121

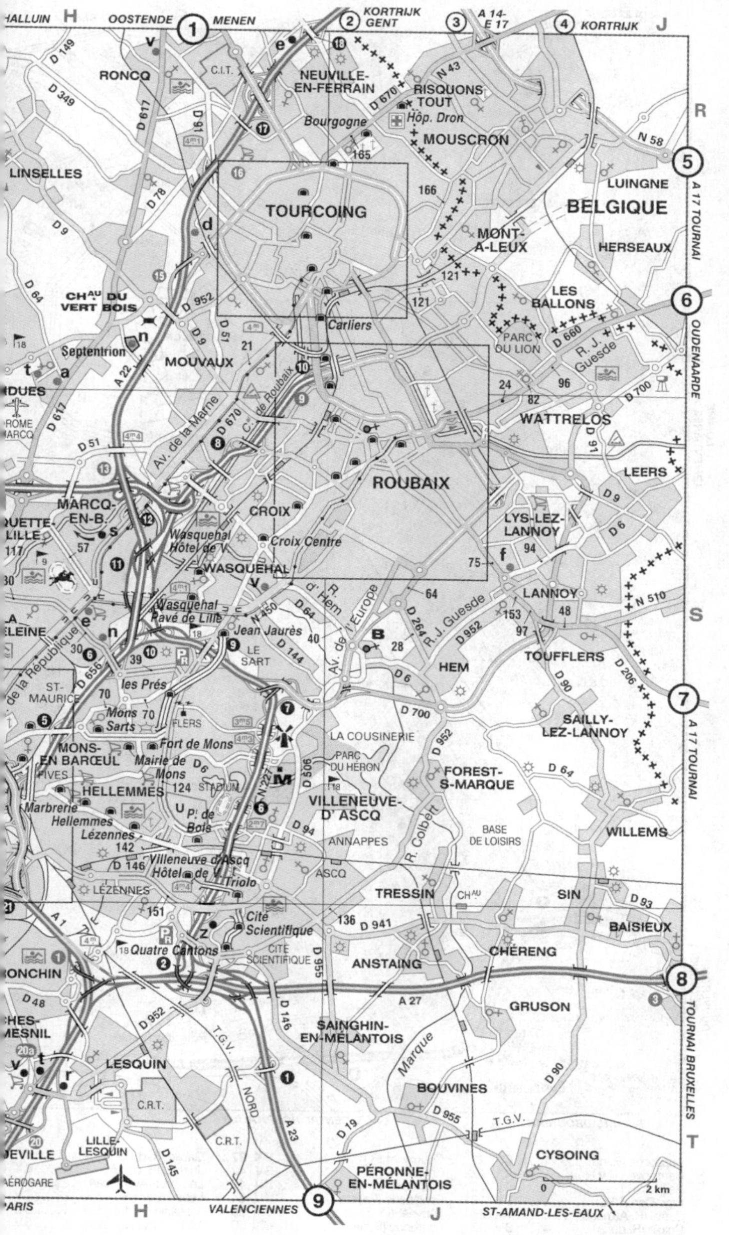
HALLUIN
OOSTENDE
MENEN
KORTRIJK GENT
A 14-E 17
KORTRIJK
RONCQ
NEUVILLE-EN-FERRAIN
RISQUONS TOUT
Hôp. Dron
Bourgogne
MOUSCRON
LINSELLES
TOURCOING
LUINGNE
BELGIQUE
MONT-A-LEUX
HERSEAUX
CH^AU DU VERT BOIS
LES BALLONS
Carliers
PARC DU LION
Septentrion
MOUVAUX
R. J. Guesde
Av. de la Marne
WATTRELOS
ROUBAIX
LEERS
MARCQ-EN-B.
CROIX
LYS-LEZ-LANNOY
Wasquehal Hôtel de V.
Croix Centre
WASQUEHAL
LANNOY
Wasquehal Pavé de Lille
Jean Jaurès
LE SART
Av. de l'Europe
R. J. Guesde
TOUFFLERS
HEM
ST-MAURICE
les Prés
Mons Sarts
FLERS
LA COUSINERIE
SAILLY-LEZ-LANNOY
MONS-EN BARŒUL
Fort de Mons
Mairie de Mons
PARC DU HERON
FOREST-S-MARQUE
HELLEMMES
STADIUM
VILLENEUVE-D' ASCQ
Marbrerie
Hellemmes
Lézennes
P.t de Bois
ANNAPPES
BASE DE LOISIRS
WILLEMS
Villeneuve d'Ascq Hôtel de V.
Triolo
ASCQ
R. Colbert
TRESSIN
SIN
LÉZENNES
Cité Scientifique
CITE SCIENTIFIQUE
BAISIEUX
Quatre Cantons
ANSTAING
CHERENG
GRUSON
SAINGHIN-EN-MÉLANTOIS
LESQUIN
Marque
BOUVINES
C.R.T.
NORD
T.G.V.
LILLE-LESQUIN
CYSOING
AÉROGARE
PÉRONNE-EN-MÉLANTOIS
PARIS
VALENCIENNES
ST-AMAND-LES-EAUX
OUDENAARDE
A 17 TOURNAI
TOURNAI BRUXELLES
2 km

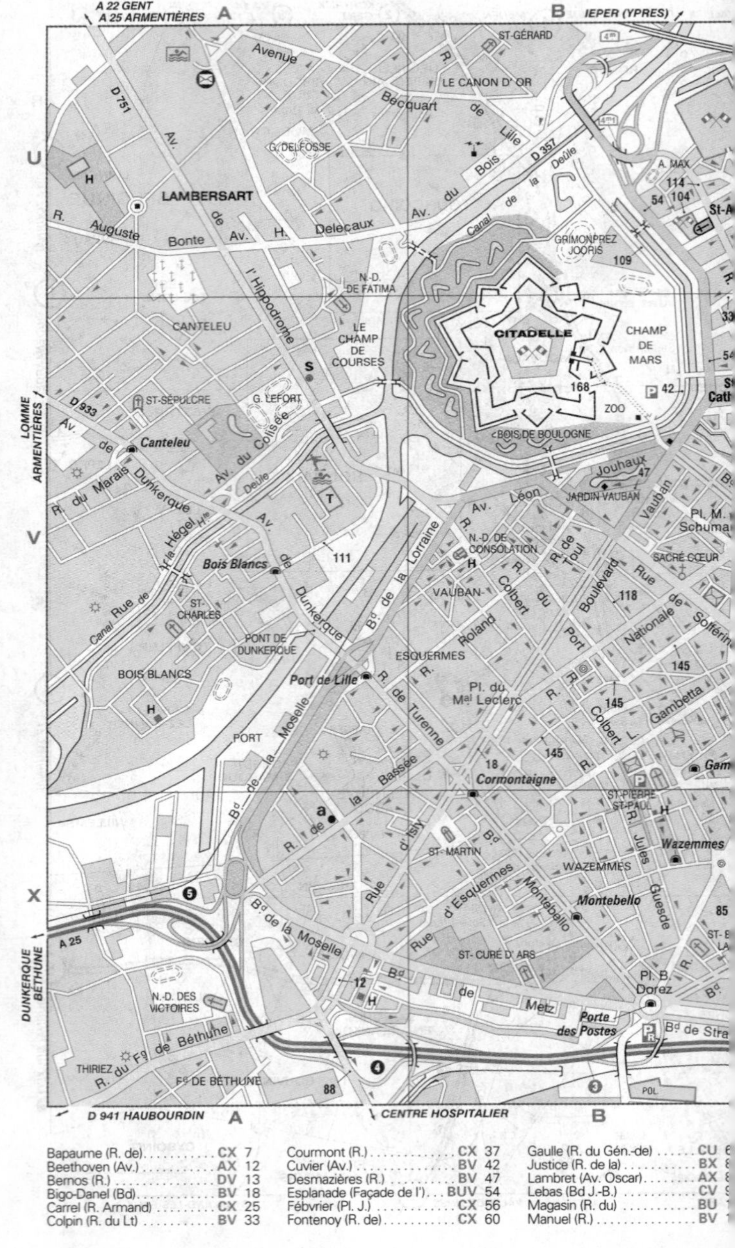

Bapaume (R. de)	CX	7	Courmont (R.)	CX	37	Gaulle (R. du Gén.-de)	CU	6
Beethoven (Av.)	AX	12	Cuvier (Av.)	BV	42	Justice (R. de la)	BX	8
Bernos (R.)	DV	13	Desmazières (R.)	BV	47	Lambret (Av. Oscar)	AX	8
Bigo-Danel (Bd)	BV	18	Esplanade (Façade de l')	BUV	54	Lebas (Bd J.-B.)	CV	9
Carrel (R. Armand)	CX	25	Fébvrier (Pl. J.)	CX	56	Magasin (R. du)	BU	1
Colpin (R. du Lt)	BV	33	Fontenoy (R. de)	CX	60	Manuel (R.)	BV	1

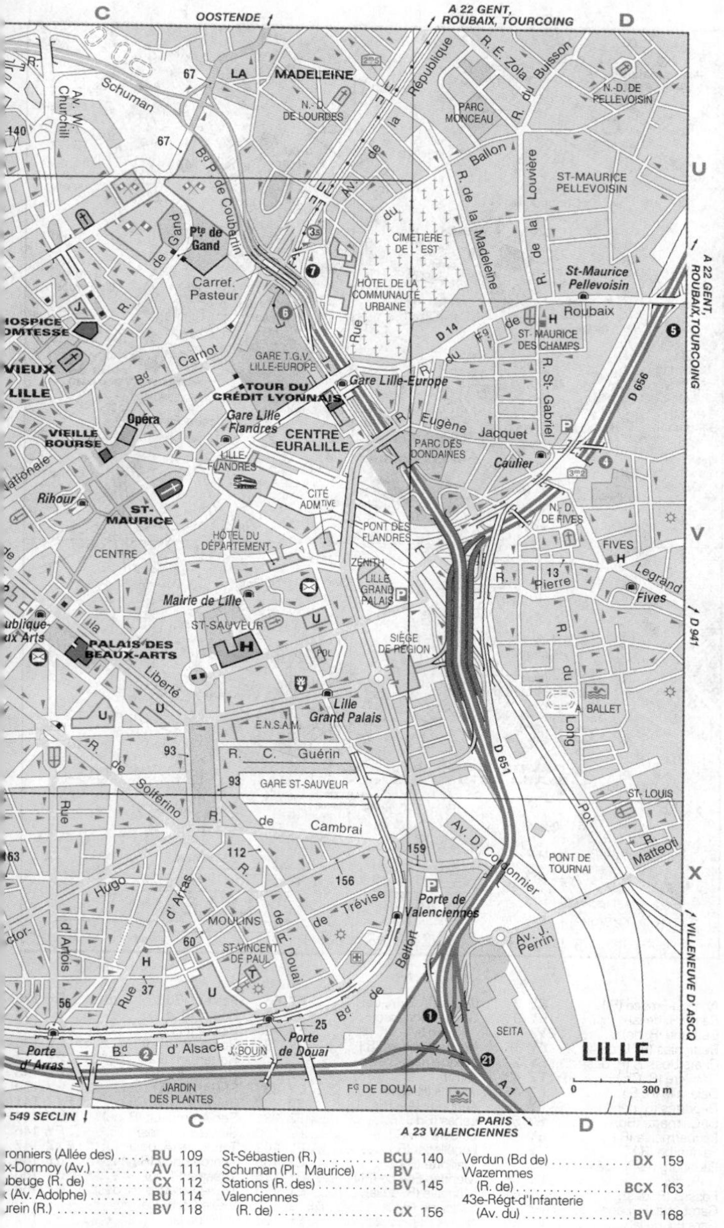

ronniers (Allée des) . . . . . BU 109
x-Dormoy (Av.). . . . . AV 111
ubeuge (R. de) . . . . CX 112
: (Av. Adolphe) . . . . BU 114
rein (R.) . . . . BV 118
St-Sébastien (R.) . . . . BCU 140
Schuman (Pl. Maurice) . . . . . BV
Stations (R. des) . . . . BV 145
Valenciennes (R. de) . . . . CX 156
Verdun (Bd de) . . . . DX 159
Wazemmes (R. de). . . . . BCX 163
43e-Régt-d'Infanterie (Av. du) . . . . BV 168

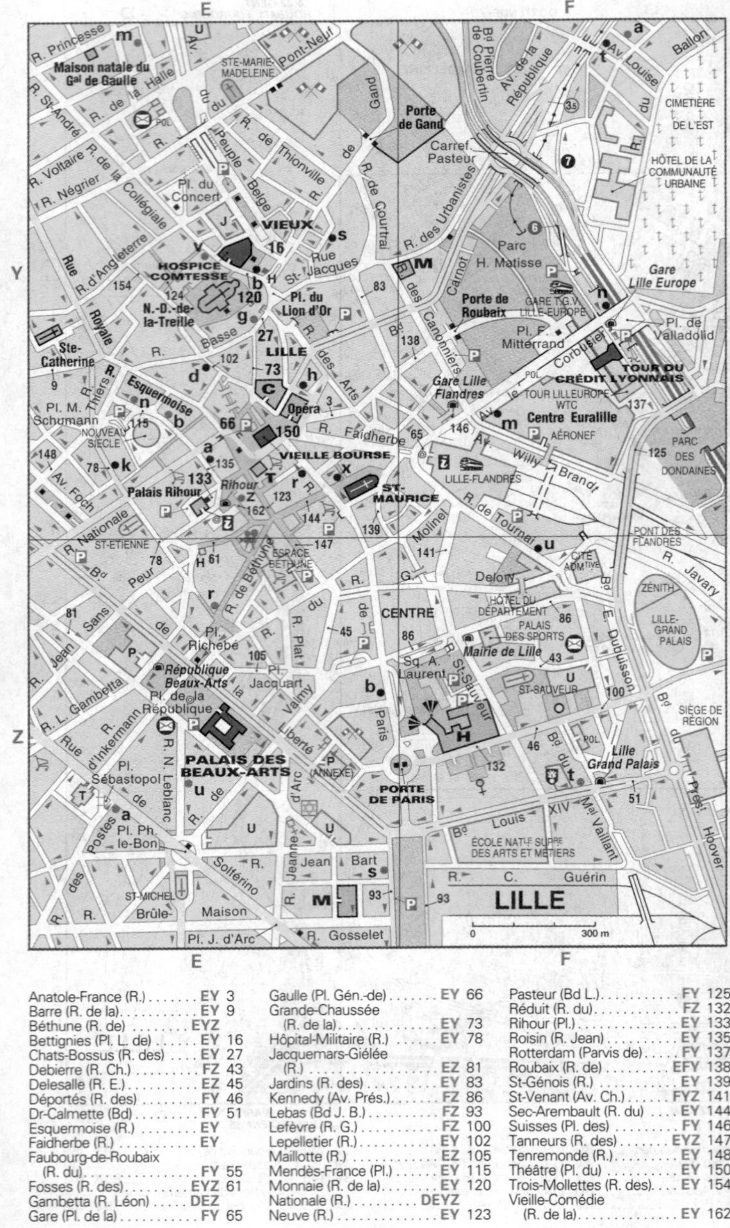

Anatole-France (R.) . . . . EY 3
Barre (R. de la). . . . . EY 9
Béthune (R. de) . . . . EYZ
Bettignies (Pl. L. de) . . . . . EY 16
Chats-Bossus (R. des) . . . . EY 27
Debierre (R. Ch.) . . . . FZ 43
Delesalle (R. E.) . . . . EZ 45
Déportés (R. des) . . . . FY 46
Dr-Calmette (Bd) . . . . FY 51
Esquermoise (R.) . . . . EY
Faidherbe (R.) . . . . EY
Faubourg-de-Roubaix (R. du). . . . . FY 55
Fosses (R. des). . . . . EYZ 61
Gambetta (R. Léon) . . . . . DEZ
Gare (Pl. de la) . . . . FY 65
Gaulle (Pl. Gén.-de) . . . . EY 66
Grande-Chaussée (R. de la). . . . . EY 73
Hôpital-Militaire (R.) . . . . . . EY 78
Jacquemars-Giélée (R.) . . . . EZ 81
Jardins (R. des) . . . . EY 83
Kennedy (Av. Prés.). . . . . . . FZ 86
Lebas (Bd J. B.) . . . . FZ 93
Lefèvre (R. G.) . . . . FZ 100
Lepelletier (R.) . . . . EY 102
Maillotte (R.) . . . . EZ 105
Mendès-France (Pl.) . . . . . . EY 115
Monnaie (R. de la). . . . . EY 120
Nationale (R.) . . . . DEYZ
Neuve (R.) . . . . EY 123
Pasteur (Bd L.). . . . . FY 125
Réduit (R. du). . . . . FZ 132
Rihour (Pl.) . . . . EY 133
Roisin (R. Jean) . . . . EY 135
Rotterdam (Parvis de) . . . . . FY 137
Roubaix (R. de) . . . . EFY 138
St-Génois (R.) . . . . EY 139
St-Venant (Av. Ch.) . . . . . . FYZ 141
Sec-Arembault (R. du) . . . . EY 144
Suisses (Pl. des) . . . . FY 146
Tanneurs (R. des) . . . . EYZ 147
Tenremonde (R.). . . . . EY 148
Théâtre (Pl. du) . . . . EY 150
Trois-Mollettes (R. des). . . . EY 154
Vieille-Comédie (R. de la). . . . . EY 162

Art Déco Romarin without rest
110 r. de la République in La Madeleine – ☎ 03 20 14 81 81 – www.hotelartdecoromarin.com – hotel-art-decoromarin@wanadoo.fr – Fax 03 20 14 81 80
p. 3 FY **t**
56 rm – †€ 120/135 ††€ 140/155, ☕ € 12
◆ This modern hotel is located on a busy avenue but with good soundproofing. Art Deco interiors spacious rooms, plush lounge and bar.

De la Paix without rest
46 bis r. de Paris – ☎ 03 20 54 63 93 – www.hotel-la-paix.com – hotelpaixlille@aol.com – Fax 03 20 63 98 97
p. 8 EY **r**
36 rm – †€ 75 ††€ 90, ☕ € 9
◆ A hotel built in 1782. The art-loving landlord displays reproductions of paintings and the mural in the breakfast room is all her own work. Snug rooms.

Des Tours without rest
27 r. des Tours – ☎ 03 59 57 47 00 – www.hotel-des-tours.com – contact@hotel-des-tours.com – Fax 03 59 57 47 99
p. 8 EY **s**
64 rm – †€ 115/130 ††€ 125/140, ☕ € 15
◆ A pleasant hotel superbly located in the heart of Old Lille, with a guarded garage and a hall and lounge adorned with contemporary paintings. Modern, practical rooms.

Brueghel without rest
parvis St-Maurice – ☎ 03 20 06 06 69 – www.hotel-brueghel.com – hotel.brueghel@nordnet.fr – Fax 03 20 63 25 27
p. 8 EY **x**
65 rm – †€ 80 ††€ 94, ☕ € 8,50
◆ Typically Flemish façade, retro charm in the hallway and lift, small fresh personalised rooms and central location.

De La Treille without rest
7/9 pl. Louise de Bettignies – ☎ 03 20 55 45 46 – www.hoteldelatreille.fr.st – hoteldelatreille@free.fr – Fax 03 20 51 51 69
p. 8 EY **b**
42 rm – †€ 70/135 ††€ 70/135, ☕ € 11
◆ With slightly-cramped yet fresh and well-appointed rooms, this hotel is perfectly located for exploring the old town. Generous buffet breakfast.

Ibis Opéra without rest
21 r. Lepelletier – ☎ 03 20 06 21 95 – www.ibishotel.com – h0902@accor.com – Fax 03 20 74 91 30
p. 8 EY **d**
59 rm – †€ 65/94 ††€ 65/94, ☕ € 8
◆ A smart traditional façade and new rooms in line with the chain's standards (modern furniture, desk space): an excellent base camp to visit the historic city centre.

La Maison Carrée
29 r. Bonte-Pollet – ☎ 03 20 93 60 42 – www.lamaisoncarree.fr – reservation@lamaisoncarree.fr
p. 6 AX **a**
5 rm ☕ – †€ 150/230 ††€ 150/230 **Table d'hôte** – Menu € 40/60
◆ Magnificent early 20C private mansion, run by contemporary art and home decoration enthusiasts. The quintessence of peacefulness, sophistication and comfort.

XXXX ✿ **A L'Huîtrière**
3 r. Chats Bossus ✉ 59800 – ☎ 03 20 55 43 41 – www.huitriere.fr – contact@huitriere.fr – Fax 03 20 55 23 10 – Closed 26 July-24 August, Sunday dinner and bank holiday dinner
p. 8 EY **g**
Rest – Menu € 45 (weekday lunch) – Carte € 75/120
Spec. Déclinaison d'huîtres plates et creuses, froides et chaudes. Lotte et andouille, ravioles au crayeux de Roncq, émulsion à la bière des 3 Monts (Oct. to April). Cramique perdu, glace à la bière.
◆ In this establishment devoted to seafood, you cannot fail but admire the decorative tiles of the shop or the new oyster bar, before venturing into three luxurious dining rooms.

La Laiterie (Benoit Bernard)
138 r. de l'Hippodrome, at Lambersart ✉ 59130 – ☎ 03 20 92 79 73 – www.lalaiterie.fr – lalaiterie@wanadoo.fr – Fax 03 20 22 16 19 – Closed 2-24 August, Sunday and Monday p. 6 AV **s**
Rest – Menu (€ 42 bi), € 48/78 – Carte € 72/100
Spec. Bar, déclinaison de cèpes, jus de persil. Millefeuille de boeuf au foie gras, artichauts poivrade. Gourmandise chocolat blanc passion.
◆ Restaurant on the outskirts of Lille. The attractive modern interior is discreet to do full justice to the chef's delicious, creative cuisine full of flavours.

Le Sébastopol (Jean-Luc Germond)
1 pl. Sébastopol – ☎ 03 20 57 05 05 – www.restaurant-sebastopol.fr – n.germond@restaurant-sebastopol.fr – Closed 2-24 August, Sunday dinner, Saturday lunch and Monday lunch p. 8 EZ **a**
Rest – Menu € 52 bi/68 – Carte € 72/80
Spec. Saint-Jacques d'Etaples (Oct. to April). Filet de sole aux jets de houblon (spring). Notre raison d'aimer la chicorée du Nord.
◆ A curtain of greenery and an unusual glass canopy adorn the façade of this friendly establishment. Delicious classical cuisine and fine wine list.

Champlain
13 r. N. Leblanc – ☎ 03 20 54 01 38 – www.lechamplain.fr – le.champlain@wanadoo.fr – Fax 03 20 40 07 28 – Closed August, Saturday lunch, Sunday dinner and Monday dinner p. 8 EZ **u**
Rest – Menu € 27 bi (weekday lunch), € 32/47
◆ Take a seat in the plush dining room or in the peaceful inner courtyard of this 19C abode to sample the first-rate cuisine which does full justice to the excellence of its produce.

Clément Marot
16 r. Pas ✉ 59800 – ☎ 03 20 57 01 10 – www.clement-marot.com – clmarot@nordnet.fr – Fax 03 20 57 39 69 – Closed Sunday evening p. 8 EY **n**
Rest – Menu (€ 18), € 36/66 bi – Carte € 42/83
◆ A small brick house run by the descendants of Clément Marot, a poet from Cahors. Modern decor, walls hung with pictures and a friendly atmosphere.

Le Colysée
201 av. Colisée ✉ 59130 Lambersart – ☎ 03 20 45 90 00 – www.le-colysee.com – contact@le-colysee.com – Fax 03 20 45 90 70 – Closed for one week in August, Saturday lunch, Monday dinner and Sunday p. 6 AV
Rest – Menu (€ 20), € 28/80 bi – Carte € 38/65
◆ The ground floor of the Colysée is home to this muted restaurant decorated in an avant-garde style (films projected onto the ceiling) in keeping with the innovative characterful cuisine.

L'Écume des Mers
10 r. Pas – ☎ 03 20 54 95 40 – www.ecume-des-mers.com – Fax 03 20 54 96 66 – Closed 20 July-30 August and Sunday dinner p. 8 EY **n**
Rest – brasserie – Menu (€ 18), € 25 (weekday dinner) – Carte € 29/56
◆ A lively atmosphere, fish caught the same day, a good oyster bar and some meat dishes for those who prefer meat: a vast brasserie with the wind in its sails!

Brasserie de la Paix
25 pl. Rihour – ☎ 03 20 54 70 41 – www.restaurantsdelille.com – contactpaix@restaurantsdelille.com – Fax 03 20 40 15 52 – Closed Sunday p. 8 EY **z**
Rest – Menu (€ 15), € 18/26 – Carte € 29/55
◆ Ceramics, woodwork, benches and tightly packed tables set the Art Deco scene of this pleasant brasserie situated near the Palais Rihour (Tourist Office). Most friendly.

Le Bistrot Tourangeau
61 bd Louis XIV ✉ 59800 – ☎ 03 20 52 74 64 – www.restochart.com – hhochard@laposte.net – Fax 03 20 85 06 39 – Closed 1-24 August, 26 December-3 January, Monday dinner, Tuesday dinner, Wednesday dinner, Saturday lunch and Sunday
Rest – Carte € 32/58 p. 8 FZ **t**
◆ A charming red façade hides a long dining room, separated from the kitchens by a pane of glass. Updated traditional repertoire, regional dishes from Tours, wine from the Loire.

XX **Le Why Not**

9 r. Maracci – 03 20 74 14 14 – www.lewhynot-restaurant.fr – lewhynot@nordnet.fr – Fax 03 20 74 14 15 – Closed 28 July-17 August, 1-6 January, Saturday lunch and Sunday p. 8 EY **m**

Rest – Menu (€ 22), € 26/35

◆ In the heart of historic Lille, this trendy-yet-friendly restaurant is set in a designer-decorated cellar. Tasty, up-to-date cooking by a globe-trotting chef.

X **L'Assiette du Marché**

61 r. Monnaie – 03 20 06 83 61 – www.assiettedumarche.com – contact@assiettedumarche.com – Fax 03 20 14 03 75 – Closed 2-24 August and Sunday

Rest – Menu (€ 16), € 20 – Carte € 24/44 p. 8 EY **v**

◆ The happy blend of old and new decoration and the glass roof covering the interior courtyard enhance this 18C Hôtel des Monnaies (Mint). Dishes with seasonal market produce.

X **Le Bistrot de Pierrot**

6 pl. Béthune – 03 20 57 14 09 – www.bistrot-de-pierrot.fr – tomaled@orange.fr – Fax 03 20 30 93 13 – Closed 10-16 August, January, Sunday and Monday

Rest – Carte € 30/45 p. 8 EZ **r**

◆ The new owners have preserved the soul and character of this authentic bistro. On the menu: a fine choice of "old-fashioned" dishes and a lighter selection for the diet conscious.

in Bondues – pop. 10 100 – alt. 37 m – ✉ 59910

Syndicat d'initiative, 266, domaine de la vigne 03 20 25 94 94

XXX **Auberge de l'Harmonie**

pl. Abbé Bonpain – 03 20 23 17 02 – www.aubergeharmonie.fr – contact@aubergeharmonie.fr – Fax 03 20 23 05 99 – Closed 20 July-10 August, Sunday dinner, Tuesday dinner, Thursday dinner and Monday p. 5 HR **t**

Rest – Menu (€ 28 bi), € 36/90 bi – Carte € 44/70

◆ Colourful and warm with rustic furniture, exposed beams, lush green terrace and seasonally varied dishes. A good blend of decor and cuisine.

XXX **Val d'Auge** (Christophe Hagnerelle)

805 av. Gén. de Gaulle – 03 20 46 26 87 – www.valdauge.com – valdauge@numericable.fr – Fax 03 20 37 43 78 – Closed Easter holidays, 28 July-17 August, 24-30 December, Sunday dinner, Monday dinner, Wednesday and public holidays

Rest – Menu (€ 46 bi), € 52 bi, € 57/70 – Carte € 60/73 p. 5 HR **a**

Spec. Foie gras d'oie grillé. Pigeon des flandres rôti sur carcasse. Moelleux au chocolat, crème glacée à la mangue.

◆ This restaurant on the main road offers a modern, pleasantly bright interior. The cuisine features a subtle blend of flavours and aromas.

in La Madeleine – pop. 22 600 – alt. 48 m – ✉ 59110

Syndicat d'initiative, 177, rue du Général-de-Gaulle 03 20 74 32 35, Fax 03 20 74 32 35

XX **L'Atelier "La Cour des Grands"**

15 r. François de Badts at la Madeleine – 03 20 74 26 33 – Fax 03 20 55 89 66 – Closed 20 July-17 August, 1 week in February, Sunday, Monday and bank holidays p. 8 FY **a**

Rest – Menu € 22 – Carte € 38/55

◆ Industrial loft decor, artwork and photography, an inventive minimalist cuisine and good choice of wines by the glass: this former garage has become the in-place of Lille.

in Marcq-en-Baroeul – pop. 38 800 – alt. 15 m – ✉ 59700

Office de tourisme, 111, avenue Foch 03 20 72 60 87, Fax 03 20 72 56 65

Mercure

157 av. Marne, via D 670: 5 km – 03 28 33 12 12 – www.mercure.com – h1099@accor.com – Fax 03 28 33 12 24 p. 5 HS **s**

125 rm – † € 85/225 †† € 95/235, ☕ € 18 – 1 suite

Rest ***L'Europe*** – *03 28 33 12 68* – Menu (€ 18), € 23 – Carte € 27/50

◆ A 1970s building surrounded by greenery near a motorway interchange. Stylish, contemporary renovated rooms. Snug sitting room and pleasant piano bar. Daily specials chalked up on the blackboard, classic menu and oyster bar.

XXX **Le Septentrion**
parc du château Vert-Bois, by D 617: 9 km – ✆ 03 20 46 26 98 – www.septentrion.fr – contact-septentrion@nordnet.fr – Fax 03 20 46 38 33 – Closed Sunday dinner, Tuesday dinner, Wednesday dinner and Monday *p. 5* HR **n**
Rest – Menu (€ 36), € 41/90
♦ Within the Prouvost-Septentrion Foundation, this former outbuilding of the Vert Bois château (complete with a brasserie) commands a pastoral view of the park. Updated cuisine.

X **La Table de Marcq**
944 av. de la République – ✆ 03 20 72 43 55 – Closed 1-26 August, Sunday dinner and Monday *p. 4* HS **e**
Rest – Menu € 14 bi (weekday lunch), € 17/32 – Carte € 32/46
♦ Formerly a café, this restaurant has been decorated in a modern vein, without however forgoing the lovely old counter. Friendly atmosphere and market-inspired menu.

in Villeneuve d'Ascq – pop. 61 300 – alt. 26 m – ✉ 59491
Office de tourisme, chemin du Chat Botté ✆ 03 20 43 55 75, Fax 03 20 91 28 28

Ascotel
av. P. Langevin-Cité Scientifique – ✆ 03 20 67 34 34 – www.ascotel.fr – ascotel@club.fr – Fax 03 20 91 39 28 *p. 5* HT **z**
83 rm – €59/91 €71/95, € 13 – 2 suites
Rest – *(Closed Saturday and Sunday)* Menu € 18 (weekdays)/28 – Carte € 29/36
♦ In the centre of the science park, a hotel complex for business trips - vast conference room, large lecture hall and functional rooms undergoing renovation. A modern dining room and traditional buffet-style dishes.

X **Le Carré des Sens**
73 av. de Flandres – ✆ 03 20 82 05 97 – restaurant@lecarredessens.eu – Closed 20 July-20 August, Sunday and Monday *p. 5* HS **v**
Rest – Menu (€ 24), € 35/70 – Carte € 64/80
♦ This house in the suburbs welcomes diners into a vast contemporary dining room (some tables are higher than the average). Updated menu. Pleasant summer terrace.

to Lille-Lesquin Airport – ✉ 59810 Lesquin

Mercure Aéroport
110 r. Jean Jaurès – ✆ 03 20 87 46 46 – www.mercure.com – h1098@accor-hotels.com – Fax 03 20 87 46 47 *p. 5* HT **r**
215 rm – €60/165 €60/165, € 15
Rest ***La Flamme*** – Menu (€ 20), € 25/45 bi – Carte € 29/46
♦ Contemporary architecture; spacious, comfortable rooms. Avoid rooms overlooking the motorway. Shuttle service to nearby airport. A friendly atmosphere, regional dishes and spit-roast meats on view at the Flamme.

Novotel Aéroport
55 rte de Douai – ✆ 03 20 62 53 53 – www.novotel.com – h0427@accor.com – Fax 03 20 97 36 12 *p. 5* HT **t**
92 rm – €75/149 €75/149, € 15 **Rest** – Carte € 28/38
♦ This low building is the chain's oldest hotel (1967). Functional rooms gradually being refurbished in the latest Novotel style. Traditional dishes and diet recipes rub shoulders in the fully redecorated restaurant.

Agena without rest
451 av du Gén.-Leclerc ✉ 59155 – ✆ 03 20 60 13 14 – www.hotel-agena.com – hotelagena@nordnet.fr – Fax 03 20 97 31 79 *p. 5* HT **v**
40 rm – €69 €74, € 9
♦ The rooms in this semi-circular building are on garden level; the quieter ones face the patio. A discreet setting, roughcast walls, simple furniture and faultless upkeep.

in Wattignies – pop. 13 800 – alt. 39 m – ✉ 59139

X **Le Cheval Blanc** AC VISA MC AE
110 r. Gén. de Gaulle – ✆ 03 20 97 34 62 – www.restaurantlechevalblanc.com – le-cheval-blanc3@wanadoo.fr – Fax 03 20 97 34 62 – Closed Saturday lunch, Sunday dinner and Wednesday p.4 GT **x**
Rest – Menu (€ 25 bi), € 32/42 – Carte € 45/64
◆ A warm welcome and decor (light colours, modern art, handsome wooden bar) and an appetising repertoire that focuses on market fresh and locally sourced produce.

in Emmerin – pop. 2 815 – alt. 24 m – ✉ 59320

La Howarderie
1 r. Fusillés – ✆ 03 20 10 31 00 – www.lahowarderie.com – contact@lahowarderie.com – Fax 03 20 10 31 09 – Closed 3-24 August, 22 December-5 January and Sunday evening p. 4 GT **e**
7 rm – †€ 90/95 ††€ 100/150, ☕ € 17
Rest – Menu (€ 14), € 28 (weekdays)/49 – Carte € 38/61
◆ One wing of this old brick farmhouse opposite the church offers a choice of elegant rooms with an individual touch and antique or period furnishings. Modern cuisine served in two intimate dining rooms.

in Capinghem – pop. 1 524 – alt. 50 m – ✉ 59160

X **La Marmite de Pierrot** P VISA MC AE
93 r. Poincaré – ✆ 03 20 92 12 41 – www.pierrot-de-lille.com – pierrot@pierrot-de-lille.com – Fax 03 20 92 72 51 – Closed Sunday dinner, Tuesday dinner, Wednesday dinner, Thursday dinner and Monday p. 4 GS **v**
Rest – Menu € 27/32 – Carte approx. € 33
◆ Rustic-style bistro specialising in pork products and tripe. Informal ambience and interior decorated with halters and other farming implements.

in St-André-Lez-Lille – pop. 10 900 – alt. 20 m – ✉ 59350

Office de tourisme, 89, rue du Général Leclerc ✆ 03 20 51 79 05, Fax 03 20 63 07 60

XXX **La Quintinie** AC P VISA MC
501 av. Mal-de-Lattre-de-Tassigny, (D 57) – ✆ 03 20 40 78 88 – www.alaquintinie.com – anita@alaquintinie.com – Fax 03 20 40 62 77 – Closed 20 July-17 August, Monday and dinner except Saturday p. 4 GS **t**
Rest – Menu (€ 29), € 45/68 – Carte € 48/80
◆ Brick house in a pretty garden with a vegetable patch. Elegant, contemporary decor inside with faïence paintings; classic cuisine.

LIMERAY – 37 Indre-et-Loire – 317 P4 – see Amboise

LIMOGES P – 87 Haute-Vienne – 325 E6 – pop. 135 100 – Built-up area 173 299 – alt. 300 m – ✉ 87000 Dordogne-Berry-Limousin 24 B2

Paris 391 – Angoulême 105 – Brive-la-Gaillarde 92 – Châteauroux 126

Limoges: ✆ 05 55 43 30 30, 8 km on the ⑦

Office de tourisme, 12, boulevard de Fleurus ✆ 05 55 34 46 87, Fax 05 55 34 19 12

de la Porcelaine Panazol Celicroux, 9 km on the Clermont-Ferrand road, ✆ 05 55 31 10 69

de Limoges Avenue du Golf, 3 km on the St-Yriex road, ✆ 05 55 30 21 02

Cathédrale St-Etienne (St Etienne Cathedral)★ - Église St-Michel-des-Lions (St Michel des Lions Church)★ - Cour du temple (Temple courtyard)★ CZ 115 - Jardins de l'évêché (Bishop's Palace gardens)★ - Musée national de la porcelaine Adrien Dubouché (Adrien Dubouché National Porcelaine Museum)★★ (porcelaines) BY - Rue de Boucherie★ - Musée de l'évêché (Bishop's Palace Museum)★ : enamels★ - Chapelle St-Aurélien (Chapel of St Aurelien)★ - Gare des Bénédictins★.

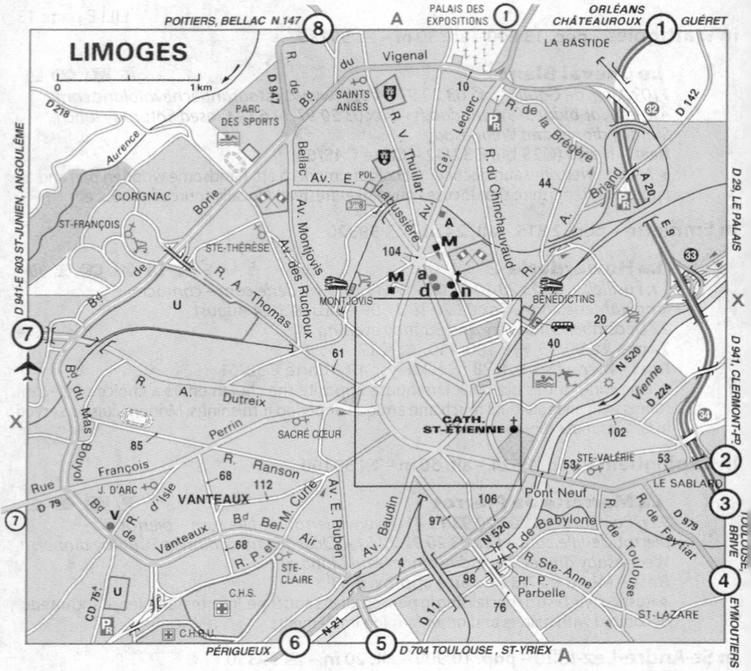

LIMOGES

Mercure Royal Limousin without rest
1 pl. République – ✆ 05 55 34 65 30 – www.mercure.com – h5955@accor.com – Fax 05 55 34 55 21 VISA CY **u**
80 rm – €85/120 €102/130, €13
◆ A tasteful blend of light wood and pastel colours characterises this hotel standing on a huge square. Three categories of rooms depending on your wish, from simple to comfortable.

Atrium without rest VISA
22 allée de Seto - Parc du Ciel – ✆ 05 55 10 75 75 – www.interhotel-atrium.com – ha8703@inter-hotel.com – Fax 05 55 10 75 76 DY **a**
70 rm – €90/115 €90/140, €13
◆ A former customs warehouse converted into a hotel offering pleasant rooms, some of which overlook the superb railway station of Limoges. Those overlooking the courtyard are quieter.

Domaine de Faugeras
allée Faugeras, 3 km northwest by Rue A-Briand and D 142 – ✆ 05 55 34 66 22 – www.faugeras.fr – infos@domainedefaugeras.fr – Fax 05 55 34 18 05 VISA AY **e**
9 rm – €95/290 €110/290, €14 – 2 suites
Rest *White Owl* – *(closed Sunday dinner and Monday)* Menu €24 (weekday lunch), €42/70 – Carte €30/63
◆ This 18C château overlooking Limoges combines history and modern comfort. Extremely well-equipped rooms, fireside lounge, wine-tasting cellar and spa. "Lounge" ambience and plate-glass windows at The White Owl.

LIMOGES

Street	Grid	No.
Aine (Pl. d')	BZ	2
Allois (R. des)	DZ	6
Amphithéâtre (R. de l')	BY	8
Barreyrrette (Pl. de la)	CZ	12
Bénédictins (Av. des)	DY	14
Betoulle (Pl. L.)	CZ	16
Boucherie (R. de la)	CZ	18
Cathédrale (R. de la)	DZ	23
Clocher (R. du)	CZ	25
Collège (R. du)	CZ	26
Consulat (R. du)	CZ	
Coopérateurs (R. des)	BY	27
Dupuytren (R.)	CZ	30
Ferrerie (R.)	CZ	33
Fonderie (R. de la)	BY	35
Fontaine-des-Barres (Pl.)	CY	37
Gambetta (Bd)	BCZ	
Giraudoux (Square Jean)	CY	42
Haute-Cité (R.)	DZ	46
Jacobins (Pl. des)	CZ	49
Jean-Jaurès (R.)	CYZ	
Louis-Blanc (Bd)	CZ	
Louvrier-de-Lajolais (R.)	BY	55
Manigne (Pl.)	CZ	57
Maupas (R. du)	DY	59
Michels (R. Charles)	CZ	63
Motte (Pl. de la)	CZ	66
Périn (Bd G.)	CY	71
Préfecture (R. de la)	CY	83
Raspail (R.)	DZ	89
Réforme (R. de la)	CY	91
République (Pl. de la)	CY	95
St-Martial (R.)	CY	107
St-Maurice (Bd)	DZ	109
St-Pierre (Pl.)	CZ	110
Stalingrad (Pl.)	CY	113
Temple (Cour du)	CZ	115
Temple (R. du)	CZ	116
Tourny (Carrefour)	CY	118
Victor-Hugo (Bd)	BY	120
Vigne-de-Fer (R.)	CZ	122
71e-Mobile (R. du)	DZ	125

Richelieu without rest

40 av. Baudin – ✆ 05 55 34 22 82 – www.hotel-richelieu.com – info@hotel-richelieu.com – Fax 05 55 34 35 36 CZ **k**

41 rm – €78/108 €88/118, €13 – 2 suites

◆ Close to the Town Hall and Media Library, this hotel combines modern comforts with a classical decor of 1930s inspiration. Extended and remodelled public areas (lounge, terrace).

Jeanne-d'Arc without rest

17 av. Gén. de Gaulle – ✆ 05 55 77 67 77 – www.hoteljeannedarc-limoges.fr – hoteljeannedarc.limoges@wanadoo.fr – Fax 05 55 79 86 75 – Closed 19 December-4 January DY **s**

50 rm – €65/82 €77/96, €8

◆ This former 19C post-house, not far from the station, features a delightfully outdated provincial atmosphere. Well-kept rooms and pleasant breakfast room.

St-Martial without rest
21 r. A. Barbès – ✆ 05 55 77 75 29 – www.hotelsaintmartiallimoges.com – sm8702@inter-hotel.com – Fax 05 55 79 27 60 AX **n**
30 rm – 🚹€ 55/81 🚹🚹€ 55/81, ☕ € 8,50
◆ This tastefully renovated hotel near the station sports a classical elegance. The modern practical rooms are faultlessly maintained. Plush sitting rooms.

Art Hôtel Tendance without rest
37 r. Armand-Barbes – ✆ 05 55 77 31 72 – www.arthoteltendance.com – arthoteltendance@orange.fr – Fax 05 55 10 25 53 AX **t**
13 rm – 🚹€ 53/62 🚹🚹€ 58/68, ☕ € 8
◆ Functional family establishment near the station. Personalised rooms according to destination (Bali, Venice, Greece, etc) in two houses separated by a courtyard.

De la Paix without rest
25 pl. Jourdan – ✆ 05 55 34 36 00 – www.phono.org – Fax 05 55 32 37 06 DY **r**
31 rm – 🚹€ 43 🚹🚹€ 60/72, ☕ € 8
◆ This late 19C building features lounges decorated with an impressive collection of phonographs worthy of a museum. Simple rooms (WC on the landing for eight rooms).

Amphitryon (Richard Lequet)
26 r. Boucherie – ✆ 05 55 33 36 39 – amphitryon87000@aol.com – Fax 05 55 32 98 50 – Closed 5-12 May, 25 August-8 September, 5-12 January, Sunday and Monday CZ **u**
Rest – Menu (€ 21), € 25 (weekday lunch), € 42/72 – Carte € 84/99
Spec. Les trois foies gras. Filet de bœuf du Limousin, sauce bordelaise et purée de pomme de terre. Paris-Brest.
◆ This half-timbered house in the heart of a picturesque village has a pleasant summer terrace and a warm interior. A creative slant on a traditional culinary repertoire.

Le Vanteaux
122 r. d'Isle – ✆ 05 55 49 01 26 – christof.aubisse@numericable.com – Closed 27 April-4 May, 2-23 August, 1st-11 January, Sunday dinner and Monday
Rest – Menu (€ 19), € 25, € 39/80 – Carte € 45/60 dinner only AX **v**
◆ Spruce façade (1815) that has been refreshed, smart interior and a terrace. Inventive menu, tempting cart of mini desserts, and at lunchtime a selection of wines available by the glass.

Le Versailles
20 pl. Aine – ✆ 05 55 34 13 39 – www.restaurateursdefrance.com – le.versailles@club-internet.fr – Fax 05 55 32 84 73 BZ **a**
Rest – brasserie – Menu € 16 (weekday lunch), € 22/29 – Carte € 21/57
◆ With the law courts as a backdrop, this brasserie founded in 1932, extended by a circular mezzanine, serves tasty simple dishes in keeping with the spirit of the establishment.

La Cuisine
21 r. Montmailler – ✆ 05 55 10 28 29 – www.restaurantlacuisine.com – lacuisine@restaurantlacuisine.com – Fax 05 55 10 28 29 – Closed Sunday, Monday and public holidays BY **a**
Rest – Menu € 17 (lunch), € 35/50 – Carte € 35/50
◆ The young chef prepares inventive dishes with exotic influences and unusual flavours such as Carambar (a chewy caramel) ice cream. Packed at lunchtimes and evenings.

La Maison des Saveurs
74 av. Garibaldi – ✆ 05 55 79 30 74 – Fax 05 55 79 30 74 – Closed 13-27 July, Saturday lunch, Sunday dinner and Monday AX **d**
Rest – Menu (€ 16), € 24/55 – Carte € 57/68
◆ This contemporary restaurant features traditional fare largely based on local produce: foie gras, farm-reared duck, Limousin meat and apples.

27
27 r. Haute-Vienne – ✆ 05 55 32 27 27 – www.le27.com – Fax 05 55 34 37 53 – Closed Sunday and public holidays CZ **a**
Rest – Menu (€ 16), € 19 (weekdays) – Carte € 33/50
◆ Glossy red tables and shelves lined with bottles set the scene in this fashionable restaurant near the market. Contemporary cuisine and a good selection of wines.

Les Petits Ventres
20 r. de la Boucherie – ✆ 05 55 34 22 90 – www.les-petits-ventres.com – emavic-sarl@wanadoo.fr – Fax 05 55 32 41 04 – Closed 20 April-3 May, 5-20 September, 8-22 February, Sunday and Monday CZ **u**
Rest – Menu (€ 17), € 24/34 – Carte € 37/44
◆ Tripe dishes and an impressive choice of menus for big and small eaters alike! Rustic, half-timbered décor hung with colourful paintings.

Le Bouche à Oreille
72 bis av. Garibaldi – ✆ 05 55 10 09 57 – w.w.w leboucheaoreille87.com – david.daudon@wanadoo.fr – Fax 05 55 10 09 57 – Closed 1st-10 January, Tuesday dinner from 15 September to 15 June, Sunday except lunch from 15 September to 15 June and Monday AX **a**
Rest – bistro – Menu (€ 18), € 24/34 – Carte € 34/45
◆ A friendly town centre bistro with a clientele of regulars. Market fresh cuisine served in a non-smoking dining room decorated in bright reds and yellows.

Chez Alphonse
5 pl. Motte – ✆ 05 55 34 34 14 – bistrot.alphonse@wanadoo.fr – bistrot.alphonse@wanadoo.fr – Fax 05 55 34 34 14 – Closed 27 July-10 August, 29 December-12 January, Sunday and public holidays CZ **e**
Rest – bistro – Menu (€ 13 bi) – Carte € 21/46
◆ In keeping with tradition, the chef of this lively bistro pays a daily visit to the market next door for produce with which to concoct his authentic repertoire.

La Table de Jean
5 r. Boucherie – ✆ 05 55 32 77 91 – Closed 25 July-9 August, 19 December-5 January, Saturday, Sunday and public holidays CZ **x**
Rest – *(number of covers limited, pre-book)* Menu (€ 18) – Carte € 30/46
◆ A fine restaurant in the historic district. Pleasant service and a minimalist decor. Tasty market fresh cooking with a choice of wines from independent winegrowers.

via ① and A 20 - ✉ 87280 Limoges

Novotel rm, VISA
2 av. d'Uzurat, ZI Nord exit, Lac d'Uzurat : 5 km – ✆ 05 44 20 20 00 – www.accorhotels.com – h0431@accor.com – Fax 05 44 20 20 10
90 rm – †€ 116 ††€ 116/127, ☕ € 14 **Rest** – Carte € 24/34
◆ On an industrial estate, a hotel with a 1970s overlooking Uzurat Lake in the centre of a 3ha park. Jogging track for clients eager to stay fit or relax. Modern dining room, terrace overlooking expanses of water; classic fare.

in St-Martin-du-Fault by ⑦, N 141, D 941 and D 20: 13 km – ✉ 87510 Nieul

Chapelle St-Martin (Gilles Dudognon)
– ✆ 05 55 75 80 17 – www.chapellesaintmartin.com – chapelle@relaischateaux.fr – Fax 05 55 75 89 50 – Closed 2 January-6 February
10 rm – †€ 80/690 ††€ 80/690, ☕ € 17 – 4 suites – ½ P € 117/252
Rest – *(closed Sunday dinner from November to March, Tuesday lunch, Wednesday lunch and Monday) (number of covers limited, pre-book)* Menu (€ 35), € 55/89 – Carte € 80/130
Spec. Foie gras, feuillantine sablée et laque à la réduction de jus de carotte-pamplemousse. Côte de veau, polenta moelleuse et légumes de saison. Mille-feuille caramel "chocolat balsamique".
◆ A plush elegant manor house in a park on the edge of a wood; guestrooms which sport colourful fabrics, sophisticated furniture and wall hangings. Well-prepared cuisine using regional produce.

LIMONEST – 69 Rhône – **327** H4 – **see Lyon**

LIMOUX – 11 Aude – **344** E4 – **pop. 9 709 – alt. 172 m** – ✉ **11300** 22 **B3**
Languedoc-Roussillon-Tarn Gorges

Paris 769 – Carcassonne 25 – Foix 70 – Perpignan 104 – Toulouse 94
Syndicat d'initiative, promenade du Tivoli ✆ 04 68 31 11 82, Fax 04 68 31 87 14

Grand Hôtel Moderne et Pigeon rm, VISA AE

1 pl. Gén.-Leclerc, (near the post office) – ✆ 04 68 31 00 25 – www.grandhotelmodernerpigeon.fr – hotelmodernepigeon@wanadoo.fr – Fax 04 68 31 12 43 – Closed Sunday evening from 15 October to 15 May

11 rm – €98/102 €125/140 – 3 suites

Rest – *(closed Sunday dinner except July-August, Tuesday lunch, Saturday lunch and Monday)* Menu (€24), €28 (weekday lunch), €39/80 – Carte €60/95

◆ This 17C mansion has been restored from top to toe. The spacious rooms are tastefully personalised and the magnificent staircase has murals and stained glass. Bar-smoking room. Attractive 1900s style dining rooms and a verdant patio-terrace; classic bourgeois cuisine.

La Maison de la Blanquette VISA

46 bis promenade du Tivoli – ✆ 04 68 31 01 63 – luciedorsimont@hotmail.com – Closed Wednesday

Rest – Menu €18 bi (weekday lunch), €27 € bi/40 bi – Carte €25/45

◆ This restaurant serves generous portions of local dishes to accompany the famous Blanquette de Limoux and other local wines. Wine shop. Wine is included in the price.

LINGOLSHEIM – 67 Bas-Rhin – **315** K5 – **see Strasbourg**

LINIÈRES-BOUTON – 49 Maine-et-Loire – **317** J4 – **pop. 96** – alt. 53 m – ✉ 49490 — 35 **C2**

Paris 293 – Nantes 155 – Angers 67 – Tours 58 – Joué-lès-Tours 85

Château de Boissimon without rest VISA

– ✆ 02 41 82 30 86 – www.chateaudeboissimon.com – contact@chateaudeboissimon.com – Open from April to October

5 rm – €130/150 €150/190

◆ This château, set in quiet wooded parkland, offers meticulously renovated rooms decorated with a host of refined details. Ideal for a romantic break.

LE LIOUQUET – 13 Bouches-du-Rhône – **340** I6 – **see La Ciotat**

LIPSHEIM – 67 Bas-Rhin – **315** J6 – **see Strasbourg**

LISIEUX – 14 Calvados – **303** N5 – **pop. 23 100 – alt. 51 m – Pilgrimage (end September)** – ✉ **14100** Normandy — 33 **C2**

Paris 179 – Alençon 94 – Caen 64 – Évreux 73 – Le Havre 60 – Rouen 93

Office de tourisme, 11, rue d'Alençon ✆ 02 31 48 18 10, Fax 02 31 48 18 11

St-Pierre cathedral ★ BY.

★ of St-Germain-de-Livet 7 km by ④.

Plan on next page

Mercure VISA AE

via ②: 2.5 km (rte de Paris) – ✆ 02 31 61 17 17 – www.accor-hotels.com – h1725@accor.com – Fax 02 31 32 33 43

69 rm – €78/99 €82/102, €13

Rest – Menu (€18), €21/23 – Carte €25/45

◆ A hotel on the outskirts of town with comfortable, well-kept rooms (sloping ceilings on the top floor). This restaurant extended by a summer terrace overlooking the swimming pool, offers buffets of hors d'œuvres and desserts.

Azur without rest VISA AE

15 r. au Char – ✆ 02 31 62 09 14 – www.azur-hotel.com – resa@azur-hotel.com – Fax 02 31 62 16 06 BYZ **b**

15 rm – €60/70 €80/90, €9

◆ Set in a 50-year-old building, spring fresh, comfortable guest rooms. Fine breakfast served in a conservatory breakfast room.

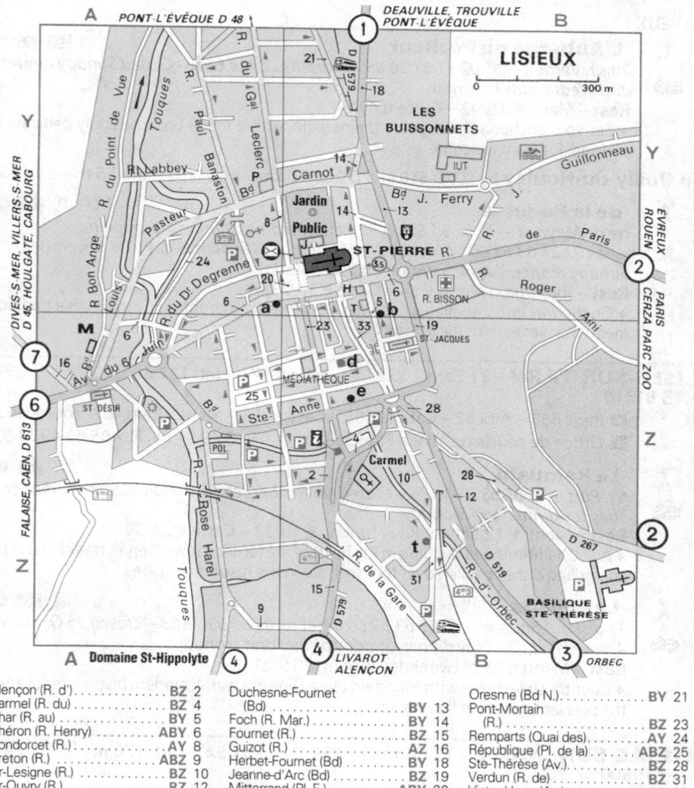

Alençon (R. d') .... BZ 2
Carmel (R. du) .... BZ 4
Char (R. au) .... BY 5
Chéron (R. Henry) .... ABY 6
Condorcet (R.) .... AY 8
Creton (R.) .... ABZ 9
Dr-Lesigne (R.) .... BZ 10
Dr-Ouvry (R.) .... BZ 12
Duchesne-Fournet (Bd) .... BY 13
Foch (R. Mar.) .... BY 14
Fournet (R.) .... BZ 15
Guizot (R.) .... AZ 16
Herbet-Fournet (Bd) .... BY 18
Jeanne-d'Arc (Bd) .... BZ 19
Mitterrand (Pl. F.) .... ABY 20
Oresme (Bd N.) .... BY 21
Pont-Mortain (R.) .... BZ 23
Remparts (Quai des) .... AY 24
République (Pl. de la) .... ABZ 25
Ste-Thérèse (Av.) .... BZ 28
Verdun (R. de) .... BZ 31
Victor-Hugo (Av.) .... BZ 33

de la Place without rest VISA AE
67 r. Henry Chéron – ☎ 02 31 48 27 27 – www.lisieux-hotel-delaplace.com
– hoteldelaplacebw@wanadoo.fr – Fax 02 31 48 27 20
– Closed 1st December-3 January ABY **a**
33 rm – †€ 47/50 ††€ 70/80, ☐ € 10
◆ A friendly welcome awaits guests in this central hotel. Refurbished rooms in bright, modern colours; some overlook the cathedral. Generous buffet breakfast.

L'Espérance VISA AE
16 bd Ste-Anne – ☎ 02 31 62 17 53 – www.lisieux-hotel.com
– booking@lisieux-hotel.com – Fax 02 31 62 34 00
– Open from mid-April to end October BZ **e**
100 rm – †€ 69/115 ††€ 79/115, ☐ € 10
Rest – Menu € 22/45 – Carte € 40/69
◆ On the main boulevard, this large Norman-style hotel built in the 1930s has regularly updated rooms with good soundproofing (double glazing). A large country fresco covers the walls of this grand dining area. Serving up-dated traditional meals.

Aux Acacias VISA
13 r. Résistance – ☎ 02 31 62 10 95 – Fax 02 31 32 59 06
– Closed Sunday dinner and Monday BZ **d**
Rest – Menu € 18 (weekdays)/46 – Carte € 64/88
◆ Pleasant Provencal-style restaurant: pastel coloured tablecloths and curtains with painted wooden furniture. Traditional cuisine, based on Normandy produce.

L'Auberge du Pêcheur VISA MC AE
2bis r. Verdun – ✆ 02 31 31 16 85 – marteltiti@aol.com – Closed Sunday dinner and Wednesday in winter BZ **t**
Rest – Menu € 16/42 – Carte € 40/80
◆ Set your anchor at this marine themed inn, with a menu unsurprisingly dedicated to seafood. Pleasant welcome.

in Ouilly-du-Houley by ②, **D 510 and D 262: 10 km – pop. 191 – alt. 55 m – ✉ 14590**

de la Paquine P VISA MC
rte de Moyaux – ✆ 02 31 63 63 80 – championlapaquine@orange.fr – Fax 02 31 63 63 80 – Closed 10-19 March, 2-10 September, 11-28 November, Sunday dinner, Tuesday dinner and Wednesday
Rest – *(pre-book)* Menu € 34 – Carte € 50/73
◆ On the way into the village, this small flower-decked countrified inn serves a traditional menu that varies with the seasons.

LISLE-SUR-TARN – 81 Tarn – 338 C7 – pop. 4 171 – alt. 127 m – ✉ 81310 29 C2

Paris 668 – Albi 32 – Cahors 105 – Castres 58 – Montauban 46 – Toulouse 51
Office de tourisme, place Paul Saissac ✆ 05 63 40 31 85, Fax 05 63 40 31 85

Le Romuald VISA MC
6 r. Port – ✆ 05 63 33 38 85 – Closed November school holidays, Sunday dinner, Tuesday dinner and Monday
Rest – Menu € 12 bi (weekday lunch), € 19/32 – Carte € 23/39
◆ A 16C half-timbered building in the heart of the fortified town. Serves traditional cuisine and grilled dishes cooked over the large fire in the rustic dining area.

Le Cépage VISA MC
15 pl. Paul-Saissac – ✆ 05 63 33 50 44 – Fax 05 63 33 98 83 – Closed 26 October-4 November, Tuesday dinner, Sunday dinner and Monday
Rest – Menu € 13 bi (weekday lunch), € 15/21
◆ Country-style dishes with a modern twist. Dine in a warm, modern bistro interior and on the pleasant terrace in fine weather.

LISSAC-SUR-COUZE – 19 Corrèze – 329 J5 – pop. 527 – alt. 170 m – ✉ 19600 24 B3

Paris 489 – Limoges 101 – Tulle 45 – Brive-la-Gaillarde 14 – Sarlat-la-Canéda 57

Château de Lissac without rest
in the village – ✆ 05 55 85 14 19 – www.chateaudelissac.com – chateaudelissac@wanadoo.fr – Fax 05 75 24 06 31
6 rm – 🛉€ 120/160 🛉🛉€ 120/160, ☕ € 10
◆ In a quiet village, this 13C, 15C and 18C château and its beautiful garden are ideally located overlooking the lake. Mod cons and unostentatious contemporary decoration.

LISSES – 91 Essonne – 312 D4 – 106 32 – see Paris, Area (Évry)

LISTRAC MEDOC – 33 Gironde – 335 G4 – pop. 2 115 – alt. 40 m – ✉ 33480 3 B1

Paris 609 – Bordeaux 38 – Lacanau-Océan 39 – Lesparre-Médoc 31

Auberge des Vignerons with rm AC rest, P VISA MC
28 av. Soulac – ✆ 05 56 58 08 68 – Fax 05 56 58 08 99 – Closed February school holidays, Saturday lunch, Sunday dinner and Monday
7 rm – 🛉€ 40 🛉🛉€ 40, ☕ € 7
Rest – Menu (€ 12), € 15 (weekday lunch), € 28/52 – Carte € 44/58
◆ Inn next to the Maison des Vins (Wine House). Traditional cuisine, wine list topped by Listrac vintages and view of the storeroom where the wine is matured. Terrace facing the vineyards.

LIVRY-GARGAN – 93 Seine-Saint-Denis – 305 G7 – 101 18 – see Paris, Area

LA LLAGONNE – 66 Pyrénées-Orientales – 344 D7 – see Mont-Louis

LLO – 66 Pyrénées-Orientales – 344 D8 – see Saillagouse

LOCHES – 37 Indre-et-Loire – 317 O6 – pop. 6 370 – alt. 80 m – ✉ 37600 Châteaux of the Loire 11 **B3**

- Paris 261 – Blois 68 – Châteauroux 72 – Châtellerault 56 – Tours 42
- Office de tourisme, place de la Marne ✆ 02 47 91 82 82, Fax 02 47 91 61 50
- de Loches-Verneuil Verneuil-sur-Indre La Capitainerie, 10 km on D 943, ✆ 02 47 94 79 48
- Medieval town★★: keep★★, St-Ours church ★, Porte Royale★, porte des cordeliers★, town hall★ Y H - Châteaux★★: recumbent statue of Agnès Sorel★, triptych★ - troglodytic quarries Vignemont★.
- Portal ★ of Chartreuse du Liget East: 10 km by ②.

LOCHES

Anciens A.F.N. (Pl. des) .... Z
Auguste (Bd Ph.) .... Z
Balzac (R.) .... YZ
Bas-Clos (Av. des) .... Y 2
Blé (Pl. au) .... Y 3
Château (R. du) .... YZ 5
Cordeliers (Pl. des) .... Y
Descartes (R.) .... Y 7
Donjon (Mail du) .... Z
Droulin (Mail) .... Z
Filature (Q. de la) .... Y 8
Foulques-Nerra (R.) .... Z 9
Gare (Av. de la) .... Y
Gaulle (Av. Gén.-de) .... Y 10
Grande-Rue .... Y 13
Grand Mail (Pl. du) .... Y 12
Lansyer (R.) .... Z 14
Louis XI (Av.) .... Y
Maquis Césario (Allée) .... Z
Marne (Pl. de la) .... Y
Mazerolles (Pl.) .... Y 15
Moulins (R. des) .... Y 16
Pactius (R. T.) .... Z 17
Picois (R.) .... Y
Ponts (R. des) .... Y 18
Porte-Poitevine (R. de la) .... Z 19
Poterie (Mail de la) .... Z
Quintefol (R.) .... YZ
République (R. de la) .... Y
Ruisseaux (R. des) .... Z 20
St-Antoine (R.) .... Y 21
St-Ours (R.) .... Z 22
Tours (R. de) .... Y
Verdun (Pl. de) .... Y
Victor-Hugo (R.) .... Y
Vigny (R. A.-de) .... Y
Wermelskirchen (Pl. de) .... Y 29

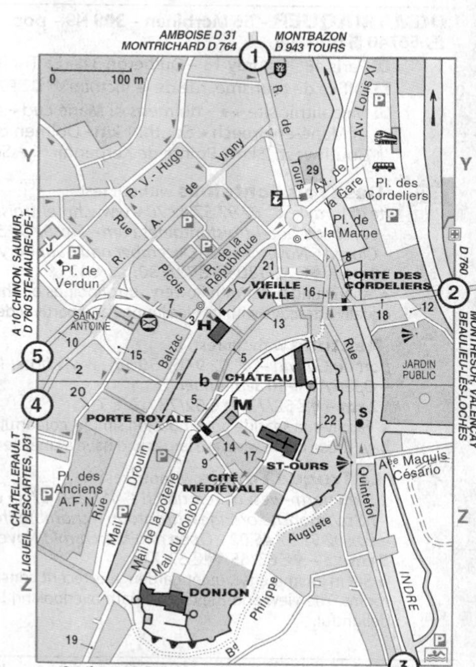

Le George Sand

39 r. Quintefol – ✆ 02 47 59 39 74 – www.hotelrestaurant-georgesand.com – contactgs@hotelrestaurant-georgesand.com – Fax 02 47 91 55 75 – Closed for the autumn school holidays and February school holidays Z **s**

19 rm – †€ 45/125 ††€ 45/125, ☕ € 11 – ½ P € 55/94

Rest – *(closed Sunday dinner, Monday lunch and Tuesday)*

Menu € 21 (weekdays)/47

◆ A 15C house on the banks of the Indre with the feel of a family inn. Rustic bedrooms, half of which overlook the river. Impressive stone spiral staircase. Pleasant restaurant with exposed beams and a fireplace, plus a delightful covered terrace with bucolic views.

Luccotel
12 r. Lézards, 1 km by ⑤ – ✆ 02 47 91 30 30 – www.luccotel.com – luccotel@wanadoo.fr – Fax 02 47 91 30 35 – Closed 11 December-12 January
69 rm – †€ 48/76 ††€ 48/76, ☕ € 8
Rest – *(closed Saturday lunch)* Menu (€ 19), € 28/40
◆ This new hotel, flanked by two annexes, overlooks the medieval town and château, which are visible from some of the rather functional rooms. The modern dining room and terrace offer a pleasant view of the town.

L'Entracte
4 r. du Château – ✆ 02 47 94 05 70 – Fax 02 47 91 55 75 – Closed Sunday dinner and Wednesday from 15 October to 15 April Y **b**
Rest – Menu € 10 (weekday lunch)/24 – Carte € 25/40
◆ This restaurant situated in a picturesque little street near the castle offers a Lyon-style atmosphere; appetising dishes chalked up on large boards.

LOCMARIAQUER – 56 Morbihan – 308 N9 – pop. 1 632 – alt. 5 m – ✉ 56740 Brittany 9 **A3**

Paris 488 – Auray 13 – Quiberon 31 – La Trinité-sur-Mer 10 – Vannes 31
Office de tourisme, rue de la Victoire ✆ 02 97 57 33 05, Fax 02 97 57 44 30
Megalithic site ★★ - dolmens of Mané Lud★ and Mané Rethual★ - Tumulus of Mané-er-Hroech★ South: 1 km - Dolmen of the Pierres Plates★ Southwest: 2 km - Pointe de Kerpenhir ≤★ Southeast: 2 km.

Des Trois Fontaines without rest
rte d'Auray – ✆ 02 97 57 42 70 – www.hotel-troisfontaines.com – contact@hotel-troisfontaines.com – Fax 02 97 57 30 59 – Closed 6 November-26 December and 6 January-7 February
18 rm – †€ 72/130 ††€ 72/130, ☕ € 12
◆ An inviting hotel with flowery surroundings on the edge of the village. The interior is equally attractive with its nice lounge and partly redecorated rooms with antiques.

Neptune without rest
port du Guilvin – ✆ 02 97 57 30 56 – www.hotel-le-neptune.fr – Open April-30 September
12 rm – †€ 52/73 ††€ 52/73, ☕ € 7
◆ Family-run seaside hotel housing simple, colourful rooms, some of which overlook the bay. Those in the wing are larger and have a small terrace.

La Troque Toupie without rest
2.5 km north-west of Kerouarch – ✆ 02 97 57 45 02 – http://monsite.orange.fr/troqtoup – chambredhotetroque@orange.fr – Fax 02 97 57 45 02 – Open mid March-mid November
5 rm ☕ – †€ 63/65 ††€ 67/71
◆ Set in an immense, quiet garden, this recent construction offers comfortable, elegant rooms. The view and the coastal path overlooking the islands of the Morbihan gulf are delightful.

LOCMINÉ – 56 Morbihan – 308 N7 – pop. 3 430 – alt. 108 m – ✉ 56500 Brittany 10 **C2**

Paris 453 – Lorient 52 – Pontivy 24 – Quimper 114 – Rennes 104 – Vannes 29
Syndicat d'initiative, place Anne de Bretagne ✆ 02 97 60 00 37, Fax 02 97 44 24 64

in Bignan East: 5 km by D 1 – pop. 2 531 – alt. 148 m – ✉ 56500

Auberge La Chouannière
6 r. G. Cadoual – ✆ 02 97 60 00 96 – Fax 02 97 44 24 58 – Closed 2-18 March, 30 June-8 July, 5-20 October, Sunday dinner, Tuesday dinner, Wednesday dinner and Monday
Rest – Menu € 23 (weekdays)/80 – Carte € 36/50
◆ The inn sign refers to Pierre Guillemot, Cadoudal's fierce lieutenant, born in this village. A discreet decor, Louis XVI-style chairs and classic cuisine.

LOCQUIREC – 29 Finistère – 308 J2 – pop. 1 293 – alt. 15 m – ✉ 29241 9 B1
Brittany

Paris 534 – Brest 81 – Guingamp 52 – Lannion 22 – Morlaix 26
Office de tourisme, place du Port ☎ 02 98 67 40 83, Fax 02 98 79 32 50
Church★ - Pointe de Locquirec★ 30 mn - Viewpoint indicator of Marc'h Sammet ≤★ West: 3 km.

Le Grand Hôtel des Bains
rest.
15 bis r. de l'Église – ☎ 02 98 67 41 02 – www.grand-hotel-des-bains.com – reception@grand-hotel-des-bains.com – Fax 02 98 67 44 60
36 rm – €137/269 €154/333, €12 – ½ P €172/189
Rest – *(dinner only)* Menu €38 – Carte €59/78
◆ The famous French film, "Hôtel de la Plage" was made here. Salt-water swimming pool, waterside flower garden, massage room and contemporary "seaside" style guestrooms. Smart restaurant with pastel panelling and seafood cuisine.

LOCRONAN – 29 Finistère – 308 F6 – pop. 799 – alt. 105 m – ✉ 29180 9 A2
Brittany

Paris 576 – Brest 66 – Briec 22 – Châteaulin 18 – Crozon 33 – Douarnenez 11 – Quimper 16
Office de tourisme, place de la Mairie ☎ 02 98 91 70 14, Fax 02 98 51 83 64
Square★★ - St-Ronan church and Le Pénity chapel ★★ - Montagne de Locronan ✻★ East: 2 km.

Le Prieuré
rm,
11 r. Prieuré – ☎ 02 98 91 70 89 – www.hotel-le-prieure.com – leprieure1@aol.com – Fax 02 98 91 77 60 – Hotel: Open 16 March-10 November, Restaurant: closed 11-30 November and February school holidays
15 rm – €52/58 €60/72, €9 – ½ P €58/63
Rest – Menu (€14), €19/48 – Carte €28/60
◆ A small family run hotel on the edge of a famous and picturesque Breton village. The rooms overlooking the garden are quieter as are those in the older wing. Traditional cuisine in a welcoming dining room embellished with exposed beams, stonework, a fireplace and furniture from the local area.

Northwest : 3 km by secondary road – ✉ 29550 Plonévez-Porzay

Manoir de Moëllien
rm,
– ☎ 02 98 92 50 40 – www.moellien.com – manmoel@aol.com – Fax 02 98 92 55 21 – Closed 12 November-20 March
18 rm – €60/72 €72/145, €12 – ½ P €60/107
Rest – *(closed Wednesday mid September-mid June) (dinner only)* Menu €28/47
◆ A fine 17C manor with extensive parkland in open country. The rooms, in separate buildings, are very quiet. Impressive fireplaces in the restaurant.

LOCTUDY – 29 Finistère – 308 F8 – pop. 4 101 – alt. 8 m – ✉ 29750 9 A2
Brittany

Paris 587 – Rennes 236 – Quimper 26 – Concarneau 40 – Douarnenez 40
Office de tourisme, place des Anciens Combattants ☎ 02 98 87 53 78, Fax 02 98 87 57 07

Auberge Pen Ar Vir
r. Cdt. Carfort – ☎ 02 98 87 57 09 – auberge.pen.arvir@wanadoo.fr – Fax 02 98 87 57 62 – Closed autumn school holidays, 5-25 January, Tuesday and Wednesday from mid-September to mid-April, Sunday dinner and Monday
Rest – Menu (€22), €29/70
◆ A recent villa set in a pretty garden (where drinks are served) by the seaside; fashionable modern interior; short menu with a strong focus on market produce and local fish.

LODÈVE – 34 Hérault – 339 E6 – pop. 7 400 – alt. 165 m – ✉ 34700 23 C2
Languedoc-Roussillon-Tarn Gorges

Paris 695 – Alès 98 – Béziers 63 – Millau 60 – Montpellier 55 – Pézenas 39
Office de tourisme, 7, place de la République ☎ 04 67 88 86 44, Fax 04 67 44 07 56
Former St-Fulcran cathedral ★ - Musée de Lodève ★ - Cirque du Bout du Monde ★.

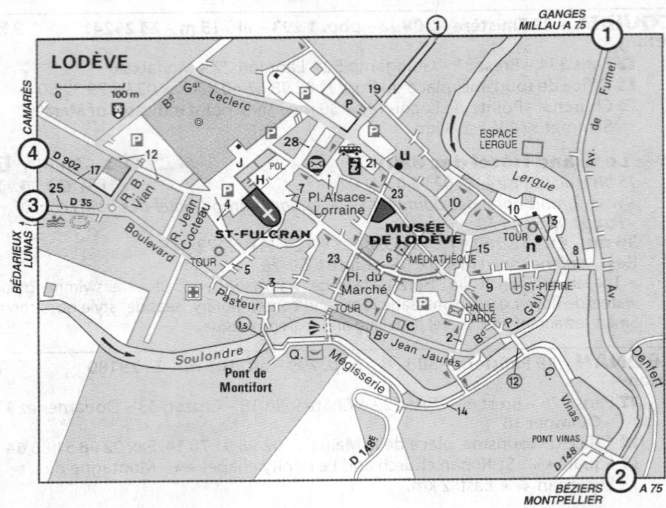

Paix

11 bd Montalangue – ☎ 04 67 44 07 46 – www.hotel-dela-paix.com – hotel-de-la-paix@wanadoo.fr – Fax 04 67 44 30 47 – Closed 15-30 November, February, Sunday evening and Monday from October to April except school holidays n

23 rm – †€ 40/50 ††€ 55/75, ☕ € 8 – 1 suite

Rest – Menu € 18/37 – Carte € 10/18

◆ On the edge of the Grands Causses, a former old post house converted into a family-run hotel. Guestrooms renovated in a clearly Provencal style: colourful and bright. Charming patio-terrace reminiscent of Andalusia: ochre walls, mosaics, tiled floor, palm trees and pool. Fine wines.

Du Nord without rest

18 bd Liberté – ☎ 04 67 44 10 08 – www.hotellodeve.com – hoteldunord.lodeve@wanadoo.fr – Fax 04 67 44 92 78 – Closed autumn school holidays and Christmas holidays u

24 rm – †€ 41/47 ††€ 46/53, ☕ € 7 – 1 suite

◆ The composer Georges Auric was born in this town centre hotel in 1899. It has been fully renovated with simple and functional rooms. Pleasant terrace.

Domaine du Canalet without rest

av. Joseph Vallot, via ③ – ☎ 04 67 44 29 33 – www.domaineducanalet.com – domaineducanalet@wanadoo.fr

4 rm – †€ 195/350 ††€ 195/350, ☕ € 18

◆ More than just a guesthouse, it is also an art gallery... works (for sale) are found throughout the premises. Personalised designer rooms. Park featuring sequoias and a stream.

in Poujols North: 6.5 km by D 609 and D 149 – pop. 152 – alt. 250 m – ✉ 34700

Le Temps de Vivre

rte de Pegairolles – ☎ 04 67 44 03 78 – Fax 04 67 44 03 78 – Closed December, January, Wednesday off season, Sunday dinner and Monday

Rest – Menu (€ 19), € 29/48 – Carte € 42/68

◆ Clinging to a hillside overlooking the Escalette valley, this restaurant has two dining rooms, one a veranda opening onto the countryside. Personalised dishes and regional wines.

LODS – 25 Doubs – 321 H4 – pop. 248 – alt. 361 m – ✉ 25930 17 C2
Burgundy-Jura

Paris 440 – Baume-les-Dames 50 – Besançon 37 – Levier 22 – Pontarlier 25 – Vuillafans 5

Truite d'Or
40 rte de Besançon – ☎ 03 81 60 95 48 – www.la-truite-dor.fr – la-truite-dor@wanadoo.fr – Fax 03 81 60 95 73 – Closed 15 December-1st February, Sunday dinner and Monday from October to June
11 rm – €48 €48, ☕ €6,50 – ½ P €52
Rest – Menu (€13), €19/44 – Carte €28/45
◆ On the edge of this picturesque village on the banks of the Loue. Once a stonemason's house, it will delight fishermen. Modest rooms. Trout takes pride of place in this regional repertoire.

LOGELHEIM – 68 Haut-Rhin – 315 I8 – see Colmar

LOGONNA-DAOULAS – 29 Finistère – 308 F5 – pop. 2 025 – alt. 45 m – ✉ 29460 9 A2

Paris 579 – Rennes 227 – Quimper 59 – Brest 26 – Morlaix 75

Le Domaine de Moulin Mer
34 rte de Moulin Mer, 1 km on D 333 – ☎ 02 98 07 24 45 – www.domaine-moulin-mer.com – info@domaine-moulin-mer.com
5 rm ☕ – €65/130 €65/130 **Table d'hôte** – Menu €40 bi
◆ On the coast road, set within a garden strewn with palm trees, this old residence dating from the beginning of the 20C hides a beautifully renovated interior. There are charming rooms reminiscent of yesteryear and a lounge/library. Menu of the day prepared by the owner, based on his inspiration and on market availability.

LOIRÉ – 49 Maine-et-Loire – 317 D3 – pop. 772 – alt. 39 m – ✉ 49440 34 B2

Paris 322 – Ancenis 35 – Angers 45 – Châteaubriant 34 – Laval 66 – Nantes 69 – Rennes 84

Auberge de la Diligence (Michel Cudraz)
4 r. de la Libération – ☎ 02 41 94 10 04 – www.diligence.fr – info@diligence.fr – Fax 02 41 94 10 04 – Closed 4-11 April, 31 July-24 August, 1st-10 January, Saturday lunch, Sunday dinner and Monday
Rest – *(number of covers limited, pre-book)* Menu €29/80 – Carte €40/66
Spec. Fricassée de langoustines. Poularde en papillote transparente et carottes au cumin. Déclinaison sur la pomme "honey crunch" de Loiré et sablé breton. **Wines** Savennières, Anjou-Villages.
◆ This 18C restaurant features a rustic dining area with a large fireplace, and serves generous personalised cuisine accompanied by an excellent selection of regional wines.

LOMENER – 56 Morbihan – 308 K8 – see Ploemeur

LA LONDE-LES-MAURES – 83 Var – 340 M7 – pop. 10 034 – alt. 24 m – ✉ 83250 41 C3

Paris 868 – Marseille 93 – Toulon 29 – La Seyne-sur-Mer 35 – Hyères 10
Office de tourisme, avenue Albert Roux ☎ 04 94 01 53 10, Fax 04 94 01 53 19

Cédric Gola
22 av. Georges-Clemenceau – ☎ 04 94 66 97 93 – Closed for one week in June, 15 November-26 December, lunch except Sunday from September to June, Monday and Tuesday
Rest – *(number of covers limited, pre-book)* Menu €35/47
◆ Modern, Provencal inspired cuisine served in a warm, bistro-style dining room. The attractive menu changes every month; 'truffle menu' also available.

LONDINIÈRES – 76 Seine-Maritime – **304** I3 – **pop.** 1 188 – **alt.** 78 m – ✉ 76660 33 **D1**

Paris 147 – Amiens 78 – Dieppe 27 – Neufchâtel-en-Bray 14 – Le Tréport 31

Syndicat d'initiative, Mairie ✆ 02 35 94 90 69, Fax 02 35 94 90 69

Auberge du Pont with rm

14 r. du Pont de Pierre – ✆ 02 35 93 80 47 – Fax 02 32 97 00 57 – Closed 1st-15 February and Monday

10 rm – €40 €40, ☕ €5

Rest – Menu (€7), €10 (weekdays)/32 – Carte €22/42

◆ This small Normandy inn is located on the banks of the Eaulne. It serves regional cuisine in a small, rustic dining room. Refurbished, practical and colourful rooms, ideal for an overnight stay.

LA LONGEVILLE – 25 Doubs – **321** I4 – **see Montbenoît**

LONGJUMEAU – 91 Essonne – **312** C3 – **101** 35 – **see Paris, Area**

LONGUES – 63 Puy-de-Dôme – **326** G9 – **see Vic-le-Comte**

LONGUEVILLE-SUR-SCIE – 76 Seine-Maritime – **304** G3 – **pop.** 923 – **alt.** 61 m – ✉ 76590 33 **D1**

Paris 183 – Dieppe 20 – Le Havre 97 – Rouen 52

Le Cheval Blanc

3 r. Guynemer – ✆ 02 35 83 30 03 – Fax 02 35 83 30 03 – Closed 10-31 August, 23 February-4 March, Sunday dinner, Monday dinner and Wednesday

Rest – Menu (€14), €24 (weekday lunch)/50 – Carte approx. €60

◆ Pleasant guesthouse in the village centre. Traditional cuisine served under the beams of a rustic dining room with fresh and bright colours.

LONGUYON – 54 Meurthe-et-Moselle – **307** E2 – **pop.** 5 782 – **alt.** 213 m – ✉ 54260 26 **B1**

Paris 314 – Metz 79 – Nancy 133 – Sedan 69 – Thionville 56 – Verdun 48

Office de tourisme, place S. Allende ✆ 03 82 39 21 21, Fax 03 82 26 44 37

in Rouvrois-sur-Othain (Meuse) South: 7.5 km by D 618 – pop. 182 – alt. 223 m – ✉ 55230

La Marmite

11 rte Nationale – ✆ 03 29 85 90 79 – gerardsilvestre55@orange.fr – Fax 03 29 85 99 23 – Closed 16-30 August, 1st-10 February, Sunday dinner, Monday and Tuesday except public holidays

Rest – Menu €15 (weekday lunch), €26/55 – Carte €40/60

◆ Authentic flavoursome recipes made with excellent local produce are the hallmark of this establishment. Inviting rustic dining room with fireplace. Affable welcome and service.

LONGWY – 54 Meurthe-et-Moselle – **307** F1 – **pop.** 14 300 – **alt.** 262 m – ✉ 54400 Alsace-Lorraine 26 **B1**

Paris 328 – Luxembourg 38 – Metz 64 – Thionville 41

Office de tourisme, place Darche ✆ 03 82 24 94 54, Fax 03 82 24 77 75

Musée municipal: collection of irons★.

in Méxy 3 km south on the N 52 – pop. 2 154 – alt. 369 m – ✉ 54135

Ibis

r. Château d'Eau – ✆ 03 82 23 14 19 – www.accorhotels.com – h2051@accor.com – Fax 03 82 25 61 06

62 rm – €57/75 €57/75, ☕ €8

Rest – Menu (€10 bi), €15 (weekdays)/25 – Carte €18/32

◆ Hotel near a busy thoroughfare. Spacious interior, excellent fixtures and fittings and contemporary furnishings. Modern rooms. Gourmet dishes and a buffet, in a classic dining area or on the terrace.

LONS-LE-SAUNIER P – **39 Jura** – **321** D6 – **pop. 17 900** – **alt. 255 m** 16 **B3**
– **Spa : early April-late Oct.** – **Casino** – ✉ **39000** Burgundy-Jura

Paris 408 – Besançon 84 – Bourg-en-Bresse 73 – Chalon-sur-Saône 61

Office de tourisme, place du 11 Novembre ☎ 03 84 24 65 01, Fax 03 84 43 22 59

du Val de Sorne Vernantois, S : 6 km on D 117 and D 41, ☎ 03 84 43 04 80

Rue du Commerce★ - Theatre★ - Pharmacie★ de l'Hôtel-Dieu (chemist's).

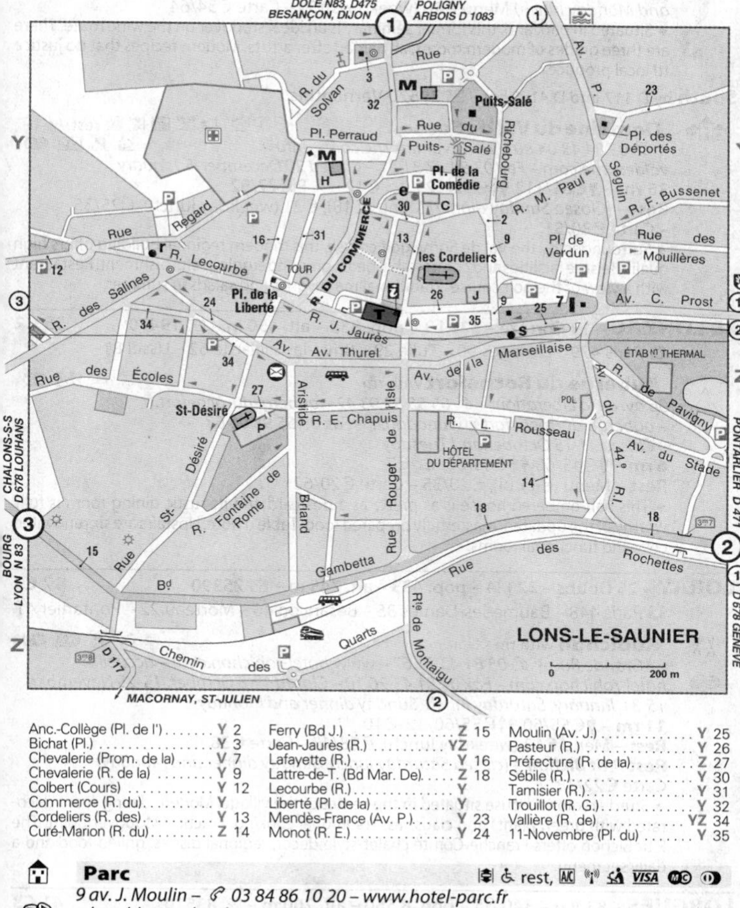

Anc.-Collège (Pl. de l') . . . . Y 2
Bichat (Pl.) . . . . Y 3
Chevalerie (Prom. de la) . . . . . Y 7
Chevalerie (R. de la) . . . . Y 9
Colbert (Cours) . . . . Y 12
Commerce (R. du) . . . . Y
Cordeliers (R. des) . . . . Y 13
Curé-Marion (R. du) . . . . Z 14
Ferry (Bd J.) . . . . Z 15
Jean-Jaurès (R.) . . . . YZ
Lafayette (R.) . . . . Y 16
Lattre-de-T. (Bd Mar. De) . . . . Z 18
Lecourbe (R.) . . . . Y
Liberté (Pl. de la) . . . . Y
Mendès-France (Av. P.) . . . . . . Y 23
Monot (R. E.) . . . . Y 24
Moulin (Av. J.) . . . . Y 25
Pasteur (R.) . . . . Y 26
Préfecture (R. de la) . . . . Z 27
Sébile (R.) . . . . Y 30
Tamisier (R.) . . . . Y 31
Trouillot (R. G.) . . . . Y 32
Vallière (R. de) . . . . YZ 34
11-Novembre (Pl. du) . . . . Y 35

Parc — rest, VISA

9 av. J. Moulin – ☎ 03 84 86 10 20 – www.hotel-parc.fr
– hotelduparc.lonslesaunier@orange.fr – Fax 03 84 24 97 28 Y **s**

16 rm – €52/60 €58/64, €8 – ½ P €67

Rest – *(closed Sunday dinner)* Menu (€15), €18/28 – Carte €18/40

◆ Two minutes from the thermal baths, this hotel (a centre for reinsertion) offers simple, functional rooms adorned with stained wooden furniture. Plain dining room and simple cuisine using regional produce.

Nouvel Hôtel without rest — P VISA AE

50 r. Lecourbe – ☎ 03 84 47 20 67 – www.nouvel-hotel-lons.fr – nouvel.hotel39@wanadoo.fr – Fax 03 84 43 27 49 – Closed 19 December-4 January Y **r**

25 rm – €40/57 €45/57, €8

◆ The owner's model ships adorn the lobby of this central hotel. The practical guestrooms are well kept; warm welcome and moderate prices.

in Chille by ① Besançon roadand D 157: 3 km – **pop. 331** – **alt. 330 m** – ✉ **39570**

Parenthèse rm, VISA

186 chemin du Pin – ☎ 03 84 47 55 44 – www.hotelparenthese.com – parenthese.hotel@wanadoo.fr – Fax 03 84 24 92 13 – Closed 20-30 December
34 rm – €93/145 €93/145, €11 – ½ P €84/111
Rest – *(closed Sunday dinner except July-August, Saturday lunch and Monday lunch)* Menu €20 (weekdays)/54 – Carte €34/64
◆ Situated in parkland, this former seminary is an ideal stopover on the wine route. There are three grades of modern rooms, all named after artists. Modern recipes that do justice to local produce.

South by D 117 and D 41: 6 km – ✉ **39570 Vernantois**

Domaine du Val de Sorne rest, VISA

– ☎ 03 84 43 04 80 – www.valdesorne.com – info@valdesorne.com – Fax 03 84 47 31 21 – Closed 20 December-5 January
35 rm – €81/112 €92/125, €12 – ½ P €77/92
Rest – *(Closed Sunday dinner)* Menu (€18), €21 (weekday lunch), €25/35 – Carte €30/51
◆ Surrounded by the Val de Sorne golf course, this modern regional building offers high quality leisure facilities and comfortable bedrooms undergoing refurbishment. Restaurant with a view of the golf course. Traditional menu; grills and salads in summer.

LE LONZAC – 19 Corrèze – 329 L3 – pop. 835 – alt. 450 m – ✉ 19470 25 C2

Paris 479 – Limoges 90 – Tulle 29 – Brive-la-Gaillarde 62 – Ussel 81

Auberge du Rochefort with rm VISA

36 av. de la Libération – ☎ 05 55 97 93 42 – aubergedurochefort.fr – auberge-du-rochefort@wanadoo.fr – Fax 05 55 98 06 63 – Closed 1st-15 October and Tuesday
6 rm – €45/60 €45/60, €7
Rest – Menu (€11 bi), €20/35 – Carte €20/62
◆ This half-timbered house is as pretty as a postcard and its rustic dining room is fully worthy of the updated, masterfully prepared food. Table d'hôte. Upstairs are six renovated cosy and functional rooms.

LORAY – 25 Doubs – 321 I4 – pop. 433 – alt. 745 m – ✉ 25390 17 C2

Paris 448 – Baume-les-Dames 35 – Besançon 46 – Morteau 22 – Pontarlier 41

Robichon with rm VISA

22 Grande Rue – ☎ 03 81 43 21 67 – www.hotel-robichon.com – accueil@hotel-robichon.com – Fax 03 81 43 26 10 – Closed 1st-8 October, 15-25 November, 15-31 January, Saturday lunch, Sunday dinner and Monday
11 rm – €55/60 €55/60, €10
Rest – Menu €13 (weekday lunch), €28/46 – Carte €38/65
Rest *P'tit Bichon* – *(closed Saturday lunch, Sunday dinner and Monday)* Carte €22/38
◆ Sturdy regional house situated in the centre of the village. Modern dining room decorated with green plants and claustras. Traditional cooking. Practical stopover point. The P'tit Bichon offers Franche-Comté chalet-style decor, regional dishes, grilled food and a daily set menu.

LORGUES – 83 Var – 340 N5 – pop. 8 550 – alt. 200 m – ✉ 83510 41 C3

French Riviera

Paris 841 – Brignoles 34 – Draguignan 12 – Fréjus 37 – St-Raphaël 41 – Toulon 72

Office de tourisme, place Trussy ☎ 04 94 73 92 37, Fax 04 94 84 34 09

La Bastide du Pin without rest VISA

1017 rte de Salernes, 1 km via D 10 – ☎ 04 94 73 90 38 – www.bastidedupin.com – bastidedupin@wanadoo.fr – Fax 04 94 73 63 01
5 rm – €80/85 €85/120
◆ A former 18C olive and wine producing estate, now a hotel providing Provençal-style guestrooms. Pool. Breakfasts served outdoors in summertime. Mediterranean inspired dishes.

XXX **Bruno** (Bruno Clément) with rm rm, VISA AE
2350 rte des Arcs, Campagne Mariette, 3 km South East via rte des Arcs – 04 94 85 93 93 – www.restaurantbruno.com – chezbruno@wanadoo.fr – Fax 04 94 85 93 99 – Closed Sunday dinner and Monday from 15 September to 15 June
6 rm – €100/306 €100/306, €35 **Rest** – (pre-book) Menu €65/130
Spec. Pomme de terre cuite en robe des champs, crème de truffe. Epaule d'agneau de lait des Pyrénées confite au four. Moelleux au chocolat et son cœur caramel truffé. **Wines** Côtes de Provence
◆ A colourful chef with a passion for truffles runs this farmhouse restaurant surrounded by vineyards. Rustic Provençal decor, serving a set menu with truffles in winter and summer. Pretty guestrooms at garden level.

XX **Le Chrissandier** VISA AE
18 cours de la République – 04 94 67 67 15 – www.lechrissandier.com – christophe.chabredier@wanadoo.fr – Fax 04 94 67 67 15 – Closed 29 June-5 July, January, Tuesday and Wednesday from October to June
Rest – Menu €29 (weekday lunch), €40/60 – Carte €60/110
◆ Traditional cuisine in tune with the seasons served in an elegant, rustic dining room with modern settings. Attractive summer terrace in a small inner courtyard.

Northwest by Salernes road, D 10 and secondary road: 8 km – 83510

Château de Berne rm, VISA AE
– 04 94 60 48 88 – www.chateauberne.com – hotel@chateauberne.com – Fax 04 94 60 48 89 – Closed January and February
18 rm – €200/580 €200/580, €20 – 1 suite
Rest – Menu (€20), €27 (lunch), €39/60 – Carte €70/85
◆ In the centre of a wine-growing estate, charming Provencal-style guestrooms, exhibitions, concerts, fitness centre, wine and cookery classes. Simple fare at lunchtime (grilled meats). More elaborate meals in the evening (market and organic produce) in a refined setting.

The red symbol?
This denotes the very essence of peace –
only the sound of birdsong first thing in the morning...

LORIENT – 56 Morbihan – 308 K8 – pop. 58 400 – Built-up area 116 174 – alt. 4 m – 56100 Brittany 9 **B2**

Paris 503 – Quimper 69 – St-Brieuc 116 – St-Nazaire 146 – Vannes 60
Lorient-Bretagne Sud: 02 97 87 21 50, 9 km on the D 162 AZ.
Office de tourisme, quai de Rohan 02 97 21 07 84, Fax 02 97 21 99 44
18 de Valqueven Quéven Lieu dit Kerruisseau, N : 8 km on D 765, 02 97 05 17 96
Submarine base★ AZ - Interior★ of N.-D.-de-Victoire church BY **E.**

Plan on following page

Mercure without rest VISA AE
31 pl. J. Ferry – 02 97 21 35 73 – www.accorhotels.com – h0873@accor.com – Fax 02 97 64 48 62 BZ **m**
58 rm – €69/116 €69/116, €13
◆ Shops, a conference centre and harbour moorings are conveniently located nearby. The lounge-bar and room decor discreetly recall the East India Company.

Cléria without rest VISA AE
27 bd Mar. Franchet d'Esperey – 02 97 21 04 59 – www.hotel-cleria.com – info@hotel-cleria.com – Fax 02 97 64 19 10 AY **f**
33 rm – €49/69 €59/79, €9
◆ The rooms of this central hotel are gradually being spruced up; those overlooking the flower-decked courtyard (where breakfast is served in summer) are quieter.

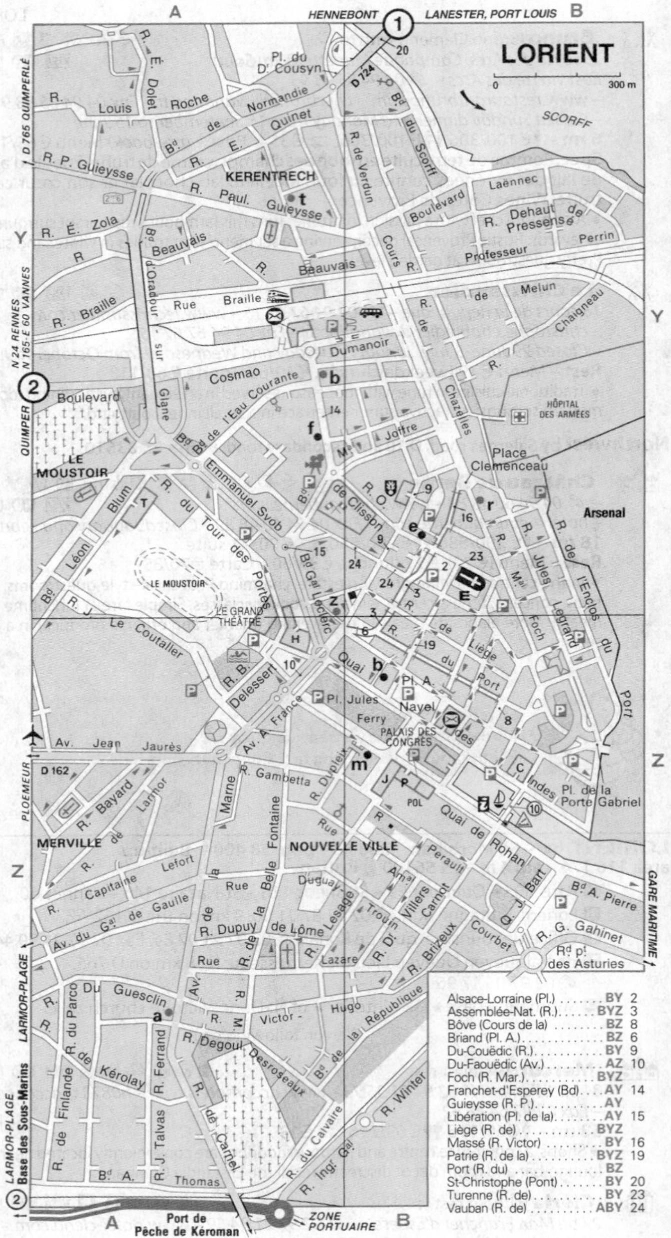
LORIENT
0
300 m
HENNEBONT
LANESTER, PORT LOUIS
SCORFF
A
B
Y
Z
1
2
D 765 QUIMPERLÉ
N 24 RENNES
N 165-E 60 VANNES
QUIMPER
PLOEMEUR
D 162
LARMOR-PLAGE
LARMOR-PLAGE
Base des Sous-Marins
GARE MARITIME
Port de
Pêche de Kéroman
ZONE
PORTUAIRE
KERENTRECH
LE MOUSTOIR
MERVILLE
NOUVELLE VILLE
Arsenal
HÔPITAL
DES ARMÉES
Place
Clemenceau
PALAIS DES
CONGRÈS
LE GRAND
THÉÂTRE
Pl. du
Dr Cousyn
Pl. Jules
Ferry
Pl. A.
Nayel
Pl. de la
Porte Gabriel
Rd pt
des Asturies
D 724
R. É. Dolet
R. Louis Roche
Bd de Normandie
R. E. Quinet
R. P. Guieysse
R. Paul Guieysse
R. de Verdun
Bd du Scorff
Laënnec
Boulevard
R. Dehaut de Pressensé
Perrin
Professeur
Cours
R. É. Zola
Bd d'Oradour-sur-Glane
R. Beauvais
Rue Braille
R. Braille
R. de Melun
R. de Chazelles
Chaigneau
Dumanoir
Cosmao
Bd de l'Eau Courante
Boulevard
Bd Emmanuel Svob
Mal Joffre
Bd Franchet
R. de Clisson
R. du Tour des Portes
Bd Léon Blum
R. J. Le Coutaller
Bd Gal Leclerc
R. de Liège
R. du Port
R. Mal Foch
R. Jules Legrand
R. de l'Enclos du Port
Quai des Indes
R. B. Delessert
Av. A. France
Av. Jean Jaurès
R. Bayard
R. de Lamor
R. Gambetta
R. Marne
Fontaine
R. Dupleix
Rue
R. Capitaine Lefort
Rue de la Belle
R. Amal Perault
Quai de Rohan
J. Bart
Bd A. Pierre
R. G. Gahinet
Av. du Gal de Gaulle
R. Dupuy de Lôme
R. Duguay-Trouin
R. Lesage
Villers
Carnot
Courbet
R. Brizeux
Rue Lazare
R. Du Guesclin
R. du Parco
R. de Kérolay
R. Ferrand
R. J. Talvas
R. de Finlande
Bd A. Thomas
R. Victor-Hugo
R. M.
R. Degoul
Desroseaux
Bd de la République
R. de Carnel
R. du Calvaire
R. Ingr Gal
R. Winter
POL
Alsace-Lorraine (Pl.) . . . . BY 2
Assemblée-Nat. (R.) . . . . . . BYZ 3
Bôve (Cours de la) . . . . BZ 8
Briand (Pl. A.) . . . . BZ 6
Du-Couëdic (R.) . . . . BY 9
Du-Faouëdic (Av.) . . . . AZ 10
Foch (R. Mar.) . . . . BYZ
Franchet-d'Esperey (Bd) . . . . AY 14
Guieysse (R. P.) . . . . AY
Libération (Pl. de la) . . . . . . AY 15
Liège (R. de) . . . . BYZ
Massé (R. Victor) . . . . BY 16
Patrie (R. de la) . . . . BYZ 19
Port (R. du) . . . . BZ
St-Christophe (Pont) . . . . BY 20
Turenne (R. de) . . . . BY 23
Vauban (R. de) . . . . ABY 24

Astoria without rest
3 r. Clisson – ✆ 02 97 21 10 23 – www.hotelastoria-lorient.com
– hotelastoria.lorient@wanadoo.fr – Fax 02 97 21 03 55
– Closed 23 December-7 January BY **e**
35 rm – †€ 60/75 ††€ 60/75, ☕ € 8,50
◆ A pleasant establishment for many reasons: warm, family welcome, simple but individually decorated rooms and art exhibitions in the breakfast room.

Central Hôtel without rest
1 r. Cambry – ✆ 02 97 21 16 52 – www.centralhotellorient.com
– centralhotel.lorient@orange.fr – Fax 02 97 84 88 94
– Closed Christmas holidays BZ **b**
21 rm – †€ 45/85 ††€ 50/85, ☕ € 8
◆ Town-centre hotel, as the name suggests, whose rooms have been successfully renovated with new materials, cheerful colours and good soundproofing.

Le Jardin Gourmand
46 r. J. Simon – ✆ 02 97 64 17 24 – www.jardin-gourmand.fr
– jardingourmandlorient@yahoo.fr – Fax 02 97 64 15 75
– Closed for the February school holidays, Sunday dinner,
Monday and Tuesday AY **t**
Rest – Menu (€ 22), € 28 (weekday lunch)/40
◆ The owner-chef gives Breton produce pride of place in her inventive recipes, escorted by a fine choice of wines, whiskies and brandies. Attractive, modern interior.

Le Quai des Arômes
1 r. Maître Esvelin – ✆ 02 97 21 60 40 – Fax 02 97 35 29 04
– Closed 5-12 April, 14-31 August, Saturday lunch and Sunday BZ **a**
Rest – Menu (€ 13), € 17/23 – Carte € 28/35
◆ A new and contemporary feel for this traditional restaurant, opposite the Palais de Justice. Grey/white colour scheme, old photos, paintings and modern furniture. Covered terrace.

Henri et Joseph (Philippe Le Lay)
4 r. Léo Le Bourgo – ✆ 02 97 84 72 12 – Closed Tuesday dinner, Wednesday dinner, Thursday dinner, Sunday and Monday except July-August AY **z**
Rest – *(pre-book)* Menu (€ 31), € 48
Spec. Consommé de crevettes et crostini de Saint-Jacques (October-November) Homard de l'Île de Groix en cocotte (June to September). Millefeuille aux fraises (June-July).
◆ An original concept for this trendy bistro with a choice of a 'masculine' or 'feminine' dish of the day, as detailed by the chef. Set menu in the evening. Charming welcome.

Le Pécharmant
5 r. Carnel – ✆ 02 97 21 33 86 – Fax 02 97 35 11 01
– Closed 13-20 April, 5-20 July, 26 October-2 November, Sunday,
Monday and public holidays AZ **a**
Rest – Menu € 17 (weekdays)/69 – Carte € 50/70
◆ The orange façade decorated with copper pans does not go unnoticed. Yet it is the generous, subtle cuisine served in this small restaurant that makes it so popular.

Le Pic
2 bd Mar. Franchet d'Esperey – ✆ 02 97 21 18 29 – restaurant-lepic.com
– restaurant.lepic@orange.fr – Fax 02 97 21 92 64 – Closed Wednesday dinner,
Saturday lunch and Sunday except public holidays AY **b**
Rest – Menu (€ 15), € 19 (weekdays)/38 – Carte € 31/45
◆ Bright red façade, smart 1940s decor (stained glass, mirrors and bar), bistro ambience, traditional menu and fresh fish daily: what more could you want!

L'Ocre Marine
8 r. Mar.-Foch – ✆ 02 97 84 05 77 – locremarine@orange.fr
– Closed 12-27 September, 1st-18 January, Saturday lunch, Wednesday dinner
and Sunday BY **r**
Rest – pancake rest. – Menu (€ 12), € 16 (weekday dinner) – Carte approx. € 21
◆ Family photos adorn this all wood, hospitable restaurant. The lady of the house's sweet and savoury pancakes are not to be missed: organic, home-grown produce only.

Northwest : 3,5 km by D 765 AY – ✉ 56100 Lorient

XXX **L'Amphitryon** (Jean-Paul Abadie)
127 r. Col. Müller – ✆ 02 97 83 34 04 – www.amphitryon-abadie.com – amphi-abadie@orange.fr – Fax 02 97 37 25 02 – Closed 26 April-11 May, 6-21 September, 1st-11 January, Sunday and Monday
Rest – Menu € 56 (weekdays)/118 – Carte € 114/165
Spec. Gratin d'étrilles au kari-gosse. Homard saisi au beurre, épices et pointe de réglisse (April to October). Fines feuilles de grué de cacao, parfait glacé au caramel et anis vert.
◆ A masterful, almost playfully inventive cuisine; superb choice of little known wines; service that is as professional as it is friendly; and a handsome modern decor.

LORRIS – 45 Loiret – 318 M4 – pop. 2 777 – alt. 126 m – ✉ 45260 — 12 C2

Châteaux of the Loire

- Paris 132 – Gien 27 – Montargis 23 – Orléans 55 – Pithiviers 45 – Sully-sur-Loire 19
- Office de tourisme, 2, rue des Halles ✆ 02 38 94 81 42, Fax 02 38 94 88 00
- N.-Dame church ★.

XX **Guillaume de Lorris**
8 Grande Rue – ✆ 02 38 94 83 55 – vanoandco@orange.fr – Fax 02 38 94 83 55 – Closed 7-20 April, 21 December-4 January, 23 February-1st March, Sunday dinner, Monday and Tuesday
Rest – *(number of covers limited, pre-book)* Menu € 28/75 – Carte € 37/49
◆ The restaurant is named after the author of the 'Roman de la Rose', born in Lorris. Sample updated fare in a cosily appointed sitting room with a pleasant decor.

LOUBRESSAC – 46 Lot – 337 G2 – pop. 458 – alt. 320 m – ✉ 46130 — 29 C1

Dordogne-Berry-Limousin

- Paris 531 – Brive-la-Gaillarde 47 – Cahors 73 – Figeac 44 – Gramat 16 – St-Céré 10
- Office de tourisme, le bourg ✆ 05 65 10 82 18
- Site★ from the château.

Le Relais de Castelnau — rm, VISA
rte de Padirac – ✆ 05 65 10 80 90 – www.relaisdecastelnau.com – rdc46@wanadoo.fr – Fax 05 65 38 22 02 – Open 1st April to end October and closed Sunday dinner and Monday in April and October
40 rm – †€ 55/76 ††€ 55/110, ☐ € 10 – ½ P € 65/85
Rest – *(closed lunch except Sunday and public holidays)* Menu € 19/48 – Carte € 33/48
◆ This modern building stands opposite the château of Castelnau-Bretenoux, which dominates the valley. Colourful, practical rooms. Panoramic views of the Bave and Dordogne valleys from the terrace and dining room.

LOUDÉAC – 22 Côtes-d'Armor – 309 F5 – pop. 9 619 – alt. 155 m – ✉ 22600 — 10 C2

Brittany

- Paris 438 – Carhaix-Plouguer 69 – Dinan 76 – Pontivy 24 – Rennes 88 – St-Brieuc 41
- Syndicat d'initiative, 1, rue Saint-Joseph ✆ 02 96 28 25 17, Fax 02 96 28 25 33

Voyageurs — rest, VISA AE
10 r. Cadélac – ✆ 02 96 28 00 47 – www.hoteldesvoyageurs.fr – hoteldesvoyageurs@wanadoo.fr – Fax 02 96 28 22 30
30 rm – †€ 56/70 ††€ 59/75, ☐ € 8,50 – ½ P € 53
Rest – *(closed 22 December-3 January, Sunday dinner and Saturday)* Menu (€ 17 bi), € 15 (weekdays)/39 – Carte € 22/40
◆ Travellers welcome! Two new prestigious guest rooms complete the functional well-kept accommodation. Friendly brasserie style restaurant with a spacious dining area. Traditional cuisine served.

LOUDUN – 86 Vienne – 322 G2 – pop. 7 173 – alt. 120 m – ✉ 86200 39 C1
Atlantic Coast

Paris 311 – Angers 79 – Châtellerault 47 – Poitiers 55 – Tours 72

Syndicat d'initiative, 2, rue des Marchands ✆ 05 49 98 15 96, Fax 05 49 98 69 49

de Loudun Roiffé Domaine de Saint Hilaire, N : 18 km on D 147, ✆ 05 49 98 78 06

Tour carrée ✳★

L'Aumônerie without rest
3 bd Mar. Leclerc – ✆ 05 49 22 63 86 – www.l-aumonerie.biz – chris.lharidon@wanadoo.fr t

4 rm – €39/44 €46/50

◆ The owner of this handsome 13C lodge cannot be faulted for her gracious welcome. Personalised rooms with antiques and bright colours and a breakfast veranda facing the garden.

LOUHANS – 71 Saône-et-Loire – 320 L10 – pop. 6 422 – alt. 179 m – ✉ 71500 8 D3
Burgundy-Jura

Paris 373 – Bourg-en-Bresse 61 – Chalon-sur-Saône 38 – Dijon 85 – Dole 76 – Tournus 31

Office de tourisme, 1, Arcade Saint-Jean ✆ 03 85 75 05 02, Fax 03 85 75 48 70

Grande-Rue★.

Le Moulin de Bourgchâteau
r. Guidon, Chalon road – ✆ 03 85 75 37 12 – www.bourgchateau.com – bourgchateau@netcourrier.com – Fax 03 85 75 45 11

19 rm – €46/51 €57/105, €10

Rest – *(closed 12 November-5 December and Monday from September to April) (number of covers limited, pre-book)* Menu €28 (weekdays)/55 – Carte €46/58

◆ This flour mill built in 1778 on the banks of the Seille is now a stylish hotel-restaurant. Gradually refurbished guestrooms. This restaurant has an original decor including a millstone, wooden beams and old stonework. Serving traditional cuisine with Italian influences due to the owners' origins.

Host. du Cheval Rouge et La Buge
rm, rest,

5 r. d'Alsace – ✆ 03 85 75 21 42 – www.hotel-chevalrouge.com – hotel-chevalrouge@wanadoo.fr – Fax 03 85 75 44 48 – Closed 16-26 June, 22 December-19 January, Sunday dinner from December to March and Monday

20 rm – €32/43 €56/59, €9

Rest – *(closed Tuesday lunch and Monday)* Menu €19 (weekdays)/43 – Carte €27/50

◆ A former post house by a busy street is now home to rooms at affordable prices. More up-to-date and comfortable in the quiet nearby wing. Traditional cuisine and regional meals served in a provincial-style atmosphere.

Barbier des Bois
rm, rm,

rte de Cuiseaux, 3.5 km south-east via D 996 – ✆ 03 85 75 55 65 – www.barbierdesbois.com – info@barbierdesbois.com – Fax 03 85 75 70 56

10 rm – €61 €72, €10

Rest – Menu €15 (weekday lunch), €20/56 – Carte €40/60

◆ This country motel provides practical, pleasant rooms with a terrace overlooking the greenery. Each guestroom sports a different colour. Lovely timbered bar. A modern interior or teak furnished terrace serving modern cuisine.

Luxury pad or humble abode?
and denote categories of comfort.

LOUPIAC – 12 Aveyron – 338 E3 – ✉ 12700 29 C1

Paris 582 – Toulouse 153 – Rodez 69 – Cahors 80 – Villefranche-de-Rouergue 24

Le Claux de Sérignac

rm, VISA

4 km south on the rte de Villefranche-de-Rouergue – ✆ 05 65 64 87 15 – www.clauxdeserignac.com – clauxdeserignac@free.fr – Fax 05 65 80 87 66

14 rm – †€ 60/110 ††€ 60/110, ☕ € 10

Rest – Menu (€ 15 bi), € 22/32 – Carte € 40/55

◆ Peaceful grounds with a pool and tennis court surround this lovely country house. It sports a tasteful, countrified decor with classical or modern rooms. Stone fireplace and exposed beams decorate the pleasant dining room.

LOURDES – 65 Hautes-Pyrénées – 342 L6 – pop. 15 100 – alt. 420 m – Major pilgrimage site – ✉ 65100 Languedoc-Roussillon-Tarn Gorges 28 A3

Paris 850 – Bayonne 147 – Pau 45 – St-Gaudens 86 – Tarbes 19

Tarbes-Lourdes-Pyrénées: ✆ 05 62 32 92 22, 10 km on the ①

Office de tourisme, place Peyramale ✆ 05 62 42 77 40, Fax 05 62 94 60 95

Lourdes Golf Club Chemin du Lac, 3 km on the Pau road, ✆ 05 62 42 02 06

Château fort (Fortified castle)★ DZ - Musée de Cire de Lourdes (Lourdes Wax Museum)★ DZ M[1] - Basilique souterraine St-Pie X (St Pie X underground basilica) CZ - Pic du Jer★.

Plans on following pages

Éliseo

rm, VISA

4 r. Reine-Astrid – ✆ 05 62 41 41 41 – www.cometolourdes.com – eliseo@cometolourdes.com – Fax 05 62 41 41 50 – Closed 12 December-6 February

197 rm – †€ 88/113 ††€ 118/168, ☕ € 15 – 7 suites – ½ P € 96/121 CZ **p**

Rest – Menu € 28 (lunch)/35 – Carte € 42/63

◆ Near the cave, a brand new establishment with large, modern, very well-equipped rooms. Souvenir shop and rooftop terraces with a panoramic view. Traditional cuisine served in modern-style spacious dining rooms.

Padoue

VISA

1 r. Reine-Astrid – ✆ 05 62 53 07 00 – www.hotelpadoue.fr – reservation@hotelpadoue.fr – Fax 05 62 53 07 01 – Open 1st April-15 October CZ **a**

155 rm ☕ – †€ 105/110 ††€ 121/125 – ½ P € 76/79

Rest – Menu (€ 14) – Carte € 21/35

◆ Located 150m from the grotto, this brand new hotel has been designed to provide all modern comforts. Large rooms, seminar room, religious gift shop and tea room. Simple, traditional cuisine served in an enormous contemporary restaurant on the first floor.

Grand Hôtel de la Grotte

VISA

66 r. de la Grotte – ✆ 05 62 94 58 87 – www.hoteldelagrotte.com – contact@hoteldelagrotte.com – Fax 05 62 94 20 50 – Open 8 April-24 October DZ **y**

80 rm – †€ 80/160 ††€ 90/170, ☕ € 16 – 7 suites – ½ P € 75/115

Rest – Menu € 26 (lunch)/32 – Carte € 50/98

Rest *Brasserie* – *✆ 05 62 42 39 34 (open 26 April-24 October)* Menu (€ 18), € 21/26 – Carte € 34/62

◆ A traditional hotel situated at the foot of the castle. Louis XVI-style rooms, some with views of the basilica. Master suite. Hushed dining rooms, serving traditional cuisine and buffet menus in summer. The Brasserie offers modern decor and a large terrace under the chestnut trees.

Gallia et Londres

rm, VISA

26 av. B. Soubirous – ✆ 05 62 94 35 44 – www.hotelgallialondres.com – contact@hotelgallialondres.com – Fax 05 62 42 24 64 – Open 12 April-19 October CZ **c**

87 rm – †€ 93/118 ††€ 120/170, ☕ € 20 – 3 suites

Rest – Menu € 24/30 – Carte € 44/60

◆ An entrancing 'old France' atmosphere in this fine hotel near the sanctuaries. Comfortable rooms, furnished in Louis XVI style. A dining room with pleasant wood-panelling, crystal chandeliers and a fresco of Venice.

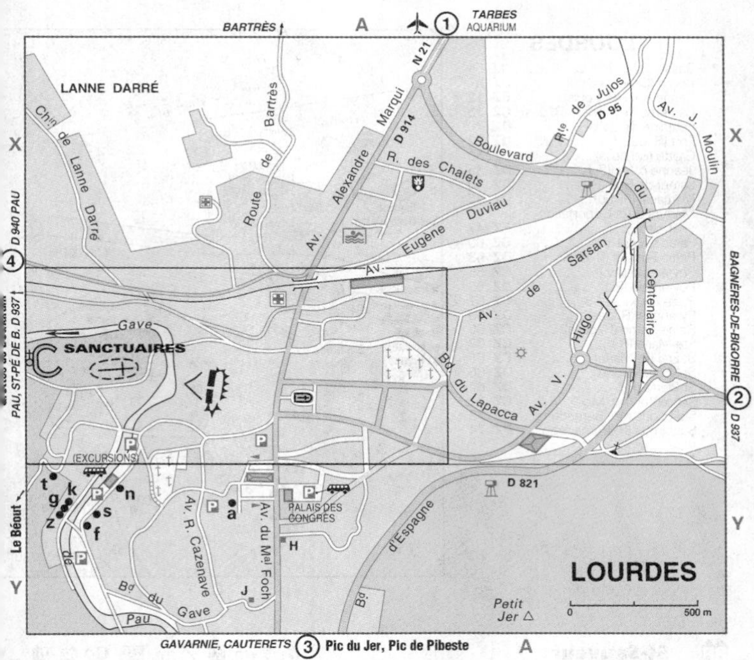

Alba rm, VISA AE

27 av. Paradis – ✆ 05 62 42 70 70 – www.hotelalba.fr – reservation@hotelalba.fr – Fax 05 62 94 54 52 – Open 2 April-30 October AY **f**

237 rm – €76 €95, €8 – ½ P €66/71

Rest – Menu €17 – Carte €20/34

◆ A vast modern building situated at the edge of the Pau stream. Comfortable rooms which are gradually being renovated, spacious lounges and a small chapel. Traditional dishes on offer in the modern-looking restaurant. Comfortable bar and shop.

Paradis rm, rest, P VISA AE

15 av. Paradis – ✆ 05 62 42 14 14 – www.hotelparadislourdes.com – info@hotelparadislourdes.com – Fax 05 62 94 64 04 – Open 15 March-1st November

300 rm – €110 €120, €15 **Rest** – Menu €29 AY **n**

◆ This riverside hotel dating from 1992 has refined decor featuring marble and oriental carpets. Spacious rooms, practical furnishings and good sound insulation. A large restaurant; refined lounges and bar with comfortable leather armchairs.

Mercure Impérial rm, rest, VISA AE

3 av. Paradis – ✆ 05 62 94 06 30 – www.mercure.com – h5445@accor-hotels.com – Fax 05 62 94 48 04 – Closed 15 December-31 January CZ **u**

93 rm – €88/135 €94/148, €12 **Rest** – Carte €32/47

◆ At the foot of the château, overlooking the mountain stream, a 1930s hotel with rooms renovated in a retro style. Panoramic roof terrace. A lovely staircase leads up to the classic style dining area and lounge with stained glass window.

Miramont rest, VISA AE

40 av. Peyramale – ✆ 05 62 94 70 00 – www.cometolourdes.com – miramont@cometolourdes.com – Fax 05 62 94 50 17 – Open 3 April-3 November AY **g**

92 rm – €53/69 €80/108, €10 – ½ P €67/81

Rest – Menu €16 – Carte €24/37

◆ Comptetely renovated modern construction. Brigth, contemporary lobby, bar and comfortable lounge: guestrooms in the same vein, with designer furniture.

LOURDES

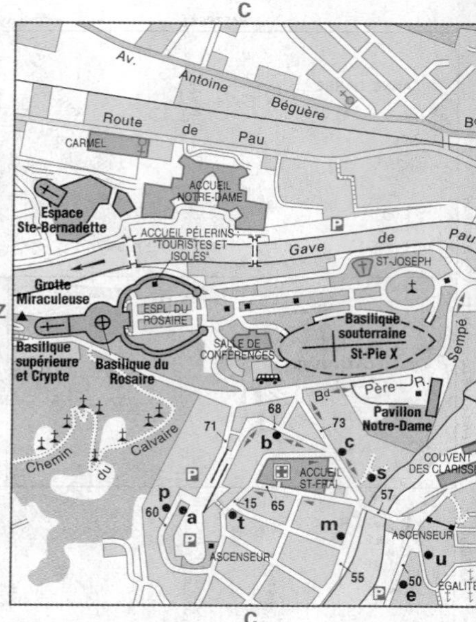

St-Sauveur

9 r. Ste-Marie – 05 62 94 25 03 – www.hotelsaintsauveur.com – contact@hotelsaintsauveur.com – Fax 05 62 94 36 52 – Closed 12 December-31 January

174 rm – €67/82 €80/110, €15 CZ **b**

Rest – Menu (€13), €18/27 – Carte €17/29

◆ Modern hotel near the sanctuaries. Huge hallway bathed in light, and modern comforts in the bedrooms. Brasserie set menu served beneath the glass roof or traditional cuisine in the elegant dining room.

Méditerranée

23 av. Paradis – 05 62 94 72 15 – www.lourdeshotelmed.com – hotelmed@aol.com – Fax 05 62 94 10 54 – Open April-October AY **s**

171 rm – €65/76 €81/95, €8

Rest – Menu (€13), €17/26 – Carte €26/37

◆ Large modern building with pleasant, well-designed rooms, a small solarium and a chapel for gathering ones thoughts. Immense, modern and functional dining room overlooking the Pau river. The bar is more intimate.

Christ-Roi

9 r. Mgr Rodhain – 05 62 94 24 98 – www.lourdes-christroi.com – hotelchristroi@wanadoo.fr – Fax 05 62 94 17 65 – Open Easter-15 October

180 rm – €59/61 €71/75, €6,50 **Rest** – Menu €20 AY **t**

◆ Pilgrims can take a lift situated a stone's throw from the hotel to reach the religious area. Modern bedrooms in a recent building. English bar. Restaurant serving traditional cuisine, mainly used by hotel residents.

Beauséjour

16 av. de la Gare – 05 62 94 38 18 – www.hotel-beausejour.com – hotel@bestwestern-beausejour.com – Fax 05 62 94 96 20 EZ **s**

45 rm – €72/95 €82/185, €11

Rest *Le Parc* – 05 62 94 73 48 – Menu (€15), €18 – Carte €27/40

◆ This small hotel adjoining the station has a renovated century-old façade, garden, opulent interior, welcoming rooms and souvenir shop. Traditional dishes served on the brasserie style restaurant-veranda or terrace overlooking the greenery.

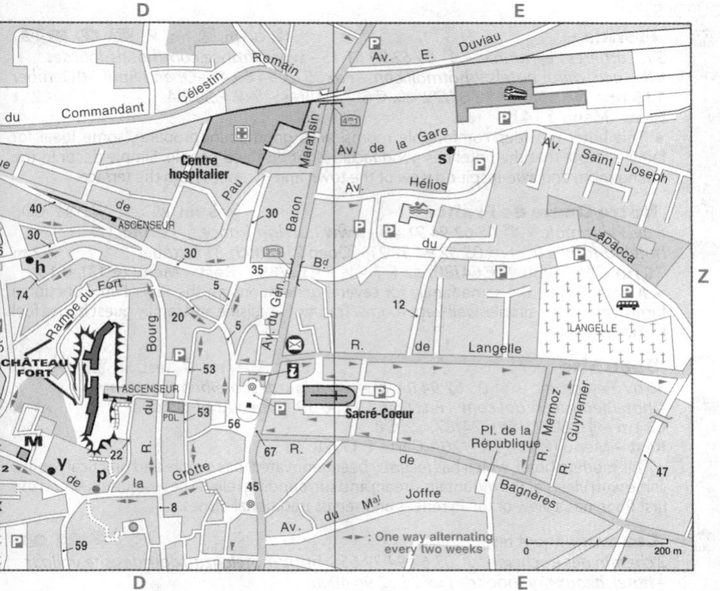

Solitude
3 passage St-Louis – ✆ 05 62 42 71 71 – www.hotelsolitude.com – contact@hotelsolitude.com – Fax 05 62 94 40 65 – Open 12 April-4 November CZ **s**
293 rm – 🚹€ 72/82 🚹🚹€ 90/110, ☕ € 15 – 4 suites – ½ P € 62/73
Rest – Menu (€ 12), € 18 – Carte € 17/29
◆ Near the entrance to the sanctuaries, this building bordering the Pau river has up-to-date rooms, one-third of which have been refurbished. A panoramic view from the small rooftop swimming pool. A rotunda dining room with a terrace overlooking the river.

Espagne
9 av. Paradis – ✆ 05 62 94 50 02 – www.hoteldespagne.com – hoteldespagne@wanadoo.fr – Fax 05 62 94 58 15 – Open 4 April-25 October CZ **e**
129 rm ☕ – 🚹€ 63/72 🚹🚹€ 78/89 – ½ P € 55/60
Rest – Menu € 19 – Carte € 26/47
◆ The name and the discreet decor of the Spanish-Moorish lounge remind you how close Spain is. Simple, functional rooms available. Choose one with a terrace. Restaurant with arched ceiling and exposed beams and the separate 'Seville' room.

Christina
42 av. Peyramale – ✆ 05 62 94 26 11 – www.hotel-christina-lourdes.com – hotel.christina@orange.fr – Fax 05 62 94 97 09 – Open 1st April-30 October
199 rm – 🚹€ 62/83 🚹🚹€ 80/116, ☕ € 8 – ½ P € 59/64 AY **z**
Rest – Menu € 14/22 – Carte € 16/22
◆ This large, white hotel is home to practical, regularly redecorated rooms. The most pleasant overlook the mountain stream and Pyrenees. Rooftop terrace and rock garden. A sizeable dining area decorated with a nautical theme, serving traditional cuisine.

Excelsior
83 bd de la Grotte – ✆ 05 62 94 02 05 – www.excelsior-lourdes.com – hotel.excelsior@wanadoo.fr – Fax 05 62 94 82 88 – Open 20 March-31 October
66 rm ☕ – 🚹€ 59/62 🚹🚹€ 81/83 – ½ P € 59/61 DZ **h**
Rest – Menu € 18/30 – Carte € 24/40
◆ Pleasant family-run restaurant. Pilgrims can choose between rooms with views of the basilica or the castle. Refined lounge and elegant bar on the ground floor. Panoramic dining room upstairs serving traditional style meals.

Florida rm, rm, VISA AE
3 r. Carrières Peyramale – 05 62 94 51 15 – www.ifrance.com/hotels-lourdes – flo_aca_mira_hotels@hotmail.com – Fax 05 62 94 69 49 – Open 3 April-30 October
115 rm – €50/54 €67/72, €6 – 2 suites – ½ P €50/54 CZ **t**
Rest – Menu €14 bi
◆ This hotel provides comfortable rooms, with good soundproofing, some ideal for families. Note that the hotel has good facilities for disabled people. Simple decor in the dining room and awe-inspiring view of the town and Pyrenees from the terrace.

Notre Dame de France rm, rest, VISA
8 av. Peyramale – 05 62 94 91 45 – www.hotelnd-france.fr – contact@hotelnd-france.fr – Fax 05 62 94 57 21 – Open 21 March-31 October CZ **m**
76 rm – €50/60 €64/80, €7 – ½ P €60/85 **Rest** – Menu (€13), €18
◆ A hotel run by the same family for several generations on the River Pau. Functional furnishings in the simple, well-kept rooms. Traditional cuisine and family guest house feel in the restaurant.

Beau Site rm, rest, VISA AE
36 av. Peyramale – 05 62 94 04 08 – www.lourdeshotelbeausite.com – hotelbeausite@aol.com – Fax 05 62 94 06 59 – Open April-October AY **k**
63 rm – €60/71 €74/87, €8
Rest – Menu (€13), €17/26 – Carte €17/28
◆ This modern hotel, which has recently been renovated, has simple and practical rooms, some with views of the mountain stream and surrounding relief. The restaurant, set on the first floor, has a view of the Pyrenees and serves traditional dishes.

Cazaux without rest VISA
2 chemin des Rochers – 05 62 94 22 65 – http://hotelcazauxlourdes.site.voila.fr – hotelcazaux@yahoo.fr – Fax 05 62 94 48 32 – Open from Easter to mid October AY **a**
20 rm – €36 €41, €6
◆ Friendly welcome and reasonable prices are the advantages of this small, family-run hotel near the food market. Good-sized, functional bedrooms.

Atrium Mondial rest, VISA
9 r. des Pélerins – 05 62 94 27 28 – atriummondialhotel@wanadoo.fr – Fax 05 62 94 70 92 – Open 10 April-15 October DZ **x**
48 rm – €40/45 €45/50, €6 **Rest** – Menu €13
◆ A spruce façade for this family guest house situated in a quiet area on the hills of the town. Simple rooms, decorated with a single crucifix. A large dining area with glass roof serving traditional meals.

Alexandra VISA AE
3 r. du Fort – 05 62 94 31 43 – cathsteph@orange.fr – Fax 05 62 46 11 06 – Closed 1st-10 July and 8-17 November DZ **p**
Rest – Menu (€10), €13/18 – Carte €35/60
◆ This discreet house with red façade is a real little miracle! Tasty, bistro-style cooking served in two unusual settings: one very colourful, the other quirky and modern.

LOURMARIN – 84 Vaucluse – **332** F11 – **pop. 1 119** – **alt. 224 m** – 84160 **Provence** 42 **E1**

Paris 732 – Apt 19 – Aix-en-Provence 37 – Cavaillon 32 – Digne-les-Bains 114
Syndicat d'initiative, avenue Philippe de Girard 04 90 68 10 77
Château★.

Le Moulin de Lourmarin VISA AE
r. du Temple – 04 90 68 06 69 – www.moulindelourmarin.com – reservation@moulindelourmarin.com – Fax 04 90 68 31 76 – Closed early January to mid-February
19 rm – €120/140 €180/230, €18 – 2 suites
Rest – Menu €32 (lunch), €52/90 – Carte €73/90
◆ An 18C oil mill in a charming setting. Delightful guestrooms with authentic Provençal charm – solidly built, decorated in muted colours and furnished with new and second-hand furniture. Restaurant in a former mill with delightful shaded terrace. Regional cuisine.

Mas de Guilles rest,
Vaugines road : 2 km – 04 90 68 30 55 – www.guilles.com – hotel@guilles.com – Fax 04 90 68 37 41 – Open early April to early November
28 rm – € 70/90 € 70/230, € 15 – ½ P € 97/177
Rest – *(dinner only)* Menu € 36/52
◆ Set amidst the vineyards is this characterful, peaceful and romantic farmhouse. It is home to bright Provençal inspired rooms, renovated in stages. Fine traditional gastronomy served in a pleasant vaulted dining room or on a vast terrace.

La Bastide de Lourmarin
rte de Cucuron – 04 90 07 00 70 – www.hotelbastide.com – info@hotelbastide.com – Fax 04 90 68 89 48 – Closed 5 January-9 February
19 rm – € 85/290 € 85/290, € 13
Rest – *(closed Tuesday lunch except July-August, Sunday dinner and Monday)* Menu (€ 22), € 28 – Carte € 30/46
◆ Recent farmhouse with local charm; fine suites and themed accommodation. Contemporary furniture, ethnic touches and the latest technology. Provençal cuisine served on the poolside terrace in summer.

Auberge La Fenière (Reine Sammut) with rm rm,
2 km via rte de Cadenet – 04 90 68 11 79 – www.reinesammut.com – reine@wanadoo.fr – Fax 04 90 68 18 60 – Closed 17 November-4 December and January
18 rm – € 150/315 € 180/380 – ½ P € 175/255
Rest – *(closed Tuesday lunch and Monday)* Menu (€ 48), € 82/130 – Carte € 100/130
Rest *Bistrot La Cour de Ferme* – Menu (€ 25), € 35
Spec. Ragoût de fèves et asperges vertes aux truffes noires (February to April). Pigeonneau fermier de Provence à l'ail confit, riz rouge aux amandes et jus épicé (spring-summer). Calissons glacés, coulis d'abricot à l'amande amère. **Wines** Côtes du Luberon rouge et blanc.
◆ A salutary refuge for lovers of fine cuisine, in this inn facing the Grand Luberon. At "La Cour de Ferme", warm ambiance in the covered part of the farm courtyard and country-style food. Elegant guestrooms with decor inspired by traditional trades. Or stay in one of two Gypsy caravans!

L'Antiquaire
9 r. Grand Pré – 04 90 68 17 29 – Fax 04 90 68 17 29 – Closed 13 November-4 December, 5-22 January, Sunday dinner from October to April, Tuesday lunch and Monday
Rest – Menu € 22 (weekday lunch), € 32/44 – Carte € 32/52
◆ In an attractive old stone house, the dining rooms sport Provençal colours. The menu specialises in a talented combination of fresh regional produce.

LOUVIERS – 27 Eure – 304 H6 – pop. 18 200 – alt. 15 m – 27400 33 D2

Normandy

Paris 104 – Les Andelys 22 – Lisieux 75 – Mantes-la-Jolie 51 – Rouen 33
Syndicat d'initiative, 10, rue du Maréchal Foch 02 32 40 04 41, Fax 02 32 61 28 85
du Vaudreuil Le Vaudreuil6 km on the Rouen road, 02 32 59 02 60
N.-Dame church ★: works of art★, porch★ BY.
Vironvay ★.

Plan on following page

Le Pré-St-Germain rm,
7 r. St-Germain – 02 32 40 48 48 – www.le-pre-saint-germain.com – le.pre.saint.germain@wanadoo.fr – Fax 02 32 50 75 60 BY **s**
30 rm – € 78 € 95, € 11 – ½ P € 115
Rest – *(Closed Saturday and Sunday)* Menu (€ 15,50), € 28/34 – Carte € 39/71
◆ This imposing residence offers rooms with a modern decor and practical facilities. Quiet, but centrally located. Traditional cuisine and blackboard suggestions in a contemporary setting or on the fine summer terrace. Fast food menu served at the bar.

LOUVIERS

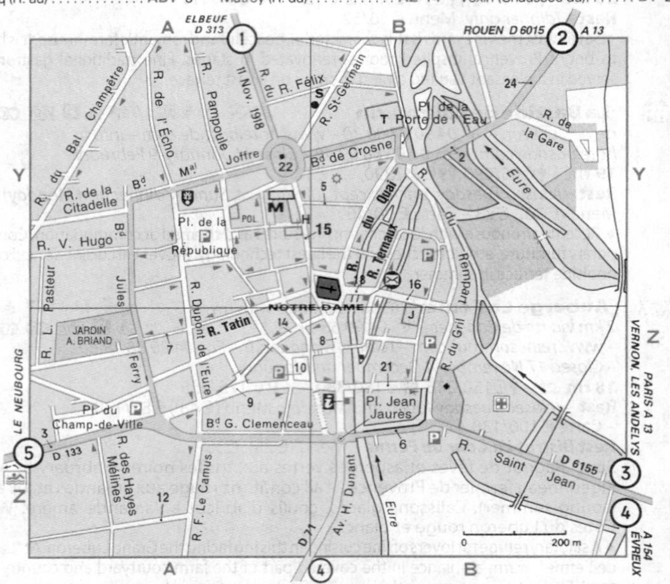

LE LUC – 83 Var – 340 M5 – pop. 8 534 – alt. 160 m – ✉ 83340 — 41 C3

French Riviera

Paris 836 – Cannes 75 – Draguignan 29 – Fréjus 41 – St-Raphaël 45 – Toulon 52

Office de tourisme, 3, place de la Liberté ✆ 04 94 60 74 51

Le Gourmandin

pl. L. Brunet – ✆ 04 94 60 85 92 – www.legourmandin.com – contact@legourmandin.com – Fax 04 94 47 91 10 – Closed 25 August-21 September, 25 February-10 March, Sunday dinner, Thursday dinner, Monday

Rest – *(pre-book Sat - Sun)* Menu € 25/45 – Carte approx. € 40

◆ This welcoming restaurant in the heart of the village serves traditional cuisine with southern touches in a warm, rustic Provencal setting.

West : 4 km by D N7 – ✉ 83340 Le Luc

La Grillade au Feu de Bois

– ✆ 04 94 69 71 20 – www.lagrillade.com – contact@lagrillade.com – Fax 04 94 59 66 11

16 rm – †€ 80/125 ††€ 80/125

Rest – Menu € 20 (weekday lunch)/50 – Carte € 35/60

◆ Just off the road, this former wine-growing farm and park is home to a hotel providing spacious rooms spread over several buildings. Italian specialities and grilled food cooked over a wood fire. Shaded terrace.

LUCELLE – 68 Haut-Rhin – 315 H12 – pop. 47 – alt. 640 m – ✉ 68480 — 1 A3

Alsace-Lorraine

Paris 472 – Altkirch 29 – Basel 41 – Belfort 56 – Colmar 98 – Delémont 17 – Montbéliard 46

Northeast : 4,5 km by D 41 and secondary road – ✉ 68480 Lucelle

Le Petit Kohlberg rm, rm, VISA
– *03 89 40 85 30 – www.petitkohlberg.com – petitkohlberg@wanadoo.fr*
– *Fax 03 89 40 89 40* **30 rm** – €56 €56, €10 – ½ P €63/66
Rest – *(closed Monday and Tuesday)* Menu €16 (weekdays)/42 – Carte €25/52
◆ This countrified establishment is ideal for a rest. Comfortable rooms in the process of being revamped. Jerseys of cycling teams decorate the breakfast room. Mountain-style dining room and terrace facing the garden. Traditional cuisine.

LUCENAY – **69 Rhône** – **327** H4 – **pop. 1 565** – **alt. 230 m** – ✉ **69480** 43 **E1**

Paris 446 – Lyon 25 – Vénissieux 38 – Villeurbanne 29

Les Tilleuls
31 rte de Lachassagne – 04 74 60 28 58 – www.lestilleuls.org – vermare@hotmail.com – Fax 04 74 60 28 58 – Closed 3-18 January
3 rm – €95 €110 – ½ P €68/70 **Table d'hôte** – Menu €32 bi
◆ Located opposite a church, this former wine estate dates back to the 17C, now featuring light rooms decorated with travel souvenirs collected by the owner. Tasty regional dishes served in a pretty dining room.

LA LUCERNE D'OUTREMER – **50 Manche** – **303** D7 – **pop. 798** 32 **A2**
– **alt. 70 m** – ✉ **50320**

Paris 332 – Caen 100 – Saint-Lô 65 – Saint-Malo 84 – Granville 16

Le Courtil de la Lucerne VISA
17 r. de la Libération, (Le Bourg) – 02 33 61 22 02
– www.lecourtildelalucerne.com – lecourtildelalucerne@wanadoo.fr
– Fax 01 33 61 22 15 – Closed 15 November-4 December, mid-February to mid-March, Sunday dinner, Tuesday from September to Easter and Wednesday
Rest – Menu €17 (weekdays), €27/35 – Carte €40/60
◆ Set in the former presbytery of a small Norman village, this simply decorated restaurant offers fine, modern cuisine.

LUCEY – **54 Meurthe-et-Moselle** – **307** G6 – **see Toul**

LUCHÉ-PRINGÉ – **72 Sarthe** – **310** J8 – **pop. 1 531** – **alt. 34 m** 35 **C2**
– ✉ **72800** Châteaux of the Loire

Paris 242 – Angers 68 – La Flèche 14 – Le Lude 10 – Le Mans 39

Syndicat d'initiative, 4, rue Paul Doumer 02 43 45 44 50, Fax 02 43 45 75 71

Auberge du Port des Roches with rm VISA
at Port des Roches, 2.5 km east on D 13 and D 214 – 02 43 45 44 48
– leportdesroches@orange.fr – Fax 02 43 45 39 61 – Closed 25 January-15 March, 17-20 August, 26 October-4 November, Sunday dinner, Tuesday lunch and Monday
12 rm – €50/58 €50/58, €8 – ½ P €54/60
Rest – Menu €24/49 – Carte €46/56
◆ Riverside garden-terrace, plush dining room and spruce colourful guestrooms. A cosy inn on the banks of the Loir to brighten your day! Elaborate traditional cuisine served on the terrace in summertime.

LUCHON – **31 H.-Gar.** – **343** B8 – **see Bagnères-de-Luchon**

LUCINGES – **74 Haute-Savoie** – **328** k3 – **pop. 1 211** – **alt. 700 m** – ✉ **74380** 46 **F1**

Paris 559 – Annecy 49 – Thonon-les-Bains 33 – Bonneville 18
– Dingy-en-Vuache 39

Le Bonheur dans Le Pré rest, rest, rm, VISA
2011 rte Bellevue – 04 50 43 37 77
– www.lebonheurdanslepre.com – lebonheurdanslepre.lucinges@wanadoo.fr
Fax 04 50 43 38 57 – Closed autumn school holidays and 21 December-15 January
8 rm – €60/80 €70/100, €9 – ½ P €55
Rest – *(closed Sunday and Monday) (dinner only) (pre-book)* Menu €30
◆ A name that holds true for this old farm, set at the foot of the village out in the countryside: garden, assured peace and quiet and pleasantly personalised rooms. Rustic dining room and wine cellar. Only one set menu focusing on local produce and depending on the market.

LUÇON – 85 Vendée – 316 I9 – pop. 9 722 – alt. 8 m – ✉ 85400 34 B3
Atlantic Coast

Paris 438 – Cholet 89 – Fontenay-le-Comte 30 – La Rochelle 43 – La Roche-sur-Yon 33

Office de tourisme, square Édouard Herriot ☎ 02 51 56 36 52, Fax 02 51 56 03 56

Notre-Dame cathedral★ - Dumaine garden★.

XXX La Mirabelle

89 bis r. de Gaulle, Sables d'Olonne road – ☎ 02 51 56 93 02 – www.restaurant-lamirabelle.com – b.hermouet@wanadoo.fr – Fax 02 51 56 35 92 – Closed Sunday dinner, Monday dinner and Tuesday except from 1st to 25 August

Rest – Menu (€ 19), € 25/65 – Carte € 45/75

◆ A welcoming establishment located 800m from the cathedral where Richelieu was made a bishop in 1608. Modern dining room and flower-decked terrace. Tasty regional cuisine.

X Au Fil des Saisons with rm

55 rte de la Roche-sur-Yon – ☎ 02 51 56 11 32 – www.aufildessaisons-vendee.com – hotel-restaurant-aufildessaisons@orange.fr – Fax 02 44 84 07 61

4 rm – †€ 47 ††€ 55, ☕ € 7 – ½ P € 52

Rest – *(Closed Saturday lunch, Sunday dinner and Monday)* Menu (€ 14), € 25/40

◆ Choose between the dining room adorned with paintings and a veranda overlooking the garden in this regional-style auberge. Contemporary cuisine. Simple, bright guestrooms.

LUC-SUR-MER – 14 Calvados – 303 J4 – pop. 3 186 – Casino 32 B2
– ✉ 14530 Normandy

Paris 249 – Arromanches-les-Bains 23 – Bayeux 29 – Cabourg 28 – Caen 18

Office de tourisme, rue du Docteur Charcot ☎ 02 31 97 33 25, Fax 02 31 96 65 09

Municipal park★.

Des Thermes et du Casino

5 r. Guyemer – ☎ 02 31 97 32 37 – www.hotelresto-lesthermes.com – hotelresto@hotelresto-lesthermes.com – Fax 02 31 96 72 57 – Open 21 March-31 October

48 rm – †€ 81/116 ††€ 81/116, ☕ € 11 – ½ P € 73/90

Rest – Menu € 27/58 – Carte € 48/70

◆ A stimulating hotel on the seafront promenade near the spa baths and casino. The rooms with balconies have a sea view. The restaurant overlooks the English channel on one side with a flower garden and apple trees on the other.

LE LUDE – 72 Sarthe – 310 J9 – pop. 4 201 – alt. 48 m – ✉ 72800 35 D2
Châteaux of the Loire

Paris 244 – Angers 63 – Chinon 63 – La Flèche 20 – Le Mans 45 – Saumur 51 – Tours 51

Office de tourisme, place François de Nicolay ☎ 02 43 94 62 20, Fax 02 43 94 62 20

Château★★.

L'Auberge Alsacienne

rest,

14 r. de la Boule-d'Or – ☎ 02 43 48 20 45 – www.auberge-alsacienne-le-lude.com – aubergealsaciennelelude@neuf.fr – Fax 02 43 48 20 42

7 rm – †€ 48/70 ††€ 52/75, ☕ € 8 – ½ P € 60/65

Rest – Menu € 12 (lunch), € 27/33 – Carte € 25/30

◆ This former convent is home to spacious, entirely refurbished and well-soundproofed rooms. The subdued, Alsace inspired decor of the restaurant gives you a foretaste of the menu: choucroute, tarte flambée and other more regional dishes. Flower-decked summer terrace.

XX La Renaissance with rm

rm, rest,

2 av. Libération – ☎ 02 43 94 63 10 – www.renaissancelelude.com – lelude.renaissance@wanadoo.fr – Fax 02 43 94 21 05 – Closed 26 October-8 November, 16 February-1st March and Sunday dinner

8 rm – †€ 47/57 ††€ 47/57, ☕ € 8

Rest – *(closed Monday)* Menu (€ 12 bi), € 16 bi (weekdays)/38 – Carte approx. € 45

◆ This restaurant, located just near the château, serves modern cuisine in a contemporary style dining area. There is also a summer terrace on the inner courtyard.

LUDES – 51 Marne – **306** G8 – **pop. 628** – **alt. 140 m** – ✉ **51500** 13 **B2**

Paris 157 – Châlons-en-Champagne 52 – Reims 15 – Épernay 22 – Tinqueux 20

Domaine Ployez-Jacquemart

8 r. Astoin – ✆ 03 26 61 11 87 – www.ployez-jacquemart.fr – contact@ployez-jacquemart.fr – Fax 03 26 61 12 20 – Closed 17 December-15 January

5 rm – €88/113 €100/125

Table d'hôte – *(closed 3-19 April, August, September and 24 October-4 November)* Menu €150 bi

◆ This mansion in the middle of a champagne vineyard celebrates the French art of living. Comfortable and refined rooms based on various themes: baroque, savannah, etc. Table d'hôte serving a house champagne dinner (on reservation).

LUMBRES – 62 Pas-de-Calais – **301** F3 – **pop. 3 744** – **alt. 45 m** – ✉ **62380** 30 **A2**

Paris 261 – Arras 81 – Boulogne-sur-Mer 43 – Calais 44 – Dunkerque 51 – St-Omer 11

Office de tourisme, rue François Cousin ✆ 03 21 93 45 46, Fax 03 21 12 15 87

Moulin de Mombreux rm, rest,

West : 2 km via Boulogne road, D 225 and minor road – ✆ 03 21 39 13 13 – www.moulindemombreux.com – contact@moulindemombreux.com – Fax 03 21 93 61 34 – Closed January, Monday lunch and Saturday lunch

24 rm – €119/135 €119/135, €15

Rest – Menu (€18), €30 – Carte €41/68

◆ Comfortable nights at this 18C windmill on the banks of the Bléquin with the murmur of a waterfall to send you to sleep, recently renovated to enhance the old style refinement. Exposed beams and rustic furniture grace the upstairs dining room.

LUNAS – 34 Hérault – **339** E6 – **pop. 647** – **alt. 281 m** – ✉ **34650** 22 **B2**

Paris 710 – Montpellier 68 – Béziers 76 – Millau 73 – Mèze 67

Office de tourisme, chemin de Reiregardi ✆ 04 67 23 76 67

Château de Lunas

r. du Château – ✆ 04 67 23 87 99 – www.chateaudelunas.fr – chateaudelunas@live.fr – Fax 04 67 23 87 99 – Closed February, Tuesday and Wednesday except July-August

Rest – Menu €23/43 – Carte €32/68

◆ This 17C château is set on the banks of the Gravezon. Contemporary artwork on the historic walls of the dining rooms. Attractive terrace. Cuisine focusing on quality produce.

LUNEL – 34 Hérault – **339** J6 – **pop. 23 900** – **alt. 6 m** – ✉ **34400** 23 **C2**
Languedoc-Roussillon-Tarn Gorges

Paris 733 – Aigues-Mortes 16 – Alès 58 – Arles 56 – Montpellier 30 – Nîmes 31

Office de tourisme, 16, cours Gabriel Péri ✆ 04 67 71 01 37, Fax 04 67 71 26 67

Chodoreille

140 r. Lakanal – ✆ 04 67 71 55 77 – www.chodoreille.fr – chodoreille@wanadoo.fr – Fax 04 67 83 19 97 – Closed 15 August-1st September, 2-19 January, Sunday and Monday

Rest – Menu €22 (weekdays), €28/53 – Carte €44/66

◆ Classic dishes with an original touch served in the contemporary dining room or shaded terrace, depending on the weather. Camargue beef a speciality.

LUNÉVILLE – 54 Meurthe-et-Moselle – **307** J7 – **pop. 19 500** – **alt. 224 m** – ✉ **54300** **Alsace-Lorraine** 27 **C2**

Paris 347 – Épinal 69 – Metz 95 – Nancy 36 – St-Dié 56 – Strasbourg 132

Office de tourisme, aile sud du Château ✆ 03 83 74 06 55, Fax 03 83 73 57 95

Château★ A - Les Bosquets park ★ AB - Panelling★ of St-Jacques church A.

LUNÉVILLE

Abbé Pierre (R. de l') . . . . A 43
Banaudon (R.) . . . . A 2
Basset (R. R.) . . . . B 3
Bosquets (R. des) . . . . B 4
Brèche (R. de la) . . . . A 5
Carnot (R.) . . . . B 7
Castara (R.) . . . . A 9
Chanzy (R.) . . . . A 10
Charier (R. G.) . . . . A 13
Charité (R. de la) . . . . A 15
Château (R. du) . . . . A 16
Erckmann (R.) . . . . B 18
Gaillardot (R.) . . . . A 20
Gambetta (R.) . . . . B 21
Haxo (R.) . . . . B 23
Lebrun (R.) . . . . B 25
Leclerc (R. Gén.) . . . . A 27
Léopold (Pl.) . . . . AB 28
République (R.) . . . . A 30
Ste-Marie (R.) . . . . A 37
St-Jacques (Pl.) . . . . A 32
St-Rémy (Pl.) . . . . A 36
Sarrebourg (R. de) . . . . A 39
Templiers (R. des) . . . . A 41
Viller (R. de) . . . . A 48
2e-Div.-de-Cavalerie (Pl. de la) A 50

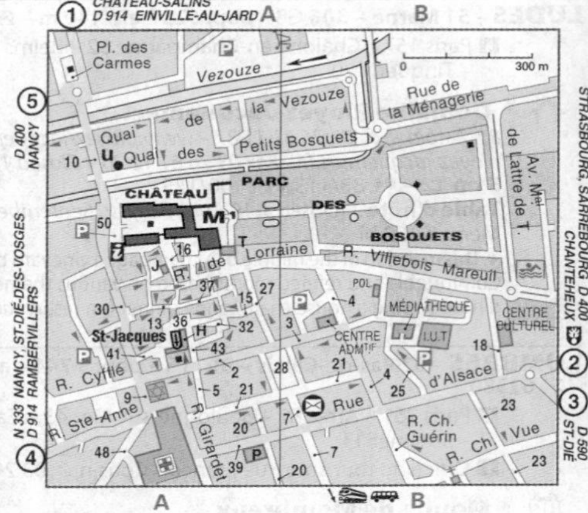

Les Pages
5 quai des Petits-Bosquets – ✆ 03 83 74 11 42 – lespages@9business.fr – Fax 03 83 73 46 63 A u
37 rm – €55/95 €65/120, €8,50 – ½ P €54/69
Rest *Le Petit Comptoir* – *✆ 03 83 73 14 55 (Closed 21-24 December, 31 December-3 January, Saturday lunch and Sunday dinner)* Menu €17 (weekdays)/35 – Carte €30/45
◆ This large group of buildings stands opposite the château. The bedrooms have quite an original modern style, which makes up for them being slightly small. The restaurant is laid out in bistro style. Simple and appetising cuisine.

in Moncel-lès-Lunéville St-Dié road by ③: 3 km – pop. 391 – alt. 234 m – ✉ 54300

Relais St-Jean
22 av. de l'Europe, on N 59 – ✆ 03 83 74 08 65 – Fax 03 83 75 33 16 – Closed 3-24 August, Sunday dinner, Wednesday dinner and Monday
Rest – Menu (€12,50), €15/25 – Carte €23/49
◆ The main dining room in this restaurant in the Meurthe valley is welcoming, furnished with wrought iron. Classic cuisine.

South by ④ then Avenue G. Pompidou and cités Ste-Anne: 5 km – ✉ 54300 Lunéville

Château d'Adoménil (Cyril Leclerc) rest,
– ✆ 03 83 74 04 81 – www.adomenil.com – adomenil@relaischateaux.com – Fax 03 83 74 21 78 – Closed 4-29 January, 15-26 February, Sunday evening from 1st November to 15 April, Tuesday from 1st November to 1st March and Monday
9 rm – €175/195 €175/220, €21 – 5 suites – ½ P €195/215
Rest – *(closed Sunday dinner from 1st November to 15 April, Tuesday except dinner from 2 March to 31 October, Wednesday lunch, Thursday lunch, Friday lunch and Monday)* Menu €49 (weekdays)/95 – Carte €76/120
Rest *Version A* – *(open Wednesday, Thursday and Friday) (lunch only)* Menu €32 – Carte €32/50
Spec. Saint-Jacques émincées crues, mascarpone, wasabi, et anis vert (November to March). Cabillaud de petite pêche et œuf poché dans un bouillon de crevettes grises. Cornets craquants de mirabelles de Lorraine et pavot bleu (20 August-20 September). **Wines** Côtes de Toul blanc et rouge.
◆ A fine 18C residence situated in an attractive park. Traditional bedrooms in the château, or Provençal-style in the outbuildings. Up-to-date cuisine in the restaurant, and a contemporary, Baroque-style decor combining dark tones with touches of colour. At lunch, version A – a bistro with large windows overlooking an English-style garden.

LURBE-ST-CHRISTAU – 64 Pyrénées-Atlantiques – 342 I6 – pop. 225 – alt. 260 m – Spa : closed, opening date unknown at present – ✉ 64660 3 **B3**

Paris 820 – Laruns 32 – Lourdes 61 – Oloron-Ste-Marie 10 – Pau 44 – Tardets-Sorholus 29

Au Bon Coin
rte des Thermes – ✆ 05 59 34 40 12 – www.thierry-lassala.com – thierrylassala@wanadoo.fr – Fax 05 59 34 46 40 – Closed 1 week in February and Sunday dinner from 20 September to 20 June
18 rm – €56/88 €58/88, €10
Rest – *(closed Sunday dinner except in July-August, Monday and Tuesday lunch)* Menu (€22 bi), €30/52
◆ Friendly family-run hotel on the edge of the forest. Comfortable and practical rooms. Those at the back are quieter. Regional, updated cuisine and Madiran wines to be enjoyed in a dining room with exposed beams and stonework, or on the veranda.

LURE – 70 Haute-Saône – 314 G6 – pop. 8 337 – alt. 290 m – ✉ 70200 Burgundy-Jura 17 **C1**

Paris 387 – Belfort 37 – Besançon 77 – Épinal 77 – Montbéliard 35 – Vesoul 30

Office de tourisme, 35, avenue Carnot ✆ 03 84 62 80 52, Fax 03 84 62 74 61

in Roye East: 2 km by Belfort road – pop. 1 219 – alt. 301 m – ✉ 70200

Le Saisonnier
56 r. de la Verrerie, N 19 – ✆ 03 84 30 46 00 – www.restaurant-lesaisonnier.com – casagrande.laurent@wanadoo.fr – Fax 03 84 30 46 00 – Closed 3 June-17 August, 15-25 February, Sunday dinner, Monday dinner and Wednesday
Rest – *(number of covers limited, pre-book)* Menu €26/60 – Carte €40/55
◆ The thick walls of this old farmhouse now house three country-style dining areas serving contemporary cuisine. Terrace-garden dining in summer.

in Froideterre Northeast: 3 km by D 486 and D 99 – pop. 358 – alt. 306 m – ✉ 70200

Hostellerie des Sources with rm
4 r. du Grand Bois – ✆ 03 84 30 34 72 – www.hostellerie-des-sources.com – hostelleriedessources@wanadoo.fr – Fax 03 84 30 29 87
5 rm – €70/119 €70/119, €10
Rest – *(closed 3 weeks in January, Sunday dinner, Monday and Tuesday) (number of covers limited, pre-book)* Menu €28/58 – Carte €38/54
◆ Spruce stone farmhouse on the edge of the Mille Étangs plateau. Elegant rustic interior. Tasty up-to-date cuisine. Accommodation is in five new contemporary styled and particularly well-equipped villas (three with private spa and sauna).

LUSSAC-LES-CHÂTEAUX – 86 Vienne – 322 K6 – pop. 2 407 – alt. 104 m – ✉ 86320 Atlantic Coast 39 **D2**

Paris 355 – Bellac 42 – Châtellerault 52 – Montmorillon 12 – Poitiers 39 – Ruffec 51

Office de tourisme, place du 11 novembre 1918 ✆ 05 49 84 57 73, Fax 05 49 84 57 73

Merovingian necropolis★ of Civaux Northwest: 6 km on D 749.

Les Orangeries
12 av. du Dr Dupont – ✆ 05 49 84 07 07 – www.lesorangeries.fr – orangeries@wanadoo.fr – Fax 05 49 84 98 82 – Closed 1st-15 March
11 rm – €55/115 €60/135, €13 – 4 suites – ½ P €69/107
Rest – *(dinner only)* Menu (€18), €28/45 bi
◆ An interior steeped in character, cosy rooms, pool, landscaped park and an orchard, are some of the many appeals of this 18C 'guesthouse'. Regional based menu reflects the location: generous, 'green' home cooking (seasonal menu, organic products).

LUTTER – 68 Haut-Rhin – 315 I12 – see Ferrette

LUTZELBOURG – 57 Moselle – 307 O6 – pop. 695 – alt. 212 m – ✉ 57820 Alsace-Lorraine 27 D2

Paris 438 – Metz 113 – Obernai 49 – Sarrebourg 20 – Sarreguemines 53 – Strasbourg 62

Syndicat d'initiative, 147, rue A.J. Konzett ✆ 03 87 25 30 19, Fax 03 87 25 33 76

Plan-incliné (slope) ★ of St-Louis-Arzviller Southwest: 3.5 km.

XX **Des Vosges** with rm VISA AE

2 r. Ackermann – ✆ 03 87 25 30 09 – www.hotelvosges.com – info@hotelvosges.com – Fax 03 87 25 42 22

10 rm – €58/68 €58/68, €8 – ½ P €68

Rest – *(closed Sunday dinner and Wednesday)* Menu (€12), €20/35 – Carte €24/42

♦ Traditional inn with terrace overlooking the canal. Panelling and original parquet in the dining area; regional cuisine and truite au bleu (trout poached in court bouillon).

LUXÉ – 16 Charente – 324 K4 – see Mansle

LUXEUIL-LES-BAINS – 70 Haute-Saône – 314 G6 – pop. 7 575 – alt. 305 m – Spa : late March to late October – Casino – ✉ 70300 Burgundy Jura 17 C1

Paris 379 – Épinal 58 – Vesoul 32 – Vittel 72

Office de tourisme, rue Victor Genoux ✆ 03 84 40 06 41, Fax 03 84 93 56 44

18 de Luxeuil Bellevue Genevrey RN 57, 11 km on the Vesoul road, ✆ 03 84 95 82 00

Hôtel du Cardinal Jouffroy★ **B** - Musée de la tour des Échevins: stele★ **M**[1] - Anc. Abbaye St-Colomban★ - Maison François1er★ **K.**

Les Sources without rest VISA AE

2 av. Jean-Moulin – ✆ 03 84 93 70 04 – www.70lessources.fr – contact@70lessources.fr – Fax 03 84 93 98 98 – Closed 20 December to 3 January

41 rm – €55/92 €65/100, €8,50

♦ Not far from the thermal springs, this entirely renovated edifice, erected in 1860, now offers 41 contemporary styled studios (with kitchenette) overlooking the park or town.

Cannes (R. des)	2
Carnot (R.)	3
Clemenceau (R. G.)	4
Gambetta (R.)	5
Genoux (R. V.)	6
Hoche (R.)	7
Jeanneney (R. J.)	8
Lavoirs (R. des)	9
Maroseli (Allées A.)	12
Morbief (R. du)	15
Thermes (Av. des)	16

LUYNES – 37 Indre-et-Loire – **317** M4 – **pop. 4 945** – **alt. 60 m** 11 **B2**
– ✉ **37230** Châteaux of the Loire

Paris 247 – Angers 115 – Chinon 41 – Langeais 15 – Saumur 56 – Tours 11

Office de tourisme, 9, rue Alfred Baugé ✆ 02 47 55 77 14, Fax 02 47 55 77 14

Church★ in the Vieux-Bourg (old town) of St-Etienne de Chigny West: 3 km.

Domaine de Beauvois rest, rest, VISA
4 km north-west via the D 49 – ✆ 02 47 55 50 11 – www.beauvois.com – beauvois@grandesetapes.fr – Fax 02 47 55 59 62
36 rm – €188/350 €188/350, €22
Rest – Menu (€19), €28 (weekday lunch), €45/75 – Carte €55/92
◆ Huge 16C and 17C manor house, nestling in a park planted with trees with a small lake. Superb guestrooms with individual touches in a country house style. Elegant dining room and intimate lounges offering modern food (dinner and on Sundays) or local dishes (at lunchtime).

A good night's sleep without spending a fortune?
Look for a Bib Hotel.

LUZ-ST-SAUVEUR – 65 Hautes-Pyrénées – **342** L7 – **pop. 1 077** 28 **A3**
– **alt. 710 m** – **Winter sports : 1 800/2 450 m** 14 – **Spa : mid-April-late October**
– ✉ **65120** Languedoc-Roussillon-Tarn Gorges

Paris 882 – Argelès-Gazost 19 – Cauterets 24 – Lourdes 32 – Pau 77 – Tarbes 51

Office de tourisme, 20, place du 8 mai ✆ 05 62 92 30 30, Fax 05 62 92 87 19

Fortified church★.

in Esquièze-Sère North – **pop. 438** – **alt. 710 m** – ✉ **65120**

Le Montaigu rest, VISA
rte de Vizos – ✆ 05 62 92 81 71 – www.hotelmontaigu.com – hotel.montaigu@wanadoo.fr – Fax 05 62 92 94 11 – Closed April, October and November
42 rm – €60/70 €70/85, €9 – ½ P €60/65
Rest – *(dinner only)* Menu €17/35 – Carte €30/42
◆ A recent establishment situated at the foot of a ruined château. Spacious, functional rooms, seven of which are brand new; some with a balcony overlooking the mountains. Traditional menu in the restaurant and bright lounge-bar area facing the garden.

Terminus without rest VISA
r. Marcadaou – ✆ 05 62 92 80 17 – hotel.terminus65120@orange.fr – Fax 05 62 92 32 89 – Closed November
16 rm – €40 €42, €6
◆ This hotel is located in a large village house, providing all-renovated and colourful guestrooms. Enjoy your breakfast in the garden on fine mornings.

LUZY – **319** G11 – **pop. 2 077** – **alt. 275 m** – ✉ **58170 Luzy** 7 **B3**

Paris 319 – Dijon 122 – Nevers 81 – Le Creusot 47 – Montceau-les-Mines 40

Syndicat d'initiative, place Chanzy ✆ 03 86 30 02 65, Fax 03 86 30 04 51

Le Morvan VISA
73 av. Dr-Dollet – ✆ 03 86 30 00 66 – www.hotelrestaurantdumorvan.fr – hotel.morvan@wanadoo.fr – Fax 03 86 30 04 92 – Closed 22 August-3 September, 1st-8 March, Saturday lunch, Sunday dinner and Wednesday
Rest – Menu €15 (weekday lunch), €22/70 – Carte €51/63
◆ The setting of this old inn oozes with charm, however it is the mouth-watering inventive cuisine of the owner/chef and pretty countrified dining room that make it so popular!

The quay of the Saône and Notre-Dame de Fourvière

LYON

Department: 69 Rhône
Michelin LOCAL map: n° 327 I5
Paris 458 – Genève 151 – Grenoble 106 – Marseille 314 – St-Étienne 61
Population: 468 400
Pop. built-up area: 1 449 000
Altitude: 175 m
Postal Code: 69000
Lyon - Rhone Valley
Carte régionale 43 E1

USEFUL INFORMATION

TOURIST OFFICE

place Bellecour 04 72 77 69 69, Fax 04 78 42 04 32

TRANSPORT

Auto-train 3635 et tapez 42 (0,34 €/mn)

AIRPORT

Lyon Saint-Exupéry 0 826 800 826 (0.15 €/min), 25 km on the ④

CASINO

at the Tour de Salvagny
le Pharaon (quai Charles-de-Gaulle in Lyon) GV

A FEW GOLF COURSES

- 18 de Lyon Chassieu Chassieu Route de Lyon, 04 78 90 84 77
- 18 de Salvagny La Tour-de-Salvagny 100 rue des Granges, 20 km on the Roanne road, 04 78 48 88 48
- 9 public de Miribel Jonage Vaulx-en-Velin Chemin de la Bletta, NE : 9 km, 04 78 80 56 20
- 18 de Mionnay-la-Dombes Mionnay Domaine de Beau Logis, N : 23 km on D 1083, 04 78 91 84 84
- 36 de Lyon Villette-d'Anthon : 25 km on D 517, D6 and D 55, 04 78 31 11 33

TO SEE

SITE

⩽★★★ of Notre-Dame de Fourvière basilicaEX
Up Garillan★ EX
⩽★ on the Saône and peninsula from Place Rouville EV

ROMAN AND GALLO-ROMAN LYON

Roman and Odéon theatresEY - Roman aqueducts EY - Musée de la civilisation gallo-romaine (Gallo-Roman Civilization Museum) ★★ : table claudienne (Claudian table)★★★ EY M10

OLD LYON

Districts of St-Jean, St-Paul and St-Georges★★★ EFXY - Rue St-Jean: Courtyard★★ at n° 28 and courtyard★of the hôtel du Gouvernement at n° 2 – Vaulted corridor★ at n° 18 rue Lainerie - Gallery★★ of hôtel Bullioud at n° 8 rue Juiverie - Hôtel Gadagne★ FX M4 : musée historique de Lyon (Lyon History Museum)★, musée lapidaire (Lapidary Museum)★, musée international de la Marionnette (International Puppet Museum)★ - Primitiale St-Jean★ (Choir★★) EFY - Maison du Crible★ at n° 16 rue du Boeuf - Theatre " FX T

THE PRESQU'ÎLE

Place Bellecour FY - Fountain★ of place des Terreaux FX - Palais St-Pierre★ FX M9 Musée des Beaux-Arts (Fine Arts Museum)★★★ FX M9 - Musée historique des tissus (Cloth History Museum) ★★★ FY M17 - Musée de l'imprimerie (Printing Museum)★★ FX M16 - Musée des Arts décoratifs (Decorative Arts Museum) ★★ FY M7

LA CROIX ROUSSE

Origins of the Lyon silk industry
Mur des Canuts (Silk Worker's Wall) **FV R** - Maison des Canuts (Silk Workers' House) **FV M5** - Ateliers de Soierie vivante (Living Silk Workshops)★ **FV E**

LEFT BANK OF THE RHÔNE

Districts: les Brotteaux, la Guillotière, Gerland, la Part-Dieu
Tête d'Or Park ★ : Rose garden ★ **GHV** - Musée d'Histoire naturelle Natural History Museum)★★ **GV M20**
- Centre d'Histoire de la Résistance et de la Déportation (Resistance and Deportation History Centre)★ **FZ M1**
Musée d'Art contemporain (Modern Art Museum)★ **GU** - Musée urbain Tony-Garnier (Tony Garnier Urban Museum)**CQ** - Halle Tony-Garnier **BQR** - Château Lumière **CQ M2**

SURROUNDING AREA

Musée de l'automobile Henri-Malartre (car museum)★★ to Rochetaillée-sur-Saône : 12 km by ⑪

City Centre (Bellecour-Terreaux)

Sofitel rm, A/C VISA MC AE
20 quai Gailleton ✉ 69002 Ⓜ Bellecour – ☎ 04 72 41 20 20 – www.sofitel.com – h0553@accor.com – Fax 04 72 40 05 50 p. 8 FY **p**
164 rm – €230/380 €230/380, €27 – 26 suites
Rest *Les Trois Dômes* – see below
Rest *Silk Brasserie* – ☎ *04 72 41 20 80* – Menu (€19), €28 bi – Carte €37/51
◆ The cuboid exterior contrasts with the luxurious interior: contemporary rooms in good taste, modern conference facilities, smart shops and a hair-dressing salon. Fashionable setting, international and regional dishes at the Silk Brasserie.

Le Royal Lyon A/C VISA MC AE
20 pl. Bellecour ✉ 69002 Ⓜ Bellecour – ☎ 04 78 37 57 31 – www.lyonhotel-leroyal.com – H2952@accor.com – Fax 04 78 37 01 36 p. 8 FY **g**
74 rm – €150/450 €150/450, €22 – 10 suites
Rest – Menu (€19), €28 – Carte €32
◆ After renovation, this 19C hotel run by the Paul Bocuse Institute has regained its former splendour. Magnificent guestrooms. The breakfast room is decorated in the manner of a kitchen. Up-to-date menu at the restaurant.

Carlton without rest A/C VISA MC AE
4 r. Jussieu ✉ 69002 Ⓜ Cordeliers – ☎ 04 78 42 56 51 – mercure.com – h2950@accor.com – Fax 04 78 42 10 71 p. 8 FX **b**
83 rm – €89/159 €99/219, €17
◆ Purple and gold prevail in this traditional hotel, decorated in the manner of an old-fashioned luxury hotel. The period lift cage has a charm of its own. Comfortable rooms.

Globe et Cécil without rest A/C VISA MC AE
21 r. Gasparin ✉ 69002 Ⓜ Bellecour – ☎ 04 78 42 58 95 – www.globeetcecilhotel.com – accueil@globeetcecilhotel.com – Fax 04 72 41 99 06 p. 8 FY **b**
60 rm – €135/140 €150/170
◆ One of the last silk-merchants of the town decorated the conference room of this hotel. Antique and modern furniture adorns the tastefully decorated rooms. Irresistible welcome.

Mercure Lyon Beaux-Arts without rest A/C VISA MC AE
75 r. Prés. E. Herriot ✉ 69002 Ⓜ Cordeliers – ☎ 04 78 38 09 50 – www.mercure.com – h2949@accor.com – Fax 04 78 42 19 19 p. 8 FX **t**
75 rm – €94/219 €104/229, €16 – 4 suites
◆ Beautiful building from 1900, most of the bedrooms are furnished in Art Deco style. Four are more unusual and are decorated by contemporary artists.

Mercure Plaza République without rest A/C VISA MC AE
5 r. Stella ✉ 69002 Ⓜ Cordeliers – ☎ 04 78 37 50 50 – www.mercure.com – h2951@accor.com – Fax 04 78 42 33 34 p. 8 FY **k**
78 rm – €99/209 €109/219, €17
◆ 19C architecture, central location, modern interior, full range of comforts and conference facilities: a hotel especially popular with its business clientele.

Grand Hôtel des Terreaux without rest VISA MC AE
16 r. Lanterne ✉ 69001 Ⓜ Hôtel de ville – ☎ 04 78 27 04 10 – www.hotel-lyon.fr – ght@hotel-lyon.fr – Fax 04 78 27 97 75 p. 6 FX **u**
53 rm – €85/90 €115/157, €12
◆ Personalised, tastefully decorated rooms, a pretty indoor pool and attentive service ensure that guests can relax to the full in this former 19C post house.

Des Artistes without rest A/C VISA MC AE
8 r. G. André ✉ 69002 Ⓜ Cordeliers – ☎ 04 78 42 04 88 – reservation@hotel-des-artistes.fr – Fax 04 78 42 93 76 p. 8 FY **r**
45 rm – €85/100 €105/140, €10
◆ The hotel is named after the "artistes" of the neighbouring Célestins theatre. Stylish rooms; a Cocteau style fresco adorns the breakfast room.

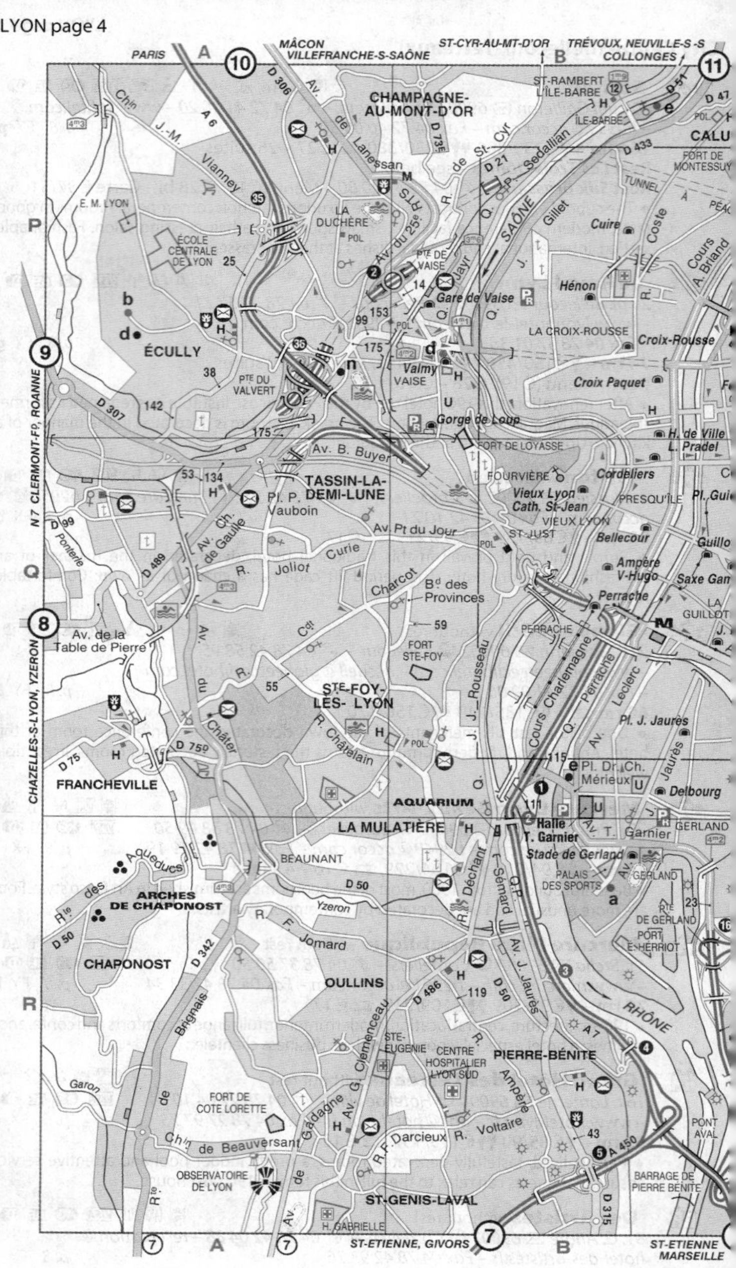
PARIS
A
10
MÂCON
VILLEFRANCHE-S-SAÔNE
ST-CYR-AU-MT-D'OR
TRÉVOUX, NEUVILLE-S-S
COLLONGES
B
11
CHAMPAGNE-AU-MONT-D'OR
ST-RAMBERT L'ÎLE-BARBE
ÎLE-BARBE
CALU
FORT DE MONTESSUY
E. M. LYON
ÉCOLE CENTRALE DE LYON
LA DUCHÈRE
Av. de Lanessan
Chin J.-M. Vianney
A 6
D 306
D 73E
R. de St-Cyr
P. Sedallian
D 21
D 433
SAÔNE
Gillet
Cuire
Coste
Cours A. Briand
Hénon
LA CROIX-ROUSSE
Croix-Rousse
Croix Paquet
Av. du 25e R.T.S.
PTE DE VAISE
Gare de Vaise
Q. Jayr
Valmy
VAISE
P
b
d
ÉCULLY
9
PTE DU VALVERT
D 307
N 7 CLERMONT-FD, ROANNE
Gorge de Loup
FORT DE LOYASSE
FOURVIÈRE
H. de Ville L. Pradel
Cordeliers
Vieux Lyon Cath. St-Jean
VIEUX LYON
PRESQU'ÎLE
Pl. Gui
ST-JUST
Bellecour
Guillo
Ampère V-Hugo
Saxe Gam
Perrache
LA GUILLOT
Av. B. Buyer
TASSIN-LA-DEMI-LUNE
Pl. P. Vauboin
Av. Ch. de Gaulle
D 99
Ponterie
D 489
R. Joliot Curie
Av. Pt du Jour
Charcot
Bd des Provinces
Q
8
Av. de la Table de Pierre
CHAZELLES-S-LYON, YZERON
FORT STE-FOY
PERRACHE
Cours Charlemagne
Q. Perrache
Av. Leclerc
Cdt
R.
STE-FOY-LÈS-LYON
R. Châtelain
J. J. Rousseau
Pl. J. Jaurès
Jaurès
Av. du Châter
D 75
D 759
FRANCHEVILLE
AQUARIUM
Pl. Dr. Ch. Mérieux
Delbourg
LA MULATIÈRE
Halle T. Garnier
Av. T. Garnier
GERLAND
Stade de Gerland
PALAIS DES SPORTS
Av. GERLAND
a
BEAUNANT
Rte des Aqueducs
ARCHES DE CHAPONOST
D 50
Yzeron
R. F. Jomard
R. Déchant
P. Sémard
Q.P.
RTE DE GERLAND
PORT E. HERRIOT
D 342
CHAPONOST
OULLINS
Av. J. Jaurès
D 486
R
Brignais
RHÔNE
A 7
Av. G. Clemenceau
STE-EUGENIE
CENTRE HOSPITALIER LYON SUD
PIERRE-BÉNITE
R. Ampère
Garon
FORT DE COTE LORETTE
Chin de Beauversant
Gadagne
R. F. Darcieux
R. Voltaire
PONT AVAL
A 450
OBSERVATOIRE DE LYON
Rte de
BARRAGE DE PIERRE BÉNITE
ST-GENIS-LAVAL
H. GABRIELLE
D 315
7
A
ST-ETIENNE, GIVORS
B
ST-ETIENNE MARSEILLE

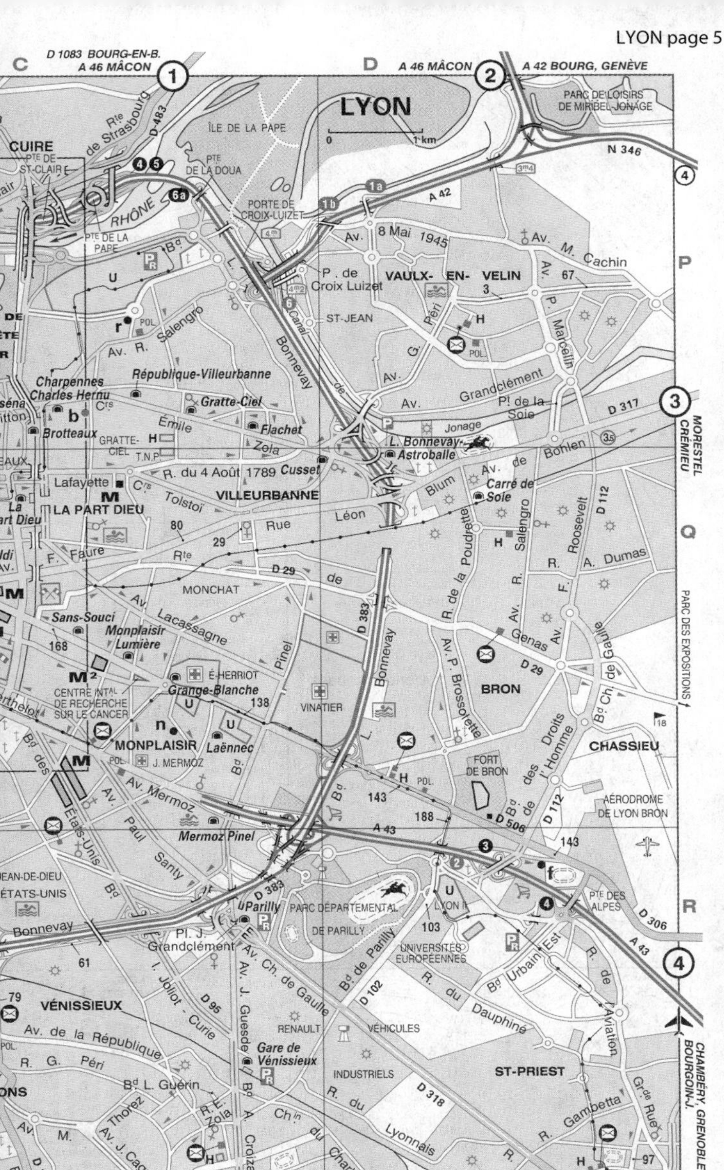
D 1083 BOURG-EN-B.
A 46 MÂCON
A 46 MÂCON
A 42 BOURG, GENÈVE
LYON
PARC DE LOISIRS DE MIRIBEL-JONAGE
ÎLE DE LA PAPE
CUIRE
N 346
A 42
VAULX-EN-VELIN
VILLEURBANNE
LA PART DIEU
MONCHAT
BRON
CHASSIEU
MONPLAISIR
VÉNISSIEUX
ST-PRIEST
PARC DÉPARTEMENTAL DE PARILLY
AÉRODROME DE LYON BRON
PARC DES EXPOSITIONS
MORESTEL CREMIEU
CHAMBÉRY, GRENOBLE BOURGOIN-J.
CORBAS
A 46 HEYRIEUX

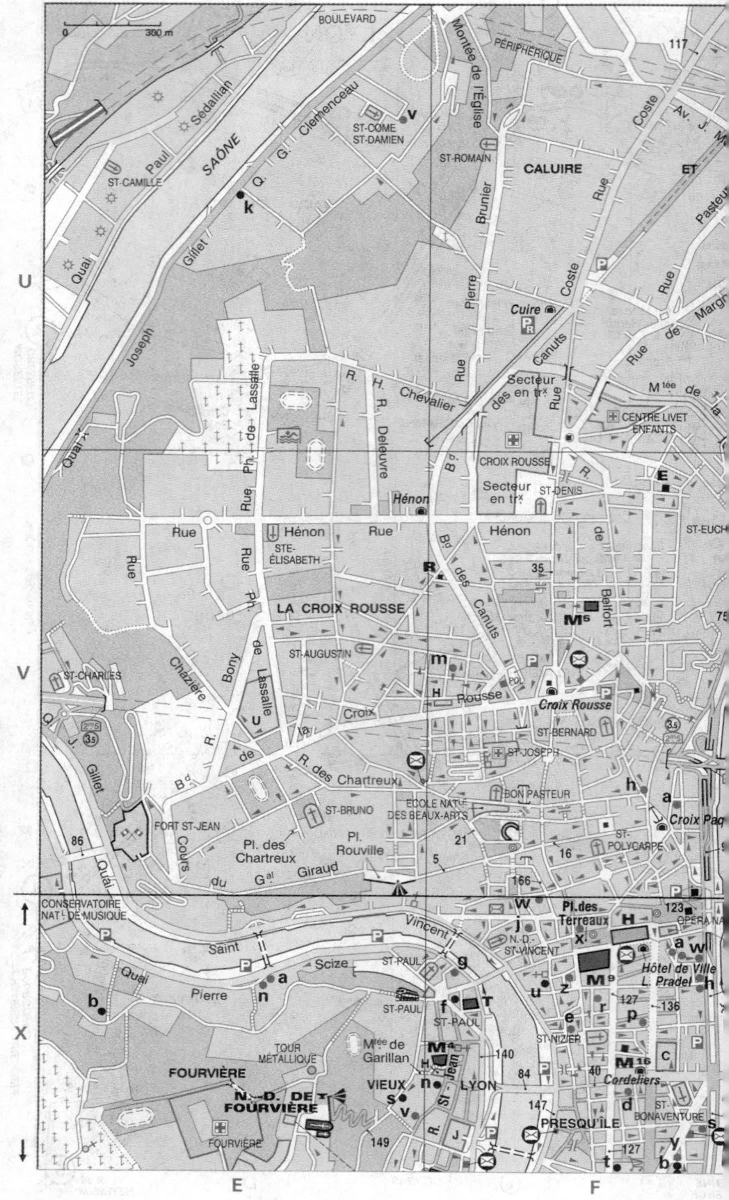
E
F
U
V
X
0
300 m
BOULEVARD
PÉRIPHÉRIQUE
Montée de l'Église
SAÔNE
Quai Paul Sédallian
Q. G. Clemenceau
ST-COME
ST-DAMIEN
ST-ROMAIN
CALUIRE
ST-CAMILLE
Quai Joseph Gillet
Rue Pierre Brunier
Rue Coste
Av. J. M
Rue Pasteur
Rue de Margn
Cuire
Rue des Canuts
Secteur en trx
M tée de la
CENTRE LIVET ENFANTS
R. H. Chevalier
R. Deleuvre
Rue Ph. de Lassalle
CROIX ROUSSE
Secteur en trx
ST-DENIS
Hénon
Rue Hénon
ST-ÉLISABETH
Bd des Canuts
Rue de Belfort
LA CROIX ROUSSE
ST-EUCH
ST-AUGUSTIN
ST-CHARLES
R. Bony
Rue Chazière
Bd de la Croix Rousse
Croix Rousse
ST-BERNARD
ST-JOSEPH
R. des Chartreux
BON PASTEUR
ECOLE NATLE DES BEAUX-ARTS
ST-BRUNO
FORT ST-JEAN
Pl. des Chartreux
Pl. Rouville
Cours du Gal Giraud
ST-POLYCARPE
Croix Paq
Q. J. Gillet
Quai Saint Vincent
CONSERVATOIRE NATL DE MUSIQUE
Quai Pierre Scize
ST-PAUL
N.-D. ST-VINCENT
Pl. des Terreaux
OPÉRA NA
Hôtel de Ville L. Pradel
ST-NIZIER
TOUR MÉTALLIQUE
Mtée de Garillan
FOURVIÈRE
N.-D. DE FOURVIÈRE
VIEUX LYON
R. St-Jean
PRESQU'ÎLE
Cordeliers
ST-BONAVENTURE
117
35
86
21
16
5
166
123
127
136
140
84
40
147
149
M5
M9
M4
M16
E
F

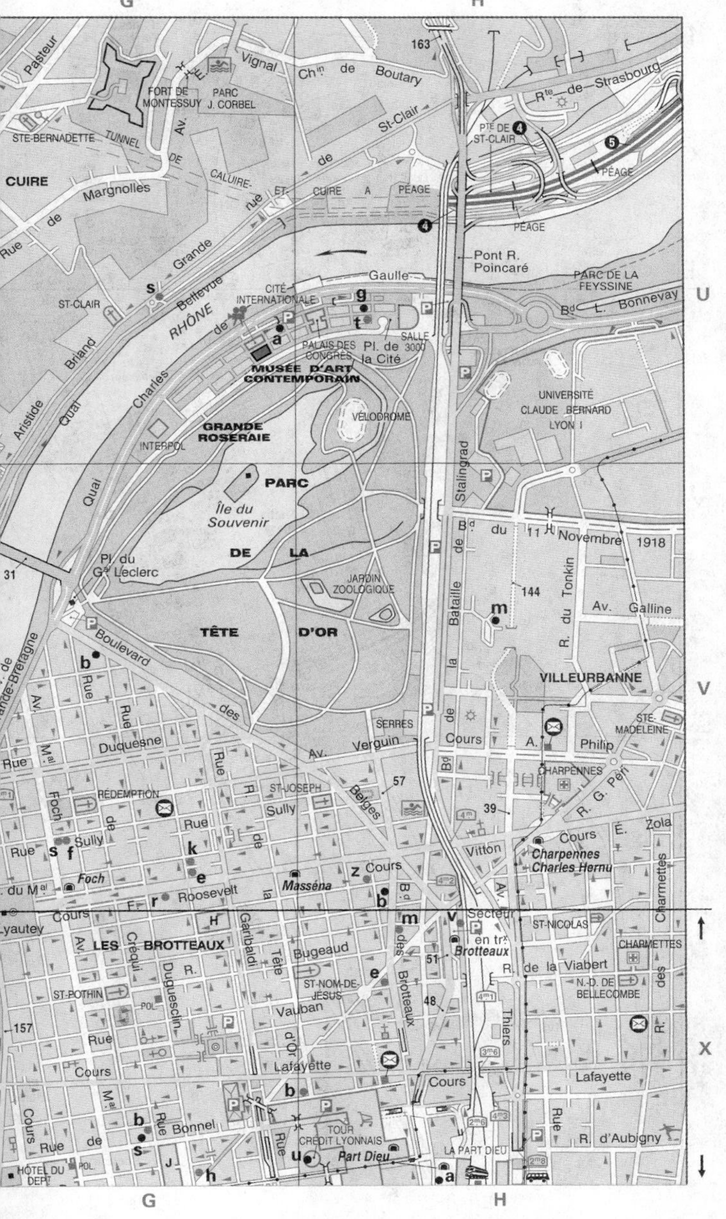

G
H
U
V
X
FORT DE MONTESSUY
PARC J. CORBEL
STE-BERNADETTE
CUIRE
ST-CLAIR
RHÔNE
CITÉ INTERNATIONALE
PALAIS DES CONGRÈS
Pl. de la Cité
SALLE 3000
MUSÉE D'ART CONTEMPORAIN
GRANDE ROSERAIE
INTERPOL
VÉLODROME
PARC
Île du Souvenir
DE LA
TÊTE D'OR
JARDIN ZOOLOGIQUE
Pont R. Poincaré
PARC DE LA FEYSSINE
UNIVERSITÉ CLAUDE BERNARD LYON I
VILLEURBANNE
SERRES
Charpennes Charles Hernu
Masséna
Foch
LES BROTTEAUX
Brotteaux
TOUR CRÉDIT LYONNAIS
Part Dieu
LA PART DIEU
HÔTEL DU DÉPT

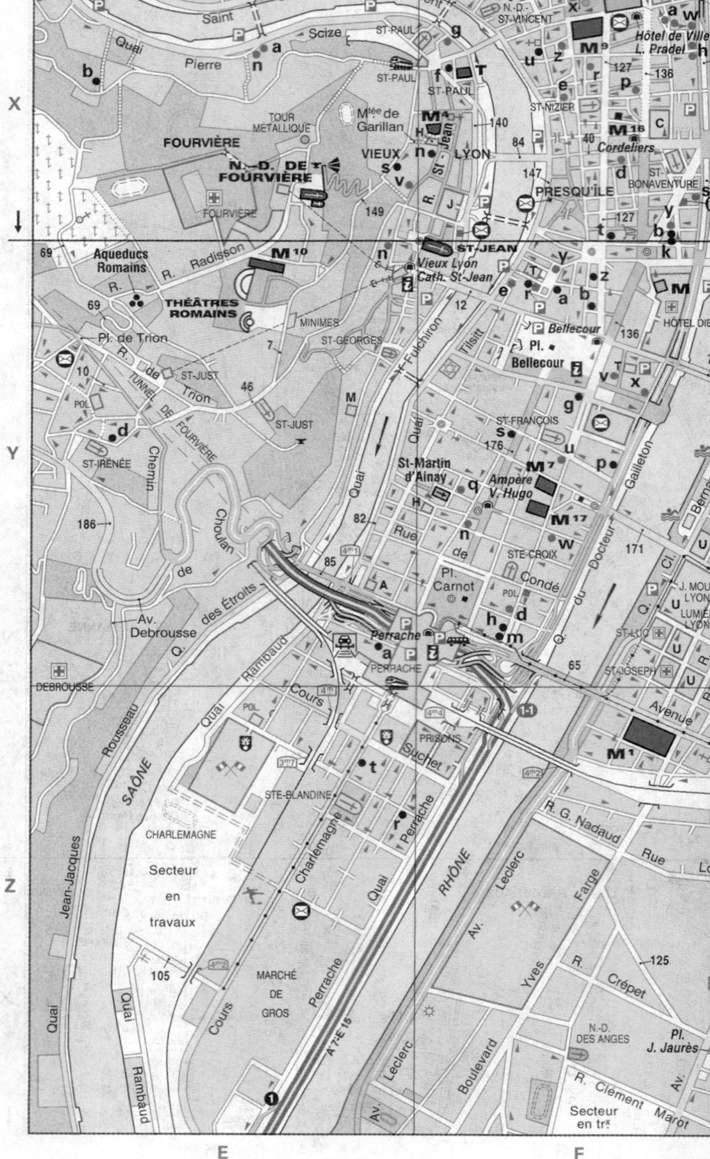
E
F
X
Y
Z
CONSERVATOIRE NATL DE MUSIQUE
Quai Pierre Scize
Saint Vincent
ST-PAUL
N.-D. ST-VINCENT
Pl. des Terreaux
OPÉRA
Hôtel de Ville L. Pradel
ST-NIZIER
TOUR MÉTALLIQUE
FOURVIÈRE
N.-D. DE FOURVIÈRE
Mtée de Garillan
VIEUX LYON
PRESQU'ÎLE
Cordeliers
ST-BONAVENTURE
ST-JEAN
Vieux Lyon Cath. St-Jean
Aqueducs Romains
R. Radisson
THÉÂTRES ROMAINS
MINIMES
ST-GEORGES
Pl. de Trion
R. de Trion
ST-JUST
TUNNEL DE FOURVIÈRE
ST-IRÉNÉE
Chemin de Choulan
Bellecour
Pl. Bellecour
HÔTEL DIEU
Tilsitt
Fulchiron
ST-FRANÇOIS
St-Martin d'Ainay
Ampère V. Hugo
Quai
Rue de Condé
STE-CROIX
Pl. Carnot
Q. du Docteur Gailleton
Av. Debrousse
Q. des Étroits
Perrache
PERRACHE
DEBROUSSE
Quai Rambaud
Cours
PRISONS
Suchet
Rousseau
SAÔNE
STE-BLANDINE
CHARLEMAGNE
Charlemagne
Secteur en travaux
Jean-Jacques
Quai Perrache
RHÔNE
R. G. Nadaud
Rue
Av. Leclerc
Farge
Yves
R. Crépet
MARCHÉ DE GROS
Cours
A7-E15
N.-D. DES ANGES
Pl. J. Jaurès
Boulevard
R. Clément Marot
Secteur en tr^x
J. MOULIN LYON
LUMIÈRE LYON
ST-LUC
ST-JOSEPH
Avenue
Q. Cl.
Bernard

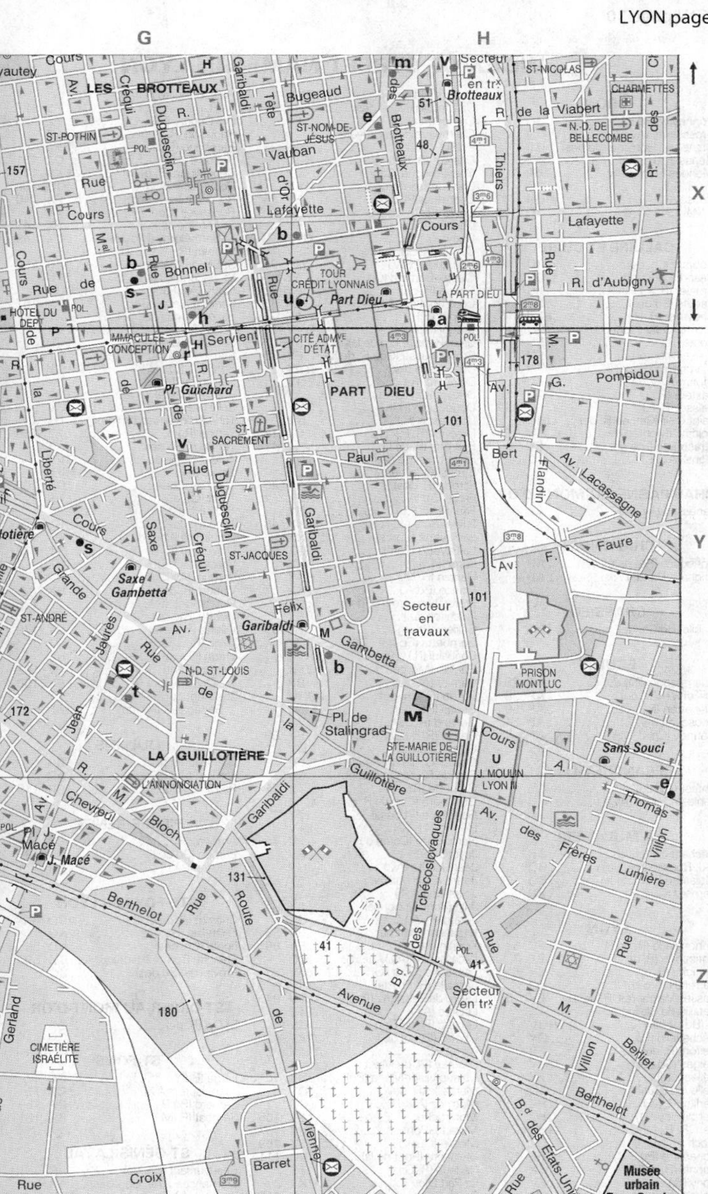
G
H
X
Y
Z
LES BROTTEAUX
Brotteaux
ST-NICOLAS
CHARMETTES
N.-D. DE BELLECOMBE
ST-NOM-DE-JÉSUS
ST-POTHIN
Bugeaud
Vauban
Lafayette
Cours Lafayette
R. de la Viabert
Thiers
R. d'Aubigny
TOUR CRÉDIT LYONNAIS
Part Dieu
LA PART DIEU
HÔTEL DU DEPT
IMMACULÉE CONCEPTION
Servient
CITÉ ADMVE D'ÉTAT
PART DIEU
Pl. Guichard
Av. G. Pompidou
ST-SACREMENT
Paul Bert
Av. Lacassagne
Flandin
Cours de la Liberté
Saxe
Créqui
Duguesclin
Garibaldi
ST-JACQUES
Av. F. Faure
Saxe Gambetta
Grande Rue de la Guillotière
ST-ANDRÉ
Félix
Cours Gambetta
Garibaldi
Secteur en travaux
PRISON MONTLUC
N-D. ST-LOUIS
Pl. de Stalingrad
STE-MARIE DE LA GUILLOTIÈRE
Sans Souci
LA GUILLOTIÈRE
L'ANNONCIATION
J. MOULIN LYON III
A. Thomas
Av. Jean Jaurès
Av. Chevreul
R. M. Bloch
Av. des Frères Lumière
Villon
Tchécoslovaques
Pl. J. Macé
J. Macé
Berthelot
Route de Vienne
Bd des Tchécoslovaques
Avenue Berthelot
Secteur en trx
Rue M. Berliet
Gerland
CIMETIÈRE ISRAÉLITE
Barret
Croix
ST-VINCENT DE PAUL
Bd des États-Unis
Musée urbain Tony-Garnier
157
51
48
178
101
172
131
41
180

INDEX OF STREET NAMES IN LYON

BRON

CALUIRE ET CUIRE

CHAMPAGNE-AU-MONT-D'OR

CHAPONOST

CHASSIEU

ÉCULLY

FRANCHEVILLE

LA MULATIÈRE

LYON

OULLINS

PIERRE-BÉNITE

STE-FOY-LÈS-LYON

ST-DIDIER-AU-MONT-D'OR

ST-FONS

ST-GÉNIS-LAVAL

ST-PRIEST

Briand (R. A.) . . . . **DR**
Dauphiné (R. du) . . . . **DR**
Gambetta (R.) . . . . **DR**
Grande-Rue . . . . **DR**
Herriot (Bd E.) . . . . **DR** 77
Lyonnais (R. du) . . . . **DR**
Maréchal (R. H.) . . . . **DR** 97
Parilly (Bd de) . . . . **DR**
Rostand (R. E.) . . . . **DR** 145
Urbain Est (Bd) . . . . **DR**

TASSIN-LA-DEMI-LUNE

Foch (Av. du Mar.) . . . . **AQ** 53
Gaulle (Av. Ch.-de) . . . . **AQ**
République (Av. de la) . . . . **AQ** 134
Vauboin (Pl. P.) . . . . **AQ**
Victor Hugo (Av.) . . . . **APQ** 175

VAULX-EN-VELIN

Allende (Av. S.) . . . . **DP** 3
Bohlen (Av. de) . . . . **DQ**
Cachin (Av. M.) . . . . **DP**
Dumas (R. A.) . . . . **DQ**
Gaulle (Av. Ch.-de) . . . . **DP** 67
Grandclément (Av.) . . . . **DP**
Marcellin (Av. P.) . . . . **DP**
Péri (Av. G.) . . . . **DP**
Roosevelt (Av. F.) . . . . **DQ**
Salengro (Av. R.) . . . . **DQ**
Soie (Pont de la) . . . . **DP**
8 Mai 1945 (Av. du) . . . . **DP**

VÉNISSIEUX

Bonnevay (Bd L.) . . . . **CR**
Cachin (Av. M.) . . . . **CR** 18
Cagne (Av. J.) . . . . **CR**
Charbonnier (Ch. du) . . . . **CDR**
Croizat (Bd A.) . . . . **CR**
Farge (Bd Y.) . . . . **CR**
Frères L. et É. Bertrand (R. des) . . . . **CR** 61
Gaulle (Av. Ch.-de) . . . . **CR**
Gérin (Bd L.) . . . . **CR**
Grandclément (Pl. J.) . . . . **CR**
Guesde (Av. J.) . . . . **CR**
Joliot Curie (Bd I.) . . . . **CR**
Péri (R. G.) . . . . **CR**
République (Av. de la) . . . . **CR**
Thorez (Av. M.) . . . . **CR**
Vienne (Rte de) . . . . **CQR**

VILLEURBANNE

Bataille de Stalingrad (Bd de la) . . . . **HUV**
Blum (R. L.) . . . . **CDQ**
Bonnevay (Bd L.) . . . . **CP**
Charmettes (R. des) . . . . **HVX**
Chirat (R. F.) . . . . **CQ** 29
Croix Luizet (Pont de) . . . . **CDP**
Dutriévoz (Av. A.) . . . . **HV** 39
Galline (Av.) . . . . **HV**
Genas (Rte de) . . . . **CDQ**
Jean-Jaurès (R.) . . . . **CQ** 80
Philip (Cours A.) . . . . **HV**
Poincaré (Pt R.) . . . . **HU**
Poudrette (R. de la) . . . . **DQ**
Rossellini (Av. R.) . . . . **HV** 144
Salengro (Av. R.) . . . . **CP**
Tolstoï (Cours) . . . . **CQ**
Tonkin (R. du) . . . . **HV**
Zola (Cours Émile) . . . . **CP**
4 Août 1789 (R. du) . . . . **CQ**
11 Novembre 1918 (Bd du) . . . . **HV**

ALPHABETICAL LIST OF HOTELS

ALPHABETICAL LIST OF RESTAURANTS

La Résidence without rest

18 r. V. Hugo ✉ 69002 Ⓜ Bellecour – ✆ 04 78 42 63 28 – www.hotel-la-residence.com – hotel-la-residence@wanadoo.fr – Fax 04 78 42 85 76 p. 8 FY **s**

67 rm – †€ 81 ††€ 81, ☕ € 7

◆ In a pedestrian street near Bellecour square, this hotel provides rooms and a lounge in a 1970s style. A few rooms are more elegant and graced with wainscoting.

Célestins without rest

4 r. Archers ✉ 69002 Ⓜ Guillotière – ✆ 04 72 56 08 98 – www.hotelcelestins.com – info@hotelcelestins.com – Fax 04 72 56 08 65 p. 8 FY **a**

25 rm – †€ 69/110 ††€ 75/120, ☕ € 8,50

◆ Hotel occupying several floors in a residential building. Brigth rooms with simple furnishings; those at the front have a view over the Fourvière hill.

Élysée Hôtel without rest

92 r. Prés. E. Herriot ✉ 69002 Ⓜ Cordeliers – ✆ 04 78 42 03 15 – www.hotel-elysee.fr – accueil@hotel-elysee.fr – Fax 04 78 37 76 49 p. 8 FY **z**

29 rm – †€ 58/69 ††€ 73/82, ☕ € 8

◆ Recently renovated, functional rooms, a central location, continental breakfasts and reasonable prices: this family establishment is popular with a business clientele.

Perrache

Grand Hôtel Mercure Château Perrache

12 cours Verdun ✉ 69002 Ⓜ Perrache – ✆ 04 72 77 15 00 – www.mercure.com – h1292@accor.com – Fax 04 78 37 06 56 p. 8 EY **a**

111 rm – †€ 95/180 ††€ 125/200, ☕ € 17 – 2 suites

Rest *Les Belles Saisons* – *(closed 25 July-25 August, weekends and public holidays)* Carte € 20/38

◆ This hotel built in 1900 has partially conserved its Art Nouveau setting: intricate wood carving in the lobby and period furniture in some of the rooms and suites. The full effect of the Majorelle style is reflected in this superb restaurant.

Charlemagne rest,

23 cours Charlemagne ✉ 69002 Ⓜ Perrache – ✆ 04 72 77 70 00 – www.charlemagne-hotel.fr – charlemagne@hotel-lyon.fr – Fax 04 78 42 94 84 p. 8 EZ **t**

116 rm – †€ 80/125 ††€ 85/135, ☕ € 10

Rest – *(closed Saturday and Sunday)* Menu € 19 bi (weekdays)/50 bi – Carte approx. € 30

◆ Two buildings home to renovated, comfortable and tastefully appointed rooms; a business centre; winter-garden style breakfast room. Modern restaurant with a pleasant terrace in summer and unpretentious, standard fare.

Axotel

12 r. Marc-Antoine Petit ✉ 69002 Ⓜ Perrache – ✆ 04 72 77 70 70 – www.hotel-axotel-perrache.fr – axotel.perrache@hotel-lyon.fr – Fax 04 72 40 00 65 p. 8 EZ **r**

126 rm – †€ 71/95 ††€ 76/95, ☕ € 9

Rest *Le Chalut* – *(closed 27 July-24 August, 21 December-4 January, Friday dinner, Saturday lunch and Sunday)* Menu € 26 – Carte € 32/47

◆ A business clientele appreciates this establishment's extensive seminar facilities. The rooms vary in size and style. As well as excellent fish dishes, there are also some meat dishes on the menu.

Verdun without rest

82 r. de la Charité ✉ 69002 Ⓜ Perrache – ✆ 04 78 37 34 71 – www.hoteldeverdun.com – reservation@hoteldeverdun.com – Fax 04 78 37 45 35 – Closed 2-16 August p. 8 FY **m**

26 rm – †€ 85/130 ††€ 95/140, ☕ € 12

◆ Hotel near the railway station, which has been modernised, but retains all the charm of the original decor. Copious breakfast. Partly non-smoking.

Des Savoies without rest

80 r. de la Charité ✉ 69002 Ⓜ Perrache – ✆ 04 78 37 66 94 – www.hotel-des-savoies.fr – hotel.des.savoies@wanadoo.fr – Fax 04 72 40 27 84

46 rm – †€ 54/74 ††€ 60/78, ☕ € 6 p. 8 FY **h**

◆ A façade embellished with Savoyard coats of arms. Small, functional and recently refurbished rooms. Good value for money. Convenient garage.

Vieux-Lyon

Villa Florentine
25 montée St-Barthélémy ✉ 69005 Ⓜ Fourvière – ✆ 04 72 56 56 56 – www.villaflorentine.com – florentine@relaischateaux.com – Fax 04 72 40 90 56
24 rm – †€ 230/470 ††€ 230/470, ☕ € 25 – 4 suites p. 6 EX **s**
Rest *Les Terrasses de Lyon* – see below
◆ On the Fourvière hill, this Renaissance-inspired abode commands a matchless view of the town. The interior sports an elegant blend of old and new.

Cour des Loges
6 r. Boeuf ✉ 69005 Ⓜ Vieux Lyon Cathédrale Saint-Jean – ✆ 04 72 77 44 44 – www.courdesloges.com – contact@courdesloges.com – Fax 04 72 40 93 61
57 rm – †€ 247/525 ††€ 247/525, ☕ € 27 – 4 suites p. 6 FX **n**
Rest *Les Loges* – *(closed July, August, Sunday and Monday) (dinner only)*
Menu € 58/85 – Carte € 70/89
Rest *Café-Épicerie* – *(closed Tuesday and Wednesday except July-August)*
Menu (€ 17) – Carte € 32/49
◆ An exceptional group of 14C-18C houses set around a splendid galleried courtyard has been decorated by contemporary designers and artists. Creative cuisine and decor with a personal touch. Tempting lunchtime menu at the Café-Épicerie.

Collège without rest
5 pl. St Paul ✉ 69005 Ⓜ Vieux Lyon Cathédrale St -Jean – ✆ 04 72 10 05 05 – www.college-hotel.com – contact@college-hotel.com – Fax 04 78 27 98 84
39 rm – †€ 115 ††€ 115/145, ☕ € 12 p. 6 FX **f**
◆ Take a trip down memory lane: old-fashioned school desks, a pommel horse and geography maps. The rooms are white, resolutely modern, with a balcony or terrace.

Du Greillon without rest
12 montée du Greillon ✉ 69009 – ✆ 06 08 22 26 33 – www.legreillon.com – contact@legreillon.com – Fax 04 72 29 10 97 – Closed 17-31 August and 18-24 February p. 8 EX **b**
4 rm ☕ – †€ 78 ††€ 110
◆ The former property of sculptor J. Chinard has been turned into a guesthouse. Pretty rooms, old furniture and ornaments, gorgeous garden and superb view of the Saône and Croix-Rousse.

La Grange de Fourvière without rest
86 r. des Macchabées ✉ 69005 Ⓜ Saint-Just – ✆ 04 72 33 74 45 – www.grangedefourviere.fr – contact@grangedefourviere.fr p. 8 EY **d**
4 rm ☕ – †€ 55/80 ††€ 65/80
◆ In the "village" of St-Irénée, this 19C barn and stables have been fully converted. Pleasant rooms, sitting room-library and small kitchen for the use of guests.

La Croix-Rousse (banks of the Saône)

Lyon Métropole
85 quai J. Gillet ✉ 69004 – ✆ 04 72 10 44 44 – www.lyonmetropole.com – metropole@lyonmetropole.com – Fax 04 72 10 44 42
118 rm – †€ 180/250 ††€ 180/250, ☕ € 18 p. 6 EU **k**
Rest *Brasserie Lyon Plage* – ✆ 04 72 10 44 30 – Menu (€ 22), € 27 – Carte € 34/53
◆ This 1980s hotel, reflected in the Olympic swimming pool, offers a superb spa, fitness facilities, tennis and squash courts, as well as golf practice areas. Modern rooms. Seafood takes pride of place on the menu of the Brasserie Lyon Plage.

Cité Internationale

Hilton
70 quai Ch.-de-Gaulle ✉ 69006 – ✆ 04 78 17 50 50 – www.hilton.com – reservations.lyon@hilton.com – Fax 04 78 17 52 52 p. 7 GU **a**
199 rm – †€ 100/435 ††€ 100/435, ☕ € 24
Rest *Blue Elephant* – *✆ 04 78 17 50 00 (closed 21 July-18 August, Saturday lunch and Sunday)* Menu € 28, € 43/55 – Carte € 59/66
Rest *Brasserie* – ✆ 04 78 17 51 00 – Menu (€ 21), € 24/42 – Carte € 40/60
◆ This impressive modern hotel built in brick and glass is equipped with a comprehensive business centre. Fully equipped bedrooms and apartments facing the Tête d'Or park or the Rhône. Thai specialities and decor at the Blue Elephant. Traditional food is to be found at the Brasserie.

De la Cité rest, VISA

22 quai Ch.-de-Gaulle ✉ 69006 – ✆ 04 78 17 86 86
– www.lyon.concorde-hotels.com – hoteldelacite@concorde-hotels.com
– Fax 04 78 17 86 99 *p. 6* HU **g**
164 rm – €95/280 €95/345, ☕ €20 – 5 suites
Rest – *(closed 1st-16 August)* Menu (€20 bi), €29 (weekday lunch)
– Carte €27/43

◆ This modern building designed by Renzo Piano stands between the Tête d'Or park and the Rhône. Bright rooms decorated in a contemporary vein. Traditional meals (buffet lunch). Terrace overlooking the patio of the Cité Internationale. Cocktail bar.

Les Brotteaux

Du Parc without rest VISA

16 bd des Brotteaux ✉ 69006 Ⓜ Brotteaux – ✆ 04 72 83 12 20
– www.hotelduparc-lyon.com – accueil@hotelduparc-lyon.com
– Fax 04 78 52 14 32 *p. 7* HV **b**
23 rm – €87/139 €97/149, ☕ €11

◆ Hotel situated between the Brotteaux train station and the Tête d'Or park. The rooms, quieter at the back, have a welcoming decor and modern fittings.

La Part-Dieu

Novotel La Part-Dieu rm, rest, VISA

47 bd Vivier-Merle ✉ 69003 Ⓜ Part Dieu – ✆ 04 72 13 51 51 – www.novotel.com
– h0735@accor.com – Fax 04 72 13 51 99 *p. 9* HX **a**
124 rm – €120/165 €120/165, ☕ €15
Rest – Menu (€21), €25 (weekdays) – Carte €24/48

◆ Two minutes from the railway station. The rooms are being progressively revamped in line with latest Novotel standards. Lounge-bar with an Internet area. This Novotel restaurant is practical for business travellers with a train to catch or between meetings.

Radisson SAS VISA

129 r. Servient, (32th Floor) ✉ 69003 Ⓜ Part Dieu – ✆ 04 78 63 55 00
– www.lyon.radissonsas.com – info.lyon@radissonsas.com
– Fax 04 78 63 55 20 *p. 7* GX **u**
245 rm – €125/285 €125/285, ☕ €21
Rest *L'Arc-en-Ciel* – *(closed 15 July-27 August, Saturday lunch and Sunday)*
Menu €44/89 – Carte €79/120
Rest *Bistrot de la Tour* – *(closed Saturday and Sunday) (lunch only)*
Menu €16 bi/20

◆ At the top of the "pencil" (100m high), interior layout inspired by the houses of old Lyons: interior courtyards and superimposed galleries. Exceptional view from some rooms. The Arc-en-Ciel is on the 32nd floor of the tower. Packed at lunchtime.

Créqui Part-Dieu rm, VISA

37 r. Bonnel ✉ 69003 Ⓜ Place Guichard – ✆ 04 78 60 20 47
– www.bestwestern-lyonpartdieu.com – directeur@hotel-crequi.com
– Fax 04 78 62 21 12 *p. 7* GX **s**
46 rm – €73/165 €73/175, ☕ €13 – 3 suites
Rest *Le Magistère* – *(Closed August, Saturday and Sunday)* Menu (€15), €18/30
– Carte €26/41

◆ The establishment is located opposite the law courts district. The renovated rooms are decorated in warm tones; those in the new wing are particularly modern in style.

La Guillotière

De Noailles without rest VISA

30 cours Gambetta ✉ 69007 Ⓜ Guillotière – ✆ 04 78 72 40 72
– www.hoteldenoailles.fr – hotel-de-noailles@wanadoo.fr – Fax 04 72 71 09 10
– Closed 31 July-24 August *p. 9* GY **s**
24 rm – €80/114 €87/129, ☕ €14

◆ The well-kept rooms open onto the inner courtyard or the garden. The garage and nearby underground station make this a handy spot.

Gerland

Novotel Gerland   rm, AC, VISA, MC, AE

70 av. Leclerc ✉ 69007 – ✆ 04 72 71 11 11 – www.novotel.com – h0736@accor.com – Fax 04 72 71 11 00   *p. 4* BQ **e**

186 rm – †€ 88/199 ††€ 88/199, ☕ € 15

Rest – Menu (€ 22), € 26 – Carte € 30/44

◆ Near Tony Garnier market and the football stadium, this Novotel has been renovated from top to toe: attractive modern rooms, hi-tech bar lounge and spacious seminar facilities. Pleasant rendering of the chain's latest style; traditional menu.

Montchat-Monplaisir

Mercure Lumière   rm, AC, VISA, MC, AE

69 cours A. Thomas ✉ 69003 Ⓜ Sans Souci – ✆ 04 78 53 76 76 – www.mercure.com – h1535@accor.com – Fax 04 72 36 97 65   *p. 9* HZ **e**

78 rm – †€ 79/200 ††€ 89/220, ☕ € 17

Rest – *(closed 8-16 August, Saturday, Sunday and public holidays)* Menu (€ 19), € 24 (weekday lunch) – Carte € 32/42

◆ Located near the Lumière film studios, this Mercure understandably pays homage to the silver screen. The practical rooms are all identical. Photos recalling the history of film adorn the contemporary dining room.

in Villeurbanne – pop. 134 800 – alt. 168 m – ✉ 69100

Congrès   AC, VISA, MC, AE

pl. Cdt Rivière – ✆ 04 72 69 16 16 – www.hoteldescongres.com – reservation@hoteldescongres.com – Fax 04 78 94 64 86 – Closed 24 December-4 January

134 rm – †€ 116/138 ††€ 127/149, ☕ € 15   *p. 7* HV **m**

Rest – *(closed Friday dinner, Saturday and Sunday)* Menu (€ 13 bi), € 20 (dinner)

◆ Concrete architecture near the Tête d'Or park. Standard 1980s decor. The Prestige rooms are more spacious and well cared for. Traditional fare in the restaurant.

Holiday Inn Garden Court   rm, AC, VISA, MC, AE

130 bd du 11 Nov. 1918 – ✆ 04 78 89 95 95 – www.holidayinn-lyon-villeurbanne.com – higcvilleurbanne@alliance-hospitality.com – Fax 04 72 43 91 55   *p. 5* CP **r**

79 rm – †€ 79/200 ††€ 79/200, ☕ € 15

Rest – *(closed Friday dinner, Sunday lunch and Saturday)* Menu (€ 13), € 22 (weekdays)/26 – Carte € 32/44

◆ The comfortable, well-appointed rooms, modular conference areas and practical location make this hotel popular with a business clientele. Bright sunny dining room and traditional menu.

in Bron – pop. 38 700 – alt. 204 m – ✉ 69500

Novotel Bron   rm, AC, P, VISA, MC, AE

260 av. J. Monnet – ✆ 04 72 15 65 65 – www.novotel.com – h0436@accor.com – Fax 04 72 15 09 09   *p. 5* DR **f**

190 rm – †€ 95/200 ††€ 95/200, ☕ € 16

Rest – Menu (€ 21), € 25 (weekdays) – Carte € 27/39

◆ Well equipped for seminars, this handy hotel now sports a decor and level of comfort in keeping with the new Novotel standards. Contemporary restaurant and traditional menu, conveniently located just outside Lyons.

Restaurants

Paul Bocuse   AC, P, VISA, MC, AE

40 r. de la Plage, near the Pont de Collonges, 12 km north along the Saône (D 433, D 51) ✉ 69660 – ✆ 04 72 42 90 90 – www.bocuse.fr – paul.bocuse@bocuse.fr – Fax 04 72 27 85 87   *p. 4* BP

Rest – Menu € 125/210 – Carte € 111/188

Spec. Soupe aux truffes noires VGE. Volaille de Bresse en vessie. Gâteau "Le Président". **Wines** Condrieu, Côte-Rôtie.

◆ The culinary world beats a path to the colourful, elegant inn of the eponymous "Monsieur Paul". His celebrated dishes in the dining room, murals of great chefs in the courtyard.

XXXX ✿ **Pierre Orsi**

3 pl. Kléber ✉ 69006 Ⓜ Masséna – ✆ 04 78 89 57 68 – www.pierreorsi.com – orsi@relaischateaux.com – Fax 04 72 44 93 34 – Closed Sunday and Monday except public holidays *p. 7* GV **e**

Rest – Menu € 60 (weekday lunch), € 85/115 – Carte € 70/135

Spec. Ravioles de foie gras de canard au jus de porto et truffes. Homard acadien en carapace "façon Pierre Orsi". Délice Geneviève (autumn). **Wines** Saint-Joseph, Pouilly-Fuissé.

◆ This venerable establishment is home to elegant dining rooms and a rose garden terrace. Fine up-to-date cuisine and good wine list.

XXX ✿ **Les Terrasses de Lyon** – Hôtel Villa Florentine

25 montée St-Barthélémy ✉ 69005 Ⓜ Fourvière – ✆ 04 72 56 56 02 – www.villaflorentine.com – lesterrassesdelyon@villaflorentine.com – Fax 04 72 56 56 04 – Closed Sunday and Monday *p. 6* EX **s**

Rest – Menu € 48 (weekday lunch)/104 – Carte € 100/144

Spec. Foie gras de canard façon "Melba". Filet mignon de veau rôti au lard fermier. Chocolat manjari à la fève de Tonka. **Wines** Crozes-Hermitage, Saint-Joseph.

◆ Breathtaking view of Lyon from the terrace. The interior and conservatory are stylish and the modern cuisine subtly enhances excellent produce.

XXX ✿✿ **Nicolas Le Bec**

14 r. Grolée ✉ 69002 Ⓜ Cordeliers – ✆ 04 78 42 15 00 – www.nicolaslebec.com – restaurant@nicolaslebec.com – Fax 04 72 40 98 97 – Closed 3-24 August, Sunday, Monday and public holidays *p. 6* FX **y**

Rest – Menu € 68 (weekday lunch), € 118/158 – Carte € 90/130

Spec. Côtes de romaine et Saint-Jacques dorées (season). Pigeonneau cuit en croûte de moutarde. Tarte au caramel mou et pralines blanches. **Wines** Mâcon, Condrieu.

◆ The muted and intimate taupe and black decor of this restaurant is eminently suited to the cuisine, which is subtle and inventive delicat. Fine wine list.

XXX ✿✿ **Mère Brazier** (Mathieu Viannay)

12 r. Royale ✉ 69001 Ⓜ Hôtel de Ville – ✆ 04 78 23 17 20 – www.lamerebrazier.fr – merebrazier@orange.fr – Fax 04 78 23 37 18 – Closed 1st-23 August, 20-28 February, Saturday and Sunday *p. 6* FV **a**

Rest – Menu (€ 31), € 35 (weekday lunch), € 55/95 – Carte € 86/124

Spec. Pâté en croûte au foie gras. Volaille de Bresse et homard sauce suprême, jus de carapace. Paris-Brest et glace aux noisettes caramélisées.

◆ This iconic Lyonnais establishment is now home to chef Mathieu Viannay. The dining room has undergone a subtle refurbishment and the charming old-fashioned decor has returned. Culinary harmony combining classical and contemporary elements.

XXX ✿ **Christian Têtedoie**

54 quai Pierre Scize ✉ 69005 – ✆ 04 78 29 40 10 – www.tetedoie.com – restaurant@tetedoie.com – Fax 04 72 07 05 65 – Closed Saturday lunch, Monday lunch and Sunday *p. 6* EX **n**

Rest – Menu € 50/82 – Carte € 60/75

Spec. Quenelle de brochet farcie aux écrevisses. Homard et tête de veau confite au jus de carotte. Sablé breton en duo de framboise et poivron doux (March to Nov.). **Wines** Crozes-Hermitage, Vin de Vienne.

◆ This carefully decorated, elegant establishment (flowers, ornaments, paintings) is on the banks of the Saône. Modern cuisine complemented by a wine list of over 700 appellations.

XXX ✿ **Les Trois Dômes** – Hôtel Sofitel

20 quai Gailleton, (8th Floor) ✉ 69002 Ⓜ Bellecour – ✆ 04 72 41 20 97 – www.les-3-domes.com – reservation@les-3-domes.com – Fax 04 72 40 05 50 – Closed 1st July-30 September, 15-23 February, Sunday and Monday *p. 8* FY **p**

Rest – Menu € 56 (weekday lunch), € 79/129 – Carte € 112/135

Spec. Millefeuille de crabe et avocat, huile parfumée au gingembre rose et citron jaune. Volaille de Bresse au citron et tomates séchées, courgette fleur et gnocchis au parmesan. Trois grands crus de chocolats. **Wines** Hermitage, Crozes-Hermitage.

◆ Admire the matchless panorama from the top floor of the Sofitel hotel, where you can also enjoy delicious contemporary cuisine matched with fine wines.

Auberge de Fond Rose (Gérard Vignat)
23 quai G. Clemenceau ✉ 69300 Caluire-et-Cuire – ✆ 04 78 29 34 61 – www.aubergedefondrose.com – contact@aubergedefondrose.com – Fax 04 72 00 28 67 – Closed autumn school holidays, 16 February-3 March, Tuesday from October to March, Sunday dinner and Monday except bank holidays *p. 6* EU **v**
Rest – Menu € 40 bi (weekday lunch), € 55/85 – Carte € 75/85
Spec. Rémoulade de grenouilles et minestrone de petits légumes. Pigeonneau cuit dans la rôtissoire et jus aux olives. Fondant tiède au chocolat guanaja et glace vanille. **Wines** Côte-Rôtie, Cornas.
◆ This handsome 1920s house features an idyllic terrace leading into the garden planted with ancient trees. Fine up-to-date menu and interesting wine list.

Léon de Lyon
1 r. Pleney, corner of r. du Plâtre ✉ 69001 Ⓜ Hôtel de ville – ✆ 04 72 10 11 12 – www.leondelyon.com – reservation@leondelyon.com – Fax 04 72 10 11 13
Rest – Menu (€ 21), € 25/32 – Carte € 32/48 *p. 8* FX **r**
◆ This institution in Lyon, now in the form of a luxurious brasserie, has lost nothing of its appeal. Excellent produce that does full justice to local gourmet specialities and delicacies.

Auberge de l'Île (Jean-Christophe Ansanay-Alex)
On Barbe Island ✉ 69009 – ✆ 04 78 83 99 49 – www.aubergedelile.com – info@aubergedelile.com – Fax 04 78 47 80 46 – Closed Sunday and Monday *p. 4* BP **e**
Rest – Menu € 95/125
Spec. Velouté de cèpes dans l'esprit d'un cappuccino, lardons de foie gras à la vapeur (autumn). Mignon d'agneau en croûte de sel, tomates "cœur de pigeon" en aigre-doux (spring-summer). Glace à la réglisse, cornet de pain d'épice. **Wines** Condrieu, Côte-Rôtie.
◆ Situated on Île Barbe, this charming 17C inn is known for its fine cuisine made from local, seasonal produce. The chef himself comes to your table to announce his legendary dish of the day.

La Rémanence
31 r. du Bât-d'Argent ✉ 69001 Ⓜ Hôtel de Ville – ✆ 04 72 00 08 08 – www.laremanence.fr – contact@laremanence.fr – Fax 04 78 39 85 10 – Closed 2-24 August, Sunday and Monday *p. 6* FX **h**
Rest – Menu € 27 (weekday lunch), € 35/69 – Carte € 45/68
◆ Near the town hall, the golden stone vaulted rooms of this restaurant were once the Jesuit refectory. Inventive cuisine rustled up by a talented young chef.

L'Alexandrin (Laurent Rigal)
83 r. Moncey ✉ 69003 Ⓜ Place Guichard – ✆ 04 72 61 15 69 – www.lalexandrin.com – laurent.rigal@lalexandrin.com – Fax 04 78 62 75 57 – Closed 2-25 August, 20-28 December, Sunday and Monday *p. 7* GX **h**
Rest – Menu € 60 bi/150
Spec. Terrine de foie gras de canard et coeur de pêche aux épices douces (15 July to 15 September). Quenelle de brochet au crémeux d'écrevisse. Madeleine au chocolat à la marmelade d'orange. **Wines** Saint-Péray, Crozes-Hermitage.
◆ A new team and new decor at this popular restaurant. Impressive choice of Côtes-du-Rhône, and regional dishes prepared with an original flair. Terrace.

Le Gourmet de Sèze (Bernard Mariller)
129 r. Sèze ✉ 69006 Ⓜ Masséna – ✆ 04 78 24 23 42 – www.le-gourmet-de-seze.com – legourmetdeseze@wanadoo.fr – Fax 04 78 24 66 81 – Closed 21-25 May, 25 July-20 August, 15-18 February, Sunday, Monday and public holidays *p. 7* HV **z**
Rest – *(number of covers limited, pre-book)* Menu (€ 25), € 37 (weekday lunch), € 47/100
Spec. Croustillants de pieds de cochon compotés à la moutarde. Saint-Jacques de la baie de Saint-Brieuc (October to March). Grand dessert du gourmet. **Wines** Saint-Aubin, Saint-Joseph.
◆ Dining room in tones of white and chocolate, furnished with medallion chairs and well-spaced round tables. Classic cuisine that is skilfully modernised, and appeals well beyond the Rue de Sèze.

XX **Cazenove** A/C VISA AE

75 r. Boileau ✉ 69006 Ⓜ Masséna – ✆ 04 78 89 82 92 – www.le-cazenove.com – orsi@relaischateaux.com – Fax 04 72 44 93 34 – Closed August, Saturday and Sunday p. 7 GV **k**

Rest – Menu € 35 (weekdays)/75 bi – Carte € 42/107

◆ Low-key ambiance and a fine Belle Époque-inspired interior: upholstered banquettes, mirrors, old-fashioned wall lighting and bronze statues. Traditional, sometimes inventive, cooking.

XX **Le Passage** A/C VISA AE

8 r. Plâtre ✉ 69001 Ⓜ Hôtel de ville – ✆ 04 78 28 11 16 – www.le-passage.com – restaurant@le-passage.com – Fax 04 72 00 84 34 – Closed August, Saturday lunch, Sunday, Monday and public holidays p. 8 FX **r**

Rest – Menu € 38/54 – Carte € 48/80

◆ Theatre seats and trompe-l'oeil backdrop in the bistro, more restrained decor in the main room and a courtyard-terrace adorned with frescoes. Reinterpreted classic repertoire.

XX **J.-C. Pequet** A/C VISA AE

59 pl. Voltaire ✉ 69003 Ⓜ Saxe Lafayette – ✆ 04 78 95 49 70 – Fax 04 78 62 85 26 – Closed August, 24 December-2 January, Saturday and Sunday p. 9 GY **v**

Rest – Menu € 29/52

◆ Decor without eccentricity and thoughtful classical cooking based on market produce: a reliable establishment with a regular clientele.

XX **Alex** A/C VISA AE

44 bd des Brotteaux ✉ 69006 Ⓜ Brotteaux – ✆ 04 78 52 30 11 – chez.alex@club-internet.fr – Fax 04 78 52 34 16 – Closed August, Sunday and Monday p. 8 HX **e**

Rest – Menu (€ 19), € 23 (weekday lunch), € 28/59 – Carte approx. € 52

◆ Restaurant whose smart, refined setting boldly allies colour, designer furniture and contemporary artworks. Menu concocted by the owner-chef from market produce.

XX **La Brunoise** A/C VISA

4 r. A. Boutin ✉ 69100 Villeurbanne Ⓜ Charpennes – ✆ 04 78 52 07 77 – www.labrunoise.fr – Fax 04 72 83 54 96 – Closed 20 July-20 August, 2-7 January, Sunday dinner, Monday dinner, Tuesday and Wednesday p. 5 CP **b**

Rest – Menu (€ 17), € 20 (weekday lunch), € 25/58 bi – Carte € 28/48

◆ The house specialities decorate the façade. Bright dining room. Modern menu inspired by classic dishes.

XX **La Tassée** A/C VISA AE

20 r. Charité ✉ 69002 Ⓜ Bellecour – ✆ 04 72 77 79 00 – www.latassee.fr – jpborgeot@latassee.fr – Fax 04 72 40 05 91 – Closed Sunday p. 8 FY **u**

Rest – Menu € 28/78 – Carte € 43/69

◆ The photos of famous clients adorn the walls of this elegant and welcoming institution of Lyon. The cuisine displays a masterful mix of tradition and modernity.

XX **Brasserie Georges** VISA AE

30 cours Verdun ✉ 69002 Ⓜ Perrache – ✆ 04 72 56 54 54 – www.brasseriegeorges.com – brasserie.georges@orange.fr – Fax 04 78 42 51 65

Rest – Menu € 20/25 – Carte € 25/42 p. 8 FZ **b**

◆ Good beer and good cheer since 1836, an Art Deco setting meticulously preserved since 1925 and relaxed ambiance: this listed brasserie is one of the landmarks of Lyons.

XX **La Voûte - Chez Léa** A/C VISA AE

11 pl. A. Gourju ✉ 69002 Ⓜ Bellecour – ✆ 04 78 42 01 33 – Fax 04 78 37 36 41 – Closed Sunday p. 8 FY **e**

Rest – Menu (€ 16), € 19 (weekday lunch), € 30/40 – Carte € 30/56

◆ One of the oldest restaurants in Lyons, it continues to brilliantly uphold the region's gastronomic traditions. Welcoming ambiance and decor. Game menu in autumn.

XX **Le Potiquet** A/C VISA AE

27 r. de l'Arbre Sec ✉ 69001 Ⓜ Hotel de ville – ✆ 04 78 30 65 44 – lepotiquet@free.fr – Closed August, Saturday lunch, Sunday and Monday p. 6 FX **w**

Rest – Menu € 29/49 – Carte € 37/46

◆ Elegance and sobriety set the scene for this pleasant family restaurant that serves up-to-date cuisine, often summery in flavour, always well prepared and sometimes surprising.

Maison Clovis AC VISA MC AE
19 bd Brotteaux ✉ 69006 Ⓜ Brotteaux – ✆ 04 72 74 44 61 – ckcloviskhoury@yahoo.fr – Closed 10-31 August, Sunday and Monday p. 7 HX **m**
Rest – Menu (€ 19), € 39/65 bi – Carte € 53/73
◆ This new establishment is greatly appreciated for its contemporary decor (grey colour scheme and designer furniture) and its gourmet cuisine. Simpler midday menu.

Argenson Gerland AC P VISA MC AE
40 allée P.-de-Coubertin, at Gerland ✉ 69007 Ⓜ Stade de Gerland – ✆ 04 72 73 72 73 – www.nordsudbrasseries.com – argenson2@wanadoo.fr – Fax 04 72 73 72 74 p. 4 BR **a**
Rest – Menu (€ 21), € 23 – Carte € 40/70
◆ One of the brasseries opened by Paul Bocuse, near the Gerland stadium. Stylish interior and pleasant shaded terrace. Traditional menu with a distinct southern flavour.

Le Nord AC VISA MC AE
18 r. Neuve ✉ 69002 Ⓜ Hôtel de ville – ✆ 04 72 10 69 69 – www.bocuse.fr – commercial@brasseries-bocuse.com – Fax 04 72 10 69 68 p. 8 FX **p**
Rest – Menu € 23 (weekdays)/33 – Carte € 26/50
◆ Authentic 1900s decor in the first of Bocuse's brasseries: banquettes, colourful tiled floor, wood panelling and spherical lamps. Traditional cuisine.

L'Est AC VISA MC AE
14 pl. J. Ferry, (Brotteaux station) ✉ 69006 Ⓜ Brotteaux – ✆ 04 37 24 25 26 – www.bocuse.fr – commercial@brasseries-bocuse.com – Fax 04 37 24 25 25 p. 9 HX **v**
Rest – Menu € 24 (weekdays)/29 – Carte € 32/50
◆ Trendy Bocuse brasserie popular with the locals. The kitchens can be seen from the dining room, miniature trains chug round above diners' heads and world cooking is on the menu.

L'Ouest AC VISA MC AE
1 quai Commerce, North via the banks of the Saône (D 51) ✉ 69009 – ✆ 04 37 64 64 64 – www.nordsudbrasseries.com – commercial@brasseries-bocuse.com – Fax 04 37 64 64 65 p. 4 BP **a**
Rest – Menu € 24 (weekdays)/29 – Carte € 35/56
◆ A distinctive modern building of wood, concrete and metal. Bar, giant screens, open kitchen, river-facing terrace and exotic dishes. Bocuse is on a western course!

33 Cité AC VISA MC AE
33 quai Charles de Gaulle ✉ 69006 – ✆ 04 37 45 45 45 – 33cite.restaurant@free.fr – Fax 04 37 45 45 46 p. 7 HU **t**
Rest – Menu (€ 19), € 23/27 – Carte € 35/53
◆ Contemporary designer setting opposite the Salle 3000 at the Cité Internationale. View of the Parc de la Tête d'Or through the large windows. Choice of modern and classic dishes.

Le Sud AC VISA MC AE
11 pl. Antonin-Poncet ✉ 69002 Ⓜ Bellecour – ✆ 04 72 77 80 00 – www.bocuse.fr – commercial@brasseries-bocuse.com – Fax 04 72 77 80 01 p. 8 FY **x**
Rest – Menu € 23 (weekdays)/28 – Carte € 33/45
◆ "Le Sud" is another of chef Paul Bocuse's creations, with Mediterranean cuisine and decor. Delightful summer terrace overlooking the square.

Le Verre et l'Assiette VISA MC
20 Grande Rue de Vaise ✉ 69009 – ✆ 04 78 83 32 25 – www.leverreetlassiette.com – leverreetlassiette@free.fr – Closed 25 July-17 August, 6-15 February, Saturday and Sunday p. 4 BP **d**
Rest – Menu (€ 19 bi), € 28 (weekdays)/42
◆ The talented chef reinvents and personalises traditional Lyon specialities as well as a few French classics. Stone and wood prevail in the modern decor. Cheerful service.

Le Contretête VISA MC AE
55 quai Pierre Scize ✉ 69005 – ✆ 04 78 29 41 29 – restaurant@tetedoie.com – Fax 04 72 07 05 65 – Closed 2-23 August, Saturday lunch and Sunday p. 6 EX **a**
Rest – Menu (€ 17) – Carte € 25/35
◆ This bistro, run by the restaurateur Christian Têtedoie, focuses on authentic home cooking. An interior decor strewn with old objects and utensils.

Le Gabion

13 bd E. Deruelle ✉ 69003 Ⓜ Part Dieu – ✆ 04 72 60 81 57 – www.legabion.fr – legabion@wanadoo.fr – Fax 04 78 60 83 18 – Closed 1st-21 August, Sunday and public holidays p. 7 HX **b**

Rest – Menu (€ 16), € 19 (lunch)/25 – Carte € 28/45

◆ Unusual modern decor with a wall of pebbles in steel mesh by the architect Chaduc. Seafood and fish dishes, sometimes with a sprinkling of Eastern spices.

Les Oliviers

20 r. Sully ✉ 69006 Ⓜ Foch – ✆ 04 78 89 07 09 – Fax 04 72 43 03 32 – Closed 1st-8 May, August, Saturday, Sunday and public holidays p. 7 GV **f**

Rest – Menu (€ 17), € 24/33 – Carte € 34/45

◆ A tiny corner of Provence hidden here in Lyon: intimate, low key dining room in warm colours and a tasty, sun-drenched cuisine.

M

47 av. Foch ✉ 69006 Ⓜ Foch – ✆ 04 78 89 55 19 – restaurant.mviannay@orange.fr – Fax 04 78 89 08 39 – Closed 1st-23 August, 20-28 February, Saturday and Sunday p. 7 GV **s**

Rest – Menu (€ 19), € 25/35

◆ This establishment is very appealing with its open plan, minimalist, faintly psychedelic interior dotted with orange arabesques. Up-to-date cuisine steeped in flavour.

Les Comédiens

2 pl. Célestins ✉ 69002 Ⓜ Bellecour – ✆ 04 78 42 08 26 – lescomedienslyon@aol.com – Closed 1st-22 August, Sunday and Monday p. 8 FY **y**

Rest – Menu € 23 (weekday lunch), € 28/48 – Carte € 30/50

◆ This restaurant is located near the Célestins theatre. A fashionable colour scheme of cream and chocolate tones. Traditional menu and a few regional dishes.

Francotte

8 pl. Célestins ✉ 69002 Ⓜ Bellecour – ✆ 04 78 37 38 64 – www.francotte.fr – p.quarre@orange.fr – Fax 04 78 38 20 35 – Closed 1st-17 August, Sunday and Monday p. 8 FY **r**

Rest – Menu € 24/32 – Carte € 33/50

◆ Brasserie-style cuisine in a bistro/bouchon-inspired setting adorned with photos of matriarchs and famous chefs from the region. Breakfasts served in the morning; tea room in the afternoon.

La Machonnerie

36 r. Tramassac ✉ 69005 Ⓜ Ampère Victor Hugo – ✆ 04 78 42 24 62 – www.lamachonnerie.com – felix@lamachonnerie.com – Fax 04 72 40 23 32 – Closed 15-30 July, 2 weeks in January, Sunday and lunch except Saturday p. 8 EY **n**

Rest – *(dinner only) (pre-book)* Menu € 20 (weekdays)/45 bi – Carte € 30/45

◆ The traditions of informal service, a friendly atmosphere and authentic regional cuisine are perpetuated in this typical neighbourhood *mâchon*. Attractive lounge devoted to jazz.

La Terrasse St-Clair

2 Grande Rue St-Clair ✉ 69300 Caluire-et-Cuire – ✆ 04 72 27 37 37 – www.terrasse-saint-clair.com – clementboucher@wanadoo.fr – Fax 04 72 27 37 38 – Closed 5-22 August, 23 December-15 January, Sunday and Monday p. 7 GU **s**

Rest – Menu (€ 18), € 30/40

◆ There is a slight air of an open-air dance hall about the restaurant and especially the terrace shaded by plane trees. Pétanque pitch.

Les Adrets

30 r. Boeuf ✉ 69005 Ⓜ Vieux Lyon Cathédrale Saint Jean – ✆ 04 78 38 24 30 – Fax 04 78 42 79 52 – Closed 13-17 April, 1st-8 May, August, 25-31 December, Saturday and Sunday p. 6 EX **v**

Rest – Menu (€ 16 bi), € 23 (weekday dinner), € 30/45 – Carte € 35/52 (dinner only)

◆ A venerable establishment in Vieux Lyons. Rustic interior with exposed beams, tiled floor and a partial view of the kitchens. Hearty traditional dishes.

L'Étage A/C VISA MC
4 pl. Terreaux, (2nd floor) ✉ 69001 Ⓜ Hôtel de ville – ✆ 04 78 28 19 59 – Fax 04 78 28 19 59 – Closed 19 July-21 August, Sunday and Monday p. 8 FX **x**
Rest – *(pre-book)* Menu € 34/56 – Carte € 55/71
◆ Located on the building's second floor (no lift), this refitted silk worker's studio has a stylish up-to-date setting and is popular with Lyon folk. Appetising, creative menu.

Le Comptoir des Marronniers A/C VISA MC AE
8 r. des Marronniers ✉ 69002 Ⓜ Bellecour – ✆ 04 72 77 10 00 – www.comptoir-des-marronniers.com – bistrotsdecuisiniers@leondelyon.com – Fax 04 72 77 10 01 – Closed 2-23 August, Monday lunch and Sunday p. 8 FY **v**
Rest – Menu (€ 20), € 23
◆ In a pedestrian street near Bellecour square, a "chef's bistro", seemingly haphazardly decorated with a profusion of objects and posters relating to cooking. Modern reasonably priced cuisine.

Cuisine & Dépendances A/C VISA MC AE
46 r. Ferrandière ✉ 69002 Ⓜ Cordeliers – ✆ 04 78 37 44 84 – www.cuisineetdependances.com – restaurant@cuisineetdependances.com – Fax 04 78 38 33 28 – Closed 1st-20 August, Sunday and Monday p. 8 FX **s**
Rest – Menu (€ 16), € 31 bi/70 – Carte approx. € 45
◆ Elongated little dining room, designer decor and welcoming lounge ambiance, serving inventive cuisine with a strong fish focus: already a firm favourite with the locals.

Cuisine & Dépendances Acte II A/C VISA MC AE
68 r. de la Charité ✉ 69002 Ⓜ Perrache – ✆ 04 78 37 45 02 – www.cuisineetdependances.com – cuisineetdependancesacte2@hotmail.fr – Fax 04 78 37 52 46 – Closed 3-18 August, Sunday and Monday p. 8 FY **d**
Rest – Menu (€ 21), € 26/70 – Carte € 40/54
◆ Hot on the heels of the first venture, Act II of this highly addictive (seafood) cuisine is offered in a modern bistro with a bold colour scheme.

Fleur de Sel A/C VISA MC AE
3 r. des Remparts-d'Ainay ✉ 69002 Ⓜ Ampère Victor Hugo – ✆ 04 78 37 40 37 – www.jofe.fr – reservation@jofe.fr – Fax 04 78 37 26 37 – Closed two weeks in August, Monday dinner, Saturday and Sunday p. 8 FY **q**
Rest – *(number of covers limited, pre-book)* Menu € 19 (weekday lunch), € 29/39 – Carte € 45/65
◆ Under new management, this trendy bistro (bright, colourful and stylish) is a picture of affability. Mediterranean gastronomy and excellent wine suggestions.

Maison Villemanzy VISA MC AE
25 montée St-Sébastien ✉ 69001 Ⓜ Croix Paquet – ✆ 04 72 98 21 21 – www.maison-villemanzy.com – maisonvillemanzy@yahoo.fr – Fax 04 72 98 21 22 – Closed 2-17 August, 20 December-11 January, Monday lunch and Sunday p. 6 FV **h**
Rest – *(pre-book)* Menu (€ 19), € 24
◆ Clinging to the slopes of the Croix Rousse this terraced house commands a splendid view of the city. Home cooking featuring basic dishes and a 1940s bistro style interior.

Le Bistrot du Palais VISA MC AE
220 r. Duguesclin ✉ 69003 Ⓜ Place Guichard – ✆ 04 78 14 21 21 – www.bistrot-du-palais.com – bistrotsdecuisiniers@leondelyon.com – Fax 04 78 14 21 22 – Closed 2-23 August, Monday dinner and Sunday p. 9 GY **r**
Rest – Menu (€ 20), € 24
◆ Attractive bistro located opposite the courthouse offering welcoming decor, pleasant enclosed terrace and traditional cooking varying in accordance with market availability.

Bernachon Passion A/C VISA MC AE
42 cours Franklin-Roosevelt ✉ 69006 Ⓜ Foch – ✆ 04 78 52 23 65 – www.bernachon.com – bernachon.chocolats@free.fr – Fax 04 78 52 67 77 – Closed 26 July-25 August, Sunday, Monday and public holidays p. 7 GV **r**
Rest – *(lunch only) (number of covers limited, pre-book)* Menu (€ 28) – Carte € 32/44
◆ This restaurant is run by Paul Bocuse's daughter and her husband, owner of the renowned chocolate shop next door. Traditional menu; dish of the day at lunchtime. Tea room.

Eskis

11 r. Chavanne ✉ 69001 Ⓜ Cordeliers – ✆ 04 78 27 86 93
– www.eskis-restaurant.com – contact@eskis-restaurant.com
– Closed 28 July-20 August, 1st-7 January, 14-22 February — p. 6 FX **e**

Rest – Menu € 25 (weekday lunch), € 29/69 – Carte € 49/63

◆ Originality is definitely the byword in this restaurant that focuses on subtly creative, adroitly prepared molecular dishes. The decor is accordingly sleek and modern.

Magali et Martin

11 r. des Augustins ✉ 69001 Ⓜ Place des Terreaux – ✆ 04 72 00 88 01
– Fax 04 72 00 28 17 – Closed 1st-21 August, 21 December-11 January,
Saturday and Sunday — p. 6 FX **j**

Rest – Menu (€ 19), € 21 (weekday lunch), € 28/50 – Carte € 36/45

◆ Magali is in charge of welcoming guests and advising them on their choice of wine, while Martin prepares cuisine inspired by local market produce. A winning duet!

Le St-Florent

106 cours Gambetta ✉ 69007 Ⓜ Garibaldi – ✆ 04 78 72 32 68 – zagonel@wanadoo.fr – Fax 04 78 72 32 68 – Closed 1st-22 August, Saturday lunch,
Monday lunch, Sunday and public holidays — p. 9 HY **b**

Rest – Menu € 15 (weekday lunch), € 22/35 – Carte € 25/49

◆ In Lyons, the Bresse embassy is at 106 rue Gambetta: from the floor to the ceiling, and the starter to the dessert, this pleasant restaurant celebrates poultry in all its forms.

Thomas

6 r. Laurencin ✉ 69002 Ⓜ Bellecour – ✆ 04 72 56 04 76
– www.restaurant-thomas.com – info@restaurant-thomas.com
– Closed 1st-15 May, 7-21 August, 24 December-2 January, Saturday and Sunday

Rest – Menu € 17 (weekday lunch), € 29/41 — p. 8 FY **w**

◆ The enthusiastic young chef proposes a theme dinner (Nice, Pork, Morocco) once a month in his inviting bistro. Take away service of cooked dishes.

Le Bistrot de St-Paul

2 quai de Bondy ✉ 69005 Ⓜ Vieux Lyon Cathédrale Saint Jean – ✆ 04 78 28 63 19
– www.bistrotdesaintpaul.fr – contact@bistrotdestpaul.fr – Fax 04 78 28 11 56
– Closed Sunday dinner — p. 6 FX **g**

Rest – Menu (€ 13), € 15 (weekday lunch)/20 – Carte € 35/50

◆ Cassoulet, duck breast, Bordeaux and Cahors wines, etc.: the essence of south-west France in this friendly bistro on an embankment of the Saône.

La Famille

18 r. Duviard ✉ 69004 Ⓜ Croix Rousse – ✆ 04 72 98 83 90 – lafamille69@orange.fr – Closed 1st-15 August, 21 December-4 January,
Sunday and Monday — p. 6 FV **m**

Rest – Menu € 16 (weekday lunch) – Carte € 21/30

◆ Old family photos adorn the walls of this relaxed restaurant. A slate lists the daily specials of traditional dishes that vary according to market availability.

LES BOUCHONS : *regional food and wines in a typical Lyonnais ambiance*

Daniel et Denise

156 r. Créqui ✉ 69003 Ⓜ Place Guichard – ✆ 04 78 60 66 53
– www.daniel-et-denise.fr – jviola@hotmail.fr – Fax 04 78 60 66 53
– Closed 24 July-25 August, Saturday, Sunday and public holidays — p. 7 GX **b**

Rest – bistro – Menu (€ 23) – Carte € 32/40

◆ Attractive well-worn setting and a relaxed informal atmosphere in this welcoming bistro, that serves traditionally prepared tasty Lyon specialities.

Le Garet

7 r. Garet ✉ 69001 Ⓜ Hôtel de ville – ✆ 04 78 28 16 94 – legaret@wanadoo.fr
– Fax 04 72 00 06 84 – Closed 24 July-24 August, 22 February-1st March,
Saturday and Sunday — p. 6 FX **a**

Rest – *(pre-book)* Menu € 18 (weekday lunch)/23 – Carte € 20/36

◆ This institution in Lyon is well-known to lovers of good cooking: calf's head, tripe, quenelles and andouillettes served in a relaxed characteristic setting.

Café des Fédérations

8 r. Major Martin ✉ 69001 Ⓜ Hôtel de ville – ✆ 04 78 28 26 00 – www.lesfedeslyon.com – yr@lesfedeslyon.com – Fax 04 72 07 74 52 – Closed 24 December-4 January and Sunday p. 6 FX **z**

Rest – *(pre-book)* Menu € 20 (lunch)/25

◆ Checked tablecloths, tightly packed tables, giant sausages hanging from the ceiling and a relaxed informal atmosphere: a genuine "bouchon" for sure!

Le Jura

25 r. Tupin ✉ 69002 Ⓜ Cordeliers – ✆ 04 78 42 20 57 – http://lejura.cartesurtables.com – Closed August, Monday from September to April, Saturday from May to September and Sunday p. 8 FX **d**

Rest – *(pre-book)* Menu (€ 18), € 25 – Carte € 26/39

◆ This authentic "bouchon", in existence since 1864, has scrupulously preserved a stylish 1930s decor. Traditional tasty dishes of Lyons.

SURROUNDING AREA

in Rillieux-la-Pape 7 km by ① D 483 and D 484 – pop. 29 300 – alt. 269 m – ✉ 69140

Larivoire (Bernard Constantin)

chemin des Îles – ✆ 04 78 88 50 92 – www.larivoire.com – bernard.constantin@larivoire.com – Fax 04 78 88 35 22 – Closed 16-31 August, Sunday dinner, Monday dinner and Tuesday

Rest – Menu (€ 36), € 50/90 – Carte € 80/100

Spec. Crème mousseuse de grenouilles aux champignons et foie gras. Viennoise de ris de veau poêlé. Composition d'un dessert tout chocolat noir. **Wines** Saint-Véran, Saint-Joseph.

◆ Three generations of the same family have been running this attractive house built in the early 20C. Refined interior, popular summer terrace and classic cuisine.

in Meyzieu 14 km by ③ and D 517 – pop. 28 500 – alt. 201 m – ✉ 69330

36 de Lyon Villette-d'AnthonNE : 12 km on D 6, ✆ 04 78 31 11 33

La Petite Auberge du Pont d'Herbens

32 r. V. Hugo – ✆ 04 78 31 41 09 – www.petite-auberge-pont-dherbens.com – direction@petite-auberge-pont-dherbens.com – Fax 04 78 04 34 93 – Closed March, Monday and Tuesday except lunch bank holidays

Rest – Menu (€ 22), € 28 bi/58 – Carte € 32/60

◆ Not far from the Grand Large Lake, this pleasant inn boasts a plush dining room and a VIP area (terrace and sitting room). Traditional repertoire and fine wine list.

in Genas 12 km east by Genas road (D 29) - DQ – pop. 11 700 – alt. 218 m – ✉ 69740

Syndicat d'initiative, 55, rue de la République ✆ 04 72 79 05 31, Fax 04 72 79 05 31

Ambassadeur

36 r. Antoine-Pinay – ✆ 04 78 40 02 02 – www.ambassadeur-hotel.fr – contact@ambassadeur-hotel.fr – Fax 04 78 90 23 53 – Closed 25 December-1st January

78 rm – € 115/135 € 115/135, € 12 – 6 suites

Rest – *(closed 1st-24 August, Saturday and Sunday)* Menu € 28 (weekdays) – Carte € 36/51

◆ A new hotel popular with business travellers for its relatively spacious, well-appointed, restful and contemporary-style bedrooms (wenge furniture). A minimalist-style restaurant serving contemporary cuisine. Japanese garden.

in Tassin-la-Demi-Lune 5 km west (A6, exit 36) - APQ – pop. 18 100 – alt. 220 m – ✉ 69160

Novotel Tassin without rest

13D av. V. Hugo – ✆ 04 78 64 68 69 – www.novotel.com – h1201@accor.com – Fax 04 78 64 61 11 p. 4 AP **n**

103 rm – € 85/150 € 85/150, € 15

◆ This modern hotel, near a large intersection not far from the Fourvière tunnel, provides good, standard Novotel-style rooms.

in Ecully 7 km west (A6, exit 36) - AP - - **pop. 18 000 – alt. 240 m –** ✉ **69130**

Les Hautes Bruyères without rest
5 chemin des Hautes Bruyères – ✆ 04 78 35 52 38 – www.lhb.hote.fr – htesbruyeres@wanadoo.fr – Fax 06 08 48 69 50 p.4 AP **d**
5 rm – €135 €135
◆ Once belonging to a nearby château and surrounded by parkland, this 19C former gardener's house offers a delightful combination of authenticity and elegance.

Saisons
Château du Vivier, 8 chemin Trouillat – ✆ 04 72 18 02 20 – www.institutpaulbocuse.com – contact@institutpaulbocuse.com – Fax 04 78 43 33 51 – Closed 3-24 August, 18 December-4 January, Wednesday dinner, Saturday and Sunday p.4 AP **b**
Rest – Menu €26 (lunch), €32/48
◆ A 19C château and grounds, home to an international catering school founded in 1990 under the leadership of Paul Bocuse. Students prepare and serve dishes.

in Charbonnières-les-Bains 8 km by ⑨ **and N 7 – pop. 4 541 – alt. 233 m –** ✉ **69260**
Lacroix Laval Park: château de la Poupée★.

Le Pavillon de la Rotonde
3 av. du Casino – ✆ 04 78 87 79 79 – www.pavillon-rotonde.com – contact@pavillon-rotonde.com – Fax 04 78 87 79 78
16 rm – €295/495 €325/525, €25
Rest ***La Rotonde*** – see below
◆ A stone's throw from the casino, a luxurious hotel with contemporary decor and discreet Art Deco touches. Spacious guestrooms with terrace giving onto the gardens. Heated indoor swimming pool and spa.

Mercure Charbonnières rest,
78 bis rte de Paris, (D 307) – ✆ 04 78 34 72 79 – www.mercure.com – h0345@accor.com – Fax 04 78 34 88 94
60 rm – €60/140 €70/150, €16
Rest – *(closed 1st-16 August, 24 December-3 January, Saturday, Sunday and public holidays)* Menu (€21), €26 (weekdays)/40 – Carte €21/40
◆ The hotel is in a strategic position, a stone's throw from the regional council. The rooms have undergone a facelift in shimmering colours. Designer restaurant lit by a large liner-style window. Menu in keeping with current taste.

Le Beaulieu without rest
19 av. Gén. de Gaulle – ✆ 04 78 87 12 04 – www.hotel-beaulieu.com – Fax 04 78 87 00 62
44 rm – €65/70 €65/75
◆ Popular with locals, the same family has been running this town centre hotel for thirty years. Recently renovated, practical rooms.

La Rotonde
at the casino Le Lyon Vert ✉ 69890 La Tour de Salvagny – ✆ 04 78 87 00 97 – www.restaurant-rotonde.com – restaurant-rotonde@g-partouche.fr – Fax 04 78 87 81 39 – Closed 1st-9 May, 1st August-2 September, Sunday and Monday
Rest – Menu €55 bi (weekday lunch), €110/155 – Carte €101/192
Spec. Rouget barbet aux champignons iodés. Canard de Challans cuit à la broche. Cannelloni de chocolat amer à la glace. **Wines** Côte-Rôtie, Condrieu.
◆ A renowned gourmet restaurant on the first floor of the casino. Elegant Art Deco-style dining room opening onto the gardens and park. Subtle cuisine and fine wine list.

L'Orangerie de Sébastien
Domaine de Lacroix Laval ✉ 69280 Marcy l'Etoile – ✆ 04 78 87 45 95 – www.orangeriedesebastien.fr – info@orangeriedesebastien.fr – Fax 04 78 87 45 96 – Closed 16 February-4 March, Sunday dinner, Monday and Tuesday
Rest – Menu €27 (weekdays)/45 – Carte €36/53
◆ The 17C castle orangery houses an elegant restaurant serving modern cuisine. Lovely terrace overlooking the gardens. Countless activities on offer on the estate.

Porte de Lyon 10 km by ⑩ (A 6-N 6 junction) – ✉ 69570 Dardilly

Novotel Lyon Nord rm, VISA MC AE
– ✆ 04 72 17 29 29 – www.novotel.com – h0437@accor.com – Fax 04 78 35 08 45
107 rm – †€ 90/121 ††€ 90/121, ☕ € 15
Rest – Menu (€ 17), € 22 – Carte € 22/36
◆ 1970s Novotel in the business park of Dardilly in the process of being brought up to the highest standards of the chain: contemporary comfort and decor. Traditional dishes served in a dining room facing the landscaped garden.

in Limonest 13 km by ⑩, A 6 and D 42 – pop. 3 007 – alt. 390 m – ✉ 69760

Laurent Bouvier VISA MC AE
25 rte du Puy d'Or, crossroads of D 306 and D 42 – ✆ 04 78 35 12 20 – www.restaurant-puydor.com – contact@restaurant-puydor.com – Fax 04 78 64 55 15 – Closed 8-24 August, 26 December-2 January, Sunday and Monday
Rest – Menu € 19 (weekdays), € 39/78 – Carte € 57/79
◆ A family-run inn entirely refurbished by Alain Vavro in a contemporary style. Creative, classic cuisine in tune with the seasons.

in St-Cyr-au-Mont-d'Or 10 km north by St-Cyr road - BP – pop. 5 385 – alt. 320 m – ✉ 69450

L'Ermitage rm, VISA MC AE
chemin de l'Ermitage, 2.5 km at Sommet du Mont Cindre – ✆ 04 72 19 69 69 – www.ermitage-college-hotel.com – contact@ermitage-college-hotel.com – Fax 04 72 19 69 71
28 rm – †€ 135 ††€ 185, ☕ € 12 – 1 suite **Rest** – Menu (€ 24), € 30/35
◆ The concept of this new hotel is to combine the extraordinary views of Lyon and the Monts-d'Or with a contemporary decor (picture windows, recycled objects). Peace and quiet guaranteed! Lyonnaise specialities served in the kitchen-cum-dining room; panoramic terrace.

in Collonges-au-Mont-d'Or 12 km north along the Saône (D 433, D 51) - BP – pop. 3 583 – alt. 176 m – ✉ 69660

see XXXXX ✿✿✿ Paul Bocuse à Lyon

at Lyon St-Exupéry Airport : 27 km on the A 43 – ✉ 69125

Espace Le Bec VISA MC AE
Lyon St-Exupéry airport – ✆ 04 72 22 71 86 – Closed Sunday
Rest – Menu (€ 20), € 26 (weekdays) – Carte € 25/35
◆ Warm, modern lounge ambiance, at this establishment named after the starred chef who creates the brasserie menu. Intimate corner tables and bar overlooking the runways. Professional service.

LYONS-LA-FORÊT – 27 Eure – 304 I5 – pop. 795 – alt. 88 m 33 D2
– ✉ 27480 Normandy

Paris 104 – Beauvais 57 – Mantes-la-Jolie 66 – Rouen 35

Office du tourisme, 20, rue de l'Hôtel de Ville ✆ 02 32 49 31 65, Fax 02 32 48 10 60

La Licorne rm, VISA MC AE
pl. de la Halle – ✆ 02 32 48 24 24 – www.hotel-licorne.com – contact@hotel-licorne.com – Fax 02 32 49 80 09
15 rm – †€ 89/175 ††€ 99/195, ☕ € 15 – 5 suites – ½ P € 125/195
Rest – *(closed Monday and Tuesday)* Menu € 29/39 – Carte € 45/80
◆ This 1610 post house, surrounded by beech trees, stands in one of France's 'most beautiful villages'. Admirably refurbished guestrooms in an elegant fashionable register. Up-to-date menu served in a dining room graced with an immense fireplace. Terrace in the garden.

Les Lions de Beauclerc
7 r. Hôtel de ville – ✆ 02 32 49 18 90 – www.lionsdebeauclerc.com – leslionsdebeauclerc@free.fr – Fax 02 32 48 27 80
6 rm – 🛉€ 59/64 🛉🛉€ 64/69, ☕ € 9 – ½ P € 60/70
Rest – crêperie – *(closed Tuesday)* Menu € 15/28 – Carte € 17/33
◆ In the heart of a delightful village, this large brick house is home to guestrooms decorated with old furniture and knick-knacks. Breakfast on the terrace in fine weather. Choice of two classical dining rooms to sample traditional dishes.

Good food without spending a fortune?
Look out for the Bib Gourmand

LYS-LEZ-LANNOY – 59 Nord – **302** H3 – **pop. 12 800 – alt. 28 m – see Roubaix**

LYS-ST-GEORGES – 36 Indre – **323** G7 – **pop. 220 – alt. 200 m** – ✉ 36230 12 **C3**

Paris 287 – Argenton-sur-Creuse 29 – Bourges 80 – Châteauroux 29 – La Châtre 22

Auberge La Forge
7 r. du Château – ✆ 02 54 30 81 68 – www.restaurantlaforge.com – contacts@restaurantlaforge.com – Fax 02 54 30 81 68 – Closed 30 June-5 July, 23 September-9 October, 3-22 January, Sunday dinner, Tuesday from September to June and Monday
Rest – Menu € 19 (weekdays), € 29/49 – Carte € 35/59
◆ The rustic decor (beams, tiles and fireplace) of this welcoming village inn is in perfect harmony with the regional cooking. Pretty verdant terrace.

MACÉ – 61 Orne – **310** J3 – **see Sées**

MACHEZAL – 42 Loire – **327** E4 – **pop. 399 – alt. 623 m** – ✉ 42114 44 **A1**

Paris 428 – Lyon 59 – Saint-Étienne 93 – Clermont-Ferrand 133 – Villeurbanne 68

Le Myrrhis
– ✆ 04 77 62 47 25 – www.lemyrrhis.fr – lemyrrhis@orange.fr – Closed 4-30 January, Sunday dinner, Monday and Tuesday
Rest – Menu € 15 (weekday lunch), € 19/35 – Carte € 38/49
◆ A motivated young couple run this pleasant restaurant near the village church. Bright colours in the dining room bring an element of gaiety to the plain decor. Modern menu.

MACHILLY – 74 Haute-Savoie – **328** K3 – **pop. 954 – alt. 525 m** – ✉ 74140 46 **F1**

Paris 548 – Annemasse 11 – Genève 21 – Thonon-les-Bains 20

Le Refuge des Gourmets
90 rte des Framboises – ✆ 04 50 43 53 87 – www.refugedesgourmets.com – chanove@refugedesgourmets.com – Fax 04 50 43 53 76 – Closed 16 August-8 September, 2-11 January, 16-25 February, Sunday dinner and Monday
Rest – Menu (€ 24), € 31/66 – Carte € 60/80
◆ Wine-bar entrance hall and elegant Belle Époque-inspired setting inside this "refuge" where gourmets can appreciate the creative, seasonal cuisine.

LA MACHINE (COL) – 26 Drôme – **332** F4 – **see St-Jean-en-Royans**

MACINAGGIO – 2B Haute-Corse – **345** F2 – **see Corse**

MÂCON Ⓟ – 71 Saône-et-Loire – **320** I12 – **pop. 34 100 – alt. 175 m** 8 **C3**
– ✉ **71000** **Burgundy-Jura**

- Paris 391 – Bourg-en-Bresse 38 – Chalon-sur-Saône 59 – Lyon 71 – Roanne 96
- Office de tourisme, 1, place Saint-Pierre ☎ 03 85 21 07 07, Fax 03 85 40 96 00
- de la Commanderie Crottet L'Aumusse, 7 km on the Bourg-en-Bresse road, ☎ 03 85 30 44 12
- de Mâcon La Salle La Salle14 km on the Tournus road, ☎ 03 85 36 09 71
- Musée des Ursulines ★ BY **M**[1] - Musée Lamartine BZ **M**[2] - Apothicary's ★ of the Hôtel-Dieu BY - ≤★ of Pont St-Laurent.
- Roche de Solutré ★★ West: 9 km - Steeple ★ of St-André de Bagé church East: 8,5 km.

MÂCON

Barre (Pl. de la) .... **AYZ** 2
Barre (R. de la) .... **BZ** 3
Dombey (R.) .... **BZ** 5
Dufour (R.) .... **BZ** 6
Gaulle (Av. Gén.-de) .. **BY** 7
Laguiche (R. Ph.) ..... **BZ** 8
Lamartine (R.) .... **BYZ** 9
Paix (Square de la) ... **BY** 10
Perrier (R.) .... **AY** 12
Poissonnière (Pl.) ..... **BZ** 13
Pont (R. du) .... **BZ** 14
Préfecture (R. de la) . **BY** 15
St-Étienne (Pl.) .... **BY** 17
St-Nizier (R.) .... **BZ** 18
Sigorgne (R.) .... **BZ** 19
Strasbourg (R. de) .... **BY** 20
Ursulines (R. des) .... **BY** 21
11-Nov.-1918 (R. du) **ABY** 22
28-Juin-1944 (R.) ..... **BY** 24

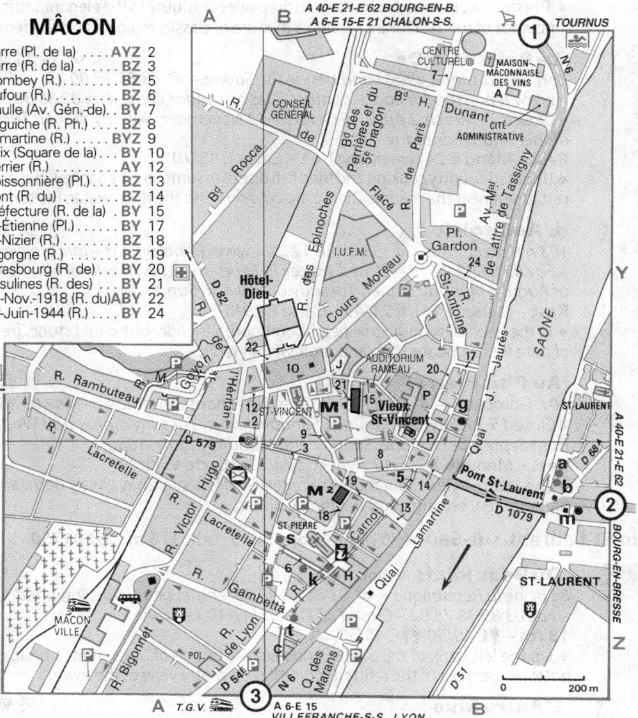

A 40-E 21-E 62 BOURG-EN-B.
A 6-E 15-E 21 CHALON-S-S.
TOURNUS
A 40-E 21-E 62
BOURG-EN-BRESSE
T.G.V.
A 6-E 15
VILLEFRANCHE-S-S., LYON

 **Park Inn**
26 r. Pierre de Coubertin , via ①: 0.5 km – ☎ 03 85 21 93 93
– www.macon.parkinn.fr – info.macon@rezidorparkinn.com
– Fax 03 85 39 11 45
64 rm – €90/124 €101/139, ☕ €13
Rest – *(Closed Sunday)* Menu (€18), €28/32 – Carte €42/57
◆ Near the marina, this chain-type hotel has refurbished rooms (most with views of the River Saône). Business clientele. Renovated contemporary dining room and bar. Poolside terrace for fine weather dining.

Du Nord without rest
313 quai Jean-Jaurès – ✆ 03 85 38 08 68 – www.hotel-dunord.com – contact@hotel-dunord.com – Fax 03 85 39 01 92 – Closed 19 December-4 January BY **g**
16 rm – †€ 52/65 ††€ 60/76, ☕ € 8
◆ A pink façade hides the best small hotel in the town, on the harbour side near the town centre. Reasonable prices, partly renovated rooms, good breakfasts.

Pierre (Christian Gaulin)
7 r. Dufour – ✆ 03 85 38 14 23 – www.restaurant-pierre.com – christian.gaulin@aliceadsl.fr – Fax 03 85 39 84 04 – Closed 19 July-11 August, 22 February-4 March, Sunday dinner, Tuesday lunch and Monday BZ **k**
Rest – Menu (€ 22), € 29 (weekday lunch), € 46/73 – Carte € 60/80
Spec. Escargots de bourgogne en coquille. Quenelles de brochet aux champignons noirs. Soufflé aux griottines confites, sorbet arrosé au kirsch. **Wines** Mâcon Uchizy, Mâcon Viré-Clessé.
◆ The stonework, wooden beams and fireplace contribute to the elegant setting and warm ambiance of this restaurant serving a mixture of classic, regional and modern cuisine.

Le Poisson d'Or
port de plaisance, via ① and beside the Saône – ✆ 03 85 38 00 88 – www.lepoissondor.com – contact@lepoissondor.com – Fax 03 85 38 82 55 – Closed 24 March-2 April, 19 October-12 November, Sunday dinner, Tuesday dinner and Wednesday
Rest – Menu € 24 (weekdays)/64 – Carte € 45/70
◆ Updated country cooking and fried fish dishes in summer. The Saône flows alongside this restaurant near the marina. Dining area overlooking the river; waterside terrace.

L'Ambroisie
103 r. Marcel-Paul – ✆ 03 85 38 12 21 – www.lambroisie.fr – lambroisie@live.fr – Fax 03 85 38 99 48 – Closed 1 week in February, 2 first weeks of May, 2 first weeks of August, Monday dinner, Tuesday dinner and Sunday
Rest – Menu (€ 15), € 21/45 – Carte € 29/67
◆ In the heart of an industrial neighbourhood, a friendly bistro (old stone, fresco) worthy of note for its updated fare and professional service.

Au P'tit Pierre
10 r. Gambetta – ✆ 03 85 39 48 84 – laurechant@hotmail.fr – Fax 03 85 22 73 78 – Closed 5-27 July, 1-4 January, Sunday dinner, Tuesday dinner and Wednesday from September to June, Sunday and Monday in July-August BZ **t**
Rest – Menu (€ 15), € 17 (weekdays)/33 – Carte € 30/39
◆ This bistro-style restaurant with a regular local clientele has a lively decor and nice table presentation, serving good traditional dishes.

in St-Laurent-sur-Saône (01Ain) – pop. 1 655 – alt. 176 m – ✉ 01750

Du Beaujolais without rest
88 pl. de la République – ✆ 03 85 38 42 06 – hotel.beaujolais@wanadoo.fr – Fax 03 85 38 78 02 – Closed 27 December-10 January BZ **m**
13 rm – †€ 45/50 ††€ 45/50, ☕ € 6
◆ On the left bank of the Saône, opposite the bridge of St-Laurent, a basic comfortable hotel where most of the refitted rooms have a pretty view of the town.

L'Autre Rive
143 quai Bouchacourt – ✆ 03 85 39 01 02 – www.lautrerive.fr – Fax 03 85 38 16 92 – Closed 21-25 December, Sunday dinner and Monday BZ **a**
Rest – Menu € 21 (weekdays)/49 – Carte € 38/48
◆ This restaurant on the river bank facing Mâcon has everything: an attractive veranda-dining room, a pleasant terrace overlooking the Saône and generous regional dishes featuring seafood.

Le Saint-Laurent
1 quai Bouchacourt – ✆ 03 85 39 29 19 – www.georgesblanc.com – saintlaurent@georgesblanc.com – Fax 03 85 38 29 77 BZ **b**
Rest – Menu € 18 (weekday lunch), € 22/46 – Carte € 37/54
◆ A terrace with a view over Mâcon, and wholesome dishes. An old-fashioned bistro over St Laurent bridge, which rose to fame when Mitterrand and Gorbatchev dined here.

to A6-N6 Mâcon-Nord interchange 7 km by ① – ✉ 71000 Mâcon

Novotel rm,

A6 motorway Mâcon North toll station Exit 28 – ✆ 03 85 20 40 00 – www.novotel.com – h0438@accor.com – Fax 03 85 20 40 33

114 rm – €105/162 €105/162, ☕ €14

Rest – Menu (€17), €22 – Carte €24/54

◆ A standard looking but practical establishment in the hotel district by the north Mâcon interchange. Ask for one of the more recent guestrooms. Functional dining room with kitchen-grill visible to all, terrace by the side of the swimming pool.

North 3 km by ① on N 6 – ✉ 71000 Mâcon

La Vieille Ferme rm,

Bd Gén. de Gaulle – ✆ 03 85 21 95 15 – www.hotel-restaurant-lavieilleferme.com – vieil.ferme@wanadoo.fr – Fax 03 85 21 95 16 – Closed 20 December-10 January

24 rm – €52 €52, ☕ €7 **Rest** – Menu €12/29 – Carte €21/34

◆ A rural stop in a park by the side of the Saône. The simple, practical guestrooms are in a new motel type building. This "old farmhouse" is home to a rustic restaurant with exposed beams, stonework and a fireplace, also featuring a charming terrace.

in Sennecé-lès-Mâcon 7,5 km by ① – ✉ 71000 Mâcon

Auberge de la Tour

604 r. Vrémontoise – ✆ 03 85 36 02 70 – www.auberge-tour.fr – aubergedelatour@wanadoo.fr – Fax 03 85 36 03 47 – Closed 26 October-9 November, 1-22 February, Tuesday lunch, Sunday dinner and Monday

24 rm – €47/53 €49/73, ☕ €10 – ½ P €56/64

Rest – Menu (€14), €19 (weekday lunch), €24/46 – Carte €23/54

◆ Simple, rustic, family-run inn next to the village lookout tower - a local curiosity. Rooms in various sizes and styles. Carefully prepared regional dishes by the chef, who loves local produce. Fine selection of Mâcon wines.

via ② Bourg-en-Bresse road – ✉ 01750 Replonges

La Huchette rm,

1089 rte de Bourg, 4.5 km, near exit n°3 of the A40 – ✆ 03 85 31 03 55 – www.hotel-lahuchette.com – lahuchette@wanadoo.fr – Fax 03 85 31 10 24 – Closed 1st-10 November

14 rm – €90/110 €105/135, ☕ €14 – ½ P €95/110

Rest – *(closed 1st- 17 November Tuesday lunch and Monday) (dinner only)* Menu €34/56 – Carte €36/60

◆ This abode, located in an attractive park, offers refurbished rooms, opening onto the garden with pool. Classic fare served beneath the beams of a rustic dining room (stone hearth, chandeliers, rural murals) or on the terrace in summer.

in Crèches-sur-Saône 8 km South by ③ and N 6 – pop. 2 833 – alt. 180 m – ✉ 71680

Syndicat d'initiative, 466, route nationale 6 ✆ 03 85 37 48 32, Fax 03 85 36 57 91

Hostellerie du Château de la Barge

rte des Bergers, 1 km northwest on the D89 – ✆ 03 85 23 93 23 – www.chateaudelabarge.fr – hotelchateaudelabarge@wanadoo.fr – Fax 03 85 23 93 39 – Closed 18 December-4 January

21 rm – €90/95 €95/105, ☕ €13

Rest – Menu €20 (weekday lunch), €25/70 bi – Carte €53/80

◆ This lovely abode, hidden in parkland surrounded by vineyards, dates back to the 17C. Tasteful contemporary guestrooms or more spacious and 'stately'. Heated pool. A stone fireplace, beams and wainscoting blend in with a modern decor.

in Hurigny 5.5 km Northeast by D 82 AY and secondary road – **pop. 1 522 – alt. 275 m** – ✉ 71870

Château des Poccards without rest
120 rte des Poccards – ✆ 03 85 32 08 27 – www.chateau-des-poccards.com – chateau.des.poccards@wanadoo.fr – Fax 03 85 32 08 19 – Open mid-March to end November
5 rm – €80/120 €80/120
◆ A château built in 1805 set in landscaped gardens. Original furnishings add individual touches to the rooms. Several lounges, one in Art Deco style. Breakfast on the terrace.

LA MADELAINE-SOUS-MONTREUIL – **62 Pas-de-Calais** – **301** D5 – **see Montreuil**

MADIÈRES – **34 Hérault** – **339** G5 – ✉ **34190 St Maurice Navacelles** 23 **C2**

Paris 705 – Lodève 30 – Montpellier 62 – Nîmes 79 – Le Vigan 20

Château de Madières rest, VISA MC AE
hamlet of Madières on the D 25 – ✆ 04 67 73 84 03 – www.chateau-madieres.com – madieres@wanadoo.fr – Fax 04 67 73 55 71 – Open 10 April-31 October
12 rm – €150/299 €150/299, €17 **Rest** – Menu €49 – Carte €52/66
◆ In the heart of a park scaling the plateau, this fine 12C château, enlarged during the Renaissance, overlooks the Vis gorges. A grandiose, authentic setting... yet cosy. Dining room with attractive stone vaulting and pleasant terrace. Sunny cuisine.

MADIRAN – **65 Hautes-Pyrénées** – **342** L1 – **pop. 476 – alt. 125 m** – ✉ 65700 28 **A2**

Paris 753 – Pau 51 – Tarbes 41 – Toulouse 154

Le Prieuré VISA MC AE
4 r. de l'Église – ✆ 05 62 31 44 52 – www.leprieure-madiran.com – restaurantleprieure@cegetel.net – Closed 5-11 January, 8-15 February, Sunday dinner, Monday and Tuesday
Rest – Menu (€13), €18 (weekdays)/25
◆ This restaurant is set in a former monastery, also home to the Madiran wine producers. Elegant, colourful decor, and modern cuisine with a fine selection of local wines.

MAFFLIERS – **95 Val-d'Oise** – **305** E6 – **pop. 1 614 – alt. 145 m** – ✉ 95560 18 **B1**

Paris 29 – Beaumont-sur-Oise 10 – Beauvais 53 – Compiègne 73 – Senlis 45

Novotel rm, rest, VISA MC AE
allée des Marronniers – ✆ 01 34 08 35 35 – www.novotel.com – h0383@accor.com – Fax 01 34 08 35 00
99 rm – €90/250 €90/250, €14 **Rest** – Menu €18 – Carte €25/40
◆ Admirably quiet and peaceful! On the way into the park, this modern wing houses rooms refurbished according to the chain's standards. A restaurant in a fine, late-18C abode serving modern fare. Terrace overlooking the countryside.

MAGALAS – **34 Hérault** – **339** E8 – **pop. 2 489 – alt. 115 m** – ✉ **34480** 22 **B2**

Paris 755 – Montpellier 82 – Béziers 17 – Narbonne 54 – Sète 71

Ô. Bontemps VISA MC
pl. de l'Église – ✆ 04 67 36 20 82 – www.o-bontemps.com – contact@o-bontemps.com – Closed 9-17 March, 11-19 May, 7-22 September, 21 December-5 January, Sunday and Monday except bank holidays
Rest – Menu (€20), €26 (weekday lunch), €30/65 – Carte €37/50
◆ The chef of this restaurant opposite the church has returned to the region where he grew up. Contemporary decor, attractive wine list and convivial atmosphere.

MAGESCQ – **40 Landes** – **335** D12 – **pop. 1 378 – alt. 28 m** – ✉ **40140** 3 **B2**

Paris 722 – Bayonne 45 – Biarritz 52 – Castets 13 – Dax 16 – Mont-de-Marsan 71

Office de tourisme, 1, place de l'Église ✆ 05 58 47 76 24, Fax 05 58 47 75 81

Relais de la Poste (Jean Coussau)
24 av. de Maremne – ✆ 05 58 47 70 25 – poste@relaischateaux.com – Fax 05 58 47 76 17 – Closed 12 November-20 December, Monday and Tuesday from October to April, Tuesday lunch, Thursday lunch and Monday from May to September
16 rm – †€ 135/365 ††€ 150/380, ☕ € 20 – 1 suite – ½ P € 165/270
Rest – *(pre-book Sat - Sun)* Menu € 58 (weekdays)/110 – Carte € 85/130
Spec. Saumon de l'Adour simplement grillé, vraie béarnaise (15 March-30 June). Magret de palombe rôtie à l'os, cuisses en salmis (Oct. to Feb.). Pistache dans tous ses états. **Wines** Jurançon, Tursan.
◆ Small castle surrounded by a large park, offering warm hospitality. Individually decorated rooms with balconies, sauna, steam room and Jacuzzi. Elegant restaurant and terrace overlooking the pine forest. Superb regional cuisine and a fine wine selection.

Côté Quillier
26 av. de Maremne – ✆ 05 58 47 79 50 – coussau@wanadoo.fr – poste@relaischateaux.com – Fax 558477617 – Closed 11 November-19 December
Rest – Menu € 28 – Carte approx. € 40
◆ Designer furniture complements the on-trend wall colours at this elegant-looking bistro. Terrace and splendid garden with skittles. Modern cuisine.

MAGLAND – 74 Haute-Savoie – 328 M4 – pop. 2 929 – alt. 513 m – ✉ 74300 46 F1

▶ Paris 583 – Annecy 68 – Genève 49 – Lyon 192

Le Relais du Mont Blanc
1 km south on D 1205 – ✆ 04 50 21 00 85 – www.lerelaisdumontblanc.com – lerelaisdumontblanc@wanadoo.fr – Fax 04 50 34 31 83 – Closed 3-23 August, 10-15 November, 28 December-3 January
21 rm – †€ 69/90 ††€ 79/110, ☕ € 10 **Rest** – *(closed Friday dinner, Saturday lunch and Sunday dinner)* Menu € 19 (weekdays)/38 – Carte € 50/76
◆ This attractive mountain chalet just 20 minutes from Mont Blanc provides renovated rooms with much wooden décor. This rustic restaurant serves tasty regional cuisine in modern style.

MAGNAC-BOURG – 87 Haute-Vienne – 325 F7 – pop. 916 – alt. 444 m – ✉ 87380 24 B2

▶ Paris 419 – Limoges 31 – St-Yrieix-la-Perche 28 – Uzerche 28
ℹ Office de tourisme, 2, place de la Bascule ✆ 05 55 00 89 91, Fax 05 55 00 78 38

Auberge de l'Étang
9 rte de la gare – ✆ 05 55 00 81 37 – www.aubergedeletang.com – ml.hermann@wanadoo.fr – Fax 05 55 48 70 74 – Closed 1-16 March, 8 November-7 December, 8-23 February, Sunday dinner and Monday except July-August
14 rm – †€ 45/55 ††€ 45/55, ☕ € 8,50
Rest – *(Closed Sunday dinner, Monday from September to June and Wednesday lunch in July-August)* Menu € 15 (weekdays)/43 – Carte € 32/60
◆ This welcoming family inn overlooking a pond stands at the entrance to the village. Recently refurbished rooms; some enjoy a view of the swimming pool and pond. Generous helpings of traditional cuisine and a pleasant summer terrace.

MAGNY-COURS – 58 Nièvre – 319 B10 – see Nevers

MAGNY-LE-HONGRE – 77 Seine-et-Marne – 312 F2 – 106 22 – see Paris, Area (Marne-la-Vallée)

MAÎCHE – 25 Doubs – 321 K3 – pop. 3 875 – alt. 777 m – ✉ 25120 17 C2

▶ Paris 498 – Besançon 75 – Belfort 60 – Montbéliard 42 – Pontarlier 61
ℹ Syndicat d'initiative, place de la Mairie ✆ 03 81 64 11 88, Fax 03 81 64 02 30

in Mancenans Lizerne 2.5 km East by D 464 and D 272 – pop. 152 – alt. 720 m – ✉ 25120

Au Coin du Bois
r. sous le rang, La Lizerne – ✆ 03 81 64 00 55 – sabrina.maire@wanadoo.fr – Fax 03 81 64 21 98 – Closed 25 July-3 August, 2-9 February, Sunday dinner, Monday dinner and Wednesday dinner
Rest – Menu (€ 14 bi), € 22/58 – Carte € 29/60
◆ Attractive chalet, surrounded by pine trees. Discreet rustic dining room and pleasant terrace serving traditional cuisine and local country dishes.

MAILLANE – 13 Bouches-du-Rhône – **340** D3 – see St-Rémy-de-Provence

MAILLEZAIS – 85 Vendée – **316** L9 – pop. 967 – alt. 6 m – ✉ 85420 35 **C3**
Atlantic Coast

Paris 443 – Nantes 129 – La Roche-sur-Yon 76 – La Rochelle 50 – Niort 33
Office de tourisme, rue du Dr Daroux ✆ 02 51 87 23 01, Fax 02 51 00 72 51

Madame Bonnet without rest
69 r. Abbaye – ✆ 02 51 87 23 00 – liliane.bonnet@wanadoo.fr – Fax 02 51 00 72 44
5 rm – €50/55 €60/68
◆ Elegant bedrooms, a decor full of history, breakfast by the fire, garden and vegetable plot, and charming hosts. What more can you ask of a bed & breakfast?

MAISONNEUVE – 15 Cantal – **330** F6 – see Chaudes-Aigues

MAISONS-ALFORT – 94 Val-de-Marne – **312** D3 – **101** 27 – see Paris, Area

MAISONS-DU-BOIS – 25 Doubs – **321** I5 – see Montbenoit

MAISONS-LAFFITTE – 78 Yvelines – **311** I2 – **101** 13 – see Paris, Area

MAISONS-LÈS-CHAOURCE – 10 Aube – **313** F5 – see Chaource

MALAUCÈNE – 84 Vaucluse – **332** D8 – pop. 2 669 – alt. 333 m 40 **B2**
– ✉ 84340 Provence

Paris 673 – Avignon 45 – Carpentras 18 – Vaison-la-Romaine 10
Office de tourisme, place de la Mairie ✆ 04 90 65 22 59, Fax 04 90 65 22 59

Le Domaine des Tilleuls without rest VISA
rte du Mont-Ventoux – ✆ 04 90 65 22 31 – www.hotel-domainedestilleuls.com – info@hotel-domainedestilleuls.com – Fax 04 90 65 16 77 – Open from March to October
20 rm – €79/81 €81/97, €11
◆ This 18C silkworm farm is now home to a charming hotel decorated in Provencal style. Favour the rooms facing the pleasant park planted with sycamores and lime trees.

La Chevalerie VISA AE
53 pl. de l'Église, (Les Remparts) – ✆ 04 90 65 11 19 – www.la-chevalerie.net – contact@la-chevalerie.net – Fax 04 90 12 69 22 – Closed 20-30 January, 20-28 February, Sunday dinner and Monday
Rest – *(number of covers limited, pre-book)* Menu (€16), €20/36 – Carte €26/44
◆ Set in a fine, imposing building, once the residence of the Princes of Orange, the restaurant is reached via the gunroom. Generous, traditional cuisine.

MALBUISSON – 25 Doubs – **321** H6 – pop. 500 – alt. 900 m – ✉ 25160 17 **C3**
Burgundy-Jura

Paris 456 – Besançon 74 – Champagnole 42 – Pontarlier 16 – St-Claude 72
Office de tourisme, 69, Grande Rue ✆ 03 81 69 31 21, Fax 03 81 69 71 94
St-Point Lake★.

Le Lac rest, VISA
65 Grande Rue – ✆ 03 81 69 34 80 – www.hotel-le-lac.fr – hotellelac@wanadoo.fr – Fax 03 81 69 35 44 – Closed 16 November-16 December
51 rm – €42/60 €50/115, €10 – 3 suites – ½ P €53/86
Rest – Menu €19 (weekdays)/45 – Carte €34/65
Rest *du Fromage* – Menu (€12), €19/22 – Carte €22/34
◆ Old house along the main village street and facing the lake on the garden side. Opulent retro interior and some modernised rooms. Generous breakfasts with home made pastries in the tea room. Regional cuisine served at le Lac. Tarts, fondues, raclette at the Restaurant du Fromage.

Beau Site VISA
– ✆ 03 81 69 70 70 – www.hotel-le-lac.fr – hotellelac@wanadoo.fr – Fax 03 81 69 35 44 – Closed 12 November-18 December
17 rm – €29/38 €38, €10
◆ Early 19C building with an entrance flanked by columns. Functional rooms. Reception at the Hôtel du Lac.

De la Poste
61 Gd Rue – 03 81 69 79 34 – www.hotel-le-lac.fr – hotellelac@wanadoo.fr – Fax 03 81 69 35 44 – Closed 16 November-16 December
10 rm – €35 €40/47, €10 – ½ P €46/50
Rest – *(closed Sunday dinner, Tuesday dinner and Monday except July-August)* Menu €10 (weekday lunch)/19 – Carte €14/40
◆ This small renovated hotel has rooms adorned with colourful furniture. Choose a quieter room facing the lake. You can expect traditional cuisine and specialities cooked on hot stone in a prettily rustic setting.

Le Bon Accueil (Marc Faivre) with rm
Grande Rue – 03 81 69 30 58 – www.le-bon-accueil.fr – marcfaivre@le-bon-accueil.fr – Fax 03 81 69 37 60 – Closed 19-29 April, 25 October-4 November, 13 December-13 January, Sunday dinner from 1st September to 14 July, Tuesday lunch and Monday
12 rm – €70 €100, €10 – ½ P €71/90
Rest – Menu (€23 bi), €32/57 – Carte €50/78
Spec. Tarte fine à la saucisse de Morteau, étuvée de poireau. Rouelle de poulet fermier au vin jaune et morilles. Cannelloni croustillant sur une poêlée de fruits (Sep. to Dec.). **Wines** Côtes du Jura, Arbois rouge.
◆ A charming restaurant with owners providing attentive service. Excellent modern cuisine; spacious and comfortable rooms.

in Granges-Ste-Marie 2 km Southwest– ✉25160 Labergement Ste Marie

Auberge du Coude
1r. du Coude – 03 81 69 31 57 – www.aubergeducoude.com – aubergeducoude@orange.fr – Fax 03 81 69 33 90 – Closed 5 November-18 December
11 rm – €54 €54, €8,50 – ½ P €54
Rest – *(closed Sunday dinner)* Menu €18/48 – Carte €35/55
◆ Located between the lakes of Saint Point and Remoray Boujeons, this house dating from 1826 has a warm atmosphere. Charming rustic bedrooms. Garden with lake. Rustic dining room with wood panelling and Louis XIII furniture. Regional cuisine.

LA MALÈNE – 48 Lozère – 330 H9 – pop. 164 – alt. 450 m – ✉ 48210 23 C1

Languedoc-Roussillon-Tarn Gorges

Paris 609 – Florac 41 – Mende 41 – Millau 44 – Sévérac-le-Château 33 – Le Vigan 77
Office de tourisme, 04 66 48 50 77
West: les Détroits★★ and cirque des Baumes★★ (by boat).

Manoir de Montesquiou
– 04 66 48 51 12 – www.manoir-montesquiou.com – montesquiou@demeures-de-lozere.com – Fax 04 66 48 50 47 – Open end March to end October
10 rm – €70/75 €70/110, €14 – 2 suites – ½ P €84/102
Rest – Menu €27/48 – Carte €42/68
◆ This 15C stone manor is rich in appeal: friendly welcome, personalised rooms (four-poster beds, period furniture) and a lovely rose garden. Regionally sourced dishes served on a pleasant terrace in fine weather.

Northeast 5,5 km on D 907bis – ✉ 48210 Ste Énimie

Château de la Caze rm, rest,
– 04 66 48 51 01 – www.chateaudelacaze.com – chateaucaze@orange.fr – Fax 04 66 48 55 75 – Open 3 April-11 November and closed Thursday in October
7 rm – €114/174 €114/174, €16 – 9 suites – €170/280 – ½ P €111/141
Rest – *(closed Thursday lunch and Wednesday)* Menu (€32), €38/82 – Carte €44/60
◆ Majestic 15C chateau in a park beside the Tarn. Exquisite, individualised bedrooms (those in the annexe are also very comfortable, but less characterful). Particularly pleasant welcome. Restaurant in an old chapel serving flavoursome modern dishes based on local produce.

MALESHERBES – 45 Loiret – 318 L2 – pop. 6 097 – alt. 108 m – ✉ 45330 12 C1

Châteaux of the Loire

Paris 75 – Étampes 26 – Fontainebleau 27 – Montargis 62 – Orléans 62 – Pithiviers 19
Office de tourisme, 19-21, pl. du Martroy 02 38 34 81 94, Fax 02.38.34.49.40
du Château d'Augerville Augerville-la-Rivière Place du Château, S : 8 km on D 410, 02 38 32 12 07

Écu de France
10 pl. Martroi – ☎ 02 38 34 87 25 – http://logis-de-france-loiret.com/ecu_de_france_malesherbes/ – ecudefrance@wanadoo.fr – Fax 02 38 34 68 99
16 rm – †€ 56/68 ††€ 56/68, ☕ € 8 – ½ P € 61/66
Rest – *(closed 1st-17 August, Thursday dinner and Sunday dinner)* Menu (€ 14), € 25 (weekdays)/50 – Carte € 25/54
Rest *Brasserie de l'Écu* – *(closed 1st-17 August, Thursday dinner and Sunday dinner)* Menu (€ 14) – Carte € 19/45
◆ This former post house, a short distance from the Château de Malesherbes, has stylish, very well kept rooms. Old beams and fireplace give this restaurant a certain cachet. Terrace in the courtyard. Fast meals in the brasserie area.

La Lilandière without rest
7 chemin de la Messe, (Hamlet of Trézan) – ☎ 02 38 34 84 51 – www.lalilandiere.com – la-lilandiere@wanadoo.fr
5 rm ☕ – †€ 56 ††€ 62
◆ Stones, beams and modern furniture combine happily in this tastefully restored former farmhouse. Lovers of fishing and canoeing will appreciate the river that runs through the garden.

MALICORNE-SUR-SARTHE – **72 Sarthe** – **310** I8 – **pop. 1 878** – **alt. 39 m** – ✉ **72270** **Châteaux of the Loire** — 35 **C2**

Paris 236 – Château-Gontier 52 – La Flèche 16 – Le Mans 32

Office de tourisme, 5, place Duguesclin ☎ 02 43 94 74 45, Fax 02 43 94 59 61

La Petite Auberge
5 pl. Duguesclin – ☎ 02 43 94 80 52 – www.petite-auberge-malicorne.fr – contact@petite-auberge-malicorne.fr – Fax 02 43 94 31 37 – Closed 22 December-28 February, dinner except Saturday September-April, Sunday dinner and Tuesday dinner May-August and Monday
Rest – Menu € 17 (weekday lunch), € 24/49 – Carte approx. € 39
◆ Summer dining on the terrace by the waterside. In winter, enjoy a meal around the 13C fireplace. Serving fine, traditional meals.

MALLING – **57 Moselle** – **307** I2 – **pop. 504** – **alt. 158 m** – ✉ **57480** — 26 **B1**

Paris 352 – Luxembourg 35 – Metz 43 – Trier 63

in Petite Hettange **1 km east on D 654** – ✉ **57480**

Olmi
11 Rte Nationale – ☎ 03 82 50 10 65 – www.olmi-restaurant.fr – relais3frontieres@wanadoo.fr – Closed 16-22 February, Tuesday dinner, Wednesday dinner and Monday
Rest – Menu € 35/70 – Carte € 50/70
◆ Located close to the border, this former truck stop has been refurbished and now offers a more contemporary decor. Classic cuisine with some Italian touches.

MALO-LES-BAINS – **59 Nord** – **302** C1 – **see Dunkerque**

LE MALZIEU-VILLE – **48 Lozère** – **330** I5 – **pop. 970** – **alt. 860 m** – ✉ 48140 — 23 **C1**

Paris 541 – Mende 51 – Millau 107 – Le Puy-en-Velay 74 – Rodez 125 – St-Flour 38

Office de tourisme, tour de Bodon ☎ 04 66 31 82 73, Fax 04.66.31.82.73

Voyageurs
rte Saugues – ☎ 04 66 31 70 08 – http://perso.orange.fr/hotel.des.voyageurs – pagesc@wanadoo.fr – Fax 04 66 31 80 36 – Closed 15 December-28 February
19 rm – †€ 52/58 ††€ 58/62, ☕ € 8 – ½ P € 50
Rest – *(closed Sunday dinner and Saturday except July-August)* Menu (€ 10), € 15/30 – Carte € 19/45
◆ In a pretty village of the Margeride, a 1970s building with functional bedrooms. A practical base from which to explore the region. Traditional and local dishes are served in this countrified dining room.

MANCENANS LIZERNE – **25 Doubs** – **321** K3 – **see Maîche**

MANCEY – 71 Saône-et-Loire – 320 I10 – pop. 377 – alt. 280 m – ✉ 71240 8 C3

Paris 373 – Dijon 102 – Mâcon 43 – Chalon-sur-Saône 34 – Le Creusot 68

Auberge du Col des Chèvres
Dulphey – ✆ 03 85 51 06 38 – aub.coldeschevres.para@wanadoo.fr – Closed 25 August-3 September, February school holidays, Sunday dinner from November to March, Tuesday except July-August and Wednesday
Rest – Menu € 18 (weekdays), € 25/30 – Carte € 21/37
◆ A small and welcoming family-run village inn where traditional cuisine with a modern twist is served in a simple rustic setting.

MANCIET – 32 Gers – 336 C7 – see Nogaro

MANDELIEU – 06 Alpes-Maritimes – 341 C6 – pop. 20 200 – alt. 4 m 42 E2
– Casino : Royal Hôtel Z – ✉ 06210 French Riviera

Paris 890 – Brignoles 86 – Cannes 9 – Draguignan 53 – Fréjus 30 – Nice 37
Office de tourisme, avenue H. Clews ✆ 04 92 97 99 27, Fax 04 93 93 64 66
de Mandelieu Route du Golf, SW : 2 km, ✆ 04 92 97 32 00
Riviera Golf Club Avenue des Amazones, SW : 2 km, ✆ 04 92 97 49 49
<★ from San Peyré hill - Site★ of the château-museum.

Plan on following page

Hostellerie du Golf rm, VISA
780 av. Mer – ✆ 04 93 49 11 66 – www.hostelleriedugolf.com – hoteldugolf@aol.com – Fax 04 92 97 04 01 Y n
55 rm – †€ 68/98 ††€ 82/122, ☐ € 9 – 16 suites – ½ P € 68/98
Rest – Menu € 24 – Carte approx. € 39
◆ Built on the riverbanks facing the famous Old Course, founded by a Russian Grand Duke in 1891. Practical rooms with a terrace or balcony. Bright dining room opening onto the garden; unpretentious fare.

Les Bruyères without rest VISA
1400 av. Fréjus – ✆ 04 93 49 92 01 – www.hotellesbruyeres.net – hotel.les.bruyeres@wanadoo.fr – Fax 04 93 49 21 55 – Closed 5-26 January Y h
14 rm – †€ 67/92 ††€ 67/92, ☐ € 10
◆ Not far from the beach and golf course; functional, well-soundproofed, neat bedrooms behind a broad modern façade enhanced by a rotunda.

Acadia without rest VISA
681 av. de la Mer – ✆ 04 93 49 28 23 – acadia-hotel.com – acadia.revotel@wanadoo.fr – Fax 04 92 97 55 54 – Closed 19 Nov. - 27 Dec. Y v
36 rm – †€ 61/90 ††€ 71/90, ☐ € 9 – 6 suites
◆ The private pontoons of this hotel located in a bend of the Siagne, opposite Robinson island, make an excellent place for a waterside stroll. The simple rooms are gradually being renovated.

Azur hôtel without rest VISA
192 av. Maréchal Juin – ✆ 04 93 49 24 24 – www.azurhotel06.com – reception@azurhotel06.com – Fax 04 92 97 68 36 – Closed 21 November-21 December Y k
48 rm – †€ 52/86 ††€ 64/106, ☐ € 9
◆ This hotel has been treated to a facelift and now offers functional, colourful rooms equipped with new bathrooms. Wi-fi, sitting room-veranda and pool with a small bar.

La Napoule – ✉ 06210

Paris 893 – Cannes 9 – Mandelieu-la-Napoule 3 – Nice 40 – St-Raphaël 34
Site★ of the château-museum.

Sofitel Royal Casino < rm, VISA
605 av. Gén.-de-Gaulle, (D 6098) – ✆ 04 92 97 70 00 – www.pullmanhotels.com – h1168@accor.com – Fax 04 93 49 51 50 Z a
213 rm – †€ 285/745 ††€ 285/745, ☐ € 24 – 2 suites
Rest *Le Féréol* – ✆ 04 92 97 70 20 – Menu € 39 (dinner) – Carte € 49/72
Rest *Terrasse du Casino* – ✆ 04 92 97 70 21 – Menu (€ 20) – Carte € 23/37
◆ After a full-scale renovation, this modern seaside complex sports a contemporary, minimalist decor. Predominantly white colour scheme in rooms, facing the sea or the golf course. A designer setting, lunchtime buffets and evening menus. The casino's Purple Lounge is the setting for a new live music restaurant concept.

LA NAPOULE

MANDELIEU-LA-NAPOULE

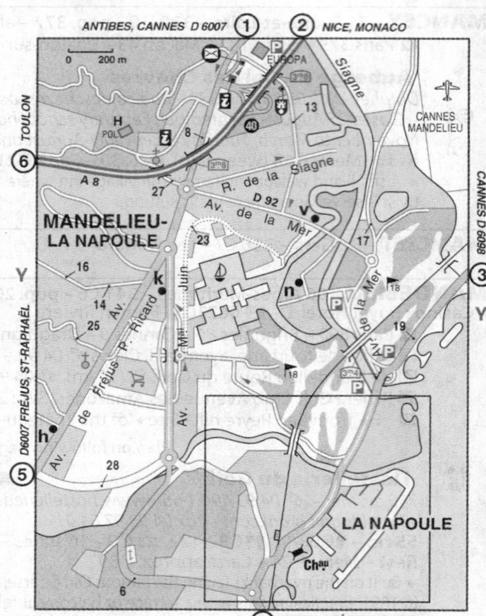

ANTIBES, CANNES D 6007
NICE, MONACO
0 200 m
EUROPA
Siagne
CANNES MANDELIEU
CANNES D 6098
TOULON
A 8
R. de la Siagne
D 92
Av. de la Mer
MANDELIEU-LA NAPOULE
Av. de Fréjus
P. Ricard
Av. Mal Juin
Av. de la Mer
D6007 FRÉJUS, ST-RAPHAËL
LA NAPOULE
Chau
D 6098 THÉOULE-S-MER
Y

0 200 m
D 6098
CASINO
LES RÉSIDENCES DU PORT
Argentière
Riou
Av. du
Av. Gal de Gaulle
PARC DÉPARTEMENTAL
Av.
Port
R. Ptit
Av. H. Clews
San Peyré
du Peyré
Bd du San
Fanfarigoule
Bd
23 Août
Av.
R. de la Plage
Château
PORT
CAPITAINERIE
LA NAPOULE
Bd J. Soustelle
PLAGE DE LA RAGUETTE
Z

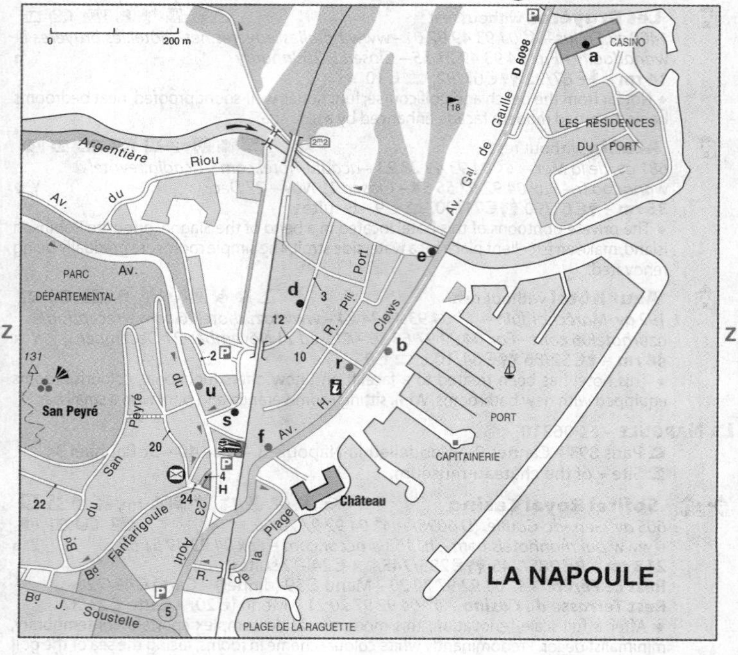

L'Ermitage du Riou

av. H. Clews – ✆ 04 93 49 95 56 – www.ermitage-du-riou.fr – hotel@ermitage-du-riou.fr – Fax 04 92 97 69 05 Z **e**

41 rm – †€ 126/331 ††€ 126/331, ☕ € 18 – 4 suites

Rest – Menu € 27/100 – Carte € 65/130

◆ This old ochre and brick Provençal abode has comfortable bedrooms overlooking the ocean or the golf course. A dining room-veranda facing the port in which traditional dishes, seafood and wines from the estate take pride of place.

Villa Parisiana without rest

5 r. Argentière – ✆ 04 93 49 93 02 – www.villaparisiana.com – villa.parisiana@orange.fr – Fax 04 93 49 62 32 – Closed 29 November-28 December and 10-15 January Z **d**

13 rm – †€ 42/69 ††€ 42/69, ☕ € 8

◆ This 1900 villa exudes charm: well renovated inviting rooms, some with sunny balconies and a summer terrace under the vines. Non-smoking.

La Corniche d'Or without rest

pl. de la Fontaine – ✆ 04 93 49 92 51 – www.cornichedor.com – info@cornichedor.com – Fax 04 93 49 71 95 Z **s**

12 rm – †€ 39/79 ††€ 44/79, ☕ € 8

◆ This hotel offers simple spruce rooms (all have balcony) with pine furnishings, new bed linen and air-conditioning (on request). Pleasant terrace and friendly staff.

L'Oasis (Stéphane, Antoine et François Raimbault)

r. J. H. Carle – ✆ 04 93 49 95 52 – www.oasis-raimbault.com – contact@oasis-raimbault.com – Fax 04 93 49 64 13 – Closed from mid-December to mid-January, Sunday and Monday Z **r**

Rest – Menu € 58 (lunch), € 77/190 – Carte € 131/216

Spec. Emietté de tourteau au guacamole en salade de langouste et pourpier à l'huile de curry. Teppanyaki d'entrecôte wagyu "souvenir d'Osaka" sauce akamiso et yuzu. Caravane de desserts. **Wines** Côtes de Provence, les Baux-de-Provence.

◆ This caravanserai for gourmet nomads is not a mirage! Discover delicious Mediterranean cuisine with oriental touches, gourmet workshops (covering cooking, patisserie and wine), as well as a lush patio and elegant setting.

La Pomme d'Amour

209 av. du 23 Août – ✆ 04 93 49 95 19 – Fax 04 93 49 95 24 – Closed 16 November-7 December, Tuesday lunch and Monday Z **u**

Rest – Menu (€ 26), € 32/55 – Carte € 44/70

◆ Discreet culinary venue in the centre of La Napoule, right next to the station. A pleasant, cosy dining room with neat table settings. Traditional and local cuisine.

Les Bartavelles

1 pl. Château – ✆ 04 93 49 95 15 – sarl-etec-bartavelles@wanadoo.fr – Fax 04 93 49 95 15 – Closed 5-26 January, Tuesday and Wednesday except dinner in July-August Z **f**

Rest – Menu (€ 22 bi), € 27/39 – Carte € 38/53

◆ This friendly informal house makes a point of serving generous traditional dishes. Dining room-veranda extended by a terrace shaded by plane trees in summer.

Le Bistrot du Port

At the port – ✆ 04 93 49 80 60 – www.bistrotduport.fr – bistrotduport@wanadoo.fr – Fax 04 93 49 69 76 – Closed 25 November-15 December, Wednesday in low season and school holidays Z **b**

Rest – Menu (€ 18), € 26/32 – Carte € 36/64

◆ To enjoy a unique view of the boats, drop anchor in this harbour bistro. Welcoming nautical interior, a veranda extended by a terrace in fine weather and excellent seafood.

MANDEREN – 57 Moselle – 307 J2 – see Sierck-les-Bains

MANE – 04 Alpes-de-Haute-Provence – 334 C9 – see Forcalquier

MANIGOD – 74 Haute-Savoie – 328 L5 – pop. 924 – alt. 950 m – ✉ 74230 46 F1

Paris 558 – Albertville 39 – Annecy 25 – Chamonix-Mont-Blanc 67 – Thônes 6

Office de tourisme, Chef-lieu ✆ 04 50 44 92 44, Fax 04 50 44 94 68

Manigod Valley ★★, French Alps

col de la Croix-Fry road : 5,5 km - ✉ 74230 Manigod

Chalet Hôtel Croix-Fry VISA MC AE

– ✆ 04 50 44 90 16 – www.hotelchaletcroixfry.com – hotelcroixfry@wanadoo.fr – Fax 04 50 44 94 87 – Open mid June-mid September and mid December to mid April

10 rm – †€ 150 ††€ 150/440, ☐ € 20 – ½ P € 140/205

Rest – *(closed Tuesday lunch, Wednesday lunch and Monday)*

Menu € 26 (weekday lunch), € 50/78 – Carte € 58/84

◆ Idyllically located in alpine meadows, this lovely chalet has been run by the same family for decades. Cosy mountain decor and adorably snug bedrooms. Friendly table d'hôte in the restaurant; panoramic terrace facing the Aravis peaks.

MANOSQUE – 04 Alpes-de-Haute-Provence – 334 C10 – pop. 21 300 – alt. 387 m – ✉ 04100 French Alps 40 B2

Paris 758 – Aix-en-Provence 57 – Avignon 91 – Digne-les-Bains 61

Office de tourisme, place du Docteur Joubert ✆ 04 92 72 16 00, Fax 04 92 72 58 98

du Lubéron Pierrevert La Grande Gardette, 7 km on the la Bastide-des-Jourdans road, ✆ 04 92 72 17 19

Old Manosque★: Porte Saunerie★, façade★ of the town hall - Sarcophagus★ and Black Virgin★ in N.-D. de Romigier church - Carzou Foundation★ M - ⋞★ du Mont d'Or Northeast: 1.5 km.

Pré St-Michel without rest VISA MC AE

1.5 km north on bd M. Bret and Dauphin road – ✆ 04 92 72 14 27 – www.presaintmichel.com – pre.st.michel@wanadoo.fr – Fax 04 92 72 53 04

24 rm – †€ 60/110 ††€ 60/110, ☐ € 10

◆ A modern, regional-style hotel with spacious rooms decorated in Provençal style, some with a private terrace. Featuring a charming view over the town.

Le Sud rm, VISA MC AE

bd Charles de Gaulle – ✆ 04 92 87 78 58 – www.hotel-lesud.com – hotelbestwesternlesud@orange.fr – Fax 04 92 72 66 60

36 rm – †€ 70/100 ††€ 80/110, ☐ € 12 – ½ P € 65/95

Rest – Menu (€ 16), € 19/28 – Carte € 24/45

◆ Business hotel, ideal for conferences, situated on the outskirts of the old town. The rooms are all identical and the lounge areas are decorated with Provencal touches. The spirit of the South is omnipresent in this restaurant (painted woodwork and sunny colours).

MANOSQUE

Arthur-Robert (R.) 2
Aubette (R. d') 3
Bret (Bd M.) 5
Chacundier (R.) 6
Cougourdelles (Bd des) 7
Dauphine (R.) 8
Giono (Av. J.) 9
Grande (R.) 10
Guilhempierre (R.) 12
Hôtel-de-Ville (Pl. de l') 13
Jean-Jacques-Rousseau (R.) 14
Marchands (R. des) 15
Mirabeau (Bd) 16
Mont-d'Or (R. du) 17
Observantins (Pl. des) 19
Ormeaux (Pl. des) 20
Paul-Martin Nalin (Bd) 21
Pelloutier (Bd C.) 22
Plaine (Bd de la) 23
République (R. de la) 26
St-Lazare (Av.) 28
Saunerie (R. de la) 30
Soubeyran (R.) 32
Tanneurs (R. des) 33
Tourelles (R. des) 34
Voland (R.) 35
Vraies-Richesses (Montée des) 36

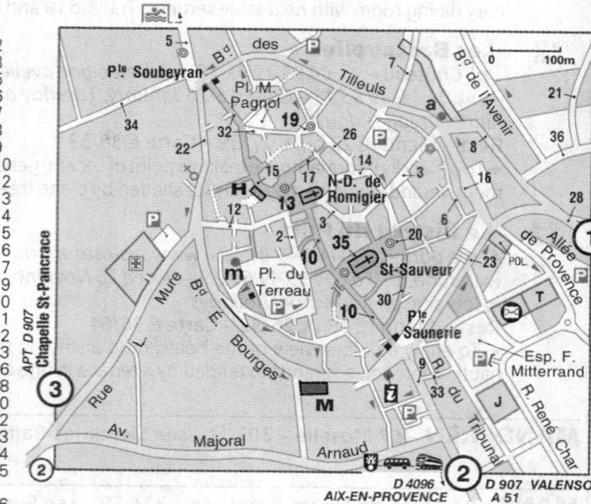

Les Monges without rest
rte d'Apt, 4 km northwest on the D 907 and minor road – 04 92 72 68 41 – www.lesmonges.com – contact@lesmonges.com – Open 15 March-30 November
5 rm – €60/75 €60/75
◆ Former barn in the middle of the country, where the writer Jean Giono would buy his cheese. Friendly welcome and fresh, functional rooms. Homemade jam and fresh eggs at breakfast.

Le Luberon VISA AE
21 bis pl. Terreau – 04 92 72 03 09 – Closed 12-26 October, Thursday dinner, Sunday dinner and Monday **m**
Rest – Menu (€ 15), € 20/55 – Carte € 37/65
◆ A small restaurant in the centre of town with a rustic dining area decorated in sunny tones. Verdant terrace providing welcome shade in summer. Southern French cuisine.

to A51 interchange 4 km by ② - **04100 Manosque**

Ibis without rest P VISA AE
– 04 92 71 18 00 – www.ibishotel.com – h5611@accor.com – Fax 04 92 72 00 45
48 rm – €55/77 €55/77, €8
◆ It's easy to find this modern building with a yellow façade. It provides functional rooms in line with the hotel chain's standards. Practical stopover option.

LE MANS P – 72 Sarthe – **310** K6 – **pop. 143 800 – Built-up area 194 825 – alt. 80 m – 72000** Châteaux of the Loire 35 **D1**

Paris 206 – Angers 97 – Le Havre 213 – Nantes 184 – Rennes 154 – Tours 85

Office de tourisme, rue de l'Étoile 02 43 28 17 22, Fax 02 43 28 12 14

18 de Sargé-lès-le-Mans Sargé-lès-le-Mans Rue du Golf, 6 km on the Bonnétable road, 02 43 76 25 07

18 des 24 Heures-Le Mans Mulsanne Route de Tours, 11 km on the Tours road, 02 43 42 00 36

24-hour race circuit and Bugatti circuit 02 43 40 24 24: 5 km by ④.

St-Julien cathedral ★★: apse★★★ - Old Le Mans★★: House of Queen Bérengère★, Gallo-Roman wall★ DV **M²** - La Couture church★: Virgin★★ - Ste-Jeanne-d'Arc church ★ - Musée de Tessé★ - Épau abbey★ BZ , 4 km by D 152 - Musée de l'Automobile★★: 5 km by ④.

Plans on following pages

Mercure Centre without rest P VISA AE
19 r. Chanzy – 02 43 40 22 40 – www.mercure.com – h5641@accor.com – Fax 02 43 40 22 31 DX **p**
73 rm – €150 €165, €14 – 5 suites
◆ Hotel (non-smokers) located in a listed building that formerly housed the Mutuelles du Mans. Practical, contemporary furnished rooms with good soundproofing.

Chantecler without rest P VISA AE
50 r. Pelouse – 02 43 14 40 00 – www.hotelchantecler.fr – hotel.chantecler@wanadoo.fr – Fax 02 43 77 16 28 – Closed 8-23 August CY **f**
32 rm – €71 €82, €10 – 3 suites
◆ Entirely non-smoking hotel. Breakfast is served in a veranda winter garden. Soothing pastel colours in the well-soundproofed rooms.

Mercure Batignolles rm, P VISA AE
17 r. Pointe – 02 43 72 27 20 – www.mercure.com – h0344@accor.com – Fax 02 43 85 96 06 AZ **b**
68 rm – €65/95 €75/105, €10
Rest – *(closed 24 December-3 January, Saturday and Sunday from September to May and Monday lunch)* Menu (€ 16), € 21
◆ Establishment housing modern, practical and well-kept rooms; those to the rear are quieter. Garden with crazy golf. Dining room decorated with photographs recalling the legendary Le Mans 24-hr race. Traditional repertory.

LE MANS

Ambroise Paré (R.) . . . . AZ 4
Ballon (R. de) . . . . AZ 6
Bertinière (R. de la) . . . . BZ 10
Brosselette (Bd P.) . . . . AZ 15
Carnot (Bd) . . . . AZ 16
Churchill (Bd W.) . . . . BZ 17
Clemenceau (Bd G.) . . . . BZ 18
Douce-Amie (R. de) . . . . BZ 22
Durand (Av. G.) . . . . BZ 26
Esterel (R. de l') . . . . BZ 30
Flore (R. de) . . . . BZ 31
Gaulle (R. du Gén.-de) . . . . . ABZ 36
Géneslay (Av. F.) . . . . ABZ 37
Grande-Maison (R. de la) . . . . . . AZ 39
Heuzé (Av. O.) . . . . AZ 42
Jean-Jaurès (Av.) . . . . BZ 43
Lefeuvre (Av. H.) . . . . AZ 44
Maillets (R. des) . . . . BZ 46
Mare (CH. de la) . . . . BZ 49
Mariette (R. de la) . . . . BZ 51
Monthéard (Av. de) . . . . BZ 55
Moulin (Av. J.) . . . . BZ 57
Négrier (Bd du Gén.) . . . . BZ 58
Néruda (R. Pablo) . . . . BZ 60
Pied-Sec (R. de) . . . . AZ 63
Pointe (R. de la) . . . . AZ 64
Prémartine (Rte de) . . . . BZ 67
Riffaudières (Bd des) . . . . AZ 73
Rondeau (R. J.) . . . . AZ 74
Rubillard (Av.) . . . . AZ 78
Schuman (Bd R.) . . . . BZ 80
Victimes du Nazisme (R. des) . . . . BZ 82
Yvré-Levêque (Ch. d') . . . . BZ 87

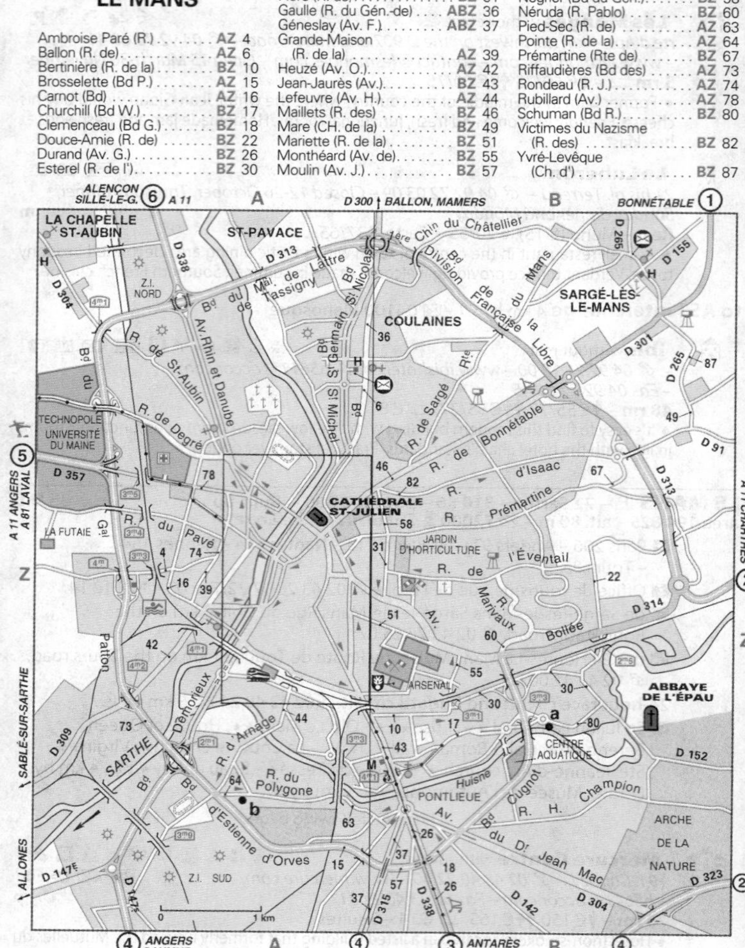

Emeraude without rest
18 r. Gastelier – ✆ 02 43 24 87 46 – www.hotel-emeraude-le-mans.com – emeraudehotel@wanadoo.fr – Fax 02 43 24 60 64 – Closed 9-23 August and 20 December-3 January CY **z**
33 rm – †€ 64/68 ††€ 68/75, ☕ € 8
◆ A warm welcome in this hotel near the station. Rooms in pastel tones. Breakfast served in the inner flower-decked courtyard on fine days.

Le Commerce without rest
41 bd de la Gare – ✆ 02 43 83 20 20 – www.commerce-hotel.fr – commerce.hotel@wanadoo.fr – Fax 02 43 83 20 21 CY **d**
31 rm – †€ 54/65 ††€ 60/65, ☕ € 8
◆ This hotel located near the station has excellent sound insulation, providing renovated and functional rooms, all very well kept.

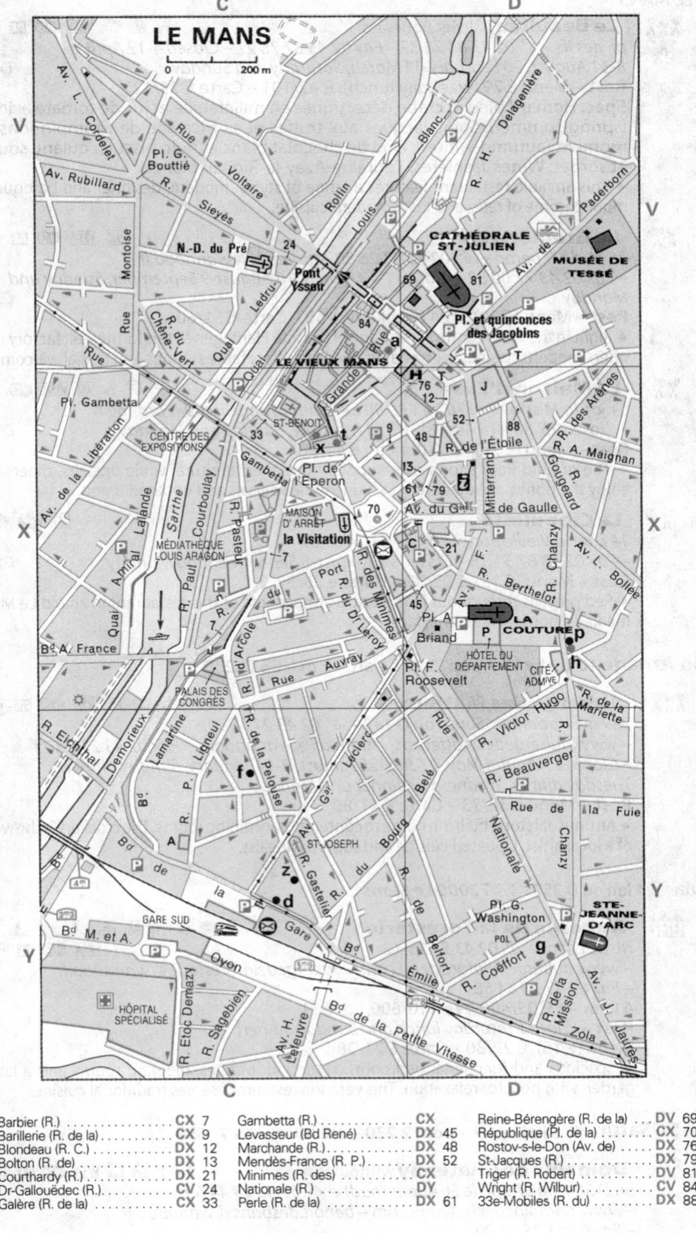

Barbier (R.)	CX	7	Gambetta (R.)	CX		Reine-Bérengère (R. de la)	DV	69
Barillerie (R. de la)	CX	9	Levasseur (Bd René)	DX	45	République (Pl. de la)	CX	70
Blondeau (R. C.)	DX	12	Marchande (R.)	DX	48	Rostov-s-le-Don (Av. de)	DX	76
Bolton (R. de)	DX	13	Mendès-France (R. P.)	DX	52	St-Jacques (R.)	DX	79
Courthardy (R.)	DX	21	Minimes (R. des)	CX		Triger (R. Robert)	DV	81
Dr-Gallouëdec (R.)	CV	24	Nationale (R.)	DY		Wright (R. Wilbur)	CV	84
Galère (R. de la)	CX	33	Perle (R. de la)	DX	61	33e-Mobiles (R. du)	DX	88

XXX **Le Beaulieu** (Olivier Boussard)
pl. des Ifs – ✆ 02 43 87 78 37 – Fax 02 43 87 78 27 – Closed 4-12 April, 8-31 August, 20 February-1st March, Saturday and Sunday DX **h**
Rest – Menu € 29 (weekday lunch), € 42/101 – Carte € 73/122
Spec. Homard bleu et crabe décortiqués en millefeuille et jus de tomate acidulé (spring-summer). Saint-Jacques aux truffes et sa fricassée de champignons du moment (autumn-winter). Duo de chocolat blanc et noir, biscuit coulant, soufflé et sorbet. **Wines** Jasnières, Touraine-Azay-le-Rideau blanc.
◆ This amiable restaurant features a range of styles (modern, designer and baroque), a monochrome of reds, and tasty modern cuisine.

XX **Le Grenier à sel**
26 pl. de l'Eperon – ✆ 02 43 23 26 30 – grenasel@wanadoo.fr – Fax 02 43 77 00 80 – Closed 1-17 March, 16 August-9 September, Sunday and Monday CX **t**
Rest – Menu (€ 20), € 24 (weekdays)/58 – Carte € 51/60
◆ Right in the town centre at the edge of the Cité Plantagenêt, this former salt factory now offers modern cuisine. Rejuvenated decor, faultless table settings and genial welcome.

XX **La Maison d'Élise**
6 r. de la Mission – ✆ 02 43 40 00 58 – lamaisondelise49@orange.fr – Closed 15 July-15 August, 15-28 February, Sunday and Monday DY **g**
Rest – Menu (€ 20), € 30 (lunch), € 40/58
◆ The ground floor sports contemporary designer furniture, while upstairs, diners can enjoy the bonus of a quiet terrace. Lunchtime specials and updated menu.

X **La Ciboulette**
14 r. de la Vieille Porte – ✆ 02 43 24 65 67 – Fax 02 43 87 51 18 – Closed 24 August-8 September and Monday CX **x**
Rest – Menu (€ 13), € 22/32 – Carte € 26/53
◆ Red prevails throughout in the bistro atmosphere of this restaurant in an old Le Mans medieval house. Traditional fare.

in Arnage **10 km by ④ – pop. 5 177 – alt. 42 m – ✉ 72230**

XXX **Auberge des Matfeux**
289 av. Nationale, South on D 147 – ✆ 02 43 21 10 71 – www.aubergedesmatfeux.fr – matfeux@wanadoo.fr – Fax 02 43 21 25 23 – Closed 27 April-4 May, 27 July-25 August, 2-14 January, Sunday dinner, Tuesday dinner, Wednesday dinner and Monday
Rest – Menu € 38/73 – Carte € 41/80
◆ An unusual stone built inn home to contemporary dining rooms. The crockery is the work of a local artist. Updated cuisine and superb wine list.

via ⑤ 4 km on D 357 – ✉ *72000 Le Mans*

Auberge de la Foresterie rm, rest,
rte de Laval – ✆ 02 43 51 25 12 – www.aubergedelaforesterie.com – aubergedelaforesterie@wanadoo.fr – Fax 02 43 28 54 58
41 rm – †€ 95/400 ††€ 110/600, ☕ € 11
Rest – *(Closed Saturday lunch and Sunday dinner)*
Menu (€ 15), € 22/30 – Carte € 21/38
◆ Spacious and functional bedrooms, reception lounges, meeting rooms and a large garden with pool for relaxation. This veranda restaurant serves traditional cuisine.

in St-Saturnin **8 km by ⑥ – pop. 2 230 – alt. 80 m – ✉ 72650**

Domaine de Chatenay without rest
on D 304, (la Chapelle St-Aubin road) – ✆ 02 43 25 44 60 – www.domainedechatenay.com – benoit.desbans@wanadoo.fr – Fax 02 43 25 21 00
8 rm ☕ – †€ 78/115 ††€ 120/138
◆ A superb 18C manor set in a 40ha estate, providing refined guestrooms with antiques and beautiful fabrics. Breakfast served in the Empire dining room.

MANSLE – 16 Charente – 324 L4 – pop. 1 527 – alt. 65 m – ✉ 16230 39 C2

Paris 421 – Angoulême 26 – Cognac 53 – Limoges 93 – Poitiers 88 – St-Jean-d'Angély 62

Office de tourisme, place du Gardoire ✆ 05 45 20 39 91, Fax 05 45 20 39 91

Beau Rivage

pl. Gardoire – ✆ 05 45 20 31 26 – www.hotel-beau-rivage-charente.com – hotel.beau.rivage.16@orange.fr – Fax 05 45 22 24 24 – Closed 16 February-10 March, 24 November-15 December, Sunday dinner and Monday lunch October-April

29 rm – †€ 55/58 ††€ 55/58, ☕ € 9

Rest – Menu € 14 (weekdays)/34 – Carte € 30/50

◆ Behind a slightly austere façade, this hotel has elegant rooms, some of which have been tastefully renovated. Garden on the banks of the Charente (canoe hire). A large dining area and terrace with a view of the river. Traditional cuisine.

in Luxé 6 km West by D 739 – pop. 756 – alt. 70 m – ✉ 16230

Auberge du Cheval Blanc

at the station – ✆ 05 45 22 23 62 – restaurantlechevalblanc@wanadoo.fr – Fax 05 45 39 94 75 – Closed 1st-10 September, February, Sunday dinner, Tuesday and Monday

Rest – Menu € 18 bi (weekday lunch), € 29/40 – Carte approx. € 37

◆ This century-old building with an attractive façade has an equally pleasant rustic dining room, decorated with flowers. Refined regional cuisine.

MANTES-LA-JOLIE – 78 Yvelines – 311 G2 – pop. 40 900 – alt. 34 m – ✉ 78200 Northern France and the Paris Region 18 A1

Paris 56 – Beauvais 69 – Chartres 78 – Évreux 46 – Rouen 80 – Versailles 47

Office de tourisme, 8 bis, rue Marie et Robert Dubois ✆ 01 34 77 10 30, Fax 01 30 98 61 49

de Guerville Guerville La Plagne, 6 km on the Houdan road, ✆ 01 30 92 45 45

de Moisson-Mousseaux Moisson Base de Loisir de Moisson, 14 km on the Vernon road and minor road, ✆ 01 34 79 39 00

de Villarceaux Chaussy Château du Couvent, N : 20 km on D 147, ✆ 01 34 67 73 83

Notre-Dame collegiate church ★★ BB.

Plan on following page

Rive Gauche

1 r. du Fort – ✆ 01 30 92 30 16 – www.rivegauchemantes.fr – rivegauche.mantes@wanadoo.fr – Fax 01 30 92 30 16 – Closed 3 August-1st September, Saturday lunch, Sunday and Monday B **a**

Rest – Menu (€ 22 bi) – Carte € 45/55

◆ Not far from the Seine, behind the Porte-aux-Prêtres, this nice little restaurant serves modern cuisine in a decor combining old and new styles.

in Mantes-la-Ville 2 km by ③ – pop. 18 200 – alt. 36 m – ✉ 78711

Le Moulin de la Reillère

171 rte Houdan – ✆ 01 30 92 22 00 – le-moulin.reillere@wanadoo.fr – Fax 01 34 97 82 85 – Closed 10 August-1st September, Saturday lunch, Sunday dinner and Monday

Rest – Menu (€ 26), € 34/51 – Carte € 40/60

◆ Pretty inn located in an old 18C mill. Pleasant, refined dining room, terrace, attractive flower garden and traditional cuisine. Friendly welcome.

in Rosay 10 km by ③ – pop. 358 – alt. 98 m – ✉ 78790

Auberge de la Truite

1 r. Boinvilliers – ✆ 01 34 76 30 52 – aubergedelatruite@wanadoo.fr – Fax 01 34 76 30 65 – Closed 25 August-9 September, 1st-13 January, Tuesday lunch, Sunday dinner and Monday

Rest – Menu € 30 (weekday lunch), € 38/60

◆ Rustic setting with art work on sale, terrace, up-to-date seasonal classic cuisine and advice on your choice of wine: what more could you want? Enjoy your meal!

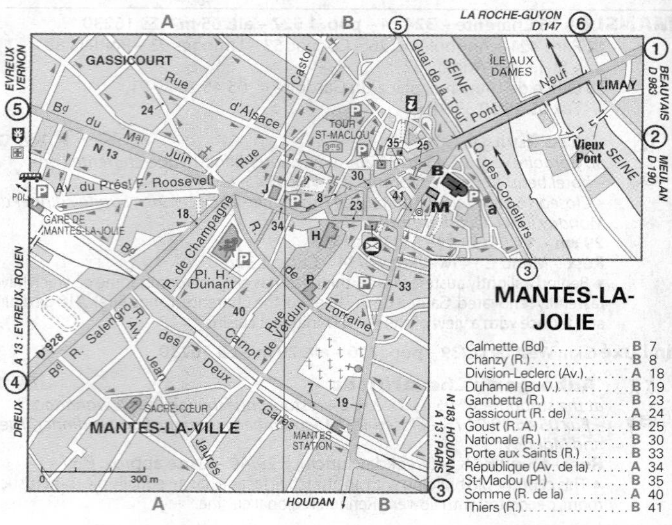

MANTES-LA-VILLE – 78 Yvelines – **311** G2 – **see Mantes-la-Jolie**

MANVIEUX – 14 Calvados – **303** I3 – **see Arromanches-les-Bains**

MANZAC-SUR-VERN – 24 Dordogne – **329** E5 – **pop. 508** – **alt. 80 m** 4 **C1**
– ✉ 24110

▶ Paris 502 – Bergerac 34 – Bordeaux 112 – Périgueux 20

Le Lion d'Or with rm
pl. de l'Église – ✆ 05 53 54 28 09 – www.lion-dor-manzac.com – lion-dor@lion-dor-manzac.com – Fax 05 53 54 25 50 – Closed 16-30 November, 1st-22 February, Sunday dinner except July-August and Monday
8 rm – †€ 48 ††€ 52/55, ☐ € 8 – ½ P € 53
Rest – Menu (€ 16 bi), € 19/34 – Carte € 29/45
♦ Bright dining room adorned with knick-knacks, serving generous, up-to-date cuisine with regional touches.

MARAIS-VERNIER – 27 Eure – **304** C5 – **see Conteville**

MARANS – 17 Charente-Maritime – **324** E2 – **pop. 4 654** – **alt. 1 m** 38 **B2**
– ✉ 17230 **Atlantic Coast**

▶ Paris 461 – Fontenay-le-Comte 28 – Niort 56 – La Rochelle 24 – La Roche-sur-Yon 60

Office de tourisme, 62, rue d'Aligre ✆ 05 46 01 12 87, Fax 05 46 35 97 36

La Porte Verte with rm
20 quai Foch – ✆ 05 46 01 09 45 – www.la-porte-verte.com – laporteverte@aol.com – Open from April to September and closed Wednesday
5 rm – †€ 46 ††€ 52/56
Rest – *(number of covers limited, pre-book)* Menu € 18/33 – Carte € 27/47
♦ This charming 19C building on the banks of the canal near the ocean port is a rustic restaurant serving regional cuisine, also providing well-kept guest rooms.

MARAUSSAN – 34 Hérault – 339 D8 – see Béziers

MARÇAY – 37 Indre-et-Loire – 317 K6 – see Chinon

MARCILLAC-LA-CROISILLE – 19 Corrèze – 329 N4 – pop. 827 25 C3
– alt. 550 m – ✉ 19320 Dordogne-Berry-Limousin

Paris 498 – Argentat 26 – Aurillac 80 – Égletons 17 – Mauriac 40 – Tulle 27

at Pont du Chambon 15 km Southeast, by D 978 (dir. Mauriac), D 60 and D 13
✉ 19320 St-Merd-de-Lapleau

Fabry (Au Rendez-vous des Pêcheurs) with rm
– ✆ 05 55 27 88 39 – www.rest-fabry.com – contact@rest-fabry.com – Fax 05 55 27 83 19 – Open 13 February-12 November and closed Sunday dinner and Monday off season
8 rm – €45 €45/50, €7
Rest – Menu €16 (weekdays)/39 – Carte €28/40
◆ A verdant backdrop to this house standing alone on the banks of the Dordogne, which for three generations has provided regional cooking, light bedrooms and friendly hospitality.

MARCILLY-EN-VILLETTE – 45 Loiret – 318 J5 – pop. 1 958 12 C2
– alt. 124 m – ✉ 45240

Paris 153 – Blois 83 – Orléans 23 – Romorantin-Lanthenay 55 – Salbris 40

La Ferme des Foucault without rest
6 km south-east on the D 64 (rte de Sennely) – ✆ 02 38 76 94 41 – www.ferme-des-foucault.com – rbeau@wanadoo.fr – Fax 02 38 76 94 41
3 rm – €75/85 €80/90
◆ This old half-timbered farmhouse is located in the heart of the Sologne forest, providing charming and spacious rooms with rustic furnishings, one of which also features a terrace.

MARCQ-EN-BAROEUL – 59 Nord – 302 G3 – see Lille

MAREUIL-CAUBERT – 80 Somme – 301 D7 – see Abbeville

MARGAUX – 33 Gironde – 335 G4 – pop. 1 391 – alt. 16 m – ✉ 33460 3 B1

Paris 599 – Bordeaux 29 – Lesparre-Médoc 42
de Margaux 5 route de l 'Île Vincent, N : 1 km, ✆ 05 57 88 87 40

Relais de Margaux
5 route de l'Île Vincent, 2.5 km north-westward – ✆ 05 57 88 38 30 – www.relais-margaux.fr – relais-margaux@relais-margaux.fr – Fax 05 57 88 31 73
92 rm – €159/199 €159/199, €21 – 8 suites
Rest *L'Île Vincent* – *(Open 1 May-30 October) (dinner only)* Menu €46/84 bi – Carte €55/90
Rest *Brasserie du Lac* – Menu (€16), €21 (lunch) – Carte €35/55
◆ Former winegrower's estate between the estuary and vineyards. Golf in the park, hi-tech spa and comfortable rooms. Smart interior, lovely terrace, modern menu and selection of local vintages. A trendy brasserie with its culinary roots in the soil. In summer, enjoy outdoor dining on the attractive terrace.

Le Pavillon de Margaux rm,
3 r. G. Mandel – ✆ 05 57 88 77 54 – www.pavillonmargaux.com – le-pavillon-margaux@wanadoo.fr – Fax 05 57 88 77 73 – Closed 21-28 December
14 rm – €75/125 €75/125, €12
Rest – *(closed 21 December-8 February, Tuesday and Wednesday from 1 November to 1 April)* Menu €15 (weekday lunch), €34/62 – Carte €43/55
◆ Handsome 19C abode surrounded by vineyards. Attractive plush sitting room and pleasant bedrooms decorated on the theme of the Médoc estates. Smart dining room and veranda facing the prestigious Margaux vineyard. Traditional menu.

Le Savoie

1 pl. Trémoille – 05 57 88 31 76 – www.lesavoie.net – Fax 05 57 88 31 76 – Closed 22-28 December, Monday dinner except from June to September and Sunday dinner

Rest – Menu (€ 15), € 28/88 – Carte € 50/69

◆ This 19C house has a pleasant interior and a patio terrace with a glass ceiling. Tasty cuisine prepared in a coal-fired oven, plus a good selection of Bordeaux wines.

in Arcins 6 km Northwest On D 2 – **pop. 357 – alt. 10 m** – ✉ **33460**

Le Lion d'Or

– 05 56 58 96 79 – Closed July, 23 December-2 January, Sunday, Monday and bank holidays

Rest – *(number of covers limited, pre-book)* Menu € 15 bi (weekdays) – Carte € 28/42

◆ Attractive rustic bistro with light wood panelling and bottle rack decor. Generous, country-style cuisine. A warm and friendly ambience guaranteed.

MARGÈS – **26 Drôme** – **332** D3 – **pop. 846 – alt. 282 m** – ✉ **26260** 43 **E2**

Paris 551 – Grenoble 92 – Hauterives 14 – Romans-sur-Isère 13 – Valence 36

Auberge Le Pont du Chalon

2 km south on D 538 – 04 75 45 62 13 – www.pontduchalon.com – pontduchalon@wanadoo.fr – Fax 04 75 45 60 19 – Closed 27 April-3 May, 17 August-2 September, 21-30 December, Sunday evening, Wednesday evening, Monday and Tuesday

9 rm – †€ 40/45 ††€ 40/45, ☕ € 6 – ½ P € 44/47

Rest – *(closed Wednesday dinner from September to May, Sunday dinner, Monday and Tuesday)* Menu (€ 12), € 18/33 – Carte € 24/35

◆ This inn built in 1900 is nestled behind a curtain of plane trees, providing a warm and refined atmosphere with modern and colourful décor. "Rustic chic" restaurant with terrace and a French bowls pitch for a game before or after your meal.

MARGUERITTES – **30 Gard** – **339** L5 – **see Nîmes**

MARIENTHAL – **67 Bas-Rhin** – **315** K4 – ✉ **67500** 1 **B1**

Paris 479 – Haguenau 5 – Saverne 42 – Strasbourg 30

Le Relais Princesse Maria Leczinska

1 r. Rothbach – 03 88 93 43 48 – Closed Saturday lunch, Sunday dinner and Wednesday

Rest – *(number of covers limited, pre-book)* Menu (€ 15), € 38/40

◆ Traditional at heart (beams, stained-glass windows, enamelled stove) but with a contemporary spirit (simple colours), this establishment offers a reduced but tasty modern menu.

MARIGNANE – **13 Bouches-du-Rhône** – **340** G5 – **pop. 33 400 – alt. 10 m** – ✉ **13700** **Provence** 40 **B3**

Paris 753 – Aix-en-Provence 24 – Marseille 26 – Martigues 16 – Salon-de-Provence 33

Marseille-Provence: 04 42 14 14 14.

Office de tourisme, 4, boulevard Frédéric Mistral 04 42 77 04 90, Fax 04 42 31 49 39

Rove underground canal ★ Southeast: 3 km.

to Marseille-Provence Airport North – ✉ **13700**

Pullman

– 04 42 78 42 78 – www.pullman-marseille-provence.com – h0541@accor.com – Fax 04 42 78 42 70

177 rm – †€ 145/345 ††€ 145/365, ☕ € 25 – 1 suite

Rest – 04 42 78 42 83 – Menu € 19/32 – Carte € 41/60

◆ This fully revamped 1970s hotel offers rooms in styles varying from Provençal to modern minimalism. Fitness facilities. Enjoy the Mediterranean cuisine and a snack menu in a pleasant, fashionable decor with a muted lounge atmosphere. Fine wine list.

Best Western
(at the airport) ✉ *13127 Vitrolles – ✆ 04 42 15 54 00 – www.bwmrs.com – info@bwmrs.com – Fax 04 42 89 69 18*
120 rm – †€ 95/179 ††€ 95/179, ☐ € 14 **Rest** – Carte € 27/45
◆ This recent building hides an unexpectedly classic interior. Louis XVI furniture in the bedrooms and crystal chandelier in the hall. Modern dining room with wood panelling. Teak terrace by the swimming pool.

Z.I. Les Estroublans **4 km Northeast by D 9 (Vitrolles road) – ✉ *13127 Vitrolles***

Novotel
24 r. de Madrid – ✆ 04 42 89 90 44 – www.novotel.com – h0442@accor.com – Fax 04 42 79 07 04
117 rm – †€ 110/160 ††€ 110/160, ☐ € 15
Rest – Menu (€ 21), € 24 – Carte € 30/38
◆ Spacious and soundproofed rooms, gradually being redone in the latest style of this chain hotel. Pretty rose garden and swimming pool. Restaurant serving traditional cuisine. Novotel café with snacks and trendy decor.

MARIGNY-ST-MARCEL – 74 Haute-Savoie – 328 I6 – pop. 621 – alt. 404 m – ✉ 74150 46 F1

Paris 536 – Aix-les-Bains 22 – Annecy 19 – Bellegarde-sur-Valserine 43 – Rumilly 6

Blanc with rm
– ✆ 04 50 01 09 50 – www.blanc-hotel-restaurant.fr – hotelblanc@wanadoo.fr – Fax 04 50 64 58 05 – Closed 28 December-5 January
16 rm – †€ 55/130 ††€ 55/130, ☐ € 11 – ½ P € 56/85
Rest – *(closed Sunday dinner and Saturday except July-August)*
Menu (€ 16), € 24/62 bi – Carte € 40/67
◆ Family-run inn with two neat dining rooms (one for winter, one for summer); classic menu. Shaded terrace giving onto the garden and pool. Pleasant rooms.

MARINGUES – 63 Puy-de-Dôme – 326 G7 – pop. 2 605 – alt. 315 m – ✉ 63350 Auvergne 6 C2

Paris 409 – Clermont-Ferrand 32 – Lezoux 16 – Riom 22 – Thiers 23 – Vichy 29

Le Clos Fleuri with rm
rte de Clermont – ✆ 04 73 68 70 46 – www.leclosfleuri.net – closfleuri63@wanadoo.fr – Fax 04 73 68 75 58 – Closed 16 February-14 March, Monday except dinner July-August, Friday dinner and Sunday dinner September-June
15 rm – †€ 45/49 ††€ 50/55, ☐ € 7 – ½ P € 54
Rest – Menu (€ 18), € 24/40 – Carte € 25/45
◆ Run by the same family for three generations, the rustic dining rooms of this house on the way out of the village, overlook the lovely garden. Regional-classic fare.

MARLENHEIM – 67 Bas-Rhin – 315 I5 – pop. 3 365 – alt. 195 m – ✉ 67520 Alsace-Lorraine 1 A1

Paris 468 – Haguenau 50 – Molsheim 13 – Saverne 18 – Strasbourg 21

Office de tourisme, 11, place du Kaufhus ✆ 03 88 87 75 80, Fax 03 88 87 75 80

Le Cerf (Michel Husser)
30 r. Gén. de Gaulle – ✆ 03 88 87 73 73 – www.lecerf.com – info@lecerf.com – Fax 03 88 87 68 08 – Closed 5-19 March
17 rm – †€ 70/255 ††€ 70/255, ☐ € 21
Rest – *(closed Tuesday and Wednesday)* Menu € 39 (weekday lunch), € 67/125 – Carte € 69/95
Spec. Presskopf de tête de veau poêlé en croustille, sauce gribiche. Choucroute au cochon de lait rôti et poché, foie gras fumé. Baba à l'alsacienne arrosé au vieux kirsch. **Wines** Riesling, Pinot gris.
◆ An old posthouse transformed into an elegant hostelry. Stylish bedrooms. Pretty flower-decked courtyard. Alsace takes pride of place in the restaurant decorated with wood panelling and paintings. Personalised cuisine focused on the produce and the region.

Hostellerie Reeb rest, rm, VISA AE
2 r. Albert Schweitzer – ✆ 03 88 87 52 70 – www.hostellerie-reeb.fr – info@hostellerie-reeb.fr – Fax 03 88 87 69 73 – Closed 2-10 January, Sunday dinner and Monday
26 rm – †€ 55 ††€ 55, ☕ € 8,50 – ½ P € 55
Rest – Menu (€ 11), € 22/60 – Carte € 25/55
Rest *La Crémaillère* – ✆ 388875270 – Menu (€ 11), € 22/38 – Carte € 32/52
◆ A half-timbered building on the doorstep of the village where the wine route starts. Comfortable, light rooms furnished in a rustic spirit (family heirlooms and local fabrics). Classic menu in tune with the plush interior. At the Crémaillère find an all-wood decor and regional fare.

MARLY-LE-ROI – **78 Yvelines** – **312** B2 – **101** 12 – **see Paris, Area**

MARMANDE – **47 Lot-et-Garonne** – **336** C2 – **pop. 17 300** – **alt. 30 m** – ✉ **47200** **Atlantic Coast** 4 **C2**

Paris 666 – Agen 67 – Bergerac 57 – Bordeaux 90 – Libourne 65

Office de tourisme, boulevard Gambetta ✆ 0553644444, Fax 0553201719

Le Capricorne without rest VISA AE
av. Hubert Ruffe, Agen road, 2 km on D 813 – ✆ 05 53 64 16 14 – www.lecapricorne-hotel.com – lecapricorne-hotel@wanadoo.fr – Fax 05 53 20 80 18 – Closed 19 December-4 January
34 rm – †€ 63 ††€ 73, ☕ € 8
◆ Built in the 1970s, this hotel is regularly spruced up: functional, well-kept, soundproofed rooms. Brand new bathrooms. Excellent value for money.

to A 62 interchange **9 km South by D 933** – ✉ **47430 Ste-Marthe**

Les Rives de l'Avance without rest VISA
Moulin de Trivail – ✆ 05 53 20 60 22 – Fax 05 53 20 98 76
16 rm – †€ 38/52 ††€ 43/58, ☕ € 6
◆ This hotel adjoining a water mill makes an unexpected peaceful and green haven so close to the motorway. Functional and colourful rooms. Lounge with a piano.

at Pont-des-Sables **5 km south by D 933** – ✉ **47200**

Syndicat d'initiative, Val de Garonne-Pont des Sables ✆ 05 53 89 25 59, Fax 05 53 93 28 03

Auberge de l' Escale VISA AE
Pont des Sables – ✆ 05 53 93 60 11 – Fax 05 53 83 09 15 – Closed 31 August-7 September, 16-23 November, 4-11 January, Wednesday dinner from September to June, Sunday dinner and Monday
Rest – Menu € 19 (weekday lunch), € 31/63 bi – Carte € 40/70
◆ This Landes house is popular with boaters on the canal. Attractive interior with fireplace (grilled meats) and summer terrace. Traditional and seasonal cuisine.

MARMANHAC – **15 Cantal** – **330** C4 – **pop. 725** – **alt. 650 m** – ✉ **15250** 5 **B3**

Paris 566 – Clermont-Ferrand 154 – Aurillac 17 – Saint-Flour 69 – Arpajon-sur-Cère 19

Château de Sédaiges without rest VISA AE
– ✆ 04 71 47 30 01 – www.chateausedaiges.com – chateau15@free.fr – Open 1st May-30 September
5 rm ☕ – †€ 110/120 ††€ 110/120
◆ This family château, typical of the Troubadour style (12C-19C), is surrounded by parkland. Charming rooms adorned with antiques and tapestries. Tasty country breakfast.

MARNE-LA-VALLÉE – **Île-de-France** – **312** E2 – **101** 19 – **see Paris, Area**

MARQUAY – 24 Dordogne – 329 H6 – pop. 558 – alt. 175 m – ✉ 24620 4 D3

Dordogne-Berry-Limousin

Paris 530 – Brive-la-Gaillarde 55 – Périgueux 60 – Sarlat-la-Canéda 12

La Condamine

rm, VISA MC AE

Meyrals road: 1 km – ✆ 05 53 29 64 08 – www.hotel-lacondamine.com – hotel.lacondamine@wanadoo.fr – Fax 05 53 28 81 59 – Open from Easter to 1st November

22 rm – € 40/58 € 40/58, € 8 – ½ P € 48/58

Rest – *(dinner only)* Menu € 16/35 – Carte € 15/30

◆ A traditional-style building overlooking the Périgord countryside. A few rooms have balconies with a view of the countryside. Simple rustic decor. Miniature golf, and boules pitch. Family guesthouse-style restaurant and terrace opening onto the garden and swimming pool.

MARSAC-SUR-DON – 44 Loire-Atlantique – 316 F2 – pop. 1 327 – alt. 50 m – ✉ 44170 34 B2

Paris 408 – Nantes 50 – St-Herblain 53 – Rezé 59 – Saint-Sébastien-sur-Loire 59

La Mérais without rest

1,3 km au Sud par D44 – ✆ 02 40 79 50 78 – www.lamerais.com – lamerais@wanadoo.fr – Open May to October

3 rm – € 45 € 58

◆ This blue schist longère (long house) set in grounds near the village has the charm of a country home. Rooms decorated in warm colours. Breakfast served on the terrace in fine weather.

MARSANNAY-LA-CÔTE – 21 Côte-d'Or – 320 J6 – see Dijon

MARSANNE – 26 Drôme – 332 C6 – pop. 1 209 – alt. 250 m – ✉ 26740 44 B3

Lyon - Rhone Valley

Paris 611 – Lyon 149 – Romans-sur-Isère 69 – Valence 48

Office de tourisme, Place Emile Loubet ✆ 04 75 90 31 59, Fax 04 75 90 31 40

Le Mas du Chatelas

rm, VISA MC

La Plaine – ✆ 04 75 52 97 31 – www.lemasduchatelas.com – philippe@lemasduchatelas.com – Fax 04 75 53 14 48

5 rm – € 85/125 € 95/135 **Table d'hôte** – Menu € 25/35 bi

◆ This 18C farmhouse provides rooms with a refined country-style décor, and romantic candle-lit dinners; terrace dining also possible.

MARSEILLAN – 34 Hérault – 339 G8 – pop. 6 199 – alt. 3 m – ✉ 34340 23 C2

Languedoc-Roussillon-Tarn Gorges

Paris 754 – Agde 7 – Béziers 31 – Montpellier 49 – Pézenas 20 – Sète 24

Office de tourisme, avenue de la Méditerranée ✆ 04 67 21 82 43, Fax 04 67 21 82 58

La Table d'Emilie

VISA MC AE

8 pl. Carnot – ✆ 04 67 77 63 59 – latabledemilie@orange.fr – Fax 04 67 01 72 02 – Closed 3-24 November, 3-15 January, Monday lunch and Thursday lunch from 1st July-30 September, Sunday dinner, Monday and Wednesday from 1st October-30 June

Rest – Menu € 19 (weekday lunch), € 28/50 – Carte € 55/62

◆ Small 12C house full of romantic charm, with exposed stonework, ogive vaults and verdant patio. Well-executed inventive cuisine based on ingredients of the day.

Le Château du Port

VISA MC AE

9 quai de la Résistance – ✆ 04 67 77 31 67 – www.chateauduport.com – Fax 04 67 77 11 30

Rest – Menu (€ 19), € 29 – Carte € 35/50

◆ A chic, contemporary bistro housed in a fine 19C residence serving seafood and regional modern cuisine. Pleasant terrace overlooking the canal.

Chez Philippe

VISA MC

20 r. Suffren – ✆ 04 67 01 70 62 – chezphilippe@club-internet.fr – Fax 04 67 01 70 62 – Closed mid-November to mid-February, Tuesday in low season and Monday

Rest – *(pre-book)* Menu (€ 21), € 28 – Carte € 30/42

◆ An attractive restaurant with a southern-French atmosphere near the Thau basin, serving Mediterranean cuisine in a colourful dining area or on the summer terrace.

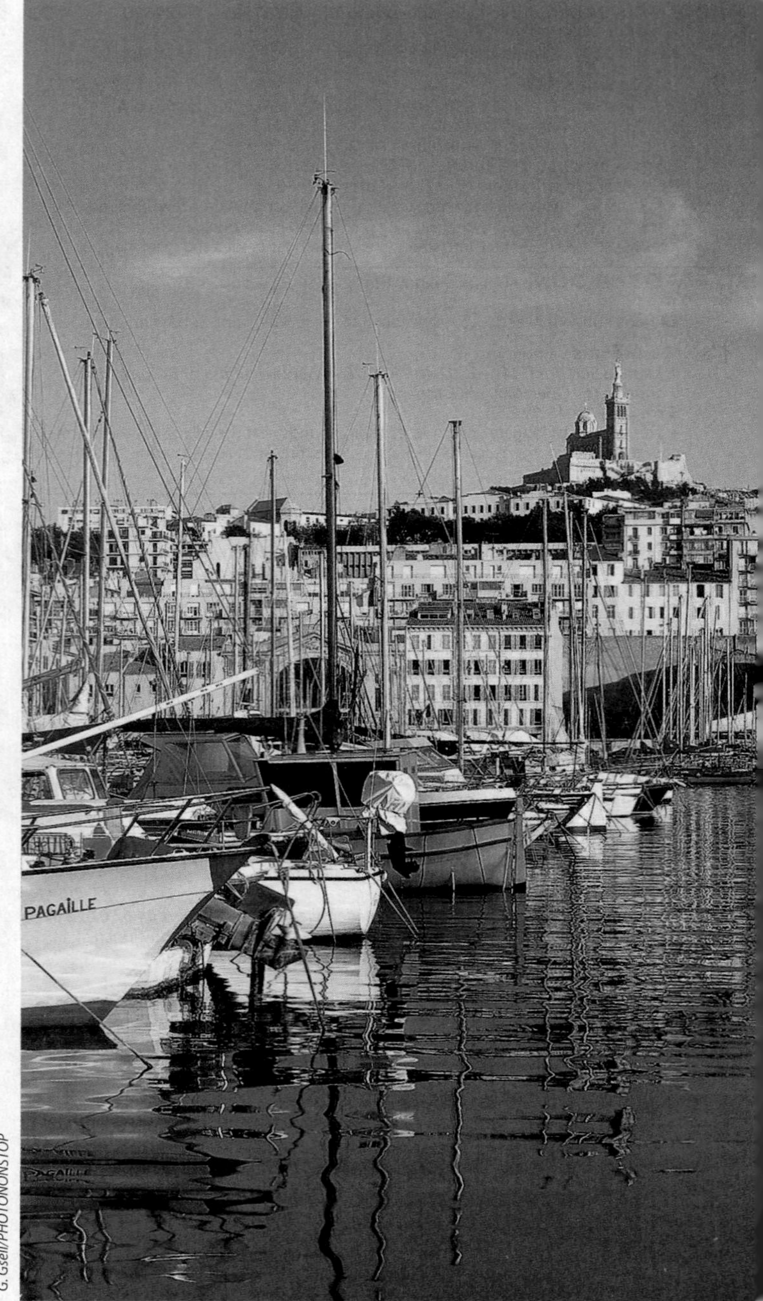

G. Gsell/PHOTONONSTOP

The old port and Notre-Dame de la Garde

MARSEILLE

Department: 13 Bouches-du-Rhône
Michelin LOCAL map: n° 340 H6 114 28
Paris 769 – Lyon 314 – Nice 189
– Torino 373 – Toulon 64
– Toulouse 405

Population: 826 700
Pop. built-up area: 1 349 772
Postal Code: ✉ 13000
Provence
Carte régionale 40 **B3**

USEFUL INFORMATION

TOURIST OFFICES

Annexe Gare Saint-Charles ✆ 04 91 50 59 18
Office de tourisme, 4, la Canebière ✆ 04 91 13 89 00, Fax 04 91 13 89 20

TRANSPORT

Auto-train ✆ 3635 et tapez 42 (0,34 €/mn)
Tunnel Prado-Carénage : péage 2007, tarif normal : 2,50 €

SEA TRANSPORT

For Château d'If: Frioul If Express boats ✆ 04 91 46 54 65
For Corsica: SNCM 61 bd des Dames (2e) ✆ 0 825 888 088 (0.15 €/mn),
Fax 04 91 56 35 86 - CMN 4 quai d'Arenc (2e) ✆ 0 810 201 320,
Fax 04 91 99 45 95

AIRPORT

Marseille-Provence ✆ 04 42 14 14 14, by ①: 28 km

A FEW GOLF COURSES

18 de Marseille-La Salette 65, impasse des Vaudrans, E : 10 km at la Valentine, ✆ 04 91 27 12 16

9 d'Allauch Allauch Domaine de Fontvieille, NE : 14 km on the Allauch road, ✆ 04 91 07 28 22

TO SEE

AROUND OLD HARBOUR

Le vieux port★★ - Quai des Belges (fish market) ET 5 - Musée d'Histoire de Marseille★ ET M3 - Musée du Vieux Marseille DET M7 - Musée des Docks romains★ DT M6 - ⩽★ from the St-Laurent viewpoint DT D - Musée Cantini★ FU M2

QUARTIER DU PANIER

Vieille Charité Centre ★★: Musée d'archéologie méditerranéenne, Musée d'Arts africains, océaniens, amérindiens MAAOA★★ DS E - Former Major Cathedral★ DS B

NOTRE-DAME-DE-LA-GARDE

⩽★★★ of the N.-D.-de -la-Garde basilica square EV

- St-Victor basilica★ (crypte★★) DU

LA CANEBIÈRE

from rue Longue-des-Capucins to cours Julien: place du Marché-des-Capucins, rue du Musée, rue Rodolph-Pollack, rue d'Aubagne, rue St-Ferréol.

QUARTIER LONGCHAMP

Musée Grobet-Labadié★★ GS M8 - Palais Longchamp★ GS: musée des Beaux-Arts★ and musée d'Histoire naturelle★

SOUTHERN DISTRICTS

Corniche Président-J.-F.-Kennedy★★ AYZ - Parc du Pharo DU

AROUND MARSEILLE

Visit of the harbour★ - Château d'If★★: ⁕★★★ off Marseille - Massif des Calanques★★ - Musée de la faïence★

Sofitel Vieux Port rm, VISA
36 bd Ch.-Livon ✉ 13007 – ✆ 04 91 15 59 00 – www.sofitel-marseille-vieuxport.com – h0542@accor.com – Fax 04 91 15 59 50 p. 6 DU **n**
134 rm – €200/500 €200/500, €26 – 3 suites
Rest ***Les Trois Forts*** – *✆ 04 91 15 59 56* – Menu (€44), €57/87 – Carte €88/110
◆ This fine hotel, overlooking the Vieux Port and its historic forts, provides spacious Provençal or contemporary rooms; some have a terrace and a sea view. Restaurant serving modern cuisine, featuring panoramic views.

Radisson SAS rest, VISA
38 quai Rive-Neuve ✉ 13007 – ✆ 04 88 92 19 50 – www.marseille.radissonsas.com – info.marseille@radissonsas.com – Fax 04 88 92 19 51 p. 6 DU **d**
189 rm – €130/395 €140/405, €25 – 10 suites
Rest – *(closed Saturday lunch and Sunday)* Menu (€25), €35 – Carte €47/61
◆ Imposing modern designer building overlooking the old port. Provençal or African influences in the hi-tech rooms. Some command picture postcard views. Softly lit trendy restaurant with Mediterranean inspired menu.

Villa Massalia VISA
17 pl. Louis-Bonnefon, au Sud du Parc Borély ✉ 13007 – ✆ 04 91 72 90 00 – www.concorde-hotels.com – villamassalia@concorde-hotels.com – Fax 04 91 72 90 01 p. 5 BZ
136 rm – €130/500 €130/500, €21 – 4 suites
Rest ***Yin Yang*** – Menu (€38 bi), €42 – Carte €40/70
◆ Ideal for a business clientele, this new hotel on the edge of the Borély park offers modern rooms that are comfortable and well-equipped. The Asian inspired décor at Yin Yang complements the fusion cuisine. Terrace opposite the race-course.

Pullman Palm Beach
200 Corniche J.-F.-Kennedy ✉ 13007 – ✆ 04 91 16 19 00 – www.pullmanhotels.com – h3485@accor.com – Fax 04 91 16 19 39 VISA p. 4 AZ **b**
160 rm – €200/325 €225/350, €25 – 10 suites
Rest ***La Réserve*** – *✆ 04 91 16 19 21* – Menu €42 bi (weekdays) – Carte €50/100
◆ Nautical in design and spirit, this modern vessel is anchored opposite Château d'If island. Comfortable rooms, well-being centre and extensive conference facilities. La Réserve features a very modern setting and updated Mediterranean food.

Le Petit Nice (Gérald Passédat) rest, P
anse de Maldormé, (160 Corniche J.-F. Kennedy) ✉ 13007 – ✆ 04 91 59 25 92 – www.passedat.fr – contact@passedat.fr – Fax 04 91 59 28 08 – Closed 1st-20 January, February and autumn school holidays VISA p. 4 AZ **d**
13 rm – €250/750 €250/750, €30 – 3 suites
Rest – *(closed Sunday and Monday)* Menu €85 (weekday lunch), €130/230 – Carte €132/220
Spec. Menu "Découverte de la mer". Anémones de mer en onctueux iodé puis en beignets légers, lait mousseux au caviar. Bouille-Abaisse comme un menu. **Wines** Vin de Table du Var, Côtes de Provence.
◆ Inventive and refined, remarkable seafood cuisine is reason to pull up a seat in this enchanting establishment. These two villas from the 1910s offer a magical sea view, modern décor and luxurious guestrooms that are personalised without being ostentatious.

New Hôtel of Marseille
71 bd Ch.-Livon ✉ 13007 – ✆ 04 91 31 53 15 – www.newhotelofmarseille.com – info@newhotelofmarseille.com – Fax 04 91 31 20 00 VISA p. 6 DU **v**
100 rm – €195/215 €215/235, €18 – 8 suites
Rest – Menu (€19), €25/39 – Carte €25/53
◆ Brand new hotel incorporating a 19C building. Low key, modern, well-equipped bedrooms, some of which command splendid views of the old port. The trendy restaurant serves food of southern and further flung inspiration.

MARSEILLE

Street	Grid	No.
Aix (R. d')	BY	
Anthoine (R. d')	AX	
Baille (Bd)	BCY	
Belsunce (Cours)	BY	
Blancarde (Bd de la)	CY	
Bompard (Bd)	AYZ	
Briançon (Bd de)	BX	13
Canebière (La)	BY	
Cantini (Av. Jules)	BCZ	
Capelette (Av. de la)	CYZ	
Castellane (Pl.)	BY	
Catalans (R. des)	AY	16
Chartreux (Av. des)	CY	17
Chave (Bd)	BCY	
Chutes Lavie (Av.)	CX	
Dunkerque (Bd de)	AX	
Duparc (Bd Françoise)	CXY	
Endoume (R. d')	AY	
Estrangin (Bd G.)	ABZ	
Fleming (Bd Alexander)	CX	
Foch (Av. Mar.)	CY	
Guesde (Pl. Jules)	BY	35
Guibal (R.)	BX	
Guigou (Bd)	BX	36
Jeanne-d'Arc (Bd)	CY	
Jean-Jaurès (Pl.)	BY	
Lazaret (Quai du)	AX	
Leclerc (Av. Gén.)	BY	
Lesseps (Bd Ferdinand de)	AX	40
Lieutaud (Cours)	BY	
Livon (Bd Charles)	AY	
Mazargues (Av. de)	BZ	
Mermoz (R. Jean)	BZ	
Michelet (Bd)	BCZ	
Moulin (Bd Jean)	CY	47
National (Bd)	BX	
Notre-Dame (Bd)	BY	
Paradis (R.)	BYZ	
Paris (Bd de)	ABX	
Pelletan (Av. C.)	BXY	
Périer (Bd)	BZ	
Plombières (Bd de)	BX	
Pologne (Pl. de)	CY	51
Pompidou (Prom. Georges)	BZ	52
Prado (Av. du)	BYZ	
Président-J.-F.-Kennedy (Corniche)	AYZ	
Pyat (R. Félix)	BX	
Rabatau (Bd)	BCZ	
République (R. de la)	ABY	
Roches (Av. des)	AZ	
Rolland (Bd Romain)	CZ	
Rolland (R. du Cdt)	BZ	
Rome (R. de)	BY	
Roucas Blanc (Chemin du)	AZ	
Rouet (R. du)	BYZ	
Ste-Marguerite (Bd)	CZ	
Ste-Marthe (Ch. de)	BX	
St-Just (Av. de)	CX	
St-Pierre (R.)	BCY	
Sakakini (Bd)	CY	
Salengro (Av. Roger)	BX	
Sartre (Av. Jean-Paul)	CX	59
Schlœsing (Bd)	CZ	
Sébastopol (Pl.)	CY	
Strasbourg (Bd)	BX	61
Teisseire (Bd R.)	CZ	
Tellène (Bd)	AY	
Timone (Av. de la)	CY	
Toulon (Av. de)	BCY	
Vallon l'Oriol (Chemin)	AZ	
Vauban (Bd)	BY	
Verdun (R. de)	CY	70

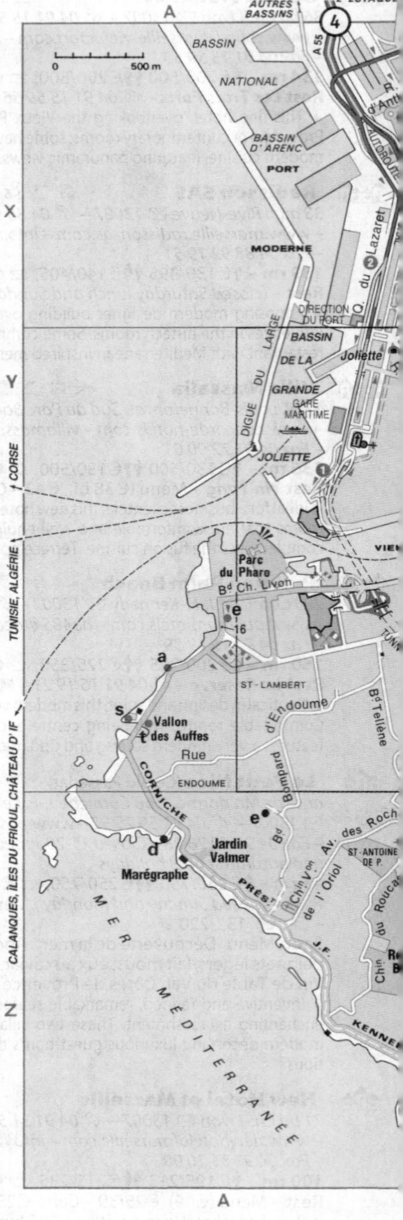

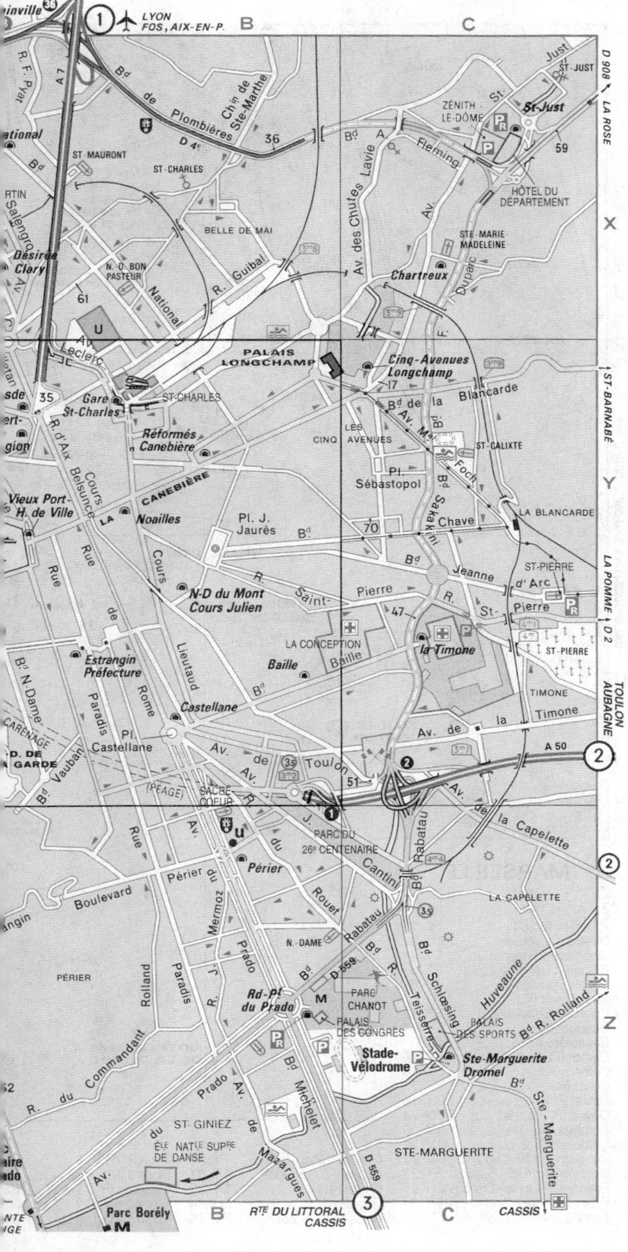
LYON
FOS, AIX-EN-P.
B
C
Bd de Plombières
Chin de Ste-Marthe
D 4c
ST-MAURONT
ST-CHARLES
BELLE DE MAI
Av. des Chutes Lavie
Bd A. Fleming
ZÉNITH - LE DÔME
St-Just
ST-JUST
HÔTEL DU DÉPARTEMENT
D 908 LA ROSE
X
STE-MARIE-MADELEINE
Chartreux
Av. Dupare
Désirée Clary
N.-D. BON PASTEUR
R. Guibal
National
PALAIS LONGCHAMP
Cinq-Avenues Longchamp
Gare St-Charles
Réformés Canebière
CANEBIÈRE
LES CINQ AVENUES
Bd de la Blancarde
Av. Mal Foch
ST-CALIXTE
Pl. Sébastopol
ST-BARNABÉ
Y
Vieux Port-H. de Ville
Noailles
Pl. J. Jaurès
Bd Chave
Bd Sakakini
LA BLANCARDE
Bd Jeanne d'Arc
ST-PIERRE
R. Saint-Pierre
N-D du Mont Cours Julien
LA CONCEPTION
la Timone
LA POMME D 2
Estrangin Préfecture
Baille
Cours Lieutaud
Rue de Rome
Castellane
Pl. Castellane
TIMONE
Av. de la Timone
TOULON AUBAGNE
A 50
Av. de Toulon
SACRÉ-CŒUR
PARC DU 26e CENTENAIRE
Av. de la Capelette
Bd Rabatau
R. J. Cantini
Périer
Boulevard Périer
Av. du Mermoz
Rouet
LA CAPELETTE
N.-DAME
PÉRIER
Prado
Paradis
Rolland
Rd-Pt du Prado
PARC CHANOT
PALAIS DES CONGRÈS
Bd Schlœsing
Huveaune
PALAIS DES SPORTS
Bd R. Rolland
Z
Stade-Vélodrome
Ste-Marguerite Dromel
R. Teisseire
R. du Commandant
Prado
Av. de Mazargues
Bd Michelet
ST-GINIEZ
ÉLE NATLE SUPRE DE DANSE
STE-MARGUERITE
Bd Ste-Marguerite
Parc Borély
RTE DU LITTORAL CASSIS
CASSIS
D 559

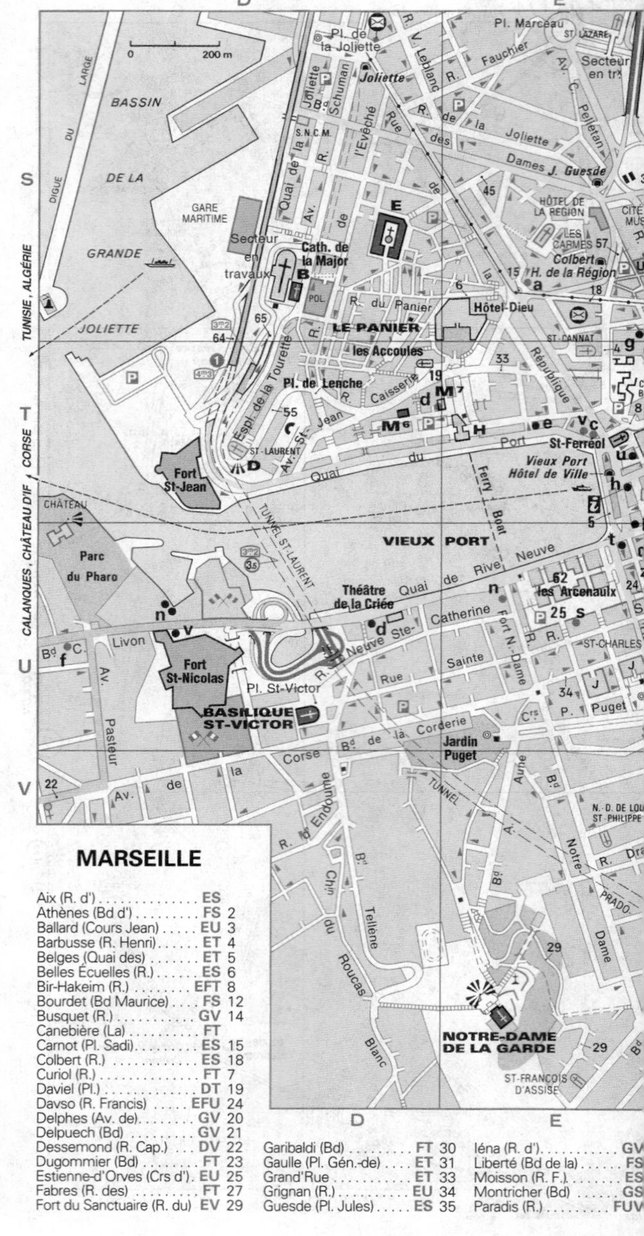
D
E
S
T
U
V
0 200 m
BASSIN
DE LA
GRANDE
JOLIETTE
DIGUE DU LARGE
GARE MARITIME
Secteur en travaux
TUNISIE, ALGÉRIE
CORSE
CALANQUES, CHÂTEAU D'IF
Pl. de la Joliette
Joliette
Bd Schuman
Quai de la Joliette
S.N.C.M.
Av. R. de l'Evêché
R. V. Leblanc
Rue de la Joliette
R. des Dames
Fauchier
Pl. Marceau
ST-LAZARE
Secteur en tx
Av. C. Pelletan
J. Guesde
HÔTEL DE LA RÉGION
CITÉ MUS.
LES CARMES
Colbert
H. de la Région
Cath. de la Major
POL.
R. du Panier
Hôtel-Dieu
LE PANIER
les Accoules
ST-CANNAT
République
Espl. de la Tourette
Pl. de Lenche
R. Caisserie
Av. St-Jean
ST-LAURENT
Fort St-Jean
Quai du Port
St-Ferréol
Vieux Port Hôtel de Ville
Ferry Boat
CHÂTEAU
Parc du Pharo
TUNNEL ST-LAURENT
VIEUX PORT
Quai de Rive Neuve
les Arcenaulx
Théâtre de la Criée
Catherine
Fort N.-Dame
ST-CHARLES
Bd C. Livon
Fort St-Nicolas
R. Neuve Ste-
Rue Sainte
Pl. St-Victor
BASILIQUE ST-VICTOR
Av. Pasteur
Crs
P. Puget
Bd de la Corderie
Jardin Puget
TUNNEL
Av. de la Corse
R. d'Endoume
Bd Aune
Bd A.
N.-D. DE LOU
ST-PHILIPPE
Notre-
PRADO
R. Dra
Bd Tellène
Chin du Roucas Blanc
Dame
NOTRE-DAME DE LA GARDE
ST-FRANÇOIS D'ASSISE

MARSEILLE

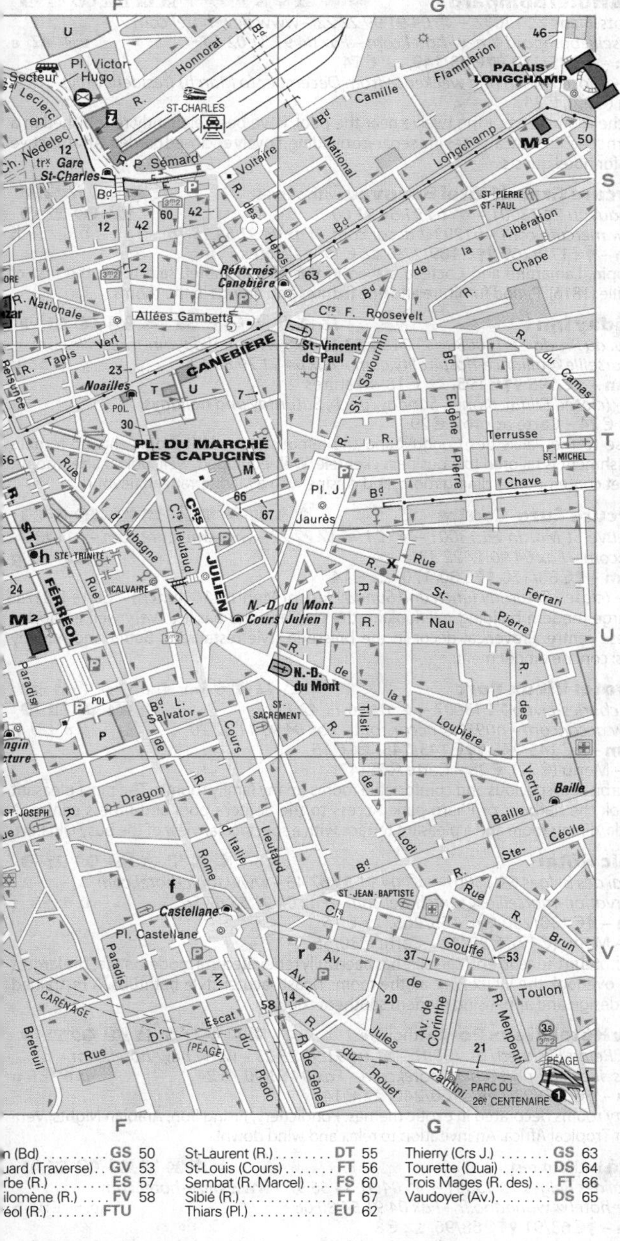

F
G

n (Bd) . . . . GS 50
uard (Traverse) . . GV 53
rbe (R.) . . . . ES 57
ilomène (R.) . . . . FV 58
éol (R.) . . . . FTU

St-Laurent (R.) . . . . DT 55
St-Louis (Cours) . . . . FT 56
Sembat (R. Marcel) . . . . FS 60
Sibié (R.) . . . . FT 67
Thiars (Pl.) . . . . EU 62

Thierry (Crs J.) . . . . GS 63
Tourette (Quai) . . . . DS 64
Trois Mages (R. des) . . . FT 66
Vaudoyer (Av.) . . . . DS 65

New Hôtel Bompard

2 r. Flots-Bleus ✉ 13007 – ☎ 04 91 99 22 22 – www.new-hotel.com – marseillebompard@new-hotel.com – Fax 04 91 31 02 14 p. 4 AZ **e**

49 rm – †€ 85/129 ††€ 85/149, ☕ € 14

Rest – *(Closed lunch and weekends from December to March) (resident only)* Menu (€ 22), € 26

◆ All the rooms, except the twelve near the pool, have been elegantly refurbished in a modern style. Provencal suites in a separate building. Lovely enclosed garden. An attractive menu for hotel guests.

Mercure Grand Hôtel Beauvau without rest

4 r. Beauvau ✉ 13001 – ☎ 04 91 54 91 00 – www.mercure.com – h1293@accor.com – Fax 04 91 54 15 76 p. 6 ET **h**

70 rm – †€ 179/269 ††€ 189/279, ☕ € 17 – 2 suites

◆ Chopin, Lamartine and Cocteau stayed in this elegant hotel, said to be the first of Marseille (1816). Period furniture and fine fixtures and fittings in the rooms.

Holiday Inn

103 av. du Prado ✉ 13008 – ☎ 04 91 83 10 10 – www.holidayinn-marseille.com – himarseille@alliance-hospitality.com – Fax 04 91 79 84 12 p. 5 BZ **u**

115 rm – †€ 195 ††€ 195, ☕ € 18 – 4 suites

Rest – *(closed Friday dinner, Sunday lunch, Saturday and holidays)* Menu € 24 – Carte approx. € 29

◆ Close to the Palais des Congrès and the famous Stade Vélodrome this up-to-date establishment is tailored to a business clientele. Well-equipped, well looked after rooms. Discreet contemporary dining room, and cuisine with a Mediterranean flavour.

Mercure Euro-Centre

1 r. Neuve-St-Martin ✉ 13001 – ☎ 04 96 17 22 22 – www.mercure.com – h1148@accor.com – Fax 04 96 17 22 33 p. 6 EST **g**

200 rm – †€ 80/170 ††€ 80/170, ☕ € 14

Rest – *(closed Saturday lunch and Sunday lunch)* Menu € 16 (lunch) – Carte € 21/35

◆ A large modern building overlooking the port and the basilica. Very well equipped business centre. Provençal decor in the brasserie-style restaurant. Buffet and midday menus; concise dinner menu.

Novotel Vieux Port

rm, rm,

36 bd charles-Livon ✉ 13007 – ☎ 04 96 11 42 11 – www.accor.com – h0911@accor.com – Fax 04 96 11 42 20 p. 6 DU **n**

110 rm – †€ 145/245 ††€ 145/245, ☕ € 15

Rest – Menu (€ 22), € 25 – Carte € 28/47

◆ Refurbished, spacious and comfortable rooms (many family rooms). The most pleasant overlook the harbour or Pharo park. Access to the Sofitel's pool and fitness centre. A veranda/dining room and a pleasant terrace with a spectacular view of the busy Old Port.

Tonic Hôtel

43 quai des Belges ✉ 13001 – ☎ 04 91 55 67 46 – www.tonic-hotel.com – reservation-marseille@tonichotel.com – Fax 04 91 55 67 56 p. 6 EU **t**

56 rm – †€ 130/230 ††€ 165/265, ☕ € 16

Rest – Menu (€ 17), € 22/42 – Carte € 30/55

◆ This hotel in the centre of Marseille has been fully renovated in a modern style. The largest rooms overlook the Vieux Port; all the rooms boast Jacuzzi style bathtubs. A restrained 1970s design and appetising modern southern cooking.

New Hôtel Vieux Port without rest

3 bis r. Reine-Élisabeth ✉ 13001 – ☎ 04 91 99 23 23 – www.new-hotel.com – marseillevieux-port@new-hotel.com – Fax 04 91 90 76 24 p. 6 ET **u**

42 rm – †€ 140/220 ††€ 160/240, ☕ € 14

◆ Pretty rooms decorated in exotic themes: Pondichery, Rising Sun, Arabian Nights, Vera Cruz or Tropical Africa. An invitation to relax and wind down!

Alizé without rest

35 quai des Belges ✉ 13001 – ☎ 04 91 33 66 97 – www.alize-hotel.com – alize-hotel@wanadoo.fr – Fax 04 91 54 80 06 p. 6 ETU **b**

39 rm – †€ 63/91 ††€ 68/96, ☕ € 8

◆ A functional, extremely well kept and fully renovated hotel, facing the famous fish market. The sixteen rooms in the front enjoy a view of the harbour.

Du Palais without rest
26 r. Breteuil ✉ 13006 – ☎ 04 91 37 78 86 – www.hotel-palais-marseille.com – hoteldupalais13@wanadoo.fr – Fax 04 91 37 91 19 p. 7 EU **a**
22 rm – †€ 98/130 ††€ 98/130, ☕ € 8,50
◆ An ideally located hotel near the old port: providing brightly coloured rooms, modern furnishings and all modern comforts. Hospitable and welcoming.

Hermès without rest
2 r. Bonneterie ✉ 13002 – ☎ 04 96 11 63 63 – www.hotelmarseille.com – hermes@hotelmarseille.com – Fax 04 96 11 63 64 p. 6 ET **e**
28 rm – †€ 77/100 ††€ 77/100, ☕ € 9
◆ Unpretentious, centrally located hotel with small well-kept rooms; those on the fifth floor have a terrace overlooking the quayside. Panoramic rooftop sun deck.

Une Table au Sud (Lionel Lévy)
2 quai du Port, (1st floor) ✉ 13002 – ☎ 04 91 90 63 53 – www.unetableausud.com – unetableausud@wanadoo.fr – Fax 04 91 90 63 86 – Closed 1st-28 August, 3-11 January, Sunday and Monday p. 6 ET **c**
Rest – Menu € 37 (weekday lunch), € 52/105 bi – Carte € 55/95
Spec. Fricassée de cèpes à l'huile de noisette et gel d'ail (Sep. to Nov.). Grosses Saint-Jacques de plongée à la moelle (Oct. to March). Castel à la betterave et réglisse (Oct. to Dec.). **Wines** Vin de Pays des Alpilles, Vin de Pays des Bouches-du-Rhône.
◆ This colourful restaurant delights both the eye and the taste buds, thanks to its inventive cuisine with delicious southern accents, as well as views of the forts and hilltop basilica.

Miramar
12 quai du Port ✉ 13002 – ☎ 04 91 91 10 40 – www.bouillabaisse.com – contact@bouillabaisse.com – Fax 04 91 56 64 31 – Closed Sunday and Monday p. 6 ET **v**
Rest – Carte € 70/90
◆ This restaurant serving bouillabaisse and other fish specialities on the Vieux Port has a very 1960s style with varnished wood and red armchairs.

L'Épuisette
Vallon des Auffes ✉ 13007 – ☎ 04 91 52 17 82 – www.l-epuisette.com – contact@l-epuisette.com – Fax 04 91 59 18 80 – Closed 5 August-5 September, Sunday and Monday p. 4 AY **s**
Rest – Menu € 55, € 85/135 bi – Carte € 80/135
Spec. Trilogie d'oeufs a la truffe. Cannelloni de poireaux et langoustines rôties. Carré d'un baba au limoncello, sorbet chocolat amer et caramel de curry. **Wines** Coteaux d'Aix-en-Provence, Côtes du Luberon.
◆ Set near the rocks in the picturesque Auffes valley, this glass fronted restaurant takes you on a pleasant culinary voyage in a light, warm and refined atmosphere. Attentive staff.

Péron
56 Corniche J.-F.-Kennedy ✉ 13007 – ☎ 04 91 52 15 22 – www.restaurant-peron.com – info@restaurant-peron.com – Fax 04 91 52 17 29 – Closed 1 week in March and 1 week in November p. 4 AY **a**
Rest – Menu € 58/72
Spec. Gambas poêlées au tandoori, guacamole, chips de radis noir. Chipirons farcis aux petits légumes, crumble de fenouil. Noisettes d'agneau en croûte de tapenade, poêlée d'artichauts poivrades.
◆ Décor like an ocean liner (red walls, exotic woods, paintings), and above all a panoramic view over the Frioul islands. Lounge atmosphere and modern, southern inspired cuisine.

Chez Fonfon
140 Vallon des Auffes ✉ 13007 – ☎ 04 91 52 14 38 – www.chez-fonfon.com – contact@chez-fonfon.com – Fax 04 91 52 14 16 – Closed 2-17 January, Monday except dinner from May to October and Sunday p. 4 AY **t**
Rest – Menu € 42/55 – Carte € 60/70
◆ A family-run establishment (1952) that is as popular for its decor as for its menu of fresh fish, bought straight off the little boats you can see bobbing down in the harbour.

XX **Des Mets de Provence "Chez Maurice Brun"** A/C VISA MC
18 quai de Rive-Neuve, (2nd Floor) ✉ 13007 – ✆ 04 91 33 35 38 – www.mauricebrun.fr – lesmets.deprovence@orange.fr – Fax 04 91 33 05 69 – Closed 9-25 August, Monday lunch, Saturday lunch and Sunday *p. 6* EU **d**
Rest – Menu (€ 25), € 60 – Carte € 40/70
◆ Reminiscent of Pagnol's Provence, this converted attic of a religious convent is located in the old port. Locally sourced menu served in a decor worthy of a museum!

XX **Michel-Brasserie des Catalans** A/C VISA MC AE
6 r. des Catalans ✉ 13007 – ✆ 04 91 52 30 63 – Fax 04 91 59 23 05 – Fermé15 February-1st March *p. 4* AY **e**
Rest – Carte € 58/88
◆ A renovated Marseille restaurant specialising in bouillabaisse, situated opposite the Catalans beach. Locals also enjoy the fish of the day on display.

XX **Le Moment Christian Ernst** A/C VISA MC AE
5 pl. Sadi Carnot ✉ 13002 – ✆ 04 91 52 47 49 – www.lemoment-marseille.com – Closed Monday dinner, Tuesday dinner and Sunday *p. 6* ES **a**
Rest – Menu (€ 19), € 25 (weekday lunch), € 35/61 – Carte € 52/61
◆ Trendy new restaurant near the old port with many facets. Find a contemporary dining room, sitting rooms upstairs, workshops, wine library and takeaway dishes. Updated menu.

XX **Les Arcenaulx** A/C VISA MC AE
25 cours d'Estienne-d'Orves ✉ 13001 – ✆ 04 91 59 80 30 – www.les-arcenaulx.com – restaurant@les-arcenaulx.com – Fax 04 91 54 76 33 – Closed 11-17 August and Sunday *p. 6* EU **s**
Rest – Menu (€ 18), € 36/55 – Carte € 36/65
◆ This original establishment, located in a 17C galley ship warehouse, includes a bookshop, publishing company, tea room and restaurant serving Mediterranean style food.

XX **Charles Livon** A/C VISA MC AE
89 bd Charles-Livon ✉ 13007 – ✆ 04 91 52 22 41 – www.charleslivon.fr – alban.gerardin@club-internet.fr – Fax 04 91 31 41 63 – Closed three weeks in August, Saturday lunch, Monday lunch and Sunday *p. 6* DU **f**
Rest – *(number of covers limited, pre-book)* Menu € 39/72 – Carte approx. € 72
◆ This establishment opposite the Palais du Pharo has a new owner and chef. Modern cuisine and wine list, both with regional accents.

XX **Cyprien** A/C VISA MC
56 av. de Toulon ✉ 13006 – ✆ 04 91 25 50 00 – www.restaurant-cyprien.com – faure.lequien@hotmail.fr – Fax 04 91 25 50 00 – Closed 2 August-1 September, 24 December-5 January, Monday dinner, Saturday lunch, Sunday and bank holidays *p. 7* GV **r**
Rest – Menu (€ 25), € 25/56 – Carte € 30/65
◆ This restaurant near the Place Castellane offers classic, tasty cuisine and a decor to match. Interior adorned with floral touches and paintings.

X **La Table du Fort** A/C VISA MC
8 r. Fort-Notre-Dame ✉ 13007 – ✆ 04 91 33 97 65 – www.latabledufort.fr – mathieulajoinie13@hotmail.fr – Closed 10-25 August, lunch and Sunday
Rest – *(dinner only)* Menu € 30 – Carte € 33/50 *p. 6* EU **n**
◆ Popular with locals, this quayside restaurant has a trendy feel with designer lamps, modern art and a host of colourful details. Innovative cuisine.

X **Le Café des Épices** VISA MC
4 r. Lacydon ✉ 13002 – ✆ 04 91 91 22 69 – cafedesepices@yahoo.fr – Closed Saturday dinner, Sunday, Monday and bank holidays *p. 6* DT **d**
Rest – *(number of covers limited, pre-book)* Menu (€ 21), € 25/43
◆ This tiny restaurant, extended by a covered terrace, serves inventive well-prepared food. In summer, meals are served on the esplanade against a backdrop of olive groves.

X **Axis** A/C VISA MC
8 r. Sainte Victoire ✉ 13006 – ✆ 04 91 57 14 70 – www.axis-restaurant.fr – axis_restaurant@yahoo.fr – Fax 04 91 57 14 70 – Closed August, 24-30 December, Saturday lunch, Monday dinner and Sunday *p. 7* FV **f**
Rest – Menu (€ 15), € 19 (lunch), € 28/35 – Carte € 28/35
◆ The seasonal, contemporary-style cuisine makes this establishment worth a detour. Modern decor, with views of the chefs in action and charming welcome.

X **Le Ventre de l'Architecte - Le Corbusier**
280 bd Michelet, (Cité Radieuse, 3rd floor), via ③ ✉ 13008 – ✆ 04 91 16 78 00 – www.hotellecorbusier.com – alban.gerardin@club-internet.fr – Fax 04 91 16 78 28 – Closed 5-20 August, 5-15 January, Sunday and Monday
Rest – Menu (€ 28), € 50/65 – Carte € 53/63
◆ The 'maison du fada' hides an unusual and stylish restaurant that opens onto a balcony (ideal for aperitifs) with a view over Marseilles and the sea in the distance. Delicious inventive cuisine.

in Plan-de-Cuques **10 km Northeast by La Rose and D 908 – pop. 10 500 – alt. 70 m – ✉ 13380**

Le César
av. G. Pompidou – ✆ 04 91 07 25 25 – www.lecesar.fr – contact@lecesar.fr – Fax 04 91 05 37 16
30 rm – †€ 98 ††€ 110/160, ☕ € 10
Rest – *(closed Sunday dinner)* Menu € 28 – Carte € 30/50
◆ Mediterranean serenity, ochre colour theme, Provencal-styled bedrooms, fitness centre and colonnaded pool: an overwhelming invitation to relax! Regional menu; light airy dining room and pleasant terrace.

MARSOLAN – 32 Gers – 336 F6 – pop. 388 – alt. 171 m – ✉ 32700 — 28 B2

▶ Paris 721 – Toulouse 115 – Auch 43 – Agen 49 – Moissac 67

Lous Grits
in the village – ✆ 05 62 28 37 10 – www.hotel-lousgrits.com – contact@hotel-lousgrits.com – Fax 05 62 28 37 59
5 rm – †€ 190/290 ††€ 190/290, ☕ € 20
Rest – *(dinner only) (residents only)* Menu € 38
◆ You feel at home in this welcoming establishment that tastefully recreates the art of living Gascon style (family furniture, knick-knacks, local pottery and mosaics, paintings). Single regional menu in the evening, served to guests around the fireplace.

MARTAINVILLE-ÉPREVILLE – 76 Seine-Maritime – 304 H5 – see Rouen

---

MARTEL – 46 Lot – 337 F2 – pop. 1 513 – alt. 225 m – ✉ 46600 — 29 C1

Dordogne-Berry-Limousin

▶ Paris 510 – Brive-la-Gaillarde 33 – Cahors 79 – Figeac 59 – St-Céré 30

Office de tourisme, place des Consuls ✆ 05 65 37 43 44, Fax 05 65 37 37 27

Place des Consuls ★ - Façade ★ of the Hotel de la Raymondie ★.

Relais Ste-Anne
r. Pourtanel – ✆ 05 65 37 40 56 – www.relais-sainte-anne.com – relais.sainteanne@wanadoo.fr – Fax 05 65 37 42 82 – Open 1st March-15 November
16 rm – †€ 45/175 ††€ 75/175, ☕ € 15 – 5 suites
Rest ***Le Patio Ste-Anne*** – *✆ 05 65 37 19 10 (open 1st April-15 Nov. and closed Wednesday lunch, Thursday lunch and Tuesday)* Menu € 37/69 – Carte € 49/73
◆ A former girls' boarding school surrounded by a garden. Old chapel, elegant lounge and guestrooms with personal touches. Charming little restaurant, just opposite the hotel, serving contemporary cuisine in a modern dining room. Small patio-terrace.

X **Auberge des Sept Tours** with rm
av de Turenne – ✆ 05 65 37 30 16 – www.auberge7tours.com – auberge7tours@wanadoo.fr – Fax 05 65 37 41 69 – Closed February holidays
8 rm – †€ 50 ††€ 50, ☕ € 8
Rest – *(closed Sunday dinner and Monday dinner 28 August-12 July, Monday lunch and Saturday lunch)* Menu (€ 14 bi), € 26/53 – Carte € 31/47
◆ Attractive veranda-dining room overlooking the countryside. Traditional menu, duck specialities and a mainly regional wine list. Rustic rooms.

MARTIEL – 12 Aveyron – 338 D4 – pop. 823 – alt. 400 m – ✉ 12200 29 C1

Paris 613 – Toulouse 134 – Rodez 63 – Cahors 49 – Villefranche-de-Rouergue 11

Les Fontaines without rest

Pleyjean, via Villeneuve road, D 76 – ✆ 05 65 29 46 70 – www.lesfontaines.net – andreacam@wanadoo.fr

3 rm – € 50/70 € 60/80

◆ Old house renovated by an English couple in a rural hamlet near the Aveyron Valley. Attractive lounge, welcoming guestrooms and rustic dining room. Copious breakfast.

MARTIGNÉ-BRIAND – 49 Maine-et-Loire – 317 G5 – pop. 1 847 – alt. 75 m – ✉ 49540 35 C2

Paris 324 – Nantes 113 – Angers 33 – Cholet 46 – Saumur 33

Château des Noyers

5 km west on D 208 – ✆ 02 41 54 09 60 – www.chateaudesnoyers.com – chateaudesnoyers@wanadoo.fr – Fax 02 41 44 32 63 – Open 1st April-15 November

5 rm – € 160 € 280 – 2 suites **Table d'hôte** – Menu € 45 bi/50 bi

◆ A listed historic monument, this 16-17C château is surrounded by a vineyard estate. It has period furniture (Louis XV and XVI, Empire, etc.), a refined décor, a swimming pool and tennis court. Fireplace and Richelieu's coat of arms in the dining room. Dungeon converted into wine store and wine-tasting in the vaults.

MARTIGUES – 13 Bouches-du-Rhône – 340 F5 – pop. 46 200 – alt. 1 m – ✉ 13500 Provence 40 B3

Paris 769 – Aix-en-Provence 45 – Arles 53 – Marseille 40

Syndicat d'initiative, rond point de l'Hôtel de Ville ✆ 04 42 42 31 10, Fax 04 42 42 31 11

Miroir aux oiseaux★ - Étang de Berre★ Z.

<★ of N.D.-des-Marins chapel, 3.5 km by ④.

Plan on next page

St-Roch

rm,

av. G. Braque – ✆ 04 42 42 36 36 – www.hotelsaintroch.com – hotel-st-roch@wanadoo.fr – Fax 04 42 80 01 80 Y **x**

63 rm – € 98 € 116

Rest – *(closed 25 December-1st January)* Menu € 21 – Carte € 23/53

◆ This hotel in the upper reaches of the 'Venice of Provence' has been refurbished. Find a modern lobby-lounge, warm red colour scheme, and up-to-date rooms. Modern restaurant and terrace with a view of a tower from 1516 (the remains of an old mill). Traditional dishes.

Le Bouchon à la Mer

19 quai L. Toulmond – ✆ 04 42 49 41 41 – lebouchonalamer@wanadoo.fr – Fax 04 42 42 14 40 – Closed Easter holidays, autumn half term holidays, February holidays, Tuesday lunch, Sunday dinner and Monday Y **v**

Rest – Menu € 44/50

◆ Located near the Miroir aux Oiseaux, a popular painter's spot, this restaurant serves classic cuisine in a charming dining area with cream and chocolate toned décor. Canal-side terrace.

Le Garage

20 av. Frédéric-Mistral – ✆ 04 42 44 09 51 – www.restaurantmartigues.com – restaurant.legarage@orange.fr – Closed 1-15 January, 10-25 August, Saturday lunch, Sunday dinner and Monday Z **a**

Rest – Menu € 26 (weekday lunch)/34 – Carte € 43/50

◆ A town centre bistro run by an enthusiastic young chef. Fashionable decor (taupe colour scheme, wenge wood tables, open kitchen) and modern menu.

MARTIGUES

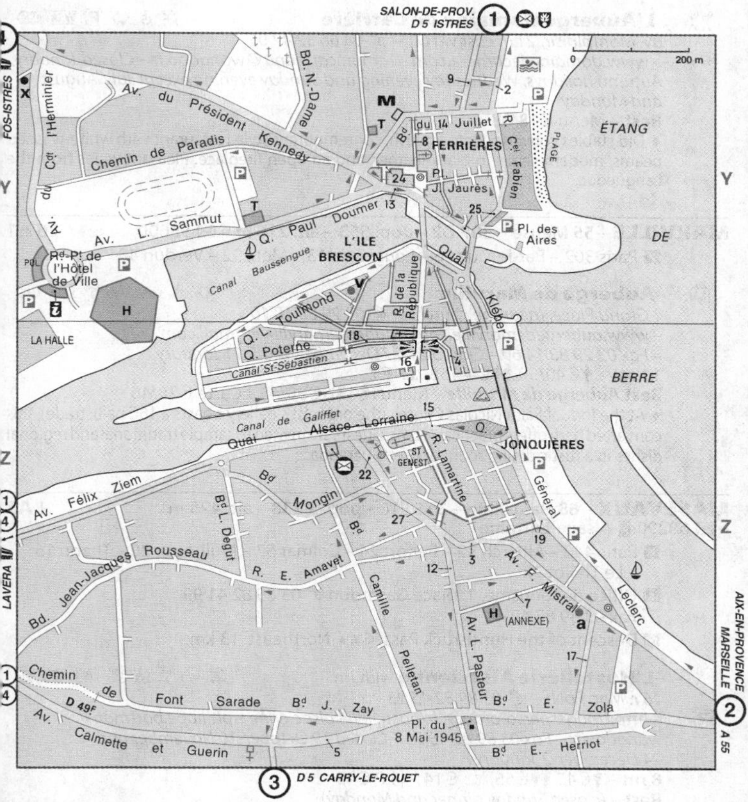

MARTILLAC – 33 Gironde – 335 H6 – see Bordeaux

MARTIN-ÉGLISE – 76 Seine-Maritime – 304 G2 – see Dieppe

LA MARTRE – 83 Var – 340 O3 – pop. 160 – alt. 984 m – ✉ 83840 41 C2

Paris 808 – Castellane 19 – Digne-les-Bains 73 – Draguignan 50 – Grasse 50

Château de Taulane rm, VISA AE

at the golf club, northeast: 4 km via D6085 –
04 93 40 60 80 – www.chateau-taulane.com – resahotel@chateau-taulane.com – Fax 04 93 60 37 48 – Open 1 April-8 November
45 rm – €129/499 €149/499, €19 – ½ P €140/275
Rest – Menu €35 (lunch) – Carte €56/76 dinner only
◆ An 18C chateau surrounded by four dovecotes, located near a 340-hectare golf course and park. Home to well-equipped, standard rooms, and simpler rooms in the secondary building. A charming restaurant and clubhouse with a snack bar. Terrace overlooking the greens.

MARVEJOLS – 48 Lozère – 330 H7 – pop. 5 501 – alt. 650 m – ✉ 48100 Languedoc-Roussillon-Tarn Gorges 23 C1

Paris 580 – Montpellier 178 – Mende 28 – Espalion 83 – Saint-Chély-d'Apcher 34

Office de tourisme, place Henri IV ✆ 04 66 32 02 14, Fax 04 66 32 02 14

L'Auberge Domaine de Carrière

VISA

av. Montplaisir, 2 km east via D1 – ✆ 04 66 32 47 05 – www.domainedecarriere.com – ramon.carmona@wanadoo.fr – Closed January, Autumn holidays, Wednesday evening and Sunday evening except July-August and Monday

Rest – Menu € 18/38

◆ Old stables converted into a plush, contemporary-style restaurant with white-washed beams, modern chairs in black leather, and an open fireplace. Pleasant wines from the Languedoc.

MARVILLE – 55 Meuse – 307 D2 – pop. 553 – alt. 216 m – ✉ 55600 26 A1

Paris 302 – Bar-le-Duc 96 – Longuyon 13 – Metz 92 – Verdun 40

Auberge de Marville

rest, VISA

1 Grand Place, (near the church) – ✆ 03 29 88 10 10 – www.aubergedemarville.com – aubergemarville@gmail.com – Fax 03 29 88 14 60 – Closed 21-27 December and 5-11 January

11 rm – €40/50 €44/58, €7

Rest *Auberge de Marville* – Menu (€ 13), € 30/45 – Carte € 28/46

◆ At the foot of Saint Nicolas Church (the organist's gallery boasts a 16C balustrade), this converted barn offers practical rooms. Guests are invited to sample traditional and regional dishes in a rustic dining room or pretty veranda.

MASEVAUX – 68 Haut-Rhin – 315 F10 – pop. 3 238 – alt. 425 m – ✉ 68290 Alsace-Lorraine 1 A3

Paris 440 – Altkirch 32 – Belfort 24 – Colmar 57 – Mulhouse 30 – Thann 15 – Le Thillot 38

Office de tourisme, 1, place Gayardon ✆ 03 89 82 41 99, Fax 03 89 82 49 44

Descent of the Hundsrück Pass ≤★★ Northeast: 13 km.

L'Hostellerie Alsacienne with rm

VISA AE

16 r. Mar. Foch – ✆ 03 89 82 45 25 – http://pagesperso-orange.fr/hostellerie.alsacienne – philippe.battman@wanadoo.fr – Fax 03 89 82 45 25 – Closed 19 October-10 November and 24 December-2 January

8 rm – €45 €55, € 14 – ½ P € 45

Rest – *(closed Sunday dinner and Monday)*

Menu (€ 11), € 13 (weekday lunch), € 26/43 – Carte € 24/50 dinner only

◆ Independent local growers and organic produce take pride of place on the menu, which features regional recipes inspired by local traditions. Alsace decor and partly refurbished rooms.

MASSERET – 19 Corrèze – 329 K2 – pop. 608 – alt. 380 m – ✉ 19510 24 B2

Paris 432 – Limoges 45 – Guéret 132 – Tulle 48 – Ussel 101

Syndicat d'initiative, le Bourg ✆ 05 55 98 24 79, Fax 05 55 73 49 69

De la Tour

A/C rest, VISA

7 pl. Marcel Champeix – ✆ 05 55 73 40 12 – www.hoteldelatourmasseret.com – hoteldelatour19@aol.com – Fax 05 55 73 49 41 – Closed Sunday evening except July-August

15 rm – €43 €43, € 6,50 – ½ P € 45

Rest – Menu (€ 14), € 19/44 – Carte € 30/55

◆ On the quiet heights of this Limousin town is a family-run hostelry with well-kept, refurbished, simple guestrooms. Spacious dining room extended by a terrace from which you can admire the 'tower', a water tower - medieval in appearance only.

MASSIAC – 15 Cantal – **330** H3 – **pop. 1 838** – **alt. 534 m** – ✉ **15500** 5 **B3**
Auvergne

Paris 484 – Aurillac 84 – Brioude 23 – Issoire 38 – Murat 37 – St-Flour 30

Office de tourisme, 24, rue du Dr Mallet ✆ 04 71 23 07 76, Fax 04 71 23 08 50

North: Gorges de l'Alagnon ★ - Site of Ste-Madeleine chapel ★ North: 2 km.

Grand Hôtel de la Poste rest, VISA
26 av. Ch. de Gaulle – ✆ 04 71 23 02 01 – www.hotel-massiac.com – hotel.massiac@wanadoo.fr – Fax 04 71 23 09 23 – Closed 15 November-22 December, Tuesday dinner and Wednesday from January to Easter
33 rm – €44/56 €44/57, €7 – ½ P €47/54
Rest – Menu €15 (weekdays)/35 – Carte €24/42
◆ Imposing building, just outside town and near the A75 exit. Comfortable rooms and a wealth of leisure activities (fitness centre, Jacuzzi, squash court). A non-smoking dining room with a fireplace serving Auvergne-inspired cuisine.

La Colombière without rest VISA AE
rte de Grenier Montgon, 1 km north on D 909 – ✆ 04 71 23 18 50 – www.hotel-lacolombiere.com – contact@hotel-lacolombiere.com – Fax 04 71 23 18 58 – Closed 15 January-1 March
30 rm – €38 €45, €6,50
◆ Recently built hotel ideally located on the road to the Gorges de l'Alagnon. Spacious functional rooms (new furniture, well-equipped bathrooms, faultless upkeep).

MASSY – 91 Essonne – **312** C3 – **101** 25 – **see Paris, Area**

MATOUGUES – 51 Marne – **306** I9 – **see Châlons-en-Champagne**

MATOUR – 71 Saône-et-Loire – **320** G12 – **pop. 1 074** – **alt. 500 m** – ✉ **71520** Burgundy-Jura 8 **C3**

Paris 405 – Charolles 28 – Cluny 24 – Lapalisse 82 – Lyon 102 – Mâcon 36 – Roanne 57

Office de tourisme, ✆ 03 85 59 72 24, Fax 03 85 59 72 24

Christophe Clément VISA
pl. de l'Église – ✆ 03 85 59 74 80 – Fax 03 85 59 75 77 – Closed 5-12 October, 14 December-13 January, dinner except Saturday from October to April, Sunday dinner and Monday
Rest – Menu (€12), €19/37 – Carte €29/45
◆ This restaurant located on the church square has an attractive façade and a distinctive sign of a rooster's head. Serving copious, traditional cuisine and an unusual house special in a rustic, country-style atmosphere.

MAUBEC – 84 Vaucluse – **332** D10 – **pop. 1 791** – **alt. 120 m** – ✉ **84660** 42 **E1**

Paris 717 – Marseille 84 – Avignon 36 – Aix-en-Provence 68 – Arles 78

La Bastide du Bois Bréant without rest VISA
501 chemin du Puits de Grandaou – ✆ 04 90 05 86 78 – www.hotel-bastide-bois-breant.com – contact@hotel-bastide-bois-breant.com – Fax 04 90 75 03 27 – Open 15 March-15 November
12 rm – €96/192 €107/192 – 1 suite
◆ Very well preserved building set in an oak forest. The place has lost none of its Provençal character and the decor in every room tells a story.

MAUBEUGE – 59 Nord – **302** L6 – **pop. 32 400** – **Built-up area 117 470** – **alt. 134 m** – ✉ **59600** Northern France and the Paris Region 31 **D2**

Paris 242 – Mons 21 – St-Quentin 114 – Valenciennes 39

Office de tourisme, place Vauban ✆ 03 27 62 11 93, Fax 03 27 64 10 23

South by Avesnes-sur-Helpe road– ✉ 59330 Beaufort

Auberge de l'Hermitage
51 rte Nationale, at 6 km on N 2 – ✆ 03 27 67 89 59 – auberge.hermitage@orange.fr – Fax 03 27 39 84 52 – Closed 28 July-13 August, 26-31 December, Sunday dinner, Tuesday dinner, Thursday dinner and Monday
Rest – Menu (€ 22), € 29 (weekdays)/72 – Carte € 45/70
◆ A welcoming brick building near the main road on the edge of the Avesnois Nature Park. Well-appointed dining room and traditional cuisine in the land of the Maroilles cheese.

Le Relais de Beaufort
8 km away on N 2 – ✆ 03 27 63 50 36 – www.lerelaisdebeaufort.fr – Fax 03 27 67 85 11 – Closed 17 August-4 September, Sunday dinner and Monday
Rest – Menu € 24/43 – Carte € 33/60
◆ Two dining rooms: one marine in style with a splendid olive tree, the other rustic and full of light. Terrace overlooking a pretty garden. Traditional menu.

MAULÉVRIER – 49 Maine-et-Loire – **317** E6 – see Cholet

MAUREILLAS-LAS-ILLAS – 66 Pyrénées-Orientales – **344** H8 22 **B3**
– pop. 2 546 – alt. 130 m – ✉ 66480 Languedoc-Roussillon-Tarn Gorges

Paris 873 – Gerona 71 – Perpignan 31 – Port-Vendres 31 – Prades 69

Syndicat d'initiative, avenue Mal Joffre ✆ 04 68 83 48 00

in Las Illas 11 km Southwest by D 13 – ✉ 66480

Hostal dels Trabucayres with rm
– ✆ 04 68 83 07 56 – Fax 04 68 83 07 56 – Open 15 April-20 October and closed Tuesday and Wednesday in low season
5 rm – †€ 32/36 ††€ 32/36, ☕ € 5,50 – ½ P € 37
Rest – *(Open 15 March-25 October)* Menu € 13 bi (weekdays)/50 bi – Carte € 24/38
◆ An old, simple inn along the GR10 footpath at the heart of a forest. Original rustic interior where the menu is based on Catalan dishes. Peace and quiet guaranteed. Basic bedrooms and two modern gîtes.

MAURIAC – 15 Cantal – **330** B3 – pop. 3 963 – alt. 722 m – ✉ 15200 5 **A3**
Auvergne

Paris 490 – Aurillac 53 – Le Mont-Dore 77 – Clermont-Ferrand 113 – Tulle 73

Office de tourisme, 1, rue Chappe d'Auteroche ✆ 04 71 67 30 26, Fax 04 71 68 25 08

Val-Saint-JeanW : 2 km, ✆ 06 07 74 22 29

Notre-Dame-des-Miracles basilica ★ - Le Vigean: shrine★ in the church Northeast: 2 km.

Barrage de l'Aigle★★: 11 km by D 678 and D105, Dordogne-Berry-Limousin

Des Voyageurs
pl. de la Poste – ✆ 04 71 68 01 01 – www.aubergevoyageurs.com – aubergevoyageurs@info.com – Fax 04 71 68 01 56 – Closed 20 April-3 May, 28 September-11 October and 21 December-5 January
18 rm – †€ 38/50 ††€ 45/60, ☕ € 6,50
Rest *La Bonne Auberge* – *(Closed Sunday dinner, Friday dinner and Saturday)* Menu € 12/35 – Carte € 21/39
◆ An unpretentious town centre establishment for weary travellers. Well-kept, above all practical bedrooms. The restaurant of the Bonne Auberge has preserved its 1980s "look". Regional and family cooking.

Auv'Hôtel without rest
4 r. du 11 Novembre – ✆ 04 71 68 19 10 – www.auv-hotel.fr – mauriac@auv-hotel.com – Fax 04 71 68 17 77 – Closed 15-28 February
14 rm – †€ 43/45 ††€ 46/49, ☕ € 8
◆ Near the Norman church N.D. des Miracles, pleasant little hotel offering functional rooms with rustic furniture.

MAUROUX – 46 Lot – **337** C5 – **see Puy-l'Évêque**

MAURY – 66 Pyrénées-Orientales – **344** G6 – **pop. 901** – **alt. 200 m** – ✉ 66460 — 22 **B3**

Paris 876 – Montpellier 179 – Perpignan 35 – Carcassonne 142 – Canet-en-Roussillon 45

Syndicat d'initiative, Avenue Jean Jaurès ✆ 04.68.50.08.54, Fax 04.68.50.08.54

Pascal Borrell
la Maison du Terroir, av. Jean Jaurès – ✆ 04 68 86 28 28 – www.maison-du-terroir.com – pascalborrell@wanadoo.fr – Fax 04 68 86 04 80 – Closed for one week in February, Sunday dinner and Monday from October to March
Rest – Menu (€ 28), € 45/65 – Carte € 75/85
Spec. Saint-Jacques en marinade au citron vert façon sashimi et caviar de hareng. Cannette de Challans braisée au sautoir et laquée au miel de garrigue (Oct. to Feb.). Macaron arabica, garniture chocolat épicé et copeaux de chocolat. **Wines** Maury, Vin de Pays des Côtes Catalanes.
♦ Contemporary restaurant decorated in typical Catalan colours, specialising in regional cuisine with an innovative twist. Shop selling wine and regional produce to whet your appetite.

MAUSSAC – 19 Corrèze – **329** N3 – **see Meymac**

MAUSSANE-LES-ALPILLES – 13 Bouches-du-Rhône – **340** D3 – **pop. 2 155** – **alt. 32 m** – ✉ **13520** — 42 **E1**

Paris 712 – Arles 20 – Avignon 30 – Marseille 81 – Martigues 44 – St-Rémy-de-Provence 10

Office de tourisme, place Laugier de Monblan ✆ 04 90 54 52 04, Fax 04 90 54 39 44

Le Pré des Baux without rest
r. Vieux Moulin – ✆ 04 90 54 40 40 – www.lepredesbaux.com – info@lepredesbaux.com – Fax 04 90 54 53 07 – Open 27 March-2 November
10 rm – †€ 95/125 ††€ 95/125, ☕ € 12
♦ The rooms are situated around a Mediterranean garden away from prying glances and noise and open directly onto private, ground-level terraces where breakfast is served.

Castillon des Baux without rest
10 bis av. de la Vallée des Baux – ✆ 04 90 54 31 93 – www.castillondesbaux.com – castillondesbaux@orange.fr – Fax 04 90 54 51 31 – Closed January
15 rm – †€ 82/130 ††€ 82/130, ☕ € 11
♦ This red ochre construction stands in a garden with olive trees and an attractive pool. Most of the spacious, pastel-decorated rooms have a balcony or a terrace.

Aurelia without rest
124 av. de la Valléee des Baux – ✆ 04 90 54 22 54 – www.bestwestern-aurelia.com – resa@bestwestern-aurelia.com – Fax 04 90 54 20 75 – 15 Mar. - 15 Nov.
39 rm – †€ 125 ††€ 125, ☕ € 11
♦ Sun drenched decor in this regionally-inspired construction. The unfussy, well-equipped rooms are more pleasant by the pool, with views of the countryside.

Val Baussenc
rm, rm, rest,
122 av. de la Vallée des Baux – ✆ 04 90 54 38 90 – www.valbaussenc.com – information@valbaussenc.com – Fax 04 90 54 33 36 – Open 1st March-31 October
21 rm – †€ 69/118 ††€ 81/118, ☕ € 11 – 1 suite – ½ P € 70/89
Rest – *(closed Wednesday) (dinner only)* Menu € 27/35 – Carte approx. € 45
♦ Provençal-style construction built with limestone from Les Baux. The bedrooms, nearly all of which have a terrace or balcony, offer views of the countryside. Small, colourful dining room and pleasant terrace under a trellis.

XX **Ou Ravi Provençau**

34 av. de la Vallée des Baux – ✆ 04 90 54 31 11 – www.ouravi.net – infos@ouravi.net – Fax 04 90 54 41 03 – Closed 15 November-15 December, Tuesday and Wednesday

Rest – Menu (€ 20 bi), € 35/55 – Carte € 40/100

◆ Authentic, generous and tasty: it's almost as if the food served in this attractive southern house came straight out of the "Reboul", the bible of Provençal cooking.

X **La Place**

65 av. de la Vallée des Baux – ✆ 04 90 54 23 31 – www.maisonsdebaumaniere.com – laplace@maisonsdebaumaniere.com – Closed January and Tuesday

Rest – Menu (€ 25), € 32

◆ Savour the intimate, trendy atmosphere of this restaurant serving tasty southern inspired cuisine in two cosy sitting rooms and a shaded terrace.

in Paradou **2 km West by D 17, Arles road – pop. 1 167 – alt. 21 m – ✉ 13520**

Le Hameau des Baux

chemin de Bourgeac – ✆ 04 90 54 10 30 – www.hameaudesbaux.com – reservation@hameaudesbaux.com – Fax 04 90 54 45 30 – Closed January and February

15 rm – **†**€ 195/280 **††**€ 195/280, € 18 – 5 suites

Rest – *(closed Sunday dinner and Wednesday) (number of covers limited, pre-book)* Menu € 45 (lunch)/53 – Carte € 48/58

◆ Superbly reconstituted Provençal hamlet surrounded by cypress and olive trees, offering extreme refinement and quiet in guestrooms with a personal touch; an address for the aesthetically-minded. The contemporary cuisine influenced by southern flavours enhances the magical appeal of the spot.

Du Côté des Olivades

lieu dit de Bourgeac – ✆ 04 90 54 56 78 – www.ducotedesolivades.com – ducotedesolivades@wanadoo.fr – Fax 04 90 54 56 79

10 rm – **†**€ 79/184 **††**€ 79/184, € 16 – ½ P € 102/156

Rest – *(number of covers limited, pre-book)* Menu € 38/55 – Carte € 35/70

◆ This restful modern villa, tucked away among olive groves, offers a warm welcome, smart designer decor, suites, a pool, spa and meeting room. At the restaurant regional dishes that vary with the seasons.

B design & Spa

1 rm – **†**€ 150/220 **††**€ 150/220, € 18 – 14 suites – **††**€ 250/550 – ½ P € 141/341

◆ Modernity at the service of comfort and well-being sums up the spirit of this new hotel on the way into the estate. Immense rooms, decorated by an interior designer. Terraces.

La Maison du Paradou

2 rte de St-Roch – ✆ 04 90 546 546 – www.maisonduparadou.com – reservations@maisonduparadou.com – Fax 04 90 54 85 83

5 rm – **†**€ 285 **††**€ 285, € 20 **Table d'hôte** – Menu € 45 bi (lunch)/75 bi

◆ An old staging post (1699) run by a British couple. Comfortable guestrooms featuring myriad individual touches and high-tech gadgetry. Library-lounge, Provençal garden and swimming pool. Table d'hôte (reservation required) beneath a shady pergola with the Alpilles as a backdrop.

X **Le Bistrot du Paradou "Chez Jean-Louis"**

57 av. de la Vallée des Baux – ✆ 04 90 54 32 70 – Fax 04 90 54 32 70 – Closed 1-9 March, Sunday and Monday in low season and dinner from October to May except Friday and Saturday

Rest – *(pre-book)* Menu € 43 bi (lunch)/49 bi

◆ This blue shuttered Provençal house is a local institution. Tasty regional fare served in a friendly decor adorned with a vast collection (2,400) of beer bottles.

If breakfast is included the symbol appears after the number of rooms.

MAYENNE – 53 Mayenne – 310 F5 – pop. 13 800 – alt. 124 m 35 C1
– ✉ 53100 Normandy

Paris 283 – Alençon 61 – Flers 56 – Fougères 47 – Laval 30 – Le Mans 89

Office de tourisme, quai de Waiblingen ✆ 02 43 04 19 37, Fax 02 43 00 01 99

Former château ≤★.

Le Grand Hôtel
VISA AE

2 r. Ambroise de Loré – ✆ 02 43 00 96 00 – www.grandhotelmayenne.com – grandhotelmayenne@wanadoo.fr – Fax 02 43 00 69 20 – Closed 10-30 August, 24 December-4 January and Saturday dinner from November to April

22 rm – †€ 69/95 ††€ 82/121, ☕ € 11 – ½ P € 79/97

Rest – *(closed Sunday from November to April and Saturday except dinner from May to October)* Menu (€ 18), € 21/61 – Carte € 47/61

◆ For about 40-years, the same family has run this centrally located hotel dating from 1850. Fully renovated rooms and a comfortable lounge and whisky bar. Two dining rooms, one with a veranda, with a view of the Mayenne. Classic menu.

La Croix Couverte with rm
rest, VISA AE

Alençon road: 2 km on N 12 – ✆ 02 43 04 32 48 – www.lacroixcouverte.com – la-croixcouverte@wanadoo.fr – Fax 02 43 04 43 69 – Closed 2-17 August, Christmas holidays, Sunday dinner, Monday and bank holidays

11 rm – †€ 50 ††€ 60, ☕ € 10

Rest – Menu (€ 16), € 20 (weekdays)/40 – Carte € 43/65

◆ Hundred-year-old house by the main road with "vintage" style dining room opening onto a pleasant terrace and garden. Unpretentious rooms, quieter to the rear.

at Fontaine-Daniel 6 km southwest by D 104 – ✉ 53100

La Forge
VISA

au bourg – ✆ 02 43 00 34 85 – www.restaurantlaforge.fr – contact@restaurantlaforge.fr – Closed 1-15 January, 1-7 September, Tuesday except dinner from June to September, Sunday dinner and Monday

Rest – Menu (€ 13), € 25/45

◆ In the village square, discover this forge converted into a contemporary restaurant. Inventive, visually refined and tasty dishes. Original wine list.

Laval road South by N 162 – ✉ 53100 Mayenne

La Marjolaine
rm, VISA AE

6.5 km on, at the Domaine du Bas-Mont – ✆ 02 43 00 48 42 – www.lamarjolaine.fr – lamarjolaine@wanadoo.fr – Fax 02 43 08 10 58

23 rm – †€ 51/120 ††€ 51/120, ☕ € 8,50 – ½ P € 70/90

Rest – *(Closed Friday dinner from 1 January to 15 April and Saturday lunch from 15 October to 15 April)* Menu € 19 (weekdays)/42 – Carte € 44/58

Rest *Le Bistrot de La Marjolaine* – *(closed Saturday, Sunday and holidays) (lunch only)* Menu (€ 14), € 17/23

◆ Old restored farm on a wooded estate near a river. Pleasant dining room with a terrace facing the park, serving up-to-date cuisine with a good wine list. Pleasant rooms. The Bistrot has wall coverings depicting peacocks, fast service and well-presented dishes.

Beau Rivage with rm
≤ VISA AE

rte de Saint-Baudelle, 4 km away – ✆ 02 43 00 49 13 – www.restaurantbeaurivage.com – fbeaurivage@9online.fr – Fax 02 43 00 49 26 – Closed Sunday dinner, public holiday dinner and Monday

8 rm – †€ 54 ††€ 68, ☕ € 8 – ½ P € 58/68

Rest – grill room – Menu (€ 14), € 18 (weekdays)/36 – Carte € 28/48

◆ Delightful and stylish open-air café atmosphere in this house with a fine shaded terrace on the banks of the Mayenne. Dishes cooked on a roasting spit. Cheerful rooms.

LE MAYET-DE-MONTAGNE – 03 Allier – 326 J6 – pop. 1 478 6 C2
– alt. 535 m – ✉ 03250 Auvergne

Paris 369 – Clermont-Ferrand 81 – Lapalisse 23 – Moulins 73 – Thiers 44 – Vichy 27

Office de tourisme, rue Roger Degoulange ✆ 04 70 59 38 40, Fax 04 70 59 37 24

Le Relais du Lac with rm

rte de Laprugne, 0.5 km south by D 7 – 04 70 59 70 23 – renécazals@orange.fr – Closed October, Monday and Tuesday

6 rm – €50/60 €50/60, €8 – ½ P €50/55

Rest – Menu €13 (weekday lunch)/22 – Carte €32/44

◆ In the heart of the Bourbonnais mountains next to a lake, this restaurant has a local flavour, with rural decor, and regional specialities. Neat and tidy rooms available.

MAZAMET – 81 Tarn – **338** G10 – **pop. 10 300** – **alt. 241 m** – ✉ **81200** 29 **C2**

Languedoc-Roussillon-Tarn Gorges

Paris 739 – Albi 64 – Carcassonne 50 – Castres 21 – Toulouse 92

Castres-Mazamet: 05 63 70 34 77, West: 14 km.

Office de tourisme, rue des Casernes 05 63 61 27 07, Fax 05 63 61 31 35

de Mazamet-la-Barouge Pont de l'Arn, N : 3 km, 05 63 61 06 72

≤★ of the gorges de l'Arnette South: 4 km.

Mets et Plaisirs rest,

7 av. Albert Rouvière – 05 63 61 56 93 – www.metsetplaisirs.com – contact@metsetplaisir.com – Fax 05 63 61 83 38 – Closed 3-23 August, 2-11 January and Sunday dinner

11 rm – €45 €55, €7 – ½ P €60

Rest – *(closed Monday)* Menu €16 (weekdays)/55

◆ This early 20C mansion is located in the town centre opposite the post office. It has well-appointed, refurbished, simple guestrooms. Elegant atmosphere in this restaurant, which was once an aristocratic home. Contemporary cuisine.

MAZAN – 84 Vaucluse – **332** D9 – **see Carpentras**

MAZAYE – 63 Puy-de-Dôme – **326** E8 – **pop. 608** – **alt. 760 m** 5 **B2**
– ✉ 63230

Paris 441 – Clermont-Fd 23 – Le Mont-Dore 32 – Pontaumur 27 – Pontgibaud 7

Auberge de Mazayes rm,

at Mazayes-Basses – 04 73 88 93 30 – www.auberge-mazayes.com – Fax 04 73 88 93 80 – Closed 15 December-25 January, Monday from October to March and Tuesday lunch

15 rm – €53/62 €65/77, €9 – ½ P €61/65

Rest – Menu €18 (weekdays)/32 – Carte €34/53

◆ This former farmhouse makes an ideal pied-à-terre for discovering the Auvergne countryside: the rural beauty of the site is only equalled by its facilities. Pretty, country-style restaurant; tasty regional dishes; lovely selection of Bordeaux and local wines.

MÉAUDRE – 38 Isère – **333** G7 – **see Autrans**

MEAULNE – 03 Allier – **326** C3 – **pop. 771** – **alt. 185 m** – ✉ **03360** 5 **B1**

Auvergne

Paris 307 – Clermont-Ferrand 126 – Moulins 96 – Montluçon 31 – Saint-Amand-Montrond 19

Au Coeur de Meaulne rest,

20 pl. de l'Eglise – 04 70 06 20 30 – www.aucoeurdemeaulne.com – info@aucoeurdemeaulne.com – Fax 04 70 06 92 58 – Closed 1 week in October, 1 week in November and 2-16 January

8 rm – €51/70 €61/70, €10 – ½ P €60/65

Rest – *(closed Tuesday except dinner July-August and Wednesday)*
Menu (€15 bi), €23/50 – Carte €35/50

◆ This renovated auberge has fresh, clean rooms, where old tree trunks from the Forêt du Tronçais take the place of bedside tables! Contemporary cuisine served in a smart dining room or, in summer, in the shade of an old horse chestnut tree.

MEAUX ⓢⓟ – 77 Seine-et-Marne – 312 G2 – pop. 49 200 – alt. 51 m – ✉ 77100 ▮ Northern France and the Paris Region

19 **C1**

▶ Paris 54 – Compiègne 68 – Melun 56 – Reims 98

ℹ Office de tourisme, 1, place Doumer ✆ 01 64 33 02 26, Fax 01 64 33 24 86

⛳18 de Meaux Boutigny Boutigny11 km on the A 140 and D 228, ✆ 01 60 25 63 98

⛳18 de la Brie Crécy-la-Chapelle Ferme de Montpichet, 16 km on the A 140 and Melun road, ✆ 01 64 75 34 44

⛳18 Disneyland Paris Magny-le-Hongre Allée de la Mare Houleuse, S : 16 km on the D5, ✆ 01 60 45 68 90

👁 Episcopal Centre ★ ABY : cathedral★ **B**, ⩽★ from ramparts terrace.

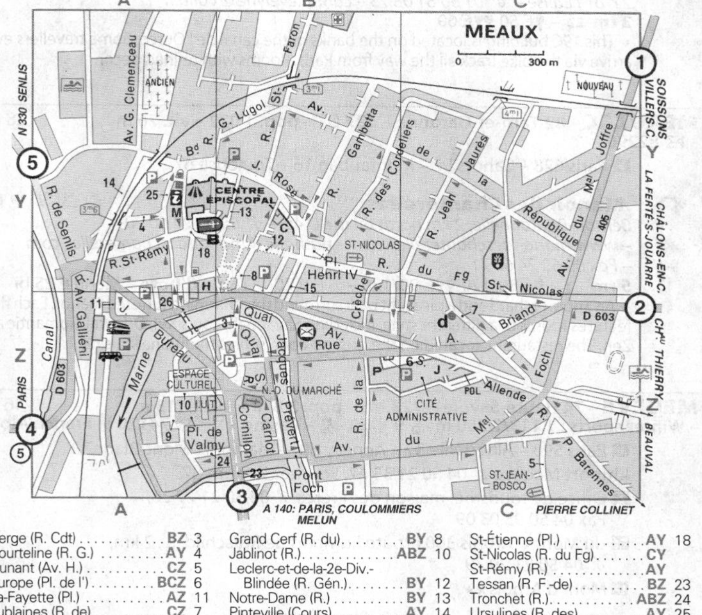

Berge (R. Cdt) . . . . BZ 3
Courteline (R. G.) . . . . AY 4
Dunant (Av. H.) . . . . CZ 5
Europe (Pl. de l') . . . . BCZ 6
La-Fayette (Pl.) . . . . AZ 11
Fublaines (R. de) . . . . CZ 7
Grande Ile (R. de la) . . . . . . AZ 9
Grand Cerf (R. du) . . . . BY 8
Jablinot (R.) . . . . ABZ 10
Leclerc-et-de-la-2e-Div.-Blindée (R. Gén.) . . . . BY 12
Notre-Dame (R.) . . . . BY 13
Pinteville (Cours) . . . . AY 14
Raoult (Cours) . . . . BY 15
St-Étienne (Pl.) . . . . AY 18
St-Nicolas (R. du Fg) . . . . . . CY
St-Rémy (R.) . . . . AY
Tessan (R. F.-de) . . . . BZ 23
Tronchet (R.) . . . . ABZ 24
Ursulines (R. des) . . . . AY 25
Victor-Hugo (Quai) . . . . AZ 26

XX La Grignotière

AC VISA MC ①

36 r. de la Sablonnière – ✆ 01 64 34 21 48 – Fax 01 64 33 93 93 – Closed August, Saturday lunch, Tuesday and Wednesday CZ **d**

Rest – Menu € 32 (weekdays)/45 – Carte € 60/74

◆ Pleasant rustic interior, where a fire often burns in the hearth. Tasty local cuisine and splendid seafood platters served all year round.

in Germigny-l'Évêque 8 km on the ①, D 405 and D 97 – pop. 1 285 – alt. 49 m – ✉ 77910

XX Hostellerie Le Gonfalon with rm

⩽ VISA MC AE ①

2 r. de l'Église – ✆ 01 64 33 16 05 – www.hotelgonfalon.com – le-gonfalon@wanadoo.fr – Fax 01 64 33 25 59

8 rm – †€ 85/120 ††€ 85/150, ☕ € 12

Rest – Menu € 35 (weekdays)/78 – Carte € 65/90

◆ Freshness and charm flood the romantic terrace of this inn on the banks of the Marne. Modern, seasonal cuisine, served by the fire in winter in the Louis XIII dining room. Very quiet rooms, some with a large private terrace on the river side.

in Poincy 5 km by ② and D 17A – pop. 723 – alt. 53 m – ✉ 77470

XX **Le Moulin de Poincy**
r. du Moulin – ☎ 01 60 23 06 80 – moulin.de.poincy@orange.fr – Fax 01 60 23 12 56 – Closed 1-24 September, 5-28 January, Monday dinner, Tuesday and Wednesday
Rest – Menu € 31/61 – Carte € 44/76
◆ Enjoy life at a gentle pace at this pretty 17C mill and garden beside the Marne. Old-style interior (flea market items, coffee pot collection) and delicious traditional cuisine.

in Trilbardou 7 km by ④ and D 27 – pop. 517 – alt. 47 m – ✉ 77450

M. et Mme. Cantin without rest
2 r. de l'Église – ☎ 01 60 61 08 75 – cantin.evelyne@voila.fr
3 rm – €50 €60
◆ This 19C building is located on the banks of the canal de l'Ourcq. Some travellers even arrive via the bike track all the way from Paris. Rooms with refined decor.

MEAUZAC – 82 Tarn-et-Garonne – 337 D7 – pop. 1 022 – alt. 76 m – ✉ 82290 28 **B2**

Paris 628 – Cahors 57 – Montauban 16 – Toulouse 67

Manoir des Chanterelles
Bernon-Boutounelle, 2 km north on the D 45 – ☎ 05 63 24 60 70 – www.manoirdeschanterelles.com – nathalie@manoirdeschanterelles.com – Fax 05 63 24 60 71
5 rm – €80/120 €90/120 – ½ P €70 **Table d'hôte** – Menu €25 bi
◆ An apple orchard and a pleasant park surround this charming turreted manor. Each floor features rooms of a different style, including Savannah, Louis XVI, Oriental, Romantic and Zen. The restaurant, located on the ground floor, serves traditional cuisine.

MEGÈVE – 74 Haute-Savoie – 328 M5 – pop. 3 878 – alt. 1 113 m – Winter sports : 1 113/2 350 m 9 70 – Casino AY – ✉ 74120 **French Alps** 46 **F1**

Paris 598 – Albertville 32 – Annecy 60 – Chamonix-Mont-Blanc 33

Altiport Megève ☎ 04 50 21 33 67, Southeast: 7 km BZ

Office de tourisme, maison des Frères ☎ 04 50 21 27 28, Fax 04 50 93 03 09

du Mont-d'Arbois 3001 route Edmond de Rotschild, E : 2 km, ☎ 04 50 21 29 79

Mont d'Arbois★★.

Plan on next page

Les Fermes de Marie
163 chemin de la Riante Colline, via ② – ☎ 04 50 93 03 10 – www.fermesdemarie.com – contact@fermesdemarie.com – Fax 04 50 93 09 84 – Open 26 June-30 August and 18 December-11 April
63 rm – €260/970 €260/970, €25 – 8 suites – ½ P €200/550
Rest – Carte €80/110
Rest *Restaurant Alpin* – *(dinner only)* Carte €48/82
◆ This hamlet of authentic Savoy farms has been carefully reconstructed. Cosy guestrooms, snug bar and superb spa. Luxurious and unique. Splendid alpine setting and up-to-date cuisine. Regional recipes in the restaurant specialising in cheese.

Lodge Park
100 r. Arly – ☎ 04 50 93 05 03 – www.lodgepark.com – contact@lodgepark.com – Fax 04 50 93 09 52 – Open 18 December-31 March AY **s**
49 rm – €370/590 €370/590, €25 – 11 suites **Rest** – Carte €45/95
◆ The remarquable decor in the bedrooms is on the theme of the Canadian lakes and gold prospectors: logs, waterfalls, hunting trophies, stone hearths ... A new take on the Adirondacks, but in a fashionable Megève style! Inventive cuisine.

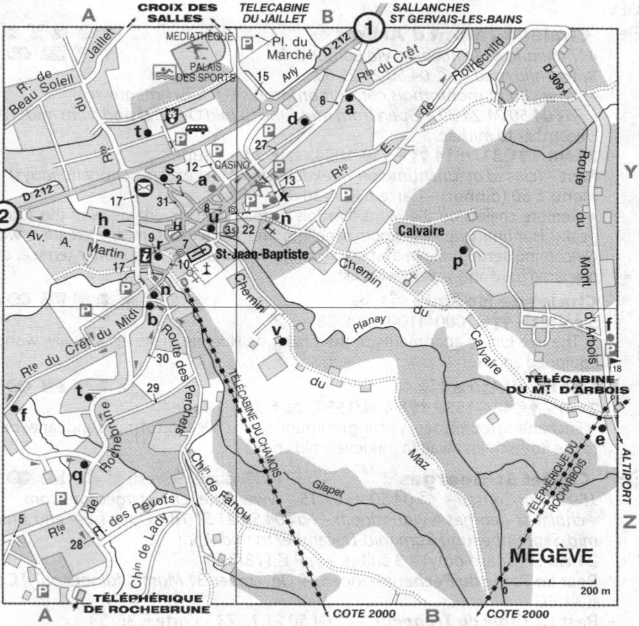

Arly (R. d') .... AY 2
Bouchet (Rte du) .... AZ 5
Église (Pl. de l') .... AY 7
Feige (R. Ch.) .... ABY 8
Martin (R. A.) .... AY 9
Monseigneur-Conseil (R.) ..... AY 10
Muffat-de-St-Amour (R. du Gén.) ... AY 12
Oberstdorf (R.) .... BY 13
Palais des Sports (Rte du) ..... ABY 15
Poste (R. de la) .... AY 17
Résistance (Pl. de la) .... AY 22
St-François (R.) .... ABY 27
Téléphérique (Rte du) .... AZ 28
Torrents (R. des) .... AZ 29
Verte (Allée) .... AZ 30
5-Rues (Passage des) .... AY 31

Le Fer à Cheval rest, VISA

36 rte Crêt d'Arbois – ✆ 04 50 21 30 39
– www.feracheval-megeve.com – fer-a-cheval@wanadoo.fr
– Fax 04 50 93 07 60 – Open mid-June to mid-September
and mid-December to mid-April BY **a**
42 rm (½ board only) – 14 suites – ½ P € 178/340
Rest – *(closed Monday off season and lunch in winter)*
Menu € 60 – Carte € 70/85
Rest *L'Alpage* – *(Open from mid December to early April)* Carte approx. € 53

◆ The chalet, built in 1938 by the village blacksmith, boasts a superb Alpine-style interior. Cosy lounges and rooms (regional furniture), luxurious bathrooms, spa. Dinner by candlelight near the fireplace in an intimate dining room. Regional cuisine at l'Alpage.

Mont-Blanc VISA

29 r. Ambroise Martin, (pl. de l'Église) – ✆ 04 50 21 20 02
– www.hotelmontblanc.com – contact@hotelmontblanc.com
– Fax 04 50 21 45 28 – Closed 19 April-5 June AY **r**
40 rm – †€ 260/360 ††€ 260/560, ☕ € 25
Rest *Les Enfants Terribles* – *(closed 1 week in September, 2 weeks in November, Wednesday, Thursday and lunch in summer)* Menu (€ 29) – Carte € 68/100

◆ Legendary doyen of Mégève hotels: "21st arrondissement of Paris" according to Cocteau, setting for Les Liaisons Dangereuses in the Vadim version ... Very pretty individual bedrooms. The restaurant/brasserie 'Les Enfants Terribles' opens its doors to you.

Chalet du Mont d'Arbois
rm,
447 chemin de la Rocaille, via Edmond de Rothschild road – ✆ 04 50 21 25 03 – www.chalet-montarbois.com – montarbois@relaischateaux.fr – Fax 04 50 21 24 79 – Open from mid June to mid October and from mid December to mid April BY **p**
23 rm – †€ 317/814 ††€ 339/1024, ☕ € 28 – 1 suite
Rest – *(closed at lunchtime on weekdays and Mon. except school holidays)*
Menu € 60 (dinner) – Carte € 80/130
◆ Remote chalets on the Mont d'Arbois plateau with superb views of the surrounding peaks. Hunting trophies, wood panelling and attractive furniture create a warm and welcoming setting. Minimalist spa. Elegant restaurant, busy summer terrace, carefully-prepared food and superb wine list.

Chalet de Noémie
5 suites – ††€ 1000/4100, ☕ € 28
◆ The five luxury apartments of the Chalet de Noémie make up a lovely, wonderfully-equipped annexe.

Chalet d'Alice
7 rm – †€ 484/1550 ††€ 484/1550, ☕ € 28 – 1 suite
◆ Enchanting rooms, a cosy sitting room and a rare collection of pipes and canes belonging to the Rothschilds await in this lovely old chalet.

Chalet St-Georges
rm, rest,
159 r. Mgr Conseil – ✆ 04 50 93 07 15 – www.hotel-chaletstgeorges.com – chalet-st-georges@wanadoo.fr – Fax 04 50 21 51 18 – Open from end June to mid-September and from mid-December to mid-April AY **n**
21 rm (½ board only) – 3 suites – ½ P € 178/310
Rest *La Table du Pêcheur* – *(open 19 December-31 March) (dinner only)* Carte € 34/60
Rest *La Table du Trappeur* – *✆ 04 50 21 15 73* – Carte € 36/53
◆ A real "doll's house" whose small bedrooms and wood-covered sitting rooms are adorned with trinkets, books, Savoyard furniture and coloured fabrics. Seafood and regional specialities at La Table du Pêcheur. Roast meats and good wine list at La Table du Trappeur.

Le Manège
15 rte Crêt du Midi, (Rochebrune roundabout) – ✆ 04 50 21 41 09 – www.hotel-le-manege.com – reservation@hotel-le-manege.com – Fax 04 50 21 44 76 – Open 20 June-31 August and 15 December-31 March AYZ **b**
15 rm – †€ 230/295 ††€ 320/420, ☕ € 18 – 18 suites – ††€ 410/630
Rest – Menu € 26 – Carte € 35/55
◆ New building a stone's throw from the resort. Cosy interior with wood and mostly red and green colour schemes. Pretty rooms with balconies, including some split-level rooms. Italian and Savoy flavours mingle in the panelled restaurant.

Au Coin du Feu
252 rte Rochebrune – ✆ 04 50 21 04 94 – www.coindufeu.com – contact@coindufeu.com – Fax 04 50 21 20 15 – Open 18 December-31 March AZ **t**
23 rm – †€ 210/265 ††€ 210/370, ☕ € 18 – ½ P € 155/235
Rest *Le Saint Nicolas* – *(dinner only)* Menu € 50
◆ Named after its welcoming fireplace, this hotel provides comfortable, well-decorated guestrooms. Larger rooms with a small lounge area are available. Traditional cuisine and cheese specialities in a setting reminiscent of a mountain inn.

La Grange d'Arly
rm,
10 r. Allobroges – ✆ 04 50 58 77 88 – www.grange-darly.com – contact@grange-darly.com – Fax 04 50 93 07 13 – Open from end June to mid September and from mid December to end March AY **t**
22 rm ☕ – †€ 138/183 ††€ 159/302 – ½ P € 113/184
Rest – *(dinner only)* Menu € 18/33
◆ A chalet surrounded by greenery not far from a river. Charming decor mingling light wood and colourful fabrics. The sloped-ceiling bedrooms are the prettiest. Smart dining room - light panelling and bright southern fabrics – regional fare.

Ferme du Golf without rest
3048 rte Edmond-de-Rothschild – ✆ 04 50 21 14 62 – www.chalet-montarbois.com – ferme.golf@sfhm.fr – Fax 04 50 21 42 82 – Open mid-June to mid-September and mid-December to early April BZ **e**
19 rm – †€ 145/245 ††€ 195/355, ☕ € 15
◆ At the foot of the Mont d'Arbois cable car, this old mountain farmhouse has pretty renovated rooms, quieter on the valley side. Welcoming lounge with fireplace and billiards. Jacuzzi.

La Chaumine without rest
36 chemin des Bouleaux, via chemin du Maz – ✆ 04 50 21 37 05 – www.hotel-lachaumine-megeve.com – lachauminemegeve@orange.fr – Fax 04 50 21 37 21 – Open 27 June-6 September and 19 December-31 March
11 rm – †€ 80/115 ††€ 90/115, ☕ € 10 BZ **v**
◆ 300m from the village and the Chamois cable car, a farm attractively restored in typical Alpine style. Smart guestrooms and evening snack service (local dishes).

Au Coeur de Megève rest, VISA
44 av. Ch. Feige – ✆ 04 50 21 25 30 – www.hotel-megeve.com – info@hotel-megeve.com – Fax 04 50 91 91 27 AY **u**
36 rm – †€ 90/250 ††€ 140/390, ☕ € 12 – 7 suites
Rest – *(closed Wednesday and Thursday off season)* Menu (€ 17), € 22 (lunch), € 33/40 – Carte € 30/47
Rest *St-Jean* – *(Open mid-December to March and Closed Monday dinner outside school holidays) (dinner only)* Carte € 35/55
◆ Elegant renovated rooms in typical Savoyard style, some of which have a view of the peaks, others of the river. In the restaurant: traditional and regional recipes, salon de thé and summer terrace. The Saint Jean offers cheese specialities.

Au Vieux Moulin
188 r. A. Martin – ✆ 04 50 21 22 29 – www.vieuxmoulin.com – hotelvieuxmoulin@orange.fr – Fax 04 50 93 07 91 – Open 15 June-15 September and 15 December-15 April AY **h**
38 rm – †€ 99/199 ††€ 99/390, ☕ € 13
Rest – *(dinner only in winter)* Menu (€ 25), € 32
◆ Two chalets with rooms renovated in a subdued pleasant alpine style. The sauna, swimming pool and beauty centre further enhance the experience. Modern decoration, fireplace and wine bar in the restaurant. Traditional dishes.

La Prairie without rest
407 r. Ch. Feige – ✆ 04 50 21 48 55 – www.hotellaprairie.com – contact@hotellaprairie.com – Fax 04 50 21 42 13 – Open 4 June-22 September and 13 December-26 April BY **d**
39 rm ☕ – †€ 95/240 ††€ 95/240
◆ At the entrance to the resort, functional bedrooms with balconies. Those in the annexe are more modern. Snack menu (regional dishes) available day and night.

Le Gai Soleil
rte Crêt du Midi – ✆ 04 50 21 00 70 – www.le-gai-soleil.fr – info@le-gai-soleil.fr – Fax 04 50 21 57 63 – Open 6 June-26 September and 20 December-11 April
21 rm ☕ – †€ 82/130 ††€ 115/175 – ½ P € 76/112 AZ **f**
Rest – *(dinner only)* Menu € 30/50
◆ This 1920s chalet has a regular clientele due to its stylishness and the beneficial effects of its small fitness centre. Bedrooms quieter at the back. Friendly rustic restaurant with regional dishes and Savoyard menus on Mondays and Thursdays.

Alp'Hôtel rest, VISA
434 rte de Rochebrune – ✆ 04 50 21 07 58 – www.alp-hotel.fr – alp.hotel@wanadoo.fr – Fax 04 50 21 13 82 – Open 1st July-20 September and 20 December-15 April AZ **q**
18 rm – †€ 47/88 ††€ 59/88, ☕ € 8,50 – ½ P € 59/75
Rest – *(closed lunch winter)* Menu € 22
◆ Halfway between the centre of the village and the Rochebrune ring road, this impeccably maintained, traditional chalet offers simple rustic decor and a friendly welcome. Well-prepared family-style cuisine and local specialities.

Le Chalet de l'Ancolie

1295 rte de Sallanches, (in Demi-Quartier), 2,5 km via ① – ✆ 04 50 21 21 37 – www.chalet-ancolie.com – contact@chalet-ancolie.com – Fax 04 50 58 95 06 – Closed 19-30 April and 3 November-4 December
10 rm – †€ 50/105 ††€ 55/120, ☕ € 8 – ½ P € 60/100
Rest – *(dinner only)* Menu € 22, € 30/38
◆ Pleasant little hotel on the road to the resort. The inside has been entirely renovated in alpine style, with minimalist, bright panelled rooms, quieter at the back. In the restaurant, traditional menu with some regional specialities.

Les Oyats without rest

771 chemin de Lady, to the South – ✆ 04 50 21 11 56 – www.lesoyats.fr – lesoyats3@wanadoo.fr – Closed mid April-mid May
3 rm ☕ – †€ 75 ††€ 86
◆ This atypical family farm has everything going for it: wood-inspired decor; home-made, solid furniture; rooms with terraces with views of the hamlet, a kitchen opening onto the stables with donkeys...

Taverne du Mont d'Arbois

2811 rte Edmond de Rothschild – ✆ 04 50 21 03 53 – www.chalet-montarbois.com – taverne-sehtma@sfhm.fr – Fax 04 50 58 93 02 – Closed May, November, Tuesday and Wednesday except school holidays BZ **f**
Rest – *(dinner only)* Menu € 38/58 bi – Carte € 39/85
Rest *L'Atelier* – *(Open 15 December-15 April) (dinner only)* Menu € 40/55
◆ A pleasant Alpine atmosphere in this fashionable chalet: a cosy setting and modern takes on traditional recipes. The dishes are roasted in the fireplace before your very eyes. Trendy setting, rustic and contemporary. Inventive menu presented on the boards.

Flocons Village

75 r. St-François – ✆ 04 50 78 35 01 AY **a**
Rest – Menu (€ 20), € 28
◆ A 19C alpine farm in the heart of the old village with two rustic dining rooms, decorated with care. Traditional 'petits plats' and local dishes.

Le Puck

31 r. Oberstdorf – ✆ 04 50 21 06 61 – Fax 04 50 93 88 53 – Closed dinner from 16 April to 30 June, Monday dinner and Sunday BY **x**
Rest – Menu (€ 25), € 30 – Carte € 31/52
◆ The Puck, set in the main ice rink, is ideal for ice hockey enthusiasts. Modern decoration with shades of grey, well-placed terrace and brasserie cuisine.

Le Vieux Megève

58 pl. de la Résistance – ✆ 04 50 21 16 44 – Fax 04 50 93 06 69 – Open 11 July-31 August and 11 December-30 March BY **n**
Rest – Carte € 30/45
◆ This (1880) chalet is reminiscent of Megève as it used to be: high-quality service, gleaming woodwork, a large fireplace, old-fashioned bed linen and regional specialities.

Le Crystobald

489 rte Nationale, via ① – ✆ 04 50 21 26 82 – lecrystobald@orange.fr – Closed 15 June-3 July, 23 November-17 December, Sunday dinner, Monday and Tuesday in low season
Rest – Menu (€ 16), € 20 (lunch), € 32/45 – Carte € 37/60
◆ This family-run chalet has a pleasant rustic atmosphere. Good contemporary cuisine in a dining room decorated in light wood or on the terrace. Friendly service.

at the top of Mont d'Arbois by cable car from Mont d'Arbois or cable car from La Princesse – ✉ 74170 St-Gervais

L'Igloo

3120 rte des Crêtes – ✆ 04 50 93 05 84 – www.ligloo.com – igloo2@wanadoo.fr – Fax 04 50 21 02 74 – Open 25 June-10 September and 17 December-20 April
12 rm (½ board only) – ½ P € 137/221 **Rest** – Carte € 50/65 lunch only
◆ At the meeting point of three cable-cars, a stunning view over the Mont-Blanc Massif. Well-chosen furniture, Jacuzzi and sauna add to the fittings of this place. The panorama from the restaurant terrace is amazing! Also, self-service for skiers.

L'idéal
– ✆ 04 50 21 31 26 – www.chalet-montarbois.com – _ideal-sehtma@shm.fr
– Fax 04 50 93 02 63 – Open mid December-mid April
Rest – *(lunch only)* Carte € 37/77
◆ Old mountain farm which is now a chic high-altitude restaurant. Impressive landscape; huge terrace and mountain cuisine.

in la Côte 2000 **8 km Southeast by Edmond de Rothschild road** - BZ – ✉ **74120 Megève**

Côte 2000
3461 rte de la Cote 2000 – ✆ 04 50 21 31 84 – c2000-sehtma@sfhm.fr
– Fax 04 50 21 59 25 – Open 2 July-9 September and 16 December-30 April
Rest – Carte € 45/70
◆ This superb Austrian chalet (a Rothschild property) was dismantled and rebuilt here in the 1960s. Large panoramic terrace and regional menu.

in Leutaz **4 km Southwest by Le Bouchet road**AZ – ✉ **74120 Megève**

Flocons de Sel (Emmanuel Renaut) with rm
1775 rte du Leutaz – ✆ 04 50 21 49 99
– www.floconsdesel.com – flocons.de.sels@wanadoo.fr – Fax 04 50 21 68 22
– Closed June, 4 November-10 December, Tuesday lunch and Wednesday lunch
6 rm – †€ 300/600 ††€ 300/600, ☕ € 20
Rest – Menu (€ 35), € 65 (lunch)/120 – Carte € 100/160
Spec. Ecrevisses du lac Léman au jus de maïs et coriandre. Féra du lac Léman, pâte de cresson et quinoa tiède. (mid Jan. to end Oct.). Ballon chocolat-gentiane .
Wines Roussette de Savoie, Mondeuse d'Arbin.
◆ Emmanuel Renaut has relocated to this group of chalets in the middle of the countryside. Delicious creative cuisine in a minimalist mountain setting. Luxurious guestrooms in contempory style (most with fireplace).

La Sauvageonne
– ✆ 04 50 91 90 81 – Fax 04 50 58 75 44 – Open 12 July-14 September and 4 December-16 April
Rest – Menu € 30 (lunch) – Carte € 65/100
◆ 1907 farm whose smart interior is adorned with paintings on sculpted wood representing alpine landscapes. Smoking lounge and selection of cigars. "Showbiz" clientele.

Le Refuge
2615 rte du Leutaz – ✆ 04 50 21 23 04 – www.refuge-megeve.com
– Fax 04 50 91 99 76 – Closed 10 June-10 July, 15 October-15 November, Tuesday in low season, Monday and Wednesday
Rest – Menu (€ 22), € 27 – Carte € 42/53
◆ Charming "refuge" located above the resort. Mountain influences in the decor and on the plate. Simple, tasty cuisine. Large panoramic terrace.

MEILLARD – **03 Allier** – **326** G4 – **pop. 249** – **alt. 340 m** – ✉ **03500** 5 **B1**

Paris 319 – Clermont-Fd 86 – Mâcon 149 – Montluçon 68 – Moulins 27 – Nevers 82

L'Auberge Gourmande
au bourg – ✆ 04 70 42 06 09 – auberge.gourmande@wanadoo.fr
– Closed 5-17 April, 20 December-8 January, Sunday dinner, Monday, Tuesday and Wednesday
Rest – *(pre-book)* Menu € 32/56 – Carte € 50/66
◆ This old regional establishement has a rather ordinary countrified interior. The outside dining area offers a view of the village's unusual church. Small, up-to-date menu. Children's play area.

Red = Pleasant. Look for the red ✗ and 🏠 symbols.

MEILLONNAS – 01 Ain – **328** F3 – **pop. 1 286 – alt. 271 m** – ✉ **01370** 44 **B1**

Paris 432 – Bourg-en-Bresse 12 – Mâcon 47 – Nantua 37 – Oyonnax 46

Auberge Au Vieux Meillonnas VISA AE

Le Mollard – ✆ 04 74 51 34 46 – www.auvieuxmeillonnas.fr – auvieuxmeillonnas@orange.fr – Fax 04 74 51 34 46 – Closed 19 August-2 September, 28 October-4 November, 17-24 February, Tuesday dinner, Sunday dinner and Wednesday

Rest – Menu € 16 (weekdays)/35 – Carte € 24/53

◆ A refreshingly unaffected inn known for its friendly atmosphere. Regional menu served in a rustic dining room, opening onto a shaded terrace and garden.

MEISENTHAL – 57 Moselle – **307** P5 – **pop. 770 – alt. 380 m** – ✉ **57960** 27 **D2**

Paris 440 – Haguenau 47 – Sarreguemines 38 – Saverne 40 – Strasbourg 62

Auberge des Mésanges VISA AE

r. des Vergers – ✆ 03 87 96 92 28 – www.aubergedesmesanges.com – hotel-restaurant.auberge-mesanges@orange.fr – Fax 03 87 96 99 14 – Closed 24 December-2 January, 12 February-1 March

20 rm – € 44/49 € 51/59, € 8,50 – ½ P € 51/60

Rest – *(closed Tuesday lunch, Sunday dinner and Monday)*
Menu € 11 (weekday lunch)/30

◆ An unpretentious family inn located in a century-old house on the edge of a forest in the North Vosges natural park. Small, functional rooms. Traditional cuisine (tarte flambée) served in a large rustic dining room.

MÉJANNES-LÈS-ALÈS – 30 Gard – **339** J4 – see Alès

MÉLISEY – 70 Haute-Saône – **314** H6 – **pop. 1 730 – alt. 330 m** – ✉ 70270 **Burgundy-Jura** 17 **C1**

Paris 397 – Belfort 33 – Besançon 92 – Épinal 63 – Lure 13 – Luxeuil-les-Bains 22

Office de tourisme, place de la Gare ✆ 03 84 63 22 80, Fax 03 84 63 26 94

La Bergeraine AC VISA AE

27 rte des Vosges – ✆ 03 84 20 82 52 – www.labergeraine.fr – labergeraine@wanadoo.fr – Fax 03 84 20 04 47 – Closed Sunday dinner, Tuesday dinner and Wednesday except holidays

Rest – Menu (€ 18), € 25/90 – Carte € 40/74

◆ A small house surrounded by flowers located on the road near a village on the Mille Étangs plateau. Modern meals served in a new decor that mingles wood, water and glass.

MELLE – 79 Deux-Sèvres – **322** F7 – **pop. 3 659 – alt. 138 m** – ✉ **79500** 39 **C2**

Paris 394 – Niort 30 – Poitiers 60 – St-Jean-d'Angély 45

Office de tourisme, 3, rue Émilien Traver ✆ 05 49 29 15 10, Fax 05 49 29 19 83

L'Argentière rm, AC rest, VISA AE

at St-Martin, on Niort road: 2 km – ✆ 05 49 29 13 22 – www.largentiere.com – hotel-retaurant.largentiere@wanadoo.fr – Fax 05 49 29 06 63 – Closed Friday dinner from 15 November to 15 March

25 rm – € 47/51 € 49/55, € 7 – ½ P € 59/63

Rest ***La Table de L'Argentière*** – *✆ 05 49 29 13 74 (Closed Sunday dinner and Monday lunch)* Menu € 16 (weekdays)/47 – Carte € 47/59

◆ The name recalls the former local silver mines. The street level pavilions feature antique-style columns, and have small, colourful rooms (quieter on the internal patio). Fine dining area where traditional cuisine is served.

XX **Les Glycines** with rm

5 pl. R.-Groussard – ✆ 05 49 27 01 11 – www.hotel-lesglycines.com – contact@hotel-lesglycines.com – Fax 05 49 27 93 45 – Closed 11-24 January and Sunday evening except in July-August

7 rm – †€ 42/55 ††€ 49/63, ☕ € 7,50 – ½ P € 53/62

Rest – Menu (€ 18), € 25/43 – Carte € 60/70

◆ Opulent dining room with contemporary decor and attractive veranda. Updated traditional cuisine and a set menu of the day served in the brasserie. Attractive guest-rooms.

MELUN Ⓟ – 77 Seine-et-Marne – **312** E4 – **pop. 38 000** – **Built-up area 107 705** – **alt. 43 m** – ✉ **77000** **Northern France and the Paris Region** 19 **C2**

Paris 47 – Fontainebleau 18 – Orléans 104 – Troyes 128

Office de tourisme, 18, rue Paul Doumer ✆ 01 64 52 64 52, Fax 01 60 56 54 31

U.C.P.A. Bois-le-Roi Bois-le-Roi Base de loisirs, 8 km on the Fontainebleau road, ✆ 01 64 81 33 31

de Greenparc Saint-Pierre-du-Perray Route de Villepècle, 15 km on the Cesson road, ✆ 01 60 75 40 60

Blue Green Golf de Villeray Saint-Pierre-du-Perray21 km on the Corbeil road, ✆ 01 60 75 17 47

Portal★ of St-Aspais church.

Vaux-le-Vicomte: chateau★★ and gardens★★★ 6 km by ②.

Plan on following page

XX **Le Mariette**

31 r. St-Ambroise – ✆ 01 64 37 06 06 – www.lemariette.fr – restaurant@lemariette.fr – Fax 01 64 37 00 47 – Closed August, Monday dinner, Saturday lunch and Sunday AZ **a**

Rest – Menu (€ 28), € 36/60 – Carte € 57/78

◆ Blue is everywhere – façade, walls and lobster aquarium – in the elegant decor of this restaurant with modern cuisine featuring seasonal food and market produce.

XX **La Melunoise**

5 r. Gâtinais – ✆ 01 64 39 68 27 – www.lamelunoise.fr – contact@lamelunoise.fr – Fax 01 64 39 81 81 – Closed August, February school holidays, Sunday dinner, Monday and Tuesday X **b**

Rest – Menu € 28/35 – Carte € 43/50

◆ Discreet house away from the traffic. Two simple, rustic dining areas separated by a small reception featuring stonework. Traditional menu.

in Crisenoy 10 km by ② – **pop. 632** – **alt. 89 m** – ✉ **77390**

XXX **Auberge de Crisenoy**

23 r. Grande – ✆ 01 64 38 83 06 – Fax 01 64 38 89 06 – Closed 20 July-10 August, 22-31 December, Sunday dinner, Wednesday dinner and Monday

Rest – Menu € 24 (weekday lunch), € 32/49 – Carte € 42/53

◆ This inn in the heart of a small village has retained its old-fashioned ambiance: bare stone, beams, a fireplace and rustic furnishings. Pleasant seasonal cooking.

in Vaux-le-Pénil 3 km Southeast – **pop. 11 500** – **alt. 60 m** – ✉ **77000**

XXX **La Table St-Just** (Fabrice Vitu)

✿ *r. de la Libération, (near the château) – ✆ 01 64 52 09 09 – www.restaurant-latablesaintjust.com – latablesaintjust@free.fr – Fax 01 64 52 09 09 – Closed 25 April-3 May, 8-29 August, 24 December-4 January, Sunday, Monday and bank holidays* X **s**

Rest – Menu € 45/95 – Carte € 62/82

Spec. Salade de homard à l'orange. Terrine de cèpes aux gambas (season). Soufflé au Grand-Marnier.

◆ An old farm formerly part of the château of Vaux le Pénil. Today it is a tastefully designed restaurant beneath a high oak framed ceiling. Fine up-to-date cuisine.

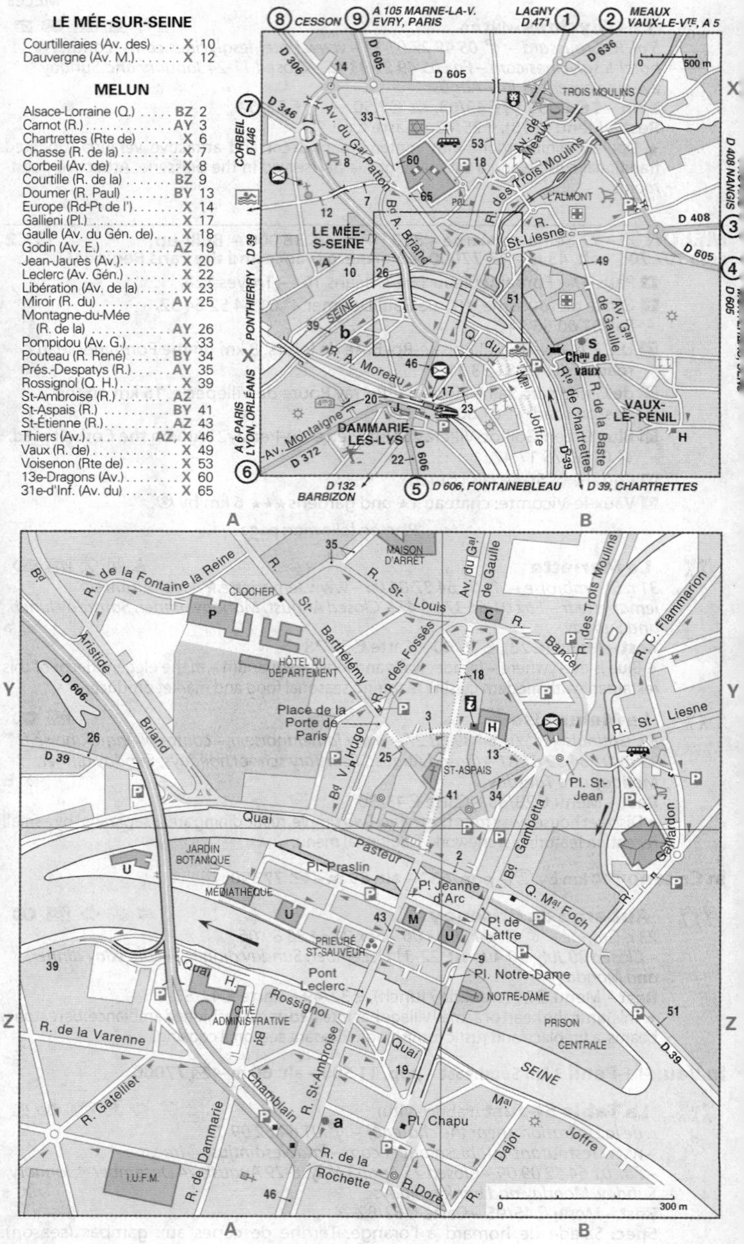
LE MÉE-SUR-SEINE
Courtilleraies (Av. des) . . . . X 10
Dauvergne (Av. M.). . . . . . . X 12
MELUN
Alsace-Lorraine (Q.) . . . . . BZ 2
Carnot (R.) . . . . AY 3
Chartrettes (Rte de) . . . . . . X 6
Chasse (R. de la) . . . . X 7
Corbeil (Av. de) . . . . X 8
Courtille (R. de la) . . . . . . BZ 9
Doumer (R. Paul) . . . . BY 13
Europe (Rd-Pt de l') . . . . . . X 14
Gallieni (Pl.) . . . . X 17
Gaulle (Av. du Gén. de) . . . . X 18
Godin (Av. E.) . . . . AZ 19
Jean-Jaurès (Av.) . . . . X 20
Leclerc (Av. Gén.) . . . . X 22
Libération (Av. de la) . . . . . X 23
Miroir (R. du) . . . . AY 25
Montagne-du-Mée (R. de la) . . . . AY 26
Pompidou (Av. G.) . . . . X 33
Pouteau (R. René) . . . . . . BY 34
Prés.-Despatys (R.) . . . . . . AY 35
Rossignol (Q. H.) . . . . X 39
St-Ambroise (R.) . . . . AZ
St-Aspais (R.) . . . . BY 41
St-Étienne (R.) . . . . AZ 43
Thiers (Av.) . . . . AZ, X 46
Vaux (R. de) . . . . X 49
Voisenon (Rte de) . . . . X 53
13e-Dragons (Av.) . . . . X 60
31e-d'Inf. (Av. du) . . . . X 65
8 CESSON
9 A 105 MARNE-LA-V. EVRY, PARIS
LAGNY D 471 1
2 MEAUX VAUX-LE-VTE, A 5
D 408 NANGIS 3
4 D 605
7 CORBEIL D 446
6 A 6 PARIS LYON, ORLEANS
PONTHIERRY D 39
5 D 606, FONTAINEBLEAU
D 132 BARBIZON
D 39, CHARTRETTES
LE MÉE-S-SEINE
DAMMARIE-LES-LYS
VAUX-LE-PÉNIL
TROIS MOULINS
L'ALMONT
Chau de vaux
SEINE
Av. du Gal Patton
Bd A. Briand
R. des Trois Moulins
Av. de Meaux
R. St-Liesne
Av. Gal de Gaulle
Q. du Mal Joffre
Rte de Chartrettes
R. de la Baste
R. A. Moreau
Av. Montaigne
0 500 m
MAISON D'ARRÊT
CLOCHER
HÔTEL DU DÉPARTEMENT
Place de la Porte de Paris
ST-ASPAIS
Pl. St-Jean
JARDIN BOTANIQUE
MÉDIATHÈQUE
Pl. Praslin
Pl. Jeanne d'Arc
Pl. de Lattre
PRIEURÉ ST-SAUVEUR
Pont Leclerc
Pl. Notre-Dame
NOTRE-DAME
PRISON CENTRALE
CITÉ ADMINISTRATIVE
Pl. Chapu
I.U.F.M.
R. de la Fontaine la Reine
Bd Aristide Briand
R. St-Louis
R. St-Barthélémy
R. des Fossés
Av. du Gal de Gaulle
R. Bancel
R. C. Flammarion
R. Gallardon
Bd Gambetta
Q. Mal Foch
Quai Pasteur
Quai H. Rossignol
Bd Chamblain
R. St-Ambroise
R. de la Varenne
R. Gatelliet
R. de Dammarie
R. de la Rochette
R. Doré
Quai Mal Joffre
R. Dajot
0 300 m

MENDE 🅿 – 48 Lozère – **330** J7 – **pop. 12 600 – alt. 731 m** – ✉ **48000**

▮ **Languedoc-Roussillon-Tarn Gorges**

▶ Paris 584 – Alès 102 – Aurillac 150 – Gap 305 – Issoire 139 – Millau 96

ℹ Office de tourisme, Place du Foirail ✆ 04 66 94 00 23, Fax 04 66 94 21 10

👁 Cathedral★ - Pont N.-Dame★.

MENDE

- Aigues-Passes (R. d') 2
- Ange (R. de l') 3
- Angiran (R. d') 4
- Arjal (R. de l') 5
- Beurre (Pl. au) 6
- Blé (Pl. au) 7
- Britexte (Bd) 8
- Capucins (Bd des) 9
- Carmes (R. des) 10
- Chanteronne (R. de) 12
- Chaptal (R.) 13
- Chastel (R. du) 14
- Collège (R. du) 18
- Droite (R.) 19
- Écoles (R. des) 20
- Épine (R. de l') 21
- Estoup (Pl. René) 22
- Gaulle (Pl. Ch.-de) 23
- Montbel (R. du Fg) 24
- Piencourt (Allée) 25
- Planche (Pont de la) 26
- Pont N.-Dame (R. du) 27
- République (Pl. et R.) 30
- Roussel (Pl. Th.) 32
- Soubeyran (Bd du) 33
- Soubeyran (R.) 34
- Soupirs (Allée des) 36
- Urbain V (Pl.) 37

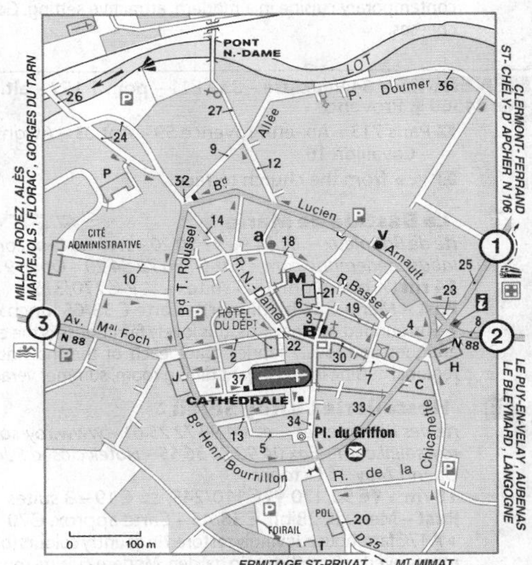

De France

9 bd L. Arnault – ✆ 04 66 65 00 04 – www.hoteldefrance-mende.com – contact@hoteldefrance-mende.com – Fax 04 66 49 30 47 – Closed 27 December-14 January **v**

24 rm – 🛉€ 70/105 🛉🛉€ 70/105, ☕ € 10 – 3 suites – ½ P € 75/88

Rest – *(closed Monday lunch in low season and Saturday lunch)*

Menu (€ 22), € 28/35 – Carte € 32/38

◆ A handsome wrought-iron gateway leads to this attractively renovated old coaching inn, which has welcomed guests since 1856. Modern dining room and charming guestrooms. Traditional cuisine served in an attractive, refurbished dining room or in the courtyard in summer.

Du Pont Roupt

av. 11-Novembre, via ③ – ✆ 04 66 65 01 43 – www.hotel-pont-roupt.com – hotel-pont-roupt@wanadoo.fr – Fax 04 66 65 22 96 – Closed 22-30 December

26 rm – 🛉€ 75/85 🛉🛉€ 75/93, ☕ € 11

Rest – *(closed Sunday except dinner 1st November-1st April and Saturday)*

Menu € 27/56 bi – Carte € 25/65

◆ Family-run hotel on the banks of the Lot. Modern fireplace and stylish armchairs in the sitting room, smart bedrooms, splendid indoor pool and illuminated well. Tasty regional dishes prepared by the same family for four generations.

Le Mazel

25 r. Collège – ✆ 04 66 65 05 33 – Open 11 April-30 September and closed Monday dinner and Tuesday **a**

Rest – Menu € 16/29 – Carte € 23/37

◆ A mural in clay moss by Loul Combes, a well-known artist, adorns one of the walls of this restaurant. Traditional family recipes.

in Chabrits 5 km Northwest by ③ and D 42 – ✉ 48000 Mende

La Safranière
hamlet of Chabrits – ✆ 04 66 49 31 54 – restaurant-la-safraniere@orange.fr – Fax 04 66 49 31 54 – Closed 1st-15 March, 7-13 September, 15-28 February, Wednesday lunch except July-August, Sunday dinner and Monday
Rest – *(pre-book)* Menu € 23 (weekdays)/50
◆ Occupying old stable buildings in the foothills of the Gévaudan, this restaurant serves contemporary cuisine in a modern, attractive setting. Good choice of wine and regional cheeses.

MÉNERBES – **84 Vaucluse** – **332** E11 – **pop. 1 157** – **alt. 224 m** – ✉ **84560** **Provence** 42 **E1**

Paris 713 – Aix-en-Provence 59 – Apt 23 – Avignon 40 – Carpentras 34 – Cavaillon 16

≤★ from the church terrace.

La Bastide de Marie rm, VISA AE
rte de Bonnieux – ✆ 04 90 72 30 20 – www.c-h-m.com – contact@labastidedemarie.com – Fax 04 90 72 54 20 – Open 9 April-3 November
14 rm (½ board only) – 5 suites – ½ P € 270/375
Rest – Menu € 85 bi (dinner) – Carte € 38/65 lunch only
◆ Surrounded by vineyards, this lovely farmhouse is the epitome of Provence. Bare stone, antiques and lovely fabrics grace each of the individually decorated rooms. Sample regional cuisine in an elegant dining room, summer veranda or on the delightful terrace.

Hostellerie Le Roy Soleil VISA AE
rte des Beaumettes – ✆ 04 90 72 25 61 – www.roy-soleil.com – reservation@roy-soleil.com – Fax 04 90 72 36 55 – Hotel: closed 5 January-1 March, Restaurant: Open 1 May-15 October
18 rm – †€ 90/170 ††€ 110/245, ☕ € 19 – 3 suites
Rest – Menu (€ 28 bi), € 38/45 – Carte approx. € 70
◆ A 17C farmhouse, lovingly restored in country colours (blue, white, red-ochre). Provencal rooms overlooking the patio garden. Modern cuisine served under vaulted ceilings in the dining room or on a flower-decked terrace.

La Bastide de Soubeyras
rte des Beaumettes – ✆ 04 90 72 94 14 – www.bastidesoubeyras.com – soubeyras@wanadoo.fr – Fax 04 90 72 94 14 – Closed February
5 rm ☕ – †€ 95/165 ††€ 95/165 **Table d'hôte** – Menu € 35 bi
◆ A charming building of dry stone, set on a hill over the village, this hotel provides Provençal-style rooms, also featuring a garden with swimming pool. One night a week, the lady of the house invites guests to taste the flavours of the Luberon.

MÉNESQUEVILLE – **27 Eure** – **304** I5 – **pop. 404** – **alt. 65 m** – ✉ **27850** **Normandy** 33 **D2**

Paris 100 – Les Andelys 16 – Évreux 53 – Gournay-en-Bray 33 – Lyons-la-Forêt 8 – Rouen 29

Le Relais de la Lieure rm, VISA AE
1 r. Gén. de Gaulle – ✆ 02 32 49 06 21 – www.relaisdelalieure.com – relais.lieure@orange.fr – Fax 02 32 49 53 87
14 rm – †€ 58 ††€ 58/66, ☕ € 8,50 – ½ P € 60
Rest – *(closed 21 December-3 January, Monday lunch, Friday from 15 October to 1 April and Sunday dinner)* Menu € 16 (weekdays)/42 – Carte € 32/53
◆ Family stop in a hamlet located alongside the magnificent forest of Lyons. Large enough bedrooms, furnished simply and well kept. Traditional meals served in a countrified dining area or on the veranda terrace in fine weather.

MENESTEROL – **24 Dordogne** – **329** B5 – **see Montpon-Ménestérol**

MENESTREAU-EN-VILLETTE – **45 Loiret** – **318** J5 – **see La Ferté-St-Aubin**

LE MÉNIL – 88 Vosges – 314 I5 – see le Thillot

LA MÉNITRÉ – 49 Maine-et-Loire – 317 H4 – pop. 1 899 – alt. 21 m – ✉ 49250 35 C2

Paris 301 – Angers 27 – Baugé 23 – Saumur 26

Syndicat d'initiative, place Léon Faye ☎ 02 41 45 67 51

Auberge de l'Abbaye

Le Port St-Maur – ☎ 02 41 45 64 67 – lasjuilliarias.jeanluc@neuf.fr – Fax 02 41 57 69 75 – Closed Sunday dinner, Monday and Tuesday

Rest – Menu (€ 19), € 36/52 – Carte € 45/60

◆ A pleasant, contemporary-style dining room in this house on an embankment overlooking the Loire. Focus on regional produce (fish from the river and fresh vegetables).

LA MÉNOUNIÈRE – 17 Charente-Maritime – 324 B4 – see île d'Oléron

MENTHON-ST-BERNARD – 74 Haute-Savoie – 328 K5 – pop. 1 659 – alt. 482 m – ✉ 74290 French Alps 46 F1

Paris 548 – Albertville 37 – Annecy 10 – Bonneville 50 – Megève 52 – Talloires 4 – Thônes 14

Office de tourisme, Chef-lieu ☎ 04 50 60 14 30, Fax 04 50 60 22 19

Château of Menthon★: ≤★ East: 2 km.

Palace de Menthon

rm, rest, VISA AE

665 rte des Bains – ☎ 04 50 64 83 00 – www.palacedementhon.com – reception@palacedementhon.com – Fax 04 54 64 83 81

63 rm – €85/99 €130/170, € 15 – 2 suites – ½ P € 93/135

Rest – Menu (€ 25 bi), € 35/40

Rest *Palace Beach* – *(Open early May to end September)* Menu (€ 30), € 35

◆ Hotel dating from 1911, recently renovated and boasting a superb view of the lake and château. Large park and comfortable bedrooms with period or Art Deco furniture. Contemporary cuisine in an elegant setting at the restaurant. Moorish decor and terrace overlooking the water at the Palace Beach.

Beau Séjour without rest

161 allée Tennis – ☎ 04 50 60 12 04 – www.hotelbeausejour-menthon.com – h.beau-sejour@laposte.net – Fax 04 50 60 05 56 – Open 15 April-end-September

18 rm – €69 €69/77, € 8

◆ Peaceful villa, surrounded by a flower garden, 100m from the lake and full of retro charm. Countrified rooms, gradually being spruced up, varied furnishings and several balconies.

La Vallombreuse without rest

VISA

534 rte Moulins, 700 m east on Col de Bluffy road – ☎ 04 50 60 16 33 – www.la-vallombreuse.com – contact@la-vallombreuse.com – Fax 04 50 64 88 87

5 rm – €67/122 €75/130

◆ In a quiet garden, this handsome 15C fortified house is home to immense rooms furnished with antique, Savoyard or period pieces. Art exhibitions in the sitting rooms.

MENTON – 06 Alpes-Maritimes – 341 F5 – pop. 27 300 – Casino : du Soleil AZ – ✉ 06500 French Riviera 42 E2

Paris 956 – Cannes 63 – Cuneo 102 – Monaco 11 – Nice 30

Office de tourisme, 8, avenue Boyer ☎ 04 92 41 76 76, Fax 04 92 41 76 78

Site★★ - Old town ★★: Parvis St-Michel★★, Façade★ of the La Conception chapel BY **B** - ≤★ of the English cemetery BX **D** - Promenade du Soleil★★, ≤★ of the Impératrice-Eugénie pier BV - Jardin de Menton★: le Val Rameh★ BV **E** - Salle des mariages (wedding room)★ of the town hall BY **H** - Musée des Beaux-Arts★ (palais Carnolès) AX **M**[1].

Jardin Hanbury★★ Vintimille, West: 2 km.

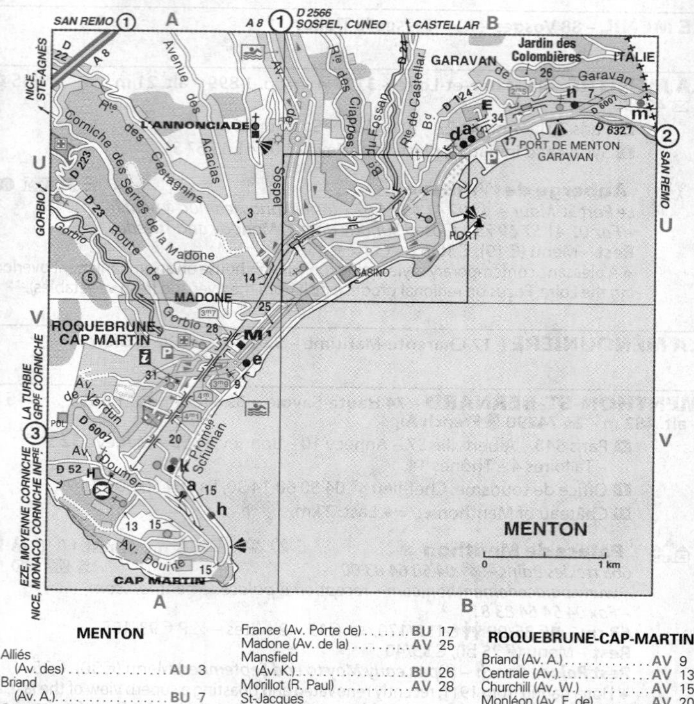

MENTON

- Alliés (Av. des) . . . . . AU 3
- Briand (Av. A.) . . . . . BU 7
- Coty (Cours René) . . . . . AU 14
- France (Av. Porte de) . . . . . BU 17
- Madone (Av. de la) . . . . . AV 25
- Mansfield (Av. K.) . . . . . BU 26
- Morillot (R. Paul) . . . . . AV 28
- St-Jacques (Av.) . . . . . BU 34

ROQUEBRUNE-CAP-MARTIN

- Briand (Av. A.) . . . . . AV 9
- Centrale (Av.) . . . . . AV 13
- Churchill (Av. W.) . . . . . AV 15
- Monléon (Av. F. de) . . . . . AV 20
- Pasteur (Av. L.) . . . . . AV 31

Riva without rest

600 promenade du Soleil – ✆ 04 92 10 92 10 – rivahotel.com – contact@rivahotel.com – Fax 04 93 28 87 87 CZ **n**

40 rm – €88/119 €88/119, €11

◆ On the seafront a new spa hotel with sun deck, Jacuzzi and summer restaurant on the roof. All the rooms have been renovated; some have sea-view balconies.

Napoléon

29 Porte de France – ✆ 04 93 35 89 50 – www.napoleon-menton.com – info@napoleon-menton.com – Fax 04 93 35 49 22 BU **a**

43 rm – €69/149 €94/149, €14 – 1 suite

Rest – *(closed 15 November-15 December, Sunday dinner and Monday off season)* Carte €37/59

◆ Elegant contemporary décor in the rooms named after famous people who have stayed in Menton (Cocteau, Sutherland, etc.). Those with sea views also have lovely teak terraces. This beach restaurant serves grilled and barbecued fish; mouthwatering ice cream menu.

Princess et Richmond

617 promenade du Soleil – ✆ 04 93 35 80 20 – www.princess-richmond.com – princess.hotel@orange.fr – Fax 04 93 57 40 20 – Closed 1 November-12 December CZ **s**

46 rm – €88/135 €88/135, €11

Rest – *(closed Monday lunch, Wednesday lunch and Tuesday)* Menu (€26), €33 – Carte approx. €37

◆ A pebble beach right outside the door, ocean liner-style lounge, and a panoramic rooftop solarium and Jacuzzi are the main attractions of this hotel. Comfortable guestrooms, some with a sea view.

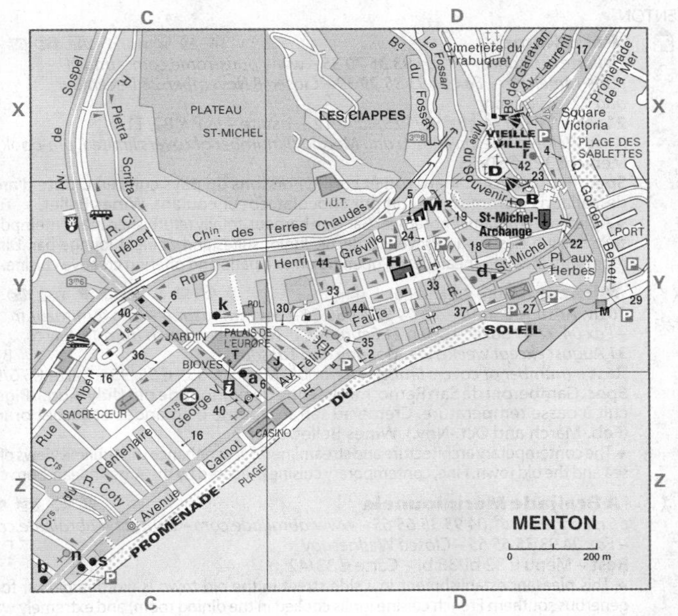

Adémar de Lantagnac (R. d')	DY 2	Guyau (R.)	DY 19	St-Michel (R.)	DY
Bonaparte (Quai)	DX 4	Logettes (R. des)	DY 22	St-Roch (Pl.)	DY 35
Bosano (R. Lt)	DY 5	Longue (R.)	DX 23	Thiers (Av.)	CY 36
Boyer (Av.)	CYZ 6	Lorédan-Larchey (R.)	DY 24	Trenca (R.)	DY 37
Édouard-VII (Av.)	CYZ 16	Monléon (Quai de)	DY 27	Verdun (Av. de)	CYZ 40
Félix-Faure (Av.)	CDY	Napoléon-III (Quai)	DY 29	Vieux-Château (R.)	DX 42
Gallieni (R. Gén.)	DY 18	Partouneaux (R.)	DY 30	Villarey (R.)	DY 44
		République (R. de la)	DY 33		

L'Aiglon rm, VISA

7 av. Madone – ✆ 04 93 57 55 55 – www.hotelaiglon.net – aiglon.hotel@wanadoo.fr – Fax 04 93 35 92 39 – Closed 23 November-20 December CZ **b**

29 rm – †€ 60/116 ††€ 71/193, ☕ € 10

Rest *Riaumont* – Menu (€ 19), € 25/49 – Carte € 29/54

◆ The sitting room of this late 19C villa boasts its original decor of paintings, mosaic and mirrors. All the rooms are different, both in style and size. A few palm trees set the backdrop of this restaurant and its pleasant terrace.

Prince de Galles rm, VISA

4 av. Gén. de Gaulle – ✆ 04 93 28 21 21 – www.princedegalles.com – hotel@princedegalles.com – Fax 04 93 35 92 91 AV **e**

64 rm – †€ 73/132 ††€ 73/132, ☕ € 12

Rest *Petit Prince* – *✆ 04 93 41 66 05 (closed 17 November-12 December)*
Menu (€ 17), € 23/36 – Carte € 30/49

◆ Claude Monet is said to have stayed in this hotel, located in the former barracks of the soldiers of the Princes de Monaco (1860). Practical rooms, choose one overlooking the sea. This restaurant has a summer terrace shaded by two large palm trees.

Chambord without rest VISA

6 av. Boyer – ✆ 04 93 35 94 19 – www.hotel-chambord.com – hotel.chambord@wanadoo.fr – Fax 04 93 41 30 55 CYZ **a**

40 rm – †€ 85/100 ††€ 100/125, ☕ € 10

◆ Practical hotel not far from the palais de l'Europe. Breakfasts are served only in the rooms, all of which are soundproofed and most of which have a balcony.

Paris Rome rm, VISA AE

79 Porte de France – ✆ 04 93 35 70 35 – www.paris-rome.com – info@paris-rome.com – Fax 04 93 35 29 30 – Closed 8 November-28 December and 12-26 January BU **n**

21 rm – †€ 64/74 ††€ 82/125, ☕ € 12 – 1 suite – ½ P € 82/113

Rest – *(closed Tuesday lunch and Monday) (number of covers limited, pre-book)* Menu (€ 32), € 50/95

Spec. Foie gras de canard rôti et confit. Poissons du pays cuits en croûte d'argile de Vallauris (summer). Biscuit pur chocolat, coeur coulant. **Wines** Bellet.

◆ A pleasant little family hotel near Garavan harbour, totally refurbished in a contemporary style, mixing classic and Provencal decor. Junior suites and opulent lounge bar. Dining room with Mediterranean decor, opening on to a patio and offering creative cuisine.

Mirazur (Mauro Colagreco) P VISA AE

30 av. Aristide Briand – ✆ 04 92 41 86 86 – www.mirazur.fr – info@mirazur.fr – Fax 04 92 41 86 87 – Open 21 February-1st November, lunch from 15 July to 31 August except weekends, Monday and Tuesday BU **m**

Rest – *(number of covers limited, pre-book)* Menu (€ 35), € 55/95 – Carte € 76/91

Spec. Gamberoni de San Remo, mousseline de pignons de pin (July-Aug.). Pigeon cuit à basse température. Crème au safran, spume d'amandes et sorbet orange (Feb.-March and Oct.-Nov.). **Wines** Bellet.

◆ The contemporary architecture and streamlined decor enhance the sublime views of the sea and the old town. Fine, contemporary cuisine prepared by the Argentinean-born chef.

A Braijade Méridiounale VISA

66 r. Longue – ✆ 04 93 35 65 65 – www.abraijade.com – contact@abraijade.com – Fax 04 93 35 65 65 – Closed Wednesday DX **r**

Rest – Menu € 32 bi/38 bi – Carte € 33/42

◆ This pleasant establishment in a side street in the old town is worth a detour for its generous southern French cuisine (grills cooked in the dining room) and extremely warm welcome.

La Cantinella VISA

8 r. Trenca – ✆ 04 93 41 34 20 – la.cantinella@free.fr – Closed January, Wednesday lunch and Tuesday except July-August DY **d**

Rest – *(number of covers limited, pre-book)* Menu € 20 (weekdays) – Carte € 25/50

◆ Nothing is too much trouble for the Sicilian-born owner, who rustles up tasty southern-inspired (Nice meets Italy) dishes with fresh market produce. Delightfully friendly.

in Monti **5 km North by Sospel road – ✉ 06500 Menton**

Pierrot-Pierrette with rm rest, P VISA

pl. de l'Église – ✆ 04 93 35 79 76 – www.pierrotpierrette.fr – pierrotpierrette@hotmail.fr – Fax 04 93 35 79 76 – Closed 3 December-12 January and Monday except holidays

6 rm (½ board only) – ½ P € 70/86

Rest – Menu € 28 (weekdays)/40 – Carte € 35/70

◆ A family inn in the hills where the hospitality is as abundant as the local cuisine. Attractive interior, renovated rooms and a loyal band of regulars.

LES MENUIRES – **73 Savoie** – **333** M6 – **alt. 1 400 m** – **Winter sports : 1 400/3 200 m** **8** **36** – ✉ **73440 St Martin de Belleville** ▌**French Alps** 46 **F2**

Paris 632 – Albertville 51 – Chambéry 101 – Moûtiers 27

Office de tourisme, immeuble Belledonne ✆ 04 79 00 73 00, Fax 04 79 00 75 06

Kaya P VISA AE

à Reberty – ✆ 04 79 41 42 00 – www.hotel-kaya.com – info@hotel-kaya.com – Fax 04 79 41 42 01 – Open December-April

24 rm (½ board only) – 22 suites – ½ P € 255/406

Rest ***Le K*** – Menu € 52 (dinner) – Carte € 29/43

◆ From quiet lounges (billiards table, fireplace) to comfortable rooms, all in a refined and contemporary style, prettily enhanced by the warmth of old wood. Sauna and steam bath. Simplified menu at lunchtime. Modern cuisine with a Savoy touch in the evenings.

L'Ours Blanc

at Reberty 2000 – 04 79 00 61 66 – www.hotel-ours-blanc.com – info@hotel-ours-blanc.com – Fax 04 79 00 63 67 – Open 5December-16 April

49 rm (½ board only) – ½ P € 78/105 **Rest** – Menu € 23/85 – Carte € 40/70

◆ This large alpine-style chalet is set on the ski slopes. It provides airy rooms with balconies, some of which are refurbished. There is a cosy sitting room with a fireplace. Fitness facilities. Warm all wood restaurant overlooking the Masse range. Regional recipes.

MERCATEL – 62 Pas-de-Calais – **301** J6 – **see Arras**

MERCUÈS – 46 Lot – **337** E5 – **see Cahors**

MERCUREY – 71 Saône-et-Loire – **320** I8 – pop. 1 310 – alt. 269 m – ✉ 71640 8 **C3**

Paris 344 – Autun 39 – Beaune 26 – Chagny 11 – Chalon-sur-Saône 13 – Mâcon 73

Hôtellerie du Val d'Or

Grande-Rue – 03 85 45 13 70 – www.le-valdor.com – contact@le-valdor.com – Fax 03 85 45 18 45 – Closed 23-28 August, 19 December-16 January, Tuesday lunch and Monday

12 rm – €77/98 €77/98, € 11 – ½ P € 87/128

Rest – Menu (€ 22), € 25 bi (lunch), € 39/76 – Carte € 53/96

◆ Former post house with a dozen rooms in a winegrowers' village on the Chalons Côte. Pleasant garden. Rustic dining room with a fireplace and bare beams.

MÉRIBEL – 73 Savoie – **333** M5 – **Winter sports : 1 450/2 950 m** 16 45 – ✉ 73550 French Alps 46 **F2**

Paris 621 – Albertville 41 – Annecy 85 – Chambéry 90 – Moûtiers 15

Office de tourisme, 04 79 08 60 01, Fax 04 79 00 59 61

Méribel B.P. 54, NE : 4 km, 04 79 00 52 67

★★★ la Saulire, ★★ Mont du Vallon, ★★ Roc des Trois marches, ★★ Tougnète.

Plan on following page

Le Grand Coeur & Spa

– 04 79 08 60 03 – www.legrandcoeur.com – grandcoeur@relaischateaux.com – Fax 04 79 08 58 38 – Open 17 December-13 April **a**

35 rm – €215/430 €205/440, € 25 – 5 suites – ½ P € 180/348

Rest – Menu € 80 (dinner), € 85/95 – Carte € 95/155

◆ An exquisite mixture of romanticism and luxury depict this splendid hotel, one of the oldest in the resort. Pale wood furnishings and pretty fabrics adorn the rooms. Cosy piano bar and spa. Arcades and pale woodwork adorn the warm restaurant, which offers carefully prepared dishes.

Allodis

at Belvédère – 04 79 00 56 00 – www.hotelallodis.com – allodis@wanadoo.fr – Fax 04 79 00 59 28 – Open 5 July-29 August and mid-December to mid-April **d**

44 rm – €300/340 €422/502, € 20 – 6 suites – ½ P € 231/271

Rest – Menu (€ 39), € 49 (dinner), € 58/79 – Carte € 75/95

◆ This chalet overlooking the resort opens onto the ski slopes. Spacious, comfortable rooms with balcony. Pool, sauna and hammam. In the evening, dine on traditional cuisine served in a plush setting. The panoramic terrace facing the valley of Méribel is perfect at lunchtime.

Le Yéti

rd-pt des Pistes – 04 79 00 51 15 – www.hotel-yeti.com – welcome@hotel-yeti.com – Fax 04 79 00 51 73 – Open 5 July-31 August and 13 December-26 April **p**

28 rm – €245 €290, € 18 – ½ P € 199/281 **Rest** – Menu € 31/45

◆ This hotel is homely yet sophisticated. Its rooms have polished woodwork, kilim rugs, and Austrian-style beds. There is also a cosy bar and sitting room, as well as a sauna, hammam and fitness facilities. Well-laid tables in the restaurant (evenings) and a south-facing terrace that is ideal at lunchtime.

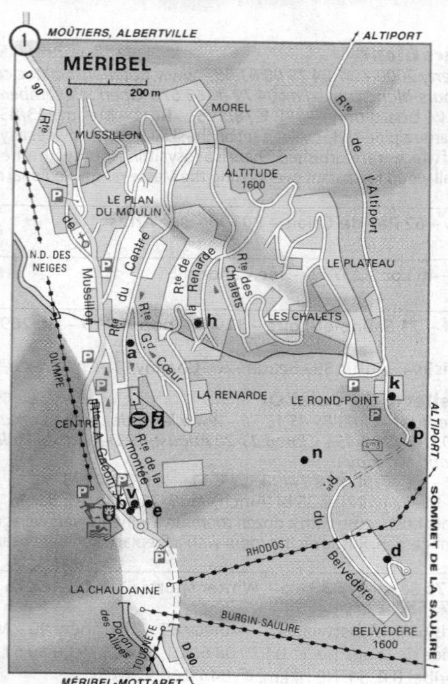

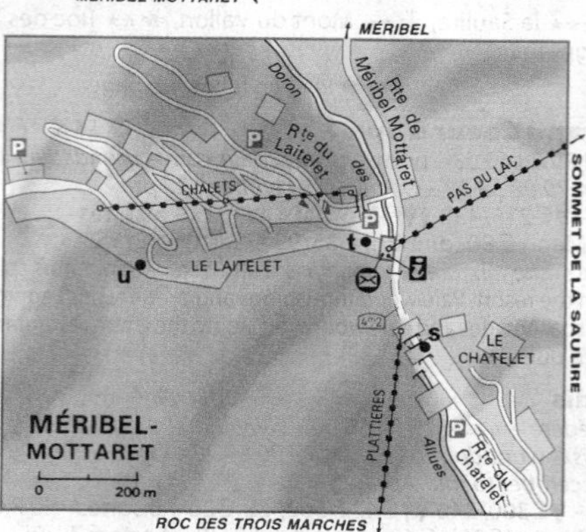

La Chaudanne 

rte de la Montée – *04 79 08 61 76* – *www.chaudanne.com*
– *infos@chaudanne.com* – *Fax 04 79 08 57 75*
– *Open June-September and 1st December-30 April*

73 rm – €259/342 €279/362 – 7 suites – ½ P €187/228

Rest – *(dinner only) (resident only)*

◆ Hotel complex at the foot of the cable car line offering both relaxation and fitness facilities: comfortable rooms, access to health spa, heated outdoor pool.

e

Marie-Blanche – rm, rest,
rte Renarde – 04 79 08 65 55 – http://www.marie-blanche.com – info@marie-blanche.com – Fax 04 79 08 57 07 – Open 7 July-26 August and 13 December-20 April **h**
21 rm – €165/225 €225/315 – ½ P €142/184
Rest – Menu €43 (dinner) – Carte €52/67
◆ This family chalet offers delightful Savoyard inspired rooms with balcony. Welcoming lounge-bar with a central fireplace and view of the mountains. Attractive terrace, airy dining room lit by large bay windows and a regional menu.

L' Éterlou rm,
rte A. Gacon – 04 79 08 89 00 – www.chaudanne.com – infos@chaudanne.com – Fax 04 79 08 57 75 – Open end November-end April and June-September **b**
42 rm – €259/342 €279/362 – 1 suite
Rest *La Grange* – *04 79 08 53 19* – Carte €50/60
Rest *Kouisena* – *04 79 08 89 23 (dinner only)* Carte €45/60
◆ A centrally located hotel with a warm, friendly atmosphere. Fitness facilities, a heated outdoor pool and comfy leather sofas in the lodge bar. Regional cuisine at La Grange. The Kouisena serves Savoyard cuisine in local costume.

L'Orée du Bois
rd-pt des Pistes – 04 79 00 50 30 – www.meribel-oree.com – contact@meribel-oree.com – Fax 04 79 08 57 52 – Open July-August and December to Easter **k**
35 rm (½ board only) – ½ P €151/173 **Rest** – Menu €39/50
◆ This friendly establishment pays tribute to Savoyard traditions. Wood-panelled rooms with balconies, and a log fire burning in the sitting room in winter. Airy dining room, panoramic terrace and traditional and regional specialities.

Le Tremplin without rest
– 04 79 08 61 76 – www.chaudanne.com – infos@chaudanne.com – Fax 04 79 08 57 75 – Open from mid-June to end September and from early December to end April **v**
41 rm – €259/342 €279/362
◆ Hidden behind this wood and stone façade are pleasant, alpine-style bedrooms. An excellent springboard for a successful stay in the Trois Vallées.

Adray Télébar
on the pistes (pedestrian access) – 04 79 08 60 26 – www.telebar-hotel.com – welcome@telebar-hotel.com – Fax 04 79 08 53 85 – Open 15 December-15 April **n**
24 rm (½ board only) – ½ P €135/170 **Rest** – Menu (€35) – Carte €40/65
◆ The friendly welcome (you are greeted by a tracked vehicle) and the very unusual location help you forget the relatively basic interior. Well-maintained rooms. Tasty home cooking and a panoramic terrace with a matchless view of the ski slopes.

Le Blanchot
3.5 km by L'Altiport road – 04 79 00 55 78 – le-blanchot@orange.fr – Fax 04 79 00 53 20 – Open 26 June-9 September, 16 December-19 April and closed Sunday dinner and Monday dinner
Rest – *(closed Sun. evening and Mon. evening)* Menu (€39) – Carte €45/70
◆ This well-situated chalet (golf in summer and Nordic skiing in winter) provides a cosy atmosphere and a terrace facing a pine forest. Contemporary menu and fine wine list.

in l'altiport Northeast: 4,5 km – ✉ **73550 Méribel-les-Allues**

Altiport Hôtel rest,
– 04 79 00 52 32 – www.altiporthotel.com – message@altiporhotel.com – Fax 04 79 08 57 54 – Open mid December-mid April
33 rm (½ board only) – ½ P €185/225 **Rest** – Menu €45 (lunch)
◆ Chalet adjacent to the altiport (flights over Mont Blanc) and golf in the summer. Well-soundproofed inviting rooms and cosy fireside sitting room. Alpine chic dining room, a superlative view of the landscape from the sunny terrace, and well-prepared traditional dishes.

in Méribel-Mottaret 6 km – ✉ 73550 Méribel les Allues

Mont Vallon rest, VISA AE

– ✆ *04 79 00 44 00 – www.hotel-montvallon.com – info@hotel-montvallon.com – Fax 04 79 00 46 93 – Open mid-December to mid-April* s

89 rm (½ board only) – 3 suites – ½ P € 185/515

Rest ***Le Chalet*** – *(dinner only)* Menu € 80

Rest ***Brasserie Le Schuss*** – Menu (€ 40), € 60 (lunch) – Carte € 50/80

◆ Warm wood and duvets create a cosy atmosphere in the rooms of this large hotel at the foot of the ski slopes. Sauna, hammam, Jacuzzi tub and squash courts. A chic welcoming decor at Le Chalet. Fast food in the brasserie at lunch; Savoyard specialities at night.

Alpen Ruitor rest, VISA AE

– ✆ *04 79 00 48 48 – www.alpenruitor.com – info@alpenruitor.com – Fax 04 79 00 48 31 – Open 12 December-17 April* t

44 rm – €230/350 €330/670 – 1 suite – ½ P € 330/670

Rest – Menu € 35 (dinner) – Carte € 25/75

◆ All the rooms boast a balcony with a view of the slopes (south) or the valley (north). Warm Tyrolean colour scheme and ambience. Pleasant fireside lounge-bar and attentive service. Regional specialities served in a dining room adorned with frescoes.

Les Arolles rest, VISA

– ✆ *04 79 00 40 40 – www.arolles.com – info@arolles.com – Fax 04 79 00 45 50 – Open 20 December-23 April* u

56 rm – €135/180 €180/280 – ½ P € 125/195

Rest – Menu (€ 20), € 25/45 – Carte € 25/35

◆ Practically on the ski slopes dotted with pine trees (also called arollas) this large chalet provides partly refurbished rooms with balcony. Recreational and relaxation facilities. Understated restaurant, large terrace and regional food.

in Allues North: 7 km by D 915^A – **pop. 1 893 – alt. 1 125 m** – ✉ **73550**

La Croix Jean-Claude VISA AE

– ✆ *04 79 08 61 05 – www.croixjeanclaude.com – lacroixjeanclaude@wanadoo.fr – Fax 04 79 00 32 72 – Closed 1st May-1st June*

16 rm – €62/124 €62/124, € 9 – ½ P € 66/97

Rest – *(closed Saturday lunch and Sunday lunch in low season)* Carte € 33/70

◆ This establishment dating from the late 1940s is one of the oldest hotels in the Trois Vallées region. Snug alpine-style rooms, inviting sitting room and bar. Restaurant with pleasant Savoyard interior. Locally inspired cooking.

MÉRIGNAC – **33 Gironde** – **335** H5 – **see Bordeaux**

MERKWILLER-PECHELBRONN – **67 Bas-Rhin** – **315** K3 – **pop. 859** – **alt. 160 m** – ✉ **67250** Alsace-Lorraine 1 **B1**

Paris 496 – Haguenau 17 – Strasbourg 51 – Wissembourg 18

Syndicat d'initiative, 1, route de Lobsann ✆ 03 88 80 72 36, Fax 03 88 80 63 33

Auberge Baechel-Brunn with rm VISA

3 rte de Soultz – ✆ 03 88 80 78 61 – www.baechel-brunn.com – baechel-brunn@wanadoo.fr – Fax 03 88 80 75 20 – Closed 11 August-4 September, 19-31 January, Sunday dinner, Monday dinner and Tuesday

5 rm – €40 €50

Rest – Menu (€ 15), € 26 (weekday lunch), € 38/50 – Carte € 40/58

◆ Old barn with a cosy, modern, well-kept interior. Classic and contemporary cuisine, blending the culinary talents of the chef-owner and his son. Charming rooms in an establishment a short walk from the restaurant. Wooded garden.

MERLETTE – **05 Hautes-Alpes** – **334** F4 – **see Orcières**

MERRY-SUR-YONNE – 89 Yonne – 319 E6 – pop. 216 – alt. 150 m – ✉ 89660 7 B2

Paris 203 – Dijon 139 – Auxerre 44 – Avallon 32 – Migennes 56

Le Charme Merry rm, VISA

30 rte de Compostelle – ✆ 03 86 81 08 46 – www.lecharmemerry.com – olivia.peron@wanadoo.fr – Fax 03 86 81 08 46 – Closed 5 January-12 March

4 rm – €120 €120 **Table d'hôte** – Menu €40 bi

◆ This establishment boasts superb contemporary style rooms (photos by the owner, designer bathrooms, quality materials, local stone). Garden, swimming pool. Up-to-date dishes served beneath the dining room's exposed rafters (open-plan kitchen).

MÉRU – 60 Oise – 305 D5 – pop. 12 712 – alt. 110 m – ✉ 60110 36 B3

Northern France and the Paris Region

Paris 60 – Beauvais 27 – Compiègne 74 – Mantes-la-Jolie 62 – Pontoise 22

18 des Templiers Ivry-le-TempleW : 9 km on D 121 and D 105, ✆ 03 44 08 73 72

Les Trois Toques VISA

21 r. P. Curie – ✆ 03 44 52 01 15 – www.lestroistoques.fr – les3toques@orange.fr – Fax 03 44 52 01 15 – Closed 1-7 August, Sunday dinner and Wednesday

Rest – Menu €18 (weekdays)/48 – Carte €39/51

◆ Updated menu prepared by the chef-patron and served in a spruced-up dining room enhanced with rustic touches.

MERVILLE FRANCEVILLE-PLAGE – 14 Calvados – 303 K4 – pop. 1 748 – alt. 2 m – ✉ 14810 32 B2

Paris 225 – Caen 20 – Beuvron-en-Auge 20 – Cabourg 7 – Lisieux 41

Office de tourisme, place de la Plage ✆ 02 31 24 23 57, Fax 02 31 24 17 49

Le Vauban without rest VISA AE

8 rte de Cabourg – ✆ 02 31 24 23 37 – www.hotel-vauban-franceville.com – hotel-levauban14@wanadoo.fr – Fax 02 31 24 54 40 – Closed 28 September-8 October, 1st-17 December, Wednesday except July-August

15 rm – €60 €, €9

◆ A family establishment near the road and not far from the beach. Simple, well-kept rooms; those in the annexe are quieter. Buffet breakfast. Pleasant reception.

MÉRY-SUR-OISE – 95 Val-d'Oise – 305 E6 – 101 4 – see Paris, Area (Cergy-Pontoise)

MESCHERS-SUR-GIRONDE – 17 Charente-Maritime – 324 E6 – pop. 2 234 – alt. 5 m – ✉ 17132 Atlantic Coast 38 B3

Paris 511 – Blaye 78 – La Rochelle 87 – Royan 12 – Saintes 45

Office de tourisme, 31, rue Paul Messy ✆ 05 46 02 70 39, Fax 05 46 02 51 65

La Forêt VISA AE

1 bd Marais – ✆ 05 46 02 79 87 – laforet-resto@wanadoo.fr – Fax 05 46 02 61 45 – Closed 21 September-2 October, 21 December-8 January, 8 February-19 March, Tuesday except dinner in July-August and Monday

Rest – Menu €26/38 – Carte €22/50

◆ On the edge of the woods, not far from the Gironde beaches; vast dining room serving fresh seafood, notably the house speciality, mouclade (mussels). Countrified decor.

MESNIÈRES-EN-BRAY – 76 Seine-Maritime – 304 I3 – see Neufchâtel-en-Bray

LE MESNIL-AMELOT – 77 Seine-et-Marne – 312 E1 – see Paris, Area

MESNIL-ST-PÈRE – 10 Aube – 313 G4 – pop. 384 – alt. 131 m 13 B3
– ✉ 10140 Northern France and the Paris Region

Paris 200 – Bar-sur-Aube 32 – Châtillon-sur-Seine 55 – St-Dizier 74 – Troyes 22

Regional Natural Park of the Forêt d'Orient★★.

XXX **Auberge du Lac - Au Vieux Pressoir** with rm — rm, rest,
5 r. du 28 août – ✆ 03 25 41 27 16 – www.au-vieux-pressoir.com – auberge.lac.p.gublin@wanadoo.fr – Fax 03 25 41 57 59 – Closed 7 December-11 January, Sunday dinner from 15 October to 15 March, Monday lunch and Tuesday lunch
21 rm – €69/73 €73/76, €13
Rest – Menu €29 (weekday lunch), €38/75 – Carte €72/98
◆ A half-timbered house typical of the Champagne region. Bright neo-rustic interior and summer terrace. Contemporary cuisine.

MESNIL-VAL – 76 Seine-Maritime – 304 H1 – ✉ 76910 33 D1

Paris 184 – Amiens 96 – Dieppe 28 – Le Tréport 6

Royal Albion without rest
1 r. de la Mer – ✆ 02 35 86 21 42 – www.treport-hotels.com et www.hotels-treport.com – evergreen2@wanadoo.fr – Fax 02 35 86 78 51 – Closed 21-27 December
20 rm – €65/74 €69/136, €9,50
◆ This cliffside abode, a former 19C barracks, sports a colonial allure and elegant interior decoration. Louis XVI, Victorian and Art Nouveau styles depict the rooms' decoration.

MESQUER – 44 Loire-Atlantique – 316 B3 – pop. 1 631 – alt. 6 m 34 A2
– ✉ 44420

Paris 460 – La Baule 16 – Nantes 86 – St-Nazaire 29 – Vannes 58

Office de tourisme, place du Marché - Quimiac ✆ 02 40 42 64 37, Fax 02 40 42 50 89

XX **La Vieille Forge**
32 r. d'Aha – ✆ 02 40 42 62 68 – www.vieilleforge.fr – keumsun@orange.fr – Closed 16-25 June, 21 September-3 October, February, Monday, Tuesday and Wednesday off season
Rest – *(dinner only in July-August except Saturday-Sunday)* Menu (€13 bi), €25/50 – Carte €30/50
◆ This former forge, from 1711, houses two dining rooms: one has a furnace and bellows while the other is modern and opens onto the garden terrace. Updated cuisine with Asian touches.

in St-Molf 3.5 km southeast by D 33, D 52 and D 252 – pop. 1 501 – alt. 10 m – ✉ 44350

Office de tourisme, 10, rue Duchesse Anne ✆ 02 40 62 58 99, Fax 02 40 62 58 74

Kervenel without rest
– ✆ 02 40 42 50 38 – ybrasselet@aol.com – Fax 02 40 42 50 38 – Open 1 April-1 October
3 rm – €50 €70
◆ Distinctive restored Breton cottage in a quiet setting. The old wheat barn houses three rooms opening onto the garden in varying styles: Louis Philippe, Louis XV and Contemporary.

MESSANGES – 40 Landes – 335 C12 – pop. 647 – alt. 8 m – ✉ 40660 3 A2

Paris 717 – Bordeaux 157 – Mont-de-Marsan 92 – Bayonne 46 – Anglet 49

Office de tourisme, route des Lacs ✆ 05 58 48 93 10, Fax 05.58.48.93.75

La Maison de la Prade without rest
av. de la Plage – ✆ 05 58 48 38 96 – www.lamaisondelaprade.com – lamaisondelaprade@orange.fr – Fax 05 58 49 26 75 – Open from March to November
16 rm – €87/115 €107/138, €12 – 2 suites
◆ Near an untamed beach, surrounded by a fine forest, this Art Deco building has been converted into a contemporary hotel. Spacious and bright rooms. Terrace beside the swimming pool.

MESSERY – 74 Haute-Savoie – 328 K2 – pop. 2 025 – alt. 428 m – ✉ 74140 46 F1

Paris 560 – Annecy 68 – Thonon-les-Bains 17 – Annemasse 23 – Cluses 52

Office de tourisme, 5, rue des Écoles ☎ 04 50 94 75 55, Fax 04 50 94 75 55

Atelier des Saveurs

7 chemin sous les Près – ☎ 04 50 94 73 40 – Closed 24 October-16 November, Sunday and Monday

Rest – Menu € 24/60 – Carte € 55/65

◆ A pleasant establishment combining a restaurant (modern decoration and small terrace) with a wine bar. Tasty traditional cuisine accompanied by fine wine.

MÉTABIEF – 25 Doubs – 321 I6 – pop. 907 – alt. 960 m – Winter sports : 1000/1423 m 20 – ✉ 25370 Burgundy-Jura 17 C3

Paris 466 – Besançon 78 – Champagnole 45 – Morez 49 – Pontarlier 18

Étoile des Neiges

rm,

4 r. Village – ☎ 03 81 49 11 21 – www.hoteletoiledesneiges.fr – contact@hoteletoiledesneiges.fr – Fax 03 81 49 26 91

23 rm – €54 €54, €6

Rest – *(closed Thursday dinner and Sunday dinner off season)*
Menu € 17/26 – Carte € 18/38

◆ A totally-renovated family hotel in a busy resort, popular both in summer and winter with mountain bikers, walkers and skiers. Pretty, wood-panelled rooms with flowered balconies. Regional food served in a welcoming dining room decorated with wood.

METZ – 57 Moselle – 307 I4 – pop. 124 200 – Built-up area 322 526 – alt. 173 m – ✉ 57000 Alsace-Lorraine 26 B1

Paris 330 – Luxembourg 62 – Nancy 57 – Saarbrücken 69 – Strasbourg 163

Metz-Nancy-Lorraine: ☎ 03 87 56 70 00, 35 km on the ③

☎ 3635 et tapez 42 (0,34 €/mn)

Office de tourisme, place d'Armes ☎ 03 87 55 53 76, Fax 03 87 36 59 43

de la Grange-aux-Ormes Marly Rue de la Grange aux Ormes, S : 3 km on D 5, ☎ 03 87 63 10 62

du Technopôle Metz 1 rue Félix Savart, 5 km on D 955, ☎ 03 87 39 95 95

de Metz Chérisey Verny Château de Cherisey, 14 km on D 913 and D 67, ☎ 03 87 52 70 18

St-Etienne cathedral ★★★ CDV - Porte des Allemands★ DV - Esplanade★ CV: St-Pierre-aux-Nonnains church ★ CX **V** - Place St-Louis★ DVX - St-Maximin church ★ DVX - Narthex★ of St-Martin church DX - ≤★ du Moyen Pont CV - Musée de la Cour d'Or★★ (archeological section ★★★) **M**[1] - Place du Général de Gaulle★.

Plans on following pages

La Citadelle (Christophe Dufossé)

rm,

5 av. Ney – ☎ 03 87 17 17 17 – www.citadelle-metz.com – contact@citadelle-metz.com – Fax 03 87 17 17 18 CX **y**

79 rm – € 185/355 € 205/375, € 21

Rest *Le Magasin aux Vivres* – *(closed 1st-18 August, 9-22 February, Sunday dinner and Monday)* Menu € 43 (weekday lunch), € 63/105 – Carte € 91/105

Spec. Cassolettes gourmandes. Bar en croûte de sel, algues iodées. Assiette dégustation "tout chocolat grand cru". **Wines** Vins de Moselle.

◆ This luxurious hotel is in the town centre. It has successfully managed to create spacious modern rooms in a military edifice built under Vauban in the 16C. The restaurant serves inventive cuisine in a minimalist decor enlivened with colourful touches.

Novotel Centre

rm,

pl. Paraiges – ☎ 03 87 37 38 39 – www.accorhotels.com/novotel_metz_centre.htm – h0589@accor.com – Fax 03 87 36 10 00 DV **t**

120 rm – € 69/149 € 69/149, € 15 **Rest** – Carte € 23/48

◆ This Novotel between the cathedral and shopping centre has been refurbished. Vast, comfortable rooms and well-equipped gym. Enjoy a pleasant break at the Novotel Café with its poolside terrace.

Cheapest 1st May

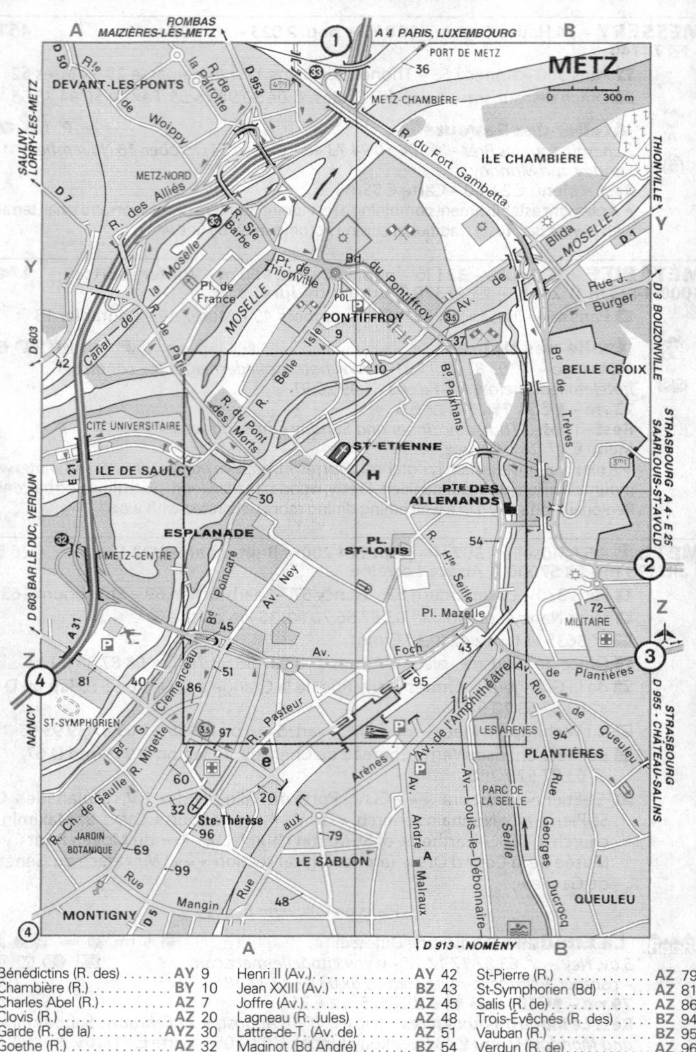

Bénédictins (R. des) .... **AY** 9	Henri II (Av.) .... **AY** 42	St-Pierre (R.) .... **AZ** 79
Chambière (R.) .... **BY** 10	Jean XXIII (Av.) .... **BZ** 43	St-Symphorien (Bd) .... **AZ** 81
Charles Abel (R.) .... **AZ** 7	Joffre (Av.) .... **AZ** 45	Salis (R. de) .... **AZ** 86
Clovis (R.) .... **AZ** 20	Lagneau (R. Jules) .... **AZ** 48	Trois-Évêchés (R. des) ..... **BZ** 94
Garde (R. de la) .... **AYZ** 30	Lattre-de-T. (Av. de) ...... **AZ** 51	Vauban (R.) .... **BZ** 95
Goethe (R.) .... **AZ** 32	Maginot (Bd André) .... **BZ** 54	Verdun (R. de) .... **AZ** 96
Grange-aux-Dames (R.) ..... **BY** 36	Nancy (Av. de) .... **AZ** 60	Verlaine (R.) .... **AZ** 97
Grilles (Pont des) .... **BY** 37	Pont-à-Mousson (R. de) ..... **AZ** 69	20e-Corps-Américain (R. du) ... **AZ** 99
Hegly (Allée V.) .... **AZ** 40	Pont-Rouge (R. du) .... **BZ** 72	

Mercure Centre

29 pl. St-Thiébault – ✆ 03 87 38 50 50 – www.mercure.com – h1233@accor.com – Fax 03 87 75 48 18 DX **d**

112 rm – €140 €150, €16

Rest – *(Closed Saturday lunch, Sunday and bank holidays)*
Menu €25 – Carte €28/43

◆ A major renovation programme is underway in this hotel built in the 1970s. The rooms are gradually being refurbished in a modern and tasteful spirit. Wine bar and restaurant decorated in a bright modern style.

METZ

Street	Grid	No.
Allemands (R. des)	DV	2
Ambroise-Thomas (R.)	CV	3
Armes (Pl. d')	DV	5
Augustins (R. des)	DX	6
Chambière (R.)	DV	10
Chambre (Pl. de)	CV	12
Champé (R. du)	DV	13
Chanoine-Collin (R. du)	DV	15
Charlemagne (R.)	CX	17
Chèvre (R. de la)	DX	19
Clercs (R. des)	CV	
Coëtlosquet (R. du)	CX	22
Coislin (R.)	DX	23
Enfer (R. d')	DV	25
En Fournirue	DV	
Fabert (R.)	CV	26
Faisan (R. du)	CV	27
La-Fayette (R.)	CX	47
Fontaine (R. de la)	DX	29
Gaulle (Pl. du Gén.-de)	DX	31
Grande-Armée (R. de la)	DV	34
Hache (R. de la)	DV	39
Jardins (R. des)	DV	
Juge-Pierre-Michel (R. du)	CV	46
Lasalle (R.)	DX	49
Lattre-de-T. (Av. de)	CX	51
Leclerc-de-H. (Av.)	CX	52
Mondon (Pl. R.)	CX	57
Paix (R. de la)	CV	61
Palais (R. du)	CV	62
Paraiges (Pl. des)	DV	63
Parmentiers (R. des)	DX	64
Petit-Paris (R. du)	CV	65
Pierre-Hardie (R. de la)	CV	66
Pont-Moreau (R. du)	CDV	70
Prés.-Kennedy (Av. J.-F.)	CX	73
République (Pl. de la)	CX	75
Ste-Croix (Pl.)	DV	83
Ste-Marie (R.)	CV	84
St-Eucaire (R.)	DV	76
St-Gengoulf (R.)	CX	77
St-Georges (R.)	CV	78
St-Louis (Pl.)	DVX	
St-Simplice (Pl.)	DV	80
St-Thiébault (Pl.)	DX	82
Salis (R. de)	CX	86
Schuman (Av. R.)	CX	
Sérot (Bd Robert)	CV	87
Serpenoise (R.)	CV	
Taison (R.)	DV	88
Tanneurs (R. des)	DV	90
Tête d'Or (R. de la)	DV	
Trinitaires (R. des)	DV	93
Verlaine (R.)	CX	97

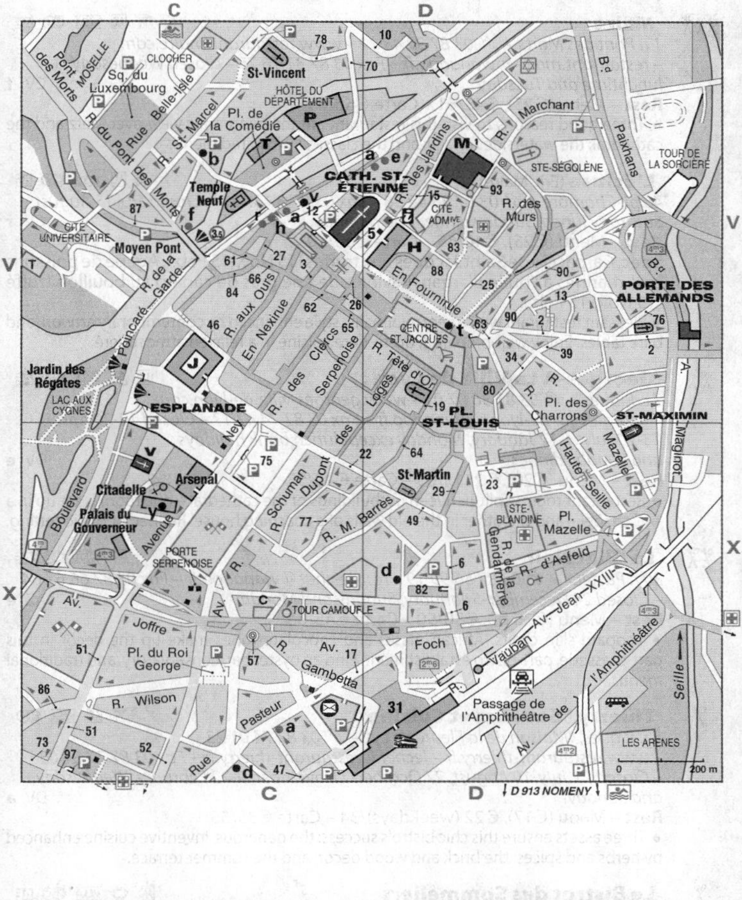

Du Théatre without rest

3 r. du Pont St-Marcel – ✆ 03 87 31 10 10 – www.hoteldutheatre-metz.com – reception@hoteldutheatre-metz.com – Fax 03 87 30 04 66 CV **b**

65 rm – †€ 89/108 ††€ 95/135, ☕ € 13 – 1 suite

◆ Recently built hotel in a choice location in the old town. Practical rooms; those overlooking the river are quieter. Fine Lorraine furniture in the hall.

De la Cathédrale without rest
25 pl. Chambre – ✆ 03 87 75 00 02 – www.hotelcathedrale-metz.fr – hotelcathedrale-metz@wanadoo.fr – Fax 03 87 75 40 75 CV **v**
30 rm – †€ 70/110 ††€ 70/110, ☕ € 11
◆ This 17C hotel once provided accommodation for Mme de Staël and Châteaubriand. The rooms are all elegant, and those in the recent extension are even more luxurious.

Escurial without rest
18 r. Pasteur – ✆ 03 87 66 40 96 – www.escurial-hotel.com – hotelescurial.metz@wanadoo.fr – Fax 03 87 63 43 61 – Closed 29 December-1st January CX **d**
36 rm – †€ 58/76 ††€ 72/84, ☕ € 9
◆ This non-smoking hotel facing the station has had a facelift. It now has a warm, brightly coloured interior and well-kept rooms (those in the rotunda are larger).

Maire
1 r. Pont des Morts – ✆ 03 87 32 43 12 – www.restaurant-maire.com – restaurant.maire@wanadoo.fr – Fax 03 87 31 16 75 – Closed Wednesday lunchtime and Tuesday CV **f**
Rest – Menu (€ 25), € 42/61 – Carte € 50/65
◆ Three good reasons to visit this restaurant are the panoramic view over Metz and the cathedral; the waterside terrace; and the classically inspired menu.

L'Écluse (Eric Maire)
45 pl. Chambre – ✆ 03 87 75 42 38 – Fax 03 87 37 30 11 – Closed 1st - 15 August, Saturday lunch, Sunday dinner and Monday CV **r**
Rest – Menu (€ 25), € 40/65 – Carte € 60/80
Spec. Carpaccio de Saint Jacques aux truffes (15 Nov.-15 Feb.). Agape de poissons crus marinés à l'huile d'argan. Ravioles de foie gras de canard au bouillon truffé (15 Nov.-15 Feb.).
◆ Pleasant restaurant with a very minimalist style enhanced by contemporary artwork and bare tables. Enjoy well-prepared, up-to-date cuisine in a relaxed atmosphere.

Georges-A La Ville de Lyon
7 r. Piques – ✆ 03 87 36 07 01 – www.georges-ville-de-lyon.com – george-ville-de-lyon@wanadoo.fr – Fax 03 87 74 47 17 – Closed 13-20 April, 13-20 July, 4-12 January, Monday except lunch bank holidays and Sunday dinner DV **e**
Rest – Menu (€ 20), € 25 bi/65 – Carte € 40/55
◆ Restaurant rooms split between outbuildings of the cathedral – one room is set up in a 14C chapel – and the other in the old walls of a coaching house. Refined or rustic setting.

Le Chat Noir
30 r. Pasteur – ✆ 03 87 56 99 19 – rest-le-chat@wanadoo.fr – Fax 03 87 66 67 64 – Closed 24 December-5 January, Sunday and Monday AZ **e**
Rest – Menu (€ 25 bi), € 30/50 – Carte € 45/60
◆ Leopard skin chairs, African masks and chocolate tones make up the decor in this part-brasserie, part-bistro establishment. Find an oyster bar, conservatory, and traditional menu.

Thierry "Saveurs et Cuisine"
5 r. Piques, "Maison de la Fleure de Ly" – ✆ 03 87 74 01 23 – www.restaurant-thierry.fr – lechef@restaurant-thierry.fr – Fax 03 87 77 81 03 – Closed 21 July-10 August, 27 October-2 November, 9-22 February, Wednesday and Sunday DV **a**
Rest – Menu (€ 17), € 22 (weekdays)/34 – Carte € 35/55
◆ Three assets ensure this chic bistro's success: the generous, inventive cuisine enhanced by herbs and spices; the brick and wood decor; and the summer terrace.

Le Bistrot des Sommeliers
10 r. Pasteur – ✆ 03 87 63 40 20 – lebistrotdessommeliers@wanadoo.fr – Fax 03 87 63 54 46 – Closed 23 December-4 January, Saturday lunch, Sunday and holidays CX **a**
Rest – Menu (€ 16) – Carte € 29/40
◆ A wine themed façade at this bistro near the station. A good choice of wines by the glass and blackboard specials based on market produce.

À côté

43 pl. de Chambre – 03 87 66 38 84 – ericmaire.acote@orange.fr – Fax 03 87 66 39 53 – Closed 1-15 August, Sunday and Monday CV **d**

Rest – Menu € 30 – Carte € 25/45

◆ The fashionable wing of 'L'Ecluse' serves modern tapas-style dishes in a laid back, trendy atmosphere. View of the kitchen and bar service.

via ① and A 31 Maizières-lès-Metz exit: 10 km – ✉ 57280 Maizières-lès-Metz

Novotel-Hauconcourt

– 03 87 80 18 18 – www.novotel.com – h0446@accor.com – Fax 03 87 80 36 00

132 rm – € 77/150 € 77/150, € 15 **Rest** – Carte € 23/32

◆ This hotel built in 1970 is enjoying a new lease of life. It now sports the chain's 'Novation' interior decor: spacious and cosy rooms, a soothing colour scheme and handsome bathrooms. Restaurant with terrace by the swimming pool.

Saarlouis road 13 km by ②, N 233 and D 954 - ✉ 57640 Ste-Barbe

Mazagran

1 rte de Boulay – 03 87 76 62 47 – www.restaurant-mazagran.com – mele-cass@orange.fr – Fax 03 87 76 79 50 – Closed 17 August-3 September, 4-13 January, Sunday dinner, Monday and Tuesday except bank holidays

Rest – Menu (€ 22), € 28/53 – Carte € 59/84

◆ This farmhouse was built for one of the soldiers who defended the Mazagran fort in Algeria in 1840. Rich, elegant dining room with a contemporary menu. Garden terrace.

in Borny by ③ and Strasbourg road: 3 km – ✉ 57070 Metz

Le Jardin de Bellevue

58 r. Claude Bernard, (near Metz 2000 Technology park) – 03 87 37 10 27 – www.jardindebellevue.com – lejardindebellevue@wanadoo.fr – Fax 03 87 37 15 45 – Closed 15-31 July, 15-25 February, Saturday lunch, Sunday dinner, Tuesday dinner and Monday

Rest – Menu € 22 (weekday lunch), € 38/62 – Carte € 56/64

◆ Chic façade for this century-old house in a residential area. Attractively set tables in a pleasant dining room and shaded terrace in high season. Modern cuisine.

in Plappeville via Avenue Henri II - AY : 7 km – pop. 2 295 – alt. 280 m – ✉ 57050

La Vigne d' Adam

50 r. Gén. de Gaulle – 03 87 30 36 68 – www.lavignedadam.com – contact@lavignedadam.com – Fax 03 87 30 79 01 – Closed 15-31 August, Christmas holiday, Tuesday dinner, Sunday and Monday

Rest – Carte € 30/67

◆ In the heart of the village, this old winegrower's house is now a trendy, modern wine bar/restaurant. Modern cuisine and a fine selection of wines.

METZERAL – 68 Haut-Rhin – 315 G8 – pop. 1 065 – alt. 480 m – ✉ 68380 1 A2

Paris 464 – Colmar 25 – Gérardmer 39 – Guebwiller 41 – Thann 43

Aux Deux Clefs

rest,

12 r. Altenhof – 03 89 77 61 48 – www.aux-deux-clefs.com – auxdeuxclefs@free.fr – Fax 03 89 77 63 88 – Closed 1st-15 March and 1st-7 November

14 rm – € 40/50 € 55/75, € 10 – ½ P € 55/65

Rest – *(closed Wednesday)* Menu € 13 (weekday lunch), € 16/65 – Carte € 30/75

◆ In the upper reaches of the village, this guesthouse-style hotel is pleasantly peaceful. The rooms have an alpine décor. Elegant dining room (classic cuisine).

MEUCON – 56 Morbihan – 308 O8 – pop. 1 268 – alt. 80 m – ✉ 56890 9 A3

Paris 464 – Vannes 8 – Lorient 62 – Ploërmel 49 – Pontivy 45

Le Tournesol

20 rte de Vannes – 02 97 44 50 50 – http://pagesperso-orange.fr/le-tournesol/ – le.tournesol@wanadoo.fr – Fax 02 97 44 65 42 – Closed 6-15 July, 14-28 September, 4-11 January, Sunday dinner, Wednesday dinner and Monday

Rest – Menu (€ 17), € 21 (weekdays)/52 – Carte € 35/56

◆ The two dining rooms in this building have been treated to a makeover with a fashionable colour scheme and wicker furniture. Appetising, up-to-the-minute menu.

MEUDON – 92 Hauts-de-Seine – 311 J3 – 101 24 – see Paris, Area

MEURSAULT – 21 Côte-d'Or – 320 I8 – see Beaune

LE MEUX – 60 Oise – 305 H4 – see Compiègne

MEXIMIEUX – 01 Ain – 328 E5 – pop. 7 217 – alt. 245 m – ✉ 01800 44 B1

Paris 458 – Bourg-en-Bresse 37 – Chambéry 120 – Genève 118 – Grenoble 125 – Lyon 38

Office de tourisme, 1, rue de Genève ✆ 04 74 61 11 11, Fax 04 74 61 00 50

La Cour des Lys

17 r. de Lyon, (rooms available) – ✆ 04 74 61 06 78 – www.la-cour-des-lys.fr – la.cour.des.lys@orange.fr – Fax 04 74 34 75 23 – Closed 23-31 March, 3-18 August, 25 October-3 November, 2-13 January, Wednesday lunch and Monday

Rest – Menu (€ 20), € 26/58 – Carte € 45/72

◆ A new chef has taken over at this local institution. Enticing menu based on Dombes culinary traditions, with a touch of modern flair. Decor typical of the region.

at Pont de Chazey-Villieu 3 km east by D 1084 – ✉ 01800 Villieu-Loyes-Mollon

La Mère Jacquet with rm

Pont de Chazey – ✆ 04 74 61 94 80 – contact@lamerejacquet.com – Fax 04 74 61 92 07 – Closed 13-19 April, 3-16 August, 21 December-3 January

19 rm – †€ 55 ††€ 75, ☕ € 8 – ½ P € 75

Rest – *(Closed Saturday lunch, Sunday dinner and Friday)*
Menu € 23 (weekdays)/45 – Carte € 51/67

◆ Inviting dining room and veranda overlooking a pretty garden. Classic cuisine with a regional focus: Mother Jacquet's traditions live on in this establishment.

MÉXY – 54 Meurthe-et-Moselle – 307 F2 – see Longwy

MEYLAN – 38 Isère – 333 H6 – see Grenoble

MEYMAC – 19 Corrèze – 329 N2 – pop. 2 627 – alt. 702 m – ✉ 19250 25 C2

Dordogne-Berry-Limousin

Paris 443 – Aubusson 57 – Limoges 96 – Neuvic 30 – Tulle 49 – Ussel 17

Office de tourisme, 1, place de l'Hôtel de Ville ✆ 05 55 95 18 43, Fax 05 55 95 66 12

Black Virgin★ in the abbey church.

Chez Françoise with rm

24 r. Fontaine du Rat – ✆ 05 55 95 10 63 – Fax 05 55 95 40 22 – Closed 24 December-1 February, Sunday dinner and Monday

4 rm – †€ 60/70 ††€ 60/70, ☕ € 8

Rest – Menu € 16 (weekday lunch), € 29/36 – Carte € 40/50

◆ Authentic home cooking and a good choice de wines await you in this 16C rustic house flanked by a tower. Regional produce shop next door.

in Maussac 9 km south by D 36 and D 1089 – pop. 385 – alt. 615 m – ✉ 19250

Europa

on D 1089 – ✆ 05 55 94 25 21 – www.hoteleuropa1.fr – hotel.europa1@orange.fr – Fax 05 55 94 26 08 – Closed 23 December-2 January

22 rm – †€ 42 ††€ 45/49, ☕ € 7 – ½ P € 45/56

Rest – *(closed Sunday off season)* Menu € 12 (weekday lunch), € 17/28 – Carte € 23/34

◆ This hotel, easily accessible from the main road, provides functional rooms with king size beds. Rooms at the rear are quieter. Traditional, unpretentious cuisine. Mostly business clientele.

MEYRONNE – 46 Lot – 337 F2 – pop. 269 – alt. 130 m – ✉ 46200 29 C1

Paris 524 – Brive-la-Gaillarde 47 – Cahors 76 – Figeac 54 – Sarlat-la-Canéda 40

La Terrasse rm, rest,

pl. de l'Eglise – ✆ 05 65 32 21 60 – www.hotel-la-terrasse.com – terrasse.liebus@wanadoo.fr – Fax 05 65 32 26 93 – Open 14 March-5 November

13 rm – €70/125 €70/125, ☕ €12 – 4 suites – ½ P €80/122

Rest – *(closed Tuesday lunch)* Menu €20 (weekday lunch), €28/50 – Carte €53/74

◆ This 11C château and adjoining old stone houses overlook the Dordogne. Rooms adorned with antique furniture. Attractive vaulted winter dining room, a more contemporary area or an idyllic shaded terrace with an arbour.

MEYRUEIS – 48 Lozère – 330 I9 – pop. 909 – alt. 698 m – ✉ 48150 23 C1

Languedoc-Roussillon-Tarn Gorges

Paris 643 – Florac 36 – Mende 57 – Millau 43 – Rodez 99 – Le Vigan 56

Office de tourisme, Tour de l'Horloge ✆ 04 66 45 60 33, Fax 04 66 45 65 27

Northwest: Gorges de la Jonte★★.

Aven Armand★★★ Northwest: 11 km - Grotte de Dargilan★★ Northwest: 8,5 km.

Château d'Ayres rest,

rte d'Ayres, 1.5 km east by D 57 – ✆ 04 66 45 60 10 – www.chateau-d-ayres.com – chateau-d-ayres@wanadoo.fr – Fax 04 66 45 62 26 – Closed 3 January-15 February

22 rm – €80/99 €99/165, ☕ €15 – 7 suites – ½ P €85/165

Rest – Menu €25/50 – Carte €55/70

◆ The blend of old-fashioned refinement and modern comfort, and the serenity of a 6-hectare park affords a sense of charm to this 12C château, a former priory imbued with Cévennes history. Vaulted dining room with a fireplace; terrace shaded by sequoias and regional dishes.

Du Mont Aigoual

34 quai Barrière – ✆ 04 66 45 65 61 – www.hotel-mont-aigoual.com – hotelmontaigoual@free.fr – Fax 04 66 45 64 25 – Open 23 March-2 November

30 rm – €57 €57/75, ☕ €8 – ½ P €56/63

Rest – *(closed Tuesday lunchtime except July-August)* Menu €20/42

◆ At the foot of the picturesque Aigoual range, this village is an ideal base to discover the Grands Causses and the Cévennes. Partly renovated rooms; swimming pool, garden. Tasty traditional cuisine served in a charming Provençal-style dining room.

De l'Europe without rest

2 quai Barrière – ✆ 04 66 45 60 05 – www.hotel-europe-meyrueis.fr – frederic-robert-48@wanadoo.fr – Fax 04 66 45 65 31 – Open 10 April-1 November

29 rm – €32/36 €37/41, ☕ €7

◆ An old family guesthouse with simple but faultlessly kept bedrooms. Access to the pool of the hotel (Mont Aigoual) next door.

Family Hôtel rest,

4 r. Barrière – ✆ 04 66 45 60 02 – www.hotel-family.com – hotel.family@wanadoo.fr – Fax 04 66 45 66 54 – Open 1st April-5 November

48 rm – €40 €49, ☕ €8 – ½ P €50

Rest – Menu €13 (weekday lunch), €17/31 – Carte €16/39

◆ Family-run hotel on the banks of the Bétuzon, a tributary of the Jonte. Practical, well-kept guestrooms. Garden and charming swimming pool with Jacuzzi on the opposite bank. Copious Lozère cuisine served in several renovated and air-conditioned dining rooms.

Grand Hôtel de France rest,

pl. J. Séquier – ✆ 04 66 45 60 07 – www.grandhotel2france.com – grandhoteldefrance@wanadoo.fr – Fax 04 66 45 67 62 – Open 12 April-30 September

45 rm – €45 €46/50, ☕ €7 – ½ P €49

Rest – *(open 30 April-30 September)* Menu €17/30 – Carte €24/38

◆ Built out of regional stone, this hotel offers small, colourful bedrooms. At the rear of hotel are a hillside garden and swimming pool. Pleasantly countrified restaurant with a fireplace and rustic furniture. Basic setting, traditional menus.

MEYZIEU – 69 Rhône – 327 J5 – see Lyon

MÈZE – 34 Hérault – 339 G8 – pop. 10 336 – alt. 20 m – ✉ 34140 23 C2

Languedoc-Roussillon-Tarn Gorges

Paris 746 – Agde 21 – Béziers 43 – Lodève 52 – Montpellier 36 – Pézenas 19 – Sète 20

Office de tourisme, 8, rue Massaloup ✆ 04 67 43 93 08, Fax 04 67 43 55 61

Gallo-Roman villa ★ of Loupian North: 1,5 km.

De la Pyramide without rest

8 promenade Sergent Jl.-Navarro – ✆ 04 67 46 61 50 – www.hoteldelapyramide.fr – la-pyramidehotel@orange.fr – Fax 04 67 78 58 93 – Closed January

22 rm – †€ 70/95 ††€ 70/95, ☕ € 9

◆ Fine Provencal house in the middle of a small park. Very comfortable rooms with minimalist decor (white walls, wrought iron furniture); balconies overlooking the Thau lake.

in Bouzigues 4 km northeast by D 613 and secondary road – pop. 1 522 – alt. 3 m – ✉ 34140

La Côte Bleue

rm, rm, VISA AE

av L. Tudesq – ✆ 04 67 78 31 42 – www.cotebleue.fr – lacotebleue0572@orange.fr – Fax 04 67 78 35 49

31 rm – †€ 60 ††€ 90, ☕ € 13

Rest – *(Closed February holiday and Wednesday in low season)*

Menu (€ 19), € 29 (weekdays)/44 – Carte € 31/58

◆ Modern building with functional bedrooms and balconies on the banks of the Thau lake, a mecca for shellfish growers. Seafood cooking with pride of place given to the famous Bouzigues oysters; try them in summer on the shady terrace.

À La Voile Blanche

rm, rm, VISA AE

1 av. Louis Tudesq – ✆ 04 67 78 35 77 – www.alavoileblanche.com – alavoileblanche@wanadoo.fr – Fax 04 67 74 44 06 – Closed 17-30 November, Tuesday and Wednesday from October to March

8 rm – †€ 65/190 ††€ 65/190, ☕ € 8 **Rest** – Menu € 20 bi – Carte € 31/59

◆ A well-designed hotel by the lake, with its oyster beds and small port. Refined, ultra-modern decor. Some bedrooms with terrace. Enjoy southern cuisine with fish and grilled shellfish to the fore. Relaxed atmosphere.

MÉZOS – 40 Landes – 335 E10 – pop. 848 – alt. 23 m – ✉ 40170 3 B2

Paris 684 – Bordeaux 124 – Mont-de-Marsan 107 – Dax 58 – Biscarrosse 44

Office de tourisme, avenue de la Gare ✆ 05 58 42 64 37, Fax 05 58 42 64 60

La Maison de Mézos without rest

VISA AE

av. de l' Océan – ✆ 05 58 42 61 38 – www.hotel-mezos.com – maisondemezos@orange.fr – Fax 05 58 42 65 29 – Closed 1 November-19 December and January

9 rm – †€ 70/165 ††€ 70/165, ☕ € 8,50

◆ This charming hotel in a small village in the Landes has a family ambience (rustic setting, shabby chic furniture). The huge garden houses a lodge, suites and caravans. Pool.

MÉZY-MOULINS – 02 Aisne – 306 D8 – pop. 494 – alt. 81 m – ✉ 02650 37 C3

Paris 103 – Amiens 221 – Laon 92 – Reims 55 – Meaux 56

Le Moulin Babet with rm

rm, VISA

8 r. du Moulin Babet – ✆ 03 23 71 44 72 – www.hotel-moulinbabet.com – lemoulinbabet@orange.fr – Fax 03 23 71 48 11 – Closed 24 December-11 January, Sunday dinner (except hotel), Tuesday and Wednesday

7 rm – †€ 70/90 ††€ 70/90, ☕ € 9 **Rest** – Menu € 31/65 – Carte € 53/61

◆ In open countryside, this mill's old wheel is still visible from the lobby. Nice contemporary rooms, and restaurant combining rustic and modern.

MIEUSSY – 74 Haute-Savoie – 328 M4 – pop. 1 983 – alt. 636 m 46 F1
– ✉ 74440 French Alps

Paris 563 – Annecy 62 – Bonneville 21 – Chamonix-Mont-Blanc 59 – Thonon-les-Bains 49

Office de tourisme, Le Pont du Diable ✆ 04 50 43 02 72, Fax 04 50 43 01 87

Accueil Savoyard
– ✆ 04 50 43 01 90 – accueil-savoyard@wanadoo.fr – Fax 04 50 43 09 59 – Closed 5-18 May and 10-25 November

8 rm – €45/50 €56, €7 – ½ P €54

Rest – *(closed Sunday)* Menu €13 (weekday lunch), €19/25 – Carte €23/38

◆ Family guesthouse type hotel in the verdant Giffre valley. Well-kept rooms, some with balcony; ask for one with a view of the mountains. A rustic dining room serving a traditional menu and Savoy specialities.

Maison des Soeurs
pl. de l'Église – ✆ 04 50 43 15 74 – www.mieussy.net – mlm@mieussy.net – Fax 04 50 43 15 74

3 rm – €52/62 €63/95

Table d'hôte – *(closed Sunday)* Menu €15 bi/22 bi

◆ This sturdily built house (1841), easily recognisable by its turquoise shutters, has long been used by nuns and colonies de vacances. Large, attractive bedrooms with personal touches. Open fireplace in the lounge. Kitchen-cum-dining room with an open fireplace where casseroles and grilled poultry are sometimes cooked.

MILLAU – 12 Aveyron – 338 K6 – pop. 21 900 – alt. 372 m 29 D2
– ✉ 12100 Languedoc-Roussillon-Tarn Gorges

Paris 636 – Albi 106 – Mende 95 – Montpellier 114 – Rodez 67

Office de tourisme, 1, place du Beffroi ✆ 05 65 60 02 42, Fax 05 65 60 95 08

Musée de Millau★ : pottery ★, maison de la Peau et du Gant ★ (1st floor) M - Viaduct ★★★.

Canyon de la Dourbie★★ 8 km by ②.

Plan on following page

Mercure
1 pl. de la Tine – ✆ 05 65 59 29 00 – www.mercure.com – h5614@accor.com – Fax 05 65 59 29 01 BY **m**

57 rm – €99/149 €109/159, €17

Rest – *(Closed Saturday and Sunday in low season)*
Menu (€13), €24/29 – Carte €24/40

◆ This renovated hotel is located in the village centre, with a modern atmosphere, providing several rooms with a view of the viaduct. This regional-style restaurant serves local cuisine.

Cévenol Hôtel
115 r. Rajol – ✆ 05 65 60 74 44 – www.cevenol-hotel.fr – contact@cevenol-hotel.fr – Fax 05 65 60 85 99 BY **k**

42 rm – €54/58 €54/58, €8 – ½ P €50/57

Rest – Menu (€12), €17 (weekdays)/37 – Carte €20/55

◆ This 1980s building, separated from the Tarn by a main road, houses functional, rather spacious rooms. New bar. The dining room opens onto a summer terrace with a small grill. Regional cuisine.

Millau Hôtel Club
via ④ and rte Montpellier – ✆ 05 65 59 71 33 – www.hotels-de-millau.com – millauhotelclub@wanadoo.fr – Fax 05 65 59 71 67 – Open 1st March-30 November

37 rm – €66 €66, €10 – ½ P €57

Rest – grill – *(closed Sunday dinner and Monday lunch)*
Menu €12 bi (lunch), €19/27 bi – Carte €25/40

◆ This modern complex located near the bypass offers functional rooms, a fitness centre, sauna, swimming pool, bowling alley and tennis court. View over Millau, the Tarn and the viaduct. Grilled food, salads and a good regional wine list on offer in the plain rotunda dining room.

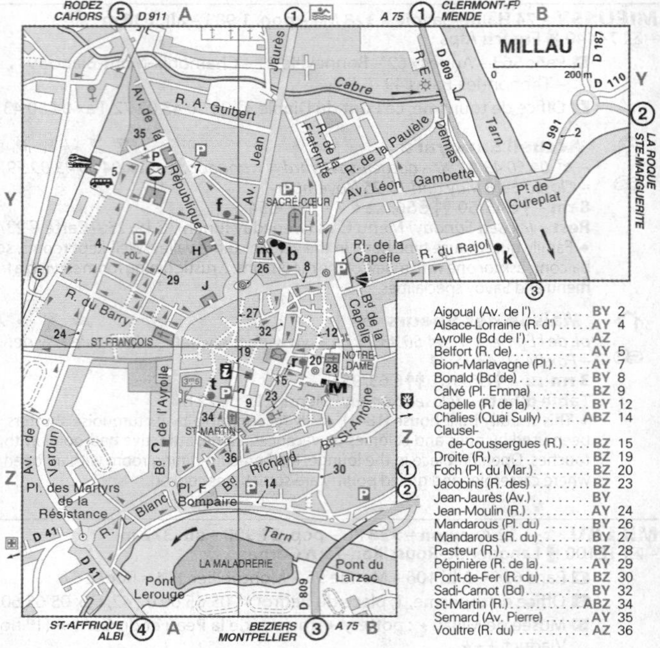

Ibis without rest

r. du Sacré Cœur – 05 65 59 29 09 – www.ibishotel.com – h5613@accor.com – Fax 05 65 59 29 01 BY **b**

46 rm – €65/99 €65/99, €10

◆ This hotel in the town centre is conveniently located for a walk along the famous viaduct. Spacious, bright and comfortable rooms.

Capion

3 r. J.-F. Alméras – 05 65 60 00 91 – www.restaurant-capion.com – restaurantcapion@wanadoo.fr – Fax 05 65 60 42 13 – Closed 1-7 January, Thursday in July-August, Tuesday dinner and Wednesday AY **f**

Rest – Menu €15/38 – Carte €33/49

◆ Town-centre establishment which is often full. Generous traditional cuisine using local products and a more exotic "menu des îles" set menu.

La Braconne

7 pl. Mar. Foch – 05 65 60 30 93 – Fax 05 65 61 88 20 – Closed Sunday dinner and Monday BZ **r**

Rest – Menu €20/41 – Carte €28/48

◆ The restaurant is located under "cover" of the columns of this picturesque square in old Millau, in a pretty 13C vaulted room. Family cooking and service.

via ④ 2 km St-Affrique road – ✉ 12100 Millau

Château de Creissels

– 05 65 60 16 59 – www.chateau-de-creissels.com – chateau-de-creissels@wanadoo.fr – Fax 05 65 61 24 63 – Closed January, February and Sunday evening from November to March

30 rm – €49/97 €63/97, €9 – 1/2 P €61/77

Rest – *(closed Sunday dinner and Monday lunch except from June to September)* Menu €24/50 – Carte €39/50

◆ This 12C château and its modern extension (1971) offer a choice between charming period and more conventional bedrooms. Stylish sitting room; billiards. Dining room with attractive stone vaulting, panoramic terrace and tasty classical cooking.

MILLY-LA-FORÊT – 91 Essonne – 312 D5 – pop. 4 746 – alt. 68 m 18 B3
– ✉ 91490 Northern France and the Paris Region

Paris 58 – Étampes 25 – Évry 31 – Fontainebleau 19 – Melun 25 – Nemours 27

Office de tourisme, 47, rue Langlois ✆ 01 64 98 83 17, Fax 01 64 98 94 80

Park★★ of the chateau de Courances★★ North: 5 km.

in Auvers (S.-et-M.) 4 km south by D 948 – ✉ 77123 Noisy on Ecole

XX **Auberge d'Auvers Galant** VISA MC AE

7 r. d'Auvers – ✆ 01 64 24 51 02 – http://perso.wanadoo.fr/auvers-galant – auvers-galant@wanadoo.fr – Fax 01 64 24 56 40 – Closed 31 August-15 September, 19 January-5 February, Sunday dinner, Monday and Tuesday
Rest – Menu € 25 (weekdays)/50 – Carte € 45/70

◆ A truly gallant place with a pleasant and colourful rustic interior. Traditional recipes (including calf's head).

MILLY-SUR-THERAIN – 60 Oise – 305 C3 – pop. 1 520 – alt. 82 m 36 A2
– ✉ 60112

Paris 91 – Compiègne 69 – Amiens 74 – Beauvais 11

XX **Hostellerie du Lac "La gourmandine"** with rm

1 r. Étangs – ✆ 03 44 81 07 52 rest, P VISA MC
– www.la-gourmandine.net – hostellerie-la-gourmandine@wanadoo.fr – Fax 03 44 81 36 60 – Closed 15 February-8 March
8 rm – †€ 65 ††€ 85, ☕ € 10 – ½ P € 70
Rest – *(Closed Saturday lunch, Sunday dinner and Monday)*
Menu (€ 18), € 29/100 bi – Carte € 36/65

◆ A 1900 lodge on the banks of a small lake surrounded by a wood. Comfortable dining room offering classic food and a brasserie section for the set menu of the day. Renovated hotel. Rooms furnished with veneered wood furniture, or more rustically.

MIMIZAN – 40 Landes – 335 D9 – pop. 6 605 – alt. 13 m – Casino 3 B2
– ✉ 40200 Atlantic Coast

Paris 692 – Arcachon 67 – Bayonne 109 – Bordeaux 109 – Dax 72 – Mont-de-Marsan 77

Office de tourisme, 38, avenue Maurice Martin ✆ 05 58 09 11 20, Fax 05 58 09 40 31

Sud Beach

L'Émeraude des Bois P VISA MC

66/68 av. Courant – ✆ 05 58 09 05 28 – www.emeraudedesbois.com – emeraudedesbois@wanadoo.fr – Fax 05 58 09 35 73 – Open 1 April-30 September
15 rm – †€ 52/57 ††€ 56/75, ☕ € 8 – ½ P € 51/55
Rest – *(open 26 April-13 September) (dinner only)* Menu € 17/42 – Carte € 19/45

◆ A pleasant hotel three minutes from the beaches of the Côte d'Argent and the large Mimizan forest. Renovated rooms (no smoking). A dining room with veranda and a pleasant shady terrace.

L'Airial without rest P VISA MC AE

6 r. Papeterie – ✆ 05 58 09 46 54 – www.hotel-airial.com – hotel.airial@aliceadsl.fr – Fax 05 58 09 32 10 – Closed Sunday dinner off season
16 rm – †€ 40/52 ††€ 45/60, ☕ € 8

◆ Warm hospitality, well-maintained bedrooms furnished in pine, rest lounges, breakfast in the garden; here is an ocean stay to remember.

de France without rest P VISA MC

18 av. de la Côte d'Argent – ✆ 05 58 09 09 01 – www.hoteldefrance-mimizan.com – hoteldefrancemimizan@orange.fr – Fax 05 58 09 47 16 – Open 1st March-20 October
21 rm – †€ 50/80 ††€ 55/80, ☕ € 6,50

◆ Not far from the beach, this small, practical hotel provides renovated rooms with simple furnishings and decorated in pastel tones. Snacks also served in high season.

MINERVE – **34 Hérault** – **339** B8 – **pop. 112** – **alt. 227 m** – ✉ **34210** 22 **B2**
Languedoc-Roussillon-Tarn Gorges

Paris 812 – Béziers 45 – Carcassonne 44 – Narbonne 33 – St-Pons 30

Syndicat d'initiative, 9, rue des Martyrs ☎ 04 68 91 81 43, Fax 04 68 91 81 43

Site★★.

Relais Chantovent with rm VISA
17 Grand'Rue – ☎ 04 68 91 14 18 – relais.chantovent@orange.fr
– Fax 04 68 91 81 99 – Open 16 March-11 November and closed Sunday dinner and Monday
5 rm – €35 €42, €6,50 – ½ P €55
Rest – Menu €21/46 – Carte €40/65
◆ In the heart of the Cathar village, an attractive family-run inn serving appetising regional cuisine. A view of the Brian gorges from the terrace. Simple guestrooms.

MIOMO – **2B Haute-Corse** – **345** F3 – **see Corse (Bastia)**

MIONNAY – **01 Ain** – **328** C5 – **pop. 2 124** – **alt. 276 m** – ✉ **01390** 43 **E1**

Paris 457 – Bourg-en-Bresse 44 – Lyon 23 – Meximieux 26
– Villefranche-sur-Saône 33

de Mionnay-la-Dombes Domaine de Beau Logis, E : 3 km, ☎ 04 78 91 84 84

Alain Chapel with rm P VISA AE
– ☎ 04 78 91 82 02 – www.alainchapel.fr – chapel@relaischateaux.com
– Fax 04 78 91 82 37 – Closed January, Friday lunch, Monday and Tuesday except public holidays
12 rm – €127/147 €127/147, €16
Rest – Menu €75 (weekday lunch), €114/157 – Carte €95/136
Spec. Pressé de tourteau et oeufs de saumon (summer). Petits rougets, cocos de Paimpol et effiloché de canard dans soupe de poissons de roche (summer-autumn). Sabayon froid au café sur sablé de muesli, transparence aux noix et gelée d'amaretto. **Wines** Morgon, Condrieu.
◆ The three tastefully decorated dining rooms sport a warm, romantic typically Bresse ambience. Classic gourmet menu. Spruce guestrooms and flower-decked garden.

MIRAMAR – **06 Alpes-Maritimes** – **341** C7 – **see Théoule-sur-Mer**

MIRAMBEAU – **17 Charente-Maritime** – **324** G7 – **pop. 1 452** 38 **B3**
– **alt. 59 m** – ✉ **17150**

Paris 515 – Bordeaux 72 – Angoulême 73 – Cognac 48 – Royan 52

Office de tourisme, 90, avenue de la République ☎ 05 46 49 62 85,
Fax 05 46 49 62 85

Château de Mirambeau rest,
1 av. des Comtes Duchatel – ☎ 05 46 04 91 20 P VISA AE
– www.chateaumirambeau.com – reservation@chateaumirambeau.com
– Fax 05 46 04 26 72 – Open 5 April-1st November
14 rm – €230/555 €230/555, €28 – 9 suites
Rest – Menu (€45), €65/90 – Carte €70/107
◆ Sumptuous lounges, antique furniture, refined guestrooms, luxury bathrooms, vast park and beautiful indoor pool: charm and elegance abound in this magnificent 19C château. Three small intimate dining rooms and a terrace overlooking the estate.

MIRANDE – **71 Saône-et-Loire** – **320** J11 – **see Fleurville**

MIRANDOL-BOURGNOUNAC – **81 Tarn** – **338** E6 – **pop. 1 069** 29 **C2**
– **alt. 393 m** – ✉ **81190**

Paris 653 – Albi 29 – Rodez 51 – St-Affrique 79
– Villefranche-de-Rouergue 39

Office de tourisme, 2, place de la Liberté ☎ 05 63 76 97 65,
Fax 05 63 76 90 11

Hostellerie des Voyageurs with rm — rest, VISA

pl. du Foirail – ✆ 05 63 76 90 10 – Fax 05 63 76 96 01 – Closed spring holiday, 24 August-9 September and dinner from 1 October to 15 April

8 rm – †€ 33 ††€ 42/52, ☕ € 6 – ½ P € 48/54

Rest – Menu € 13 bi (weekdays)/33 – Carte € 26/50

◆ Building with a discreet façade, also home to the village café. Large country-style dining area and generous family cooking based on slow-cooked dishes. Flower-decked terrace.

MIREBEL – 39 Jura – 321 E6 – pop. 230 – alt. 580 m – ✉ 39570 — 16 B3

Paris 419 – Champagnole 17 – Lons-le-Saunier 17

Mirabilis — P VISA

41 Grande Rue – ✆ 03 84 48 24 36 – www.lemirabilis.com – lemirabilis@wanadoo.fr – Fax 03 84 48 22 25 – Closed 2-10 January, Tuesday and Wednesday from September to June and Monday

Rest – Menu (€ 13), € 20/50 – Carte € 26/37

◆ Dating from 1760, this family residence is well equipped with indoor and outdoor activities for children. Elegant dining room overlooking the terrace and garden. Modern, regional cuisine.

MIREPOIX – 09 Ariège – 343 J6 – pop. 3 060 – alt. 308 m – ✉ 09500 — 29 C3

Languedoc-Roussillon-Tarn Gorges

Paris 753 – Carcassonne 52 – Castelnaudary 34 – Foix 37 – Limoux 33 – Pamiers 25

Office de tourisme, place Maréchal Leclerc ✆ 05 61 68 83 76, Fax 05 61 68 89 48

Place principale★★.

Relais Royal — VISA AE

8 r. Mar. Clauzel – ✆ 05 61 60 19 19 – www.relaisroyal.com – relaisroyal@relaischateaux.com – Fax 05 61 60 14 15 – Closed 3 January-11 February

5 rm ☕ – †€ 200/290 ††€ 200/290 – 3 suites

Rest – *(Closed Tuesday lunch, Wednesday lunch and Thursday lunch from November to Easter, Tuesday dinner, Saturday lunch and Monday)*
Menu € 37/95 – Carte approx. € 75

◆ This lovely residence (1742) used to be the home of the Mayor. A large staircase leads to the spacious rooms decorated with stylish furniture and modern equipment. Small, plush dining room where you can enjoy appetising, modern recipes.

La Maison des Consuls without rest — VISA AE

6 pl. du Mar. Leclerc – ✆ 05 61 68 81 81 – www.maisondesconsuls.com – hotel@maisondesconsuls.com – Fax 05 61 68 81 15

8 rm – †€ 80/95 ††€ 80/155, ☕ € 16

◆ This old 14C courthouse is now a hotel with personalised rooms (one suite with a terrace) embellished with a mix of medieval- and contemporary-style furniture. Views over the square and a patio.

Les Minotiers — AC P VISA

av. Mar. Foch – ✆ 05 61 69 37 36 – www.lesminotiers.com – info@lesminotiers.com – Fax 05 61 69 48 55

27 rm – †€ 45 ††€ 49/57, ☕ € 7

Rest – *(closed Saturday lunch except July-August)* Menu € 16/36 – Carte € 32/55

◆ A brand new hotel within the walls of an old flourmill. Soft tones and modern equipment in the simple but comfortable guestrooms. Unpretentious and reasonably priced traditional cuisine.

Le Comptoir Gourmand — VISA

cours Mar. de Mirepoix – ✆ 05 61 68 19 19 – www.lecomptoirgourmand.com – comptoir.gourmand@wanadoo.fr – Fax 05 61 68 19 19 – Closed Tuesday and Wednesday from September to June, Sunday and lunch

Rest – Menu € 28/35 – Carte € 28/45

◆ The enticing, refined and traditional cuisine served here is based on ingredients and wines sourced from small local producers. Boutique at the entrance to the restaurant. Summer terrace.

MIRMANDE – 26 Drôme – **332** C5 – **pop. 507** – **alt. 204 m** 44 **B3**
Lyon - Rhone Valley

Paris 603 – Lyon 141 – Valence 42 – Romans-sur-Isère 61 – Montélimar 21
Syndicat d'initiative, place du Champ de Mars ☎ 04 75 63 10 88, Fax 04 75 63 10 88

La Capitelle rm, VISA MC AE
Le Rempart – ☎ 04 75 63 02 72 – www.lacapitelle.com – capitelle@wanadoo.fr – Fax 04 75 63 02 50 – Closed 15 December-15 February and Tuesday except July-August
12 rm – †€ 80/130 ††€ 85/150, ☕ € 12 – ½ P € 85/125
Rest – *(closed Wednesday lunch except July-August)*
Menu (€ 19), € 39/53 – Carte € 50/60 dinner only
◆ This former silkworm farm, lit by mullioned windows, was once the home of Cubist André Lhote. Beautiful antique furniture in the rooms. The monumental stone fireplace is the soul of this vaulted dining room. The terrace commands a view of the orchards and hills.

MISSILLAC – 44 Loire-Atlantique – **316** D3 – **pop. 4 557** – **alt. 44 m** 34 **A2**
– ✉ **44780** Brittany

Paris 436 – Nantes 62 – Redon 24 – St-Nazaire 37 – Vannes 55
Office de tourisme, la Chinoise ☎ 02 40 88 35 14
Altar-piece★ in the church - Site★ of the château de la Bretesche West: 1 km.

La Bretesche rm, VISA MC AE
Domaine de la Bretesche, la Baule road – ☎ 02 51 76 86 96 – www.bretesche.com – bretesche@relaischateaux.com – Fax 02 40 66 99 47
32 rm – †€ 155/440 ††€ 155/440, ☕ € 27 – ½ P € 154/296
Rest – *(closed February and lunch except Sunday)* Menu € 56/106 – Carte € 93/115
Rest *Le Club* – brasserie *(closed dinner 15 October-31 March)* Menu (€ 19), € 24 – Carte € 35/55
Spec. Ravioles de thon rouge au chèvre frais (May-Sep.). Saint-Pierre cuit sur peau et tartare d'huître. Carré de chocolat à la menthe des marais. **Wines** Muscadet de Sèvre-et-Maine sur lie.
◆ A world of fairy stories in the heart of La Brière... Converted outbuildings opposite a crenelated chateau surrounded by moats. Refined restaurant, pleasant courtyard terrace and delicious modern recipes. A modern brasserie spirit reigns in the club, perfect for hurried diners.

MITTELBERGHEIM – 67 Bas-Rhin – **315** I6 – **pop. 653** – **alt. 220 m** 2 **C1**
– ✉ **67140** Alsace-Lorraine

Paris 499 – Barr 2 – Erstein 24 – Molsheim 23 – Sélestat 21 – Strasbourg 41
Syndicat d'initiative, 2, rue Principale ☎ 03 88 08 01 66, Fax 03 88 08 01 66

Am Lindeplatzel VISA MC
71 r. Principale – ☎ 03 88 08 10 69 – Fax 03 88 08 45 08 – Closed 25 August-3 September, 20-30 November, 9-28 February, Monday lunch, Wednesday dinner and Thursday
Rest – Menu € 23/58 – Carte € 43/60
◆ Establishment located in a beautiful village, popular for its traditional and contemporary dishes, as well as its regional specialities with an up-to-the-minute focus.

Gilg with rm VISA MC AE
1 r. Rotland – ☎ 03 88 08 91 37 – www.hotel-gilg.com – hotel.gilg@orange.fr – Fax 03 88 08 45 17 – Closed 29 June-14 July, 5-28 January, Tuesday and Wednesday
19 rm – †€ 55 ††€ 58/87, ☕ € 8 **Rest** – Menu € 29/68 – Carte € 40/60
◆ Beautiful house (1614) in the style of the Low Rhineland, located in the town centre. The original winstub, home to the first pâté vigneron (winegrower's meat pie), or so they say, has been transformed into a restaurant with an Alsatian setting.

MITTELHAUSBERGEN – 67 Bas-Rhin – **315** K5 – **see Strasbourg**

MITTELHAUSEN – 67 Bas-Rhin – 315 J4 – pop. 546 – alt. 185 m – ✉ 67170 1 B1

Paris 478 – Haguenau 21 – Saverne 22 – Strasbourg 24

À l'Étoile rest, VISA AE

12 r. La Hey – ✆ 03 88 51 28 44 – www.hotel-etoile.net – hotelrestaurant.etoile@wanadoo.fr – Fax 03 88 51 24 79 – Closed 1st-14 January

24 rm – €48 €55/63, ☕ €7 – ½ P €62

Rest – *(closed 12 July-5 August, 1st-14 January, Sunday dinner and Monday)* Menu (€12), €19/42 – Carte €22/49

◆ New building with a flower-filled facade and a regional look far from the busy main roads. Functional bedrooms renovated in stages. Warm and welcoming dining rooms decorated with old wood panelling.

MITTELWIHR – 68 Haut-Rhin – 315 H8 – pop. 780 – alt. 210 m – ✉ 68630 2 C2

Paris 445 – Colmar 10 – Kaysersberg 6 – Ribeauvillé 403 – Sélestat 20

Le Mandelberg without rest VISA AE

chemin du Mandelberg – ✆ 03 89 49 09 49 – http://monsite.wanadoo.fr/hotelmandelberg.fr – hotelmandelberg@wanadoo.fr – Fax 03 89 49 09 48 – Closed 5 January-1st February

18 rm – €70/110 €80/110, ☕ €10

◆ A neo-Alsatian-style establishment in the heart of the "Midi of Alsace", so named due to its microclimate. Comfortable, spacious rooms, some overlooking the vineyards.

Le Mittelwihr without rest VISA AE

19 rte du Vin – ✆ 03 89 49 09 90 – http://monsite.wanadoo.fr/hotelmittelwihr.fr – hotelmittelwihr@wanadoo.fr – Fax 03 89 86 02 29 – Closed February

15 rm – €65/110 €65/110, ☕ €10

◆ On the wine route, a brand-new, traditionally constructed house where a typically generous local breakfast is served after a comfortable night.

La Table de Mittelwihr VISA AE

rte du Vin – ✆ 03 89 78 61 40 – www.la-table-de-mittelwihr.com – latabledemittelwihr@wanadoo.fr – Fax 03 89 86 01 66 – Closed 2-24 November, Tuesday lunch and Monday

Rest – Menu €17 (weekday lunch), €30/45 – Carte €39/49

◆ Enjoy modern local cuisine in the rather original contemporary interior architecture (curved wooden beams) or on the pleasant summer terrace.

MIZOËN – 38 Isère – 333 J7 – see le Freney-d'Oisans

MOËLAN-SUR-MER – 29 Finistère – 308 J8 – pop. 6 841 – alt. 58 m – ✉ 29350 Brittany 9 B2

Paris 523 – Carhaix-Plouguer 66 – Concarneau 27 – Lorient 27 – Quimper 50 – Quimperlé 10

Office de tourisme, 20, place de l'Église ✆ 02 98 39 67 28, Fax 02 98 39 63 93

Manoir de Kertalg without rest VISA

Riec-sur-Belon road 3 km westward via the D 24 and private path – ✆ 02 98 39 77 77 – www.manoirdekertalg.com – kertalg@free.fr – Fax 02 98 39 72 07 – Open 12 April-12 November

9 rm – €115/210 €115/250, ☕ €14

◆ Sweet serenity reigns at this historic abode nestling in a wooded estate, which will appeal to art lovers (painting exhibitions). Refurbished decor in elegant style.

Les Moulins du Duc rm, VISA AE

2 km north-westward – ✆ 02 98 96 52 52 – www.hotel-moulins-du-duc.com – moulin.duc@wanadoo.fr – Fax 02 98 96 52 53 – Open 1st March-30 November

26 rm – €81/198 €81/198, ☕ €15

Rest – *(closed Sunday dinner and Monday in March and November, Monday lunch and Tuesday lunch from April to end October)* Menu €38/69 – Carte €44/64

◆ A leafy park with a tranquil lake, a 16C mill, plus guestrooms in attractive small houses by the river. This former mill, with its original workings on display in the lounge, is now home to a restaurant serving traditional cuisine. Riverside veranda.

MOERNACH – 68 Haut-Rhin – 315 H11 – see Ferrette

MOIRAX – 47 Lot-et-Garonne – 336 F5 – see Agen

MOISSAC – 82 Tarn-et-Garonne – 337 C7 – pop. 12 300 – alt. 76 m – ✉ 82200 Languedoc-Roussillon-Tarn Gorges 28 **B2**

Paris 632 – Agen 57 – Auch 87 – Cahors 63 – Montauban 31 – Toulouse 71

Office de tourisme, 6, place Durand de Bredon ✆ 05 63 04 01 85, Fax 05 63 04 27 10

d'Espalais Valence-d'Agen L'Ilôt, 20 km on the Agen road, ✆ 05 63 29 04 56

St-Pierre church★: south portal ★★★, cloister★★★, christ★.
Boudou ✳★ 7 km by ③.

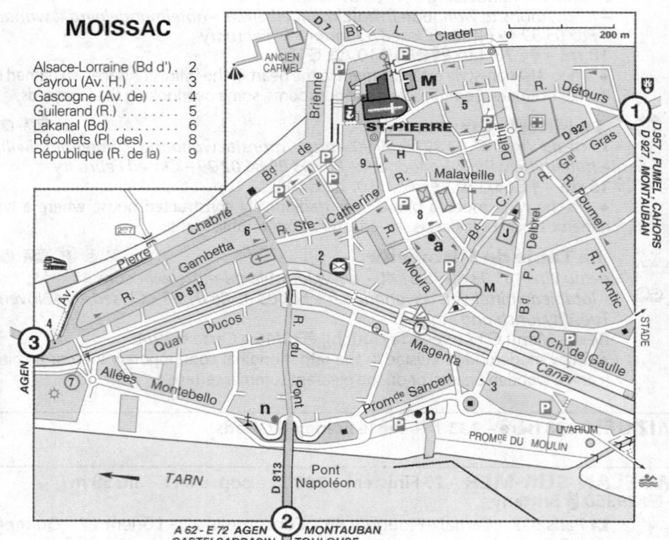

Le Moulin de Moissac rm, VISA AE b

Esplanade du Moulin – ✆ 05 63 32 88 88 – www.lemoulindemoissac.com – hotel@lemoulindemoissac.com – Fax 05 63 32 02 08

36 rm – †€ 75 ††€ 75/150, ☕ € 12

Rest – *(closed Saturday lunchtime and Sunday)*

Menu € 24 (weekday lunch), € 38/55 – Carte € 72/84

◆ This mill dates back to the 15. It has been transformed many times and now has a pleasantly-decorated interior and pretty, themed rooms (sea, countryside and mountains). Simple and elegant restaurant overlooking the Tarn; traditional menu.

Le Chapon Fin without rest VISA AE a

3 pl. des Récollets – ✆ 05 63 04 04 22 – www.lechaponfin-moissac.com – info@lechaponfin-moissac.com – Fax 05 63 04 58 44

23 rm – †€ 45/80 ††€ 45/80, ☕ € 9

◆ Located on the market square, just a stone's throw from the Romanesque abbey. Classically decorated, functional guestrooms and warm welcome.

XX **Le Pont Napoléon-La Table de Nos Fils** with rm
2 allées Montebello – 05 63 04 01 55
– www.le-pont-napoleon.com – lepontnapoleon@orange.fr – Fax 05 63 04 34 44
– Closed 2-12 November, 15-28 February, Monday lunch from October to April, Wednesday lunch and Tuesday n
12 rm – €40/45 €50/54, €8
Rest – Menu (€28), €34/42 – Carte €42/54
◆ This restaurant is located opposite the Pont Napoléon on the banks of the Tarn. Pleasantly up-to-the-minute decor with paintings on the wall, antiques and objets d'art. Modern cuisine.

North 9 km by D 7 - ✉ ***82400 St-Paul-Espis***

Le Manoir St-Jean rest,
at St-Jean-de-Cornac – 05 63 05 02 34 – www.manoirsaintjean.com
– info@manoirsaintjean.com – Fax 05 63 05 07 50
– Closed 1st-24 November and 4-18 January
1 rm – €100/170 €100/170, €13 – 9 suites – €140/190 – ½ P €95/130
Rest – *(closed Sunday dinner and Monday from 1st October-15 May) (pre-book)*
Menu (€28), €38/70
◆ This 19C manor house owes much of its character to its many antiques. The rooms-suites are decorated on various themes: Art Deco, marine, etc. Pleasant garden and pool. Comfortable dining room in which regional dishes take pride of place.

MOISSAC-BELLEVUE – 83 Var – 340 M4 – see Aups

MOISSIEU-SUR-DOLON – 38 Isère – 333 C5 – pop. 625 – alt. 350 m – ✉ 38270 44 B2

Paris 511 – Grenoble 78 – Lyon 55 – La Tour-du-Pin 53 – Vienne 25

Domaine de la Colombière
– 04 74 79 50 23 – www.lacolombiere.com
– colombieremoissieu@hotmail.com – Fax 04 74 79 50 25
– Closed 26-30 December, 15 February-1 March, Sunday dinner and Monday except bank holidays
20 rm – €93/125 €105/149, €15 – 1 suite – ½ P €91/102
Rest – Menu €35/67 – Carte €42/65
◆ An impressive 1820 house surrounded by a 4ha park. Large, well-equipped rooms decorated on the theme of famous painters (copies produced by the artist-landlady). A large restaurant with private dining room, country terrace and modern menu.

MOLINES-EN-QUEYRAS – 05 Hautes-Alpes – 334 J4 – pop. 325 – alt. 1 750 m – Winter sports : 1 750/2 900 m 15 – ✉ 05350 French Alps 41 C1

Paris 724 – Briançon 44 – Gap 87 – Guillestre 27 – St-Véran 6

Office de tourisme, Clot la Chalpe 04 92 45 83 22, Fax 04 92 45 80 79

Château-Queyras: site★★, fort Queyras★, geological space★, Northwest: 8 km.

Le Chamois
– 04 92 45 83 71 – www.hotel-lechamois.com – contact@hotel-lechamois.com
– Fax 04 92 45 80 58 – Open 20 April-30 September, 24 October-1 November and 25 December-31 March
17 rm – €55/62 €55/62, €9 – ½ P €56/61
Rest – *(closed for lunch from 25 December to 31 March and Monday)*
Menu €16/26 – Carte €37/48
◆ Here everything is reminiscent of the mountain environment: the rustic-style bedrooms (six with balconies) and the warm and simple hospitality. Traditional meals served in a dining area with a view of the mountains.

MOLINEUF – 41 Loir-et-Cher – 318 E6 – see Blois

MOLITG-LES-BAINS – 66 Pyrénées-Orientales – 344 F7 – pop. 213 — 22 B3
– alt. 607 m – Spa : early April-late Nov. – ✉ 66500
Languedoc-Roussillon-Tarn Gorges

Paris 896 – Perpignan 50 – Prades 7 – Quillan 56

Syndicat d'initiative, route des Bains ✆ 04 68 05 03 28, Fax 04 68 05 01 13

Château de Riell rm,
– ✆ *04 68 05 04 40 – riell@relaischateaux.com*
– Fax 04 68 05 04 37 – Open 29 March-2 November
16 rm – € 145/350 € 145/350, € 19 – 3 suites
Rest – *(closed lunch except weekends)* Menu € 48 (lunch) – Carte € 83/90
◆ Built in wooded parkland and baroque in spirit, this 19C Catalan 'folly' has snug personalised bedrooms. There are seven others in little cottages. Smart bodega atmosphere in this dining room and terrace surrounded by lush vegetation.

Grand Hôtel Thermal rest,
– ✆ *04 68 05 00 50 – www.chainethermale.fr*
– molitglesbains@chainethermale.fr – Fax 04 68 05 02 91
– Open 29 March-6 December
34 rm – € 125/165 € 125/165, € 13 – 5 suites – ½ P € 87/135
Rest – *(closed Saturday lunch and Sunday lunch)*
Menu € 32 – Carte € 40/60 lunch only
◆ In a lakeside park, this hotel offers colourful rooms refurbished in a tasteful Catalan style. A few spacious and very attractive suites. One of the dining rooms is in an old chocolate factory. Classic menu.

MOLLANS-SUR-OUVÈZE – 26 Drôme – 332 E8 – pop. 950 — 44 B3
– alt. 280 m – ✉ 26170 French Alps

Paris 676 – Carpentras 30 – Nyons 21 – Vaison-la-Romaine 13

Le St-Marc rest,
av. de l'Ancienne Gare – ✆ *04 75 28 70 01 – www.saintmarc.com*
– le-saint-marc@club-internet.fr – Fax 04 75 28 78 63 – Open 10 April-3 November
30 rm – € 62/86 € 62/86, € 9 – ½ P € 64/76
Rest – *(dinner only)* Menu € 27/33
◆ This Provencal-style house, fronted by a garden, lies at the foot of Mont Ventoux. Rooms enlivened by colourful fabrics. A rustic restaurant with an open fireplace, serving southern French cuisine and featuring a pleasant shaded and floral terrace.

MOLLÉGÈS – 13 Bouches-du-Rhône – 340 E3 – pop. 2 171 – alt. 55 m — 42 E1
– ✉ 13940

Paris 704 – Avignon 24 – Cavaillon 9 – Marseille 80 – Saint-Rémy-de-Provence 12

Mas du Capoun with rm rm, rm,
27 av. des Paluds – ✆ *04 90 26 07 12 – www.masducapoun.fr – lemasducapoun@orange.fr – Fax 04 90 26 08 17 – Rest closed 1st-14 November and mid February to mid March hotel: Open mid March to mid October*
6 rm – € 75/85 € 85/95
Rest – *(closed Tuesday dinner, Saturday lunch and Wednesday)*
Menu (€ 16), € 22 bi (weekday lunch)/33
◆ Refined farmhouse with bright dining room where you can enjoy modern dishes, served under the exposed beams of the chic, rustic barn. Pretty guestrooms with private terrace.

MOLLKIRCH – 67 Bas-Rhin – 315 I5 – pop. 920 – alt. 320 m – ✉ 67190 — 1 A2

Paris 485 – Molsheim 11 – Saverne 35 – Strasbourg 40

Fischhutte
30 rte de la Fischhutte, rte Grendelbruch: 3,5 km – ✆ *03 88 97 42 03*
– www.fischhutte.com. – fischhutte@wanadoo.fr – Fax 03 88 97 51 85
– Closed 16 March-8 April and 20 July-4 August
18 rm – € 60/70 € 70/145, € 10 – ½ P € 70/100
Rest – *(closed Monday and Tuesday)*
Menu (€ 15), € 34 (weekdays)/54 – Carte € 26/48
◆ A country hotel in the Magel valley. Comfortable rooms with modern decor. Some offer a view of the Vosges forest. Brasserie area flanking a smart dining room. Regional menu and game in season.

MOLSHEIM – 67 Bas-Rhin – 315 I5 – pop. 9 452 – alt. 180 m – ✉ 67120 Alsace-Lorraine 1 A1

Paris 477 – Lunéville 94 – St-Dié 79 – Saverne 28 – Sélestat 37 – Strasbourg 32

Office de tourisme, 19, place de l'Hôtel Ville ☎ 03 88 38 11 61, Fax 03 88 49 80 40

La Metzig★ - Jésuites church ★.

Frescoes★ of St-Ulrich chapel North: 3.5 km.

Diana rm, rm, VISA

pont de la Bruche – ☎ 03 88 38 51 59 – www.hotel-diana.com – info@hotel-diana.com – Fax 03 88 38 87 11

60 rm – †€ 95/118 ††€ 95/132, ☕ € 11 – 4 suites

Rest – *(Closed 15-31 July, 23-31 December and Sunday dinner)*
Menu (€ 26 bi), € 40 bi (weekdays)/44 – Carte € 48/65

◆ A 1970s hotel decorated with numerous works of art. Rooms remodelled in an uncluttered modern style. Spa, fitness facilities, lounge and garden. Restaurant with a modern menu and beautiful wine cellar.

Le Bugatti without rest VISA

r. de la Commanderie – ☎ 03 88 49 89 00 – www.hotel-le-bugatti.com – info@hotel-le-bugatti.com – Fax 03 88 38 36 00 – Closed 24 December-1st January

48 rm – †€ 56/62 ††€ 56/62, ☕ € 7 – 1 suite

◆ The modern architecture of the Bugatti, near the factories of the legendary marque, houses practical rooms, renovated in a contemporary spirit.

LES MOLUNES – 39 Jura – 321 F8 – pop. 130 – alt. 1 274 m – ✉ 39310 16 B3

Paris 485 – Genève 49 – Gex 30 – Lons-le-Saunier 74 – St-Claude 16

Le Pré Fillet rm, VISA

rte des Moussières – ☎ 03 84 41 62 89 – www.hotel-leprefillet.com – leprefillet@wanadoo.fr – Fax 03 84 41 64 75 – Closed 26 April-2 May, 18 October-15 December, Sunday dinner and Monday

15 rm – †€ 55 ††€ 55, ☕ € 7 – ½ P € 55

Rest – Menu (€ 14 bi), € 21/40 – Carte € 15/50

◆ Unpretentious yet pleasant hostelry (non-smoking) in a mountain setting. Well-kept rooms, sauna and Jacuzzi with view over the countryside. Regional fare generously served; good local and Burgundy wine list.

MONACO (PRINCIPALITY) – 341 F5 – 115 27 – see the end of the guide

MONCEL-LÈS-LUNÉVILLE – 54 Meurthe-et-Moselle – 307 K7 – see Lunéville

MONCOUTANT – 79 Deux-Sèvres – 322 C4 – pop. 3 019 – alt. 180 m – ✉ 79320 38 B1

Paris 403 – Bressuire 16 – Cholet 49 – Niort 54 – La Roche-sur-Yon 79

Syndicat d'initiative, 18, avenue du Maréchal Juin ☎ 05 49 72 78 83, Fax 05 49 72 89 09

St-Pierre rm, VISA

rte de Niort – ☎ 05 49 72 88 88

30 rm – †€ 49/53 ††€ 59/62, ☕ € 7 – ½ P € 44/49

Rest – *(Closed Friday dinner and Sunday dinner)*
Menu (€ 14 bi), € 19/45 – Carte € 30/50

◆ The dining room of this recent construction with wooden facade faces due south. Wood frame ceiling and garden view (small pond). Functional rooms.

MONDEMENT-MONTGIVROUX – 51 Marne – 306 E10 – see Sézanne

MONDOUBLEAU – 41 Loir-et-Cher – 318 C4 – pop. 1 509 – alt. 170 m – ✉ 41170 Châteaux of the Loire 11 B2

Paris 170 – Blois 62 – Chartres 74 – Châteaudun 40 – Le Mans 64 – Orléans 92

Office de tourisme, 2, rue Bizieux ☎ 02 54 80 77 08, Fax 02 54 80 77 08

Le Grand Monarque
2 r. Chrétien – 02 54 80 92 10 – legrandmonarque@wanadoo.fr – Fax 02 54 80 77 40 – Closed 26 October-4 November, 24 December-4 January, Sunday except lunch from March to December and Monday
12 rm – €53 €53, €9 – ½ P €59
Rest – Menu (€20 bi), €24/28 – Carte approx. €40
◆ Alongside a region dear to the Kings of France, an old posthouse to welcome you... in princely style! Cool bedrooms await you. Modern dining room with well laid and well spaced tables. Pleasant terrace under the wisteria. Traditional cooking.

MONDRAGON – **84 Vaucluse** – **332** B8 – **pop. 3 363** – **alt. 40 m** – ✉ 84430 40 **A2**

Paris 640 – Avignon 45 – Montélimar 40 – Nyons 41 – Orange 17

La Beaugravière with rm
N 7 – 04 90 40 82 54 – www.beaugraviere.com – labeaugraviere84@wanadoo.fr – Fax 04 90 40 91 01 – Closed 15-30 September, Sunday dinner and Monday
4 rm – €65/100 €65/100, €8
Rest – Menu €28/110 – Carte €50/125
◆ This Provencal restaurant has a fine dining room with fireplace and shaded terrace. It serves classic cuisine with truffle specialties in season, and an excellent wine list.

MONEIN – **64 Pyrénées-Atlantiques** – **342** I3 – **pop. 4 393** – **alt. 154 m** – ✉ 64360 3 **B3**

Paris 799 – Pau 23 – Navarrenx 20 – Oloron-Sainte-Marie 21 – Orthez 29

L'Auberge des Roses
quartier Loupien – 05 59 21 45 63 – aubergedesroses@orange.fr – Fax 05 59 21 45 63 – Closed 6-29 July, 21 February-10 March, Monday and Wednesday
Rest – Menu €23 (weekdays)/35 – Carte €30/43
◆ Located in a residential district, this restaurant is surrounded by vines (Jurançon). Enjoy appetising modern cuisine in well-decorated dining rooms or on the shaded terrace.

MONESTIER-DE-CLERMONT – **38 Isère** – **333** G8 – **pop. 921** – **alt. 825 m** – ✉ **38650** **French Alps** 45 **C2**

Paris 598 – Grenoble 36 – La Mure 29 – Serres 72 – Sisteron 107

Office de tourisme, 103 bis, Grand Rue 04 76 34 15 99, Fax 04 76 34 15 99

Au Sans Souci
at St-Paul-lès- Monestier, 2 km northwest on D 8 - alt. 800 – 04 76 34 03 60 – www.au-sans-souci.com – au.sans.souci@club-internet.fr – Fax 04 76 34 17 38 – Closed Sunday evening and Monday
12 rm – €43 €60/75, €8
Rest – Menu (€15), €19 (weekdays)/49 – Carte €38/48
◆ Unlike "the passing trade," you will enjoy tarrying in this old sawmill covered in virginia creeper. Rustic bedrooms. A family-run business since 1934, serving tasty cuisine prepared with market produce.

Piot
7 chemin des Chambons – 04 76 34 07 35 – www.hotel-piot.fr – hotepiot@club-internet.fr – Fax 04 76 34 12 74 – Open 15 March-15 November and closed Tuesday dinner and Monday except July-August and Tuesday lunch
14 rm – €40/50 €45/58, €8,50 – ½ P €60
Rest – Menu (€16), €19 (weekdays)/33 – Carte €35/60
◆ Impressive 1912 villa in a small park planted with century-old pines. Simple, well-kept bedrooms and friendly atmosphere. Spacious, recently decorated dining room, pleasant terrace shaded by conifers and traditional cooking.

LE MONÊTIER-LES-BAINS – **05 Hautes-Alpes** – **334** H3 – **see Serre-Chevalier**

LA MONGIE – 65 Hautes-Pyrénées – **342** N5 – **Winter sports : 1 800/2 500 m** 3 41 – ✉ 65200 Bagneres de Bigorre 28 **A3**
Languedoc-Roussillon-Tarn Gorges

Paris 853 – Bagnères-de-Bigorre 25 – Bagnères-de-Luchon 72 – Tarbes 48

Office de tourisme, place de la Grenouillere ✆ 05 62 91 94 15, Fax 05 62 95 33 13

Le Taoulet ≤★★ North by cable car - Col du Tourmalet★★: 4 km.

Pic du Midi de Bigorre★★★.

Northeast 8 km by D 918 – ✉ 65710 Campan

La Maison d'Hoursentut rest, VISA
– ✆ *05 62 91 89 42 – www.maison-hoursentut.com – contact@maison-hoursentut.com – Fax 05 62 91 88 13*
13 rm – €60/65 €60/65, €8 – ½ P €58/61
Rest – *(dinner only) (number of covers limited, pre-book)* Menu €20
◆ Contemporary, mountain-style décor and a warm atmosphere in this small hotel providing charming rooms, a lounge with fireplace and a pretty garden with a Norwegian-style bath. The menu is announced by the waiters. Featuring a terrace on the banks of the Adour.

MONHOUDOU – 72 Sarthe – **310** K5 – **pop. 199** – **alt. 130 m** – ✉ 72260 35 **D1**

Paris 199 – Alençon 30 – Le Mans 42 – Nantes 223

Château de Monhoudou rest, VISA AE
2 km south on the D 117 and minor road – ✆ *06 83 35 39 12 – www.monhoudou.com – info@monhoudou.com – Fax 02 43 33 11 58*
5 rm – €100/160 €100/160 – ½ P €92/122
Table d'hôte – Menu €42 bi/69 bi
◆ In the midst of an English style park (free roaming animals), this beautiful Renaissance château (16-18C) has been in the same family for 19 generations. Large, elegant rooms with antique furniture, lounge with fireplace and library. Meals are prepared by the lady of the house.

MONNAIE – 37 Indre-et-Loire – **317** N4 – **pop. 3 835** – **alt. 113 m** – ✉ 37380 11 **B2**

Paris 227 – Château-Renault 15 – Tours 16 – Vouvray 10

Au Soleil Levant A/C VISA AE
53 r. Nationale – ✆ *02 47 56 10 34 – www.achat-touraine.com/ausoleillevant. – didier.frebout@orange.fr – Fax 02 47 56 19 97 – Closed 2 weeks in September, Thursday dinner, Sunday dinner and Monday*
Rest – Menu €26/42 – Carte €39/49
◆ This inn on the way through the town is well known for its tasty updated cooking: a hearty stop on the doorstep of the Angers marsh and woodlands.

MONPAZIER – 24 Dordogne – **329** G7 – **pop. 533** – **alt. 180 m** – ✉ 24540 Dordogne-Berry-Limousin 4 **C2**

Paris 575 – Bergerac 47 – Périgueux 75 – Sarlat-la-Canéda 50 – Villeneuve-sur-Lot 46

Office de tourisme, place des Cornières ✆ 05 53 22 68 59, Fax 05 53 74 30 08

Place des Cornières★.

Edward 1er ≤ VISA AE
5 r. St-Pierre – ✆ *05 53 22 44 00 – www.hoteledward1er.com – info@hoteledward1er.com – Fax 05 53 22 57 99 – Open 13 March-14 November*
10 rm – €54/82 €68/158, €12 – 2 suites – ½ P €72/130
Rest – *(open 1st April-31 October and closed Wednesday except July-August) (dinner only) (pre-book)* Menu €30/38
◆ This 19C gentleman's house offers a taste of the good life. High ceilings, mouldings, period furniture and wall hangings. Spacious rooms with a view. Every day the chef creates a set menu based on Périgord produce.

Bistrot 2
Foirail Nord – 05 53 22 60 64 – www.bistrot2.fr – info@bistrot2.fr – Fax 05 53 58 36 27 – Closed 21 November-6 December, 1-13 February, Friday dinner, Saturday lunch, Sunday and Monday from November to April
Rest – Menu (€ 15), € 19 (weekday lunch)/23 – Carte € 23/29
◆ Part of the Edward I's team has taken over this new contemporary bistro, offering enticingly reinterpreted regional recipes. Terrace shaded by wisteria.

MONTAGNAT – 01 Ain – 328 E3 – pop. 1 421 – alt. 262 m – ✉ 01250 44 B1

Paris 447 – Lyon 84 – Bourg-en-Bresse 8 – Mâcon 55 – Oyonnax 56

Au Pot de Grès
2013 rte du Village – 04 74 51 67 05 – franck.provillard@free.fr – Fax 04 74 51 67 05 – Closed Easter holidays, autumn half-term holidays, Sunday dinner, Monday and Tuesday
Rest – Menu (€ 10), € 14 (weekday lunch), € 24/45 – Carte € 34/47
◆ This inviting country home welcomes guests into a dining room lit by an open fire. The chef cleverly reinvents regional dishes using fine produce.

MONTAGNE – 33 Gironde – 335 K5 – pop. 1 684 – alt. 80 m – ✉ 33570 4 C1

Paris 541 – Agen 129 – Bordeaux 41 – Bergerac 61 – Libourne 11

Le Vieux Presbytère
pl. de l'Église – 05 57 74 65 33 – www.restaurant-montagne-st-emilion.com – levieuxpresbytere@orange.fr – Closed 4-27 January, Tuesday and Wednesday
Rest – Menu (€ 16 bi), € 24/54 bi
◆ A restaurant in a former presbytery at the foot of a Romanesque chapel. Cosy, rustic setting, fine courtyard terrace, traditional cuisine and local wines.

MONTAGNE-DU-SEMNOZ – 74 Haute-Savoie – 328 J6 – ✉ 74000 46 F1

French Alps

Paris 552 – Aix-les-Bains 43 – Albertville 60 – Annecy 17 – Chambéry 59

Crêt de Châtillon ✻ ★★★ (**access** by D 41: from Annecy 20 km or from Leschaux Pass 14 km, then 15 mn).

on D 41 – ✉ 74000 Annecy

Les Rochers Blancs
near the summit, alt. 1650 – 04 50 01 23 60 – lesrochersblancs@wanadoo.fr – Fax 04 50 01 40 68 – Closed 15 September-15 December and 15 April-10 June
15 rm – €45 €60/64, €9 – ½ P €60
Rest – *(closed November)* Menu € 18/25 – Carte € 27/35
◆ At an altitude of 1650m, this chalet enjoys an outstanding view and matchless peace and quiet. Renovated rooms in the local style. Restaurant decorated in pure alpine tradition, cuisine in the same vein. Terrace.

MONTAGNY – 42 Loire – 327 E3 – pop. 1 115 – alt. 530 m – ✉ 42840 44 A1

Paris 408 – Lyon 70 – Montbrison 78 – Roanne 15 – St-Étienne 96 – Thizy 7

L'Air du Temps
1 r. de la République – 04 77 66 11 31 – www.lairdutemps42.fr – restaurant.lairdutemps@orange.fr – Fax 04 77 66 15 63 – Closed Sunday dinner and Monday
Rest – Menu € 16 (weekday lunch), € 25/56 – Carte € 35/50
◆ Pastel hues, a contemporary decor and well-spaced round tables in the dining room of this restaurant on the first floor of an old café. Cooking suited to current tastes.

MONTAGNY-LÈS-BEAUNE – 21 Côte-d'Or – 320 J8 – see Beaune

MONTAIGU – 85 Vendée – 316 I6 – pop. 4 822 – alt. 40 m – ✉ 85600 34 B3

Paris 389 – Cholet 36 – Fontenay-le-Comte 88 – Nantes 37 – La Roche-sur-Yon 39

Office de tourisme, 6, rue Georges Clemenceau ✆ 02 51 06 39 17, Fax 02 51 06 39 17

Vendée Memorial ★★: le logis de la Chabotterie★ (historical rooms★★) Southwest: 14 km, le chemin de la Mémoire des Lucs★ Southwest: 24 km **Atlantic Coast.**

at Pont de Sénard 7 km north by N 137 and D 77 – ✉ 85600 St-Hilaire-de-Loulay

Le Pont de Sénard rm, VISA AE
– ✆ 02 51 46 49 50 – www.hotel-pontdesenard.fr – hotel.senard@free.fr – Fax 02 51 94 11 11 – Closed 3-21 August, 30 October-6 November and 26-31 December
25 rm – †€ 52 ††€ 70, ☕ € 8,50 – ½ P € 65
Rest – *(Closed Friday dinner from October to April and Sunday dinner)*
Menu € 23/58 – Carte € 57/84
◆ This hotel overlooking the River Maine has a loyal following drawn here by the delightful, bucolic location, good seminar facilities, and guestrooms which are gradually being renovated. Veranda-dining room and attractive rustic terrace overlooking the river.

MONTAIGUT-LE-BLANC – 63 Puy-de-Dôme – 326 F9 – see Champeix

MONTAREN-ET-ST-MÉDIERS – 30 Gard – 339 L4 – see Uzès

MONTARGIS – 45 Loiret – 318 N4 – pop. 15 700 – alt. 95 m – ✉ 45200 Burgundy-Jura 12 D2

Paris 109 – Auxerre 81 – Bourges 117 – Orléans 73 – Sens 50

Office de tourisme, rue du Port ✆ 02 38 98 00 87, Fax 02 38 98 82 01

de Vaugouard Fontenay-sur-Loing Chemin des Bois, 9 km on the Fontainebleau road, ✆ 02 38 89 79 09

Collection Girodet★ of the museum **M**[1].

Plan on following page

Ibis rm, VISA AE
2 pl. V. Hugo – ✆ 02 38 98 00 68 – www.ibishotel.com – h0861@accor.com – Fax 02 38 89 14 37 Z **b**
59 rm – †€ 56/69 ††€ 56/69, ☕ € 8
Rest *Brasserie de la Poste* – Menu (€ 12), € 21/29 – Carte € 20/43
◆ The bedrooms in this modern and practical hotel provide the chain's usual services. Those on the third floor are particularly well-suited for families. A pleasant retro-style restaurant with glass roof, elegant lighting and red bench seating. Serves bistro-style meals.

Central without rest VISA AE
2 r. Gudin – ✆ 02 38 85 03 07 – www.hotel-montargis.com – info@hotel-montargis.com – Fax 02 38 98 33 39 – Closed 25 December-1st January
12 rm – †€ 48/54 ††€ 60, ☕ € 7 Z **a**
◆ Once a monastery, this fine residence in the town centre was converted into a hotel in the late 20C and renovated in 2004. A carved oak staircase leads to the simple, clean guestrooms.

Dorèle without rest VISA AE
222 r. Émile Mengin – ✆ 02 38 07 18 18 – www.leshotelsdorele.com – contact@leshotelsdorele.com – Fax 02 38 07 18 19 Y **t**
51 rm – †€ 49/65 ††€ 55/65, ☕ € 7
◆ A recent cubic-looking construction in the area around the train station. The rather small rooms are well thought out and have good soundproofing. Comfortable lounge.

MONTARGIS

Anatole-France (Bd) . . . . Y 2
Ancien Palais (R.) . . . . Z 3
Baudin (Bd Paul) . . . . YZ 4
Belles Manières (Bd) . . . . Z 5
Bon-Guillaume (R. du) . . . . . . Z 6
Carnot (R. Lazare) . . . . Y 8
Cormenin (R.) . . . . Z 12
Decourt (R. E.) . . . . Y 13
Dr-Roux (R. du) . . . . Y 15
Dr-Szigeti (Av. du) . . . . Y 16
Dorée (R.) . . . . Z
Ferry (Pl. Jules) . . . . Z 20
Fg de la Chaussée (R. du) YZ 17
Fg d'Orléans (R. du) . . . . . . YZ 18
Jean-Jaurès (R.) . . . . Y 21
Kléber (R.) . . . . Y 22
Laforge (R. R.) . . . . Z 23
Lamy (R. Jean) . . . . Y 24
Longeard (R. du) . . . . Y 26
Moulin à Tan (R.du) . . . . Z 28
Pêcherie (R. de la) . . . . Z 30
Poterne (R. de la) . . . . Z 32
Pougin-de-la-Maisonneuve (R.) . . . . Z 33
Prés.-Roosevelt (R.) . . . . Y 34
République (Pl. de la) . . . . Z 36
Sédillot (R.) . . . . Y 37
Tellier (R. R.) . . . . Z 39
Vaublanc (R. de) . . . . Z 41
Verdun (Av. de) . . . . Y 42
18-Juin-1940 (Pl. du) . . . . Z 45

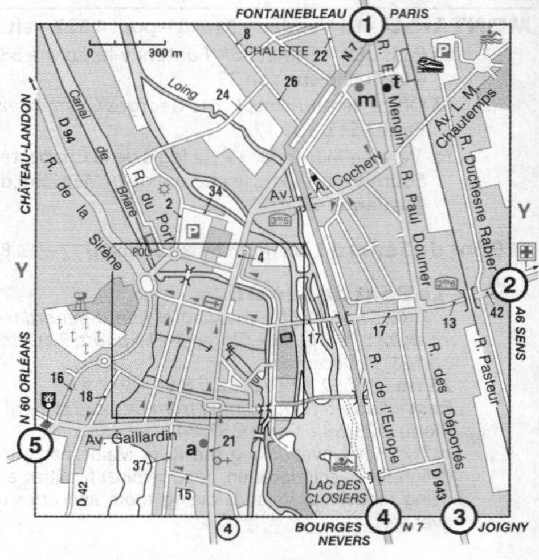

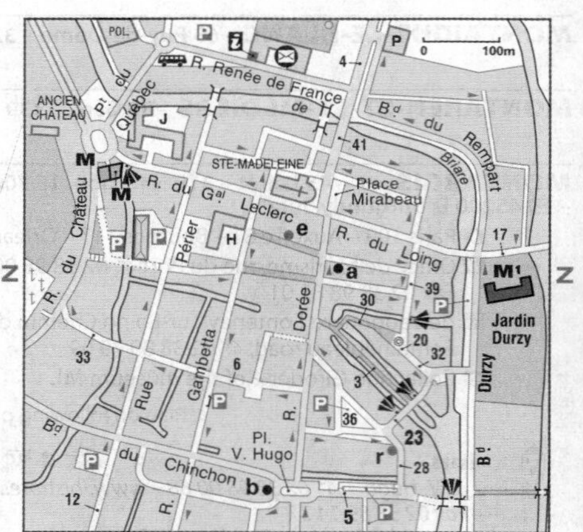

ⅩⅩⅩ **La Gloire** (Jean-Claude Martin) with rm — rest, VISA AE
✿ *74 av. Gén. de Gaulle – ✆ 02 38 85 04 69 – www.lagloire-montargis.com – contact@lagloire-montargis.com – Fax 02 38 98 52 32 – Closed 17 August-3 September, 16 February-11 March, Tuesday and Wednesday* Y **m**
10 rm – †€ 50 ††€ 62/80, ☕ € 9,50
Rest – Menu € 32 (weekdays)/55 – Carte € 68/103
Spec. Salade de homard. Papillote de Saint-Pierre à la ventrèche. Chariot de desserts. **Wines** Sancerre, Menetou-Salon.
◆ Classic setting with bouquets of flowers and a friendly welcome. This establishment is indeed the 'glory' of Montargis. Subtly updated and generous cuisine. Comfortable guest-rooms.

ⅩⅩ **L'Agrappe Cœur** — P VISA AE
22 r. Jean Jaurès – ✆ 02 38 85 22 65 – www.restaurant-agrappecoeur.com – Closed August, Sunday dinner, Tuesday dinner and Monday Y **a**
Rest – Menu € 21 (weekdays)/37 – Carte € 47/71
◆ Enjoy a pleasant bistro atmosphere in the first dining room adorned with a fine 1930s wooden counter. The other three rooms have a more low-key decor.

Les Dominicaines

6 r. du Dévidet – ✆ 02 38 98 10 22 – www.restaurant-lesdominicaines.com – odile.freddy@wanadoo.fr – Fax 02 38 98 41 41 – Closed 16-31 August, Saturday lunch, Sunday and public holidays Z **e**

Rest – *(pre-book)* Menu (€ 19), € 33 – Carte € 37/70

◆ Displaying Dominican stained-glass windows in the entrance, this restaurant revives the town's history. Cuisine based on seafood and on the Provence region, with fish specialities.

in Amilly 5 km by ③ – pop. 11 800 – alt. 110 m – ✉ 45200

Le Belvédère without rest

192 r. Jules Ferry – ✆ 02 38 85 41 09 – http://perso.wanadoo.fr/hbelvedere – h.belvedere@wanadoo.fr – Fax 02 38 98 75 63 – Closed 9-23 August and 20 December-3 January

24 rm – €52/65 €58/65, ☕ € 7

◆ This family-run hotel, fronted by a flower garden, faces the village school. The small, comfortable and peaceful rooms have personal touches.

in Conflans-sur-Loing 7 km by ③ – pop. 356 – alt. 100 m – ✉ 45700

Auberge de Conflans

– ✆ 02 38 94 75 46 – Fax 02 38 94 75 46 – Closed 10-31 August, 20-28 December, February, Tuesday dinner, Wednesday dinner, Thursday dinner, Sunday dinner and Monday

Rest – Menu (€ 13 bi), € 21/32 – Carte € 46/58

◆ Charming and elegant village inn with a rustic atmosphere. The gracious owner maintains the conviviality with refined traditional dishes.

Ferrières road by ①, N 7 and secondary road – ✉ 45210 Fontenay-sur-Loing

Domaine de Vaugouard

chemin des Bois – ✆ 02 38 89 79 00 – www.vaugouard.com – info@vaugouard.com – Fax 02 38 89 79 01 – Closed 20-30 December

67 rm – € 140/240 € 140/240, ☕ € 18 – ½ P € 165/215

Rest – Menu (€ 21), € 49/55 – Carte € 30/45

◆ Attractive 18C château in the heart of a golf course. Comfortable, elegant rooms (renovated). Those in the annexe are larger. Small, opulent dining rooms, terrace facing the golf course, and classic cuisine.

MONTAUBAN Ⓟ – 82 Tarn-et-Garonne – 337 E7 – pop. 53 200 – alt. 98 m – ✉ 82000 Languedoc-Roussillon-Tarn Gorges 28 **B2**

Paris 627 – Agen 86 – Albi 73 – Auch 86 – Cahors 64 – Toulouse 53

Office de tourisme, place Prax Paris ✆ 05 63 63 60 60, Fax 05 63 63 65 12

des Aiguillons Route de Loubejac, N : 8 km on D 959, ✆ 05 63 31 35 40

Old Montauban★: portal★ of Hôtel Lefranc-de-Pompignan Z **E** - Musée Ingres★ - Place Nationale★ - Last dying Centaur★ (bronze by Bourdelle) **B.**

Pente d'eau de Montech★: 15 km by ③ and D 928.

Plan on following page

Crowne Plaza

6-8 quai de Verdun – ✆ 05 63 22 00 00 – www.crowneplaza-montauban.com – contact@cp-montauban.com – Fax 05 63 22 00 01 Z **t**

80 rm – € 147/210 € 147/210, ☕ € 20 – 4 suites

Rest *La Table des Capucins* – *(closed 9-23 August and Sunday)* Menu € 30 (weekday lunch), € 42/85 – Carte € 60/80

Spec. Dégustation autour de la tomate (spring-summer). Ris de veau aux truffes. Soufflé au Grand Marnier. **Wines** Vin de Pays des Côtes du Tarn, Vin de Pays du Comté Tolosan.

◆ Although the decor and comfort are very contemporary, the monastic aura of this listed convent (1630) has been well preserved. Fully equipped spa to re-energise both body and soul and creative cuisine with a strong focus on flavour and authenticity.

MONTAUBAN

Abbaye (R. de l') . . . . Z
Alsace-Lorraine (Bd) . . . . . . X 3
Arago (R.) . . . . Z
Banque (R. de la) . . . . Z
Barbazan (R.) . . . . Z
Bourdelle (Pl.) . . . . Z 4
Bourjade (Pl. L.) . . . . Z 6
Briand (Av. A.) . . . . Y 7
Cambon (R.) . . . . Z 9
Carmes (R. des) . . . . Z 10
Chamier (Av.) . . . . Y 12
Cladel (R. L.) X
Comédie (R. de la) . . . . Z 13
Consul-Dupuy (Allée du) . . . Z 14
Coq (Pl. du) . . . . Z 16
Dr-Alibert (R.) X
Dr-Lacaze (R. du) . . . . Z 19
Doumerc (Bd B.) X
Foch (Pl. du Mar.) . . . . Z
Fort (R. du) . . . . Z
Gambetta (Av.) . . . . YZ
Garrisson (Bd G.) . . . . YZ
Gaulle (Av. Ch.-de) . . . . Y 25
Grand'Rue Sapiac . . . . Z
Grand'Rue Villenouvelle . . . . X 28
Guibert (Pl.) . . . . Z 29
Herriot (Av. É.) . . . . Y 30
Hôtel-de-Ville (R. de l') . . . . Z 31
Ingres (R. D.) X
Jourdain (R. A.) . . . . Z
Lacapelle (Fg) . . . . YZ
Lafon (R. du Pasteur L.) . . . Y 34
Lafon (R. Mary) . . . . Z 32
Lagrange (R. L.) . . . . YZ 35
Leclerc (Pl. du Gén.) . . . . . . Z
Libération (Pl. de la) X
Lycée (R. du) . . . . Z
Malcousinat (R.) . . . . Z 36
Mandoune (R. de la) . . . . . . Z
Marceau-Hamecher (Av.) . . . Y 37
Marre (R. H.) . . . . Z
Martyrs (Carrefour des) . . . Z 46
Marty (Pl. A.) . . . . XY
Mayenne (Av.) . . . . Y 50
Michelet (R.) . . . . Z 51
Midi-Pyrénées (Bd) . . . . Z 52
Monet (R. J.) . . . . Z 53
Montauriol (Bd) . . . . Y
Montmurat (Q. de) . . . . Z 54
Mortarieu (Allées de) . . . . . Z 56
Moustier (Fg du) . . . . Z
Nationale (Pl.) . . . . Z
Notre-Dame (R.) . . . . Z 60
Piquard (Sq Gén.) . . . . Z 62
Pouvillon (R. E.) . . . . Z
Prax-Paris (Pl.) . . . . Z
République (R. de la) . . . . . Z 63
Résistance (R. de la) . . . . . . Z 64
Roosevelt (Pl. F.) . . . . Z 66
Ste-Claire (R.) . . . . Z
St-Jean (R.) . . . . X 67
Sapiac (Pont de) . . . . YZ 68
Sarrail (R. Gén.) . . . . Y 70
Verdun (Q. de) . . . . Z 71
10e-Dragons (Av. du) X
11e-Rég.-d'Infanterie (Av. du) . . . . X 73
19-Août-1944 (Av. du) . . . . . X 75
22-Septembre (Pl. du) . . . . . Z 76

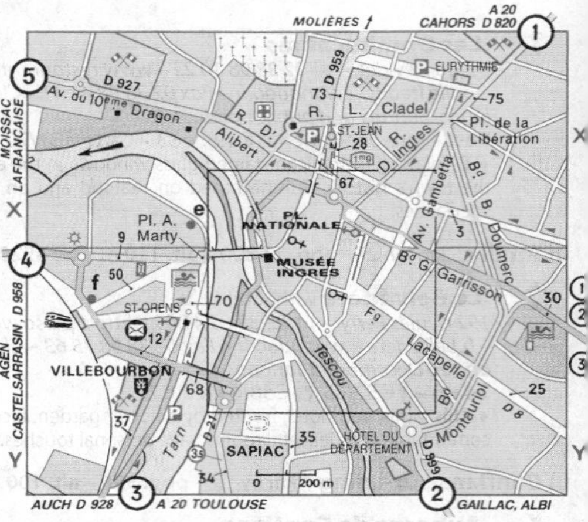

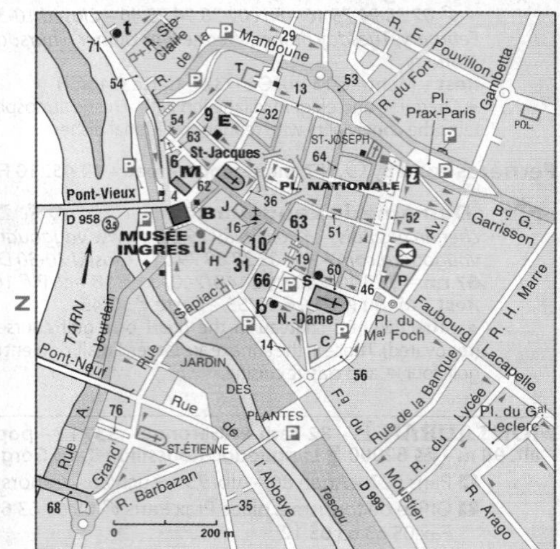

Mercure

12 r. Notre-Dame – ✆ 05 63 63 17 23 – h2183@accor.com – Fax 05 63 66 43 66 Z **s**

44 rm – †€ 94/117 ††€ 104/127, ☕ € 12

Rest – Menu € 15/35 – Carte approx. € 35

◆ This 18C private mansion was completely renovated in 1999. The rooms are spacious and contemporary and are well sound-proofed. The dining room furnished in Louis XVI-style is topped by a vast glass roof.

Du Commerce without rest

9 pl. Roosevelt – ✆ 05 63 66 31 32 – www.hotel-commerce-montauban.com – info@hotel-commerce-montauban.com – Fax 05 63 66 31 28 – Closed 22 December-3 January Z **b**

27 rm – †€ 57/60 ††€ 57/79, ☕ € 9

◆ A large, 18C hotel near the cathedral with a reception and lounge featuring lovely antique furniture. Simple, well-kept guestrooms and colourfully decorated bathrooms.

XXX **Les Saveurs d'Ingres** A/C VISA MC

13 r. Hôtel de Ville – ✆ 05 63 91 26 42 – www.saveursdingres.com
– Closed 18-25 May, 17 August-1st September and Sunday Z **u**

Rest – Menu € 28 (lunch), € 42/75 – Carte € 60/70

◆ This restaurant's name pays tribute to the Montauban artist (Ingres museum nearby). Pleasant vaulted dining room with modern furniture. Local dishes with personal touches.

XX **La Cuisine d'Alain** A/C VISA MC AE

29 r. Roger Salengro, (opposite the station) – ✆ 05 63 66 06 66
– www.hotel-restaurant-orsay.com – cuisinedalain@wanadoo.fr
– Fax 05 63 66 19 39 – Closed 1st-9 May, 1st-20 August, 20 December-5 January, Monday lunch, Saturday lunch and Sunday Y **f**

Rest – Menu € 24 bi (weekday lunch), € 36/65 – Carte € 45/60

◆ Dining room and lounge adorned with still life paintings, china and flower arrangements. Attractive terrace. Traditional cuisine; extensive choice of desserts.

XX **Au Fil de l'Eau** A/C VISA MC

14 quai Dr Lafforgue – ✆ 05 63 66 11 85 – www.aufildeleau82.com
– aufildeleau82@wanadoo.fr – Fax 05 63 91 97 56
– Closed 16-23 February, Wednesday dinner except July-August, Sunday except lunch from September to June and Monday X **e**

Rest – Menu (€ 18), € 35/55 – Carte € 43/70

◆ This old-style house in a quiet street is home to a spacious and modern restaurant serving traditional meals and with a good selection of regional wines.

Good food and accommodation at moderate prices?
Look for the Bib symbols: red Bib Gourmand for food,
blue Bib Hotel for hotels.

MONTAUBAN-SUR-L'OUVÈZE – 26 Drôme – 332 G8 – pop. 113 – alt. 719 m – ✉ 26170 45 **C3**

Paris 705 – Apt 68 – Carpentras 64 – Lyon 243

La Badiane VISA MC AE

Hamlet of Ruissas, 3 km north-east – ✆ 04 75 27 17 74
– www.la-badiane-sejours.com – la-badiane@club-internet.fr – Fax 04 75 27 17 74
– Open from Easter to 1st November

7 rm – € 108/123 € 121/136

Rest – table d'hôte – *(closed Wednesday and Sunday) (dinner only) (residents only)* Menu € 29

◆ Originally a barn, this hotel located in the Drôme mountains has been restored with originality. Individually-styled rooms, pool, sauna and relaxation facilities. Family cuisine served in a charming dining area with a Mediterranean touch or on the terrace.

MONTAUROUX – 83 Var – 340 P4 – pop. 4 526 – alt. 364 m – ✉ 83440 French Riviera 41 **C3**

Paris 890 – Cannes 36 – Draguignan 37 – Fréjus 30 – Grasse 21

Office de tourisme, place du Clos ✆ 04 94 47 75 90, Fax 04 94 47 61 97

Grasse road 3 km Southeast – ✉ 83340 Montauroux

XX ✿ **Auberge des Fontaines d'Aragon** (Eric Maio) P VISA MC AE

D 37 – ✆ 04 94 47 71 65
– www.fontaines-daragon.com – ericmaio@club-internet.fr – Fax 04 94 39 85 23
– Closed 26 October-5 November, 4-27 January, Monday and Tuesday

Rest – Menu (€ 28), € 52/95

Spec. Hamburger de figues, foie gras de canard poêlé et focaccia aux truffes (August-September). Pigeon en croûte farci de truffes, blettes et foie gras. Tarte au citron contemporaine (January to March). **Wines** Vin de Pays du Var, Côtes de Provence.

◆ Delicious, modern cuisine served in an elegant Provencal style dining room or on the delightful terrace: a great place for a meal on the way to St Cassien lake.

MONTBARD – 21 Côte-d'Or – **320** G4 – **pop. 5 815 – alt. 221 m** 8 **C2**
– ✉ **21500** Burgundy-Jura

Paris 240 – Autun 87 – Auxerre 81 – Dijon 81 – Troyes 100

Office de tourisme, place Henri Vincenot ✆ 03 80 92 53 81, Fax 03 80 89 17 38

Parc Buffon★.

Abbaye de Fontenay★★★ East: 6 km by D 905.

L'Écu

7 r. A. Carré – ✆ 03 80 92 11 66 – www.hotel-de-l-ecu.fr – snc.coupat@wanadoo.fr – Fax 03 80 92 14 13 – Closed 21 February-8 March, Friday dinner, Sunday dinner and Saturday from 11 November to 8 March

23 rm – €62/68 €76/90, €11 – ½ P €74/85 **Rest** – Menu €21/45

◆ This 16C former post house provides a friendly welcome, country-style hospitality and features standard rooms and public areas. Restaurant serving traditional cuisine under the vaulted ceiling of the former stables or in the stylish dining area. Courtyard terrace.

in St-Rémy **3 km west on the D 905 – pop. 814 – alt. 207 m – ✉ 21500**

La Mirabelle

1 r. de la Brenne – ✆ 03 80 92 40 69 – lamirabelle2@free.fr – Closed 19 August-21 September and 24 December-6 January

Rest – *(number of covers limited, pre-book)* Menu €19 (weekdays), €28/38 – Carte €44/61

◆ Near the canal, this former salt warehouse is home to a fine stone-vaulted dining room. Warm ambiance and tasty traditional cooking.

MONTBAZON – 37 Indre-et-Loire – **317** N5 – **pop. 3 713 – alt. 59 m** 11 **B2**
– ✉ **37250** Châteaux of the Loire

Paris 247 – Châtellerault 59 – Chinon 41 – Loches 33 – Saumur 73 – Tours 15

Office de tourisme, esplanade du Val de l'Indre ✆ 02 47 26 97 87, Fax 02 47 26 22 42

Château d'Artigny

2 km southwest by D 17 – ✆ 02 47 34 30 30 – www.artigny.com – artigny@grandesetapes.fr – Fax 02 47 34 30 39

61 rm – €165/480 €165/480, €22 – 2 suites

Rest – Menu (€50 bi), €60 (dinner), €90/125 bi – Carte €50/80

◆ This château with its wooded grounds and French-style gardens was designed in the 1920s by the perfumer Coty. Pure classical style and omnipresent splendour. Classic cuisine, excellent selection of wines and vintage armagnacs.

Moulin d' Artigny

7 rm – €90 €90, €22

◆ This pretty riverside pavilion, 800m from the château, offers rustic, less luxurious accommodation in a bucolic vein.

Domaine de la Tortinière

rte de Ballan-Veigné, 2 km north on D 910 and D 287 – ✆ 02 47 34 35 00 – www.tortiniere.com – domaine.tortiniere@wanadoo.fr – Fax 02 47 65 95 70 – Closed 20 December-28 February

25 rm – €130/170 €130/270, €17 – 5 suites – ½ P €125/195

Rest – *(closed Sunday dinner from November to March) (pre-book)* Menu (€32 bi), €39 bi (lunch), €43/60 – Carte €43/53

◆ A Second Empire château in the grounds of a park overlooking the Indre. Elegant bedrooms full of charm. Pleasant swimming pool. Classic, tasteful dining rooms, opening onto the valley landscape. Modern menu.

Chancelière "Jeu de Cartes"

1 pl. Marronniers – ✆ 02 47 26 00 67 – www.lachanceliere.fr – lachanceliere@lachanceliere.fr – Fax 02 47 73 14 82 – Closed 9-26 August, 2-15 January, Sunday and Monday except public holidays

Rest – Menu €36/42

Spec. Crumble de saumon et avruga au chèvre frais (spring-summer). Escalopes de foie gras aux figues (autumn). Gâteau du prélat. **Wines** Montlouis, Bourgueil.

◆ An elegant regional-style building featuring a range of interior styles, including a cosy dining area with colourful décor. Inventive and classic cuisine.

West 5 km by D 910, D 287 and D 87 – ✉ **37250 Montbazon**

XX **Le Moulin Fleuri** with rm

rte du Ripault – 02 47 26 01 12 – www.moulin-fleuri.com – lemoulinfleuri@wanadoo.fr – Fax 02 47 34 04 71 – Closed 17-25 December, from 22 January to end February, Sunday dinner from 12 November to 30 March, Thursday lunch and Monday

10 rm – €78 €78/113, €11

Rest – Menu (€22), €31/51 – Carte approx. €41

◆ This 16C former flourmill was once powered by a branch of the Indre River. Traditional recipes with a local flavour, superb cellar with over 800 wines, and waterside terrace. Classically furnished guestrooms with views of the river or garden.

Look out for red symbols, indicating particularly pleasant establishments.

MONTBÉLIARD – 25 Doubs – **321** K1 – **pop. 26 500** – **Built-up area 113 059** – **alt. 325 m** – ✉ **25200** Burgundy-Jura 17 **C1**

Paris 477 – Belfort 22 – Besançon 76 – Mulhouse 60 – Vesoul 60

Office de tourisme, 1, rue Henri-Mouhot 03 81 94 45 60, Fax 03 81 94 14 04

de Prunevelle Dampierre-sur-le-Doubs Ferme des Petits Bans, 8 km on the Besançon road, 03 81 98 11 77

Old Montbéliard★: hôtel Beurnier-Rossel★ - Sochaux: Musée de l'aventure Peugeot★★.

Plan on following page

Bristol without rest

2 r. Velotte – 03 81 94 43 17 – www.hotel-bristol-montbeliard.com – hotel.bristol@wanadoo.fr – Fax 03 81 94 15 29 Z **b**

48 rm – €58/66 €63/72, €8

◆ A meticulously renovated 1930s hotel. Pretty interior decor, cosy rooms and an authentic tea room (many varieties of tea).

Aux Relais Verts rm,

le Pied des Gouttes – 03 81 90 10 69 – www.hotelrelaisvert.net – hotelrelaisvert@wanadoo.fr – Fax 03 81 90 15 18 – Closed 24 December-4 January X **v**

64 rm – €72/93 €72/93, €8 – ½ P €93/116

Rest *Le Tire Bouchon* – *(closed Saturday lunch and Sunday)*

Menu €18/44 – Carte €28/78

◆ A modern hotel in an urban development zone with small functional rooms that are arranged around a patio, or in a new wing where they are warmer and more spacious. Houseplants and paintings enliven the subdued decor in the dining room.

XXX **Le St-Martin** (Olivier Prevot-Carme)

1 r. Gén. Leclerc – 03 81 91 18 37 – lesaintmartin.montbeliard@orange.fr – Fax 03 81 91 18 37 – Closed 2-8 March, 1st-24 August, 1st-5 January, Saturday, Sunday and public holidays Z **u**

Rest – Menu €29 (weekdays)/65 – Carte €45/59

Spec. Fricassée de grenouilles au beurre demi-sel (spring). Féra aux morilles et risotto au vin jaune (spring and autumn). Crème de mascarpone au vin jaune et morilles. **Wines** Côtes du Jura-Savagnin, Klevener de Heiligenstein.

◆ This old house hides a charming restaurant that is both intimate and luxurious. Fairly inventive regional cuisine, a menu that changes in line with the market and fish specialities.

XX **Joseph**

17 r. de Belfort – 03 81 91 20 02 – Fax 03 81 91 88 99 – Closed 14-31 August, Sunday and Monday Z **a**

Rest – Carte €50/61

◆ Charming welcome from the owners of this well-presented restaurant. Traditional cuisine (some local dishes) based on fresh, seasonal produce.

MONTBÉLIARD

MONTBENOÎT – 25 Doubs – 321 I5 – pop. 282 – alt. 804 m – ✉ 25650 17 C2
Burgundy-Jura

Paris 464 – Besançon 61 – Morteau 17 – Pontarlier 15

Office de tourisme, 8, rue du Val Saugeais ✆ 03 81 38 10 32, Fax 03 81 38 10 32

Former abbey★: stalls★★, abbey church niche★★.

in La Longeville 5.5 km North by D 131 – pop. 591 – alt. 900 m – ✉ 25650

Le Crêt l'Agneau

Les Auberges – ✆ 03 81 38 12 51 – www.lecret-lagneau.com – lecret.lagneau@wanadoo.fr

5 rm – †€ 70 ††€ 79/102 **Table d'hôte** – Menu € 26/29 bi

◆ This 17C farmhouse in the countryside with very well-kept rooms, is run by a dynamic pair. Cosy ambiance particular to houses in the region. Local-style cuisine, cooked with care, and homemade bread.

in Maisons-du-Bois 4 km Southwest on D 437 – pop. 494 – alt. 810 m – ✉ 25650

Du Saugeais

– ✆ 03 81 38 14 65 – www.hotel-du-saugeais.com – Fax 03 81 38 11 27 – Closed 15-30 January, Sunday dinner and Monday

Rest – Menu € 15 (weekdays)/38 – Carte € 25/40

◆ Family roadside inn serving regional specialities in a country style dining room.

MONTBOUCHER-SUR-JABRON – 26 Drôme – 332 B6 – see Montélimar

MONTBRAS – 55 Meuse – 307 F7 – pop. 27 – alt. 315 m – ✉ 55140 26 B2

Paris 290 – Metz 117 – Bar-le-Duc 61 – Nancy 66 – Vandœuvre-lès-Nancy 52

Hostellerie de l'Isle en Bray without rest

3 r. des Erables – ✆ 03 29 90 49 90 – www.chateau-montbras.com – contact@hib.com – Fax 03 29 90 82 23 – Open Easter-1st November

5 rm – †€ 70 ††€ 90/120 – 2 suites

◆ A superb listed Renaissance château (parkland, parade courtyard, chapel) with stylish, spacious, comfortable and beautifully peaceful rooms. Sweeping views of the countryside.

MONTBRISON – 42 Loire – 327 D6 – pop. 14 589 – alt. 391 m 44 A2
– ✉ 42600 Lyon - Rhone Valley

Paris 444 – Lyon 103 – Le Puy-en-Velay 99 – Roanne 68 – St-Étienne 45 – Thiers 68

Office de tourisme, cloître de Cordeliers ✆ 04 77 96 08 69, Fax 04 77 96 20 88

de Savigneux-les-Étangs Savigneux Gaia concept Savigneux, E : 4 km on D 496, ✆ 04 77 58 70 74

Superflu Golf Club Saint-Romain-le-Puy Domaine des Sucs, SE : 8 km on D 8, ✆ 04 77 76 93 41

Interior★ of N.-D.-d'Espérance collegiate church.

La Roseraie

61 av. Alsace-Lorraine, (opposite the station) – ✆ 04 77 58 15 33 – www.restaurantlaroseraie.com – j-p.tholoniat@wanadoo.fr – Fax 04 77 58 93 88 – Closed 14-25 April, 16 August-6 September, 13 January-4 February, Sunday dinner, Tuesday dinner and Wednesday

Rest – Menu (€ 15), € 18 (weekdays)/56 – Carte € 19/54

◆ In the former terminus (1896), modern fare made with local produce is served. Enjoy in a colourful dining room or on the veranda or terrace in the shade of a lime tree.

in Savigneux 2 km East by D 496 – pop. 3 066 – alt. 382 m – ✉ 42600

Marytel without rest
95 rte de Lyon – ✆ 04 77 58 72 00 – www.hotel-marytel.com – hm4203@inter-hotel.com – Fax 04 77 58 42 81
47 rm – †€ 48/85 ††€ 53/95, ☕ € 8
◆ Practical roadside hotel. A new wing, the Relais Alice, offers very modern rooms equipped with the latest hi-tech gadgets. Double-glazing throughout.

Yves Thollot
93 rte de Lyon – ✆ 04 77 96 10 40 – www.yves-thollot.com – mail@yves-thollot.com – Fax 04 77 58 31 92 – Closed 3-24 August, 15-28 February, Sunday dinner, Tuesday dinner and Monday
Rest – Menu € 23/58 – Carte € 40/58
◆ A modern house surrounded by greenery. Several large dining rooms and a shaded terrace invite guests to sample simply prepared, hearty traditional meals.

in St-Romain-le-Puy 8 km southeast on the D 8 and D 107 – pop. 2 803 – alt. 405 m – ✉ 42610

Sous le Pic-La Pérolière without rest
20 r. Jean-Moulin – ✆ 04 77 76 97 10 – www.laperoliere.com – laperoliere@wanadoo.fr – Fax 04 77 76 97 10 – Closed 2 January-28 February
4 rm ☕ – †€ 49/62 ††€ 59/72
◆ A haven of peace and quiet at the foot of an 11C priory. Antique and wrought iron furniture adorn this late 19C Forèze farmhouse. Breakfast is served in the conservatory overlooking the garden in summer.

MONTCEAU-LES-MINES – 71 Saône-et-Loire – 320 G9 8 C3

– pop. 19 400 – Built-up area 92 000 – alt. 285 m – ✉ 71300 Burgundy-Jura

Paris 333 – Autun 47 – Chalon-sur-Saône 46 – Mâcon 69 – Moulins 100
Office de tourisme, 16, rue Carnot ✆ 03 85 69 00 00, Fax 03 85 69 00 01
du Château d'Avoise Montchanin 9 rue de Mâcon, 14 km on the Chalon-sur-Saône road, ✆ 03 85 78 19 19
Mont-St-Vincent: tower ☀★★ 12 km by ②.

Plan on next page

Nota Bene
70 quai Jules Chagot – ✆ 03 85 69 10 15 – www.notabene.fr – nota.bene.hotel@wanadoo.fr – Fax 03 85 69 10 20 AZ **b**
46 rm – †€ 39/62 ††€ 62/72, ☕ € 7 – ½ P € 55/82
Rest – Menu (€ 14), € 18/30 – Carte € 20/32
◆ Set opposite the canal bridge, this hotel has a distinctive light wood façade. Comfortable rooms; those in the annexe are more spacious. Squash courts and gym. Wide choice of traditional dishes served in the restaurant.

Le France (Jérôme Brochot)
7 pl. Beaubernard – ✆ 03 85 67 95 30 – www.jeromebrochot.com – lefrance@jeromebrochot.com – Fax 03 85 67 95 44 – Closed 2-10 March, 3-24 August, 5-12 January, Saturday lunch, Sunday dinner and Monday AZ **k**
Rest – Menu (€ 20), € 40/80 – Carte € 49/80
Spec. Filet de bœuf charolais confit et rond de gite en carpaccio. Sandre de Saône en croustillant de chèvre sec du Charolais (from April to July). Sorbet au foin et galette croustillante d'épeautre. **Wines** Rully, Givry
◆ This restaurant in the upper part of town houses an elegant, contemporary dining room in beige and white tones. Inventive cuisine with a classic underpinning.

in Galuzot 5 km southwest by ③ and D 974 – ✉ 71230 St-Vallier

Le Moulin
– ✆ 03 85 57 18 85 – Closed 19 August-2 September, 18 February-4 March, Sunday dinner, Tuesday dinner and Wednesday
Rest – Menu (€ 16), € 20/39 – Carte € 20/50
◆ This restaurant on the banks of the attractive Canal du Centre features a country-style dining area, and another room with a more refined and modern atmosphere. Serves traditional meals.

MONTCEAU-LES-MINES

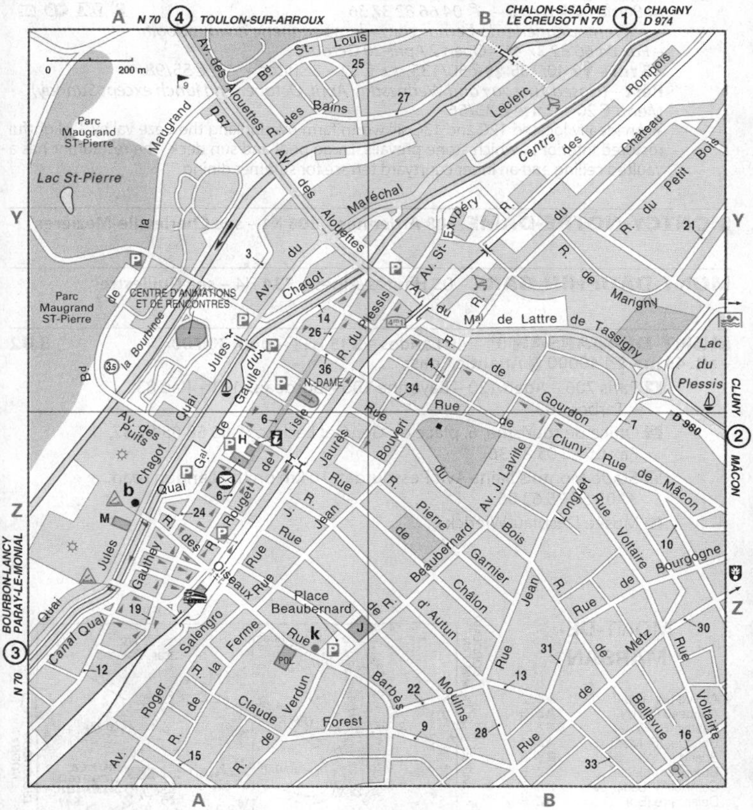

MONTCENIS – 71 Saône-et-Loire – 320 G9 – see le Creusot

MONTCHAUVET – 78 Yvelines – 311 F2 – pop. 290 – alt. 100 m – ✉ 78790 18 A2

Paris 67 – Dreux 33 – Évreux 47 – Mantes-la-Jolie 16 – Rambouillet 39 – Versailles 49

XX **La Jument Verte** VISA MC AE

6 pl. de l'Église – ☎ 01 30 93 43 60 – Fax 01 30 93 49 20 – Closed 1st-15 September and 15-28 February

Rest – Carte € 42/55

◆ Named after a novel by Marcel Aymé, this restaurant has a terrace on the village square and country style interior (exposed beams, stone and fireplace).

MONTCHENOT – 51 Marne – 306 G8 – see Reims

MONTCLUS – 30 Gard – 339 L3 – pop. 161 – alt. 94 m – ✉ 30630 23 D1

▶ Paris 657 – Alès 46 – Avignon 58 – Bagnols-sur-Cèze 24 – Pont-St-Esprit 25

La Magnanerie de Bernas

rm, P VISA MC AE

at Bernas, 2 km east – ✆ 04 66 82 37 36 – www.magnanerie-de-bernas.com – lamagnanerie@wanadoo.fr – Fax 04 66 82 37 41 – Open 2 April-20 October

15 rm – †€ 40/105 ††€ 50/135, ☕ € 12 – 2 suites – ½ P € 55/98

Rest – *(closed Tuesday and Wednesday April, October and lunch except Sunday)* Menu € 20 – Carte € 33/56

◆ An ideally located 12C and 13C silkworm farm overlooking the Cèze valley. Delightful restored interior in which stone prevails. Large pool and sun deck. The restaurant has a vaulted ceiling and an inner courtyard terrace for summer dining.

MONTCY-NOTRE-DAME – 08 Ardennes – 306 K4 – see Charleville-Mézières

MONT-DAUPHIN-GARE – 05 Hautes-Alpes – 334 H4 – see Guillestre

MONT-DE-MARSAN Ⓟ – 40 Landes – 335 H11 – pop. 30 700 – alt. 43 m – ✉ 40000 Atlantic Coast 3 B2

▶ Paris 706 – Agen 120 – Bayonne 106 – Bordeaux 131 – Pau 83 – Tarbes 103

ℹ Office de tourisme, 6, place du Général Leclerc ✆ 05 58 05 87 37, Fax 05 58 05 87 36

⛳18 Stade Montois Saint-Avit Pessourdat, 10 km on the Langon road, ✆ 05 58 75 63 05

👁 Musée Despiau-Wlérick★.

MONT-DE-MARSAN

Alsace-Lorraine (R. d') . . . AZ 2
Auribeau (Bd d') . . . AZ 3
Bastiat (R. F.) . . . ABZ
Bosquet (R. Mar.) . . . AZ 4
Briand (R. A.) . . . BY 5
Brouchet (Allées) . . . BZ 6
Carnot (Av. Sadi) . . . BZ 7
Delamarre (Bd) . . . BZ 8
Despiau (R. Ch.) . . . AZ 9
Farbos (Allées Raymond) . BZ 10
Gambetta (R. L.) . . . BZ 12
Gaulle (Pl. Ch.-de) . . . BY 13
Gourgues (R. D.-de) . . . BY 14
Landes (R. L.-des) . . . BZ 15
Lasserre (R. Gén.) . . . AZ 16
Lattre-de-Tassigny (Bd de) BY 17
Leclerc (Pl. du Gén.) . . . BZ 18
Lesbazeilles (R. A.) . . . BZ 19
Martinon (R.) . . . BZ 20
Pancaut (Pl. J.) . . . AZ 21
Poincaré (Pl. R.) . . . AY 22
Président-Kennedy (Av. du) . . . BZ 23
Ruisseau (R. du) . . . AZ 24
St-Jean-d'Août (R.) . . . AY 25
St-Roch (Pl.) . . . BZ 26
Victor-Hugo (R.) . . . BY 27
8-Mai-1945 (R. du) . . . BY 28
34e-d'Inf. (Av. du) . . . BZ 29

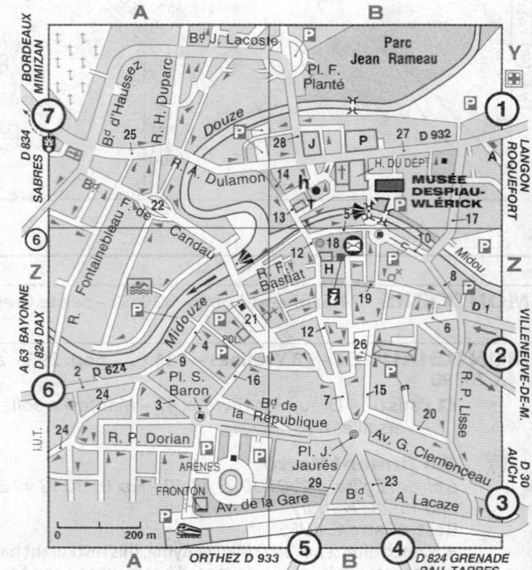

Le Renaissance rm, rm, VISA AE

225 av. de Villeneuve, 2 km via ② – ✆ 05 58 51 51 51 – www.le-renaissance.com – lerenaissance@wanadoo.fr – Fax 05 58 75 29 07

28 rm – 🚹€ 61/82 🚹🚹€ 68/92, ☕ € 8 – 1 suite

Rest – *(closed Sunday except lunch from June to October, Saturday and bank holidays)* Menu (€ 23), € 29/51 – Carte € 32/52

◆ Located slightly out of town, this modern hotel is popular with business clients. The functional rooms are quieter on the garden side. Most have been redecorated. A pleasant restaurant with a view of the pond, serving traditional cuisine with a modern touch.

Abor rm, VISA

112 chemin de Lubet, Grenade road, 3 km on ④ ✉ 40280 – ✆ 05 58 51 58 00 – www.aborhotel.com – contact@aborhotel.com – Fax 05 58 75 78 78

68 rm – 🚹€ 61/72 🚹🚹€ 68/88, ☕ € 8,50 – ½ P € 57/74

Rest – *(closed 24 December-5 January, Saturday lunch and Sunday lunch)* Menu (€ 13), € 16 (weekday lunch), € 23/37 – Carte € 24/51

◆ A modern building on the outskirts of the capital of the Marsan region with small, practical, soundproofed bedrooms. Decor without frills, but careful maintenance. Restaurant with colourful décor, serving traditional cuisine and buffet options.

Richelieu rest, VISA AE

3 r. Wlérick – ✆ 05 58 06 10 20 – www.citotel.com – le.richelieu@wanadoo.fr – Fax 05 58 06 00 68 BY **h**

29 rm – 🚹€ 47/64 🚹🚹€ 60/80, ☕ € 8,50 – ½ P € 52/68

Rest – *(Closed 2-11 January, Friday dinner from 24 July to 18 September, Sunday dinner and Saturday)* Menu (€ 18), € 20 (weekdays)/42 – Carte approx. € 42

◆ A central hotel, near the Despiau Wlérick sculpture museum. The well-kept rooms are plain and modern and are gradually being redecorated. This restaurant is set up like a brasserie.

Les Clefs d'Argent (Christophe Dupouy) VISA

333 av. des Martyrs de la Résistance, via ⑥ – ✆ 05 58 06 16 45 – www.clefs-dargent.com – lesclefsdargent@orange.fr – Closed Christmas holidays and in August, Sunday dinner and Monday

Rest – Menu € 20 bi (weekday lunch), € 40/90 bi – Carte € 56/62

Spec. Foie gras de canard des Landes et pommes confites. Homard thermidor. Flognarde aux pommes et lait de poule à l'amaretto.

◆ This unassuming yet charming establishment serves tasty up-to-date dishes, full of authentic delicacy. Several cosy dining rooms, recently redecorated.

in Uchacq-et-Parentis by ⑦ : **7 km – pop. 568 – alt. 50 m – ✉ 40090**

Didier Garbage VISA

N 134 – ✆ 05 58 75 33 66 – www.restaudidiergarbage.fr – restau.didier.garbage@wanadoo.fr – Fax 05 58 75 22 77 – Closed 2-20 January, Tuesday dinner, Sunday dinner and Monday

Rest – Menu € 25/75 bi – Carte € 61/85

Rest *Bistrot* – Menu € 12/28

◆ Rustic interior, wooden tables and old knick-knacks. The establishment's reputation and conviviality are popular with the locals. Regional cuisine and vintages in the cellar. Equally rustic, the Bistrot offers regional dishes.

MONTDIDIER – **80 Somme** – **301** I10 – **pop. 6 029** – **alt. 82 m** – ✉ **80500** **Northern France and the Paris Region** 36 **B2**

Paris 108 – Compiègne 36 – Amiens 39 – Beauvais 49 – Péronne 48 – St-Quentin 65

Office de tourisme, 5, place du Général-de-Gaulle ✆ 03 22 78 92 00, Fax 03 22 78 00 88

Dijon

1 pl. 10 Août 1918, (Breteuil road) – ✆ 03 22 78 01 35 – d.vanoverschelde@wanadoo.fr – Fax 03 22 78 27 24 – Closed 10-30 August, 8-21 February and Sunday evening

19 rm – €42 €68, €7,50 – ½ P €60

Rest – *(closed Sunday dinner and Saturday)*

Menu (€14), €17 (weekdays), €20/29 – Carte €35/52

◆ This hotel, near the railway station, offers a carefully-arranged rustic setting. All rooms have been renovated. Those at the front have double-glazing. Charming service. Traditional food in the birthplace of Parmentier, the famous potato promoter.

LE MONT-DORE – 63 Puy-de-Dôme – 326 D9 – pop. 1 427 5 B2

– alt. 1 050 m – Winter sports : 1 050/1 850 m 2 18 – Spa : early April-mid Oct. – Casino Z – ✉ 63240 Auvergne

Paris 462 – Aubusson 87 – Clermont-Ferrand 43 – Issoire 49 – Ussel 56

Office de tourisme, avenue du Maréchal Leclerc ✆ 04 73 65 20 21, Fax 04 73 65 05 71

du Mont-Dore2 km on the Tour d'Auvergne road, ✆ 04 73 65 00 79

Thermal establishment: galerie César★, concourse ★ - Puy de Sancy ★★★ 5 km by ② then 1 h. return by cable car and hiking - Funiculaire du capucin★.

Col de la Croix-St-Robert ★★ 6,5 km by ②.

Plan on next page

Panorama — rest, VISA

27 av. de la Libération – ✆ 04 73 65 11 12 – www.hotel-le-panorama.com – contact@hotel-le-panorama.com – Fax 04 73 65 20 80 – Open 1st May-6 October and 22 December-10 March Z **u**

39 rm – €70/125 €70/125, €11 – ½ P €64/91

Rest – *(dinner only in winter)* Menu €19, €22/55 – Carte €38/48

◆ A 1960s building overlooking the railway station, near the 'Chemin des Artistes'. Modern rooms. Fine panoramic pool. Relaxing fireside bar. Warm atmosphere and traditional cuisine in the restaurant.

Le Castelet — rest, VISA AE

av. M. Bertrand – ✆ 04 73 65 05 29 – www.lecastelet-montdore.com – hotel-le-castelet@orange.fr – Fax 04 73 65 27 95 – Open 15 May-4 October and 20 December-21 March Y **t**

35 rm – €55/68 €59/78, €10 – ½ P €51/67 **Rest** – Menu €22

◆ A 1920s house with a contemporary feel to the lobby-lounge. Soberly decorated bedrooms; those facing the garden are brighter and more cheerful. Two dining rooms, one of which is decorated with an Asian touch. Regional menu.

De Russie — VISA

3 r. Favart – ✆ 04 73 65 05 97 – www.lerussie.com – hotelderussie@orange.fr – Fax 04 73 65 22 10 Y **a**

32 rm – €60/75 €60/75, €9 – 1 suite – ½ P €55/63

Rest – Menu (€18) – Carte €31/40

◆ This hotel is named after the Russian clientele who flocked to the area in the heyday of thermal spas. Renovated hotel dating from 1902, perfect for skiers (shuttle bus to the slopes). After a day walking or skiing, enjoy comforting regional dishes served in a wood-panelled room.

Parc — rest, VISA AE

r. Meynadier – ✆ 04 73 65 02 92 – www.hotelduparc-montdore.com – hotelduparc.md@wanadoo.fr – Fax 04 73 65 28 36 – Open 2 May-10 October and 26 December-29 March Z **k**

37 rm – €49/53 €53/58, €7 – ½ P €43/51

Rest – *(residents only)* Menu €16

◆ A century-old building in the centre of the famous thermal spa, where the Gauls used to take the waters. Practical and successfully-renovated rooms. Pretty mouldings, high ceiling, restored parquet and a lovely fireplace characterise this pleasant dining room.

LE MONT-DORE

Apollinaire (R. S.) . . . . Y 2
Artistes (Chemin des) . . . . Z
Banc (R. Jean) . . . . Y 3
Belges (Av. des). . . . . Y
Bertrand (Av. M.). . . . . Y
Chazotte (R. Capitaine) . . . . . . Y 4
Clemenceau (Av.) . . . . Z 5
Clermont (Av. de) . . . . Y 7
Crouzets (Av. des). . . . . Y
Déportés (R. des) . . . . Z 8
Dr-Claude (R.) . . . . Y
Duchâtel (R.) . . . . Z 9
Favart (R.). . . . . Y 12
Ferry (Av. J.) . . . . YZ
Gaulle (Pl. Ch.-de) . . . . Y 14
Guyot-Dessaigne (Av.) . . . . Y 15
Latru (R.) . . . . Y
Lavialle (R.) . . . . Y
Leclerc (Av. du Gén.). . . . . Y
Libération (Av. de la) . . . . YZ
Melchi-Roze (Chemin) . . . . Y
Meynadier (R.) . . . . YZ
Mirabeau (Bd) . . . . Y
Montlosier (R.) . . . . Y 19
Moulin (R. Jean) . . . . Z 20
Panthéon (Pl. du) . . . . Z 22
Pasteur (R.) . . . . Y
Ramond (R.) . . . . Z 24
République (Pl. de la) . . . . Z 26
Rigny (R.) . . . . Z 28
Sand (Allée G.) . . . . YZ 29
Sanistas (R. F.) . . . . Y
Verrier (R. P.) . . . . Y
Wilson (Av.) . . . . Y
19-Mars-1962 (R. du) . . . . Y 32

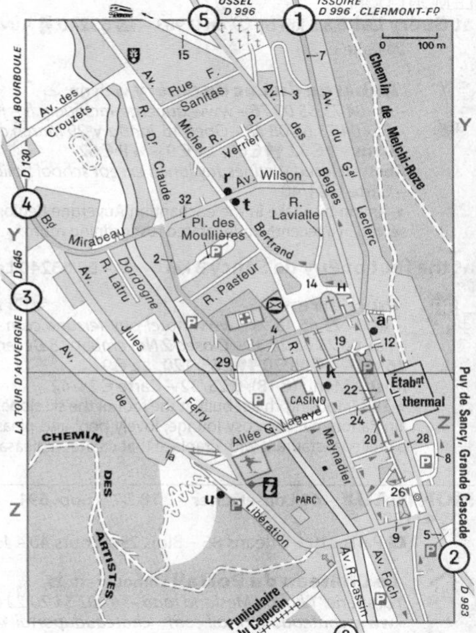

Le Wilson without rest — VISA

1 av. Wilson – ✆ 04 73 65 00 06 – www.residence-wilson.com – residencewilson@free.fr – Fax 04 73 65 27 95 – Closed 1st April-15 May and 7 October-20 December — Y r

16 rm – †€ 49/60 ††€ 57/60, ☕ € 7

◆ A large, early-20C villa, housing functional and well-equipped studio flats, available for one night or longer stays.

Les Charmettes without rest — VISA

30 av. G. Clemenceau, via ② – ✆ 04 73 65 05 49 – www.hotellescharmettes.com – charmettes-lemontdore@wanadoo.fr – Fax 04 73 65 20 28 – Closed 3-27 June and 4 November-12 December

21 rm – †€ 43/46 ††€ 50/55, ☕ € 8

◆ Hotel facing in the direction of the majestic Puy de Sancy. Small, simple rooms are available here for a faithful hiker clientèle.

La Closerie de Manou without rest

Le Genestoux, 3 km via ⑤ and D 996 – ✆ 04 73 65 26 81 – www.lacloseriedemanou.com – lacloseriedemanou@club-internet.fr – Fax 04 73 65 58 34 – Open from April to mid October

5 rm ☕ – †€ 55/65 ††€ 85/90

◆ This regional style 18C Auvergne building is a real wonder. The spacious cosy rooms all have personal details. Great hospitality.

Le Pitsounet — VISA

Le Genestoux, 3km by ⑤ on D 996 – ✆ 04 73 65 00 67 – aubergelepitsounet@wanadoo.fr – Fax 04 73 65 06 22 – Closed from mid October to mid December, Sunday dinner and Monday except July-August and February

Rest – Menu € 17 (weekdays)/33 – Carte € 20/35

◆ This chalet at the side of a main road offers a rural atmosphere with two rustic dining rooms, copious regional food and reasonable prices.

at Guéry Lake 8.5 km by ① on D 983 – ✉ 63240 Auvergne

Lake★.

Auberge du Lac de Guéry with rm
– *04 73 65 02 76 – www.auberge-lac-guery.fr – jean.leclerc2@wanadoo.fr – Fax 04 73 65 08 78 – Open 15 January-29 March and 6 April-11 October*
10 rm – €52 €60, €9 – ½ P €62
Rest – *(closed Wednesday lunch except school holidays)* Menu €19/45 – Carte €24/40
◆ An inn by a lake in the enchanting Auvergne Regional Volcano Park. Regional cuisine served in a recently redecorated rustic dining room.

at the foot of Puy de Sancy 3 km by ② – ✉ 63240 Le Mont-Dore

Puy Ferrand
rest, VISA
– *04 73 65 18 99 – www.hotel-puy-ferrand.com – info@hotel-puy-ferrand.com – Fax 04 73 65 28 38 – Closed 2 November-18 December*
36 rm – €60/70 €65/120, €9
Rest – Menu (€18), €25/32 – Carte €25/42
◆ This imposing chalet built at the foot of the ski slopes offers you a deep breath of fresh air. Panoramic bar, cosy lounge, lovely pool and pleasantly-redecorated rooms. Wood-panelled restaurant with fireplace that creates a pleasant, mountain-style atmosphere.

MONTEAUX – 41 Loir-et-Cher – 318 D7 – pop. 691 – alt. 62 m – ✉ 41150 11 **A1**

Paris 210 – Orléans 85 – Blois 25 – Tours 40 – Joué-lès-Tours 51

Le Château du Portail without rest
VISA
à Besnerie, 1 km on Mesland road – 02 54 70 22 88 – www.chateauduportail.com – chateauduportail@orange.fr – Fax 02 54 70 22 32 – Closed 15 December-15 January
5 rm – €150/180 €150/180
◆ Ideally located for visiting the chateaux of the Loire, between Blois and Amboise. Luxurious 17C-18C residence with formal garden and rooms with antique furniture.

MONTECH – 82 Tarn-et-Garonne – 337 D8 – pop. 5 065 – alt. 100 m – ✉ 82700 28 **B2**

Paris 643 – Toulouse 50 – Montauban 14 – Colomiers 56 – Tournefeuille 57

La Maison de l'Eclusier
VISA
The Port – 05 63 65 37 61 – www.lamaisondeleclusier.com – Fax 05 63 65 37 61 – Closed 28 June-6 July, 31 August-4 September, 1st-16 January, Tuesday lunch in July-August, Sunday dinner from September to June, Saturday lunch and Monday
Rest – Menu (€13), €23 (weekday lunch), €27/38 – Carte €28/40
◆ An old lock keeper's house and pretty terrace by the canal side. Tasty traditional fare from a blackboard menu; small but well chosen cellar and fine selection of wines by the glass.

MONTEILS – 82 Tarn-et-Garonne – 337 F6 – see Caussade

MONTÉLIER – 26 Drôme – 332 D4 – pop. 3 172 – alt. 219 m – ✉ 26120 43 **E2**

Paris 567 – Crest 27 – Romans-sur-Isère 13 – Valence 12

La Martinière
VISA AE
ZA La Pimpie, Chabeuil road – 04 75 59 60 65 – www.a-lamartiniere.com – la-martiniere@wanadoo.fr – Fax 04 75 59 69 20
30 rm – €52 €58, €8 – ½ P €54
Rest – Menu €16 (weekdays)/62 – Carte €20/69
◆ This hotel is housed in a contemporary building, with redecorated rooms and a lovely swimming pool. Modern Provençal dining area with covered terrace. Traditional cuisine and a good selection of Bordeaux wines.

MONTÉLIMAR – 26 Drôme – **332** B6 – **pop. 33 800** – **alt. 90 m** – ✉ **26200** 44 **B3**
Lyon - Rhone Valley

Paris 602 – Avignon 83 – Nîmes 108 – Le Puy-en-Velay 132 – Valence 47

Office de tourisme, allées Provençales ✆ 04 75 01 00 20, Fax 04 75 52 33 69

de La Valdaine Montboucher-sur-Jabron Château du Monard, E : 4 km on D 540, ✆ 04 75 00 71 33

de la Drôme provençale Clansayes 21 km on N 7 and Nyons road, ✆ 04 75 98 57 03

Allées provençales★ - Musée de la Miniature★ **M.**

Site★★ du Château de Rochemaure★, 7 km by ④.

MONTÉLIMAR

Street	Zone	No.
Adhémar (R.)	Z	2
Aygu (Av.)	Z	4
Baudina (R.)	Y	5
Blanc (Pl. L.)	Z	6
Bourgneuf (R.)	Y	8
Carmes (Pl. des)	Y	9
Chemin Neuf (R. du)	Z	10
Clercs (Pl. des)	Y	12
Corneroche (R.)	Y	14
Cuiraterie (R.)	Z	15
Desmarais (Bd Marre)	Y	17
Dormoy (Pl. M.)	Z	18
Espoulette (Av. d')	Z	19
Europe (Pl. de l')	Z	21
Fust (Pl. du)	Y	23
Gaulle (Bd Gén.-de)	Z	25
Juiverie (R.)	Y	28
Julien (R. Pierre)	YZ	
Loubet (Pl. Émile)	Z	29
Loubet (R. Émile)	Z	30
Meyer (R. M.)	Y	32
Monnaie-Vieille (R.)	Y	34
Montant-au-Château (R.)	Y	35
Planel (Pl. A.)	Z	37
Poitiers (R. Diane de)	Z	38
Porte Neuve (R.)	Z	39
Prado (Pl. du)	Y	41
Puits Neuf (R. du)	Y	42
Rochemaure (Av. de)	Y	47
St-Martin (Montée)	Y	50
St-Pierre (R.)	Y	51
Villeneuve (Av. de)	Y	54

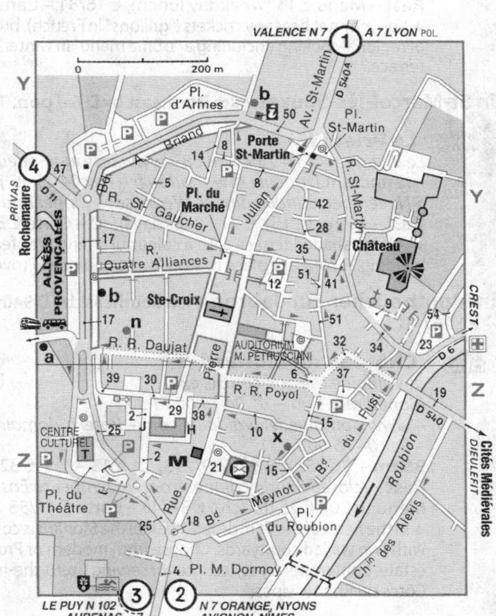

Sphinx without rest

19 bd Desmarais – ✆ 04 75 01 86 64 – www.sphinx-hotel.fr – reception@sphinx-hotel.fr – Fax 04 75 52 34 21 – Closed 23 December-11 January Y **b**

24 rm – †€ 50/59 ††€ 57/79, ☕ € 7

◆ The pretty courtyard, warm parquet floors and wood panelling give an undeniable charm to this 17C mansion located opposite the typical Provençal streets. Fairly quiet rooms.

Du Parc without rest

27 av. Ch. de Gaulle – ✆ 04 75 01 00 73 – hotelduparc-montelimar.com – hotelduparc26@wanadoo.fr – Fax 04 75 51 27 93 Y **a**

16 rm – †€ 60 ††€ 60, ☕ € 8

◆ This welcoming little hotel is opposite the park and near the station and town centre. Well-kept rooms. Breakfasts served in a warm dining room or on the terrace.

Les Senteurs de Provence

202 rte de Marseille, via ② – ✆ 04 75 01 43 82 – lsdp.restaurant@wanadoo.fr – Fax 04 75 01 21 81 – Closed Thursday dinner, Sunday, Monday, Tuesday and Wednesday

Rest – Menu (€ 12), € 16 (weekdays)/34 – Carte € 28/48

◆ Adorned in Provençal colours (ochre and orange) and decked in wrought iron furniture, this restaurant serves modern cuisine with a distinct southern flavour.

X **Petite France**

34 imp. Raymond Daujat – ☎ 04 75 46 07 94 – Closed 13 July-4 August, 21-25 December, Sunday and Monday Y **n**

Rest – Menu (€ 15), € 21/30 – Carte € 27/43

◆ This restaurant in the old town is named after a district of Strasbourg. Sample traditional fare in a vaulted room adorned with a fresco.

X **Le Grillon**

40 r. Cuiraterie – ☎ 04 75 01 79 02 – Fax 04 75 01 79 02 – Closed 10-25 July, 23-28 December, Thursday dinner, Sunday dinner and Monday Z **x**

Rest – Menu € 14 (weekday lunch), € 16/31 – Carte € 30/45

◆ You may not hear any crickets ("grillons" in French), but you'll certainly taste the flavours of regional cooking (including a "truffle menu" in winter) in the rustic dining area or on the terrace.

in St-Marcel-lès-Sauzet 7 km Northeast by D 6 – pop. 1 116 – alt. 110 m – ✉ 26740

XX **Le Prieuré**

Le Village – ☎ 04 75 46 78 68 – www.restau-le-prieure.com – restaurant.leprieure@wanadoo.fr – Fax 04 75 46 10 96 – Closed 15 October-5 November, Sunday dinner, Wednesday dinner and Monday

Rest – Menu (€ 15), € 21 (weekdays)/42 – Carte € 39/73

◆ A large shaded terrace with a colourful dining area feature in this lovely regional stone building. A pleasant place to stop for a traditional, Provencal meal.

in Montboucher-sur-Jabron 4 km Southeast by D 940 – pop. 1 823 – alt. 124 m – ✉ 26740

Château du Monard rm,

at Valdaine the golf course, exit Montélimar-Sud – ☎ 04 75 00 71 30 – www.domainedelavaldaine.com – hotel@domainedelavaldaine.com – Fax 04 75 00 71 31

35 rm – †€ 75/168 ††€ 89/213, ☕ € 13 – ½ P € 82/135

Rest – *(closed Sunday dinner from November to Easter)*
Menu (€ 20), € 25 (lunch), € 34/46 – Carte € 41/53

◆ In the heart of the Parc de la Valdaine, the Monard is comprised of a Renaissance château with two walled courtyards. Choose from modern or Provençal rooms. Golf course on the estate. Contemporary styled interior serving up-to-the-minute cuisine and a fine choice of Côtes du Rhône wines.

on N 7 7.5 km by ② – ✉ 26780 Châteauneuf-du-Rhône

XXX **Pavillon de l'Étang**

N 7 – ☎ 04 75 90 76 82 – www.lepavillondeletang.fr – pavillondeletang@orange.fr – Fax 04 75 90 72 39 – Closed 25 October-10 November, 5-15 January, Wednesday dinner, Sunday dinner and Monday

Rest – *(number of covers limited, pre-book)* Menu (€ 25 bi), € 36/70 bi – Carte € 40/65

◆ The pastoral setting and warm welcome are the main assets of this house, located in the middle of the countryside. Truffle menu in season.

via ② 9 km by N 7 and D 844, Donzère road – ✉ 26780 Malataverne

Domaine du Colombier rest,

– ☎ 04 75 90 86 86 – www.domaine-colombier.com – reservation@domainecolombier.com – Fax 04 75 90 79 40

20 rm – †€ 100/150 ††€ 120/200, ☕ € 17 – 3 suites

Rest – Menu (€ 31), € 51/85 – Carte € 83/91

◆ This farmhouse is the epitome of calm and elegance. A tasteful, low-key decor in each of the individually styled rooms, pool and flower-decked park. Contemporary-style dining rooms, pleasant courtyard terrace and up-to-date cuisine.

MONTENACH – **57 Moselle – 307** J2 – **see Sierck-les-Bains**

MONTESQUIOU – 32 Gers – 336 D8 – pop. 586 – alt. 214 m – ✉ 32320 28 **A2**

Paris 783 – Toulouse 112 – Auch 33 – Tarbes 60 – Aureilhan 57

Office de tourisme, Mairie ✆ 05 62 70 91 18, Fax 05 62 70 80 16

Maison de la Porte Fortifiée

in the village – ✆ 05 62 70 97 06 – www.porte-fortifiee.eu – maison@porte-fortifiee.eu – Fax 05 62 70 97 06 – Closed 4 January-20 March

4 rm – †€ 60/70 ††€ 80/120 – ½ P € 69/84 **Table d'hôte** – Menu € 29/39

◆ Establishment located near the 13C fortified gate of a peaceful village overlooking the valley. Fireplaces and period furniture personalise the large rooms. Terrace-garden. Gascon or exotic dishes in the table d'hôtes (dinner by reservation).

MONTEUX – 84 Vaucluse – 332 C9 – see Carpentras

MONTFAUCON – 25 Doubs – 321 G3 – see Besançon

MONTFAVET – 84 Vaucluse – 332 C10 – see Avignon

MONTFORT-EN-CHALOSSE – 40 Landes – 335 F12 – pop. 1 210 – alt. 110 m – ✉ 40380 Atlantic Coast 3 **B3**

Paris 744 – Aire-sur-l'Adour 57 – Dax 19 – Hagetmau 27 – Mont-de-Marsan 43 – Orthez 29

Office de tourisme, 25, place Foch ✆ 05 58 98 58 50, Fax 05 58 98 58 01

Musée de la Chalosse★.

Aux Tauzins rest, AC VISA MC

rte d'Hagetmau – ✆ 05 58 98 60 22 – www.auxtauzins.com – auxtauzins@wanadoo.fr – Fax 05 58 98 45 79 – Closed 1st-15 October, February, Sunday evening and Monday except July-August

16 rm – †€ 57 ††€ 76, € 8 – ½ P € 74

Rest – *(closed Monday lunchtime in July-August)* Menu (€ 16), € 22/42 – Carte € 50/60

◆ Family-run hotel offering simple, well-kept rooms, some of them with a balcony and a view of the Chalosse vales. Garden with miniature golf and pool. Country-style panoramic restaurant with wisteria covered terrace and regional specialities.

MONTFORT-L'AMAURY – 78 Yvelines – 311 G3 – pop. 3 133 – alt. 185 m – ✉ 78490 Northern France and the Paris Region 18 **A2**

Paris 46 – Dreux 36 – Houdan 18 – Mantes-la-Jolie 31 – Rambouillet 19 – Versailles 29

Syndicat d'initiative, 3, rue Amaury ✆ 01 34 86 87 96, Fax 01 34 86 87 96

du Domaine du Tremblay Le Tremblay-sur-Mauldre Place de l'Eglise, E : 8 km, ✆ 01 34 94 25 70

Church★ - Former cemetery★ - Château ruins ≤★.

Saint-Laurent without rest VISA MC AE

2 pl. Lebreton – ✆ 01 34 57 06 66 – www.hotelsaint-laurent.com – reception@hotelsaint-laurent.com – Fax 01 34 86 12 27 – Closed 1st-23 August

15 rm – †€ 99 ††€ 109, € 12

◆ This superb 17C manor house has been tastefully renovated, now providing rooms, some with private terrace, others on the top floor with original wooden beams.

MONTGENEVRE – 05 Hautes-Alpes – 334 I3 – pop. 466 – alt. 1 850 m – ✉ 05100 41 **C1**

Paris 757 – Marseille 274 – Gap 99 – Briançon 13

Office de tourisme, route d'Italie ✆ 04 92 21 52 52, Fax 04.92.21.92.45

Le Chalet Blanc

hamlet of l'Obélisque – ☎ 04 92 44 27 02 – www.hotellechaletblanc.com – info@hotellechaletblanc.com – Fax 04 92 46 05 29 – Closed 18-31 May and 19 October-15 November

32 rm – **†**€ 72/400 **††**€ 80/500

Rest – *(closed Monday and Tuesday in low season)*
Menu (€ 32), € 45/75 – Carte € 42/90

◆ This lavish hotel, the latest addition to the resort, is proud of its exclusive status. Flawless comfort and tasteful interior decoration that combines traditional alpine materials (stone, wood) with a contemporary style. The restaurant is located in a separate chalet, accessible from the outside.

MONTGIBAUD – 19 Corrèze – 329 J2 – pop. 234 – alt. 460 m – ✉ 19210 — 24 B2

Paris 434 – Arnac-Pompadour 15 – Limoges 47 – St-Yrieix-la-Perche 23 – Tulle 21 – Uzerche 25

Le Tilleul de Sully

– ☎ 05 55 98 01 96 – Fax 05 55 98 01 96 – Closed 21 December-11 January, Tuesday dinner in low season, Sunday dinner and Monday except public holidays

Rest – *(number of covers limited, pre-book)* Menu € 14 (weekday lunch), € 18/36 – Carte € 39/45

◆ A country restaurant near an old linden tree, serving as a pilgrim stopover on the Santiago de Compostela route. Rustic dining area with fireplace. Traditional fare.

MONTGRÉSIN – 60 Oise – 305 G6 – see Chantilly

LES MONTHAIRONS – 55 Meuse – 307 D4 – see Verdun

MONTHIEUX – 01 Ain – 328 C5 – pop. 578 – alt. 295 m – ✉ 01390 — 43 E1

Paris 443 – Lyon 31 – Bourg-en-Bresse 38 – Meximieux 26 – Villefranche-sur-Saône 19

Le Gouverneur

D 6 – ☎ 04 72 26 42 00 – www.golfgouverneur.fr – info@golfgouverneur.fr – Fax 04 72 26 42 20 – Closed 22-31 December

53 rm – **†**€ 95/115 **††**€ 105/125, ☕ € 12

Rest – *(closed Sunday dinner from 1st October to 31 March) (dinner only)*
Menu (€ 20 bi), € 35/40 – Carte € 39/51

◆ Out in the countryside, this former 14C property of the Governor of the Dombes has a new wing housing stylish modern rooms. Nine and 18-hole golf courses and fishing. Attractive, modern dining rooms (one overlooks the golf course); traditional menus.

MONTHION – 73 Savoie – 333 L4 – see Albertville

MONTI – 06 Alpes-Maritimes – 341 F5 – see Menton

MONTIGNAC – 24 Dordogne – 329 H5 – pop. 3 023 – alt. 77 m – ✉ 24290 Dordogne-Berry-Limousin — 4 D1

Paris 513 – Brive-la-Gaillarde 39 – Limoges 126 – Périgueux 54 – Sarlat-la-Canéda 25

Office de tourisme, place Bertran-de-Born ☎ 05 53 51 82 60, Fax 05 53 50 49 72

Grottes de Lascaux★★ Southeast: 2 km.

Le Thot, Cro-magnon area★ South: 7 km - Église★★ de St-Amand de Coly East: 7 km.

Relais du Soleil d'Or rm, VISA

16 r. 4 Septembre – ✆ 05 53 51 80 22 – www.le-soleil-dor.com – soleil-or@wanadoo.fr – Fax 05 53 50 27 54
32 rm – €68/101 €68/101, ☕ €13 – ½ P €72/93
Rest – *(closed Sunday dinner and Monday from 4 November to 16 March)* Menu (€23), €28/56 – Carte €44/68
Rest *Le Bistrot* – *(closed Sunday dinner and Monday from 4 November to 16 March)* Menu €12,50 – Carte €16/34
◆ A former coaching inn in the centre of the small Périgord town. In the annexe, the comfortable rooms have discreet modern touches; most of them overlook a peaceful park. Restaurant-veranda offering a traditional menu. Simple meals offered at Le Bistrot.

Hostellerie la Roseraie VISA

11 pl. d'Armes – ✆ 05 53 50 53 92 – www.laroseraie-hotel.com – hotelroseraie@wanadoo.fr – Fax 05 53 51 02 23 – Open 3 April-1st November
14 rm (½ board only) – €75/115 €85/180 – ½ P €80/145
Rest – *(closed lunch weekdays off season)* Menu €23/50 – Carte €39/50
◆ In the heart of the medieval village, this 19C hotel on the banks of the Vézère provides cosy, personalised rooms and a lovely rose garden. Stylish dining room, pleasant shaded terrace and traditional menu.

MONTIGNY – 76 Seine-Maritime – 304 F5 – see Rouen

We try to be as accurate as possible when giving room rates.
But prices are open to change,
so please check rates when booking.

MONTIGNY-LA-RESLE – 89 Yonne – 319 F4 – pop. 581 – alt. 155 m – ✉ 89230 7 B1

Paris 170 – Auxerre 14 – St-Florentin 19 – Tonnerre 32

Le Soleil d'Or VISA

N77 – ✆ 03 86 41 81 21 – www.lesoleil-dor.com – le-soleil-dor@wanadoo.fr – Fax 03 86 41 86 88 – Closed Sunday evening in January and February
16 rm – €57 €60, ☕ €10 – ½ P €57
Rest – Menu (€12), €26/70 – Carte €50/70
◆ A former coaching inn on the main road, this hotel provides practical rooms to the rear in the converted outbuildings. Slightly reminiscent of a motel in layout. Traditional cuisine served in a colourful setting; lovely little wainscoted sitting room.

MONTIGNY-LE-BRETONNEUX – 78 Yvelines – 311 I3 – 101 22 – see Paris, Area (St-Quentin-en-Yvelines)

MONTIGNY-LE-ROI – 52 Haute-Marne – 313 M6 – pop. 2 173 – alt. 404 m – ✉ 52140 14 C3

Paris 296 – Bourbonne-les-Bains 21 – Chaumont 35 – Langres 23 – Neufchâteau 50

Arcombelle rest, VISA

25 av. de Lierneux – ✆ 03 25 90 30 18 – www.hotelmoderne.fr – arcombelle@orange.fr – Fax 03 25 90 71 80 – Closed weekends in January and Sunday dinner from October to March
24 rm – €63/86 €63/86, ☕ €9 **Rest** – Menu €21/44 – Carte €35/46
◆ Building located at a crossroads with well-kept, soundproofed rooms (some renovated), equipped with modern furniture. Family atmosphere. 1980s-style dining room. Large choice of menus, including a small traditional menu.

MONTIGNY-LÈS-ARSURES – 39 Jura – 321 E5 – pop. 267 – alt. 400 m – ✉ 39600 16 B2

Paris 417 – Besançon 46 – Lons-le-Saunier 42 – Dole 59 – Pontarlier 55

Château de Chavanes without rest
r. St-Laurent – ☎ 03 84 37 47 95 – www.chateau-de-chavanes.com – fdechavanes@chateau-de-chavanes.com – Fax 03 84 37 47 65 – Open April-November
5 rm – †€ 75/90 ††€ 125/150
◆ Substantial renovations have left this château, dating back to 1708, eminently comfortable and tasteful. Find antique furniture, a modern organic wine cellar and a terrace overlooking the garden and vineyards.

MONTIGNY-SUR-AVRE – 28 Eure-et-Loir – 311 C3 – pop. 256 – alt. 140 m – ✉ 28270 11 B1

Paris 111 – Alençon 85 – Argentan 86 – Chartres 52 – Dreux 35 – Verneuil-sur-Avre 9

Moulin des Planches rm,
149 chemin du Moulin des Planches, 1.5 km northeast on the D 102 – ☎ 02 37 48 25 97 – www.moulin-des-planches.fr – moulin.des.planches@wanadoo.fr – Closed 13 July-16 August, Sunday dinner and Monday
18 rm – †€ 58/99 ††€ 64/115, € 10 **Rest** – Menu € 32/75 – Carte € 65/74
◆ A mill on the Avre, in the heart of the countryside. Bedrooms are equipped with period furniture and mostly have views of the river, while a few overlook the park. The country restaurant is full of character, with its tiled floor, patina beams and brick walls. Modern cuisine.

MONTIPOURET – 36 Indre – 323 H7 – pop. 569 – alt. 200 m – ✉ 36230 12 C3

Paris 295 – Châteauroux 28 – Issoudun 37 – Orléans 169

in La Brande 5 km northeast by D49 and secondary road - ✉ 36230 Montipouret

Maison Voilà
– ☎ 02 54 31 17 91 – www.maisonvoila.com – maisonvoila@yahoo.com
4 rm – †€ 60 ††€ 80 **Table d'hôte** – Menu € 25
◆ A 19C farmhouse in the countryside with a fine garden of fruit trees. Attractive interiors, with cosy rooms, many featuring old-style furnishings. Enjoy a meal in the company of the owners around the fireplace or on the terrace in summer. International cuisine served.

MONTJEAN-SUR-LOIRE – 49 Maine-et-Loire – 317 D4 – pop. 2 687 – alt. 44 m – ✉ 49570 Châteaux of the Loire 34 B2

Paris 324 – Angers 28 – Ancenis 30 – Châteaubriant 64 – Château-Gontier 56 – Cholet 43

Office de tourisme, rue d'Anjou ☎ 02 41 39 07 10, Fax 02 41 39 03 38

Le Fief des Cordeliers without rest
lieu-dit Bellevue – ☎ 02 41 43 96 09 – www.logis.lefiefdescordeliers.com – logis@lefiefdescordeliers.com – Fax 01 70 24 77 82
4 rm – †€ 50/60 ††€ 60/70
◆ Discover the mild Angers climate at this 15C former Cordeliers convent. Classical rooms and family suites, splendid vista of the Loire and the valley.

Auberge de la Loire with rm rest,
2 quai des Mariniers – ☎ 02 41 39 80 20 – www.aubergedelaloire.com – contacts@aubergedelaloire.com – Fax 02 41 39 80 20 – Closed 17 August-2 September, Christmas holidays, Sunday dinner from September to March and Wednesday
8 rm – †€ 49 ††€ 59, € 8 – ½ P € 62 **Rest** – Menu € 20/36 – Carte € 39/67
◆ A welcoming, family inn on the banks of the Loire. Here you can enjoy delicious, traditional food using fresh products, many from the local fishermen. Simple, well-kept rooms, half of which overlook the river.

MONTLIARD – 45 Loiret – **318** L3 – see Bellegarde

MONTLIOT – 21 Côte-d'Or – **320** H2 – see Châtillon-sur-Seine

MONTLIVAULT – 41 Loir-et-Cher – **318** F6 – **pop. 1 337** – **alt. 77 m** – ✉ **41350** 11 **B2**

Paris 180 – Blois 13 – Olivet 58 – Orléans 56

La Maison d'à Côté (Ludovic Laurenty) with rm
25 rte de Chambord – ✆ 02 54 20 62 30 – www.lamaisondacote.fr – contact@lamaisondacote.fr – Fax 02 54 20 58 55 – Closed 15 December-1st February, Wednesday lunch and Tuesday
8 rm – €78/88 €78/88, € 9 – ½ P € 80/86 **Rest** – Menu (€ 22 bi), € 35/52
Spec. Goujonnettes de bar au concassé de tomate et fenouil. Poitrine de pigeonneau facon tajine et citron confit. Soupe de fraises gariguette au maury.
◆ New owners and a new team for this renovated village inn. The chef prepares interesting dishes with harmonious flavours. Contemporary guestrooms and pleasant upstairs patio.

Red = Pleasant. Look for the red and symbols.

MONT-LOUIS – 66 Pyrénées-Orientales – **344** D7 – **pop. 284** – **alt. 1 565 m** – ✉ **66210** **Languedoc-Roussillon-Tarn Gorges** 22 **A3**

Paris 867 – Andorra-la-Vella 90 – Font-Romeu-Odeillo-Via 10 – Perpignan 81

Syndicat d'initiative, 3, rue Lieutenant Pruneta ✆ 04 68 04 21 97

Ramparts ★ - Lacs des Bouillouses ★.

in la Llagonne 3 km North by D 118 – **pop. 285** – **alt. 1 600 m** – ✉ **66210**

Corrieu rest,
– ✆ 04 68 04 22 04 – www.hotel-corrieu.com – hotel.corrieu@wanadoo.fr – Fax 04 68 04 16 63 – Open 6 June-19 September, 19 December-4 January and 9 January-16 March
18 rm – €56/78 €62/84, € 10 – ½ P € 56/70
Rest – *(closed Thursday lunch except during school holidays)*
Menu (€ 17), € 24 (weekdays)/38 – Carte € 27/42
◆ Run by the same family since 1882, this old coaching inn has peaceful, simply furnished rooms and have views of the Pyrenees. New tennis facilities. Refurbished restaurant with simple, classic fare.

MONTLOUIS – 18 Cher – **323** K4 – **pop. 115** – **alt. 180 m** – ✉ **18160** 12 **C3**

Paris 277 – Orléans 152 – Bourges 39 – Châteauroux 56 – Vierzon 68

Domaine de Varennes
– ✆ 02 48 60 11 86 – www.domaine-de-varennes.com – lumet.varennes@wanadoo.fr – Closed 5 January-20 March
5 rm – €65/90 €70/100 **Table d'hôte** – Menu € 27 bi
◆ Nothing is missing from this charming establishment: flawless greeting, comfort, tasteful decor and superb grounds (quiet parkland, pool and golf course).

MONTLOUIS-SUR-LOIRE – 37 Indre-et-Loire – **317** N4 – **pop. 10 381** – **alt. 60 m** – ✉ **37270** **Châteaux of the Loire** 11 **B2**

Paris 235 – Amboise 14 – Blois 49 – Château-Renault 32 – Loches 39 – Tours 11

Office de tourisme, place François Mitterrand ✆ 02 47 45 00 16, Fax 02 47 45 87 10

Château de la Bourdaisière without rest
– 02 47 45 16 31
– www.chateaulabourdaisiere.com – contact@chateaulabourdaisiere.com
– Fax 02 47 45 09 11 – Open 1st April-1st November
20 rm – €136/236 €137/237, €15
◆ Built by François I for his mistress, the chateau was later home to Gabrielle d'Estrées, the favourite of Henri IV. Individually furnished rooms, park and vegetable garden.

MONTLUÇON – 03 Allier – 326 C4 – pop. 39 700 – alt. 220 m – 03100 Auvergne

5 **B1**

Paris 327 – Bourges 97 – Clermont-Ferrand 112 – Limoges 155 – Moulins 82
Office de tourisme, 67 ter, boulevard de Courtais 04 70 05 11 44, Fax 04 70 03 89 91
du Val de Cher Nassigny 1 route du Vallon, N : 20 km on D 2144, 04 70 06 71 15
Interior ★ of St-Pierre church (Sainte Madeleine★★) CYZ - Château esplanade ★.

Plan on next page

Des Bourbons rest, VISA AE
47 av. Marx Dormoy – 04 70 05 28 93 – www.hotel-des-bourbons.fr
– hoteldesbourbons@wanadoo.fr – Fax 04 70 05 16 92 BZ **a**
44 rm – €54/59 €57/63, €7 – ½ P €52/58
Rest – *(closed 27 July-23 August, Sunday dinner and Monday)* Menu €24/40 – Carte €25/45
Rest *Brasserie Pub 47* – *04 70 05 22 79 (closed 20 July-20 August, Sunday dinner and Monday)* Menu (€16), €24/40 – Carte €25/45
◆ Fine late-19C hotel, opposite the railway station, housing renovated rooms with functional and discreet pre-1940s style furniture, along with well-kept, colourful bathrooms. Traditional menu served in a modern setting. Simple dishes offered at the Brasserie.

Grenier à Sel with rm VISA AE
pl. des Toiles – 04 70 05 53 79 – www.legrenierasel.com – info@legrenierasel.com – Fax 04 70 05 87 91 – Closed autumn half-term holidays, February holidays, Saturday lunch in winter, Sunday dinner September-June and Monday except dinner July-August CZ **n**
7 rm – €75/105 €110/125, €10 **Rest** – Menu €22/67 – Carte €51/73
◆ A restaurant housed in an Old Montluçon mansion. The dining room is decorated with numerous trinkets, and is refined down to the smallest details. Cooking suited to current tastes.

Safran d'Or VISA AE
12 pl. des Toiles – 04 70 05 09 18 – Closed 30 August-6 September, Sunday dinner, Tuesday dinner and Monday CZ **u**
Rest – Menu (€18), €21 bi/35 – Carte €45/55
◆ This small restaurant has a cheerful, imitation-marble exterior, and bistro-type furnishings in the main dining room and the vaulted basement. Traditional cuisine.

Le Plaisir des Marais VISA
152 av. Albert Thomas, 1.5 km via ⑥ – 04 70 03 49 74 – Fax 04 70 03 49 74 – Closed 1 week in August, Tuesday dinner, Sunday dinner and Monday
Rest – Menu (€16), €20/27
◆ This restaurant, with a smart pink facade, enlivens the Marais suburban district. Traditional cuisine at reasonable prices. Country interior. Warm reception.

in St-Victor 7 km by ① – pop. 1 957 – alt. 212 m – 03410

Le Jardin Délice VISA AE
6 rte de Paris – 04 70 28 80 64 – www.jardindelice.com – lejardindelice@orange.fr – Fax 04 70 02 00 73 – Closed 1st-20 July
25 rm – €50 €50, €7 – ½ P €65
Rest – *(closed Wednesday)* Menu €18, €29/48 – Carte €56/71
◆ This hotel near the motorway offers contemporary-style rooms on the ground floor with an interior garden. Faultless upkeep. Updated traditional dishes served in a pleasantly modern setting. Lovely summer terrace.

MONTLUÇON

Barathon (R.) . . . . CZ 2
Beaulieu (R. de) . . . . AX 4
Blanzat (R. de) . . . . AX 5
Château (R. du) . . . . CZ 6
Châtelet (Pont du) . . . . AX 8
Courtais (Bd de) . . . . BCZ
Desmoulins (R. C.) . . . . AX 9
Dienat (R. du) . . . . AX 10
Egalité (R. de l') . . . . AX 12
Einstein (R. A.) . . . . AX 13
Faucheroux (R.) . . . . AX 14
Favières (Quai) . . . . BY 15
Fontaine (R. de la) . . . . CZ 16
Forges (R. Porte) . . . . CZ 17
Jean-Jaurès (Pl.) . . . . CZ 18
Menut (R. L.) . . . . CY 22
Nègre (Av. J.) . . . . AX 24
Notre-Dame (Pl.) . . . . CZ 25
Notre-Dame (R.) . . . . CZ 26
Pamparoux (R.) . . . . AX 27
Petit (R. P.) . . . . CY 30
Picasso (R. P.) . . . . CY 31
Piquand (R. E.) . . . . BZ 32
République (Av.) . . . . BY
St-Pierre (Pl.) . . . . BCZ 35
St-Pierre (R. Fg) . . . . BY 36
St-Roch (R.) . . . . BCZ 38
Semard (R. P.) . . . . AX 40
Serruriers (R.) . . . . BCZ 42
Thomas (Av. A.) . . . . AX 45
Verrerie (R. et Pl. de la) . . . . . AX 46
Victor-Hugo (R.) . . . . AX 47
Villon (R. P.) . . . . AX 49
Voltaire (R.) . . . . AX 50
5 Piliers (R. des) . . . . CZ 52

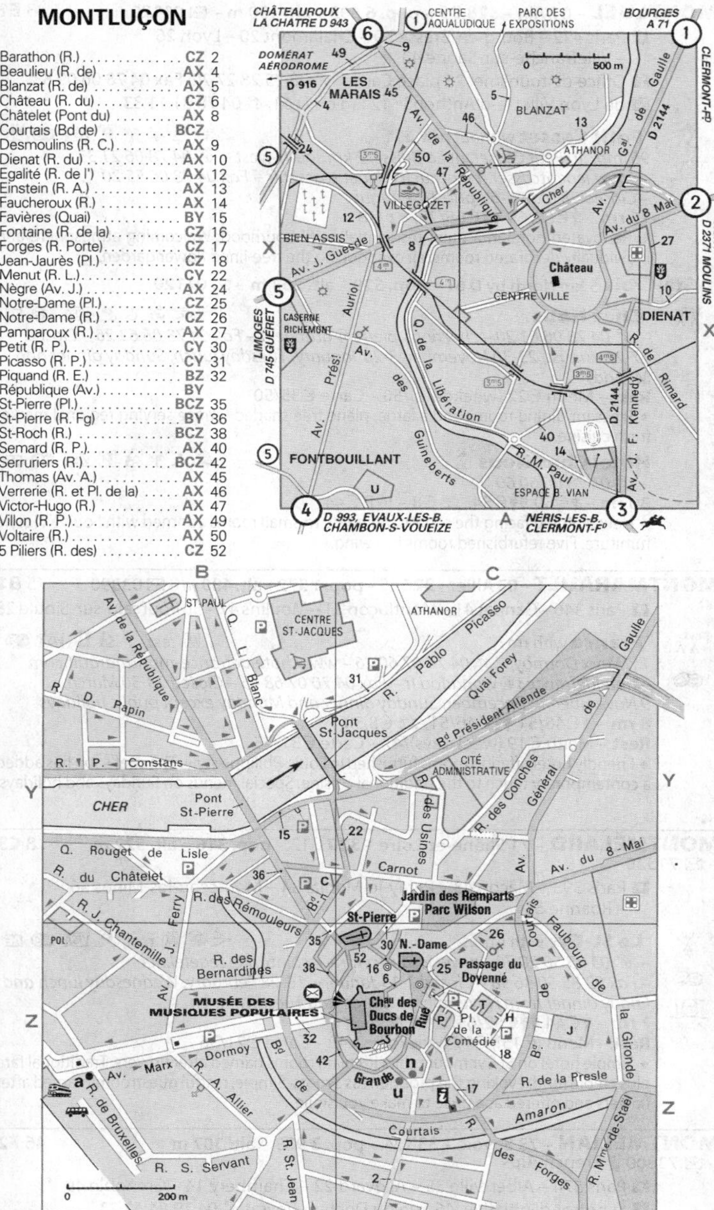

MONTLUEL – 01 Ain – 328 D5 – pop. 6 505 – alt. 190 m – ✉ 01120 43 E1

Paris 472 – Bourg-en-Bresse 59 – Chalamont 20 – Lyon 26 – Villefranche-sur-Saône 43

Office de tourisme, 28 place Carnot ✆ 08 75 28 27 72, Fax 04 78 06 09 53

de Lyon Villette-d'AnthonS : 12 km on D 61, ✆ 04 78 31 11 33

Petit Casset without rest

96 imp. du Petit Casset, at La Boisse, 2 km south-west – ✆ 04 78 06 21 33 – www.lepetitcasset.fr – accueil@lepetitcasset.fr – Fax 04 78 06 55 20 – Closed 28 March-6 April, 9-24 August

16 rm – €62/69 €65/75, €8

◆ Renovated hotel in a quiet residential neighbourhood. Welcoming atmosphere and individually decorated rooms, all overlooking the tree-lined flower garden.

in Ste-Croix 5 km North by D 61 – pop. 529 – alt. 263 m – ✉ 01120

Chez Nous

– ✆ 04 78 06 61 20 – cheznous-pierre@orange.fr – Fax 04 78 06 63 26 – Closed 17-24 August, 23-30 November, 3-20 January, Tuesday lunch, Sunday dinner and Monday

Rest – Menu €22 (weekdays)/50 – Carte €35/50

◆ Pleasant dining rooms and a large, plane tree shaded terrace serving regional market fresh cuisine.

Hôtel Chez Nous

– ✆ 04 78 06 60 60

30 rm – €50 €54, €8 – ½ P €44

◆ New building facing the restaurant, home to small rooms adorned with Louis XVI style furniture. Five refurbished rooms in a wing.

MONTMARAULT – 03 Allier – 326 E5 – pop. 1 572 – alt. 480 m – ✉ 03390 5 B1

Paris 346 – Gannat 41 – Montluçon 31 – Moulins 47 – St-Pourçain-sur-Sioule 28

France with rm rest,

1 r. Marx Dormoy – ✆ 04 70 07 60 26 – www.hoteldefrance-montmarault.com – hoteldefrance3@wanadoo.fr – Fax 04 70 07 68 45 – Closed 23-30 March, 9 November-1st December, Sunday dinner and Monday except public holidays

8 rm – €46/51 €46/51, €8,50

Rest – Menu €19 (weekdays)/47 – Carte €31/45

◆ Friendly hotel offering rooms furnished in Louis-Philippe style. The chef's son has added a contemporary touch to the traditional cuisine. Special menus on Sundays and holidays.

MONTMÉLARD – 71 Saône-et-Loire – 320 G12 – pop. 316 – alt. 522 m – ✉ 71520 8 C3

Paris 393 – Mâcon 43 – Paray-le-Monial 34 – Montceau-les-Mines 56 – Roanne 53

Le St-Cyr with rm rest,

– ✆ 03 85 50 20 76 – www.lesaintcyr.fr – lesaintcyr@cegetel.net – Fax 03 85 50 36 98 – Closed 2-13 January, 16-28 February, Wednesday lunch and Friday dinner from November to March and Tuesday lunch

7 rm – €44 €52/65, €7

Rest – Menu (€15), €17 (weekdays)/40 – Carte €21/36

◆ Simple hotel on St Cyr mountain with plain rooms named after flowers. Traditional fare plus creole food, evoking the proprietress's roots. Simple, restful guestrooms named after flowers and offered at a price to make you smile.

MONTMÉLIAN – 73 Savoie – 333 J4 – pop. 3 933 – alt. 307 m – ✉ 73800 French Alps 46 F2

Paris 574 – Albertville 35 – Allevard 22 – Chambéry 14 – Grenoble 49

Syndicat d'initiative, 46, rue du Docteur Veyrat ✆ 04 79 84 42 23, Fax 04 79 84 42 23

du Granier Apremont Apremont Chemin de Fontaine Rouge, W : 8 km on D 201, ✆ 04 79 28 21 26

✻★★ from the rock.

George

11 quai de l'Isère, (D 1006) – 04 79 84 05 87 – www.hotelgeorge.fr – infos@hotelgeorge.fr – Fax 04 79 84 40 14
11 rm – €34 €42, €6,50 – ½ P €55
Rest – snack – *(closed 1st-15 July and Autumn holidays) (dinner only) (residents only)* Menu €17
◆ A former 18C salt granary on the roadside. Corridors decorated with old tools, leading to simple, refurbished and well-soundproofed rooms. Small, simple restaurant and menu of the day.

MONTMERLE-SUR-SAÔNE – **01 Ain** – **328** B4 – **pop. 3 584** – **alt. 170 m** – ✉ **01090** 43 **E1**

Paris 419 – Bourg-en-Bresse 44 – Lyon 48 – Mâcon 34 – Villefranche-sur-Saône 13

Emile Job

12 r. du Pont – 04 74 69 33 92 – www.hotelemilejob.com – contact@hotelemilejob.com – Fax 04 74 69 49 21 – Closed 29 February-18 March, 25 October-19 November, Sunday dinner from October to May, Tuesday lunch from June to September and Monday
22 rm – €70/80 €70/80, €8 – ½ P €80
Rest – Menu €21 (weekdays)/55 – Carte €48/70
◆ Regional style house on the banks of the Saône that has preserved its family atmosphere. Classic or more modern rooms (refurbished and colourful). Plush, elegant restaurant and shaded terrace; classic menu and local specialities.

MONTMIRAIL – **84 Vaucluse** – **332** D9 – **see Vacqueyras**

MONTMORENCY – **95 Val-d'Oise** – **305** E7 – **101** 5 – **see Paris, Area**

MONTMORILLON – **86 Vienne** – **322** L6 – **pop. 6 898** – **alt. 100 m** – ✉ **86500** Atlantic Coast 39 **D2**

Paris 354 – Bellac 43 – Châtellerault 56 – Limoges 88 – Niort 123 – Poitiers 51

Office de tourisme, 2, place du Maréchal Leclerc 05 49 91 11 96, Fax 05 49 91 11 96

Notre-Dame church: frescoes★ in the Ste-Catherine crypt.

Hôtel de France et Lucullus rm, rest

4 bd de Strasbourg – 05 49 84 09 09 – www.le-lucullus.com – lucullus.hoteldefrance@wanadoo.fr – Fax 05 49 84 58 68 – Closed 12 November- 5 December
35 rm – €47 €50, €9 – ½ P €50
Rest – *(closed 12 November-6 December, Sunday dinner, Monday, Tuesday and Wednesday)* Menu (€12), €20/46 – Carte €29/45
Rest ***Bistrot de Lucullus*** – *(closed Saturday dinner and Sunday)* Menu €12
◆ Near the bridge over the Gartempe, a regional building with spacious, practical and brightly coloured guestrooms. Sunny decor and carefully prepared cuisine that varies with the seasons. Simpler meals served at the Bistrot de Lucullus for the busy clientele.

MONTNER – **66 Pyrénées-Orientales** – **344** H6 – **pop. 290** – **alt. 127 m** – ✉ **66720** 22 **B3**

Paris 860 – Perpignan 28 – Amélie-les-Bains-Palalda 60 – Font-Romeu-Odeillo-Via 82 – Prades 37

Auberge du Cellier with rm rest,

1 r. Ste Eugénie – 04 68 29 09 78 – www.aubergeducellier.com – contact@aubergeducellier.com – Fax 04 68 29 10 61 – Closed 12 November-16 December, Monday from November to March, Tuesday and Wednesday
8 rm – €54 €61, €9
Rest – Menu €24 (weekday lunch), €39/79 – Carte €55/67
◆ A wine inspired restaurant located in a former wine cellar, hence its name. Fine Côtes du Roussillon wine list. Updated regional cuisine.

MONTOIRE-SUR-LE-LOIR – 41 Loir-et-Cher – 318 C5 – pop. 4 186 11 B2
– alt. 65 m – ✉ 41800 Châteaux of the Loire

Paris 186 – Blois 52 – La Flèche 81 – Le Mans 70 – Vendôme 19

Syndicat d'initiative, 16, pl. Clemenceau ✆ 02 54 85 23 30, Fax 02 54 85 23 87

St-Gilles chapel ★: frescoes★★ - Bridge ≤★.

in Lavardin 2 km Southeast by D 108 – pop. 262 – alt. 78 m – ✉ 41800

Relais d'Antan VISA
6 pl. du Capt.-du-Vigneau – ✆ 02 54 86 61 33 – Fax 02 54 85 06 46
– Closed 27 September-21 October, 21 February-17 March, Sunday dinner from October to May, Monday and Tuesday
Rest – Menu € 29/40
◆ This rustic inn stands in a picturesque village. One of its dining rooms is adorned with wall paintings inspired by the Middle Ages. Pleasant terrace on the banks of the Loir.

MONTPELLIER Ⓟ – 34 Hérault – 339 I7 – pop. 248 000 – Built-up area 287 981 – alt. 27 m – ✉ 34000 Languedoc-Roussillon-Tarn Gorges 23 C2

Paris 758 – Marseille 173 – Nice 330 – Nîmes 55 – Toulouse 242

Montpellier-Méditerranée ✆ 04 67 20 85 00 Southeast by ③: 7 km.

Office de tourisme, 30, allée Jean de Latre de Tassigny ✆ 04 67 60 60 60, Fax 04 67 60 60 61

18 de Fontcaude Juvignac Route de Lodève, 8 km on the Lodève road, ✆ 04 67 45 90 10

18 de Coulondres Saint-Gély-du-Fesc 72 rue des Erables, 12 km on the Ganges road, ✆ 04 67 84 13 75

18 Montpellier Massane Baillargues Domaine de Massane, 13 km on the Nîmes road, ✆ 04 67 87 87 89

Old Montpellier★★: hôtel de Varennes★ FY **M²**, hôtel des Trésoriers de la Bourse★ FY **Q**, rue de l'Ancien Courrier★ EFY **4** - Promenade du Peyrou★★: ≤★ from the upper terrace - Quartier Antigone★ - Musée Fabre★★ FY - Musée Atger★ (in the faculté de médecine) EX - Musée languedocien★ (in the Hôtel des trésoriers de France) FY **M¹**.

Château de Flaugergues★ East: 3 km - Château de la Mogère★ East: 5 km by D 24 DU.

Plans on following pages

Sofitel Antigone rest, VISA AE
1 r. Pertuisanes – ✆ 04 67 99 72 72 – www.pullmanhotels.com – h1294@accor.com – Fax 04 67 65 17 50 CU **v**
89 rm – †€ 220/260 ††€ 220/260, ☕ € 22 – 1 suite
Rest – Menu (€ 43), € 46 – Carte € 44/58
◆ This hotel, located in the business district designed by Ricardo Bofill, has been newly renovated to fit in. Comfortable rooms. Roof terrace with swimming pool. Bar; gym. The restaurant is located on the eighth floor, serving contemporary cuisine.

Holiday Inn Métropole rm, AC P VISA AE
3 r. Clos René – ✆ 04 67 12 32 32
– www.holidayinn-montpellier.com – himontpellier@alliance-hospitality.com
– Fax 04 67 92 13 02 FZ **a**
80 rm – †€ 140/210 ††€ 140/210, ☕ € 18
Rest – *(closed Saturday and Sunday)* Menu (€ 20), € 28 – Carte € 32/45
◆ This building, dating from 1898, is said to have been the home of Queen Helena of Italy. Functional bedrooms, modern bar and shaded garden-terrace. Simple modern decor in this restaurant featuring superb ceiling mouldings.

Mercure Antigone rm, AC VISA AE
285 bd Aéroport International – ✆ 04 67 20 63 63 – www.mercure.com – h1544@accor.com – Fax 04 67 20 63 64 DU **f**
114 rm – †€ 130 ††€ 150, ☕ € 13 – 9 suites
Rest – *(Closed Saturday lunch and Sunday)* Menu € 25/29 – Carte approx. € 43
◆ This hotel near the neo-classical Antigone district provides modern, spacious rooms, most with king size beds. Fine furnishings. This circular restaurant offers pleasant colonial decor. Thematic gourmet evenings.

Mercure Centre
218 r. Bastion Ventadour – ✆ 04 67 99 89 89 – www.amphimercure.fr – h3043@accor.com – Fax 04 67 99 89 88 CU **q**
120 rm – †€ 89/130 ††€ 89/140, ☕ € 13
Rest – *(closed Saturday and Sunday)* Carte approx. € 34
◆ An attractive, resolutely modern interior with art on display and a library for guests. The rooms are a little small, however. A modern restaurant serving southern cuisine and small selection of Languedoc wines.

New Hôtel du Midi without rest
22 bd Victor Hugo – ✆ 04 67 92 69 61 – www.new-hotel.com – montpelliermidi@new-hotel.com – Fax 04 67 92 73 63 FZ **b**
44 rm – †€ 135 ††€ 155, ☕ € 12
◆ A fine early-20C building in the centre of town, providing cosy, comfortable rooms renovated in modern style. Colourful bathrooms.

D'Aragon without rest
10 r. Baudin – ✆ 04 67 10 70 00 – www.hotel-aragon.fr – info@hotel-aragon.fr – Fax 04 67 10 70 01 – Closed from 1st-18 January FY **a**
12 rm – †€ 69/75 ††€ 104/134, ☕ € 10
◆ This charming building is home to a small, new hotel providing well-kept and comfortable rooms personalised with junk shop finds. Pleasant veranda where breakfast is served.

Le Guilhem without rest
18 r. J.-J. Rousseau – ✆ 04 67 52 90 90 – www.leguilhem.com – contact@leguilhem.com – Fax 04 67 60 67 67 EY **a**
35 rm – †€ 85/183 ††€ 96/183, ☕ € 12
◆ A group of 16C and 17C houses with cosy rooms; those on the top floor have a view of the cathedral. Breakfast served on the terrace. Non-smoking throughout.

Du Parc without rest
8 r. A. Bège – ✆ 04 67 41 16 49 – www.hotelduparc-montpellier.com – hotelduparcmtp@wanadoo.fr – Fax 04 67 54 10 05 BT **k**
19 rm – †€ 46/75 ††€ 53/90, ☕ € 11
◆ A former 18C manor house close to the historic town centre, providing pleasant, individually styled rooms, and a courtyard terrace for breakfast in summer. Friendly service.

Hôtelience without rest
1149 r. de la Croix-Verte – ✆ 04 67 41 55 00 – www.hotelience-montpellier.com – montpellier01@hotelience.com – Fax 04 67 41 55 01
75 rm – †€ 85/105 ††€ 85/105, ☕ € 12 – 21 suites
◆ New modern hotel located near the university. Comfortable rooms (standard or suite) with minimalist decor. Designer style in the pleasant breakfast room.

Du Palais without rest
3 r. Palais – ✆ 04 67 60 47 38 – www.hoteldupalais-montpellier.fr – hoteldupalais2@wanadoo.fr – Fax 04 67 60 40 23 EY **m**
26 rm – †€ 64 ††€ 69/81, ☕ € 12
◆ A fine, century-old building near the law courts. Attentive touches in the small, cosy rooms (fresh flowers, chocolates, etc.). Efficient soundproofing.

Ulysse without rest
338 av. St-Maur – ✆ 04 67 02 02 30 – www.hotel-ulysse.fr – hotelulysse@free.fr – Fax 04 67 02 16 50 – Closed 21 December-4 January CT **b**
23 rm – †€ 54/59 ††€ 64/70, ☕ € 7,50
◆ Stylish bedrooms, with wrought-iron furniture in this spotless hotel appreciated by guests for its pleasant atmosphere. Quiet residential setting.

Les Troënes without rest
17 av. É. Bertin-Sans, via Ave Charles Flahaut and Ganges road, towards Hôpitaux-Faculté (hospitals) ✉ 34090 – ✆ 04 67 04 07 76 – www.hotel-les-troenes.fr – hotel-les-troenes@wanadoo.fr – Fax 04 67 61 04 43
14 rm – †€ 49/51 ††€ 56/58, ☕ € 8
◆ This welcoming and homely family house is linked to the town centre by tram. Pleasant rooms which are immaculately kept. Non-smoking hotel.

MONTPELLIER

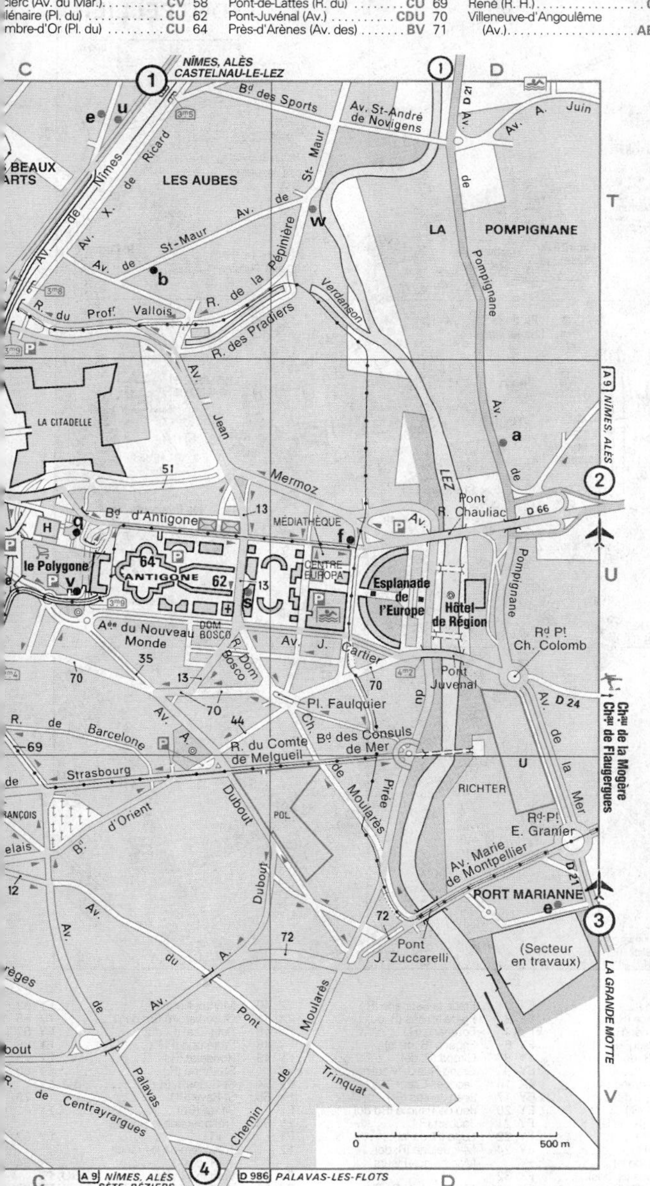

C
D
NÎMES, ALÈS
CASTELNAU-LE-LEZ
Bd des Sports
Av. St-André de Novigens
Av. A. Juin
D 21
BEAUX ARTS
LES AUBES
Av. de Nîmes
Av. X. de Ricard
Av. de St-Maur
R. de St-Maur
R. de la Pépinière
R. du Profr Vallois
R. des Pradiers
Verdanson
LA POMPIGNANE
Av. de Pompignane
T
LA CITADELLE
Av. Jean Mermoz
LEZ
A 9 NÎMES, ALÈS
Pont R. Chauliac
D 66
Bd d'Antigone
MÉDIATHÈQUE
le Polygone
ANTIGONE
CENTRE EUROPA
Esplanade de l'Europe
Hôtel de Région
U
Aée du Nouveau Monde
DOM BOSCO
R. Dom Bosco
Av. J. Cartier
Rd Pt Ch. Colomb
Pont Juvénal
D 24
Pl. Faulquier
R. de Barcelone
R. du Comte de Melgueil
Bd des Consuls de Mer
Chau de la Mogère
Chau de Flaugergues
Strasbourg
Ch. de Moularès
Dubout
Pirée
RICHTER
Av. de la Mer
Rd Pt E. Granier
Bd d'Orient
POL
Av. Marie de Montpellier
PORT MARIANNE
Pont J. Zuccarelli
(Secteur en travaux)
LA GRANDE MOTTE
Av. du Pont
Av. de Palavas
Moularès
Chemin de Trinquat
R. de Centrayrargues
V
0
500 m
A 9 NÎMES, ALÈS
SÈTE, BÉZIERS
D 986 PALAVAS-LES-FLOTS

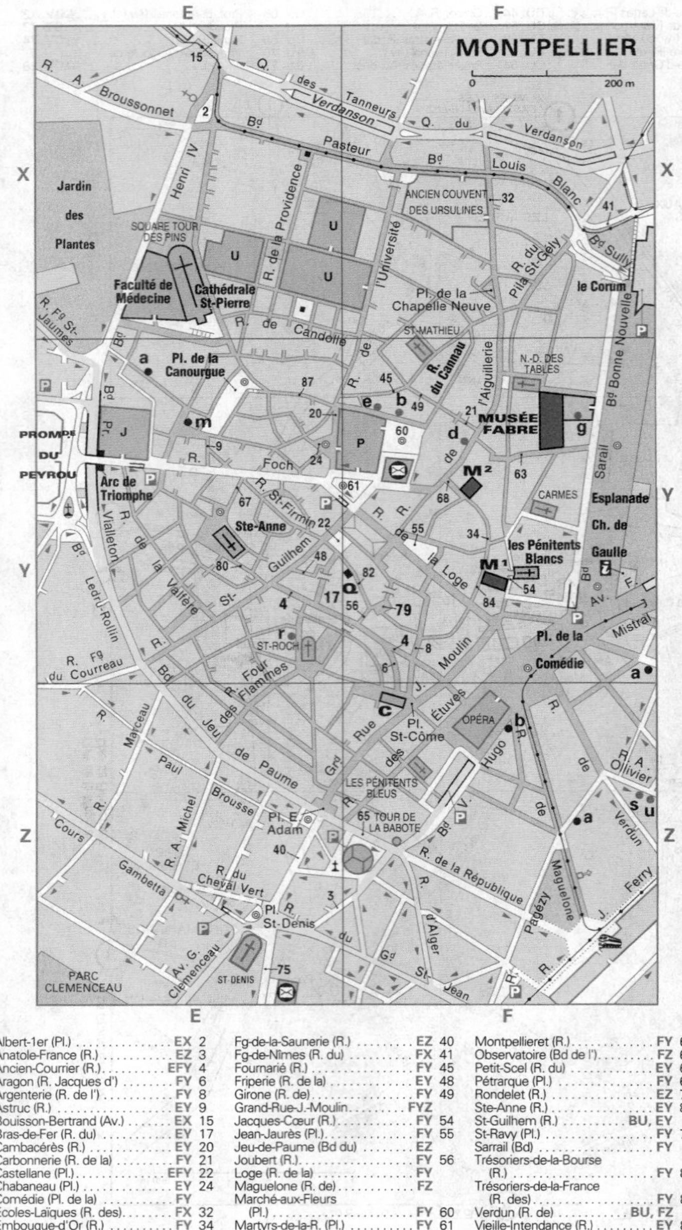

MONTPELLIER
0
200 m
E
F
X
Y
Z
R. A. Broussonnet
Q. des Tanneurs
Verdanson
Q. du Verdanson
Bd Pasteur
Bd Louis Blanc
Bd Henri IV
Jardin des Plantes
SQUARE TOUR DES PINS
Faculté de Médecine
Cathédrale St-Pierre
R. de la Providence
R. de Candolle
l'Université
ANCIEN COUVENT DES URSULINES
R. du Pila St-Gely
Pl. de la Chapelle Neuve
le Corum
Bd Sully
Bd Bonne Nouvelle
ST-MATHIEU
R. du Cannau
l'Aiguillerie
N.-D. DES TABLES
MUSÉE FABRE
Pl. de la Canourgue
R. Fg St-Jaumes
PROMDE DU PEYROU
Arc de Triomphe
R. Foch
R. St-Firmin
Ste-Anne
R. de la Valfère
R. St-Guilhem
R. de la Loge
CARMES
Esplanade Ch. de Gaulle
les Pénitents Blancs
Bd Sarrail
Av. F. Mistral
Pl. de la Comédie
Bd Ledru-Rollin
R. Fg du Courreau
Bd du Jeu de Paume
R. des Four des Flammes
ST-ROCH
Grd Rue J. Moulin
Pl. St-Côme
R. des Étuves
OPÉRA
R. V. Hugo
R. de Verdun
R. A. Ollivier
LES PÉNITENTS BLEUS
TOUR DE LA BABOTE
Pl. E. Adam
R. Marceau
R. Paul Brousse
R. A. Michel
Cours Gambetta
R. du Cheval Vert
Pl. St-Denis
R. du Gd St-Jean
R. d'Alger
R. de la République
R. Maguelone
R. Pagézy
R. J. Ferry
Av. G. Clemenceau
ST-DENIS
PARC CLEMENCEAU
Bd V. Hugo

XXXX **Le Jardin des Sens** (Jacques et Laurent Pourcel) with rm
🌻🌻 *11 av. St-Lazare – ✆ 04 99 58 38 38 – www.jardindessens.com – contact@jardindessens.com – Fax 04 99 58 38 39* CT **e**

13 rm – €170/235 €170/235, €22 – 2 suites

Rest – *(closed 2-15 January, Monday lunch, Wednesday lunch and Sunday) (number of covers limited, pre-book)* Menu €50, €80/190 – Carte €117/212

Spec. Pressé de homard et légumes au jambon de canard, mangue et melon. Filet de loup cuit au four, petits cannelloni de céleri, jus de crustacés et escalope de foie gras. Soufflé au chocolat mi-amer, ganache tiède et glace vanille. **Wines** Vin de Pays de l'Hérault doux, Coteaux du Languedoc.

◆ The unusual loft-style dining room provides a view of the spiral garden: all five senses will be amazed, both by the cuisine and by the setting. Modern-style, very luxurious guest-rooms decorated with paintings from the Pourcel brothers' collection. Suite with private swimming pool.

XXX **Cellier Morel**
27 r. Aiguillerie, (Maison de la Lozère) – ✆ 04 67 66 46 36 – www.celliermorel.com – contact@celliermorel.com – Fax 04 67 66 23 61 – Closed 1st-23 August, Monday lunch, Wednesday lunch, Saturday lunch, Sunday and public holidays FY **d**

Rest – Menu (€32), €49/95 – Carte €70/91

◆ A vaulted, 13C dining room with fine designer decor, and a delightful courtyard-terrace enclosed by an 18C mansion. Inventive Lozère cuisine and fine wine list.

XX **La Réserve Rimbaud**
820 av. St-Maur – ✆ 04 67 72 52 53 – www.reserve-rimbaud.com – contact@reserve-rimbaud.com – Fax 04 67 02 02 77 – Closed 8-24 August, 3-13 January, Saturday lunch, Sunday dinner and Monday DT **w**

Rest – Menu (€24), €29/45 – Carte approx. €45

◆ A new lease of life for this restaurant, established in 1835, with dining room and terrace overlooking the Lez. Charming, southern style cuisine and good regional wines.

XX **Castel Ronceray**
130 r. Castel Ronceray, via ⑤ – ✆ 04 67 42 46 30 – www.lecastelronceray.fr – lecastelronceray@free.fr – Fax 04 67 27 41 96 – Closed 16 August-4 September, 21 February-1st March, Sunday and Monday

Rest – Menu (€28 bi), €44/67 – Carte €60/74

◆ A large shady garden screens this 19C Napolean III-style family mansion. Elegant, personalised interior. Traditional cuisine and well recommended wines.

XX **Les Vignes**
2 r. Bonnier d'Alco – ✆ 04 67 60 48 42 – www.lesvignesrestaurant.com – germaintasselli@hotmail.fr – Fax 04 67 60 48 42 – Closed 3-24 August and Sunday FY **e**

Rest – Menu (€24), €35/56 – Carte €42/53

◆ Walk down the stairs to the elegant dining area with a vaulted ceiling in this small restaurant located behind the prefecture building. Regional cuisine.

XX **Le Séquoïa**
148 r. de Galata, at Port Marianne – ✆ 04 67 65 07 07 – www.restaurantsequoia.com – Fax 04 67 64 50 23 – Closed 22 December-1st January, Saturday lunch and Sunday DV **e**

Rest – Menu (€29), €35/45 – Carte €40/55

◆ A trendy restaurant in the Port Marianne quarter on the left bank of the Lez. It has a modern setting, terrace overlooking the Jacques-Cœur basin and cuisine of various origins.

XX **Prouhèze Saveurs**
728 av. de la Pompignane – ✆ 04 67 79 43 34 – prouhezesaveurs@wanadoo.fr – Fax 04 67 79 71 94 – Closed 21 July-25 August, Wednesday dinner, Saturday lunch, Sunday, Monday and Tuesday DU **a**

Rest – Menu (€18), €27/32

◆ Restaurant run by the Prouhèze family (formely in the Aubrac region), featuring typical southern French colours and serving good, simple regional dishes around the fireplace in winter or on the terrace in summer.

La Compagnie des Comptoirs

51 av. Frédéric Delmas – ✆ 04 99 58 39 29 – www.lacompagniedescomptoirs.com – peyrinmickaelcdc@hotmail.fr – Fax 04 99 58 39 28 – Closed Tuesday lunch, Saturday lunch and Monday CT **u**

Rest – Menu (€ 25), € 36 – Carte € 30/40

◆ Hip decor inspired by the French-Indian trading company in this restaurant with a charming, partly covered terrace. The menu has Far Eastern and southern flavours.

Kinoa

6 r. des Sœurs Noires – ✆ 04 67 15 34 38 – restaurantkinoa@yahoo.fr – Fax 04 67 15 34 33 – Closed 10-23 November, Sunday and Monday EY **r**

Rest – Menu (€ 18 bi), € 28 (weekdays)/38 – Carte € 45/52

◆ Elegant modern setting and a charming terrace overlooking a small, shaded square next to an old church. Modern cuisine and a diet menu (no cream, alcohol or sugar).

Tamarillos

2 pl. Marché aux Fleurs – ✆ 04 67 60 06 00 – www.tamarillos.biz – info@tamarillos.biz – Fax 04 67 60 06 01 – Closed 28 October-4 November, 22-28 February, Monday lunch, Wednesday lunch and Sunday FY **b**

Rest – *(number of covers limited, pre-book)* Menu (€ 28), € 38/90 – Carte € 54/80

◆ Fruit and flowers are the inspiration for both the cuisine and decor of this unusual restaurant. A chef who was twice winner of the French dessert championship runs it.

Verdi

10 r. A. Ollivier – ✆ 04 67 58 68 55 – gunara1952@libero.it – Fax 04 67 58 28 47 – Closed Sunday FZ **s**

Rest – Menu (€ 15), € 19/28 – Carte approx. € 40

◆ This small, simple and relaxed Italian restaurant, close to the railway station, is decorated with Verdi and Opera posters. Italian and fish specialities. Wine shop.

L'Olivier

12 r. A. Ollivier – ✆ 04 67 92 86 28 – www.restaurant-lolivier.fr – contact@restaurant-lolivier.fr – Fax 04 67 92 10 65 – Closed 25 July-17 August, Sunday and Monday FZ **u**

Rest – *(pre-book)* Menu (€ 21), € 36/58 – Carte € 57/71

◆ Narrow dining room near the station, lined with mirrors and tightly packed tables, for convivial meals in a modernised setting. Classic cuisine served.

Insensé

39 bd Bonne-Nouvelle – ✆ 04 67 58 97 78 – www.jardindessens.com – insense.sebastien@gmail.com – Fax 04 67 02 08 19 – Closed Tuesday dinner and Thursday dinner from September to June, Sunday dinner and Monday FY **g**

Rest – Menu (€ 21), € 28

◆ Restaurant set within the walls of the Fabre Museum. The Pourcel brothers have set up this modern, designer establishment that has quickly made its mark. Up-to-date cuisine.

in Castries – pop. 5 146 – alt. 70 m – ✉ 34160

Syndicat d'initiative, 19, rue Sainte Catherine ✆ 04 99 74 01 77, Fax 04 99 74 01 77

Disini

1 r. des Carrières – ✆ 04 67 41 97 86 – www.disini-hotel.com – contact@disini-hotel.com – Fax 04 67 41 97 16

15 rm – † € 120/160 †† € 120/160, ☕ € 15 – 1 suite

Rest – *(closed Saturday lunch, Sunday dinner and Monday)* Menu (€ 19), € 25 (weekday lunch), € 32/75 – Carte € 53/69

◆ A brand-new hotel set amid a tranquil forest of evergreen oak. Individually furnished guestrooms with ethnic touches (Asia and Africa), soft lighting and high-tech comforts. Contemporary dishes in an eastern-inspired setting at the restaurant.

in Castelnau-le-Lez 7 km by ① and N 113 – pop. 15 000 – alt. 60 m – ✉ 34170

Domaine de Verchant
1 bd Philippe-Lamour – ✆ 04 67 07 26 00
– www.domainedeverchant.com – reservation@verchant.com
– Fax 04 67 07 26 01 – Closed 5-18 January
15 rm – €190/250 €190/900, €30 – 1 suite
Rest – *(number of covers limited, pre-book)*
Menu €25 (weekday lunch) – Carte €40/65
◆ An impressive wine domaine set in parkland. The interior, by the architect of the Murano and Kube hotels in Paris, blends Italian design with high-tech gadgetry. Superb guest-rooms. Up-to-date menu accompanied by wines from the estate.

in Baillargues – pop. 6 026 – alt. 23 m – ✉ 34670

Golf Hôtel de Massane
at the Massane Golf Course – ✆ 04 67 87 87 87
– www.massane.com – contact@massane.com – Fax 04 67 87 87 90
32 rm – €101/114 €119/135, €14
Rest – Menu (€22), €27/39 – Carte €29/50
◆ Vast hotel complex with extensive leisure and relaxation facilities. Featuring spacious rooms with Camargue-style decor. A contemporary style restaurant overlooking the golf course, serving modern meals and a good selection of regional wines.

via ② 5 km : A9 exit 29 and D172[E] – ✉ 34000 Montpellier

Le Mas des Brousses
540 r. Mas des Brousses – ✆ 04 67 64 18 91 – lemasdesbrousses@free.fr
– Fax 04 67 64 18 89 – Closed lunch from 1st to 20 August, Saturday lunch, Sunday dinner and Monday
Rest – Menu (€19), €24 (weekday lunch), €45/65 – Carte €50/60
◆ Pleasant 16C house covered in Virginia creeper and surrounded by a garden with terrace and pool. Inviting and spacious interior in warm colours. Traditional cuisine.

near A9-Montpellier-Sud interchange 2 km by ④ – ✉ 34000 Montpellier

Novotel
125 bis av. Palavas – ✆ 04 99 52 34 34 – www.accorhotels.com – h0450@accor.com – Fax 04 99 52 34 33
163 rm – €99/142 €99/165, €14
Rest – Menu (€18), €22 – Carte €20/45
◆ This typical motel, close to an interchange, houses bedrooms in conformity with chain standards, which are gradually being renovated. Wifi. Pleasant modern restaurant with poolside terrace service in summer.

in Lattes 5 km by ④ – pop. 16 600 – alt. 3 m – ✉ 34970

Office de tourisme, 679, avenue de Montpellier ✆ 04 67 22 52 91, Fax 04 67 22 52 91

Domaine de Soriech
opposite Z.A.C. Soriech, near the D 189 and D 21 roundabout – ✆ 04 67 15 19 15
– www.domaine-de-soriech.fr – michel.loustau@domaine-de-soriech.fr
– Fax 04 67 15 58 21 – Closed 2-15 February, Sunday dinner and Monday
Rest – Menu (€23 bi), €30 (weekday lunch), €35/76 – Carte €65/95
◆ A fine villa inspired by 1970s California architecture with designer decor, modern artwork and giant palm and pine trees in a delightful park. Quality regional cuisine.

Le Mazerand
Mas De Causse CD 172 – ✆ 04 67 64 82 10 – www.le-mazerand.com – info@le-mazerand.com – Fax 04 67 20 10 73 – Closed Saturday lunch, Sunday dinner and Monday
Rest – Menu (€23), €30/61 – Carte €45/80
◆ The new modern decor of this mansion house harmonises well with its past (vaults and ceilings with exposed woodwork). Regional cuisine is served. Attractive tiered terraces.

Le Bistrot d'Ariane

at Port Ariane – ✆ 04 67 20 01 27 – lebistrotdariane@free.fr – Fax 04 67 15 03 25 – Closed 20 December-4 January and Sunday except public holidays

Rest – Menu (€ 14), € 20 (weekdays)/39 – Carte € 40/58

◆ A subtle Art Deco style with a brasserie atmosphere in this attractive restaurant popular with the locals. Terrace overlooking the port. Nice menu of regional wines.

in Juvignac 6 km by ⑥, Millau road – pop. 5 592 – alt. 32 m – ✉ 34990

Golf Hôtel

rm,

rte de Lodève, at the international golf club – ✆ 04 67 45 90 00 – www.golfhotelmontpellier.com – info@golfhotelmontpellier.com – Fax 04 67 45 90 20

46 rm – €84 €112 – 40 suites **Rest** – Carte € 26/36

◆ This hotel is popular with golfers at the Juvignac course. Most of the rooms provide a view of the greens, some also feature a terrace. New suites. Modern dining room and quick snacks in the club house.

MONTPEZAT-DE-QUERCY – 82 Tarn-et-Garonne – 337 E6 – pop. 1 407 – alt. 275 m – ✉ 82270 Dordogne-Berry-Limousin 28 **B1**

Paris 600 – Cahors 29 – Montauban 39 – Toulouse 91

Office de tourisme, boulevard des Fossés ✆ 05 63 02 05 55, Fax 05 63 02 05 55

Les Trois Terrasses without rest

r. de la Libération – ✆ 05 63 02 66 21 – www.trois-terrasses.com – info@trois-terrasses.com – Fax 05 63 64 01 62 – Open 1st April-26 October

4 rm – €110/150 €110/150

◆ A pleasant stay in this 18C Provencal farmhouse with its blend of old and new furnishings. Rooms and terraced garden with a view overlooking the countryside.

Domaine de Lafon

Pech de Lafon, 4 km south via rte de Mirabel, D 20 and D 69 – ✆ 05 63 02 05 09 – www.domainedelafon.com – micheline.perrone@domainedelafon.com – Closed 15 February-15 March and 15-30 November

3 rm – €60/63 €73/81 – ½ P € 62/66 **Table d'hôte** – Menu € 25 bi

◆ This 19C building features a 360-degree view of the surrounding valleys. Providing rooms with the owner's work on display, and featuring fine fabrics. A charming library is located in the old pigeon coop. Traditional cuisine served.

MONTPON-MÉNESTÉROL – 24 Dordogne – 329 B5 – pop. 5 585 – alt. 93 m – ✉ 24700 4 **C1**

Paris 532 – Bergerac 40 – Libourne 43 – Périgueux 56 – Ste-Foy-la-Grande 23

Office de tourisme, place Clemenceau ✆ 05 53 82 23 77, Fax 05 53 81 86 74

in Ménestérol 1 km North – ✉ 24700 Montpon-Ménestérol

Auberge de l'Eclade

Coutras road – ✆ 05 53 80 28 64 – auberge-de-leclade@wanadoo.fr – Fax 05 53 80 28 64 – Closed Monday dinner, Tuesday dinner and Wednesday

Rest – Menu (€ 22 bi), € 28 bi/60 – Carte € 45/65

◆ Fine, personalised cuisine, a lengthy wine list, good choice of whiskies, pleasant modern décor and summer terrace: the locals think a lot of this restaurant.

MONT-PRÈS-CHAMBORD – 41 Loir-et-Cher – 318 F6 – pop. 3 242 – alt. 108 m – ✉ 41250 11 **B1**

Paris 184 – Blois 12 – Bracieux 8 – Orléans 63 – Romorantin-Lanthenay 35

Le St-Florent without rest

14 r. Chabardière – ✆ 02 54 70 81 00 – www.hotel-saint-florent.com – info@hotel-saint-florent.com – Fax 02 54 70 78 53

19 rm – €50 €56/62, € 8 – ½ P € 54/57

◆ The village is adjacent to the Boulogne Forest and Chambord Park. This vast house with a family feel has bright bedrooms, with sloping ceilings on the top floor.

Les Délices du St-Florent
14 r. Chabardière – ✆ 02 54 70 73 17 – lesdelicesdusaintflorent@wanadoo.fr – Fax 02 54 70 88 50 – Closed 15-30 November, 25-31 January, one week in February, Tuesday from October to March and Monday
Rest – Menu (€ 15), € 26/46 – Carte € 42/49
◆ Classic and creative cooking in this restaurant run by an energetic young couple. A press and rafters enhance the appealing rustic decor.

MONTRÉAL – 32 Gers – 336 D6 – pop. 1 238 – alt. 131 m – ✉ 32250 28 A2
Languedoc-Roussillon-Tarn Gorges

Paris 725 – Agen 57 – Auch 59 – Condom 16 – Mont-de-Marsan 65 – Nérac 27
Office de tourisme, pl. de l'hôtel de ville ✆ 05 62 29 42 85, Fax 05 62 29 42 46
de Guinlet Eauze, S : 12 km on D 29, ✆ 05 62 09 80 84

Daubin
(opposite the church) – ✆ 05 62 29 44 40 – daubin.bernard@wanadoo.fr – Fax 05 62 29 49 94 – Closed Sunday dinner, Monday and Tuesday
Rest – Menu € 16 (weekday lunch), € 26/58 – Carte € 49/70
◆ This welcoming, family-run village restaurant has been operating for three generations, serving tasty regional cuisine and local wines and featuring a terrace shaded by plane trees.

MONTREDON – 11 Aude – 344 F3 – see Carcassonne

MONTREUIL – 62 Pas-de-Calais – 301 D5 – pop. 2 428 – alt. 54 m 30 A2
– ✉ 62170 Northern France and the Paris Region

Paris 232 – Abbeville 49 – Arras 86 – Boulogne-sur-Mer 38 – Calais 73 – Lille 116
Office de tourisme, 21, rue Carnot ✆ 03 21 06 04 27, Fax 03 21 06 57 85
Site★ - Citadel★: ←★★ - Ramparts★ - St-Saulve church ★.

Château de Montreuil (Christian Germain)
4 chaussée des Capucins – ✆ 03 21 81 53 04 – www.chateaudemontreuil.com – reservation@chateaudemontreuil.com – Fax 03 21 81 36 43 – Closed 13 December-5 February, Tuesday lunch and Monday except July-August and Thursday lunch
12 rm – †€ 150/300 ††€ 150/300, ☕ € 18 – 4 suites – ½ P € 215/248
Rest – Menu € 38 (weekday lunch), € 75/95 – Carte € 75/85
Spec. Huîtes normandes de Saint-Vaast, espuma glacé à la ciboulette. Pigeonneau de Licques et foie gras dans l'esprit d'un hochepot flamand. Soufflé chaud aux fruits de la passion, sorbet Campari-orange.
◆ This elegant residence is located inside the ramparts. Refined rooms, adorned with period furniture, overlook a landscaped garden. Modern food with exotic and Mediterranean touches enhanced by a fine wine list.

Hermitage
pl. Gambetta – ✆ 03 21 06 74 74 – www.hermitage-montreuil.com – contact@hermitage-montreuil.com – Fax 03 21 06 74 75
57 rm – †€ 85/130 ††€ 85/160, ☕ € 15
Rest *Le Jéroboam* – 1 r. des Juifs, cours de l'hermitage, *✆ 03 21 86 65 80 (closed January, Monday except dinner in July-August and Sunday)* Menu € 17 (weekday lunch), € 25/64 – Carte € 40/75
◆ A fine, restored building, built under Napoleon III. Low-key bar and large rooms with discreet modern furniture. A modern menu accompanied by wines from small farmers can be found at this very designer restaurant with a wine-bar setting.

Coq Hôtel
rm,
2 pl. de la Poissonnerie – ✆ 03 21 81 05 61 – www.coqhotel.fr – arsene.pousset@wanadoo.fr – Fax 03 21 86 46 73 – Closed 21 December-6 February
19 rm – †€ 118 ††€ 138, ☕ € 21 – ½ P € 102/114
Rest – *(closed Sunday except July-August) (dinner only)*
Menu € 34/65 – Carte € 45/85
◆ This building with a refined façade of red brick is located on a small square in the town centre, providing charming rooms with modern style. This restaurant features two dining areas with parquet, a fireplace, and simple furnishings. Serves traditional cuisine.

Darnétal with rm — rm, VISA

pl. Darnétal – ✆ 03 21 06 04 87 – Fax 03 21 86 64 67 – Closed 22 June-10 July, 21 December-1st January, Monday and Tuesday

4 rm – €35 €60, ☕ €5 **Rest** – Menu €22 (weekdays)/38 – Carte €36/52

◆ This rustic inn on one of the squares of the upper town is decorated with many paintings, old trinkets and copperware. Convivial atmosphere and traditional cooking.

Froggy's Tavern — VISA AE

51 bis pl. du Gén. de Gaulle – ✆ 03 21 86 72 32 – www.froggystavern.com – contact@lagrenouillere.fr – Closed 20 December-4 February

Rest – grill room – Menu €18/24 – Carte €24/35

◆ Authenticity and conviviality guaranteed at this old granary loft built from wood and stone. Andouillettes and pork loins turn on the spit.

in La Madelaine-sous-Montreuil 3 km West by D 139 and secondary road – pop. 162 – alt. 7 m – ✉ 62170

Auberge de la Grenouillère (Alexandre Gauthier) with rm — P VISA AE

– ✆ 03 21 06 07 22 – www.lagrenouillere.fr – contact@lagrenouillere.fr – Fax 03 21 86 36 36 – Closed 20 December-4 February, Tuesday and Wednesday except July-August

4 rm – €125/135 €125/135, ☕ €10

Rest – Menu €33 (lunch), €55/95 – Carte €70/80

Spec. Grenouilles (season). Homard rôti fumé minute. Crêpes Suzette.

◆ This Picardy style farmhouse on the banks of the Canche is adorned with old sideboards, copperware and murals depicting frogs having a meal. In the kitchen, father and son create modern cuisine. Carefully selected wine list.

in Inxent 9 km North On D 127 – pop. 158 – alt. 28 m – ✉ 62170

Auberge d'Inxent with rm — P VISA

318 r. de la Vallée de la Course – ✆ 03 21 90 71 19 – auberge.inxent@wanadoo.fr – Fax 03 21 86 31 67 – Closed 22 June-10 July, 16 November-4 February, Tuesday and Wednesday

5 rm – €68/75 €68/75, ☕ €10 – ½ P €60/86

Rest – Menu €16/39 – Carte €19/45

◆ This former presbytery converted into a restaurant has fine furniture and a warm family atmosphere. It offers regional cuisine and an extensive wine list.

MONTREUIL – 93 Seine-Saint-Denis – 311 k2 – 101 17 – see Paris, Area

---

MONTREUIL-BELLAY – 49 Maine-et-Loire – 317 I6 – pop. 4 112 – alt. 50 m – ✉ 49260 Châteaux of the Loire — 35 C2

Paris 335 – Angers 54 – Châtellerault 70 – Chinon 39 – Cholet 61 – Poitiers 80 – Saumur 16

Office de tourisme, place du Concorde ✆ 02 41 52 32 39, Fax 02 41 52 32 35

Château★★ - Site★.

Hostellerie St-Jean — P VISA

432 r. Nationale – ✆ 02 41 52 30 41 – http://hostellerie-saint-jean.site.tc – ludoviccottet@orange.fr – Closed Wednesday dinner in low season, Sunday dinner and Monday

Rest – Menu (€14), €18/33 – Carte €25/50

◆ Located at the centre of the small, fortified, Medieval town; the cosy country-style main dining room is friendly and simple, while the lounge is more modern.

The ✿ award is the crème de la crème.
This is awarded to restaurants which are really worth travelling miles for!

MONTREUIL-L'ARGILLÉ – 27 Eure – 304 C8 – pop. 783 – alt. 170 m – ✉ 27390 33 C2

Paris 178 – L'Aigle 26 – Argentan 50 – Bernay 22 – Évreux 56 – Lisieux 33 – Vimoutiers 27

De Courteilles without rest
r. André Zalkin, rte d'Orbec, D 438, rte d'Orbec – ✆ 02 32 47 41 41 – www.hoteldecourteilles.com – b.borde@hoteldecourteilles.com – Fax 02 32 47 41 51
20 rm – †€ 48 ††€ 48, ☐ € 6
◆ An informal atmosphere in this new hotel, built away from the road. Functional bedrooms with varnished wooden furniture.

MONTREVEL-EN-BRESSE – 01 Ain – 328 D2 – pop. 1 994 – alt. 215 m – ✉ 01340 44 B1

Paris 395 – Bourg-en-Bresse 18 – Mâcon 25 – Pont-de-Vaux 22 – St-Amour 24 – Tournus 36

Office de tourisme, place de la Grenette ✆ 04 74 25 48 74, Fax 04 74 25 48 74

Léa (Louis Monnier)
10 rte d'Etrez – ✆ 04 74 30 80 84 – www.restaurant-lea.com – lea.montrevel@free.fr – Fax 04 74 30 85 66 – Closed 26 June-11 July, 22 December-15 January, Monday except July-August, Sunday dinner and Wednesday
Rest – *(number of covers limited, pre-book)* Menu € 28 (weekday lunch), € 36/70 – Carte € 60/90
Spec. Gâteau de foies blonds. Poularde de Bresse à la crème et aux morilles. Glace vanille aux éclats de nougatine, crème arabica. **Wines** Viré-Clessé, Fleurie.
◆ Classic gourmet menu served in a welcoming inn. Plants, paintings and knick-knacks (prevalence of poultry!) lend the dining room a chocolate-box feel.

Le Comptoir
9 Grande Rue – ✆ 04 74 25 45 53 – www.restaurant-lea.com – lea.montrevel@free.fr – Fax 04 74 30 85 66 – Closed 25 June-9 July, 17 December-7 January, Sunday dinner, Tuesday dinner and Wednesday
Rest – Menu € 18/31 – Carte € 23/37
◆ The Comptoir sports numerous authentic details such as bench seating, posters, mirrors and a mouth-watering bistro menu. Several regional dishes.

Bourg-en-Bresse road 2 km South on D 975 – ✉ 01340 Montrevel-en-Bresse

Pillebois
– ✆ 04 74 25 48 44 – www.hotellepillebois.com – lepillebois@wanadoo.fr – Fax 04 74 25 48 79 – Closed Sunday evening from November to March
31 rm – †€ 80/85 ††€ 85/90, ☐ € 9 – 1 suite – ½ P € 70/73
Rest *L'Aventure* – *(Closed Saturday lunch and Sunday dinner from November to March)* Menu € 20 (weekdays)/56 – Carte € 41/51
◆ This hotel has a modern look and Bresse charm with its red brick and wood. Functional, well-kept rooms. The ethnic decor of this restaurant invites you to travel as you sample the interesting menu of reinterpreted regional classics. Poolside terrace.

MONTRICHARD – 41 Loir-et-Cher – 318 E7 – pop. 3 451 – alt. 62 m – ✉ 41400 Châteaux of the Loire 11 A1

Paris 220 – Blois 37 – Châteauroux 85 – Châtellerault 95 – Loches 33 – Tours 43 – Vierzon 80

Syndicat d'initiative, 1, rue du Pont ✆ 02 54 32 05 10, Fax 02 54 32 28 80

Keep★: ✻★★.

Le Bellevue
24 quai de la République – ✆ 02 54 32 06 17 – www.hotel-le-bellevue41.com – contact@hotel-le-bellevue41.com – Fax 02 54 32 48 06 – Closed Friday, Saturday and Sunday from 23 November to 20 December
35 rm – †€ 80/110 ††€ 88/125, ☐ € 13 – 3 suites – ½ P € 73/93
Rest – *(closed on Friday from October to April)* Menu (€ 17), € 21/55 – Carte € 44/57
◆ The name says it all: most of the rooms, furnished in Wengé and pear wood, offer a panoramic view of the Cher. Three suites in a neighbouring villa. Restaurant with lovely wood panelling, bay windows facing the delightful valley and traditional food.

in Chissay-en-Touraine 4 km West by D 176 – pop. 1 005 – alt. 63 m – ✉ 41400

Château de Chissay
– ✆ 02 54 32 32 01 – chissay@leshotelsparticuliers.com – Fax 02 54 32 43 80
– Open mid-March to mid-November
23 rm – †€ 130/230 ††€ 130/230, ☕ € 15 – 9 suites
Rest – Menu (€ 25), € 42/65 – Carte € 48/85
◆ This 15C château has welcomed some illustrious guests, including Charles VII, Louis XI and de Gaulle. Spacious rooms with character, especially the troglodyte. Elegant restaurant (ribbed vaults, wood panelling and Louis XIII-style furniture) serving modern food.

MONTRICOUX – 82 Tarn-et-Garonne – 337 F7 – pop. 1 024 – alt. 113 m – ✉ 82800 29 C2

Paris 618 – Cahors 51 – Gaillac 39 – Montauban 25 – Villefranche-de-Rouergue 58

Les Gorges de l'Aveyron
Le Bugarel – ✆ 05 63 24 50 50 – www.gorges-aveyron.com – gorges-aveyron@orange.fr – Fax 05 63 24 50 51 – Closed 9-27 March, 7-18 December, 4-29 January, Tuesday except from 15 June to 15 September
Rest – Menu (€ 29), € 34/41 – Carte € 51/66
◆ A section of this modern villa has been converted into a restaurant. The bright and comfortable dining room opens onto a park, overlooking the Aveyron. Standard dishes.

MONTROND-LES-BAINS – 42 Loire – 327 E6 – pop. 4 608 – alt. 356 m – Spa : late March-late Nov. – Casino – ✉ 42210 Lyon - Rhone Valley 44 A2

Paris 447 – Lyon 69 – Montbrison 15 – Roanne 58 – St-Étienne 31 – Thiers 80

Office de tourisme, avenue des Sources ✆ 04 77 94 64 74, Fax 04 77 94 59 59

du Forez Domaine de Presles, S : 12 km on D 1082 and D 16, ✆ 04 77 30 86 85

Hostellerie La Poularde (Gilles Etéocle) rm,
2 r. de St-Étienne – ✆ 04 77 54 40 06 – www.la-poularde.com – la-poularde@wanadoo.fr – Fax 04 77 54 53 14 – Closed 3-25 August, 1st-20 January, Tuesday lunch, Sunday dinner and Monday
7 rm – †€ 82 ††€ 112, ☕ € 21 – 9 suites
Rest – *(pre-book weekends)* Menu (€ 56 bi), € 63 (weekdays)/123 – Carte € 90/110
Spec. Foie gras d'oie d'hier et d'aujourd'hui. Agneau de lait. Soufflé chaud à la Chartreuse. **Wines** Saint-Joseph blanc et rouge.
◆ A 1732 post house in the thermal spa of Forez. Choose from a personalised bedroom or apartments and duplexes overlooking the pool. Wine shop. Tempting menus in the restaurant: classic dishes updated with a contemporary touch and an excellent wine list.

Motel du Forez without rest
37 rte de Roanne – ✆ 04 77 54 42 28 – www.motelduforez.com – motelduforez@orange.fr – Fax 04 77 94 66 58 – Closed 16-23 August, 25 December-3 January and Sunday from November to February
18 rm – †€ 42 ††€ 52, ☕ € 7,50
◆ This Fifties hotel has comfortable, soundproofed bedrooms with pine furniture, well protected from the noise of the road. Extremely well-kept. Family hospitality.

Carré Sud
4 rte de Lyon – ✆ 04 77 54 42 71 – carre-sud.com – carresudfs@orange.fr – Fax 04 77 54 52 85 – Closed Wednesday lunch and Sunday
Rest – Menu (€ 17), € 26 (weekday lunch), € 30/57 – Carte € 50/90
◆ Suggestions on the specials board at lunch, more substantial menu in the evening. Market-inspired cuisine based around spices and Mediterranean flavours. Summer terrace.

MONTROUGE – 92 Hauts-de-Seine – 311 J3 – 101 25 – see Paris, Area

LE MONT-ST-MICHEL – 50 Manche – 303 C8 – pop. 41 – alt. 10 m – ✉ 50170 Normandie Cotentin, Brittany 32 A3

Paris 359 – Alençon 135 – Avranches 23 – Dinan 58 – Fougères 45 – Rennes 68 – St-Malo 55

Office de tourisme, boulevard de l'Avancée ✆ 02 33 60 14 30, Fax 02 33 60 06 75

Abbey★★★: La Merveille★★★, Cloister★★★ - Ramparts★★ - Grande-Rue★ - Abbey gardens★ - Mont-St-Michel Bay ★★.

Auberge St-Pierre

– ✆ 02 33 60 14 03 – www.auberge-saint-pierre.fr – aubergesaintpierre@wanadoo.fr – Fax 02 33 48 59 82 – Closed 30 December - 1st January

21 rm – †€ 99/106 ††€ 110/163, ☕ € 14

Rest – Menu (€ 19), € 23/62 – Carte € 22/42

◆ This 15C half-timbered inn is home to a restaurant and small well-kept bedrooms. The latter are bigger in an adjacent wing and offer sea views. You have a choice between a brasserie on the road side, a dining room upstairs or the terrace built against the ramparts.

in la Digue 2 km South On D 976 – ✉ 50170 Le Mont-St-Michel

Relais St-Michel

rm, VISA

– ✆ 02 33 89 32 00 – www.lemontsaintmichel.info – hotel@relais-st-michel.fr – Fax 02 33 89 32 01

32 rm – †€ 160/280 ††€ 160/280, ☕ € 15 – 7 suites – ½ P € 160/240

Rest – Menu (€ 15), € 25 (lunch), € 35/65 – Carte € 45/70

◆ The abbey in the background and elegant English-style furniture add to this establishment's charm. Large rooms with balcony or terrace. A dining room with a view of the famous Mount. Traditional cuisine.

Mercure

rm, VISA

La Caserne rte du Mont Saint Michel – ✆ 02 33 60 14 18 – www.le-mont-saint-michel.com – h1263@accor.com – Fax 02 33 60 39 28 – Open 7 February-10 November

100 rm – †€ 71/105 ††€ 79/115, ☕ € 12

Rest *Le Pré Salé* – Menu € 20/52 – Carte € 27/70

◆ This hotel complex, along the Couesnon and at the dyke's initial section, offers mostly identical and practical bedrooms with the chain's new design. Taste the renowned salt meadow lamb in the bright, spacious dining room.

De la Digue

rest, rm, VISA

– ✆ 02 33 60 14 02 – www.lemontsaintmichel.info – hotel-de-la-digue@wanadoo.fr – Fax 02 33 60 37 59

35 rm – †€ 65 ††€ 85, ☕ € 9 – ½ P € 85/95

Rest – Menu € 15/28 – Carte € 35/55

◆ Since 1877, the dyke has linked Mont-St-Michel to the mainland. The long, coastal hotel offers refurbished bedrooms of various sizes. The dining room and terrace command fine views of the Mont-St-Michel. Traditional cooking, seafood specialities.

Le Relais du Roy

rm, VISA

La Digue – ✆ 02 33 60 14 25 – www.le-relais-du-roy.com – reservation@le-relais-du-roy.com – Fax 02 33 60 37 69 – Closed 7 February-6 March

27 rm – †€ 70/101 ††€ 70/101, ☕ € 10

Rest – Menu (€ 14), € 19/40 – Carte € 32/53

◆ Hotel in an old farmhouse next to the sea wall. It dates from the end of the 18C and has more recent extensions. Functional rooms that are quieter on the riverside and to the rear. Traditional menu with Pré Salé lamb and seafood to the fore. The Breton fireplaces are 14C and 15C.

MONTSALVY – 15 Cantal – 330 C6 – pop. 890 – alt. 800 m – ✉ 15120 Auvergne 5 B3

Paris 586 – Aurillac 31 – Entraygues-sur-Truyère 14 – Figeac 57 – Rodez 56

Office de tourisme, rue du Tour-de-Ville ✆ 04 71 46 94 82, Fax 04 71 46 94 83

Puy-de-l'Arbre ❋★ Northeast: 1.5 km.

L'Auberge Fleurie with rm
place du Barry – ✆ 04 71 49 20 02 – www.auberge-fleurie.com – aubergefleuriecantal@orange.fr – Fax 04 71 49 29 65 – Closed 8-15 June, 28 September-5 October, Sunday evening and Monday except July-August
7 rm – €49/62 €49/62, €8 – ½ P €49/61
Rest – Menu €14 (weekday lunch), €24/29 – Carte €25/35
◆ The charm of yesteryear happily rubs shoulders with contemporary elegance in this smart inn where the chef rustles up tasty updated country fare. Excellent wine cellar. Attractive, very calm colonial-style guestrooms and delicious breakfasts.

MONT-SAXONNEX – 74 Haute-Savoie – 328 L4 – pop. 1 477 – alt. 1 000 m – ✉ 74130 — 46 F1

Paris 572 – Lyon 189 – Annecy 57 – Genève 38 – Vernier 55
Office de tourisme, 294 route de l'Eglise ✆ 04 50 96 97 27, Fax 04 50 96 97 63

Jalouvre
45 rte Gorge du Cé – ✆ 04 50 96 90 67 – www.iletait3fois.com – info@iletait3fois.com – Fax 04 50 96 91 41 – Closed 5-20 January
14 rm – €60 €75, €8 **Rest** – Menu €20/37 – Carte €30/44
◆ This completely renovated hotel in a quiet, mountain-village location offers comfortable, modern rooms decorated in the style of a contemporary chalet. Modern cuisine served in a wood-dominated decor. Panoramic views, plus a terrace under the shade of a lime tree.

LES MONTS-DE-VAUX – 39 Jura – 321 E6 – see Poligny

MONTSÉGUR – 09 Ariège – 343 I7 – see Lavelanet

MONTSERET – 11 Aude – 344 H4 – pop. 401 – alt. 92 m – ✉ 11200 — 22 B3

Paris 811 – Montpellier 115 – Carcassonne 50 – Perpignan 68 – Béziers 56

Le Relais de Montséret rm, rm,
1 r. Bufolenc – ✆ 04 68 43 29 51 – www.relais-de-montseret.com – relaisdemontseret@aliceadsl.fr – Fax 04 68 43 29 52 – Closed 12 November-18 December
6 rm – €69 €85, €9 – ½ P €65/73
Rest – *(closed Thursday lunch and Wednesday except in July-August)*
Menu (€15 bi), €19 bi (weekday lunch), €25/39 – Carte €30/38
◆ A characterful establishment set within the walls of an old barn. Rustic, Mediterranean-style rooms. Swimming pool. The wine-loving owner suggests regional wines to go with the traditional daily specials served in the restaurant.

MONTSOREAU – 49 Maine-et-Loire – 317 J5 – pop. 503 – alt. 77 m – ✉ 49730 Châteaux of the Loire — 35 C2

Paris 292 – Angers 75 – Châtellerault 65 – Chinon 18 – Poitiers 82 – Saumur 11 – Tours 56
Office de tourisme, avenue de la Loire ✆ 02 41 51 70 22
✳★★ from the viewpoint.
Candes St-Martin★: Collégiales★.

La Marine de Loire without rest
9 av. de la Loire – ✆ 02 41 50 18 21 – www.hotel-lamarinedeloire.com – resa@hotel-lamarinedeloire.com – Fax 02 41 50 19 26 – Closed in January
8 rm – €140/180 €140/180, €13 – 3 suites
◆ This hotel on the banks of the Loire is home to a flower-decked interior garden and delightful rooms. Large Jacuzzi swim tub and massages on request. Sunday brunch.

Le Bussy without rest
4 r. Jeanne d'Arc – ✆ 02 41 38 11 11 – www.hotel-lebussy.fr – hotel.lebussy@wanadoo.fr – Fax 02 41 38 18 10 – Open mid February-mid November
12 rm – €60 €80/90, €10
◆ Most of the rooms in this 18C house face the pretty castle of La Dame de Monsoreau, whose lover was Bussy. "Troglodyte" breakfast room.

Diane de Méridor
12 quai Ph. de Commines – ✆ 02 41 51 71 76 – www.restaurant-dianedemeridor.com – dianedemeridor@wanadoo.fr – Fax 02 41 51 17 17 – Closed 17-30 November, 8 January-8 February, Tuesday and Wednesday
Rest – Menu (€ 15), € 28/43 bi – Carte € 58/71
◆ Behind the old tufa façade of this restaurant is a dining room with views of the Loire. The brick-coloured walls are embellished with paintings. Elegant traditional cuisine.

MOOSCH – 68 Haut-Rhin – 315 G9 – pop. 1 818 – alt. 390 m – ✉ 68690 1 A3

Paris 469 – Strasbourg 128 – Colmar 53 – Mulhouse 29 – Belfort 48

Aux Trois Rois
35 r. du Gén. de Gaulle – ✆ 03 89 82 34 66 – www.aux-trois-rois.com – contact@aux-trois-rois.com – Fax 03 89 82 39 27 – Closed 29 December-14 January, Monday and Tuesday
Rest – Menu (€ 13), € 32/55 bi – Carte € 45/55
◆ A restaurant with a specials board that focuses on fish and seafood. Typically Alsatian-style (wood panelling, stained glass) or more dining rooms. Shaded terrace.

MORANGIS – 91 Essonne – 312 D3 – 101 35 – see Paris, Area

MOREILLES – 85 Vendée – 316 J9 – pop. 310 – alt. 5 m – ✉ 85450 34 B3

Paris 443 – Nantes 103 – La Roche-sur-Yon 50 – La Rochelle 42 – Fontenay-le-Comte 43

Le Château de l'Abbaye
– ✆ 02 51 56 17 56 – www.chateau-moreilles.com – daniellerenard@hotmail.com – Fax 02 51 56 30 30
5 rm – 🚹€ 79/109 🚹🚹€ 89/159, ☕ € 12 – ½ P € 95/115
Table d'hôte – Menu € 39
◆ A romantic château built on the ruins of an abbey where Richelieu officiated. Elegant rooms (antique furniture and family heirlooms), attractive sitting rooms and attentive service. Table d'hôte ambiance and generous portions of good family cooking.

MORET-SUR-LOING – 77 Seine-et-Marne – 312 F5 – pop. 4 477 – alt. 50 m – ✉ 77250 Northern France and the Paris Region 19 C3

Paris 74 – Fontainebleau 11 – Melun 28 – Nemours 17 – Sens 44

Office de tourisme, 4 bis, place de Samois ✆ 01 60 70 41 66, Fax 01 60 70 82 52

de la Forteresse Thoury-Férottes Domaine de la Forteresse, SW : 15 km on D 218 and D 22, ✆ 01 60 96 95 10

Site★.

Auberge de la Terrasse
40 r. Pêcherie – ✆ 01 60 70 51 03 – www.auberge-terrasse.com – aubergedelaterrasse@wanadoo.fr – Fax 01 60 70 51 69 – Closed 19 October-10 November, Friday dinner, Sunday dinner and Monday
17 rm – 🚹€ 41/63 🚹🚹€ 55/77, ☕ € 10 – ½ P € 65
Rest – Menu (€ 22), € 31/51 – Carte € 42/60
◆ An old building on the banks of the River Loing. Providing small, well-kept rooms with sound-proofed windows. Rustic-style dining room and terrace overlooking the river often painted by Alfred Sisley. Serving traditional cuisine.

Le Relais de Pont-Loup
14 r. Peintre Sisley – ✆ 01 60 70 43 05 – pontloup@wanadoo.fr – Fax 01 60 70 22 54 – Closed Tuesday from October to April, Sunday dinner and Monday
Rest – *(pre-book weekends)* Menu € 28 (weekdays)/38 – Carte € 53/74
◆ Bricks, beams, fireplace and roasting spit make up the decor in this restaurant that is reached via the kitchens. Terrace facing the garden that winds down to the Loing.

XX **Hostellerie du Cheval Noir** with rm
47 av. J. Jaurès – ✆ 01 60 70 80 20 – www.chevalnoir.fr – infos@chevalnoir.fr – Fax 01 60 70 80 21 – Closed 27 July-11 August, 25 January-9 February, Monday lunch and Tuesday lunch
1 rm – €90/145 €105/175, €12 – ½ P €92/127
Rest – Menu (€20), €30/90 – Carte €60/90
◆ This former 18C post house is opposite the gateway to the old fortified town. It serves inventive 'sugar and spice' cuisine.

MOREY-ST-DENIS – 21 Côte-d'Or – 320 J6 – pop. 696 – alt. 275 m – ✉ 21220 8 D1

Paris 318 – Beaune 30 – Dijon 16

Castel de Très Girard rm, VISA AE
7 r. de Très Girard – ✆ 03 80 34 33 09 – www.castel-tres-girard.com – info@castel-tres-girard.com – Fax 03 80 51 81 92 – Closed 15-26 November and 15 February-5 March
9 rm – €79/187 €79/187, €15
Rest – Menu (€25), €27 (lunch), €42/83 – Carte €61/80 dinner only
◆ This lovely 18C mansion, formerly a wine press, offers spacious, comfortable rooms. Pleasant garden and swimming pool. Menu in keeping with current tastes. Rustic, trendy decor and a lovely summer terrace.

MORGAT – 29 Finistère – 308 E5 – ✉ 29160 Crozon Brittany 9 A2

Paris 590 – Brest 62 – Châteaulin 38 – Douarnenez 42 – Morlaix 84 – Quimper 52

Large grottoes★.

Le Grand Hôtel de la Mer VISA AE
av. de la Plage – ✆ 02 98 27 02 09 – thierry.regnier@belambra-vvf.fr – Fax 02 98 27 02 39 – Open 3 April-3 October
78 rm – €48/91 €56/125, €15 – ½ P €49/110
Rest – *(Closed lunch except Sunday and Monday except dinner in July-August)* Menu €22/39
◆ A Belle Époque ambiance pervades in this hotel, run by the Belambra-VVF group. Simple rooms overlooking the sea or the garden planted with palm trees. A large dining room for half-board guests and a more intimate restaurant. Both rooms overlook Douarnenez bay.

Julia rest, VISA AE
43 r. de Tréflez – ✆ 02 98 27 05 89 – www.hoteljulia.fr – contact@hoteljulia.fr – Fax 02 98 27 23 10 – Open April-3 November
15 rm – €51/140 €51/140, €9 – 1 suite – ½ P €59/103
Rest – *(Closed lunch from Tuesday to Friday except July-August and Monday)* Menu €25, €33/60 – Carte €33/65
◆ Situated in a quiet residential area, this hotel is gradually being renovated to provide modern levels of comfort (to date, four large, contemporary-style bedrooms and a brand new seminar room). "Boarding house" atmosphere in the circular dining room. Regional recipes.

De la Baie without rest VISA
46 bd Plage – ✆ 02 98 27 07 51 – www.presquile-crozon.com – hotel.de.la.baie@presquile-crozon.com – Fax 02 98 26 29 65
26 rm – €45/50 €50/60, €7
◆ A small, simple hotel with well-maintained rooms, revamped in bright colours. Some enjoy a view of the sea, as does the attractive breakfast room.

MORILLON – 74 Haute-Savoie – 328 N4 – see Samoëns

MORLAÀS – 64 Pyrénées-Atlantiques – 342 K2 – pop. 4 121 – alt. 287 m – ✉ 64160 Atlantic Coast 3 B3

Paris 767 – Pau 15 – Tarbes 37

Office de tourisme, place Sainte-Foy ✆ 05 59 33 62 25, Fax 05 59 33 62 25

Portal★ of Sainte-Foy church.

Le Bourgneuf with rm

3 r. Bourg Neuf – ✆ 05 59 33 44 02 – courbet.daniel@wanadoo.fr – Fax 05 59 33 07 74 – Closed 15 October-8 November, Sunday dinner and Saturday

12 rm – €43 €47, ☕ €5

Rest – Menu (€10), €15 bi (weekdays)/40 – Carte €25/45

◆ Regional cuisine served in a renovated rustic decor. Dishes of the day also served at the bar. The small, practical and spruced up rooms are in a new building.

MORLAIX – **29 Finistère** – **308** H3 – **pop. 15 800** – **alt. 7 m** 9 **B1**
– ✉ **29600** **Brittany**

Paris 538 – Brest 61 – Quimper 78 – St-Brieuc 86

Office de tourisme, place des Otages ✆ 02 98 62 14 94, Fax 02 98 63 84 87

de Carantec Carantec Rue de Kergrist, N : 13 km on the D73, ✆ 02 98 67 09 14

Old Morlaix★: Viaduct★ - Grand'Rue★ - Interior★ of "Reine Anne" (Queen Anne) house - Virgin★ in St-Mathieu church - Rose★ in the musée des Jacobins★.

Calvaire★★ de Plougonven★ 12 km by D 9.

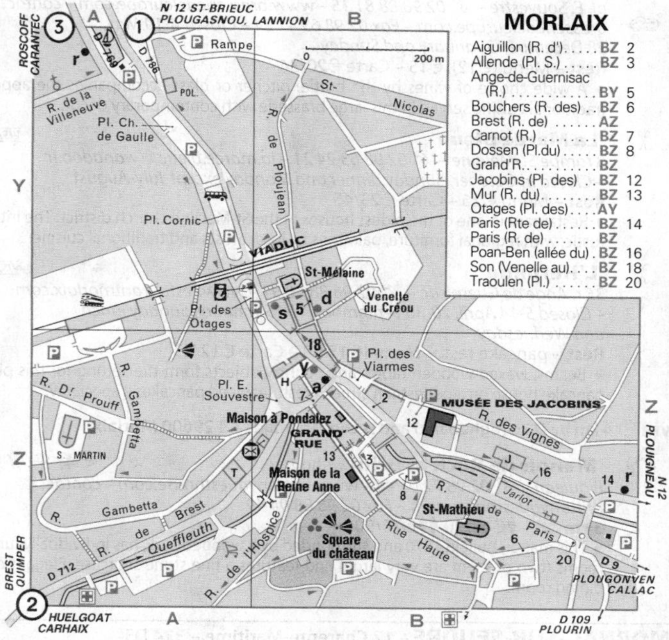

De l'Europe without rest

1 r. Aiguillon – ✆ 02 98 62 11 99 – www.hotel-europe-com.fr – reservations@hotel-europe-com.fr – Fax 02 98 88 83 38 – Closed 17 December-3 January BZ **a**

59 rm – €75/250 €110/250, ☕ €8,50

◆ The hall and staircase of this 200-year old building have fine carved 17C wooden-panelling. Choose a refurbished room with prettier decor. Cheerful hospitality.

Du Port without rest
3 quai de Léon – ✆ 02 98 88 07 54 – www.lhotelduport.com – info@lhotelduport.com – Fax 02 98 88 43 80 – Closed 20 December-4 January AY **r**
25 rm – 🚹€ 54/60 🚹🚹€ 62/82, ☕ € 9
◆ A 19C Breton house facing the marina. Practical rooms, which are all modernised and well-soundproofed. Some have a view of the quayside and viaduct.

Les Bruyères without rest
3 km via Plouigneau road, east on the D712 – ✆ 02 98 88 08 68 – www.hotel-morlaix.com – hotellesbruyeres@wanadoo.fr – Fax 02 98 88 66 54
32 rm – 🚹€ 49/71 🚹🚹€ 49/74, ☕ € 8
◆ A low level, typical 1970s building providing fully refurbished rooms (practical furnishings and lively colours) and welcoming breakfast room.

Manoir de Coat Amour
rte de Paris – ✆ 02 98 88 57 02 – www.gites-morlaix.com – stafford.taylor@wanadoo.fr – Fax 02 98 88 57 02 BZ **r**
6 rm ☕ – 🚹€ 70/78 🚹🚹€ 80/115 **Table d'hôte** – Menu € 32 bi/47 bi
◆ Set above the town, this regional-style 19C manor is surrounded by a floral park. Providing plush and spacious rooms with antique furnishings. Table d'hôte on some evenings during the week.

Brasserie de l'Europe
pl. E. Souvestre – ✆ 02 98 88 81 15 – www.brasseriedeleurope.com – contact@brasseriedeleurope.com – Fax 02 98 63 47 24 – Closed 4-10 May, 28 December-3 January and Sunday BZ **y**
Rest – Menu (€ 12), € 15 – Carte € 20/34
◆ A wide choice of wines by the bottle, pitcher or glass accompanies the appetising traditional cuisine served in this large brasserie with contemporary decor.

La Marée Bleue
3 rampe St-Mélaine – ✆ 02 98 63 24 21 – la.maree.bleue@wanadoo.fr – Closed in October, Sunday dinner and Monday except July-August BY **s**
Rest – Menu € 26 – Carte € 23/45
◆ Restaurant in one of the oldest houses in the St-Mélaine church district. The interior is rustic, with regional furniture, paintings by local artists and traditional cuisine.

L'Hermine
35 r. Ange de Guernisac – ✆ 02 98 88 10 91 – www.restaurantmorlaix.com – Closed 5-14 April, 20-30 September, 1st-15 January, Sunday lunch and Wednesday BY **d**
Rest – pancake rest. – Menu (€ 15 bi) – Carte € 12/23
◆ Beams, waxed wooden tables and country objects form the setting for this pleasant pancake house on a pedestrian street. Fresh seaweed pancakes a speciality.

via ① 4 km by D 76 (right bank) and secondary road - ✉ 29600 Morlaix

Manoir de Roch ar Brini without rest
Ploujean – ✆ 02 98 72 01 44 – www.brittanyguesthouse.com – contact@brittanyguesthouse.com – Fax 02 98 88 04 49
3 rm ☕ – 🚹€ 65/70 🚹🚹€ 70/90
◆ This manor, built in 1870 and surrounded by a wooded park, has individually furnished rooms (two of them are very large) and features a fine stone staircase. Elegant original dining room.

MORNAC-SUR-SEUDRE – 17 Charente-Maritime – 324 D5 38 A3
– pop. 682 – alt. 5 m – ✉ 17113 Poitou Charentes Vendée

Paris 508 – Poitiers 175 – La Rochelle 66 – Rochefort 36 – Saintes 38

Le Mornac without rest
21 r. des Halles – ✆ 05 46 22 63 20 – www.le-mornac.com – le-mornac@orange.fr – Fax 05 46 22 63 20 – Closed 14 January-4 February
5 rm ☕ – 🚹€ 55/70 🚹🚹€ 60/75
◆ Handsome 18C abode converted into a guesthouse by a charming couple of Dutch origin. Cosy rooms in which guests will immediately feel at home. Garden, terrace, pool.

MORNAS – 84 Vaucluse – **332** B8 – **pop. 2 248** – **alt. 37 m** – ✉ **84550** 40 **A2**
Provence

Paris 646 – Avignon 40 – Bollène 12 – Montélimar 47 – Nyons 46 – Orange 12

Le Manoir
16 av. Jean Moulin – ✆ 04 90 37 00 79 – www.hotel-le-manoir.com – info@lemanoir-mornas.fr – Fax 04 90 37 10 34 – Closed 1st January-12 February, Sunday dinner, Monday and Tuesday from October to May
23 rm – €55 €55/95, €8 – ½ P €63/83
Rest – *(closed Tuesday lunch and Monday)* Menu (€18), €28/50 – Carte €37/46
◆ At the foot of a sheer cliff, this stylish 18C abode sports a charming 1940s decor and a family feel. Each of the rooms boasts its own personal tasteful style. Rustic dining room and delightfully shaded patio terrace. Traditional cooking.

MORSBRONN-LES-BAINS – 67 Bas-Rhin – **315** K3 – **pop. 568** – **alt. 200 m** – ✉ **67360** 1 **B1**

Paris 489 – Haguenau 11 – Sarreguemines 68 – Strasbourg 44 – Wissembourg 28

Office de tourisme, 1, route de Haguenau ✆ 03 88 05 82 40, Fax 03 88 94 20 04

La Source des Sens
19 rte Haguenau – ✆ 03 88 09 30 53 – www.lasourcedessens.fr – contact@lasourcedessens.fr – Fax 03 88 09 35 65 – Closed 16-31 July, January, Sunday dinner and Monday
16 rm – €45/150 €55/160, €12 – 1 suite – ½ P €65/130
Rest – Menu €15 (weekday lunch), €25/65 – Carte €50/65
◆ An in vogue establishment: minimalist design, dark wood, Japanese light fixtures in the rooms and an extensive wellness centre. In the restaurant, a plasma screen broadcasts action live from the kitchens. Modern decor and creative dishes.

MORTAGNE-AU-PERCHE – 61 Orne – **310** M3 – **pop. 4 156** – **alt. 260 m** – ✉ **61400** Normandy 33 **C3**

Paris 153 – Alençon 39 – Chartres 80 – Lisieux 89 – Le Mans 73 – Verneuil-sur-Avre 40

Office de tourisme, Halle aux Grains ✆ 02 33 85 11 18, Fax 02 33 83 34 37

De Bellême Saint-Martin Bellême Les Sablons, S : 17 km on D 938, ✆ 02 33 73 12 79

Panelling★ of N.-Dame church.

Du Tribunal
4 pl. Palais – ✆ 02 33 25 04 77 – www.hotel-tribunal.fr – hotel.du.tribunal@wanadoo.fr – Fax 02 33 83 60 83
21 rm – €60/85 €60/105, €9
Rest – Menu (€17), €25/48 – Carte €36/57
◆ This delightful 13C and 18C flower-decked house offers guests a choice of comfortable rooms, renovated in a modern, very tasteful style. Elegant dining room where the culinary offerings include boudin noir (black pudding), a speciality of Mortagne. Terrace and interior garden.

in Pin-la-Garenne 9 km South by Bellême road on D 938 – pop. 619 – alt. 158 m – ✉ 61400

La Croix d'Or
6 r. de la Herse – ✆ 02 33 83 80 33 – www.lacroixdor.free.fr – lacroixdor@free.fr – Fax 02 33 83 06 03 – Closed 3 February-4 March, Tuesday dinner and Wednesday
Rest – Menu (€10), €19/45 – Carte €26/48
◆ Friendly inn alongside the main road through the village. A log fire adds warmth and welcome to the rustic dining room in wintertime. Traditional fare.

MORTAGNE-SUR-GIRONDE – 17 Charente-Maritime – **324** F7 – **pop. 1 001** – **alt. 51 m** – ✉ **17120** Atlantic Coast 38 **B3**

Paris 509 – Blaye 59 – Jonzac 30 – Pons 26 – La Rochelle 115 – Royan 34 – Saintes 36

Syndicat d'initiative, 1, place des Halles ✆ 05 46 90 52 90, Fax 05 46 90 52 90

Chapel★ of the St-Martial hermitage South : 1,5 km.

La Maison du Meunier without rest
36 quai de l'Estuaire, (at the port) – ✆ 05 46 97 75 10
– www.maisondumeunier.com – info@maisondumeunier.com
– Fax 05 46 92 25 54
5 rm – **†**€ 60 **††**€ 60
◆ Modern art, old photos and even an old motorbike decorate this house that once belonged to a miller. Attractive personalised rooms and delightful welcome.

MORTEAU – **25 Doubs** – **321** J4 – **pop. 6 339** – **alt. 780 m** – ✉ **25500** 17 **C2**
Burgundy-Jura

Paris 468 – Basel 121 – Belfort 88 – Besançon 65 – Neuchâtel 42 – Pontarlier 31

Office de tourisme, place de la Halle ✆ 03 81 67 18 53, Fax 03 81 67 62 34

La Guimbarde without rest
10 pl. Carnot – ✆ 03 81 67 14 12 – www.la-guimbarde.com – info@la-guimbarde.com – Fax 03 81 67 48 27
25 rm – **†**€ 51/100 **††**€ 56/100, € 8
◆ Imposing 19C building with updated rooms; only the breakfast room has kept its rustic appearance. Piano bar in the lounge at weekends.

Auberge de la Roche (Philippe Feuvrier)
at Pont de la Roche, 3 km southwest by D 437 ✉ 25570 – ✆ 03 81 68 80 05 – pfeuvrier@wanadoo.fr – Fax 03 81 68 87 64 – Closed 1st-14 July, 1st-7 February, Tuesday dinner, Sunday dinner and Monday
Rest – Menu € 27, € 43/78 – Carte € 68/91
Spec. Foie gras d'oie au naturel à la gelée d'huître (November to April). Paillasson de grosses langoustines au beurre d'orange. Moelleux et macaron au chocolat.
Wines Château-Châlon, Côtes du Jura-Trousseau.
◆ A warm welcome and updated Franche Comté cuisine have brought renown to this restaurant in the Haut Doubs countryside. Aperitifs and coffee are served on the terrace.

in Grand'Combe-Châteleu **5 km Southwest by D 437 and D 47** – **pop. 1 322** – **alt. 760 m** – ✉ **25570**

Old farmhouses★.

Faivre
2, bas de Grand'Combe – ✆ 03 81 68 84 63 – Fax 03 81 68 87 80 – Closed Sunday dinner and Monday
Rest – Menu € 18 bi (weekday lunch), € 25/60 – Carte € 25/65
◆ A large Comté house in a picturesque hamlet with attractive old farmhouses. Rustic setting where regulars sample regional dishes, including the renowned Morteau sausage, the 'Jesus'.

in Combes **7 km West by D 48 and secondary road** – **pop. 689** – **alt. 935 m** – ✉ **25500**

L'Auberge de la Motte
at la Motte – ✆ 03 81 67 23 35 – www.auberge-de-la-motte.fr – auberge.delamotte@orange.fr – Fax 03 81 67 63 45 – Closed one week in November and December except school holidays
7 rm – **†**€ 45/48 **††**€ 45/48, € 6,50
Rest – *(closed lunch from Monday to Friday and Sunday dinner)* Menu € 17/20 – Carte € 20/28
◆ Restored regional style farmhouse dating from 1808. Wood panelled rooms with modern furniture. Simple regional menu with the emphasis on local produce. Summer terrace.

MORTEMART – **87 Haute-Vienne** – **325** C4 – **pop. 125** – **alt. 300 m** – ✉ **87330** **Dordogne-Berry-Limousin** 24 **A1**

Paris 388 – Bellac 14 – Confolens 31 – Limoges 41 – St-Junien 20

Syndicat d'initiative, Château des Ducs ✆ 05 55 68 98 98

XX **Le Relais** with rm VISA

1 pl. Royale – 05 55 68 12 09 – dominique.pradeau189@wanadoo.fr – Fax 05 55 68 12 09 – Closed February, Tuesday except 15 July-31 August and Monday

5 rm – € 48 € 55, € 8 – ½ P € 65

Rest – Menu € 20 (weekdays)/48 – Carte € 35/58

◆ A pleasant country restaurant with exposed beams, bare stonework and fireplace. Opposite the lovely food market. Tasty traditional cuisine, and simple but attractive rooms.

MORTHEMER – **86 Vienne** – **322** J6 – **86300** 39 **C2**

Poitou Charentes Vendée

Paris 370 – Poitiers 33 – Châtellerault 70 – Buxerolles 35 – Chauvigny 17

X **La Passerelle** VISA

2 r. du Baron de Soubeyran – 05 49 01 13 33 – Fax 05 49 01 13 33 – Closed 2-9 March, 14-28 September, Sunday, Monday except lunch public holidays and Wednesday dinner

Rest – Menu € 12 bi (weekday lunch), € 25/45 – Carte € 40/50

◆ The majestic chateau of Morthemer dominates this tiny country house reached via a footbridge (hence the name). Rustic interior, traditional fare made from fresh produce.

MORZINE – **74 Haute-Savoie** – **328** N3 – **pop. 2 948** – **alt. 960 m** – **Winter sports : 1 000/2 100 m** **6** **61** – **74110** French Alps 46 **F1**

Paris 586 – Annecy 84 – Cluses 26 – Genève 58 – Thonon-les-Bains 31

Office de tourisme, 23, Place du Baraty 04 50 74 72 72, Fax 04 50 79 03 48

Avoriaz Office du Tourisme Avoriaz, E : 12 km on D 338, 04 50 74 11 07

Le Pléney★ by cable car, pointe du Nyon★ by cable car - Télésiège de Chamoissière (Chamoissière chairlift)★★.

Plan on following page

Le Samoyède VISA AE

– 04 50 79 00 79 – www.hotel-lesamoyede.com – info@hotel-lesamoyede.com – Fax 04 50 79 07 91 – Open end June to end September and 15 December-15 April B **g**

30 rm – € 59/105 € 70/280, € 13 – ½ P € 82/187

Rest *L'Atelier* – *(closed lunch except Sunday and public holidays)* Menu € 38/68 – Carte € 45/65

◆ Most of the spacious guestrooms (four which are brand new) in this large chalet face west, and have views of the ski slopes. Elegant ambience and innovative cuisine.

Le Dahu rest, VISA

293 chemin du Mas Métout – 04 50 75 92 92 – www.dahu.com – info@dahu.com – Fax 04 50 75 92 50 – Open 20 June-10 September and 20 December-15 April B **z**

39 rm – € 45/135 € 70/210, € 14 – 8 suites – ½ P € 70/160

Rest – *(closed lunch winter except school holidays and Tuesday dinner 20 December-15 April)* Menu € 28/50

◆ Family hotel dominating the valley on the right bank of the Dranse. Cosy mountain accommodation, often with balcony. A good place to recharge one's batteries. Panoramic restaurant with an original menu.

Champs Fleuris VISA AE

– 04 50 79 14 44 – www.hotel-champs-fleuris.com – info@hotel-champs-fleuris.fr – Fax 04 50 79 27 75 – Open 25 June-10 September and 15 December-11 April A **f**

47 rm – € 100/265 € 100/265, € 12 – 6 suites – ½ P € 89/174

Rest – Menu € 25 (lunch), € 31/35

◆ Ideally situated at the foot of the Le Pléney cable car. Spacious guestrooms, most of which have been renovated in Alpine style. Lounge with fireplace and a view over the ski slopes. Traditional cuisine served in a refurbished dining room.

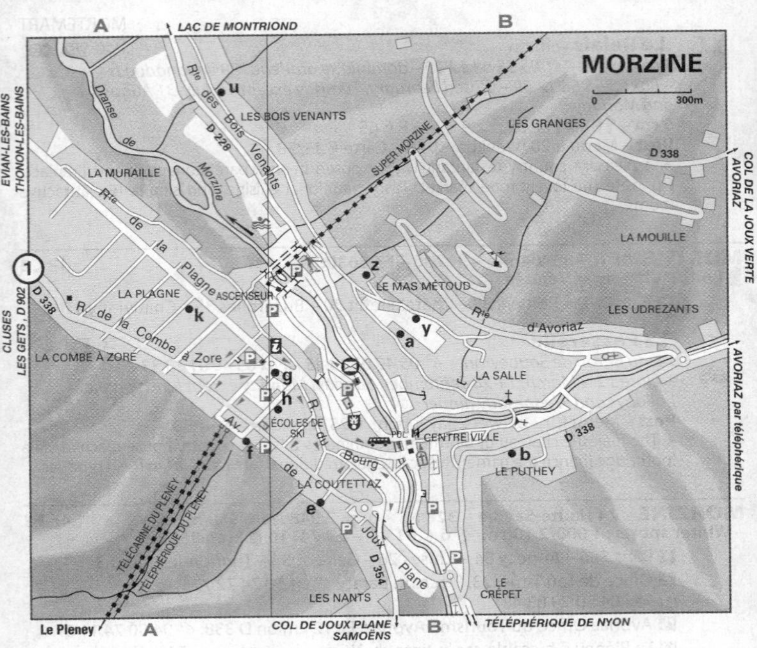

La Bergerie without rest

– ✆ 04 50 79 13 69 – www.hotel-bergerie.com
– info@hotel-bergerie.com – Fax 04 50 75 95 71
– Open 27 June-13 September and 19 December-20 April B **h**

27 rm – †€ 70/200 ††€ 115/310, ☕ € 12

◆ An inviting chalet, with a young, family atmosphere, where guests quickly feel at home. Traditional Alpine decor. Heated swimming pool open all year.

Chalet Philibert

rm, rest, VISA

480 rte des Putheys – ✆ 04 50 79 25 18 – www.chalet-philibert.com
– info@chalet-philibert.com – Fax 04 50 79 25 81 – Open 15 June-15 September and 1st December-20 April B **b**

25 rm (½ board only) – ½ P € 94/132

Rest ***Le Restaurant du Chalet*** – *(open 18 December-20 April) (dinner only)*
Menu € 32, € 45/55

◆ A chalet renovated according to the Savoy tradition, using old materials gleaned from neighbouring farms. Comfortable rooms, most of which have balconies. The emphasis is on contemporary cuisine in this friendly restaurant, which has an attractive vaulted dining room

La Clef des Champs

rm, rest, VISA

av. Joux-Plane – ✆ 04 50 79 10 13
– www.clefdeschamps.com – hotel@clefdeschamps.com – Fax 04 50 79 08 18
– Open 30 June-2 September and 20 December-13 April B **e**

30 rm – †€ 80/130 ††€ 80/150, ☕ € 10 – ½ P € 69/89

Rest – Menu (€ 20), € 25

◆ This chalet, located at the foot of the ski slopes, has attractive, intricately carved wooden balconies. Three categories of rooms, refurbished in Alpine style. Choose between regional specialities and international cuisine in this restaurant, attractively furnished in polished pine.

L'Hermine Blanche
414 chemin du Mas Metout – 04 50 75 76 55 – www.hermineblanche.com – info@hermineblanche.com – Fax 04 50 74 72 47 – Open 5 July-1st September and 20 December-18 April — B **y**
25 rm – €47/64 €58/84, €9 – ½ P €59/78
Rest – *(dinner only)* Menu €25
◆ Near the road to Avoriaz, this attractive chalet offers simple, fresh and welcoming rooms, all with a balcony. A pleasant half-covered swimming pool and jacuzzi face the garden. Residents can choose from a range of international dishes prepared by the Italian chef.

Fleur des Neiges
– 04 50 79 01 23 – www.chalethotelfleurdesneiges.com – info@chalethotelfleurdesneiges.com – Fax 04 50 75 95 75 – Open 1st July-10 September and 20 December-15 April — A **k**
31 rm – €40/72 €50/100, €10 – ½ P €50/95 **Rest** – Menu €20/30
◆ This fully renovated establishment offers cosy rooms with pine furniture and snug duvets. Leisure facilities: fitness centre, sauna, tennis court and pool. A panelled dining room in winter. In summer, service in the garden. Set menu.

Les Côtes
265 chemin de la Salle – 04 50 79 09 96 – www.hotel-lescotes.com – info@hotel-lescotes.com – Fax 04 50 75 97 38 – Open 3 July-31 August and 20 December-11 April — B **a**
4 rm – €60/83 €60/83, €8 – 19 suites – €75/136 – ½ P €57/82
Rest – *(dinner only) (residents only)* Menu €21/24
◆ This double chalet, with carved wooden balconies, is well situated on a south-facing slope. Simple but well-kept rooms and studio apartments. Good choice of leisure activities, including an attractive glass-covered swimming pool.

L'Ours Blanc
522 chemin Martenant – 04 50 79 04 02 – www.oursblanc-morzine.com – info@oursblanc-morzine.com – Fax 04 50 75 97 82 – Open 5 July-7 September and 22 December-10 April — A **u**
22 rm – €48/66 €60/78, €9 – ½ P €58/70
Rest – *(dinner only) (residents only)* Menu €22
◆ Standard south-facing chalet, set away from the centre. Clean, attractive and simply furnished guestrooms, some of which have balconies. Hospitable welcome. This restaurant only serves one menu - fondue and raclette twice a week.

in Avoriaz 14 km East by D 338 – 74110
Office de tourisme, place centrale 04 50 74 02 11, Fax 04 50 74 24 29

Les Dromonts
pedestrian access – 04 50 74 08 11 – www.christophe-leroy.com – info@christophe-leroy.com – Fax 04 50 74 02 79 – Open 15 December-28 April
29 rm (½ board only) – 6 suites – ½ P €115/350
Rest *Table du Marché* – Menu €29 (weekdays)/89 – Carte €65/93
◆ Cosy contemporary rooms, intimate lounges, bar and an ultra-modern fireplace. This famous hotel opened in 1965 and remains as popular as ever. Smart bistro interior and a specials board at the Table du Marché.

MOSNAC – 17 Charente-Maritime – 324 G6 – see Pons

MOSNES – 37 Indre-et-Loire – 317 P4 – pop. 757 – alt. 70 m – 37530 — 11 A1

Paris 211 – Orléans 86 – Tours 37 – Blois 26 – Joué-lès-Tours 48

Domaine des Thômeaux — rm, rest,
12 r. des Thômeaux – 02 47 30 40 14 – www.domainedesthomeaux.fr – hotel@domainedesthomeaux.fr – Fax 02 47 30 43 32
27 rm – €78/130 €78/130, €11
Rest – Menu (€15), €20/24 – Carte €25/38
◆ This brick and tufa stone château offers rooms decorated on the theme of cities around the world. Relaxation and leisure activities in the spa and Fantasy Forest theme park. World cuisine served in a cosy setting or on a large terrace.

LA MOTHE-ACHARD – 85 Vendée – 316 G8 – pop. 2 340 – alt. 20 m – ✉ 85150 34 **B3**

Paris 446 – Nantes 90 – La Roche-sur-Yon 25 – Challans 40 – Les Sables-d'Olonne 19

Office de tourisme, 56, rue G. Clémenceau ✆ 02 51 05 90 49, Fax 02.51.05.95.51

Domaine de Brandois
La Forêt, Near to the extraordinary garden – ✆ 02 51 06 24 24 – www.domainedebrandois.com – contact@domainedebrandois.com – Fax 02 51 06 37 87
39 rm – €95/150 €95/150, ☕ €12
Rest – *(Closed Sunday dinner from October to April)* Menu (€29), €37
◆ A former agricultural school, this small château (1868) has been converted into a resolutely modern hotel. Guestrooms with a designer or more restrained feel. Spacious grounds plus a swimming pool. The ambience in this restaurant is a successful mix of the old and modern. Traditional cuisine.

LA MOTTE – 83 Var – 340 O5 – pop. 2 772 – alt. 79 m – ✉ 83920 41 **C3**

Paris 864 – Cannes 54 – Fréjus 25 – Marseille 118

Office de tourisme, 25, boulevard André Bouis ✆ 04 94 84 33 76

Le Mas du Père without rest
280 chemin du Péré – ✆ 04 94 84 33 52 – www.lemasdupere.com – le.mas.du.pere@club-internet.fr – Fax 04 94 84 33 52
3 rm ☕ – €78/105 €78/105
◆ A high-perched village is home to this Provençal farmstead surrounded by greenery. Cosy rooms with private terraces. Lovely view of the Maures range from the pool.

LA MOTTE-AU-BOIS – 59 Nord – 302 D3 – see Hazebrouck

MOTTEVILLE – 76 Seine-Maritime – 304 F4 – see Yvetot

MOUCHARD – 39 Jura – 321 E5 – pop. 1 188 – alt. 285 m – ✉ 39330 16 **B2**

Paris 397 – Arbois 10 – Besançon 38 – Dole 35 – Lons-le-Saunier 48 – Salins-les-Bains 9

Chalet Bel'Air with rm — rest, VISA
7 pl. Bel Air – ✆ 03 84 37 80 34 – www.besac.com/chaletbelair/ – bruno.gatto@wanadoo.fr – Fax 03 84 73 81 18 – Closed 22-29 June, 20 November-15 December, Sunday dinner and Wednesday except school holidays
9 rm – €53 €53, ☕ €10
Rest – Menu (€18), €24/75 – Carte €42/69
Rest *Rôtisserie* – Menu €24/38 – Carte €25/38
◆ 1970s chalet with a kitsch interior offering an accommodating welcome. Classic menu and mouth-watering dessert trolley. At the Rôtisserie, meat is roasted in front of diners in the huge fireplace; terrace overlooking the road.

MOUDEYRES – 43 Haute-Loire – 331 G4 – pop. 104 – alt. 1 177 m – ✉ 43150 6 **C3**

Paris 565 – Aubenas 64 – Langogne 58 – Le Puy-en-Velay 26

Le Pré Bossu
– ✆ 04 71 05 10 70 – www.auberge-pre-bossu.com – sarl.le-pre-bossu@wanadoo.fr – Fax 04 71 05 10 21 – Open 1st May-30 October and closed Monday in May, September and October
6 rm – €105/155 €105/155, ☕ €17 – ½ P €105/125
Rest – *(dinner only)* Menu €40/68
◆ Attractive stone cottage at the entrance to a picturesque mountain village. Most of the rooms have a private sitting room; breakfast near the fireplace. Pleasant country restaurant; dishes prepared using home-grown and local produce.

MOUGINS – 06 Alpes-Maritimes – 341 C6 – pop. 19 500 – alt. 260 m – ✉ 06250 French Riviera

42 **E2**

Paris 902 – Antibes 13 – Cannes 8 – Grasse 12 – Nice 31 – Vallauris 8

Office de tourisme, 15, avenue Jean Charles Mallet ✆ 04 93 75 87 67, Fax 04 92 92 04 03

Royal Mougins Golf Club 424 avenue du Roi, 3.5 km on D 35, ✆ 04 92 92 49 69

de Cannes Mougins 175 avenue du Golf, SW : 8 km, ✆ 04 93 75 79 13

Site★ - N.-D. de Vie hermitage: site★, ≤★ Southeast: 3.5 km - Musée de l'Automobiliste★ Northwest: 5 km.

Le Mas Candille

rm, VISA

bd C. Rebuffel – ✆ 04 92 28 43 43 – www.lemascandille.com – candille@relaischateaux.com – Fax 04 92 28 43 40

39 rm – €300/665 €300/665, € 28 – 1 suite – ½ P € 250/433

Rest *Le Candille* – *(closed January, Tuesday lunch and Monday)* Menu € 54 bi (lunch), € 80/130 – Carte € 124/152

Rest *Pergola* – *(open 1st May-30 September and closed evenings except July-August)* Carte € 63/82

Spec. Tatin de foie gras à l'Armagnac. Déclinaison d'agneau de lait de Provence, poivron grillé et tagliatelle de courgette. Sphère ivoire à la feuille d'or, poelée de mangue au basilic. **Wines** Vin de Pays des Alpes Maritimes, Côtes de Provence.

◆ A fine 18C farmhouse and its more modern extension, located in the heart of a 4-hectare Mediterranean-style park. Fine rooms with peace and quiet guaranteed. Japanese-style spa. Le Candille boasts a delightful, panoramic terrace and delicious up-to-date food.

Royal Mougins Golf Resort

VISA

424 av. du Roi Mougins – ✆ 04 92 92 49 69 – www.royalmougins.fr – Fax 04 92 92 49 72

29 suites – €190/490 **Rest** – Menu € 55, € 45/70

◆ New luxury hotel with simple, modern interior, which fits well into its surroundings. The latest technology, sumptuous beds and suites with large terraces. High-end spa facilities. Modern cuisine in the restaurant or on the terrace overlooking the course.

De Mougins

rm, VISA

205 av. du Golf, 2.5 km via Antibes road – ✆ 04 92 92 17 07 – www.hotel-de-mougins.com – info@hotel-de-mougins.com – Fax 04 92 92 17 08

50 rm – €170/275 €180/285, € 20 – 1 suite

Rest – *(closed Sunday and Monday from November to March)* Menu (€ 43), € 75/132 bi – Carte € 75/132

◆ Hotel with spacious Provençal-style rooms in various houses dotted around the garden of lavender, rosemary and orange trees. A stylish restaurant extended by summer terrace shaded by an old ash tree. Regional recipes.

Le Manoir de l'Étang

rm, rm, VISA

66 allée du Manoir, 3 km via Antibes road – ✆ 04 92 28 36 00 – www.manoir-de-letang.com – manoir.etang@wanadoo.fr – Fax 04 92 28 36 10 – Open April-October

19 rm – €125/275 €125/275, € 17 – 2 suites

Rest – Menu € 39 (lunch) – Carte € 55/70

◆ A 19C building with a nearby pond featuring water lilies in summer, visible from most of the rooms. Elegant interior, a blend of the old and the new. 4-hectare park. Italian cuisine, including antipasti, pasta and Mediterranean fish.

Les Muscadins without rest

VISA

18 bd Courteline – ✆ 04 92 28 43 43 – www.hotel-mougins-muscadins.com – info@lemascandille.com – Fax 04 92 28 43 40 – Open March-October

11 rm – €130/340 €130/340, € 17

◆ This charming residence on the outskirts of the village offers attractively personalised rooms and access to the spa and swimming pool of Mas Candille.

XXXX **Le Moulin de Mougins** with rm

av. Notre-Dame-de-vie, at Notre-Dame-de-Vie, 2.5 km southeast by D 3 – ☎ 04 93 75 78 24 – www.moulindemougins.com – reservation@moulindemougins.com – Fax 04 93 90 18 55

11 rm – †€ 185/470 ††€ 185/470, ☕ € 20

Rest – Menu (€ 74 bi), € 98/180 – Carte € 120/200

◆ Change of proprietor at this 16C oil mill set amidst gardens and dry stone walls. Romanic interior blending the contemporary with the Provençal. Pleasant terrace.

XX **L'Amandier de Mougins**

pl. des Patriotes, (in the village) – ☎ 04 93 90 00 91 – www.amandier.fr – phouc@ics.fr – Fax 04 92 92 89 95

Rest – Menu € 25 (lunch), € 34/44 – Carte € 53/83

◆ A 14C oil press building on the outskirts of the village dear to Picasso and Man Ray. Provençal interior, adorned with mosaics and modern paintings. Regional dishes.

X **Brasserie de la Méditerranée**

pl. du Commandant Lamy, in the village – ☎ 04 93 90 03 47 – www.restaurantlamediterranee.com – lamediterranee2@wanadoo.fr – Fax 04 93 75 72 83 – Closed 8 January-13 February, Tuesday and Wednesday in low season

Rest – bistro – *(pre-book)* Menu € 26 (lunch), € 38/50 – Carte € 40/78

◆ Pleasant restaurant, with a bistro-type decor, on the picturesque main square. You can savour Mediterranean-inspired up-to-date cuisine.

X **Le Bistrot de Mougins**

pl. du village – ☎ 04 93 75 78 34 – la.ballatore@free.fr – Fax 04 93 75 25 52 – Closed 27 November-27 December, Wednesday except lunch in July-August and Tuesday

Rest – *(pre-book)* Menu (€ 22), € 36/49 – Carte € 57/70

◆ This restaurant-bistro, fitted out in a pleasant vaulted cellar, makes a welcome change from the inevitable Mougins terraces. Smart, rustic interior and Provençal cooking.

MOUILLERON-EN-PAREDS – 85 Vendée – 316 K7 – pop. 1 236 – alt. 101 m – ✉ 85390 Atlantic Coast 34 B3

Paris 426 – Nantes 95 – La Roche-sur-Yon 53 – Cholet 70 – Bressuire 40

Office de tourisme, 13, place de Lattre de Tassigny ☎ 02 51 00 32 32

La Boisnière without rest

– ☎ 02 51 51 36 39 – www.laboisniere.com – laboisniere@wanadoo.fr – Fax 251513639

5 rm ☕ – †€ 70 ††€ 80/90

◆ Comfort is the key word in this restored farmhouse dominating the Chemin de la colline des Moulins: spruce, recent well-equipped rooms, faultless upkeep and lovely pool.

MOULICENT – 61 Orne – 310 N3 – pop. 286 – alt. 335 m – ✉ 61290 33 C3

Paris 148 – Caen 134 – La Ferté-Bernard 51 – Nogent-le-Rotrou 35

Château de la Grande Noë without rest

500 m west on D 289 – ☎ 02 33 73 63 30 – www.chateaudelagrandenoe.com – contact@chateaudelagrandenoe.com – Open from April to November

3 rm ☕ – †€ 80/100 ††€ 100/120

◆ A family-run hotel set in a large park, providing a fine welcome. Individually furnished rooms in an old-fashioned style (ornaments) and a pleasant dining area adorned with 18C wooden panelling.

Hotels and restaurants change every year, so change your Michelin guide every year!

MOULIHERNE – 49 Maine-et-Loire – 317 J4 – pop. 874 – alt. 80 m – ✉ 49390 35 C2

Paris 282 – Nantes 150 – Angers 63 – Saumur 31 – La Flèche 33

Le Cèdre de Monnaie
La Verrie, 4.5 km south on Longué road and Forestière road – ✆ 02 41 67 09 27 – www.cedredemonnaie.com – cedredemonnaie@gmail.com – Fax 02 41 67 09 27 – Closed 31 December-1st March
5 rm – €45 €57 **Table d'hôte** – Menu €20 bi
◆ On the edge of the Monnaie forest, this site is perfect for nature lovers. Authentically rustic rooms in a converted barn and breakfasts in the former cowshed. The table d'hôte is installed in the attractive kitchen with fireplace; home cooking.

MOULIN-DE-MALFOURAT – 24 Dordogne – 329 D7 – see Bergerac

MOULINS P – 03 Allier – 326 H3 – pop. 20 700 – alt. 240 m – ✉ 03000 6 C1
Auvergne

Paris 294 – Bourges 101 – Clermont-Ferrand 105 – Nevers 56 – Roanne 98

Office de tourisme, 11, rue François Péron ✆ 04 70 44 14 14, Fax 04 70 34 00 21

de Moulins-Les Avenelles Toulon-sur-Allier Les Avenelles, 7 km on the Vichy road, ✆ 04 70 44 02 39

Notre-Dame cathedral ★: triptych★★★, stained-glass windows★★ - Jacquemart Statue ★ - Mausoleum of the Duke of Montmorency★ (visitation chapel) - Musée d'Art et d'Archéologie★★.

Plan on following page

Le Parc — AC rest, P VISA MC
31 av. Gén.-Leclerc – ✆ 04 70 44 12 25 – www.hotel-moulins.com – hotelrestaurant.leparc03@wanadoo.fr – Fax 04 70 46 79 35 – Closed 27 July-19 August and 21 December-5 January BX a
26 rm – €46/75 €46/75, €8 – ½ P €52/60
Rest – *(closed Sunday dinner and Saturday)* Menu €22 (weekdays)/47 – Carte €35/55
◆ This family establishment, located near a park and the railway station, bends over backwards to make your stay pleasant. Well-kept rooms, some of which have been refurbished. Attractively decorated dining room where carefully prepared traditional food is served.

XXX **Le Clos de Bourgogne** with rm — AC P P VISA MC
83 r. de Bourgogne – ✆ 04 70 44 03 00 – www.closdebourgogne.fr – contact@closdebourgogne.fr – Fax 04 70 44 03 33 – Closed 17 August-4 September, 22-29 December and Sunday from October to March DY n
11 rm – €80/170 €80/170, €13
Rest – *(closed Saturday lunch, Sunday dinner and Monday)* Menu (€22), €39/60 – Carte €55/68
◆ This 18C residence set in greenery away from the town centre combines charm and refinement. Personalised attractive guestrooms. Tasty, modern food.

XXX **Des Cours** — AC VISA MC AE
36 cours J. Jaurès – ✆ 04 70 44 25 66 – www.restaurant-des-cours.com – patrick.bourhy@wanadoo.fr – Fax 04 70 20 58 45 – Closed 28 April-8 May, 26 August-8 September, Tuesday dinner except from June to August and Wednesday DY x
Rest – Menu €20/50 – Carte €55/63
◆ This restaurant worth visiting in the administrative office district offers two elegant, plush dining rooms. Contemporary cuisine. Terrace.

XX **Le Trait d'Union** — AC VISA MC
16 r. Gambetta – ✆ 04 70 34 24 61 – Closed 15-31 July, 20-28 February, Sunday except public holidays and Monday DZ t
Rest – Menu €22 (weekday lunch), €34/43 – Carte €55/68
◆ Wicker chairs, modern pictures and furnishings, flowers and well-set tables: a contemporary feel in harmony with the young chef-patron's up-to-date cuisine.

MOULINS

Allier (Pl. d') . . . . CDZ
Allier (R. d') . . . . DYZ
Alsace-Lorraine (Av. d') . . . BX 3
Ancien Palais (R.) . . . . DY 4
Bourgogne (R. de) . . . BV, DY 6
Bréchimbault (R.) . . . . DZ 7
Cerf-Volant (R. du) . . . . BV 8
Clermont-Ferrand (Rte de) AX 10
Desboutins (R. M.) . . . . BX 16
Fausses Braies (R. des) . . . DY 19
Flèche (R. de la) . . . . DZ 20
Grenier (R.) . . . . DY 25
Horloge (R. de l') . . . . DZ 26
Hôtel de Ville (Pl. de l') . . . DY 27
Jeu de Paume (R. du) . . . . BV 28
Leclerc (Av. Général) . . . . . BX 30
Libération (Av. de la) . . . . . AX 31
Montilly (Rte de) . . . . AX 32
Orfèvres (R. des) . . . . DY 33
Pascal (R. Blaise-) . . . . CZ 34
Péron (R. F.) . . . . DY 35
République (Av. de la) . . . . BX 36
Tanneries (R. des) . . . BV, DV 38
Tinland (R. M.) . . . . CY 39
Vert Galant (R. du) . . . . . CDY 40
4 Septembre (R. du) . . . . . DZ 42

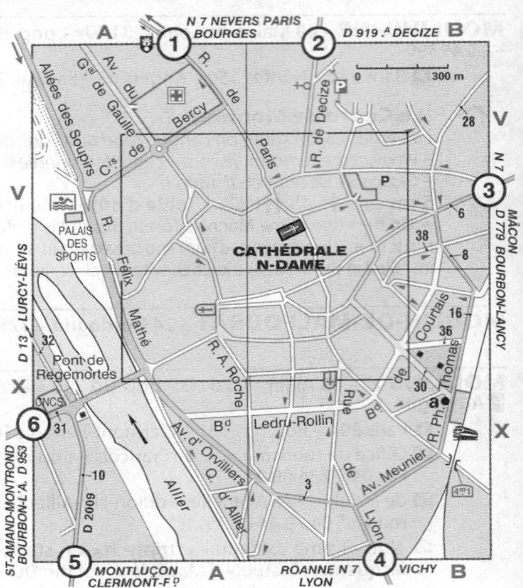

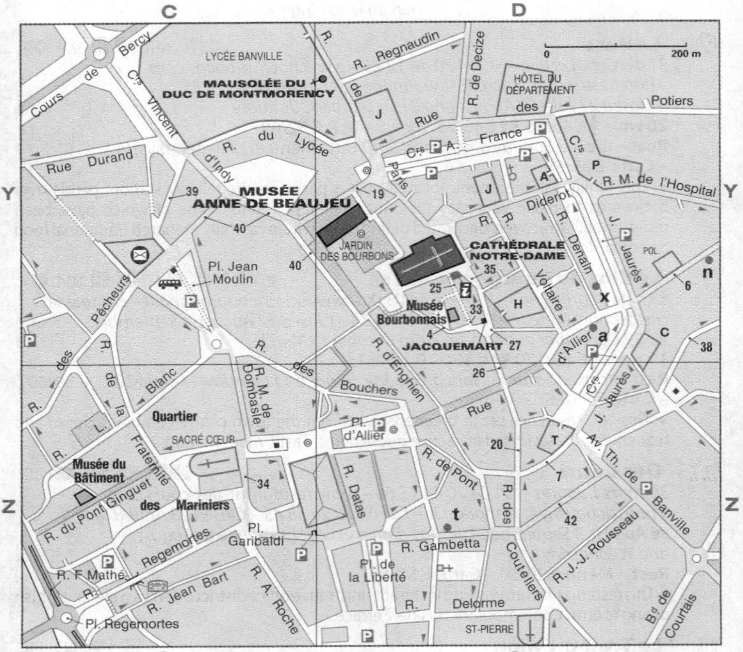

LYCÉE BANVILLE

MAUSOLÉE DU DUC DE MONTMORENCY

MUSÉE ANNE DE BEAUJEU

JARDIN DES BOURBONS

CATHÉDRALE NOTRE-DAME

HÔTEL DU DÉPARTEMENT

Musée Bourbonnais

JACQUEMART

Pl. Jean Moulin

Quartier SACRÉ CŒUR

Musée du Bâtiment

Pl. d'Allier

Pl. Garibaldi

Pl. de la Liberté

Pl. Regemortes

ST-PIERRE

9/7 Olivier Mazuelle
97 r. d'Allier – ✆ 04 70 35 01 60 – restaurant97om@orange.fr – restaurant97om@orange.fr – Closed 1 week in July, 2 weeks in August, Monday dinner, Saturday lunch and Sunday DY **a**
Rest – Menu (€ 15), € 22/40 – Carte € 35/45
◆ A minimalist atmosphere reigns in this tasteful, modern interior (light greens, amply spaced wooden tables and plants). Up-to-the-minute recipes made with regional produce.

Paris road **8 km by ① – ✉ 03460 Trevol**

Mercure
RN 7 – ✆ 04 70 46 84 84 – www.mercure.com – H0827@accor.com – Fax 04 70 46 84 80
42 rm – †€ 48/87 ††€ 58/97, ☕ € 13 **Rest** – Menu (€ 21), € 25 bi/42
◆ Despite being on a busy road, the hotel's modern, renovated rooms all look out onto a small park and swimming pool to the rear. A restaurant with terrace, serving traditional cuisine and great wines at reasonable prices.

in Coulandon **8 km by ⑥ and D 945 – pop. 680 – alt. 250 m – ✉ 03000**

Le Chalet
26 rte du Chalet, 2 km north-east – ✆ 04 70 46 00 66 – www.hotel-lechalet.fr – chalet.montegut@wanadoo.fr – Fax 04 70 44 07 09 – Closed 21 December-7 January
28 rm – †€ 49/55 ††€ 71/78, ☕ € 10 – ½ P € 63
Rest ***Montégut*** – Menu € 18 (weekdays)/45 – Carte € 34/50
◆ In the heart of the countryside, establishment set within the grounds of a park with lake. Quiet, charmingly provincial guestrooms split between the chalets and the old stables. Sober, modern dining room. In summer, a calm terrace opens onto the countryside.

La Grande Poterie
9 r. de la Grande-Poterie, 3 km south-west – ✆ 04 70 44 30 39 – www.lagrandepoterie.com – jcpompon@lagrandepoterie.com – Fax 04 70 44 30 39 – Open 15 March-31 October
4 rm ☕ – †€ 56 ††€ 68 **Table d'hôte** – Menu € 28 bi/30 bi
◆ A former farmhouse, restored, in a park with well-kept trees and flower beds. Rooms feature pastel colours, with a calm and pleasant atmosphere. This restaurant serves specialties from the Auvergne region.

Auberge Saint-Martin
Le Bourg – ✆ 04 70 46 06 10 – www.auberge-saint-martin03.com – Fax 04 70 46 06 10 – Closed 20 December-3 January, Sunday dinner, Monday dinner and Tuesday dinner
Rest – Menu € 11 bi (weekday lunch), € 16/26 – Carte € 20/35
◆ This inn, also a grocer's-bar-bread depot, is a focal point in the village. Serving no-frills traditional dishes in a country-style dining room.

MOULINS-LA-MARCHE – 61 Orne – 310 L3 – pop. 774 – alt. 257 m – ✉ 61380 33 C3

▶ Paris 156 – L'Aigle 19 – Alençon 50 – Argentan 45 – Mortagne-au-Perche 17
ℹ Syndicat d'initiative, 1, Grande Rue ✆ 02 33 34 45 98

Le Dauphin
66 Grande Rue – ✆ 02 33 34 50 55 – www.hotel-ledauphin.fr – createur-dinstant@hotel-ledauphin.fr – Fax 02 33 34 25 35
7 rm – †€ 55/60 ††€ 60/75, ☕ € 8
Rest – *(closed Sunday dinner and Monday except public holidays)*
Menu (€ 11 bi), € 21/55 – Carte € 28/46
◆ A warm atmosphere, whether in the Jean Gabin country style or more rustic dining room. Varied cuisine: regional or modern (with a Guadeloupe influence) dishes and of course, the ubiquitous sauerkraut. Rooms redecorated in a simple but refined style with charming results.

LE MOULLEAU – 33 Gironde – 335 D7 – see Arcachon

MOURÈZE – 34 Hérault – 339 F7 – pop. 168 – alt. 200 m – ✉ 34800 23 **C2**
Languedoc-Roussillon-Tarn Gorges

Paris 717 – Bédarieux 22 – Clermont-l'Hérault 8 – Montpellier 50
Cirque★★.

Navas "Les Hauts de Mourèze" without rest
Cirque dolomitique – ☎ 04 67 96 04 84
– Fax 04 67 96 25 85 – Open 28 March-1st November
16 rm – €42/45 €52/64, €6
◆ Rustic rooms without TV and telephone for more peace and quiet. Parkland and the superb Dolomite cirque nearby. A relaxing stay guaranteed.

MOURIÈS – 13 Bouches-du-Rhône – 340 E3 – pop. 2 752 – alt. 13 m 42 **E1**
– ✉ 13890

Paris 713 – Avignon 36 – Arles 29 – Marseille 75 – Martigues 38
Office de tourisme, 2, rue du Temple ☎ 04 90 47 56 58,
Fax 04 90 47 67 33

Terriciaë without rest
rte de Maussane (D 17) – ☎ 04 90 97 06 70 – www.hotelterriciae.fr
– terriciaehotel@aol.com – Fax 04 90 47 63 85
31 rm – €82 €98, €12 – 4 suites
◆ In a peaceful setting, this brand new hotel offers Provençal style rooms, some overlooking the pool, others split-level or junior suites. Terrace and garden with olive trees.

Le Vallon du Gayet rm, rm,
rte Servannes – ☎ 04 90 47 50 63
– www.levallondegayet.com – wcarre@aol.com – Fax 04 90 47 64 31
24 rm – €86/96 €96/112, €11
Rest – *(closed from end November to end January, Monday, Tuesday lunch, Wednesday lunch in winter and lunch in summer)* Menu €25 – Carte €32/64
◆ All rooms in this farmhouse, nestled at the foot of the Alpilles, have a small garden-level loggia with the exception of the most recent, more spacious rooms. Food grilled on a wood fire in a rustic setting. Terrace shaded by a century-old pine tree.

MOUSSEY – 10 Aube – 313 E4 – see Troyes

MOUSTIERS-STE-MARIE – 04 Alpes-de-Haute-Provence – 334 F9 41 **C2**
– pop. 705 – alt. 631 m – ✉ 04360 French Alps

Paris 783 – Aix-en-Provence 90 – Digne-les-Bains 47 – Draguignan 61
– Manosque 50
Office de tourisme, place de l'Église ☎ 04 92 74 67 84, Fax 04 92 74 60 65
Site★★ - Church ★ - Musée de la Faïence★.
Grand Canyon du Verdon★★★ -Lac de Ste-Croix★★.

Bastide de Moustiers rm, rm,
Chemin de Quinson, to the south of the village,
via D 952 and secondary road – ☎ 04 92 70 47 47
– www.bastide-moustiers.com – contact@bastide-moustiers.com
– Fax 04 92 70 47 48 – Closed March, 4 January-28 February, Tuesday and Wednesday from November to March and Monday except public holidays
12 rm – €190/400 €190/400, €20
Rest – *(number of covers limited, pre-book)* Menu €55/75 – Carte €60/75 lunch only
Spec. Artichauts cuisinés en barigoule, lard croustillant et riquette (March to October). Agneau de pays rôti au pèbre d'aï et garniture de saison (April to October). Nougat glacé au miel de lavande (May to August). **Wines** Coteaux Varois en Provence, Bandol.
◆ A 17C master earthenware maker's country house, converted into an inn. Attractive Provençal rooms, high-tech equipment and a superb park (deer farm and vegetable garden). An intimate atmosphere amid unusual furnishings. Handsome terrace. Fine Mediterranean cuisine.

Les Restanques de Moustiers without rest
rte des Gorges du Verdon, 500 m on the rte de Castellane – ✆ 04 92 74 93 93 – www.hotel-les-restanques.com – contact@hotel-les-restanques.com – Fax 04 92 74 52 91 – Open 16 March-15 November
18 rm – 🛉€ 59/85 🛉🛉€ 59/85, ☕ € 8 – 2 suites
◆ Two minutes from the village, this new establishment offers relatively spacious rooms, some of which have a terrace or balcony. Chinaware adorns the breakfast room.

Le Colombier without rest
500 m on the rte de Castellane – ✆ 04 92 74 66 02 – www.le-colombier.com – infos@le-colombier.com – Fax 04 92 74 66 70 – Open from mid-March to mid-November
22 rm – 🛉€ 66/70 🛉🛉€ 78/90, ☕ € 10
◆ This hotel is ideally located at the entrance to the Grand Canyon of Verdon. Tastefully decorated guestrooms, most with a private terrace. Jacuzzi and small pool.

Le Clos des Iris without rest
Chemin de Quinson, South of the village, via D 952 and secondary road – ✆ 04 92 74 63 46 – www.closdesiris.fr – closdesiris@wanadoo.fr – Fax 04 92 74 63 59 – Closed December and January
9 rm – 🛉€ 65/70 🛉🛉€ 65/70, ☕ € 10
◆ Smart Provençal rooms (no TV), private terraces, pleasant Mediterranean garden, charming and friendly welcome (a peaceful hotel with a number of plus points.

La Ferme Rose without rest
chemin de Peyrengue, to the south of the village, via Ste-Croix-du-Verdon road – ✆ 04 92 75 75 75 – www.lafermerose.com – contact@lafermerose.com – Fax 04 92 73 73 73 – Open 28 March-14 November
12 rm – 🛉€ 78/150 🛉🛉€ 78/150, ☕ € 10
◆ Friendly 'guest house' feel to this old farm at the foot of the village. Furniture from here and there, knickknacks and diverse collections, all make it unusual and endearing.

La Bonne Auberge
rte de Castellane, (in the village) – ✆ 04 92 74 66 18 – www.bonne-auberge-moustiers.com – labonneauberge@club-internet.fr – Fax 04 92 74 65 11 – Open 1st April-31 October
19 rm – 🛉€ 49/56 🛉🛉€ 60/80, ☕ € 8 – ½ P € 60/65
Rest – *(closed Sunday dinner and Monday off season, Saturday lunch, Tuesday lunch and Thursday lunch 15 June-15 September)* Menu € 19/39 – Carte € 38/48
◆ This hotel, just a stone's throw from the Verdon Gorges, has light practical rooms. Magnificent overflow pool. Discreetly decorated, rustic-style dining room; traditional food and regional dishes.

La Bouscatière
chemin Marcel Provence – ✆ 04 92 74 67 67 – www.labouscatiere.com – bonjour@labouscatiere.com – Fax 04 92 74 65 72
5 rm – 🛉€ 115/140 🛉🛉€ 115/210, ☕ € 16 **Table d'hôte** – Menu € 35/90
◆ This fine 18C building set into the cliffside provides luxury, calm and simplicity. Individually furnished rooms, a walled garden, and regional dishes served at the table d'hôte.

La Ferme Ste-Cécile
1.5 km on Castellane road – ✆ 04 92 74 64 18 – www.ferme-ste-cecile.com – patcrespin@aol.com – Closed 15 November-20 February, Sunday dinner except July-August and Monday
Rest – Menu (€ 27), € 36
◆ This old farmhouse has retained its original rustic charm, with old stone work and a fireplace in the dining room, and a large terrace. Serving regional dishes and good wines by the glass.

Treille Muscate
pl. de l'Église – ✆ 04 92 74 64 31 – www.restaurant-latreillemuscate.com – la.treille.muscate@wanadoo.fr – Fax 04 92 74 63 75 – Open 11 February-14 November and closed Wednesday except lunch off season and Thursday except July-August
Rest – Menu € 27/39 – Carte € 52/69
◆ Small, attractive Provençal bistro. A vine-covered footbridge links the dining room with the attractive terrace, which is shaded by an old plane tree and overlooks the church square.

MOUTHIER-HAUTE-PIERRE – 25 Doubs – **321** H4 – **pop. 314** – alt. 450 m – ✉ 25920 Burgundy-Jura 17 **C2**

▶ Paris 442 – Baume-les-Dames 55 – Besançon 39 – Pontarlier 23 – Salins-les-Bains 42

◉ Belvédère de Mouthier (viewpoint) ≤★★ Southeast: 2.5 km - Gorges de Nouailles★ Southeast: 3.5 km - Belvédère du moine de la vallée (viewpoint)★★.

La Cascade

4 rte des Gorges de Noailles – ✆ 03 81 60 95 30 – www.hotel-lacascade.fr – hotellacascade@wanadoo.fr – Fax 03 81 60 94 55 – Open 20 March-2 November

16 rm – †€ 55 ††€ 67, ☕ € 9 – ½ P € 56/65 **Rest** – Menu € 18/45

◆ Hotel facing the Loue valley housing modern, well-kept rooms, some with a small balcony. At breakfast time: bread, croissants and jam, all home-made. Regional cuisine served in the panoramic dining room.

MOÛTIERS – 73 Savoie – **333** M5 – **pop. 3 936** – **alt. 480 m** – ✉ **73600** French Alps 46 **F2**

▶ Paris 607 – Albertville 26 – Chambéry 76 – St-Jean-de-Maurienne 85

ℹ Office de tourisme, place Saint-Pierre ✆ 04 79 24 04 23, Fax 04 79 24 56 05

Le Coq Rouge

115 pl. A. Briand – ✆ 04 79 24 11 33 – www.lecoqrouge.com – restaurant@lecoqrouge.com – Fax 04 79 24 11 33 – Closed 27 June-20 July, Sunday and Monday

Rest – Menu (€ 13), € 29/46 – Carte € 44/69

◆ The decor of this engaging house, dating from 1735, is eminently fanciful: collection of cockerels and artwork by the owner-chef. Seasonal, sometimes unusual, cuisine.

La Voûte

172 Grande rue – ✆ 04 79 24 23 23 – restaurantlavoute.com – vivet.falcoz.antoine@wanadoo.fr – Fax 04 79 06 04 75 – Closed 21 April-11 May, 14-28 September, 4-11 January, Sunday dinner, Wednesday dinner and Monday

Rest – Menu (€ 15), € 20 (weekday lunch), € 26/28 – Carte € 30/64

◆ In a pedestrian street, just 50m from the cathedral, this pleasant restaurant sports an alpine decor of beams and woodwork. Culinary repertory in keeping with modern tastes.

MOUZON – 08 Ardennes – **306** M5 – **pop. 2 554** – **alt. 160 m** – ✉ **08210** Northern France and the Paris Region 14 **C1**

▶ Paris 261 – Carignan 8 – Charleville-Mézières 41 – Longwy 62 – Sedan 17 – Verdun 64

ℹ Syndicat d'initiative, place du Colombier ✆ 03 24 26 56 11

◉ Notre-Dame church ★.

Les Échevins

33 r. Charles de Gaulle – ✆ 03 24 26 10 90 – www.restaurant-lesechevins.com – lesechevins@orange.fr – Closed Sunday dinner, Monday dinner and Wednesday dinner

Rest – Menu € 19 (weekday lunch), € 26/51 – Carte € 32/46

◆ A welcoming rustic restaurant in a 17C half-timbered building. Well-priced, daily-changing menus with precise cooking and direct flavours. Impeccable service.

MUHLBACH-SUR-MUNSTER – 68 Haut-Rhin – **315** G8 – **pop. 760** – alt. 460 m – ✉ 68380 Alsace-Lorraine 1 **A2**

▶ Paris 462 – Colmar 24 – Gérardmer 37 – Guebwiller 45

Perle des Vosges

22 rte Gaschney – ✆ 03 89 77 61 34 – www.perledesvosges.net – perledesvosges@wanadoo.fr – Fax 03 89 77 74 40 – Closed 2 January-1 February

45 rm – †€ 40/117 ††€ 40/117 – ½ P € 45/83

Rest – Menu (€ 9), € 19/65 bi – Carte € 47/58

◆ At the foot of the Hohneck, this hotel boasts a panoramic fitness centre. Modern rooms, some in Alsatian style, most of which overlook the Vosges. The dining room with a summer terrace extension has a slightly solemn air.

MUIDES-SUR-LOIRE – 41 Loir-et-Cher – 318 G5 – pop. 1 157 – alt. 82 m – ✉ 41500 11 B2

▶ Paris 169 – Orléans 48 – Blois 20 – Châteauroux 109

ℹ Syndicat d'initiative, place de la Libération ✆ 02 54 87 58 36, Fax 02 54 87 58 36

Château de Colliers without rest

rte de Blois, RD 951 – ✆ 02 54 87 50 75 – www.chateau-colliers.com – contact@chateau-colliers.com – Fax 02 54 87 03 64

5 rm – †€ 118 ††€ 133/169 – 1 suite

◆ The most beautiful chateaux in France are to be found on the banks of the Loire. This one enchants its guests with its antique paintings and period furnishings.

XX Auberge du Bon Terroir

20 r. 8-Mai – ✆ 02 54 87 59 24 – Fax 02 54 87 59 19 – Closed 23 November-8 December, 4-26 January, Monday and Tuesday

Rest – Menu € 25 (weekdays)/60 – Carte € 45/65

◆ Traditional menus and Loire Valley specialities in one of the dining rooms or on the terrace in the shade of a lime tree.

MULHOUSE – 68 Haut-Rhin – 315 I10 – pop. 110 900 – Built-up area 234 445 – alt. 240 m – ✉ 68100 Alsace-Lorraine 1 A3

▶ Paris 465 – Basel 34 – Belfort 43 – Freiburg-im-Breisgau 59 – Strasbourg 122

✈ Basel Mulhouse Freiburg (Euro-Airport) by ③: 27 km, ✆ 03 89 90 31 11, ✆ 061 325 3111 from Switzerland, ✆ 0761 1200 3111 from Germany.

✆ 3635 et tapez 42 (0,34 €/mn)

ℹ Office de tourisme, 9, avenue du Maréchal Foch ✆ 03 89 35 48 48, Fax 03 89 45 66 16

Parc zoologique et botanique (zoo and botanic parc) ★★ - Town hall★★ FY H[1], musée historique (history museum) ★★ - Stained glass windows★ of St-Étienne temple - Musée de l'automobile- Schlumpf collection ★★★ BU - Musée français du chemin de fer★★★ AV - Musée de l'Impression sur étoffes★ FZ M[6] - Electropolis: musée de l'énergie électrique (electric power museum)★ AV M[2].

Musée du Papier peint (Wallpaper Museum)★: collection★★ at Rixheim East: 6 km DV M[7].

Plans on following pages

Bristol without rest

18 av. de Colmar – ✆ 03 89 42 12 31 – www.hotelbristol.com – hbristol@club-internet.fr – Fax 03 89 42 50 57 FY e

85 rm – †€ 60/125 ††€ 70/170, € 10 – 5 suites

◆ Hotel close to the historic town centre, offering large, modern rooms; some have been renovated, personalised and equipped with lavish bathrooms (Versace tiles).

Parc

26 r. Sinne – ✆ 03 89 66 12 22 – www.hotelduparc-mulhouse.com – contact@hotelduparc-mulhouse.com – Fax 03 89 66 42 44 FZ p

76 rm – †€ 110/225 ††€ 130/245, € 19 – 2 suites

Rest – *(closed 14 July-15 August)* Menu (€ 24 bi), € 45 (dinner), € 55/70 – Carte € 49/72

◆ A luxurious hotel in the 1930s, this establishment has retained the charm of a bygone era (Chaplin-themed piano bar for example). Refined, comfortable guestrooms. Art deco style restaurant and traditional cuisine.

Mercure Centre

4 pl. Gén. de Gaulle – ✆ 03 89 36 29 39 – www.mercure.com – h1264-gm@accor.com – Fax 03 89 36 29 49 FZ b

92 rm – †€ 134/215 ††€ 144/220, € 15

Rest – Menu (€ 14) – Carte € 27/34

◆ A 1970s hotel near the Fabric Print Museum. Comfortable rooms, mostly refurbished, a cosy bar and a small Japanese inspired garden-terrace. Traditional menu, completed by dishes of the day and Alsatian specialities.

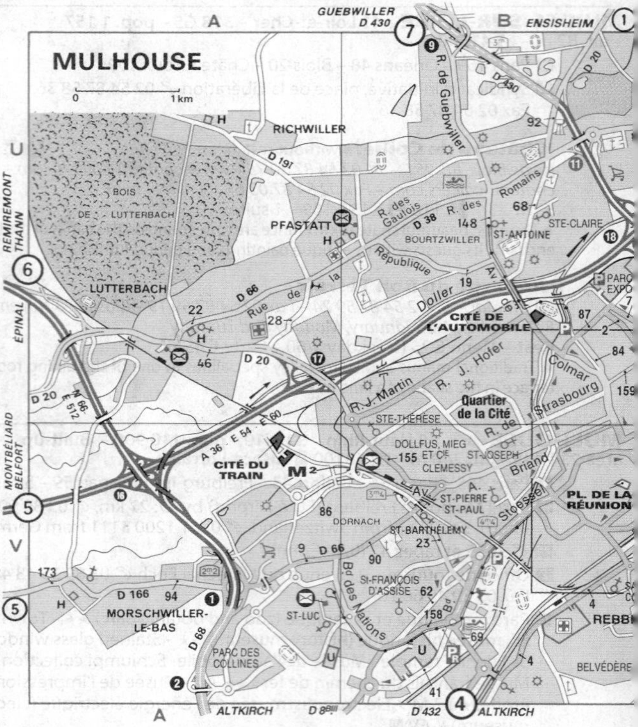

Agen (R. d')	BU 2	Brunstatt (R. de)	BV 23	Ile Napoléon (R. de l')	CU 58
Alliés (Bd des)	BCU 3	Dollfus (Av. Gustave)	CV 27	Illberg (R. de l')	BV 62
Altkrich (Av.)	BV 4	Dornach (R. de)	AU 28	Ilot (R. de l')	DU 63
Bâle (Rte de)	CU 7	Fabrique (R. de la)	CU 36	Jardin-Zoologique (R. du)	CV 64
Bartholdi (R.)	CV 8	Frères-Lumière (R. des)	BV 41	Juin (R. A.)	CU 66
Belfort (R. de)	AV 9	Gambetta (Bd Léon)	CV 42	Katz (Allée Nathan)	CU 67
Belgique (Av. de)	CU 12	Gaulle (R. du Gén.-de)	AU 46	Kingersheim (R. de)	BU 68
Bourtz (R. Sébastien)	BU 19	Hardt (R. de la)	CV 51	Lagrange (R. Léo)	BV 69
Briand (R. Aristide)	AU 22	Hollande (Av. de)	CU 57	Lefèbvre (R.)	BU 73

Kyriad Centre without rest
15 r. Lambert – ✆ 03 89 66 44 77
– www.hotel-mulhouse.com – kyriad@hotel-mulhouse.com
– Fax 03 89 46 30 66 FY **a**
60 rm – €51/65 €51/65, ☕ €10
◆ Smart practical bedrooms renovated in contemporary style; particularly spacious and comfortable in the business category. Breakfast on the terrace in summer.

Il Cortile (Stefano D'Onghia)
11 r. Franciscains – ✆ 03 89 66 39 79
– www.ilcortile-mulhouse.fr – ilcortile-mulhouse@orange.fr
– Fax 03 89 36 07 97 – Closed 18 August-1st September, 12-26 January, Sunday and Monday EY **a**
Rest – Menu €29 (weekday lunch), €59/75 – Carte €66/84
Spec. Spaghetti de mozzarella et légumes d'été (summer). Caille farcie au foie gras, cerises et pistaches de Sicile. Tiramisu aux fruits de saison.
◆ Quintessential Italy, from the creative cuisine and fine choice of wines (by the glass) to the contemporary interior and the lovely courtyard-terrace.

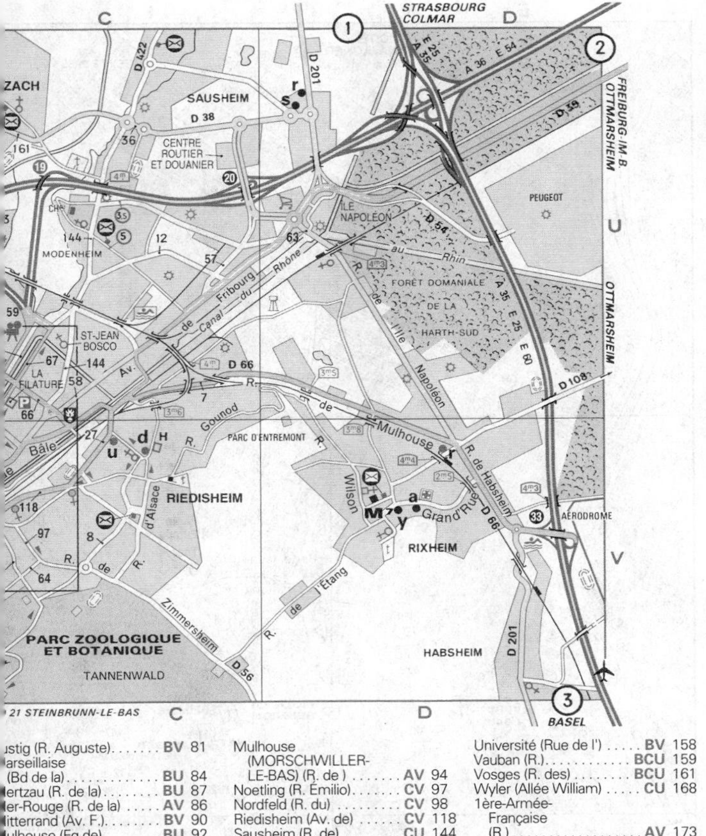

ıstig (R. Auguste). . . . . . . **BV** 81
ıarseillaise
(Bd de la). . . . . **BU** 84
ıertzau (R. de la). . . . . **BU** 87
ıer-Rouge (R. de la) . . . . . **AV** 86
ıitterrand (Av. F.). . . . . **BV** 90
ıulhouse (Fg de). . . . . **BU** 92
ıulhouse (ILLZACH)
(R. de). . . . . **CU** 93

Mulhouse
(MORSCHWILLER-
LE-BAS) (R. de) . . . . **AV** 94
Noetling (R. Émilio). . . . . . . **CV** 97
Nordfeld (R. du) . . . . **CV** 98
Riedisheim (Av. de) . . . . . . **CV** 118
Sausheim (R. de) . . . . **CU** 144
Soultz (R. de) . . . . **BU** 148
Thann (R. de) . . . . **BV** 155

Université (Rue de l') . . . . . **BV** 158
Vauban (R.). . . . . **BCU** 159
Vosges (R. des) . . . . **BCU** 161
Wyler (Allée William) . . . . . **CU** 168
1ère-Armée-
Française
(R.) . . . . **AV** 173
9e-Div.-d'Infanterie-Col.
(R.) . . . . **CV** 175

XX **Poincaré II**

6 porte Bâle – ✆ 03 89 46 00 24
– www.lepoincare2.com – Fax 03 89 56 33 15
– Closed Saturday and Sunday FY**m**

Rest – bistro – Menu € 19/60 bi
– Carte € 39/69

◆ A pleasant dining room with a view of the chefs conjuring up traditional cuisine. Extensive cellar of Bordeaux and Loire wines.

XX **Oscar**

1 av. Maréchal Joffre – ✆ 03 89 45 25 09
– www.bistrot-oscar.com – bistrot.oscar@wanadoo.fr
– Fax 03 89 45 23 65 – Closed 1st-23 August, 20 December-5 January, Saturday and Sunday FZ **x**

Rest – bistro – Menu € 22 (weekdays)/35 – Carte € 30/50

◆ Appetising bistro cuisine, daily specials listed on a blackboard, served in a cosy brasserie. Busy atmosphere and friendly service. Fine list of estate wines.

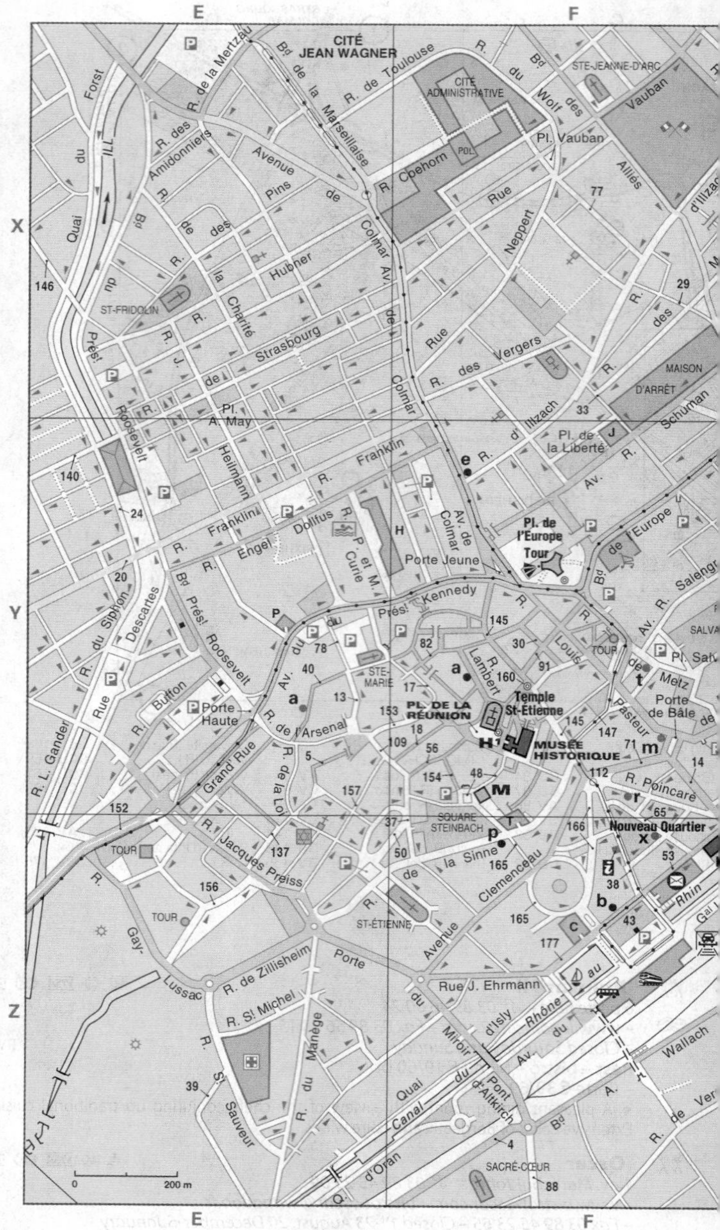

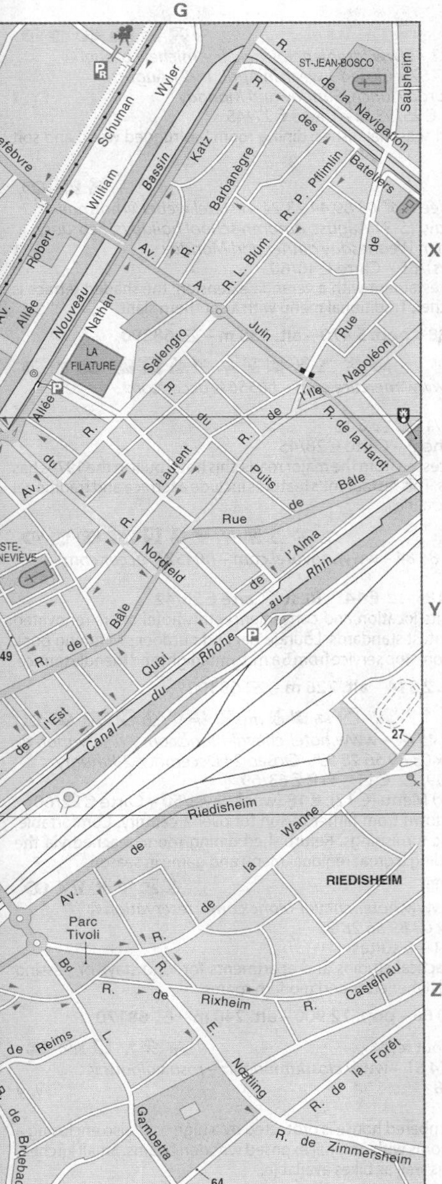

MULHOUSE

Altkrich (Av. d') . . . . FZ 4
Augustins (Passage des) . . EY 5
Bonbonnière (R.) . . . . EY 13
Bonnes-Gens (R. des) . . . . . FY 14
Bons-Enfants (R. des) . . . . . FY 17
Boulangers (R. des) . . . . FY 18
Briand (Av. Aristide) . . . . . . EY 20
Cloche (Quai de la) . . . . EY 24
Colmar (Av. de) . . . . EFXY
Dollfus (Av. Gustave) . . . . . GY 27
Dreyfus (R. du Capit.) . . . . . FX 29
Engelmann (R.) . . . . FY 30
Ensisheim (R. d') . . . . FX 33
Fleurs (R. des) . . . . FYZ 37
Foch (Av. du Mar.) . . . . FZ 38
Fonderie (R. de la) . . . . EZ 39
Franciscains (R. des) . . . . . . EY 40
Gaulle (Pl. du Gén.-de) . . . . . FZ 43
Guillaume-Tell (Pl. et R.) . . . FY 48
Halles (R. des) . . . . FZ 50
Henner (R. J.-J.) . . . . FZ 53
Henriette (R.) . . . . FY 56
Jardin-Zoologique (R. du) . . GZ 64
Joffre (Av. du Mar.) . . . . . . FYZ 65
Lambert (R.) . . . . FY
Lattre-de-Tassigny
(Av. Mar.-de) . . . . FY 71
Loisy (R. du Lt de) . . . . FX 77
Lorraine (R. de la) . . . . EY 78
Maréchaux (R. des) . . . . FY 82
Montagne (R. de la) . . . . FZ 88
Moselle (R. de la) . . . . FY 91
Président-Kennedy
(Av. du) . . . . EFY
Raisin (R. du) . . . . EFY 109
République (Pl. de la) . . . . . FY 112
Riedisheim (Pont de) . . . . . . FZ 119
Ste-Claire (R.) . . . . EZ 137
Ste-Thérèse (R.) . . . . EY 140
Sauvage (R. du) . . . . FY 145
Schoen (R. Anna) . . . . EX 146
Somme (R. de la) . . . . FY 147
Stalingrad (R. de) . . . . FY 149
Stoessel (Bd Charles) . . . . EYZ 152
Tanneurs (R. des) . . . . EFY 153
Teutonique (Passage) . . . . . . FY 154
Tour-du-Diable (R.) . . . . EZ 156
Trois-Rois (R. des) . . . . EY 157
Victoires (Pl. des) . . . . FY 160
Wicky (Av. Auguste) . . . . . . FZ 165
Wilson (R.) . . . . FYZ 166
Zuber (R.) . . . . FY 172
17-Novembre (R. du) . . . . . FZ 177

La Table de Michèle
16 r. Metz – ✆ 03 89 45 37 82 – www.latabledemichele.fr – michele.brouet@wanadoo.fr – Fax 03 89 45 37 82 – Closed 1 week in April, 1st-21 August, 22 December-4 January, Saturday lunch, Sunday and Monday FY **t**
Rest – bistro – Menu (€ 18), € 25/55 bi – Carte € 27/45
◆ Michèle concocts classic and seasonal dishes; dining room has rugged wood and soft lighting.

L'Estérel
83 av. de la 1ère Division Blindée – ✆ 03 89 44 23 24 – esterel.weber@hotmail.fr – Closed 1 week spring holiday, 15-31 August, autumn school holidays, February school holidays, Sunday dinner, Wednesday dinner and Monday V **t**
Rest – Menu € 24 (weekdays)/65 – Carte € 40/60
◆ Near the zoo, a small rustic restaurant with a veranda extension; the shaded terrace is extremely popular in fine weather. Traditional menu with a southern slant.

in Sausheim **3 km north on the D 38 – pop. 5 470 – alt. 238 m – ✉ 68390**

Mercure
D 442 – ✆ 03 89 61 87 87 – www.mercure.com – h0556@accor.com – Fax 03 89 61 88 40 DU **r**
100 rm – €65/145 €75/155, ☕ €15
Rest – Menu (€ 15), € 17 (lunch) – Carte € 28/45
◆ In a shopping area readily accessed from the major roads, this hotel built in the 1970s has large practical, well-kept rooms. This restaurant's features include a terrace and traditional menu comprising Alsatian specialities.

Novotel
r. Île Napoléon – ✆ 03 89 61 84 84 – www.novotel.com – h0452@accor.com – Fax 03 89 61 77 99 DU **s**
77 rm – €73/185 €73/185, ☕ € 14 **Rest** – Carte € 28/42
◆ An interesting stopover for its location and convenience, this hotel offers renovated rooms in line with the chain's latest standards. Lounge-bar and outdoor swimming pool. Restaurant appreciated for its non-stop service from 6 a.m. to midnight and friendly terrace.

in Baldersheim **8 km by ① – pop. 2 514 – alt. 226 m – ✉ 68390**

Au Cheval Blanc
27 r. Principale – ✆ 03 89 45 45 44 – www.hotel-cheval-blanc.com – reservation@hotel-cheval-blanc.com – Fax 03 89 56 28 93 – Closed 24 December-2 January
82 rm – €60/80 €70/109, ☕ €11 – ½ P €63/69
Rest – *(closed Sunday dinner)* Menu (€ 12), € 18 (weekdays)/50 – Carte € 22/60
◆ Alsatian-style hotel passed down from father to son for over a century. Comfortable, good quality rooms with rustic furnishings. Refurbished dining room, reached via the village café. Wide choice, including a great regional menu and game in season.

Au Vieux Marronnier
300 m – ✆ 03 89 36 87 60 – www.hotel-cheval-blanc.com – reservation@hotel-cheval-blanc.com – Fax 03 89 56 28 93
8 rm – €88 €88, ☕ €11 – 6 suites
◆ Recent building offering practical studios and apartments for long stays or passing families: space, well-equipped kitchenettes and modern rooms.

in Rixheim **3 km southeast on the D 66 – pop. 12 900 – alt. 240 m – ✉ 68170**

Le Clos du Mûrier without rest
42 Grand'Rue – ✆ 03 89 54 14 81 – www.closdumurier.fr – rosa.volpatti@orange.fr – Fax 03 89 64 47 08 DV **y**
5 rm ☕ – €76 €84
◆ This well-restored 16C half-timbered house is protected by a high wall, also enclosing a floral garden. Quite spacious rooms with original exposed wooden beams. Small kitchen, ironing and washing facilities, as well as bikes available.

La Grange à Élise without rest
68 Grand-Rue – ✆ 03 89 54 20 71 – www.grange-elise.com – contact@grange-elise.com – Fax 03 69 77 48 71 DV **a**
5 rm ☕ – €72 €94
◆ In the heart of the village, this former barn has been tastefully renovated, losing nothing of its rustic appeal (earthenware stove). Cosy rooms named after flowers. Friendly service.

XXX **Le Manoir**

65 av. Gén.-de-Gaulle – ✆ 03 89 31 88 88 – www.runser.fr – manoirrunser@orange.fr – Fax 03 89 31 88 89 – Closed Sunday except public holidays DV **r**

Rest – Menu (€ 20), € 25/75 – Carte € 51/94

◆ A lovely 1900 house surrounded by a walled garden. Abstract artwork adorns the modern interior. The menu features a regional slant, enhanced by seasonal touches.

in Riedisheim **2 km Southeast by D 56 and D 432 – pop. 11 900 – alt. 225 m – ✉ 68400**

XXX ✿ **La Poste** (Jean-Marc Kieny)

7 r. Gén. de Gaulle – ✆ 03 89 44 07 71 – www.restaurant-kieny.com – contacts@restaurant-kieny.com – Fax 03 89 64 32 79 – Closed 1st-20 August, Sunday dinner, Tuesday lunch and Monday CV **d**

Rest – Menu (€ 26), € 26 bi (weekdays)/80 – Carte € 50/75

Spec. Tapas alsaciens. Blanc de barbue masqué d'une bolognaise de homard (spring-summer). Vacherin contemporain vanille-framboise. **Wines** Pinot blanc, Riesling.

◆ A welcoming coaching inn established in 1850. Here six generations have passed on the secrets of a classic cuisine, blending Alsatian tradition with a contemporary touch.

XX **Auberge de la Tonnelle**

61 r. Mar.-Joffre – ✆ 03 89 54 25 77 – auberge.latonnelle@orange.fr – Fax 03 89 64 29 85 – Closed Sunday dinner and public holidays dinners CV **u**

Rest – Menu € 28 (weekdays) – Carte € 49/66

◆ In a residential area, this large regional building has a well-lit dining room serving traditional dishes which vary with the seasons.

in Zimmersheim **5 km Southeast by D 56 – pop. 996 – alt. 290 m – ✉ 68440**

X **Jules**

5 r. de Mulhouse – ✆ 03 89 64 37 80 – www.restojules.fr – info@restojules.fr – Fax 03 89 64 03 86 – Closed 21 February-2 March and Saturday lunch

Rest – *(pre-book)* Menu (€ 15) – Carte € 35/55

◆ Meat and seafood specialities (fishmongers next door), delicious homemade pastries and wide choice of wine by the glass: this busy contemporary bistro is often full to bursting.

in Landser **11 km Southeast by Parc zoologique road, Bruebach, D 21 and D 6 BIS – pop. 1 592 – alt. 230 m – ✉ 68440**

XXX ✿ **Hostellerie Paulus** (Hervé Paulus)

4 pl. Paix – ✆ 03 89 81 33 30 – hostellerie.paulus@orange.fr – Fax 03 89 26 81 85 – Closed 2-17 August, Saturday lunch, Sunday dinner and Monday

Rest – *(number of covers limited, pre-book)* Menu € 29 (weekday lunch), € 59/79 – Carte € 70/85

Spec. Terrine de foie gras de canard à la compote de rhubarbe (spring). Perdreau aux choux et foie gras (winter). Gratin de fruits rouges (summer). **Wines** Muscat, Riesling.

◆ This half-timbered house with oriel window has been revamped in a sober manner and the modernisation has not detracted from its original charm. Skilfully updated country cooking.

in Froeningen **9 km Southwest by D 8BIII - BV – pop. 606 – alt. 256 m – ✉ 68720**

Auberge de Froeningen

2 rte Illfurth – ✆ 03 89 25 48 48 – www.aubergedefroeningen.com – aubergedefroeningen@orange.fr – Fax 03 89 25 57 33 – Closed 18-31 August, 12-31 January, Tuesday from November to April, Sunday evening and Monday

7 rm – †€ 59 ††€ 69, ☕ € 9

Rest – Menu (€ 13), € 16 (weekday lunch), € 25/60 – Carte € 29/59

◆ An inviting inn typical of the region. Antique furniture, effective soundproofing and excellent upkeep of the rooms, none of which have TVs. Ideal to recharge your batteries! Dining rooms with character, local cuisine and "Alsace Day" on Thursdays.

MUNSTER – 68 Haut-Rhin – 315 G8 – pop. 5 108 – alt. 400 m – ✉ 68140 Alsace-Lorraine 1 A2

Paris 458 – Colmar 19 – Guebwiller 40 – Mulhouse 60 – St-Dié 54 – Strasbourg 96

Office de tourisme, 1, rue du Couvent ✆ 03 89 77 31 80, Fax 03 89 77 07 17

Soultzbach-les-Bains: altars ★★ in the church East: 7 km.

Verte Vallée
10 r. A. Hartmann, (La Fecht park) – ✆ 03 89 77 15 15 – www.vertevallee.com – contact@vertevallee.fr – Fax 03 89 77 17 40 – Closed 3-27 January
108 rm – €83/130 €83/130, €15 – 9 suites – ½ P €79/125
Rest – Menu €25/50 – Carte €33/49
◆ A large, modern hotel with a spa centre and leisure facilities. The comfortable rooms have been refurbished in an Alsatian or more modern style. Pleasant garden on the banks of the Fecht. Classic cuisine and fine wine list in this establishment.

Deybach without rest
4 r. du Badischhof, 1 km on Colmar road (D 417) – ✆ 03 89 77 32 71 – www.hotel-deybach.com – accueil@hotel-deybach.com – Fax 03 89 77 52 41 – Closed Monday in low season and Sunday evening
16 rm – €42 €46/55, €8
◆ The friendly reception and warm atmosphere set this roadside family hotel apart. Practical and extremely well-kept rooms. Small bar and garden (deck chairs).

A l'Agneau d'Or
2 r. St-Grégoire – ✆ 03 89 77 34 08 – www.martinfache.com – info@martinfache.com – Fax 03 89 77 34 08 – Closed Monday and Tuesday
Rest – *(number of covers limited, pre-book)* Menu €36 – Carte €42/50
◆ A regional-style building in the heart of the village, home to a restaurant serving a blend of traditional and regional cuisine. Game served in season. A cheerful atmosphere.

in Wihr-au-Val 6 km east on the D 417 – pop. 1 177 – alt. 330 m – ✉ 68230

Nouvelle Auberge (Bernard Leray)
rte de Colmar – ✆ 03 89 71 07 70 – www.nauberge.com – la.nouvelle.auberge@wanadoo.fr – Closed 1st-15 July, autumn half-term holidays, February holidays, Sunday dinner, Monday and Tuesday
Rest – Menu €30/55 – Carte €47/53
Rest – ***Brasserie*** *(lunch only)* Menu €10 (weekdays) – Carte approx. €21
Spec. Soupe d'escargots au jus de persil. Demi-pigeonneau rôti et escalope de foie gras chaud de canard. Kougelhopf façon pain perdu.
◆ The chef of this post house serves classical fare with an emphasis on simplicity and respect for produce, served in pleasantly countrified rooms upstairs. Daily specials at the brasserie on the ground floor.

MURAT – 15 Cantal – 330 F4 – pop. 2 053 – alt. 930 m – ✉ 15300 Auvergne 5 B3

Paris 520 – Aurillac 48 – Brioude 59 – Issoire 74 – Le Puy-en-Velay 121 – St-Flour 23

Office de tourisme, 2, rue du fauboug Notre-Dame ✆ 04 71 20 09 47, Fax 04 71 20 21 94

Site ★★ - Church ★ of Albepierre-Bredons South: 2 km.

East 4 km by N 122, Clermont-Ferrand road – ✉ 15300 Murat

Le Jarrousset
– ✆ 04 71 20 10 69 – www.restaurant-le-jarrousset.com – info@restaurant-le-jarrousset.com – Fax 04 71 20 15 26 – Closed 15 November-1st February, Monday and Tuesday except July-August
Rest – Menu (€16), €22/73 bi – Carte approx. €45
◆ This stylish stone inn offers a contemporary dining room, and a more intimate room facing the countryside. Appetising up-to-date menu made with regional produce.

LA MURAZ – 74 Haute-Savoie – **328** K4 – pop. 804 – alt. 630 m – ✉ 74560 46 **F1**

Paris 545 – Annecy 33 – Annemasse 11 – Thonon-les-Bains 41

XX **L'Angélick** VISA

– *04 50 94 51 97 – www.angelick.fr – info@angelick.com – Fax 04 50 94 59 05 – Closed 10-20 August, 22 December-6 January, Sunday dinner, Monday, Tuesday and lunch in week*
Rest – Menu (€ 25), € 35/85 bi – Carte € 56/65
◆ Colourful restaurant with wrought-iron and leather seating, well-set tables and a terrace with an unusual fountain, serving inventive cuisine.

MURBACH – 68 Haut-Rhin – **315** G9 – see Guebwiller

MUR-DE-BARREZ – 12 Aveyron – **338** H1 – pop. 837 – alt. 790 m – ✉ 12600 Languedoc-Roussillon-Tarn Gorges 29 **D1**

Paris 567 – Aurillac 38 – Rodez 73 – St-Flour 56

Office de tourisme, 12, Grand' Rue 05 65 66 10 16, Fax 05 65 66 31 90

Auberge du Barrez rm, P VISA AE

av. du Carladez – 05 65 66 00 76 – www.aubergedubarrez.com – auberge.du.barrez@wanadoo.fr – Fax 05 65 66 07 98 – Closed 4 January-12 February
18 rm – € 42/60 € 58/78, € 8,50 – ½ P € 57/69
Rest – *(closed Monday lunch)* Menu € 15 (weekdays), € 25/41 – Carte € 32/44
◆ This large house provides rooms of varying sizes; all are contemporary and practical. Flower garden. Pleasant modern dining area with some tables offering a view of the countryside and generous portions of tasty fare.

MÛR-DE-BRETAGNE – 22 Côtes-d'Armor – **309** E5 – pop. 2 084 – alt. 225 m – ✉ 22530 Brittany 10 **C2**

Paris 457 – Carhaix-Plouguer 50 – Guingamp 47 – Loudéac 20 – Pontivy 17 – St-Brieuc 44

Office de tourisme, place de l'Église 02 96 28 51 41, Fax 02 96 26 35 31

Rond-Point du lac ★ - Guerlédan lake ★★ West: 2 km.

XXX **Auberge Grand'Maison** (Christophe Le Fur) with rm VISA AE

1 r. Léon-le-Cerf – 02 96 28 51 10 – www.auberge-grand-maison.com – auberge-grand-maison@wanadoo.fr – Fax 02 96 28 52 30 – Closed 6-21 October, 2-13 January, 16-28 February, Sunday dinner and Tuesday lunch off season and Monday
9 rm – € 48/90 € 55/98, € 11 – ½ P € 77/98
Rest – Menu (€ 27), € 46/90 – Carte € 70/110
Spec. Mikado de langoustines en tempura. Lieu jaune jaune doré au sautoir et chair de tourteau. Tarte « autrement » au chocolat et mousseux framboise, glace carambar.
◆ This establishment lost nothing of its old Brittany inn atmosphere when it modernised its dining room. Modern, creative menu featuring excellent produce. Spacious, cosy guestrooms.

MURO – 2B Haute-Corse – **345** C4 – see Corse

MUS – 30 Gard – **339** K6 – pop. 1 176 – alt. 53 m – ✉ 30121 Provence 23 **C2**

Paris 737 – Arles 52 – Montpellier 37 – Nîmes 26

La Paillère P

26 av. du Puits Vieux – 04 66 35 55 93 – www.paillere.com – welcome@paillere.com
5 rm – € 70 € 80 **Table d'hôte** – Menu € 25/25
◆ Relax in style in this charming 17C home that wears its age with grace. Provençal or Eastern inspired furnishings and plush sitting rooms. Tree-lined patio terrace. A copious breakfast served. Mediterranean dishes made for guests by reservation.

MUSSIDAN – 24 Dordogne – **329** D5 – **pop. 2 831 – alt. 50 m** 4 **C1**
– ✉ 24400 Dordogne-Berry-Limousin

Paris 526 – Angoulême 84 – Bergerac 26 – Libourne 59 – Périgueux 39

Office de tourisme, place de la République ✆ 05 53 81 73 87, Fax 05 53 81 73 87

Relais de Gabillou

1.5 km on rte de Périgueux – ✆ 05 53 81 01 42 – relaisdegabillou@hotmail.com – Fax 05 53 81 01 42 – Closed 22-29 June, 16 November-14 December, dinner from 3 to 31 January, Sunday dinner in low season and Monday

Rest – Menu (€ 13), € 16 (weekdays)/45 – Carte € 33/58

◆ The atmosphere of this roadside hotel is rustic; the dining hall is enhanced by a huge stone fireplace and a shaded terrace invites relaxation. Regional cuisine.

Le Clos Joli

7 km west on D 6089 and secondary road – ✆ 05 53 81 00 24 – www.leclosjoli.fr – le-clos-joli@wanadoo.fr – Closed 16-24 April, 26 October-4 November, 29 December-4 January, Tuesday and Wednesday

Rest – Menu (€ 13), € 30/42 – Carte € 35/65

◆ In open country, this charming old presbytery has a pretty dining room and shaded terrace. Southern menu which is regularly varied.

in Sourzac 4 km east by D 6089 – **pop. 1 032 – alt. 50 m** – ✉ 24400

Le Chaufourg en Périgord without rest

– ✆ 05 53 81 01 56 – www.lechaufourg.com – info@lechaufourg.com – Closed 7 January-10 February

5 rm – †€ 175/340 ††€ 175/340, ☕ € 16 – 4 suites

◆ This 17C residence, with incredible romantic charm, takes great care over its decor. Discreetly luxurious bedrooms, guesthouse atmosphere and lovely garden.

MUSSY-LA-FOSSE – 21 Côte-d'Or – **320** G4 – **see Vénarey-les-Laumes**

MUTIGNY – 51 Marne – **306** G8 – **pop. 221 – alt. 221 m** – ✉ **51160** 13 **B2**
Northern France and the Paris Region

Paris 150 – Châlons-en-Champagne 33 – Épernay 9 – Reims 32

North 2 km on the D 271 - ✉ 51160 Mutigny

Manoir de Montflambert without rest

– ✆ 03 26 52 33 21 – www.manoirdemontflambert.fr – contact@manoirdemontflambert.fr – Fax 03 26 59 71 08

5 rm ☕ – †€ 95 ††€ 110

◆ The personalised rooms of this 17C manor house, furnished with lovely old pieces, overlook a courtyard, vineyards or woodland. Immense grounds complete with a large pond.

MUTZIG – 67 Bas-Rhin – **315** I5 – **pop. 5 976 – alt. 190 m** – ✉ **67190** 1 **A1**
Alsace-Lorraine

Paris 479 – Obernai 11 – Saverne 30 – Sélestat 38 – Strasbourg 32

L'Ours de Mutzig

rm, VISA AE

pl. Fontaine – ✆ 03 88 47 85 55 – www.loursdemutzig.com – hotel@loursdemutzig.com – Fax 03 88 47 85 56

47 rm – †€ 49/85 ††€ 49/85, ☕ € 11

Rest – *(Closed Thursday)* Menu (€ 10), € 16/34 – Carte € 20/45

◆ Built in 1900, this brasserie with a blue façade once belonged to Mutzig brewery. Now a hotel providing some recently built rooms in a pleasant modern style. Traditional menu and light dining room in the restaurant. Dotted here and there are... teddy bears.

LE MUY – 83 Var – **340** O5 – **pop. 8 716 – alt. 27 m** – ✉ **83490** 41 **C3**

Paris 861 – Marseille 132 – Toulon 77 – Antibes 59 – Cannes 48

Office de tourisme, 6, route de la Bourgade ✆ 04 94 45 12 79, Fax 04 94 45 06 67

North 3 km on the Callas road

Château des Demoiselles without rest
2040 rte de Callas – ☎ 06 43 84 06 06 – www.chateaudesdemoiselles.com – resa@chateaudesdemoiselles.com – Fax 04 94 85 91 64 – Closed 14 January-6 February
5 rm – †€ 132/222 ††€ 150/240
◆ An avenue of plane trees leads to this Provencal building (1830) in a vineyard. Updated 18C-style decor with personal touches. Wines from the vineyard; table d'hote by reservation.

NACONNE – 42 Loire – 327 E5 – see Feurs

NAINVILLE-LES-ROCHES – 91 Essonne – 312 D4 – pop. 502 – alt. 77 m – ✉ 91750 19 **C2**

Paris 49 – Boulogne-Billancourt 49 – Montreuil 50 – Saint-Denis 62

Le Clos des Fontaines without rest
3 r. de l'Église – ☎ 01 64 98 40 56 – www.closdesfontaines.com – soton@closdesfontaines.com – Fax 01 64 98 40 56
5 rm – †€ 75/90 ††€ 90/110
◆ Located in a large park, this former presbytery now provides peaceful rooms, all individually furnished. Deluxe breakfast served in a modern dining area.

NAJAC – 12 Aveyron – 338 D5 – pop. 744 – alt. 315 m – ✉ 12270 29 **C1**
Languedoc-Roussillon-Tarn Gorges

Paris 629 – Albi 51 – Cahors 85 – Gaillac 51 – Rodez 71 – Villefranche-de-Rouergue 20

Office de tourisme, place du Faubourg ☎ 05 65 29 72 05, Fax 05 65 29 72 29

The Fortress★: ≤★.

Les Demeures de Longcol
6 km north-east on D 39 and D 638 – ☎ 05 65 29 63 36 – www.longcol.com – longcol@wanadoo.fr – Fax 05 65 29 64 28 – Open April-October
18 rm – †€ 145/190 ††€ 145/190, € 15 – ½ P € 123/145
Rest – *(dinner only) (number of covers limited, pre-book)* Menu € 35
◆ A property with a medieval ambience in a bucolic setting on the banks of the Aveyron. Rustic guestrooms with a hint of the Orient, well-tended garden and infinity swimming pool-belvedere. A single menu which varies according to the season, with an emphasis on organic ingredients and exotic flavours.

Le Belle Rive rest,
at Roc du Pont, 3 km northwest by D 39 – ☎ 05 65 29 73 90 – www.lebellerive.com – hotel.bellerive.najac@wanadoo.fr – Fax 05 65 29 76 88 – Open 1st April-31 October and closed Sunday evening in October
20 rm – †€ 59 ††€ 59, € 10
Rest – *(closed Sunday dinner and Monday lunch in October)* Menu (€ 11), € 20/50 – Carte € 40/50
◆ Run by the same family for five generations, this hotel is pleasantly located on the banks of the River Aveyron. Regularly redecorated rooms. Cuisine with a regional flavour is served in the restaurant, on the veranda or on the large, shaded terrace in fine weather.

L'Oustal del Barry with rm rm,
pl. du Bourg – ☎ 05 65 29 74 32 – www.oustaldelbarry.com – oustaldelbarry@wanadoo.fr – Fax 05 65 29 75 32 – Open 1st April-1st November
17 rm – †€ 45/48 ††€ 54/76, € 10 – ½ P € 63/72
Rest – *(closed Monday lunch and Tuesday lunch except from mid-June to mid-September)* Menu (€ 16), € 19 (weekday lunch), € 24/50 bi – Carte € 68/98
◆ A welcoming hotel in a lovely hillside village. Comfortable country-chic dining room. Delicious modern cuisine. Fetching renovated guestrooms.

NALZEN – 09 Ariège – 343 I7 – see Lavelanet

NANCY 🅿 – 54 Meurthe-et-Moselle – **307** I6 – **pop. 106 300** – **Built-up area 331 363** – **alt. 206 m** – ✉ **54000** **Alsace-Lorraine** 26 **B2**

Paris 314 – Dijon 216 – Metz 57 – Reims 209 – Strasbourg 154
Metz-Nancy-Lorraine: ✆ 03 87 56 70 00, by ⑥: 43 km.
✆ 3635 et tapez 42 (0,34 €/mn)
Office de tourisme, place Stanislas ✆ 03 83 35 22 41, Fax 03 83 35 90 10
de Nancy Pulnoy Pulnoy 10 rue du Golf, 17 km on the Château-Salins road and D 83, ✆ 03 83 18 10 18
de Nancy Liverdun Aingeray, NW : 17 km on D 90, ✆ 03 83 24 53 87
Place Stanislas★★★, Arc de Triomphe★ BY **B** - Place de la Carrière★ and Palais du Gouverneur★ BX **R** - Palais ducal★★: musée historique lorrain★★★ - Les Cordeliers church and convent ★: recumbent figure of Philippe de Gueldre★★ - Porte de la Craffe★ - N.-D.-de-Bon-Secours church ★ EX - Front★ of St-Sébastien church - Museums: Beaux-Arts★★ BY **M**³, Ecole de Nancy★★ DX **M**⁴, tropical aquarium★ of the museum-aquarium CY **M**⁸ - Jardin botanique du Montet★ DY.
Basilica ★★ of St-Nicolas-de-Port by ②: 12 km.

Plans on following pages

Park Inn VISA
11 r. Raymond Poincaré – ✆ 03 83 39 75 75 – www.nancy-parkinn.fr – info.nancy@rezidorparkinn.com – Fax 03 83 32 78 17 AY **r**
192 rm – €119/139 €129/149, ☕ €15
Rest – *(Closed 10-25 August, 15-31 December, Saturday, Sunday and public holidays)* Menu (€21), €24 (lunch)/30 – Carte €25/35
◆ This hotel is superbly located in the heart of the business district and within easy reach of the historic centre. Spacious, practical and well-appointed rooms. Light bathes the dining room whose menu is poised between brasserie and traditional.

D'Haussonville without rest VISA
9 r. Mgr Trouillet – ✆ 03 83 35 85 84 – www.hotel-haussonville.fr – direction@hotel-haussonville.fr – Fax 03 83 32 78 96 – Closed 3-25 August and 1st-18 January
3 rm – €140/160 €140/160, ☕ €16 – 4 suites – €190/230 AX **g**
◆ This handsome 16C mansion is the epitome of refinement. Find plush rooms with original fireplaces and parquet flooring, as well as a grand piano in the lovely sitting room.

Des Prélats without rest VISA
56 pl. Mgr Ruch – ✆ 03 83 30 20 20 – www.hoteldesprelats.com – contact@hoteldesprelats.com – Fax 03 83 30 20 21 – Closed 24 December-4 January
42 rm – €84/209 €104/249, ☕ €12 CY **r**
◆ This superb 17C mansion backs onto the cathedral. It boasts spacious rooms overflowing with character and sophistication (antiques and curios).

Mercure Centre Stanislas without rest VISA
5 r. Carmes – ✆ 03 83 30 92 60 – www.mercure.com – h1068@accor.com – Fax 03 83 30 92 92 BY **m**
80 rm – €87/177 €125/187, ☕ €17
◆ This hotel is in the heart of Nancy's shopping district. It offers comfortable, contemporary rooms, which are individually appointed with Art Nouveau inspired furniture. Small wine bar.

Crystal without rest VISA
5 r. Chanzy – ✆ 03 83 17 54 00 – www.bestwestern-hotel-crystal.com – hotelcrystal.nancy@wanadoo.fr – Fax 03 83 17 54 30 – Closed 24 December-4 January AY **a**
58 rm – €95/130 €95/130, ☕ €12
◆ The rooms of this family-run establishment are all equally pleasant and impeccably maintained. The most recent sport an attractive contemporary decor. Sitting room-bar.

Maison de Myon VISA
7 r. Mably – ✆ 03 83 46 56 56 – www.maisondmyon.com – contact@maisondemyon.com – Fax 03 83 46 90 90 CY **s**
5 rm ☕ – €110 €130 **Table d'hôte** – Menu €30 bi/50 bi
◆ This handsome 18C residence is now a maison d'hôte. The tasteful interior marries antiques and designer furniture, rare ornaments and elegant fabrics. Library in a converted stable. Cooking lessons, wine tasting, etc.

XXX **Le Capucin Gourmand**

31 r. Gambetta – ✆ 03 83 35 26 98 – www.lecapu.com – info@lecapu.com – Fax 03 83 35 99 29 – Closed 8-24 August, Saturday and Sunday BY **m**

Rest – Menu (€ 19), € 29/76 – Carte € 62/74

◆ The dining room of this Nancy institution sports a tasteful mixture of monochrome beiges, woodwork and carvings. The updated cuisine varies with the seasons.

XXX ✿ **Le Grenier à Sel** (Patrick Frechin)

28 r. Gustave-Simon – ✆ 03 83 32 31 98 – www.legrenierasel.eu – patrick.frechin@free.fr – Fax 03 83 35 32 88 – Closed 21 July-9 August, Sunday and Monday BY **x**

Rest – Menu € 32 (weekday lunch), € 45/65 – Carte € 92/102

Spec. Langoustines rôties, déclinaison de légumes crus et cuits. Pigeonneau poché aux griottines de Fougerolles. Profiteroles aux framboises et chocolat (summer).

◆ This restaurant is on the first floor of one of the city's oldest houses. It sports a low-key, cosy, contemporary decor, perfectly suited to the chef's personal and inventive cuisine.

XX **La Maison dans le Parc**

3 r. Ste-Catherine – ✆ 03 83 19 03 57 – www.lamaisondansleparc.com – contact@lamaisondansleparc.com – Closed 27 April-3 May, 10-16 August, 4-24 January, Sunday, Monday and Tuesday CY **s**

Rest – Menu € 29 (lunch)/35 – Carte € 65/79

◆ After a chic facelift, this 19C abode sports a monochrome of greys and John Hutton furniture. Table d'hôte and terrace facing lovely parkland. Beautifully presented meals and wines to match.

XX **La Toq'**

1 r. Mgr Trouillet – ✆ 03 83 30 17 20 – www.latoqueblanche.fr – restaurant@latoqueblanche.fr – Closed for the Easter holidays, 27 July-17 August, February school holidays, Sunday dinner and Monday ABY **z**

Rest – Menu € 20 (weekday lunch), € 26/70 – Carte € 58/79 lunch only

◆ The bare stones and old vaults provide an elegant backdrop to the contemporary furnishings and mauve colour scheme. Intimate ambience and updated recipes.

XX **Les Agaves**

2 r. Carmes – ✆ 03 83 32 14 14 – les-agaves.durand-gilles@wanadoo.fr – Closed 1st-15 August, Monday dinner, Wednesday dinner and Sunday BY **u**

Rest – Menu (€ 22), € 27 (weekdays) – Carte € 40/55

◆ The chef prepares recipes of southern inspiration, mixing Italian and Mediterranean notes. Fine choice of trans-alpine wines. Choice of a plush or more bistro-style dining room.

XX **Les Petits Gobelins**

18 r. Primatiale – ✆ 03 83 35 49 03 – Fax 03 83 37 41 49 – Closed 1st-23 August, 2-24 January, Sunday and Monday CY **z**

Rest – Menu (€ 19), € 24 (weekdays)/62 – Carte € 50/60

◆ A welcoming restaurant in an 18C edifice. A handsome contemporary interior combined with up-to-date cooking (homemade ice-creams and bread) and a great wine cellar.

X **V Four**

10 r. St-Michel – ✆ 03 83 32 49 48 – bruno.faonio@numericable.fr – Fax 03 83 32 49 48 – Closed 14-22 September, 26 February-3 March, Sunday dinner and Monday BX **r**

Rest – *(number of covers limited, pre-book)* Menu (€ 18), € 26/39 – Carte € 48/76

◆ A small, modern, bistro-style dining area serving fine up-to-date cuisine. A charming restaurant located in a pedestrian backstreet, very popular with locals.

X **Chez Tanésy "Le Gastrolâtre"**

23 Grande Rue – ✆ 03 83 35 51 94 – Closed 13-19 April, 17-30 August, 1 week in January, Tuesday lunch, Sunday and Monday BY **v**

Rest – bistro – *(number of covers limited, pre-book)* Menu € 30/42 – Carte € 48/65

◆ A bistro atmosphere and decor add character to this establishment in the old town. The menu is authentic and tempting: offal, truffles (in season), homemade ice-creams, etc.

JARVILLE-LA-MALGRANGE

Street	Grid	No.
République (R. de la)	EX	76

LAXOU

Street	Grid	No.
Europe (Av. de l')	DX	32
Poincaré (R. R.)	DX	71
Résistance (Av. de la)	CV	78
Rhin (Av. du)	CV	79

NANCY

Street	Grid	No.
Adam (R. Sigisbert)	BX	2
Albert-1er (Bd)	DV	3
Anatole-France (Av.)	DV	6
Armée-Patton (R.)	DV	7
Auxonne (R. d')	DV	8
Barrès (R. Maurice)	CY	10
Bazin (R. H.)	CY	13
Benit (R.)	BY	14
Blandan (R. du Sergent)	DX	15
Braconnot (R.)	BX	19
Carmes (R. des)	BY	20
Chanoine-Jacob (R.)	AX	23
Chanzy (R.)	AY	24
Cheval-Blanc (R. du)	BY	25
Clemenceau (Bd G.)	EX	26
Craffe (R. de la)	AX	27
Croix de Bourgogne (Espl.)	AZ	28
Dominicains (R. des)	BY	29
Erignac (R. C.)	BY	31
La-Fayette (Pl. de)	BY	47
Foch (Av.)	DV	34
Gambetta (R.)	BY	36
Gaulle (Pl. Gén.-de)	BX	37
Grande-Rue	BXY	
Haussonville (Bd d')	DX	38
Haut-Bourgeois (R.)	AX	39
Héré (R.)	BY	40
Ile de Corse (R. de l')	CY	41
Jeanne-d'Arc (R.)	DEX	44
Jean-Jaurès (Bd)	EX	43
Keller (R. Ch.)	AX	46
Linnois (R.)	EX	49
Louis (R. Baron)	AXY	50
Loups (R. des)	AX	51
Majorelle (R. Louis)	DX	52
Mazagran (R.)	AY	54
Mengin (Pl. Henri)	BY	55
Mgr-Ruch (Pl.)	CY	63
Molitor (R.)	CZ	60
Monnaie (R. de la)	BY	62
Mon-Désert (R. de)	ABZ	61
Mouja (R. du Pont)	BY	64
Nabécor (R. de)	EX	65
Oudinot (R. Maréchal)	EX	68
Poincaré (R. H.)	AY	69
Poincaré (R. R.)	AY	70
Point-Central	BY	72
Ponts (R. des)	BYZ	73
Primatiale (R. de la)	CY	74

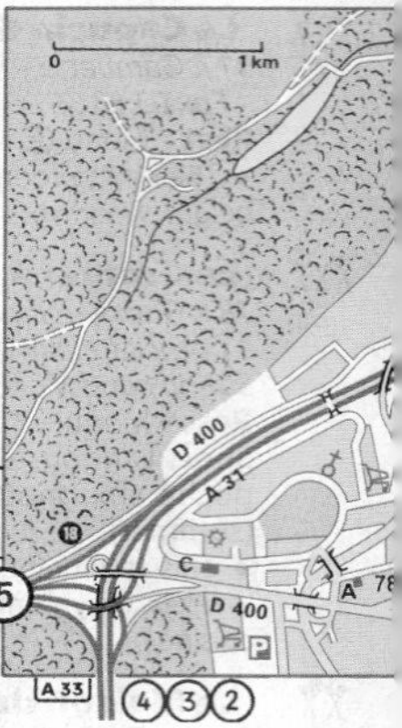

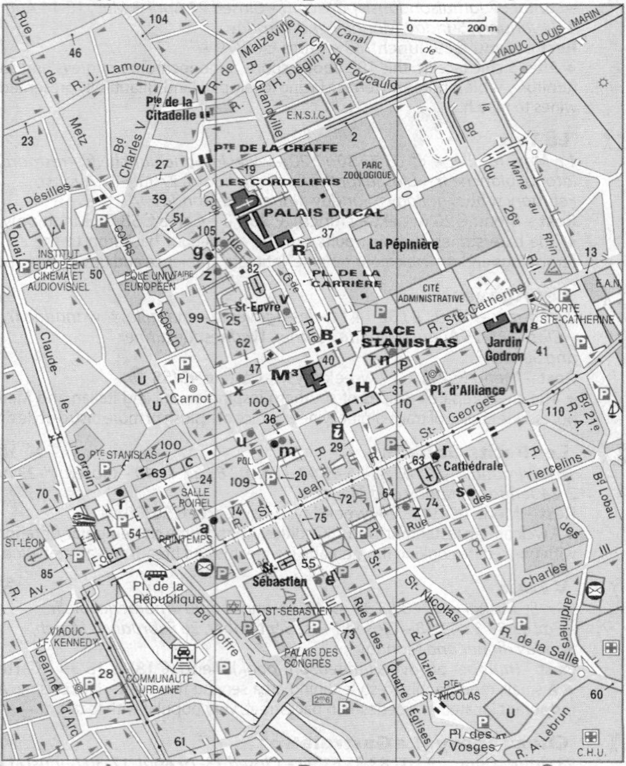

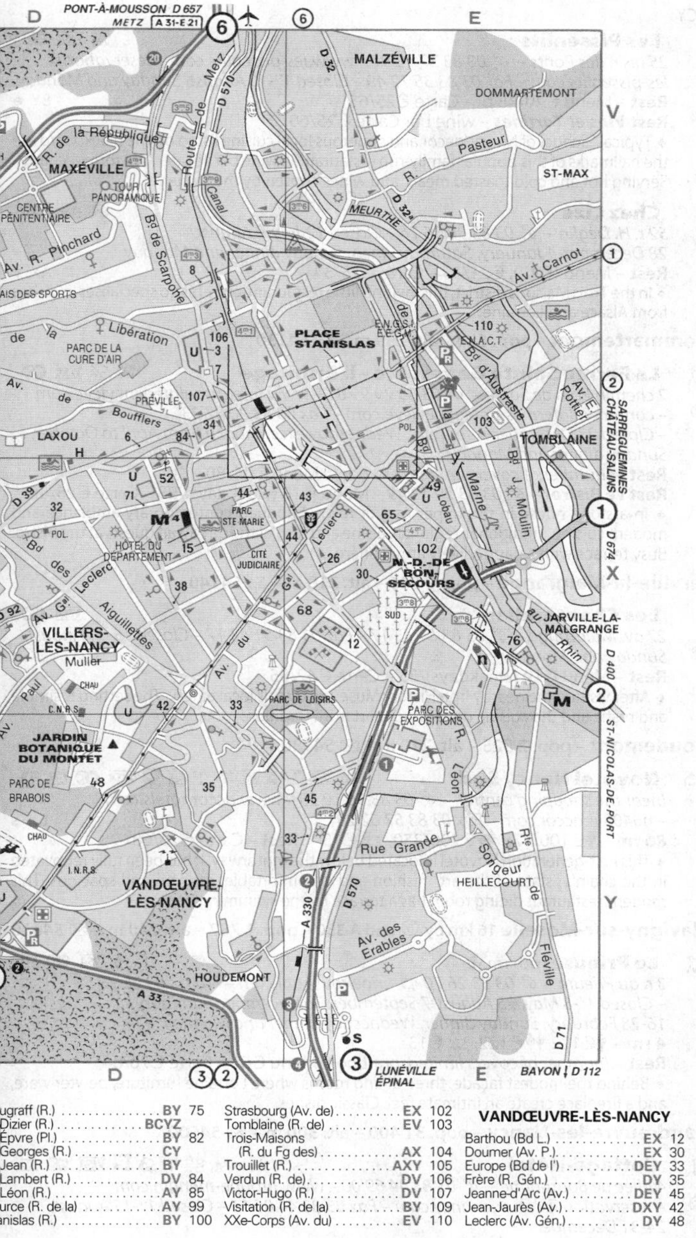

ugraff (R.)	BY	75
Dizier (R.)	BCYZ	
Épvre (Pl.)	BY	82
Georges (R.)	CY	
Jean (R.)	BY	
Lambert (R.)	DV	84
Léon (R.)	AY	85
urce (R. de la)	AY	99
anislas (R.)	BY	100
Strasbourg (Av. de)	EX	102
Tomblaine (R. de)	EV	103
Trois-Maisons (R. du Fg des)	AX	104
Trouillet (R.)	AXY	105
Verdun (R. de)	DV	106
Victor-Hugo (R.)	DV	107
Visitation (R. de la)	BY	109
XXe-Corps (Av. du)	EV	110

VANDŒUVRE-LÈS-NANCY

Barthou (Bd L.)	EX	12
Doumer (Av. P.)	EX	30
Europe (Bd de l')	DEY	33
Frère (R. Gén.)	DY	35
Jeanne-d'Arc (Av.)	DEY	45
Jean-Jaurès (Av.)	DXY	42
Leclerc (Av. Gén.)	DY	48

Les Pissenlits

25 bis r. des Ponts – ☏ 03 83 37 43 97 – www.les-pissenlits.com – reservation@les-pissenlits.com – Fax 03 83 35 72 49 – Closed 1st-15 August, Sunday and Monday
Rest – Menu € 20/38 bi – Carte € 25/65 BY **e**
Rest *Vins et Tartines* – wine bar Carte € 25/60
◆ Typical "School of Nancy" decor and generous local cuisine listed on the blackboard are the hallmarks of this popular family-run restaurant. A wine bar, located in a former chapel. Serving hot and cold toasted meals, and wines chosen by the owner.

Chez Lize

52 r. H. Déglin – ☏ 03 83 30 36 26 – Closed 12 July-9 August, 28 December-4 January, Saturday lunch, Sunday dinner and Monday
Rest – Menu (€ 17), € 21/25 – Carte € 25/34 AX **v**
◆ In the Trois Maisons district, this inviting little restaurant-cum-bistro specialises in dishes from Alsace and Lorraine.

in Dommartemont – pop. 654 – alt. 299 m – ✉ 54130

La Ferme Sainte Geneviève - L'Ermitage

2 chemin Pain de Sucre – ☏ 03 83 29 99 81 – www.lafermesaintegenevieve.com – contact@lafermesaintegenevieve.com – Fax 03 83 20 87 23 – Closed 23 December-6 January, Wednesday except lunch from April to October, Sunday dinner and Monday
Rest – *(number of covers limited, pre-book)* Menu € 45/80
Rest *Le Bistrot* – ☏ 03 83 29 13 49 – Menu € 18 (weekdays)/28 – Carte € 25/40
◆ In a stone house in the upper part of town. Subdued contemporary ambiance and modern cuisine. Traditional, regional cuisine and dish of the day await guests at the Bistro. Busy terrace with a happy, lively atmosphere.

in Jarville-la-Malgrange – pop. 9 546 – alt. 210 m – ✉ 54140

Les Chanterelles

27 av. Malgrange – ☏ 03 83 51 43 17 – Fax 03 83 51 43 17 – Closed 15-31 August, Sunday and Monday EX **n**
Rest – Menu € 19 (weekdays)/35 – Carte € 42/55
◆ After visiting the nearby Iron History Museum, try this local eatery. The setting is simple and rustic and the cuisine does not depart from tradition.

in Houdemont – pop. 2 525 – alt. 270 m – ✉ 54180

Novotel Nancy Sud

(near the shopping centre) – ☏ 03 83 56 10 25 – www.accorhotels.com – h0408@accor.com – Fax 03 83 57 62 20 EY **s**
86 rm – 🚹€ 100/175 🚹🚹€ 200/350, ☕ € 15 **Rest** – Carte € 26/68
◆ This first-generation Novotel is located below the motorway. It has been fully renovated in the chain's "state-of-the art" fashion and is comfortable, modern and spacious. This modern restaurant dining room has a terrace by the swimming pool.

in Flavigny-sur-Moselle 16 km by ③ and A 330 – pop. 1 787 – alt. 240 m – ✉ 54630

Le Prieuré with rm

3 r. du Prieuré – ☏ 03 83 26 70 45 – rjoelroy@aol.com – Fax 03 83 26 75 51 – Closed 1st-8 May, 25 August-7 September, 30 December-6 January, 16-28 February, Sunday dinner, Wednesday dinner and Monday
4 rm – 🚹€ 122 🚹🚹€ 122, ☕ € 13
Rest – *(number of covers limited, pre-book)* Menu € 61 – Carte € 70/84
◆ Behind the modest façade, three dining rooms where Lorraine furniture, pewter ware, and a fireplace create an intimate feel. Classic dishes.

in Vandœuvre-lès-Nancy – pop. 31 400 – alt. 300 m – ✉ 54500

Cottage-Hôtel

rest,

4 allée de Bourgogne – ☏ 03 83 44 69 00 – www.groupe-mengin.com – reservation@cottagenancy.com – Fax 03 83 44 06 14 – Closed 1st-15 August, 24-31 December
55 rm – 🚹€ 47/58 🚹🚹€ 47/58, ☕ € 8 – ½ P € 44/48
Rest – *(Closed Sunday dinner)* Menu € 17/35 bi – Carte € 20/45
◆ These small practical rooms located in two recent buildings are close to the racecourse and technopole. Traditional fare served in an airy dining room-cum-veranda.

in Neuves-Maisons 14 km by ④ – **pop. 6 951 – alt. 230 m – ✉ 54230**

XX **L'Union** VISA MC AE

1 r. A. Briand – ✆ 03 83 47 30 46 – Fax 03 83 47 33 42 – Closed two weeks in August, in January and Monday
Rest – Menu € 27/38 – Carte € 45/60
◆ A small restaurant in a pretty, colourful house, once the village café. Traditional cuisine served in two pleasantly simple dining rooms. Shady terrace.

NANS-LES-PINS – **83 Var** – **340** J5 – **pop. 3 159** – **alt. 380 m** – ✉ **83860** 40 **B3**

Paris 794 – Aix-en-Provence 44 – Brignoles 26 – Marseille 42 – Toulon 71

Office de tourisme, 2, cours Général-de-Gaulle ✆ 04 94 78 95 91, Fax 04 94 78 60 07

de la Sainte-Baume Domaine de Châteauneuf, N : 4 km on D 80, ✆ 04 94 78 60 12

Domaine de Châteauneuf rm, rm, rest, P P VISA MC AE

3 km north on D 560 –
✆ 04 94 78 90 06 – www.domaine-de-chateauneuf.com
– chateauneuf@relaischateaux.com – Fax 04 94 78 63 30
– Open 15 March-15 November
29 rm – € 157/256 € 196/390, € 19 – 1 suite
Rest – *(closed at lunchtime on weekdays)* Menu € 40/78 – Carte € 55/70
◆ Napoleon I is believed to have stayed in this 18C residence, now run by an couple with extensive hospitality experience. Refined rooms with period furniture. Historic frescoes in one of the salons. Dine in the classical dining room or terrace on a regional menu (more elaborate in the evening).

XX **Château de Nans** with rm P VISA MC AE

quartier du Logis, 3 km via D 560 (rte d'Auriol) – ✆ 04 94 78 92 06
– www.chateau-de-nans.com – info@chateau-de-nans.com – Fax 04 94 78 60 46
– Hotel: Open 1st April-30 October, Restaurant: closed 24 November-3 December, from mid-February to mid-March, Tuesday except July-August and Monday
7 rm – € 106 € 122/183 **Rest** – Menu (€ 28), € 48/59 – Carte € 48/59
◆ Small, elegant 19C Château, by the road opposite the St Baume golf course. Enjoy modern cuisine in the classic setting of the dining room or on the terrace. Comfortably personalised rooms, those in the towers are more original. Grounds and pool.

NANTERRE – **92 Hauts-de-Seine** – **311** J2 – **101** 14 – **see Paris, Area**

A. Le Bot/PHOTONONSTOP

The Castle of the Dukes

NANTES

Department: 44 Loire-Atlantique
Michelin LOCAL map: n° **316** G4
Paris 381 – Angers 88 – Bordeaux 325 – Quimper 233 – Rennes 109

Population: 281 800
Pop. built-up area: 575 000
Altitude: 8 m – **Postal Code:** 44000
Brittany
Carte régionale 34 **B2**

USEFUL INFORMATION

TOURIST OFFICE

7, rue de Valmy 08 92 46 40 44, Fax 02 40 89 11 99

TRANSPORT

Auto-train 3635 and type 42 (0,34 €/mn)

AIRPORT

International Nantes-Atlantique 02 40 84 80 00, 10 km on the D 85 BX

A FEW GOLF COURSES

- de Nantes Erdre Chemin du Bout des Landes, N : 6 km on D 69, 02 40 59 21 21
- de Carquefou Carquefou Boulevard de l'Epinay, N : 9 km on D 337, 02 40 52 73 74
- de Nantes Vigneux-de-Bretagne RD 81, NW : 16 km on D 965 and D 81, 02 40 63 25 82

TO SEE

SOUVENIRS OF THE DUKES OF BRITANNY

Château★★: tour de la Couronne d'Or (Golden Crown Tower)★★, well★★ **HY** - Interior★★ of Cathedral St-Pierre-et-St-Paul: tomb of François II★★, cenotaph of Lamoricière★ **HY**

18C NANTES

Former Île Feydeau★ **GZ**

19C TOWN

Passage Pommeraye★ **GZ** 150 - Quartier Graslin★ **FZ** - Cours Cambronne★ **FZ** - Jardin des Plantes★ **HY**

MUSEUMS

Musée des Beaux-Arts★★ **HY** - Muséum d'histoire naturelle★★ **FZ** M4 - Musée Dobrée★ **FZ** - Musée archéologique★ M3 - Musée Jules-Verne★ **BX** M1

Grand Hôtel Mercure AC rm, VISA MC AE
4 r. Couëdic – 02 51 82 10 00 – www.mercure.com – H1985@accor.com – Fax 02 51 82 10 10 p. 7 GZ **m**
152 rm – €95/240 €105/250, €16 – 10 suites
Rest – *(Closed Saturday, Sunday and public holidays)* Menu (€15 bi) – Carte €22/38
◆ Attractive 19C façade, glass roofed hall and cosy piano bar. Rooms with Art Deco style furniture and travel photographs. Restaurant decorated in a modern, bistro style. Spontaneous cuisine and a selection of wines by the glass.

Novotel Cité des Congrès rm, AC rm, VISA MC AE
3 r. Valmy – 02 51 82 00 00 – www.novotel.fr – h1571@accor.com – Fax 02 51 82 07 40 p. 7 HZ **t**
103 rm – €129/180 €129/180, €15 – 2 suites **Rest** – Carte €23/38
◆ The hotel is next to the Cité des Congrès, providing large renovated rooms, some with a pleasant view of the St-Félix canal. Children's play area. Grill area for all to see, "Novotel" menu and daily specials.

Mercure Île de Nantes AC P VISA MC AE
15 bd A. Millerand 44200 – 02 40 95 95 95 – www.mercure.com – H0555@accor.com – Fax 02 40 48 23 83 p. 5 CX **a**
100 rm – €90/165 €95/170, €15
Rest – *(Closed Christmas holidays, Friday dinner, Saturday, Sunday and public holidays)* Menu (€14), €17 (weekday lunch) – Carte €25/31
◆ A 1970s hotel on the banks of the Loire. Spacious rooms, typical of the chain, over half of which overlook the river. Modern bar and spruced up low-key restaurant decor, serving a plancha menu.

Holiday Inn Garden Court rm, AC rest, rest, VISA MC AE
1 bd Martyrs Nantais 44200 – 02 40 47 77 77 – www.hotelinn-nantes.com – hotel.inn.nantes@orange.fr – Fax 02 40 47 36 52 p. 7 HZ **v**
108 rm – €69/260 €69/260, €14
Rest – *(closed Christmas holidays, Sunday lunch, Saturday and public holidays)* Menu (€20) – Carte €29/36
◆ On the Île de Nantes, near the tramway is the ideal location for this non-smoking hotel, which has been fully refurbished. Spacious, air-conditioned rooms. Comfortable modern dining room. Pergola shaded service in summer.

L'Hôtel without rest VISA MC AE
6 r. Henri IV – 02 40 29 30 31 – www.nanteshotel.com – lhotel@mageos.com – Fax 02 40 29 00 95 – Closed 24 December-2 January p. 7 HY **z**
31 rm – €79/150 €90/160, €10
◆ A contemporary style lobby provides a stylish entrance to this hotel. The clean lines continue in the bedrooms facing the château or overlooking the garden.

All Seasons Centre without rest AC VISA MC AE
3 r. Couëdic – 02 40 35 74 50 – www.accorhotels.com – allseasons.nantes@orange.fr – Fax 02 40 20 09 35 p. 7 GZ **h**
65 rm – €90/165 €110/195
◆ Close to Place Royale, a recent hotel with contemporary, discreet, well-cared-for rooms; those on the top floor have a view over the Nantes rooftops.

Graslin without rest VISA MC AE
1 r. Piron – 02 40 69 72 91 – www.hotel-graslin.com – info@hotel-graslin.com – Fax 02 40 69 04 44 p. 6 FZ **v**
47 rm – €75/115 €75/115, €11
◆ This hotel is currently being renovated and has two types of rooms. Choose those which are redecorated, streamlined and Art deco in style. The others have pine furnishings.

Pommeraye without rest VISA MC AE
2 r. Boileau – 02 40 48 78 79 – www.hotel-pommeraye.com – info@hotel-pommeraye.com – Fax 02 40 47 63 75 p. 7 GZ **t**
50 rm – €54/124 €59/124, €9,50
◆ Hotel located a stone's throw from the famous Passage Pommeraye and Rue Crébillon shops. This town centre establishment has a sophisticated contemporary decor.

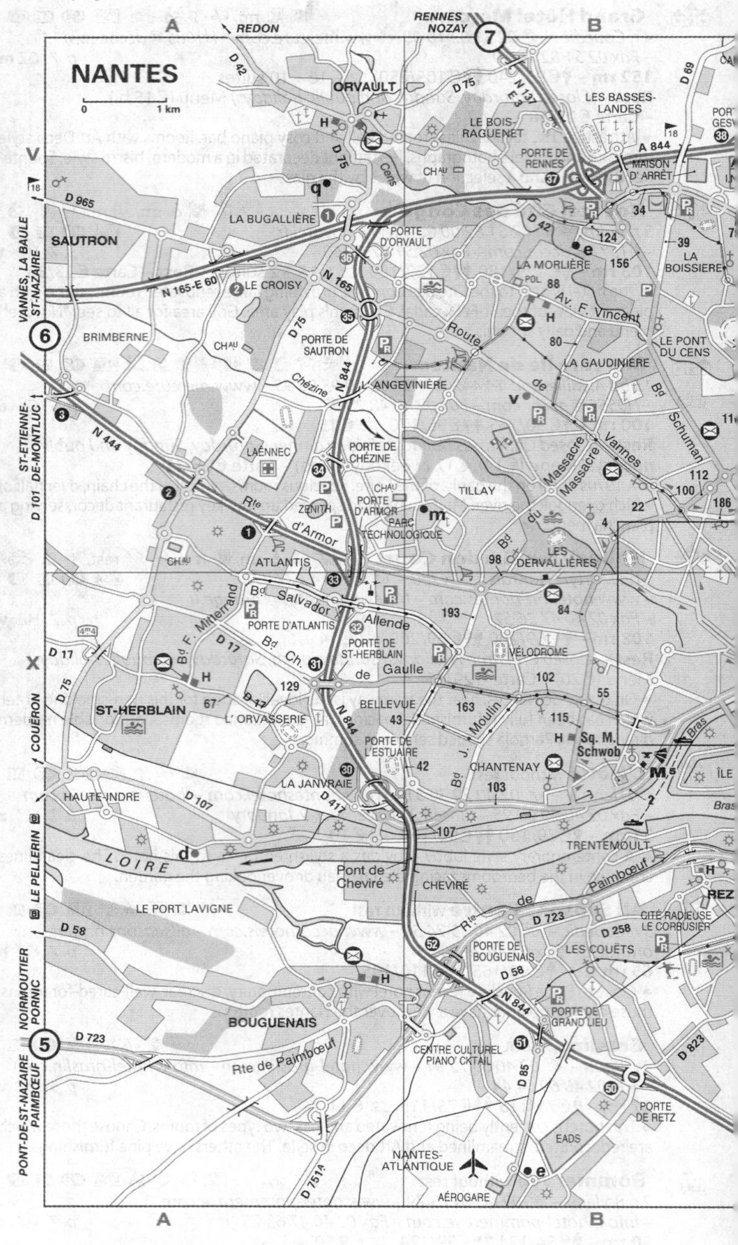
NANTES
0 1 km
REDON
RENNES NOZAY
7
ORVAULT
LES BASSES-LANDES
LE BOIS-RAGUENET
PORTE DE RENNES
A 844
MAISON D' ARRÊT
SAUTRON
LA BUGALLIÈRE
PORTE D'ORVAULT
N 165-E 60
LE CROISY
LA MORLIÈRE
Av. F. Vincent
LA BOISSIERE
BRIMBERNE
PORTE DE SAUTRON
LE PONT DU CENS
LA GAUDINIÈRE
L'ANGEVINIÈRE
VANNES, LA BAULE ST-NAZAIRE
6
ST-ETIENNE-DE-MONTLUC D 101
N 444
Route de Vannes
Bd du Massacre
Bd Schuman
LAËNNEC
PORTE DE CHÉZINE
TILLAY
ZENITH
PORTE D'ARMOR
PARC TECHNOLOGIQUE
Rte d'Armor
ATLANTIS
LES DERVALLIÈRES
Bd Salvador Allende
PORTE D'ATLANTIS
PORTE DE ST-HERBLAIN
Bd F. Mitterrand
Bd Ch. de Gaulle
VÉLODROME
ST-HERBLAIN
L'ORVASSERIE
BELLEVUE
Bd J. Moulin
Sq. M. Schwob
PORTE DE L'ESTUAIRE
CHANTENAY
LA JANVRAIE
HAUTE-INDRE
ÎLE
COUËRON
LE PELLERIN
LOIRE
TRENTEMOULT
Pont de Cheviré
CHEVIRÉ
Rte de Paimbœuf
REZ
LE PORT LAVIGNE
CITÉ RADIEUSE LE CORBUSIER
LES COUËTS
PORTE DE BOUGUENAIS
NOIRMOUTIER PORNIC
BOUGUENAIS
PORTE DE GRAND LIEU
5
CENTRE CULTUREL PIANO' CKTAIL
PONT-DE-ST-NAZAIRE PAIMBŒUF
Rte de Paimbœuf
PORTE DE RETZ
EADS
NANTES-ATLANTIQUE
AÉROGARE

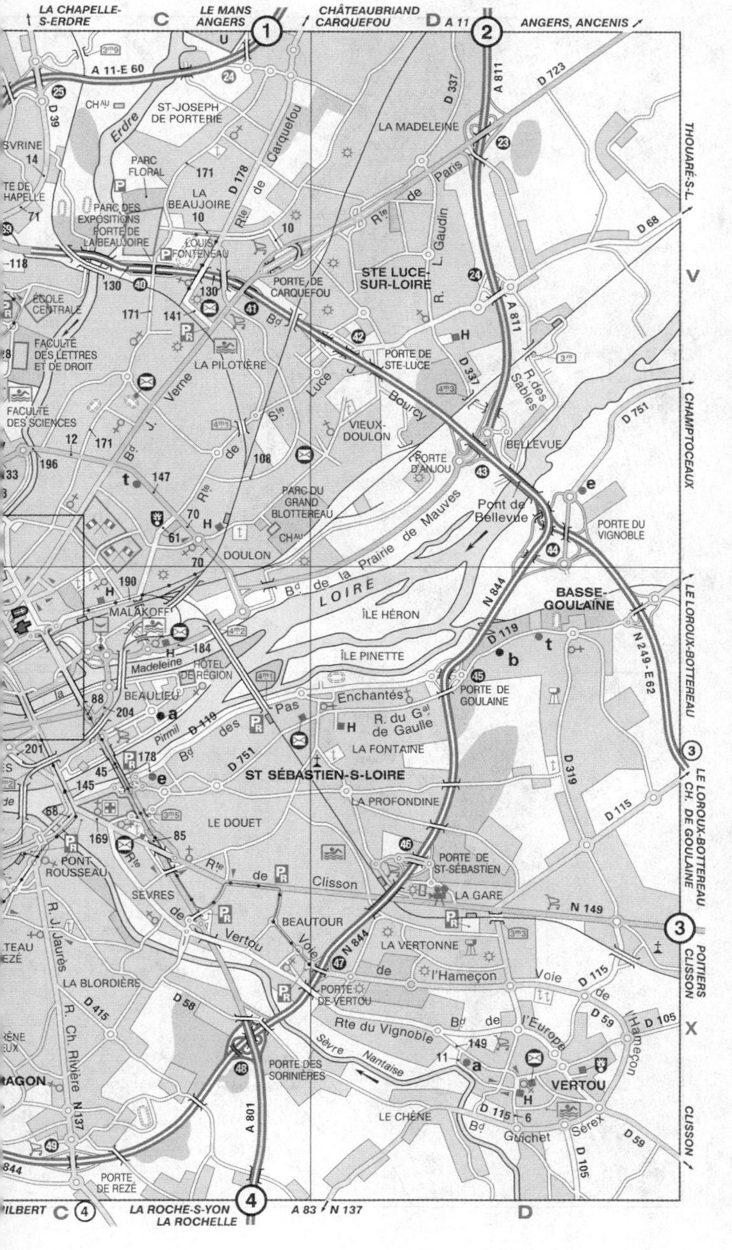
LA CHAPELLE-S-ERDRE
LE MANS ANGERS
CHÂTEAUBRIAND CARQUEFOU
A 11
ANGERS, ANCENIS
THOUARÉ-S-L.
CHAMPTOCEAUX
LE LOROUX-BOTTEREAU
LE LOROUX-BOTTEREAU CH. DE GOULAINE
POITIERS CLISSON
CLISSON
LA ROCHE-S-YON LA ROCHELLE
A 83
N 137
A 11-E 60
D 39
ST-JOSEPH DE PORTERIE
Erdre
PARC FLORAL
LA BEAUJOIRE
PARC DES EXPOSITIONS
PORTE DE LA BEAUJOIRE
LOUIS FONTENEAU
ÉCOLE CENTRALE
FACULTÉ DES LETTRES ET DE DROIT
FACULTÉ DES SCIENCES
LA PILOTIÈRE
Bd J. Verne
Rte de Carquefou
D 178
D 337
A 811
D 723
D 68
LA MADELEINE
Rte de Paris
R. L. Gaudin
STE LUCE-SUR-LOIRE
PORTE DE CARQUEFOU
PORTE DE STE-LUCE
Bd J. Bourcy
Rte de Ste Luce
VIEUX-DOULON
R. des Sables
BELLEVUE
D 751
PORTE D'ANJOU
PARC DU GRAND BLOTTEREAU
Pont de Bellevue
PORTE DU VIGNOBLE
DOULON
MALAKOFF
Bd de la Prairie de Mauves
LOIRE
ÎLE HÉRON
ÎLE PINETTE
N 844
BASSE-GOULAINE
D 119
PORTE DE GOULAINE
N 249-E 62
Madeleine
HÔTEL DE RÉGION
BEAULIEU
Pirmil
Bd des Pas Enchantés
R. du Gal de Gaulle
LA FONTAINE
ST SÉBASTIEN-S-LOIRE
D 319
D 115
LA PROFONDINE
LE DOUET
PORTE DE ST-SÉBASTIEN
LA GARE
N 149
PONT ROUSSEAU
SÈVRES
Rte de Clisson
Rte de Vertou
BEAUTOUR
LA VERTONNE
Voie de l'Hameçon
Voie de Hameçon
R. J. Jaurès
LA BLORDIÈRE
D 415
D 58
PORTE DE VERTOU
Bd de l'Europe
D 59
D 105
Rte du Vignoble
Sèvre Nantaise
PORTE DES SORINIÈRES
VERTOU
R. Ch. Rivière
N 137
A 801
LE CHÊNE
Bd Guichet Sérex
PORTE DE REZÉ
C
D
V
X

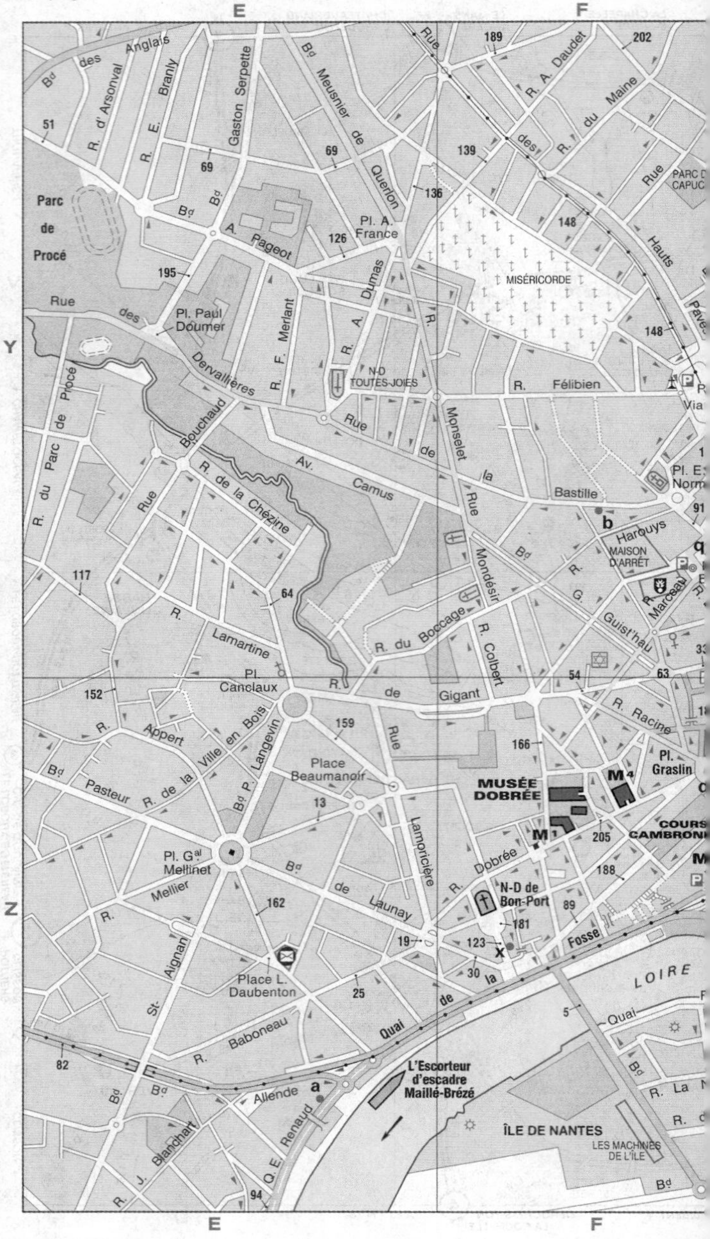

E F

Bd des Anglais
R. d' Arsonval
R. E. Branly
Gaston Serpette
Bd Meusnier de Querlon
Rue
189
R. A. Daudet
202
R. du Maine
des
Rue
Hauts
Pavé
51
69
69
139
136
148
PARC DES CAPUCINS
Parc de Procé
Bd A. Pageot
Pl. A. France
126
R. A. Dumas
195
MISÉRICORDE
Rue des Dervallières
Pl. Paul Doumer
R. F. Merlant
R.
148
Y
R. du Parc de Procé
N-D TOUTES-JOIES
R. Félibien
Via
Bouchaud
Rue de la Bastille
Monselet
Av. Camus
Pl. E. Normand
Rue
R. de la Chézine
Rue
91
b
Harouys
MAISON D'ARRÊT
q
Bd
Mondésir
R. G. Guist'hau
R. Marceau
117
64
R. Lamartine
R. du Boccage
R. Colbert
Pl. Canclaux
R. de Gigant
54
63
152
159
R. Racine
R. Appert
R. de la Ville en Bois
Bd P. Langevin
Rue
166
Pl. Graslin
Place Beaumanoir
MUSÉE DOBRÉE
M4
Bd Pasteur
13
M1
205
COURS CAMBRONNE
Pl. Gal Mellinet
Bd de Launay
Lamoricière
R. Dobrée
188
Mellier
162
N-D de Bon-Port
89
N
R.
St-Aignan
19
123
181
x
Fosse
Place L. Daubenton
25
30
la
LOIRE
Quai de
5
Quai
R. Baboneau
82
R.
L'Escorteur d'escadre Maillé-Brézé
Bd
R. La
a
Bd Allende
Bd
R.
ÎLE DE NANTES
R. J. Blanchart
Q. E. Renaud
LES MACHINES DE L'ÎLE
Bd
R.
94

E F

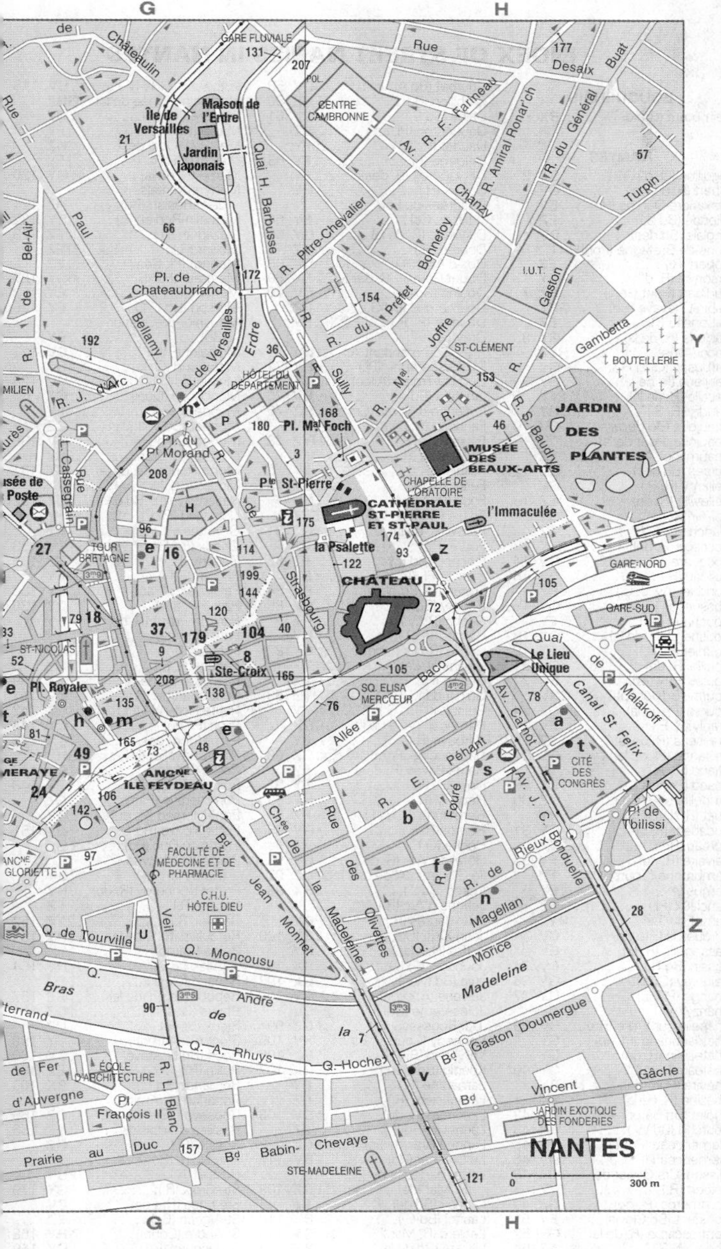
G
H
Y
Z
GARE FLUVIALE
CENTRE CAMBRONNE
Île de Versailles
Maison de l'Erdre
Jardin japonais
Quai H. Barbusse
R. Pitre-Chevalier
Av. R. F. Farineau
R. Amiral Ronar'ch
R. du Général Buat
Rue Desaix
Turpin
Chanzy
Bonnefoy
R. du Préfet
Joffre
Gaston
I.U.T.
Gambetta
ST-CLÉMENT
BOUTEILLERIE
JARDIN DES PLANTES
R. S. Baudry
MUSÉE DES BEAUX-ARTS
CHAPELLE DE L'ORATOIRE
l'Immaculée
Pl. Mal Foch
Pl. St-Pierre
CATHÉDRALE ST-PIERRE ET ST-PAUL
la Psalette
CHÂTEAU
HÔTEL DU DÉPARTEMENT
Pl. de Chateaubriand
Q. de Versailles
Erdre
Bellamy
Paul
Bel-Air
Rue de Châteaulin
R. J. d'Arc
Pl. du Pt Morand
Rue L. Cassegrain
Musée de la Poste
TOUR BRETAGNE
ST-NICOLAS
Pl. Royale
Ste-Croix
Strasbourg
GARE-NORD
GARE-SUD
Le Lieu Unique
Quai de Malakoff
Canal St Felix
Av. Carnot
Av. J. C. Bonduelle
CITÉ DES CONGRÈS
Pl. de Tbilissi
SQ. ELISA MERCŒUR
Allée Baco
ANCNE ÎLE FEYDEAU
R. E. Péhant
Fouré
R. de Rieux
R. de Magellan
Rue des Olivettes
Chée de la Madeleine
Bd Jean Monnet
FACULTÉ DE MÉDECINE ET DE PHARMACIE
C.H.U. HÔTEL DIEU
R. G. Veil
Q. de Tourville
Q. Moncousu
Q. André
Q. Morice
Bras de la Madeleine
Q. A. Rhuys
Q. Hoche
Bd Gaston Doumergue
Bd Vincent Gâche
JARDIN EXOTIQUE DES FONDERIES
ÉCOLE D'ARCHITECTURE
de Fer
d'Auvergne
Pl. François II
R. L. Blanc
Prairie au Duc
Bd Babin-Chevaye
STE-MADELEINE
ANCNE GLORIETTE
NANTES
0
300 m

INDEX OF STREET NAMES IN NANTES

St-Pierre (Cours) . . . . HY 174
St-Pierre (Pl.) . . . . GY 175
St-Rogatien (R.) . . . . HY 177
St-Sébastien (Côte) . . . . . . CX 178
Salengro (Pl. R.) . . . . GY 180
Sanitat (Pl. du) . . . . FZ 181
Santeuil (R.) . . . . GY 183
Sarrebrück (Bd de) . . . . . . CX 184
Say (R. L.) . . . . BV 186
Schuman (Bd R.) . . . . BV
Scribe (R.) . . . . FZ 187
Serpette (Bd G.) . . . . EY
Sibille (R. M.) . . . . FZ 188
Simon (R. Jules) . . . . EY 189
Stalingrad (Bd de) . . . . CX 190
Strasbourg (R. de) . . . . GY
Sully (R.) . . . . HY
Talensac (R.) . . . . GY 192
Tbilissi (Pt de) . . . . ZH
Tertre (Bd du) . . . . BX 193
Thomas (Bd A.) . . . . EY 195
Tortière (Pont de la) . . . . . . CV 196
Tourville (Quai de) . . . . GZ
Turpin (R. Gaston) . . . . HY
Vannes (Rte de) . . . . BV
Veil (R. G.) . . . . GZ
Verdun (R. de) . . . . GY 199
Versailles (Quai de) . . . . GY
Vertou (Rte de) CX
Viarme (Pl.) . . . . FY
Victor-Hugo (Bd) . . . . CX 201
Villebois-Mareuil (R.) . . . . . FY 202
Ville-en-Bois (R. de la) . . . . EZ
Viviani (R. René) . . . . CX 204
Voltaire (R.) . . . . FZ 205
Waldeck-Rousseau (Pl.) . GHY 207
50-Otages (Crs des) . . . . GYZ 208

ORVAULT

Ferrière (Av. de la) . . . . BV 80
Goupil (Av. A.) . . . . BV 88
Mendès-France (Bd) . . . . . BV 124
Rennes (Rte de) . . . . BV 156
Vannes (Rte de) . . . . BV
Vincent (Av. F.) . . . . BV

REZÉ

Gaulle (Bd Gén.-de) . . . . . . CX 87
Jean-Jaurès (R.) CX
Rivière (R. Ch.) CX

STE-LUCE-SUR-LOIRE

Bellevue (Pont de) . . . . DV

Gaudin (R. L.) . . . . DV
Sables (R. des) . . . . DV

ST-HERBLAIN

Allende (Bd S.) . . . . ABX
Armor (Rte d') . . . . AV
Dr-Boubée
(R. du) . . . . AX 67
Gaulle (Av. Ch.-de) . . . . AX
Massacre (Bd du) . . . . BV
Mitterrand (Bd F.) . . . . AX
Monnet (R. J.) . . . . AX 125

ST-SÉBASTIEN-SUR-LOIRE

Clisson (Rte de) . . . . CDX
Gaulle (R. du Gén.-de) . . . . DX
Pas-Enchantés (Bd des) . CDX

VERTOU

Arnaud (R. A.) . . . . DX 6
Beauséjour (R.) . . . . DX 11
Europe (Bd de l') . . . . DX
Guichet Sérex (Bd) . . . . DX
Pont de l'Arche (R. du) . . . . DX 149
Vignoble (Rte du) . . . . DX

Des Colonies without rest
5 r. Chapeau Rouge – ✆ 02 40 48 79 76 – www.hoteldescolonies.fr – hoteldescolonies@free.fr – Fax 02 40 12 49 25 p. 7 GZ **e**
38 rm – €56/75 €63/75, €11
◆ This hotel located in a small side street has a reception area that features art on display. Contemporary rooms in bright colours (good linen).

L'Atlantide (Jean-Yves Guého)
16 quai E. Renaud ✉ 44100 – ✆ 02 40 73 23 23 – www.restaurant-atlantide.net – jygueho@club-internet.fr – Fax 02 40 73 76 46 – Closed 25 July-24 August, 24 December-2 January, Saturday lunch, Sunday and public holidays p. 6 EZ **a**
Rest – Menu €32 bi (lunch), €60/95 – Carte €70/85
Spec. Grenouilles meunières et brandade d'anguilles fumées en colonne de moëlle (March to September). Poitrine de pigeonneau rôtie à la broche, homard de pays en tronçon, jus corsé (April to September). Sphère du nouveau monde, chocolat framboises. **Wines** Muscadet de Sèvre-et-Maine sur lie, Savennières.
◆ This contemporary restaurant at the top of a modern building offers a splendid view of the town and river. Original cuisine and good Loire wine list.

L'Océanide
2 r. P. Bellamy – ✆ 02 40 20 32 28 – www.restaurant-oceanide.com – Fax 02 40 48 08 55 – Closed 27 July-17 August, Sunday and Monday p. 7 GY **n**
Rest – Menu €21 (weekdays)/65 – Carte €40/65
◆ Restaurant with an attractive counter, wood panelling, benches and paintings, offering seafood and a fine wine list.

La Poissonnerie
4 r. Léon Maître – ✆ 02 40 47 79 50 – lestroisas@orange.fr – Closed 4-26 August, 21 December-7 January, Saturday lunch, Sunday and Monday p. 7 GZ **e**
Rest – Menu (€15), €43 – Carte €35/58
◆ The name says it all: the sea is an integral part of this restaurant, both in its decor with shades of blue and nautical objects, and in the fish and seafood cuisine. Good choice of Muscadet wine.

L'abélia
125 bd des Poilus – ✆ 02 40 35 40 00 – www.restaurantlabelia.com – restaurant.abelia@neuf.fr – Closed 4-24 August, Christmas holidays, Sunday and Monday p. 5 CV **t**
Rest – Menu (€26), €31/65 bi
◆ Friendly welcome at this fine house dating from 1900. Modern food served in the warm coloured dining rooms, featuring parquet and tiled flooring and exposed stone.

XX **Félix**

1 r. Lefèvre Utile – ✆ 02 40 34 15 93 – www.brasseriefelix.com – contact@felixbrasserie.com – Fax 02 40 34 46 23 *p. 7* HZ **a**

Rest – Menu (€ 16) – Carte € 33/46

◆ This brasserie is popular with the locals, with a contemporary atmosphere, a terrace overlooking the St Félix canal and serving tempting brasserie cuisine.

XX **La Cigale**

4 pl. Graslin – ✆ 02 51 84 94 94 – www.lacigale.com – lacigale@lacigale.com – Fax 02 51 84 94 95 *p. 6* FZ **d**

Rest – Menu (€ 15), € 18/28 – Carte € 25/46

◆ Inaugurated in 1895, this famous brasserie has had a multitude of celebrated customers. The superb setting (mosaics, wood panelling, etc.) is the epitome of Modern Style ornamentation.

XX **Christophe Bonnet**

6 r. Mazagran – ✆ 02 40 69 03 39 – www.christophebonnet.com – info@christophebonnet.com – Closed 28 July-31 August, 1st-9 January, Sunday and Monday *p. 6* FZ **x**

Rest – Menu € 30 bi (weekday lunch), € 38/120 bi

◆ The chef's inventive cuisine is the inspiration behind the redecorated rooms at this aubergine-coloured façade's restaurant.

XX **Le Rive Gauche**

10 côte St-Sébastien ✉ 44200 – ✆ 02 40 34 38 52 – www.restaurant-lerivegauche.com – rive.gauche@wanadoo.fr – Fax 02 40 33 21 20 – Closed 13-19 April, 26 July-18 August, 24 December-2 January, Saturday lunch, Sunday dinner and Monday *p. 5* CX **e**

Rest – Menu (€ 25), € 33/110 bi – Carte approx. € 40

◆ Long, low house with a veranda overlooking the quayside, the Loire and Beaulieu island. Modern setting and carefully laid tables offering up-to-date food.

X **Maison Baron Lefèvre**

33 r. de Rieux – ✆ 02 40 89 20 20 – baron-lefevre@wanadoo.fr – Fax 02 40 89 20 22 – Closed 3-22 August, Sunday and Monday *p. 7* HZ **n**

Rest – Menu (€ 15), € 18 (weekday lunch)/25 – Carte € 35/60

◆ New style brasserie and fine foods deli (hams, wine and other produce) set in a warehouse that was formerly a market gardener's shop. Refined decor, mezzanine.

X **Les Temps Changent**

1 pl. A. Briand – ✆ 02 51 72 18 01 – les.temps.changent@wanadoo.fr – Fax 02 51 88 91 82 – Closed 3-23 August, Saturday and Sunday *p. 6* FY **q**

Rest – Menu € 25 (lunch), € 42/50

◆ This restaurant's name describes the seasonal suggestions in one of the set menus of this chic bistro, where the atmosphere gets cosier in the evening. Two hundred wines available.

X **Le 1**

1 r. Olympe-de-Gouges, (on the corner of quai F. Mitterand) – ✆ 02 40 08 28 00 – www.leun.fr – contact@leun.fr – Fax 02 40 08 28 68 *p. 7* GZ **c**

Rest – Menu (€ 17), € 23 (weekday lunch)/28 – Carte € 30/45

◆ Establishment founded by 'seasoned' chefs on the island of Nantes. A fashionable brasserie concept with an open kitchen and bar. Modern and updated regional cuisine.

X **L'Embellie**

14 r. Armand Brossard – ✆ 02 40 48 20 02 – www.restaurantlembellie.com – francoisproquin@yahoo.co.uk – Fax 02 72 01 72 25 – Closed August, Sunday and Monday *p. 7* GY **e**

Rest – Menu (€ 15), € 24/52 – Carte € 39/56

◆ Sensible prices, modern recipes prepared with care, a small selection of well-selected wines and a warm, modern interior: L'Embellie is the place to be!

X **Le Gressin**

40 bis r. Fouré – ✆ 02 40 48 26 24 – le.gressin@orange.fr – Fax 02 40 48 26 24 – Closed 5-20 August, Monday dinner and Sunday *p. 7* HZ **f**

Rest – Menu (€ 15), € 20/31

◆ Little local restaurant with exposed walls, rustic furnishings and art on display. Traditional set menus that change with the seasons.

A ma Table
11 r. Fouré – 02 40 47 01 18 – amatable@aliceadsl.fr – Closed 1st-20 August, February school holidays, Saturday and Sunday p. 7 HZ **s**
Rest – Menu (€ 16), € 21
◆ Fans of petit beurre Nantais will enjoy this bistro, located next to the old Lu biscuit factory. Old photos of the area, retro posters and simple, good quality, market based cuisine.

Les Capucines
11 bis r. Bastille – 02 40 20 41 58 – www.restaurant-capucines.com – restaurantlescapucines@wanadoo.fr – Fax 02 51 72 02 96 – Closed 1st-24 August, Saturday lunch, Monday dinner and Sunday p. 6 FY **b**
Rest – Menu € 12 (lunch)/30 – Carte € 29/35
◆ Informal restaurant with three retro bistro style dining rooms (two of which open onto a patio). Traditional seasonal dishes and specialities from southwest France.

SURROUNDING AREA

on the banks of the Erdre 11 km by D 178 or exit n° 24 of A 11 motorway and La Chantrerie road- CV

Manoir de la Régate
155 rte Gachet 44300 Nantes – 02 40 18 02 97 – www.manoir-regate.com – info@manoir-regate.com – Fax 02 40 25 23 36 – Closed 26-30 December, Sunday dinner and Monday
Rest – Menu € 20 (weekdays)/70 – Carte € 68/89
◆ Fine 19C residence with comfortable, contemporary atmosphere. Meals served in one of the dining rooms or on the pleasant terrace overlooking the gardens. Modern menu.

Auberge du Vieux Gachet
rte Gachet 44470 Carquefou – 02 40 25 10 92 – www.aubergeduvieuxgachet.com – Fax 02 40 18 03 92 – Closed Sunday dinner and Monday
Rest – Menu (€ 20), € 24 (weekday lunch), € 35/85 – Carte € 57/70
◆ An old farm which gives you the impression of being in the country, although it is very close to town. Old beams, rustic atmosphere and a terrace on the banks of the Erdre.

Angers road on the N 23 or exit 23 of the A 11 motorway- DV – 44470 Carquefou

Novotel Carquefou
rm, rest,
4 allée des sapins, 11 km: Belle Etoile roundabout – 02 28 09 44 44 – www.novotel.com – H0410@accor.com – Fax 02 28 09 44 54
79 rm – €65/145 €65/145, € 14
Rest – Menu (€ 21) – Carte € 24/46
◆ This 1970s hotel is close to major roads and has simple, functional rooms. Half of which have been refurbished to the chain's latest standards. The modern dining room opens onto the terrace and pool.

Bords de Loire road on the D 751 DV, exit 44 Porte du Vignoble

Villa Mon Rêve
9 km 44115 Basse-Goulaine – 02 40 03 55 50 – www.villa-mon-reve.com – contact@villa-mon-reve.com – Fax 02 40 06 05 41 – Closed 17-30 November, February school holidays, Sunday dinner and Tuesday p. 5 DV **e**
Rest – Menu (€ 23), € 32/78 bi – Carte € 42/74
◆ This 1900 establishment with shady tables to the front is between the Loire and the market gardens. Timeless atmosphere, regional cuisine, nice selection of Muscadets.

Auberge Nantaise
at 13 km, at the Bout des Ponts 44450 St-Julien-de-Concelles – 02 40 54 10 73 – Fax 02 40 36 83 28 – Closed 10-21 July, Sunday dinner and Monday
Rest – Menu (€ 14), € 17 (weekdays)/50 – Carte € 50/65
◆ Modern upstairs dining room whose picture windows overlook the Loire. Ground floor with a colourful setting. Regional menu including frogs, fish in light butter sauce, etc.

XX **La Divate**

11 km, at Boire-Courant ✉ 44450 St-Julien-de-Concelles – ✆ 02 40 54 19 66 – Fax 02 40 36 58 39 – Closed 20 August-7 September, February half-term holidays, Sunday dinner, Monday dinner, Tuesday dinner and Wednesday

Rest – Menu (€ 13), € 15 (weekday lunch), € 19/40 – Carte € 53/61

◆ Loire Valley specialities are served in this small country house set on the riverbank. Stonework and wood create an attractive rustic setting.

X **Clémence**

at 15 km, at la Chebuette ✉ 44450 St-Julien-de-Concelles – ✆ 02 40 36 03 18 – wwww.restaurantclemence.fr – contact@restaurantclemence.fr – Fax 02 40 36 03 18 – Closed 10-30 August, Sunday dinner and Monday

Rest – Menu (€ 16 bi), € 27/69 – Carte approx. € 44

◆ Refurbished house in a refined setting. It is here that the chef Clémence Lefeuvre (1860-1932) created the famous beurre blanc, still present in the inventive regional cuisine.

in Basse-Goulaine **10 km by D 119 – pop. 7 927 – alt. 22 m – ✉ 44115**

L'Orangerie du Parc without rest

195 r. Grignon, (D 119) – ✆ 02 40 54 91 30 – www.gites-de-france-44.fr/lorangerie – lorangerieduparc@voila.fr – Fax 02 40 54 91 30 *p. 5* DX **b**

5 rm – †€ 62/67 ††€ 75/81

◆ The orangery of a residence formerly owned by a minister under Napoleon III. With five charming rooms on the ground floor (four with separate sleeping area).

in Haute-Goulaine **14 km by ③ and D 119 – pop. 5 394 – alt. 41 m – ✉ 44115**

XXX **Manoir de la Boulaie** (Laurent Saudeau)

33 r. Chapelle St Martin – ✆ 02 40 06 15 91 – www.manoir-de-la-boulaie.fr – reservation@manoir-de-la-boulaie.fr – Fax 02 40 54 56 83 – Closed 27 July-20 August, 21 December-14 January, Sunday dinner, Monday and Wednesday

Rest – Menu € 39 (weekday lunch), € 69/130 – Carte € 95/130

Spec. Spirale de spaghetti au ris de veau et langoustines. Tronçon de rouget aux huîtres, compotée de chorizo Iberico. Tomate, framboise, yuzu (summer). **Wines** Muscadet de Sèvre-et-Maine, Savennières.

◆ This fine, large 1920s residence, surrounded by a park and vineyards, is popular with people from Nantes due to its delicious, inventive cuisine. Good selection of Muscadet wine.

in La Haie-Fouassière **15 km by ③, D 149 and D 74 – pop. 3 917 – alt. 25 m – ✉ 44690**

Château du Breil without rest

r. du Breil – ✆ 02 40 36 71 55 – http://lebreil.monsite.orange.fr – lebreil@wanadoo.fr – Closed December and January

5 rm – †€ 100 ††€ 140

◆ This Nantes folly built in 1863 is set in the centre of a vineyard estate with wooded park, pool and lounge-library. Comfortable rooms with period furniture.

XX **Le Cep de Vigne**

at the north station: 1 km on the D 74 – ✆ 02 40 36 93 90 – Fax 02 51 71 60 69 – Closed February holiday, Sunday dinner, Monday dinner, Tuesday dinner and Wednesday

Rest – Menu (€ 15), € 23 bi (weekdays)/52 – Carte € 52/70

◆ The facade of this restaurant is decorated with a vine theme. Two of the three dining rooms have been refurbished, one has a veranda. Rustic lounge. Choice of Muscadet wines.

in Vertou **10 km by D 59 exit porte de Vertou – pop. 21 200 – alt. 32 m – ✉ 44120**

Office de tourisme, place du Beau Verger ✆ 02 40 34 94 36, Fax 02 40 34 06 86

XX **Monte-Cristo**

Chaussée des Moines – ✆ 02 40 34 40 36 – www.monte-cristo.fr – le.monte.cristo@orange.fr – Fax 02 40 03 26 20 – Closed 26-30 October, 27 December-4 January, Wednesday dinner, Sunday dinner and Monday

Rest – Menu (€ 19), € 25 – Carte € 32/54 *p. 5* DX **a**

◆ Dumas penned the first lines of the Count of Monte Cristo here. Brand new modern decor and terrace with broad views of the Sèvre. Modern cooking.

in Château-Thébaud **18 km by ③, D 149, D74 and D63 – pop. 2 731 – alt. 58 m – ✉ 44690**

Auberge la Gaillotière
La Gaillotière – ✆ 02 28 21 31 16 – www.auberge-la-gaillotiere.fr – contact@ auberge-la-gaillotiere.fr – Fax 02 28 21 31 17 – Closed 27 July-12 August, 2 February-4 March, Tuesday dinner and Wednesday
Rest – Menu € 13 (weekday lunch), € 18/26
◆ An inn isolated in the middle of the vineyards of the Nantes area. Traditional, seasonal market dishes and local wine served in a simple rustic setting.

La Roche-sur-Yon road **12 km by ④ and D 178 – ✉ 44840 Les Sorinières**

Abbaye de Villeneuve
– ✆ 02 40 04 40 25 – www.abbayedevilleneuve.com – villeneuve@ leshotelsparticuliers.com – Fax 02 40 31 28 45
21 rm – €95/195 €95/195, € 15 – ½ P € 98/148
Rest – Menu (€ 25), € 35/65 – Carte € 45/80
◆ An 18C residence built on the remains of a medieval abbey. Some tombstones decorate the lobby. Very traditional rooms; smaller rustic rooms on the second floor. Guests pass through cloisters to reach this restaurant. The dining room opens onto the park.

to Nantes-Atlantique International Airport **exit 51 porte de Grandlieu - Bouguenais – ✉ 44340 Bouguenais**

Océania
– ✆ 02 40 05 05 66 – www.oceaniahotels.com – oceania.nantes@ oceaniahotels.com – Fax 02 40 05 12 03 p. 4 BX **e**
87 rm – €175 €175, € 15 – 2 suites
Rest – *(closed Saturday lunch and Sunday lunch)* Menu € 21/30 – Carte € 37/52
◆ Imposing contemporary facade lined with pilasters. Practical rooms refurbished in a clean modern style. Shuttle linking the hotel to the airport. Pleasant lounge with fireplace, large dining room and terrace by the swimming pool.

in Bouaye **15 km by D 751A - AX – pop. 5 505 – alt. 16 m – ✉ 44830**

Office de tourisme, 2, pl. du Bois Jacques ✆ 02 40 65 53 55, Fax 02 51 70 59 84

Kyriad
rte de Nantes – ✆ 02 40 65 43 50 – www.champsdavaux.com – info@ champsdavaux.com – Fax 02 40 32 64 83 – Closed 24 December-3 January
44 rm – €72/82 €72/120, € 12 – ½ P € 64/66
Rest ***Les Champs d'Avaux*** – *(closed Sunday dinner)* Menu (€ 17), € 21 (weekdays)/73 – Carte € 35/70
◆ All the rooms in this modern building are contemporary and have double glazing. Some on the ground floor open onto the garden. Children's play area. Pleasant restaurant opening onto a garden. Traditional and regional dishes.

in Haute-Indre **10 km West by D 107, exit porte de l'Estuaire – ✉ 44610 Indre**

Belle Rive
8 pl. Jean Saillant – ✆ 02 40 86 01 07 – restarant.bellerive@wanadoo.fr – Fax 02 40 86 01 07 – Closed 21 July-24 August, 22-25 December, Saturday lunch, Sunday dinner, Monday dinner, Tuesday dinner and Wednesday p.4 AX **d**
Rest – Menu (€ 16), € 25 (weekdays)/32
◆ Restaurant near the small port of Haute Indre located on the Loire. Chocolate coloured dining room with matching tablecloths and chairs where market inspired food is served.

in Coueron **15 km by D 107, exit porte de l'Estuaire – pop. 18 500 – alt. 13 m – ✉ 44220**

François II
5 pl. Aristide Briand – ✆ 02 40 38 32 32 – www.francois2.com – solennjeromeE@ aol.com – Fax 02 40 38 32 32 – Closed 13-16 April, 27 July-20 August, 1st-4 November, 15-21 February, Sunday dinner, Tuesday dinner, Thursday dinner and Monday
Rest – Menu (€ 12), € 14 (weekday lunch), € 21/50 – Carte € 38/56
◆ The name pays tribute to the Duke of Brittany, father of Anne, who died in Couëron. Rustic style decor (exposed stonework, carpets and tapestries) and copious traditional food.

in St-Herblain 8 km West – pop. 43 900 – alt. 8 m – ✉ 44800

La Marine
esplanade de la Bégraisière – ✆ 02 40 95 26 66 – www.hotel-marine.fr – hotelmarine@wanadoo.fr – Fax 02 40 46 85 70 p. 4 BV **m**
24 rm – †€ 54/85 ††€ 61/85, ☕ € 8
Rest – *(closed Saturday lunch and Sunday)* Menu (€ 14), € 16 (lunch)/37 – Carte € 26/36
◆ Guests are assured a warm welcome in this hotel set in the heart of a large, peaceful garden. The spacious rooms are classically furnished and all identical. Dining room-veranda opening onto greenery; traditional food.

Les Caudalies
229 rte de Vannes – ✆ 02 40 94 35 35 – www.restaurant-lescaudalies.com – restaurant.les-caudalies@wanadoo.fr – Fax 02 40 40 89 90 – Closed 26 July-26 August, 15-25 February, Sunday dinner, Monday and Wednesday p. 4 BV **v**
Rest – Menu € 19 (weekdays), € 28/40 – Carte € 30/37
◆ A 1980s roadside villa with two small, discreet dining rooms. Cuisine based on market produce draws on specialities from all the regions of France.

in Orvault 6 km by N 137 exit porte de Rennes – pop. 24 000 – alt. 45 m – ✉ 44700

Le Domaine d'Orvault rest,
24 chemin des Marais-du-Cens – ✆ 02 40 76 84 02 – www.domaine-orvault.com – contact@domaine-orvault.com – Fax 02 40 76 04 21 p. 4 BV **e**
40 rm ☕ – †€ 88/116 ††€ 100/116
Rest – *(Closed Sunday from 15 October to 1st April)* Menu (€ 26), € 34/58 – Carte € 34/48
◆ Despite its appearance, this villa tucked away in a green setting dates from the 1970s. Large rooms furnished in various styles; choose one of the more modern. Contemporary restaurant with terrace shaded by lime trees. Modern cuisine.

Du Parc without rest
92 r. de la Garenne – ✆ 02 40 63 04 79 – www.hotel-du-parc-nantes.com – parc.hotel@wanadoo.fr – Fax 02 40 63 62 99 – Closed 6-26 August and 23 December-1st January p. 4 AV **q**
30 rm ☕ – †€ 60 ††€ 76/84
◆ Surrounded by woodland, this entirely revamped hotel offers tastefully decorated modern rooms, which are well soundproofed and faultlessly looked after. Sitting room-cum-library.

NANTILLY – 70 Haute-Saône – **314** B8 – see Gray

NANTOUX – 21 Côte-d'Or – **320** I7 – pop. 186 – alt. 295 m – ✉ 21190 7 **A3**

Paris 326 – Dijon 55 – Chalon-sur-Saône 37 – Le Creusot 48 – Beaune 9

Domaine de la Combotte without rest
r. de Pichot – ✆ 03 80 26 02 66 – www.lacombotte.com – info@lacombotte.com
5 rm ☕ – †€ 80/100 ††€ 105/130
◆ In the centre of a winegrowing village, this cluster of recent houses offers large rooms decorated on a wine theme. Special truffle packages in season.

NANTUA – 01 Ain – **328** G4 – pop. 3 902 – alt. 479 m – ✉ 01130 45 **C1**
Burgundy-Jura

Paris 476 – Aix-les-Bains 79 – Annecy 67 – Bourg-en-Bresse 52 – Genève 67 – Lyon 93

Office de tourisme, place de la Déportation ✆ 04 74 75 00 05, Fax 04 74 75 06 83

St-Michel church★ : Martyre de St-Sébastien★★ by E. Delacroix - Lake★.

La cuivrerie★ de Cerdon.

L'Embarcadère ⚓ rm, **P** VISA

av. Lac – ☎ 04 74 75 22 88 – www.hotelembarcadere.com – contact@hotelembarcadere.com – Fax 04 74 75 22 25

49 rm – †€ 59/73 ††€ 59/73, ☕ € 10

Rest – *(closed 20 December-5 January)* Menu € 25 (weekdays)/65 – Carte € 70/80

◆ Half the rooms overlook the lake and they have all been treated to a tasteful makeover in warm colours. The attractive panoramic view and the delicious regional cuisine are the main appeals of the restaurant, reached by a covered walkway.

in Brion **Northwest: 5 km by D 1084 and D 979 – pop. 511 – alt. 475 m – ✉ 01460**

Bernard Charpy **P** VISA

1 r. la Croix-Chalon – ☎ 04 74 76 24 15 – Fax 04 74 76 22 36 – Closed 17-25 May, 9 August-7 September, 26 December-4 January, Saturday lunch, Sunday dinner and Monday

Rest – Menu € 21 (weekday lunch), € 25/40 – Carte € 49/61

◆ The recently revamped contemporary dining room with timber ceiling serves enticing traditional fare, including a splendid selection of fresh fish.

in La Cluse **Northwest: 3.5 km by D 1084 – ✉ 01460 Montréal-la-Cluse**

Lac Hôtel without rest **P** VISA AE

22 av. Bresse – ☎ 04 74 76 29 68 – www.lac-hotel.com – lac-hotel@wanadoo.fr – Fax 04 74 76 13 70 – Closed 1st-8 August and 1st November-31 December

28 rm – †€ 38/44 ††€ 38/47, ☕ € 7

◆ Well kept, practical rooms with good soundproofing at unbeatable prices. An attractive location within easy reach of the main road. Internet access available.

LA NAPOULE – 06 Alpes-Maritimes – 341 C6 – see Mandelieu

NARBONNE – 11 Aude – 344 J3 – pop. 51 300 – alt. 13 m – ✉ 11100 Languedoc-Roussillon-Tarn Gorges

22 **B3**

Paris 787 – Béziers 28 – Carcassonne 61 – Montpellier 96 – Perpignan 64

☎ 3635 et tapez 42 (0,34 €/mn)

Office de tourisme, 31, rue Jean Jaurès ☎ 04 68 65 15 60, Fax 04 68 65 59 12

St-Just-et-St-Pasteur cathedral★★ (Treasure-house: tapestry portraying the Creation★★) - Donjon Gilles Aycelin★ ✻★ **H** - Choir★ of St-Paul basilica - Palais des Archevêques★ BY : musée d'Art et d'Histoire★ - Musée archéologique★ - Musée lapidaire★ BZ - Pont des marchands★.

Plan on following page

Novotel rm, **P** VISA AE

130 r. de l'Hôtellerie, Plaisance Industrial Estate 3 km via ③, Perpignan road – ☎ 04 68 42 72 00 – www.novotel.com – H0412@accor.com – Fax 04 68 42 72 10

96 rm – †€ 90/150 ††€ 90/150, ☕ € 15 **Rest** – Carte € 19/29

◆ This chain hotel is regularly renovated, providing a practical stop-off on the way to Spain. Comfortable rooms provided. Modern restaurant with a pergola shaded terrace and garden planted with yew and pine trees. Regional wines.

La Résidence without rest VISA AE

6 r. du 1er Mai – ☎ 04 68 32 19 41 – www.hotelresidence.fr – hotellaresidence@free.fr – Fax 04 68 65 51 82 – Closed 20 January-15 February AY **r**

26 rm – †€ 60/79 ††€ 66/115, ☕ € 9

◆ Jean Marais, Louis de Funès, Georges Brassens, Michel Serrault: a prestigious visitors' book in this traditional hotel in a 19C residence.

de France without rest VISA AE

6 r. Rossini – ☎ 04 68 32 09 75 – www.hotelnarbonne.com – accueil@hotelnarbonne.com – Fax 04 68 65 50 30 – Closed 1st February-1st March BZ **s**

15 rm – †€ 32/68 ††€ 36/70, ☕ € 7

◆ Functional, well kept rooms on either side of a small inner courtyard. The archaeology museum, with a collection of Roman paintings, is 500m away.

NARBONNE

Anatole-France (Av.) . . . . . . AYZ 2
Ancienne Porte de Béziers (R. de l') . . . . BY 4
Ancien Courrier (R. de l') . . . BY 3
Blum (Sq. Th.-Léon) . . . . BY 6
Cabirol (R.) . . . . AZ 7
Chennebier (R.) . . . . AY 9
Concorde (Pont de la) . . . . . . AY 10
Condorcet (Bd) . . . . BY 12
Courier (R. P.-L.) . . . . BZ 13
Crémieux (R. B.) . . . . BZ 15
Deymes (R. du Lt-Col.) . . . . . BY 16
Droite (R.) . . . . BY
Escoute (Pont de l') . . . . AY 17
Fabre (R. Gustave) . . . . AY 18
Foch (Av. Mar.) . . . . BY 19
Garibaldi (R.) . . . . BY 20
Gaulle (Bd Gén.-de) . . . . BY 21
Gauthier (R. Armand) . . . . . . BY 22
Hôtel de Ville (Pl. de l') . . . . BYZ
Jacobins (R. des) . . . . BZ 23
Jean-Jaurès (R.) . . . . AY 24
Joffre (Bd Mar.) . . . . AYZ 25
Liberté (Pont de la) . . . . BZ 27
Lion d'Or (R. du) . . . . AY 28
Louis-Blanc (R.) . . . . BY 29
Luxembourg (R. du) . . . . AZ 30
Major (R. de la) . . . . BZ 31
Maraussan (R.) . . . . AZ 32
Marchands (Pont des) . . . . . BZ 36
Michelet (R.) . . . . BY 33
Mirabeau (Cours) . . . . BZ 35
Pyrénées (Av. des) . . . . AY 37
Pyrénées (Pl. des) . . . . AZ 39
Rabelais (R.) . . . . AZ 40
République (Crs de la) . . . . . BZ 41
Salengro (Pl. R.) . . . . BY 43
Sermet (Av. E.) . . . . BY 44
Toulouse (Av. de) . . . . AZ 45
Voltaire (Pont) . . . . AY 47

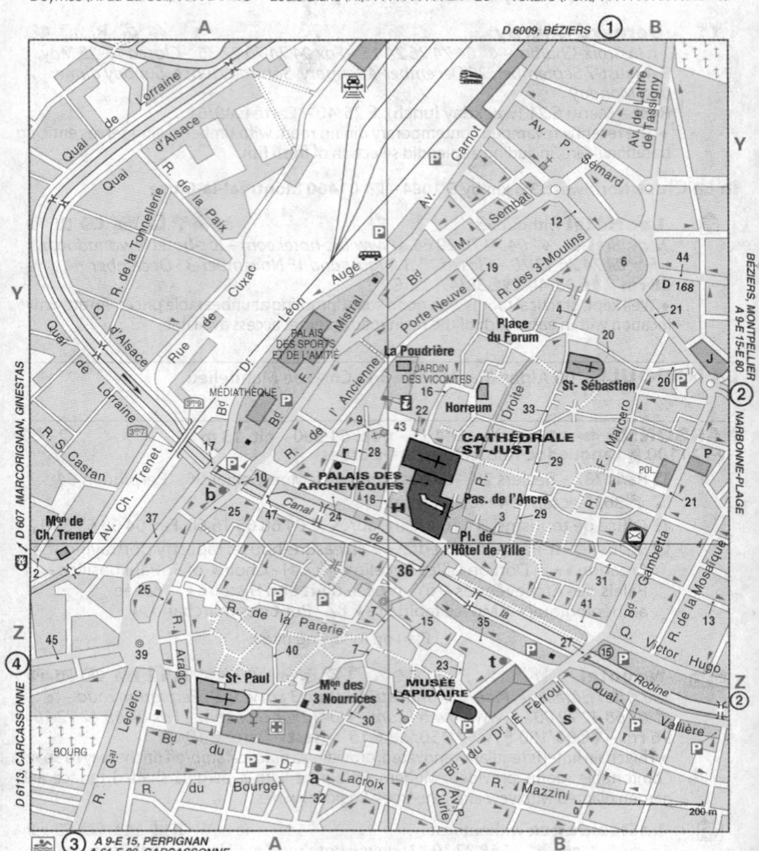

XXX ✿ **La Table St-Crescent** (Lionel Giraud)
68 av. Gén. Leclerc, at the Palais du Vin via ③ – ✆ 04 68 41 37 37 – www.la-table-saint-crescent.com – saint-crescent@wanadoo.fr – Fax 04 68 41 01 22 – Closed Saturday lunch, Sunday dinner and Monday
Rest – Menu (€ 23 bi), € 45 bi/79 bi – Carte € 64/85
Spec. Cube de foie gras des Landes, purée de céleri rave et truffe. Volaille sphérique au foie gras, quintessence de parmesan. Compression d'un vacherin à la fraise des bois, glace basilic. **Wines** Minervois, Corbières.
◆ Elegant, designer décor in this medieval oratory, with vine-covered terrace. Tasty, inventive cuisine and Languedoc-Roussillon wines.

XX **Le Petit Comptoir**
4 bd Mar. Joffre – ✆ 04 68 42 30 35 – www.petitcomptoir.com – camille@petitcomptoir.com – Fax 04 68 41 52 71 – Closed 26 July-10 August, 1st-7 January, Sunday and Monday AY **b**
Rest – Menu € 17 (weekday lunch), € 27/59 bi – Carte € 30/55
◆ Traditional recipes with a southern flavour and efficient attentive service: this pleasant 1930s bistro-style restaurant is often fully booked.

X **L'Estagnol**
5 bis cours Mirabeau – ✆ 04 68 65 09 27 – fabricemeynadier@wanadoo.fr – Fax 04 68 32 23 38 – Closed Monday dinner and Sunday BZ **t**
Rest – Menu (€ 12), € 19/33 – Carte € 22/45
◆ A modernised brasserie serving cuisine with a regional flavour made with produce from the next-door covered market. Pretty view of the canal from the first floor.

X **Le 26**
8 bd Dr-Lacroix – ✆ 04 68 41 46 69 – www.restaurantle26.fr – restole26@free.fr – Closed Saturday lunch, Sunday and Monday AZ **a**
Rest – Menu (€ 15), € 24/35 – Carte € 38/50
◆ Traditional cuisine prepared by the owner is served in the sober dining room (parquet flooring and stone walls) of this friendly and welcoming restaurant.

in Coursan **7 km by ① – pop. 6 059 – alt. 6 m – ✉ 11110**

Syndicat d'initiative, 10 bis, avenue Jean Jaurès ✆ 04 68 33 60 86, Fax 04 68 33 60 86

XX **L'Os à Table**
88 av. Jean Jaurès, Salles d'Aude road – ✆ 04 68 33 55 72 – http://perso.wanadoo.fr/losatable-coursan – losatable-coursan@wanadoo.fr – Fax 04 68 33 35 39 – Closed 14-30 September, Tuesday lunch, Sunday dinner and Monday
Rest – Menu € 25/46 – Carte € 30/47
◆ This restaurant is housed in a small mansion on the edge of the village near the Aude river. Well-lit dining areas decorated in pastel tones, serving traditional cuisine, fine choice of wines.

in l'Hospitalet **10 km by ② Narbonne-Plage road (D 168) – ✉ 11100**

Château l'Hospitalet
– ✆ 04 68 45 28 50 – www.gerard-bertrand.com – chateau.hospitalet@gerard-bertrand.com – Fax 04 68 45 28 78 – Closed 2-26 January and Sunday from October to March
38 rm – †€ 80/110 ††€ 90/120, ☕ € 15
Rest – (closed Sunday dinner and Monday from October to March) Menu € 29 bi – Carte € 29/60
◆ A hotel linked to a wine estate, including several craft workshops. Fine interior decoration and updated rooms. Regional menu and wines from its own estate are served in a former sheepfold.

in Bages **8 km by ③, D 6009 and D 105 – pop. 755 – alt. 30 m – ✉ 11100**

Syndicat d'initiative, 8, rue des Remparts ✆ 04 68 42 81 76, Fax 04 68 42 81 76

Les Palombières d'Estarac
Estarac, to the south-west – ✆ 04 68 42 45 56 – www.palombieres-estarac.com – estarac@wanadoo.fr – Fax 04 68 42 45 56
4 rm ☕ – †€ 62/122 ††€ 72/132 **Table d'hôte** – Menu € 27 bi
◆ This restored farmhouse surrounded by scrubland is home to cheerful, fresh personalised rooms: "Ocean", "Soleillad" and "Olivine". Serving Mediterranean dishes, this restaurant has a dining area overlooking parkland; roaring fire in winter.

XX **Le Portanel**
la Placette – ✆ 04 68 42 81 66 – jean-christophe.rousseau4@wanadoo.fr – Fax 04 68 41 75 93 – Closed Sunday dinner 15 September-15 July and Monday
Rest – Menu (€ 20 bi), € 25/40 – Carte € 36/65
◆ Mediterranean inspired cuisine using fresh local produce and distinctive flavours served in a former fisherman's house. Exhibition-sale of art and veranda with a view of the harbour.

in Ornaisons 14 km by ④, D 6113 and D 24 – **pop. 1 111 – alt. 34 m** – ✉ **11200**

Le Relais du Val d'Orbieu

on D 24 – ☎ 04 68 27 10 27 – www.relaisduvaldorbieu.com – contact@relaisdurvaldorbieu.com – Fax 04 68 27 52 44 – Closed 15 November-1st February and Sunday in November and February

18 rm – €65/120 €75/165, ☕ €17 – 2 suites – ½ P €80/130

Rest – *(dinner only)* Menu (€25), €39/49

◆ This former windmill, standing in the middle of the Corbières vineyards, features attractive bedrooms laid out around the fine patio. Good leisure facilities. Traditional cooking and regional wine selection served under a pretty pergola in summer.

LA NARTELLE – **83 Var** – **340** O6 – **see Ste-Maxime**

NASBINALS – **48 Lozère** – **330** G7 – **pop. 502** – **alt. 1 180 m** – **Winter sports : 1 240/1 320 m** 1 – ✉ **48260** **Languedoc-Roussillon-Tarn Gorges** 22 **B1**

Paris 573 – Aurillac 105 – Aumont-Aubrac 24 – Mende 57 – Rodez 64 – St-Flour 53

Office de tourisme, Village ☎ 04 66 32 55 73, Fax 04 66 32 55 73

Relais de l'Aubrac

au Pont de Gournier, (D 12 - D 112 junction), 4 km via D 12 – ☎ 04 66 32 52 06 – www.relais-aubrac.com – relais-aubrac@wanadoo.fr – Fax 04 66 32 56 58 – Open beg. March-mid November

27 rm – €49/70 €49/70, ☕ €8 – ½ P €47/60

Rest – Menu (€14), €20/33 – Carte €18/40

◆ This large house, popular with walkers and anglers, is next to a bridge over the Bès. Informal atmosphere, practical rooms and breakfast on the veranda. Regional cuisine (aligot) served in a rustic interior or on the terrace. Friendly service.

NATZWILLER – **67 Bas-Rhin** – **315** H6 – **pop. 599** – **alt. 500 m** – ✉ **67130** 2 **C1**

Paris 422 – Barr 25 – Molsheim 31 – St-Dié 43 – Strasbourg 59

Auberge Metzger with rm

55 r. Principale – ☎ 03 88 97 02 42 – www.hotel-aubergemetzger.com – auberge.metzger@wanadoo.fr – Fax 03 88 97 93 59 – Closed 29 June-6 July, 21-25 December, 6-26 January, Sunday dinner and Monday except July-August

16 rm – €57 €67/77, ☕ €10 – ½ P €75/84

Rest – Menu (€14), €20/58 – Carte €28/45

◆ The flower-decked façade gives on to a pleasant family inn, well known for its tasty regional cuisine. Paved courtyard with terrace. Comfortable guestrooms.

NAVARRENX – **64 Pyrénées-Atlantiques** – **342** H5 – **pop. 1 138** – **alt. 125 m** – ✉ **64190** 3 **B3**

Paris 787 – Pau 43 – Mourenx 15 – Oloron-Ste-Marie 23 – Orthez 22 – Peyrehorade 44

Office de tourisme, place des Casernes ☎ 05 59 66 54 80, Fax 05 59 66 54 80

Du Commerce

pl. des Casernes – ☎ 05 59 66 50 16 – www.hotel-commerce.fr – hotel.du.commerce@wanadoo.fr – Fax 05 59 66 52 67

24 rm – €65 €72, ☕ €8 – ½ P €72/86

Rest – Menu €11 (weekday lunch), €17/35 – Carte €33/65

◆ Entirely renovated regional-style abodes in the heart of a small, walled town founded in 1316. The delightfully rustic decor and comfortable rooms are most appreciable. The dining room is done in a country style with bright colours. Regional cuisine.

NEAUPHLE-LE-CHÂTEAU – **78 Yvelines** – **311** H3 – **pop. 2 973** – **alt. 185 m** – ✉ **78640** **Northern France and the Paris Region** 18 **A2**

Paris 38 – Dreux 42 – Mantes-la-Jolie 32 – Rambouillet 24 – Versailles 21

Syndicat d'initiative, 14, place du Marché ☎ 01 34 89 78 00, Fax 01 34 89 78 00

Domaine du Verbois rest, **P**
38 av. de la République – ☎ 01 34 89 11 78 VISA MC AE
– www.hotelverbois.com – verbois@hotelverbois.com – Fax 01 34 89 57 33
– Closed 9-21 August and 21-28 December
22 rm – †€ 105 ††€ 115/180, ☕ € 12 – ½ P € 149
Rest – *(closed Sunday dinner)* Menu € 39/49
◆ This stylish home dating from the late 19C is surrounded by a park and dominates the Mauldre valley. It offers customized bedrooms, with period or contemporary furnishings. Traditional cuisine in several elegant rooms or on the shaded terrace, overlooking the countryside.

Le Clos St-Nicolas without rest **P** VISA MC
33 r. St-Nicolas – ☎ 01 34 89 76 10 – www.clos-saint-nicolas.com
– mariefrance.drouelle@wanadoo.fr – Fax 01 34 89 76 10
5 rm ☕ – †€ 90 ††€ 96
◆ Very convivial family atmosphere in this fine 19C house. Pretty colour themed rooms (yellow, green, red) and breakfast on the veranda opposite the flower-filled park.

NÉGREVILLE – 50 Manche – 303 C3 – pop. 813 – alt. 70 m – ✉ 50260 — 32 A1

▶ Paris 342 – Caen 108 – Saint-Lô 72 – Cherbourg 22 – Équeurdreville-Hainneville 28

Northeast 5 km by D 146 and D 62 - ✉ 50260 Négreville

Château de Pont Rilly without rest **P** VISA MC
– ☎ 02 33 40 47 50 – www.chateau-pont-rilly.com
– chateau-pont-rilly@wanadoo.fr
5 rm ☕ – †€ 150 ††€ 150
◆ A perfectly preserved 18C château surrounded by formal, French-style gardens. Antique furniture and a rustic ambience add to the charm. Beautiful guestrooms with a fireplace.

NÉRIS-LES-BAINS – 03 Allier – 326 C5 – pop. 2 728 – alt. 364 m – Spa : early April-late Oct. – Casino – ✉ 03310 Auvergne — 5 B1

▶ Paris 336 – Clermont-Ferrand 86 – Montluçon 9 – Moulins 73
ℹ Office de tourisme, carrefour des Arènes ☎ 04 70 03 11 03, Fax 04 70 09 05 29
⛳18 de Sainte-Agathe Villebret, 4 km on the Montluçon road, ☎ 04 70 03 21 77

NÉRIS-LES-BAINS

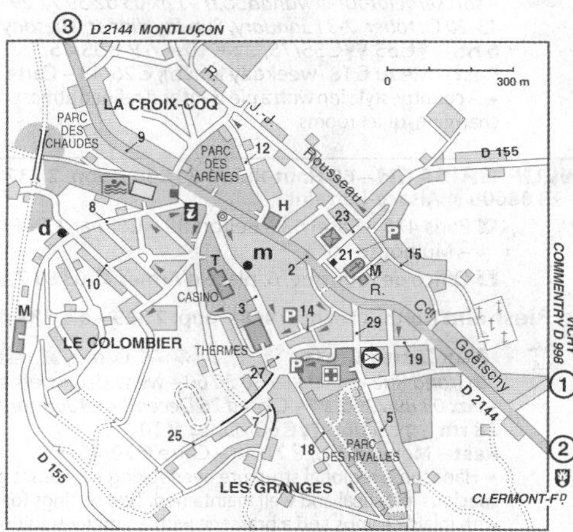

Mona Lisa rm, rest, VISA
40 r. Boisrot-Desserviers – ☎ 04 70 08 79 80 – www.monalisahotels.com – resa-neris@monalisahotels.com – Fax 04 70 08 79 81 **m**
59 rm – †€ 70/85 ††€ 70/85, ☕ € 11 – ½ P € 61/69
Rest – *(closed lunch except public holidays)* Menu € 18
◆ Behind the Belle Époque facade of this hotel located opposite the casino lie air-conditioned comfort, contemporary style, and the latest technology. A restaurant with soberly dressed tables and designer furniture in keeping with the chef's modern cuisine.

Le Garden rm, VISA
12 av. Marx Dormoy – ☎ 04 70 03 21 16 – http://monsite.wanadoo.fr/hotellegarden – hotel.le.garden@wanadoo.fr – Fax 04 70 03 10 67 – Closed 26-31 December, 28 January-8 March **d**
19 rm – †€ 48/70 ††€ 48/70, ☕ € 7 – ½ P € 48/55
Rest – *(closed Sunday dinner and Monday from November to March)* Menu (€ 15), € 17/38 – Carte € 18/43
◆ This villa, in a garden in bloom, was converted into a hotel, and lies near the centre of the resort. Modern and regularly redecorated bedrooms. This stylish dining room, appreciated for its brightness and cheerfulness, serves simple cuisine.

NÉRONDES – 18 Cher – 323 M5 – pop. 1 515 – alt. 200 m – ✉ 18350 12 **D3**

Paris 240 – Bourges 37 – Montluçon 84 – Nevers 33 – St-Amand-Montrond 44

la Vallée de Germigny Saint-Hilaire-de-Gondilly Domaine de Villefranche, NE : 9 km on D 6, ☎ 02 48 80 23 43

Le Lion d'Or with rm rest, VISA
pl. de la Mairie – ☎ 02 48 74 87 81 – Fax 02 48 74 92 63 – Closed 31 August-6 September, 19-25 October, Sunday dinner and Wednesday
10 rm – †€ 50 ††€ 50/55, ☕ € 8,50 – ½ P € 52
Rest – Menu € 20/40 – Carte € 55/73
◆ Family-run, town centre inn, offering a stylish, rustic dining room, serving traditional cuisine. Renovated rooms, with the quietest ones at the back.

NESTIER – 65 Hautes-Pyrénées – 342 O6 – pop. 171 – alt. 500 m – ✉ 65150 28 **A3**

Paris 789 – Auch 74 – Bagnères-de-Luchon 45 – Lannemezan 14 – St-Gaudens 24

Relais du Castéra with rm VISA
place du calvaire – ☎ 05 62 39 77 37 – www.hotel-castera.com – sarl.sergelatour@wanadoo.fr – Fax 05 62 39 77 29 – Closed 2-10 June, 13-20 October, 2-31 January, Sunday dinner, Tuesday dinner and Monday
6 rm – †€ 55 ††€ 55/75, ☕ € 10 – ½ P € 55/75
Rest – Menu € 18 (weekday lunch), € 26/48 – Carte € 45/56
◆ A country-style inn with a pleasant and refined atmosphere. Locally inspired cuisine and charming, quiet rooms.

NEUF-BRISACH – 68 Haut-Rhin – 315 J8 – pop. 2 237 – alt. 197 m – ✉ 68600 Alsace-Lorraine 2 **C2**

Paris 475 – Basel 63 – Belfort 80 – Colmar 17 – Freiburg-im-Breisgau 35 – Mulhouse 40

Office de tourisme, 6, place d'Armes ☎ 03 89 72 56 66, Fax 03 89 72 91 73

in Biesheim North: 3 km by D 468 – pop. 2 329 – alt. 189 m – ✉ 68600

Aux Deux Clefs rest, rest, VISA
50 Grand Rue – ☎ 03 89 30 30 60 – www.deux-clefs.com – info@deux-clefs.com – Fax 03 89 72 92 94 – Closed 26 December-4 January
28 rm – †€ 58/68 ††€ 68/85, ☕ € 10
Rest – Menu (€ 11), € 21/48 – Carte € 20/48
◆ Handsome regional structure overlooking a pleasant garden. The rooms are relatively spacious, practical and well maintained. Two settings for your meal. A plush dining room with inlaid ceilings and a brasserie with a simpler traditional menu.

NEUFCHÂTEAU – 88 Vosges – 314 C2 – pop. 7 056 – alt. 300 m 26 B3
– ✉ 88300 Alsace-Lorraine

Paris 321 – Belfort 158 – Chaumont 57 – Épinal 75 – Langres 78 – Verdun 106

Office de tourisme, 3, Parking des Grandes Ecuries ✆ 03 29 94 10 95, Fax 03 29 94 10 89

Town hall★ staircase - Stone group★ in St-Nicolas church.

L'Eden rm, rm, VISA MC AE

r. 1ère Armée Française – ✆ 03 29 95 61 30 – www.leden.fr – hotel-eden@wanadoo.fr – Fax 03 29 94 03 42

27 rm – †€ 45/80 ††€ 50/85, ☕ € 8,50

Rest – *(closed 2-15 January, Sunday dinner and Monday lunch)* Menu (€ 15), € 25/45 – Carte € 32/54

◆ A recent hotel with comfortable, colourful rooms of various sizes. The rooms on the top floor boast Jacuzzi bathtubs. A plush dining room, decorated mainly in blue and ochre. Up-to-the-minute menu.

Romain VISA MC

74 av. Kennedy – ✆ 03 29 06 18 80 – Fax 03 29 06 18 80 – Closed 16-31 August, 14-28 February, Sunday dinner and Monday

Rest – Menu (€ 12,50), € 18/34 – Carte € 26/47

◆ A roadside restaurant, with a vast, bright and modern dining room. Traditional, country menu with a few regional specialities and seafood.

NEUFCHÂTEL-EN-BRAY – 76 Seine-Maritime – 304 I3 – pop. 4 937 33 D1
– alt. 99 m – ✉ 76270 Normandy

Paris 133 – Rouen 50 – Abbeville 57 – Amiens 72 – Dieppe 40 – Gournay-en-Bray 37

Office de tourisme, 6, place Notre-Dame ✆ 02 35 93 22 96, Fax 02 32 97 00 62

de Saint-Saëns Saint-Saëns Domaine du Vaudichon, SW : 17 km on D 6028 and D 929, ✆ 02 35 34 25 24

Forêt d'Eawy★★ 10 km Southwest.

Les Airelles with rm VISA MC AE

2 passage Michu, (near the church) – ✆ 02 35 93 14 60 – les-airelles-sarl@wanadoo.fr – Fax 02 35 93 89 03 – Closed autumn half-term holidays, February half-term holidays, Sunday dinner September-June, Tuesday lunch and Monday except July-August and except hotel

14 rm – †€ 50/68 ††€ 50/68, ☕ € 8 – ½ P € 55/64

Rest – Menu € 17 (weekdays)/42 – Carte € 39/61

◆ This restaurant is in an attractive, traditional town centre edifice. It is home to two simple, modern dining areas, and a summer terrace in the small garden. Up-to-date cuisine.

in Mesnières-en-Bray Northwest: 5.5 km by D 1 – pop. 884 – alt. 65 m – ✉ 76270

Château★.

Auberge du Bec Fin VISA MC AE

1 r. du Château – ✆ 02 35 94 15 15 – www.aubergedubecfin.fr – christophe-pillorget@wanadoo.fr – Fax 02 35 94 42 14 – Closed Sunday dinner, Tuesday dinner and Wednesday

Rest – Menu (€ 13), € 16 (weekdays)/43 – Carte € 37/55

◆ Traditional cuisine takes pride of place in the attractive cream and brown modern interior. Seasonal, market-fresh cuisine to suit current tastes.

NEUFCHÂTEL-EN-SAOSNOIS – 72 Sarthe – 310 K 4 – pop. 763 35 D1
– alt. 190 m – ✉ 72600

Paris 200 – Nantes 228 – Le Mans 56 – Alençon 15 – Argentan 66

Les Étangs de Guibert rm, VISA MC

2 km east on the minor road – ✆ 02 43 97 15 38 – www.lesetangsdeguibert.com – relais_des_etangs_de_guibert@voila.fr – Fax 02 43 33 22 99

15 rm – †€ 52/100 ††€ 52/100, ☕ € 10

Rest – Menu € 21 (weekdays)/41 – Carte € 26/54

◆ Tucked away in the countryside, the peace and quiet of this old farmstead and private lake (fishing possible) are very pleasant. Spruce, quiet rooms. An opportunity to sample modern cuisine, enlivened with exotic spices in a spacious rustic room or on the waterside terrace.

NEUFCHÂTEL-SUR-AISNE – 02 Aisne – 306 G6 – pop. 461 37 D2
– alt. 59 m – ✉ 02190

Paris 163 – Laon 46 – Reims 22 – Rethel 33 – Soissons 60

de Menneville Menneville La Haie Migaut, SW : 3 km, ✆ 03 23 79 79 88

XX Le Jardin

22 r. Principale – ✆ 03 23 23 82 00 – www.restaurant-le-jardin.com – lejardint@wanadoo.fr – Fax 03 23 23 84 05 – Closed 2 weeks in September, 3 weeks in January, Sunday dinner, Monday and Tuesday

Rest – Menu (€ 18), € 26/53 – Carte € 45/61

◆ A "lawned" floor, flowered walls, plants, a veranda facing flower beds - the restaurant lives up to its name. Menus according to the market produce available.

NEUILLÉ-LE-LIERRE – 37 Indre-et-Loire – 317 O3 – pop. 711 11 B2
– alt. 92 m – ✉ 37380

Paris 217 – Amboise 16 – Château-Renault 10 – Montrichard 34 – Reugny 5 – Tours 27

XX Auberge de la Brenne with rm

19 r. de la République – ✆ 02 47 52 95 05 – www.auberge-brenne.com – hotel.brenne@wanadoo.fr – Fax 02 47 52 29 43 – Closed 23 November-2 December, 1st February-10 March

5 rm – †€ 60/90 ††€ 60/90, ☕ € 15

Rest – *(closed Sunday dinner 15 September-15 June, Tuesday and Wednesday) (pre-book weekends)* Menu (€ 20), € 25 (weekdays)/50 – Carte € 44/73

◆ The owners of this inviting village inn gracefully welcome diners into an attractive dining room. Traditional dishes. Comfortable guestrooms in a 1900 house 50m away.

NEUILLY-LE-REAL – 03 Allier – 326 H4 – pop. 1 324 – alt. 260 m 6 C1
– ✉ 03340

Paris 313 – Mâcon 128 – Moulins 16 – Roanne 82 – Vichy 48

XX Logis Henri IV

13 r. du 14 Juillet – ✆ 04 70 43 87 64 – Closed September, 15-28 February, Sunday dinner and Monday

Rest – Menu (€ 15), € 21 (weekday lunch), € 31/51

◆ This 16C, former hunting lodge is adorned with floor-tiles and a timber frame that give it lots of character. Traditional cooking.

NEUVÉGLISE – 15 Cantal – 330 F5 – pop. 1 133 – alt. 938 m – ✉ 15260 5 B3

Paris 528 – Aurillac 78 – Espalion 66 – St-Chély-d'Apcher 42 – St-Flour 17

Office de tourisme, le Bourg ✆ 04 71 23 85 43, Fax 04 71 23 86 40

Château d'Alleuze★★: site★★ Northeast: 14 km, **Auvergne-Rhone Valley**

in Cordesse East: 1,5 km on D 921 – ✉ 15260 Neuvéglise

X Relais de la Poste with rm

– ✆ 04 71 23 82 32 – www.relaisdelaposte.com – relais.poste@wanadoo.fr – Fax 04 71 23 86 23 – Open 4 April-4 November

9 rm – †€ 50/70 ††€ 60/75, ☕ € 10 – ½ P € 60/70

Rest – *(closed Monday lunch except July-August)* Menu (€ 15), € 18 (weekday lunch), € 26/48 – Carte € 22/53

◆ A recent establishment with rustic decor including fireplace and attractive wood panelling. Children's play area. Generous and simple regional fare.

NEUVES-MAISONS – 54 Meurthe-et-Moselle – 307 H7 – see Nancy

NEUVILLE-DE-POITOU – 86 Vienne – 322 H4 – pop. 4 058 39 C1
– alt. 116 m – ✉ 86170

Paris 335 – Châtellerault 36 – Parthenay 41 – Poitiers 16 – Saumur 82 – Thouars 51

Office de tourisme, 28, place Joffre ✆ 05 49 54 47 80, Fax 05 49 54 18 66

La Roseraie

78 r. A. Caillard – ✆ 05 49 54 16 72 – www.laroseraiefrance.fr – info@laroseraiefrance.fr

5 rm – €59/71 €64/82 **Table d'hôte** – Menu €28 bi

◆ This mid-19C mansion has a garden with rose bushes and vines (small producer of Pineau de Charentes). Personalised rooms. International cuisine (the owners come from Zimbabwe and England) served on the terrace or in an elegant dining room.

St-Fortunat

4 r. Bangoura-Moridé – ✆ 05 49 54 56 74 – www.saintfortunat.com – fabien.dupont6@voila.fr – Fax 05 49 53 18 02 – Closed 10-23 August, Sunday dinner, Monday and public holidays

Rest – Menu (€15), €22 (lunch), €38/57 – Carte €42/52

◆ Contemporary dining room adorned with a tapestry, leading onto a courtyard-terrace and veranda. Designer table settings and modern cuisine.

If breakfast is included the symbol appears after the number of rooms.

NEUVILLE-ST-AMAND – **02 Aisne** – **306** B4 – **see St-Quentin**

NEUZY – **71 Saône-et-Loire** – **320** E11 – **see Digoin**

NÉVACHE – **05 Hautes-Alpes** – **334** H2 – **pop. 326** – **alt. 1 640 m** – ✉ **05100** 41 **C1**

Paris 693 – Briançon 21 – Le Monêtier-les-Bains 35 – Montgenèvre 25

Office de tourisme, Ville Haute ✆ 04 92 20 02 20, Fax 04 92 20 51 72

Le Chalet d'En Hô rm, rest,

hameau des Chazals – ✆ 04 92 20 12 29 – www.chaletdenho.com – chaletdenho@orange.fr – Fax 04 92 20 59 70 – Open 30 May-12 September, 24-31 October and 19 December-2 March

14 rm – €100/110 €130/147, €12 – ½ P €85/95

Rest – *(dinner only)* Menu €30

◆ The wood panelling, Provencal quilting, cushions and photos create a cosy atmosphere at this chalet set in a peaceful and attractive landscape. The charming decor of the dining room is based on mountain activities of times past. Traditional cuisine.

NEVERS – **58 Nièvre** – **319** B10 – **pop. 38 200** – **Built-up area 100 556** – **alt. 194 m** – **St Bernadette's pilgrimage from April to October : St Gildard's convent** – ✉ **58000** **Burgundy-Jura** 7 **A2**

Paris 236 – Bourges 70 – Clermont-Ferrand 161 – Orléans 167

du Nivernais Magny-Cours Le Bardonnay, E : 2 km on D 200, ✆ 03 86 58 18 30

Circuit Automobile permanent to Magny-Cours ✆ 03 86 21 80 00, by ④ : 12 km.

St-Cyr and Ste-Juliette cathedral ★★ - Palais ducal★ - St-Étienne church ★ - Façade★ of Ste-Marie chapel - Porte du Croux★ - Nevers earthenware ★ of the musée municipal Frédéric Blandin **M¹**.

Circuit de Nevers-Magny-Cours: musée Ligier F1★.

Plan on following page

Mercure Pont de Loire rm,

quai Médine – ✆ 03 86 93 93 86 – www.alpha-hotellerie.com – h3480@accor.com – Fax 03 86 59 43 29 Z **a**

59 rm – €92 €102, €12 **Rest** – Menu €23/32 – Carte €30/39

◆ Pleasantly located on the banks of the Loire. Comfortable bar with piano. Attractive rooms, some of which offer a delightful view of the river. Panoramic dining room and huge terrace. Regionally inspired cuisine and wine list.

NEVERS

Street	Square	No.
Ardilliers (R. des)	Y	2
Banlay (R. du)	V	3
Barre (R. de la)	Y	4
Bourgeois (R. Mlle)	V	5
Champ-de-Foire (R. du)	Z	6
Charnier (R. du)	Y	7
Chauvelles (R. des)	V	8
Cloître-St-Cyr (R. du)	Z	9
Colbert (Av.)	Y	10
Coquille (Pl. G.)	Y	12
Docks (R. des)	V	13
Fer (R. du)	Y	47
Fonmorigny (R.)	Y	48
Francs-Bourgeois (R. des)	Y	14
Gaulle (Av. Gén.-de)	YZ	
Gautron-du-Coudray (Bd)	V	15
Jacobins (R. des)	Z	16
Lattre-de-Tassigny (Bd Mar.-de)	V	17
Mancini (Pl.)	Y	50
Mantoue (Quai de)	Z	18
Marceau (Av.)	Y	19
Midi (R. du)	Z	20
Mirangron (R.)	Y	49
Mitterrand (R. F.)	YZ	
Nièvre (R. de)	Y	21
Ouches (R. des)	YZ	22
Pelleterie (R. de la)	Y	24
Petit-Mouësse (R. du)	X	26
Porte-du-Croux (R. de la)	Z	51
Préfecture (R. de la)	Y	27
Récollets (R. des)	Z	52
Remigny (R. de)	Y	28
Renardats (R. des)	V	30
République (Bd de la)	X	32
République (Pl. de la)	Z	34
Roy (R. C.)	Y	36
St-Martin (R.)	Y	38
St-Sébastien (Pl.)	Y	39
Tillier (R. C.)	Z	40
Vaillant-Couturier (R. Paul)	V	42
14-Juillet (R. du)	Z	45

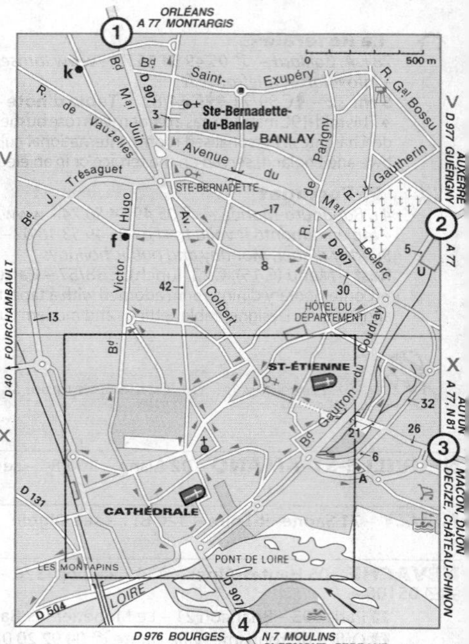

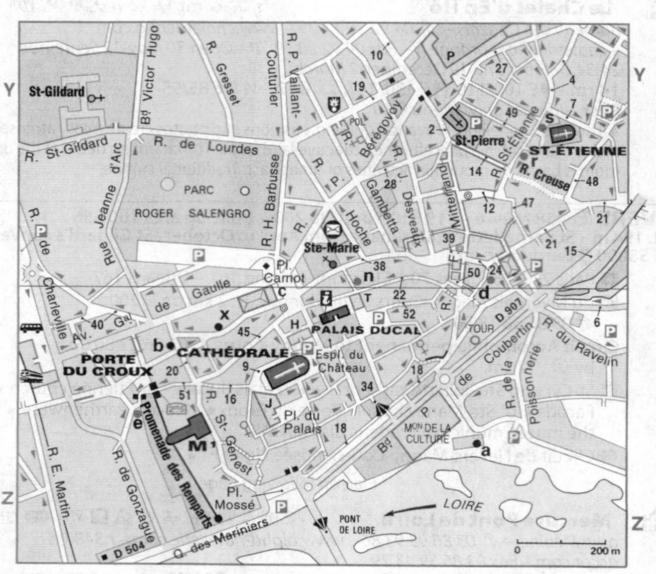

De Diane
38 r. du Midi – ✆ 03 86 57 28 10 – www.bestwesterndiane-nevers.com – diane.nevers@wanadoo.fr – Fax 03 86 59 45 08 – Closed 20 December-4 January Z **b**
30 rm – €86 €102, ☕ €11
Rest – *(closed Friday lunch and Sunday)* Menu (€ 17), € 20/29
◆ This former residence near the station houses sizeable, renovated rooms, furnished with care. The breakfast room is in a 14C tower. The restaurant offers classic food and a discreet setting.

Ibis
r. du Plateau de la Bonne Dame, via ④ – ✆ 03 86 37 56 00 – www.ibishotel.com – h0947@accor.com – Fax 03 86 37 64 48
56 rm – €60/95 €60/100, ☕ €8,50
Rest – *(dinner only)* Menu € 18/22
◆ This hotel is located on the left bank, near the Loire bridge. The recently refurbished rooms are quieter on the car park side. Traditional meals offered in a refurbished dining room or on the terrace.

Molière without rest
25 r. Molière – ✆ 03 86 57 29 96 – www.hotel-moliere-nevers.com – contact@hotel-moliere-nevers.com – Fax 03 86 36 00 13 V **k**
18 rm – €47 €52, ☕ €7
◆ A warm welcome at this clean and simple hotel situated in a residential area. You can choose between rustic or modern bedrooms.

Jean-Michel Couron
21 r. St-Étienne – ✆ 03 86 61 19 28 – www.jm-couron.com – info@jm-couron.com – Fax 03 86 36 02 96 – Closed 13 July-4 August, 2-8 January, 15-22 February, Sunday dinner, Tuesday lunch and Monday Y **r**
Rest – *(number of covers limited, pre-book)* Menu € 23 (weekdays)/53 – Carte € 65/78
Spec. Tarte de tomates au chèvre frais et jambon du Morvan. Pièce de bœuf charolais. Soupe tiède de chocolat aux épices et palmiers feuilletés. **Wines** Pouilly-Fumé, Sancerre.
◆ In the old quarter of Nevers. One of the three tiny dining rooms is under the 14C vaults of the former St. Etienne church cloister. Fine, inventive cuisine.

La Botte de Nevers
r. du Petit Château – ✆ 03 86 61 16 93 – labottedenevers@wanadoo.fr – Fax 03 86 36 42 22 – Closed Sunday dinner, Tuesday lunch and Monday Y **n**
Rest – Menu (€ 19), € 23/52 – Carte € 36/65
◆ The attractive wrought-iron sign, a medieval-style setting and swords decorating the staircase echo the reference to the Duke of Never's famous final sword thrust.

L'Assiette
7 bis r. F. Gambon – ✆ 03 86 36 24 99 – Closed 17 August-7 September, dinner from Monday to Thursday and Sunday Y **d**
Rest – Menu (€ 15) – Carte € 25/35
◆ An original concept for this delightful establishment: theme dishes (starter, main dish, cheese) made from fresh produce. Modern blue and chocolate decor.

Orléans road by ① – ✉ **58640 Varennes-Vauzelles**

Le Bengy
25 rte de Paris, 4.5 km via D 907 – ✆ 03 86 38 02 84 – www.le-bengy-restaurant.com – lebengyrestaurant@wanadoo.fr – Fax 03 86 38 29 00 – Closed 27 July-19 August, 1st-5 January, 22 February-10 March, Sunday and Monday
Rest – Menu € 19 (weekdays)/31 – Carte € 30/47
◆ A fashionable colour scheme, contemporary lines, leather, wrought iron and plants create the soothing Japanese inspired setting of this often fully booked restaurant. Modern menu.

in Sauvigny-les-Bois 10 km by ③ D 978 and D 18 – pop. 1 515 – alt. 210 m – ✉ 58160

XX **Moulin de l'Étang**

64 rte de l'Étang – ✆ 03 86 37 10 17 – www.moulindeletang.fr – restaurant@moulindeletang.fr – Fax 03 86 37 12 06 – Closed 1st-20 August, February school holidays, Sunday dinner, Wednesday dinner and Monday

Rest – Menu € 20/41 – Carte € 28/50

◆ At the edge of the village and near the lake, this former dairy houses a rustic dining room (beams, old clock and art exhibition). Modern menu.

Moulins road 3 km by ④, on N 7 – ✉ 58000 Challuy

XX **La Gabare**

171 rte de Lyon – ✆ 03 86 37 54 23 – www.restaurant-lagabare.fr – Fax 03 86 37 64 49 – Closed 12 July-11 August, Sunday dinner and Monday

Rest – Menu € 19 (weekdays)/26 – Carte € 32/59

◆ A finely-restored old farmhouse offering two rustic dining rooms with exposed beams, colourful walls and a large fireplace. Terrace with flowers for a meal outside in fine weather.

in Magny-Cours 12 km by ④, Moulins road – pop. 1 486 – alt. 205 m – ✉ 58470

Holiday Inn

Ferme du domaine de Bardonnay – ✆ 03 86 21 22 33 – www.holidayinn-nevers.com – himagnycours@alliance-hospitality.com – Fax 03 86 21 22 03

70 rm – †€ 98 ††€ 98, ☕ € 18 **Rest** – Menu (€ 13), € 18 – Carte € 27/50

◆ Located near a motor-racing circuit and golf course. The original farmhouse has been extended with a modern bedroom wing. Some rooms overlook the swimming pool or greens. Bright dining room opening onto a vast terrace. Traditional cuisine.

NÉVEZ – 29 Finistère – 308 I8 – pop. 2 542 – alt. 40 m – ✉ 29920 9 B2

Paris 547 – Rennes 196 – Quimper 40 – Lorient 51 – Lanester 51

Office de tourisme, place de l' Église ✆ 02 98 06 87 90, Fax 02 98 06 73 09

X **Le Bistrot de l'Écailler**

au port de Kerdruc, 3 km east par D 77 and secondary road – ✆ 02 98 06 78 60 – claudie@huitres-cadoret.com – Fax 02 98 06 78 60 – Open mid-April to end September and closed Tuesday and Wednesday except dinner in July-August

Rest – Menu € 45 – Carte € 34/48

◆ An attractive bistro specialising in fish and seafood with a terrace overlooking the port and the Aven. Superb seafood platters, daily suggestions, lobster and chips, and an imaginative wine list.

in Raguenès-Plage 4 km south on the minor road – ✉ 29920

Ar Men Du

– ✆ 02 98 06 84 22 – www.men-du.com – contact@men-du.com – Fax 02 98 06 76 69 – Closed 1st-13 March, 2 November-21 December and 2 January-1st March

14 rm – †€ 80 ††€ 100/125, ☕ € 13 – 1 suite

Rest – *(closed Tuesday lunch and Wednesday lunch) (pre-book)* Menu (€ 28 bi), € 37/75 – Carte € 54/80

◆ In a conservation area overlooking the ocean, this 1970s neo-Breton house has a distinctly maritime feel. Guestrooms decorated in nautical style, sea views and peaceful surroundings. Fish and seafood specialities, with views of Île Raguénès in the distance. Good choice of wines by the glass.

Your opinions are important to us:
please write and let us know about your discoveries
and experiences – good and bad!

NEXON – 87 Haute-Vienne – 325 E6 – pop. 2 385 – alt. 359 m – ✉ 87800 — 24 B2

▶ Paris 416 – Limoges 27 – Saint-Junien 56 – Panazol 27 – Isle 27

ℹ Office de tourisme, Conciergerie du Château ✆ 05 55 58 28 44, Fax 05 55 58 23 56

XX **Les Chaumières** with rm

Domaine des Landes, 2 km via D 11 – ✆ 05 55 58 25 26 – www.les-chaumieres.com – jfcane@les-chaumieres.com – Fax 05 55 58 25 25

3 rm – †€ 70 ††€ 70, ☕ € 8

Rest – *(closed Sunday dinner, Monday and Tuesday) (pre-book)* Menu € 35/40

◆ Pretty thatched cottage in a garden with old trees. Warm, elegant interior, friendly welcome and contemporary cuisine which varies with the seasons. Guest rooms in an outhouse for a peaceful extension to your stay.

NEYRAC-LES-BAINS – 07 Ardèche – 331 H5 – ✉ 07380 — 44 A3

▶ Paris 606 – Alès 92 – Aubenas 16 – Montélimar 56 – Privas 45 – Le Puy-en-Velay 75

XX **Du Levant**

Meyras – ✆ 04 75 36 41 07 – www.hotel-levant.com – info@hotel-levant.com – Fax 04 75 36 48 09 – Open 29 March-21 November and closed Tuesday except dinner in July-August, Sunday dinner and Monday

Rest – Menu (€ 19 bi), € 25/55

◆ In the same family since 1885, this inn specialises in appetising regional dishes with a modern slant and a fine wine list. Panoramic half-rustic, half-designer room, terrace.

NÉZIGNAN-L'ÉVÈQUE – 34 Hérault – 339 F8 – see Pézenas

H. Le Gac/MICHELIN

Old Nice

NICE

P **Department:** 06 Alpes-Maritimes
Michelin LOCAL map: n° **341** E5 **115**]26]27
Paris 927 – Cannes 33 – Genova 192 – Lyon 471 – Marseille 189 – Torino 210

Population: 383 400
Pop. built-up area: 1 003 450
Altitude: 6 m – **Postal Code:** ✉ 06000
French Riviera
Carte régionale 42 **E2**

USEFUL INFORMATION

TOURIST OFFICES

Office de tourisme, 5, promenade des Anglais ✆ 08 92 70 74 07
Office de tourisme, Aéroport ✆ 08 92 70 74 07

TRANSPORT

Auto-train ✆ 3635 et tapez 42 (0,34 €/mn)

SEA TRANSPORT

For Corsica:
SNCM - Ferryterranée quai du Commerce ✆ 0 825 888 088 (0.15 €/mn) JZ
CORSICA FERRIES Port de Commerce ✆ 04 92 00 42 93, Fax 04 92 00 42 94

AIRPORT

Nice-Côte-d'Azur ✆ 0820 423 333 (0.12 €/min), 6 km AU

CASINO

Ruhl, 1 promenade des Anglais FZ
Le Palais de la Méditerannée, 15 promenade des Anglais FZ

TO SEE

THE SEA FRONT AND OLD NICE

Site★★ - Promenade des Anglais★★ - ⩽★★ of the château - Interior ★ of St-Martin church - St-Augustin **HY** - St-Jacques church ★ **HZ** - Monumental staircase ★ of the palais Lascaris **HZ**V - Interior ★ of Ste-Réparate cathedral **HZ** - decorations★ of the Annonciation chapel **HZ** B - Altar-pieces★ of the Miséricorde chapel ★ **HZ** D

CIMIEZ

Musée Marc-Chagall★★ **GX** - Musée Matisse★★ **HV** M^{4} - Franciscan monastery★: primitive Niçois paintings★★ in the church **HV** K - Gallo-Roman archeological site ★

WESTERN DISTRICTS

Musée des beaux-Arts (Jules Chéret)★★ **DZ** - Musée d'Art naîf A.Jakovsky★ **AU** M^{10} - Giant greenhouse★ of the Phoenix Park ★ **AU** - Musée des Arts asiatiques★★

PROMENADE DU PAILLON

Musée d'Art moderne et d'Art contemporain★★ **HY** M^{2} - Palais des Arts, du Tourisme et des Congrès (Arts, Tourism and Congress Centre) (Acropolis)★ **HJX**

OTHER SIGHTS

St-Nicolas Russian Orthodox Cathedral ★ **EXY** - Mosaic★ by Chagall in the Law Faculty **DZ** U - Musée Masséna★ **FZ** M^{3}

Negresco
37 promenade des Anglais – ✆ 04 93 16 64 00
– www.hotel-negresco-nice.com
– direction@hotel-negresco.com
– Fax 04 93 88 35 68 *p. 6* FZ **k**
128 rm – €290/590 €290/590, €30 – 9 suites
Rest *Chantecler* – see below
Rest *La Rotonde* – Menu (€31), €36 – Carte €37/93
◆ Built in 1913 by Henri Negresco, son of a Romanian inn keeper, this palace, or rather, this mythical and majestic museum hotel, is brimming with works of art and grandeur. The Rotonde: an unusual brasserie with a merry-go-round decor, wooden horses and automatons.

Palais de la Méditerranée rm, rest,
13 promenade des Anglais – ✆ 04 92 14 77 00
– http://palais.concorde-hotels.fr – reservation-pdlm@concorde-hotels.com
– Fax 04 92 14 77 14 *p. 6* FZ **g**
176 rm – €180/875 €180/875, €27 – 12 suites
Rest *Le Padouk* – *✆ 04 92 14 76 00 (Closed 10 January-2 February, Sunday and Monday except July-August)* Menu €35, €49/75 – Carte €69/85
Rest *Pingala Bar* – *✆ 04 92 14 76 01 (lunch only)* Carte €45/56
◆ This famous building with a listed Art Deco façade now houses a new hotel offering soberly modern, spacious and luxurious rooms. The Padouk offers Asian and southern-inspired food. The Pingala Bar offers simple Niçoise dishes in a chic setting.

Radisson SAS rm,
223 promenade des Anglais – ✆ 04 97 17 71 77
– www.nice.radissonsas.com
– info.nice@radissonsas.com – Fax 04 93 71 21 71 *p. 4* AU **n**
331 rm – €140/235 €140/235, €22 – 13 suites
Rest – Menu (€31), €39 (lunch) – Carte €51/61
◆ Hotel in the spirit of the times, with modern architecture, large stylish bedrooms (Urban, Chilli and Ocean themes), designer bar, fitness suite and rooftop terrace pool. Comfortable dining room decorated in blue and lemon tones; local cuisine.

Méridien rest,
1 promenade des Anglais – ✆ 04 97 03 44 44
– www.lemeridien.com/nice – mail.nice@lemeridien.com
– Fax 04 97 03 44 45 *p. 6* FZ **d**
316 rm – €155/525 €155/525, €23 – 2 suites
Rest *Le Colonial Café* – *✆ 04 97 03 40 36* – Carte €16/28
Rest *La Terrasse du Colonial* – *✆ 04 97 03 40 37* – Carte €56/66
◆ On offer at this luxury hotel: the heated rooftop pool overlooking the Baie des Anges, attractive rooms progressively redecorated, beauty salon and high-tech meeting rooms. Minimalist furnishings, warm colours and soft lighting at the Colonial Café. A superb sea view at the Terrasse.

Élysée Palace rm,
59 promenade des Anglais – ✆ 04 93 97 90 90 – www.elyseepalace.com
– info@elyseepalace.com – Fax 04 93 44 50 40 *p. 6* EZ **d**
143 rm – €110/285 €110/285, €21 – 2 suites
Rest *Le Caprice* – Menu (€23), €45 – Carte €38/61
◆ The highlight of this futuristic architecture is a giant bronze Venus. An Art Deco-style decor, extremely comfortable amenities, excellent soundproofing and a rooftop pool. Appetising regional menu served on the terrace in summer.

Boscolo Hôtel Plaza
12 av. de Verdun – ✆ 04 93 16 75 75 – www.boscolohotels.com
– reservation@nice.boscolo.com – Fax 04 93 88 61 11 *p. 7* GZ **u**
174 rm – €270/549 €270/549, €20 – 8 suites
Rest – *(closed Sunday and Monday from November to March)*
Menu (€17 bi), €26/36 – Carte €51/71
◆ An imposing hotel, adjacent to the Albert I garden. Spacious bedrooms. Roof terrace offering a fine view of the Mediterranean. Fully equipped for seminars. A dining room in warm colours and large panoramic terrace with town views.

INDEX OF STREET NAMES IN NICE

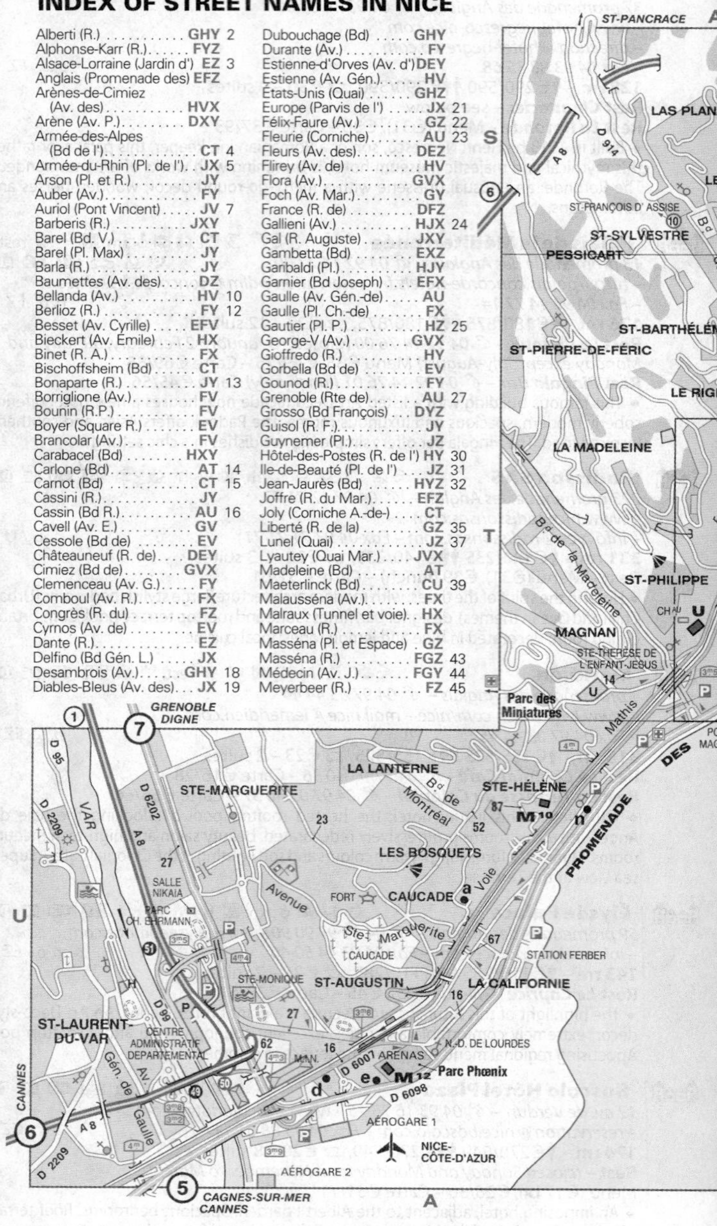

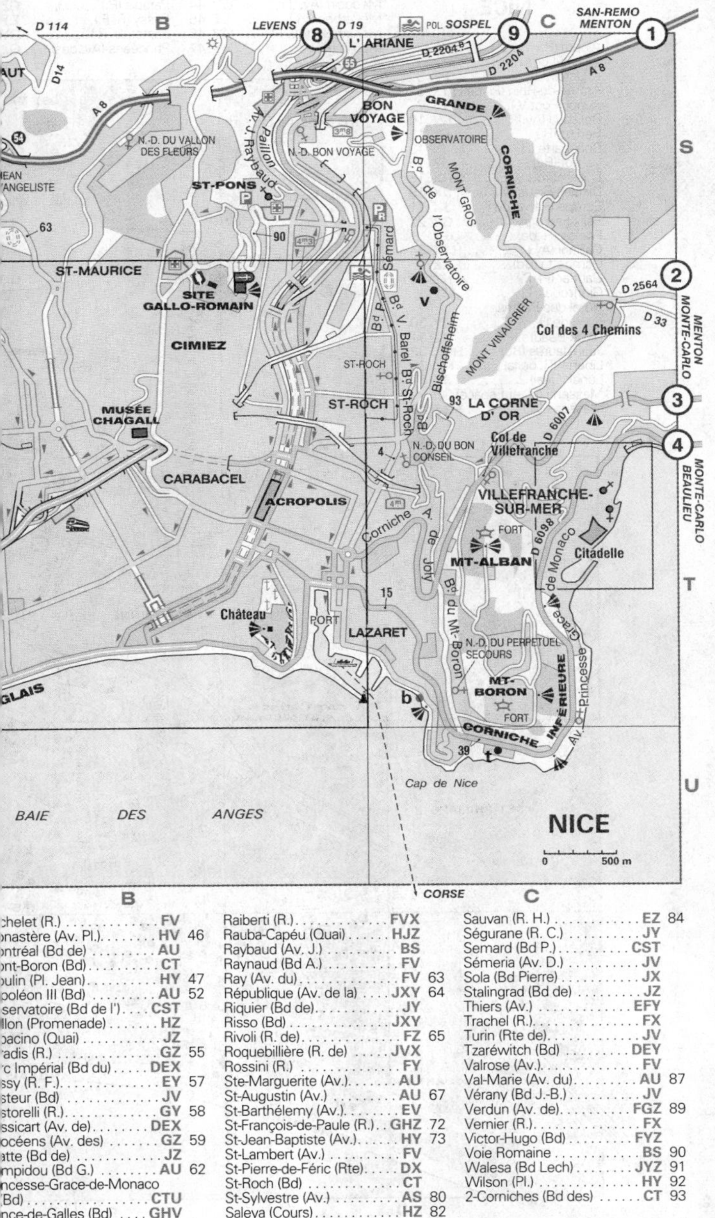

D 114
B
LEVENS
8
D 19
POL. SOSPEL
9
C
SAN-REMO
MENTON
1
L' ARIANE
D 2204 B
D 2204
A 8
D14
A 8
54
N.-D. DU VALLON DES FLEURS
BON VOYAGE
GRANDE
N.-D. BON VOYAGE
OBSERVATOIRE
CORNICHE
MONT GROS
S
Av. J. Raybaud
Paillon
Bd de l'Observatoire
ST-PONS
63
90
ST-MAURICE
SITE GALLO-ROMAIN
Bd P. Sémard
V
2
D 2564
D 33
MENTON
MONTE-CARLO
MONT VINAIGRIER
Col des 4 Chemins
CIMIEZ
Bd V. Barel
ST-ROCH
Bischoffsheim
Bd St-Roch
ST-ROCH
93
LA CORNE D' OR
3
MUSÉE CHAGALL
D 6007
Col de Villefranche
4
N.-D. DU BON CONSEIL
MONTE-CARLO
BEAULIEU
CARABACEL
VILLEFRANCHE-SUR-MER
ACROPOLIS
Corniche A. de Joly
FORT
D 6098
Bd de Monaco
Citadelle
MT-ALBAN
T
15
Château
PORT
LAZARET
Bd du Mt-Boron
N.-D. DU PERPETUEL SECOURS
Grace
Princesse
Av.
INFÉRIEURE
GLAIS
b
MT-BORON
FORT
CORNICHE
39
t
Cap de Nice
U
BAIE DES ANGES
NICE
0
500 m
CORSE
B
C

NICE

Alberti (R.) . . . . GHY 2
Alsace-Lorraine
(Jardin d') . . . . EZ 3
Armée-du-Rhin (Pl. de l') JX 5
Auriol (Pont V.). . . . . . . JV 7
Bellanda (Av.) . . . . HV 10
Berlioz (R.) . . . . FY 12
Bonaparte (R.) . . . . JY 13
Carnot (Bd) . . . . JZ 15
Desambrois (Av.). . . . GHX 18
Diables-Bleus (Av. des). JX 19
Europe (Parvis de l') . . . JX 21
Félix-Faure (Av.). . . . . . GZ 22
France (R. de) . . . . DFZ
Gallieni (Av.) . . . . HJX 24
Gambetta (Bd) . . . . . . EXZ
Gautier (Pl. P.) . . . . HZ 25
Gioffredo (R.) . . . . HY
Hôtel-des-Postes
(R. de l') . . . . HY 30
Ile-de-Beauté (Pl.) . . . . . JZ 31
Jean-Jaurès (Bd) . . . . HYZ 32
Liberté (R. de la) . . . . . . GZ 35
Lunel (Quai) . . . . JZ 37
Masséna (Pl. et Espace) GZ
Masséna (R.) . . . . FGZ 43
Médecin (Av. J.) . . . . . FGY 44
Meyerbeer (R.) . . . . FZ 45
Monastère (Av. Pl.). . . . HV 46
Moulin (Pl. J.) . . . . HY 47
Paradis (R.) . . . . GZ
Passy (R. F.). . . . . EY
Pastorelli (R.). . . . . GY
Phocéens (Av. des). . . . GZ

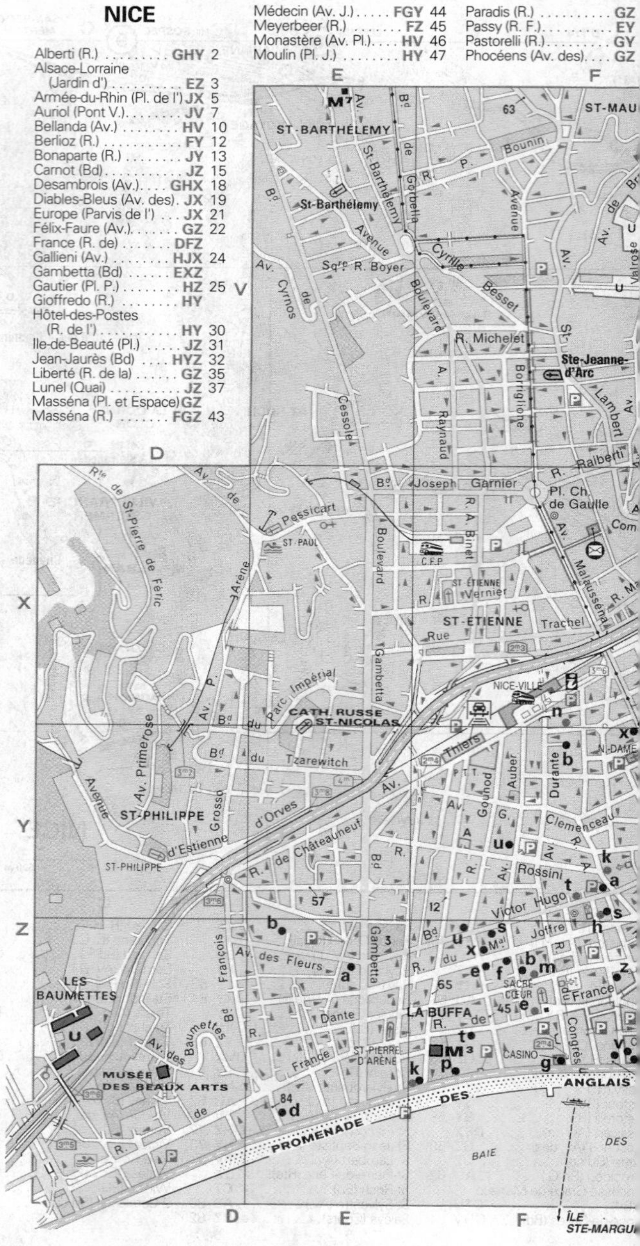

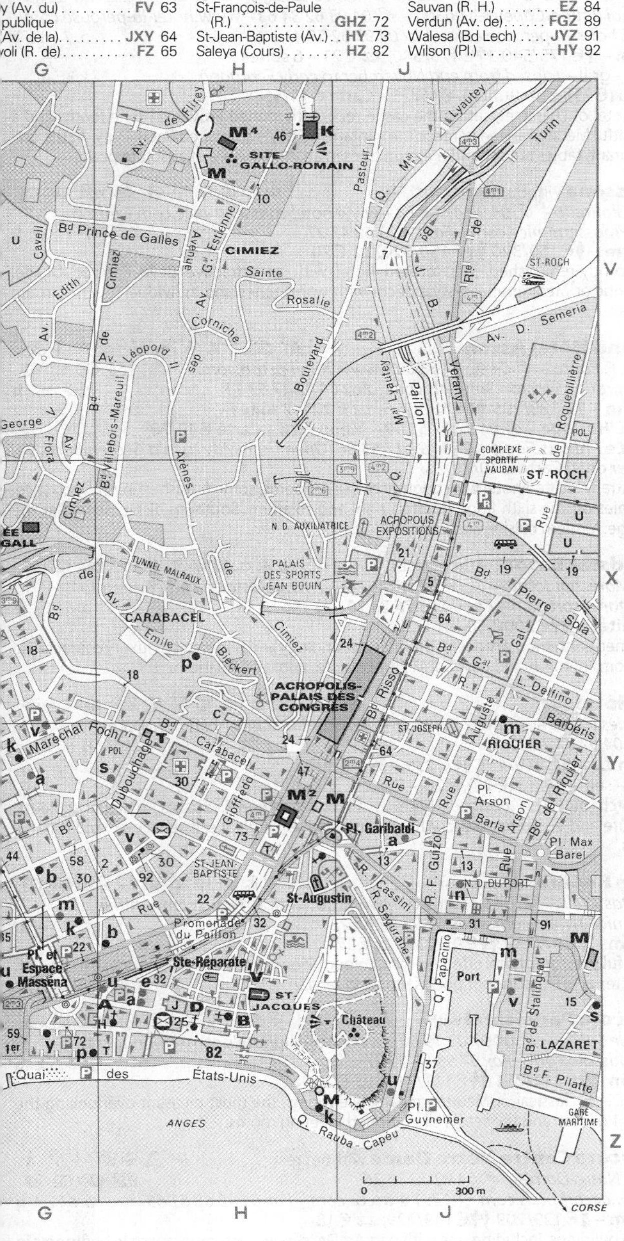

SITE GALLO-ROMAIN
CIMIEZ
Bd Prince de Galles
ST-ROCH
COMPLEXE SPORTIF VAUBAN
ACROPOLIS EXPOSITIONS
N. D. AUXILIATRICE
PALAIS DES SPORTS JEAN BOUIN
TUNNEL MALRAUX
CARABACEL
ACROPOLIS-PALAIS DES CONGRÈS
ST-JOSEPH
RIQUIER
Pl. Garibaldi
ST-JEAN-BAPTISTE
St-Augustin
Promenade du Paillon
Ste-Réparate
Pl. et Espace Masséna
ST-JACQUES
Château
N. D. DU PORT
Port
LAZARET
GARE MARITIME
Quai des États-Unis
ANGES
Q. Rauba-Capeu
Pl. Guynemer
300 m
CORSE

La Pérouse
11 quai Rauba-Capéu ✉ 06300 – ✆ 04 93 62 34 63 – www.hotel-la-perouse.com – lp@hotel-la-perouse.com – Fax 04 93 62 59 41 p. 7 HZ **k**
54 rm – €175/540 €175/540, ☕ €21 – 6 suites
Rest – grill – *(closed from end November to early February)*
Menu (€25), €40 (lunch), €45/75 – Carte €45/55
◆ A hotel of character, set on the castle rock, with refined Provençal-style rooms and a delightful Mediterranean garden. The vantage point view inspired Raoul Dufy. At the grill restaurant, tables are set under lemon trees in an atmosphere of absolute peace.

Masséna without rest
58 r. Gioffredo – ✆ 04 92 47 88 88 – www.hotel-massena-nice.com – info@hotel-massena-nice.com – Fax 04 93 62 43 27 p. 7 GZ **k**
110 rm – €150/320 €150/320, ☕ €20
◆ Recently-refurbished, well-located hotel with an attractive Belle Époque façade. Romantic or Mediterranean-style décor with warm tones and individual touches in the rooms.

Grand Hôtel Aston
12 av. F. Faure – ✆ 04 92 17 53 00 – www.hotel-aston.com – reservation@aston.3ahotels.com – Fax 04 92 17 53 11 p. 7 HZ **b**
147 rm – €180/295 €180/295, ☕ €22 – 2 suites
Rest *L'Horloge* – *✆ 04 92 17 53 09* – Menu €26 – Carte €40/70
Rest *Le Phileas Fogg* – *✆ 04 92 17 53 86 (Open from May to mid-September) (dinner only)* Carte €40/70
◆ Centrally located hotel with brightly coloured rooms, some furnished in Art Deco style. Balconies on the sixth floor. Rooftop pool and solarium. Southern dishes served at the Horloge. Modern cuisine and view of the sea.

Goldstar Resort without rest
45 r. Maréchal Joffre – ✆ 04 93 16 92 77 – www.goldstar-resort.com – info@goldstar-resort.com – Fax 04 93 76 23 30 p. 6 FZ **e**
56 suites – €200/550, ☕ €20
◆ Refined contemporary decor, the latest technology and understated luxury characterise the rooms of this brand new hotel. Fitness suite, pool and solarium.

Hi Hôtel
3 av. des Fleurs – ✆ 04 97 07 26 26 – www.hi-hotel.net – hi@hi-hotel.net – Fax 04 97 07 26 27 p. 6 EZ **a**
37 rm ☕ – €219/419 €239/439 – 1 suite
Rest – self – Menu (€22), €26 – Carte €23/32
◆ Watch out! This designer hotel is all but traditional. Spaces, material, colours, furniture and equipment; everything is innovative. Original self-service of cold organic dishes.

Nice Riviera without rest
45 r. Pastorelli – ✆ 04 93 92 69 60 – www.hotel-nice-riviera.com – info@hotel-nice-riviera.com – Fax 04 93 92 69 22 p. 7 GY **b**
122 rm – €97/239 €97/239, ☕ €17
◆ This fully restored hotel offers elegant, colourful rooms (red and yellow tones), some with sunny terrace. Small indoor pool, sauna and Jacuzzi.

Boscolo Park Hôtel without rest
6 av. de Suède – ✆ 04 97 03 19 00 – www.boscolohotels.com – manager@park.boscolo.com – Fax 04 93 82 29 27 p. 6 FZ **a**
104 rm – €111/711 €111/711, ☕ €20
◆ Art Deco, classical or Mediterranean-style rooms, the most pleasant overlooking the Albert 1 garden and the sea. Well-equipped meeting rooms.

Mercure Centre Notre Dame without rest
28 av. Notre-Dame – ✆ 04 93 13 36 36 – www.accorhotels.com – h1291@accor.com – Fax 04 93 62 61 69 p. 6 FXY **q**
200 rm – €129/209 €149/229, ☕ €18
◆ Two buildings, including one with part Art Deco, part contemporary style bedrooms in a pretty garden. Beauty parlour and pool on the roof terrace.

Splendid rest, VISA MC AE
50 bd V. Hugo – 04 93 16 41 00 – www.splendid-nice.com – info@splendid-nice.com – Fax 04 93 16 42 70 p. 6 FZ **u**
128 rm – €175/265 €195/265, €16 – 15 suites
Rest – Menu €25/80 – Carte €35/60
◆ Fine views over Nice from the small rooftop pool and solarium. Refurbished rooms vary in size and many have a balcony. Spa. Restaurant and panoramic terrace on the roof.

Le Grimaldi without rest VISA MC AE
15 r. Grimaldi – 04 93 16 00 24 – www.le-grimaldi.com – zedde@le-grimaldi.com – Fax 04 93 87 00 24 p. 6 FY **s**
46 rm – €85/210 €95/240, €15
◆ Provençal furniture, wrought iron and beautiful Pierre Frey fabrics add a personal touch to the rooms with small terraces on the top floor. Cosy hall-bar-lounge.

Villa Victoria without rest P VISA MC AE
33 bd V. Hugo – 04 93 88 39 60 – www.villa-victoria.com – contact@villa-victoria.com – Fax 04 93 88 07 98 – Closed 14-28 December p. 6 FZ **s**
38 rm – €75/190 €90/210, €15
◆ A beautiful old building with a southern feel. Choose a room with a balcony overlooking the attractive Mediterranean garden. Those on the road side are well soundproofed.

Windsor rest, VISA MC AE
11 r. Dalpozzo – 04 93 88 59 35 – www.hotelwindsornice.com – contact@hotelwindsornice.com – Fax 04 93 88 94 57 p. 6 FZ **f**
57 rm – €80/185 €90/185, €12 – ½ P €80/128
Rest – *(closed Sunday) (dinner only)* Menu €30 – Carte €30/40
◆ This hotel has a particular attraction: 27 'artists' rooms in a tribute to contemporary art. The most recent is by O. Nottellet. Exotic garden and well-being centre (steam bath, massages, sauna). Snacks served in the bar and, in summer, amid the palm trees and bougainvilleas.

Mercure Promenade des Anglais without rest
2 r. Halévy – 04 93 82 30 88 – www.mercure.com – H0360-RE@accor.com – Fax 04 93 82 18 20 VISA MC AE p. 6 FZ **q**
122 rm – €89/249 €99/259, €16
◆ Hotel set in the Ruhl casino building. Comfortable, refurbished rooms decorated in gaming-inspired style. Breakfast room with view over the Promenade des Anglais.

Petit Palais without rest P VISA MC AE
17 av. E. Bieckert – 04 93 62 19 11 – www.petitpalaisnice.fr – reservation@petitpalaisnice.com – Fax 04 93 62 53 60 p. 7 HX **p**
25 rm – €80/90 €90/170, €15
◆ Sacha Guitry lived in this 1900s villa, perched on the Cimiez Hill. Most of the bedrooms have a view looking down on the rooftops of the old quarter of Nice and the Baie des Anges.

Brice rm, VISA MC AE
44 r. Mar. Joffre – 04 93 88 14 44 – www.nice-hotel-brice.com – info@nice-hotel-brice.com – Fax 04 93 87 38 54 p. 6 FZ **x**
58 rm – €90/120 €107/147, €13
Rest – *(open June to September and closed Monday) (dinner only)*
Menu €28 – Carte €29/45
◆ This hotel's functional and well-kept rooms are protected from traffic noise by a flower-decked garden-terrace. Asian-influenced decor in the bar and Internet connection. Unpretentious family cooking served outside in fine weather.

Alba without rest VISA MC AE
41 av. Jean Médecin – 04 93 88 02 88 – www.hotellalba.com – reservation@hotellalba.com – Fax 04 93 88 55 03 p. 6 FXY **x**
35 rm – €98/123 €113/185, €13
◆ This town-centre hotel has been successfully renovated with its very well-equipped and soundproofed rooms now sporting trendy decor (grey and brown tones).

Aria without rest
15 av. Auber – ✆ 04 93 88 30 69 – www.aria-nice.com – reservation@aria-nice.com – Fax 04 93 88 11 35 p. 6 FY **u**
26 rm – €84/94 €94/124, ☕ €13 – 4 suites
◆ In the heart of the musicians' district, good-sized rooms, well-soundproofed and with classic or Provençal-style furnishings; choose one overlooking the little square.

De Flore without rest
2 r. Maccarani – ✆ 04 92 14 40 20 – www.hoteldeflore-nice.fr – info@hoteldeflore-nice.fr – Fax 04 92 14 40 21 p. 6 FZ **z**
64 rm – €82/150 €94/165, ☕ €13 – 3 suites
◆ Wrought-iron furniture, wicker chairs and colours of the south in the cheery, functional rooms. A patio for breakfast in a typical Mediterranean setting.

Anis Hôtel
50 av. Lanterne ✉ 06200 – ✆ 04 93 18 29 00 – www.hotel-anis.com – info@hotel-anis.com – Fax 04 93 83 31 16 p. 4 AU **a**
42 rm – €106/150 €118/150, ☕ €10
Rest – *(closed Sunday dinner and Monday)*
Menu (€12), €17 (weekdays)/27 – Carte €10/45
◆ Hidden in a quiet residential area, this establishment has plenty going for it: renovated, well-soundproofed rooms, a pleasant pool and reasonable prices. Enjoy regional cuisine on the terrace or in a dining room in southern colours.

Durante without rest
16 av. Durante – ✆ 04 93 88 84 40 – www.hotel-durante.com – info@hotel-durante.com – Fax 04 93 87 77 76 – Closed January p. 6 FY **b**
28 rm – €70/130 €70/150, ☕ €10
◆ The calm of this cul-de-sac lets guests sleep with windows open, in rooms that face a sweet-smelling orange-tree garden. Non-smoking throughout.

Nautica without rest
38 r. Barbéris – ✆ 04 92 00 21 21 – www.hotelnautica.com – reservation@hotelnautica.com – Fax 04 92 00 21 22 p. 7 JXY **m**
87 rm – €90/134 €90/134, ☕ €11
◆ This fully renovated hotel is located near the harbour and has chosen a nautical decor. Practical, well-soundproofed rooms, impeccably kept.

Les Cigales without rest
16 r. Dalpozzo – ✆ 04 97 03 10 70 – www.hotel-lescigales.com – infos@hotel-lescigales.com – Fax 04 97 03 10 71 p. 6 FZ **b**
19 rm – €75/120 €80/135, ☕ €12
◆ This former mansion, with a pretty, finely worked façade has a pleasant little courtyard terrace. Functional and colourful rooms, with sloping ceilings on the top floor.

Mercure Marché aux Fleurs without rest
91 quai des Etats-Unis – ✆ 04 93 85 74 19 – www.mercure.com – H0962@accor.com – Fax 04 93 13 90 94 p. 6 GZ **p**
49 rm – €97/273 €107/283, ☕ €14
◆ Polished furniture and beige and chocolate tones in the warm, well-equipped rooms, six of which have sea views. Friendly, efficient welcome.

Armenonville without rest
20 av. Fleurs – ✆ 04 93 96 86 00 – www.hotel-armenonville.com – nice@hotel-armenonville.com – Fax 04 93 44 66 53 p. 6 EZ **b**
12 rm – €39/99 €49/99, ☕ €11
◆ This 1900s villa and its pretty garden stand in a cul-de-sac in the old Russian émigrés district. Furnishings from the Negresco Hotel personalise the rooms which are being gradually updated.

De la Fontaine without rest
49 r. France – ✆ 04 93 88 30 38 – www.hotel-fontaine.com – hotel-fontaine@webstore.fr – Fax 04 93 88 98 11 p. 6 FZ **t**
29 rm – €77/105 €90/145, ☕ €10
◆ Hotel standing in a busy shopping street. For peace and quiet, choose a room on the small patio with fountain, where breakfast is served in season.

Star Hôtel without rest
14 r. Biscarra – 04 93 85 19 03 – www.hotel-star.com – info@hotel-star.com – Fax 04 93 13 04 23 – Closed 12 November-25 December p. 7 GY **k**
24 rm – €45/59 €55/79, €6
◆ Small, plain but clean rooms, some with balcony. Quite a simple establishment, but benefiting from a central location and reasonable prices.

Villa la Lézardière
87 bd de l'Observatoire 06300 – 04 93 56 22 86 – www.villa-nice.com – rpaauw@free.fr – Fax 04 93 56 22 86 p. 5 CT **v**
5 rm – €90/130 €100/170 **Table d'hôte** – Menu €40 bi
◆ This Provençal-style villa on the Grande Corniche has magnificent views over the town and Alps. Personalised rooms, pool and large enclosed garden. Traditional or Thai cuisine.

Chantecler – Hôtel Negresco
37 promenade des Anglais – 04 93 16 64 00 – www.hotel-negresco-nice.com – chantecler@hotel-negresco.com – Fax 04 93 88 35 68 – Closed 3 January-3 February, Monday and Tuesday except public holidays p. 6 FZ **k**
Rest – Menu €50 (lunch), €95/135 – Carte €95/145
Spec. Langoustines rôties au piment d'Espelette, croustillant de tête de veau. Dos de loup sauvage en croûte d'herbes, émulsion de coquillages. Carré d'agneau rôti en spirale d'herbes, fleur de courgette en tempura. **Wines** Bellet, Vin de Pays des Alpes-Maritimes.
◆ A French Regency-style setting enhanced by wood panelling, Aubusson tapestries, old masters and damask or lampas silk curtains. Up-to-date cuisine with personal touches.

L'Ane Rouge
7 quai Deux-Emmanuel 06300 – 04 93 89 49 63 – www.anerougenice.com – anerouge@free.fr – Fax 04 93 26 51 42 – Closed February school holidays, Thursday lunch and Wednesday p. 7 JZ **m**
Rest – Menu (€26), €36 (weekdays)/78 – Carte €64/87
◆ This restaurant, facing the marina and château, offers tasty surf'n'turf dishes in a warm and recently redecorated dining room.

Les Viviers
22 r. A. Karr – 04 93 16 00 48 – www.les-viviers-nice.com – viviers.bretons@wanadoo.fr – Fax 04 93 16 04 06 – Closed Saturday lunch and Sunday p. 6 FY **k**
Rest – Menu €35 (lunch), €52/85 – Carte €39/101
◆ An elegant dining room with light wood panelling or a 1900s-style bistro: two decors but the same cuisine, based on fish, seafood and dishes of the day.

L'Univers-Christian Plumail
54 bd J. Jaurès 06300 – 04 93 62 32 22 – www.christian-plumail.com – plumailunivers@aol.com – Fax 04 93 62 55 69 – Closed Saturday lunch, Monday lunch and Sunday p. 7 HZ **u**
Rest – *(pre-book)* Menu (€22), €44/70 – Carte €60/86
Spec. Socca, mousse de panisse et pois chiches, crustacé rôti au jambon serrano. Loup de ligne rôti à l'orange. Palet au chocolat et noix caramélisées. **Wines** Bellet, Côtes de Provence.
◆ Canvasses and modern sculptures embellish this much frequented restaurant in Nice; here one can enjoy personalised local cuisine but booking is often advisable.

Jouni "Atelier du Goût" (Jouni Tormanen)
60 bd. F.Pilatte, (1st floor) – 04 97 08 14 80 – www.jouni.fr – contact@jouni.fr – Fax 04 92 04 23 02 – Closed 9 November-2 December, weekday lunch, Sunday and Monday p. 5 CT **b**
Rest – Menu €65 (lunch), €100/150 – Carte €88/102
Rest ***Bistrot de la Réserve*** – Menu (€30), €65/105 bi – Carte €65/80
Spec. Moelleux de homard et courgettes violon (summer). Pêche du jour (Jan. to Nov.). Tarte aux chocolats fondants (Jan. to Nov.).
◆ From here you have a ringside seat to admire the port and the sea. On the site of the famous 'Réserve', it has a pretty Art Deco setting, roof terrace and delicious, refined, Mediterranean inspired cuisine. Bistro on the ground floor in a contemporary, lounge style setting.

XX **Keisuke Matsushima**
22 ter r. de France – ✆ 04 93 82 26 06 – www.keisukematsushima.com – info@keisukematsushima.com – Fax 04 92 00 08 49 – Closed Saturday lunch, Monday lunch and Sunday p. 6 FZ **e**
Rest – Menu € 35 (lunch), € 65/130 – Carte € 80/130
Spec. Saint-Jacques et navets en carpaccio, vinaigrette aigre-douce (Nov. to March). Selle d'agneau de Sisteron "Nissa la Bella" (Jan. to April). Cannelloni d'ananas à la mousse de noix de coco, meringue citron vert. **Wines** Bellet, Bandol.
◆ Formerly Kei's Passion, the restaurant may have grown in size and has a different decor (fashionable, minimalist) but the cuisine is just as creative and the service faultless. Table d'hôte by reservation.

XX **Aphrodite**
10 bd Dubouchage – ✆ 04 93 85 63 53 – www.restaurant-aphrodite.com – reception@restaurant-aphrodite.com – Fax 04 93 80 10 41 – Closed 1st-24 January, Sunday and Monday p.7 HY **s**
Rest – Menu € 25 (lunch), € 35/95 – Carte € 55/75
◆ Clean designer lines, wood, red leather and alcove tables: chic, cosy and contemporary decor match the chef's individual cooking style.

XX **Les Épicuriens**
6 pl. Wilson – ✆ 04 93 80 85 00 – Fax 04 93 85 65 00 – Closed August, Saturday lunch and Sunday p. 7 HY **v**
Rest – Carte € 30/52
◆ Regional menu and tasty blackboard specials attract a loyal clientele to this warm, panelled restaurant. Terrace on the square.

XX **L'Allegro**
6 pl. Guynemer ✉ 06300 – ✆ 04 93 56 62 06 – sarl.divin@orange.fr – Fax 04 93 56 38 28 – Closed 1st-6 January, lunch in August, Saturday lunch and Sunday p. 7 JZ **u**
Rest – Menu € 19 (weekday lunch), € 23/54 – Carte € 34/59
◆ Freshly prepared pasta and ravioli dishes from the open kitchen, served in an exuberant decor of fresco trompe-l'oeils showing "Commedia dell'arte" characters.

XX **Brasserie Flo**
4 r. S. Guitry – ✆ 04 93 13 38 38 – www.flonice.com – dbarrau@groupeflo.fr – Fax 04 93 13 38 39 p. 7 GYZ**m**
Rest – Menu (€ 19), € 24/34 bi – Carte € 29/63
◆ A parterre of tables and troop of waiters at the ready: the bell rings and the deep-red curtain goes up on the kitchens of this brasserie housed in a 1930 theatre.

XX **Stéphane Viano**
26 bd. Victor Hugo – ✆ 04 93 82 48 63 – vianostephane@wanadoo.fr – Closed Sunday p. 6 FY **t**
Rest – Menu (€ 22) – Carte € 32/45
◆ Easily recognisable by its long veranda furnished with Provençal-blue chairs, this fashionable restaurant also has a dining room with a vaulted ceiling and black and white decor. Typical Nice dishes given a modern twist.

XX **Les Pêcheurs**
18 quai des Docks – ✆ 04 93 89 59 61 – www.lespecheurs.com – lespecheurs@aliceadsl.fr – Closed January, Monday and Tuesday from October to May, Thursday lunch and Wednesday from June to September p. 7 JZ **v**
Rest – Menu € 28/38 – Carte € 41/77
◆ Enjoy local and more exotic fish and seafood dishes on the summer terrace with views of the port, or in the dining room refurbished by the new owners.

XX **L'Aromate**
20 av. Mar. Foch – ✆ 04 93 62 98 24 – www.laromate.fr – mickaelgracieux@hotmail.com – Fax 04 93 62 98 24 – Closed January, Sunday and Monday
Rest – *(dinner only)* Menu € 50/70 – Carte € 60/70 p. 7 GY **v**
Rest *Le Grain de Riz de l'Aromate* – *(lunch only)* Menu (€ 25), € 35 – Carte € 38/48
◆ Updated traditional setting – the small room at the entrance has a view of kitchen – offering inventive evening meals. Simpler market cuisine served at lunch (two set-price menus and an à la carte menu), based around risotto, meat and fish.

Luc Salsedo
14 r. Maccarani – ✆ 04 93 82 24 12 – www.restaurant-salsedo.com – contact@restaurant-salsedo.com – Fax 04 93 82 93 68 – Closed 1st-25 January, lunch in July-August, Thursday lunch, Saturday lunch and Wednesday p. 6 FY **h**
Rest – Menu (€ 26), € 44/65
◆ Mediterranean shades, a colourful abstract mural and Asian furniture give this small dining room particular appeal. Modern cuisine with Provençal touches.

Bông-Laï
14 r. Alsace-Lorraine – ✆ 04 93 88 75 36 p. 6 FX **n**
Rest – Menu € 20/39 – Carte € 30/70
◆ A long dining room, unsurprisingly Oriental decorations yet an intimate atmosphere. Vietnamese family cooking, accompanied by a few Chinese dishes.

Kamogawa
18 r. de la Buffa – ✆ 04 93 88 75 88 – Closed Sunday lunch and Monday
Rest – Menu € 33, € 36/65 – Carte € 38/60 p. 7 GYZ **m**
◆ This typical Japanese restaurant (all the staff are from Japan) is highly successful thanks to its simple, traditional recipes served in a simple setting.

Mireille
19 bd Raimbaldi – ✆ 04 93 85 27 23 – Closed 4-12 May, 3-19 August, 4-10 January, Monday and Tuesday p. 7 GX **d**
Rest – Carte approx. € 31
◆ Restaurant with Spanish decor and a Provençal name, in the heart of the Italian "Nissa"! The paella (only main dish available) is presented on copper crockery.

Lou Pistou
4 r. Raoul Bosio ✉ 06300 – ✆ 04 93 62 21 82 – nicisa@gmail.com – Closed 14-22 March, 1st-15 November, Saturday and Sunday p. 7 HZ **a**
Rest – taverne – Carte € 29/38
◆ Located next to the Palace of Justice, this lawyers' "canteen" serves simple regional dishes, in a rather small dining room. Friendly reception.

La Casbah
3 r. Dr Balestre – ✆ 04 93 85 58 81 – Closed July, August, Sunday dinner and Monday p. 7 GY **a**
Rest – Carte € 22/38
◆ Small family restaurant offering a choice of homemade mainly couscous dishes and lamb specialities. North African pastries for dessert.

La Merenda
4 r. Raoul Bosio – Closed 1st-8 March, 25 July-10 August, Saturday and Sunday
Rest – *(limited number of covers)* Carte € 31/38 p. 7 HZ **a**
◆ Uncomfortable stools, no telephone and credit cards are not accepted. Despite all of this, crowds flock to La Merenda every day to sample its authentic Niçois cuisine!

in l'Aire St-Michel North: 9 km by Boulevard de Cimiez – ✉ 06100 Nice

Au Rendez-vous des Amis
176 av. Rimiez ✉ 06100 – ✆ 04 93 84 49 66 – www.rdvdesamis.fr – contact@rdvdesamis.fr – Fax 04 93 52 62 09 – Closed 26 October-26 November, 8-24 February, Tuesday except July-August and Wednesday
Rest – Menu (€ 19), € 24 – Carte € 29/37
◆ The warm reception and ambiance of this restaurant confirm the promise in its name! Tasty, typically local dishes with menus purposely limited. Delightful shaded terrace.

to Nice-Côte-d'Azur Airport 7 km – ✉ 06200 Nice

Park Inn Nice rm,
179 bd René Cassin – ✆ 04 93 18 34 00 – www.nice-rezidorparkinn.com – reservations.nice@rezidorparkinn.com – Fax 04 93 71 40 63 p. 4 AU **d**
151 rm – †€ 115/160 ††€ 125/455, ☕ € 18
Rest – Menu (€ 19 bi), € 32 bi (weekdays)/50 bi – Carte € 36/46
◆ This hotel near the airport has pleasant, contemporary rooms, repainted in various colours depending on the floor (red, green, blue or yellow). Modern restaurant (traditional menu) and poolside snack bar in summer.

Novotel Arenas rm, VISA AE

455 promenade des Anglais – ✆ 04 93 21 22 50 – www.novotel.com – h0478@accor.com – Fax 04 93 21 63 50 *p. 4* AU **e**

131 rm – †€ 90/250 ††€ 90/250, ☕ € 15 **Rest** – Carte € 24/54

◆ Rooms progressively updated in a trendy style: modern furniture in grey and chocolate tones. Good soundproofing and numerous conference rooms. An unusually intimate dining room serving traditional cuisine.

in St-Isidore by ⑦: 13 km – ✉ **06200**

Servotel VISA AE

30 av. A. Verola – ✆ 04 93 29 99 00 – www.servotel-nice.fr – info@servotel-nice.fr – Fax 04 93 29 99 01

84 rm – †€ 71/148 ††€ 81/178, ☕ € 13 – 2 suites – ½ P € 65/84

Rest – *(Closed Saturday and Sunday)* Menu € 23/33 – Carte € 47/69

◆ New hotel near a shopping centre. Well-equipped functional rooms, ideal for business travellers. Lounge with fireplace and seminar facilities. A modern dining room with southern shades, serving simple traditional cuisine.

The sun's out – let's eat alfresco!
Look for a terrace:

NIEDERBRONN-LES-BAINS – 67 Bas-Rhin – 315 J3 – pop. 4 329 – alt. 190 m – Spa : early April-late Nov. – Casino – ✉ 67110 Alsace-Lorraine 1 **B1**

Paris 460 – Haguenau 23 – Sarreguemines 55 – Saverne 40 – Strasbourg 52

Office de tourisme, 6, place de l'Hôtel de Ville ✆ 03 88 80 89 70, Fax 03 88 80 37 01

Mercure without rest VISA AE

av. Foch – ✆ 03 88 80 84 48 – www.mercure.com – h5548@accor.com – Fax 03 88 80 84 40

59 rm – †€ 59/89 ††€ 59/98, ☕ € 12 – 5 suites

◆ This establishment houses large, refined, renovated rooms and suites. Good soundproofing. Modern-style bar-lounge. Pleasant peaceful garden planted with trees.

Le Bristol A/C rest, rm, VISA AE

4 pl. de l'Hôtel-de-Ville – ✆ 03 88 09 61 44 – www.lebristol.com – hotel.lebristol@wanadoo.fr – Fax 03 88 09 01 20

29 rm – †€ 50/55 ††€ 60/70, ☕ € 8,50 – ½ P € 60/65

Rest – Menu (€ 10), € 15/42 – Carte € 27/40

◆ This family hotel is in the centre of the spa resort: most of the rooms have been refurbished (wood furniture and bright colours) and well soundproofed. Traditional cooking served in a plush dining room overflowing onto the veranda on busy days.

Du Parc rm, VISA AE

r. de la République – ✆ 03 88 09 01 42 – www.parchotel.net – parchotel1@orange.fr – Fax 03 88 09 05 80

40 rm – †€ 52/70 ††€ 65/80, ☕ € 9 – ½ P € 59/68

Rest – Menu (€ 12), € 20/55 – Carte € 26/45

◆ This hotel under new management is comprised of two buildings in a busy street. Regularly refurbished, very well-kept and admirably appointed rooms. Traditional cuisine served in an Alsace-style dining area or under the trees in fine weather.

L'Atelier du Sommelier VISA AE

35 r. des Acacias, 2 km on towards the sports complex – ✆ 03 88 09 06 25 – www.atelierdusommelier.com – stephane.knecht@wanadoo.fr – Closed 10-23 August, 15 February-1st March, Saturday lunch, Monday and Tuesday

Rest – Menu € 28/50 – Carte € 34/53

◆ This bright restaurant harbours a rustic charm honouring Bacchus: pale wood furniture, stained glass windows, wine crates and vintages on display (for sale). Refined cuisine and a rich wine list.

NIEDERSCHAEFFOLSHEIM – 67 Bas-Rhin – 315 K4 – pop. 1 248 – alt. 185 m – ✉ 67500 1 B1

Paris 473 – Haguenau 7 – Saverne 35 – Strasbourg 28

Au Bœuf Rouge with rm rest, VISA MC AE
39 r. du Gén. de Gaulle – ☎ 03 88 73 81 00 – www.boeufrouge.com – auboeufrouge.hotel@wanadoo.fr – Fax 03 88 73 89 71 – Closed 14 July-5 August and 8-23 February
13 rm – †€ 70 ††€ 72/74, ☐ € 10 – ½ P € 68/74
Rest – *(closed Sunday dinner, Tuesday lunch and Monday)*
Menu € 30 (weekdays)/72 – Carte € 64/76
◆ The same family has been welcoming guests to this renowned Alsatian restaurant since 1880. Elegant, classic-style dining room with wooden panelling. Cuisine bourgeoise with a modern twist.

NIEDERSTEINBACH – 67 Bas-Rhin – 315 K2 – pop. 139 – alt. 225 m – ✉ 67510 Alsace-Lorraine 1 B1

Paris 460 – Bitche 24 – Haguenau 33 – Lembach 8 – Strasbourg 66 – Wissembourg 23

Cheval Blanc rest, rest, VISA MC
11 r. Principale – ☎ 03 88 09 55 31 – www.hotel-cheval-blanc.fr – contact@hotel-cheval-blanc.fr – Fax 03 88 09 50 24 – Closed 17 June-2 July, 23 November-3 December and February
25 rm – †€ 50/66 ††€ 63/75, ☐ € 11 – 1 suite – ½ P € 58/64
Rest – *(closed Thursday)* Menu € 20 (weekdays), € 25/57 – Carte € 30/66
◆ Traditional and family-run inn with a luxurious interior: charming, perfectly-kept rooms and warm lounges. Plentiful breakfasts. In the restaurant, you can savour hearty, regional cooking in a rustic Alsatian setting in wooden "stubes".

in Wengelsbach Northwest: 5 km by D 190 – ✉ 67510

Au Wasigenstein VISA MC
32 r. Principale – ☎ 03 88 09 50 54 – www.wasigenstein-wengelsbach.com – wasigenstein@wanadoo.fr – Fax 03 88 09 50 54 – Closed from mid-January to end February, Wednesday and Thursday from November to February, Monday and Tuesday except public holidays
Rest – Menu € 12 (weekday lunch), € 21/30 – Carte € 17/35
◆ Small family business in a peaceful and charming village. One of the dining rooms, with a pleasant country-style decor, is adorned with an earthenware stove. Fine terrace.

NIEUIL – 16 Charente – 324 N4 – pop. 927 – alt. 150 m – ✉ 16270 39 C2

Paris 434 – Angoulême 42 – Confolens 24 – Limoges 66 – Nontron 58 – Ruffec 34

East 2 km on the D 739 and minor road - ✉ 16270 Nieuil

Château de Nieuil without rest VISA MC AE
– ☎ 05 45 71 36 38 – www.chateaunieuilhotel.com – chateaunieuilhotel@wanadoo.fr – Fax 05 45 71 46 45 – Open March-November
11 rm – †€ 117/185 ††€ 130/275, ☐ € 16 – 3 suites
◆ A Renaissance château, once a hunting lodge used by Francis I, in a vast wooded park. Handsome Empire, Art deco, classical, etc. rooms.

La Grange aux Oies VISA MC AE
in the château grounds – ☎ 05 45 71 81 24 – www.grange-aux-oies.com – info@grange-aux-oies.com – Fax 05 45 71 81 25 – Closed 30 March-10 April, 2-28 November and 5-16 January
Rest – Menu (€ 26 bi), € 48 bi – Carte € 40/55
◆ Pleasant dining room combining modern decor with stone features in the former stables of the Château de Nieuil. Up-to-date cuisine in keeping with the setting.

NIEUL – 87 Haute-Vienne – 325 E5 – pop. 1 545 – alt. 396 m – ✉ 87510 24 B2

Paris 391 – Limoges 16 – Bellac 27 – Guéret 86

Les Justices with rm

3 km south-east on Limoges road – ✆ 05 55 75 84 54 – Closed Sunday dinner, Monday and public holidays dinner

3 rm – †€ 46 ††€ 46, ☕ € 8

Rest – *(number of covers limited, pre-book)* Menu € 26/32 – Carte € 26/41

◆ With its collections of porcelain, brightly dressed costume dolls, engraved glass and exotic plants, the decor in this restaurant is homely, if a little twee. Traditional cuisine. Clean, retro-style guestrooms.

NIEULLE-SUR-SEUDRE – 17 Charente-Maritime – 324 D5 38 A2 – pop. 713 – alt. 3 m – ✉ 17600

Paris 503 – Poitiers 170 – La Rochelle 60 – Rochefort 30 – Saintes 32

Le Logis de Port Paradis

12 r. de Port Paradis – ✆ 05 46 85 37 38 – www.portparadis.com – logis.portparadis@wanadoo.fr

5 rm ☕ – †€ 66 ††€ 70 **Table d'hôte** – Menu € 29 bi

◆ The delightful rooms of this house typical of the Charentes region feature bedheads made out of old wood or slate salvaged from oyster farming sheds. Dine with the owners on regional dishes and hearty 100% homemade breakfasts.

NÎMES P – 30 Gard – 339 L5 – pop. 144 000 – Built-up area 148 889 23 C3 – alt. 39 m – ✉ 30000 Provence

Paris 706 – Lyon 251 – Marseille 123 – Montpellier 58

Nîmes-Arles-Camargue: ✆ 04 66 70 49 49, 12 km on the ⑤

Office de tourisme, 6, rue Auguste ✆ 04 66 58 38 00, Fax 04 66 58 38 01

de Nimes Vacquerolles 1075 chemin du Golf, 6 km on D 999, ✆ 04 66 23 33 33

de Nimes Campagne Route de Saint Gilles, 11 on the airport road, ✆ 04 66 70 17 37

Amphitheatre★★★ - Maison Carrée★★★ - Jardin de la Fontaine★★: Tour Magne★, ≤★ - Interior★ of the Jesuits chapel DU B - Carré d'Art★ - Musée d'Archéologie★ M[1] - Musée du Vieux Nîmes M[3] - Musée des Beaux-Arts★ M[2].

Plans on following pages

Jardins Secrets without rest

3 r. Gaston-Maruejols – ✆ 04 66 84 82 64 – www.jardinssecrets.net – contact@jardinssecrets.net – Fax 04 66 84 27 47 BY m

12 rm – †€ 195/380 ††€ 195/380, ☕ € 25 – 3 suites

◆ An 18C interior tastefully updated and modernised. Magnificent poolside garden planted with fragrant Mediterranean species and a splendid spa. A rare find in the town centre!

Imperator Concorde

quai de la Fontaine – ✆ 04 66 21 90 30 – www.hotel-imperator.com – hotel.imperator@wanadoo.fr – Fax 04 66 67 70 25 AX g

60 rm ☕ – †€ 152/246 ††€ 173/267 – 3 suites – ½ P € 117/164

Rest – Menu € 30 bi/55 – Carte € 49/59

◆ This 1929 abode is laid out around a pretty Florentine patio with a fountain. Gradually renovated interior: spruced up rooms and a sitting room full of the opulence of yesteryear. Elegant restaurant, arranged as a gallery around the charming courtyard. Classic food.

Vatel

140 r. Vatel via av. Kennedy AY – ✆ 04 66 62 57 57 – www.hotelvatel.com – hotel@vatel.fr – Fax 04 66 62 57 50

46 rm – †€ 120/230 ††€ 130/230, ☕ € 12

Rest *Les Palmiers* – *(closed August, Sunday dinner, Monday and lunch except Sunday)* Menu € 30/54 – Carte € 52/73

Rest *Le Provençal* – Menu (€ 20), € 25/58

◆ Students from the Ecole Hotelière work hard for your wellbeing. Rooms are spacious and comfortable with marble bathrooms. Classic, Southern-style food and a lovely view of the town can be found at Les Palmiers. Bountiful Provençal-inspired buffets.

NÎMES

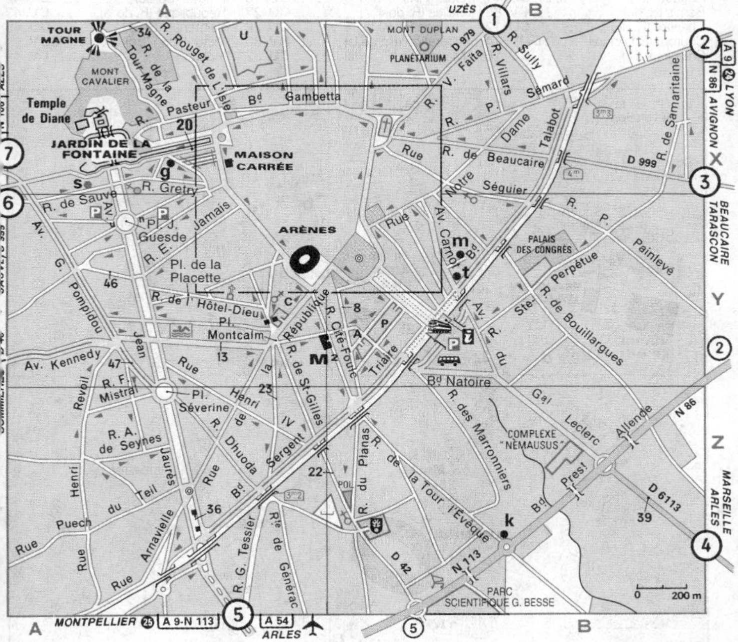

Novotel Atria Nîmes Centre

5 bd de Prague – ✆ 04 66 76 56 56
– accorhotels.com
– h0985@accor.com – Fax 04 66 76 56 59 DV **f**

119 rm – 🚹€ 95/185 🚹🚹€ 95/185, ☕ € 15 – 7 suites
Rest – Menu (€ 16), € 22 (weekdays) – Carte € 19/45

◆ The rooms of this hotel, refurbished from top to toe, are greatly appreciated by business guests, as is its conference centre. Modern interior and fine view of Nîmes from the top floor. Breakfast served on the patio. Restaurant in line with the chain's requirements.

La Maison de Sophie without rest

31 av. Carnot – ✆ 04 66 70 96 10 – www.hotel-lamaisondesophie.com
– lamaisondesophie@orange.fr
– Fax 04 66 36 00 47 BY **t**

8 rm – 🚹€ 140 🚹🚹€ 160/290, ☕ € 16

◆ Marble lobby, fine staircase, period stained glass, cosy sitting rooms and libraries: a pleasant homeliness pervades Sophie's plush 1900s-style property.

New Hôtel La Baume without rest

21 r. Nationale – ✆ 04 66 76 28 42 – www.new-hotel.com
– nimeslabaume@new-hotel.com
– Fax 04 66 76 28 45 DU **b**

34 rm – 🚹€ 110/200 🚹🚹€ 140/230, ☕ € 12

◆ This pleasant private mansion is embellished with a charming open-air square courtyard, a vaulted breakfast room and warm, tastefully renovated guestrooms.

NÎMES

Street	Grid	No.
Arènes (Bd des)	CV	2
Aspic (R. de l')	CUV	
Auguste (R.)	CU	4
Bernis (R. de)	CV	6
Chapitre (R. du)	CU	12
Courbet (Bd Amiral)	DUV	14
Crémieux (R.)	DU	16
Curaterie (R.)	DU	17
Daudet (Bd Alphonse)	CU	18
Fontaine (Quai de la)	CU	20
Gambetta (Bd)	CDU	
Grand'Rue	DU	24
Guizot (R.)	CU	26
Halles (R. des)	CU	27
Horloge (R. de l')	CU	28
Libération (Bd de la)	DV	30
Madeleine (R. de la)	CU	32
Maison Carrée (Pl. de la)	CU	33
Marchands (R. des)	CU	35
Nationale (R.)	CDU	
Perrier (R. Gén.)	CU	
Prague (Bd de)	DV	42
République (R. de la)	CV	43
Saintenac (Bd E.)	DU	45
Victor-Hugo (Bd)	CUV	
Violettes (R.)	CV	49

L'Orangerie rm, AC, VISA, MC, AE

755 r. Tour-de-l'Évêque – ✆ 04 66 84 50 57
– www.orangerie.fr
– info@orangerie.fr – Fax 04 66 29 44 55 BZ **k**

37 rm – †€ 79/149 ††€ 79/149, ☕ € 10 – ½ P € 67/102

Rest – Menu (€ 18), € 24/28 – Carte € 32/49

◆ Built in the style of an old farmhouse. Pretty Provençal decorated rooms (some have terraces and others Jacuzzis), six are brand new. Traditional menu rich in regional produce.

Le Pré Galoffre without rest AC, P, VISA, MC, AE

rte de Générac, 6 km south on the D 13 – ✆ 04 66 29 65 41
– www.lepregaloffre.com – lepregaloffre@wanadoo.fr
– Fax 04 66 38 23 49

27 rm – †€ 60/80 ††€ 60/80, ☕ € 10

◆ All the charm of a 17C residence combined with a contemporary layout. Simple, modern and well-kept rooms. Fine swimming pool. Pleasant welcome.

Kyriad without rest AC, VISA, MC, AE

10 r. Roussy – ✆ 04 66 76 16 20 – www.hotel-kyriad-nimes.com
– contact@hotel-kyriad-nimes.com – Fax 04 66 67 65 99 DU **n**

28 rm – †€ 69/85 ††€ 72/85, ☕ € 8,50

◆ A pleasant town centre hotel: practical garage, small, cheerful, well-soundproofed rooms (two with a terrace and view over the Nîmes rooftops), endearing welcome.

XXX **Le Lisita** (Olivier Douet)

2 bd des Arènes – ✆ 04 66 67 29 15 – www.lelisita.com – restaurant@lelisita.com – Fax 04 66 67 25 32 – Closed Sunday and Monday CV **h**

Rest – Menu (€ 27), € 35 (lunch), € 54/78 – Carte € 77/94

Spec. Brandade de morue à la fleur de thym et copeaux de truffes. Filet de taureau sauté, jus à l'huile d'olive. Biscuit chocolat-caramel sauce praliné. **Wines** Costières de Nîmes.

◆ An enviable location near the arenas. Gourmet dishes with a southern twist are served in the tasteful, modern interior of the stone built dining room or on the terrace beneath plane trees.

XX **Aux Plaisirs des Halles**

4 r. Littré – ✆ 04 66 36 01 02 – www.auxplaisirsdeshalles.com – Fax 04 66 36 08 00 – Closed 8-15 June, autumn school holidays and February school holidays, Sunday and Monday CU **r**

Rest – Menu (€ 22), € 27/60 – Carte € 60/75

◆ A handsome modern dining room (panelling, designer furniture) and a pleasant flower-decked patio for summer dining. Generous tasty cuisine; fine list of regional wines.

XX **Le Bouchon et L'Assiette**

5 bis r. de Sauve – ✆ 04 66 62 02 93 – www.bouchon-assiette.fr – bouchon-assiette@orange.fr – Fax 04 66 62 03 57 – Closed14 July-15 August, 2-17 January, Tuesday and Wednesday AX **s**

Rest – Menu (€ 17), € 27/45 – Carte € 34/41

◆ This restaurant has a particularly well-designed décor with paintings and antique objects, as well as a very friendly welcome. Tasty seasonal cooking at the table.

XX **Le Magister**

5 r. Nationale – ✆ 04 66 76 11 00 – www.le-magister-a-table.com – le.magister@wanadoo.fr – Fax 04 66 67 21 05 – Closed Monday lunch DU **q**

Rest – Menu (€ 21), € 36/47 – Carte € 40/55

◆ Art exhibitions adorn the well worn, wood panelled walls of this welcoming chalet type restaurant. Appetising regional fare.

XX **Shogun**

38 bd Victor-Hugo – ✆ 04 66 27 59 88 – restaurant.shogun@wanadoo.fr – Fax 04 66 64 23 92 – Closed 25 May-1st June, 2-24 August, 13-20 September, 17-25 January, Sunday and Monday CV **v**

Rest – Menu € 14 bi (lunch), € 20 € bi/48 – Carte € 44/67

◆ People come from far and near to sample the talented creations of the chef and the Sushi master. Find the inimitable art of hospitality in this feng shui restaurant.

XX **Le Darling**

40 r. Madeleine – ✆ 04 66 67 04 99 – www.ledarling.com – restaurantledarling@wanadoo.fr – Fax 04 66 67 04 99 – Closed 1st-23 July, 31 December-10 January, lunch except Sunday October-May and Wednesday CU **p**

Rest – *(number of covers limited, pre-book)* Menu € 42/60 – Carte € 58/71

◆ Smart contemporary interior for this in vogue establishment: stone vaults, gold leaf embellished fresco, and creative cuisine with successfully unusual combinations.

X **L'Exaequo**

11 r. Bigot – ✆ 04 66 21 71 96 – www.exaequorestaurant.com – l.exaequo@wanadoo.fr – Fax 04 66 21 77 96 – Closed 15-25 August, Saturday lunch and Sunday CV **a**

Rest – Menu (€ 16), € 20 (weekday lunch), € 26/75 bi – Carte approx. € 45

◆ Near the arenas, a distinctive lounge ambience in reds and oranges (background music and designer furniture), delightful patio with water sprays, and current cuisine.

X **Le Marché sur la Table**

10 r. Littré – ✆ 04 66 67 22 50 – Fax 04 66 76 19 78 – Closed Sunday and Monday CU **d**

Rest – Menu € 39 – Carte approx. € 35

◆ A friendly little restaurant offering bistro cuisine based on fresh ingredients, sourced by the owner every morning in the local market.

in Marguerittes by ② and D 981: 8 km – pop. 8 692 – alt. 60 m – ✉ 30320

L'Hacienda rm, rest, VISA
Le Mas de Brignon, south-east: 2 km on minor road
– ✆ 04 66 75 02 25 – www.hotel-hacienda-nimes.fr – contact@hotel-hacienda-nimes.fr – Fax 04 66 75 45 58
– Open mid March-end November
12 rm – €82/142 €92/162, €15 – ½ P €96/136
Rest – *(dinner only)* Menu €34/44 – Carte €52/65
◆ Tucked away in the countryside, this secluded house offers quiet, spacious rooms furnished in a charming Provencal style. The two dining rooms, one for winter and one for summer, command a direct view of the kitchen and pool. Tasty, updated traditional fare.

in Garons by ⑤, D 42 and D 442: 9 km – pop. 3 692 – alt. 90 m – ✉ 30128

Alexandre (Michel Kayser) VISA AE
2 r. X.-Tronc – ✆ 04 66 70 08 99 – www.michelkayser.com
– restaurant.alexandre@wanadoo.fr – Fax 04 66 70 01 75
– Closed 23 August-8 September, 4-12 January, 15-27 February, Tuesday from September to June, Sunday except lunch from September to June and Monday
Rest – Menu €64 (weekdays)/124 – Carte €86/149
Spec. Île flottante aux truffes de Provence (Sep. to April). Filet de taureau de manade, lasagne aux deux céleris acidulés et câpres. L'écrin des desserts "Alexandre". **Wines** Costières de Nîmes.
◆ Tasty Provençal cooking in elegant and resolutely modern dining rooms, opening onto a magnificent garden. Good choice of Languedoc-Roussillon wine.

NIORT – 79 Deux-Sèvres – **322** D7 – **pop. 57 900** – **alt. 24 m** 38 **B2**
– ✉ **79000** **Atlantic Coast**

Paris 408 – Bordeaux 184 – Nantes 142 – Poitiers 76 – La Rochelle 65

Office de tourisme, 16, rue du Petit Saint-Jean ✆ 05 49 24 18 79, Fax 05 49 24 98 90

de Niort Chemin du Grand Ormeau, S : 3 km near the racecourse, ✆ 05 49 09 01 41

Keep★: salle de la chamoiserie et de la ganterie (shammy leather and glove room)★ - Le Pilori★.

Le Marais Poitevin★★.

Plan on next page

Mercure rm, rest, VISA AE
80 bis av. de Paris – ✆ 05 49 24 29 29 – www.mercure.com – hotel.mercure@mercure-niort.fr – Fax 05 49 28 00 90 BY **a**
79 rm – €63/112 €75/135, €13
Rest – Menu (€20), €26/29 – Carte €36/51
◆ Welcoming contemporary hotel near the town centre. It offers large, well-presented rooms and a garden with pool. Warm, modern dining room-veranda and terrace service in fine weather. À la carte menu and daily specials.

Le Grand Hôtel without rest VISA AE
32 av. de Paris – ✆ 05 49 24 22 21 – www.grandhotelniort.com
– grandhotel-niort@wanadoo.fr – Fax 05 49 24 42 41 BY **v**
39 rm – €66/99 €69/102, €9
◆ Town centre establishment with double-glazing. Even so, the rooms overlooking the small garden are quieter. Full breakfast buffet and some garage parking available.

Ambassadeur without rest VISA AE
82 r. de la Gare – ✆ 05 49 24 00 38 – www.ambassadeur-hotel.com
– info@ambassadeur-hotel.com – Fax 05 49 24 94 38 – Closed 26 December-3 January BZ **b**
32 rm – €52 €62, €7
◆ The rooms in this hotel near the station are practical and well kept. They have modern furnishings, warm colours and good soundproofing.

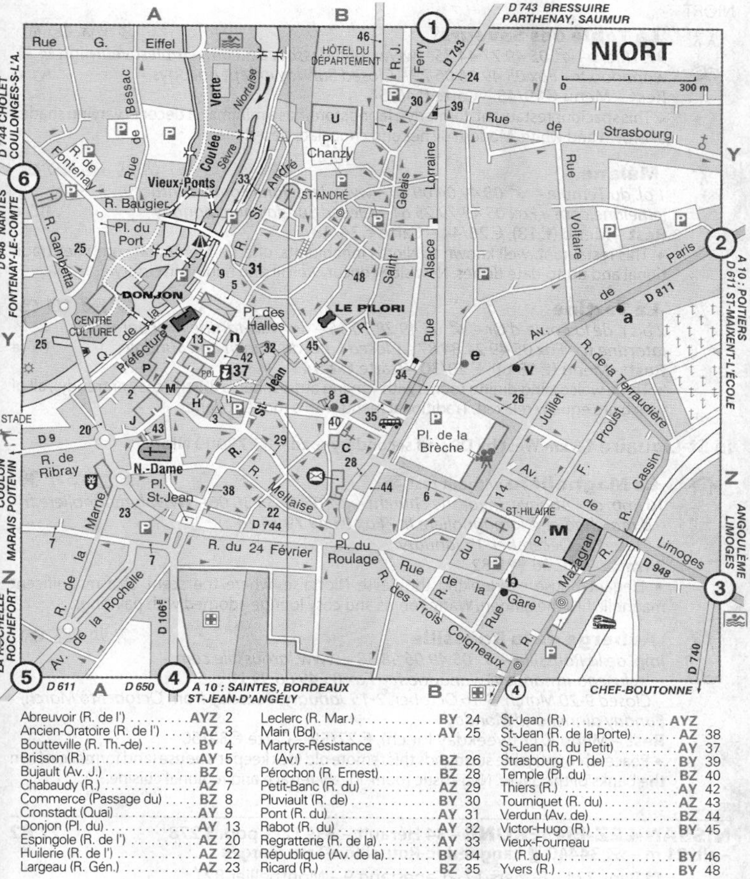

NIORT

Sandrina without rest
43 av. St-Jean d'Angély, ④ – ✆ 05 49 79 28 42
– www.hotel-sandrina.com – hotelsandrina@wanadoo.fr
– Fax 05 49 73 10 85 – Closed 26 December-4 January
18 rm – †€ 52 ††€ 54, ☕ € 7
◆ Family hotel in the town centre offering colourful, functional and immaculately kept rooms. Closed car park available.

XXX **La Belle Étoile**
115 quai M. Métayer, near ring road West -AY- Ouest : 2.5 km
– ✆ 05 49 73 31 29 – www.la-belle-etoile.fr
– info@la-belle-etoile.fr – Fax 05 49 09 05 59
– Closed Sunday dinner, Wednesday dinner and Monday
Rest – Menu (€ 23), € 30/65 – Carte € 46/77
◆ Along the Sèvre, this house is isolated from the road by a screen of greenery. Elegant dining room and shaded terrace. Fine collection of old vintage wine bottles.

La Table des Saveurs

9 r. Thiers – 05 49 77 44 35 – www.tabledessaveurs.com – tablesaveurniort@wanadoo.fr – Fax 05 49 16 06 29 – Closed Sunday except holidays AY **n**

Rest – Menu € 19/45 – Carte € 40/56

◆ This spacious restaurant, formerly a fabric store, has a minimalist decor in varying shades of brown and white. Modern dishes and chocolate desert menu.

Mélane

1 pl. du Temple – 05 49 04 00 40 – www.lemelane.com – contact@lemelane.com – Fax 05 49 79 25 61 – Closed Sunday and Monday BZ **a**

Rest – Menu (€ 18), € 26/44 – Carte € 34/48

◆ This restaurant, well known to Niort's inhabitants, offers a menu that combines traditional and up-to-date dishes. New sleek decor, well lit and minimalist in style.

La Tartine

2 bis r. de la Boule-d'Or – 05 49 28 20 15 – www.la-tartine.fr – contact@latartine.fr – Fax 05 49 24 84 87 – Closed Saturday lunch and Sunday BY **e**

Rest – Menu (€ 13 bi), € 20/30 – Carte € 22/41

◆ Three welcoming dining rooms with varying atmospheres (bistro, cosy or trendy), all of which are equally relaxed. Traditional menu with a modern slant.

in St-Liguaire 4,5 km West by D9 and secondary road – 79000 Niort

La Magnolière without rest

16 imp. de l'Abbaye, (near the church) – 05 49 35 36 06 – www.lamagnoliere.fr – a.marchadier@lamagnoliere.fr – Fax 05 49 79 14 28 – Closed 22 December-1st January

3 rm – €76 €82

◆ Elegant house overlooking the Sèvre Niortaise, where the scent of a magnificent magnolia fills the garden. Warm rooms and cosy lounge adorned with paintings.

Auberge de la Roussille

imp. de la Roussille – 05 49 06 98 38 – www.laroussille.com – leclusegourmande@wanadoo.fr – Fax 05 49 06 99 10 – Closed 9-20 March, 5-16 October, 2-15 January, Tuesday from October to March, Sunday dinner and Monday

Rest – Menu € 17 (weekday lunch), € 22/59 – Carte € 32/60

◆ Peaceful countryside surrounds this remote old lock keeper's house (and former café) on the banks of the Sèvre. Neo-rustic room, lovely terrace and regional cuisine.

NISSAN-LEZ-ENSERUNE – 34 Hérault – 339 D9 – pop. 3 278 – alt. 21 m – 34440 Languedoc-Roussillon-Tarn Gorges 22 **B2**

Paris 774 – Béziers 12 – Capestang 9 – Montpellier 82 – Narbonne 17

Office de tourisme, square Rene Dez 04 67 37 14 12, Fax 04.67.37.14.12

Oppidum d'Ensérune★: museum★, ≤★ Northwest: 5 km.

Résidence rm,

35 av. Cave – 04 67 37 00 63 – www.hotel-residence.com – contact@hotel-residence.com – Fax 04 67 37 68 63 – Closed 11 December-4 January

18 rm – €62/72 €62/72, € 10 – ½ P € 67/72

Rest – Menu (€ 16), € 21 (weekday lunch), € 28/48 – Carte € 35/53

◆ Fine residence at the heart of a small village. Rooms are gradually being updated; those in the wing (a former 19C winegrower's house) are larger. In fine weather, enjoy a meal on the pleasant shaded terrace opposite the pool.

Le Plô without rest

7 av. de la Cave – 04 67 37 38 21 – www.bedbreakfast-nissan.com – patry.c@wanadoo.fr – Fax 04 67 37 38 21 – Open April-December

4 rm – €45/70 €45/80, € 6

◆ In the village centre, this impressive manor house is a hotel providing spacious rooms with a calm atmosphere and plenty of light. Pleasant hospitality provided.

NITRY – 89 Yonne – **319** G5 – **pop. 402** – **alt. 240 m** – ✉ **89310** 7 **B1**

Paris 195 – Auxerre 36 – Avallon 23 – Vézelay 31

Auberge la Beursaudière

9 chemin de Ronde – ☎ 03 86 33 69 69 – www.beursaudiere.com – message@beursaudiere.com – Fax 03 86 33 69 60 – Closed 5-23 January

11 rm – €75/115 €75/115, ☕ €10

Rest – Menu (€12), €20/42 – Carte €25/45

◆ Guestrooms with character, breakfast rooms with vaulted ceilings and a medieval pigeon loft: the conversion of this old priory outbuilding has been particularly successful. Carefully-laid tables and country-style decor with staff in regional costume. Regional food and well-stocked cellar.

NOAILHAC – 81 Tarn – **338** G9 – **pop. 808** – **alt. 222 m** – ✉ **81490** 29 **C2**

Paris 730 – Toulouse 90 – Albi 55 – Béziers 99 – Carcassonne 61 – Castres 12

Hostellerie d'Oc

av. Charles Tailhades – ☎ 05 63 50 50 37 – hostelleriedoc@orange.fr – Fax 05 63 50 50 37 – Closed 7-21 September, 5-29 January, Wednesday dinner and Monday

Rest – Menu €11 bi (weekdays), €17/33 – Carte €23/43

◆ Former coaching inn converted into a restaurant, housing rustic dining rooms. Regional cooking mainly using local produce.

NOAILLY – 42 Loire – **327** D3 – **pop. 737** – **alt. 240 m** – ✉ **42640** 44 **A1**

Paris 395 – Lyon 98 – Roanne 13 – Vichy 68

Château de la Motte

La Motte Nord, 1,5 km – ☎ 04 77 66 64 60 – www.chateaudelamotte.net – chateaudelamotte@wanadoo.fr – Fax 04 77 66 68 10 – Open March-15 November

6 rm ☕ – €77/108 €85/115 – ½ P €65/81

Table d'hôte – *(closed Sunday dinner)* Menu €28 bi

◆ This 18-19C château nestles in sumptuous parkland. The bedrooms, decorated with period furniture, are named after famous authors. The most unusual room, Lamartine, has a round bathtub in the tower. Home-grown produce takes pride of place on the traditional menu. Theme stays.

NOCÉ – 61 Orne – **310** N4 – **see Bellême**

NOEUX-LES-MINES – 62 Pas-de-Calais – **301** I5 – **pop. 12 100** – **alt. 29 m** – ✉ **62290** **Northern France and the Paris Region** 30 **B2**

Paris 208 – Arras 28 – Béthune 5 – Bully-les-Mines 8 – Doullens 49 – Lens 17 – Lille 38

d'Olhain Houdain Parc départemental de Nature, S : 11 km on D 65 and D 301, ☎ 03 21 02 17 03

Carrefour des Saveurs

94 rte Nationale – ☎ 03 21 26 74 74 – david.wojtkowiak@wanadoo.fr – Fax 03 21 27 12 14 – Closed 20 July-16 August, Wednesday dinner, Sunday dinner and Monday

Rest – Menu (€17), €21 (weekdays)/48 – Carte €44/68

◆ This restaurant has a convivial dining room with stone and brick walls. Serving a range of appetising modern meals.

NOGARO – 32 Gers – **336** B7 – **pop. 1 969** – **alt. 98 m** – ✉ **32110** 28 **A2**

Paris 729 – Agen 88 – Auch 63 – Mont-de-Marsan 45 – Pau 72 – Tarbes 69

Office de tourisme, 81, rue Nationale ☎ 05 62 09 13 30, Fax 05 62 08 88 21

Solenca rest,

rte d'Auch – ✆ 05 62 09 09 08 – www.solenca.com – info@solenca.com – Fax 05 62 09 09 07

48 rm – †€ 59/90 ††€ 65/90, ☕ € 8 – ½ P € 54/115

Rest – Menu € 13 (weekday lunch), € 16/37 – Carte € 30/53

◆ A pleasant stop in the heart of the Gers. All the identically decorated rooms are well kept and practical. Lovely pool surrounded by a tree-lined garden. Countrified restaurant and a terrace facing the greenery. Regionally inspired cuisine.

in Manciet **Northeast: 9 km by N 124 – pop. 788 – alt. 131 m – ✉ 32370**

La Bonne Auberge with rm

Pl. du Pesquerot – ✆ 05 62 08 50 04 – labonneauberge32@orange.fr – Fax 05 62 08 58 84 – Closed 23 December-3 January, Sunday dinner and Monday

14 rm – †€ 42 ††€ 52, ☕ € 8 – ½ P € 58 **Rest** – Menu € 25/50 – Carte € 48/82

◆ This century-old building is home to a restaurant with two comfortable dining areas, one on the veranda and the other with a fireplace, wooden panelling and a collection of armagnac on display.

NOGENT – 52 Haute-Marne – 313 M5 – pop. 4 113 – alt. 410 m – ✉ 52800 Northern France and the Paris Region 14 C3

Paris 289 – Bourbonne-les-Bains 35 – Chaumont 24 – Langres 25 – Neufchâteau 53

Syndicat d'initiative, place du Général de Gaulle ✆ 03 25 03 69 18, Fax 03 25 03 69 18

Musée de la coutellerie de l'espace Pelletier - Musée du patrimoine coutelier.

Le Commerce rm,

pl. Gén. de Gaulle – ✆ 03 25 31 81 14 – www.relais-sud-champagne.com – hotelcommerce.nogent@wanadoo.fr – Fax 03 2531 74 00 – Closed 23 December-3 January and Sunday

18 rm – †€ 68 ††€ 68, ☕ € 9 – ½ P € 78

Rest – *(Closed Saturday from October to March and Sunday)*
Menu (€ 11), € 20/30 – Carte € 29/48

◆ A good overnight stop opposite the town hall and near the Musée de la Coutellerie. Recently renovated rooms furnished in Louis Philippe style. Regional cuisine served to a choice of backdrop: the traditional restaurant or the more relaxed brasserie.

NOGENT-LE-ROI – 28 Eure-et-Loir – 311 F4 – pop. 4 067 – alt. 93 m – ✉ 28210 Northern France and the Paris Region 11 B1

Paris 77 – Ablis 35 – Chartres 28 – Dreux 19 – Maintenon 10 – Rambouillet 26

Syndicat d'initiative, Mairie ✆ 02 37 51 23 20

du Château de Maintenon Maintenon 1 route de Gallardon, SE : 8 km on D 983, ✆ 02 37 27 18 09

Relais des Remparts

2 pl. du Marché aux Légumes – ✆ 02 37 51 40 47 – www.relais-des-remparts.com – twagner1@club-internet.fr – Fax 02 37 51 40 47 – Closed 6-27 August, 17 February-3 March, Monday dinner from November to February, Sunday dinner, Tuesday dinner and Wednesday

Rest – Menu € 20 (weekdays), € 27/38 – Carte € 30/40

◆ The keys to this restaurant's success are tasty traditional cuisine, pleasant, efficient service and a harmoniously decorated and comfortable dining room.

NOGENT-LE-ROTROU – 28 Eure-et-Loir – 311 A6 – pop. 11 700 – alt. 116 m – ✉ 28400 Normandy 11 B1

Paris 146 – Alençon 65 – Chartres 54 – Châteaudun 55 – Le Mans 76

Office de tourisme, 44, rue Villette-Gaté ✆ 02 37 29 68 86, Fax 02 37 29 68 86

NOGENT-LE-ROTROU

Bouchers (R. des) .... Z 2
Bourg-le-Comte (R.) .... Z 3
Bretonnerie (R.) .... Z
Château-St-Jean (R.) .... Z
Croix-la-Comtesse (R.) ...... Y
Deschanel (R.) .... YZ
Dr-Desplantes (R.) .... Z 8
Foch (Av. Mar.) .... Y 9
Fuye (R. de la) .... YZ 10
Giroust (R.) .... Y 12
Gouverneur (R.) .... YZ 13
Marches-St-Jean (R. des) .... Z 14
Paty (R. du) .... Z 15
Poupardières (R. des) .... Z 16
Prés (Av. des) .... Y
République (Pl. de la) ...... Z 17
Rhône (R. de) .... Z 18
St-Hilaire (R.) .... Y
St-Laurent (R.) .... Z 20
St-Martin (R.) .... Y
Sully (R. de) .... YZ 23
Villette-Gaté (R.) .... Y 25

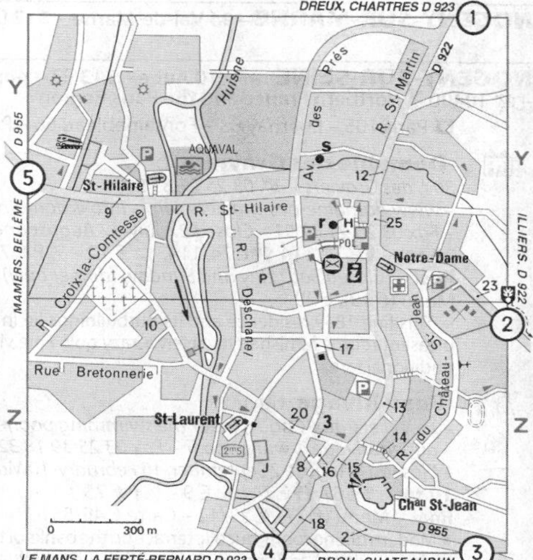

Brit Hôtel du Perche without rest VISA AE
r. de la Bruyère via ⑤ – ☎ 02 37 53 43 60 – www.hotel-du-perche.com – hotelduperche@brithotel.fr – Fax 02 37 53 43 69
40 rm – †€ 49/56 ††€ 56/68, ☕ € 6,50
◆ A modern building on the outskirts of the town with bright, cosy bedrooms furnished in a Provençal spirit. Buffet breakfast.

Sully without rest VISA AE
51 r. des Viennes – ☎ 02 37 52 15 14 – www.hotelsullynogent.fr – hotel.sully@wanadoo.fr – Fax 02 37 52 15 20 – Closed 2 weeks in August and Christmas holidays
42 rm – †€ 56/59 ††€ 66/69, ☕ € 7 Y **s**
◆ Reasonably priced establishment located in a peaceful neighbourhood. The name refers to the Duke of Sully, whose tomb can be seen in the Hôtel Dieu.

Au Lion d'Or without rest VISA
28 pl. St-Pol – ☎ 02 37 52 01 60 – www.hotel-chartres-le-mans.com – hotelauliondor@wanadoo.fr – Fax 02 37 52 23 82 – Closed 1-22 August, 26 December-3 January and 13-20 February Y **r**
18 rm – †€ 47/67 ††€ 55/67, ☕ € 6,50
◆ Practically located in the town centre, this former post house sports refurbished, functional and well-kept rooms (small bathrooms).

L' Alambic VISA
20 av. de Paris, at Margon 1.5 km via ① – ☎ 02 37 52 19 03 – joel.tremeaux@wanadoo.fr – Closed 5-26 August, 20 February-4 March, Wednesday dinner, Sunday dinner and Monday
Rest – Menu € 15 (weekdays)/42 – Carte € 40/58
◆ This former "roadside café" is now a smart restaurant housing dining rooms in bright shades of red, green and yellow. Traditional cuisine, including a speciality: calf's head.

in L'Ambition 10 km by ③ and D 955 – ✉ **28480 Vichères**

Les Vallées du Perche rm, VISA AE
– ☎ 02 37 29 47 58 – www.auberge-vallees-du-perche.fr – lesvalleesduperche@aliceadsl.fr – Fax 02 37 29 91 55 – Closed 2 weeks in July and 2-16 January
14 rm – †€ 38 ††€ 48, ☕ € 6,50
Rest – *(closed Sunday dinner, Monday lunch and Tuesday lunch)*
Menu (€ 12), € 19/30 – Carte € 25/40
◆ Unpretentious inn home to simple, well-soundproofed rooms decked in pine, cane and wrought iron. Countrified restaurant (beams, whitewashed walls, fireplace) and traditional cuisine. Sample the house speciality of fillet of duck in goat's cheese and honey.

NOGENT-SUR-MARNE – 94 Val-de-Marne – 312 D2 – 101 27 – see Paris, Area

NOGENT-SUR-SEINE – 10 Aube – 313 B3 – pop. 5 984 – alt. 67 m 13 A2
– ✉ 10400 Northern France and the Paris Region

Paris 105 – Épernay 83 – Fontainebleau 66 – Provins 19 – Sens 47 – Troyes 56

Domaine des Graviers
30 r. des Graviers – ☎ 03 25 21 81 90
– www.domaine-des-graviers.com – info@domaine-des-graviers.com
– Fax 03 25 21 81 91 – Closed 27 July-17 August and 21 December-4 January
26 rm – †€ 74/114 ††€ 74/114, ☕ € 12 – ½ P € 75/95
Rest – *(Closed Saturday and Sunday) (dinner only) (resident only)*
Menu (€ 19), € 29
◆ This fine 1899 residence and its outbuildings lie in a 17-ha park. Elegant lounge and pleasant rooms furnished diversely. Crazy golf. Fine view of the estate's venerable trees; traditional fare.

Beau Rivage with rm
20 r. Villiers-aux-Choux, (near the swimming pool) – ☎ 03 25 39 84 22
– aubeaurivage@wanadoo.fr – Fax 03 25 39 18 32
– Closed 17 August-2 September, 15 February-10 March, Sunday dinner and Monday
10 rm – †€ 62 ††€ 74, ☕ € 9 – ½ P € 75
Rest – Menu (€ 17), € 22/42 – Carte € 45/55
◆ Modern dining room, bucolic terrace on the banks of the Seine, fine cooking (modernised regional cuisine) and spruce rooms: these are the plus points of the Beau Rivage.

Auberge du Cygne de la Croix
22 r. Ponts – ☎ 03 25 39 91 26 – www.cygne-de-la-croix.fr – cygnedelacroix@wanadoo.fr – Fax 03 25 39 81 79 – Closed 20 December-5 January, 15-23 February, Tuesday dinner and Wednesday dinner from October to March, Sunday dinner and Monday dinner
Rest – Menu € 20 (weekday lunch), € 26/50 – Carte € 35/65
◆ A former 16C coaching inn, where two countrified dining rooms (the one at the rear is lighter) a peaceful courtyard-terrace and traditional recipes await.

NOIRLAC – 18 Cher – 323 K6 – see St-Amand-Montrond

NOIRMOUTIER (ÎLE) – 85 Vendée – 316 C6 – see Île de Noirmoutier

NOISY-LE-GRAND – 93 Seine-Saint-Denis – 305 G7 – 101 18 – see Paris, Area

NOIZAY – 37 Indre-et-Loire – 317 O4 – pop. 1 099 – alt. 56 m 11 B2
– ✉ 37210

Paris 230 – Amboise 11 – Blois 44 – Tours 21 – Vendôme 49

Château de Noizay
Promenade de Waulsort – ☎ 02 47 52 11 01 – www.chateaudenoizay.com
– noizay@relaischateaux.com – Fax 02 47 52 04 64 – Closed 17 January-25 March
19 rm – †€ 150/290 ††€ 150/290, ☕ € 21 – ½ P € 168/238
Rest – *(closed Tuesday lunch, Wednesday lunch and Thursday lunch)*
Menu (€ 39), € 52/77 – Carte € 66/72
◆ This 16C château is nestled in a park, dominating the village and its vineyards. Large rooms with personal touches and fine furniture. Those in the outbuilding are more modern. The restaurant is comprised of elegant plush rooms serving up-to-date cuisine and Loire Valley wines.

NOLAY – 21 Côte-d'Or – 320 H8 – pop. 1 490 – alt. 299 m – ✉ 21340 7 A3
Burgundy-Jura

Paris 316 – Autun 30 – Beaune 20 – Chalon-sur-Saône 34 – Dijon 64

Office de tourisme, 24, rue de la République ☎ 03 80 21 80 73, Fax 03 80 21 80 73

site★ of the Château de la Rochepot East: 5 km - Site★ of the Cirque du Bout-du-Monde Northeast: 5 km.

Du Parc rest, VISA

3 pl. Hôtel-de-Ville – 03 80 21 78 88 – hotel.restaurant.du.parc.nolay@orange.fr – Fax 03 80 21 86 39 – Open 15 March-30 November

14 rm – €61/64 €64/96, €7 – ½ P €59/72

Rest – *(open 1st April-30 November)* Menu (€15), €18 (weekday lunch), €28/39 – Carte €25/45

◆ A former 16C coaching inn. It offers small, fresh and well-soundproofed bedrooms, with simple furniture. Exposed framework in the second-floor rooms. A small rustic dining room with beams and a fireplace. Pleasant terrace courtyard

De la Halle without rest VISA

pl. des Halles – 03 80 21 76 37 – www.terroirs-b.com/lahalle – noelle.pocheron@wanadoo.fr – Fax 03 80 21 76 37

13 rm – €53 €58, €7

◆ The two main buildings, set on either side of an interior courtyard decked with flowers, face the 14C covered market. Rather modest, but well-kept bedrooms, which are bigger at the back.

Le Burgonde A/C VISA

35 r. de la République – 03 80 21 71 25 – jean-noel.aprikian764@orange.fr – Fax 03 80 21 86 41 – Closed mid-February to mid-March, Sunday dinner, Tuesday dinner and Wednesday

Rest – Menu (€13), €20/40 – Carte €27/55

◆ The owners have retained the original floorboards and shop windows of what was once an antique dealer. Resulting in an attractive, colourful restaurant, with a reasonably priced concise menu.

LES NONIÈRES – 26 Drôme – 332 G5 – alt. 282 m – ✉ 26410 45 C3

Paris 648 – Die 25 – Gap 84 – Grenoble 73 – Valence 91

Le Mont-Barral VISA

– 04 75 21 12 21 – www.hotelmontbarral-vercors.com – mtbarral@aol.com – Fax 04 75 21 12 70 – Open 1 March-11 November and closed Tuesday dinner and Wednesday in low season

19 rm – €52/59 €52/59, €8 – ½ P €53/60

Rest – Menu (€16), €18 (lunch), €25/40 – Carte €28/40

◆ A mountain stopping place for Upper Drôme hikers. Bedrooms fitted out in the newly-built extension are bigger. Modest rustic-style restaurant. Traditional dishes and a "country" menu.

NONTRON – 24 Dordogne – 329 E2 – pop. 3 458 – alt. 260 m – ✉ 24300 Dordogne-Berry-Limousin 4 C1

Paris 454 – Angoulême 45 – Libourne 135 – Limoges 68 – Périgueux 50 – Rochechouart 42

Office de tourisme, 3, avenue du Général Leclerc 05 53 56 25 50, Fax 05 53 60 34 13

Grand Hôtel VISA

3 pl. A. Agard – 05 53 56 11 22 – www.hotel-pelisson-nontron.com – grand-hotel-pelisson@wanadoo.fr – Fax 05 53 56 59 94 – Closed Sunday evening October-June

23 rm – €53 €65, €6,50 – ½ P €63

Rest – Menu €23 (weekdays)/55 – Carte €25/60

◆ Old-style hospitality is maintained in this former post house with an Old France atmosphere. Regularly maintained and spotless. Regional dishes served in a rustic dining room or on the terrace overlooking the garden.

NONZA – 2B Haute-Corse – 345 F3 – see Corse

NOTRE-DAME-DE-BELLECOMBE – 73 Savoie – 333 M3 – pop. 510 – alt. 1 150 m – Winter sports : 1 150/2 070 19 – ✉ 73590 French Alps 46 F1

Paris 585 – Albertville 25 – Annecy 54 – Chambéry 76 – Chamonix-Mont-Blanc 43

Office de tourisme, Chef Lieu 04 79 31 61 40, Fax 04 79 31 67 09

Ferme de Victorine

Le Planay, 3 km east by Les Saisies road – ✆ 04 79 31 63 46 – www.la-ferme-de-victorine.com – Closed 7-25 June, 11 November-16 December, Sunday dinner and Monday from April to June and from September to November

Rest – Menu (€ 22), € 27/50 – Carte € 40/65

◆ A perfect replica of a traditional mountain house (all-wood decor, antiques). Tasty regional cooking, which is faithful to the seasons: fish in summer, game in autumn.

NOTRE-DAME-DE-BONDEVILLE – 76 Seine-Maritime – 304 G5 – see Rouen

NOTRE-DAME-DE-GRAVENCHON – 76 Seine-Maritime – 304 D5 33 C2

– pop. 8 618 – alt. 35 m – ✉ 76330 Normandy

Paris 176 – Bolbec 14 – Le Havre 40 – Rouen 51 – Yvetot 25

Pascal Saunier

1 av. Amiral Grasset – ✆ 02 35 38 60 67 – www.hotelpascalsaunier.com – info@hotelpascalsaunier.com – Fax 02 35 38 30 64

29 rm – €71/105 €78/110, € 10

Rest – *(closed August, Friday dinner, Saturday and Sunday)*

Menu (€ 25 bi) – Carte € 30/45

◆ A big half-timbered residence (1930) surrounded by a peaceful garden with bright, functional, pastel-coloured rooms. A terrace lengthens the modern style dining room and the blackboard menu of traditional cooking changes daily.

NOTRE-DAME-DE-LIVAYE – 14 Calvados – 303 M5 – pop. 130 33 C2

– alt. 27 m – ✉ 14340

Paris 185 – Caen 36 – Le Havre 86 – Lisieux 16 – Hérouville-Saint-Clair 39

Aux Pommiers de Livaye

– ✆ 02 31 63 01 28 – http://bandb.normandy.free.fr – bandb.normandy@wanadoo.fr – Closed mid November-beg. February

5 rm – €75 €89 **Table d'hôte** – Menu € 25/35

◆ A drive lined in apple trees leads to this peaceful Normandy farmhouse built in 1720. Personalised rooms adorned with a mixture of antique or period furniture. Homemade breakfast. Regional cuisine served in an authentic rustic dining room. Small scale cider production.

NOTRE-DAME-DE-MONTS – 85 Vendée – 316 D6 – pop. 1 528 34 A3

– alt. 6 m – ✉ 85690

Paris 457 – Challans 22 – Nantes 72 – Noirmoutier-en-l'Île 26 – La Roche-sur-Yon 66

Office de tourisme, 6, rue de la Barre ✆ 02 51 58 84 97, Fax 02 51 58 15 56

La Barre-de-Monts: Centre de découverte du Marais breton-vendéen North: 6 km **Atlantic Coast.**

L'Orée du Bois

rm,

14 r. Frisot – ✆ 02 51 58 84 04 – www.oree-du-bois.com – hoteloreedubois@aol.com – Open from Easter to end September

30 rm – €52/70 €54/72, € 8 – ½ P € 53/59

Rest – *(dinner only) (resident only)* Menu € 18/26

◆ Bright, practical accommodation occupying three buildings around a swimming pool, in a residential district. Those on the ground floor have a terrace.

NOTRE-DAME D'ORSAN – 18 Cher – 323 J6 – see le Châtelet

NOTRE-DAME-DU-GUILDO – 22 Côtes-d'Armor – 309 I3 10 C1

– pop. 3 187 – alt. 52 m – ✉ 22380

Paris 427 – Rennes 94 – Saint-Brieuc 49 – Saint-Malo 32

Château du Val d' Arguenon without rest

1 km east on D 786 ✉ 22380 St-Cast – ✆ 02 96 41 07 03 – www.chateauduval.com – chateau@chateauduval.com – Open Easter-end October

5 rm – 🛉€ 90/140 🛉🛉€ 95/160

◆ This fine family-run residence (16C-18C) nestles in a park that runs down to the sea. Stylish interior with period furniture in the lounge and rooms.

NOTRE-DAME-DU-HAMEL – **27 Eure** – **304** D8 – **pop. 203** – **alt. 200 m** – ✉ **27390** 33 **C2**

Paris 158 – L'Aigle 21 – Argentan 48 – Bernay 28 – Évreux 55 – Lisieux 40 – Vimoutiers 28

XXX **Le Moulin de la Marigotière**

D 45 – ✆ 02 32 44 58 11 – www.moulin-marigotiere.com – contact@moulin-marigotiere.com – Fax 02 32 44 40 12 – Closed 23 February-5 March, Monday dinner except July-August, Sunday dinner, Tuesday dinner and Wednesday

Rest – Menu € 30 (weekday lunch), € 40/75 – Carte € 50/85

◆ Former mill converted into a restaurant, where you can enjoy traditional meals in a stylish atmosphere. Pretty park where the Charentonne flows in the background.

NOTRE-DAME-DU-PÉ – **72 Sarthe** – **310** H8 – **pop. 483** – **alt. 73 m** – ✉ **72300** 35 **C2**

Paris 262 – Angers 51 – La Flèche 28 – Nantes 140

La Reboursière

1 km south on the D 134 and minor road – ✆ 02 43 92 92 41 – www.lareboursiere.fr.st – gilles-chappuy@wanadoo.fr – Fax 02 43 92 92 41

4 rm – 🛉€ 70 🛉🛉€ 78 – ½ P € 60 **Table d'hôte** – Menu € 27 bi

◆ This restored mid-19C farmhouse surrounded by a park guarantees peaceful nights. Large guestrooms, furnished with antiques. Traditional cuisine, served with a smile, in an authentic rustic setting.

NOUAN-LE-FUZELIER – **41 Loir-et-Cher** – **318** J6 – **pop. 2 500** – **alt. 113 m** – ✉ **41600** 12 **C2**

Paris 177 – Blois 59 – Cosne-sur-Loire 74 – Gien 56 – Lamotte-Beuvron 8 – Orléans 44

Syndicat d'initiative, place de la Gare ✆ 02 54 88 76 75

Les Charmilles without rest

D 122-rte Pierrefitte-sur-Sauldre – ✆ 02 54 88 73 55 – www.hotel-les-charmilles.com – hotel.lescharmilles@tele2.fr – Fax 02 54 88 74 55 – Closed February

12 rm – 🛉€ 41 🛉🛉€ 51/54, € 7 – 1 suite

◆ A tasteful, early-20C residence nestled in a park with a pond. You'll sleep in rustic-style rooms, which are spacious and well kept. Home-made pastries.

XX **Le Dahu**

14 r. H. Chapron – ✆ 02 54 88 72 88 – www.restaurantledahu.com – ledahu.restaurant@wanadoo.fr – Fax 02 54 88 21 28 – Closed 9 March-3 April, 12 November-4 December, 5 January-2 February, Tuesday dinner from 1 October to 15 April, Wednesday and Thursday

Rest – Carte € 48/55

◆ In the middle of a lush garden (summer terrace), an old shepherd's dwelling converted into a restaurant. Sitting under the exposed framework of the rustic dining room, you'll really feel in the country!

Look out for red symbols, indicating particularly pleasant establishments.

NOUILHAN – 65 Hautes-Pyrénées – 342 M4 – pop. 178 – alt. 196 m – ✉ 65500 28 A2

Paris 771 – Pau 47 – Tarbes 24 – Toulouse 144

Les 3B
8 rte des Pyrénées, D 935 – ☎ 05 62 96 79 78 – www.hoteldes3b.com – restaurantdes3b@wanadoo.fr – Fax 05 62 31 84 52
7 rm – €40/45 €40/45, ☕ €6 – ½ P €45
Rest – *(closed Wednesday)* Menu (€12), €20/26 – Carte €30/40 (dinner only)
◆ A former family farmstead by the roadside, now converted into a hotel. Comfortable, well-equipped guestrooms; ask for one with a terrace overlooking the rear. Traditional recipes based on market-fresh produce served in the countrified dining room.

LE NOUVION-EN-THIÉRACHE – 02 Aisne – 306 E2 – pop. 2 850 – alt. 185 m – ✉ 02170 37 D1

Paris 198 – Avesnes-sur-Helpe 20 – Guise 21 – Hirson 25 – St-Quentin 49 – Vervins 27

Syndicat d'initiative, Hôtel de Ville ☎ 03 23 97 98 06, Fax 03 23 97 98 04

Paix rm,
37 r. J. Vimont-Vicary – ☎ 03 23 97 04 55 – www.hotel-la-paix.fr – la.paix.pierrart@wanadoo.fr – Fax 03 23 98 98 39 – Closed 17 August-2 September, 26 December-2 January, 15 February-2 March and Sunday evening
15 rm – €60/68 €60/75, ☕ €10 – ½ P €55/78
Rest – *(closed Saturday lunch, Sunday dinner and Monday)*
Menu (€15), €20 (weekdays)/50 – Carte €36/50
◆ A well-kept hotel, whose various bedrooms are fitted out differently. Some have been redecorated in a more modern style. Warm welcome. Bricks, mirrors, pastel tones and ornaments make up the attractive decor of the dining room. Classic menu.

NOUZERINES – 23 Creuse – 325 J2 – see Boussac

NOVALAISE – 73 Savoie – 333 H4 – see Aiguebelette-le-Lac

NOVES – 13 Bouches-du-Rhône – 340 E2 – pop. 4 845 – alt. 42 m – ✉ 13550 Provence 42 E1

Paris 688 – Arles 38 – Avignon 14 – Carpentras 33 – Cavaillon 17 – Marseille 86 – Orange 36

Office de tourisme, place Jean Jaurès ☎ 04 90 92 90 43, Fax 04 90 92 90 43

Auberge de Noves (Robert Lalleman)
rte de Châteaurenard, 2 km via D 28 – ☎ 04 90 24 28 28 – www.aubergedenoves.com – resa@aubergedenoves.com – Fax 04 90 24 28 00
21 rm – €190/400 €190/400, ☕ €22 – 2 suites – ½ P €195/283
Rest – *(closed Sunday and Monday)* Menu (€45), €68/115 – Carte €70/120
Spec. Foie gras de canard. Carré d'agneau aux herbes de la colline. Crème d'enfance au romarin. **Wines** Châteauneuf du Pape, Palette.
◆ This noble 19C residence, nestling in an extensive park, houses spacious rooms with varied decor (including one in the old chapel). Elegant restaurant with a charming terrace. Modern recipes with Provencal flavours; simpler menu at lunchtime.

NOYAL-MUZILLAC – 56 Morbihan – 308 Q9 – pop. 2 193 – alt. 52 m – ✉ 56190 10 C3

Paris 456 – La Baule 44 – St-Nazaire 52 – Vannes 30

Manoir de Bodrevan
to the north-east: 2 km on the D 153 and minor road – ☎ 02 97 45 62 26 – www.manoir-bodrevan.com – contact@manoir-bodrevan.com
6 rm – €77/149 €77/149, ☕ €14 **Rest** – *(pre-book)* Menu €35
◆ A former 16C hunting lodge converted into a charming hotel in a rural setting. Warm welcome, relaxed atmosphere and comfortable, elegant rooms with a personal touch.

NOYALO – 56 Morbihan – **308** O9 – **pop. 685** – ✉ **56450** 9 **A3**

Paris 468 – Rennes 116 – Vannes 15 – La Baule 75

XX **L'Hortensia** with rm — rest, VISA

18 r. Ste-Brigitte – 02 97 43 02 00 – www.lhortensia.com – lhortensia@orange.fr – Fax 02 97 43 67 25 – Closed Monday except July-August

5 rm – †€ 62/76 ††€ 62/76, € 8 – ½ P € 63/70

Rest – Menu € 29/100 bi – Carte € 51/85

◆ 19C stone farmhouse converted into a restaurant. Up-to-the-minute dishes served to a background of modern art with a view of the well-stocked wine cellar. Spacious guest-rooms decorated on the theme of hydrangeas.

NOYAL-SUR-VILAINE – 35 Ille-et-Vilaine – **309** M6 – **see Rennes**

NOYANT-DE-TOURAINE – 37 Indre-et-Loire – **317** M6 – **see Ste-Maure-de-Touraine**

NOYANT-LA-GRAVOYÈRE – 49 Maine-et-Loire – **317** D2 – **pop. 1 767** – **alt. 95 m** – ✉ **49520** 34 **B2**

Paris 321 – Angers 51 – Laval 52 – Nantes 81

XX **Le Petit Manoir** — P VISA

Le Prieuré de St-Blaise – 02 41 61 20 70 – www.lagazettedupetitmanoir.blogspot.com – lepetitmanoir49@hotmail.com – Closed 15-30 July, 15-28 February, Wednesday dinner, Saturday lunch, Sunday dinner, Monday and Tuesday

Rest – *(number of covers limited, pre-book)* Menu € 16 (weekday lunch), € 19/70 – Carte € 23/54

◆ An Anglo-French couple run this restaurant in a building that was first a priory (13C), and then a manor house (17C) and farm. Modern cuisine in a rustic setting.

NOYON – 60 Oise – **305** J3 – **pop. 14 471** – **alt. 52 m** – ✉ **60400** 37 **C2**

Northern France and the Paris Region

Paris 108 – Amiens 67 – Compiègne 29 – Laon 53 – St-Quentin 47 – Soissons 40

Office de tourisme, place Bertrand Labarre 03 44 44 21 88, Fax 03 44 93 08 53

Notre-Dame cathedral ★★ - Ourscamps abbey ★ 5 km by N 32.

Le Cèdre without rest — P VISA AE

8 r. de l'Évêché – 03 44 44 23 24 – www.hotel-lecedre.com – reservation@hotel-lecedre.com – Fax 03 44 09 53 79

35 rm – †€ 66 ††€ 77, € 8

◆ Modern red brick hotel, in keeping with the style of the town, offering warm and successfully-renovated rooms. Most of them offer a view of the cathedral.

XXX **Saint Eloi** with rm — rest, VISA AE

81 bd Carnot – 03 44 44 01 49 – www.hotelsainteloi.fr – reception@hotelsainteloi.fr – Fax 03 44 09 20 90 – Closed 1st-15 August, Saturday lunch and Sunday dinner

23 rm – †€ 60 ††€ 77, € 9 **Rest** – Menu € 38/100 bi – Carte € 74/80

◆ Restaurant with an elegant decor in a lovely 19C manor. Mouldings, warm lighting and comfortable Louis XV-style chairs in the dining room. Guest rooms in an annex.

XX **Dame Journe** — AC VISA

2 bd Mony – 03 44 44 01 33 – www.damejourne.fr – damejourne@wanadoo.fr – Fax 03 44 09 59 68 – Closed 7-20 September, 5-12 January, Sunday dinner, Tuesday dinner, Wednesday dinner, Thursday dinner and Monday

Rest – Menu € 22 (weekday lunch), € 27/39 – Carte € 32/70

◆ This restaurant with a regular clientele has a warm, well-cared-for setting: Louis XVI-style armchairs and wood panelling. Good choice of menus offering traditional cuisine.

NUAILLÉ – 49 Maine-et-Loire – **317** E6 – see Cholet

NUEIL-LES-AUBIERS – 79 Deux-Sèvres – **316** M6 – **pop. 4 492** 38 **B1**
– **alt. 120 m** – ✉ **79250**

Paris 364 – Bressuire 15 – Cholet 29 – Poitiers 100

Le Moulin de la Sorinière rest, rest, VISA AE
southwest: 2 km by D 33, Cerizay road and C 3 – 05 49 72 39 20 – www.hotel-moulin-soriniere.com – moulin-soriniere@wanadoo.fr – Fax 05 49 72 90 78 – Closed 20 April-4 May, 20 October-5 November and 1-6 January
8 rm – €46/50 €52/57, €8
Rest – *(closed Sunday dinner and Monday)* Menu (€15), €26/33
◆ Old 19C mill, restored while preserving its rustic charm. Rooms with a floral theme. A river flows through the kitchen garden. Up-to-date cuisine served in the renovated former barn or on the waterside terrace.

NUITS-ST-GEORGES – 21 Côte-d'Or – **320** J7 – **pop. 5 335** 8 **D1**
– **alt. 243 m** – ✉ **21700** **Burgundy-Jura**

Paris 320 – Beaune 22 – Chalon-sur-Saône 45 – Dijon 22 – Dole 67

Office de tourisme, 3, rue Sonoys 03 80 62 11 17, Fax 03 80 61 30 98

La Gentilhommière VISA AE
13 vallée de la Serrée, Meuilley road, west: 1.5 km – 03 80 61 12 06 – www.lagentilhommiere.fr – contact@lagentilhommiere.fr – Fax 03 80 61 30 33 – Closed mid December-end January
31 rm – €90/200 €90/200, €15
Rest *Le Chef Coq* – *(closed Wednesday lunchtime, Saturday lunchtime and Tuesday)* Menu (€23), €49 (dinner), €57/62 – Carte €65/75 dinner only
◆ A 16C hunting lodge with a recently completed wing. Choose the personalised rooms, which are more comfortable. Some rooms have views of the park and river. Modern cuisine accompanied by fine vintage Burgundy wines at the Chef Coq.

Hostellerie St-Vincent rm, VISA AE
r. Gén. de Gaulle – 03 80 61 14 91 – www.hostellerie-st-vincent.com – hostellerie.st.vincent@club-internet.fr – Fax 03 80 61 24 65 – Closed Christmas holidays and Sunday from December to March
23 rm – €72/95 €79/105, €11
Rest *L'Alambic* – *03 80 61 35 00 (Closed 21-28 December, Sunday dinner in low season and Monday lunch)* Menu €23/46 – Carte €35/65
◆ A recent building with practical, well-soundproofed rooms. Shop selling regional produce. A restaurant, with a superb still, is in a cellar built with stones from the old Beaune prison! Regional cuisine; good selection of local wines.

La Cabotte VISA AE
24 Grand Rue – 03 80 61 20 77 – www.resto.fr/lacabotte/ – la.cabotte@orange.fr – Closed 20-26 April, 26 July-9 August, 3-18 January, Monday lunch, Saturday lunch and Sunday
Rest – *(number of covers limited, pre-book)* Menu €27/39 – Carte €49/63
◆ The dining room has exposed beams and stonework, modern lighting and rustic furniture, with a view of the kitchen. Inspired modern dishes and a good wine list.

in Curtil-Vergy Northwest: 7 km by D 25, D 35 and secondary road – **pop. 104**
– **alt. 350 m** – ✉ **21220**

Manassès without rest VISA AE
r. Guillaume de Tavanes – 03 80 61 43 81 – www.ifrance.com/hotelmanasses – yves.chaley@aliceadsl.fr – Fax 03 80 61 42 79 – Open from March to November
12 rm – €75/100 €75/100, €12
◆ Beautiful regional residence with a collection of rustic furniture and home to a vine museum. The Price of Wales himself was once a guest! Generous breakfast.

NYONS – 26 Drôme – 332 D7 – pop. 7 108 – alt. 271 m – ✉ 26110 44 B3

Provence

Paris 653 – Alès 109 – Gap 106 – Orange 43 – Sisteron 99 – Valence 98

Office de tourisme, place de la Libération ✆ 04 75 26 10 35, Fax 04 75 26 01 57

Old Nyons★: Rue des Grands Forts★ - Pont Roman (old bridge)★.

NYONS

Autiero (Pl.) 2
Chapelle (R. de la) 3
Digue (Promenade de la) 4
Liberté (R. de la) 6
Maupas (R.) 8
Petits Forts (R. des) 10
Randonne (R.) 12
Résistance (R.de la) 14

La Caravelle without rest

8 r. Antignans, by the dyke promenade – ✆ 04 75 26 07 44 – www.lacaravelle-nyons.com – Fax 04 75 26 07 40 – Open 31 March-1 November

11 rm – †€ 79/89 ††€ 79/99, ☕ € 8,50

◆ This handsome 1930s villa boasts unusual architecture and a garden planted with Indian bean trees. Well-kept rooms, some with portholes taken from an old warship.

Une Autre Maison

pl. de la République – ✆ 04 75 26 43 09 – www.uneautremaison.com – nyons@uneautremaison.com – Fax 04 75 26 93 69 – Closed 15 November-8 January d

10 rm – †€ 60/150 ††€ 60/150, ☕ € 15 – ½ P € 80/125

Rest – *(dinner only)* Menu € 38

◆ This 'other house' combines the charm and appeal of the 19C with today's comforts and quest for well-being. Exquisite, individually decorated rooms, enchanting garden and pool. Updated seasonal cuisine served in a faultlessly stylish interior or on the terrace.

Le Petit Caveau

9 r. V. Hugo – ✆ 04 75 26 20 21 – www.petit-caveau.com – Fax 04 75 26 07 28 – Closed 28 December-22 January, Wednesday dinner in low season, Sunday dinner and Monday u

Rest – *(number of covers limited, pre-book)* Menu € 25/55 – Carte € 60/75

◆ Charming vaulted dining room, a stone's throw from the main square, with an intimate and refined atmosphere. Modern cuisine with southern touches. Good choice of wines by the glass.

Gap road by ①: 7 km on D 94 – ✉ 26110 Nyons

La Charrette Bleue

– ✆ 04 75 27 72 33 – www.lacharrettebleue.net – Fax 04 75 27 76 14 – Closed 15 December-31 January, Sunday dinner from October to March, Tuesday from September to June and Wednesday

Rest – Menu € 20 (weekday lunch), € 27/45 – Carte € 33/57

◆ The blue cart perched on the roof of this 18C former post house is impossible to miss! Limestone building, delightful, countrified interior, regional cuisine and a fine wine list.

Orange road by ③ On D 94 – ✉ 26110 Nyons

La Bastide des Monges without rest

4 km – ✆ 04 75 26 99 69 – www.bastidedesmonges.com – lesmonges@wanadoo.fr – Fax 04 75 26 99 70

9 rm – †€ 74/87 ††€ 74/87, ☕ € 10

◆ An 18C former convent converted into a hotel. With prettily decorated rooms in varying styles, overlooking the vineyards or garden. Delightful welcome and lovely terrace.

OBERHASLACH – 67 Bas-Rhin – 315 H5 – pop. 1 773 – alt. 270 m – ✉ 67280 Alsace-Lorraine 1 A1

▶ Paris 482 – Molsheim 16 – Saverne 32 – St-Dié 57 – Strasbourg 45

ℹ Syndicat d'initiative, 22, rue du Nideck ✆ 03 88 50 90 15, Fax 03 88 48 75 24

Hostellerie St-Florent

28 r. Nideck – ✆ 03 88 50 94 10 – www.hostellerie-saint-florent.com – ganjoueff.s@hostellerie-saint-florent.com – Fax 03 88 50 99 61 – Closed Sunday evening and Monday

20 rm – †€ 43/49 ††€ 49, ☕ € 9 – ½ P € 49

Rest – Menu (€ 10), € 21/45 – Carte € 30/50

◆ Alsatian residence offering bright rooms (with sloping ceilings on the third floor) and Louis-Philippe-style furniture. Elegant Rhenish-style dining room with its coffered ceiling and wooden panelling.

OBERLARG – 68 Haut-Rhin – 315 H12 – pop. 150 – alt. 525 m – ✉ 68480 1 A3

▶ Paris 462 – Mulhouse 44 – Belfort 46 – Montbéliard 42

Auberge de la Source de la Largue

19 r. Principale – ✆ 03 89 40 85 10 – Fax 03 89 08 19 86 – Closed Tuesday, Wednesday and Thursday

Rest – Menu (€ 18), € 22 (lunch) – Carte € 23/34

◆ A small village inn run by the same family for four generations. The regional menu includes fried carp, veal brawn and tripe.

OBERNAI – 67 Bas-Rhin – 315 I6 – pop. 10 800 – alt. 185 m – ✉ 67210 Alsace-Lorraine 1 A2

▶ Paris 488 – Colmar 50 – Molsheim 12 – Sélestat 27 – Strasbourg 31

ℹ Office de tourisme, place du Beffroi ✆ 03 88 95 64 13, Fax 03 88 49 90 84

◉ Place du Marché★★ - Town hall★ **H** - Chapelle Tower ★ **L** - Former covered wheat market ★ **D** - Old houses★.

Plan on next page

Le Parc

169 rte Ottrott, west on D 426 – ✆ 03 88 95 50 08 – www.hotel-du-parc.com – info@hotel-du-parc.com – Fax 03 88 95 37 29 – Closed 1st-13 July

56 rm – †€ 125/150 ††€ 135/250, ☕ € 19 – 6 suites

Rest *La Table* – *(closed 15 December-15 January, Sunday dinner, Monday and lunch except Sunday)* Menu € 50, € 55/75 – Carte € 60/90

Rest *Stub* – *(closed Sunday and Monday) (lunch only)* Carte € 25/45

◆ This large, half-timbered residence offers rooms of varying levels of comfort and style. Fitness centre, spa, world massages (Alsace, Latin America, India). A refined atmosphere and classic food are to be found at La Table. Alsatian specialities at the Stub.

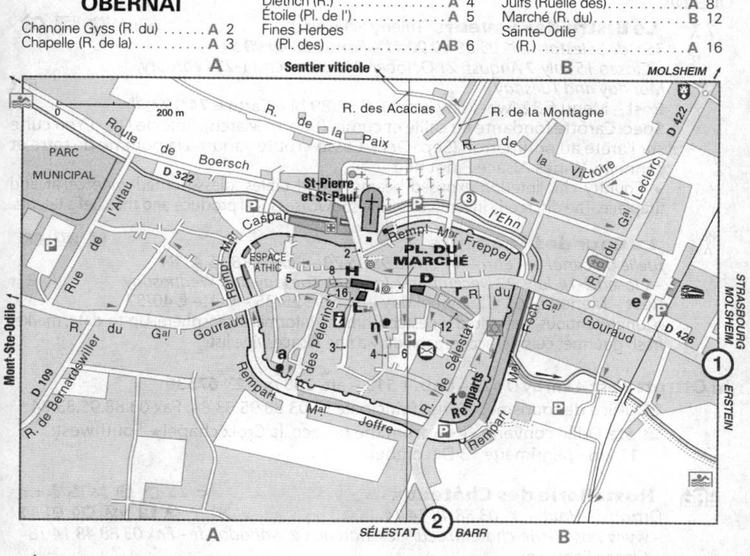

A la Cour d'Alsace

3 r. Gail – ☎ 03 88 95 07 00 – www.cour-alsace.com – info@cour-alsace.com – Fax 03 88 95 19 21 – Closed 24 December-26 January

49 rm – €79/146 €128/189, ☕ €17 – 4 suites — A **a**

Rest *Jardin des Remparts* – *(closed 23 December-6 March, 27 July-28 August, Thursday lunch, Friday lunch, Saturday lunch, Sunday dinner, Monday, Tuesday and Wednesday)* Menu €49/92 – Carte €44/82

Rest *Caveau de Gail* – *(closed Thursday dinner)* Menu (€27), €31 – Carte €37/56

◆ Former property of the Barons of Gail with a central courtyard and wing. Comfortable rooms decorated in a soothing monochrome of beiges. Well-being centre and spa. Stylish dining room and reinvented up-to-date cuisine. Regional cuisine at the Caveau de Gail.

Le Colombier without rest

6 r. Dietrich – ☎ 03 88 47 63 33 – www.hotel-colombier.com – info@hotel-colombier.com – Fax 03 88 47 63 39

44 rm – €88/142 €88/142, ☕ €11 – 8 suites — A **n**

◆ The regional style façade of this house in the heart of the historic town hides a distinctly contemporary look. Some rooms have balconies.

Les Jardins d'Adalric without rest

19 r. Mar. Koenig, via ① – ☎ 03 88 47 64 47 – www.jardins-adalric.com – jardins.adalric@wanadoo.fr – Fax 03 88 49 91 80

46 rm – €75/95 €85/95, ☕ €12

◆ Modern building, away from the town centre, with well-kept rooms. Plush breakfast room with bay window, extended by a poolside terrace. Pool; garden.

La Fourchette des Ducs (Nicolas Stamm)

6 r. de la Gare – ☎ 03 88 48 33 38 – www.lesgrandestablesdumonde.com – Fax 03 88 95 44 39 – Closed 28 July-12 August, 1st-8 January, 23 February-8 March, Sunday dinner, Monday and lunch except Sunday — B **e**

Rest – *(number of covers limited, pre-book)* Menu €89/120 – Carte €121/164

Spec. Duo de langoustines au caviar d'aquitaine, mousse de chou-fleur. Pigeonneau d'alsace, suprêmes et cuisses, réduction au chocolat. Ganache aux épices et chocolat, crème moka et caramel mou. **Wines** Riesling, Pinot gris.

◆ Inventive cuisine served in two rooms: one with marquetry by Charles Spindler and lighting by René Lalique for winter, and for summer, a modern Baccarat room with internal courtyard.

Le Bistro des Saveurs (Thierry Schwartz)
35 r. de Sélestat – ✆ 03 88 49 90 41 – Fax 03 88 49 90 51
– Closed 15 July-7 August, 21 October-8 November, 11-28 February, Monday and Tuesday B t
Rest – Menu € 32 (weekday lunch), € 62/89 bi – Carte € 74/127
Spec. Carotte fondante au caillé et cumin (Sep. to March). Sole de l'Île d'Yeu cuite sur l'arête au potimarron (Sep.-Oct.). Casse-croûte yaourt à la pomme de terre et cannelle. **Wines** Alsace Pinot noir.
◆ Country chic interior: exposed beams, round tables, glass-fronted wine cellar and fireplace. The discreetly inventive cuisine showcases local produce and the chef's talents.

La Cour des Tanneurs
ruelle du canal de l'Ehn – ✆ 03 88 95 15 70 – Fax 03 88 95 43 84
– Closed 2-14 July, 22 December-2 January, Tuesday and Wednesday B r
Rest – Menu (€ 16), € 20 (weekday lunch), € 25/35 – Carte € 40/52
◆ Unpretentious, well cared for establishment. Informal atmosphere. Up-to-date, market fresh gourmet cuisine, accompanied by a fine Alsace wine list.

in Ottrott West: 4 km by D 426 – pop. 1 513 – alt. 268 m – ✉ 67530
Office de tourisme, 46, rue Principale ✆ 03 88 95 83 84, Fax 03.88.95.83.84
Ste-Odile convent: ✳★★ from the terrace, la Croix chapel★ Southwest: 11 km - pilgrimage 13 December.

Hostellerie des Châteaux rm,
Ottrott-le-Haut – ✆ 03 88 48 14 14
– www.hostellerie-chateaux.eu – leschateaux@wanadoo.fr – Fax 03 88 48 14 18
– Closed February
67 rm – € 120/125 € 125/520, € 18 – ½ P € 133/220
Rest – *(closed 26 July-10 August, Sunday dinner, Tuesday lunch and Monday in low season)* Menu € 38 (lunch), € 59/90 – Carte € 59/98
◆ This hostelry is ideal for those in need of a little pampering: spa and beauty centre, stunning indoor pool. All wood, Alsace inspired rooms. Classic fare served in a restaurant made up of three low-key, snug dining rooms.

Beau Site
Ottrott-le-Haut – ✆ 03 88 48 14 30 – www.hotel-beau-site.fr – lebeausiteott@wanadoo.fr – Fax 03 88 48 14 18 – Closed February
18 rm – € 78/98 € 98/170, € 15 – ½ P € 99/135
Rest – *(closed 5-19 July, Sunday dinner, Monday and Tuesday)*
Menu € 21 (weekdays)/54 – Carte € 31/69
◆ Large half-timbered house with an oriel window. Comfortable rooms, some with balconies. Those on the top floor are spacious and individually decorated. This luxury winstub, adorned by works by Spindler, focuses on regional delicacies.

Le Clos des Délices rm,
17 rte Klingenthal, 1 km northwest on the D 426 – ✆ 03 88 95 81 00
– www.leclosdesdelices.com – contact@leclosdesdelices.com
– Fax 03 88 95 97 71
22 rm – € 99/119 € 99/160, € 16 – 1 suite
Rest – *(closed Sunday dinner)* Menu € 29 (weekday lunch), € 40/69
– Carte € 45/74
◆ This lovely ivy clad inn by the roadside boasts individually decorated, well-soundproofed rooms. Terrace overlooking the grounds. Small spa. Light, spacious restaurant overlooking woodland. Discreetly creative classic menu.

À l'Ami Fritz rm, rm,
Ottrott-le-Haut – ✆ 03 88 95 80 81 – www.amifritz.com – ami-fritz@wanadoo.fr
– Fax 03 88 95 84 85 – Closed 11-31 January
21 rm – € 80/110 € 80/135, € 13 – 1 suite – ½ P € 79/115
Rest – *(closed 1st-10 July, 11-31 January and Wednesday)*
Menu € 26/63 – Carte € 36/56
◆ Regional style construction offering comfortable rooms with personal touches. The establishment's name recalls Erckmann Chatrian's novel, as well as the owners' name. Inviting restaurant with a winstub feel, serving tasty regional cuisine.

Aux Chants des Oiseaux without rest
Ottrott-le-Haut – ✆ 03 88 95 87 39 – www.chantsdesoiseaux.com – ami-fritz@wanadoo.fr – Fax 03 88 95 84 85 – Closed 1-12 July and 11 January-4 February
16 rm – †€ 77/98 ††€ 77/106, ☕ € 13
◆ Regional style house in the middle of the countryside. Pleasant colourful rooms. Wainscoted, timber-roofed breakfast room and poolside terrace.

Domaine Le Moulin rm, rest,
Klingenthal road, north-west: 1 km on D 426
– ✆ 03 88 95 87 33 – www.domaine-le-moulin.com – domaine.le.moulin@wanadoo.fr – Fax 03 88 95 98 03 – Closed 23 December-20 January
23 rm – †€ 60 ††€ 72/80, ☕ € 14 – 3 suites – ½ P € 67/76
Rest – *(closed Saturday lunch, Sunday dinner and Monday lunch)*
Menu (€ 16), € 25 bi/57 – Carte € 25/50
◆ The Wine Route passes by this hotel, behind which lies an immense park with a river and small lake. Snug rooms and, in the wing, spacious more modern duplex apartments. Regional menu in the restaurant and terrace facing the forest.

OBERSTEIGEN – 67 Bas-Rhin – **315** H5 – ✉ **67710** Alsace-Lorraine 1 **A1**

Paris 466 – Molsheim 27 – Sarrebourg 32 – Saverne 16 – Strasbourg 39 – Wasselonne 13

Mossig Valley ★ East: 2 km.

Hostellerie Belle Vue rest, rest,
16 rte de Dabo – ✆ 03 88 87 32 39
– www.hostellerie-belle-vue.com – hostellerie.belle-vue@wanadoo.fr
– Fax 03 88 87 37 77 – Open 4 April-1 January and closed Sunday dinner and Monday in low season except bank holidays
25 rm – †€ 75/90 ††€ 80/90, ☕ € 10 – 2 suites – ½ P € 70/80
Rest – Menu (€ 18), € 25/40 – Carte € 30/55
◆ This hostelry, in the heart of Saverne forest, offers a magnificent view of the valley. Comfortable rooms with period furnishings. Wellness centre, garden and pool. Large, regional style dining room and flower-decked summer terrace. Traditional menu.

OBERSTEINBACH – 67 Bas-Rhin – **315** K2 – **pop. 225** – **alt. 239 m** – ✉ **67510** Alsace-Lorraine 1 **B1**

Paris 458 – Bitche 22 – Haguenau 35 – Strasbourg 68 – Wissembourg 25

Anthon with rm
40 r. Principale – ✆ 03 88 09 55 01 – www.restaurant-anthon.fr – info@restaurant-anthon.fr – Fax 03 88 09 50 52 – Closed January, Tuesday and Wednesday
10 rm – †€ 48/65 ††€ 65, ☕ € 10 – ½ P € 75
Rest – Menu € 25/65 – Carte € 31/61
◆ A half-timbered house (1860) with an elegant, round dining room, facing the garden. Local cuisine. Redecorated guestrooms, including two that have beds set into wooden alcoves.

OBJAT – 19 Corrèze – **329** J4 – **pop. 3 400** – **alt. 131 m** – ✉ **19130** 24 **B3**

Paris 467 – Brive-la-Gaillarde 21 – Limoges 79 – Tulle 45 – Uzerche 30

Office de tourisme, place Charles de Gaulle ✆ 05 55 25 96 73, Fax 05 55 25 97 45

De France
av. G. Clemenceau, (towards the station) – ✆ 05 55 25 80 38
– http://pagesperso-orange.fr/hoteldefrance.objat – hoteldefrance.objat@wanadoo.fr – Fax 05 55 25 91 87 – Closed 15 September-5 October, 23 December-2 January and Saturday
27 rm – †€ 35 ††€ 45, ☕ € 7 – ½ P € 42
Rest – *(closed Sunday dinner and Saturday)* Menu € 14 (weekdays)/34 – Carte € 30/40
◆ Charming welcome in this family hotel near the station. The rooms are simple and functional and are progressively being equipped with air-conditioning. Renovated restaurant opening onto an inner courtyard. Regional specialities on the menu.

La Tête de L'Art
53 av. J. Lascaux – 05 55 25 50 42 – latetedelart@wanadoo.fr – Closed 23 June-9 July, 2-5 November, 3-13 February, Tuesday dinner and Wednesday
Rest – Menu (€ 15), € 18 (weekday lunch), € 28/40 – Carte € 28/40
◆ With a history of combining art and taste, this more simple family-run restaurant organises exhibitions of paintings and sculptures by local artists. Traditionally inspired cuisine.

OFFRANVILLE – 76 Seine-Maritime – **304** G2 – **see Dieppe**

OGNES – 02 Aisne – **306** B5 – **see Chauny**

L'OIE – 85 Vendée – **316** J7 – **pop. 1 045** – **alt. 102 m** – ✉ **85140** 34 **B3**
Paris 394 – Cholet 40 – Nantes 62 – Niort 94 – La Roche-sur-Yon 29

Le Grand Turc rest, rm,
33 r. Nationale – 02 51 66 08 74 – www.hotel-legrandturc.fr – legrandturc@wanadoo.fr – Fax 02 51 66 14 13 – Closed 24 December-8 January
19 rm – €54 €68, € 8
Rest – *(Closed Saturday dinner and Sunday)* Menu € 19/38 – Carte € 37/66
◆ The sign depicts Mameluke Amakuc, chief guard of Napoleon I when the latter visited the inn. The rooms behind are functional and well kept. One room is devoted to traditional fare, while the other features a buffet and dish of the day.

OINVILLE-SOUS-AUNEAU – 28 Eure-et-Loir – **311** G5 – **pop. 313** – **alt. 150 m** – ✉ **28700** 12 **C1**
Paris 77 – Chartres 20 – Montigny-le-Bretonneux 50 – Orléans 88

Caroline Lethuillier without rest
2 r. des Prunus, in Cherville, 2 km west – 02 37 31 72 80 – www.cherville.com – info@cherville.com – Fax 02 37 31 38 56
4 rm – €48/53 €58/62
◆ The rooms in the loft of this old farmhouse, dating back to 1800, have red floor tiles, beams, themed decoration and family furniture. Delicious homemade breakfasts.

OISLY – 41 Loir-et-Cher – **318** F7 – **pop. 333** – **alt. 120 m** – ✉ **41700** 11 **A1**
Paris 208 – Tours 61 – Blois 27 – Châteauroux 80 – Romorantin-Lanthenay 32

St-Vincent
in the village – 02 54 79 50 04 – Fax 02 54 79 50 04 – Closed 2-25 January, Tuesday except lunch from Easter to September and Wednesday
Rest – Menu € 25/43 – Carte € 47/60
◆ The contemporary cuisine attracts gourmets to this country-style restaurant with its sign depicting the patron saint of winegrowers. Tasting of local wines.

OIZON – 18 Cher – **323** L2 – **pop. 734** – **alt. 230 m** – ✉ **18700** 12 **C2**
Paris 179 – Bourges 54 – Cosne-sur-Loire 35 – Gien 29 – Orléans 66 – Salbris 38 – Vierzon 50

Les Rives de l'Oizenotte
at Nohant lake, east: 1 km – 02 48 58 06 20 – www.lesrivesdeloizenotte.fr – oizenotte.g@infonie.fr – Fax 02 48 58 28 97 – Closed 2-8 September, 21 December-17 January, Monday and Tuesday
Rest – *(number of covers limited, pre-book)* Menu € 19 bi (weekdays)/29 bi
◆ Renovated regional restaurant beside a lake with a pretty waterside terrace. Modern rooms with pale wood panelling, and décor on a fishing theme.

OLEMPS – 12 Aveyron – **338** H4 – **see Rodez**

OLÉRON (ÎLE) – 17 Charente-Maritime – **324** C4 – **see île d'Oléron**

OLIVET – 45 Loiret – **318** I4 – see Orléans

LES OLLIÈRES-SUR-EYRIEUX – 07 Ardèche – **331** J5 – pop. 883 – alt. 200 m – ✉ 07360 44 **B3**

Paris 593 – Le Cheylard 28 – Lamastre 33 – Montélimar 53 – Privas 19 – Valence 34

Office de tourisme, grande rue ✆ 04 75 66 30 21, Fax 04 75 66 20 31

Le Truffolier AC VISA

D 120 – ✆ 04 75 66 20 32 – www.letruffolier.net – letruffolier@wanadoo.fr – Fax 04 75 66 20 63 – Closed 8-16 June, 28 September-13 October, 10 November-15 March, Monday except lunch in July-August and Sunday dinner except bank holidays

Rest – Menu € 15/36 – Carte € 28/54

◆ A rustic dining room serving traditional, unpretentious cuisine; simple hospitality in this family inn in the Eyrieux valley.

OLMETO – 2A Corse-du-Sud – **345** C9 – see Corse

OLMETO PLAGE – 2A Corse-du-Sud – **345** C9 – see Olmeto

OLORON-STE-MARIE – 64 Pyrénées-Atlantiques – **342** I5 – pop. 10 992 – alt. 224 m – ✉ 64400 Atlantic Coast 3 **B3**

Paris 809 – Bayonne 105 – Mont-de-Marsan 101 – Pau 34

Office de tourisme, allée du Comte de Tréville ✆ 05 59 39 98 00, Fax 05 59 39 43 97

Portal★★ of Ste-Marie church.

OLORON-STE-MARIE

Barthou (R. Louis) . . . . B
Bellevue (Promenade) . . . . . B 2
Biscondau (R. du) . . . . B 3
Bordelongue (R. A.) . . . . B 4
Camou (R.) . . . . B
Casamayor-Dufaur (R.) . . . . A 5
Cathédrale (R. de la) . . . . . . A 6
Dalmais (R.) . . . . B 7
Derême (Av. Tristan) . . . . . . A 8
Despourrins (R.) . . . . A 9
Gabe (Pl. Amédée) . . . . B 10
Gambetta (Pl.) . . . . B 12
Jaca (Pl.) . . . . A 13
Jeliote (R.) . . . . B 14
Lattre-de-Tassigny (Av. du Mar.de) . . . . A 23
Mendiondou (Pl. Léon) . . . . B 15
Moureu (Av. Charles et Henri) . . . A 16
Oustalots (Pl. des) . . . . A 18
Pyrénées (Bd des) . . . . A 19
Résistance (Pl. de la) . . . . . B 20
St-Grat (R.) . . . . A 22
Toulet (R. Paul-Jean) . . . . . . A 24
Vigny (Av. Alfred de) . . . . . . A 26
4-Septembre (Av. du) . . . . . . A 28
14-Juillet (Av. du) . . . . A 30

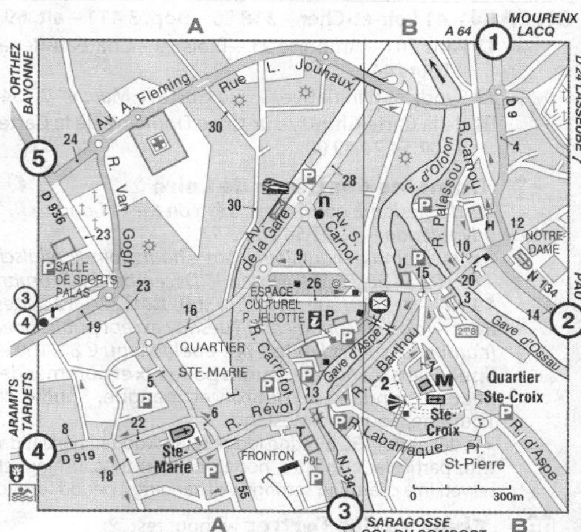

Alysson VISA

bd des Pyrénées ✉ 64400 – ✆ 05 59 39 70 70 – www.alysson-hotel.fr – alysson.hotel@wanadoo.fr – Fax 05 59 39 24 47 A **r**

47 rm – †€ 72/102 ††€ 80/110, ☕ € 12 – 1 suite – ½ P € 68/83

Rest – *(closed 19 December-4 January, 20-28 February, Friday dinner from October to April, Saturday except dinner from May to September)* Menu € 22 (weekday lunch), € 27/45 – Carte € 55/70

◆ A modern hotel with spacious, functional rooms (some with hydromassage baths) and well-equipped conference rooms. Light wood and contemporary furniture in the vast dining room opening onto a garden.

La Paix without rest

24 av. Sadi-Carnot – ✆ 05 59 39 02 63 – www.hotel-oloron.com – hoteloloron@aliceadsl.fr – Fax 05 59 39 98 20 A **n**

24 rm – †€ 48/53 ††€ 48/63, ☕ € 8

◆ This family-run establishment, in the railway station area, has been renovated. Cheerful, colourful and very well-kept rooms.

OMIÉCOURT – **80 Somme** – **301** K9 – **pop. 235** – **alt. 85 m** – ✉ **80320** 37 **B2**

Paris 128 – Amiens 64 – Saint-Quentin 39 – Compiègne 53 – Tergnier 63

Château d'Omiécourt without rest

4 r. du Bosquet – ✆ 03 22 83 01 75 – www.chateau-omiecourt.com – thezy@terre-net.fr – Fax 03 22 83 09 56

5 rm ☕ – †€ 70/80 ††€ 95/105

◆ Guests are welcomed by the sixth generation of owners of this family château. Personalised rooms furnished with antiques. Driving range in the grounds and counter-current pool.

OMONVILLE-LA-PETITE – **50 Manche** – **303** A1 – **pop. 132** – **alt. 33 m** – ✉ **50440** 32 **A1**

Paris 380 – Barneville-Carteret 45 – Cherbourg 25 – Nez de Jobourg 7 – St-Lô 101

La Fossardière without rest

– ✆ 02 33 52 19 83 – www.lafossardiere.fr – Fax 02 33 52 73 49 – Open 15 March-15 November

8 rm – †€ 61 ††€ 74, ☕ € 9

◆ Several houses with refurbished rooms in a pleasant hamlet near Omonville, the village where Jacques Prévert is buried. Breakfast is served in the former bakery.

ONZAIN – **41 Loir-et-Cher** – **318** E6 – **pop. 3 411** – **alt. 69 m** – ✉ **41150** 11 **A1**

Paris 201 – Amboise 21 – Blois 19 – Château-Renault 24 – Montrichard 23 – Tours 44

Syndicat d'initiative, 3, rue Gustave Marc ✆ 02 54 20 78 52

de la Carte Chouzy-sur-Cisse Domaine de la Carte, SW : 6 km on D 952, ✆ 02 54 20 49 00

Domaine des Hauts de Loire

Rte de Mesland, north-west: 3 km on the D 1 and private road – ✆ 02 54 20 72 57 – www.domainehautsloire.com – hauts-loire@relaischateaux.com – Fax 02 54 20 77 32 – Closed 1st December-20 February

19 rm – †€ 130/300 ††€ 130/300, ☕ € 22 – 12 suites – ½ P € 210/550

Rest – *(closed Monday and Tuesday except public holidays) (number of covers limited, pre-book)* Menu € 80/160 – Carte € 100/160

Spec. Filets d'anguille, jeunes poireaux et pommes de terre aux aromates. Pigeonneau au fondant de potiron et mangue. Soufflé chaud au citron vert. **Wines** Touraine, Touraine Mesland.

◆ A delightful 19C hunting lodge set in wooded parkland with a lake. Personalised rooms with particular character, hot-air balloon trips, fishing, etc. Appetising modern cuisine served in a charming setting: wall hangings, period furniture, beams and fireplace.

Château des Tertres without rest

11 bis r. de Meuves – ✆ 02 54 20 83 88 – www.chateau-tertres.com – contact@chateau-tertres.fr – Fax 02 54 20 89 21 – Open 1 April-18 October

18 rm – †€ 68 ††€ 72/80, ☕ € 10

◆ A Second Empire country seat in a magnificent 5-ha park. Rooms are either Napoleon III or Louis-Philippe in style; those in a nearby cottage are original and contemporary in design.

OPIO – **06 Alpes-Maritimes** – **341** C5 – **pop. 2 070** – **alt. 300 m** – ✉ **06650** 42 **E2**

Paris 911 – Cannes 17 – Digne-les-Bains 125 – Draguignan 74 – Grasse 9 – Nice 31

Syndicat d'initiative, route Village ✆ 04 93 77 23 18

Le Mas des Géraniums

1 km at San Peyre, east on D 7 – ✆ 04 93 77 23 23 – www.le-mas-des-geranium.com – info@le-mas-des-geraniums.com – Fax 04 93 77 76 05 – Closed 2 November-18 December, Tuesday and Wednesday

Rest – Menu € 18 (weekday lunch), € 25/45 – Carte € 42/65

◆ Traditional cuisine served in a cosy, rustic dining room or on the shady, flower-decked terrace with a view of the old village. Arbour, tall palm tree and olive trees in the garden.

ORADOUR-SUR-GLANE – 87 Haute-Vienne – 325 D5 – pop. 2 025 – alt. 275 m – ✉ 87520 Dordogne-Berry-Limousin 24 B2

Paris 408 – Angoulême 85 – Bellac 26 – Confolens 33 – Limoges 25 – Nontron 66

Office de tourisme, place du Champ de Foire ✆ 05 55 03 13 73, Fax 05 55 03 13 73

"Martyred village "whose inhabitants were slaughtered in June 1944.

La Glane

8 pl. Gén. de Gaulle – ✆ 05 55 03 10 43 – www.hotel-de-la-glane.oradoursurglane.com – Fax 05 55 03 15 42

10 rm – †€ 44 ††€ 46, ☕ € 8 – ½ P € 46

Rest – *(closed 15 December-28 February and Saturday)*

Menu (€ 13), € 15/29 – Carte € 25/50

◆ In the busy central square of the rebuilt village, hotel offering small, modest but well kept rooms. Guests eat shoulder to shoulder in this rustic restaurant offering starter and dessert buffets and simple grill-based main courses.

Le Milord

10 av. du 10-Juin – ✆ 05 55 03 10 35 – www.hotel-le-milord-oradoursurglane.fr – Fax 05 55 03 21 76 – Closed Sunday dinner, Monday dinner, Tuesday dinner and Wednesday dinner

Rest – Menu € 13 (weekdays)/41 – Carte € 27/40

◆ The brasserie-style dining room has beige velvet banquettes and simply decorated tables set close together. Simple but generous traditional cuisine.

ORADOUR-SUR-VAYRES – 87 Haute-Vienne – 325 C6 – pop. 1 530 – alt. 322 m – ✉ 87150 24 A2

Paris 433 – Limoges 40 – Saint-Junien 23 – Panazol 45 – Isle 36

Office de tourisme, 3, avenue du 8 Mai 1945 ✆ 05 55 78 22 21, Fax 05 55 78 27 32

La Bergerie des Chapelles

– ✆ 05 55 78 29 91 – www.domainedeschapelles.com – info@domainedeschapelles.com – Fax 05 55 71 70 19 – Closed in November and in January

7 rm – †€ 60/85 ††€ 70/95, ☕ € 9 – ½ P € 70/86

Rest – *(closed Sunday dinner and Monday off season)* Carte € 18/38

◆ A converted sheep barn in the middle of the country, now quiet and cosy accommodation with impressive bathrooms and terraces overlooking the park. Contemporary cuisine served in a modernised rustic backdrop of dark walls adorned with large paintings.

ORANGE – 84 Vaucluse – 332 B9 – pop. 29 000 – alt. 97 m – ✉ 84100 Provence 42 E1

Paris 655 – Alès 84 – Avignon 31 – Carpentras 24 – Nîmes 56

Office de tourisme, 5, cours Aristide Briand ✆ 04 90 34 70 88, Fax 04 90 34 99 62

d'Orange Route de Camaret, 4 km on the Mt-Ventoux road, ✆ 04 90 34 34 04

Théâtre antique★★★ - Arc de Triomphe★★ - Colline St-Eutrope ≤★.

ORANGE

Arc de Triomphe (Av. de l') AY
Artaud (Av. A.) . . . . ABY
Blanc (R. A.) . . . . BZ
Briand (Crs A.) . . . . AYZ
Caristie (R.) . . . . BY 2
Châteauneuf (R. de) . . . . . BZ 3
Clemenceau (Pl. G.) . . . . . BY 4
Concorde (R. de la) . . . . . . BY
Contrescarpe (R. de la) . . . . BY
Daladier (Bd E.) . . . . ABY
Fabre (Av. H.) . . . . BY
Frères-Mounet (Pl. des) . . . BY 5
Guillaume-le-Taciturne (Av.) . . . . BY
Herbes (Pl. aux) . . . . BY 7
Lacour (R.) . . . . AY
Leclerc (Av. Gén.) . . . . BZ
Levade (R. de la) . . . . BY
Mistral (Av. F.) . . . . BY 9
Noble (R. du) . . . . ABY
Pourtoules (Cours) . . . . BZ
Pourtoules (R.) . . . . BZ 12
Princes d'Orange-Nassau (Mtée des) . . . . AZ
République (Pl. de la) . . . . BY 14
République (R. de la) . . . . BY 16
Roch (R. Madeleine) . . . . . BZ 18
St-Clement (R.) . . . . AZ
St-Florent (R.) . . . . BY 20
St-Jean (R.) . . . . AY
St-Martin (R.) . . . . AY 22
Tanneurs (R. des) . . . . AY 24
Thermes (Av. des) . . . . AZ
Tourre (R. de) . . . . AZ 26
Victor-Hugo (R.) . . . . AY

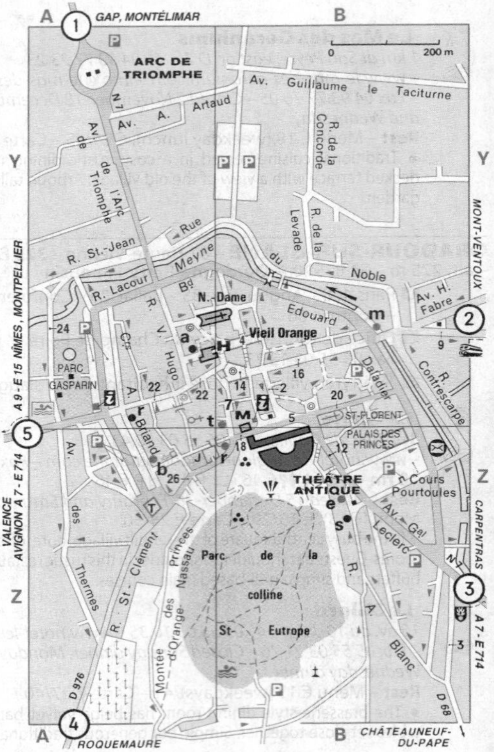

Park Inn rm, VISA MC AE

rte Caderousse, on the ⑤ – ✆ 04 90 34 24 10 – www.orange.parkinn.fr – info.orange@rezidorparkinn.com – Fax 04 90 34 85 48

99 rm – †€ 89/145 ††€ 89/145, ☕ € 12 **Rest** – Menu € 24/29 – Carte € 35/60

◆ The Provençal decorated rooms, attractive sitting room and excellent service of this modern establishment appeals both to a business clientele and to tourists. Sundrenched cuisine served on a poolside terrace in summer.

Arène rm, VISA MC AE

pl. Langes – ✆ 04 90 11 40 40 – www.hotel-arene.fr – reservation@hotel-arene.fr – Fax 04 90 11 40 45 AY **a**

35 rm – †€ 56/145 ††€ 76/170, ☕ € 8

Rest – *(closed dinner except Wednesday and Sunday)* Menu (€ 12) – Carte € 18/25

◆ This impressive edifice built in the 1800s stands on a pedestrian square shaded by plane trees. Provençal inspired or 'executive' (more contemporary, comfortable and well appointed) rooms. A choice of regional or Italian menus in these two restaurants.

Le Glacier without rest VISA MC AE

46 cours A. Briand – ✆ 04 90 34 02 01 – www.le-glacier.com – info@le-glacier.com – Fax 04 90 51 13 80 – Closed 19 December-4 January, Friday, Saturday and Sunday from November to February AY **r**

28 rm – †€ 49/89 ††€ 49/130, ☕ € 8

◆ A strong family atmosphere is evident in this hotel passed down from father to son for the past three generations. Small air-conditioned bedrooms (except three) gradually being renovated in Provençal style.

St-Jean without rest
1 cours Pourtoules – ✆ 04 90 51 15 16 – www.hotelsaint-jean.com – hotel.saint-jean@wanadoo.fr – Fax 04 90 11 05 45 – Closed 20 December-4 January
22 rm – †€ 55/65 ††€ 55/80, ☕ € 7 BZ **s**
◆ Former 17C post house backing onto St Eutrope Hill in the heart of the Roman city. Unusual sitting room hewn out of the rock and rooms of varying sizes.

Justin de Provence without rest
chemin Mercadier – ✆ 04 90 69 57 94 – www.justin-de-provence.com – contact@justin-de-provence.com – Fax 04 90 29 67 43
5 rm ☕ – †€ 90/180 ††€ 110/195
◆ This quintessential Provençal farmhouse has a guesthouse ambience. It boasts opulent Art Deco or nostalgic guestrooms, a snug sitting room and a bistro worthy of Pagnol.

Le Parvis
55 cours Pourtoules – ✆ 04 90 34 82 00 – le-parvis2@wanadoo.fr – Fax 04 90 51 18 19 – Closed 8 November-1st December, 10 January-1st February, Sunday and Monday BZ **e**
Rest – Menu (€ 12), € 18 (lunch), € 27/47
◆ Warm colours, beams and contemporary art create a tasteful atmosphere in this restaurant. Gourmet cuisine with a Provençal note, local vegetables and spices.

Le Monteverdi
443 bd E. Daladier – ✆ 04 90 29 53 77 – monteverdi84000@gmail.com – Fax 04 90 29 53 77 – Closed Saturday lunch BY **m**
Rest – Menu € 15 (weekday lunch)/25 – Carte € 30/47
◆ The modern innovative decor matches the cuisine. The chef concocts inventive updated dishes using high quality produce. Tables d'hôte and sitting room.

Le Forum
3 r. de Mazeau – ✆ 04 90 34 01 09 – Fax 04 90 34 01 09 – Closed 20 August-3 September, 23 February-5 January, Saturday lunch, Sunday dinner and Monday
Rest – Menu € 19 (weekday lunch), € 22/38 – Carte € 24/45 BY **t**
◆ A delightful little restaurant tucked away in a narrow lane near the antique theatre. Elegant Provençal style decor and a traditional repertory of regional inspiration.

Alons'O Bistro
58 cours Aristide-Briand – ✆ (00-04) 04 90 29 69 27 – alonsobistro@orange.fr – Fax 04 90 70 05 62 – Closed Wednesday dinner from September to April, Thursday except dinner from May to August and Saturday lunch AZ **b**
Rest – Menu (€ 19 bi), € 28
◆ Despite its unassuming entrance, this restaurant hides a vibrant, colourful Provençal interior. Local produce takes pride of place on the concise, updated menu.

La Rom'Antique
5 pl. Sylvain – ✆ 04 90 51 67 06 – cedricbremond@aol.com – Fax 04 90 51 67 06 – Closed 18 October-2 November, 1-25 January, Sunday dinner from October to May, Saturday lunch and Monday BZ **r**
Rest – Menu (€ 15), € 20/38 – Carte € 35/45 dinner only
◆ Sundrenched menu and a mouth-watering choice of desserts in this small, rustic-modern establishment. Slate of lunchtime specials. The terrace overlooks the antique theatre.

via ① N 7 and secondary road: 4 km – ✉ 84100 Orange

Le Mas des Aigras - Table du Verger with rm
Chemin des Aigras, (Russamp Est) – ✆ 04 90 34 81 01 rm,
– www.masdesaigras.com – mas-des-aigras@orange.fr – Fax 04 90 34 05 66 – Closed 19 October-5 November., 8-25 February, Tuesday and Wednesday from October to March
10 rm – †€ 75/120 ††€ 75/120, ☕ € 13 – ½ P € 81/103
Rest – *(closed Monday lunch, Wednesday lunch and Saturday lunch from April to September) (number of covers limited, pre-book)*
Menu € 20 (weekday lunch), € 30/55 – Carte € 52/74
◆ Pleasant stone farmhouse set amid vineyards and fields. The chef rustles up, partly in front of diners, tasty recipes based on organic produce. Tasteful decor and attractive terrace. The rooms, decked in Provençal colours, are undergoing renovation.

in Sérignan-du-Comtat **by ①, N 7 and D 976: 8 km – pop. 2 362 – alt. 80 m – ✉ 84830**

XXX ✿ **Le Pré du Moulin** (Pascal Alonso) with rm
rte Ste-Cécile les Vignes – ✆ 04 90 70 14 55 rest, VISA MC
– www.predumoulin.com – info@predumoulin.com – Fax 04 90 70 05 62 – Closed Sunday dinner, Tuesday lunch and Monday from mid-September to May and Monday lunch and Tuesday lunch from May to mid-September
11 rm – †€ 110/230 ††€ 110/230, ☕ € 15 – ½ P € 115/170
Rest – Menu € 39/79 – Carte € 74/94
Spec. Raviole ouverte aux truffes du Tricastin et artichauts sautés (Nov. to March). Pigeon farci au chou et foie gras. Soufflé chaud au Grand Marnier. **Wines** Côtes du Rhône.
◆ A mill and a school in former times, this village house exades country charm. Tempting market-fresh dishes steeped in the flavours of Provence. Shaded terrace. Spacious, peaceful guestrooms of various sizes and styles.

ORBEC – 14 Calvados – 303 O5 – pop. 2 400 – alt. 110 m – ✉ 14290 33 C2
Normandy

Paris 173 – L'Aigle 38 – Alençon 80 – Argentan 53 – Bernay 18 – Caen 85 – Lisieux 21
Office de tourisme, 6, rue Grande ✆ 02 31 32 56 68, Fax 02 31 32 04 37
Old manor ★.

XXX **Au Caneton** VISA MC AE
32 r. Grande – ✆ 02 31 32 73 32 – Fax 02 31 62 48 91 – Closed 31 August-16 September, 4-19 January, Sunday dinner and Monday
Rest – *(number of covers limited, pre-book)* Menu € 23 (weekdays)/78 – Carte € 60/100
◆ A 17C house in the centre of the village with two low-key dining rooms decorated with copperware and a collection of antique plates. Classic cuisine.

X **L'Orbecquoise** VISA MC
60 r. Grande – ✆ 02 31 62 44 99 – herve.doual@wanadoo.fr – Fax 02 31 62 44 99 – Closed 25 June-12 July, Wednesday except lunch 15 July-15 September and Thursday
Rest – Menu (€ 14), € 18/32 – Carte € 35/45
◆ Rustic inn occupying a 17C residence. Old postcards and photos of the town decorate the dining room walls. Regional cuisine.

ORBEY – 68 Haut-Rhin – 315 G8 – pop. 3 608 – alt. 550 m – Winter sports : see "Le Bonhomme" – ✉ 68370 Alsace-Lorraine 1 A2

Paris 434 – Colmar 23 – Gérardmer 42 – Munster 21 – St-Dié 37 – Sélestat 35
Office de tourisme, 48, rue du Général-de-Gaulle ✆ 03 89 71 30 11, Fax 03 89 71 34 11

Bois Le Sire et son Motel P VISA MC AE
20 r. Ch. de Gaulle – ✆ 03 89 71 25 25 – www.bois-le-sire.fr – boislesire@bois-le-sire.fr – Fax 03 89 71 30 75 – Closed 4 January-6 February
35 rm – †€ 53/82 ††€ 53/82, ☕ € 10 – 1 suite – ½ P € 59/73
Rest – *(closed Monday except July-August)* Menu (€ 10), € 17/50 – Carte € 22/50
◆ This hotel is made up of two buildings with practical rooms. Choose the motel rooms, which are quieter and more spacious. Fitness area, sauna, Jacuzzi. Stylish wainscoting and furniture in the restaurant, which serves simple, traditional fare.

Aux Bruyères rm, P VISA MC AE
35 r. Ch. de Gaulle – ✆ 03 89 71 20 36 – www.auxbruyeres.com – info@auxbruyeres.com – Fax 03 89 71 35 30 – Open 3 April-25 October and 15-31 December
29 rm – †€ 42 ††€ 42/65, ☕ € 8 – ½ P € 41/56
Rest – *(closed Wednesday lunch and Thursday lunch in season)* Menu (€ 11), € 14/38 bi – Carte € 21/38
◆ This family house with tea room has functional bedrooms and three family suites. Rooms in the lodge face the garden. Muted dining room, summer terrace and regional food.

in Basses-Huttes South: 4 km by D 48 – ✉ 68370 Orbey

Wetterer rm, VISA AE
– *03 89 71 20 28 – www.hotel-wetterer.com – info@hotel-wetterer.com – Fax 03 89 71 36 50 – Closed 8 March-2 April, 4-26 November and 4 January-5 February*
15 rm – €37/42 €46/63, €8 – ½ P €44/49
Rest – *(Closed Wednesday)* Menu (€14), €16/35 – Carte €18/36
◆ Built in the heart of superb forest and mountain scenery, this 1960s hotel offers practical, well-kept rooms. Peace and quiet guaranteed! Rustic-chic dining room with rafters, fireplace and silverware. Classic repertory.

in Pairis 3 km southwest by D 48" – ✉ 68370 Orbey

Lac Noir (Black Lake) ★: ≤★ 30 mn West: 5 km.

Le Domaine de Pairis VISA
233 Pairis – 03 89 71 20 15 – www.pairis.fr – info@pairis.fr – Fax 03 89 71 39 90 – Closed 12-27 November and 10-25 January
14 rm – €59 €69/89, €10 – ½ P €68/78
Rest – *(closed Sunday dinner and lunch Monday-Saturday)*
Menu €23/40 – Carte €21/47
◆ Simply and tastefully decorated rooms: minimalist, ecru coloured furniture offset by colourful paintings and rugs. Organic farm produce and homemade jams. Regional menu and wine list (Alsace, Burgundies and clarets).

Bon Repos VISA
235 Pairis – 03 89 71 21 92 – www.aubonrepos.com – au-bon-repos@wanadoo.fr – Fax 03 89 71 24 51 – Open 8 February-19 October, 19 December-3 January and closed Wednesday
16 rm – €46/51 €46/51, €8 – ½ P €48/53
Rest – *(dinner only except Sunday)* Menu €16/34 – Carte €20/43
◆ On the lake road, a small family inn giving onto a peaceful garden. Simple, practical rooms; those in the annexe are more peaceful, overlooking a forest of fir trees. Welcoming rustic style dining room offering regional cooking.

ORCHIES – 59 Nord – 302 H5 – pop. 8 172 – alt. 40 m – ✉ 59310 31 C2

Paris 219 – Denain 28 – Douai 20 – Lille 29 – Tournai 20 – Valenciennes 30

Syndicat d'initiative, 42, rue Jules Roch 03 20 64 86 32, Fax 03 20 64 86 32

Le Manoir rm, VISA AE
Hameau de Manneville, D 549: west via route Seclin – 03 20 64 68 68 – www.manoir.net – contact@manoir.net – Fax 03 20 64 68 69 – Closed 1st-28 August
34 rm – €75/120 €75/120, €9
Rest – *(Closed 26-31 December, Friday dinner, Saturday lunch, Sunday dinner and bank holiday dinner)* Menu (€17), €23/40 – Carte €24/60
◆ This hotel, located between a busy road and the motorway, offers modern rooms with good sound insulation. Linked to the hotel by a covered passage, the Manoir restaurant includes a cosy bar and three intimate, rustic-style dining rooms.

La Chaumière VISA
685 r. Henri Fiévet, 3 km south on the D 957, rte Marchiennes – 03 20 71 86 38 – Fax 03 20 61 65 91 – Closed 1st-15 September, February, Sunday dinner and Monday
Rest – Menu (€14), €30/82 bi – Carte €41/67
◆ Horses feature prominently among the animal ornaments, adding to the rustic feel of this restaurant. Classic fare, fine cheese platter and excellent choice of Bordeaux.

ORCIÈRES – 05 Hautes-Alpes – 334 F4 – pop. 810 – alt. 1 446 m – Winter sports : to Orcières-Merlette 1 850/2 650 m 2 26 – ✉ 05170 41 C1

French Alps

Paris 676 – Briançon 109 – Gap 32 – Grenoble 113 – La Mure 73

Office de tourisme, maison du Tourisme 04 92 55 89 89, Fax 04 92 55 89 64

Vallée du Drac Blanc★★ Northwest: 14 km.

in Merlette North: 5 km by D 76 – ✉ 05170 Orcières

Les Gardettes with rm — rm, VISA
– *☎ 04 92 55 71 11 – www.gardettes.com – info@gardettes.com – Fax 04 92 55 77 26 – Open 6 December-26 April and 26 June-10 September*
15 rm – €56/99 €56/99, ☕ €8 – ½ P €49/73
Rest – *(closed 1 - 15 Dec)* Menu €23/34 – Carte €25/46
◆ A family-run restaurant in a converted cattle shed. Pretty, typically Alpine decoration and regional dishes with a personal touch. Small rooms.

ORCINES – 63 Puy-de-Dôme – **326** F8 – **see Clermont-Ferrand**

ORCIVAL – 63 Puy-de-Dôme – **326** E8 – **pop. 256** – **alt. 840 m** – ✉ 63210 Auvergne 5 **B2**

Paris 441 – Aubusson 82 – Clermont-Ferrand 27 – Le Mont-Dore 17 – Ussel 55
Office de tourisme, le bourg ☎ 04 73 65 89 77, Fax 04 73 65 89 78
Notre-Dame basilica ★★.

Roche without rest — VISA
– *☎ 04 73 65 82 31 – Fax 04 73 65 94 15 – Closed 11 November-25 December and Monday off season*
8 rm – €35 €38, ☕ €6
◆ This establishment facing the basilica houses small, simple and well-kept rooms that are gradually being redecorated. Small garden at the back.

If breakfast is included the ☕ symbol appears after the number of rooms.

ORGELET – 39 Jura – **321** D7 – **pop. 1 740** – **alt. 500 m** – ✉ 39270 16 **B3**

Paris 434 – Besançon 104 – Lons-le-Saunier 20 – Bourg-en-Bresse 68 – Oyonnax 42

La Valouse — VISA AE
12 r. des Fossés, (opposite the church) – ☎ 03 84 25 54 80 – www.hotel-restaurant-jura.com – lavalouse@wanadoo.fr – Fax 03 84 25 54 70 – Closed 24 December-20 January and Sunday dinner
14 rm – €53/58 €73/78, ☕ €8 – ½ P €68
Rest – Menu (€14), €16/48 bi – Carte €30/50
◆ This non-smoking family hotel has just been fully renovated. The simple and well-soundproofed rooms are modern and colourful. Updated local cuisine, or dish of the day available in adjoining café.

ORGEVAL – 78 Yvelines – **311** H2 – **101** 11 – **see Paris, Area**

ORGON – 13 Bouches-du-Rhône – **340** F3 – **pop. 2 913** – **alt. 90 m** – ✉ 13660 Provence 42 **E1**

Paris 712 – Aix-en-Provence 58 – Avignon 29 – Marseille 72
Office de tourisme, place de la Liberté ☎ 04 90 73 09 54, Fax 04 90 73 09 54

Le Mas de la Rose — rm, VISA AE
Eygalières road, 4 km south-westward along the D 24b – ☎ 04 90 73 08 91 – www.mas-rose.com – contact@mas-rose.com – Fax 04 90 73 31 03 – Closed 4 January-26 February
8 rm – €170/280 €170/280, ☕ €18 – 1 suite
Rest – *(Open 21 May-30 September) (dinner only) (residents only)* Menu €55
◆ In a bucolic setting, these 17C sheep barns have been tastefully converted. Provencal style rooms with individual touches. Superb landscaped garden with a pool. Elegant, rustic-contemporary decor and seasonal cuisine.

Domaine de Saint-Véran without rest
rte de Cavaillon, 1.5 km north on the D 26 – ✆ 04 90 73 32 86 – www.avignon-et-provence.com/chambres-hotes/domaine-saint-veran – d1jour@wanadoo.fr – Closed January and February
5 rm – €70/80 €80/100
◆ Fine house, nestling in a large park planted with umbrella pine and cypress trees. Tastefully decorated interior, well-kept rooms, cosy lounge, pool, etc.

Auberge du Parc VISA
rte de la Gare – ✆ 04 90 73 35 85 – www.aubergeduparc.net – info@aubergeduparc.net – Fax 04 90 73 39 60 – Closed 15-30 November and Saturday lunch
Rest – *(number of covers limited, pre-book)* Menu (€ 20), € 39/59 – Carte € 49/69
◆ At the bottom of rocky cliffs in the foothills of the Alpilles, this large warm residence surrounded by greenery has a colourful dining room and small terrace. Modern cuisine.

"Rest" appears in red for establishments with a ✿ (star) or ☺ (Bib Gourmand).

ORLÉANS – 45 Loiret – 318 I4 – pop. 113 200 – Built-up area 263 292 – alt. 100 m – ✉ 45000 **Châteaux of the Loire** 12 **C2**

Paris 132 – Caen 311 – Clermont-Ferrand 295 – Le Mans 143 – Tours 118

Office de tourisme, 2, place de l'Étape ✆ 02 38 24 05 05, Fax 02 38 54 49 84

de Limère Ardon 1411 allée de la Pomme de Pin, S : 9 km on D 326, ✆ 02 38 63 89 40

d'Orléans Donnery Donnery Domaine de la Touche, E : 17 km on N 460, ✆ 02 38 59 25 15

de Sologne La Ferté-Saint-Aubin Route de Jouy-le-Potier, 24 km S : on N 20 and D 18, ✆ 02 38 76 57 33

de Marcilly Marcilly-en-Villette Domaine de la Plaine, 18 SE : on D 14 and D 108, ✆ 02 38 76 11 73

Ste-Croix cathedral ★★: panelling★★ - Maison de Jeanne d'Arc (Joan of Arc's House)★ **V** - Quai Fort-des-Tourelles ≤★ EZ **60** - Musée des Beaux-Arts★★ **M**[1] - Musée Historique et Archéologique★ **M**[2] - Muséum★.

Olivet: La Source floral park ★★ Southeast: 8 km CZ.

Plans on following pages

Mercure rm, rm, VISA
44 quai Barentin – ✆ 02 38 62 17 39 – www.mercure.com – h0581@accor.com – Fax 02 38 53 95 34 DZ **t**
111 rm – €85/160 €100/175, € 15
Rest – *(Closed Saturday lunch, Sunday lunch and bank holiday lunch)* Menu (€ 17) – Carte approx. € 28
◆ The spacious, soundproofed rooms of this hotel now sport the latest design of the Mercure chain (modern furniture); those on the top floor command a view of the Loire. Boat-styled decor for this restaurant; collection of plates on a boating theme.

D'Arc without rest VISA
37 r. de la République – ✆ 02 38 53 10 94 – www.hoteldarc.fr – hotel.darc@wanadoo.fr – Fax 02 38 81 77 47 EY **g**
35 rm – €86/126 €99/163, € 12
◆ Hotel with an original façade and Art Nouveau inspired arch. It houses redecorated rooms with Louis Philippe style furniture, which are all non-smoking. The period lift is worthy of a museum.

Des Cèdres without rest VISA
17 r. Mar. Foch – ✆ 02 38 62 22 92 – www.hoteldescedres.com – contact@hoteldescedres.com – Fax 02 38 81 76 46 – Closed 24 December-5 January DY **b**
32 rm – €64/69 €66/82, € 8,50
◆ Out of the town centre, this quiet hotel offers relatively spacious rooms adorned with cane furniture. Sitting room/veranda facing a garden planted with cedar trees.

ORLÉANS

Antigna (R.) . . . . DY 4
Bannier (R.) . . . . DY
Bothereau (R. R.) . . . . FY 14
Bourgogne (Fg de) . . . . . . FZ 15
Bourgogne (R. de) . . . . . . EFZ
Brésil (R. du) . . . . FY 16
Bretonnerie (R. de la) . . . DEY 17
Briand (Bd A.) . . . . FY 19
Champ-de-Mars (Av.) . . . . DZ 25
Charpenterie (R. de la) . . . . EZ 34
Châtelet (Square du) . . . . . EZ 32
Chollet (R. Théophile) . . . . EY 36
Claye (R. de la) . . . . FY 38
Coligny (R.) . . . . FZ 39
Croix-de-la-Pucelle (R.) . . . EZ 43
Dauphine (Av.) . . . . EZ 47
Dolet (R. Étienne) . . . . EZ 49
Ducerceau (R.) . . . . EZ 51
Dupanloup (R.) . . . . EFY 53
Escures (R. d') . . . . EY 55
Étape (Pl. de l') . . . . EY 56
Ételon (R. de l') . . . . FY 57
Folie (R. de la) . . . . FZ 58
Fort-des-Tourelles (Q.) . . . . EZ 60
Gaulle (Pl. du Gén.-de) . . . . DZ 65
Hallebarde (R. de la) . . . . . . DY 70
Hôtelleries (R. des) . . . . EZ 71
Jeanne d'Arc (R.) . . . . EY
Lin (R. au) . . . . EZ 81
Loire (Pl. de la) . . . . EZ 85
Madeleine (R. Fg) . . . . DZ 88
Manufacture (R. de la) . . . . . FY 89
Motte-Sanguin (Bd de la) . . FZ 95
N.-D.-de-Recouvrance (R.) DZ 97
Oriflamme (R. de l') . . . . FZ 98
Parisie (R.) . . . . EZ 100
Poirier (R. du) . . . . EZ 106
Pothier (R.) . . . . EZ 112
Prague (Quai) . . . . DZ 113
Pressoir (R. du) . . . . FY 115
Pte-Madeleine (R.) . . . . DY 108
Pte-St-Jean (R.) . . . . DY 109
Rabier (R. F.) . . . . EY 117
République (Pl.) . . . . EZ 121
République (R. de la) . . . . . . EY
Roquet (R.) . . . . EZ 124
Royale (R.) . . . . EZ 125
Ste-Catherine (R.) . . . . EZ 135
Ste-Croix (Pl.) . . . . EYZ 139
St-Euverte (Bd) . . . . FYZ 126
St-Euverte (R.) . . . . FY 127
Secrétain (Av. R.) . . . . DZ 140
Segellé (Bd P.) . . . . FY 141
Tabour (R. du) . . . . EZ 145
Tour Neuve (R. de la) . . . . . FZ 147
Verdun (Bd de) . . . . DY 152
Vieux-Marché (Pl.) . . . . DZ 159
Weiss (R. L.) . . . . FY 160
6-Juin 1944 (Pl. du) . . . . . . FY 162

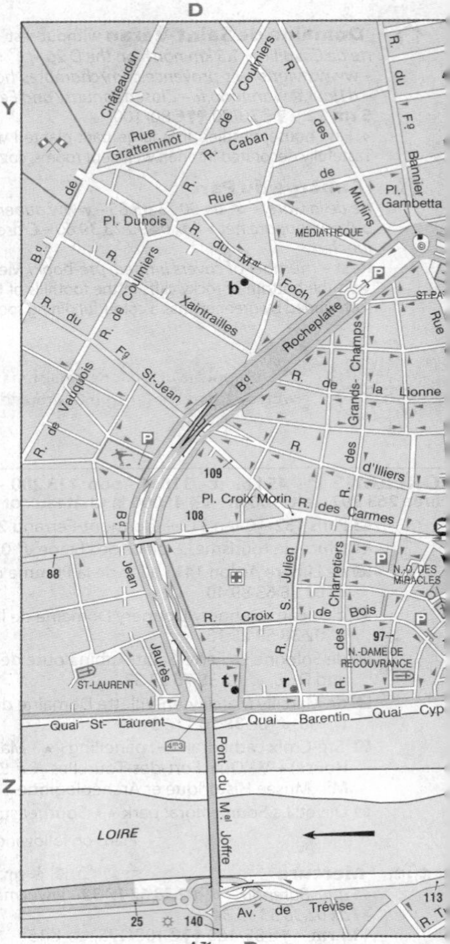

D'Orléans without rest
6 r. A. Crespin – ☎ 02 38 53 35 34 – www.hoteldorleans.fr
– hotel.orleans@wanadoo.fr
– Fax 02 38 53 68 20 EY **t**
18 rm – †€ 55/70 ††€ 65/80, ☕ € 8
◆ Two buildings set around a courtyard and linked together by the breakfast room. The rooms (new bedding) and communal areas are being renovated.

Marguerite without rest
14 pl. du Vieux Marché – ☎ 02 38 53 74 32
– www.hotel-orleans.fr – hotel.marguerite@wanadoo.fr
– Fax 02 38 53 31 56 – Closed 26 December-3 January DZ **f**
25 rm – †€ 54/65 ††€ 63/79, ☕ € 7
◆ This hotel is being progressively enhanced: tastefully refurbished interior and rooms (contemporary furnishings, flatscreen TV, wifi) with excellent soundproofing.

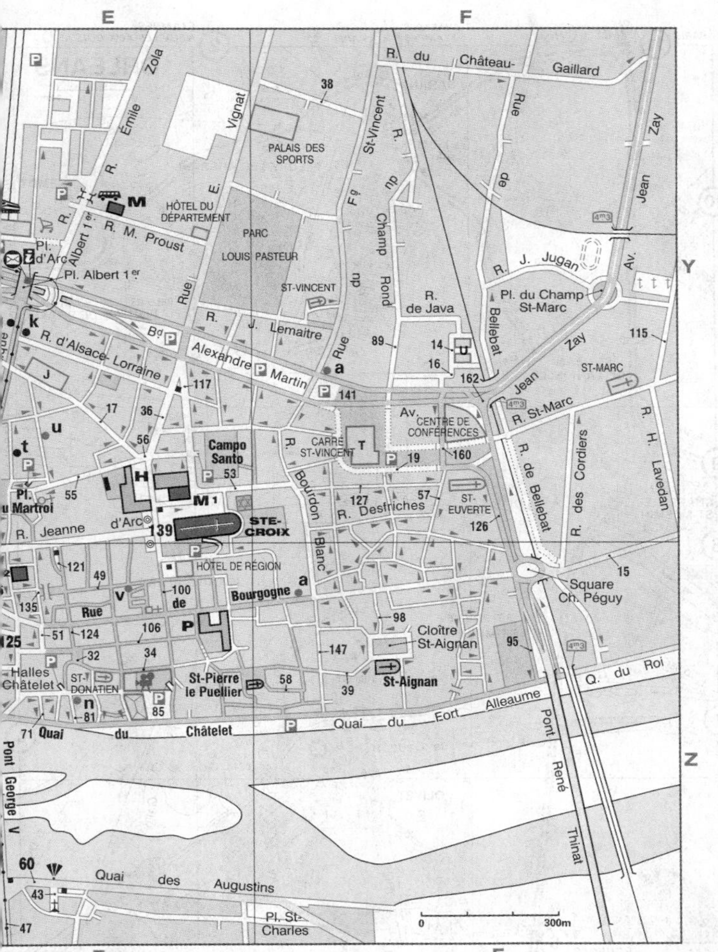

De l'Abeille without rest

64 r. d'Alsace-Lorraine – ✆ 02 38 53 54 87 – www.hoteldelabeille.com – hoteldelabeille@wanadoo.fr – Fax 02 38 62 65 84 EY **k**

28 rm – †€ 47/95 ††€ 62/95, ☕ € 9

◆ This town-centre hotel offers small and stylish rooms; the majority have been redecorated. Personalised decoration with a choice of colours and hand-picked old furniture.

L'Épicurien

54 r. Turcies – ✆ 02 38 68 01 10 – Fax 02 38 68 19 02 – Closed 1-10 May, 3 weeks in August, 25 December-1 January, Saturday lunch in July and August, Sunday and Monday DZ **r**

Rest – Menu € 25 (weekdays)/65 – Carte € 50/65

◆ Epicureans can be found in this old house with rustic dining rooms enlivened by shades of yellow, exposed beams and drawings of fruit. Modern cuisine.

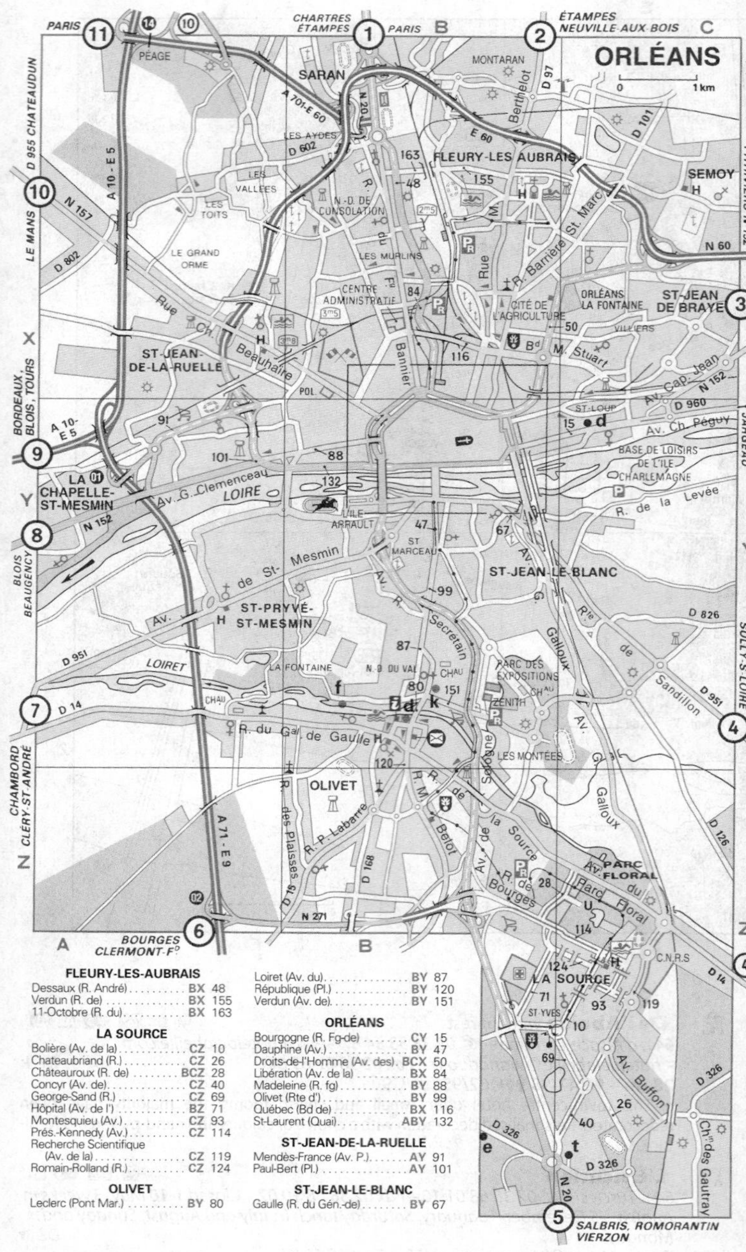

FLEURY-LES-AUBRAIS

Dessaux (R. André) . . . . BX 48
Verdun (R. de) . . . . BX 155
11-Octobre (R. du) . . . . BX 163

LA SOURCE

Bolière (Av. de la) . . . . CZ 10
Chateaubriand (R.) . . . . CZ 26
Châteauroux (R. de) . . . . BCZ 28
Concyr (Av. de) . . . . CZ 40
George-Sand (R.) . . . . CZ 69
Hôpital (Av. de l') . . . . BZ 71
Montesquieu (Av.) . . . . CZ 93
Prés.-Kennedy (Av.) . . . . CZ 114
Recherche Scientifique (Av. de la) . . . . CZ 119
Romain-Rolland (R.) . . . . CZ 124

OLIVET

Leclerc (Pont Mar.) . . . . BY 80
Loiret (Av. du) . . . . BY 87
République (Pl.) . . . . BY 120
Verdun (Av. de) . . . . BY 151

ORLÉANS

Bourgogne (R. Fg-de) . . . . CY 15
Dauphine (Av.) . . . . BY 47
Droits-de-l'Homme (Av. des) . BCX 50
Libération (Av. de la) . . . . BX 84
Madeleine (R. fg) . . . . BY 88
Olivet (Rte d') . . . . BY 99
Québec (Bd de) . . . . BX 116
St-Laurent (Quai) . . . . ABY 132

ST-JEAN-DE-LA-RUELLE

Mendès-France (Av. P.) . . . . AY 91
Paul-Bert (Pl.) . . . . AY 101

ST-JEAN-LE-BLANC

Gaulle (R. du Gén.-de) . . . . BY 67

Eugène
24 r. Ste-Anne – 02 38 53 82 64 – Fax 02 38 54 31 89 – Closed 25 July-17 August, 25 December-4 January, Saturday and Sunday EY **u**
Rest – Menu € 23/69 – Carte € 38/60
◆ This little restaurant is well known by the people of Orleans who hurry here to relish the savours of the Southern French cuisine. Pleasant and warm setting.

La Vieille Auberge
2 fg Saint-Vincent – 02 38 53 55 81 – lavieilleauberge45@orange.fr – Closed Saturday lunch, Monday in July-August and Sunday dinner FY **a**
Rest – Menu (€ 18), € 25 (weekdays)/49 – Carte € 40/62
◆ A new team has taken over this establishment and the up-to-date cuisine is now focused on the produce. Dine in its still stylish interior or outdoors in the pleasant garden.

La Dariole
25 r. Etienne Dolet – 02 38 77 26 67 – Fax 02 38 77 26 67 – Closed 3-23 August, Saturday, Sunday and dinner except Tuesday and Friday EZ **v**
Rest – *(number of covers limited, pre-book)* Menu (€ 18), € 22
◆ This 15C half-timbered house serves tasty cuisine with personal touches. Dine in the smart, rustic dining room or on the small summer terrace opening onto a little square.

Chez Jules
136 r. de Bourgogne – 02 38 54 30 80 – Fax 02 38 54 08 47 – Closed 6-21 July, Monday lunch, Saturday lunch and Sunday FZ **a**
Rest – Menu (€ 17), € 23/31 – Carte € 46/57
◆ This small, rustic and economic establishment distinguishes itself from the numerous neighbouring restaurants by its extremely warm welcome and generous helpings of reworked traditional dishes.

in St-Jean-de-Braye East: 4 km - CXY – **pop. 18 600 – alt. 108 m – ✉ 45800**

Novotel Orléans St-Jean-de-Braye rm,
145 av. de Verdun, (N 152) – 02 38 84 65 65 – www.novotel.com – H1075@accor.com – Fax 02 38 84 66 61
107 rm – †€ 120/125 ††€ 125/145, ☕ € 18
Rest – Menu € 38 (lunch), € 59/90 – Carte € 59/98
◆ Latest generation of Novotel rooms, garden and pool, children's play area and a location on the edge of a forest: such are a few of the pleasant features of this Novotel. Restaurant serving traditional cuisine.

Promotel without rest
117 fg Bourgogne – 02 38 53 64 09 – www.hotelpromotel.net – hotelpromotel@orange.fr – Fax 02 38 53 13 22 – Closed 1-23 August and 22 December-5 January CY **d**
83 rm – †€ 57/59 ††€ 60/62, ☕ € 8,50
◆ The most modern of these two buildings, well soundproofed, lies on a busy road; the other offers a shaded garden. Rooms are spacious and practical.

Les Toqués
71 chemin du Halage – 02 38 86 50 20 – lestoques@noos.fr – Fax 02 38 84 30 96 – Closed August, Sunday and Monday
Rest – Menu € 20 (weekday lunch), € 30/45
◆ Beside the Loire, this former inn that has been very prettily converted, has a modern and lively interior, delightful summer terrace, appetising modern menu... Chapeau Les Toqués!

in La Source Southeast: 11 km- BCZ – **✉ 45100 Orléans**

Novotel Orléans La Source rm, rm,
2 r. H. de Balzac, (crossroads N20-D326, Concyr road) – 02 38 63 04 28 – www.novotel.com – h0419@accor.com – Fax 02 38 69 24 04 CZ **t**
119 rm – †€ 89/142 ††€ 89/142, ☕ € 15 **Rest** – Carte € 30/50
◆ The modern rooms (modular furniture) of this Novotel have been renovated in keeping with the chain's latest concept. Children's play area. The stylish restaurant offers a pleasant view of the pool and garden. Minimalist cuisine and diet recipes.

at Limère Park **Southeast: 13 km by N 20 and D 326 – ✉ 45160 Ardon**

Domaine des Portes de Sologne
200 allée des 4 vents rm,
– ✆ 02 38 49 99 99 – www.portes-de-sologne.com – resa@portes-de-sologne.com – Fax 02 38 49 99 00 BZ **e**
117 rm – €123 €137, ☕ €11 – 14 suites
Rest – Menu (€21), €28/48 – Carte €45/66
◆ Hotel complex, in the middle of the countryside, near a golf course and balneotherapy centre. Simply decorated rooms, charming cottages (two-floor family accommodation) and conference facilities. Modern and opulent restaurant serving updated cuisine; summer terrace.

in Olivet **South: 5 km via Avenue Loiret and banks of the Loiret – pop. 20 700 – alt. 100 m – ✉ 45160** **Châteaux of the Loire**

Office de tourisme, 236, rue Paul Genain ✆ 02 38 63 49 68, Fax 02 38 63 50 45

Le Rivage with rm
635 r. Reine Blanche – ✆ 02 38 66 02 93 – http://monsite.wanadoo.fr/le.rivage.olivet – hotel-le-rivage.jpb@wanadoo.fr – Fax 02 38 56 31 11 – Closed 25 December-20 January BY **f**
17 rm – €85 €85, ☕ €13 – ½ P €85/103
Rest – *(closed Saturday lunch and Sunday dinner from November to April)* Menu €28 (weekdays)/62 – Carte €48/82
◆ Handsome villas and old mills: take full advantage of the pastoral scene on the banks of the Loiret from the brigth veranda/dining room or the waterside terrace.

Laurendière
68 av. Loiret – ✆ 02 38 51 06 78 – http://lalaurendiere.new.fr – lalaurendiere@wanadoo.fr – Fax 02 38 56 36 20 – Closed 6-22 July, 15-24 February, Monday dinner, Tuesday dinner and Wednesday BY **k**
Rest – Menu €23/49 – Carte €48/66
◆ Traditional cuisine and a fine choice of wines (many from the Loire) await you in this colourful restaurant located in an old, regional style house.

L'Eldorado
10 r. M.-Belot – ✆ 02 38 64 29 74 – www.camus-eldorado.com – eldorado45@wanadoo.fr – Fax 02 38 69 14 33 BY **d**
Rest – Menu €28/50
◆ The décor of this former open-air café falls in line with its up-to-date and refined cuisine, and the terrace beside the Loiret is always charming... Delightful from A to Z.

in la Chapelle-St-Mesmin **West: 4 km - AY – pop. 9 282 – alt. 101 m – ✉ 45380**

Orléans Parc Hôtel without rest
55 rte d'Orléans – ✆ 02 38 43 26 26 – www.orleansparchotel.com – lucmar@aol.com – Fax 02 38 72 00 99 – Closed 22 December-6 January AY **v**
33 rm – €61 €77/92, ☕ €9
◆ Simply decorated, comfortable rooms (choose one overlooking the Loire), a welcoming lounge and breakfast room. The attractive, shady riverside park is ideal for a pleasant stroll.

Côté Saveurs
55 rte d'Orleans – ✆ 02 38 72 29 51 – resto.cs@free.fr – Fax 02 38 72 29 67 – Closed 1-16 March, 2-17 August and 20-28 December AY **v**
Rest – Menu (€19), €29 – Carte €45/58
◆ Elegant 19C house with gardens. The interior combines classic (mouldings and panelling) with modern (red leather armchairs). Current cuisine.

ORLY (Aéroports de Paris) – **91 Essonne** – **312** D3 – **101** 26 – **see Paris, Area**

ORMOY-LA-RIVIÈRE – **91 Essonne** – **312** B5 – **see Étampes**

ORNAISONS – 11 Aude – **344** I3 – see Narbonne

ORNANS – 25 Doubs – **321** G4 – **pop. 4 106** – **alt. 355 m** – ✉ **25290** 16 **B2**
Burgundy-Jura

Paris 428 – Baume-les-Dames 42 – Besançon 26 – Morteau 48 – Pontarlier 37

Office de tourisme, 7, rue Pierre Vernier ✆ 03 81 62 21 50, Fax 03 81 62 02 63

Grand Pont ≤★ - West: Vallée de la Loue (Loue Valley)★★ - Le Château (Castle) ≤★ North: 2.5 km.

De France
r. P. Vernier – ✆ 03 81 62 24 44 – www.hoteldefrance-ornans.com – contact@hoteldefrance-ornans.com – Fax 03 81 62 12 03 – Closed 6-22 November, 18 December-25 January, Saturday and Sunday from November to April
26 rm – †€ 65 ††€ 85, ☕ € 9 – 1 suite – ½ P € 80
Rest – *(Closed Saturday and Sunday from November to April and Monday lunch from April to November)* Menu € 19 (weekdays)/45 – Carte € 45/60
◆ A traditional hotel in a village known as the Pearl of the Loue. Rooms of varying sizes gradually being renovated, and fine suites. Private, world-renowned fly fishing course. A pleasant restaurant in an elegant rustic setting facing the Great Bridge over the Loue.

Courbet
34 r. P. Vernier – ✆ 03 81 62 10 15 – www.restaurantlecourbet.com – restaurantlecourbet@wanadoo.fr – Fax 03 81 62 13 34 – Closed Christmas holidays, 15 February-17 March, Sunday dinner, Tuesday lunch and Monday
Rest – Menu € 19/39
◆ A few feet from the house where Courbet was born, the dining room where delicious modern cuisine is served, pays homage to the painter with reproductions. Terrace on the Loue.

in Saules 6 km northeast by D 492 – **pop. 191** – **alt. 585 m** – ✉ **25580**

La Griotte
27 b Grande Rue – ✆ 03 81 57 17 71 – Fax 03 81 57 17 71 – Closed 24 August-30 September, 8 February-3 March, Tuesday from November to March, Sunday dinner and Wednesday
Rest – *(number of covers limited, pre-book)* Menu € 14/30 – Carte € 28/52
◆ The gamble has paid off for this new restaurant located in a former coaching inn. It has kept a friendly welcome, simple setting, and reasonably priced regional cuisine.

OROUET – 85 Vendée – **316** E7 – see St-Jean-de-Monts – ✉ **85160**

ORPIERRE – 05 Hautes-Alpes – **334** C7 – **pop. 318** – **alt. 682 m** – ✉ **05700** **French Alps**

Paris 689 – Château-Arnoux 47 – Digne-les-Bains 72 – Gap 55 – Serres 20 – Sisteron 33

Office de tourisme, le Village ✆ 04 92 66 30 45, Fax 04 92 66 32 52

in Bégües Southwest: 4,5 km – ✉**05700 Orpierre**

Le Céans
rte des Princes d'Orange – ✆ 04 92 66 24 22 – www.le-ceans.fr.st – le.ceans@gmail.com – Fax 04 92 66 28 29 – Open 15 March-1st November and closed Wednesday October-15 April
21 rm – †€ 45/90 ††€ 45/90, ☕ € 8 – ½ P € 43/57
Rest – Menu € 16/37 – Carte € 19/46
◆ Set in the centre of a hamlet in the Massif des Baronnies. This establishment has small rooms and family lodges dotted around a country park that stretches down to the river. A restaurant with a guesthouse atmosphere, and family cooking based on regional specialities. Street-facing terrace.

ORSCHWILLER – 67 Bas-Rhin – **315** I7 – **pop. 564** – **alt. 240 m** 2 **C1**
– ✉ 67600

Paris 441 – Colmar 22 – St-Dié 44 – Sélestat 7 – Strasbourg 61

Le Fief du Château rm, VISA AE

20 Grand' rue – ✆ 03 88 82 56 25 – www.fief-chateau.com – fiefduchateau@evc.net – Fax 03 88 82 26 24 – Closed 3-10 March, 30 June-5 July, 27 October-3 November

8 rm – €40 €48, €7 – ½ P €48

Rest – *(closed Wednesday)* Menu (€9), €19/26 – Carte €25/40

◆ A late-19C, regional style house with a pretty, flower-decked facade in a typical village on the Alsace wine route. Simple, refurbished rooms. Restaurant with a rustic feel, a friendly welcome and Alsatian cuisine.

ORTHEZ – 64 Pyrénées-Atlantiques – **342** H4 – **pop. 10 200** – **alt. 55 m** 3 **B3**
– ✉ 64300 **Atlantic Coast**

Paris 765 – Bayonne 74 – Dax 39 – Mont-de-Marsan 57 – Pau 47

Office de tourisme, rue Bourg-Vieux ✆ 05 59 38 32 84, Fax 05 59 69 12 00

de Salies-de-Béarn Salies-de-Béarn Quartier Hélios, 17 km on the Bayonne road, ✆ 05 59 38 37 59

Pont Vieux★.

Au Temps de la Reine Jeanne rm, rest, VISA AE

44 r. Bourg-Vieux – ✆ 05 59 67 00 76 – www.reine-jeanne.fr – reine.jeanne.orthez@wanadoo.fr – Fax 05 59 69 09 63

30 rm – €58/88 €66/110, €8,50

Rest – *(Closed Sunday dinner from 18 October to 20 March)* Menu €25/65 – Carte €42/53

◆ Former 18C and 19C residences housing small rooms set around a covered patio. The neighbouring building offers modern, larger and more comfortable rooms. Pleasant, rustic restaurant. Traditional menu and jazz evenings with dinner in the season.

ORVAULT – 44 Loire-Atlantique – **316** G4 – **see Nantes**

OSNY – 95 Val-d'Oise – **305** D6 – **106** 5 – **101** 2 – **see Paris, Area (Cergy-Pontoise)**

OSTHOUSE – 67 Bas-Rhin – **315** J6 – **pop. 946** – **alt. 155 m** – ✉ **67150** 1 **B2**

Paris 502 – Obernai 17 – Offenburg 35 – Sélestat 23 – Strasbourg 32

À la Ferme without rest VISA

10 r. du Château – ✆ 03 90 29 92 50 – www.hotelalaferme.com – hotelalaferme@wanadoo.fr – Fax 03 90 29 92 51

7 rm – €86/135 €90/135, €15

◆ Former 18C farmhouse and stables, offering peaceful, smart and spacious rooms with a personal touch. Attentive service too.

A l'Aigle d'Or VISA AE

– ✆ 03 88 98 06 82 – www.hotelalaferme.com – hotelalaferme@wanadoo.fr – Fax 03 88 98 81 75 – Closed 3 weeks in August, Christmas holidays, February holidays, Monday and Tuesday

Rest – Menu €33 (weekdays)/68 – Carte €50/80

Rest *Winstub* – Carte €25/35

◆ The family goes to great lengths to welcome you in this warm, elegant and refined restaurant (wood panelling and attractive painted coffered ceiling). Classic cuisine. The Winstub offers a relaxed atmosphere and fairly plush decor serving Alsatian specialities.

OSTWALD – 67 Bas-Rhin – **315** K5 – **see Strasbourg**

OTTROTT – 67 Bas-Rhin – **315** I6 – **see Obernai**

OUCHAMPS – 41 Loir-et-Cher – 318 E7 – pop. 807 – alt. 92 m – ✉ 41120 11 A1

Paris 199 – Blois 18 – Montrichard 19 – Romorantin-Lanthenay 40 – Tours 57

Château de Fougères-sur-Bièvre★ Northwest: 5 km, **Châteaux of the Loire**

Relais des Landes

1.5 km north on D 7 – ✆ 02 54 44 40 40 – www.relaisdeslandes.com – info@relaisdeslandes.com – Fax 02 54 44 03 89 – Open 7 March-30 November

28 rm – €103/124 €124/154, ☕ €15 – ½ P €113/139

Rest – *(dinner only except weekends and bank holidays)*

Menu €40/47 bi – Carte €44/56

◆ This fine 17C manor house stands in extensive grounds with an ornamental lake. Quite large, country smart rooms; private terrace for the duplex. Cosy, countrified lounge-bar. Beautiful rustic dining room (fireplace, fresco) and veranda facing the garden.

OUCQUES – 41 Loir-et-Cher – 318 E5 – pop. 1 420 – alt. 127 m – ✉ 41290 11 B2

Paris 160 – Beaugency 30 – Blois 27 – Châteaudun 30 – Orléans 62 – Vendôme 21

Syndicat d'initiative, Mairie ✆ 02 54 23 11 00, Fax 02 54 23 11 04

Du Commerce with rm — rest,

9 r. de Beaugency – ✆ 02 54 23 20 41 – www.hotel-commerce-oucques.com – hotelrestaurantcommerce@wanadoo.fr – Fax 02 54 23 02 88 – Closed 20 December-5 January, 2-10 March, Sunday dinner and Monday except July-August and bank holidays

11 rm – €63 €69, ☕ €10 – ½ P €67

Rest – *(pre-book Sat - Sun)* Menu €22/62 – Carte €49/70

◆ A 1970s-style dining room with attentive service, serving well-prepared up-to-date cuisine. Highly colourful and well-kept guestrooms.

The red symbol?
This denotes the very essence of peace –
only the sound of birdsong first thing in the morning...

OUESSANT (ÎLE) – 29 Finistère – 308 A4 – see Île d' Ouessant

OUHANS – 25 Doubs – 321 H5 – pop. 376 – alt. 600 m – ✉ 25520 17 C2

Paris 450 – Besançon 48 – Pontarlier 18 – Salins-les-Bains 40

Source of the Loue★★★ North: 2.5 km then 30 mn - Belvédère du Moine de la Vallée (viewpoint) ✻★★ Northwest: 5 km - Belvédère de Renédale (viewpoint) ≤★ Northwest: 4 km then 15 mn, **Burgundy-Jura.**

Les Sources de la Loue

9 grande Rue, (in the village) – ✆ 03 81 69 90 06 – www.sources-de-la-loue.com – hotel-des-sources-loue@wanadoo.fr – Fax 03 81 69 93 17 – Hotel: Open Easter-11 November and closed 20-30 September

14 rm ☕ – €54/64 €54/64 – ½ P €60/64

Rest – *(Closed 20-30 September, 20 December-1 February, Saturday lunch and Sunday dinner)* Menu €14 (weekday lunch), €26/33

◆ A large square house, in the centre of the village, with rather large, simply furnished and well-maintained rooms with double-glazing. Restaurant with a country-style decor; summer terrace and Franche-Comté dishes.

OUILLY-DU-HOULEY – 14 Calvados – 303 N4 – see Lisieux

OUISTREHAM – 14 Calvados – **303** K4 – **pop. 9 209** – **Casino : Riva Bella** – ✉ **14150** ▮ **Normandy** 32 **B2**

Paris 234 – Arromanches-les-Bains 33 – Bayeux 44 – Cabourg 20 – Caen 16

Office de tourisme, esplanade Lofi ☎ 02 31 97 18 63, Fax 02 31 96 87 33

St-Samson church ★.

Du Phare

10 pl. Gén.-de-Gaulle – ☎ 02 31 97 13 13 – www.hotelduphare.fr – hotelduphare@wanadoo.fr – Fax 02 31 97 14 57 – Closed 23 December-1st January

19 rm – †€ 53/62 ††€ 53/62, ☕ € 6

Rest – *(closed for dinner from October to May and Wednesday from mid-September to May)* Menu (€ 11), € 21 – Carte € 11/36

◆ A hotel run by the same family for six generations that is strategically located near the locks and opposite the ferry terminal. Simple, well-kept rooms. Brasserie type food served in a remodelled and modernised dining room-veranda.

Le Normandie

71 av. M. Cabieu, au port d'Ouistreham – ☎ 02 31 97 19 57 – www.lenormandie.com – hotel@lenormandie.com – Fax 02 31 97 20 07 – Closed 1 January-4 February

22 rm – †€ 68/75 ††€ 68/75, ☕ € 10 – ½ P € 70

Rest – Menu (€ 17), € 22/34 – Carte € 23/43

◆ This imposing house near the ferry terminal has rather small, practical rooms. Enjoy the buffet breakfast in a classic setting. Revamped in a more contemporary style, this restaurant offers daily specials that pay tribute to seafood.

La Mare Ô Poissons

68 r. E.-Herbline – ☎ 02 31 37 53 05 – www.lamareopoissons.fr – info@lamareopoissons.fr – Fax 02 31 37 49 61

Rest – Menu (€ 18 bi), € 29/47 – Carte € 34/53

◆ Restaurant accessed via a delicatessen. Quietly refined dining rooms (taupe and chocolate decor, displays of artwork and sculpture). Individual fish and seafood dishes.

La Table d'Hôtes

10 av. du Gén.-Leclerc – ☎ 02 31 97 18 44 – latabledhotes@orange.fr – Fax 02 31 97 18 44 – Closed 25 October-5 November and 15-25 February

Rest – Menu (€ 19), € 31

◆ Simple setting at a warm restaurant where guests are welcomed as friends. Traditional dishes on the menu, which the chef changes daily according to the market and inspiration.

in Riva-Bella – ✉ **14150 Ouistreham**

Riva Bella

av. Cdt Kieffer – ☎ 02 31 96 40 40 – www.hotelrivabella.fr – ouistreham@thalazur.fr – Fax 02 31 96 45 45 – Closed 11-26 December

89 rm – †€ 115 ††€ 150/160, ☕ € 13

Rest – Menu (€ 17 bi), € 29 – Carte € 40/70

◆ Large beachside hotel complex housing a thalassotherapy centre near the casino. Simple, standardised rooms, some with a sea view. Traditional cuisine, low calorie set menus and seafood platters in the restaurant.

Mercure

37 r. des Dunes – ☎ 02 31 96 20 20 – www.mercure.com – h1967@accor.com – Fax 02 31 97 10 10

49 rm – †€ 75/80 ††€ 85/90, ☕ € 10 **Rest** – Menu € 16/22 – Carte € 24/49

◆ Modern building a stone's throw from the harbour. Cruise ship cabins were the inspiration for the decor in the guestrooms. Sea inspired paintings. Refurbished restaurant with lively colours serving traditional cuisine.

De la Plage without rest

39 av. Pasteur – ☎ 02 31 96 85 16 – www.hotel-ouistreham.com – info-hoteldelaplage@wanadoo.fr – Fax 02 31 97 37 46 – Closed 8-26 February

17 rm – †€ 48/58 ††€ 64/77, ☕ € 9

◆ A late-19C, Anglo-Norman villa in a quiet street near the beach. Stylish bedrooms, the more spacious ones more suitable for families. Attractive garden.

St-Georges

51 av. Andry – ✆ 02 31 97 18 79 – www.hotel-le-saint-georges.com – saint-georges.hotel@wanadoo.fr – Fax 02 31 96 08 94 – Closed 4-26 January, Sunday dinner and Monday lunch from October to March

18 rm – †€ 66/69 ††€ 69/75, ☕ € 9 – ½ P € 74

Rest – Menu (€ 17), € 24/40 – Carte € 35/50

◆ Building dating from 1894 with rather small, but well-kept rooms overlooking either the seafront and casino, or the garden. Buffet breakfast. Restaurant with panoramic vistas offering traditional cuisine based on fish and seafood.

LES OURSINIÈRES – 83 Var – 340 L7 – see le Pradet

OUSSON-SUR-LOIRE – 45 Loiret – 318 N6 – pop. 758 – alt. 158 m – ✉ 45250 12 D2

Paris 165 – Orléans 96 – Gien 19 – Montargis 51 – Châlette-sur-Loing 52

Le Clos du Vigneron

18 rte Nationale 7 – ✆ 02 38 31 43 11 – www.hotel-clos-du-vigneron.com – leclosduvigneron@orange.fr – Fax 02 38 31 14 84 – Closed 23 December-4 February, Sunday dinner, Tuesday dinner and Wednesday

8 rm – †€ 58 ††€ 58, ☕ € 8 **Rest** – Menu (€ 18), € 28/48 – Carte € 35/47

◆ This regional style establishment, which has recently undergone total renovation, offers comfortable modern rooms. Those in the annexe are all ground floor with a pleasant garden. Up-to-date cuisine served in a simply decorated dining room.

OUZOUER-SUR-LOIRE – 45 Loiret – 318 L5 – pop. 2 637 – alt. 140 m – ✉ 45570 12 C2

Paris 151 – Gien 16 – Montargis 45 – Orléans 54 – Pithiviers 55 – Sully-sur-Loire 9

L'Abricotier

106 r. Gien – ✆ 02 38 35 07 11 – Fax 02 38 35 07 11 – Closed 26 July-12 August, Sunday dinner, Wednesday dinner and Monday

Rest – *(number of covers limited, pre-book)* Menu (€ 19 bi), € 24/39 – Carte € 45/55

◆ A courteous welcome, cosy provincial atmosphere and tasty traditional dishes inspired by market produce are the plus points of this inn situated in the centre of the village.

OYONNAX – 01 Ain – 328 G3 – pop. 23 200 – alt. 540 m – ✉ 01100 45 C1

Burgundy-Jura

Paris 484 – Bourg-en-Bresse 60 – Nantua 19

Syndicat d'initiative, 1, rue Bichat ✆ 04 74 77 94 46, Fax 04 74 77 68 27

La Toque Blanche

11 pl. Émile Zola – ✆ 04 74 73 42 63 – www.latoqueblanche-oyonnax.com – la.toqueblanche@club-internet.fr – Fax 04 74 73 76 48 – Closed 22 July-20 August, 2-10 January, Saturday lunch, Sunday dinner and Monday

Rest – Menu € 20/70 – Carte € 39/65

◆ A restaurant with an attractive decor brightened up with warm colours. Its cuisine blends elements from the Bresse, Jura and Lyon regions.

at Genin Lake Southeast: 10 km by D 13 – ✉ 01130 Charix

Site★ of the lake.

Auberge du Lac Genin with rm

– ✆ 04 74 75 52 50 – www.lac-genin.fr – lacgenin@wanadoo.fr – Fax 04 74 75 51 15 – Closed 19 October-4 December, Sunday dinner and Monday

3 rm – †€ 48/58 ††€ 48/58, ☕ € 6

Rest – Menu € 12 (weekday lunch), € 16/20 – Carte € 19/35

◆ This lakeside inn is surrounded by peace and quiet. Smart dining room with fireplace and frequently packed terrace. Rooms refurbished in a modern alpine spirit.

OZENAY – 71 Saône-et-Loire – see Tournus

OZOIR-LA-FERRIÈRE – 77 Seine-et-Marne – 312 F3 – 106 33 – 101 30 – see Paris, Area

PACY-SUR-EURE – 27 Eure – 304 I7 – pop. 4 826 – alt. 40 m – ✉ 27120 Normandy 33 **D2**

Paris 81 – Dreux 38 – Évreux 20 – Louviers 33 – Mantes-la-Jolie 28 – Rouen 62 – Vernon 14

Office de tourisme, place Dufay ✆ 02 32 26 18 21, Fax 02 32 36 96 67

Altina
rte de Paris – ✆ 02 32 36 13 18 – www.hotelaltina.com – altinasa@aol.com – Fax 02 32 26 05 11
29 rm – €55/63 €58/66, €8
Rest – Menu €13, €21/39 – Carte €26/45
◆ Located in a business district, this establishment has large, simple and contemporary rooms. Live jazz in the piano bar on Friday evenings. A friendly welcome and traditional, reasonably priced menus await guests.

L' Etape de la Valllée
1 r. Edouard Isambard – ✆ 02 32 36 12 77 – www.etapedelavallee.com – etapedelavallee@wanadoo.fr – Fax 02 32 36 22 74
15 rm – €56/82 €66/90, €8,50
Rest – *(closed Sunday dinner and Monday)* Menu (€19), €29/49 – Carte €37/66
◆ A large, splendid riverside villa. Two kinds of rooms available: cosy with personal touches at the front or more functional and renovated to the rear. Traditional restaurant with a warm setting; bay windows overlooking the River Eure.

in Cocherel Northwest: 6,5 km by D 836 – ✉ 27120 Houlbec-Cocherel

La Ferme de Cocherel with rm
8 r. Aristide Briand – ✆ 02 32 36 68 27 – Fax 02 32 26 28 18 – Closed 31 August-23 September, 5-21 January, Tuesday and Wednesday except bank holidays
3 rm – €120 €120/145, €12 – ½ P €112/125
Rest – *(number of covers limited, pre-book)* Menu €40/58 – Carte €84/121
◆ Enjoy the intimate fireside dining room, pleasant rotunda and flower-decked garden of this attractive, 18C Normandy house. Classic seasonal fare and fine cheese platter.

Do not confuse X with ✿!
X defines comfort, while stars are awarded for the best cuisine, across all categories of comfort.

PADIRAC – 46 Lot – 337 G2 – pop. 185 – alt. 360 m – ✉ 46500 29 **C1**

Paris 531 – Brive-la-Gaillarde 50 – Cahors 68 – Figeac 41 – Gramat 10 – St-Céré 17

Syndicat d'initiative, village ✆ 05 65 33 47 17, Fax 05 65 33 47 17

Gouffre de Padirac★★ North: 2,5 km, Dordogne-Berry-Limousin

L'Auberge de Mathieu
rte du gouffre, 2 km – ✆ 05 65 33 64 68 – http://perso.wanadoo.fr/auberge.mathieu – auberge.mathieu@gmail.com – Fax 05 65 33 64 68 – Open 1st April-15 November
5 rm – €52 €52/64, €7 – ½ P €55/65
Rest – Menu (€15), €18/34 – Carte €24/48
◆ Located just a couple of hundred metres from the entrance to the Gouffre de Padirac, this auberge offers guests unpretentious service and accommodation that is basic but functional. Regional dishes speedily served in the pastel-coloured dining room or on the shady terrace.

PAILHEROLS – 15 Cantal – 330 E5 – pop. 167 – alt. 1 000 m – ✉ 15800 5 B3

Paris 558 – Aurillac 32 – Entraygues-sur-Truyère 45 – Murat 39 – Vic-sur-Cère 14

Auberge des Montagnes
rm, VISA MC

– ✆ 04 71 47 57 01 – www.auberge-des-montagnes.com – info@auberge-des-montagnes.com – Fax 04 71 49 63 83 – Closed 11 November-20 December

23 rm – €50/70 €50/70, €8 – ½ P €47/60

Rest – *(closed 7 October-20 December and Tuesday)* Menu €21 (weekdays), €26/36 – Carte €25/40

◆ This prettily restored farmhouse offers numerous leisure activities (Turkish bath, climbing wall, etc.). Attractive wood-panelled rooms; those in the wing are more spacious. Welcoming dining rooms, including a conservatory; well-prepared, generous portions of Auvergne cuisine.

PAIMPOL – 22 Côtes-d'Armor – 309 D2 – pop. 7 756 – alt. 15 m 10 C1 – ✉ 22500 Brittany

Paris 494 – Guingamp 29 – Lannion 33 – St-Brieuc 46

Office de tourisme, 19, rue du Général Leclerc ✆ 02 96 20 83 16, Fax 02 96 55 11 12

Beauport abbey★ 2 km by D 786 - Tour de Kerroc'h ≤★ 3 km by D 789 then 15 mn.

Pointe de Minard★★ 11 km by D 786.

K'Loys
rm, VISA MC AE

21 quai Morand – ✆ 02 96 20 40 01 – www.k-loys.com – hotelkloys@orange.fr – Fax 02 96 20 72 68

17 rm – €85 €85/200, €8 **Rest** – Menu €19/38 – Carte €20/40

◆ This former ship owner's residence facing the harbour is now a characterful hotel. Find antique furnished guestrooms, a plush sitting room and veranda breakfast room. Marine bistro serving pancakes and seafood; wharfside terrace.

Goëlo without rest
VISA MC AE

quai Duguay-Trouin – ✆ 02 96 20 82 74 – www.legoelo.com – contact@legoelo.com – Fax 02 96 20 58 93 – Closed 16-25 January

32 rm – €45/51 €60/75, €7

◆ Set on the marina quayside, this recent building commands a view of the masts. Small but comfortable and well-kept rooms. Buffet breakfast. Friendly welcome.

De la Marne with rm
AC rest, P VISA MC AE

30 r. de la Marne – ✆ 02 96 20 82 16 – www.hotelrestaurantdelamarne.com – hotel.marne22.restaurant@wanadoo.fr – Fax 02 96 20 92 07 – Closed 4-20 October, 15-24 February, Tuesday from October to March, Sunday dinner and Monday

9 rm – €57 €57, €9 – ½ P €67 **Rest** – Menu €29/85 bi

◆ Half way between the railway station and the town centre, this regional construction serves appetising 'surf n' turf' menus in a relaxing atmosphere. Attentive service. Practical guestrooms.

La Vieille Tour
VISA MC AE

13 r. de l'Église – ✆ 02 96 20 83 18 – lavieilletour@orange.fr – Fax 02 96 20 90 41 – Closed 22 June-3 July, Sunday dinner and Wednesday dinner except July-August and Monday

Rest – Menu (€17), €30/51 – Carte €53/78

◆ Charming 16C inn in the heart of historic Paimpol. A wooden staircase leads up to the main rustic and stylish dining room. Traditional menu and simpler bistro formula at midday.

La Cotriade
≤ VISA MC

16 quai Armand Dayot – ✆ 02 96 20 81 08 – www.la-cotriade.com – contact@la-cotriade.com – Fax 0296551094 – Closed 29 June-3 July, 22 November-7 December, 7-22 February, Sunday in low season, Monday except dinner in high season, Wednesday lunch and Saturday lunch in high season

Rest – Menu (€19), €25 (weekday lunch) – Carte €44/60

◆ Small, modernised bistro with a slightly Japanese decor and a wharfside terrace. A concise slate displays a choice of updated recipes that vary with the tides and seasons.

in Ploubazlanec 3.5 km north by D 789 – **309** D2 – **pop. 3 321** – **alt. 60 m** – ✉ **22620**

Les Agapanthes without rest
1 r. Adrien Rebours – ☎ 02 96 55 89 06 – www.hotel-les-agapanthes.com – contact@hotel-les-agapanthes.com – Fax 02 96 55 79 79 – Closed 5 January-2 February
21 rm – €43/70 €43/70, €8
◆ This house dating back to 1768 and flanked by a recent wing, offers nautical inspired, well-kept rooms that are more spacious in the new section. Terrace facing the bay.

PAIMPONT – 35 Ille-et-Vilaine – **309** I6 – **pop. 1 614** – **alt. 159 m** – ✉ **35380** Brittany 10 **C2**

Paris 393 – Bruz 37 – Cesson-Sévigné 54 – Rennes 42

Syndicat d'initiative, 5, esplanade de Brocéliande ☎ 02 99 07 84 23, Fax 02 99 07 84 24

La Corne de Cerf without rest
Le Cannée, 2 km south – ☎ 02 99 07 84 19 – http://corneducerf.beld.net – Closed January
3 rm – €48 €56
◆ The legendary Brocéliande Forest is only a stone's throw from this long house, decorated like an artist's home. Cheerful rooms. Homemade organic bread and jams at breakfast.

PAIRIS – 68 Haut-Rhin – **315** G8 – **see Orbey**

LE PALAIS – 56 Morbihan – **308** M10 – **see Belle-Île-en-Mer**

PALAVAS-LES-FLOTS – 34 Hérault – **339** I7 – **pop. 6 048** – **alt. 1 m** – Casino – ✉ **34250** Languedoc-Roussillon-Tarn Gorges 23 **C2**

Paris 763 – Aigues-Mortes 26 – Montpellier 17 – Nîmes 60 – Sète 33

Office de tourisme, Phare de la Méditerranée ☎ 04 67 07 73 34, Fax 04 67 07 73 58

Former★ aguelone cathedral Southwest: 4 km.

Brasilia without rest
9 bd Joffre – ☎ 04 67 68 00 68 – www.brasilia-palavas.com – hotel@brasilia-palavas.com – Fax 04 67 68 40 41 – Closed 1st December-2 January
22 rm – €52/106 €53/107, €8
◆ This seafront hotel has had a contemporary style makeover. Practical rooms refurbished in a fashionable spirit, all with a balcony or terrace.

Amérique Hôtel without rest
av. F. Fabrège – ☎ 04 67 68 04 39 – www.hotelamerique.com – hotel.amerique@wanadoo.fr – Fax 04 67 68 07 83
49 rm – €57/72 €57/72, €8
◆ A hotel made up of two buildings separated by an avenue leading to the sea. Practical guestrooms, gradually refurbished in a modern style. Pool and Jacuzzi.

L'Escale
5 bd Sarrail, (left bank) – ☎ 04 67 68 24 17 – www.restaurant-lescale.com – rizzotti@club-internet.fr – Fax 04 67 68 24 17 – Closed Wednesday September-June except holidays, Wednesday lunch and Thursday lunch July-August
Rest – Menu €22 bi (weekday lunch), €29/65 – Carte €45/55
◆ The elegant dining hall and veranda offer a fine view of the beach. Appetising up-to-date cuisine largely inspired by the nearby sea.

Le Saint-Georges
4 bd Maréchal-Foch, (next to the casino) – ☎ 04 67 68 31 38 – le-st-georges.palavas@wanadoo.fr – Closed 28 June-6 July, Saturday lunch, Sunday dinner and Monday
Rest – Menu (€19), €24/34 – Carte €46/60
◆ In this enticing little bistro, find a friendly welcome, laidback atmosphere and traditional 'surf n' turf' recipes based on fresh produce.

PALEYRAC – 24 Dordogne – **329** G7 – see Buisson-de-Cadouin

LA PALMYRE – 17 Charente-Maritime – **324** C5 – ✉ 17570 38 **A3**

Paris 519 – La Rochelle 80 – Royan 16

Office de tourisme, 2, avenue de Royan ✆ 05 46 22 41 07, Fax 05 46 22 52 69

Palmyr'hotel

2 allée des Passereaux – ✆ 05 46 23 65 65 – www.monalisahotels.com – resa-palmyre@monalisahotels.com – Fax 05 46 22 44 13 – Open 4 April-3 November

46 rm – €95 €95, €11 – ½ P €74

Rest – Menu €19/37 – Carte €25/36

◆ Not far from the zoo, forest and beaches, this hotel complex offers functional rooms, almost all of which have a balcony. A few duplex rooms. Contemporary low-key decor and a terrace that is teeming in fine weather.

LA PALUD-SUR-VERDON – 04 Alpes-de-Haute-Provence 41 **C2**
– **334** G10 – **pop. 314** – **alt. 930 m** – ✉ **04120** French Alps

Paris 796 – Castellane 25 – Digne-les-Bains 65 – Draguignan 60 – Manosque 68

Syndicat d'initiative, le Château ✆ 04 92 77 32 02, Fax 04 92 77 32 02

Viewpoints: Trescaïre★★, 5 km, Escalès★★★, 7 km by D952 then D 23 - Point Sublime★★★, ⩤ on the Grand Canyon du Verdon Northeast: 7.5 km then 15 mn.

Des Gorges du Verdon

1 km south on the rte de la Maline – ✆ 04 92 77 38 26 – www.hotel-des-gorges-du-verdon.fr – info@hotel-des-gorges-du-verdon.fr – Fax 04 92 77 35 00 – Open 10 April-18 October

27 rm – €120/310 €135/370 – 3 suites – ½ P €83/200

Rest – *(dinner only)* Menu €34

◆ This hillside hotel stands near a village, popular with hikers. Rooms decked in colourful fabrics, and there are duplex family rooms and lovely suites. Hammam, Jacuzzi and pool. The menu is inspired by the region and served in a setting that also reflects local traditions.

PAMIERS – 09 Ariège – **343** H6 – **pop. 14 800** – **alt. 280 m** 29 **C3**
– ✉ **09100** Languedoc-Roussillon-Tarn Gorges

Paris 745 – Auch 147 – Carcassonne 76 – Castres 106 – Foix 20 – Toulouse 70

Office de tourisme, boulevard Delcassé ✆ 05 61 67 52 52, Fax 05 34 01 00 39

De France

rm, rest,

5 cours Joseph Rambaud – ✆ 05 61 60 20 88 – www.hotel-de-france-pamiers.com – contact@hotel-de-france-pamiers.com – Fax 05 61 67 29 48

31 rm – €50/60 €60/75, €8 – ½ P €50/63

Rest – *(closed Monday lunch, Saturday lunch and Sunday)*
Menu €18 (weekdays)/75 – Carte €59/76

◆ Located close to the town centre, the Hotel de France has benefited from a welcome makeover. Rooms are gradually being upgraded in a contemporary style with wood furniture. In The restaurant, a new sleek setting with artwork, photos and trendy furniture. Tasty cuisine with a personal touch.

De la Paix

rest,

4 pl. A. Tournier – ✆ 05 61 67 12 71 – www.hoteldelapaix-pamiers.com – info@hoteldelapaix-pamiers.com – Fax 05 61 60 61 02 – Closed 24 December-8 January

15 rm – €46/52 €52/57, €8 – ½ P €47/50

Rest – *(Closed Sunday dinner from October to May)*
Menu (€13), €16/35 – Carte €35/60

◆ Colourful rooms, furnished rustically or practically in this former post house. The warm atmosphere of bygone days pervades the dining room crowned by its superb (and original) moulded ceiling dating from 1760.

PANAZOL – 87 Haute-Vienne – **325** E5 – **pop.** 10 076 – **alt.** 302 m – ✉ 87350 24 **B2**

▶ Paris 395 – Limoges 5 – Saint-Junien 39 – Isle 9 – Saint-Yrieix-la-Perche 43

Domaine du Forest without rest

1 allée de Forest, 5 km north-east on N 141 and Golf de la Porcelaine road – ✆ 05 55 31 33 68 – www.domainedeforest.com – domainedeforest@wanadoo.fr – Fax 05 55 31 85 08

5 rm – †€ 95 ††€ 105

◆ A lovely drive leads up to this peaceful 18C manor. Plush sitting rooms and comfortable, meticulously decorated bedrooms. Tennis courts, fitness, sauna, Jacuzzi.

PANISSIÈRES – 42 Loire – **327** F5 – **pop.** 2 850 – **alt.** 641 m – ✉ 42360 44 **A1**

▶ Paris 448 – Lyon 62 – Saint-Étienne 65 – Villeurbanne 66

ℹ Office de tourisme, 1, rue de la République ✆ 04 77 28 67 70, Fax 04 77 28 82 18

La Ferme des Roses

Le Clair – ✆ 04 77 28 63 63 – http://lafermedesroses.free.fr – jednostka.arabians@free.fr

5 rm – †€ 44 ††€ 54/59 **Table d'hôte** – Menu € 17 bi

◆ This former farmhouse (1813) is well known for its friendly atmosphere, as well as the landlord's twin passions: Arab thoroughbreds, that he trains, and roses. Very well-equipped modern rooms. Local cuisine washed down with Forez wines.

LE PARADOU – 13 Bouches-du-Rhône – **340** D3 – see Maussane-les-Alpilles

PARAMÉ – 35 Ille-et-Vilaine – **309** J3 – see St-Malo

PARAY-LE-MONIAL – 71 Saône-et-Loire – **320** E11 – **pop.** 9 066 – **alt.** 245 m – ✉ 71600 Burgundy-Jura 7 **B3**

▶ Paris 360 – Mâcon 67 – Montceau-les-Mines 37 – Moulins 67 – Roanne 55

ℹ Office de tourisme, 25, avenue Jean-Paul II ✆ 03 85 81 10 92, Fax 03 85 81 36 61

◉ Sacré-Coeur basilica ★★ - Town hall ★ H.

PARAY-LE-MONIAL

Alsace-Lorraine (Pl.) 2
Billet (R.) 3
Chapelains (Allée des) 5
Charolles (Av. de) 6
Commerce (Quai du) 7
Dauphin-Louis (Bd) 8
Desrichard (R. Louis) 9
Deux ponts (R.) 12
Dr-Griveaud (R.) 13
Four (R. du) 14
Gaulle (Av. Ch.-de) 15
Guignault (Pl.) 17
Industrie (Quai de l') 18
Jean-Jaurès (Cours) 20
Lamartine (Pl.) 21
Paix (R. de la) 23
Regnier (Bd H.-de) 26
République (R.) 27
St-Vincent (R.) 28
Victor-Hugo (R.) 29
Visitation (R.) 30

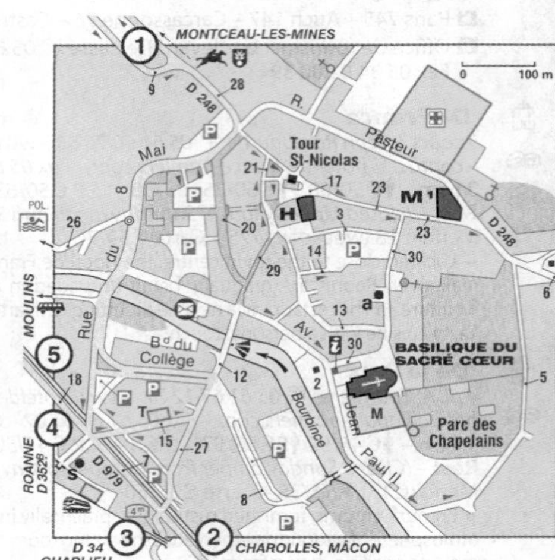

Le Parada without rest
Bb. Champ Bossu, via ①, Montceau road – 03 85 81 91 71 – www.hotel-leparada.com – leparada@wanadoo.fr – Fax 03 85 81 91 70
30 rm – €46/55 €55/70, €8
◆ A recently built hotel just outside town with spacious rooms (non-smoking). Breakfast on the veranda. Automatic payment and key delivery terminal in the evening.

Terminus
27 av. de la Gare – 03 85 81 59 31 – www.terminus-paray.fr – hotel.terminus@club-internet.fr – Fax 03 85 81 38 31 – Closed November school holidays and Sunday s
16 rm – €46 €62, €8 – ½ P €50
Rest – *(dinner only)* Menu (€14), €18 – Carte €28/44
◆ A typical 1900s station hotel, well renovated and easily recognisable by its candy pink façade. Period hall and comfortable rooms with fine bathrooms. Traditional cuisine served on the terrace in the shade of lime trees in summer.

Grand Hôtel de la Basilique rest,
18 r. de la Visitation – 03 85 81 11 13 – www.hotelbasilique.com – resa@hotelbasilique.com – Fax 03 85 88 83 70 – Open 2 April-27 October a
54 rm – €35/50 €42/57, €7 – ½ P €40/47
Rest – Menu (€14), €15/40 – Carte €19/44
◆ Four generations of the same family have managed this hotel and offer rooms that are being gradually renovated. Many overlook the basilica. Meals are served in a bright dining room reflecting the countryside and local tradition.

in Sermaize-du-Bas 12,5 km by ③ by D 34 then D 458 to Poisson dir. St -Julien-de-Civry – ✉ 71600 Poisson

M. Mathieu without rest
– 03 85 81 06 10 – mp.mathieu@laposte.net – Open 15 March-11 November
5 rm – €45 €50/60
◆ At this former hunting lodge in yellow stonework, a round tower leads to the clean rooms that are personalised with antique furniture. Pleasant welcome.

in Poisson 8 km by ③ On D 34 – pop. 575 – alt. 300 m – ✉ 71600

La Poste et Hôtel La Reconce with rm rm, rest,
– 03 85 81 10 72 – la.reconce@wanadoo.fr – Fax 03 85 81 64 34 – Closed 28 September-15 October, 1st February-6 March, Monday and Tuesday except dinner July-August
7 rm – €60 €68/112, €11
Rest – Menu (€17), €28/88 bi – Carte €45/60
◆ Old Charolais residence offering traditional, updated cuisine of predominantly local produce. Terrace shaded by plane trees. Attractively decorated and peaceful rooms.

via ⑤ 4 km on N 79 – ✉ 71600 Paray-le-Monial

Le Charollais
– 03 85 81 03 35 – www.lecharollais.fr – candussol@aol.com – Fax 03 85 81 50 31
20 rm – €53 €59, €7 **Rest** – grill – Menu (€16), €19 – Carte €24/50
◆ Motel style establishment with fresh, clean and variously arranged rooms that overlook a park with a children's play area. Charolais meat and pizzas cooked on a wood fire. Veranda and terrace.

PARC du FUTUROSCOPE – **86 Vienne – 322** I4 – **see Poitiers**

PARCEY – **39 Jura – 321** C4 – **see Dole**

H. Le Gac/MICHELIN

La place de la Concorde

PARIS and OUTSKIRTS

Department: 75 Ville-de-Paris
Population: 2 166 000
Pop. built-up area: 11 577 000
Altitude: 30 m
Postal Code: ✉ 75000
Carte régionale 21 **D2**

USEFUL INFORMATION

TOURIST OFFICES

25 rue des Pyramides (1er) ✆ 08 92 68 30 00 (0,34 €/mn) commun à tous les bureaux
20 bd Diderot Gare de Lyon (12e)
18 rue de Dunkerque Gare du Nord (10e)
place du Tertre Montmartre (18e)
Carroussel du Louvre (1er)
Anvers sur le terre-plein face au 72 bd de Rochechouard (18e)
Clemenceau angle av. des Champs-Elysées/av. de Marigny (8e)

BUREAUX DE CHANGE

Most banks are open from 9 am to 4.30 pm, except Sat, Sun and public holidays
to Orly-Sud Airport: 6.30 am to 11 pm
to Paris-Charles-de-Gaulle Airport: 6 am to 11.30 pm

TRANSPORT

Paris airport links: Info cars Air France (Air France coach information) ✆ 0 892 350 820 (0.34 €/min)(Roissy-Charles-de-Gaulle 1 and Charles-de-Gaulle2/Orly) departing from Étoile, Invalides and Montparnasse terminal.Info Bus R.A.T.P. ✆ 3246 (0.34 €/min).
Roissy-Bus, departing from Opéra 9e Orly-Bus, departing from pl. Denfert-Rochereau 14e : by rail (RER) ✆ 3246 (0.34 €/min).
Bus-Métro: see Paris Michelin Map No. 56. The bus allows a good view of the city, especially on short journeys.
Taxi: flag down a vacant cab – Taxi ranks – day and night: telephone calls
Auto-train: information ✆ 3635 and enter 42 (00.34 €/min)

POSTES-TÉLÉPHONE (post office and telephone services)

Each district has a post office branch open until 19:00, Saturday from 08:00 to 12:00 – closed on Sunday
Post Office open 24 hours: 52 r. du Louvre 1er ✆ 01 40 28 20 00

AIRLINE COMPANY

Air France : 49 av. de l'Opéra 2e ✆ 3654 (0,34 €/mn)

CAR BREAKDOWN SERVICE

There are non-stop repair workshops and breakdown services in Paris and the Paris Area Police stations will inform you of the nearest repairman

MICHELIN in Paris

Services de Tourisme (Tourist Services)
46 Av. de Breteuil - 75324 PARIS CEDEX 07 - ✆ 01 45 66 12 34, Fax 01 45 66 11 63.
Open Monday to Fridat from 08:45 to 16:30 (16:00 on Friday)
Michelin on-line shop: www.michelin.fr tab: "voyage et déplacements" (travel and business trips), heading: Cartes et Guides (Maps and Guides), and Espace Michelin (Michelin Area) on the 1st floor of BHV Rivoli, Rue de Rivoli, 75004 PARIS (métro station: Hôtel de Ville)

PRACTICAL INFORMATION

TOURIST INFORMATION

Paris "Welcome" Office (Office de Tourisme de Paris) : ✆ 0 892 683 000 (0,34 €/mn) Pyramides (Main Office) 25 r. des Pyramides 1st, Gare de Lyon 20 bd Diderot, Gare du Nord 18 r. de Dunkerque, Montmartre place du Tertre 18th, Carroussel du Louvre 1st, Anvers 72 bd de Rochechouard 18th, Clemenceau corner of av. des Champs-Elysées and av. Marigny 8th.

FOREIGN EXCHANGE OFFICES

Banks : close at 4.30 pm and at week-end
Orly Sud Airport : daily 6.30 am to 11 pm
Charles-de-Gaulle Airport : daily 6 am to 11.30 pm

TRANSPORT

Airports : Roissy-Charles-de-Gaulle ✆ 3950 (0,34 €/mn) – Orly Aérogare ✆ 3950 (0,34 €/mn)

Bus-Underground : for full details see the Michelin Plan de Paris n°56. The Underground is quicker but the bus is better for sightseeing and more pratical for the short distances

Taxis : may be hailed in the street when showing the illuminated sign-available, day and night all taxi ranks or called by telephone

POSTAL SERVICE

Local post offices: open Mondays to Fridays 8 am to 7 pm - Saturdays 8 am to noon
General Post Office, 52 r. du Louvre 1st : open 24 hours ✆ 01 40 28 20 00

AIRLINES

AMERICAN AIRLINES : Roissy-Charles-de-Gaulle airport T2a ✆ 01 55 17 43 41
DELTA AIRLINES : 2 r. Robert Esnault-Pelterie 7th ✆ 0 811 640 005
UNITED AIRLINES : Roissy-Charles- de-Gaulle airport, T1 gate 36 ✆ 0 810 72 72 72
BRITISH AIRWAYS : Roissy-Charles- de-Gaulle airport, T2b ✆ 0 825 825 400
AIR FRANCE : 49 av. de l'Opéra 2nd ✆ 36 54 (0,34 €/mn)

BREAKDOWN SERVICE

Some garages in central and outer Paris operate a 24-hour breakdown service. If you break down, the police are usually able to help by indicating the nearest one.

TIPPING

In France, in addition to the usual people who are tipped (the barber or ladies'hairdresser, hat-check girl, taxi-driver, doorman, porter, et al.), the ushers in Paris theaters ans cinemas, as well as the custodians of the "men's" and "ladies" in all kinds of establishments, expect a small gratuity.
In restaurants, the tip ("service") is always included in the bill to the tune of 15%. However you may choose to leave in addition the small change in your plate, especially if it is a place you would like to come back to, but there is no obligation to do so.

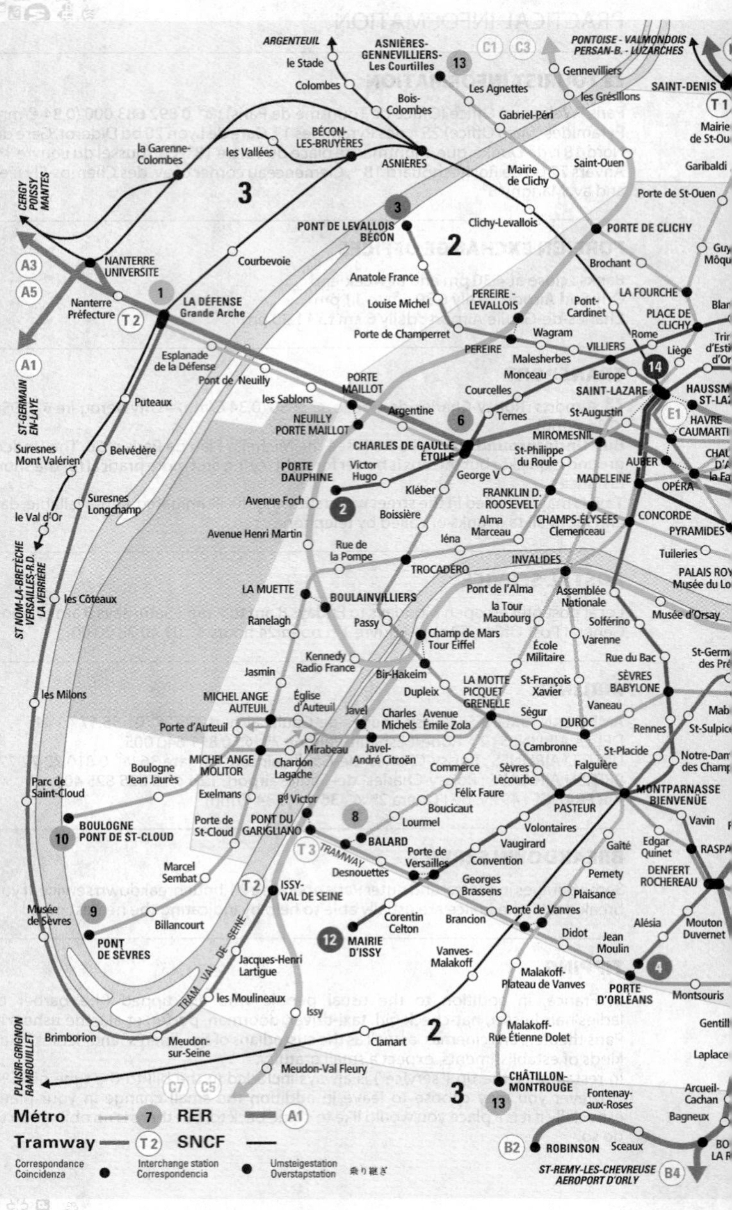
ARGENTEUIL
le Stade
Colombes
ASNIÈRES-
GENNEVILLIERS-
Les Courtilles
13
C1
C3
PONTOISE - VALMONDOIS
PERSAN-B. - LUZARCHES
Gennevilliers
Les Agnettes
les Grésillons
SAINT-DENIS
T1
Bois-
Colombes
Gabriel-Péri
Mairie
de St-Ou
BÉCON-
LES-BRUYÈRES
la Garenne-
Colombes
les Vallées
ASNIÈRES
Mairie
de Clichy
Saint-Ouen
Garibaldi
CERGY
POISSY
MANTES
3
Porte de St-Ouen
3
PONT DE LEVALLOIS
BÉCON
Clichy-Levallois
PORTE DE CLICHY
2
A3
A5
NANTERRE
UNIVERSITE
Courbevoie
Brochant
Anatole France
LA FOURCHE
1
Nanterre
Préfecture
T 2
LA DÉFENSE
Grande Arche
Louise Michel
PEREIRE -
LEVALLOIS
Pont-
Cardinet
PLACE DE
CLICHY
Porte de Champerret
Wagram
Rome
A1
Esplanade
de la Défense
PEREIRE
VILLIERS
Liège
Malesherbes
14
Pont de Neuilly
Monceau
Europe
ST-GERMAIN
EN-LAYE
Puteaux
les Sablons
PORTE
MAILLOT
Courcelles
SAINT-LAZARE
HAUSSM
ST-LA
NEUILLY
PORTE MAILLOT
Argentine
6
Ternes
St-Augustin
E1
HAVRE
CAUMARTI
Suresnes
Mont Valérien
Belvédère
CHARLES DE GAULLE
ÉTOILE
MIROMESNIL
St-Philippe
du Roule
AUBER
PORTE
DAUPHINE
Victor
Hugo
George V
MADELEINE
OPÉRA
Suresnes
Longchamp
Avenue Foch
2
Kléber
FRANKLIN D.
ROOSEVELT
le Val d'Or
Boissière
Alma
Marceau
CHAMPS-ÉLYSÉES
Clemenceau
CONCORDE
Avenue Henri Martin
Iéna
PYRAMIDES
ST NOM-LA-BRETÈCHE
VERSAILLES-R.D.
LA VERRIERE
Rue de
la Pompe
Tuileries
TROCADÉRO
INVALIDES
PALAIS ROY
Musée du Lo
LA MUETTE
BOULAINVILLIERS
Pont de l'Alma
Assemblée
Nationale
les Côteaux
la Tour
Maubourg
Musée d'Orsay
Ranelagh
Passy
Solférino
Champ de Mars
Tour Eiffel
Varenne
École
Militaire
Kennedy
Radio France
Rue du Bac
Jasmin
Bir-Hakeim
LA MOTTE
PICQUET
GRENELLE
St-François
Xavier
SÈVRES
BABYLONE
les Milons
MICHEL ANGE
AUTEUIL
Église
d'Auteuil
Dupleix
Javel
Charles
Michels
Avenue
Émile Zola
Ségur
Vaneau
Porte d'Auteuil
DUROC
Rennes
St-Sulpice
Javel-
André Citroën
Mirabeau
Cambronne
St-Placide
MICHEL ANGE
MOLITOR
Chardon
Lagache
Commerce
Sèvres
Lecourbe
Falguière
Notre-Dam
des Champ
Boulogne
Jean Jaurès
Parc de
Saint-Cloud
Exelmans
Bd Victor
Félix Faure
MONTPARNASSE
BIENVENÜE
8
Boucicaut
PASTEUR
BOULOGNE
PONT DE ST-CLOUD
10
Porte de
St-Cloud
PONT DU
GARIGLIANO
Lourmel
Vavin
Volontaires
BALARD
Gaîté
Edgar
Quinet
T3
TRAMWAY
Vaugirard
Porte de
Versailles
Convention
Marcel
Sembat
Desnouettes
Pernety
DENFERT
ROCHEREAU
T2
ISSY-
VAL DE SEINE
Georges
Brassens
Plaisance
Porte de Vanves
Musée
de Sèvres
9
Billancourt
Corentin
Celton
Brancion
Alésia
Mouton
Duvernet
TRAM VAL DE SEINE
PONT
DE SÈVRES
12
MAIRIE
D'ISSY
Didot
Jean
Moulin
Jacques-Henri
Lartigue
Vanves-
Malakoff
4
Malakoff-
Plateau de Vanves
PORTE
D'ORLÉANS
Montsouris
les Moulineaux
Issy
Gentill
2
Malakoff-
Rue Étienne Dolet
PLAISIR-GRIGNON
RAMBOUILLET
Brimborion
Meudon-
sur-Seine
Clamart
Laplace
Meudon-Val Fleury
CHÂTILLON-
MONTROUGE
C7
C5
3
13
Fontenay-
aux-Roses
Arcueil-
Cachan
Métro
7
RER
A1
Bagneux
Tramway
T2
SNCF
B2
ROBINSON
Sceaux
Correspondance
Coincidenza
Interchange station
Correspondencia
Umsteigestation
Overstapstation
乗り継ぎ
ST-REMY-LES-CHEVREUSE
AEROPORT D'ORLY
B4

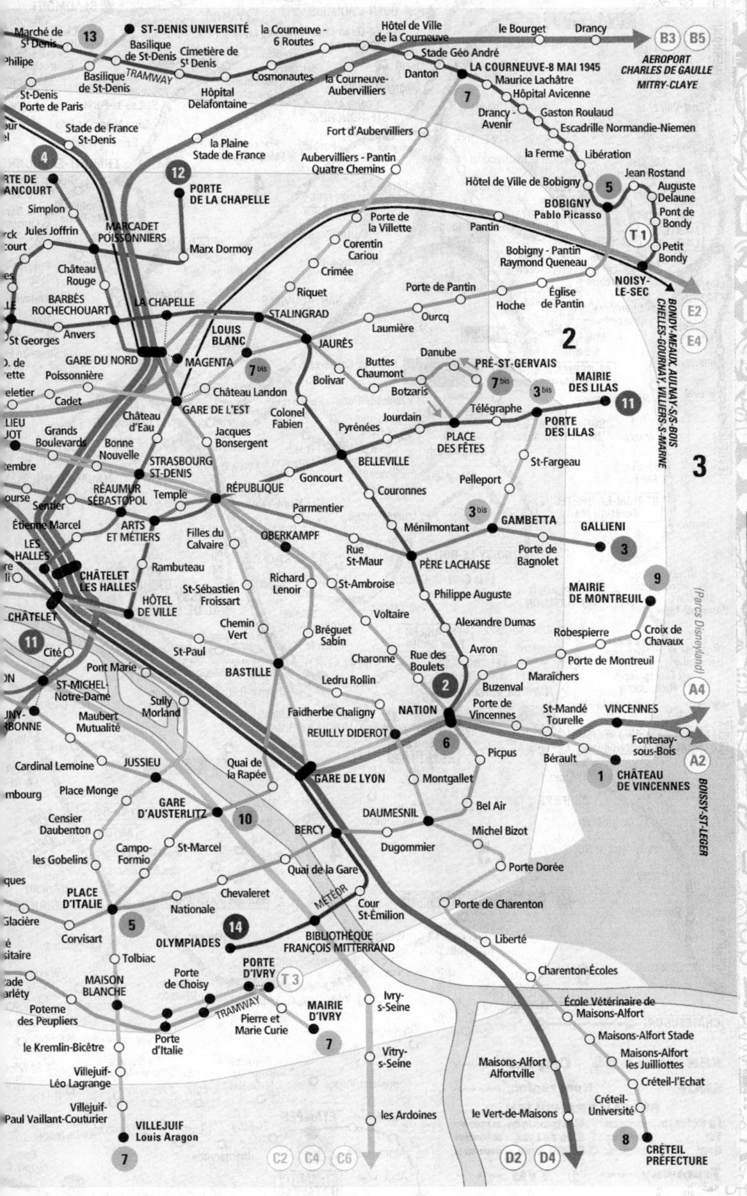
Marché de St Denis
13
ST-DENIS UNIVERSITÉ
la Courneuve - 6 Routes
Hôtel de Ville de la Courneuve
le Bourget
Drancy
B3
B5
AEROPORT CHARLES DE GAULLE
MITRY-CLAYE
Basilique de St-Denis
Cimetière de St Denis
Stade Géo André
LA COURNEUVE-8 MAI 1945
Basilique de St-Denis
TRAMWAY
Cosmonautes
la Courneuve-Aubervilliers
Danton
Maurice Lachâtre
Hôpital Avicenne
St-Denis Porte de Paris
Hôpital Delafontaine
7
Drancy - Avenir
Gaston Roulaud
Escadrille Normandie-Niemen
Stade de France St-Denis
la Plaine Stade de France
Fort d'Aubervilliers
la Ferme
Libération
4
Aubervilliers - Pantin Quatre Chemins
Jean Rostand
12
PORTE DE LA CHAPELLE
Hôtel de Ville de Bobigny
5
Auguste Delaune
Simplon
BOBIGNY Pablo Picasso
Pont de Bondy
Jules Joffrin
MARCADET POISSONNIERS
Porte de la Villette
Pantin
T 1
Corentin Cariou
Marx Dormoy
Bobigny - Pantin Raymond Queneau
Petit Bondy
Château Rouge
Crimée
NOISY-LE-SEC
Riquet
Porte de Pantin
Église de Pantin
BARBÈS ROCHECHOUART
LA CHAPELLE
STALINGRAD
Hoche
BONDY-MEAUX, AULNAY-S/S-BOIS
CHELLES-GOURNAY, VILLIERS-S-MARNE
E2
Anvers
LOUIS BLANC
Laumière
Ourcq
St Georges
JAURÈS
2
E4
GARE DU NORD
MAGENTA
7 bis
Danube
PRÉ-ST-GERVAIS
Poissonnière
Buttes Chaumont
Bolivar
Botzaris
7 bis
3 bis
MAIRIE DES LILAS
Cadet
Château Landon
11
GARE DE L'EST
Colonel Fabien
Télégraphe
Château d'Eau
Jourdain
Pyrénées
PORTE DES LILAS
Grands Boulevards
Bonne Nouvelle
Jacques Bonsergent
PLACE DES FÊTES
BELLEVILLE
St-Fargeau
3
STRASBOURG ST-DENIS
Goncourt
Pelleport
RÉAUMUR SÉBASTOPOL
Temple
RÉPUBLIQUE
Couronnes
Sentier
Parmentier
3 bis
GAMBETTA
Étienne Marcel
ARTS ET MÉTIERS
Filles du Calvaire
Ménilmontant
GALLIENI
OBERKAMPF
LES HALLES
Rue St-Maur
Porte de Bagnolet
3
PÈRE LACHAISE
CHÂTELET LES HALLES
Rambuteau
Richard Lenoir
St-Ambroise
9
MAIRIE DE MONTREUIL
St-Sébastien Froissart
Philippe Auguste
HÔTEL DE VILLE
(Parcs Disneyland)
CHÂTELET
Voltaire
Chemin Vert
Bréguet Sabin
Alexandre Dumas
Croix de Chavaux
Robespierre
11
Cité
St-Paul
Charonne
Rue des Boulets
Avron
Porte de Montreuil
Pont Marie
BASTILLE
Maraîchers
Ledru Rollin
2
Buzenval
A4
ST-MICHEL-Notre-Dame
Sully Morland
Porte de Vincennes
St-Mandé Tourelle
VINCENNES
Maubert Mutualité
Faidherbe Chaligny
NATION
REUILLY DIDEROT
6
Fontenay-sous-Bois
Picpus
Bérault
Cardinal Lemoine
JUSSIEU
Quai de la Rapée
A2
1
CHÂTEAU DE VINCENNES
GARE DE LYON
Montgallet
BOISSY-ST-LEGER
Place Monge
GARE D'AUSTERLITZ
10
Bel Air
Censier Daubenton
DAUMESNIL
BERCY
Michel Bizot
Campo-Formio
St-Marcel
Dugommier
les Gobelins
Quai de la Gare
Porte Dorée
PLACE D'ITALIE
Chevaleret
MÉTÉOR
Nationale
Cour St-Émilion
Porte de Charenton
Glacière
5
Corvisart
14
OLYMPIADES
BIBLIOTHÈQUE FRANÇOIS MITTERRAND
Liberté
Tolbiac
PORTE D'IVRY
T 3
Charenton-Écoles
MAISON BLANCHE
Porte de Choisy
Ivry-s-Seine
École Vétérinaire de Maisons-Alfort
TRAMWAY
MAIRIE D'IVRY
Poterne des Peupliers
Pierre et Marie Curie
Maisons-Alfort Stade
Porte d'Italie
7
le Kremlin-Bicêtre
Vitry-s-Seine
Maisons-Alfort Alfortville
Maisons-Alfort les Juilliottes
Villejuif-Léo Lagrange
Créteil-l'Echat
Villejuif-Paul Vaillant-Couturier
les Ardoines
le Vert-de-Maisons
Créteil-Université
VILLEJUIF Louis Aragon
8
CRÉTEIL PRÉFECTURE
7
C2
C4
C6
D2
D4

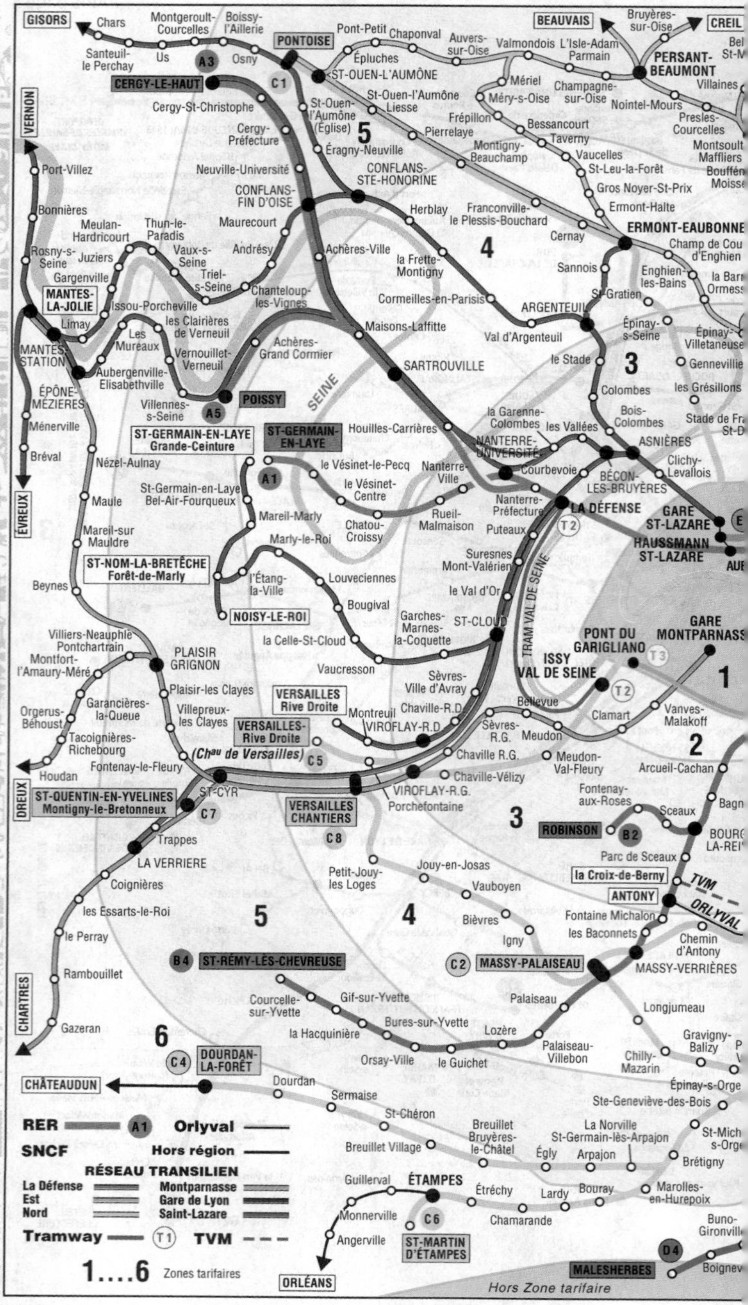

GISORS
Chars
Santeuil-le Perchay
Montgeroult-Courcelles
Us
Boissy-l'Aillerie
Osny
A3
PONTOISE
C1
Pont-Petit
Chaponval
Épluches
Auvers-sur-Oise
Valmondois
L'Isle-Adam Parmain
BEAUVAIS
Bruyères-sur-Oise
CREIL
PERSANT-BEAUMONT
CERGY-LE-HAUT
ST-OUEN-L'AUMÔNE
Mériel
Méry-s-Oise
Champagne-sur-Oise
Nointel-Mours
Villaines
Presles-Courcelles
Cergy-St-Christophe
St-Ouen-l'Aumône (Église)
St-Ouen-l'Aumône Liesse
Frépillon
Bessancourt
Taverny
Montsoult Maffliers
VERNON
Cergy-Préfecture
5
Pierrelaye
Éragny-Neuville
Montigny-Beauchamp
Vaucelles
St-Leu-la-Forêt
Port-Villez
Neuville-Université
CONFLANS-STE-HONORINE
Gros Noyer-St-Prix
CONFLANS-FIN D'OISE
Ermont-Halte
Bonnières
Meulan-Hardricourt
Thun-le-Paradis
Maurecourt
Herblay
Franconville-le Plessis-Bouchard
ERMONT-EAUBONNE
Rosny-s-Seine
Juziers
Vaux-s-Seine
Andrésy
Achères-Ville
4
Cernay
Champ de Courses d'Enghien
Gargenville
Triel-s-Seine
la Frette-Montigny
Sannois
Enghien-les-Bains
MANTES-LA-JOLIE
Issou-Porcheville
Chanteloup-les-Vignes
St-Gratien
Cormeilles-en-Parisis
ARGENTEUIL
Limay
Les Mureaux
les Clairières de Verneuil
Maisons-Laffitte
Épinay-s-Seine
Épinay-Villetaneuse
Val d'Argenteuil
MANTES-STATION
Aubergenville-Elisabethville
Vernouillet-Verneuil
Achères-Grand Cormier
SARTROUVILLE
le Stade
3
Gennevilliers
ÉPÔNE-MÉZIÈRES
SEINE
Colombes
les Grésillons
Villennes-s-Seine
POISSY
A5
Ménerville
la Garenne-Colombes
Bois-Colombes
les Vallées
Stade de France St-Denis
ST-GERMAIN-EN-LAYE Grande-Ceinture
ST-GERMAIN-EN-LAYE
Houilles-Carrières
NANTERRE-UNIVERSITÉ
ASNIÈRES
Bréval
Nézel-Aulnay
A1
le Vésinet-le-Pecq
Nanterre-Ville
Courbevoie
BÉCON-LES-BRUYÈRES
Clichy-Levallois
ÉVREUX
St-Germain-en-Laye Bel-Air-Fourqueux
le Vésinet-Centre
Maule
Nanterre-Préfecture
LA DÉFENSE
GARE ST-LAZARE
Mareil-Marly
Chatou-Croissy
Rueil-Malmaison
Puteaux
T2
HAUSSMANN ST-LAZARE
Mareil-sur Mauldre
Marly-le-Roi
ST-NOM-LA-BRETÈCHE Forêt-de-Marly
Suresnes Mont-Valérien
l'Étang-la-Ville
Louveciennes
le Val d'Or
Beynes
Bougival
TRAM VAL DE SEINE
NOISY-LE-ROI
Garches-Marnes-la-Coquette
ST-CLOUD
PONT DU GARIGLIANO
GARE MONTPARNASSE
Villiers-Neauphle Pontchartrain
la Celle-St-Cloud
ISSY VAL DE SEINE
T3
Montfort-l'Amaury-Méré
PLAISIR GRIGNON
Vaucresson
Sèvres-Ville d'Avray
1
Plaisir-les Clayes
VERSAILLES Rive Droite
Bellevue
Garancières-la-Queue
Chaville-R.D.
Clamart
Vanves-Malakoff
Orgerus-Béhoust
Villepreux-les Clayes
Montreuil
VIROFLAY-R.D.
VERSAILLES-Rive Droite
Sèvres-R.G.
Meudon
2
Tacoignières-Richebourg
(Chau de Versailles)
C5
Chaville R.G.
Meudon-Val-Fleury
Arcueil-Cachan
Houdan
Fontenay-le-Fleury
Chaville-Vélizy
DREUX
ST-QUENTIN-EN-YVELINES Montigny-le-Bretonneux
ST-CYR
VIROFLAY-R.G.
Porchefontaine
Fontenay-aux-Roses
Bagneux
C7
VERSAILLES CHANTIERS
3
Sceaux
Trappes
C8
ROBINSON
B2
BOURG-LA-REINE
LA VERRIERE
Petit-Jouy-les Loges
Jouy-en-Josas
Parc de Sceaux
Coignières
Vauboyen
la Croix-de-Berny
TVM
ANTONY
ORLYVAL
les Essarts-le-Roi
5
4
Bièvres
Fontaine Michalon
le Perray
Igny
les Baconnets
Chemin d'Antony
B4
ST-RÉMY-LÈS-CHEVREUSE
C2
MASSY-PALAISEAU
MASSY-VERRIÈRES
CHARTRES
Rambouillet
Courcelle-sur-Yvette
Gif-sur-Yvette
Palaiseau
Longjumeau
Bures-sur-Yvette
Gazeran
la Hacquinière
Lozère
Gravigny-Balizy
6
Orsay-Ville
le Guichet
Palaiseau-Villebon
Chilly-Mazarin
C4
DOURDAN-LA-FORÊT
CHÂTEAUDUN
Dourdan
Épinay-s-Orge
Sermaise
Ste-Geneviève-des-Bois
St-Chéron
Breuillet Bruyères-le-Châtel
La Norville St-Germain-lès-Arpajon
St-Michel-s-Orge
RER
A1
Orlyval
SNCF
Hors région
Breuillet Village
Égly
Arpajon
Brétigny
RÉSEAU TRANSILIEN
La Défense
Montparnasse
Est
Gare de Lyon
Nord
Saint-Lazare
Guillerval
ÉTAMPES
Étréchy
Lardy
Bouray
Marolles-en-Hurepoix
Chamarande
Monnerville
C6
Buno-Gironville
Tramway
T1
TVM
Angerville
ST-MARTIN D'ÉTAMPES
D4
1....6
Zones tarifaires
ORLÉANS
MALESHERBES
Boigneville
Hors Zone tarifaire

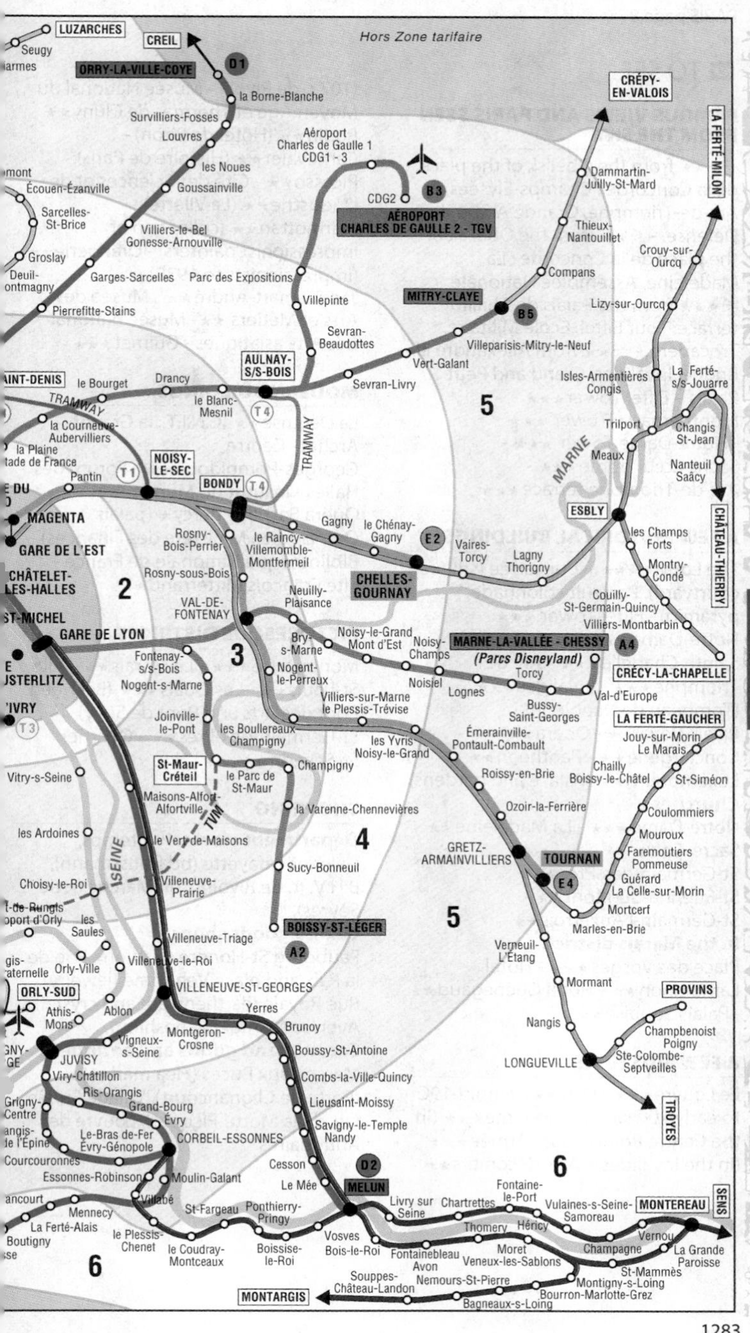

Hors Zone tarifaire
LUZARCHES
CREIL
Seugy
ORRY-LA-VILLE-COYE
D1
la Borne-Blanche
Survilliers-Fosses
Louvres
les Noues
Goussainville
Écouen-Ézanville
Sarcelles-
St-Brice
Villiers-le-Bel
Gonesse-Arnouville
Groslay
Deuil-
Garges-Sarcelles
Parc des Expositions
Pierrefitte-Stains
Aéroport
Charles de Gaulle 1
CDG1 - 3
CDG2
B3
AÉROPORT
CHARLES DE GAULLE 2 - TGV
Villepinte
Sevran-
Beaudottes
MITRY-CLAYE
B5
Villeparisis-Mitry-le-Neuf
Vert-Galant
Sevran-Livry
CRÉPY-
EN-VALOIS
LA FERTÉ-MILON
Dammartin-
Juilly-St-Mard
Thieux-
Nantouillet
Compans
Crouy-sur-
Ourcq
Lizy-sur-Ourcq
Isles-Armentières
Congis
La Ferté-
s/s-Jouarre
Trilport
Changis
St-Jean
Meaux
Nanteuil
Saâcy
MARNE
ESBLY
CHÂTEAU-THIERRY
AULNAY-
S/S-BOIS
le Bourget
Drancy
le Blanc-
Mesnil
T4
TRAMWAY
la Courneuve-
Aubervilliers
la Plaine
Pantin
T1
NOISY-
LE-SEC
BONDY
MAGENTA
GARE DE L'EST
Rosny-
Bois-Perrier
le Raincy-
Villemomble-
Montfermeil
Gagny
le Chénay-
Gagny
E2
Vaires-
Torcy
Lagny
Thorigny
les Champs
Forts
Montry-
Condé
CHELLES-
GOURNAY
Rosny-sous-Bois
Neuilly-
Plaisance
Couilly-
St-Germain-Quincy
Villiers-Montbarbin
CHÂTELET-
LES-HALLES
2
5
VAL-DE-
FONTENAY
GARE DE LYON
Bry-
s-Marne
Noisy-le-Grand
Mont d'Est
Noisy-
Champs
MARNE-LA-VALLÉE - CHESSY
(Parcs Disneyland)
A4
Fontenay-
s/s-Bois
3
Nogent-
le-Perreux
Noisiel
Torcy
CRÉCY-LA-CHAPELLE
Nogent-s-Marne
Lognes
Bussy-
Saint-Georges
Val-d'Europe
Villiers-sur-Marne
le Plessis-Trévise
LA FERTÉ-GAUCHER
Joinville-
le-Pont
les Boullereaux
Champigny
les Yvris
Noisy-le-Grand
Émerainville-
Pontault-Combault
Jouy-sur-Morin
Le Marais
St-Maur-
Créteil
le Parc de
St-Maur
Champigny
Roissy-en-Brie
Chailly
Boissy-le-Châtel
St-Siméon
Vitry-s-Seine
Maisons-Alfort-
Alfortville
la Varenne-Chennevières
Ozoir-la-Ferrière
Coulommiers
TVM
les Ardoines
le Vert-de-Maisons
4
Mouroux
SEINE
GRETZ-
ARMAINVILLIERS
TOURNAN
Faremoutiers
Pommeuse
Sucy-Bonneuil
Choisy-le-Roi
Villeneuve-
Prairie
E4
Guérard
La Celle-sur-Morin
Mortcerf
les
Saules
BOISSY-ST-LÉGER
5
Marles-en-Brie
Villeneuve-Triage
A2
Verneuil-
L'Étang
Orly-Ville
Villeneuve-le-Roi
Mormant
PROVINS
ORLY-SUD
VILLENEUVE-ST-GEORGES
Athis-
Mons
Ablon
Yerres
Brunoy
Nangis
Champbenoist
Poigny
Vigneux-
s-Seine
Montgeron-
Crosne
JUVISY
Boussy-St-Antoine
LONGUEVILLE
Ste-Colombe-
Septveilles
Viry-Châtillon
Combs-la-Ville-Quincy
Ris-Orangis
Grigny-
Centre
Grand-Bourg
Évry
Lieusaint-Moissy
TROYES
Le-Bras de-Fer
Évry-Génopole
CORBEIL-ESSONNES
Savigny-le-Temple
Nandy
Courcouronnes
Cesson
D2
6
Essonnes-Robinson
Moulin-Galant
Le Mée
MELUN
Fontaine-
le-Port
Villabé
Mennecy
St-Fargeau
Ponthierry-
Pringy
Livry sur
Seine
Chartrettes
Vulaines-s-Seine-
Samoreau
MONTEREAU
SENS
La Ferté-Alais
Thomery
Héricy
Boutigny
le Plessis-
Chenet
le Coudray-
Montceaux
Boissise-
le-Roi
Vosves
Bois-le-Roi
Fontainebleau
Avon
Moret
Veneux-les-Sablons
Champagne
Vernou
La Grande
Paroisse
6
Souppes-
Château-Landon
Nemours-St-Pierre
Montigny-s-Loing
St-Mammès
Bourron-Marlotte-Grez
MONTARGIS
Bagneaux-s-Loing

TO SEE

FAMOUS VIEWS AND PARIS SEEN FROM THE SKY

⩽★★★ from the Obelisk of the place de la Concorde : Champs-Élysées, Arc-de-Triomphe, Grande Arche de la Défense. - ⩽★★ from the Obelisk of the place de la Concorde : La Madeleine, Assemblée Nationale. - ⩽★★★ from the Palais de Chaillot terrace: Tour Eiffel, École Militaire, Trocadéro. - ⩽★★ from Allexandre III Bridge: Invalides, Grand and Petit Palais – Eiffel Tower★★★ - Montparnasse Tower ★★★ - Notre-Dame Tower ★★★ - Sacré-Cœur dome★★★ - Arc-de-Triomphe terrace★★★

A FEW HISTORICAL BUILDINGS

The Louvre★★★ (cour carrée (square courtyard), Perrault colonnade, pyramid) - Eiffel Tower ★★★ - Notre-Dame★★★ - Sainte-Chapelle★★★ - Arc de Triomphe★★★ - Invalides★★★ (Tombeau de Napoléon) - Palais-Royal★★ - Opéra★★ - Conciergerie★★ - Panthéon★★ - Luxembourg★★ (Palace and gardens)
Churches :
Notre-Dame★★★ - La Madeleine★★ - Sacré-Coeur★★ - St-Germain-des-Prés★★ - St-Étienne-du-Mont★★ - St-Germain-l'Auxerrois★★
In the Marais district:
Place des Vosges★★★ - Hôtel Lamoignon★★ - Hôtel Guénégaud★★ - Palais Soubise★★

A FEW MUSEUMS

Le Louvre★★★ - Orsay★★★ (mid-19C to early 20C s.) - Art moderne★★★ (in the Centre Pompidou) - Armée★★★ (in the Invalides) - Arts décoratifs★★ (107 r. de Rivoli) - Musée National du Moyen Âge et Thermes de Cluny★★ - Rodin★★ (Hôtel de Biron) - Carnavalet★★ (Histoire de Paris) - Picasso★★ - Cité des Sciences et de l'Industrie★★ (La Vilette) - Marmottan★★ (collection of Impressionist painters) - Orangerie★★ (Impressionists to 1930) - Jacquemart-André★★ - Musée des Arts et Métiers ★★- Musée national des Arts asiatiques - Guimet★★★

MODERN BUILDINGS

La Défense★★ (C.N.I.T., la Grande Arche) - Centre Georges-Pompidou★★★ - Forum des Halles - Institut du Monde Arabe★ - Opéra Bastille - Bercy★ (palais Omnisports, Ministère des Finances) - Bibliothèque Nationale de France - Site François Mitterrand★

PICTURESQUE DISTRICTS

Montmartre★★★ - Le Marais★★★ - Île St-Louis★★ - Les Quais★★★ (Between Pont des Arts and Pont de Sully) - St-Germain-des-Prés★★ - Quartier St-Séverin★★

SHOPPING

Department stores: Printemps, Galeries Lafayette (bd Haussmann), B.H.V. (r. de Rivoli), Bon Marché (r. de Sèvres).
Luxury goods shops:
Faubourg St-Honoré (fashion), Rue de la Paix and place Vendôme (jewelry), Rue Royale (earthenware and crystal), Avenue Montaigne (fashion).
Secondhand goods and antiques:
Marché aux Puces (Flea market)★ (Porte de Clignancourt), Village Suisse (av. de la Motte-Picquet), Louvre des Antiquaires.

ALPHABETICAL OF HOTELS

A

B

C

O
Page

P
Page

Q
Page

R
Page

ALPHABETICAL OF RESTAURANTS

A

B

C

PARIS page 16

STARRED ESTABLISHMENTS

✿✿✿ 2009

			Page
	Alain Ducasse au Plaza Athénée - 8e	XXXXX	85
	L'Ambroisie *(Bernard Pacaud)* - 4e	XXXX	52
	Arpège *(Alain Passard)* - 7e	XXX	72
	Astrance *(Pascal Barbot)* - 16e	XXX	120
N	**Le Bristol** - 8e	XXXXX	85
	Guy Savoy - 17e	XXXX	127
	Ledoyen - 8e	XXXXX	85
	le Meurice - 1er	XXXXX	43
	Pierre Gagnaire - 8e	XXXX	86
	Le Pré Catelan - 16e	XXXX	124

✿✿ 2009

	Les Ambassadeurs - 8e	XXXXX	84
	Apicius - 8e	XXXXX	85
	L'Atelier de Joël Robuchon - 7e	X	74
	Carré des Feuillants - 1er	XXXX	43
	Le "Cinq" - 8e	XXXXX	84
N	**L'Espadon** - 1er	XXXXX	43
N	**Gordon Ramsay au Trianon** - Versailles	XXXX	173
	Le Grand Véfour - 1er	XXXX	43
	Hélène Darroze-La Salle à Manger - 6e	XXX	65
	Lasserre - 8e	XXXXX	85
	Michel Rostang - 17e	XXXX	127
	Relais Louis XIII - 6e	XXX	64
	Senderens - 8e	XXX	86
	La Table de Joël Robuchon - 16e	XXX	120
	Taillevent - 8e	XXXXX	85

✿ 2009

N	**Agapé** - 17e	XX	128
	Aida - 7e	X	76
N	**L'Angélique** - Versailles	XX	173
	L'Angle du Faubourg - 8e	XX	88
N	**L'Arôme** - 8e	X	90
	Auberge des Saints Pères - Aulnay-sous-Bois	XXX	136
	Auberge du Château "Table des Blot" - Dampierre-en-Yvelines	XXX	146
	Auguste - 7e	XX	73
	Au Trou Gascon - 12e	XX	103
	Bath's - 17e	X	129
	La Belle Époque - Châteaufort	XXX	143
	Benoit - 4e	XX	53
N	**Bigarrade** - 17e	X	129
	La Braisière - 17e	XX	128
	La Bretèche - Saint-Maur-des-Fossés	XXX	165
	Le Camélia - Bougival	XXX	137
	Le Céladon - 2e	XXX	48
	Le Chiberta - 8e	XXX	86
	Au Comte de Gascogne - Boulogne-Billancourt	XXX	138
	Dominique Bouchet - 8e	X	90
N	**Ducoté Cuisine** - Boulogne-Billancourt	XX	139
	L'Escarbille - Meudon	XX	155
N	**etc...** - 16e	XX	122
	Les Fables de La Fontaine - 7e	X	75
N	**Fogón** - 6e	XX	66
	Gaya Rive Gauche par Pierre Gagnaire - 7e	X	74
	Gérard Besson - 1er	XXX	43
	La Grande Cascade - 16e	XXXX	124
	Hiramatsu - 16e	XXXX	120
	Il Vino d'Enrico Bernardo - 7e	XX	72
	Jacques Cagna - 6e	XXX	64

Rising stars

For ✿✿

BIB GOURMAND

Outskirts

PLEASANT HOTELS

Outskirts

PLEASANT RESTAURANTS

		Page
Alain Ducasse au Plaza Athénée - 8e	XXXXX ✿✿✿	85
Les Ambassadeurs - 8e	XXXXX ✿✿	84
L'Ambroisie - 4e	XXXX ✿✿✿	52
Apicius - 8e	XXXXX ✿✿	85
L'Atelier de Joël Robuchon - 7e	X ✿✿	74
Le Bristol - 8e	XXXXX ✿✿✿	85
Le "Cinq" - 8e	XXXXX ✿✿	84
L'Espadon - 1er	XXXXX ✿✿	43
La Grande Cascade - 16e	XXXX ✿	124
Le Grand Véfour - 1er	XXXX ✿✿	43
Il Vino d'Enrico Bernardo - 7e	XX ✿	72
Le Jules Verne - 7e	XXX ✿	71
Lasserre - 8e	XXXXX ✿✿	85
Laurent - 8e	XXXX ✿	86
Ledoyen - 8e	XXXXX ✿✿✿	85
le Meurice - 1er	XXXXX ✿✿✿	43
1728 - 8e	XX	87
Paris - 6e	XXX ✿	64
Le Pré Catelan - 16e	XXXX ✿✿✿	124
Le Restaurant - 6e	XX ✿	65
Taillevent - 8e	XXXXX ✿✿	85
La Tour d'Argent - 5e	XXXXX ✿	57

Outskirts

L' Auberge de l'Élan - Cernay-la-Ville	X	143
Auberge Ravoux - Auvers-sur-Oise	X	136
Cazaudehore - Saint-Germain-en-Laye	XXX	165
L'Escarbille - Meudon	XX ✿	155
Gordon Ramsay au Trianon - Versailles	XXXX ✿✿	173
La Gueulardière - Ozoir-la-Ferrière	XXX	159
Le Pouilly - Sénart	XXX ✿	168
Tastevin - Maisons-Laffitte	XXX ✿	152

MENUS FOR LESS THAN €30

Outskirts

OUTDOOR DINING

Outskirts

PRIVATE DINING ROOMS

Outskirts

BRASSERIES

Outskirts

BISTROS

Outskirts

TRADITIONAL DISHES

Coq au vin

Restaurant		Page
La Biche au Bois - 12e	X	104
Bourgogne - Maisons-Alfort	XX	152
Chez René - 5e	X	58
Le Coq de la Maison Blanche - Saint-Ouen	XX	166
Le Mesturet - 2e	X	49
Moissonnier - 5e	X	58
Quincy - 12e	X	104

Escargots

Restaurant		Page
Allard - 6e	X	67
Au Boeuf Couronné - 19e	XX	133
Au Bourguignon du Marais - 4e	X	53
Au Moulin à Vent - 5e	X	58
Au Petit Riche - 9e	XX	95
Au Pouilly Reuilly - Le Pré-Saint-Gervais	X	160
Le Ballon des Ternes - 17e	XX	129
Benoit - 4e	XX ✿	53
Bistrot St-Honoré - 1er	X	45
Bourgogne - Maisons-Alfort	XX	152
Gallopin - 2e	XX	48
La Petite Marmite - Livry-Gargan	XX	151
Petit Marguery - 13e	XX	105
Pharamond - 1er	X	45
Le Pré Cadet - 9e	X ☺	96
Le Sarladais - 8e	XX	88
Vaudeville - 2e	XX	48

Fish and seafood

Restaurant		Page
Au Pied de Cochon - 1er	XX	44
Le Ballon des Ternes - 17e	XX	129
Le Bistrot de Marius - 8e	X	91
Bistrot du Dôme - 14e	X	109
Bofinger - 4e	XX	53
La Cagouille - 14e	X	110
La Coupole - 14e	XX	108
Dessirier - 17e	XX	128
Le Dôme - 14e	XXX	108
Le Duc - 14e	XXX	108
L'Écaille de la Fontaine - 2e	X	49
L'Ecailler du Bistrot - 11e	X	101
Les Embruns - 1er	X	45
L'Espadon Bleu - 6e	X	66
Les Fables de La Fontaine - 7e	X ✿	75
Gallopin - 2e	XX	48
Gaya Rive Gauche par Pierre Gagnaire - 7e	X ✿	74
Goumard - 1er	XX	44
L'Huîtrier - 17e	X	130
Jarrasse L'Ecailler de Paris - Neuilly-sur-Seine	XX	157
Le Divellec - 7e	XXX ✿	72
La Luna - 8e	XX	89
La Marée Denfert - 14e	X	109
La Marée Passy - 16e	X	123
Marius - 16e	XX	122
Marius et Janette - 8e	XX	89
Marty - 5e	XX	57
Méditerranée - 6e	XX	65
Pétrus - 17e	XXX	128
Prunier - 16e	XXX	121
Rech - 17e	XX	128
La Rotonde - 6e	X	66
Terminus Nord - 10e	XX	99
35 ° Ouest - 7e	X	76
Vin et Marée - 7e	XX	74
Vin et Marée - 11e	XX	100
Vin et Marée - 14e	XX	108

Grills

Restaurant		Page
L'A.O.C. - 5e	X	58
Au Boeuf Couronné - 19e	XX	133
Au Pied de Cochon - 1er	XX	44
Bofinger - 4e	XX	53
Bistrot St-Honoré - 1er	X	45
La Coupole - 14e	XX	108
La Maison de L'Aubrac - 8e	X	91
Quincy - 12e	X	104
Severo - 14e	X	110

Soufflés

Restaurant		Page
L'Amuse Bouche - 14e	X	109
Cigale Récamier - 7e	XX	72
Le Soufflé - 1er	XX	44

Tête de veau

Restaurant		Page
Au Boeuf Couronné - 19e	XX	133
Au Petit Riche - 9e	XX	95
Au Pouilly Reuilly - Le Pré-Saint-Gervais	X	160
Benoit - 4e	XX ✿	53
Chez Georges - 17e	XX	129
Chez Jacky - 13e	XX	105
Louis Vins - 5e	X	58
Manufacture - Issy-les-Moulineaux	XX	150
Marty - 5e	XX	57
Pamphlet - 3e	XX	51
Petit Marguery - 13e	XX	105

PARIS page 32

Restaurant	Category	Page
Le Pré Cadet - 9e	X ☺	96
Ribouldingue - 5e	X ☺	59
Stella Maris - 8e	XXX ✿	87
Vaudeville - 2e	XX	48

CUISINE BY TYPE

Antilles, Réunion, Seychelles

Restaurant	Category	Page
Coco de Mer - 5e	X	59
La Table de Babette - 16e	XX	121
La Table d'Erica - 6e	X	68

Belgian

Restaurant	Category	Page
Graindorge - 17e	XX ☺	128

Chinese

Restaurant	Category	Page
Impérial Choisy - 13e	X ☺	106
Le Lys d'Or - 12e	X	104
Les Pâtes Vivantes - 9e	X	97
Tang - 16e	XX	122
Tsé Yang - 16e	XX	121
Village d'Ung et Li Lam - 8e	XX	90

Chinese, Thai and Vietnamese

Restaurant	Category	Page
Le Panoramic de Chine - Carrières-sur-Seine	X	140
Thiou - 7e	XX	73

Greek

Restaurant	Category	Page
Les Délices d'Aphrodite - 5e	X	58
Mavrommatis - 5e	XX	57

Indian

Restaurant	Category	Page
Indra - 8e	XX	88
Jodhpur Palace - 12e	XX	103
New Jawad - 7e	XX	73
Ratn - 8e	XX	89
Yugaraj - 6e	XX	65

Italian

Restaurant	Category	Page
L'Altro - 6e	X	68
Les Cailloux - 13e	X ☺	105
Conti - 16e	XX	122

Tripes

Restaurant	Category	Page
Pharamond - 1er	X	45
Ribouldingue - 5e	X ☺	59

Restaurant	Category	Page
Delizie d'Uggiano - 1er	XX	44
L'Enoteca - 4e	X	54
Fontanarosa - 15e	XX	113
Giulio Rebellato - 16e	XX	122
I Golosi - 9e	X	96
Montefiori - 17e	X	129
L'Osteria - 4e	X	54
Le Perron - 7e	X	76
Romain - 9e	XX	95
La Romantica - Clichy	XXX	144
Romantica Caffé - 7e	X	75
Sormani - 17e	XXX	127
Le Stresa - 8e	X	90
Le Vinci - 16e	XX	123

Japanese

Restaurant	Category	Page
Aida - 7e	X ✿	76
Azabu - 6e	X	68
Benkay - 15e	XXX	112
Bi Zan - 2e	X	49
Hanawa - 8e	XX	89
Hotaru - 9e	XX	95
Isami - 4e	X	54
Kaï - 1er	X	45
Kaiseki - 15e	X	115
Kinugawa - 1er	XX	45
Koetsu - 2e	X	49
Momoka - 9e	X	97
Ozu - 16e	XX	122
Tampopo - 16e	X	124
Tsukizi - 6e	X	68
Yanasé - 15e	X	113
Yen - 6e	X	66
Zen - 1er	X ☺	46

Korean

Restaurant	Category	Page
Bibimbap - 5e	X	59
Gwon's Dining - 15e	X	115
Sa Mi In - 7e	X	77
Shin Jung - 8e	X	91

Lebanese

North African

Portuguese

Russian

Scandinavian

Spanish

Thai

Tibetan

Turkish

Vietnamese

DINNER AFTER THE THEATRE

→ last orders in brackets

OPEN AT WEEK ENDS

PARIS page 36

Outskirts

ROOMS FOR LESS THAN €93

Outskirts

NEIGHBOURHOODS AND ARRONDISSEMENTS

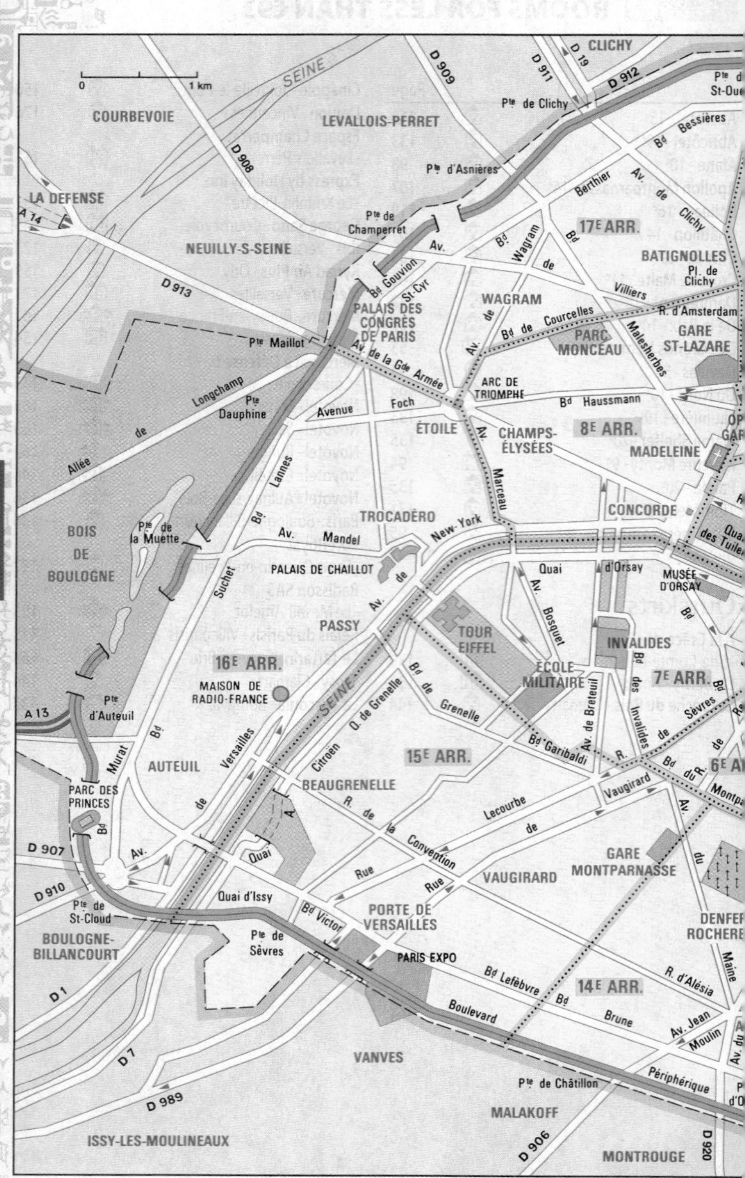

G12: These co-ordinates refer to **Michelin maps Paris** n° **54, Paris with index** n° **55, Paris North to South** n° **56**, and **Paris by Arrondissement** n° **57**
In these publications you will also find the closest car parks to the selected establishment.

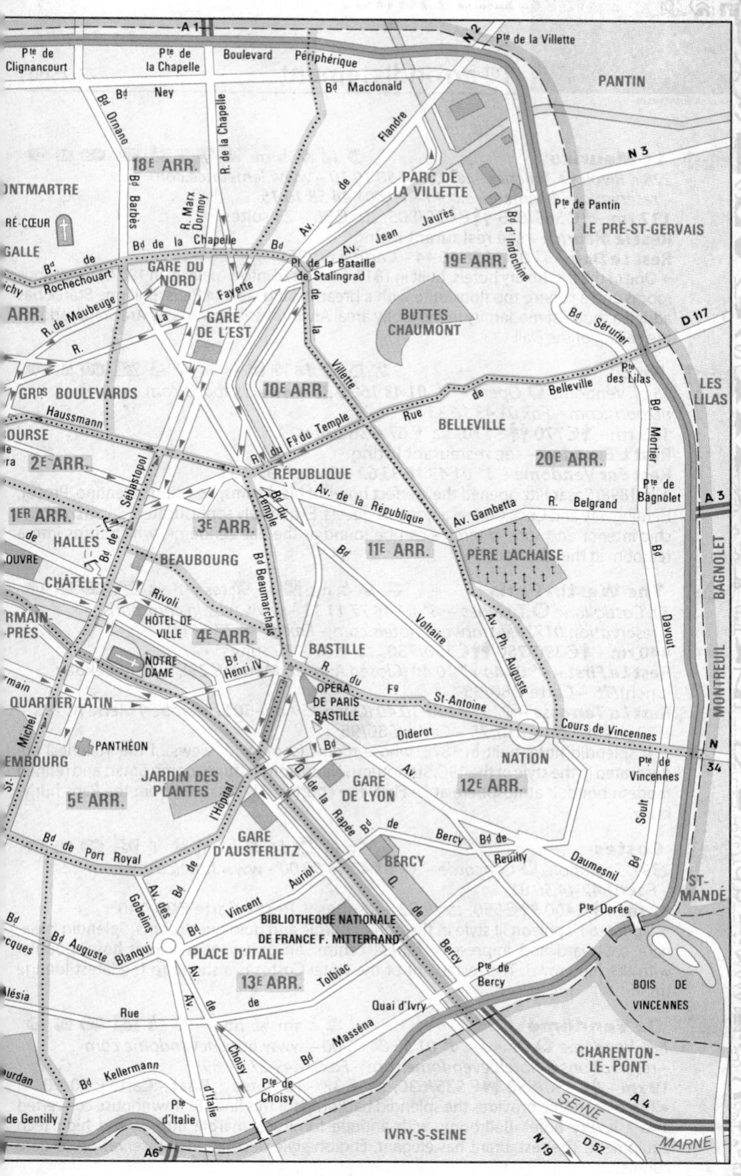

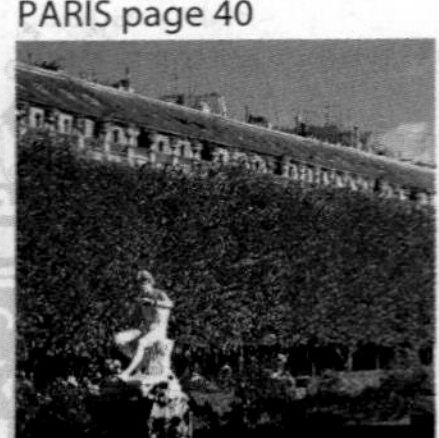
S. Sauvignier/MICHELIN

Palais-Royal • Louvre-Tuileries • Les Halles

1st arrondissement ✉ 75001

Le Meurice rm, VISA
228 r. Rivoli Ⓜ Tuileries – ✆ 01 44 58 10 10 – www.lemeurice.com – reservations@lemeurice.com – Fax 01 44 58 10 15 G 12
137 rm – †€ 565/665 ††€ 625/805, ☕ € 36 – 23 suites
Rest *le Meurice* – see restaurant listing
Rest *Le Dali* – *✆ 01 44 58 10 44* – Carte € 60/95
◆ One of the first luxury hotels, built in 1817, converted into a "palace" in 1907. Sumptuous rooms and a superb top floor suite with a breathtaking view of Paris. Philippe Starck has added a touch of modernity in the lobby area. An impressive canvas by Ara Starck adorns the ceiling of the Dali.

Ritz VISA
15 pl. Vendôme Ⓜ Opéra – ✆ 01 43 16 30 30 – www.ritzparis.com – resa@ritzparis.com – Fax 01 43 16 33 75 G 12
123 rm – †€ 770 ††€ 770, ☕ € 67 – 36 suites
Rest *L'Espadon* – see restaurant listing
Rest *Bar Vendôme* – *✆ 01 43 16 33 63* – Carte € 92/131
◆ In 1898, César Ritz opened the 'perfect hotel' of his dreams, boasting Valentino, Proust, Hemingway and Coco Chanel among its guests. Exquisitely sophisticated. Superb pool. A chic interior and superb terrace can be found at the Bar Vendôme, which turns into a tearoom in the afternoon.

The Westin Paris rm, rest, VISA
3 r. Castiglione Ⓜ Tuileries – ✆ 01 44 77 11 11 – www.westin.com/paris – reservation.01729@starwoodhotels.com – Fax 01 44 77 14 60 G 12
440 rm – †€ 390/750 ††€ 390/750, ☕ € 37 – 29 suites
Rest *Le First* – *✆ 01 44 77 10 40 (Closed August)* Menu (€ 29), € 32 (weekday lunch)/75 – Carte € 80/95
Rest *La Terrasse* – *✆ 01 44 77 10 40 (Open 15 April-30 September)* Menu (€ 29), € 32 (weekday lunch)/75 – Carte € 80/95
◆ A splendid hotel built in 1878, whose rooms (some with views of the Tuileries) are decorated in the style of the 19C. Sumptuous Napoleon III sitting rooms. Smart and refined modern boudoir atmosphere at Le First. The courtyard is secluded from the Paris hurly-burly.

Costes rm, VISA
239 r. St-Honoré Ⓜ Concorde – ✆ 01 42 44 50 00 – www.hotelcostes.com – Fax 01 42 44 50 01 G 12
82 rm – †€ 400 ††€ 550, ☕ € 32 – 3 suites **Rest** – Carte € 80/140
◆ Updated Napoleon III style in the hotel's purple and gold guestrooms. Splendid Italianate courtyard and impressive fitness centre. An extravagant luxury hotel popular with the hip crowd. The restaurant of the Hôtel Costes is a shrine to the latest lounge trend.

De Vendôme rm, rm, VISA
1 pl. Vendôme Ⓜ Opéra – ✆ 01 55 04 55 00 – www.hoteldevendome.com – reservations@hoteldevendome.com – Fax 01 49 27 97 89 G 12
19 rm – †€ 450/550 ††€ 535/630, ☕ € 32 – 10 suites **Rest** – Carte € 70/90
◆ Place Vendôme provides the splendid backdrop for this fine 18C townhouse converted into a luxury hotel. Bedrooms with antique furniture, marble fittings and high tech equipment. The restaurant has elegant, English-style decoration and serves up-to-date cuisine.

Renaissance Paris Vendôme
4 r. Mont-Thabor Ⓜ *Tuileries – ✆ 01 40 20 20 00 – www.renaissanceparisvendome.com – francereservations@marriotthotels.com – Fax 01 40 20 20 01* G 12
97 rm – †€ 330/620 ††€ 330/620, ☕ € 29 – 12 suites
Rest *Pinxo* – see restaurant listing
◆ A 19C building converted into a contemporary hotel with interesting decor from the 1930s to 1950s. Honey and chocolate tones and wood predominate in the high-tech bedrooms. Attractive Chinese bar.

Castille Paris
33 r. Cambon Ⓜ *Madeleine – ✆ 01 44 58 44 58 – www.castille.com – reservations@castille.com – Fax 01 44 58 44 00* G 12
91 rm – †€ 260/820 ††€ 260/820, ☕ € 28 – 17 suites
Rest *Il Cortile* – 37 r. Cambon, *✆ 01 44 58 45 67 (closed August, 24-30 December, Saturday and Sunday)* Menu (€ 38), € 48/95 – Carte € 53/80
◆ Delightful Venetian-inspired decor in the Opéra wing, with black and white chic in the Rivoli wing (in reverence to nearby fashion house Chanel). Il Cortile serves Italian cuisine in a Villa d'Este-style dining room. Attractive patio-terrace.

Regina
2 pl. des Pyramides Ⓜ *Tuileries – ✆ 01 42 60 31 10 – www.regina-hotel.com – reservation@regina-hotel.com – Fax 01 40 15 95 16* H 13
120 rm – †€ 375 ††€ 375, ☕ € 32 – 10 suites
Rest – Menu (€ 34) – Carte € 35/55
◆ The Art Nouveau decor of this 1900 hotel has been preserved. Superb lobby and the rooms, rich in antique furniture, are quieter on the patio side; some offer views of the Eiffel Tower. Dining room with a pretty Majorelle fireplace and popular courtyard-terrace.

Cambon without rest
3 r. Cambon Ⓜ *Concorde – ✆ 01 44 58 93 93 – www.hotelcambon.com – info@hotelcambon.com – Fax 01 42 60 30 59* G 12
40 rm – †€ 230/290 ††€ 330/370, ☕ € 19 – 2 suites
◆ Between the gardens of the Tuileries and Rue St-Honoré, pleasant rooms combining contemporary furniture, attractive engravings and old paintings. Regular clientele.

Royal St-Honoré without rest
221 r. St-Honoré Ⓜ *Tuileries – ✆ 01 42 60 32 79 – www.hotel-royal-st-honore.com – rsh@hroy.com – Fax 01 42 60 47 44* G 12
72 rm – †€ 340/390 ††€ 390/440, ☕ € 22
◆ An opulent-looking 19C building on the site of the former Hôtel de Noailles. Elegant and refined guestrooms, with Louis XVI decor in the breakfast room. Cosy bar.

Meliá Vendôme without rest
8 r. Cambon Ⓜ *Concorde – ✆ 01 44 77 54 00 – www.solmelia.com – Fax 01 44 77 54 01* G 12
83 rm – †€ 379 ††€ 399, ☕ € 28 – 4 suites
◆ Smart, restrained decor in tones of red and gold. Bedrooms with period furniture, elegant lounge with a Belle Époque glass roof, chic bar and attractive breakfast area.

Washington Opéra without rest
50 r. Richelieu Ⓜ *Palais Royal – ✆ 01 42 96 68 06 – www.washingtonopera.com – hotel@washingtonopera.com – Fax 01 40 15 01 12* G 13
36 rm – †€ 190/275 ††€ 245/335, ☕ € 13
◆ Former townhouse of the Marquise de Pompadour. Directoire or 'Gustavian'-style rooms. The 6th floor terrace offers beautiful views over the gardens of the Palais-Royal.

Mansart without rest
5 r. des Capucines Ⓜ *Opéra – ✆ 01 42 61 50 28 – www.esprit-de-france.com – mansart@espritfrance.com – Fax 01 49 27 97 44* G 12
57 rm – †€ 160 ††€ 170/345, ☕ € 13
◆ Close to Place Vendôme, this hotel pays homage to Mansart, architect to Louis XIV. Classic rooms furnished in Empire or Directoire style. A more modern lobby-lounge.

Opéra Richepanse without rest
14 r. Chevalier de St-George Ⓜ Madeleine – ✆ 01 42 60 36 00 – www.richepanse.com – hotel@richepanse.com – Fax 01 42 60 13 03 G 12
38 rm – †€ 250/444 ††€ 250/444, ☕ € 18
◆ The hotel has been fully renovated and furnished in Art Deco style. Harmonious, well-appointed bedrooms, some with views of the Madeleine. Vaulted breakfast room in the basement.

Novotel Les Halles rest,
8 pl. M.-de-Navarre Ⓜ Châtelet – ✆ 01 42 21 31 31 – www.novotelparisleshalles.com – h0785@accor.com – Fax 01 40 26 05 79
280 rm – †€ 195/309 ††€ 215/330, ☕ € 18 – 5 suites H 14
Rest – *(closed Sunday lunch and Saturday)* Carte € 20/45
◆ A central location near the St Eustache church and Forum des Halles, meeting facilities and renovated minimalist-style rooms are the main selling points at this modern hotel. Traditional menu and grill in the restaurant; bar open until 2am.

Britannique without rest
20 av. Victoria Ⓜ Châtelet – ✆ 01 42 33 74 59 – www.hotel-britannique.fr – mailbox@hotel-britannique.fr – Fax 01 42 33 82 65 J 14
39 rm – †€ 128/160 ††€ 152/279, ☕ € 13
◆ Founded by an English family during the reign of Queen Victoria, this hotel has retained its elegantly British Imperial charm and refined exotic feel. Charming lounge.

Thérèse without rest
5 r. Thérèse Ⓜ Pyramides – ✆ 01 42 96 10 01 – www.hoteltherese.com – info@hoteltherese.com – Fax 01 42 96 15 22 G 13
43 rm – †€ 155/320 ††€ 155/320, ☕ € 13
◆ The charm of this hotel lies in its refined contemporary decor of paintings, attractive fabrics and pastel shades. Vaulted breakfast room occupying the former cellars.

Relais St-Honoré without rest
308 r. St Honoré Ⓜ Tuileries – ✆ 01 42 96 06 06 – www.relaissainthonore.com – relaissainthonore@wanadoo.fr – Fax 01 42 96 17 50 G 12
15 rm – †€ 203 ††€ 203/340, ☕ € 13
◆ This 17C building is home to quiet, antique furnished rooms with exposed beams (except first floor). Breakfasts in the rooms only.

Molière without rest
21 r. Molière Ⓜ Palais Royal Musée du Louvre – ✆ 01 42 96 22 01 – www.hotel-moliere.fr – info@hotel-moliere.fr – Fax 01 42 60 48 68
32 rm – †€ 145/170 ††€ 170/190, ☕ € 14 G 13
◆ The hotel is named after the famous playwright, born in this street in 1622. Cosy and quite spacious non-smoking rooms with period furniture. Double-glazing.

Relais du Louvre without rest
19 r. Prêtres-St-Germain-l'Auxerrois Ⓜ Louvre Rivoli – ✆ 01 40 41 96 42 – www.relaisdulouvre.com – contact@relaisdulouvre.com – Fax 01 40 41 96 44 H 14
20 rm – †€ 125 ††€ 170, ☕ € 13 – 1 suite
◆ A stylish, quiet and well-maintained hotel behind a narrow 18C façade. Colourful yet refined guestrooms offering modern comfort. Attractive suite on the top floor.

Place du Louvre without rest
21 r. Prêtres-St-Germain-L'Auxerrois Ⓜ Louvre Rivoli – ✆ 01 42 33 78 68 – www.espritdefrance.com – hpl@espritfrance.com – Fax 01 42 33 09 95
20 rm – †€ 125/200 ††€ 154/200, ☕ € 13 H 14
◆ Stylish rooms, each bearing the name of a painter, in the shadow of the St-Germain-l'Auxerrois church. Breakfast is served in a 14C vaulted cellar which was once connected to the Louvre.

Aux Ducs de Bourgogne without rest
19 r. Pont-Neuf Ⓜ Châtelet – ✆ 01 42 33 95 64 – www.paris-hotel-bourgogne.com – bourgogne@paris-inn.com – Fax 01 40 39 01 25 H 14
50 rm – †€ 150/290 ††€ 150/290, ☕ € 15
◆ Situated in a 19C building, the well-soundproofed rooms are graced with period furniture. Recent, functional bathrooms. Plush sitting room.

Louvre Ste-Anne without rest
32 r. Ste-Anne Ⓜ Pyramides – ☎ 01 40 20 02 35 – www.louvre-ste-anne.fr – contact@louvre-ste-anne.fr – Fax 01 40 15 91 13 G 13
20 rm – €116/130 €135/190, €12
◆ In a street lined with Japanese restaurants, this hotel has small but well-equipped rooms decorated in pastel shades. Vaulted breakfast room.

le Meurice – Hôtel Le Meurice
228 r. Rivoli Ⓜ Tuileries – ☎ 01 44 58 10 55 – www.lemeurice.com – restaurant@lemeurice.com – Fax 01 44 58 10 76 – Closed 1st-30 August, 20 February-7 March, Saturday and Sunday G 12
Rest – Menu €90 (lunch)/220 – Carte €205/290
Spec. Poulet à la bouteille "Aniel Zélie" généreusement truffé, salade de jeunes pousses (winter). Dos de saumon de l'Adour confit, chou aux écorces d'orange et fumet au genièvre. Fuseaux croustillants au chocolat lacté, truffe blanche à la fleur de sel.
◆ Dining room in the style of Louis XIV, inspired by the château of Versailles, and talented modern cuisine by Yannick Alleno: a palace for gourmets!

L'Espadon – Hôtel Ritz
15 pl. Vendôme Ⓜ Opéra – ☎ 01 43 16 30 80 – www.ritzparis.com – espadon@ritzparis.com – Fax 01 43 16 33 75 G 12
Rest – Menu €80 (lunch), €105/340 bi – Carte €170/266
Spec. Emietté de tourteau, jaune d'oeuf fumé et caviar impérial. Sole aux coquillages, confit de pommes de terre au beurre demi-sel. Millefeuille "Tradition Ritz", crème glacée caramel.
◆ In this magical setting, amidst gold and drapery, Michel Roth's faultlessly classic cuisine finds its true expression. Impeccable service.

Le Grand Véfour
17 r. Beaujolais Ⓜ Palais Royal – ☎ 01 42 96 56 27 – www.grand-vefour.com – grand.vefour@wanadoo.fr – Fax 01 42 86 80 71 – Closed 20-24 April, 2-31 August, 24 December-1st January, Friday dinner, Saturday and Sunday G 13
Rest – Menu €88 (lunch)/268 – Carte €210/230
Spec. Ravioles de foie gras, crème foisonnée truffée. Parmentier de queue de bœuf aux truffes. Palet noisette et chocolat au lait, glace au caramel brun et prise de sel de Guérande.
◆ Many famous personalities have dined in the elegant Directoire-style *salons* of this luxurious restaurant, located in the gardens of the Palais-Royal. Innovative cuisine created by an inspired chef.

Carré des Feuillants (Alain Dutournier)
14 r. Castiglione Ⓜ Tuileries – ☎ 01 42 86 82 82 – www.carredesfeuillants.fr – carredesfeuillants@orange.fr – Fax 01 42 86 07 71 – Closed August, Saturday and Sunday G 12
Rest – Menu €58 (lunch)/175 – Carte €137/176
Spec. Huîtres de Marennes, caviar d'Aquitaine et algues marines (except summer). Turbot sauvage rôti, riz noir et asperges vertes (spring-summer). Cerises burlat en jubilé façon "forêt verte" (summer).
◆ A modern restaurant on the site of the former Feuillants convent enhanced by contemporary works of art. The up-to-date menu shows distinct Gascon influences and there is a superb choice of wines and armagnacs.

Gérard Besson
5 r. Coq Héron Ⓜ Louvre Rivoli – ☎ 01 42 33 14 74 – www.gerardbesson.com – gerard.besson4@libertysurf.fr – Fax 01 42 33 85 71 – Closed 25 July-24 August, Monday lunch, Saturday lunch and Sunday H 14
Rest – Menu (€70), €130 – Carte €125/160
Spec. Fricassée de homard "Georges Garin". Gibier (early Oct. to mid Dec.). Fenouil confit aux épices, glace vanille de tahiti.
◆ Elegant restaurant near Les Halles decorated in beige tones with still life paintings and Jouy wall hangings. Reinterpreted classic cuisine, game specialities and a fine wine list.

XXX **Macéo**
15 r. Petits-Champs Ⓜ *Bourse – ✆ 01 42 97 53 85 – www.maceorestaurant.com – info@maceorestaurant.com – Fax 01 47 03 36 93 – Closed 1-17 August, Saturday lunch, Sunday and bank holidays* G 13
Rest – Menu (€ 27), € 32 (weekdays)/60 – Carte € 50/62
◆ Lively French Second Empire setting: period mirrors combine with modern furnishings. Updated cuisine, a vegetarian menu and international wine list. Friendly lounge-bar.

XX **Goumard**
9 r. Duphot Ⓜ *Madeleine – ✆ 01 42 60 36 07 – www.goumard.com – goumard.philippe@wanadoo.fr – Fax 01 42 60 04 54* G 12
Rest – Menu (€ 29), € 39/49 bi – Carte € 49/70
◆ Esteemed 100-year-old Parisian restaurant where major artists including Majorelle, Lalique and Labouret have enhanced the Art Deco setting. Fine seafood menu.

XX **Palais Royal**
110 Galerie de Valois - Jardin du Palais Royal Ⓜ *Bourse – ✆ 01 40 20 00 27 – www.restaurantdupalaisroyal.com – palaisrest@aol.com – Fax 01 40 20 00 82 – Closed 21 December-10 January and Sunday* G 13
Rest – Carte € 50/75
◆ Beneath the windows of Colette's apartment, an Art Deco-style restaurant with an idyllic terrace, opening onto the Palais-Royal garden.

XX **Pierre au Palais Royal**
10 r. Richelieu Ⓜ *Palais Royal – ✆ 01 42 96 09 17 – www.pierreaupalaisroyal.com – pierreaupalaisroyal@wanadoo.fr – Fax 01 42 96 26 40 – Closed August, Saturday lunch and Sunday* H 13
Rest – Menu (€ 33), € 39/54
◆ Change of course for this establishment: a dining room redecorated in black and white, in a simple, chic effect, and dishes inspired by the southwest, a region that the owner promotes with passion.

XX **Au Pied de Cochon**
6 r. Coquillière Ⓜ *Châtelet-Les Halles – ✆ 01 40 13 77 00 – www.pieddecochon.com – pieddecochon@blanc.net – Fax 01 40 13 77 09* H 14
Rest – Menu € 26 – Carte € 35/66
◆ Famous Parisian brasserie well known among night owls since it opened in 1947. Long, traditional menu (pauper's platter, seafood).

XX **Le Soufflé**
36 r. Mont-Thabor Ⓜ *Tuileries – ✆ 01 42 60 27 19 – c_rigaud@club.fr – Fax 01 42 60 54 98 – Closed 3-24 August, 21 February-7 March, Sunday and bank holidays* G 12
Rest – Menu (€ 25 bi), € 31/36 – Carte € 40/50
◆ For over 40 years this elegant restaurant near the Tuileries has devoted itself to soufflés. Find a savoury and sweet menu totally dedicated to this culinary creation.

XX **Delizie d'Uggiano**
18 r. Duphot Ⓜ *Madeleine – ✆ 01 40 15 06 69 – www.delizieduggiano.com – losapiog@wanadoo.fr – Fax 01 40 15 03 90 – Closed 5-20 August, Saturday lunch and Sunday* G 12
Rest – Menu € 30 bi (weekday lunch), € 36/89 bi – Carte € 46/79
◆ Main dining room on the first floor with attractive Tuscany-inspired decor. Wine bar and delicatessen on the ground floor. All is dedicated to Italian cuisine.

XX **Au Gourmand**
17 r. Molière Ⓜ *Pyramides – ✆ 01 42 96 22 19 – www.augourmand.fr – Fax 01 42 96 05 72 – Closed 21-25 May, 10-17 August, 24-28 December, Saturday lunch, Sunday and bank holidays* G13
Rest – Menu € 30/105 – Carte € 65/80
◆ Traditional cuisine with a contemporary twist (including a menu based on Joël Thiébault's famous vegetables) prepared by a self-taught chef. Knowledgeable sommelier and friendly, welcoming ambience.

Saudade
34 r. Bourdonnais Ⓜ *Pont Neuf – ✆ 01 42 36 03 65 – Fax 01 42 36 30 71 – Closed 15-31 August and Sunday* H 14
Rest – Menu € 22 bi (lunch) – Carte € 35/59
◆ Enjoy an authentic Portuguese meal in the heart of Paris, in this restaurant decorated with azulejos tiles. Sample typical dishes and Lusitanian wines to the sound of fados.

Pinxo – Hôtel Renaissance Paris Vendôme
9 r. d'Alger Ⓜ *Tuileries – ✆ 01 40 20 72 00 – www.pinxo.fr – Fax 01 40 20 72 02 – Closed 3 weeks in August* G 12
Rest – Menu (€ 32 bi) – Carte € 48/70
◆ A restaurant with minimalist furniture, black and white shades, an open kitchen and understated but stylish decoration, serving simple, tasty dishes à la Dutournier.

Kinugawa
9 r. Mont Thabor Ⓜ *Tuileries – ✆ 01 42 60 65 07 – http://kinugawa.free.fr – higashiuchi.kinugawa@free.fr – Fax 01 42 60 45 21 – Closed 24 December-6 January and Sunday* G 12
Rest – Menu € 32 (lunch), € 75/125 – Carte € 54/125
◆ Japanese cuisine served on the first floor dining room with a contemporary, Japanese look: paintings, refined lines and discreet colours. Sushi bar on the ground floor.

L'Atelier Berger
49 r. Berger Ⓜ *Louvre Rivoli – ✆ 01 40 28 00 00 – www.restaurant-atelierberger.com – atelierberger@wanadoo.fr – Fax 01 40 28 10 65 – Closed Saturday lunchtime and Sunday* H 14
Rest – Menu € 37/69 – Carte € 37/55
◆ Opposite the Jardin des Halles, the modern first floor dining room is popular with locals who come here to enjoy the modern menu and fine wine list. Smoking room.

Willi's Wine Bar
13 r. Petits-Champs Ⓜ *Bourse – ✆ 01 42 61 05 09 – www.williswinebar.com – info@williswinebar.com – Fax 01 47 03 36 93 – Closed 9-24 August, Sunday and bank holidays* G 13
Rest – Menu (€ 21), € 27 (lunch)/35
◆ A collection of posters created for the establishment by modern artists decorates this very friendly wine bar. Bistro cuisine and carefully selected wines.

Pharamond
24 r. de la Grande-Truanderie Ⓜ *Châtelet-Les -Halles – ✆ 01 40 28 45 18 – www.pharamond.fr – dorabineau@wanadoo.fr* H 15
Rest – Menu (€ 19), € 29 – Carte € 43/92
◆ An institution dating back to the heyday of Les Halles. The Pharamond still serves traditional dishes (tripe and offal a speciality). Authentic 1900s decor.

Bistrot St-Honoré
10 r. Gomboust Ⓜ *Pyramides – ✆ 01 42 61 77 78 – bistrotsthonore@orange.fr – Fax 01 42 61 74 10 – Closed 24 December-2 January and Sunday* G 13
Rest – Menu € 28 – Carte € 30/77
◆ Despite its typically Parisian feel, this small bistro showcases the gastronomic traditions and wines of Burgundy, in a warm setting and relaxed atmosphere.

Les Embruns
4 r. Sauval Ⓜ *Louvre Rivoli – ✆ 01 40 26 08 07 – magalie.granjon@gmail.com – Closed 1-21 August, Sunday and Monday* H 14
Rest – *(number of covers limited, pre-book)* Menu (€ 25), € 35 (weekdays)/50 – Carte € 44/62
◆ From the small rustic dining room of this friendly establishment you can observe the chef at work, producing dishes using the freshest fish from Brittany's ports.

Kaï
18 r. du Louvre Ⓜ *Louvre Rivoli – ✆ 01 40 15 01 99 – Closed one week in April, three weeks in August, one week to Christmas, Sunday lunch and Monday*
Rest – Menu € 28 (lunch), € 31/135 – Carte € 16/38 H 14
◆ Simple, minimalist decor in traditional Japanese style in this restaurant specialising in dishes from Tokyo (fish and charcoal-grilled meats). Desserts by Pierre Hermé.

Zen

8 r. de L'Echelle Ⓜ *Palais Royal – ☎ 01 42 61 93 99 – www.restaurant-zen.fr.cc – mondial.paris@wanadoo.fr – Fax 01 40 20 92 91 – Closed 10-20 August* H 13

Rest – Menu (€ 12), € 18 (lunch), € 30/60 – Carte € 20/30

◆ Japanese restaurant with typically extensive menu, yet refreshingly untraditional in its decor: clean curving lines, white and acid green colour scheme.

Baan Boran

43 r. Montpensier Ⓜ *Palais Royal – ☎ 01 40 15 90 45 – www.baan-boran.com – baan.boran@orange.fr – Fax 01 40 15 90 45 – Closed Saturday lunchtime and Sunday* G 13

Rest – Menu (€ 16), € 45 (dinner) – Carte € 30/40

◆ An Asian venue opposite the Palais-Royal, with a modern setting enlivened by numerous orchids and serving Thai wok specialities.

Chez La Vieille "Adrienne"

1 r. Bailleul Ⓜ *Louvre Rivoli – ☎ 01 42 60 15 78 – Fax 01 42 60 15 78 – Closed 1-25 August, Saturday and Sunday* H 14

Rest – *(pre-book)* Menu € 26 (weekday lunch) – Carte € 40/61

◆ This restaurant is under new management, but the traditional dishes (pot-au-feu, kidneys), well-worn setting and friendly atmosphere have made its reputation continue.

Lescure

7 r. Mondovi Ⓜ *Concorde – ☎ 01 42 60 18 91 – Closed August, Christmas holidays, Saturday and Sunday* G 11

Rest – Menu € 24 bi – Carte € 28/35

◆ A rustic inn near Place de la Concorde. Closely packed diners enjoy generous portions of specialities from southwest France at a communal table.

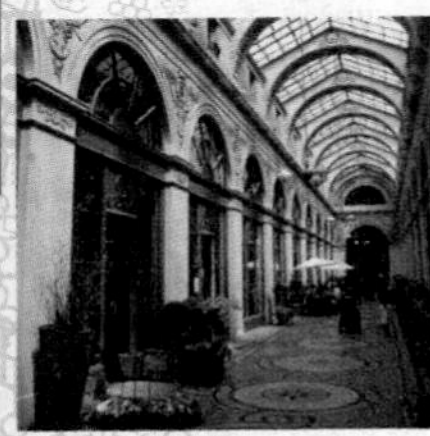

S. Sauvignier/MICHELIN

Bourse • Sentier

2nd arrondissement

✉ 75002

Park Hyatt

5 r. de la Paix Ⓜ *Opéra – ☎ 01 58 71 12 34 – www.paris.vendome.hyatt.fr – paris.vendome@hyatt.com – Fax 01 58 71 12 35* G 12

168 rm – †€ 800 ††€ 800, ☕ € 48 – 22 suites

Rest Le Pur' Grill – see restaurant listing

Rest *Les Orchidées* – *☎ 01 58 71 10 61 (lunch only)* Carte € 61/123

◆ This group of five Haussmannian buildings has been converted into an ultra-modern luxury hotel with contemporary decor by Ed Tuttle. Collection of modern art, a spa and high-tech equipment throughout. Cuisine in keeping with current tastes, served to diners beneath a glass roof.

Westminster

13 r. de la Paix Ⓜ *Opéra – ☎ 01 42 61 57 46 – www.hotelwestminster.com – resa.westminster@warwickhotels.com – Fax 01 42 60 30 66* G 12

102 rm – †€ 280/630 ††€ 280/630, ☕ € 28 – 22 suites

Rest *Le Céladon* – see restaurant listing

Rest *Le Petit Céladon* – *☎ 01 47 03 40 42 (closed August, Monday, Tuesday, Wednesday, Thursday and Friday)* Menu € 55

◆ In was in 1846 that this elegant hotel took the name of its most loyal guest, the Duke of Westminster. Sumptuous rooms, luxurious apartments. The hall is redecorated every season. The Céladon becomes the Petit Céladon at the weekend, with a simplified menu and more relaxed service.

Édouard VII without rest
39 av. Opéra Ⓜ Opéra – ✆ 01 42 61 56 90 – www.edouard7hotel.com – info@edouard7hotel.com – Fax 01 42 61 47 73 G 13
71 rm – †€ 220/360 ††€ 250/500, ☕ € 25 – 7 suites
◆ Edward VII, Prince of Wales liked to stay here on his trips through Paris. Spacious, luxurious rooms. Dark wood panelling and stained glass decorate the bar.

Mercure Stendhal without rest
22 r. D. Casanova Ⓜ Opéra – ✆ 01 44 58 52 52 – www.mercure.com – h1610@accor.com – Fax 01 44 58 52 00 G 12
20 rm – †€ 270/410 ††€ 290/420, ☕ € 17
◆ On the trail of the famous writer, stay in the "Red and Black" suite of this stylish residence. Smart, personalised rooms and snug lounge-bar with fireplace.

L'Horset Opéra without rest
18 r. d'Antin Ⓜ Opéra – ✆ 01 44 71 87 00 – www.hotelhorsetopera.com – reservation@hotelhorsetopera.com – Fax 01 42 66 55 54 G 13
54 rm ☕ – †€ 180/265 ††€ 195/295
◆ Colourful wall hangings, warm wood panelling and fine furnishings add style to the rooms of this traditional hotel a short distance from the Garnier Opera House. Cosy lounge.

Noailles without rest
9 r. de la Michodière Ⓜ Quatre Septembre – ✆ 01 47 42 92 90 – www.hoteldenoailles.com – goldentulip.denoailles@wanadoo.fr – Fax 01 49 24 92 71 G 13
58 rm – †€ 205/265 ††€ 215/280, ☕ € 15 – 4 suites
◆ Bold contemporary elegance behind a pretty façade. Minimalist decor in the rooms, most of which open onto a patio-terrace. Fashionable lounges.

États-Unis Opéra without rest
16 r. d'Antin Ⓜ Opéra – ✆ 01 42 65 05 05 – www.hotel-paris-opera.com – us-opera@wanadoo.fr – Fax 01 42 65 93 70 G 13
45 rm – †€ 110/222 ††€ 135/255, ☕ € 12
◆ Nestled by a quiet street, this hotel in a 1930s building offers modern, comfortable rooms. Breakfast is served in the inviting English-style bar.

Victoires Opéra without rest
56 r. Montorgueil Ⓜ Etienne Marcel – ✆ 01 42 36 41 08 – www.victoiresopera.com – hotel@victoiresopera.com – Fax 01 45 08 08 79 G 14
24 rm – †€ 214 ††€ 214, ☕ € 12
◆ In a lively and fashionable pedestrian shopping street this trendy establishment offers tasteful, elegant, snug rooms. Breakfast is served in a lovely vaulted room.

Malte Opéra without rest
63 r. de Richelieu Ⓜ Quatre Septembre – ✆ 01 44 58 94 94 – www.astotel.com – hotel.malte@astotel.com – Fax 01 42 86 88 19 G 13
64 rm – †€ 176/240 ††€ 176/240, ☕ € 14
◆ Lovely 17C building facing the National Library. Appealing inner patio, classically decorated rooms (quieter overlooking the courtyard) and a plush peaceful lounge.

Favart without rest
5 r. Marivaux Ⓜ Richelieu Drouot – ✆ 01 42 97 59 83 – www.hotel-favart.com – favart.hotel@wanadoo.fr – Fax 01 40 15 95 58 F 13
37 rm ☕ – †€ 102/130 ††€ 135/160
◆ The artist Goya stayed in this charming hotel of timeless appeal. The rooms to the front, facing the Opéra-Comique, are the most pleasant.

Vivienne without rest
40 r. Vivienne Ⓜ Grands Boulevards – ✆ 01 42 33 13 26 – www.hotel-vivienne.com – paris@hotel-vivienne.com – Fax 01 40 41 98 19 F 14
45 rm – †€ 62/116 ††€ 77/116, ☕ € 10
◆ Family-run establishment two minutes from the Grands Boulevards. Spacious rooms in varying styles. Some have a balcony, others a terrace, but only one has a view of the rooftops of Paris.

Le Pur' Grill – Hôtel Park Hyatt
5 r. de la Paix Opéra – 01 58 71 10 60 – www.paris.vendome.hyatt.fr – paris.vendome@hyatt.com – Closed August G 12
Rest – *(dinner only)* Menu € 135/300 bi – Carte € 97/185
Spec. Sashimi de langoustines sur l'idée d'une pinacolada. Bar de ligne confit à l'huile d'olive, supions, sauce tonato. Sablé breton au beurre demi-sel, marmelade figues et cassis, crème glacée au shizo.
◆ Simplicity and refinement best describe the modern menu served in the chic and contemporary rotunda-shaped dining room (kitchen in full view). Attractive summer terrace.

Le Céladon – Hôtel Westminster
15 r. Daunou Opéra – 01 47 03 40 42 – www.leceladon.com – cmoisand@leceladon.com – Fax 01 42 61 33 78 – Closed August, Saturday and Sunday
Rest – Menu € 55 (weekday lunch), € 82/110 – Carte € 90/120 G 12
Spec. Thon rouge et sardine bretonne marinés et rôtis à la chermoula. Turbot côtier rôti au beurre salé, salade de charlotte grillée. Chocolat, sablé à la fleur de sel et sabayon.
◆ Sophisticated decor that combines Regency-style furniture and a collection of Chinese porcelain. Cuisine in line with current tastes.

La Fontaine Gaillon
pl. Gaillon Quatre Septembre – 01 47 42 63 22 – www.la-fontaine-gaillon.com – lafontainegaillon@cegetel.net – Fax 01 47 42 82 84 – Closed 1-23 August, Saturday and Sunday G 13
Rest – Menu € 43 (weekday lunch), € 49/58 – Carte € 60/70
◆ Seafood dishes and wine selection supervised by the actor Gérard Depardieu in a graceful, 17C townhouse. Stylish decor and terrace with central fountain.

Drouant
16 pl. Gaillon Quatre Septembre – 01 42 65 15 16 – www.drouant.com – a.westermann@orange.fr – Fax 01 49 24 02 15 G 13
Rest – Menu € 43 (lunch)/54 – Carte € 56/86
◆ Under the auspices of Antoine Westermann, the legendary Goncourt restaurant is enjoying a new lease of life: elegant, opulent, yet uncluttered decor, dotted with antiques and a modern menu.

Le Versance
16 r. Feydeau Bourse – 01 45 08 00 08 – www.leversance.fr – contact@leversance.fr – Fax 01 45 08 47 99 – Closed August, 24 December-5 January, Saturday lunch, Sunday and Monday F 14
Rest – Menu (€ 32 bi), € 38 bi (weekday lunch) – Carte € 54/71
◆ A tasteful combination of elegant modern (white/grey tones, designer furniture) and period decor (exposed beams, stained glass). Contemporary cuisine from a globetrotting chef.

Gallopin
40 r. N.-D.-des-Victoires Bourse – 01 42 36 45 38 – www.brasseriegallopin.com – administration@brasseriegallopin.com – Fax 01 42 36 10 32 G 14
Rest – Menu (€ 25), € 30/36 bi – Carte € 30/50
◆ Named after its former owners, this brasserie opposite the Palais Brongniart, sports a plush, Victorian (1876) decor. Speedy service and excellent choice of bistro-style dishes.

Vaudeville
29 r. Vivienne Bourse – 01 40 20 04 62 – www.vaudevilleparis.com – Fax 01 40 20 14 35 G 14
Rest – Menu € 24/32 – Carte € 35/60
◆ This large brasserie with its sparkling Art Deco details in pure Parisian style has become the 'canteen' of numerous journalists. It is also especially lively after theatre performances. Classical menu.

Liza
14 r. de la Banque Bourse – 01 55 35 00 66 – www.restaurant-liza.com – info@restaurant-liza.com – Fax 01 40 15 04 60 – Closed Saturday lunch and Sunday evening G 14
Rest – Menu € 18 (weekday lunch), € 23/50 – Carte € 35/70
◆ Stylish Lebanese address (oriental designer decor with a "lounge" feel) offering a refined interpretation of traditional dishes.

Chez Georges
1 r. du Mail Ⓜ *Bourse – ✆ 01 42 60 07 11 – Closed August, Christmas holidays, Saturday, Sunday and bank holidays* G 14
Rest – Carte € 50/81
◆ The historic façade sets the scene for the style and spirit of the establishment: a genuine 1900 Parisian bistro. Traditional cuisine, fine wine list and faultless service.

Aux Lyonnais
32 r. St-Marc Ⓜ *Richelieu Drouot – ✆ 01 42 96 65 04 – www.esprit-bistrot.com – auxlyonnais@online.fr – Fax 01 42 97 42 95 – Closed 26 July-24 August, 24 December-2 January, Saturday lunch, Sunday and Monday* F 13
Rest – *(pre-book)* Menu € 32 – Carte € 40/49
◆ This bistro founded in 1890 offers delicious, intelligently updated Lyonnais recipes. Delightfully retro setting: bar counter, banquettes, bevelled mirrors and mouldings.

Le Mesturet
77 r. de Richelieu Ⓜ *Bourse – ✆ 01 42 97 40 68 – www.lemesturet.com – lemesturet@wanadoo.fr – Fax 01 42 97 40 68* G 13
Rest – Menu (€ 21), € 27/34
◆ Authentic regional produce, generous traditional dishes, fine choice of wines and friendly welcome: this old-fashioned style bistro is often completely full.

Pierrot
18 r. Étienne Marcel Ⓜ *Etienne Marcel – ✆ 01 45 08 00 10 – Fax 01 42 77 35 92 – Closed 9-28 August and Sunday* H 15
Rest – Menu € 50 bi/70 bi
◆ Bistro in the Sentier district offering a discovery tour of the flavours of the Aveyron. Free-range meat from the Aubrac, duck confit, foie gras, etc. Pavement terrace.

Silk & Spice
6 r. Mandar Ⓜ *Sentier – ✆ 01 44 88 21 91 – www.groupsilkandspice.com – paris@groupsilkandspice.com – Fax 01 42 21 36 25* G 14
Rest – Menu € 21 (lunch), € 32/60 – Carte € 48/61
◆ Elegant and intimate setting at this Thai restaurant with orchids, tropical wood and low-key lighting.

Bi Zan
56 r. Ste-Anne Ⓜ *Quatre Septembre – ✆ 01 42 96 67 76* G 13
Rest – Menu (€ 20), € 60/150 – Carte € 60/250
◆ Popular address (the name refers to a mountainous region of Japan) in minimalist style. Sushi counter, intimate upstairs dining room and interesting saké list.

L'Ecaille de la Fontaine
15 r. Gaillon Ⓜ *Quatre Septembre – ✆ 01 47 42 02 99 – Fax 01 47 42 82 84 – Closed 1-23 August, Saturday and Sunday* G 13
Rest – *(number of covers limited, pre-book)* Menu (€ 23) – Carte € 35/45
◆ Oysters and seafood to take away or sample in the delightful little room, decorated with souvenir photos of actor Gérard Depardieu, the owner.

Dalva
48 r. d'Argout Ⓜ *Sentier – ✆ 01 42 36 02 11 – www.dalvarestaurant.fr – Closed Sunday* G 14
Rest – Menu (€ 14), € 28/35
◆ A bright red façade, a few tables on the pavement, decorative touches from here and there... This friendly bistro stands out from the crowd with its market-inspired cooking at reasonable prices.

Koetsu
42 r. Ste-Anne Ⓜ *Quatre Septembre – ✆ 01 40 15 99 90 – Fax 01 40 15 99 59 – Closed Sunday* G 13
Rest – Menu (€ 15), € 16/55 bi – Carte € 28/48
◆ In a street crammed with Japanese restaurants, this establishment proposes sushi, sashimi and yakitori in a typically minimalist decor.

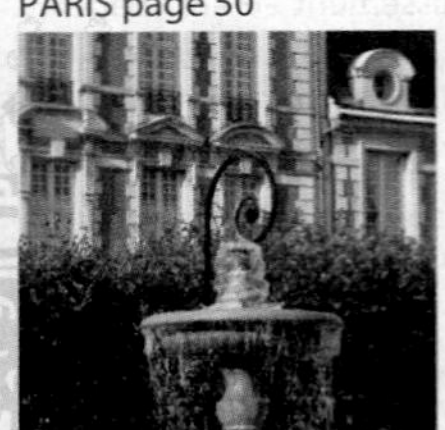
S. Sauvignier/MICHELIN

Le Haut Marais • Temple

3rd arrondissement ✉ 75003

Pavillon de la Reine without rest
28 pl. des Vosges Ⓜ Bastille – ✆ 01 40 29 19 19 – www.pavillon-de-la-reine.com – contact@pavillon-de-la-reine.com – Fax 01 40 29 19 20 J 17
41 rm – †€ 380/480 ††€ 450/480, ☕ € 30 – 16 suites
◆ Behind one of the 36 brick houses lining the Place des Vosges stand two buildings, one of which is 17C, housing elegant rooms on the courtyard or (private) garden side.

Murano
13 bd du Temple Ⓜ Filles du Calvaire – ✆ 01 42 71 20 00 – www.muranoresort.com – paris@muranoresort.com – Fax 01 42 71 21 01
49 rm – †€ 440/2500 ††€ 440/2500, ☕ € 26 – 2 suites H 17
Rest – Menu (€ 30) – Carte € 49/151
◆ The Murano is a trendy hotel that stands out from the crowd with its immaculate designer decor, play of colours, high-tech equipment and pop-art bar (150 types of vodka). The restaurant has a colourful contemporary style, fusion cuisine and a DJ at the decks.

Du Petit Moulin without rest
29 r. du Poitou Ⓜ St-Sébastien Froissart – ✆ 01 42 74 10 10 – www.hoteldupetitmoulin.com – contact@hoteldupetitmoulin.com – Fax 01 42 74 10 97 H 16
17 rm – †€ 190/350 ††€ 190/350, ☕ € 15
◆ For this hotel in the Marais, Christian Lacroix has designed a unique and refined decor, playing on the contrasts between traditional and modern. Each room has a different design. Cosy bar.

Little Palace without rest
4 r. Salomon de Caus Ⓜ Réaumur Sébastopol – ✆ 01 42 72 08 15 – www.littlepalacehotel.com – info@littlepalacehotel.com – Fax 01 42 72 45 81 G 15
53 rm – †€ 170/230 ††€ 190/265, ☕ € 15 – 4 suites
◆ A charming address with decor combining Belle Époque and contemporary styles. Attractive guestrooms; those on the fifth and sixth floors have a balcony with views of Paris.

Des Archives without rest
87 r. des Archives Ⓜ Temple – ✆ 01 44 78 08 00 – www.hoteldesarchives.com – contact@hoteldesarchives.com – Fax 01 44 78 08 10 H 16
19 rm – †€ 155/185 ††€ 155/215, ☕ € 12 – 2 suites
◆ Charming hotel near the National Archives with small yet prettily decorated and contemporary rooms. Modern lounge lobby.

Austin's without rest
6 r. Montgolfier Ⓜ Arts et Métiers – ✆ 01 42 77 17 61 – www.hotelaustins.com – austins.amhotel@wanadoo.fr – Fax 01 42 77 55 43 G 16
29 rm – †€ 108/112 ††€ 148/155, ☕ € 9
◆ In a quiet street facing the Arts et Métiers museum. The rooms are decorated in red or yellow and are warm and bright. Some have original exposed beams.

Ambassade d'Auvergne
22 r. Grenier St-Lazare Ⓜ Rambuteau – ✆ 01 42 72 31 22 – www.ambassade-auvergne.com – info@ambassade-auvergne.com – Fax 01 42 78 85 47 H 15
Rest – Menu (€ 22 bi), € 30 – Carte € 31/47
◆ True ambassadors of a province rich in flavours and traditions: Auvergne style furniture and décor, produce, recipes and local wines.

Pamphlet
38 r. Debelleyme Ⓜ Filles du Calvaire – ✆ 01 42 72 39 24 – pamphlet@wanadoo.fr – Fax 01 42 72 12 53 – Closed 1-8 May, 7-23 August, 1-15 January, Saturday lunch, Monday lunch and Sunday H 17
Rest – Menu € 35 – Carte € 50/80
◆ Charming address smack in the middle of the Marais. Rustic decor brightened with pretty colours, engravings and bullfighting posters. Updated market cuisine. Friendly welcome.

Food & Beverage
14 r. Charlot Ⓜ St-Sébastien Froissart – ✆ 01 42 78 02 31 – www.foodandbeverage.fr – fabien-renaud@hotmail.fr – Fax 01 42 78 02 51 – Closed August, Saturday lunch and Sunday H 16
Rest – Menu (€ 15), € 19 (weekday lunch), € 27/32 – Carte approx. € 37
◆ Orange and brown tones, bare stone and clean lines at this contemporary address. Traditional dishes, specialities from the Southwest and a selection of wines from Cahors.

Le Carré des Vosges
15 r. St-Gilles Ⓜ Chemin Vert – ✆ 01 42 71 22 21 – www.lecarredesvosges.fr – lecarredesvosges@yahoo.fr – Fax 01 41 17 09 33 – Closed 5-25 August, 1-10 January, Saturday lunch, Monday lunch and Sunday G 17
Rest – Menu (€ 21), € 27 (weekday lunch)/40 – Carte € 38/60
◆ A stone's throw from the Rue des Franc-Bourgeois and its trendy boutiques, this friendly district bistro has a modern look. Well-prepared market cuisine with fish to the fore.

Pramil
9 r. Vertbois Ⓜ Temple – ✆ 01 42 72 03 60 – apramil@free.fr – Closed 5-10 May, 17-31 August, Sunday lunch and Monday G 16
Rest – Menu (€ 20), € 31 – Carte € 30/40
◆ The simplicity of the decor (white orchids, artwork) in this family bistro contrasts with the warm welcome and the generous portions of market cuisine.

Café des Musées
49 r. de Turenne Ⓜ Chemin Vert – ✆ 01 42 72 96 17 – cafe.des.musees@orange.fr – Fax 01 44 59 38 68 – Closed 1st-7 January and 7-27 August J 17
Rest – Menu (€ 14), € 21 – Carte € 22/43
◆ Between the Carnavalet and Picasso museums, this bistro is Parisian through and through and gets everything right: hearty seasonal cooking, served in a convivial atmosphere.

S. Sauvignier/MICHELIN

Île de la Cité • Île St-Louis • Le Marais • Beaubourg

4th arrondissement ✉ 75004

Bourg Tibourg without rest
19 r. Bourg Tibourg Ⓜ Hôtel de Ville – ✆ 01 42 78 47 39 – www.hotelbourgtibourg.com – hotel@bourgtibourg.com – Fax 01 40 29 07 00
30 rm – †€ 180 ††€ 230/360, ☕ € 16 J 16
◆ The lovely personalised guestrooms in this boutique hotel are decorated in a variety of styles (neo-Gothic, Baroque or Oriental). A little gem in the heart of the Marais quarter.

Duo without rest
11 r. Temple Ⓜ Hôtel de Ville – ✆ 01 42 72 72 22 – www.duoparis.com – contact@duoparis.com – Fax 01 42 72 03 53 J 15
56 rm – †€ 130/240 ††€ 200/480, ☕ € 15 – 2 suites
◆ The trendily refurbished second wing with its warm vivid tones has given new life to this hotel that is full of character. The same family has run it for three generations. Fitness facilities.

Villa Mazarin without rest
6 r. des Archives Ⓜ *Hôtel de Ville – ✆ 01 53 01 90 90 – www.villamazarin.com – paris@villamazarin.com – Fax 01 53 01 90 91* J 15
29 rm – †€ 140/380 ††€ 140/380, ☕ € 12
◆ With its high tech equipment (wifi, flat screen TVs) and mix of modern and period furniture, this comfortable hotel near the Hôtel de Ville combines tradition and modernity.

Deux Îles without rest
59 r. St-Louis-en-l'Île Ⓜ *Pont Marie – ✆ 01 43 26 13 35 – www.hoteldesdeuxiles.com – info@hoteldesdeuxiles.com – Fax 01 43 29 60 25* K 16
17 rm – †€ 155/165 ††€ 195, ☕ € 12
◆ A few yards from the capital's most popular ice-cream parlour, this establishment has comfortable, cane furnished, peaceful rooms and cosy lounges (one of which is vaulted and one with a fireplace).

Beaubourg without rest
11 r. S. Le Franc Ⓜ *Rambuteau – ✆ 01 42 74 34 24 – www.hotelbeaubourg.com – sa.beaubourg@wanadoo.fr – Fax 01 42 78 68 11* H 15
28 rm – †€ 120/150 ††€ 130/150, ☕ € 9
◆ Nestled in a tiny street behind the Georges-Pompidou Centre. Some of the friendly, well-soundproofed rooms have exposed stone walls and wooden beams.

Caron de Beaumarchais without rest
12 r. Vieille-du-Temple Ⓜ *Hôtel de Ville – ✆ 01 42 72 34 12 – www.carondebeaumarchais.com – hotel@carondebeaumarchais.com – Fax 01 42 72 34 63* J 16
19 rm – †€ 125/170 ††€ 130/170, ☕ € 12
◆ Figaro's creator lived on this historic Marais street, and the stylish decoration in this charming hotel pays a faithful tribute to him. Small, comfortable rooms.

Bretonnerie without rest
22 r. Ste-Croix-de-la-Bretonnerie Ⓜ *Hôtel de Ville – ✆ 01 48 87 77 63 – www.bretonnerie.com – hotel@bretonnerie.com – Fax 01 42 77 26 78* J 16
29 rm – †€ 135/190 ††€ 135/190, ☕ € 10
◆ Some of the rooms in this elegant 17C mansion in the Marais include four-poster beds and exposed beams. Vaulted ceiling in the breakfast room.

Lutèce without rest
65 r. St-Louis-en-l'Île Ⓜ *Pont Marie – ✆ 01 43 26 23 52 – www.hoteldelutece.com – info@hoteldelutece.com – Fax 01 43 29 60 25* K 16
23 rm – †€ 155 ††€ 195, ☕ € 12
◆ The rustic charm of this mansion on the Île St-Louis is particularly popular with American visitors. Modernised guestrooms with a country feel, plus attractive old woodwork in the lounge.

Castex without rest
5 r. Castex Ⓜ *Bastille – ✆ 01 42 72 31 52 – www.castexhotel.com – info@castexhotel.com – Fax 01 42 72 57 91* K 17
30 rm – †€ 120 ††€ 120/150, ☕ € 10
◆ Very Grand Siècle setting in this residence renovated from top to toe: toile de Jouy prints, traditional red tiles and Louis XIII furniture make you forget that the rooms are small.

L'Ambroisie (Bernard Pacaud)
9 pl. des Vosges Ⓜ *St-Paul – ✆ 01 42 78 51 45 – Closed August, 23 February-11 March, Sunday and Monday* J 17
Rest – Carte € 240/360
Spec. Feuillantine de langoustines aux graines de sésame. Escalopines de bar à l'émincé d'artichaut, caviar "oscietre gold". Tarte fine sablée au chocolat, glace vanille.
◆ Under the arcades of the Place des Vosges, royal decor and subtle cuisine, close to perfection. The name is most appropriate: ambrosia was the food of the gods of Antiquity.

XX **Benoit**
✿
20 r. St-Martin Ⓜ Châtelet-Les Halles – ✆ 01 42 72 25 76 – www.esprit-bistrot.com – restaurant.benoit@wanadoo.fr – Fax 01 42 72 45 68 – Closed 26 July-25 August and 25 February-2 March J 15

Rest – Menu € 38 (lunch) – Carte € 55/84

Spec. Escargots en coquille, beurre d'ail et fines herbes. Filet de sole nantua, épinards à peine crémés. Tête de veau traditionnelle sauce ravigote.

◆ Alain Ducasse runs this chic and lively bistro, one of the oldest in Paris. Traditional cuisine, respecting the traditions of this authentic and delightful establishment.

XX **Le Dôme du Marais**
53 bis r. Francs-Bourgeois Ⓜ Rambuteau – ✆ 01 42 74 54 17 – www.ledomedumarais.fr – ledomedumarais@hotmail.com – Fax 01 42 77 78 17 – Closed 2-27 August, 1-7 January, Sunday and Monday H 16-J 16

Rest – Menu (€ 19), € 25 (lunch), € 36/100 bi – Carte approx. € 58

◆ Tables are arranged under the pretty dome in the old sales room of the Crédit Municipal, and in a second dining room that resembles a winter garden. Modern cuisine.

XX **Bofinger**
5 r. Bastille Ⓜ Bastille – ✆ 01 42 72 87 82 – www.bofingerparis.com – eberne@groupeflo.fr – Fax 01 42 72 97 68 J 17

Rest – Menu (€ 25), € 32 – Carte € 35/65

◆ The famous clients and remarkable decor have bestowed enduring renown on this brasserie created in 1864. The interior boasts a finely worked cupola, and a room on the first floor decorated by Hansi.

X **Mon Vieil Ami**
69 r. St-Louis-en-l'Île Ⓜ Pont Marie – ✆ 01 40 46 01 35 – www.mon-vieil-ami.com – mon.vieil.ami@wanadoo.fr – Fax 01 40 46 01 35 – Closed 1st-20 August, 1st-20 January, Monday and Tuesday K 16

Rest – Menu € 41 – Carte € 42/55 lunch only

◆ In this old house with a refurbished interior on Île St Louis, sample tasty, traditional recipes infused with modern touches and Alsatian culinary influences.

X **Au Bourguignon du Marais**
52 r. François-Miron Ⓜ St-Paul – ✆ 01 48 87 15 40 – Fax 01 48 87 17 49 – Closed 11-31 August, 19 January-1 February, Sunday and Monday J 16

Rest – Carte € 40/62

◆ Located between the Hôtel de Ville and Saint Paul, the cuisine can be summed up in two words: regional and generous. Appealing setting and fine wine list.

X **Le Gaigne**
12 r. Pecquay Ⓜ Rambuteau – ✆ 01 44 59 86 72 – www.restaurantlegaigne.fr – legaigne@restaurantlegaigne.fr – Fax 01 44 59 81 32 – Closed August, Sunday lunch and Tuesday H 16

Rest – Menu (€ 16), € 22 (weekday lunch), € 39/54 bi – Carte € 47/57

◆ Discreet establishment in a quiet Marais street, well worth a visit for its delicious modern cooking. Intimate dining room decorated in sober style.

X **Le Fin Gourmet**
42 r. St-Louis-en-l'Île Ⓜ Pont Marie – ✆ 01 43 26 79 27 – www.lefingourmet.fr – contact@lefingourmet.fr – Fax 01 43 26 96 08 – Closed 15 July-15 August, 2-15 January, Monday and Tuesday K 16

Rest – Menu € 20 (lunch), € 36 € bi – Carte € 48/56

◆ Enjoy to the full the charm of this semi-historic, semi-contemporary restaurant run by a young and enthusiastic team. Elegant setting for up-to-date cuisine.

X **b4**
6 square Ste-Croix-de-la-Bretonnerie Ⓜ Hôtel de Ville – ✆ 01 42 72 16 19 – www.b4resto.com – b4resto@b4resto.com – Fax 01 42 72 16 19 – Closed Sunday dinner and Monday J 15

Rest – Menu (€ 14), € 55 (dinner) – Carte € 35/56

◆ In the heart of the gay district, ultra-contemporary restaurant (white furniture, grey walls, blue-tinged lighting in the evening) offering an up-to-date menu.

L'Osteria AC VISA MC AE
10 r. Sévigné Ⓜ *St-Paul – ✆ 01 42 71 37 08 – Closed Monday lunch, Saturday dinner and Sunday* J 16
Rest – *(pre-book)* Carte € 35/100
◆ No name or menu appears on the façade of this trattoria frequented by a faithful band of regulars and celebrities (if the autographs and drawings are anything to go by!). Tasty, seasonal Italian cuisine.

Les Fous de l'Île AC VISA MC AE
33 r. des Deux-Ponts Ⓜ *Pont Marie – ✆ 01 43 25 76 67 – www.lesfousdelile.com – contact@lesfousdelile.com – Fax 01 55 42 96 04* K 16
Rest – Menu (€ 21), € 26
◆ Modern bistro in the heart of the Île St Louis. The hen ornaments showcased on the walls enhance the otherwise typical decor. Well thought out menu.

L'Enoteca AC VISA MC AE
25 r. Charles V Ⓜ *St-Paul – ✆ 01 42 78 91 44 – www.enoteca.fr – enoteca@enoteca.fr – Fax 01 44 59 31 72 – Closed 10-23 August, 24-26 December and lunch in August* J 16
Rest – *(pre-book)* Menu (€ 14 bi), € 30/45 bi – Carte € 33/42
◆ A 16C building housing a restaurant whose superb wine list of about 500 Italian wines is its main asset. Italian dishes and very lively atmosphere.

Isami AC VISA MC
4 quai d'Orléans Ⓜ *Pont Marie – ✆ 01 40 46 06 97 – Closed 3-25 August, Sunday and Monday* K 16
Rest – *(number of covers limited, pre-book)* Carte € 60/150
◆ A very discreet Japanese restaurant that serves a fine choice of raw fish (sushi and sashimi specialities). Very plain decor: some tables and a counter, as in Japan.

Suan Thai VISA MC AE
41 r. Ste-Croix -de-la-Bretonnerie – ✆ 01 42 77 10 20 – suan.thai@yahoo.fr
Rest – Menu (€ 14), € 18/28 – Carte € 37/61 - *Closed monday* J 15
◆ An authentique taste of Thailand in a discreetly exotic setting. Reservations are often required, given the reasonable prices and popularity of this local eatery.

Ph. Gajic/MICHELIN

Quartier Latin • Jardin des Plantes • Mouffetard

5th arrondissement ✉ 75005

Villa Panthéon without rest AC VISA MC AE
41 r. des Écoles Ⓜ *Maubert Mutualité – ✆ 01 53 10 95 95 – www.leshotelsdeparis.com – pantheon@leshotelsdeparis.com – Fax 01 53 10 95 96* K 14
59 rm – †€ 160/380 ††€ 195/450, ☕ € 18
◆ The reception, guestrooms and bar (fine selection of whiskies) have a British feel created by parquet floors, colourful hangings, exotic wooden furniture and Liberty style light fixtures.

Les Rives de Notre-Dame without rest AC VISA MC AE
15 quai St-Michel Ⓜ *St-Michel – ✆ 01 43 54 81 16 – www.rivesdenotredame.com – hotel@rivesdenotredame.com – Fax 01 43 26 27 09* J 14
10 rm – †€ 170/550 ††€ 170/550, ☕ € 14
◆ Splendidly preserved 16C edifice whose spacious Provençal-style rooms all overlook the Seine and Notre Dame. Top floor penthouse.

Royal St-Michel without rest
3 bd St-Michel Ⓜ *St-Michel – ✆ 01 44 07 06 06 – www.hotelroyalsaintmichel.com – hotelroyalsaintmichel@wanadoo.fr – Fax 01 44 07 36 25* K 14
39 rm – †€ 169/260 ††€ 179/290, ☕ € 15
◆ On the Boulevard St Michel, opposite the fountain of the same name, this hotel enjoys an excellent location in the heart of the lively Latin Quarter. Attractive, modern rooms.

Panthéon without rest
19 pl. Panthéon Ⓜ *Luxembourg – ✆ 01 43 54 32 95 – www.hoteldupantheon.com – reservation@hoteldupantheon.com – Fax 01 43 26 64 65* L 14
36 rm – †€ 89/300 ††€ 99/310, ☕ € 13
◆ The cosy or Louis XVI-style rooms command a view of the dome of the Pantheon. Attractive lounge and vaulted breakfast room.

Des Grands Hommes without rest
17 pl. Panthéon Ⓜ *Luxembourg – ✆ 01 46 34 19 60 – www.hoteldesgrandshommes.com – reservation@hoteldesgrandshommes.com – Fax 01 43 26 67 32* L 14
31 rm – †€ 80/310 ††€ 90/310, ☕ € 13
◆ Facing the Panthéon, pleasant hotel decorated in Directoire style (antique furnishings). Over half the rooms overlook the final resting place of some of France's most eminent citizens.

Tour Notre-Dame without rest
20 r. Sommerard Ⓜ *Cluny la Sorbonne – ✆ 01 43 54 47 60 – www.tour-notre-dame.com – reservation@la-tour-notre-dame.com – Fax 01 43 26 42 34* K 14
48 rm – †€ 110/190 ††€ 120/250, ☕ € 13
◆ This hotel is very well situated, almost adjoining the Cluny museum. Comfortable, recently-renovated rooms. Those at the back are quieter.

Grand Hôtel St-Michel without rest
19 r. Cujas Ⓜ *Luxembourg – ✆ 01 46 33 33 02 – www.grand-hotel-st-michel.com – grand.hotel.st.michel@wanadoo.fr – Fax 01 40 46 96 33* K 14
47 rm – †€ 170/290 ††€ 170/350, ☕ € 17 – 1 suite
◆ Hotel in a Haussmannian building offering comfortable rooms adorned with painted furniture. Napoleon III-style lounge. Breakfast served beneath a vaulted ceiling.

Notre Dame without rest
1 quai St-Michel Ⓜ *St-Michel – ✆ 01 43 54 20 43 – http://www.hotel-paris-notredame.com/ – hotel.denotredame@libertysurf.fr – Fax 01 43 26 61 75* K 14
26 rm – †€ 159/199 ††€ 159/199, ☕ € 7
◆ The cosy little rooms in this hotel have all been refurbished and are air-conditioned and well appointed. Most rooms have a view over Notre-Dame cathedral.

Relais St-Jacques without rest
3 r. Abbé de l'Épée Ⓜ *Luxembourg – ✆ 01 53 73 26 00 – www.relais-saint-jacques.com – info@relais-saint-jacques.com – Fax 01 43 26 17 81* L 14
22 rm – †€ 189/370 ††€ 189/370, ☕ € 17
◆ Rooms of various styles (Directoire, Louis Philippe, etc.), a glass-roofed breakfast room, Louis XV lounge and 1920s bar, make this a stylish hotchpotch hotel!

St-Christophe without rest
17 r. Lacépède Ⓜ *Place Monge – ✆ 01 43 31 81 54 – www.saint-christophe-hotel.com – saintchristophe@wanadoo.fr – Fax 01 43 31 12 54* L 15
31 rm – †€ 103/126 ††€ 113/138, ☕ € 9
◆ The naturalist Lacépède gave his name to this street, a reminder of the proximity of the Jardin des Plantes. Small, rustic-style rooms; all are non-smoking.

Sully St-Germain without rest
31 r. des Écoles Ⓜ *Maubert Mutualité – ✆ 01 43 26 56 02 – www.hotelsullysaintgermain.com – sully@sequanahotels.com – Fax 01 43 29 74 42* K 15
61 rm – †€ 90/155 ††€ 100/165, ☕ € 10
◆ Perhaps it is the proximity of the Middle Ages museum that inspires the medieval decor in this establishment. Glass-roofed sitting room.

Jardin de Cluny without rest
9 r. Sommerard Ⓜ Maubert Mutualité – ✆ 01 43 54 22 66 – www.hoteljardindecluny.com – reservation@hoteljardindecluny.com – Fax 01 40 51 03 36 K 14
40 rm – †€ 139/369 ††€ 169/369, ☕ € 14
◆ Non-smoking hotel which has been awarded an 'Ecolabel'. Nicely up-to-date rooms and breakfast buffet served in a large vaulted dining room with exposed stone.

Select without rest
1 pl. Sorbonne Ⓜ Cluny la Sorbonne – ✆ 01 46 34 14 80 – www.selecthotel.fr – info@selecthotel.fr – Fax 01 46 34 51 79 K 14
67 rm ☕ – †€ 195/275 ††€ 195/275
◆ Staunchly contemporary hotel in the heart of the student quarter of Paris. Bar and lounges disposed around a patio with a cactus garden. Some rooms offer views over the rooftops.

Du Levant without rest
18 r. Harpe Ⓜ St-Michel – ✆ 01 46 34 11 00 – www.hoteldulevant.com – hlevant@club-internet.fr – Fax 01 46 34 25 87 K 14
47 rm ☕ – †€ 73/135 ††€ 118/160
◆ Pleasant guestrooms in this hotel built in 1875 in the heart of the Latin Quarter. Admire photos from the 1920s in the corridors, as well as the mural in the breakfast room.

Albe without rest
1 r. Harpe Ⓜ St-Michel – ✆ 01 46 34 09 70 – www.albehotel.fr – albehotel@wanadoo.fr – Fax 01 40 46 85 70 K 14
45 rm – †€ 150/170 ††€ 180/225, ☕ € 11
◆ Attractive, modern hotel with smallish, yet nicely-arranged and cheerful rooms. With the Latin quarter and the Île de la Cité close by, Paris is at your doorstep!

Agora St-Germain without rest
42 r. Bernardins Ⓜ Maubert Mutualité – ✆ 01 46 34 13 00 – www.agorasaintgermain.com – resa@agora-paris-hotel.com – Fax 01 46 34 75 05 K 15
39 rm – †€ 149 ††€ 189/195, ☕ € 11
◆ This hotel near the St-Nicolas-du-Chardonnet church has benefited from a recent facelift. Cosy bedrooms, with those facing the courtyard generally quieter. Charming stone-walled breakfast room.

Grandes Écoles without rest
75 r. Cardinal-Lemoine Ⓜ Cardinal Lemoine – ✆ 01 43 26 79 23 – www.hotel-grandes-ecoles.com – Hotel.Grandes.Ecoles@orange.fr – Fax 01 43 25 28 15 L 15
51 rm – †€ 115/135 ††€ 115/140, ☕ € 9
◆ Three houses with an old-fashioned charm (rooms without TV), prized for their peaceful location right at the heart of the Latin Quater. Breakfast in the garden in summer.

Dacia-Luxembourg without rest
41 bd St-Michel Ⓜ Cluny la Sorbonne – ✆ 01 53 10 27 77 – www.hoteldacia.com – info@hoteldacia.com – Fax 01 44 07 10 33 K 14
38 rm – †€ 95/140 ††€ 120/162, ☕ € 11
◆ In the heart of the Latin Quarter, a warm and well-kept establishment. Attractive white quilted bedspreads in the rooms (two with canopy beds). Breakfast served in a vaulted dining room.

Henri IV without rest
9 r. St-Jacques Ⓜ St-Michel – ✆ 01 46 33 20 20 – www.hotel-henri4.com – info@hotel-henri4.com – Fax 01 46 33 90 90 K 14
23 rm – †€ 165 ††€ 185, ☕ € 12
◆ Almost all the attractive guestrooms in this hotel overlook the chevet of St Séverin church. Traditional floor tiles, antique furniture and a fireplace grace the charming lounge.

Minerve without rest
13 r. des Écoles Ⓜ Maubert Mutualité – ✆ 01 43 26 26 04 – www.parishotelminerve.com – resa@parishotelminerve.com – Fax 01 44 07 01 96 L 15
54 rm – †€ 93/179 ††€ 107/179, ☕ € 9
◆ This building, from 1864, offers a pleasant entrance hall (exposed stone and period furniture) and small, well-kept and rooms full of character.

The Five without rest
3 r. Flatters Ⓜ *Gobelins – ✆ 01 43 31 74 21 – www.thefivehotel.com – contact@thefivehotel.com – Fax 01 43 31 61 96* M 14
24 rm – €165/202 €195/232, €15 – 1 suite
◆ Five, as in the fifth arrondissement and the five senses, the inspiration for this designer hotel. Restful and original guestrooms (colour themes, scents...).

Pierre Nicole without rest
39 r. Pierre Nicole Ⓜ *Port Royal – ✆ 01 43 54 76 86 – www.hotel-pierre-nicole.com – hotelpierre-nicole@voila.fr – Fax 01 43 54 22 45 – Closed 1-23 August*
33 rm – €85/90 €95/110, €7 M 13
◆ The name pays tribute to the Port-Royal moralist. Small but well-kept and reasonably-priced, practical rooms. The Luxembourg gardens are nearby.

St-Jacques without rest
35 r. des Écoles Ⓜ *Maubert Mutualité – ✆ 01 44 07 45 45 – www.paris-hotel-stjacques.com – hotelsaintjacques@wanadoo.fr – Fax 01 43 25 65 50*
36 rm – €97 €105/189, €10 K 15
◆ Modern comfort allies with old-style charm in the rooms of this hotel. Library with 18C and 19C works. Breakfast room with Roaring Twenties cabaret-style decor.

Familia without rest
11 r. des Écoles Ⓜ *Cardinal Lemoine – ✆ 01 43 54 55 27 – www.familiahotel.com – hotelfamilia@wanadoo.fr – Fax 01 43 29 61 77* L-K 15
30 rm – €83/125 €95/125, €6
◆ Notre Dame and the Collège des Bernardins provide the backdrop for rustic rooms adorned with sepia frescoes of the monuments of Paris. Family-style breakfast room.

Devillas without rest
4 bd St-Marcel Ⓜ *St-Marcel – ✆ 01 43 31 37 50 – www.hoteldevillas.com – info@hoteldevillas.com – Fax 01 43 31 96 03* M 16
40 rm – €85/106 €92/120, €10
◆ Renovated and well-equipped rooms in this hotel situated in a street near La Pitié-Salpêtrière hospital. For more quiet, reserve at the back.

La Tour d'Argent
15 quai Tournelle Ⓜ *Maubert Mutualité – ✆ 01 43 54 23 31 – www.latourdargent.com – resa@latourdargent.com – Fax 01 44 07 12 04 – Closed August and Monday* K 16
Rest – Menu €75 (lunch) – Carte €250/300
Spec. Quenelles de brochet "André Terrail". Caneton "Tour d'Argent". Crêpes "Belle Epoque".
◆ The 'skyline' dining room offers a magnificent view of Notre Dame cathedral. Exceptional wine list, famous Challans duck and a celebrity clientele since the 16C. An institution!

La Truffière
4 r. Blainville Ⓜ *Place Monge – ✆ 01 46 33 29 82 – www.latruffiere.com – restaurant.latruffiere@wanadoo.fr – Fax 01 46 33 64 74 – Closed 20-26 December, Sunday and Monday* L 15
Rest – Menu (€24), €28 (weekday lunch), €50/125 – Carte €99/110
◆ A 17C house home to three dining rooms. One is rustic with bare beams and the other two are vaulted. Traditional cuisine from southwest France and a fine wine list.

Mavrommatis
42 r. Daubenton Ⓜ *Censier Daubenton – ✆ 01 43 31 17 17 – www.mavrommatis.fr – info@mavrommatis.fr – Fax 01 43 36 13 08 – Closed 15 August-15 September, Sunday and Monday* M 15
Rest – Menu (€28), €39/49 – Carte €55/75
◆ The ambassador of Greek cuisine in Paris. Nothing clichéd, just tasteful, elegant, comfortable surroundings and attentive service. Summer terrace lined with olive trees.

Marty
20 av. Gobelins Ⓜ *Les Gobelins – ✆ 01 43 31 39 51 – www.marty-restaurant.com – restaurant.marty@wanadoo.fr – Fax 01 43 37 63 70 – Closed August*
Rest – Menu €35 – Carte €38/65 M 15
◆ This restaurant has pleasant 1930s decor including mahogany wood panelling, hand-picked antique furniture and paintings. Traditional menu and seafood dishes.

Atelier Maître Albert
1 r. Maître Albert Ⓜ *Maubert Mutualité – ✆ 01 56 81 30 01 – www.ateliermaitrealbert.com – ateliermaitrealbert@guysavoy.com – Fax 01 53 10 83 23 – Closed 25 July-17 August, Christmas holidays, Saturday lunch and Sunday lunch* K 15

Rest – Menu (€ 29) – Carte € 45/55

◆ A huge medieval fireplace and spits for roast meat take pride of place in this handsome interior designed by J M Wilmotte. Guy Savoy is responsible for the mouth-watering menu.

Les Délices d'Aphrodite
4 r. Candolle Ⓜ *Censier Daubenton – ✆ 01 43 31 40 39 – www.mavrommatis.fr – info@mavrommatis.fr – Fax 01 43 36 13 08* M 15

Rest – Carte € 35/50

◆ Convivial tavern with a holiday atmosphere. Find photos of sunny landscapes, an ivy covered ceiling and the rich, sun-drenched flavours of the Greek-Cypriot cuisine.

La Table de Fabrice
13 quai de la Tournelle Ⓜ *Pont-Marie – ✆ 01 44 07 17 57 – www.restaurantlatabledefabrice.com – latabledefabrice@orange.fr – Fax 01 43 25 37 55 – Closed 5-25 August, Saturday lunch and Sunday* K 16

Rest – Menu € 40 (lunch) – Carte € 55/80

◆ A charming small restaurant in a 17C edifice. Provincial atmosphere and views of the banks of the Seine from the first floor. A set menu and seasonal specials on a blackboard.

Chez René
14 bd St-Germain Ⓜ *Maubert Mutualité – ✆ 01 43 54 30 23 – Fax 01 43 54 33 57 – Closed August, 24 December-1 January, Sunday and Monday* K 15

Rest – Carte € 35/70

◆ Lively atmosphere guaranteed by a loyal team in this local institution. Authentic bistro décor: bench seats, mirrors and copper bars. Summer terrace.

Moissonnier
28 r. Fossés-St-Bernard Ⓜ *Jussieu – ✆ 01 43 29 87 65 – Fax 01 43 29 87 65 – Closed August, Sunday and Monday* K 15

Rest – Menu € 24 (weekday lunch) – Carte € 32/45

◆ The typical decor of this bistro has not been altered for years: gleaming bar, patina on the walls and bench seats. Jugs of Beaujolais and a definite flavour of Lyons in the cuisine.

Itinéraires
5 r. de Pontoise Ⓜ *Maubert Mutualité – ✆ 01 46 33 60 11 – Fax 01 40 26 44 91 – Closed 4-25 August, 20-29 December, Sunday and Monday* K 15

Rest – *(booking essential)* Menu (€ 29), € 36

◆ Deservedly much-talked-about bistro proposing fine modern cuisine in a contemporary setting. Charcuterie and tapas served at the counter in the evening.

Au Moulin à Vent
20 r. Fossés-St-Bernard Ⓜ *Jussieu – ✆ 01 43 54 99 37 – www.au-moulinavent.com – alexandra.damas@au-moulinavent.com – Fax 01 40 46 92 23 – Closed 2-26 August, 31 December-8 January, Saturday lunch, Sunday and Monday* K 15

Rest – Carte € 50/100

◆ Nothing has changed in this Parisian bistro since 1948. The decor has developed a well-worn sheen over the years and meat specialities have been added to the traditional menu.

Louis Vins
9 r. Montagne-Ste-Geneviève Ⓜ *Maubert Mutualité – ✆ 01 43 29 12 12 – www.fifi.fr – louisvins@orange.fr* K 15

Rest – Menu (€ 24), € 27

◆ A warm Belle époque-style decor (walnut counter, mirrors, murals), in which you can enjoy generous bistro-type dishes and a fine wine list.

L' A.O.C.
14 r. des Fossés St-Bernard Ⓜ *Maubert Mutualité – ✆ 01 43 54 22 52 – www.restoaoc.com – aocrestaurant@wanadoo.fr – Closed August, Sunday and Monday* K 16

Rest – Menu (€ 21 bi), € 32 (dinner) – Carte € 34/52

◆ A restaurant for meat lovers, all of controlled origin and matured by the owner himself. Rotisserie at the entrance and fuss-free bistro.

Ribouldingue

VISA MC

10 r. St-Julien le Pauvre Ⓜ Maubert Mutualité – ✆ 01 46 33 98 80 – Fax 01 43 54 09 34 – Closed 9-31 August, 27 December-4 January, Sunday and Monday K 14

Rest – Menu € 29

◆ This pleasant bistro has an unusual theme: it specialises in offal (brain, tongue, tripe etc.) but also serves classic dishes.

Petit Pontoise

AC VISA MC AE

9 r. Pontoise Ⓜ Maubert Mutualité – ✆ 01 43 29 25 20 K 15

Rest – Carte € 35/45

◆ A stone's throw from the Quays of the Seine and Notre-Dame, local bistro decorated in the style of the 1950's. Menu suggestions chalked on the slate. Regular clientele.

Les Oudayas

AC VISA MC

34 Bd St-Germain Ⓜ Maubert Mutualité – ✆ 01 43 29 97 38 K 15

Rest – Menu € 23/45 – Carte € 30/47

◆ A stone's throw from the Institut du Monde Arabe, this restaurant takes its name from the Kasbah in Rabat, and reproduces a Moroccan atmosphere. Refined specialities, lounge atmosphere and tearoom.

Papilles

VISA MC

30 r. Gay Lussac Ⓜ Luxembourg – ✆ 01 43 25 20 79 – www.lespapillesparis.com – lespapilles@hotmail.fr – Fax 01 43 25 24 35 – Closed Easter holidays, 1st-21 August, 1st-8 January, Sunday and Monday L 14

Rest – Menu (€ 22), € 31 – Carte € 30/38 lunch

◆ Bistro, cellar and grocer's: on one side are wine racks, on the other shelves with jars of southwest specialities and in the middle...you can enjoy market-inspired food!

Christophe

VISA MC

8 r. Descartes Ⓜ Maubert Mutualité – ✆ 01 43 26 72 49 – www.christopherestaurant.fr – Closed Wednesday and Thursday L 15

Rest – Menu (€ 16) – Carte € 40/55

◆ This simply furnished bistro serves fine cuisine with individual touches. Fish and pork figure prominently on the excellent menu.

Coco de Mer

VISA MC

34 bd St-Marcel Ⓜ St-Marcel – ✆ 01 47 07 06 64 – www.cocodemer.fr – contact@cocodemer.fr – Fax 01 43 31 45 75 – Closed 2 weeks in August, Monday lunch and Sunday M 16

Rest – Menu € 30 – Carte € 28/36

◆ Fed up with the weather? Take a trip to the Seychelles: ti-punch in bare feet on the fine sand of the veranda, and typical island dishes with fresh fish delivered weekly.

Bibimbap

VISA MC

32 bd de l'Hôpital Ⓜ Gare d'Austerlitz – ✆ 01 43 31 27 42 – www.bibimbap.fr – kwonyoungchul@hotmail.com – Fax 01 72 27 18 21 – Closed Sunday M 16

Rest – Menu € 10 (lunch), € 12/25

◆ A simple Korean establishment offering authentic cuisine in an unpretentious setting.

Lhassa

VISA MC

13 r. Montagne Ste-Geneviève Ⓜ Maubert Mutualité – ✆ 01 43 26 22 19 – Fax 01 42 17 00 08 – Closed Mon. K 15

Rest – Menu € 13/21 – Carte € 22/30

◆ As the name suggests, this little restaurant is entirely devoted to Tibet: colourful fabrics, craftwork, photos of the Dalai Lama and Tibetan specialities.

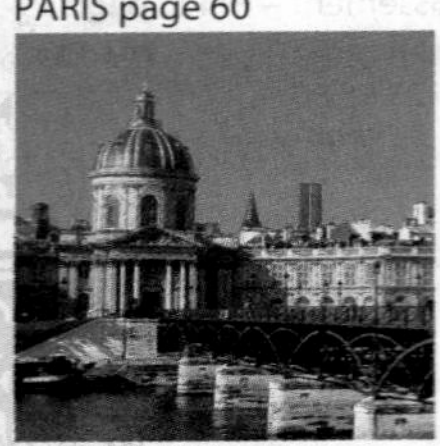
S. Sauvignier/MICHELIN

St-Germain-des-Prés • Odéon • Jardin du Luxembourg

6th arrondissement ✉ 75006

Lutetia
45 bd Raspail Ⓜ *Sèvres Babylone – ☎ 01 49 54 46 46 – www.lutetia-paris.com – lutetia-paris@lutetia-paris.com – Fax 01 49 54 46 00* K 12
231 rm – €450/600 €460/610, €28 – 11 suites
Rest *Paris* – see restaurant listing
Rest *Brasserie Lutetia* – ☎ *01 49 54 46 76* – Menu (€38), €43 – Carte €60/73
◆ Built in 1910, this luxury hotel on the Left Bank has lost none of its sparkle. It happily blends Art Deco fixtures with contemporary details (sculptures by César, Arman, etc). Refurbished rooms. Popular with well-heeled Parisians, the Brasserie Lutetia is renowned for its seafood.

Victoria Palace without rest
6 r. Blaise-Desgoffe Ⓜ *St-Placide – ☎ 01 45 49 70 00 – www.victoriapalace.com – info@victoriapalace.com – Fax 01 45 49 23 75* L 11
62 rm – €273/620 €273/620, €18
◆ Small luxury hotel with undeniable charm: toiles de Jouy, Louis XVI-style furniture and marble bathrooms in the rooms. Paintings, red velvet and porcelain in the lounges.

D'Aubusson without rest
33 r. Dauphine Ⓜ *Odéon – ☎ 01 43 29 43 43 – www.hoteldaubusson.com – reservations@hoteldaubusson.com – Fax 01 43 29 12 62* J 13
49 rm – €275/305 €275/305, €25
◆ A 17C townhouse with character, offering elegant, renovated rooms with Versailles parquet and Aubusson tapestries. Jazz evenings at the Café Laurent at the weekend.

Relais Christine without rest
3 r. Christine Ⓜ *St-Michel – ☎ 01 40 51 60 80 – www.relais-christine.com – contact@relais-christine.com – Fax 01 40 51 60 81* J 14
51 rm – €380/780 €380/780, €30
◆ Breakfast is served in a 13C vaulted room of this mansion, built on a medieval site. Handsome cobbled courtyard, fitness facilities, and rooms with a personal touch.

Relais St-Germain
9 carrefour de l'Odéon Ⓜ *Odéon – ☎ 01 44 27 07 97 – www.hotelrsg.com – hotelrsg@wanadoo.fr – Fax 01 46 33 45 30* K 13
22 rm – €180/220 €230/285
Rest *Le Comptoir* – see restaurant listing
◆ Elegant hotel comprising three 17C buildings. Polished beams, shimmering fabrics and antique furniture.

Bel Ami St-Germain des Prés without rest
7 r. St-Benoit Ⓜ *St-Germain des Prés – ☎ 01 42 61 53 53 – www.hotel-bel-ami.com – contact@hotel-bel-ami.com – Fax 01 49 27 09 33* J 13
112 rm – €245/620 €245/620, €25
◆ This attractive building may well be 19C in origin but the era of Maupassant is long gone! Resolutely modern interior where minimalist luxury rubs shoulders with hi-tech gadgets and a relaxed ambience.

Le Six without rest
14 r. Stanislas Ⓜ *Notre-Dame des Champs – ☎ 01 42 22 00 75 – www.hotel-le-six.com – info@hotel-le-six.com – Fax 01 42 22 00 95*
37 rm – €199/525 €199/525, €22 – 4 suites L 12
◆ Contemporary hotel at the crossroads of Luxembourg, St-Germain-des-Prés and Montparnasse. Spacious (non-smoking) rooms decorated in warm tones. Small spa.

Buci without rest
22 r. Buci Ⓜ Mabillon – ✆ 01 55 42 74 74 – www.buci-hotel.com – reservations@buci-hotel.com – Fax 01 55 42 74 44 J 13
24 rm – †€ 190/220 ††€ 220/335, ☕ € 18 – 5 suites
◆ An elegant midnight blue façade gives an idea of the tone of this boutique hotel. The stylish guestrooms have canopies on the beds and English period furniture, while others sport a more contemporary look.

L'Abbaye without rest
10 r. Cassette Ⓜ St-Sulpice – ✆ 01 45 44 38 11 – www.hotel-abbaye.com – hotel.abbaye@wanadoo.fr – Fax 01 45 48 07 86 K 12
40 rm ☕ – †€ 232/261 ††€ 427/472 – 4 suites
◆ Hotel in a former 18C convent combining old-world charm with modern comfort. Pleasant veranda, duplex apartment with a terrace, and stylish rooms. Some overlook a delightful patio.

Littré without rest
9 r. Littré Ⓜ Montparnasse Bienvenüe – ✆ 01 53 63 07 07 – www.hotellittreparis.com – hotellittre@hotellittreparis.com – Fax 01 45 44 88 13 L 11
88 rm – †€ 315 ††€ 315/550, ☕ € 20 – 2 suites
◆ Classic building, halfway between Saint Germain des Prés and Montparnasse. The stylish rooms are all very comfortable. Magnificent view from the top floor.

L'Hôtel
13 r. des Beaux-Arts Ⓜ St-Germain-des-Prés – ✆ 01 44 41 99 00 – www.l-hotel.com – stay@l-hotel.com – Fax 01 43 25 64 81 J 13
20 rm – †€ 280/370 ††€ 345/740, ☕ € 18 – 4 suites
Rest Le Restaurant – see restaurant listing
◆ This hotel is where Oscar Wilde passed away, leaving an unpaid bill behind him. It sports a vertiginous well of light and an extravagant decor by Garcia (Baroque, French Empire and Oriental).

Esprit Saint-Germain without rest
22 r. Saint-Sulpice Ⓜ Mabillon – ✆ 01 53 10 55 55 – www.espritsaintgermain.com – contact@espritsaintgermain.com – Fax 01 53 10 55 56 K 13
28 rm – †€ 320/790 ††€ 320/790, ☕ € 26
◆ Elegant and contemporary rooms pleasantly combining red, chocolate and beige colours with modern paintings and furniture; bathrooms with slate walls.

Pas de Calais without rest
59 r. des Saints-Pères Ⓜ St-Germain-des-Prés – ✆ 01 45 48 78 74 – www.hotelpasdecalais.com – infos@hotelpasdecalais.com – Fax 01 45 44 94 57 J 12
38 rm – †€ 145/160 ††€ 155/180, ☕ € 15
◆ The hotel lobby is lit by a glass ceiling and has a beautiful vertical garden made up of orchids. Lovely rooms with individual touches; exposed beams on the top floor.

Madison without rest
143 bd St-Germain Ⓜ St-Germain des Prés – ✆ 01 40 51 60 00 – www.hotel-madison.com – resa@hotel-madison.com – Fax 01 40 51 60 01 J 13
52 rm ☕ – †€ 175/195 ††€ 235/255
◆ Camus loved to stay at this hotel with its elegant rooms. Choose one on the top floors, refurbished in a chic, cosy, modern style. Some rooms have views of the church.

Left Bank St-Germain without rest
9 r. de l'Ancienne Comédie Ⓜ Odéon – ✆ 01 43 54 01 70 – www.paris-hotels-charm.com – reservation@hotelleftbank.com – Fax 01 43 26 17 14 K 13
31 rm ☕ – †€ 160/260 ††€ 170/280
◆ Wainscoting, damask, Jouy drapes, Louis XIII style furniture and half-timbered walls set the scene. Some rooms command views of Notre Dame.

La Villa d'Estrées et Résidence des Arts without rest
17 r. Gît le Coeur Ⓜ Saint-Michel – ✆ 01 55 42 71 11 – www.villadestrees.com – resa@villadestrees.com – Fax 01 55 42 71 00
21 rm – †€ 175/325 ††€ 175/325, ☕ € 12 J 14
◆ These two buildings are decorated in Napoleon III style, updated with modern details by a protegé of the designer Garcia. Cosy, well-appointed bedrooms and apartments.

La Villa without rest
29 r. Jacob Ⓜ St-Germain des Prés – ✆ 01 43 26 60 00 – www.villa-saintgermain.com – hotel@villa-saintgermain.com – Fax 01 46 34 63 63 J 13
31 rm – †€ 280/510 ††€ 280/510, ☕ € 22
◆ The façade is 19C but the interior is staunchly smart and contemporary: wenge furniture, rich fabrics and soft lighting set the scene.

Sénat without rest
10 r. de Vaugirard Ⓜ Luxembourg – ✆ 01 43 54 54 54 – www.hotelsenat.com – reservations@hotelsenat.com – Fax 01 43 54 54 55 K 14
35 rm – †€ 185/265 ††€ 185/265, ☕ € 15 – 6 suites
◆ The stylish black façade, and immense grey vases topped with clusters of mistletoe, set the scene in this smart, contemporary hotel. Very pleasant rooms.

Ste-Beuve without rest
9 r. Ste-Beuve Ⓜ Notre-Dame des Champs – ✆ 01 45 48 20 07 – www.parishotelcharme.com – saintebeuve@wanadoo.fr – Fax 01 45 48 67 52
22 rm – †€ 155/215 ††€ 199/315, ☕ € 15 L 12
◆ The intimate atmosphere of this establishment makes it feel like a private home. The guestrooms have been renovated in a tasteful modern style; bathrooms in black and white.

Millésime without rest
15 r. Jacob Ⓜ St-Germain des Prés – ✆ 01 44 07 97 97 – www.millesimehotel.com – reservation@millesimehotel.com – Fax 01 46 34 55 97 J 13
21 rm – †€ 190 ††€ 220, ☕ € 16
◆ Colours of the south and select furniture and fabrics create a warm atmosphere in the splendid rooms at this hotel. Superb 17C staircase, patio and fine vaulted dining room.

Des Académies et des Arts without rest
15 r. de la Grande-Chaumière Ⓜ Vavin – ✆ 01 43 26 66 44 – www.hoteldesacademies.com – reservation@hoteldesacademies.com – Fax 01 40 46 86 85 L 12
20 rm – †€ 183/294 ††€ 183/294, ☕ € 15
◆ The walls of this creative and artistic hotel are adorned with white figures painted by Jérôme Mesnager and sculptures by Sophie de Watrigant. Elegant, well-appointed guestrooms.

Relais Médicis without rest
23 r. Racine Ⓜ Odéon – ✆ 01 43 26 00 60 – www.relaismedicis.com – reservation@relaismedicis.com – Fax 01 40 46 83 39 K 13
16 rm ☕ – †€ 142/172 ††€ 172/258
◆ A hint of Provence enhances the rooms of this hotel near the Odeon theatre; those overlooking the patio are quieter. Interesting antique furniture.

Au Manoir St-Germain-des-Prés without rest
153 bd St-Germain Ⓜ St-Germain des Prés – ✆ 01 42 22 21 65 – www.paris-hotels-charm.com – reservation@hotelaumanoir.com – Fax 01 45 48 22 25 J 12
28 rm ☕ – †€ 200 ††€ 300
◆ This elegant hotel facing the Flore and Deux Magots (famous St Germain des Prés cafés) has been fully renovated. It retains its bourgeois charm with murals, wood panelling and antiques.

St-Grégoire without rest
43 r. Abbé-Grégoire Ⓜ St-Placide – ✆ 01 45 48 23 23 – www.hotelsaintgregoire.com – hotel@saintgregoire.com – Fax 01 45 48 33 95 L 12
20 rm – †€ 195/250 ††€ 250/300, ☕ € 14
◆ Elegant and welcoming decor at this establishment. Two of the rooms have small leafy terraces. Attractive vaulted breakfast room.

Villa des Artistes without rest
9 r. Grande-Chaumière Ⓜ Vavin – ✆ 01 43 26 60 86 – www.villa-artistes.com – hotel@villa-artistes.com – Fax 01 43 54 73 70 L 12
55 rm – †€ 109/270 ††€ 129/350, ☕ € 15
◆ The name pays tribute to the artists who embellished the history of the Montparnasse district. Some rooms have been renovated on the theme of 20C artists.

Artus without rest
34 r. de Buci Ⓜ Mabillon – ✆ 01 43 29 07 20 – www.artushotel.com – info@artushotel.com – Fax 01 43 29 67 44 J 13
27 rm ☕ – †€ 195/305 ††€ 195/305
◆ Contemporary yet intimate, with modern bedrooms ornamented with antiques, an attractive vaulted cellar, designer bar, and paintings from nearby galleries on display.

Relais St-Sulpice without rest
3 r. Garancière Ⓜ St-Sulpice – ✆ 01 46 33 99 00 – www.relais-saint-sulpice.com – relaisstsulpice@wanadoo.fr – Fax 01 46 33 00 10 K 13
26 rm – †€ 178/217 ††€ 178/217, ☕ € 12
◆ Appealing hotel not far from the Sénat and the Luxembourg gardens housing spacious, well-decorated rooms. Those at the back are very quiet.

De Fleurie without rest
32 r. Grégoire de Tours Ⓜ Odéon – ✆ 01 53 73 70 00 – www.hotel-de-fleurie.fr – bonjour@hotel-de-fleurie.fr – Fax 01 53 73 70 20 K 13
29 rm – †€ 135/215 ††€ 175/320, ☕ € 13
◆ Spruce 18C facade adorned with statues in niches. Elegant rooms with soft tones, enhanced by woodwork. Choose the quieter rooms overlooking the courtyard.

Prince de Conti without rest
8 r. Guénégaud Ⓜ Odéon – ✆ 01 44 07 30 40 – www.prince-de-conti.com – princedeconti@wanadoo.fr – Fax 01 44 07 36 34 J 13
26 rm – †€ 165/280 ††€ 165/280, ☕ € 13
◆ This 18C building adjoining the Hotel de la Monnaie has a charming lounge full of interesting features; refined bedrooms; and a bright duplex decorated with precious objects.

Clos Médicis without rest
56 r. Monsieur Le Prince Ⓜ Odéon – ✆ 01 43 29 10 80 – www.hotelclosmedicisparis.com – message@hotelclosmedicisparis.com – Fax 01 43 54 26 90 K 14
37 rm – †€ 145/300 ††€ 180/300, ☕ € 13 – 1 suite
◆ Hotel dating from 1773 a few feet from the Marie de Médicis garden. The modern interior, warm tones, soft lighting and attention to detail makes it ideal for a relaxing stay.

Odéon without rest
3 r. Odéon Ⓜ Odéon – ✆ 01 43 25 90 67 – www.odeonhotel.fr – odeon@odeonhotel.fr – Fax 01 43 25 55 98 K 13
33 rm – †€ 130 ††€ 190/270, ☕ € 12
◆ The façade, stone walls and exposed beams bear witness to the age of this building (17C). Personalised guestrooms, some with views of the Eiffel Tower.

Odéon St-Germain without rest
13 r. St-Sulpice Ⓜ Odéon – ✆ 01 43 25 70 11 – www.paris-hotel-odeon.com – reservation@paris-hotel-odeon.com – Fax 01 43 29 97 34 K 13
27 rm – †€ 156/250 ††€ 182/370, ☕ € 14
◆ The interior of this 16C house is varied to say the least: old brass or four-poster beds, bric-a-brac from antique markets, etc. Tiny lush garden.

Prince de Condé without rest
39 r. de Seine Ⓜ Mabillon – ✆ 01 43 26 71 56 – www.prince-de-conde.com – princedeconde@wanadoo.fr – Fax 01 46 34 27 95 J 13
11 rm – †€ 195 ††€ 195/280, ☕ € 13
◆ An intimate hotel close to numerous art galleries. Cosy rooms with stone walls, fine vaulted cellar and lounge-library.

Régent without rest
61 r. Dauphine Ⓜ Odéon – ✆ 01 46 34 59 80 – www.hotelleregent.com – hotel.leregent@wanadoo.fr – Fax 01 40 51 05 07 J 13
24 rm – †€ 140/175 ††€ 140/250, ☕ € 14
◆ Tall façade dating from 1769. The rooms are cosy and well equipped. The charming breakfast room with exposed stone walls is located in the basement.

Bréa without rest
14 r. Bréa Ⓜ Vavin – ✆ 01 43 25 44 41 – www.jardinlebrea-paris-hotel.com – brea.hotel@wanadoo.fr – Fax 01 44 07 19 25 L 12
23 rm – †€ 110/195 ††€ 130/220, ☕ € 13
◆ Two renovated buildings joined by an attractive, glass-roofed, winter garden room. Spacious, well-equipped rooms, dressed with English Designer's Guild fabrics.

De Sèvres without rest
22 r. Abbé-Grégoire Ⓜ St-Placide – ✆ 01 45 48 84 07 – www.hoteldesevres.com – info@hoteldesevres.com – Fax 01 42 84 01 55 K 11-12
31 rm – †€ 99/129 ††€ 115/145, ☕ € 13
◆ This peaceful, renovated hotel near the Bon Marché offers modern rooms. The breakfast room overlooks a tiny courtyard decked with flowers. Temporary exhibitions in the lounge.

Le Clément without rest
6 r. Clément Ⓜ Mabillon – ✆ 01 43 26 53 60 – www.hotel-clement.fr – info@hotel-clement.fr – Fax 01 44 07 06 83 K 13
28 rm – †€ 123/144 ††€ 123/144, ☕ € 11
◆ Opposite the St Germain market, this hotel with an elegant grey facade has been in the same family for three generations. Reasonably priced, well-kept rooms.

Paris – Hôtel Lutetia
45 bd Raspail Ⓜ Sèvres Babylone – ✆ 01 49 54 46 90 – www.lutetia-paris.com – lutetia-paris@lutetia-paris.com – Fax 01 49 54 46 00 – Closed August, 24-30 December, Saturday, Sunday and bank holidays K 12
Rest – Menu € 60 bi (weekday lunch), € 80/130 – Carte € 65/145
Spec. Homard breton au tartare de betterave, tétragone à l'huile de noisette. Langoustines dorées, fleurs de courgettes aux girolles et aux amandes fraîches. Fruits rouges et noirs, palet de noix de coco, coque de sucre filé, jus chaud à la fraise.
◆ In keeping with the style of the hotel, the Sonia Rykiel Art Deco dining room reproduces one of the lounges from the Normandie ocean liner. Inspired up-to-date cuisine.

Jacques Cagna
14 r. Grands Augustins Ⓜ St-Michel – ✆ 01 43 26 49 39 – www.jacques-cagna.com – restaurant@jacques-cagna.com – Fax 01 43 54 54 48 – Closed 1st-26 August, Monday lunch, Saturday lunch and Sunday J 14
Rest – Menu € 45 (lunch)/100 – Carte € 104/170
Spec. Langoustines de l'atlantique en croustillant. Gibier (season). Paris-Brest au praliné à l'ancienne.
◆ Located in one of the oldest buildings in Paris, the comfortable dining room boats massive rafters, 16C woodwork and Flemish paintings. Refined cuisine.

Relais Louis XIII (Manuel Martinez)
8 r. Grands Augustins Ⓜ Odéon – ✆ 01 43 26 75 96 – www.relaislouis13.com – contact@relaislouis13.com – Fax 01 44 07 07 80 – Closed August, 22 December-3 January, Sunday and Monday J 14
Rest – Menu (€ 50), € 80 (weekday dinner), € 110/170 bi – Carte € 141/166
Spec. Ravioli de homard breton, foie gras et crème de cèpes. Caneton challandais rôti entier aux épices douces et fortes. Millefeuille à la vanille bourbon.
◆ The building dates from the 16C and there are three Louis XIII-style dining rooms with balustrades, tapestries and open stonework. Subtle and up-to-date cuisine.

Hélène Darroze-La Salle à Manger
4 r. d'Assas Ⓜ Sèvres Babylone – ✆ 01 42 22 00 11 – reservation@helenedarroze.com – Fax 01 42 22 25 40 K 12
Rest – *(1st floor) (closed lunch from 20 July to 30 August, Sunday and Monday)* Menu € 72 (lunch), € 175/280 – Carte € 111/189
Rest ***Le Salon*** – *(closed 27 July-30 August, Sunday and Monday)* Menu (€ 25), € 88/180 – Carte € 45/110
Spec. Riz carnaroli acquarello noir et crémeux, chipirons au chorizo et tomates confites, jus au persil, émulsion de parmesan. Grosses langoustines bretonnes rôties aux épices tandoori, mousseline de carottes aux agrumes. Pigeonneau fermier de Racan flambé au capucin et foie gras de canard des Landes grillé au feu de bois.
◆ Modern, low-key décor in tones of aubergine and orange, where you can enjoy delicious cuisine and wines from the southwest. On the ground floor, Hélène Darroze presides over the Salon, serving tapas and snacks with a rustic Landes accent.

Le Restaurant – Hôtel L'Hôtel
13 r. des Beaux-Arts Ⓜ St-Germain-des-Prés – ✆ 01 44 41 99 01 – www.lerestaurantparis.com – eat@l-hotel.com – Fax 01 43 25 64 81 – Closed 4-29 August, 21-29 December, Sunday and Monday J 13
Rest – Menu (€ 42), € 95/155 bi – Carte € 95/130
Spec. Cèpe en ravioles et grillé, truffe marinée et jus corsé de champignons (autumn). Bar de ligne, chou fleur, œufs de hareng fumé et poutargue. Fraise des bois, cheese cake et sorbet citron (spring).
◆ Inside the hotel, this restaurant simply known as 'Le Restaurant' has a décor created by Jacques Garcia and a small indoor courtyard. Refined, modern cuisine.

Sensing
19 r. Bréa Ⓜ Vavin – ✆ 01 43 27 08 80 – www.restaurant-sensing.com – contact@restaurantsensing.com – Fax 01 43 26 99 27 – Closed August, Monday lunch and Sunday L 12
Rest – Menu (€ 25), € 55 bi (lunch), € 75 € bi/140 bi – Carte € 59/73
◆ A short menu with refined, contemporary dishes prepared using excellent produce and served in an uncluttered, ultra-stylish setting. Run by the famous French chef, Guy Martin.

Bastide Odéon
7 r. Corneille Ⓜ Odéon – ✆ 01 43 26 03 65 – www.bastide-odeon.com – reservation@bastide-odeon.com – Fax 01 44 07 28 93 – Closed 3-25 August, Sunday and Monday K 13
Rest – Menu (€ 26 bi), € 41
◆ Near the Luxembourg Gardens, a pleasant, comfortable restaurant with decor reminiscent of a Provençal farm. Private room upstairs. Mediterranean specialities.

Méditerranée
2 pl. Odéon Ⓜ Odéon – ✆ 01 43 26 02 30 – www.la-mediterranee.com – la.mediterranee@wanadoo.fr – Fax 01 43 26 18 44 – Closed 22-28 December K 13
Rest – Menu (€ 27), € 34 – Carte € 38/69
◆ Mediterranean cuisine is served in two dining rooms decorated with frescos depicting the sea, as well as a veranda facing the Théâtre de l'Europe.

Yugaraj
14 r. Dauphine Ⓜ Odéon – ✆ 01 43 26 44 91 – Fax 01 46 33 50 77 – Closed August, Monday lunch and Thursday lunch J 14
Rest – Menu (€ 19), € 28/66 – Carte € 36/48
◆ New look but the same refinement at this highly acclaimed Indian restaurant with its museum-like decor (wood panelling, silks and antiques). Comprehensive menu.

Alcazar
62 r. Mazarine Ⓜ Odéon – ✆ 01 53 10 19 99 – www.alcazar.fr – contact@alcazar.fr – Fax 01 53 10 23 23 J 13
Rest – Menu (€ 26 bi), € 32 bi (lunch), € 35/43 – Carte € 40/66
◆ Sir Conrad's establishment attracts fans of electro-chic atmospheres and modern tastes. The glass wall, mezzanine and view of the kitchens give the location its individuality.

Les Bouquinistes

53 quai Grands Augustins Ⓜ St-Michel – ✆ 01 43 25 45 94 – www.guysavoy.com – bouquinistes@guysavoy.com – Fax 01 43 25 23 07 – Closed 5-23 August, 23 December-5 January, Saturday lunch and Sunday J 14

Rest – Menu (€ 26 bi), € 40 bi/120 bi – Carte € 70/95

◆ Opposite the second-hand bookstalls of the embankments, enjoy original cuisine in a jazzy decor by D Humair. Designer furnishings, coloured lamps and abstract artwork.

Fogon (Juan Alberto Herráiz)

45 quai des Grands-Augustins Ⓜ St-Michel – ✆ 01 43 54 31 33 – www.fogon.fr – Closed 15-31 August, Monday and lunch except weekends 23 December-3 January J 14

Rest – Menu € 44/49 – Carte € 46/55

Spec. Jambon de porc Ibérique. Riz dans une paella aux langoustines. Tapas sucrés.

◆ Spanish cuisine (tapas, paëllas) revisited with flair and ingenuity, using top-quality produce and served in a contemporary designer setting.

Yen

22 r. St-Benoît Ⓜ St-Germain des Prés – ✆ 01 45 44 11 18 – restau.yen@wanadoo.fr – Fax 01 45 44 19 48 – Closed 2 weeks in August and Sunday J 13

Rest – Menu (€ 38), € 58 – Carte € 30/65

◆ Two dining rooms with highly refined Japanese decor, the one on the first floor is slightly warmer in style. Pride of place on the menu for the chef's speciality: soba (buckwheat noodles).

La Rotonde

105 bd Montparnasse Ⓜ Vavin – ✆ 01 43 26 68 84 – Fax 01 46 34 52 40 L 12

Rest – Menu € 18 bi (weekday lunch), € 35/45 – Carte € 35/70

◆ The history of this typical Parisian brasserie is printed on the back of the menu. It has served many famous people since 1903. An ideal place for a meal after an evening out at the theatre.

La Marlotte

55 r. du Cherche-Midi Ⓜ St-Placide – ✆ 01 45 48 86 79 – www.lamarlotte.com – Fax 01 44 07 28 93 K 12

Rest – Menu (€ 23 bi) – Carte € 30/65

◆ Near the Bon Marché, a pleasant local restaurant where you may rub shoulders with publishers and politicians. Long dining room, rustic decor and traditional cuisine.

L'Épi Dupin

11 r. Dupin Ⓜ Sèvres Babylone – ✆ 01 42 22 64 56 – www.epidupin.com – lepidupin@wanadoo.fr – Fax 01 42 22 30 42 – Closed 1st-24 August, Monday lunch, Saturday and Sunday K 12

Rest – *(number of covers limited, pre-book)* Menu (€ 25 bi), € 34

◆ Beams and stonework for character, closely-packed tables for conviviality and delicious cuisine to delight the palate; this pocket-handkerchief-sized restaurant has captivated people in the Bon Marché area.

L'Espadon Bleu

25 r. Grands Augustins Ⓜ St-Michel – ✆ 01 46 33 00 85 – www.jacques-cagna.com – espadonbleu6@yahoo.fr – Fax 01 43 54 54 48 – Closed August, Monday lunch, Saturday lunch and Sunday J 14

Rest – Menu (€ 25), € 32 (weekdays) – Carte € 30/70

◆ Pleasant restaurant specialising in fish and seafood dishes. Swordfish (the establishment's namesake) adorn the walls painted in southern shades, and the mosaic tables.

Joséphine "Chez Dumonet"

117 r. du Cherche-Midi Ⓜ Duroc – ✆ 01 45 48 52 40 – Fax 01 42 84 06 83 – Closed Saturday and Sunday L 11

Rest – Carte € 35/70

◆ An authentic Twenties-style establishment with its counter, bench seating and gleaming bistro decor. A good wine list and traditional cuisine.

Ze Kitchen Galerie (William Ledeuil)
4 r. Grands Augustins Ⓜ St-Michel – ☎ 01 44 32 00 32 – www.zekitchengalerie.fr – zekitchen.galerie@wanadoo.fr – Fax 01 44 32 00 33 – Closed Saturday lunchtime and Sunday J 14
Rest – Menu (€ 29 bi), € 35 (weekday lunch)/76 – Carte approx. € 65
Spec. Bouillon Thaï de crustacé, ravioli de langoustine. Saint Jacques grillées, condiment kumquat-citron caviar. Financier châtaigne, chocolat, coco et émulsion cacahuète.
◆ Tempting fusion menu influenced by Asia, refined interior with a loft atmosphere, contemporary paintings and visible kitchens: Ze Kitchen is 'ze' hip place to be on the Left Bank.

Allard
1 r. l'Eperon Ⓜ St-Michel – ☎ 01 43 26 48 23 – Fax 01 46 33 04 02 – Closed 2-23 August J 14
Rest – Menu (€ 25), € 34 – Carte € 45/85
◆ This 1900 bistro offers home-made-type dishes, a friendly atmosphere, a period bar, engravings and paintings depicting scenes of everyday life in Burgundy.

Le Comptoir – Hôtel Relais-St-Germain
9 carr. de l'Odéon Ⓜ Odéon – ☎ 01 44 27 07 97 – www.hotelrsg.com – hotelrsg@wanadoo.fr – Fax 01 46 33 45 30 K 13
Rest – *(number of covers limited, pre-book)* Menu € 50 (weekday dinner) – Carte € 35/80 lunch only
◆ In this pleasant little bistro, Yves Camdeborde offers tasty, generous traditional cuisine, including specialities from Southwest France. Authentic 1930s decor.

Rôtisserie d'en Face
2 r. Christine Ⓜ Odéon – ☎ 01 43 26 40 98 – www.jacques-cagna.com – la-rotisserie@orange.fr – Closed Saturday lunchtime and Sunday J 14
Rest – Menu (€ 26), € 31 (weekday lunch) – Carte € 39/63
◆ Pleasant Jacques Cagna bistro across the street from his eponymous restaurant. Relaxed atmosphere and discreetly elegant decor in varying shades of ochre.

La Maison du Jardin
27 r. Vaugirard Ⓜ Rennes – ☎ 01 45 48 22 31 – Fax 01 45 48 22 31 K 12
Rest – *(pre-book)* Menu € 26/31
◆ In a setting between bistro and provincial inn, this establishment serves tasty updated traditional dishes. Short, reasonably-priced wine list.

L'Épigramme
9 r. l'Éperon ✉ 75006 Ⓜ Odéon – ☎ 01 44 41 00 09 – Fax 01 44 41 00 09 – Closed for three weeks in August, one week at Christmas, Sunday and Monday K 14
Rest – *(number of covers limited, pre-book)*
Menu (€ 22), € 28 (lunch)/30
◆ The tasty updated bistro menu, warm interior decoration (stone and beams) and moderate prices, explain the popularity of this often fully booked restaurant.

Les Terrines de Gérard Vié
97 r. du Cherche-Midi Ⓜ Duroc – ☎ 01 42 22 19 18 – Fax 01 42 22 19 18 – Closed 2 weeks in August, Sunday and Monday L 11
Rest – Menu (€26 b.i.), €36
◆ This new affable bistro focuses on traditional recipes and terrines, rustled up by a chef who rose to fame in a Versailles restaurant. Selection of naturally-produced wines.

Fish La Boissonnerie
69 r. de Seine Ⓜ Odéon – ☎ 01 43 54 34 69 – Fax 01 46 34 63 41 – Closed 10-17 August, 21 December-2 January and Monday C 1
Rest – Menu (€ 11), € 24 (lunch)/37
◆ Former fish shop with mosaic façade, now a fully-fledged, authentic gastropub. Bistro cuisine with a changing market menu. Good wine list.

Azabu

3 r. A. Mazet Ⓜ *Odéon – ✆ 01 46 33 72 05 – Closed 19-27 April, Sunday lunch and Monday* J 13

Rest – Menu (€ 19), € 39/59 – Carte € 45/60

◆ Modern Japanese cuisine served in a small, simple, contemporary dining room, or at the bar opposite the teppanyaki (cooking hob).

Aux Charpentiers

10 r. Mabillon Ⓜ *Mabillon – ✆ 01 43 26 30 05 – auxcharpentiers@wanadoo.fr – Fax 01 46 33 07 98* K13

Rest – Menu (€ 20 bi) – Carte € 36/55

◆ This establishment was once the headquarters of the Carpenters Guild (1874-1970) and has the photographs, engravings and models to prove it. Traditional dishes.

La Table de Fès

5 r. Ste-Beuve Ⓜ *Notre Dame des Champs – ✆ 01 45 48 07 22 – Fax 01 45 49 47 88 – Closed 24 July-27 August and Sunday* L 12

Rest – *(dinner only)* Carte € 35/60

◆ Frescoes (oasis, desert and gardens) and craftwork from Morocco adorn the dining room. Authentic North African cuisine focused on couscous.

Le Bistrot de L' Alycastre

2 r. Clément Ⓜ *Mabillon – ✆ 01 43 25 77 66 – jmlemmery@hotmail.com – Fax 01 43 25 77 66 – Closed 10-30 August, February holiday, Sunday lunch, Monday lunch and Tuesday lunch* K 13

Rest – Menu (€ 34) – Carte € 46/60

◆ An enthusiastic chef has taken over this chic bistro opposite the St Germain market. Simple, modern and tasty cuisine with quality service. Popular terrace.

L'Altro

16 r.du Dragon Ⓜ *St-Germain-des-Prés – ✆ 01 45 48 49 49 – www.laltro.fr – laltro@sljcohen.fr – Fax 01 45 80 96 36 – Closed 14-23 August and 21-27 December* J 12

Rest – Menu (€ 17), € 22 (weekday lunch) – Carte € 25/55

◆ Italian dishes in a part-bistro, part-New York loft décor (black banquettes, white-tiled walls, glass kitchen). Laid-back, trendy atmosphere.

Le Timbre

3 r. Ste-Beuve Ⓜ *Notre-Dame des Champs – ✆ 01 45 49 10 40 – www.restaurantletimbre.com – Closed 1-7 May, 27 July-23 August and Christmas holidays, Sunday and Monday* L 12

Rest – *(number of covers limited, pre-book)* Menu (€ 22), € 26/30 – Carte € 32/38 dinner only

◆ Pleasant little bistro, as big as a postage stamp, and often packed to the gunnels. Daily specials prepared by a British chef in an open kitchen.

La Table d'Erica

6 r. Mabillon Ⓜ *Mabillon – ✆ 01 43 54 87 61 – www.tablederica.com – alatablederica@gmail.com – Closed August, Sunday and Monday*

Rest – Menu (€ 13), € 29 – Carte € 32/50 K 13

◆ Cross the footbridge to La Table d'Erica for a taste of the exotic! A concise, typically Creole menu, with fish from the Caribbean, spicy chicken and curried specialities.

Le Carré de Marguerite

87 r. d'Assas Ⓜ *Port Royal – ✆ 01 43 26 33 61 – www.lecarredemarguerite.fr – restaurant@lecarredemarguerite.fr – Closed Saturday lunch, Sunday and Monday* L 13-M 13

Rest – Menu (€ 19), € 22 (lunch) – Carte € 36/46

◆ A homely air pervades this establishment with its old furniture, grocery store style shelves and knick-knacks. Market-fresh menu renewed daily.

Tsukizi

2 bis r. des Ciseaux Ⓜ *St-Germain-des-Prés – ✆ 01 43 54 65 19 – Closed Sunday lunch and Monday* K 13

Rest – Menu (€ 16) – Carte € 30/75

◆ Sit at the counter, just like in Japan, in the small and rather modest dining area at this traditional restaurant, and watch the chef prepare sushi and other Japanese specialities.

Vivre en Italien.

S. Sauvignier/MICHELIN

Tour Eiffel • École Militaire • Invalides

7th arrondissement

✉ 75007

Pont Royal without rest
7 r. Montalembert Ⓜ *Rue du Bac – ✆ 01 42 84 70 00 – www.hotel-pont-royal.com – hpr@hotel-pont-royal.com – Fax 01 42 84 71 00*
J 12
65 rm – €410 €550, ☕ €27 – 10 suites
◆ Bold colours and mahogany walls adorn the bedrooms; the romance of the salad days of St-Germain-des-Prés with all the comfort of an elegant "literary hotel"!

Duc de St-Simon without rest
14 r. St-Simon Ⓜ *Rue du Bac – ✆ 01 44 39 20 20 – www.hotelducdesaintsimon.com – duc.de.saint.simon@wanadoo.fr – Fax 01 45 48 68 25*
J 11
34 rm – €225/290 €250/290, ☕ €15
◆ Cheerful colours, wood panelling, antique furniture and objects. The atmosphere here is that of a beautiful house of olden times, with the additional appeal of a friendly welcome and peaceful surroundings.

Montalembert
3 r. Montalembert Ⓜ *Rue du Bac – ✆ 01 45 49 68 68 – www.montalembert.com – welcome@montalembert.com – Fax 01 45 49 69 49*
J 12
56 rm – €340/520 €340/520, ☕ €24 – 7 suites **Rest** – Carte €56/87
◆ Dark wood, leather, glass and steel, with tobacco, plum and lilac-coloured decor. The rooms combine all the components of contemporary style. Designer dining room, terrace protected by a boxwood partition, and cuisine for appetites large and small!

K+K Hotel Cayré without rest
4 bd Raspail Ⓜ *Rue du Bac – ✆ 01 45 44 38 88 – www.kkhotels.com/cayre – reservations@kkhotels.fr – Fax 01 45 44 98 13*
J 12
125 rm – €248/406 €280/448, ☕ €26
◆ The discreet Haussmann façade contrasts with the elegant designer rooms within. Fitness centre (with sauna), elegant lounge and bar serving simple bistro-style dishes.

Le Bellechasse without rest
8 r. de Bellechasse Ⓜ *Musée d'Orsay – ✆ 01 45 50 22 31 – www.lebellechasse.com – info@lebellechasse.com – Fax 01 45 51 52 36*
H 11
34 rm – €290/390 €340/390, ☕ €21
◆ Top couturier Christian Lacroix designed the rooms of this hotel. He has joyfully mixed colour with antique and modern details to create an almost dreamlike but distinctly fashionable setting.

Saint Vincent without rest
5 r. Pré aux Clercs Ⓜ *Rue du Bac – ✆ 01 42 61 01 51 – www.hotel-st-vincent.com – reservation@hotel-st-vincent.com – Fax 01 42 61 01 54*
J 12
22 rm – €210/240 €210/240, ☕ €13 – 2 suites
◆ A delightful luxury hotel in the heart of the Left Bank. This 18C private mansion is home to warm, spacious rooms appointed in a Napoleon III spirit.

Bourgogne et Montana without rest
3 r. de Bourgogne Ⓜ *Assemblée Nationale – ✆ 01 45 51 20 22 – bourgogne-montana.com – bmontana@bourgogne-montana.com – Fax 01 45 56 11 98*
H 11
28 rm ☕ – €180/200 €200/290 – 4 suites
◆ Elegance and beauty fill every room of this discreet 18C hotel. The top floor rooms offer superb views over the "Palais-Bourbon" (French Parliament buildings).

Le Walt without rest
37 av. de La Motte-Picquet Ⓜ *Ecole Militaire* – ✆ *01 45 51 55 83*
– www.lewaltparis.com – lewalt@inwoodhotel.com – Fax 01 47 05 77 59
25 rm – †€ 275/325 ††€ 295/345, ☕ € 19 J 9
◆ The imposing reproductions of classical masterpieces and "panther" or "zebra" bedspreads add originality to the comfortable, contemporary rooms.

Le Tourville without rest
16 av. Tourville Ⓜ *Ecole Militaire* – ✆ *01 47 05 62 62 – www.hoteltourville.com*
– hotel@tourville.com – Fax 01 47 05 43 90 J 9
28 rm – †€ 150/350 ††€ 150/350, ☕ € 15 – 2 suites
◆ A pleasing mix of primary and pastel tones, of modern and period furniture sets the scene in this cosy hotel. Four bedrooms with terrace, breakfast in a vaulted cellar.

Verneuil without rest
8 r. Verneuil Ⓜ *Rue du Bac* – ✆ *01 42 60 82 14 – www.hotelverneuil.com – info@hotelverneuil.com – Fax 01 42 61 40 38* J 12
26 rm ☕ – †€ 157 ††€ 200/260
◆ This old building on the Left Bank is decorated in the style of a private house. Elegant rooms adorned with 18C prints. Serge Gainsbourg lived opposite.

Lenox St-Germain without rest
9 r. de l'Université Ⓜ *St-Germain des Prés* – ✆ *01 42 96 10 95*
– www.lenoxsaintgermain.com – hotel@lenoxsaintgermain.com
– Fax 01 42 61 52 83 J 12
32 rm – †€ 135/180 ††€ 160/295, ☕ € 14 – 2 suites
◆ A discreetly luxurious Art Deco style depicts this hotel. Rooms are a little on the small side but attractively decorated. "Egyptian" frescoes adorn the breakfast room. Pleasant bar.

D'Orsay without rest
93 r. Lille Ⓜ *Solférino* – ✆ *01 47 05 85 54 – www.esprit-de-france.com – orsay@espritfrance.com – Fax 01 45 55 51 16* H 11
41 rm – †€ 155/210 ††€ 177/370, ☕ € 13
◆ The hotel occupies two handsome, late-18C buildings. Attractive classical style rooms and welcoming lounge overlooking a small leafy patio.

De Suède Saint Germain without rest
31 r. Vaneau Ⓜ *Rue du Bac* – ✆ *01 47 05 00 08 – www.hoteldesuede.com*
– hoteldesuede@aol.com – Fax 01 47 05 69 27 J 11
39 rm – †€ 129/195 ††€ 129/300, ☕ € 13
◆ Flanked by ministries, this family-run 18C hotel offers Louis XVI-style rooms. Some command a view of the gardens of the prime minister's Matignon residence.

Muguet without rest
11 r. Chevert Ⓜ *Ecole Militaire* – ✆ *01 47 05 05 93 – www.hotelmuguet.com*
– muguet@wanadoo.fr – Fax 01 45 50 25 37 J 9
43 rm – †€ 106 ††€ 140, ☕ € 10
◆ Hotel spruced up in a classic spirit. Sitting room furnished in Louis Philippe style, well-appointed rooms (seven overlook the Eiffel Tower or the Invalides), veranda and small garden.

Eiffel Park Hôtel without rest
17bis r. Amélie Ⓜ *La Tour Maubourg* – ✆ *01 45 55 10 01 – www.eiffelpark.com*
– reservation@eiffelpark.com – Fax 01 47 05 28 68 J 9
36 rm – †€ 135/260 ††€ 135/260, ☕ € 12
◆ From the Indian and Chinese artefacts to the ethnic fabrics, exoticism reigns throughout this elegant hotel. Even more unusual, it boasts a rooftop summer terrace complete with beehives.

Relais Bosquet without rest
19 r. Champ-de-Mars Ⓜ *Ecole Militaire* – ✆ *01 47 05 25 45*
– www.hotelrelaisbosquet.com – hotel@relaisbosquet.com – Fax 01 45 55 08 24
40 rm – †€ 135/185 ††€ 155/210, ☕ € 15 J 9
◆ This discreet hotel has a prettily furnished Directoire style interior. The classic style rooms feature the same attention to detail with thoughtful little touches.

Splendid Tour Eiffel without rest
29 av. Tourville Ⓜ Ecole Militaire – ☎ 01 45 51 29 29 – www.hotel-splendid-paris.com – reservation@hotel-splendid-paris.com – Fax 01 44 18 94 60 J 9
48 rm – €145/165 €165/225, €12
◆ Haussmannian building, housing elegant rooms adorned with contemporary furnishings. Most of them offer a splendid view, some a glimpse of the Eiffel Tower. Cosy lounge-bar.

Londres Eiffel without rest
1 r. Augereau Ⓜ Ecole Militaire – ☎ 01 45 51 63 02 – www.londres-eiffel.com – info@londres-eiffel.com – Fax 01 47 05 28 96 J 8
30 rm – €165 €185, €14
◆ Cosy hotel done up in warm colours near the leafy paths of the Champ-de-Mars. The second building, reached through a small courtyard, has quieter rooms.

Du Cadran without rest
10 r. du Champ-de-Mars Ⓜ Ecole Militaire – ☎ 01 40 62 67 00 – www.hotelducadran.com – info@cadranhotel.com – Fax 01 40 62 67 13 J 9
41 rm – €150/230 €150/230, €13
◆ This hotel near the lively Rue Cler market is in store for a total makeover. Contemporary style in all the rooms, 17C fireplace in the sitting room, and vaulted dining room.

St-Germain without rest
88 r. du Bac Ⓜ Rue du Bac – ☎ 01 49 54 70 00 – www.hotel-saint-germain.fr – info@hotel-saint-germain.fr – Fax 01 45 48 26 89 J 11
29 rm – €150/240 €150/240, €12
◆ Empire, Louis-Philippe, high-tech design, antique objects, contemporary paintings - the charm of variety. Comfortable library, patio pleasant in summer.

De Varenne without rest
44 r. Bourgogne Ⓜ Varenne – ☎ 01 45 51 45 55 – www.hoteldevarenne.com – info@hoteldevarenne.com – Fax 01 45 51 86 63 J 10
25 rm – €125/177 €135/197, €10
◆ A quietly located hotel adorned with French Empire and Louis XVI style furniture. In summer, breakfast is served in a small, leafy courtyard.

Champ-de-Mars without rest
7 r. du Champ-de-Mars Ⓜ Ecole Militaire – ☎ 01 45 51 52 30 – www.hotelduchampdemars.com – reservation@hotelduchampdemars.com – Fax 01 45 51 64 36 J 9
25 rm – €89 €95, €8
◆ Small hotel with an English atmosphere, between the Champ-de-Mars and the Invalides. Dark green façade, cosy rooms (soon to be renovated) and neat "Liberty" style decor.

Bersoly's without rest
28 r. de Lille Ⓜ Musée d'Orsay – ☎ 01 42 60 73 79 – www.bersolyshotel.com – hotelbersolys@wanadoo.fr – Fax 01 49 27 05 55 – Closed 10-21 August J 13
16 rm – €130/140 €150/170, €10
◆ Impressionist nights in this 17C building in which each room honours an artist whose works are displayed in the nearby Musée d'Orsay (Renoir, Gauguin, etc.).

France without rest
102 bd de la Tour Maubourg Ⓜ Ecole Militaire – ☎ 01 47 05 40 49 – www.hoteldefrance.com – hoteldefrance@wanadoo.fr – Fax 01 45 56 96 78 J 9
60 rm – €90/160 €110/160, €12
◆ Two buildings with a guesthouse feel. Modernised rooms overlooking the Hôtel des Invalides on the street side, quieter on the courtyard side.

Le Jules Verne
2nd floor Eiffel Tower, private lift, South pillar Ⓜ Bir-Hakeim – ☎ 01 45 55 61 44 – www.lejulesverne-paris.com – Fax 01 47 05 29 41 J 7
Rest – Menu €85 (weekday lunch), €165/200 – Carte €190/242
Spec. Pressé de volaille et foie gras. Pavé de turbot aux girolles. Ecrou au chocolat et praliné croustillant.
◆ Although the views of Paris remain the same, the décor in this famous restaurant in the Eiffel Tower has been modernised. For a truly memorable experience, book a window table.

Arpège (Alain Passard)
84 r. de Varenne Ⓜ Varenne – ✆ 01 45 51 47 33 – www.alain-passard.com – arpege.passard@wanadoo.fr – Fax 01 44 18 98 39 – Closed Saturday and Sunday J 10
Rest – Menu € 135 (lunch)/360 – Carte € 190/285
Spec. Couleur, saveur, parfum et dessin du jardin, cueillette éphémère. Volaille de pays "Grande Tradition". Tarte aux pommes bouquet de rose.
◆ Choose the elegant modern dining room, with rare wood and glass decorations by Lalique, rather than the basement. Savour dazzling vegetable garden-based cuisine by a master chef and poet of the land.

Le Divellec (Jacques Le Divellec)
107 r. Université Ⓜ Invalides – ✆ 01 45 51 91 96 – ledivellec@noos.fr – Fax 01 45 51 31 75 – Closed 25 July-25 August, 25 December-2 January and Sunday H 10
Rest – Menu € 55 – Carte € 110/205
Spec. Emincé de langoustines aux truffes. Gros turbot de ligne rôti. Harmonie des compotes.
◆ This restaurant, devoted to outstanding seafood, is just a stone's throw from Les Invalides and offers its prosperous clientèle a feeling of the ocean in the centre of Paris. Classic, somewhat outdated décor.

Pétrossian
144 r. de l'Université Ⓜ Invalides – ✆ 01 44 11 32 32 – Fax 01 44 11 32 35 – Closed August, Sunday and Monday H 10
Rest – Menu € 35 (lunch)/90 – Carte € 65/110
◆ The Petrossians have treated Parisians to caviar from the Caspian sea since 1920. Above the boutique, inventive cuisine is served in a comfortable, elegant dining room.

Il Vino d'Enrico Bernardo
13 bd La Tour-Maubourg Ⓜ Invalides – ✆ 01 44 11 72 00 – www.ilvinobyenricobernardo.com – info@ilvinobyenricobernardo.com – Fax 01 44 11 72 01 H 10
Rest – Menu € 50 bi (lunch), € 95 € bi/1000 bi – Carte € 90/140
Spec. Calamars poêlés, caviar d'aubergine et poivrons confits (summer). Duo d'agneau, ballotines et côtelettes rôties, purée de petits pois et légumes croquants (spring). Melon et abricots en salade, coulis de fruits exotiques, glace au fromage blanc et miel (summer).
◆ Choose the wine and let the meal take care of itself! In his chic designer restaurant, the Best Sommelier 2004 reverses the trend by linking the food to the wine.

Le Violon d'Ingres (Christian Constant et Stéphane Schmidt)
135 r. St-Dominique Ⓜ Ecole Militaire – ✆ 01 45 55 15 05 – www.leviolondingres.com – violondingres@wanadoo.fr – Fax 01 45 55 48 42 – Closed in August, Sunday and Monday J 8
Rest – Menu € 49 (weekdays)/65 – Carte € 49/60
Spec. Foie gras d'oie brioché, gelée au pinot noir. Suprême de bar croustillant aux amandes, ravigote aux câpres de Sicile. Feuillantine au chocolat guanaja
◆ This elegant dining room in the style of a contemporary bistro is a meeting point for gourmets, attracted by quality cuisine that enhances the produce and respects the seasons.

Les Ombres
27 quai Branly Ⓜ Alma Marceau – ✆ 01 47 53 68 00 – www.lesombres.fr – ombres.restaurant@elior.com – Fax 01 47 53 68 18 H 8
Rest – Menu € 38 (lunch)/95 – Carte € 38/95
◆ This restaurant enjoys fine views of the Eiffel Tower and its nocturnal illuminations from the roof-terrace of the Musée du Quai Branly. Contemporary dining.

Cigale Récamier
4 r. Récamier Ⓜ Sèvres Babylone – ✆ 01 45 48 86 58 – Closed Sun K 12
Rest – Carte € 55/65
◆ A welcoming establishment with a clientele of writers and editors. Classic cuisine and sweet and savoury soufflé specialities, renewed every month. Peaceful terrace.

XX **153 Grenelle** A/C VISA MC AE
153 r. de Grenelle Ⓜ *La Tour Maubourg – ✆ 01 45 51 54 12 – jjjouteux@gmail.com* J 9
Rest – Menu (€ 25), € 35 (weekdays)/59 – Carte approx. € 60
◆ Taken over by a new chef, this restaurant has been treated to a soothing, elegant, classical interior (grey colour scheme, fresh flowers, artwork). Traditional fare.

XX ✿ **Vin sur Vin** A/C VISA MC
20 r. de Monttessuy Ⓜ *Pont de l'Alma – ✆ 01 47 05 14 20 – Closed 1-11 May, August, 24 December-6 January, Monday except dinner from September to March, Saturday lunch and Sunday* H 8
Rest – *(number of covers limited, pre-book)* Carte € 88/138
Spec. Galette de pied de cochon. Ris de veau de lait français. Soufflé chaud.
◆ Warm welcome, elegant decor, delicious traditional dishes and extensive wine list (600 vintages) – full marks for this restaurant close to the Eiffel Tower!

XX **Tante Marguerite** A/C VISA MC AE
5 r. Bourgogne Ⓜ *Assemblée Nationale – ✆ 01 45 51 79 42 – www.bernard-loiseau.com – tante.marguerite@bernard-loiseau.com – Fax 01 47 53 79 56 – Closed August, Saturday and Sunday* H 11
Rest – Menu € 47
◆ Not far from the Palais Bourbon, Tante Marguerite offers tasty, traditional cuisine in a calm ambiance.

XX **Chez les Anges** A/C VISA MC AE
54 bd de la Tour Maubourg Ⓜ *La Tour Maubourg – ✆ 01 47 05 89 86 – www.chezlesanges.com – mail@chezlesanges.com – Fax 01 47 05 45 56 – Closed Saturday and Sunday* J 10
Rest – Menu (€ 25), € 34/40 – Carte € 44/73
◆ A trendy atmosphere, minimalist contemporary decor and long counter where you can take a seat to sample the tasty cuisine, half-traditional, half-modern.

XX **New Jawad** A/C VISA MC AE
12 av. Rapp Ⓜ *Ecole Militaire – ✆ 01 47 05 91 37 – Fax 01 45 50 31 27* H 8
Rest – Menu € 16/42 – Carte € 21/42
◆ Pakistani and Indian specialities, attentive service and a plush, cosy setting characterise this restaurant in the vicinity of the Pont de l'Alma.

XX **Thiou** A/C VISA MC AE
49 quai d'Orsay Ⓜ *Invalides – ✆ 01 40 62 96 50 – Fax 01 40 62 97 30 – Closed August, Saturday lunch and Sunday* H 9
Rest – Carte € 45/90
◆ Thiou is the nickname of the lady chef of this restaurant, often mentioned in the press, whose regular customers include celebrities. Thai dishes served in a discreetly exotic, comfortable dining room.

XX **La Cuisine** A/C VISA MC AE
14 bd La Tour-Maubourg Ⓜ *Invalides – ✆ 01 44 18 36 32 – www.lacuisine.lesrestos.com – lacuisine@lesrestos.com – Fax 01 44 18 30 42 – Closed Saturday lunch* H 10
Rest – Menu (€ 28), € 42 – Carte € 56/82
◆ A charming decor of sunny colours, paintings, mirrors, banquettes and upholstered chairs provides a warm setting for the chef's tasty dishes.

XX ✿ **Auguste** (Gaël Orieux) A/C VISA MC AE
54 r. Bourgogne Ⓜ *Varenne – ✆ 01 45 51 61 09 – www.restaurantauguste.fr – orieux.gael@wanadoo.fr – Fax 01 45 51 27 34 – Closed 3-24 August, Saturday and Sunday* J 10
Rest – Menu € 35 (lunch) – Carte € 62/94
Spec. Huitres creuses en gelée à la diable. Rouget de roche au confit de poivrons doux. Soufflé au chocolat pur caraïbes
◆ The pleasant colourful decor of this up-to-date establishment is the setting for a cuisine that is as flavourful as it is inventive. A fine tribute to Auguste Escoffier.

XX **Le Clarisse** AE VISA MC AE
29 r. Surcouf Ⓜ *La Tour Maubourg – ✆ 01 45 50 11 10 – www.leclarisse.fr – olivier.maria@leclarisse.fr – Fax 01 45 50 11 14 – Closed August, Saturday lunch and Sunday* H 9
Rest – Menu (€ 29), € 35 – Carte € 54/70
◆ Near Les Invalides, this contemporary restaurant sports a simple and refined interior dominated by shades of black and white. Intimate lounge on the first floor. Contemporary menu that changes with the seasons.

XX **Le Bamboche** AC VISA MC AE
15 r. Babylone Ⓜ *Sèvres Babylone – ✆ 01 45 49 14 40 – www.lebamboche.com – lebamboche@aol.com – Fax 01 45 49 14 44 – Closed 27 July-9 August and Sunday lunch* K 11
Rest – Menu (€ 28), € 35 (weekdays)/80 – Carte € 75/90
◆ A discreet and seductive address a stone's throw from the Bon Marché. The contemporary decor of the dining room is the setting for creative food. Attentive service.

XX **Le Petit Bordelais** VISA MC AE
22 r. Surcouf Ⓜ *Invalides – ✆ 01 45 51 46 93 – www.lepetit-bordelais.com – contact@le-petit-bordelais.fr – Fax 01 45 50 30 11 – Closed 26 July-18 August, Sunday and Monday* H 9
Rest – Menu € 19 (lunch), € 33/45 – Carte € 48/66
◆ New address offering a good choice of wines by the glass, particularly Bordeaux. Intimite decor in red and moka tones, velvet banquettes.

XX **D'Chez Eux** AC VISA MC AE
2 av. Lowendal Ⓜ *Ecole Militaire – ✆ 01 47 05 52 55 – www.chezeux.com – contact@chezeux.com – Fax 01 45 55 60 74 – Closed 1st-18 August and Sunday* J 9
Rest – Menu € 42 (lunch) – Carte € 55/75
◆ For 40 years customers have been seduced by this restaurant where hearty dishes from Auvergne and southwest France are served by waiters in smocks in a "provincial inn" atmosphere.

XX **L'Esplanade** AC VISA MC AE
52 r. Fabert Ⓜ *La Tour Maubourg – ✆ 01 47 05 38 80* J 9
Rest – Carte € 55/80
◆ This Costes establishment is ideally located opposite the Invalides. Unusual ball-and-canon décor, very Napoleon III. Trendy fusion brasserie menu.

XX **Vin et Marée** AC VISA MC AE
71 av. Suffren Ⓜ *La Motte Picquet Grenelle – ✆ 01 47 83 27 12 – www.vin-et-maree.com – vmsuffren@orange.fr – Fax 01 53 86 98 26* K 8
Rest – Menu (€ 21) – Carte € 30/50
◆ A modern brasserie style (bench seating, mirrors and copperware) in seaside colours. The blackboard menu offers fish and seafood only.

X **L'Atelier de Joël Robuchon** AC VISA MC
5 r. Montalembert Ⓜ *Rue du Bac – ✆ 01 42 22 56 56 – www.joel-robuchon.com – latelierdejoelrobuchon@wanadoo.fr – Fax 01 42 22 97 91 – Open from 11.30am to 3.30pm and 6.30pm to midnight. Reservations only possible for certain services: please enquire* J 12
Rest – Menu € 120 – Carte € 57/123
Spec. Langoustines en papillote croustillante au basilic. Caille caramélisée farcie de foie gras et pomme purée. Chocolat "sensation", sorbet ivoire et crémeux araguani.
◆ An original concept in a chic décor designed by Rochon: no tables, just high stools in a row facing the counter, where you can sample fine, modern cuisine, served tapas style.

X **Gaya Rive Gauche par Pierre Gagnaire** AC VISA MC AE
44 r. Bac Ⓜ *Rue du Bac – ✆ 01 45 44 73 73 – www.pierre-gagnaire.com – p.gagnaire@wanadoo.fr – Fax 01 45 44 73 73 – Closed Saturday lunch and Sunday* J 12
Rest – Menu (€ 38) – Carte € 70/95
Spec. Chair de tourteau à la gelée de fenouil au citron. Poêlée de langoustines à la coriandre fraîche. Gâteau au chocolat.
◆ In this delightful contemporary and relaxed bistro with a grey-blue décor designed by Christian Ghion, you are served a succession of creative seafood dishes.

Au Bon Accueil
14 r. Monttessuy Ⓜ Pont de l'Alma – ✆ 01 47 05 46 11 – www.aubonaccueilparis.com – mail@chezlesanges.com – Fax 01 45 56 15 80 – Closed 7-20 August, Saturday and Sunday H 8

Rest – Menu € 27/31 – Carte € 54/75

◆ Beneath the shadow of the Eiffel Tower, this modern restaurant offers delicious up-to-date dishes pleasantly reflecting the changing seasons.

Les Fables de La Fontaine (Sébastien Gravé)
131 r. Saint-Dominique Ⓜ Ecole Militaire – ✆ 01 44 18 37 55 – www.lesrestaurantsdeconstant.com – violondingres@wanadoo.fr – Fax 01 44 18 37 57 J 8

Rest – Menu (€ 35 bi), € 80 – Carte € 56/78

Spec. Fine tarte de rouget façon pissaladière. Saint-Jacques à la plancha à l'écrasé de topinambour et châtaigne. Gâteau basque.

◆ Bistro dedicated to seafood set in a small dining room (brown tones, bench seats, tiles and blackboards) and on a summer terrace. Short, well though-out menu and good wines available by the glass.

L'Agassin
8 r. Malard Ⓜ La Tour Maubourg – ✆ 01 47 05 18 18 – lagassin@free.fr – Fax 01 45 55 64 41 – Closed August, Sunday and Monday H 9

Rest – Menu € 23 (lunch)/34

◆ The Agassin, the lowest bud on a vine branch, sets the tone of this new, minimalist, contemporary bistro (dark wood and light walls) serving up-to-date cuisine.

Nabuchodonosor
6 av. Bosquet Ⓜ Alma Marceau – ✆ 01 45 56 97 26 – www.nabuchodonosor.net – rousseau.e@wanadoo.fr – Fax 01 45 56 98 44 – Closed 1-24 August, Saturday lunch and Sunday H 9

Rest – Menu (€ 23), € 29/50 bi – Carte € 40/68

◆ The sign honours the largest champagne bottle. Walls adorned with Sienna earthenware, oak panels and nebuchadnezzars add decorative effect. Market cuisine.

Bistrot de Paris
33 r. Lille Ⓜ Musée d'Orsay – ✆ 01 42 61 16 83 – amicorrestauration@orange.fr – Fax 01 49 27 06 09 – Closed August, 24 December-1st January, Sunday and Monday J 12

Rest – Carte € 26/60

◆ André Gide was once a regular of this former "soup kitchen". The 1900 decor, revised by Slavik, shimmers with copperware and mirrors. Bistro ambiance and cuisine.

Les Olivades
41 av. Ségur Ⓜ Ségur – ✆ 01 47 83 70 09 – Fax 01 42 73 04 75 – Closed August, Saturday lunch, Monday lunch, Sunday and public holidays K 9

Rest – Menu (€ 22), € 28/70 – Carte € 45/57

◆ A restaurant where olive oil flows freely with appetising up-to-date dishes based on fresh produce. Attractive photos enhance the contemporary decor.

Le Clos des Gourmets
16 av. Rapp Ⓜ Alma Marceau – ✆ 01 45 51 75 61 – www.closdesgourmets.com – closdesgourmets@wanadoo.fr – Fax 01 47 05 74 20 – Closed 1-25 August, Sunday and Monday H 8

Rest – Menu (€ 25), € 29 (lunch)/35

◆ Many regulars love this discreet restaurant decorated in warm colours. The tempting menu varies according to the availability of market produce.

Romantica Caffé
96 bd de la Tour Maubourg Ⓜ École Militaire – ✆ 01 44 18 36 37 – www.laromantica.fr – laromantica@wanadoo.fr – Fax 01 44 18 39 40 J 9

Rest – Menu € 29 (weekday lunch)/39 – Carte € 35/59

◆ The Parisian annex of La Romantica (in Clichy) offers refined Italian cuisine in a contemporary setting (stonework, bottle racks, Venetian mirrors) ; terrace facing Les Invalides.

Le Perron
6 r. Perronet Ⓜ St-Germain des Prés – ✆ 01 45 44 71 51 – cadoniroberto@hotmail.com – Fax 01 45 44 71 51 – Closed in August and Sunday J 12

Rest – Carte € 43/52

◆ Discreet trattoria in the heart of Saint Germain des Prés. Rustic setting with exposed stonework and beams. Italian, mainly Sardinian and Venetian, cuisine.

Florimond
19 av. La Motte-Picquet Ⓜ Ecole Militaire – ✆ 01 45 55 40 38 – Fax 01 45 55 40 38 – Closed 27 July-17 August, 24-27 December-1-4 January, Saturday lunch and Sunday J 9

Rest – Menu € 22 (lunch)/36 – Carte € 47/64

◆ Pocket-sized restaurant named after Monet's gardener in Giverny. Bistro decor, popular with locals for its tasty traditional cooking.

Gorille Blanc
11bis r. Chomel Ⓜ Sèvres Babylone – ✆ 01 45 49 04 54 – legorilleblanc@orange.fr – Fax 01 45 49 04 54 – Closed Sunday K 12

Rest – Menu (€ 20) – Carte € 29/48

◆ A welcoming refuge a stone's throw from the Bon Marché. Regulars enjoy the sunny décor, bistro style and traditional Southwestern cuisine.

Pasco
74 bd La Tour Maubourg Ⓜ La Tour Maubourg – ✆ 01 44 18 33 26 – www.restaurantpasco.com – restaurant.pasco@wanadoo.fr – Fax 01 44 18 34 06 J 9

Rest – Menu (€ 21), € 26 – Carte € 32/45

◆ Mainly Mediterranean cuisine with market produce served in a relaxed atmosphere and a setting of brick walls and ochre shades.

Fontaine de Mars
129 r. St-Dominique Ⓜ Ecole Militaire – ✆ 01 47 05 46 44 – www.fontainedemars.com – lafontainedemars@orange.fr – Fax 01 47 05 11 13 J 9

Rest – Carte € 36/82

◆ This name of this perfectly restored 1930s bistro recalls the nearby fountain dedicated to the warrior god. Terrace under the arcades; traditional and southwestern cuisine.

Café de l'Alma
5 av. Rapp Ⓜ Alma Marceau – ✆ 01 45 51 56 74 – www.cafe-de-l-alma.com/ – cafedelalma@wanadoo.fr – Fax 01 45 51 10 08 H 8

Rest – Carte € 40/70

◆ A stylish, resolutely contemporary dining room by François Champsaur, the new idol of the interior decoration world. Up-to-date dishes and elegant cuisine.

35 ° Ouest
35 r. Verneuil Ⓜ Rue du Bac – ✆ 01 42 86 98 88 – 35degresouest@orange.fr – Fax 01 42 86 00 65 – Closed 2-24 August, Sunday and Monday J 12

Rest – *(number of covers limited, pre-book)* Menu (€ 30 bi) – Carte € 45/85

Spec. Friture d'éperlans sauce tartare. Saint-Pierre rôti aux girolles et pommes de terre ratte. Sablé breton aux pommes caramélisées.

◆ This modern, tastefully designed restaurant sports a grey and green colour scheme and a handsome bar. Inventive seafood cuisine full of flavour.

Aida (Koji Aida)
1 r. Pierre Leroux Ⓜ Vaneau – ✆ 01 43 06 14 18 – www.aidaparis.com – Fax 01 43 06 14 18 – Closed 3 weeks in August, February school holidays and Monday K 11

Rest – *(dinner only) (number of covers limited, pre-book)* Menu € 140/160

Spec. Foie gras chaud, radis blanc cuit vapeur et miso de Kyoto. Chateaubriand cuit au teppanyaki. Wagashi.

◆ A Zen feel to this discreet Japanese restaurant with a bar counter and private dining room. Choice of omakase menus, and a rich list of Burgundy wines chosen by the passionate chef.

P'tit Troquet
28 r. de l'Exposition Ⓜ *Ecole Militaire – ✆ 01 47 05 80 39 – Fax 01 47 05 80 39 – Closed August, Saturday lunch, Monday lunch and Sunday* J 9
Rest – *(number of covers limited, pre-book)* Menu (€ 20), € 32 – Carte approx. € 42
◆ This bistro is certainly as small as its name suggests! But it has so much going for it: a nostalgic charm (old advertisements, soda siphons and period bar counter), friendly atmosphere and tasty market fresh cuisine.

L'Affriolé
17 r. Malar Ⓜ *Invalides – ✆ 01 44 18 31 33 – Closed 3 weeks in August, Sunday and Monday* H 9
Rest – Menu € 19 bi (lunch), € 23/34
◆ This bistro's chef prepares seasonal dishes with fresh market produce, which are announced as daily specials on the blackboard or in a set menu that changes every month.

Chez l'Ami Jean
27 r. Malar Ⓜ *La Tour Maubourg – ✆ 01 47 05 86 89 – Fax 01 45 55 41 82 – Closed August, 23 December-2 January, Sunday and Monday* H 9
Rest – Menu € 34
◆ Chez l'Ami Jean offers tasty, copious dishes, with market produce, and from Southwest France (game specialities in season) in a warm, Basque Country setting.

Oudino
17 r. Oudinot Ⓜ *Vaneau – ✆ 01 45 66 05 09 – www.oudino.com – Fax 01 45 66 53 35 – Closed 9-19 August, 25 December-2 January, Saturday lunch and Sunday* K 11
Rest – Menu € 18 (lunch) – Carte € 26/36
◆ Take a pleasant gourmet break near French government ministry buildings. Dining room with slight Art Deco touches and bistro-type dishes displayed on a blackboard.

Léo Le Lion
23 r. Duvivier Ⓜ *Ecole Militaire – ✆ 01 45 51 41 77 – http://restaurantleolelion.site.voila.fr – restaurantleolelion@hotmail.com – Fax 01 45 51 41 77 – Closed August, 25 December-1st January, Sunday and Monday* J 9
Rest – Carte € 43/55
◆ A 1930's bistro with a charcoal grill. Fish dishes claim the lion's share of the menu all year round; but in season game too evokes a murmur of sheer delight!

Sa Mi In
74 av. Breteuil Ⓜ *Sèvres-Lecourbe – ✆ 01 47 34 58 96 – Fax 01 47 34 58 96* K 10
Rest – Menu € 18, € 25/50
◆ This small, authentic Korean restaurant offers tasty, exotic flavours in a refined and intimate setting. Vegetarian menu.

Café Constant
139 r. St-Dominique Ⓜ *Ecole Militaire – ✆ 01 47 53 73 34 – www.lesrestaurantsdeconstant.com – violondingres@wanadoo.fr – Fax 01 45 55 48 42 – Closed Sunday and Monday* J 8
Rest – Menu (€ 16) – Carte € 30/40
◆ This Christian Constant address is housed in an old café convivial. Good value gourmet bistro cuisine.

Les Cocottes
135 r. St-Dominique Ⓜ *Ecole Militaire – www.lesrestaurantsdeconstant.com – violondingres@wanadoo.fr – Closed Sunday* J 8
Rest – Carte € 24/45
◆ The concept of this friendly establishment, more bar (high counter) than restaurant, lies in its reinvented bistro cuisine, served in cast-iron casserole dishes. No booking.

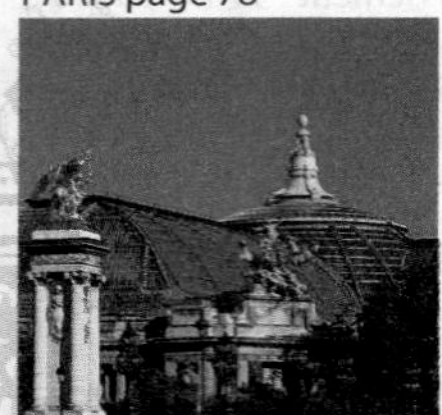
S. Sauvignier/MICHELIN

Champ-Élysées • Concorde • Madeleine

8th arrondissement ✉ 75008

Plaza Athénée

25 av. Montaigne ✉ 75008 Ⓜ Alma Marceau – ✆ 01 53 67 66 65 – www.plaza-athenee-paris.com – reservations@plaza-athenee-paris.com – Fax 01 53 67 66 66 G 9

146 rm – €595/650 €740/790, €50 – 45 suites

Rest *Alain Ducasse au Plaza Athénée* et ***Le Relais Plaza*** – see below

Rest *La Cour Jardin* – restaurant-terrace – *✆ 01 53 67 66 02 (open mid May-mid September)* Carte €82/118

◆ The luxury Parisian hotel par excellence: sumptuous Classic or Art Deco style rooms, afternoon teas with music in the Gobelins gallery, stunning designer bar, and luxurious Dior beauty salon. The charming, greenery-filled terrace of La Cour Jardin opens when the weather turns nice.

Four Seasons George V

rm,

31 av. George-V Ⓜ George V – ✆ 01 49 52 70 00 – www.fourseasons.com/paris – reservation.paris@fourseasons.com – Fax 01 49 52 70 10 G 8

197 rm – €770/1520 €770/1520, €49 – 48 suites

Rest *Le Cinq* – see below

Rest *La Galerie* – *✆ 01 49 52 30 01* – Carte €95/157

◆ Completely renovated in an 18C style, the George V has luxurious bedrooms, which are extremely spacious by Paris standards. Beautiful collections of art work and a superb spa. In summer, the tables at La Galerie are set out in the delightful interior courtyard.

Le Bristol

112 r. Fg St-Honoré Ⓜ Miromesnil – ✆ 01 53 43 43 00 – www.lebristolparis.com – resa@lebristolparis.com – Fax 01 53 43 43 01 F 10

123 rm – €650 €710/1200, €55 – 38 suites

Rest *Le Bristol* – see below

◆ 1925 luxury hotel set around a magnificent garden. Sumptuous rooms, mainly Louis XV or Louis XVI-style with an exceptional "boat" swimming pool on the top floor.

Crillon

10 pl. de la Concorde Ⓜ Concorde – ✆ 01 44 71 15 00 – www.crillon.com – crillon@crillon.com – Fax 01 44 71 15 02 G 11

119 rm – €770 €770/1220, €49 – 28 suites

Rest *Les Ambassadeurs* – see below

Rest *L'Obélisque* – *✆ 01 44 71 15 15* – Menu €54 – Carte €54/110

◆ This 18C townhouse has kept its sumptuous, decorative features. The bedrooms, decorated with wood-furnishings, are magnificent. A French style luxury hotel through-and-through.

Fouquet's Barrière

46 av. George-V Ⓜ George V – ✆ 01 40 69 60 00 – www.fouquets-barriere.com – hotelfouquets@lucienbarriere.com – Fax 01 40 69 60 35 F 8

86 rm – €710/1190 €710/1190, €46 – 21 suites

Rest *Fouquet's* – see below

Rest *Le Diane* – *(closed 19 July-10 August, 3-11 January, Sunday and Monday)* Menu €68 (weekday lunch), €90/135 – Carte €109/155

◆ The latest hotel of the Barrière group offers 16,000m² of luxury: décor bearing the Garcia stamp, modern comfort, high technology, spa and garden. A hushed ambience at Le Diane with its brightly-lit niches adorned with flowers. Contemporary cuisine.

Lancaster
7 r. Berri Ⓜ *George V – ✆ 01 40 76 40 76 – www.hotel-lancaster.fr – restaurant@hotel-lancaster.fr – Fax 01 40 76 40 00* F 9
46 rm – †€ 270/320 ††€ 425/520, ☕ € 37 – 11 suites
Rest *La Table du Lancaster* – see below
◆ Boris Pastoukhoff paid for his lodging in this hotel with paintings, thus adding richly to this former mansion's stylish décor. Its discreet luxury was also beloved by Marlene Dietrich.

Hilton Arc de Triomphe
51 r. de Courcelles Ⓜ *Courcelles – ✆ 01 58 36 67 00 – www.hilton.fr – reservations.adt@hilton.com – Fax 01 58 36 67 84* E 9
463 rm – †€ 295/650 ††€ 295/650, ☕ € 30 – 50 suites
Rest *Safran* – *✆ 01 58 36 67 96* – Menu € 40 (lunch) – Carte € 50/75
◆ This new hotel, inspired by the liners of the 1930s, has successfully created their luxurious and refined atmosphere. Elegant Art Deco rooms designed by Jacques Garcia, patio with a fountain, fitness centre etc. At Safran, contemporary cuisine influenced by the flavours and scents of Asia.

Champs-Élysées Plaza without rest
35 r. de Berri Ⓜ *George V – ✆ 01 53 53 20 20 – www.champselyseesplaza.com – info@champselyseesplaza.com – Fax 01 53 53 20 21* F 9
35 rm – †€ 490/690 ††€ 490/690, ☕ € 24 – 10 suites
◆ The spacious and elegant rooms of this refurbished hotel sport a happy marriage of period and more contemporary furniture. Lovely sitting room with fireplace. Fitness facilities.

Balzac without rest
6 r. Balzac Ⓜ *George V – ✆ 01 44 35 18 00 – www.hotelbalzac.com – reservation-balzac@jjwhotels.com – Fax 01 44 35 18 05* F 8
57 rm – †€ 420/500 ††€ 470/550, ☕ € 38 – 13 suites
◆ Hotel completely refurbished in luxury style, with neo-Classical décor, a vibrant colour scheme and references to the writer Balzac. Period furniture and high-tech facilities in the guestrooms.

Hyatt Regency
24 bd Malhesherbes Ⓜ *Madeleine – ✆ 01 55 27 12 34 – www.paris.madeleine.hyatt.com – paris.madeleine@hyatt.com – Fax 01 55 27 12 35* F 11
86 rm – †€ 295/515 ††€ 330/545, ☕ € 42
Rest *Café M* – *(closed Sunday dinner)* Menu (€ 35 bi), € 47 (weekdays)/54
◆ A distinctly contemporary interior that is both restrained and warm depicts this hotel: lobby-sitting rooms by Eiffel, spacious personalised rooms and a sauna and hammam. The delicious modern cuisine served at the Café M make it very popular. Champagne bar in the evening.

Napoléon
40 av. Friedland Ⓜ *Charles de Gaulle-Etoile – ✆ 01 56 68 43 21 – www.hotelnapoleonparis.com – napoleon@hotelnapoleon.com – Fax 01 47 66 82 33* F 8
101 rm – †€ 540/640 ††€ 540/640, ☕ € 26 – 30 suites
Rest – *(closed dinner, Saturday and Sunday)* Carte € 55/80
◆ A stone's throw from Place de l'Étoile, this hotel-museum honours the emperor's memory via autographs, figurines and paintings from the period. Plush Directoire- or Empire-style rooms. A traditional menu served in the restrained, cosy, wainscoted restaurant.

San Régis
12 r. J. Goujon Ⓜ *Champs-Elysées Clemenceau – ✆ 01 44 95 16 16 – www.hotel-sanregis.fr – message@hotel-sanregis.fr – Fax 01 45 61 05 48* G 9
41 rm – †€ 350/745 ††€ 465/745, ☕ € 36 – 3 suites
Rest – *(closed August and Sunday)* Menu € 40 (weekday lunch) – Carte € 49/63
◆ This 1857 townhouse has been remodelled with taste. A fine staircase adorned with stained glass and statues leads to delightful guestrooms furnished with a diverse range of furniture. The hotel's exquisitely appointed restaurant occupies a subdued but luxurious and exclusive lounge-library.

Vernet
25 r. Vernet Ⓜ *Charles de Gaulle-Etoile* – ✆ *01 44 31 98 00 – www.hotelvernet.com – reservations@hotelvernet.com – Fax 01 44 31 85 69*
50 rm – †€ 290/340 ††€ 290/340, ☕ € 30 – 9 suites F 8
Rest *Les Élysées* – ✆ *01 44 31 98 98* – Menu (€ 35), € 45 (lunch) – Carte € 51/73
◆ A fine building dating from the 1920s, with a dressed-stone façade and wrought-iron balconies. Empire- or Louis XVI-style rooms. Fashionable bar and grill. Both the chic, bistro-style traditional cuisine and the glass-roofed dining room and bar have a modern feel.

Bedford
17 r. de l'Arcade Ⓜ *Madeleine* – ✆ *01 44 94 77 77 – www.hotel-bedford.com – reservation@hotel-bedford.com – Fax 01 44 94 77 97* F 11
135 rm – †€ 172 ††€ 228, ☕ € 19 – 10 suites
Rest – *(Closed August, Saturday, Sunday and bank holidays) (lunch only)*
Menu (€ 34), € 42 – Carte € 63/75
◆ This hotel, built in 1860 in the well-heeled Madeleine district, offers guests tastefully decorated rooms of varying size. 1900s-style decor with an abundance of decorative, stucco motifs and a lovely cupola. The restaurant room is the Bedford's real jewel.

De Vigny
9 r. Balzac Ⓜ *George V* – ✆ *01 42 99 80 80 – www.hoteldevigny.com – reservation@hoteldevigny.com – Fax 01 42 99 80 40* F 8
26 rm – †€ 290/395 ††€ 290/440, ☕ € 39 – 11 suites
Rest *Baretto* – *(closed 15-24 August)* Menu € 60 bi/95 bi – Carte € 54/84
◆ A discreet stylish hotel close to the Champs-Elysées. The snug rooms are graced with personalised touches including a few four-poster beds. Cosy fireside lounge. The Baretto serves traditional cuisine in a stylish, low-key atmosphere and Art Deco setting.

Crowne Plaza Champs Elysées
64 av. Marceau Ⓜ *George V* – ✆ *01 44 43 36 36 – www.crowneplazaparischampselysees.com – reservations@crowneplazaparischampselysees.com – Fax 0142 84 10 30* F 8
56 rm – †€ 450/1500 ††€ 450/1500, ☕ € 30
Rest – *(Opening planned in spring)*
◆ Luxurious designer hotel a stone's throw from Place de l'Étoile. The décor combines high-tech, contemporary furniture and reproductions of Italian Renaissance frescoes and sketches.

Marriott
70 av. des Champs-Élysées Ⓜ *Franklin D. Roosevelt* – ✆ *01 53 93 55 00 – www.marriott.com/pardt – mhrs.pardt.ays@marriotthotels.com – Fax 01 53 93 55 01* F 9
174 rm – †€ 355/775 ††€ 355/775, ☕ € 29 – 18 suites
Rest *Sur les Champs* – ✆ *01 53 93 55 44 (Closed Saturday lunch and Sunday lunch)* Menu (€ 35), € 45 – Carte € 65/90
◆ Enjoy American efficiency combined with lavish comfort in this smart hotel. Most of the guestrooms overlook the Champs-Élysées. Traditional dishes and grills are served in the contemporary decor of the restaurant (red and chocolate tones) and on the terrace.

La Trémoille
14 r. Trémoille Ⓜ *Alma Marceau* – ✆ *01 56 52 14 00 – www.hotel-tremoille.com – reservation@hotel-tremoille.com – Fax 01 40 70 01 08* G 9
90 rm – †€ 315/485 ††€ 370/570, ☕ € 37 – 3 suites
Rest *Louis2* – *(closed Saturday lunch, Sunday and holidays)* Menu (€ 35), € 48/68 – Carte € 49/70
◆ The hotel has been successfully refurbished with contemporary decor combining the old and the ultra-modern, the latest high-tech equipment, and marble bathrooms with Portuguese tiles. Refurbished, comfortable and lit up by a skylight, the Louis 2 serves modern cuisine.

De Sers
41 av. Pierre 1er de Serbie Ⓜ *George V* – ✆ *01 53 23 75 75 – www.hoteldesers.com – contact@hoteldesers.com – Fax 01 53 23 75 76* G 8
49 rm ☕ – †€ 299/550 ††€ 299/550 – 3 suites
Rest – *(closed August)* Menu (€ 29) – Carte € 50/85
◆ Successfully refurbished late-19C townhouse. While the hall has kept its original character, the rooms are thoroughly modern. The food reflects current tastes and is served in a designer dining room or, in summer, on the pleasant terrace.

François 1er without rest
7 r. Magellan Ⓜ *George V – ✆ 01 47 23 44 04 – www.the-paris-hotel.com – hotel@hotel-francois1er.fr – Fax 01 47 23 93 43* F 8
40 rm – †€ 300/390 ††€ 325/490, ☕ € 22 – 2 suites
◆ Carrara marble, mouldings, curios, antique furniture and a plethora of paintings set the lavish decor created by French architect Pierre Yves Rochon. Substantial buffet breakfasts.

Sofitel le Faubourg
15 r. Boissy d'Anglas Ⓜ *Concorde – ✆ 01 44 94 14 14 – www.sofitel.com – h1295-gr@accor.com – Fax 01 44 94 14 28* G 11
163 rm – †€ 450/550 ††€ 550/850, ☕ € 32 – 10 suites
Rest *Café Faubourg* – *(closed August, Saturday lunch and Sunday lunch)* Menu € 37 – Carte € 58/70
◆ This Sofitel is housed in two buildings, one 18C, the other 19C. Rooms with high-tech facilities; a 1930s bar; plus a lounge with a glass roof. Trendy decor, relaxing interior garden and modern cuisine at the Café Faubourg.

Daniel
8 r. Frédéric Bastiat Ⓜ *St-Philippe du Roule – ✆ 01 42 56 17 00 – www.hoteldanielparis.com – danielparis@relaischateaux.com – Fax 01 42 56 17 01* F 9
25 rm – †€ 350/500 ††€ 420/500, ☕ € 27 – 1 suite
Rest – *(closed 31 July-31 August, Saturday and Sunday)* Menu € 40/80 – Carte € 50/73
◆ This hotel likes to travel! Furniture and objects brought back from all over the world combined with a variety of patterned fabrics create a refined and welcoming decor for Parisian globetrotters.

Bradford Élysées without rest
10 r. St-Philippe-du-Roule Ⓜ *St-Philippe du Roule – ✆ 01 45 63 20 20 – www.astotel.com – hotel.bradford@astotel.com – Fax 01 45 63 20 07* F 9
50 rm – †€ 290/545 ††€ 290/545, ☕ € 22
◆ Marble fireplaces, mouldings, brass beds, 1940s decor and a 100-year-old lift – quintessential Parisian charm combined with all mod cons (LCD screens).

Royal without rest
33 av. Friedland Ⓜ *Charles de Gaulle-Etoile – ✆ 01 43 59 08 14 – www.royal-hotel.com – rh@royal-hotel.com – Fax 01 45 63 69 92* F 8
58 rm – †€ 250/270 ††€ 340/360, ☕ € 22
◆ The partially renovated rooms sport a subdued, updated classical decor and have excellent soundproofing. Some command a view of the Arc de Triomphe.

Sofitel Champs-Élysées
8 r. J. Goujon Ⓜ *Champs-Elysées Clemenceau – ✆ 01 40 74 64 64 – www.sofitel-champselysees-paris.com – h1184-re@accor.com – Fax 01 40 74 79 66* G 9
40 rm – †€ 410/500 ††€ 410/510, ☕ € 27
Rest *Les Signatures* – ✆ *01 40 74 64 94 (Closed 1-23 August, 25 December-3 January, Saturday, Sunday and bank holidays) (lunch only)* Menu (€ 36), € 41/49 – Carte € 52/61
◆ A Second Empire building shared with the Press Club of France. The rooms have a contemporary new look and are equipped with state-of-the-art facilities. Business centre. Minimalist decor and a lovely terrace. A restaurant popular with journalists.

Radisson SAS Champs-Élysées
78 av. Marceau Ⓜ *Charles de Gaulle-Etoile – ✆ 01 53 23 43 43 – www.champselysees.paris.radissonsas.com – reservations.paris@radissonsas.com – Fax 01 53 23 43 44* F 8
46 rm – †€ 300/600 ††€ 300/700, ☕ € 29
Rest *La Place* – *(closed 1-23 August, 25 December-3 January, Saturday and Sunday)* Menu € 50/80 – Carte € 65/84
◆ A new hotel occupying the former headquarters of Louis Vuitton. Restful, contemporary rooms, high-tech equipment (plasma TVs) and excellent soundproofing. Updated menu and small courtyard terrace at La Place restaurant.

Powers without rest
52 r. François 1er Ⓜ Franklin D. Roosevelt – ✆ 01 47 23 91 05
– www.hotel-powers.com – contact@hotel-powers.com
– Fax 01 49 52 04 63 G 9
50 rm – †€ 240/650 ††€ 240/650, ☕ € 25
◆ The well-equipped rooms are appealingly stylish with mouldings, fireplaces, bronze clocks and chandeliers, etc. Cosy lounges and an English club style bar.

Franklin Roosevelt without rest
18 r. Clément-Marot Ⓜ Franklin D. Roosevelt – ✆ 01 53 57 49 50
– www.hroosevelt.com – hotel@hroosevelt.com
– Fax 01 53 57 49 59 G 9
47 rm – †€ 310/400 ††€ 310/400, ☕ € 25 – 1 suite
◆ This hotel of Victorian charm cuts a fine figure. Refined decor depicted by an abundance of rare wood, chintz, leather and marble. Pleasant bar.

Chateaubriand without rest
6 r. Chateaubriand Ⓜ George V – ✆ 01 40 76 00 50
– www.hotelchateaubriand.com – welcome@hotelchateaubriand.com
– Fax 01 40 76 09 22 F 9
28 rm – †€ 190/450 ††€ 205/590, ☕ € 22
◆ Original paintings, furniture from around the world and marble bathrooms adorn the guestrooms, each with their own individual charm. Breakfasts facing the interior courtyard.

Relais Monceau without rest
85 r. Rocher Ⓜ Villiers – ✆ 01 45 22 75 11 – www.relais-monceau.com
– relaismonceau@wanadoo.fr – Fax 01 45 22 30 88 E 11
51 rm – †€ 170/240 ††€ 170/240, ☕ € 12
◆ A modern hotel between the Parc Monceau and the Gare St Lazare. Contemporary rooms endowed with rustic charm. Lounge-library, plus a bar which opens onto an attractive small patio.

Marignan
12 r. Marignan Ⓜ Franklin D. Roosevelt – ✆ 01 40 76 34 56
– www.hotelmarignan.fr – contact@hotelmarignan.fr
– Fax 01 40 76 34 34 G 9
73 rm – †€ 470/845 ††€ 470/845, ☕ € 27
Rest – Menu € 47 (weekdays) – Carte € 60/85
◆ Located a stone's throw from the Champs-Élysées. Charming bedrooms with Directoire period furnishings, and comfortable duplexes with work areas designed with business visitors in mind.

Chambiges Élysées without rest
8 r. Chambiges Ⓜ Alma Marceau – ✆ 01 44 31 83 83 – www.hotelchambiges.com
– reservation@hotelchambiges.com – Fax 01 40 70 95 51 G 9
32 rm ☕ – †€ 280/320 ††€ 280/320 – 2 suites
◆ Wood panelling, lovely hangings and fabrics and period furniture depict the cosy romantic allure of this fully renovated hotel. Cosy rooms and a pretty interior garden.

Pershing Hall rm,
49 r. Pierre Charron Ⓜ George V – ✆ 01 58 36 58 00 – www.pershinghall.com
– info@pershinghall.com – Fax 01 58 36 58 01 G 9
20 rm – †€ 329/470 ††€ 329/470, ☕ € 26 – 6 suites
Rest – Menu (€ 49), € 59 – Carte € 60/90
◆ Once the home of General Pershing, then a veterans club and finally a charming hotel designed by Andrée Putman. Chic interior, original and enchanting hanging garden. Behind the curtain of glass beads, the decor is trendy and the cuisine fashionable. Lounge evenings.

Le A without rest
4 r. d'Artois Ⓜ St-Philippe du Roule – ✆ 01 42 56 99 99
– www.hotel-le-a-paris.com – hotel-le-a@wanadoo.fr
– Fax 01 42 56 99 90 F 9
25 rm – †€ 365/660 ††€ 365/660, ☕ € 23 – 1 suite
◆ F. Hybert, a visual artist, and F. Méchiche, an interior designer, masterminded this trendy hotel (or gallery, perhaps?) in black and white. Relaxing lounge-library and bar-lounge.

De l'Arcade without rest
9 r. Arcade Ⓜ Madeleine – ✆ 01 53 30 60 00 – www.hotel-arcade.com – reservation@hotel-arcade.com – Fax 01 40 07 03 07 F 11
48 rm – †€ 168/190 ††€ 203/420, ☕ € 13
◆ The marble and wood panels in the hall and lounges, and the soft colours and carefully-chosen furniture in the rooms, all contribute to the charm of this elegant and discreet hotel near the Madeleine.

Monna Lisa
97 r. La Boétie Ⓜ St-Philippe du Roule – ✆ 01 56 43 38 38 – www.hotelmonnalisa.com – contact@hotelmonnalisa.com – Fax 01 45 62 39 90 F 9
22 rm – †€ 250/280 ††€ 250/280, ☕ € 22
Rest *Caffe Ristretto* – *(closed 3-24 August, 20-28 December, Saturday and Sunday)* Menu (€ 26) – Carte € 48/66
◆ This fine hotel built in 1860 is a showpiece for audacious Italian design. Larger rooms on the street side. The Caffe Ristretto offers a delicious journey through the specialities of the Italian peninsula in a wonderfully modern setting.

Le 123 without rest
123 r. du Faubourg St Honoré Ⓜ St-Philippe du Roule – ✆ 01 53 89 01 23 – www.astotel.com – hotel.le123@astotel.com – Fax 01 45 61 09 07 F 9
41 rm – †€ 269/420 ††€ 309/450, ☕ € 24
◆ Contemporary decor and a mixture of styles, materials and colours. The personalised rooms, which are decorated with fashion sketches, are as appealing as they are unusual.

Le Lavoisier without rest
21 r. Lavoisier Ⓜ St-Augustin – ✆ 01 53 30 06 06 – www.hotellavoisier.com – info@hotellavoisier.com – Fax 01 53 30 23 00 F 11
27 rm – †€ 179/300 ††€ 179/300, ☕ € 14 – 3 suites
◆ Contemporary rooms, cosy little library-cum-lounge also serving as a bar, and a vaulted breakfast room are the hallmarks of this hotel in the St-Augustin district.

Élysées Mermoz without rest
30 r. J. Mermoz Ⓜ Franklin D. Roosevelt – ✆ 01 42 25 75 30 – www.hotel-elyseesmermoz.com – hotel@emhotel.com – Fax 01 45 62 87 10 F 10
22 rm – †€ 110/199 ††€ 122/229, ☕ € 12 – 5 suites
◆ This cosy hotel has rooms in sunny colours or shades of grey; varnished wood panelling and blue stone in the bathrooms, as well as a cane furnished conservatory lounge.

Le Vignon without rest
23 r. Vignon Ⓜ Madeleine – ✆ 01 47 42 93 00 – www.levignon.com – reservation@hotelvignon.com – Fax 01 47 42 04 60 F 12
28 rm – †€ 190/330 ††€ 195/360, ☕ € 20
◆ A friendly, discreet hotel just a few steps from Place de la Madeleine. Cosy rooms – those on the top floor have been refurbished in a distinctly contemporary style.

Mercure Opéra Garnier without rest
4 r. de l'Isly Ⓜ St Lazare – ✆ 01 43 87 35 50 – www.mercure.com – h1913@accor.com – Fax 01 43 87 03 29 F 12
140 rm – †€ 180/360 ††€ 180/360, ☕ € 16
◆ Practically located between St Lazare train station and the big department stores. Practical rooms and buffet breakfast served in a small inner garden in summertime.

St-Augustin without rest
9 r. Roy Ⓜ St Augustin – ✆ 01 42 93 32 17 – www.astotel.com – hotel.staugustin@astotel.com – Fax 01 42 93 19 34 F 11
63 rm – †€ 176/240 ††€ 176/240, ☕ € 14
◆ This renovated hotel in a quiet district has a modern, attractive interior decor. Pleasant contemporary-style guestrooms furnished with dark wood and bright colours.

Élysées Céramic without rest
34 av. Wagram Ⓜ Ternes – ✆ 01 42 27 20 30 – www.elysees-ceramic.com – info@elysees-ceramic.com – Fax 01 46 22 95 83 E 8
57 rm – †€ 195/205 ††€ 220/230, ☕ € 12
◆ The Art Nouveau glazed stoneware façade (1904) is an architectural gem. The interior lives up to the same standard with furniture and decor in the same spirit. Several balconies.

Atlantic without rest
44 r. de Londres Ⓜ *St-Lazare – ✆ 01 43 87 45 40 – www.atlanticparis.fr – contact@atlanticparis.fr – Fax 01 42 93 06 26* E 12
82 rm – †€ 160/210 ††€ 160/210, ☕ € 16
◆ Wavy lines, paintings and boat models... A few discreet touches of the sea enliven this hotel's contemporary decor. Vast glassed-in lounge and bar.

Astoria Opéra without rest
42 r. de Moscou Ⓜ *Rome – ✆ 01 42 93 63 53 – www.astotel.com – hotel.astoria@astotel.com – Fax 01 42 93 30 30* D 11
86 rm – †€ 124/220 ††€ 124/220, ☕ € 14
◆ This hotel in the Europe quarter seems particularly popular with a business clientele. Lounge embellished with modern paintings. Breakfast room with a glass roof.

West-End without rest
7 r. Clément-Marot Ⓜ *Alma Marceau – ✆ 01 47 20 30 78 – www.hotel-west-end.com – contact@hotel-west-end.com – Fax 01 47 20 34 42* G 9
49 rm ☕ – †€ 295/500 ††€ 295/500
◆ Old lithographs, original paintings and modern fittings await you in the simple, chic rooms of this peaceful hotel. Some offer a glimpse of the Eiffel Tower.

Cordélia without rest
11 r. Greffulhe Ⓜ *Madeleine – ✆ 01 42 65 42 40 – www.cordelia-paris-hotel.com – hotelcordelia@wanadoo.fr – Fax 01 42 65 11 81* F 12
30 rm – †€ 155/185 ††€ 185/205, ☕ € 15
◆ Hotel with warm, welcoming rooms of various sizes, a nice vaulted room for breakfast and a lounge with fireplace and wood panelling.

Arioso without rest
– ✆ 01 53 05 95 00 – www.arioso-hotel.com – info@arioso-hotel.com – Fax 01 40 06 04 21 F 10
28 rm – †€ 145/215 ††€ 160/275, ☕ € 15
◆ This fine, well-situated Haussmann building offers small, cosy rooms. Pleasant lounge-library. Breakfast room overlooking an inner courtyard.

Alison without rest
21 r. de Surène Ⓜ *Madeleine – ✆ 01 42 65 54 00 – www.hotelalison.com – hotel.alison@orange.fr – Fax 01 42 65 08 17* F 11
34 rm – †€ 96/172 ††€ 118/192, ☕ € 10
◆ A family hotel in a quiet street near the Théâtre de la Madeleine with an entrance hall decorated with modern paintings. Neat and tidy, functional bedrooms, with attic-style rooms on the 6th floor.

Le "Cinq" – Hôtel Four Seasons George V
31 av. George V Ⓜ *George V – ✆ 01 49 52 71 54 – www.fourseasons.com – lecinq.par@fourseasons.com – Fax 01 49 52 71 81* G 8
Rest – Menu € 85 (lunch), € 155/220 – Carte € 225/340
Spec. Tartine de pied et oreille de porc. Pithiviers de gibier (season). Macaron au caramel.
◆ The superb dining room, a majestic evocation of the Grand Trianon, opens onto a delightful interior garden. Refined atmosphere, good wine list and classic cuisine.

Les Ambassadeurs – Hôtel Crillon
10 pl. Concorde Ⓜ *Concorde – ✆ 01 44 71 16 16 – www.crillon.com – ambassadeurs@crillon.com – Fax 01 44 71 15 02 – Closed August, Sunday and Monday* G 11
Rest – Menu € 92 (weekday lunch)/220 – Carte € 168/273
Spec. Blanc à manger d'œuf et truffe noire (Jan. to March). Pigeonneau désossé, foie gras de canard et jus à l'olive. Comme un vacherin aux fruits de saison.
◆ This splendid dining room was once the ballroom of an 18C mansion. Sophisticated, inventive cuisine and a superb wine list.

Alain Ducasse au Plaza Athénée – Hôtel Plaza Athénée
25 av. Montaigne Ⓜ *Alma Marceau –*
01 53 67 65 00 – www.alain-ducasse.com – adpa@alain-ducasse.com – Fax 01 53 67 65 12 – Closed 17 July-25 August, 18-30 December, Monday lunch, Tuesday lunch, Wednesday lunch, Saturday and Sunday G 9
Rest – Menu € 260/360 – Carte € 215/395
Spec. Caviar oscietre d'Iran, langoustines rafraîchies. Volaille de Bresse, sauce Albufera (15 Oct.-31 Dec.). Fraises des bois en coupe rafraîchie.
◆ The sumptuous regency décor has been redone with a mind to design and organza. Inventive dishes from a talented team coached by Ducasse and 1001 selected wines: the palatial life!

Ledoyen
8 av. Dutuit (carré Champs-Élysées) Ⓜ *Champs Elysées Clemenceau –*
01 53 05 10 01 – simiand@ledoyen.com – Fax 01 47 42 55 01 – Closed 3-25 August, Monday lunch, Saturday and Sunday G 10
Rest – Menu € 88 (lunch), € 199/299 – Carte € 160/285
Spec. Grosses langoustines bretonnes, émulsion d'agrumes. Blanc de turbot de ligne juste braisé, pommes rattes truffées. Croquant de pamplemousse cuit et cru au citron vert.
◆ This neo-classical lodge built on the Champs Élysées in 1792 offers delicious cuisine, magnificent Napoleon III décor and a view of the gardens designed by Hittorff.

Le Bristol – Hôtel Bristol
112 r. Fg St-Honoré Ⓜ *Miromesnil – 01 53 43 43 00 – www.lebristolparis.com – resa@lebristolparis.com – Fax 01 53 43 43 01* F 10
Rest – Menu € 95 (lunch)/220 – Carte € 124/230
Spec. Macaronis farcis, truffe noire, artichaut et foie gras de canard. Poularde de Bresse cuite en vessie aux écrevisses. Précieux chocolat nyangbo, cacao liquide et fine tuile croustillante.
◆ With its splendid wood panelling, the winter dining room resembles a small theatre. The summer dining room overlooks the hotel's charming garden. Dazzling cuisine.

Apicius (Jean-Pierre Vigato)
20 r. d'Artois Ⓜ *St-Philippe du Roule – 01 43 80 19 66 – www.restaurant-apicius.com – restaurant-apicius@wanadoo.fr – Fax 01 44 40 09 57 – Closed August, Saturday, Sunday and public holidays*
Rest – Menu € 160 – Carte € 130/190 F 9
Spec. Déclinaison sur le thème des langoustines. Tourte de canard façon grande cuisine bourgeoise. Grand dessert au caramel.
◆ This elegant restaurant, in a townhouse with garden, boasts a fine interior blending classical, rococo and contemporary styles. Up-to-date cuisine and superb wine list.

Taillevent
15 r. Lamennais Ⓜ *Charles de Gaulle-Etoile – 01 44 95 15 01 – www.taillevent.com – mail@taillevent.com – Fax 01 42 25 95 18 – Closed 25 July-24 August, Saturday, Sunday and bank holidays* F 9
Rest – *(number of covers limited, pre-book)* Menu € 80 (lunch)/190 – Carte € 128/219
Spec. Epeautre du pays de Sault en risotto, cuisses de grenouilles dorées. Langoustines royales croustillantes, marmelade d'agrumes et thé vert. Tarte renversée au chocolat et au café grillé.
◆ Panelling and works of art adorn this former private residence dating from the 19C. It was once home to the Duke of Morny, and is now a guardian of French haute cuisine. Exquisite dishes and magnificent wine list.

Lasserre
17 av. F.-D.-Roosevelt Ⓜ *Franklin D. Roosevelt – 01 43 59 53 43 – www.restaurant-lasserre.com – lasserre@lasserre.fr – Fax 01 45 63 72 23 – Closed August, Saturday lunch, Monday lunch, Tuesday lunch, Wednesday lunch and Sunday* G 10
Rest – Menu € 75 (lunch)/185 – Carte € 130/180
Spec. Macaroni à la truffe et au foie gras. Pigeon André Malraux. Timbale Elysée Lasserre.
◆ Considered an institution by Parisian gourmets, the neo-Classical dining room features objets d'art and an amazing retractable roof. Classic menu; superb wine list.

Laurent

41 av. Gabriel Ⓜ Champs Elysées Clemenceau – ✆ 01 42 25 00 39 – www.le-laurent.com – info@le-laurent.com – Fax 01 45 62 45 21 – Closed 23 December-5 January, Saturday lunch, Sunday and bank holidays

Rest – Menu € 80/160 – Carte € 136/225 G 10

Spec. Araignée de mer dans ses sucs en gelée, crème de fenouil. Flanchet de veau de lait braisé, blettes à la moelle et au jus (April to Oct.). Glace vanille minute en corolle.

◆ A stone's throw from the Champs Élysées, this former hunting lodge belonging to Louis XIV with its elegant shaded terraces has a loyal following. Traditional cuisine and a fine wine list.

Pierre Gagnaire

6 r. Balzac Ⓜ George V – ✆ 01 58 36 12 50 – www.pierre-gagnaire.com – p.gagnaire@wanadoo.fr – Fax 01 58 36 12 51 – Closed Sunday lunch and Saturday F 8

Rest – Menu € 105/255 – Carte € 230/449

Spec. Gelée de poivron doux au citron, thon rouge confit et foie gras de canard. Galinette de Palamos braisée et poêlée de blettes aux petits pois. Le dessert "Rouge".

◆ The low key, chic, contemporary décor (light wood panelling, modern art) pales before the unrestrained score played by a spellbinding chef/jazz player. Music maestro please!

La Table du Lancaster – Hôtel Lancaster

7 r. Berri Ⓜ George V – ✆ 01 40 76 40 18 – www.hotel-lancaster.fr – restaurant@hotel-lancaster.fr – Fax 01 40 76 40 00 F 9

Rest – Menu (€ 52), € 95 (lunch)/150 – Carte € 92/143

Spec. Cuisses de grenouilles au tamarin, chou-fleur en copeaux. Pièce de thon au ponzu, sur un riz "koshi hikari". Soufflé au citron et sirop au miel d'acacia.

◆ Inventive food supervised by Michel Troisgros, and a pleasant, contemporary setting (Chinese prints) opening onto the garden.

Maison Blanche

15 av. Montaigne Ⓜ Alma Marceau – ✆ 01 47 23 55 99 – www.maison-blanche.fr – reservations@maison-blanche.fr – Fax 01 47 20 09 56 – Closed Saturday lunch and Sunday lunch G 9

Rest – Menu (€ 45), € 55 (weekday lunch) – Carte € 95/185

◆ On top of the Théâtre des Champs Élysées, whose loft-duplex design features a huge glass roof facing the golden dome of Les Invalides. Languedoc-inspired cuisine.

Le Chiberta

3 r. Arsène-Houssaye Ⓜ Charles de Gaulle-Etoile – ✆ 01 53 53 42 00 – www.lechiberta.com – chiberta@guysavoy.com – Fax 01 45 62 85 08 – Closed 1st-23 August, Christmas holidays, Saturday lunch and Sunday

Rest – Menu € 60/155 bi – Carte € 86/124 F 8

Spec. Crème de carotte "citronnelle-gingembre" et gambas éclatées aux épices. Lièvre à la royale et gratin de macaroni aux champignons sauvages (Oct. to Dec.). Soufflé vanille et glace caramel.

◆ A serene atmosphere, soft lighting and clean-lined décor designed by J.M. Wilmotte (dark colours and unusual wine bottle walls) provide the setting for inventive cuisine supervised by Guy Savoy.

Senderens

9 pl. de la Madeleine Ⓜ Madeleine – ✆ 01 42 65 22 90 – www.senderens.fr – restaurant@senderens.fr – Fax 01 42 65 06 23 – Closed 2-24 August

Rest – Menu € 110/150 bi – Carte € 89/120 G 11

Rest *Bar le Passage* – ✆ 01 42 65 56 66 – Menu € 36 – Carte € 39/52

Spec. Langoustines croustillantes, coriandre et livèche. Morue des îles Féroé en brandade et pousses de salade. Fine dacquoise au poivre de Séchouan, marmelade de citron confit, glace au gingembre.

◆ This luxurious establishment, which is always extremely lively, boasts a successful marriage of designer furniture and Art Nouveau wood panelling by Majorelle. Creative cuisine and a fine choice of accompanying wines. The Bar Le Passage has a lounge atmosphere and eclectic menu offering tapas, sushis, etc.

XXX **Fouquet's**

99 av. Champs Élysées Ⓜ George V – ✆ 01 40 69 60 50 – www.lucienbarriere.com – fouquets@lucienbarriere.com – Fax 01 40 69 60 35 F 8

Rest – Menu € 78 – Carte € 76/188

◆ A listed dining room, updated by J. Garcia, a terrace that is popular come summer or winter and brasserie cuisine: Fouquet's has been catering to the jet set since 1889.

XXX **El Mansour**

7 r. Trémoille Ⓜ Alma Marceau – ✆ 01 47 23 88 18 – www.elmansour.fr – Fax 01 40 70 13 53 – Closed Monday lunch and Sunday G 9

Rest – Carte € 43/69

◆ This plush Moroccan restaurant, located in the heart of Paris' well-heeled district, is lined with warm wood panels and brightened with Eastern touches. Generous North African dishes.

XXX **Stella Maris** (Tateru Yoshino)

4 r. Arsène Houssaye Ⓜ Charles de Gaulle-Etoile – ✆ 01 42 89 16 22 – www.tateruyoshino.com – stella.maris.paris@wanadoo.fr – Fax 01 42 89 16 01 – Closed 10-22 August, Saturday lunch, Sunday and bank holidays F 8

Rest – Menu € 49 (weekday lunch), € 99/130 – Carte € 119/163

Spec. Millefeuille de thon rouge mariné, aubergine, tapenade et caviar français. Tête de veau en cocotte, crête de coq et œuf frit. Kouing-aman façon Penthièvre.

◆ A pleasant restaurant with a refined decor and warm welcome near the Arc de Triomphe. Classic French cuisine with a modern touch added by a skilful Japanese chef.

XX **1728**

8 r. d'Anjou Ⓜ Madeleine – ✆ 01 40 17 04 77 – www.restaurant-1728.com – restaurant1728@wanadoo.fr – Fax 01 42 65 53 87 – Closed 5-25 August, Sunday and public holidays G 11

Rest – Menu (€ 35) – Carte € 55/121

◆ An 18C town house where La Fayette lived from 1827 until his death. Modern cuisine with an international accent served in stylish rooms adorned with panelling and period furniture.

XX **Spoon**

12 r. Marignan Ⓜ Franklin D. Roosevelt – ✆ 01 40 76 34 44 – www.spoon.tm.fr – spoon-paris@hotelmarignan.fr – Fax 01 40 76 34 37 – Closed August, 25 December-3 January, Saturday and Sunday G 9

Rest – Menu € 36, € 80/120 bi – Carte approx. € 69

◆ A smart designer decor and an open kitchen set the fun scene by Alain Ducasse, whose fusion menu mingles with more traditional dishes. Exceptional wines from around the globe.

XX **Les Saveurs de Flora**

36 av. George V Ⓜ George V – ✆ 01 40 70 10 49 – www.lessaveursdeflora.com – lessaveursdeflora@wanadoo.fr – Fax 01 47 20 52 87 – Closed August, Saturday lunch and Sunday G 8

Rest – Menu (€ 29), € 32 (lunch), € 38/98 bi – Carte € 60/100

◆ Flora, the proprietress, welcomes guests in a fashionable, understated decor that mingles old and new. Inventive cuisine that blends tradition and distant flavours.

XX **Tante Louise**

41 r. Boissy-d'Anglas Ⓜ Madeleine – ✆ 01 42 65 06 85 – www.bernard-loiseau.com – tante.louise@bernard-loiseau.com – Fax 01 42 65 28 19 – Closed August, Saturday, Sunday and public holidays

Rest – Menu € 38 (lunch)/42 – Carte € 46/72 F 11

◆ The name refers to the former Parisian-born owner of this restaurant, which serves traditional cuisine alongside typical Burgundy specialities. Subdued Art Deco decor.

XX **Citrus Étoile**

6 r. Arsène-Houssaye Ⓜ Charles de Gaulle-Étoile – ✆ 01 42 89 15 51 – www.citrusetoile.fr – info@citrusetoile.fr – Fax 01 42 89 28 67 – Closed 8-19 August, 21 December-3 January, Saturday, Sunday and holidays

Rest – Menu € 49/120 – Carte € 88/118 F 8

◆ Chef Gilles Épié invites you to sample rich cuisine that is full of new flavours inspired by his travels in California and Japan. Elegant, simple décor and a delicious welcome.

XX **L'Angle du Faubourg**
195 r. Fg St-Honoré Ⓜ Ternes – ✆ 01 40 74 20 20 – www.taillevent.com – resa@angledufaubourg.com – Fax 01 40 74 20 21 – Closed August, Saturday, Sunday and bank holidays E 9
Rest – Menu € 38/75 – Carte € 63/93
Spec. Sablé de thon aux épices. Saint-Jacques rôties à la vanille bourbon. Macaron moelleux à la banane et passion.
◆ On the corner of Rue du Faubourg-St-Honoré and Rue Balzac, this modern bistrot serves skilfully updated classic cuisine in line with current tastes.

XX **Bistrot du Sommelier**
97 bd Haussmann Ⓜ St-Augustin – ✆ 01 42 65 24 85 – www.bistrotdusommelier.com – bistrot-du-sommelier@noos.fr – Fax 01 53 75 23 23 – Closed 1-30 August, 24 December-4 January, Saturday and Sunday F 11
Rest – Menu (€ 33), € 39 (lunch), € 65 € bi/110 bi – Carte € 52/62
◆ This bistro of free-flowing Bacchanalian pleasure belongs to Philippe Faure-Brac, elected World's Best Sommelier in 1992.

XX **Market**
15 av. Matignon Ⓜ Franklin D. Roosevelt – ✆ 01 56 43 40 90 – www.jean-georges.com – prmarketsa@aol.com – Fax 01 43 59 10 87
Rest – Menu (€ 34) – Carte € 53/80 F 10
◆ A trendy establishment with a prestigious location. Wood and marble decor, including African masks in niches. Mixed cuisine (French, Italian and Asian).

XX **La Table d'Hédiard**
21 pl. Madeleine Ⓜ Madeleine – ✆ 01 43 12 88 99 – www.hediard.fr – latablehediard@hediard.fr – Fax 01 43 12 88 98 – Closed Sunday F 11
Rest – Carte € 58/86
◆ A touch of exoticism in the decor and cuisine with a thousand spices; it's an invitation to a culinary "safari" – but have a peek at the appetising aisles in the famous luxury food shop first.

XX **Indra**
10 r. Cdt-Rivière Ⓜ St-Philippe du Roule – ✆ 01 43 59 46 40 – www.restaurant-indra.com – indrarest@wanadoo.fr – Fax 01 42 25 70 32 – Closed Saturday lunchtime and Sunday F 9
Rest – Menu € 40 (lunch), € 44/65 – Carte € 40/60
◆ In one of France's first Indian restaurants (1976), a delightful decor of patchwork walls and finely carved wood panels sets the charming scene for an extensive menu of Indian specialities.

XX **Le Sarladais**
2 r. Vienne Ⓜ St-Augustin – ✆ 01 45 22 23 62 – www.lesarladais.com – Fax 01 45 22 23 62 – Closed 30 April-10 May, August, 24-31 December, Saturday except dinner from 20 September to 30 April, Sunday and bank holidays E 11
Rest – Menu € 38/64 – Carte € 48/124
◆ Wainscoting, a warm colour scheme, artwork and freshly cut flowers characterise this comfortable dining room that serves hearty specialities from the Périgord region.

XX **Le Relais Plaza** – Hôtel Plaza Athénée
25 av. Montaigne Ⓜ Alma Marceau – ✆ 01 53 67 64 00 – www.plaza-athenee-paris.com – reservation@plaza-athenee-paris.com – Fax 01 53 67 66 66 – Closed August G 9
Rest – Menu € 50 – Carte € 68/148
◆ The chic, intimate 'local' for the nearby fashion houses. Timeless atmosphere and beautiful 1930s decor inspired by the Normandie cruise ship. Classic, refined cuisine.

XX **Fermette Marbeuf 1900**
5 r. Marbeuf Ⓜ Alma Marceau – ✆ 01 53 23 08 00 – www.fermettemarbeuf.com – fermettemarbeuf@blanc.net – Fax 01 53 23 08 09 G 9
Rest – Menu (€ 20), € 32 – Carte € 36/78
◆ One must reserve a table to enjoy the Art Nouveau decor of this glass dining hall dating back to 1898 and discovered by chance in the course of renovation. Classic cuisine.

XX **Marius et Janette**

4 av. George V Ⓜ Alma Marceau – ✆ 01 47 23 41 88 – www.mariusjanette@yahoo.fr – Fax 01 47 23 07 19 G 8

Rest – Menu € 48 – Carte € 90/140

◆ The name of this restaurant recalls Robert Guédiguian's films and Marseille's Estaque quarter. Elegant nautical deco, a pleasant street terrace and seafood fare.

XX **Hanawa**

26 r. Bayard Ⓜ Franklin D. Roosevelt – ✆ 01 56 62 70 70 – www.kinugawa-hanawa.com – hanawa2007@free.fr – Fax 01 56 62 70 71 – Closed Sunday G 9

Rest – Menu (€ 54), € 85/115 – Carte € 65/115

◆ Covering 1,100m², this sober, refined restaurant (wood, fresh flowers) offers a choice of Japanese (first floor) and French (basement) cuisine, with teppanyaki tables and a sushi bar.

XX **Maxan**

37 r. Miromesnil Ⓜ Miromesnil – ✆ 01 42 65 78 60 – www.rest-maxan.com – rest.maxan@wanadoo.fr – Fax 01 49 24 96 17 – Closed 3-25 August, 24 December-3 January, Monday dinner, Saturday lunch and Sunday

Rest – Menu (€ 30), € 45 – Carte € 50/77 F 10

◆ The contemporary decor designed by Pierre Pozzi is tastefully restrained (white or colourful striped walls and bistro-style furnishings). Updated authentic cuisine.

XX **Chez Catherine**

3 r. Berryer Ⓜ George V – ✆ 01 40 76 01 40 – www.restaurantchezcatherine.com – Fax 01 40 76 03 96 – Closed Friday dinner and Sunday dinner from November to February F 9

Rest – Menu € 44/70

◆ Elegant modern dining room, opening onto the kitchens and partly crowned by a glass roof. A stylish, yet cosy restaurant serving updated cuisine.

XX **La Luna**

69 r. Rocher Ⓜ Villiers – ✆ 01 42 93 77 61 – www.restaurant-laluna.fr – laluna75008@yahoo.fr – Fax 01 40 08 02 44 – Closed 1-24 August and Sunday

Rest – Carte € 87/110 E 11

◆ An Art Deco setting, peaceful ambience and fine cuisine based on fish and seafood delivered fresh from the Atlantic.

XX **Al Ajami**

58 r. François 1er Ⓜ George V – ✆ 01 42 25 38 44 – www.ajami.com – ajami@free.fr – Fax 01 42 25 38 39 G 9

Rest – Menu (€ 20), € 28 (weekdays)/48 – Carte € 35/60

◆ This temple of traditional Lebanese cuisine is the Parisian branch of a Beirut establishment in operation since 1920. Near East decor, family ambiance and many regulars.

XX **Palace Élysées**

20 r. Quentin-Bauchart Ⓜ Georges V – ✆ 01 40 70 19 17 – www.palace-elysee.com – celine@palace-elysee.com – Fax 01 40 70 18 06 – Closed Sunday F 8

Rest – Menu (€ 19), € 55/120 – Carte € 70/145

◆ This spacious venue is the epitome of lounge atmosphere with its trendy design featuring immaculately white classic and modern furniture, ultra-violet lighting, photographs, a bar and food to match.

XX **Ratn**

9 r. de la Trémoille Ⓜ Alma Marceau – ✆ 01 40 70 01 09 – www.restaurantratn.com – contact@restaurantratn.com – Fax 01 40 70 01 22 G 9

Rest – Menu (€ 21), € 39 (weekdays) – Carte € 50/60

◆ A genuine Indian restaurant serving delicately spiced cuisine. Traditional and elegant decor with gold-coloured fabrics and carved wooden panelling. Friendly service.

XX **L'Étoile Marocaine**

56 r. Galilée Ⓜ Georges V – ✆ 01 47 20 44 43 – www.etoilemarocaine.com – contact@etoilemarocaine.com – Fax 01 47 23 53 75 – Closed Saturday lunch

Rest – Menu € 25 (weekday lunch) – Carte € 36/64 F 8

◆ This restaurant honouring the Moroccan tradition has it all : an intimate dining room, Eastern décor (mosaics, sculpted wood panelling, embossed copper trays) ans atmospheric music.

Village d'Ung et Li Lam

10 r. J. Mermoz Ⓜ Franklin D. Roosevelt – ✆ 01 42 25 99 79 – menez.lam@orange.fr – Fax 01 42 25 12 06 – Closed Saturday lunchtime and Sunday lunchtime

Rest – Menu € 19/35 – Carte € 25/35 F 10

◆ Ung and Li welcome you into a very original Asian setting: suspended aquariums and a flooring of glass and sand tiles. Chinese-Thai cuisine.

Dominique Bouchet

11 r. Treilhard Ⓜ Miromesnil – ✆ 01 45 61 09 46 – www.dominique-bouchet.com – dominiquebouchet@yahoo.fr – Fax 01 42 89 11 14 – Closed in August, Saturday, Sunday and bank holidays E 10

Rest – *(pre-book)* Menu (€ 46) – Carte € 57/97

Spec. Croustillant de tête de veau aux poireaux et oeufs mimosa. Macaroni de homard sur purée de champignons et coulis de carapaces. Pêche glacée et crème brûlée a la vanille bourbon (June-Sept.).

◆ Tasteful contemporary decor, a friendly atmosphere and delicious, traditionally-based cuisine using market produce are the hallmarks of this small, successful and trendy restaurant.

L'Arôme

3 r. St-Philippe-du-Roule Ⓜ St-Philippe-du-Roule – ✆ 01 42 25 55 98 – www.larome.fr – contact@larome.fr – Fax 01 42 25 55 97 – Closed 2-23 August, 19-28 December, Saturday and Sunday F 9

Rest – Menu (€ 29), € 36 (lunch), € 70/114 bi – Carte € 55/75

Spec. Cannelloni de tourteau décortiqué et daïkon au pamplemousse. Foie gras de canard poêlé au cacao amer. Tarte aux pommes façon tatin.

◆ A chic 'neo-bistro' run by Eric Martins (in the dining room) and Thomas Boullault (in the kitchen). Simple decor in shades of coral pink and taupe. Open kitchen. Modern cuisine.

Le Stresa

7 r. Chambiges Ⓜ Alma Marceau – ✆ 01 47 23 51 62 – Closed August, 20 December-3 January, Saturday and Sunday G 9

Rest – *(pre-book)* Carte € 70/120

◆ Golden Triangle trattoria frequented by a very jet-set clientele. Paintings by Buffet and compressed sculptural art by César – artists also appreciate the Italian cuisine here.

Bistro de l'Olivier

13 r. Quentin Bauchart Ⓜ George V – ✆ 01 47 20 78 63 – bistrotdelolivier@orange.fr – Fax 01 47 20 74 58 – Closed August, Saturday lunch and Sunday G 8

Rest – *(number of covers limited, pre-book)* Menu (€ 29), € 35 – Carte € 35/75

◆ Provençal fabrics and paintings recalling southern France brighten the very warm dining room in this restaurant near Avenue George V. Mediterranean cuisine.

Chez Cécile la Ferme des Mathurins

17 r. Vignon Ⓜ Madeleine – ✆ 01 42 66 46 39 – www.chezcecile.com – cecile@chezcecile.com – Closed August, Saturday lunch and Sunday F 12

Rest – bistro – Menu (€ 32), € 36 (lunch), € 38/59

◆ Generous portions of fine, traditional cuisine are served in this authentic Parisian bistro, which has a loyal clientele. Lively atmosphere and often fully booked.

Café Lenôtre - Pavillon Elysée

10 av. Champs-Elysées Ⓜ Champs Elysées Clemenceau – ✆ 01 42 65 85 10 – www.lenotre.fr – webmaster@lenotre.fr – Fax 01 42 65 76 23 – Closed 3 weeks in August, 1 week in February, Monday dinner and Sunday dinner from November to February G 10

Rest – Carte € 45/65

◆ This elegant pavilion built for the 1900 World Fair has been treated to a make over. It houses a boutique, a catering school and a distinctly modern restaurant.

Aoki Makoto

19 r. Jean Mermoz Ⓜ Mirosmenil – ✆ 01 43 59 29 24 – Fax 01 43 59 29 24 – Closed 9-23 August, 23 December-3 January, Saturday lunch and Sunday F 10

Rest – Menu (€ 21,50), € 40 (dinner)/60 – Carte € 58/78

◆ Disregard the misleading name (it comes from the Japanese chef) at this discreet and convivial restaurant with a bistro look; the food is French, and delicious.

La Maison de L'Aubrac
37 r. Marbeuf Ⓜ Franklin D. Roosevelt – ✆ 01 43 59 05 14 – www.maison-aubrac.fr – miguel.aubrac@orange.fr – Fax 01 42 25 29 87
Rest – Menu (€ 30), € 45 – Carte € 37/56 G 9
◆ Aveyron farmhouse-style decor, generous portions of rustic cuisine (with an emphasis on Aubrac beef) and an excellent wine list: a piece of Aubrac just a stone's throw from the Champs-Élysées.

SYDR
6 r. de Tilsitt Ⓜ Charles de Gaulle-Etoile – ✆ 01 45 72 41 32 – Fax 01 45 72 41 79 – Closed 3 weeks in August, Saturday lunch, Monday dinner and Sunday
Rest – Menu (€ 12 bi), € 28/48 – Carte € 36/48 F 8
◆ This post-modern cider bar created by Alain Dutournier and Philippe Sella is extremely minimalist in style. Regional cuisine with a modern twist, plus a bar offering tapas and cider tastings.

Devez
5 pl. de l'Alma Ⓜ Alma Marceau – ✆ 01 53 67 97 53 – www.devezparis.com – contact@devezparis.com – Fax 01 47 23 09 48 G 8
Rest – Carte € 36/59
◆ The landlord, also a cattle breeder, clearly loves his region; up-to-date cuisine based on tasty Aubrac meat. Fine modern interior and table d'hôte.

Le Bistrot de Marius
6 av. George V Ⓜ Alma Marceau – ✆ 01 40 70 11 76 – Fax 01 40 70 17 08 G 8
Rest – Menu (€ 28) – Carte € 40/65
◆ Small, tightly packed and simply laid tables, brightly coloured Provencal decor and seafood cuisine. Southern French harbour atmosphere.

L'Évasion
7 pl. St-Augustin Ⓜ Saint Augustin – ✆ 01 45 22 66 20 – restaurantlevasion@orange.fr – Fax 01 40 75 04 32 F 11
Rest – Carte € 40/70
◆ The bistro-wine bar with a typical décor (old-style counter, profusion of bottles, blackboard on the wall) boasts a superb selection of vintage wines, accompanied by market-based dishes.

L'Atelier des Compères
56 r. Galilée Ⓜ George V – ✆ 01 47 20 75 56 – www.atelierdescomperes.com – contact@atelierdescomperes.com – Closed August, Christmas holidays, Saturday, Sunday and holidays F 8
Rest – *(number of covers limited, pre-book)* Carte € 43/55
◆ A chic café-style address in a paved courtyard with a roof that opens in summer. Appetising daily specials based around market availability.

Daru
19 r. Daru Ⓜ Courcelles – ✆ 01 42 27 23 60 – www.daru.fr – restaurant.daru@wanadoo.fr – Fax 01 47 54 08 14 – Closed August and Sunday E 9
Rest – Menu € 28 (weekday lunch)/34 – Carte € 60/90
◆ Founded in 1918, Daru was the first Russian grocery store in Paris. Today it still offers customers a choice of zakouskis, blinis and caviar in its red and black interior.

Le Bouco
10 r. Constantinople Ⓜ Europe – ✆ 01 42 93 73 33 – www.lebouco.com – info@lebouco.com – Fax 01 42 93 95 44 – Closed August, Saturday, Sunday and bank holidays E 11
Rest – *(number of covers limited, pre-book)* Menu (€ 22), € 29/37 bi – Carte € 32/55
◆ Rugby posters and souvenirs, the owner's passion, adorn this local bistro. It serves hearty fare, made with Basque and southwest produce.

Shin Jung
7 r. Clapeyron Ⓜ Rome – ✆ 01 45 22 21 06 – jung6161@aol.com – Closed Sunday lunchtime and lunchtime public holidays D 11
Rest – Menu (€ 9), € 14/23 – Carte € 20/35
◆ The minimalist decor in this restaurant includes calligraphy paintings on the walls. The focus here is on South Korean cuisine and raw fish. Friendly welcome.

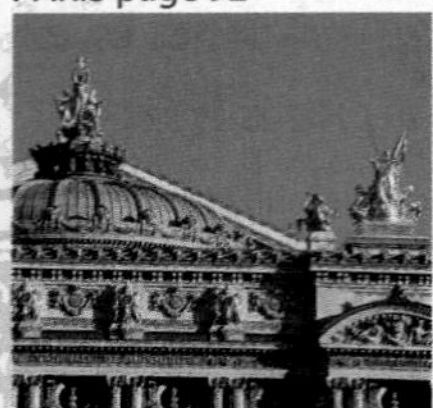
S. Sauvignier/MICHELIN

Opéra • Grands Boulevards

9th arrondissement ✉ 75009

Intercontinental Le Grand

2 r. Scribe Ⓜ *Opéra – ✆ 01 40 07 32 32 – www.ichotelsgroupe.com – legrand@ihg.com – Fax 01 42 66 12 51* F 12

442 rm – †€ 360/750 ††€ 360/750, ☕ € 38 – 28 suites

Rest *Café de la Paix* – see restaurant listing

◆ This illustrious luxury hotel, opened in 1862, was refurbished in 2003. An admirable mix of Second Empire style and modern comforts.

Scribe

1 r. Scribe Ⓜ *Opéra – ✆ 01 44 71 24 24 – www.hotel-scribe-paris.com – h0663@accor.com – Fax 01 42 65 39 97* F 12

204 rm – †€ 570/1150 ††€ 570/1150, ☕ € 35 – 9 suites

Rest *Café Lumière* – Carte € 63/152

◆ Housed in a grand Haussmann style building, this hotel has been completely renovated and is much appreciated for its discreet luxury. The world première of the Lumière brothers' first film screening was held here in 1895. Spa. Cosy, slightly British ambiance at the Café Lumière, brightened by a glass roof. Modern menu.

Millennium Opéra

12 bd Haussmann Ⓜ *Richelieu Drouot – ✆ 01 49 49 16 00 – www.millenniumhotels.com – opera@millenniumhotels.fr – Fax 01 49 49 17 00* F 13

157 rm – †€ 180/500 ††€ 200/550, ☕ € 25 – 6 suites

Rest *Brasserie Haussmann* – ✆ *01 49 49 16 64* – Menu (€ 19 bi) – Carte € 29/55

◆ This 1927 hotel has lost none of its period lustre. Tastefully appointed rooms with Art Deco furniture. Modern facilities. Carefully renovated with modern decor, and typical brasserie fare at the Brasserie Haussman.

Ambassador

16 bd Haussmann Ⓜ *Richelieu Drouot – ✆ 01 44 83 40 40 – www.hotelambassador-paris.com – ambass@concorde-hotels.com – Fax 01 44 83 40 57* F 13

294 rm – †€ 200/500 ††€ 200/500, ☕ € 28 – 8 suites

Rest *16 Haussmann* – ✆ *01 48 00 06 38* – Menu (€ 32), € 44/52 – Carte € 48/59

◆ Painted panels, crystal chandeliers and antiques adorn this elegant hotel dating from the 1920s. The renovated rooms are decorated in simple, contemporary style; the others somewhat more traditional. At 16 Haussmann, the royal blue and gold colour scheme is enhanced by light-coloured wood, red Starck chairs and views of the lively boulevard through the large windows.

Pavillon de Paris without rest

7 r. Parme Ⓜ *Liège – ✆ 01 55 31 60 00 – www.pavillondeparis.com – mail@pavillondeparis.com – Fax 01 55 31 60 01* D 12

30 rm – †€ 215/240 ††€ 270/296, ☕ € 21

◆ Contemporary-style hotel in a quiet street. The rooms are on the small side, but have a sober, luxurious decor and a pleasant intimate atmosphere. Japanese garden in the mini-courtyard.

Villa Opéra Drouot without rest

2 r. Geoffroy Marie Ⓜ *Grands Boulevards – ✆ 01 48 00 08 08 – drouot@leshotelsdeparis.com – Fax 01 48 00 80 60* F 14

29 rm – †€ 129/310 ††€ 139/320, ☕ € 20

◆ A surprising and subtle blend of Baroque decor and the latest in elegant comfort in these rooms embellished with wall hangings, velvets, silks and wood panelling.

Jules without rest
49 r. La Fayette Ⓜ Le Peletier – ✆ 01 42 85 05 44 – www.hoteljules.com – info@hoteljules.com – Fax 01 49 95 06 60 F 14
101 rm – †€ 285/500 ††€ 285/500, ☕ € 20
◆ This hotel has embraced contemporary design without sacrificing any of its inherent elegance. Bright and lively breakfast room (orange decor with floral motif). Gym.

Astra Opéra without rest
29 r. Caumartin Ⓜ Havre Caumartin – ✆ 01 42 66 15 15 – www.astotel.com – hotel.astra@astotel.com – Fax 01 42 66 98 05 F 12
82 rm – †€ 225/295 ††€ 255/345, ☕ € 22
◆ Haussmann-style building with large, comfortable rooms. Bright lounge with a glass roof and contemporary art on the walls. Welcoming breakfast room.

St-Pétersbourg without rest
33 r. Caumartin Ⓜ Havre Caumartin – ✆ 01 42 66 60 38 – www.hotelsaintpetersbourg.com – info@hotelpeters.com – Fax 01 42 66 53 54 E 12
100 rm ☕ – †€ 141/210 ††€ 181/267
◆ A large, traditional, family-run hotel. Elegant entrance with chandeliers and a marble floor, numerous lounges and meeting rooms. Spacious guestrooms.

Lorette Opéra without rest
36 r. Notre-Dame de Lorette Ⓜ St-Georges – ✆ 01 42 85 18 81 – www.astotel.com – hotel.lorette@astotel.com – Fax 01 42 81 32 19 E 13
84 rm – †€ 136/240 ††€ 136/240, ☕ € 14
◆ The decor in this completely renovated hotel is a harmonious mix of bare stone and designer style. Pleasant, contemporary rooms; breakfast is served in the cellar with its vaulted ceiling.

Villathéna without rest
23 r. d'Athènes Ⓜ St-Lazare – ✆ 01 44 63 07 07 – www.villathena.com – reservation@villathena.com – Fax 01 44 63 07 60 E 12
43 rm – †€ 119/385 ††€ 119/385, ☕ € 17
◆ Housed in the former Social Security offices, this brand-new hotel has a resolutely contemporary feel. Lobby decorated in red, white and black; well-appointed guestrooms with light wood furniture.

Richmond Opéra without rest
11 r. Helder Ⓜ Chaussée d'Antin – ✆ 01 47 70 53 20 – paris@richmond-hotel.com – Fax 01 48 00 02 10 F 13
59 rm – †€ 136/151 ††€ 156/171, ☕ € 10
◆ The spacious, elegant rooms almost all give onto the courtyard. The lounge is rather grandly decorated in the Empire style.

Opéra Franklin without rest
19 r. Buffault Ⓜ Cadet – ✆ 01 42 80 27 27 – www.operafranklin.com – info@operafranklin.com – Fax 01 48 78 13 04 E 14
67 rm – †€ 146/203 ††€ 189/247, ☕ € 13
◆ Located in a quiet street, this business hotel is built around a central courtyard. Large lobby with a glass roof and bar. Functional, simply decorated rooms.

ATN without rest
21 r. d'Athènes Ⓜ St-Lazare – ✆ 01 48 74 00 55 – www.atnhotel.fr – atn@atnhotel.fr – Fax 01 42 81 04 75 E 12
36 rm – †€ 139/350 ††€ 149/360, ☕ € 11
◆ Situated a stone's throw from St-Lazare station, completely refurbished hotel in a trendy, contemporary style. Quality materials and attention to detail add to the appeal.

9HOTEL without rest
14 r. Papillon Ⓜ Cadet – ✆ 01 47 70 78 34 – www.le9hotel.com – info@le9hotel.com – Fax 01 40 22 91 00 E 14
35 rm – †€ 140/280 ††€ 140/280, ☕ € 15
◆ Renovated in sober designer style, this hotel has a pleasant lounge with art books and international press. Rooms are fairly small but functional, with contemporary furniture and mood lighting.

Caumartin Opéra without rest
27 r. Caumartin Ⓜ Havre Caumartin – ✆ 01 47 42 95 95 – www.astotel.com – hotel.caumartin@astotel.com – Fax 01 47 42 88 19 F 12
40 rm – €155/240 €165/240, €14
◆ This small hotel in the Grand Magasins district has had a complete face-lift. Contemporary-style guestrooms with immaculate white bathrooms.

Grand Hôtel Haussmann without rest
6 r. Helder Ⓜ Opéra – ✆ 01 48 24 76 10 – www.hotelhaussmann.com – ghh@club-internet.fr – Fax 01 48 00 97 18 F 13
59 rm – €145/225 €160/225, €15
◆ Hiding behind this discreet facade are cosy rooms of different sizes with a personal touch; all look out to the back and are gradually being renovated.

Anjou Lafayette without rest
4 r. Riboutté Ⓜ Cadet – ✆ 01 42 46 83 44 – www.hotelanjoulafayette.com – hotel.anjou.lafayette@wanadoo.fr – Fax 01 48 00 08 97 E 14
39 rm – €98/170 €118/190, €12
◆ Near the leafy Square Montholon, with its Second Empire wrought-iron gates, this hotel offers guests comfortable, soundproofed rooms decorated in warm tones.

Les Trois Poussins without rest
15 r. Clauzel Ⓜ St-Georges – ✆ 01 53 32 81 81 – www.les3poussins.com – h3p@les3poussins.com – Fax 01 53 32 81 82 E 13
40 rm – €106/156 €109/171, €10
◆ Elegant rooms offering several levels of comfort. View of Paris from the top floors. Prettily vaulted breakfast room. Small courtyard-terrace.

Opéra d'Antin without rest
75 r. de Provence Ⓜ Chaussée d'Antin – ✆ 01 48 74 12 99 – www.paris-inn.com – operadantin@paris-inn.com – Fax 01 48 74 16 14 – Reopening planned in spring after refurbishment F 12
30 rm – €145/195 €145/195, €13
◆ A restored hotel near the famous Galeries Lafayette. A breakfast room with a glass roof and pleasant rooms in an Art deco style.

Langlois without rest
63 r. St-Lazare Ⓜ Trinité – ✆ 01 48 74 78 24 – www.hotel-langlois.com – info@hotel-langlois.com – Fax 01 49 95 04 43 E 12
24 rm – €110/120 €140/150, €13 – 3 suites
◆ Built in 1870, the building first housed a bank and then a hotel from 1896 on. Art nouveau, Art deco or Fifties-style rooms – all with a character of their own.

Bergère Opéra without rest
34 r. Bergère Ⓜ Grands Boulevards – ✆ 01 47 70 34 34 – www.astotel.com – hotel.bergere@astotel.com – Fax 01 47 70 36 36 F 14
134 rm – €124/220 €165/220, €14
◆ Between the Grands Boulevards, Opéra and Drouot auction house. A panoramic lift takes you up to the refurbished rooms.

Mercure Monty without rest
5 r. Montyon Ⓜ Grands Boulevards – ✆ 01 47 70 26 10 – www.mercure.com – hotel@mercuremonty.com – Fax 01 42 46 55 10 F 14
69 rm – €75/250 €90/275, €18
◆ Beautiful façade dating from the 1930s, Art Deco setting at the front desk, and the hotel chain's standard equipment characterise this Mercure located in view of the Folies Bergère.

Acadia without rest
4 r. Geoffroy Marie Ⓜ Grands Boulevards – ✆ 01 40 22 99 99 – www.astotel.com – hotel.acadia@astotel.com – Fax 01 40 22 01 82 F 14
36 rm – €124/220 €165/220, €14
◆ In a lively district which is busy day and night, this spotless small hotel has well-equipped rooms with double-glazing.

Villa Opéra Lamartine without rest
39 r. Lamartine Ⓜ Notre-Dame-de-Lorette – ☏ 01 48 78 78 58 – www.villa-opera-lamartine.com – lamartineopera@wanadoo.fr – Fax 01 48 74 65 15 E 14
28 rm – €80/130 €90/190, €12
◆ This hotel, a stones' throw from Notre-Dame-de-Lorette church, elegantly evokes the Romantic authors of Paris. Tasteful rooms and breakfast served under a fine vaulted stone ceiling.

du Pré without rest
10 r. P. Sémard Ⓜ Poissonnière – ☏ 01 42 81 37 11 – www.leshotelsdupre.com – hotel@duprehotels.com – Fax 01 40 23 98 28 E 15
40 rm – €102/105 €125/130, €12
◆ Functional, attractively coloured rooms, a lounge furnished with Chesterfield sofas, plus a breakfast room and bistro-style bar.

Monterosa without rest
30 r. La Bruyère Ⓜ St-Georges – ☏ 01 48 74 87 90 – www.hotelmonterosaparis.com – hotel.monterosa@wanadoo.fr – Fax 01 42 81 01 12 – Closed 19-26 December E 13
36 rm – €80/110 €95/145, €9
◆ Intimate hotel in the Nouvelle Athènes neighbourhood, decorated in warm red and yellow tones and wood panelling. Pleasant lounge bar.

Café de la Paix – Intercontinental Le Grand
12 bd Capucines Ⓜ Opéra – ☏ 01 40 07 36 36 – www.cafedelapaix.fr – info@cafedelapaix.fr – Fax 01 40 07 36 13 F 12
Rest – Menu (€37), €47 (lunch)/85 – Carte €62/100
◆ Fine murals, gold wainscoting and French Second Empire-inspired furniture: this famous luxury brasserie, open from 7am to midnight is still the place to meet in Paris.

Jean
8 r. St-Lazare Ⓜ Notre-Dame-de-Lorette – ☏ 01 48 78 62 73 – www.restaurantjean.fr – chezjean@wanadoo.fr – Fax 01 48 78 66 04 – Closed 27 July-17 August, 23-27 February, Saturday and Sunday E 12
Rest – Menu €46 (lunch), €65/85 – Carte €70/77
Spec. Foie gras, risotto et figues au vinaigre de Xérès (season). Pigeon et ravioles de foie de volaille au jus chocolaté (season). Pêche de vigne pochée au vin blanc (season).
◆ Tempting modern cuisine served in this redecorated restaurant. The bistro spirit has made way for a cosy atmosphere (striped fabrics, flowery motifs, mosaic floor). Lounge on the first floor.

Romain
40 r. St-Georges Ⓜ St-Georges – ☏ 01 48 24 58 94 – restaurant_romain@yahoo.fr – Fax 01 42 47 09 75 – Closed August, Sunday and Monday E 13
Rest – Menu €36 – Carte €40/65
◆ This restaurant nestled behind Notre-Dame-de-Lorette offers a concise Italian menu, including excellent charcuterie and home-made pasta, accompanied by wines from the various regions.

Au Petit Riche
25 r. Le Peletier Ⓜ Richelieu Drouot – ☏ 01 47 70 68 68 – www.aupetitriche.com – aupetitriche@wanadoo.fr – Fax 01 48 24 10 79 – Closed Saturday from 14 July to 20 August and Sunday F 13
Rest – Menu (€25), €31/37 bi – Carte €32/64
◆ Bench seats in red velvet, etched mirrors, and elegant tables: the charm of the sitting room that was the height of fashion in the 19C remains intact here. Cuisine inspired by the Tours region and a good choice of wines from the Loire valley.

Hotaru
18 r. Rodier Ⓜ Notre-Dame-de-Lorette – ☏ 01 48 78 33 74 – www.hotaru.fr – Closed Sunday and Monday E 14
Rest – Menu (€23), €35/60 – Carte €33/60
◆ No-frills decor at this new Japanese restaurant installed in a former inn. Traditional, fish-based cuisine.

Casa Olympe A/C VISA MC

48 r. St-Georges Ⓜ St-Georges – ✆ 01 42 85 26 01 – www.casaolympe.com – info@casaolympe.com – Closed 1st-12 May, 1st-25 August, 23 December-3 January, Saturday and Sunday E 13

Rest – *(number of covers limited, pre-book)* Menu (€ 33), € 42

◆ Two small ochre coloured rooms with tightly packed tables. Traditional dishes that Olympe – Dominique Versini, cuisine icon of the 1980s – interprets in her own way.

La Petite Sirène de Copenhague VISA MC AE

47 r. N.-D. de Lorette Ⓜ St-Georges – ✆ 01 45 26 66 66 – Closed 1-31 August, 23 December-2 January, Saturday lunch, Sunday and Monday E 13

Rest – *(pre-book)* Menu € 29 (lunch)/34 – Carte € 43/71

◆ A tasteful dining room, colour washed walls and soft Danish lighting set the scene for original recipes from Andersen's homeland. Attentive service.

Carte Blanche A/C VISA MC AE

6 r. Lamartine Ⓜ Cadet – ✆ 01 48 78 12 20 – www.restaurantcarteblanche.com – rest.carteblanche@free.fr – Fax 01 48 78 12 21 – Closed 27 July-17 August, 22-28 February, Saturday lunch and Sunday E 14

Rest – Menu (€ 28), € 37/42

◆ The owners of this restaurant are great travellers: photos and souvenirs from their trips around the world can be seen in the dining room. Exotic tableware and cuisine that shows French and international influence.

Villa Victoria A/C VISA MC AE

52 r. Lamartine Ⓜ Notre-Dame-de-Lorette – ✆ 01 48 78 60 05 – www.la-villa-victoria.com – victoria52@orange.fr – Fax 01 48 78 60 05 – Closed August and Sunday E 13

Rest – Menu (€ 25), € 33/38 – Carte € 33/40

◆ This neo-bistro with a warm interior (visible stonework, small, tightly packed tables, menus and wines listed on a blackboard) offers reinvented traditional cuisine. Delicious home-made bread.

I Golosi A/C VISA MC

6 r. Grange Batelière Ⓜ Richelieu Drouot – ✆ 01 48 24 18 63 – i.golosi@wanadoo.fr – Fax 01 45 23 18 96 – Closed 8-20 August, Saturday dinner and Sunday

Rest – Carte € 25/45 F 14

◆ On the 1st floor, Italian designer decor with a minimalism made up for by the joviality of the service. Café, shop and little spot for tasting things on the ground floor. Italian cuisine.

Le Pré Cadet A/C VISA MC AE

10 r. Saulnier Ⓜ Cadet – ✆ 01 48 24 99 64 – Fax 01 73 77 39 49 – Closed 1st-8 May, 3-21 August, 24 December-1st January, Saturday lunch and Sunday F 14

Rest – *(number of covers limited, pre-book)* Menu € 30 – Carte € 50/70

◆ This friendly, convivial restaurant in the vicinity of the 'Folies' is renowned for hearty, mistic such as tête de veau - its pride and joy. Very good coffee list.

Sizin VISA MC

47 r. St-Georges Ⓜ St-Georges – ✆ 01 44 63 02 28 – www.sizin-restaurant.com – ekilic@free.fr – Closed August and Sunday E 13

Rest – Menu (€ 15) – Carte € 28/35

◆ This welcoming restaurant, decorated with old prints and Izmir earthenware, offers a variety of rich Turkish dishes.

Georgette VISA MC AE

29 r. St-Georges Ⓜ Notre-Dame-de-Lorette – ✆ 01 42 80 39 13 – Closed Easter holidays, August, autumn half-term holidays, Saturday, Sunday and Monday

Rest – Menu (€ 24) – Carte € 35/50 E 13

◆ With its multicoloured formica tables and vinyl-covered chairs, this restaurant has a pleasant retro air. Bistro cuisine with excellent vegetables to the fore.

L'Oriental
47 av. Trudaine Ⓜ Pigalle – ✆ 01 42 64 39 80 – www.loriental-restaurant.com – Fax 01 42 64 39 80
E 14
Rest – Menu € 32 – Carte € 25/40
◆ An oriental but more restrained decor for this restaurant transferred from the rue des Martyrs to avenue Trudaine. Fragrant Moroccan cuisine.

Spring
28 r. Tour d'Auvergne Ⓜ Cadet – ✆ 01 45 96 05 72 – www.springparis.fr – freshsnail@free.fr – Closed 2 weeks in August, Christmas holidays, Tuesday lunch, Wednesday lunch, Saturday, Sunday and Monday
E 14
Rest – *(number of covers limited, pre-book)* Menu € 35/42
◆ Single set menu according to the market, and the chef's inspiration, at this local table d'hote that is full of personality. Wines selected from small producers.

L'Office
3 r. Richer Ⓜ Poissonnière – ✆ 01 47 70 67 31 – Fax 01 47 70 67 31 – Closed August, 21 December-5 January, Saturday lunch, Sunday, Monday, Tuesday and Wednesday
F 15
Rest – *(number of covers limited, pre-book)* Menu (€ 16), € 31
◆ Modish new restaurant with simple, sober decor. The self-taught chef offers a well-structured and attractively priced menu based around market produce.

Radis Roses
68 r. Rodier Ⓜ Anvers – ✆ 01 48 78 03 20 – www.radis-roses.com – radisroses@tele2.fr – Fermé1-15 August, Sunday except dinner in winter and Monday
E 14
Rest – *(pre-book)* Carte € 27/34
◆ A pleasant, slightly trendy, little establishment serving cuisine specialising in dishes from the Drome. Charming service; plain, tasteful decor.

Les Diables au Thym
35 r. Bergère Ⓜ Grands Boulevards – ✆ 01 47 70 77 09 – www.lesdiablesauthym.com – lesdiablesauthym@orange.fr – Fax 01 47 70 77 09 – Closed 3 weeks in August, Saturday and Sunday
F14
Rest – Menu (€ 22) – Carte € 36/49
◆ A simple bistro-style restaurant (with some contemporary paintings) near the Musée Grévin. Up-to-date seasonal cuisine; choice of organic wines on the blackboard.

Momoka
5 r. Jean-Baptiste Pigalle Ⓜ Trinité d'Estienne d'Orves – ✆ 01 40 16 19 09 – masayohashimoto@aol.com – Fax 01 40 16 19 09 – Closed August, Saturday lunch, Sunday and Monday
E 13
Rest – Menu € 29 (lunch), € 39/49
◆ Book ahead for this tiny restaurant run by a Franco-Japanese couple, where Masayo creates delicious Japanese dishes which change daily. Authentic setting and homely atmosphere.

Les Pâtes Vivantes
46 r. du Faubourg-Montmartre Ⓜ Le Peletier – ✆ 01 45 23 10 21 – www.lespatesvivantes.com – flx369@126.com – Fax 01 42 22 84 89 – Closed August and Sunday
F 14
Rest – Menu (€ 12,50), € 15 – Carte € 20/30
◆ Unlike the usual caterers, this discreet Chinese cafeteria, which fills up very quickly, features authentic specialities from Northern China. Noodles handmade right in front of you.

Ph. Gagic/MICHELIN

Gare de l'Est • Gare du Nord • Canal St-Martin

10th arrondissement ✉ 75010

Mercure Terminus Nord without rest
12 bd Denain Ⓜ *Gare du Nord – ☎ 01 42 80 20 00 – www.mercure.com – h2761@accor.com – Fax 01 42 80 63 89* E 16
236 rm – €148/298 €178/348, €16
◆ A sympathetic renovation has restored this 19C hotel to its former glory. Art Nouveau stained glass, "British" decor and a cosy atmosphere give it the air of an elegant Victorian mansion.

Holiday Inn Opéra rm, VISA AE
38 r. de l'Échiquier Ⓜ *Bonne Nouvelle – ☎ 01 42 46 92 75 – www.holiday-inn.com/paris-opera – information@hi-parisopera.com – Fax 01 42 47 03 97* F 15
92 rm – €159/499 €159/499, €20
Rest – *(closed Saturday lunch and Sunday)* Menu (€25), €35/39 bi – Carte approx. €40
◆ A step away from the Grands Boulevards and their string of theatres and brasseries. This hotel offers large rooms decorated in the style of the Belle Époque. The dining room is an authentic gem from the year 1900: mosaics, glass roof, woodwork and fine Art Nouveau furniture.

Paris-Est without rest
4 r. du 8 Mai 1945 Ⓜ *Gare de l'Est – ☎ 01 44 89 27 00 – www.bestwestern-hotelparisest.com – hotelparisest.bestwestern@autogrill.net – Fax 01 44 89 27 49* E 16
45 rm – €114/150 €114/150, €13
◆ Although just next to the train station, this establishment offers quiet rooms, facing the back courtyard, which have been renovated and soundproofed.

Eurostars Panorama without rest
9 r. des Messageries Ⓜ *Poissonnière – ☎ 01 47 70 44 02 – www.eurostarshotels.com – info@eurostarspanorama.com – Fax 01 40 22 91 09* F 14
43 rm – €100/540 €100/540, €10
◆ Brand new hotel in ultra-contemporary style. Designer decor with references to French culture.

Albert 1er without rest
162 r. Lafayette Ⓜ *Gare du Nord – ☎ 01 40 36 82 40 – www.albert1erhotel.com – paris@albert1erhotel.com – Fax 01 40 35 72 52* E 16
55 rm – €110/125 €130/145, €15
◆ Hotel where the well-designed modern rooms are equipped with double glazing and have the advantage of being continually redone. Convivial atmosphere.

Du Nord without rest
47 r. Albert Thomas Ⓜ *Jacques Bonsergent – ☎ 01 42 01 66 00 – www.hoteldunord-leparivelo.com – contact@hoteldunord-leparivelo.com – Fax 01 42 01 92 10* F 16
24 rm – €70/80 €70/80, €8
◆ Rustic charm at this hotel on a quiet street. Small but individually decorated guestrooms and attractive vaulted breakfast room. Bicycles available for loan.

Alane without rest
72 bd Magenta Ⓜ *Gare de l'Est – ☎ 01 40 35 83 30 – www.alane-paris-hotel.com – alanehotel@wanadoo.fr – Fax 01 46 07 44 03* F 16
32 rm – €68/125 €75/135, €10
◆ Conveniently located hotel opposite the Gare de l'Est. Small, well-kept rooms with simple decor; those on the top floor with sloping ceilings. Attractive lounge with cane furnishings.

XX **Terminus Nord** AC VISA MC AE
23 r. Dunkerque M Gare du Nord – ✆ 01 42 85 05 15 – www.terminusnord.com – Fax 01 40 16 13 98 E 16
Rest – Menu (€ 25), 32 – Carte € 35/45
◆ High ceilings, frescoes, posters and sculptures are reflected in the mirrors of this brasserie that successfully mixes Art Deco and Art Nouveau. Cosmopolitan clientele.

X **Café Panique** VISA MC AE
12 r. des Messageries M Poissonnière – ✆ 01 47 70 06 84 – www.cafepanique.com E 15
Rest – Menu € 20 (lunch)/33 – Carte approx. € 44
◆ Former textile workshop converted into a loft-style restaurant: skylight, mezzanine, temporary exhibitions and modern dishes from an open-plan kitchen.

X **Chez Michel** VISA MC
10 r. Belzunce M Gare du Nord – ✆ 01 44 53 06 20 – Fax 01 44 53 61 31 – Closed 2 weeks in August, Monday lunch, Saturday and Sunday E 15
Rest – Menu € 32/55
◆ Unpretentious and popular retro-style bistro proposing delicious traditional dishes, with a slight Breton slant (the chef's origins and name!) Excellent game in season.

X **Chez Casimir** VISA MC
6 r. Belzunce M Gare du Nord – ✆ 01 48 78 28 80 – Closed 10-20 August, 21 December-1 January, Saturday and Sunday E 15
Rest – Menu (€ 22), € 26 (lunch)/29 – Carte approx. € 38
◆ One hundred percent bistro ambiance in the simple but fresh cuisine and decor (panelling, copper, checked tablecloths, etc) of this pleasant establishment.

X **Urbane** VISA MC
12 r. Arthur-Groussier M Goncourt – ✆ 01 42 40 74 75 – www.myspace.com/urbaneparis – urbane.resto@gmail.com – Closed 2 weeks in August, Saturday lunch, Sunday and Monday E 18
Rest – Menu (€ 15), € 20 (lunch)/30
◆ A trendy, yet simply decorated restaurant (white walls, bistro-style furniture, imitation leather banquettes and industrial lamps). Modern dishes with an emphasis on quality ingredients.

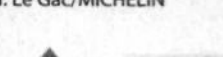
H. Le Gac/MICHELIN

Nation • Voltaire • République

11th arrondissement ✉ 75011

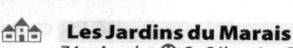

Les Jardins du Marais rm, AC VISA MC AE
74 r. Amelot M St-Sébastien Froissart – ✆ 01 40 21 20 00 – www.homeplazza.com – resabastille@homeplazza.com – Fax 01 47 00 82 40 H 17
201 rm – †€ 180/350 ††€ 180/350, ☕ € 20 – 64 suites
Rest – *(closed Sunday)* Menu (€ 22) – Carte € 36/60
◆ Partly listed buildings overlooking an old cul-de-sac with small, private terraces. Designer entrance hall and bar, and Art Deco touches in the bedrooms.

Le Général without rest AC VISA MC AE
5 r. Rampon M République – ✆ 01 47 00 41 57 – www.legeneralhotel.com – info@legeneralhotel.com – Fax 01 47 00 21 56 G 17
46 rm – †€ 150/170 ††€ 185/245, ☕ € 18 – 3 suites
◆ A pleasant hotel with a very sleek and simple contemporary decor near the Place de la République. Small business centre, basement gym and sauna.

Le Standard Design without rest
29 r. des Taillandiers Ⓜ Bastille – ✆ 01 48 05 30 97 – www.standard-design-hotel-paris.com – reservation@standard-design-hotel-paris.com – Fax 01 47 00 29 26 J 18
36 rm – €125/160 €150/210, €15
◆ A contemporary interior in black and white with touches of colour in the bedrooms. Bright breakfast room under sloping ceilings.

Le Patio St-Antoine without rest
289bis r. fg St-Antoine Ⓜ Nation – ✆ 01 40 09 40 00 – www.homeplazza.com – resanation@homeplazza.com – Fax 01 40 09 11 55 K 20
89 rm – €250/295 €250/295, €18
◆ Practical rooms (with kitchenette) overlooking two quiet, flower-decked patios. Buffet breakfast served in a room decorated in warm tones.

Marais Bastille without rest
36 bd Richard Lenoir Ⓜ Bréguet Sabin – ✆ 01 48 05 75 00 – www.bestwestern.com/fr/maraisbastille – maraisbastille@wanadoo.fr – Fax 01 43 57 42 85 J 18
36 rm – €89/100 €109/145, €13
◆ The hotel runs along the boulevard, which has covered the Canal St Martin since 1860. Tastefully decorated rooms, those at the rear are quieter.

Grand Prieuré without rest
20 r. Grand Prieuré Ⓜ Oberkampf – ✆ 01 47 00 74 14 – www.hotelgrandprieure.fr – gprieure@yahoo.fr – Fax 01 49 23 06 64 G 17
32 rm – €150/169 €169, €8,50
◆ This hotel has been fully refurbished in a smart, contemporary urban style. Find a white colour scheme, woodwork, designer furniture and immense photos of Paris over the bed heads.

Grand Hôtel Français without rest
223 bd Voltaire Ⓜ Nation – ✆ 01 43 71 27 57 – www.grand-hotel-francais.fr – grand-hotel-francais@wanadoo.fr – Fax 01 43 48 40 05 K 20
36 rm – €155/160 €155/160, €10
◆ Small but modern rooms, refurbished in keeping with modern tastes. Find comfortable bedding, thick carpets and tasteful, plain furniture. Well soundproofed.

Nord et Est without rest
49 r. Malte Ⓜ Oberkampf – ✆ 01 47 00 71 70 – www.paris-hotel-nordest.com – info@hotel-nord-est.com – Fax 01 43 57 51 16 G 17
45 rm – €101 €101, €8,50
◆ The warm family atmosphere and reasonable prices draw regulars to this hotel near Place de la République. Ask for one of the refurbished rooms, which have a more modern style.

Croix de Malte without rest
5 r. Malte Ⓜ Oberkampf – ✆ 01 48 05 09 36 – www.hotelcroixdemalte-paris.com – hotelcroixdemalte@orange.fr – Fax 01 43 57 02 54 H 17
29 rm – €75/95 €80/100, €10
◆ Colourful furniture and large posters of parrots in the rather quiet bedrooms. Pleasant breakfast rooms served in a conservatory.

Vin et Marée
276 bd Voltaire Ⓜ Nation – ✆ 01 43 72 31 23 – www.vin-et-maree.com – vmvoltaire@orange.fr – Fax 01 40 24 00 23 K 21
Rest – Menu (€21), €35 – Carte €36/64
◆ Depending on the catch, this brasserie serves seafood specials that are chalked up on the blackboard daily. Rear dining room with view of the kitchens.

Mansouria
11 r. Faidherbe Ⓜ Faidherbe Chaligny – ✆ 01 43 71 00 16 – www.fatemahalreceptions.com – lollisoraya@yahoo.fr – Fax 01 40 24 21 97 – Closed 10-18 August, Monday lunch, Tuesday lunch and Sunday K 19
Rest – *(pre-book)* Menu €30/46 bi – Carte €30/50
◆ Run by a former ethnologist, well-known in Paris in the field of Moroccan cuisine. The delicate, aromatic dishes are prepared by women and served in a Moorish decor.

Chardenoux
Ⓜ *Charonne – ✆ 01 43 71 49 52 – Fax 01 43 71 80 89* K 20
Rest – Menu (€ 24), € 29 – Carte € 38/50
◆ Reopened under the chef Cyril Lignac on its 100th anniversary, this bistro is bringing back traditional cuisine. Decor of yesteryear: marble counter, zinc bar and painted ceiling.

Astier
44 r. J.-P. Timbaud Ⓜ *Parmentier – ✆ 01 43 57 16 35 – www.restaurant-astier.com – restaurant.astier@wanadoo.fr* G 18
Rest – *(pre-book)* Menu (€ 20), € 26 (lunch)/31
◆ A relaxed atmosphere reigns in this lively traditional bistro. Set menu complemented by daily specials chalked on a board. Extensive wine list with around 400 labels.

Villaret
13 r. Ternaux Ⓜ *Parmentier – ✆ 01 43 57 75 56 – Closed August, 24 December-4 January, Saturday lunch and Sunday* H 18
Rest – Menu (€ 22), € 27/50 – Carte € 42/55
◆ This simple but characterful bistro has hit on a winning formula: a friendly atmosphere, good, seasonal cuisine and a fine selection of wines.

Auberge Pyrénées Cévennes
106 r. Folie-Méricourt Ⓜ *République – ✆ 01 43 57 33 78 – Closed 30 July-20 August, Saturday lunch, Sunday and public holidays* G 17
Rest – Menu € 30 – Carte € 33/81
◆ This establishment, popular with good food lovers, has hanging hams, sausages and peppers, as well as nourishing Lyon specialities (tripe). Frank, friendly welcome and a rustic decor.

Bistrot Paul Bert
18 r. Paul Bert Ⓜ *Faidherbe Chaligny – ✆ 01 43 72 24 01 – Closed August, Sunday and Monday* K 19/K 20
Rest – *(pre-book)* Menu (€ 18), € 23/34
◆ In addition to an intriguing wine list, this pleasant bistro is popular for its wholesome family cooking, full of flavour and generosity.

Le Chateaubriand
129 av. Parmentier Ⓜ *Goncourt – ✆ 01 43 57 45 95 – anomalia@voila.fr – Closed 15-31 August, Saturday lunch, Sunday and Monday* G 18
Rest – Menu € 16 (weekday lunch)/43 – Carte € 34/49
◆ Updated cuisine, high quality produce (more creative set menu in the evening), and a simple retro decor: these are the ingredients of this trendy bistro, well covered by the media.

Le Temps au Temps
13 r. Paul-Bert Ⓜ *Faidherbe Chaligny – ✆ 01 43 79 63 40 – Fax 01 43 79 63 40 – Closed 2-25 August, 20-29 December, Sunday and Monday* K 19
Rest – Menu € 18 (weekday lunch)/32
◆ Simplicity seems to be the guideline of this delightful and well-reputed establishment (bookings advisable). Characteristic decor, seasonal blackboard menu.

Au Vieux Chêne
7 r. Dahomey Ⓜ *Faidherbe Chaligny – ✆ 01 43 71 67 69 – Closed 11-20 April, 25 July-18 August, 24 December-4 January, Saturday and Sunday* K 19
Rest – Menu (€ 14), € 17 (lunch)/32 – Carte € 37/48
◆ This neighbourhood bistro is invariably packed thanks to its authentic cuisine and decor. Enticing wine list at very moderate prices.

L'Écailler du Bistrot
22 r. Paul-Bert Ⓜ *Faidherbe Chaligny – ✆ 01 43 72 76 77 – Closed August, Sunday and Monday* K 19
Rest – Menu € 18 (weekday lunch)/50 – Carte € 38/73
◆ Super fresh seafood is this restaurant's main selling point. Catch of the day specials and lobster available year round. Enjoy the nautical ambience par excellence and the fine wine list.

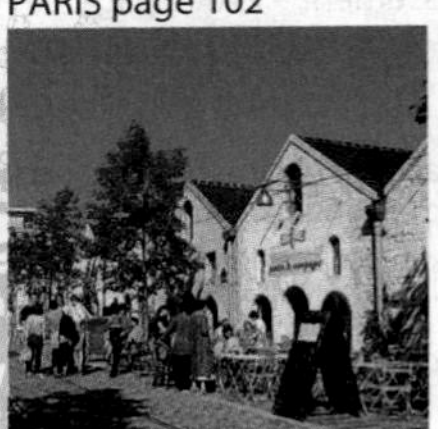
S.Sauvignier/MICHELIN

Bastille • Bercy • Gare de Lyon

12th arrondissement ✉ 75012

Paris Bercy Pullman

1 r. Libourne Ⓜ Cour St-Emilion – ✆ 01 44 67 34 00 – www.pullmanhotels.com – h2192@accor.com – Fax 01 44 67 34 01 NP 20

395 rm – €410/490 €410/490, ☕ €27

Rest *Café Ké* – *(closed 4-25 August, 22-29 December, Saturday and Sunday)* Menu (€29), €36 – Carte €49/81

◆ A beautiful glass façade, contemporary interior in shades of brown, beige and blue, and modern facilities. Some of the rooms enjoy views across Paris. The elegant Café Ké is a pleasant option in the Bercy village. Modern cuisine; Sunday brunch.

Novotel Gare de Lyon

2 r. Hector Malot Ⓜ Gare de Lyon – ✆ 01 44 67 60 00 – www.novotel.com – h1735@accor.com – Fax 01 44 67 60 60 L 18

253 rm – €155/250 €155/250, ☕ €16

Rest – Menu (€20) – Carte €24/45

◆ This modern hotel overlooking a tranquil square offers comfortable, typical Novotel-style guestrooms; those on the sixth floor have a terrace. 24-hour swimming pool and well-designed children's area. Brasserie style restaurant (modern decor, benches, bay windows) and traditional fare.

Novotel Bercy

85 r. Bercy Ⓜ Bercy – ✆ 01 43 42 30 00 – h0935@accor.com – Fax 01 43 45 30 60 M 19

151 rm – €110/255 €110/255, ☕ €15 **Rest** – Carte €26/47

◆ The bright rooms in this Novotel are decorated in the chain's new "Novation" style. The nearby Parc de Bercy occupies the site of an old wine depot. Dining room/veranda and popular terrace in summertime. Traditional menu.

Mercure Gare de Lyon without rest

2 pl. Louis Armand Ⓜ Gare de Lyon – ✆ 01 43 44 84 84 – www.mercure.com – h2217@accor.com – Fax 01 43 47 41 94 L 18

315 rm – €160/294 €175/310, ☕ €18

◆ The modern architecture of this hotel contrasts with the nearby belfry of the Gare de Lyon. The bedrooms are furnished in ceruse wood and have the benefit of good sound-proofing. Wine bar.

Paris Bastille without rest

67 r. Lyon Ⓜ Bastille – ✆ 01 40 01 07 17 – www.hotelparisbastille.com – infosbastille@wanadoo.fr – Fax 01 40 01 07 27 K 18

37 rm – €170/260 €182/260, ☕ €13

◆ Up-to-date comfort, modern furnishings and carefully chosen colour schemes characterise the rooms in this hotel facing the Opéra.

Claret

44 bd Bercy Ⓜ Bercy – ✆ 01 46 28 41 31 – www.hotel-claret.com – reservation@hotel-claret.com – Fax 01 49 28 09 29 M 19

52 rm – €115/155 €135/235, ☕ €12 – ½ P €104/120

Rest – Menu (€14), €18 (weekdays)/40 – Carte €26/40

◆ This former coaching inn is one of the last vestiges of Bercy in the olden days. The cosy rooms have retained their exposed beams. Dining room in pretty ochre and terracotta colours, serving bistro dishes and Lyon specialities. Terrace.

Terminus Lyon without rest VISA AE
19 bd Diderot Ⓜ Gare de Lyon – ✆ 01 56 95 00 00 – www.hotelterminuslyon.com – info@hotelterminuslyon.com – Fax 01 43 44 09 00 L 18
60 rm – †€ 85/129 ††€ 119/129, ☕ € 11
◆ Opposite the Gare de Lyon, this well maintained hotel has plainly furnished rooms. Larger rooms overlooking the road and quieter ones overlook the courtyard. Room service possible.

Pavillon Bercy Gare de Lyon without rest VISA AE
209 r. Charenton Ⓜ Dugommier – ✆ 01 43 40 80 30 – www.leshotelsdeparis.com – bercy@leshotelsdeparis.com – Fax 01 43 40 81 30 M 20
48 rm – †€ 94/225 ††€ 99/230, ☕ € 9
◆ This modern corner building stands next to the métro, a stone's throw from the town hall of the 12th arrondissement. Small, bright and functional rooms with light wood furniture.

XXX **L'Oulette** VISA AE
15 pl. Lachambeaudie Ⓜ Cour St-Emilion – ✆ 01 40 02 02 12 – www.l-oulette.com – info@l-oulette.com – Fax 01 40 02 04 77 – Closed 8-23 August, Saturday and Sunday N 20
Rest – Menu € 41/90 bi – Carte € 55/86
◆ In the revived Bercy quarter, this firmly contemporary restaurant offers an inventive cuisine with southwestern touches. Sheltered terrace behind the thuya trees.

XX **Au Trou Gascon** VISA AE
40 r. Taine Ⓜ Daumesnil – ✆ 01 43 44 34 26 – www.autrougascon.fr – trougascon@orange.fr – Fax 01 43 07 80 55 – Closed August, Saturday and Sunday M 21
Rest – Menu € 36 (lunch)/50 – Carte € 53/70
Spec. Gambas "plancha", royale de foie gras et émulsion de châtaignes (autumn-winter). Suprême de pigeonneau flanqué de foie gras et cuisse effilochée en cannelloni potager (spring-summer). Macaron à la rose, fraises des bois andalouses et litchis (winter-spring).
◆ The decor of this old 1900 bistro combines period mouldings, designer furniture and grey hues. On the menu: Landes and Chalosse produce, seafood and southwestern wines.

XX **Le Janissaire** VISA AE
22 allée Vivaldi Ⓜ Daumesnil – ✆ 01 43 40 37 37 – www.lejanissaire.fr – karamanmus@hotmail.com – Fax 01 43 40 38 39 – Closed Saturday lunchtime and Sunday M 20
Rest – Menu € 13 (weekday lunch), € 25/45 – Carte € 25/44
◆ Turkish ambience and cuisine, as the sign indicates, showing an elite soldier of the Ottoman infantry. Pass the threshold of the Sublime Porte!

XX **Jodhpur Palace** VISA
42 allée Vivaldi Ⓜ Daumesnil – ✆ 01 43 40 72 46 – www.jodhpurpalace.com – jodhpur_palace@yahoo.fr – Fax 01 43 40 17 02 M 20
Rest – Menu (€ 14), € 25/29 – Carte € 32/46
◆ Simple, fresh and exotic decor in this Indian restaurant with friendly service and reasonably priced cuisine. Quiet terrace.

X **La Gazzetta** VISA AE
29 r. de Cotte Ⓜ Ledru Rollin – ✆ 01 43 47 47 05 – www.lagazzetta.fr – team@lagazzetta.fr – Fax 01 43 47 47 17 – Closed August, Sunday and Monday K 19
Rest – Menu (€ 16), € 37 (dinner)/49 – Carte € 45/64 dinner only
◆ A trendy all-in-one restaurant (restaurant, wine bar and café with foreign newspapers available) with a Mediterranean ambience. Fine southern cuisine.

X **Ô Rebelle** VISA AE
24 r. Traversière Ⓜ Gare de Lyon – ✆ 01 43 40 88 98 – www.o-rebelle.fr – info@o-rebelle.fr – Fax 01 43 40 88 99 – Closed 4-26 August, 24 December-1st January, Saturday lunch and Sunday L 18
Rest – Menu € 36/52 – Carte € 38/60
◆ Inventive cuisine with an original combination of flavours, international wine list and a colourful Australian style decor: more globetrotter than rebel perhaps!

Jean-Pierre Frelet
25 r. Montgallet Ⓜ *Montgallet – ✆ 01 43 43 76 65 – jean-pierre.frelet@orange.fr – Closed 3-31 August, Saturday lunch and Sunday* L 20
Rest – Menu (€ 20), € 28 (dinner) – Carte € 42/55
◆ This small neighbourhood restaurant has a friendly, authentic atmosphere. Minimalist decor, tightly packed tables; generous portions of seasonal cuisine.

Quincy
28 av. Ledru-Rollin Ⓜ *Gare de Lyon – ✆ 01 46 28 46 76 – www.lequincy.fr – Fax 01 46 28 46 76 – Closed August, Saturday, Sunday and Monday* L 17
Rest – Carte € 60/85
◆ A warm atmosphere in this rustic bistrot serving hearty cusine which, like "Bobosse" the jovial owner, has plenty of character.

La Biche au Bois
45 av. Ledru-Rollin Ⓜ *Gare de Lyon – ✆ 01 43 43 34 38 – Closed 20 July-20 August, 23 December-2 January, Monday lunch, Saturday and Sunday* K 18
Rest – Menu € 26/36
◆ Tightly packed tables at this discrete restaurant, where the attentive service and lively atmosphere work their charm. Traditional cuisine generously served. Game in season.

Le Lys d'Or
5 pl. Col-Bourgoin Ⓜ *Reuilly Diderot – ✆ 01 44 68 98 88 – www.lysdorming.com – lysdorming@hotmail.fr – Fax 01 44 68 98 80* L 19
Rest – Menu (€ 15 bi), € 24/29 – Carte € 25/35
◆ Enjoy traditional Chinese cuisine from four different regions (Szechuan, Shangai, Canton and Beijing) in this attractive restaurant. Interior garden with small streams and fountains.

L'Auberge Aveyronnaise
40 r. Lamé Ⓜ *Cour St-Emilion – ✆ 01 43 40 12 24 – lesaubergistes@hotmail.fr – Fax 01 43 40 12 15 – Closed 2-18 August* N 20
Rest – Menu (€ 19), € 24 (weekday lunch)/26
◆ Modern bistro-cum-brasserie, and as the name suggests, specialities from Aveyron feature prominently. Large modern-rustic dining rooms and pleasant terrace.

S. Sauvignier/MICHELIN

Place d'Italie • Gare d'Austerlitz • Bibliothèque nationale de France

13th arrondissement ✉ 75013

Holiday Inn Bibliothèque de France without rest
21 r. Tolbiac Ⓜ *Bibliothèque F. Mitterrand – ✆ 01 45 84 61 61 – www.holiday-inn.com/paris-tolbiac – hibdf@wanadoo.fr – Fax 01 45 84 43 38* P 18
71 rm – †€ 127/187 ††€ 127/187, ☕ € 14
◆ In a busy street 20m from the métro station, this hotel offers comfortable, well-kept rooms with double glazing. Simple dishes available in the evening.

Mercure Place d'Italie without rest
25 bd Blanqui Ⓜ *Place d'Italie – ✆ 01 45 80 82 23 – www.mercure.com – h1191@accor.com – Fax 01 45 81 45 84* P 15
50 rm – †€ 160/300 ††€ 170/310, ☕ € 17
◆ This hotel, near the Manufacture des Gobelins tapestry museum, offers warm, well-soundproofed and functional rooms.

Demeure without rest
51 bd St-Marcel Ⓜ Les Gobelins – ✆ 01 43 37 81 25 – www.hotel-paris-lademeure.com – la_demeure@netcourrier.com – Fax 01 45 87 05 03
37 rm – †€ 125/165 ††€ 145/202, ☕ € 13 – 6 suites M 16
◆ An attentive welcome at this family-run establishment. Modern rooms, cosy sitting room and appetising breakfast buffet. Lovely collection of old Paris photos.

Résidence Vert Galant without rest
43 r. Croulebarbe Ⓜ Les Gobelins – ✆ 01 44 08 83 50 – www.vergalant.com – hotel.vert.galant@gmail.com – Fax 01 44 08 83 69 N 15
15 rm – †€ 90/100 ††€ 95/150, ☕ € 9
◆ Countryside in the heart of Paris: a pleasant residence with quiet and charming rooms, all looking out onto a private garden planted with vines.

La Manufacture without rest
8 r. Philippe-de-Champagne Ⓜ Place d'Italie – ✆ 01 45 35 45 25 – www.hotel-la-manufacture.com – reservation@hotel-la-manufacture.com – Fax 01 45 35 45 40 N 16
56 rm – †€ 115/165 ††€ 145/165, ☕ € 12
◆ Friendly service and elegant decor are the main features of this well-maintained hotel. Guestrooms somewhat on the small side. Breakfast room with a Provençal atmosphere.

Chez Jacky
109 r. du Dessous-des-Berges Ⓜ Bibliothèque F. Mitterrand – ✆ 01 45 83 71 55 – www.chezjacky.fr – contact@chezjacky.fr – Fax 01 45 86 57 73 – Closed August, 24 December-5 January, Saturday, Sunday and holidays P 18
Rest – Menu € 39 (weekdays)/65 – Carte € 60/75
◆ This restaurant affirms its status as a very French provincial tavern with its exposed beams and colourful artwork. Traditional cuisine served graciously.

Petit Marguery
9 bd Port-Royal Ⓜ Les Gobelins – ✆ 01 43 31 58 59 – www.petitmarguery.fr – gm@petitmarguery.com – Fax 01 43 36 73 34 M 15
Rest – Menu (€ 23), € 26 (lunch), € 35/65 bi
◆ This restaurant, with a friendly atmosphere, offers pleasant 1940s-style dining rooms. The typical bistro-type dishes and game in season are popular with a wide following of regulars.

BIOart
3 quai François-Mauriac Ⓜ Bibliothèque F. Mitterrand – ✆ 01 45 85 66 88 – www.restaurantbioart.fr – evenement@bioart.fr – Closed 25 December-1st January
Rest – Menu (€ 34), € 46 – Carte € 46/56 N 19
◆ A huge split-level health food restaurant with an environmental bent, next to the Bibliothèque Nationale de France. Zen/feng-shui décor with soundproofed picture windows overlooking the Seine.

L'Avant Goût
26 r. Bobillot Ⓜ Place d'Italie – ✆ 01 53 80 24 00 – www.lavangout.com – Fax 01 53 80 00 77 – Closed 3-25 August, Sunday and Monday P 15
Rest – *(number of covers limited, pre-book)* Menu (€ 14 bi), € 31 – Carte € 46/54
◆ This modern bistro is often crowded. The reasons for its success? How about dishes made from market produce, a good wine list and a relaxed atmosphere.

Les Cailloux
58 r. des Cinq-Diamants Ⓜ Corvisart – ✆ 01 45 80 15 08 – www.lescailloux.fr – lescailloux@sljcohen.fr – Fax 01 45 80 96 36 – Closed for one week in August and at Christmas P 15
Rest – *(booking advisable)* Menu (€ 14 bi), € 18 bi (weekday lunch) – Carte € 23/46
◆ The Butte des Cailles is home to many restaurants, including this laidback Italian bistro decorated in a monochrome of browns. Good food at good prices.

L'Ourcine
92 r. Broca Ⓜ Les Gobelins – ✆ 01 47 07 13 65 – Fax 01 47 07 18 48 – Closed 1 week February school holidays, 1 week spring school holidays, 13 July-25 August, Sunday and Monday N 14
Rest – Menu (€ 24), € 32
◆ Simple, modern decor in this restaurant with a friendly atmosphere. Inspired, seasonal cuisine chalked up on a blackboard.

Impérial Choisy
32 av. de Choisy Ⓜ Porte de Choisy – ✆ 01 45 86 42 40 – cdm13@free.fr – Fax 01 45 83 93 34 R 17
Rest – Carte € 25/50
◆ Authentic and popular Chinese restaurant, much appreciated by regulars for its delicious Cantonese specialities.

Lao Lane Xang 2
102 av. d'Ivry Ⓜ Tolbiac – ✆ 01 58 89 00 00 P 16
Rest – Menu (€ 11 bi) – Carte € 18/30
◆ Enjoy the flavours of Laos, Vietnam and Thailand at this family restaurant in the Chinatown of Paris. Simple contemporary décor, with a more Asian look upstairs.

Sukhothaï
12 r. Père Guérin Ⓜ Place d'Italie – ✆ 01 45 81 55 88 – Closed 3-23 August, Monday lunch and Sunday P 15
Rest – Menu (€ 12 bi), € 21/25 – Carte € 20/34
◆ The name is a reminder of the former capital of a 13-14C Thai kingdom. Chinese and Thai food served under the watchful eye of Buddha (handmade sculptures).

Bambou
70 r. Baudricourt Ⓜ Les Olympiades – ✆ 01 45 70 91 75 – Closed 1st-15 August and Monday P 17
Rest – Carte € 15/30
◆ They're flocking to this little Vietnamese restaurant, where the flavourful cuisine gives diners a welcome change of scenery.

J.-P. Clapham/MICHELIN

Montparnasse • Denfert-Rochereau • Parc Montsouris

14th arrondissement ✉ 75014

Méridien Montparnasse
19 r. Cdt Mouchotte Ⓜ Montparnasse Bienvenüe – ✆ 01 44 36 44 36 – www.lemeridien.com/montparnasse – meridien.montparnasse@lemeridien.com – Fax 01 44 36 49 00 M 11
918 rm – €159/600 €159/600, € 25 – 35 suites
Rest *Montparnasse'25* – see below
Rest *Justine* – ✆ 01 44 36 44 00 – Menu € 42 – Carte € 45/70
◆ The spacious rooms in this glass and concrete building have been redone in a modern spirit with Art Deco details. Beautiful view of the capital from the top floors. At Justine's, winter garden decor, green terrace and buffet menus.

Concorde Montparnasse
40 r. Cdt Mouchotte Ⓜ Gaîté – ✆ 01 56 54 84 00 – www.concorde-montparnasse.com – montparnasse-booking@concorde-hotels.com – Fax 01 56 54 84 84 M 11
354 rm – €150/500 €150/500, € 21 **Rest** – Carte € 52/60
◆ This hotel, on Place de Catalogne, was treated to a facelift recently. Calm and refined rooms, interior garden, fitness centre and bar. Exotic wood and colourful fabrics grace this modern, low-key restaurant, serving a modern menu.

Aiglon without rest
232 bd Raspail Ⓜ Raspail – ✆ 01 43 20 82 42 – www.aiglon.com – aiglon@espritfrance.com – Fax 01 43 20 98 72 M 12
36 rm – €145/195 €145/195, € 12 – 10 suites
◆ This one time home to Giacometti and Bunuel is gradually being modernised. Bright colours and stylish details (mosaic bathrooms, photos) set the scene for the new decor.

Villa Royale Montsouris without rest
144 r. Tombe-Issoire Ⓜ Porte d'Orléans – ✆ 01 56 53 89 89 – www.leshotelsdeparis.com – montsouris@leshotelsdeparis.com – Fax 01 56 53 89 80 R 12
36 rm – €99/230 €109/290, ☕ €15
◆ A change of atmosphere is guaranteed for guests in this hotel, astutely decorated in Andalusian and Moorish style. Rooms are small but very cosy, named after Moroccan towns.

Lenox Montparnasse without rest
15 r. Delambre Ⓜ Vavin – ✆ 01 43 35 34 50 – www.hotellenox.com – hotel@lenoxmontparnasse.com – Fax 01 43 20 46 64 M 12
52 rm – €150/310 €150/310, ☕ €16
◆ Establishment noted for its elegance: plush, low-key bar and sitting rooms, personalised stylish rooms, pleasant suites on the sixth floor.

Nouvel Orléans without rest
25 av. Gén. Leclerc Ⓜ Mouton Duvernet – ✆ 01 43 27 80 20 – www.hotelnouvelorleans.com – nouvelorleans@aol.com – Fax 01 43 35 36 57 P 12
46 rm – €110/145 €110/190, ☕ €12
◆ The name comes from the Porte d'Orléans, 800m away. In this entirely renovated hotel, modern furniture and warm colourful materials decorate the rooms.

Mercure Raspail Montparnasse without rest
207 bd Raspail Ⓜ Vavin – ✆ 01 43 20 62 94 – www.mercure.com – h0351@accor.com – Fax 01 43 27 39 69 M 12
63 rm – €170/220 €175/220, ☕ €14
◆ Enjoy an overnight stay in this Haussmann building near the famous Montparnasse brasseries. Fully refurbished, modern rooms graced with pale wood furniture.

Delambre without rest
35 r. Delambre Ⓜ Edgar Quinet – ✆ 01 43 20 66 31 – www.hoteldelambre.com – delambre@club-internet.fr – Fax 01 45 38 91 76 M 12
30 rm – €90/170 €95/170, ☕ €11
◆ André Breton stayed in this hotel located in a quiet street close to Montparnasse railway station. The decor is modern, the rooms simple but bright, and many are spacious.

Midi without rest
4 av. René Coty Ⓜ Denfert Rochereau – ✆ 01 43 27 23 25 – midi-hotel-paris.com – info@midi-hotel-paris.com – Fax 01 43 21 24 58 N 13
45 rm – €88/108 €108/168, ☕ €12
◆ Near Place Denfert Rochereau find soundproofed rooms, some with hydromassage baths, and organic breakfasts: what more could you want!

Châtillon without rest
11 square Châtillon Ⓜ Porte d'Orléans – ✆ 01 45 42 31 17 – www.hotelchatillon.fr – chatillon.hotel@wanadoo.fr – Fax 01 45 42 72 09 P 11
31 rm – €85 €85, ☕ €7
◆ A place frequented by regulars who appreciate its peace and quiet. Spacious well-maintained guestrooms overlooking a square at the end of a cul-de-sac. Friendly atmosphere.

De la Paix without rest
225 bd Raspail Ⓜ Raspail – ✆ 01 43 20 35 82 – www.hoteldelapaix.com – resa@hoteldelapaix.com – Fax 01 43 35 32 63 M 12
39 rm – €79/107 €84/120, ☕ €9
◆ The hotel is furnished in a 1970s style offering comfortable, well-kept rooms, progressively redecorated in a modern style. Delightful welcome.

Apollon Montparnasse without rest
91 r. Ouest Ⓜ Pernety – ✆ 01 43 95 62 00 – www.apollon-montparnasse.com – apollonm@wanadoo.fr – Fax 01 43 95 62 10 N 10-11
33 rm – €70/98 €85/125, ☕ €11
◆ Gradually renovated family hotel near the station. Tastefully decorated rooms, a smiling welcome, and a quiet location in a side street.

Cécil without rest
47 r. Beaunier Ⓜ Porte d' Orléans – ✆ 01 45 40 93 53 – www.cecilhotel.net – cecil-hotel@wanadoo.fr – Fax 01 45 40 43 26 R 12
25 rm – €98/148 €98/148, ☕ €10
◆ A hotel full of charm in a quiet street near Montsouris park. Furniture and hand picked objects lend each room its own personality. Lounge-library and small garden.

Montparnasse'25 – Hôtel Méridien Montparnasse
19 r. Cdt Mouchotte Ⓜ Montparnasse Bienvenüe – ✆ 01 44 36 44 25 – www.lemeridien.com/montparnasse – meridien.montparnasse@lemeridien.com – Fax 01 44 36 49 03 – Closed 1-10 May, 13 July-31 August, 22 December-4 January, Saturday, Sunday and bank holidays M 25
Rest – Menu €50/110 – Carte €110/133
Spec. Saint Jacques et ormeaux, crème de chou fleur au caviar (season). Sole au jus d'étrilles (season). Gaufre, crème légère et châtaigne (season).
◆ The modern setting based around black lacquer may surprise but this restaurant turns out to be comfortable and warm. Contemporary cuisine, superb cheese boards.

Le Dôme
108 bd Montparnasse Ⓜ Vavin – ✆ 01 43 35 25 81 – Fax 01 42 79 01 19 – Closed Sunday and Monday in August LM 12
Rest – Carte €85/150
◆ A temple of literary and artistic bohemian life in the Twenties has been turned into a stylish and trendy Left-Bank brasserie, with its Art Deco style intact. Fish and seafood.

Le Duc
243 bd Raspail Ⓜ Raspail – ✆ 01 43 20 96 30 – restaurantleduc@orange.fr – Fax 01 43 20 46 73 – Closed 2-24 August, 24 December-2 January, Saturday lunch, Sunday and Monday M 12
Rest – Menu €55 (lunch) – Carte €90/120
◆ Fish and seafood served amid a yacht cabin decor of mahogany panelling, wall lights with a marine theme and gleaming copperware.

Pavillon Montsouris
20 r. Gazan Ⓜ Cité Universitaire – ✆ 01 43 13 29 00 – Fax 01 43 13 29 02 – Closed February half-term holidays and Sunday dinner from mid September to Easter R 14
Rest – Menu €51 – Carte €67/89
◆ This Belle Epoque lodge in Montsouris Park offers a calm country atmosphere in the centre of Paris. Pretty glass roof, colonial type decoration and lush green terrace.

La Coupole
102 bd Montparnasse Ⓜ Vavin – ✆ 01 43 20 14 20 – www.flobrasseries.com – jtosi@groupeflo.fr – Fax 01 43 35 46 14 L 12
Rest – Menu €36 – Carte €35/70
◆ The spirit of Montparnasse lives on in this immense Art Deco brasserie, opened in 1927. The 24 pillars were decorated by artists of the period, while the cupola sports a new contemporary fresco.

Vin et Marée
108 av. Maine Ⓜ Gaîté – ✆ 01 43 20 29 50 – www.vin-et-maree.com – vmmaine@orange.fr – Fax 01 43 27 84 11 N 11
Rest – Menu €21 – Carte €30/50
◆ Fish and seafood, the restaurant's specialities, are chalked up every day on the slate, depending on Neptune's humour. Dining rooms decorated in nautical style.

Monsieur Lapin
11 r. R. Losserand Ⓜ Gaîté – ✆ 01 43 20 21 39 – www.monsieur-lapin.fr – franck.enee@wanadoo.fr – Fax 01 43 21 84 86 – Closed August, Saturday lunch, Sunday lunch and Monday N 11
Rest – *(number of covers limited, pre-book)* Menu (€25), €29 (weekday lunch), €35/45 – Carte €45/56
◆ Just like the March Hare in Alice in Wonderland, Mr. Rabbit is everywhere: in the decor of the dining room and on a menu which makes good use of a wide choice of sauces.

XX **Les Vendanges** VISA MC AE D

40 r. Friant Ⓜ Porte d'Orléans – ✆ 01 45 39 59 98 – www.lesvendanges-paris.com – Fax 01 45 39 74 13 – Closed 31 July-30 August, 24 December-3 January, Saturday and Sunday R 11

Rest – Menu (€ 25), € 35

◆ The façade, decorated with clusters of grapes, hints at what is to come - a superb wine cellar (vintage clarets). Updated cuisine redolent of southwest France.

X **Millésimes 62** VISA MC AE

13 pl. Catalogne Ⓜ Gaîté – ✆ 01 43 35 34 35 – www.millesimes62.com – millesimes62@orange.fr – Fax 01 43 20 26 21 – Closed 1-17 August, Saturday lunch and Sunday M 11

Rest – Menu (€ 20), € 25 (weekdays)/35

◆ Appealing restaurant with modern decor, near the great hotels and theatres of the Montparnasse area. Enjoy its tasty dishes, made with market produce, and at friendly prices.

X **La Marée Denfert** VISA MC AE

83 av. Denfert-Rochereau Ⓜ Denfert Rochereau – ✆ 0143 54 99 86 – www.lamareepassy.com – paudou@orange.fr – Closed Saturday lunch and Sunday N 13

Rest – Carte € 42/48

◆ New seafood restaurant whose elegant red and white decor boasts matching velvet seats and model boats. Fish of the day chalked up on a slate.

X **La Régalade** AC VISA MC

49 av. J. Moulin Ⓜ Porte d'Orléans – ✆ 01 45 45 68 58 – la_regalade@yahoo.fr – Fax 01 45 40 96 74 – Closed 25 July-20 August, 1st-10 January, Monday lunch, Saturday and Sunday R 11

Rest – *(pre-book)* Menu € 32

◆ A welcoming smile, tasty country cuisine and a simple decor are the assets of this small bistro near the Porte de Châtillon.

X **L'Assiette** VISA MC

181 r. du Château Ⓜ Mouton Duvernet – ✆ 01 43 22 64 86 – Fax 01 43 20 54 66 – Closed Monday and Tuesday N 11

Rest – *(pre-book)* Menu (€ 25) – Carte € 40/50

◆ David Rathgeber, formerly the chef at Benoit, has taken over this well-worn bistro. Short menu of fine classic cuisine, slightly bourgeois in style.

X **La Cerisaie** VISA MC

70 bd E. Quinet Ⓜ Edgar Quinet – ✆ 01 43 20 98 98 – Fax 01 43 20 98 98 – Closed 1st-11 May, 11 July-17 August, 19 December-4 January, Saturday and Sunday N 13

Rest – *(pre-book)* Menu (€ 23), € 34/40

◆ A tiny restaurant in the heart of the Breton quarter. Every day, the owner chalks up on a blackboard the carefully prepared south-western dishes.

X **À La Bonne Table** AC VISA MC AE D

42 r. Friant Ⓜ Porte d'Orléans – ✆ 01 45 39 74 91 – Fax 01 45 43 66 92 – Closed 12 July-2 August, 20 December-3 January, Saturday lunch and Sunday R 11

Rest – Menu € 26 (lunch)/30 – Carte € 41/56

◆ The chef, originally from Japan, prepares traditional French cuisine enhanced with Japanese flair. Comfortable, long dining room in a 1940s style.

X **L'Amuse Bouche** VISA MC D

186 r. Château Ⓜ Mouton Duvernet – ✆ 01 43 35 31 61 – Closed 1st-20 August, Sunday and Monday N 11

Rest – Menu (€ 21 bi) – Carte approx. € 32

◆ Tightly packed tables and orange walls decorated with saucepans... a simple, small restaurant serving tasty traditional cuisine and soufflé specialities.

X **Bistrot du Dôme** AC VISA MC AE

1 r. Delambre Ⓜ Vavin – ✆ 01 43 35 32 00 – Closed Sunday and Monday in August M 12

Rest – Carte € 46/52

◆ The wing of the Dôme also specialises in fish and seafood. A relaxed atmosphere in the large dining room, the ceiling of which is decorated with vine leaves.

La Cagouille
VISA AE

10 pl. Constantin-Brancusi Ⓜ *Gaité – ✆ 01 43 22 09 01 – www.la-cagouille.fr – la-cagouille@wanadoo.fr – Fax 01 45 38 57 29* M 11

Rest – Menu (€ 26), € 42 bi – Carte € 35/70

◆ The tasteful setting (wood panelling, pulleys, old ship rigging) and fine, simply prepared seafood are a perfect match. Terrace on a quiet little square.

L'Ordonnance
VISA MC

51 r. Hallé Ⓜ *Mouton Duvernet – ✆ 01 43 27 55 85 – fredericchalette@orange.fr – Fax 01 43 20 64 72 – Closed August, Christmas holidays, Saturday except dinner in Winter and Sunday* P 12

Rest – Menu € 24 (weekdays)/30

◆ A stone's throw from Place Michel Audiard, this warm, modern establishment serves tasty traditional cuisine in a good-humoured atmosphere.

L'Atelier d'Antan
VISA MC AE

9 r. L.-Robert Ⓜ *Raspail – ✆ 01 43 21 36 19 – pascal.dantan@hotmail.fr – Closed Saturday lunch and Sunday* N 12

Rest – Menu (€ 15), € 18 (lunch)/34

◆ The bistro style, smiling staff and friendly atmosphere are well suited to the tasty traditional cuisine. A particularly pleasant establishment.

La Cantine du Troquet
VISA MC

100 r. de l'Ouest Ⓜ *Pernety* N 10

Rest – Menu (€ 20), € 30 – Carte € 25/35

◆ This canteen breathes conviviality (no reservations, no telephone) and is the simpler, sister establishment to the Troquet. Red banquettes, wooden tables and daily blackboard specials.

L'Entêtée
VISA MC

4 r. Danville Ⓜ *Denfert Rochereau – ✆ 01 40 47 56 81 – www.myspace.com/entetee – entetee@gmail.com – Closed August, Saturday lunch, Sunday and Monday* N 12

Rest – *(number of covers limited, pre-book)* Menu (€ 20), € 25 (lunch), € 30

◆ "Entêtée" (stubborn) could be just the name of this discreet bistro or it could also refer to the chef's character... Generous dishes, perfumed with herbs and spices.

Les Fils de la Ferme
VISA MC

5 r. Mouton-Duvernet Ⓜ *Mouton Duvernet – ✆ 01 45 39 39 61 – www.filsdelaferme.com – jc.dutter@noos.fr – Fax 01 45 39 39 61 – Closed three weeks in August, Sunday dinner and Monday* N 12

Rest – Menu (€ 19), € 28

◆ A discreet contemporary bistro (yellow tones, exposed stonework) run by two brothers, one in the kitchen, the other in the dining room. Seasonal dishes.

Le Jeu de Quilles
A/C VISA MC

45 r. Boulard Ⓜ *Mouton Duvernet – ✆ 01 53 90 76 22 – Closed 3 weeks in August, Sunday and Monday* N 12

Rest – *(lunch only) (pre-book)* Carte € 39/47

◆ With its deli corner in the entrance and kitchen at the far end of the tiny dining area, this lively bistro really gets your appetite going. Short blackboard menu with fine ingredients; convivial atmosphere to spare.

Severo
A/C VISA MC

8 r. des Plantes Ⓜ *Mouton Duvernet – ✆ 01 45 40 40 91 – Closed 11-19 April, 25 July-23 August, 24 December-4 January, 13-21 February, Saturday, Sunday and bank holidays* N 11

Rest – Carte € 33/56

◆ Products from Auvergne (meat, charcuterie) take centre stage on the daily slate menu of this friendly bistro. The wine list is enticingly eclectic.

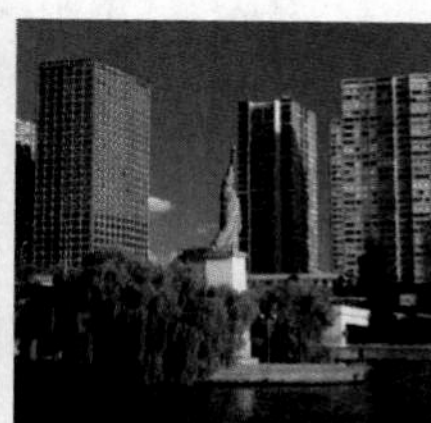
H. Le Gac/MICHELIN

Porte de Versailles • Vaugirard • Beaugrenelle

15th arrondissement ✉ 75015

Pullman Rive Gauche

8 r. L. Armand Ⓜ Balard – ✆ 01 40 60 30 30 – www.pullman-hotels.com – h0572@accor.com – Fax 01 40 60 30 00 VISA MC AE D N 5

606 rm – †€ 141/430 ††€ 141/430, ☕ € 27 – 12 suites

Rest *Brasserie* – Menu € 28 (weekday lunch) – Carte € 39/66

◆ Hotel opposite the heliport which has been refurbished with the business traveller in mind. Modern, identical, soundproofed rooms. Upper floors have a lovely view over western Paris. Simple cuisine in the brasserie, English style bar, panoramic breakfast room.

Novotel Tour Eiffel

61 quai de Grenelle Ⓜ Charles Michels – ✆ 01 40 58 20 00 – www.novotel.com – h3546@accor.com – Fax 01 40 58 24 44 VISA MC AE D K 6

758 rm – †€ 260/450 ††€ 260/450, ☕ € 22 – 6 suites

Rest *Benkay* – see below

Rest *Tour Eiffel Café* – ✆ 01 40 58 20 75 – Menu (€ 25), € 40/48 bi – Carte € 29/55

◆ A hotel overlooking the Seine with comfortable modern rooms (wood, light shades), most of which have views of the river. High-tech conference centre. Pleasant, minimalist decor and modern cuisine.

Mercure Suffren Tour Eiffel

20 r. Jean Rey Ⓜ Bir-Hakeim – ✆ 01 45 78 50 00 – www.mercure.com – h2175@accor.com – Fax 01 45 78 91 42 VISA MC AE D J 7

405 rm – †€ 175/310 ††€ 190/310, ☕ € 20

Rest – Menu (€ 24 bi) – Carte € 30/45

◆ This modern building in the heart of the capital stands out with its verdant reception and environs. Rooms are perfectly soundproofed and some have views of the Eiffel Tower. The dining room opens onto a pleasant terrace surrounded by trees and greenery.

Novotel Vaugirard

257 r. Vaugirard Ⓜ Vaugirard – ✆ 01 40 45 10 00 – www.novotel.com – h1978@accor.com – Fax 01 40 45 10 10 VISA MC AE D M 9

187 rm – †€ 109/350 ††€ 109/350, ☕ € 16 **Rest** – Carte € 20/47

◆ In the heart of the 15th arrondissement, this establishment has been well thought out for a business clientele. Simple, functional rooms in accordance with the chain's lines. Numerous items of seminar equipment. The Novotel Café serves traditional cuisine and some grilled specialities.

Océania without rest

52 r. Oradour sur Glane Ⓜ Porte de Versailles – ✆ 01 56 09 09 09 – www.oceaniahotels.com – oceania.paris@oceaniahotels.com – Fax 01 56 09 09 19 VISA MC AE D P 6

232 rm – †€ 270 ††€ 285, ☕ € 17 – 18 suites

◆ Modern comfort in an elegant, contemporary setting. This new hotel offers well-equipped bedrooms, a relaxation centre and an exotic terrace-garden.

Novotel Gare Montparnasse

17 r. Cotentin Ⓜ Montparnasse Bienvenüe – ✆ 01 53 91 23 75 – h5060@accor.com – Fax 01 53 91 23 76 VISA MC AE D M 10

197 rm – †€ 160/400 ††€ 160/400, ☕ € 16 – 2 suites

Rest – Menu (€ 21 bi) – Carte € 25/45

◆ A brand-new hotel near the railway station with guestrooms decorated in a minimalist, contemporary style (high-tech facilities and good soundproofing). Generous buffet breakfast.

Holiday Inn Montparnasse without rest
10 r. Gager Gabillot Ⓜ Vaugirard – ✆ 01 44 19 29 29
– www.holiday-inn.fr/paris-mountain – reservations@hiparis-montparnasse.com
– Fax 01 44 19 29 39 M 9
60 rm – †€ 90/99 ††€ 310/340, ☕ € 14
◆ A modern building located in a quiet street. Spacious lobby and contemporary lounge with a glass pyramid roof. Identical, functional rooms.

Eiffel Cambronne without rest
46 r. Croix-Nivert Ⓜ Av. Emile Zola – ✆ 01 56 58 56 78
– www.eiffelcambronne.com – hotel@eiffefcambronne.com – Fax 01 56 58 56 79
31 rm – †€ 119/189 ††€ 119/189, ☕ € 13 L 8
◆ Comfy armchairs and an open fire add to the warm ambience of the hotel's lounge-lobby. Average-sized rooms; those to the rear are quieter. Copious breakfast served in the inner courtyard.

Mercure Paris XV without rest
6 r. St-Lambert Ⓜ Boucicaut – ✆ 01 45 58 61 00 – accor.com – h0903@accor.com
– Fax 01 45 54 10 43 M 7
56 rm – †€ 135/161 ††€ 140/167, ☕ € 14
◆ A hotel located 800m from the Porte de Versailles. The reception, lounges and comfortable, well-kept rooms are in contemporary style.

Aberotel without rest
24 r. Blomet Ⓜ Volontaires – ✆ 01 40 61 70 50 – www.aberotel.com – aberotel@wanadoo.fr – Fax 01 40 61 08 31 L 9
28 rm – †€ 80/130 ††€ 90/150, ☕ € 8
◆ A popular hotel with stylish rooms and an inner courtyard for summer breakfasts. It has a pleasant lounge adorned with paintings on wood of playing cards.

Benkay – Novotel Tour Eiffel
61 quai de Grenelle Ⓜ Bir-Hakeim – ✆ 01 40 58 21 26 – www.restaurant-benkay.com
– reservations@restaurant-benkay.com – Fax 01 40 58 21 30 K 6
Rest – Menu € 35 (lunch), € 55/150 – Carte € 84/162
◆ Elegant Japanese setting on the top floor of a hotel overlooking the Seine. Teppanyaki counter (prepared on the hot plate in front of guests) and kaiseki (table service).

Le Quinzième Cuisine Attitude
14 r. Cauchy Ⓜ Javel – ✆ 01 45 54 43 43 – www.restaurantlequinzieme.com
– resa@lequinzieme.com – Fax 01 45 57 22 96 – Closed 10-20 August, Monday lunch, Saturday lunch and Sunday L 5
Rest – Menu (€ 45), € 110/155 bi – Carte € 80/110
◆ A trendy setting, a "chef's table" with a view of the kitchen, and delicious modern cuisine; a seductive recipe from Cyril Lignac, star of the TV cookery show "Oui Chef!".

La Gauloise
59 av. La Motte-Picquet Ⓜ La Motte Picquet Grenelle – ✆ 01 47 34 11 64
– Fax 01 40 61 09 70 K 8
Rest – brasserie – Menu (€ 24) – Carte € 33/45
◆ This 1900 brasserie must have seen many celebrities pass through, judging from the signed photos on the walls. A pleasant, kerbside terrace.

Thierry Burlot "Le Quinze"
8 r. Nicolas Charlet Ⓜ Pasteur – ✆ 01 42 19 08 59 – Fax 01 45 67 09 13
– Closed 15 July-15 August, Saturday and Sunday L 10
Rest – Menu € 28 (lunch)/35 – Carte € 30/54
◆ The inventive and careful, seasonal based cuisine is served in a peaceful and refined atmosphere with subdued lighting. The sleek, simple setting is punctuated with a wall covered in gold leaf.

Caroubier
82 bd Lefebvre Ⓜ Porte de Vanves – ✆ 01 40 43 16 12
– www.restaurant-lecaroubier.com – Fax 01 40 43 16 12
– Closed 18 July-20 August and Monday P 8
Rest – Menu € 19 (weekday lunch)/30 – Carte € 31/48
◆ Modern decor enhanced with touches of the oriental. A family atmosphere and warm welcome presage generous helpings of sun-gorged Moroccan cuisine.

XX **Fontanarosa**

28 bd Garibaldi Ⓜ Cambronne – ✆ 01 45 66 97 84 – www.fontanarosa-ristorante.eu – contact@fontanarosa-ristorante.eu – Fax 01 47 83 96 30 L 9

Rest – Menu (€ 17), € 21 (weekday lunch)/30 – Carte € 34/65

◆ This authentic trattoria spirits you far away from the bustle of Paris. Enjoy good Italian cuisine with a focus on Sardinian specialities. Outdoor terrace in summer.

XX **La Dînée**

85 r. Leblanc Ⓜ Balard – ✆ 01 45 54 20 49 – www.restaurant-ladinee.com – contact@restaurant-ladinee.com – Fax 01 40 60 73 76 – Closed Saturday and Sunday M 5

Rest – Menu (€ 36), € 39

◆ Up-to-the-minute dining room decorated with contemporary pictures and offering fashionable cuisine. Grill menu served in the adjoining bistro.

XX **Erawan**

76 r. Fédération Ⓜ La Motte Picquet Grenelle – ✆ 01 47 83 55 67 – Fax 01 47 34 85 98 – Closed 3 weeks in August and Sunday K 8

Rest – Menu € 14 bi (lunch), € 20/29 – Carte € 20/40

◆ Carved wood, pastel shades and Asian curios set the scene for this restrained restaurant. Delicious Thai cuisine and staff in national costume; delightful welcome.

XX **L'Épopée**

89 av. Émile-Zola Ⓜ Charles Michels – ✆ 01 45 77 71 37 – www.lepopee.fr – lepopee@hotmail.fr – Fax 01 45 77 71 37 – Closed 9-17 August, 24 December-5 January and Sunday L 7

Rest – Menu (€ 24), € 35

◆ Despite the grandeur of its name (The Epic), this is a small, convivial restaurant. Regulars keep coming back for its excellent wine list and traditional cuisine.

X **Stéphane Martin**

67 r. des Entrepreneurs Ⓜ Charles Michels – ✆ 01 45 79 03 31 – www.stephanemartin.com – resto.stephanemartin@free.fr – Closed 19-27 April, 1st-24 August, 20 December-4 January, Sunday and Monday L 7

Rest – Menu (€ 17), € 22 (weekday lunch)/35 – Carte € 50/64

◆ This inviting restaurant with a library theme (mural of bookshelves), serves up-to-date market fresh cuisine.

X **Bernard du 15**

62 r. des Entrepreneurs Ⓜ Charles Michels – ✆ 01 40 59 09 27 – Closed Saturday lunch, Monday lunch and Sunday L 7

Rest – Menu (€ 24), € 34 – Carte € 34/54

◆ A classical restaurant (round tables and white tablecloths, cream-coloured walls decorated with landscapes) where the chef updates classic dishes with his creative use of spices.

X **Bistro d'Hubert**

41 bd Pasteur Ⓜ Pasteur – ✆ 01 47 34 15 50 – www.bistrodhubert.com – message@bistrodhubert.com – Fax 01 45 67 03 09 – Closed Monday lunch, Saturday lunch, Sunday and holidays L 10

Rest – Menu (€ 28), € 36 – Carte € 40/80

◆ Jars and bottles on the shelves, gingham tablecloths, a direct view of the kitchens and gleaming copperware - the decor of this bistro is reminiscent of a Landes farmhouse.

X **Yanasé**

75 r. Vasco-de-Gamma Ⓜ Lourmel – ✆ 01 42 50 07 20 – www.yanase.fr – yanase@orange.fr – Fax 01 42 50 07 90 – Closed 2-19 August, 24 December-4 January, Saturday lunch and Sunday N 6

Rest – Menu (€ 20 bi), € 38 (dinner)/58 – Carte € 38/61

◆ A minimalist interior in Yanasé (Japanese cedar) serving typical Japanese grilled dishes, prepared in front of diners on a charcoal-fired "robata" barbecue.

X **Afaria**

15 r. Desnouettes Ⓜ Convention – ✆ 01 48 56 15 36 – Fax 01 48 56 15 36 – Closed 23-28 December, 2-24 August, Sunday and Monday lunch N 7

Rest – Menu (€ 22), € 26 (weekday lunch)/45 – Carte € 34/50

◆ Find tasty, well-prepared, creative cuisine in this bistro inspired restaurant (striped tablecloths and large mirrors). Drinks and tapas at the bar.

Beurre Noisette VISA AE

68 r. Vasco de Gama Ⓜ Lourmel – ✆ 01 48 56 82 49 – Fax 01 48 28 59 38 – Closed 1st-24 August, 1st-7 January, Sunday and Monday N 6

Rest – Menu (€ 22), € 30 (weekday lunch), € 32/40

◆ Two contemporary-style rooms decorated in warm tones serving market-inspired cuisine (dishes chalked on a blackboard). Good choice of wines by the glass.

Le Grand Pan VISA

20 r. Rosenwald Ⓜ Plaisance – ✆ 01 42 50 02 50 – Fax 01 42 50 02 66 – Closed 1 week in May, 10-30 August, Christmas holidays, Saturday and Sunday N 9

Rest – Menu (€ 20), € 28 (lunch)/32

◆ Old-fashioned Parisian bistro (copper-topped bar, wood tables and blackboards) decorated in warm shades of brown. Meat specialities (game in season) and soup starter.

Kim Anh AC VISA

51 av. Emile Zola Ⓜ Charles Michels – ✆ 01 45 79 40 96 – Closed 9-23 August and Monday L 7

Rest – *(dinner only)* Menu € 37/50 – Carte € 43/71

◆ The restaurant is protected from the avenue by a screen of bushes. Simple setting and aromatic tasty Vietnamese cuisine.

Le Troquet VISA

21 r. François Bonvin Ⓜ Cambronne – ✆ 01 45 66 89 00 – Fax 01 45 66 89 83 – Closed 1 week in May, 1st-24 August, 24 December-1st January, Sunday and Monday L 9

Rest – Menu € 30 (lunch), € 32/42

◆ An authentic Parisian bar: single set menu shown on a blackboard, retro-style dining room and tasty market based cuisine. For locals... and others!

Le Cristal de Sel VISA

13 r. Mademoiselle Ⓜ Commerce – ✆ 01 42 50 35 29 – restaurant@lecristaldesel.fr – Fax 01 42 50 35 29 – Closed August, Christmas holidays, Sunday and Monday L8

Rest – Menu (€ 20) – Carte € 39/58

◆ Appetising contemporary dishes are listed on blackboards on the walls of this bright, simple restaurant. No set menu but quality cuisine based on fresh produce.

La Villa Corse AC VISA AE

164 bd Grenelle Ⓜ La Motte Picquet Grenelle – ✆ 01 53 86 70 81 – www.lavillacorse.com – lavillacorse@wanadoo.fr – Fax 01 53 86 90 73 – Closed Sunday K 8

Rest – Menu € 25 (lunch) – Carte € 45/60

◆ Each of the three charming dining rooms in this Corsican restaurant has a different atmosphere: library, lounge-bar and terrace. Flavoursome cuisine and wines from the island.

Le Mûrier VISA

42 r. Olivier de Serres Ⓜ Convention – ✆ 01 45 32 81 88 – lepimpecmartin@yahoo.fr – Closed 9-23 August, Saturday lunch and Sunday N 8

Rest – Menu (€ 19), € 21 (lunch)/25

◆ Pleasant restaurant near the rue de la Convention shopping area, serving traditional dishes in a dining room decorated with old posters.

Le Bélisaire VISA

2 r. Marmontel Ⓜ Vaugirard – ✆ 01 48 28 62 24 – Fax 01 48 28 62 24 – Closed 1st-8 March, 2-23 August, 24 December-3 January, Saturday lunch and Sunday M 8

Rest – Menu € 22 (weekday lunch), € 32/42

◆ This well-presented bistro has built up a strong reputation in the neighbourhood thanks to its excellent contemporary-style cuisine and quality service.

Le Dirigeable VISA AE

37 r. d' Alleray Ⓜ Vaugirard – ✆ 01 45 32 01 54 – Closed 1st-24 August, 24-31 December, Sunday and Monday M 9

Rest – Menu (€ 19), € 22 (lunch) – Carte € 30/52

◆ Relaxed atmosphere, unpretentious setting and traditional dishes at attractive prices at this neighbourhood eaterie.

Jadis
208 r. de la Croix Nivert Ⓜ Convention – ✆ 01 45 57 73 20 – Fax 01 45 57 18 67 – Closed 3 week in August, Saturday and Sunday M 7
Rest – Menu €32
◆ This restaurant with a bistro feel is the image of its promising and pleasant young chef-owner. Modern menu that changes with the season.

L'Os à Moelle
3 r. Vasco-de-Gama Ⓜ Lourmel – ✆ 01 45 57 27 27 – th.faucher@laposte.net – Fax 01 45 57 28 00 – Closed 3 to 25 August, Sunday and Monday M 6
Rest – Menu (€ 21), € 28 (weekday lunch)/35
◆ Paradise for good food lovers. A small room painted in sunny colours and a menu on a blackboard. Delicious bistro-style, market-fresh cuisine.

Du Marché
59 r. Dantzig Ⓜ Porte de Versailles – ✆ 01 48 28 31 55 – Fax 01 48 28 18 31 – Closed August, Sunday and Monday P 8
Rest – Menu (€ 26), € 30
◆ The setting of this pleasant bistro near the Georges-Brassens park evokes the charm of the 1950s. Savoury dishes from the south-west served in a warmly simple atmosphere.

Le Gastroquet
10 r. Desnouettes Ⓜ Convention – ✆ 01 48 28 60 91 – Fax 01 45 33 23 70 – Closed 20 July-31 August, 23 December-3 January, Saturday in summer and Sunday N 7
Rest – Menu € 22 (weekdays)/29 – Carte € 51/61
◆ A family-run bistro, popular with local gourmets and visitors to the Porte de Versailles exhibition centre, serving carefully-prepared traditional dishes.

Gwon's Dining
51 r. Cambronne Ⓜ Cambronne – ✆ 01 47 34 53 17 – gwonsdining@gmail.com – Fax 01 47 34 09 93 – Closed Sunday and bank holidays lunch L 9
Rest – Menu (€ 19) – Carte € 34/40
◆ The tasteful contemporary décor with Asian touches here and there creates a soothing atmosphere (despite the crowds) where you can enjoy the typical Korean cuisine.

Kaiseki
– ✆ 01 45 54 48 60 – www.kaiseki.com – le_chef@kaiseki.com – Fax 01 45 54 78 38 L 5
Rest – Menu € 60 (lunch), € 80/200 – Carte € 30/150
◆ An atypical restaurant that can be a bit disconcerting due to the creative chef's surprising Japanese cuisine. Minimalist décor and shared tables. A unique experience.

Le Pételˆ
4 r. Pétel Ⓜ Vaugirard – ✆ 01 45 32 58 76 – www.lepetel.com – millemarie@noos.fr – Fax 01 45 32 58 76 – Closed 25 July-15 August, Sunday and Monday L 8
Rest – Menu (€ 19) – Carte € 32/38
◆ This friendly neighbourhood bistro is invariably packed in the evenings. Traditional market-inspired cuisine chalked up on a blackboard.

Banyan
24 pl. E. Pernet Ⓜ Félix Faure – ✆ 01 40 60 09 31 – www.lebanyan.com – lebanyan@noos.fr – Fax 01 40 60 09 20 L 7
Rest – Menu € 25 (weekday lunch), € 35/55 – Carte € 33/52
◆ Take your taste buds on holiday to this small Thai restaurant, which prepares subtly-flavoured cuisine. Pleasant modern setting and families welcome.

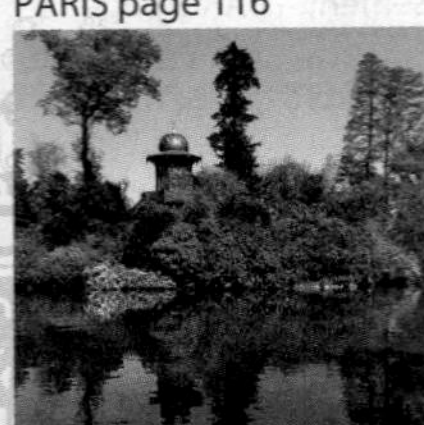
G. Targat/MICHELIN

Trocadéro • Étoile • Passy • Bois de Boulogne

16th arrondissement ✉ 75016

Raphael
17 av. Kléber ✉ 75116 Ⓜ Kléber – ✆ 01 53 64 32 00 – www.raphael-hotel.com – reservation@raphael-hotel.com – Fax 01 53 64 32 01 F 7
45 rm – †€ 345/505 ††€ 345/605, ☕ € 39 – 37 suites
Rest *La Salle à Manger* – *(closed August, Saturday and Sunday)* Carte € 50/200
Rest *Les Jardins Plein Ciel* – restaurant-terrace – *✆ 01 53 64 32 30 (open from May to September and closed Saturday lunch and Sunday)* Menu € 75 (weekdays)
◆ The Raphael, built in 1925, offers a superb wood-panelled gallery, refined rooms, a rooftop terrace with a panoramic view and a trendy English bar. Superb dining room in Grand Hotel style. A lovely view of Paris and traditional cuisine in the Jardins Plein Ciel (seventh floor).

St-James Paris
43 av. Bugeaud ✉ 75116 Ⓜ Porte Dauphine – ✆ 01 44 05 81 81 – www.saint-james-paris.com – contact@saint-james-paris.com – Fax 01 44 05 81 82 F 5
38 rm – †€ 390/660 ††€ 510/660, ☕ € 32 – 10 suites
Rest – *(closed Saturday, Sunday and public holidays)* Menu (€ 55) – Carte € 75/200
◆ Beautiful private townhouse built in 1892 by Mrs. Thiers, in the heart of a leafy garden. Majestic staircase, spacious rooms and a bar-library with the atmosphere of an English club.

Renaissance Parc-Trocadéro
55 av. R. Poincaré ✉ 75116 Ⓜ Victor Hugo – ✆ 01 44 05 66 66 – www.marriott.com – restaurant.lerelais@renaissancehotels.com – Fax 01 44 05 66 00 G 6
116 rm – †€ 229/690 ††€ 249/750, ☕ € 27 – 4 suites
Rest *Le Relais du Parc* – *✆ 01 44 05 66 10 (closed August, Christmas holidays, Saturday lunch, Sunday and Monday)* Menu € 59 (lunch)/85 – Carte € 50/90
◆ The rooms are elegant and pleasingly British in atmosphere. All are well equipped (with Wifi) and distributed around a garden terrace. Part of the bar decor is by Arman. The ground floor boasts an elegant, contemporary dining room that opens onto a delightful tree-lined courtyard-terrace. Well prepared, seasonal cuisine.

Sofitel Baltimore
88 bis av. Kléber ✉ 75116 Ⓜ Boissière – ✆ 01 44 34 54 54 – www.baltimore-sofitel-paris.com – h2789@accor.com – Fax 01 44 34 54 44 G 7
103 rm – †€ 470/890 ††€ 470/890, ☕ € 26 – 1 suite
Rest *Table du Baltimore* – see restaurant listing
◆ Simple furniture, trendy fabrics, old photos of the city of Baltimore: the contemporary decor of the rooms contrasts with the architecture of this 19C building.

Costes K. without rest
81 av. Kléber ✉ 75116 Ⓜ Trocadéro – ✆ 01 44 05 75 75 – www.hotelcostesk.com – reception@hotelcostesk.com – Fax 01 44 05 74 74 G 7
83 rm – †€ 300/350 ††€ 350/400, ☕ € 20
◆ This hotel by Ricardo Bofill is ultra-modern. It invites you to enjoy the discreet calm of its vast rooms with their pure lines, laid out around a Japanese-style patio.

Keppler without rest
10 r. Keppler ✉ 75116 Ⓜ George V – ✆ 01 47 20 65 05 – www.keppler.fr – hotel@keppler.fr – Fax 01 47 23 02 29 F 8
34 rm – †€ 325/350 ††€ 350/390, ☕ € 22 – 5 suites
◆ This luxurious, sophisticated establishment is the work of designer Pierre-Yves Rochon. A magical blend of styles, materials and light sets the tone in the lobby and rooms.

Square
3 r. Boulainvilliers ✉ 75016 Ⓜ Mirabeau – ✆ 01 44 14 91 90
– www.hotelsquare.com – reservation@hotelsquare.com
– Fax 01 44 14 91 99 K 5
20 rm – €320 €320, ☕ €25 – 2 suites
Rest *Zébra Square* – *✆ 01 44 14 91 91* – Menu €32 – Carte €45/60
◆ A jewel of contemporary architecture opposite the Maison de la Radio. Curves, colours, high-tech facilities and abstract paintings: a hymn to modern art! Trendy decor with striped theme in the restaurant and contemporary cuisine on the menu.

Trocadero Dokhan's without rest
117 r. Lauriston ✉ 75116 Ⓜ Trocadéro – ✆ 01 53 65 66 99
– www.dokhans-sofitel-paris.com – reservation@dokhans.com
– Fax 01 53 65 66 88 G 6
45 rm – €450/500 €450/500, ☕ €27 – 4 suites
◆ Attractive town house (1910) with Palladian architecture and neo-Classical interior decor. 18C celadon wood panelling in the cosy lounges and intimate champagne bar.

Sezz without rest
6 av. Frémiet ✉ 75016 Ⓜ Passy – ✆ 01 56 75 26 26 – www.hotelsezz.com
– mail@hotelsezz.com – Fax 01 56 75 26 16 J 6
22 rm – €285/340 €335/470, ☕ €25 – 5 suites
◆ Revamped hotel in a modern style: spacious, minimalist interior (shades of grey, giant vases), hi-tech gadgets and attentive staff. Steam bath and Jacuzzi.

La Villa Maillot without rest
143 av. Malakoff ✉ 75116 Ⓜ Porte Maillot – ✆ 01 53 64 52 52
– www.lavillamaillot.fr – resa@lavillamaillot.fr – Fax 01 45 00 60 61 F 6
39 rm – €230/415 €230/415, ☕ €28 – 3 suites
◆ A step away from Porte Maillot. Soft colours, a high level of comfort and good soundproofing in the rooms. Glassed-in space for breakfasts, opening onto the greenery.

Pergolèse without rest
3 r. Pergolèse ✉ 75116 Ⓜ Argentine – ✆ 01 53 64 04 04
– www.hotelpergolese.com – hotel@pergolese.com
– Fax 01 53 64 04 40 E 6
40 rm – €230 €260/390, ☕ €18
◆ Restrained 16th arrondissement chic on the outside hides a successful designer interior combining mahogany, glass bricks, chrome and bright colours. Breakfast facing a pleasant patio.

Élysées Régencia without rest
41 av. Marceau ✉ 75116 Ⓜ George V – ✆ 01 47 20 42 65 – www.regencia.com
– info@regencia.com – Fax 01 49 52 03 42 G 8
43 rm – €195/275 €215/295, ☕ €19
◆ Tastefully renovated in a designer style, this hotel offers modern, stylish rooms (blue, fuchsia or aniseed), an elegant sitting room, and a bar/library (red and chocolate coloured wainscoting).

Waldorf Trocadero without rest
97 r. Lauriston ✉ 75116 Ⓜ Boissière – ✆ 01 45 53 83 30
– www.hotelwaldorftrocadero.com – trocadero@hotelswaldorfparis.com
– Fax 01 47 55 92 52 G 7
44 rm – €300/350 €320/440, ☕ €20
◆ This former townhouse between the Arc de Triomphe and Trocadéro offers new facilities and a pretty modern decor. Rooms of various sizes.

Alexander without rest
102 av. V. Hugo ✉ 75116 Ⓜ Victor Hugo – ✆ 01 56 90 61 00
– www.solmelia.com – melia.alexander@solmelia.com
– Fax 01 56 90 61 01 G 6
61 rm – €179/399 €179/399, ☕ €28
◆ An elegant building on a chic avenue. The rooms are well proportioned, comfortable and recently refurbished; those to the rear are quieter.

Garden Élysée without rest

12 r. St-Didier ✉ 75116 Ⓜ Boissière – ✆ 01 47 55 01 11 – www.paris-hotel-gardenelysee.com – garden.elysee@wanadoo.fr – Fax 01 47 27 79 24 G 7

46 rm – 🛉€ 190/495 🛉🛉€ 200/620, ☕ € 22

◆ Set back from the street, in the calm of a green inner courtyard where breakfast is served in summer, up-to-date rooms and a pretty lounge lined with carved wood panels.

Bassano without rest

15 r. Bassano ✉ 75116 Ⓜ George V – ✆ 01 47 23 78 23 – www.hotel-bassano.com – info@hotel-bassano.com – Fax 01 47 20 41 22 G 8

33 rm – 🛉€ 195/275 🛉🛉€ 215/295, ☕ € 19 – 1 suite

◆ Cosy atmosphere, wrought-iron furniture, sunny fabrics -it feels like being at a friend's home in Provence, but is only a few hundred metres from the Champs-Elysées.

Kléber without rest

7 r. Belloy ✉ 75116 Ⓜ Boissière – ✆ 01 47 23 80 22 – www.kleberhotel.com – kleberhotel@wanadoo.fr – Fax 01 49 52 07 20 G 7

23 rm – 🛉€ 99/299 🛉🛉€ 99/299, ☕ € 14 – 1 suite

◆ The sitting rooms of this 1853 hotel have Louis XV style furniture, original frescoes and old paintings. Exposed stonework and parquet floors in the guestrooms.

Montfleuri without rest

21 av. Grande Armée ✉ 75116 Ⓜ Charles de Gaulle-Etoile – ✆ 01 45 00 33 65 – www.montfleuri.fr – montfleuri@wanadoo – Fax 01 45 00 06 36 F7

42 rm – 🛉€ 230/250 🛉🛉€ 270/290, ☕ € 14 – 3 suites

◆ Two steps from the Arc de Triomphe, this hotel has been entirely redecorated in a modern style. Peaceful, refined rooms in muted tones, elegantly furnished and adorned with fine fabrics.

Étoile Résidence Impériale without rest

155 av. de Malakoff ✉ 75116 Ⓜ Porte Maillot – ✆ 01 45 00 23 45 – www.residenceimperiale.com – reservation@residenceimperiale.com – Fax 01 45 01 88 82 E 6

37 rm – 🛉€ 100/260 🛉🛉€ 100/260, ☕ € 14

◆ Well-soundproofed hotel, with theme rooms (Africa, Asia, etc.). Some have retained their exposed beams, while others open onto the patio.

Passy Eiffel without rest

10 r. de Passy ✉ 75016 Ⓜ Passy – ✆ 01 45 25 55 66 – www.passyeiffel.com – contact@passyeiffel.com – Fax 01 42 88 89 88 J 6

49 rm – 🛉€ 96/160 🛉🛉€ 110/185, ☕ € 13

◆ In a busy street, a family hotel with practical, well-kept rooms that overlook either the street (some enjoy a view of the Eiffel Tower) or a pretty flower-decked patio.

Chambellan Morgane without rest

6 r. Keppler ✉ 75116 Ⓜ George V – ✆ 01 47 20 35 72 – www.hotel-paris-morgane.com – chambellan-morgane@wanadoo.fr – Fax 01 47 20 95 69 GF 8

20 rm – 🛉€ 110/165 🛉🛉€ 130/185, ☕ € 14

◆ Small hotel with character whose rooms sport Provençal colours and brand new bathrooms. Prettily spruced up Louis XVI lobby and sitting room.

Victor Hugo without rest

19 r. Copernic ✉ 75116 Ⓜ Victor Hugo – ✆ 01 45 53 76 01 – www.victorhugohotel.com – paris@victorhugohotel.com – Fax 01 45 53 69 93 G 7

75 rm – 🛉€ 159/255 🛉🛉€ 178/395, ☕ € 18

◆ This hotel in a quiet district across from the Passy reservoirs has rooms with traditional furniture and, on the top floor, balconies offering unobstructed views.

Floride Étoile without rest

14 r. St-Didier ✉ 75116 Ⓜ Boissière – ✆ 01 47 27 23 36 – www.floride-paris-hotel.com – floride.etoile@wanadoo.fr – Fax 01 47 27 82 87 G 7

63 rm – 🛉€ 125/240 🛉🛉€ 145/240, ☕ € 16

◆ A stone's throw from Trocadéro. The renovated rooms are comfortable; those on the courtyard side are smaller but more tranquil. Stylishly furnished lounge decorated with flowers.

Résidence Foch without rest
10 r. Marbeau ✉ 75116 Ⓜ Porte Maillot – ✆ 01 45 00 46 50 – www.residencefoch.com – residence@foch.com – Fax 01 45 01 98 68 F 6
25 rm – †€ 140/200 ††€ 140/200, ☕ € 13
◆ This small family type hotel is not far from the aristocratic Avenue Foch. There is a pleasant breakfast room and practical, nicely decorated bedrooms.

Windsor Home without rest
3 r. Vital ✉ 75016 Ⓜ La Muette – ✆ 01 45 04 49 49 – www.windsorhomeparis.fr – whparis@wanadoo.fr – Fax 01 45 04 59 50 H 6
8 rm – †€ 130/170 ††€ 140/180, ☕ € 11
◆ This charming, hundred-year-old residence with a garden in front is decorated like a private house: antique furniture, mouldings, light colours and contemporary touches.

Du Bois without rest
11 r. du Dôme ✉ 75116 Ⓜ Kléber – ✆ 01 45 00 31 96 – www.hoteldubois.com – reservations@hoteldubois.com – Fax 01 45 00 90 05 F 7
39 rm – †€ 117/325 ††€ 117/325, ☕ € 15
◆ This hotel stands in the street, where Baudelaire passed away. Entirely refurbished, it is a happy marriage of Parisian charm and tasteful contemporary decor.

Gavarni without rest
5 r. Gavarni ✉ 75116 Ⓜ Passy – ✆ 01 45 24 52 82 – www.gavarni.com – reservation@gavarni.com – Fax 01 40 50 16 95 J 6
25 rm – †€ 110/180 ††€ 160/200, ☕ € 15
◆ This red-brick building offers rooms that are small but delightfully snug and well equipped; those on the two top floors are the cosiest.

Queen's without rest
4 r. Bastien Lepage ✉ 75016 Ⓜ Michel Ange Auteuil – ✆ 01 42 88 89 85 – www.hotel-queens-hotel.com – info@hotel-queens-hotel.com – Fax 01 40 50 67 52 K 4
22 rm – †€ 90/102 ††€ 130/145, ☕ € 9
◆ Modern paintings brighten the attractive hall and most of the rooms, which are small but smartly designed.

Nicolo without rest
3 r. Nicolo ✉ 75116 Ⓜ Passy – ✆ 01 42 88 83 40 – www.hotel-nicolo.fr – hotel.nicolo@wanadoo.fr – Fax 01 42 24 45 41 J 6
28 rm ☕ – †€ 130/146 ††€ 140/175
◆ One reaches this venerable establishment by a peaceful back courtyard. Indonesian or antique furniture and Asian trinkets adorn the rooms, most of which have been renovated.

Marceau Champs Élysées without rest
37 av. Marceau ✉ 75016 Ⓜ George V – ✆ 01 47 20 43 37 – www.hotelmarceau.com – info@hotelmarceau.com – Fax 01 47 20 14 76 G 8
30 rm – †€ 138/198 ††€ 148/208, ☕ € 12
◆ Refurbished rooms with marble bathrooms await behind this classic façade on a busy avenue. Lounge-breakfast room on the 1st floor.

Boileau without rest
81 r. Boileau ✉ 75016 Ⓜ Exelmans – ✆ 01 42 88 83 74 – www.hotel-boileau.com – info@hotel-boileau.com – Fax 01 45 27 62 98 M 3
31 rm – †€ 55/77 ††€ 65/105, ☕ € 9
◆ Brittany and Maghreb figure among the canvasses and antique trinkets; tiny flower-decked patio and rustic furnishings. A welcoming hotel with discreetly personalised rooms.

Le Hameau de Passy without rest
48 r. Passy ✉ 75016 Ⓜ La Muette – ✆ 01 42 88 47 55 – www.hameaudepassy.com – hameau.passy@wanadoo.fr – Fax 01 42 30 83 72 J 5-6
32 rm ☕ – †€ 132 ††€ 146
◆ An impasse leads to this discreet hamlet with its charming inner courtyard overrun with greenery. Quiet nights ensured in the small rooms which are nevertheless up-to-date and well-maintained.

Au Palais de Chaillot without rest
35 av. R. Poincaré ✉ 75116 Ⓜ Trocadéro – ☎ 01 53 70 09 09 – www.hotel-palaisdechaillot.com – palaisdechaillot-hotel@magic.fr – Fax 01 53 70 09 08 G 6
28 rm – †€ 119 ††€ 134, ☕ € 9
◆ Beautiful location near Trocadéro for this family-run hotel. Small, functional rooms (quieter at the back). Friendly welcome.

XXXX **Hiramatsu**
52 r. Longchamp ✉ 75116 Ⓜ Trocadéro – ☎ 01 56 81 08 80 – www.hiratamatsu.co.jp – paris@hiramatsu.co.jp – Fax 01 56 81 08 81 – Closed 1st-30 August, 1st-8 January, Saturday and Sunday G 7
Rest – *(number of covers limited, pre-book)* Menu € 48 (lunch), € 95/130 – Carte € 104/125
Spec. Gourmandise de homard et pigeon fumé. Fines lamelles d'agneau, compotée d'oignons blancs et jus de truffe au thym. Gâteau au chocolat "Hiramatsu".
◆ Despite the Japanese name, Hiramatsu honours French cuisine with inventiveness and talent. High-class gastronomy in an extremely elegant setting decorated with flowers. Magnificent wine list.

XXX **Astrance** (Pascal Barbot)
4 r. Beethoven ✉ 75016 Ⓜ Passy – ☎ 01 40 50 84 40 – Closed 1-3 March, 1-5 May, 30 May-3 June, 11-15 July, August, 1st-8 November, Christmas holidays, Saturday, Sunday and Monday J 7
Rest – *(number of covers limited, pre-book)* Menu € 70 (lunch), € 120/290 bi
Spec. Agrumes, herbes sauvages, fleurs et coquillages. Langoustines, girolles, concombre et pistache. Chocolat blanc et framboise.
◆ In an intimate decor, sample the inventive cuisine of a chef at the height of his art in the 'surprise menu'. Equally outstanding wine and service. An unforgettable culinary experience.

XXX **Relais d'Auteuil** (Patrick Pignol)
31 bd. Murat ✉ 75016 Ⓜ Michel Ange Molitor – ☎ 01 46 51 09 54 – pignol-p@wanadoo.fr – Fax 01 40 71 05 03 – Closed August, Christmas holidays, Monday lunchtime, Saturday lunchtime and Sunday L 3
Rest – Menu € 60 (lunch), € 110/149 – Carte € 120/185
Spec. Ravioles de Saint-Jacques à la truffe (season). Ris de veau rissolé au beurre de cardamome. Madeleines cuites minute, glace miel et noix.
◆ Intimate setting in neutral tones enhancing modern paintings and sculptures. Carefully-prepared classic cuisine and an excellent wine list (magnificent selection of Burgundy wines).

XXX **La Table de Joël Robuchon**
16 av. Bugeaud ✉ 75116 Ⓜ Victor Hugo – ☎ 01 56 28 16 16 – latabledejoelrobuchon@wanadoo.fr – Fax 01 56 28 16 78 F 6
Rest – Menu € 55 bi (lunch)/150 – Carte € 60/155
Spec. Langoustine en papillotes croustillantes au basilic. Caille au foie gras et caramélisée avec une pomme-purée truffée. "Chocolat tendance" crème onctueuse au chocolat araguani, glace chocolat au biscuit Oréo.
◆ In this elegant setting you are sure to enjoy your meal: sample tapas style snacks and classic dishes subtly updated by Joël Robuchon.

XXX **Le Pergolèse** (Stéphane Gaborieau)
40 r. Pergolèse ✉ 75116 Ⓜ Porte Maillot – ☎ 01 45 00 21 40 – www.lepergolese.com – le-pergolese@wanadoo.fr – Fax 01 45 00 81 31 – Closed 3 weeks in August, Saturday and Sunday F 6
Rest – Menu € 42 bi/95 – Carte € 75/110
Spec. Ravioli de langoustines, duxelles de champignons, émulsion de crustacés au foie gras. Aiguillette de Saint-Pierre meunière, cannelloni farcis aux multi saveurs. Feuilles d'ananas en raviole, fruits exotiques et sorbet fromage blanc.
◆ Yellow wall hangings, light wood panelling and surprising sculptures reflect in the mirrors, forming an elegant decor a step away from select Avenue Foch. Impeccable classic cuisine.

XXX ✿ **La Table du Baltimore** – Hôtel Sofitel Baltimore
1 r. Léo Delibes ✉ 75016 Ⓜ Boissière – ✆ 01 44 34 54 34 – www.hotel-baltimore-paris.com – h2789-fb@accor.com – Fax 01 44 34 54 44 – Closed August, Saturday and Sunday G 7
Rest – Menu € 48 bi (lunch)/75 – Carte € 62/85
Spec. Le tourteau. La volaille. Le chocolat.
◆ Period wood panelling, modern furnishings, warm colours and a collection of drawings characterise this restaurant. Gourmet up-to-date cuisine.

XXX **Prunier**
16 av. Victor-Hugo Ⓜ Charles de Gaulle-Etoile – ✆ 01 44 17 35 85 – www.caviarhouse-prunier.com – maison-prunier3@wanadoo.fr – Fax 01 44 17 90 10 – Closed August, Sunday and bank holidays F 7
Rest – Menu € 59 (lunch)/175 – Carte € 69/159
◆ Superb listed Art Deco interior (black marble, mosaics, stained glass) at this institution, created in 1925 by the architect Boileau. Excellent fish and seafood (caviar, salmon etc).

XXX **Les Arts**
9 bis av. d'Iéna ✉ 75116 Ⓜ Iéna – ✆ 01 40 69 27 53 – www.sodexho-prestige.fr – restaurant.am@sodexho-prestige.fr – Fax 01 40 69 27 08 – Closed 24 July-24 August, 24 December-2 January, Saturday and Sunday G 7
Rest – Menu € 41 – Carte € 65/85
◆ Hotel in a townhouse built in 1892, "gadzarts" (ENSAM graduates) house since 1925. The dining room (colonnades, mouldings, paintings) and garden-terrace are now open to the public.

XXX ✿ **Passiflore** (Roland Durand)
33 r. Longchamp ✉ 75116 Ⓜ Trocadéro – ✆ 01 47 04 96 81 – www.restaurantpassiflore.com – passiflore@club-internet.fr – Fax 01 47 04 32 27 – Closed 20 July-20 August, Monday lunch, Saturday lunch and Sunday G 7
Rest – Menu € 42 (lunch), € 49/65 – Carte € 50/60
Spec. Gratin de macaroni au foie gras. Tournedos de pied de cochon. Fraîcheur d'aloe vera à l'orange.
◆ An unassumingly elegant decor of ethnic inspiration (yellow tones and wood panelling) and a classic, personalised cuisine combine to rejoice the taste buds of Parisian society.

XX **Cristal Room Baccarat**
11 pl. des Etats-Unis ✉ 75116 Ⓜ Boissière – ✆ 01 40 22 11 10 – cristalroom@baccarat.fr – Fax 01 40 22 11 99 – Closed Sun G 7
Rest – Menu (€ 59), € 99 bi/200 bi – Carte € 80/120
◆ This mansion was used by M-L de Noailles and now belongs to Baccarat. It offers a Starck decor and modern dishes at V.I.P. prices. Beauty can be far from reasonable!

XX **Tsé Yang**
25 av. Pierre 1er de Serbie ✉ 75116 Ⓜ Iéna – ✆ 01 47 20 70 22 – www.tseyang.fr – Fax 01 47 20 75 34 G 8
Rest – Menu € 49/59 – Carte € 45/90
◆ Two interior designers have revamped this chic temple of traditional Chinese cuisine. Black dominates the decor with gold coffered ceiling, attractive settings, etc.

XX **Pavillon Noura**
21 av. Marceau ✉ 75116 Ⓜ Alma Marceau – ✆ 01 47 20 33 33 – noura@noura.fr – Fax 01 47 20 60 31 G 8
Rest – Menu € 36, € 56/64 – Carte € 40/55
◆ Elegant room whose walls are adorned with Levantine frescoes. Lebanese influence in evidence, with traditional selection of little hot and cold dishes and glasses of arack.

XX **La Table de Babette**
32 r. Longchamp ✉ 75016 Ⓜ Trocadéro – ✆ 01 45 53 00 07 – www.tabledebabette.com – tabledebabette@wanadoo.fr – Fax 01 45 53 00 15 – Closed Saturday lunch, Sunday and holidays lunch G 7
Rest – Menu € 22 (lunch) – Carte € 30/60
◆ Babette invites guests to sample her skilful interpretation of French West Indies cuisine. Cosy dining room with musical ambiance at the weekend.

XX **Conti** AC VISA MC AE

72 r. Lauriston ✉ 75116 Ⓜ Boissière – ✆ 01 47 27 74 67 – Fax 01 47 27 37 66 – Closed 3-23 August, 25 December-1 January, Saturday, Sunday and bank holidays

Rest – Menu € 34 – Carte € 47/75 G 7

◆ Red and black predominate in this restaurant's decor, where mirrors and crystal chandeliers glitter. Italian cuisine; wonderful wine list.

XX **6 New-York** AC VISA MC AE

6 av. New-York ✉ 75016 Ⓜ Alma Marceau – ✆ 01 40 70 03 30 – www.6newyork.fr – 6newyork@wanadoo.fr – Fax 01 40 70 04 77 – Closed August, Saturday lunch and Sunday H 8

Rest – Menu € 30 (lunch) – Carte € 42/64

◆ The sign gives you a clue to the address but does not tell you that this stylish bistro prepares dishes perfectly suited to its modern and refined setting.

XX **etc...** AC VISA MC AE

2 r. La Pérouse ✉ 75016 Ⓜ Kléber – ✆ 01 49 52 10 10 – etc@groupeepicure.com – Fax 01 49 52 10 11 – Closed Saturday lunch and Sunday G 7

Rest – Menu € 68 bi (lunch) – Carte approx. € 85

Spec. Fraîcheur de tourteau. Noix d'entrecôte de boeuf Hereford, laquée de soja-ciboulette. Caramel au goût de carambar glacé.

◆ Stylish new address in monochrome tones from chef Christian Le Squer (Ledoyen). Top-notch modern cooking with a seasonal slant.

XX **Giulio Rebellato** AC VISA MC AE

136 r. Pompe ✉ 75116 Ⓜ Victor Hugo – ✆ 01 47 27 50 26 – jrebellato@hotmail.com – Closed 3 weeks in August G 6

Rest – Menu € 33 (weekday lunch) – Carte € 50/80

◆ The warm, Venetian-inspired decor by Garcia includes fine fabrics, old prints and glittering mirrors. Northern Italian cuisine.

XX **Tang** AC VISA MC

125 r. de la Tour ✉ 75116 Ⓜ Rue de la Pompe – ✆ 01 45 04 35 35 – www.restaurant-tang.fr – charlytang16@yahoo.fr – Fax 01 45 04 58 19 – Closed 1-24 August, Monday lunch and Sunday H 5

Rest – Menu (€ 39 bi) – Carte € 70/139

◆ A high-ceiling dining room lit by large bay windows and a classic decor with Asian touches. Chinese and Thai specialties.

XX **Chez Géraud** VISA MC

31 r. Vital ✉ 75016 Ⓜ La Muette – ✆ 01 45 20 33 00 – Fax 01 45 20 46 60 – Closed August, 23 December-5 January, Saturday and Sunday H 5

Rest – Menu € 32 – Carte € 48/75

◆ The façade and the inside mural, both in Longwy earthenware tiles, are most eye-catching. Stylish bistro setting for traditional cuisine that highlights game in season.

XX **Bistro de la Muette** AC VISA MC AE

10 chaussée de la Muette ✉ 75016 Ⓜ La Muette – ✆ 01 45 03 14 84 – www.bistrocie.fr – bistro@bistrocie.fr – Fax 01 42 88 31 63 J 5

Rest – Menu (€ 27), € 38 bi

◆ The very attractive, all-inclusive formula of this elegant bistro explains part of its appeal in the neighbourhood. Warm, modern decor in brown colours. Veranda.

XX **Ozu** AC VISA MC AE

5 av. Albert de Mun ✉ 75116 Ⓜ Iéna – ✆ 01 40 69 23 90 – www.ozurestaurants.com – info@cineaqua.fr – Fax 01 40 69 23 01

Rest – Menu (€ 28), € 45 bi (lunch), € 65/85 – Carte € 46/63 H 7

◆ Unusual setting in the CinéAqua complex of the Trocadéro with samurai costumes, flat screens, a huge aquarium, and a sushi and sashimi counter. Creative Japanese inspired menu.

XX **Marius** VISA MC AE

82 bd Murat ✉ 75016 Ⓜ Porte de St-Cloud – ✆ 01 46 51 67 80 – restaurant.marius@orange.fr – Fax 01 40 71 83 75 – Closed August, Saturday lunch and Sunday

Rest – Carte € 45/70 M 2

◆ Yellow velvet chairs, light walls, fabric blinds and large mirrors are the main decorative features in the dining room-veranda of this seafood restaurant. Select wine list.

XX **Le Vinci** A/C VISA MC AE

23 r. P. Valéry ✉ 75116 Ⓜ Victor Hugo – ✆ 01 45 01 68 18 – levinci@wanadoo.fr – Fax 01 45 01 60 37 – Closed 2-24 August, Saturday and Sunday F 7

Rest – Carte € 45/75

◆ Tasty Italian cuisine, pleasant colourful interior and friendly service (a highly-prized establishment a step away from the chic shopping in Avenue Victor-Hugo.

XX **A et M Restaurant** A/C VISA MC AE

136 bd Murat ✉ 75016 Ⓜ Porte de St-Cloud – ✆ 01 45 27 39 60 – am-bistrot-16@wanadoo.fr – Fax 01 45 27 69 71 – Closed August, Saturday lunch and Sunday M 3

Rest – Menu (€ 23), € 30

◆ Fashionable bistro close to the Seine. Tasteful contemporary décor in shades of cream and browns, designer lighting and carefully prepared up-to-date cuisine.

XX **L'Acajou** A/C VISA MC AE

35bis r. Jean-de-la-Fontaine ✉ 75016 Ⓜ Jasmin – ✆ 01 42 88 04 47 – www.l-acajou.com – jeanimbert.acajou@hotmail.fr – Fax 01 42 88 95 12 – Closed August, Saturday lunch and Sunday K 5

Rest – Menu (€ 28), € 35/40 bi – Carte € 50/70

◆ Up-to-date, well-presented food, modern decor with old wood panelling and pleasant service at this family-run establishment.

X **La Villa Corse** A/C VISA MC AE

141 av. Malakoff Ⓜ Porte Maillot – ✆ 01 40 67 18 44 – www.lavillacorse.com – lavillacorserivedroite@wanadoo.fr – Fax 01 40 67 18 19 – Closed Sunday E 6

Rest – Menu € 25 bi (lunch)/35 bi – Carte € 50/65

◆ The right bank sibling of the "Villa" in the 15th arrondissement. Corsican cuisine served in a large dining room and mezzanine with a relaxed, trendy ambience.

X **La Marée Passy** A/C VISA MC AE

71 av P. Doumer ✉ 75016 Ⓜ La Muette – ✆ 01 45 04 12 81 – paudou@orange.fr – Fax 01 45 04 00 50 H 5

Rest – Carte € 45/60

◆ The warm, red toned, wood-panelled dining room decorated with navigation tools is the perfect setting for the seafood-based menu (one daily special meat dish).

X **Le Petit Pergolèse** A/C VISA MC

38 r. Pergolèse ✉ 75016 Ⓜ Porte Maillot – ✆ 01 45 00 23 66 – Fax 01 45 00 44 03 – Closed August, Saturday and Sunday F 6

Rest – Carte € 50/70

◆ Tightly-packed tables in this chic bistro in the 16th arrondissement. Contemporary decor, open kitchens and modern culinary repertoire.

X **Essaouira** VISA MC

135 r. Ranelagh ✉ 75016 Ⓜ Ranelagh – ✆ 01 45 27 99 93 – Fax 01 45 27 56 36 – Closed August, Monday lunch and Sunday J 4

Rest – Menu (€ 16) – Carte € 35/55

◆ The former Mogador lent its name to this Moroccan restaurant decorated with a mosaic fountain, carpets and craftwork. Couscous, tajine and méchoui, just like back home!

X **La Table Lauriston** A/C VISA MC AE

129 r. Lauriston ✉ 75016 Ⓜ Trocadéro – ✆ 01 47 27 00 07 – Fax 01 47 27 00 07 – Closed 1-24 August, Saturday lunch and Sunday G 6

Rest – Menu € 25 (lunch) – Carte € 45/70

◆ This restaurant in a fashionable district of Paris focuses on simplicity and quality; lovely traditional food to be enjoyed in a modern bistro-style decor.

X **Chaumette** VISA MC AE

7 r. Gros ✉ 75016 Ⓜ Mirabeau – ✆ 01 42 88 29 27 – Fax 01 42 88 26 89 – Closed 8-24 August, 23 December-3 January, Saturday lunch and Sunday K 5

Rest – Menu (€ 21), € 25 (lunch) – Carte € 37/55

◆ The epitome of an old-fashioned bistro. It has dark woodwork, well-laid tables, an authentic bar and a traditional menu popular with the well-heeled clientèle.

Rosimar

26 r. Poussin ✉ 75016 Ⓜ Michel Ange Auteuil – ✆ 01 45 27 74 91 – Fax 01 45 20 75 05 – Closed August, 24-31 December, Saturday, Sunday, bank holidays and dinner except Friday K 3

Rest – Menu € 40 bi – Carte € 42/67

◆ This enlarged dining room contains all the savours of traditional Spain. "Hombre"! A nice little family affair!

Tokyo Eat

13 av. du Président Wilson ✉ 75016 Ⓜ Iéna – ✆ 01 47 20 00 29 – tokyoeat@palaisdetokyo.com – Fax 01 47 20 05 62 – Closed Monday G 8

Rest – Menu (€ 20) – Carte € 35/65

◆ The temple of contemporary art - Palais de Tokyo - offers an interesting, industrial inspired stage of untreated concrete, a live DJ, unusual lighting, fusion cuisine and Sunday brunch.

Tampopo

66 r. Lauriston ✉ 75116 Ⓜ Boissière – ✆ 01 47 27 74 52 – contact@restaurant-tampopo.fr – Fax 01 47 55 17 84 – Closed August, Saturday lunch and Sunday G 7

Rest – *(number of covers limited, pre-book)* Menu (€ 18) – Carte € 35/50

◆ Simple, traditional, family setting at Tampopo (Japanese for 'dandelion'). Sushi, sashimi, grills and tempura on the menu at this small Japanese restaurant.

Oscar

6 r. Chaillot Ⓜ Iéna – ✆ 01 47 20 26 92 – fredmartinod@orange.fr – Fax 01 47 20 27 93 – Closed 5-20 August, Saturday lunch and Sunday G 8

Rest – Menu (€ 23) – Carte € 35/45

◆ This bistro, with a discreet façade, tightly packed tables and a blackboard with daily specials, does not need to advertise to attract a clientele from well beyond the area.

in the Bois de Boulogne – ✉ 75016

Le Pré Catelan

rte Suresnes ✉ 75016 – ✆ 01 44 14 41 14 – www.lenotre.fr – leprecatelan-restaurant@lenotre.fr – Fax 01 45 24 43 25 – Closed 2-24 August, 25 October-2 November, 21 February-8 March, Sunday and Monday H 2

Rest – Menu € 85 (weekday lunch), € 180/240 – Carte € 195/250

Spec. Homard breton rôti, pois gourmands au parfum d'ail, câpres et champignons. Bar poêlé recouvert de sésame doré acidulé et caviar d'Aquitaine. Pomme soufflée croustillante et crème glacée au carambar.

◆ Based on classic recipes that pay homage to the produce, Frédéric Anton's inventive cuisine is perfectly accomplished. Elegant Napoleon III pavilion with décor by Pierre-Yves Rochon.

La Grande Cascade

allée de Longchamp ✉ 75016 – ✆ 01 45 27 33 51 – www.grandecascade.com – grandecascade@wanadoo.fr – Fax 01 42 88 99 06 A 2

Rest – Menu € 79/185 – Carte € 131/200

Spec. Fleurs de courgette ivres de girolles. Bar de ligne nacré aux algues et beurre demi-sel. Chaud-froid d'un chocolat pure origine "Praïa".

◆ A Parisian paradise at the foot of the Grande Cascade (10m!) in the Bois de Boulogne. Delicately distinctive cuisine served in the 1850 pavilion or on the splendid terrace.

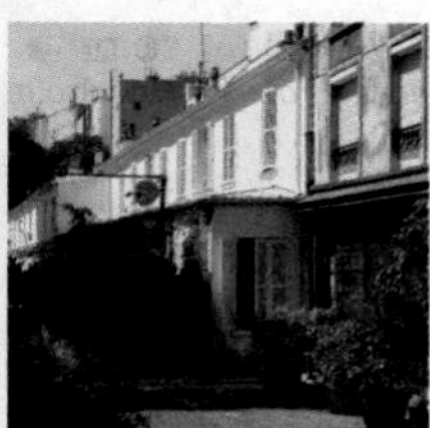
S. Sauvignier/MICHELIN

Palais des Congrès • Wagram • Ternes • Batignolles

17th arrondissement

✉ 75017

Le Méridien Étoile

rm, VISA

81 bd Gouvion St-Cyr Ⓜ *Neuilly-Porte Maillot – ✆ 01 40 68 34 34 – www.lemeriden.com/etoile – guest.etoile@lemeridien.com – Fax 01 40 68 31 31*

1025 rm – €175/475 €175/475, €25 – 21 suites E 6

Rest *L'Oneroc* – *✆ 01 40 68 30 40 (closed from end July to end August, 20-28 December, Saturday and Sunday)* Menu (€35), €44 (weekdays)/75 – Carte €52/90

Rest *La Terrasse du Jazz* – *✆ 01 40 68 30 42* – Carte €25/49

◆ Facilities at this huge hotel include a jazz club, bar, boutiques and an impressive conference centre. Black granite and shades of beige predominate in the contemporary-style guestrooms. The Orenoc reflects current tastes in food, and has warm, colonial-style decor. An updated menu and live music with the Sunday brunch at the Jazz Club Lounge.

Concorde Lafayette

VISA

3 pl. Gén. Koenig Ⓜ *Porte Maillot – ✆ 01 40 68 50 68 – www.concorde-lafayette.com – booking@concorde-hotels.com – Fax 01 40 68 50 43* E 6

931 rm – €150/600 €150/600, €28 – 21 suites

Rest – *✆ 01 40 68 51 19* – Menu (€35), €45 (lunch) – Carte €46/69

◆ This 33-floor tower, part of the city's convention centre, offers wonderful views of Paris from most of its spacious and comfortable rooms, as well as from the panoramic bar. Eat as much as you like at the buffet of the La Fayette restaurant.

Splendid Étoile

rm, VISA

1bis av. Carnot Ⓜ *Charles de Gaulle-Etoile – ✆ 01 45 72 72 00 – www.hsplendid.com – sales@groupefrontenac.com – Fax 01 45 72 72 01*

54 rm – €310/400 €310/400, €25 – 3 suites F 7

Rest *Le Pré Carré* – *✆ 01 46 22 57 35 (Closed 8-23 August, Saturday lunch and Sunday)* Menu €34 (dinner) – Carte €37/65

◆ Beautiful classical façade with wrought-iron balconies. Spacious rooms full of character, embellished with Louis XV furnishings; some look out onto the Arc de Triomphe. Two mirrors reflect the infinite elegance of this restaurant's decor, featuring dark wood panelling and subdued orchid lights.

Ampère

rm, VISA

102 av. Villiers Ⓜ *Pereire – ✆ 01 44 29 17 17 – www.hotelampere.com – resa@hotelampere.com – Fax 01 44 29 16 50* D 8

96 rm – €260/400 €260/400, €17

Rest *Le Jardin d'Ampère* – *✆ 01 44 29 16 54 (closed August and Sunday dinner)* Menu (€38) – Carte €58/77

◆ The main features of this 4-star hotel are the elegant piano bar opening onto a verdant terrace, wi-fi Internet access and comfortable contemporary rooms (some overlooking the interior courtyard). Elegant decor and pleasant terrace at the Jardin d'Ampère. Dinner concerts in fine weather.

Balmoral without rest

VISA

6 r. Gén. Lanrezac Ⓜ *Charles de Gaulle-Etoile – ✆ 01 43 80 30 50 – www.hotel-balmoral.com – hotel@hotelbalmoral.fr – Fax 01 43 80 51 56* E 7

57 rm – €135/145 €150/185, €10

◆ A personalised welcome and calm atmosphere characterise this old hotel (1911) a stone's throw from the Étoile. Brightly coloured bedrooms, and elegant wood panelling in the lounge.

Regent's Garden without rest
6 r. P. Demours Ⓜ *Ternes – ✆ 01 45 74 07 30 – hotel.regents.garden@wanadoo.fr – Fax 01 40 55 01 42* E 7
39 rm – †€ 290/440 ††€ 290/440, ☕ € 19
◆ Townhouse commissioned by Napoleon III for his doctor, now fully refurbished in a boutique hotel style. Fashionable bedrooms, Japanese garden, and Ecolabel certified.

Novotel Porte d'Asnières
34 av. Porte d'Asnières Ⓜ *Pereire – ✆ 01 44 40 52 52 – www.novotel.com – h4987@accor.com – Fax 01 44 40 44 23* C 9
139 rm – †€ 99/235 ††€ 99/235, ☕ € 16 **Rest** – Menu (€ 22), € 28
◆ Modern architecture near the ring road but very well soundproofed. The rooms from the seventh floor upwards command a fine view of Paris' rooftops. A contemporary decor in this restaurant serving brasserie-style meals.

Banville without rest
166 bd Berthier Ⓜ *Porte de Champerret – ✆ 01 42 67 70 16 – www.hotelbanville.fr – info@hotelbanville.fr – Fax 01 44 40 42 77* D 8
38 rm – †€ 215/310 ††€ 215/310, ☕ € 20
◆ Tastefully restored building from 1926. Elegant lobby and lounges and particularly refined rooms with personal (Provencal) touches. Live jazz on Tuesday evenings in the piano bar.

Waldorf Arc de Triomphe without rest
36 r. Pierre Demours Ⓜ *Ternes – ✆ 01 47 64 67 67 – www.hotelswaldorfparis.com – arc@hotelswaldorfparis.com – Fax 01 40 53 91 34* D 8
44 rm – †€ 320/460 ††€ 340/460, ☕ € 20
◆ Attractively refurbished, elegant contemporary rooms. Good fitness centre, a small pool, sauna and steam bath: ideal after a hard day's work or sightseeing!

Villa Alessandra without rest
9 pl. Boulnois Ⓜ *Ternes – ✆ 01 56 33 24 24 – www.villa-alessandra.com – alessandra@leshotelsdeparis.com – Fax 01 56 33 24 30* E 8
49 rm – †€ 310 ††€ 320, ☕ € 18
◆ This Ternes quarter hotel is on a delightful quiet little square and is appreciated for its calm. Colours of southern France in the rooms, with wrought-iron beds and painted wood furniture.

Amarante Arc de Triomphe without rest
25 r. Th.-de-Banville Ⓜ *Pereire – ✆ 01 47 63 76 69 – www.jjwhotels.com – amarante-arcdetriomphe@jjwhotels.com – Fax 01 43 80 63 96* D 8
50 rm – †€ 140/250 ††€ 140/250, ☕ € 22
◆ This hotel has Directoire-style rooms which are popular with its business clientele. Attic-type rooms on the top floor, with some rooms opening onto the patio.

Princesse Caroline without rest
1bis r. Troyon Ⓜ *Charles de Gaulle-Etoile – ✆ 01 58 05 30 00 – www.hotelprincessecaroline.fr – contact@hotelprincessecaroline.fr – Fax 01 42 27 49 53* E 8
53 rm – †€ 158 ††€ 158, ☕ € 18
◆ In a small street just off the Étoile, this hotel pays homage to Caroline Murat, sister of Napoleon I. Light, cosy and well-appointed rooms; those overlooking the inner courtyard are very quiet.

Champerret Élysées without rest
129 av. Villiers Ⓜ *Porte de Champerret – ✆ 01 47 64 44 00 – www.champerret-elysees.fr – reservation@champerret-elysees.fr – Fax 01 47 63 10 58* D 7
45 rm – †€ 99/150 ††€ 99/150, ☕ € 15
◆ Located at Porte de Champerret, this hotel offers colourful rooms (those overlooking the courtyard are quieter). Breakfast buffet served to a trompe l'oeil view of Paris.

Magellan without rest
17 r. J.-B. Dumas Ⓜ Porte de Champerret – ✆ 01 45 72 44 51 – www.hotelmagellan.com – paris@hotelmagellan.com – Fax 01 40 68 90 36 D 7
72 rm – †€ 103/137 ††€, ☕ € 14
◆ Large, functional rooms in a handsome edifice dating from 1900. Breakfast is served in the small pavilion at the end of the garden in summer. Art Deco-style lounge.

Mercure Wagram Arc de Triomphe without rest
3 r. Brey Ⓜ Charles de Gaulle-Etoile – ✆ 01 56 68 00 01 – www.mercure.com – h2053@accor.com – Fax 01 56 68 00 02
43 rm – †€ 195/260 ††€ 205/270, ☕ € 14 E 8
◆ This new Mercure between Étoile and Ternes offers a warm welcome and cosy little rooms with pale wood panels and pretty fabrics that create a nautical atmosphere.

Tilsitt Étoile without rest
23 r. Brey Ⓜ Charles de Gaulle-Etoile – ✆ 01 43 80 39 71 – www.tilsitt.com – info@tilsitt.com – Fax 01 47 66 37 63 E 8
38 rm – †€ 140 ††€ 170, ☕ € 13
◆ The hotel is located on a quiet street in the Étoile quarter. Snug, cosy rooms (a few tiny terraces), appealing breakfast room and designer decor lounge bar.

Champlain without rest
99 bis r. de Rome Ⓜ Rome – ✆ 01 42 27 49 52 – www.hotelchamplainparis.com – hotelchamplainparis@jjwhotels.com D 11
51 rm – †€ 170/190 ††€ 190/230, ☕ € 16
◆ Recently refurbished hotel near St Lazare station. Welcoming bar and sitting room and elegant contemporary rooms; the top two floors command matchless views over Montmartre.

Monceau Élysées without rest
108 r. Courcelles Ⓜ Courcelles – ✆ 01 47 63 33 08 – www.monceau-elysees.com – monceau-elysees@wanadoo.fr – Fax 01 46 22 87 39 E 9
29 rm – †€ 89/175 ††€ 99/235, ☕ € 11
◆ This hotel close to the Parc Monceau offers guests personalised rooms decorated with salmon colours and printed and/or more contemporary fabrics. Stone-vaulted breakfast room.

Guy Savoy
18 r. Troyon Ⓜ Charles de Gaulle-Etoile – ✆ 01 43 80 40 61 – www.guysavoy.com – reserv@guysavoy.com – Fax 01 46 22 43 09 – Closed August, 24 December-2 January, Saturday lunch, Sunday and Monday E 8
Rest – Menu € 275/345 – Carte € 140/270
Spec. Huîtres en nage glacée. Bar en écailles grillées aux épices douces. Noir (dessert).
◆ Glasswork, leather and Wenge, works by great names in contemporary art, African sculptures and refined, inventive cuisine make this the inn for the 21C par excellence.

Michel Rostang
20 r. Rennequin Ⓜ Ternes – ✆ 01 47 63 40 77 – www.michelrostang.com – rostang@relaischateaux.com – Fax 01 47 63 82 75 – Closed 3-25 August, Monday lunch, Saturday lunch and Sunday D 8
Rest – Menu € 78 (lunch), € 165/285 – Carte € 133/222
Spec. Carte des truffes et "sandwichs" à la truffe (15 Dec. to mid-March). Grosse sole de ligne meunière, marinière de coquillages au curry mauri. Tarte chaude au chocolat amer.
◆ Wainscoting, Robj statuettes, works by Lalique, and Art Deco stained glass make this both a luxurious and unusual setting. Exquisite cuisine and outstanding wine list.

Sormani
4 r. Gén. Lanrezac Ⓜ Charles de Gaulle-Etoile – ✆ 01 43 80 13 91 – sasormani@wanadoo.fr – Fax 01 40 55 07 37 – Closed 1st-25 August, Saturday, Sunday and public holidays E 7
Rest – Carte € 60/200
◆ Latin charm predominates in this restaurant near the Place de l'Etoile, with its new decor (red tones and Murano-glass chandeliers), dolce vita atmosphere and Italian cuisine.

Pétrus
12 pl. Mar. Juin Ⓜ Pereire – ✆ 01 43 80 15 95 – Fax 01 47 66 49 86 – Closed 5-25 August D 8
Rest – Carte € 45/85
◆ The former nautical decor has given way to an equally flawless new minimalist look. Particularly attentive service and reinterpreted versions of a classic repertory.

La Braisière (Jacques Faussat)
54 r. Cardinet Ⓜ Malesherbes – ✆ 01 47 63 40 37 – labraisiere@free.fr – Fax 01 47 63 04 76 – Closed 26 July-23 August, 1st-10 January, Saturday lunch and Sunday D 9
Rest – Menu € 38 (lunch)/110 – Carte € 53/65
Spec. Gâteau de pomme de terre au foie gras et aux girolles (season). Saint-Jacques poêlées (autumn-winter). Figues rôties aux fruits d'automne, crème de marrron et épices de la joie (season).
◆ Comfortable, modern restaurant decorated in a tasteful restrained style. The menu is influenced by the cuisine of southwest France, changes with the seasons and the chef's inspiration.

Dessirier
9 pl. Mar. Juin Ⓜ Pereire – ✆ 01 42 27 82 14 – www.restaurantdessirier.com – reservation@restaurantdessirier.com – Fax 01 47 66 82 07 – Closed 10-17 August, Saturday and Sunday in July-August D 8
Rest – Carte € 62/97
◆ One of the chef Michel Rostang's six Paris bistros. Impressive seafood menu and beautiful oyster display. Lively atmosphere and brasserie style interior.

Rech
62 av. des Ternes Ⓜ Ternes – ✆ 01 45 72 29 47 – www.esprit-bistrot.com – restaurant.rech@free.fr – Fax 01 45 72 41 60 – Closed 26 July-24 August, 24 December-1 January, Sunday and Monday E7
Rest – Menu € 34 (lunch)/55 – Carte € 50/85
◆ Recently renovated, Art Deco-inspired dining rooms (mirrors, stained glass) at this venerable restaurant. Principally fine fish and seafood specialities, but the odd meat dish too.

Timgad
21 r. Brunel Ⓜ Argentine – ✆ 01 45 74 23 70 – www.timgad.fr – contact@timgad.fr – Fax 01 40 68 76 46 E 7
Rest – Menu € 69 bi/113 bi – Carte € 40/85
◆ Delve into the past splendour of the city of Timgad: the elegant Moorish decor of the rooms was carried out by Moroccan stucco-workers. Fragrant North African cuisine.

La Maison de Charly
97 bd Gouvion-St-Cyr Ⓜ Porte Maillot – ✆ 01 45 74 34 62 – www.lamaisondecharly.fr – Fax 01 55 37 90 21 – Closed August and Monday
Rest – Menu (€ 29), € 34 E 6
◆ An ochre façade, olive trees, elegant Moorish decor and a palm tree beneath the glass ceiling provide the typical decor for this restaurant serving varied couscous, tajine and pastilla dishes.

Agapé
51 r. Jouffroy-d'Abbans Ⓜ Wagram – ✆ 01 42 27 20 18 – www.agape-paris.fr – www.agape-paris@orange.fr – Fax 01 43 80 68 09 D 9
Rest – *(closed August, Saturday and Sunday)* Menu € 39 (lunch), € 77/110 – Carte € 57/79
Spec. Veau cru-fumé de Corrèze, citron vert-vanille et fines herbes. Pigeonneau de Sologne, endive carmine et abricot. Chocolat-café Panama.
◆ This new restaurant, whose name means love in Greek, will appeal to gourmets. It has a chic, minimalist decor and a concise enticing menu.

Graindorge
15 r. Arc de Triomphe Ⓜ Charles de Gaulle-Etoile – ✆ 01 47 54 00 28 – le.graindorge@wanadoo.fr – Closed 1st-15 August, Saturday lunch and Sunday
Rest – Menu (€ 24), € 28 (weekdays), € 34/50 – Carte € 44/50 E 7
◆ Here you can choose between beer and wine, generous Flemish cuisine and appealing market dishes in an attractive Art Deco setting.

Meating
122 av.de Villiers Ⓜ Pereire – ✆ 01 43 80 10 10 – www.meating.abemadi.com – chezmichelpereire@wanadoo.fr – Fax 01 43 80 31 42 – Closed Sunday and Monday B 2
Rest – Menu € 34 – Carte € 50/75
◆ A trendy steakhouse in a chic district where the chef sources the best cuts of meat and cooks them to your exact requirement. Classic dishes also available.

Le Ballon des Ternes
103 av. Ternes Ⓜ Porte Maillot – ✆ 01 45 74 17 98 – leballondesternes@fr.oleane.com – Fax 01 45 72 18 84 E 6
Rest – Carte € 40/65
◆ No, you have not had a glass of wine too many! The table set upside down on the ceiling is part of the 1900 decor of this brasserie next to the Palais des Congrès.

Chez Georges
273 bd Péreire Ⓜ Porte Maillot – ✆ 01 45 74 31 00 – www.chez-georges.com – chez-georges@hotmail.fr – Fax 01 45 72 18 84 E 6
Rest – bistro – Carte € 42/75
◆ An institution in Paris since 1926, the ambience and decor of this brasserie are perfectly in keeping with its appetising bistro cuisine. Menu and daily suggestions.

Chez Léon
32 r. Legendre Ⓜ Villiers – ✆ 01 42 27 06 82 – chezleon32@wanadoo.fr – Fax 01 46 22 63 67 – Closed 26 July-24 August, 24 December-4 January, Saturday, Sunday and holidays D 10
Rest – Menu (€ 24), € 32 (lunch)/34
◆ One of the establishment's three dining rooms now sports a new contemporary bistro decor. The cuisine also mingles modernity and tradition. Friendly, lively ambience.

Bigarrade (Christophe Pelé)
106 r. Nollet Ⓜ Brochant – ✆ 01 42 26 01 02 – www.bigarrade.fr – restobigarrade@orange.fr – Closed August, Christmas holidays, Monday lunch, Saturday and Sunday C 11
Rest – *(number of covers limited, pre-book)* Menu € 35 (lunch), € 45/65
Spec. Menus du marché.
◆ No à la carte here but simply a choice of two set "surprise" menus composed of tasting-size portions. Seductive, creative cuisine and an open-plan kitchen with views of the chef at work.

Bath's
25 r. Bayen Ⓜ Ternes – ✆ 01 45 74 74 74 – www.baths.fr – contact@baths.fr – Fax 01 45 74 71 15 – Closed August, Sunday and bank holidays E 7
Rest – Menu (€ 28), € 42 (weekdays) – Carte € 50/70
Spec. Cassolette d'oeufs brouillés. Filet de boeuf de Salers aux épices douces. Riz au lait, compotée d'ananas.
◆ Contemporary artwork, and sculpture by the owner grace the modern decor of this restaurant, enhanced by an orange and black colour scheme. Tasty market-fresh cuisine.

Caïus
6 r. d'Armaillé Ⓜ Charles de Gaulle-Etoile – ✆ 01 42 27 19 20 – Fax 01 40 55 00 93 – Closed Saturday and Sunday E 7
Rest – Menu (€ 23), € 39
◆ Every day, the chef of this smart bistro chalks up his new personalised recipes made with spices and 'forgotten' produce. Minimalist modern decor.

Montefiori
19 r. de l'Etoile Ⓜ Charles de Gaulle-Etoile – ✆ 01 55 37 90 00 – www.montefiori.fr – montesiori@wanadoo.fr – Closed 1-23 August, 24 December-4 January, Saturday lunch, Monday dinner and Sunday E 8
Rest – Menu (€ 17), € 22 (lunch) – Carte € 30/50
◆ This former bakery with a listed façade serves high quality Italian specialities amid a contemporary red and green decor.

Karl & Erick
20 r. de Tocqueville Ⓜ Villiers – ✆ 01 42 27 03 71 – vandevelde17@orange.fr – Closed 1-24 August, Saturday lunch, Sunday and Monday D 10
Rest – Menu (€ 24) – Carte € 37/57
◆ A set of twins – one in the dining room, one in the kitchen – run this bistro with the feel of a contemporary loft. Well-presented modern bistro daily specials.

Table des Oliviers
38 r. Laugier Ⓜ Pereire – ✆ 01 47 63 85 51 – www.latabledesoliviers.fr – latabledesoliviers@hotmail.fr – Fax 01 47 63 85 81 – Closed early August, Saturday lunch and Sunday D 7-8
Rest – Menu (€ 24), € 32 – Carte € 50/58
◆ This restaurant decked in warm southern colours serves Provençal cuisine drenched in the flavours of olive oil, thyme and basil. Only the chirping of the crickets is lacking!

Bistrot Niel
75 av. Niel Ⓜ Pereire – ✆ 01 42 27 88 44 – lebistrotdeniel@aol.com – Fax 01 42 27 32 12 – Closed Saturday lunch and Sunday D 8
Rest – Menu € 30 (lunch)/35 – Carte € 43/61
◆ A modern bistro that is both chic and welcoming. The cuisine here is focused on seafood dishes, updated with a hint of spice.

Le Café d'Angel
16 r. Brey Ⓜ Charles de Gaulle-Etoile – ✆ 01 47 54 03 33 – Fax 01 47 54 03 33 – Closed 1-21 August, 24 December-2 January, Saturday, Sunday and bank holidays E 8
Rest – Menu (€ 22), € 26 – Carte € 42/56
◆ A small establishment evocative of Parisian bistros of yesteryear: a retro setting with banquettes, pottery on the walls and traditional dishes marked on a blackboard.

Le Clou
132 r. Cardinet Ⓜ Malesherbes – ✆ 01 42 27 36 78 – www.restaurant-leclou.fr – le.clou@wanadoo.fr – Fax 01 42 27 89 96 – Closed 1-24 August and Sunday C 10
Rest – Menu € 22 (weekday lunch), € 29/33 – Carte € 33/45
◆ This bistro combines sophistication with affability. Find tightly packed tables, reinterpreted regional dishes (mainly Poitou) depending on the seasons, and prestigious wines.

Chez Mathilde-Paris XVII
41 r. Guersant Ⓜ Porte Maillot – ✆ 01 45 74 75 27 – www.chezmathilde.fr – contact@chezmathilde.fr – Closed 26 July-26 August, 24 December-1st January, Saturday and Sunday D 7
Rest – Carte approx. € 25
◆ The chef's bistro-style market based cuisine is listed on a blackboard. A modest family-run restaurant far from the Parisian trendy set.

L'Huîtrier
16 r. Saussier-Leroy Ⓜ Ternes – ✆ 01 40 54 83 44 – alainbunel17@free.fr – Fax 01 40 54 83 86 – Closed August and Monday E 8
Rest – Carte € 40/70
◆ As you enter, the oyster bar will make your mouth water. Enjoy the shellfish, elbow to elbow, in a discreetly modern dining room.

L'Entredgeu
83 r. Laugier Ⓜ Porte de Champerret – ✆ 01 40 54 97 24 – Fax 01 40 54 96 62 – Closed 25 April-7 May, 5-25 August, 22-29 December, Sunday and Monday D 7
Rest – Menu (€ 24), € 32
◆ Friendly welcome, decor with touches of south western France, lively atmosphere, menu chalked up on a blackboard, market fresh cuisine and a tongue-twisting name to boot.

Caves Petrissans
30 bis av. Niel Ⓜ Pereire – ✆ 01 42 27 52 03 – cavespetrissans@noos.fr – Fax 01 40 54 87 56 – Closed August, Saturday, Sunday and bank holidays
Rest – *(pre-book)* Menu € 35 – Carte € 42/56 D 8
◆ Céline, Abel Gance and Roland Dorgelès loved to visit these cellars, which are over a century old and now double as a wine shop and restaurant. Tasty, bistro style cooking.

S. Sauvignier/MICHELIN

Montmartre • Pigalle

18th arrondissement ✉ 75018

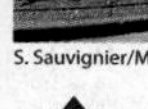

Terrass'Hôtel
12 r. J. de Maistre Ⓜ *Place de Clichy – ✆ 01 46 06 72 85 – www.terrass-hotel.com – reservation@terrass-hotel.com – Fax 01 44 92 34 30* C 13
98 rm – €280/330 €280/330, €17
Rest *Le Diapason* – *✆ 01 44 92 34 00 (closed Sunday dinner16 September-30 April and Saturday lunch)* Menu (€22), €29/35 bi – Carte €45/63
◆ Situated at the foot of the Sacré-Coeur basilica, this hotel has stunning views of Paris from its upper-floor rooms and top-floor terrace. Elegant interior adorned with ornaments and wood panelling. Plain, contemporary decor (in sands, greys and black) at the Diapason. Cuisine in the same modern and refined style.

Kube
1 passage Ruelle Ⓜ *La Chapelle – ✆ 01 42 05 20 00 – www.kubehotel.com – paris@kubehotel.com – Fax 01 42 05 21 01* C 16
41 rm – €250/275 €300/325, €25
Rest – Menu (€19), €25 (lunch)/41 – Carte €35/53
◆ The 19C façade belies this hotel's 21C high-tech designer interior. The bar – built entirely from ice (-10°C) – makes for an unusual and unforgettable experience. Very trendy concept also in the lounge restaurant: modern menu and finger food.

L'Hôtel Particulier without rest
23 av. Junot Ⓜ *Lamarck Caulaincourt – ✆ 01 53 41 81 40 – www.hotel-particulier-montmartre.com – hotelparticulier@orange.fr*
4 rm – €390 €390, €20 – 1 suite C 13
◆ This striking Directoire residence is a haven of peace in the heart of Montmartre. Discreet entrance on a cobblestone passage, lush garden, intimate atmosphere, artistic décor.

Relais Montmartre without rest
6 r. Constance Ⓜ *Abbesses – ✆ 01 70 64 25 25 – www.relaismontmartre.fr – contact@relaismontmartre.fr – Fax 01 70 64 25 00* D 13
26 rm – €155/195 €155/195, €13
◆ Discover the unexpected charm of this quiet, country-style residence in a lively district close to Pigalle. Stylish, classical decor and modern facilities.

Holiday Inn Garden Court Montmartre without rest
23 r. Damrémont Ⓜ *Lamarck Caulaincourt – ✆ 01 44 92 33 40 – www.holiday-inn.com/parismontmart – hiparmm@aol.com – Fax 01 44 92 09 30* C 13
54 rm – €140/170 €160/190, €13
◆ A recently built hotel with renovated, functional rooms on a typically steep Montmartre street. The breakfast room opens onto a small terrace.

Mercure Montmartre without rest
3 r. Caulaincourt Ⓜ *Place de Clichy – ✆ 01 44 69 70 70 – www.mercure.com – h0373@accor.com – Fax 01 44 69 70 71* D 12
305 rm – €205 €215, €15
◆ A stone's throw from the famous Moulin Rouge, the hotel lobby is decorated on the theme of Montmartre and its painters. The rooms on the top three floors enjoy lovely views of the rooftops of Paris.

Timhotel without rest
11 r. Ravignan Ⓜ *Abbesses – ✆ 01 42 55 74 79 – www.timhotel.com – montmartre.manager@timhotel.fr – Fax 01 42 55 71 01* D 13
59 rm – €85/130 €85/210, €8,50
◆ Smart, functional hotel on one of the neighbourhood's most charming squares. The rooms on the 4th and 5th floors have been renovated and offer superb views of the capital.

Roma Sacré Coeur without rest
101 r. Caulaincourt Ⓜ Lamarck Caulaincourt – ✆ 01 42 62 02 02 – www.hotelromasacre.fr – hotelroma@wanadoo.fr – Fax 01 42 54 34 92
57 rm – †€ 80/120 ††€ 95/145, ☕ € 8 C 14
◆ This hotel has a charming location in Montmartre, with a garden to the front, typical flights of steps to the side and Sacré-Cœur above. Attractive, brightly coloured guestrooms.

Damrémont without rest
110 r. Damrémont Ⓜ Jules Joffrin – ✆ 01 42 64 25 75 – www.damremont-paris-hotel.com – hotel.damremont@wanadoo.fr – Fax 01 46 06 74 64 B 13
35 rm – †€ 65/140 ††€ 75/140, ☕ € 7
◆ Near Montmartre, the functional bedrooms are quieter on the courtyard side; they are not very large but well looked after and appealing. Small sitting room.

Le Moulin de la Galette
83 r. Lepic Ⓜ Abbesses – ✆ 01 46 06 84 77 – www.lemoulindelagalette.fr – reservation@lemoulindelagalette.fr – Fax 01 46 06 84 78 C 13
Rest – Menu (€ 17), € 25 (lunch), € 50/60 – Carte € 50/70
◆ A windmill in 1622, then a popular dance hall painted by Renoir and Toulouse-Lautrec, this place has been remodelled and is now a bistro-style restaurant with a plant filled terrace.

Au Clair de la Lune
9 r. Poulbot Ⓜ Abbesses – ✆ 01 42 58 97 03 – www.auclairdelalune.fr – herve.kerfant@free.fr – Fax 01 42 55 64 74 – Closed 17 August-15 September, Monday lunch and Sunday D 14
Rest – Menu € 32 – Carte € 37/65
◆ Situated behind Place du Tertre, this restaurant takes its name from a French nursery rhyme. Classical cuisine served in a friendly atmosphere with frescoes of old Montmartre on the walls.

Au Poulbot Gourmet
39 r. Lamarck Ⓜ Lamarck Caulaincourt – ✆ 01 46 06 86 00 – bistro@poulbot.com – Closed August, Monday lunch and Sunday C 14
Rest – Menu (€ 14), € 18 (lunch)/35 – Carte € 35/42
◆ The bistro's sign depicts the kids of Montmartre sketched by Poulbot. Under new management, it now provides a friendly setting, traditional menu and updated recipes (evenings).

Chéri bibi
15 r. André-del-Sarte Ⓜ Barbès Rochechouart – ✆ 01 42 54 88 96 – Closed 3 weeks in August and Sunday D 14
Rest – *(dinner only)* Menu (€ 19), € 24
◆ Trendy, lively establishment, slightly bohemian in feel. Shabby chic furniture from the 1950s and an old zinc counter. Old family recipes and personal touches.

Miroir
94 r. des Martyrs Ⓜ Abbesses – ✆ 01 46 06 50 73 – miroir.restaurant@gmail.com – Closed 2-24 August, 23-28 December, Sunday dinner, Monday and bank holidays
Rest – Menu (€ 25), € 32 D 13-D 14
◆ A young, professional team run this modern bistro. Contemporary dining room with glass roof, seasonal offerings on the blackboard menu and fine wine list.

La Table d'Eugène
18 r. Eugène-Sue Ⓜ Jules Joffrin – ✆ 01 42 55 61 64 – Closed 2-25 August, 20-29 December, Sunday and Monday C 14
Rest – *(pre-book)* Menu (€ 25), € 32
◆ This simple bistro (mouldings and pastel tones) has a regularly changing menu with intelligent and well-presented seasonal cuisine.

Le Café qui Parle
24 r. Caulaincourt ✉ 75018 Ⓜ Lamarck Caulaincourt – ✆ 01 46 06 06 88 – Closed August, Sunday dinner and Wednesday C 13
Rest – Menu (€ 13), € 17 – Carte € 28/34
◆ Sample skilfully updated, classic cuisine in a convivial ambience and chocolate coloured decor. Brunch served on Sundays. Exhibitions.

Ph. Gajic/MICHELIN

Parc de la Villette • Parc des Buttes Chaumont

19th arrondissement ✉ 75019

Holiday Inn rm, rest, VISA
216 av. J. Jaurès Ⓜ Porte de Pantin – ✆ 01 44 84 18 18 – www.holidayinn-parisvillette.com – hilavillette@alliance-hospitality.com – Fax 01 44 84 18 20 C 21
182 rm – †€ 240 ††€ 240, ☕ € 18
Rest – *(closed Saturday and Sunday)* Menu € 28 – Carte € 31/51
◆ Modern construction across from the Cité de la Musique. Spacious and soundproofed rooms, offering modern comfort (mahogany furniture). Meeting rooms, auditorium and gym. Designer cafeteria décor and a brasserie menu: Small verdant terrace.

Laumière without rest VISA
4 r. Petit Ⓜ Laumière – ✆ 01 42 06 10 77 – www.hotel-lelaumiere.com – lelaumiere@wanadoo.fr – Fax 01 42 06 72 50 D 19
54 rm – †€ 60/72 ††€ 61/75, ☕ € 8,50
◆ Yearning for some greenery? This simple, well-kept hotel will rejuvenate you with its pretty garden (where breakfast is served) and the nearby Buttes-Chaumont park.

Crimée without rest VISA
188 r. Crimée Ⓜ Crimée – ✆ 01 40 36 75 29 – www.hotelcrimee.com – hotelcrimee19@wanadoo.fr – Fax 01 40 36 29 57 C 18
31 rm – †€ 66/72 ††€ 68/75, ☕ € 7
◆ Hotel 300m from the Ourcq Canal. The well-soundproofed and air-conditioned rooms have functional furniture and some overlook a small garden.

Abricôtel without rest VISA
15 r. Lally Tollendal Ⓜ Jaurès – ✆ 01 42 08 34 49 – www.abricotel.fr – abricotel@wanadoo.fr – Fax 01 42 40 83 95 D 18
39 rm – †€ 52/55 ††€ 65, ☕ € 7
◆ This little family business giving onto a busy street offers small simple rooms that are functional and reasonably priced.

Relais des Buttes VISA
86 r. Compans Ⓜ Botzaris – ✆ 01 42 08 24 70 – aurelaisdesbutteschaumont@yahoo.fr – Fax 01 42 03 20 44 – Closed August, 24 December-3 January, Saturday lunch and Sunday E 20
Rest – Menu € 34 – Carte € 52/74
◆ Close to Buttes Chaumont park. In winter, the up-to-date dining room with fireplace is most welcome, while the peaceful courtyard terrace is ideal in summer. Classic menu.

Au Boeuf Couronné VISA
188 av. Jean Jaurès Ⓜ Porte de Pantin – ✆ 01 42 39 44 44 – www.rest-gj.com – boeuf.couronne@laposte.net C 20
Rest – Menu € 32 bi – Carte € 35/60
◆ This establishment opposite the former Villette market is as successful as ever. Generous portions (heaven for meat lovers), friendly service and a vintage decor.

L'Hermès VISA
23 r. Mélingue Ⓜ Pyrénées – ✆ 01 42 39 94 70 – lhermes@wanadoo.fr – Closed Easter holidays, August, February holidays, Wednesday lunch, Sunday and Monday F 20
Rest – Menu € 17 (lunch)/33 – Carte € 35/58
◆ A charming Provencal ambience of ochre, wood and colourful tableware. Generous, bistro-style dishes highlighted on the daily specials board. A popular local address.

La Violette

11 av. Corentin Cariou Ⓜ Corentin Cariou – ✆ 01 40 35 20 45 – www.restaurant-laviolette.com – restolaviolette@free.fr – Closed 18-22 May, 9-24 August, 25 December-3 January, Saturday and Sunday B 19

Rest – *(number of covers limited, pre-book)* Carte € 35/53

◆ A friendly welcome and atmosphere, trendy decor (black and white colour scheme, purple bench, walls covered with bottle racks), and tasty contemporary cuisine.

La Cave Gourmande

10 r. Gén. Brunet Ⓜ Botzaris – ✆ 01 40 40 03 30 – lacavegourmande@wanadoo.fr Fax 01 40 40 03 30 – Closed 1-24 August, February holiday, Saturday lunch and Sunday

Rest – Menu (€ 31), € 36 E 20

◆ A friendly ambience, decorative bottle racks, wooden tables and market-inspired dishes are the main features of this pleasant bistro near the Buttes-Chaumont park.

S. Sauvignier/MICHELIN

Cimetière du Père Lachaise • Gambetta • Belleville

20th arrondissement ✉ 75020

Mama Shelter

109 r. de Bagnolet Ⓜ Gambetta – ✆ 01 43 48 48 48 – www.mamashelter.com – paris@mamashelter.com – Fax 01 44 54 38 66 H 22

171 rm – †€ 79/169 ††€ 89/179, ☕ € 15 – 1 suite **Rest** – Carte € 30/65

◆ The original décor at this vast new hotel was created by the imaginative Starck. At the cutting edge of modern design, it sports a look that is both streamlined and whimsical. Large lounge bar.

Palma without rest

77 av. Gambetta Ⓜ Gambetta – ✆ 01 46 36 13 65 – www.paris-hotel-palma.com – hotel.palma@wanadoo.fr – Fax 01 46 36 03 27 G 21

32 rm – †€ 67/74 ††€ 76/80, ☕ € 7

◆ A stone's throw from Place Gambetta and the Père Lachaise cemetery, this hotel offers small, slightly old-fashioned rooms decorated in 1970s style.

Les Allobroges

71 r. Grands-Champs Ⓜ Maraîchers – ✆ 01 43 73 40 00 – Closed 3-25 August, Sunday dinner and Monday **Rest** – Menu € 20 (weekdays)/34 K 22

◆ Step off the beaten track to discover this friendly restaurant close to Porte de Montreuil. Simple, pretty decor and copious modern cuisine prepared by the new chef.

Le Bistrot des Soupirs "Chez les On"

49 r. Chine Ⓜ Gambetta – ✆ 01 44 62 93 31 – Fax 01 44 62 77 83 – Closed 1-8 May, 5-25 August, 25 December-1 January, Sunday and Monday

Rest – Menu € 17 (lunch) – Carte € 29/43 G 21

◆ Next to the picturesque Soupirs lane, Auvergne and Lyons specialities take pride of place in this pleasant countrified inn. Resolutely jovial in spirit.

Le Baratin

3 r. Jouye-Rouve Ⓜ Pyrénées – ✆ 01 43 49 39 70 – Closed August, Saturday lunch, Sunday and Monday **Rest** – *(pre-book)* Menu € 17 – Carte € 31/40 F 19

◆ Enticing dishes chalked up on the blackboard, reasonable prices, choice of fine wines...it's easy to understand the appeal of this neighbourhood bistro.

La Boulangerie

15 r. des Panoyaux – ✆ 01 43 58 45 45 – Fax 01 43 58 45 46 G 20

Rest – Menu (€ 14), € 32

◆ The stylish old bistro décor at this restaurant – originally a bakery – charms regulars and tourists alike. Copious dishes and good wine list at reasonable prices.

Ph. Gajic/MICHELIN

Outskirts of Paris

cartes 18-21

"40 Km around the city"

ANTONY – **92 Hauts-de-Seine** – **311** J3 – **101** 25 – **pop. 60 000** – **alt. 80 m** 20 **B3** – ✉ **92160**

Paris 13 – Bagneux 6 – Corbeil-Essonnes 28 – Nanterre 23 – Versailles 16

Syndicat d'initiative, place Auguste Mounié ✆ 01 42 37 57 77, Fax 01 46 66 30 80

Sceaux: park★★ and musée de l'Île-de-France★ North: 4 km - Châtenay-Malabry: St-Germain-l'Auxerrois church ★, Chateaubriand House★ Northwest: 4 km, **Île de France**

De Berny without rest VISA AE
129 av. A.-Briand – ✆ 01 46 11 43 90 – www.hotel-berny.com – hoteldeberny@netgdi.com – Fax 01 46 74 96 46
40 rm – €79/130 €79/140, €12 – 4 suites
◆ Not far from La Croix de Berny, this recent hotel sports a restrained sitting room, well-equipped guestrooms and a few suites. The decor and furnishings are contemporary in spirit.

XX **L'Amandier** A/C VISA
8 r. de l'Église – ✆ 01 46 66 22 02 – www.restaurant-lamandier.fr – colpart.eric@neuf.fr – Closed 5-25 August, 25 December-1st January, Saturday lunch, Sunday dinner and Monday **Rest** – Menu €25 (weekday lunch)/34 – Carte €38/50
◆ This restaurant in old Antony houses a spacious and comfortable dining room that is half-classical, half-contemporary. The inventive menu is regularly updated.

X **La Tour de Marrakech** A/C VISA AE
72 av. Division Leclerc – ✆ 01 46 66 00 54 – Fax 01 46 66 12 99 – Closed Aug. and Mon.
Rest – Menu €23 (weekday lunch) – Carte €25/45
◆ Quintessential Morocco from the Moorish decor to the delicately prepared dishes of North Africa. Friendly welcome and attentive service.

ARGENTEUIL – **95 Val-d'Oise** – **305** E7 – **101** 14 – **pop. 102 400** – **alt. 33 m** 20 **B1** – ✉ **95100** **Northern France and the Paris Region**

Paris 16 – Chantilly 38 – Pontoise 20 – St-Germain-en-Laye 19

XXX **La Ferme d'Argenteuil** VISA AE
2 bis r. Verte – ✆ 01 39 61 00 62 – www.lafermedargenteuil.com – info@lafermedargenteuil.com – Fax 01 30 76 32 31 – Closed August, Monday dinner, Tuesday dinner, Wednesday dinner and Sunday
Rest – Menu €38/70 – Carte €60/70
◆ Two sisters run this inn, slightly out of the centre. Amélia welcomes guests into the entirely redecorated dining room, while Marie oversees the updated cuisine.

ASNIÈRES-SUR-SEINE – **92 Hauts-de-Seine** – **311** J2 – **101** 15 – **pop. 82 800** 20 **B1** – **alt. 37 m** – ✉ **92600** **Northern France and the Paris Region**

Paris 10 – Argenteuil 6 – Nanterre 8 – Pontoise 26 – St-Denis 8 – St-Germain-en-Laye 20

XXX **Van Gogh** P VISA AE
2 quai Aulagnier, (access via the Cimetière des Chiens (pet cemetery)) – ✆ 01 47 91 05 10 – www.levangogh.com – levangogh@wanadoo.fr – Fax 01 47 93 00 93 – Closed Sunday dinner
Rest – Menu (€32), €39 – Carte €47/90
◆ This is where Van Gogh immortalised the banks of the Seine. Modern, pleasure boat setting, summer terrace overlooking the water, fish direct from the Atlantic and pleasant service.

XX **La Petite Auberge** VISA

118 r. Colombes – ✆ 01 47 93 33 94 – lapetite.auberge@orange.fr – Fax 01 47 93 33 94 – Closed 6-24 August, Sunday dinner, Wednesday dinner and Monday

Rest – Menu € 30

◆ A small roadside inn with a pleasant atmosphere. Old objects, paintings and a collection of plates decorate the rustic dining room. Traditional cuisine.

Red = Pleasant. Look for the red and symbols.

AULNAY-SOUS-BOIS – **93 Seine-Saint-Denis** – **305** F7 – **101** 18 – **pop. 81 200** 21 **D1** – **alt. 46 m** – ✉ **93600**

Paris 19 – Bobigny 9 – Lagny-sur-Marne 23 – Meaux 30 – St-Denis 16 – Senlis 38

Novotel rm, rest, VISA AE

65 r. Michel Ange, (carrefour de l'Europe, N 370) – ✆ 01 58 03 90 90 – www.novotel.com – h0387@accor.com – Fax 01 58 03 90 99

139 rm – †€ 80/300 ††€ 80/300, € 14

Rest – *(Closed Saturday and Sunday)* Menu € 18/22 – Carte € 25/49

◆ Classical chain hotel made up of a café (brasserie menu), garden with pool, and a 'cyber terrace'. The rooms have been partly refurbished. Modern dining room; garden dining in fine weather.

XXX **Auberge des Saints Pères** (Jean-Claude Cahagnet) VISA AE

212 av. Nonneville – ✆ 01 48 66 62 11 – www.auberge-des-saints-peres.com – aubergedessaintsperes@orange.fr – Fax 01 48 66 67 44 – Closed 3-9 March, 4-24 August, 10-15 November, Wednesday dinner and Saturday and Sunday

Rest – Menu € 41/85 bi – Carte € 51/72

Spec. Queues de langoustines sur une tartine de cochon (July-Sept.) Turbot sauvage poché à l'émultion de lait fumé et Cécina craquant (July-Sept.). Cube de chocolat, lait d'amande et myrtille (July-Sept.).

◆ This establishment has been treated to a more modern interior decor. A perfect backdrop to the chef's creative talent, enhanced by herbs fresh from the garden.

AUVERS-SUR-OISE – **95 Val-d'Oise** – **305** E6 – **106** 6 – **101** 3 – **pop. 6 938** 18 **B1** – **alt. 30 m** – ✉ **95430** Northern France and the Paris Region

Paris 36 – Beauvais 52 – Chantilly 35 – Compiègne 84 – L'Isle-Adam 7 – Pontoise 10

Office de tourisme, rue de la Sansonne ✆ 01 30 36 10 06, Fax 01 34 48 08 47

Van Gogh House★ - Journey-show at the time of the Impressionists★ in the château of Léry.

XXX **Hostellerie du Nord** with rm rm, VISA

6 r. Gén. de Gaulle – ✆ 01 30 36 70 74 – www.hostelleriedunord.fr – contact@hostelleriedunord.fr – Fax 01 30 36 72 75 – Closed Sunday dinner

8 rm – †€ 99/129 ††€ 129/189, € 14

Rest – *(closed Saturday lunch and Monday)* Menu (€ 49 bi), € 59/79 – Carte € 59/69

◆ Famous painters once stayed in this former post house. The works of art adorning the dining room and bedrooms are a reminder of this rich past. Traditional cuisine.

X **Auberge Ravoux** VISA AE

(opposite the town hall) – ✆ 01 30 36 60 60 – www.maisondevangogh.fr – info@vangoghfrance.com – Fax 01 30 36 60 61 – Open mid-March to mid-November and closed Wednesday dinner, Thursday dinner, Monday and Tuesday

Rest – *(number of covers limited, pre-book)* Menu (€ 28), € 37 – Carte € 50/57

◆ A warm atmosphere and the generous cuisine of the 19C artists' cafés in the inn where Van Gogh lived towards the end of his life. Visit the painter's little bedroom (€5).

BAGNOLET – 93 Seine-Saint-Denis – **305** F7 – **101** 17 – **pop. 33 900** 21 **C2**
– alt. 96 m – ✉ 93170

Paris 8 – Bobigny 6 – Lagny-sur-Marne 32 – Meaux 39

Novotel Porte de Bagnolet
1 av. de la République, (Porte de Bagnolet junction) –
01 49 93 63 00 – www.novotel.com – h0380@accor.com – Fax 01 43 62 55 58
609 rm – €135/280 €135/280, €15 – 7 suites
Rest – Menu (€22) – Carte €25/30
◆ Near the ring road, this hotel, one of the first opened by the chain, has been fully renovated from top to toe. Functional, modern rooms. Business people, groups and tourists from all over the world cross paths at this restaurant, open very late.

BOIS-COLOMBES – 92 Hauts-de-Seine – **311** J2 – **101** 15 – **pop. 26 700** 20 **B1**
– alt. 37 m – ✉ 92270

Paris 12 – Nanterre 6 – Pontoise 25 – St-Denis 11 – St-Germain-en-Laye 19

Le Chefson
17 r. Ch. Chefson – 01 42 42 12 05 – Fax 01 47 80 51 68 – Closed 1st-28 August, 1 week in February, Monday dinner, Saturday and Sunday
Rest – bistro – *(number of covers limited, pre-book)* Menu (€19), €25/35
◆ The bistro ambience and simple, generous and traditional cuisine contribute to the charm of this establishment, popular with locals. Daily market specials on the blackboard.

BOUGIVAL – 78 Yvelines – **311** I2 – **101** 13 – **pop. 8 416** – **alt. 40 m** 20 **A2**
– ✉ 78380 **Northern France and the Paris Region**

Paris 21 – Rueil-Malmaison 5 – St-Germain-en-Laye 6 – Versailles 8 – Le Vésinet 5

Syndicat d'initiative, 10, rue du Général Leclerc 01 39 69 21 23, Fax 01 39 69 37 65

Holiday Inn
10-12 r. Yvan Tourgueneff, (D 113) – 01 30 08 18 28 – www.holiday-inn.com – holidayinn.parvb@hotels-res.com – Fax 01 30 08 18 38
181 rm – €100/270 €100/270, €18
Rest – Menu (€28) – Carte €31/54
◆ This 1970s building, with its original facade, has had a fully-renovated interior, rearranged around a patio. Spacious rooms, including ten with period furniture that overlook the River Seine. The restaurant has a sunny decor and offers traditional cuisine with southern flavours.

Villa des Impressionnistes without rest
15 quai Rennequin Sualem, (D 113) –
01 30 08 40 00 – www.villa-impressionnistes.fr – villa.impression@wanadoo.fr – Fax 01 39 18 58 89
50 rm – €115/165 €135/180, €15 – 1 suite
◆ Selected objects and furniture, bright colours and reproduction paintings (the charming decor of this recent hotel reflects the Impressionist past of the Bougival quayside.

La Vasconia without rest
7 r. de la Butte-de-la-Celle – 01 39 69 03 93 – www.la-vasconia.com – jppilard@free.fr
3 rm – €65 €85
◆ The entrance to this house in a peaceful residential area is through a large garden full of flowers and trees. The stylish rooms all have a personal touch (with old furniture).

Le Camélia (Thierry Conte)
7 quai G. Clemenceau – 01 39 18 36 06 – www.lecamelia.com – info@lecamelia.com – Fax 01 39 18 00 25 – Closed 22 February-2 March, 19-27 April, 26 July-24 August, Sunday and Monday
Rest – Menu €45/75 – Carte €90/110
Spec. Royale de foie gras aux champignons. Gibier (season). Fondant chocolat griottes et framboises (summer).
◆ A smart façade near Ivan Tourgueniev's Datcha-museum. Classic cuisine served in a modern, warm and colourful setting. Fine French wine selection.

BOULOGNE-BILLANCOURT – 92 Hauts-de-Seine – **311** J2 – **101** 24 – pop. 110 300 – alt. 35 m – ✉ 92100 Northern France and the Paris Region 20 **B2**

Paris 10 – Nanterre 9 – Versailles 11

Musée départemental Albert-Kahn★: gardens★ - Musée Paul Landowski★.

Radisson SAS VISA AE
33 av. E. Vaillant – ✆ 01 46 08 85 00 – www.boulogne.radissonsas.com – info.boulogne@radissonsas.com – Fax 01 46 08 85 01
170 rm – €150/345 €150/345, €24
Rest *A O C* – *(closed 4-25 August and Saturday)* Menu (€35) – Carte €38/68
◆ Respect for the environment and local community is this hotel's leitmotif, from the choice of building materials and facilities, to the involvement of the staff. The AOC opens onto a patio-terrace planted with vines. Up-to-date cuisine.

Mercure Porte de St-Cloud rm, VISA AE
37 pl. René Clair – ✆ 01 49 10 49 10 – www.mercure.com – h6188@accor.com – Fax 01 46 08 26 16
180 rm – €145/275 €165/295, €19 – 4 suites
Rest *Croisette Café* – *✆ 01 49 10 49 50 (closed Friday dinner, Saturday, Sunday and holidays)* Menu (€22) – Carte €38/48
◆ Modern glass building housing renovated, comfortable rooms. Fully equipped business centre and lounge-bar adorned with photos of stars by the Harcourt studio. Murals depicting some 400 famous show business personalities enliven the café.

Acanthe without rest VISA AE
9 rd-pt Rhin et Danube – ✆ 01 46 99 10 40 – www.quality-acanthe-paris.com – hotel-acanthe@france-paris.com – Fax 01 46 99 00 05
69 rm – €195/225 €195/225, €16 – 1 suite
◆ Near the Boulogne studios and the unusual gardens of the Albert-Kahn museum, this well-soundproofed hotel has rooms renovated in a modern style. Pleasant flowered patio.

Sélect Hôtel without rest P VISA AE
66 av. Gén.-Leclerc – ✆ 01 46 04 70 47 – www.select-hotel.fr – reception@select-hotel.fr – Fax 01 46 04 07 77
61 rm – €90/130 €100/140, €12
◆ This comfortable establishment is on the main Paris to Versailles road. Its well-soundproofed rooms are in Art Nouveau style in the main wing or Art Deco in the annexe.

Paris without rest VISA AE
104 bis r. Paris – ✆ 01 46 05 13 82 – www.hotel-paris-boulogne.com – contact@hotel-paris-boulogne.com – Fax 01 48 25 10 43
31 rm – €78 €86, €9
◆ Situated in a quiet area, this simple family hotel is perfectly turned out. The small rooms are practical and well-soundproofed. A pleasant welcome from the owners.

Au Comte de Gascogne (Henri Charvet) VISA AE
89 av. J.-B. Clément – ✆ 01 46 03 47 27 – www.comtedegascogne.com – aucomtedegasc@aol.com – Fax 01 46 04 55 70 – Closed 3-18 August, Monday dinner, Saturday lunch and Sunday
Rest – Menu €58 (lunch)/120 – Carte €108/172
Spec. Ballotine de tourteau en feuille de chou. Ragoût de homard aux pommes de terre safranées. Glace vanille bourbon et madeleines chaudes.
◆ The conservatory decor with its mass of lush exotic plants is perfect for appreciating the excellent modern cuisine prepared by the chef-owner. Interesting selection of wines.

L'Auberge VISA AE
86 av. J.-B. Clément – ✆ 01 46 05 67 19 – www.restaurant-boulogne-billancourt.com – legoux.cyrille@9business.fr – Fax 01 46 05 14 24 – Closed 27 July-20 August, Saturday lunch, Sunday dinner and Monday
Rest – Menu (€32), €36/60
◆ Pastel and sunny tones, exposed beams and stonework at this charming inn. Enjoy updated classic cuisine, prepared with the seasons in mind.

XX **Ducoté Cuisine** (Julien Ducoté)
112 av. Victor Hugo – ✆ 01 48 25 49 20 – Closed August, Sunday and Monday
Rest – Menu € 43/85 – Carte € 60/80
Spec. Mousseline de sandre et langoustines rôties. Ris de veau et gratin de macaroni soubise. Millefeuille à la vanille bourbon.
◆ A youthful team manages this contemporary-style restaurant. Subtle modern touches enhance the flavoursome and carefully prepared cuisine.

LE BOURGET – **93 Seine-Saint-Denis** – **305** F7 – **101** 17 – **pop. 12 500** – **alt. 47 m** – ✉ **93350** **Northern France and the Paris Region** 21 **C1**

Paris 13 – Bobigny 6 – Chantilly 38 – Meaux 41 – St-Denis 8 – Senlis 38

Musée de l'Air et de l'Espace★★.

Novotel
2 r. Perrin, (Pont Yblon au Blanc-Mesnil Industrial Park) ✉ 93150 – ✆ 01 48 67 48 88 – www.novotel.com – h0388@accor-hotels.com – Fax 01 45 91 08 27
143 rm – † € 125/280 †† € 125/280, ☕ € 14
Rest – Menu (€ 19) – Carte € 24/40
◆ In a business park near the airport, this hotel is nonetheless protected by greenery. The renovated rooms are in keeping with "Novation" standards. Photos illustrating the history of aviation adorn the restaurant. Terrace and pool.

BRIE-COMTE-ROBERT – **77 Seine-et-Marne** – **312** E3 – **101** 39 – **pop. 14 500** – **alt. 90 m** – ✉ **77170** **Northern France and the Paris Region** 19 **C2**

Paris 30 – Brunoy 10 – Évry 20 – Melun 18 – Provins 63

Syndicat d'initiative, place Jeanne d'Evreux ✆ 01 64 05 30 09, Fax 01 64 05 68 18

Clément Ader Gretz-Armainvilliers Domaine du Château Péreire, NE : 12 km on D 216, ✆ 01 64 07 34 10

de Marolles en Brie Marolles-en-Brie Mail de la Justice, NW : 6 km, ✆ 01 45 95 18 18

ASPTT Paris Golf des Corbuches Lésigny Ferme des Hyverneaux, N : 6 km on N 104, ✆ 01 60 02 07 26

du Réveillon Lésigny Ferme des Hyverneaux, N : 6 km on N 104, ✆ 01 60 02 17 33

Window★ of the church apse.

À la Grâce de Dieu
79 r. Gén.-Leclerc, (D 619) – ✆ 01 64 05 00 76 – www.gracededieu.com – gracedie@wanadoo.fr – Fax 01 64 05 60 57
16 rm – † € 45 †† € 52/70, ☕ € 8,50
Rest – *(closed Sunday evening)* Menu € 22/42 – Carte € 39/55
◆ This 17C coaching inn was the last stop before possible encounters with highwaymen. It has retained a rather pessimistic name but now offers modern comfort. This restaurant is reminiscent of an old country inn (Louis XIII furniture). Traditional cuisine.

BRY-SUR-MARNE – **94 Val-de-Marne** – **312** E2 – **101** 18 – **pop. 15 000** – **alt. 40 m** – ✉ **94360** 21 **D2**

Paris 16 – Créteil 12 – Joinville-le-Pont 5 – Nogent-sur-Marne 3 – Vincennes 9

Syndicat d'initiative, 2, grande rue ✆ 01 48 82 30 30, Fax 01 45 16 90 02

XX **L'Auberge du Pont de Bry**
3 av. Gén. Leclerc – ✆ 01 48 82 27 70 – Closed August, 1st-15 January, Wednesday evening, Sunday evening and Monday
Rest – Menu € 39 – Carte € 37/67
◆ This discreet is inn home to a comfortable modern dining room in pastel colours with a veranda extension. Tempting up-to-date cuisine made with fresh produce.

CARRIÈRES-SUR-SEINE – **78 Yvelines** – **311** J2 – **101** 14 – **pop. 15 300** – **alt. 52 m** – ✉ **78420** 20 **A1**

▶ Paris 19 – Argenteuil 8 – Nanterre 7 – Pontoise 28 – St-Germain-en-Laye 7

⛳9 de l'Île Fleurie Carrières sur Seine, ✆ 01 39 52 61 61

✗ **Le Panoramic de Chine**

1 r. Fermettes – ✆ 01 39 57 64 58 – Jeanpierre.limy@orange.fr – Jeanpirre.limy@orange.fr – Fax 01 39 15 17 68 – Closed August, 24-31 December, Sunday dinner and Monday

Rest – Menu € 22 (weekdays) – Carte € 25/48

◆ The pagoda entrance and resolutely Asian-style interior decoration of this 1920s house is an invitation to taste its Chinese, Thai and Vietnamese cuisine. Summer terrace.

CERGY-PONTOISE Ⓟ – **95 Val-d'Oise** – **305** D6 – **106** 5 – **101** 2 – **pop. 178 656** – ✉ **95** ▌**Northern France and the Paris Region** 18 **B1**

▶ Paris 35 – Mantes-la-Jolie 40 – Pontoise 3 – Rambouillet 60 – Versailles 33

⛳18 de Cergy-Pontoise Vauréal 2 allée de l'Obstacle d'Eau, W : 7 km on D 922, ✆ 01 34 21 03 48

⛳27 d'Ableiges Ableiges Chaussée Jules César, NW : 14 km on the Ableiges road, ✆ 01 30 27 97 00

⛳18 de Gadancourt Gadancourt 20 km on the Rouen road, ✆ 01 34 66 12 97

CERGY-PRÉFECTURE

Arts (Pl. des) . . . Z 2
Boucle (R. de la) . . . Y 3
Bourgognes (R. des) . . . Z 5
Chênes Émeraude . . . Y 13
Columbia (Square) . . . Y 14
Diapason (Square du) . . . Y 17
Écureuil (R. de l') . . . Y 19
Étoile (Allée de l') . . . Y 21
Galeries (R. des) . . . Y 24
Gare (R. de la) . . . Z 25
Grouettes (Av. des) . . . Z 33
Herbes (R. aux) . . . Y 34
Italiens (R. des) . . . Y 39
Marché Neuf (R. du) . . . Y 43
Pays de France (R. des) . . . Y 52
Pergola (Pl. de la) . . . Z 53
Platanes (Allée des) . . . Z 59
Préfecture (Parvis de la) . . . Z 63
Préfecture (R. de la) . . . Z 64
Prieuré (R. du) . . . Z 66
Théâtre (Allée du) . . . Z 71
Traversière (R.) . . . Y 74
Verger (R. du) . . . Z 77
Villarceaux (R. de) . . . Z 81

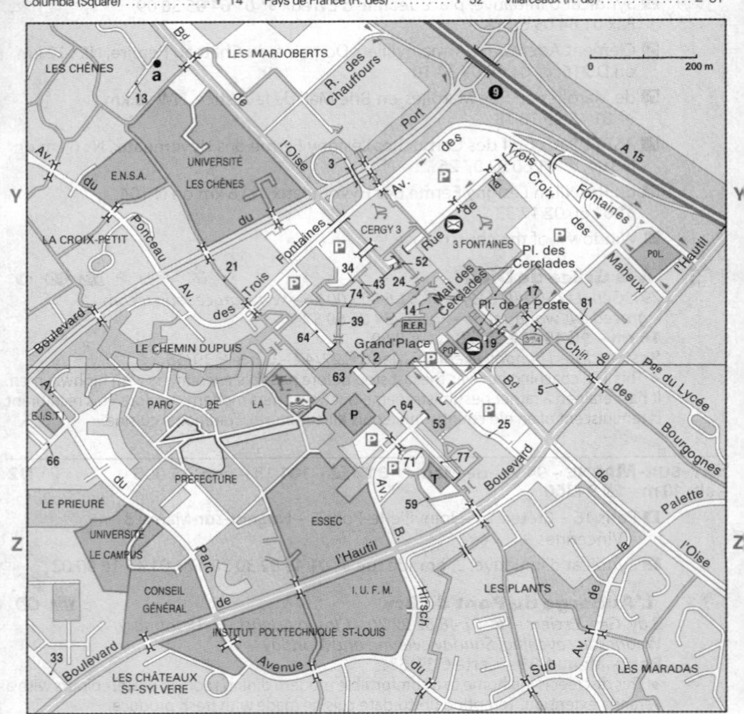

CERGY-PONTOISE

Bougara (Av. Rédouane) . . . **BV** 4	Constellation (Av. de la) . . . . **AV** 13	Mitterrand (Av. Fr.). . . . . . . **BVX** 45
Bouticourt (Bd Ch.). . . . . **BV** 6	Delarue (Av. du Gén.-G.) . . . **BV** 15	Moulin à Vent (Bd du) . . . . . **AV** 47
	Genottes (Av. des) . . . . **AV** 28	Petit Albi (R. du) . . . . **AV** 55
	Lavoye (R. Pierre). . . . . **BV** 40	Verdun (Av. de). . . . . **BX** 76
	Mendès-France (Mail) . . . . . **AX** 44	Viosne (Bd de la) . . . . **BVX** 83

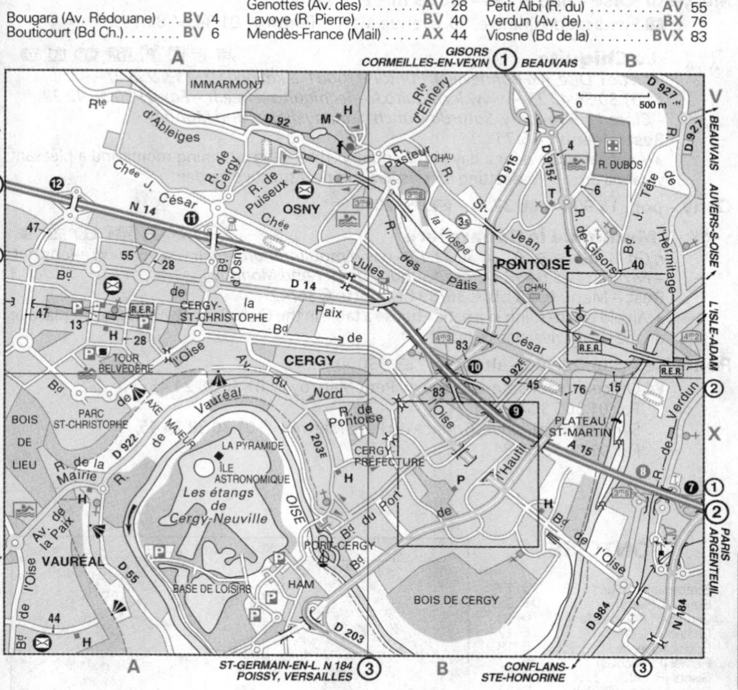

Cergy – pop. 54 600 – alt. 30 m – ✉ 95000

Mercure without rest

3 r. Chênes Émeraude, on bd de l'Oise – ✆ 01 34 24 94 94 – www.mercure.com – h3452@accor.com – Fax 01 34 24 95 15 Y a

56 rm – †€ 145 ††€ 155, ☕ € 14

◆ Behind the restored façade is a modern hotel with large, extremely well-equipped rooms with period furniture. Choose the quieter rooms at the back.

Cormeilles-en-Vexin by ①: 10 km – pop. 954 – alt. 111 m – ✉ 95830

XX Maison Cagna

rte de Dieppe – ✆ 01 34 66 61 56 – www.maison-cagna.fr – contact@maison-cagna.fr – Fax 01 34 66 40 31 – Closed for three weeks in August, 23-27 December, Sunday except bank holidays and Monday

Rest – Menu € 32 (weekday lunch)/65 bi – Carte approx. € 52

◆ Today, Mr Cagna's children run the restaurant in this attractive Vexin house. Warm country setting (exposed stonework and beams) enhanced by modern highlights. Refined cuisine.

Hérouville Northeast by D 927: 8 km – pop. 559 – alt. 120 m – ✉ 95300

X Les Vignes Rouges

3 pl. de l'Église – ✆ 01 34 66 54 73 – www.vignesrouges.fr – Fax 01 34 66 20 88 – Closed 3-12 May, 5-27 August, Toussaint holiday, Sunday dinner, Monday and Tuesday

Rest – Menu € 38 – Carte € 52/80

◆ A typical Île de France house named after a painting by Van Gogh. Veranda facing the church. Exhibition of paintings by a local artist. Traditional dishes.

Méry-sur-Oise – pop. 9 190 – alt. 29 m – ✉ 95540

Syndicat d'initiative, 30, avenue Marcel Perrin ✆ 01 34 64 85 15

Le Chiquito

93 r. de l' Oise, (La Bonneville), Pontoise road1 .5 km on D 922 ✉ 95540 – ✆ 01 30 36 40 23 – www.lechiquito.fr – lechiquito@free.fr – Fax 01 30 36 42 22 – Closed 2-9 January, Saturday lunch, Sunday dinner and Monday

Rest – Menu € 56/71

◆ An ideal address for a day in the country! Three elegant dining rooms and a pleasant veranda provide the setting for classical cuisine. Attractive garden.

Osny – pop. 15 900 – alt. 37 m – ✉ 95520

Moulin de la Renardière

r. Gd Moulin – ✆ 01 30 30 21 13 – www.moulinrenardiere.fr – severine@e-leos.net – Fax 01 34 25 04 98 – Closed Sunday dinner and Monday AV **f**

Rest – Menu (€ 28 bi), € 36/69 bi – Carte € 36/42

◆ An old mill nestling in a park. Choose a table in the Grain Room with its fine fireplace or on the shady, riverside terrace.

Pontoise – pop. 28 500 – alt. 48 m – ✉ 95000

Office de tourisme, 6, place du Petit Martroy ✆ 01 30 38 24 45, Fax 01 30 73 54 84
Syndicat d'initiative, 6, place du Petit Martroy ✆ 01 30 38 24 45, Fax 01 30 73 54 84

PONTOISE

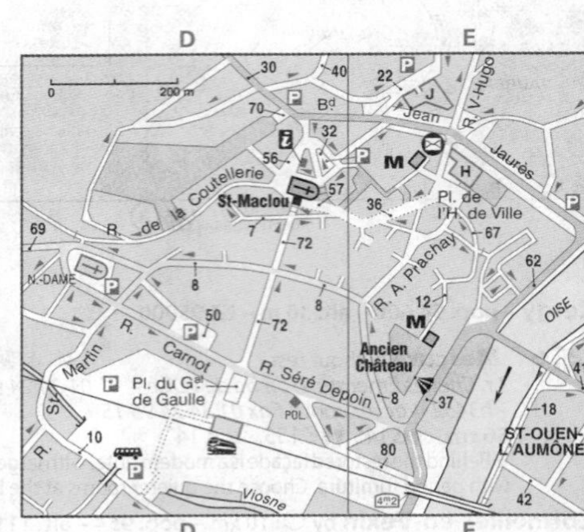

Auberge du Cheval Blanc

47 r. Gisors – ✆ 01 30 32 25 05 – www.chevalblanc95.com – aubergeduchevalblanc95@wanadoo.fr – Closed 27 July-16 August, Saturday lunch, Sunday and Monday BV **t**

Rest – Menu (€ 35), € 39 – Carte € 50/60

◆ Contemporary setting with works by local artists on display. Modern cuisine accompanied by a good selection of wines from small producers. Summer terrace.

CERNAY-LA-VILLE – 78 Yvelines – **311** H3 – **106** 29 – **101** 31 – **pop. 1 641** – alt. 170 m – ✉ 78720 18 **B2**

Paris 45 – Chartres 52 – Longjumeau 31 – Rambouillet 12 – Versailles 25

Abbey ★ of Vaux-de-Cernay West: 2 km, **Île de France.**

Abbaye des Vaux de Cernay rm, rest,
2.5 km west on the D 24 – 01 34 85 23 00 VISA
– www.abbayedecernay.com – reception.cernay@leshotelsparticuliers.com
– Fax 01 34 85 11 60
54 rm – €120/315 €120/315, €18 – 3 suites
Rest – Menu (€28), €50/88 – Carte €55/90
◆ A magnificent 12C Cistercian abbey, reached via parkland. Find Gothic lounges and vast guestrooms with antique and more modern furnishings. Traditional cuisine served in the amazing dining room with a superb vaulted ceiling.

La Ferme des Vallées without rest VISA
west: 3.5 km on the D24 – 01 30 46 32 42 – www.lafermedesvallees.com
– vallees@leshotelsparticuliers.com – Fax 01 30 46 32 23
30 rm – €97/245 €97/245, €15
◆ This old farmhouse on the estate of Vaux de Cernay Abbey now houses variously furnished rooms with roof windows. Simpler rooms in the wing, a former sheepfold.

in La Celle-les-Bordes South: 4 km by D 72 – pop. 842 – alt. 125 m – ✉ 78720

L'Auberge de l'Élan VISA
5 r. du Village (Les Bordes) – 01 34 85 15 55 – www.laubergedelelan-78.com
– aubergelan@wanadoo.fr – Fax 01 34 85 15 55 – Closed 10-31 August,
19-26 December, 20-26 February, Sunday dinner, Tuesday and Wednesday
Rest – Menu (€28), €38/100
◆ This old village house has been renovated but retains its warm rustic feel. Traditional cuisine, highlighting regional produce. Grocer's next door.

CHARENTON-LE-PONT – **94 Val-de-Marne** – **312** D3 – **101** 26 – **pop. 27 800** 21 **C2**
– alt. 45 m – ✉ 94220

Paris 8 – Alfortville 3 – Ivry-sur-Seine 4

Novotel Atria rest, VISA
5 pl. Marseillais – 01 46 76 60 60 – www.novotel.com – h1549@accor.com
– Fax 01 49 77 68 00
132 rm – €153/215 €153/215, €14 – 1 suite
Rest – Menu (€23), €37/45 – Carte approx. €21
◆ This hotel offers rooms in compliance with the chain's style and is fully equipped for meetings and seminars, from individual desks to a large conference room. Modern restaurant dining room and traditional cuisine.

CHÂTEAUFORT – **78 Yvelines** – **311** I3 – **101** 22 – **pop. 1 453** – **alt. 153 m** 20 **A3**
– ✉ 78117

Paris 28 – Arpajon 28 – Chartres 75 – Versailles 15

National Guyancourt 2 avenue du Golf, NW : 7 km on D 36, 01 30 43 36 00

La Belle Époque (Philippe Delaune) VISA
10 pl. Mairie – 01 39 56 95 48 – www.labelleepoque78.fr
– Fax 01 39 56 99 93 – Closed 2-24 August, 21-28 December, Sunday and Monday
Rest – Menu €36 (weekdays)/56 – Carte €58/70
Spec. Pavé de thon rouge mi-cuit au coulis de roquette. Filet de Saint Pierre meunière et augergines confites. Tiramisu au café et pain épicé aux cerises amarena.
◆ The name evokes the style of the decor: zinc bar, beams and copper pans. Guests enjoy seasonal cuisine. Shaded terrace overlooking the Chevreuse Valley.

CLAMART – **92 Hauts-de-Seine** – **311** J3 – **101** 25 – **pop. 49 800** – **alt. 102 m** 20 **B2**
– ✉ 92140

Paris 10 – Boulogne-Billancourt 7 – Issy-les-Moulineaux 4 – Nanterre 15 – Versailles 13

Syndicat d'initiative, 22, rue Paul Vaillant Couturier 01 46 42 17 95, Fax 01.46.42.44.30

La Brèche du Bois without rest VISA
7 pl. J. Hunebelle – 01 46 42 29 06 – www.hotel-brechedubois.com
– brechebois@aol.com – Fax 01 46 42 00 05
30 rm – €59/62 €68/72, €7
◆ Practical guestrooms in this hotel in a tree-filled district not far from Clamart's woodlands. Rooms are quieter at the rear.

Trosy without rest
41 r. P. Vaillant-Couturier – ✆ 01 47 36 37 37 – www.hoteldutrosy.com – hoteltrosy@aol.com – Fax 01 47 36 88 38
40 rm – †€ 40/56 ††€ 40/62, ☕ € 7
◆ This modern building features functional well-kept rooms; ask for one overlooking the quieter courtyard side. Family atmosphere.

CLICHY – 92 Hauts-de-Seine – **311** J2 – **101** 15 – **pop. 56 600 – alt. 30 m** 20 **B1** – ✉ 92110

Paris 9 – Argenteuil 8 – Nanterre 9 – Pontoise 26 – St-Germain-en-Laye 21
Office de tourisme, 61, rue Martre ✆ 01 47 15 31 61, Fax 01 47 15 30 29

Holiday Inn
2 r. 8 mai 1945 – ✆ 01 76 68 77 00 – www.holidayinn.com/parisclichy – hipclichy@ihg.com – Fax 01 76 68 77 01
270 rm ☕ – †€ 175/400 ††€ 175/400
Rest – *(Closed Sunday lunch and Saturday)* Menu (€ 16) – Carte € 27/49
◆ Despite its location close to the ring-road, the rooms in this hotel are quiet, thanks to excellent soundproofing. Modern architecture, harmonious rooms and state-of-the-art facilities.

Europe without rest
52 bd Gén. Leclerc – ✆ 01 47 37 13 10 – www.hotel-residence-europe.com – europe.hotel@wanadoo.fr – Fax 01 40 87 11 06
83 rm – †€ 110/140 ††€ 120/150, ☕ € 10
◆ Renovated brick building (1920) offering comfortable rooms with a soothing yet fashionable decoration. Fully equipped, high quality leisure and fitness area.

Résidence Europe without rest
15 r. Pierre Curie – ✆ 01 47 37 13 10 – www.hotel-residence-europe.com – europe.hotel@wanadoo.fr – Fax 01 40 87 11 06
28 rm – †€ 100/150 ††€ 110/160, ☕ € 10
◆ In a peaceful street, this establishment has refurbished rooms with limed furniture. The plush breakfast room serves a morning buffet.

La Romantica
73 bd J. Jaurès – ✆ 01 47 37 29 71 – www.laromantica.fr – laromantica@wanadoo.fr – Fax 01 47 37 76 32 – Closed Saturday lunchtime and Sunday
Rest – Menu € 38 (weekday lunch), € 48/80 – Carte € 49/92
◆ A business clientele appreciates the Italian gourmet cuisine and fine wine list of this smart establishment. The décor mingles classical, Roman and rustic elements. Flower-decked courtyard terrace.

La Barrière de Clichy
1 r. Paris – ✆ 01 47 37 05 18 – labarrieredeclichy@free.fr – Fax 01 47 37 77 05 – Closed August, Saturday, Sunday and bank holidays
Rest – Menu € 33/42 – Carte € 35/45
◆ This alluring restaurant is elegant, light and minimalist. Seasonal menu that caters to modern tastes and a market-sourced menu that changes daily.

COLOMBES – 92 Hauts-de-Seine – **312** C2 – **101** 14 – **pop. 81 400 – alt. 38 m** 20 **B1** – ✉ 92700

Paris 19 – Nanterre 9 – Boulogne-Billancourt 19 – Montreuil 23 – Argenteuil 4

Courtyard by Marriott
91 bd Charles de Gaulle – ✆ 01 47 69 59 49 – www.marriott.com – cy.colombes@courtyard.com – Fax 01 47 69 59 20
150 rm – †€ 99/259 ††€ 99/259, ☕ € 17
Rest – *(closed Saturday lunch and Sunday lunch)*
Menu (€ 15) – Carte € 24/37 dinner only
◆ This new building has functional guestrooms and a gym. The lobby, heated by an open fireplace, is home to the Market, serving self-service snacks and refreshments. Seasonal, contemporary cuisine prepared by the chef in full view of diners.

Conflans-Ste-Honorine – 78 Yvelines – 311 I2 – 101 3 – pop. 33 700 18 **B1**
– alt. 25 m – ✉ 78700 Northern France and the Paris Region

Paris 38 – Mantes-la-Jolie 39 – Poissy 10 – Pontoise 8 – Versailles 27

Office de tourisme, 1, rue René Albert ✆ 01 34 90 99 09, Fax 01 39 19 80 77

≤★ from the château park terrace - Musée de la Batellerie.

Au Bord de l'Eau

15 quai Martyrs-de-la-Résistance – ✆ 01 39 72 86 51 – Closed 8-24 August, 23 December-3 January, Monday and dinner except Saturday

Rest – Menu € 29 (weekday lunch), € 42/59

◆ Boat name plaques and navigation instruments: The interior of this family restaurant on the quays of the Seine renders homage to river craft.

Corbeil-Essonnes – 91 Essonne – 312 D4 – 101 37 – pop. 40 900 18 **B2**
– alt. 37 m – ✉ 91100

Paris 36 – Fontainebleau 37 – Créteil 27 – Évry 6 – Melun 24

Syndicat d'initiative, 36, rue Saint-Spire ✆ 01 64 96 23 97, Fax 01 60 88 05 37

Blue Green Golf de Villeray Saint-Pierre-du-PerrayE : 6 km, ✆ 01 60 75 17 47

de Greenparc Saint-Pierre-du-Perray Route de Villepècle, NE : 6 km on D 947, ✆ 01 60 75 40 60

in Coudray-Montceaux Southeast: 6 km by N 7 – pop. 2 800 – alt. 81 m – ✉ 91830

Mercure

rte de Milly-la-Forêt – ✆ 01 64 99 00 00 – h0977@accor-hotels.com – Fax 01 64 93 95 55

125 rm – €127 €137, €15 **Rest** – Carte € 25/35

◆ Archery, golf and handball, etc., as well as a fine conference centre: this hotel's sports and business facilities are just as appreciated by families as by business guests. Modern dining room/veranda and terrace overlooking the forest and countryside.

Courbevoie – 92 Hauts-de-Seine – 311 J2 – 101 15 – pop. 84 000 20 **B1**
– alt. 28 m – ✉ 92400 Northern France and the Paris Region

Paris 10 – Asnières-sur-Seine 4 – Levallois-Perret 4 – Nanterre 5 – St-Germain-en-Laye 17

George Sand without rest

18 av. Marceau – ✆ 01 43 33 57 04 – reception@georgesandhotel.net – Fax 01 47 88 59 38

31 rm – €90/145 €90/145, €12

◆ It is worth staying in this hotel, with a pretty Art Deco facade, for its refined interior reminiscent of the world of George Sand, 19C furniture and romantic lounge where Chopin's music is played.

Central without rest

99 r. Cap. Guynemer – ✆ 01 47 89 25 25 – www.central-courbevoie-hotel.com – central-ladefense@wanadoo.fr – Fax 01 46 67 02 21

55 rm – €98/107 €98/107, €7

◆ The sound-proofed bedrooms and public areas of this family-run hotel near La Défense have been revamped in a pleasantly modern style.

quartier Charras

Mercure La Défense 5 rm,

18 r. Baudin – ✆ 01 49 04 75 00 – www.mercure.com – h1546@accor.com – Fax 01 47 68 83 32

507 rm – €75/230 €90/245, €18 – 5 suites

Rest ***Le Bistrot de l'Echanson*** *– ✆ 01 49 04 75 85 (closed Friday evening, Sunday lunchtime and Saturday)* Menu (€ 15) – Carte € 20/36

◆ Recently renovated functional rooms behind the original circular arc façade. From the eighth floor up some have a view of Paris or La Défense. Gym, steam room and solarium. Designer décor and warm atmosphere at the Bistrot de l'Échanson.

at Bécon Park

Les Trois Marmites

215 bd St-Denis – ✆ 01 43 33 25 35 – Fax 01 43 33 25 35 – Closed August, Saturday, Sunday and public holidays

Rest – *(lunch only)* Menu (€ 34), € 39/69

◆ Popular with a business clientele, this small neighbourhood restaurant near the quays is situated opposite Bécon Park and Roybet Fould Museum (works by Carpeaux). Traditional fare.

CRÉTEIL P – **94 Val-de-Marne** – **312** D3 – **101** 27 – **pop. 89 000** – **alt. 48 m** 21 **C2**
– ✉ 94000 **Northern France and the Paris Region**

Paris 14 – Bobigny 22 – Évry 32 – Lagny-sur-Marne 29 – Melun 35

de Marolles-en-Brie Marolles-en-Brie Mail de la Justice, SE : 10 km, ✆ 01 45 95 18 18

d'Ormesson Ormesson-sur-Marne Chemin du Belvédère, E : 15 km, ✆ 01 45 76 20 71

Town hall ★: square ★.

Novotel

rm,

r. Jean Gabin, (at the lake) – ✆ 01 56 72 56 72 – www.novotel.com – h0382@accor.com – Fax 01 56 72 56 73

110 rm – †€ 59/200 ††€ 59/200, ☕ € 14 **Rest** – Menu (€ 26) – Carte € 30/50

◆ The major attraction of this Novotel is its location overlooking the lake (leisure centre and jogging trail). The rooms have been refurbished according to the chain's charter. A resolutely modern-style restaurant, enlivened by plasma screens. Traditional cuisine.

DAMPIERRE-EN-YVELINES – **78 Yvelines** – **311** H3 – **101** 31 – **pop. 1 128** 18 **B2**
– **alt. 100 m** – ✉ **78720**

Paris 38 – Chartres 57 – Longjumeau 32 – Rambouillet 16 – Versailles 21

Office de tourisme, 9, Grande Rue ✆ 01 30 52 57 30, Fax 01 30 52 52 43

de Forges-les-Bains Forges-les-Bains Route du Général Leclerc, SE : 14 km, ✆ 01 64 91 48 18

Château de Dampierre ★★, **Northern France and the Paris Region**

Auberge du Château "Table des Blot" (Christophe Blot) with rm

rest,

1 Grande rue – ✆ 01 30 47 56 56 – www.latabledesblot.com – Fax 01 30 47 51 75 – Closed 17-31 August, 21-29 December, Sunday dinner, Monday and Tuesday

11 rm – †€ 80/90 ††€ 80/90, ☕ € 8

Rest – Menu € 37 (weekdays)/65

Spec. Foie fras poché au vin rouge. Travers de cochon confit aux épices (Oct. to March). Soufflé au chocolat, cacao mi-cuit et mousse.

◆ Attractive and well-decorated 17C inn where old and new combine harmoniously. The chef's talents unite with the rhythm of the seasons to produce creative dishes. Warm welcome. Pretty, country house style bedrooms.

Les Écuries du Château

2 Grande Rue, (at the chateau) – ✆ 01 30 52 52 99 – www.lesecuriesduchateau.com – contact@lesecuriesduchateau.com – Fax 01 30 52 59 90 – Closed 16 February-4 March, 31 July-21 August, Tuesday and Wednesday

Rest – Menu (€ 30), € 42/50 – Carte approx. € 55

◆ The saddlery of Dampierre château provides a magical setting for this restaurant. Guests enjoy traditional cuisine in a rustic and cosy decor and views over parkland.

Auberge St-Pierre

1 r. Chevreuse – ✆ 01 30 52 53 53 – Fax 01 30 52 58 57 – Closed August, Sunday dinner, Tuesday dinner and Monday

Rest – Menu (€ 25), € 30

◆ The half-timbered façade of this characteristic country inn sets the scene. A lovely fireplace and bare beams grace the dining room. Traditional menu.

LA DÉFENSE – 92 Hauts-de-Seine – 311 J2 – 101 14 – ✉ 92400 Paris 20 **B1**

Paris 10 – Courbevoie 1 – Nanterre 4 – Puteaux 2

District★★: view★ of the square.

Pullman La Défense rm, rest,

11 av. Arche, Défense 6 exit ✉ 92081 – ✆ 01 47 17 50 00 VISA

– www.pullman-hotels.com – h3013@accor.com – Fax 01 47 17 56 78

368 rm – €410 €410, €27 – 16 suites

Rest *Avant Seine* – grill room – *✆ 01 47 17 50 99 (Closed 7-30 August, 19 December-3 January, Friday dinner, Saturday, Sunday and bank holidays)* Carte approx. €52

◆ Beautiful architecture, resembling a ship's hull, a combination of glass and ochre stonework. Spacious, elegant rooms, lounges and very well-equipped auditorium (with simultaneous translation booths). The Avant Seine offers you quality designer décor and spit-roast dishes.

Renaissance rm, VISA

60 Jardin de Valmy, on the circular road, exit La Défense 7 ✉ 92918 – ✆ 01 41 97 50 50 – www.renaissancehotels.com/parld – francereservation@mariott.com – Fax 01 41 97 51 51

324 rm – €159/490 €159/490, €25 – 3 suites

Rest – *(closed Saturday lunch, Sunday lunch and holidays lunch)*

Menu €32 (weekday lunch) – Carte €51/68

◆ Luxurious sophistication defines this contemporary hotel at the foot of the Grande Arche: quality materials, flawless comfort and inviting, perfectly equipped guestrooms. In the restaurant, all wood features with a 1940s brasserie atmosphere overlooking the gardens of Valmy.

Hilton La Défense rm, VISA

2 pl. de la Défense ✉ 92053 – ✆ 01 46 92 10 10 – www.hilton.com – parldhirm@hilton.com – Fax 01 46 92 10 50

142 rm – €255/360 €255/360, €27 – 6 suites

Rest *Coté Parvis* – Carte €48/81

◆ Hotel situated within the CNIT complex. Some of the rooms have been particularly designed with the business traveller in mind: work, rest, relaxation and Jacuzzi tubs in the bathrooms. At Côté Parvis, modern cuisine and a fine view of the Arch of La Défense.

Sofitel Centre VISA

34 cours Michelet, via ring road, La Défense 4 exit ✉ 92060 Puteaux – ✆ 01 47 76 44 43 – http://www.sofitel-paris-ladefense.com – h0912@sofitel.com – Fax 01 47 76 72 10

150 rm – €140/495 €140/495, €27 – 1 suite

Rest *L'Italian Lounge* – *✆ 01 47 76 72 40* – Menu (€40), €55/98 bi Carte €55/89

◆ The scalloped façade of this hotel blends in among the skyscrapers of La Défense. Spacious, well-equipped rooms, which sport a fashionable look. A contemporary setting for Mediterranean cuisine and a fine wine list.

Novotel La Défense rm, VISA

2 bd Neuilly, Défense 1 exit – ✆ 01 41 45 23 23 – www.novotel.com – h0747@accor.com – Fax 01 41 45 23 24

280 rm – €290/390 €290/490, €16 **Rest** – Carte €22/45

◆ This hotel is at the foot of La Défense, a genuine open-air museum. Some of the renovated rooms overlook Paris. Trendy new Novotel Café-style bar. Contemporary decor in the restaurant, whose cuisine evolves with the seasons.

DRAVEIL – 91 Essonne – 312 D3 – 101 36 – pop. 29 300 – alt. 55 m – ✉ 91210 21 **C3**

Paris 23 – Corbeil Essonnes 11 – Créteil 14 – Versailles 30

Syndicat d'initiative, place de la République ✆ 01 69 03 09 39, Fax 01 69 42 50 02

XX **Gibraltar** VISA

61 av. Libert – ✆ 01 69 42 32 05 – www.legibraltar.fr – legibraltars@wanadoo.fr – Fax 01 69 52 06 82 – Closed Sunday dinner

Rest – Menu (€13), €17 (weekdays)/38 – Carte €38/50

◆ Set sail for Gibraltar... on the banks of the Seine! Updated recipes served on a pleasant terrace overlooking the river or in the recently renovated dining room.

ENGHIEN-LES-BAINS – 95 Val-d'Oise – 305 E7 – 101 5 – pop. 12 300 20 **B1**
– alt. 45 m – Spa : all year – Casino – ✉ **95880** **Northern France and the Paris Region**

Paris 17 – Argenteuil 7 – Chantilly 34 – Pontoise 22 – St-Denis 7 – St-Germain-en-Laye 25

Office de tourisme, 81, rue du Général-de-Gaulle ✆ 01 34 12 41 15, Fax 01 39 34 05 76

de Domont Montmorency Domont Route de Montmorency, N : 8 km, ✆ 01 39 91 07 50

Lake ★ - Deuil-la-Barre: historiated capitals ★ of Notre-Dame church Northeast: 2 km.

Grand Hôtel Barrière

VISA MC AE

85 r. Gén. de Gaulle – ✆ 01 39 34 10 00 – www.grand-hotel-enghien.fr – grandhotelenghien@lucienbarriere.com – Fax 01 39 34 10 01

37 rm – €234/260 €234/260, ☕ €19 – 6 suites

Rest *L'Aventurine* – *(closed 3-16 August, Sunday dinner, Monday and Tuesday)* Menu €45/95 – Carte €68/86

◆ One of France's largest spa and fitness centres, this hotel has a classic, understated elegance. Stylish, individually decorated rooms. Pleasant restaurant with wood panelling and silk hangings serving up to the minute cuisine. Terrace.

Du Lac

rm, VISA MC AE

89 r. Gén. de Gaulle – ✆ 01 39 34 11 00 – www.hotel-du-lac-enghien.com – hoteldulac@lucienbarriere.com – Fax 01 39 34 11 01

138 rm – €234/328 €234/328, ☕ €15 – 3 suites

Rest – *(closed Saturday lunch)* Menu (€22), €29 – Carte €40/66

◆ This recent hotel sports a holiday resort feel. Comfortable rooms with a lake view (those on the garden side are quieter). Access to the spa and fitness facilities possible. The modern dining room is pleasantly intimate. Attractive waterside summer terrace.

Aux Saveurs d'Alice

AC VISA MC AE

32 bd d'Ormesson – ✆ 01 34 12 78 36 – www.auxsaveursdalice.com – auxsaveursdalice@orange.fr – Fax 01 34 12 22 78 – Closed 5-25 August, Sunday dinner, Wednesday dinner and Monday

Rest – Menu (€22 bi), €28 bi – Carte approx. €38

◆ This town centre restaurant is mainly appreciated for its simple classic cuisine made with fresh produce. Three discreetly rustic dining rooms.

ÉVRY P **– 91 Essonne – 312 D4 – 101 37 –** ✉ **91000** 18 **B2**
Northern France and the Paris Region

Paris 32 – Chartres 80 – Créteil 30 – Étampes 36 – Fontainebleau 36 – Melun 23

La Résurrection cathedral ★ - 5 May-Jan. Epiphanies (Exhibition).

All Seasons

rm, AC rest, VISA MC AE

52 bd Coquibus, (opposite the cathedral) – ✆ 01 69 47 30 00 – www.all-seasons-hotels.com – H1986@accor.com – Fax 01 69 47 30 10 – Closed 31 July-23 August and 23 December-3 January

110 rm ☕ – €105 €115

Rest – *(closed Friday dinner, Saturday, Sunday and holidays)* Menu (€20) – Carte approx. €30

◆ On a busy boulevard facing the Cathedral of the Resurrection, a hotel with quite spacious, well-soundproofed rooms, equipped with a functional office area. Traditional menu in the restaurant.

in Courcouronnes – pop. 14 500 – alt. 80 m – ✉ **91080**

de Bondoufle Bondoufle Départementale 31, W : 3 km, ✆ 01 60 86 41 71

Canal

AC VISA MC

31 r. du Pont Amar, (near the hospital) – ✆ 01 60 78 34 72 – Fax 01 60 79 22 72 – Closed August, 19-27 December, Saturday and Sunday

Rest – Menu €20/28 – Carte €35/45

◆ Small brasserie, a little old-fashioned. Enjoy the hearty cuisine giving pride of place to pork products (pigs' trotters). Only fresh produce.

in Lisses – **pop. 7 206** – **alt. 86 m** – ✉ **91090**

Espace Léonard de Vinci rest,
av. Parcs – ✆ *01 64 97 66 77* – *www.leonard-de-vinci.com* VISA MC AE
– *contact@leonard-de-vinci.com* – *Fax 01 64 97 59 21*
74 rm – †€ 100/110 ††€ 100/110, ☕ € 10 **Rest** – Carte € 30/40
◆ Football pitches, squash courts, pools, steam bath, Jacuzzi tub, fitness facilities and a balneotherapy centre! And practical rooms for a well earned rest after so much activity. Brasserie or plush classical restaurant. Live jazz on Saturday evenings.

GAGNY – **93 Seine-Saint-Denis** – **305** G7 – **101** 18 – **pop. 37 600** – **alt. 70 m** 21 **D1**
– ✉ **93220**

Paris 17 – Bobigny 11 – Raincy 3 – St-Denis 18

Syndicat d'initiative, 1, avenue Jean-Jaurès ✆ 01 43 81 49 09

Le Vilgacy VISA
45 av. H. Barbusse – ✆ *01 43 81 23 33* – *www.vilgacy.com* – *vilgacy@orange.fr*
– *Fax 01 43 81 23 33* – *Closed 27 July-20 August, 15-25 February, Sunday dinner, Tuesday dinner and Monday except bank holidays*
Rest – Menu (€ 24), € 33 – Carte € 50/62
◆ Guests cannot fail to appreciate the modern decor of the two rooms (exhibited paintings for purchase) and, in summer, the garden terrace. Savoury traditional cuisine.

LA GARENNE-COLOMBES – **92 Hauts-de-Seine** – **311** J2 – **101** 14 20 **D1**
– **pop. 27 500** – **alt. 40 m** – ✉ **92250**

Paris 13 – Argenteuil 7 – Asnières-sur-Seine 5 – Courbevoie 2 – Nanterre 4 – Pontoise 27

Syndicat d'initiative, 24, rue d'Estienne-d'Orves ✆ 01 47 85 09 90

L'Instinct VISA MC AE
1 r. Voltaire – ✆ *01 56 83 82 82* – *www.restaurant-linstinct.com* – *Fax 01 47 82 09 53*
– *Closed 9-26 August, Monday dinner, Saturday lunch and Sunday*
Rest – *(pre-book)* Menu € 34
◆ Opposite the covered market, a distinctive modern and colourful decor sets the scene in the bright dining room and splendid bar. Up-to-date cuisine.

GRESSY – **77 Seine-et-Marne** – **312** F2 – **101** 10 – **pop. 813** – **alt. 98 m** 19 **C1**
– ✉ **77410**

Paris 32 – Meaux 20 – Melun 56 – Senlis 35

Le Manoir de Gressy rm, rest,
– ✆ *01 60 26 68 00* – *www.manoirdegressy.com* VISA MC AE
– *information@manoirdegressy.com* – *Fax 01 60 26 45 46*
– *Closed 24 December-5 January*
87 rm – †€ 210/290 ††€ 210/290, ☕ € 19
Rest – Menu € 46/140 bi – Carte € 47/57
◆ On the site of an 18C fortified farmstead, this manor house sports an attractive blend of styles. Individualised bedrooms all overlook the garden and pool. Well worn walls and parquet flooring in the large dining room, where seasonal cuisine and buffets are served.

ISSY-LES-MOULINEAUX – **92 Hauts-de-Seine** – **311** J3 – **101** 25 20 **B2**
– **pop. 62 600** – **alt. 37 m** – ✉ **92130** **Northern France and the Paris Region**

Paris 8 – Boulogne-Billancourt 3 – Clamart 4 – Nanterre 11 – Versailles 14

Office de tourisme, esplanade de l'Hôtel de Ville ✆ 01 41 23 87 00, Fax 01 41 23 87 07

Musée de la Carte à jouer★.

La Table des Montquartiers VISA MC
5 chemin Montquartiers – ✆ *01 46 44 05 45* – *www.crayeres-montquartiers.com*
– *contact@crayeres-montquartiers.com* – *Fax 01 46 45 66 55* – *Closed August, 24-27 December, Saturday, Sunday and bank holidays*
Rest – *(lunch only)* Menu (€ 35), € 40
◆ Venture into this unusual setting - the galleries of a former chalk quarry - and discover a magnificent wine list enhanced by a seasonally inspired menu.

XX **River Café**
Pont d'Issy, 146 quai Stalingrad – ✆ 01 40 93 50 20 – www.lerivercafe.net – reservation@lerivercafe.net – Fax 01 41 46 19 45
Rest – Menu € 35
◆ A former oil barge moored opposite Île St Germain. Market fresh menu, a colonial inspired decor and valet car parking. A gourmet trip in store!

XX **L'Île**
Parc Île St-Germain, 170 quai Stalingrad – ✆ 01 41 09 99 99 – www.restaurant-lile.com – v.fresneau@restaurant-lile.com – Fax 01 41 09 99 19
Rest – Menu € 44 bi/69 bi – Carte € 41/70
◆ This former barracks, located on an island on the Seine, is now home to a trendy restaurant, much in favour with the local showbiz crowd. Seasonal produce takes pride of place on the menu.

XX **Manufacture**
20 espl. Manufacture, (opposite 30 Rue E. Renan) – ✆ 01 40 93 08 98 – www.restaurantmanufacture.com – restaurantmanufacture@wanadoo.fr – Fax 01 40 93 57 22 – Closed 5-20 August, 25 December-1 January, Saturday and Sunday
Rest – Menu (€ 29), € 36
◆ This former tobacco factory (1904) has been successfully converted into a modern designer-inspired restaurant with an attractive terrace. Updated menu catering to today's tastes.

X **Coquibus**
16 av. de la République – ✆ 01 46 38 75 80 – www.coquibus.com – reservation@coquibus.com – Fax 01 41 08 95 80 – Closed Sunday
Rest – Menu (€ 18) – Carte € 25/45
◆ Wood-panelling, colourful artwork and terracotta cockerels lend this friendly restaurant the appearance of a 1930s brasserie. Traditional cuisine based on market produce.

JANVRY – **91 Essonne** – **312** B4 – **101** 33 – **pop. 605** – **alt. 160 m** – ✉ **91640** 18 **B2**

▶ Paris 35 – Briis s/s Forges 4 – Dourdan 20 – Palaiseau 19

XX **Bonne Franquette**
1 r. du Marchais – ✆ 01 64 90 72 06 – www.bonnefranquette.fr – info@bonnefranquette.fr – Fax 01 64 90 53 63 – Closed 4-25 May, 1-28 September, 21 December-11 January, Saturday lunch, Sunday dinner and Monday
Rest – Menu € 35
◆ Former post house opposite the 17C château of an attractive village in the Paris area. Two large blackboards show daily specials served in a warm rustic setting.

JOINVILLE-LE-PONT – **94 Val-de-Marne** – **312** D3 – **101** 27 – **pop. 17 100** – **alt. 49 m** – ✉ **94340** 21 **D2**

▶ Paris 12 – Créteil 7 – Lagny-sur-Marne 22 – Maisons-Alfort 5 – Vincennes 6
ℹ Office de tourisme, 23, rue de Paris ✆ 01 42 83 41 16, Fax 01 49 76 92 98

Kyriad Prestige rm,
16 av. Gén. Gallieni – ✆ 01 48 83 11 99 – www.kyriadprestige.fr – joinvillelepont@kyriadprestige.fr – Fax 01 48 89 51 58
89 rm – †€ 103/133 ††€ 103/133, ☕ € 14
Rest – Menu (€ 20), € 27 – Carte € 27/43
◆ Contemporary architecture with spacious, soundproofed rooms equipped with a small sitting room for relaxation or an office for working. Pleasant modern dining room and buffet meals.

Cinépole without rest
8 av. Platanes – ✆ 01 48 89 99 77 – www.cinepole.com – cinepole@wanadoo.fr – Fax 01 48 89 43 92
34 rm – †€ 61/63 ††€ 61/63, ☕ € 8
◆ The hotel's name conjures up memories of the old Joinville cinema studios. Practical, well-kept rooms. A tiny patio where breakfast is served in the summer.

LE KREMLIN-BICÊTRE – 94 Val-de-Marne – 312 D3 – 101 26 21 C2
– pop. 25 000 – alt. 60 m – ✉ 94270

Paris 5 – Boulogne-Billancourt 11 – Évry 28 – Versailles 23

Novotel Porte d' Italie

22 r. Voltaire – ✆ 01 45 21 19 09 – www.novotel.com – h5586@accor.com – Fax 01 45 21 12 60

168 rm – €115/170 €115/170, €15 **Rest** – Carte €20/45

◆ This recently built hotel with a simple, polished granite façade is just five minutes from Place d'Italie and offers rooms that meet the chain's latest standards. Restaurant with a trendy decor. Traditional cuisine.

Express by Holiday Inn without rest

1-3 r. Elisée Reclus – ✆ 01 47 26 26 26 – reservation@porteditalie.hiexpress.com – Fax 01 47 26 16 66

89 rm – €70/230 €79/230

◆ Hotel with a simple red brick façade near the French capital's southern districts. Small rooms lined with light wood panelling and colourful fabrics.

LEVALLOIS-PERRET – 92 Hauts-de-Seine – 311 J2 – 101 15 20 B1
– pop. 62 800 – alt. 30 m – ✉ 92300

Paris 9 – Argenteuil 8 – Nanterre 8 – Pontoise 27 – St-Germain-en-Laye 20

Evergreen Laurel

rm,

8 pl. G. Pompidou – ✆ 01 47 58 88 99 – www.evergreenhotel-paris.com – pardos@evergreen-hotels.com – Fax 01 47 58 88 99

337 rm – €330/480 €330/480, €19 – 1 suite

◆ Luxury, elegance and light: a brand new hotel designed with businessmen in mind. The spacious rooms have pleasant rosewood furniture. Restaurant undergoing restructure before reopening.

Espace Champerret without rest

26 r. Louise Michel – ✆ 01 47 57 20 71 – www.hotel-espace-champerret.com – espace.champerret.hotel@wanadoo.fr – Fax 01 47 57 31 39

39 rm – €55/86 €60/93, €8

◆ In summer breakfast is served in the courtyard which separates the two buildings of this hotel; the one at the rear is quieter. The refurbished rooms are soundproofed and well kept.

Les Autodidactes

9 pl, Jean Zay – ✆ 01 47 39 54 02 – autodidactes.restaurant@wanadoo.fr – Fax 01 47 39 59 99 – Closed August, 24 December-1st January, Monday dinner, Wednesday dinner, Saturday, Sunday and holidays

Rest – Menu €35 – Carte €43/55

◆ The landlord is also an artist and displays his very colourful paintings in the restaurant dining room. Pleasant shaded terrace and short menu including seasonal market produce.

LIVRY-GARGAN – 93 Seine-Saint-Denis – 305 G7 – 101 18 21 D1
– pop. 40 900 – alt. 60 m – ✉ 93190

Paris 19 – Aubervilliers 14 – Aulnay-sous-Bois 4 – Bobigny 8 – Meaux 26 – Senlis 42

Office de tourisme, 5, place François Mitterrand ✆ 01 43 30 61 60, Fax 01 43 30 48 41

La Petite Marmite

8 bd de la République – ✆ 01 43 81 29 15 – www.la-petite-marmite-93.com – contact@la-petite-marmite-93.com – Fax 01 43 02 69 59 – Closed 5-27 August, Sunday dinner and Wednesday

Rest – Menu €35/60 – Carte €56/68

◆ This restaurant serves generous, traditional cuisine in a pleasant, country-style setting. The terrace in the interior courtyard is decorated with frescoes.

LONGJUMEAU – 91 Essonne – **312** C3 – **101** 35 – **pop. 20 900** – **alt. 78 m** – ✉ **91160** 20 **B3**

Paris 20 – Chartres 70 – Dreux 84 – Évry 15 – Melun 41 – Orléans 113 – Versailles 27

XX **St-Pierre**

42 r. F. Mitterrand – ✆ 01 64 48 81 99 – www.lesaintpierre.com – saint-pierre@wanadoo.fr – Fax 01 69 34 25 53 – Closed 27 July-18 August, Monday dinner, Wednesday dinner, Saturday lunch and Sunday
Rest – Menu € 33/46 – Carte € 43/58
◆ The owners love to share their passion for products from Gers: duck and foie gras lead the way, followed by south western dishes, all served in a warm, rustic setting.

MAISONS-ALFORT – 94 Val-de-Marne – **312** D3 – **101** 27 – **pop. 53 300** – **alt. 37 m** – ✉ **94700** **Northern France and the Paris Region** 21 **C2**

Paris 10 – Créteil 4 – Évry 34 – Melun 39

XX **La Bourgogne**

164 r. J. Jaurès – ✆ 01 43 75 12 75 – www.restaurantlabourgogne.com – restaurant.labourgogne@orange.fr – Fax 01 43 68 05 86 – Closed 8-20 August, 24 December-1st January, Saturday lunch and Sunday
Rest – Menu € 32/49 bi – Carte € 40/68
◆ Smiling staff and a provincial country inn atmosphere where modern cuisine is made with market fresh produce. Regional specialities for the regulars.

MAISONS-LAFFITTE – 78 Yvelines – **311** I2 – **101** 13 – **pop. 22 600** – **alt. 38 m** – ✉ **78600** **Northern France and the Paris Region** 20 **A1**

Paris 21 – Mantes-la-Jolie 38 – Poissy 9 – Pontoise 17 – St-Germain-en-Laye 8 – Versailles 19

Office de tourisme, 41, avenue de Longueil ✆ 01 39 62 63 64, Fax 01 39 12 02 89

Château★.

XXX **Tastevin** (Michel Blanchet)

9 av. Eglé – ✆ 01 39 62 11 67 – letastevin78@wanadoo.fr – Fax 01 39 62 73 09 – Closed 3-26 August, 22 February-8 March, Monday and Tuesday
Rest – Menu € 45 (weekday lunch)/95 – Carte € 92/121
Spec. Foie gras sous toutes ses formes. Gibier (season). Assiette du maître chocolatier.
◆ Mansion on the edge of the park with attentive service, high quality produce and a fine wine list.

X **La Plancha**

5 av. St-Germain – ✆ 01 39 12 03 75 – Fax 01 34 93 43 46 – Closed 1-11 March, 20 July-20 August, Sunday dinner, Tuesday dinner and Wednesday
Rest – Menu € 36/75 – Carte € 60/75
◆ Restaurant with a wanderlust feel, set near the station. A rather eccentric menu, offering recipes that successfully combine French, Spanish and Japanese ingredients.

MARLY-LE-ROI – 78 Yvelines – **312** B2 – **101** 12 – **pop. 16 600** – **alt. 90 m** – ✉ **78160** 20 **A2**

Paris 24 – Bougival 5 – St-Germain-en-Laye 5 – Versailles 9

Office de tourisme, 2, avenue des Combattants ✆ 01 39 16 16 35, Fax 01 39 16 16 01

XX **Le Village**

3 Grande Rue – ✆ 01 39 16 28 14 – tomohiro.uido@club-internet.fr – Fax 01 39 58 62 60 – Closed 3-24 August, Saturday lunch, Sunday dinner and Monday
Rest – *(number of covers limited, pre-book)* Menu € 39/75 – Carte € 109/148
◆ Appealing restaurant-inn in Old Marly. The Japanese chef skilfully mixes flavours from the Land of the Rising Sun with French classics.

MARNE-LA-VALLÉE – Île-de-France – **312** E2 – **101** 19 – **pop. 246 607** 19 **C2**
– ✉ 77206 Northern France and the Paris Region

Paris 27 – Meaux 29 – Melun 40

de Bussy-Saint-Georges Bussy-Saint-Georges Promenade des Golfeurs, ☎ 01 64 66 00 00

de Torcy Torcy Base Régionale de loisirs, N : 5 km, ☎ 01 64 80 80 90

Disneyland Paris Magny-le-Hongre Allée de la Mare Houleuse, ☎ 01 60 45 68 90

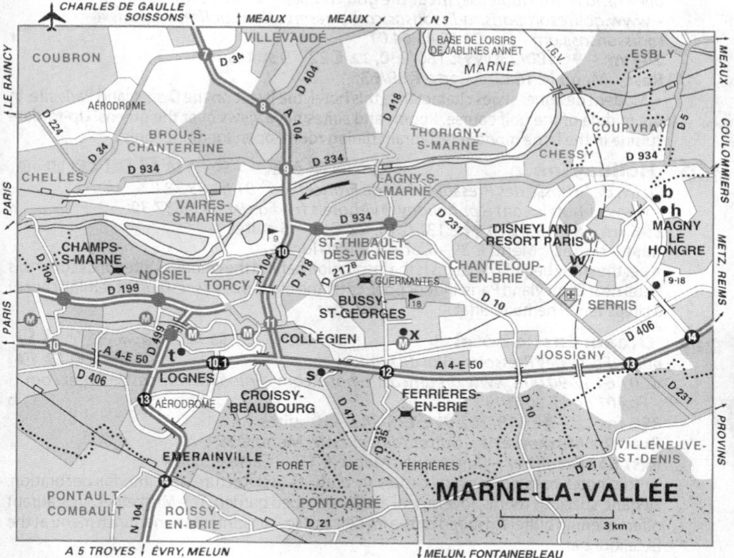

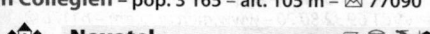

in Bussy-St-Georges – pop. 16 980 – alt. 105 m – ✉ 77600

Tulip Inn Marne la Vallée rm, VISA AE
44 bd A. Giroust – ☎ *01 64 66 11 11*
– *www.tulipinnmarnelavallee.com* – *tulip.reservations@wanadoo.fr*
– *Fax 01 64 66 29 05* **x**
87 rm – †€ 129 ††€ 129, ☕ € 12
Rest – *(closed Saturday lunch and Sunday)* Menu (€ 17), € 20 – Carte € 34/43
◆ Part of a large real estate complex opposite the RER station, a hotel with functional, well-soundproofed rooms. The bar is decorated in Louisiana style. Traditional menu enlivened with Italian notes served in the pastel coloured dining room.

in Collégien – pop. 3 165 – alt. 105 m – ✉ 77090

Novotel rm, P VISA AE
(exit 12) – ☎ *01 64 80 53 53* – *www.accor-hotels.com* – *h0385@accor.com*
– *Fax 01 64 80 48 37* **s**
195 rm – †€ 120/130 ††€ 133/143, ☕ € 15 **Rest** – Carte € 22/42
◆ This hotel caters for business clients and corporate meetings. The renovated rooms have a modern decor with wooden furniture and pretty colours. Traditional restaurant in a designer decor or on the poolside terrace. Simple dishes at the Novotel Café.

in Disneyland Resort Paris **access by A 4 motorway and Disneyland slip road** – ✉ **77777**

Disneyland Paris ★★★ (see Green Guide of Northern France and the Paris Region)- Hotel booking centre: ✆ (00 33) 08 25 30 60 30 (0.15 €/mn), Fax (00 33) 01 64 74 57 50 - Disneyland Resort Paris hotels offer daily packages including room price and entrance to theme parks - These prices change according to the season - we recommend that you contact the booking centre.

in Magny-le-Hongre – pop. 3 720 – alt. 117 m – ✉ **77700**

Radisson

allée de la Mare-Houleuse, (near the golf course) – ✆ *01 60 43 64 00 – www.golfresort.paris.radissonsas.com – reservations.golfresort.paris@radissonsas.com – Fax 01 60 43 64 01* **r**

241 rm – †€ 180/230 ††€ 180/230, ☐ € 22 – 9 suites

Rest – Menu (€ 16 bi) – Carte € 39/63

◆ Modern designer styles characterise this hotel, the latest on the Disneyland Paris site, in the middle of the golf course. Rooms and suites have views over the greens. Up-to-date cuisine in the large modern restaurant dining room (open for dinner only).

Holiday Inn

20 av. de la Fosse des Pressoirs, (Val de France) – ✆ *01 64 63 38 02 – www.vi-hotels.com – pr.holiday@vi-hotels.fr – Fax 01 64 63 37 39* **h**

396 rm – †€ 135/210 ††€ 135/210, ☐ € 10 – 5 suites

Rest – buffet – Menu € 29 – Carte € 24/34 lunch

◆ Let the show begin! The circus is the inspiration behind the colourful interior decor of this hotel near Disneyland Paris. Indoor pool. Enter the big top at this restaurant reminiscent of a circus tent. Themed buffet.

Dream Castle hôtel

40 av. Fosse des Pressoirs , (Val de France) – ✆ *01 64 17 90 00 – www.dreamcastle-hotel.com – info@dreamcastle-hotel.com – Fax 01 64 17 90 10* **b**

396 rm ☐ – †€ 118/242 ††€ 128/242 – 10 suites

Rest *The Musketeer's* – buffet *(dinner only)* Menu € 29

Rest *Bar Excalibur* – *(lunch only)* Menu (€ 15) – Carte € 33/54

◆ This hotel pays homage to castles in both its architecture and interior decoration. Elegant, spacious rooms, lovely pool and landscaped garden. The Musketeer's restaurant offers evening buffets inspired by the market and seasons. International lunch menu at the Excalibur bar.

in Serris – pop. 2 320 – alt. 129 m – ✉ **77700**

L'Élysée Val d'Europe

rm,

7 cours Danube, (opposite the RER station) – ✆ *01 64 63 33 33 – www.hotelelysee.com – info@hotelelysee.com – Fax 01 64 63 33 30* **w**

152 rm – †€ 120/160 ††€ 130/170, ☐ € 12

Rest – Menu (€ 17), € 22 – Carte € 30/38

◆ Fine Haussman-style building set around two interior courtyards. Fine tropical conservatory topped by a Baltard-style glass roof. Spacious, well thought out rooms. Traditional menu served in the restaurant or on the terrace on the square in summer.

MASSY – **91 Essonne** – **312** C3 – **101** 25 – **pop. 40 500 – alt. 78 m –** ✉ **91300** 20 **B3**

Paris 19 – Arpajon 19 – Évry 20 – Palaiseau 4 – Rambouillet 45

Mercure

rest,

21 av. Carnot, (TGV station) – ✆ *01 69 32 80 20 – www.mercure.com – h1176@accor.com – Fax 01 69 32 80 25*

116 rm – †€ 69/175 ††€ 79/185, ☐ € 14

Rest – *(closed August, Christmas holidays, Friday dinner, Saturday and Sunday)* Carte approx. € 32

◆ A resolutely modern hotel ideally located between TGV (high speed trains) and RER (suburban trains) stations. Functional (30 have been redone), well-soundproofed rooms, new bathrooms. A modern dining room serving traditional seasonal cuisine.

LE MESNIL-AMELOT – **77 Seine-et-Marne** – **312** E1 – **101** 9 – **pop. 682** – **alt. 80 m** – ✉ **77990** 19 **C1**

Paris 34 – Bobigny 25 – Goussainville 15 – Meaux 28 – Melun 67

Radisson SAS
r. de la Chapelle – ✆ 01 60 03 63 00 – www.radissonsas.com – radisson.sas@hotels-res.com – Fax 01 60 03 74 40
240 rm – €90/650 €90/650, ☕ €20
Rest – Menu (€27), €29 (weekdays) – Carte €34/57
◆ Glass building near Roissy airport with many assets. Including leisure and conference facilities, lounge bar and modern rooms. Large brasserie with modern decor and terrace; buffet of starters.

MEUDON – **92 Hauts-de-Seine** – **311** J3 – **101** 24 – **pop. 44 200** – **alt. 100 m** – ✉ **92190** **Northern France and the Paris Region** 20 **B2**

Paris 11 – Boulogne-Billancourt 4 – Clamart 4 – Nanterre 12 – Versailles 10

Terrace★: ✱★ - Meudon forest ★.

L'Escarbille (Régis Douysset)
8 r. Vélizy – ✆ 01 45 34 12 03 – www.lescarbille.fr – contact@lescarbille.fr – Fax 01 46 89 04 75 – Closed 14 August-1 September, 24 December-5 January, 20 February-9 March, Sunday and Monday
Rest – Menu €44/61
Spec. Poêlée de girolles, moelle et cébette (June to Nov.). Pigeon en crapaudine jus lié au foie gras. Truffes fondantes au chocolat, kumquats confits.
◆ This century-old establishment near the station has had a facelift. Find a renovated façade, well-turned out interior and fine seasonal cuisine in tune with today's tastes.

MONTMORENCY – **95 Val-d'Oise** – **305** E7 – **101** 5 – **pop. 21 500** – **alt. 82 m** – ✉ **95160** **Northern France and the Paris Region** 18 **B1**

Paris 19 – Enghien-les-Bains 4 – Pontoise 24 – St-Denis 9

Office de tourisme, 1, avenue Foch ✆ 01 39 64 42 94, Fax 01 39 34 95 29

St-Martin collegiate church ★.

Château d'Écouen★★: musée de la Renaissance★★ (Hanging of David and Bathsheba★★★).

Au Coeur de la Forêt
av. Repos de Diane, and access via forest road – ✆ 01 39 64 99 19 – www.aucoeurdelaforet.com – au.coeur.de.la.foret@wanadoo.fr – Fax 01 34 28 17 52 – Closed August, 15-25 February, Thursday dinner, Sunday dinner and Monday
Rest – Menu €43
◆ A welcoming decor in two rustic rooms, one of which is very spacious with rafters and a fireplace. Shaded summer terrace. Simple, traditional menu in tune with the seasons.

MONTREUIL – **93 Seine-Saint-Denis** – **311** K2 – **101** 17 – **pop. 100 600** – **alt. 70 m** – ✉ **93100** **Northern France and the Paris Region** 21 **C2**

Paris 11 – Bobigny 10 – Boulogne-Billancourt 18 – Argenteuil 28 – Saint-Denis 15

Office de tourisme, 1, rue Kléber ✆ 01 41 58 14 09, Fax 01 41 58 14 13

Villa9Trois
28 r. Colbert – ✆ 01 48 58 17 37 – www.villa9trois.com – stephane@villa9trois.com – Closed Sunday dinner
Rest – Menu €39/44 – Carte €55/65
◆ A haven of greenery in the middle of the suburbs, the villa offers a relaxed meal in modern surroundings. Large terrace in the garden.

MONTROUGE – **92 Hauts-de-Seine** – **311** J3 – **101** 25 – **pop. 44 100** – **alt. 75 m** – ✉ **92120** 20 **B2**

Paris 5 – Boulogne-Billancourt 8 – Longjumeau 18 – Nanterre 16 – Versailles 16

Mercure rm, VISA AE

13 r. F.-Ory – 01 58 07 11 11 – www.accorhotels.com – h0374@accor.com – Fax 01 58 07 11 21

181 rm – €135/175 €145/195, €15 – 7 suites

Rest – *(closed Saturday and Sunday)* Menu (€19), €26 – Carte €28/36

◆ Large building, set slightly away from the ring road, housing tasteful, well-soundproofed and air-conditioned modern rooms. Renovated dining room in a contemporary style, enlivened with vegetable themed lithographs (Traditional cuisine).

MORANGIS – **91 Essonne** – **312** D3 – **101** 35 – **pop. 11 500** – **alt. 85 m** – ✉ **91420** 21 **C3**

Paris 21 – Évry 14 – Longjumeau 5 – Versailles 23

XXX **Sabayon** VISA AE

15 r. Lavoisier – 01 69 09 43 80 – www.restaurantlesabayon.com – von-moos.claude@wanadoo.fr – Fax 01 64 48 27 28 – Closed 1st-29 August, Monday dinner, Tuesday dinner, Wednesday dinner, Saturday lunch and Sunday

Rest – Menu €43/80

◆ With its ochre walls, yellow lacquered ceilings, modern canvases, and plants, this restaurant is a ray of sunshine on a slightly drab industrial estate. Contemporary cuisine.

NANTERRE P – **92 Hauts-de-Seine** – **311** J2 – **101** 14 – **pop. 87 800** – **alt. 35 m** – ✉ **92000** 20 **B1**

Paris 13 – Beauvais 81 – Rouen 124 – Versailles 15

Syndicat d'initiative, 4, rue du Marché 01 47 21 58 02, Fax 01 47 25 99 02

Mercure La Défense Parc rm, VISA AE

r. des 3 Fontanot – 01 46 69 68 00 – www.mercure.com – h1982@accor.com – Fax 01 47 25 46 24

160 rm – €86/235 €101/250, €16 – 25 suites

Rest – *(Closed 18 July-21 August, 24-27 December, 31 December-4 January, Sunday lunch, Friday dinner and Saturday)*

Menu (€24), €31/47 bi – Carte approx. €31

◆ A modern building and annex next to the André Malraux park. Modern-style furniture and full facilities. Ask for a renovated room. International cuisine served in a cosy and comfortable dining room boasting a line of modern furniture.

NEUILLY-SUR-SEINE – **92 Hauts-de-Seine** – **311** J2 – **101** 15 – **pop. 61 100** – **alt. 34 m** – ✉ **92200** Northern France and the Paris Region 20 **B1**

Paris 9 – Argenteuil 10 – Nanterre 6 – Pontoise 29 – St-Germain-en-Laye 18 – Versailles 17

Courtyard by Marriott rm, VISA AE

58 bd V. Hugo – 01 55 63 64 65 – www.courtyard.com/parcy – cy.parcy.dosm@courtyard.com – Fax 01 55 63 64 66

242 rm – €179/239 €179/239, €22 – 69 suites

Rest – Menu (€22) – Carte €30/70

◆ An imposing 1970s hotel near the American Hospital offering every modern comfort. Fine rooms, trendy atmosphere in the lobby and bar, and terraces. Traditional cuisine and Sunday brunch, served in a pleasant, modern setting.

Paris Neuilly without rest VISA AE

1 av. Madrid – 01 47 47 14 67 – www.hotel-paris-neuilly.com – h0883@accor.com – Fax 01 47 47 97 42

74 rm – €145/260 €160/275, €17 – 6 suites

◆ The rooms are decorated in a variety of styles. Breakfast is served on a covered patio decorated with a fresco representing the Palacio Real in Madrid built by François I in 1528.

Jardin de Neuilly without rest
5 r. P. Déroulède – ✆ 01 46 24 22 77 – www.hoteljardindeneuilly.com – reservation@hoteljardindeneuilly.com – Fax 01 46 37 14 60
29 rm – †€ 175/255 ††€ 220/355, ☕ € 16
◆ A 19C mansion 300m from Porte Maillot. The rooms are individually decorated and furnished with antiques. Some overlook the garden: the countryside on the doorstep of Paris!

De la Jatte without rest
4 bd Parc – ✆ 01 46 24 32 62 – www.hoteldelajatte.com – hoteldelajatte@wanadoo.fr – Fax 01 46 40 77 31
69 rm – †€ 98/250 ††€ 98/250, ☕ € 12 – 2 suites
◆ On the Île de la Jatte, once popular with painters, today there is a trendy hotel. Designer décor (trendy colours, dark wood), pleasant veranda.

Neuilly Park Hôtel without rest
23 r. M. Michelis – ✆ 01 46 40 11 15 – www.hotelneuillypark.com – hotel@neuillypark.com – Fax 01 46 40 14 78
30 rm – †€ 145/185 ††€ 165/185, ☕ € 11
◆ This Sablons district hotel has been fully renovated. Small rooms with Art Nouveau-style furniture and drapes. Charming service.

Foc Ly
79 av. Ch. de Gaulle – ✆ 01 46 24 43 36 – www.focly.com – Fax 01 46 24 70 58 – Closed 1st-23 August
Rest – Menu (€ 23) – Carte € 40/120
◆ Two lions frame the entrance to this restaurant with a pagoda-terrace façade. Redecorated modern interior. Chinese and Thai cuisine.

La Truffe Noire (Patrice Hardy)
2 pl. Parmentier – ✆ 01 46 24 94 14 – www.truffenoire.net – patchef.hardy@wanadoo.fr – Fax 01 46 24 94 60 – Closed 1st-25 August, Saturday and Sunday
Rest – Menu € 40/140 – Carte € 75/140
Spec. Salade de pommes de terre fumées et lamelles de truffe. Lièvre à la royale et polenta blanche (15 Oct.-15 Dec.). Crème glacée et soufflé à la truffe.
◆ This attractive, recently-renovated establishment celebrates the "black gold", but also Parmentier, who grew the first French potatoes in the Sablons district.

Jarrasse L'Ecailler de Paris
4 av. de Madrid – ✆ 01 46 24 07 56 – www.jarrasse.com – reservation@jarrasse.com – Fax 01 40 88 35 60 – Closed 1 week in August
Rest – *(pre-book)* Menu € 42 – Carte € 50/90
◆ Dining rooms fully redecorated in a modern style: contemporary materials and pastel colours create a relaxed atmosphere. Fish and seafood dishes, and an oyster bar.

Le Bistrot d'à Côté Neuilly
4 r. Boutard – ✆ 01 47 45 34 55 – www.bistrotboutarde.com – reservation@bistrotboutarde.com – Fax 01 47 45 15 08 – Closed 9-17 August, Saturday lunch and Sunday
Rest – Menu (€ 30), € 43
◆ Relaxed service, wood panelling, collection of old coffee-grinders, daily specials chalked on a blackboard, and wine served "à la ficelle" (you pay for what you drink): a "genuine imitation bistro".

À la Coupole
3 r. Chartres – ✆ 01 46 24 82 90 – Closed spring school holidays, August, Saturday and Sunday
Rest – Carte € 40/50
◆ Miniature cars and lorries made in Madagascar from recovered metal decorate the simple dining room of this family-run restaurant. Traditional cuisine and oysters in season.

Aux Saveurs du Marché
4 r. de l'Eglise – ✆ 01 47 45 72 11 – auxsaveursdumarche@wanadoo.fr – Fax 01 46 37 72 13 – Closed 3-23 August, Saturday and Sunday
Rest – Carte € 43/52
◆ Pre-1940s style bistro, near the market, with velvet bench seating and an original wood and mirror ceiling. Blackboard displayed devilishly-tasty dishes. Very busy at lunchtime.

NOGENT-SUR-MARNE – **94 Val-de-Marne** – **312** D2 – **101** 27 – **pop. 30 400** – **alt. 59 m** – ✉ **94130** **Northern France and the Paris Region** 21 **D2**

Paris 14 – Créteil 10 – Montreuil 6 – Vincennes 6

Office de tourisme, 5, avenue de Joinville ✆ 01 48 73 73 97, Fax 01 48 73 75 90

Mercure Nogentel rm, rm, VISA MC AE

8 r. du Port – ✆ 01 48 72 70 00 – www.lecanotiernogentel.com – h1710@accor.com – Fax 01 48 72 86 19

60 rm – €128 €145, €15

Rest ***Le Canotier*** – *(closed 5-20 August and Sunday dinner)*

Menu (€36) – Carte approx. €42

◆ A hotel on the banks of the Marne with modern rooms. The spirit of Nogent is still present on the river bank ideal for a walk among the flowers. The spacious dining room with nautical decor enjoys a view of the marina. Traditional fare.

NOISY-LE-GRAND – **93 Seine-Saint-Denis** – **305** G7 – **101** 18 – **pop. 61 600** – **alt. 82 m** – ✉ **93160** **Northern France and the Paris Region** 21 **D2**

Paris 19 – Bobigny 17 – Lagny-sur-Marne 14 – Meaux 38

Syndicat d'initiative, 167, rue Pierre Brossolette ✆ 01 43 04 51 55, Fax 01 43 03 79 48

Mercure VISA MC AE

2 bd Levant – ✆ 01 45 92 47 47 – www.mercure.com – h1984@accor.com – Fax 01 45 92 47 10

192 rm – €112/145 €118/151, €14

Rest – *(closed Friday dinner, Saturday, Sunday and holidays)*

Menu (€16 bi), €26 – Carte approx. €35

◆ A modern building with a glass façade that reflects the panoramic lifts as they go up and down. Spacious, functional rooms. A brasserie-style restaurant with a wall covered in multicoloured stars. Inner courtyard terrace.

Novotel Atria rest, VISA MC AE

2 allée Bienvenue-quartier Horizon – ✆ 01 48 15 60 60 – www.accorhotels.com – h1536@accor.com – Fax 01 43 04 78 83

144 rm – €91/179 €101/189, €14 **Rest** – Menu (€20) – Carte €23/45

◆ A fully renovated, contemporary building in a business district. Practical, spruce rooms in keeping with the chain's standards. Spacious dining room serving 'Lenôtre' cuisine. Children's play area in garden.

L'Amphitryon VISA MC AE

56 av. A. Briand – ✆ 01 43 04 68 00 – http://amphitryon.over-blog.com – nicole.guerineau@wanadoo.fr – Fax 01 43 04 68 10 – Closed 5-26 August, February half-term holidays, Saturday lunch and Sunday dinner

Rest – Menu €26 (weekdays)/41 – Carte €41/49

◆ Melon-coloured walls and multi-coloured china set the tone of this elegant restaurant dining room. The food is traditional and served quickly and with a smile.

ORGEVAL – **78 Yvelines** – **311** H2 – **101** 11 – **pop. 5 359** – **alt. 100 m** – ✉ **78630** 18 **B1**

Paris 32 – Mantes-la-Jolie 28 – Pontoise 22 – St-Germain-en-Laye 11 – Versailles 22

de Villennes Villennes-sur-Seine Route d'Orgeval, N : 2 km, ✆ 01 39 08 18 18

Moulin d'Orgeval VISA MC AE

r. de l'Abbaye, 1.5 km south – ✆ 01 39 75 85 74 – www.moulindorgeval.com – contact@moulindorgeval.com – Fax 01 39 75 48 52

14 rm – €140 €165, €15

Rest – *(Closed 20 December-3 January and Sunday dinner)*

Menu (€36), €46/72 – Carte €36/74

◆ This former mill set in a 5ha park with trees and a pond offers peace and relaxation. Cosy rooms and English-style bar. Rustic restaurant dining room and pleasant waterside terrace in the summer. Traditional dishes.

ORLY (AÉROPORTS DE PARIS) – **91 Essonne** – **312** D3 – **101** 26 – **pop. 21 646** – **alt. 89 m** – ✉ **94390** 21 **C3**

Paris 16 – Corbeil-Essonnes 24 – Créteil 14 – Longjumeau 15 – Villeneuve-St-Georges 9

Aérogare Sud ✆ 03 36 68 15 15

Hilton Orly

near Orly Sud airport ✉ 94544 – ✆ 01 45 12 45 12 – www.hilton.fr – Fax 01 45 12 45 00

351 rm – €130 €130, €19

Rest – brasserie – Menu (€27) – Carte €41/64

◆ A popular choice for corporate clients, this 1960s hotel has a designer interior, discreet yet elegant bedrooms and state of the art business facilities. Modern, entirely revamped decor and a classic menu.

Mercure

aérogare ✉ 94547 – ✆ 01 49 75 15 50 – www.mercure.com – h1246-re@accor.com – Fax 01 49 75 15 51

192 rm – €110/220 €120/230, €15

Rest – Menu (€15) – Carte approx. €32

◆ Convenient for travellers between flights. Smiling staff, pleasant verdant setting and above all, well-kept, gradually refurbished rooms. Bar snacks and traditional dishes adapted to the timetables of travellers in transit.

in Orly-ville – **pop. 20 900** – **alt. 71 m** – ✉ **94310**

Kyriad Air Plus

58 voie Nouvelle – ✆ 01 41 80 75 75 – www.hotelairplus.com – Fax 01 41 80 12 12

72 rm – €65/82 €65/82, €8,50

Rest – *(Closed August, Saturday and Sunday)* Menu €13/16 – Carte €32/38

◆ Frequented by numerous airline crews on stopovers. English style pub with an aeronautical atmosphere. The nearby Parc Méliès is popular with jogging enthusiasts. Classic repertory served in an interior devoted to aircraft.

See also at **Rungis**

OZOIR-LA-FERRIÈRE – **77 Seine-et-Marne** – **312** F3 – **106** 33 – **101** 30 – **pop. 20 100** – **alt. 110 m** – ✉ **77330** 19 **C2**

Paris 34 – Coulommiers 42 – Lagny-sur-Marne 22 – Melun 29 – Sézanne 84

Syndicat d'initiative, 43, avenue du Général-de-Gaulle ✆ 01 64 40 10 20, Fax 01 64 40 09 91

XXX **La Gueulardière**

66 av. Gén. de Gaulle – ✆ 01 60 02 94 56 – www.la-gueuladière.com – gueulardiere@orange.fr – Fax 01 60 02 98 51 – Closed 1st-15 September and Sunday dinner

Rest – Menu €38/78 – Carte €58/102

◆ This town centre inn serves classic cuisine in two elegant dining rooms or under a pergola on the terrace in summer.

LE PERREUX-SUR-MARNE – **94 Val-de-Marne** – **312** E2 – **101** 18 – **pop. 32 200** – **alt. 50 m** – ✉ **94170** 21 **D2**

Paris 16 – Créteil 12 – Lagny-sur-Marne 23 – Villemomble 6 – Vincennes 7

Office de tourisme, 75, avenue Ledru Rollin ✆ 01 43 24 26 58, Fax 01 43 24 02 10

XXX **Les Magnolias** (Jean Chauvel)

48 av. de Bry – ✆ 01 48 72 47 43 – www.lesmagnolias.com – jcmagno@wanadoo.fr – Fax 01 48 72 22 28 – Closed August, Saturday lunch, Sunday and Monday

Rest – Menu (€41), €58/92

Spec. Tagliatelles de seiche et bouillon d'algues corsé de citron vert. Agneau en crumble végétal, croque romaine à l'huile d'olive vierge. Cassant chocolat blanc-noir envoûté de passion onctueuse.

◆ An elegant setting of light wood fixtures adorned with contemporary art and amusing armchairs in which to sample the equally light hearted, inventive cuisine.

LE PRÉ ST-GERVAIS – 93 Seine-Saint-Denis – **305** F7 – **101** 16 – **pop. 17 000** 21 **C1** – **alt. 82 m** – ✉ **93310**

▶ Paris 8 – Bobigny 6 – Lagny-sur-Marne 33 – Meaux 38 – Senlis 47

Au Pouilly Reuilly
68 r. A. Joineau – ✆ 01 48 45 14 59 – Fax 01 48 45 93 93 – Closed Saturday lunchtime and Sunday
Rest – Menu € 29 – Carte € 45/81
◆ A pre-war bistro decor, a cheerful atmosphere and fortifying cuisine, with an emphasis on offal. The Paris smart set tend to congregate here.

PUTEAUX – 92 Hauts-de-Seine – **311** J2 – **101** 14 – **pop. 42 300** – **alt. 36 m** 20 **B1** – ✉ **92800**

▶ Paris 11 – Nanterre 4 – Pontoise 30 – St-Germain-en-Laye 17 – Versailles 15

Vivaldi without rest
5 r. Roque de Fillol – ✆ 01 47 76 36 01 – www.hotelvivaldi.com – vivaldi@hotelvivaldi.com – Fax 01 47 76 11 45
27 rm – †€ 88/162 ††€ 94/194
◆ This hotel, standing on a peaceful street near the town hall, is home to refurbished rooms equipped with functional furniture. Breakfast on the patio in summertime.

La Table d'Alexandre
7 bd Richard-Wallace – ✆ 01 45 06 33 63 – latabledalexandre@9business.fr – Fax 01 45 06 33 63 – Closed 2-24 August, Saturday, Sunday and holidays
Rest – Menu € 26 (weekdays)/35 – Carte approx. € 37
◆ The red façade of this pleasant restaurant cannot be missed. Classic interior decor enhanced by a few contemporary details. Tasty seasonally inspired updated menu.

Good food and accommodation at moderate prices?
Look for the Bib symbols: red Bib Gourmand for food,
blue Bib Hotel for hotels.

ROISSY-EN-FRANCE (PARIS AIRPORTS) – 95 Val-d'Oise – **305** G6 – **101** 8 19 **C1** – **pop. 2 564** – **alt. 85 m** – ✉ **95700**

▶ Paris 26 – Chantilly 28 – Meaux 38 – Pontoise 39 – Senlis 28
✈ Charles-de-Gaulle ✆ 03 36 68 15 15.
ℹ Office de tourisme, 40, avenue Charles-de-Gaulle ✆ 01 34 29 43 14, Fax 01 34 29 43 33

Z. I. Paris Nord II – ✉ 95912

Hyatt Regency
351 av. Bois de la Pie – ✆ 01 48 17 12 34 – www.paris.charlesdegaulle.hyatt.com – cdg@hyattintl.com – Fax 01 48 17 17 17
376 rm – †€ 130/560 ††€ 130/560, € 27 – 12 suites
Rest – buffet – Menu € 56 – Carte € 43/62
◆ Spectacular, contemporary architecture in a good location close to the airport. Large, stylish bedrooms equipped with ultra-modern facilities for its predominantly corporate guests. Enjoy buffet cuisine or classic à la carte choices in the Hyatt Regency's glass-ceilinged restaurant.

in l'aérogare nº 2

Sheraton
– ✆ 01 49 19 70 70 – www.sheraton.com/parisairport – Fax 01 49 19 70 71
252 rm – †€ 199/599 ††€ 199/599, € 30
Rest ***Les Étoiles*** *– ✆ 01 41 84 64 54 (Closed 25 July-30 August, Saturday, Sunday and bank holidays)* Menu € 57 – Carte € 60/86
Rest ***Les Saisons*** – Menu € 35 (weekday lunch) – Carte € 40/55
◆ Leave your plane or train and take a trip on this "luxury liner" with its futuristic architecture. Decor by Andrée Putman, a view of the runways, absolute quiet and refined rooms. Les Étoiles offers modern cuisine and beautiful contemporary setting. Brasserie dishes at Les Saisons.

in Roissypole

Hilton
– ✆ 01 49 19 77 77 – www.hilton.fr – events.parischarlesdegaulleairport@hilton.com – Fax 01 49 19 77 78
385 rm – †€ 239/729 ††€ 239/729, ☕ € 25
Rest *Les Aviateurs* – ✆ 01 49 19 77 95 – Carte € 35/85
◆ Daring architecture, space and light are the main features of this hotel. Its ultra-modern facilities make it an ideal place in which to work and relax. The Aviateurs offers a small choice of brasserie dishes.

Pullman
Zone centrale Ouest – ✆ 01 49 19 29 29 – www.pullmanhotels.com – h0577-gm@accor.com – Fax 01 49 19 29 00
342 rm – †€ 110/550 ††€ 110/550, ☕ € 27 – 8 suites
Rest *L'Escale* – Menu € 31/45 – Carte € 30/72
◆ A personal welcome, comfortable atmosphere, conference rooms, an elegant bar and well-looked-after rooms are the advantages of this hotel between two airport terminals. A pleasant port of call dedicated to travel, this restaurant offers a menu of world flavours.

in Roissy-Ville

Courtyard by Marriott
allée du Verger – ✆ 01 34 38 53 53
– www.marriott.com – mhrs.parmc.sales.mgr@marriott.com – Fax 01 34 38 53 54
300 rm – †€ 149/550 ††€ 149/550, ☕ € 22 – 4 suites
Rest – Menu (€ 27), € 33 – Carte € 43/70
◆ Behind its colonnaded white façade, this establishment has modern facilities perfectly in tune with the requirements of businessmen transiting through Paris. Themed brasserie menu served in a large and carefully decorated dining room.

Millennium
allée du Verger – ✆ 01 34 29 33 33 – www.millenniumhotels.com – sales.cdg@mill-cop.com – Fax 01 34 29 03 05
239 rm – †€ 380 ††€ 380/500, ☕ € 20
Rest – Menu (€ 16 bi) – Carte € 28/46
◆ Bar, Irish pub, fitness centre, attractive swimming pool, conference rooms, and spacious bedrooms with one floor specially equipped for businessmen: a hotel with good facilities. International cuisine and brasserie buffet or fast food served at the bar.

Novotel Convention et Wellness
allée des Vergers – ✆ 01 30 18 20 00
– www.novotel.com – h5418-fo@accor.com – Fax 01 34 29 95 60
282 rm – †€ 109/350 ††€ 109/350, ☕ € 19 – 7 suites
Rest – Menu (€ 20), € 25 (weekdays) – Carte approx. € 27
◆ The latest arrival in the hotel zone at Roissy offers impressive services: extensive seminar facilities, kids' corner and comprehensive wellness centre. Lenôtre brasserie dishes available twenty-four hours a day at Novotel Café and Côté Jardin.

Mercure
allée des Vergers – ✆ 01 34 29 40 00 – www.mercure.com – h1245@accor.com – Fax 01 34 29 00 18
203 rm – †€ 79/250 ††€ 89/260, ☕ € 18 **Rest** – Menu (€ 20) – Carte € 28/42
◆ This hotel has a meticulous decor comprising Provençal style in the hall, old-fashioned zinc in the bar and spacious rooms in light wood. A contemporary menu that changes with the seasons served in the pleasant dining room or on the terrace overlooking the garden.

ROSNY-SOUS-BOIS – **93 Seine-Saint-Denis** – **305** F7 – **101** 17 – **pop. 40 900** – **alt. 80 m** – ✉ **93110** 21 **D2**

Paris 14 – Bobigny 8 – Le Perreux-sur-Marne 5 – St-Denis 16

AS Golf de Rosny-sous-Bois 12 rue Raspail, ✆ 01 48 94 01 81

Quality Hôtel Golf

4 r. Rome – ✆ 01 48 94 33 08 – www.rosnysousbois.quality-hotel.fr – qualityhotel.rosny@wanadoo.fr – Fax 01 48 94 30 05

97 rm – €140/160 €150/170, €12 – ½ P €170/190

Rest *Le Vieux Carré* – *(closed August, 25 December-1st January, Friday dinner, Saturday, Sunday and holidays)* Menu €27/30 – Carte €28/46

◆ A hotel on the golf course, with architecture and interior decoration reminiscent of Louisiana. Spacious, comfortable rooms. The sign and the furniture of Le Vieux Carré evoke New Orleans. Terrace facing the golf course.

RUEIL-MALMAISON – **92 Hauts-de-Seine** – **311** J2 – **101** 14 – **pop. 77 800** 20 **A1**
– **alt. 40 m** – ✉ **92500** **Northern France and the Paris Region**

Paris 16 – Argenteuil 12 – Nanterre 3 – St-Germain-en-Laye 9 – Versailles 12

Office de tourisme, 160, avenue Paul Doumer ✆ 01 47 32 35 75, Fax 01 47 14 04 48

de Rueil-Malmaison 25 Boulevard Marcel Pourtout, ✆ 01 47 49 64 67

Château de Bois-Préau★ - Church ★ organ - Malmaison: château ★★ museum.

Novotel Atria

21 av. Ed. Belin – ✆ 01 47 16 60 60 – www.novotel.com – h1609@accorhotel.com – Fax 01 47 51 09 29

118 rm – €150/320 €150/320, €16 **Rest** – Carte €15/35

◆ A modern building in the Rueil 2000 business district near the RER station. Contemporary, well-appointed guestrooms. Conference centre. A restaurant with a modern setting and an up-to-date menu with a healthy focus.

Le Bonheur de Chine

6 allée A. Maillol, (opposite 35 Ave J. Jaurès in Suresnes) – ✆ 01 47 49 88 88 – www.bonheurdechine.com – bonheurdechine@wanadoo.fr – Fax 01 47 49 48 68 – Closed Mon.

Rest – Menu €23 (weekday lunch), €38/59 – Carte €30/70

◆ Furniture and other elements of decoration from the Far East form the authentic setting for this restaurant full of the flavour of Chinese cuisine.

RUNGIS – **94 Val-de-Marne** – **312** D3 – **101** 26 – **pop. 5 644** – **alt. 80 m** 21 **C3**
– ✉ **94150**

Paris 14 – Antony 5 – Corbeil-Essonnes 30 – Créteil 13 – Longjumeau 12

in Pondorly **access: from Paris, A6 and Orly slip road; from the provinces, A6 and Rungis exit** – ✉ **94150 Rungis**

Holiday Inn

4 av. Charles Lindbergh – ✆ 01 49 78 42 00 – www.holidayinn-parisorly.com – hiorly@alliance-hospitality.com – Fax 01 45 60 91 25

169 rm – €113/319 €131/338

Rest – *(closed school holidays, Friday dinner, Saturday, Sunday and holidays)* Menu (€25), €30/55 – Carte €30/50

◆ This chain hotel on the motorway offers the usual high levels of comfort in its spacious, sound-proofed and well-appointed rooms decorated in harmonious tones. The up-to-date dining room sports a few discreet Art Deco touches. Traditional dishes.

Novotel

Zone du Delta, 1 r. Pont des Halles – ✆ 01 45 12 44 12 – www.novotel.com – h1628@accor.com – Fax 01 45 12 44 13

181 rm – €79/179 €79/179, €15 – 5 suites

Rest – *(closed Sunday lunch and Saturday)* Carte €24/46

◆ The comfortable rooms in this vast glass building are contemporary in design with the added benefit of double-glazing. Swimming pool with adjoining terrace. The restaurant dining room and the Novotel Café have both adopted the same colourful, designer decor.

SACLAY – 91 Essonne – 312 C3 – **101** 24 – **pop. 3 013 – alt. 147 m** 20 **A3**
– ✉ **91400**

Paris 27 – Antony 14 – Chevreuse 13 – Montlhéry 16 – Versailles 12

Novotel rm, rest,
r. Charles Thomassin – ✆ 01 69 35 66 00
– www.novotel.com – h0392@accor.com – Fax 01 69 41 01 77
137 rm – €79/160 €79/160, € 14 **Rest** – Carte € 23/47
◆ A 19C manor house and old farmstead comprise the Novotel Saclay. Rooms in keeping with the chain's standards and extensive sports facilities. Attractive restaurant overlooking the pool and century-old woodland.

ST-CLOUD – 92 Hauts-de-Seine – 311 J2 – **101** 14 – **pop. 29 200 – alt. 63 m** 20 **B2**
– ✉ **92210** Northern France and the Paris Region

Paris 12 – Nanterre 7 – Rueil-Malmaison 6 – St-Germain 16 – Versailles 10

du Paris Country Club 1 rue du Camp Canadien, (Racecourse), ✆ 01 47 71 39 22

Park★★ (Grand fountain★★) - Stella Matutina church ★.

Quorum rm, rest, VISA
2 bd République – ✆ 01 47 71 22 33 – www.hotel-quorum-paris.com
– hotel-quorum@club-internet.fr – Fax 01 46 02 75 64
58 rm – €100/125 €105/135, € 10
Rest – *(closed August, Saturday and Sunday)* Menu (€ 21) – Carte approx. € 35
◆ A building with rooms renovated in 2007, just two minutes from the beautiful St Cloud park. Minimalist furniture with a few pieces by Starck. Modern spacious dining room with purple chairs. Traditional cuisine.

L'Heureux Père VISA
47 bis Bd Semard – ✆ 01 46 02 09 43 – www.lheureuxpere.com – lheureuxpere@wanadoo.fr – Fax 01 46 02 93 28 – Closed 8-30 August
Rest – Menu (€ 19), € 24 (weekday lunch) – Carte € 35/52
◆ Traditional culinary boundaries vanish in this establishment. The chef enjoys surprising his clientele with unusual combinations of Creole-inspired flavours and spices. Flower-decked terrace.

Le Garde-Manger VISA
21 r. d'Orléans – ✆ 01 46 02 03 66 – www.legardemanger.com – restaurant@legardemanger.com – Fax 01 46 02 11 55 – Closed Mon on public holidays and Sun
Rest – Carte € 30/37
◆ After a temporary move, this establishment has regained its original address and a brand new decor. Find a generous bistro cuisine and tempting wine list.

ST-DENIS – 93 Seine-Saint-Denis – 305 F7 – **101** 16 – **pop. 96 600** 21 **C1**
– alt. 33 m – ✉ **93200** Northern France and the Paris Region

Paris 11 – Argenteuil 12 – Beauvais 70 – Bobigny 11 – Chantilly 31 – Pontoise 27 – Senlis 44

Office de tourisme, 1, rue de la République ✆ 01 55 87 08 70, Fax 01 48 20 24 11

Basilica★★★ - Stade de France★.

ST-GERMAIN-EN-LAYE – 78 Yvelines – 311 I2 – **101** 13 – **pop. 41 000** 20 **A1**
– alt. 78 m – ✉ **78100** Northern France and the Paris Region

Paris 25 – Beauvais 81 – Dreux 66 – Mantes-la-Jolie 36 – Versailles 13

Office de tourisme, Maison Claude Debussy, 38, rue au Pain ✆ 01 34 51 05 12, Fax 01 34 51 36 01

de Joyenval Chambourcy Chemin de la Tuilerie, on the Mantes road: 6 km on D 160, ✆ 01 39 22 27 50

Terrace★★ - English garden★ - Château★: musée des Antiquités nationales★★ - Musée Maurice Denis★.

ST-GERMAIN-EN-LAYE

Bonnenfant (R. A.) . . . . **AZ** 3
Coches (R. des) . . . . **AZ** 4
Denis (R. M.) . . . . **AZ** 5
Detaille (Pl. É.) . . . . **AY** 6
Gde-Fontaine (R. de la) . . . . . **AZ** 10
Giraud-Teulon (R.) . . . . **BZ** 9
Loges (Av. des) . . . . **AY** 14
Malraux (Pl. A.) . . . . **BZ** 16
Marché-Neuf (Pl. du) . . . . **AZ**
Mareil (Pl.) . . . . **AZ** 19
Pain (R. au) . . . . **AZ** 20
Paris (R. de) . . . . **AZ**
Poissy (R. de) . . . . **AZ** 22
Pologne (R. de) . . . . **AY** 23
Surintendance
(R. de la) . . . . **AY** 28
Victoire (Pl. de la) . . . . **AY** 30
Vieil-Abreuvoir (R. du) . . . . . . **AZ** 32
Vieux-Marché (R. du) . . . . **AZ** 33

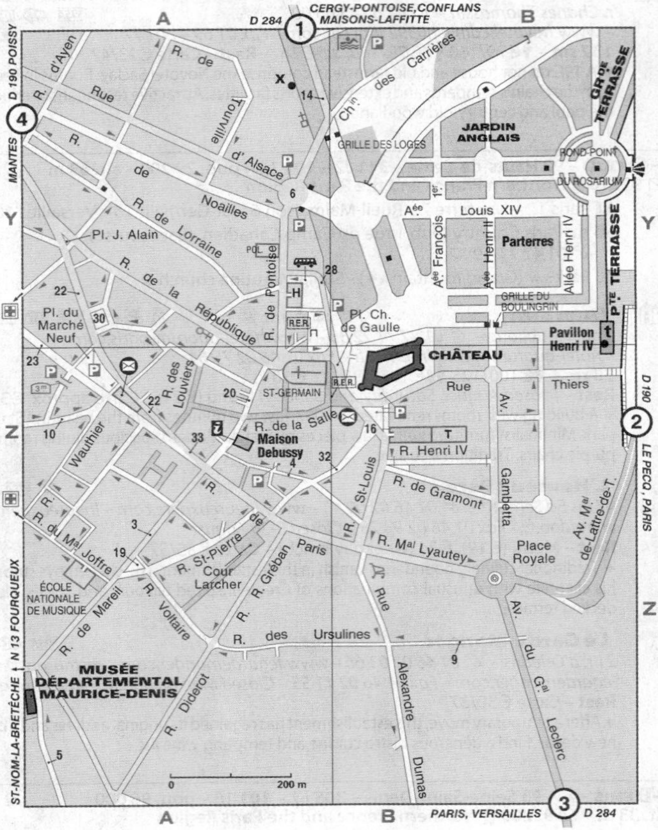

Pavillon Henri IV ⚘ ≤ rest, **P** VISA AE

21 r. Thiers – ✆ 01 39 10 15 15
– www.pavillonhenri4.fr
– reservation@pavillonhenri4.fr
– Fax 01 39 73 93 73 BYZ **t**

42 rm – €130/250 €130/250, ☕ €17
Rest – *(closed 1-22 August, 19-30 December, Saturday lunch and Sunday dinner)*
Carte €57/79

◆ Finished in 1604 under Henry IV, this building was the birthplace of the future king, Louis XIV. A high-class atmosphere in the nicely refurbished lounges and rooms. The comfortable dining room has superb views over the River Seine valley and Paris.

Ermitage des Loges VISA

11 av. Loges – ✆ 01 39 21 50 90 – www.ermitage-des-loges.com – hotel@ermitagedesloges.com – Fax 01 39 21 50 91 AY **x**

56 rm – €100/133 €119/151, €13

Rest – *(closed August)* Menu €22 bi (weekday lunch), €34/52 – Carte €40/65

◆ Hotel made up of two buildings on the edge of the St Germain forest. The main building dates from the 19C. Rooms in the modern annexe have views over the garden. The large dining room is decorated on an aeronautical theme.

via ① and D 284: 2.5 km – ✉ 78100 St-Germain-en-Laye

La Forestière rest, VISA

1 av. Prés. Kennedy – ✆ 01 39 10 38 38 – www.cazaudehore.fr – cazaudehore@relaischateaux.com – Fax 01 39 73 73 88

25 rm – €165/175 €205/215, €20 – 5 suites

Rest *Cazaudehore* – see restaurant listing

◆ Charm and comfort are on the menu at this captivating hotel surrounded by trees. The choice of colours and attractive modern furniture make the rooms more personal and cosy.

Cazaudehore – Hôtel La Forestière VISA

1 av. Prés. Kennedy – ✆ 01 30 61 64 64 – www.cazaudehore.fr – cazaudehore@relaischateaux.com – Fax 01 39 73 73 88 – Closed Sunday dinner from November to March and Monday

Rest – Menu (€47), €59 (dinner) – Carte €52/77

◆ Chic and cosy atmosphere, contemporary decor, delightful terrace shaded by acacias, well-prepared cuisine and fine wine list. A family-run establishment since 1928.

ST-MANDÉ – 94 Val-de-Marne – 312 D2 – 101 27 – pop. 22 000 – alt. 50 m – ✉ 94160 21 C2

Paris 7 – Créteil 10 – Lagny-sur-Marne 29 – Maisons-Alfort 6 – Vincennes 2

L'Ambassade de Pékin VISA

6 av. Joffre – ✆ 01 43 98 13 82 – Fax 01 43 28 31 93

Rest – Menu €14 (weekday lunch), €24/32 – Carte €18/70

◆ A restaurant particularly appreciated for its unusual Chinese, Vietnamese and Thai cuisine. Dine in a wood-panelled dining room, adorned with an aquarium of lobsters and exotic fish.

L'Ambre d'Or VISA

44 av. du Gén. de Gaulle – ✆ 01 43 28 23 93 – Fax 01 43 28 23 93 – Closed 21-25 April, 4-24 August, Sunday and Monday

Rest – Menu (€27), €33 – Carte €81/88

◆ Discreet restaurant opposite the town hall. The dining room tastefully combines old beams with modern furniture. Seasonal up-to-date menu.

ST-MAUR-DES-FOSSÉS – 94 Val-de-Marne – 312 D3 – 101 27 – pop. 75 200 – alt. 38 m – ✉ 94100 21 D2

Paris 12 – Créteil 6 – Nogent-sur-Marne 6

La Renaissance VISA

8 pl. des Marronniers – ✆ 01 48 85 91 74 – ederle.bernard@wanadoo.fr – Fax 01 48 83 04 67 – Closed Tuesday dinner, Sunday dinner and Monday

Rest – Menu (€18), €25 (weekday lunch), €28/41

◆ Out of the town centre, this inviting house sports a colourful interior. Classic menu enhanced by a number of old-fashioned recipes (beef stew, calf's head).

in La Varenne-St-Hilaire – ✉ 94210

La Bretèche VISA

171 quai Bonneuil – ✆ 01 48 83 38 73 – www.labreteche.fr – contact@labreteche.fr – Fax 01 42 83 63 19 – Closed 2-16 August, 22 February-8 March, Sunday dinner and Monday

Rest – Menu €35 (weekdays)/60 – Carte €88/118

Spec. Thon rouge mi-cuit à la crème de wasabi, caviar d'Aquitaine. Pomme de ris de veau doré aux champignons des bois. Macaron noisette, crème glacée à la rose et fruits rouges.

◆ This restaurant on the banks of the Marne is appreciated for its elegant decor and tasty modern cuisine. Attractive terrace for outdoor dining in summer.

Entre Terre et Mer
15 r. St-Hilaire – ✆ 01 55 97 04 98 – Closed 19 July-20 August, Sunday dinner and Monday
Rest – Carte € 42/60
◆ A tiny restaurant worth a stop over to sample its carefully prepared, fresh fish and seafood dishes. Charming colourful decor, adorned with paintings by local artists.

Faim et Soif
28 r. St-Hilaire – ✆ 01 48 86 55 76 – Fax 01 48 86 55 76 – Closed Sunday and Monday
Rest – Carte € 61/74
◆ A new shamelessly trendy establishment: grey façade, contemporary art, designer furniture and a plasma screen in place of a slate. Updated, minimalist cuisine.

ST-OUEN – 93 Seine-Saint-Denis – **305** F7 – **101** 16 – **pop. 43 400** – **alt. 36 m** 21 **C1** – ✉ **93400**

Paris 9 – Bobigny 12 – Chantilly 46 – Meaux 49 – Pontoise 26 – St-Denis 5

Office de tourisme, 30, avenue Gabriel Péri ✆ 01 40 11 77 36, Fax 01 40 11 01 70

Manhattan
115 av. G. Péri – ✆ 01 41 66 40 00 – www.hotel-le-manhattan.com – reservation@hotel-le-manhattan.com – Fax 01 41 66 40 66
126 rm – †€ 158/190 ††€ 168/200, ☕ € 14 – ½ P € 168/190
Rest – *(Closed August, Saturday, Sunday and bank holidays)*
Menu (€ 20), € 25 (weekdays) – Carte approx. € 46
◆ A glass and stone modern building housing bright and practical rooms. Quieter at the back. Dining room-veranda perched on the eighth floor of the hotel, serving traditional dishes.

Le Coq de la Maison Blanche
37 bd J. Jaurès – ✆ 01 40 11 01 23 – www.lecoqdelamaisonblanche.com – coqmaisonblanche@orange.fr – Fax 01 40 11 67 68 – Closed 11-14 July, 10-15 August and Sunday
Rest – Menu € 32 – Carte € 44/80
◆ Authentic 1950s decor, traditional cooking, efficient service and long-standing customers. Just like being in a film of the period.

Le Soleil
109 av. Michelet – ✆ 01 40 10 08 08 – www.restaurantlesoleil.com – lesoleil2@orange.fr – Fax 01 47 05 44 02
Rest – *(lunch only)* Menu (€ 26), € 28 (weekdays), € 32/48 bi – Carte € 40/70
◆ A pleasant bistro with an amusing mixture of antique furniture and trinkets, reminding us that the Marché aux Puces (Flea Market) is nearby. Generous traditional dishes.

St-Prix – 95 Val-d'Oise – **305** E6 – **101** 5 – **pop. 7 214** – **alt. 70 m** 18 **B1** – ✉ **95390**

Paris 26 – Cergy 22 – Paris 15 36 – Paris 20 28 – Paris 18 22

Hostellerie du Prieuré without rest
74 r. A.-Rey – ✆ 01 34 27 51 51 – www.hosteldeprieure.com – contact@hosteldeprieure.com – Fax 01 39 59 21 12
8 rm – †€ 115 ††€ 115, ☕ € 15 – 1 suite
◆ A former village bistro dating from the 17C. Eight spacious and charming rooms that lead you to dream: some dedicated to romance, others to far off countries... Generous breakfasts.

À La Grâce de Dieu
r. de l'Église – ✆ 01 39 59 08 00 – www.grace-dieu.com – contact@grace-dieu.com – Fax 01 39 59 21 12 – Closed Sunday dinner and Monday
Rest – Menu € 30/44 – Carte € 40/50
◆ At the foot of the church, this large establishment houses three dining rooms, a veranda and a terrace. The chef offers an ever changing contemporary menu. Good wine list.

ST-QUENTIN-EN-YVELINES – 78 Yvelines – 311 H3 – 101 21 – pop. 116 082 18 B2

Northern France and the Paris Region

Paris 33 – Houdan 33 – Palaiseau 28 – Rambouillet 21 – Versailles 14

Blue Green Golf St-Quentin-en-Yvelines Trappes Base de loisirs, 01 30 50 86 40

National Guyancourt 2 avenue du Golf, 01 30 43 36 00

Montigny-le-Bretonneux – pop. 34 200 – alt. 162 m – 78180

Mercure rm, VISA MC AE D

9 pl. Choiseul – 01 39 30 18 00 – www.mercure.com – h1983@accor.com – Fax 01 30 57 15 22

74 rm – €155/180 €165/190, €16

Rest – *(Closed 31 July-23 August, 18 December-3 January, Friday dinner, Saturday and Sunday)* Menu (€16 bi) – Carte €34/41

◆ This hotel with refurbished, minimalist style rooms is part of a real estate complex. Low-key lounge-bar with designer decor and plasma screen. The redecorated restaurant offers traditional dishes and shaded summer terrace.

Voisins-le-Bretonneux – pop. 12 400 – alt. 163 m – 78960

Remains of Port-Royal des Champs abbey ★ Southwest: 4 km.

Novotel St-Quentin Golf National rm, VISA MC AE D

au Golf National, 2 km east on the D 36 78114 – 01 30 57 65 65 – www.novotel.com – h1139@accor.com – Fax 01 30 57 65 00

131 rm – €109/179 €109/179, €15 – 1 suite **Rest** – Carte €19/42

◆ This modern hotel is ideally located on a golf course. Friendly service, contemporary decor in the bedrooms, and leisure facilities including pool, solarium and tennis court. Modern decor served in a designer setting with trendy ambiance at the Novotel Café.

Port Royal without rest VISA MC

20 r. H. Boucher – 01 30 44 16 27 – www.hotelportroyal.com – didiercadoret@wanadoo.fr – Fax 01 30 57 52 11 – Closed 1-16 August and 23 December-3 January

40 rm – €76 €80, €8

◆ This calm and convivial hotel, on the edge of the Chevreuse Valley, houses perfectly well kept and simply furnished rooms. Pleasant garden planted with trees.

STE-GENEVIÈVE-DES-BOIS – 91 Essonne – 312 C4 – 101 35 – pop. 33 900 – alt. 78 m – 91700 Northern France and the Paris Region 18 B2

Paris 27 – Arpajon 10 – Corbeil-Essonnes 18 – Étampes 30 – Évry 10 – Longjumeau 9

La Table d'Antan VISA MC AE

38 av. Gde Charmille du Parc, (near the Town Hall) – 01 60 15 71 53 – www.latabledantan.fr – table-antan@wanadoo.fr – Closed 3-24 August, Tuesday dinner, Wednesday dinner, Sunday dinner and Monday

Rest – Menu €31/48 – Carte €40/60

◆ This pleasant restaurant in a residential district sports a warm atmosphere and a plush décor. Classic cuisine and specialities of southwest France; list of whiskies.

SÉNART – 312 E4 – 101 39 – pop. 93 069 19 C2

Northern France and the Paris Region

Paris 38 – Boulogne-Billancourt 50 – Montreuil 39 – Argenteuil 67 – Saint-Denis 50

le Plessis-Picard – 77550

La Mare au Diable VISA MC AE D

– 01 64 10 20 90 – www.lamareaudiable.fr – mareaudiable@wanadoo.fr – Fax 01 64 10 20 91 – Closed 28 July-13 August, Tuesday dinner, Sunday dinner and Monday

Rest – Menu €25 (weekday lunch), €45/55 – Carte €38/69

◆ This 15C house covered in ampelopsis was visited by George Sand. The interior, with patinated beams and with a fireplace, does not lack character.

Pouilly-le-Fort – ✉ **77240**

XXX **Le Pouilly**
1 r. de la Fontaine – ✆ 01 64 09 56 64 – www.lepouilly.fr – contact@lepouilly.fr – Fax 01 64 09 56 64 – Closed 9 August-11 September, 21-28 December, Sunday dinner and Monday
Rest – Menu € 30 bi (weekday lunch), € 48/75 – Carte € 75/90
Spec. Foie gras de canard. Filet de lièvre (autumn). Velouté de chocolat chaud.
◆ In this old farm, exposed stonework, tapestries and a fireplace make up a decor full of charm, also featuring a garden terrace. Delicious modern cuisine.

St-Pierre-du-Perray – **pop. 7 733** – **alt. 88 m** – ✉ **91280**
de Greenparc route de Villepècle, ✆ 01 60 75 40 60

Novotel
golf de Greenparc – ✆ 01 69 89 75 75 – www.novotel.com – h1783-gm@accor.com – Fax 01 69 89 75 50
78 rm – €80/130 €80/130, € 14 – 2 suites
Rest – Menu (€ 20), € 25 (weekdays) – Carte € 20/43
◆ Modern hotel perfect for a quiet, relaxing stay, with golf course, swimming pool and gym. Half of the 'Harmonie' style rooms overlook the fairways. Some rooms have a balcony. Contemporary-style dining room and lounge overlooking the golf course. Classic menu.

SUCY-EN-BRIE – **94 Val-de-Marne** – **312** E3 – **101** 28 – **pop. 26 200** – **alt. 96 m** – ✉ **94370** 21 **D2**
Paris 21 – Créteil 6 – Chennevières-sur-Marne 4
Château de Gros Bois★: furniture★★ South: 5 km,
Northern France and the Paris Region

quartier les Bruyères Southeast: 3 km – ✉ **94370 Sucy-en-Brie**

Le Tartarin
carrefour de la Patte d'Oie – ✆ 01 45 90 42 61 – www.auberge-tartarin.com – aubergetartarin@gmail.com – Fax 09 55 17 42 61 – Closed August and Sunday dinner
12 rm – €55 €65, € 8,50
Rest – *(closed Thursday dinner, Monday, Tuesday and Wednesday)*
Menu € 22/49 – Carte € 35/53
◆ Three generations of the same family have reigned over this former hunting lodge on the outskirts of the forest with a warm, country atmosphere. Swans take pride of place in the dining room (trophies, stuffed animals). Traditional cuisine.

XX **Le Clos de Sucy**
17 r. Porte – ✆ 01 45 90 29 29 – leclosdesucy@wanadoo.fr – Fax 01 45 90 29 29 – Closed 3-25 August, 22-25 December, Saturday lunch, Sunday dinner and Monday
Rest – Menu (€ 23), € 35/45 – Carte € 42/61
◆ A dining room that is both elegant and countrified, with its half-timbered partitions, exposed beams and wine-coloured shades. Traditional cuisine with personal touches.

XX **Terrasse Fleurie**
1 r. Marolles – ✆ 01 45 90 40 07 – www.laterrassefleurie.com – terrasse.fleurie@wanadoo.fr – Fax 01 45 90 40 07 – Closed 27 July-21 August, Sunday dinner, Monday dinner, Tuesday dinner, Thursday dinner and Wednesday
Rest – Menu (€ 19 bi), € 27/40
◆ Situated in a pavilion, this restaurant serves simple, generous food in a country-style dining room or on the pleasant flowered terrace.

SURESNES – **92 Hauts-de-Seine** – **311** J2 – **101** 14 – **pop. 43 400** – **alt. 42 m** – ✉ **92150** **Northern France and the Paris Region** 20 **B2**
Paris 12 – Nanterre 4 – Pontoise 32 – St-Germain-en-Laye 13 – Versailles 14
Office de tourisme, 50, boulevard Henri Sellier ✆ 01 41 18 18 76, Fax 01 41 18 18 78
Fort du Mont Valérien (Mémorial National de la France combattante).

 **Novotel**

7 r. Port aux Vins – 01 40 99 00 00 – www.novotel.com – h1143@accor.com – Fax 01 45 06 60 06

112 rm – €95/230 €95/230, €16 – 1 suite **Rest** – Carte €23/45

◆ A recently renovated hotel in a quiet street near the Seine. Rooms whose smart, fashionable decor is depicted by bright, tasteful soothing colours. Traditional cuisine at the restaurant or snack-bar food at the Novotel Café.

Les Jardins de Camille

70 av. Franklin Roosevelt – 01 45 06 22 66 – www.les-jardins-de-camille.fr – lesjardinsdecamille@free.fr – Fax 01 47 72 42 25 – Closed Sunday evening

Rest – Menu €42/60 – Carte €58/70

◆ Magnificent view of Paris and La Défense from the dining room (huge bay windows and mirrors) and terrace. Fine selection of Burgundies and wines from the rest of the world.

THIAIS – **94 Val-de-Marne** – **312** D3 – **101** 26 – **pop. 28 200** – **alt. 60 m** – 94320 21 **C2**

Paris 18 – Créteil 7 – Évry 27 – Melun 37

Ophélie la Cigale Gourmande

82 av. de Versailles – 01 48 92 59 59 – luclamass@free.fr – Closed 4-28 August, 22-31 December, Wednesday dinner, Saturday lunch, Sunday dinner and Monday

Rest – Menu €32 (weekday lunch), €37/55

◆ A little corner of Provence at the gates of Paris! Tasty, updated Mediterranean cuisine prepared with fresh produce. Served in a simple but smart and colourful decor.

TREMBLAY-EN-FRANCE – **93 Seine-Saint-Denis** – **305** G7 – **101** 18 – **pop. 35 300** – **alt. 60 m** – 93290 21 **D1**

Paris 24 – Aulnay-sous-Bois 7 – Bobigny 13 – Villepinte 4

in Tremblay-Vieux-Pays

Le Cénacle

1 r. de la Mairie – 01 48 61 32 91 – Fax 01 48 60 43 89 – Closed August, Saturday, Sunday and holidays

Rest – Menu €38/68 – Carte €60/87

◆ Behind this cheerful façade with red blinds there are two lovely rooms with painted beams, ochre colour schemes, impressionist paintings, Louis XV–style chairs and a shellfish aquarium. Traditional cuisine.

TRIEL-SUR-SEINE – **78 Yvelines** – **311** I2 – **101** 10 – **pop. 11 700** – **alt. 20 m** – 78510 **Northern France and the Paris Region** 18 **B1**

Paris 39 – Mantes-la-Jolie 27 – Pontoise 18 – Rambouillet 55 – St-Germain-en-Laye 12

St-Martin church ★.

St-Martin

2 r. Galande, (opposite the post office) – 01 39 70 32 00 – restaurantsaintmartin.com – Closed 3 weeks in August, Christmas holidays, Wednesday and Sunday

Rest – *(number of covers limited, pre-book)* Menu (€17), €20 (weekday lunch), €32/55 – Carte €35/55

◆ The restaurant stands next to a truly lovely 13C gothic church; here one can enjoy modernised traditional cooking in a pleasant rustic-style decor.

VANVES – **92 Hauts-de-Seine** – **311** J3 – **101** 25 – **pop. 26 800** – **alt. 61 m** – 92170 20 **B2**

Paris 7 – Boulogne-Billancourt 5 – Nanterre 13

Syndicat d'initiative, 2, rue Louis Blanc 01 47 36 03 26, Fax 01 47 36 06 63

Mercure Paris Porte de Versailles Expo

36-38 r. Moulin – ✆ 01 46 48 55 55 – www.mercure.com – h0375@accor.com – Fax 01 46 48 56 56

388 rm – €152/295 €162/305, ☕ €17 **Rest** – Carte €30/60

◆ Plant-filled patio-lobby with translucent ceiling at this hotel with modern rooms, decorated in warm colours. Modern decor, contemporary furniture and simply laid tables in the restaurant. Brasserie-style menu.

Pavillon de la Tourelle

10 r. Larmeroux – ✆ 01 46 42 15 59 – www.pavillontourelle.fr – pavillontourelle@wanadoo.fr – Fax 01 46 42 06 27 – Closed 27 July-27 August, February holiday, Sunday dinner and Monday

Rest – Menu (€37), €53 bi – Carte €43/71

◆ This house on the edge of the park is home to an elegant restaurant decorated in pastels with fresh flowers, chandeliers and attractively laid tables. Traditional cuisine.

VAUCRESSON – **92 Hauts-de-Seine** – **311** I2 – **101** 23 – **pop. 8 547** – **alt. 160 m** – ✉ 92420 20 **A2**

Paris 18 – Mantes-la-Jolie 44 – Nanterre 11 – St-Germain-en-Laye 11 – Versailles 5

Stade Francais 129 av. de la Celle St Cloud, N : 2 km, ✆ 01 47 01 15 04

Etang de St-Cucufa★ Northeast: 2,5 km - Institut Pasteur - Musée des Applications de la Recherche★ to Marnes-la-Coquette Southwest: 4 km, **Northern France and the Paris Region.**

see plan of Versailles

Auberge de la Poularde

36 bd Jardy, (near the motorway), D 182 – ✆ 01 47 41 13 47 – auberge.lapoularde@free.fr – Fax 01 47 41 13 47 – Closed August, February school holidays, Sunday evening, Tuesday evening and Wednesday U **a**

Rest – Menu €30 – Carte €45/68

◆ A friendly welcome and impeccable service single out this inn with a charming provincial atmosphere. The menu is classic, particularly based on Bresse poultry dishes.

VÉLIZY-VILLACOUBLAY – **78 Yvelines** – **311** J3 – **101** 24 – **pop. 20 600** – **alt. 164 m** – ✉ 78140 20 **B2**

Paris 19 – Antony 12 – Chartres 81 – Meudon 8 – Versailles 6

Holiday Inn

av. de l'Europe, (near Vélizy II shopping centre) – ✆ 01 39 46 96 98 – www.holidayinn-parisvelizy.com – hivelizy@alliance-hospitality.com – Fax 01 34 65 95 21

182 rm – €250/510 €250/510, ☕ €20 **Rest** – Menu €31 – Carte €33/55

◆ This hotel has spacious, comfortable, well-soundproofed and regularly redecorated rooms. Choose a room away from the motorway. Exposed beams in the comfortable dining room of the restaurant.

VERSAILLES Ⓟ – **78 Yvelines** – **311** I3 – **101** 23 – **pop. 87 100** – **alt. 130 m** – ✉ 78000 **Northern France and the Paris Region** 20 **A2**

Paris 22 – Beauvais 94 – Dreux 59 – Évreux 90 – Melun 65 – Orléans 129

Office de tourisme, 2 bis, avenue de Paris ✆ 01 39 24 88 88, Fax 01 39 24 88 89

du Stade Français Vaucresson 129 av. de la Celle St Cloud, 7 km on the Rueil road, ✆ 01 47 01 15 04

de Saint-Aubin Saint-Aubin Route du Golf, 17 km on the Chevreuse road, ✆ 01 69 41 25 19

de Feucherolles Feucherolles Sainte Gemme, 17 km on the Mantes road (D 307), ✆ 01 30 54 94 94

du haras de jardy Marnes-la-Coquette Boulevard de Jardy, NE : 9 km, ✆ 01 47 01 35 80

Château★★★ - Gardens★★★ (Great fountains★★★ and night fairs★★★ in summer) - Ecuries Royales★ - Trianon★★ - Musée Lambinet★ Y **M.**

Jouy-en-Josas: la Diège★ (statue) in the church, 7 km by ③.

VERSAILLES

Bellevue (Av. de) . . . . U 2
Coste (R.) . . . . V 9
Dr-Schweitzer (Av. du) . . . . . . U 12
Franchet-d'Esperey (Av. du Mar.) . . . . U 15
Glatigny (Bd de) . . . . U 19
Leclerc (Av. du Gén.) . . . . V 22
Marly-le-Roi (R. de) . . . . U 26
Mermoz (R. Jean) . . . . V 27
Moxouris (R.) . . . . U 29
Napoléon III (Rte) . . . . U 30
Pelin (R. L.) . . . . U 32
Porchefontaine (Av.) . . . . V 33
Pottier (R.) . . . . U 35
Rocquencourt (Av. de) . . . . . . U 39
St-Antoine (Allée) . . . . V 40
Sports (R. des) . . . . U 43
Vauban (R.) . . . . V 45

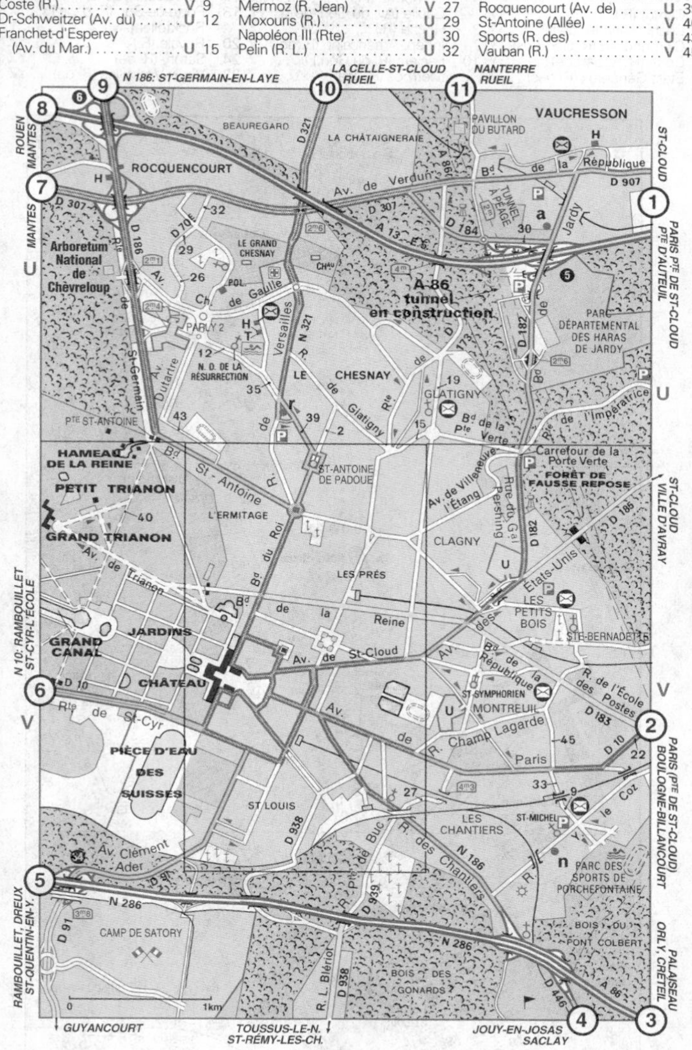

Trianon Palace rm, rm,

1 bd de la Reine – ✆ 01 30 84 50 00

– www.trianonpalace.fr – reservation.01104@westin.com – Fax 01 30 84 50 01

199 rm – €250/730 €250/730, €38 – 17 suites X **r**

Rest Gordon Ramsay au Trianon – see restaurant listing

Rest – *✆ 01 30 84 55 56* – Menu €55 bi (weekday lunch) – Carte €55/73

◆ This classical style luxury hotel standing on the edge of the grounds of the château has very comfortable, contemporary style guestrooms. Excellent spa. Up-to-date menu and summer terrace at the Veranda.

VERSAILLES

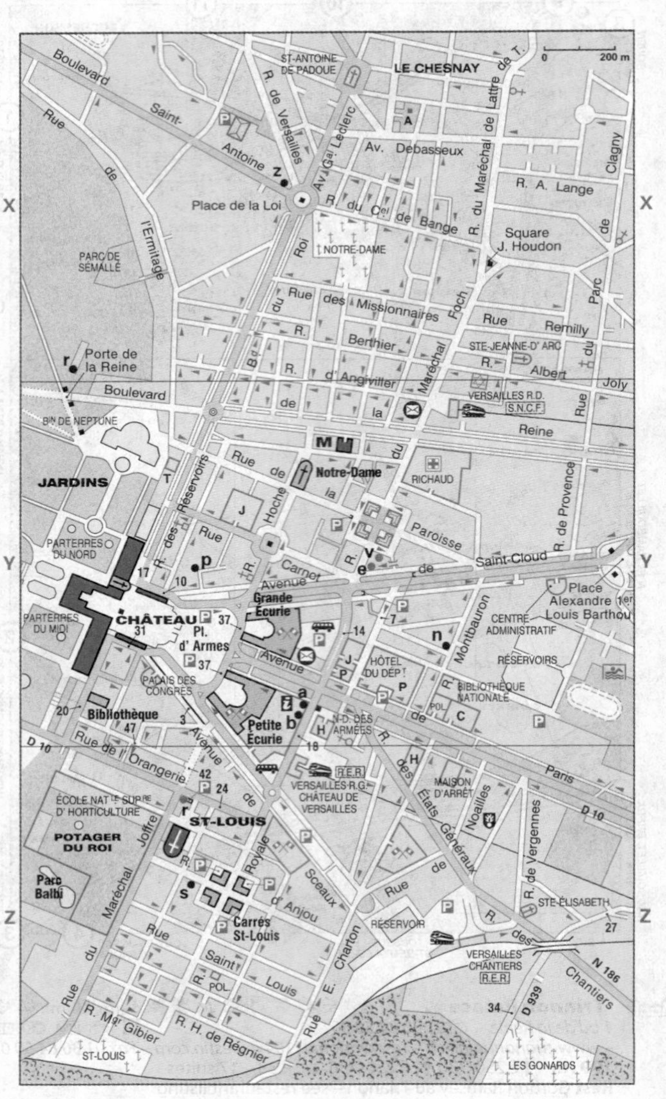

Boulevard Saint-Antoine
Rue de l'Ermitage
ST-ANTOINE DE PADOUE
R. de Versailles
Av. Gal Leclerc
LE CHESNAY
0 200 m
Av. Debasseux
R. du Maréchal de Lattre de T.
Clagny
R. A. Lange
Place de la Loi
R. du Cel de Bange
NOTRE-DAME
Square J. Houdon
Parc de Clagny
PARC DE SÉMALLÉ
Bd du Roi
Rue des Missionnaires
Rue Remilly
R. Berthier
Maréchal Foch
STE-JEANNE-D' ARC
R. Albert Joly
Porte de la Reine
R. d'Angiviller
Boulevard de la Reine
VERSAILLES R.D.
S.N.C.F.
Rue du Parc
Bin DE NEPTUNE
Rue de la Paroisse
Notre-Dame
RICHAUD
JARDINS
R. des Réservoirs
Rue Hoche
Rue Carnot
R. de Provence
PARTERRES DU NORD
Avenue de Saint-Cloud
Grande Écurie
CHÂTEAU
Pl. d' Armes
PARTERRES DU MIDI
Place Alexandre 1er
Louis Barthou
CENTRE ADMINISTRATIF
Montbauron
RÉSERVOIRS
HÔTEL DU DÉPT
BIBLIOTHÈQUE NATIONALE
PALAIS DES CONGRÈS
Avenue de Paris
Bibliothèque
Petite Écurie
N.-D. DES ARMÉES
D 10
Rue de l'Orangerie
Avenue de Sceaux
VERSAILLES R.G. CHÂTEAU DE VERSAILLES
R.E.R.
MAISON D'ARRÊT
R. des États Généraux
Noailles
ÉCOLE NATLE SUPRE D' HORTICULTURE
POTAGER DU ROI
ST-LOUIS
R. de Vergennes
Rue Royale
Parc Balbi
Rue du Maréchal Joffre
R. d'Anjou
Rue de Noailles
STE-ÉLISABETH
Carrés St-Louis
RÉSERVOIR
R. des Chantiers
Rue Saint Louis
Rue E. Charton
VERSAILLES CHANTIERS
N 186
D 939
POL.
R. Mgr Gibier
R. H. de Régnier
LES GONARDS
X
Y
Z

Pullman rm,
2 bis av. de Paris – 01 39 07 46 46 – www.pullman-hotels.com – h1300@accor.com Y a
146 rm – €180/395 €180/395, €27 – 6 suites
Rest – Menu (€30), €38 – Carte €40/60
◆ Only the gateway remains of the old artillery riding school. Elegant, designer lounge-lobby and guestrooms renovated in a modern style. Warm colours in the bar and restaurant. Cuisine using flavours from France and abroad.

Le Versailles without rest
7 r. Ste-Anne – 01 39 50 64 65 – www.hotel-le-versailles.fr – info@hotel-le-versailles.fr – Fax 01 39 02 37 85 Y p
45 rm – €123/154 €133/164, €14
◆ Near the peace and quiet of the château, this establishment has been fully renovated in an Art Deco style. Ornate and colourful themed rooms (travel, dreams, love, etc) invite guests to relax.

La Résidence du Berry without rest
14 r. Anjou – 01 39 49 07 07 – www.hotel-berry.com – resa@hotel-berry.com – Fax 01 39 50 59 40 Z s
38 rm – €140/165 €150/165, €14
◆ A fine 18C building between the Carrés St Louis and the Potager du Roi with intimate rooms with a personal touch. Elegant and cosy bar-billiards room. Small garden.

Mercure without rest
19 r. Ph. de Dangeau – 01 39 50 44 10 – www.mercure.com – hotel@mercure-versailles.com – Fax 01 39 50 65 11 Y n
60 rm – €79/122 €79/132, €10
◆ In a quiet area, an establishment with particularly practical rooms. Well-furnished lobby giving onto a pleasant breakfast room.

Ibis without rest
4 av. Gén. de Gaulle – 01 39 53 03 30 – www.ibishotel.com – h1409@accor.com – Fax 01 39 50 06 31 Y b
85 rm – €69/115 €69/115, €8
◆ Recently refurbished hotel near the château and town hall, offering the chain's latest standards of comfort. Poppy red rooms, which are functional and attractive.

Trianon Palace – Hôtel Trianon Palace
1 bd de la Reine – 01 30 84 55 55 – www.gordonramsay.com – trianon@gordonramsay.com – Fax 01 30 84 55 57 – Closed 26 July-25 August, 3-11 January, 21 February-1st March, Sunday and Monday X r
Rest – *(dinner only)* Menu €150 – Carte €120/150
Spec. Pressé de chevreuil écossais, foie gras, cèpes et truffes du Périgord. Filet de boeuf Angus aux girolles, sauce vin rouge. Chocolat croustillant, fruit de la passion et praliné noisette.
◆ On the edge of the château gardens, a classic, very elegant location with contemporary decor. Subtle, inventive and harmonious cuisine. Excellent selection of Burgundy wines.

Le Valmont
20 r. au Pain – 01 39 51 39 00 – www.levalmont.com – levalmont@wanadoo.fr – Fax 01 39 51 39 00 – Closed Sunday evening and Monday Y v
Rest – Menu (€23), €33 – Carte €56/79
◆ A captivating façade, Louis XVI style chairs and paintings of Île de France landscapes: a pleasant location to enjoy cuisine with a personal touch. Summer terrace.

L'Angélique (Régis Douysset)
27 av. Saint-Cloud – 01 30 84 98 85 – contact@langelique.fr – Closed 16 August-1st September, 24 December-4 January, 21 February-9 March, Sunday and Monday Y d
Rest – Menu €38
Spec. Croque monsieur de foie gras. Paleron de bœuf, légumes de saison, raifort et moelle. Tarte aux pommes, crème glacée à la vanille.
◆ The unassuming walls and angelic decor of this establishment may well hide Versailles' latest up-and-coming gourmet restaurant. An enticing menu composed with market-fresh, seasonal produce.

XX **Le Potager du Roy**
1 r. Mar.-Joffre – ☎ 01 39 50 35 34
– Fax 01 30 21 69 30
– Closed Sunday and Monday Z r
Rest – Menu (€ 27), € 34 (weekdays)/42
◆ Delightfully retro setting and meat and fish dishes with the vegetables in pride of place. Hardly surprising as the name refers to the nearby King's Vegetable Garden!

XX **Zin's à l'étape gourmande**
125 r. Yves Le Coz – ☎ 01 30 21 01 63 – www.arti-zins.fr
– contact@arti-zins.fr – Closed for three weeks in August, Saturday lunch, Sunday and Monday V n
Rest – *(number of covers limited, pre-book)* Menu € 42
◆ In the Porchefontaine district, find cuisine prepared using the freshest market produce and a fine choice of wines from regional producers.

in Chesnay – pop. 29 600 – alt. 120 m – ✉ 78150

Novotel Château de Versailles
4 bd St-Antoine – ☎ 01 39 54 96 96
– www.novotel.com – h1022@accor.com – Fax 01 39 54 94 40 X z
105 rm – €99/175 €99/175, ☐ € 14
Rest – *(closed Saturday lunch and Sunday lunch)*
Menu (€ 18), € 23 – Carte € 25/34
◆ Hotel at the entrance to the town, on the place de la Loi. Functional and well-soundproofed rooms lead off an atrium made into a lounge (numerous green plants). Restaurant with modern, bistro style interior and traditional menu.

LE VÉSINET – 78 Yvelines – **311** I2 – **101** 13 – **pop. 16 400 – alt. 44 m – ✉ 78110** 20 **A1**

Paris 19 – Maisons-Laffitte 9 – Pontoise 23 – St-Germain-en-Laye 4 – Versailles 12

Syndicat d'initiative, 60, boulevard Carnot ☎ 01 30 15 47 00

Auberge des Trois Marches
15 r. J. Laurent, (pl. de l'église) – ☎ 01 39 76 10 30
– www.auberge-des-3-marches.com – aubergedes3marches@yahoo.fr
– Fax 01 39 76 62 58
15 rm – €90/105 €100/115, ☐ € 11
Rest – *(Closed 12-21 August, Sunday dinner and Monday lunch)*
Menu (€ 18) – Carte € 41/58
◆ Quiet guesthouse in an area with a village atmosphere (church, market). Functional rooms which are gradually being renovated. Impeccably maintained and a friendly welcome. A fresco recalling scenes from the 1930s decorates the dining room.

VILLE D'AVRAY – 92 Hauts-de-Seine – **311** J3 – **101** 24 – **pop. 11 200 – alt. 130 m – ✉ 92410** 20 **B2**

Paris 14 – Antony 16 – Boulogne-Billancourt 5 – Neuilly-sur-Seine 10 – Versailles 6

Les Étangs de Corot
53 r. de Versailles – ☎ 01 41 15 37 00 – www.etangs-corot.com
– contact@etangs-corot.com
– Fax 01 41 15 37 99
43 rm – €185/245 €215/285, ☐ € 20
Rest *Le Corot* – *(closed Sunday dinner, Monday and Tuesday) (pre-book)*
Menu € 37 – Carte € 65/82
Rest *Les Paillottes* – *(open June-September)* Carte € 45/57
◆ This delightful hamlet beside a lake inspired the painter Camille Corot. It is now home to a charming hotel boasting elegant, personalised rooms. Cosy decor, garden views and creative menu at the Corot. A late 19C atmosphere and bistro cuisine at the waterside Paillottes.

VILLENEUVE-LA-GARENNE – 92 Hauts-de-Seine – 311 J2 – 101 15 21 **C1**
– pop. 24 900 – alt. 30 m – ✉ 92390

Paris 13 – Nanterre 14 – Pontoise 23 – St-Denis 3 – St-Germain-en-Laye 24

XX **Les Chanteraines** VISA AE

av. 8 Mai 1945 – ✆ 01 47 99 31 31 – leschanteraines@wanadoo.fr – Fax 01 41 21 31 17 – Closed August, Saturday and Sunday

Rest – Menu € 36 – Carte € 45/60

◆ This restaurant is set in the modern complex next to Chanteraines park. Up-to-date cuisine served in a dining room with a veranda, and on the summer terrace facing the lake.

VILLENEUVE-LE-ROI – 94 Val-de-Marne – 312 D3 – 101 26 – pop. 18 400 21 **C3**
– alt. 100 m – ✉ 94290

Paris 20 – Créteil 9 – Arpajon 29 – Corbeil-Essonnes 21 – Évry 16

XX **Beau Rivage** AC VISA AE

17 quai de Halage – ✆ 01 45 97 16 17 – beaurivage94290@orange.fr – beaurivage94290@orange.fr – Fax 01 49 61 02 60 – Closed 15 August-4 September, Tuesday evening, Wednesday evening, Sunday evening and Monday

Rest – Menu € 39 – Carte approx. € 55

◆ As the name indicates, the Beau Rivage is on the riverside; choose a table near the picture windows for a view of the Seine. A modern setting and traditional cuisine.

VILLEPARISIS – 77 Seine-et-Marne – 312 E2 – 101 19 – pop. 23 400 19 **C1**
– alt. 72 m – ✉ 77270

Paris 26 – Bobigny 15 – Chelles 10 – Tremblay-en-France 5

Relais du Parisis P VISA AE

2 av. Jean Monnet – ✆ 01 64 27 83 83 – www.relaisduparisis.com – relaisduparisis@wanadoo.fr – Fax 01 64 27 94 49

44 rm – †€ 49/69 ††€ 49/69, ☕ € 9 – ½ P € 49/59

Rest – *(closed 1-28 August)* Menu (€ 14), € 20/27 – Carte € 32/46

◆ This practical and functional hotel in an industrial estate, near a bypass, houses small, well-kept and simply furnished rooms. Traditional cuisine with influences from southwestern France, served in the large dining room or on the summer terrace.

XX **La Bastide** VISA

15 av. J. Jaurès – ✆ 01 60 21 08 99 – la_bastide@cegetel.net – Fax 01 60 21 08 99 – Closed 3 weeks in August, 22 February-1 March, Monday dinner, Saturday lunch and Sunday

Rest – *(pre-book Sat - Sun)* Menu € 22 (weekday lunch), € 29/46 – Carte € 47/72

◆ Pleasant town centre inn with jolly, rustic decor (beams, fireplace, yellow walls), warm welcome and seasonal cuisine.

VINCENNES – 94 Val-de-Marne – 312 D2 – 101 17 – pop. 47 200 – alt. 51 m 21 **C2**
– ✉ 94300

Paris 7 – Créteil 11 – Lagny-sur-Marne 26 – Meaux 47 – Melun 45 – Senlis 48

Office de tourisme, 11, avenue de Nogent ✆ 01 48 08 13 00, Fax 01 43 74 81 01

Château★★ - Bois de Vincennes★★: Zoo★★, Parc floral de Paris★★, Musée des Arts d'Afrique et d'Océanie★, **Paris.**

St-Louis without rest AC VISA AE

2 bis r. R. Giraudineau – ✆ 01 43 74 16 78 – www.hotel-paris-saintlouis.com – saint-louis@paris-hotel-capital.com – Fax 01 43 74 16 49

25 rm – †€ 98/140 ††€ 112/160, ☕ € 13

◆ This building near the château houses elegant, period furnished rooms. Some ground floor rooms, which open onto the small garden, have basement bathrooms.

Daumesnil Vincennes without rest

50 av. Paris – ✆ 01 48 08 44 10 – www.hotel-daumesnil.com – info@hotel-daumesnil.com – Fax 01 43 65 10 94

50 rm – †€ 87/109 ††€ 111/194, ☕ € 12

◆ A pleasant Provençal-style decor enlivens this hotel, which is situated on a busy avenue. The breakfast room on a veranda opens onto a small patio.

Donjon without rest

22 r. Donjon – ✆ 01 43 28 19 17 – www.hotel-donjon-vincennes.fr – info@hotel-donjon-vincennes.fr – Fax 01 49 57 02 04 – Closed 18 July-25 August

25 rm – †€ 65/70 ††€ 70/80, ☕ € 7

◆ A town centre establishment with rather small, spick and span rooms. Pleasantly furnished breakfast and sitting rooms.

La Rigadelle

23 r. de Montreuil – ✆ 01 43 28 04 23 – Fax 01 43 28 04 23 – Closed 28 July-17 August, 20-28 December, Sunday and Monday

Rest – *(number of covers limited, pre-book)* Menu (€ 24), € 33/51 – Carte € 42/67

◆ The stylish dining room is tiny with mirrors making it appear more spacious. The cuisine is in keeping with modern taste, with the accent on fish.

VIRY-CHÂTILLON – 91 Essonne – **312** D3 – **101** 36 – **pop. 30 600** – **alt. 34 m** – ✉ 91170 21 **C3**

▶ Paris 26 – Corbeil-Essonnes 15 – Évry 8 – Longjumeau 10 – Versailles 29

Dariole de Viry

21 r. Pasteur – ✆ 01 69 44 22 40 – www.dariole-de-viry.fr – la-dariole-de-viry@wanadoo.fr – Closed Saturday lunch, Sunday dinner and Monday

Rest – Menu € 25 (weekday lunch)/38

◆ Seasonal, traditional cuisine at this restaurant, whose façade is painted in chocolate tones. Recently re-decorated, attractive dining room.

Marcigny

27 r. D. Casanova – ✆ 01 69 44 04 09 – Closed Saturday lunch, Sunday dinner and Monday

Rest – Menu € 26 (weekday lunch)/36

◆ The Marcigny bears the name of a Burgundy village. Friendly atmosphere, attentive service, traditional French and Burgundian cuisine, accompanied by home-baked bread. A popular restaurant which is often full.

Look out for red symbols, indicating particularly pleasant establishments.

PARTHENAY – 79 Deux-Sèvres – **322** E5 – **pop. 10 466** – **alt. 175 m** – ✉ 79200 **Atlantic Coast** 38 **B1**

▶ Paris 377 – Bressuire 32 – Niort 42 – Poitiers 50 – Thouars 41

Office de tourisme, 8, rue de la Vau Saint-Jacques ✆ 05 49 64 24 24, Fax 05 49 64 52 29

Château des Forges Les Forges Domaine des Forges, SE : 23 km on D 59 and D 121, ✆ 05 49 69 91 77

⩽★ from the Pont-Neuf - ⩽★ of the hôtel de ville terrace - Bridge and St-Jacques gateway★ Y **B** - Rue de la Vau-St-Jacques★ Y - St-Pierre church★ Parthenay-le-Vieux 1.5 km on the ④

Plan on next page

St-Jacques without rest

13 av. 114ᵉ R.I. – ✆ 05 49 64 33 33 – www.hotel-parthenay.com – hotel.st.jacques@aliceadsl.fr – Fax 05 49 94 00 69 Z **a**

46 rm – †€ 47/90 ††€ 47/90, ☕ € 8

◆ Nestling beneath the citadel, this 1980s building has been admirably renovated. Extremely simple but new rooms; those at the rear are quieter.

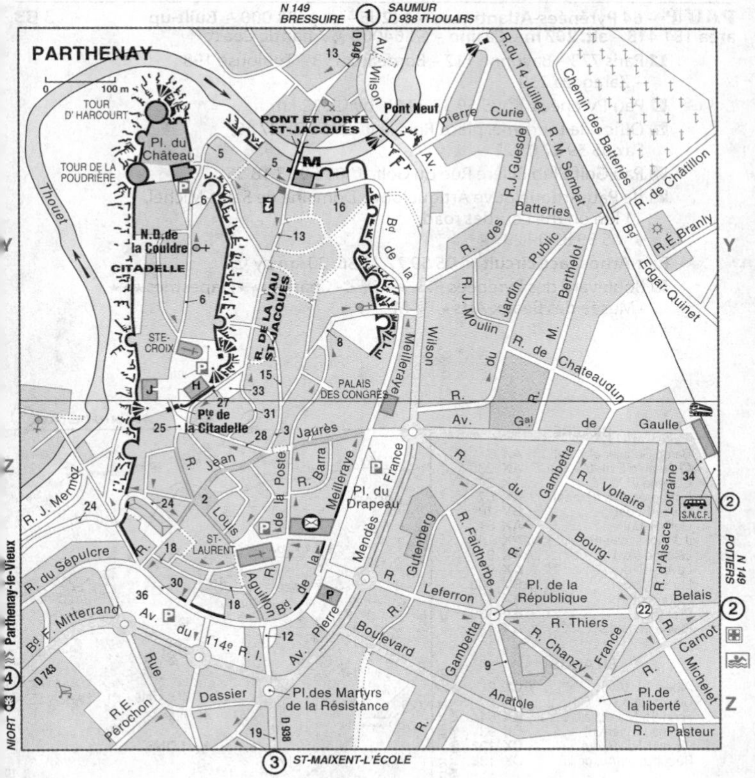

PARTHENAY

Aguillon (R. Louis) . . . . Z
Bancs (Pl. des) . . . . Z 2
Bombarde (R.) . . . . Z 3
Château (R. du) . . . . Y 5
Citadelle (R. de la) . . . . Y 6
Cordeliers (R. des) . . . . Y 8
Denfert-Rochereau (R.) . . . . Z 9
Donjon (Pl. du) . . . . Z 12
Faubourg St-Jacques (R. du) . . . . . . Y 13
Férolle (R.) . . . . Y 15
Godineau (R.) . . . . Y 16
Jean-Jaurès (R.) . . . . Z
J.-J. Rousseau (R.) . . . . Z 18
Marchioux (R. du) . . . . Z 19
Michelet (Pl.) . . . . Z 22
Niquet (R. Gaston) . . . . Z 24
Picard (Pl. Georges) . . . . Z 25
Place (R. de la) . . . . YZ 27
Saunerie (R. de la) . . . . Z 28
Sires-de-Parthenay (Bd des) . . . . . . Z 30
Vauvert (Pl. du) . . . . Y 33
Vau (R. des) . . . . YZ 31
Victor-Hugo (R.) . . . . Z 34
11-Novembre (Pl. du) . . . . Z 36

North 8 km on the N 149 and D 127

Château de Tennessus without rest
– ✆ *05 49 95 50 60 – www.tennessus.com – tennessus@orange.fr*
– Fax 05 49 95 50 62
3 rm – †€ 110/140 ††€ 120/145
◆ This well-restored 14C fortress will take you back to the Middle Ages. Enjoy the lovely preserved architecture and rustic interior, steeped in character.

PARVILLE – **27 Eure** – **304** G7 – **see Évreux**

PASSENANS – **39 Jura** – **321** D6 – **see Poligny**

PATRIMONIO – **2B Haute-Corse** – **345** F3 – **see Corse**

PAU Ⓟ – 64 Pyrénées-Atlantiques – **342** J5 – **pop. 83 000** – **Built-up area 181 413** – **alt. 207 m** – **Casino** – ✉ **64000** Atlantic Coast 3 **B3**

- Paris 773 – Bayonne 112 – Bordeaux 198 – Toulouse 198 – Zaragoza 236
- Pau-Pyrénées: ✆ 05 59 33 33 00, by ①: 12 km.
- Office de tourisme, place Royale ✆ 05 59 27 27 08, Fax 05 59 27 03 21
- Pau Golf Club Billère Rue du Golf, ✆ 05 59 13 18 56
- de Pau-Artiguelouve Artiguelouve Domaine de Saint-Michel, 11 km on the Lourdes road, ✆ 05 59 83 09 29

Pau-Arnos race circuit ✆ 05 59 77 11 36, 20 km by ⑦.

- Boulevard des Pyrénées ✳★★★ DEZ - Château★★: tapestries★★★ - Musée des Beaux-Arts★ EZ **M.**

BILLÈRE

- Baron Séguier (Av. du) . . . . **AX** 7
- Château d'Este (Av. du) . . . . **AX** 23
- Claverie (R.) . . . . **AX** 24
- Entrepreneurs (R. des) . . . . **AX** 57
- Galas (R. de) . . . . **BV** 70
- Golf (R. du) . . . . **AX** 81
- J.J. Rousseau (R.) . . . . **AX** 145
- Lalanne (Av.) . . . . **AVX** 91
- Lavoir (R. du) . . . . **AX** 95
- Lons (Av. de) . . . . **ABV** 100
- Piedmont (R.) . . . . **AX** 129
- Pilar (R.) . . . . **BV** 130
- Plaine (R. de la) . . . . **AX** 132

BIZANOS

- Albert 1er (Av.) . . . . **BCX** 2
- Clemenceau (R. G.) . . . . **BX** 27
- Foch (R. Maréchal) . . . . **BX** 64
- Larribau (Chemin) . . . . **CX** 93
- Pic du Midi (R. du) . . . . **CX** 127
- République (Av. de la) . . . . **CX** 138

GELOS

- Barthou (R. L.) . . . . **BX** 9
- Gélos (Av. de) . . . . **BX** 80
- Leclerc (Av. du Maréchal) . . **BX** 96
- Vallée Heureuse (Av. de la) **BX** 162

JURANÇON

- Cambot (Av. G.) . . . . **AX** 17
- Corps Franc Pommiès (Av. du) . . . . **AX** 36
- Espagne (Pont d') . . . . **AX** 58
- Gaulle (R. Ch.-de) . . . . **AX** 77
- Ollé-Laprune . . . . **AX** 115

LESCAR

- Carrérot (Av.) . . . . **AV** 19
- Coustettes (Chemin des) . . **AV** 42
- Lacau (R.) . . . . **AV** 89
- Santos-Dumont (Av.) . . . . **AV** 147
- Vigné (Côte du) . . . . **AV** 168

LONS

- Ampère (Av. André-Marie) . **AV** 3
- Ariste (R.) . . . . **AV** 6
- Château (R. du) . . . . **AV** 22
- Dassault (Av. Marcel) . . . . **AX** 45
- Ecoles (R. des) . . . . **AV** 51
- Église (R. de l') . . . . **AV** 53
- Frères Farman (Bd des) . . . **AV** 67
- Frères Mongolfier (Av. des) **AX** 68
- Mairie (R. de la) . . . . **AV** 103
- Moulin (Av. du) . . . . **AV** 110
- Pau (Av. de) . . . . **AV** 125
- Souvenir (R. du) . . . . **AV** 152

PAU

- Bérard (Cours Léon) . . . . **BV** 12

Parc Beaumont

1 av. Edouard VII – ✆ 05 59 11 84 00 – www.hotel-parc-beaumont.com – resa@hotel-parc-beaumont.com – Fax 05 59 11 85 00 FZ **b**

69 rm – 🚹€ 205/390 🚹🚹€ 205/390, ☕ € 21 – 11 suites

Rest *Le Jeu de Paume* – Menu (€ 30), € 40/85 – Carte € 60/80

◆ Whether they overlook the town or Beaumont Park, the designer-decorated rooms (some for families) are comfortable and stylish. Relax in the pool, Jacuzzi tub and spa. The restaurant's welcoming decor overlooks a picture of greenery. South-facing terrace.

Villa Navarre

59 av. Trespoey – ✆ 05 59 14 65 65 – www.accorhotels.com – h5677@accor.com – Fax 05 59 14 65 64 BX **a**

26 rm – 🚹€ 177/319 🚹🚹€ 197/339, ☕ € 18 – 4 suites

Rest – *(closed Sunday dinner)* Menu (€ 24), € 47/57 bi – Carte € 47/58

◆ A distinctly British atmosphere reigns in this lovely 1865 mansion and its recent extension, hidden in the heart of a 2ha park. Large, well-kept guestrooms. The sophisticated dining room opens onto the countryside; updated culinary register.

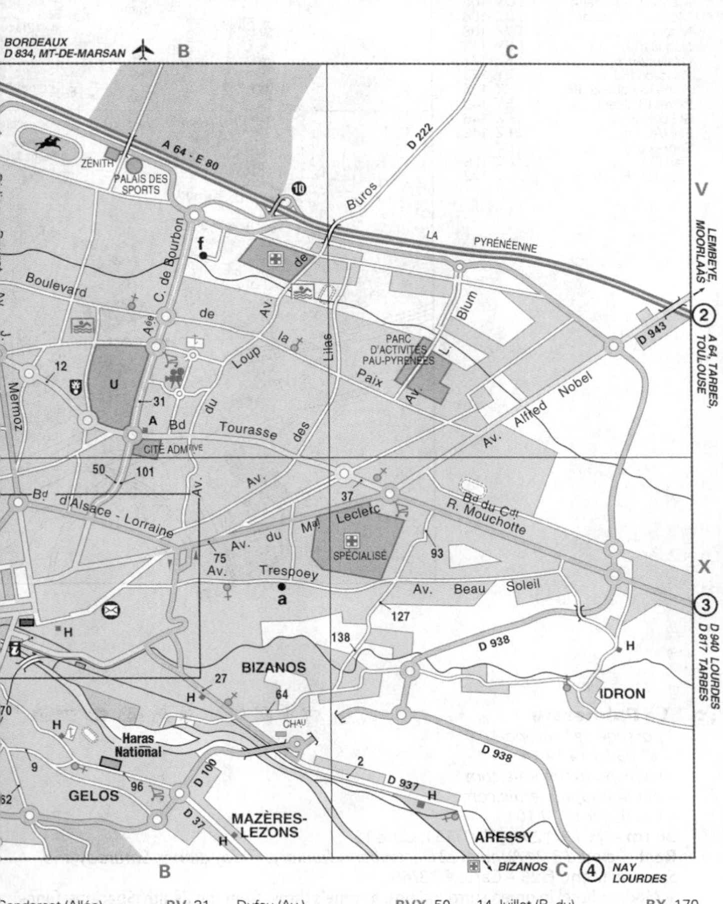

Condorcet (Allée) . . . . **BV** 31
Corps Franc Pommiès et du 49e R.I. (Bd) . . . . . **CX** 37
Dufau (Av.) . . . . **BVX** 50
Gaulle (Av. Gén.-de) . . . . . **BV** 75
Lyautey (Cours) . . . . **BVX** 101
14 Juillet (R. du) . . . . **BX** 170

PAU

Barthou (R. Louis) . . . . **EFZ**
Bernadotte (R.) . . . . **DZ** 14
Bordenave-d'Abère (R.) . . . . **DZ** 15
Cassin (R. René) . . . . **EY** 20
Clemenceau (Pl. Georges) . . **EZ** 25
Clemenceau (R. Georges) . . **FZ** 28
Cordeliers (R. des) . . . . **EZ** 33
Despourrins (R.) . . . . **EY** 47
Ducasse (R. Amiral) . . . . **DY** 48
Espalungue (R. d') . . . . **DZ** 59
Gambetta (R.) . . . . **EZ** 72
Gassion (R.) . . . . **DZ** 73
Gaulle (Av. Gén.-de) . . . . **FY** 75
Gramont (Pl.) . . . . **DZ** 84
Henri-IV (R.) . . . . **DZ** 87
Jeanne-d'Arc (R.) . . . . **DY** 88
Lalanne (R. Mathieu) . . . . . . **EZ** 92
Lespy (R.) . . . . **EFY** 98
Mermoz (Av. Jean) . . . . **DY** 105
Monnaie (Pl. de la) . . . . **DZ** 106
Monnet (R. J.) . . . . **EYZ** 108
Nogue (R.) . . . . **EY** 113
Ossau (Av. d') . . . . **EZ** 121
Palassou (R.) . . . . **EY** 123
Reine-Marguerite (Pl.) . . . . . . **EZ** 135
Réveil (R. Jean) . . . . **EY** 140
St-Louis (R.) . . . . **EZ** 146
Say (Av. L.) . . . . **EFZ** 149
Serviez (R.) . . . . **EZ**
Tran (R.) . . . . **EZ** 158
218e-R.I. (R. du) . . . . **DY** 172

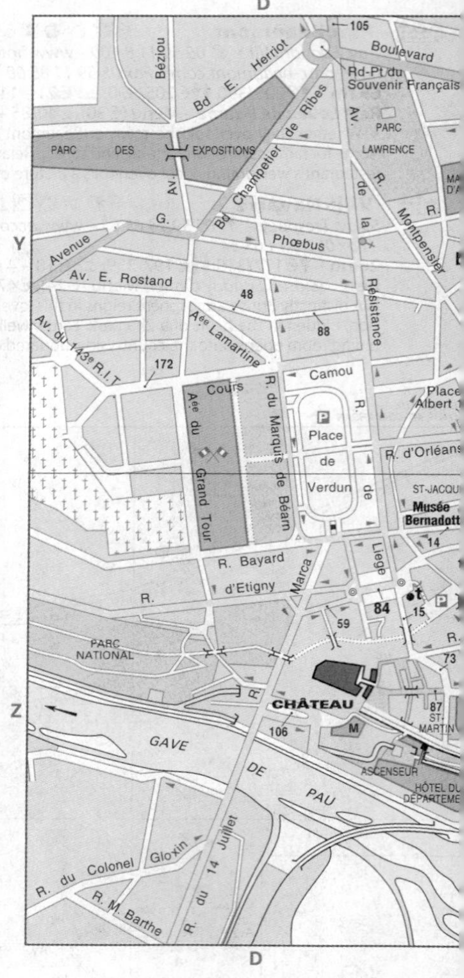

La Palmeraie
1 passage de l'Europe
– ✆ 05 59 14 14 14
– www.paupalmeraie.com
– info@paupalmeraie.com
– Fax 05 59 14 14 10 BV **f**
36 rm – †€ 83/129 ††€ 91/151, ☕ € 15
Rest – *(closed 3-24 August, 22 December-6 January, Friday dinner, Saturday and Sunday)* Menu € 25 – Carte € 33/46
◆ Modern hotel in green surroundings, a stone's throw from the Zenith. Spacious, functional rooms, decorated in pastel shades. The tastefully refurbished dining room leads onto a shaded terrace. Traditional cuisine.

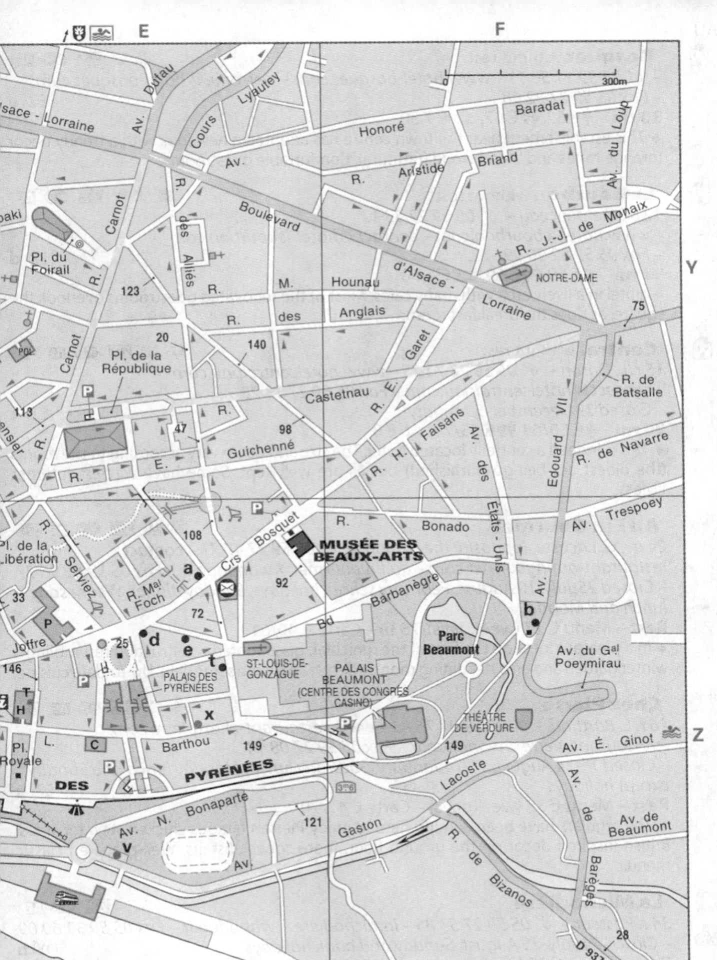

Continental

2 r. Mar. Foch – ✆ 05 59 27 69 31 – www.bestwestern-continental.com – hotel@ bestwerstern-continental.com – Fax 05 59 27 99 84 EZ **a**

74 rm – 🚹€ 68/98 🚹🚹€ 68/98, ☕ € 9

Rest – *(closed August, Saturday and Sunday)* Menu (€ 12), € 20/25 – Carte € 22/35

◆ Pau's luxury hotel (1912) has retained its period hall and lounges, affording it a certain nostalgia. Refurbished colourful rooms, four of which are circular (in a tower). Dining room brightened with colours and mirrors. Traditional food.

Hôtel de Gramont without rest

3 pl. Gramont – ✆ 05 59 27 84 04 – www.hotelgramont.com – hotelgramont@ wanadoo.fr – Fax 05 59 27 62 23 – Closed 20 December-3 January DZ **t**

34 rm – 🚹€ 60/86 🚹🚹€ 86/126, ☕ € 10 – 2 suites

◆ This former 17C coaching inn is said to be the oldest hotel in Pau. Tastefully refurbished rooms overlooking the street or the Hédas Valley. Generous breakfast buffet; billiards sitting room.

Bosquet without rest
– ✆ 05 59 11 50 11 – www.hotel-bosquet.com – welcome@hotel-bosquet.com
– Fax 05 59 27 22 98 EZ **e**
30 rm – †€ 62 ††€ 67, ☕ € 7,50
◆ This establishment near the town centre has adopted a new look with a trendy décor (orange tones and blond wood furniture). Comfortable guestrooms.

Le Bourbon without rest
12 pl. Clemenceau – ✆ 05 59 27 53 12
– www.hotel-lebourbon.com – contact@hotel-lebourbon.com
– Fax 05 59 82 90 99 EZ **d**
33 rm – †€ 59 ††€ 69, ☕ € 6,50
◆ Hotel in a lively area with many cafés. Most of the renovated guestrooms overlook the square, as does the breakfast room.

Central without rest
15 r. L. Daran – ✆ 05 59 27 72 75 – www.hotelcentralpau.com
– contact@hotelcentralpau.com – Fax 05 59 27 33 28
– Closed 29 December-5 January EZ **t**
26 rm – †€ 50/63 ††€ 55/79, ☕ € 8
◆ This is indeed a centrally located hotel. The size and decor vary according to the rooms (the oldest are being refurbished) but all are well kept. Some have wireless Internet access.

Au Fin Gourmet
24 av. G. Lacoste, (opposite the station) – ✆ 05 59 27 47 71 – contact@restaurant-aufingourmet.com – au.fin.gourmet@wanadoo.fr – Fax 05 59 82 96 77 – Closed 25 July-10 August, February school holidays, Sunday dinner, Wednesday lunch and Monday EZ **v**
Rest – Menu € 27 (weekdays)/75 bi – Carte € 40/61
◆ In a pleasant location the foot of the funicular, glass-roofed construction resembling a winter garden and an older dining room redecorated in the same vein. Up-to-date cuisine.

Chez Pierre
16 r. L. Barthou – ✆ 05 59 27 76 86 – www.restaurant-chez-pierre.com
– restaurant.pierre@wanadoo.fr – Fax 05 59 27 08 14
– Closed 1st-14 August, 1st-14 January, Saturday lunch, Monday lunch and Sunday except holidays EZ **x**
Rest – Menu € 35 (weekdays) – Carte € 47/70
◆ The regulars have been coming here to enjoy Pierre's famous chicken stew for years! British inspired decor on the ground floor, more sober upstairs. Well-prepared classic menu.

La Michodière
34 r. Pasteur – ✆ 05 59 27 53 85 – lamichodiere@wanadoo.fr – Fax 05 59 33 60 09
– Closed 24 July-25 August, Sunday and bank holidays DY **b**
Rest – Menu € 15 (weekday lunch)/27 – Carte € 32/75
◆ Behind the pebbled facade are two dining rooms; the one with wood panelling reveals the chefs at work in the kitchen. Modern setting and dishes made with market produce.

La Planche de Boeuf
30 r. Pasteur – ✆ 05 59 27 62 60 – Fax 05 59 27 62 60 – Closed August, Sunday evening, Wednesday evening and Monday EY **s**
Rest – Menu € 26/38 – Carte € 30/45
◆ This inviting old house makes you want to venture inside. The tables near the fireplace are greatly appreciated in winter. Friendly welcome and traditional cuisine.

La Table d'Hôte
1 r. du Hédas – ✆ 05 59 27 56 06 – la-table-dhote@wanadoo.fr
– Fax 05 59 27 56 06 – Closed Christmas holidays, Monday except dinners in July-August and Sunday EZ **k**
Rest – Menu (€ 19), € 24/31
◆ Brick, beams and pebbles give a country atmosphere to this former 17C tannery, nestling in a small medieval street. Pleasant atmosphere. Local cuisine.

in Jurançon : 2 km – pop. 7 087 – alt. 177 m – ✉ 64110

XXX ✿ **Chez Ruffet** (Stéphane Carrade)
3 av. Ch. Touzet – ✆ 05 59 06 25 13 – www.restaurant-chezruffet.com – chez.ruffet@wanadoo.fr – Fax 05 59 06 52 18 – Closed Sunday and Monday AX **e**
Rest – *(pre-book)* Menu € 28 bi (weekday lunch), € 66/130 bi – Carte € 100/130
Spec. Foie frais de canard poché au jus de raisin (autumn). Filet de rouget fumé, rôti aux chipirons crus marinés (summer). Gâteau de crespères, mousse au Grand Marnier et glace Nutella. (autumn). **Wines** Jurançon, Madiran.
◆ Guests to this old regional farmhouse are captivated by its authentic (stonework, well polished wood) blend of elegance and informality. Excellent updated regional cuisine.

in Lescar Northwest: 7.5 km by D 817 and D 601 – pop. 9 439 – alt. 179 m – ✉ 64230
Office de tourisme, place Royale ✆ 05 59 81 15 98, Fax 05 59 81 12 54

La Terrasse
1 r. Maubec – ✆ 05 59 81 02 34 – laterrasselescar@wanadoo.fr – Fax 05 59 81 08 77 – Closed 30 July-24 August and 21 December-5 January
20 rm – †€ 49 ††€ 53, ☕ € 8 – ½ P € 48
Rest – *(closed Saturday lunch and Sunday)* Menu € 28 – Carte € 35/50
◆ A pleasant place to stay (once a stopover for pilgrims) in a quiet side street. Simple rooms with sturdy wooder furniture. Exhibitions of paintings in the restaurant and traditional cuisine.

PAUILLAC – 33 Gironde – **335** G3 – pop. 5 242 – alt. 20 m – ✉ 33250 3 **B1**
Atlantic Coast

Paris 625 – Arcachon 113 – Blaye 16 – Bordeaux 54 – Lesparre-Médoc 23
Office de tourisme, La Verrerie ✆ 05 56 59 03 08, Fax 05 56 59 23 38
château Mouton Rothschild★: musée★★ Northwest: 2 km.

✿✿ **Château Cordeillan Bages** rm,
61 r. des vignerons, 1 km south on D 2 – ✆ 05 56 59 24 24 – www.cordeillanbages.com – cordeillan@relaischateaux.fr – Fax 05 56 59 01 89 – Closed 20 December-13 February
28 rm – †€ 199/517 ††€ 199/517, ☕ € 24 – ½ P € 242/430
Rest – *(closed Saturday lunch, Monday and Tuesday)*
Menu € 90 (lunch)/175 – Carte € 105/125
Spec. Huître semi-prise à cru, longuet iodé et caviar. Pigeon au thé, pâtes fraîches fumées, copeaux de fenouil cru. Brioche crue et lait en fermentation. **Wines** Pauillac, Graves.
◆ This attractive 17C country mansion is in the heart of the vineyards. It has fine guestrooms and a cosy ambience. Daring and inventive cuisine in the restaurant.

France et Angleterre
3 quai Albert Pichon – ✆ 05 56 59 01 20 – www.hoteldefrance-angleterre.com – contact@hoteldefrance-angleterre.com – Fax 05 56 59 02 31 – Closed 18 December-11 January
29 rm – †€ 57/90 ††€ 57/90, ☕ € 10
Rest – *(closed Sunday from November to February)*
Menu (€ 15), € 20/40 – Carte € 42/54
◆ A 19C building, situated on the quayside with practical, well-renovated rooms. Those at the front have an attractive view of the Gironde estuary. A modern dining room and veranda with a menu based on traditional and regional recipes.

Vignoble
20 rm – †€ 87/100 ††€ 87/103, ☕ € 10 – ½ P € 76/80
◆ This modern annex contains functional rooms, decorated on a vineyard theme. Balcony or ground-floor terrace with greenery. Fully-equipped seminar area.

X **Café Lavinal**
at Bages, pl. Desquet – ✆ 05 57 75 00 09 – www.villagedebages.com – cafe.lavinal@bordeauxsaveurs.com – Fax 05 57 75 00 10 – Closed 24 December-1st February and Sunday dinner
Rest – Menu (€ 14), € 25/35 – Carte € 28/40
◆ A neo-retro bistro which opened its doors in 2006 in the centre of Pauillac, where the Argentinian chef presides over a predominantly traditional menu. Daily specials and wines from local estates.

PAVILLON (COL) – 69 Rhône – **327** F3 – see Cours

PAYRAC – 46 Lot – **337** E3 – **pop. 626** – **alt. 320 m** – ✉ 46350 28 **B1**

Paris 530 – Brive-la-Gaillarde 53 – Cahors 48 – Figeac 60 – Sarlat-la-Canéda 32

Syndicat d'initiative, avenue de Toulouse ✆ 05 65 37 94 27, Fax 05 65 37 94 27

Hostellerie de la Paix

– ✆ 05 65 37 95 15 – www.escalotel.com/hostlapaix – host.la.paix@escalotel.com – Fax 05 65 37 90 37 – Open March-October

50 rm – †€ 49/59 ††€ 55/65, ☕ € 8 – ½ P € 45/52

Rest – Menu € 16/30 – Carte € 22/46

◆ This former post house has an attractive stone facade. Most of the renovated rooms face away from the road. Restaurant dining rooms and veranda serving recipes from the Quercy region (chicken in verjuice, tourin soup, etc.).

PÉGOMAS – 06 Alpes-Maritimes – **341** C6 – **pop. 6 296** – **alt. 18 m** – ✉ 06580 42 **E2**

Paris 896 – Cannes 12 – Draguignan 59 – Grasse 9 – Nice 41 – St-Raphaël 38

Office de tourisme, 287, avenue de Grasse ✆ 04 92 60 20 70, Fax 04 92 60 20 66

Le Bosquet without rest

chemin des Périssols, Mouans-Sartoux road – ✆ 04 92 60 21 20 – www.hoteldubosquet.com – hotel.lebosquet@wanadoo.fr – Fax 04 92 60 21 49 – Closed 15 January-1st February

23 rm – †€ 50/65 ††€ 65/70, ☕ € 7

◆ A warm welcome and a restful environment in a wooded park await in this small, well-kept hotel where you will be treated to home-made jams. Rooms or studios available.

L'Écluse

Chemin de l'écluse, beside the Siagne – ✆ 04 93 42 22 55 – www.restaurant-lecluse.com – ecluse@wanadoo.fr – Fax 04 93 40 72 65 – Closed November, weekdays from 30 September to 15 April and Monday from 16 April to 30 September

Rest – Menu (€ 18), € 27/31 – Carte € 30/40

◆ A restaurant appreciated for its simplicity, relaxed atmosphere and large waterside terrace reminiscent of an open-air café. Traditional cuisine.

in St-Jean Southeast: 2 km by D 9 – ✉ **06550 La Roquette-sur-Siagne**

Les Chasseurs without rest

1175 av. République – ✆ 04 92 19 18 00 – hoteldeschasseurs@wanadoo.fr – Fax 04 92 19 19 61 – Closed 23 October-15 November and 20-31 December

17 rm ☕ – †€ 46 ††€ 62/72

◆ Simple rooms, rather old but impeccably well kept; the rooms at the rear are quieter. A reasonably-priced overnight stay not far from Cannes!

PEILLON – 06 Alpes-Maritimes – **341** F5 – **pop. 1 336** – **alt. 200 m** – ✉ 06440 **French Riviera** 42 **E2**

Paris 947 – Contes 14 – L'Escarène 14 – Menton 38 – Monaco 29 – Nice 20 – Sospel 34

Syndicat d'initiative, 620, avenue de l'Hôtel de Ville ✆ 04 93 91 98 34, Fax 04 93 79 87 65

Village★ - Frescoes★ in the Pénitents Blancs chapel.

Auberge de la Madone (Christian and Thomas Millo)

– ✆ 04 93 79 91 17 – www.auberge-madone-peillon.com – auberge.de.la.madone@wanadoo.fr – Fax 04 93 79 99 36 – Closed 6 November-22 December and Wednesday

14 rm – †€ 90/180 ††€ 95/200, ☕ € 24 – 3 suites – ½ P € 125/135

Rest – Menu (€ 32 bi), € 49 (weekdays)/90 – Carte € 73/99

Spec. Tourte d'herbes sauvages, escalope de foie gras poêlé. Duo d'agneau des Alpilles, carré rôti à la fleur de thym et épaule confite. Macaron à la blette, compotée de pomme-poire, glace niçoise. **Wines** Bellet, Côtes de Provence.

◆ Well-kept, quiet rooms are a feature of this characterful hotel surrounded by a flower garden. Fine regionally inspired cuisine is served in an attractive Provençal dining room or on a pleasant terrace facing the delightful village perched on its rocky peak.

Lou Pourtail

3 pl. A. Arnulf, welcome to the Auberge de la Madone – 04 93 79 91 17 – Closed 9 November-25 December, 15-31 January and Wednesday
6 rm – €44/69 €44/69, €13
Rest – *(open May-September) (lunch only)* Carte €20/39
◆ The charm of an old house with whitewashed walls, vaulted or high ceilings and country furniture – inside the village walls. Simple rooms without TV. Small rustic dining room and summer garden terrace serving dishes made with local produce.

PEISEY-NANCROIX – 73 Savoie – 333 N4 – pop. 614 – alt. 1 320 m – ✉ 73210 French Alps 45 D2

Paris 635 – Albertville 55 – Bourg-St-Maurice 13
Office de tourisme, place de Roscanvel 04 79 07 94 28, Fax 04 79 07 95 34

La Vanoise rm, VISA

at Plan Peisey – 04 79 07 92 19 – www.hotel-la-vanoise.com – hotel-la-vanoise@wanadoo.fr – Fax 04 79 07 97 48 – Open 1st July-31 August and 18 December-28 April
33 rm – €70/90 €85/130, €12 – ½ P €70/106
Rest – Menu €24/32 – Carte €27/37
◆ Attractive view of the Bellecôte dome from this establishment. The rooms sport a fetching alpine style and those facing south have a balcony. Well-being centre. Warm wainscoting, Savoyard menus and a log fire - no doubt about it, you're in the mountains!

PELVOUX (Commune) – 05 Hautes-Alpes – 334 G3 – pop. 404 – alt. 1 260 m – Winter sports : 1 250/2 300 m 7 – ✉ 05340 French Alps 41 C1

Paris 702 – L'Argentière-la-Bessée 11 – Briançon 22 – Gap 84 – Guillestre 32
Route des Choulières: ★★ E.

Ailefroide – alt. 1 510 m – ✉ 05340 Pelvoux

Pré de Madame Carle: landscape★★ Nortwest: 6 km.

Chalet Hôtel d'Ailefroide rest, VISA

– 04 92 23 32 01 – www.chalets-hotels.com – contact@chalethotel-ailefroide.com – Fax 04 92 23 49 97 – Open 13 June-6 September
24 rm – €45/52 €58/72 – ½ P €47/54
Rest – Menu €20/23 – Carte €21/32
◆ A small hotel well known to hikers. Accommodation is in simple, not very large rooms, some with a new mountain-style look. Sauna and jacuzzi. A friendly, invigorating restaurant, whether near the fireplace or in the garden.

PÉNESTIN – 56 Morbihan – 308 Q10 – pop. 1 527 – alt. 20 m – ✉ 56760 10 C3

Paris 458 – La Baule 29 – Nantes 84 – La Roche-Bernard 18 – St-Nazaire 43 – Vannes 48
Office de tourisme, allée du Grand Pré 02 99 90 37 74, Fax 02 99 90 47 08
Pointe du Bile ★ South: 5 km, Brittany

Loscolo VISA

Pointe de Loscolo, 4 km southwest – 02 99 90 31 90 – www.hotelloscolo.com – hotelloscolo@neuf.fr – Fax 02 99 90 32 14 – Open 30 April-5 October
14 rm – €49/101 €57/109, €14 – ½ P €78/104
Rest – *(closed Wednesday) (dinner only) (residents only)* Menu €35
◆ You are in the home of the inventor of the oyster-opening machine! Enjoy a peaceful, invigorating stay in discreetly appointed rooms, most of which face the sea. Dining room in soft shades and dishes based on ocean flavours.

PENHORS – 29 Finistère – 308 E7 – see Pouldreuzic

PENNEDEPIE – 14 Calvados – 303 N3 – see Honfleur

PENVÉNAN – 22 Côtes-d'Armor – **309** C2 – **pop. 2 580** – **alt. 70 m** – ✉ 22710 9 **B1**

▶ Paris 521 – Guingamp 34 – Lannion 16 – St-Brieuc 70 – Tréguier 8

ℹ Syndicat d'initiative, 12, place de l'Église ✆ 02 96 92 81 09

Le Crustacé VISA MC

2 r. de la Poste – ✆ 02 96 92 67 46 – Closed Monday in July-August, Sunday dinner, Tuesday dinner and Wednesday from September to June

Rest – Menu € 17/37 – Carte € 31/62

◆ Small welcoming family-run restaurant, opposite the church, with a simple and well-kept rustic dining room. Traditional cuisine and seafood.

Luxury pad or humble abode?
and denote categories of comfort.

PENVINS – 56 Morbihan – **308** O9 – see Sarzeau

PERI – 2A Corse-du-Sud – **345** C7 – see Corse

PÉRIGNAC – 17 Charente-Maritime – **324** H6 – see Pons

PÉRIGNAC – 16 Charente – **324** K7 – **pop. 508** – **alt. 164 m** – ✉ 16250 39 **C3**

▶ Paris 485 – Poitiers 147 – Angoulême 28 – Cognac 51 – Soyaux 32

Château de Lerse [P]

2 km south by D 10 – ✆ 05 45 60 32 81 – www.chateaudelerse.com – fl.lafargue@wanadoo.fr – Open May-September

3 rm – †€ 80/100 ††€ 90/110 **Table d'hôte** – Menu € 25 bi/35 bi

◆ This small, fortified 13C château, surrounded by acres of countryside, extends a friendly welcome. Spacious, classically-decorated guestrooms. Regional cuisine and garden produce served in a period dining room (huge fireplace and family portraits).

PÉRIGNAT-LÈS-SARLIÈVE – 63 Puy-de-Dôme – **326** F8 – see Clermont-Ferrand

PÉRIGNY – 86 Vienne – **322** H5 – see Poitiers

PÉRIGUEUX [P] – 24 Dordogne – **329** F4 – **pop. 29 600** – **alt. 86 m** – ✉ 24000 Dordogne-Berry-Limousin 4 **C1**

▶ Paris 482 – Agen 138 – Bordeaux 128 – Limoges 96 – Poitiers 198

ℹ Office de tourisme, 26, place Francheville ✆ 05 53 53 10 63, Fax 05 53 09 02 50

18 de Périgueux Marsac-sur-l'Isle Domaine de Saltgourde, 5 km on the Angoulême road, ✆ 05 53 53 02 35

◉ St-Front cathedral★★, Saint-Étienne de la Cité church★ - Quartier St-Front★★★: rue Limogeanne★ BY, Renaissance staircase★ of Hôtel de Lestrade (rue de la sagesse) BY - Galerie Daumesnil★ opposite 3 de la rue Limogeanne - Musée du Périgord★★ CY **M²**.

Plans on following pages

Mercure without rest VISA MC AE

7 pl. Francheville – ✆ 05 53 06 65 00 – www.mercure.com – h6237@accor.com – Fax 05 53 07 20 33 BZ **e**

66 rm – †€ 85/95 ††€ 97/107, € 16

◆ This brand-new hotel with a dressed stone façade enjoys a good location opposite a park and a multiplex cinema. Pleasant, contemporary-style rooms.

Bristol without rest
37 r. A. Gadaud – ✆ 05 53 08 75 90 – www.bristolfrance.com – hotel@bristolfrance.com – Fax 05 53 07 00 49 – Closed 20 December-3 January BY **u**
29 rm – €60/68 €66/77, €8
◆ This hotel, near the town centre and tourist highlights, is home to gradually refurbished rooms of fine proportions (except 6) with good soundproofing. Impeccably kept.

Le Rocher de l'Arsault
15 r. L'Arsault – ✆ 05 53 53 54 06 – rocher.arsault@wanadoo.fr – Fax 05 53 08 32 32 – Closed 6 July-2 August, 2-8 January, Sunday dinner and Wednesday CY **s**
Rest – Menu (€20), €28/81 – Carte €42/60
◆ A long building against the rock. Stylish, colourful dining room with one wall showing exposed stonework. Pleasant private rooms. Regionally sourced cuisine.

Le Clos St-Front
5, 7 r. de la Vertu – ✆ 05 53 46 78 58 – www.leclossaintfront.com – leclossaintfront@wanadoo.fr – Fax 05 53 46 78 20 – Closed February school holidays, Sunday dinner and Monday except from June to September CY **r**
Rest – Menu (€20), €27 (weekdays)/62 – Carte €46/52
◆ Immense fireplaces and contemporary art adorn this very pleasant restaurant. Terrace shaded by lime trees. The cuisine is an interesting mixture of exotic and regional accents.

Hercule Poireau
2 r. Nation – ✆ 05 53 08 90 76 – romainsauvage@hotmail.com – Closed 5-18 January, Tuesday dinner in Winter and Wednesday CZ **r**
Rest – Menu €21/38 – Carte €41/58
◆ In the rustic 16C dining room (timber and stonework) or old cellar (16C vaulting) you will taste regional recipes reinterpreted and updated by the chef.

La Taula
3 r. Denfert-Rochereau – ✆ 05 53 35 40 02 – lataula@laposte.net – Fax 05 53 35 40 02 – Closed 1st-9 March, 1-7 July and Monday in low season BZ **k**
Rest – Menu (€18), €30/36 – Carte €47/54
◆ Welcoming long restaurant serving tasty local cuisine; the name is local dialect for table.

Le Fou du Roy
2 r. Montaigne – ✆ 05 53 09 43 77 – Closed Saturday lunch and Sunday BY **a**
Rest – *(number of covers limited, pre-book)* Menu (€20), €25/36 – Carte €50/60
◆ A hospitable welcome, rustic interior and modern cuisine. Seafood takes pride of place on the table. Theme menus, including a special scallop menu in season.

Le Grain de Sel
7 r. des Farges – ✆ 05 53 53 45 22 – alainbanier.@hotmail.fr – Closed 28 June-20 July, 20 December-4 January, Sunday and Monday BZ **t**
Rest – Menu (€19), €26/48 – Carte €49/61
◆ Venture over the threshold of this traditional house in a narrow lane of old Périgueux. It serves up-to-date dishes in a classical, slightly rustic setting. Located near the cathedral.

L'Essentiel (Eric Vidal)
8 r. de la Clarté – ✆ 05 53 35 15 15 – eric.vidal24@wanadoo.fr – Fax 05 53 35 15 15 – Closed Easter holidays, 7-15 July, autumn school holidays, 31 December-15 January, Sunday and Monday BZ **n**
Rest – *(number of covers limited, pre-book)* Menu €27 (weekday lunch), €37/75 bi – Carte €37/68
Spec. Lasagne de poireaux aux truffes du Périgord, foie gras rôti. (mid December to early March). Demi-pigeon rôti et caramélisé à la goutte de sang. Beignet de chocolat chaud coulant aux fruits de saison. **Wines** Pécharmant, Monbazillac.
◆ The unassuming façade hides two small dining rooms and an excellent surprise: up-to-date, extremely refined cuisine and an outstanding selection of regional wines.

PÉRIGUEUX

Street	Grid	No.
Abreuvoir (R. de l')	CY	2
Amphithéâtre (R. de l')	AZ	3
Arènes (Bd des)	AZ	6
Aubergerie (R.)	BZ	9
Barbecane (R.)	CY	12
Barbusse (Av. Henri)	AY	13
Bride (R. de la)	BZ	15
Bugeaud (Pl.)	BZ	
Calvaire (R. du)	BZ	16
Cavaignac (Av.)	AZ	18
Cité (R. de la)	ABZ	23
Clarté (R. de la)	BZ	24
Claütre (Pl. de la)	BZ	26
Clos-Chassaing	BY	27
Coderc (Pl. du)	BYZ	28
Condé (R.)	BZ	29
Constitution (R. de la)	CY	30
Daumesnil (Av. et Pl.)	BCZ	32
Daumesnil (Galerie)	BYZ	31
Durand (Rd-Pt Charles)	AZ	34
Eguillerie (R.)	BY	35
Fénelon (Cours)	BZ	
Goudeau (Pl. Émile)	CY	36
Hôtel de Ville (Pl. de l')	BZ	37
Lammary (R.)	BY	38
Limogeanne (R.)	BY	
Maurois (Pl. André)	BY	39
Miséricorde (R. de la)	BY	40
Mobiles-de-Coulmiers (R.)	AY	41
Montaigne (Bd M.)	BYZ	
Montaigne (Cours et Pl. M.)	BYZ	
Notre-Dame (R.)	CY	42
Port-de-Graule (R. du)	CYZ	44
Port (Allée du)	AY	43
Président-Wilson (R. du)	AY	
République (R. de la)	BYZ	45
Sagesse (R. de la)	BY	46
Ste-Marthe (R.)	CZ	50
St-Pierre-ès-Liens (R.)	ABZ	47
St-Roch (R.)	BZ	48
St-Silain (Pl.)	BY	49
Sully (R.)	BZ	53
Taillefer (R.)	BZ	
Talleyrand-Périgord (R.)	CZ	54
Théâtre (Espl. du)	BY	55
Turenne (R. de)	AZ	60
15e-Régt-de-Tirailleurs-Algériens (R. du)	AZ	61
50e-Régt-d'Infanterie (Av. du)	AZ	62

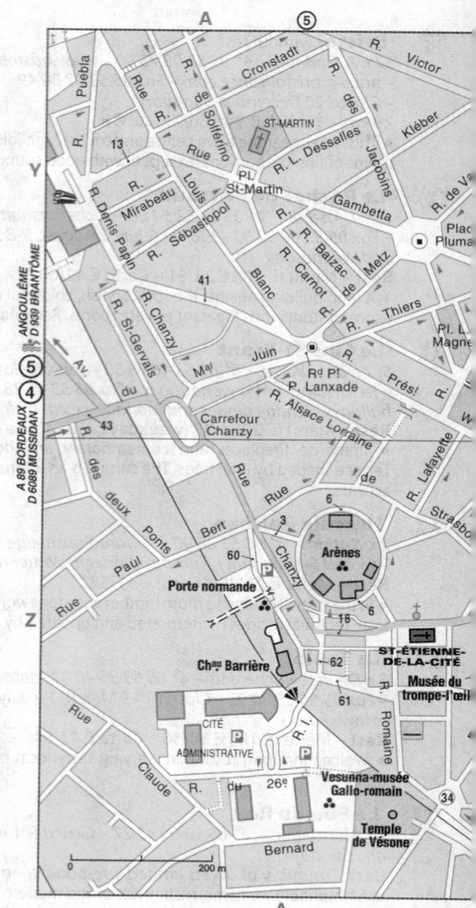

in Chancelade by ⑤, D 710 and D 1: 5.5 km – pop. 3 865 – alt. 88 m – ✉ 24650

Abbey★.

Château des Reynats

15 av. des Reynats – ✆ *05 53 03 53 59*
– www.chateau-hotel-perigord.com
– reynats@chateau-hotel-perigord.com
– Fax 05 53 03 44 84

45 rm – †€ 88/250 ††€ 88/250, ☕ € 14 – 5 suites – ½ P € 82/170

Rest – *(closed 2-26 January, Saturday lunch, Monday lunch and Sunday)*
Menu € 28 (weekday lunch), € 48/65 – Carte € 78/99

◆ A fine 19C château nestling in a wooded park. Rooms with attractive personal touches; those in the wing have just been refurbished, are smaller and have a more restrained decor. The dining room is in keeping with the chateau spirit. Updated regional fare.

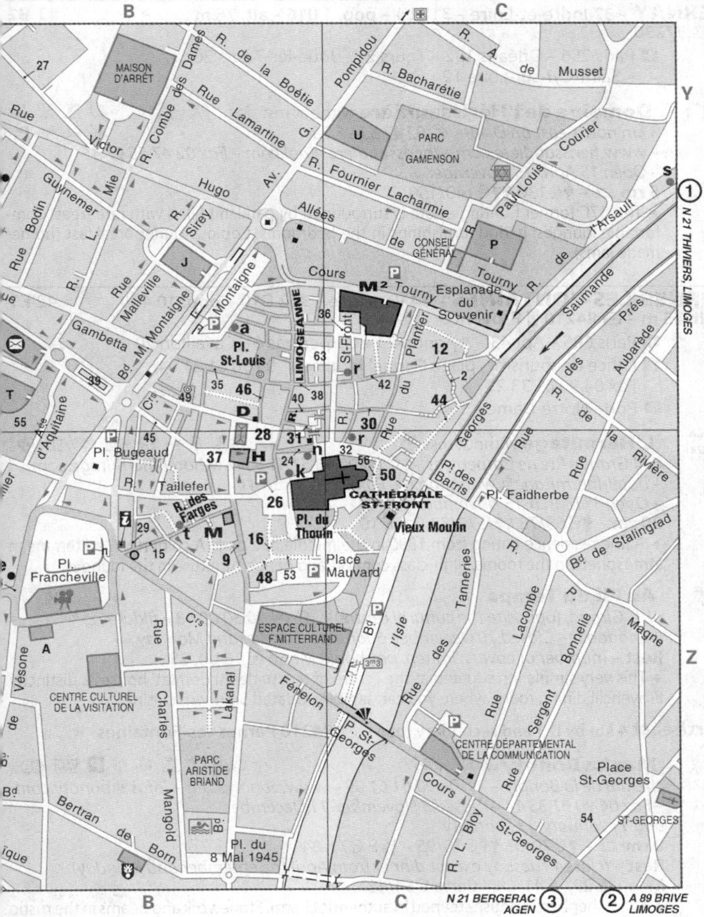

in Champcevinel North: 5 km via Avenue G. Pompidou CY – **pop. 2 486** – **alt. 210 m** – ✉ 24750

XXX **La Table du Pouyaud** VISA MC

rte de Paris, D 8 – ✆ 05 53 09 53 32 – www.pouyaud.com
– tablepouyaud@yahoo.fr – Fax 05 53 09 50 48
– Closed Sunday dinner, Monday dinner and Tuesday

Rest – Menu € 25 (weekday lunch), € 32/75 – Carte € 57/97

◆ Comfortable restaurant in a former farmhouse. Yellow walls adorned with paintings, attractive cane chairs and well-laid round tables. Regional produce takes pride of place.

PERNAND-VERGELESSES – 21 Côte-d'Or – 320 J7 – see Beaune

Red = Pleasant. Look for the red X and 🏠 symbols.

PERNAY – 37 Indre-et-Loire – 317 L4 – pop. 1 016 – alt. 76 m – ✉ 37230 11 B2

Paris 256 – Orléans 132 – Tours 21 – Joué-lès-Tours 26 – Saint-Cyr-sur-Loire 19

Domaine de l'Hérissaudière without rest
3 km north-east on D 48 – 02 47 55 95 28 – www.herissaudiere.com – lherissaudiere@aol.com – Fax 02 47 55 97 45 – Open 15 April-15 November
5 rm – €130 €140/150
◆ This 17C former hunting estate is surrounded by parkland filled with rare trees. Comfortable lounges; period furnishings in the bedrooms. Copious buffet breakfast (home-made jams).

PERNES-LES-FONTAINES – 84 Vaucluse – 332 D10 – pop. 10 400 – alt. 75 m – ✉ 84210 Provence 42 E1

Paris 685 – Apt 43 – Avignon 23 – Carpentras 6 – Cavaillon 20

Office de tourisme, place Gabriel Moutte 04 90 61 31 04, Fax 04 90 61 33 23

Porte Notre-Dame★.

L'Hermitage without rest
614 Grande Rte de Carpentras – 04 90 66 51 41 – www.hotel-lhermitage.com – hotel-lhermitage@wanadoo.fr – Fax 04 90 61 36 41 – Open 1st March-15 November
20 rm – €65/78 €70/83, €10
◆ A fine residence dating from 1890 in the middle of a park. A colourful Mediterranean atmosphere in the rooms, high-class comfort and period furniture in the lounges.

Au Fil du Temps
pl. L. Giraud, (opposite the cultural centre) – 04 90 30 09 48 – fildutemp@wanadoo.fr – Closed 20 December-6 January, Sunday and Monday
Rest – *(number of covers limited, pre-book)* Menu (€16 bi), 25
◆ This very simple inn situated at the centre of the 'perle du Comtat' houses a distinctly Provençal dining room, where you can sample updated Southern cuisine.

Northeast 4 km by D 1 and secondary road – ✉ 84210 Pernes-les-Fontaines

Mas La Bonoty with rm
chemin de la Bonoty – 04 90 61 61 09 – www.bonoty.com – infos@bonoty.com – Fax 04 90 61 35 14 – Closed 8 November-11 December and 11 January-13 February
8 rm – €70/95 €70/95 – ½ P €71/84
Rest – *(closed Tuesday except dinner from April to September and Monday)* Menu (€22), €41/68 – Carte €54/68
◆ A 17C shepherd's house steeped in authentic charm. Stonework and beams in the rustic dining room. Good quality local seasonal produce on the menu. Provençal-style rooms.

PÉRONNAS – 01 Ain – 328 E3 – see Bourg-en-Bresse

PÉRONNE – 80 Somme – 301 K8 – pop. 8 213 – alt. 52 m – ✉ 80200 Northern France and the Paris Region 37 C1

Paris 141 – Amiens 58 – Arras 48 – Doullens 54 – St-Quentin 30

Office de tourisme, 16, place André Audinot 03 22 84 42 38, Fax 03 22 85 51 25

Historial de la Grande Guerre★★.

St-Claude
42 pl. du Cdt-L.-Daudré – 03 22 79 49 49 – www.hotelsaintclaude.com – hotel.saintclaude@wanadoo.fr – Fax 03 22 79 10 57
40 rm – €60/80 €80/105, €10 – 2 suites – ½ P €105
Rest – Menu (€15), €26 – Carte €19/46
◆ Totally renovated town centre hotel with spacious, comfortable rooms decorated in sober style.

in Rancourt 10 km north on the ND 1017 – pop. 176 – alt. 143 m – ✉ 80360

Le Prieuré
24 rte nationale – ✆ 03 22 85 04 43 – www.hotel-le-prieure.fr – contact@ hotel-le-prieure.fr – Fax 03 22 85 06 69
27 rm – €65/71 €68/73, ☕ €8 – ½ P €65/68
Rest – Menu €20 bi (weekdays)/43 – Carte €35/56
◆ Moorish-style architecture for this hotel with personalised rooms, the larger ones being located at the rear. A Scottish bar just through an arch. Brick and stone walls add to the elegance of the dining room; regional and traditional fare.

Aire d'Assevillers 15 km south on the Amiens road (D 1029) and minor road then A 1 – ✉ 80200 Péronne

Mercure
– ✆ 03 22 85 78 30 – www.mercure-peronne.com – mercure-peronne@ wanadoo.fr – Fax 03 22 85 78 31
79 rm – €81/107 €98/130, ☕ €14
Rest – grill – Menu €16/19 – Carte €31/42
◆ An imposing 1970s building with large functional rooms, gradually being renovated and refitted. Good soundproofing. The restaurant is open from 11am to 11pm. Grilled meats and starter buffet.

PÉROUGES – 01 Ain – 328 E5 – pop. 1 189 – alt. 290 m – ✉ 01800 44 B1

Lyon - Rhone Valley

Paris 460 – Bourg-en-Bresse 39 – Lyon 37 – Villefranche-sur-Saône 58
Syndicat d'initiative, entrée de la Cité ✆ 04 74 46 70 84, Fax 04 74 46 70 84
de la Sorelle Villette-sur-Ain Domaine de Gravagneux, N : 12 km on D 984, ✆ 04 74 35 47 27
The town★★: place de la Halle★★★.

Ostellerie du Vieux Pérouges
pl. du Tilleul – ✆ 04 74 61 00 88 – www.hostelleriedeperouges.com – thibaut@ ostellerie.com – Fax 04 74 34 77 90 – Closed 15 February-1st March
13 rm – €127 €200/240, ☕ €16 – 2 suites – ½ P €150/165
Rest – Menu €40/62 – Carte €52/80
◆ Appealing Gothic-Renaissance buildings dotted about the village. Guestrooms combining antique furniture (some with four-poster beds) with modern comforts. The restaurant's decor ranges from medieval to comfortably plush. Regional dishes including the famous galette.

Le Pavillon
– Closed two weeks in February
13 rm – €84/95 €124/156, ☕ €16 – ½ P €115/138
◆ A few metres from the Ostellerie, Le Pavillon has practical and more simply furnished rooms. Those in the extension are more comfortable.

PERPIGNAN P – 66 Pyrénées-Orientales – 344 I6 – pop. 115 000 – Built-up area 162 678 – alt. 60 m – Casino : at Port-Barcarès – ✉ 66000 22 B3

Languedoc-Roussillon-Tarn Gorges

Paris 848 – Andorra-la-Vella 170 – Béziers 94 – Montpellier 156 – Toulouse 204
Perpignan-Rivesaltes: ✆ 04 68 52 60 70, 3 km on the ①
Office de tourisme, place Armand Lanoux ✆ 04 68 66 30 30, Fax 04 68 66 30 26
Le Castillet★ - Sea lodge★ BY **K** - Town hall★ BY **H** - St-Jean cathedral ★ - Palais des rois de Majorque★ - Musée numismatique Joseph-Puig★ - Place Arago: maison Julia★.

Plans on following pages

Villa Duflot
rd-pt Albert Donnezan, 3 km via ④, towards the motorway – ✆ 04 68 56 67 67 – www.villa-duflot.com – contact@villa-duflot.com – Fax 04 68 56 54 05
24 rm – €150/190 €150/190, ☕ €17
Rest – Menu (€25 bi), €31 bi (weekday lunch) – Carte €43/51
◆ A light elegant setting (contemporary statues) and spacious Art Deco furnished rooms overlooking the patio or the park: a haven of greenery, unusually located - in a shopping area! The charm of the south of France in the cuisine and the restaurant faces the pool.

PERPIGNAN

Alsace-Lorraine (R.) . . . . . BY 2
Anciens-Combattants-d'Indochine (Pl. des) . . BY 3
Ange (R. de l') . . . . BZ 4
Arago (Pl.) . . . . BZ 5
Argenterie (R. de l') . . . . . BY 6
Barre (R. de la) . . . . BY 7
Bartissol (R. E.) . . . . BY 8
Batllo (Quai F.) . . . . BY 9
Castillet (R. du) . . . . BY 21
Clemenceau (Bd G.) . . . . . . BY
Cloche d'Or (R. de la) . . BYZ 22
Côte des Carmes (R.) . . . CZ 23
Fabriques d'En Nabot (R. des) . . . . BY 24
Fabriques d'En Nadal (R. des) . . . . BY 25
Fontaine-Neuve (R.) . . . . CZ 26
Fontfroide (R.) . . . . BY 27
Gambetta (Pl.) . . . . BY 28
Grande la Monnaie (R.) . . BZ 31
Lattre-de-Tassigny (Quai de) . . . . BZ 32
Loge (R. et Pl. de la) . . . . BY 33
Louis-Blanc (R.) . . . . . . ABY 34
Marchands (R. des) . . . . . BY 35
Mermoz (Av. J.) . . . . CZ 36
Mirabeau (R.) . . . . BY 37
Payra (R. J.) . . . . BY 38
Péri (Pl. Gabriel) . . . . BZ 39
Petite la Monnaie (R.) . . . BZ 40
Porte d'Assaut (R.) . . . . . BZ 41
Porte de Canet (R.) . . . . . CZ 42
Remparts la Réal (R. des) BZ 43
République (Pl. de la) . . . BZ 44
Résistance (Pl. de la) . . . BY 45
Révolution Française (R. de la) . . . . CY 46
Rigaud (Pl.) . . . . BZ 47
Sadi-Carnot (Quai) . . . . . . BY 50
St-Jean (R.) . . . . BY 52
Théâtre (R. du) . . . . BZ 55
Trois-Journées (R. des) . . BY 58
Vauban (Quai) . . . . BY 60
Verdun (Pl. de) . . . . BY 64
Victoire (Pl. de la) . . . . . . BY 67
Vielledent (R. J.) . . . . CZ 69
Waldeck-Rousseau (R.) . . . CZ 72

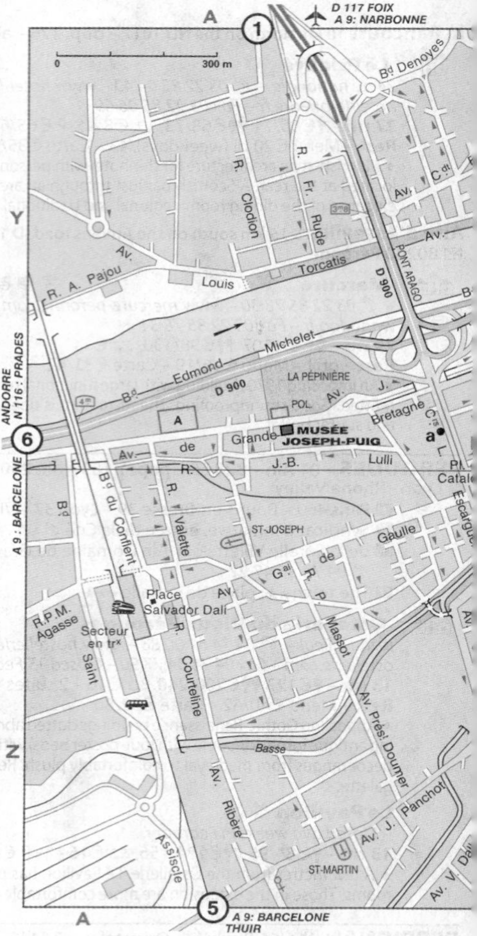

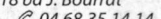

Park Hôtel

18 bd J. Bourrat
– ✆ 04 68 35 14 14
– www.parkhotel-fr.com
– contact@parkhotel-fr.com
– Fax 04 68 35 48 18

CY **y**

69 rm – †€ 80/140 ††€ 80/140, ☕ € 11 – ½ P € 66/88

Rest *Le Chap'* – *✆ 04 68 35 31 16 (Closed 26 July-10 August, 2-25 January, Monday lunch, Friday lunch, Saturday lunch and Sunday)* Menu (€ 28 bi), € 30/50 – Carte € 35/65

Spec. Cuisses de grenouilles à la bière et crème de cresson au chamalow à l'orange. Carré d'agneau de lait, chartreuse d'aubergine aux épices. Soufflé chaud au chocolat et Grand Marnier.

◆ Spain beckons in this hotel near Bir Hakeim square. Colourful, well-kept rooms (some with Majorcan beds) at Le Chap', minimalist modern decor of mineral and vegetal elements, grey and beige colour scheme, glazed wine cellar and flat screens.

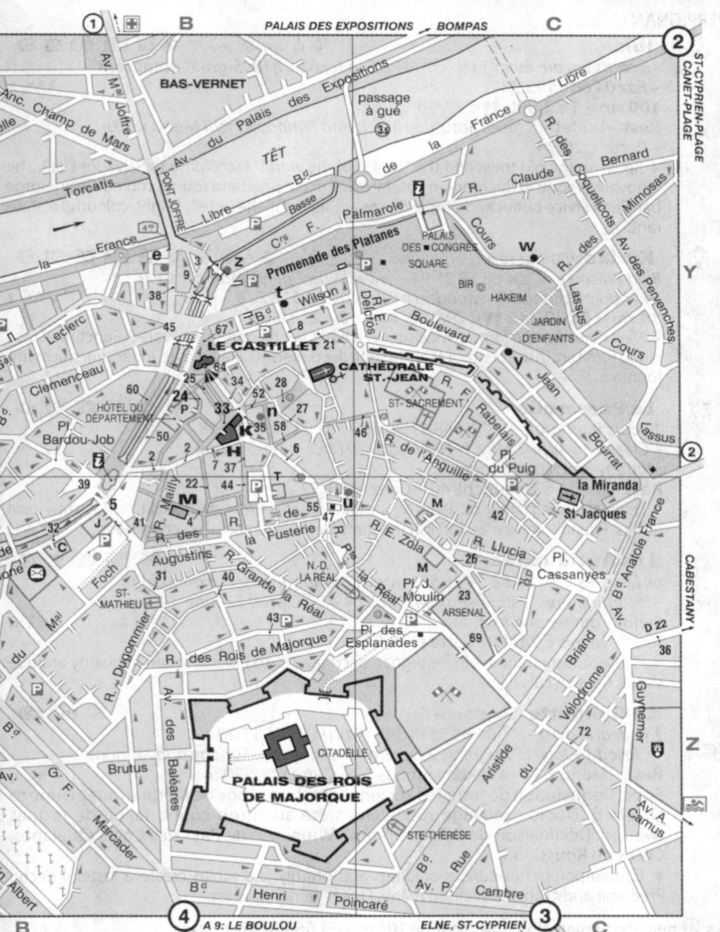

Le Mas des Arcades

rm, VISA

840 av. d'Espagne, via ④: 2 km on the N 9 ✉ 66100 – ✆ 04 68 85 11 11 – www.hotel-mas-des-arcades.fr – contact@hotel-mas-des-arcades.fr – Fax 04 68 85 21 41 – **62 rm** – €85/125 €85/125, ☕ €12 – 3 suites – ½ P €83/103 **Rest** – Menu (€20), €28/48 – Carte €43/64

◆ Recently renovated with fashionable lobby and sitting rooms. Spruce rooms, half of which boast balconies and overlook the pool. Tennis courts. Restaurant leading onto a glass-roofed terrace; traditional dishes and grilled food served in summer.

New Christina

rm, rest, VISA

51 cours Lassus – ✆ 04 68 35 12 21 – www.hotel-newchristina.com – info@hotel-newchristina.com – Fax 04 68 35 67 01 – Closed 21 December-4 January
25 rm – €68/95 €75/115, ☕ €10 CY **w**
Rest – *(Closed 16 July-1st September, Friday, Saturday and Sunday) (dinner only)*
Menu (€16), 22

◆ Functional, simple rooms with pebbledashed walls. Leisure facilities include a small rooftop swimming pool, jacuzzi, hammam and bar. A modern bistro-style dining room and traditional dishes on a blackboard.

Ibis rm, VISA

16 cours Lazare Escarguel – ☎ 04 68 35 62 62 – h1045-gm@accor.com – Fax 04 68 35 13 38 AY **a**

100 rm – †€ 77/90 ††€ 77/90, ☐ € 8

Rest – buffet – *(closed Saturday lunch and Sunday lunch)* Menu (€ 10) – Carte € 26/34

♦ Between the old town and the "centre of the world" (according to Salvador Dali). The renovated rooms in this modern hotel are well maintained and soundproofed. Cosy lounge bar. Self-service buffet and simple dishes are served in the hotel's bright, colourful restaurant.

Kyriad without rest VISA

8 bd Wilson – ☎ 04 68 59 25 94 – www.kyriad-perpignan-centre.fr – kyriad.perpignan@wanadoo.fr – Fax 04 68 61 57 70 BY **t**

38 rm – †€ 79/140 ††€ 79/150, ☐ € 10 – 11 suites

♦ New name for the former Windsor, which has been entirely renovated. Functional rose wood furniture in the bedrooms and a suite decorated in Catalan style. Inner courtyard with fountain.

La Passerelle VISA

1 cours Palmarole – ☎ 04 68 51 30 65 – Fax 04 68 51 90 58 – Closed 26 April-3 May, 9-16 August, 20 December-3 January, Monday lunch and Sunday BY **z**

Rest – Menu € 25 (lunch)/40 – Carte € 39/52

♦ This welcoming family business on the River Basse serves fish specialities plus a few local dishes. Friendly service and stylish maritime decor (Murano glass chandelier).

Les Antiquaires VISA

pl. Desprès – ☎ 04 68 34 06 58 – www.lesantiquairesperpignan.fr.gd – lesantiquaires@sfr.fr – Fax 04 68 35 04 47 – Closed 22 June-14 July, Sunday dinner and Monday BZ **u**

Rest – Menu € 24/43 – Carte € 31/55

♦ Pleasant restaurant in old Perpignan decorated with objects found in nearby antique shops. Catalan cuisine.

La Galinette (Christophe Comes) VISA

23 r. Jean Payra – ☎ 04 68 35 00 90 – Fax 04 68 35 15 20 – Closed 15 July-15 August, 22 December-5 January, Sunday and Monday

Rest – Menu € 19 (weekday lunch)/55 – Carte € 52/80 BY **e**

Spec. Dégustation de tomates anciennes et thon rouge de Méditerranée (June to October). Dorade sauvage rôtie sans arête au citron confit, tajine de racines (winter). Déclinaison de fraises (spring). **Wines** Vin de Pays des Côtes Catalanes, Côtes du Roussillon.

♦ Contemporary furniture, mouldings and prettily laid tables create a tasteful decor. Predominantly fish and seafood menu. Fine regional wine list.

via ① near Perpignan-Nord interchange 10 km – ✉ 66600 Rivesaltes

Novotel rm, VISA

– ☎ 04 68 64 02 22 – www.accor.com – h0424@accor.com – Fax 04 68 64 24 27

56 rm – †€ 95/148 ††€ 95/148, ☐ € 14

Rest – Menu € 20 (weekdays) – Carte € 22/40

♦ Surrounded by greenery, this Novotel offers relaxation and comfort just off the motorway. The large, functional rooms have been partly renovated to give a contemporary, minimalist look. Catalan-style bar. The restaurant overlooks the pool, with terrace and barbecues in summer.

in Cabestany 5 km by ③ and D22[c] – **pop. 8 230 – alt. 35 m – ✉ 66330**

Les Deux Mas rm, VISA

1 r. Madeleine Brès, opposite Médipôle – ☎ 04 68 50 08 08 – www.les2mas.com – contact@les2mas.com – Fax 04 68 62 32 54

32 rm – †€ 65/88 ††€ 85/108, ☐ € 10 – 1 suite – ½ P € 67/78

Rest – Menu € 19 (weekday lunch), € 25/44 – Carte € 30/60

♦ An unusual hotel: a distinctive mural on the façade depicts a sleeping woman; small colourful bedrooms with Moorish touches surround an Andalusian patio. Simple Catalan dishes served in a sunny setting.

LE PERREUX-SUR-MARNE – **94 Val-de-Marne** – **312** E2 – **106** 20 – **101** 18 – **see Paris, Area**

PERRIER – **63 Puy-de-Dôme** – **326** G9 – **see Issoire**

LE PERRIER – **85 Vendée** – **316** E6 – **see Challans**

A good night's sleep without spending a fortune?
Look for a Bib Hotel .

PERROS-GUIREC – **22 Côtes-d'Armor** – **309** B2 – **pop. 7 614** 9 **B1**
– alt. 60 m – Casino A – ✉ **22700** **Brittany**

Paris 527 – Lannion 12 – St-Brieuc 76 – Tréguier 19

Office de tourisme, 21, place de l'Hôtel de Ville ✆ 02 96 23 21 15, Fax 02 96 23 04 72

Romanesque nave★ of the church B - Pointe du château ⩽★ - Viewpoint indicator ⩽★ B **E** - Sentier des douaniers (customs officers' path)★★ - N.-D. de la Clarté chapel ★ 3 km by ② - Semaphore ⩽★ 3.5 km by ②.

Ploumanach★★: municipal park ★★, rocks★★ - Sentier des Douaniers★★.

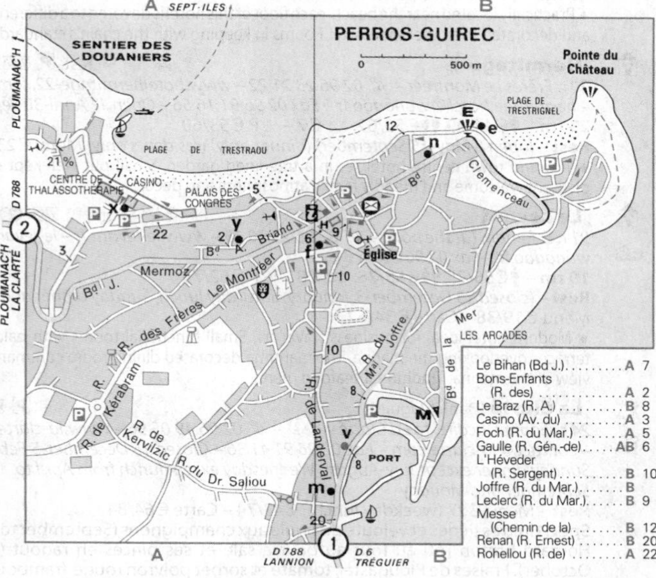

L'Agapa ⩽ rest,
12 r. des Bons-Enfants – ✆ *02 96 49 01 10* VISA
– www.lagapa.com – hotel@lagapa.com – Fax 02 96 91 16 36 A **y**
47 rm – €160/420 €160/420, ☕ €18 – 1 suite
Rest ***Le Belouga*** – *(closed 3-27 December and 7-31 January)* Menu (€25 bi), €45/77 bi – Carte €60/116

◆ This glass, steel and granite hotel overlooking the sea offers minimalist designer rooms. Relaxed comfort and hi-tech facilities. Superb spa. At the Le Belouga fine modern seafood menu served with complementary wines.

Le Manoir du Sphinx

67 chemin de la Messe – 02 96 23 25 42 – www.lemanoirdusphinx.com – lemanoirdusphinx@wanadoo.fr – Fax 02 96 91 26 13 – Closed 16 November-2 December and 17 January-25 February B **e**

20 rm – €110/114 €110/128, €10 – ½ P €104/121

Rest – *(closed Sunday dinner from October to March except school holidays, Monday lunch and Friday lunch except public holidays)* Menu €30/50 – Carte €47/60

◆ This delightful Belle Époque villa overlooks the sea. The British style rooms have views of the bay and islands. The charming garden stretches down to the rocks. A plush, panoramic veranda-dining room serving modern cuisine and seafood.

Les Feux des Îles

rm,

53 bd Clemenceau – 02 96 23 22 94 – www.feux-des-iles.com – feuxdesiles2@wanadoo.fr – Fax 02 96 91 07 30 – Closed 15-19 March, 4-12 October, 21 December-4 January, Sunday dinner and Friday dinner (except hotel) from October to May B **n**

18 rm – €92/102 €115/140, €12 – ½ P €95/115

Rest – *(dinner only except Sunday)* Menu €26/65 – Carte €36/58

◆ A family-run hotel made up of a stone house and recently-built annex, whose larger and more modern rooms have a sea view. Some have direct access to the garden. Traditional and seafood dishes are served in the dining room facing the islands' 'lights'.

Mercure without rest

100 av. du Casino – 02 96 91 22 11 – accorhotels.com – H0476@accor.com – Fax 02 96 91 24 78 A **x**

49 rm – €65/111 €70/116, €12

◆ Practically located near the beach, each floor of this hotel is devoted to a different sea bird and decorated in a different colour. Rooms in keeping with the chain's standards.

Hermitage

rest,

20 r. Frères Le Montréer – 02 96 23 21 22 – www.hotelhermitage-22.com – hermitage.hotel@wanadoo.fr – Fax 02 96 91 16 56 – Open 1st April-30 September

23 rm – €44/49 €52/62, €7 – ½ P €53/60 B **f**

Rest – *(open 8 May-15 September) (dinner only) (residents only)* Menu €23

◆ A grand town centre hotel set in a tree-lined garden. Small but well-kept rooms. A pleasant welcome and friendly family atmosphere and decor.

Le Levant

rm,

91 r. E. Renan, (at the port) – 02 96 23 20 15 – www.le-levant.fr – le-levant@wanadoo.fr – Fax 02 96 23 36 31 B **m**

19 rm – €55/75 €55/78, €8 – ½ P €62/73

Rest – *(closed 23 December-3 January, Saturday lunch, Sunday dinner and Friday)* Menu €19/38 – Carte €34/62

◆ Modern hotel ideal for business travellers. Small functional rooms with balconies or terraces overlooking the marina. The maritime decorated dining room commands a fine view of the marina. Traditional seafood menu.

La Clarté (Daniel Jaguin)

24 r. Gabriel Vicaire, to La Clarté via ② – 02 96 49 05 96 – www.la-clarte.com – contact@la-clarte.com – Fax 02 96 91 41 36 – Closed 15 December-5 February, Sunday dinner except July-August, Wednesday except lunch from April to September and Monday

Rest – Menu €27 (weekday lunch), €42/74 – Carte €64/84

Spec. Huîtres tièdes et velouté de poule aux champignons (September to March). Homard breton rôti au four au beurre salé et ses pinces en ragoût (April to October). Fraises de Plougastel, tomate et sorbet poivron rouge-framboise (June to September).

◆ This pretty pink granite house, very popular with the locals, is rightly proud of its stylish new modern decor and bright colour scheme. Tasty seafood menu.

Au Bon Accueil

11 r. Landerval – 02 96 23 25 77 – www.aubonacceuil-perros.com – au-bon-accueil@wanadoo.fr – Fax 02 96 23 12 66 – Closed 28 December-8 January

Rest – *(closed Sunday dinner and Monday except July-August)* Menu (€17), €26/37 – Carte €32/52 B **v**

◆ Panoramic restaurant in a contemporary spirit occupying a modern villa overlooking the marina. Traditional cuisine.

in Ploumanach 6 km by ② – ✉ **22700 Perros-Guirec**

Rocks★★ - Municipal park★★.

Castel Beau Site (P) VISA AE

plage St-Guirec – ✆ 02 96 91 40 87 – www.castelbeausite.com – infos@castelbeausite.com – Fax 02 96 91 66 37 – Closed 1st March-2 April

34 rm – †€ 110/450 ††€ 110/450, ☕ € 15

Rest – Menu € 34 (dinner)/48 – Carte € 43/67

◆ This 1930s pink granite building stands on the sea front, right on the beach. The refurbished comfortable guestrooms enjoy lovely sea views. Modern cuisine. In summer, brasserie and seafood menu at midday.

Parc rest, (P) VISA

174 pl. St-Guirec – ✆ 02 96 91 40 80 – www.hotelduparc.com – hotel.du.parclacotriade@wanadoo.fr – Fax 02 96 91 60 48 – Closed 11 November-20 December, Saturday lunch and Sunday dinner except school holidays

10 rm – †€ 49/55 ††€ 49/55, ☕ € 8 – ½ P € 55/60

Rest – Menu € 15/37 – Carte € 27/54

◆ A pink granite family house and lovely garden in the centre of the village, a stone's throw from the beach and famous rocks. Small, well-kept rooms. Seafood served on large terraces or in the maritime dining room. Pancakes.

PERTUIS – 84 Vaucluse – **332** G11 – **pop. 18 600 – alt. 246 m** – ✉ **84120** 40 **B2**

Provence

Paris 747 – Aix-en-Provence 23 – Apt 36 – Avignon 76 – Digne-les-Bains 97 – Manosque 36

Office de tourisme, place Mirabeau ✆ 04 90 79 15 56, Fax 04 90 09 59 06

Sévan Parc Hôtel P VISA AE

rte de Manosque, 1.5 km east – ✆ 04 90 79 19 30 – www.sevanparchotel.com – hotel-sevan@orange.fr – Fax 04 90 79 35 77

46 rm – †€ 90/130 ††€ 110/150, ☕ € 12

Rest *L'Olivier* – *✆ 04 90 79 08 19 (closed 1st January-7 February, Sunday dinner, Monday except dinner in July-August and Wednesday)* Menu (€ 19), € 30/50 – Carte approx. € 44

Rest *La Paillote* – *✆ 04 90 09 63 67 (closed mid December-mid January and Tuesday)* Menu € 14 bi (weekday lunch) – Carte € 24/40

◆ At the foot of the Luberon massif, surrounded by flower-decked grounds, this hotel overlooks a peaceful, green landscape. Sun-drenched rooms of Provençal inspiration. The Olivier serves regional cuisine in an inviting contemporary decor. La Paillotte serves grilled meats and Tex-Mex dishes in a laidback atmosphere. Poolside terrace.

Château Grand Callamand without rest (P) VISA AE

rte de Loubière, 2 km on Léon-Arnoux street – ✆ 04 90 09 61 00 – www.chateaugrandcallamand.fr – chateaugrandcallamand@wanadoo.fr – Fax 04 90 09 61 00

3 rm ☕ – †€ 130/160 ††€ 130/160 – 1 suite

◆ This splendid 16C stronghold stands amidst vineyards. Delightful welcome, peaceful atmosphere, pool, terrace facing Ste Victoire Mountain and exquisitely tasteful rooms.

Le Boulevard AC VISA AE

50 bd Pecout – ✆ 04 90 09 69 31 – www.restaurant-le-boulevard.com et www.restaurant-leboulevard.com – leboulevard-bontoux@wanadoo.fr – Fax 04 90 09 09 48 – Closed 1st-12 July, February school holidays, Sunday dinner, Tuesday dinner and Wednesday

Rest – *(number of covers limited, pre-book)* Menu € 19/35 – Carte € 35/44

◆ A town centre restaurant in an attractive old house. A discreetly rustic dining room upstairs provides the backdrop to traditional cuisine that evolves with the seasons.

PETIT-BERSAC – 24 Dordogne – **329** C4 – **pop. 177** – **alt. 90 m** – ✉ 24600 39 **C3**

Paris 501 – Bordeaux 121 – Périgueux 50 – Angoulême 49 – Soyaux 47

Château Le Mas de Montet
– *05 53 90 08 71 – www.lemasdemontet.com – reception@lemasdemontet.com – Fax 05 53 90 66 92*
10 rm – €175/435 €175/435
Rest – Menu €45 (dinner) – Carte €60/90
◆ Sought after surroundings for this magnificent Renaissance château: fine grounds, swimming pool, kitchen garden, and terrace. The interior seduces you both by its romantic nature and its refinement. Traditional cuisine served in the 'Chatelaine' dining room.

Good food without spending a fortune?
Look out for the Bib Gourmand

PETITE-HETTANGE – 57 Moselle – **307** I2 – **see Malling**

LA PETITE-PIERRE – 67 Bas-Rhin – **315** H3 – **pop. 604** – **alt. 340 m** – ✉ 67290 Alsace-Lorraine 1 **A1**

Paris 433 – Haguenau 41 – Sarreguemines 48 – Sarre-Union 24 – Strasbourg 57

Office de tourisme, 2a, rue du Château 03 88 70 42 30, Fax 03 88 70 41 08

La Clairière rm, rest,
63 rte d'Ingwiller, D 7: 1.5 km – 03 88 71 75 00 – www.laclairiere.com – info@laclairiere.com – Fax 03 88 70 41 05
50 rm – €111/135 €165/190, €17 – 4 suites – ½ P €128/154
Rest – *(dinner only)* Menu €35 – Carte approx. €35
◆ Tucked away in the forest, this modern hotel is dedicated to well being. Find an outdoor pool overlooking a teak deck, 950m2 spa, and a 'challenge' circuit for conference guests. Spacious guestrooms and a British-style bar. Modern decor, wholesome cuisine and organic wines.

Lion d'Or rest,
15 r. Principale – 03 88 01 47 57 – www.liondor.com – contact@liondor.com – Fax 03 88 01 47 50 – Closed March
42 rm – €57/70 €80/106, €12 – ½ P €76/89
Rest – Menu (€12), €19 (weekdays)/65 – Carte €30/75
◆ Ideal for those in need of a real break. A country hotel complete with an arbrothérapie (tree treatment) centre. The rooms in the old house are very soothing. Regional cuisine served in the dining room overlooking the city and forest.

Des Vosges rm, rest, rm,
30 r. Principale – 03 88 70 45 05 – www.hotel-des-vosges.com – hotel-des-vosges@wanadoo.fr – Fax 03 88 70 41 13 – Closed 16-31 July and 22 February-20 March
30 rm – €58 €68/84, €10 – ½ P €63/72
Rest – *(closed Tuesday off season)* Menu €24 (weekdays)/57 – Carte €29/58
◆ Snug, well-kept rooms in varying styles (some Alsatian). Pleasant wellness centre. Traditional and regional dishes are served in a dining room with a view of the valley. Well-chosen wine list of old vintages.

in Graufthal 11 km Southwest by D 178 and D 122 – ✉ 67320 Eschbourg

Le Cheval Blanc
19 r. Principale – 03 88 70 17 11 – www.auchevalblanc.net – restaurant@auchevalblanc.net – Fax 03 88 70 12 37 – Closed 1st-15 September, 1st-21 January, Monday dinner, Wednesday dinner and Tuesday
Rest – Menu (€24), €27/38 – Carte €35/50
◆ This appealing inn, decorated in a somewhat jumbled rustic style, serves regional dishes. Attractive tiled stove in one of the dining rooms.

Au Vieux Moulin with rm
7 rue du Vieux Moulin – 03 88 70 17 28 – www.auvieuxmoulin.eu – auvieux.moulin@orange.fr – Fax 03 88 70 11 25 – Closed 15 February-3 March, 25 June-7 July
14 rm – €52/72 €52/72, €8 – ½ P €52
Rest – *(closed Monday except residents)* Menu €11 (weekday lunch), €15/34 – Carte €22/45
◆ This establishment offers a warm welcome in a hamlet whose peacefulness was proclaimed by Erckman and Chatrian. Alsatian family cooking served in a light-filled dining room. Small, comfortable rooms in the process of refurbishment.

LE PETIT-PRESSIGNY – 37 Indre-et-Loire – 317 O7 – pop. 326 – alt. 80 m – 37350 — 11 B3

Paris 290 – Le Blanc 38 – Châtellerault 36 – Châteauroux 68 – Poitiers 73 – Tours 61

La Promenade (Jacky Dallais)
11 r. du Savoureulx – 02 47 94 93 52 – Fax 02 47 91 06 03 – Closed 22 September-7 October, 5 January-4 February, Sunday dinner, Monday and Tuesday
Rest – Menu €40/85 – Carte €58/114
Spec. Poireaux grillés en vinaigrette et ravioles de jaune de poule truffées. Côte de cochon fermier, beurre de genièvre et tombée d'oignons blancs. Fraises soufflées à la violette (summer). **Wines** Touraine.
◆ This inn has a very contemporary dining room (with the look of an old covered market), and another that is more classic. Tasty modern cuisine with touches from the Tours region, and a good wine list.

LE PETIT QUEVILLY – 76 Seine-Maritime – 304 G5 – see Rouen

PETRETO-BICCHISANO – 2A Corse-du-Sud – 345 C9 – see Corse

PEYRAT-LE-CHÂTEAU – 87 Haute-Vienne – 325 H6 – pop. 1 009 – alt. 426 m – 87470 Dordogne-Berry-Limousin — 25 C2

Paris 409 – Aubusson 45 – Guéret 52 – Limoges 53 – Tulle 81 – Ussel 79 – Uzerche 58

Office de tourisme, 1, rue du Lac 05 55 69 48 75, Fax 05 55 69 47 82

at Vassivière Lake – 23460 Royère-de-Vassivière

Centre d'art contemporain de l'île de Vassivière (Modern art centre) ★★

Au Golf du Limousin
rest,
at Auphelle, (Lake Vassivière) – 05 55 69 41 34 – www.hotel-gorlfdulimousin.fr – hotel-golfdulimousin@wanadoo.fr – Fax 05 55 69 49 16 – Open 1st February-14 November
18 rm – €44/54 €44/54, €8 – ½ P €44/54
Rest – *(dinner only)* Menu €19
◆ This hotel, perched at an altitude of 650m, enjoys views of the lake. Simple but well-maintained and spacious guestrooms, with attic-style accommodation on the second floor. Traditional cuisine served in an attractive dining room or on the terrace in summer.

PÉZENAS – 34 Hérault – 339 F8 – pop. 8 511 – alt. 15 m – 34120 — 23 C2
Languedoc-Roussillon-Tarn Gorges

Paris 734 – Agde 22 – Béziers 24 – Lodève 39 – Montpellier 55 – Sète 38

Office de tourisme, place Gambetta 04 67 98 36 40, Fax 04 67 98 96 80

Old Pézenas★★: Hôtels of Lacoste★, Alfonce★, Malibran★.

XX **L'Entre Pots**

8 av. Louis-Montagne – ✆ 04 67 90 00 00 – www.restaurantentrepots.com – entre-pots@orange.fr – Fax 04 67 90 17 42 – Closed autumn school holidays, spring holidays, Sunday and Monday

Rest – Menu (€ 21), € 29 – Carte € 35/45

◆ Fresh seasonal cuisine blending regional traditions and contemporary styles, a pretty, modern and intimate interior, peaceful courtyard/terrace and service with a smile: let it work its magic on you....

X **Le Pré Saint Jean**

18 av. Mar. Leclerc – ✆ 04 67 98 15 31 – leprest.jean@wanadoo.fr – Fax 04 67 98 89 23 – Closed Thursday dinner except July August, Sunday dinner and Monday

Rest – Menu € 25/46 – Carte € 35/55

◆ This discreet busy roadside façade hides a welcoming winter conservatory dining room. Updated regional cuisine and fine local wine list.

in Nézignan-l'Évêque South: 5 km by D 609 and D 13 – pop. 1 259 – alt. 40 m – ✉ 34120

Hostellerie de St-Alban rm, rest,

31 rte Agde – ✆ 04 67 98 11 38 – www.saintalban.com – info@saintalban.com – Fax 04 67 98 91 63 – Open 14 February-14 November

13 rm – †€ 82/127 ††€ 98/195, ☕ € 15 – ½ P € 96/143

Rest – *(closed Thursday lunch and Wednesday except April-October)* Menu (€ 24), € 34/44 – Carte € 42/60

◆ Attractive 19C family mansion, nestling in a charming flower garden. The sometimes original rooms, equipped with wrought-iron furniture, are spacious and colourful. Restaurant with an immaculate decor and modern works of art, serving traditional Mediterranean dishes.

PEZENS – 11 Aude – **344** F3 – see Carcassonne

PÉZILLA-LA-RIVIÈRE – 66 Pyrénées-Orientales – **344** H6 – pop. 2 957 – alt. 75 m – ✉ 66370 22 **B3**

Paris 857 – Argelès-sur-Mer 35 – Le Boulou 25 – Perpignan 12 – Prades 35

X **L'Aramon Gourmand**

127 av. du Canigou, Baho road, D 614 – ✆ 04 68 92 43 59 – http://restaurant.aramon.free.fr – philippe.coste66@wanadoo.fr – Fax 04 68 92 43 59 – Closed for 1 week at the end of September, 16-22 February, Sunday dinner, Tuesday dinner and Wednesday

Rest – Menu (€ 20), € 27/37

◆ Roussillon flavours and dishes in the charming red and yellow dining room, furnished with solid wood chairs, or outdoors under the mulberry and plane trees. Wine cellar on view.

PFAFFENHOFFEN – 67 Bas-Rhin – **315** J3 – pop. 2 677 – alt. 170 m – ✉ 67350 Alsace-Lorraine 1 **B1**

Paris 457 – Haguenau 16 – Sarrebourg 55 – Sarre-Union 50 – Saverne 30 – Strasbourg 37

Musée de l'Imagerie peinte et populaire alsacienne★.

XX **De l'Agneau** with rm rest, rm,

3 r. de Saverne – ✆ 03 88 07 72 38 – www.hotel-restaurant-delagneau.com – anne.ernwein@wanadoo.fr – Fax 03 88 72 20 24 – Closed 3-10 March, 16-23 June, 7-28 September, Sunday dinner, Tuesday except lunch from September to May and Monday

12 rm – †€ 55/61 ††€ 55/73, ☕ € 13 – ½ P € 60/89

Rest – Menu (€ 14), € 27/71 bi – Carte € 42/62

◆ This 1769 inn, now run by the seventh generation, offers traditional cuisine and a substantial wine list. Summer terrace in an internal flower-filled courtyard. Smart rooms.

PFULGRIESHEIM – 67 Bas-Rhin – 315 K5 – see Strasbourg

PHALSBOURG – 57 Moselle – 307 O6 – pop. 4 630 – alt. 365 m 27 D2
– ✉ 57370 Alsace-Lorraine

Paris 435 – Metz 110 – Sarrebourg 17 – Sarreguemines 50 – Strasbourg 59

Office de tourisme, 30, place d'Armes ✆ 03 87 24 42 42, Fax 03 87 24 42 87

Erckmann-Chatrian rm, rest, VISA
pl. d'Armes – ✆ 03 87 24 31 33 – hotel.rest.e.chatrian@wanadoo.fr – Fax 03 87 24 27 81
16 rm – €67 €78, €12 **Rest** – Menu €21/58 – Carte €20/38
◆ Old house with a stylish, flower-decked façade. The good sized rooms sport period furniture and some have a small lounge area. Traditional meals to be enjoyed in a dining room lined with dark wood panelling or in a brasserie atmosphere.

Au Soldat de l'An II (Georges Schmitt) with rm rm, VISA AE
1 rte Saverne – ✆ 03 87 24 16 16 – www.soldatan2.com – info@soldatan2.com – Fax 03 87 24 18 18 – Closed 13-24 April, 27 July-6 August, 26 October-6 November, 4-22 January, Sunday dinner, Tuesday lunch and Monday
7 rm – €150 €150, €22 – ½ P €185
Rest – Menu €40 bi, €88/129 – Carte €91/103
Spec. Foie gras d'Alsace selon l'air du temps. Poisson de mer sauvage flambé. Île flottante aux truffes. **Wines** Gewurztraminer, Riesling.
◆ Trinkets and the soldier guarding the entrance to this former barn are reminiscent of the days of French Revolution patriots. Up-to-date cuisine and fine wine list. Comfortable guestrooms with refined decor in the house next door.

in Bonne-Fontaine East: 4 km by D 604 and secondary road ✉ 57370 Danne-et-Quatre-Vents

Notre-Dame de Bonne Fontaine VISA AE
212 rte Bonne-Fontaine – ✆ 03 87 24 34 33 – www.notredamebonnefontaine.com – ndbonnefontaine@aol.com – Fax 03 87 24 24 64 – Closed 11-30 January and 14-21 February
34 rm – €53/63 €65/78, €9,50 – ½ P €63/69
Rest – *(closed Sunday dinner in January, February, March and November)* Menu (€12), €20/47 bi – Carte €20/47
◆ The same family has been running this hotel, nestling in a forest close to a pilgrimage centre, for several generations. Simple rooms. Pretty walks under the pine trees. A veranda-dining room and shaded terrace serving traditional regional dishes.

PHILIPPSBOURG – 57 Moselle – 307 Q5 – pop. 539 – alt. 215 m 27 D1
– ✉ 57230

Paris 450 – Haguenau 29 – Strasbourg 58 – Wissembourg 42

Office de tourisme, 186, rue de Baerenthal ✆ 03 87 06 56 12, Fax 03 87 06 51 48

Au Tilleul VISA
24 rte de Niederbronn – ✆ 03 87 06 50 10 – au.tilleul.issler@wanadoo.fr – Fax 03 87 06 58 89 – Closed January, Monday dinner, Tuesday dinner and Wednesday
Rest – Menu €12 (weekday lunch), €17/51 – Carte €26/50
◆ The entrance to this family inn has a bar where dishes of the day are served, while traditional cuisine is proposed in the rustic-style dining room.

in l'étang de Hanau Northwest: 5 km by D 662 and secondary road – ✉ 57230 Philippsbourg

Small lake★, **Alsace-Lorraine-Champagne**

Beau Rivage without rest VISA
– ✆ 03 87 06 50 32 – www.hotel-beau-rivage-fr.com – Fax 03 87 06 57 46 – Closed 2 weeks in November and February
22 rm – €40/49 €59/89, €8
◆ The rooms of this hotel, isolated in the countryside, look out onto a pond or forest. Some have Alsatian furniture, while others facing the water often have a balcony.

PIANA – 2A Corse-du-Sud – **345** A6 – **see Corse**

LE PIAN-MÉDOC – **33 Gironde** – **335** H5 – **pop. 5 248** – **alt. 36 m** – ✉ **33290** 3 **B1**

Paris 578 – Bordeaux 20 – Mérignac 18 – Pessac 24 – Talence 29

Golf du Médoc Hôtel

chemin de Courmanteau, in Louens – ✆ 05 56 70 31 31 – www.hotelgolfdumedoc.com – contact@hotelgolfdumedoc.com – Fax 05 56 70 78 78

79 rm – €70/190 €85/205, ☕ €17

Rest – Menu (€14), €39 (dinner)/50 – Carte €25/50

◆ Hotel complex built on the famous Médoc golf course. Modern, spacious and practical rooms. Small well-being centre with pool. Lunch at the clubhouse and dinner at the Terroir. Terrace overlooking the course.

PIERRE-BUFFIERE – **87 Haute-Vienne** – **325** F6 – **pop. 1 131** – **alt. 330 m** – ✉ **87260** 24 **B2**

Paris 415 – Limoges 22 – Brantôme 84 – Guéret 107 – Tulle 67

Office de tourisme, place du 8 Mai 1945 ✆ 05 55 00 94 33, Fax 05 55 00 94 33

La Providence

pl. Adeline – ✆ 05 55 00 60 16 – www.hotel-limoges.net – laprovidence@hotel-limoges.net – Fax 05 55 00 98 69 – Closed January, Sunday dinner and Monday lunch from 15 November to 15 March

14 rm – €55/95 €55/115, ☕ €10

Rest – Menu €20/70 – Carte €37/70

◆ This family run hotel borders the main square of a Limousin village. Comfortable, modern and well-kept guestrooms. The restaurant offers simple traditional dishes in an unpretentious dining room adorned with rustic furniture.

PIERREFITTE-EN-AUGE – **14 Calvados** – **303** N4 – **see Pont-L'Évêque**

PIERREFITTE-SUR-SAULDRE – **41 Loir-et-Cher** – **318** J6 – **pop. 854** – **alt. 125 m** – ✉ **41300** 12 **C2**

Paris 185 – Orléans 52 – Aubigny-sur-Nère 23 – Blois 73 – Bourges 55 – Salbris 13

Syndicat d'initiative, 10, place de l'Église ✆ 02 54 88 67 15, Fax 02 54 88 67 15

Le Lion d'Or

1 pl. de l'Église – ✆ 02 54 88 62 14 – liondor41@orange.fr – Fax 02 54 88 62 14 – Closed 1st-10 March, 31 August-23 September, 15-23 February, Wednesday dinner and Thursday dinner in low season, Monday and Tuesday except public holidays

Rest – Menu €32/40 – Carte approx. €50

◆ Timber-framed walls, beams and a collection of old china form an authentic rustic setting for this attractive Sologne house. A pretty garden/terrace. Regional menu.

PIERREFONDS – **60 Oise** – **305** I4 – **pop. 2 039** – **alt. 81 m** – ✉ **60350** 37 **C2**

Northern France and the Paris Region

Paris 82 – Beauvais 78 – Compiègne 15 – Soissons 31 – Villers-Cotterêts 18

Office de tourisme, place de l'Hôtel de Ville ✆ 03 44 42 81 44, Fax 03 44 42 86 31

Château ★★ - St-Jean-aux-Bois: church ★ West: 6 km.

in Chelles 4.5 km East by D 85 – **pop. 412** – **alt. 75 m** – ✉ **60350**

Relais Brunehaut with rm

3 r. de l'Église – ✆ 03 44 42 85 05 – Fax 03 44 42 83 30

11 rm – €50 €62/65, ☕ €9 – ½ P €69/72

Rest – *(closed 15 January-15 February, Tuesday lunch and Monday from 15 April to 15 November, Wednesday lunch and Thursday lunch from 16 November to 15 April)* Menu €26 (weekdays)/41 – Carte €63/70

◆ The watermill with its large wheel and the inn are set around an attractive, flower-decked courtyard. The mill houses pleasant rooms, while the inn offers a rustic dining room.

in St-Jean-aux-Bois : 6 km by D 85 – pop. 324 – alt. 71 m – ✉ 60350

XXX **Auberge A la Bonne Idée** with rm rm, VISA
3 r. Meuniers – ✆ 03 44 42 84 09 – www.a-la-bonne-idee.fr
– a-la-bonne-idee.auberge@wanadoo.fr – Fax 03 44 42 80 45
– Closed 5 January-2 February, Sunday dinner and Monday from October to April
21 rm – †€ 80/155 ††€ 80/155, ☕ € 10 – ½ P € 85/125
Rest – Menu € 31 (weekdays)/75 – Carte € 70/80
◆ Restaurant in a charming village. Country interior, with beams, old stonework and a fireplace. Terrace facing a flower garden and classic cuisine.

PIERREFORT – 15 Cantal – 330 F5 – pop. 1 002 – alt. 950 m – ✉ 15230 5 B3

Paris 540 – Aurillac 64 – Entraygues-sur-Truyère 55 – Espalion 62 – St-Flour 29

Office de tourisme, 29, avenue Georges Pompidou ✆ 04 71 23 38 04, Fax 04 71 23 94 55

Du Midi VISA
5 av. G. Pompidou – ✆ 04 71 23 30 20 – www.hoteldumidi-pierrefort.com – info@hoteldumidi-pierrefort.com – Fax 04 71 23 39 34 – Closed 22 December-11 January
13 rm – †€ 47/49 ††€ 49/51, ☕ € 7
Rest – Menu (€ 11), € 15 (weekdays)/40 – Carte € 28/53
◆ Meeting facilities, children's play area, baby changing-room: this central establishment is as popular with business travellers as with families: small, brightly-decorated guestrooms and pleasant atmosphere. Vaulted dining rooms and excellent regional cuisine.

PIERRELATTE – 26 Drôme – 332 B7 – pop. 12 100 – alt. 50 m – ✉ 26700 Lyon - Rhone Valley 44 B3

Paris 624 – Bollène 17 – Montélimar 23 – Nyons 45 – Orange 33 – Pont-St-Esprit 17

Office de tourisme, place du Champ de Mars ✆ 04 75 04 07 98, Fax 04 75 98 40 65

Ferme aux crocodiles (Crocodile farm) ★, South: 4 km by N 7 until interchange with D 59.

Du Tricastin without rest VISA AE
r. Caprais-Favier – ✆ 04 75 04 05 82 – www.hoteldutricastin.com
– hoteltriscastin@orange.fr – Fax 04 75 04 19 36
13 rm – †€ 42/44 ††€ 46/48, ☕ € 6,50
◆ In a quiet street near the town centre, a spruce façade giving onto well-equipped rooms. Impeccably kept and attentive service.

Du Centre without rest AC VISA AE
6 pl. de l'Église – ✆ 04 75 04 28 59 – www.hotelducentre26.com – info@hotelducentre26.com – Fax 04 75 96 97 97 – Closed 21 December-3 January
26 rm – †€ 54 ††€ 54/57, ☕ € 7,50
◆ This former abbey houses simple, good-sized rooms that are gradually being renovated. Pleasant breakfast room. Very friendly welcome.

PIERRE-PERTHUIS – 89 Yonne – 319 F7 – see Vézelay

PIETRANERA – 2B Haute-Corse – 345 F3 – see Corse (Bastia)

PIGNA – 2B Haute-Corse – 345 C4 – see Corse (Île-Rousse)

LE PIN-AU-HARAS – 61 Orne – 310 J2 – pop. 366 – alt. 202 m – ✉ 61310 33 C2

Paris 183 – Caen 78 – Alençon 47 – Lisieux 68 – Argentan 14

XX **La Tête au Loup** VISA
– ✆ 02 33 35 57 69 – www.lateteauloup.fr – lateteauloup@wanadoo.fr
– Closed 23 June-6 July and 19 December-11 January
Rest – Menu (€ 25), € 28/46 – Carte € 40/57
◆ A bright modern setting depicts the veranda, while the room at the rear is smarter in style. Matchless view of the valley from the terrace. Traditional cuisine and island recipes.

PINEY – 10 Aube – **313** F3 – **pop. 1 252** – **alt. 116 m** – ✉ 10220 13 **B3**

Paris 192 – Troyes 22 – St-Dizier 149 – Sézanne 80

Office de tourisme, Maison du Parc ✆ 03 25 43 38 88, Fax 03 25 41 54 09

Le Tadorne rm, VISA

1 pl. de la Halle – ✆ 03 25 46 30 35 – www.le-tadorne.com – le.tadorne@wanadoo.fr – Fax 03 25 46 36 49 – Closed 1st-8 January, 21 February-8 March and Sunday dinner from October to Easter

26 rm – €59 €65, €9 – ½ P €65

Rest – Menu (€12), €19/49 – Carte €30/60

◆ Pretty timber framed houses with beams set around a poolside terrace. Some of the small rooms have a sitting room area, and some are air-conditioned. Wood dominates the country-style dining room complete with mezzanine floor.

LE PIN-LA-GARENNE – 61 Orne – **310** M4 – **see Mortagne-au-Perche**

PINSOT – 38 Isère – **333** J5 – **see Allevard**

PIOGGIOLA – 2B Haute-Corse – **345** C4 – **see Corse**

PIRIAC-SUR-MER – 44 Loire-Atlantique – **316** A3 – **pop. 2 254** – **alt. 7 m** – ✉ 44420 Brittany 34 **A2**

Paris 462 – La Baule 17 – Nantes 88 – La Roche-Bernard 33 – St-Nazaire 31

Office de tourisme, 7, rue des Cap-Horniers ✆ 02 40 23 51 42, Fax 02 40 23 51 19

Pointe du Castelli ≤★ Southwest: 1 km.

De la Poste VISA

26 r. de la Plage – ✆ 02 40 23 50 90 – www.piriac-hoteldelaposte.com – hoteldelaposte.piriac@wanadoo.fr – Fax 02 40 23 68 96 – Open 13 February-8 November

12 rm – €62/70 €62/70, €9 – ½ P €60

Rest – *(closed 13 February-31 March except weekends and school holidays)* Menu (€20), €26/42 – Carte €31/44

◆ In the centre of a small picturesque fishing port with attractive 17C houses is this 1930s villa. Recently redecorated rooms. Classic dishes to be enjoyed in a warm dining room or on the terrace.

PISCIATELLO – 2A Corse-du-Sud – **345** C8 – **see Corse (Ajaccio)**

PITHIVIERS – 45 Loiret – **318** K2 – **pop. 9 242** – **alt. 115 m** – ✉ 45300 Châteaux of the Loire 12 **C1**

Paris 82 – Chartres 74 – Fontainebleau 46 – Montargis 46 – Orléans 44

Office de tourisme, 1, mail Ouest ✆ 02 38 30 50 02, Fax 02 38 30 55 00

Le Relais de la Poste VISA

10 Mail Ouest – ✆ 02 38 30 40 30 – www.le-relais-de-la-poste.com – le-relais-de-la-poste@wanadoo.fr – Fax 02 38 30 47 79

41 rm – €54 €59, €8 – ½ P €60

Rest – *(closed Sunday dinner)* Menu €18/32 – Carte €30/48

◆ This large building in the town centre was once a post house and offers spacious, wood-panelled rooms decorated with rustic furniture. Light wood panelling and a fireplace make this dining room very welcoming. Traditional food.

Aux Saveurs Lointaines VISA

1 pl. Martroi – ✆ 02 38 30 18 18 – auxsaveurslointaines.com – hsnguyen55@gmail.com – Closed Sunday dinner and Monday

Rest – Menu €14 (weekday lunch) – Carte €14/25

◆ Bamboo curtains, woven straw objects and teak and wrought-iron furniture decorate this family restaurant dedicated to Vietnamese food. Exotic fruit specialities.

PIZAY – 69 Rhône – **327** H3 – **see Belleville**

PLAGE DE CALALONGA – 2A Corse-du-Sud – 345 E11 – see Corse (Bonifacio)

PLAILLY – 60 Oise – 305 G6 – pop. 1 646 – alt. 100 m – ✉ 60128 19 C2

Paris 40 – Beauvais 69 – Chantilly 16 – Compiègne 46 – Meaux 36 – Pontoise 48 – Senlis 16

La Gentilhommière VISA MC AE

25 r. Georges Bouchard, (behind the church) – ✆ 03 44 54 30 20 – http://lagentilhommiere-plailly.neuf.fr – alain.gouraud@wanadoo.fr – Fax 03 44 54 31 27 – Closed 4-25 August, 23 February-9 March, Saturday lunch, Sunday dinner, Monday and Tuesday

Rest – Menu € 25 (weekday lunch), € 34/44 – Carte € 52/62

◆ Former 17C post house beside the bell tower. Fireplace, beams and copperware emphasise the rustic nature of the dining room. Traditional menu and daily suggestions.

LA PLAINE-SUR-MER – 44 Loire-Atlantique – 316 C5 – pop. 2 517 – alt. 26 m – ✉ 44770 34 A2

Paris 438 – Nantes 58 – Pornic 9 – St-Michel-Chef-Chef 7 – St-Nazaire 28

Office de tourisme, square du Fort Gentil ✆ 02 40 21 52 52

Pointe de St-Gildas ★ West: 5 km, **Atlantic Coast**

Anne de Bretagne (Philippe Vételé) P VISA MC AE

at Port de Gravette, 3 km northwest – ✆ 02 40 21 54 72 – www.annedebretagne.com – bienvenue@annedebretagne.com – Fax 02 40 21 02 33 – Closed from beg. January to mid February

20 rm – †€ 125/320 ††€ 135/320, ☕ € 18 – ½ P € 149/216

Rest – *(closed Tuesday except dinner in season, Sunday dinner from November to March and Monday)* Menu € 55 bi (weekday lunch), € 59/110

Spec. Marinière de palourdes et couteaux. Dos de bar cuit à basse température. Dacquoise réglisse, marmelade d'orange. **Wines** Muscadet de Sèvre et Maine sur lie, Fiefs Vendéens.

◆ White house on the dunes, most of whose rooms have been recently spruced up in a minimalist style (lovely furniture and contemporary art). Sea or garden view. Minimalist modern restaurant whose bay windows command views of the sea. Seafood menu and fine wine list.

PLAISIANS – 26 Drôme – 332 E8 – pop. 183 – alt. 612 m – ✉ 26170 44 B3

Paris 690 – Carpentras 44 – Nyons 33 – Vaison-la-Romaine 27

Auberge de la Clue AC P

pl. de l'Église – ✆ 04 75 28 01 17 – laclue@libertysurf.fr – Fax 04 75 28 29 17 – Open 1st April-18 October, weekend and public holidays from November to March except February and closed Sunday dinner except July-August and Monday

Rest – Menu € 26/32 – Carte € 32/45

◆ Regulars of this pleasant restaurant often travel long distances to enjoy the tasty local dishes. Dining room with Provençal colours. Terrace facing the Mont Ventoux.

PLANCOËT – 22 Côtes-d'Armor – 309 I3 – pop. 2 934 – alt. 41 m – ✉ 22130 10 C2

Paris 417 – Dinan 17 – Dinard 20 – St-Brieuc 46 – St-Malo 26

Syndicat d'initiative, 1, rue des Venelles ✆ 02 96 84 00 57

Maxime et Jean-Pierre Crouzil et Hôtel L'Ecrin with rm

20 les quais – ✆ 02 96 84 10 24 AC rest, P VISA MC AE

– www.crouzil.com – jean-pierre.crouzil@wanadoo.fr – Fax 02 96 84 01 93 – Closed 1st-15 October, 10 January-1st February, Sunday dinner except July-August, Tuesday except in July-August and Monday

7 rm – †€ 75 ††€ 120/160, ☕ € 23 – ½ P € 85/145

Rest – *(pre-book weekends)* Menu € 25 (weekdays)/130 – Carte approx. € 90

Spec. Saint-Jacques dorées au sautoir, tomates confites au basilic. Homard breton rôti, brûlé au lambic. Soufflé chaud aux poires et sorbet williamine.

◆ Plancoët, famous for its mineral water and hostelry since the 19C, boasts an elegant restaurant serving Brittany inspired cuisine. Shop selling homemade produce. The hotel offers classically opulent and well-kept guestrooms.

PLAN-DE-CUQUES – 13 Bouches-du-Rhône – 340 H5 – see Marseille

PLAN-DE-LA-TOUR – 83 Var – 340 O5 – pop. 2 524 – alt. 69 m – ✉ 83120 41 C3

Paris 859 – Cannes 68 – Draguignan 36 – Fréjus 28 – St-Tropez 24 – Ste-Maxime 10

Office de tourisme, 1, rue du 19 mars 1962 ✆ 04 94 43 01 50, Fax 04 94 43 75 08

Mas des Brugassières without rest

1.5 km south on Grimaud road – ✆ 04 94 55 50 55 – www.mas-des-brugassieres.com – mas.brugassieres@free.fr – Fax 04 94 55 50 51 – Open 10 April-25 November

12 rm – €75/90 €80/98, ☕ €9

◆ Attractive farmstead in the heart of the Maures massif. Personalised rooms decorated in a Provençal style. Some have a terrace, while others overlook the garden.

PLAN-DU-VAR – 06 Alpes-Maritimes – 341 E4 – ✉ 06670 Levens 41 D2

Paris 941 – Antibes 38 – Cannes 48 – Nice 32 – Puget-Théniers 35 – Vence 26

Gorges de la Vésubie★★★ Northeast - Chaudan defile★★ North: 2 km.

Bonson: site★, ≤★★ from the church terrace, **French Riviera**

Cassini

231 av. Porte des Alpes, D 6202 – ✆ 04 93 08 91 03 – www.restaurantcassini.com – restaurantcassini@wanadoo.fr – Fax 04 93 08 45 48 – Closed 10-25 November, 10-25 February, Tuesday dinner, Wednesday dinner, Thursday dinner from 15 September to 15 June, Sunday dinner and Monday

Rest – Menu (€ 19), € 39/68 bi – Carte € 29/58

◆ The same family has run this roadside inn in the heart of the village for four generations. The dining room has recently been treated to a facelift. Traditional menu.

PLANGUENOUAL – 22 Côtes-d'Armor – 309 G3 – pop. 1 736 – alt. 76 m – ✉ 22400 10 C2

Paris 449 – Rennes 96 – Saint-Brieuc 19 – Saint-Malo 89 – Plérin 21

Manoir de la Hazaie without rest

2.5 km south-east on D 59 – ✆ 02 96 32 73 71 – www.manoir-hazaie.com – manoir.hazaie@wanadoo.fr – Fax 02 96 32 79 72

6 rm – € 116/130 € 130/240, ☕ € 14

◆ This 16C granite manor house and its tree-lined park are ideal for a country break. Period furnished rooms decorated with great attention to detail (spa bath tubs).

PLANPRAZ – 74 Haute-Savoie – 328 O5 – see Chamonix-Mont-Blanc

PLAPPEVILLE – 57 Moselle – 307 H4 – see Metz

PLATEAU-D'ASSY – 74 Haute-Savoie – 328 N5 – ✉ 74480 46 F1

French Alps

Paris 597 – Annecy 83 – Bonneville 41 – Chamonix-Mont-Blanc 23 – Megève 20

Office de tourisme, 1133,av. Jacques Arnaud ✆ 04 50 58 80 52, Fax 04 50 93 83 74

✻★★★ - Church ★: decoration★★ - Pavillon de Charousse ✻★★ West: 2.5 km then 30 mn - Lac Vert (Green Lake)★ Northeast: 5 km - Plaine-Joux ≤★★ Northeast: 5.5 km.

Tourisme without rest

6 r. d'Anterne ✉ 74190 – ✆ 04 50 58 80 54 – www.hotel-letourisme.com – hotel.le.tourisme@wanadoo.fr – Fax 04 50 93 82 11 – Closed 25 June-10 July, 23 October-13 November and Wednesday

15 rm – € 25 € 32/49, ☕ € 6

◆ This PMU (betting office) hotel-bar has basic, well-kept rooms, half of which look out over Mont Blanc. Pleasant terrace with panoramic views where breakfast is served in summer.

PLAZAC – 24 Dordogne – **329** H5 – **pop. 686** – **alt. 110 m** – ✉ **24580** 4 **D1**

Paris 530 – Bordeaux 170 – Périgueux 38 – Brive-la-Gaillarde 60 – Sarlat-la-Canéda 35

Béchanou

4 km north by D 6 and secondary road – ✆ 05 53 50 39 52 – www.bechanou.com – info@bechanou.com

5 rm – €80 €90 **Table d'hôte** – Menu €25 bi

◆ An old stone residence located at the end of a steep path, offering tranquillity and a breathtaking view of the valley. Simple rooms that preserve the nature of the location. Swimming pool. Tempting home cooking served in a rustic dining room or on the terrace.

PLÉLO – 22 Côtes-d'Armor – **309** E3 – **pop. 2 631** – **alt. 110 m** – ✉ **22170** 10 **C1**

Paris 470 – Lannion 54 – Rennes 118 – Saint-Brieuc 22

Au Char à Bancs with rm

Moulin de la ville Geffroy, 1 km north on D 84 – ✆ 02 96 74 13 63 – www.aucharabanc.com – charabanc@wanadoo.fr – Fax 02 96 74 13 03 – Closed January

5 rm – €60/80 €65/90

Rest – *(closed weekdays off season and Tuesday July-August)* Carte €15/25

◆ A friendly and welcoming auberge which serves dishes prepared using the farm's own produce (including hearty soups cooked over an open fire) at the wooden dining table. Cosy rooms with exposed beams and pretty, retro-style bathrooms.

PLÉNEUF-VAL-ANDRÉ – 22 Côtes-d'Armor – **309** G3 – **pop. 3 895** – **alt. 52 m** – **Casino : the Rotonde at Val-André** – ✉ **22370** 10 **C1**

Paris 446 – Dinan 43 – Erquy 9 – Lamballe 16 – St-Brieuc 28 – St-Cast 30 – St-Malo 51

Office de tourisme, 1, rue Winston Churchill ✆ 02 96 72 20 55, Fax 02 96 63 00 34

de Pleneuf-Val-André Rue de la plage des Vallées, 1 km E : on D 515, ✆ 02 96 63 01 12

in Val-André 2 km West – ✉ **22370 Pléneuf-Val-André** **Brittany**

Pointe de Pléneuf★ North 15 mn - Tour of the Pointe de Pléneuf ≤★★ North 30 mn.

Georges without rest

131 r. Clemenceau – ✆ 02 96 72 23 70 – www.partouche.fr – hotel-georges@g-partouche.fr – Fax 02 96 72 23 72 – Open end March to 10 November, Christmas holidays and February holidays

24 rm – €64/81 €74/91, €9

◆ This hotel in the heart of the seaside resort, sports simple, bright, practical rooms. Pleasant updated decor throughout.

Grand Hôtel du Val André

80 r. Amiral Charner – ✆ 02 96 72 20 56 – www.grand-hotel-val-andre.fr – monsejour@grand-hotel-val-andre.fr – Fax 02 96 63 00 24 – Closed 2-26 January

39 rm – €71/81 €85/106, €10 – ½ P €96/101

Rest – *(closed Tuesday lunch, Sunday dinner and Monday)* Menu (€17), €29/50 – Carte €45/70

◆ A traditional hotel built in 1895 on the sea front. Cane-furnished, regularly refurbished guestrooms. Sunlit restaurant and waterside terrace. Extensive menu that does full justice to sea produce.

Au Biniou

121 r. Clemenceau – ✆ 02 96 72 24 35 – Closed 7 December-7 January, February, Tuesday and Wednesday except July-August

Rest – Menu (€17), €26/34 – Carte €50/56

◆ A modern, sea themed interior serving inventive recipes made from the best fish and shellfish.

LE PLESSIS-PICARD – 77 Seine-et-Marne – **312** E4 – see Paris, Area (Sénart)

PLESTIN-LES-GRÈVES – 22 Côtes-d'Armor – 309 A3 – pop. 3 569 – alt. 45 m – ✉ 22310 Brittany 9 B1

Paris 528 – Brest 79 – Guingamp 46 – Lannion 18 – Morlaix 24 – St-Brieuc 77

Syndicat d'initiative, place de la Mairie ✆ 02 96 35 61 93, Fax 02 96 54 12 54

Lieue de Grève★ - Corniche de l'Armorique (cliff road) ★ North: 2 km.

Les Panoramas without rest P VISA
rte Corniche Nord: 5.5 km via D 42 – ✆ 02 96 35 63 76 – www.lespanoramas.fr – hotel.les.panoramas@wanadoo.fr – Fax 02 96 35 09 10 – Closed 2 January-15 March
13 rm – €35 €40/58, €6
◆ A practical hotel overlooking Beg Douar harbour. Most of the rooms have bow windows commanding a fine view of St Efflam beach and the Bruyères coastline.

PLEUDIHEN-SUR-RANCE – 22 Côtes-d'Armor – 309 K3 – pop. 2 516 – alt. 62 m – ✉ 22690 10 D2

Paris 395 – Rennes 59 – Saint-Brieuc 71 – Saint-Malo 22 – Granville 86

Manoir de St-Meleuc without rest P VISA
St-Meleuc – ✆ 02 96 83 34 26 – www.manoir-de-saint-meleuc.com – manoir_de_saint_meleuc@yahoo.fr
4 rm – €95 €140/180
◆ Skilfully renovated small 15C manor, in the heart of a 2.5-hectare park. Breakfast served in a large dining room with exposed beams and stonework, and old-style guestrooms.

PLÉVEN – 22 Côtes-d'Armor – 309 I4 – pop. 597 – alt. 80 m – ✉ 22130 10 C2

Paris 431 – Dinan 24 – Dinard 28 – St-Brieuc 38 – St-Malo 34

Ruins of the château de la Hunaudaie★ Southwest: 4 km, Brittany

Manoir de Vaumadeuc without rest P VISA AE
– ✆ 02 96 84 46 17 – www.vaumadeuc.com – manoir@vaumadeuc.com – Fax 02 96 84 40 16 – Open from Easter to 1st November
13 rm – €80/175 €105/210, €12
◆ A 15C manor nestling in a park. Wood panelling, fireplace and period furniture are part of the characterful decor. The second floor rooms are cosy and have sloping ceilings.

PLEYBER-CHRIST – 29 Finistère – 308 H3 – pop. 2 882 – alt. 131 m – ✉ 29410 Brittany 9 B1

Paris 548 – Brest 55 – Châteaulin 47 – Morlaix 12 – Quimper 67 – St-Pol-de-Léon 26

De la Gare rm, P VISA AE
2 r. Parmentier – ✆ 02 98 78 43 76 – www hotel-pleyber.com – hotelgare@wanadoo.fr – Fax 02 98 78 49 78 – Closed 22 December-14 January and Sunday except July-August
8 rm – €50/53 €53/57, €7,50
Rest – *(closed Saturday lunch and Sunday)* Menu €14 (weekday lunch), €21/38 – Carte €20/38
◆ Practical family hotel opposite the station. Functional rooms, which are not spacious but are very well kept, and pleasant little lounge overlooking a garden. Very simple restaurant, serving generous traditional cuisine at a reasonable price.

PLOBSHEIM – 67 Bas-Rhin – 315 K6 – see Strasbourg

PLOEMEUR – 56 Morbihan – 308 K8 – pop. 18 700 – alt. 45 m – ✉ 56270 9 B2

Paris 509 – Concarneau 51 – Lorient 6 – Quimper 68 – Vannes 65

Office de tourisme, 25, place de l'Église ✆ 02 97 85 27 88

de Ploemeur-Océan Saint Jude Kerham, W : 8 km on D 162, ✆ 02 97 32 81 82

Le Haut du Panier

20 bd de L'Atlantique, Le Couregant, 3 km south on the D 152 – 02 97 82 88 60 – lehautdupanier@yahoo.fr – Closed autumn school holidays, Tuesday from October to May and Wednesday

Rest – Carte € 33/50

◆ This 'basket' is laden with lovely seasonal produce, chalked up on a slate. Dishes are served in a modern interior or on the terrace facing the beach. Friendly staff.

in Lomener **4 km South by D 163 – ✉ 56270 Ploemeur**

Le Vivier

9 r. de Bergervir – 02 97 82 99 60 – www.levivier-lomener.com – info@levivier-lomener.com – Fax 02 97 82 88 89 – Closed 27 December-4 January

14 rm – €76/94 €88/106, €9 – ½ P €92/100

Rest – *(closed Sunday dinner except July-August)* Menu €25 (weekdays)/46 – Carte €38/60

◆ This hotel, anchored to a rock is dedicated to Neptune. Find a superb view of the sea and the Isle of Groix from modern, welcoming rooms, two of which have a terrace. Restaurant that all but bathes its toes in the water – small wonder seafood is its speciality!

PLOËRMEL – 56 Morbihan – 308 Q7 – pop. 7 525 – alt. 93 m – ✉ 56800 10 C2

Paris 417 – Lorient 88 – Loudéac 47 – Rennes 68 – Vannes 46

Office de tourisme, 5, rue du Val 02 97 74 02 70, Fax 02 97 73 31 82

du Lac-au-Duc Le Clos Hazel, N : 2 km on D 8, 02 97 73 64 64

Le Roi Arthur

rm, rest,

at Duc lake: 1.5 km by D 8 – 02 97 73 64 64 – www.hotelroiarthur.com – info@hotelroiarthur.com – Fax 02 97 73 64 50 – Closed February school holidays

46 rm – €83/164 €96/204, €13 – ½ P €88/141

Rest – Menu (€21), €33/45 – Carte €34/51

◆ This hotel stands in a park with a lake and golf course. Opt for one of the more comfortable, recently refurbished guestrooms with their new contemporary decor. Take a seat at a round table to enjoy up-to-date dishes, as a tribute to the legend.

PLOGOFF – 29 Finistère – 308 D6 – pop. 1 388 – alt. 70 m – ✉ 29770 9 A2

Paris 610 – Audierne 11 – Douarnenez 32 – Pont-l'Abbé 43 – Quimper 48

Ker-Moor

plage du Loch, 2.5 km on Audierne road – 02 98 70 62 06 – www.hotel-kermoor.com – kermoor.h.rest@wanadoo.fr – Fax 02 98 70 32 69 – Closed 7 January-12 February

12 rm – €50/85 €50/85, €9 – ½ P €68/88

Rest – *(closed Sunday dinner and Monday off season)* Menu (€17), €19 (weekdays)/45 – Carte €25/80

◆ Only the road separates this neo-Breton house from the sea. The furniture and view vary according to the room: some have terraces overlooking the waves. Try the house speciality, lobster cooked in cider (by reservation), while admiring Audierne Bay.

PLOMBIÈRES-LES-BAINS – 88 Vosges – 314 G5 – pop. 1 936 – alt. 429 m – Spa : mid March-mid Nov. – Casino – ✉ 88370 Alsace-Lorraine 27 C3

Paris 378 – Belfort 79 – Épinal 38 – Gérardmer 43 – Vesoul 54 – Vittel 61

Office de tourisme, 1, place Maurice Janot 03 29 66 01 30, Fax 03 29 66 01 94

La Feuillée Nouvelle ←★ 5 km - Semousse Valley ★.

Le Prestige Impérial

rm,

av. des Etats-Unis – 03 29 30 07 07 – www.plombieres-les-bains.com – residences.napoleon@plombieres-les-bains.com – Fax 03 29 30 07 08

80 rm – €80 €136, €11 – 2 suites – ½ P €103

Rest – Menu €24 (weekdays)/48 – Carte €30/51

◆ A light, glass roofed lobby leads into this Napoleon III hotel, linked to the thermal spas of the town. Art Deco-style rooms. The restaurant has been fully renovated and offers modern food.

PLOMEUR – 29 Finistère – 308 F7 – pop. 3 351 – alt. 33 m – ✉ 29120 9 A2
Brittany

Paris 579 – Douarnenez 39 – Pont-l'Abbé 6 – Quimper 26
Office de tourisme, 1, place de l'Église ✆ 02 98 82 09 05

La Ferme du Relais Bigouden without rest
à Pendreff, Guilvinec road: 2.5 km – ✆ 02 98 58 01 32 – www.hotel-bigouden.com – Fax 02 98 82 09 62 – Closed 1st December-15 January
16 rm – †€ 54 ††€ 58, ☕ € 8
◆ An old farmhouse in the Bigouden region with discreet, comfortable rooms all overlooking the garden. The breakfast room has its original charm.

Hotels and restaurants change every year,
so change your Michelin guide every year!

PLOMODIERN – 29 Finistère – 308 F5 – pop. 2 101 – alt. 60 m – ✉ 29550 9 A2

Paris 559 – Brest 60 – Châteaulin 12 – Crozon 25 – Douarnenez 18 – Quimper 28
Syndicat d'initiative, place de l'Église ✆ 02 98 81 27 37, Fax 02 98 81 59 91
Altar-pieces★ of Ste-Marie-du-Ménez-Hom chapel North: 3.5 km - Framework★ of St-Côme chapel Northwest: 4.5 km.
Ménez-Hom ※★★★ North: 7 km by D 47, Brittany

Pors-Morvan
3 km eastward by secondary road – ✆ 02 98 81 53 23 – www.porz-morvan.fr – christian.nicolas19@wanadoo.fr – Fax 02 98 81 28 61 – Open April-October, for the autumn school holidays and Christmas holidays
12 rm – †€ 50 ††€ 50, ☕ € 6 **Rest** – pancake rest. – Carte € 10/25
◆ Nature lovers will appreciate this 1830 farmhouse. The outbuildings house small rooms overlooking the quiet countryside. Garden and pond. A crêperie in an old timber-framed barn with a rustic decor and attractive fireplace.

Auberge des Glazicks (Olivier Bellin)
7 r. de la Plage – ✆ 02 98 81 52 32 – www.auberge-des-glazicks.com – aubergedesglazicks@orange.fr – Fax 02 98 81 57 18 – Closed 17-31 March, 15 October-30 November, Monday and Tuesday
Rest – Menu € 48/150 – Carte € 102/141
Spec. Langoustine rôtie en involtini de tête de cochon. Raviole de Saint-Jacques et foie gras (mid-September to end-March). Oeufs à la neige version 2008.
◆ This former blacksmith's has a dramatic view over Douarnenez bay. Inventive cuisine is served in a charming dining room where blue and white predominate.

PLOUBALAY – 22 Côtes-d'Armor – 309 J3 – pop. 2 488 – alt. 32 m – ✉ 22650 Brittany 10 C1

Paris 412 – Dinan 18 – Dol-de-Bretagne 35 – Lamballe 36 – St-Brieuc 56 – St-Malo 15
Water tower ※★★: 1 km Northeast.

De la Gare
4 r. Ormelets – ✆ 02 96 27 25 16 – restaurantdelagare3@wanadoo.fr – Fax 02 96 82 63 22 – Closed 23 June-2 July, 1st-15 October, 15-28 February, Monday dinner and Tuesday dinner from September to June, Tuesday lunch and Monday in July-August and Wednesday
Rest – Menu € 25/52 – Carte € 38/60
◆ Modern surf n' turf cuisine served in two dining rooms: one with a rustic feel and the other with a view over the small garden. Pleasant welcome and service.

PLOUBAZLANEC – 22 Côtes-d'Armor – 309 D2 – see Paimpol

PLOUER-SUR-RANCE – 22 Côtes-d'Armor – 309 J3 – pop. 3 058 10 D2
– alt. 62 m – ✉ 22490 Brittany

Paris 397 – Dinan 13 – Dol-de-Bretagne 20 – Lamballe 53 – St-Brieuc 70 – St-Malo 23

Manoir de Rigourdaine without rest
(at Rigourdaine), 3 km on Langrolay road and secondary road – 02 96 86 89 96 – www.hotel-rigourdaine.fr – hotel.rigourdaine@wanadoo.fr – Fax 02 96 86 92 46 – Open from early April to mid-November

19 rm – €68/82 €68/82, €8

◆ A well-restored old farmhouse overlooking the Rance estuary whose ancestral beams, large open fireplace and country furniture give the establishment particular character. Very peaceful.

PLOUGASNOU – 29 Finistère – 308 I2 – pop. 3 217 – alt. 55 m 9 B1
– ✉ 29630

Paris 550 – Rennes 198 – Quimper 100 – Lannion 34 – Morlaix 17

Syndicat d'initiative, place du Général Leclerc 02 98 67 31 88, Fax 02.98.67.31.88

Ar Velin Avel
4 rte de Kerlevenez – 02 98 67 81 35 – www.arvelinavel.com – arvelinavel@hotmail.com

4 rm – € 135/270 € 150/270, € 20 **Table d'hôte** – Menu € 30/60

◆ An exceptional setting for a luxurious sojourn: plush sitting room, theme-decorated rooms (Asia, sea, romanticism), sauna and massages. Bucolic site overlooking the bay. At the table d'hôte, sumptuous 'surf n' turf' menu and majestic breakfast (sometimes with caviar).

PLOUGASTEL-DAOULAS – 29 Finistère – 308 E4 – pop. 12 900 9 A2
– alt. 113 m – ✉ 29470 Brittany

Paris 596 – Brest 12 – Morlaix 60 – Quimper 64

Office de tourisme, 4 bis, place du Calvaire 02 98 40 34 98, Fax 02 98 40 68 85

Calvary★★ - Site★ of St-Jean chapel Northeast: 5 km - Kernisi ❋★ Southwest: 4.5 km.

Pointe de Kerdéniel ❋★★ Southwest: 8.5 km then 15 mn.

Le Chevalier de l'Auberlac'h
5 r. Mathurin Thomas – 02 98 40 54 56 – chevalierauberlach@voila.fr – Fax 02 98 40 65 16 – Closed Monday except lunch July-August and Sunday dinner

Rest – Menu € 18 (weekday lunch), € 24 € bi/41 – Carte € 30/47

◆ Stained glass, wooden beams, an open fireplace, wrought-iron chandelier and armour all combine to create a medieval ambience in this restaurant. Pleasant summer terrace in a small, enclosed garden.

PLOUGONVEN – 29 Finistère – 308 I3 – pop. 3 199 – alt. 176 m 9 B1
– ✉ 29640 Brittany

Paris 535 – Lannion 38 – Morlaix 12 – Rennes 183

La Grange de Coatélan
Coatélan, 4 km west on the D 109 – 02 98 72 60 16 – www.lagrangedecoatelan.com – la-grange-de-coatelan@wanadoo.fr – Fax 02 98 72 60 16 – Closed Christmas holidays

5 rm – €42/60 €50/70 **Table d'hôte** – *(pre-book)* Menu € 22/24

◆ This very peaceful 16C Breton farmhouse lies in the middle of the countryside. The panelled rooms are of various sizes and are located in the outbuildings. Restaurant offering local cuisine (single menu) in the rustic setting of an old barn.

PLOUGOUMELEN – 56 Morbihan – 308 N9 – pop. 2 083 – alt. 27 m – ✉ 56400 9 A3

▶ Paris 475 – Vannes 14 – Auray 10 – Lorient 49

Crêperie de Keroyal

3 imp. Keroyal, 1 km west by secondary road – ✆ 02 97 24 03 81 – www.creperie-keroyal.com – creperie-keroyal@wanadoo.fr – Fax 02 97 24 03 81 – Closed 9 March-2 April, 2 November-17 December, Monday in low season and Tuesday lunch

Rest – Carte € 10/18

◆ Crêperie in an old cottage. Here you can enjoy sweet and savoury pancakes mainly made with organic produce. Children's play area.

PLOUGRESCANT – 22 Côtes-d'Armor – 309 C1 – pop. 1 402 – alt. 53 m – ✉ 22820 Brittany 9 B1

▶ Paris 514 – Guingamp 38 – Lannion 23 – Rennes 162

Manoir de Kergrec'h without rest

– ✆ 02 96 92 59 13 – www.manoirdekergrech.com – kergrec.h@wanadoo.fr – Fax 02 96 92 51 27

8 rm – €100 €110

◆ Former 17C Episcopal manor house stands in extensive grounds stretching down to the seashore. Stylish lounge, guestrooms graced with family heirlooms and well-prepared breakfast by the fireside.

PLOUHARNEL – 56 Morbihan – 308 M9 – pop. 1 865 – alt. 21 m – ✉ 56340 Brittany 9 B3

▶ Paris 492 – Rennes 141 – Vannes 32 – Lorient 50 – Lanester 44

Office de tourisme, rond-point de l'Océan ✆ 02 97 52 32 93, Fax 02 97 52 49 87

Carnac Lodge without rest

Kerhueno – ✆ 02 97 58 30 30 – www.carnaclodge.com – contact@carnaclodge.com – Fax 02 97 58 31 33 – Closed 5 January-5 February

20 rm – €65/135 €65/135, €9

◆ Between Carnac and Plouharnel, this hotel, set in a quiet garden, offers rooms whose decoration features a clever blend of 1980s furnishings with modern details.

PLOUIDER – 29 Finistère – 308 F3 – pop. 1 871 – alt. 74 m – ✉ 29260 9 A1

▶ Paris 582 – Brest 36 – Landerneau 21 – Morlaix 46 – St Pol de Léon 28

La Butte

10 r. de la Mer – ✆ 02 98 25 40 54 – www.labutte.fr – info@labutte.fr – Fax 02 98 25 44 17 – Closed 28 January-21 February

22 rm – €60/112 €65/116, € 12 – ½ P € 72/104

Rest – *(closed Sunday dinner and Monday)* Menu € 24 (weekdays)/68 – Carte € 35/97

◆ This modern building houses spacious, functional and well-kept rooms. Those at the rear overlook a pleasant garden and command a view of the bay of Goulven. The traditional cuisine does full justice to the region's wealth of seafood and country produce.

PLOUIGNEAU – 29 Finistère – 308 I3 – pop. 4 278 – alt. 156 m – ✉ 29610 9 B1

▶ Paris 530 – Rennes 177 – Quimper 96 – Lannion 32 – Morlaix 14

Manoir de Lanleya without rest

manoir de Lanleya, 4 km north along the D 64 and secondary road – ✆ 02 98 79 94 15 – www.manoir-lanleya.com – manoir.lanleya@wanadoo.fr – Fax 02 98 79 94 15

5 rm – €66 €71

◆ This very well-restored 16C manor house (non-smoking) has pretty, antique-furnished rooms, flower-filled courtyard and wonderful riverside garden. Charming welcome.

PLOUMANACH – 22 Côtes-d'Armor – 309 B2 – see Perros-Guirec

PLUVIGNER – 56 Morbihan – **308** M8 – **pop. 6 315** – **alt. 87 m** – ✉ **56330** 10 **C2**

Paris 482 – Rennes 131 – Vannes 36 – Lorient 38 – Lanester 33

Syndicat d'initiative, place Saint-Michel ✆ 02 97 24 79 18, Fax 02 97 24 92 44

Domaine de Kerbarh VISA

r. de Kerbarh, rte de Ste Anne – ✆ 02 97 59 40 15 – www.domaine-dekerbarh.com – accueil@domaine-dekerbarh.com – Fax 02 97 59 40 15

5 rm – €100/280 €100/280, €15 **Table d'hôte** – Menu €30 bi

◆ Renovated farm with personalised rooms (bright colours, oriental furniture, high tech equipment, wood burning stove). Sauna, steam room, hot tub and pool for relaxation. Generous brunch-style breakfast and traditional table d'hôte in the evening.

LE POËT-LAVAL – 26 Drôme – **332** D6 – see Dieulefit

POGGIO-MEZZANA – 2B Haute-Corse – **345** F5 – see Corse

LE POINÇONNET – 36 Indre – **323** G6 – see Châteauroux

POINCY – 77 Seine-et-Marne – **312** G2 – see Meaux

POINTE DE MOUSTERLIN – 29 Finistère – **308** G7 – see Fouesnant

POINTE DE ST-MATHIEU – 29 Finistère – **308** C5 – see le Conquet

POINTE DU GROUIN – 35 Ille-et-Vilaine – **309** K2 – see Cancale

POINTE-DU-RAZ ★★★ – 29 Finistère – **308** C6 – ✉ 29770 Plogoff 9 **A2**
Brittany

Paris 614 – Douarnenez 37 – Pont-l'Abbé 48 – Quimper 53

☼★★.

in La Baie des Trépassés by D 784 and secondary road: 3.5 km – ✉ Cleden Cap Sizun

De La Baie des Trépassés rest, VISA

– ✆ 02 98 70 61 34 – hoteldelabaie@aol.com – Fax 02 98 70 35 20 – Open 15 February-10 November

27 rm – €39/77 €39/77, €11 – ½ P €62/81

Rest – *(closed Monday from 15 September to 15 June except school holidays)*
Menu €20/60 – Carte €35/85

◆ A location popular with tourists in the daytime but quiet in the evening. Small partially refurbished rooms; choose one with a sea view. The tightly packed tables of the restaurant have views of the Raz point. Traditional cooking inspired by the sea.

POINT-SUBLIME – 04 Alpes-de-Haute-Provence – **334** G10 – ✉ **04120 Rougon** **French Alps** 41 **C2**

Paris 803 – Castellane 18 – Digne-les-Bains 71 – Draguignan 53 – Manosque 76

≤★★★ on Grand Canyon du Verdon 15 mn - Couloir Samson★★ South: 1,5 km - Rougon ≤★ North: 2,5 km - Clue de Carejuan★ East: 4 km.

Viewpoints Southwest: of Escalès★★★ 9 km, Trescaïre★★ 8 km, Tilleul★★ 10 km, Glacières★★ 11 km, Imbut★★ 13 km.

✗ **Auberge du Point Sublime** with rm ⋞ 🏠 ⇸ ⚟ rest, P VISA MC

D 952 – ✆ 04 92 83 60 35 – pointsublime@nordnet.fr – Fax 04 92 83 74 31
– Open Easter-mid October
13 rm – †€ 61 ††€ 61, ☕ € 8 – ½ P € 60
Rest – *(closed Thursday lunch except 14 July-15 August and Wednesday)*
Menu (€ 16), € 23/31 – Carte approx. € 44

◆ A pleasant family-run inn near a belvedere, where meals (regional cuisine) are served in a pretty rustic setting or on the shaded terrace. Simple rooms.

For a pleasant stay in a charming hotel, look for the red 🏠 ... 🏠🏠🏠🏠🏠 symbols.

POISSON – **71 Saône-et-Loire** – **320** E11 – **see Paray-le-Monial**

POITIERS P – **86 Vienne** – **322** H5 – **pop. 89 200** – **Built-up area 119 371** – **alt. 116 m** – ✉ **86000** **Atlantic Coast** 39 **C1**

- Paris 335 – Angers 134 – Limoges 126 – Nantes 215 – Niort 76 – Tours 102
- Poitiers-Biard-Futuroscope: ✆ 05 49 30 04 40 AV.
- Office de tourisme, 45, place Charles-de-Gaulle ✆ 05 49 41 21 24, Fax 05 49 88 65 84
- 18 de Poitiers Mignaloux-Beauvoir 635 route de Beauvoir, 8 km on the Lussac-les-Châteaux road, ✆ 05 49 55 10 50
- 27 du Haut-Poitou Saint-Cyr Parc des Loisirs de Saint Cyr, 22 km on the Châtellerault road, ✆ 05 49 62 53 62
- N.-D.-la-Grande church ★★: front★★★ - St-Hilaire-le-Grand church ★★ - St-Pierre cathedral ★ - Ste-Radegonde church ★ **D** - St-Jean baptistry ★ - Great hall★ of the Palais de Justice (law courts) **J** - Boulevard Coligny ⋞★ - Musée Ste-Croix★★ - Statue of N-D-des-Dunes: ⋞★.
- Futuroscope Park ★★★: 12 km by ①.

Plans on following pages

🏠🏠 **Le Grand Hôtel** without rest ⚘ ⇅ ♿ AC 📶 🏃 🚗 VISA MC AE D

28 r. Carnot – ✆ 05 49 60 90 60 – www.grandhotelpoitiers.fr
– grandhotelpoitiers@wanadoo.fr – Fax 05 49 62 81 89 CZ **k**
41 rm – †€ 68/70 ††€ 78/86, ☕ € 12 – 6 suites

◆ Centrally located but with a peaceful courtyard, the hotel is decorated in a warm Art Deco style. Comfortable rooms and large terrace where breakfast is served in summer.

🏠🏠 **De l'Europe** without rest ⛍ ⇅ ♿ 📶 🏃 P 🚗 VISA MC AE

39 r. Carnot – ✆ 05 49 88 12 00 – www.hotel-europe-poitiers.com
– reservations@hotel-europe-poitiers.com – Fax 05 49 88 97 30
– Closed 24 December-3 January CZ **n**
88 rm – †€ 54/85 ††€ 60/89, ☕ € 8

◆ Three buildings (the oldest dating from 1810) arranged around an interior courtyard, located close to the pedestrianised area. The rooms are decorated in various styles (contemporary, Louis-Philippe, Oriental etc).

🏠 **Come Inn** 🏠 Fo ♿ rm, ⇸ ⚟ rest, 📶 🏃 P VISA MC

13 r. Albin Haller, (République 2 industrial estate) – ✆ 05 49 88 42 42
– www.hotelcomeinn.com – come-inn@wanadoo.fr – Fax 05 49 88 42 44
– Closed 24 July-13 August and 24 December-5 January AV **d**
44 rm – †€ 45 ††€ 52, ☕ € 8
Rest – *(closed Saturday and Sunday)* Menu (€ 13), € 15

◆ A practical location on a business park near the Aquitaine motorway. Functional bedrooms decorated in restrained style. Restrained contemporary decor provides the backdrop for a traditional menu.

POITIERS

Aérospatiale (R. de l') . . . . . . **AV** 3
Allende (R. Salvador) . . . . . . **BX** 7
Blaiserie (R. de la) . . . . **AV** 9
Ceuille-Mirebalaise (R.) . . . . **AV** 19
Coligny (Bd) . . . . **BX** 23
Demi-Lune (Carr. de la) . . . . **AV** 27
Fg-Ceuille-Mirebalaise (R. du) . . . . **AV** 29
Fg-du-Pont-Neuf (R. du) . . . . **BX** 30
Fg-St-Cyprien (R. du) . . . . . . **AX** 31
Fief-de-Grimoire (R.) . . . . **AX** 33
Gibauderie (R. de la) . . . . **BX** 39
Guynemer (R.) . . . . **AX** 43
Maillochon (R. de) . . . . **AX** 54
Miletrie (R. de la) . . . . **BX** 57
Montbernage (R. de) . . . . **BV** 58
Montmidi (R. de) . . . . **AX** 62
Pierre-Levée (R.) . . . . **BX** 69
Rataudes (R. des) . . . . **AX** 70
Schuman (Av. R.) . . . . **BV** 88
Vasles (Rte de) . . . . **AX** 93

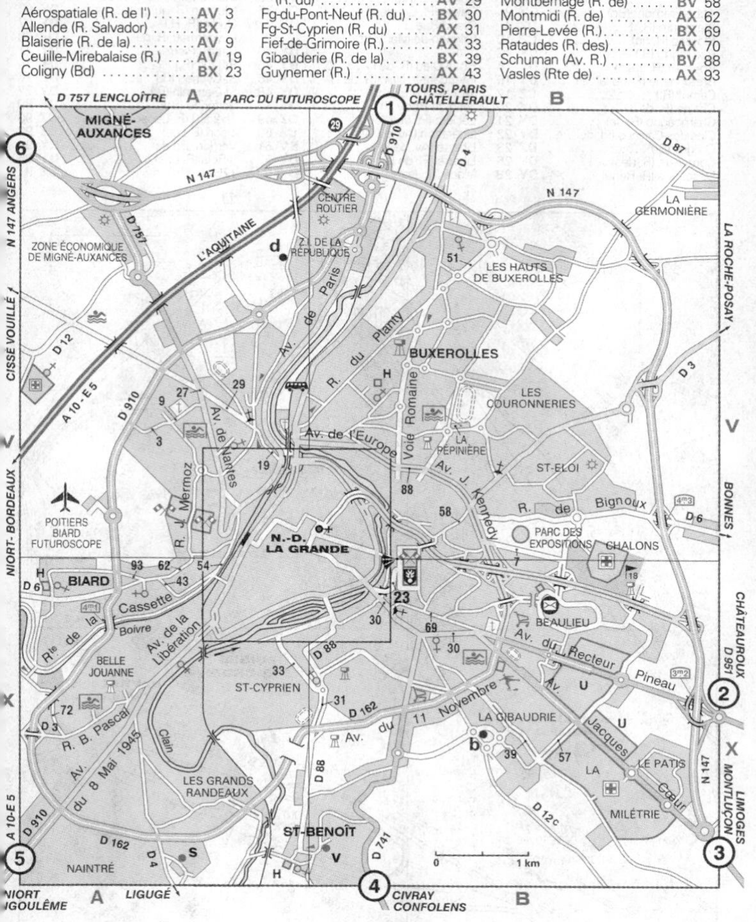

Gibautel without rest
2 r. de la Providence, Nouaillé road – ✆ 05 49 46 16 16 – hotel.gibautel@wanadoo.fr – Fax 05 49 46 85 97 — BX **b**
36 rm – †€ 47/49 ††€ 52/54, ☕ € 6
◆ Simple rooms, breakfast buffets and reasonable prices: a useful place to stop in an area away from the centre where several treatment establishments are located.

Le Poitevin
76 r. Carnot – ✆ 05 49 88 35 04 – http://le-poitevin.fr – contact@le-poitevin.fr – Fax 05 49 52 88 05 – Closed 18 April-4 May, 6-26 July, 23 December-4 January and Sunday dinner — CZ **r**
Rest – Menu (€ 12), € 26/40 – Carte € 35/60
◆ Restaurant in a shopping street, made up of three small dining rooms with rustic or modern decor. Traditional and regional cuisine.

POITIERS

Street	Grid	No.
Abbé-Frémont (Bd)	DY	2
Alexandre (R. J.)	DZ	4
Blossac (R. de)	CZ	10
Boncenne (R.)	CDY	12
Bouchet (R. Jean)	DY	14
Bretonnerie (R. de la)	DY	16
Carnot (R.)	CZ	17
Chaine (R. de la)	DY	20
Champagne (R. de)	DY	21
Clos-des-Carmes (Pl. du)	DY	22
Coligny (Bd)	DZ	23
Cordeliers (R. des)	DY	25
Descartes (R. René)	DY	28
Fg-du-Pont-Neuf	DZ	30
Gabillet (R. H.)	DY	34
Gambetta (R.)	DY	35
Gaulle (Pl. Ch.-de)	DY	36
Grand-Rue	DY	
Grignon-de-Montfort (R.)	DY	40
Hôtel-Dieu (R. de l')	DY	45
Intendant-le-Nain (R. de l')	DY	46
Jeanne-d'Arc (Bd)	DY	48
Jean-de-Berry (Pl.)	DY	47
Leclerc (Pl. du Mar.)	DZ	49
Libération (Av. de la)	CZ	50
Liberté (Av. de la)	BV	51
Liberté (Pl. de la)	DY	52
Macé (R. Jean)	DY	53
Marché-Notre-Dame (R. du)	DYZ	55
Marne (R. de la)	CY	56
Mouton (R. du)	DY	63
Oudin (R. H.)	DY	67
Puygarreau (R. du)	DZ	70
Rat (R. Pierre)	DY	71
Riffault (R.)	DY	74
St-Cyprien (R.)	DZ	76
St-Germain (R.)	DY	77
Solférino (Bd)	CY	89
Thezard (R. Léopold)	CZ	90
Tison (Bd de)	CZ	92
Verdun (Bd de)	CY	94
3-Rois (R. des)	DY	95
125e-R.-I. (R. du)	CZ	97

in Chasseneuil-du-Poitou 9 km by ① – ✉ **86360 Chasseneuil-du-Poitou – pop. 3 845 – alt. 75 m**

Office de tourisme, place du Centre ✆ 05 49 52 83 64, Fax 05 49 52 59 31

Château Clos de la Ribaudière rm, rest, P VISA

10 r. du Champ de Foire, in the village –
✆ 05 49 52 86 66 – www.ribaudiere.com – ribaudiere@ribaudiere.com
– Fax 05 49 52 86 32
41 rm – †€ 85/129 ††€ 106/152, ☕ € 13 – ½ P € 95/104
Rest – Menu € 31/57 – Carte € 48/67

◆ An attractive 19C residence in its own park beside the Clain. Elegant and spacious rooms in the castle and more standard ones in the annexe. The delightful dining room-veranda and terrace overlook the garden with its pond. Modern cuisine.

Mercure Alisée
D 910, 14 r. du Commerce – 05 49 52 90 41 – h0425@accor.com – Fax 05 49 52 51 72 – Closed 21 December-4 January
80 rm – €75/88 €87/103, €13
Rest ***Les 3 Garçons*** – *05 49 37 86 09 (closed Monday dinner, Saturday lunch and Sunday)* Menu (€10), €13 (weekdays)/24 – Carte €26/37
◆ The corridors, decorated so as to resemble a paved street, lead to large functional rooms, some of which look over the peaceful garden. Changing menus on the boards, friendly brasserie-style setting. Cosy lounge and fine library.

Futuroscope Park 12 km by ① – ✉ **Chasseneuil-du-Poitou**

Novotel Futuroscope
Téléport 4 – 05 49 49 91 91 – contact@novotel-futuroscope.biz – Fax 05 49 49 91 90
115 rm – €100/110 €127/190, €14
Rest – Menu €23/32 – Carte €26/39
◆ This elegant glass and steel building is in perfect harmony with the futuristic environment of the theme park. Modern functional rooms. The large restaurant overlooking the swimming pool and the piano bar have a decor reminiscent of the cinema.

Plaza Futuroscope
av. du Futuroscope Téléport 1 – 05 49 49 07 07 – www.hotel-plaza-futuroscope.com – reservation@plaza-futuroscope.com – Fax 05 49 49 55 49
274 rm – €95/140 €105/150
Rest ***Relais Plaza*** – Menu (€19), €26/32 – Carte €33/49
◆ Equally well-suited to business and tourist guests. A railway feel to the lobby. Comfortable rooms (VIP category is available) and a fitness centre. Traditional cuisine served in a restrained modern decor.

Mercure Aquatis Futuroscope
av. Jean Monnet, Téléport 3 ✉ 86962 – 05 49 49 55 00 – h2773@accor.com – Fax 05 49 49 55 01
140 rm – €79/89 €84/94, €14
Rest – Menu (€14), €18 – Carte approx. €25
◆ A minimalist silhouette contrasts with the strange architecture of Futuroscope. Practical rooms; those in the new wing are more spacious. A huge restaurant with columns, arcades and statues; traditional dishes and small menu featuring roast meats.

Ibis Futuroscope
av. Thomas Edison – 05 49 49 90 00 – www.ibishotel.com – h1193@accor.com – Fax 05 49 49 90 09
140 rm – €53/72 €53/72, €8 **Rest** – Menu €19
◆ With its practical rooms, comfortable bar lounge and conference rooms, this Ibis hotel will appeal both to businessmen and to fans of the fourth dimension. In the restaurant there is a boat-style decor and buffet meals featuring seafood.

in Lavoux 15 km by ② and D 1 – pop. 1 103 – alt. 126 m – ✉ 86800

Logis du Château du Bois Dousset
– 05 49 44 20 26 – mariediane1012@yahoo.fr – Fax 05 49 44 20 26
3 rm – €70/80 €80/90 **Table d'hôte** – Menu €30 bi
◆ This 400ha family estate includes a château, magnificent formal garden and Louis XIII-style lodge. The latter houses comfortable ground-floor rooms and a luxurious suite. Restaurant serving produce from the vegetable garden and Poitou specialities.

Limoges road 10 km by ③, N 147 and secondary road – ✉ **86550 Mignaloux**

Manoir de Beauvoir
635 rte de Beauvoir, at the golf course – 05 49 55 47 47 – www.manoirdebeauvoir.com – resa-poitiers@monalisahotels.com – Fax 05 49 55 31 95
41 rm – €99 €99, €12 – 4 suites – ½ P €82
Rest – Menu €29 – Carte €31/50
◆ The rooms are in the 19C house; the apartments with kitchenettes are in the annexe. A 90ha park and an 18-hole golf course. The Manoir offers diners the choice between a wood-panelled dining room and the more British style in the clubhouse.

in St-Benoît 4 km south of map by D 88 – pop. 6 859 – alt. 77 m – ✉ 86280

Office de tourisme, 18, rue Paul Gauvin ✆ 05 49 88 42 12, Fax 05 49 56 08 82

Passions et Gourmandises (Richard Toix)

6 r. du Square – ✆ 05 49 61 03 99
– www.passionsetgourmandises.com – info@passionsetgourmandises.com
– Closed 2-11 January, Sunday dinner, Wednesday lunch and Monday

Rest – Menu (€ 18), € 25 (weekday lunch), € 35/70 – Carte € 60/80 BX **v**

Spec. Huîtres à l'échalote. Langoustine à la plancha légèrement fumée et sabayon de mangue (September-January). Tube croustillant chocolat-café et crème glacée au cognac (winter). **Wines** Haut-Poitou rouge.

◆ Tempting modern cuisine in a bright, spacious, contemporary setting. Pretty terrace beside the stream.

Ligugé road 4 km South of map by D 4 – ✉ 86280 St-Benoît

L'Orée des Bois with rm

13 r. de Naintré – ✆ 05 49 57 11 44 – oreedesbois@free.fr – Fax 05 49 43 21 40
– Closed Saturday lunch, Sunday dinner and Monday AX **s**

12 rm – †€ 47 ††€ 54, ☕ € 7 – ½ P € 59

Rest – Menu € 17 (weekdays)/55 – Carte approx. € 43

◆ A Virginia creeper-clad house at the heart of the Clain Valley. Two rustic style dining rooms serving traditional cuisine. Renovated, sober and spotless rooms with rustic furniture.

Angoulême road 6 km by ⑤, Hauts-de-Croutelle exit – ✉ 86240 Croutelle

La Chênaie

Les Hauts de Croutelle, at La Berlanderie, Lejat street – ✆ 05 49 57 11 52
– www.la-chenaie.com – restaurantlachenaie@wanadoo.fr – Fax 05 49 57 11 51
– Closed 20 July-9 August, February holidays, Sunday dinner and Monday

Rest – Menu € 20/40 – Carte € 41/65

◆ An old, attractively restored farmhouse standing back from the road. The smart dining room overlooks a garden with ancient oak trees. Modern cuisine.

Niort road 7 km by ⑤ – ✉ 86240 Ligugé

Le Bois de la Marche rm, rest,

junction of N10 and D611 – ✆ 05 49 53 10 10
– www.bois-de-la-marche.com – boisdelamarche@wanadoo.fr
– Fax 05 49 55 32 25

53 rm – †€ 62/78 ††€ 73/129, ☕ € 11 – ½ P € 69/89

Rest – Menu € 22 (weekdays)/49 – Carte € 41/50

◆ A short drive from the Western world's oldest monastery (Ligugé), the hotel is a large, modern building in a park planted with trees. Rooms are being gradually refurbished. Most of them are furnished in Louis XV style. Traditional and Périgord dishes served on the huge terrace, weather permitting.

in Périgny 17 km by ⑥, N 149 and secondary road – ✉ 86190 Vouillé

Château de Périgny

40 r. des Coteaux – ✆ 05 49 51 80 43 – www.chateau-perigny.com – info@chateau-perigny.com – Fax 05 49 51 90 09

43 rm – †€ 78/128 ††€ 88/148, ☕ € 14 – 1 suite – ½ P € 88/96

Rest – Menu (€ 18), € 32/58 – Carte € 49/77

◆ A Renaissance château in a vast park. The pretty rooms have period furniture. Those in the outbuildings are more modern. Restaurant looking out over a delightful patio, where tables are set in summer. Modern recipes.

POLIGNY – 05 Hautes-Alpes – 334 E4 – pop. 275 – alt. 1 062 m – ✉ 05500 41 **C1**

Paris 658 – Gap 19 – Marseille 199 – Vizille 71

Le Chalet des Alpages

Les Forestons, 1.5 km to the west – ✆ 04 92 23 08 95
– www.lechaletdesalpages.com – lechaletdesalpages@gmail.com

5 rm ☕ – †€ 70/100 ††€ 90/120 – ½ P € 70/85 **Table d'hôte** – Menu € 25 bi

◆ This building, with an area of 6,000m, has numerous assets: Alpine-style rooms, some with a balcony, fitness room, hot outdoor tub and clear view of the Noyer Pass, Faraud Barrier and Old Chaillol. Cuisine combining both local and Provençal flavours.

POLIGNY – 39 Jura – 321 E5 – pop. 4 377 – alt. 373 m – ✉ 39800 16 B3
Burgundy-Jura

Paris 397 – Besançon 57 – Dole 45 – Lons-le-Saunier 30 – Pontarlier 63

Office de tourisme, 20, place des Déportés ✆ 03 84 37 24 21, Fax 03 84 37 22 37

Collegiate church ★ - Culée de Vaux★ South: 2 km - Cirque de Ladoye ≤★★ South: 2 km.

in Monts de Vaux **Southeast: 4,5 km by Genève road – ✉ 39800 Poligny**

≤★.

Hostellerie des Monts de Vaux ≤ rest, P VISA MC AE
– ✆ 03 84 37 12 50 – www.hostellerie.com – mtsvaux@hostellerie.com – Fax 03 84 37 09 07 – Closed 27 October-28 December, Tuesday except dinner July-August and Wednesday lunch
10 rm – †€ 115/190 ††€ 125/250, ☕ € 15 – ½ P € 160/190
Rest – Menu € 28 (lunch), € 33/80 – Carte € 44/74
◆ Sitting in grounds overlooking the remoteness of the Vaux, this old farmhouse has elegant rooms which exude charm. Recently added business meeting facility. Classic and regional cuisine enhanced by a fine selection of regional vintages.

in Passenans **Southwest: 11 km by D 1083 and D 57 – pop. 300 – alt. 320 m – ✉ 39230**

Revermont ≤ rm, P VISA MC AE
600 rte de Revermont – ✆ 03 84 44 61 02 – www.domaine-du-revermont.fr – schmit-revermont@wanadoo.fr – Fax 03 84 44 64 83 – Closed 20 December-1st March
28 rm – †€ 67/99 ††€ 67/106, ☕ € 12 – ½ P € 69/89
Rest – Menu (€ 16), € 23/78 bi – Carte € 27/60
◆ A 1970s building on a hillside overlooking the vineyards. Practical rooms; the best (with balcony or terrace) overlook the pool. A rustic dining room (beams, exposed stonework, fireplace) and updated Franche Comté cuisine.

POLLIAT – 01 Ain – 328 D3 – pop. 2 336 – alt. 260 m – ✉ 01310 44 B1

Paris 415 – Bourg-en-Bresse 12 – Lyon 74 – Mâcon 26 – Villefranche-sur-Saône 53

De la Place with rm — A/C rest, P VISA MC
51 pl. de la Mairie – ✆ 04 74 30 40 19 – hoteldelaplacepolliat@orange.fr – Fax 04 74 30 42 34 – Closed 24 July-14 August, 2-16 January, Sunday evening and Monday
7 rm – †€ 47 ††€ 50, ☕ € 8 – ½ P € 52
Rest – *(closed Thursday dinner, Sunday dinner and Monday)* Menu € 18 (weekdays)/54 – Carte € 27/47
◆ Decor in bright colours (rustic or wrought iron furniture) where tasty and generous regional cuisine is served with a smile. Renovated rooms.

POLMINHAC – 15 Cantal – 330 D5 – pop. 1 156 – alt. 650 m – ✉ 15800 5 B3

Paris 553 – Aurillac 15 – Murat 34 – Vic-sur-Cère 5

Syndicat d'initiative, rue de la Gare ✆ 04 71 47 48 36, Fax 04 71 47 58 56

Au Bon Accueil ≤ A/C rest, P VISA MC
– ✆ 04 71 47 40 21 – www.hotel-bon-accueil.com – info@hotel-bon-accueil.com – Fax 04 71 47 40 13 – Closed 15 October-1st December, Sunday evening and Monday
23 rm – †€ 38/48 ††€ 43/55, ☕ € 6,50 – ½ P € 38/45 **Rest** – Menu € 11/26
◆ The architecture may be ordinary but the hotel deserves its name: smiles and friendliness are the bywords. Spruce, particularly practical rooms. The restaurant overlooks the Cère valley and its mountainous backdrop; regional food.

LA POMARÈDE – 11 Aude – **344** C2 – **pop. 166** – **alt. 304 m** 22 **A2**
– ✉ 11400

Paris 728 – Auterive 49 – Carcassonne 49 – Castres 38 – Gaillac 72 – Toulouse 57

XXX ✿ **Hostellerie du Château de la Pomarède** (Gérald Garcia) with rm
Château de la Pomarède – ✆ *04 68 60 49 69* – rest, P VISA MC AE
– www.hostellerie-lapomarede.fr – hostellerie-lapomarede@wanadoo.fr
– Fax 04 68 60 49 71 – Closed 26 October-24 November and 15 January-15 March
14 rm – †€ 85/110 ††€ 150/225, ☕ € 18
Rest – *(closed Sunday dinner from December to April, Monday and Tuesday)*
Menu (€ 25), € 42/89 – Carte € 68/92
Spec. Bonbons de foie gras et ormeaux du Cotentin sauce aigre douce. Pommes de ris de veau, queues de langoustines et carottes fanes glacéés. Pequillos farcis à la marmelade d'orange et fruits secs. **Wines** Malepère, Corbières.
◆ Elegant dining room with exposed beams, panoramic terrace and spacious modern guestrooms in the outbuildings of an 11C Cathar château. Inventive cuisine and regional wine list.

POMMERIT-JAUDY – 22 Côtes-d'Armor – **309** C2 – **pop. 1 152** 9 **B1**
– **alt. 74 m** – ✉ 22450

Paris 510 – Rennes 157 – Saint-Brieuc 62 – Lannion 20 – Morlaix 73

Château de Kermezen without rest P VISA MC AE
2 km west on secondary road – ✆ *02 96 91 35 75 – micheldekermel@kermezen.com – Fax 02 96 91 35 75*
5 rm ☕ – †€ 85/90 ††€ 90/110
◆ Faultlessly hospitable family mansion set in vast wooded grounds (complete with chapel). Stylish guestrooms, and magnificent 15C and 16C Breton rustic furniture in the breakfast room.

POMMEUSE – 77 Seine-et-Marne – **312** H3 – **see Coulommiers**

POMMIERS – 69 Rhône – **327** H4 – **pop. 2 109** – **alt. 315 m** – ✉ 69480 43 **E1**

Paris 442 – Lyon 32 – Villeurbanne 45 – Vénissieux 45 – Caluire-et-Cuire 36

X **Les Terrasses de Pommiers** P VISA MC
La Buisante – ✆ *04 74 65 05 27 – www.terrasses-de-pommiers.com*
– Fax 04 74 65 05 27 – Closed 26 October-10 November, 22 February-9 March, Monday and Tuesday
Rest – Menu (€ 19 bi), € 28/52 – Carte € 40/55
◆ Enjoy fine views of the Saône valley and the Monts du Lyonnais through the windows of the wood-floored, covered terrace, which comes into its own in summer. Modern seasonal menu.

PONS – 17 Charente-Maritime – **324** G6 – **pop. 4 442** – **alt. 39 m** 38 **B3**
– ✉ 17800 Atlantic Coast

Paris 493 – Blaye 64 – Bordeaux 97 – Cognac 24 – La Rochelle 99 – Royan 43 – Saintes 22

Syndicat d'initiative, place de la République ✆ 05 46 96 13 31, Fax 05 46 96 34 52

Keep★ of the former château - Hospice des Pèlerins★ Southwest by D 732 - Panelling★ of the château d'Usson 1 km by D 249.

De Bordeaux rm, VISA MC
1 av. Gambetta – ✆ *05 46 91 31 12 – www.hotel-de-bordeaux.com – info@hotel-de-bordeaux.com – Fax 05 46 91 22 25 – Closed Christmas holidays, Saturday lunch and Sunday evening from October to March*
16 rm – †€ 53 ††€ 65, ☕ € 10 – ½ P € 58
Rest – Menu € 18/49 – Carte € 37/52
◆ In a street in the town centre, this hundred-year-old hotel has been renovated and boasts small, attractive guestrooms and an English-style bar. Opening onto a charming patio-terrace, this restaurant's decor is in pleasant harmony with the creative cuisine. Extensive choice of cognacs.

in Pérignac Northeast: 8 km by Cognac road – pop. 972 – alt. 41 m – ✉ 17800

XX **La Gourmandière**
42 av. de Cognac – ✆ 05 46 96 36 01 – www.la-gourmandiere-perignac.com – lagourmandiere.perignac@wanadoo.fr – Closed 23 November-3 December, 26 January-4 February, Tuesday and Wednesday from October to mid-June except public holidays and Sunday dinner from mid-June to September
Rest – Menu (€ 15), € 26/58 – Carte € 39/56
◆ A pretty village cottage redecorated by its young owners in a warm modern spirit. Inviting terrace overlooking the garden and up-to-date menu.

in Mosnac South: 11 km by Bordeaux road and D 134 – pop. 448 – alt. 23 m – ✉ 17240

Moulin du Val de Seugne
– ✆ 05 46 70 46 16 – www.valdeseugne.com – moulin@valdeseugne.com – Fax 05 46 70 48 14 – Closed 2 January-10 February
rm, VISA AE
14 rm – †€ 105/165 ††€ 105/165, ☕ € 13 – ½ P € 89/119
Rest – Menu (€ 21), € 29/79 – Carte € 50/90
◆ Elegant hostelry on the banks of the River Seugne. Refined rooms, adorned with antique furniture and luxury bathrooms. Lounge opening onto the mill's machinery. Pleasant restaurant and terrace overlooking the river. Regional products on sale in the shop.

Do not confuse X with ✿!
X defines comfort, while stars are awarded for the best cuisine, across all categories of comfort.

PONT (LAC) – 21 Côte-d'Or – **320** G5 – see Semur-en-Auxois

PONTAILLAC – 17 Charente-Maritime – **324** D6 – see Royan

PONT-A-MOUSSON – 54 Meurthe-et-Moselle – **307** H5 – pop. 14 100 – alt. 180 m – ✉ 54700 Alsace-Lorraine 26 **B2**

- Paris 325 – Metz 31 – Nancy 30 – Toul 48 – Verdun 66
- Office de tourisme, 52, place Duroc ✆ 03 83 81 06 90, Fax 03 83 82 45 84
- Place Duroc★ - Former Prémontrés abbey ★.

X **Le Fourneau d'Alain**
64 pl. Duroc, (1st floor) – ✆ 03 83 82 95 09 – www.lefourneaudalain.com – lefourneaudalain@neuf.fr – Fax 03 83 82 95 09 – Closed 1st-7 May, 1st-15 August, Wednesday dinner, Sunday dinner and Monday
VISA
Rest – Menu € 28/53 – Carte € 34/46
◆ A discreetly contemporary restaurant on the main square, on the first floor of one of the 16C arcaded houses. Tables are well laid out and the service unpretentious.

PONTARLIER – 25 Doubs – **321** I5 – pop. 18 700 – alt. 838 m – ✉ 25300 Burgundy-Jura 17 **C2**

- Paris 462 – Besançon 60 – Dole 88 – Lausanne 67 – Lons-le-Saunier 82
- Office de tourisme, 14 bis, rue de la Gare ✆ 03 81 46 48 33, Fax 03 81 46 83 32
- Pontarlier Les Étraches La Grange des Pauvres, E : 8 km on D 47, ✆ 03 81 39 14 44
- Portal★ of the former Annonciades chapel.
- Grand Taureau ✳★★ by ②: 11 km.

PONTARLIER

Arçon (Pl. d') . . . . A 2
Augustins (R. des) . . . . B 3
Bernardines (Pl. des) . . . . . . AB 4
Capucins (R. des) . . . . A 7
Crétin (Pl.) . . . . B 8
Écorces (R. des) . . . . A 12
Gambetta (R.) . . . . B 13
Halle (R. de la) . . . . B 15
Industrie (R. de l') . . . . B 16
Latttre-de-Tassigny (Pl. Mar.-de) . . . . B 19
Mathez (R. Jules) . . . . B 26
Mirabeau (R.) . . . . B 27
Moulin Parnet (R. du) . . . . A 29
Pagnier (Pl. J.) . . . . B 30
République (R. de la) . . . . . . AB
Ste-Anne (R.) . . . . AB 35
St-Étienne (R. du Fg) . . . . B
St-Pierre (Pl.) . . . . A
Salengro (Pl. R.) . . . . A 36
Tissot (R.) . . . . AB 37
Vannolles (R. de) . . . . B 38
Vieux-Château (R. du) . . . . A 39
Villingen-Schwenningen (Pl. de) . . . . A 40

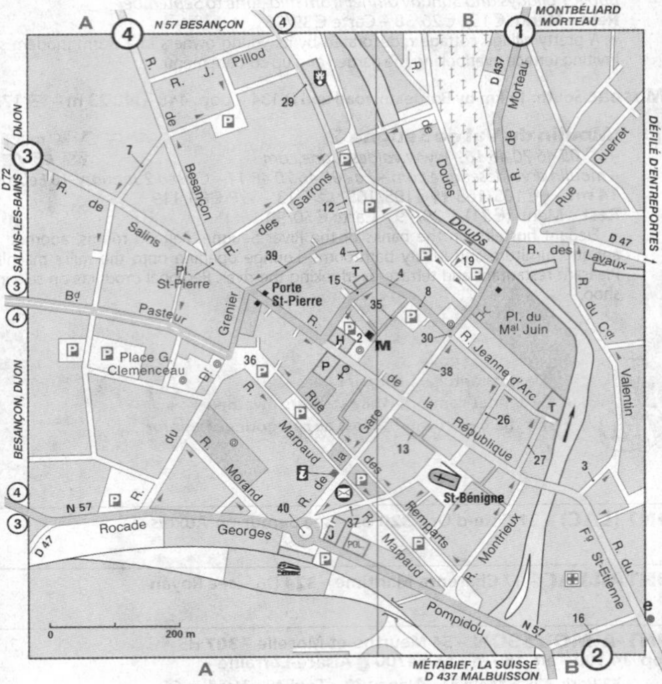

XX **L'Alchimie**

1 av. Armée de l'Est – ✆ 03 81 46 65 89
– www.l-alchimie.com – restau-lalchimie@wanadoo.fr
– Fax 03 81 39 08 75
– Closed 19-29 April, 13 July-2 August, 2-12 January, Sunday dinner, Tuesday dinner and Wednesday B **e**

Rest – Menu (€ 20), € 39/54 – Carte € 52/58

◆ The alchemist chef prepares his inventive dishes by 'transmuting' local produce, spices and exotic flavours. Redecorated in a trendy style.

in Doubs by ④: 2 km – pop. 2 405 – alt. 813 m – ✉ 25300

X **Le Doubs Passage**

11 Gde Rue, D 130 – ✆ 03 81 39 72 71
– http://monsite.wanadoo.fr/ledoubspassage/
– ledoubspassage@wanadoo.fr
– Fax 03 81 39 72 71
– Closed 20 August-1st September, Sunday dinner, Wednesday dinner and Monday

Rest – Menu € 18/30 – Carte € 25/38

◆ A family inn on the banks of the Doubs. Well decorated dining room with parquet flooring, soft lighting and a profusion of plants and flowers. Traditional cuisine.

PONTAUBAULT – 50 Manche – 303 D8 – pop. 469 – alt. 25 m – ✉ 50220 32 A3

Paris 345 – Avranches 9 – Dol-de-Bretagne 35 – Fougères 38 – Rennes 78 – St-Malo 60

Les 13 Assiettes

6 rte de la Quintine, north: 1 km on the D 43E (former Avranches road) – ✆ 02 33 89 03 03 – www.hotel-le-mont-saint-michel.com – 13assiettes@wanadoo.fr – Fax 02 33 89 03 06

39 rm – €65/75 €77/87, € 10 – ½ P € 61/66

Rest – Menu € 18 (weekdays)/63 – Carte € 25/48

◆ The rooms in the bungalows have simple furnishings. Those in the main building are larger with the same level of comfort but more modern (a few family-sized rooms). Bright restaurant giving onto a garden terrace with pool and palm trees. Traditional dishes.

PONTAUBERT – 89 Yonne – 319 G7 – see Avallon

PONT-AUDEMER – 27 Eure – 304 D5 – pop. 8 981 – alt. 15 m – ✉ 27500 Normandy 32 B3

Paris 164 – Caen 74 – Évreux 68 – Le Havre 44 – Lisieux 36 – Rouen 52

Office de tourisme, place Maubert ✆ 02 32 41 08 21, Fax 02 32 57 11 12

Stained-glass windows★ of St-Ouen church.

PONT-AUDEMER

Street	No.
Canel (R. Alfred)	2
Carmélites (R. des)	3
Clemencin (R. Paul)	5
Cordeliers (R. des)	6
Delaquaize (R. S.)	7
Déportés (R. des)	8
Épée (R. de l')	9
Félix-Faure (Quai)	
Ferry (R. Jules)	
Gambetta (R.)	13
Gaulle (Pl. Général-de)	14
Gillain (Pl. Louis)	16
Goulley (Pl. J.)	
Jean-Jaurès (R.)	18
Joffre (R. Mar.)	19
Kennedy (Pl.)	
Leblanc (Quai R.)	20
Maquis-Surcouf (R.)	21
Maubert (Pl.)	22
Mitterrand (Quai François)	23
N.-D.-du-Pré (R.)	
Pasteur (Bd)	
Place-de-la-Ville (R.)	24
Pot-d'Étain (Pl. du)	25
Président-Coty (R. du)	26
Président-Pompidou (Av. du)	
République (R. de la)	27
Sadi-Carnot (R.)	
St-Ouen (Impasse)	29
Seule (R. de la)	30
Thiers (R.)	32
Verdun (Pl. de)	34
Victor-Hugo (Pl.)	35

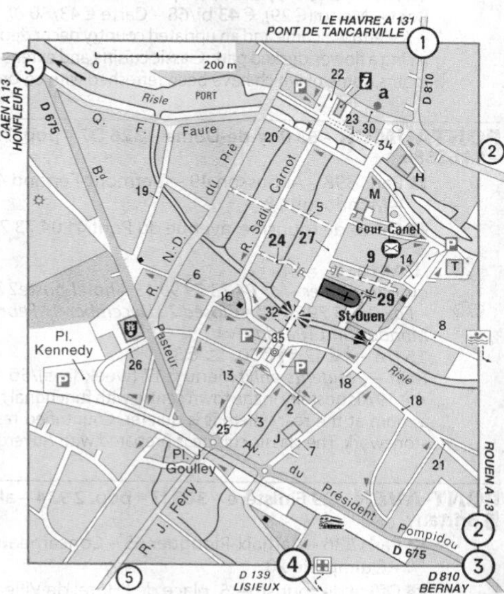

Belle Isle sur Risle

112 rte de Rouen, via ② – ✆ 02 32 56 96 22 – www.bellile.com – hotelbelle-isle@wanadoo.fr – Fax 02 32 42 88 96 – Open 18 March-15 November and 30 December-3 January

20 rm – €100/137 €115/259, € 18

Rest – *(closed Monday lunch, Tuesday lunch and Wednesday lunch)* Menu € 30 (weekday lunch), € 39/64 – Carte € 50/75

◆ Attractive ivy clad mansion built in 1856 on an islet of the Risle in a landscaped 2ha park (river fishing). The rooms, of various sizes, have pretty personal touches. This restaurant has a quiet terrace amid trees, which are over two-centuries-old.

XX **Erawan**

4 r. Sëule – ✆ 02 32 41 12 03 – Closed August and Wednesday a

Rest – Menu € 20 – Carte € 25/44

◆ The menu is 100% Thai and the setting 75% Norman: a surprising melting pot in this restaurant on the banks of the Risle.

Southeast by ② and D 39: 5 km – ✉ 27500 Pont-Audemer

XXX **Au Jardin d'Eden**

rte Condé-s-Risle – ✆ 02 32 57 01 52 – www.aujardindeden.fr – aujardindeden@wanadoo.fr – Fax 02 32 41 42 01 – Closed 11-29 January, Tuesday dinner and Monday except July-August and Sunday dinner

Rest – Menu (€ 20), € 28 (weekdays)/75 – Carte € 52/100

◆ This fine Norman house, converted into a restaurant, lies on an artificial peninsula in the middle of a big lake. Modern decor and traditional menu.

in Campigny by ③ and D 29: 6 km – pop. 818 – alt. 121 m – ✉ 27500

XXX **Le Petit Coq aux Champs** with rm

– ✆ 02 32 41 04 19 – www.lepetitcoqauxchamps.fr – le.petit.coq.aux.champs@wanadoo.fr – Fax 02 32 56 06 25 – Closed 17-24 November, January, Sunday dinner and Monday 1st November-31 March

12 rm – †€ 139 ††€ 139/159, ☕ € 13 – ½ P € 124/132

Rest – Menu (€ 29), € 43 bi/68 – Carte € 43/80

◆ A warm welcome and an updated country decor depict this Normandy cottage. Terrace facing a flower-decked park. Classic cuisine and extensive wine list. Calm and comfortable rooms, some of which have been refreshed with co-ordinated bedding.

PONTAUMUR – 63 Puy-de-Dôme – 326 D7 – pop. 755 – alt. 535 m – ✉ 63380 5 B2

Paris 398 – Aubusson 49 – Clermont-Ferrand 42 – Le Mont-Dore 49 – Montluçon 68

Office de tourisme, avenue du Pont ✆ 04 73 79 73 42, Fax 04 73 73 73 36

Poste

av. Marronnier – ✆ 04 73 79 90 15 – hotel-poste2@wanadoo.fr – Fax 04 73 79 73 17 – Closed 20 December-1st February, Sunday dinner, Monday and Tuesday

15 rm – †€ 42 ††€ 50, ☕ € 8

Rest – *(residents only)* Menu € 17 (weekdays)/50 – Carte € 30/55

◆ A 1970s hostelry in the town centre with functional rooms of standard comfort. Choose a room at the rear where it is quieter. Countrified restaurant dominated by wood and stonework. The classic cuisine is prepared with Auvergne produce.

PONT-AVEN – 29 Finistère – 308 I7 – pop. 2 934 – alt. 18 m – ✉ 29930 9 B2

Brittany

Paris 536 – Carhaix-Plouguer 65 – Concarneau 15 – Quimper 36 – Quimperlé 20

Office de tourisme, 5, place de l'Hôtel de Ville ✆ 02 98 06 04 70, Fax 02 98 06 17 25

Walk in the Bois d'Amour★.

Les Ajoncs d'Or

1 pl. Hôtel de Ville – ✆ 02 98 06 02 06 – www.ajoncsdor-pontaven.com – ajoncsdor@aol.com – Fax 02 98 06 18 91 – Closed 19-26 October, February, Sunday evening and Monday from October to May

20 rm – †€ 56 ††€ 56/85, ☕ € 8 – ½ P € 58

Rest – *(closed Monday from October to May and Sunday dinner)* Menu (€ 18), € 26/47 – Carte € 39/57

◆ Gauguin apparently stayed in this Breton house (1892) during his last stay in Pont-Aven. Stylish, soundproofed rooms named after painters; charming welcome. Bright dining room adorned with art (for sale), summer terrace and traditional cuisine.

Mimosas

1 square Théodore-Botrel – ✆ 02 98 06 00 30 – www.hotels-pont-aven.com – hotelmimosas@wanadoo.fr – Fax 02 98 06 01 54 – Closed 12 November-17 December

10 rm – €65 €65, ☕ €8

Rest – *(closed Tuesday and Wednesday from October to March except school holidays)* Menu (€ 14), € 20/39 – Carte € 31/102

◆ Pleasant, family-run hotel near the Pont Aven harbour. Smart, well-kept rooms (chinzy fabrics) with uninterrupted views over the boats. Rustic decor in keeping with the unpretentious, traditional seafood cuisine.

Moulin de Rosmadec (Frédéric Sebilleau) with rm

near the bridge, town centre – ✆ 02 98 06 00 22 – www.moulinderosmadec.com – moulinderosmadec@wanadoo.fr – Fax 02 98 06 18 00 – Closed 18-31 October and February school holidays

5 rm – € 80/90 € 90, ☕ € 12

Rest – *(closed Sunday dinner in low season and Wednesday)* Menu € 35/76 – Carte € 64/75

Spec. Langoustines en kadaïf, sucs de tomates à l'huile d'olive. Rôti décortiqué aux pâtes fraîches parfumées à l'estragon. Petit macaron rosé au citron vert et framboise (May to October).

◆ Copperware, ceramics and Breton furnishings adorn one of the rooms of this astonishing 15C stone and wood mill; the veranda overlooks the garden and the Aven. "Surf and turf" menu.

Sur le Pont ...

11 pl. Paul-Gauguin – ✆ 02 98 06 16 16 – moulinderosmadec@wanadoo.fr – Closed Tuesday dinner in low season, Sunday dinner except July-August and Wednesday

Rest – Menu (€ 19), € 23 (weekday lunch)/29 – Carte € 42/53

◆ A rather hip restaurant providing enjoyable, informal cuisine in what was the location for the famous French film 'Galettes de Pont-Aven'.

Concarneau road West: 4 km by D 783 – ✉ 29930 Pont-Aven

La Taupinière (Guy Guilloux)

Croissant St André – ✆ 02 98 06 03 12 – www.la-taupiniere.com – lataupiniere@wanadoo.fr – Fax 02 98 06 16 46 – Closed 16-24 March, 20 September-14 October, Monday and Tuesday

Rest – Menu € 53/85 – Carte € 72/150

Spec. Crépinettes de tourteau et araignée de mer. Panaché de poissons du marché aux légumes de saison (spring-summer). Soufflé chocolat amer aux framboises (spring-summer).

◆ This cottage has an elegant dining room enlivened by the glow of the stoves. The cuisine is classical with fish specialities playing a major role. Tempting wine list.

PONTCHARTRAIN – 78 Yvelines – 311 H3 – ✉ 78760 18 A2

Paris 37 – Dreux 42 – Mantes-la-Jolie 32 – Montfort-l'Amaury 10 – Versailles 20

Isabella Plaisir Sainte Appoline, E : 3 km, ✆ 01 30 54 10 62

Domaine de Thoiry★★ Northwest: 12 km, **Northern France and the Paris Region**

L'Arpège

41 rte de Paris – ✆ 01 34 89 02 45 – www.arpege78.com – societearpege@aol.com – Fax 01 34 89 58 24 – Closed 2-31 August

11 rm – € 80/95 € 80/95, ☕ € 10 – ½ P € 125

Rest – *(closed Saturday lunch, Sunday and Monday)* Menu (€ 24), € 32 (weekday lunch), € 48/53 – Carte approx. € 51

◆ This former coaching inn offers either modern and practical or slightly countrified rooms. Cosy lounge and piano-bar with jazz at weekends. Pleasant dining room, low-key atmosphere and cuisine with a contemporary touch.

XX **Bistro Gourmand** VISA AE

7 rte Pontel, (N 12) – ✆ 01 34 89 25 36 – bistro.gourmand@free.fr – Fax 08 72 64 48 31 – Closed 9-16 March, 27 July-17 August, Sunday dinner, Wednesday dinner and Monday

Rest – Menu € 38/48

◆ In a new decor of electric blue seating and red walls, seafood and seasonal dishes take pride of place on the menu.

in Ste-Apolline East: 3 km by N 12 and D 134 – ✉ **78370 Plaisir**

XXX **La Maison des Bois** P VISA AE

av. d'Armorique – ✆ 01 30 54 23 17 – www.lamaisondesbois.fr – maison.des.bois@wanadoo.fr – Fax 01 30 68 92 26 – Closed 4-25 August, Sunday dinner and Thursday

Rest – Menu € 36 (lunch) – Carte € 47/71

◆ Two refined dining rooms in a rustic-style residence: the largest room, less countrified in style, gives onto the garden. Traditional menu.

PONT-CROIX – 29 Finistère – **308** E6 – **pop. 1 699 – alt. 25 m** – ✉ 29790 Brittany 9 **A2**

Paris 602 – Rennes 251 – Quimper 40 – Brest 105 – Concarneau 64

Office de tourisme, rue Laënnec ✆ 02 98 70 40 38, Fax 02 98 70 40 38

L'Orée du Cap without rest

29 r. du Goyen – ✆ 02 98 70 47 10 – www.oreeducapsizun.com – jean-yves.merrien@wanadoo.fr

4 rm – †€ 45/49 ††€ 48/60

◆ A welcoming house with two distinct styles: one modern, the other rustic with Breton furnishings. Cosy, immaculately-kept rooms. Flower-decked garden.

PONT-DE-BRIQUES – 62 Pas-de-Calais – **301** C3 – see Boulogne-sur-Mer

---

PONT-DE-CHAZEY-VILLIEU – 01 Ain – **328** E5 – see Meximieux

PONT-DE-CHERUY – 38 Isère – **333** E3 – **pop. 4 591 – alt. 220 m** – ✉ 38230 44 **B1**

Paris 486 – Belley 57 – Bourgoin-Jallieu 22 – Grenoble 89 – Lyon 35 – Meximieux 22

Bergeron rest, P VISA

3 r. Giffard, near the church – ✆ 04 78 32 10 08 – www.hotelbergeron.com – hotel.bergeron@wanadoo.fr – Fax 04 78 32 11 70

17 rm – †€ 39 ††€ 45, € 6

Rest – *(closed Saturday and Sunday) (dinner only) (residents only)* Menu € 12

◆ A modest but well-kept hotel. The rustic-style rooms are more spacious in the main house and quieter overlooking the garden. Those in the wing are simpler. In the evening guests sit down in a countrified dining room to sample a set menu.

PONT-DE-DORE – 63 Puy-de-Dôme – **326** H7 – see Thiers

PONT-DE-FILLINGES – 74 Haute-Savoie – **328** L4 – see Bonne

PONT-DE-L'ARCHE – 27 Eure – **304** G6 – **pop. 3 898 – alt. 20 m** – ✉ 27340 Normandy 33 **D2**

Paris 114 – Les Andelys 30 – Elbeuf 15 – Évreux 36 – Louviers 12 – Rouen 19

De la Tour without rest P VISA AE

41 quai Foch – ✆ 02 35 23 00 99 – www.hoteldelatour.org – hotel-de-la-tour@wanadoo.fr – Fax 02 35 23 46 22 – Closed 8-15 August

18 rm – †€ 82 ††€ 82, € 9

◆ Two spruce semi-detached houses backed up against the ramparts. Well-kept individually decorated rooms with bright colours and period furniture. Family ambience.

XX **La Pomme**
Les Damps 1.5 km on the bank of the river Eure – ✆ 02 35 23 00 46 – www.laubergedelapomme.com – william.boquelet@orange.fr – Fax 02 35 23 52 09
Rest – Menu € 30 (weekday lunch), € 42/65 – Carte approx. € 73
◆ This restaurant is a handsome Normandy half-timbered abode on the banks of the Eure. It serves up-to-date cuisine in a cosy, discreetly countrified look.

PONT-DE-L'ISÈRE – 26 Drôme – 332 C3 – see Valence

LE PONT-DE-PACÉ – 35 Ille-et-Vilaine – 309 L6 – see Rennes

PONT-DE-POITTE – 39 Jura – 321 E7 – pop. 619 – alt. 450 m 16 **B3**
– ✉ 39130 Burgundy-Jura

Paris 423 – Champagnole 34 – Genève 92 – Lons-le-Saunier 17

X **Ain** with rm VISA AE
18 pl. Fontaine – ✆ 03 84 48 30 16 – www.hoteldelain.fr – hoteldelain@wanadoo.fr – Fax 03 84 48 36 95 – Closed 24 December-2 February, Sunday dinner and Friday
9 rm – †€ 38 ††€ 42/45, ☕ € 8 – ½ P € 48
Rest – Menu (€ 13), € 18/40 – Carte € 35/45
◆ Stone house surrounded by greenery on the banks of the Ain. Country chic dining room and summer terrace for wholesome regional cooking.

PONT-DE-ROIDE – 25 Doubs – 321 K2 – pop. 4 619 – alt. 351 m 17 **C2**
– ✉ 25150 Burgundy-Jura

Paris 478 – Belfort 36 – Besançon 77 – La Chaux-de-Fonds 55 – Porrentruy 29

X **La Tannerie** VISA AE
1 pl. Gén. de Gaulle – ✆ 03 81 92 48 21 – dominique.autran@wanadoo.fr – Fax 03 81 92 47 79 – Closed 25 June-5 July, 23 December-7 January, Sunday dinner, Thursday dinner and Wednesday
Rest – Menu € 11 (weekday lunch), € 18/24 – Carte € 22/49
◆ This family restaurant serves traditional dishes, trout from the fish tank and blackboard specials in a warm dining room or on a terrace overlooking the river.

PONT-DE-SALARS – 12 Aveyron – 338 I5 – pop. 1 525 – alt. 700 m 29 **D1**
– ✉ 12290

Paris 651 – Albi 86 – Millau 47 – Rodez 25 – St-Affrique 56 – Villefranche-de-Rouergue 71

Office de tourisme, place de la Mairie ✆ 05 65 46 89 90, Fax 05 65 46 81 16

Des Voyageurs rest, P VISA
1 av. Rodez – ✆ 05 65 46 82 08 – hotel-d-voyageurs.com – hotel-des-voyageurs@wanadoo.fr – Fax 05 65 46 89 99 – Open 2 March-23 October and closed Sunday dinner and Monday from October to June
27 rm – †€ 42/46 ††€ 42/58, ☕ € 9 – ½ P € 44/59
Rest – *(closed 24 October-14 November, 20 January-1st March, dinner from November to January, Sunday dinner and Monday from October to June)* Menu (€ 13), € 17 bi (weekday lunch), € 26/40 – Carte € 21/56
◆ Friendly welcome guaranteed at this hotel in the centre of the village. The light, spacious rooms to the front have been renovated; the others, 1970s in style, await their turn. Two dining rooms: one rustic and one modern in style, serving local dishes.

PONT-DES-SABLES – 47 Lot-et-Garonne – 336 C3 – see Marmande

PONT-DE-VAUX – 01 Ain – 328 C2 – pop. 2 043 – alt. 177 m 44 **B1**
– ✉ 01190

Paris 380 – Bourg-en-Bresse 40 – Lons-le-Saunier 69 – Mâcon 24

Office de tourisme, 2, rue Maréchal de Lattre de Tassigny ✆ 03 85 30 30 02, Fax 03 85 30 68 69

Le Raisin with rm
2 pl. M.-Poisat – 03 85 30 30 97 – www.leraisin.com – hotel.leraisin@wanadoo.fr – Fax 03 85 30 67 89 – Closed 5 January-5 February, Sunday dinner except July-August, Tuesday lunch and Monday
18 rm – €64 €64, €9 **Rest** – Menu €27/67 – Carte €47/65
◆ An establishment in the traditional Savoy Bresse style with an elegant, rustic dining room. Tasty regional cuisine. Spacious, quiet guestrooms at the rear.

Les Platanes with rm
at Quatre-Vents – 03 85 30 32 84 – www.hotelplatanes.com – hotel-des-platanes@wanadoo.fr – Fax 03 85 30 32 15 – Closed 20 February-20 March, Friday lunch and Thursday
8 rm – €57 €58/68, €9 – ½ P €52/56
Rest – Menu (€18), €26/65 – Carte €26/65
◆ Smart rustic dining room with fine terrace under plane trees, serving generous Bourg-en-Bresse cuisine. Modern guestrooms make this inn a pleasant place for a break.

in St-Bénigne **Northeast: 2 km on D 2 – pop. 1 108 – alt. 208 m – ✉ 01190**

St-Bénigne
– 03 85 30 96 48 – Fax 03 85 30 96 48 – Closed 2-10 November, 21 December-12 January, 8-24 February, Monday and dinner except Saturday
Rest – Menu €13 (weekday lunch), €21/36 – Carte €28/47
◆ The chef rustles up regional dishes and the house speciality is frogs' legs. Served either in a countrified, or another more stylish dining room.

PONT-D'HÉRAULT – **30 Gard** – **339** H5 – **see le Vigan**

PONT-D'OUILLY – **14 Calvados** – **303** J6 – **pop. 1 038** – **alt. 65 m** – ✉ **14690** **Normandy** 32 **B2**

Paris 230 – Briouze 24 – Caen 41 – Falaise 20 – Flers 21 – Villers-Bocage 37 – Vire 39

Syndicat d'initiative, boulevard de la Noë 02 31 69 29 86

Oëtre Rock ★★ South: 6,5 km.

Du Commerce
8 r. de la Vème République – 02 31 69 80 16 – www.relaisducommerce.com – relaisducommerce@wanadoo.fr – Fax 02 31 69 78 08 – Closed 2-12 October, 2-27 January, Sunday dinner and Monday
12 rm – €60/70 €60/70, €10 – ½ P €75
Rest – Menu €16 (weekday lunch), €25/53 – Carte €32/90
◆ This fully renovated hotel in a charming village of Swiss Normandy is enjoying a new lease of life. Spruce, well-kept rooms. Seafood and traditional dishes, such as calf's head, served in a classical interior or on the terrace.

PONT-DU-BOUCHET – **63 Puy-de-Dôme** – **326** D7 – ✉ **63770 Les Ancizes Comps** 5 **B2**

Paris 390 – Clermont-Ferrand 39 – Pontaumur 13 – Riom 36 – St-Gervais-d'Auvergne 18

Méandre de Queuille ★★ Northeast: 11,5 km then 15 mn, **Auvergne-Rhone Valley**

La Crémaillère
Pont du Bouchet – 04 73 86 80 07 – www.hotel-restaurant-cremaillere.com – la-cremaillere63@wanadoo.fr – Fax 04 73 86 93 17 – Closed 18 December-25 January, Friday evening, Sunday evening and Saturday in low season
16 rm – €44/48 €46/48, €8 – ½ P €44/49
Rest – Menu €15 (weekdays)/42 – Carte €22/47
◆ A breath of fresh air in this family-run lakeside inn. A pleasant welcome and highly attentive staff. Spotless rooms. Rustic style dining room and regional cooking.

PONT-DU-CASSE – **47 Lot-et-Garonne** – **336** G4 – **see Agen**

PONT-DU-CHAMBON – 19 Corrèze – 329 N4 – see Marcillac-la-Croisille

PONT-DU-CHÂTEAU – 63 Puy-de-Dôme – 326 G8 – pop. 8 874 – alt. 365 m – ✉ 63430 Auvergne
5 **B2**

Paris 418 – Billom 13 – Clermont-Ferrand 16 – Riom 21 – Thiers 37

Syndicat d'initiative, rond-point de Montboissier ✆ 04 73 83 37 42, Fax 04 73 83 37 42

L'Estredelle
rm, VISA MC

24 r. Pont – ✆ 04 73 83 28 18 – www.hotel-estredelle.com – estredelle@wanadoo.fr – Fax 04 73 83 55 23 – Closed 27 July-9 August, 21 December-4 January, Sunday dinner and public holidays dinner

44 rm – †€ 44 ††€ 47, ☕ € 7 – ½ P € 42

Rest – Menu (€ 13), € 19/31 – Carte € 23/41

◆ A new hotel in the former river craft district. Functional rooms split over three pavilions; eight of them (reservation required) overlook the Allier. The dining room and terrace command a fine view of an 18C bridge.

Auberge du Pont
VISA MC

70 av. Dr Besserve – ✆ 04 73 83 00 36 – www.auberge-du-pont.com – info@auberge-du-pont.com – Fax 04 73 83 36 71 – Closed 15 August-7 September, 1st-11 January, Sunday dinner, Tuesday dinner and Wednesday

Rest – Menu (€ 16), € 20 (weekday lunch), € 28/95 bi – Carte € 52/69

◆ A former canal boat post house (1809) on the banks of the Allier. Coloured brick walls, pale green wood panelling and varnished parquet decorate the dining room. Terrace facing the bridge.

Le Calliope
AC VISA MC

6 r. de la Poste – ✆ 04 73 83 50 03 – restaurant-calliope.com – lecalliope@orange.fr – Closed 4 August-1st September, 19 January-3 February, Sunday dinner, Monday and Wednesday

Rest – Menu (€ 17), € 27/46 – Carte approx. € 39

◆ A modern restaurant in the town centre with a distinctive and elegant façade. The menu here is a fusion of the traditional and contemporary.

PONT-DU-GARD – 30 Gard – 339 M5 – ✉ 30210 Vers Pont du Gard
23 **D2**

Provence

Paris 688 – Alès 48 – Arles 40 – Avignon 26 – Nîmes 25 – Orange 38 – Pont-St-Esprit 41

Roman aqueduct bridge★★★.

Colombier
VISA MC AE

24 av. du Pont du Gard, (right bank), 1 km east on the D 981 – ✆ 04 66 37 05 28 – hotelresto.colombier@free.fr – Fax 04 66 37 35 75

18 rm – †€ 42 ††€ 52, ☕ € 8 – ½ P € 47

Rest – Menu (€ 14), € 18/28 – Carte € 24/32

◆ Hundred-year-old house with attractive gallery-terrace where breakfast is served. The upstairs rooms have just been successfully renovated. Dining room with Provençal decor and traditional, no-frills food.

in Castillon-du-Gard **Northeast: 4 km by D 19 and D 228 – pop. 1 115 – alt. 90 m – ✉ 30210**

Le Vieux Castillon
AC VISA MC AE

r. Turion Sabatier – ✆ 04 66 37 61 61 – www.vieuxcastillon.com – vieuxcastillon@relaischateaux.com – Fax 04 66 37 28 17 – Closed 2 January-14 February

32 rm – †€ 195/385 ††€ 195/385, ☕ € 20 – 3 suites – ½ P € 182/304

Rest – *(closed Monday lunch and Tuesday lunch)* Menu (€ 53), € 80 (dinner), € 94/116 – Carte € 75/111 dinner only

Spec. Châtaigne en soupe crémeuse, sucettes de pigeonneau rôti (automne-hiver). Noisette de chevreuil flambé au cognac (autumn-winter). Sphère au chocolat, biscuit crémeux au marron, glace au rhum. **Wines** Châteauneuf-du-Pape, Coteaux du Languedoc.

◆ Tiered patios and terraces make this a charming hotel in the heart of a medieval hilltop village. Rooms with personal touches. Exposed beams and Provencal colours are the main decorative features of the restaurant where you can enjoy delicious, sun-gorged food.

XX **L'Amphitryon**

pl. 8 Mai 1945 – ✆ 04 66 37 05 04 – Closed Tuesday except July-August and Wednesday

Rest – Menu € 31 (weekday lunch), € 45/57 – Carte € 60/86

◆ A vaulted ceiling and rough stonework in these dining rooms in an old sheepfold. An attractive patio for summertime meals. Modernised regional cuisine and a friendly atmosphere.

in Collias **West: 7 km by D 981, D 112 and D 3 – pop. 829 – alt. 45 m – ✉ 30210**

Hostellerie Le Castellas rm, VISA AE

Grand'rue – ✆ 04 66 22 88 88 – www.lecastellas.fr – info@lecastellas.fr – Fax 04 66 22 84 28 – Closed 5 January-2 April

15 rm – € 60/130 € 90/210, € 17 – 2 suites – ½ P € 154/200

Rest – *(closed Saturday lunch and Wednesday except public holidays)* Menu (€ 20), € 30 (weekday lunch), € 58/105 – Carte € 85/150

Spec. Contraste de foie gras en trois versions. Bœuf race "Aubrac". Nage tremblotante de melon et pastèque à la verveine (summer). **Wines** Costières de Nîmes, Côtes du Rhône Villages.

◆ These Gard-style, dressed stone houses date from the 17C and surround a patio. Choose from the fine guestrooms in various sizes and styles. Friendly welcome. Vaulted dining rooms opening onto the garden. Perfectly accomplished modern cuisine based on classic dishes.

Le Gardon VISA

Campchestève – ✆ 04 66 22 80 54 – www.hotel-le-gardon.com – auberge-le-gardon@wanadoo.fr – Fax 04 66 22 88 98 – Open 27 February-4 November

14 rm – € 67/77 € 67/96, € 10 – ½ P € 62/68

Rest – *(closed at lunchtime from Monday to Friday)* Menu € 21/34 – Carte € 30/44

◆ This recent hotel lined by an olive grove provides a pleasant break amid sweet-scented gorse. Garden, pool and comfortable wrought iron furnished rooms. Market fresh southern French cooking served on the veranda or terrace. Everything is homemade!

in Vers-Pont-du-Gard **3.5 km north on the D 19 and D 112 – pop. 1 509 – alt. 40 m – ✉ 30210**

XX **Lisa M** with rm VISA

3 pl. de la Madone – ✆ 04 66 22 92 12 – www.lisam.fr – info@lisam.fr – Fax 04 66 22 92 12 – Closed 15 January-15 February, Wednesday and Sunday from 15 October to 15 February, Monday and Tuesday

4 rm – € 120 € 140

Rest – *(dinner only) (number of covers limited, pre-book)* Menu € 52/59

◆ This old house is a little jewel: romantic decor, ivory and pearl grey tones, pale floor tiles, vaulted ceilings, patio and small pool. Modern and creative single set menu. Personalised rooms.

PONT-EN-ROYANS – 38 Isère – 333 F7 – pop. 878 – alt. 197 m – ✉ 38680 French Alps

43 **E2**

Paris 604 – Grenoble 63 – Lyon 143 – Valence 45

Office de tourisme, Grande rue ✆ 04 76 36 09 10, Fax 04 76 36 09 24

Du Musée de l'Eau VISA

pl. Breuil – ✆ 04 76 36 15 53 – www.musee-eau.com – musee.eau@wanadoo.fr – Fax 04 76 36 97 32

31 rm – € 39 € 46/59, € 7 – ½ P € 46/51

Rest – Menu (€ 13), € 16 (weekday lunch), € 23/34 – Carte € 23/34

◆ Big renovated building overlooking the Bourne. Small rooms with modern-style furniture; some have a view of the mountain and perched village. Simple dining room extended by a terrace with sprays. Bottled water bar.

LE PONTET – 84 Vaucluse – 332 C10 – see Avignon

PONTGIBAUD – 63 Puy-de-Dôme – 326 E8 – pop. 768 – alt. 735 m – ✉ 63230 Auvergne 5 B2

Paris 432 – Aubusson 68 – Clermont-Ferrand 23 – Le Mont-Dore 37 – Riom 26 – Ussel 68

Office de tourisme, rue du Commerce ☎ 04 73 88 90 99, Fax 04 73 88 90 09

XX **Poste** with rm — AC rest, VISA MC

pl. de la République – ☎ 04 73 88 70 02 – h.delaposte@yahoo.fr – Fax 04 73 88 79 74 – Closed 2-28 January, 7-23 February, Sunday dinner and Monday from October to May

10 rm – †€ 41/49 ††€ 41/49, ☕ € 6 – ½ P € 45

Rest – Menu (€ 13 bi), € 20/35 – Carte € 30/48

◆ This regional-style house in the heart of a quiet country town is over a century old. Well polished parquet flooring, chandeliers, plush table settings and floral paintings.

in La Courteix East: 4 km on D 941B – ✉ 63230 St-Ours

XXX **L'Ours des Roches** — P VISA MC AE

– ☎ 04 73 88 92 80 – www.oursdesroches.com – oursdesroches@wanadoo.fr – Fax 04 73 88 75 07 – Closed 2-24 January, Tuesday October-March, Sunday dinner and Monday except public holidays

Rest – Menu (€ 20 bi), € 27/65 – Carte € 39/81

◆ A restaurant under the archways of an old sheepfold. Decor with an unusual blend of rustic and contemporary styles. Terrace.

PONTHIERRY – 77 Seine-et-Marne – 312 E4 – ✉ 77310 St Fargeau Ponthierry 19 C2

Paris 44 – Corbeil-Essonnes 12 – Étampes 35 – Fontainebleau 20 – Melun 12

XX **Auberge du Bas Pringy** — P VISA MC

at Pringy - D 607 – ☎ 01 60 65 57 75 – aubergedubaspringy@orange.fr – Fax 01 60 65 48 57 – Closed 28 April-6 May, 28 July-26 August, Sunday dinner, Tuesday and Wednesday

Rest – Menu € 25/38 – Carte € 55/77

◆ A pleasant country roadside inn; summer terrace with plants and flowers. Up-to-date cuisine, using truffles and mushrooms in season.

PONTIVY – 56 Morbihan – 308 N6 – pop. 13 508 – alt. 99 m – ✉ 56300 Brittany 10 C2

Paris 460 – Lorient 59 – Rennes 110 – St-Brieuc 58 – Vannes 53

Syndicat d'initiative, 61, rue du Général de Gaulle ☎ 02 97 25 04 10, Fax 02 97 25 63 69

de Rimaison Bieuzy, S : 15 km on D 768, ☎ 02 97 27 74 03

Old houses★.

Plan on following page

Rohan without rest — P VISA MC AE

90 r. Nationale – ☎ 02 97 25 02 01 – www.hotelpontivy.com – contact@hotelpontivy.com – Fax 02 97 25 02 85 Z u

16 rm – †€ 60/82 ††€ 74/100, ☕ € 12

◆ A fine, late-19C residence on the main street of an area built by Napoleon. Rooms tastefully renovated in various styles and based on a number of themes (Oriental, romantic, cinema, comic books etc). Courtyard planted with trees.

L'Europe without rest — P VISA MC AE

12 r. F. Mitterrand – ☎ 02 97 25 11 14 – www.hotellerieurope.com – hoteleuropepontivy@wanadoo.fr – Fax 02 97 25 48 04 – Closed 25-31 December Z t

18 rm – †€ 60/82 ††€ 75/140, ☕ € 10

◆ Large, pleasant house dating from the reign of Napoleon III. Breakfast is served in the impressive breakfast room, and in summer beneath a glass dome. The guestrooms to the rear are quieter.

PONTIVY

Anne-de-Bretagne (Pl.) . . . . . . Y 2
Caïnain (R.) . . . . Z 3
Couvent (Q. du) . . . . Y 4
Dr-Guépin (R. du) . . . . Y 5
Fil (R. du) . . . . Y 6
Friedland (R. de) . . . . Y 8
Gaulle (R. du Gén.-de) . . . . Y 9
Le Goff (R.) . . . . Z 16
Jean-Jaurès (R.) . . . . Z 10
Lamennais (R. J.-M. de) . . . . . Z 13
Lorois (R.) . . . . Y 17
Marengo (R.) . . . . Z 19
Martray (Pl. du) . . . . Y 20
Mitterrand (R. François) . . . . . Z 24
Nationale (R.) . . . . YZ
Niémen (Q.) . . . . Y 27
Plessis (Q. du) . . . . YZ 29
Pont (R. du) . . . . Y 28
Presbourg (Q.) . . . . Y 32
Récollets (Q. des) . . . . Y 33
Viollard (Bd) . . . . Z 38

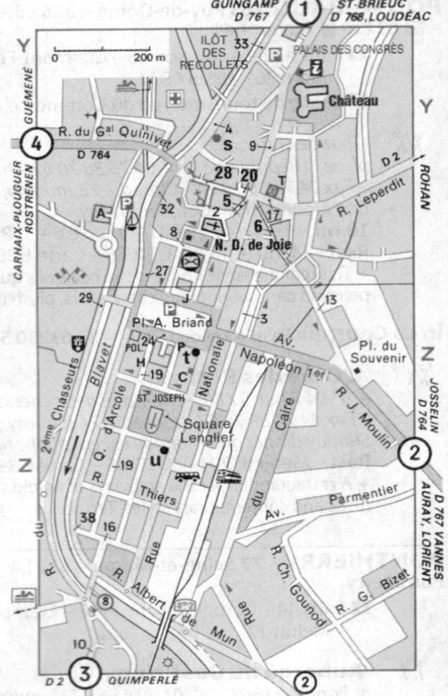

XX **Pommeraie** VISA MC AE

17 quai Couvent – ✆ 02 97 25 60 09
– restaurant.lapommeraie@wanadoo.fr – Fax 02 97 25 75 93
– Closed 12-19 April, 16-31 August, 26 December-4 January, Sunday and Monday Y s

Rest – Menu (€ 19), € 26/58 – Carte € 33/52

◆ A yellow façade and warm colours in the spruce dining room and flower-decked courtyard: this restaurant on the banks of the Blavet is an absolute symphony of colour. Modern dishes.

in Quelven by ③, D 2 and Guern road (D 2[B]): 10 km – ✉ **56310 Guern**

Auberge de Quelven P VISA MC

at la Chapelle – ✆ 02 97 27 77 50 – aubergedequelven@laposte.net
– Closed Wednesday

8 rm – †€ 50 ††€ 55, ☕ € 6 **Rest** – Carte € 7/17

◆ Long granite house facing a 15C chapel in a peaceful hamlet. Small, discreet and well-kept rooms. Cheerful reception. The menu of this rustic restaurant and crêperie focuses on Brittany galettes and crêpes.

PONT-L'ABBÉ – 29 Finistère – **308** F7 – **pop. 8 001** – **alt. 5 m** – ✉ **29120** **Brittany** 9 **A2**

Paris 573 – Douarnenez 33 – Quimper 20

Office de tourisme, square de l'Europe ✆ 02 98 82 37 99, Fax 02 98 66 10 82

Manoir de Kerazan★ 3 km by ② - Calvary★★ of N.-D.-de-Tronoën chapel West: 8 km.

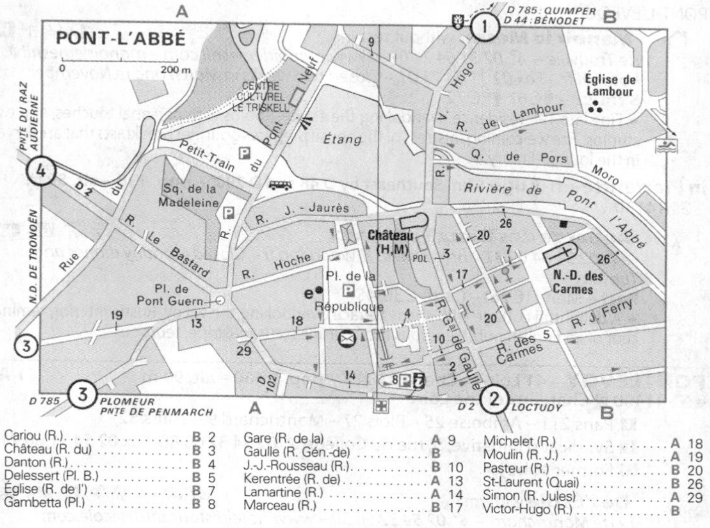

Cariou (R.) . . . . B 2
Château (R. du) . . . . B 3
Danton (R.) . . . . B 4
Delessert (Pl. B.) . . . . B 5
Église (R. de l') . . . . B 7
Gambetta (Pl.) . . . . B 8
Gare (R. de la) . . . . A 9
Gaulle (R. Gén.-de) . . . . B
J.-J.-Rousseau (R.) . . . . B 10
Kerentrée (R. de) . . . . A 13
Lamartine (R.) . . . . A 14
Marceau (R.) . . . . B 17
Michelet (R.) . . . . A 18
Moulin (R. J.) . . . . A 19
Pasteur (R.) . . . . B 20
St-Laurent (Quai) . . . . B 26
Simon (R. Jules) . . . . A 29
Victor-Hugo (R.) . . . . B

De Bretagne rm, VISA MC AE

24 pl. de la République – ✆ 02 98 87 17 22 – www.hoteldebretagne29.com – hoteldebretagne29@orange.fr – Fax 02 98 82 39 31 A **e**

18 rm – †€ 52/62 ††€ 57/67, ☕ € 8 – ½ P € 66/70

Rest – *(closed Monday lunch)* Menu (€ 13), € 16 (weekday lunch), € 25/50 – Carte € 26/54

◆ The small, unpretentious rooms of this family-run hotel in the town centre are simply furnished but well-kept, offering a calm and practical stopover. Seafood takes pride of place in a rustic-style dining room or on the terrace in an inner courtyard.

PONT-L'ÉVÊQUE – 14 Calvados – 303 N4 – pop. 4 163 – alt. 12 m – ✉ 14130 Normandy 32 **A3**

Paris 190 – Caen 49 – Le Havre 43 – Rouen 78 – Trouville-sur-Mer 12

Office de tourisme, 16, rue Saint-Michel ✆ 02 31 64 12 77, Fax 02 31 64 76 96

de Saint-Julien, SE : 3 km on D 579, ✆ 02 31 64 30 30

The belle époque of the motor-car★ South by D 48.

Le Lion d'Or without rest VISA MC AE

8 pl. Calvaire – ✆ 02 31 65 01 55 – www.leliondorhotel.com – info@leliondorhotel.com – Fax 02 31 64 90 10

25 rm – †€ 69/120 ††€ 69/160, ☕ € 10

◆ This former 17C post house has simple, mainly duplex rooms (wrought iron furniture). Breakfast served in the lounge bar, which is decorated with junk shop finds.

in St-Martin-aux-Chartrains 3 km by D 677, towards Deauville – pop. 351 – alt. 13 m – ✉ 14130

Mercure VISA MC AE

– ✆ 02 31 64 40 40 – www.hoteldeauville.fr – mercurepontleveque@wanadoo.fr – Fax 02 31 64 40 41

63 rm – †€ 69/122 ††€ 77/135, ☕ € 13

Rest – *(closed Saturday lunch and Sunday lunch except in July-August)* Menu € 21 – Carte € 25/38

◆ Modern hotel set in the peace of a park with a small lake: comfortable rooms (some of them larger) that are classically furnished and well kept. Several meeting rooms. Dining room with large bay windows. Brasserie-type food and terrace.

Manoir le Mesnil without rest

rte Trouville – ✆ 02 31 64 71 01 – www.manoirlemesnil.com – manoirlemesnil@hotmail.fr – Fax 02 31 64 71 01 – Closed two weeks in March and in November

5 rm – €67 €72

◆ Fine late 19C residence overlooking the estate. Rooms with personal touches, and two studios. The welcoming mistress of the house prepares gourmet breakfasts that are served in the lounge-library.

in Pierrefitte-en-Auge 5 km Southeast by D 48 and D 280^A – **pop. 136 – alt. 59 m** – ✉ 14130

Auberge des Deux Tonneaux

– ✆ 02 31 64 09 31 – brettetwells@wanadoo.fr – Closed Monday dinner and Tuesday

Rest – Menu (€26) – Carte €30/45

◆ A delightful cottage with shady terrace overlooking the valley. Rustic interior, reminiscent of an English pub. Generous local cuisine (sausage, tripe, teurgoule).

PONTLEVOY – 41 Loir-et-Cher – **318** E7 – **pop. 1 460 – alt. 99 m** 11 **A1**
– ✉ 41400 Châteaux of the Loire

Paris 211 – Amboise 25 – Blois 27 – Montrichard 9 – Tours 52

Syndicat d'initiative, 5, rue du Collège ✆ 02 54 32 60 80, Fax 02 54 71 60 71

Former abbey★.

De l'École with rm

12 rte Montrichard – ✆ 02 54 32 50 30 – www.hotelrestaurantdelecole.com – hoteldelecole@orange.fr – Fax 02 54 32 33 58 – Closed 16 November-15 December, 23 February-19 March, Sunday dinner and Monday

11 rm – €60 €62/77, €13 – ½ P €67

Rest – *(pre-book weekends)* Menu €24/56 – Carte €36/60

◆ Attractive Loire-region house with two rustic dining rooms, one with a fireplace. Flower garden for summer meals by a fountain. Dishes based on local produce. Old-fashioned rooms.

PONTOISE – 95 Val-d'Oise – **305** D6 – **106** 5 – **101** 3 – **see Paris, Area (Cergy-Pontoise)**

PONT-RÉAN – 35 Ille-et-Vilaine – **309** L6 – ✉ 35580 Guichen 10 **D2**

Paris 361 – Châteaubriant 57 – Fougères 67 – Nozay 60 – Rennes 16 – Vitré 56

Auberge de Réan

86 rte de Redon – ✆ 02 99 42 24 80 – www.auberge-de-rean.com – auberge.de.rean@wanadoo.fr – Fax 02 99 42 28 66 – Closed Sunday dinner and Monday

Rest – Menu (€15 bi), €29/55 – Carte €34/51

◆ Breton house on the banks of the Vilaine, facing an 18C stone bridge. Pleasant dining room with warm decor and terrace with riverside view.

PONT-ST-PIERRE – 27 Eure – **304** H5 – **pop. 1 063 – alt. 15 m** 33 **D2**
– ✉ 27360 Normandy

Paris 106 – Les Andelys 20 – Évreux 47 – Louviers 23 – Pont-de-l'Arche 12 – Rouen 22

Church★ panelling - Côte des Deux-Amants ≤★★ Southwest: 4.5 km then 15 mn - Ruins of Fontaine-Guérard abbey★ Northeast: 3 km.

Auberge de l'Andelle

– ✆ 02 32 49 70 18 – Fax 02 32 49 59 43 – Closed 22 December-6 January and Tuesday dinner

Rest – Menu €23/65 – Carte €43/73

◆ A rustic setting complete with stone fireplace and a multitude of nooks and crannies explain the appeal of this Normandy inn. Traditional menu.

PONT-STE-MARIE – 10 Aube – **313** E4 – **see Troyes**

PONT-SCORFF – 56 Morbihan – 308 K8 – pop. 3 012 – alt. 42 m 9 B2
– ✉ 56620 Brittany

Paris 503 – Lanester 13 – Lorient 13 – Rennes 152

Syndicat d'initiative, rue de Lorient ✆ 02 97 32 50 27, Fax 02 97 32 59 96

XX **Laurent Le Berrigaud** VISA AE
Le Moulin des Princes – ✆ 02 97 32 42 07 – laurent.le-berrigaud@wanadoo.fr – Fax 02 97 32 50 02 – Closed 27 October-3 November, 1st-12 January and Monday
Rest – Menu (€ 29 bi), € 39/57 – Carte € 60/80
◆ This riverside restaurant has a pretty decor combining old stonework, art and flower arrangements. Waterside terrace, tasty, inventive cuisine and a charming welcome.

LES PONTS-NEUFS – 22 Côtes-d'Armor – 309 G3 – ✉ 22400 10 C2
Morieux

Paris 441 – Dinan 51 – Dinard 52 – Lamballe 9 – St-Brieuc 15 – St-Malo 58

XX **La Cascade** VISA AE
4 r. des Ponts Neufs, on D 786 – ✆ 02 96 32 82 20 – restaurantlacascade.com – la.cascade.jamme@wanadoo.fr – Fax 02 96 32 70 74 – Closed Tuesday dinner, Wednesday dinner and Thursday dinner 16 September-14 June, Sunday dinner and Monday
Rest – Menu € 23 (weekday lunch), € 32/46 – Carte € 35/60
◆ The dining room of this restaurant enjoys views of a small lake. Rustic yet contemporary decor and tempting traditional cuisine.

PORNIC – 44 Loire-Atlantique – 316 D5 – pop. 13 500 – alt. 20 m 34 A2
– Casino : le Môle – ✉ 44210 Atlantic Coast

Paris 429 – Nantes 49 – La Roche-s-Yon 89 – Les Sables-d'Olonne 93 – St-Nazaire 30

Office de tourisme, place de la Gare ✆ 02 40 82 04 40, Fax 02 40 82 90 12

de Pornic Avenue Scalby Newby, W : 1 km, ✆ 02 40 82 06 69

Alliance rest, VISA AE
de la Source beach, 1 km south – ✆ 02 40 82 21 21 – www.thalassopornic.com – info.resa@thalassopornic.com – Fax 02 40 82 80 89 – Closed 1st-15 December
118 rm – †€ 120/240 ††€ 145/260, ☕ € 16 – 2 suites
Rest *La Source* – Menu (€ 23), € 32 – Carte € 43/54
Rest *La Terrasse* – *(booking advisable)* Menu (€ 23), € 32 – Carte € 48/54
◆ Modern hotel and thalassotherapy centre facing the sea. Large rooms (30 of which are brand new) with terraces and deck chairs. Contemporary, rotunda dining room (former casino) commanding a stunning sea view. Classic and diet cuisine. Exclusively fish and seafood menu served in a minimalist decor.

Auberge La Fontaine aux Bretons VISA
chemin des Noëlles, 3 km southeast by La Bernerie road – ✆ 02 51 74 07 07 – www.auberge-la-fontaine.com – auberge@auberge-la-fontaine.com – Fax 02 51 74 15 15 – Closed in January
11 rm – †€ 85/121 ††€ 85/121, ☕ € 12 – 12 suites – ††€ 103/143
Rest – *(closed Sunday dinner and Monday off season except holidays)* Menu (€ 20), € 29/48 – Carte € 29/50
◆ The fountain refreshed the Breton pilgrims of St Jacques. Today, this inn offers pleasant rooms with balconies, located in a former farmhouse (1867). Vineyard, kitchen garden and rustic-style restaurant. Traditional cuisine.

Beau Soleil without rest VISA
70 quai Leray – ✆ 02 40 82 34 58 – www.annedebretagne.com/beausoleil – beausoleil@annedebretagne.com – Fax 02 40 82 43 00
17 rm – †€ 55/113 ††€ 55/113, ☕ € 9
◆ A modern building opposite the harbour and castle. Rooms are not spacious but functional and well kept. Breakfast served on Pornic pottery tableware.

Les Alizés without rest
44 r. Général de Gaulle – ☎ 02 40 82 00 51 – www.hotel-alizes-pornic.com – alizes@brithotel.fr – Fax 02 40 82 87 32
29 rm – †€ 60/75 ††€ 60/75, ☕ € 8
◆ Recently constructed hotel with practical rooms, located in a busy street. Choose one of the rooms at the rear, which are quieter. Those next to the street have triple glazing.

Beau Rivage
Birochère beach, 2.5 km southeast – ☎ 02 40 82 03 08 – www.restaurant-beaurivage.com – info@restaurant-beaurivage.com – Fax 02 51 74 04 24 – Closed 15 December-31 January, Tuesday except July-August and Monday
Rest – Menu (€ 26), € 37/80 – Carte € 48/90
◆ Boat models, shellfish and other maritime artefacts adorn this restaurant overlooking the sea. Predominance of fish and seafood, accompanied by a fine selection of Muscadets. Gourmet food shop.

Le Bistrot
pl. Petit Nice – ☎ 02 40 82 51 25 – Fax 02 40 64 94 81 – Closed mid-November to mid-December, Wednesday dinner, Sunday dinner except public holidays and school holidays and Thursday
Rest – Menu (€ 14), € 19 (weekday lunch)/31
◆ Inside, there is contemporary, bistro-style decor with nautical touches; outside the terrace faces the castle. Menu offering seafood recipes and traditional dishes.

in Ste-Marie **West: 3 km – ✉ 44210 Pornic**

Les Sablons
13 r. Sablons – ☎ 02 40 82 09 14 – www.hotelesablons.com – contact@hotelesablons.com – Fax 02 40 82 04 26
28 rm – †€ 55/70 ††€ 55/90, ☕ € 9 – ½ P € 57/75
Rest – *(closed 15 December-15 January, Sunday dinner, Tuesday lunch and Monday except 1st June-15 September)* Menu (€ 15), € 20/41 – Carte € 31/51
◆ A 1970s hotel midway between the village and the beach. Simply decorated rooms (some with a sea view) in a family guesthouse spirit. Colourful and flower-filled dining room; in summer, tables are pleasantly placed in the garden.

PORNICHET – 44 Loire-Atlantique – 316 B4 – pop. 10 423 – alt. 12 m – Casino – ✉ 44380 Brittany
34 **A2**

Paris 444 – La Baule 6 – Nantes 70 – St-Nazaire 11
Office de tourisme, 3, boulevard de la République ☎ 02 40 61 33 33, Fax 02 40 11 60 88

Sud Bretagne
42 bd de la République – ☎ 02 40 11 65 00 – www.hotelsudbretagne.com – contact@hotelsudbretagne.com – Fax 02 40 61 73 70
25 rm – †€ 100/180 ††€ 120/200, ☕ € 14 – 4 suites
Rest – *(closed Sunday off season)* Menu € 48/75 – Carte € 50/70
◆ Hotel run by the same family since 1912. All rooms are attractively decorated along a theme, echoed by the fabrics, furniture and objects. Indoor Jacuzzi pool and massages on request. Stylish dining room, charming terrace, and seafood menu.

Villa Flornoy
7 av. Flornoy, near the Town Hall – ☎ 02 40 11 60 00 – www.villa-flornoy.com – hotflornoy@aol.com – Fax 02 40 61 86 47 – Closed December and January
30 rm – †€ 60/110 ††€ 60/110, ☕ € 9 – ½ P € 54/79
Rest – *(open 1st April-30 September) (dinner only)* Carte € 30/38
◆ In a residential district, this large villa is arranged like a cottage and has pastel colours, period furniture and English china. Pretty personalised rooms. Spacious, light dining room; set menu featuring traditional dishes.

Ibis rm, rest,
66 bd Océanides – ✆ 02 51 73 13 13 – www.hotelibis-labaule.com – h1171-gm@accor.com – Fax 02 40 61 74 74
88 rm – €64/121 €64/167, €10
Rest *Entre Terre et Mer* – Menu (€ 15 bi), € 20/24 – Carte € 22/33
◆ The rooms in this Ibis hotel are clean and simple. Direct access to the thalassotherapy centre next door. An ocean liner atmosphere created by nautical menus, wooden blinds and bay windows. Traditional menus and diet dishes.

Le Régent rest,
150 bd Océanides – ✆ 02 40 61 04 04 – www.le-regent.fr – hotel@le-regent.fr – Fax 02 40 61 06 06
23 rm – €77/170 €77/170, €11
Rest *Grain de Folie* – *(closed 1st-24 January, Sunday dinner except July-August)* Menu (€ 16), € 25/40 – Carte € 32/48
◆ Early 20C family home with the Atlantic on the horizon. Pleasant, well-kept rooms. A fashionably decorated trendy restaurant, whose predominantly black interior is enhanced by splashes of colour; metal veranda overlooking the sea. Up-to-the-minute menu.

PORQUEROLLES (ÎLE) – **83 Var** – **340** M7 – **see Île de Porquerolles**

PORT-CAMARGUE – **30 Gard** – **339** J7 – **see Grau-du-Roi**

PORT-CROS (ÎLE) – **83 Var** – **340** N7 – **see Île de Port-Cros**

PORT-DE-CARHAIX – **29 Finistère** – **308** J5 – **see Carhaix**

PORT-DE-GAGNAC – **46 Lot** – **337** H2 – **see Bretenoux**

PORT-DE-LA-MEULE – **85 Vendée** – **316** B7 – **see Île d'Yeu**

PORT-DE-LANNE – **40 Landes** – **335** D13 – **pop. 808** – **alt. 28 m** – ✉ **40300** 3 **B3**

Paris 747 – Bayonne 29 – Biarritz 37 – Dax 23 – Mont-de-Marsan 77 – Peyrehorade 7

La Vieille Auberge without rest
66 pl. de la Liberté – ✆ 05 58 89 16 29 – www.vieille-auberge.izispot.com – vieille.auberge@wanadoo.fr – Fax 05 58 89 12 89 – Open from beg. May to end September
8 rm – €49/69 €69/78, €8 – 2 suites
◆ This delightful rustic inn houses a small museum dedicated to local traditions. The guestrooms are housed in cottages around the flower garden (pool). Friendly welcome.

PORT-DE-SALLES – **86 Vienne** – **322** J7 – **see l'Isle-Jourdain**

PORT-DE-SECHEX – **74 Haute-Savoie** – **328** L2 – **see Thonon-les-Bains**

PORTEL-DES-CORBIÈRES – **11 Aude** – **344** I4 – **pop. 1 097** – **alt. 32 m** – ✉ **11490** 22 **B3**

Paris 810 – Perpignan 50 – Béziers 50 – Carcassonne 61 – Narbonne 18

Domaine de la Pierre Chaude without rest
Les Campets, on Durban road – ✆ 04 68 48 89 79 – www.lapierrechaude.com – lapierrechaude@yahoo.fr – Closed 4 January-28 February
5 rm – €85/95 €85/120
◆ Old 18C wine and spirit store surrounded by scrubland. Spacious southern-style rooms with wrought iron, mosaics, terra cotta and whitewashed walls. Flower decked terrace, home-made breakfasts.

XX **La Bergerie**

at Château de Lastours, 2 km south by secondary road – ✆ 04 68 48 64 77 – www.labergerie-corbieres.com – pgspringer@yahoo.fr – Closed 1st-20 January, Monday, Tuesday and Sunday dinner in low season

Rest – Menu € 24/32

◆ An old farm building on the wine estate of Château de Lastours, AOC Corbières. Wines from the estate and up-to-date food served in a handsome vaulted dining room.

PORT-EN-BESSIN – 14 Calvados – **303** H3 – **pop. 2 005 – alt. 10 m** – ✉ 14520 Port en Bessin Huppain ▮ Normandy — 32 **B2**

Paris 275 – Bayeux 10 – Caen 41 – Cherbourg 92 – St-Lô 43

Office de tourisme, quai Baron Gérard ✆ 02 31 22 45 80, Fax 02 31 51 28 29

La Chenevière

1.5 km south on D 6 – ✆ 02 31 51 25 25 – www.lacheneviere.com – reservation@lacheneviere.fr – Fax 02 31 51 25 20 – Closed February

26 rm – †€ 202/410 ††€ 202/410, ☕ € 21 – 3 suites

Rest – *(dinner only)* Menu € 50/90 – Carte € 78/137

◆ A stately 19C home and outbuildings set in lovely grounds. Tasteful guestrooms decked in pastel colours. Snug sitting rooms and exotically decorated cellar bar. The plush dining room has all the character you would except.

Mercure

chemin du Colombier, on the golf course, 2 km west by D 514 – ✆ 02 31 22 44 44 – www.mercure.com – h1215@accor.com – Fax 02 31 22 36 77 – Closed 17 December-15 January

70 rm – †€ 80/150 ††€ 90/185, ☕ € 14 – ½ P € 75/100

Rest – Menu (€ 22), € 27/75 – Carte € 31/51

◆ An ideally-situated hotel complex on the edge of a golf course. Peaceful nights in renovated, practical, modern rooms. A veranda-dining room serving traditional cuisine and a club house with a small brasserie-type menu.

X **L' Écailler**

2 r. Bayeux, (at the port) – ✆ 02 31 22 92 16 – lecailler@msn.com – Fax 02 31 22 90 38 – Closed 5 January-12 February, Monday and Tuesday

Rest – Menu (€ 19), € 23 (weekdays) – Carte € 40/80

◆ Attractive maritime decor, a terrace overlooking the harbour and a scaling bench at the entrance. The appetising menu focuses on fresh shellfish and seafood.

X **Fleur de Sel**

6 quai Félix Faure – ✆ 02 31 21 73 01 – Fax 02 31 21 73 01 – Closed 23 December-1st February, Tuesday from October to Easter and Wednesday

Rest – Menu € 17/35 – Carte € 23/48

◆ This harbour restaurant specialises in simple dishes based on seafood. Daily suggestions on a slate. Rustic decor downstairs and nautical upstairs (view of Vauban Tower).

PORT-GOULPHAR – 56 Morbihan – **308** L11 – **see Belle-Île-en-Mer**

PORT-GRIMAUD – 83 Var – **340** O6 – ✉ **83310 Cogolin** ▮ French Riviera — 41 **C3**

Paris 867 – Brignoles 63 – Fréjus 27 – Hyères 47 – St-Tropez 9 – Ste-Maxime 8 – Toulon 66

≤★ tower of the ecumenical church.

Giraglia

on the beach – ✆ 04 94 56 31 33 – www.hotelgiraglia.com – message@hotelgiraglia.com – Fax 04 94 56 33 77 – Open from mid-May to end September

49 rm – †€ 280/430 ††€ 280/430, ☕ € 21 – 10 suites

Rest – Menu € 56 (dinner) – Carte € 35/85

◆ Bright Provençal style rooms, either overlooking the gulf or marina, many with a balcony. During the summer use water transport to travel around the resort. The dining room and the flowered terraces command a panoramic view of the sea. Mediterranean inspired cuisine.

Suffren without rest
16 pl. du Marché – ✆ 04 94 55 15 05 – www.hotelleriedusoleil.com – lesuffren@hotelleriedusoleil.com – Fax 04 94 55 15 06 – Open 3 April-31 October
19 rm ☕ – 🚹€ 75/165 🚹🚹€ 75/255
◆ In the heart of the lakeside resort in a semi-pedestrian sector, this hotel pays tribute to Provence. The rooms have well-worn furniture and bright colours, some of which boast balconies.

PORTICCIO – 2A Corse-du-Sud – 345 B8 – see Corse

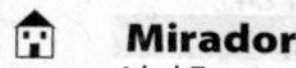

PORTIRAGNES – 34 Hérault – 339 F9 – pop. 3 094 – alt. 10 m – ✉ 34420 23 C2

Paris 762 – Montpellier 72 – Agde 13 – Béziers 13 – Narbonne 51
Office de tourisme, place du Bicentenaire ✆ 04 67 90 92 51, Fax 04 67 90 92 51

Mirador
4 bd Front-de-Mer, at Portiragnes-Plage – ✆ 04 67 90 91 33 – www.hotel-le-mirador.com – hotel_le_mirador@hotmail.com – Fax 04 67 90 88 80 – Open 1st February-31 October
16 rm – 🚹€ 49/113 🚹🚹€ 49/113, ☕ € 8 – ½ P € 53/85
Rest *Saveurs du Sud* – *✆ 04 67 90 97 67 (closed at lunchtime from Mon. to Thurs.)* Menu (€ 16), € 21/50 – Carte € 41/67
◆ Family-run hotel on the waterside offering functional, well-kept rooms. Choose those with terraces overlooking the waves. Traditional cuisine with southern touches served in a modern dining room-veranda.

PORTIVY – 56 Morbihan – 308 M9 – see Quiberon

PORT-JOINVILLE – 85 Vendée – 316 B7 – see Île d'Yeu

PORT-LA-NOUVELLE – 11 Aude – 344 J4 – pop. 5 610 – alt. 2 m – Casino – ✉ 11210 Languedoc-Roussillon-Tarn Gorges 22 B3

Paris 813 – Montpellier 120 – Carcassonne 81 – Perpignan 49 – Béziers 60
Syndicat d'initiative, place Paul Valéry ✆ 04 68 48 00 51, Fax 04 68 40 33 66

Méditerranée
bd Front-de-Mer – ✆ 04 68 48 03 08 – www.hotelmediterranee.com – hotel.mediterranee@wanadoo.fr – Fax 04 68 48 53 81 – Closed 4 January-4 February
30 rm – 🚹€ 62/88 🚹🚹€ 62/94, ☕ € 8 – ½ P € 60/76
Rest – *(closed 5-15 November, 4 January-4 February, Friday dinner and Sunday dinner from 9 November to 7 February)* Menu € 13/48 – Carte € 22/55
◆ Seaside construction on the promenade facing the beach. Well-proportioned and equipped rooms; ask for one with a balcony overlooking the sea to enjoy the view. Cuisine focused on seafood. Pavement terrace.

PORT-LESNEY – 39 Jura – 321 E4 – pop. 506 – alt. 251 m – ✉ 39600 Burgundy-Jura 16 B2

Paris 401 – Arbois 12 – Besançon 36 – Dole 39 – Lons-le-Saunier 51 – Salins-les-Bains 10

Château de Germigney
r. Edgar-Faure – ✆ 03 84 73 85 85 – www.chateaudegermigney.com – germigney@relaischateaux.com – Fax 03 84 73 88 88 – Closed 1st January-5 February
20 rm – 🚹€ 130 🚹🚹€ 200/350, ☕ € 15 – ½ P € 138/213
Rest – *(closed Monday lunch and Tuesday lunch)* Menu € 39 (lunch), € 60/99 – Carte € 70/99
Spec. Ravioli de foie gras poêlé. Volaille de Bresse cuite en terrine lutée, pomme de terre boulangère au vin jaune. Moelleux au chocolat et praliné croustillant.
Wines Arbois, Côtes du Jura.
◆ Manor house set in fine parkland with ecological swimming pool (naturally filtered lake water). Large personalised rooms and sophisticated lounge. Cuisine combining the best of Provence and the Jura served in a vaulted dining room, in the orangery or on the terrace.

Le Bistrot "Pontarlier"
pl. 8 Mai 1945 – ✆ 03 84 37 83 27 – www.chateaudegermigney.com – germigney@relaischateaux.com – Fax 03 84 73 88 88 – Closed 1st January-5 February, Monday to Thursday from October to April, Thursday and Wednesday except July-August
Rest – bistro – Menu € 22 – Carte € 28/37
◆ Bistro-style cuisine in this restaurant on the banks of the Loue. The dining room is decorated with various knick-knacks, including fishing rods. Pleasant terrace shaded by a tulip tree.

PORT-LEUCATE – **11 Aude** – **344** J5 – **see Leucate**

PORT-LOUIS – **56 Morbihan** – **pop. 2 927** – **alt. 5 m** – ✉ **56290** 9 **B2**

Paris 505 – Vannes 50 – Lorient 19 – Pontivy 61 – Quimper 84

Office de tourisme, 1, rue de la Citadelle ✆ 02 97 82 52 93, Fax 02 97 82 14 75

Avel Vor (Patrice Gahinet)
25 r. Locmalo – ✆ 02 97 82 47 59 – Fax 02 97 82 47 59 – Closed 30 June-8 July, 29 September-15 October, 25 January-11 February, Sunday dinner, Monday and Tuesday
Rest – Menu € 29 (weekdays)/88 – Carte € 74/106
Spec. Saint-Jacques saisies, foie gras de canard poêlé (October to February). Homard bleu cuit dans sa carapace (June to September). Pomme rôtie à la cannelle, crème mascarpone, glace vanille (October to May).
◆ A sea breeze (avel vor in Breton) blows in this restaurant near the port. It offers freshly caught fish, a contemporary decor with nautical touches, and a view of the sea.

PORT-MANECH – **29 Finistère** – **308** I8 – ✉ **29920 Nevez** **Brittany** 9 **B2**

Paris 545 – Carhaix-Plouguer 73 – Concarneau 18 – Quimper 44 – Quimperlé 29

Du Port
30 r. Aven – ✆ 02 98 06 82 17 – www.hotelduport.com – hotel.du.port@wanadoo.fr – Fax 02 98 06 62 70 – Open 1st April-30 September and 23 October-1st November
31 rm – € 42/60 € 45/68, € 8 – ½ P € 49/60
Rest – *(closed for lunch in low season, Saturday lunch and Wednesday in July-August)* Menu € 20/50 – Carte € 27/80
◆ At the confluence of the Aven and Belon estuaries. The larger of the pleasant and simply furnished rooms are to be found in the annexe. Good home cooking served in a dining room veranda or terrace facing the small port. Shellfish in season.

PORT-MORT – **27 Eure** – **304** I6 – **pop. 1 008** – **alt. 19 m** – ✉ **27940** 33 **D2**

Paris 89 – Les Andelys 11 – Évreux 33 – Rouen 55 – Vernon-sur-Eure 12

Auberge des Pêcheurs
– ✆ 02 32 52 60 43 – www.auberge-des-pecheurs.com – auberge-des-pecheurs@wanadoo.fr – Fax 02 32 52 07 62 – Closed 3-23 August, January, Sunday dinner, Monday dinner and Tuesday
Rest – Menu (€ 17), € 22 (weekdays)/31
◆ The Seine meanders near this inn, home to a spacious, rustic dining room with a veranda facing the garden. Traditional repertory.

PORT -NAVALO – **56 Morbihan** – **308** N9 – **see Arzon**

PORTO – **2A Corse-du-Sud** – **345** B6 – **see Corse**

PORTO-POLLO – **2A Corse-du-Sud** – **345** B9 – **see Corse**

PORTO-VECCHIO – **2A Corse-du-Sud** – **345** E10 – **see Corse**

PORTSALL – 29 Finistère – **308** C3 – ✉ **29830** Brittany 9 **A1**

Paris 616 – Rennes 263 – Quimper 98 – Brest 29 – Landerneau 46

La Demeure Océane without rest VISA
20 r. Bar Al Lan – ☎ 02 98 48 77 42 – www.demeure-oceane.fr – la-demeure-oceane@wanadoo.fr – Fax 02 98 48 04 15 – Open 16 February-14 October
7 rm – €55/65 €60/70
◆ An early-20C house located in a quiet district above the port. Attractive lounge-veranda overlooking the garden; bedrooms with sea views; and an English-style dining room.

PORT-SUR-SAÔNE – 70 Haute-Saône – **314** E6 – **pop. 2 773** – **alt. 228 m** – ✉ **70170** 16 **B1**

Paris 347 – Besançon 61 – Bourbonne-les-Bains 46 – Épinal 75 – Gray 51 – Vesoul 13

Office de tourisme, rue de la Rézelle ☎ 03 84 78 10 66, Fax 03 84 78 18 09

in Vauchoux South: 3 km by D 6 – **pop. 124** – **alt. 210 m** – ✉ **70170**

Château de Vauchoux (Jean-Michel Turin) VISA
Vallée de la Saône road – ☎ 03 84 91 53 55 – Fax 03 84 91 65 38 – Closed 23-28 February, Monday and Tuesday
Rest – *(pre-book)* Menu €75/125
Spec. Foie gras d'oie au pain d'épice. Pigeonneau rôti au gingembre "Edwige Feuillère". Plaisir des Gâtines. **Wines** Charcenne.
◆ This former hunting lodge has no lack of charm. From the flower-decked grounds, striking Louis XV dining room to the generous classical cuisine and fine wine cellar, very well stocked with Bordeaux.

PORT-VENDRES – 66 Pyrénées-Orientales – **344** J7 – **pop. 4 579** – **alt. 3 m** – ✉ **66660** Languedoc-Roussillon-Tarn Gorges 22 **B3**

Paris 881 – Perpignan 32

Office de tourisme, 1, quai François Joly ☎ 04 68 82 07 54, Fax 04 68 82 62 95

Tour Madeloc ✻★★ Southwest: 8 km then 15 mn.

Les Jardins du Cèdre rm, rm, VISA
29 rte Banyuls – ☎ 04 68 82 01 05 – www.lesjardinsducedre.com – contact@lesjardinsducedre.com – Fax 04 68 82 22 13 – Closed 15 November-20 December and 7 January-1st February
19 rm – €59/110 €59/110, €9 – 1 suite – ½ P €65/95
Rest – *(Closed Monday lunch, Wednesday lunch and Tuesday)* Menu (€18), €35/46 – Carte €46/60
◆ The garden of this hotel is very attractive: view of the harbour and sea, palm trees, old cedar of Lebanon and pretty pool. Modern rooms with pleasant colour schemes. Stylish restaurant and charming terrace. À la carte and set menus of modern dishes.

Côte Vermeille VISA
quai Fanal, direction la criée – ☎ 04 68 82 05 71 – Fax 04 68 82 05 71 – Closed 1st-7 July, 5 January-2 February, Sunday and Monday except July-August
Rest – Menu €29 bi (weekday lunch), €36/58 – Carte €55/65
◆ Restaurant in the fishing harbour: the chef is only a few feet away from the best of the days catch. Mediterranean flavours. His brother runs the dining room.

LA POTERIE – 22 Côtes-d'Armor – **309** H4 – **see Lamballe**

POUANÇAY – 86 Vienne – **322** F2 – **pop. 243** – **alt. 73 m** 39 **C1**

Paris 348 – Poitiers 75 – Saumur 29 – Bressuire 56 – Thouars 26

Trésor Belge
1 allée du Jardin Secret – ☎ 05 49 98 72 25 – www.tresorbelge.com – info@tresorbelge.com – Closed 1st-7 July, 1st-7 September, January, Monday and Tuesday
Rest – *(number of covers limited, pre-book)* Menu (€25 bi), €30/59 – Carte €38/48
◆ An outpost of Flemish cuisine serving delicious Belgian specialities to be washed down with traditional Belgian beer (choice of 40!). Friendly relaxed atmosphere.

POUGUES-LES-EAUX – 58 Nièvre – 319 B9 – pop. 2 509 – alt. 198 m – Casino – ✉ 58320 Burgundy-Jura 7 A2

Paris 225 – Auxerre 123 – Bourges 65 – Nevers 12

Syndicat d'initiative, 42, avenue de Paris ✆ 03 86 58 75 69, Fax 03 86 90 96 05

Hôtel des Sources without rest

r. Mignarderie – ✆ 03 86 90 11 90 – www.hoteldessources.fr – contact@hoteldessources.fr – Fax 03 86 90 11 91

29 rm – €60 €60, €11

◆ Quiet hotel in a residential district a stone's throw from the casino. Spacious and well-equipped rooms. Friendly service provided.

POUILLON – 40 Landes – 335 F13 – pop. 2 746 – alt. 28 m – ✉ 40350 3 B3

Paris 742 – Dax 16 – Mont-de-Marsan 69 – Orthez 28 – Peyrehorade 15

Syndicat d'initiative, chemin de Lahitte ✆ 05 58 98 38 93, Fax 05 58 98 30 67

L'Auberge du Pas de Vent

281 av. du pas de Vent – ✆ 05 58 98 34 65 – www.auberge-dupasdevent.com – sophiedubern@cegetel.net – Fax 05 58 98 34 65 – Closed 26 October-13 November, 22 February-8 March, Sunday dinner, Monday dinner, Tuesday dinner and Wednesday

Rest – Menu € 12 (weekday lunch), € 23/40 – Carte € 35/55

◆ The chef of this pleasant country inn uses age-old recipes for the regional dishes. Adjacent ninepins play area.

POUILLY-EN-AUXOIS – 21 Côte-d'Or – 320 H6 – pop. 1 438 – alt. 390 m – ✉ 21320 Burgundy-Jura 8 C2

Paris 270 – Avallon 66 – Beaune 42 – Dijon 44 – Montbard 59

Office de tourisme, le Colombier ✆ 03 80 90 74 24, Fax 03 80 90 74 24

du Château de Chailly Chailly s/Armançon, W : 6 km on D 977, ✆ 03 80 90 30 40

Poste with rm

pl. de la Libération – ✆ 03 80 90 86 44 – www.hoteldelapostepouilly.fr – hoteldelapostepouilly@orange.fr – Fax 03 80 90 75 99 – Closed 10-30 November, Sunday dinner and Monday

6 rm – €49/61 €49/61, €7

Rest – Menu (€ 13 bi), € 18/43 – Carte € 24/43

◆ A stone inn set by the main square of this small Burgundy town. The veranda-dining room sports a classical country style. Traditional, regionally influenced cuisine. Spacious unassuming guestrooms.

in Chailly-sur-Armançon 6.5 km west by D 977bis – pop. 270 – alt. 387 m – ✉ 21320

Château de Chailly rm, rm,

– ✆ 03 80 90 30 30 – www.chailly.com – reservation@chailly.com – Fax 03 80 90 30 00 – Closed 13 December-22 January and 7-20 February

37 rm – €215/295 €260/340, € 20 – 8 suites

Rest *L'Armançon* – *(closed Sunday and Monday) (dinner only)* Menu € 60/100

Rest *Le Rubillon* – *(closed dinner except Sunday and Monday)* Menu (€ 33), € 42 – Carte € 44/55

◆ One façade of the château has rich Renaissance decoration, the other is a reminder that this was once a medieval fortress. Extensive grounds and superb golf course. L'Armançon offers both a classic menu and decor. The Rubillon offers a terrace facing the pool, serving buffets and traditional dishes.

POUILLY-LE-FORT – 77 Seine-et-Marne – 312 E4 – see Paris, Area (Sénart)

POUILLY-SOUS-CHARLIEU – 42 Loire – 327 D3 – pop. 2 674 – alt. 264 m – ✉ 42720 44 A1

▶ Paris 393 – Charlieu 5 – Digoin 43 – Roanne 15 – Vichy 75

XXX **Loire**
r. de la Berge – ✆ 04 77 60 81 36 – www.restauloire.fr – restoloire@yahoo.fr – Fax 04 77 60 76 06 – Closed 21 September-10 October, 4-28 January, Sunday dinner, Tuesday except dinner in July-August and Monday
Rest – Menu € 22 (weekdays)/70 – Carte € 30/70
◆ This inn which formerly served simple meals has become an elegant restaurant with a terrace overlooking the garden. Traditional meals served.

POUILLY-SUR-LOIRE – 58 Nièvre – 319 A8 – pop. 1 746 – alt. 168 m – ✉ 58150 Burgundy-Jura 7 A2

▶ Paris 200 – Bourges 58 – Clamecy 54 – Cosne-sur-Loire 18 – Nevers 38 – Vierzon 80

ℹ Syndicat d'initiative, 17, quai Jules Pabiot ✆ 03 86 39 54 54, Fax 03 86 39 54 55

Relais de Pouilly rm, rm, VISA
rte de Mesves-sur-Loire, 3 km south on D 28A – ✆ 03 86 39 03 00 – www.relaisdepouilly.com – info@relaisdepouilly.com – Fax 03 86 39 07 47
24 rm – †€ 55/68 ††€ 72/78, ☕ € 10 – ½ P € 72/76
Rest – Menu (€ 14), € 19/36 – Carte € 25/40
◆ A hotel poised between the wine producing town and a motorway service area (pedestrian access). Rooms are modern, soundproofed and overlook the Loire. Restaurant looking out over the garden, regional menu, buffets, grilled food and a selection of Pouilly wines.

POUJOLS – 34 Hérault – 339 E6 – see Lodève

POULDREUZIC – 29 Finistère – 308 E7 – pop. 1 814 – alt. 51 m – ✉ 29710 9 A2

▶ Paris 587 – Audierne 17 – Douarnenez 17 – Pont-l'Abbé 15 – Quimper 25
ℹ Syndicat d'initiative, rue de la Mer ✆ 02 98 54 49 90

in Penhors west: 4 km by D 40 – ✉ 29710 Pouldreuzic

Breiz Armor VISA
at the beach – ✆ 02 98 51 52 53 – www.breiz-armor.fr – breiz-armor@wanadoo.fr – Fax 02 98 51 52 30 – Open 4 April-15 October and 26-31 December
36 rm – †€ 70/82 ††€ 70/82, ☕ € 9 – ½ P € 71/80
Rest – *(closed Monday except dinner July-August)* Menu € 16 (weekday lunch), € 21/79 – Carte € 22/55
◆ A modern, seafront building with well-kept rooms. The delightful museum (shells, birds), billiards table, sundeck, fitness facilities, sauna, bicycles, and laundry are a few of the establishment's attractions. Regional and seafood recipes are served in this restaurant with a breathtaking sea view.

LE POULDU – 29 Finistère – 308 J8 – ✉ 29360 Clohars Carnoet Brittany 9 B2

▶ Paris 521 – Concarneau 37 – Lorient 25 – Moëlan-sur-Mer 10 – Quimper 61 – Quimperlé 14

St-Maurice: site★ and ≤★ of bridge Northeast: 7 km.

Le Panoramique without rest VISA
at Kérou beach – ✆ 02 98 39 93 49 – www.hotel-panoramique.fr – poulduramique@orange.fr – Fax 02 98 96 90 16 – Open 3 April-5 November
25 rm – †€ 47/63 ††€ 47/63, ☕ € 9
◆ Clean, functional guestrooms in this hotel where breakfast is served in a bright sea-facing dining room. Reading/sitting rooms with bar and TV.

POURVILLE-SUR-MER – 76 Seine-Maritime – 304 G2 – see Dieppe

POUZAY – 37 Indre-et-Loire – **317** M6 – **see Ste-Maure-de-Touraine**

LE POUZIN – 07 Ardèche – **331** K5 – **pop. 2 668 – alt. 90 m** – ✉ **07250** 44 **B3**

Paris 590 – Lyon 127 – Privas 16 – Valence 28 – Romans-sur-Isère 48

La Cardinale

– *04 75 41 20 39 – www.lacardinale.net – lacardinale@orange.fr – Fax 04 75 43 45 66 – Closed 23 October-9 November and 21 December-7 January*

10 rm – €90/195 €105/245, €15

Rest – *(closed Monday, Tuesday and Wednesday from October to June) (dinner only) (pre-book)* Carte €49/60

◆ This stone house and pool are surrounded by a park planted with rare tree species. The ground floor rooms (superb bathrooms) open onto a terrace. Traditional cuisine served in a cosy, fashionable setting.

PRADES – 66 Pyrénées-Orientales – **344** F7 – **pop. 6 221** 22 **B3**
– alt. 360 m – ✉ **66500** Languedoc-Roussillon-Tarn Gorges

Paris 892 – Mont-Louis 36 – Olette 16 – Perpignan 46 – Vernet-les-Bains 11

Office de tourisme, 4, rue des Marchands 04 68 05 41 02, Fax 04 68 05 21 79

de Marcevol Arboussols Le Hameau de Marcevol, Northeast: 10 km by D 35, 04 68 96 18 08

St-Michel-de-Cuxa abbey ★★ South: 3 km - Village of Eus★ Northeast: 7 km.

Pradotel without rest

av. Festival, On the beltway – 04 68 05 22 66 – pradotel66@orange.fr – Fax 04 68 05 23 22

39 rm – €50/62 €54/72, €8,50

◆ A contemporary functional building. To the rear, a fine view of the Canigou from the balconies. Terraces for the poolside ground floor rooms are a new feature.

Hexagone rm,

rd-pt de Molitg, on the bypass – 04 68 05 31 31 – www.hotelhexagone.fr – hotelhexagone@cegetel.net – Fax 04 68 05 24 89

30 rm – €50/62 €56/68, €8

Rest – *(closed Saturday and Sunday) (dinner only) (residents only)* Menu €17

◆ Identical, simple and well-kept rooms: a practical address in this town renowned for its music festival.

in Clara South 5 km by D 35 – ✉ **66500**

Les Loges du Jardin d'Aymeric

7 rue du Canigou – 04 68 96 08 72 – www.logesaymeric.com – jardin.aymeric@wanadoo.fr – Fax 04 68 96 08 72 – Closed January

3 rm – €55/75 €65/85

Table d'hôte – *(closed Tuesday dinner and Wednesday from October to May)* Menu €30

◆ Tucked away in a pleasant village at the foot of the Canigou, this establishment has spacious rooms which are sober yet bright. Good pool in the flowered garden. Regional family fare in a charming rustic setting typical of the region.

LE PRADET – 83 Var – **340** L7 – **pop. 10 100 – alt. 1 m** – ✉ **83220** 41 **C3**
French Riviera

Paris 842 – Draguignan 76 – Hyères 11 – Toulon 10

Office de tourisme, place Général-de-Gaulle 04 94 21 71 69, Fax 04 94 08 56 96

Musée de la mine de Cap Garonne: large room★, 3 km South by D 86.

in Oursinières South: 3 km by D 86 – ✉ **83320 Le Pradet**

L'Escapade without rest

Port des Oursières 1 r. de la Tartane – 04 94 08 39 39 – www.hotel-escapade.com – info@hotel-escapade.com – Fax 04 94 08 52 60 – Open 6 March-3 November

9 rm – €125/215 €125/215, €13 – 1 suite

◆ Small houses 100 m from the sea in a beautiful garden. Rooms decorated in Tyrolean style. The pretty breakfast room looks out on to the swimming pool. Pleasant welcome.

XX **La Chanterelle**

50 r. de la Tartane – ✆ 04 94 08 52 60 – www.hotel-escapade.com – chanterelle@nerim.net – Closed 2 November-5 December, 4 January-5 March, Monday and Tuesday from September to April

Rest – Menu € 39 (weekdays)/49 – Carte € 50/59

◆ The dining room has a carved wood ceiling and coloured stained-glass windows representing still life subjects. Pleasant flower garden. Modern regional cuisine.

PRALOGNAN-LA-VANOISE – 73 Savoie – 333 N5 – pop. 756 – alt. 1 425 m – Winter sports : 1 410/2 360 m 1 13 – ✉ 73710 French Alps 45 D2

Paris 634 – Albertville 53 – Chambéry 103 – Moûtiers 28

Office de tourisme, avenue de Chasseforêt ✆ 04 79 08 79 08, Fax 04 79 08 76 74

Site★ - La Vanoise National Park ★★ - La Chollière★ Southwest: 1.5 km then 30 mn - Mont Bochor ≤★ by cable car.

Les Airelles rest, VISA AE

1 km north, Les Darbelays – ✆ 04 79 08 70 32 – www.hotel-les-airelles.fr – hotellesairelles@free.fr – Fax 04 79 08 73 51 – Open 6 June-18 September and 19 December-16 April

21 rm – †€ 50/70 ††€ 73/95, ☕ € 8 – ½ P € 52/74

Rest – Menu € 21/24 – Carte € 23/30

◆ An attractive 1980s chalet located on the edge of Granges Forest. Refurbished chalet-style rooms, whose balconies offer a fine mountain view. A warm, regional-style restaurant with cheese specialities (tartiflettes, fondues, gratins, etc.).

De la Vanoise rm, VISA AE

– ✆ 04 79 08 70 34 – www.hoteldelavanoise.fr – hotel@la-vanoise.com – Fax 04 79 08 75 79 – Open mid June-mid September and 20 December-20 April

32 rm – †€ 39/52 ††€ 78/104, ☕ € 9 – ½ P € 60/93

Rest – Menu (€ 15), € 18/35 – Carte € 20/40

◆ At the centre of the resort and near the ski lifts. All the simple wood-panelled rooms (a few duplexes) have a balcony. Sauna. Traditional, Savoyard or vegetarian dishes in an alpine decor of pale wood panelling and floral fabrics.

Du Grand Bec rest, VISA

– ✆ 04 79 08 71 10 – www.hoteldugrandbec.fr – grand_bec@wanadoo.fr – Fax 04 79 08 72 22 – Open 1st June-18 September and 19 December-13 April

39 rm – †€ 55/80 ††€ 60/120, ☕ € 10 – ½ P € 52/74

Rest – Menu € 20/40 – Carte € 22/48

◆ A regional-style hotel, dominated by the Grand Bec mountain, on the outskirts of the resort. Alpine-style rooms with a balcony (12 have a sitting room). Restaurant in warm colours, facing the village and peaks. Traditional menu with Savoy dishes.

PRA-LOUP – 04 Alpes-de-Haute-Provence – 334 H6 – see Barcelonnette

LE PRARION – 74 Haute-Savoie – 328 N5 – see les Houches

PRATS-DE-MOLLO-LA-PRESTE – 66 Pyrénées-Orientales – 344 F8 – pop. 1 141 – alt. 740 m – ✉ 66230 Languedoc-Roussillon-Tarn Gorges 22 B3

Paris 905 – Céret 32 – Perpignan 64

Office de tourisme, place du Foiral ✆ 04 68 39 70 83, Fax 04 68 39 74 51

High town★.

Bellevue rest, VISA AE

pl. du Foiral – ✆ 04 68 39 72 48 – www.hotel-le-bellevue.fr – info@hotel-le-bellevue.fr – Fax 04 68 39 78 04 – Closed 1st December-14 February, Tuesday and Wednesday except from 1st April to 6 November

17 rm – †€ 42/54 ††€ 50/70, ☕ € 8 – ½ P € 43/59

Rest – Menu € 22/50 – Carte € 35/55

◆ Situated on the market square, this regional-style hotel has simply furnished rooms, some of which have been refurbished. Views of the mountain and the ramparts of the medieval town. Menu offering appetising Catalan recipes in a dining room decorated in pastel shades.

in La Preste : 8 km – ✉ **66230 Prats-de-Mollo-la-Preste – Spa : beg. April-mid Nov.**

Ribes
rest, VISA

– *04 68 39 71 04 – www.hotel-ribes.com – info@hotel-ribes.com*
– Fax 04 68 39 78 02 – Open 12 April-20 October
16 rm – €46/49 €46/55, €8,50 – ½ P €40/46
Rest – Menu (€11), €17/29 – Carte €28/38
◆ This farmhouse surrounded by meadows is now a pleasant, family-run hotel. The modest, well-maintained rooms have been gradually renovated. The panoramic restaurant overlooking the valley serves traditional Catalan cuisine based on produce from the family farm.

Le Val du Tech
VISA

– *04 68 39 71 12 – www.hotel-levaldutech.com – val.du.tech@wanadoo.fr*
– Fax 04 68 39 78 07 – Open 25 April-24 October
25 rm – €34/37 €50/56, €7 – ½ P €48/51
Rest – Menu (€12), €16/26
◆ This small hotel situated on the hillside near the spa is popular with hikers and spa visitors alike. Very simple guestrooms, some of which have no shower or WC. Traditional cuisine served in a large dining room with a discreetly rustic, Catalan-style setting.

PRATZ – 39 Jura – 321 E8 – pop. 554 – alt. 682 m – ✉ 39170 — 16 B3

Paris 460 – Besançon 130 – Lons-le-Saunier 47 – Genève 113 – Bourg-en-Bresse 84

Les Louvières
VISA AE

– *03 84 42 09 24 – www.leslouvieres.com – info@leslouvieres.com*
– Fax 03 84 42 09 24 – Closed 21 December-31 January, Sunday dinner, Monday and Tuesday
Rest – Menu €28 (weekday lunch), €34/46
◆ Isolated farmhouse that has been beautifully renovated with a contemporary decor that does not detract from the warm mountain style. Modern cuisine, world wines. Pleasant welcome.

LE PRAZ – 73 Savoie – 333 M5 – see Courchevel

LES PRAZ-DE-CHAMONIX – 74 Haute-Savoie – 328 O5 – see Chamonix-Mont-Blanc

---

PRAZ-SUR-ARLY – 74 Haute-Savoie – 328 M5 – pop. 1 349 – alt. 1 036 m – Winter sports : 1 036/2 070 m 12 – ✉ 74120 — 46 F1

Paris 602 – Albertville 28 – Chambéry 79 – Chamonix-Mont-Blanc 37 – Megève 5

Office de tourisme, 04 50 21 90 57, Fax 04 50 21 98 08

La Griyotire
VISA

rte La Tonnaz – 04 50 21 86 36 – www.griyotire.com – hotel@griyotire.com
– Fax 04 50 21 86 34 – Open 13 June-12 September and 13 December-12 April
16 rm – €102/116 €102/116, €11 – ½ P €91/98
Rest – *(dinner only)* Menu €29/35 – Carte €30/46
◆ An elegant Savoy-style chalet, which is quiet despite its central location. Attractive, cosy bedrooms and a comfortable lounge with open fireplace. Hammam, sauna and massage available. Attractive mountain interior, classic and regional cuisine, cheese specialities.

PREIGNAC – 33 Gironde – 335 J7 – see Langon

The sun's out – let's eat alfresco!
Look for a terrace:

PRENOIS – 21 Côte-d'Or – **320** J5 – see Dijon

LE PRÉ-ST-GERVAIS – 93 Seine-Saint-Denis – **305** F7 – **101** 16 – see Paris, Area

LA PRESTE – 66 Pyrénées-Orientales – **344** F8 – see Prats-de-Mollo

PRINGY – 74 Haute-Savoie – **328** J5 – see Annecy

PRIVAS P – 07 Ardèche – **331** J5 – pop. 8 681 – alt. 300 m – ✉ 07000 44 **B3**
Lyon - Rhone Valley

Paris 596 – Montélimar 34 – Le Puy-en-Velay 91 – Valence 41
Office de tourisme, 3, place du Général-de-Gaulle ✆ 04 75 64 33 35, Fax 04 75 64 73 95
Site ★.

PRIVAS

Bacconnier (R. L.) . . . . . B 2
Boeufs (Pl. aux) . . . . . A 3
Champ de Mars (Pl. du) . . . . . B 5
Coux (Av. de) . . . . . B 7
Durand (R. H.) . . . . . B 10
Esplanade (Cours de l') . . . . . B 9
Faugier (Av. C.) . . . . . A 12
Filliat (R. P.) . . . . . B 14
Foiral (Pl. du) . . . . . A 16
Gaulle (Pl. Ch.-de) . . . . . B 17
Hôtel de Ville (Pl. de l') . . . . . B 18
Mobiles (Bd des) . . . . . B 20
Ouvèze (Chemin de la) . . . . . B 22
Petit Tournon (Av. du) . . . . . B 24
République (R. de la) . . . . . B 26
St-Louis (Cours) . . . . . A 28
Vanel (Av. du) . . . . . B 30

La Chaumette
av. Vanel – ✆ *04 75 64 30 66* – *www.hotelchaumette.fr* – *hotelchaumette@wanadoo.fr* – *Fax 04 75 64 88 25* – *Closed for the autumn school holidays and 2-15 January* B **e**
36 rm – †€ 63/87 ††€ 79/102, ☕ € 13 – ½ P € 72/81
Rest – *(closed Sunday except dinner from June to mid-October and Saturday lunch)* Menu (€ 23), € 35/58 – Carte € 49/63
◆ A welcoming hotel with a southern French feel opposite the Conseil Général building. Public areas decorated in ochre tones, with bedrooms that are being renovated in stages. Modern cuisine served in a contemporary, southern French-style dining room or on the terrace overlooking the swimming pool.

Les Châtaigniers

Plaine du Lac – ✆ 04 75 66 39 60 – www.leschataigners.fr – hotel.chataigniers@free.fr – Fax 04 75 64 68 76

82 rm – €46/51 €49/54, €8 – ½ P €48/53

Rest – Menu €18 (weekday lunch), €21/32 – Carte €26/41

◆ With its functional, air-conditioned rooms, this hotel is an ideal stopover on the way to the Coiron massif. Breakfast is served in the bar or on the terrace. A menu offering traditional recipes is offered in the light dining room.

in Rochessauve 11 km by ③, D 2 and D 999 – **pop. 378 – alt. 300 m** – ✉ **07210**

Château de Rochessauve

– ✆ 04 75 65 07 06 – www.chateau-de-rochessauve.com – vialley@wanadoo.fr – Closed 1st January to Easter

5 rm – €100 €110/120

Table d'hôte – *(closed Thursday)* Menu €20 bi/40 bi

◆ The Ardèche mountains form the backdrop to this very peaceful château, whose rooms have a refined atmosphere. Meals, prepared with local produce, are served in the dining room decorated with collector's items or on the patio in summer.

PROJAN – 32 Gers – **336** A8 – **pop. 146 – alt. 157 m** – ✉ **32400** 28 **A2**

Paris 742 – Pau 42 – Tarbes 60 – Toulouse 169

Le Château de Projan

– ✆ 05 62 09 46 21 – www.chateau-de-projan.com – infos@chateau-de-projan.com – Fax 05 62 09 44 08 – Closed autumn school holidays, 20-27 December, February and Sunday in low season

7 rm – €95/100 €110/160, €12 – ½ P €85/99

Rest – *(dinner only)* Menu €32/75

◆ A guesthouse atmosphere in this château nestling in a hilltop park. Fine antique furniture and modern paintings adorn the rooms and lounges. Bright dining room extended by a terrace, serving regional dishes. Cooking lessons available.

PROPRIANO – **2A Corse-du-Sud** – **345** C9 – **see Corse**

PROVINS – **77 Seine-et-Marne** – **312** I4 – **pop. 11 600 – alt. 91 m** – ✉ **77160** **Northern France and the Paris Region** 19 **D2**

Paris 88 – Châlons-en-Champagne 98 – Fontainebleau 55 – Sens 47

Office de tourisme, chemin de Villecran ✆ 01 64 60 26 26, Fax 01 64 60 11 97

High town★★ AV: ramparts★★ AY, Caesar tower ★★: ≤★, Grange aux Dîmes★ AV **E** - Place du Chatel★ - Central portal ★ and group of statues★★ in St-Ayoul church BV - Choir ★ of St-Quiriace collegiate church AV - Musée de Povins et du Provinois: collections of sculptures and pottery★ **M.**

St-Loup-de-Naud: portal★★ of church★ 7 km by ④.

Plan on next page

Aux Vieux Remparts

3 r. Couverte - ville haute – ✆ 01 64 08 94 00 – www.auxvieuxremparts.com – info@auxvieuxremparts.com – Fax 01 60 67 77 22 – Closed from end December to mid-January AV **b**

32 rm – €80/265 €95/275, €16

Rest – Menu €28 (weekdays)/90 – Carte €65/85

Rest *Le Petit Ecu* – Menu (€15), €19 (weekdays)/23 – Carte €25/33

◆ This hotel, located in the heart of the medieval town, offers guests modern rooms in varying sizes. Some benefit from a mezzanine. Classic cuisine in the dining rooms, one inspired by the Middle Ages; the other, rustic. Summer terrace. Traditional menu at the Petit Ecu.

PROVINS

Alips (R. Guy) . . . . **AX**
Anatole-France (Av.) . . . . **AV** 2
Arnoul (R. Victor) . . . . **BX** 3
Balzac (Pl. Honoré-de) . . . . . . **BVX** 4
Bellevue (Rampe de) . . . . **BX**
Bordes (R. des) . . . . **BX** 7
Bourquelot (R. Félix) . . . . **BV** 8
Bray (Rte de) . . . . **AX**
Briand (R. Aristide) . . . . **BX**
Canal (R. du) . . . . **AX**
Carnot (Bd) . . . . **BX**
Champbenoist (Rte de) . . . . . . **BX** 13
Changis (R. de) . . . . **BX** 14
Châtel (Pl. du) . . . . **AV** 18
Chomton (Bd Gilbert) . . . . **AX** 19
Collège (R. du) . . . . **ABV** 23
Cordonnerie (R. de la) . . . . **BV** 24
Courloison (R.) . . . . **BV** 27
Couverte (R.) . . . . **AV** 28
Delort (Rue du Gén.) . . . . **BVX** 29
Desmarets (R. Jean) . . . . **AV** 30
Dromigny (R. Georges) . . . . **AX**
Esternay (R. d') . . . . **BX**
Ferté (Av. de la) . . . . **BV** 33
Fourtier-Masson (R.) . . . . **BX** 35
Friperie (R. de la) . . . . **BV** 37
Garnier (R. Victor) . . . . **BX** 39
Gd-Quartier-Gén. (Bd du) . . . . **BX** 42
Hugues-le-Grand (R.) . . . . **BX** 43
Jacobins (R. des) . . . . **BV** 44
Jean-Jaurès (Av.) . . . . **BX**
Leclerc (Pl. du Mar.) . . . . **BV** 47
Malraux (Av. André) . . . . **AVY**
Michelin (R. Maximilien) . . . . . . **AX**
Nanteuil (Rte de) . . . . **BV**
Nocard (R. Edmond) . . . . **BVX** 54
Opoix (R. Christophe) . . . . **BV** 57
Palais (R. du) . . . . **AV** 59
Pasteur (Bd) . . . . **BV**
Plessier (Bd du Gén.) . . . . **BVX** 64
Pompidou (Av. G.) . . . . **BV** 67
Pont-Pigy (R. du) . . . . **BV** 68
Prés (R. des) . . . . **BV** 69
Rebais (R.) . . . . **BV**
Remparts (Allée des) . . . . **AV** 72
Ste-Croix (R.) . . . . **BV**
St-Ayoul (Pl.) . . . . **BV** 73
St-Jean (R.) . . . . **AV** 74
St-Quiriace (Pl.) . . . . **AV** 77
St-Syllas (Rampe) . . . . **BV**
Souvenir (Av. du) . . . . **BV** 78
Val (R. du) . . . . **BV** 79
Verdun (Av. de) . . . . **BV** 82
Voulzie (Av. de la) . . . . **BX** 85
29e-Dragons (Pl. du) . . . . **BV** 84

PRUNETE – 2B Haute-Corse – **345** F6 – see Corse (Cervione)

PUGIEU – 01 Ain – **328** G6 – see Belley

PUJAUDRAN – 32 Gers – **336** I8 – see l'Isle-Jourdain

PUJAUT – 30 Gard – **339** N4 – **pop. 3 723** – **alt. 70 m** – ✉ **30131** 23 **D2**

Paris 683 – Montpellier 98 – Nîmes 52 – Avignon 14 – Arles 79

XX **Entre Vigne et Garrigue** (Serge Chenet) with rm rest, P VISA MC AE
7 chemin des Falaises, 2 km southwest – ✆ 04 90 95 20 29 – www.vigne-et-garrigue.com – contact@vigne-et-garrigue.com – Fax 04 90 95 20 29 – Closed January, Sunday dinner and Monday
4 rm – €85/135 €85/135
Rest – *(number of covers limited, pre-book)* Menu (€ 26), € 37/55
Spec. Nage de homard et langoustines. Effiloché de lièvre façon royale (season). Mousseux au chocolat arabica, sorbet cacao.
◆ The authentic setting of a remote Provencal farm located between cliffs and vineyards, combined with tasty classic cuisine. There are two set menus to choose from. Simple decor; terrace. Personalised guestrooms with a guesthouse feel.

PUJOLS – 47 Lot-et-Garonne – 336 G3 – see Villeneuve-sur-Lot

PUJOLS – 33 Gironde – 335 K6 – pop. 580 – alt. 60 m – ✉ 33350 4 C2

Paris 560 – Bordeaux 51 – Mérignac 68 – Pessac 63

Les Gués Rivières

rest,

5 pl. du Gén. de Gaulle – ✆ 05 57 40 74 73
– http://perso.orange.fr/margotte.olivier – margotte.olivier@wanadoo.fr
– Fax 05 57 40 73 26 – Closed 23 December-4 January
4 rm – †€ 68 ††€ 68 **Table d'hôte** – Menu (€ 18), € 20/25

◆ This house, lining the main village square, offers colourful and tastefully-furnished rooms. Gargantuan breakfasts and regional dishes are served on the magnificent terrace facing the vineyards and St Émilion, weather permitting.

La Poudette

VISA

La Rivière, (on D17) – ✆ 05 57 40 71 52 – www.lapoudette.com – la-poudette@wanadoo.fr – Closed March, Sunday dinner and Tuesday except July-August and Monday
Rest – Menu (€ 28), € 33

◆ Despite its difficult access, simple façade and unfussy interior, this house surrounded by a wild garden serves fine modern and seasonal cuisine.

PULIGNY-MONTRACHET – 21 Côte-d'Or – 320 I8 – see Beaune

PULVERSHEIM – 68 Haut-Rhin – 315 H9 – pop. 2 819 – alt. 235 m – ✉ 68840 1 A3

Paris 473 – Belfort 51 – Colmar 34 – Guebwiller 13 – Mulhouse 11 – Thann 18

in l'Écomusée 2,5 km Northwest – ✉ 68190 Ungersheim

Les Loges de l'Écomusée

VISA AE

– ✆ 03 89 74 44 95 – www.ecomusee-alsace.fr – hotel.loges@ecomusee-alsace.fr
– Fax 03 89 74 44 68 – Closed January-February, Monday and Tuesday except July-August
40 rm – †€ 50 ††€ 62, ☕ € 7
Rest ***La Taverne*** – *✆ 03 89 74 44 49 (closed Sunday dinner and Monday)*
Menu € 20 (weekdays)/35 – Carte approx. € 30

◆ A reconstruction of a traditional local village near the entrance to the open-air museum: rooms are modern and located in half-timbered houses, decorated in Alsatian style. A hybrid of brasserie and winstub offering regional fare (fresh trouts, local wines) in a spacious setting.

PUTEAUX – 92 Hauts-de-Seine – 311 J2 – 101 14 – see Paris, Area

PUYCELCI – 81 Tarn – 338 C7 – pop. 494 – alt. 258 m – ✉ 81140 29 C2

Paris 637 – Albi 44 – Gaillac 25 – Montauban 40 – Rodez 107 – Toulouse 62

Office de tourisme, chapelle Saint-Roch ✆ 05 63 33 20 47, Fax 05 63 33 19 25

L'Ancienne Auberge

rm, VISA AE

pl. de l'Eglise – ✆ 05 63 33 65 90 – www.ancienne-auberge.com – caddack@aol.com – Fax 05 63 33 21 12
9 rm – †€ 70/150 ††€ 70/150, ☕ € 12
Rest – *(closed Sunday dinner and Monday)* Menu € 24/35 – Carte € 26/45

◆ An inn with character occupying a 13C residence at the heart of a fortified village. Rooms with personal touches and magnificent open fireplace in the lounge. Stone arches and late-19C stained glass bring character to the restaurant.

LE PUY-DE-DÔME – 63 Puy-de-Dôme – 326 E8 – see Clermont-Ferrand

LE PUY-EN-VELAY P – 43 Haute-Loire – 331 F3 – pop. 19 300 – alt. 629 m – ✉ 43000 Lyon - Rhone Valley 6 C3

Paris 539 – Clermont-Ferrand 129 – Mende 87 – St-Étienne 76

Office de tourisme, 2, place du Clauzel ✆ 04 71 09 38 41, Fax 04 71 05 22 62

du Puy-en-Velay Ceyssac Sénilhac, W : 7 km on D 590, ✆ 04 71 09 17 77

Site★★★ - L'île aux trésors★★★ BY : Notre-Dame cathedral★★★, cloister★★ - Religious art treasure-house★★ in the États du Velay - St-Michel d'Aiguilhe AY - Liberal arts painting of the Reliques chapel★★ - Old town★ - Rocher Corneille ←★ - Musée Crozatier: collection of lapidary★, lace★.

Polignac★: ✳★ 5 km by ③.

Plan on following page

Du Parc

4 av. C. Charbonnier – ✆ 04 71 02 40 40 – www.hotel-du-parc-le-puy.com – francoisgagnaire@wanadoo.fr – Fax 04 71 02 18 72 AZ s

15 rm – †€ 75/195 ††€ 75/195, ☕ € 11

Rest ***François Gagnaire*** – see below

◆ This well-renovated hotel, near Vinay Garden, offers practical, modern and appealing guestrooms. Sitting rooms and breakfast room with terrace and bar.

Regina

rm, AC rest, VISA MC AE

34 bd Mar. Fayolle – ✆ 04 71 09 14 71 – wwww.hotelregina.com – contact@hotelrestregina.com – Fax 04 71 09 18 57 BZ d

25 rm – †€ 53/57 ††€ 65/92, ☕ € 9 – 3 suites – ½ P € 62/65

Rest – *(closed Sunday dinner 15 November-15 March)* Menu (€ 17), € 22 (weekdays)/60 bi – Carte € 42/62

◆ This 1905 building is now a hotel that is being gradually renovated. The pleasant rooms, painted in bright colours, are all different and often spacious (some have a Jacuzzi). A cheerful, colourful and comfortable dining room. Traditional cuisine.

Le Brivas

rm, P VISA MC AE

2 av. Charles Massot, at Vals-près-le-Puy ✉ 43750 – ✆ 04 71 05 68 66 – www.hotel-le-brivas.com – brivas@wanadoo.fr – Fax 04 71 05 65 88 – Closed 19 December-12 January, Friday dinner, Sunday dinner from 15 October to 15 April and Saturday lunch

48 rm – †€ 63/85 ††€ 63/85, ☕ € 8,50 – ½ P € 54/65

Rest – Menu € 15 (lunch), € 19/43 – Carte € 22/41

◆ A modern hotel offering functional comfort in a residential district to the south of Le Puy. Pleasant riverside terrace-garden. Fitness area. Traditional cuisine based on local produce, served in a contemporary setting.

Le Val Vert

rm, P VISA MC AE

6 av. Baptiste Marcet, 1.5 km on the N 88 and rte Mende via ② – ✆ 04 71 09 09 30 – www.hotelvalvert.com – info@hotelvalvert.com – Fax 04 71 09 36 49 – Closed 25 December-9 January

23 rm – †€ 45/58 ††€ 45/58, ☕ € 9

Rest – *(closed Saturday lunch from November to June)* Menu (€ 15 bi), € 20/40 – Carte € 40/48

◆ The busy Mende road passes through verdant country. Partially refurbished colourful rooms, some decorated in an Italian style. Well soundproofed. Large picture windows overlooking the village bring light to the attractive dining room.

Dyke Hôtel without rest

VISA MC

37 bd Mar. Fayolle – ✆ 04 71 09 05 30 – www.dykehotel.fr – dyke.hotel@wanadoo.fr – Fax 04 71 02 58 66 – Closed 18 December-5 January BZ r

15 rm – †€ 39/51 ††€ 43/55, ☕ € 6,50

◆ The town is protected by its famous basalt dykes. Simple soundproofed rooms; choose one overlooking the lane. Cordial welcome.

LE PUY-EN-VELAY

Street	Square	No.
Aiguières (R. Porte)	AZ	2
Becdelièvre (R.)	AY	3
Bouillon (R. du)	BY	5
Card.-de-Polignac (R.)	BY	8
Chamarlenc (R. du)	AY	10
Charbonnier (Av. C.)	AZ	12
Chaussade (R.)	BZ	
Chênebouterie (R.)	AY	13
Clair (Bd A.)	AZ	14
Collège (R. du)	BZ	17
Consulat (R. du)	AY	19
Courrerie (R.)	AZ	20
Crozatier (R.)	BZ	23
Dr-Chantemesse (Bd)	AY	24
Fayolle (Bd Mar.)	BZ	
Foch (Av. Mar.)	BZ	
For (Pl. du)	BY	27
Gambetta (Bd)	AY	29
Gaulle (Av. Gén.-de)	ABZ	30
Gouteyron (R.)	AY	31
Grangevieille (R.)	AY	32
Martouret (Pl. du)	ABZ	34
Monteil (R. A.-de)	AY	35
Pannessac (R.)	AY	
Philibert (R.)	AY	36
Pierret (R.)	BZ	37
Plot (Pl. du)	AZ	38
Raphaël (R.)	AY	39
République (Bd de la)	BY	40
Roche-Taillade (R.)	AY	42
Saint-François-Régis (R.)	BY	43
Saint-Georges (R.)	BY	45
Saint-Gilles (R.)	AZ	
Saint-Jean (R. du Fg)	BY	46
Saint-Louis (Bd)	AZ	
Saint-Maurice (Pl.)	AY	47
Séguret (R.)	AY	48
Tables (Pl. des)	AY	49
Tables (R. des)	AY	52
Vallès (R. J.)	BY	54
Vaneau (R.)	AY	55
Verdun (R.)	BY	58

François Gagnaire – Hôtel Du Parc
4 av. C. Charbonnier – ☎ 04 71 02 75 55 – www.francois-gagnaire-restaurant.com – francoisgagnaire@wanadoo.fr – Fax 04 71 02 18 72 – Closed end June-early July, early November, in January, Tuesday lunch and Monday AZ **a**
Rest – Menu (€ 27), € 33 (weekdays)/134 bi – Carte € 70/90
Spec. Gaspacho de lentilles vertes du Puy à la truffe (summer). Souris d'agneau "noire du Velay" confite aux écorces d'orange et coriandre (autumn-winter). Les perles rouges du Velay et crèmeux à la verveine verte (été). **Wines** Saint-Joseph, Condrieu.
◆ The modern elegant restaurant, decorated with Raoul Dufy lithographs, serves delightful, personalised cuisine, made with local and more exotic produce.

Tournayre
12 r. Chênebouterie – ☎ 04 71 09 58 94 – www.restaurant-tournayre.com – info@restaurant-tournayre.com – Fax 04 71 02 68 38 – Closed 1st-7 September, 2-31 January, Wednesday dinner, Sunday dinner and Monday AY **f**
Rest – Menu € 23/66 – Carte € 50/70
◆ Ribbed vaulted ceilings, exposed stone, woodwork and frescoes make up the decor of this 16C former chapel. Generous Auvergne dishes.

Le Poivrier
69 r. Pannessac – ☎ 04 71 02 41 30 – www.lepoivrier.fr – lepoivrier@orange.fr – Fax 04 71 02 59 25 – Closed Sunday except dinner in August, Monday dinner and Tuesday dinner AY **v**
Rest – Menu € 15 (weekday lunch), € 22/35 – Carte € 28/44
◆ This restaurant has been redesigned in a rather trendy minimalist style, without losing its convivial feel. Haute Loire beef specialities. Photography exhibition.

Lapierre
6 r. Capucins – ☎ 04 71 09 08 44 AZ **u**
Rest – *(closed Tuesday dinner from November to February) (number of covers limited, pre-book)* Menu (€ 15), € 20/29 – Carte € 27/34
◆ This popular gourmet venue has food based on organic produce and the inevitable Puy lentils. The decor consists of bistro furniture, painted panelling and fabrics in shades of grey.

Bambou et Basilic
18 r. Grangevieille – ☎ 04 71 09 25 59 – www.bambou-basilic.com – delphineabrial@hotmail.com – Fax 04 71 09 25 59 – Closed Sunday and Monday AY **b**
Rest – Menu (€ 18), € 24/45
◆ The young chef draws inspiration from all four corners of the world to create a personal inventive cuisine that can surprise at times. An establishment on the way up.

in Espaly-St-Marcel 3 km by ③ – pop. 3 586 – alt. 650 m – ✉ 43000

L'Ermitage without rest
73 av. de l'Ermitage, Clermont-Ferrand road – ☎ 04 71 07 05 05 – www.hotelermitage.com – contact@hotelermitage.com – Fax 04 71 07 05 00 – Closed January and February
20 rm – †€ 50/75 ††€ 50/75, ☕ € 10
◆ The terrace of this hotel commands a panoramic view of the Puy. Practical, quiet rooms; those facing south overlook the countryside.

L'Ermitage
73 av. de l'Ermitage, Clermont-Ferrand road – ☎ 04 71 04 08 99 – bruno.chartier@wanadoo.fr – Fax 04 71 04 25 72 – Closed 19-26 October, 11 January-8 February, Sunday dinner and Monday
Rest – Menu (€ 18), € 22 (weekdays), € 30/49 – Carte € 37/63
◆ This attractively restored farmhouse has retained its rustic character and cosy feel. Meals served by the open fire in winter. Good traditional cuisine.

If breakfast is included the ☕ symbol appears after the number of rooms.

PUY-GUILLAUME – 63 Puy-de-Dôme – 326 H7 – pop. 2 668 – alt. 285 m – ✉ 63290 6 C2

Paris 374 – Clermont-Ferrand 53 – Lezoux 27 – Riom 35 – Thiers 15 – Vichy 21

Relais Hôtel de Marie rm, rm, VISA
av. E. Vaillant – ✆ 04 73 94 18 88 – www.hotel-marie.com – hotel.marie@wanadoo.fr – Fax 04 73 94 73 98 – Closed Sunday dinner and Monday
14 rm – €38/48 €38/53, €6,50
Rest – Menu €12 (weekday lunch), €18/36 – Carte €23/38
◆ Convenient for an overnight stay. The hotel has been restored and modernised with small, modern, functional rooms, quieter on the car park side. Fresh, simple restaurant where traditional and regional dishes are served.

PUY-L'ÉVÊQUE – 46 Lot – 337 C4 – pop. 2 178 – alt. 130 m – ✉ 46700 28 B1

Dordogne-Berry-Limousin

Paris 601 – Agen 71 – Cahors 31 – Gourdon 41 – Sarlat-la-Canéda 52 – Villeneuve-sur-Lot 43

Syndicat d'initiative, place de la Truffière ✆ 05 65 21 37 63, Fax 05 65 21 37 63

Bellevue rm, VISA
pl. Truffière – ✆ 05 65 36 06 60 – www.lothotel-bellevue.com – hotelbellevue.puyleveque@wanadoo.fr – Fax 05 65 36 06 61 – Closed 15-30 November and 4 January-2 February
11 rm – €68/96 €68/96, €12 – ½ P €70/86
Rest *Côté Lot* – *(closed Tuesday except October-June, Sunday except July-September and Monday)* Menu €25 (lunch), €35/46
Rest *L'Aganit* – brasserie *(closed Tuesday except October-June, Sunday except July-September and Monday)* Menu €14 (weekday lunch)/20 – Carte €21/33
◆ The hotel, situated on a spur overlooking the Lot, lives up to its name. Rooms are spacious, contemporary and personalised. Inventive cuisine at the Côté Lot restaurant and a generous view of the valley. A conservatory, local dishes and brasserie style are to be found at L'Aganit.

in Touzac 8 km West by D 8 – pop. 341 – alt. 75 m – ✉ 46700

Château de Bonaguil ★★ North: 10,5 km.

De la Source Bleue rm, VISA
– ✆ 05 65 36 52 01 – www.sourcebleue.com – sourcebleue@wanadoo.fr – Fax 05 65 24 65 69 – Open 1st April-2 November
12 rm – €89/110 €89/120, €10 – 1 suite – ½ P €82/97
Rest – *(closed for lunch except Saturday and Sunday)* Menu €32/39 – Carte €39/45
◆ Several 14C mills in a pretty bamboo grove on the banks of the Lot have been converted into a hotel with elegant, minimalist and peaceful rooms. This restaurant occupies a 17C outbuilding with fine beams and stone walls. Contemporary cuisine.

in Mauroux 12 km Southwest by D 8 and D 5 – pop. 417 – alt. 213 m – ✉ 46700

Syndicat d'initiative, le Bourg ✆ 05 65 30 66 70, Fax 05 65 36 49 64

Hostellerie le Vert rm, rm, VISA
Lieu dit "Le Vert" – ✆ 05 65 36 51 36 – www.hotellevert.com – info@hotellevert.com – Fax 05 65 36 56 84 – Open 1st April-31 October
7 rm – €85/130 €85/130, €10 – ½ P €83/105
Rest – *(closed Thursday) (dinner only)* Carte €43/49
◆ Enjoy warm hospitality at this 14C Quercy farm in the middle of the countryside. Personalised rooms with a mix of period and rustic furniture. Traditional cuisine with a modern twist is on offer beneath the dining room's rustic beams.

in Anglars-Juillac 8 km East by D 811 and D 67 – pop. 342 – alt. 98 m – ✉ 46140

Clau del Loup with rm VISA
Métairie Haute, D 8 – ✆ 05 65 36 76 20 – www.claudelloup.com – Fax 05 65 36 76 29 – Closed Tuesday dinner and Wednesday dinner in low season
5 rm – €100/120 €100/120, €12 – ½ P €96/107
Rest – Menu €17 bi (weekday lunch), €29/65 – Carte €35/52
◆ A lovely residence (1818) in a shady and flowered garden. Modern food served in a wonderful dining room or on the terrace, under old plane trees. Comfortable and attractive rooms, furnished in varying styles.

PUYMIROL – 47 Lot-et-Garonne – 336 G4 – pop. 920 – alt. 153 m – ✉ 47270 ▮ Atlantic Coast 4 **C2**

Paris 649 – Agen 17 – Moissac 35 – Villeneuve-sur-Lot 30

Syndicat d'initiative, 7, place Maréchal Leclerc ✆ 05 53 67 80 40, Fax 05 53 95 32 38

Michel Trama

52 r. Royale – ✆ 05 53 95 31 46 – www.aubergade.com – trama@aubergade.com – Fax 05 53 95 33 80 – Closed three weeks in November, Sunday dinner and Monday in low season, Monday lunch in high season and Tuesday lunch

9 rm – €270/500 €270/500, ☕ €30 – 1 suite

Rest – Menu €76 (weekdays)/225 – Carte €120/210

Spec. Papillote de pomme de terre en habit vert à la truffe. Hamburger de foie gras chaud aux cèpes. Assiette des cinq sens. **Wines** Buzet, Côtes de Duras.

◆ Luxuriously renovated 13C (former residence of the counts of Toulouse) and 17C houses. Lavish bedrooms designed by Garcia. An unusual 'wall of scents', an exuberant Baroque dining room, cloister-terrace, well-stocked wine cellar and delightfully inventive cuisine.

PUYRAVAULT – 17 Charente-Maritime – 324 F3 – see Surgères

PUY-ST-PIERRE – 05 Hautes-Alpes – 334 H3 – see Briançon

PUY-ST-VINCENT – 05 Hautes-Alpes – 334 G4 – pop. 285 – alt. 1 325 m – Winter sports : 1 400/2 700 m 16 – ✉ 05290 ▮ French Alps 41 **C1**

Paris 700 – L'Argentière-la-Bessée 10 – Briançon 21 – Gap 83 – Guillestre 30

Office de tourisme, les Alberts ✆ 04 92 23 58 42

Les Prés ★ Southeast: 2 km - ★ Vallouise church North: 4 km.

La Pendine

at Prés, 1 km east on the D 404 – ✆ 04 92 23 32 62 – www.lapendine.com – contact@lapendine.com – Fax 04 92 23 46 63 – Open 20 June-31 August and 16 December-6 April

25 rm – €47/65 €56/92, ☕ €9 – ½ P €56/69

Rest – Menu (€14), €20 (lunch), €25/37 – Carte €33/48

◆ The wooden fronted hotel, dominating the village, offers guestrooms decorated in an alpine style (some have a balcony). Enjoy traditional dishes in the restaurant as you admire the matchless vista of Vallouise Valley and the Ecrins range.

Saint-Roch

at Prés, 1 km east on the D 404 – ✆ 04 92 23 32 79 – www.hotel-st-roch.com – info@hotel-st-roch.com – Fax 04 92 23 45 11 – Open 20 June-31 August and 20 December-5 April

15 rm – €90/94 €90/94, ☕ €12 – ½ P €75/90

Rest – self – Menu €22/37 – Carte €37/64

◆ This 1970s building is ideally situated at the foot of the slopes. The large rooms are simply but practically furnished and those facing south boast a balcony. Beautiful panoramic view from the restaurant and the terrace; self-service lunchtime menu in winter.

PYLA-SUR-MER – 33 Gironde – 335 D7 – ✉ 33115 ▮ Atlantic Coast 3 **B2**

Paris 648 – Arcachon 8 – Biscarrosse 34 – Bordeaux 66

Syndicat d'initiative, 2, avenue Ermitage ✆ 05 56 54 02 22, Fax 05 56 22 58 84

Dune du Pilat★★.

See plan of Arcachon urban area.

Maminotte without rest

av. Acacias – ✆ 05 57 72 05 05 – hotel-maminotte@wanadoo.fr – Fax 05 57 72 06 06 – Closed 1st January-5 February AY **n**

12 rm – €60/120 €60/120, ☕ €9

◆ Villa in a residential area near the beach with rustic rooms, many of them updated. Some with balcony overlooking the pine trees.

XX **L'Authentic d'Éric Thore** VISA

35 bd de l'Océan – ✆ 05 56 54 07 94 – Closed 1st-10 March, Tuesday and Wednesday except school holidays AY e

Rest – Menu € 20 (weekday lunch)/32 – Carte € 44/70

◆ Renovated in a charming holiday spirit, inspired by the wood cabins of the Arcachon region. Pergola for dining in fine weather. Creative cuisine from the chef-patron.

QUARRÉ-LES-TOMBES – 89 Yonne – 319 G7 – pop. 714 – alt. 457 m 7 B2
– ✉ 89630 **Burgundy-Jura**

Paris 233 – Auxerre 73 – Avallon 18 – Château-Chinon 49 – Clamecy 49 – Dijon 118

Syndicat d'initiative, rue des Ecoles ✆ 03 86 32 22 20, Fax 03.86.32.23.43

Du Nord rest, VISA

25 pl. de l'Église – ✆ 03 86 32 29 30 – www.hoteldunord-morvan.com – Fax 03 86 32 29 31 – Closed 3 November-16 February, Wednesday dinner and Thursday

8 rm – †€ 45/55 ††€ 60/75, ☕ € 9 – 2 suites – ½ P € 55/68

Rest – Menu € 23 (weekdays)/39 – Carte € 31/39

◆ This old hotel opposite the well-known church was saved by a local charitable association. Small, functional, redecorated rooms. The restaurant has a bistro style, retro atmosphere and appropriate, traditional food.

XX **Le Morvan** with rm rm, VISA

6 r. des Écoles, opposite the public park – ✆ 03 86 32 29 29 – www.le-morvan.fr – reservation@le-morvan.fr – Fax 03 86 32 29 28 – Closed 6-16 October, 1st December-10 March, Wednesday lunch in March, October and November, Monday and Tuesday

8 rm – †€ 48/68 ††€ 54/74, ☕ € 10 – ½ P € 60/70

Rest – Menu € 22/50 – Carte € 38/57

◆ Warm welcome at this lovely inn where you can savour carefully prepared modern dishes in a pleasant dining room with exposed beams. Comfortable guestrooms.

in Lavaults 5 km Southeast by D 10 – ✉ **89630 Quarré-les-Tombes**

XXX **Auberge de l'Âtre** with rm VISA

– ✆ 03 86 32 20 79 – www.auberge-de-latre.com – laubergedelatr@free.fr – Fax 03 86 32 28 25 – Closed 15 June-1st July, 16 February-12 March, Tuesday and Wednesday

7 rm – †€ 58/72 ††€ 75/95, ☕ € 10

Rest – *(pre-book)* Menu € 33 (weekdays)/58 – Carte € 48/75

◆ Rustic local farmhouse in the heart of the countryside, offering large, classic rooms. Local cuisine (specialising in mushrooms), complemented by vintage Bordeaux wines.

QUATRE-ROUTES-D'ALBUSSAC – 19 Corrèze – 329 L5 25 C3
– alt. 600 m – ✉ 19380 Albussac

Paris 492 – Aurillac 72 – Brive-la-Gaillarde 27 – Mauriac 67 – St-Céré 36 – Tulle 18

Roche de Vic ✻★ South: 2 km then 15 mn, **Dordogne-Berry-Limousin**

Roche de Vic VISA

– ✆ 05 55 28 15 87 – rochedevic.fr – rochevic@orange.fr – Fax 05 55 28 01 09 – Closed 1st-8 October, 2 January-15 March and Monday except July-August

11 rm – †€ 47/50 ††€ 47/60, ☕ € 7 – ½ P € 55/60

Rest – *(closed Sunday dinner and Monday from October to March)* Menu (€ 12), € 17 (weekday lunch), € 22/40 – Carte € 28/55

◆ A 1950s country house. Neat, discreetly furnished rooms in the style of the period; those overlooking the garden are more attractive. Children's play area. Regional recipes to be sampled before or after you admire the panorama at Roche de Vic.

QUÉDILLAC – 35 Ille-et-Vilaine – **309** J5 – **pop. 1 036** – **alt. 85 m** – ✉ 35290 10 **C2**

Paris 389 – Dinan 30 – Lamballe 45 – Loudéac 57 – Ploërmel 46 – Rennes 39

Le Relais de la Rance with rm
6 r. de Rennes – ✆ 02 99 06 20 20 – relaisdelarance@21s.fr – Fax 02 99 06 24 01 – Closed 20 December-20 January, Friday evening and Sunday evening
13 rm – †€ 57/72 ††€ 57/72, ☕ € 10 – ½ P € 68/78
Rest – Menu (€ 18), € 22/70 – Carte € 44/60
◆ Granite village house offering an elegant restaurant with frescoes, period furniture and carefully set tables. Traditional cuisine and menu based on local produce.

LES QUELLES – 67 Bas-Rhin – **315** G6 – see Schirmeck

QUELVEN – 56 Morbihan – **308** M6 – see Pontivy

QUEND – 80 Somme – **301** C6 – **pop. 1 378** – **alt. 5 m** – ✉ 80120 36 **A1**

Paris 209 – Amiens 91 – Boulogne-sur-Mer 58 – Abbeville 35 – Outreau 60
Office de tourisme, 8 bis, avenue Vasseur ✆ 09 63 40 47 15, Fax 03 22 23 32 04

Les Augustines without rest
18 rte de la plage Monchaux – ✆ 03 22 23 54 26 – www.hotel-augustines.com – hoteldesaugustines@wanadoo.fr – Fax 03 22 24 10 53
15 rm – †€ 65/78 ††€ 65/78, ☕ € 10
◆ This hotel offers small ground floor rooms identically decorated in light colours. A friendly establishment ideal for a visit to this lovely region.

QUENZA – 2A Corse-du-Sud – **345** D9 – see Corse

QUESTEMBERT – 56 Morbihan – **308** Q9 – **pop. 6 272** – **alt. 100 m** – ✉ 56230 Brittany 10 **C3**

Paris 445 – Ploërmel 32 – Redon 34 – Rennes 96 – La Roche-Bernard 23 – Vannes 29
Office de tourisme, 15, rue des Halles ✆ 02 97 26 56 00, Fax 02 97 26 54 55

Le Bretagne et sa Résidence (Alain Orillac) with rm
r. St-Michel – ✆ 02 97 26 11 12 – www.residence-le-bretagne.com – lebretagne@wanadoo.fr – Fax 02 97 26 12 37 – Closed 16-30 November and 12 January-2 February
9 rm – †€ 70/90 ††€ 90/150, ☕ € 15 – ½ P € 125/145
Rest – *(closed Sunday dinner and Tuesday lunch from October to April and Monday) (pre-book)* Menu (€ 28), € 50/100 – Carte € 77/135
Spec. Huîtres en paquets sous un beurre mousseux à l'estragon. Ris de veau rôti en cocotte. Boule fondante au chocolat, poire pochée à la vanille (October to December). **Wines** Muscadet de Sèvre et Maine sur lie.
◆ A restaurant with an elegant wood-panelled dining room and winter garden. Inventive cuisine. Comfortable guestrooms in the annexe.

QUETTEHOU – 50 Manche – **303** E2 – **pop. 1 475** – **alt. 14 m** – ✉ 50630 Normandy 32 **A1**

Paris 345 – Barfleur 10 – Cherbourg 29 – St-Lô 66 – Valognes 16
Office de tourisme, place de la Mairie ✆ 02 33 43 63 21, Fax 02 33 43 63 21

Demeure du Perron without rest
rte de St-Vaast – ✆ 02 33 54 56 09 – www.demeureduperron.com – hotel@demeureduperron.com – Fax 02 33 43 69 28 – Closed Sunday from 15 November to 31 March
20 rm – †€ 52/72 ††€ 52/72, ☕ € 6
◆ A number of pavilions dotted around an attractive garden where breakfast is served in summer. Well-cared for rooms of varying styles and sizes (recent or more rustic).

Auberge de Ket Hou VISA AE
17 r. de Gaulle – ✆ 02 33 54 40 23 – aubergedekethou@wanadoo.fr – Fax 02 33 54 02 11 – Closed Sunday dinner and Monday
Rest – Menu (€ 15), € 19/43 – Carte € 30/50
◆ This roadside country inn offers traditional cuisine in a countrified interior of old stone and wood.

LA QUEUE-EN-BRIE – 94 Val-de-Marne – **312** E3 – **101** 29 – see Paris, Area

---

QUÉVEN – 56 Morbihan – **308** K8 – **pop. 8 753** – **alt. 50 m** – ✉ 56530 9 **B2**
Paris 505 – Rennes 154 – Vannes 61 – Lorient 9 – Lanester 9

Manoir de Kerlebert
r. de Kerlebert – ✆ 02 97 80 22 37 – www.manoir-kerlebert.com – manoirkerlebert@wanadoo.fr – Fax 02 97 80 20 83
4 rm – €50 €60
Table d'hôte – *(Closed Tuesday, Thursday, Saturday and Sunday)* Menu € 25 bi
◆ In the midst of a park, this pretty 17C longère (long house), renovated during the 1950s, offers a refined and tasteful interior. Lounge, billiards room, and library. Romantic or maritime rooms. Seafood served in the evenings (guests only).

QUEYRIÈRES – 43 Haute-Loire – **331** G3 – **pop. 311** – **alt. 1 110 m** – ✉ 43260 6 **C3**
Paris 563 – Clermont-Ferrand 149 – Le Puy-en-Velay 22 – Saint-Étienne 67 – Firminy 51

La Boria delh Castel
Le bourg – ✆ 04 71 57 70 81 – www.laboria-queyrieres.com – contact@laboria-queyrieres.com – Fax 04 71 57 70 81
4 rm – €46 €52 – ½ P € 63 **Table d'hôte** – Menu € 18 bi
◆ A restored stone farmhouse at the foot of the basalt rock. Attractive bedrooms, a small craft museum and a table d'hôte offering rustic cuisine based on organic produce.

QUIBERON – 56 Morbihan – **308** M10 – **pop. 5 073** – **alt. 10 m** – **Casino** – ✉ 56170 **Brittany** 9 **B3**
Paris 505 – Auray 28 – Concarneau 98 – Lorient 47 – Vannes 47
Office de tourisme, 14, rue de Verdun ✆ 08 25 13 56 00, Fax 02 97 30 58 22
Côte sauvage★★ Northwest: 2.5 km.

Plan on next page

Sofitel Thalassa rest, VISA AE
pointe de Goulvars – ✆ 02 97 50 20 00 – www.accorthalassa.com – h0557@accor-hotels.com – Fax 02 97 50 46 32 – Closed 4-24 January B **a**
133 rm – € 147/284 € 168/347, € 25 – 17 suites – ½ P € 140/231
Rest – Menu € 55 – Carte € 58/77
◆ For a breath of sea air, a pleasantly situated hotel complex facing the beach and with direct access to the Thalassotherapy centre. Rooms on the sea side are more spacious. Traditional dishes and choices for healthy eating, seafood selections top the list.

Sofitel Diététique rm, VISA AE
pointe de Goulvars – ✆ 02 97 50 20 00 – h0562@accor.com – Fax 02 97 30 47 63 – Closed 4-24 January B **v**
78 rm (½ board only) – 2 suites – P € 285/415
Rest – dietetic rest. – *(residents only)*
◆ This hotel is particularly popular with guests from the thalassotherapy institute (direct access). Every room has a loggia facing the sea. Health focused menus.

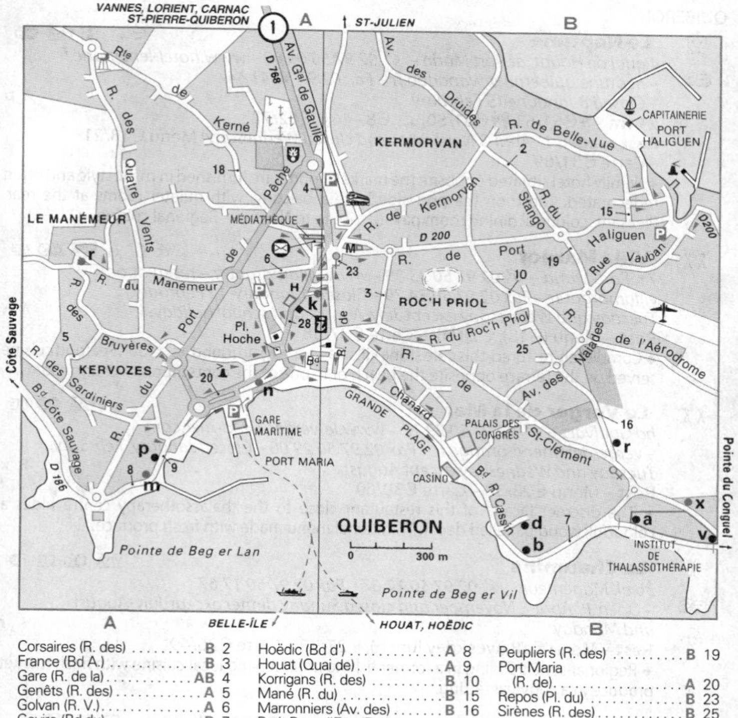

Bellevue rest, VISA

r. Tiviec – 02 97 50 16 28 – www.bellevuequiberon.com – bienvenue@bellevuequiberon.com – Fax 02 97 30 44 34 – Open April-September

B **d**

38 rm – €54/103 €60/120, €10 – ½ P €62/92

Rest – Menu €26/30 – Carte €27/38

◆ Ordinary architecture but a spring-like interior: a wide palette of colours in the rooms which have terraces, some with a sea view. Daily menu and small, traditional à la carte menu served in a bright dining room.

La Petite Sirène without rest VISA

15 bd R. Cassin – 02 97 50 17 34 – www.hotel-lapetitesirene.fr – info@hotel-lapetitesirene.fr – Fax 02 97 50 03 73 – Open 1st April-4 October and 23 October-11 November

B **b**

14 rm – €62/96 €62/96, €11

◆ This hotel, on the headland of Beg er Vil, has well-equipped rooms with renovated bathrooms and loggias facing the sea.

Ibis rest, VISA

av. Marronniers, (Pointe de Goulvars) – 02 97 30 47 72 – www.hotelibis-quiberon.com – h0909@accor.com – Fax 02 97 30 55 78

95 rm – €69/121 €69/121, €10

B **r**

Rest – *(closed 5-23 January)* Menu €19/24 – Carte €30/50

◆ Located just a stone's throw from the sea, the Ibis offers simply furnished bedrooms, some of which are split-level. Contemporary-style lounge-bar. Traditional and (upon request) more health-conscious dishes on offer in the wood-panelled dining room.

Le Neptune

4 quai de Houat, at Port Maria – ✆ 02 97 50 09 62 – www.hotel-leneptune.fr – neptune.quiberon@wanadoo.fr – Fax 02 97 50 41 44 – Closed 8 January-15 February A **p**

21 rm – †€ 51/63 ††€ 61/80, ☕ € 8 – ½ P € 62/72

Rest – *(open 1st April-5 November and closed Wednesday)* Menu € 18/21 – Carte € 31/69

◆ Family hotel situated opposite the market. Rooms are furnished in rustic style and often redecorated. Those on the port side have a balcony, with quieter rooms at the rear. Pleasant, colourful dining room paying tribute to Neptune. Regional cuisine.

Villa Margot

7 r. Port-Maria – ✆ 02 97 50 33 89 – www.villamargot.fr – reservation@villamargot.fr – Fax 02 97 50 34 79 – Closed 4 January-12 February, Tuesday and Wednesday except July-August and school holidays A **n**

Rest – Menu (€ 18), € 28/42 – Carte € 37/58

◆ Completely restored, this pale stone villa has once again found its colour. Seafood cuisine served on the terrace opposite the beach or in one of the contemporary dining rooms.

Le Verger de la Mer

bd Goulvars – ✆ 02 97 50 29 12 – www.le-verger-de-la-mer.com – vergerdelamer@orange.fr – Fax 02 97 50 29 06 – Closed January, February, Tuesday and Wednesday except August B **x**

Rest – Menu € 23/38 – Carte € 30/60

◆ The discreet facade of this restaurant close to the thalassotherapy centre hides a colourful, wood panelled decor. Traditional menu made with fresh produce.

La Chaumine

36 pl. Manémeur – ✆ 02 97 50 17 67 – Fax 02 97 50 17 67 – Open 1st April-8 November and closed Sunday dinner except July-August and Monday A **r**

Rest – Menu € 18 (weekday lunch), € 27/38 – Carte € 26/49

◆ Regional-style building in a former fishing area, serving local cuisine with fresh market produce in a convival setting.

in St-Pierre-Quiberon **5 km North by D 768 – pop. 2 204 – alt. 12 m – ✉ 56510**

Pointe du Percho ← ★ Northwest: 2,5 km.

De la Plage

25 quai d'Orange – ✆ 02 97 30 92 10 – www.hotel-la-plage.com – bienvenue@hotel-la-plage.com – Fax 02 97 30 99 61 – Open early April-end-September

37 rm – †€ 52/120 ††€ 52/120, ☕ € 12 – 5 suites – ½ P € 58/92

Rest – *(closed lunch except Saturday and Sunday)* Menu € 25/35 – Carte € 34/54

◆ Family-run hotel located on the beach. Recently-renovated rooms, some with a balcony on the bay side. Restaurant offering a traditional menu with a seafood focus and a lovely view of the Atlantic.

in Portivy **6 km north by D 768 and secondary road – ✉56150 St-Pierre-Quiberon**

Le Petit Hôtel du Grand Large with rm

11 quai St-Ivy – ✆ 02 97 30 91 61 – www.lepetithoteldugrandlarge.fr – contact@lepetithoteldugrandlarge.fr – Fax 02 97 30 72 52 – Closed 10 November-26 December

6 rm – †€ 90/125 ††€ 90/125, ☕ € 9

Rest – *(closed Tuesday and Wednesday except dinner in season)* Menu € 38

◆ Fresh produce, particularly non-farmed fish and seafood, is favoured by the proprietor-chef of this maritime-influenced bistro. All the bedrooms in this charming family-run inn have been refurbished by an interior designer, affording views of the sea and this small port on the Côte Sauvage.

QUIÉVRECHAIN – **59 Nord** – **302** K5 – see Valenciennes

QUILINEN – **29 Finistère** – **308** G6 – see Quimper

QUILLAN – 11 Aude – 344 E5 – pop. 3 445 – alt. 291 m – ✉ 11500 22 A3
Languedoc-Roussillon-Tarn Gorges

Paris 797 – Andorra la Vella 113 – Carcassonne 52 – Foix 64 – Limoux 28 – Perpignan 76

Office de tourisme, square André Tricoire ✆ 04 68 20 07 78, Fax 04 68 20 04 91

Défilé de Pierre Lys★ South: 5 km.

La Chaumière A/C rm, VISA MC AE

25 bd Ch. de Gaulle – ✆ 04 68 20 02 00 – www.pyren.fr – lachaumiere@pyren.fr – Fax 04 68 20 27 06

18 rm – †€ 60/80 ††€ 70/95, ☕ € 10

Rest – Menu (€ 19), € 24 (weekdays)/55 – Carte € 40/46

◆ This vast, round building has been fully renovated and offers spacious, modern rooms. Ideal as a stopover or for longer stays. The roomy dining room has kept its rustic atmosphere (fireplace, beams). Semi-classic, semi-traditional cuisine.

Cartier A/C rest, VISA MC AE

31 bd Ch. de Gaulle – ✆ 04 68 20 05 14 – www.hotelcartier.com – contact@hotelcartier.com – Fax 04 68 20 22 57 – Closed 15 January-28 February

28 rm – †€ 49/65 ††€ 49/65, ☕ € 8,50 – ½ P € 56/62

Rest – *(closed 15 December-20 March and Saturday lunch October-April)* Menu (€ 15 bi), € 18/30 – Carte € 26/35

◆ An early 20C building situated on a busy boulevard. A family hotel with simple, but well-kept and soundproofed rooms. A rustic-style dining room with an open fireplace. Aude specialities: rabbit with garlic, cassoulet and rouzolle (sausage meat soup).

Canal with rm VISA MC

36 bd Ch. de Gaulle – ✆ 04 68 20 08 62 – www.hotel-canal.com – hotel-canal@wanadoo.fr – Fax 04 68 20 27 96 – Closed 2-31 January, Sunday dinner and Monday except July-August

12 rm – †€ 34/36 ††€ 40/42, ☕ € 7 – ½ P € 43/46

Rest – *(closed Sunday dinner and Monday)* Menu € 13 (weekdays)/32 – Carte € 24/37

◆ A regional house on the town's main street that invites you to try its traditional and local cuisine in an informal atmosphere. Modest accommodation.

QUIMPER Ⓟ – 29 Finistère – 308 G7 – pop. 64 900 – Built-up area 120 441 – alt. 41 m – ✉ 29000 Brittany 9 B2

Paris 564 – Brest 73 – Lorient 67 – Rennes 215 – St-Brieuc 130

Quimper-Cornouaille: ✆ 02 98 94 30 30, by ⑥: 8 km AX.

Office de tourisme, place de la Résistance ✆ 02 98 53 04 05, Fax 02 98 53 31 33

St-Corentin cathedral★★ - Old Quimper★: Rue Kéréon★ ABY - Jardin de l'Évêché ≤★ BZ **K** - Mont-Frugy ≤★ ABZ - Musée des Beaux-Arts★★ BY **M¹** - Musée départemental breton★ BZ **M²** - Musée de la faïence★ AX **M³** - Boat trip along the Odet★★ 1 h 30 - Festival de Cornouaille★ (end of July).

Plans on following pages

Océania A/C P VISA MC AE

17 r. Poher, Kerdrézec complex via the Bénodet road ⑤ – ✆ 02 98 90 46 26 – www.oceaniahotels.com – oceania.quimper@oceaniahotels.com – Fax 02 98 53 01 96

92 rm – †€ 76/140 ††€ 76/140, ☕ € 13

Rest – *(closed Christmas holidays)* Menu (€ 17), € 20/25 – Carte € 19/31

◆ Chain hotel in a commercial district pleasantly surrounded by greenery. Large revamped rooms which are well designed and equipped. Contemporary dining room with slightly cramped tables. Poolside terrace.

Manoir-Hôtel des Indes without rest P VISA MC AE

1 allée de Prad ar C'hras, on the ⑦ and D 765 – ✆ 02 98 64 86 96 – www.manoir-hoteldesindes.com – sergeant.olivier@wanadoo.fr – Fax 02 98 64 82 58

14 rm – †€ 90/230 ††€ 100/260, ☕ € 15

◆ Hotel whose name honours its former owner, a sailor on the French-India trading routes. Fine bedrooms with an exotic theme. Parkland, pool and sauna.

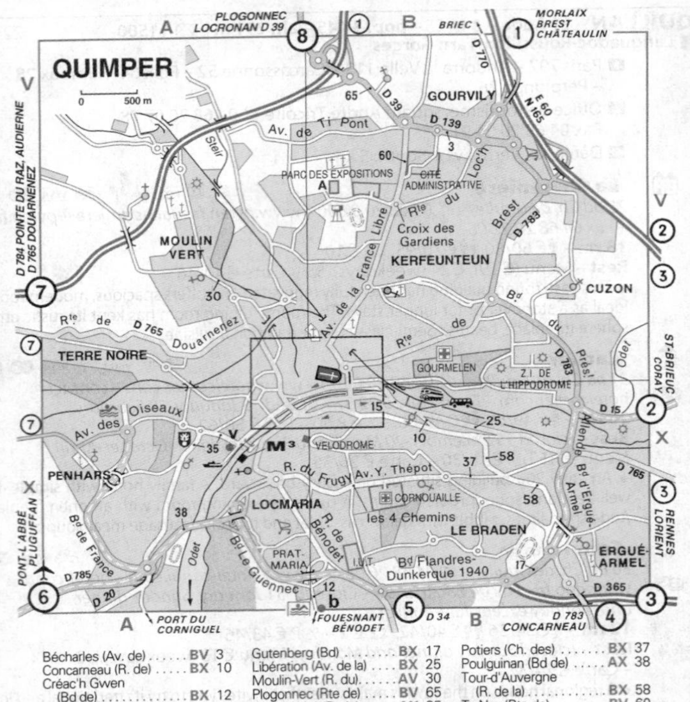

Bécharles (Av. de)	BV	3	Gutenberg (Bd)	BX	17	Potiers (Ch. des)	BX	37
Concarneau (R. de)	BX	10	Libération (Av. de la)	BX	25	Poulguinan (Bd de)	AX	38
Créac'h Gwen (Bd de)	BX	12	Moulin-Vert (R. du)	AV	30	Tour-d'Auvergne (R. de la)	BX	58
Gare (Av. de la)	BX	15	Plogonnec (Rte de)	BV	65	Ty-Nay (Rte de)	BV	60
			Pont-l'Abbé (R. de)	AX	35			

Kregenn without rest
13 r. des Réguaires – ☎ 02 98 95 08 70 – www.hotel-kregenn.fr – information@kregenn.fr – Fax 02 98 53 85 12 BZ **t**
30 rm – †€ 80/180 ††€ 95/200, ☕ € 13 – 2 suites
◆ Recently renovated, this friendly hotel on a quiet street in the town centre has simply decorated, modern rooms, some of which have Jacuzzis.

Gradlon without rest
30 r. Brest – ☎ 02 98 95 04 39 – www.hotel-gradlon.com – contact@hotel-gradlon.com – Fax 02 98 95 61 25 – Closed 12 December-11 January
20 rm – †€ 82/135 ††€ 82/160, ☕ € 12 BY **a**
◆ Pleasant guestrooms with individual touches, most of which overlook a pretty flower-decked courtyard, as does the veranda on which breakfast is served. Attentive service.

Le Logis du Stang without rest
allée de Stang-Youen, via r. Ch. Le Goffic, to the East on the map – ☎ 02 98 52 00 55 – www.logis-du-stang.com – logis-du-stang@wanadoo.fr – Fax 02 98 52 00 55 – Closed 20 December-5 February
3 rm ☕ – †€ 52/75 ††€ 68/80
◆ This 19C manor house, surrounded by a charming enclosed garden, has been tastefully renovated. Three delightful bedrooms, two of which occupy the old barn. Good attention to detail.

Les Acacias
85 bd Creac'h Gwen – ☎ 02 98 52 15 20 – www.les-acacias-quimper.monsite.orange.fr – acacias-qper@orange.fr – Fax 02 98 10 11 48 – Closed August, Sunday dinner and Saturday BX **b**
Rest – Menu € 20 (weekdays)/48 – Carte € 30/60
◆ This restaurant occupies a charming modern house with an attractive flower garden. Classic cuisine is served in a bright, contemporary-style dining room.

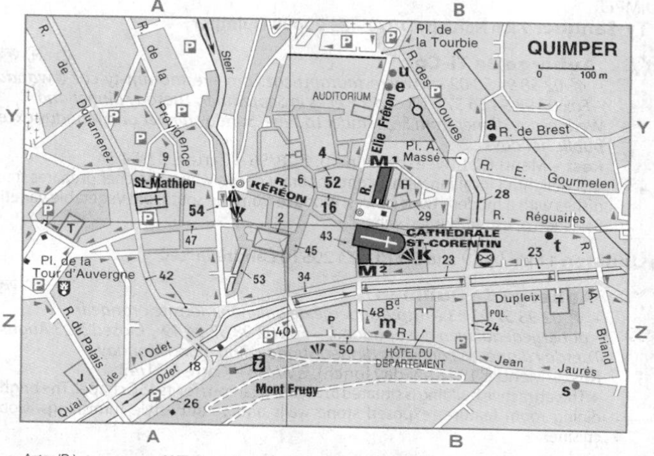

Astor (R.) .... AYZ 2	Kerguélen (Bd Amiral de) .... BZ 23	Ronarc'h (R. Amiral) .... AZ 42
Beurre (Pl. au) .... BY 4	Locmaria (Allées) .... AZ 26	Ste-Catherine (R.) .... BZ 48
Boucheries (R. des) .... BY 6	Luzel (R.) .... BY 28	Ste-Thérèse (R.) .... BZ 50
Chapeau-Rouge (R. du) .... AY 9	Mairie (R. de la) .... BY 29	St-Corentin (Pl.) .... BZ 43
Guéodet (R. du) .... BY 16	Parc (R. du) .... ABZ 34	St-François (R.) .... BZ 45
Le Hars (R. Th.) .... BZ 24	Résistance-et-du-Gén.-de-Gaulle (Pl. de la) .... AZ 40	St-Mathieu (R.) .... AZ 47
Jacob (Pont Max) ...... AZ 18		Sallé (R. du) .... BY 52
Kéréon (R.) .... ABY		Steir (Quai du) .... AZ 53
		Terre-au-Duc (Pl.) .... AY 54

XX L'Ambroisie

VISA MC

49 r. Elie Fréron – ✆ 02 98 95 00 02 – www.ambroisie-quimper.com – gilbert.guyon@wanadoo.fr – Fax 02 98 95 00 02 – Closed Sunday dinner except from 14 July to 25 August and Monday BY **u**

Rest – Menu € 23 (weekday lunch), € 37/65 – Carte approx. € 63

◆ A small modern dining room hung with original paintings on wood. Traditional, regional cuisine with the emphasis on local products.

X Fleur de Sel

VISA MC

1 quai Neuf – ✆ 02 98 55 04 71 – www.fleur-de-sel-quimper.com – Fax 02 98 55 04 71 – Closed 24 December-2 January, Saturday lunch and Sunday

Rest – Menu € 22 bi (weekday lunch), € 27/37 bi – Carte € 29/50 AX **v**

◆ This restaurant located in a picturesque part of town serves traditional cuisine in a dining room overlooking the River Odet.

X Ailleurs

VISA MC

43 r. Elie Fréron – ✆ 02 98 95 56 32 – contact@restaurant-ailleurs.com – Fax 02 98 95 56 32 – Closed 26 August-3 September and 23-29 December, Saturday lunch, Monday lunch and Sunday BY **e**

Rest – Menu (€ 15), € 25/35 – Carte € 37/50

◆ Inspired by a love of travel, the chef here produces seasonal international dishes, with a strong Asian influence. Good selection of wines from around the world to accompany your meal.

X L'Assiette

VISA MC

5 bis r. J. Jaurès – ✆ 02 98 53 03 65 – Closed 24 August-7 September and Sunday

Rest – Menu (€ 15), € 24 BZ **s**

◆ A pleasant family restaurant situated between the station and the town centre. Bistro-cum-brasserie decor and attractively laid tables. Simple, freshly cooked traditional dishes.

X La VIIe Vague

VISA MC

72 r. J. Jaurès – ✆ 02 98 53 33 10 – 7emevague@free.fr – Fax 02 98 52 23 85 – Closed 1st-15 August, Saturday and Sunday BZ **m**

Rest – Menu (€ 16), € 21/28 – Carte € 31/47 dinner only

◆ This popular restaurant has a simple, restful and trendy decor, a relaxing terrace and delicious regional cuisine (themed menu based on the number 7 in the evening).

in Ty-Sanquer **7 km North by D 770 – ✉ 29000 Quimper**

XX **Auberge de Ti-Coz**

– ✆ *02 98 94 50 02 – www.restaurantticoz.com – restaurant-ty-coz@wanadoo.fr – Fax 02 98 94 56 37 – Closed 2 weeks in September, Tuesday dinner and Wednesday dinner from September to June, Sunday dinner and Monday except public holidays*

Rest – Menu € 21 (weekday lunch), € 28/56 – Carte € 37/54

◆ A delightful local inn with a contemporary decor, where the chef prepares traditional dishes with a modern twist (spices, produce from the south, old vegetable varieties etc). Selection of estate-bottled wines.

in Quilinen **11 km by ① and D 770 – ✉ 29510 Landrevarzec**

X **Auberge de Quilinen**

– ✆ *02 98 57 93 63 – http://auberge.de.quilinen.monsite.orange.fr – aubergedequilinen@wanadoo.fr – Fax 02 98 57 94 49 – Closed 3-23 August, Tuesday dinner, Wednesday dinner, Sunday dinner and Monday*

Rest – Menu € 19 (weekday lunch), € 27/36 – Carte € 31/43

◆ This attractive building is situated in a hamlet famous for its 15C chapel. The bright, rustic dining room features exposed stone walls and country-style furnishings. Good local cuisine.

Southeast **5 km by boulevard Poulguinan** - AX - **and D 20 – ✉ 29700 Pluguffan**

XXX **La Roseraie de Bel Air** (Lionel Hénaff)

r. Boissière – ✆ *02 98 53 50 80 – www.roseraie.de.bel.air.com – roseraie-de-bel-air@wanadoo.fr – Fax 02 98 53 50 80 – Closed 3-13 May, 6 September-2 October, Sunday and Monday*

Rest – Menu € 25 (weekday lunch), € 48/95

Spec. Poissons de petits bateaux. Agneau des prés salés de la rivière de Pont-l'Abbé (March to September). Fruits rouges de la région (spring-summer).

◆ This is a fine 19C Brittany residence. A warmly attractive ambiance pervades the long dining hall with its two tall granite fireplaces. Reinterpreted regional cuisine.

QUIMPERLÉ – 29 Finistère – 308 J7 – pop. 10 900 – alt. 30 m   9 B2

– ✉ 29300 **Brittany**

- Paris 517 – Carhaix-Plouguer 57 – Concarneau 32 – Pontivy 76 – Quimper 49 – Rennes 169
- Office de tourisme, 45, place Saint-Michel ✆ 02 98 96 04 32, Fax 02 98 96 16 12
- Ste-Croix church★★ - Rue Dom-Morice★.

Le Vintage without rest

20 r. Bremond d'Ars – ✆ *02 98 35 09 10 – www.hotelvintage.com – hotelvintage@orange.fr – Fax 02 98 35 09 29*

10 rm – †€ 60 ††€ 85/115, ☕ € 11

◆ This contemporary hotel devoted to wine has a beautiful 19C facade. Rooms with personal touches, including unique murals and contemporary furniture.

XX **Le Bistro de la Tour**

2 r. Dom Morice – ✆ *02 98 39 29 58 – www.hotelvintage.com – bistrodelatour@orange.fr – Fax 02 98 39 21 77 – Closed Sunday lunch in July-August, Sunday dinner off season, Monday except dinners in July-August and Saturday lunch*

Rest – Menu (€ 22), € 31/61 bi – Carte € 36/42

◆ This cosy old-fashioned bistro (ornaments, paintings, bottles) serves generous portions of food ranging from traditional to regional. Fine wine list. Gourmet grocers next-door.

X **La Cigale Egarée**

Villeneuve-Braouic on Lorient road – ✆ *02 98 39 15 53 – www.lacigaleegaree.com – lacigale29@yahoo.fr – Closed November school holidays, Sunday and Monday*

Rest – *(number of covers limited, pre-book)* Menu (€ 17), € 21 (weekday lunch), € 35/70 – Carte € 39/59

◆ The "Lost Cricket" is an atypical restaurant in an ochre-coloured house with a garden. Avant-garde cuisine served to an attractive neo-Provençal backdrop.

Northeast 6 km by Arzano road and D 22 – ✉ 29300 Arzano

Château de Kerlarec — rest, P
rte d'Arzano – ☎ 02 98 71 75 06 – www.chateau-de-kerlarec.com – chateau-de-kerlarec@orange.fr – Fax 02 98 71 74 55 – Closed 23-27 December
5 rm – †€ 115 ††€ 125/160 **Table d'hôte** – Menu € 30/55
◆ This château with authentic charm dating from the French Second Empire has a carefully decorated interior and attentive proprietors (fine linen and courtesy tray). The table d'hôte (by reservation only) offers pancakes, plates of seafood and local dishes.

QUINCIÉ-EN-BEAUJOLAIS – 69 Rhône – 327 G3 – pop. 1 121 – alt. 325 m – ✉ 69430 — 43 E1

Paris 428 – Beaujeu 6 – Bourg-en-Bresse 55 – Lyon 57 – Mâcon 33 – Roanne 66

Le Mont-Brouilly — rm, rest, P VISA MC AE
Le Pont des Samsons, 2,5 km east on D 37 – ☎ 04 74 04 33 73 – www.hotelbrouilly.com – contact@hotelbrouilly.com – Fax 04 74 04 30 10 – Closed 21-28 December, 1st February-2 March, Sunday evening and Monday from October to May
28 rm – †€ 65/70 ††€ 70/73, € 8,50
Rest – *(closed Sunday dinner from October to May, Tuesday lunch and Monday)* Menu (€ 18), € 23/46 – Carte € 34/45
◆ This 1980s hotel stands at the foot of Mont Brouilly in the midst of vineyards. Practical, identically decorated rooms. The vast dining room has a pleasant view of the garden; traditional food served.

QUINÉVILLE – 50 Manche – 303 E2 – pop. 303 – alt. 29 m – ✉ 50310 — 32 A1
Normandy

Paris 338 – Barfleur 21 – Carentan 31 – Cherbourg 37 – St-Lô 59
Office de tourisme, 17, avenue de la Plage ☎ 02 33 21 40 29, Fax 02 33 21 61 39

Château de Quinéville — rm, P VISA MC AE
– ☎ 02 33 21 42 67 – www.chateau-de-quineville.com – chateau.quineville@wanadoo.fr – Fax 02 33 21 05 79 – Open 31 March-2 November
30 rm – †€ 65/165 ††€ 65/165, € 11
Rest – *(dinner only)* Menu € 33 – Carte € 33/50
◆ The rooms, relatively plain for the most part, are larger and more recent in the former stables than in the 18C château. The park has Roman remains, a 14C tower, greenhouses and a lake. A dining room of character overlooking a lovely green setting. Traditional cuisine.

QUINGEY – 25 Doubs – 321 F4 – pop. 1 217 – alt. 275 m – ✉ 25440 — 16 B2

Paris 397 – Besançon 23 – Dijon 84 – Dole 36 – Gray 54

La Truite de la Loue — VISA MC
2 rte de Lyon – ☎ 03 81 63 60 14 – www.latruitedelaloue.com – latruitedelaloue@wanadoo.fr – Fax 03 81 63 84 77 – Closed January, 23 February-4 March, Tuesday dinner and Wednesday from October to May
10 rm – †€ 40 ††€ 52, € 7 – ½ P € 47 **Rest** – Menu € 19/47 – Carte € 20/57
◆ Family guesthouse on the banks of the Loue offering functional rooms of various sizes. A small country dining room with windows overlooking the river. Regional cuisine and specialities based on trout from the tank on the premises.

QUINSON – 04 Alpes-de-Haute-Provence – 334 E10 – pop. 350 – alt. 370 m – ✉ 04500 French Alps — 41 C2

Paris 804 – Aix-en-Provence 76 – Brignoles 44 – Castellane 72 – Digne-les-Bains 62
Syndicat d'initiative, rue Saint-Esprit ☎ 04 92 74 01 12, Fax 04 92 74 01 12

Relais Notre-Dame rm, P VISA MC

– ✆ 04 92 74 40 01 – www.relaisnotredame.com – relaisnotredame@orange.fr – Fax 04 92 74 02 10 – Hotel: Open 30 March-15 November and closed Monday and Tuesday; Restaurant: Closed 15 December-15 February, Monday dinner and Tuesday

12 rm – †€ 50/58 ††€ 58/65, ☕ € 9 – ½ P € 60/65 **Rest** – Menu € 26/42

◆ On the road to the Verdon gorges, a family-run hotel next to the Prehistory Museum. Pretty garden. Gradually refurbished rooms in a contemporary Provençal style. Countrified dining room and peaceful, green terrace. Regional cuisine, truffles in season.

QUINTIN – 22 Côtes-d'Armor – **309** E4 – **pop. 2 797** – **alt. 180 m** 10 **C2**
– ✉ **22800** Brittany

Paris 463 – Lamballe 35 – Loudéac 31 – St-Brieuc 18

Office de tourisme, 6, place 1830 ✆ 02 96 74 01 51, Fax 02 96 74 06 82

Du Commerce VISA MC

2 r. Rochonen – ✆ 02 96 74 94 67 – www.hotelducommerce-quintin.com – valerie@hotelducommerce-quintin.com – Fax 02 96 74 00 94 – Closed Friday lunch from 14 July to 18 August, Friday evening from 19 August to 13 July, Sunday evening and Monday

11 rm ☕ – †€ 57 ††€ 69/80 – ½ P € 56/62

Rest – Menu € 15 (weekdays)/46 bi – Carte € 47/57

◆ This 18C granite building was formerly a post house. Classic, well-kept guestrooms, each of which is named after an exotic spice. Dining room adorned with handsome panelling and a fireplace bearing the coat of arms of Brittany.

RABAT-LES-TROIS-SEIGNEURS – 09 Ariège – **343** H7 – see Tarascon-sur-Ariège

---

RAMATUELLE – 83 Var – **340** O6 – **pop. 2 271** – **alt. 136 m** – ✉ **83350** 41 **C3**
French Riviera

Paris 873 – Fréjus 35 – Le Lavandou 34 – St-Tropez 10 – Ste-Maxime 15 – Toulon 70

Office de tourisme, place de l'Ormeau ✆ 04 98 12 64 00, Fax 04 94 79 12 66

Col de Collebasse ≤★ South: 4 km.

Le Baou rm, P VISA MC AE

av. Gustave Etienne – ✆ 04 98 12 94 20 – www.hostellerielebaou.com – hostellerie.lebaou@wanadoo.fr – Fax 04 98 12 94 21 – Open beg. May-end September

39 rm – †€ 200/370 ††€ 200/370, ☕ € 21 – 2 suites

Rest ***La Terrasse*** – *(dinner only)* Carte € 65/95

◆ Le Baou (peak in Provençal dialect), dominating Pampelonne cove, is aptly named. Spacious, contemporary rooms all with a balcony and fine view. An elegant dining room and panoramic terrace overlooking the village and sea.

La Vigne de Ramatuelle without rest P VISA MC AE

rte de La Croix-Valmer, at 3 km – ✆ 04 94 79 12 50 – www.hotel-vignederamatuelle.com – contact@hotel-vignederamatuelle.com – Fax 04 94 79 13 20 – Open 4 April-18 October

14 rm – †€ 125/295 ††€ 125/295, ☕ € 15

◆ Charm, tranquillity and the feel of a private house depict this villa amid vineyards. Find contemporary rooms with terrace, a summer lounge and a pool in the garden.

L'Ecurie du Castellas et H. Lou Castellas with rm P VISA MC

rte du Moulins de Paillas – ✆ 04 94 79 11 59 – www.lecurieducastellas.com – lecurieducastellas@wanadoo.fr – Fax 04 94 79 21 04

16 rm ☕ – †€ 55/180 ††€ 55/180 **Rest** – Menu € 28/65 – Carte € 50/65

◆ As you sample the appetising regional cuisine, feast your eyes on the charming Provençal dining room and sweeping view of countryside and sea.

in la Bonne Terrasse 5 km East by D 93 and Camarat road – ✉ 83350 Ramatuelle

X **Chez Camille** P VISA MC

Bonne Terrasse district – ✆ 04 98 12 68 98 – www.chezcamille.fr – Open 9 April-11 October and closed Friday lunch and Tuesday

Rest – *(pre-book in high season and weekends)* Menu € 42/75

◆ Father and sons have succeeded one another in the kitchens of this waterside restaurant since 1913. Popular for its bouillabaisse (spicy fish stew) and grilled fish.

RAMBERVILLERS – 88 Vosges – 314 H2 – pop. 5 647 – alt. 287 m – ✉ 88700

27 **C3**

▶ Paris 407 – Epinal 27 – Lunéville 36 – Nancy 68 – St-Dié-des-Vosges 29

ℹ Syndicat d'initiative, 2, place du 30 Septembre ✆ 03 29 65 49 10, Fax 03 29 65 25 20

XX **Mirabelle** VISA MC

6 r. de l'Église – ✆ 03 29 65 37 37 – Closed 16 August-20 September, January and Wednesday

Rest – *(lunch only)* Menu (€ 15), € 38/50 – Carte € 41/80

◆ A warm informal welcome in this tiny restaurant decorated in the colours of Lorraine. Culinary classics on the menu such as calf's head, the chef's speciality.

RAMBOUILLET – 78 Yvelines – 311 G4 – pop. 25 400 – alt. 160 m – ✉ 78120 Northern France and the Paris Region

18 **A2**

▶ Paris 53 – Chartres 42 – Mantes-la-Jolie 50 – Orléans 93 – Versailles 35

ℹ Office de tourisme, place de la Libération ✆ 01 34 83 21 21, Fax 01 34 83 21 31

18 de Forges-les-Bains Forges-les-Bains Route du Général Leclerc, E : 22 km on D 906 and D 24, ✆ 01 64 91 48 18

◉ Château ★ panelling - Park★★: laiterie de la Reine (Queen's dairy)★ Z **B** - chaumière aux coquillages★ Z **E** - Bergerie nationale★ Z - Rambouillet forest★.

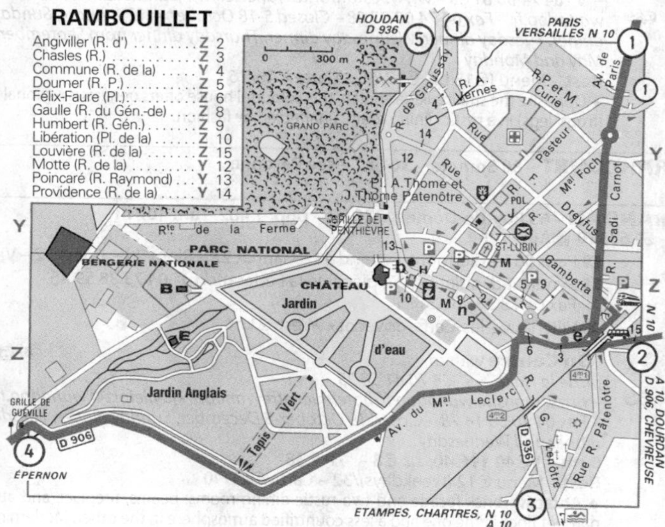

Mercure Relays du Château without rest
1 pl. de la Libération – ✆ 01 34 57 30 00 – www.mercure-rambouillet.com – relays@mercure-rambouillet.com – Fax 01 30 46 23 91 Z **b**
83 rm – €85/155 €90/170, ☕ €14
◆ A superbly renovated 16C coaching inn, situated opposite the château. The interior decor mixes old and new, while the bedrooms are comfortable and well-equipped.

Cheval Rouge
78 r. Gén. de Gaulle – ✆ 01 30 88 80 61 – www.cheval-rouge.fr – cpommier@aol.com – Fax 01 34 83 91 60 – Closed Tuesday dinner and Wednesday Z **n**
Rest – Menu (€28), €34 – Carte €42/50
◆ The restaurant is widely appreciated for its Provençal decor and traditional cuisine. At midday on week days, the veranda-dining room offers a brasserie-type set menu.

L'Huître sur le Zinc
15 r. Chasles – ✆ 01 30 46 22 58 – www.lhuitresurlezinc.fr – lhuitresurlezinc@wanadoo.fr – Closed 1st-21 August, 15-31 December, Sunday and Monday
Rest – Menu €39 (weekday lunch) – Carte €46/70 Z **e**
◆ This restaurant exclusively offers seafood and fish from the adjacent fishmonger's, run by the chef-landlord's brother. Pleasant sea-themed decoration and fine garden-terrace.

in Gazeran 5 km by ④ – **pop. 1 176 – alt. 162 m – ✉ 78125**

Villa Marinette
20 av. Gén. de Gaulle – ✆ 01 34 83 19 01 – www.villamarinette.fr – villamarinette@wanadoo.fr – Fax 01 30 88 83 65 – Closed Sunday dinner, Tuesday lunch and Monday
Rest – Menu €29 (weekday lunch)/60 – Carte €52/65
◆ The warm, well-kept dining room and terrace in a delightful walled garden offer tasty dishes prepared by the chef. Cosy rooms.

RAMONVILLE-ST-AGNE – 31 Haute-Garonne – 343 G3 – see Toulouse

---

RANCÉ – 01 Ain – 328 C5 – pop. 633 – alt. 282 m – ✉ 01390 43 E1

Paris 437 – Bourg-en-Bresse 44 – Lyon 32 – Villefranche-sur-Saône 13

De Rancé
– ✆ 04 74 00 81 83 – www.restaurantderance.com – jeanmarc.martin3@wanadoo.fr – Fax 04 74 00 87 08 – Closed 5-18 October, 4-17 January, Sunday dinner, Tuesday dinner, Wednesday dinner, Thursday dinner from September to May and Monday
Rest – Menu (€13 bi), €17/55 – Carte €26/76
◆ Opposite the small village church, this colourful house offers generous regional cuisine (frogs' legs) in a rustic dining room, unaffected by fashion.

RANCOURT – 80 Somme – 301 K7 – see Péronne

RANDAN – 63 Puy-de-Dôme – 326 H6 – pop. 1 462 – alt. 407 m – ✉ 63310 Auvergne 6 C2

Paris 367 – Clermont-Ferrand 41 – Gannat 22 – Riom 26 – Thiers 32 – Vichy 15

Syndicat d'initiative, 27, place de la Fédération ✆ 04 73 38 59 45, Fax 04 73 38 25 15

Villeneuve-les-Cerfs: dovecot★ West: 2 km.

Du Centre with rm
pl. de la Halle – ✆ 04 70 41 50 23 – http//monsite.wanadoo.fr/hotelducentre_randan – jay.lefort@wanadoo.fr – Fax 04 70 56 14 78 – Closed 19 October-5 December, Sunday dinner, Tuesday dinner and Wednesday
9 rm – €40 €40, ☕ €8 – ½ P €38
Rest – Menu €12 (weekdays)/32 – Carte €21/40
◆ Attractive brick facade and two rustic dining rooms: beams, fireplace and attractive parquet floor in the one and a less countrified atmosphere in the other. Modern rooms.

RÂNES – 61 Orne – 310 H3 – pop. 964 – alt. 237 m – ✉ 61150 32 B3
Normandy

Paris 212 – Alençon 40 – Argentan 20 – Bagnoles-de-l'Orne 20 – Falaise 34
Syndicat d'initiative, Mairie ☎ 02 33 39 73 87, Fax 02 33 39 79 77

St-Pierre
6 r. de la Libération – ☎ 02 33 39 75 14 – www.hotelsaintpierreranes.com – info@hotelsaintpierreranes.com – Fax 02 33 35 49 23
12 rm – €55 €62, €9 – ½ P €68
Rest – *(closed Friday dinner)* Menu (€18), €25/46 – Carte approx. €43
◆ Fine regional-style house whose small, well-cared for rustic rooms have individual touches and are decorated in warm colours. The cuisine, inspired by local produce, has tripe and frogs legs in pride of place on the menu. Warm welcome.

RASTEAU – 84 Vaucluse – 332 C8 – see Vaison-la-Romaine

RATTE – 71 Saône-et-Loire – 320 L10 – pop. 365 – alt. 201 m – ✉ 71500 8 D3
Paris 386 – Dijon 111 – Mâcon 97 – Chalon-sur-Saône 47 – Bourg-en-Bresse 72

Le Chaudron
in the town – ☎ 03 85 75 57 81 – www.lechaudron.fr – Fax 03 85 75 19 35 – Closed 19 January-3 February, Tuesday and Wednesday
Rest – Menu (€13), €16 bi (weekday lunch), €27/45 – Carte €40/58
◆ A good stopping point on a very busy road. This inn with simple rustic decor is characterised by a friendly welcome, attentive service and traditional cuisine.

RAULHAC – 15 Cantal – pop. 348 – alt. 740 m – ✉ 15800 5 B3
Paris 571 – Clermont-Ferrand 156 – Aurillac 31 – Saint-Flour 73 – Arpajon-sur-Cère 27

Château de Courbelimagne
4 km south on the Mur-de-Barrez road (D 600) – ☎ 04 71 49 58 25 – http//:perso.wanadoo.fr/courbelimagne/ – jean-louis.welsch@wanadoo.fr – Fax 04 71 49 58 25
5 rm – €75 €75/105 **Table d'hôte** – Menu €27
◆ In a romantic park, this manor of character dates from the 16-19C. It features period furniture, a collection of rare dried flowers (1850) and personalised rooms. Naturopathy treatments. Creative and organic local cuisine is available to guests in the evenings.

LE RAULY – 24 Dordogne – 329 D7 – see Bergerac

LE RAYOL-CANADEL-SUR-MER – 83 Var – 340 N7 – pop. 508 – alt. 100 m – ✉ 83820 41 C3
Paris 886 – Fréjus 49 – Hyères 35 – Le Lavandou 13 – St-Tropez 27
Office de tourisme, place Michel Goy ☎ 04 94 05 65 69, Fax 04 94 05 51 80
Rayol Estate Mediterranean Garden★★

Le Bailli de Suffren
Le Rayol – ☎ 04 98 04 47 00 – www.lebaillidesuffren.com – infos@lebaillidesuffren.com – Fax 04 98 04 47 99 – Open 15 April-15 October
54 rm – €189/443 €189/443, €24
Rest *Praya* – *(open from mid-April to mid-October, closed dinner from end June to September)* Menu €52/85 – Carte €74/89
Rest *L'Escale* – *(open 15 May-30 September) (lunch only except from mid-June to end August)* Carte €44/55
◆ Superb view over the Hyères islands from this attractive seafront hotel. Spacious and refined rooms with a balcony or terrace. Private beach. Refined Provençal dining room with panoramic terrace at the Praya. Traditional cuisine with a modern twist in a contemporary setting at l'Escale.

X **Le Relais des Maures** with rm
av. Ch. Koeklin, La Canadel – ✆ 04 94 05 61 27 – www.lerelaisdesmaures.fr – lerelaisdesmaures@wanadoo.fr – Fax 04 94 05 65 29 – Closed 8 November-31 January, lunch in July-August, Sunday dinner and Monday in low season
12 rm – 🛉€ 65/85 🛉🛉€ 65/85, ☕ € 8 **Rest** – Menu € 28/48 – Carte € 37/51
◆ Small family inn near the sea serving reasonably priced traditional cuisine. Meals served on the terrace or in the bistro-style dining room. Small, plain and rustic bedrooms; those on the second floor have sea views.

RÉ (ÎLE) – **17 Charente-Maritime** – **324** B2 – **see Île de Ré**

RÉALMONT – **81 Tarn** – **338** F8 – **pop. 3 081** – **alt. 212 m** – ✉ **81120** 29 **C2**
Paris 704 – Albi 21 – Castres 24 – Graulhet 18 – Lacaune 57 – St-Affrique 84 – Toulouse 78
Office de tourisme, 8, place de la République ✆ 05 63 79 05 45, Fax 05 63 79 05 36

XX **Les Secrets Gourmands**
72 av. Gén. de Gaulle, (D 612) – ✆ 05 63 79 07 67 – les-secrets-gourmands@wanadoo.fr – Fax 05 63 79 07 69 – Closed 25-31 August, 10-31 January, Sunday dinner and Tuesday
Rest – Menu € 21 (weekdays), € 29/52 – Carte € 41/50
◆ Three cosy, refined dining rooms enlivened with modern paintings and opening onto a pleasant summer terrace. Tasty modern cuisine.

REDON – **35 Ille-et-Vilaine** – **309** J9 – **pop. 9 461** – **alt. 10 m** 10 **C3**
– ✉ **35600** **Brittany**
Paris 410 – Nantes 78 – Rennes 65 – St-Nazaire 53 – Vannes 59
Office de tourisme, place de la République ✆ 02 99 71 06 04, Fax 02 99 71 01 59
Tower★ of St-Sauveur church.

XX **La Bogue**
3 r. Etats – ✆ 02 99 71 12 95 – Fax 02 99 71 12 95 – Closed 29 June-7 July, 1 week in November, Sunday dinner and Monday
Rest – Menu € 23/60 – Carte € 42/68
◆ The restaurant dining room (moulded wood panelling and Louis XIII chairs) hosts regional painting exhibitions. Simple, light, traditional fare.

La Gacilly road **3 km north on the D 873** – ✉ **35600 Redon**

XX **Moulin de Via**
– ✆ 02 99 71 05 16 – www.lemoulindevia.fr – moulindevia@orange.fr – Fax 02 99 71 08 36 – Closed 5-22 March, September, Wednesday from October to June, Sunday dinner, Tuesday dinner and Monday
Rest – Menu € 25/65
◆ Country furniture, beams and a fireplace contribute to the rural charm of this old watermill in a green setting. A shady terrace opening onto the garden.

REICHSTETT – **67 Bas-Rhin** – **315** K5 – **see Strasbourg**

REILHAC – **43 Haute-Loire** – **331** C3 – **see Langeac**

REIMS – **51 Marne** – **306** G7 – **pop. 184 800** – **Built-up area 215 581** 13 **B2**
– **alt. 85 m** – ✉ **51100** **Northern France and the Paris Region**
Paris 144 – Bruxelles 218 – Châlons-en-Champagne 48 – Lille 208
Reims-Champagne: ✆ 03 26 07 15 15, 7 km on the D 74 U.
Office de tourisme, 2, rue Guillaume de Machault ✆ 03 26 77 45 00, Fax 03 26 77 45 19
de Reims-Champagne Gueux Château des Dames de France, 9 km on the Paris road, ✆ 03 26 05 46 10
Notre-Dame cathedral ★★★ - St-Rémi basilica ★★: interior★★★ - Palais du Tau★★ BY **V** - Caves de Champagne (cellars)★★ BCX, CZ - Place Royale★ - Porte Mars★ - Hôtel de la Salle★ BY **R** - Foujita chapel ★ - Library★ of the former Collège des Jésuites BZ **C** - Musée St-Rémi★★ CZ **M**[4] - Musée-hôtel Le Vergeur★ BX **M**[3] - Musée des Beaux-Arts★ BY **M**[2].
Fort de la Pompelle (German helmets★) 9 km by ③.

REIMS

Berthelot (Bd M.) . . . . U 5
Brébant (Av.) . . . . U 8
Brimontel (R. de) . . . . U 10
Carré (R. du Gén.) . . . . UV 20
Champagne (Av. de) . . . . V 22
Cognacq-Jay (R.) . . . . V 25
Danton (R.) . . . . U 30
Dr-Lemoine (R.) . . . . U 35
Europe (Av. de l') . . . . V 42
Farman (Av. Henri) . . . . V 43
Maison-Blanche (R.) . . . . V 64
Paris (Av. de) . . . . V 69
Pompidou (Av. G.) . . . . V 71
Robespierre (Bd) . . . . U 74
Tinqueux (R. de) . . . . V 87
Vaillant-Couturier (Av.) . . . . . . V 89
Witry (Rte de) . . . . U 91
Zola (R. Émile) . . . . U 92

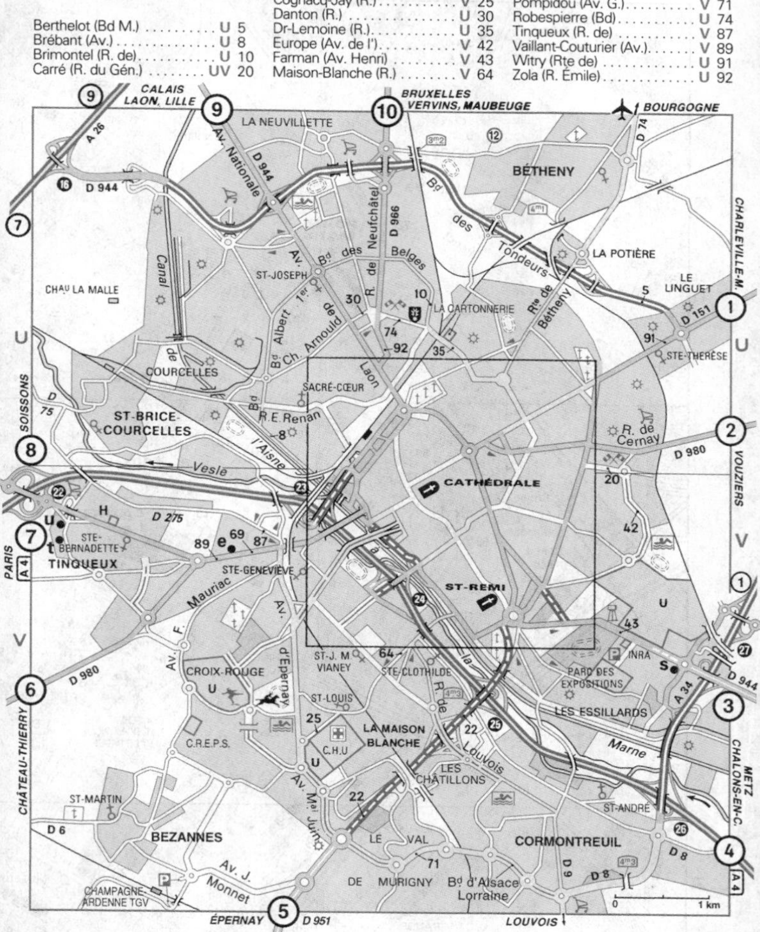

Château les Crayères

64 bd Henry Vasnier – ✆ 03 26 82 80 80
– www.lescrayeres.com – crayeres@relaischateaux.com
– Fax 03 26 82 65 52
– Closed 3-27 January

CZ **a**

17 rm – †€ 350/810 ††€ 350/810, ☕ € 30 – 3 suites
Rest – *(closed Monday and Tuesday) (number of covers limited, pre-book)*
Menu € 70 (weekday lunch), € 185/305 bi – Carte € 140/176
Spec. Langoustine royale. Menu champagne. Pamplemousse rose au biscuit rose de Reims. **Wines** Champagne.

◆ A charming residence and small lodge set in a landscaped park. Chandeliers, panelling, moulding and period furniture in the beautiful bedrooms. Delicious, seasonal cuisine served with good wine and champagnes.

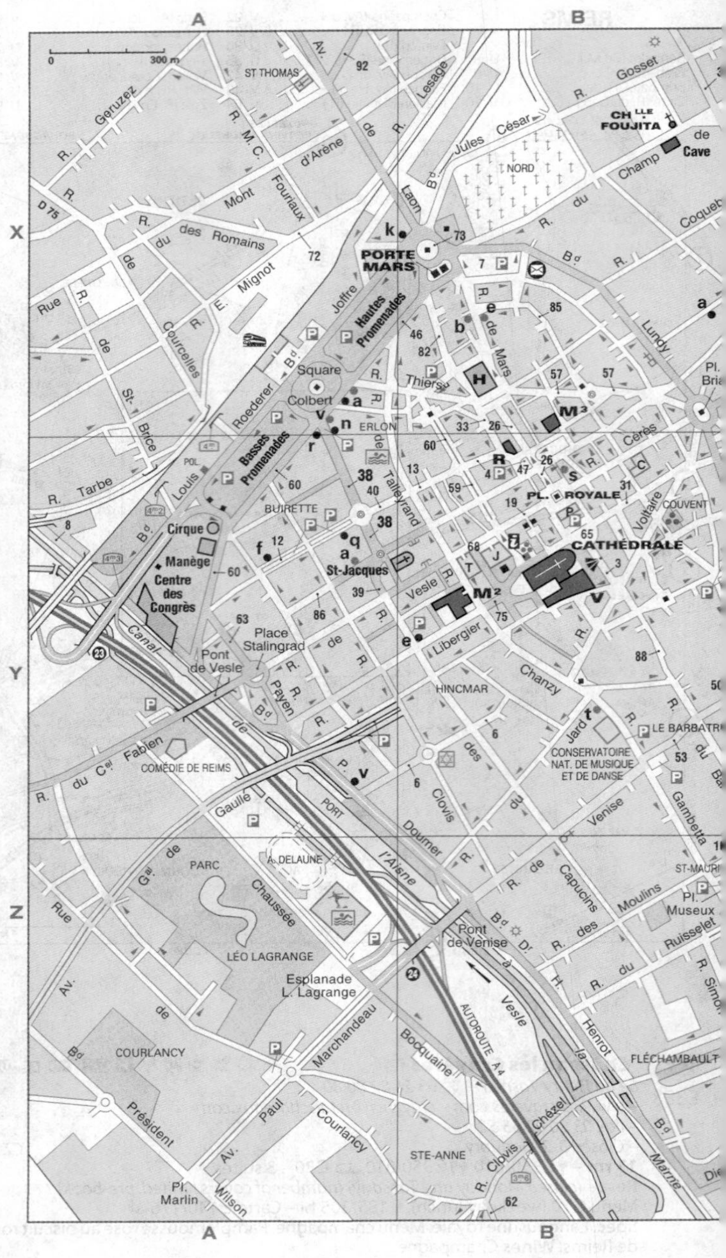
A
B
X
Y
Z
0
300 m
ST THOMAS
Av. de Laon
92
R. Lesage
R. Gosset
CH^LLE FOUJITA
Cave
Champ de
R. Geruzez
R. M. C. Fouriaux
Mont d'Arène
Bd Jules César
NORD
R. du Coquebert
D 75
R. du des Romains
72
PORTE MARS
73
7
Bd
R. Lundy
R. de Courcelles
Rue de St-Brice
R. E. Mignot
Bd Joffre
Hautes Promenades
46
82
R. de Mars
85
57
Pl. Bria
Square Colbert
R. Thiers
H
M³
Bd Roederer
Basses Promenades
ERLON
33
26
60
R. Cérès
R. Tarbe
POL.
Louis
60
BUIRETTE
38
40
R. de Talleyrand
13
59
4
47
26
PL. ROYALE
31
R. Voltaire
COUVENT
C
19
8
Bd
Cirque
Manège
Centre des Congrès
60
f
12
q
a
St-Jacques
68
J
T
65
CATHÉDRALE
3
39
R. Vesle
M²
75
V
63
86
Canal
Pont de Vesle
Place Stalingrad
R. de R.
R. Libergier
e
R. Chanzy
88
R. Payen
Bd
HINCMAR
Jard
R. R.
LE BARBATRE
23
R. du Cel Fabien
COMÉDIE DE REIMS
R.
6
R. des Clovis
CONSERVATOIRE NAT. DE MUSIQUE ET DE DANSE
53
R. du Bar
P. v
6
Gaulle
PORT
Doumer
du Venise
Gambetta
St-MAURI
PARC
A. DELAUNE
Ga de
Chaussée
l'Aisne
R. de Capucins
Moulins
Pl. Museux
Rue
R.
Bd Dr
R. des
Ruisselet
Pont de Venise
LÉO LAGRANGE
24
Vesle
R. du
R. Simon
Esplanade L. Lagrange
Av. de
Marchandeau
AUTOROUTE A4
H. Henrot
la
Bocquaine
COURLANCY
Bd
FLÉCHAMBAULT
Président
Paul
Courlancy
Chézel
Bd
Marne
Av.
STE-ANNE
R. Clovis
Pl. Marlin
Wilson
62

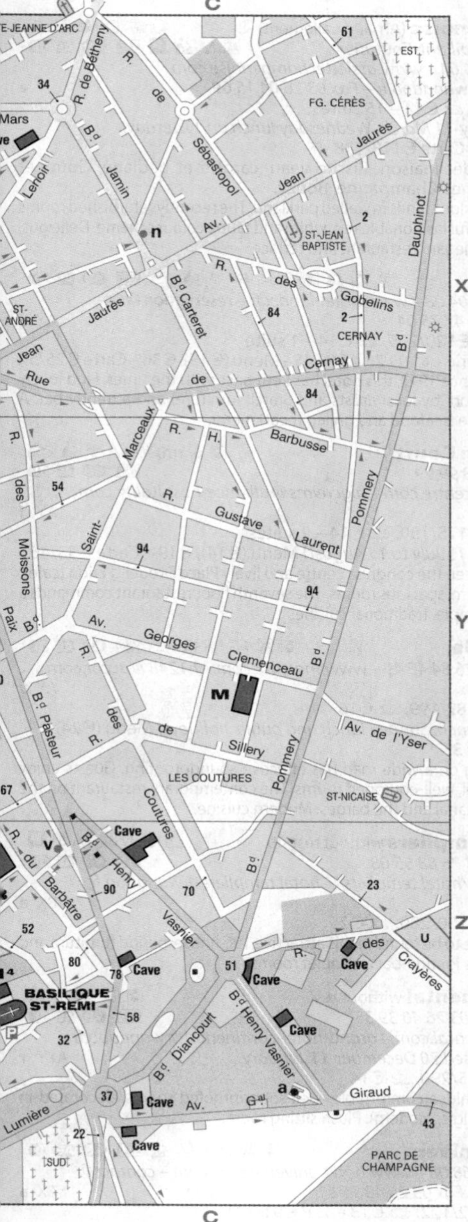
C
E-JEANNE D'ARC
R. de Betheny
34
Mars
Lenoir
Bd Jamin
R. de Sébastopol
61
EST
FG. CÉRÈS
Av. Jean Jaurès
n
2
ST-JEAN BAPTISTE
Dauphinot
R. des Gobelins
ST-ANDRÉ
Jean Jaurès
Bd Carteret
84
2
CERNAY
Bd
Rue de Cernay
84
Marceaux
R. H. Barbusse
R. des Moissons
54
Saint-
R. Gustave Laurent
Pommery
94
94
Bd Paix
Av. Georges Clemenceau
Bd
M
R. des
Bd Pasteur
R. de Sillery
Av. de l'Yser
Pommery
LES COUTURES
ST-NICAISE
67
Couture
Cave
R. du Barbâtre
Bd Henry
V
90
70
Bd
23
Vasnier
52
80
78
Cave
51
Cave
R. des Crayères
Cave
U
BASILIQUE ST-REMI
58
32
Bd Diancourt
Bd Henry Vasnier
Cave
37
Cave
Av. Gal Giraud
a
Lumière
22
Cave
43
SUD
PARC DE CHAMPAGNE
X
Y
Z
C

REIMS

L'Assiette Champenoise (Arnaud Lallement) rm,
at Tinqueux, 40 av. Paul Vaillant-Couturier
51430 – 03 26 84 64 64 – www.assiettechampenoise.com
– assiette.champenoise@wanadoo.fr – Fax 03 26 04 15 69 V **e**
40 rm – €160 €160, €14 – 15 suites
Rest – *(closed 22 February-11 March, Wednesday lunch and Tuesday)*
Menu (€68), €130/155 – Carte €118/138
Spec. Langoustines en déclinaison. Ris de veau, carotte et badiane. Goûts et textures du chocolat. **Wines** Champagne, Bouzy.
◆ This elegant late 19C mansion stands in walled parkland. The recently refurbished rooms have been treated to a tasteful fashionable red, white and taupe colour scheme. Delicious, modern food served in an elegant restaurant and terrace.

De la Paix
9 r. Buirette – 03 26 40 04 08 – www.hotel-lapaix.fr – reservation@hotel-lapaix.fr – Fax 03 26 47 75 04 AY **q**
168 rm – €120/205 €120/205, €14 – 1 suite
Rest *Café la Paix* – brasserie – *03 26 47 00 45* – Menu (€15), €36 – Carte €25/52
◆ Run by the same family since 1912, this hotel has kept pace with the times. Find lovely contemporary rooms (artwork by local artists and Starck furniture) and a trendy bar. A designer decor and brasserie (seafood and grilled meat) menu.

Holiday Inn Garden Court rm,
46 r. Buirette – 03 26 78 99 99
– www.holidayinn-reims-centre.com – higcreims@alliance-hospitality.com
– Fax 03 26 78 99 90 AY **f**
80 rm – €125/150 €125/150, €14 – 2 suites
Rest – *(closed lunch from 15 July to 15 August)* Menu (€14), €19 – Carte €33/46
◆ A practical location between the congress centre and lively Place Drouet d'Erlon (cafés, restaurants, cinemas). Modern, spacious rooms. The seventh floor restaurant commands a sweeping view of Reims. Simple, traditional cuisine.

Mercure-Cathédrale
31 bd P. Doumer – 03 26 84 49 49 – www.mercure.com – h1248@accor.com
– Fax 03 26 84 49 84 AY **v**
126 rm – €78/194 €82/199, €16
Rest – *(closed Saturday lunch, Sunday lunch and public holidays)* Menu (€24), €30/33 – Carte approx. €35
◆ This large 1970s building on a wide road has effective soundproofing. Guests enjoy peaceful nights in functional, well-equipped rooms. The contemporary restaurant on the first floor has a view of the canal and the barges. Modern cuisine.

Grand Hôtel des Templiers without rest
22 r. des Templiers – 03 26 88 55 08
– http://perso.wanadoo.fr/hotel.templiers/ – hotel.templiers@wanadoo.fr
– Fax 03 26 47 80 60 BX **a**
18 rm – €190/280 €190/280, €25
◆ Luxury and refinement are to be found in this attractive 19C house: period furniture and opulent fabrics. A bourgeois lounge-bar and quiet rooms.

Grand Hôtel Continental without rest
93 pl. Drouet d'Erlon – 03 26 40 39 35
– www.grandhotelcontinental.com – grand-hotel-continental@wanadoo.fr
– Fax 03 26 47 51 12 – Closed 20 December-11 January AXY **r**
50 rm – €79/290 €95/290, €14
◆ The lovely 1862 façade hides comfortable, well-soundproofed rooms, decorated in varying styles (classic, nostalgic, modern). Plush sitting room.

Grand Hôtel de l'Univers rest,
41 bd Foch – 03 26 88 68 08 – www.hotel-univers-reims.com – contact@hotel-univers-reims.com – Fax 03 26 40 95 61 AX **a**
42 rm – €73/79 €112/122, €13 – ½ P €91/131
Rest *Au Congrès* – Menu €23 – Carte €23/37
◆ This Art Deco establishment (1932) with comfortable, well-soundproofed rooms is 150m from the 13C cathedral. Cosy lounge-bar. Elegant dark wood panelling in the restaurant. Classic recipes.

Crystal without rest
86 pl. Drouet d'Erlon – ✆ 03 26 88 44 44 – www.hotel-crystal.fr – reservation@hotel-crystal.fr – Fax 03 26 47 49 28 – Closed 24 December-3 January
31 rm – †€ 58/65 ††€ 63/75, ☕ € 9 AXY **n**
◆ This town centre hotel stands at the end of a passage offering matchless peace and quiet. Spruced up, well-kept rooms. Breakfast in a small garden in summer.

Porte Mars without rest
2 pl. de la République – ✆ 03 26 40 28 35 – www.hotelportemars.com – hotel.porte-mars@wanadoo.fr – Fax 03 26 88 92 12 AX **k**
24 rm – †€ 82/89 ††€ 90/98, ☕ € 12
◆ The wood-panelled rooms are perfectly soundproofed and air-conditioned. A snug lounge with a fireplace. Gourmet breakfast served in a conservatory.

De la Cathédrale without rest
20 r. Libergier – ✆ 03 26 47 28 46 – www.hotel-cathedrale-reims.fr – hoteldelacathedrale@wanadoo.fr – Fax 03 26 88 65 81 BY **e**
17 rm – †€ 54/62 ††€ 62/71, ☕ € 7
◆ A corner building with simple, well-kept rooms that are gradually being updated. Breakfast is served in a room decorated with the work of local artists.

Le Millénaire (Laurent Laplaige)
– ✆ 03 26 08 26 62 – www.lemillenaire.com – reservations@lemillenaire.com – Fax 03 26 84 24 13 – Closed Saturday lunch and Sunday BY **s**
Rest – Menu € 32 (weekdays)/80 – Carte € 85/95
Spec. Crabe royal et tourteau. Ris de veau de lait et pied de cochon rissolés dans une pomme de terre croustillante. Moelleux au chocolat fort et griottines. **Wines** Champagne.
◆ Modern restaurant redecorated in bright colours and with contemporary artwork. Tasty, up-to-the-minute cuisine.

Le Foch (Jacky Louazé)
37 bd Foch – ✆ 03 26 47 48 22 – www.lefoch.com – jacky.louaze@orange.fr – Fax 03 26 88 78 22 – Closed 22 February-9 March, 20 July-17 August, Saturday lunch, Sunday dinner and Monday AX **a**
Rest – Menu € 33 (weekdays)/80 – Carte € 75/95
Spec. Raviole virtuelle de Saint-Jacques et huîtres Marennes-Oléron (mid-October to mid-April). Bar de ligne cuit en terre d'argile de Vallauris. La part des anges (September to November). **Wines** Champagne blanc de blancs.
◆ The restaurant borders the Promenades (shaded 18C courtyards). Refurbished dining hall, now in a fine, modern style. Up-to-date cuisine based on classic dishes.

La Vigneraie
14 r. Thillois – ✆ 03 26 88 67 27 – www.vigneraie.com – lavigneraie@wanadoo.fr – Fax 03 26 40 26 67 – Closed 27 July-17 August, 8-22 February, Sunday dinner, Wednesday lunch and Monday AY **a**
Rest – *(number of covers limited, pre-book)* Menu (€ 17), € 25 (weekday lunch), € 33/66 – Carte € 56/76
◆ Behind a glass façade, a stylish dining room decorated with works by a local artist. A good wine list featuring champagnes accompanies the modern seasonal dishes.

Flo
96 pl. Drouet d'Erlon – ✆ 03 26 91 40 50 – www.floreims.com – _idarocha@groupeflo.fr – Fax 03 26 91 40 54 AX **v**
Rest – brasserie – Menu (€ 19), € 30 – Carte € 30/50
◆ A traditional brasserie menu is served in an Art Deco inspired interior (period mosaic floor in one room) with wainscoting and chandeliers. The rotunda terrace is packed in summertime.

Au Petit Comptoir
17 r. de Mars – ✆ 03 26 40 58 58 – au.petit.comptoir@wanadoo.fr – Fax 03 26 47 26 19 – Closed in August, Christmas holidays, Sunday and Monday BX **b**
Rest – Menu (€ 18 bi) – Carte € 37/45
◆ This restaurant has a simple modern interior, decorated with paintings. Generous, updated bistro cuisine. Regional and international wines.

Brasserie Le Boulingrin
48 r. de Mars – ✆ 03 26 40 96 22 – www.boulingrin.fr – boulingrin@wanadoo.fr – Fax 03 26 40 03 92 – Closed Sunday BX **e**
Rest – Menu € 19 bi/25 – Carte € 24/46
◆ This Reims brasserie, an institution in the town since 1925, is renowned for its Art Deco interior, cheerful atmosphere and wholesome cuisine made with fresh produce.

Le Jamin
18 bd Jamin – ✆ 03 26 07 37 30 – www.lejamin.com – eurl-jamin@wanadoo.fr – Fax 03 26 02 09 64 – Closed 11-26 August, 19 January-2 February, Sunday dinner and Monday CX **n**
Rest – Menu (€ 14 bi), € 21 bi/31 – Carte € 27/42
◆ A small unpretentious local restaurant that is both low-key and generous. Traditional menu and daily specials on a slate, moderate prices and friendly efficient service.

Les Charmes
11 r. Brûlart – ✆ 03 26 85 37 63 – www.restaurantlescharmes.fr – jgoyeux@club-internet.fr – Fax 03 26 36 21 00 – Closed 23 April-3 May, 27 July-17 August, 1st-4 January, Monday dinner, Saturday lunch and Sunday CZ **v**
Rest – Menu € 15 (weekday lunch), € 25/34 – Carte approx. € 32
◆ A pleasant family-run restaurant adorned with painted wood panels near the cellars of the city's main champagne houses and the St-Remi basilica. Good choice of whiskies.

La Table Anna
6 r. Gambetta – ✆ 03 26 89 12 12 – www.latableanna.com – latableanna@wanadoo.fr – Fax 03 26 89 12 12 – Closed spring school holidays, 20 July-15 August, 23 December-2 January, Sunday dinner and Monday
Rest – Menu (€ 13 bi), € 24 – Carte € 29/41 BY **t**
◆ The 'chef-artist' has some of his own paintings on the walls and dresses the windows; his wife Anna is in charge of the dining room. Delightful cuisine.

Châlons-en-Champagne road 3 km to ③ – ✉ 51100 Reims

Mercure-Parc des Expositions
– ✆ 03 26 05 00 08 – www.accorhotels.com – h0363@accor.com – Fax 03 26 85 64 72 V **s**
100 rm – €69/149 €79/159, ☕ € 16
Rest – *(closed Saturday lunch, Sunday lunch and public holidays lunch)*
Menu (€ 20) – Carte € 23/50
◆ A 1970s building, which is gradually being updated, with bright and well-kept rooms. Restaurant, extended by a veranda, terrace and pool, serving traditional meals and daily specials.

in Sillery 11 km by ③ and D 8E – pop. 1 564 – alt. 90 m – ✉ 51500

Le Relais de Sillery
3 r. de la Gare – ✆ 03 26 49 10 11 – Fax 03 26 49 12 07 – Closed 16 August-9 September, 2-9 January, 9-22 February, Tuesday dinner, Sunday dinner and Monday
Rest – Menu € 21 (weekdays)/65 – Carte € 63/75
◆ Elegant inn (panelling, artwork) with terrace offering views of the Vesle. Classic dishes using excellent produce; impressive wine list.

in Montchenot 11 km by ⑤ – ✉ 51500 Villers-Allerand

Grand Cerf (Dominique Giraudeau et Pascal Champion)
50 rte Nationale – ✆ 03 26 97 60 07 – giraudeau.lucie@orange.fr – Fax 03 26 97 64 24 – Closed 10-31 August, February school holidays, Sunday dinner, Tuesday dinner and Wednesday
Rest – Menu € 37 (weekdays)/84 – Carte € 72/100
Spec. Homard-melon (May to September) ou homard-poire (October to April). Pied de cochon farci au ris de veau sauce truffe. Crêpes au beurre demi-sel aux truffes, glace à la truffe (December to March). **Wines** Champagne, Bouzy.
◆ This inn at the foot of the Montagne de Reims has two elegant, wood-panelled dining rooms with one on a veranda giving onto the garden. Appetizing classic cuisine.

via ⑦ 6 km, A 4 motorway, Tinqueux exit – ✉ 51430 Tinqueux

Novotel rm, P VISA
– ✆ *03 26 08 11 61 – www.novotel.com – h0428@accor.com*
– Fax 03 26 08 72 05 V **u**
127 rm – †€ 113/143 ††€ 113/143, ☕ € 14 **Rest** – Carte € 23/42
◆ Impeccable hotel dating from the 1970s set in an industrial estate, whose rooms have been updated in a minimalist style. Large bistro-style dining room overlooking the swimming pool. Grill menu.

Tip Top without rest P VISA
1 av. d'A.F.N. – ✆ 03 26 83 84 85 – www.tiptop-hotel.com – info@tiptop-hotel.com – Fax 03 26 49 58 25 V **t**
66 rm – †€ 63 ††€ 68, ☕ € 8
◆ A recently opened hotel near the motorway with functional, well-kept rooms. Sitting room-library and buffet breakfasts served in a contemporary setting.

REIPERTSWILLER – 67 Bas-Rhin – 315 I3 – pop. 961 – alt. 230 m 1 A1
– ✉ 67340 Alsace-Lorraine

Paris 450 – Bitche 19 – Haguenau 33 – Sarreguemines 48 – Saverne 32 – Strasbourg 54

La Couronne rest, P VISA
13 r. Wimmenau – ✆ 03 88 89 96 21
– www.hotel-la-couronne.com
– sb.kuhm@wanadoo.fr – Fax 03 88 89 98 22
– Closed 15 June-2 July, 2-13 November, 3-13 February
16 rm – †€ 48/55 ††€ 52/63, ☕ € 12 – ½ P € 57/62
Rest – *(closed Wednesday dinner except from June to September, Sunday dinner from October to February, Wednesday and Thursday in January-February, Monday and Tuesday)* Menu (€ 9), € 19 (weekday lunch), € 25/48 – Carte € 33/60
◆ The façade of this regional style construction sports an unusual wrought iron sculpture. Tasteful rooms and a stunning view of the countryside from the rear. At the restaurant, classic cuisine served in a sumptuous decor of Art Nouveau inspired walnut panelling.

LA REMIGEASSE – 17 Charente-Maritime – 324 C4 – see île d'Oléron

---

REMIREMONT – 88 Vosges – 314 H4 – pop. 8 104 – alt. 400 m 27 C3
– ✉ 88200 Alsace-Lorraine

Paris 413 – Belfort 70 – Colmar 80 – Épinal 28 – Mulhouse 81 – Vesoul 66

Office de tourisme, 2, rue Charles-de-Gaulle ✆ 03 29 62 23 70, Fax 03 29 23 96 79

Rue Ch.-de-Gaulle★ - Crypt★ of St-Pierre abbey church.

Plan on following page

Du Cheval de Bronze without rest VISA
59 r. Ch. de Gaulle – ✆ 03 29 62 52 24 – hotel-du-cheval-de-bronze@wanadoo.fr – Fax 03 29 62 34 90 – Closed in November B **s**
35 rm – †€ 30 ††€ 38/58, ☕ € 7
◆ A hotel in an old post house under the picturesque town centre arcades. Modest, well kept, rustic style rooms. Excellent value for money.

Le Clos Heurtebise P VISA
13 chemin des Capucins, via r. Capit. Flayelle B – ✆ 03 29 62 08 04 – Fax 03 29 62 38 80 – Closed 31 August-15 September, 4-19 January, Sunday dinner and Monday
Rest – Menu € 18 (weekdays)/60 – Carte € 51/60
◆ This south-facing establishment in the upper part of the town serves unfussy, classic cuisine embellished with local and Mediterranean influences. Pleasant terrace.

REMIREMONT

Abbaye (Pl. de l') . . . . A 2
Calvaire (Av. du). . . . . A 3
Courtine (R. de la) . . . . A
Écoles (R. des) . . . . A 5
États-Unis (R. des) . . . . A 6
Franche-Pierre (R.) . . . . A 7
Gaulle (R. Ch.-de) . . . . AB
Prêtres (R. des) . . . . B 14
Utard (Pl. H.) . . . . A 15
Xavée (R. de la) . . . . A 16
5e-et-15e-B.C.P. (R. des) . . . . B 18

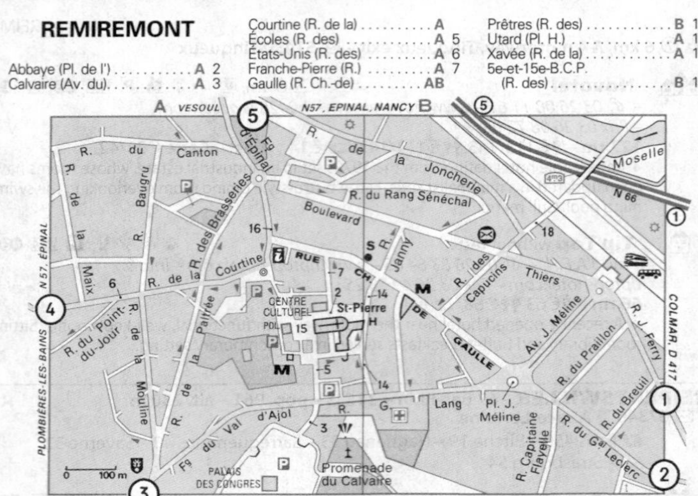

in Girmont-Val-d'Ajol 7 km southeast by D 23, D 57 and secondary road – pop. 273 – alt. 650 m – ✉ 88340

La Vigotte
131 lieu-dit la Vigotte – ✆ 03 29 24 01 82 – www.vigotte.com – contact@vigotte.com – Fax 03 29 24 04 55 – Closed 9-28 March, 7-18 December, Tuesday and Wednesday
25 rm – †€ 36/76 ††€ 45/95, ☕ € 8 – ½ P € 50/65 **Rest** – Menu € 23
◆ Old Vosges farmhouse set amidst forest and ponds. Tasteful rooms decorated with sponge painted walls, attractive furniture and paintings. Enjoy traditional dishes in an ambiance reminiscent of a family house in the country (large fireplace).

REMOULINS – 30 Gard – 339 M5 – pop. 1 996 – alt. 27 m – ✉ 30210 23 D2

Provence

Paris 685 – Alès 50 – Arles 37 – Avignon 23 – Nîmes 23 – Orange 34 – Pont-St-Esprit 40

Office de tourisme, place des Grands Jours ✆ 04 66 37 22 34, Fax 04 66 37 22 34

in St-Hilaire-d'Ozilhan 4.5 km Northeast by D792 – pop. 656 – alt. 55 m – ✉ 30210

L'Arceau
1 r. Arceau – ✆ 04 66 37 34 45 – www.hotel-arceau.com – contact@hotel-arceau.com – Fax 04 66 37 33 90 – Closed 20 December-14 February, Sunday dinner, Tuesday lunch and Monday from 1st October to Easter
23 rm – †€ 80/85 ††€ 80/85, ☕ € 9 **Rest** – Menu € 25/60 – Carte € 30/60
◆ 18C residence with a fine stone façade in a village set amongst vineyards and scrubland. Well-kept, simply furnished and quite spacious rooms. Part-traditional, part-regional cuisine served in a Provençal coloured, neo-rustic dining room or on a shaded terrace.

RENAISON – 42 Loire – 327 C3 – pop. 2 798 – alt. 387 m – ✉ 42370 44 A1

Lyon - Rhone Valley

Paris 385 – Chauffailles 43 – Lapalisse 39 – Roanne 11 – St-Étienne 90 – Thiers 74 – Vichy 56

Syndicat d'initiative, 50, route de Roanne ✆ 04 77 62 17 07

Town★ of St-Haon-le-Châtel North: 2 km - Barrage de la Tache: rocher-belvédère★ West: 5 km.

Central
8 r. du 10 Août 1944 – ✆ 04 77 64 25 39 – hotelcentral.renaison@orange.fr – Fax 04 77 62 13 09 – Closed February holidays
9 rm – †€ 40 ††€ 40/55, ☕ € 6
Rest – *(closed Wednesday)* Menu € 11 bi (weekday lunch), € 20/34 – Carte € 25/35
◆ This family hotel situated on the village square, houses small, unpretentious rooms with good bedding and modern bathrooms. Tasty regional fare served on a terrace in fine weather.

La Ferme d'Irène without rest
Platelin – ✆ 04 77 64 29 12 – www.platelin.com – contact@platelin.com – Fax 04 77 62 14 79
3 rm ☕ – †€ 67 ††€ 72
◆ Peacefully located 19C farmhouse in open countryside. Very cosy lounge (grand piano, earthenware stove). Stylish rooms located in the former cowshed and hen house.

Jacques Cœur
15 r. Roanne – ✆ 04 77 64 25 34 – Fax 04 77 64 43 88 – Closed 23 March-7 April, 7-18 September, Sunday dinner, Monday and Tuesday
Rest – Menu € 20 (weekdays)/40 – Carte € 37/46
◆ "Nothing is impossible if you set your mind to it": this restaurant illustrates the motto of Charles VII's famous Treasurer, with its 1946 murals and modern-style decor. Pretty terrace.

St-Haon-le-Vieux 3 km North by D 8 – pop. 859 – alt. 424 m – ✉ 42370

Auberge du Bon Accueil
La Croix Lucas – ✆ 04 77 64 40 72 – auberge-bon-accueil2@wanadoo.fr – Closed 13-22 April, 24 August-2 September, 26-30 October, 4-31 January, Wednesday except July-August, Monday and Tuesday
Rest – Menu € 20/52 – Carte € 31/53
◆ This inn set by the side of the main road has a small garden in front of it. Sober, rustic dining room and traditional, well-presented food.

"Rest" appears in red for establishments with a ✿ (star) or ☺ (Bib Gourmand).

RENNES P – 35 Ille-et-Vilaine – **309** L6 – **pop. 210 500** – **Built-up area 272 263** – **alt. 40 m** – ✉ **35000** Brittany — 10 **D2**

Paris 349 – Angers 129 – Brest 246 – Caen 185 – Le Mans 155 – Nantes 108
Rennes-St-Jacques: ✆ 02 99 29 60 00, 8 km on the ⑦
Office de tourisme, 11, rue Saint-Yves ✆ 02 99 67 11 11, Fax 02 99 67 11 00
18 de la Freslonnière Le Rheu7 km on the Ploërmel road, ✆ 02 99 14 84 09
18 de Cicé Blossac Bruz Domaine de Cicé-Blossac, 10 km on the Redon road, ✆ 02 99 52 79 79
9 de Cesson-Sévigné Cesson-Sévigné Île de Tizé, E : 11 km on D 96, ✆ 02 99 83 26 74
27 de Rennes Saint-Jacques Saint-Jacques-de-la-Lande Le Temple du Cerisier, 11 km on the Redon road, ✆ 02 99 30 18 18
Old Rennes★★ - Jardin du Thabor★★ - Palais de justice (law courts)★★ - Altar-piece★★ inside★ St-Pierre cathedral AY - Museums: de Bretagne★, des Beaux-Arts★ BY **M**.

Plans on following pages

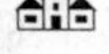

Mercure Colombier — rm, — ABZ **m**
1 r. Cap. Maignan – ✆ 02 99 29 73 73 – www.mercure.com – h1249@accor.com – Fax 02 99 29 54 00
142 rm – †€ 55/255 ††€ 67/297, ☕ € 16 **Rest** – *(dinner only)* Carte € 15/40
◆ This Mercure has undergone a large-scale refurbishment. Rooms are partly done up. The décor in the lobby and wine bar (informal dining) evokes the Brocéliande forest.

RENNES

Bourgeois (Bd L.) .... DV 3
Canada (Av. du) .... CV 6
Churchill (Av. Sir W.) .... CU 13
Combes (Bd E.) .... DV 14
Duchesse-Anne (Bd de la) .. DU 15
Guilloux (R. L.) .... CU 23
Laennec (Bd) .... DU 31
Leroux (Bd Oscar) .... DV 36
Lorient (R. de) .... CU 38
Maginot (Av. du Sergent) .. DU 39
Pompidou (Bd G.) .... CV 55
St-Brieuc (R. du) .... CU 64
St-Jean-Baptiste de la Salle (Bd) .... CU 70
Strasbourg (Bd de) .... DU 83
Ukraine (Allée d') .... CV 84
Vitré (Bd de) .... DU 87
Yser (Bd de l') .... CV 88
3-Croix (Bd des) .... CU 89

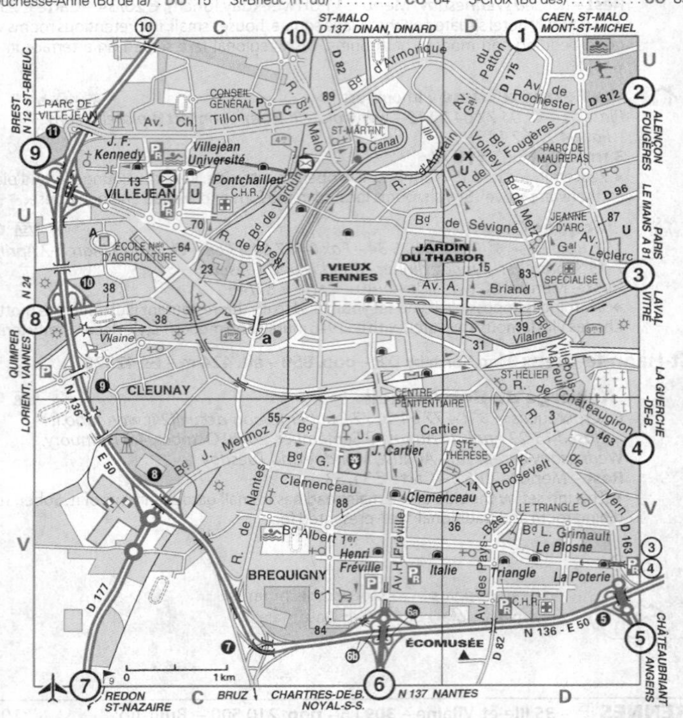

Le Coq-Gadby rm, VISA

156 r. Antrain – ✆ 02 99 38 05 55 – www.lecoq-gadby.com – lecoq-gadby@wanadoo.fr – Fax 02 99 38 53 40 DU **x**

22 rm – €130/280 €180/330, € 18 – 2 suites

Rest *La Coquerie* – *(closed 12-20 April, 26 July-25 August, 25 October-2 November, 27 December-4 January, 21 February-1st March, Wednesday lunch, Sunday and Monday)* Menu (€ 30 bi), € 35 (weekday lunch), € 49/70 bi – Carte € 66/75

Spec. Légumes racines et fruits de saison à l'huile d'argan. Canard colvert rôti, jus d'une sangria. Sablé breton à la cannelle, fraises et framboises au sirop d'agrumes. **Wines** Savennières, Pouilly-Fumé.

◆ Charming grouping of buildings dating from the 17C with refined rooms and suites. There is an eco spa and organic treatments, as well as cooking and flower arranging classes. Artwork and cockerel trinkets decorate La Coquerie where classic cuisine is served. Pool.

Anne de Bretagne without rest VISA

12 r. Tronjolly – ✆ 02 99 31 49 49 – www.hotel-rennes.com – hotelannedebretagne@wanadoo.fr – Fax 02 99 30 53 48 – Closed 24 December-3 January AZ **q**

42 rm – €68/120 €68/120, € 10

◆ Hotel dating from the 1970s close to the historic town centre. Modern lobby, pleasant bar and spacious, well-equipped contemporary bedrooms.

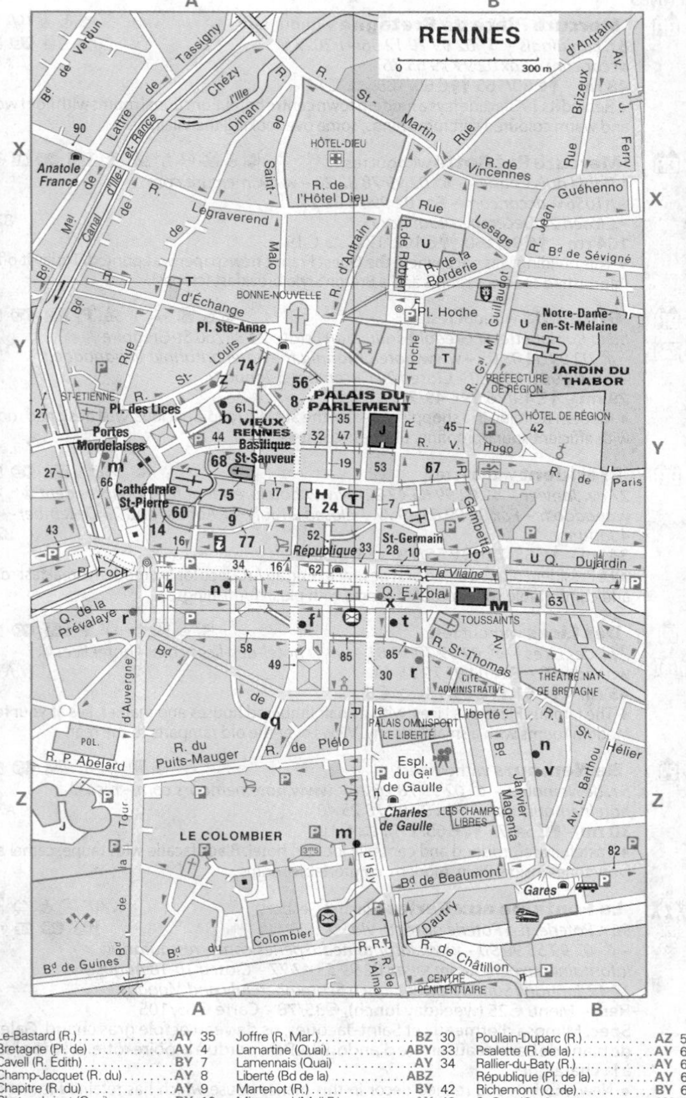

Le-Bastard (R.)	AY	35
Bretagne (Pl. de)	AY	4
Cavell (R. Édith)	BY	7
Champ-Jacquet (R. du)	AY	8
Chapitre (R. du)	AY	9
Chateaubriant (Quai)	BY	10
Dames (R. des)	AY	14
Duguay-Trouin (Quai)	AY	16
Du-Guesclin (R.)	AY	17
Estrées (R. d')	AY	19
La-Fayette (R.)	AY	32
Hôtel-de-Ville (Pl. de l')	AY	24
Ille-et-Rance (Quai)	AY	27
Jean-Jaurès (R.)	BY	28
Joffre (R. Mar.)	BZ	30
Lamartine (Quai)	ABY	33
Lamennais (Quai)	AY	34
Liberté (Bd de la)	ABZ	
Martenot (R.)	BY	42
Mitterrand (Mail F.)	AY	43
Monnaie (R. de la)	AY	44
Motte-Fablet (R.)	AY	46
Motte (Cont. de la)	BY	45
Nationale (R.)	ABY	47
Nemours (R. de)	AZ	49
Orléans (R. d')	AY	52
Palais (Pl. du)	BY	53
Pont-aux-Foulons (R. du)	AY	56
Poullain-Duparc (R.)	AZ	58
Psalette (R. de la)	AY	60
Rallier-du-Baty (R.)	AY	61
République (Pl. de la)	AY	62
Richemont (Q. de)	BY	63
St-Cast (Quai)	AY	66
St-Georges (R.)	BY	67
St-Guillaume (R.)	AY	68
St-Michel (R.)	AY	74
St-Sauveur (R.)	AY	75
St-Yves (R.)	AY	77
Solférino (Bd)	BZ	82
Vasselot (R.)	AZ	85
41e-d'Infanterie (R.)	AX	90

Mercure Place de Bretagne without rest
6 r. Lanjuinais – ✆ 02 99 79 12 36 – h2027@accor.com – Fax 02 99 79 65 76 AY **n**
48 rm – †€ 60/165 ††€ 60/185, ☕ € 14
◆ Behind its 19C façade lays a modern town centre hotel. Functional rooms with light wood and warm coloured soft furnishings, some overlooking the Vilaine.

Mercure Pré Botté without rest
r. Paul Louis Courier – ✆ 02 99 78 82 20 – www.mercure.com – h1056@accor.com – Fax 02 99 78 82 21 – Closed 24 December-4 January BZ **t**
104 rm – †€ 90/160 ††€ 102/172, ☕ € 19
◆ This building was once where the Ouest France newspaper was printed. Today it offers refurbished spacious rooms and a Breton style breakfast (crepes).

Britannia without rest
bd la Robiquette, St Grégoire Industrial Estate ✉ 35760 St-Grégoire – ✆ 02 99 54 03 03 – www.hotelbritannia.fr – hotel.britannia@wanadoo.fr – Fax 02 99 54 03 80 – Closed 24 December-3 January
29 rm – †€ 49/76 ††€ 49/76, ☕ € 9
◆ Modern building in a shopping area on the St Malo road. Spacious, well designed rooms with efficient soundproofing. Business clientele.

Président without rest
27 av. Janvier – ✆ 02 99 65 42 22 – www.hotelpresident.fr – hotelpresident@wanadoo.fr – Fax 02 99 65 49 77 – Closed 24 July-17 August and 23 December-4 January BZ **n**
34 rm – †€ 55/72 ††€ 55/78, ☕ € 8,50
◆ Le Président offers a blend of styles, including an Art Deco lobby, modern breakfast room and comfortable soundproofed rooms with plush furnishings.

Des Lices without rest
7 pl. des Lices – ✆ 02 99 79 14 81 – www.hotel-des-lices.com – hotel.lices@wanadoo.fr – Fax 02 99 79 35 44 AY **b**
45 rm – †€ 61 ††€ 65/73, ☕ € 8
◆ The famous Place des Lices, with its half timbered houses and market, lies at your feet. Modern rooms with a small balcony. Views over the old ramparts to the rear.

De Nemours without rest
5 r. de Nemours – ✆ 02 99 78 26 26 – www.hotelnemours.com – resa@hotelnemours.com – Fax 02 99 78 25 40 AZ **f**
30 rm – †€ 54/75 ††€ 65/110, ☕ € 10
◆ Tastefully refurbished and centrally located hotel. Black facade with taupe, camel and ivory tones inside. Plain, modern, comfortable rooms.

La Fontaine aux Perles (Rachel Gesbert)
96 r. Poterie, (La Poterie district), via ④ – ✆ 02 99 53 90 90 – www.lafontaineauxperles.com – restaurant@lafontaineauxperles.com – Fax 02 99 53 47 77 – Closed 10-18 August, 1st-12 January, Sunday except lunch September-July and Monday
Rest – Menu € 25 (weekday lunch), € 35/78 – Carte € 85/105
Spec. Mimosa d'ormeaux et Saint-Jacques, ris de veau et foie gras chaud. Galette de blanc de barbue au tartare d'andouille. Pain perdu à la poire rôtie, crème glacée à la châtaigne.
◆ New, modern and refined decor in this manor house which has retained it original, themed guestrooms (champagne, wine, Rennes football club). Personalised cuisine. Delightful terrace in a leafy garden.

L'Ouvrée
18 pl. Lices – ✆ 02 99 30 16 38 – www.louvree.com – restaurantlouvree@wanadoo.fr – Fax 02 99 30 16 38 – Closed 13-20 April, 27 July-17 August, Saturday lunch, Sunday dinner and Monday AY **z**
Rest – Menu € 15/34 – Carte € 42/52
◆ Built in 1659, this house is a Rennes institution. The classic style of decor continues in the kitchen. Wine inspired suppers which change on a monthly basis.

XX **Le Guehennec**

33 r. Nantaise – ✆ 02 99 65 51 30 – www.leguehennec.com – Fax 02 99 65 68 26 – Closed 2 weeks in August, Saturday lunch, Monday dinner and Sunday AY **m**

Rest – Menu € 20 (weekday lunch), € 38/48 – Carte € 62/74

◆ A fine combination of light wooden panelling and modern furniture in chocolate shades help to make this restaurant most appealing. Modern cuisine with market produce.

XX **Le Galopin**

21 av. Janvier – ✆ 02 99 31 55 96 – www.le-galopin.fr – legalopin.rennes@orange.fr – Fax 02 99 31 08 95 – Closed August, Saturday lunch and Sunday BZ **v**

Rest – Menu € 18 (weekdays)/46 – Carte € 35/60

◆ Old fashioned wooden frontage contrasts with the dynamic atmosphere inside: modern decor and young staff serving brasserie cuisine and surf and turf (lobster).

X **Le Quatre B**

4 pl. Bretagne – ✆ 02 99 30 42 01 – www.quatreb.fr – quatreb@wanadoo.fr – Fax 02 99 30 42 01 – Closed Monday lunch, Saturday lunch and Sunday

Rest – Menu (€ 12), € 16 (weekday lunch), € 20/27 – Carte € 32/47 AYZ **r**

◆ Refined dining room with red banquettes, modern chairs and large, floral themed canvasses. Pleasant terrace. The contemporary style successfully extends to the cuisine.

X **Autre Sens**

11 r. Armand Rebillon – ✆ 02 99 14 25 14 – Fax 02 99 14 26 00 – Closed 22 July-8 August, Saturday lunch and Sunday CU **b**

Rest – Menu € 18 (lunch), € 27/30

◆ Restaurant refurbished in a contemporary bistro style next to the Ille and Rance canal. Two waterside terraces (the smaller of which is raised). Tempting modern menu.

X **Léon le Cochon**

1 r. Mar. Joffre – ✆ 02 99 79 37 54 – www.leonlecochon.com – Fax 02 99 79 07 35 BY **x**

Rest – Menu (€ 13 bi) – Carte € 31/50

◆ If you're in the mood for pork, try Léon's excellent dishes, served in a relaxed modern décor (floodlit trees, apple green timbers). Grilled pork and fish.

X **Le Petit Sabayon**

16 r. Trente – ✆ 02 99 35 02 04 – lepetitsabayon@free.fr – Closed 2-9 March, 24 August-8 September, Saturday lunch, Sunday dinner and Monday CU **a**

Rest – *(number of covers limited, pre-book)* Menu € 16 (weekday lunch), € 24/32 – Carte € 32/39

◆ Discretely tucked away restaurant in a quiet area of town. The locals come to enjoy the appetising cuisine made using market produce served in the pleasant dining room.

X **Les Carmes**

2 r. Carmes – ✆ 02 99 79 28 95 – lescarmes.rennes@free.fr – Fax 02 99 79 28 95 – Closed Sunday dinner and Monday BZ **r**

Rest – Menu (€ 15), € 30/65 bi – Carte € 32/47

◆ This restaurant with a chocolate coloured facade comes highly recommended. The young chef prepares modern cuisine served in a contemporary setting.

in St-Grégoire 3 km North by D82 – pop. 7 977 – alt. 45 m – ✉ 35760

XXX **Le Saison** (David Etcheverry)

1 imp. Vieux Bourg, (near the church) – ✆ 02 99 68 79 35 – www.le-saison.com – contact@le-saison.com – Fax 02 99 68 92 71 – Closed 3-24 August, 3-10 January, Sunday dinner and Monday

Rest – Menu (€ 27), € 38/75 – Carte € 60/87

Spec. Trois dimensions pour une étrille de roche (September to January). Noisettes de cochon de lait, tomato-cèpes et tartine d'abats (September to November). Tubes de potimarron au vieux bourbon et mûres sauvages (September to November).

◆ Large, rebuilt long house surrounded by a garden. Tasty modern cuisine in a contemporary dining room (beige and chocolate shades); pleasant terrace.

in Cesson-Sévigné 6 km by ③ – pop. 15 800 – alt. 28 m – ✉ 35510

Germinal
rest, VISA AE

9 cours Vilaine, in the village – ✆ 02 99 83 11 01 – le-germinal@wanadoo.fr – Fax 02 99 83 45 16 – Closed 23 December-4 January

18 rm – †€ 80/100 ††€ 90/160, ☐ € 12

Rest – *(closed Sunday)* Menu (€ 18), € 22 (weekday lunch), € 32/55 – Carte € 43/64

◆ This family hotel occupying a former mill is set son a stretch of the Vilaine reached via a bridge. Renovated rooms and communal areas. Lovely dining room/veranda decorated in a modern style and a superb modern terrace facing the river. Traditional menu.

L'Adresse
VISA AE

32 cours Vilaine – ✆ 02 99 83 82 06 – www.restaurant-ladresse.com – Closed 2-24 August, 9-15 February, Monday dinner, Saturday lunch and Sunday

Rest – Menu (€ 14 bi), € 17 bi (weekday lunch), € 27/45 – Carte € 24/42

◆ Small, old style café with waterside terrace shaded by wisteria. A bistro style repertoire is served with Brittany specialities to the fore.

in Noyal-sur-Vilaine 12 km by ③ – pop. 4 794 – alt. 75 m – ✉ 35530

Auberge du Pont d'Acigné (Sylvain Guillemot)
P VISA AE

rte d'Acigné: 3 km – ✆ 02 99 62 52 55 – www.auberge-du-pont-dacigne.com – pont.d.acigne@wanadoo.fr – Fax 02 99 62 21 70 – Closed 1 week in April, 2-21 August, 2-8 January, Saturday lunch, Sunday dinner and Monday

Rest – Menu € 26 (weekday lunch), € 38/75 – Carte € 80/110

Spec. Craquant de homard (June to September). Saint-Jacques poêlées et céleri confit (October to March). Gaufres de figues fraîches (August to October).

◆ Good regional cuisine served in a lovely dining area or on the terrace overlooking the Vilaine. Views of the village. Excellent range of wines by the glass.

Hostellerie Les Forges with rm
rm, P VISA AE

22 av. du Gén. de Gaulle – ✆ 02 99 00 51 08 – sarl.lesforges@orange.fr – Fax 02 99 00 62 02 – Closed 1st-24 August, 19-28 February, Friday dinner, Sunday dinner and public holidays dinner

12 rm – †€ 40/45 ††€ 40/55, ☐ € 7

Rest – Menu € 15 (weekday lunch), € 20/35 – Carte € 40/46

◆ This captivating roadside hotel has two dining rooms, one with a rustic decor and attractive fireplace. Simple, modern and comfortable bedrooms.

St-Nazaire road 8 km by ⑦ – ✉35170 Bruz

Kerlann
rm, rest, P VISA AE

– ✆ 02 99 05 95 80 – www.kerlann.fr – direction@hotel-kerlann.fr – Fax 02 99 05 94 10

52 rm – †€ 80/150 ††€ 80/150, ☐ € 12 – 3 suites – ½ P € 75/109

Rest – *(Closed August, 24 December-4 January, Saturday and Sunday)* Menu (€ 19), € 26/29 – Carte € 35/47

◆ Modern building located between the airport and Cicé golf course. The rooms, laid out around a patio, are comfortable and colourful. Asian inspired suites. Brasserie style snacks in a setting with Chinese touches.

Le Rheu 8 km by ⑧ and D 224 – pop. 6 920 – alt. 30 m – ✉ 35650

Le Relais Fleuri
P VISA

Les Landes d'Apigné – ✆ 02 99 14 60 14 – www.hotel-restaurant-lerelaisfleuri.fr – hotel.lerelaisfleuri@wanadoo.fr – Fax 02 99 14 60 03 – Closed 10-30 August and 24 December-3 January

24 rm – †€ 48/75 ††€ 56/80, ☐ € 7

Rest – Menu (€ 13), € 15 (weekday lunch), € 18/28 – Carte approx. € 33

◆ The new owners of this inn serve traditional cuisine. Modernised rooms offer contemporary comforts.

Lorient road 6 km by ⑧, N 24 – ✉ 35650 Le Rheu

XXX **Manoir du Plessis** with rm rm, VISA MC AE
– ✆ 02 99 14 79 79 – www.manoirduplessis.fr – info@manoirduplessis.fr
– Fax 02 99 14 69 60 – Closed 10-17 August and 28 December-4 January
5 rm – †€ 95 ††€ 100, ☕ € 12
Rest – *(closed Saturday lunch, Sunday dinner and Monday)*
Menu € 17 (weekday lunch), € 23/38 – Carte approx. € 48
◆ A family mansion set in a park. Parquet floors, wood panelling, fireplaces, Louis XVI -style chairs and an attractive terrace create an ideal setting to enjoy your meal.

LA RÉOLE – **33 Gironde** – **335** K7 – **pop. 4 218** – **alt. 44 m** – ✉ **33190** 4 **C2**

Paris 649 – Bordeaux 74 – Casteljaloux 42 – Duras 25 – Libourne 45 – Marmande 33

Office de tourisme, 18, rue Peysseguin ✆ 05 56 61 13 55, Fax 05 56 71 25 40

XX **Aux Fontaines** VISA MC
8 r. de Verdun – ✆ 05 56 61 15 25 – Fax 05 56 61 15 25 – Closed 15 November-1st December, 28 February-8 March, Sunday dinner, Wednesday dinner and Monday in low season
Rest – *(number of covers limited, pre-book)* Menu € 20/45
◆ Restaurant in a large town centre building constructed against a hill. In summer meals are served on the attractive garden terrace. Traditional cuisine.

LA RÉPARA-AURIPLES – **26 Drôme** – **332** D6 – **see Crest**

RESTONICA (GORGES) – **2B Haute-Corse** – **345** D6 – **see Corse (Corte)**

RETHONDES – **60 Oise** – **305** I4 – **see Compiègne**

REUGNY – **03 Allier** – **326** C4 – **pop. 269** – **alt. 204 m** – ✉ **03190** 5 **B1**

Paris 312 – Bourbon-l'Archambault 43 – Montluçon 15 – Montmarault 45 – Moulins 64

XX **La Table de Reugny** AC VISA MC
25 rte de Paris – ✆ 04 70 06 70 06 – www.restaurant-reugny.com – info@restaurant-reugny.com – Fax 04 70 06 77 52 – Closed 24 August-6 September, 2-9 January, Sunday dinner, Monday and Tuesday
Rest – Menu (€ 16), € 21 (weekdays), € 28/47 – Carte approx. € 28
◆ Behind the imposing façade of this roadside restaurant is a welcoming dining room decorated in red and a terrace overlooking the garden. Enticing contemporary cuisine.

REUILLY-SAUVIGNY – **02 Aisne** – **306** D8 – **pop. 234** – **alt. 78 m** – ✉ 02850 37 **C3**

Paris 109 – Épernay 34 – Château-Thierry 16 – Reims 50 – Soissons 46 – Troyes 116

XXX **Auberge Le Relais** (Martial Berthuit) with rm AC rm, P VISA MC AE
2 r. de Paris – ✆ 03 23 70 35 36
– www.relaisreuilly.com – auberge.relais.de.reuilly@wanadoo.fr
– Fax 03 23 70 27 76 – Closed 16 August-3 September, 2 February-5 March, Tuesday and Wednesday
7 rm – †€ 75/92 ††€ 80/98, ☕ € 15
Rest – Menu € 32 (weekdays)/82 – Carte € 82/100
Spec. Langoustines poêlées, râpée de pomme granny-smith. Noix de ris de veau au sautoir, échalote fumée et vinaigrette de légumes au miel et citron. Autour de la figue (September-October). **Wines** Coteaux Champenois, Champagne.
◆ Elegant new interior, attractive veranda surrounded by greenery and a delicate cuisine that subtly blends tradition and modernity: a smart inn with boundless appeal.

REVEL – 31 Haute-Garonne – 343 K4 – pop. 8 648 – alt. 210 m 29 C2
– ✉ 31250 Languedoc-Roussillon-Tarn Gorges

Paris 727 – Carcassonne 46 – Castelnaudary 21 – Castres 28 – Gaillac 62 – Toulouse 54

Office de tourisme, place Philippe VI de Valois ✆ 05 34 66 67 68, Fax 05 34 66 67 67

Du Midi
34 bd Gambetta – ✆ 05 61 83 50 50 – www.hotelrestaurantdumidi.com – contact@hotelrestaurantdumidi.com – Fax 05 61 83 34 74 – Closed 23-29 November

17 rm – †€ 49/55 ††€ 49/70, ☕ € 7 – ½ P € 51/56

Rest – *(closed 23-30 March, 12 November-6 December, Sunday dinner and Monday lunch from October to June except public holidays)*
Menu (€ 14), € 23/45 bi – Carte € 32/48

◆ Situated on a busy boulevard, this 19C post house offers a variety of rooms. Those at the rear are quieter. Bright dining room serving a combination of local produce with traditional cuisine.

in St-Ferréol 3 km Southeast by D 629 – ✉ 31250

Bassin de St-Ferréol★.

La Comtadine
rm, rest, VISA MC AE

Lieu dit l'Hermitage – ✆ 05 61 81 73 03 – www.lacomtadine.com – contact@lacomtadine.com – Fax 05 34 66 53 28

9 rm – †€ 65/80 ††€ 65/80, ☕ € 9

Rest – *(dinner only) (residents only)* Menu € 25 bi

◆ A restored peaceful little hotel, just a stone's throw from the lake. Bright modern rooms, enhanced with antique furniture. Non-smoking. Cuisine with a distinctly regional accent.

REVENTIN-VAUGRIS – 38 Isère – 333 C5 – see Vienne

REVIGNY-SUR-ORNAIN – Meuse – 307 A6 – pop. 3 206 – alt. 144 m 26 A2
– ✉ 55800

Paris 239 – Bar-le-Duc 18 – St-Dizier 30 – Vitry-le-François 36

Syndicat d'initiative, rue du Stade ✆ 03 29 78 73 34, Fax 03 29 78 73 34

La Maison Forte without rest
6 pl. Henriot-du-Coudray – ✆ 03 29 70 78 94 – www.lamaisonforte.fr – caroline_cheurlin@hotmail.com

5 rm ☕ – †€ 65 ††€ 80

◆ This 18C edifice was formerly the property of the Duke of Bar and then the Duke of Lorraine. Characterful rooms and homemade breakfasts (jams and fresh fruit pies).

RÉVILLE – 50 Manche – 303 E2 – pop. 1 198 – alt. 12 m – ✉ 50760 32 A1

Paris 351 – Carentan 44 – Cherbourg 30 – St-Lô 72 – Valognes 22

La Pernelle ※★★ of the blockhouse West: 3 km - Pointe de Saire: blockhouse ≤★ Southeast: 2,5 km, Normandy

La Villa Gervaiserie without rest
VISA MC

17 rte des Monts – ✆ 02 33 54 54 64 – www.lagervaiserie.com – la.gervaiserie@wanadoo.fr – Fax 02 33 54 73 00 – Open from April to mid-November

10 rm – †€ 85/114 ††€ 85/114, ☕ € 8,50

◆ Facing the beach, all this hotel's rooms have a balcony or terrace with a view of the sea or Tatihou Island. Pleasant modern decoration and considerate welcome. Fine wooded garden.

Au Moyne de Saire with rm
VISA MC

15 r. Général de Gaulle – ✆ 02 33 54 46 06 – www.au-moyne-de-saire.com – au.moyne.de.saire@wanadoo.fr – Fax 02 33 54 14 99 – Closed 21-29 December and Monday

12 rm – †€ 44 ††€ 50/85, ☕ € 8 – ½ P € 45/60

Rest – Menu € 17 (weekdays)/33 – Carte € 24/75

◆ A family inn that extends a warm welcome to guests. Tasteful refined interior, traditional and Norman cuisine. Small, well-kept rooms.

REY – 30 Gard – **339** G4 – **see Le Vigan**

REZÉ – 44 Loire-Atlantique – **316** G4 – **see Nantes**

LE RHEU – 35 Ille-et-Vilaine – **309** L6 – **see Rennes**

LE RHIEN – 70 Haute-Saône – **314** H6 – **see Ronchamp**

RHINAU – 67 Bas-Rhin – **315** K7 – **pop. 2 613 – alt. 158 m** – ✉ **67860** 1 **B2**

Paris 525 – Marckolsheim 26 – Molsheim 38 – Obernai 28 – Sélestat 28 – Strasbourg 39

Office de tourisme, 35, rue du Rhin ✆ 03 88 74 68 96, Fax 03 88 74 83 28

Au Vieux Couvent (Alexis Albrecht) VISA MC AE

– ✆ 03 88 74 61 15 – www.vieuxcouvent.fr – restaurant@vieuxcouvent.fr – Fax 03 88 74 89 19 – Closed 29 June-17 July, 12-16 October, two weeks in February-March, Monday dinner, Tuesday and Wednesday

Rest – Menu € 35 (weekdays)/138 bi – Carte € 66/100

Spec. Faux millefeuille de saumon fumé minute. Dos de bar sauvage rôti, légumes de notre potager (summer-autumn). Baba au kirsch et trois chantillys vertes.
Wines Riesling, Pinot blanc.

◆ The name of the restaurant invites contemplation, and the interior reinforces this. Graceful welcome. Inventive cuisine using herbs and flowers grown with passion by the chef.

RIANS – 83 Var – **340** J4 – **pop. 4 127 – alt. 406 m** – ✉ **83560** 40 **B3**

Paris 770 – Aix-en-Provence 40 – Avignon 100 – Manosque 33 – Marseille 69 – Toulon 77

Office de tourisme, place du Posteuil ✆ 04 94 80 33 37, Fax 04 94 80 33 37

La Roquette P VISA MC

1 km via Manosque road – ✆ 04 94 80 32 58 – Fax 04 94 80 32 58 – Closed 29 June-5 July, 18-25 November, 2-13 January, Sunday dinner, Wednesday and dinner in winter except Saturday and Sunday

Rest – Menu € 28/48

◆ A family residence serving a regional menu, which changes with the seasons. Three discreetly Provencal dining rooms and pleasant terrace under an arbour.

RIANTEC – 56 Morbihan – **308** L8 – **pop. 4 910 – alt. 4 m** – ✉ **56670** 9 **B2**

Paris 503 – Rennes 152 – Vannes 59 – Lorient 16 – Lanester 14

La Chaumière de Kervassal without rest P

3 km north of Kervassal – ✆ 02 97 33 58 66 – www.tymaya.com – gonzague.watine@wanadoo.fr – Fax 02 97 33 58 66 – Open April-mid October

3 rm – †€ 75 ††€ 75

◆ This former home of the vassal, after whom Kervassal is named, welcomes guests to its cosy sitting room and classic or more modern guestrooms. Pretty garden.

RIBEAUVILLÉ – 68 Haut-Rhin – **315** H7 – **pop. 4 948 – alt. 240 m – Casino** – ✉ **68150** Alsace-Lorraine 2 **C2**

Paris 439 – Colmar 16 – Mulhouse 60 – St-Dié 42 – Sélestat 14

Grand'Rue★★: tour des Bouchers★.

Riquewihr★★★ - Château du Haut-Ribeaupierre: ❋★★ - Château de St-Ullrich★: ❋★★.

RIBEAUVILLÉ

Abbé-Kremp (R. de l') . . . . A 2
Château (R. du) . . . . A 3
Flesch (R.) . . . . B 5
Fontaine (R. de la) . . . . A 6
Frères-Mertian (R. des) . . . . . . A 7
Gaulle (Av. du Gén.-de) . . . . . . B 9
Gouraud (Pl.) . . . . B 10
Grand'Rue . . . . AB
Grand'Rue de l' Eglise . . . . A 21
Halle aux Blés (R. de la) . . . . . B 12
Hôtel de Ville (Pl. de l') . . . . . A 13
Ortlieb (R.) . . . . B 14
Ste-Marie-aux-Mines (Rte) . . . . A 15
Sinne (Pl. de la) . . . . A 16
Synagogue (R. de la) . . . . B 17
Tanneurs (R. des) . . . . B 18

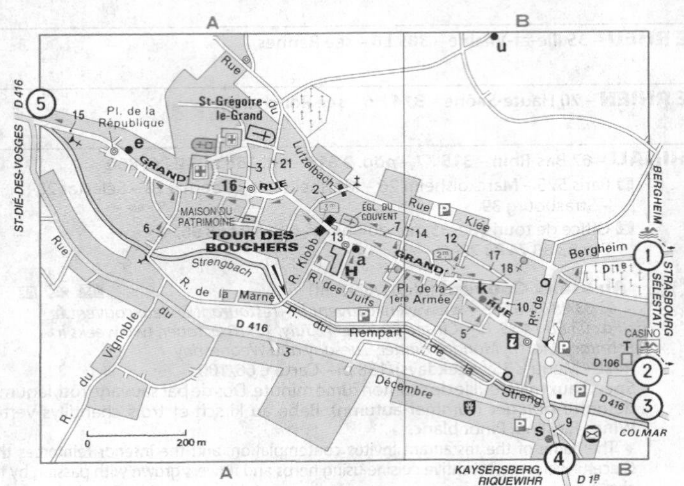

Le Clos St-Vincent rm, VISA
Bergheim road, 1.5 km north-east by secondary road – ☎ 03 89 73 67 65 – www.leclossaintvincent.com – reception.leclos@wanadoo.fr – Fax 03 89 73 32 20 – Open 15 March-15 December B u
20 rm – €120/215 €140/215, €15 – 4 suites
Rest – *(closed Tuesday) (dinner only)* Menu €40/55
◆ Admire the superb view over the Alsace plain from this peaceful 1960s house among the vineyards. Vast, comfortable rooms, four of which have been recently renovated. Dining room and terrace with splendid panoramic views. Traditional cuisine.

Le Ménestrel without rest VISA
27 av. Gén. de Gaulle, via ④ – ☎ 03 89 73 80 52 – www.menestrel.com – menestrel2@wanadoo.fr – Fax 03 89 73 32 39
29 rm – €63/73 €73/99, €15
◆ Pleasantly upgraded rooms, some with balcony. The owner, a pastry chef, prepares the breakfast pastries and jams himself.

La Tour without rest VISA
1 r. de la Mairie – ☎ 03 89 73 72 73 – www.hotel-la-tour.com – info@hotel-la-tour.com – Fax 03 89 73 38 74 – Closed 4 January-12 March A a
31 rm – €67/89 €73/100, €9
◆ An old winery offering bright, practical rooms. The most recent have been treated to a contemporary Vosgian makeover; those overlooking the attractive courtyard are very quiet.

Cheval Blanc VISA
122 Grand'Rue – ☎ 03 89 73 61 38 – www.cheval-blanc-alsace.fr – cheval-blanc-ribeauville@wanadoo.fr – Fax 03 89 73 37 03 – Closed 12-22 November and 6 January-12 February A e
23 rm – €56 €56, €8 – ½ P €55
Rest – *(closed Tuesday lunchtime and Wednesday)* Menu (€11 bi), €18/40 – Carte €25/46
◆ The façade of this Alsace building is decked with flowers in the summer. Rustic interior; modest rooms, those at the rear are quieter; a lounge with fireplace. Slightly extravagant Alsace atmosphere in this restaurant serving traditional cuisine.

XX **Au Relais des Ménétriers** VISA MC
10 av. Gén. de Gaulle – ✆ 03 89 73 64 52 – Fax 03 89 73 69 94 – Closed 14-29 July, Thursday dinner, Sunday dinner and Monday B s
Rest – Menu € 12 (weekday lunch), € 23/37 – Carte € 37/52
◆ Pride of place to regional specialities using locally grown vegetables and traditional Alsace crockery (authentic *baeckoeffe* dishes). Pleasant rustic décor.

X **Wistub Zum Pfifferhüs** VISA MC
14 Grand'Rue – ✆ 03 89 73 62 28 – Closed 1st-12 March, 1st-14 July, 25 January-21 February, Thursday from November to July and Wednesday B k
Rest – *(pre-book)* Menu € 26 – Carte € 34/52
◆ A charming "winstub" with a friendly authentic atmosphere, particularly on Pfifferdaj (Minstrels' Day). Retro decor and appetising local cuisine.

Ste-Marie-aux-Mines road 4 km by ⑤ **on D 416 – ✉ 68150**

XX **Au Valet de Cœur et Hostel de la Pépinière** with rm ♿ rm, ⚡
– ✆ 03 89 73 64 14 – www.valetdecoeur.fr – reception@valetdecoeur.fr – Fax 03 89 73 88 78 P VISA MC AE D
16 rm – †€ 55/99 ††€ 80/99, ☕ € 10 – ½ P € 85/105
Rest – *(closed Tuesday lunch, Sunday dinner and Monday)*
Menu € 34 (weekdays)/85 – Carte € 60/82
Spec. Bâtonnet de foie gras de canard. Homard en trois façons. Soufflé aux fruits de saison. **Wines** Riesling, Gewurztraminer.
◆ This regional style building in a forest clearing serves modern cuisine, complemented by regional dishes. Bright dining room that has been elegantly redecorated. Charming rooms.

RIBÉRAC – 24 Dordogne – 329 D4 – pop. 4 123 – alt. 68 m – ✉ 24600 4 C1
Dordogne-Berry-Limousin

Paris 505 – Angoulême 58 – Barbezieux 58 – Bergerac 52 – Libourne 65 – Périgueux 39

Office de tourisme, place Charles-de-Gaulle ✆ 05 53 90 03 10, Fax 05 53 91 35 13

Rêv'Hôtel without rest ♿ ⚡ P VISA MC
rte de Périgueux, 1.5 km – ✆ 05 53 91 62 62 – www.rev-hotel.fr – contact@rev-hotel.fr – Fax 05 53 91 48 96
29 rm – †€ 42/62 ††€ 47/67, ☕ € 6
◆ A recent building in a small mixed housing development. Rooms are functional, well-kept and are all on the ground floor.

LES RICEYS – 10 Aube – 313 G6 – pop. 1 395 – alt. 180 m – ✉ 10340 13 B3
Northern France and the Paris Region

Paris 210 – Bar-sur-Aube 48 – St-Florentin 58 – Tonnerre 37 – Troyes 46

Office de tourisme, 14, place des Héros de la Résistance ✆ 03 25 29 15 38, Fax 03 25 29 15 38

XX **Le Magny** with rm ♿ ⚡ P VISA MC
rte de Tonnerre, (D 452) – ✆ 03 25 29 38 39 – www.le-magny.com – lemagny@wanadoo.fr – Fax 03 25 29 11 72 – Closed 29 August-9 September, 24 January-6 March, Tuesday except from May to September and Wednesday
12 rm – †€ 63/77 ††€ 63/77, ☕ € 9 – ½ P € 65/72
Rest – Menu € 15/40 – Carte € 28/47
◆ In the fief of the famous Rosé wine, this country-style restaurant is in a carefully-restored stone residence. The welcome is warm, menus traditional and rooms comfortable.

RICHELIEU – 37 Indre-et-Loire – 317 K6 – pop. 2 165 – alt. 40 m – ✉ 37120 11 A3
Châteaux of the Loire

Paris 299 – Joué-lès-Tours 60 – Orléans 175 – Poitiers 66

Office de tourisme, 7, Place Louis XIII ✆ 02 47 58 13 62, Fax 02 47 58 29 86

La Maison without rest
6 r. Henri Proust – 02 47 58 29 40 – www.lamaisondemichele.com – lamaisondemichele@yahoo.com – Fax 02 47 58 29 40 – Open 15 April-30 September
4 rm – €90 €110
◆ A fine well-bred house, offering spacious rooms with antique furniture, striped wallpaper and large beds. Pretty garden adorned with a bamboo patch.

RIEC-SUR-BELON – **29 Finistère** – **308** I7 – **pop. 4 129** – **alt. 65 m** – ✉ 29340 9 **B2**

Paris 529 – Carhaix-Plouguer 61 – Concarneau 20 – Quimper 43 – Quimperlé 13

Office de tourisme, 2, rue des Gentilshommes 02 98 06 97 65, Fax 02 98 06 93 73

at Port de Belon **4 km south by C 3 and C 5 – ✉ 29340 Riec-sur-Belon**

Chez Jacky VISA
port du Belon – 02 98 06 90 32 – www.chez-jacky.com – chez.jacky@wanadoo.fr – Fax 02 98 06 49 72 – Open Easter to end September and closed Sunday dinner and Monday except public holidays
Rest – *(pre-book in high season)* Menu €18/80 – Carte €24/59
◆ An attractive oyster farmer's house on the banks of the Belon. Rustic dining room with a menu focused entirely on fish and seafood. Terrace with pleasant views. The property has its own oyster basin.

RIEUMES – **31 Haute-Garonne** – **343** E4 – **pop. 3 237** – **alt. 270 m** – ✉ 31370 28 **B2**

Paris 712 – Toulouse 39 – Auch 56 – Foix 75

Auberge les Palmiers rm, rm, VISA AE
13 pl. du Foirail – 05 61 91 81 01 – www.auberge-lespalmiers.com – auberge_lespalmiers@yahoo.fr – Fax 05 61 91 56 36 – Closed 24 August-7 September, 30 October-4 November and 24 December-3 January
12 rm – €56 €62, €8 – ½ P €63
Rest – *(closed Sunday dinner and Monday)* Menu (€12), €15 (weekday lunch), €24/32 – Carte €35/50
◆ This welcoming 19C edifice (non-smoking) sports a happy blend of rustic furniture and contemporary details. Superb junior suite with its own private sauna. Spruce interior. Traditional menu enriched with regional dishes.

RIEUPEYROUX – **12 Aveyron** – **338** F5 – **pop. 2 045** – **alt. 750 m** – ✉ 12240 29 **C1**

Paris 632 – Albi 54 – Carmaux 38 – Millau 94 – Rodez 36 – Villefranche-de-Rouergue 24

Office de tourisme, 28, rue de l'Hom 05 65 65 60 00

Du Commerce P VISA AE
60 r. l'Hom – 05 65 65 53 06 – www.logis-commerce-hotel.com – hotel.j.b.delmas@wanadoo.fr – Fax 05 65 81 43 72 – Closed 27 September-6 October, 27 December-2 February, Friday evening (except hotel), Sunday evening and Monday except from 15 June to 15 September
22 rm – €50 €50/60, €8 – ½ P €52
Rest – Menu (€12), €15 (weekday lunch), €18/38 – Carte €25/40
◆ A family-run hotel with renovated rooms that are functional and well kept. Those looking onto the garden and pool are quieter. Try Tripoux du Ségala (tripe), Aveyron veau de lait (veal) or kebabs.

RIGNY – **70 Haute-Saône** – **314** B8 – **see Gray**

RILLIEUX-LA-PAPE – **69 Rhône** – **327** I5 – **see Lyon**

RIMBACH-PRÈS-GUEBWILLER – **68 Haut-Rhin** – **315** G9 – **see Guebwiller**

RIMONT – 09 Ariège – **343** F7 – **pop. 512** – **alt. 525 m** – ✉ **09420** 28 **B3**

▶ Paris 765 – Auch 136 – Foix 32 – St-Gaudens 56 – St-Girons 14 – Toulouse 92

Domaine de Terrac

4 km east on D 117 and secondary road – ✆ 05 61 96 39 60 – www.chambresdhotesariege.com – domainedeterrac@wanadoo.fr – Closed January and February

5 rm – 👤€ 75 👥€ 90, ☕ € 5 **Table d'hôte** – Menu € 30 bi

◆ This magnificently restored former farmhouse cannot fail to appeal. It offers charming and peaceful rooms; two of them have a terrace overlooking the valley. Regional cuisine, augmented by vegetarian and Indian dishes.

De la Poste

pl. 8-Mai – ✆ 05 61 96 33 23 – restaurantdelaposte@orange.fr – Fax 05 61 96 33 23 – Closed 25-30 August, 15 February-1st March, Monday dinner, Tuesday dinner and Wednesday dinner except July-August

Rest – Menu (€ 12), € 21/29 – Carte € 32/45

◆ Retro façade behind which is a bright rustic restaurant with a warm ambiance. Simple, unfussy traditional cuisine.

RIOM – 63 Puy-de-Dôme – **326** F7 – **pop. 18 000** – **alt. 363 m** – ✉ **63200** **Auvergne** 5 **B2**

▶ Paris 407 – Clermont-Ferrand 15 – Montluçon 102 – Thiers 45 – Vichy 39

ℹ Office de tourisme, 27 place de la Fédération ✆ 04 73 38 59 45, Fax 04 73 38 25 15

◉ N.-D.-du-Marthuret church★ : Virgin with bird ★★★ - Maison des Consuls★ **K** - Courtyard ★ of the hôtel Guimeneau **B** - Ste-Chapelle★ of the palais de justice(law courts) **N** - Courtyard ★ of the town hall **H** - Tour de l'Horloge★ **R** - Museums: Régional d'Auvergne★ **M^1**, Mandet★ **M^2**.

◉ Mozac: capitals★★, church★★ treasure-house★ 2 km by ④ - Marsat: Black Virgin★★ in church S-W: 3 km by D 83.

RIOM

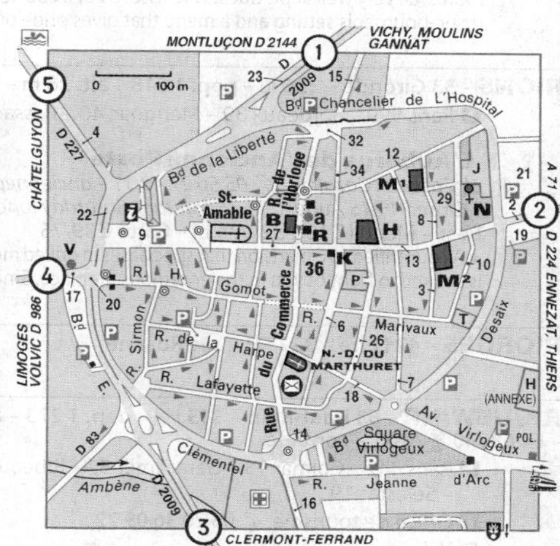

Le Moulin de Villeroze

144 rte Marsat, south-west of Le Plan on the D 83 – ✆ 04 73 38 62 23 – www.le-moulin-de-villeroze.fr – Fax 04 73 38 62 23 – Closed 17 August-4 September, Wednesday dinner, Sunday dinner and Monday

Rest – Menu € 22/48 – Carte € 55/75

◆ This mill built at the end of the 19C houses two welcoming, contemporary dining rooms with exposed beams. Shady terrace; modern menu.

Le Flamboyant
21 bis r. de l'Horloge – ✆ 04 73 63 07 97 – www.restaurant-le-flamboyant.com – restaurant.leflamboyant@wanadoo.fr – Fax 04 73 64 17 36 – Closed Sunday dinner and Monday a
Rest – Menu € 22 bi (weekday lunch), € 28/58 bi – Carte approx. € 45
◆ Admire the inner courtyards of the townhouses lining the street before entering the colourful restaurant with its low-key modern decor. Up-to-date cuisine.

Le Magnolia
11 av. Cdt Madeline – ✆ 04 73 38 08 25 – www.lemagnolia.fr – magnolia-gastronomie@wanadoo.fr – Fax 04 73 38 09 29 – Closed 1st-15 March, 2-16 August, Sunday dinner, Saturday lunch and Monday v
Rest – Menu (€ 18 bi), € 24 (weekdays)/42 – Carte € 38/46
◆ This restaurant sports a distinctive modern style, featuring brushed cement, exotic wood, burgundy walls and an original layout. Modern cuisine.

RIOM-ÈS-MONTAGNES – 15 Cantal – 330 D3 – pop. 2 727 – alt. 840 m – ✉ 15400 5 B3

Paris 506 – Aurillac 80 – Clermont-Ferrand 91 – Ussel 46
Office de tourisme, 1, avenue Fernand Brun ✆ 04 71 78 07 37, Fax 04 71 78 16 87

St-Georges
5 r. Cap. Chevalier – ✆ 04 71 78 00 15 – www.hotel-saint-georges.com – hotel.saint-georges@wanadoo.fr – Fax 04 71 78 24 37 – Closed 15-30 January
14 rm – €32/35 €44/52, € 8,50 – ½ P € 38/43
Rest – *(closed Sunday dinner and Monday lunch from 15 September to 30 June)* Menu (€ 10), € 14 (weekdays)/27 – Carte € 23/33
◆ This late-19C stone house in the village centre has small, refurbished, well-equipped rooms, all very well kept. Guests are assured of a courteous welcome. At the restaurant, a rustic-bourgeois setting and a menu that gives pride of place to Cantal dishes.

RIONS – 33 Gironde – 335 I6 – pop. 1 518 – alt. 96 m – ✉ 33410 3 B2

Paris 599 – Bordeaux 39 – Mérignac 46 – Pessac 42 – Talence 36

L'Auberge de l'Ancienne Poste
pl. Cazeaux Cazalet – ✆ 05 56 27 43 31 – ancienneposte@hotmail.fr – Closed 1st-15 August, 1st-15 January, Saturday lunch, Sunday dinner and Monday
Rest – Menu (€ 16), € 29/75 bi – Carte € 39/75
◆ A countrified 19C mansion that specialises in grilled meats. Notably the rib of beef, which is cooked in front of you in the enormous fireplace. Smiling, friendly welcome.

RIORGES – 42 Loire – 327 D3 – see Roanne

RIQUEWIHR – 68 Haut-Rhin – 315 H8 – pop. 1 273 – alt. 300 m – ✉ 68340 Alsace-Lorraine 2 C2

Paris 442 – Colmar 15 – Gérardmer 52 – Ribeauvillé 5 – St-Dié 46 – Sélestat 19
Office de tourisme, ✆ 08 20 36 09 22
Village★★★.

Plan on next page

Le Schoenenbourg without rest
r. Schoenenbourg – ✆ 03 89 49 01 11 – www.hotel-schoenenbourg.fr – schoenenbourg@calixo.net – Fax 03 89 47 95 88 – Closed 5-30 January B r
58 rm – €79/129 €81/135, € 13 – 4 suites
◆ Built in the 1980s, backing onto a vineyard, the hotel offers comfortable, simply decorated rooms. Large heated pool and a peaceful environment.

RIQUEWIHR

Cerf (R. du) . . . . A 2	Couronne (R. de la) . . . . B 8	St-Nicolas (R.) . . . . A 13
Château (Cour du) . . . . B 3	Dinzheim (R. de) . . . . A 9	Strasbourg (Cour de) . . . . A 15
Cheval (R. du) . . . . A 4	Écuries (R. des) . . . . B 12	3-Églises (R. des) . . . . B 17
Cordiers (R. des) . . . . A 6		

Riquewihr without rest

rte de Ribeauvillé – ✆ 03 89 86 03 00 – www.hotel-riquewihr.fr – reservation@hotel-riquewihr.fr – Fax 03 89 47 99 76 – Closed 1st January to mid-February B

44 rm – †€ 61/87 ††€ 61/92, ☕ € 11 – 6 suites

◆ A large, neo-Alsatian style building on a road winding through the vineyards. Rooms are comfortable and well kept, mini fitness centre and generous breakfast buffet.

À l'Oriel without rest

3 r. des Ecuries Seigneuriales – ✆ 03 89 49 03 13 – www.hotel-oriel.com – info@hotel-oriel.com – Fax 03 89 47 92 87 B **a**

22 rm – †€ 69 ††€ 79/99, ☕ € 12

◆ In a quiet little street, this 16C hotel has an attractive façade with an oriel window. Rustic personalised rooms, some with boat beds, and cosier to the rear. Bar in the converted cellar.

Le B. Espace Suites without rest

48 r. Gén. de Gaulle – ✆ 03 89 86 54 55 – www.jlbrendel.com – suites@jlbrendel.com – Fax 03 89 47 87 30 A **t**

5 rm – †€ 118/150 ††€ 118/250, ☕ € 16

◆ Four rooms in a former vintner's house with attractive wine-coloured façade. The decor cleverly incorporates the ancient walls, designer furniture, luxury and refinement.

Table du Gourmet (Jean-Luc Brendel)

5 r. 1ère Armée – ✆ 03 89 49 09 09 – www.jlbrendel.com – table@jlbrendel.com – Fax 03 89 49 04 56 – Closed 4 January-13 February, Wednesday except dinner from April to mid-November, Thursday lunch and Tuesday A **u**

Rest – Menu € 45 (weekdays)/92 – Carte € 60/90

Spec. Grenouilles en beignets d'amandes, émulsion amande, pommes aigres (autumn). Porcelet rôti et laqué sur choucroute de radis. Crème malabar sur fraises rôties (summer). **Wines** Pinot gris, Riesling.

◆ A contemporary red and black decor sets the scene for the delightfully amusing cuisine, made from only the finest, albeit sometimes very unusual, produce.

XXX **Auberge du Schoenenbourg**

r. de la Piscine – ✆ 03 89 47 92 28 – www.auberge-schoenenbourg.com – auberge-schoenenbourg@wanadoo.fr – Fax 03 89 47 89 84 – Closed 19-26 August, 3-29 January, lunch except Sunday, Monday and Wednesday dinner B **m**

Rest – Menu € 29/81 – Carte € 48/70

◆ A welcoming family home and terrace extension facing the vineyard and ramparts. Succulent cuisine using home-grown produce and herbs from the garden.

XX **Le Sarment d'Or** with rm

rm, VISA

4 r. du Cerf – ✆ 03 89 86 02 86 – www.riquewihr-sarment-dor.com – info@riquewihr-sarment-dor.com – Fax 03 89 47 99 23 – Closed 16-24 November and 2-24 March A **f**

9 rm – †€ 60 ††€ 70/80, ☐ € 8

Rest – *(closed Tuesday lunch, Sunday dinner and Monday)*

Menu € 20/55 – Carte € 41/52

◆ Light-coloured wood, exposed beams, fireplace and antiques set the scene for this 17C establishment's carefully prepared traditional cuisine. Cosy bedrooms.

X **La Grappe d'Or**

VISA

1 r. Ecuries Seigneuriales – ✆ 03 89 47 89 52 – www.restaurant-grappedor.com – rest.grappe.or@wanadoo.fr – Fax 03 89 47 85 91 – Closed 25 June-10 July, January, Wednesday from February to March and Thursday B **a**

Rest – Menu € 16 (weekday lunch), € 20/36 – Carte € 25/44

◆ This welcoming house from 1554 has two dining rooms with well-worn walls, one adorned with rustic tools and the other with a pretty earthenware stove. Locally sourced menu.

X **d'Brendelstub**

AC VISA AE

48 r. Gén. de Gaulle – ✆ 03 89 86 54 54 – www.jlbrendel.com – stub@jlbrendel.com – Fax 03 89 47 87 30 – Closed 12-29 January A **b**

Rest – Menu (€ 14), € 20/37 – Carte € 23/39

◆ Local specialities, roast meats and good Alsatian wines by the glass in a pleasant contemporary winstub ambiance; themed musical evenings.

in Zellenberg **1 km East by D 3 – pop. 397 – alt. 300 m – ✉ 68340**

XXX **Maximilien** (Jean-Michel Eblin)

AC P VISA AE

19a rte Ostheim – ✆ 03 89 47 99 69 – www.le-maximilien.com – Fax 03 89 47 99 85 – Closed 25 August-8 September, 23 February-9 March, Friday lunch, Sunday dinner and Monday

Rest – Menu € 32 (weekday lunch), € 46/82 – Carte € 64/86

Spec. Œuf mollet aux queues d'écrevisses et écume d'asperge verte. Poitrine de pigeon rôtie et homard. Millefeuille rhubarbe et fraises, sorbet fraise au poivre de sichuan (April to September). **Wines** Riesling, Pinot gris.

◆ An Alsatian-style hillside restaurant. The elegant dining room offers attractive views of the vineyards, succulent dishes and a fine choice of wines.

X **Auberge du Froehn**

AC VISA AE

5 rte Ostheim – ✆ 03 89 47 81 57 – Fax 03 89 47 80 28 – Closed 1st-18 March, 29 June-3 July, 9-18 November, Tuesday and Wednesday

Rest – Menu (€ 12), € 23/39 – Carte € 37/49

◆ This inn, typical of the region, pays homage to the vineyard (and vintage of the same name) that dominates the village. Rustic cellar decor, friendly atmosphere and regional cuisine.

RISCLE – 32 Gers – **336** B8 – **pop. 1 701** – **alt. 105 m** – ✉ **32400** 28 **A2**

Paris 739 – Aire-sur-l'Adour 17 – Auch 71 – Mont-de-Marsan 49 – Pau 59 – Tarbes 55

Syndicat d'initiative, 6, place du foirail ✆ 05 62 69 74 01, Fax 05 62 69 86 07

XX **Le Pigeonneau**

VISA

36 av. Adour – ✆ 05 62 69 85 64 – Fax 05 62 69 85 64 – Closed 22 June-7 July, 1 week in January, Sunday dinner, Monday and Tuesday

Rest – Menu (€ 15) – Carte € 34/45

◆ Old floor tiles and ochre shades emphasise the warmth of this restaurant in the Adour valley. Contemporary cuisine, including pigeon-based dishes.

RISOUL – 05 Hautes-Alpes – **334** H5 – **pop. 622 – alt. 1 117 m** 41 **C1**
– ✉ 05600

Paris 716 – Briançon 37 – Gap 61 – Guillestre 4 – St-Véran 35

Office de tourisme, Risoul 1850 ✆ 04 92 46 02 60, Fax 04 92 46 01 23

Belvédère de l'Homme de Pierre ✳★★ South: 15 km **French Alps**

La Bonne Auberge rest, rest, VISA
in the village – ✆ 04 92 45 02 40 – Closed April-May, 20 September-26 December and from Monday to Thursday in January
25 rm – €41/61 €56/61, €8 – ½ P €51/55
Rest – *(dinner only in winter)* Menu €16/24
◆ A large chalet set just outside the village. Rooms with a pretty view of the Mont Dauphin fort, built by Vauban. A fairly discreet decor and family guesthouse atmosphere in the restaurant with a panoramic view of the Guillestrois.

RIVA-BELLA – 14 Calvados – **303** K4 – **see Ouistreham-Riva-Bella**

RIVE-DE-GIER – 42 Loire – **327** G6 – **pop. 14 600 – alt. 225 m** 44 **B2**
– ✉ 42800 **Lyon - Rhone Valley**

Paris 494 – Lyon 38 – Montbrison 65 – Roanne 105 – St-Étienne 23 – Thiers 128 – Vienne 27

Hostellerie La Renaissance with rm VISA AE
41 r. A. Marrel – ✆ 04 77 75 04 31 – restaurant.larenaissance@wanadoo.fr – Fax 04 77 83 68 58 – Closed 2 weeks in August, 4-10 January, Sunday dinner, Wednesday dinner and Monday
5 rm – €48/56 €48/56, €12 **Rest** – Menu €30/88 – Carte €50/70
◆ Rustic furniture, contemporary objects and colourful paintings provide the decor in this dining room overlooking the garden-terrace. Contemporary cuisine.

in Ste-Croix-en-Jarez 10 km Southeast by D 30 – **pop. 405 – alt. 450 m** – ✉ 42800

Le Prieuré with rm rest, VISA AE
– ✆ 04 77 20 20 09 – prieure.bl@orange.fr – Fax 04 77 20 20 80 – Closed 2 January-13 February
4 rm – €55 €70, €10 – ½ P €70
Rest – *(closed Monday)* Menu (€15), €18 (weekdays)/40
◆ A restaurant in a converted charterhouse on the edge of an unusual village. A countrified dining room; regional cuisine and home-made sausage and cooked meats.

RIVEDOUX-PLAGE – 17 Charente-Maritime – **324** C3 – **see Île de Ré**

LA RIVIÈRE – 33 Gironde – **335** J5 – **see Libourne**

LA RIVIÈRE-ST-SAUVEUR – 14 Calvados – **303** N3 – **see Honfleur**

LA RIVIÈRE-THIBOUVILLE – 27 Eure – **304** E7 – **alt. 72 m** 33 **C2**
– ✉ 27550 Nassandres

Paris 140 – Bernay 15 – Évreux 34 – Lisieux 39 – Pont-Audemer 34 – Rouen 51

Le Manoir du Soleil d'Or VISA
23 Côte de Paris – ✆ 02 32 44 90 31 – www.manoirdusoleildor.com – lemanoirdusoleildor@orange.fr – Fax 02 32 44 90 31 – Closed Sunday dinner and Wednesday
Rest – Menu (€21 bi), €25/52 – Carte €38/51
◆ Norman mansion offering a clear view of the Risle Valley from its terrace and elegant dining room. Modern cuisine.

L'Auberge de la Vallée VISA
7 rte Brionne-Nassandres – ✆ 02 32 44 21 73 – Closed 24 December-1st January, dinner from Monday to Wednesday and Sunday
Rest – Menu €13 (weekdays)/24 – Carte approx. €28
◆ This restaurant, occupying a fine half-timbered building, houses two country dining rooms, adorned with a collection of wicker baskets. Up-to-date cuisine.

RIXHEIM – 68 Haut-Rhin – **315** I10 – **see Mulhouse**

ROAIX – 84 Vaucluse – **332** D8 – **see Vaison-la-Romaine**

ROANNE – 42 Loire – **327** D3 – **pop. 35 700** – **Built-up area 104 892** 44 **A1**
– **alt. 265 m** – ✉ **42300** **Lyon - Rhone Valley**

Paris 395 – Clermont-Ferrand 115 – Lyon 84 – St-Étienne 85

Roanne-Renaison: ✆ 04 77 66 83 55, by D 9 AV : 5 km.

Office de tourisme, 8, place de Lattre de Tassigny ✆ 04 77 71 51 77, Fax 04 77 71 07 11

du Roannais Villerest7 km on the Thiers road, ✆ 04 77 69 70 60

Musée Joseph-Déchelette: Revolutionary earthenware ★.

Belvédère de Commelle-Vernay ≤★: 7 km South via quai Sémard BV.

Plan on next page

Troisgros (Michel Troisgros)
pl. de la Gare – ✆ *04 77 71 66 97* – *www.troisgros.com* – *info@troisgros.com* – *Fax 04 77 70 39 77* – *Closed 4-19 August, February school holidays, Monday lunch from October to February, Tuesday and Wednesday* CX **r**
11 rm – †€ 190 ††€ 190/375, ☕ € 27 – 5 suites
Rest – *(number of covers limited, pre-book)* Menu € 95 (weekday lunch), € 155/195 – Carte € 170/250
Spec. Mezzaluna de pomme de terre à la truffe. Rouget barbet et carmine aigrelette. Soufflé à la rhubarbe fraîche. **Wines** Pouilly-Fuissé, Saint-Joseph.
◆ Superb designer rooms, a gourmet library, collections of contemporary paintings - a railway station hotel 21st century style! The Troisgros restaurant, with a three-star rating since 1968, offers excellent, subtly reinterpreted cuisine and a splendid wine list.

Le Grand Hôtel without rest
18 cours de la République, (opposite the station) – ✆ *04 77 71 48 82* – *www.grand-hotel-roanne.fr* – *granotel@wanadoo.fr* – *Fax 04 77 70 42 40*
31 rm – †€ 62/78 ††€ 72/92, ☕ € 12 CX **f**
◆ An early-20C building offering well-maintained guestrooms with diverse decor (modern furnishings, wrought iron, wicker and bright colours). Comfortable lounge-bar.

L'Astrée
17 bis cours République, (opposite the station) – ✆ *04 77 72 74 22* – *Closed 15-28 March, 27 July-16 August, Saturday and Sunday* CX **f**
Rest – Menu (€ 21), € 25 (weekdays)/80 – Carte approx. € 70
◆ A comfortable, pleasant contemporary decor with wood panelling and paintings by local artists. Personalised cuisine – in homage to the lovers, Astrée and Céladon!

Le Relais Fleuri
allée Claude Barge – ✆ *04 77 67 18 52* – *www.perso.orange.fr/lerelaisfleuri/pub* – *relaisfleuri@orange.fr* – *Closed Sunday dinner, Tuesday and Wednesday*
Rest – Menu € 20/46 – Carte € 48/65 BV **v**
◆ One of the dining rooms of this former café (1900) boasts a glass dome roof. Attractive shaded garden for the summer months. Up-to-date cuisine.

Le Central
20 cours République, (opposite the station) – ✆ *04 77 67 72 72* – *restaurant.lecentral@wanadoo.fr* – *Fax 04 77 72 57 67* – *Closed 2-22 August, 24 December-1st January, Sunday and Monday* CX **r**
Rest – bistro – *(pre-book)* Menu (€ 21), € 26 (lunch)/29 – Carte € 39/50
◆ Shelves of gourmet products provide the original decor for this bistro-cum-delicatessen serving simple, tasty cuisine. A friendly atmosphere guaranteed!

in Coteau (right bank of the Loire) – **pop. 7 065** – **alt. 350 m** – ✉ **42120**

Des Lys
133 av. de la Libération – ✆ *04 77 68 46 44* – *www.hotel-des-lys.com* – *hotel.deslys@orange.fr* – *Fax 04 77 72 23 50* – *Closed 2-24 August, 20 December-4 January, Saturday lunch and Sunday* BV **e**
18 rm ☕ – †€ 78/98 ††€ 87/107 **Rest** – Menu (€ 12), € 15/25 – Carte € 25/39
◆ A new team has taken over this hotel from the family that had run it for three generations. Find 1980s and more modern style rooms. Traditional cuisine in the restaurant.

ROANNE

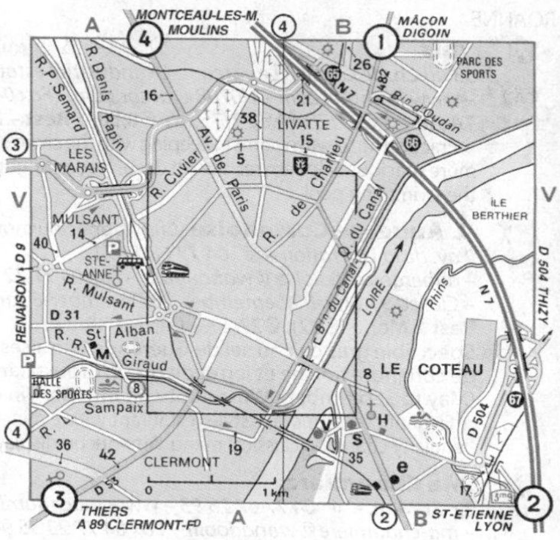

MONTCEAU-LES-M.
MOULINS
MÂCON
DIGOIN
PARC DES SPORTS
LIVATTE
LES MARAIS
MULSANT
STE-ANNE
ÎLE BERTHIER
LE COTEAU
HALLE DES SPORTS
CLERMONT
THIERS
A 89 CLERMONT-Fd
ST-ETIENNE
LYON
RENAISON D 9
D 504 THIZY
LOIRE

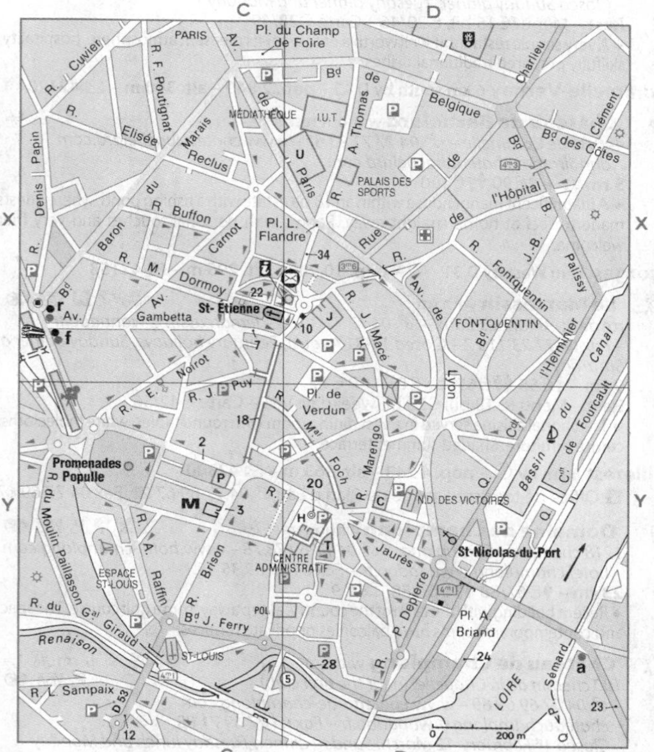

Ibis rm,
53 bd Ch. de Gaulle, (Le coteau – BV industrial estate) – 04 77 68 36 22 – www.ibishotel.com – H0708@accor.com – Fax 04 77 71 24 99
74 rm – €57/75 €57/75, €8,50 **Rest** – Menu €10/25 – Carte €20/32
◆ Practical hotel with rooms in keeping with the chain's standards (the latest are somewhat more spacious). Modern restaurant decorated in bright colours, plus a terrace overlooking the swimming pool.

L'Auberge Costelloise (Christophe Souchon)
2 av. de la Libération – 04 77 68 12 71 – auberge-costelloise@wanadoo.fr – Fax 04 77 72 26 78 – Closed 9 August-2 September, 26 December-8 January, Sunday and Monday
Rest – Menu (€22), €27/53 – Carte €38/72 DY **a**
Spec. Foie gras cuit au sel de Guérande et fraises au vinaigre. Bar rôti à l'infusion de coriandre fraîche et jarret de bœuf. Croustillant de fraises et crème à la vanille (May to September). **Wines** Côte Roannaise, Vin de Pays d'Urfé.
◆ Elegant contemporary-style restaurant with a mini-veranda on the banks of the Loire. Regularly changing classical menu. Artwork on display.

Ma Chaumière
3 r. St-Marc – 04 77 67 25 93 – www.machaumiere.fr – ma-chaumiere@wanadoo.fr – Fax 04 77 23 35 94 – Closed Sunday dinner, Tuesday dinner and Monday BV **s**
Rest – Menu (€15 bi), €20/46 – Carte €28/49
◆ A very simple restaurant well worth a detour for its pleasant atmosphere, hospitality and skilfully prepared traditional dishes.

in Commelle-Vernay **6 km south by D 43 – pop. 2 849 – alt. 340 m – ✉ 42120**

Château de Bachelard without rest
440 rte de Commelle – 04 77 71 93 67 – www.chateaubachelard.com – dhnoirard@chateaubachelard.com
5 rm – €90 €100
◆ A magnificent manor house within an 18-ha estate with a fishing pond, where guests are made to feel at home straight away. Rooms with personal touches and very friendly welcome.

in Riorges **3 km West by D 31** - AV – **pop. 10 200 – alt. 295 m – ✉ 42153**

Le Marcassin with rm
rte de St-Alban-les-Eaux – 04 77 71 30 18 – lemarcassin@wanadoo.fr – Fax 04 77 23 11 22 – Closed 17-31 August, February holidays, Sunday dinner and Saturday
9 rm – €55 €65, €8 – ½ P €72
Rest – Menu (€18 bi), €23 bi (weekdays)/55 – Carte €42/56
◆ Traditional cuisine served in a vast dining room with round tables, white tablecloths and ceruse furniture. Shaded summer terrace.

in Villerest **6 km by ③ – pop. 4 243 – alt. 363 m – ✉ 42300**

Office de tourisme, plage du Plan d'Eau 04 77 69 67 21, Fax 04 77 69 67 22

Domaine de Champlong without rest
1218 chemin de Champlong – 04 77 69 78 78 – www.hotel-champlong.com – hotel.champlong@wanadoo.fr – Fax 04 77 69 35 45
23 rm – €67/88 €67/88, €9
◆ Recent building with the calm of the country, a step away from a golf course. The spacious and contemporary rooms have balconies or private terraces.

Château de Champlong with rm
100 chemin de la Chapelle, (near the golf club) – 04 77 69 69 69 – www.chateau-de-champlong.com – chateauchamplong@wanadoo.fr – Fax 04 77 69 71 08 – Closed 1st February-12 March, Sunday dinner, Tuesday lunch and Monday
12 rm – €85/145 €85/145, €12
Rest – Menu (€26), €36/90 bi – Carte €50/60
◆ A handsome 18C residence in attractive grounds. The "painting room" is worth a look with its old canvases, parquet floor and imposing fireplace. Elegant lounges. Original cuisine. Brand new guestrooms built over the restaurant.

ROBION – 84 Vaucluse – 332 D10 – pop. 3 941 – alt. 140 m – ✉ 84440 42 E1

▶ Paris 713 – Aix-en-Provence 69 – Avignon 31 – Marseille 82

ℹ Office de tourisme, Place Clément Gros ✆ 04 90 05 84 31, Fax 04 90 06 08 79

L'Escanson

450 av. Aristide-Briand – ✆ 04 90 76 59 61 – www.lescanson.fr – info@lescanson.fr – Closed 2 January-2 February, lunch in July, Wednesday lunch and Tuesday

Rest – *(number of covers limited, pre-book)* Menu (€ 18), € 25/37 – Carte € 36/44

◆ Pastel colours and wrought iron lend a Provençal flavour to this small restaurant. Gourmet, traditional cuisine spiced up with a zest of creativity. Shaded terrace.

ROCAMADOUR – 46 Lot – 337 F3 – pop. 633 – alt. 279 m – ✉ 46500 29 C1

Dordogne-Berry-Limousin

▶ Paris 531 – Brive-la-Gaillarde 54 – Cahors 60 – Figeac 47 – St-Céré 31

ℹ Office de tourisme, L'Hospitalet ✆ 05 65 33 22 00, Fax 05 65 33 22 01

Site★★★ - Ramparts ✻★★★ - Tapestries★ in the town hall - Black Virgin★ in Notre-Dame chapel - Musée d'Art sacré★ M¹ - Musée du Jouet ancien automobile: pedal cars - L'Hospitalet ✻★★: Féerie du rail: model★ by ②.

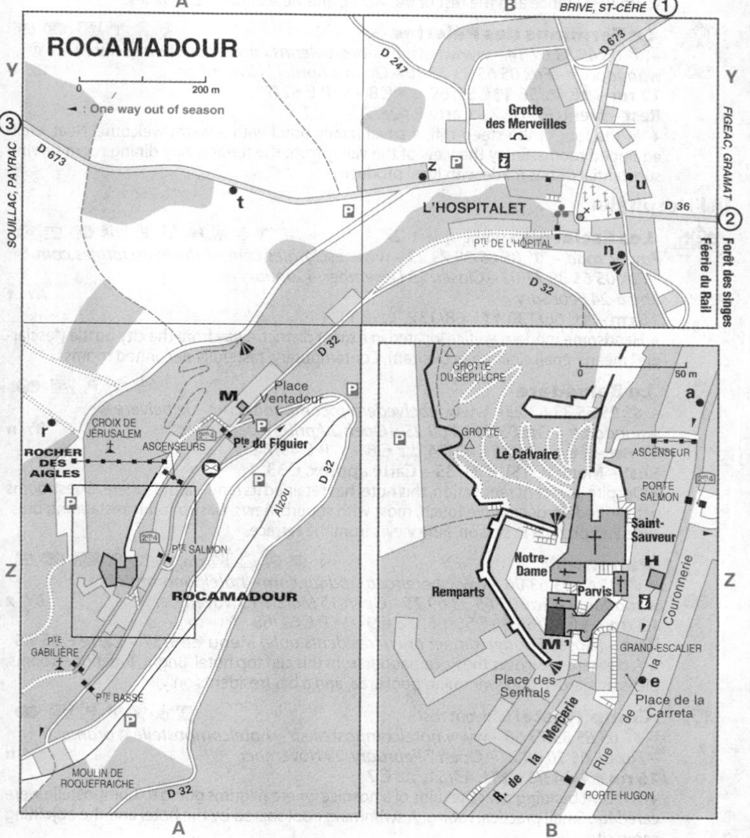

at the château

Château — rm, AZ r
rte du château – 05 65 33 62 22 – www.hotelchateaurocamadour.com – hotelchateaurocamadour@wanadoo.fr – Fax 05 65 33 69 00 – Open 28 March-12 November
58 rm – €66/88 €70/102, €10 – ½ P €70/87
Rest – Menu (€15), €25/49 – Carte €38/66
◆ Away from tourist hustle and bustle, a contemporary hotel with spacious, functional rooms. The peaceful atmosphere, swimming pool, tennis court and garden are much appreciated. 50 m from the hotel, the restaurant serves regional cuisine; modern decor and a terrace in the shade of truffle oaks.

In the Cité

Beau Site — rm, BZ a
– 05 65 33 63 08 – www.bestwestern-beausite.com – info@bestwestern-beausite.com – Fax 05 65 33 65 23 – Open 9 February-11 November
38 rm – €42/93 €53/108, €13 – ½ P €71/82
Rest ***Jehan de Valon*** – Menu €18 (lunch), €26/56 – Carte €35/70
◆ In the heart of the town, a 15C house with an attractive, medieval-style lobby and rooms of character. A more modern decor in the annex. Traditional dishes and wines from southwest France and the rest of the world; fine view of the Alzou Valley.

Le Terminus des Pélerins — BZ e
– 05 65 33 62 14 – www.terminus-des-pelerins.com – hotelterm.pelerinsroc@wanadoo.fr – Fax 05 65 33 72 10 – Open 4 April-1st November
12 rm – €46/56 €51/69, €8 – ½ P €62/71
Rest – Menu €17/32 – Carte €42/72
◆ At the foot of the steep cliff, a small family hotel with a warm welcome. Neat, well-equipped rooms. Enjoy the view of the valley from the terrace. Airy dining room serving substantial dishes made with local produce.

in l'Hospitalet

Les Esclargies without rest — AY t
Payrac road – 05 65 38 73 23 – www.esclargies.com – infos@esclargies.com – Fax 05 65 39 71 07 – Closed 23 December-4 January and 6-24 February
16 rm – €66/130 €68/132, €11
◆ Handsome modern edifice located in a quiet district, away from the city bustle ("esclargie" means small clearing in Occitan). Contemporary, tastefully decorated rooms.

Le Belvédère — BY n
– 05 65 33 63 25 – www.lebelvedere-rocamadour.com – le.belvere@wanadoo.fr – Fax 05 65 33 69 25 – Open 2 April-31 December
17 rm – €43/74 €43/74, €8 – ½ P €49/64
Rest – Menu (€15), €21/35 – Carte approx. €33
◆ Despite its recent renovation, this hotel has retained its family atmosphere. Guestrooms with a modern decorative touch, most with superb views. Gastronomic restaurant; brasserie and pizzeria in season. Fine views from the terrace.

Panoramic — rm, BY z
– 05 65 33 63 06 – www.hotelrocamadour.com – hotelpanoramic@wanadoo.fr – Fax 05 65 33 69 26 – Open 15 March-15 November
12 rm – €55/65 €55/66, €9 – ½ P €62/68
Rest – *(closed Friday) (dinner only) (residents only)* Menu €19/37 – Carte €35/65
◆ A pleasant view over the Rocamadour from this cliff top hotel. Bright, functional rooms, pleasant garden and swimming pool area, and a bar (residents only).

Comp'Hostel without rest — BY u
– 05 65 33 73 50 – www.hotelcompostelle.fr – hotelcompostelle@orange.fr – Fax 05 65 10 68 21 – Open 7 February-29 November
15 rm – €43/51 €43/51, €7
◆ A recent building near the ruins of a hospice where pilgrims going to Compostelle were cared for. Small practical rooms. A swimming pool shared by the hotel and the adjoining camp site.

Brive road 2.5 km by ① and by D 673 – ✉ 46500 Rocamadour

Troubadour – rest,
– ✆ *05 65 33 70 27 – www.hotel-troubadour.com – hoteltroubadour@wanadoo.fr – Fax 05 65 33 71 99 – Open 15 February-15 November*
10 rm – €60/98 €60/98, €12 – 2 suites – ½ P €70/85
Rest – *(closed July-August) (dinner only) (residents only)* Menu €26/37
◆ This old farmhouse located in a peaceful garden has been attractively renovated, providing pleasant, well-kept rooms. Billiard room in the old bake house. Swimming pool.

Le Roc du Berger
Bois de Belveyre – ✆ 05 65 33 19 99 – www.rocduberger.com – rocduberger@wanadoo.fr – Fax 05 65 33 72 46 – Open from end March to end September and Saturday dinner and Sunday lunch in October
Rest – Menu €13/27 – Carte €19/57
◆ A terrace under truffle oaks, a busy atmosphere, simple service and, on the table, exclusively regional farm produce, prepared over a charcoal fire.

in la Rhue 6 km by ① Brive road by D 673, D 840 and secondary road – ✉ 46500 Rocamadour

Domaine de la Rhue without rest
– ✆ *05 65 33 71 50 – www.domainedelarhue.com – domainedelarhue@wanadoo.fr – Fax 05 65 33 72 48 – Open 11 April-17 October*
14 rm – €75/145 €75/145, €8,50
◆ Large, personalised rooms in elegantly-restored 19C stables. Superb rustic lounge with fireplace. Summertime breakfast dining on the terrace. Swimming pool.

Payrac road 4 km by ③, D 673 and secondary road – ✉ 46500 Rocamadour

Les Vieilles Tours
– ✆ *05 65 33 68 01 – www.vieillestours-rocamadour.com – les.vieillestours@wanadoo.fr – Fax 05 65 33 68 59 – Open 29 March-11 November*
16 rm – €73/160 €73/160, €12 **Rest** – *(dinner only)* Menu €25/39
◆ Pleasant welcome, peace and quiet and a refined country atmosphere at this former hunting lodge. The 13C falcon house shelters the prettiest bedroom. Park with views over the valley. Two dining rooms, one more rustic; modern cuisine.

ROCBARON – 83 Var – 340 L6 – pop. 3 180 – alt. 376 m – ✉ 83136 41 C3

Paris 832 – Marseille 79 – Toulon 35 – La Seyne-sur-Mer 43 – Hyères 36

La Maison de Rocbaron
3 r. St-Sauveur, (opposite the town hall) – ✆ 04 94 04 24 03 – www.maisonderocbaron.com – contact@maisonderocbaron.com – Open 1st March-15 November
5 rm – €78/108 €78/108 **Table d'hôte** – Menu €35
◆ Warm atmosphere in this family house, formerly a barn, surrounded by greenery. Personalised rooms, pool and quiet garden. Table d'hote using local produce.

LA ROCHE-BERNARD – 56 Morbihan – 308 R9 – pop. 796 – alt. 38 m – ✉ 56130 Brittany 10 C3

Paris 444 – Nantes 70 – Ploërmel 55 – Redon 28 – St-Nazaire 37 – Vannes 42
Office de tourisme, 14, rue du Docteur Cornudet ✆ 02 99 90 67 98, Fax 02 99 90 67 99
de la Bretesche Missillac Domaine de la Bretesche, SE: 11 km, ✆ 02 51 76 86 86
Pont du Morbihan★.

Le Manoir du Rodoir
rte de Nantes – ✆ 02 99 90 82 68 – www.lemanoirdurodoir.com – lemanoirdurodoir@wanadoo.fr – Fax 02 99 90 76 22 – Closed 15 January-1st March
24 rm – €85/130 €85/130, €13
Rest – *(closed lunch July-August, Saturday lunch, Monday lunch and Sunday)* Menu (€19), €20 (lunch)/39 – Carte €30/50
◆ A 2 ha park surrounds this former foundry, now a hotel offering comfortable, spacious guestrooms, attic-style on the 2nd floor. A concise menu offering a fusion of ingredients and dishes from France, Asia, Mediterranean Europe and South America. Rustic decor.

L'Auberge Bretonne (Jacques Thorel) with rm
2 pl. Duguesclin – ✆ 02 99 90 60 28 – www.auberge-bretonne.com – aubbretonne@relaischateaux.com – Fax 02 99 90 85 00 – Closed 15 November-15 January except hotel and except public holidays
11 rm – €100/280 €100/280, ☕ €17 – ½ P €200/265
Rest – *(closed Monday lunch, Tuesday lunch, Friday lunch and Thursday)* Menu €35 (weekdays), €95/137
Spec. Truffe de Saint-Jacques et bouillon d'asperge (October to March). Homard de nos côtes, pommes confites. Les délices de Solange.
◆ Elegant restaurant occupying three flower-decked Breton houses. Galleried dining room surrounding a vegetable garden. " Surf'n Turf" menu plus an astonishing wine list.

ROCHECHOUART – 87 Haute-Vienne – 325 B6 – pop. 3 808 – alt. 260 m – ✉ 87600 Dordogne-Berry-Limousin

24 **A2**

Paris 433 – Limoges 43 – Saint-Junien 12 – Panazol 50 – Isle 44

Office de tourisme, 6, rue Victor Hugo ✆ 05 55 03 72 73

De France
7 pl. O-Marquet – ✆ 05 55 03 77 40 – www.hoteldefrance-rochechouart.fr – contact@hoteldefrance-rochechouart.fr – Fax 05 55 03 03 87 – Closed 1st-7 January and Sunday dinner
14 rm – €38/45 €45/55, ☕ €8 **Rest** – Menu €13/34 – Carte €24/47
◆ This family-run town centre inn has been treated to a makeover and offers simple, clean and practical rooms decorated in a modern spirit. The chef-patron rustles up regional inspired recipes served in a neo-rustic dining room.

ROCHECORBON – 37 Indre-et-Loire – 317 N4 – see Tours

ROCHEFORT – 17 Charente-Maritime – 324 E4 – pop. 26 300 – alt. 12 m – Spa : mid March-early Dec. – ✉ 17300 Atlantic Coast

38 **B2**

Paris 475 – Limoges 221 – Niort 62 – La Rochelle 38 – Royan 40 – Saintes 44

Access Pont de Matrou: no toll.

Office de tourisme, avenue Sadi-Carnot ✆ 05 46 99 08 60, Fax 05 46 99 52 64

du pays Rochefortais Saint-Laurent-de-la-Prée 1608 route Impériale, NW : 7 km on D 137, ✆ 05 46 84 56 36

Quartier de l'Arsenal★ - Corderie royale (royal rope factory)★★ - Pierre Loti House★ AZ - Musée d'Art et d'Histoire★ AZ **M²** - Les Métiers de Mercure★ (museum) BZ **D.**

Plan on next page

La Corderie Royale
r. Audebert, (near the Corderie Royale) – ✆ 05 46 99 35 35 – www.corderieroyale.com – corderie.royale@wanadoo.fr – Fax 05 46 99 78 72 – Closed 18 December-20 January and Sunday dinner from November to March BY **h**
42 rm – €80/175 €80/175, ☕ €11 – 3 suites – ½ P €79/158
Rest – *(closed Saturday lunch, Sunday dinner and Monday from November to March)* Menu (€30), €36/66 – Carte €47/84
◆ An overnight hotel, steeped in history, within the walls of the old royal gunnery on the banks of the Charente and the port. Spacious rooms with a good level of comfort. Up-to-the-minute cuisine served on a veranda/dining room with views over the river.

Les Remparts rest,
43 av. C. Pelletan, (at the Thermal Baths) – ✆ 05 46 87 12 44 – www.hotelrempart.com – hotel.remparts.rochefort@eurothermes.com – Fax 05 46 83 92 62 – Closed 5-18 January BY **s**
73 rm – €52/65 €54/67, ☕ €7 – ½ P €51/58
Rest – Menu (€14), €18/23 – Carte €25/35
◆ This 1980s building is regularly renovated and has direct access to the thermal baths and Emperor's spring. Large, functional rooms. Classic fare is served in this vast dining room that opens onto a terrace.

ROCHEFORT

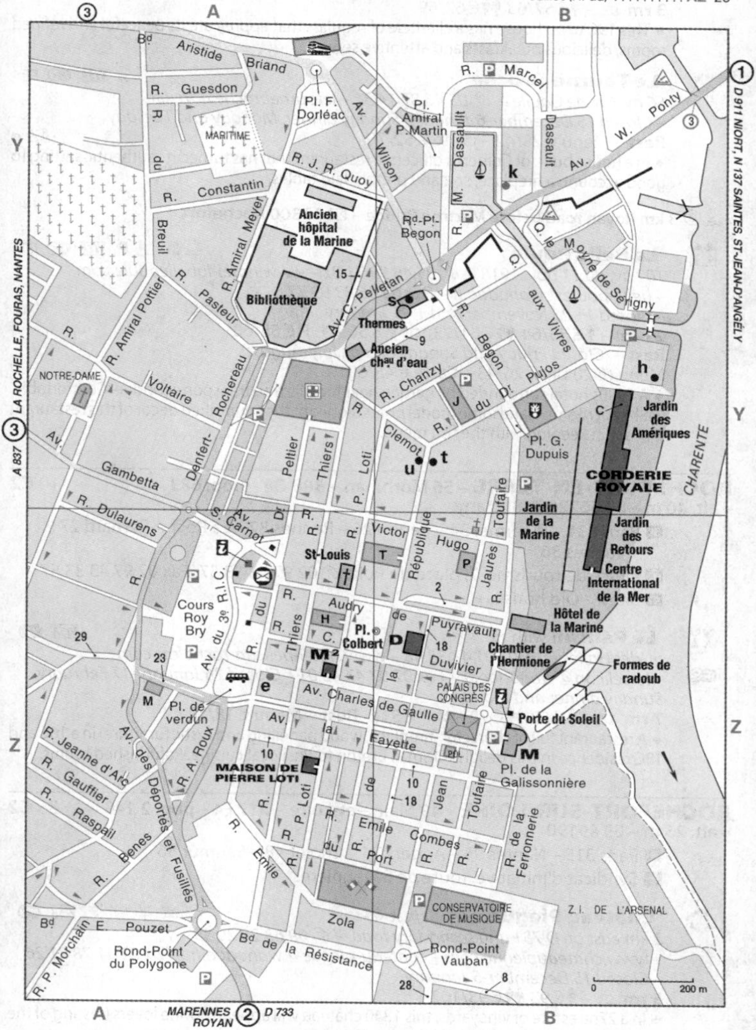

Roca Fortis without rest

14 r. de la République – ✆ 05 46 99 26 32 – www.hotel-rocafortis.com – hotel-rocafortis@wanadoo.fr – Fax 05 46 99 26 62 – Closed January

16 rm – †€ 44/49 ††€ 53/62, ☕ € 6 BY **t**

◆ Two regional houses set around a courtyard where breakfast is served in summer. Attractively-renovated interior (antique furniture, modern tones); very quiet back bedrooms.

Palmier sur Cour without rest
55 r. de la République – ✆ 05 46 99 55 54 – www.palmiersurcour.com – palmiersurcour@wanadoo.fr – Closed 20 December-12 February BY **u**
3 rm – ♦€ 57/63 ♦♦€ 62/69
◆ This 19C town house has a clientele of regulars that appreciate its peaceful and refined rooms, delicious breakfasts and attentive service.

Le Tourne-Broche VISA AE
56 av. Ch. de Gaulle – ✆ 05 46 87 14 32 – letournebroche@free.fr – Closed 15 December-6 January, Sunday dinner, Monday and Tuesday
Rest – Menu € 28/42 – Carte € 52/70 AZ **e**
◆ In a house built for Colbert's officers, a restaurant that has turned its authentic setting to good account: a fireplace, spit and prettily-laid tables.

via ② 3 km Royan road before Martrou Bridge – ✉ 17300 Rochefort

La Belle Poule P VISA AE
102 av. du 11 nov. 1918 – ✆ 05 46 99 71 87 – www.hotel-labellepoule.com – belle-poule@wanadoo.fr – Fax 05 46 83 99 77 – Closed 1st-22 November and 1st-5 January
21 rm – ♦€ 55/64 ♦♦€ 61/73, € 8,50 – ½ P € 55/60
Rest – *(Closed Friday and Sunday except July-August)*
Menu (€ 20 bi), € 26/43 – Carte € 45/60
◆ A 1980s hotel surrounded by garden near the Martrou transporter bridge. Comfortable, well-kept rooms. Handsome model boats highlight the countrified decor of this restaurant and are in keeping with the fish menu.

ROCHEFORT-EN-TERRE – 56 Morbihan – 308 Q8 – pop. 683 – alt. 40 m – ✉ 56220 Brittany 10 C2

Paris 431 – Ploërmel 34 – Redon 26 – Rennes 82 – La Roche-Bernard 27 – Vannes 36
Office de tourisme, 7, place du Puits ✆ 02 97 43 33 57, Fax 02 97 43 33 57
Site★ - Old houses★.

Le Pélican with rm VISA
pl. des Halles – ✆ 02 97 43 38 48 – www.hotel-pelican-rochefort.com – le.pelican@wanadoo.fr – Fax 02 97 43 42 01 – Closed 26 January-17 February, Sunday dinner and Monday
7 rm – ♦€ 62 ♦♦€ 72 – ½ P € 51 **Rest** – Menu € 18/38
◆ A restaurant full of character (fireplace, wood panelling and rustic furniture) in a 16C and 18C residence in this delightful small Breton town. Local cuisine. Refurbished rooms.

ROCHEFORT-SUR-LOIRE – 49 Maine-et-Loire – 317 F4 – pop. 2 140 – alt. 25 m – ✉ 49190 35 C2

Paris 315 – Nantes 95 – Angers 24 – Cholet 48 – Saumur 86
Syndicat d'initiative, route de Savennières

Château Pieguë without rest P VISA
2 km east on D 751 and secondary road – ✆ 09 63 20 20 39 – www.chateaupiegue.com – chateau-piegue@wanadoo.fr – Fax 02 41 78 71 26 – Closed 15 December-5 January
5 rm – ♦€ 93 ♦♦€ 93/102
◆ In a 27ha estate of vineyards, this 1840 château will appeal to wine lovers (tasting of the estate wine). Contemporary minimalist rooms. Homemade breakfasts.

ROCHEFORT-SUR-NENON – 39 Jura – 321 D4 – see Dôle

ROCHEGUDE – 26 Drôme – 332 B8 – pop. 1 346 – alt. 121 m – ✉ 26790 44 B3

Paris 641 – Avignon 46 – Bollène 8 – Carpentras 34 – Nyons 31 – Orange 17

Château de Rochegude
– *04 75 97 21 10 – www.chateaurochegude.com*
– *rochegude@relaischateaux.com – Fax 04 75 04 89 87*
24 rm – €160/195 €160/195, €20 – 1 suite
Rest – *(closed Monday off season)* Menu (€22), €35/115 – Carte €35/200
♦ An 11C fortress, altered in the 18C, dominates the Côtes du Rhône vineyards. Sympathetically restored rooms and deer park. Modern cuisine – simpler dishes at lunchtime – and a fine selection of wines served in the comfortable restaurant.

LA ROCHE-L'ABEILLE – 87 Haute-Vienne – 325 E7 – pop. 591 – alt. 400 m – ✉ 87800

24 **B2**

Paris 423 – Limoges 34 – Saint-Junien 63 – Panazol 34 – Isle 34

Le Moulin de la Gorce (Pierre Bertranet) with rm
– *05 55 00 70 66 – www.moulindelagorce.com*
– *moulingorce@relaischateaux.com – Fax 05 55 00 76 57*
– *Open 13 February-14 November and closed Monday except dinner from 11 July to mid-August, Wednesday lunch and Tuesday*
10 rm – €85/225 €85/225, €18
Rest – Menu (€50 bi), €75/145 bi
Spec. Œufs brouillés aux truffes, mouillettes de pain brioché. Carré de veau fermier du Limousin "élevé sous la mère". Puits d'amour aux framboises de Juillac (May to October). **Wines** Bergerac.
♦ A fine 16C mill with outbuildings located on the edge of a pond in a pleasant country park. Characterful interior and carefully prepared classical cuisine. Rooms are individually styled.

ROCHE-LEZ-BEAUPRÉ – 25 Doubs – 321 G3 – see Besançon

LA ROCHELLE Ⓟ – 17 Charente-Maritime – 324 D3 – pop. 77 300 – Built-up area 116 157 – alt. 1 m – Casino AX – ✉ 17000 Atlantic Coast

38 **A2**

Paris 472 – Angoulême 150 – Bordeaux 183 – Nantes 141 – Niort 65

Access to Île de Ré via ③. **toll** bridge in 2007: car(return) 16.50 (in season) 9.00 (off season), car and caravan 27.00 (in season), 15.00 (off season), lorry 18.00 to 45.00, motorcycle 2.00, free for pedestrians and bicycles.
Information from Régie d'Exploitation des Ponts : 05 46 00 51 10, Fax 05 46 43 04 71.

la Rochelle-Île-de-Ré: 05 46 42 30 26, Northwest: 4,5 km AV.

Office de tourisme, Le Gabut 05 46 41 14 68, Fax 05 46 41 99 85

de La Prée La Rochelle Marsilly, N : 11 km on D 105, 05 46 01 24 42

Old harbour ★★: tour St-Nicolas★, ❋★★ of the tour de la Lanterne★ - Old quarter ★★: Town hall★ Z **H**, Hôtel de la Bourse★ Z **C**, Porte de la Grosse Horloge★ Z **N**, Grande-rue des Merciers★ - Maison Henry II★, arcades★ de la rue du Minage, rue Chaudrier★, rue du Palais★, rue de l'Escale★ - Aquarium★★ CDZ - Museums: Nouveau Monde★ CDY**M⁷**, Beaux-Arts★ CDY **M²** - d'Orbigny-Bernon★ (history of La Rochelle and ceramics) Y **M⁸**, Automates★ (place de Montmartre★★) Z **M¹**, maritime★: Neptunéa C **M⁵** - Muséum d'Histoire naturelle★★ Y.

Plans on following pages

Champlain-France Angleterre without rest
30 r. Rambaud – 05 46 41 23 99
– *www.hotelchamplain.com – larochelle@hotelchamplain.com*
– *Fax 05 46 41 15 19*
CY **b**
36 rm – €92/125 €110/125, €12 – 4 suites
♦ Once a private residence, the hotel has a pleasant, romantic garden. A fine central staircase leads to spacious, superbly-furnished rooms.

LA ROCHELLE

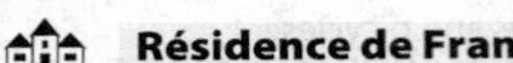

Résidence de France

43 r. Minage – ✆ 05 46 28 06 00 – www.hotel-larochelle.com – info@hotel-larochelle.com – Fax 05 46 28 06 03 DY **x**

5 rm – €110/170 €110/170, ☕ €15 – 11 suites – €150/400

Rest – *(closed Sunday and Monday) (dinner only)* Menu €25 – Carte approx. €30

◆ A fine 16C abode houses this establishment (part of a hotel residence). Well thought out decor, spacious and serene. Exhibitions of local artists' work. Furniture inspired by the 18C in the dining room, which opens onto a patio-terrace.

Masqhôtel without rest

17 r. Ouvrage à Cornes – ✆ 05 46 41 83 83 – www.masqhotel.com – info@masqhotel.com – Fax 05 46 07 04 43 DZ **t**

76 rm – €108/168 €108/168, ☕ €14

◆ Contemporary Indonesian art adorns the walls of this new hotel in a quiet side street near the station. Designer furniture, chic minimalist and hi-tech ambiance.

Novotel

av. Porte Neuve – ✆ 05 46 34 24 24 – www.novotel.com – h0965@accor.com – Fax 05 46 34 58 32 CY **t**

94 rm – €115/150 €130/170, ☕ €14

Rest – *(closed Saturday and Sunday off season)* Menu (€17), €22 (weekday lunch) – Carte €20/40

◆ Renovated from top to toe, this glass building surrounded by a park offers contemporary and minimalist rooms equipped with state-of-the-art fittings. Restaurant opening onto the swimming pool; traditional dishes, and snacks at the bar.

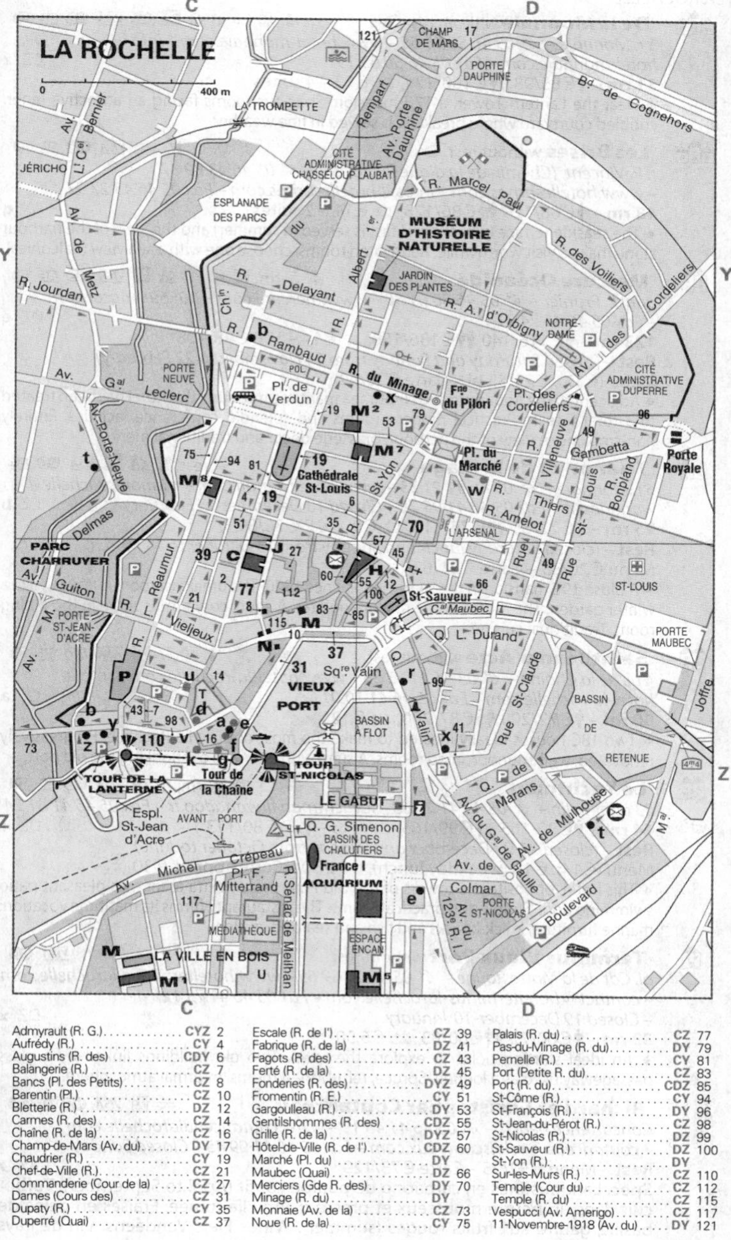

LA ROCHELLE
0
400 m
C
D
Y
Z
LA TROMPETTE
CHAMP DE MARS
PORTE DAUPHINE
Bd de Cognehors
Rempart
Av. Porte Dauphine
CITÉ ADMINISTRATIVE CHASSELOUP LAUBAT
ESPLANADE DES PARCS
R. Marcel Paul
MUSÉUM D'HISTOIRE NATURELLE
JARDIN DES PLANTES
R. des Voiliers
Cordeliers
JÉRICHO
Av. Lt Cel Bernier
Av. de Metz
R. Jourdan
R. Delayant
R. A. d'Orbigny
NOTRE-DAME
R. Rambaud
R. du Minage
Fne du Pilori
Pl. des Cordeliers
CITÉ ADMINISTRATIVE DUPERRE
PORTE NEUVE
Av. Gal Leclerc
Pl. de Verdun
Av. Porte-Neuve
Cathédrale St-Louis
St-Yon
Pl. du Marché
R. Gambetta
Porte Royale
R. Thiers
R. Amelot
L'ARSENAL
R. Bonpland
Rue St-Louis
Rue Villeneuve
Delmas
PARC CHARRUYER
Av. Guiton
Réaumur
R. L. Vieljeux
St-Sauveur
Cal Maubec
Q. L. Durand
ST-LOUIS
PORTE MAUBEC
PORTE ST-JEAN-D'ACRE
Sqre Valin
VIEUX PORT
BASSIN A FLOT
Rue St-Claude
BASSIN DE RETENUE
Joffre
Valin
TOUR DE LA LANTERNE
Tour de la Chaîne
TOUR ST-NICOLAS
LE GABUT
Q. de Marans
Av. de Mulhouse
Espl. St-Jean d'Acre
AVANT PORT
Q. G. Simenon
BASSIN DES CHALUTIERS
France I
AQUARIUM
Av. Michel Crépeau
Pl. F. Mitterrand
R. Sénac de Meilhan
Av. du Gal de Gaulle
Av. de Colmar
PORTE ST-NICOLAS
Av. du 123e R. I.
Boulevard
MÉDIATHÈQUE
ESPACE ENCAN
LA VILLE EN BOIS

De la Monnaie without rest
3 r. Monnaie – ☎ 05 46 50 65 65 – www.hotel-monnaie.com – info@hotel-monnaie.com – Fax 05 46 50 63 19 CZ **z**
31 rm – †€ 85/98 ††€ 108/124, ☐ € 13 – 4 suites
◆ Near the Lantern Tower, a 17C mansion. Spacious rooms facing an attractive inner, cobbled courtyard where breakfast is served in fine weather.

Les Brises without rest
r. P. Vincent, (Chemin de la digue Richelieu) – ☎ 05 46 43 89 37 – www.hotellesbrises.com – infos@hotellesbrises.com – Fax 05 46 43 27 97
48 rm – †€ 68/128 ††€ 86/128, ☐ € 11 – 2 suites AX **q**
◆ The seaside terrace (where breakfast is served in summer) and the view of the harbour alone make a visit worthwhile. Renovated rooms; choose one with a sea view (balconies).

Mercure Océanide rm,
quai L. Prunier – ☎ 05 46 50 61 50 – www.mercure.com – h0569@accor.com – Fax 05 46 41 24 31 DZ **e**
123 rm – †€ 116/140 ††€ 136/156, ☐ € 14 – ½ P € 98/108
Rest – *(closed Saturday and Sunday from 14 November to 22 February)*
Menu (€ 17), € 23/55 bi – Carte € 25/42
◆ Adjacent to the Aquarium and Neptunea maritime museum, this hotel has been treated to a total facelift. Practical modern rooms and splendid conference facilities. Entirely non-smoking. A view of the harbour, brasserie decor and traditional menu.

Trianon et de la Plage rest,
6 r. Monnaie – ☎ 05 46 41 21 35 – www.hoteltrianon.com – trianonlarochelle@wanadoo.fr – Fax 05 46 41 95 78 – Closed 18 December-1st February CZ **b**
25 rm – †€ 72/85 ††€ 76/110, ☐ € 9 – ½ P € 76/89
Rest – *(closed Saturday lunch and Sunday from 15 October to 15 March)*
Menu € 20/35 – Carte € 21/62
◆ A plush 19C mansion in the same hands since 1920. The breakfast room is laid out like a winter garden. The rooms at the rear are quieter. A snug, cosy atmosphere in the dining room. Traditional cuisine.

Saint Jean d'Acre without rest
4 pl. de la Chaine – ☎ 05 46 41 73 33 – www.hotel-la-rochelle.com – info@hotel-la-rochelle.com – Fax 05 46 41 10 01 CZ **a**
60 rm – †€ 72/200 ††€ 87/200, ☐ € 12
◆ Two 18C houses ideally located to make the most of busy La Rochelle. Progressively renovated, well-soundproofed rooms. A suite with a terrace overlooking the old port.

Le Yachtman rm,
23 quai Valin – ☎ 05 46 41 20 68 – leyachtman@wanadoo.fr – Fax 05 46 41 81 24
44 rm – †€ 89/165 ††€ 99/165, ☐ € 13 – ½ P € 80/113 DZ **r**
Rest – *(closed 21-27 December and Sunday from October to June)*
Menu (€ 14), € 18 (weekday lunch), € 24/30 – Carte approx. € 30
◆ This hotel, opposite the towers of the Old Port, has an extra asset – its pleasant patio swimming pool. Simple and practical rooms. The restaurant affirms its maritime vocation: marine furniture, knick-knacks and fish and seafood cuisine.

Terminus Vieux Port without rest
pl. Cdt de la Motte Rouge – ☎ 05 46 50 69 69 – www.hotelterminus-larochelle.com – contact@hotelterminus-larochelle.com – Fax 05 46 41 73 12 – Closed 19 December-10 January DZ **x**
33 rm – †€ 60/72 ††€ 60/83, ☐ € 6,50
◆ An ideal starting point to explore the town. Two old buildings linked by a glass passageway used as a lounge. Spruce, refurbished rooms. Informal atmosphere.

Richard et Christopher Coutanceau
Concurrence beach – ☎ 05 46 41 48 19 – www.coutanceaularochelle.com – coutanceau@relaischateaux.com – Fax 05 46 41 99 45 – Closed Sunday
Rest – Menu € 52/95 – Carte € 73/129 AX **r**
Spec. Langoustines en carpaccio de poulpe confit (April to September). Turbot cuit dans un beurre mousseux et préssé d'anguille fumée. Fraises en gelée de basilic, gaufre aux fruits rouges (summer). **Wines** Fiefs Vendéens, Vin de Pays Charentais.
◆ A refined, rotunda dining room overlooking the harbour and ocean is the elegant backdrop to fine cuisine with an emphasis on fresh seafood.

XX **Les Flots**
1 r. Chaîne – ✆ 05 46 41 32 51 – www.gregorycoutanceau.com – contact@les-flots.com – Fax 05 46 41 90 80 CZ **g**
Rest – Menu € 28 (lunch), € 39/76 – Carte € 56/83
◆ An 18C tavern, at the foot of the Tour de la Chaîne. A rustic setting, modernised in a nautical style. Seafood with an inventive slant and magnificent wine list (900 choices).

XX **Le Comptoir du Sud**
4 pl. Chaîne – ✆ 05 46 41 06 08 – www.lecomptoirdusud.com – lcomptoirdusud@orange.fr – Fax 05 46 41 79 77 – Closed 5 January-5 February CZ **e**
Rest – Menu (€ 18), € 21/33 – Carte € 37/45
◆ A slight southern touch in the decor and menu of this restaurant opposite the Chain Tower. Interesting selection of wines from the Mediterranean basin.

XX **Le Comptoir des Voyages**
22 r. St-Jean-du-Pérot – ✆ 05 46 50 62 60 – www.gregorycoutanceau.com – contact@lecomptoirdesvoyages.com – Fax 05 46 41 90 80 CZ **d**
Rest – Menu (€ 19 bi) – Carte € 30/51
◆ Take a gourmet voyage without moving from the warm, contemporary decor of the "Comptoir" serving dishes prepared with spices from distant lands; selection of world wines.

X **Les Orchidées**
24 r. Thiers – ✆ 05 46 41 07 63 – www.restaurant-les-orchidees.com – hottlet_y@alicepro.fr – Fax 05 46 50 05 16 – Closed 27 July-7 August DY **w**
Rest – Menu (€ 22), € 28/77 – Carte € 45/85
◆ A family bistro near the market and off the main tourist track. The chef prepares traditional dishes; the orchids on show in the dining room are his other passion.

X **André**
pl. Chaîne – ✆ 05 46 41 28 24 – www.barandre.com – barandre@blanc.net – Fax 05 46 41 64 22 CZ **f**
Rest – Menu (€ 25), € 33/37 – Carte € 40/50
◆ For three generations, the same family has run this local institution renowned for its seafood. Ten dining rooms with a pronounced nautical decor and unusual objects.

X **Le Champêtre**
22 r. Verdière – ✆ 05 46 41 12 17 – Closed 26 October-1st November, Monday in low season and Sunday CZ **u**
Rest – Menu (€ 23), € 33/43 – Carte € 45/52
◆ Near the port, but away from the tourist track, this small restaurant has two dining rooms, one rustic and the other, modern and colourful (on the first floor). Well-presented modern cuisine.

X **L'Entracte**
35 r. St-Jean-du-Pérot – ✆ 05 46 52 26 69 – www.gregorycoutanceau.com – contact@lentracte.net – Fax 05 46 41 90 80 CZ **v**
Rest – Menu € 21 bi – Carte € 30/51
◆ This establishment under the Coutanceau banner offers a contemporary bistro atmosphere while guarding a sense of the nostalgic (wood panelling, brass wall lamps, old posters). Modern dishes.

in Aytré **5 km by ② – pop. 8 687 – ✉ 17440**

XXX **La Maison des Mouettes**
1 r. Claires, (1st floor) – ✆ 05 46 44 29 12 – www.lamaisondesmouettes.fr – reservation-mouettes@orange.fr – Fax 05 46 34 66 01
Rest – Menu € 36/78 – Carte € 65/101
Rest *Version Original* – Menu € 22
◆ This large seaside villa has comfortable, modern dining room with a superb panoramic view on the 1st floor. Modern cuisine served. Trendy lounge ambiance and decor and a simple, appetising menu.

Look out for red symbols, indicating particularly pleasant establishments.

LA ROCHE-POSAY – **86 Vienne** – **322** K4 – **pop. 1 522** – **alt. 112 m** 39 **D1**
– **Spa : late Jan.-mid Dec.** – **Casino** – ✉ **86270** Atlantic Coast

Paris 325 – Le Blanc 29 – Châteauroux 76 – Loches 49 – Poitiers 61 – Tours 92

Office de tourisme, 14, boulevard Victor Hugo ✆ 05 49 19 13 00, Fax 05 49 86 27 94

du Connetable Parc Thermal, S : 2 km on D 3, ✆ 05 49 86 25 10

Les Loges du Parc without rest
10 pl. de la République – ✆ 05 49 19 40 50 – www.la-roche-posay.info – loges@la-roche-posay.info – Fax 05 49 19 40 51 – Open 10 April-11 October
44 rm – €84/106 €102/127, €10 – 33 suites
◆ This huge Belle Epoque structure offers classic hotel accommodation suitable for short breaks or longer stays. Jazz and Egypt are the themes of two superb suites; countless leisure activities.

St-Roch rm, rm, VISA
4 cours Pasteur – ✆ 05 49 19 49 00 – www.resorthotel-larocheposay.fr – contact@la-roche-posay.info – Fax 05 49 19 49 40 – Closed 14 December-15 January
37 rm – €49/78 €67/94, €8,50 – ½ P €60/73
Rest – Menu (€22), €28/36 – Carte €35/57
◆ Those come to take the waters appreciate this centrally-located hotel's direct access to Saint-Roch thermal baths. Practical rooms, some of which overlook the garden. Traditional cuisine in a fresh and bright dining room, which also offers a children's play area.

LE ROCHER – **07 Ardèche** – **331** H6 – **see Largentière**

ROCHESERVIÈRE – **85 Vendée** – **316** G6 – **pop. 2 691** – **alt. 58 m** 34 **B3**
– ✉ **85620**

Paris 415 – La Roche-sur-Yon 34 – Nantes 34 – Saint-Herblain 42

Office de tourisme, 21, rue du Péplu ✆ 02 51 94 94 05, Fax 02 51 94 94 28

Le Château du Pavillon without rest
r. Gué-Baron – ✆ 02 51 06 55 99 – www.le-chateau-du-pavillon.com – annie.gilbert.rio@orange.fr – Fax 02 51 06 55 99 – Open 30 April-15 September
4 rm – €80/120 €80/120, €8,50
◆ This château from 1885, set inside a park with a pond, combines charm, elegance and comfort. Truly romantic rooms and nursery for children under ten.

ROCHESSAUVE – **07 Ardèche** – **331** J5 – **see Privas**

LA ROCHE-SUR-FORON – **74 Haute-Savoie** – **328** K4 – **pop. 8 538** 46 **F1**
– **alt. 548 m** – ✉ **74800** French Alps

Paris 553 – Annecy 34 – Bonneville 8 – Genève 26 – Thonon-les-Bains 42

Office de tourisme, place Andrevetan ✆ 04 50 03 36 68, Fax 04 50 03 31 38

Old town ★★.

Le Foron without rest VISA
imp. de l'Étang, (Le Dragiez Industrial Estate), D 1203 – ✆ 04 50 25 82 76 – www.hotel-le-foron.com – lf7405@inter-hotel.com – Fax 04 50 25 81 54 – Closed 22 December-4 January and Sunday
26 rm – €55/57 €62/65, €8
◆ A practical spot, this small hotel in the Roche-sur-Foron industrial area has functional, soundproofed, well-kept rooms.

LA ROCHE-SUR-YON Ⓟ – **85 Vendée** – **316** H7 – **pop. 50 600** 34 **B3**
– **alt. 75 m** – ✉ **85000** Atlantic Coast

Paris 418 – Cholet 69 – Nantes 68 – Niort 91 – La Rochelle 77

Office de tourisme, rue Clemenceau ✆ 02 51 36 00 85, Fax 02 51 36 90 27

de La Domangère Nesmy La Roche sur Yon, S : 8 km on D 746 and D 85, ✆ 02 51 07 65 90

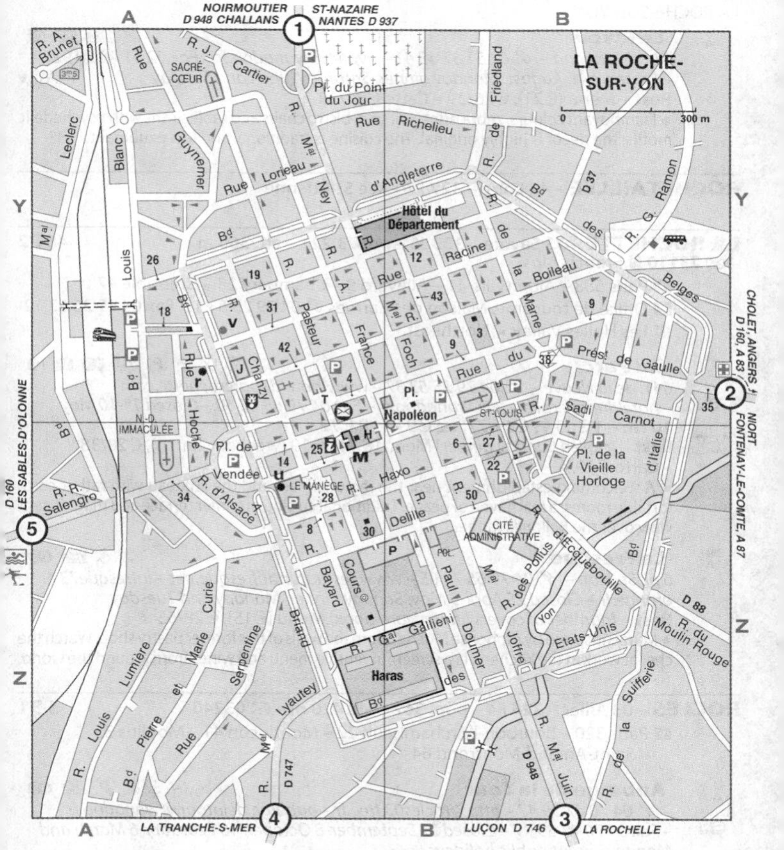

LA ROCHE-SUR-YON

Street	Grid	No.	Street	Grid	No.	Street	Grid	No.
Albert-1er (Pl.)	BY	3	La-Fayette (R.)	AZ	25	Molière (R.)	AY	31
Allende (R. Salv.)	AY	4	Gambetta (Av.)	AY	18	Poincaré (R. Raymond)	AZ	34
Baudry (R. Paul)	BZ	6	Gén.-de-Castelnau (R.)	AY	19	Pompidou (R. G.)	BY	35
Bérégovoy (R. P.)	AZ	8	Halles (R. des)	BZ	22	Résistance (Pl. de la)	BY	38
Berthelot (R. M.)	BY	9	Manuel (R.)	AY	26	Verdun (R. de)	AY	42
Bossuet (R.)	BY	12	Marché (R. du)	BYZ	27	Victor-Hugo (R.)	BY	43
Carnot (R. Sadi)	BY		Mazurelle (Esplanade J.)	AZ	28	93e-R.I. (R. du)	BZ	50
Clemenceau (R. G.)	AZ	14	Mitterrand (Pl. F.)	AZ	30			

Mercure rm, VISA

117 bd A. Briand – ☎ 02 51 46 28 00 – www.mercure.com – h1552@accor.com – Fax 02 51 46 28 98 AZ **u**

67 rm – †€ 72/106 ††€ 76/118, ☕ € 14

Rest – Menu (€ 18), € 22/28 bi – Carte € 39/50

◆ Midway between the station and Place Napoléon, this recent hotel has spacious, practical and well-soundproofed rooms. A glass roofed breakfast room. Simple dishes in a traditional vein served in a restaurant or terrace, beneath boat sails.

Napoléon without rest VISA

50 bd A. Briand – ☎ 02 51 05 33 56 – www.hotel-le-napoleon.fr – hotel-nap@wanadoo.fr – Fax 02 51 62 01 69 – Closed 23 December-1st January AY **r**

29 rm – †€ 74/92 ††€ 84/102, ☕ € 10

◆ Despite the hotel's proximity to a busy road, its well-kept rooms (renovated in stages) are surprisingly quiet. Copious breakfasts served in a room decorated in Empire style.

Le Rivoli

31 bd A. Briand – 02 51 37 43 41 – rivoli4@wanadoo.fr – Fax 02 51 46 20 92 – Closed 3-16 August, Monday dinner, Saturday lunch and Sunday AY **v**

Rest – Menu (€ 21), € 26/39 – Carte € 31/38

◆ Flamboyant colours, zebra print wall seat, bistro chairs and tablecloths with psychedelic motifs: the decor is highly original. The cuisine is traditional and less exuberant.

ROCHETAILLÉE – 42 Loire – 327 F7 – see St-Étienne

LA ROCHETTE – 73 Savoie – 333 J5 – pop. 3 221 – alt. 360 m – ✉ 73110 French Alps 46 F2

Paris 588 – Albertville 41 – Allevard 9 – Chambéry 28 – Grenoble 47

Office de tourisme, Maison des Carmes 04 79 25 53 12, Fax 04 79 25 53 12

Les Huiles Valley ★ Northeast.

Du Parc

64 r. de la Neuve – 04 79 25 53 37 – www.hotelduparcrochette.com – hotelduparc.rochette@wanadoo.fr – Fax 04 79 65 07 60 – Closed 1st-10 May

10 rm – €60 €69/77, € 9 – ½ P € 72

Rest – *(closed Sunday dinner)* Menu (€ 14), € 19 (weekday lunch), € 28/38 – Carte € 29/49

◆ A welcoming establishment near the regional park and the château with rather comfortable rooms: a real haven of peace. Traditional cuisine, summer terrace and magnificent view over the Bellones range.

La Fresque

6 pl. St-Jean – 04 79 65 78 05 – www.restaurantlafresque.net – lafresque73@orange.fr – Closed 25 April-5 May, Sunday dinner, Monday and Tuesday

Rest – *(number of covers limited, pre-book)* Menu (€ 15), € 28/55

◆ Murals inspired by Alphonse Mucha adorn the walls of this former pastry shop. Watch the chef at work in the kitchen via a screen. Inventive menu and wines from around the world.

ROCLES – 03 Allier – 326 F4 – pop. 362 – alt. 420 m – ✉ 03240 5 B1

Paris 320 – Bourbon-l'Archambault 22 – Montluçon 41 – Moulins 35 – Saint-Amand-Montrond 64

Auberge de la Tour

– 04 70 47 39 47 – http://rocles03.free.fr – auberge.delatour@wanadoo.fr – Fax 04 70 47 39 47 – Closed 22 September-8 October, 18 February-6 March and Monday except public holidays

Rest – Menu € 16 (weekdays)/45 – Carte € 30/50

◆ This old cafe, dating from 1893 and recognisable by its tower, stands opposite a 12C church. Bright dining room-veranda and terrace overlooking the garden. Modern cuisine.

RODEZ P – 12 Aveyron – 338 H4 – pop. 23 900 – alt. 635 m – ✉ 12000 Languedoc-Roussillon-Tarn Gorges 29 C1

Paris 623 – Albi 76 – Aurillac 87 – Clermont-Ferrand 213

Rodez-Marcillac: 05 65 76 02 00, by ③: 12 km.

Office de tourisme, place Foch 05 65 75 76 77, Fax 05 65 68 78 15

du Grand Rodez Onet-le-Château Route de Marcillac, N : 4 km on D 901, 05 65 78 38 00

Steeple★★★ of N.-Dame cathedral ★★ - Musée Fenaille★★ BZ **M**[1] - Wooden galleries★ of the Jesuits chapel.

Plan on next page

La Ferme de Bourran without rest

r. Berlin, in Bourran 1.5 km via ③ – 05 65 73 62 62 – www.fermedebourran.com – contact@fermedebourran.com – Fax 05 65 73 14 15

7 rm – € 100/140 € 120/180, € 15

◆ Seven rooms are available in this old farmstead perched on a hillside. Contemporary decoration, comfort, calm and state-of-the-art equipment. Table d'hôte breakfast.

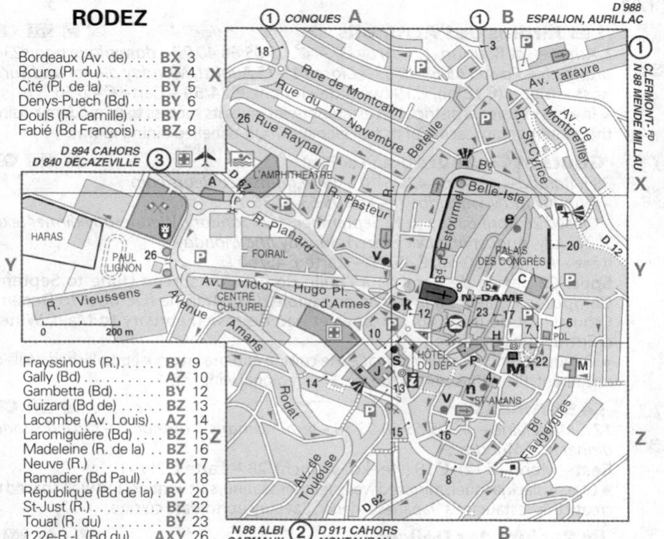

 Biney without rest
r. Victoire-Massol – ✆ 05 65 68 01 24 – www.hotel-biney.com – hotel.biney@wanadoo.fr – Fax 05 65 75 22 98 BY **k**
26 rm – †€ 72 ††€ 82/141, ☕ € 13 – 2 suites
◆ Although some rooms are slightly small, all are individual and rather charming with painted wooden furniture, attractive coloured fabrics and comfortable bedding. Hammam and sauna.

 La Tour Maje without rest
bd Gally – ✆ 05 65 68 34 68 – www.hotel-tour-maje.fr – tourmaje@orange.fr – Fax 05 65 68 27 56 BZ **s**
40 rm – †€ 55/70 ††€ 60/80, ☕ € 10 – 3 suites
◆ A 1970s hotel backing onto a 15C tower where the rustic-style suites are located (with exposed stone walls). Simple rooms; those on the fifth floor are Provençal in style.

 Ibis without rest
46 r. St-Cyrice – ✆ 05 65 76 10 30 – www.ibis.com – h2748-gm@accor.com – Fax 05 65 76 10 33 BX **a**
45 rm – †€ 64/74 ††€ 64/74, ☕ € 7,50
◆ In the heart of a totally renovated district, this chain hotel has small, functional rooms, some with balcony. Meeting rooms and lounge-bar.

 Du Midi
1 r. Béteille – ✆ 05 65 68 02 07 – www.hotelmidi.com – hotel.du.midi@wanadoo.fr – Fax 05 65 68 66 93 – Closed Christmas holidays ABY **v**
34 rm – †€ 54 ††€ 60, ☕ € 7 – ½ P € 54
Rest – *(closed Saturday lunch and Sunday)* Menu € 12/28 – Carte € 22/39
◆ The hotel's location close to the cathedral is ideal for sightseeing on foot. Simple, functional rooms which are quiet on the courtyard side and soundproofed at the front. Restaurant serving traditional dishes, salads, grills and the inevitable aligot.

 Deltour without rest
6 r. Bruxelles, in Bourran, 1,5 km via ③ – ✆ 05 65 73 03 03 – www.deltourhotel.com – hoteldeltourrodezb@wanadoo.fr – Fax 05 65 73 03 05 – Closed 21 December-7 January
39 rm – †€ 52 ††€ 52, ☕ € 8 – 3 suites
◆ This new hotel caters for a business clientele, with bright, functional rooms which are comfortable, well sound-proofed and simply decorated.

XX **Les Jardins de l'Acropolis**

r. Athènes, at Bourran, 1.5 km by ③ – 05 65 68 40 07 – dominique.panis234@orange.fr – Fax 05 65 68 40 67 – Closed 1st-15 August, Monday dinner and Sunday

Rest – Menu (€ 18 bi), € 19 (weekday lunch), € 24/59 – Carte € 42/56

◆ In a busy business district, this establishment owes its success to its modern cuisine and the contemporary cachet of its two elegant wood-panelled dining rooms.

XX **Goûts et Couleurs** (Jean-Luc Fau)

38 r. Bonald – 05 65 42 75 10 – www.goutsetcouleurs.com – jean-luc.fau@wanadoo.fr – Fax 05 65 42 75 10 – Closed 26 April-6 May, 1-12 September, 4-27 January, Wednesday dinner (except June, July, August and December), Sunday and Monday BY **e**

Rest – Menu (€ 30 bi), € 35/75 – Carte € 45/60

Spec. Carpaccio de gambas à l'huile de fleur de sureau (June to September). Compotée de lièvre à la royale en raviole de châtaigne (October to December). Croustillant de miel aux agrumes et eau de rose (February to May). **Wines** Vin d'Entraygues et du Fel.

◆ Originality and creativity pervade the cuisine and the artwork embellished walls of this restaurant. Pleasant summer terrace. Fine regional wine list.

XX **Le St-Amans**

12 r. Madeleine – 05 65 68 03 18 – lesaintamans@orange.fr – Closed Sunday dinner and Monday BZ **v**

Rest – Menu (€ 12), € 18 (weekday lunch)/28 – Carte € 29/41

◆ Glossy black lacquer, mirrored walls, leather seating, soft lighting and well-spaced tables create this restaurant's 'Japanese' decor. Savoury up-to-date cuisine.

X **Le Parfum des Délices**

24 pl. du Bourg – 05 65 68 95 00 – www.leparfumdesdelices.fr – Fax 05 65 68 08 25 – Closed 15 August-7 September, 7-23 February, Sunday, Monday and dinner from Tuesday to Thursday BZ **n**

Rest – Menu (€ 13), € 24/39

◆ Three dining areas (room, vaulted cellar and terrace) decorated in a contemporary style with aubergine walls and dark wood. Spices and herbs feature prominently in the food. Tea room.

Espalion road by ① and D 988

Causse Comtal rest,

12 km – 05 65 74 90 98 – www.bestwester@caussecomtal.com – contact@caussecomtal.com – Fax 05 65 46 92 69 – Closed Saturday lunch and Sunday dinner in low season

120 rm – €76 €86, € 12 – 2 suites – ½ P € 75/90

Rest – Menu (€ 22), € 28/52 – Carte € 18/52

◆ This modern building, isolated in the middle of the causse (limestone plateau), has a large stone tower. It has extensive leisure facilities. Practical, colourful rooms. A fresh, cheerful restaurant, with small summer terrace and traditional dishes.

in Olemps 3 km West by ② – pop. 3 020 – alt. 580 m – ✉ 12510

Les Peyrières rm,

22 r. Peyrières – 05 65 68 20 52 – www.hotel-les-peyrieres.com – contact@hotel-les-peyrieres.com – Fax 05 65 68 47 88 – Closed Sunday dinner

60 rm – €75 €75/110, € 10

Rest – *(closed Sunday dinner and Monday lunch)* Menu (€ 14), € 20 (weekdays)/40 – Carte € 49/63

◆ This long contemporary villa in the residential suburb of Rodez has simple, well-kept rooms. Pleasant welcome. Three dining rooms serving traditional dishes. Terrace overlooking the pool.

Conques road North AX D 901

Hostellerie de Fontanges

rte de Conques, at 4 km – 05 65 77 76 00 – www.hostellerie-fontanges.com – fontanges.hotel@wanadoo.fr – Fax 05 65 42 82 29

43 rm – €59/75 €65/85, € 10 – 5 suites – ½ P € 75/85

Rest – *(closed Saturday lunch and Sunday dinner from November to Easter)* Menu (€ 20), € 24/45 – Carte € 50/60

◆ Large, attractive 16C-17C residence surrounded by parkland and a golf course. Subdued decor in the renovated rooms; suites personalised with period furniture. French manor house-style dining room with veranda extension. Regional cuisine and extensive wine list.

 **Château de Labro** without rest
Onet village, 7 km on the D 901 and D 568 – 05 65 67 90 62 – www.chateaulabro.fr – chateau.labro@wanadoo.fr – Fax 05 65 67 45 79
14 rm – €110/130 €110/200
◆ This chateau and park are simply divine: romantic rooms with beautiful old furniture and modern bathrooms, and a swimming pool in the old orchard. Breakfast served among the antique shop finds.

ROISSY-EN-FRANCE – **95 Val-d'Oise** – **305** G6 – **101** – see Paris, Area

---

ROLLEBOISE – **78 Yvelines** – **311** F1 – **pop. 401** – **alt. 20 m** – ✉ **78270** 18 **A1**

Paris 65 – Dreux 45 – Mantes-la-Jolie 9 – Rouen 72 – Vernon 15 – Versailles 56

La Corniche de Rolleboise
5 rte de la Corniche – 01 30 93 20 00 – www.domainedelacorniche.com – corniche@wanadoo.fr – Fax 01 30 42 27 44
34 rm – €120/250 €120/250, €15 – 2 suites – ½ P €103/168
Rest – *(closed Sunday dinner from November to end March)*
Menu (€27 bi), €67 (dinner) – Carte €34/92
◆ This folly, built by Leopold II of Belgium for his last love, dominates the Seine. Modern rooms in the main building and extensions. Panoramic summer pool. Contemporary restaurant and terrace with view of the river. Modern cuisine.

ROMAGNIEU – **38 Isère** – **333** G4 – **pop. 1 374** – **alt. 298 m** – ✉ **38480** 45 **C2**

Paris 539 – Grenoble 57 – Chambéry 35 – Lyon 109

Auberge les Forges de la Massotte
655 chemin des Forges, West 2 km,exit ⑩ on A 43 – 04 76 31 53 00 – www.aubergemassotte.com – lesforgesdelamassotte@wanadoo.fr – Fax 04 76 31 53 02 – Closed autumn and Easter school holidays
5 rm – €58 €68, €9 – ½ P €66
Rest – *(closed Sunday) (dinner only) (residents only)* Menu €29
◆ The walls of this former forge now house pretty rooms furnished in a solid wood Savoyard or Dauphine style. Peace and quiet, faultless service and hearty breakfasts. Half-regional, half-traditional set menu served in a countrified dining room.

ROMANÈCHE-THORINS – **71 Saône-et-Loire** – **320** I12 – **pop. 1 767** – **alt. 187 m** – ✉ **71570** **Lyon - Rhone Valley** 8 **C3**

Paris 406 – Chauffailles 46 – Lyon 55 – Mâcon 17 – Villefranche-sur-Saône 24
"Le Hameau du vin" ★★ Touroparc Zoo and Amusement Park★.

Les Maritonnes rm,
rte Fleurie, near the station – 03 85 35 51 70 – www.maritonnes.com – contact@maritonnes.com – Fax 03 85 35 58 14 – Closed 17-30 December
25 rm – €80/130 €90/175, €15 – ½ P €85/115
Rest – *(closed Sunday dinner, Monday and Tuesday lunch from mid-October to early March)* Menu (€15), €35/70 – Carte €58/80
◆ Peaceful hotel in a large, Virginia creeper clad hotel and nestled in flower-filled parkland. Choose a recently redecorated bedroom. Traditional meals enjoyed with the famous local Moulin-à-Vent vintage wine.

ROMANS-SUR-ISÈRE – **26 Drôme** – **332** D3 – **pop. 33 700** – **alt. 162 m** – ✉ **26100** **Lyon - Rhone Valley** 43 **E2**

Paris 558 – Die 78 – Grenoble 81 – St-Étienne 121 – Valence 20 – Vienne 73
Office de tourisme, place Jean Jaurès 04 75 02 28 72, Fax 04 75 05 91 62
de Valence Saint-Didier Saint-Didier-de-Charpey15 km on the Crest road, 04 75 59 67 01
Hangings★★ of St-Barnard collegiate church - Shoe collection of ★ the musée international de la chaussure (international shoe museum) - Musée diocésain d'Art sacré★ to Mours-St-Eusèbe, 4 km by ①.

ROMANS-SUR-ISÈRE

Clercs (R. des) . . . . CY 4
Cordeliers (Côtes des) . . . . . . CY
Écosserie (R. de l') . . . . BY 8
Faure (Pl. M.) . . . . BY
Fontaine des Cordeliers (R.) . CY 10
Gailly (Pl. E.) . . . . BY
Guilhaume (R.) . . . . AZ 12
Herbes (Pl. aux) . . . . BY 14
Jacquemart (Côte) . . . . BY 15
Jacquemart (R.) . . . . AZ 16
Massenet (Pl.) . . . . CY 17
Mathieu-de-la-Drôme (R.) . . . CY 18
Merlin (R.) . . . . CY 20
Mouton (R. du) . . . . BY 22
Palestro (R.) . . . . AZ 24
Perrot-de-Verdun (Pl.) . . . . . . BY 26
Sabaton (R.) . . . . CY 28
Ste-Marie (R.) . . . . CY 29
Semard (Av. P.) . . . . AZ 30
Trois Carreaux (R.) . . . . CY 32
Victor-Hugo (Av.) . . . . AZ 34

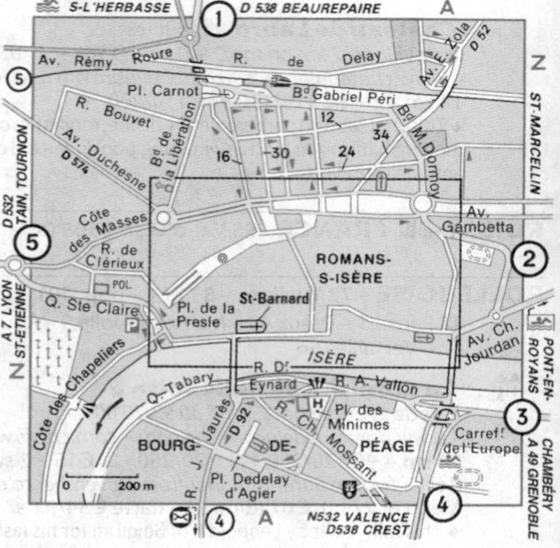

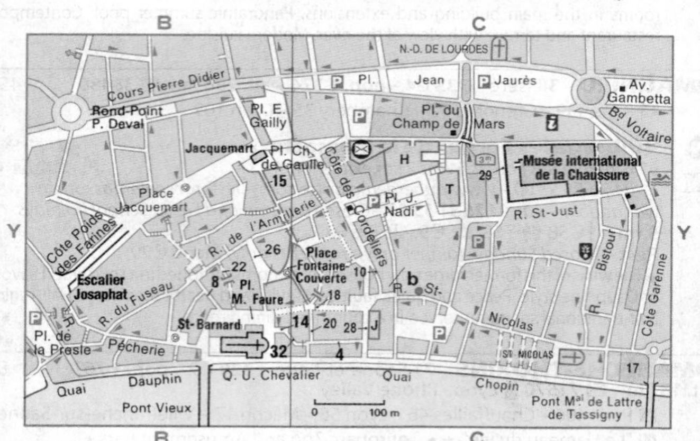

L'Orée du Parc without rest
6 av. Gambetta, via ② – ✆ 04 75 70 26 12 – www.hotel-oreeparc.com – hotoree-parc@wanadoo.fr – Fax 04 75 05 08 23 – Closed 11-18 October, 27 December-3 January and 6-22 February
10 rm – †€ 80/111 ††€ 83/115, ☕ € 10
◆ This fine, well-bred 1920s edifice offers pretty rooms named after flowers and with modern personal touches. Good breakfasts served on the veranda or garden (pool). Non-smoking only.

Mandrin
70 r. St-Nicolas – ✆ 04 75 02 93 55 – destrait.emmanuel@wanadoo.fr – Fax 04 75 02 93 55 – Closed 3-25 August, 15-23 February, Sunday and Monday CY **b**
Rest – Menu € 20/38 – Carte € 26/35
◆ Mandrin, a famous French smuggler, is said to have found refuge in this house dating from 1754. The terracotta floor, exposed beams, half-timbering and rolled pebbles give the restaurant dining room a medieval feel. Traditional menu and paella upon request.

in l'Est 4 km by ② and D 92N – ✉ 26750 St-Paul-lès-Romans

Karene
St Verant district – ☎ 04 75 05 12 50 – www.hotelkarene.com – contact@hotelkarene.com – Fax 04 75 05 25 17 – Closed 22 December-1st January
23 rm – €58/60 €67/72, €10
Rest – *(closed Friday, Saturday, Sunday and public holidays) (dinner only) (residents only)* Menu €17 – Carte approx. €28
◆ This former company head office converted into a hotel, is set away from the road and offers functional rooms. Some have air-conditioning. Friendly welcome and traditional dishes served in a dining room adorned with copies of Van Gogh paintings.

in Châtillon-St-Jean 11 km by ② – pop. 1 156 – alt. 198 m – ✉ 26750

Maison Forte de Clérivaux without rest
– ☎ 04 75 45 32 53 – www.clerivaux.fr – contact@clerivaux.fr – Fax 04 75 71 45 43 – Closed 3 January-3 March
4 rm – €60 €65
◆ These harmoniously renovated 16C and 17C buildings situated in a rustic location have retained much of their old style. Terraces and lovely garden where breakfast is served under the arbour in summer.

in Granges-lès-Beaumont 6 km by ⑤ – pop. 963 – alt. 155 m – ✉ 26600

Les Cèdres (Jacques Bertrand)
Le Village – ☎ 04 75 71 50 67 – www.restaurantlescedres.fr – Fax 04 75 71 64 39 – Closed 14-22 April, 17 August-2 September, 21 December-5 January, Sunday dinner, Monday and Tuesday
Rest – *(number of covers limited, pre-book)* Menu €40 (weekday lunch), €80/110 – Carte €70/90
Spec. Saint-Jacques à la plancha aux graines de sésame torréfiées (winter). Turbot rôti sur l'arête, jus de viande à la moelle de bœuf (spring). Tarte sablée au chocolat guanaja, sorbet cacao amer (autumn-winter). **Wines** Hermitage, Crozes Hermitage.
◆ Welcoming village house offering delicious contemporary cuisine in an elegant dining room. Good choice of Côtes-du-Rhône wines. Lounge with a fireplace. Well-kept garden.

in St-Paul-lès-Romans 8 km by ② – pop. 1 626 – alt. 171 m – ✉ 26750

La Malle Poste
Le Village – ☎ 04 75 45 35 43 – lamalle.poste@wanadoo.fr – Fax 04 75 71 40 48 – Closed 27 July-22 August, 2-17 January, Sunday dinner, Tuesday dinner and Monday
Rest – Menu €32/62
◆ Cleverly inventive cuisine, respectful of the seasons and locality. Very fine wine list (over 350 labels). Warm, simple dining room.

ROMILLY-SUR-SEINE – 10 Aube – 313 C2 – pop. 14 100 – alt. 76 m 13 B2 – ✉ 10100

Paris 124 – Châlons-en-Champagne 76 – Nogent-sur-Seine 18 – Sens 65 – Troyes 39

Office de tourisme, 27, rue Saint-Laurent ☎ 03 25 24 87 80

Auberge de Nicey
24 r. Carnot – ☎ 03 25 24 10 07 – www.denicey.com – contact@denicey.com – Fax 03 25 24 47 01 – Closed 22 December-4 January
23 rm – €85/99 €119/139, €13 – ½ P €96/109
Rest – *(closed Saturday lunch, Sunday lunch and Monday lunch in August and Sunday dinner)* Menu €23 (weekdays)/45 – Carte €40/57
◆ This comfortable hotel, with functional and well-soundproofed rooms, is located near the railway station. Annex bedrooms are bigger. Two elegant dining rooms, adorned with colourful artwork. Traditional culinary register.

ROMORANTIN-LANTHENAY – 41 Loir-et-Cher – 318 H7 12 C2
– pop. 17 400 – alt. 93 m – ✉ 41200 Châteaux of the Loire

Paris 202 – Blois 42 – Bourges 74 – Orléans 67 – Tours 95 – Vierzon 38

Office de tourisme, place de la Paix ✆ 02 54 76 43 89, Fax 02 54 76 96 24

Old houses★ B - View of bridges★ - Musée de Sologne★ M².

ROMORANTIN-LANTHENAY

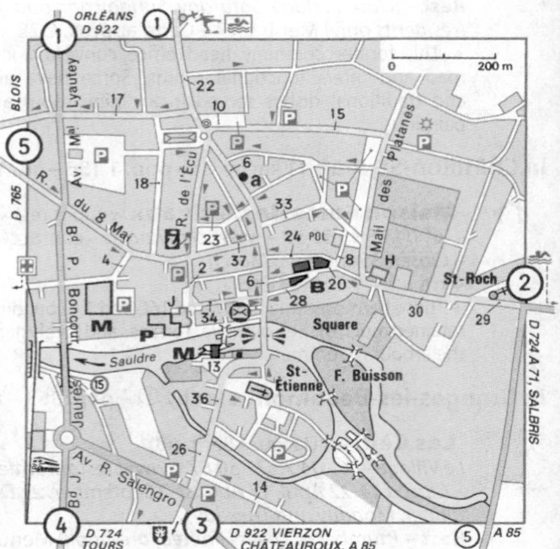

Grand Hôtel du Lion d'Or (Didier Clément) rm, rm,
69 r. Clemenceau – ✆ 02 54 94 15 15
– www.hotel-liondor.fr – liondor@relaischateaux.com – Fax 02 54 88 24 87
– Closed 16 February-26 March and 15-26 November a
13 rm – †€ 170 ††€ 170/400, ☕ € 24 – 3 suites
Rest – *(closed Tuesday lunch) (number of covers limited, pre-book)*
Menu € 98/155 – Carte € 115/165
Spec. Cuisses de grenouilles à la rocambole. Pigeon farci façon babylonienne. Brioche caramélisée, sorbet angélique. **Wines** Cour-Cheverny, Bourgueil.
◆ Founded in 1774, this hotel sports one Renaissance and one Napoleon III façade. Period fixtures (panelling, balconies) are combined with modern furniture in the rooms. Updated cuisine and a good choice of Loire wines served in three rooms or on the summer terrace.

Pyramide rm,
r. Pyramide, by ① – ✆ 02 54 76 26 34 – www.hotelapyramide.com
– lapyramide@wanadoo.fr – Fax 02 54 76 22 28
66 rm – †€ 49 ††€ 59, ☕ € 10 – ½ P € 46
Rest – *(closed 21 December-6 January and Friday lunch)*
Menu € 17 (weekdays)/31 – Carte € 23/45
◆ Modern building near a cultural complex. Functional rooms which are all identical, in a modern style. Traditional meals are served in the simple dining room or on the terrace behind the restaurant.

Auberge le Lanthenay with rm rest,
9 r. Notre Dame du Lieu, 2.5 km by ① and D 922 – ✆ 02 54 76 09 19
– lelanthenay@orange.fr – Fax 02 54 76 72 91 – Closed 2-26 January, Friday lunch, Sunday dinner and Monday
10 rm – †€ 52/55 ††€ 52/55, ☕ € 8 – ½ P € 55
Rest – *(number of covers limited, pre-book)*
Menu € 23 (weekdays)/52 – Carte € 28/48
◆ Pleasant place to spend the night in a picturesque hamlet, where you'll discover good cuisine combined with quiet surroundings. The dining room is more intimate than the veranda.

RONCE-LES-BAINS – 17 Charente-Maritime – 324 D5 – ✉ 17390 38 A2
La Tremblade ▌ **Atlantic Coast**

Paris 505 – Marennes 9 – Rochefort 31 – La Rochelle 68 – Royan 27

Office de tourisme, place Brochard ✆ 05 46 36 06 02, Fax 05 46 36 38 17

Le Grand Chalet VISA

2 av. La Cèpe – ✆ 05 46 36 06 41 – www.legrandchalet.net – frederic.moinardeau@wanadoo.fr – Fax 05 46 36 38 87 – Closed 4 November-10 February

26 rm – †€ 46/85 ††€ 46/85, ☐ € 12 – ½ P € 55/75

Rest – *(closed Sunday dinner in low season, Monday except dinner in high season and Tuesday)* Menu € 26/48

◆ A hotel from 1850 overlooking the sea with direct access to the beach. Some of the simple rooms have a fine view of the Île d'Oléron, others face the hotel garden. In the restaurant some tables have a pleasant view of the ocean. Traditional cuisine.

RONCHAMP – 70 Haute-Saône – 314 H6 – pop. 2 924 – alt. 380 m 17 C1
– ✉ 70250 ▌ **Burgundy-Jura**

Paris 399 – Belfort 22 – Besançon 88 – Lure 12 – Luxeuil-les-Bains 31 – Vesoul 42

Office de tourisme, 14, place du 14 Juillet ✆ 03 84 63 50 82, Fax 03 84 63 50 82

Notre-Dame-du-Haut Chapel★★.

in Rhien 3 km North – ✉ 70250 Ronchamp

Rhien Carrer rm, rm, VISA

14 r. d'Orière – ✆ 03 84 20 62 32 – www.ronchamp.com – carrer@ronchamp.com – Fax 03 84 63 57 08

19 rm – †€ 42 ††€ 50, ☐ € 8 – ½ P € 43

Rest – *(closed Sunday dinner from October to March)*
Menu (€ 8,50), € 12 (weekdays)/42 – Carte € 25/55

◆ Family hotel not far from the Chapelle Notre Dame du Haut, a masterpiece by Le Corbusier. Comfortable quiet guestrooms, more recent in the wing. The restaurant menu honours the region through local specialities. Terrace.

in Champagney 4.5 km East by D 4 – pop. 3 501 – alt. 370 m – ✉ 70290

Le Pré Serroux VISA

4 av. Gén. Brosset – ✆ 03 84 23 13 24 – www.lepreserroux.com – lepreserroux@wanadoo.fr – Fax 03 84 23 24 33 – Closed 22 December-12 January and Sunday

25 rm – †€ 65 ††€ 70, ☐ € 10 – ½ P € 60

Rest – *(closed Saturday lunch, Monday lunch, lunch in August and Sunday)*
Menu € 15 (weekday lunch), € 23/40 – Carte € 30/50

◆ This pleasant hotel sports a quaint personalised decor that includes Peugeot mopeds and sewing machines. Some of the comfortable rooms are decorated in a regional style. Indoor pool. The Art Nouveau inspired dining room is the setting for traditional cuisine and a fine wine list.

RONCQ – 59 Nord – 302 G3 – see Lille

LE ROND-D'ORLÉANS – 02 Aisne – 306 B5 – see Chauny

ROOST-WARENDIN – 59 Nord – 302 G5 – see Douai

ROPPENHEIM – 67 Bas-Rhin – 315 M3 – pop. 956 – alt. 117 m 1 B1
– ✉ 67480

Paris 503 – Haguenau 25 – Karlsruhe 41 – Strasbourg 48 – Wissembourg 35

A l'Agneau VISA

11 r. Principale – ✆ 03 88 86 40 08 – Closed 26 April-4 May, 12 July-10 August, 20 December-4 January, Sunday and Monday

Rest – *(dinner only except Saturday)* Carte € 20/55

◆ A typical Alsace style house, popular for its generous meals (traditional cooking and grills) and very cheerful atmosphere. Showcase for regional products.

ROQUEBILLIÈRE – 06 Alpes-Maritimes – 341 E3 – pop. 1 634 – alt. 650 m – ✉ 06450   41 D2

Paris 889 – Marseille 245 – Nice 58 – Cuneo 132 – San Remo 106

Le Provençal
5 r. des Héros-de-14-18, (opposite the church) – ☎ 04 93 05 13 13 – www.restaurant-le-provencal.com – jeromecornillon@hotmail.fr – Closed 12 November-12 December, February school holidays, Tuesday and Wednesday except July-August
Rest – Menu € 13 (lunch), € 24/30
◆ Decorated in Provençal style, this restaurant serves traditional French cuisine with an emphasis on seasonal garden and market produce.

ROQUEBRUNE-CAP-MARTIN – 06 Alpes-Maritimes – 341 F5 – pop. 11 692 – alt. 257 m – ✉ 06190 French Riviera   42 E2

Paris 953 – Menton 3 – Monaco 9 – Monte-Carlo 7 – Nice 26

Office de tourisme, 218, avenue Aristide Briand ☎ 04 93 35 62 87, Fax 04 93 28 57 00

Perched village★★: rue Moncollet★, ✻★★ from the keep★ - Cap Martin ≤★★ X - ≤★★ from the belvédère du Vistaëro (viewpoint) Southwest: 4 km.

Site★ of Gorbio North: 8 km by D 50.

Plans: see Menton.

Vista Palace ≤ rm, rest,
Grande Corniche, 4 km by ③ La Turbie road D 2564 – ☎ 04 92 10 40 00 – www.vistapalace.com – info@vistapalace.com – Fax 04 93 35 18 94
64 rm – †€ 200/360 ††€ 300/440, ☕ € 25 – 4 suites
Rest *Le Vistaero* – *☎ 04 92 10 40 20 (dinner only)* Menu € 58/85 – Carte € 74/92
Rest *La Corniche* – *(lunch only)* Carte € 50/60
◆ This ultra-modern hotel, with its daring architecture and luxurious decorations, overlooks the Riviera. Beauty salon, panoramic swimming pool and terraced botanical garden. At Le Vistaero modern cuisine and a view that will take your breath away. Southern-inspired recipes at La Corniche.

Victoria without rest ≤
7 promenade Cap-Martin – ☎ 04 93 35 65 90 – www.hotelmenton.com/hotel-victoria – Fax 04 93 28 27 02 – Closed 8 January-8 February   AV **k**
32 rm – †€ 81/119 ††€ 81/119, ☕ € 11
◆ A hotel in a residential building. Rooms have mainly rattan and bamboo furniture and balconies on the seafront side. Lounge-bar decorated in colonial style. Charming reception.

Alexandra without rest ≤
93 av. W. Churchill – ☎ 04 93 35 65 45 – www.alexandrahotel.fr – info@alexandrahotel.fr – Fax 04 93 57 96 51   AV **a**
40 rm – †€ 65/102 ††€ 75/202, ☕ € 10
◆ In this typical 1960s/1970s balconied seaside building, ask for a room with a sea view (top floors); rooms being gradually refurbished.

Le Roquebrune without rest ≤
100 av. J. Jaurès, via ③ and Monaco road (D6098) via Basse Corniche – ☎ 04 93 35 00 16 – www.le-roquebrune.com – leroquebrune@wanadoo.fr – Fax 04 93 28 98 36
5 rm ☕ – †€ 90/110 ††€ 115/195
◆ Guests are welcomed as friends in this charming house overlooking waves. The brand new rooms are refined and restful (some have garden-terraces).

Les Deux Frères with rm ≤ rm,
pl. des Deux Frères, in the village, 3.5 km via ③ – ☎ 04 93 28 99 00 – www.lesdeuxfreres.com – info@lesdeuxfreres.com – Fax 04 93 28 99 10 – Closed 1 week in March and 15 November-15 December
10 rm – †€ 75 ††€ 75/110, ☕ € 10 – ½ P € 98
Rest – *(closed Sunday dinner, Tuesday lunch and Monday)*
Menu € 28 bi (lunch)/48 – Carte € 48/83
◆ A former local school, on the little square with its sea view, has been turned into a restaurant. Contemporary dishes. Pretty themed rooms ("Africa", "Wedding", etc.).

XX **L'Hippocampe**
44 av. W. Churchill – ✆ 04 93 35 81 91 – l-hippocampe.restaurant@orange.fr – Fax 04 93 35 81 91 – Closed 3 November-27 December, lunch from June to October and Monday AV **h**
Rest – *(pre-book)* Menu € 32/39 – Carte € 47/80
◆ This family-run waterfront restaurant reserves one of its terraces for bathers at lunchtime. Fillet of sole is the speciality (Bouillabaisse and coq au vin by request).

ROQUEBRUNE-SUR-ARGENS – **83 Var** – **340** O5 – **pop. 11 349** – **alt. 13 m** – ✉ **83520** 41 **C3**

Paris 869 – Marseille 141 – Toulon 85 – Antibes 56 – Cannes 45

Syndicat d'initiative, 12, avenue Gabriel Péri ✆ 04 94 19 89 89, Fax 04 94 19 89 80

XX **Les Templiers**
3 pl. Alfred-Perrin – ✆ 04 94 45 12 52 – templierrestaurant@gmail.com – Fax 04 94 45 12 52 – Closed January, February, Saturday in high season, Tuesday from November to May and Monday
Rest – Menu (€ 18), € 38 (dinner)/68 – Carte € 78/89
◆ Unusual place in the medieval village centre. Dining room with candy-coloured decor. Personalised cuisine. Wines from Switzerland, the owners' homeland.

LA ROQUEBRUSSANNE – **83 Var** – **340** K5 – **pop. 1 973** – **alt. 365 m** – ✉ **83136** 41 **C3**

Paris 810 – Aix-en-Provence 61 – Aubagne 48 – Brignoles 15 – Toulon 35

Office de tourisme, 15, rue Georges Clemenceau ✆ 04 94 86 82 11

Auberge de la Loube
pl. de l'Église – ✆ 04 94 86 81 36 – www.aubergedelaloube.fr – aubergedelaloube@orange.fr – Closed March, November, January and Tuesday from October to May
8 rm – †€ 70/80 ††€ 70/80, ☕ € 6,50 – ½ P € 75/88
Rest – Menu € 27/57 – Carte € 67/81
◆ This brightly coloured inn facing the church has rooms that are being gradually renovated. Simple Provencal restaurant (painted wooden and cast iron furniture). Pleasant shaded terrace. Modern menu.

LA ROQUE-D'ANTHÉRON – **13 Bouches-du-Rhône** – **340** G3 – **pop. 4 722** – **alt. 183 m** – ✉ **13640** **Provence** 42 **E1**

Paris 726 – Aix-en-Provence 29 – Cavaillon 34 – Manosque 60 – Marseille 58

Office de tourisme, 3, cours Foch ✆ 04 42 50 70 74, Fax 04 42 50 70 76

Silvacane abbey ★★ East: 2 km.

Mas de Jossyl
rm, rest,
av. du Parc – ✆ 04 42 50 71 00 – www.masdejossyl.fr – jossyl.mas@wanadoo.fr – Fax 04 42 50 75 94 – Closed 23 August-4 September and 6-21 February
28 rm – †€ 70/128 ††€ 72/136, ☕ € 8
Rest – *(closed Sunday dinner, Monday lunch and Tuesday lunch off season)* Menu € 14 (weekday lunch), € 20/36 – Carte € 30/45
◆ In front of the 17C Château de Florans, this recent hotel in regional style has spacious, functional, soundproofed rooms. Recent modern wing and leisure centre. Bright, refurbished dining room and tree-lined terrace. Traditional menu.

ROQUEFORT – **40 Landes** – **335** J10 – **pop. 1 903** – **alt. 69 m** – ✉ **40120** **Atlantic Coast** 3 **B2**

Paris 667 – Bordeaux 107 – Mont-de-Marsan 23 – Saint-Pierre-du-Mont 31 – Aire-sur-l'Adour 40

Syndicat d'initiative, place du Soleil d'Or ✆ 05 58 45 50 46, Fax 05 58 45 53 63

Le Logis de St-Vincent rest, VISA
76 r. Laubaner – ✆ 05 58 45 75 36 – www.logis-saint-vincent.com – contact@logis-saint-vincent.com – Fax 05 58 45 73 59 – Closed 19-26 April, 27 August-2 September, 25 October-2 November and 1st-20 January
6 rm – €67/112 €67/112, €11 – 1 suite – ½ P €73/95
Rest – *(closed Sunday) (pre-book)* Menu €30/50
◆ This lovingly restored 19C townhouse has regained its sparkle. Original parquet flooring, stone walls, soft colours and period furniture give it a sense of individuality. Charming dining room, courtyard/garden with exotic trees and a regional menu.

ROQUEFORT-LES-PINS – 06 Alpes-Maritimes – 341 D6 – pop. 6 175 – alt. 184 m – ✉ 06330 42 E2

Paris 912 – Cannes 18 – Grasse 14 – Nice 25

Syndicat d'initiative, Centre Culturel R D 2085 ✆ 04 93 09 67 54

Auberge du Colombier VISA AE
in Colombier, Nice road, via D2085 – ✆ 04 92 60 33 00 – www.auberge-du-colombier.com – info@auberge-du-colombier.com – Fax 04 93 77 07 03 – Closed 5 January-12 February
20 rm – €55/115 €65/130, €8 – 2 suites
Rest – *(closed Tuesday from October to March)* Menu €23/39 – Carte €50/70
◆ A house tucked away in a leafy park dominating the valley. The rooms, which are being progressively refurbished, have well-worn wooden furniture. The rustic dining room and pleasant terrace facing the garden are the backdrop to traditional cuisine.

Auberge du Clos des Pins VISA AE
35 rte Notre Dame – ✆ 04 93 77 00 23 – www.aubergeclosdespins.com – aubergeclosdespins@orange.fr – Closed Saturday lunch, Sunday dinner and Wednesday
Rest – Menu €34 – Carte €31/49
◆ Charming auberge facing a roundabout adorned with fountains. Lounge with fireplace, Provençal-style dining room, attractive terrace and contemporary menu created by two chefs, one from Australia and the other from the Vosges.

Red = Pleasant. Look for the red and symbols.

LA ROQUE-GAGEAC – 24 Dordogne – 329 I7 – pop. 449 – alt. 85 m – ✉ 24250 Dordogne-Berry-Limousin 4 D3

Paris 535 – Brive-la-Gaillarde 71 – Cahors 53 – Périgueux 71 – Sarlat-la-Canéda 9

Office de tourisme, le Bourg ✆ 05 53 29 17 01, Fax 05 53 31 24 48

Site★★.

La Belle Étoile with rm rest, VISA AE
in the village – ✆ 05 53 29 51 44 – www.belleetoile.fr – hotel.belle-etoile@wanadoo.fr – Fax 05 53 29 45 63 – Open 1st April-1st November
15 rm – €50/65 €50/75, €9 – ½ P €78
Rest – *(closed Wednesday lunch and Monday)* Menu (€22), €27/43
◆ Traditional and modern dishes to enjoy in the lovely dining rooms or under the arbour of the terrace overlooking the Dordogne. Comfortable guestrooms.

Auberge La Plume d'Oie with rm VISA
Le Bourg – ✆ 05 53 29 57 05 – www.aubergelaplumedoie.com – laplumedoie@wanadoo.fr – Closed 15 November-20 December, 10 January to beg. March, Tuesday lunch off season and Monday except dinner in July-August
4 rm – €80/85 €80/90, €14
Rest – *(number of covers limited, pre-book)* Menu €32/65 – Carte €64/75
◆ Pleasantly restored old residence with a rustic yet stylish restaurant (exposed stone and beams, view of passing barge traffic). Modern cuisine. Small but comfortable guestrooms.

Vitrac road Southeast by D 703 – ✉ 24250 La-Roque-Gageac

Le Périgord rest,
3 km – ✆ 05 53 28 36 55 – www.hotelleperigord.eu – bienvenue@hotelleperigord.eu – Fax 05 53 28 38 73 – Closed 1st January-28 February
39 rm – †€ 59/69 ††€ 59/69, ☕ € 8 – ½ P € 58/63
Rest – *(closed Monday and Tuesday except May-15 October)*
Menu € 20/40 – Carte € 44/52
◆ This regional country home, surrounded by a big garden, stands at the foot of the walled town of Domme. Rustic-inspired, simple rooms, faultless upkeep. Updated cuisine based on Périgord specialities (as you would expect from the name of the restaurant!) Dining room-veranda and summer terrace.

Les Prés Gaillardou
rte D46 – ✆ 05 53 59 67 89 – www.lespresgaillardou.com – restau.presgaillardou@wanadoo.fr – Fax 05 53 59 67 89 – Closed Wednesday
Rest – Menu (€ 17), € 21/29 – Carte € 32/40
◆ Farm converted into a restaurant. Its three small dining rooms have stone walls and beams and there is an enclosed garden with a pleasant terrace. Local cuisine served.

ROQUEMAURE – 30 Gard – 339 N4 – pop. 5 207 – alt. 19 m – ✉ 30150 Provence

23 **D2**

Paris 665 – Alès 76 – Avignon 18 – Nîmes 47 – Orange 12 – Pont-St-Esprit 32
Office de tourisme, 1, cours Bridaine ✆ 04 66 90 21 01, Fax 04 66 90 21 01

Le Clément V
6 r. P. Semard, Nîmes road – ✆ 04 66 82 67 58 – http://hotel-clementv.com – hotel.clementv@wanadoo.fr – Fax 04 66 82 84 66 – Closed 22 December-28 January
21 rm ☕ – †€ 62/72 ††€ 67/78
Rest – *(dinner only) (residents only)* Menu € 19 (dinner)/25
◆ The Château of Roquemaure was Pope Clement V's last residence. The hotel is being renovated bit by bit, with simple and colourful rooms. At the rear, these are more spacious but lack balconies.

LA ROQUE-SUR-PERNES – 84 Vaucluse – 332 D10 – pop. 425 – alt. 250 m – ✉ 84210

42 **E1**

Paris 697 – Avignon 34 – Marseille 99 – Salon-de-Provence 49

Château la Roque
chemin du Château – ✆ 04 90 61 68 77 – www.chateaularoque.com – chateaularoque@wanadoo.fr – Fax 04 90 61 68 78 – Closed 8-31 January
5 rm – †€ 120/170 ††€ 120/240, ☕ € 18 – ½ P € 110/180
Rest – *(closed Sunday) (dinner only) (residents only)* Menu € 40/60
◆ The renovation of this 11C château has preserved its authentic appeal. Spacious guest-rooms. Tiered terraces and heated pool overlooking the valley. The owner is also the chef and meals are served in the Templar Room or garden.

ROQUETTE-SUR-SIAGNE – 06 Alpes-Maritimes – 341 C6 – pop. 4 445 – alt. 12 m – ✉ 06550

42 **E2**

Paris 912 – Marseille 165 – Nice 44 – Antibes 20 – Cannes 12

La Terrasse
484 av. de la République, (Saint Jean district) – ✆ 04 92 19 04 88 – www.restaurantlaterrasse-06.com – resterrasse.roq@orange.fr – Closed 25 December-4 January, Saturday lunch, Sunday and public holidays
Rest – Menu (€ 21 bi), € 25 bi (weekday lunch), € 35/45 – Carte € 48/60
◆ Moderately priced, creative cuisine served in a bright, Mediterranean-inspired dining room (exotic wood, plants, palm trees).

ROSAY – 78 Yvelines – 311 G2 – see Mantes-la-Jolie

ROSBRUCK – 57 Moselle – 307 M4 – see Forbach

ROSCOFF – 29 Finistère – 308 H2 – pop. 3 732 – alt. 7 m – Casino 9 B1
– ✉ 29680 Brittany

Paris 563 – Brest 66 – Landivisiau 27 – Morlaix 27 – Quimper 100

Office de tourisme, 46, rue Gambetta ✆ 02 98 61 12 13, Fax 02 98 69 75 75

N.-D.-de-Croaz-Batz church ★ - Exotic garden★.

Plan on next page

Le Brittany rm, VISA AE

bd Ste Barbe – ✆ 02 98 69 70 78 – www.hotel-brittany.com – hotel.brittany@wanadoo.fr – Fax 02 98 61 13 29 – Open 24 March-11 November Z **a**

24 rm – †€ 140/495 ††€ 140/495, ☕ € 19 – 2 suites

Rest *Le Yachtman* – *(closed Monday) (dinner only) (number of covers limited, pre-book)* Menu € 59, € 72/120 – Carte € 65/85

Spec. Tourteau décortiqué, tapenade d'artichaut et herbes fraîches (May to November). Interprétation du cochon de lait de Bretagne (June to November). Dessert autour de l'artichaut (June to November).

◆ Fine 17C manor house which was entirely dismantled and reconstructed on Roscoff harbour. Very pretty rooms (antique or contemporary furnishings) and attentive service. View over the Île de Batz and fine seafood cuisine in the elegant dining room of the yachtman.

Talabardon rest, VISA AE

27 pl. Lacaze Duthiers, (near the church) – ✆ 02 98 61 24 95 – www.talabardon.fr – hotel.talabardon@wanadoo.fr – Fax 02 98 61 10 54 – Open mid-February to November Y **b**

37 rm – †€ 85/120 ††€ 95/205, ☕ € 14 – ½ P € 81/111

Rest – *(closed Sunday dinner and Thursday)* Menu (€ 22), € 28/50 – Carte € 45/80

◆ This fully renovated family establishment overlooks the sea. The rooms have a tasteful and stylish contemporary look; the most popular enjoy a view of the ocean. Fish and seafood served in the restaurant, with views over the sea.

Thalasstonic rm, VISA AE

r. V. Hugo, (Y) – ✆ 02 98 29 20 20 – www.thalasso.com – thalasstonic.roscoff@thalasso.com – Fax 02 98 29 20 19 – Closed 6-26 December

74 rm – †€ 69/144 ††€ 72/144, ☕ € 12 **Rest** – Menu € 26 – Carte € 23/38

◆ This establishment has direct access to the thalassotherapy centre, a wealth of services and practical rooms (the most spacious have a south-facing balcony). Admire the sun setting over the Île de Batz from the restaurant: guest house and diet menus.

La Résidence without rest VISA

14 r. Johnnies – ✆ 02 98 69 74 85 – hotel.laresidence.roscoff@orange.fr – Fax 02 98 69 78 63 – Open 1st April-15 November Y **f**

31 rm – †€ 38/58 ††€ 45/78, ☕ € 8

◆ Traditional building between the harbour and the church and separated from the road by a flower garden. Well-presented bedrooms with south-facing balconies. Non-smoking.

Armen Le Triton without rest VISA AE

r. du Dr. Bagot – ✆ 02 98 61 24 44 – www.hotel-le-triton.com – resa@hotel-letriton.com – Fax 02 98 69 77 97 Z **u**

44 rm – †€ 49/55 ††€ 56/72, ☕ € 8

◆ This establishment offers a peaceful stay two steps from the spa centre and beaches. Rooms are more spacious on the tennis court side. Breakfast room looking onto the garden.

Aux Tamaris without rest VISA

49 r. É. Corbière – ✆ 02 98 61 22 99 – www.hotel-aux-tamaris.com – contact@hotel-aux-tamaris.com – Fax 02 98 69 74 36 – Open 15 February-15 November

26 rm – †€ 58/85 ††€ 58/85, ☕ € 8,50 Y **d**

◆ This Breton-style house, from 1935, offers sea or countryside-themed rooms, some with sea view. Panoramic breakfast room.

Du Centre VISA AE

le Port – ✆ 02 98 61 24 25 – www.chezjanie.com – contact@chezjanie.com – Fax 02 98 61 15 43 – Closed mid November-mid February Y **a**

16 rm – †€ 59/124 ††€ 59/124, ☕ € 10

Rest – *(closed Sunday dinner and Tuesday except July-August)*
Menu (€ 14 bi) – Carte € 26/35

◆ This hotel near the post office is down by the port. Tastefully appointed rooms: uncluttered decor, sober furniture and grey walls adorned with poem extracts. Seafood, grilled meats and salads make up the menu of this bar-restaurant facing the Channel.

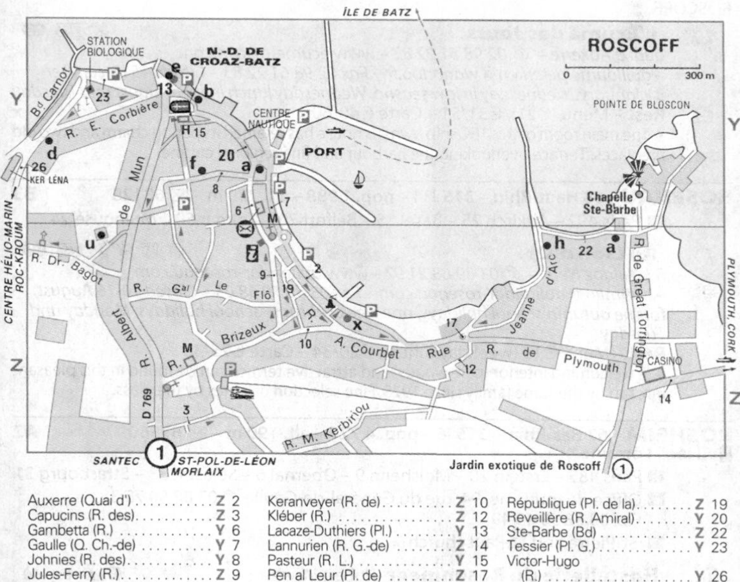

Auxerre (Quai d') . . . . . Z 2	Keranveyer (R. de) . . . . . Z 10	République (Pl. de la) . . . . . Z 19
Capucins (R. des) . . . . . Z 3	Kléber (R.) . . . . . Z 12	Reveillère (R. Amiral) . . . . . Y 20
Gambetta (R.) . . . . . Y 6	Lacaze-Duthiers (Pl.) . . . . . Y 13	Ste-Barbe (Bd) . . . . . Z 22
Gaulle (Q. Ch.-de) . . . . . Y 7	Lannurien (R. G.-de) . . . . . Z 14	Tessier (Pl. G.) . . . . . Y 23
Johnies (R. des) . . . . . Y 8	Pasteur (R. L.) . . . . . Y 15	Victor-Hugo (R.) . . . . . Y 26
Jules-Ferry (R.) . . . . . Z 9	Pen al Leur (Pl. de) . . . . . Z 17	

Ibis without rest
17 pl. Lacaze Duthiers, (church square) – ☎ 02 98 61 22 61 – ibishotel.com – h1109@accor.com – Fax 02 98 61 11 94 Y e
40 rm – €58/89 €58/89, ☕ €8
◆ In the centre of Roscoff. Small rooms which conform to the chain's standards, some with views of the Channel. Not a great deal of charm, but well-kept and reasonably priced.

Bellevue without rest
bd Sainte Barbe – ☎ 02 98 61 23 38 – www.hotel-bellevue-roscoff.fr – hotelbellevue.roscoff@wanadoo.fr – Fax 02 98 61 11 80 – Open from mid-March to mid-November and from 25 December to 3 January Z h
18 rm – €60/80 €60/80, ☕ €8
◆ Vista of the sea from the breakfast room and from most of the slightly cramped and simple yet well-kept rooms. The others look out over a flower patio. Adjoining pub-bar.

Le Temps de Vivre (Jean-Yves Crenn) rm,
pl. de l'Église – ☎ 02 98 61 27 28 – www.letempsdevivre.net – contact@letempsdevivre.net – Fax 02 98 61 19 46 – Closed two weeks in March, two weeks in October, 4-13 January, Tuesday except dinner from April to December, Sunday dinner and Monday Y e
Rest – Menu €39 (weekdays)/105 – Carte €69/115
Spec. Huîtres tièdes, foie gras, pomme et jus de laitue. Bar, Saint-Pierre et turbot. Sablé breton et bonbon de pomme.
◆ The Channel backdrop makes an elegant setting for enjoying the inventive cuisine based on local fish accompanied by a fine wine list. A recipe for success!

Le Temps de Vivre
pl. de l'Église – ☎ 02 98 19 33 19 – contact@letempsdevivre.net – Fax 02 98 19 33 00 – Closed 1st-15 October
15 rm – €95/268 €95/268, ☕ €14
◆ Spacious rooms in a very refined style (with stone, wenge and oak), in privateer houses around a flower-clad patio. Some overlook the sea.

XX **L'Écume des Jours**
quai d'Auxerre – ✆ 02 98 61 22 83 – www.ecume-roscoff.com – guillaume.peterken@wanadoo.fr – Fax 02 98 61 22 83 – Closed 15 December-31 January, Wednesday in low season, Wednesday lunch in July-August and Tuesday
Rest – Menu (€ 21), € 31/51 – Carte € 40/60 Z **x**
◆ The main room of this 16C ship owner's house has retained its period charm and two old fireplaces. Terrace overlooking the harbour and fine regional cuisine.

ROSENAU – **68 Haut-Rhin** – **315** J11 – **pop. 1 988** – **alt. 230 m** – ✉ **68128** 1 **B3**

Paris 492 – Altkirch 25 – Basel 15 – Belfort 70 – Colmar 59 – Mulhouse 24

XX **Au Lion d'Or**
5 r. Village Neuf – ✆ 03 89 68 21 97 – www.auliondor-rosenau.com – baumlin@auliondor-rosenau.com – Fax 03 89 70 68 05 – Closed 10-16 August, for the autumn school holidays, one week February school holidays, Monday and Tuesday
Rest – Menu € 13 (weekday lunch), € 20/34 – Carte € 25/38
◆ A welcoming interior (pale woods) and attractive terrace can be found in this pleasant inn, run by the same family since 1928. Fine selection of wines by the glass.

ROSHEIM – **67 Bas-Rhin** – **315** I6 – **pop. 4 721** – **alt. 190 m** – ✉ **67560** 1 **A2**
Alsace-Lorraine

Paris 485 – Erstein 20 – Molsheim 9 – Obernai 6 – Sélestat 33 – Strasbourg 31

Office de tourisme, 94, rue du Général-de-Gaulle ✆ 03 88 50 75 38, Fax 03 88 50 45 49

St-Pierre and St-Paul church ★.

Hostellerie du Rosenmeer (Hubert Maetz) rest,
45 av. de la Gare, 2 km northeast on D 35 – ✆ 03 88 50 43 29 – www.le-rosenmeer.com – info@le-rosenmeer.com – Fax 03 88 49 20 57 – Closed 20 July-4 August and 16 February-10 March
20 rm – † € 40/50 †† € 61/98, ☕ € 10 – ½ P € 76/89
Rest – *(closed Sunday dinner, Monday and Wednesday)* Menu € 35 bi (weekday lunch), € 49 € bi/76 – Carte € 47/80
Rest *Winstub d'Rosemer* – *(closed Sunday and Monday)* Menu (€ 8,50), € 30 bi/38 bi – Carte € 22/48
Spec. Escalope de foie de canard poêlée, jus de racines de primevères et son cappuccino. Dos de sandre cuit sur écorce de sapin à la purée d'orties. Forêt noire servie dans un verre, griottes d'Alsace. **Wines** Riesling, Muscat.
◆ Alsatian-style hotel on the banks of a stream, after which the hotel is named. Practical rooms, some classic and others rustic or modernised. Airy restaurant (pale wood, plum and slate colour scheme) serving inventive, regionally inspired cuisine. The small winstub has been spruced up.

XX **Auberge du Cerf**
120 r. Gén. de Gaulle – ✆ 03 88 50 40 14 – www.aubergeducerf-rosheim.com – Fax 03 88 50 40 14 – Closed 25 January-7 February, Sunday dinner and Monday
Rest – Menu (€ 12), € 16/40 – Carte € 26/50
◆ In the centre of a wine-growing village, this inn decked out with flowers has two small dining areas serving classic and regional cuisine.

X **La Petite Auberge** with rm rest,
41 r. Gén. de Gaulle – ✆ 03 88 50 40 60 – www.petiteauberge.fr – christophevasconi@wanadoo.fr – Fax 03 88 48 00 90 – Closed 22-28 June, Wednesday and Thursday
7 rm – † € 47 †† € 47, ☕ € 7 **Rest** – Menu € 22/38 – Carte € 29/59
◆ This small Alsatian-style building on the main thoroughfare is home to a rustic-style restaurant. The hotel Lys offers rooms equipped with kitchenettes, 50m away.

LA ROSIÈRE – **14 Calvados** – **303** I4 – **see Arromanches-les-Bains**

LA ROSIÈRE 1850 – **73 Savoie** – **333** O4 – **alt. 1 850 m** – **Winter sports : 1 100/2 600 m** 20 – ✉ **73700 Montvalezan** **French Alps** 45 **D2**

Paris 657 – Albertville 76 – Bourg-St-Maurice 22 – Chambéry 125

Relais du Petit St-Bernard

– ✆ 04 79 06 80 48 – www.petit-saint-bernard.com – info@petit-saint-bernard.com – Fax 04 79 06 83 40 – Open 27 June-6 September and 12 December-25 April

20 rm – €37/53 €46/76, €7,50 – ½ P €51/72

Rest – Menu €17/20 – Carte €16/40

◆ Located at the foot of ski runs, this big chalet is an inn-restaurant and souvenir shop rolled into one. Simple, rustic rooms, some with panoramic balconies. Enjoy brasserie-type food with snowy peaks in the background.

LES ROSIERS-SUR-LOIRE – 49 Maine-et-Loire – 317 H4 – pop. 2 245 – alt. 22 m – ✉ 49350 Châteaux of the Loire — 35 C2

Paris 304 – Angers 32 – Baugé 27 – Bressuire 66 – Cholet 80 – La Flèche 45 – Saumur 18

Syndicat d'initiative, place du Mail ✆ 02 41 51 90 22, Fax 02 41 51 90 22

La Toque Blanche

2 rue Quarte, (Angers road) – ✆ 02 41 51 80 75 – Fax 02 41 38 06 38 – Closed 12 November-3 December, 1st-22 January, Tuesday and Wednesday

Rest – Menu €27 bi (weekday lunch), €37/53

◆ A classically decorated dining room with large windows overlooking the river. Traditional cuisine, regional specialities and a choice of Loire Valley wines.

Au Val de Loire

pl. de l'Église – ✆ 02 41 51 80 30 – www.au-val-de-loire.com – info@vau-val-de-loire.com – Fax 02 41 51 95 00 – Closed 15 February-15 March, Thursday dinner, Sunday dinner and Monday

Rest – Menu €25/42 – Carte €30/54

◆ Herbs and flowers provide a fresh touch to the traditional cuisine served in this family-run hotel and restaurant. Redecorated dining rooms and simple rooms available.

ROSNY-SOUS-BOIS – 93 Seine-Saint-Denis – 305 F7 – 101 17 – see Paris, Area

---

ROSPEZ – 22 Côtes-d'Armor – 309 B2 – see Lannion

ROSTRENEN – 22 Côtes-d'Armor – 309 C5 – pop. 3 397 – alt. 216 m – ✉ 22110 — 9 B2

Paris 485 – Quimper 71 – St-Brieuc 58 – Carhaix-Plouguer 22 – Pontivy 38

Office de tourisme, 6, rue Gilbert ✆ 02 96 29 02 72, Fax 02 96 29 02 72

L'Eventail des Saveurs

3 pl. Bourg Coz – ✆ 02 96 29 10 71 – leventail-des-saveurs@wanadoo.fr – Fax 02 96 29 34 75 – Closed Tuesday dinner from September to May, Sunday dinner, Wednesday dinner and Monday

Rest – Menu (€15), €28/48 – Carte €38/53

◆ A fine selection of regional fare with a modern twist, concocted by an enthusiastic self-taught chef. Choose between an elegant minimalist (beige and chocolate) or brasserie decor.

ROUBAIX – 59 Nord – 302 H3 – pop. 97 600 – alt. 27 m – ✉ 59100 — 31 C2
Northern France and the Paris Region

Paris 232 – Kortrijk 23 – Lille 15 – Tournai 20

Office de tourisme, 12, place de la Liberté ✆ 03 20 65 31 90, Fax 03 20 65 31 83

du Sart Villeneuve-d'Ascq 5 rue Jean Jaurès, S : 5 km, ✆ 03 20 72 02 51

de Brigode Villeneuve-d'Ascq 36 avenue du Golf, S : 6 km, ✆ 03 20 91 17 86

de Bondues Bondues Château de la Vigne, 8 km on D 9, ✆ 03 20 23 20 62

Centre des archives du monde du travail (Labour-related Archive Centre) BX **M**[1] - La Piscine (Swimming pool)★★, Musée d'Art et d'Industrie (Museum of Art and Industry)★ - Chapelle d'Hem (Chapel of Hem)★ (walls-stained glass windows★★ by Manessier) 5 km, see map of Lille JS **B**.

Access and exits: See plan of Lille

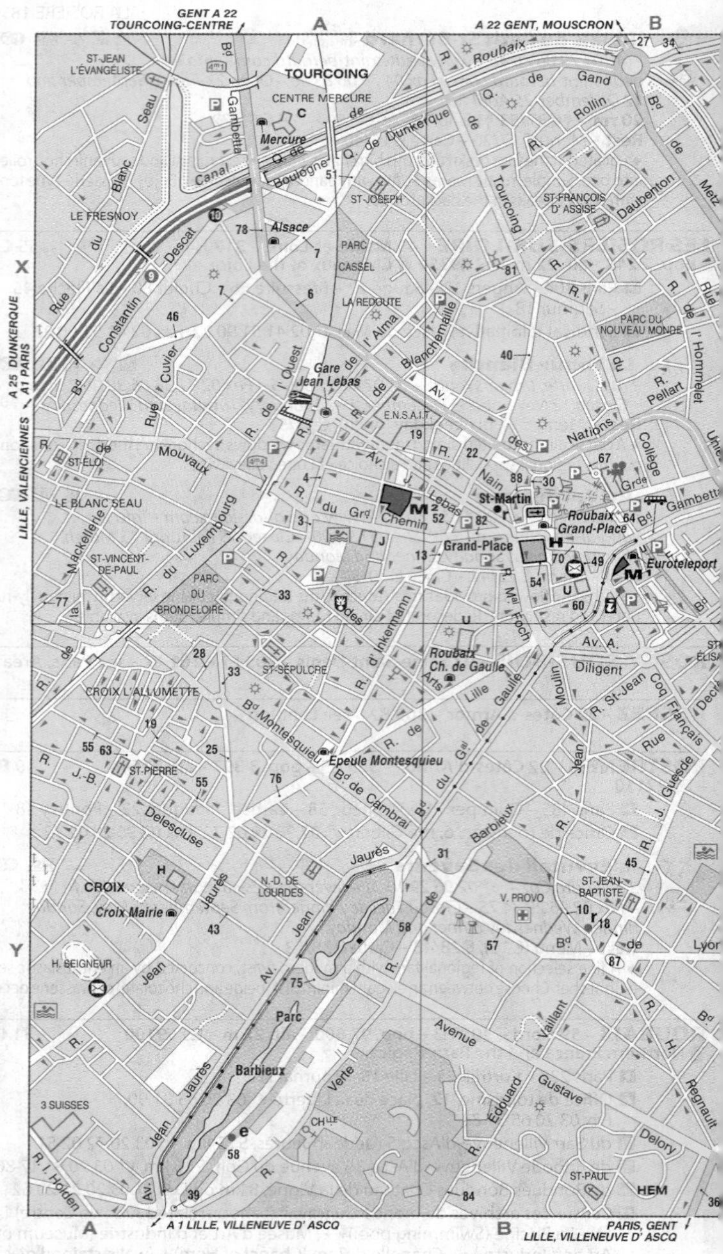

GENT A 22
TOURCOING-CENTRE
A
A 22 GENT, MOUSCRON
B
TOURCOING
CENTRE MERCURE
Mercure
Alsace
ST-JEAN L'ÉVANGÉLISTE
LE FRESNOY
ST-JOSEPH
PARC CASSEL
LA REDOUTE
ST-FRANÇOIS D' ASSISE
PARC DU NOUVEAU MONDE
Gare Jean Lebas
E.N.S.A.I.T.
St-Martin
Roubaix Grand-Place
Grand-Place
Euroteleport
ST-ÉLOI
LE BLANC SEAU
ST-VINCENT-DE-PAUL
PARC DU BRONDELOIRE
ST-SÉPULCRE
Roubaix Ch. de Gaulle
CROIX L'ALLUMETTE
ST-PIERRE
Epeule Montesquieu
CROIX
Croix Mairie
N.-D. DE LOURDES
V. PROVO
ST-JEAN-BAPTISTE
H. BEIGNEUR
Parc Barbieux
3 SUISSES
ST-PAUL
HEM
A 25 DUNKERQUE
A1 PARIS
LILLE, VALENCIENNES
X
Y
A
A 1 LILLE, VILLENEUVE D' ASCQ
B
PARIS, GENT
LILLE, VILLENEUVE D' ASCQ

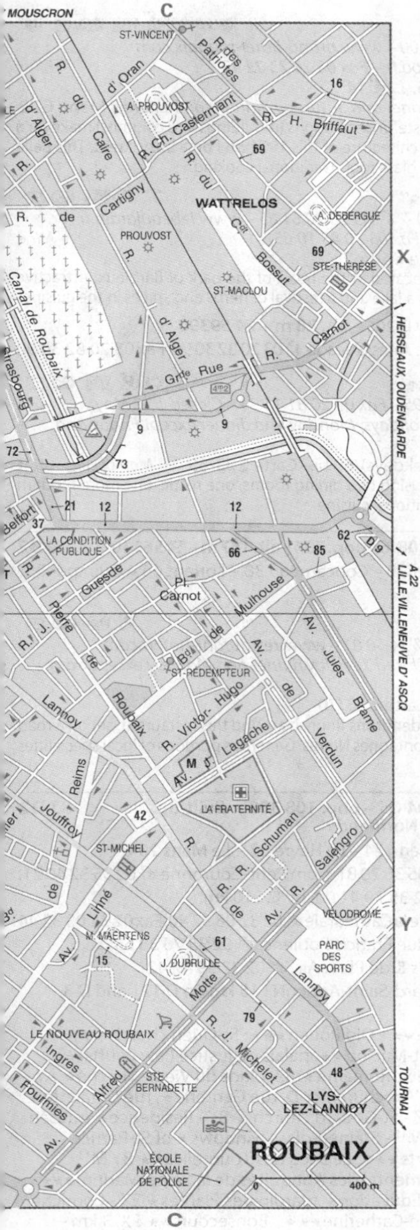

CROIX

Cheuvreuil (R.)	AY	19
Gaulle (Av. du Gén.-de)	AY	43
Kléber (R.)	AY	55
Liberté (Pl. de la)	AY	63
Raspail (R.)	AX	77

HEM

Europe (Av. de l')	BY	36
Schuman (R. Robert)	BY	84

LYS-LEZ-LANNOY

Guesde (R. Jules)	CY	48

ROUBAIX

Abreuvoir (Pl. de l')	AX	3
Alouette (R. de l')	AX	4
Alsace (Av. d')	AX	6
Armentières (Bd d')	AX	7
Avelghem (R. d')	CX	9
Beaumont (R. de)	BY	10
Beaurepaire (Bd du)	CX	12
Bois (R. du)	BX	13
Braille (R. Louis)	CY	15
Cateau (Bd du)	BY	18
Champier (R. Louise et Victor)	AX	19
Colmar (Bd de)	CX	21
Communauté-Urbaine (R.)	BX	22
Constantine (R. de)	BX	24
Courbet (R. Amiral)	AY	25
Couteaux (Bd des)	BX	27
Cugnot (R.)	AY	28
Curé (R. du)	BX	30
Douai (Bd de)	ABY	31
Épeule (R. de l')	AXY	33
Faidherbe (Pl. du Gén.)	CX	37
Fer-à-Cheval (Carr. du)	AY	39
Fosse-aux-Chênes (R.)	BX	40
Fraternité (Pl. de la)	CY	42
Goujon (R. Jean)	BY	45
Gounod (R. Ch.)	AX	46
Grande-Rue	BCX	
Grand-Place	BX	
Halle (R. de la)	BX	49
Halluin (Bd d')	AX	51
Hospice (R. de l')	BX	52
Hôtel-de-Ville (R. de l')	BX	54
Lacordaire (Bd)	BY	57
Laine (Bd de la)	BX	34
Lannoy (R. de)	BCY	
Lebas (Av. J.)	ABX	
Leclerc (Bd Gén.)	BX	60
Leconte-Baillon (R.)	CY	61
Leers (R. de)	CX	62
Liberté (Pl. de la)	BX	64
Molière (R.)	CX	66
Monnet (R. J.)	BX	67
Motte (R. Pierre)	BX	70
Nadaud (R.)	CX	72
Le Nôtre (Av.)	AY	58
Nyckès (Pont)	CX	73
Peuple-Belge (Av. du)	AY	75
Prof.-Langevin (R. du)	AY	76
République (Bd de la)	AX	78
Rousseau (R. J.-J.)	CY	79
St-Maurice (R.)	BX	81
Sarrail (R. du Gén.)	BX	82
Sévigné (R. de)	CX	85
Travail (Pl. du)	BY	87
Vieil-Abreuvoir (R. du)	BX	88

WATTRELOS

Briffaut (R. Henri)	CX	16
Monge (R.)	CX	69

Le Grand Hôtel
22 av. J. Lebas – ✆ 03 20 73 40 00 – www.grand-hotel-roubaix.com – grand.hotel.roubaix@wanadoo.fr – Fax 03 20 73 22 42 BX **r**
93 rm – €75/105 €75/115, €14
Rest – *(closed August, Friday dinner and Saturday dinner) (dinner only)* Menu €22
◆ An huge reception lobby and tasteful decorations (mouldings and columns) make for a smart interior to match the fine architecture of this 19C hotel on a busy street. This Belle Epoque dining room is lit by a big glass roof. Traditional cooking.

Le Beau Jardin "saveurs"
av. Le Nôtre, (The Parc Barbieux) – ✆ 03 20 20 61 85 – www.lebeaujardin.fr – restaurant@lebeaujardin.fr – Fax 03 20 45 10 65 AY **e**
Rest – Menu (€21), €29 – Carte €50/67
◆ This restaurant is matchlessly located at the heart of the park of Barbieux. Attractive contemporary dining room facing a lake and a festival of herbs and spices in the cuisine.

in Lys-lez-Lannoy 5 km southeast by D 206 – alt. 28 m – ✉ 59390
Syndicat d'initiative, 130, rue Jules Guesde ✆ 03 20 82 30 90, Fax 03 20 82 30 90

Auberge de la Marmotte
5 r. J.-B. Lebas – ✆ 03 20 75 30 95 – Fax 03 20 81 16 34 – Closed 1st-8 May, 1st-22 August, February school holidays, Monday and dinner except Friday and Saturday
Rest – Menu (€15 bi), €19 (weekdays)/69 bi – Carte €33/65 *Map of Lille* JS **f**
◆ Brick regional-style building housing two dining rooms, one rustic, one more modern and a small, intimate lounge. Traditional cuisine.

ROUDOUALLEC – **56 Morbihan** – **308** I6 – **pop. 704** – **alt. 167 m** – ✉ **56110** 9 **B2**
Paris 520 – Carhaix-Plouguer 29 – Concarneau 38 – Lorient 64 – Quimper 35 – Vannes 113

Bienvenue
84 r. Nicolas Le Grand – ✆ 02 97 34 50 01 – www.restaurant-hotels.com – le.bienvenue@wanadoo.fr – Closed Tuesday dinner and Monday except from June to August
Rest – Menu (€13), €20/72 – Carte €35/70
◆ Banks of hydrangeas and rhododendrons flourish around this restaurant, set on a road running through a village in the Montagnes Noires. Generous portions of local specialities on the menu.

ROUEN P – **76 Seine-Maritime** – **304** G5 – **pop. 108 300** – **Built-up area 389 862** – **alt. 12 m** – ✉ **76000** Normandy 33 **D2**
Paris 134 – Amiens 122 – Caen 124 – Le Havre 87 – Le Mans 204
Ferry: from Dieppedalle ✆ 02 35 36 20 81; from Petit-Couronne ✆ 02 35 32 40 21.
Rouen-Vallée de Seine: ✆ 02 35 79 41 00, by ③: 10 km.
Office de tourisme, 25, place de la Cathédrale ✆ 02 32 08 32 40, Fax 02 32 08 32 44
de Rouen Mont-St-Aignan Rue Francis Poulenc, ✆ 02 35 76 38 65
De Léry Poses Base de Loisirs & de Plein Air, ✆ 02 32 59 47 42
de la Forêt-Verte Bosc-Guérard-Saint-AdrienN : 15 km on D 121 and D 3, ✆ 02 35 33 62 94
★★ Notre-Dame cathedral ★★★ - Old Rouen★★★: St-Ouen church ★★, St-Maclou church ★★ Aître St-Maclou★★, palais de justice (law courts)★★, rue du Gros-Horloge★★, rue St-Romain★★ BZ, place du Vieux-Marché★ AY, - Window★★ of Ste-Jeanne-d'Arc church AY **D**, rue Ganterie★, rue Damiette★ CZ - 35, rue Martainville★ CZ - St-Godard church ★ BY - Residence★ (musée national de l'Éducation) CZ **M**[15] - Stained-glass windows★ of St-Patrice church - Museums: Beaux-Arts★★★, Le Secq des Tournelles★★ BY **M**[13], Ceramics★★ BY **M**[3], départemental des Antiquités de la Seine-Maritime★★ CY **M**[1] - Musée national de l'Éducation★ - Jardin des Plantes★ EX - Corniche (cliff road)★★★ de la Côte Ste-Catherine★★★ - Bonsecours★★ FX, 3 km - Centre Universitaire (university) ☼★★ EV.
St-Martin de Boscherville: former abbey church of St-Georges★★, 11 km by ⑦.

Plans on following pages

Mercure Champ de Mars rm, VISA
12 av. A. Briand – ✆ 02 35 52 42 32 – www.rouen-hotel.fr – h1273@accor.com – Fax 02 35 08 15 06 CZ **j**
139 rm – †€ 95/160 ††€ 110/175, ☕ € 17
Rest – *(closed 13 July-23 August, Sunday lunch and Saturday)*
Menu (€ 20 bi), € 25 – Carte € 36/45
◆ This modern hotel lies on a busy boulevard along the Seine. Its comfortable rooms are very popular with business clients. Modern restaurant, facing the Champ de Mars esplanade. Traditional cooking. Live jazz on some Friday evenings.

Mercure Centre without rest VISA
7 r. de la Croix de Fer – ✆ 02 35 52 69 52 – www.mercure.com – h1301@accor.com – Fax 02 35 89 41 46 BZ **f**
125 rm – †€ 109/220 ††€ 119/240, ☕ € 16 – 1 suite
◆ This half-timbered edifice in the pedestrian district of historic Rouen is devoted to literature. Some of the rooms enjoy a view of the famous cathedral.

Du Vieux Marché without rest VISA
15 r. Pie – ✆ 02 35 71 00 88 – www.bestwestern-hotel-vieuxmarche.com – hotelduvieuxmarche@wanadoo.fr – Fax 02 35 70 75 94 AY **h**
48 rm – †€ 111/118 ††€ 127/132, ☕ € 13
◆ Two minutes from the square, this cluster of houses just off the road provides welcoming rooms decorated in an English style. Cosy sitting room and sundeck terrace.

De Dieppe rest, VISA
pl. B. Tissot, (opposite the station) – ✆ 02 35 71 96 00 – www.hotel-dieppe.fr – hotel.dieppe@hoteldedieppe.fr – Fax 02 35 89 65 21 BY **z**
41 rm – †€ 89 ††€ 99, ☕ € 11
Rest ***Le Quatre Saisons*** – *(closed 21 July-10 August and Saturday lunch)*
Menu (€ 15), € 23/58 – Carte € 46/67
◆ The same family has run this hotel opposite the station since 1880. Diversely furnished rooms, all of which are fully equipped. Famed for its Rouen duck recipe, the restaurant pays homage to local traditions.

Suitehotel without rest VISA
10 quai de Boisguibert – ✆ 02 32 10 58 68 – www.suite-hotel.com – H6342@accor.com – Fax 02 32 10 58 69 EV **t**
80 rm – †€ 99/134 ††€ 99/134, ☕ € 13
◆ This recent hotel is home to contemporary style rooms that are spacious and light. Equally well suited to business travellers and families (kitchenettes).

Dandy without rest VISA
93 bis r. Cauchoise – ✆ 02 35 07 32 00 – www.hotels-rouen.net – contact@hotels-rouen.net – Fax 02 35 15 48 82 AY **p**
18 rm – †€ 80/105 ††€ 105/125, ☕ € 11
◆ This hotel is located in a pedestrian street leading to the Place du Vieux Marché. It has classical rooms with Louis XV and Louis XVI style furniture. Pleasant breakfast room.

De l'Europe VISA
87 r. aux Ours – ✆ 02 32 76 17 76 – www.h-europe.fr – europe-hotel@wanadoo.fr – Fax 02 32 76 17 77 – Closed 19 December-4 January AZ **e**
22 rm – †€ 60/75 ††€ 80/95, ☕ € 10 – ½ P € 60/80
Rest – *(closed 18 July-23 August, Saturday and Sunday)*
Menu (€ 13), € 23 (weekdays)/33
◆ Modern building splendidly located in the historic quarter. Functional rooms; those on the top floor command a fine view of the town. Tastefully laid tables and traditional cuisine.

Le Cardinal without rest VISA
1 pl. Cathédrale – ✆ 02 35 70 24 42 – www.cardinal-hotel.fr – hotelcardinal.rouen@wanadoo.fr – Fax 02 35 89 75 14 – Closed 25 December-15 January and public holidays BZ **r**
18 rm – †€ 54/68 ††€ 64/89, ☕ € 8
◆ Located next to Notre Dame Cathedral, a Gothic masterpiece. All the small pastel coloured rooms of this family-run hotel are well kept. Breakfast on the terrace in summer.

ROUEN

Street	Grid	No.
Alliés (Av. des)	DX	4
Ango (R. Jean)	EV	7
Béthencourt (Quai de)	EV	14
Bicheray (Av. du Cdt)	DV	15
Boisguilbert (Quai de)	EV	18
Bois-des-Dames (Av. du)	EV	17
Bonsecours (Rte de)	EV	21
Briand (R. Aristide)	DX	33
Brossolette (Bd)	DX	34
Bruyères (Rond-Point des)	EX	36
Caen (Av. de)	EV	37
Canteleu (Rte de)	DV	39
Carnot (Av.)	DV	40
Chasselièvre (R.)	EV	52
Clères (Chemin de)	EV	54
Coquelicots (R. des)	EX	55
Corneille (R. Pierre)	EX	58
Corniche (Rte de la)	FV	60
Darnétal (Rte de)	FV	64
Duclair (R. de)	DV	69
Elbeuf (R. d')	EX	75
Europe (Av. de l')	EV	78
Europe (Bd de l')	EVX	79
La-Fayette (R.)	EV	103
Felling (Av. de)	EX	82
Flaubert (Pt)	EX	83
Fond-du-Val (Allée du)	EV	85
France (Quai de)	DV	87
Gaulle (Bd Charles-de)	DX	88
Grand'Mare (Av. de la)	FV	92
Grand-Cours (Av. du)	EX	91
Jean-Jaurès (Av.)	DX	97
Jean-Jaurès (Bd)	DV	99
Leclerc-de-Hauteclocque (Av. du Gén.)	DX	106
Leclerc (Av. Général)	DV	105
Lesseps (Bd Ferdinand-de)	EV	107
Maréchal-Juin (Av. du)	FV	109
Martyrs-de-la-Résistance (R. des)	DV	110
Mont-Riboudet (Av. du)	EV	112
Nansen (R.)	DV	114
Paris (Rte de)	FX	158
Pène (R. Annie-de)	FV	118
Quatre-Mares (Grande R. de)	EV	122
Renard (R. du)	EV	125
République (R. de la)	FV	126
République (R. de la BONSECOURS)	EX	160
Rondeaux (Av. Jean)	EV	131
Roosevelt (Bd Franklin)	DX	132
Ste-Lucie (Rond-Point)	DX	135
Siegfried (Bd André)	EV	142
Sotteville (R. de)	EX	145
Verdun (Bd de)	EV	150
Verdun (Bd de GRAND-QUEVILLY)	DX	165
11-Novembre (Bd du)	EX	157

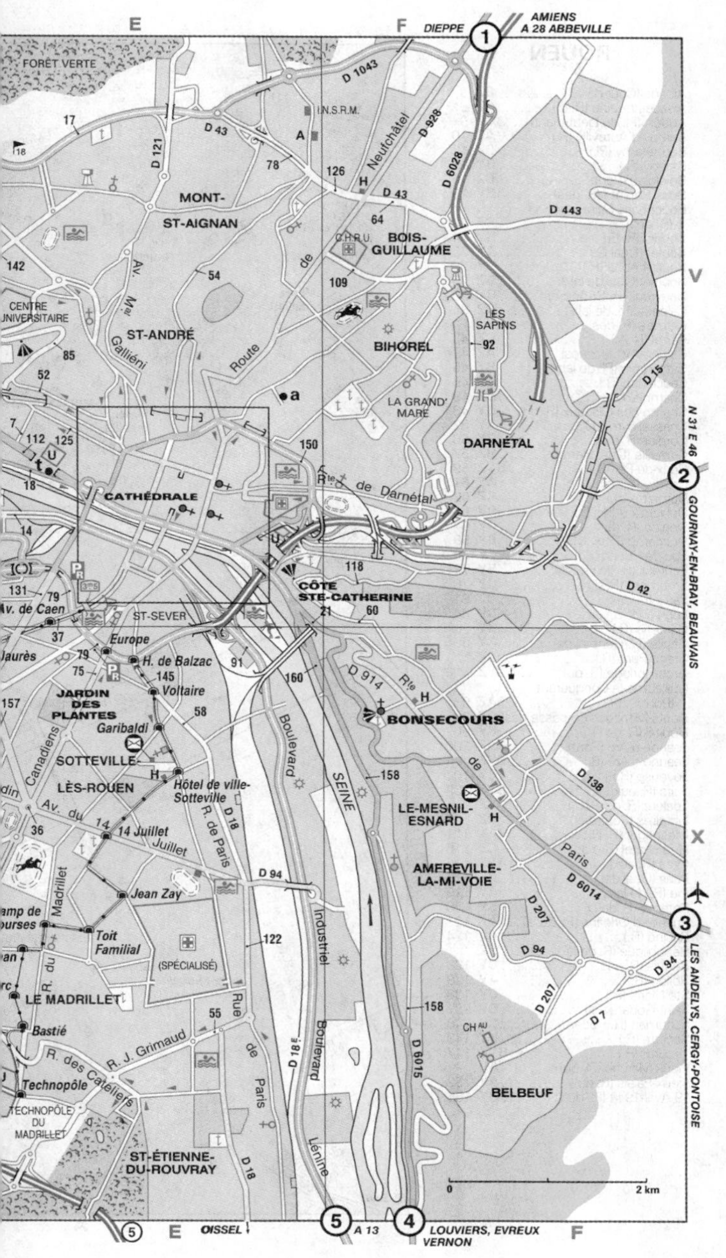

DIEPPE
AMIENS
A 28 ABBEVILLE
FORÊT VERTE
MONT-
ST-AIGNAN
BOIS-
GUILLAUME
CENTRE
UNIVERSITAIRE
ST-ANDRÉ
BIHOREL
LES SAPINS
LA GRAND' MARE
DARNÉTAL
CATHÉDRALE
CÔTE
STE-CATHERINE
ST-SEVER
JARDIN
DES
PLANTES
SOTTEVILLE-
LÈS-ROUEN
BONSECOURS
LE-MESNIL-
ESNARD
AMFREVILLE-
LA-MI-VOIE
LE MADRILLET
TECHNOPÔLE
DU
MADRILLET
ST-ÉTIENNE-
DU-ROUVRAY
BELBEUF
SEINE
GOURNAY-EN-BRAY, BEAUVAIS
LES ANDELYS, CERGY-PONTOISE
N 31 E 46
OISSEL
A 13
LOUVIERS, EVREUX
VERNON
2 km

ROUEN

Rue	Carré	N°
Albane (Cour d')	BZ	3
Alsace-Lorraine (R. d')	CZ	6
Aubert (Pl. du Lieutenant)	CZ	9
Barbey-d'Aurevilly (R.)	AZ	10
Barthélemy (Pl.)	BZ	12
Belfroy (R.)	BY	13
Boieldieu (Pont)	BZ	16
Bons-Enfants (R. des)	ABY	19
Boucheries-Saint-Ouen (R. des)	CZ	22
Boudin (R. E.)	BY	24
Boulet (Quai G.)	AY	25
Bourg-l'Abbé (R.)	CY	27
Bourse (Quai de la)	BZ	28
Bouvreuil (R. St-André)	BY	30
Calende (Pl. de la)	BZ	35
Carmes (R. des)	BYZ	
Carrel (R. A.)	CZ	42
Cartier (Av. Jacques)	AZ	43
Cathédrale (Pl. de la)	BZ	45
Cauchoise (R.)	AY	46
Champlain (Av.)	BZ	49
Champ-des-Oiseaux (R. du)	BY	48
Chasselièvre (R.)	AY	52
Cordier (R. du)	BY	56
Corneille (Quai Pierre)	BZ	57
Croix-de-Fer (R.)	BYZ	59
Crosne (R. de)	AY	61
Damiette (R.)	CZ	63
Delacroix (Allée Eugène)	BY	66
Donjon (R. du)	BY	67
Duchamp (Espl. M.)	BY	68
Eau-de-Robec (R.)	CZ	70
Écureuil (R. de l')	BY	72
Ernemont (R. d')	CY	76
Faulx (R. des)	CZ	81
Foch (Pl.)	BY	84
Ganterie (R.)	BY	
Gaulle (Pl. Général-de)	CY	89
Grand-Pont (R.)	BZ	
Gros-Horloge (R. du)	ABYZ	
Guillaume-le-Conquérant (Pont)	AZ	93
Hauts-Mariages (Impasse des)	CZ	94
Hôpital (R. de l')	BY	96
Jeanne-d'Arc (Pont)	AZ	100
Jeanne-d'Arc (R.)	BYZ	
Joyeuse (R.)	CY	101
Juifs (R. aux)	BYZ	102
Leclerc (R. du Gén.)	BZ	
Libraires (Cour des)	BZ	108
Mesnager (R. Nicolas)	AY	111
Neufchatel (Rte de)	CY	115
Ours (R. aux)	ABZ	116
Paris (Quai de)	BZ	117
Pie (R. de la)	AY	119
Poterne (R. de la)	BY	120
Pucelle-d'Orléans (Pl. de la)	AZ	121
Racine (R.)	AY	124
République (R. de la)	BZ	
Requis (R. des)	CY	128
Rollon (R.)	AY	129
Ste-Marie (R.)	CY	138
Saint-Godard (Pl.)	BY	137
Schuman (R. Robert)	CS	140
Socrate (R.)	BY	143
Thouret (R.)	BYZ	147
Vieux-Marché (Pl. du)	AY	
Vieux-Palais (R. du)	AY	152
19-Avril-1944 (Pl. du)	BY	155

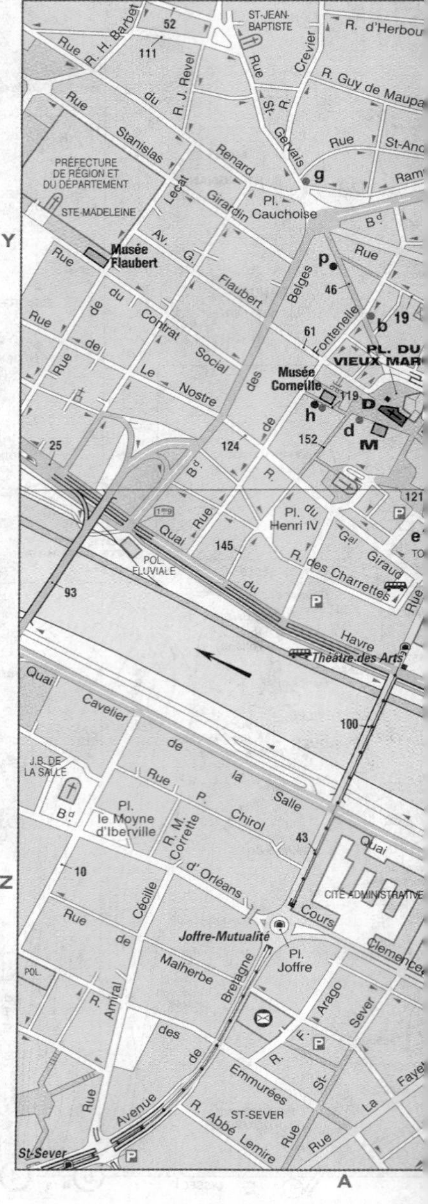

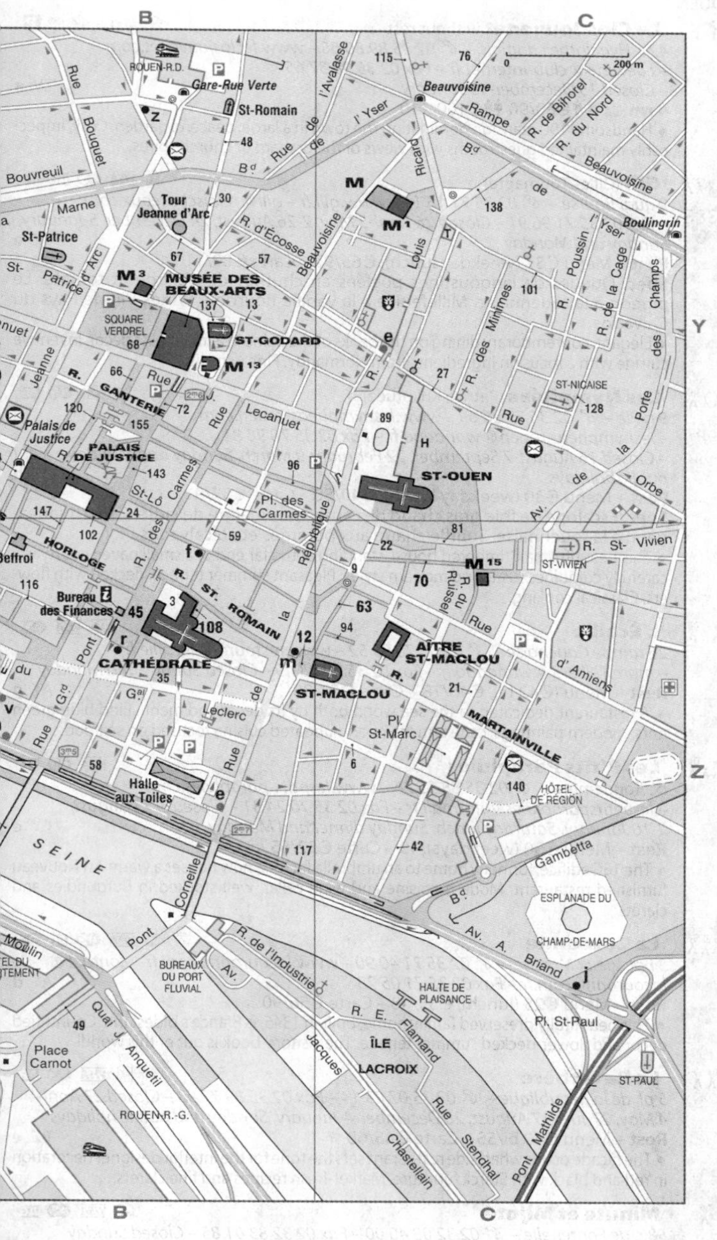

B
C
Y
Z
ROUEN-R.D.
Gare-Rue Verte
St-Romain
Rue Bouquet
Bouvreuil
Marne
Tour Jeanne d'Arc
St-Patrice
St-Patrice
d'Arc
Jeanne
MUSÉE DES BEAUX-ARTS
M 3
SQUARE VERDREL
ST-GODARD
M 13
R. GANTERIE
Rue J. Lecanuet
Palais de Justice
PALAIS DE JUSTICE
R. St-Lô
Rue des Carmes
Pl. des Carmes
HORLOGE
Beffroi
Bureau des Finances
R. des
R. ST. ROMAIN
CATHÉDRALE
Rue de la République
Pont
G[d]
Rue
Gal Leclerc
Halle aux Toiles
SEINE
Corneille
Pont
Moulin
BUREAUX DU PORT FLUVIAL
Av.
R. de l'Industrie
Quai J. Anquetil
Place Carnot
ROUEN-R.-G.
R. de l'Avalasse
Rue de l'Yser
B[d] de l'Yser
Beauvoisine
Rue Beauvoisine
Ricard
Rampe
Beauvoisine
R. de Bihorel
R. du Nord
Boulingrin
Louis
R. Louis Ricard
R. Poussin
R. de la Cage
Champs des
R. des Minimes
ST-NICAISE
Rue de la Porte
Orbe
Av. de
ST-OUEN
H
R. St-Vivien
ST-VIVIEN
M 15
R. du Ruissel
Rue d'Amiens
AÎTRE ST-MACLOU
ST-MACLOU
R. MARTAINVILLE
Pl. St-Marc
HÔTEL DE RÉGION
Gambetta
B[d]
ESPLANADE DU CHAMP-DE-MARS
Av. A. Briand
HALTE DE PLAISANCE
R. E. Flamand
ÎLE LACROIX
Jacques
Rue Chastellain
Rue Stendhal
Pont Mathilde
Pl. St-Paul
ST-PAUL
M
M 1
115
76
0
200 m
48
30
138
67
57
101
137
13
68
66
27
72
120
155
89
143
128
96
147
24
102
59
81
22
9
70
116
45
3
108
63
94
12
35
21
6
58
140
42
117
49
Z
e
f
r
m
j

Le Clos Jouvenet without rest
42 r. Hyacinthe Langlois – ✆ 02 35 89 80 66 – www.leclosjouvenet.com – cdewitte@club-internet.fr – Fax 02 35 98 37 65 – Closed 15 December-15 January EV **a**
4 rm – €80/90 €100/110
◆ Handsome 19C mansion dominating the town in a large, peaceful garden. Cosy, impeccably maintained guestrooms with views of the orchard or church spires.

Gill (Gilles Tournadre)
9 quai Bourse – ✆ 02 35 71 16 14 – www.gill.fr – gill@relaischateaux.com – Fax 02 35 71 96 91 – Closed 26 April-5 May, 2-26 August, 24 December-5 January, Sunday and Monday BZ **a**
Rest – Menu €37 (weekday lunch), €65/92 – Carte €80/110
Spec. Queues de langoustines poêlées en chutney de poivron et tomate. Le pigeon à la rouennaise. Millefeuille à la vanille Bourbon. **Wines** Vin de Pays du Calvados.
◆ Elegant, contemporary dining on the banks of the Seine in a minimalist decor. Inventive cuisine with a focus on ingredients from Normandy. Fine wine list.

Les Nymphéas (Patrice Kukurudz)
9 r. Pie – ✆ 02 35 89 26 69 – www.lesnympheas-rouen.com – lesnympheas.rouen@wanadoo.fr – Fax 02 35 70 98 81 – Closed 16 August-7 September, 22 February-9 March, Sunday and Monday except public holidays AY **h**
Rest – Menu €30 (weekday lunch), €40/50 – Carte €57/91
Spec. Escalope de foie gras chaud de canard au vinaigre de cidre. Canard sauvageon à la rouennaise. Soufflé chaud aux pommes et au calvados.
◆ This beautiful, half-timbered house, standing at the far end of a small paved courtyard, carefully combines rustic and modern styles. Pleasant summer terrace, decked with flowers. Classical cooking.

L'Écaille
26 rampe Cauchoise – ✆ 02 35 70 95 52 – www.restaurant-lecaille.fr – marc.Tellier3@wanadoo.fr – Fax 02 35 70 83 49 – Closed Sunday and Monday
Rest – Menu (€42 bi), €48/78 – Carte €73/88 AY **g**
◆ A restaurant dedicated to the sea world both by its decor and menu. Find blue-green tints, modern paintings, cane armchairs, and updated cuisine focused on seafood.

Les P'tits Parapluies
pl. Rougemare – ✆ 02 35 88 55 26 – www.lesptits-parapluies.com – lespetitsparapluies@hotmail.fr – Fax 02 35 70 24 31 – Closed 3-23 August, 2-10 January, Saturday lunch, Sunday dinner and Monday CY **e**
Rest – Menu €30 (weekdays)/49 – Carte €52/65
◆ The 16C edifice, formerly home to an umbrella factory, now houses a warm Art Nouveau furnished restaurant. Modern cuisine and wine cellar, well stocked in Burgundies and clarets.

La Couronne
31 pl. Vieux Marché – ✆ 02 35 71 40 90 – www.lacouronne.com.fr – contact@lacouronne.com.fr – Fax 02 35 71 05 78 AY **d**
Rest – Menu €25 (lunch), €35/48 – Carte €56/90
◆ This beautifully preserved family home, built in 1345, is France's oldest inn. Countrified decor and flower-decked summer terrace. The visitors' book is out of this world!

Le Reverbère
5 pl. de la République – ✆ 02 35 07 03 14 – Fax 02 35 89 77 93 – Closed 27 April-4 May, 27 July-17 August, 28 December-4 January, Sunday and public holidays
Rest – Menu €40 bi/55 – Carte €45/68 BZ **e**
◆ The façade of this wharf side restaurant sets the tone for the interior designer decoration in red and black with Starck furniture. Market-fresh recipes and fine clarets.

Minute et Mijoté
58 r. de Fontenelle – ✆ 02 32 08 40 00 – Fax 02 32 83 01 85 – Closed Sunday
Rest – Menu (€16), €20/30 AY **b**
◆ Behind a colourful façade, this former 19C brasserie sports a simple, bistro inspired decor of knick-knacks. Menu based on the seasons and market availability.

Le 37

37 r. St-Étienne-des-Tonneliers – ✆ 02 35 70 56 65 – Fax 02 35 71 96 91 – Closed 26 April-4 May, 2-25 August, 24 December-4 January, Sunday and Monday

Rest – Menu (€ 19 bi) – Carte approx. € 36 BZ **v**

◆ This chef skilfully prepares an updated menu and daily specials, which are chalked up on a blackboard. Enjoy the trendy bistro decor and relaxed atmosphere. So 37 is a lucky number!

in Martainville-Épreville 3.5 km south on the D 13, D 43 and minor road – pop. 611 – alt. 152 m – ✉ 76116

Sweet Home

534 r. des Marronniers, access via the Coquetier cul-de-sac – ✆ 02 35 23 76 05 – http://jy.aucreterre.free.fr – jean-yves.aucreterre@libertysurf.fr – Fax 02 35 23 76 05

4 rm – 🛉€ 48 🛉🛉€ 52/90 **Table d'hôte** – Menu € 16 bi/52

◆ An imposing edifice, at the end of a cul-de-sac, providing charming and romantic rooms, each in a different colour. Excellent breakfast and warm hospitality.

in Petit Quevilly 3 km southwest – pop. 22 200 – alt. 5 m – ✉ 76140

Les Capucines

16 r. J. Macé – ✆ 02 35 72 62 34 – capucines@cegetel.net – Fax 02 35 03 23 84 – Closed 3 weeks in August, Saturday lunch, Sunday dinner and Monday DX **s**

Rest – Menu € 27/52 – Carte € 50/70

◆ In the same family since 1957, this Rouen establishment is the epitome of hospitality. The modern decor and terrace appeal to a business clientele. Updated menu.

in Montigny 10 km by ⑦, D 94[E] and D 86 – pop. 1 147 – alt. 110 m – ✉ 76380

Le Relais de Montigny

r. Lieutenant Aubert – ✆ 02 35 36 05 97 – www.relais-de-montigny.com – info@le-relais-de-montigny.com – Fax 02 35 36 19 60

20 rm – 🛉€ 55 🛉🛉€ 80/86, ☕ € 10 – ½ P € 69/73

Rest – *(Closed Saturday lunch)* Menu € 28/37 – Carte € 38/47

◆ A 1960s hotel built in the upper reaches of a small village. Practical rooms, most of which have balconies overlooking a pleasant flower-decked garden. A lush green terrace adds the finishing touch to a traditional meal in summertime.

in Notre-Dame-de-Bondeville 8 km northwest – pop. 7 296 – alt. 25 m – ✉ 76960

Les Elfes

303 r. Longs Vallons – ✆ 02 35 74 36 21 – elfes2@wanadoo.fr – Fax 02 35 75 27 09 – Closed 15 July-17 August, 26 December-2 January, Sunday dinner, Monday dinner, Tuesday dinner and Wednesday dinner DV **n**

Rest – Menu (€ 17), € 21 (weekday lunch), € 23/42 – Carte € 33/68

◆ This welcoming regional inn, located below a railway line, sports rustic furniture and colourful tablecloths. Traditional cuisine.

ROUFFACH – 68 Haut-Rhin – 315 H9 – pop. 4 491 – alt. 204 m – ✉ 68250 Alsace-Lorraine 1 A3

Paris 479 – Basel 61 – Belfort 57 – Colmar 16 – Guebwiller 10 – Mulhouse 28 – Thann 26

Office de tourisme, place de la République ✆ 03 89 78 53 15, Fax 03 89 49 75 30

Alsace Golf Club Moulin de Biltzheim, E : 2 km on D 8, ✆ 03 89 78 52 12

Château d'Isenbourg

rte de Plaffenheim – ✆ 03 89 78 58 50 – www.isembourg.com – isenbourg@grandesetapes.fr – Fax 03 89 78 53 70

39 rm – 🛉€ 130/405 🛉🛉€ 130/405, ☕ € 24 – 2 suites

Rest – Menu (€ 27), € 33 (weekday lunch), € 50/88 – Carte € 73/107

◆ This 18C château overlooking the old town is surrounded by vineyards. Large, slightly antiquated, plush bedrooms. Sports facilities (fitness centre, tennis court) and a recently opened spa. The château offers two dining options: a 14C vaulted cellar or a classic dining room.

A la Ville de Lyon without rest
r. Poincaré – ✆ 03 89 49 62 49 – villedelyon@villes-et-vignoble.com
– Fax 03 89 49 76 67
48 rm – †€ 59/145 ††€ 59/145, ☕ € 8,50
◆ An attractive façade refurbished in Renaissance style. The newly renovated rooms have a cosy, contemporary and country-style appearance; the older rooms are more functional. Mosaic swimming pool.

Philippe Bohrer
r. Poincaré – ✆ 03 89 49 62 49 – www.villes-et-vignoble.com – villedelyon@villes-et-vignoble.com – Fax 03 89 49 76 67 – Closed 9-22 March and 27 July-9 August
Rest – *(closed Monday lunch, Wednesday lunch and Sunday)* Menu € 27/85 – Carte € 51/67
Rest *Brasserie Chez Julien* – ✆ 03 89 49 69 80 – Menu € 10/30 – Carte € 25/50
Spec. Tranche de foie gras de canard à la gelée au gewurztraminer. Queue et pince de homard caramélisées, knödel et écume de citron confit. Tendre goûter chocolat carambar façon "sortie d'école". **Wines** Riesling, Pinot noir.
◆ Sample a personalised, inventive cuisine accompanied by a well-stocked cellar (fine selection of Alsace wines) in a country-chic interior of pinewood. At Chez Julien, an elegant, friendly brasserie atmosphere in what used to be a cinema.

in Bollenberg 6 km southwest by D 83 and secondary road – ✉ 68250 Westhalten

Auberge au Vieux Pressoir
– ✆ 03 89 49 60 04 – www.bollenberg.com – info@bollenberg.com
– Fax 03 89 49 76 16 – Closed 21-27 December and Sunday dinner from mid-November to mid-March
Rest – Menu € 28 bi (weekday lunch), € 39/75 bi – Carte € 50/70
◆ The Alsace setting of this winegrower's house is dominated by fine cupboards and a collection of antique arms. Well-prepared regional dishes and tasting of the local vintages.

ROUFFIAC-TOLOSAN – 31 Haute-Garonne – **343** H3 – see Toulouse

---

LE ROUGET – 15 Cantal – **330** B5 – **pop. 964** – **alt. 614 m** – ✉ 15290 5 **A3**
Paris 549 – Aurillac 25 – Figeac 41 – Laroquebrou 15 – St-Céré 37 – Tulle 74

Des Voyageurs
– ✆ 04 71 46 10 14 – www.hotel-des-voyageurs.com – info@hotel-des-voyageurs.com – Fax 04 71 46 93 89 – Closed 1st-8 March, 10-18 October, 23-27 December and 15-27 February
24 rm – †€ 57/60 ††€ 57/60, ☕ € 8 – ½ P € 56/59
Rest – *(closed Sunday dinner 15 September-1st May)*
Menu € 12 (weekday lunch), € 20/32 – Carte € 28/42
◆ Lively stone building in a small Cantal village. The view from the bedrooms, currently being refurbished, will delight nature lovers. Classically laid out restaurant, pleasant terrace, and a combination of local and traditional cuisine.

ROULLET – 16 Charente – **324** K6 – see Angoulême

LE ROURET – 06 Alpes-Maritimes – **341** D5 – **pop. 3 763** – **alt. 350 m** – ✉ 06650 42 **E2**
Paris 913 – Cannes 19 – Grasse 10 – Nice 28 – Toulon, 136

Du Clos without rest
3 chemin des Écoles – ✆ 04 93 40 78 85 – www.hotel-du-clos.com – contact@hotel-du-clos.com – Fax 04 93 70 64 42
11 rm – †€ 120/250 ††€ 120/250, ☕ € 15
◆ Set in the upper village, this Provencal building and converted barn are set in tranquil parkland planted with olive trees. Personalised rooms with a country inn feel.

XX **Le Clos St-Pierre** (Daniel Ettlinger) VISA MC AE
pl. de l'Église – ✆ 04 93 77 39 18 – www.le-clos-saint-pierre.com – contact@le-clos-saint-pierre.com – Fax 04 93 42 48 30 – Closed 14 December-7 January, February holiday, Tuesday and Wednesday
Rest – *(number of covers limited, pre-book)* Menu € 33 (weekday lunch)/57
Spec. Asperges vertes du pays, œuf mollet et pancetta grillée (May-June). Selle d'agneau de Sisteron rôtie au four. Figues rôties au vin rouge et porto (August-September). **Wines** Côtes de Provence.
◆ On the church square, this welcoming inn serves delicious Mediterranean-inspired food (single set menu that changes daily). Tasteful Provençal interior and pretty terrace.

LES ROUSSES – **39 Jura** – **321** G8 – **pop. 3 018** – **alt. 1 110 m** – **Winter sports : 1 100/1 680 m** ⛷ **40** – ✉ **39220** **Burgundy-Jura** 16 **B3**

Paris 461 – Genève 45 – Gex 29 – Lons-le-Saunier 64 – Nyon 25 – St-Claude 31
Office de tourisme, Fort des Rousses ✆ 03 84 60 02 55, Fax 03 84 60 52 03
des Rousses Route du Noirmont, E : 1 km on D 29, ✆ 03 84 60 06 25
du Mont Saint-JeanE : 1 km on D 29, ✆ 03 84 60 09 71
Gorges de la Bienne★ West: 3 km.

Chamois P VISA MC
230 montée du Noirmont – ✆ 03 84 60 01 48 – www.lechamois.org – info@lechamois.org – Fax 03 84 60 39 38 – Closed 14 April-4 May
11 rm – €61 €62, ☕ € 10 – ½ P € 56
Rest – Menu € 18 (weekday lunch), € 24/54 – Carte € 32/55
◆ An isolated (non-smoking) chalet above the Rousses ski resort. A warm, contemporary interior in which wood prevails. Peaceful rooms, equipped with a DVD player. A view of the countryside, attractive table settings and creative cuisine.

Redoute P VISA MC AE
357 rte Blanche – ✆ 03 84 60 00 40 – www.hotellaredoute.com – info@hotellaredoute.com – Fax 03 84 60 04 59 – Closed 5 April-6 May and 11 October-4 December
25 rm – €49/68 €49/68, ☕ €8 – ½ P € 52/63
Rest – Menu € 16/35 – Carte € 22/45
◆ This family-run hotel enjoys a good location, despite being near the road. Clean, light and well-soundproofed guestrooms with no frills. A large dining room with exposed beams and wrought-iron chandeliers. Local cuisine.

Du Village without rest VISA MC
344 r. Pasteur – ✆ 03 84 34 12 75 – www.hotelvillage.fr – herve.girod397@orange.fr – Fax 03 84 34 12 76
10 rm – €45/53 €49/61, ☕ € 6,50
◆ A small, functional hotel with a central location and fresh, brightly coloured bedrooms. The breakfast room is also used as a lounge. Reception closed between noon and 5pm.

by D 25 5 km southwest – ✉ **39200 Prémanon**

Darbella P VISA MC AE
551 rte Darbella – ✆ 03 84 60 78 30 – www.darbella.com – hotelladarbella@wanadoo.fr – Fax 03 84 60 76 01 – Open 1st June-1st October and 1st December-30 April
16 rm – €39/65 €52/75, ☕ €6 – ½ P € 48/62
Rest – *(closed Monday and Tuesday off season)* Menu (€ 13), € 18/30 – Carte € 25/49
◆ Skiers and walkers appreciate this hotel near a ski lift leading to the Rousses domain. Refurbished and well cared for rooms; some designed for families. A small, rustic style dining room serving appetising regional and cheese dishes.

ROUSSILLON – **84 Vaucluse** – **332** E10 – **pop. 1 280** – **alt. 360 m** – ✉ **84220** **Provence** 42 **E1**

Paris 720 – Apt 11 – Avignon 46 – Bonnieux 12 – Carpentras 41 – Cavaillon 25 – Sault 31
Office de tourisme, place de la poste ✆ 04 90 05 60 25, Fax 04 90 05 63 31
Site★★.

Le Clos de la Glycine rm,
pl. de la Poste – ✆ 04 90 05 60 13 – www.luberon-hotel.com – le.clos.de.la.glycine@wanadoo.fr – Fax 04 90 05 75 80
9 rm – €105/155 €105/175, ☕ €13 – 1 suite – ½ P €114/149
Rest *David* – *(Closed 15 November-15 December, 15 January-13 February, Sunday dinner, Thursday lunch and Wednesday from 15 October to 15 April) (pre-book weekends)* Menu €33, €48/52
◆ Charming hotel in the high-perched village. Comfortable rooms with a magnificent view of the Giant's Causeway and Mount Ventoux. Panoramic terrace under the wisteria and Provençal dishes at restaurant David.

Les Sables d'Ocre without rest
rte d'Apt – ✆ 04 90 05 55 55 – www.roussillon-hotel.com – sablesdocre@orange.fr – Fax 04 90 05 55 50 – Open from March to November
22 rm – €69/82 €69/82, ☕ €10
◆ This recently-built and inviting farmhouse, set in the heart of Ochre Country, combines modern comfort and Provençal decoration. Cheerful painted metal furniture throughout.

Le Piquebaure-Côté Soleil
rte de Gordes, the Estrayas district – ✆ 04 90 05 79 65 – restaurant.piquebaure@wanadoo.fr – Closed 12 November-10 December, January, Wednesday in low season and Tuesday
Rest – *(number of covers limited, pre-book)* Menu €30/59 – Carte €34/54
◆ This restaurant takes its name from one of the rocks marking the Ochre circuit. Chic country interior and covered terrace on the valley side. Market-fresh cuisine.

ROUSSILLON – 38 Isère – 333 B5 – pop. 7 813 – alt. 200 m – ✉ 38150 — 44 B2

Paris 505 – Annonay 24 – Grenoble 92 – St-Étienne 68 – Tournon-sur-Rhône 44 – Vienne 19

Office de tourisme, place de l'Edit ✆ 04 74 86 72 07, Fax 04 74 29 74 76

Médicis without rest
r. Fernand Léger – ✆ 04 74 86 22 47 – www.hotelmedicis.fr – info@hotelmedicis.fr – Fax 04 74 86 48 05
15 rm – €52 €61, ☕ €9
◆ Modern hotel in a quiet residential district with spacious, functional rooms; tiled floors but good soundproofing. Lounge with a large-screen TV.

ROUTOT – 27 Eure – 304 E5 – pop. 1 340 – alt. 140 m – ✉ 27350 — 33 C2

Normandy

Paris 148 – Bernay 45 – Évreux 68 – Le Havre 57 – Pont-Audemer 19 – Rouen 36

La Haye-de-Routot: thousand-year-old yew trees★ North: 4 km.

L'Écurie
pl. de la Mairie – ✆ 02 32 57 30 30 – Fax 02 32 57 30 30 – Closed Sunday dinner, Tuesday dinner, Wednesday dinner and Monday
Rest – Menu (€15), €20 (weekdays)/40 – Carte €48/58
◆ This former post house is opposite the covered market. It has a lounge with a stone fireplace and two (rustic or modern) dining rooms. Traditional cuisine.

ROUVRES-EN-XAINTOIS – 88 Vosges – 314 E3 – pop. 297 – alt. 330 m – ✉ 88500 — 26 B3

Paris 357 – Épinal 42 – Lunéville 58 – Mirecourt 9 – Nancy 51 – Neufchâteau 34 – Vittel 19

Burnel rm,
22 r. Jeanne d'Arc – ✆ 03 29 65 64 10 – www.burnel.fr – hotelburnelleluth@wanadoo.fr – Fax 03 29 65 68 88 – Closed 18-31 December and Sunday evening in low season
21 rm – €50/55 €60/79, ☕ €9 – 2 suites – ½ P €53/60
Rest – *(closed Sunday dinner except from 12 July to 20 September, Saturday lunch and Monday lunch)* Menu (€10), €15 (weekdays), €28/48 – Carte approx. €40
◆ Spacious, very comfortable, countrified rooms. Some overlook the small flower-decked garden. Classic cuisine based on market produce is offered in a dining room renovated in a neo-rustic style.

ROUVROIS-SUR-OTHAIN – **55 Meuse** – **307** E2 – **see Longuyon (M.-et-M.)**

ROYAN – **17 Charente-Maritime** – **324** D6 – **pop. 18 100** – **alt. 20 m** – **Casino : Royan Pontaillac** A – ✉ **17200** **Atlantic Coast** 38 **A3**

Paris 504 – Bordeaux 121 – Périgueux 183 – Rochefort 40 – Saintes 38

Office de tourisme, rond-point de la Poste ✆ 05 46 05 04 71, Fax 05 46 06 67 76

de Royan Saint-Palais-sur-Mer Maine Gaudin, 7 km on the St-Palais-sur-Mer road, ✆ 05 46 23 16 24

Seafront ★ - Notre-Dame church /I★ **E** - Corniche★ and Conche★ de Pontaillac.

Plans on following pages

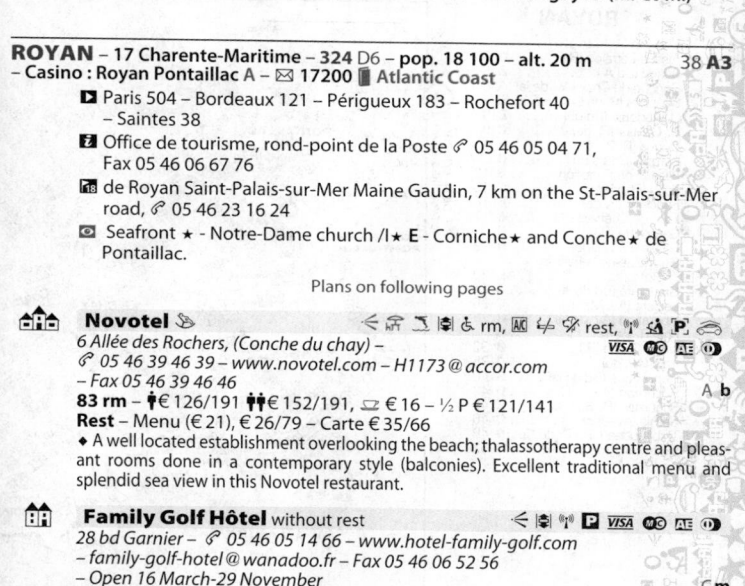

Novotel
6 Allée des Rochers, (Conche du chay) – ✆ 05 46 39 46 39 – www.novotel.com – H1173@accor.com – Fax 05 46 39 46 46
rm, rest, VISA MC AE D — A **b**
83 rm – †€ 126/191 ††€ 152/191, ☕ € 16 – ½ P € 121/141
Rest – Menu (€ 21), € 26/79 – Carte € 35/66
◆ A well located establishment overlooking the beach; thalassotherapy centre and pleasant rooms done in a contemporary style (balconies). Excellent traditional menu and splendid sea view in this Novotel restaurant.

Family Golf Hôtel without rest
VISA MC AE D
28 bd Garnier – ✆ 05 46 05 14 66 – www.hotel-family-golf.com – family-golf-hotel@wanadoo.fr – Fax 05 46 06 52 56 – Open 16 March-29 November — C **m**
30 rm – †€ 70 ††€ 70/107, ☕ € 10
◆ This seafront establishment is regularly spruced up. Half of its rather spacious bedrooms have a sea view. Breakfast served on the terrace in summer.

Les Bleuets without rest
AC VISA MC AE
21 façade de Foncillon – ✆ 05 46 38 51 79 – www.hotel-les-bleuets.com – info@hotel-les-bleuets.com – Fax 05 46 23 82 00 – Closed 18 December-3 January — B **d**
16 rm – †€ 45/70 ††€ 50/100, ☕ € 8
◆ Subdued nautical-inspired decor, well-renovated rooms, view of the sea (balconies) or the garden: a pleasant establishment between the harbour and the town centre.

Rêve de Sable without rest
VISA MC AE
10 pl. Foch – ✆ 05 46 06 52 25 – www.revedesable.com – contact@revedesable.fr – Fax 05 46 06 49 87 – Closed 1st-18 October — C **z**
11 rm – †€ 50/80 ††€ 50/80, ☕ € 7
◆ Family-run hotel near the beach and town centre. Bright, well-equipped rooms, some of which overlook the sea. Décor occasionally maritime related (fishing nets). Patio (breakfast).

XX **Les Filets Bleus**
AC VISA MC
14 r. Notre-Dame – ✆ 05 46 05 74 00 – Closed 28 June-12 July, 25 October-8 November, 3-10 January, Monday lunch and Sunday — B **s**
Rest – Menu (€ 14), € 18 (weekday lunch), € 25/48 – Carte € 40/80
◆ Restaurant dedicated to seafood and decorated to resemble a boat: blue and white colour scheme, wood, portholes, storm lamps. Special lobster menu in season.

XX **Le Relais de la Mairie**
AC VISA MC AE
1 r. du Chay – ✆ 05 46 39 03 15 – alain-gedoux@wanadoo.fr – Fax 05 46 39 03 15 – Closed 17 November-7 December, Thursday dinner, Sunday dinner and Monday — A **k**
Rest – Menu (€ 13), € 16 (weekdays)/35 – Carte € 27/57
◆ Restrained light interior, pleasantly set tables, traditional menu and family service: this little-known establishment is popular with the locals.

ROYAN

Alsace-Lorraine (R.) . . . . B 3
Briand (Bd A.) . . . . B 5
Conche-du-Chay (Av. de la). A 6
Desplats (R. du Colonel) . . . B 7
Dr-Audouin (Bd du) . . . . B 8
Dr-Gantier (Pl. du) . . . . C 9
Dugua (R. P.) . . . . B 10
Europe (Cours de l') C
Façade de Foncillon . . . . . . B 12
Foch (Pl. Mar.) . . . . C 15
Foncillon (R. de) . . . . B 16
Font-de-Cherves (R.) . . . . . . B 17
Gambetta (R.) . . . . B
Gaulle (Pl. Ch.-de) . . . . B 19
Germaine-de-la-Falaise (Bd) . . . . AB 20
Grandière (Bd de la) . . . . C 21
Leclerc (Av. Mar.) . . . . C 26
Libération (Av. de la) . . . . . . C 28
Loti (R. Pierre) . . . . B
Notre-Dame (R.) . . . . B 32
Parc (Av. du) . . . . C 35
République (Bd de la) . . . . . B 40
Rochefort (Av. de) . . . . B 42
Schuman (Pl. R.) . . . . B 45
Semis (Av. des) . . . . C 46
Thibeaudeau (Rd-Pt du Cdt.) B 48
5-Janvier-1945 (Bd du) . . . . B 52

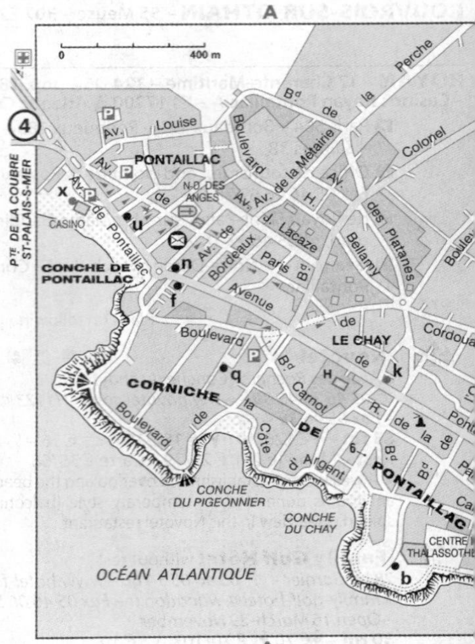

in Pontaillac – ✉ 17640

Pavillon Bleu et Résidence de Saintonge rest, P VISA
12 allée des Algues – ☎ 05 46 39 00 00
– www.le-pavillon-bleu.com – le.pavillon.bleu@wanadoo.fr – Fax 05 46 39 07 00
– Open 10 April-20 September A q
37 rm – €38/46 €49/69, €8 – 5 suites – ½ P €51/61
Rest – Menu €19 (weekday lunch), €28/35
◆ A substantial renovation programme is underway to breathe new life into this family establishment. The rooms already reveamped are contemporary and pleasant. Traditional cuisine with a marine flavour and a fine selection of Bordeaux wines.

Miramar without rest VISA
173 av. Pontaillac – ☎ 05 46 39 03 64 – www.miramar-pontallac.com
– miramaroyan@wanadoo.fr – Fax 05 46 39 23 75 A n
27 rm – €63/162 €63/162, €10
◆ This well-maintained 1950s building is just across the road from Royan's most fashionable beach. Rather spacious rooms, choose one facing the sea.

Grand Hôtel de Pontaillac without rest VISA AE
195 av. Pontaillac – ☎ 05 46 39 00 44
– www.monalisahotels.com – resa-royan@monalisahotels.com
– Fax 05 46 39 04 05 A u
40 rm – €95 €95, €12
◆ This hotel undergoing renovation overlooks Pontaillac Beach. The breakfast room and about half the bedrooms command a fine view of the Atlantic.

Belle-Vue without rest P VISA
122 av. Pontaillac – ☎ 05 46 39 06 75 – www.bellevue-pontaillac.com
– belle-vueroyan@wanadoo.fr – Fax 05 46 39 44 92 – Open from April to October
22 rm – €49/79 €49/79, €7 A f
◆ Situated on an avenue, a vast modernised 1950s villa. The average-sized rooms are prudently rustic and well-kept; ask for one overlooking the sea. Family ambiance.

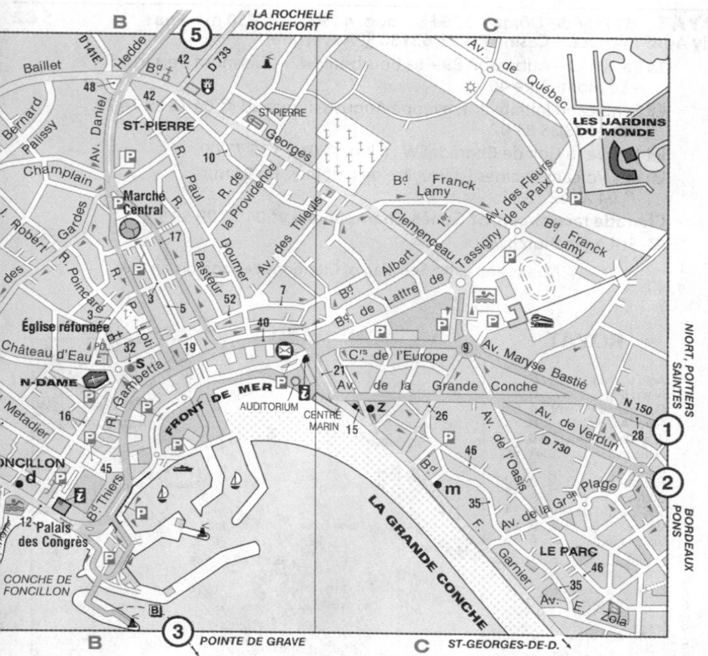

XX **La Jabotière** VISA MC AE

espl. Pontaillac – ✆ 05 46 39 91 29 – Fax 05 46 38 39 93
– Closed 12-18 October, 20-27 December, January, Wednesday dinner, Sunday dinner and Monday A x

Rest – Menu € 17 (lunch), € 20/56 – Carte € 56/81

◆ A plush yet rustic beachside restaurant overlooking the Atlantic. Traditional menu and fish; bistro-style lunches.

St-Palais road 3.5 km by ④ – ✉ 17640 Vaux-sur-Mer

Résidence de Rohan without rest VISA MC

Conche de Nauzan – ✆ 05 46 39 00 75 – www.residence-rohan.com
– info@residence-rohan.com – Fax 05 46 38 29 99 – Open 26 March-10 November

44 rm – †€ 70/134 ††€ 70/134, ☕ € 11

◆ This handsome 19C residence once housed the Duchess of Rohan's literary salon. It is augmented by a villa in a park overlooking the beach. Romantic rooms, lovely period furniture.

in St-Georges-de-Didonne 2 km au Sud-Est du plan par Bd F. Garnier – pop. 5 059 – alt. 7 m – ✉ 17110

Office de tourisme, 7, boulevard Michelet ✆ 05 46 05 09 73, Fax 05 46 06 36 99

Colinette et Costabela VISA MC

16 av. de la Grande Plage – ✆ 05 46 05 15 75 – www.colinette.fr – infos@colinette.fr – Fax 05 46 06 54 17 – Closed 20 December-20 January

21 rm – †€ 49/110 ††€ 49/110, ☕ € 8 – ½ P € 53/70

Rest – *(closed lunch from October to March)* Menu (€ 13), € 17/24 – Carte € 28/40

◆ 1930s villa-cum-guesthouse between the pine trees and beach. Light practical rooms, somewhat larger in the adjacent building.

ROYAT – 63 Puy-de-Dôme – **326** F8 – **pop. 4 797** – **alt. 450 m** – **Spa : early April-mid Oct.** – **Casino** B – ✉ **63130** ▌**Auvergne** 5 **B2**

- Paris 423 – Aubusson 89 – La Bourboule 47 – Clermont-Ferrand 5 – Le Mont-Dore 40
- Syndicat d'initiative, 1, avenue Auguste Rouzaud ☎ 04 73 29 74 70, Fax 04 73 35 81 07
- Nouveau Golf de CharadeSW : 6 km, ☎ 04 73 35 73 09
- des Volcans Orcines La Bruyère des Moines, N : 9 km, ☎ 04 73 62 15 51

Charade race circuit, St Genès-Champanelle ☎ 04 73 29 52 95.

- St-Léger church ★.

Access and exits: See plan of Clermont-Ferrand urban area.

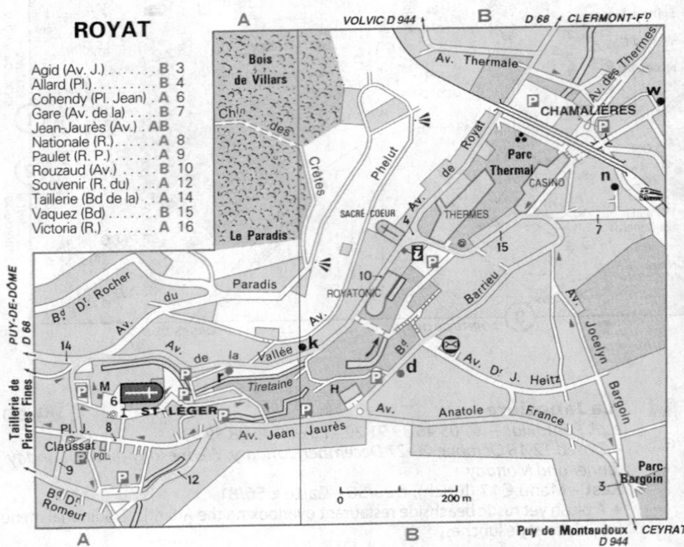

Royal St-Mart

av. de la Gare – ☎ 04 73 35 80 01 – www.hotel-auvergne.com – contact@hotel-auvergne.com – Fax 04 73 35 75 92 – Closed mid December-end January B **n**

55 rm – †€ 57/120 ††€ 65/125, ☕ € 10 – ½ P € 57/100

Rest – *(open early April to end October)* Menu € 29/32 – Carte € 25/56

◆ This hotel has been in the same family since 1853. The building, in the shade of cedars, has various types of rooms. Choose one on the garden side. Plush lounge. View of the lawn terrace from the veranda dining room. Classic fare.

Le Chatel rest,

20 av. Vallée – ☎ 04 73 29 53 00 – www.hotel-le-chatel.com – info@hotel-le-chatel.com – Fax 04 73 29 53 29 – Closed mid-December to mid-January, Saturday and Sunday from November to March B **k**

25 rm – †€ 57 ††€ 63, ☕ € 9 – 5 suites – ½ P € 54

Rest – Menu (€ 13 bi), € 18/40 – Carte € 26/40

◆ An old building with well-kept rooms opposite a park on the banks of the Tiretaine. The largest rooms occupy a neighbouring house. Renovated suites. Pleasant dining room. Traditional and regional cooking, as well as slimline set menus.

🏠 **Château de Charade** without rest
5 km south-west on D 941 and D 5 – ✆ 04 73 35 91 67 – www.chateau-de-charade.com – chateau-de-charade@orange.fr – Fax 04 73 29 92 09 – Open 31 March-7 November
5 rm – 🚹€ 70/78 🚹🚹€ 70/78, ☕ € 6
◆ Château, dating from the 17C and 19C, on the edge of the Royat golf course. The rooms, all of which overlook the park, are decorated with antique furniture. Attractive lounge and billiard table.

XXX **La Belle Meunière** with rm — VISA MC AE
25 av. Vallée – ✆ 04 73 35 80 17 – www.la-belle-meuniere.com – info@la-belle-meuniere.com – Fax 04 73 35 67 85 – Closed 17-31 August, 15-22 February, Saturday lunch, Sunday dinner and Monday — A **r**
6 rm – 🚹€ 55/70 🚹🚹€ 65/95, ☕ € 12 – ½ P € 75/95
Rest – Menu (€ 17), € 29/85 – Carte € 43/80
◆ Situated on the banks of the Tiretaine, this restaurant serves innovative cuisine influenced by Asia and the Auvergne. Napoleon III decor, with Art Nouveau stained glass and chinoiseries. The romantic liaison between La Belle Meunière and General Boulanger has inspired the 19C decor of the hotel's bedrooms.

X **L'Hostalet** — VISA MC AE
47 bd Barrieu – ✆ 04 73 35 82 67 – Closed 11 January-9 March, Sunday and Monday except bank holidays — B **d**
Rest – Menu € 18 (weekday lunch), € 25/36 – Carte € 24/39
◆ The timeless traditional dishes and an extensive wine list are appreciated by the regulars of this family restaurant with a slightly antiquated decor.

ROYE – 80 Somme – 301 J9 – pop. 6 529 – alt. 88 m – ✉ 80700 — 36 **B2**

Northern France and the Paris Region

Paris 113 – Compiègne 42 – Amiens 44 – Arras 75 – St-Quentin 61

XXX ✿ **La Flamiche** (Marie-Christine Borck-Klopp) — AC VISA MC
20 pl. Hôtel de Ville – ✆ 03 22 87 00 56 – www.laflamiche.fr – restaurantlaflamiche@wanadoo.fr – Fax 03 22 78 46 77 – Closed for three weeks in August, one week in early January, Sunday dinner, Tuesday lunch and Monday
Rest – Menu € 35/178 bi – Carte € 40/65
Spec. Flamiche aux poireaux (October to May). Colvert des marais (season). Paris-Brest.
◆ Artwork on display in the pleasant dining rooms in Picardy style. Modern cuisine with regional touches.

XX **Le Florentin Hôtel Central** with rm — AC rest, rm, VISA MC AE
36 r. d'Amiens – ✆ 03 22 87 11 05 – www.leflorentin.com – devauxd@clubinternet.fr – Fax 03 22 87 42 74 – Closed 11-25 August, Sunday dinner and Monday
8 rm – 🚹€ 45 🚹🚹€ 50, ☕ € 6 **Rest** – Menu € 16/42 – Carte € 30/50
◆ Restaurant with a red brick façade and Italian-inspired decor including columns, mouldings, marble and frescoes. Traditional cuisine. Functional rooms.

XX **Le Roye Gourmet** — VISA MC
1 pl. de la République – ✆ 03 22 87 10 87 – leroye.gourmet@orange.fr – Closed 11-23 August, 2-10 January, Sunday dinner and Monday
Rest – Menu € 17/45 – Carte € 30/65
◆ Situated on a pretty square, this restaurant specialises in regionally-inspired classical cuisine. One dining room is furnished in contemporary style; the other is adorned with paintings.

X **Hostellerie La Croix d'Or** — VISA MC
123 r. St-Gilles – ✆ 03 22 87 11 57 – www.lacroixdor80.fr – contact@lacroixdor80.fr – Fax 03 22 87 09 81 – Closed Monday dinner, Wednesday dinner, Thursday dinner, Sunday dinner and Tuesday
Rest – Menu (€ 12), € 20/38 – Carte € 29/58
◆ A pleasant country atmosphere reigns within the walls of this inn, at the town entrance. Tasty classic cuisine.

ROYE – 70 Haute-Saône – **314** H6 – see Lure

LE ROZIER – 48 Lozère – **330** H9 – **pop. 149** – **alt. 400 m** – ✉ **48150** 22 **B1**
Languedoc-Roussillon-Tarn Gorges

Paris 632 – Florac 57 – Mende 63 – Millau 23 – Sévérac-le-Château 23 – Le Vigan 72

Office de tourisme, route de Meyrueis ✆ 05 65 62 60 89, Fax 05 65 62 60 27

Terrasses du Truel ≤★ East: 3,5 km - Gorges du Tarn★★★.

Chaos de Montpellier-le-Vieux★★★ South: 11,5 km - Corniche du Causse Noir ≤★★ Southeast: 13 km then 15 mn.

Grand Hôtel de la Muse et du Rozier
rte des Gorges, in La Muse (D 907), right bank of the Tarn ✉ 12720 Peyreleau (Aveyron) – ✆ 05 65 62 60 01 – www.hotel-delamuse.fr – info@hotel-delamuse.fr – Fax 05 65 62 63 88 – Open 3 April-11 November
38 rm – €85/110 €85/165, ☕ €13 **Rest** – Menu €33/65 – Carte €52/74
◆ A private beach on the banks of the Tarn in the garden of this venerable grand hotel. The contemporary minimalist interior enhances the magnificent surrounding countryside. A creative menu focusing on local produce; riverside terrace.

Doussière without rest
– ✆ 05 65 62 60 25 – www.hotel-doussiere.com – galtier.christine@libertysurf.fr – Fax 05 65 62 65 48 – Open Easter-10 November
20 rm – €46/58 €48/62, ☕ €9
◆ Two village buildings standing on either side of the Jonte with the older bedrooms situated in the wing. Pleasant view from the breakfast room. Fitness centre.

RUCH – 33 Gironde – **335** K6 – **pop. 507** – **alt. 100 m** – ✉ **33350** 4 **C1**

Paris 609 – Bordeaux 66 – Pessac 77 – Talence 71 – Villenave-d'Ornon 65

Le Domaine de Blaignac
3 lieu dit de Blaignac – ✆ 05 57 40 54 57 – www.domainedeblaignac.com – reservation@domainedeblaignac.com – Fax 05 57 40 54 57
5 rm ☕ – €58/62 €64/68 **Table d'hôte** – Menu €25 bi
◆ In the heart of the Entre deux Mers region, orchards and vineyards surround this historic winegrower's home. Spruce, well-kept guestrooms. Regional wines accompany the home cooking at the table d'hôtes.

RUE – 80 Somme – **301** D6 – **pop. 3 075** – **alt. 9 m** – ✉ **80120** 36 **A1**
Northern France and the Paris Region

Paris 212 – Abbeville 28 – Amiens 77 – Berck-Plage 22 – Le Crotoy 8

Office de tourisme, 10, place Anatole Gosselin ✆ 03 22 25 69 94, Fax 03 22 25 76 26

St-Esprit chapel ★: interior★★.

in St-Firmin 3 km west by D 4 – ✉ **80550 Le Crotoy**

Auberge de la Dune rm, rm,
1352 r. de la Dune – ✆ 03 22 25 01 88 – www.auberge-de-la-dune.com – contact@auberge-de-la-dune.com – Fax 03 22 25 66 74 – Closed December
11 rm – €65 €65, ☕ €10 – ½ P €58
Rest – Menu (€13), €18 (weekdays)/40 – Carte €21/45
◆ Isolated in the fields, this small inn is not far from the ornithological park. Rooms are sober, modern and practical; extremely well kept. Country-style dining room serving traditional cuisine and some local specialities.

RUEIL-MALMAISON – 92 Hauts-de-Seine – **311** J2 – **101** 14 – **see Paris, Area**

RUILLÉ-FROID-FONDS – 53 Mayenne – **310** F7 – **see Château-Gontier**

RULLY – 71 Saône-et-Loire – **320** I8 – **pop. 1 463** – **alt. 220 m** – ✉ **71150** 8 **C3**

Paris 332 – Autun 43 – Beaune 20 – Chalon-sur-Saône 16 – Le Creusot 32

Le Vendangerot with rm

6 pl. Ste-Marie – ✆ 03 85 87 20 09 – www.vendangerot.com – laurence_armand@hotmail.fr – Fax 03 85 91 27 18 – Closed 1st February-15 March, Tuesday and Wednesday

14 rm – †€ 53 ††€ 53, ☕ € 7

Rest – Menu € 18 (weekdays)/47 – Carte € 50/58

◆ A village inn with a flower-decked façade facing a public garden. Dining room decorated with old photos relating to wine-growing. Regional specialities. Bedrooms with traditional charm.

RUMILLY – 74 Haute-Savoie – **328** I5 – **pop. 12 400** – **alt. 334 m** 45 **C1**
– ✉ **74150** **French Alps**

Paris 530 – Aix-les-Bains 21 – Annecy 19 – Bellegarde-sur-Valserine 37 – Genève 64

Office de tourisme, 4, place de l'Hôtel de Ville ✆ 04 50 64 58 32, Fax 04 50 01 03 53

Boîte à Sel

27 r. Pont-Neuf – ✆ 04 50 01 02 52 – Fax 04 50 01 42 11 – Closed 1st-15 August, 1st-15 January, Thursday dinner, Sunday dinner and Monday

Rest – Menu (€ 13), € 23/30 – Carte € 26/37

◆ Modest restaurant in a busy street serving bistro-style cuisine. Friendly welcome and landscape garden trompe-l'œil decor.

RUNGIS – 94 Val-de-Marne – **312** D3 – **101** 26 – **see Paris, Area**

RUOMS – Ardèche – **331** I7 – **pop. 2 189** – **alt. 121 m** – ✉ **07120** 44 **A3**
Lyon - Rhone Valley

Paris 651 – Alès 54 – Aubenas 24 – Pont-St-Esprit 49

Syndicat d'initiative, rue Alphonse Daudet ✆ 04 75 93 91 90, Fax 04 75 39 78 91

Labeaume★ West: 4 km - Défilé de Ruoms★.

Le Savel with rm

rte des Brasseries – ✆ 04 75 39 60 02 – www.ardechehotelsavel.com – hotel-le-savel@wanadoo.fr – Fax 04 75 39 76 02

14 rm – †€ 54/68 ††€ 54/68, ☕ € 8 – ½ P € 53/60

Rest – *(closed 14-30 September, Friday, Saturday from October to April and Sunday) (dinner only) (number of covers limited, pre-book)* Menu € 25

◆ The owner of this handsome bourgeois abode (1890) in the heart of a park has a passion for good regional produce. A nostalgic decor for meals and neat rooms.

RUPT-SUR-MOSELLE – 88 Vosges – **314** H5 – **pop. 3 560** – **alt. 424 m** 27 **C3**
– ✉ **88360**

Paris 423 – Belfort 58 – Colmar 80 – Épinal 38 – Mulhouse 68 – St-Dié 63 – Vesoul 61

Centre rest,

30 r. de l'Église – ✆ 03 29 24 34 73 – www.hotelrestaurantducentre.com – hotelcentreperry@wanadoo.fr – Fax 03 29 24 45 26 – Closed 1st-8 May, 2-9 June, 6-13 October, Christmas holidays, Saturday lunch, Sunday dinner and Monday

8 rm – †€ 46/57 ††€ 56/72, ☕ € 8 – ½ P € 50/58

Rest – Menu (€ 14), € 25/48 – Carte € 36/79

◆ A characteristic Moselle house near the church and on the doorstep of the Parc Régional des Ballons des Vosges. Clean, comfortable rooms. The roasting spit in the simple dining room is now purely decorative. Traditional seasonal cooking.

Relais Benelux-Bâle
VISA

69 r. de Lorraine – 03 29 24 35 40 – www.benelux-bale.com – contact@benelux-bale.com – Fax 03 29 24 40 47 – Closed 27 July-5 August, 20 December-5 January and Sunday dinner
10 rm – €40/52 €45/62, €8 – ½ P €41/44
Rest – Menu (€13), €20/33 – Carte €28/48
◆ Rather inviting fully soundproofed roadside chalet. Light, simple and well-equipped bedrooms. The restaurant has been run by the same family since 1921 and offers traditional and regional cooking. Pleasant terrace.

RUSTREL – 84 Vaucluse – **332** F10 – **pop. 645** – **alt. 400 m** – ✉ **84400** 40 **B2**
Provence

Paris 747 – Aix-en-Provence 66 – Marseille 94 – Salon-de-Provence 70

La Forge without rest
Notre-Dame-des-Anges, 2 km via Apt road and minor road – 04 90 04 92 22 – www.laforge.com.fr – laforge@laforge.com.fr – Fax 04 88 10 05 76 – Open 1st March-15 November
5 rm – €115 €120 – 1 suite
◆ A former foundry, partly converted into a welcoming guesthouse, in the depths of what is nicknamed the Provencal Colorado. Large guestrooms; garden filled with flowers.

ROEUX – 62 Pas-de-Calais – **301** K6 – **see Arras**

LES SABLES-D'OLONNE – 85 Vendée – **316** F8 – **pop. 15 200** 34 **A3**
– **alt. 4 m** – **Casinos : des Pins** CY, **des Atlantes** AZ – ✉ **85100** Atlantic Coast

Paris 456 – Cholet 107 – Nantes 102 – Niort 115 – La Roche-sur-Yon 36
Office de tourisme, 1, promenade Joffre 02 51 96 85 85, Fax 02 51 96 85 71
des Olonnes Olonne-sur-Mer6 km on the Roche-sur-Yon road, 02 51 33 16 16
de Port-Bourgenay Talmont-Saint-HilaireS : 17 km, 02 51 23 35 45
Le Remblai★.

Plans on next page

Mercure
rest, VISA

on Tanchet Lake, 2.5 km via coast road – 02 51 21 77 77 – www.accorthalassa.com – H1078@accor.com – Fax 02 51 21 77 80 – Closed 4-18 January CY **f**
100 rm – €109/234 €124/234, €13 – ½ P €92/159
Rest – Menu (€18 bi), €27/31 – Carte €30/40
◆ A modern building located within the thalassotherapy centre. Renovated modern bedrooms, decorated in the colours of the Vendée Globe race (overlooking the lake or pine forest). Panoramic restaurant and terrace; traditional and diet menus.

Atlantic Hôtel
VISA

5 prom. Godet – 02 51 95 37 71 – www.atlantichotel.fr – info@atlantichotel.fr – Fax 02 51 95 37 30 BY **e**
30 rm – €69/146 €79/146, €12 – ½ P €71/106
Rest *Le Sloop* – *(closed 20 December-4 January, Friday and Sunday October-April) (dinner only)* Menu €24, €34/40 – Carte €38/50
◆ A 1970s hotel with practical very well-kept bedrooms, some with sea view. The lounge, arranged around the indoor swimming pool, is topped by partially sliding glass roof. Beautiful ocean vista from the restaurant, decorated to look like a ship's cabin.

Arundel without rest
VISA

8 bd F. Roosevelt – 02 51 32 03 77 – ww.arundel-hotel.fr – contact@arundel-hotel.fr – Fax 02 51 32 86 28 AZ **k**
42 rm – €75/115 €90/135, €12
◆ This hotel, well-located opposite the casino, takes its name from a keep that became a lighthouse. Practical comfortable rooms, with balconies on the sea side.

LES SABLES D'OLONNE

Arago (Bd) . . . . **BY** 4
Baudry (R. P.). . . . . **BY** 5
Beauséjour (R.) . . . . **BY** 7
Briand (Av. A.) . . . . **CY** 9
Castelnau (Bd de) . . . . **BY** 12
Château-d'Olonne (Rte de) . . **CY** 13
Dr-Canteleau (R. du) . . . . **AY** 19
Dr-Schweitzer (R. du) . . . . **CY** 22
Doumer (Av. P.). . . . . **CY** 23
Estienne-d'Orves (Rd-Pt H. d') **AY** 25
Fricaud (R. D.) . . . . **BY** 26
Gabaret (Av. A.). . . . . **BY** 27
Godet (Prom. G.) . . . . **BY** 29
Ile Vertine (Bd de l') . . . . **AY** 32
Nouch (Corniche du). . . . . **AY** 43
Nouettes (R. des) . . . . **CY** 44
Président-Kennedy (Prom.). . . . . **CY** 48
Rhin-et-Danube (Av.) . . . . **CY** 50
St-Nicolas (R.) . . . . **AY** 55
Sauniers (R. des). . . . . **AY** 57
Souvenir Français (Bd du) . . . **AY** 58

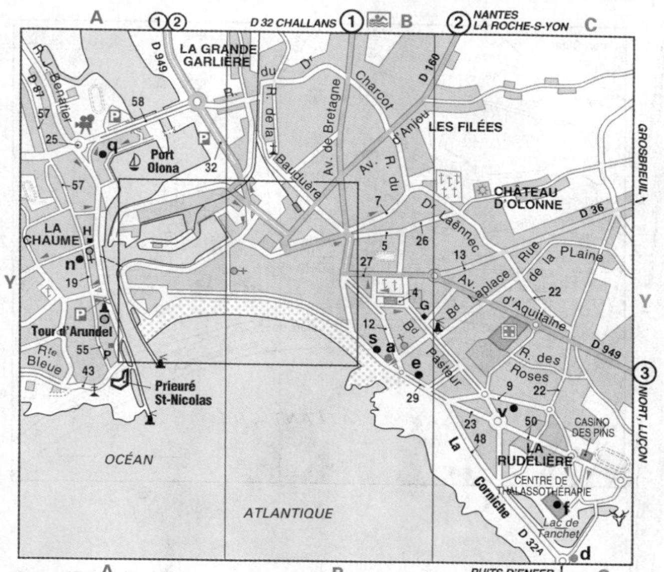

Les Roches Noires without rest
12 promenade G. Clemenceau – ✆ 02 51 32 01 71 – www.bw-lesrochesnoires.com – info@bw-lesrochesnoires.com – Fax 02 51 21 61 00 BY **s**
37 rm – †€ 60/126 ††€ 60/126, ☕ € 10
◆ In the heart of the bay are these practical, airy and well-soundproofed rooms (several balconies). The breakfast room offers a lovely sea view.

Admiral's without rest
pl. Jean-David Nau, at Port Olona – ✆ 02 51 21 41 41 – www.admiralhotel.fr – info@admiralhotel.fr – Fax 02 51 32 71 23 AY **q**
33 rm – †€ 63/92 ††€ 63/92, ☕ € 8,50
◆ A recent building near the salt marshes. Spacious, quiet rooms with loggias; some have a view over the marina, the starting line for the famous Vendée Globe race.

Le Calme des Pins without rest
43 av. A. Briand – ✆ 02 51 21 03 18 – www.calmedespins.com – calmedespins@wanadoo.fr – Fax 02 51 21 59 85 – Open 1st March-31 October CY **v**
45 rm – †€ 60/68 ††€ 64/88, ☕ € 9 – ½ P € 61/75
◆ In a residential district, two modern buildings flank an attractive 1900 villa. Revamped lobby-reception and partially refurbished, practical and well-kept rooms.

Antoine
60 r. Napoléon – ✆ 02 51 95 08 36 – www.antoinehotel.com – antoinehotel@club-internet.fr – Fax 02 51 23 92 78 – Open from mid March to mid October AZ **a**
20 rm – †€ 55/70 ††€ 55/70, ☕ € 8 – ½ P € 55/60
Rest – *(dinner only) (residents only)* Menu € 23
◆ This former property (18C) of a ship builder stands half way between the port and the beach. Simple, well proportioned rooms overlooking a small patio. Informal ambience.

LES SABLES D'OLONNE

Bauduère (R. de la) . . . . **BZ** 6
Bisson (R.) . . . . **AZ** 8
Caisse-d'Épargne (R. de la) . . **AZ** 10
Collineau (Pl. du Gén.) . . . . . . **BZ** 14
Commerce (Pl. du) . . . . **AZ** 15
Digue (Pl. de la) . . . . **BZ** 17
Dingler (Quai) . . . . **AZ** 18
Église (Pl. de l') . . . . **AZ** 24
Gabaret (Av. A.) . . . . **BZ** 27
Gaulle (R. Gén.-de) . . . . **BZ**
Guynemer (R.) . . . . **BZ**
Halles (R. des) . . . . **AZ** 30
Hôtel-de-Ville (R. de l') . . . . . . **AZ**
Leclerc (R. Mar.) . . . . **ABZ** 33
Liberté (Pl. de la) . . . . **BZ** 35
Louis-XI (Pl.) . . . . **BZ** 36
Nationale (R.) . . . . **BZ**
Navarin (Pl.) . . . . **AZ** 40
Palais-de-Justice (Pl.) . . . . **AZ** 46
Roosevelt (Bd F.) . . . . **AZ** 53
Travot (R.) . . . . **BZ** 60

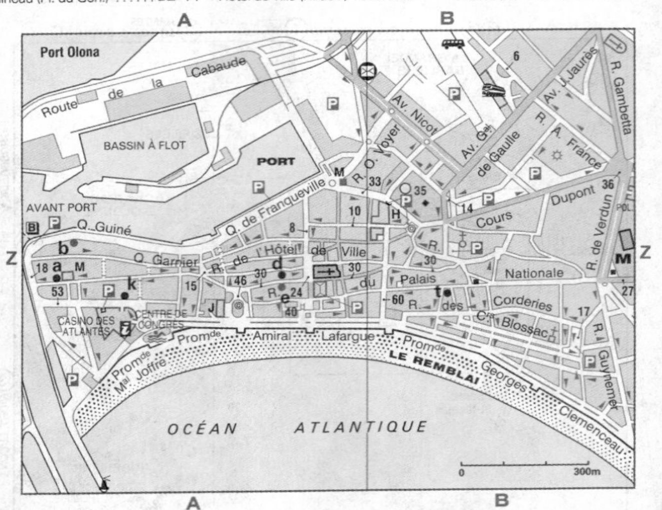

Les Embruns without rest

33 r. Lt Anger – ☎ 02 51 95 25 99 – www.hotel-lesembruns.com – info@hotel-lesembruns.com – Fax 02 51 95 84 48 – Open 1st March-3 November AY **n**

21 rm – †€ 46/58 ††€ 50/60, ☕ € 8

♦ This little-known hotel is located in the picturesque La Chaume district. A very warm welcome; small yet smart and well-kept bedrooms.

Arc en Ciel without rest

13 r. Chanzy – ☎ 02 51 96 92 50 – www.arcencielhotel.com – info@arcencielhotel.com – Fax 02 51 96 94 87 – Open 11 April-20 September BZ **t**

37 rm – †€ 62/89 ††€ 62/89, ☕ € 10

♦ Two minutes from the beach, this hotel offers practical rooms in pastel shades. Breakfast served in a well restored Belle Epoque room. Lounge with internet access.

Maison Richet without rest

25 r. de la Patrie – ☎ 02 51 32 04 12 – www.maison-richet.fr – infos@maison-richet.fr – Fax 02 51 23 72 63 – Closed 1st December-31 January AZ **d**

17 rm – †€ 58/71 ††€ 58/71, ☕ € 8,50

♦ Agreeable family establishment with a guesthouse atmosphere. Snug relaxing rooms, pretty patio and cosy sitting room with a collection of guides and globes.

Loulou Côte Sauvage

19 rte Bleue, at La Chaume AY – ☎ 02 51 21 32 32 – www.louloucotesauvage.com – loulou.cotesauvage@orange.fr – Fax 02 51 23 97 86 – Closed 20 November-19 December, February school holidays, Sunday dinner, Monday and Wednesday

Rest – Menu € 25 (weekdays)/64 – Carte € 41/86

♦ These former fish tanks set in the rock now house a restaurant. The dining room overlooks the sea and wild coastline. Generous portions of seafood.

XX **Le Puits d'Enfer**

56 bd de Lattre de Tassigny, via the cliff road – ✆ 02 51 21 52 77 – puits.enfer@ wanadoo.fr – Fax 02 51 21 52 77 – Closed 10-31 January and dinner during the week from November to March

Rest – Menu (€ 16), € 21 (weekdays)/44 – Carte € 40/60

◆ Restaurant facing the sea, decorated in modern minimalist style (wood, slate and designer furniture). Traditional, regionally inspired cuisine with a focus on spices and market-fresh produce.

XX **Le Clipper**

19 bis quai Guiné – ✆ 02 51 32 03 61 – www.leclipper.com – le_clipper@ alicepro.fr – Fax 02 51 95 21 28 – Closed 15 February-3 March, 20 November-17 December, Wednesday except from 15 June to 15 September, Thursday lunch and Tuesday AZ **b**

Rest – Menu € 20 (weekdays)/35 – Carte € 42/78

◆ This restaurant stands out from the many others on the harbour-side by its decor of mahogany-coloured parquet floor and Louis XVI chairs. Traditional and seafood dishes.

X **La Pilotine**

7 et 8 promenade Clemenceau – ✆ 02 51 22 25 25 – pvp.pilotine@tele2.fr – Fax 02 51 96 96 10 – Closed Sunday, Monday and Tuesday except July-August BY **a**

Rest – Menu € 16 (weekdays), € 24/46 – Carte € 44/76

◆ A seafront restaurant serving reasonably priced fish and seafood. New, colourful decor and charming service.

X **La Flambée**

81 r. des Halles – ✆ 02 51 96 92 35 – laflambeerestaurant@orange.fr – Fax 02 51 96 92 35 – Closed Sunday and Monday AZ **e**

Rest – Menu (€ 20 bi), € 36/43

◆ In the market district a little out of town, this establishment takes special care of its guests. Enjoy fine seasonal cuisine using local produce, an attentive welcome and a warm, modern decor.

in l'anse de Cayola 7 km southeast by la Corniche – ✉ 85180 Château-d'Olonne

XXX **Cayola**

76 promenade Cayola – ✆ 02 51 22 01 01 – www.rest-lecayola.com – Fax 02 51 22 08 28 – Closed January, Sunday dinner and Monday except public holidays

Rest – Menu € 38/95 – Carte € 67/75

Spec. Gâteau tiède de tourteau au gingembre. Sole sablaise aux senteurs de livèche. Figues rôties aux fruits secs et glace aux cèpes (October-November).

Wines Fiefs Vendéens blanc et rouge.

◆ Behind the shelter of large bay windows, admire the sea as you sample updated cooking. Veranda facing an overflow pool.

SABLES-D'OR-LES-PINS – 22 Côtes-d'Armor – 309 H3 – ✉ 22240 10 C1

Frehel Brittany

Paris 437 – Dinan 42 – Dol-de-Bretagne 60 – Lamballe 26 – St-Brieuc 39 – St-Malo 40

18 des Sables-d'Or Fréhel Sables d'Or les Pins, S : 1 km, ✆ 02 96 41 42 57

La Voile d'Or - La Lagune (Maximin Hellio) rm,

allée des Acacias – ✆ 02 96 41 42 49 – www.la-voile-dor.fr – la-voile-dor@wanadoo.fr – Fax 02 96 41 55 45 – Closed 21 December-15 February

21 rm – †€ 80/95 ††€ 95/225, ☕ € 15

Rest – *(closed Tuesday lunch, Wednesday lunch and Monday)*

Menu € 36 (weekday lunch), € 52/99 – Carte € 77/95

Spec. Saint-Jacques au chou-fleur et caviar d'Aquitaine (October to April). Homard au parfum de vadouvan et d'hibiscus (May to October). Fraises de Saint-Potan à l'angélique (May to September).

◆ At the entrance to the resort, spacious rooms decorated in a pleasant modern style, some facing the River Aber. Designer restaurant with view of the lagoon or the kitchens. Creative regional cuisine with an emphasis on local produce.

Diane rm,

allée des Acacias – ✆ 02 96 41 42 07 – www.hoteldiane.fr – hoteldiane@orange.fr – Fax 02 96 41 42 67 – Closed 3 January-7 February

47 rm – †€ 78/106 ††€ 78/108, ☕ € 11 – ½ P € 76/91

Rest – *(closed Sunday dinner, Monday lunch and Tuesday lunch from October to April except school holidays)* Menu € 24/47 – Carte € 35/60

◆ Big local-style building, along the main street and a stone's throw from the sea. Functional rooms. Rustic dining room and veranda serving up-to-date dishes, flavoured with home-grown herbs.

Le Manoir St-Michel without rest

38 r. de la Carquois, 1.5 km east via D 34 – ✆ 02 96 41 48 87 – www.hotel-bretagne.de – manoir-st-michel@fournel.de – Fax 02 96 41 41 55 – Open 30 March-5 November

20 rm – †€ 47/110 ††€ 47/118, ☕ € 6

◆ Fine 16C manor, overlooking the beach, surrounded by a vast park with an ornamental lake (fishing allowed). The spacious and cosy bedrooms have retained their charm of yesteryear.

SABLÉ-SUR-SARTHE – 72 Sarthe – **310** G7 – **pop. 12 300 – alt. 29 m** – ✉ 72300 Châteaux of the Loire — 35 **C1**

Paris 252 – Angers 64 – La Flèche 27 – Laval 44 – Le Mans 61 – Mayenne 60

Office de tourisme, place Raphaël-Elizé ✆ 02 43 95 00 60, Fax 02 43 92 60 77

de Sablé Solesmes Domaine de l'Outinière, S : 6 km on D 159, ✆ 02 43 95 28 78

Parfum d'Epices

1 r. Plaisance, rte de Laval – ✆ 02 43 92 94 14 – stchupin@wanadoo.fr – Closed 1st-9 March, 31 August-14 September and Monday except public holidays

Rest – Menu (€ 16), € 19 (weekdays)/42 – Carte € 37/50

◆ The name of this restaurant evokes a perfume of spices that will take you on a journey to distant lands. Regional recipes with Creole spices and flavours, served in a colourful jazz-themed interior.

in Solesmes 3 km northeast by D 22 – pop. 1 333 – alt. 28 m – ✉ 72300

Statues of the "Saints of Solesmes" ★★ in the abbey church ★ (Gregorian chant) - Bridge ≤★.

Le Grand Hôtel

16 pl. Dom Guéranger – ✆ 02 43 95 45 10 – www.grandhotelsolesmes.com – solesmes@grandhotelsolesmes.com – Fax 02 43 95 22 26 – Closed 26 December-2 January

30 rm – †€ 85/106 ††€ 90/140, ☕ € 12 – 2 suites – ½ P € 95/107

Rest – *(closed Saturday lunch from November to March and Sunday dinner from October to March)* Menu (€ 21), € 27/66 – Carte € 46/69

◆ A comfortable hotel, facing St Pierre Abbey, where you can hear Gregorian chants. Pretty renovated lounges, spacious colourful guestrooms, sometimes with a balcony. The restaurant's spruce sunlit dining room serves classical modernised dishes.

SABLET – 84 Vaucluse – **332** D8 – **pop. 1 249 – alt. 147 m** – ✉ 84110 — 40 **A2**

Paris 670 – Avignon 41 – Marseille 127 – Montélimar 67

Syndicat d'initiative, 8, rue du Levant ✆ 04 90 46 82 46, Fax 04 90 46 82 46

Les Abeilles with rm

4 rte de Vaison – ✆ 04 90 12 38 96 – www.abeilles-sablet.com – js@abeilles-sablet.com – Fax 04 90 12 12 70 – Closed 15 November-27 December, 15-25 February, Sunday except lunch from April to September and Monday

5 rm – †€ 60/85 ††€ 90/120, ☕ € 18 **Rest** – Menu (€ 19), € 32/58

◆ Attractive contemporary dining room, tastefully adorned with works by local artists. Fresh market produce takes pride of place in the traditional menu. Charming, well-appointed rooms.

SABRES – 40 Landes – **335** G10 – **pop. 1 107** – **alt. 78 m** – ✉ **40630** 3 **B2**
Atlantic Coast

Paris 676 – Arcachon 92 – Bayonne 111 – Bordeaux 94 – Mimizan 41 – Mont-de-Marsan 36

Ecomusée★ de la grande Lande Northwest: 4 km.

Auberge des Pins rm, rm, VISA MC AE
r. de la piscine – ✆ 05 58 08 30 00 – www.aubergedespins.fr – aubergedespins@wanadoo.fr – Fax 05 58 07 56 74 – Closed 3 weeks in January, Monday except dinner in July-August and Sunday dinner except July-August
25 rm – †€ 60/80 ††€ 65/140 – ½ P € 70/110
Rest – Menu € 19 (weekday lunch), € 25/66 – Carte € 45/70
◆ A large half-timbered Landes house in an attractive wooded park. Attractive, renovated, personalised rooms; those in the annex are simpler. A cosy lounge. Wood panelling and regional antique furniture make this restaurant special. Local cuisine.

SACHÉ – 37 Indre-et-Loire – **317** M5 – **see Azay-le-Rideau**

SACLAY – 91 Essonne – **312** C3 – **101** 24 – **see Paris, Area**

SAGELAT – 24 Dordogne – **329** H7 – **see Belves**

SAIGNON – 84 Vaucluse – **332** F10 – **see Apt**

SAILLAGOUSE – 66 Pyrénées-Orientales – **344** D8 – **pop. 971** 22 **A3**
– **alt. 1 309 m** – ✉ **66800** Languedoc-Roussillon-Tarn Gorges

Paris 855 – Bourg-Madame 10 – Font-Romeu-Odeillo-Via 12 – Mont-Louis 12 – Perpignan 93

Office de tourisme, Mairie ✆ 04 68 04 15 47, Fax 04 68 04 19 58

Gorges du Sègre★ East: 2 km.

Planes (La Vieille Maison Cerdane) VISA MC AE
6 pl. Cerdagne – ✆ 04 68 04 72 08 – www.planotel.fr – hotelplanes@wanadoo.fr – Fax 04 68 04 75 93 – Closed 10-20 March and 5 November-20 December
19 rm – †€ 45/60 ††€ 55/70, € 7 – ½ P € 53/62
Rest – *(closed Sunday dinner and Monday in low season)*
Menu € 22/48 – Carte € 30/50
◆ This former post house in the heart of the village is now a veritable institution. Gradually renovated rooms. Generous local cooking served in a welcoming regional setting. Brasserie-bar serving dishes at the counter and house specialities.

Planotel VISA MC AE
5 r. Torrent – ✆ 04 68 04 72 08 – www.planotel.fr – hotelplanes@wanadoo.fr – Fax 04 68 04 75 93 – Open June-September and school holidays
20 rm – †€ 52/62 ††€ 62/72, € 8 – ½ P € 59/69
◆ This 1970s building is ideal if you want to relax in quiet surroundings. Recently refurbished bedrooms with balconies (except two). Swimming pool with sliding roof.

in Llo 3 km east by D 33 – **pop. 148** – **alt. 1 424 m** – ✉ **66800**

Site★.

L'Atalaya rest, VISA MC
– ✆ 04 68 04 70 04 – www.atalaya66.com – atalaya66@orange.fr – Fax 04 68 04 01 29 – Open Easter-15 October
13 rm – †€ 98 ††€ 98/163, € 14
Rest – *(closed for lunch except Saturday and Sunday)* Carte € 50/65
◆ A pretty inn perched on the Cerdan mountainside. Endearing personalised guesthouse atmosphere. Panoramic pool. Classic country fare, romantic atmosphere (Catalan furniture, piano, bottled fruit) and magnificent view as far as Spain.

ST-ADJUTORY – 16 Charente – 324 M5 – pop. 314 – alt. 192 m – ✉ 16310 — 39 C3

Paris 472 – Poitiers 134 – Angoulême 33 – Saint-Junien 48 – Soyaux 36

Château du Mesnieux

Le Mesnieux – ✆ 05 45 70 40 18 – www.chateaudumesnieux.com – contact@chateaudumesnieux.com

4 rm – €70/85 €80/95 **Table d'hôte** – Menu €25 bi

◆ This small château is set in hilly grounds, ideal for long walks. Fine country-style sitting room and spacious bedrooms furnished with antiques. Meals are served at the family dining table in front of a huge fireplace.

ST-AFFRIQUE – 12 Aveyron – 338 J7 – pop. 7 507 – alt. 325 m – ✉ 12400 Languedoc-Roussillon-Tarn Gorges — 29 D2

Paris 662 – Albi 81 – Castres 92 – Lodève 66 – Millau 25 – Rodez 80

Office de tourisme, boulevard de Verdun ✆ 05 65 98 12 40, Fax 05 65 98 12 41

Roquefort-sur-Soulzon: Roquefort cellars★, rocher St-Pierre ≤★.

Le Moderne

VISA

54 av. A. Pezet – ✆ 05 65 49 20 44 – www.lemoderne.com – hotel-restaurant-le-moderne@wanadoo.fr – Fax 05 65 49 36 55 – Closed 19-25 October and 19 December-19 January

Rest – Menu (€16), €20/57 – Carte €36/54

◆ Cheese lovers will adore this house whose cheese board features no less than 12 different Roquefort cheeses. Regionally sourced menu.

ST-AFFRIQUE-LES-MONTAGNES – 81 Tarn – 338 F9 – pop. 706 – alt. 244 m – ✉ 81290 — 29 C2

Paris 741 – Albi 55 – Carcassonne 53 – Castres 12 – Toulouse 75

Domaine de Rasigous

rm, P VISA

2 km south on D 85 – ✆ 05 63 73 30 50 – www.domainederasigous.com – info@domainederasigous.com – Fax 05 63 73 30 51 – Open 10 March-20 November

6 rm – €95 €105, €12 – 2 suites – ½ P €90

Rest – *(closed Wednesday) (dinner only) (residents only)* Menu €29

◆ This 19C abode is a peaceful haven, due to its isolated, green surroundings and limited number of rooms. Paintings and sculptures bear witness to the owner's love of art.

ST-AGNAN – 58 Nièvre – 319 H8 – pop. 159 – alt. 525 m – ✉ 58230 — 7 B2

Paris 242 – Autun 53 – Avallon 33 – Clamecy 63 – Nevers 98 – Saulieu 15

La Vieille Auberge

rm, P VISA AE

– ✆ 03 86 78 71 36 – www.vieilleauberge.com – lvasaintagnan@aol.com – Fax 03 86 78 71 57 – Open 15 February-4 November

8 rm – €45 €47, €8,50 – ½ P €50/55

Rest – *(closed Monday and Tuesday)* Menu (€20), €28/49 – Carte €21/44

◆ Former café and grocer's shop in a hamlet near a lake, converted into a family-run inn. Attractive, colourful rooms with recently redone bathrooms. Rustic dining room with a stone fireplace. Attentive service and authentic regional cooking.

ST-AGRÈVE – 07 Ardèche – 331 I3 – pop. 2 588 – alt. 1 050 m – ✉ 07320 Lyon - Rhone Valley — 44 A2

Paris 582 – Aubenas 68 – Lamastre 21 – Privas 64 – Le Puy-en-Velay 51 – St-Étienne 69

Office de tourisme, Grand'Rue ✆ 04 75 30 15 06, Fax 04 75 30 60 93

Mont Chiniac ≤★★.

Domaine de Rilhac with rm

2 km southeast by D 120, D 21 and secondary road – 04 75 30 20 20 – www.domaine-de-rilhac.com – hotel_rilhac@yahoo.fr – Fax 04 75 30 20 00 – Closed 20 December-mid-March, Tuesday evening, Thursday lunch and Wednesday

7 rm – €105/125 €105/125, €14 – ½ P €115/121

Rest – Menu €25 (weekday lunch), €40/78 – Carte €54/68

◆ You're sure to find rest in this old farmhouse in the Ardèche countryside. It overlooks the Gerbier de Jonc and has stylish rooms. Cooking in tune with current tastes.

Faurie (Philippe Bouissou) with rm

36 av. des Cévennes – 04 75 30 11 45 – www.hotelfaurie.fr – philippebouissou@hotelfaurie.fr – Fax 04 75 29 23 88

3 rm – €90/130 €90/130, €20

Rest – *(number of covers limited, pre-book)* Menu €85

Spec. Les girolles et l'amande (autumn). La saucisse et la rhubarbe (spring-summer). Feuilleté framboise et crème de marron (summer).

◆ An unusual establishment with a retro interior, peppered with quirky touches. The chef draws inspiration from his kitchen garden in order to create his daily menu. Don't forget to book!

Les Cévennes with rm

rest, VISA

10 pl. de la République – 04 75 30 10 22 – rochedy07@orange.fr – Fax 04 75 29 83 06 – Closed 16-20 September, 12-26 November Monday dinner and Tuesday

6 rm – €50 €55, €10 – ½ P €56/66

Rest – Menu (€12), €14 (weekday lunch), €24/36 – Carte €30/40

◆ Modest but well-kept family hotel serving regional dishes in a wooden dining area, with simple quick meals served in the café. Modern rooms available.

If breakfast is included the symbol appears after the number of rooms.

ST-AIGNAN – 41 Loir-et-Cher – 318 F8 – pop. 3 542 – alt. 115 m – ✉ 41110 ▌Châteaux of the Loire 11 A2

Paris 221 – Blois 41 – Châteauroux 65 – Romorantin-Lanthenay 36 – Tours 62 – Vierzon 70

Office de tourisme, 60, rue Constant Ragot 02 54 75 22 85, Fax 02 54 75 50 26

Crypt★★ in the church★ - Zoo Parc de Beauval★ South: 4 km.

Les Jardins de Beauval

(in the zoo), parc de Beauval, 4 km on the D 675 – 02 54 75 60 00 – www.lesjardinsdebeauval.com – infos@lesjardinsdebeauval.com – Fax 02 54 75 60 01 – Closed 4-31 January

92 rm – €88/180 €88/180, €12 **Rest** – Menu €25 – Carte €37/46

◆ New complex made up of five villas in a landscaped garden at the foot of an animal reserve. Exotic interior of Indonesian inspiration. Classical rooms, suites and club. Buffets served in a spacious dining room opening onto a terrace.

Hostellerie Le Clos du Cher

2 r. Paul Boncour, North : 1 km via D 675 ✉ 41140 Noyers sur Cher – 02 54 75 00 03 – www.closducher.com – accueil@closducher.com – Fax 02 54 75 03 79 – Closed 26 October-8 November and 21 December-3 January

10 rm – €65/95 €65/95, €10 – ½ P €66/81

Rest – *(closed Friday lunch, Saturday lunch and Sunday dinner from October to March)* Menu €16 (weekday lunch), €28/38 – Carte €24/48

◆ A mansion dating from the 19C in a quiet wooded park with classic rooms and offering themed weekends (wine, Valentine's Day, etc). Family atmosphere and traditional cuisine in the restaurant decorated in sunny colours.

ST-ALBAN-DE-MONTBEL – 73 Savoie – 333 H4 – see Aiguebelette-le-Lac

ST-ALBAN-LES-EAUX – 42 Loire – 327 C3 – pop. 939 – alt. 410 m – ✉ 42370 44 **A1**

Paris 390 – Lapalisse 45 – Montbrison 56 – Roanne 12 – St-Étienne 86 – Thiers 56 – Vichy 61

Le Petit Prince

in the village – ✆ 04 77 65 87 13 – www.restaurant.lepetitprince.fr – lp-prince@orange.fr – Fax 04 77 65 96 88 – Closed 17 August-3 September, 26 October-2 November, Sunday dinner, Monday and Tuesday

Rest – Menu (€ 22), € 27/54

◆ The great, great aunts of the current owner created this delightful restaurant in 1805. Entrance through a terrace shaded by lime trees. Delicious inventive cuisine.

Undecided between two equivalent establishments?
Within each category,
establishments are classified in our order of preference.

ST-ALBAN-LEYSSE – 73 Savoie – 333 I4 – see Chambéry

ST-ALBAN-SUR-LIMAGNOLE – 48 Lozère – 330 I6 – pop. 1 544 – alt. 950 m – ✉ 48120 23 **C1**

Paris 552 – Espalion 72 – Mende 40 – Le Puy-en-Velay 75 – St-Chély-d'Apcher 12

Syndicat d'initiative, Rue de l'hôpital ✆ 04 66 31 57 01, Fax 04 66 31 58 70

Relais St-Roch

chemin du Carreirou – ✆ 04 66 31 55 48 – www.relais-saint-roch.fr – rsr@relais-saint-roch.fr – Fax 04 66 31 53 26 – Open 10 April-2 November

9 rm – €118/198 €118/198, € 15 – ½ P € 128/178

Rest *La Petite Maison* – see restaurant listing

◆ This 19C, pink granite manor house has delightful, well-appointed bedrooms decorated with personal touches. Comfortable lounge. Attractive heated swimming pool in the garden.

La Petite Maison – Hôtel St-Roch

av. Mende – ✆ 04 66 31 56 00 – www.la-petite-maison.fr – rsr@relais-saint-roch.fr – Fax 04 66 31 53 26 – Open 10 April-1st November and closed Monday except dinner in July-August, Tuesday lunch and Wednesday lunch

Rest – Menu (€ 24), € 28/69 – Carte € 48/78

◆ Regional fare served in a warm, romantic decor. Bison and trout specialities, fine whisky selection assembled by the owner.

ST-AMAND-MONTROND – 18 Cher – 323 L6 – pop. 11 800 – alt. 160 m – ✉ 18200 Dordogne-Berry-Limousin 12 **C3**

Paris 282 – Bourges 52 – Châteauroux 65 – Montluçon 56 – Nevers 70

Office de tourisme, place de la République ✆ 02 48 96 16 86, Fax 02 48 96 46 64

Noirlac abbey ★★ 4 km by ⑥.

Château de Meillant★★ 8 km by ①.

Plan on next page

Mercure L'Amandois

rm, rest,

7 r. H. Barbusse – ✆ 02 48 63 72 00 – www.mercure.com – h1890@accor.com – Fax 02 48 96 77 11 B r

43 rm – €65 €75, € 10 **Rest** – Menu € 18/25 – Carte € 31/39

◆ A chain hotel with a family atmosphere and 16 recent, well-equipped rooms. The guestrooms in the older building have enjoyed a recent facelift. Modern dining room with the standard Mercure menu options.

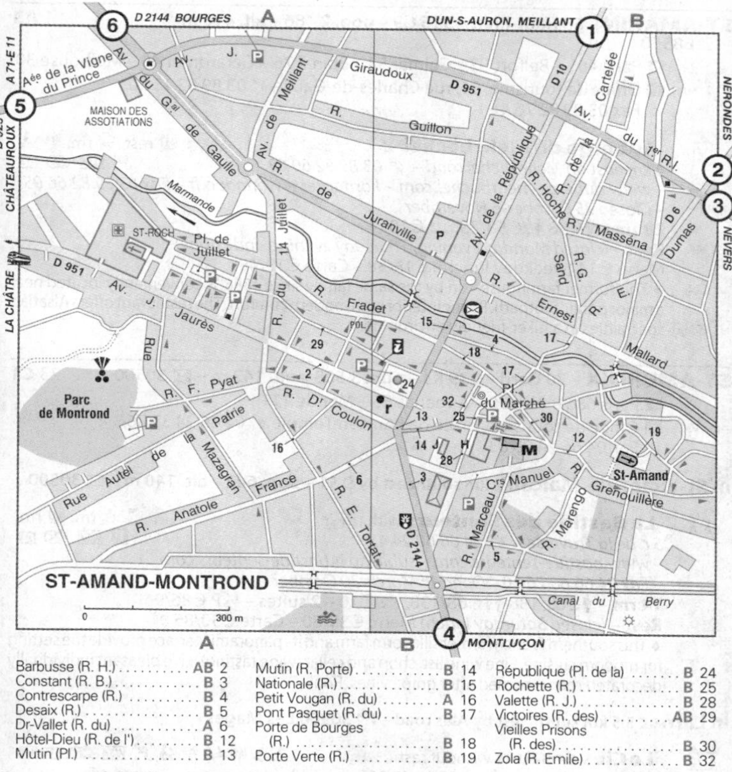

in Noirlac 4 km by ⑥ and D 35 – ✉ 18200 Bruère Allichamps

Auberge de l'Abbaye de Noirlac

– ✆ 02 48 96 22 58 – http://aubergeabbayenoirlac.free.fr
– aubergeabbayenoirlac@free.fr – Fax 02 48 96 86 63
– Open 20 February-17 November and closed Tuesday dinner and Wednesday except July-August

Rest – Menu € 21 (weekdays), € 26/34 – Carte € 40/60

◆ A 12C travellers' chapel, converted into a small inn. Dining room with beams and floor-tiles. Terrace facing the Cistercian abbey. Country cooking.

in Bruère-Allichamps 8.5 km by ⑥ – pop. 580 – alt. 170 m – ✉ 18200

Les Tilleuls

rte de Noirlac – ✆ 02 48 61 02 75 – www.hotel-restaurant-tilleuls.com
– eric.brendel18@orange.fr – Fax 02 48 61 08 41
– Closed 15-30 November, 20-28 December, 8-16 March, Sunday from mid-September to mid-June and Monday

11 rm – †€ 56/58 ††€ 56/58, ☕ € 9

Rest – Menu € 20 bi (weekday lunch), € 24/90 bi – Carte € 45/63

◆ This peacefully-situated hotel on the tourist trail along the Cher river, provides small well-kept rooms overlooking the countryside. Take a seat at a table in the Tilleuls and settle in to enjoy a delightful meal at a very reasonable price. Garden terrace.

ST-AMARIN – 68 Haut-Rhin – 315 G9 – pop. 2 486 – alt. 410 m – ✉ 68550 — 1 A3

Paris 461 – Belfort 52 – Colmar 53 – Épinal 76 – Gérardmer 40 – Mulhouse 30

Office de tourisme, 81, rue Charles-de-Gaulle ✆ 03 89 82 13 90, Fax 03 89 82 76 44

Auberge du Mehrbächel — rest, rm, P VISA MC AE

4 km east on Mehrbächel road – ✆ 03 89 82 60 68 – www.auberge-mehrbachel.com – kornacker@wanadoo.fr – Fax 03 89 82 66 05 – Closed 25 October-6 November

23 rm – €58 €58/75, €10

Rest – *(closed Monday evening, Thursday evening and Friday)*

Menu €14 (weekday lunch), €18/38 – Carte €19/45

◆ This former farmhouse, run by the same family since 1886, is conveniently located near a major public footpath. Rustic interior with modern comfort. The restaurant offers Alsatian specialities in a hiker-friendly environment.

ST-AMBROIX – 30 Gard – 339 K3 – pop. 3 508 – alt. 142 m – ✉ 30500 — 23 C1

Paris 686 – Alès 20 – Aubenas 56 – Mende 111

Office de tourisme, place de l'Ancien Temple ✆ 04 66 24 33 36, Fax 04 66 24 05 83

in St-Victor-de-Malcap 2 km southeast by D 51 – pop. 642 – alt. 140 m – ✉ 30500

La Bastide des Senteurs with rm — rm, rm, P VISA MC AE

5 r. de la Traverse – ✆ 04 66 60 24 45 – www.bastide-senteurs.com – subileau@bastide-senteurs.com – Fax 04 66 60 26 10 – Open 1st March-30 October

14 rm – €68/138 €68/138, €10 – 2 suites – ½ P €86/96

Rest – *(closed Saturday lunch)* Menu €35/80 – Carte €50/85

◆ This southern French former silkworm farm and its panoramic terrace provide the setting for modern cuisine. Fine wine list, shop and cellar (wine tasting). Five pleasant individually decorated rooms named after grape vines. Pool.

in Larnac 3.5 km southwest by Alès road – ✉ 30960 Les Mages

Le Clos des Arts without rest — P VISA MC AE

Domaine Villaret – ✆ 04 66 25 40 91 – www.closdesarts.com – contact@closdesarts.com – Fax 04 66 25 40 92

13 rm – €53/58 €53/58, €8

◆ This former 17C spinning mill offers spacious, new, suberly decorated guestrooms, a stylish vaulted breakfast room and an art gallery (sculptures).

ST-AMOUR-BELLEVUE – 71 Saône-et-Loire – 320 I12 – pop. 460 – alt. 306 m – ✉ 71570 — 8 C3

Paris 402 – Bourg-en-Bresse 48 – Lyon 63 – Mâcon 13 – Villefranche-sur-Saône 32

Auberge du Paradis — rm, VISA MC AE

Le Plâtre Durand – ✆ 03 85 37 10 26 – www.aubergeduparadis.fr – info@aubergeduparadis.fr – Closed January

8 rm – €105 €105/200, €14

Rest – *(closed Friday lunch, Sunday dinner, Monday and Tuesday)* Menu €48

◆ The original and contemporary guestrooms are decorated with taste and character. Counter-current pool, reading room and excellent breakfast. Far-flung flavours provide inspiration for the cuisine (set menu), served in a romantic setting.

Chez Jean-Pierre — VISA MC AE

Le Plâtre Durand – ✆ 03 85 37 41 26 – restaurant.jeanpierre@wanadoo.fr – Fax 03 85 37 18 40 – Closed 22 December-11 January, Sunday dinner, Wednesday and Thursday

Rest – Menu €20/48 – Carte €44/53

◆ A pleasant country inn in a wine-making village. The dining room has a blue glazed fireplace, large butcher's block and a lobster tank. Shaded, flower-decked terrace.

ST-ANDIOL – 13 Bouches-du-Rhône – 340 E3 – pop. 3 138 – alt. 55 m – ✉ 13670 42 E1

Paris 692 – Avignon 19 – Aix-en-Provence 63 – Arles 36 – Marseille 80

Syndicat d'initiative, avenue Alphonse Daudet ☎ 04 90 95 48 95, Fax 04 32 61 08 79

Le Berger des Abeilles
– ☎ 04 90 95 01 91 – www.bergerabeilles.com – abeilles13@aol.com – Fax 04 90 95 48 26 – Closed Monday from November to March
9 rm – **†**€ 75/108 **††**€ 95/168 – ½ P € 80/90 **Rest** – Menu (€ 18 bi), € 30/59
◆ This remote, little country Provençal farmhouse offers rustic, well-kept rooms. Three ground-floor rooms open onto the peaceful garden. Dining room in sunny tones and terrace shaded by a majestic plane tree. Regional cuisine.

ST-ANDRÉ-DE-ROQUELONGUE – 11 Aude – 344 I4 – pop. 959 – alt. 72 m – ✉ 11200 22 B3

Paris 821 – Béziers 53 – Montpellier 112 – Perpignan 71

Demeure de Roquelongue
53 av. de Narbonne – ☎ 04 68 45 63 57 – www.demeure-de-roquelongue.com – contact@demeure-de-roquelongue.com – Open 1st March-30 November
5 rm – **†**€ 95/135 **††**€ 95/135 **Table d'hôte** – Menu € 25
◆ This elegant, former wine growers' house (1885) boasts an exquisite lush green patio. Tastefully decorated rooms with antique furniture and old-fashioned bathrooms. Cosy sitting room.

ST-ANDRÉ-DE-VALBORGNE – Gard – 339 H4 – pop. 368 – alt. 450 m – ✉ 30940 23 C1

Paris 653 – Alès 53 – Mende 69 – Millau 81

Office de tourisme, les Quais ☎ 04 66 60 32 11, Fax 04 66 60 32 11

Bourgade with rm
pl. de l'Église – ☎ 04 66 56 69 32 – www.restaurant-bourgade.com – info@restaurant-bourgade.com – Fax 04 66 25 81 92 – Closed Tuesday, Wednesday and Thursday in low season, Sunday dinner and Monday except 15 June-15 September
10 rm – **†**€ 50/70 **††**€ 55/75, € 9 – ½ P € 60/70
Rest – Menu (€ 20), € 28/75 – Carte € 44/66
◆ This welcoming 17C-coaching inn has a terrace scented with wisteria. Market fresh cuisine is offered and suited to current tastes. A few small practical rooms.

ST-ANDRÉ-LEZ-LILLE – 59 Nord – 302 G4 – see Lille

ST-ANDRÉ-LES-VERGERS – 10 Aube – 313 E4 – see Troyes

ST-ANTHÈME – 63 Puy-de-Dôme – 326 K9 – pop. 781 – alt. 950 m – ✉ 63660 6 C2

Paris 461 – Ambert 23 – Clermont-Ferrand 100 – Feurs 50 – Montbrison 24 – St-Étienne 57

Office de tourisme, place de l'Aubépin ☎ 04 73 95 47 06, Fax 04 73 95 41 06

in Raffiny 5 km south by D 261 – ✉ 63660 St-Romain

Au Pont de Raffiny
– ☎ 04 73 95 49 10 – www.hotel-pont-raffiny.com – hotel.pont.raffiny@wanadoo.fr – Fax 04 73 95 80 21 – Closed 1st January to 15 March, Sunday dinner and Monday except July-August
11 rm – **†**€ 35/37 **††**€ 43/51, € 8 – ½ P € 47/51
Rest – Menu (€ 13), € 17 (weekdays)/35 – Carte € 27/38
◆ This country inn, occupying a stone building on the road through the hamlet, offers cosy rooms with wood panelling. Two chalets, 50 m away, with private gardens. Pool and fitness area. Spacious, rustic restaurant (beams, fireplace and fountain); regional recipes.

ST-ANTOINE-L'ABBAYE – 38 Isère – 333 E6 – pop. 959 – alt. 339 m 43 **E2**
– ✉ 38160 Lyon - Rhone Valley

Paris 553 – Grenoble 66 – Romans-sur-Isère 26 – St-Marcellin 12 – Valence 49
Office de tourisme, place Ferdinand Gilibert ✆ 04 76 36 44 46, Fax 04 76 36 40 49
Abbey church ★.

Auberge de l'Abbaye
Mail de l'Abbaye – ✆ 04 76 36 42 83 – www.auberge-abbaye.com – leydierl@wanadoo.fr – Fax 04 76 36 46 13 – Closed 5 January-5 February, Monday and Tuesday except lunch 1st July-19 September and Sunday dinner
Rest – Menu € 23/51 – Carte € 20/45
◆ Pretty house (14C), at the centre of a Medieval village. Warm, Louis XIII-style interior and terrace overlooking the abbey-church, where you can savour standard cooking.

ST-ARCONS-D'ALLIER – 43 Haute-Loire – 331 D3 – pop. 182 6 **C3**
– alt. 560 m – ✉ 43300

Paris 515 – Brioude 37 – Mende 87 – Le Puy-en-Velay 34 – St-Flour 60

Les Deux Abbesses
– ✆ 04 71 74 03 08 – www.lesdeuxabbesses.com – abbesses@relaischateaux.com – Fax 04 71 74 05 30 – Open 9 April-1st November
6 rm (½ board only) – 6 suites – ½ P € 230/330
Rest – *(dinner only) (number of covers limited, pre-book)* Menu € 65
◆ A delightful hotel with rooms spread around several houses in this magnificent hilltop village. Romantic atmosphere, well-kept garden, massage room and swimming pool. A seasonal menu is served every evening in the château. Classic cuisine given a contemporary or exotic twist.

ST-AUBIN-DE-LANQUAIS – 24 Dordogne – 329 E7 – pop. 265 4 **C1**
– alt. 110 m – ✉ 24560

Paris 548 – Bergerac 13 – Bordeaux 101 – Périgueux 56

L'Agrybella without rest
pl. de l'Église – ✆ 05 53 58 10 76 – www.agrybella.fr.st – legall.ma@wanadoo.fr – Closed January and February
5 rm – €85 €85
◆ This appealing 18C residence, next to the church, houses unusual themed rooms named: Coloniale, Rétro, Marine, Périgourdine and Surprise (suite devoted to the circus). A real success.

ST-AUBIN-DE-MÉDOC – 33 Gironde – 335 G5 – pop. 5 567 3 **B1**
– alt. 29 m – ✉ 33160

Paris 592 – Angoulème 132 – Bayonne 193 – Bordeaux 19 – Toulouse 261

Le Pavillon de St-Aubin
rte de Lacanau – ✆ 05 56 95 98 68 – www.thierry-arbeau.com – pavillon.saintaubin@wanadoo.fr – Fax 05 56 05 96 65 – Closed Sunday dinner
12 rm – €70/85 €75/85, € 10
Rest – *(closed 18-31 August, 2-7 January, Saturday lunch, Sunday dinner and Monday)* Menu (€ 26), € 37/62
◆ This colonial-inspired modern hotel is a nice stop on an itinerary through upper Médoc. Basic rooms, prettily coloured. Pleasant restaurant with sunny colours, fireplace, knick-knacks, carefully prepared tables. Traditional cuisine.

ST-AVÉ – 56 Morbihan – 308 O8 – see Vannes

ST-AVIT-DE-TARDES – 23 Creuse – pop. 194 – alt. 560 m – ✉ 23200 25 **C2**

Paris 415 – Limoges 151 – Guéret 55 – Ussel 67 – Aubusson 16

Le Moulin de Teiteix
– ✆ 05 55 67 34 18 – http://perso.wanadoo.fr/moulin-de-teiteix – yvette.louisbrun@wanadoo.fr
5 rm – €55 €75 – 1 suite **Table d'hôte** – Menu € 22 bi
◆ On the banks of a stream full of fish, this peaceful 19C mill extends a rustic welcome to guests. Spacious rooms decorated individually. The traditional cuisine served at the table d'hôte is made with regional produce.

ST-AVOLD – 57 Moselle – 307 L4 – pop. 16 900 – alt. 260 m – ✉ 57500 27 C1

Alsace-Lorraine

Paris 372 – Metz 46 – Saarbrücken 33 – Sarreguemines 29 – Strasbourg 127

Office de tourisme, 28, rue des Américains ✆ 03 87 91 30 19, Fax 03 87 92 98 02

de Faulquemont Faulquemont Avenue Jean Monnet, SW : 16 km on D 20, ✆ 03 87 81 30 52

Carved group★ in St-Nabor church.

Mine-image★ of Freyming-Merlebach Northeast: 10 km.

North : **2.5 km on D 633 (near A 4 junction) – ✉ 57500 St-Avold**

Novotel & rm, VISA AE

RN 33 – ✆ 03 87 92 25 93 – www.novotel.com – h0433@accor.com – Fax 03 87 92 02 47

61 rm – †€ 59/129 ††€ 59/129, ☕ € 14 **Rest** – Menu € 16/20 – Carte € 26/51

◆ This Novotel on the edge of the forest offers spacious and regularly redecorated bedrooms; the best and quietest ones overlook the swimming pool. Fitness course. A meal without surprises at this restaurant. Summer terrace overlooking the trees.

ST-AY – 45 Loiret – 318 H4 – pop. 3 016 – alt. 100 m – ✉ 45130 12 C2

Paris 140 – Orléans 13 – Blois 48 – Châteaudun 52 – Pithiviers 55 – Vendôme 63

Syndicat d'initiative, Mairie ✆ 02 38 88 44 44, Fax 02 38 88 82 14

La Grande Tour VISA AE

21 rte Nationale – ✆ 02 38 88 83 70 – www.lagrandetour.com – contact@lagrandetour.com – Fax 02 38 80 68 05 – Closed 10-27 August, Wednesday dinner, Sunday dinner and Monday

Rest – Menu (€ 17), € 25/66 – Carte € 49/58

◆ The Marquise de Pompadour used to stay in this former post-house which has retained all its character. Terrace opening onto a garden with a fountain. Contemporary-style cuisine.

ST-AYGULF – 83 Var – 340 P5 – ✉ 83370 French Riviera 41 C3

Paris 872 – Brignoles 69 – Draguignan 35 – Fréjus 6 – St-Raphaël 9 – Ste-Maxime 14

Office de tourisme, place de la Poste ✆ 04 94 81 22 09, Fax 04 94 81 23 04

Cap Riviera without rest VISA AE

3022 av. de la Corniche d'Azur – ✆ 04 94 81 21 42 – www.frejus-hotel.com – info@hotelcapriviera.com – Fax 04 94 81 72 39 – Open 16 March-14 October

20 rm – †€ 54/135 ††€ 54/135, ☕ € 8

◆ Family-run hotel on the coast overlooking the sea. Recent rooms decorated in a contemporary style; those overlooking the patio are quieter. Snacks served in season.

ST-BARD – 23 Creuse – 325 L5 – pop. 101 – alt. 640 m – ✉ 23260 25 D2

Paris 423 – Limoges 158 – Guéret 63 – Ussel 54 – Aubusson 23

Château de Chazelpaud

D 941 – ✆ 05 55 67 33 03 – http://membres.lycos.fr/chazelpaud/ – chazelpaud@aol.com – Fax 05 55 67 30 25 – Open April-September

5 rm ☕ – †€ 65/70 ††€ 70/85 **Table d'hôte** – Menu € 25

◆ A delightful neo-Renaissance folly with Italian mosaics, high ceilings and large personalised bedrooms with frescoes in the bathrooms. Panelled dining room embellished with a magnificent sculpted fireplace.

ST-BAZILE-DE-MEYSSAC – 19 Corrèze – 329 L5 – pop. 156 – alt. 230 m – ✉ 19500 25 **C3**

Paris 514 – Limoges 125 – Tulle 37 – Brive-la-Gaillarde 28 – Sarlat-la-Canéda 80

Le Manoir de la Brunie without rest

– ✆ 05 55 84 23 07 – *www.manoirlabrunie.com – appierre@wanadoo.fr*

3 rm – †€ 90/110 ††€ 90/110

◆ The garden of this 18C manor is perfect for relaxing. The lobby-sitting room with fireplace and breakfast room is adorned with period furniture. The bedrooms are in the same style.

ST-BEAUZEIL – 82 Tarn-et-Garonne – 337 B5 – pop. 122 – alt. 181 m – ✉ 82150 28 **B1**

Paris 631 – Agen 32 – Cahors 55 – Montauban 64 – Villeneuve-sur-Lot 23

Château de l'Hoste rm, rm, VISA AE

rte d'Agen, (D 656) – ✆ *05 63 95 25 61 – www.chateaudelhoste.com – mail@chateaudelhoste.com – Fax 05 63 95 25 50*

26 rm – †€ 75/185 ††€ 82/185, € 12 – ½ P € 83/120

Rest – *(closed Sunday dinner, Monday lunch and Thursday lunch mid October-end March)* Menu (€ 24), € 30 (weekdays)/55 – Carte approx. € 35

◆ Pretty 17C manor surrounded by a wooded park, in the heart of the Quercy countryside. Pleasant and comfortable non-smoking rooms. The dining room combines both a country and aristocratic atmosphere. Terrace in the park.

ST-BÉNIGNE – 01 Ain – 328 C2 – see Pont-de-Vaux

ST-BENOIT – 86 Vienne – 322 I5 – see Poitiers

ST-BENOÎT-SUR-LOIRE – 45 Loiret – 318 K5 – pop. 1 876 – alt. 126 m – ✉ 45730 Châteaux of the Loire 12 **C2**

Paris 166 – Bourges 92 – Châteauneuf-sur-Loire 10 – Gien 32 – Montargis 43 – Orléans 42

Office de tourisme, 44, rue Orléanaise ✆ 02 38 35 79 00, Fax 02 38 35 10 45

Basilica★★.

Germigny-des-Prés: church ★★ mosaic ★ Northwest: 6 km.

Grand St-Benoît VISA AE

7 pl. St-André – ✆ *02 38 35 11 92 – www.hoteldulabrador.fr – hoteldulabrador@wanadoo.fr – Fax 02 38 35 13 79 – Closed 1st-9 March, 17 August-1st September, 19 December-4 January, Saturday lunch, Sunday dinner and Monday*

Rest – *(number of covers limited, pre-book)* Menu (€ 18), € 26/51 – Carte € 50/56

◆ A dining room with exposed beams and contemporary furniture and a terrace on the pedestrian square of the village where the poet, Max Jacob is buried. Carefully prepared modern cuisine.

ST-BERNARD – 01 Ain – 328 B5 – pop. 1 282 – alt. 250 m – ✉ 01600 43 **E1**

Paris 443 – Lyon 29 – Bourg-en-Bresse 57 – Villeurbanne 37

Le Clos du Chêne rm, VISA AE

370 chemin du Carré – ✆ *04 74 00 45 39 – www.leclosduchene.com – contact@leclosduchene.com – Fax 04 74 08 03 51 – Closed 1st February-15 March*

5 rm – †€ 118/139 ††€ 124/145 – ½ P € 86/97

Table d'hôte – *(closed Saturday and Tuesday)* Menu € 35 bi

◆ On the banks of the Saône, this establishment has cosy, romantic rooms that combine the appeal of a country home with modern fixtures and fittings. The decor has an equestrian theme.

ST-BOIL – 71 Saône-et-Loire – 320 I10 – pop. 406 – alt. 240 m – ✉ 71390 8 C3

Paris 357 – Chalon-sur-Saône 23 – Cluny 27 – Montceau-les-Mines 37 – Mâcon 50

XX **Auberge du Cheval Blanc** with rm rm, rest, P VISA MC AE
– ✆ *03 85 44 03 16 – Fax 03 85 44 07 25*
– Closed 1st February-15 March and Wednesday
11 rm – †€ 75 ††€ 75, ☕ € 12 – ½ P € 80 **Rest** – *(dinner only)* Menu € 41
◆ Two buildings, separated by a road. A fine residence (1870) with refreshing rooms on one side, and a family inn, serving copious regional cooking, on the other.

ST-BÔMER-LES-FORGES – 61 Orne – 310 F3 – pop. 954 – alt. 250 m – ✉ 61700 32 B3

Paris 261 – Caen 88 – Alençon 73 – Flers 16 – Argentan 58

Château de la Maigraire without rest P
2 km east on D 260 – ✆ 02 33 38 09 52
– http://chateaudelamaigraire.monsite.orange.fr – la.maigraire@wanadoo.fr
– Fax 02 33 38 09 52
3 rm ☕ – †€ 90 ††€ 100
◆ The owners of this country château (1860) enjoy sharing their lovingly decorated sitting rooms and tasteful, theme-decorated guestrooms (Marie Antoinette, Blue Bird, etc.).

ST-BONNET-EN-CHAMPSAUR – 05 Hautes-Alpes – 334 E4 – pop. 1 644 – alt. 1 025 m – ✉ 05500 French Alps 41 C1

Paris 652 – Gap 16 – Grenoble 90 – La Mure 50

Office de tourisme, place Grenette ✆ 04 92 50 02 57, Fax 04 92 50 02 57

La Crémaillère P VISA MC
4 rte de la Motte – ✆ 04 92 50 00 60 – www.alacremaillere.com
– hautesalpescremaillere@orange.fr – Fax 04 92 50 01 57
23 rm – †€ 52/63 ††€ 52/63, ☕ € 8 – ½ P € 53/59
Rest – Menu (€ 13 bi), € 20 – Carte € 21/43
◆ Large chalet, surrounded by a garden, on the edge of the Écrins National Park. Mostly south facing rooms, with the Massif du Champsaur and Pic de l'Aiguille in the distance. Local dishes to be enjoyed in a large and bright dining room or on the terrace.

ST-BONNET-LE-CHÂTEAU – 42 Loire – 327 D7 – pop. 1 492 – alt. 870 m – ✉ 42380 Lyon - Rhone Valley 44 A2

Paris 484 – Ambert 48 – Montbrison 31 – Le Puy-en-Velay 66 – St-Étienne 34

Syndicat d'initiative, 7, place de la République ✆ 04 77 50 52 48, Fax 04 77 50 13 46

Collegiate church apse ≤★ - Chemin des Murailles★.

Le Béfranc P VISA MC
7 rte d'Augel – ✆ 04 77 50 54 54 – www.hotel-lebefranc.com – info@hotel-lebefranc.com – Closed 20-27 October, 2 February-2 March, Sunday dinner and Monday except July-August
17 rm – †€ 43 ††€ 50, ☕ € 7 – ½ P € 48/57
Rest – Menu (€ 13 bi), € 18/37 – Carte € 26/39
◆ On the outskirts of a locality known as "La perle du Forez", this former gendarmerie today houses a fine and...honest hotel! The rooms are well-kept. Choice of traditional dishes served at mealtimes.

XX **La Calèche** VISA MC
2 pl. Cdt Marey – ✆ 04 77 50 15 58 – www.restaurantlacaleche.fr
– caleche.restaurant@orange.fr – Fax 04 77 50 15 58 – Closed 2-16 January, 10-25 February, Monday dinner October-March, Sunday dinner, Tuesday dinner and Wednesday
Rest – Menu (€ 22), € 32/55
◆ Restaurant in a protected 17C building spread over three dining rooms with colourful decor. Contemporary cuisine to which the chef adds his personal touch.

ST-BONNET-LE-FROID – 43 Haute-Loire – 331 I3 – pop. 222 6 D3
– alt. 1 126 m – ✉ 43290

Paris 555 – Annonay 27 – Le Puy-en-Velay 58 – St-Étienne 51 – Valence 68 – Yssingeaux 31

Office de tourisme, place de la Mairie ✆ 04 71 65 64 41, Fax 04 71 65 64 41

Le Clos des Cimes

in the village – ✆ 04 71 59 93 72 – www.regismarcon.fr – contact@regismarcon.fr – Fax 04 71 59 93 40 – Closed 23 December-13 February, Monday from November to June and Tuesday

12 rm – €160/240 €160/240, ☕ €20

Rest ***Bistrot la Coulemelle*** – *✆ 04 71 65 63 62* – Menu (€21), €27/40

◆ Le Clos has personalised rooms, as elegant as they are cosy, overlooking the valley. Delicious regional dishes await you in the country chic decor of the Bistrot. See also Régis and Jacques Marcon's restaurant below.

Le Fort du Pré

rm, rest,

rte du Puy – ✆ 04 71 59 91 83 – www.le-fort-du-pre.fr – info@le-fort-du-pre.fr – Fax 04 71 59 91 84 – Closed 30 August-3 September, 18 December-4 March, Sunday dinner and Monday except July-August

34 rm – €52/90 €69/120, ☕ €10 – ½ P €65/90

Rest – Menu (€19), €25/65 – Carte €40/55

◆ Restored farmhouse much frequented for its leisure activities (covered pool, fitness centre, games room). Simple, colourful and practical rooms. Veranda-dining room which opens onto the countryside and well-prepared regional dishes.

Régis et Jacques Marcon with rm

rm, rest,

Larsiallas, in the upper reaches of the village – ✆ 04 71 59 93 72 – www.regismarcon.fr – contact@regismarcon.fr – Fax 04 71 59 93 40 – Open 12 April-19 December and closed Monday dinner from November to June, Tuesday and Wednesday

10 rm – €350 €350, ☕ €25

Rest – *(pre-book)* Menu €115, €135/190 – Carte €177/202

Spec. Cassoulet de homard aux lentilles vertes du Puy. Menu "champignons" (spring and autumn). Tarte soufflée à la châtaigne. **Wines** Saint-Joseph, Vin de Pays des Coteaux de l'Ardèche.

◆ This restaurant, wonderfully combining stone, wood and glass, overlooks the surrounding hills. An ideal setting for delicious cuisine inspired by local Auvergne produce (mushrooms). Elegant (non-smoking) rooms overlooking the countryside.

André Chatelard

pl. aux Champignons – ✆ 04 71 59 96 09 – www.restaurant-chatelard.com – restaurant-chatelard@wanadoo.fr – Fax 04 71 59 98 75 – Closed 5 January-5 March, Sunday dinner, Monday and Tuesday

Rest – Menu €19 (weekdays), €26/72 – Carte €31/56

◆ A solid country house, renowned for its delicious and well-presented regional cuisine. Neo-rustic dining rooms, lounge with fireplace and small garden with terrace. Tempting dessert trolley.

ST-BONNET-TRONÇAIS – 03 Allier – 326 D3 – pop. 789 – alt. 224 m 5 B1
– ✉ 03360 Auvergne

Paris 313 – Clermont-Ferrand 137 – Moulins 60 – Montluçon 44 – Saint-Amand-Montrond 26

in Tronçais 2 km southeast by D 250 – ✉ 03360

Le Tronçais

rest,

12 av. Nicolas Rambourg, on D 978 – ✆ 04 70 06 11 95 – www.letroncais.com – contact@letroncais.com – Fax 04 70 06 16 15 – Open 1st March-30 November and closed Sunday dinner, Tuesday lunch and Monday in March-April and October-November

12 rm – €48 €55, ☕ €8 – ½ P €53 **Rest** – Menu €24/37 – Carte €29/54

◆ With park, lake and the Tronçais forest nearby, this hotel offers a peaceful retreat. Guestrooms of varying size in the main building and annexe. Large, attractive dining room where the focus is on traditional dishes.

ST-BRANCHS – 37 Indre-et-Loire – 317 N5 – pop. 2 211 – alt. 97 m – ✉ 37320
11 **B2**

Paris 259 – Orléans 135 – Tours 24 – Joué-lès-Tours 19 – Saint-Cyr-sur-Loire 29

Le Diable des Plaisirs VISA MC

2 av. des Marronniers – ☎ 02 47 26 33 44 – www.restaurant-lediabledesplaisirs.com – lediabledesplaisirs@club-internet.fr – Closed Sunday dinner and Wednesday

Rest – Menu (€ 17), € 22 (weekdays)/36 – Carte € 42/57

◆ Enjoy the colourful, playful and nostalgic ambiance of this restaurant set in an old classroom outside the village centre. Friendly welcome; modern cuisine.

ST-BREVIN-LES-PINS – 44 Loire-Atlantique – 316 C4 – pop. 12 055 – alt. 9 m – Casino – ✉ 44250 Atlantic Coast
34 **A2**

Paris 442 – Nantes 57 – Saint-Herblain 62 – Saint-Nazaire 15

Office de tourisme, 10, rue de l'Église ☎ 02 40 27 24 32, Fax 02 40 39 10 34

Du Beryl VISA MC AE

55 bd de l'Océan – ☎ 02 28 53 20 00 – www.groupe-emeraude.com – resa.stbrevin@hotelduberyl.com – Fax 02 28 53 20 20

94 rm – €89/120 €89/120, € 11 – ½ P € 68/82

Rest – Menu (€ 16), € 19 (lunch), € 25/41 – Carte € 28/43

◆ Modern seafront hotel, built where the casino once stood. The spacious and well-soundproofed rooms are adorned with light wood furniture and good bedding. A minimalist, fashionable decor and an ocean view form the backdrop to classic dishes.

ST-BRICE-EN-COGLÈS – 35 Ille-et-Vilaine – 309 N4 – pop. 2 395 – alt. 105 m – ✉ 35460
10 **D2**

Paris 343 – Avranches 34 – Fougères 17 – Rennes 57 – St-Malo 65

Office de tourisme, 7, place Charles-de-Gaulle ☎ 02 99 97 85 44

Le Lion d'Or rm, rest, VISA MC AE

r. Chateaubriant – ☎ 02 99 98 61 44 – www.hotel-leliondor.fr – le-lion-dor3@wanadoo.fr – Fax 02 99 97 85 66

30 rm – €62/67 €62/67, € 8,50

Rest – *(closed Sunday dinner except from 1st May to 30 September)* Menu (€ 11), € 16 (weekdays)/30 – Carte € 20/43

◆ This old, granite fronted coach house is home to simple rooms that are however regularly refurbished. Comfortable restaurant with a veranda serving traditional and local dishes. Brasserie section at lunchtime.

ST-BRIEUC P – 22 Côtes-d'Armor – 309 F3 – pop. 46 700 – Built-up area 121 237 – alt. 78 m – ✉ 22000 Brittany
10 **C2**

Paris 451 – Brest 144 – Quimper 127 – Rennes 101 – St-Malo 71

St-Brieuc-Armor: ☎ 02 96 94 95 00, 10 km by ①.

Office de tourisme, 7, rue Saint-Gouéno ☎ 08 25 00 22 22, Fax 02 96 61 42 16

Club la Crinière Lamballe Manoir de la Ville Gourio, 15 km on the Lamballe road and D 786, ☎ 02 96 32 72 60

St-Étienne cathedral ★ - Tertre Aubé (mound) ≤★ BV.

Plan on following page

De Clisson without rest VISA MC AE

36 r. Gouët – ☎ 02 96 62 19 29 – www.hoteldeclisson.com – contact@hoteldeclisson.com – Fax 02 96 61 06 95 AY **e**

25 rm – €58/72 €72/120, € 8,50

◆ This white building, away from the town centre, extends a charming welcome. Rooms furnished in various styles; those with spa bathtubs are larger. Pretty garden.

ST-BRIEUC

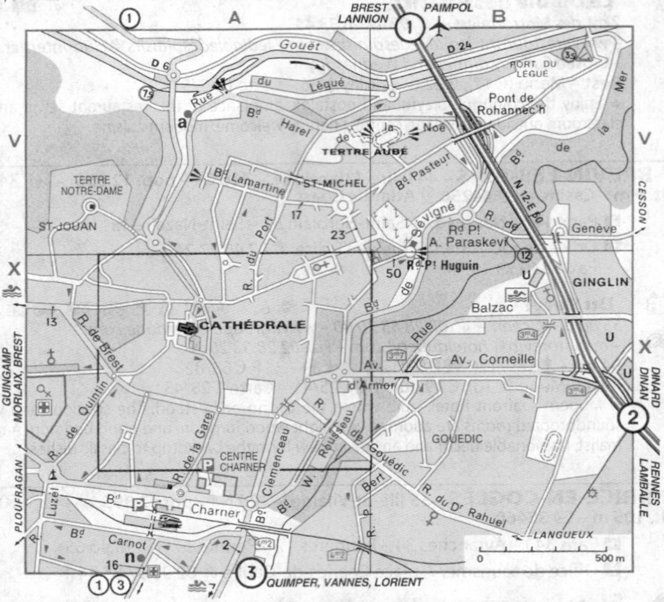

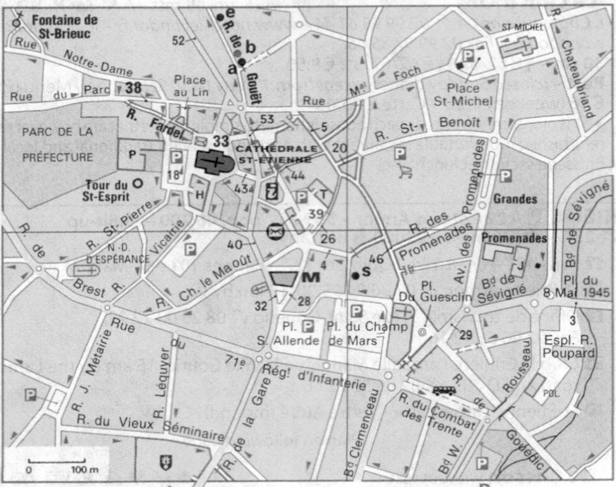

Ker Izel without rest VISA MC AE
20 r. Gouët – ✆ 02 96 33 46 29 – www.hotel-kerizel.com – bienvenue@hotel-kerizel.com – Fax 02 96 61 86 12 – Closed 25 October-11 November and 26 December-2 January AY **a**
22 rm – €41/47 €54/61, ☕ €8
◆ In the heart of the historic centre, it is believed to be the oldest hotel in St-Brieuc. Small guestrooms, under the eaves on the second floor, and well kept. Small garden and pool.

Champ de Mars without rest VISA MC
13 r. Gén. Leclerc – ✆ 02 96 33 60 99 – www.hotel-saint-brieuc.fr – hoteldemars@wanadoo.fr – Fax 02 96 33 60 05 – Closed Christmas holidays BZ **s**
21 rm – €46/52 €56/59, ☕ €8
◆ This town centre hotel is conveniently located near a large public car park. Practical, identically decorated guestrooms. A few individual touches personalise this simple hotel.

Aux Pesked (Mathieu Aumont) P VISA MC AE
59 r. Légué – ✆ 02 96 33 34 65 – www.auxpesked.com – contact@maisonphare.com – Fax 02 96 33 65 38 – Closed 27 April-4 May, 31 August-14 September, 2-18 January, Saturday lunch, Sunday dinner and Monday AV **a**
Rest – Menu (€ 19), € 23 (weekday lunch), € 38/63 – Carte approx. € 69
Spec. Saint-Jacques au garam massala et jus de betterave (mid-Oct.-end-April). Filet de Saint-Pierre, poudre d'orange et mousseux de coco de Paimpol au lard fumé. (end July-end Oct.). Tarte fine au chocolat et mandarine confite. (Oct. to April).
◆ A warm, contemporary dining room with the Vallée du Gouët as a backdrop. Fine, market-inspired modern menu with a focus on *pesked* (fish in Breton).

Amadeus VISA MC
22 r. Gouët – ✆ 02 96 33 92 44 – Fax 02 96 61 42 05 – Closed 2-20 August, 15-27 February, Monday lunch, Saturday lunch and Sunday AY **b**
Rest – Menu € 17 (weekday lunch), € 20/65 – Carte € 58/68
◆ This family-run restaurant has retained its antique charm (stonewalls, beautiful timbered ceiling) after a minimalist makeover. Up-to-the-minute menu.

Ô Saveurs VISA MC AE
10 r. J. Ferry – ✆ 02 96 94 05 34 – www.osaveurs-restaurant.com – lavigne@osaveurs-restaurant.com – Closed two weeks in August, in January, Saturday lunch, Tuesday dinner and Sunday AX **n**
Rest – Menu (€ 15), € 27/51 – Carte € 39/51
◆ Located behind the station, this restaurant boasts a stylish black and white interior suited to its seasonally inspired cuisine. Charming welcome and service.

Youpala Bistrot (Jean-Marie Baudic) VISA MC
5 r. Palasne de Champeaux, South-west via Boulevard Charner – ✆ 02 96 94 50 74 – www.youpala-bistrot.com – infos@youpala-bistrot.com – Fax 02 96 75 46 50 – Closed 1st-16 June, 31 August-16 September, 1st-19 January, Sunday dinner, Monday and Tuesday
Rest – *(number of covers limited, pre-book)* Menu (€ 19), € 24 (weekday lunch), € 49/59 bi
Spec. Produits de saison autour de la mer et des légumes.
◆ Rustic modern bistro with colourful decor. The creative chef prepares an unexpected menu based on market produce, honouring Breton seafood.

L'Air du Temps VISA MC
4 r. Gouët – ✆ 02 96 68 58 40 – www.airdutemps.fr – contact@airdutemps.fr – Closed 6-18 April, 1st-15 September, 1st-15 January, Sunday and Monday
Rest – Menu (€ 13), € 16 – Carte € 35/58
◆ Choose between the pleasant rustic-contemporary ground floor or the minimalist decor upstairs. Culinary repertory enhanced by sun-drenched herbs and spices.

in Sous-la-Tour 3 km northeast by Port Légué and D 24 BV – ✉ **22190 Plérin**

La Maison du Phare without rest VISA MC
93 r.de la Tour – ✆ 06 84 81 54 41 – www.maisonphare.com – contact@maisonphare.com – Closed 27 April-3 May and 1st-14 September
5 rm – €75/90 €90/110, ☕ €8
◆ This 19C house, clinging to the cliff and near the harbour, offers an attractive, stylish and modern interior. Guestrooms with personal touches (terrace, balcony, patio).

XX **La Vieille Tour** (Nicolas Adam)
75 r. de la Tour – ✆ 02 96 33 10 30 – www.la-vieille-tour.com – ugho777@aol.com – Fax 02 96 33 38 76 – Closed 16-31 August, 2-11 January, February school holidays, Saturday lunch, Sunday and Monday
Rest – *(number of covers limited, pre-book)* Menu € 27, € 38/77 – Carte € 72/110
Spec. "Mac'Adam" de foie gras chaud aux Saint-Jacques et cèpes (Sept. to Dec.). Turbot sauvage au thym et laurier. Tarte coulante au chocolat manjari et sorbet menthe poivrée.
◆ Very contemporary setting based around light and a variety of materials (glass, wenge wood), in perfect harmony with the fine seafood flavours at this country house facing the channel.

in Cesson 3 km east by Rue Genève BV – ✉ 22000

XXX **La Croix Blanche**
61 r. de Genève – ✆ 02 96 33 16 97 – Fax 02 96 62 03 50 – Closed 3-24 August, February school holidays, Sunday dinner and Monday
Rest – Menu € 22/88 – Carte € 50/60
◆ Restaurant in a residential area with several comfortable, individually decorated dining rooms overlooking the garden. Set menu with fish playing a starring role.

XX **Manoir le Quatre Saisons**
61 chemin Courses – ✆ 02 96 33 20 38 – www.manoirquatresaisons.fr – manoirlequatresaisons@hotmail.com – Fax 02 96 33 77 38 – Closed 2-17 March, 12-27 October, Sunday dinner and Monday
Rest – Menu (€ 18), € 25/69 – Carte approx. € 65
◆ Country inn, nestling in a small valley that leads to the sea. Traditional cuisine served in two spruce dining rooms with pretty Art Nouveau details.

ST-CALAIS – 72 Sarthe – 310 N7 – pop. 3 589 – alt. 155 m – ✉ 72120 — 35 D1
Châteaux of the Loire

Paris 188 – La Ferté-Bernard 33 – Le Mans 47 – Tours 66 – Vendôme 32
Office de tourisme, place de l'Hôtel de ville ✆ 02 43 35 82 95, Fax 02 43 35 15 13
Front★ of Notre-Dame church.

la Ferté-Bernard road 3 km North by D 1

Château de la Barre
– ✆ 02 43 35 00 17 – htttp://chateaudelabarre.com – info@chateaudelabarre.com – Fax 02 43 35 00 17 – Closed 10 January-10 February
5 rm – †€ 130 ††€ 150/450, ☕ € 15
Table d'hôte – *(closed Sunday dinner, Monday dinner, Wednesday dinner and Friday dinner)* Menu € 65 bi
◆ This fine château, surrounded by a 40-ha park, has belonged to the same family since the 15C. The refined rooms, with individual touches, boast authentic antique furniture. Fine cuisine served in a dining room adorned with a magnificent dresser.

ST-CANADET – 13 Bouches-du-Rhône – 340 H4 – ✉ 13610 — 40 B3

Paris 765 – Marseille 46 – Aix-en-Provence 18 – Avignon 93 – Toulon 100

Campagne le Bec without rest
– ✆ 04 42 61 97 05 – www.campagnelebec.com – campagnelebec@hotmail.com – Fax 04 42 61 97 05
4 rm ☕ – †€ 110/150 ††€ 110/150
◆ A remote country location for this family house (former sheepfold). Relaxed ambience. Baroque or personalised guestrooms. Meals by request. Pool.

ST-CANNAT – 13 Bouches-du-Rhône – 340 G4 – pop. 4 634 – alt. 216 m – ✉ 13760 **Provence** — 40 B3

Paris 731 – Aix-en-Provence 17 – Cavaillon 39 – Manosque 65 – Marseille 46
Syndicat d'initiative, avenue Pasteur ✆ 04 42 57 34 65, Fax 04 42 50 82 01

South 2 km by Éguilles road and secondary road – ✉ 13760 St-Cannat

Mas de Fauchon – rm, rm, VISA
1666 chemin de Berre – ☎ 04 42 50 61 77 – www.mas-de-fauchon.fr – contact@masdefauchon.fr – Fax 04 42 57 22 56
16 rm – †€ 125/240 ††€ 125/240, ☕ € 15 – 2 suites
Rest – Menu (€ 20), € 38/60 – Carte € 50/70
◆ Surrounded by a pine forest, this 17C sheepfold oozes with charm: extremely comfortable, plush Provençal inspired rooms with terraces. Peace and quiet guaranteed. Appealing rustic dining room serving traditional cuisine.

ST-CAPRAISE-DE-LALINDE – 24 Dordogne – 329 E6 – see Lalinde

ST-CAST-LE-GUILDO – 22 Côtes-d'Armor – 309 I3 – pop. 3 420 – alt. 52 m – ✉ 22380 Brittany

10 **C1**

Paris 427 – Avranches 91 – Dinan 32 – St-Brieuc 50 – St-Malo 31

Office de tourisme, place Charles-de-Gaulle ☎ 02 96 41 81 52, Fax 02 96 41 76 19

de Saint-Cast Pen-Guen Chemin du Golf, S : 4 km, ☎ 02 96 41 91 20

Pointe de St-Cast ≤★★ - Pointe de la Garde ≤★★ - Pointe de Bay ≤★ South: 5 km.

Ker Flore VISA
40 r. Rioust des Villes Audrains, in the village, near the church – ☎ 02 96 81 03 79 – ker.flore@wanadoo.fr – Closed 21 December-2 February, Sunday dinner, Tuesday dinner and Wednesday dinner except July-August and Monday
Rest – Menu (€ 13), € 20/26 – Carte € 24/38
◆ Restaurant in a country setting with brightly coloured walls and objets d'art. Traditional dishes inspired by the market.

ST-CÉRÉ – 46 Lot – 337 H2 – pop. 3 540 – alt. 152 m – ✉ 46400 Dordogne-Berry-Limousin

29 **C1**

Paris 531 – Aurillac 62 – Brive-la-Gaillarde 51 – Cahors 80 – Figeac 44 – Tulle 54

Office de tourisme, 13, avenue Francois de Maynard ☎ 05 65 38 11 85, Fax 05 65 38 38 71

de Montal Saint-Jean-LespinasseW : 3 km on D 807, ☎ 05 65 10 83 09

Site★ - Jean Lurçat tapestries ★ in the casino - Jean Lurçat workshop-museum ★ - Château de Montal★★ West: 3 km.

Cirque d'Autoire★: ≤★★ via Autoire (site★) West: 8 km.

Les Trois Soleils de Montal (Frédérik Bizat) ≤ rm, VISA
Gramat road, 2 km via D 673 – ☎ 05 65 10 16 16 – www.lestroissoleils.fr.st – lestroissoleils@wanadoo.fr – Fax 05 65 38 30 66 – Closed 1st December-31 January
26 rm – †€ 85/119 ††€ 95/119, ☕ € 14 – 4 suites – ½ P € 95/124
Rest – *(closed Sunday dinner, Tuesday lunch and Monday from October to March, Monday lunch April-September)* Menu € 32 (weekday lunch), € 42/78 – Carte € 62/78
Spec. Saint-Jacques rôties, petits gâteaux de topinambour et truffe (Oct. to April). Carré d'agneau, tomates, aubergines confites et jus d'herbes. Soufflé chaud à l'orange et chocolat. **Wines** Pécharmant, Cahors.
◆ This large house near the Château de Montal enjoys a peaceful location within a park in the middle of the country. Spacious, modern guestrooms. Delicious contemporary cuisine served in an elegant dining room embellished with 19C paintings.

De France VISA
av. François de Maynard, rte d'Aurillac – ☎ 05 65 38 02 16 – www.lefrance-hotel.com – lefrance-hotel@wanadoo.fr – Fax 05 65 38 02 98 – Closed 20 December-25 January and Friday dinner 15 October-8 February
18 rm – †€ 44/48 ††€ 50/54, ☕ € 8 – ½ P € 51/54
Rest – *(dinner only except Sunday)* Menu € 24/50 – Carte € 33/58
◆ Two minutes from the town centre, this hotel has simple, rustic rooms (choose one overlooking the garden). Comfortable, rustic-style restaurant with a shaded terrace. Traditional dishes with a focus on the cuisine of Quercy.

Villa Ric rm, VISA

Leyme road, 2.5 km on D 48 – 05 65 38 04 08 – www.villaric.com – hotel.jpric@libertysurf.fr – Fax 05 65 38 00 14 – Open 4 April-11 November
5 rm – €75 €75/105, €10 – ½ P €75/105
Rest – *(dinner only) (number of covers limited, pre-book) (residents only)*
Menu €36/40
◆ Establishment nestled against the side of a hill with cosy bedrooms decorated in pastel tones. Restful setting and a guesthouse ambience. Modern cuisine served in a bright dining room. Terrace with panoramic views of the valley.

ST-CERGUES – 74 Haute-Savoie – 328 K3 – pop. 2 513 – alt. 615 m – ✉ 74140 46 F1

Paris 547 – Annecy 54 – Annemasse 9 – Bonneville 25 – Genève 19 – Thonon-les-Bains 21

De France with rm VISA

1044 r. Allobroges – 04 50 43 50 32 – www.hoteldefrance74.com – hoteldefrance74@wanadoo.fr – Fax 04 50 94 66 45 – Closed 6-23 April, 21 August-7 September, Sunday dinner, Wednesday lunch and Monday
18 rm – €54/64 €57/67, €9 – ½ P €60/65
Rest – Menu (€13), €20 (weekdays)/52 – Carte €35/66
◆ Run by four generations of the same family, this hotel is rightly proud of its decor, welcome and cuisine. Elegant restaurant, pleasant garden-terrace and modern rooms.

ST-CERNIN-DE-LARCHE – 19 Corrèze – 329 J5 – pop. 558 – alt. 300 m – ✉ 19600 24 B3

Paris 492 – Limoges 104 – Tulle 48 – Brive-la-Gaillarde 17 – Sarlat-la-Canéda 54

Le Moulin de Laroche without rest

La Roche Ouest, 1,5 km par D 59 – 05 55 85 40 92 – Fax 05 55 85 34 66 – Open 15 March-15 November
6 rm – €57/75 €60/75
◆ Set in a park on a small hill, this farmhouse (1693) and its watermill meet all the conditions for a tranquil stay. Antique or period furniture.

ST-CHAMAS – 13 Bouches-du-Rhône – 340 F4 – pop. 7 268 – alt. 15 m – ✉ 13250 Provence 40 A3

Paris 738 – Arles 43 – Marseille 50 – Martigues 26 – Salon-de-Provence 16

Office de tourisme, Place Saint Pierre 04 90 50 90 54, Fax 04 90 50 90 10

Embarden without rest

rte de Grans – 06 84 95 57 16 – www.embarben.fr – claude.dunan@9online.fr
6 rm – €50/60 €80/100
◆ This manor house, set in grounds home to grazing sheep and a water feature, offers characterful, delightfully 1940s rooms. Cottage garden, orchard and pool. Country life at its best!

Le Rabelais VISA

8 r. A. Fabre, (town centre) – 04 90 50 84 40 – www.restaurant-le-rabelais.com – le.rabelais@wanadoo.fr – Fax 04 90 50 84 40 – Closed Sunday dinner, Wednesday dinner and Monday
Rest – Menu €26 (lunch), €39/60 – Carte €26/39
◆ This restaurant, near the former powder factory, is housed in the attractive 17C corn mill with a vaulted ceiling. Pleasant terrace decked with flowers. Inventive cuisine.

A good night's sleep without spending a fortune?
Look for a Bib Hotel.

ST-CHAMOND – 42 Loire – 327 G7 – pop. 35 500 – alt. 388 m 44 **B2**
– ✉ 42400 Lyon - Rhone Valley

Paris 505 – Feurs 55 – Lyon 50 – Montbrison 53 – St-Étienne 11 – Vienne 38

Office de tourisme, 23, avenue de la Libération ✆ 04 77 31 04 41, Fax 04 77 22 04 34

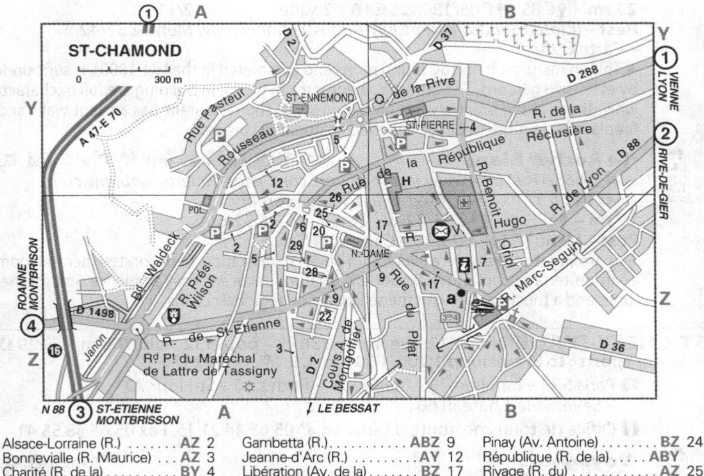

Alsace-Lorraine (R.)	AZ	2	Gambetta (R.)	ABZ	9	Pinay (Av. Antoine)	BZ	24
Bonnevialle (R. Maurice)	AZ	3	Jeanne-d'Arc (R.)	AY	12	République (R. de la)	ABY	
Charité (R. de la)	BY	4	Libération (Av. de la)	BZ	17	Rivage (R. du)	AZ	25
Delay (Bd François)	AYZ	5	Liberté (Pl. de la)	AZ	20	Sabotin (R.)	AZ	26
Dorian (Pl.)	AZ	6	Montgolfier (Crs A.-de)	AZ		Timbaud (R. P.)	AZ	28
Dugas-Montbel (R.)	BZ	7	Morel (Pl. Germain)	AZ	22	Trois Frères (R. des)	AZ	29

 **Les Ambassadeurs** rest, VISA

28 av. de la Libération – ✆ 04 77 22 85 80 – www.ambassadeurs-thomasson.com – lesambassadeurs42@orange.fr – Fax 04 77 31 96 95 BZ **a**

16 rm – €53/58 €53/60, €8

Rest – *(closed 8-11 May, 27 July-25 August, 1st-5 January, Saturday lunch, Sunday dinner and Saturday)* Menu €23 (weekday lunch), €32/50 – Carte €54/67

◆ Modern establishment now in the hands of an experienced young couple. The simple rooms are due to be refurbished soon. The chef concocts tasty, modern cuisine with inventive touches, while his wife oversees customer satisfaction in the dining room.

ST-CHARTIER – 36 Indre – 323 H7 – see La Châtre

ST-CHÉLY-D'APCHER – 48 Lozère – 330 H6 – pop. 4 468 22 **B1**
– alt. 1 000 m – ✉ 48200

Paris 540 – Aurillac 106 – Mende 45 – Le Puy-en-Velay 85 – Rodez 114 – St-Flour 36

Office de tourisme, place du 19 mars 1962 ✆ 04 66 31 03 67, Fax 04 66 31 30 30

Les Portes d'Apcher VISA

rte de St Flour, 1.5 km north on D 809 – ✆ 04 66 31 00 46 – lesportes48200@hotmail.fr – Fax 04 66 31 28 85 – Closed 22 December-17 January

16 rm – €55 €55, €8 – ½ P €51

Rest – *(Closed Friday dinner and Saturday lunch from 1st November to 1st April)* Menu (€16), €18/55 – Carte €30/60

◆ There are at least two good reasons for stopping at this simple and modern hotel: a nearby motorway access and a fine view of the Aubrac and Margeride. A rotunda dining room with timbered ceiling. Regional cuisine.

in La Garde 9 km north by D 809 – ✉ 48200 Albaret-Ste-Marie

Château d'Orfeuillette rm, VISA

at Exit 32 of the A 75, on the D809, towards La Garde – ✆ 04 66 42 65 65 – www.chateauorfeuillette.com – orfeuillette48@aol.com – Fax 04 66 42 65 66 – Closed 18-26 December

23 rm – €85 €85/180, €16 – 2 suites – ½ P €92/115

Rest – *(Closed Sunday except July-August) (dinner only)* Menu €32/42 – Carte €23/41

◆ This château, built on 16C foundations and completed in the late 1800s, is surrounded by extensive gardens. The attractive bedrooms in the main building are full of character, while those in the orangery are simpler in style. The restaurant has ancient walls and a fireplace but a modern decor, suited to its updated cuisine.

Le Rocher Blanc rest, VISA

– ✆ 04 66 31 90 09 – www.lerocherblanc.com – hotel@lerocherblanc.com – Fax 04 66 31 93 67 – Closed January and February

19 rm – €53/82 €53/82, €8,50 – ½ P €52/66

Rest – Menu (€14), €23/56 – Carte €21/50

◆ Charming stopover where everything points to relaxation. Redecorated themed rooms, a garden, terrace, pool and relaxation area. Natural decor and cosy ambience. Soft southern tones and a touch of daring in the seasonal and regional cuisine.

ST-CHÉLY-D'AUBRAC – 12 Aveyron – 338 J3 – pop. 532 – alt. 700 m – Winter sports : to Brameloup 1 200/1 390 m 9 – ✉ 12470 29 D1

Paris 589 – Espalion 20 – Mende 74 – Rodez 50 – St-Flour 70 – Sévérac-le-Château 60

Office de tourisme, route d'Espalion ✆ 05 65 44 21 15, Fax 05 65 48 55 41

Voyageurs rm, VISA

av. Aubrac – ✆ 05 65 44 27 05 – www.hotel-conserverie-aubrac.com – contact@hotel-conserverie-aubrac.com – Fax 05 65 44 21 67 – Open 11 April-26 June, 6 July-14 October and closed Wednesday except July-August

7 rm – €45 €45/50, €7 – ½ P €47/50

Rest – *(open 11 April-26 June, 6 July-30 September and closed Wednesday except for dinner in July-August)* Menu €17/24 – Carte €26/39

◆ Remote country villages can afford pleasant surprises! A small family guesthouse, with simple, pretty and well-kept bedrooms. Tasty homemade Aveyron cooking (tripoux, aligot, etc.). Cottage canning industry.

ST-CHRISTOL – 84 Vaucluse – 332 F9 – alt. 856 m – ✉ 84390 40 B2

Paris 737 – Carpentras 53 – Cavaillon 63 – Marseille 113

Le Lavandin VISA

Apt road, 3 km south-west – ✆ 04 90 75 09 18 – www.hotel-lavandin.com – le-lavandin2@wanadoo.fr – Fax 04 90 75 09 17 – Open 16 March-14 November

32 rm – €55/70 €65/85, €10 **Rest** – *(dinner only)* Menu €18/28

◆ On the Plateau d'Albion, set between fields of lavender and an oak tree forest, this hotel offers clean functional rooms. Some have a private terrace, while others can accommodate families. Restaurant offering both traditional and regional cuisine.

ST-CIERS-DE-CANESSE – 33 Gironde – 335 H4 – pop. 764 – alt. 40 m – ✉ 33710 3 B1

Paris 548 – Blaye 10 – Bordeaux 45 – Jonzac 54 – Libourne 41

Citadelle de Blaye★ Northwest: 8 km, **Pyrenees Aquitaine**

La Closerie des Vignes rm, VISA

village Arnauds, 2 km north by D 250 and D 135 – ✆ 05 57 64 81 90 – www.hotel-restaurant-gironde.com – la-closerie-des-vignes@wanadoo.fr – Fax 05 57 64 94 44 – Open 4 April-31 October

9 rm – €85/96 €85/96, €10 – ½ P €80/85

Rest – *(closed Tuesday) (dinner only)* Menu €35

◆ Modern house, surrounded by Blaye vineyards. Spacious and quiet bedrooms, equipped with simple, modern furniture. Panelled dining room with views over the vine stock and garden. Simple, traditional cuisine.

ST-CIRQ-LAPOPIE – 46 Lot – 337 G5 – pop. 215 – alt. 320 m – ✉ 46330 Dordogne-Berry-Limousin 29 **C1**

Paris 574 – Cahors 26 – Figeac 44 – Villefranche-de-Rouergue 37

Office de tourisme, place du Sombral ✆ 05 65 31 29 06, Fax 05 65 31 29 06

Site★★ - Remains of the former château ≤★★ - Le Bancourel ≤★ - Bouziès: chemin de halage du Lot(towpath)★ Northwest: 6,5 km.

Auberge du Sombral "Les Bonnes Choses" VISA AE

– ✆ 05 65 31 26 08 – www.lesombral.com – marionhardeveld@yahoo.fr – Fax 05 65 30 26 37 – Open 2 April-14 November and closed Thursday except 1st July-30 September

8 rm – €50/78 €72/78, €8

Rest – *(closed Thursday except 1st July-30 September and dinner except Friday and Saturday)* Menu (€16), €19 (lunch), €25/35 – Carte €25/37

◆ A family inn in the heart of a picturesque, medieval hillside village. Small simple rooms. The breakfast room sports a countrified decor of old tiles and a fireplace. Restaurant offering local cuisine.

Le Gourmet Quercynois A/C VISA

r. de la Peyrolerie – ✆ 05 65 31 21 20 – www.restaurant-legourmetquercynois.com – Fax 05 65 31 36 78 – Closed mid-November to mid-December and January

Rest – Menu (€15), €20/36 – Carte €32/51

◆ This cosy restaurant in a 17C house offers local cuisine focusing on duck. There is a small wine museum and a shop selling regional products.

in Tour-de-Faure 2 km east by D 8 – **pop. 353 – alt. 137 m** – ✉ **46330**

Les Gabarres without rest P VISA

– ✆ 05 65 30 24 57 – www.hotel-les-gabarres.com – hotel.les.gabarres@wanadoo.fr – Fax 05 65 30 25 85 – Open Easter-15 October

28 rm – €54 €54, €8

◆ Modern hotel located on the banks of the Lot, at the foot of a picturesque hilltop village. Practical rooms and a swimming pool.

Maison Redon without rest P

– ✆ 05 65 30 24 13 – www.maisonredon.com – patrice@maisonredon.com – Closed January and February

5 rm – €59/69 €64/74

◆ At the foot of a beautiful listed village, this 18C ivy-clad manor house welcomes guests into a warm interior. Recent rooms furnished with antiques. Pool.

ST-CLAIR – 83 Var – 340 N7 – see le Lavandou

ST-CLAR – 32 Gers – 336 G6 – pop. 969 – alt. 150 m – ✉ 32380 28 **B2**

Languedoc-Roussillon-Tarn Gorges

Paris 706 – Agen 49 – Auch 37 – Toulouse 79

Office de tourisme, 2, place de la Mairie ✆ 05 62 66 34 45, Fax 05 62 66 31 69

La Garlande without rest

pl. de la Mairie – ✆ 05 62 66 47 31 – www.lagarlande.com – contact@lagarlande.com – Fax 05 62 66 47 70 – Open 21March-2 November

3 rm – €49/61 €57/68

◆ This residence, opposite the 13C covered market, offers attractive and peaceful rooms (antique furniture, tapestries, floor tiles, parquet flooring, etc). Reading room and delightful flower-filled garden.

ST-CLAUD – 16 Charente – 324 M4 – pop. 1 094 – alt. 144 m – ✉ 16450 39 **C2**

Paris 437 – Poitiers 111 – Angoulême 44 – Saint-Junien 38 – Soyaux 46

Logis de la Broue P

r. Abbé-Rousselot – ✆ 05 45 71 43 96 – www.logisdelabroue.com – sylviane.casper@wanadoo.fr

3 rm – €80 €90 **Table d'hôte** – Menu €25 bi

◆ A very well restored former vineyard property with some parts dating back to the 15C. Elegant salon decorated with an original Aubusson tapestry. Charming old rooms. Parkland; pool. Locally inspired cuisine served in a rustic dining room.

ST-CLAUDE – **39 Jura** – **321** F8 – **pop. 12 303** – **alt. 450 m** 16 **B3**
– ✉ **39200** **Burgundy-Jura**

Paris 465 – Annecy 88 – Genève 60 – Lons-le-Saunier 59

Office de tourisme, 1, avenue de Belfort ☎ 03 84 45 34 24, Fax 03 84 41 02 72

de la Valserine Mijoux La Pellagrue, 24 km on the Genève road, ☎ 04 50 41 31 56

Site★★ - St-Pierre cathedral★: stalls★★ Z - Exhibittion of pipes, diamonds and fine stone Z **E**.

Georges du Flumen★ by ② - Morez Road ⩽★★ 7 km by ①.

ST-CLAUDE

Abbaye (Pl. de l') . . . . . . **Z** 2
Belfort (Av. de) . . . . **Y** 3
Christin (Pl.) . . . . **Y** 5
Gambetta (R.) . . . . **Z** 6
Janvier (R. A.) . . . . **Z** 7
Lamartine (R.) . . . . **Y** 9
Louis-XI (Pl.) . . . . **Z** 12
Marché (R. du) . . . . **Z** 20
Pré (R. du) . . . . **YZ**
République (Bd de la) . . **Y** 23
Rosset (R.) . . . . **Z** 24
Victor-Hugo (R.) . . . . . . **Y** 25
Voltaire (Pl.) . . . . **Y** 26
9-Avril-1944 (Pl. du) . . . . **Y** 27

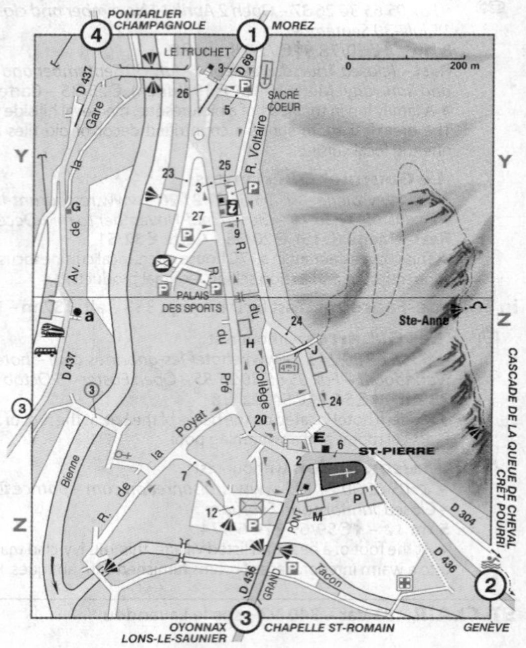

Jura rest, VISA AE
40 av. de la Gare – ☎ *03 84 45 24 04* – *www.jurahotel.com* – *info@jurahotel.com* – *Fax 03 84 45 58 10* Z **a**
35 rm – €48/58 €51/63, ☕ €8 – ½ P €48/58
Rest – *(closed 22 December-5 January and Sunday dinner)* Menu (€14), €18 (weekdays)/27 – Carte €26/37
◆ Practical, unpretentious hotel dominating the river opposite the station. Small rooms (half are for non smokers); some have a small terrace. The restaurant commands a fine view of the town and the River Bienne.

ST-CLÉMENT-DES-BALEINES – **17 Charente-Maritime** – **324** A2 – **see Île de Ré**

ST-CLÉMENT-LES-PLACES – **69 Rhône** – **327** F5 – **pop. 536** 44 **A1**
– **alt. 625 m** – ✉ **69930**

Paris 458 – Lyon 54 – Saint-Étienne 69 – Villeurbanne 63 – Lyon 03 56

L'Auberge de Saint-Clément ⩽ VISA
in the village – ☎ *04 74 26 03 83* – *Closed 15-30 August, 25-31 December, Wednesday and dinner except Friday and Saturday*
Rest – Menu €17 (weekday lunch)/23
◆ Situated in a village in the Monts du Lyonnais, this peaceful auberge boasts views of the surrounding countryside (attractive terrace). Delicious bistro-style cuisine made with local produce.

ST-CLOUD – 92 Hauts-de-Seine – 311 J2 – 101 14 – see Paris, Area

ST-CRÉPIN-ET-CARLUCET – 24 Dordogne – 329 I6 – pop. 463 – alt. 262 m – ✉ 24590 Dordogne-Berry-Limousin 4 D3

Paris 519 – Bordeaux 196 – Brive-la-Gaillarde 40 – Sarlat-la-Canéda 12

Les Charmes de Carlucet without rest
Carlucet – ✆ 05 53 31 22 60 – www.carlucet.com – lescharmes@carlucet.com – Fax 05 53 31 22 60 – Open 1st March-12 November
4 rm – €79/99 €79/119
◆ This perfectly restored and peaceful Périgord residence offers simple and spacious rooms. Two of them have dormer windows. Attentive welcome.

ST-CYPRIEN – 66 Pyrénées-Orientales – 344 J7 – pop. 8 573 – alt. 5 m – Casino – ✉ 66750 Languedoc-Roussillon-Tarn Gorges 22 B3

Paris 859 – Céret 31 – Perpignan 17 – Port-Vendres 20
Office de tourisme, quai A. Rimbaud ✆ 04 68 21 01 33, Fax 04 68 21 98 33
de Saint-Cyprien Saint-Cyprien-Plage Mas d'Huston, N : 1 km, ✆ 04 68 37 63 63

in St-Cyprien-Plage 3 km northeast by D 22 – ✉ 66750 St-Cyprien

Mas d'Huston
r. Jouy d'Arnaud, at the golf course – ✆ 04 68 37 63 63 – www.saintcyprien-golfresort.com – contact@saintcyprien-golfresort.com – Fax 04 68 37 64 64
50 rm – €129/200 €129/200, €14 – ½ P €108
Rest *Le Mas* – Menu €28 (lunch), €35/50 – Carte €58/76
Rest *L'Eagle* – brasserie *(Closed dinner except from Thursday to Saturday in summer)* Carte €20/39
◆ Henri Quinta has renovated this hotel and furnished the modern rooms (with balcony or terrace) in his trademark brightly coloured striped linen. Classic menu and a trendy decor at the Mas. Simple cuisine and designer setting at the Eagle.

in St-Cyprien-Sud 3 km – ✉ 66750 St-Cyprien

L'Île de la Lagune
bd de l'Almandin – ✆ 04 68 21 01 02 – www.hotel-ile-lagune.com – contact@hotel-ile-lagune.com – Fax 04 68 21 06 28
18 rm – €155/225 €155/225, €18 – 4 suites – ½ P €136/173
Rest *L'Almandin* – Menu €30 bi (weekday lunch), €49/105 – Carte €75/87
Spec. Marbré de foie gras de canard aux artichauts et jambon jabugo. Suquet de baudroie et gambas, pommes de terre dans un bouillon de poisson. Chocolat mangaro, ganache et dacquoise, mousse chocolat noir. **Wines** Collioure blanc, Côtes du Roussillon.
◆ Recently constructed, regional style building, on a small marina island. Functional rooms with balconies. Free launch to the beach in season. Tasty seasonal cuisine, based on reinterpreted local specialities. Terrace veranda.

La Lagune
28 av. Armand Lanoux – ✆ 04 68 21 24 24 – www.hotel-lalagune.com – contact@hotel-lalagune.com – Fax 04 68 37 00 00 – Open 3 April-10 November
49 rm – €87/146 €87/178, €12 – ½ P €79/109
Rest – Menu €26/33 bi
◆ A hotel on the beach, part of a residential complex that was designed for a "club" clientèle. Practical rooms overlooking the pool or the lagoon. Billiards room. Musical events and meals served on the terrace in summer. Simple cuisine.

ST-CYR-AU-MONT-D'OR – 69 Rhône – 327 I5 – see Lyon

ST-CYR-EN-TALMONDAIS – 85 Vendée – 316 H9 – pop. 338 – alt. 31 m – ✉ 85540 34 B3

Paris 444 – La Rochelle 57 – Luçon 14 – La Roche-sur-Yon 30 – Les Sables-d'Olonne 38
Syndicat d'initiative, Mairie ✆ 02 51 30 82 82, Fax 02 51 30 88 29

Auberge de la Court d'Aron
1 allée des Tilleuls – ✆ 02 51 30 81 80 – www.court-d-aron.com – d.orizet@wanadoo.fr – Closed 24 November-10 December, 19 January-4 February, Monday in July-August, Sunday dinner and Wednesday in low season
Rest – Menu (€ 14), € 23/43 – Carte € 27/43
◆ This auberge occupies the stables of the château of the same name. Welcoming rustic interior, covered terrace, and garden.

ST-CYR-SUR-MER – 83 Var – 340 J6 – pop. 11 562 – alt. 10 m – ✉ 83270 French Riviera

40 **B3**

Paris 810 – Bandol 8 – Le Beausset 10 – Brignoles 70 – Marseille 40 – Toulon 23

Office de tourisme, place de l'Appel du 18 Juin, les Lecques ✆ 04 94 26 73 73, Fax 04 94 26 73 74

de Frégate Route de Bandol, S : 3 km on D 559, ✆ 04 94 29 38 00

Les Lecques – ✉ 83270 St-Cyr-sur-Mer

Grand Hôtel des Lecques
24 av. du Port – ✆ 04 94 26 23 01 – www.lecques-hotel.com – info@lecques-hotel.com – Fax 04 94 26 10 22
60 rm – †€ 61/195 ††€ 68/216, ☕ € 14
Rest – Menu € 35 – Carte € 35/80
◆ An elegant Belle Époque abode in the middle of flower-decked grounds. Rooms with bright decor on the upper floors; those at the front are preferable. Enjoy traditional cuisine in the winter garden or on the attractive terrace.

Bandol road 4 km by D 559 – ✉ 83270 St-Cyr-sur-Mer

Dolce Frégate rm,
– ✆ 04 94 29 39 39 – www.dolcefregate.com – reservation-fregate@dolce.com – Fax 04 94 29 39 40
100 rm – †€ 289/339 ††€ 289/399, ☕ € 22 – 33 suites
Rest *Le Mas des Vignes* – *✆ 04 94 29 39 47 (closed Sunday and Monday) (dinner only)* Menu € 55/90 – Carte € 60/86
Rest *Restanque* – *✆ 04 94 29 38 18 (lunch only)* Menu € 31 – Carte approx. € 28
◆ Built on a quiet hillside, this regional-style, contemporary structure commands magnificent sea views. Provençal-style rooms, leisure and seminar facilities. Warm, cosy decor and updated traditional menu at the Mas de Vignes. Relaxed dining at the Restanque. Delightful terrace.

ST-DALMAS-DE-TENDE – 06 Alpes-Maritimes – 341 G3 – see Tende

ST-DALMAS-VALDEBLORE – 06 Alpes-Maritimes – 341 E3 – see Valdeblore

ST-DENIS-DE-L'HOTEL – 45 Loiret – 318 J4 – pop. 2 730 – alt. 115 m – ✉ 45550

12 **C2**

Paris 153 – Orléans 19 – Gien 48 – Montargis 52 – Pithiviers 37

Le Dauphin without rest
3 av. des Fontaines – ✆ 02 38 46 29 29 – www.hotel-le-dauphin.fr – hotel.le.dauphin@wanadoo.fr – Fax 02 38 59 07 63 – Closed 2 weeks in August and 26 December-3 January
21 rm – †€ 47 ††€ 54, ☕ € 7
◆ On the road to the Loire castles, this pleasant family hotel offers welcoming and well-kept rooms equipped with practical furniture.

ST-DENIS-LE-FERMENT – 27 Eure – 304 K6 – see Gisors

ST-DÉSIRAT – 07 Ardèche – 331 K2 – pop. 719 – alt. 130 m – ✉ 07340 43 E2

Paris 533 – Lyon 71 – Privas 83 – Saint-Étienne 53 – Valence 44

La Désirade

rte de la syrah – ✆ 04 75 34 21 88 – www.desirade-fr.com – contact@desirade-fr.com – Closed December and January

6 rm – €40 €59 – ½ P €45

Table d'hôte – *(closed Sunday and Wednesday) (pre-book)* Menu €19

◆ This hotel, a stone's throw from the Musée de l'Alambic, occupies a family house dating from 1860. Stylish bedrooms, each named after a flower. A well-maintained hotel with a friendly welcome and attractive, shaded garden-terrace. The cuisine prepared by the owner of this property has a strong focus on local products.

ST-DIDIER – 35 Ille-et-Vilaine – 309 N6 – see Châteaubourg

ST-DIDIER – 84 Vaucluse – 332 D9 – see Carpentras

ST-DIDIER-DE-LA-TOUR – 38 Isère – 333 F4 – see La Tour-du-Pin

ST-DIDIER-EN-VELAY – 43 Haute-Loire – 331 H2 – pop. 3 302 – alt. 830 m – ✉ 43140 6 D3

Paris 538 – Le Puy-en-Velay 55 – St-Étienne 25 – St-Agrève 45

Office de tourisme, 11, rue de l'ancien Hôtel de Ville ✆ 04 71 66 25 72, Fax 04 71 61 25 83

Auberge du Velay

Grand'place – ✆ 04 71 61 01 54 – fabrice.lafite@wanadoo.fr – Fax 04 71 61 15 80 – Closed 1 week in September, 1 week in January, Tuesday dinner, Thursday dinner and Wednesday in winter, Sunday dinner and Monday

Rest – Menu €15 (weekdays)/46 – Carte €50/75

◆ This appealing inn, where local dishes have been served for three centuries, was taken over in 2005 by a creative young chef. Unusual table settings (pewter).

ST-DIÉ-DES-VOSGES – 88 Vosges – 314 J3 – pop. 21 800 – alt. 350 m – ✉ 88100 Alsace-Lorraine 27 C3

Paris 397 – Colmar 53 – Épinal 53 – Mulhouse 108 – Strasbourg 97

Office de tourisme, 8, quai du Mal de L. de Tassigny ✆ 03 29 42 22 22, Fax 03 29 42 22 23

St-Dié cathedral ★ - Gothic cloister★.

Plan on following page

Ibis

rm, rm

5 quai Jeanne d'Arc – ✆ 03 29 42 24 22 – www.ibishotel.com – h1102@accor.com – Fax 03 29 55 49 15 B a

58 rm – €59/85 €59/85, €8 **Rest** – *(dinner only)* Carte approx. €21

◆ Chain hotel on the banks of the Meurthe whose rooms, although a little cramped, have been refurbished in a contemporary style. Opt for one overlooking the river. Restaurant with bistro atmosphere (wood decor and beer bar look); concise, improvised menu.

Voyageurs

22 r. Hellieule – ✆ 03 29 56 21 56 – lesvoyageurs88@wanadoo.fr – Closed Sunday dinner and Monday A u

Rest – Menu (€17), €21/32 – Carte €34/48

◆ In a bright, yellow coloured decor, this establishment serves traditional cuisine based on market fresh produce. Homemade desserts. Concise list of mainly Alsace wines.

La Table de Manaïs with rm

64 r. d'Alsace – ✆ 03 29 56 11 71 – Fax 03 29 56 45 06 – Closed Sunday

10 rm – €45 €47/50, €8,50 B v

Rest – Menu (€16,50), €22/35 – Carte €32/49

◆ This restaurant is located on a shopping street. Relaxed decor, light colours and tasty, classic menu that varies with the seasons. Small rooms.

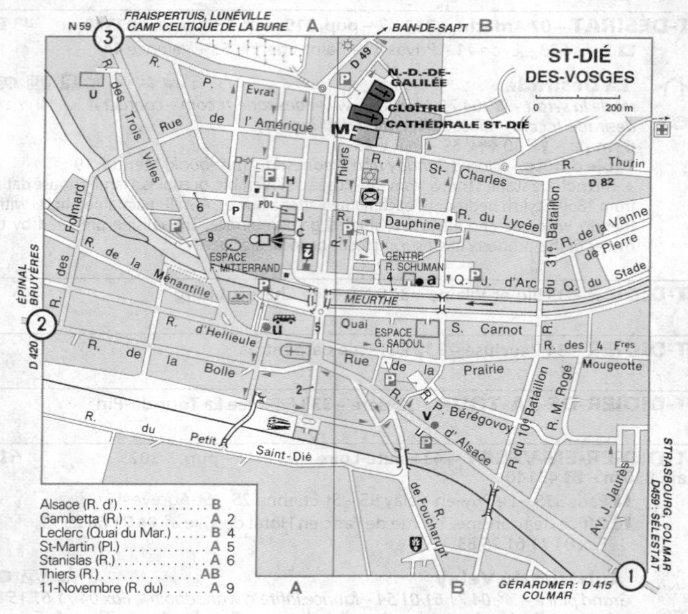

ST-DISDIER – 05 Hautes-Alpes – 334 D4 – pop. 134 – alt. 1 024 m 40 B1
– ✉ 05250 ▌French Alps

▶ Paris 643 – Gap 46 – Grenoble 81 – La Mure 41

◉ La Souloise defile ★ N.

La Neyrette

– ✆ 04 92 58 81 17 – www.la-neyrette.com – info@la-neyrette.com
– Fax 04 92 58 89 95 – Open 2 February-14 April and 1st May-10 October

12 rm – 🛉€ 58 🛉🛉€ 70/83, ☕ € 8,50 – ½ P € 63/70

Rest – *(dinner only)* Menu € 23/35 – Carte € 28/42

◆ Lovely little inn in a garden, with an ornamental pool for fetching one's trout for dinner! Rooms decorated with a mountain flowers theme. The rustic dining room is housed in a converted mill. Generous regional cuisine.

ST-DIZIER – 52 Haute-Marne – 313 J2 – pop. 26 700 – alt. 147 m 14 C2
– ✉ 52100 ▌Northern France and the Paris Region

▶ Paris 212 – Bar-le-Duc 26 – Chaumont 74 – Nancy 99 – Troyes 86

ℹ Office de tourisme, 4, avenue de Belle-Forêt-sur-Marne ✆ 03 25 05 31 84, Fax 03 25 06 95 51

Plan on next page

La Gentilhommière

29 r. J. Jaurès – ✆ 03 25 56 32 97 – restaurantlagentilhommiere@orange.fr
– Fax 03 25 06 32 66 – Closed 1st-24 August, 1st-18 March, Saturday lunch, Sunday dinner and Monday A u

Rest – Menu (€ 18), € 24/32 – Carte € 40/60

◆ Establishment situated behind a low boxwood hedge with warm, elegant dining room in beige and yellow tones. Bright veranda. Well-prepared market cuisine.

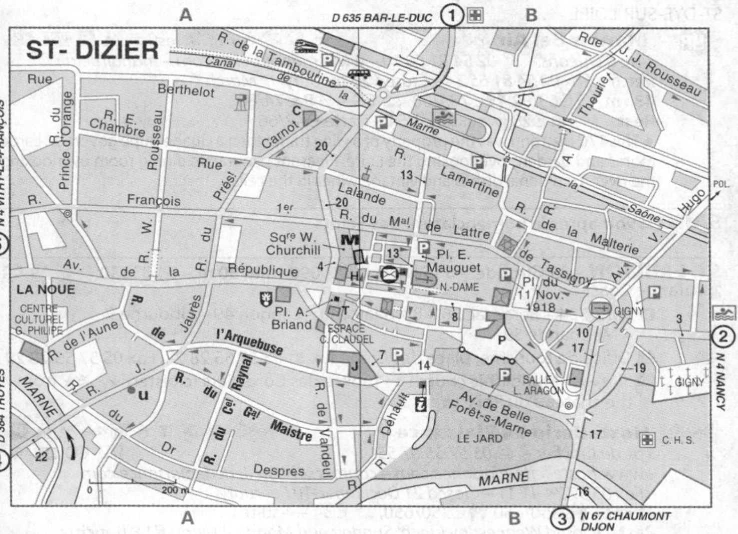

ST-DIZIER

Alsace-Lorraine (Av. d')	B	3	
Cartier (Av. M.)	A	4	
Commune de Paris (R. de la)	AB	7	
Gambetta (R.)	B	8	
Gaulle (Pl. du Gén.-de)	B	10	
Giros (R. E.)	B	13	
Liberté (Pl. de la)	B	14	
Pasteur (Av.)	B	17	
Paul Bert (R.)	B	16	
République (Av. de la)	A		
Tanneurs (R. des)	B	19	
Verdun (Av. de)	A	20	
Vergy (R. de)	A	22	

Look out for red symbols, indicating particularly pleasant establishments.

ST-DONAT-SUR-L'HERBASSE – 26 Drôme – 332 C3 – pop. 3 497 – alt. 202 m – ✉ 26260 Lyon - Rhone Valley — 43 E2

Paris 545 – Grenoble 92 – Hauterives 20 – Romans-sur-Isère 13 – Valence 27

Office de tourisme, 32, avenue Georges Bert ✆ 04 75 45 15 32, Fax 04 75 45 20 42

XXX **Chartron** with rm — A/C VISA MC

av. Gambetta – ✆ 04 75 45 11 82 – www.restaurant-chartron.com – info@restaurant-chartron.com – Fax 04 75 45 01 36 – Closed 1st-17 September, 2-8 January, Wednesday except dinner in July-August and Tuesday

8 rm – †€ 60/80 ††€ 80/120, ☕ € 10 **Rest** – Menu € 30/85

◆ Big stone building, enlarged by a glass rotunda. Large modern dining room, serving up-to-date cuisine and dishes with truffles, in season. Rooms with modern decor.

X **La Mousse de Brochet** — A/C VISA MC

pl. de la Marne – ✆ 04 75 45 10 47 – Fax 04 75 45 10 47 – Closed 25 June-16 July, 23 January-13 February, dinner during the week from September to May, Sunday dinner and Monday

Rest – Menu € 18 bi/56

◆ After admiring the collegiate's organ, take a break in this former café, with a slightly bijou-type decor, to enjoy a Mousse de Brochet, the speciality of the house.

ST-DOULCHARD – 18 Cher – 323 K4 – see Bourges

ST-DYÉ-SUR-LOIRE – 41 Loir-et-Cher – 318 F6 – pop. 1 063 – alt. 96 m – ✉ 41500 Châteaux of the Loire — 11 B2

Paris 173 – Beaugency 21 – Blois 17 – Orléans 52 – Romorantin-Lanthenay 45

Office de tourisme, 73, rue Nationale ✆ 02 54 81 65 45, Fax 02 54 81 65 45

Manoir Bel Air rm, rest,
1 rte d'Orléans – ✆ 02 54 81 60 10 – www.manoirbelair.com – manoirbelair@free.fr – Fax 02 54 81 65 34 – Closed 20 January-1st March
43 rm – €68/82 €78/200, €9 – ½ P €74/80
Rest – Menu €28 (weekdays)/54 – Carte €42/66
◆ This 17C mansion was the property of a wine trader then a Guadeloupe governor. Large rooms and gardens overlooking the Loire. Pleasant panoramic dining room overlooking the river. Traditional dishes and vintage wines in the cellar.

SAINTE voir après la nomenclature des Saints

ST-ÉMILION – 33 Gironde – 335 K5 – pop. 2 090 – alt. 30 m – ✉ 33330 4 C1

Atlantic Coast

Paris 584 – Bergerac 58 – Bordeaux 40 – Langon 49 – Libourne 9 – Marmande 59

Office de tourisme, place des Créneaux ✆ 05 57 55 28 28, Fax 05 57 55 28 29

Site★★ - Monolithic church★ - Cloître des Cordeliers (cloister) ★ - ★ from the château du Roi tower.

Hostellerie de Plaisance
5 pl. du Clocher – ✆ 05 57 55 07 55 – www.hostellerie-plaisance.com – contact@hostelleriedeplaisance.com – Fax 05 57 74 41 11 – Closed 21 December-10 February
21 rm – €350/650 €350/650, €34 – 4 suites
Rest – *(closed Wednesday lunch, Sunday and Monday)* Menu €58 (lunch), €110/130 – Carte €105/165
Spec. Foie gras de canard poêlé et champignons. Agneau, piquillos et pomelos. Fraises mara des bois et gelée à la citronnelle. **Wines** Saint-Emilion.
◆ In the heart of the city, find luxury and tranquillity in these two 14C pale stone houses, linked by their gardens. They are home to comfortable, personalised rooms. Fine, flavourful cuisine and an impressive Saint-Emilion wine list at the restaurant.

Palais Cardinal rm,
pl. 11-novembre-1918 – ✆ 05 57 24 72 39 – www.palais-cardinal.com – hotel@palais-cardinal.com – Fax 05 57 74 47 54 – Open April-November
27 rm – €69/148 €84/212, €15 – ½ P €80/144
Rest – *(closed Tuesday lunch, Thursday lunch and Wednesday)* Menu €27/42
◆ The hotel occupies part of the residence once occupied by a cardinal in the 14C. The rooms in the recent wing are large and refined. Pretty little garden and pleasant swimming pool. A stylishly furnished restaurant serving traditional dishes and Saint-Emilion from the family estate.

Au Logis des Remparts without rest
18 r. Guadet – ✆ 05 57 24 70 43 – www.logisdesremparts.com – contact@logisdesremparts.com – Fax 05 57 74 47 44 – Closed 15 December-31 January
17 rm – €78/160 €78/185, €14 – 3 suites
◆ Two houses (14C and 17C) with modern rooms furnished with a personal touch. Breakfast veranda, terrace, and an attractive pool in the garden on the edge of the vineyards.

Auberge de la Commanderie without rest
r. des Cordeliers – ✆ 05 57 24 70 19 – www.aubergedelacommanderie.com – contact@aubergedelacommanderie.com – Fax 05 57 74 44 53 – Closed 20 December-20 February
17 rm – €75 €75/140, €11
◆ This former 17C commandery is now home to a hotel with compact yet smart bedrooms refurbished in contemporary style. Those in the annexe are larger and more suited to families.

Le Tertre
5 r. Tertre de la Tente – ✆ 05 57 74 46 33 – Fax 05 57 74 49 87 – Closed 12 November-4 February, Thursday in February-March and Wednesday
Rest – Menu (€20), €29/65 – Carte €55/92
◆ Next to the church, this countrified restaurant features a shellfish tank at the back, and a little wine cellar carved into the rock. Traditional fare and Bordeaux wines.

Clos du Roy
– 05 57 74 41 55 – www.leclosduroy.fr – contact@leclosduroy.fr
– Fax 05 56 72 88 99
Rest – Menu (€ 28), € 38/80 – Carte € 60/75
◆ A pale stone establishment off the tourist circuit. Dining rooms combining the rustic-styled and the contemporary. Carefully done up-to-date cuisine.

Libourne road 4 km by D 243 – ✉ **33330 St-Émilion**

Château Grand Barrail rm, rest,
– 05 57 55 37 00 – www.grand-barrail.com
– hotelgrandbarrail@hotels-emeraude.com – Fax 05 57 55 37 49
37 rm – € 290/330 € 290/330, € 24 – 5 suites
Rest – Menu (€ 30), € 50/65 – Carte € 72/102
◆ A tastefully restored 19C château in grounds (with a lake) hidden amid the vines. Refined bedrooms, beautiful spa, fitness centre and swimming pool for the summer months. One of the three magnificent dining rooms boasts a Moorish decor. Modern cuisine and a splendid wine list.

ST-ÉTIENNE P – 42 Loire – **327** F7 – **pop. 175 500 – Built-up area 291 960 – alt. 520 m** – ✉ **42000** **Lyon - Rhone Valley** 44 **A2**

Paris 517 – Clermont-Ferrand 147 – Grenoble 154 – Lyon 61 – Valence 122

St-Étienne-Bouthéon: 04 77 55 71 71, by ⑤: 15 km.

Office de tourisme, 16, avenue de la Libération 08 92 70 05 42, Fax 04 77 49 39 03

de St-Étienne 62 rue Saint Simon, 18 km on the Annonay raod and D 501, 04 77 32 14 63

Old St-Etienne★ - Musée d'Art moderne★★ T **M²** - Puits Couriot (coal mine), musée de la mine★ AY - Musée d'Art et d'Industrie★★ - Site of the "Manufacture des Armes et Cycles de St-Étienne": planetarium★.

Plans on following pages

Mercure Parc de l'Europe
r. Wuppertal, south - east of plan, via cours Fauriel – 04 77 42 81 81
– www.mercure.com – h1252@accor.com – Fax 04 77 42 81 89 V **a**
120 rm – € 59/149 € 69/159, € 17
Rest ***La Ribandière*** – *(Closed 1st-24 August, 24 December-4 January)*
Menu (€ 22 bi) – Carte € 30/47
◆ This hotel has been given a new lease of life: decor based on a theatrical theme, individually furnished rooms, new bathrooms and pleasant lounge and bar. This contemporary restaurant shows off produce from the Forez region and Côtes-du-Rhône wines.

Du Golf rm,
67 r. St Simon face au golf par r. Revollier T – 04 77 41 41 00
– www.hoteldugolf42.com – resa@hoteldugolf42.com – Fax 04 77 38 28 16
48 rm – € 110/126 € 127/147, € 14 – 5 suites
Rest – Menu (€ 17), € 21/36 – Carte € 32/39
◆ Fully refurbished hotel in a modern style, mixing design and functionality. Well located on a hill facing the town golf course and the Forez plain. Poolside terrace. Modern rotunda-style dining room overlooking the golf course. Traditional cuisine.

Du Midi without rest
19 bd. Pasteur – 04 77 57 32 55 – www.hotelmidi.fr
– contact@hotelmidi.fr – Fax 04 77 57 28 00 – Closed 26 July-24 August and 27 December-5 January V **e**
33 rm – € 62/79 € 75/100, € 10
◆ Two buildings linked by a pleasant lounge adorned with an unusual fireplace. Smallish but practical, soundproofed and well-kept rooms.

XXX **Nouvelle** (Stéphane Laurier) AC VISA MC AE
30 r. St-Jean – ✆ 04 77 32 32 60 – www.nouvelle.fr – Fax 04 77 41 77 00 – Closed 10-24 August, Sunday and Monday BY **v**
Rest – Menu € 30, € 37/95
Spec. Foie gras de canard poêlé au concombre et melon (spring-summer). Endives au jambon, foie gras et truffe noire (winter). Figues rôties au balsamique, sorbet romarin. **Wines** Côtes du Forez.
◆ Modern furniture, a grey and brown colour scheme, a conservatory and old paintings - a setting that is both minimalist and relaxing; inventive cuisine.

XXX **André Barcet** AC VISA MC AE
19bis cours V. Hugo – ✆ 04 77 32 43 63 – www.restaurantandrebarcet.com – restaurantbarcet@wanadoo.fr – Fax 04 77 32 23 93 – Closed 15 July-9 August, Sunday dinner and Wednesday BZ **u**
Rest – Menu (€ 22), € 36/68 – Carte € 58/74
◆ Elegant facade near the covered market. A comfortable English-style lounge precedes a refined dining room, enhanced by flowers, where one can enjoy a classic menu.

XXX **A la Table des Lys** VISA MC AE
5 cours Fauriel – ✆ 04 77 25 48 55 – Fax 04 77 37 62 75 – Closed 1st-23 August, Saturday and Sunday CZ **q**
Rest – Menu € 25 (weekday lunch), € 34/78 – Carte € 50/89
◆ The new chef-owner thought of everything when he took over this restaurant: small rooms refurbished in a simple, contemporary style, and light, modern, tasty cuisine.

XX **Evohé** VISA MC AE
10 pl. Villeboeuf – ✆ 04 77 32 70 22 – Fax 04 77 32 91 52 – Closed 20-25 May, 31 July-26 August, Monday dinner, Saturday lunch and Sunday CZ **n**
Rest – Menu € 20 bi/39 – Carte € 35/42
◆ Restaurant overlooking a garden and near the Cultural Centre. The coloured walls are hung with paintings for sale, and the dining area has an intimate feel.

XX **Régency** AC VISA MC AE
17 bd J. Janin – ✆ 04 77 74 27 06 – alexis.bessette@laposte.net – Fax 04 77 74 98 24 – Closed August, 1st-9 January, Saturday and Sunday BX **r**
Rest – Menu (€ 23), € 32/49 – Carte € 45/55
◆ Cheery facade, colourful dining room in sharp yellow and orange tones, beautiful red-brick vaulting. The market and the season influence the menu.

X **Corne d'Aurochs** VISA MC
18 r. Michel Servet – ✆ 04 77 32 27 27 – www.cornedaurochs.fr – bruno.billamboz@wanadoo.fr – Fax 04 77 32 72 56 – Closed 1st-12 May, 19 July-31 August, Saturday lunch, Monday and Sunday BY **a**
Rest – Menu (€ 15 bi), € 18 (weekday lunch), € 21/40 – Carte € 26/45
◆ This wood-fronted bistro has a unique interior with a collection of pastrymaking whisks and book-festival lithographs. Lyon-style cuisine.

in Sorbiers 10 km north by D 106, N 82 and D 3 – pop. 7 399 – alt. 560 m – ✉ 42290

Office de tourisme, 2, avenue Charles-de-Gaulle ✆ 04 77 01 11 42, Fax 04 77 53 07 27

X **Le Valjoly** P VISA MC
9 r. de l'Onzon – ✆ 04 77 53 60 35 – www.levaljoly.free.fr – levaljoly@free.fr – Closed 1-14 August, Sunday dinner and Monday
Rest – Menu (€ 15), € 18 (weekday lunch), € 27/50 – Carte € 26/56
◆ A welcome with a smile, pretty floral decoration and colourful touches make up for the passing traffic noise and simple setting in this inn, which offers a traditional cuisine.

in Rochetaillée 8 km southeast by D 8 – ✉ 42100

XX **Yves Genaille** AC VISA MC AE
3 r. du Parc – ✆ 04 77 32 88 48 – www.restaurant-grenaille.fr – restaurant.genaille@wanadoo.fr – Fax 04 77 32 88 48 – Closed 19-27 April, August, dinner off season, Saturday lunch, Sunday dinner, Tuesday dinner and Monday
Rest – grill room – *(pre-book)* Menu € 25 (weekday lunch), € 30/60 – Carte € 46/58
◆ One wall of the panoramic dining room in this restaurant located in the centre of the village is emblazoned with culinary awards. Contemporary cuisine and rotisserie dishes.

ST-ÉTIENNE

Rue	Carré	N°
Aciéries (R. des)	T	2
Barrouin (R.)	T	13
Crozet-Boussingault (R.)	V	22
Daguerre (Bd)	UV	24
Déchaud (R. H.)	V	25
Dr-F.-Merlin (R. du)	T	30
Drs-Charcot (R. des)	V	31
Drs-H.-et-B.-Muller (R. des)	T	32
Dunkerque (R. de)	V	36
Fraissinette (Bd A.-de)	V	45
Franchet-d'Esperey (Bd Mar.)	U	46
Gauthier-Dumont (R.)	U	48
Grignard (R. V.)	T	55
Marx (Bd Karl)	UV	67
Oddé (R. C.)	T	78
Ogier (R. J.-B.)	U	79
Paré (R. A.)	V	131
Passementiers (R. des)	V	82
Pasteur (Bd)	V	83
Péri (R. G.)	V	84
Pompidou (Bd G.)	T	88
Revollier (R. J.-F.)	T	92
Robespierre (R.)	V	95
Rochetaillée (Av. de)	V	98
Scheurer-Kestner (R.)	T	104
Terrenoire (R. de)	U	110
Valbenoite (Bd)	UV	119
Verdun (Av. de)	T	120
Vivaraize (R. de la)	V	125
8-Mai-1945 (Bd du)	T	127
11-Novembre (R. du)	V	128
38e-R.-I. (Bd du)	U	130

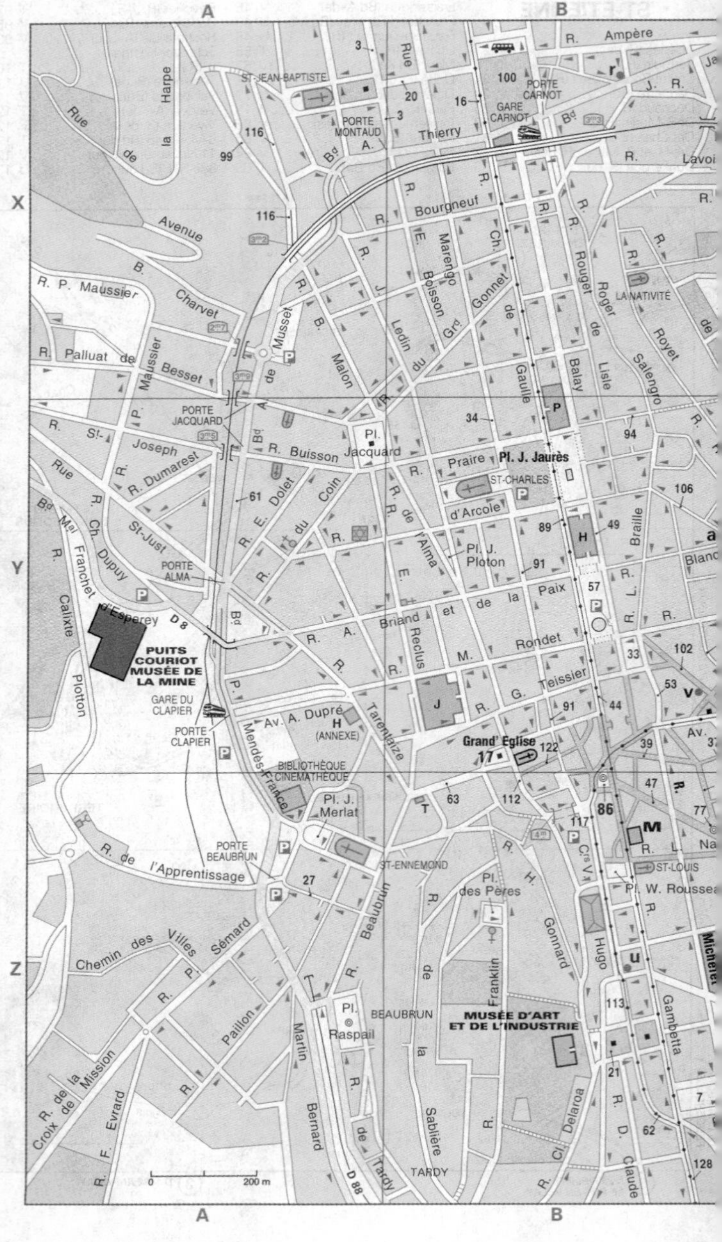
A
B
X
Y
Z
R. Ampère
ST-JEAN-BAPTISTE
PORTE MONTAUD
PORTE CARNOT
GARE CARNOT
Rue de la Harpe
Avenue B. Charvet
R. P. Maussier
R. Palluat de Besset
Thierry
Bourgneuf
R. J. Ledin
R. B. Malon
Bd de Musset
R. E. Boisson
Marengo
Gonnet
Ch. de Gaulle
Rouget de Lisle
Roger Salengro
R. Balay
LA NATIVITÉ
Royet
PORTE JACQUARD
Pl. Jacquard
R. Buisson
R. St-Joseph
R. Dumarest
Rue St-Just
R. E. Dolet
R. du Coin
Pl. J. Jaurès
Praire
ST-CHARLES
d'Arcole
R. de l'Alma
Pl. J. Ploton
Braille
Bd Mal Franchet d'Esperey
R. Ch. Dupuy
R. Calixte Plotton
PORTE ALMA
D 8
PUITS COURIOT MUSÉE DE LA MINE
GARE DU CLAPIER
PORTE CLAPIER
R. A. Briand
E. Reclus
Paix
M. Rondet
R. G. Teissier
Av. A. Dupré
H (ANNEXE)
Tarentaize
Grand' Église
Mendès-France
BIBLIOTHÈQUE CINÉMATHÈQUE
Pl. J. Merlat
ST-ENNEMOND
R. de l'Apprentissage
PORTE BEAUBRUN
R. Beaubrun
Pl. des Pères
R. H. Gonnard
Crs V. Hugo
ST-LOUIS
Pl. W. Rousseau
Chemin des Villes
R. P. Sémard
R. Paillon
Pl. Raspail
BEAUBRUN
R. Martin Bernard
R. de la Sablière
Franklin
MUSÉE D'ART ET DE L'INDUSTRIE
Cl. Delaroa
Gambetta
R. D. Claude
R. de la Croix de Mission
R. F. Evrard
R. de Tardy
D 88
TARDY
0
200 m

ST-ÉTIENNE

Street	Grid	No.
Albert-1er (Bd)	ABX	3
Anatole-France (Pl.)	BZ	7
Badouillère (R. de la)	CZ	9
Barbusse (R. H.)	CZ	12
Bérard (R. P.)	BCY	14
Bergson (R.)	BX	16
Boivin (Pl.)	BY	17
Chavanelle (Pl.)	CZ	18
Clovis-Hugues (R.)	BX	20
Comte (Pl. Louis)	BZ	21
Denfert-Rochereau (Av.)	CY	26
Descours (R.)	AZ	27
Dorian (Pl.)	BY	33
Dormoy (R. M.)	BXY	34
Dupré (R. G.)	BY	37
Durafour (R. A.)	CZ	38
Escoffier (R. D.)	BY	39
Fougerolle (R.)	CZ	41
Fourneyron (Pl.)	CY	42
Foy (R. Gén.)	BY	44
Frappa (R. J.)	BZ	47
Gambetta (R.)	BZ	
Gaulle (R. Ch.-de)	BXY	
Gérentet (R.)	BY	49
Gervais (R. E.)	CY	50
Gillet (R. F.)	BY	52
Grand Moulin (R. du)	BY	53
Guesde (Pl. J.)	BY	56
Hôtel-de-Ville (Pl. de l')	BY	57
Jacob (R.)	CX	58
Krumnow (Bd F.)	AY	61
Leclerc (R. du Gén.)	BZ	62
Libération (Av. de la)	BCY	
Loubet (Av. du Président E.)	BZ	63
Martyrs-de-Vingré (R. des)	BYZ	66
Michelet (R.)	BYZ	
Moine (Pl. Antonin)	CYZ	68
Moulin (Pl. J.)	CY	72
Mulatière (R. de la)	CZ	75
Neuve (Pl.)	BZ	77
Peuple (Pl. du)	BZ	86
Pointe-Cadet (R.)	BCZ	87
Président-Wilson (R.)	BY	89
République (R. de la)	BCY	
Résistance (R. de la)	BY	91
Rivière (R. du Sergent)	CX	93
Robert (R.)	BY	94
Ruel (R. A.)	AX	99
Sadi-Carnot (Pl.)	BX	100
St-Jean (R.)	BY	102
Sauzéa (Cours H.)	CY	103
Servet (R. M.)	BY	106
Stalingrad (Square de)	CY	109
Théâtre (R. du)	BYZ	112
Thomas (Pl. A.)	BZ	113
Tilleuls (R. des)	AX	116
Ursules (Pl. des)	BZ	117
Valbenoite (Bd)	CZ	119
Villeboeuf (Pl.)	CZ	123
Ville (R. de la)	BY	122
11-Novembre (R. du)	BZ	128

in St-Priest-en-Jarez 4 km northwest -T – **pop. 5 812 – alt. 605 m** – ✉ **42270**

Clos Fleuri
76 av. A. Raimond – ✆ 04 77 74 63 24 – www.closfleuri.fr – f.deville@closfleuri.fr – Fax 04 77 79 06 70 – Closed 11-18 August, 2-7 January, Wednesday dinner, Sunday dinner and Monday T **u**
Rest – Menu (€ 20), € 27/70 – Carte € 52/62
◆ A large flower-decked villa with an elegant dining room with cane furniture and shaded terraces. Contemporary cuisine.

Du Musée
musée d'Art moderne la Terrasse – ✆ 04 77 79 24 52 – Fax 04 77 79 92 07 – Closed 10-25 August, Wednesday dinner and Sunday dinner T **s**
Rest – Menu € 10/37 – Carte € 27/37
◆ Food for the mind, then food for the tummy...or vice versa, depending on your appetite! The Museum of Modern Art's bistro serves its menu based on market produce in a determinedly contemporary décor.

in La Fouillouse 8.5 km northwest by N 82 – **pop. 4 326 – alt. 438 m** – ✉ **42480**

La Route Bleue
40 r. du Vernay – ✆ 04 77 30 12 09 – Fax 04 77 30 27 16 – Closed 14 July-20 August, February half term holidays and Saturday
Rest – *(lunch only)* Menu € 17 (weekdays)/35 – Carte € 40/57
◆ This creeper covered, unpretentious restaurant-cum-inn, excels in copious helpings of traditional home cooking.

ST-ÉTIENNE-DE-BAÏGORRY – 64 Pyrénées-Atlantiques – 342 D5 – pop. 1 602 – alt. 163 m – ✉ 64430 Atlantic Coast 3 A3

Paris 813 – Biarritz 51 – Cambo-les-Bains 31 – Pau 116 – St-Jean-Pied-de-Port 11

Office de tourisme, place de l'Église ✆ 05 59 37 47 28, Fax 05 59 37 49 58

St-Etienne church ★.

Arcé
col d'Ispéguy road – ✆ 05 59 37 40 14 – www.hotel-arce.com – reservations@hotel-arce.com – Fax 05 59 37 40 27 – Open mid March-mid November
20 rm – †€ 70/75 ††€ 125/145, ☕ € 11 – 3 suites – ½ P € 100/105
Rest – *(closed Wednesday lunch and Monday lunch from 15 September to 15 July except public holidays) (pre-book Sat - Sun)* Menu € 29/43 – Carte € 47/55
◆ Situated on the banks of the River Nivelle, this attractive auberge was formerly a café where pelota was played. Lovely garden and pool on the opposite bank. Large, well-maintained guestrooms. The restaurant occupies a converted *trinquet* (pelota hall). Terrace shaded by plane trees. Regional dishes and wines from Irrouléguy.

ST-ÉTIENNE-DE-FURSAC – 23 Creuse – 325 G4 – see La Souterraine

ST-ÉTIENNE-DU-VAUVRAY – 27 Eure – 304 H6 – pop. 706 – alt. 13 m – ✉ 27430 33 D2

Paris 105 – Rouen 28 – Évreux 35 – Sotteville-lès-Rouen 29 – Saint-Étienne-du-Rouvray 25

La Ferme
rte de Crémonville, 2.5 km southwest on the D 77 and minor road – ✆ 02 32 59 14 22 – manoir.haute.cremonville@orange.fr – Fax 02 32 40 79 32 – Closed 1st-20 August and 24 December-1 January
Rest – *(number of covers limited, pre-book)* Menu € 28 – Carte € 30/50
◆ Fine, renovated 18C Norman farmhouse. Country-style ambiance in the restaurant with traditional style cuisine respectful of the seasons. Blackboard specials.

ST-ÉTIENNE-LA-THILLAYE – 14 Calvados – 303 M4 – pop. 437 – alt. 20 m – ✉ 14950 32 A3

Paris 198 – Caen 45 – Le Havre 47 – Lisieux 28 – Hérouville-Saint-Clair 48

La Maison de Sophie without rest VISA

– *02 31 65 69 97 – www.lamaisondesophie.fr – sophie@lamaisondesophie.fr – Fax 02 31 65 69 98 – Closed January, Sunday and Monday except school holidays*

5 rm – €170 €170

◆ A former presbytery dating from 1789, perfectly preserved with a park and small French style garden. Charming guestrooms designed around various themes associated with music and scents.

ST-ÉTIENNE-LÈS-REMIREMONT – 88 Vosges – 314 H4 – see Remiremont

ST-EUTROPE-DE-BORN – 47 Lot-et-Garonne – 336 G2 – see Cancon

ST-EVROULT-NOTRE-DAME-DU-BOIS – 61 Orne – 310 L2 – pop. 438 – alt. 355 m – ✉ 61550 Normandy 33 C2

Paris 155 – Argentan 42 – Caen 91 – Lisieux 52

Le Relais de l'Abbaye rm, VISA AE

r. principale – 02 33 84 19 00 – lerelaisdelabbaye@orange.fr – Fax 02 33 84 19 04

11 rm – €40/45 €50/60, €8

Rest – *(closed Sunday dinner and Friday)* Menu (€11), €23/37 – Carte €23/37

◆ Fully renovated hotel in the main street of a village known for its old Norman abbey. Functional and well-soundproofed rooms. Restaurant set under an original pyramid-shaped glass roof. Traditional cuisine.

ST-FARGEAU – 89 Yonne – 319 B6 – pop. 1 693 – alt. 175 m – ✉ 89170 Burgundy-Jura 7 A2

Paris 180 – Auxerre 45 – Clamecy 48 – Gien 41

Office de tourisme, 3, place de la République 03 86 74 10 07, Fax 03 86 74 10 07

Château★.

Les Grands Chênes without rest VISA

Les Berthes-Bailly, 4.5 km south by D 18 – 03 86 74 04 05 – www.hotel-de-puisaye.com – contact@hotel-de-puisaye.com – Fax 03 86 74 11 41 – Closed 20 December-4 January and 6-22 February

13 rm – €69/74 €69/74, €8,50

◆ Somewhere between a guest house and a charming residence, this luxurious building full of character has colourful rooms. It is located near the Guédelon medieval construction site (where they are building a château-fort).

ST-FÉLIX-LAURAGAIS – 31 Haute-Garonne – 343 J4 – pop. 1 354 – alt. 332 m – ✉ 31540 Languedoc-Roussillon-Tarn Gorges 29 C2

Paris 716 – Auterive 46 – Carcassonne 58 – Castres 38 – Gaillac 71 – Toulouse 43

Syndicat d'initiative, place Guillaume de Nogaret 05 62 18 96 99

Site★.

Auberge du Poids Public (Claude Taffarello) with rm A/C VISA AE

rte de Toulouse, fg. St Roch – 05 62 18 85 00 – www.auberge-du-poidspublic.com – poidspublic@wanadoo.fr – Fax 05 62 18 85 05 – Closed January and autumn half-term holidays

12 rm – €65/68 €70/102, €12 – ½ P €73/90

Rest – *(closed Sunday dinner except July-August)*
Menu (€25), €30/72 – Carte €58/79

Spec. Foie gras de canard en trois préparations. Pigeonneau du lauragais en croûte d'épices. Macarons chocolat-caramel et fruits rouges. **Wines** Minervois, Vin de Pays des Côtes du Tarn.

◆ An agreeable semi-rustic, semi-modern decor with a collection of old tools and a panoramic view of the countryside in this delightful inn. Excellent up-to-date menu with a regional slant. Ask for a room with a view of the Lauragais plain.

ST-FERRÉOL – 31 Haute-Garonne – 343 K4 – see Revel

ST-FIRMIN – 80 Somme – 301 C6 – see Rue

ST-FLORENT – 2B Haute-Corse – 345 E3 – see Corse

ST-FLORENTIN – 89 Yonne – 319 F3 – pop. 5 076 – alt. 120 m 7 B1
– ✉ 89600 Burgundy-Jura

Paris 169 – Auxerre 32 – Chaumont 145 – Dijon 172 – Sens 45 – Troyes 51

Syndicat d'initiative, 8, rue de la Terrasse ☎ 03 86 35 11 86, Fax 03 86 35 11 86

Church★ stained-glass windows **E.**

Les Tilleuls
rm, VISA MC AE

3 r. Decourtive – ☎ 03 86 35 09 09 – www.hotel-les-tilleuls.com – lestilleuls.stflorentin@wanadoo.fr – Fax 03 86 35 36 90 – Closed 17-24 November, 24 December-4 January, 16 February-15 March, Sunday dinner and Monday from mid-September to mid-June

9 rm – †€ 51 ††€ 58, ☕ € 9

Rest – *(closed Monday from mid-June to mid-September)* Menu (€ 17) – Carte € 41/58

◆ A family hotel converted from a Capuchin monastery dating back to 1635. Some of the comfortable rooms overlook a shady garden with lime trees. A pleasant restaurant enhanced by coloured beams; greenery predominates on the terrace and the cuisine is traditional.

ST-FLOUR – 15 Cantal – 330 G4 – pop. 6 625 – alt. 783 m 5 B3
– ✉ 15100 Auvergne

Paris 513 – Aurillac 70 – Issoire 67 – Le Puy-en-Velay 94 – Rodez 111

Office de tourisme, 17 bis, place d'Armes ☎ 04 71 60 22 50, Fax 04 71 60 05 14

Site★★ - Cathedral ★ - Brassard★ in the musée de la Haute Auvergne **H.**

Plan on next page

Lower town

Grand Hôtel de l'Étape
VISA MC AE

18 av. de la République, via ② – ☎ 04 71 60 13 03 – www.hotel-etape.com – info@hotel-etape.com – Fax 04 71 60 48 05 – Closed Sunday evening except July-August

23 rm – †€ 50/58 ††€ 58/77, ☕ € 9

Rest – *(closed Sunday dinner and Monday except July-August)* Menu (€ 16 bi), € 23/30 – Carte € 30/47

◆ A family-run, 1970s establishment. Spacious and practical rooms; choose one with a mountain view. There is a Seventies feel to the restaurant serving authentic regional cuisine. Most of the vegetables come from the establishment's cottage garden.

Auberge de La Providence
rm, P VISA MC AE

1 r. Château d'Alleuze, via D 40 (south of plan) – ☎ 04 71 60 12 05 – www.auberge-providence.com – info@auberge-providence.com – Fax 04 71 60 33 94 – Closed 15 November-5 January B t

12 rm – †€ 57 ††€ 60/75, ☕ € 9 – ½ P € 48/50

Rest – *(closed Sunday lunch, Friday and Saturday in winter and Sunday dinner) (dinner only) (residents only)* Menu (€ 20), € 28 – Carte € 30/40

◆ Slightly out of the centre, this welcoming family inn has modest, but well-kept, soundproofed rooms (two with terrace). The large sideboard, its wood worn smooth with age, gives character to the country restaurant; simple recipes with a regional flavour.

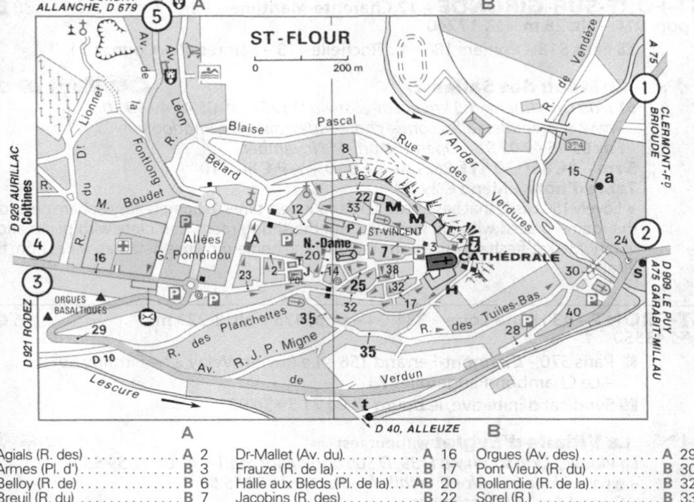

Agials (R. des)	A	2	Dr-Mallet (Av. du)	A	16	Orgues (Av. des)	A	29
Armes (Pl. d')	B	3	Frauze (R. de la)	B	17	Pont Vieux (R. du)	B	30
Belloy (R. de)	B	6	Halle aux Bleds (Pl. de la)	AB	20	Rollandie (R. de la)	B	32
Breuil (R. du)	B	7	Jacobins (R. des)	B	22	Sorel (R.)	B	33
Cardinal Bernet (R. du)	B	8	Lacs (R. des)	A	23	Traversière (R.)	B	38
Collège (R. du)	A	12	Liberté (Pl. de la)	B	24	Tuiles Haut (R. des)	AB	35
Collégiale (R. de la)	A	14	Marchande (R.)	B	25	11-Novembre (Av. du)	B	40
Delorme (Av. du Cdt)	B	15	Odilon-de-Mercoeur (Pl.)	B	28			

St-Jacques rest, VISA

8 pl. de la Liberté – ✆ 04 71 60 09 20 – www.hotelsaintjacques.com – info@hotelsaintjacques.com – Fax 04 71 60 33 81 – Closed 9 November-3 January and Friday dinner from January to Easter B **s**

28 rm – †€ 46 ††€ 54, ☕ € 8

Rest – *(closed Saturday lunch, Sunday dinner and Monday)* Carte € 21/36

Rest ***Grill*** – *(closed Friday dinner and Saturday lunch)* Menu (€ 12) – Carte € 21/36

◆ This establishment, on a small square, used to be a stop on the route to Compostella. A few family rooms and an attractive view of the upper town from the swimming pool. A colourful restaurant offering dishes from the Indian Ocean area. Bistro style and traditional dishes at the Grill.

L'Ander VISA

6 av. du Cdt Delorme – ✆ 04 71 60 21 63 – www.hotel-ander.com – info@hotel-ander.com – Fax 04 71 60 46 40 – Closed 20 January-8 March B **a**

23 rm – †€ 48 ††€ 48/57, ☕ € 9 – ½ P € 48/52

Rest – Menu € 14/36 – Carte € 18/37

◆ Dominated by the upper town and cathedral, this welcoming hotel is enjoying a new lease of life. It sports an updated countrified decor and has practical, tastefully decorated rooms. The owner's cooking has a distinct preference for regional, traditional recipes.

in St-Georges by ②, **D 909 and secondary road: 5 km – pop. 1 128 – alt. 860 m – ✉ 15100**

Le Château de Varillettes rest, VISA

– ✆ 04 71 60 45 05 – www.chateaudevarillettes.com – varillettes@leshotelsparticuliers.com – Fax 04 71 60 34 27 – Open May to September

12 rm – †€ 135/195 ††€ 135/195, ☕ € 15 – 1 suite – ½ P € 115/145

Rest – Menu € 35/45 – Carte € 40/65

◆ Treat yourself to the charm of yesteryear and the comfort of today in this 15C château, a summer residence of the bishops of St-Flour. Ask for a room with a view over the medieval garden. The vaulted restaurant dining room with its old fireplace is full of character.

ST-FORT-SUR-GIRONDE – 17 Charente-Maritime – 324 F7 – pop. 914 – alt. 28 m – ✉ 17240 38 **B3**

Paris 518 – Poitiers 186 – La Rochelle 115 – Saintes 45 – Cognac 51

Château des Salles

61 r. du Gros Chêne, 1.5 km north-east via D 125 – ✆ 05 46 49 95 10 – www.chateaudessalles.com – chateaudessalles@wanadoo.fr – Fax 05 46 49 02 81 – Open 1st April-1st November

5 rm – €86/130 €86/130, €10 – ½ P €86/110

Table d'hôte – Menu €29/38

◆ Lovely 15C castle that has been altered countless times. A homely atmosphere pervades the rooms, graced with old furniture, and the sitting room, complete with piano and a library. Market-fresh produce using regional and home-grown vegetables, wines from the estate.

ST-FRONT – 43 Haute-Loire – 331 G4 – pop. 475 – alt. 1 223 m – ✉ 43550 6 **C3**

Paris 570 – Clermont-Ferrand 156 – Le Puy-en-Velay 27 – Firminy 69 – Le Chambon-Feugerolles 73

Syndicat d'initiative, le bourg ✆ 04 71 59 54 93

La Vidalle d'Eyglet without rest

La Vidalle, 7 km south via D 39, D 500 and minor road – ✆ 04 71 59 55 58 – www.vidalle.fr – infos@vidalle.fr – Fax 04 71 59 55 58 – Open 4 April-15 September

5 rm – €90/100 €100/110

◆ An attractive restored farmhouse surrounded by fields. Pretty rooms, lounge-cum-library and painting studio (courses available). Skiing straight from the door in winter.

ST-GALMIER – 42 Loire – 327 E6 – pop. 5 705 – alt. 400 m – Casino – ✉ 42330 Lyon - Rhone Valley 44 **A2**

Paris 457 – Lyon 82 – Montbrison 25 – Montrond-les-Bains 11 – Roanne 68 – St-Étienne 24

Office de tourisme, Le Cloître, 3, boulevard Cousin ✆ 04 77 54 06 08, Fax 04 77 54 06 07

Vierge du Pilier★ and triptych★ in the church.

La Charpinière

rm,

– ✆ 04 77 52 75 00 – www.lacharpiniere.com – charpiniere.hot.rest@wanadoo.fr – Fax 04 77 54 18 79 – Closed Sunday dinner

49 rm – €79/120 €79/120, €13 – ½ P €68/88

Rest *La Closerie de la Tour* – Menu (€18), €26/50 – Carte €31/65

◆ A vast walled park surrounds this small manor house clad in Virginia creeper. Countless leisure activities. The rooms are above all practical. Winter garden style restaurant serving up-to-date recipes and a menu that varies with the seasons.

Hostellerie du Forez

6 r. Didier Guetton – ✆ 04 77 54 00 23 – www.hostellerieduforez.com – contact@hostellerieduforez.com – Fax 04 77 54 07 49

16 rm – €53/57 €62/67, €9

Rest – *(Closed 10-30 August, 21 December-4 January, Sunday dinner and Monday lunch)* Menu (€13), €16 (weekdays)/35 – Carte €25/47

◆ Now an inn, this abode, which is in perfect condition, used to be a post house in the 19C. Well-kept functional rooms, currently in the process of renovation. Updated menu served in a rustic dining room.

Le Bougainvillier

Pré Château – ✆ 04 77 54 03 31 – www.restaurant-bougainvillier.com – bougain@wanadoo.fr – Fax 04 77 94 95 93 – Closed 28 July-25 August, 9-23 February, Wednesday dinner, Sunday dinner and Monday

Rest – *(pre-book)* Menu €29 (weekdays)/62 – Carte €57/69

◆ Treat yourself to a gourmet treat in this impressive bourgeois home. The restaurant is made up of three rooms, one of which leads into the garden. Appetising contemporary cuisine.

ST-GATIEN-DES-BOIS – 14 Calvados – 303 N3 – pop. 1 163 – alt. 149 m – ✉ 14130 — 32 **A3**

▶ Paris 195 – Caen 58 – Le Havre 36 – Deauville 10 – Honfleur 13 – Lisieux 27

Le Clos Deauville St-Gatien — rest, VISA
4 r. des Brioleurs – ✆ 02 31 65 16 08 – www.clos-st-gatien.fr – hotel@clos-st-gatien.fr – Fax 02 31 65 10 27
58 rm – †€ 81/194 ††€ 81/194, ☕ € 13 – ½ P € 85/140
Rest *Le Michels* – Menu (€ 21), € 31/75 – Carte € 38/63
◆ An old farmhouse and outbuildings set in a tree lined garden. Spruced up guestrooms and a wide variety of leisure and seminar facilities. Original beams and half-timbering constitute the charm of this restaurant. Traditional fare.

ST-GAUDENS – 31 Haute-Garonne – 343 C6 – pop. 10 800 – alt. 405 m – ✉ 31800 ▮ Languedoc-Roussillon-Tarn Gorges — 28 **B3**

▶ Paris 766 – Bagnères-de-Luchon 48 – Tarbes 68 – Toulouse 94
ℹ Office de tourisme, 2, rue Thiers ✆ 05 61 94 77 61, Fax 05 61 94 77 50
◉ Boulevards des Pyrénées ≤★ - Viewpoints★.

Du Commerce — rm, rm, VISA
2 av. de Boulogne – ✆ 05 62 00 97 00 – www.commerce31.com – hotel.commerce@wanadoo.fr – Fax 05 62 00 97 01 – Closed 18 December-11 January
48 rm – †€ 57/75 ††€ 57/75, ☕ € 9 – ½ P € 53/63
Rest – Menu € 21/37 – Carte € 27/53
◆ A modern hotel located a stone's throw from the town centre. Functional rooms in a variety of styles, all with air-conditioning. Sunny colours, a happy blend of old and new, and cuisine where cassoulet takes pride of place.

ST-GENIEZ-D'OLT – 12 Aveyron – 338 J4 – pop. 2 019 – alt. 410 m – ✉ 12130 ▮ Languedoc-Roussillon-Tarn Gorges — 29 **D1**

▶ Paris 612 – Espalion 28 – Florac 80 – Mende 68 – Rodez 46 – Sévérac-le-Château 25
ℹ Office de tourisme, Le Cloître ✆ 05 65 70 43 42, Fax 05 65 70 47 05

Hostellerie de la Poste — VISA
3 pl. Gén de Gaulle – ✆ 05 65 47 43 30 – www.hoteldelaposte12.com – hotel@hoteldelaposte12.com – Fax 05 65 47 42 75 – Open from Easter to 1 November
50 rm – †€ 50/55 ††€ 60/65, ☕ € 8
Rest *Le Rive Gauche* – Menu (€ 12), € 25/42 – Carte € 36/51
◆ Different types of rooms of varying size and comfort in this centrally-located hotel, which occupies a number of separate buildings, surrounded by greenery. Popular with groups. The Rive Gauche's regional menu can be enjoyed in its dining rooms or on the terrace by the swimming pool.

ST-GENIS-POUILLY – 01 Ain – 328 J3 – pop. 7 237 – alt. 445 m – ✉ 01630 — 46 **F1**

▶ Paris 524 – Bellegarde-sur-Valserine 28 – Bourg-en-Bresse 100 – Genève 12 – Gex 10
ℹ Office de tourisme, 11 rue de Gex ✆ 04 50 42 29 37, Fax 04 50 28 32 94
⛳ des Serves Route de Meyrin, E : 2 km on D 984, ✆ 04 50 42 16 48

L'Amphitryon — VISA
– ✆ 04 50 20 64 64 – www.saint-genis-pouilly.com/amphitryon – Fax 04 50 42 06 98 – Closed 28 July-20 August, 28 December-18 February, Tuesday dinner, Sunday dinner and Monday
Rest – Menu (€ 20), € 33/55 – Carte € 50/69
◆ The unassuming facade of this modern pavilion hides the impressive dining area with frescos, vaulted ceiling and small antique-style statues. Classic cuisine and good selection of wines.

ST-GENIX-SUR-GUIERS – 73 Savoie – 333 G4 – pop. 1 817 45 C2
– alt. 235 m – ✉ 73240

Paris 513 – Belley 22 – Chambéry 34 – Grenoble 58 – Lyon 74

Office de tourisme, rue du faubourg ☎ 04 76 31 63 16,
Fax 04 76 31 71 30

in Champagneux 4 km northwest by D 1516 – pop. 471 – alt. 214 m – ✉ 73240

Les Bergeronnettes rm, VISA MC AE

Le Bourg, near the church – ☎ 04 76 31 50 30 – www.silencehotel.com – gourjux@orange.fr – Fax 04 76 31 61 29 – Closed 26 December-1st January

18 rm – €70 €70, € 10 – ½ P € 70

Rest – *(closed Sunday dinner)* Menu € 14/36 – Carte € 19/46

◆ A country hotel nestling in lush green countryside, home to spacious, well-kept rooms. Buffet breakfasts. Modern restaurant serving simply prepared regional cuisine (frogs' legs). Terrace under a marquee.

ST-GEORGES – 15 Cantal – 330 G4 – see St-Flour

ST-GEORGES-DE-DIDONNE – 17 Charente-Maritime – 324 D6 – see Royan

ST-GEORGES-D'ESPÉRANCHE – 38 Isère – 333 D4 – pop. 2 982 44 B2
– alt. 400 m – ✉ 38790

Paris 496 – Bourgoin-Jallieu 25 – Grenoble 92 – Lyon 40 – Vienne 22

Castel d'Espéranche VISA MC AE

14 rte Lafayette – ☎ 04 74 59 18 45 – www.castel-esperanche.com – info@castel-esperanche.com – Fax 04 74 59 04 40 – Closed 27 October-8 November, 9-27 February, Monday, Tuesday and Wednesday

Rest – Menu € 18 (weekdays)/54 – Carte € 45/58

◆ Restaurant partly in the 13C guard tower, with a few of its vestiges embellishing the dining rooms. Regional cuisine and "medieval" menu.

ST-GEORGES-DES-SEPT-VOIES – 49 Maine-et-Loire – 317 H4 35 C2
– pop. 570 – alt. 83 m – ✉ 49350

Paris 314 – Nantes 127 – Angers 30 – Saumur 27 – La Flèche 71

Auberge de la Sansonnière with rm rest, rest, VISA MC AE

(near the Town Hall) – ☎ 02 41 57 57 70 – www.auberge-sansonniere.com – contact@auberge-sansonniere.com – Fax 02 41 57 51 38 – Closed 9-25 March, 3 weeks in November, 1 week in January, Sunday dinner and Monday

7 rm – €60/75 €60/75, € 8,50 – ½ P € 53/61

Rest – Menu (€ 12), € 17/36 – Carte € 30/48

◆ A real gem of an inn in this prettily restored former priory. Modern bistro feel (stonework, beams, bright colours) and appetising, updated traditional cuisine. Small guestrooms that are as charming as they are welcoming.

ST-GEORGES-SUR-CHER – 41 Loir-et-Cher – 318 D8 – pop. 2 268 11 A1
– alt. 70 m – ✉ 41400

Paris 225 – Blois 40 – Orléans 102 – Tours 40

Prieuré de la Chaise without rest

8 r. Prieuré – ☎ 02 54 32 59 77 – www.prieuredelachaise.com – prieuredelachaise@yahoo.fr – Fax 02 54 32 69 49

5 rm – €60 €65

◆ Charming 16C château, surrounded by a park. Rooms with red floor tiles and antique furniture. Dining room with pleasant log fire in winter.

ST-GERMAIN-DE-JOUX – 01 Ain – 328 H3 – pop. 494 – alt. 507 m – ✉ 01130 45 C1

Paris 487 – Bellegarde-sur-Valserine 13 – Belley 61 – Bourg-en-Bresse 63 – Nantua 13

Reygrobellet with rm
D 1084 – ✆ 04 50 59 81 13 – reygrobellet@orange.fr – Fax 04 50 59 83 74 – Closed 4-21 July, 26 October-10 November, 23 February-4 March, Wednesday dinner in low season, Sunday dinner and Monday
10 rm – €53/65 €53/65, €8,50
Rest – Menu €22 (weekdays)/59 – Carte €39/70
◆ In addition to its comfortable, countrified interior, this house is popular for its generous portions of classic dishes and lovely desserts. Partially refurbished simple rooms.

ST-GERMAIN-DES-VAUX – 50 Manche – 303 A1 – pop. 422 – alt. 59 m – ✉ 50440 32 A1

Paris 383 – Barneville-Carteret 48 – Cherbourg 28 – Nez de Jobourg 7 – St-Lô 104
Baie d'Ecalgrain ★★ South: 3 km - Port de Goury ★ Northwest: 2 km.
Nez de Jobourg ★★ South: 7.5 km then 30 mn - ≤ ★★ on Vauville cove Southeast: 9.5 km by Herqueville, **Normandy.**

Le Moulin à Vent
10 rte de Port Racine, (Hamlet of Danneville), 1.5 km east via D 45 – ✆ 02 33 52 75 20 – www.le-moulin-a-vent.fr – contact@le-moulin-a-vent.fr – Fax 02 33 52 22 57 – Closed 27 November-27 December and Wednesday
Rest – *(pre-book)* Menu €26/37 – Carte €29/43
◆ This inn enjoys an attractive and remote location at the tip of the Cotentin peninsula. Modern cuisine served in a contemporary dining room with superb views.

ST-GERMAIN-DU-BOIS – 71 Saône-et-Loire – 320 L9 – pop. 1 890 – alt. 210 m – ✉ 71330 Burgundy-Jura 8 D3

Paris 367 – Chalon-sur-Saône 33 – Dole 58 – Lons-le-Saunier 29 – Mâcon 75 – Tournus 40

Hostellerie Bressane
2 rte de Sens – ✆ 03 85 72 04 69 – www.giot-hostelleriebressane.fr – la.terrinee4@wanadoo.fr – Fax 03 85 72 07 75 – Closed Sunday evening except July-August and Monday
9 rm – €48 €52, €6 – ½ P €54
Rest – Menu (€13), €20/37 – Carte €32/43
◆ Imposing 18C construction with a renovated interior in regional style. Guestrooms with character, more peaceful at the rear. Generous portions of traditional, unfussy cuisine at reasonable prices.

ST-GERMAIN-EN-LAYE – 78 Yvelines – 311 I2 – 101 13 – see Paris, Area

ST-GERMAIN-LÈS-ARLAY – 39 Jura – 321 D6 – pop. 521 – alt. 255 m – ✉ 39210 16 B3

Paris 398 – Besançon 74 – Chalon-sur-Saône 58 – Dole 46 – Lons-le-Saunier 11

Hostellerie St-Germain with rm
635 Grande rue – ✆ 03 84 44 60 91 – www.hostelleriesaintgermain.com – hoststgermain@wanadoo.fr – Fax 03 84 44 63 64
7 rm – €57/72 €57/72, €9 – ½ P €64
Rest – *(Closed Tuesday except in high season and Monday)* Menu (€18), €23/60 – Carte €43/62
◆ Worth a detour for its regional cuisine matched by a fine selection of Jura wines. Elegantly rustic setting; well-presented rooms (quieter on the terrace side).

ST-GERMER-DE-FLY – 60 Oise – 305 B4 – pop. 1 732 – alt. 105 m – ✉ 60850 Northern France and the Paris Region 36 A2

Paris 92 – Les Andelys 40 – Beauvais 26 – Gisors 21 – Gournay-en-Bray 8 – Rouen 58
Syndicat d'initiative, 11, place de Verdun ✆ 03 44 82 62 74, Fax 03 44 82 23 56
Church ★ - ≤ ★ of the D 129 Southeast: 4 km.

Auberge de l'Abbaye

5 pl. de L'Abbaye – ☎ 03 44 82 50 73 – Fax 03 44 82 64 54 – Closed 27 July-9 August, 23 February-8 March, Sunday dinner, Monday dinner, Tuesday dinner and Wednesday

Rest – Menu € 16 bi (weekdays)/33

◆ The ivy-covered facade of this restaurant facing the abbey conceals a large dining room with exposed beams. Traditional and regional cuisine. Tearoom.

ST-GERVAIS – 33 Gironde – 335 I4 – pop. 1 392 – alt. 39 m – ✉ 33240 3 B1

Paris 543 – Bordeaux 29 – Mérignac 38 – Pessac 44

Au Sarment

50 r. la Lande – ☎ 05 57 43 44 73 – www.au-sarment.com – contact@au-sarment.com – Fax 05 57 43 90 28 – Closed February holiday, Saturday lunch, Sunday dinner and Monday

Rest – Menu € 39/59 – Carte € 48/76

◆ A fine country house, plain and bright décor, now a restaurant whose landlord and chef, of Caribbean origin, prepares up-to-date dishes with Creole touches. Terrace.

ST-GERVAIS-D'AUVERGNE – 63 Puy-de-Dôme – 326 D6 – pop. 1 344 – alt. 725 m – ✉ 63390 Auvergne 5 B2

Paris 377 – Aubusson 72 – Clermont-Ferrand 55 – Gannat 41 – Montluçon 47 – Riom 39

Office de tourisme, rue du Général Desaix ☎ 04 73 85 80 94

Castel Hôtel 1904

r. du Castel – ☎ 04 73 85 70 42 – www.castel-hotel-1904.com – castel.hotel.1904@wanadoo.fr – Fax 04 73 85 84 39 – Open April-11 November

15 rm – †€ 59 ††€ 65/79, ☕ € 10 – ½ P € 55/59

Rest – *(Closed Monday lunch)* Menu € 31/60

Rest – Menu (€ 14), € 18 – Carte approx. € 30

◆ This enchanting 17C residence offers recently refurbished rooms decorated with period furnishings. Warm welcome from the family that has been at the helm since 1904. Simple meals at the Comptoir. The other restaurant offers traditional dishes in a dining room with delightful old world charm.

Le Relais d'Auvergne

Châteauneuf road – ☎ 04 73 85 70 10 – www.relais-auvergne.com – relais.auvergne.hotel@wanadoo.fr – Fax 04 73 85 85 66 – Open from March to November and closed Sunday dinner and Monday in October, November and March

12 rm – †€ 54/57 ††€ 55/68, ☕ € 7 – ½ P € 51/53

Rest – Menu (€ 13), € 19/36 – Carte € 23/41

◆ The profusion of old furniture and objects from the region (on sale in the shop) depicts the old-fashioned atmosphere. Personalised guestrooms and handsome, country-style dining room serving traditional dishes and local specialities.

ST-GERVAIS-EN-VALLIÈRE – 71 Saône-et-Loire – 320 J8 – pop. 346 – alt. 203 m – ✉ 71350 7 A3

Paris 324 – Beaune 16 – Chalon-sur-Saône 24 – Dijon 57 – Mâcon 84 – Nevers 164

in Chaublanc 3 km Northeast by D 94 and D 183 – ✉ 71350 St-Gervais-en-Vallière

Le Moulin d'Hauterive

rm, rest,

8 r. du Moulin – ☎ 03 85 91 55 56 – www.moulinhauterive.com – info@moulinhauterive.com – Fax 03 85 91 89 65 – Closed 1st December-12 February, Wednesday dinner, Tuesday from October to May and Wednesday in June and September

10 rm – †€ 70/139 ††€ 109/139, ☕ € 15 – 10 suites

Rest – *(closed Sunday dinner from November to May, Tuesday lunch in July-August, Tuesday, Wednesday, Thursday from September to June and Monday)* Menu (€ 25), € 40/62 – Carte € 54/77

◆ Located in the heart of the countryside, this old flour mill on the banks of the Dheune was built in the 12C by the monks of Cîteaux Abbey. Rooms with a personal touch, fine antique furniture. Two plush dining rooms and a pretty riverside terrace; wine shop.

ST-GERVAIS-LES-BAINS – 74 Haute-Savoie – 328 N5 – pop. 5 276 46 F1
– alt. 820 m – Winter sports : 1 400/2 000 m 2 25 – Spa : all year – Casino – ✉ 74170 French Alps

Paris 597 – Annecy 84 – Bonneville 42 – Chamonix-Mont-Blanc 25 – Megève 12

✆ 3635 et tapez 42 (0,34 €/mn)

Office de tourisme, 43, rue du Mont-Blanc ✆ 04 50 47 76 08, Fax 04 50 47 75 69

Route du Bettex★★★ 8 km by ③ then D 43.

ST-GERVAIS-LES-BAINS LE FAYET

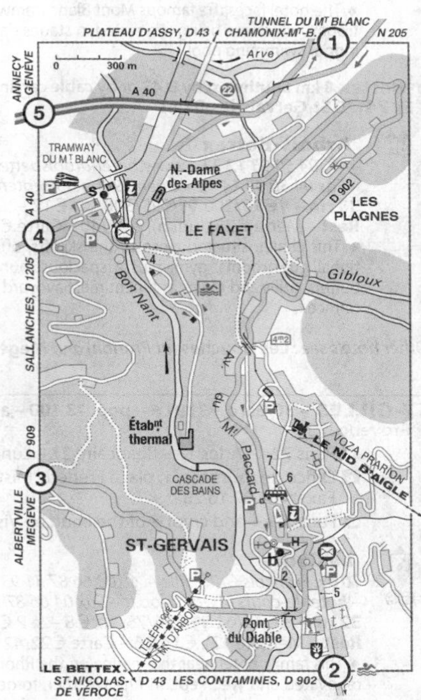

Val d'Este VISA AE
pl. de l'Église – ✆ 04 50 93 65 91 – www.hotel-valdeste.com – hotelvaldeste@voila.fr – Fax 04 50 47 76 29 – Closed 12 November-15 December **b**
14 rm – †€ 56/86 ††€ 56/86, ☕ € 8 – ½ P € 58/74
Rest *Le Sérac* – see restaurant listing
◆ This hotel in the centre of the resort has well-soundproofed guestrooms which are gradually being renovated. Those with a view of the mountains have a bathtub.

Le Sérac – Hôtel Val d'Este VISA
pl. de l'Église – ✆ 04 50 93 80 50 – www.serac-restaurant.com – Closed 19 April-7 May, 8-26 November, Wednesday except dinner in summer, Monday lunch and Thursday lunch **b**
Rest – Menu € 25/65 – Carte € 38/46
◆ With the mountains as a backdrop, this restaurant combines regional specialities with Mediterranean cuisine. Chocolate lovers won't be able to resist the dessert menu!

in Fayet 4 km northwest by D 902 – ✉ 74190

Office de tourisme, 104, avenue de la gare ✆ 04 50 93 64 64, Fax 04 50 78 38 48

Deux Gares

50 impasse des deux Gares – ✆ 04 50 78 24 75 – www.hotel2gares.com – hotel.2gares@wanadoo.fr – Fax 04 50 78 15 47 – Closed 25 April-3 May, 26 September-4 October and 1st November-18 December

28 rm – €42/47 €52/56, €8 – 2 suites – ½ P €45/48

Rest – *(dinner only) (resident only)* Menu €15/17

◆ The hotel faces the famous Mont Blanc tramway station. Small, simply furnished guestrooms which are being renovated in stages - ask for one of the most recent. Attractive indoor swimming pool.

in Bettex 8 km Southwest by D 43 or by cable car, intermediate station – ✉ 74170 St-Gervais-les-Bains

Arbois-Bettex

– ✆ 04 50 93 12 22 – www.hotel-arboisbettex.com – arboisbettex@wanadoo.fr – Fax 04 50 93 14 42 – Open 29 June-5 September and 20 December-19 April

33 rm – €75/200 €95/300, €12 – ½ P €115/190

Rest – Menu €28 (lunch), €38/40 – Carte €40/53

◆ This chalet, situated close to the ski-lifts, offers a superb view of Mont Blanc. Functional guestrooms, gym, plus a spacious lounge decorated in Austrian style. Salads, buffets, grills and roasts at lunchtime; Savoyard specialities in the evening. South-facing terrace.

Other hotels see : **Les Houches** *(at Prarion) and* **Megève** *(summit of Mont d'Arbois)*

ST-GILLES – 30 Gard – 339 L6 – pop. 13 100 – alt. 10 m – ✉ 30800 23 D2

Provence

Paris 724 – Arles 18 – Beaucaire 27 – Lunel 31 – Montpellier 64 – Nîmes 20

Office de tourisme, 1, place Frédéric Mistral ✆ 04 66 87 33 75, Fax 04 66 87 16 28

Façade★★ and crypt★ of the church - Vis de St-Gilles★.

Le Cours

10 av. François Griffeuille – ✆ 04 66 87 31 93 – www.hotel-le-cours.com – hotel-le-cours@wanadoo.fr – Fax 04 66 87 31 83 – Open 11 March-9 December

32 rm – €46/62 €56/75, €8 – ½ P €49/60

Rest – Menu (€12), €14/36 – Carte €22/42

◆ This family hotel near the marina on the Rhône canal offers small, practical rooms, all renovated and well kept. In fine weather, forget the dining room-veranda and sit at a terrace table, shaded by plane trees. Regional fare.

Domaine de la Fosse rm, rest,

rte de Sylvéréal, 7km on via D 179, D 202 crossroads – ✆ 04 66 87 05 05 – www.domaine-de-la-fosse.com – alain.abecassis@orange.fr – Fax 04 66 87 40 90

5 rm – €120 €135/145 – ½ P €100/125 **Table d'hôte** – Menu €35 bi

◆ In the heart of a Camargue rice growing estate, this former Templar stronghold (17C) offers antique furnished rooms, often with feature sloping ceilings. Sauna, steam bath, Jacuzzi.

ST-GILLES-CROIX-DE-VIE – 85 Vendée – 316 E7 – pop. 7 189 – alt. 12 m – Casino : Le Royal Concorde – ✉ 85800 Atlantic Coast 34 A3

Paris 462 – Cholet 112 – Nantes 79 – La Roche-sur-Yon 44 – Les Sables-d'Olonne 29

Office de tourisme, boulevard de l'Égalité ✆ 02 51 55 03 66, Fax 02 51 55 69 60

des Fontenelles L'Aiguillon-sur-Vie Route de Coëx, E : 11 km on D 6, ✆ 02 51 54 13 94

Le Casier

pl. du Vieux Port – ✆ 02 51 55 01 08 – www.lecasier.com – restaurant.lecasier@orange.fr – Closed 20 December-3 March and Monday

Rest – Carte € 20/41

◆ Friendly nautical-inspired bistro decor, simple well-prepared seafood; the chef of this former pork butcher's shop near the quays has successfully swapped his apron for a chef's hat.

in Sion-sur-l'Océan 5 km west by the Corniche Vendéenne – ✉ 85270

Frédéric without rest

25 r. des Estivants – ✆ 02 51 54 30 20 – www.hotel-frederic.com – info@hotel-frederic.com – Fax 02 51 54 11 68

13 rm – †€ 64/120 ††€ 64/120, ☕ € 12

◆ This attractive 1930s villa has been modernised without losing any of its former character. Ask for one of the rooms with a sea view. Delightfully old-fashioned oyster bar.

ST-GINGOLPH – 74 Haute-Savoie – **328** N2 – **pop. 626** – **alt. 385 m** – ✉ **74500** ▮ **French Alps** — 46 **F1**

Paris 560 – Annecy 102 – Évian-les-Bains 19 – Montreux 21 – Thonon-les-Bains 28

Aux Ducs de Savoie

r. 23 Juillet 44 – ✆ 04 50 76 73 09 – www.ducdesavoie.net – ducsdesavoie@orange.fr – Closed 4-20 January, 17-24 February, Tuesday except July-August and Monday

Rest – Menu € 19 (weekdays)/64 – Carte € 37/65

◆ Just below the village, this chalet is surrounded by plane trees. Shaded terrace facing the lake, traditional cuisine prepared with skill.

ST-GIRONS – 09 Ariège – **343** E7 – **pop. 6 552** – **alt. 398 m** – ✉ **09200** ▮ **Languedoc-Roussillon-Tarn Gorges** — 28 **B3**

Paris 774 – Auch 123 – Foix 45 – St-Gaudens 43 – Toulouse 101

Office de tourisme, place Alphonse Sentein ✆ 05 61 96 26 60, Fax 05 61 96 26 69

Eychenne — rest,

8 av. P. Laffont – ✆ 05 61 04 04 50 – www.ariege.com/hotel-eychenne – hotel-eychenne@wanadoo.fr – Fax 05 61 96 07 20 – Closed December, January, Sunday dinner and Monday except bank holidays from November to end March

42 rm – †€ 53/58 ††€ 71/205, ☕ € 11 – ½ P € 70/138

Rest – Menu € 28/57 – Carte € 30/50

◆ A converted post house with a pleasant, bourgeois atmosphere. Careful interior decor and antique furniture in the rooms. Some have a view of the Pyrenees. Personalised welcome. Traditional fare and fine terrace in the midst of a lovely garden.

Château de Beauregard — rest, rest,

av. de la Résistance – ✆ 05 61 66 66 64 – www.chateaubeauregard.net – contact@chateaubeauregard.net – Fax 05 34 14 07 93 – Closed 1-22 March and 6 November-1 December

10 rm – †€ 60/200 ††€ 60/200, ☕ € 10 – 3 suites – ½ P € 70/140

Rest *Auberge d'Antan* – *(closed Monday except in summer)* Menu € 29/40

◆ This small 19C château and its hunting lodge are surrounded by a peaceful, pleasant park and rose garden. Charming retro-style rooms (period furniture). Rustic decor and traditional fare cooked on a wood fire at the Auberge d'Antan.

La Clairière

av. de la Résistance – ✆ 05 61 66 66 66 – www.hotel-clairiere.com – reservation@hotel-clairiere.com – Fax 05 34 14 30 30

19 rm – †€ 58/68 ††€ 58/68, ☕ € 9 – ½ P € 63/68

Rest – Menu (€ 23), € 29/64 – Carte approx. € 42

◆ Set in a park, this unusual modern construction has a shingle roof reaching to the ground. It offers comfortable rooms, most with panelling. Restaurant offering modern cuisine and a good selection of Languedoc-Roussillon wines. Poolside terrace.

ST-GRÉGOIRE – **35 Ille-et-Vilaine** – **309** L6 – **see Rennes**

ST-GUÉNOLÉ – **29 Finistère** – **308** E8 – ✉ **29760 Penmarch** ▮ **Brittany** 9 **A2**

Paris 587 – Douarnenez 47 – Guilvinec 8 – Pont-l'Abbé 14 – Quimper 34

Office de tourisme, Pl. du Mar. Davout ☎ 02 98 58 81 44, Fax 02 98 58 86 62

Musée préhistorique★ - ≤★★ of Eckmühl lighthouse★ South: 2.5 km - Penmarch ★ church Southeast: 3 km - Pointe de la Torche ≤★ Northeast: 4 km.

Sterenn ≤ rest, VISA

plage de la Joie – ☎ 02 98 58 60 36 – www.hotel-sterenn.com – contact@hotel-sterenn.com – Fax 02 98 58 71 28 – Closed January

16 rm – €46/98 €46/98, ☕ €11 – ½ P €65/98

Rest – *(closed Monday)* Menu (€15), €22/39 – Carte €25/65

◆ Large building (1978) facing the beach, with a slate roof. Simple, tidy rooms and the Côte Sauvage nature reserve for a backdrop.

Les Ondines VISA AE

90 r. Pasteur, le phare d'Eckmühl road – ☎ 02 98 58 74 95 – www.lesondines.com – hotel@lesondines.com – Fax 02 98 58 73 99 – Open 3 April-15 November and closed Tuesday except July-August

14 rm – €52/68 €52/68, ☕ €8 – ½ P €52/62

Rest – Menu €17/40 – Carte €30/65

◆ No through road leads to this Breton establishment a step away from the sea, at the far tip of the Bigouden region. Pleasant rooms with marine-style decor. Dining room-veranda where the sea reigns over everything, even the sauerkraut!

La Mer with rm rest, VISA

184 r. F. Péron – ☎ 02 98 58 62 22 – sannierloic@orange.fr – Fax 02 98 58 53 86 – Closed 16-30 November, 20 January-10 February

10 rm – €50/66 €50/66, ☕ €9 – ½ P €70/78

Rest – *(Closed Sunday dinner and Tuesday dinner in low season and Monday except dinner in high season)* Menu €22 (weekdays)/52 – Carte €54/71

◆ This restaurant, situated on the first floor of a country house, offers a lovely view over the bay. Regional recipes honour the local fishermen.

ST-GUILHEM-LE-DESERT – **34 Hérault** – **339** G6 – **pop. 241** – **alt. 89 m** – ✉ **34150** 23 **C2**

Paris 726 – Montpellier 41 – Lodève 31 – Millau 90

Office de tourisme, 3, parc d'activités de Calamcé ☎ 04 67 57 58 83

Le Guilhaume d'Orange rm, rm, VISA

2 av. Guillaume d'Orange – ☎ 04 67 57 24 53 – www.guillaumedorange.com – contact@guilhaumedorange.com – Fax 04 67 60 38 56 – Closed 15-23 December and Wednesday

10 rm – €67/87 €87/97, ☕ €7,50 – ½ P €57/72

Rest – Menu €19/26 – Carte approx. €35

◆ This building near the Herault gorges has been carefully restored, thus retaining its original character. Charming, delightfully romantic rooms, yet with mod cons. Simple family cooking served in the dining room or on the pleasant terrace.

ST-GUIRAUD – **34 Hérault** – **339** F6 – **see Clermont-l'Hérault**

ST-HAON – **43 Haute-Loire** – **331** E4 – **pop. 376** – **alt. 1 000 m** – ✉ **43340** ▮ **Auvergne** 6 **C3**

Paris 559 – Langogne 25 – Mende 68 – Le Puy-en-Velay 29

Auberge de la Vallée with rm ≤ VISA

– ☎ 04 71 08 20 73 – auberge-de-la-vallée.fr – aubergevallee43@wanadoo.fr – Fax 04 71 08 29 21 – Closed 1st January-20 March, Sunday dinner and Monday from October to April

10 rm – €40 €47, ☕ €8 – ½ P €46 **Rest** – Menu €17/38 – Carte €25/44

◆ Unassuming family-run inn in an alpine village. Large, plainly decorated restaurant serving regionally inspire cuisine. Neat rooms.

ST-HAON-LE-VIEUX – 42 Loire – **327** C3 – see Renaison

ST-HERBLAIN – 44 Loire-Atlantique – **316** G4 – see Nantes

ST-HILAIRE-DE-BRETHMAS – 30 Gard – **339** J4 – see Alès

ST-HILAIRE-DES-LOGES – 85 Vendée – **316** L9 – pop. 1 788 – alt. 48 m – ✉ 85240 35 **C3**

Paris 444 – Nantes 130 – La Roche-sur-Yon 77 – Niort 34 – Bressuire 53

Le Pantagruelion VISA MC

9 r. Octroi – ✆ 02 51 00 59 19 – lepantagruelion@wanadoo.fr
– Fax 02 51 51 29 55 – Closed Saturday lunch, Sunday dinner and Wednesday
Rest – Menu (€ 17), € 21/28 – Carte € 35/48
◆ A beamed ceiling, stone walls and floor matting add to the pleasant rustic feel of this restaurant serving appetising traditional cuisine based on ingredients sourced from local producers.

ST-HILAIRE-D'OZILHAN – 30 Gard – **339** M5 – see Remoulins

ST-HILAIRE-DU-HARCOUËT – 50 Manche – **303** F8 – pop. 4 273 – alt. 70 m – ✉ 50600 Normandy 32 **A3**

Paris 339 – Alençon 100 – Avranches 27 – Caen 102 – Fougères 29 – Laval 66 – St-Lô 69

Office de tourisme, place du Bassin ✆ 02 33 79 38 88, Fax 02 33 79 38 89

Centre d'Art Sacré★.

Le Cygne et Résidence rm, rest, P VISA MC AE

99 r. Waldeck Rousseau, Fougères road –
✆ 02 33 49 11 84 – www.hotel-le-cygne.fr – contact@hotel-le-cygne.fr
– Fax 02 33 49 53 70 – Closed Friday dinner and Sunday dinner from October to Easter
30 rm – €54 €68, € 9 – ½ P € 60/80
Rest – Menu € 17/72 bi – Carte € 35/80
◆ Family style accommodation in a pleasant, middle-class residence of recent construction. Soberly furnished rooms; quieter to the rear. Seafood and Normandy dishes on the menu. Good wine list. Terrace on the garden side.

ST-HILAIRE-LE-CHÂTEAU – 23 Creuse – **325** I5 – pop. 273 – alt. 453 m – ✉ 23250 25 **C1**

Paris 385 – Guéret 27 – Le Palais-sur-Vienne 56 – Limoges 64

East 3 km by D 941 (Aubenas road), D10 and secondary road ✉ 23250 St-Hilaire-le-Château

Château de la Chassagne P

La Chassagne – ✆ 05 55 64 55 75 – www.chateau-lachassagne.com – m.fanton@aliceadsl.fr – Fax 05 55 64 55 75
4 rm – €95 €140 **Table d'hôte** – Menu € 30 bi
◆ Fine 15C and 17C château, nestling in a park with grazing horses. A spiral staircase serves the refined rooms, including one with magnificent exposed timberwork.

ST-HILAIRE-ST-FLORENT – 49 Maine-et-Loire – **317** I5 – see Saumur

ST-HIPPOLYTE – 25 Doubs – **321** K3 – pop. 936 – alt. 380 m – ✉ 25190 Burgundy-Jura 17 **C2**

Paris 490 – Basel 93 – Belfort 48 – Besançon 89 – Montbéliard 32 – Pontarlier 71

Office de tourisme, place de l'Hôtel de Ville ✆ 03 81 96 58 00

Site★ - Le Dessoubre Valley ★ S.

Le Bellevue

rte de Maîche – ✆ 03 81 96 51 53 – www.hotel.bellevue.free.fr – hotel.bellevue@free.fr – Fax 03 81 96 52 40 – Closed 2-16 January, Sunday dinner and Friday dinner from September to April

16 rm – €54/60 €57/68, €10 – ½ P €59/67

Rest – *(closed Monday lunch)* Menu (€12), €25/35 – Carte €32/49

◆ Former hostelry on the banks of the Dessoubre. Gradually spruced up rooms, the most recent of which are under the eaves. Enjoy river fish or game depending on the season in the charming dining room or on the panoramic terrace.

ST-HIPPOLYTE – 68 Haut-Rhin – 315 I7 – pop. 1 049 – alt. 234 m – ✉ 68590 Alsace-Lorraine — 2 C1

Paris 439 – Colmar 21 – Ribeauvillé 8 – St-Dié 42 – Sélestat 10 – Villé 18

Château du Haut-Koenigsbourg★★: ✳★★ Northwest: 8 km.

Le Parc

rm, rest,

6 r. du Parc – ✆ 03 89 73 00 06 – www.le-parc.com – hotel-le-parc@wanadoo.fr – Fax 03 89 73 04 30 – Closed 29 June-9 July and 11 January-5 February

26 rm – €75 €88/140, €14 – 5 suites – ½ P €90/125

Rest – *(closed Sunday dinner, Monday and Tuesday)* Menu (€36), €45/70

Rest *Winstub Rabseppi-Stebel* – *(closed Mon. lunch and Tues. lunch)* Menu (€10), €20/70 – Carte €32/62

◆ A riot of colour inside and outside this hotel, located opposite a park. Gradually renovated elegant rooms and extensive leisure facilities. Up-to-date cuisine in the restaurant. Alsatian specialities and wines are served in the winstub.

Hostellerie Munsch Aux Ducs de Lorraine

rm, rest,

– ✆ 03 89 73 00 09 – www.hotel-munsch.com – hotel.munsch@wanadoo.fr – Fax 03 89 73 05 46 – Closed 15-30 November and mid January-mid February

40 rm – €50/70 €80/124, €12 – ½ P €82/104

Rest – *(Closed 29 June-10 July, Tuesday dinner and Wednesday)* Menu €16 (weekday lunch), €23/56 – Carte €23/56

◆ Striking Alsatian-style inn. Individual rooms some with a balcony, overlooking the Haut-Koenigsbourg Castle or the vineyards. Sculpted wood and a flower-decked terrace. Traditional cuisine and house wines.

ST-HUBERT – 57 Moselle – 307 I3 – pop. 233 – alt. 220 m – ✉ 57640 — 27 C1

Paris 336 – Luxembourg 63 – Metz 21 – Saarbrücken 69

La Ferme de Godchure without rest

r. Principale – ✆ 03 87 77 03 96 – www.lafermedegodchure.fr – godchure@wanadoo.fr

4 rm – €75/95 €75/95

◆ A former Cistercian farm, on the edge of a country village, with a barn converted into a guesthouse. Rooms with personal touches; friendly welcome, attentive service. Small spa.

ST-ISIDORE – 06 Alpes-Maritimes – 341 E5 – see Nice

ST-JACQUES-DES-BLATS – 15 Cantal – 330 E4 – pop. 330 – alt. 990 m – ✉ 15800 — 5 B3

Paris 536 – Aurillac 32 – Brioude 76 – Issoire 91 – St-Flour 39

L'Escoundillou

rm, rest,

Route de la Gare – ✆ 04 71 47 06 42 – www.hotel-escoundillou.com – hotel-escoundillou@wanadoo.fr – Fax 04 71 47 00 97 – Closed 15 November-20 December, Friday dinner and Saturday from 15 October to 15 November

12 rm – €43 €46, €8 – ½ P €45/48 **Rest** – Menu €14/24

◆ A little hiding-place ("escoundillou" in the local dialect) on a picturesque country road, ideal for nature-lovers. Bright, clean rooms. Bright, airy, modern dining room serving locally sourced produce.

Le Brunet

– 04 71 47 05 86 – *www.hotel-brunet.com* – *hotel.brunet@wanadoo.fr* – *Fax 04 71 47 04 27*
15 rm – €43/55 €43/55, €7 – ½ P €43/55
Rest – Menu €16/30 – Carte approx. €21
◆ Recent buildings in the local style below the village. Well thought-out rooms, often with balconies facing the Cère valley. Auvergne specialities served in a sober decor or on the terrace overlooking the meadows in summer.

Le Griou

– 04 71 47 06 25 – *www.hotel-griou.com* – *hotel.griou@wanadoo.fr* – *Fax 04 71 47 00 16 – Closed 20 October-20 December*
16 rm – €45/53 €45/53, €7 – ½ P €45/49
Rest – Menu €15/32 – Carte €23/30
◆ Surrounded by the Cantal hills, this family-run guesthouse boasts a pleasant garden to the rear, overlooking the river. Simple rooms. Dining room overlooking the countryside. Auvergne stews and pountis take pride of place on the menu.

ST-JAMES – 50 Manche – 303 E8 – pop. 2 917 – alt. 100 m – ✉ 50240 — 32 A3
Normandy

Paris 357 – Avranches 21 – Fougères 29 – Rennes 69 – St-Lô 78 – St-Malo 61

Office de tourisme, 21, rue de la Libération 02 33 89 62 12, Fax 02.33.89.62.09

American cemetery

Normandie

2 pl. Bagot – 02 33 48 31 45 – *www.hotel-normandiehotel.com* – *Normandie-hotel.saint-james@hotmail.fr* – *Fax 02 33 48 31 37* – *Closed 20 December-5 January and Sunday evening except holidays*
10 rm – €33/45 €35/55, €6,50 – ½ P €49/53
Rest – Menu €16/24 – Carte €19/43
◆ Village inn on the borders of Brittany and Normandy. The discreetly furnished rooms are larger on the first floor. A restaurant with a rustic setting and predominantly seafood menu. Daily lunchtime specials served at the busy counter.

ST-JEAN – 06 Alpes-Maritimes – 341 C6 – see Pégomas

ST-JEAN-AUX-AMOGNES – 58 Nièvre – 319 D9 – pop. 462 – alt. 230 m – ✉ 58270 — 7 B2

Paris 252 – Bourges 81 – Château-Chinon 51 – Clamecy 61 – Nevers 16

Le Relais de Bourgogne

– 03 86 58 61 44 – *Fax 03 86 58 61 44 – Closed 2-22 January, Sunday dinner and Wednesday*
Rest – Menu €23/40 – Carte €31/50
◆ The recently-renovated facade of this village building conceals a warm country-style interior, with a veranda overlooking the pleasant garden terrace. Traditional meals served.

ST-JEAN-AUX-BOIS – 60 Oise – 305 I4 – see Pierrefonds

ST-JEAN-CAP-FERRAT – 06 Alpes-Maritimes – 341 E5 – pop. 2 103 – alt. 12 m – ✉ 06230 French Riviera — 42 E2

Paris 935 – Menton 25 – Nice 8

Office de tourisme, 59, avenue Denis Semeria 04 93 76 08 90, Fax 04 93 76 16 67

Site of the Villa Ephrussi-de-Rothschild★★ **M** : Musée Île de France (Île de France Museum)★★, gardens★★ - Phare ✳★★ - Pointe de St-Hospice : ≤★ of the chapel, footpath★ - Promenade Maurice-Rouvier★.

ST-JEAN-CAP-FERRAT

Albert-1er (Av.) 2
Gaulle (Bd Gén.-de) 6
Grasseuil (Av.). 7
Libération (Bd) 9
Mermoz (Av. J.) 12
Passable (Ch. de) 13
Phare (Av. du) 14
Prince-Rainier III de Monaco (Av.) 3
Puncia (Av. de la) 15
Sabatier (Av. Marie-Louise) . . 5
St-Jean (Pont) 16
Sauvan (Bd H.) 17
Semeria (Av. D.) 18
Verdun (Av. de). 20
Vignon (Av. C.) 21

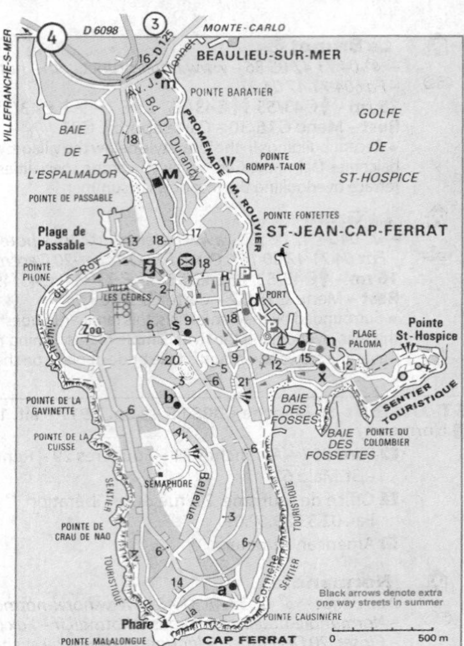

Grand Hôtel du Cap Ferrat

71 bd Gén.de Gaulle, at Cap-Ferrat – ☎ 04 93 76 50 50
– www.grand-hotel-cap-ferrat.com – reserv@grand-hotel-cap-ferrat.com
– Fax 04 93 76 04 52 – Closed 1 March-30 April **a**

49 rm – €250/1550 €250/1550, ☕ €45 – 24 suites
Rest *Le Cap* – *(closed for lunch except weekends)* Menu €135 – Carte €137/217
Rest *Club Dauphin* – swimming pool rest. *(lunch only)* Menu (€60) – Carte €88/106

Spec. Lasagne au caviar d'aubergine, jeunes poireaux à l'huile d'olive. Dos d'agneau "allaiton" de l'Aveyron, aubergine et kumquat. Tendance chocolat à l'orange, sorbet cacao. **Wines** Vin de Pays du Var, Bandol.

◆ A private (air-conditioned) funicular railway transports guests across a superb park to the infinity pool of this fully renovated luxury hotel (1908). Sea views. Luxurious restaurant, magnificent terrace and classic cuisine. At the Club Dauphin, meals are served overlooking the Club's pool.

Royal Riviera

3 av. J. Monnet – ☎ 04 93 76 31 00 – www.royal-riviera.com
– resa@royal-riviera.com – Fax 04 93 01 23 07
– Closed 29 November-17 January **m**

94 rm – €250/1415 €250/1415, ☕ €36 – 3 suites
Rest *Le Panorama* – *(dinner only in July-August)* Menu €53 – Carte €89/139
Rest *La Pergola* – swimming pool rest. *(open mid-April to mid-October)* *(lunch only)* Carte €46/109

◆ Early 20C luxury hotel with a handsome waterside garden. Elegant rooms, most overlooking the sea (contemporary Provençal décor in the Orangerie). Elegant, quiet dining rooms are to be found at the Panorama. A buffet and grilled meats at Le Pergola, brunch on Sundays.

La Voile d'Or
7 av. Jean Mermoz, at the port – 04 93 01 13 13 – www.lavoiledor.fr – reservation@lavoiledor.fr – Fax 04 93 76 11 17 – Open early April to early October
45 rm – €196/890 €270/890 f
Rest – Menu (€48 bi), €85/110 – Carte €110/190
◆ Ideal location opposite the marina, seafront swimming pools and a studied decor means that a pleasant stay is guaranteed. Panoramic dining room, lovely summer terrace and classic menu. Snacks served on the beach.

Brise Marine without rest
av. J. Mermoz – 04 93 76 04 36 – www.hotel-brisemarine.com – info@hotel-brisemarine.com – Fax 04 93 76 11 49 – Open from February to October
16 rm – €150/178 €150/178, €14 x
◆ An 1878 Italian-style villa overlooking a quiet street. Elegant rooms; in summer breakfast is served on the terrace overlooking the garden of ornamental fruit trees.

Le Panoramic without rest
3 av. Albert 1er – 04 93 76 00 37 – www.hotel-lepanoramic.com – info@hotel-lepanoramic.com – Fax 04 93 76 15 78 – Closed 15 November-25 December
20 rm – €145 €145/175, €12 s
◆ The name of this 1950s family hotel says it all: exceptional view of the gulf, the headland and the town. Simple, somewhat old-fashioned but well-kept rooms with balcony.

Clair Logis without rest
12 av. Prince Rainier III de Monaco – 04 93 76 51 81 – www.hotel-clair-logis.fr – hotel.clair.logis@orange.fr – Fax 04 93 76 51 82 – Closed 10 November-20 December and 10 January-6 March b
18 rm – €90/115 €105/175, €13
◆ General de Gaulle was one of the famous guests at this Provençal villa tucked away in a pretty park. Characterful rooms, simpler comforts in the annexe.

La Table du Cap (Laurent Poulet)
2 av. Denis-Séméria – 04 93 76 03 97 – www.laurentpoulet.com – latableducap@laurentpoulet.com – Fax 04 93 76 05 39 – Open March-October and closed Monday and Tuesday d
Rest – *(number of covers limited, pre-book)* Menu (€25 bi), €37 (lunch), €47 € bi/80 – Carte €70/130
Spec. Tartare d'un filet de Saint Pierre et barigoule de fenouil. Cœur de queue de lotte rôtie au romarin. "Cécile", le tout chocolat !
◆ Attractive restaurant that hosts contemporary art and sculpture exhibitions. Shaded terrace. Updated, inventive look at Provençal culinary classics.

Capitaine Cook
11 av. J. Mermoz – 04 93 76 02 66 – Fax 04 93 76 02 66 – Closed 4 November-26 December, Thursday lunch and Wednesday n
Rest – Menu €26/31 – Carte €44/66
◆ A spruce restaurant tucked away on the headland with tightly packed tables in the rustic dining room or small terrace. Traditional cuisine with a seafood bias.

ST-JEAN D'ALCAS – 12 Aveyron – 338 K7 – 12250 29 D2
Languedoc-Roussillon-Tarn Gorges

Paris 677 – Toulouse 170 – Rodez 118 – Millau 35 – Saint-Affrique 14

Le Moulin de Gauty without rest
– 05 65 97 51 90 – www.moulindegauty.com – contact@moulindegauty.com
4 rm – €70/110 €80/120
◆ This former mill in a rural setting is the perfect place to recharge your batteries. Stylish modern bedrooms plus an attractive riverside garden. Pool and mountain bikes available.

ST-JEAN-D'ANGÉLY – 17 Charente-Maritime – 324 G4 – pop. 7 491 – alt. 25 m – 17400 Atlantic Coast 38 B2

Paris 444 – La Rochelle 72 – Niort 48 – Royan 69 – Saintes 36

Office de tourisme, 8, rue Grosse Horloge 05 46 32 04 72, Fax 05 46 32 20 80

ST-JEAN-D'ANGÉLY

Abbaye (R. de l') . . . . A 2
Aguesseau (R. d') . . . . A 3
Bancs (R. des) . . . . A 4
Bourcy (R. Pascal) . . . . B 6
Cumont (Bd P.-de) . . . . B 8
Dubreuil (R. L. A.) . . . . A 10
Gambetta (R.) . . . . A
Grosse Horloge (R.) . . . . B 12
Gymnase (R. du) . . . . B 13
Hôtel de Ville (Pl. de l') . . . . . . B 14
Jacobins (R. des) . . . . B 16
Libération (Square de la) . . . . . B 17
Maréchal-Leclerc (Av. du) . . . . B 19
Maréchaux (R. des) . . . . AB 20
Porte de Niort (R. de la) . . . . . B 24
Port Mahon (Av. du) . . . . AB 25
Regnaud (R.) . . . . A 27
Remparts (R. des) . . . . B 28
Rose (R.) . . . . B 29
Taillebourg (Fg) . . . . A
Texier (R. Michel) . . . . A 31
Tourneur (R. L.) . . . . B 32
Tour Ronde (R.) . . . . B 33
Verdun (R. de) . . . . A 35
3-Frères-Gautreau (R. des) . . . A 37
4-Septembre (R. du) . . . . B 39
11-Novembre (R. du) . . . . . . AB 40

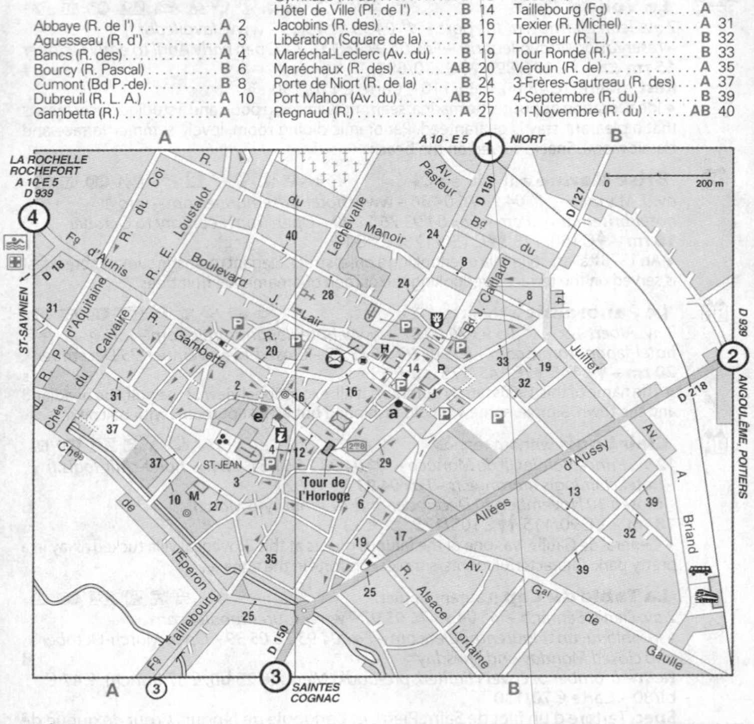

🏠 **De la Place** rm, VISA

pl. Hôtel de Ville – ✆ 05 46 32 69 11 – www.hoteldelaplace.net – paris.mail.sinclair@wanadoo.fr – Fax 05 46 32 08 44 – Closed autumn school holidays and 1st-21 January B **a**

10 rm – †€ 48/60 ††€ 58/64, ☕ € 6,50

Rest – Menu (€ 12), € 18/47 – Carte € 32/48

◆ In the heart of the town and near the historic centre, this family-run hotel offers simple, well-soundproofed rooms. Renovation underway. Cuisine with a contemporary touch served in a bistro style dining room.

XX **Le Scorlion** VISA

5 r. Abbaye – ✆ 05 46 32 52 61 – robertcr@hotmail.com – Fax 05 46 59 99 90 – Closed 14-20 April, 28 October-12 November, 23 February-8 March, Wednesday dinner October-May, Sunday dinner and Monday A **e**

Rest – Menu (€ 15), € 17/48

◆ This pleasant, comfortable restaurant inside a former royal abbey successfully mixes old and new. Culinary register in keeping with current taste.

ST-JEAN-DE-BLAIGNAC – 33 Gironde – 335 K6 – pop. 374 – alt. 50 m – ✉ 33420 4 **C1**

▶ Paris 592 – Bergerac 56 – Bordeaux 40 – Libourne 17 – La Réole 29

XX **Auberge St-Jean** VISA

8 r. du Pont – ✆ 05 57 74 95 50 – Fax 05 57 84 51 57 – Closed 7-19 December, Tuesday dinner in winter, Wednesday except lunch in high season and Sunday dinner

Rest – Menu (€ 28), € 46 – Carte € 60/80

◆ Former post house facing the Dordogne. A plush sitting room adorned with copperware leads into two tasteful dining rooms that include a covered terrace. Modern-classic menu.

ST-JEAN-DE-BRAYE – 45 Loiret – 318 I4 – see Orléans

ST-JEAN-DE-LUZ – 64 Pyrénées-Atlantiques – **342** C4 – **pop. 13 300** – alt. 3 m – Casino ABY – ✉ 64500 ▮ Atlantic Coast 3 **A3**

Paris 785 – Bayonne 24 – Biarritz 18 – Pau 129 – San Sebastián 31

Office de tourisme, place du Maréchal Foch ✆ 05 59 26 03 16, Fax 05 59 26 21 47

de Chantaco Route d'Ascain, 2 km on the Ascain road, ✆ 05 59 26 14 22

de la Nivelle Ciboure Place William Sharp, S : 3 km on D 704, ✆ 05 59 47 18 99

Harbour★ – St-Jean-Baptiste church ★★ – Maison Louis-XIV★ **N** – Corniche basque (cliff road)★★ by ④ – Sémaphore de Socoa ≤★★ 5 km by ④.

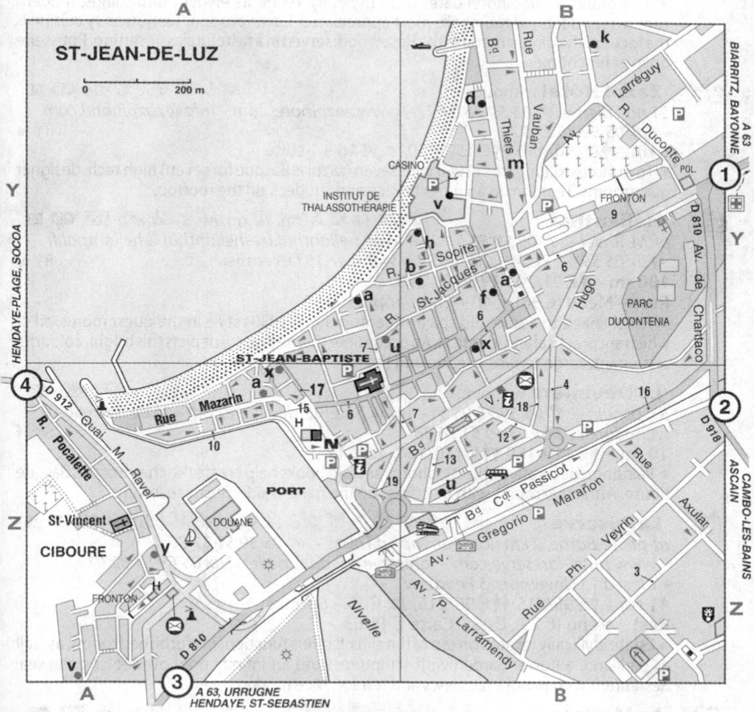

Bibal (R. F.) **BZ** 3	Infante (Quai de l') **AZ** 10	République (R. de la) **AZ** 17
Chauvin-Dragon (R.) **BZ** 4	Jaurréguiberry (Av.) **BZ** 12	Salagoity (R. de) **BZ** 18
Elizaga (Sq.) **BY** 9	Labrouche (Av.) **BZ** 13	Verdun (Av. de) **AZ** 19
Gambetta (R.) **AZ, BY** 6	Louis-XIV (Pl.) **AZ** 15	Victor-Hugo (Bd) **BYZ**
Garat (R.) **AYZ** 7	Pyrénées (Av. des) **BZ** 16	

Parc Victoria

5 r. Cépé, via bd Thiers and Quartier du Lac road – ✆ 05 59 26 78 78 – www.parcvictoria.com – parcvictoria@relaischateaux.com – Fax 05 59 26 78 08 – Open 15 March-14 November and 19 December-3 January

13 rm – ♦€ 140/320 ♦♦€ 170/360, ☕ € 20 – 5 suites – ½ P € 138/233

Rest ***Les Lierres*** – *(closed lunch except weekends and bank holidays)* Menu € 40/85 – Carte € 70/95

◆ Beautiful late-19C villa and outhouses nestling in a flower-decked park (pool and Jacuzzi). Plush Art Deco interior. Suites with a small private garden. Restaurant in a verdant setting with two small dining rooms (conservatory or 1930s style).

Grand Hôtel rest,

43 bd Thiers – ✆ 05 59 26 35 36
– www.luzgrandhotel.fr – reservation@luzgrandhotel.fr – Fax 05 59 51 99 84
52 rm – €170/320 €170/320, €30 – 3 suites BY **d**
Rest *Le Rosewood* – *(closed Monday and Tuesday) (dinner only)* Menu €45/110 – Carte €75/110
Rest *La Rôtisserie* – *(closed dinner from Wednesday to Sunday)* Menu €45/70 – Carte €75/110
Spec. Cannelloni de mangue et chair de tourteau à la coriandre (15 May to 15 Sep.). Suprême de Saint-Pierre au croustillant de boudin des Aldudes. Soufflé chaud et gaspacho pomme verte, sorbet manzana (15 Sep. to 15 Feb.). **Wines** Irouléguy.
◆ This grand seaside hotel dates from the early 1900s. Its elegant furnishings, modern comforts and refined rooms are most appreciated. Luxurious spa. Tasty, trendy cuisine is the focus of the dinner menu at the Rosewood, served in a tasteful classic setting. Rotisserie open at lunchtime.

Zazpi Hôtel without rest

21 bd Thiers – ✆ 05 59 26 07 77 – www.zazpihotel.com – info@zazpihotel.com – Fax 05 59 26 27 77 BY **a**
6 rm – €150/450 €150/450, €16 – 1 suite
◆ Townhouse dating from 1900 with seven (zazpi is Basque for seven) high tech, designer guestrooms. Tearoom in an inner terrace and sundeck on the rooftop.

Hélianthal rm, rm,

pl. M. Ravel – ✆ 05 59 51 51 51 – www.helianthal.fr – helianthal@helianthal.fr – Fax 05 59 51 51 54 – Closed 29 November-19 December BY **v**
100 rm – €91/201 €113/273, €15
Rest – Menu (€36), €40 – Carte approx. €50
◆ Hotel linked to a splendid spa (residents only). A 1930s style in the guest rooms, all of which are practical and identical. An ocean liner theme (fresco) depicts this bright, colourful restaurant. Large terrace overlooking the bay.

La Devinière without rest

5 r. Loquin – ✆ 05 59 26 05 51 – www.hotel-la-deviniere.com – la.deviniere.64@wanadoo.fr – Fax 05 59 51 26 38 BY **f**
10 rm – €110/180 €110/180, €12
◆ Paintings, decorative objects, photos and old books help create the charm of this Basque house. Attractive rooms with balconies on the garden side. Rustic tearoom.

La Réserve

rd-pt Ste-Barbe, 2 km north on the bd Thiers – ✆ 05 59 51 32 00 – www.hotel-lareserve.com – lareserve@wanadoo.fr – Fax 05 59 51 32 01 – Closed 15 November-5 February
41 rm – €95/215 €95/215, €15 – 6 suites
Rest – Menu (€25), €45 – Carte €46/63
◆ Estate idyllically located on top of the cliffs. It offers functional, refurbished rooms, as well as parkland, a flower garden with sculptures, and an infinity pool overlooking the sea. Restaurant with panoramic views and terrace. Nice modern menu.

La Marisa without rest

16 r. Sopite – ✆ 05 59 26 95 46 – www.hotel-lamarisa.com – info@hotel-lamarisa.com – Fax 05 59 51 17 06 – Closed 3 January-11 February
16 rm – €85/99 €90/160, €11 BY **b**
◆ A warm welcome awaits you in this hotel providing rooms furnished with hand picked antiques or items imported from Asia. Delicious breakfasts facing a lovely floral patio.

De la Plage rm, rm,

promenade J. Thibaud – ✆ 05 59 51 03 44 – www.hoteldelaplage.com – reservation@hoteldelaplage.com – Fax 05 59 51 03 48 – Closed 4 January-12 February and 15 November-17 December AY **a**
22 rm – €88/169 €88/169
Rest *Le Brouillarta* – *✆ 05 59 51 29 51 (closed Sunday dinner and Monday except July-August)* Menu (€25) – Carte €32/45
◆ Large, well-located seaside hotel facing the beach. Practical modern rooms, most of which face the sea. A bistro atmosphere and a fine view of the bay of Saint Jean de Luz. Simple regional fare.

Les Almadies without rest
58 r. Gambetta – 05 59 85 34 48 – www.hotel-les-almadies.com – hotel.lesalmadies@wanadoo.fr – Fax 05 59 26 12 42 – Closed 12 November-5 December BY **x**
7 rm – €85/105 €95/130, €12
◆ Tasteful restoration of this engaging small hotel, decorated with a happy mix of old and new. Immaculate rooms, faintly ethnic-inspired breakfast room and small flowered terrace.

Colbert without rest
3 bd du Cdt Passicot – 05 59 26 31 99 – www.hotelcolbertsaintjeandeluz.com – contact@hotelcolbertsaintjeandeluz.com – Fax 05 59 51 05 61 – Closed 29 November-8 January BZ **u**
34 rm – €72/126 €77/141, €13
◆ This newly decorated hotel, opposite the station, sports a discreet contemporary look (pale wood and shades of brown). Comfortable rooms. Buffet breakfast.

Villa Bel Air without rest
rest,
60 promenade J. Thibaud – 05 59 26 04 86 – www.hotel-bel-air.com – belairhotel@wanadoo.fr – Fax 05 59 26 62 34 – Open 3 April-15 November
21 rm – €84/147 €84/166, €10 BY **h**
◆ A slight boarding house feel to this large Basque seaside villa built in 1850. Cosy lounge and well-kept rooms, most overlooking the beach.

Les Goëlands
rest,
4 av. Etcheverry – 05 59 26 10 05 – www.hotel-lesgoelands.com – reception@hotel-lesgoelands.com – Fax 05 59 51 04 02 – Closed 18-26 December
33 rm (½ board only in July-August) – €40/60 €69/130 – ½ P €68/100 BY **k**
Rest – *(Open 9 April-3 November) (residents only)* Menu €21
◆ Calm, family guesthouse atmosphere in a residential area. These two charming Basque villas dating from 1902 have been well renovated. Antiques and charming interior.

Villa Argi-Eder without rest
av. Napoléon III, 3 km on ①, D 810 and secondary road – 05 59 54 81 65 – www.chambresdhotes-argi-eder.com – villa-argi-eder.@wanadoo.fr – Fax 05 59 51 26 51
4 rm – €55 €55, €6
◆ A peaceful and friendly hotel, a stone's throw from the beach. Quiet, spacious ground floor rooms opening onto private terraces, where breakfast is served.

Le Kaïku
17 r. République – 05 59 26 13 20 – Fax 05 59 51 07 47 – Closed 15-30 November, 15-30 January, Monday lunch in July-August, Tuesday and Wednesday except July-August AZ **x**
Rest – Menu (€25), €35/75 – Carte €40/58
◆ This restaurant, situated partly in the basement of the oldest house in Saint Jean de Luz (16C) has an excellent reputation locally. Seafood and contemporary fare.

Zoko Moko
6 r. Mazarin – 05 59 08 01 23 – zokomoko@hotmail.com – Fax 05 59 51 01 77
Rest – Menu (€19), €25 (weekday lunch), €42/50 AZ **a**
◆ Elegant, contemporary decor and Mediterranean food peppered with exotic flavours are the features of this 'quiet spot' (zoko moko in Basque) set in an 18C house.

Petit Grill Basque "Chez Maya"
2 r. St-Jacques – 05 59 26 80 76 – Fax 05 59 26 80 76 – Closed 20 December-25 January, Thursday lunch, Monday lunch and Wednesday
Rest – Menu €22/30 – Carte €40/50 AY **u**
◆ Authentic Basque inn with Louis Floutier frescoes and plates, copperware and an amusing manual ventilation system. Timeless regional cuisine.

Olatua
30 bd Thiers – 05 59 51 05 22 – www.olatua.fr – olatua@wanadoo.fr – Fax 05 59 51 32 99 BY **m**
Rest – Menu (€14), €35
◆ A local institution serving updated Basque fare in a refreshing, colourful interior. Blue and yellow colour scheme indoors, sheltered summer terrace and small covered garden outdoors.

in Urrugne 4 km by ③ – **pop. 7 759** – **alt. 34 m** – ✉ **64122**

Office de tourisme, place René Soubelet ☎ 05 59 54 60 80, Fax 05 59 54 63 49

Château d'Urtubie without rest
– ☎ *05 59 54 31 15 – www.chateaudurtubie.fr – chateaudurtubie@wanadoo.fr – Fax 05 59 54 62 51 – Open April-October*
10 rm – €75/150 €85/160, ☕ €11
◆ On the road to Spain, a 14C fortress, modified through the ages. Now a museum and country inn, it has rooms of character with period furniture.

Auberge Chez Maïté with rm
rest, VISA
pl. de la Mairie – ☎ 05 59 26 14 62 – www.auberge-chezmaite.com – aubergechezmaite@orange.fr – Fax 05 59 26 64 20 – Closed 10 November-14 December and 5 January-15 February
7 rm – €75/120 €95/150, ☕ €10 – ½ P €95/115
Rest – *(closed Sunday dinner and Monday)* Menu €29 – Carte €43/52
◆ On the town hall square, a small dining room decorated in the Basque style, where you will sample some traditional cooking from the Southwest shoulder to shoulder. New and fairly spacious rooms, decorated in shades of red and white and fully-equipped.

in Ciboure 1 km by ④ – **pop. 6 282** – **alt. 3 m** – ✉ **64500**

Office de tourisme, 27, quai Maurice Ravel ☎ 05 59 47 64 56, Fax 05 59 47 64 55

N.-D. de Socorri chapel: site★ 5 km by ③.

see plan of St-Jean-de-Luz

Chez Dominique
VISA
15 quai M. Ravel – ☎ 05 59 47 29 16 – Fax 05 59 47 29 16 – Closed 2 weeks in March, 2 weeks in December, Tuesday from November to March, Sunday dinner and Monday AZ **y**
Rest – Menu €30 (weekdays) – Carte €48/65
◆ On the quayside stand the birthplace of Maurice Ravel (at no. 27) and this welcoming restaurant with its pleasant marine decor lit by fishermen's lights. Seafood and regional wines.

Chez Mattin
VISA
63 r. E. Baignol – ☎ 05 59 47 19 52 – Fax 05 59 47 05 57 – Closed 14 July-30 August, Sunday except bank holidays and Monday
Rest – Carte €28/48 AZ **v**
◆ This rustic restaurant set in an old country house is marked by a family ambience. Choice of fish dishes depending on the day's catch; typically local cuisine.

in Socoa 3 km by ④ – ✉ **64122**

Iguski-Begui without rest
8 chemin d'Atalaya – ☎ 06 63 08 03 93 – www.iguski-begui.com – info@iguski-begui.com – Fax 05 59 47 21 19
4 rm – €65 €65, ☕ €8
◆ This attractive house, overlooking the Rhune and the bay of St Jean de Luz, offers rooms with individual touches. Choose Sémaphore for a view of the Socoa lighthouse.

Pantxua
VISA
At the Socoa harbour – ☎ 05 59 47 13 73 – Fax 05 59 47 01 54 – Closed 15-30 November, 5-31 January and Tuesday
Rest – Menu €27 (weekdays) – Carte €30/65
◆ Numerous canvases by Basque painters hang on the dining room walls. The popular veranda and terrace open onto the bay. Fresh fish takes pride of place at the table.

ST-JEAN-DE-MAURIENNE – 73 Savoie – 333 L6 – pop. 8 731 – alt. 556 m – ✉ 73300 French Alps 46 F2

Paris 635 – Albertville 62 – Chambéry 75 – Grenoble 105

Office de tourisme, place de la Cathédrale ☎ 04 79 83 51 51, Fax 04 79 83 42 10

Ciborium★ and stalls★★ of St-Jean-Baptiste cathedral.

St-Georges without rest
334 r. de la République – ✆ 04 79 64 01 06 – www.hotel-saintgeorges.com – info@hotel-saintgeorges.com – Fax 04 79 59 84 84
30 rm – †€ 50/53 ††€ 63/66, ☕ € 9
◆ In a calm setting near the town centre, welcoming hotel built in 1866. Spacious, well-furnished and recently-renovated rooms; home-made jam at breakfast. Reasonable prices.

Nord rest, VISA MC AE
pl. Champ de Foire – ✆ 04 79 64 02 08 – www.hoteldunord.net – info@hoteldunord.net – Fax 04 79 59 91 31 – Closed 4-19 April, 24 October-8 November, Sunday dinner except July-August and Monday lunch
19 rm – †€ 41/45 ††€ 58/60, ☕ € 8,50 – ½ P € 50
Rest – Menu (€ 15), € 25/52 – Carte € 30/70
◆ A former coaching inn near the Cathédrale St Jean Baptiste and the Musée Opinel. All the spacious rooms have been renovated. Restaurant set under the stone vaults of an old stable, serving modern and traditional cuisine prepared with local produce. Good wine list.

Dorhotel without rest
r. L. Sibué – ✆ 04 79 83 23 83 – www.dorhotel.com – info@dorhotel.com – Fax 04 79 83 23 00
41 rm – †€ 43/55 ††€ 50/57, ☕ € 7,50
◆ A practical hotel with functional rooms, 500 m from the station. Buffet menu for breakfast, served in a large modern dining room.

ST-JEAN-DE-MONTS – **85 Vendée** – **316** D7 – **pop. 7 599** – **alt. 16 m** – **Casino : La Pastourelle** – ✉ **85160** **Atlantic Coast** 34 **A3**

Paris 451 – Cholet 123 – Nantes 73 – La Roche-sur-Yon 61 – Les Sables-d'Olonne 47
Office de tourisme, 67, esplanade de la Mer ✆ 08 26 88 78 87, Fax 02 51 59 87 87
de Saint-Jean-de-Monts Avenue des Pays de la Loire, W : 2 km, ✆ 02 51 58 82 73

Mercure rm, VISA MC AE
16 av. Pays de Monts – ✆ 02 51 59 15 15 – www.mercure-st-jean.com – hotelmercurestjean@wanadoo.fr – Fax 02 51 59 91 03 – Closed 3 January-1st February
44 rm – †€ 94/168 ††€ 100/176, ☕ € 14
Rest – *(Closed Sunday lunch from 1st November to 19 December)* Menu (€ 17), € 27/38 – Carte € 29/50
◆ Well located near the beach, golf course and thalassotherapy spa resort. Comfortable rooms, all with balconies. Choose from the classic or diet menu. Fine view over the pine forest.

De la Forêt without rest VISA MC
13 r. Pouvreau – ✆ 02 51 58 00 36 – www.hotel-de-la-foret.fr – hotel.foret@gmail.com – Closed January and February
16 rm – †€ 64/103 ††€ 64/103, ☕ € 10
◆ This hotel, near the forest, has just been fully renovated. The colourful and well-soundproofed rooms occupy several houses around a small pool.

L'Espadon VISA MC AE
8 av. de la forêt – ✆ 02 51 58 03 18 – www.hotel-espadon.com – info@hotel-espadon.com – Fax 02 51 59 16 11
27 rm – †€ 54/77 ††€ 54/77, ☕ € 8,50 – ½ P € 55/65
Rest – *(closed mid-November to early February, Sunday dinner and Monday except from June to September)* Menu € 13 bi (weekday lunch), € 22/35 – Carte € 25/43
◆ Located on the wide avenue down to the beach, this 1970s building has small but well-kept rooms (most with a balcony). Two pleasantly bright dining rooms serving seafood cuisine.

Le Robinson rm, VISA MC AE
28 bd Gén. Leclerc – ✆ 02 51 59 20 20 – www.hotel-lerobinson.com – infos@hotel-lerobinson.com – Fax 02 51 58 88 03 – Closed December and January
66 rm – †€ 52/70 ††€ 52/77, ☕ € 8,50 – ½ P € 52/68
Rest – Menu (€ 12), € 16 (weekdays)/45 – Carte € 25/47
◆ Occupying several buildings centred around a patio, the rooms are being renovated in stages and vary in comfort. Fine indoor pool and small weights room. Three welcoming dining rooms serving seafood.

La Cloche d'Or rest, VISA AE

26 av. des Tilleuls – ✆ 02 51 58 00 58 – www.laclochedor.com – la-cloche-dor@voila.fr – Fax 02 51 58 82 85 – Closed 16 December-7 February

21 rm – †€ 46/75 ††€ 46/75, ☕ € 8 – ½ P € 46/64

Rest – Menu € 14 (weekdays)/32 – Carte € 25/41

◆ Half way between the centre of town and the beach, this quiet establishment is ideally located for walking. The well-kept rooms are a little narrow yet practical. Simply furnished in a rustic style. Classic cuisine.

Le Petit St-Jean AC P VISA

128 rte Notre-Dame-de-Monts – ✆ 02 51 59 78 50 – Closed Sunday dinner and Wednesday

Rest – Menu (€ 18), € 24/38 – Carte € 29/44

◆ Stone, beams, ornaments, copperware and old furniture decorate this inn where you are served local dishes featuring seafood.

La Quich'Notte P VISA AE

200 rte Notre-Dame-de-Monts – ✆ 02 51 58 62 64 – ferdi.quichnotte@hotmail.fr – Open 21 March-15 September and closed Tuesday lunch, Saturday lunch and Monday except July-August

Rest – Menu € 24/35 – Carte € 25/45

◆ Local dishes (frogs' legs and eel) served in a cosy setting in a Vendée "bourrine" dating back to the 19C. The glass rotunda is used on crowded days.

in Orouet 7 km southeast on D 38 – ✉ **85160**

La Chaumière AC rest, P VISA AE

103 av. Orouët – ✆ 02 51 58 67 44 – www.chaumierehotel.fr – hotelchaumiere@wanadoo.fr – Fax 02 51 58 98 12 – Closed 16 November-2 February

32 rm – †€ 47/67 ††€ 47/67, ☕ € 8 – ½ P € 48/57

Rest – *(closed Sunday dinner and Monday from October to March)* Menu (€ 12), € 18/32 – Carte € 24/47

◆ Long building with thatched gables, set in a large garden with indoor-outdoor swimming pool. The rooms are small, but spruce and well kept (a few have a balcony). The neo-rustic dining areas feature exposed beams. Traditional menu.

ST-JEAN-DE-SIXT – 74 Haute-Savoie – 328 L5 – pop. 1 212 – alt. 963 m – ✉ 74450 French Alps 46 F1

Paris 561 – Annecy 28 – Bonneville 22 – Chamonix-Mont-Blanc 76 – La Clusaz 4 – Genève 48

Office de tourisme, ✆ 04 50 02 70 14, Fax 04 50 02 78 78

Défilé des Étroits★ Northwest: 3 km.

Beau Site P VISA

La Ruaz – ✆ 04 50 02 24 04 – www.hotelbeausite.biz – hotelbeausite@hotmail.com – Fax 04 50 02 35 82 – Open 7 June-12 September and 19 December-13 April

15 rm – †€ 40/60 ††€ 55/80, ☕ € 8 – ½ P € 47/71

Rest – Menu (€ 14), € 18/24 – Carte € 24/32

◆ This hotel has two types of room - Savoyard, with panelling and warm furnishings, or modern and functional. In any case, peace and quiet assured. The bay windows of the restaurant command a pretty view of the village. Family cooking.

ST-JEAN-DU-BRUEL – 12 Aveyron – 338 M6 – pop. 690 – alt. 520 m – ✉ 12230 Languedoc-Roussillon-Tarn Gorges 29 D2

Paris 676 – Lodève 43 – Millau 40 – Montpellier 97 – Rodez 108 – Le Vigan 36

Office de tourisme, 32, Grand'Rue ☎ 05 65 62 23 64, Fax 05 65 62 12 82

Gorges de la Dourbie★★ Northeast: 10 km.

Du Midi-Papillon

pl. du Manège – ☎ 05 65 62 26 04 – Fax 05 65 62 12 97 – Open 31 March-11 November

18 rm – €36/64 €36/64, €6 – ½ P €41/57

Rest – Menu €15 (weekdays), €23/41 – Carte €24/44

◆ This cosy, romantic establishment along the Dourbie combines a faultless welcome with individually decorated, comfortable rooms. The appetising local fare will delight the taste buds, and for the eye, a splendid view over the river and medieval bridge.

ST-JEAN-EN-ROYANS – 26 Drôme – 332 E3 – pop. 2 895 – alt. 250 m – ✉ 26190 French Alps 43 E2

Paris 584 – Die 62 – Romans-sur-Isère 28 – Grenoble 71 – St-Marcellin 20 – Valence 44

Office de tourisme, 13, place de l'Église ☎ 04 75 48 61 39, Fax 04 75 47 54 44

at col de la Machine 11 km southeast by D 76 – alt. 1 011 m – ✉ 26190

Combe Laval★★★.

Du Col de la Machine

rest,

– ☎ 04 75 48 26 36 – www.hotel-coldelamachine.com – jfaravello@aol.com – Fax 04 75 48 29 12 – Closed 9-21 March, 24 October-1st November, 29 November-27 December, 5-17 January, Tuesday dinner and Wednesday except July-August and school holidays

11 rm – €53/56 €59/62, €10 – ½ P €63/66

Rest – *(closed Wednesday lunch in July-August)* Menu €18/42 – Carte €30/60

◆ At the start of the vertiginous Combe Laval road, this establishment has been in the same family since 1848. The majority of the rooms have been renovated (mountain style décor). Garden at the edge of the forest. Chalet style dining room. Attentive welcome and service.

ST-JEAN-LE-THOMAS – 50 Manche – 303 C7 – pop. 395 – alt. 20 m – ✉ 50530 32 A2

Paris 350 – Avranches 16 – Granville 18 – St-Lô 71 – St-Malo 82 – Villedieu-les-Poêles 37

Syndicat d'initiative, 21, place Pierre le Jaudet ☎ 02 33 70 90 71, Fax 02 33 70 90 71

Des Bains

8 allée Clemenceau – ☎ 02 33 48 84 20 – www.hdesbains.fr – hdbains@orange.fr – Fax 02 33 48 66 42 – Open 31 March-2 November and closed Wednesday in October

25 rm – €50/80 €58/80, €8 – ½ P €57/68

Rest – *(closed Wednesday lunch and Thursday lunch except from 14 July to 31 August)* Menu (€12), €16 (weekdays)/35 – Carte €24/47

◆ The same family has greeted guests here since 1912 in this group of village houses. Old-fashioned rooms, simply furnished. Garden with swimming pool. An immense flower-decked rustic dining room with a pretty bar. 'Surf n'turf' cuisine.

ST-JEAN-PIED-DE-PORT – 64 Pyrénées-Atlantiques – 342 E6 – pop. 1 511 – alt. 159 m – ✉ 64220 Atlantic Coast 3 B3

Paris 817 – Bayonne 54 – Biarritz 55 – Pau 106 – San Sebastián 96

Office de tourisme, 14, place Charles-de-Gaulle ☎ 05 59 37 03 57, Fax 05 59 37 34 91

Route of the pilgrims ★ of Santiago de Compostella.

ST-JEAN-PIED-DE-PORT

Çaro (Rte de) 2
Çitadelle (R. de la) 4
Église (R. de l') 6
Espagne (R. d') . . . .
France (R.) 12
Fronton (Av. du) 15
Gaulle (Pl. Ch.-de) 16
Liberté (R. de la) 17
St-Jacques (Ch. de) 18
St-Michel (Rte de) 21
Trinquet (Pl. du) 24
Uhart (R. d') 27
Zuharpeta (R.) 30

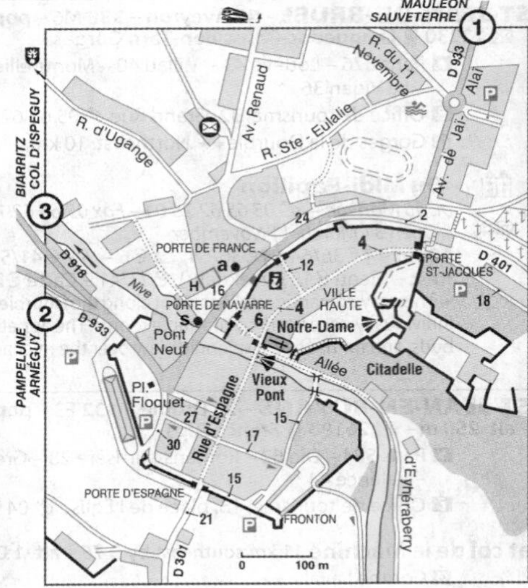

Les Pyrénées (Philippe and Firmin Arrambide) rm, VISA

pl. Ch. de Gaulle – ☎ 05 59 37 01 01
– www.hotel-les-pyrenees.com – pyrenees@relaischateaux.com
– Fax 05 59 37 18 97 – Closed 20 November-22 December, 5-28 January, Monday dinner from November to March and Tuesday from 20 September to 30 June except public holidays a

14 rm – 🚹€ 110/260 🚹🚹€ 160/260, ☕ € 16 – 4 suites – ½ P € 160/220
Rest – *(pre-book in high season and Sat - Sun)* Menu € 45/105
– Carte € 60/110

Spec. Assiette de langoustines aux quatre façon. Saumon sauvage de l'Adour grillé, sauce béarnaise. Gratin de fraises des bois du jardin (July to Sep.). **Wines** Jurançon sec, Irouléguy.

◆ A former coaching inn with spacious, elegant rooms (beautiful bathrooms). Swimming pool in luxuriant verdant surroundings. Fine Basque cuisine from a father and son team served in the contemporary dining room or on the veranda.

Central rm, VISA

pl. Ch. de Gaulle – ☎ 05 59 37 00 22 – Fax 05 59 37 27 79
– Open 11 March-30 November and closed Tuesday from March to June s

12 rm – 🚹€ 58/74 🚹🚹€ 62/77, ☕ € 9 – ½ P € 60/68
Rest – Menu € 21/46 – Carte € 40/70

◆ As its name suggests, this hotel is located a stone's throw from the citadel. A two-century-old polished staircase leads to the spacious traditional guestrooms. Enjoy local cuisine in the dining room-veranda or on the tiny terrace on the banks of the Nive.

in Esterençuby 8 km south by D 301 – pop. 382 – alt. 229 m – ✉ 64220

Artzain Etchea VISA

rte d'Iraty, 1km – ☎ 05 59 37 11 55 – www.artzain-etchea.com
– info@artzain-etchea.fr – Fax 05 59 37 20 16 – Open 2 March-19 November and closed Tuesday and Wednesday except in season

11 rm – 🚹€ 50 🚹🚹€ 50, ☕ € 6,50 – ½ P € 47 **Rest** – *(resident only)*

◆ This large white building, built on the mountainside, overlooks the Nive. Simple, well-kept rooms; some with balconies. Hunting and fishing packages. Dining room with exposed beams and pastoral photos. Basque cuisine.

Les Sources de la Nive
at Béherobie – 05 59 37 10 57 – source.nive@wanadoo.fr – Fax 05 59 37 39 06 – Closed January and Tuesday off season

26 rm – €50 €50, €5 – ½ P €45 **Rest** – Menu €14/30 – Carte €19/43
◆ This small hotel on the banks of the Nive is the perfect base for nature-lovers. Simply furnished but well-maintained guestrooms, renovated gradually. Dining room decorated in Basque style, plus a veranda overlooking the river. Regional cuisine.

in Aincille by ① and D 18: 7 km – pop. 118 – alt. 253 m – 64220

Pecoïtz with rm rest,
rte d'Iraty – 05 59 37 11 88 – pecoitzjp@orange.fr – Fax 05 59 37 35 42 – Open 1st April-1st January and closed Wednesday dinner and Thursday except school holidays
14 rm – €45/48 €45/48, €5 – ½ P €45
Rest – Menu €16/33 – Carte €23/35
◆ Copious home cooking with a regional flavour served in a colourful setting (one dining room with a view over the countryside). Simple bedrooms.

ST-JEAN-ST-MAURICE-SUR-LOIRE – 42 Loire – 327 D4 44 A1
– 42155 Lyon - Rhone Valley

Paris 406 – Lyon 95 – Roanne 15 – Vichy 79

L'Échauguette
– 04 77 63 15 89 – www.echauguette-alex.com – contact@echauguette-alex.com
4 rm – €57 €67/77 **Table d'hôte** – Menu €27 bi
◆ These three maisonnettes open onto the calm waters of the Villerest Lake. The rooms are tastefully decorated in various styles and benefit from a separate entrance. Meals served in an open kitchen or on the terrace, weather permitting.

ST-JEAN-SAVERNE – 67 Bas-Rhin – 315 I4 – see Saverne

ST-JEAN-SUR-VEYLE – 01 Ain – 328 C3 – pop. 1 009 – alt. 200 m 44 B1
– 01290

Paris 402 – Bourg-en-Bresse 32 – Mâcon 12 – Villefranche-sur-Saône 45

La Petite Auberge
Le bourg – 03 85 31 53 92 – www.chefscuisiniers-ain.com – lapetiteaubergeperonnet@wanadoo.fr – Closed 1st-15 September, 31 December-19 January, Tuesday dinner, Sunday dinner and Monday
Rest – Menu (€12 bi), €20 bi/41 – Carte €41/50
◆ The inviting dining room of this half-timbered building (red brick, beams and art by local artists) forms the backdrop to regional specialities.

ST-JOACHIM – 44 Loire-Atlantique – 316 C3 – pop. 3 772 – alt. 5 m 34 A2
– 44720 Brittany

Paris 435 – Nantes 61 – Redon 40 – St-Nazaire 14 – Vannes 64

Tour of Fédrun island ★ West: 4.5 km - Barge trip★★.

La Mare aux Oiseaux (Eric Guérin) with rm
Île de Fedrun – 02 40 88 53 01 – www.mareauxoiseaux.fr – courriel@mareauxoiseaux.fr – Fax 02 40 91 67 44 – Closed Monday lunch
10 rm – €130/160 €130/160, €12
Rest – Menu €38/80 – Carte approx. €74
Spec. Grosses crevettes en tzatziki. Saint-Pierre à la plancha comme un poulet rôti. Tarte fine au citron.
◆ Lovely cottage surrounded by the Brière marshland, ideal for bird watchers and food lovers. Surprising, inventive and occasionally disconcerting cuisine. Pleasant rooms.

ST-JOSSE – 62 Pas-de-Calais – **301** C5 – **pop. 1 170** – **alt. 35 m** 30 **A2**
– ✉ **62170** **Northern France and the Paris Region**

Paris 223 – Lille 144 – Arras 94 – Boulogne-sur-Mer 39 – Abbeville 49

Le Relais de St-Josse VISA AE

17 Grand'Place, (near the church) – ✆ 03 21 94 61 75 – www.le-relais-de-st-josse.com – contact@le-relais-de-st-josse.com – Fax 03 21 84 88 72 – Closed 5 January-12 February, Wednesday dinner and Sunday dinner in low season and Thursday

Rest – Menu (€ 20), € 29/39 – Carte € 34/43

◆ With its colourful façade and London taxi cab parked outside, this auberge definitely catches the eye. Fine contemporary cuisine served in an attractive dining room with parquet flooring and library.

in Moulinel 2 km northeast by D 145 – ✉ **62170 St-Josse**

Auberge du Moulinel P VISA AE

116 chaussée de l'Avant Pays – ✆ 03 21 94 79 03 – www.aubergedumoulinel.com – aubergedumoulinel@free.fr – Fax 03 21 09 37 14 – Closed 5-25 January, Sunday dinner, Monday and Tuesday except July-August

Rest – Menu (€ 20), € 28 (weekdays)/49 – Carte € 60/72

◆ This inn, set away from busy roads, offers three pleasant dining rooms, serving up-to-date cuisine with market produce.

ST-JOUAN-DES-GUÉRETS – 35 Ille-et-Vilaine – **309** K3 – **pop. 2 484** 10 **D1**
– **alt. 31 m** – ✉ **35430**

Paris 398 – Rennes 65 – Saint-Malo 10 – Granville 89 – Dinan 28

La Malouinière des Longchamps without rest P VISA AE

1.5 km east on the D 204 – ✆ 02 99 82 74 00 – www.malouiniere.com – contact@malouiniere.com – Fax 02 99 82 74 14 – Closed 4 January-6 February

15 rm – €79/198 €99/198, € 15

◆ This farmhouse lost in the country is the perfect place for a peaceful break. Find a flower-filled garden, pool, and spa. Modern rooms; more traditional duplex apartments in the annexe.

ST-JOUIN-BRUNEVAL – 76 Seine-Maritime – **304** A4 – **pop. 1 782** 33 **C1**
– **alt. 110 m** – ✉ **76280**

Paris 202 – Fécamp 25 – Le Havre 20 – Rouen 92

Le Belvédère P VISA AE

– ✆ 02 35 20 13 76 – www.restaurant-lebelvedere.com – Closed 4 January-4 February, Sunday dinner, Wednesday dinner and Thursday

Rest – Menu € 21 (weekdays)/40 – Carte € 46/65

◆ You can enjoy an impressive panoramic view of the cliffs and the sea, while savouring traditional dishes as well as fish and seafood specialities. Neat contemporary decor.

ST-JULIEN-AUX-BOIS – 19 Corrèze – **329** N5 – **pop. 490** – **alt. 594 m** 25 **C3**
– ✉ **19220**

Paris 524 – Aurillac 53 – Brive-la-Gaillarde 66 – Mauriac 29 – St-Céré 60 – Tulle 50 – Ussel 63

Auberge de St-Julien-aux-Bois with rm P VISA AE

1 rte des Pierres Blanches – ✆ 05 55 28 41 94 – www.auberge-saint-julien.com – auberge_st_julien@hotmail.com – Fax 05 55 28 37 85 – Closed February school holidays, Sunday dinner, Wednesday in low season and Wednesday lunch in July-August

6 rm – €42 €49/56, € 7 – ½ P € 47/50

Rest – Menu (€ 14), € 16/48 – Carte € 25/37

◆ This village house makes a point of serving healthy organic produce; the desserts are German in style. Country setting; the pretty rooms are graced with fresh flowers.

ST-JULIEN-CHAPTEUIL – 43 Haute-Loire – 331 G3 – pop. 1 886 – alt. 815 m – ✉ 43260 Lyon - Rhone Valley 6 C3

Paris 559 – Lamastre 52 – Privas 88 – Le Puy-en-Velay 20 – St-Agrève 32 – Yssingeaux 17

Office de tourisme, place Saint-Robert ✆ 04 71 08 77 70, Fax 04 71 08 42 20

Site★ - Montagne du Meygal★: Grand Testavoyre ✻★★ Northeast: 14 km then 30 mn.

XX **Vidal** VISA MC AE

18 pl. du Marché – ✆ 04 71 08 70 50 – www.restaurant-vidal.com – info@restaurant-vidal.com – Fax 04 71 08 40 14 – Closed 27-30 June, 1st-4 September and 13 January – 21 February

Rest – *(closed Tuesday dinner off season, Thursday dinner and Monday)* Menu € 28/75 – Carte € 58/80

Rest *Bistrot de Justin* – bistro *(closed Sunday and Monday) (lunch only)* Menu € 15 bi – Carte € 15/25

◆ Murals depicting the region, lace table mats, pale wooden furniture and old doors embellish the decor of this rustic restaurant in the Velay region.

ST-JULIEN-DE-CREMPSE – 24 Dordogne – 329 E6 – see Bergerac

ST-JULIEN-D'EMPARE – 12 Aveyron – 338 E3 – see Capdenac-Gare

ST-JULIEN-DU-SAULT – 89 Yonne – 319 C3 – pop. 2 380 – alt. 82 m – ✉ 89330

Paris 137 – Dijon 187 – Auxerre 40 – Sens 25 – Montereau-Fault-Yonne 68

XX **Les Bons Enfants** VISA MC AE

4 pl. de la Mairie – ✆ 03 86 91 17 38 – www.bonsenfants.fr – bonsenfants@orange.fr – Fax 03 86 91 14 19 – Closed 18 January-7 February, Tuesday lunch, Sunday dinner and Monday

Rest – *(number of covers limited, pre-book)* Menu € 39 (weekday lunch), € 44/77 – Carte € 53/72

Rest – *(closed Sunday dinner)* Menu (€ 16), € 19 (weekday lunch)/28

◆ Imposing establishment in the centre of the village proposing creative cuisine with a vegetable focus. Carefully-prepared traditional dishes at the Bistrot.

ST-JULIEN-EN-CHAMPSAUR – 05 Hautes-Alpes – 334 E5 – pop. 275 – alt. 1 050 m – ✉ 05500

Paris 658 – Gap 17 – Grenoble 95 – La Mure 55 – Orcières 21

XX **Les Chenets** with rm AC rest, VISA MC AE

in the village – ✆ 04 92 50 03 15 – les-chenets.com – les-chenets@wanadoo.fr – Fax 04 92 50 73 06 – Closed April, 11 November-27 December, Sunday dinner and Wednesday off season

18 rm – †€ 26/30 ††€ 39/45, ☕ € 7 – ½ P € 43/46

Rest – Menu € 21/37 – Carte € 35/45

◆ Restaurant in the heart of the green Champsaur area with decor pleasantly combining wood, stone and glass. Traditional cuisine and fine local specialities. A few rooms available.

ST-JULIEN-EN-GENEVOIS – 74 Haute-Savoie – 328 J4 – pop. 10 691 – alt. 460 m – Casino – ✉ 74160 46 F1

Paris 525 – Annecy 35 – Bonneville 36 – Genève 11 – Nantua 56 – Thonon-les-Bains 47

Office de tourisme, 2, place du Crêt ✆ 04 50 04 71 63, Fax 04 50 04 89 76

in Archamps 5 km east by A40, 13.1 exit – pop. 1 693 – alt. 535 m – ✉ 74160

Porte Sud de Genève P VISA MC AE

parc d'affaire international, (Site d'Archamps) – ✆ 04 50 31 16 06 – www.bestwesternportesudgeneve.com – hotel-portesudgva@site-archamps.com – Fax 04 50 31 29 71

90 rm – †€ 108/158 ††€ 119/169, ☕ € 15

Rest – Menu (€ 26), € 31 – Carte approx. € 40

◆ A modern hotel set in the heart of the Franco-Swiss technology belt. The contemporary rooms are both relaxing and well thought out for business guests. A bright dining room, a terrace facing the garden and traditional recipes.

in Bossey 7 km east by D 1206 – pop. 664 – alt. 438 m – ✉ 74160

XXX **La Ferme de l'Hospital** (Jean-Jacques Noguier)
rte du golf – ✆ 04 50 43 61 43 – www.ferme-hospital.com – jjnoguier@wanadoo.fr – Fax 04 50 95 31 53 – Closed 1st-16 August, 1st-15 February, Sunday and Monday
Rest – *(pre-book)* Menu (€ 38), € 50/75 – Carte € 60/80
Spec. Ravioles de foie gras cèpes et truffes. Foie gras de canard rôti. Macarons orange-Grand Marnier-hysope. **Wines** Chignin-Bergeron, Mondeuse.
◆ This 17C farmhouse was once the property of the Geneva hospital. Interiors have a lot of character. Pleasant terrace, up-to-date cuisine and carefully selected wines.

Annecy road 9.5 km south by N 201 – ✉ 74350 Cruseilles

Rey without rest
131 rte d'Annecy, on the Mont Sion pass – ✆ 04 50 44 13 29 – www.hotelrey.com – contact@hotel-rey.com – Fax 04 50 44 05 48 – Closed 13-20 April, 7-22 September and 27 December-11 January
30 rm – †€ 61/64 ††€ 72/75, ☕ € 9
◆ Hidden from the road by a swathe of greenery, this hotel offers practical, cheerful rooms, quieter to the rear. Breakfast served on the veranda overlooking the garden.

ST-JULIEN-LE-FAUCON – 14 Calvados – 303 M5 – pop. 670 – alt. 40 m – ✉ 14140 33 C2

Paris 192 – Caen 41 – Falaise 32 – Lisieux 14

X **Auberge de la Levrette**
48 r. Lisieux – ✆ 02 31 63 81 20 – aubergedelalevrette@orange.fr – Fax 02 31 63 97 05 – Closed 18-24 March, 18-24 November, 22-29 December, Monday and Tuesday except bank holidays
Rest – Menu (€ 14 bi), € 20/25 – Carte € 23/45
◆ Formerly a post house, this characteristic half-timbered house, built in 1550, has a small museum devoted to mechanical musical instruments. Seasonal menu.

ST-JULIEN-MOLIN-MOLETTE – 42 Loire – 327 G8 – see Annonay

ST-JULIEN-SUR-CHER – 41 Loir-et-Cher – 318 H8 – pop. 663 – alt. 110 m – ✉ 41320 12 C2

Paris 227 – Blois 51 – Bourges 66 – Châteauroux 62 – Vierzon 25

X **Les Deux Pierrots**
9 r. Nationale – ✆ 02 54 96 40 07 – Closed August, Monday and Tuesday
Rest – Menu (€ 24), € 27/40
◆ This village inn has a rustic style dining area with exposed beams, opening onto the vegetable garden in summer. Simple and traditional cuisine.

ST-JULIEN-VOCANCE – 07 Ardèche – pop. 257 – alt. 680 m – ✉ 07690 44 B2

Paris 553 – Saint-Étienne 56 – Valence 68 – Annonay 18

XX **Julliat**
Le Marthouret – ✆ 04 75 34 71 61 – www.restaurant-julliat.com – contact@restaurant-julliat.com – Fax 04 75 34 79 19 – Closed 2-9 January, 4-25 February, Tuesday and Wednesday
Rest – Menu (€ 22), € 31/63
◆ This old, prettily restored house is a happy blend of contemporary decoration and old stone work where you are served appetising, modern food.

ST-JUNIEN – 87 Haute-Vienne – 325 C5 – pop. 11 500 – alt. 240 m – ✉ 87200 Dordogne-Berry-Limousin 24 A2

Paris 416 – Angoulême 73 – Bellac 34 – Confolens 27 – Limoges 32

Office de tourisme, place du Champ de Foire ✆ 05 55 02 17 93, Fax 05 55 02 94 31

de Saint-Junien Les Jouberties, W : 4 km, ✆ 05 55 02 96 96

Collegiate church ★.

Le Relais de Comodoliac

22 av. Sadi-Carnot – ✆ 05 55 02 27 26 – www.comodoliac.com – comodoliac@wanadoo.fr – Fax 05 55 02 68 79 – Closed 27 February-7 March
29 rm – †€ 56 ††€ 72, ☕ € 9 – ½ P € 65
Rest – *(closed Sunday dinner October-Easter)* Menu € 17 (weekdays)/39 – Carte € 38/47
◆ This building at the entrance to the town dates back to the 1970s. It is separated from the road by a pretty garden. Book one of the refurbished, modern rooms. A veranda dining room opening onto a delightful terrace. Classic menu.

South : 2 km by Rochechouart road, D 675 and secondary road – ✉ 87200 St-Junien

Lauryvan
200 allée du Bois au Boeuf – ✆ 05 55 02 26 04 – www.lauryvan.fr – lauryvan@nomade.fr – Fax 05 55 02 25 29 – Closed 2-7 January, Sunday dinner, Monday and dinners public holidays
Rest – Menu € 28 (weekdays)/56 – Carte € 27/49
◆ Pavilion in an area of thick vegetation, near a pond. The dining room (non-smoking on Sundays and public holidays) serves low priced regional dishes and classic fare. Garden terrace.

ST-JUST-ET-VACQUIERES – 30 Gard – 339 K4 – pop. 260 – alt. 190 m – ✉ 30580 23 C1

Paris 699 – Montpellier 104 – Nîmes 54 – Alès 18 – Orange 75

Mas Vacquières without rest
hameau de Vacquières – ✆ 04 66 83 70 75 – www.masvac.com – info@masvac.com
5 rm ☕ – †€ 80/120 ††€ 85/145
◆ This typical house, tucked away in a lane of the hamlet, is set in a delightfully peaceful garden. Spotless, pleasant rooms and generous breakfasts (terrace).

ST-JUSTIN – 40 Landes – 335 J11 – pop. 845 – alt. 90 m – ✉ 40240 3 B2

Paris 694 – Aire-sur-l'Adour 38 – Casteljaloux 49 – Dax 84 – Mont-de-Marsan 25 – Pau 89

Office de tourisme, place des Tilleuls ✆ 05 58 44 86 06, Fax 05 58 44 86 06

France with rm
pl. des Tilleuls – ✆ 05 58 44 83 61 – hoteldefrance.stjustin@orange.fr – Fax 05 58 44 83 89 – Closed 22 November-7 December, Sunday and Monday
8 rm – †€ 40 ††€ 40, ☕ € 7
Rest – Menu € 28/40 – Carte € 34/48
Rest ***Bistrot*** – *(closed Saturday dinner, Sunday, Monday and public holidays)* Menu € 15 (weekdays)/34 – Carte € 34/48
◆ The building is under the arcades of the medieval square where, in season, a terrace operates. Copious and traditional cuisine. Home-made jams at breakfast. Village café atmosphere and blackboard menu at the Bistrot.

ST-JUST-ST-RAMBERT – 42 Loire – 327 E7 – pop. 14 900 – alt. 380 m – ✉ 42170 44 A2

Paris 542 – St Etienne 17 – Lyon 81 – Montbrison 18 – Roanne 74

Office de tourisme, place de la Paix ✆ 04 77 52 05 14, Fax 04 77 52 15 91

Le Neuvième Art (Christophe Roure)
pl. 19 Mars 1962 – ✆ 04 77 55 87 15 – www.leneuviemeart.com – le.neuvieme.art@wanadoo.fr – Fax 04 77 55 80 77 – Closed 9 August-2 September, 23-29 December, 8-23 February, Sunday and Monday
Rest – *(number of covers limited, pre-book)* Menu € 65/115 – Carte € 80/88
Spec. Barrette de foie gras mi-cuit et "flanby" à la fève de tonka. Grosse langoustine bretonne pochée dans un bouillon d'infusion. Pureté et géométrie d'une mousse chocolat intense, "after eight" glacé. **Wines** Vin de Pays d'Urfé, Côtes du Forez.
◆ A centre of creativity for flavoursome contemporary cuisine. With a designer setting and premium attentive service, this former railway station is full of surprises!

ST-LARY – 09 Ariège – 343 D7 – pop. 153 – alt. 692 m – ✉ 09800 28 B3

Paris 786 – Bagnères-de-Luchon 48 – St-Gaudens 36 – St-Girons 24 – Salies-du-Salat 197

Auberge de l'Isard

r. des Bains – ☎ 05 61 96 72 83 – www.hotel.logis.ariege.com – aubergeisard@aol.fr – Fax 05 61 96 73 71 – Open from March to November and closed Monday

8 rm – †€ 38/40 ††€ 40/42, ☕ € 6 – ½ P € 45

Rest – Menu € 18/29 – Carte € 22/42

◆ Pleasant well-maintained hotel which also houses the village bar and a shop selling regional produce. Rustic decor in the well-equipped rooms. Separated by a stream from the hotel, the restaurant serves traditional fare.

ST-LARY-SOULAN – 65 Hautes-Pyrénées – 342 N8 – pop. 1 084 28 A3

– alt. 820 m – Winter sports : 1 680/2 450 m 2 30 – Spa : early April-late Oct. – ✉ 65170 Languedoc-Roussillon-Tarn Gorges

Paris 830 – Arreau 12 – Auch 103 – Bagnères-de-Luchon 44 – St-Gaudens 66 – Tarbes 74

Office de tourisme, 37, rue Vincent Mir ☎ 05 62 39 50 81, Fax 05 62 39 50 06

La Pergola

rm, VISA MC AE

25 r. Vincent Mir – ☎ 05 62 39 40 46 – www.hotellapergola.fr – jean-pierre.mir@wanadoo.fr – Fax 05 62 40 06 55

22 rm – †€ 62/77 ††€ 69/111, ☕ € 11 – ½ P € 64/91

Rest *L'Enclos des Saveurs* – *(closed November)* Menu (€ 14), € 32/52 – Carte € 43/56

◆ A peaceful house set in a garden. Large rooms with elegant personal touches. Seven of them have a terrace or balcony with a view of the mountain peaks. Attentive service. Up-to-date menu and local dishes available at the Enclos des Saveurs.

Les Arches without rest

VISA MC AE

15 av. des Thermes – ☎ 05 62 49 10 10 – www.hotel-les-arches.com – contact@hotel-les-arches.com – Fax 05 62 49 10 15 – Closed 1st-16 November

30 rm – †€ 50/70 ††€ 50/70, ☕ € 8,50

◆ Modern architecture housing small, functional rooms with contemporary furniture. Welcoming breakfast room and pleasant fireside lounge.

Aurélia

VISA MC

chemin de St Lary, at Vielle-Aure – ☎ 05 62 39 56 90 – www.hotel-aurelia.com – hotel-aurelia@wanadoo.fr – Fax 05 62 39 43 75 – Closed 27 September-14 December

20 rm – †€ 41/45 ††€ 49/56, ☕ € 7,50 – ½ P € 48/54 **Rest** – *(resident only)*

◆ Family hotel with good leisure facilities near the thermal baths. Comfortable rooms with sloping ceilings on the third floor; two duplex rooms also available. Regional cuisine in the restaurant (residents only) prepared by the owner's young son.

De la Neste

rest, VISA MC

– ☎ 05 62 39 42 79 – www.hotel-delaneste.com – hoteldelaneste@wanadoo.fr – Fax 05 62 39 58 77 – Closed 15 April-31 May and 15 October-2 December

17 rm – †€ 48/57 ††€ 48/57, ☕ € 8 – 3 suites – ½ P € 49/58

Rest – *(dinner only) (residents only)*

◆ This quietly located hotel is pleasantly set alongside a river, next to a thermal and leisure centre. Large, comfortable rooms, some with dormer windows. Regional dishes served in a convivial atmosphere.

Pons "Le Dahu"

rest, VISA MC

4 r. Coudères – ☎ 05 62 39 43 66 – hotelpons.com – hotelpons@wanadoo.fr – Fax 05 62 40 00 86 – Closed 20 April-3 May

39 rm – †€ 55/60 ††€ 65/70, ☕ € 8 – ½ P € 56

Rest – Menu € 15 (weekdays)/25 – Carte € 20/41

◆ These 1950s buildings are set in a residential area near the cable car and town centre. The largest rooms are in the annexe and all have balconies. Tasty and copious traditional dishes can be enjoyed in a guesthouse atmosphere.

XX **La Grange**
Autun road – 05 62 40 07 14 – hotel-angleterre-arreau.com – contact@angleterre-arreau.com – Fax 05 62 98 69 66 – Closed 27 April-10 May, in June, in November, Tuesday and Wednesday except dinner in high season
Rest – Menu € 20/45 – Carte € 49/61
◆ This old barn was converted into a comfortable and pretty restaurant with a warm wooden decor. In winter, attractive flames in the fireplace. Regional menus.

ST-LATTIER – 38 Isère – 333 E7 – pop. 1 031 – alt. 170 m – ✉ 38840 — 43 E2

Paris 571 – Grenoble 67 – Romans-sur-Isère 13 – St-Marcellin 15 – Valence 34

Le Lièvre Amoureux
La Gare – 04 76 64 50 67 – www.lelievreamoureux.com – lelievreamoureux@wanadoo.fr – Closed 12-22 August and 10-20 February
5 rm – †€ 65 ††€ 75, ☕ € 10 **Table d'hôte** – *(closed Sunday)* Menu € 40/65
◆ This former hunting lodge was successfully renovated to provide three fine, spacious rooms with personal touches, as well as two duplexes. This dining room has a large fireplace and offers tasty local Dauphinois dishes.

X **Auberge du Viaduc** with rm
D1092 (hamlet of La Rivière) – 04 76 64 51 65 – www.auberge-du-viaduc.new.fr – auberge.du.viaduc@wanadoo.fr – Fax 04 76 64 30 93 – Closed 28 November-15 January, Sunday dinner December-April, Tuesday (except hotel), Wednesday lunch June-September and Monday
7 rm – †€ 82/122 ††€ 82/122, ☕ € 10
Rest – *(number of covers limited, pre-book)* Menu € 29/59 – Carte € 36/72
◆ Long-standing family residence, opening onto a pleasant garden. Intimate dining rooms, with a veranda and a log fire in winter. Pretty regional furniture in the rooms.

X **Brun** with rm
Les Fauries, D 1092 – 04 76 64 54 08 – www.hotel-brun.com – contact@hotel-brun.com – Fax 04 76 64 31 78 – Closed 12-30 October, 18 February-5 March and Sunday dinner
10 rm – †€ 47 ††€ 57, ☕ € 7 – ½ P € 47
Rest – Menu (€ 14), € 18 (weekdays)/45 – Carte € 38/45
◆ A country restaurant extended by a fine terrace shaded by linden trees on the banks of the Isère. Accommodation in a building 400 m away.

ST-LAURENT-DE-CERDANS – 66 Pyrénées-Orientales – 344 G8 – pop. 1 267 – alt. 675 m – ✉ 66260 Languedoc-Roussillon-Tarn Gorges — 22 B3

Paris 901 – Céret 28 – Perpignan 60

Syndicat d'initiative, 7, rue Joseph Nivet 04 68 39 55 75, Fax 04 68 39 59 59

Southwest 6.5 km by D 3 and secondary road – ✉ 66260 St-Laurent-de-Cerdans

Domaine de Falgos
– 04 68 39 51 42 – www.falgos.com – contact@falgos.com – Fax 04 68 39 52 30 – Open 15 March-11 November
25 rm ☕ – †€ 96/134 ††€ 139/209 – 7 suites **Rest** – Carte € 39/50
◆ Situated in an isolated spot on the Spanish border, this old mountain farmhouse has been redeveloped into a hotel complex with a golf course and fitness centre. Cosy, spacious and well-appointed guestrooms. Brasserie-style menu at lunchtime and traditional cuisine in the evening. Summer terrace overlooking the golf course.

ST-LAURENT-DE-LA-SALANQUE – 66 Pyrénées-Orientales – 344 I6 – pop. 8 224 – alt. 2 m – ✉ 66250 — 22 B3

Paris 845 – Elne 26 – Narbonne 62 – Perpignan 19 – Quillan 80 – Rivesaltes 12

Syndicat d'initiative, place Gambetta 04 68 28 31 03

Fort de Salses★★ Northwest: 9 km, Languedoc-Roussillon-Tarn Gorges

XX **Le Commerce** with rm — AC rest, VISA MC

2 bd de la Révolution – ✆ 04 68 28 02 21 – www.lecommerce66.com – contact@lecommerce66.com – Fax 04 68 28 39 86 – Closed 26 October-17 November, 16 February-3 March, Sunday dinner except July-August and Monday except dinner in July-August

11 rm – †€ 51 ††€ 51, ☕ € 8,50 – ½ P € 53

Rest – Menu (€ 19), € 28/39 – Carte € 40/63

◆ At the centre of the village, regional fare served in a rustic dining room painted in bright yellow colours. Small rooms with Catalan furniture.

ST-LAURENT-DE-MURE – 69 Rhône – 327 J5 – pop. 4 745 – alt. 252 m – ✉ 69720 — 43 E1

▶ Paris 478 – Lyon 19 – Pont-de-Chéruy 16 – La Tour-du-Pin 38 – Vienne 38

Hostellerie Le St-Laurent — rm, P P VISA MC AE

8 r. Croix Blanche – ✆ 04 78 40 91 44 – www.lesaintlaurent.fr – le.st.laurent@wanadoo.fr – Fax 04 78 40 45 41 – Closed 1st-3 May, 8-10 May, 22-24 May, 12-14 July, 1st-23 August, 26 December-3 January, Friday dinner, Saturday, Sunday dinner and bank holiday evenings

30 rm – †€ 70/126 ††€ 70/126, ☕ € 8,50

Rest – Menu € 26 (weekdays)/63 – Carte € 45/63

◆ A fine 18C Dauphiné abode nestling in wooded parkland. The simple rooms vary in size, but those in the annexe are smaller. In summer, meals are served on the terrace under a 300 year-old lime tree.

ST-LAURENT-DES-ARBRES – 30 Gard – 339 N4 – pop. 2 017 – alt. 60 m – ✉ 30126 — 23 D2

▶ Paris 673 – Alès 70 – Avignon 20 – Nîmes 47 – Orange 22

ℹ Office de tourisme, Tour de Ribas ✆ 04 66 50 10 10, Fax 04 66 50 10 10

Le Saint-Laurent without rest — AC P VISA MC AE

pl. de l'Arbre – ✆ 04 66 50 14 14 – www.lesaintlaurent.biz – info@lesaintlaurent.biz – Fax 04 66 50 46 30 – Closed 3 weeks in November

9 rm – †€ 95/165 ††€ 95/195, ☕ € 16 – 1 suite

◆ This former wine-grower's house, nestling in the village, is full of character and carefully decorated. Antique furniture, cosy rooms and a pretty inner courtyard. A real little treasure.

Felisa without rest — P VISA MC

6 r. Barris – ✆ 04 66 39 99 84 – www.maison-felisa.com – information@maison-felisa.com – Open 3 April-3 January

5 rm ☕ – †€ 120/160 ††€ 120/160

◆ A zen spirit reigns over this stone abode (1830) that offers massages, yoga and a pool. Minimalist rooms (on the theme of fragrances) and a trendy, youthful ambience.

ST-LAURENT-DU-PONT – 38 Isère – 333 H5 – pop. 4 479 – alt. 410 m – ✉ 38380 French Alps — 45 C2

▶ Paris 560 – Chambéry 29 – Grenoble 34 – La Tour-du-Pin 42 – Voiron 15

ℹ Office de tourisme, place de la Mairie ✆ 04 76 06 22 55, Fax 04 76 06 21 21

◉ Gorges du Guiers Mort★★ Southeast: 2 km - Site★ of the Chartreuse de Curière Southeast: 4 km.

XX **La Blache** — VISA MC

2 pl. du 10ème Groupement – ✆ 04 76 55 29 57 – Closed 27 April-12 May, 31 August-15 September, 4-19 January, Sunday dinner, Monday and Tuesday

Rest – Menu € 30/53 – Carte € 34/57

◆ Unusual wooden armchairs adorn this tasteful establishment in a former train station near the Guiers Mort gorge. The market fresh menu changes with the seasons.

ST-LAURENT-DU-VAR – 06 Alpes-Maritimes – 341 E5 – pop. 30 400 – alt. 18 m – ✉ 06700 French Riviera 42 E2

Paris 919 – Antibes 16 – Cagnes-sur-Mer 5 – Cannes 26 – Grasse 31 – Nice 10 – Vence 16

Syndicat d'initiative, 18-19, route du Bord de Mer ✆ 04 93 31 31 21, Fax 04 93 14 92 83

Corniche du Var★ North.

See plan of NICE urban area

in Cap 3000

Novotel rm, VISA MC AE

40 av. de Verdun – ✆ 04 93 19 55 55 – www.novotel.com – h0414@accor-hotels.com – Fax 04 93 19 55 59

103 rm – €89/189 €89/189, €15 **Rest** – Carte €32/45

◆ A recently renovated modern hotel in a suburban shopping area near Nice-Côte-d'Azur Airport. Choose between an outside table in a haven of greenery, or the cool air-conditioned dining room much appreciated when it is scorching hot.

in Port St-Laurent

Holiday Inn Resort rm, VISA MC AE

167 promenade Flots Bleus – ✆ 04 93 14 80 00 – resort@wanadoo.fr – Fax 04 93 07 21 24

124 rm – €350/380 €385/415, €23

Rest ***Chez Panisse*** – Menu €22/31 bi – Carte €36/60

◆ A prestigious international hotel right on the beach, with a carefully kept modern look. The spacious and well-equipped rooms have a view of the sea or of the countryside. Seaside resort ambiance, traditional cuisine and spit-roasted meats.

La Mousson VISA MC AE

promenade Flots Bleus – ✆ 04 93 31 13 30 – barthelemi.eric@wanadoo.fr – Closed 25 December-1st January

Rest – Menu (€25), €31 (weekday lunch)/45 – Carte €40/55 dinner only

◆ Thai savours and exotic spices transport you to the kingdom of Siam during your meal, while you are pleasantly seated in this seafront restaurant.

ST-LAURENT-DU-VERDON – 04 Alpes-de-Haute-Provence – 334 E10 – pop. 92 – alt. 468 m – ✉ 04500 41 C2

Paris 806 – Brignoles 49 – Castellane 70 – Digne-les-Bains 59 – Manosque 37

Le Moulin du Château rm, rest, VISA MC

– ✆ 04 92 74 02 47 – www.moulin-du-chateau.com – info@moulin-du-chateau.com – Fax 04 92 74 02 97 – Open 14 March-8 November

10 rm – €69/109 €75/115, €9 – 1 suite – ½ P €77/97

Rest – *(closed Mon and Thu) (dinner only) (residents only)* Menu €32

◆ Delightful 17C olive oil mill, now a hotel with modern guestrooms and a sitting room facing the millstone. Relaxing garden and admirable ecological ethic (rainwater tank, organic produce, etc.). Regional breakfasts and Provençal dinners (residents only).

ST-LAURENT-LA-GÂTINE – 28 Eure-et-Loir – 311 F3 – pop. 452 – alt. 134 m – ✉ 28210 11 B1

Paris 77 – Évreux 66 – Orléans 121 – Versailles 57

Clos St-Laurent without rest

6 r. de l'Église – ✆ 02 37 38 24 02 – www.clos-saint-laurent.com – james@clos-saint-laurent.com – Closed 22 December-5 January

4 rm – €68 €73

◆ The former farm building houses four large guestrooms, tastefully decorated in a smart rustic style. Charming breakfast room and garden-terrace.

ST-LAURENT-SUR-SAÔNE – 01 Ain – 328 C3 – see Mâcon

ST-LÉON – 47 Lot-et-Garonne – 336 D4 – pop. 293 – alt. 80 m – ✉ 47160 4 C2

Paris 667 – Bordeaux 107 – Agen 43 – Villeneuve-sur-Lot 44 – Marmande 35

Le Hameau des Coquelicots without rest

at Goutte d'Or, 2 km south on D 285 – ✆ 05 53 84 06 13 – www.lehameaudescoquelicots.com – contact@lehameaudescoquelicots.com – Fax 05 53 84 06 13

5 rm – €120 €130

◆ Three houses in the heart of the countryside. Add to the tranquil location a charming welcome and a refined décor comprised of natural materials and works of art. Kitchen garden and ecological swimming pool.

ST-LÉONARD-DE-NOBLAT – 87 Haute-Vienne – 325 F5 – pop. 4 667 – alt. 347 m – ✉ 87400 Dordogne-Berry-Limousin 24 B2

Paris 407 – Aubusson 68 – Brive-la-Gaillarde 99 – Guéret 62 – Limoges 21

Office de tourisme, place du Champ de Mars ✆ 05 55 56 25 06, Fax 05 55 56 36 97

Church ★: steeple ★★.

Relais St-Jacques VISA

6 bd A. Pressemane – ✆ 05 55 56 00 25 – www.lerelaissaintjacques.com – le.relais.st.jacques@orange.fr – Fax 05 55 56 19 87 – Closed 24 December-3 January, 23 February-15 March, Sunday dinner and Monday lunch from October to May

7 rm – €50 €50, €7 – ½ P €52

Rest – Menu €15 bi (weekday lunch), €19/37 – Carte €33/47

◆ Traditional building in an avenue skirting the town centre. Small fresh rooms, simply furnished and well-maintained. Simply decorated dining room serving traditional cooking and country dishes. Hospitable welcome.

Le Grand St-Léonard with rm VISA AE

23 av. Champs de Mars – ✆ 05 55 56 18 18 – www.hotelrestaurantlegrandsaintleonard-limousin.com – grandsaintleonard@wanadoo.fr – Fax 05 55 56 98 32 – Closed 20 December-20 January, Monday except dinner 15 June-15 September and Tuesday lunch

14 rm – €57/61 €57/61, €11

Rest – Menu (€15), €26/61 – Carte €56/65

◆ This former post house sports a pleasant provincial atmosphere. Classic dishes served in a sophisticated rustic décor: collection of cake moulds and Limoges chinaware. Prettily provincial, sometimes antiquated, rooms.

ST-LIGUAIRE – 79 Deux-Sèvres – 322 C7 – see Niort

ST-LÔ – 50 Manche – 303 F5 – pop. 19 600 – alt. 20 m – ✉ 50000 Normandy 32 A2

Paris 296 – Caen 62 – Cherbourg 80 – Laval 154 – Rennes 141

Office de tourisme, place Général-de-Gaulle ✆ 02 33 77 60 35, Fax 02 33 77 60 36

Centre Manche Saint-Martin-d'Aubigny Le Haut Boscq, 20 km on D 900, ✆ 02 33 45 24 52

Haras national ★ - Hanging of the Love of Gombaut and Macée in the musée des Beaux-Arts.

Plan on next page

Mercure VISA AE

1 av. Briovère – ✆ 02 33 05 10 84 – www.mercure.com – h1072@accor.com – Fax 02 33 56 46 92 A v

67 rm – €85/105 €95/115, €13

Rest – *(Closed Sunday) (dinner only)* Menu €16/31 – Carte €22/52

◆ Two hotels have been joined together to create this relatively contemporary establishement facing the ramparts. New or recently redone rooms with a good level of comfort. Traditional cuisine with regional touches.

ST-LÔ

Alsace-Lorraine (R.) . . . . **A** 2
Baltimore (R. de) . . . . **A** 3
Beaucoudray (R. de) . . . . **A** 5
Belle (R. du) . . . . **A** 7
Briovère (Av. de) . . . . **A** 8
Champ-de-Mars (Pl.) . . . . **B** 9
Feuillet (R. Octave) . . . . **A** 12
Gaulle (Pl. Gén.-de) . . . . **A** 13
Gerhardt (R. Gén.) . . . . **B** 14
Grimouville (R. de) . . . . **A** 16
Havin (R.) . . . . **A** 17
Houssin-Dumanoir (R.) . . . . . . **A** 18
Lattre-de-T. (R. Mar.-de) . . . . . **B** 19
Leclerc (R. Mar.) . . . . **B**
Mesnilcroc (R. du) . . . . **B** 22
Neufbourg (R. du) . . . . **B** 23
Notre-Dame (Parvis) . . . . **A** 24
Noyers (R. des) . . . . **A** 27
Poterne (R. de la) . . . . **A** 28
Ste-Croix (Pl.) . . . . **B** 30
St-Thomas (R.) . . . . **A**
Torteron (R.) . . . . **A**
Vieillard-de-Boismartin (R.) . . . **B** 31
80e-et-136e-Territorial (R. des) **A** 33

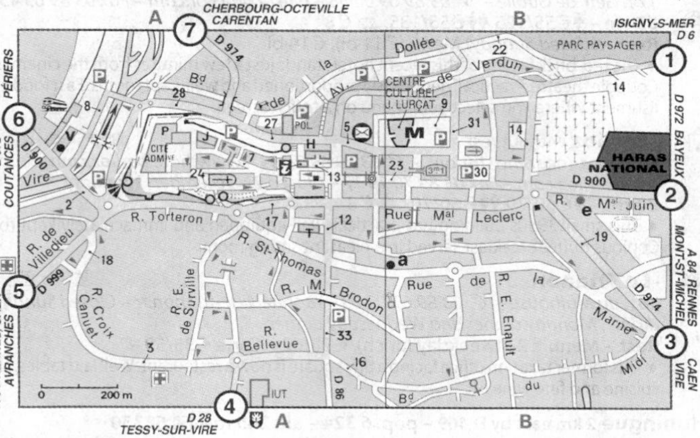

XX Le Péché Mignon
VISA MC AE D

84 r. Mar. Juin – ✆ 02 33 72 23 77 – http://le-peche-mignon.monsite.wanadoo.fr – restaurant-le-peche-mignon@wanadoo.fr – Fax 02 33 72 27 58 – Closed 14 July-1st August, 16-22 February and Monday B **e**

Rest – Menu (€ 12), € 17/50 – Carte € 38/50

♦ This restaurant offers two small, simple but comfortable dining rooms in a building near the national stud farm. Traditional meals with a touch of modernity.

in Calvaire 7 km by ② and D 972 – ✉ 50810 St-Pierre-de-Semilly

XXX La Fleur de Thym
P VISA MC AE

– ✆ 02 33 05 02 40 – www.la-fleur-de-thym.com – contact@la-fleur-de-thym.com – Fax 02 33 56 29 32 – Closed 16-31 August, 2-19 January, Saturday lunch, Sunday dinner and Monday

Rest – Menu € 21 (weekdays)/60 – Carte € 45/81

♦ This old farmstead has a shaded summer terrace that is well protected from the traffic noise of the nearby road. Classic repertoire enhanced by southern flavours.

ST-LOUBÈS – 33 Gironde – 335 I5 – pop. 7 639 – alt. 28 m – ✉ 33450 3 B1

Paris 568 – Bordeaux 18 – Créon 20 – Libourne 18 – St-André-de-Cubzac 15

X Le Coq Sauvage with rm
AC rest, VISA MC AE

71 av. du Port-Cavernes, in Cavernes, north-west : 4 km – ✆ 05 56 20 41 04 – www.lecoqsauvage.com – coq.sauvage@wanadoo.fr – Fax 05 56 20 44 76 – Closed 8-23 August and 19 December-3 January

6 rm – †€ 50 ††€ 60, ☕ € 7 – ½ P € 48

Rest – *(closed Saturday and Sunday)* Menu (€ 17), € 27 – Carte € 32/43

♦ Charming rustic house on the marina, with the Dordogne beyond. Regional dishes served on the pleasant patio in summer. Quiet rooms.

Good food without spending a fortune?
Look out for the Bib Gourmand

ST-LOUIS – 68 Haut-Rhin – 315 J11 – pop. 19 961 – alt. 250 m – ✉ 68300 1 B3

Paris 498 – Altkirch 29 – Basel 5 – Belfort 76 – Colmar 65 – Ferrette 24 – Mulhouse 30

Ibis
17 r. Gén. de Gaulle – ☎ 03 89 69 06 58 – h5612@accor.com – Fax 03 89 69 45 03
65 rm – €55/125 €55/135, ☕ €8
Rest – *(closed Sunday)* Menu (€11 bi), €14 bi
◆ The red-brick façade of this recent hotel stands just a few minutes from the cinemas and Coupole theatre. Practical, generously proportioned and well-kept rooms. Fast food establishment where you select your menu on a touch screen.

Berlioz without rest
r. Henner, (near the station) – ☎ 03 89 69 74 44 – www.hotelberlioz.com – info@hotelberlioz.com – Fax 03 89 70 19 17 – Closed 22 December-3 January
20 rm – €60/70 €60/70, ☕ €8
◆ This small 1930s building has practical, well-equipped and immaculately kept rooms. Copious buffet breakfast served in a pleasant sitting room.

Le Trianon
46 r. du Mulhouse – ☎ 03 89 67 03 03 – raphael@le-trianon.fr – Closed Sunday dinner, Monday dinner and Wednesday dinner
Rest – Menu €21 (weekday lunch), €28/62 – Carte €35/59
◆ This former taxation office facing a tiny square is now a restaurant. Well laid tables, classic cuisine and fine wine list.

in Huningue 2 km east by D 469 – pop. 6 324 – alt. 245 m – ✉ 68330

Tivoli
15 av. de Bâle – ☎ 03 89 69 73 05 – www.tivoli.fr – info@tivoli.fr – Fax 03 89 67 82 44
41 rm – €58/85 €63/99, ☕ €10 – ½ P €63/86
Rest *Philippe Schneider* – *(Closed 23 July-16 August and 23 December-6 January)* Menu €24/47 – Carte €37/64
◆ A stone's throw from the Swiss and German borders. The renovated rooms sport a modern decor. The others remain up to date and well kept. A relatively plush restaurant serving modern cuisine, and a trendier room with a blackboard menu.

in Village-Neuf 3 km northeast by D 66 and D 21 – pop. 3 444 – alt. 240 m – ✉ 68128

Office de tourisme, 81, rue Vauban ☎ 03 89 70 04 49, Fax 03 89 67 30 80

Au Cerf
72 r. Gén. de Gaulle – ☎ 03 89 67 12 89 – lorpasc.martin@wanadoo.fr – lorpasc.martin@wanadoo.fr – Fax 03 89 69 85 57 – Closed 14 July-10 August, 24 December-1st January, Thursday dinner, Sunday dinner and Monday
Rest – Menu €11 (weekday lunch), €18/42 – Carte €25/45
◆ Near the Alsatian Petite Camargue – see above, a family inn of rustic inspiration adorned with hunting trophies. Traditional cuisine and asparagus and game specialities in season.

in Hésingue 4 km west by D 419 – pop. 2 265 – alt. 290 m – ✉ 68220

Au Boeuf Noir
2 r. de Folgensbourg – ☎ 03 89 69 76 40 – www.boeufnoir.com – giuggiola.auboeufnoir@orange.fr – Fax 03 89 67 77 29 – Closed 18-25 March, 18-31 August, Saturday lunch, Sunday and Monday
Rest – Menu (€36 bi), €48/64 – Carte €47/73
◆ Near a busy junction, pleasant restaurant with modern paintings by the artist owner. Carefully prepared modern dishes.

ST-LOUP-DE-VARENNES – 71 Saône-et-Loire – 320 J9 – see Chalon-sur-Saône

ST-LUNAIRE – 35 Ille-et-Vilaine – 309 J3 – see Dinard

ST-LUPERCE – 28 Eure-et-Loir – 311 D5 – see Chartres

ST-LYPHARD – 44 Loire-Atlantique – 316 C3 – pop. 4 030 – alt. 12 m – ✉ 44410 Brittany 34 **A2**

Paris 447 – La Baule 17 – Nantes 73 – Redon 43 – St-Nazaire 22

Office de tourisme, place de l'Eglise ☎ 02 40 91 41 34, Fax 02 40 91 34 96

Church steeple ✳ ★★.

Les Chaumières du Lac et Auberge Les Typhas

rte Herbignac – ☎ 02 40 91 32 32 rest, VISA MC AE
– www.leschaumieresdulac.com – info@leschaumieresdulac.com
– Fax 02 40 91 30 33 – Closed 23 December-17 January
20 rm – †€ 64/74 ††€ 64/110, ☕ € 10
Rest – *(Closed Wednesday lunch and Tuesday)* Menu (€ 15), € 20 (weekday lunch), € 22/44 – Carte € 48/96
◆ Hamlet of thatch roofed cottages in the Brière Regional Nature Park. Vast rooms, some refurbished. Excellent breakfasts featuring farm produce. Pleasant, renovated dining room leading onto a terrace. Modern-style cuisine.

St-Nazaire road 3 km south by D 47 – ✉ 44410 St-Lyphard

Auberge le Nézil

VISA MC AE
– ☎ 02 40 91 41 41 – www.aubergelenezil.com – aubergelenezil@wanadoo.fr
– Fax 02 40 91 45 39 – Closed 5-12 October, 16 November-14 December, Wednesday dinner from October to May, Sunday dinner and Monday
Rest – Menu (€ 20), € 27/49 – Carte € 30/65
◆ Well-kept country inn on the edge of the Grande Brière marshland. Tasty classic cuisine, made with local produce, served in the pleasant garden-terrace in summer.

in Bréca 6 km south by D 47 and secondary road – ✉ 44410 St-Lyphard

Auberge de Bréca

VISA MC AE
D 47 – ☎ 02 40 91 41 42 – www.auberge-breca.com – aubergedebreca@wanadoo.fr – Fax 02 40 91 37 41 – Closed 4-24 January, Sunday dinner and Monday except July-August
Rest – Menu (€ 20), € 28/54 – Carte € 35/80
◆ This Brière cottage (1903) is today a warm regional restaurant with a lovely veranda. Garden and terrace overlooking the marshland in fine weather.

ST-MACAIRE – 33 Gironde – 335 J7 – see Langon

ST-MACLOU – 27 Eure – 304 C5 – pop. 463 – alt. 114 m – ✉ 27210 32 **A3**

Paris 179 – Le Grand-Quevilly 67 – Le Havre 35 – Rouen 73

La Crémaillère with rm

VISA MC AE
– ☎ 02 32 41 17 75 – Fax 02 32 42 50 90 – Closed 30 June-9 July, 12-21 November, Tuesday dinner and Wednesday; hotel open 15 April-15 October
3 rm – †€ 30 ††€ 46, ☕ € 6,50 – ½ P € 52
Rest – Menu (€ 11), € 14 (weekdays)/38 – Carte € 39/58
◆ Charming, flower-decked little inn in the heart of the village. Pleasant brightly coloured and wood-panelled dining room that opens onto a summer terrace. Creative regional cuisine.

ST-MAIXENT-L'ÉCOLE – 79 Deux-Sèvres – 322 E6 – pop. 6 602 – alt. 85 m – ✉ 79400 Atlantic Coast 38 **B2**

Paris 383 – Angoulême 106 – Niort 24 – Parthenay 30 – Poitiers 52

Syndicat d'initiative, porte Châlon ☎ 05 49 05 54 05, Fax 05 49 05 76 25

du Petit Chêne Mazières-en-GâtineW : 20 km on D 6, ☎ 05 49 63 20 95

Abbey church ★ - Musée du sous-officier (collection of uniforms★).

Le Logis St-Martin

VISA MC AE
chemin Pissot – ☎ 05 49 05 58 68 – www.logis-saint-martin.com – contact@logis-saint-martin.com – Fax 05 49 76 19 93
12 rm – †€ 110/155 ††€ 125/180, ☕ € 16 – 1 suite – ½ P € 120/155
Rest – *(Closed Saturday lunch, Tuesday lunch and Monday except dinner in high season)* Menu (€ 35), € 48/78 – Carte € 52/75
◆ This 17C stately home, which has been tastefully restored, nestles in a park by the River Sèvre. Individually decorated rooms. This refurbished restaurant is very refined and cosy in style, and makes the most of the beams and the old fireplace. Classic dishes.

in Soudan 7.5 km east on the N 11 – pop. 399 – alt. 155 m – ✉ 79800

Musée des Tumulus de Bougon★★.

L'Orangerie

10 rte de l'Atlantique – ✆ 05 49 06 56 06 – www.lorangerie79.com – orangerie79@orange.fr – Fax 05 49 06 56 10 – Closed 2 weeks in January, Monday lunch in July-August, Sunday dinner and Monday from September to June

Rest – Menu € 15 (weekdays)/45 – Carte € 46/58

◆ Under new management, this restaurant by a busy highway is enjoying a breath of fresh air: dining room leading into the garden and updated traditional repertory.

ST-MAIXME-HAUTERIVE – 28 Eure-et-Loir – 311 D4 – pop. 349 – alt. 194 m – ✉ 28170 11 B1

Paris 105 – Chartres 31 – Évreux 61 – Orléans 112

La Rondellière

11 r. de la Mairie – ✆ 02 37 51 68 26 – www.ferme-rondelliere.com – jeanpaul.langlois@wanadoo.fr – Fax 02 37 51 08 53

4 rm – †€ 33 ††€ 42 **Table d'hôte** – *(Closed Sunday dinner)* Menu € 15 bi

◆ The spacious and well-arranged rooms occupy the former haylofts of this farm that is still in the cereal business. Guaranteed peace and quiet and friendly welcome. Table d'hôte serving dishes prepared with home-grown vegetable-garden produce (booking essential).

ST-MALO – 35 Ille-et-Vilaine – 309 J3 – pop. 49 600 – alt. 5 m – Casino AXY – ✉ 35400 Brittany 10 D1

Paris 404 – Avranches 68 – Dinan 32 – Rennes 70 – St-Brieuc 71

Dinard-Pleurtuit-St-Malo: ✆ 02 99 46 18 46, by ③: 14 km.

Office de tourisme, esplanade Saint-Vincent ✆ 08 25 13 52 00, Fax 02 99 56 67 00

Ramparts★★★ - Château★★: musée d'Histoire de la ville et d'Ethnographie du pays malouin★ M², Quic-en-Groigne tower ★ DZ E - Fort national★: ≤★★ 15 mn - Stained-glass windows★ of St-Vincent cathedral - Mystères de la mer (Mysteries of the sea) ★★ (aquarium) via ③ - Rothéneuf: musée-manoir Jacques-Cartier★, 3 km by ① - St Servan sur Mer: corniche d'Aleth (cliff road) ≤★, tour Solidor★, views of the parc des Corbières★, belvédère du Rosais (Viewpoint)★.

Plans on following pages

Intra muros

Central

6 Gde-Rue – ✆ 02 99 40 87 70 – www.bestwestern-hotelcentral-saintmalo.com – centralbw@wanadoo.fr – Fax 02 99 40 47 57 DZ **n**

50 rm – †€ 60/108 ††€ 80/130, € 11 – 3 suites

Rest – Menu € 17/32 – Carte € 33/54

◆ In the heart of the pirate capital and with well-kept practical rooms, the Central is the ideal base from which to discover St Malo's charms. Restaurant serving seafood with fishing tackle decorating the walls.

Ajoncs d'Or without rest

10 r. Forgeurs – ✆ 02 99 40 85 03 – www.st-malo-hotel-ajoncs-dor.com – hotel-ajoncs-dor@wanadoo.fr – Fax 02 99 40 80 70 – Closed December and January DZ **a**

22 rm – †€ 74/150 ††€ 94/150, € 13

◆ Rooms with individual touches (nautical pictures) in a quiet street in the old town. Wood panelled breakfast room decorated with prints.

Hôtel du Louvre without rest

2 r. Marins – ✆ 02 99 40 86 62 – www.hoteldulouvre-saintmalo.com – contact@hoteldulouvre-saintmalo.com – Fax 02 99 40 86 93 DZ **b**

50 rm – †€ 70/125 ††€ 79/139, € 12

◆ Plain, modern decor in this hotel renovated from top to bottom. Dark wood, paintings, pastel coloured walls and warm feature colours in the rooms and breakfast room.

La Cité without rest
26 r. Ste-Barbe – 02 99 40 55 40 – www.hotelcite.com – hotelcite-stmalo@wanadoo.fr – Fax 02 99 40 10 04 DZ **v**
41 rm – €50/88 €69/133, €12
◆ Building in the old town with functional, well-sized rooms. Enjoy breakfast served under the exposed beams with views over the ramparts.

San Pedro without rest
1 r. Ste-Anne – 02 99 40 88 57 – www.sanpedro-hotel.com – hotelsanpedro@wanadoo.fr – Fax 02 99 40 46 25 – Open 1st March-15 November DZ **f**
12 rm – €48/50 €57/71, €8
◆ This small hotel is a stone's throw from Bon Secours beach. Wonderful warm welcome. Tiny but perfectly maintained rooms. Impeccable breakfast.

Le Croiseur without rest
2 pl. de la Poissonnerie – 02 99 40 80 40 – www.hotel-le-croiseur.com – hotel.le.croiseur@free.fr – Fax 02 99 56 83 76 – Closed 11 November-1st January DZ **h**
14 rm – €55/65 €59/72, €7
◆ Brown leather and wenge furniture endow this hotel with a contemporary minimalist look. In summer, breakfast is served on a pretty cobbled square complete with occasional fishmonger.

Le Chalut (Jean-Philippe Foucat)
8 r. Corne de Cerf – 02 99 56 71 58 – Fax 02 99 56 71 58 – Closed Monday and Tuesday DZ **d**
Rest – *(number of covers limited, pre-book)* Menu €25 (weekday lunch), €40/70 – Carte €53/68
Spec. Feuilles de lotte et chair de tourteau marinés. Etuvé de Saint-Pierre à la coriandre fraîche. Délice glacé au pur malt.
◆ Beautiful facade recalling the sailors' life, a convivial interior and refined seafood cuisine: three good reasons to stop by!

Delaunay
6 r. Ste-Barbe – 02 99 40 92 46 – www.restaurant-delaunay.com – bdelaunay@orange.fr – Closed mid-January to mid-February, Monday in low season and Sunday DZ **x**
Rest – *(dinner only)* Menu €35 – Carte €38/64
◆ This small dining area with wine coloured facade is situated amid several other restaurants, and has been newly refurbished. Numerous paintings on display. Modern menu.

A la Duchesse Anne (Serge Thirouard)
5 pl. Guy La Chambre – 02 99 40 85 33 – Fax 02 99 40 00 28 – Closed December, January, Sunday evening in low season, Monday lunch and Wednesday DZ **e**
Rest – Menu €78 – Carte €47/95
Spec. Gratin de langoustines à l'estragon. Homard à l'armoricaine. Tarte tatin.
◆ A St Malo institution (1945) with beautiful mosaic and fresco interior. Old style classic cuisine.

Gilles
2 r. Pie qui boit – 02 99 40 97 25 – Fax 02 99 40 97 25 – Closed Thursday in low season and Wednesday DZ **t**
Rest – *(number of covers limited, pre-book)* Menu (€21), €26/40
◆ The impressive rampart walk is guaranteed to work up an appetite. This discreet restaurant with large bay windows serves carefully prepared modern cuisine.

L'Ancrage
7 r. J. Cartier – 02 99 40 15 97 – Fax 02 23 18 03 61 – Closed 4 January-4 February, Tuesday and Wednesday except July-August DZ **r**
Rest – Menu €16/36 – Carte €50/71
◆ Informally served meals at this fish and seafood restaurant, situated right against the ramparts. Nautical decor on the ground floor, pretty vaulted dining room upstairs.

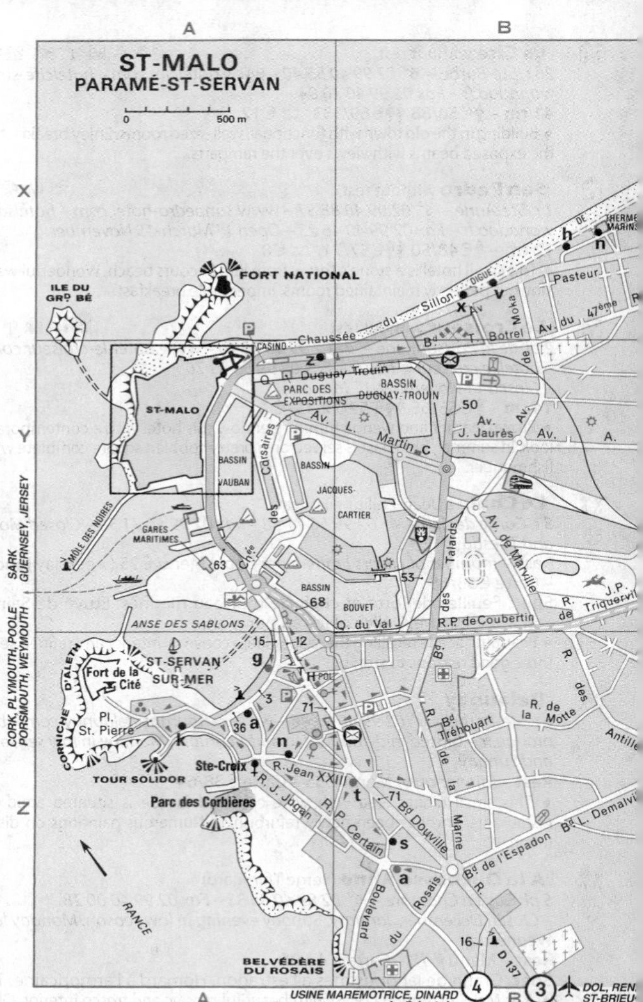

St-Malo Est and Paramé – ✉ 35400 St-Malo

Grand Hôtel des Thermes ≤ ◁ rm, AC

100 bd Hébert – ☎ 02 99 40 75 75 VISA MC AE D
– www.thalassotherapie.com – resa@thalassotherapie.com – Fax 02 99 40 76 00
– Closed 3-17 January BX **n**

169 rm – †€ 80/172 ††€ 140/422, ☕ € 20 – 7 suites
Rest *Le Cap Horn* – ☎ 02 99 40 75 40 – Menu € 29 (weekdays)/56
– Carte € 50/65
Rest *La Verrière* – Menu (€ 23), € 34/43 – Carte € 35/45

◆ This old 19C palace on the seafront includes a thalassotherapy centre (six seawater pools and top class treatments). All the rooms are of a good size. Beautiful view of the English Channel; classic menu. Belle Epoque decor and diet cuisine at the Verrière.

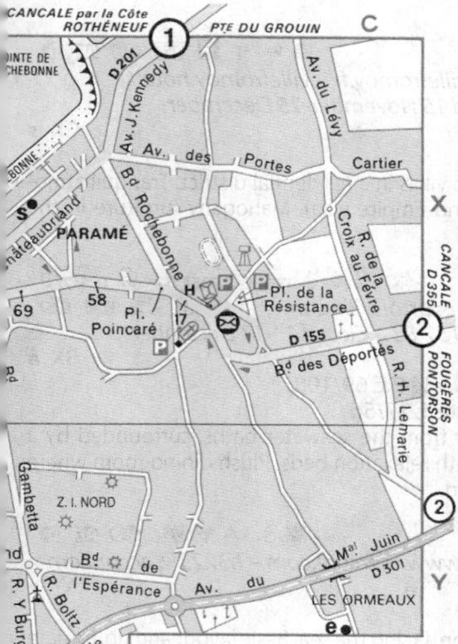

Bardelière (R. M. de la) ..... **CZ** 2
Bas-Sablons (R. des) ..... **AZ** 3
Broussais (R.) ..... **DZ**
Cartier (R. J.) ..... **DZ** 5
Chartres (R. de) ..... **DZ** 6
Chateaubriand (Pl.) ..... **DZ** 8
Clemenceau (R. Georges) ..... **AZ** 12
Cordiers (R. des) ..... **DZ** 13
Dauphine (R.) ..... **AZ** 15
Dinan (R. de) ..... **DZ**
Doutreleau (R.) ..... **BZ** 16
Flaubert (R. G.) ..... **CX** 17
Forgeurs (R. du) ..... **DZ** 18
Fosse (R. de la) ..... **DZ** 19
Herbes (Pl. aux) ..... **DZ** 25
Lamennais (Pl. Fr.) ..... **DZ** 28
Mettrie (R. de la) ..... **DZ** 35
Mgr-Duchesne (Pl.) ..... **AZ** 36
Pilori (Pl. du) ..... **DZ** 38
Poids-du-Rois (Pl. du) ..... **DZ** 39
Poissonnerie (Pl. de la) ..... **DZ** 42
Porcon-de-la-Barbinais (R.) ..... **DZ** 43
République (Bd de la) ..... **BY** 50
Roosevelt (Av. F.) ..... **BY** 53
St-Benoist (R.) ..... **DZ** 56
St-Vincent (R.) ..... **DZ** 57
Schuman (R. du Président-Robert) ..... **CX** 58
Tabarly (Chaussée Eric) ..... **AY** 63
Trichet (Q. de) ..... **AY** 68
Umbricht (R. du R. P.) ..... **CX** 69
Vauban (Pl.) ..... **DZ** 70
Ville-Pépin (R.) ..... **ABZ** 71

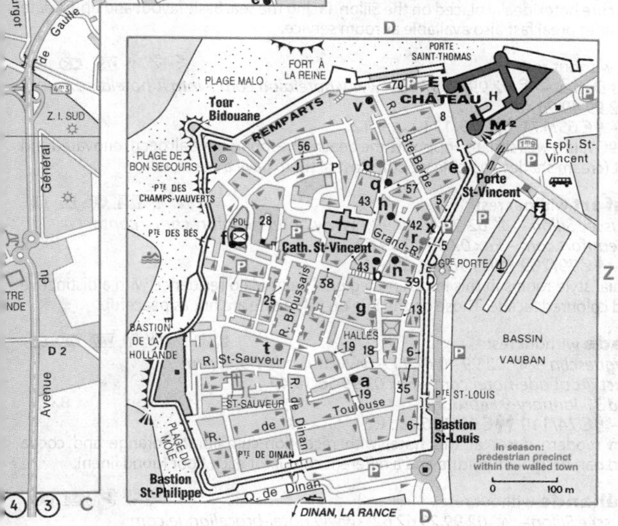

Alexandra

138 bd Hébert – ✆ 02 99 56 11 12
– alexandra.hotel@wanadoo.fr
– Fax 02 99 56 11 12
– Closed January

BX **h**

31 rm – €83/147 €95/173, ☕ €14 – ½ P €94/126
Rest – Menu €24/72 – Carte €28/50

◆ The rooms, with terraces or bay windows, enjoy a pretty view of the bay or the city rooftops. Sunny and functional setting, decorated with model ships. A brasserie style restaurant offering a traditional menu inspired by the sea.

La Villefromoy without rest
7 bd Hébert – ☎ 02 99 40 92 20 – www.villefromoy.fr – villefromoy.hotel@wanadoo.fr – Fax 02 99 56 79 49 – Closed 15 November-25 December and 3 January-4 February CX **s**
26 rm – †€ 89/175 ††€ 89/175, ☐ € 13
◆ A charming welcome awaits at these two villas in a residential district. Tranquil atmosphere in the lounge (in the French Second Empire villa). Mahogany furniture in the rooms.

Grand Hôtel Courtoisville rm, rest, rest,
69 bd Hébert – ☎ 02 99 40 83 83 – www.courtoisville.com – hotel@courtoisville.com – Fax 02 99 40 57 83 – Closed 1st-17 December and 3 January-4 February BX **a**
45 rm – †€ 66/169 ††€ 66/169, ☐ € 13 – ½ P € 69/108
Rest – Menu € 18 (lunch), € 25/32 – Carte € 27/56
◆ Early 20C family-run guesthouse not far from the seawater baths, surrounded by a garden. Spacious and quiet rooms, most with relaxation beds. Plush dining room where you can enjoy traditional dishes and seafood.

Mercure without rest
36 chaussée Sillon – ☎ 02 23 18 47 47 – www.mercure.com – h3225@accor.com – Fax 02 23 18 47 48 AY **z**
51 rm – †€ 73/150 ††€ 81/195, ☐ € 14
◆ A Mercure hotel ideally placed on the Sillon, facing the sea. Basic layout and up-to-date decor. Buffet breakfast also available as room service.

Alba without rest
17 r. des Dunes – ☎ 02 99 40 37 18 – www.hotelalba.com – info@hotelalba.com – Fax 02 99 40 96 40 BX **v**
22 rm – †€ 65/171 ††€ 79/171, ☐ € 12
◆ This 19C villa is well situated opposite the beach. The rooms have all been renovated and are light (cream shades and pale wood). Most of them have a sea view.

Beaufort without rest
25 chaussée Sillon – ☎ 02 99 40 99 99 – www.hotel-beaufort.com – contact@hotel-beaufort.com – Fax 02 99 40 99 62 BX **x**
22 rm – †€ 79/209 ††€ 79/209, ☐ € 13
◆ Colonial style rooms in this imposing regional Saint Malo residence with a distinctive mustard coloured façade. Those on the Rue du Sillon side are not as peaceful.

Aubade without rest
8 pl. Duguesclin – ☎ 02 99 40 47 11 – www.aubade-hotel.com – contact@aubade-hotel.com – Fax 02 99 56 10 49 – Closed 31 January-9 February BXY
20 rm – †€ 74/110 ††€ 90/136, ☐ € 11
◆ Warm modern decor at this hotel with reception-cum-library, orange and cocoa coloured bar, designer furniture and a different colour for each floor (good linen).

Brocéliande without rest
43 chaussée Sillon – ☎ 02 99 20 62 62 – www.hotel-broceliande.com – logis.broceliande@wanadoo.fr – Fax 02 99 40 42 47 – Open March-mid November BX **v**
9 rm – †€ 85/115 ††€ 90/160, ☐ € 12
◆ This large 19C residence now offers B&B style-accommodation. Each room is decorated with Laura Ashley fabrics and bears the name of a Broceliande hero. A hospitable welcome awaits you.

La Malouinière du Mont Fleury without rest
2 r. Montfleury – ☎ 02 23 52 28 85 – www.lemontfleury.com – bob.haby@wanadoo.fr – Fax 02 23 52 28 85 CY **e**
4 rm ☐ – †€ 75 ††€ 75/105
◆ Beautiful St Malo house dating from the 18C set in a peaceful garden. Quiet rooms (two of them duplex) decorated with various themes – the sea, the Orient, China and America.

in St-Servan-sur-Mer – ✉ 35400 St Malo

Valmarin without rest
7 r. Jean XXIII – ☎ 02 99 81 94 76 – www.levalmarin.com – levalmarin@wanadoo.fr – Fax 02 99 81 30 03 AZ **n**
12 rm – †€ 100/145 ††€ 100/145, ☕ € 11
◆ Elegant residence providing individually decorated rooms, named after famous local people. The most attractive rooms afford views of the peaceful wooded park.

Manoir du Cunningham without rest
9 pl. Mgr Duchesne – ☎ 02 99 21 33 33 – www.st-malo-hotel-cunningham.com – cunningham@wanadoo.fr – Fax 02 99 21 33 34 – Open from mid-March to mid-November, weekends, Christmas and February holidays AZ **a**
13 rm – †€ 90/190 ††€ 90/190, ☕ € 10
◆ Appealing Anglo-Norman pseudo-mansion facing the Sablons cove. The spacious rooms, named after islands, are pleasant, if a little outmoded; most command sea views.

L'Ascott without rest
35 r. Chapitre – ☎ 02 99 81 89 93 – www.ascotthotel.com – informations@ascotthotel.com – Fax 02 99 81 77 40 – Closed 5-22 January BZ **s**
10 rm – †€ 85/100 ††€ 100/155, ☕ € 13
◆ A pleasant blend of contemporary decor (designer furniture) and antique features (chandeliers and paintings) in this charming mansion in a residential district.

La Rance without rest
15 quai Sébastopol, (Solidor port) – ☎ 02 99 81 78 63 – www.larancehotel.com – hotel-la-rance@wanadoo.fr – Fax 02 99 81 44 80 – Open beg. February-mid November AZ **k**
11 rm – †€ 60/88 ††€ 60/88, ☕ € 9
◆ This Hotel in the Solidor district has small, personalised bedrooms overlooking the sea. It is undergoing gradual renovation, and you will be received as if by friends.

Le St-Placide (Luc Mobihan)
6 pl. Poncel – ☎ 02 99 81 70 73 – www.lesaintplacide.com – imobihan@wanadoo.fr – Closed 14 June-2 July, 9-20 November, 15-25 February, Wednesday except dinner from 14 July to 15 August and Tuesday BZ **a**
Rest – Menu € 26 (weekday lunch), € 42/82 – Carte € 69/86
Spec. Risotto homard-bacon (spring-summer). Pigeonneau rôti au thé fumé (autumn-winter). Retour sur la tarte au citron meringuée.
◆ In the contemporary decor of this small restaurant, the chef gives free reign to his imagination. Modern cuisine, friendly welcome and service.

Les Corbières
6 pl. Mgr Juhel – ☎ 02 99 82 07 46 – www.lescorbieres-saintmalo.fr – restaurantlescorbieres@yahoo.fr – Closed 18-30 June, 5-30 November, 15-28 February, Tuesday except dinner in July-August and Monday BZ **t**
Rest – *(number of covers limited, pre-book)* Menu € 25 (weekday lunch), € 36/55 – Carte approx. € 40
◆ A discreet brown facade hides this restaurant with a modern feel (Murano lighting) in the heart of the Corbières district. Aesthetically pleasing and inventive cuisine.

La Gourmandise
2 r. des Bas-Sablons – ☎ 02 99 21 93 53 – www.lagourmandise.book.fr – steve.delamaire@wanadoo.fr – Fax 02 99 21 93 53 – Closed 22 December-28 December, 15-21 February, Tuesday dinner, Saturday lunch and Sunday AZ **g**
Rest – Menu (€ 15), € 24/44 – Carte € 49/64
◆ This simple restaurant is located behind the Sablons cove in the St Servan district. It offers seasonal cuisine with Mediterranean accents. Warm welcome.

Rennes road 3 km by ③ and Ave Gén. de Gaulle – ✉ 35400 St-Malo

La Grassinais rm, rest, rm, P VISA MC AE
12 allée Grassinais – ✆ 02 99 81 33 00 – www.saint-malo-hebergement.com – manoirdelagrassinais@wanadoo.fr – Fax 02 99 81 60 90 – Closed 20 December-31 January
29 rm – €58/79 €58/89, €9 – ½ P €61/76
Rest – *(closed Saturday lunch and Monday from September to mid-July, Sunday dinner except in August)* Menu (€19), €24/39 – Carte €39/51
◆ Just outside St-Malo, this former farm has been prettily restored. Modern, comfortable, refurbished rooms, warm, panelled dining room and traditional gourmet recipes prepared with great care.

ST-MANDÉ – 94 Val-de-Marne – 312 D2 – 101 27 – see Paris, Area

ST-MARC-A-LOUBAUD – 23 Creuse – 325 I5 – pop. 131 – alt. 705 m – ✉ 23460 25 C2

▶ Paris 411 – Aubusson 24 – Guéret 54 – Limoges 78 – Tulle 87 – Ussel 57

Les Mille Sources P VISA MC
in the village – ✆ 05 55 66 03 69 – Fax 05 55 66 03 69 – Open from Easter to mid-November and closed Sunday dinner and Monday except school holidays
Rest – *(pre-book)* Menu €35/49 – Carte approx. €58
◆ A pleasantly converted farm where you will be welcomed as long-lost friends. Ducks from Challans and legs of lamb are roasted in the period fireplace in the attractive rustic dining room.

ST-MARCEL-DU-PÉRIGORD – 24 Dordogne – 329 F6 – pop. 140 – alt. 160 m – ✉ 24510 4 C1

▶ Paris 538 – Bordeaux 144 – Périgueux 58 – Bergerac 26 – Sarlat-la-Canéda 55

Auberge Lou Peyrol VISA MC
au bourg – ✆ 05 53 24 09 71 – www.loupeyrol.com – fiona.wavrin@wanadoo.fr – Closed for one week in March, 15 November-15 December, Monday in winter and Tuesday
Rest – Menu €27/38 – Carte €34/42
◆ Périgord inn with extremely rustic charm serving seasonal, regional cuisine. Terrace shaded by an ancient lime tree.

ST-MARCEL-EN-DOMBES – 01 Ain – 328 C5 – pop. 1 202 – alt. 265 m – ✉ 01390 43 E1

▶ Paris 440 – Bourg-en-Bresse 36 – Lyon 30 – Meximieux 21 – Villefranche-sur-Saône 26

La Colonne VISA MC
– ✆ 04 72 26 11 06 – Fax 04 72 08 59 24 – Closed 18 December-18 January, Monday dinner and Tuesday
Rest – Menu €16 (weekday lunch), €20/38 – Carte €27/47
◆ The name of this hotel refers to the 16C stone column standing in the middle of the dining room (oak wood panelling and French-style ceiling). Regional cuisine. Garden-terrace.

ST-MARCEL-LÈS-SAUZET – 26 Drôme – 332 B6 – see Montélimar

ST-MARCELLIN – 38 Isère – 333 E7 – pop. 6 955 – alt. 282 m – ✉ 38160 Lyon - Rhone Valley 43 E2

▶ Paris 570 – Die 76 – Grenoble 55 – Valence 46 – Vienne 71 – Voiron 47

Office de tourisme, 2, avenue du Collège ✆ 04 76 38 53 85, Fax 04 76 38 17 32

La Tivollière

Château du Mollard – ✆ 04 76 38 21 17 – www.lativolliere.com – restaurant.lativolliere@orange.fr – Fax 04 76 38 94 51 – Closed Thursday dinner, Sunday dinner and Monday

Rest – Menu € 30/49

Rest *Face B* – *(Closed Monday and dinner except Friday and Saturday)* Menu (€ 18), € 21 (weekday lunch) – Carte € 30/45

◆ A restaurant with a rather unexpected modern decor in a 15C castle overlooking the town. The shaded terrace offers a glimpse of the Vercors. At Face B, bistro dishes at lunch during the week, tapas and lounge feel at weekends.

ST-MARTIAL-DE-NABIRAT – 24 Dordogne – 329 I7 – pop. 513 – alt. 175 m – ✉ 24250 4 D2

Paris 556 – Bordeaux 213 – Périgueux 82 – Cahors 43 – Sarlat-la-Canéda 20

Le St-Martial

au bourg – ✆ 05 53 29 18 34 – www.lesaintmartial.com – le-saint-martial@aliceadsl.fr – Fax 05 53 29 73 45 – Closed Monday lunch from mid-July to end August, Tuesday and Wednesday except dinner from 16 July to 31 August

Rest – Menu (€ 25), € 32/60 – Carte € 48/63

◆ With its wrought iron furniture, the terrace on the village square invites you to sit down. Inside, find a modern decor and contemporary cuisine.

ST-MARTIN-AUX-CHARTRAINS – 14 Calvados – 303 N4 – see Pont-L'Évêque

ST-MARTIN-DE-BELLEVILLE – 73 Savoie – 333 M5 – pop. 3 080 – alt. 1 450 m – Winter sports : 1 450/2 850 m 9 37 – ✉ 73440 46 F2

French Alps

Paris 624 – Albertville 44 – Chambéry 93 – Moûtiers 20

Office de tourisme, immeuble L'Épervière ✆ 04 79 00 20 00, Fax 04 79 08 91 71

St-Martin

– ✆ 04 79 00 88 00 – www.hotel-stmartin.com – hotelsaintmartin@orange.fr – Fax 04 79 00 88 39 – Open 16 December-14 April

27 rm (½ board only) – 5 suites – ½ P € 98/205

Rest *Le Grenier* – Carte € 39/79

◆ This pretty chalet with a stone-slab roof is tastefully decorated. Warm wood decor and modern facilities in the rooms, all of which have balconies. Local dishes and daily specials announced on large blackboards. Savoyard atmosphere.

L'Edelweiss

r. St-François – ✆ 04 79 08 96 67 – www.hotel-edelweiss73.com – hoteledelweiss@wanadoo.fr – Fax 04 79 08 90 40 – Open 10 July-31 August and 20 December-26 April

16 rm – †€ 90/108 ††€ 120/160 – ½ P € 98/112

Rest – Menu € 30 (dinner)/45 – Carte € 45/80

◆ The mountain spirit flourishes at the Edelweiss. All the rooms are well kept, and some have been renovated. Sauna much appreciated by skiers. A traditional restaurant open during the summer season.

La Bouitte (René et Maxime Meilleur) with rm

at St-Marcel, 2 km South-East – ✆ 04 79 08 96 77 – www.la-bouitte.com – info@la-bouitte.com – Fax 04 79 08 96 03 – Open 1st July-3 September and 2 December-30 April

8 rm – †€ 180/215 ††€ 266/278

Rest – *(closed Monday in summer)* Menu € 59/165 – Carte € 85/140

Spec. Demi-lobe de foie gras de canard grillé, figues rôties et balsamique verdi. Pomme de ris de veau caramélisée, poire et beaufort, fumée de chêne. Pêches blanches et jaunes cuites façon risotto, feuilles de fenouil et chocolat. **Wines** Chignin-Bergeron, Vin de Savoie passerillé

◆ With its pretty, old chalet-style decor, creative, sweet and savoury cooking using mountain herbs and faultless hospitality, La Bouitte is a real Savoyard delight. Stunning alpine inspired rooms.

XX **Étoile des Neiges**

r. St-Martin – ✆ 04 79 08 92 80 – www.hotel-edelweiss73.com – hoteledelweiss@wanadoo.fr – Fax 04 79 08 90 40 – Open 10 July-30 August, and 20 December-25 April

Rest – Menu € 30 (dinner)/45 – Carte € 45/80

◆ Traditional restaurant and summer terrace. Dining rooms with a mountain setting warmed by a central fireplace. Upstairs mezzanine.

X **Le Montagnard**

– ✆ 04 79 01 08 40 – www.le-montagnard.com – info@le-montagnard.com – Open 1st July-31 August and 15 December-15 May and closed lunch in July-August

Rest – Menu (€ 21) – Carte € 38/70

◆ This pleasant and lively restaurant, on the village heights, has a warm mountain decor of rough woodwork, limewashed walls, solid furniture and old tools. Local dishes.

ST-MARTIN-DE-LONDRES – 34 Hérault – 339 H6 – pop. 2 159 – alt. 194 m – ✉ 34380 Languedoc-Roussillon-Tarn Gorges — 23 C2

▶ Paris 744 – Montpellier 25 – Le Vigan 37

ℹ Office de tourisme, Maison de Pays ✆ 04 67 55 09 59, Fax 04 67 55 70 91

XXX **Les Muscardins**

19 rte des Cévennes – ✆ 04 67 55 75 90 – www.les-muscardins.fr – thierry.rousset@wanadoo.fr – Fax 04 67 55 70 28 – Closed 5 February-8 March, Monday and Tuesday except bank holidays

Rest – Menu (€ 29), € 44/76 – Carte € 74/94

◆ The dining room and side lounge have been decorated in warm tones. Colourful paintings on the walls. Cuisine in keeping with modern taste. Catering service.

South 12 km by D 32, D 127 and D 127E6 – ✉ **34380 Argelliers**

XX **Auberge de Saugras** with rm

Domaine de Saugras – ✆ 04 67 55 08 71 – www.aubergedesaugras.fr – auberge.saugras@wanadoo.fr – Fax 04 67 55 04 65 – Closed 3-26 August, 21 December-6 January, Monday lunch in July-August, Tuesday except dinner in July-August and Wednesday

7 rm – †€ 45/85 ††€ 45/85, ☕ € 7 – ½ P € 59/79

Rest – *(pre-book)* Menu € 20 (weekdays)/59 – Carte € 25/95

◆ Standing alone in the midst of countryside, this 12C stone-built farmhouse offers generous local cuisine, pleasant terrace and functional guestrooms.

ST-MARTIN-D'ENTRAUNES – 06 Alpes-Maritimes – 341 B3 – pop. 88 – alt. 1 050 m – ✉ 06470 — 41 C2

▶ Paris 778 – Barcelonnette 50 – Castellane 66 – Digne-les-Bains 104 – Nice 108

Hostellerie de la Vallière

le village – ✆ 04 93 05 59 59 – www.hotel-lavalliere.com – info@hotel-lavalliere.com – Fax 04 93 05 59 60 – Open 15 April-30 October

10 rm (½ board only) – ½ P € 46 **Rest** – Menu € 21/25 – Carte € 25/35

◆ Hikers and weary urbanites appreciate this colourful inn that faces the Mercantour massif. Countrified decor and unpretentious comfort (no TV) in the rooms. Traditional meals in a dining room extended by a small terrace.

ST-MARTIN-DE-LA-PLACE – 49 Maine-et-Loire – 317 I5 – pop. 1 130 – alt. 80 m – ✉ 49160 — 35 C2

▶ Paris 314 – Nantes 147 – Angers 60 – Saumur 11 – La Flèche 70

ℹ Syndicat d'initiative, Mairie ✆ 02 41 38 43 06, Fax 02 41 38 09 93

Domaine de la Blairie rm, rest,

5 r. de la Mairie – ✆ 02 41 38 42 98 – www.hotel-blairie.com – contact@hotel-blairie.com – Fax 02 41 38 41 20 – Closed 15 December-15 February and Sunday dinner from 15 November to 15 March

44 rm – †€ 39/54 ††€ 57/83, ☕ € 9

Rest – *(closed Sunday dinner 15 November-15 March, Wednesday and Thursday)* Menu (€ 14), € 18/32 – Carte € 28/42

◆ This tufa stone construction offers practical, well-kept rooms spread over three buildings. Both the nearby Saumur village and the large garden with pool are refreshingly peaceful. Attractively priced traditional cuisine served in a warm setting.

ST-MARTIN-DE-RÉ – 17 Charente-Maritime – 324 B2 – see Île de Ré

ST-MARTIN-DU-FAULT – 87 Haute-Vienne – 325 E5 – see Limoges

ST-MARTIN-DU-TOUCH – 31 Haute-Garonne – 343 G3 – see Toulouse

ST-MARTIN-DU-VAR – 06 Alpes-Maritimes – 341 E5 – pop. 2 197 41 D2
– alt. 110 m – ✉ 06670

Paris 938 – Antibes 34 – Cannes 44 – Nice 28 – Puget-Théniers 40 – Vence 22

XXX ✿ **Jean-François Issautier**

3 km Nice road (D 6202) – 04 93 08 10 65 – www.issautier.fr – restaurant@issautier.fr – Fax 04 93 29 19 73 – Closed 26 October-4 November, early January to early February, Sunday dinner, Monday and Tuesday

Rest – Menu € 43/115 – Carte € 75/118

Spec. Pied de cochon cuit croustillant. Cul d'agneau rôti rosé, jus de menthe et légumes du marché. Tarte au chocolat fort en goût "araguani" et glace vanille.
Wines Bellet, Côtes de Provence.

◆ A conifer hedge separates this discreet restaurant from the road. Classic and regional repertoire served in an elegant high-ceilinged dining room.

ST-MARTIN-EN-BRESSE – 71 Saône-et-Loire – 320 K9 – pop. 1 792 8 C3
– alt. 192 m – ✉ 71620

Paris 353 – Beaune 48 – Chalon-sur-Saône 18 – Dijon 86 – Dôle 56 – Lons-le-Saunier 48

XX **Au Puits Enchanté** with rm rest,

1 pl. René Cassin – 03 85 47 71 96 – www.aupuitsenchante.com – chateau.jacky@wanadoo.fr – Fax 03 85 47 74 58 – Closed 9-17 March, 21-29 September, 23 November-1st December, 5-23 January, Sunday dinner, Monday and Tuesday

13 rm – †€ 51/61 ††€ 51/61, ☕ € 9 – ½ P € 52/58

Rest – Menu € 21/48 – Carte € 28/38

◆ In the heart of the town, this country house bends over backwards to make guests feel at home. Generous country cooking made with local produce. Rooms for overnight stays.

ST-MARTIN-LA-MÉANNE – 19 Corrèze – 329 M4 – pop. 359 25 C3
– alt. 500 m – ✉ 19320

Paris 510 – Aurillac 67 – Brive-la-Gaillarde 54 – Mauriac 48 – St-Céré 53 – Tulle 32 – Ussel 65

Barrage du Chastang ★ Southeast: 5 km, Dordogne-Berry-Limousin

X **Des Voyageurs** with rm

pl. Mairie – 05 55 29 11 53 – www.hotellesvoyageurs.com – info@hotellesvoyageurs.com – Fax 05 55 29 27 70 – Open 28 March-11 November and closed Sunday dinner and Monday except from May to September

8 rm – †€ 43/46 ††€ 43/56, ☕ € 7 – ½ P € 44/50

Rest – Menu (€ 17), € 22/36 – Carte € 40/46

◆ Time stands still in this charming stone inn that serves earthy food in an authentic country setting, or in summer, in the garden stretching out to a pond (fishing).

ST-MARTIN-LE-BEAU – 37 Indre-et-Loire – 317 O4 – pop. 2 606 11 B2
– alt. 55 m – ✉ 37270 Châteaux of the Loire

Paris 231 – Amboise 9 – Blois 45 – Loches 34 – Tours 20

XX **Auberge de la Treille** with rm

2 r. d'Amboise – 02 47 50 67 17 – www.auberge-de-la-treille.com – auberge-de-la-treille@wanadoo.fr – Fax 02 47 50 20 14 – Closed 1st-9 March, 25 October-4 November, Sunday dinner and Wednesday except July-August

8 rm – †€ 50 ††€ 50, ☕ € 8 – ½ P € 56

Rest – Menu (€ 13), € 20/40 – Carte € 33/40

◆ A stone's throw from the Touraine Aquarium. Modern menu served in the two rustic, half-timbered dining rooms. Simple bedrooms, which are bright and colourful.

ST-MARTIN-LE-GAILLARD – 76 Seine-Maritime – **304** I2 – pop. 323 – alt. 60 m – ✉ 76260 Normandy 33 **D1**

Paris 168 – Amiens 99 – Dieppe 27 – Eu 12 – Neufchâtel-en-Bray 34 – Rouen 87

Moulin du Becquerel
2 r. des Moulins, Northwest : 1.5 km on D 16 – *✆ 02 35 86 74 94 – www.moulindubecquerel.fr – moulindubecquerel@free.fr – Closed 20 January-6 March, Sunday dinner, Monday, Tuesday and Wednesday except July-August and holidays*
Rest – Menu € 20/44 – Carte € 31/52
◆ A peaceful riverside Normandy house. Rustic interior and pleasant terrace in the garden. Traditional cuisine based on seasonal market produce.

ST-MARTIN-VÉSUBIE – 06 Alpes-Maritimes – **341** E3 – pop. 1 300 – alt. 1 000 m – ✉ 06450 French Riviera 41 **D2**

Paris 845 – Antibes 73 – Barcelonnette 111 – Cannes 83 – Menton 88 – Nice 66

Office de tourisme, place Félix Faure ✆ 04 93 03 21 28, Fax 04 93 03 21 44

Venanson : ≤★, Frescoes ★ of St-Sébastien chapel South: 4,5 km.

Le Boréon★★ (waterfall★) North : 8 km - Cirque★★ du vallon de la Madone de Fenestre Northeast : 12 km.

Gelas without rest
27 r. Dr Cagnoli – ✆ 04 93 03 21 81 – www.hotel-gelas.com – contact@hotel-gelas.com – Fax 04 93 03 24 87 – Closed November
10 rm – 🚹€ 68 🚹🚹€ 68, ☕ € 9
◆ Charming welcome in this family establishment renovated by a skiing enthusiast. Panelled rooms and breakfast in a winter sports setting or on the terrace.

ST-MATHIEU-DE-TRÉVIERS – 34 Hérault – **339** I6 – pop. 4 341 – alt. 81 m – ✉ 34270 23 **C2**

Paris 761 – Marseille 176 – Montpellier 22 – Nice 334 – Nîmes 53 – Toulouse 261

Lennys
266 av. Louis Cancel, D 17 – ✆ 04 67 55 37 97 – restaurant.lennys@wanadoo.fr – Fax 04 67 54 71 82 – Closed 6-30 September, 10-19 January, Saturday lunch, Sunday dinner and Monday
Rest – Menu (€ 21), € 45/84 – Carte € 72/85
◆ Pleasant inn near the St Loup Peak, after which the local wine is named. Mediterranean setting, shaded terrace, and skilfully inventive cuisine.

ST-MATHURIN – 85 Vendée – **316** F8 – pop. 1 256 – alt. 30 m – ✉ 85150 34 **A3**

Paris 451 – Nantes 95 – La Roche-sur-Yon 29 – Challans 66 – Les Sables-d'Olonne 10

Le Château de la Millière without rest
La Millière – ✆ 02 51 22 73 29 – www.chateau-la-milliere.com – chateaudelamilliere@club-internet.fr – Open 1st May-30 September
3 rm ☕ – 🚹€ 92 🚹🚹€ 100
◆ This romantic 19C château has extensive grounds with a swimming pool, ponds, bridle paths and barbecue. The building has retained its original character, while still providing modern levels of comfort.

ST-MAUR-DES-FOSSÉS – 94 Val-de-Marne – **312** D3 – **101** 27 – see Paris, Area

ST-MAURICE-DE-SATONNAY – 71 Saône-et-Loire – **320** I11 – pop. 394 – alt. 250 m – ✉ 71260 8 **C3**

Paris 400 – Dijon 129 – Mâcon 17 – Chalon-sur-Saône 61 – Bourg-en-Bresse 49

Auberge des Grenouillats
Le Bourg – 03 85 33 40 50 – les.grenouillats@orange.fr – Closed 1st-9 March, 25 October-5 November, 20 December-4 January, 6-22 February, Tuesday dinner and Wednesday
Rest – *(number of covers limited, pre-book)* Carte € 32/38
◆ This small bistro in the old village café offers, among other things, regional specialities (frogs' legs, Charolais beef) at reasonable prices. Terrace under plane trees.

ST-MAXIMIN-LA-STE-BAUME – 83 Var – 340 K5 – pop. 13 900 – alt. 289 m – 83470 Provence

40 **B3**

Paris 793 – Aix-en-Provence 44 – Marseille 51 – Toulon 55
Office de tourisme, Hôtel de Ville 04 94 59 84 59, Fax 04 94 59 82 92

Couvent Royal
pl. Jean Salusse – 04 94 86 55 66 – www.hotelfp-saintmaximin.com – contact@hotelfp-saintmaximin.com – Fax 04 94 59 82 82
67 rm – € 99/109 € 122/159, € 12
Rest – Menu € 39/55 – Carte € 45/55
◆ An unusual hotel adjoining a 13C basilica. The monks' cells have been converted into snug rooms. Traditional dishes served in the lovely chapter house or in fine weather, on the terrace giving onto the cloister.

ST-MÉDARD – 46 Lot – 337 D4 – pop. 164 – alt. 170 m – 46150

28 **B1**

Paris 571 – Cahors 17 – Gourdon 34 – Villeneuve-sur-Lot 59

Gindreau (Alexis Pélissou)
– 05 65 36 22 27 – http://perso.wanadoo.fr/le.gindreau – le.gindreau@wanadoo.fr – Fax 05 65 36 24 54 – Closed 16 March-8 April, 19 October-12 November, Wednesday lunch from December to March, Monday and Tuesday
Rest – *(pre-book Sat - Sun)* Menu € 38 (weekdays)/115 – Carte € 69/103
Spec. Truffes fraîches (Dec. to March). Agneau fermier du Quercy. Soufflé "alliance de la truffe et du Marasquin". **Wines** Vins de Pays du Lot blanc et rouge.
◆ Old village school elegantly turned into two pastel coloured dining rooms. Chestnut trees shade the terrace. Tasty contemporary menu with a strong regional influence.

ST-MÉDARD-EN-JALLES – 33 Gironde – 335 G5 – pop. 27 000 – alt. 22 m – 33160

3 **B1**

Paris 591 – Blaye 62 – Bordeaux 18 – Jonzac 97 – Libourne 48 – Saintes 129

Tournebride
55 r. Alexis Puyo, at Hastignan – 05 56 05 09 08 – le.tournebride@hotmail.fr – Fax 05 56 05 09 08 – Closed Wednesday dinner, Sunday dinner and Monday
Rest – Menu € 14 (weekday lunch), € 19/36 – Carte € 27/35
◆ Refurbished dining room, prettily decorated with a fresco of the Arcachon Bay. The other dining room has a wine and vine theme. Regional specialities.

ST-MICHEL-EN-L'HERM – 85 Vendée – 316 I9 – pop. 1 948 – alt. 9 m – 85580

34 **B3**

Paris 453 – La Rochelle 46 – Luçon 15 – La Roche sur Yon 47 – Les Sables-d'Olonne 54
Syndicat d'initiative, 5, place de l'Abbaye 02 51 30 21 89, Fax 02 51 30 21 89

La Rose Trémière
4 r. de l'Église – 02 51 30 25 69 – rose.tremiere@wanadoo.fr – Fax 02 51 30 25 69 – Closed 5-20 October, 15 February-4 March, Tuesday except July-August, Sunday dinner and Monday
Rest – Menu € 18 (weekdays), € 24/47 – Carte € 31/47
◆ Period house with a pleasant dining room decorated in a tastefully rustic style, with tables laid out around the central fireplace. Traditional cuisine.

ST-MICHEL-ESCALUS – 40 Landes – 335 D11 – pop. 231 – alt. 23 m – ✉ 40550 3 **B2**

Paris 721 – Bayonne 67 – Bordeaux 135 – Dax 30

La Bergerie-St-Michel without rest

St-Michel, on the D 142, Castets road – ✆ 05 58 48 74 04 – www.bergeriestmichel.fr – bergerie-saintmichel@wanadoo.fr – Fax 05 58 48 74 04

4 rm – †€ 75/85 ††€ 95/130

◆ The Landes Forest surrounds this magnificently restored former farmhouse. Very comfortable rooms, decorated with contemporary paintings. Copious breakfasts.

Hotels and restaurants change every year, so change your Michelin guide every year!

ST-MICHEL-MONT-MERCURE – 85 Vendée – 316 K7 – pop. 1 875 – alt. 284 m – ✉ 85700 Atlantic Coast 34 **B3**

Paris 383 – Bressuire 36 – Cholet 35 – Nantes 85 – Pouzauges 7 – La Roche-sur-Yon 52

✳★★ from the church steeple.

Château de la Flocellière

La Flocellière, 2 km east – ✆ 02 51 57 22 03 – www.flocellierecastle.com – flocelliere.chateau@wanadoo.fr – Fax 02 51 57 75 21

5 rm – †€ 155/205 ††€ 175/305, € 12 **Table d'hôte** – Menu € 54 bi/61 bi

◆ This building full of history was a major Lower Poitou fortress during the Middle Ages. It now houses spacious and peaceful rooms, overlooking the park. Those inside the keep are magnificent. Medieval or Renaissance-themed evening meals in a breathtaking 16C dining room.

Auberge du Mont Mercure

8 r. l'Orbrie, (near the church) – ✆ 02 51 57 20 26 – www.aubergemontmercure.com – contact@aubergemontmercure.com – Fax 02 51 57 78 67 – Closed autumn and February school holidays, Monday dinner from September to June, Tuesday dinner and Wednesday

Rest – Menu € 15 (weekdays)/35 – Carte € 21/36

◆ Perched on top of the hill, this family-run inn benefits from a large panoramic view over the Vendée. Children's play area.

ST-MIHIEL – 55 Meuse – 307 E5 – pop. 4 816 – alt. 228 m – ✉ 55300 Alsace-Lorraine 26 **B2**

Paris 287 – Metz 63 – Nancy 66 – Bar-le-Duc 35 – Toul 52 – Verdun 36

Office de tourisme, rue du Palais de Justice ✆ 03 29 89 06 47, Fax 03 29 89 06 47

de Madine Nonsard Base de Loisirs, NE : 25 km on D 901 and D 179, ✆ 03 29 89 56 00

Sepulchre★★ in St-Étienne church - Swoon of the Virgin★ in St-Michel church.

in Heudicourt-sous-les-Côtes 15 km northeast by D 901 and D 133 – pop. 187 – alt. 240 m – ✉ 55210

Butte de Montsec: ✳★★, monument★ South: 13 km.

Lac de Madine rm,

22 r. Charles de Gaulle – ✆ 03 29 89 34 80 – www.hotel-lac-madine.com – hotel-lac-madine@wanadoo.fr – Fax 03 29 89 39 20 – Closed 20-28 December, 2 January-13 February

41 rm – †€ 55/95 ††€ 55/95, € 10 – ½ P € 58/78

Rest – *(closed Monday lunch)* Menu € 23/35 – Carte € 40/60

◆ Old renovated house near a lake offering spruce modern rooms, ten of which boast a spa bathtub. Those in the wing overlook the garden. Traditional menu served in a light dining room beneath fine timberwork. Shaded terrace.

ST-NAZAIRE – 44 Loire-Atlantique – **316** C4 – pop. 68 200 – Built-up area 136 886 – alt. 4 m – ✉ 44600 Brittany

Paris 435 – La Baule 19 – Nantes 61 – Vannes 79

Access Pont de Saint-Nazaire: no toll.

Office de tourisme, boulevard de la Légion d'Honneur ☎ 02 40 22 40 65, Fax 02 40 22 19 80

de Savenay Savenay Le Chambeau, 27 km on the Nantes road, ☎ 02 40 56 88 05

de Guérande Guérande Ville Blanche, 22 km on the Guérande road, ☎ 02 40 60 24 97

Submarine base ★ - Dry dock "Louis-Joubert" ★ - Terrace with a panoramic view ★ **B** - St-Nazaire-St-Brévin road bridge ★ by ①.

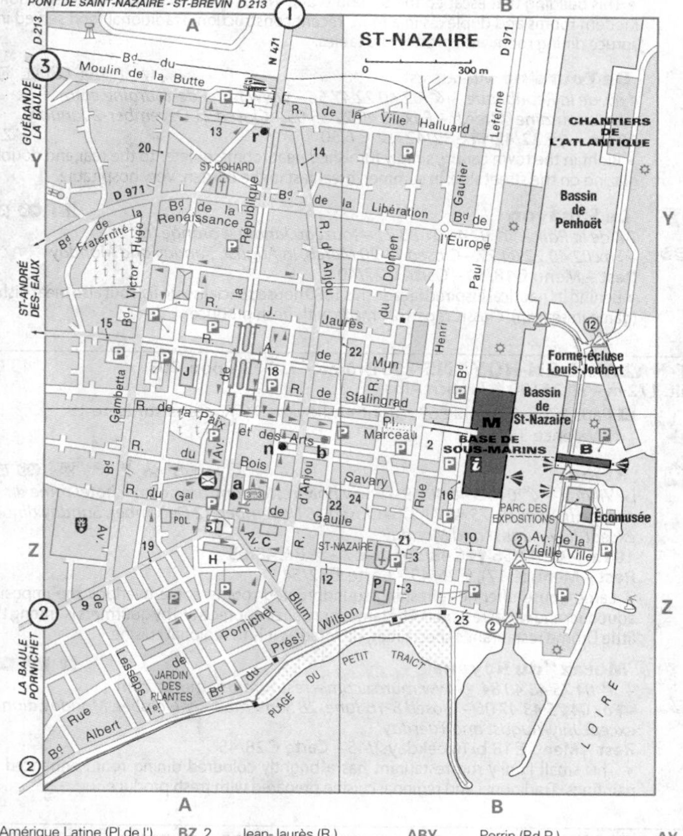

Amérique Latine (Pl.de l') . . . **BZ** 2
Auriol (R. Vincent) . . . . **BZ** 3
Blancho (Pl. F.) . . . . **AZ** 5
Chêneveaux (R.) . . . . **AZ** 9
Coty (Bd René) . . . . **BZ** 10
Croisic (R. du) . . . . **AZ** 12
Herminier (Av. Cdt-l') . . . . **AY** 13
Ile-de-France (R. de l') . . . . . . **AY** 14
Jean-Jaurès (R.) . . . . **ABY**
Lechat (R. A. B.) . . . . **AY** 15
Légion-d'Honneur (Bd de la) . . . . **BZ** 16
Martyrs-de-la-Résistance (Pl. des) . . . . **AY** 18
Mendès-France (R.) . . . . **AZ** 19
Paix et des Arts (R. de la) . . **AYZ**
Perrin (Bd P.) . . . . **AY** 20
Quatre Z'Horloges (Pl. des) . . . . **BZ** 21
République (Av. de la) . . . . **AYZ**
Salengro (R. R.) . . . . **AYZ** 22
Verdun (Bd de) . . . . **BZ** 23
28-Février-1943 (R. du) . . . . **BZ** 24

Le Berry
1 pl. Pierre Semard – 02 40 22 42 61 – www.hotel-du-berry.fr – berry.hotel@wanadoo.fr – Fax 02 40 22 45 34 – Closed 23 December-4 January AY **r**
27 rm – €75/133 €75/145, €12
Rest – *(Closed 27 July-16 August)* Menu €20 (weekdays)/30 – Carte €29/47
Rest *Brasserie* – *(Closed Sunday lunch and Saturday)* Menu (€14), €15/30 – Carte €24/44
◆ This post-war hotel standing opposite the station, offers cheerful, well-soundproofed rooms. Light, pleasant restaurant serving traditional cuisine; lobster tank. The Brasserie serves daily set dishes, chalked up on a slate, and jugs of Loire wines.

Au Bon Accueil
39 r. Marceau – 02 40 22 07 05 – www.au-bon-accueil44.com – au-bon-accueil44@wanadoo.fr – Fax 02 40 19 01 58 – Closed 20 July-9 August and February holiday AZ **n**
17 rm – €84/160 €84/190, €9 – ½ P €74/109
Rest – *(closed Sunday evening)* Menu (€18), €25/57 – Carte €38/69
◆ This building that escaped the Second World War is home to simple, well-kept rooms. Modern rooms and duplexes in a more recent construction. Traditional food served in a spruce dining room with prettily laid tables.

De Touraine without rest
4 av. de la République – 02 40 22 47 56 – www.hotel-de-touraine.com – hoteltouraine@free.fr – Fax 02 40 22 55 05 – Closed 21 December-2 January
18 rm – €32/42 €32/42, €6,50 AZ **a**
◆ Right in the town centre, simply furnished neat rooms; quieter to the rear and double-glazing on the street side. In summer, breakfast in the garden. Very hospitable.

Le Sabayon
7 r. de la Paix – 02 40 01 88 21 – touzeau.landry@orange.fr – Fax 02 40 22 04 77 – Closed 1st-20 March, in August, Sunday and Monday AZ **b**
Rest – Menu €18/50 – Carte €27/40
◆ Behind its nautical inspired façade this 1880 house specialises in fish but also meat dishes (game in season). Classic repertory made with fresh produce.

ST-NAZAIRE-EN-ROYANS – 26 Drôme – 332 E3 – pop. 703 – alt. 172 m – 26190 French Alps 43 E2

Paris 576 – Grenoble 69 – Pont-en-Royans 9 – Romans-sur-Isère 19 – Valence 35

Rome
rest,
Le Village – 04 75 48 40 69 – www.hotelrestaurantrome.com – hotel.rome@orange.fr – Fax 04 75 48 31 17 – Closed 16 November-12 December, Sunday dinner except July-August and Monday
10 rm – €47/56 €48/56, €7 – ½ P €48/65
Rest – Menu (€17), €26/45 – Carte €32/54
◆ Large house offering refreshing soundproofed rooms; some overlook the imposing aqueduct and water reservoir. The famous ravioli so appreciated by gourmets is among this little Drôme restaurant's specialities, devoted as it is to regional cuisine.

Muraz "du Royans"
– 04 75 48 40 84 – www.muraz.com – restaurant@muraz.com – Fax 04 75 48 47 06 – Closed 8-16 June, 28 September-27 October, Monday dinner except July-August and Tuesday
Rest – Menu €18 bi (weekdays)/45 – Carte €28/45
◆ This small family-run restaurant has a brightly coloured dining room enhanced by paintings. Traditional and regional cuisine prepared with fresh produce.

ST-NECTAIRE – 63 Puy-de-Dôme – 326 E9 – pop. 675 – alt. 700 m – Spa – Casino – 63710 Auvergne 5 B2

Paris 453 – Clermont-Ferrand 43 – Issoire 27 – Le Mont-Dore 24
Office de tourisme, les Grands Thermes 04 73 88 50 86, Fax 04 73 88 40 48
Church★★: treasure-house★★ - Puy de Mazeyres ✲★ East: 3 km then 30 mn.

Mercure
Les Bains Romains – 04 73 88 57 00 – www.hotel-bains-romains.com – h1814-gm@accor.com – Fax 04 73 88 57 02
71 rm – €80/100 €90/110, €14 **Rest** – Menu (€23) – Carte €30/40
◆ Old thermal baths and wooded grounds provide a nostalgic backdrop to this enchanting hotel. The comfortable rooms have been or are being refurbished. The pastel coloured dining room sports a refined low-key atmosphere. Meals served around the pool in summer.

ST-NEXANS – 24 Dordogne – 329 E7 – see Bergerac

ST-NIZIER-LE-BOUCHOUX – 01 Ain – 328 D2 – pop. 713 – alt. 216 m – ✉ 01560

44 **B1**

Paris 394 – Lyon 126 – Bourg-en-Bresse 43 – Chalon-sur-Saône 55 – Mâcon 40

La Closerie
Jassans, (1.5 km south by D 97 and secondary road) – 04 74 52 96 67 – www.lacloserie.net – francois.bongard@wanadoo.fr – Fax 04 74 52 96 67
5 rm – €50 €55 **Table d'hôte** – Menu €21 bi
◆ Located in the heart of the Bresse woodland, this charming farmhouse dating from 1830 has kept its half-timbering and delightful rural setting. Fresh and personalised rooms, named after flowers.

ST-OMER – 62 Pas-de-Calais – 301 G3 – pop. 14 900 – alt. 23 m – ✉ 62500 Northern France and the Paris Region

30 **B2**

Paris 257 – Arras 77 – Boulogne-sur-Mer 52 – Calais 43 – Ieper 57 – Lille 65

Office de tourisme, 4, rue du Lion d'Or 03 21 98 08 51, Fax 03 21 98 08 07

Saint-Omer Golf Club Acquin Chemin des Bois, 15 km on the Boulogne-sur-Mer road, 03 21 38 59 90

Cathedral district★★ : cathédrale Notre-Dame (Notre-Dame Cathedral)★★ - Hôtel Sandelin and museum★ AZ - Anc. Chapelle des Jésuites (Former Jesuit chapel)★ AZ **B** - Jardin public (Public garden)★ AZ.

Boat lift of Les Fontinettes★ Southeast: 5,5 km - Coupole d'Helfaut-Wizernes★★, South: 5 km.

Plan on following page

St-Louis
rest,
25 r. d'Arras – 03 21 38 35 21 – www.hotel-saintlouis.com – contact@hotel-saintlouis.com – Fax 03 21 38 57 26 – Closed 18 December-5 January
30 rm – €63 €75, €9 – ½ P €63 BZ **s**
Rest – *(closed for lunch from 13 July to 23 August, Saturday lunch and Sunday lunch)* Menu €17 (weekdays)/31 – Carte €22/36
◆ This pleasant arcaded hotel, formerly a post house, is close to the cathedral district. Warm, practical rooms; those in the annexe have been recently renovated. Dining room furnished in modern brasserie style. Traditional menu.

Le Bretagne
2 pl. du Vainquai – 03 21 38 25 78 – www.hotellebretagne.com – accueil@hotellebretagne.com – Fax 03 21 93 51 22 – Closed 1st-18 January BY **r**
70 rm – €70 €70/120, €9
Rest – *(Closed Saturday lunch, Sunday dinner and bank holiday dinner)* Menu €15/25 – Carte €22/54
◆ This imposing modern building, pleasantly situated in the town centre, houses extremely well-kept rooms. Red velvet benches, mirrors and wall lights bring a Parisian brasserie style to this restaurant; traditional food.

Le Cygne
8 r. Caventou – 03 21 98 20 52 – www.restaurantlecygne.fr – Fax 03 21 95 57 12 – Closed 10 August-1st September, Sunday dinner and Monday except bank holidays
Rest – Menu (€15), €18 (weekdays)/50 – Carte €36/73 AZ **e**
◆ The bright, stylish dining room, preceded by a reception area with a fireplace, leads onto a terrace. Well-prepared traditional dishes.

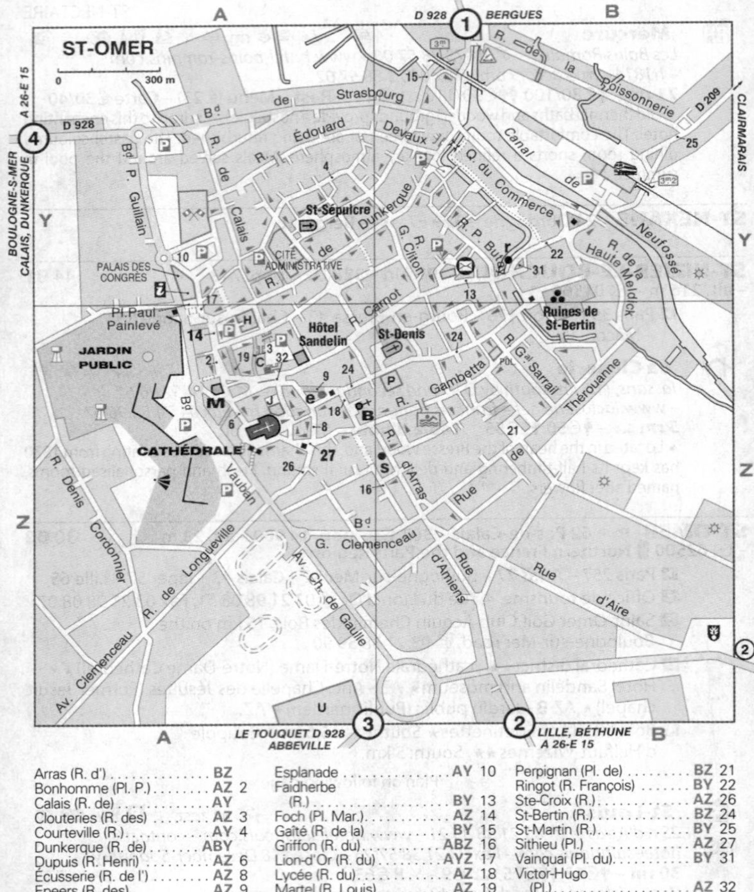

Arras (R. d') . . . . BZ
Bonhomme (Pl. P.) . . . . AZ 2
Calais (R. de) . . . . AY
Clouteries (R. des) . . . . AZ 3
Courteville (R.) . . . . AY 4
Dunkerque (R. de) . . . . ABY
Dupuis (R. Henri) . . . . AZ 6
Écusserie (R. de l') . . . . AZ 8
Epeers (R. des) . . . . AZ 9
Esplanade . . . . AY 10
Faidherbe (R.) . . . . BY 13
Foch (Pl. Mar.) . . . . AZ 14
Gaîté (R. de la) . . . . BY 15
Griffon (R. du) . . . . ABZ 16
Lion-d'Or (R. du) . . . . AYZ 17
Lycée (R. du) . . . . AZ 18
Martel (R. Louis) . . . . AZ 19
Perpignan (Pl. de) . . . . BZ 21
Ringot (R. François) . . . . BY 22
Ste-Croix (R.) . . . . AZ 26
St-Bertin (R.) . . . . BZ 24
St-Martin (R.) . . . . BY 25
Sithieu (Pl.) . . . . AZ 27
Vainquai (Pl. du) . . . . BY 31
Victor-Hugo (Pl.) . . . . AZ 32

in Blendecques 4 km by ② and D 211 – pop. 5 018 – alt. 25 m – ✉ 62575

Le St-Sébastien

2 pl. de la Libération – ✆ 03 21 38 13 05 – saint-sebastien@wanadoo.fr – Fax 03 21 39 77 85 – Closed 22-30 December, Sunday dinner, Monday and public holiday dinner

Rest – Menu (€ 15), € 17/37 – Carte € 36/49

◆ A good address to be found in a small suburb of the Audomarois agglomeration: friendly welcome, rustic well-kept decor and good, traditional recipes.

in Tilques 6 km by ④, D 943 and secondary road – pop. 993 – alt. 27 m – ✉ 62500

Château Tilques

– ✆ 03 21 88 99 99 – www.chateautilques.com – chateau-tilques.hotel@najeti.com – Fax 03 21 38 34 23 – **53 rm** – €145/460 €145/460, € 19

Rest – *(closed for lunch except Saturday and Sunday)* Menu (€ 20), € 39/72 – Carte € 67/77

◆ Brick-built château (1891) in grounds with pond, swans and peacocks. Period furniture in the rooms, more modern in the annexe. The old stables house the restaurant. Smart setting and classic cuisine.

ST-OUEN – 93 Seine-Saint-Denis – **305** F7 – **101** 16 – **see Paris, Area**

ST-OUEN – 41 Loir-et-Cher – **318** D5 – **see Vendôme**

ST-OUEN-LES-VIGNES – 37 Indre-et-Loire – **317** O4 – **see Amboise**

ST-PAIR-SUR-MER – 50 Manche – **303** C7 – **see Granville**

ST-PALAIS – 64 Pyrénées-Atlantiques – **342** F5 – **pop. 1 874 – alt. 50 m** 3 **B3**
– ✉ **64120** Atlantic Coast

Paris 788 – Bayonne 52 – Biarritz 63 – Dax 60 – Pau 74 – St-Jean-Pied-de-Port 32

Office de tourisme, place Charles-de-Gaulle ✆ 05 59 65 71 78, Fax 05 59 65 69 15

La Maison d'Arthezenea

42 r. du Palais de Justice – ✆ 05 59 65 85 96 – www.gites64.com/maison-darthezenea – francois.barthaburu@wanadoo.fr – Fax 05 59 65 85 96 – Open April-December

4 rm – €63 €73 **Table d'hôte** – Menu € 25 bi

◆ Fine stone-built residence in a pretty garden, where you will be made to feel at home. The rooms, adorned with antique furniture, have different colour schemes and names. The table d'hôte serves tasty specialities (home-made foie gras, lamb sweetbread and flambéd woodpigeon in season).

XX **Trinquet** with rm rest, VISA

31 r. du Jeu de Paume – ✆ 05 59 65 73 13 – www.le-trinquet-saint-palais.com – hoteltrinquet.saintpalais@wanadoo.fr – Fax 05 59 65 83 84 – Closed 13 April-4 May and 18 September-6 October

9 rm – €57 €57/67, €7

Rest – *(closed Sunday dinner and Monday)* Menu (€ 12) – Carte € 26/45

◆ This recently rejuvenated house located on the main square boasts an authentic 'trinquet' (hall for playing Pelote Basque) dating from 1891. Regional menu served in a modern interior. Rooms refurnished in a modern style.

ST-PALAIS-SUR-MER – 17 Charente-Maritime – **324** D6 – **pop. 3 343** 38 **A3**
– **alt. 5 m** – ✉ **17420** Atlantic Coast

Paris 512 – La Rochelle 82 – Royan 6

Office de tourisme, 1, avenue de la République ✆ 05 46 23 22 58, Fax 05 46 23 36 73

La Grande Côte★★ Northwest: 3 km - Zoo de la Palmyre★★ Northwest: 10 km.

Primavera

rm, VISA AE

12 r. Brick, via av. Gde Côte – ✆ 05 46 23 20 35 – www.hotel-primavera.com – contact@hotel-primavera.com – Fax 05 46 23 28 78 – Closed 15 November-15 December

40 rm – €75/135 €75/135, € 14 – 2 suites

Rest – *(closed Tuesday lunch, Wednesday lunch and Monday)* Menu € 25/48 – Carte € 38/90

◆ An elegant 1900 "folly" of medieval inspiration and two superbly situated annexes in a peaceful park overlooking the sea. Comfortable rooms. Refined partly panoramic restaurant. Traditional sea-inspired cuisine.

Ma Maison de Mer

VISA

21 av. du Platin – ✆ 05 46 23 64 86 – www.mamaisondemer.com – reservations@mamaisondemer.com – Fax 05 46 23 64 86

5 rm – €65/90 €75/155

Table d'hôte – *(open July-August)* Menu € 30 bi/50 bi

◆ Surrounded by a garden and pine forest and only 300 m from the beach. An English family now runs this comfortable establishment, whose lovely sea-theme decor is enchanting. Breakfast is prepared with fresh market produce.

Les Agapes

8 r. M. Vallet – ☎ 05 46 23 10 23 – www.les-agapes.fr – patrick.morin25@wanadoo.fr – Fax 05 46 23 09 23 – Closed autumn school holidays, January and Monday

Rest – Menu (€ 18), € 25/48 – Carte approx. € 53

◆ Modern interior and pleasant terrace at this restaurant near the market. In the kitchens, the chef concocts refined traditional recipes, some creatively reinterpreted.

Le Flandre

av. Tamaris, rte de la Palmyre – ☎ 05 46 23 36 16 – www.leflandre.com – yves.minot@wanadoo.fr – Fax 05 46 23 48 95 – Closed 16 November-31 January, Tuesday and Wednesday from October to March

Rest – Menu (€ 17), € 22/39 – Carte € 30/60

◆ This restaurant, nestling in the Palmyre forest, asserts its nautical roots with an upturned ship's hull ceiling, lobster aquarium and seafood on the menu.

ST-PAL-DE-MONS – 43 Haute-Loire – 331 H2 – pop. 1 748 – alt. 840 m – ✉ 43620

6 **D3**

▶ Paris 516 – Clermont-Ferrand 177 – Le Puy-en-Velay 57 – Saint-Étienne 35 – Saint-Chamond 43

Les Feuillantines

La Vialatte – ☎ 04 71 75 63 25 – www.lesfeuillantines.com – contact@lesfeuillantines.com – Fax 04 71 75 63 24 – Closed 27 April-3 May, 3-23 August, 1-4 January and Sunday

12 rm – †€ 59 ††€ 62, ☕ € 8 – ½ P € 58/61

Rest – *(closed Sunday dinner and Friday)* Menu (€ 20) – Carte € 31/54

◆ Opened in 2006, most of this hotel's rooms overlook the valley and peaks. Spacious and practical comfort (some with balcony). Fine bucolic views from the restaurant's large bay windows.

ST-PATERNE – 72 Sarthe – 310 J4 – see Alençon

ST-PATRICE – 37 Indre-et-Loire – 317 K5 – see Langeais

ST-PAUL – 06 Alpes-Maritimes – 341 D5 – pop. 3 336 – alt. 125 m – ✉ 06570 French Riviera

42 **E2**

▶ Paris 922 – Antibes 18 – Cagnes-sur-Mer 7 – Cannes 28 – Grasse 22 – Nice 21 – Vence 4

ℹ Office de tourisme, 2, rue Grande ☎ 04 93 32 86 95, Fax 04 93 32 60 27

◉ Site ★ - Ramparts ★ - Maeght Foundation ★★.

Le Saint-Paul

86 r. Grande, (in the village) – ☎ 04 93 32 65 25 – www.lesaintpaul.com – stpaul@relaischateaux.com – Fax 04 93 32 52 94 – Closed January

16 rm – †€ 250/820 ††€ 250/820, ☕ € 28 – 3 suites

Rest – *(closed Wednesday lunch and Tuesday from November to March)* Menu (€ 48), € 70/100 – Carte € 110/130

Spec. Paupiette d'aubergine et cabillaud farcie à la chair d'araignée de mer. Lasagne de homard et pousses de salade poêlées. Surprise chocolatée. **Wines** Côtes de Provence, Bellet.

◆ High in a medieval village; beautiful stonework, frescoes, a fountain and colourful furniture make for a refined ambiance in this 16C abode. Flavoursome cuisine that follows the seasons; elegant vaulted dining room and verdant terrace.

La Colombe d'Or

rm,

pl. Ch. de Gaulle – ☎ 04 93 32 80 02 – www.la-colombe-dor.com – contact@la-colombe-dor.com – Fax 04 93 32 77 78 – Closed 26 October-18 December and 5-15 January

15 rm – †€ 230/290 ††€ 230/290, ☕ € 15 – 11 suites **Rest** – Carte € 36/80

◆ This hotel-museum, appreciated by both artists and celebrities, has a superb collection of modern paintings and sculptures. "Old Provence" setting and rooms with personal touches. Deliciously shady outdoor terrace and a comfortable dining room decorated with faultless taste.

Le Mas de Pierre
2320 rte des Serres, 2 km southward –
04 93 59 00 10 – www.lemasdepierre.com – info@lemasdepierre.com
– Fax 04 93 59 00 59
46 rm – € 230/770 € 230/770, € 29 – 2 suites
Rest – *(closed Monday and Tuesday from October to March)* Menu (€ 50), € 75 – Carte € 70/98
◆ The elegant rooms are located in five bastides set around a splendid pool in the heart of a lush green garden. Luxury, comfort and well being (spa). Two smart dining rooms or outdoor dining. Traditional fare in the evening and spit roast meat at lunchtime.

La Toile Blanche with rm
rm, VISA
826 chemin Pounchounière – 04 93 32 74 21 – www.toileblanche.com – info@toileblanche.com – Fax 04 93 32 87 43
6 rm – € 150/255 € 150/255, € 15
Rest – *(open 15 June-15 September) (dinner only) (number of covers limited, pre-book)* Menu € 55
◆ Appetising fixed menu (evenings only) with an emphasis on inventive, contemporary cuisine. Outdoor dining in the summer months. Pleasant guestrooms with modern furnishings and a backdrop of grey and Provençal tones. Garden with swimming pool.

via La Colle-sur-Loup road – ✉ 06570 St-Paul

Mas d'Artigny
rm,
chemin des Salettes, 3 km Hauts de St-Paul road –
04 93 32 84 54 – www.mas-artigny.com – mas@grandesetapes.fr
– Fax 04 93 32 95 36
55 rm – € 165/560 € 165/560, € 27 – 30 suites
Rest – Menu € 49 (dinner), € 75/95 – Carte € 35/75
◆ Audacious hotel complex in a park enjoying a view extending as far as the Baie des Anges. Apartments with private pools, an immense lavish spa and sculpture park. Panoramic dining room and terrace; culinary repertoire dominated by seafood.

La Grande Bastide without rest
VISA
1350 rte de la Colle – 04 93 32 50 30 – www.la-grande-bastide.com – stpaullgb@wanadoo.fr – Fax 04 93 32 50 59 – Closed 26 November-20 December and 15 January-15 February
14 rm – € 145/315 € 145/315, € 19 – 2 suites
◆ This well-restored 18C mas extends a friendly welcome to guests. Pretty Provençal-style rooms with a balcony, view of the pool or greenery; generous breakfasts.

Les Vergers de St Paul without rest
VISA
940 Route de la Colle – 04 93 32 94 24
– www.vergersdesaintpaul.com – h.vergers@wanadoo.fr – Fax 04 93 32 91 07
17 rm – € 110/175 € 125/245, € 14
◆ A hotel nestling in a garden offering a view over St Paul. The tasteful rooms, with a terrace or a balcony, overlook the pool and sport white walls, striped fabrics and parquet floors.

Le Hameau without rest
VISA
528 rte de la Colle at 500 m. – 04 93 32 80 24 – www.le-hameau.com – lehameau@wanadoo.fr – Fax 04 93 32 55 75 – Open 13 February-15 November
15 rm – € 105/220 € 120/220, € 16 – 2 suites
◆ Rustic-styled setting, terraced gardens and small tastefully furnished rooms make up this former Provençal farm's charm. Surrounded by pretty little white cottages. Hamman, Jacuzzi.

Hostellerie des Messugues without rest
VISA
allée des Lavandes, 500m, Gardettes district by Route de la Fondation Maeght – 04 93 32 53 32
– www.messugues.com – info@messugues.com – Fax 04 93 32 94 15
– Open 1 April-31 October
15 rm – € 85/140 € 85/140, € 11
◆ A well-restored Mediterranean villa and original swimming pool in a quiet pine grove. A striking effect in the corridors: the doors of the rooms come from a 19C prison!

South 4 km by D 2 and secondary road - ✉ 06570 St-Paul

Les Bastides de St-Paul without rest
880 Chemin Blaquières (D 336 – Cagnes-Vence trunk road) – ☎ 04 92 02 08 07 – www.hotelbastides.fr – contact@hotelbastides.fr – Fax 04 93 20 50 41
20 rm – †€ 75/95 ††€ 85/145, ☕ € 15
◆ Set back a little from a busy road, a colourful establishment with spacious, functional rooms with good soundproofing. A trefoil-shaped pool.

ST-PAUL-DES-LANDES – 15 Cantal – **330** B5 – **pop. 1 100** – **alt. 554 m** – ✉ 15250 5 **A3**

Paris 544 – Aurillac 13 – Figeac 59 – St-Céré 49

Voyageurs
– ☎ 04 71 46 38 43 – www.lesvoyageurs15ifrance.com – nelly.beguin@wanadoo.fr – Fax 04 71 46 38 08 – Closed 23-31 August, 22 December-5 January, Saturday from September to May and Monday dinner
Rest – Menu (€ 12 bi), € 28 (weekdays) – Carte € 20/30
◆ This hotel looks onto the town's main street; the atmosphere is warm and friendly. The cooking is 100% home-made to match the rustic decor of the dining hall. Summer terrace.

ST-PAUL-DOUEIL – 31 Haute-Garonne – **343** B8 – **see Bagnères-de-Luchon**

ST-PAUL-LÈS-DAX – 40 Landes – **335** E12 – **see Dax**

ST-PAUL-LÈS-ROMANS – 26 Drôme – **332** D3 – **see Romans-sur-Isère**

ST-PAUL-TROIS-CHATEAUX – 26 Drôme – **332** B7 – **pop. 7 892** – **alt. 90 m** – ✉ 26130 Lyon - Rhone Valley 44 **B3**

Paris 628 – Montélimar 28 – Nyons 39 – Orange 33 – Vaison-la-Romaine 34 – Valence 73
Office de tourisme, place Chausy ☎ 04 75 96 59 60, Fax 04 75 96 90 20
St-Paul cathedral ★ - Barry ≤★★ South: 8 km.

Villa Augusta
14 r. Serre Blanc – ☎ 04 75 97 29 29 – www.villaaugusta.fr – contact@villaaugusta.fr – Fax 04 75 97 29 27 – Closed 4-24 January
23 rm – †€ 120/230 ††€ 120/230, ☕ € 18 – 1 suite
Rest *David Mollicone* – *(closed Sunday dinner and Monday except July-August)* Menu € 28 (weekday lunch), € 45/75 – Carte € 62/72
◆ Lovely, 19C residence in a superb, leafy garden. The decoration artfully combines bright colours and old and new styles; non-smoking rooms. Elegant, modern dining room, charming terrace and creative cuisine.

L'Esplan
pl. l'Esplan – ☎ 04 75 96 64 64 – www.esplan-provence.com – saintpaul@esplan-provence.com – Fax 04 75 04 92 36 – Closed 19 December-11 January
36 rm – †€ 69/100 ††€ 69/119, ☕ € 11
Rest – *(Closed Sunday from October to April) (dinner only)* Menu € 26/70 – Carte € 56/98
◆ This 16C mansion in the heart of the town has a beautiful contemporary interior and well cared for rooms decorated in warm colours. Restaurant brightened up by pastel hues. Original recipes focusing on herbs, flowers and home-grown plants.

Vieille France-Jardin des Saveurs
1.2 km La Garde Adhémar road – ☎ 04 75 96 70 47 – www.restaurant-vieillefrance-jardindessaveurs.com – vieillefrance.jardindessaveurs@wanadoo.fr – Fax 04 75 96 70 47 – Closed for one week in April, one week in October, lunch except Sunday in July-August, Monday and Tuesday
Rest – *(number of covers limited, pre-book)* Menu € 25 (weekday lunch), € 39/115 – Carte € 49/57
◆ Provençal farmhouse in the countryside. Warm contemporary decor, pleasant shady terrace, tasty Mediterranean cuisine and fine Côtes-du-Rhône wine list. Seasonal menu with truffles.

L et Lui

2 r. Charles-Chaussy – ✆ 04 75 46 61 14 – www.letlui.com – letlui@orange.fr – Closed 1-8 March, 15-23 November, 3-7 January, Friday lunch and Saturday lunch in summer, Wednesday dinner and Thursday dinner in winter, Sunday and Monday

Rest – Menu (€ 22), € 27 (weekday lunch), € 37/52

◆ In this establishment, Cathy tends the garden and Cedric does the cooking... Inventive, unusual dishes, based on produce from the kitchen garden. Each month, the wine cellar pays homage to a different winegrower. Vivid interior.

ST-PÉE-SUR-NIVELLE – 64 Pyrénées-Atlantiques – 342 C4 – pop. 5 106 – alt. 30 m – ✉ 64310 3 A3

Paris 785 – Bayonne 22 – Biarritz 17 – Cambo-les-Bains 17 – Pau 129 – St-Jean-de-Luz 14

Office de tourisme, place du Fronton ✆ 05 59 54 11 69, Fax 05 59 85 86 38

L' Auberge Basque (Cédric Béchade) with rm

Quartier Helbarron, D307 (old St-Pée road to St-Jean-de-Luz) – ✆ 05 59 51 70 00 – www.aubergebasque.com – contact@aubergebasque.com – Fax 05 59 51 70 17 – Closed 29 June-6 July, 23 November-1 December, 26 January-25 February

11 rm – €110/240 €110/240, € 28

Rest – *(closed Tuesday lunch and Monday)* Menu € 43/85 – Carte € 59/89

Spec. Oeuf poché en fine gelée d'une piperade. Agneau de Castille moelleux et caramélisé à la sauge. Reine claude, pannacotta au citron et melon d'Espagne, sucette à l'anis.

◆ Forget the typical farmhouse of yesteryear. This modern inn has a bright, minimalist dining room and terrace with views of the countryside. Updated regional cuisine. Spacious and cosy guestrooms.

Le Fronton

quartier Ibarron, St-Jean-de-Luz road – ✆ 05 59 54 10 12 – jeanbaptiste.daguerre@wanadoo.fr – Fax 05 59 54 18 09 – Closed 10 February-20 March, lunch in August, Sunday dinner, Monday, Tuesday, Wednesday and Thursday

Rest – Menu € 37/43 – Carte € 43/50

◆ Traditional cuisine with an emphasis on market produce and fresh fish is served in the comfortable, conservatory-style formal dining room. Terrace.

ST-PÉRAY – 07 Ardèche – 331 L4 – pop. 6 963 – alt. 124 m – ✉ 07130 43 E2

Paris 562 – Lamastre 35 – Privas 39 – Tournon-sur-Rhône 15 – Valence 4

Office de tourisme, 45, rue la République ✆ 04 75 40 46 75, Fax 04 75 40 55 72

Ruins of château de Crussol: site★★★ and ★★ Southeast: 2 km.

Saint-Romain-de-Lerps ★★★ Northwest: 9,5 km by D 287,

Auvergne-Rhone Valley.

in Soyons 7 km south by D 86 – pop. 1 936 – alt. 106 m – ✉ 07130

Domaine de Soyons

D 86, 670 Nîmes road – ✆ 04 75 60 83 55 – www.ledomainedesoyons.com – info@ledomainedesoyons.fr – Fax 04 75 60 85 21 – Closed 26 October-2 November and 2-10 January

28 rm – €96/171 €112/208, € 18

Rest – Menu (€ 21), € 26 (lunch), € 34/63 – Carte € 52/70

◆ A warm friendly atmosphere pervades this beautiful 19C dwelling surrounded by a verdant park (300-year-old cedar tree). Empire-style furniture in the rooms. Tasty, modern recipes served in a pleasant dining room with a veranda.

ST-PÈRE – 89 Yonne – 319 F7 – see Vézelay

ST-PHILBERT-DE-GRAND-LIEU – 44 Loire-Atlantique – 316 G5 34 B2
– pop. 6 253 – alt. 10 m – ✉ 44310 Atlantic Coast

Paris 405 – Nantes 27 – Niort 150 – Rennes 138 – La Roche-sur-Yon 50 – Tours 218

Office de tourisme, place de l'Abbatiale ✆ 02 40 78 73 88, Fax 02 40 78 83 42

La Bosselle rest, rm, VISA AE

8 r. du Port – ✆ 02 40 78 73 47 – www.la-bosselle.fr – info@restaurant-hotel-la-bosselle.fr – Fax 02 40 78 01 85

14 rm – †€ 56 ††€ 56, ☕ € 8 – ½ P € 65

Rest – Menu € 13 (weekday lunch), € 24/37 – Carte € 26/40

◆ Recently built family-run hotel near the abbey church offering simple and well-laid out rooms, quieter at the back. Fully refurbished restaurant with food grilled in the fireplace, local produce and freshwater fish specialities from the lake.

ST-PHILBERT-DES-CHAMPS – 14 Calvados – 303 N4 – see Breuil-en-Auge

ST-PHILIBERT – 56 Morbihan – 308 N9 – pop. 1 442 – alt. 15 m 9 A3
– ✉ 56470

Paris 489 – Rennes 137 – Vannes 29 – Lorient 50 – Lanester 45

Le Galet VISA

rte de la Trinité-sur-Mer, 1.2 km north by D 28 and D 781 – ✆ 02 97 55 00 56 – www.legalet.fr – contact@legalet.fr – Fax 02 97 55 19 77

21 rm – †€ 65/125 ††€ 65/125, ☕ € 12 – 2 suites

Rest – *(dinner only) (resident only)* Menu € 23

◆ A quiet night's sleep is guaranteed in this hotel surrounded by a garden just two minutes from La Trinité sur Mer. Tastefully redecorated hotel; modern bedrooms. Simple dining room for a midday snack and a single set menu in the evenings.

ST-PIERRE-CANIVET – 14 Calvados – 303 K6 – see Falaise

ST-PIERRE-D' ALBIGNY – 73 Savoie – 333 J4 – pop. 3 583 46 F2
– alt. 410 m – ✉ 73250

Paris 596 – Lyon 137 – Chambéry 29 – Annecy 77 – Aix-les-Bains 45

Office de tourisme, place de l'Europe ✆ 04 79 25 19 38, Fax 04 79 71 44 55

Château des Allues

Les Allues – ✆ 06 75 38 61 56 – www.chateaudesallues.com – info@chateaudesallues.com – Closed 30 March-10 April and 1st November-15 December

5 rm ☕ – †€ 95/120 ††€ 110/150

Table d'hôte – *(closed Monday and Tuesday)* Menu € 42 bi

◆ Everything is done for the well-being of the guests in this extremely tastefully renovated old manor. Mountain views, large rooms in either an old-fashioned or contemporary style. Garden vegetables are used in the dishes served at the table d'hôte.

ST-PIERRE-DE-CHARTREUSE – 38 Isère – 333 H5 – pop. 848 46 F2
– alt. 885 m – Winter sports : 900/1 800 m 1 13 – ✉ 38380 French Alps

Paris 571 – Belley 62 – Chambéry 39 – Grenoble 28 – La Tour-du-Pin 52 – Voiron 25

Office de tourisme, place de la Mairie ✆ 04 76 88 62 08, Fax 04 76 88 68 78

Town hall terrace ≤★ - Prairie de Valombré ≤★ West: 4 km - Site★ of Perquelin East: 3 km - La Correrie: musée Cartusien★ of the Grande Chartreuse convent Northwest: 3,5 km - Decoration★ of St-Hugues-de-Chartreuse church South: 4 km.

Beau Site rest,
Le Bourg – 04 76 88 61 34 – www.hotelbeausite.com – hotel.beausite@libertysurf.fr – Fax 04 76 88 64 69 – Closed 2April-2 May and 15 October-26 December
26 rm – €45/75 €55/75, €10 – ½ P €55/72
Rest – *(closed Tuesday lunch, Sunday dinner and Monday)* Menu €17/31 – Carte €21/42
♦ This century-old hotel boasts a collection of paintings by local painter Peter Rahmsdorf. Simple but comfortable rooms. Swimming pool with a view of the valley. Spacious dining room, panoramic terrace and traditional dishes.

ST-PIERRE-DE-JARDS – 36 Indre – 323 H4 – pop. 131 – alt. 148 m – ✉ 36260 12 C3

Paris 232 – Bourges 35 – Issoudun 22 – Romorantin-Lanthenay 40 – Vierzon 21

Les Saisons Gourmandes
pl. des Tilleuls – 02 54 49 37 67 – Fax 02 54 49 37 67 – Closed 19 October-4 November, 4-27 January, Monday except lunch from September to June, Tuesday dinner and Wednesday except July-August, Sunday dinner in July-August
Rest – Menu €22/41 – Carte €29/47
♦ The dining room of this characteristic house has retained its period beams, today painted Berry blue. Inviting terrace and well-designed traditional menu.

ST-PIERRE-DE-MANNEVILLE – 76 Seine-Maritime – 304 F5 – pop. 728 – alt. 6 m – ✉ 76113 Normandy 33 C2

Paris 150 – Évreux 72 – Rouen 18 – Sotteville-lès-Rouen 20

Manoir de Villers without rest
30 rte de Sahurs – 02 35 32 07 02 – www.manoirdevillers.com – contact@manoirdevillers.com – Fax 02 35 32 07 02 – Closed 15 December-15 January
4 rm – €130/160 €140/160, €9
♦ This fabulous 19C manor house has the air of a museum. Period decor in the public areas; rooms with parquet flooring and fine antique furniture.

ST-PIERRE-DES-CHAMPS – 11 Aude – 344 G4 – pop. 158 – alt. 146 m – ✉ 11220 22 B3

Paris 808 – Perpignan 84 – Carcassonne 41 – Narbonne 41

La Fargo rm, rm,
– 04 68 43 12 78 – www.lafargo.fr – contact@lafargo.fr – Fax 04 68 43 29 20 – Closed 21 December-23 February
12 rm – €75/105 €75/125, €8
Rest – *(closed Monday)* Menu €30 – Carte €39/60
♦ This old forge hidden in the Corbières is ideal for a relaxing healthy stay (non-smoking). Rooms are tastefully furnished, with Indonesian details. Pleasant, shady terrace and rustic-style dining room.

ST-PIERRE-D'OLÉRON – 17 Charente-Maritime – 324 C4 – see île d'Oléron

ST-PIERRE-DU-MONT – 14 Calvados – 303 G3 – pop. 78 – alt. 25 m – ✉ 14450 32 B2

Paris 291 – Caen 58 – Saint-Lô 58 – Bayeux 29 – Valognes 58

Le Château Saint Pierre without rest
1 km à l'Ouest sur D 514 – 02 31 22 63 79 – www.chambresdhotes-bayeuxarromanchesgrancamp.com – chateaustpierre@orange.fr
4 rm – €55 €70
♦ An ideal base to visit the Normandy landing beaches. Set in a garden, this 1600 château sports a countrified interior and comfortable rooms. Normandy breakfast.

ST-PIERRE-DU-PERRAY – 91 Essonne – 312 D4 – 101 38 – see Paris, Area (Sénart)

ST-PIERRE-LA-NOAILLE – 42 Loire – 327 D2 – see Charlieu

ST-PIERRE-LÈS-AUBAGNE – 13 Bouches-du-Rhône – 340 I6 – see Aubagne

ST-PIERREMONT – 88 Vosges – 314 H2 – pop. 158 – alt. 251 m – ✉ 88700 27 **C2**

Paris 366 – Lunéville 24 – Nancy 56 – St-Dié 43

Le Relais Vosgien rest, VISA AE

9 Grande Rue – ✆ 03 29 65 02 46 – relais.vosgien@wanadoo.fr – Fax 03 29 65 02 83 – Closed 10-22 January

20 rm – €55/108 €60/118, ☕ €11 – 6 suites – ½ P €60/80

Rest – *(closed Sunday dinner)* Menu (€20), €28/66 – Carte €38/61

◆ In the country, close to a pond, this old restored farmhouse with its family atmosphere is also a service-station and bar-tabac. The garden facing rooms are the most modern. Traditional dishes served in a rustic dining room or out on the terrace.

ST-PIERRE-QUIBERON – 56 Morbihan – 308 M9 – see Quiberon

ST-PIERRE-SUR-DIVES – 14 Calvados – 303 L5 – pop. 3 701 – alt. 30 m – ✉ 14170 Normandy 33 **C2**

Paris 194 – Caen 35 – Hérouville-Saint-Clair 34 – Lisieux 27

Syndicat d'initiative, 23, rue Saint-Benoist ✆ 02 31 20 97 90, Fax 02 31 20 36 02

Auberge de la Dives with rm VISA

27 bd Collas – ✆ 02 31 20 50 50 – auberge-de-la-dives@wanadoo.fr – Fax 02 31 20 50 50 – Closed 15 November-7 December, 15-30 March, Sunday dinner from 17 November to 31 March, Monday dinner and Tuesday

5 rm – €36 €40, ☕ €6,50 **Rest** – Menu (€15), €20/40 – Carte €34/50

◆ This countrified inn, whose terrace overlooks the River Dive, serves traditional cuisine with a clear focus on Normandy produce. Simple rooms upstairs.

ST-POL-DE-LÉON – 29 Finistère – 308 H2 – pop. 7 121 – alt. 60 m – ✉ 29250 Brittany 9 **B1**

Paris 557 – Brest 62 – Brignogan-Plages 31 – Morlaix 21 – Roscoff 6

Office de tourisme, Pavillon du Tourisme ✆ 02 98 69 05 69, Fax 02 98 69 01 20

de Carantec Carantec Rue de Kergrist, S : 10 km on D 58, ✆ 02 98 67 09 14

Steeple★★ of Kreisker chapel ★: ✻★★ from the tower - of the former cathedral★ - Rocher Ste-Anne: ≤★ downhill.

France without rest VISA AE

29 r. des Minimes – ✆ 02 98 29 14 14 – www.hotel-saint-pol.com – hotel.de.france.finistere@wanadoo.fr – Fax 02 98 29 10 57 – Closed 5-20 January

22 rm – €45/60 €55/75, ☕ €6

◆ A quiet side street is the setting for this elegant regional abode dating from the 1930s. Well-kept practical rooms; ask for one giving onto the garden.

Auberge La Pomme d'Api VISA AE

49 r. Verderel – ✆ 02 98 69 04 36 – yannick.lebeaudour@free.fr – Fax 02 98 29 06 53 – Closed 12-30 November, Sunday dinner and Monday except July-August

Rest – Menu (€17 bi), €23 bi (weekday lunch), €28/75 bi – Carte €55/80

◆ Beams, stone and a huge fireplace make up this 16C Breton lodging's rustic-styled setting. "Surf and turf" cuisine, mixing seafood, spices and exotic flavours.

ST-PONS – Ardèche – **331** J6 – **pop. 203 – alt. 350 m** – ✉ **07580** 44 **B3**

Paris 621 – Aubenas 24 – Montélimar 21 – Privas 24 – Valence 66

Hostellerie Gourmande "Mère Biquette"
Les Allignols, 4 km north on secondary road – ✆ 04 75 36 72 61 – www.merebiquette.fr – info@merebiquette.fr – Fax 04 75 36 76 25 – Closed 12 November-10 February, Sunday dinner from October to March, Monday lunch, Tuesday lunch and Wednesday lunch
15 rm – €63/112 €63/112, €10 **Rest** – Menu €22/45 – Carte €28/50
◆ Quiet and nature lovers will appreciate this Ardèche farm nestled between the vines and sweet chestnut trees. Practical rooms, more spacious in the new wing. Regional dishes served in the dining room/veranda with views over the valley.

ST-PONS – **04 Alpes-de-Haute-Provence** – **334** H6 – **see Barcelonnette**

ST-PONS-DE-THOMIÈRES – **34 Hérault** – **339** B8 – **pop. 2 195** – **alt. 301 m** – ✉ **34220** **Languedoc-Roussillon-Tarn Gorges** 22 **B2**

Paris 750 – Béziers 54 – Carcassonne 64 – Castres 54 – Lodève 73 – Narbonne 53
Office de tourisme, place du Foirail ✆ 04 67 97 06 65, Fax 04 67 97 95 07
Grotte de la Devèze ★ Southwest: 5 km.

in Courniou **6 km southwest on the N 112** – **pop. 619** – **alt. 362 m** – ✉ **34220**

L' Assiette Gourmande
av. de l'Occitanie – ✆ 04 67 97 52 11 – lassiettecourniou@orange.fr – Closed Monday and dinner in low season except Friday and Saturday
Rest – Menu €14 (weekday lunch), €19/24 – Carte €30/45
◆ Attractive restaurant with a friendly ambiance. Traditional cuisine with a modern twist prepared by the chef who hails from the Alps region.

ST-PORCHAIRE – **17 Charente-Maritime** – **324** E5 – **pop. 1 335** – **alt. 16 m** – ✉ **17250** 38 **B2**

Paris 474 – La Rochelle 56 – Niort 77 – Rochefort 27 – Royan 36 – Saintes 16

Le Bruant with rm rest, rm, VISA
76 r. Nationale – ✆ 05 46 94 65 36 – www.lebruant.com – lebruantotel@aol.com – Fax 05 46 94 71 00 – Closed 3-26 November, Sunday dinner and Monday
5 rm – €50 €55, €8 **Rest** – Menu €20/45 – Carte €25/60
◆ This house, built in typical Charente style, is resolutely modern in feel, with its chic, country-style decor and wonderful attention to detail. Attractive, flower-decked terrace. The modern decor in the rooms is made up of bright colours, animal sculptures and flowers.

ST-PORQUIER – **82 Tarn-et-Garonne** – **337** D7 – **pop. 1 271** – **alt. 95 m** – ✉ **82700** 28 **B2**

Paris 651 – Colomiers 60 – Montauban 18 – Toulouse 55

Les Hortensias without rest VISA
r. Ste-Catherine – ✆ 05 63 31 85 57 – www.chambres-hotes-leshortensias.com – bernard-barthe075@orange.fr
3 rm – €60 €60
◆ This pink-brick house offers colourful rooms. You will also appreciate the former wine store where breakfast is now served, as well as the pleasant flower garden.

ST-PÔTAN – **22 Côtes-d'Armor** – **309** I3 – **pop. 735** – **alt. 55 m** – ✉ **22550** 10 **C1**

Paris 429 – Rennes 79 – Saint-Brieuc 46 – Saint-Malo 35

Auberge du Manoir VISA
31 r. du 19 mars 1962 – ✆ 02 96 83 72 58 – Closed 16-29 September, 15-28 February, Tuesday and Wednesday
Rest – Menu (€13), €32/56 – Carte €35/57
◆ A pleasant gourmet stop-over in this welcoming house, located in the village. Appealing lunchtime daily specials and a longer traditional menu to be discovered in the neo-rustic dining room.

ST-POURÇAIN-SUR-SIOULE – 03 Allier – 326 G5 – pop. 5 046 – alt. 234 m – ✉ 03500 Auvergne 5 **B1**

Paris 325 – Montluçon 66 – Moulins 33 – Riom 61 – Roanne 79 – Vichy 28

Office de tourisme, 29, rue Marcellin Berthelot ✆ 04 70 45 32 73, Fax 04 70 45 60 27

de Briailles 15 rue de Metz, E : 3 km, ✆ 04 70 45 49 49

Ste-Croix church ★ - Musée de la Vigne et du Vin★.

Le Chêne Vert

bd Ledru-Rollin – ✆ 04 70 47 77 00 – www.hotel-restaurant-chene-vert.com – hotel.chenevert@wanadoo.fr – Fax 04 70 47 77 39 – Closed 4-26 January

29 rm – †€ 50/65 ††€ 59/67, ☕ € 8

Rest – *(closed Sunday dinner in low season and Monday except dinner in high season)* Menu € 18 (weekdays)/38 – Carte € 26/46

◆ Two types of rooms: contemporary and less so - 1970s style - while awaiting an upcoming renovation. A little gallery exhibits regional products. Smart dining room and pleasant terrace. Traditional cuisine complemented by local wines.

ST-PRIEST-BRAMEFANT – 63 Puy-de-Dôme – 326 H6 – pop. 791 – alt. 290 m – ✉ 63310 6 **C2**

Paris 365 – Clermont-Ferrand 49 – Riom 34 – Thiers 26 – Vichy 13

Château de Maulmont

1.5 km south on D 59 – ✆ 04 70 59 14 95 – www.chateau-maulmont.com – info@chateau-maulmont.com – Fax 04 70 59 11 88 – Open 16 March-1st November

19 rm – †€ 95/185 ††€ 95/185, ☕ € 14 – 3 suites

Rest – *(closed Tuesday lunch, Sunday dinner and Monday)* Menu (€ 25), € 42 (dinner), € 54/95 – Carte € 56/83 dinner only

◆ You can enjoy the tranquillity at this château by stepping back to the 19C, when it was altered by Adélaïde, the sister of Louis-Philippe. Period furniture, wood panelling, French style garden, etc.

ST-PRIEST-EN-JAREZ – 42 Loire – 327 F7 – see St-Étienne

ST-PRIEST-TAURION – 87 Haute-Vienne – 325 F5 – pop. 2 613 – alt. 255 m – ✉ 87480 Dordogne-Berry-Limousin 24 **B2**

Paris 387 – Bellac 47 – Bourganeuf 33 – Limoges 15 – La Souterraine 53

- ≤★ of Montméry Park North: 9 km by D 44.

Relais du Taurion with rm

2 chemin des Contamines – ✆ 05 55 39 70 14 – Fax 05 55 39 67 63 – Closed 12 December-12 January, Sunday dinner and Monday

6 rm – †€ 53 ††€ 53, ☕ € 9 – ½ P € 60

Rest – Menu € 23 (weekdays)/44 – Carte € 48/55

◆ A bourgeois home surrounded by a large garden. Traditional fare served on the terrace or in a spruce dining room adorned with fresh flowers and paintings. Small rustic rooms (non-smoking).

ST-PRIVAT-DES-VIEUX – 30 Gard – 339 J4 – see Alès

ST-PRIX – 71 Saône-et-Loire – 320 E8 – pop. 230 – alt. 464 m – ✉ 71990 7 **B2**

Paris 308 – Dijon 107 – Le Creusot 41 – Montceau-les-Mines 54

Chez Franck et Francine

Le bourg – ✆ 03 85 82 45 12 – chez-franck-et-francine@wanadoo.fr – Closed January, Sunday dinner and Monday

Rest – *(number of covers limited, pre-book)* Menu € 38/46

◆ Village restaurant with a family atmosphere. Simply-decorated dining room arranged around a fireplace. Up-to-date cuisine with personal touches.

ST-PRIX – 95 Val-d'Oise – 305 E6 – 101 5 – see Paris, Area

ST-PUY – 32 Gers – 336 E6 – pop. 567 – alt. 171 m – ✉ 32310 28 A2

Paris 731 – Agen 52 – Auch 32 – Toulouse 107

La Lumiane VISA

Grande rue – ✆ 05 62 28 95 95 – www.lalumiane.com – info@lalumiane.com – Fax 05 62 28 59 67

5 rm – †€ 42/58 ††€ 50/66 **Table d'hôte** – Menu € 23 bi

◆ Next to the 12C church, this 17C dignitary's house offers fine, stylishly rustic rooms, a peaceful reading room and pleasant flower garden. The table d'hôte menu is dominated by local dishes.

ST-QUAY-PORTRIEUX – 22 Côtes-d'Armor – 309 F3 – pop. 3 036 – alt. 25 m – Casino – ✉ 22410 Brittany 10 C1

Paris 470 – Étables-sur-Mer 3 – Guingamp 29 – Lannion 54 – Paimpol 26 – St-Brieuc 22

Office de tourisme, 17 bis, rue Jeanne d'Arc ✆ 02 96 70 40 64, Fax 02 96 70 39 99

des Ajoncs d'OrW : 7 km, ✆ 02 96 71 90 74

Ker Moor without rest VISA AE

13 r. Prés. Le Sénécal – ✆ 02 96 70 52 22 – www.ker-moor.com – hotelkermoor@orange.fr – Fax 02 96 70 50 49 – Open 15 March-15 December

27 rm – †€ 107/159 ††€ 107/159, € 12

◆ This century-old villa with a Moorish touch is perched on top of a low cliff. Rooms have balconies and offer a fine view of the sea.

Gerbot d'Avoine AC rest, VISA

2 bd Littoral – ✆ 02 96 70 40 09 – www.gerbotdavoine.com – gerbotdavoine@wanadoo.fr – Fax 02 96 70 34 06 – Closed 2 January-12 February

18 rm – †€ 68/78 ††€ 68/125, € 12 – ½ P € 72/105

Rest – *(closed Sunday dinner, Monday and Tuesday from November to March)* Menu € 42/88 bi – Carte € 55/83

◆ A Breton house in a seaside resort. Some of the rooms overlook the English Channel. Two dining rooms, one facing the sea - from which the chef draws his inspiration.

Le Saint-Quay with rm VISA

72 bd. Foch – ✆ 02 96 70 40 99 – www.lesaintquay.fr – lestquayhotel@orange.fr – Fax 02 96 70 34 04 – Closed 10-14 May, 17-27 November, 12-20 January and Tuesday in season

7 rm – †€ 45/58 ††€ 52/58, € 7,50 **Rest** – Menu € 22/59 – Carte € 53/78

◆ Small family-run restaurant with a simple neo-rustic setting. Savour traditional cuisine listed on a blackboard. Simple refurbished rooms.

ST-QUENTIN – 02 Aisne – 306 B3 – pop. 57 100 – Built-up area 103 781 – alt. 74 m – ✉ 02100 Northern France and the Paris Region 37 C2

Paris 165 – Amiens 81 – Charleroi 161 – Lille 113 – Reims 99

Office de tourisme, espace Victor Basch ✆ 03 23 67 05 00, Fax 03 23 67 78 71

de Saint-Quentin-Mesnil Mesnil-Saint-Laurent Rue de Chêne de Cambrie, SE : 10 km on D 12, ✆ 03 23 68 19 48

Basilica★ - Town hall ★ - Collection of portraits by Maurice Quentin de La Tour★★ at the musée Antoine-Lécuyer.

Plan on following page

Le Grand Hôtel without rest VISA AE

6 r. Dachery – ✆ 03 23 62 69 77 – www.grand-hotel2.cabanova.fr – grand-hotel2@wanadoo.fr – Fax 03 23 62 53 52 – Closed for three weeks in August and two weeks in December BZ **n**

24 rm – †€ 72 ††€ 90, € 9

◆ This large building at the foot of the hill has spacious, functional rooms reached by a panoramic lift.

ST-QUENTIN

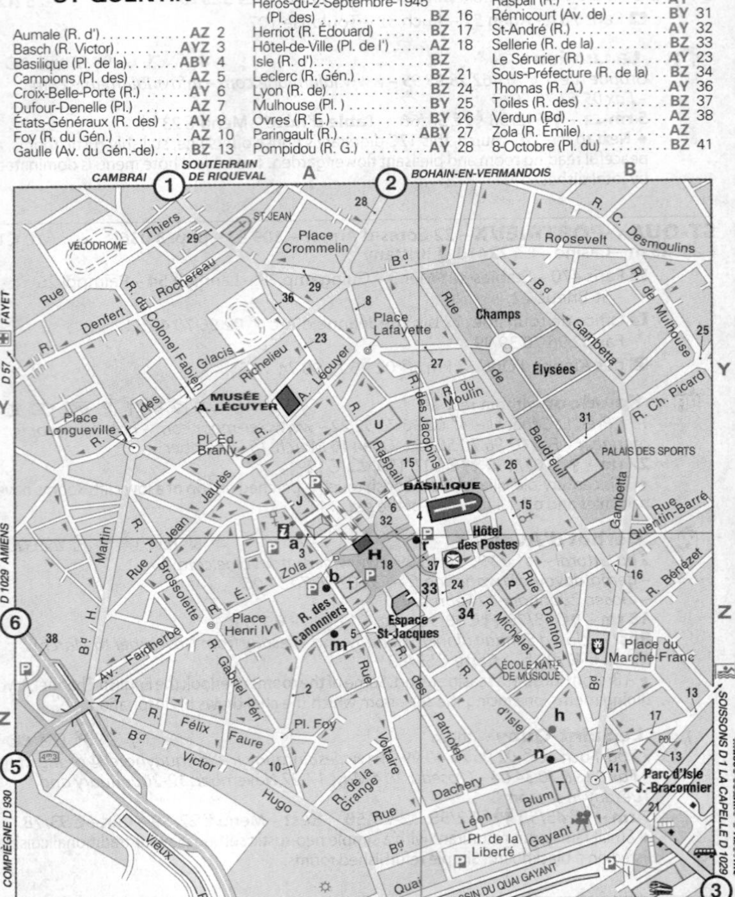

Des Canonniers without rest
15 r. Canonniers – ✆ 03 23 62 87 87 – www.hotel-canonniers.com – lescanonniers@aol.com – Fax 03 23 62 87 86 – Closed 3-16 August and Sunday dinner AZ **m**
7 rm – †€ 52/92 ††€ 62/102, ☕ € 13
◆ The entrance to this stately home is via a pretty cobbled courtyard. Quiet rooms with personal touches (kitchenette). Lovely wainscoted sitting rooms facing the park.

Ibis without rest
14 pl. Basilique – ✆ 03 23 67 40 40 – h1641@accor.com – Fax 03 23 67 84 90 ABZ **r**
76 rm – †€ 65/70 ††€ 65/70, ☕ € 8
◆ Ideally located in the heart of town, this elegant redbrick building offers rooms that are spacious for an Ibis.

Mémorial without rest
8 r. Comédie – 03 23 67 90 09 – 03 23 62 34 96 – contact@hotel-memorial.com – Fax 03 23 62 34 96 AZ **b**
18 rm – €55/87 €55/95, €8,50
◆ This old townhouse boasts a large tree-lined inner courtyard. Each of the rooms (renovation underway) is individually decorated (double glazing on the street side).

Villa d'Isle
111-113 r.d'Isle – 03 23 67 08 09 – www.villadisle.com – Fax 03 23 67 06 07 – Closed Saturday lunch, Sunday dinner and Monday BZ **h**
Rest – Menu (€ 16 bi), € 23 bi/32
◆ A lovely conservatory, period ornaments and modern fixtures and fittings: this old home skilfully mixes references to the past with modern touches. Mouth-watering bistro menu.

Auberge de l'Ermitage
331 rte de Paris, 3 km by ⑤ – 03 23 62 42 80 – auberge.ermitage@wanadoo.fr – Fax 03 23 64 29 28 – Closed 3-14 August, 1 week in February, Saturday lunch, Sunday dinner and Wednesday
Rest – Menu (€ 22), € 28 (weekdays)/53 – Carte € 50/60
◆ An inn whose façade, terrace and freshly painted exterior cannot fail but catch the eye. Tasty traditional dishes served in a pleasantly neat, rustic décor.

Le Rouget Noir
19 r. Victor-Basch – 03 23 62 44 44 – www.lerougetnoir.com – lerougenoir@wanadoo.fr – Fax 03 23 07 87 98 – Closed Saturday lunch and Sunday dinner AYZ **a**
Rest – Menu (€ 18 bi), € 29/36 – Carte € 37/53
◆ This handsome contemporary establishment is unsurprisingly done up in red and black and adorned with original works by an artist friend of the chef. Flavoursome cuisine.

in Neuville-St-Amand 3 km by ③ and D 12 – pop. 859 – alt. 82 m – ✉ 02100

Château
rm, rm,
11 r. de la Fontaine – 03 23 68 41 82 – www.chateauneuvillestamand.com – chateaudeneuville.st.amand@wanadoo.fr – Fax 03 23 68 46 02 – Closed 2-24 August, 21 December-4 January, Saturday lunch, Sunday dinner and Monday
15 rm – €71 €82, €12 **Rest** – Menu €29/58 – Carte €50/65
◆ A well-tended park surrounds this restored manor house, endowing it with a welcome peaceful atmosphere. Personalised rooms with spacious bathrooms. At meal times, the chef concocts traditional fare from fresh, good quality produce.

in Holnon 6 km by ⑥ and D 1029 – pop. 1 334 – alt. 102 m – ✉ 02760

Le Pot d'Étain
rm,
D 1029 – 03 23 09 34 35 – info@lepotdetain.fr – Fax 03 23 09 34 39
30 rm – €63 €85, €10 – ½ P €75
Rest – Menu (€ 18 bi), € 22 bi (weekdays)/42 – Carte € 40/76
◆ This hacienda-style lodge and motel lies at the entrance to the town, offering functional, well-soundproofed rooms. Huge rustic-style dining room with a summer terrace. Traditional à la carte and set menus.

ST-QUENTIN-EN-YVELINES – 78 Yvelines – **311** H3 – **106** 29 – **101** 21 – see Paris, Area

---

ST-QUENTIN-LA-POTERIE – 30 Gard – **339** L4 – see Uzès

ST-QUENTIN-SUR-LE-HOMME – 50 Manche – **303** E8 – see Avranches

---

ST-QUIRIN – 57 Moselle – **307** N7 – pop. 826 – alt. 305 m – ✉ 57560 27 **D2**
Alsace-Lorraine

Paris 433 – Baccarat 40 – Lunéville 56 – Phalsbourg 34 – Sarrebourg 19 – Strasbourg 91

Syndicat d'initiative, Mairie 03 87 08 60 34, Fax 03 87 08 66 44

XX **Hostellerie du Prieuré** with rm

163 r. Gén. de Gaulle – ✆ 03 87 08 66 52 – www.saintquirin.com – leprieure@laposte.net – Fax 03 87 08 66 49 – Closed 24-31 July, 26 October-4 November, 16-28 February, Saturday lunch, Tuesday dinner and Wednesday

8 rm – †€ 45/50 ††€ 45/50, ☕ € 7

Rest – Menu (€ 12), € 25/70 – Carte € 30/64

◆ An 18C former convent in the heart of a village popular with hikers. Traditional dishes served in colourful dining rooms. Practical rooms for an overnight stay, located in a characteristic family home two minutes away.

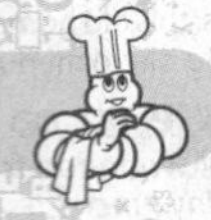

"Rest" appears in red for establishments with a ✿ (star) or ☺ (Bib Gourmand).

ST-RAPHAËL – 83 Var – 340 P5 – pop. 32 700 – Casino Z – ✉ 83700 41 **C3**

French Riviera

Paris 870 – Aix-en-Provence 121 – Cannes 42 – Fréjus 4 – Toulon 93

Office de tourisme, rue Waldeck Rousseau ✆ 04 94 19 52 52, Fax 04 94 83 85 40

Esterel Latitudes 745 Boulevard Darby, E : 5 km, ✆ 04 94 52 68 30

de Cap Estérel BP 940 - Cap Estérel, E : 3 km, ✆ 04 94 82 55 00

Collection of jars★ in the archeological museum **M.**

Plan on next page

Access and exits: See plan of Fréjus.

La Marina

port Santa-Lucia (Palais des Congrès), via ① – ✆ 04 94 95 31 31 – www.bestwestern-lamarina.com – hotel@bestwestern-lamarina.com – Fax 04 94 82 21 46

100 rm – †€ 99/145 ††€ 99/145, ☕ € 12 **Rest** – Carte € 25/35

◆ The rooms have either a blue or red colour scheme with a modern-style decor. Most have a balcony and some command a view of the pool or the marina. Restaurant with a summer wharfside terrace. Traditional, unpretentious menu.

Continental without rest

100 promenade René Coty – ✆ 04 94 83 87 87 – www.hotels-continental.com – info@hotels-continental.com – Fax 04 94 19 20 24 – Open from February to early November and 21 December-2 January Z **e**

44 rm – †€ 75/229 ††€ 75/229, ☕ € 13

◆ Opposite the beach, in the lively part of town, this hotel occupies the first floor of a huge white neo-Classical building. Comfortable bright rooms, the best ones face the sea.

Excelsior

193 bd F. Martin, (Promenade R. Coty) – ✆ 04 94 95 02 42 – www.excelsior-hotel.com – info@excelsior-hotel.com – Fax 04 94 95 33 82 Z **h**

36 rm ☕ – †€ 60/190 ††€ 125/190

Rest – Menu (€ 23), € 30 (weekday lunch), € 35/55 – Carte € 35/75

◆ Characterful hotel two minutes from the town centre. It has a small, English style pub on the ground floor. Rooms overlook St Raphael bay or the town. Regional cuisine served on the terrace overlooking the Mediterranean in fine weather.

Santa Lucia without rest

418 Corniche D'Or, via ① – ✆ 04 94 95 23 00 – www.hotelsantalucia.fr – contact@hotelsantalucia.fr – Fax 04 94 19 49 79 – Closed 21 December-31 January

12 rm ☕ – †€ 69/139 ††€ 84/154

◆ Family hotel with a liner inspired decor and immaculate rooms, each of which is reminiscent of a far off destination (Louisiana, China, Kenya). Those at the rear command a sea view.

ST-RAPHAËL

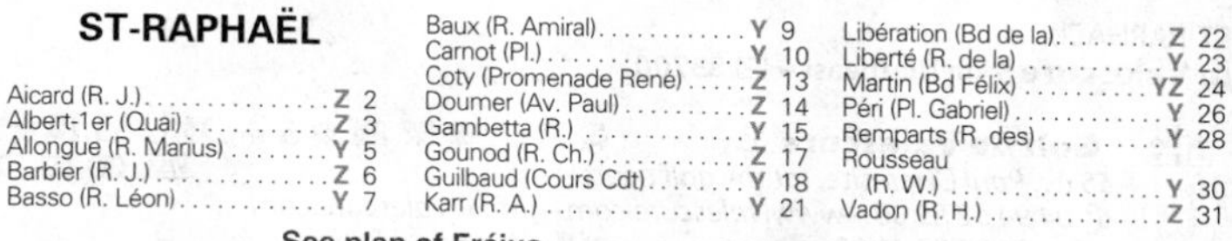

Aicard (R. J.)	Z	2
Albert-1er (Quai)	Z	3
Allongue (R. Marius)	Y	5
Barbier (R. J.)	Z	6
Basso (R. Léon)	Y	7
Baux (R. Amiral)	Y	9
Carnot (Pl.)	Y	10
Coty (Promenade René)	Z	13
Doumer (Av. Paul)	Z	14
Gambetta (R.)	Y	15
Gounod (R. Ch.)	Z	17
Guilbaud (Cours Cdt)	Y	18
Karr (R. A.)	Y	21
Libération (Bd de la)	Z	22
Liberté (R. de la)	Y	23
Martin (Bd Félix)	YZ	24
Péri (Pl. Gabriel)	Y	26
Remparts (R. des)	Y	28
Rousseau (R. W.)	Y	30
Vadon (R. H.)	Z	31

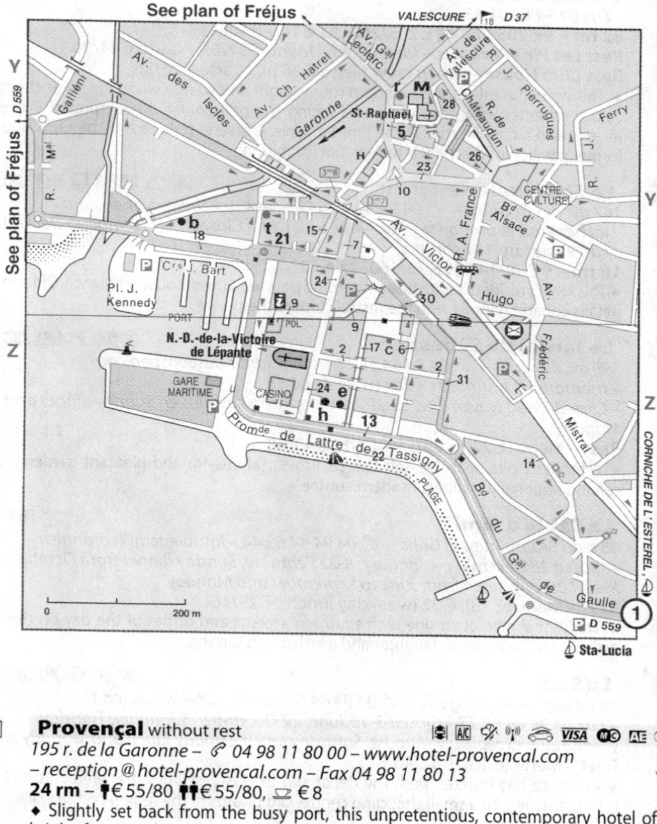

Provençal without rest

195 r. de la Garonne – ✆ 04 98 11 80 00 – www.hotel-provencal.com – reception@hotel-provencal.com – Fax 04 98 11 80 13 Y **b**

24 rm – †€ 55/80 ††€ 55/80, ☕ € 8

◆ Slightly set back from the busy port, this unpretentious, contemporary hotel offers bright, functional and faultlessly kept rooms. Friendly welcome.

XXX **L'Arbousier**

6 av. de Valescure – ✆ 04 94 95 25 00 – www.arbousier.net – arbousier.restaurant@wanadoo.fr – Fax 04 94 81 83 04 – Closed 22 December-6 January, February holiday, Tuesday except dinner in high season and Monday Y **r**

Rest – Menu € 30, € 44/59 – Carte approx. € 80

◆ In fine weather, head for the terrace, a delightful oasis of greenery, shaded by magnolia and strawberry trees. Seasonal produce takes pride of place on the Provençal inspired menu.

X **La Cave**

23 r. Thiers – ✆ 04 94 95 79 62 – www.la-cave-restaurant.com – lacaverestaurant@aol.com – Fax 04 94 53 93 35 – Closed 1-7 June and 5-26 January Y **t**

Rest – Menu (€ 18 bi), € 29/39 – Carte € 46/59

◆ The chef at this contemporary bistro offers market cuisine and old-fashioned dishes, as prepared a hundred years ago. Fine wine cellar and a gourmet grocery shop next door.

in Valescure 5 km Northeast – ✉ **83700**

Golf de Valescure
55 av. Paul L'Hermite, (at the golf course) –
04 94 52 85 00 – www.valescure.com – info@valescure.com
– Fax 04 94 82 41 88
62 rm – €205/260 €205/260, €16 – 8 suites
Rest ***Les Pins Parasols*** – *(dinner only)* Menu €37/65 – Carte €44/80
Rest ***Club House*** – *(lunch only)* Menu €26 bi – Carte €26/36
◆ This hotel has refurbished modern rooms (light and wenge wood, beige or chocolate colour scheme) with private terraces facing the golf course. Reinterpreted Provençal recipes and a cosy interior at the Pins Parasols. Brasserie-style fare in the Club House, a former pavilion of the 1900 International Exhibition.

La Chêneraie without rest
167 av. des Gondins – 04 94 44 48 84 – www.lacheneraie.jimdo.com – lacheneraie@orange.fr – Fax 04 94 51 21 71 – Closed 1st November-5 December and 19 January-13 February
10 rm – €58/145 €73/160, €12
◆ This 1890's residence with fine garden and pool has a guesthouse ambience. Old and new details cohabit happily with the restful colour scheme.

Le Jardin de Sébastien
599 av. des golfs – 04 94 44 66 56 – www.jardindesebastien.com – thomar83@hotmail.fr – Fax 04 94 44 66 56 – Closed 11-30 November, 15-30 January, Thursday dinner, Sunday dinner and Monday
Rest – Menu (€22), €28/58 – Carte €43/68
◆ A modern villa near the golf course. Provençal interior and pleasant garden-terrace serving regionally inspired, modern cuisine.

La Table d' Emi
85 r. du Bruant, rte des Golfs – 04 94 44 63 44 – latabledemi@orange.fr – Closed 28 December-4 January, 8-22 February, Sunday dinner from October to May, Tuesday lunch from June to September and Monday
Rest – Menu (€18), €22 (weekday lunch), €29/46
◆ Traditional market cuisine with southern accents and dishes of the day on the slate. Artwork by the owners' daughter and a lush green terrace.

Le Sud
16 bd Darby, rte des golfs – 04 94 44 67 86 – le-sud@wanadoo.fr – Fax 04 94 44 68 73 – Closed 3-10 June, 22 December-5 January, Tuesday, Wednesday except July -August, Saturday lunch, Sunday lunch and Monday lunch
Rest – Menu (€18), €32/40
◆ Provence has inspired both the decor and the tasty, skilfully prepared cuisine in this restaurant, next to a small shopping centre. Old photos of the region on the walls.

in Dramont 6 km by ① – ✉ **83530 Agay**

Sol e Mar
90 Bd 36ème Division Texas, rte de la Corniche d'Or – 04 94 95 25 60 – www.monalisahotels.com – resa-agay@monalisahotels.com – Fax 04 94 83 83 61 – Open 15 March-11 November
45 rm – €99/170 €99/210, €12 – 5 suites
Rest – Carte €37/48
◆ A genuine seaside hotel, most of whose subdued rooms command views of the Îles d'Or, beach-sundeck and seawater overflow pool, which is cut directly into the coastal rock. Restaurant with a panoramic view topped by a sunroof and extended by a fine terrace overlooking the sea.

ST-RÉMY – **71 Saône-et-Loire** – **320** J9 – **see Chalon-sur-Saône**

ST-RÉMY – **21 Côte-d'Or** – **320** G4 – **see Montbard**

ST-RÉMY-DE-CHARGNAT – 63 Puy-de-Dôme – 326 G9 – see Issoire

ST-RÉMY-DE-PROVENCE – 13 Bouches-du-Rhône – 340 D3 42 **E1**
– pop. 10 251 – alt. 59 m – ✉ 13210 Provence

- Paris 702 – Arles 25 – Avignon 20 – Marseille 89 – Nîmes 45
- Office de tourisme, place Jean Jaurès ✆ 04 90 92 05 22, Fax 04 90 92 38 52
- de Servanes Mouriès Domaine de Servanes, SE : 17 km, ✆ 04 90 47 59 95
- Le plateau des Antiques★★: Mausoleum★★, Arc municipal★, Glanum★ 1km by ③ - Cloister★ of the former St-Paul-de-Mausole monastery by ③ - Hôtel de Sade: lapidary deposit★ **L** - Donation Mario Prassinos★ **S.**
- ✳★★ of La Caume 7 km by ③.

ST-RÉMY-DE-PROVENCE

Street	Zone	No.
Commune (R.)	Z	2
Estrine (R.)	YZ	3
La-Fayette (R.)	Z	6
Hoche (R.)	Z	4
Libération (Av. de la)	Y	7
Mauron (Av. Ch.)	Y	8
Mirabeau (Bd)	YZ	9
Nostradamus (R.)	Y	10
Parage (R.)	Y	12
Pelletan (R. C.)	YZ	14
Résistance (Av.)	Z	15
Roux (R.)	Z	16
Salengro (R. R.)	Y	18
8 Mai 1945 (R. du)	Z	20

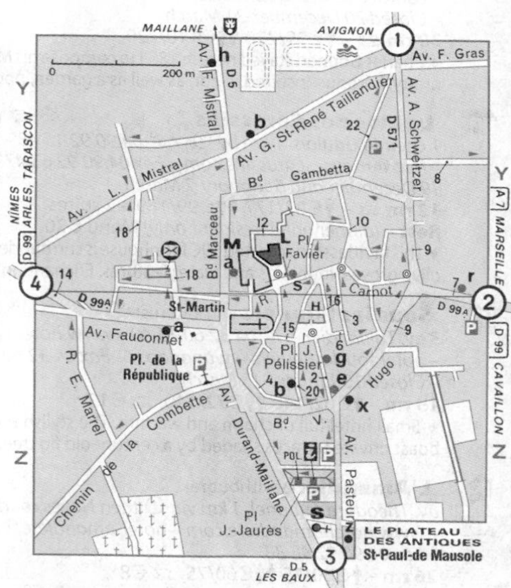

 **Hostellerie du Vallon de Valrugues**
chemin Canto Cigalo, 1 km by ② – ✆ 04 90 92 04 40
– www.vallondevalrugues.com – resa@vallondevalrugues.com
– Fax 04 90 92 44 01 – Closed 11 January-11 February
53 rm – †€ 190/240 ††€ 190/310, ☕ € 23 – 7 suites
Rest Marc de Passorio – see restaurant listing
Rest ***Bistrot Gourmand***– Menu € 29 bi – Carte € 30/40
◆ A large villa surrounded by greenery in a residential district. Luxurious decor, refurbished rooms and full leisure facilities. Mediterranean cuisine at the Bistrot.

 **Le Château des Alpilles**
rm, rm, rest,
2 km west by D 31 – ✆ 04 90 92 03 33
– www.chateaudesalpilles.com – chateau.alpilles@wanadoo.fr
– Fax 04 90 92 45 17 – Open 13 March-4 January
16 rm – †€ 124/139 ††€ 180/399, ☕ € 20 – 4 suites
Rest – *(closed Thursday lunch and Wednesday in low season)* Menu (€ 20), € 26 (weekday lunch)/42 – Carte € 42/57
◆ Splendid 19C abode surrounded by grounds planted with three-century-old plane trees. Attractively decorated rooms, ranging from classical in the main wing to modern in the outbuildings. Happily poised between plush opulence and the 1970s, the restaurant serves regional food.

Les Ateliers de l'Image
36 bd V. Hugo – 04 90 92 51 50 – www.hotelphoto.com – info@hotelphoto.com – Fax 04 90 92 43 52 – Closed from early December to end February Z **x**
28 rm – €175/380 €175/380, €19 – 4 suites
Rest – *(closed Tuesday and Wednesday in low season)* Menu (€19), €44 (dinner)/62 – Carte €55/75
◆ A park in the town centre provides the backdrop to this 'hotel workshop' devoted to photography (exhibitions, gallery, photo lab). Stylish, minimalist rooms (half boast a terrace) and unique tree cabin suite. The restaurant has a choice of sushi or a Provence style menu.

Gounod without rest
18 pl. de la République – 04 90 92 06 14 – www.hotel-gounod.com – contact@hotel-gounod.com – Fax 04 90 92 56 54 – Closed 20 December-31 March Z **a**
30 rm – €99/220 €110/220
◆ Charles Gounod stayed here in 1863 to compose his Mireille opera. Refined atmosphere, pretty, Baroque-inspired decor, as well as a garden, pool and cosy tearoom.

Le Mas des Carassins
1 chemin Gaulois, 1 km by ③ – 04 90 92 15 48 – www.masdescarassins.com – info@masdescarassins.com – Fax 04 90 92 63 47 – Closed 29 November-19 December and 6 January-7 March
12 rm – €87/177 €99/189 – 2 suites
Rest – *(dinner only) (resident only)* Menu €30
◆ This faultlessly decorated 19C farmhouse is surrounded by lavender, thyme, lemon trees, olive groves, fountains and water features. Enchanting Provençal style rooms.

Sous les Figuiers without rest
3 av. Taillandier – 04 32 60 15 40 – www.hotel-charme-provence.com – hotel.souslesfiguiers@wanadoo.fr – Fax 04 32 60 15 39 – Closed 10 January-13 March Y **b**
13 rm – €62/140 €72/140, €12
◆ Small hotel full of charm and warmth. The stylish rooms (quilts and antique furniture) boast private terraces shaded by a century-old fig tree. Painting workshop.

L'Amandière without rest
av. Théodore Aubanel, 1 km via ① then Noves road – 04 90 92 41 00 – www.hotel-amandiere.com – hotel-amandiere@wanadoo.fr – Fax 04 90 92 48 38
26 rm – €60/75 €60/75, €8
◆ This Provencal villa boasts a pleasant wooded flower garden. Peaceful and practical rooms with balcony or terrace. Breakfast served in a winter garden.

Van Gogh without rest
1 av. J. Moulin par ② – 04 90 92 14 02 – www.hotel-vangogh.com – vangoghhot@aol.com – Fax 04 90 92 09 05 – Open 15 March-20 October
21 rm – €65/85 €65/85, €8
◆ This simple town centre hotel features rooms decorated with a Provençal note. Those on the first floor have dormer windows. Attractive poolside terrace.

Du Soleil without rest
35 av. Pasteur – 04 90 92 00 63 – www.hotelsoleil.com – info@hotelsoleil.com – Fax 04 90 92 61 07 – Open 30 March-11 November Z **z**
24 rm – €64/80 €64/80, €8
◆ Buildings over a century old (converted factory), around a vast enclosed courtyard (terrace, fountain, garden, pool). Peaceful, unostentatious rooms.

Le Chalet Fleuri without rest
15 av. Frédéric Mistral – 04 90 92 03 62 – le.chalet.fleuri@orange.fr – Fax 04 90 92 60 28 – Closed January Y **h**
12 rm – €64/80 €64/110, €10
◆ A friendly establishment two minutes from the town centre. Cheerful, practical rooms. In summertime, breakfast in the garden (chestnut, pine, lime and palm trees).

Canto Cigalo without rest
8 chemin Canto-Cigalo, 1 km via ② – 04 90 92 14 28 – www.cantocigalo.com – hotel.cantocigalo@wanadoo.fr – Fax 04 90 92 24 48
20 rm – €68/84 €68/84, €8
◆ Tucked away in a peaceful neighbourhood, this house hides a warm and vibrant interior. Rustic Provençal-style guestrooms. Pool and terrace overlooking the Alpilles.

La Maison du Village without rest
10 r. du 8 mai 1945 – 04 32 60 68 20 – www.lamaisonduvillage.com – contact@lamaisonduvillage.com – Fax 04 32 60 68 21 Z **b**
5 rm – €150/210 €150/210, €12
◆ This 18C house in the heart of the historic centre is delightfully decorated. Superb rooms and enchanting courtyard-terrace.

Mas de Figues
rm, rm, VISA
Vieux chemin d'Arles, 3 km via chemin de la Combette – 04 32 60 00 98 – www.masdesfigues.com – info@masdesfigues.com – Fax 04 32 60 00 95 – Open March to November
5 rm – €99/150 €130/200, €20 – 2 suites – ½ P €95/140
Table d'hôte – *(pre-book)* Menu €28
◆ Old Provençal farmhouse surrounded by lavender and olive trees. Rooms with four-poster beds named after Alphonse Daudet's characters. Southern French cuisine made from farm grown produce. Stylish setting (large table, timber structure).

Marc de Passorio – Hostellerie du Vallon de Valrugues
chemin Canto Cigalo, 1 km by ② – 04 90 92 04 40 – www.restaurant-marcdepassorio.com – resa@vallondevalrugues.com – Fax 04 90 92 44 01 – Closed 11 January-11 February, Sunday dinner and Monday in low season
Rest – *(number of covers limited, pre-book)* Menu €58/98 – Carte €113/124
Spec. Langoustines à la poudre d'orange. Selle d'agneau et cannelloni d'aubergine. Tarte renversée au chocolat noir et blanc.
◆ Elegant atmosphere in the restaurant, which opens onto a flower-decked terrace. Regional dishes, based on the best local produce.

La Maison Jaune (François Perraud)
15 r. Carnot – 04 90 92 56 14 – www.lamaisonjaune.info – lamaisonjaune@wanadoo.fr – Closed 2 January-2 February, Sunday dinner in winter, Tuesday lunch from June to September and Monday Y **s**
Rest – *(number of covers limited, pre-book)* Menu €36/66 – Carte €58/85
Spec. Asperges vertes de Provence, poutargue et herbes en vinaigrette (spring). Pigeon rôti au vin des Baux, légumes à l'huile de noisette. Fruits rouges, rhubarbe, vieux vinaigre balsamique et sorbet (summer). **Wines** Les Baux-de-Provence.
◆ Overlooking the old town, this beautiful abode has a large shaded upstairs terrace with teak furniture and a roof of local tiles. Delicious modern Provençal cuisine.

Alain Assaud
13 bd Marceau – 04 90 92 37 11 – Open 15 March-15 November and closed Thursday lunch, Saturday lunch and Wednesday Y **a**
Rest – Menu €28/44 – Carte €45/65
◆ Pleasant rustic style restaurant (exposed stone and beams, paintings, old clock) with a country buffet and traditional food menu with a southern French touch.

Le Bistrot Découverte
19 bd Victor Hugo – 04 90 92 34 49 – www.bistrotdecouverte.com – Fax 04 32 61 09 77 – Closed January, Sunday dinner except July-August and Monday
Rest – Menu (€16), €30 – Carte €32/52 Z **e**
◆ The characterful bistro and veranda-terrace serve traditional Provençal dishes. Splendid stone vaulted cellar with a fine wine list to be sampled on the spot or taken home.

L'Aile ou la Cuisse
5 r. Commune – 04 32 62 00 25 – laileoulacuisse@orange.fr – Fax 04 32 62 00 25 – Closed 3 January-16 February, Sunday from October to June and Monday Z **g**
Rest – Menu (€19) – Carte €47/67 dinner only
◆ Set in the refectory of a former convent, this restaurant has a lot of appeal. Find a chic, refined interior, superb patio terrace, tasty bistro cuisine and pastries on sale.

at Domaine de Bournissac 11 km by ②, D 30 and D 29 – ✉ 13550 Paluds-des-Noves

La Maison de Bournissac (Christian Peyre)
montée d'Eyragues – ☎ 04 90 90 25 25 – www.lamaison-a-bournissac.com – bournissac@wanadoo.fr – Fax 04 90 90 25 26 – Closed 3 January-10 February
13 rm – †€ 145/190 ††€ 145/190, ☕ € 17 – 3 suites
Rest – *(closed Monday and Tuesday from October to April)* Menu € 45/120 – Carte € 85/115
Spec. Foie gras de canard en trois façons (Sep. to Dec.). Rouget barbet, raviole d'olive taggiasche et encornet à la plancha (Sep. to Dec.). Chocolat araguani et poire, croustillant au praliné. **Wines** Côtes du Luberon, Les Baux-de-Provence.
◆ This old farmhouse, standing on a hillside amid vineyards and olive groves, overlooks the Lubéron, Alpilles and Ventoux. Snug sitting rooms and romantic bedrooms. Regional gourmet fare, warmly decorated dining room and terraces (one on a patio shaded by fig trees).

in Verquières 11 km by ②, D 30 and D 29 – **pop. 786 – alt. 48 m** – ✉ **13670**

Le Croque Chou
pl. de l'Église – ☎ 04 90 95 18 55 – www.le-croque-chou.fr – folzfamily@le-croque-chou.fr – Closed Tuesday lunch from 15 June to 15 September, Sunday dinner and Wednesday dinner from 15 September to 15 June and Monday
Rest – *(pre-book)* Menu € 22/80 bi – Carte € 54/88
◆ Old ivy clad sheepcote serving inventive, sun drenched dishes made from high quality produce. Countrified interior and tree-lined terrace.

via ④ **4,5 km and Les Baux road D 27** – ✉ **13210 St-Rémy-de-Provence**

Domaine de Valmouriane
– ☎ 04 90 92 44 62 – www.valmouriane.com – info@valmouriane.com – Fax 04 90 92 37 32 – Closed 17 November-4 December and 5 January-5 February
13 rm – †€ 145/320 ††€ 145/320, ☕ € 18 – 1 suite
Rest – Menu € 30 (lunch), € 55/80 – Carte € 40/60
◆ This comfortable farmhouse amid pine trees lies at the foot of the Alpilles. Bar with piano and fireplace, spacious, period furnished rooms. Wellness centre (open-air massages). Vaulted, colourful dining room serving up-to-date and theme cuisine.

in Maillane 7 km Northwest by D 5 – **pop. 2 013 – alt. 14 m** – ✉ **13910**

L'Oustalet Maïanen
– ☎ 04 90 95 74 60 – www.oustaletmaianen.com – contact@oustaletmaianen.com – Fax 04 90 95 76 17 – Closed 23 June-2 July, November to January, Tuesday lunch in July-August, Saturday lunch from April to September, Sunday dinner except July-August, Tuesday and Wednesday
Rest – Menu (€ 19), € 27/40 – Carte € 38/60
◆ A pleasant restaurant opposite the former home of the poet Mistral. Provençal dining room, arboured terrace and tasty regional cuisine.

ST-RÉMY-DU-PLAIN – 35 Ille-et-Vilaine – 309 M4 – pop. 698 – alt. 108 m – ✉ 35560

10 **D2**

Paris 383 – Rennes 38 – Saint-Malo 58 – Fougères 40 – Vitré 44

La Haye d'Irée
1.5 km south on D 90 and D 12 – ☎ 02 99 73 62 07 – www.chateaubreton.com – m.deprevoisin@orange.fr – Open April-October
4 rm ☕ – †€ 60/70 ††€ 85/115 **Table d'hôte** – Menu € 20/25
◆ This granite house set in a large garden (lake, pool and rose garden) has an old fashioned atmosphere: lounge with fireplace, stonework, beams and antique filled rooms. Traditional meals (reservation required) served in a rustic dining room.

ST-RIQUIER – 80 Somme – 301 E7 – see Abbeville

ST-ROMAIN – 21 Côte-d'Or – **320** I8 – **pop. 243** – **alt. 350 m** – ✉ **21190** 7 **A3**

▶ Paris 330 – Dijon 59 – Chalon-sur-Saône 41 – Le Creusot 50 – Beaune 13

X **Les Roches** with rm VISA

pl. de la Mairie – ☎ 03 80 21 21 63 – www.les-roches.fr – lesroches.sarl@wanadoo.fr – Fax 03 80 21 66 93 – Closed 20 December-26 January, Monday and Tuesday

8 rm – €65 €65, ☕ €10 – ½ P €85

Rest – Carte €29/41

◆ Friendly establishment proposing well-prepared traditional and regional cuisine in a bistro setting. Simply-decorated rooms, practical for an overnight halt.

ST-ROMAIN-LE-PUY – 42 Loire – **327** D6 – **see Montbrison**

ST-ROME-DE-TARN – 12 Aveyron – **338** J6 – **pop. 817** – **alt. 360 m** 29 **D2**

▶ Paris 660 – Millau 21 – Rodez 68 – Toulouse 170

ℹ Syndicat d'initiative, place du Terral ☎ 05 65 62 50 89, Fax 05 65 58 44 00

Les Raspes rm, VISA

av. Denis Affre – ☎ 05 65 58 11 44 – www.aveyron.com-hebergement.hotel – lesraspes@wanadoo.fr – Fax 05 65 58 11 45 – Closed 26 October-4 November

16 rm – €65/70 €75/95, ☕ €9 – ½ P €70/85

Rest – *(Closed Sunday dinner from October to May, Saturday lunch and Monday)* Menu €20/49 – Carte €25/65

◆ This traditional stone house in the high-perched village was originally a convent. Today its cells are cosy, well-cared for elegant rooms. Attractive dining room and terrace, where guests enjoy local dishes with a southern accent.

ST-SATUR – 18 Cher – **323** N2 – **see Sancerre**

ST-SATURNIN – 63 Puy-de-Dôme – **326** F9 – **pop. 1 115** – **alt. 520 m** – ✉ **63450** Auvergne 5 **B2**

▶ Paris 438 – Clermont-Ferrand 24 – Cournon-d'Auvergne 18 – Riom 37 – Chamalières 25

Château de Saint-Saturnin P VISA

– ☎ 04 73 39 39 64 – www.chateaudesaintsaturnin.com – chateaudesaintsaturnin@yahoo.fr – Fax 04 73 39 30 86 – Open 27 March-8 November

5 rm – €150/210 €150/210, ☕ €15 **Table d'hôte** – Menu €42 bi/54 bi

◆ Step back in time to the Middle Ages in this 13C château that dominates the village. Refined rooms and suites (Duchess, Louis III) furnished with antiques. Regionally-inspired bourgeois cooking served to guests in the evenings in a vaulted dining room.

ST-SATURNIN – 72 Sarthe – **310** J6 – **see Le Mans**

ST-SATURNIN-DE-LUCIAN – 34 Hérault – **339** F6 – **see Clermont-l'Hérault**

ST-SATURNIN-LÈS-APT – 84 Vaucluse – **332** F10 – **pop. 2 479** – **alt. 420 m** – ✉ **84490** Provence 42 **E1**

▶ Paris 728 – Apt 9 – Avignon 55 – Carpentras 44 – Manosque 50

XXX **Domaine des Andéols** with rm rest, P VISA

D2 – ☎ 04 90 75 50 63 – www.domainedesandeols.com – info@domaine-des-andeols.com – Fax 04 90 75 43 22 – Open 12 February-14 November, 14 December-2 January and closed Tuesday lunch, Sunday dinner and Monday in low season

10 rm – €260/350 €645/1220, ☕ €25

Rest – Menu (€42), €53/95 – Carte €67/105

◆ A truly magical place in the heart of the Luberon. This establishment offers a designer setting with open kitchens, personalised apartments and an indoor pool with steam bath.

ST-SAUD-LACOUSSIÈRE – 24 Dordogne – **329** F2 – **pop. 861** 4 **C1**
– **alt. 370 m** – ✉ **24470**

Paris 443 – Brive-la-Gaillarde 105 – Châlus 23 – Limoges 57 – Nontron 16 – Périgueux 62

Hostellerie St-Jacques VISA AE
– ✆ *05 53 56 97 21 – hostellerie-st-jacques.com – hostellerie.st.jacques@wanadoo.fr – Fax 05 53 56 91 33 – Open 2 March-30 November and closed Monday lunch, Tuesday lunch, Wednesday lunch from 16 June to 14 September, Sunday evening, Monday and Tuesday from 15 September to 15 June*
12 rm – €80/210 €80/210, ☕ €13 – 1 suite
Rest – Menu (€28 bi), €40/80 – Carte €75/85
◆ Once a stopover on the old pilgrimage route to Santiago de Compostela, this hotel surrounded by greenery has delightful, individually furnished bedrooms, a swimming pool and a flower garden. Traditional cuisine, good wine list and shaded terrace.

ST-SAUVANT – 17 Charente-Maritime – **324** G5 – **see Saintes**

ST-SAUVES-D'AUVERGNE – 63 Puy-de-Dôme – **326** D9 – **see La Bourboule**

ST-SAUVEUR-DE-MONTAGUT – 07 Ardèche – **331** J5 44 **B3**
– **pop. 1 161** – **alt. 218 m** – ✉ **07190**

Paris 597 – Le Cheylard 24 – Lamastre 29 – Privas 24 – Valence 38
Syndicat d'initiative, quartier de la Tour ✆ 04 75 65 43 13, Fax 04 75 65 43 13

Le Montagut with rm VISA
pl. de l'Église – ✆ 04 75 65 40 31 – www.lemontagut.fr – lemontagut@orange.fr – Closed 14-30 June, Tuesday dinner, Sunday dinner and Monday except July-August
4 rm – €45 €45, ☕ €6
Rest – Menu (€16), €20 (weekdays)/40 – Carte €33/39
◆ Regional flavours on the menu at this family-run inn in an Ardèche village. Simply decorated dining room and a large terrace under a canopy. Small, functional rooms.

ST-SAVIN – 65 Hautes-Pyrénées – **342** L7 – **see Argelès-Gazost**

ST-SAVIN – 86 Vienne – **322** L5 – **pop. 913** – **alt. 76 m** – ✉ **86310** 39 **D1**
Atlantic Coast

Paris 344 – Poitiers 44 – Belac 62 – Châtellerault 48 – Montmorillon 19
Wall paintings ★★★ of the Abbey ★★.

De France rm, rest, VISA AE
38 pl. de la République – ✆ 05 49 48 19 03 – www.hoteldefrance86.fr – hotel-saint-savin@wanadoo.fr – Fax 05 49 48 97 07 – Closed 21 December-5 January
11 rm – €48 €48, ☕ €7 – ½ P €45
Rest – *(Closed Saturday except dinner in July-August and Sunday)* Menu (€13), €18/21 – Carte approx. €20
◆ This hotel is set in a country house on the village square. Practical, often spacious rooms, decorated with taste. Warm tones brighten this restaurant serving traditional and regional fare.

Christophe Cadieu VISA
15 r. de l'Abbaye – ✆ 05 49 48 17 69 – www.cadieu-86.com – restaurantcadieu@orange.fr – Fax 05 49 48 17 69 – Closed 15 June-2 July, 22 September-8 October, 5-21 January, Wednesday except lunch from May to October, Sunday dinner and Monday
Rest – Menu (€22), €40/70
Spec. Foie gras de canard confit. Homard, ris de veau ou lapin du Poitou. (according to the season). Chocolat ou fruit. **Wines** Touraine, Vin de Pays de la Vienne.
◆ This converted barn near the abbey is now a comfortable restaurant with a pleasant rustic atmosphere, pretty tables and appetising modern cuisine.

ST-SEINE-L'ABBAYE – 21 Côte-d'Or – 320 I5 – pop. 365 – alt. 451 m 8 C2
– ✉ 21440 Burgundy-Jura

Paris 289 – Autun 78 – Dijon 28 – Châtillon-sur-Seine 57 – Montbard 48

Office de tourisme, place de l'Église ☎ 03 80 35 07 63, Fax 03 80 35 07 63

Dolce Chantilly Salives Larçon, N : 32 km on D 16, ☎ 03 80 75 68 54

La Poste rm,

17 r. Carnot – ☎ 03 80 35 00 35 – www.postesoleildor.fr – contact@postesoleildor.fr – Fax 03 80 35 07 64 – Closed 20 December-3 January and Sunday

15 rm – €58/78 €66/88, €10

Rest – *(dinner only)* Menu €20, €30/35 bi – Carte €28/45

◆ Louis XIV is said to have stayed in this former post house, appreciated for its peaceful shaded garden. Relatively spacious rooms (refurbishing in progress), pool. The restaurant, adorned with a fine fireplace, has retained all its rustic character. Traditional cuisine.

ST-SERNIN-DU-BOIS – 71 Saône-et-Loire – 320 G8 – see Le Creusot

ST-SERNIN-SUR-RANCE – 12 Aveyron – 338 H7 – pop. 530 29 D2
– alt. 300 m – ✉ 12380 Languedoc-Roussillon-Tarn Gorges

Paris 694 – Albi 50 – Castres 69 – Lacaune 29 – Rodez 83 – St-Affrique 32

Syndicat d'initiative, avenue d'Albi ☎ 05 65 99 29 13, Fax 05 65 97 60 77

Carayon

pl. du Fort – ☎ 05 65 98 19 19 – www.hotel-carayon.com – contact@hotel-carayon.fr – Fax 05 65 99 69 26 – Closed Tuesday lunch, Sunday evening, Monday except July-August and public holidays

74 rm – €39/77 €39/116, €8 – ½ P €48/86

Rest – Menu €15 (weekdays)/54 bi – Carte €23/46

◆ Several types of room in this hotel offering numerous leisure activities, the majority in the main building, the rest in various outbuildings within the grounds (dovecote, fisherman's house, chalet and pavilion). Copious local cuisine is served in two bright and spacious dining rooms or on the terrace.

ST-SERVAN-SUR-MER – 35 Ille-et-Vilaine – 309 K3 – see St-Malo

ST-SEURIN-DE-CADOURNE – 33 Gironde – 335 G3 – pop. 767 3 B1
– alt. 10 m – ✉ 33180

Paris 623 – Bordeaux 65 – Saint-Médard-en-Jalles 55 – Le Bouscat 61 – Eysines 56

Syndicat d'initiative, espace Paul Daumains ☎ 05 56 59 84 14, Fax 05.53.94.77.63

Réal

6 r. Clément-Lemaignan – ☎ 05 56 59 31 04 – http://perso.orange.fr/real-en-medoc – real-en-medoc@wanadoo.fr – Fax 05 56 59 31 04

5 rm – €56 €66 **Table d'hôte** – Menu €25 bi

◆ Peaceful grounds planted with ancient trees surround this delightful family home, a former wine estate. Cosy guestrooms. Bread oven, iconography workshop. Traditional table d'hôte and regional wines in a bourgeois decor.

ST-SEURIN-D'UZET – 17 Charente-Maritime – 324 F6 – pop. 572 38 B3
– alt. 47 m – ✉ 17120

Paris 516 – Poitiers 183 – La Rochelle 113 – Rochefort 67 – Saintes 49

Blue Sturgeon

3 r. de la Cave – ☎ 05 46 74 17 18 – www.bluesturgeon.com – reservations@bluesturgeon.com – Open from March to October

5 rm – €95/120 €95/120 **Table d'hôte** – Menu €35/95

◆ The English owner, an interior decorator, has skilfully restored this 17C wine-grower's barn. A happy blend of old and new including a number of "home-made" paintings, garden and small lake. Splendid high ceilings and painted beams set the scene in the dining room.

ST-SIFFRET – 30 Gard – 339 L4 – see Uzès

ST-SILVAIN-BELLEGARDE – 23 Creuse – 325 K5 – pop. 220 – alt. 535 m – ✉ 23190 25 D1

Paris 413 – Limoges 148 – Guéret 53 – Montluçon 75 – Ussel 66

Les Trois Ponts rm, P VISA MC

– *05 55 67 12 14 – www.lestroisponts.nl – info@lestroisponts.nl – Fax 05 55 67 12 14*

5 rm – €53 €80 **Table d'hôte** – Menu €28

◆ A Dutch couple have renovated this old mill on the banks of the Tardes, preserving its authenticity. Cosy bedrooms with a Provençal feel. Good choice of leisure facilities. A warm friendly atmosphere at the fine table d'hôte.

ST-SORLIN-D'ARVES – 73 Savoie – 333 K6 – pop. 333 – alt. 1 550 m – ✉ 73530 French Alps 45 C2

Paris 657 – Albertville 84 – Le Bourg-d'Oisans 50 – Chambéry 97 – St-Jean-de-Maurienne 22

Office de tourisme, Champ Rond 04 79 59 71 77, Fax 04 79 59 75 50

Site★ of St-Jean-d'Arves church Southeast: 2.5 km.

Col de la Croix de Fer ★★ West: 7.5 km then 15 mn - Col du Glandon ★ then Combe d'Olle★★ West: 10 km.

Beausoleil rest, P VISA MC AE

Le Pré – 04 79 59 71 42 – www.hotel-beausoleil.com – info@hotel-beausoleil.com – Fax 04 79 59 75 25 – Open 1st July-31 August and 20 December-18 April

21 rm (½ board only) – ½ P €69/81

Rest – Menu (€14), €20/29 – Carte €16/30

◆ This truly peaceful chalet stands at the foot of the ski runs, in the upper part of town. Refreshing, functional rooms. Dining room with a modern setting, panoramic terrace and Savoyard cuisine.

ST-SORNIN – 17 Charente-Maritime – 324 E5 – pop. 328 – alt. 16 m – ✉ 17600 Atlantic Coast 38 B2

Paris 500 – La Rochelle 56 – Poitiers 167 – Rochefort 26

La Caussolière without rest P

10 r. du Petit Moulin – 05 46 85 44 62 – www.caussoliere.com – reservations@caussoliere.com – Fax 05 46 85 44 62 – Open from March to October

4 rm – €60 €69

◆ This 19C farmhouse opens onto a magnificent garden with an ornamental pool. All the cosy rooms have a separate entrance. Friendly welcome.

ST-SULIAC – 35 Ille-et-Vilaine – 309 K3 – pop. 901 – alt. 30 m – ✉ 35430 Brittany 10 D1

Paris 396 – Rennes 62 – Saint-Malo 14 – Granville 87 – Dinan 26

La Ferme du Boucanier VISA MC

2 r. de l'Hôpital – 02 23 15 06 35 – simonpitou@wanadoo.fr – Fax 02 99 19 51 32 – Closed end December to early January, Wednesday except dinner from May to September, Thursday lunch in low season and Tuesday

Rest – Menu (€15), €28/40 – Carte €28/40

◆ Two restaurants in one: in summer, a 1940s room serving updated dishes full of spices; in winter, a regional decor with fireplace for spit roasts and rustic cuisine. A gourmet delight!

ST-SULPICE – 81 Tarn – 338 C8 – pop. 6 402 – alt. 112 m – ✉ 81370 29 C2

Paris 666 – Albi 46 – Castres 54 – Montauban 44 – Toulouse 32

Office de tourisme, parc Georges Spenale 05 63 41 89 50, Fax 05 63 40 23 30

de Palmola Buzet-sur-Tarn Route d'Albi, W : 9 km on N 88, 05 61 84 20 50

XX **Auberge de la Pointe**

D 988 – ☎ 05 63 41 80 14 – www.aubergelapointechabbert.com – chabbert.patrick@wanadoo.fr – Fax 05 63 41 90 24 – Closed 28 September-16 October, 4-22 January, Thursday lunch in July-August, Tuesday dinner from September to June, Sunday dinner and Wednesday

Rest – Menu (€ 16), € 23/46 – Carte € 33/50

◆ Old coaching inn with a pink façade and fine rustic interior. Inviting, shady terrace overlooking the Tarn. Traditional cuisine.

ST-SULPICE-LE-VERDON – 85 Vendée – 316 H6 – pop. 701 – alt. 65 m – ✉ 85260 Atlantic Coast

34 **B3**

Paris 430 – Nantes 45 – Angers 130 – Cholet 51 – La Roche-sur-Yon 31

Office de tourisme, Logis de la Chabotterie ☎ 02 51 43 48 18

XXX **Thierry Drapeau Logis de la Chabotterie**

– ☎ 02 51 09 59 31 – www.restaurant-thierrydrapeau.com – restaurant.thierrydrapeau@wanadoo.fr – Fax 02 51 09 59 27 – Closed 30 June-13 July, 27 October-9 November, 26-30 December, Sunday dinner, Tuesday dinner and Monday

Rest – Menu (€ 37 bi), € 62/115 bi – Carte € 68/81

Spec. Homard poêlé au beurre demi-sel. Poularde sauce albufera, sushi de légumes de pot-au-feu et foie gras. Framboises et glace à la crème brulée (May to Sep.). **Wines** Fiefs Vendéens Vix.

◆ Within the walls of a residence/museum close to where the Vendée war ended, you will find delicious modern cuisine in a rustic, timber framed setting.

ST-SULPICE-SUR-LÈZE – 31 Haute-Garonne – 343 F5 – pop. 1 771 – alt. 200 m – ✉ 31410

28 **B2**

Paris 709 – Auterive 14 – Foix 53 – St-Gaudens 66 – Toulouse 36

XX **La Commanderie**

pl. Hôtel de Ville – ☎ 05 61 97 33 61 – www.lacommanderie.venez.fr – la-commanderie2@wanadoo.fr – Fax 05 61 97 32 60 – Closed for the Toussaint holiday, 23-30 December, February holiday, Tuesday and Wednesday

Rest – Menu € 21 (weekday lunch), € 35/60

◆ Fine decor mixing ancient and modern, friendly service and a subtle combination of flavours on the menu, in a former 13C Templar building.

ST-SYLVESTRE-CAPPEL – 59 Nord – 302 C3 – see Cassel

ST-SYMPHORIEN – 72 Sarthe – 310 I6 – pop. 532 – alt. 135 m – ✉ 72240

35 **C1**

Paris 231 – Laval 65 – Le Mans 28 – Nantes 201

X **Relais de la Charnie**

4 pl. Louis des Cars – ☎ 02 43 20 72 06 – relais.charnie@wanadoo.fr – Fax 02 43 20 70 59 – Closed 27 July-10 August, 15-22 February, Sunday dinner and Monday

Rest – Menu € 16/26 – Carte € 30/52

◆ The rustic dining room of this former post house has a slightly old world atmosphere and is graced by beams and a big fireplace. Traditional cuisine.

ST-THÉGONNEC – 29 Finistère – 308 H3 – pop. 2 562 – alt. 83 m – ✉ 29410 Brittany

9 **B1**

Paris 549 – Brest 50 – Châteaulin 50 – Morlaix 13 – Quimper 70 – St-Pol-de-Léon 28

Parish enclosure★★ - Guimiliau: Parish enclosure ★★, Southwest: 7,5 km.

Auberge St-Thégonnec

6 pl. de la Mairie – ✆ 02 98 79 61 18 – www.aubergesaintthegonnec.com – contact@aubergesaintthegonnec.com – Fax 02 98 62 71 10 – Closed 19 December-10 January and Sunday from September to March

19 rm – †€ 75/95 ††€ 85/110, ☕ € 11 – ½ P € 75/95

Rest – Menu (€ 22), € 26 (weekdays)/46 – Carte € 50/60

◆ A Breton establishment facing the church and its famous enclosure. Modern rooms, most overlooking the garden. Carefully prepared traditional dishes and a regionally inspired decor of furniture and paintings at the restaurant.

Ar Presbital Koz

18 r. Lividic – ✆ 02 98 79 45 62 – http://ar.presbital.koz.free.fr – ar.presbital.koz@orange.fr – Fax 02 98 79 48 47

5 rm ☕ – †€ 47 ††€ 55 – ½ P € 44

Table d'hôte – *(closed 10 July-20 August, Sunday and public holidays)*

Menu € 22 bi

◆ This former presbytery (1750) is certainly peaceful. The cosy good-sized rooms have been carefully decorated by the landlord. Traditional cuisine with a subtly spicy twist. Table d'hôte menu.

ST-THIBAULT – 18 Cher – **323** N2 – see Sancerre

ST-THIERRY – 51 Marne – 306 F7 – pop. 572 – alt. 140 m – ✉ 51220 13 B2

Paris 149 – Châlons-en-Champagne 64 – Reims 18 – Soissons 66 – Laon 43

Le Clos du Mont d'Hor without rest

8 r. du Mont-d' Hor – ✆ 03 26 03 12 42 – www.mhchampagne.com – info@mhchampagne.com – Fax 03 26 03 02 80

6 rm – †€ 90 ††€ 90, ☕ € 7

◆ Discover the secrets of champagne in this beautiful restored farmhouse surrounded by vineyards. Comfortable (split level) rooms decorated on a travel theme.

ST-THOMÉ – 07 Ardèche – 331 J6 – pop. 386 – alt. 140 m – ✉ 07220 44 B3

Paris 628 – Lyon 165 – Privas 46 – Montélimar 19 – Orange 59

La Bastide Bernard without rest

at Chasser, 1.5 km south-east on D 107 – ✆ 06 83 34 60 54 – www.bastidebernard.com – bastide@bastidebernard.com – Fax 04 75 96 45 34 – Closed 20 December-5 January and 1 week in March

4 rm ☕ – †€ 50/75 ††€ 85

◆ This hillside house commands a fine view over Saint Thomé. Uncluttered, spacious, light rooms. Pleasant breakfast terrace and pool with sun loungers.

ST-TROJAN-LES-BAINS – 17 Charente-Maritime – **324** C4 – see île d'Oléron

---

ST-TROPEZ – 83 Var – 340 O6 – pop. 5 635 – alt. 4 m – ✉ 83990 41 C3

French Riviera

Paris 872 – Aix-en-Provence 123 – Cannes 73 – Draguignan 47 – Fréjus 34 – Toulon 69

Office de tourisme, 40, rue Gambetta ✆ 08 92 68 48 28, Fax 04 94 55 98 59

de Sainte-Maxime Sainte-Maxime Route du Débarquement, 16 km on the Ste-Maxime road, ✆ 04 94 55 02 02

Gassin Golf Country Club Gassin Route de Ramatuelle, S : 9 km on D 93, ✆ 04 94 55 13 44

Harbour★★ - Musée de l'Annonciade★★ - Môle Jean Réveille ≤★ - Citadel★: ≤★ of the ramparts, ✻★★ of the musée de la Citadelle - Ste-Anne chapel ≤★ South: 1 km via av. P. Roussel.

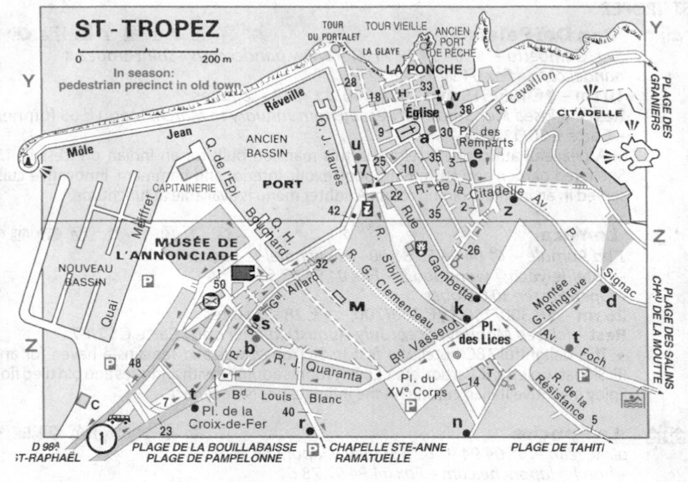

Aire du Chemin (R.)	Y	2	Herbes (Pl. aux)	Y	17	Péri (Quai Gabriel)	Z	32
Aumale (Bd d')	Y	3	Hôtel de ville (Pl. de l')	Y	18	Ponche (R. de la)	Y	33
Belle Isnarde (Rte de la)	Z	5	Laugier (R. V.)	Y	22	Portail Neuf (R. du)	YZ	35
Blanqui (Pl. Auguste)	Z	7	Leclerc (Av. Général)	Z	23	Remparts (R. des)	Y	38
Clocher (R. du)	Y	9	Marché (R. du)	Y	25	Roussel (Av. Paul)	Z	40
Commerçants (R. des)	Y	10	Miséricorde (R.)	Z	26	Suffren (Quai)	Y	42
Grangeon (Av.)	Z	14	Mistral (Quai Frédéric)	Y	28	8-Mai-1945 (Av. du)	Z	48
Guichard (R. du Cdt)	Y	15	Ormeau (Pl. de l')	Y	30	11-Novembre (Av. du)	Z	50

Byblos
av. P. Signac – ✆ 04 94 56 68 00 – www.byblos.com – saint-tropez@byblos.com – Fax 04 94 56 68 01 – Open 9 April-1st November Z **d**
51 rm – €325/500 €420/900, ☕ €36 – 44 suites
Rest *Spoon-Byblos* – see below
Rest *Le B* – *✆ 04 94 56 68 19 (closed Sunday and Monday except July-August) (dinner only)* Menu €52 – Carte €53/82
◆ A hamlet of colourful houses dotted around gardens and patios, this luxurious Provençal village is one of St Tropez's most exclusive hotels. Sumptuous spa. The 'B' specialises in up-to-the-minute cuisine (finger food and tapas at dinner), served around an indoor poolside terrace. Luxury combined with a relaxed, friendly ambience.

Résidence de la Pinède
1 km via ①, at Bouillabaisse beach – ✆ 04 94 55 91 00 – www.residencepinede.com – reservation@residencepinede.com – Fax 04 94 97 73 64 – Open 10 April-18 October
35 rm – €395/1335 €395/1335, ☕ €28 – 4 suites
Rest – *(dinner only)* Menu €95, €150/210 – Carte €130/200
Spec. Déclinaison sur les légumes varois (season). Pagre cuit à l'unilatérale, gamberoni et ormeaux rôtis. Accord pomme verte-combava. **Wines** Palette, Bellet.
◆ This elegant seaside abode combines luxury and well being. Cosy, individually decorated rooms. Private beach and jetty. Fine contemporary cuisine served in a quietly refined dining room or on the shaded terrace opposite the ocean.

La Bastide de St-Tropez
Carles road: 1 km on av. P. Roussel – ✆ 04 94 55 82 55 – www.bastide-saint-tropez.com – contact@bastidesaint-tropez.com – Fax 04 94 97 21 71 – Closed 2 January-12 February
18 rm – €247/651 €247/651, ☕ €28 – 8 suites **Rest** – Menu €55/80
◆ Elegant St Tropez house and four farmsteads set in a beautifully quiet, lush green Mediterranean garden (lovely pool). Tastefully decorated rooms with terrace or balcony. Classical decor and modern cuisine in the restaurant with veranda, facing greenery.

Pan Deï Palais
52 r. Gambetta – ✆ 04 94 17 71 71 – www.pandei.com – saint-tropez@pandei.com – Fax 04 94 17 71 72 Z **v**
10 rm – €195/515 €195/1040, €32 – 2 suites
Rest – *(closed Monday and Tuesday from January to March)* Menu €65 (dinner) – Carte €50/110
◆ A peaceful atmosphere reigns in this mansion built for an Indian princess in 1835. Sheltered garden and swimming pool, exotic interior and hammam. Innovative cuisine served in an intimate dining room. A lighter menu is available at lunchtime.

Le Yaca
1 bd Aumale – ✆ 04 94 55 81 00 – www.hotel-le-yaca.fr – hotel-le-yaca@wanadoo.fr – Fax 04 94 97 58 50 – Open Easter-30 October Y **e**
26 rm – €300/700 €300/700, €28 – 2 suites
Rest – *(closed Monday except July-August) (dinner only)* Carte €57/87
◆ This delightful 18C hotel, the first in St Tropez, was and remains a haven for artists (P. Signac, Colette, B. Bardot, etc.). Lovely rooms adorned with antiques and old tiled floors. Enjoy inventive Italian cuisine on the intimate poolside terrace.

La Ponche
pl. Révelin – ✆ 04 94 97 02 53 – www.laponche.com – hotel@laponche.com – Fax 04 94 97 78 61 – Open 15 February-1st November Y **v**
17 rm – €145/300 €170/490, €19 – 1 suite
Rest – Menu €27 (lunch)/40 – Carte €45/85
◆ Romy Schneider and many other celebrities stayed in this charming hotel. It is made up of colourful old fishermen's houses in the picturesque Ponche district. Provence can be felt in the decor and dishes of this restaurant. Terrace.

Y without rest
av. Paul Signac – ✆ 04 94 55 55 15 – hotel-le-yaca.fr – hotel-le-y@wanadoo.fr – Fax 04 94 55 55 19 – Closed 14 April-21 May, 30 October-26 December and 3-31 January Z **d**
11 rm – €295/525 €295/525, €28 – 2 suites
◆ This Provençal building is at the foot of the citadel. It houses very comfortable modern rooms with 1960s inspired furniture designed by Gio Ponti.

Domaine de l'Astragale
1,5 km by ①, chemin de la Gassine ✉ 83580 Gassin – ✆ 04 94 97 48 98 – www.lastragale.com – message@lastragale.com – Fax 04 94 97 16 01 – Open mid-May to end September
rm, rm,
50 rm – €310/455 €310/455, €21 – 16 suites
Rest – Menu €56 – Carte €60/85
◆ Villa with colourful extensions set around two pools. Spacious rooms with balcony or terrace. New suites, some with a Jacuzzi. Traditional cuisine served in a small, elegant dining room or under an open-air pavilion.

La Mistralée
1 av. Gén. Leclerc – ✆ 04 98 12 91 12 – www.hotel-mistralee.fr – contact@hotel-mistralee.fr – Fax 04 94 43 48 43 Z **t**
8 rm – €190/790 €190/790, €25 – 2 suites
Rest – *(closed 10 October-30 April except week-end)* Carte €30/98
◆ Former pied-à-terre of Alexandre, hairdresser to the stars, this villa (1850) surrounded by a garden, retains the Baroque style he favoured decorated guestrooms. Individually (Morocco, Chanel, etc.). Restaurant serving Provençal and oriental cuisine in a classical dining room.

La Maison Blanche without rest
pl. des Lices – ✆ 04 94 97 52 66 – www.hotellamaisonblanche.com – Fax 04 94 97 89 23 – Closed February Z **k**
9 rm – €180/890 €180/890, €32
◆ Far from the madding St Tropez crowds, this characterful house is home to predominantly white, romantic rooms. Champagne bar lounge and exquisite terrace.

Pastis without rest
61 av. Gén. Leclerc, via ① – ✆ 04 98 12 56 50 – www.pastis-st-tropez.com – reception@pastis-st-tropez.com – Fax 04 94 96 99 82 – Closed 30 November-27 December
9 rm – †€ 150/600 ††€ 175/600, ☕ € 20
◆ Antique, Provençal and contemporary furnishings and objets d'art: each room of this hotel is unique. Those overlooking the pool and palm trees in the garden are quieter.

Le Mandala without rest
av. P. Signac – ✆ 04 94 97 68 22 – /www.lemandala.net – contact@lemandala.net – Fax 04 94 97 77 48 Z **a**
12 rm – †€ 190/490 ††€ 190/690, ☕ € 25 – 1 suite
◆ Hotel in the spirit of the times with contemporary design, clean lines, white and grey tones and minimalist ambience. Landscaped terrace and small swimming pool.

Des Lices without rest
av. Augustin Grangeon – ✆ 04 94 97 28 28 – www.hoteldeslices.com – contact@hoteldeslices.com – Fax 04 94 97 59 52 – Open 28 March-11 November and 29 December-6 January Z **n**
42 rm – †€ 95/305 ††€ 140/380, ☕ € 16
◆ Near Place des Lices, this family-run establishment has kept pace with contemporary fashions. An updated Provençal style prevails in the rooms.

La Bastide du Port without rest
port du Pilon, via ① – ✆ 04 94 97 87 95 – www.bastideduport.com – bastide-du-port@wanadoo.fr – Fax 04 94 97 91 00 – 1st April-5 November
27 rm – †€ 135/185 ††€ 145/200, ☕ € 12
◆ This immense hotel near the town centre offers light, fresh rooms either overlooking the sea or in the rear for more peace and quiet. Breakfast on the terrace in summertime.

Mouillage without rest
port du Pilon, via ① – ✆ 04 94 97 53 19 – www.hotelmouillage.fr – contact@hotelmouillage.fr – Fax 04 94 97 50 31 – Closed mid November-mid December
12 rm – †€ 100/240 ††€ 100/240, ☕ € 17
◆ Drop anchor just a cable's length from Pilon harbour in this hotel decorated in warm Provençal colours. Rooms pay tribute to travel (Morocco, Asia, etc.).

Playa without rest
57 r. Allard – ✆ 04 98 12 94 44 – www.playahotelsttropez.com – playahotel@aol.com – Fax 04 98 12 94 45 – Open from March to October Z **s**
16 rm – †€ 95/134 ††€ 95/247, ☕ € 10
◆ Stunningly located establishment in the heart of St Tropez. Comfortable rooms, decorated in southern colours; those to the rear are quieter.

Lou Cagnard without rest
av. P. Roussel – ✆ 04 94 97 04 24 – www.hotel-lou-cagnard.com – Fax 04 94 97 09 44 – Closed 1st November-27 December Z **r**
19 rm – †€ 54/67 ††€ 65/130, ☕ € 10
◆ This ancient St Tropez house, two minutes from the centre, offers colourful Provençal-style rooms. In summer, breakfast is served in the shade of the mulberry trees.

Spoon Byblos – Hôtel Byblos
av. du Mar. Foch – ✆ 04 94 56 68 20 – www.byblos.com – saint-tropez@byblos.com – Fax 04 94 56 68 01 – Open 10 April-26 October Z **t**
Rest – *(closed Tuesday and Wednesday off season) (dinner only)* Menu € 89 – Carte € 60/122
◆ Welcome to the Mediterranean version of the Parisian 'Spoon', Ducasse's playful concept. Designer decor and soft lighting set the stage for creative cuisine. World wine list.

Le Girelier
quai Jean-Jaurès – ✆ 04 94 97 03 87 – www.legirelier.fr – aimestoesser@hotmail.fr – Fax 04 94 97 43 86 – Open 15 March-30 October Y **u**
Rest – Menu € 39 – Carte € 70/95
◆ Perfect to watch the yachts in the busy marina, this recently refurbished, modern brasserie specialises in seafood and shellfish.

L'Auberge des Maures VISA MC AE
4 r. du Dr-Boutin – ✆ 04 94 97 01 50 – www.aubergedesmaures.com – aubergedesmaures@wanadoo.fr – Fax 04 94 97 67 24 – Open 2 March-29 November
Rest – *(dinner only)* Menu € 49 – Carte € 55/78 Z **b**
◆ Two steps from old harbour, the rustic inspired, regularly spruced-up decor of this welcoming inn is quite striking. Regionally inspired cuisine.

Le Banh Hoï AC VISA MC AE
12 r. Petit St-Jean – ✆ 04 94 97 36 29 – banh-hoi@wanadoo.fr – Fax 04 98 12 91 47 – Open 3 April-4 October Y **a**
Rest – *(dinner only)* Carte € 58/75
◆ Dimmed lighting, walls and ceiling painted with black lacquer, and Asian decorative objects make up the setting of this house where you will be offered Vietnamese and Thai cuisine.

South-East by Avenue Foch - Z – ✉ **83990 St-Tropez**

La Tartane Saint-Amour AC P VISA MC AE
Salins road – ✆ 04 94 97 21 23 – www.hotel-latartane.com – reservations@latartane.fr – Fax 04 94 97 09 16 – Open Easter-14 October
24 rm – €275/460 €315/935, ☕ €29 – 4 suites **Rest** – Carte € 60/110
◆ The ideal spot to recharge flagging batteries: tastefully decorated rooms (on African, seaside, etc. themes), pool and small spa. Asian specialities in a fashionable Baroque decor, up-to-date menu on the terrace and sushi bar with evening drinks.

Benkiraï AC P VISA MC AE
11 chemin du Pinet, at 3 km – ✆ 04 94 97 04 37 – www.hotel-benkirai.com – info@hotel-benkirai.com – Fax 04 94 97 04 98 – Open beg. April-mid October
39 rm – €240/650 €240/650, ☕ €25 **Rest** – Carte € 55/80
◆ Studied modernity sums up the decor, the work of designer Patrick Jouin. Sleek bedrooms with open-plan bathrooms. Distinctive contemporary dining room and poolside terrace serving Thai cuisine.

La Bastide des Salins without rest AC P VISA MC
chemin des Salins, 4 km – ✆ 04 94 97 24 57 – www.bastidedessalins.com – info@labastidedessalins.com – Fax 04 94 54 89 03 – Open from March to October
14 rm – €200/700 €200/700, ☕ €27
◆ This venerable, welcoming country house combines the appeal of a secluded, tree-lined flower garden and delightful Provençal rooms. Lovely poolside terrace.

South-East by Avenue Paul Roussel and Tahiti road

Château de la Messardière rm, AC rest, P VISA MC AE
2 km on ✉ 83990 – ✆ 04 94 56 76 00 – www.messardiere.com – hotel@messardiere.com – Fax 04 94 56 76 01 – Open 21 March-3 November
75 rm – €240/840 €240/840, ☕ €25 – 40 suites
Rest – *(closed Monday dinner except from June to August)* Menu € 50 (lunch)/105 – Carte € 62/99
◆ In a 10ha pinewood overlooking the bay, this 19C château and luxurious villas are grouped around a patio. Ochre colours and oriental touches. Beauty therapy and swimming pool. Elegant Provençal dining room and superb panoramic terrace facing the sea. Up-to-date menu.

Ferme d'Augustin without rest AC P VISA MC AE
plage de Tahiti, 4 km ✉ 83350 Ramatuelle – ✆ 04 94 55 97 00 – www.fermeaugustin.com – info@fermeaugustin.com – Fax 04 94 97 59 76 – Open April-October
46 rm – €120/660 €165/660, ☕ €14
◆ This quiet, family establishment in a rustic Provençal-style is 100m from Tahiti beach. The rooms are in several houses dotted around the garden. Snacks available.

St-Vincent rm, AC rm, P VISA MC AE
4 km ✉ 83350 – ✆ 04 94 97 36 90 – www.hotelsaintvincent.com – hotelsaintvincent@wanadoo.fr – Fax 04 94 54 80 37 – Open 2 April-11 October
20 rm ☕ – €130/170 €170/250
Rest – swimming pool rest. – *(open 1st May-15 September)* Carte € 33/45
◆ In the peaceful setting of a vineyard, four Provençal houses decorated with oleanders. Spacious rooms some with terrace. Beautiful garden. Sun flavoured recipes, grilled food and salads served by the pool.

Mas Bellevue rm, VISA

2 km ✉ 83990 – ☎ 04 94 97 07 21 – www.masbellevue.com – masbellevue@wanadoo.fr – Fax 04 94 97 61 07 – Open 4 April-2 November
47 rm – €95/495 €95/495 – ½ P €80/280
Rest – swimming pool rest. – Carte €39/69
◆ Dominating the bay of Pampelonne, this Provençal farmhouse and bungalows are set in tranquil parkland. Choice of spacious rooms with balconies or gypsy caravans. Rustic dining room and terrace where a small menu is served at lunchtime and a more substantial choice is on offer for dinner.

La Figuière rm, rm, VISA

rte de Tahiti, 4 km ✉ 83350 – ☎ 04 94 97 18 21 – www.hotel-lafiguiere.com – la.figuiere@wanadoo.fr – Fax 04 94 97 68 48 – Open 2 April-4 October
41 rm – €110/150 €140/180, €15
Rest – swimming pool rest. – Carte €50/90
◆ On the coast road amid vineyards, this venerable Provençal farmhouse offers delightful rooms decorated with antiques (several duplex rooms). Poolside terrace shaded by mulberry trees serving simple traditional fare.

Ramatuelle road by ① and D 93le – ✉ **83350 Ramatuelle**

Villa Marie rm, VISA

chemin Val Rian – ☎ 04 94 97 40 22 – www.villamarie.fr – contact@villamarie.fr – Fax 04 94 97 37 55 – Open 25 April-5 October
42 rm – €350/1200 €350/1200, €31
Rest – Menu €90 (dinner) – Carte €60/150
◆ A refined and enchanting villa nestling in a pine forest overlooking Pampelonne Bay. Appealing, slightly Baroque restaurant in tones of beige with open kitchen, shaded terrace and sun-drenched cuisine.

La Romarine rm, rm, VISA

quartier des Marres, (Beach road), 3 km on via secondary road – ☎ 04 94 97 32 26 – www.hotel-laromarine.net – hromarine@aol.com – Fax 04 94 97 44 45 – Open 3 April-4 October
18 rm – €105/140 €160/235, €12 – 9 suites
Rest – swimming pool rest. – *(open July-August)* Carte €34/47
◆ This hacienda-style village hotel is set in a park designed for relaxation and leisure. It contains spacious rooms and villas, which are particularly well suited to families. Simple poolside meals served in July and August.

Les Bouis rm, rest, VISA

on secondary road – ☎ 04 94 79 87 61 – www.hotel-les-bouis.com – hotellesbouis@aol.com – Fax 04 94 79 85 20 – Open 25 March-15 September
23 rm – €170/218 €218/240, €14
Rest – swimming pool rest. – *(open 15 April-30 September) (lunch only) (residents only)* Carte €12/18
◆ Well located in the hinterland of St Tropez, this hotel set in pinewoods overlooks the sea. Spruce Provençal-style rooms with terrace or balcony. Home cooking and grilled meats served by the pool in season.

via ① **and secondary road** – ✉ **83580 Gassin**

Villa Belrose rm, VISA

bd des Crêtes, 3 km – ☎ 04 94 55 97 97 – www.villabelrose.com – info@villa-belrose.com – Fax 04 94 55 97 98 – Open 10 April-23 October
40 rm – €220/500 €280/890, €32 – 3 suites
Rest – *(closed lunch July-August)* Menu (€55), €95/125 – Carte €84/124
Spec. Légumes tendres d'une salade niçoise (season). Rougets dans la bouillabaisse (spring). Les grands crus de chocolat. **Wines** Côtes de Provence.
◆ Ideal location for this villa-hotel with three terraces facing the sea. Opulent interior and very comfortable rooms. Elegant restaurant in a Florentine style with a pleasant terrace overlooking the gulf. Up-to-date gourmet menu.

ST-UZE – **26 Drôme** – **332** C2 – see St-Vallier

ST-VAAST-LA-HOUGUE – 50 Manche – 303 E2 – pop. 2 080 – alt. 4 m – ✉ 50550 Normandy 32 A1

Paris 347 – Carentan 41 – Cherbourg 31 – St-Lô 68 – Valognes 19

Office de tourisme, 1, place Général de Gaulle ☎ 02 33 23 19 32, Fax 02 33 54 41 37

La Granitière without rest

74 r. Mar. Foch – ☎ 02 33 54 58 99 – www.hotel-la-granitiere.com – contact@hotel-la-granitiere.com – Fax 02 33 20 34 91

9 rm – €57/108 €75/108, €10

◆ A resort and a fishing village, "St-Va" is home to this fine old house of grey granite where you will really feel at home. Individually styled rooms and cosy lounge.

France et Fuchsias rest, VISA

20 r. Mar. Foch – ☎ 02 33 54 40 41 – www.france-fuchsias.com – reception@france-fuchsias.com – Fax 02 33 43 46 79 – Closed 30 November-9 December, 4 January-20 February, Monday from October to May and Tuesday from November to March

35 rm – €50/132 €50/132, €11 – ½ P €60/99

Rest – Menu (€20), €29/60 – Carte €51/60

◆ Pleasant family hotel where fuchsias abound in an elegant garden of palm trees, mimosas and eucalypti. Simple rooms; larger and more recent in the annexe. Dining room-veranda, attractive terrace and good traditional cooking enhanced by local specialities.

Le Chasse Marée VISA

8 pl. Gén. de Gaulle – ☎ 02 33 23 14 08 – Closed January to mid-February, Tuesday and Monday except lunch in low season

Rest – Menu €17 (weekday lunch), €21/32 – Carte €38/72

◆ Photos of boats and pennants left by sailing guests decorate this pleasant little restaurant and terrace on the port. Fish from the local catch.

ST-VALERY-EN-CAUX – 76 Seine-Maritime – 304 E2 – pop. 4 782 – alt. 5 m – Casino – ✉ 76460 Normandy 33 C1

Paris 190 – Bolbec 46 – Dieppe 35 – Fécamp 33 – Le Havre 80 – Rouen 59 – Yvetot 31

Office de tourisme, Maison Henri IV ☎ 02 35 97 00 63, Fax 02 35 97 32 65

Falaise d'Aval ←★ West: 15 mn.

Du Casino P VISA

14 av. Clemenceau – ☎ 02 35 57 88 00 – www.hotel-casino-saintvalery.com – contact@hotel-casino-saintvalery.com – Fax 02 35 57 88 88

76 rm – €76/95 €83/147, €12 – ½ P €74/81

Rest – Menu (€18), €22/40 – Carte €27/47

◆ This modern hotel overlooking the harbour has modern, functional rooms, popular with business travellers and tourists. Updated country cooking using local and seafood produce served in a large bright dining room.

Les Remparts without rest VISA

4 r. des Bains – ☎ 02 35 97 16 13 – Fax 02 35 97 19 89 – Closed 1st-10 January

15 rm – €40 €46/56, €8

◆ Small, pleasant hotel, near the sea and cliffs. Perfectly well-kept rooms, adorned with period furniture (1930s style). Very friendly welcome.

La Maison des Galets without rest VISA

22 cour Le Perrey – ☎ 02 35 97 11 22 – www.lamaisondesgalets.fr – geraldinecouture@hotmail.com – Fax 02 35 97 05 83 – Closed 7-21 January

14 rm – €43/50 €65/80, €11

◆ Family-run hotel facing the sea. Public room (antiques, objets d'art, palm trees and fireplace) with beautiful sea views. Modern rooms with sea theme.

Du Port ← VISA

quai d'Amont – ☎ 02 35 97 08 93 – Fax 02 35 97 28 32 – Closed Sunday dinner, Thursday dinner except July-August and Monday

Rest – Menu €25/45 – Carte €52/83

◆ Views of the boats coming and going from this pleasant harbour restaurant. Seafood caught by the local fishermen and traditional dishes. Classic decor.

Southeast 7 km by D 20 and D 70 - ✉ 76740 Ermenouville

Château du Mesnil Geoffroy without rest
2 r. Dame Blanche – ☎ 02 35 57 12 77
– www.chateau-mesnil-geoffroy.com – contact@chateau-mesnil-geoffroy.com
– Fax 02 35 57 10 24
5 rm – †€ 85/120 ††€ 85/120, ☕ € 11
◆ Step back to the time of Madame de Pompadour at this 18C château set in a park with a rose garden. Authentic Louis XV style rooms, objets d'art from the period, landscaped gardens.

ST-VALERY-SUR-SOMME – 80 Somme – 301 C6 – pop. 2 805 – alt. 27 m – ✉ 80230 **Northern France and the Paris Region** 36 **A1**

▶ Paris 206 – Abbeville 18 – Amiens 71 – Blangy-sur-Bresle 45 – Le Tréport 25

ℹ Office de tourisme, 2, place Guillaume-Le-Conquérant ☎ 03 22 60 93 50, Fax 03 22 60 80 34

◉ Digue-promenade★ - Marins chapel ≤★ - Ecomusée Picarvie★ - La baie de Somme★★.

Du Cap Hornu rm, VISA MC AE
2 km north on the Cap Hornu – ☎ 03 22 60 24 24 – www.baiedesomme.fr
– cap.hornu@baiedesomme.fr – Fax 03 22 26 85 13
91 rm ☕ – †€ 78/89 ††€ 88/98 – ½ P € 63/72
Rest – Menu € 22/39 – Carte € 22/45
◆ A group of regional style houses in a large park overlooking the Somme bay. Recently decorated and eco-friendly rooms (some with mezzanine floors). Pool, tennis. Traditional country cooking, served in classic dining rooms.

Du Port et des Bains rest, rm, VISA MC AE
1 quai Balvet – ☎ 03 22 60 80 09 – hotel.hpb@wanadoo.fr – Fax 03 22 60 77 90
– Closed 15 November-6 December and 2-25 January
16 rm – †€ 55 ††€ 65/80, ☕ € 9
Rest – Menu € 16 (weekdays), € 20/35 – Carte € 28/40
◆ Well located near the harbour, this hotel has lovely views of the bay. Bright colours and cane furniture in the rooms. Paintings of St-Valery in the early 20C decorate the restaurant. Traditional dishes and seafood.

Picardia without rest VISA MC AE
41 quai Romerel – ☎ 03 22 60 32 30 – http://hotel.picardia.akeonet.com
– hotel.picardia@akeonet.com – Fax 03 22 60 76 69 – Closed 5-30 January
18 rm ☕ – †€ 57/85 ††€ 95/108
◆ This welcoming country house stands next to the small medieval quarter. Bright and spacious guestrooms - those with a mezzanine are perfect for families.

Le Relais Guillaume de Normandy rest, rest, VISA MC AE
46 quai Romerel – ☎ 03 22 60 82 36
– www.relaisguillaumedenormandy.akeonet.com
– relaisguillaumedenormandy@akeonet.com – Fax 03 22 60 81 82
– Closed 14 December-10 January and Tuesday except from 14 July to 18 August
14 rm – †€ 55/60 ††€ 64/80, ☕ € 10 – ½ P € 64/72
Rest – Menu € 19/43 – Carte € 30/55
◆ Guillaume (William) left St Valéry to conquer England. This pretty brick manor facing the bay of the Somme houses practical rooms, some renovated. A classic menu is served in the panoramic dining room, which offers a view of the sea and the pleasant covered terrace.

Le Nicol's VISA MC
15 r. La Ferté – ☎ 03 22 26 82 96 – nicols@wanadoo.fr – Fax 03 22 60 97 46
– Closed 17-27 November, 5 January-5 February, Wednesday dinner, Thursday dinner 18 November to 28 March and Monday
Rest – Menu € 15/49 – Carte € 25/76
◆ This restaurant in a central shopping street has a lovely regional facade and a warm, rustic dining area serving traditional meals with an emphasis on produce from the sea.

ST-VALLIER – 26 Drôme – 332 B2 – pop. 4 051 – alt. 135 m – ✉ 26240 43 E2
Lyon - Rhone Valley

Paris 526 – Annonay 21 – St-Étienne 61 – Tournon-sur-Rhône 16 – Valence 35 – Vienne 41

Office de tourisme, avenue Désiré Valette ✆ 04 75 23 45 33, Fax 04 75 23 44 19

d'Albon Saint-Rambert-d'Albon Château de Senaud, N : 9 km on N 7 and D 122, ✆ 04 75 03 03 90

Le Bistrot d'Albert
116 av. J. Jaurès, (Lyon road) – ✆ 04 75 23 01 12 – bistrot.albert@wanadoo.fr – Fax 04 75 23 38 82 – Closed 2 weeks in August and 2 weeks in February
Rest – Menu € 15/26 – Carte € 27/35
◆ High ceilings, a luminous veranda and tasty market-based cuisine: friendly atmosphere guaranteed in this bistro near the station.

Northeast 8 km by N 7, D 122 and D 132 – ✉ 26140 Albon

Domaine des Buis
rte de St-Martin-des-Rosiers – ✆ 04 75 03 14 14 – www.domaine-des-buis.com – info@domaine-des-buis.com – Fax 04 75 03 14 14 – Closed 15 December-15 February
7 rm – €95/110 €95/150, ☕ € 12
Rest – *(dinner only) (residents only)* Menu € 30
◆ In parkland surrounded by hills, this 18C abode has the aroma of cedar and magnolia. Spacious rooms decorated with English furniture. Guesthouse atmosphere. The lady of the house concocts traditional dishes served in a plush dining room.

in St-Uze 6 km east on the D 51 – pop. 1 783 – alt. 189 m – ✉ 26240

Philip Liversain
23 r. P. Sémard – ✆ 04 75 03 52 58 – Fax 04 75 03 52 63 – Closed 13 July-4 August, Sunday dinner and Monday
Rest – Menu (€ 12), € 16/36
◆ This former 19C post house is both refreshingly cool and bathed in sunshine. A light colour scheme (wrought iron and colourful tablecloths) and a market-fresh menu.

ST-VALLIER-DE-THIEY – 06 Alpes-Maritimes – 341 C5 – pop. 3 142 – alt. 730 m – ✉ 06460 French Riviera 42 E2

Paris 907 – Cannes 29 – Castellane 52 – Draguignan 57 – Grasse 12 – Nice 47

Syndicat d'initiative, 10, place du Tour ✆ 04 93 42 78 00, Fax 04 93 42 78 00

Pas de la Faye ≤★★ Northwest: 5 km - Grotte de Beaume Obscure★ South: 2 km - Col de la Lèque ≤★ Southwest: 5 km.

Le Relais Impérial
2 et 4 pl. Cavalier Fabre, Napoléon road – ✆ 04 92 60 36 36 – www.relaisimperial.com – info@relaisimperial.com – Fax 04 92 60 36 39
29 rm – €42/48 €48/78, ☕ € 8 – ½ P € 53/65
Rest – Menu (€ 15), € 19 (weekday lunch), € 27/43 – Carte € 29/49
Rest *Le Grill du Relais* – pizzeria – ✆ *04 92 60 36 30* – Menu € 15 (weekday lunch)/20 – Carte € 26/44
◆ This former coaching inn along the Route Napoléon (the Emperor stopped here on 2 March, 1815) has small, partly-renovated, rustic rooms. Traditional cuisine served in a Louis XIII style dining room or on the veranda. Pizzas and simple dishes at the Grill.

ST-VÉRAN – 05 Hautes-Alpes – 334 J4 – pop. 290 – alt. 2 042 m – the highest commune in Europe – Winter sports : 1 750/3 000 m 15 – ✉ 05350 French Alps 41 C1

Paris 729 – Briançon 49 – Guillestre 32

Office de tourisme, la ville ✆ 04 92 45 82 21, Fax 04 92 45 84 52

Old village★★ - Musée du Soum★.

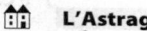

L'Astragale rest, VISA

– *04 92 45 87 00 – www.astragale.eu – contact@astragale.eu – Fax 04 92 45 87 10 – Open 18 June-31 August and 18 December-31 March*
21 rm – €88/179 €100/258, €15 – ½ P €74/155
Rest – *(dinner only)* Menu €26
◆ This modern and regularly revamped chalet has considerable charm, with its mountain-style setting, large comfortable rooms (all with a video player) and view of the mountain peaks:. A welcoming dining room with fireplace. Tea room.

ST-VÉRAND – **71 Saône-et-Loire** – **320** I12 – **pop. 183** – **alt. 300 m** – ✉ 71570 8 **C3**

Paris 401 – Bourg-en-Bresse 49 – Lyon 66 – Mâcon 14 – Villefranche-sur-Saône 35

Auberge du St-Véran rest, VISA

La Roche – 03 85 23 90 90 – www.auberge-saint-veran.com – direction@auberge-saint-veran.com – Fax 03 85 23 90 91 – Closed 3 weeks in January, Tuesday except dinner in high season and Monday
11 rm – €57 €70, €10 – ½ P €70
Rest – Menu (€15 bi), €25 (weekdays)/52 – Carte €36/60
◆ Old water mill with real country charm in the heart of the vineyards. The comfortable bedrooms have all been named after local vintages. Regional cuisine served in a rustic-style restaurant, with a terrace overlooking the swimming pool. Traditional cuisine and good choice of Mâcon and Beaujolais wines.

ST VIANCE – **19 Corrèze** – **329** J4 – **pop. 1 595** – **alt. 119 m** – ✉ **19240** 24 **B3**
Dordogne-Berry-Limousin

Paris 479 – Limoges 90 – Tulle 45 – Brive-la-Gaillarde 12 – Sarlat-la-Canéda 67

Auberge sur Vézère VISA

Le bourg – 05 55 84 28 23 – www.aubergesurvezere.com – aubergesurvezere@wanadoo.fr – Fax 05 55 84 42 47 – Closed 20 December-31 January and Sunday except July-August
10 rm – €60/65 €65/68, €8,50 – ½ P €55/60
Rest – *(closed Saturday lunch, Sunday dinner and Monday) (pre-book)* Menu (€21), €27
◆ This small country inn at the entrance to the village is run by a friendly Franco-British couple. Functional but well-appointed guestrooms. The menu served in the Provençal-style dining room or under the trees on the terrace is resolutely contemporary.

ST-VIATRE – **41 Loir-et-Cher** – **318** I6 – **pop. 1 188** – **alt. 107 m** – ✉ 41210 12 **C2**

Paris 179 – Orléans 53 – Blois 106 – Vierzon 53 – Fleury-les-Aubrais 60

Villepalay without rest

2 km on Nouan le Fuzelier road – 02 54 88 22 35 – www.digikom.fr/villepalay – navucet@wanadoo.fr – Closed March
3 rm – €55/65 €60/70
◆ A warm welcome at this old Soulogne farm with bucolic charm. Well turned out bedrooms and organic breakfast.

ST-VICTOR – 03 Allier – **326** C4 – **see Montluçon**

ST-VICTOR-DE-MALCAP – 30 Gard – **339** K3 – **see St-Ambroix**

ST-VICTOR-DES-OULES – 30 Gard – **339** L4 – **see Uzès**

ST-VINCENT – 43 Haute-Loire – **331** F3 – **pop. 938** – **alt. 605 m** 6 **C3**
– ✉ 43800

Paris 543 – La Chaise-Dieu 37 – Le Puy-en-Velay 18 – St-Étienne 76

XX **La Renouée** VISA MC
at Cheyrac, 2 km northward along the D 103 – ✆ 04 71 08 55 94 – auberge.larenouee@laposte.net – Closed for the autumn school holidays, 5 January-7 March, Tuesday dinner, Wednesday dinner and Thursday dinner from 15 October to 31 March, Sunday dinner and Monday
Rest – Menu € 19 (weekday lunch), € 26/46 – Carte € 19/43
◆ A 100-year-old establishment with a little garden in front. A huge stone hearth and a lovely cherry wood dresser adorn the redecorated dining room. Creative regional fare.

ST-VINCENT-DE-TYROSSE – 40 Landes – **335** D13 – **pop. 5 955** 3 **B3**
– **alt. 24 m** – ✉ 40230

Paris 743 – Anglet 32 – Bayonne 29 – Bordeaux 157

Office de tourisme, placette du Midi ✆ 05 58 77 12 00, Fax 05 58 77 12 00

XXX **Le Hittau** P VISA MC AE
1 r. du Nouaou – ✆ 05 58 77 11 85 – hittau@orange.fr – Closed 1st-9 July, 21 October-5 November, 19 February-12 March, Tuesday except 14 July-30 August and Wednesday
Rest – Menu € 36/75 – Carte approx. € 50
◆ This former sheepcote has a certain charm, with its exposed timberwork and monumental fireplace. Pleasant garden terrace. Up-to-date cuisine using regional produce.

ST-VINCENT-SUR-JARD – 85 Vendée – **316** G9 – **pop. 1 184** 34 **B3**
– **alt. 10 m** – ✉ 85520 **Atlantic Coast**

Paris 454 – Luçon 34 – La Rochelle 70 – La Roche-sur-Yon 35 – Les Sables-d'Olonne 23

Syndicat d'initiative, place de l'Eglise ✆ 02 51 33 62 06, Fax 02 51 33 01 23

L'Océan rm, AC rest, P VISA MC
1 km south: (near Clemenceau's house) – ✆ 02 51 33 40 45 – www.hotel-restaurant-ocean.com – hotel.locean@wanadoo.fr – Fax 02 51 33 98 15 – Closed 16 November-28 February and Wednesday from October to March
37 rm – †€ 53/71 ††€ 53/87, ☕ € 8 – ½ P € 54/74
Rest – Menu € 22/60 – Carte € 25/50
◆ Not far from the beach, the impressive seaside villa has been run by the same family for three generations. Simple rooms, garden shaded by pine trees and veranda for breakfasts. The restaurant serves a classic repertoire emphasising seafood.

X **Le Chalet St-Hubert** P VISA MC
rte de Jard – ✆ 02 51 33 40 33 – www.le-chalet-saint-hubert.com – lechaletsthubert@orange.fr – Closed Thursday dinner, Sunday dinner and Monday from September to June
Rest – Menu € 17/33 – Carte € 24/78
◆ An old house with a wood-panelled dining room serving traditional cuisine with the emphasis on fish and seafood.

ST-YBARD – 19 Corrèze – **329** K3 – see Uzerche

ST-YORRE – 03 Allier – **326** H6 – see Vichy

STE-ANNE-D'AURAY – 56 Morbihan – **308** N8 – **pop. 2 067** 9 **A3**
– **alt. 42 m** – ✉ 56400 **Brittany**

Paris 475 – Auray 7 – Hennebont 33 – Locminé 27 – Lorient 44 – Quimperlé 58 – Vannes 16

Office de tourisme, 26, rue de Vannes ✆ 02 97 57 69 16, Fax 02 97 57 79 22

Treasure-house★ of the basilica - Pardon (26 July).

L'Auberge
56 r. de Vannes – ✆ 02 97 57 61 55 – www.auberge-larvoir.com – auberge-jl-larvoir@wanadoo.fr – Fax 02 97 57 69 10
16 rm – €60/89 €60/89, €10 – 2 suites – ½ P €65/80
Rest – *(closed Wednesday lunch in winter)* Menu €25/85 – Carte €38/100
◆ Two types of decor and two distinct atmospheres. A focus on Art Deco in the hotel, with its rosewood and burr elm, Mucha and Lempicka reproductions, and Lalique wall lamps. The restaurant adopts a Breton style and serves modern cuisine.

Myriam without rest
35 bis r. Parc – ✆ 02 97 57 70 44 – www.hotellemyriam.com – contact@hotellemyriam.com – Fax 02 97 57 63 49 – Open 15 February-15 November
30 rm – €50/60 €50/60, €8
◆ This 1970s hotel in a pleasant residential area provides simple updated rooms and a breakfast area with marine decor.

STE-ANNE-DU-CASTELLET – 83 Var – 340 J6 – see le Castellet

STE-ANNE-LA-PALUD (Chapel) – 29 Finistère – 308 F6 – alt. 65 m – ✉ 29550 Brittany 9 A2

Paris 584 – Brest 68 – Châteaulin 20 – Crozon 27 – Douarnenez 12 – Quimper 24

Pardon (enf of August).

De la Plage
at the beach – ✆ 02 98 92 50 12 – www.plage.com – laplage@relaischateaux.com – Fax 02 98 92 56 54 – Open 4 April-2 November
23 rm – €187/336 €187/336, €19 – 1 suite
Rest – Menu €54/96 – Carte €75/100
◆ Shorefront location at the foot of the chapel, surrounded by flower-filled gardens. The guestrooms and suites have views of the bay. At the restaurant, enjoy traditional dishes overlooking the sea.

STE-CÉCILE – 71 Saône-et-Loire – 320 H11 – pop. 273 – alt. 250 m – ✉ 71250 8 C3

Paris 391 – Charolles 35 – Cluny 8 – Mâcon 22 – Roanne 73

L'Embellie
– ✆ 03 85 50 81 81 – www.lembellie.com – sarl.delagrange@wanadoo.fr – Fax 03 85 50 81 81 – Closed 23 June-11 July, 27 October-21 November, Sunday dinner except July-August, Tuesday except lunch September-June and Wednesday
Rest – Menu (€12), €17 (weekdays)/39 – Carte €25/47
◆ A restaurant occupying former stone stables that have retained all their rustic character, with exposed beams, ashwood furniture and warm winter fireplace. Pleasant shaded summer terrace with a view of the Carmel (convent). Classic cuisine.

STE-CÉCILE-LES-VIGNES – 84 Vaucluse – 332 C8 – pop. 2 142 – alt. 108 m – ✉ 84290 40 A2

Paris 646 – Avignon 47 – Bollène 13 – Nyons 26 – Orange 17 – Vaison-la-Romaine 19

La Farigoule with rm
26 cours M. Trintignant – ✆ 04 90 30 89 89 – www.lafarigoule.net – farigoule.raphael@wanadoo.fr – Fax 04 90 30 78 00 – Closed 1st-30 March and 22 November-7 December
9 rm – €55 €75 – ½ P €65
Rest – *(closed Sunday dinner and Monday except July-August)* Menu €18 (weekdays)/39 – Carte €38/46
◆ This pleasant inn is in the heart of the Côtes du Rhône vineyards. It offers tempting regional dishes served beneath a lush arbour or in the cosy dining room. Delightful rooms with personal touches.

Campagne, Vignes et Gourmandises

Suze-la-Rousse road – ✆ 04 90 63 40 11 – www.restaurant-cvg.com – sylfernandes@wanadoo.fr – Fax 04 90 63 40 25 – Closed 29 March-7 April, 25 October-4 November, 20 December-19 January, Tuesday in low season, Sunday dinner and Monday

Rest – *(number of covers limited, pre-book)* Menu (€ 17), € 22/55 – Carte € 44/71

◆ Vineyards encircle this modest farmhouse, built in a quiet residential neighbourhood. Countrified dining room and lovely terrace. Up-to-date cuisine with southern accents.

Good food and accommodation at moderate prices?
Look for the Bib symbols: red Bib Gourmand for food,
blue Bib Hotel for hotels.

STE-COLOMBE – 84 Vaucluse – 332 E9 – see Bédoin

STE-CROIX – 01 Ain – 328 D5 – see Montluel

STE-CROIX-DE-VERDON – 04 Alpes-de-Haute-Provence – 334 E10 41 **C2**
– pop. 138 – alt. 530 m – ✉ 04500 French Alps

Paris 780 – Brignoles 59 – Castellane 59 – Digne-les-Bains 51 – Manosque 44 – Salernes 35

L'Olivier

in the village – ✆ 04 92 77 87 95 – www.l-olivier-restaurant.com – Fax 04 92 77 87 95 – Open from mid February to mid November and closed Monday and Tuesday except July-August

Rest – Menu € 28/42 – Carte € 45/61

◆ This restaurant, in a village clinging to the cliff, invites you to discover well-presented modern cuisine. Terrace-veranda with a splendid view of Lake Sainte Croix.

STE-CROIX-EN-JAREZ – 42 Loire – 327 G7 – see Rive-de-Gier

STE-CROIX-EN-PLAINE – 68 Haut-Rhin – 315 I8 – see Colmar

STE-ÉNIMIE – 48 Lozère – 330 I8 – pop. 512 – alt. 470 m – ✉ 48210 23 **C1**
Languedoc-Roussillon-Tarn Gorges

Paris 612 – Florac 27 – Mende 28 – Meyrueis 30 – Millau 57 – Sévérac-le-Château 49

Office de tourisme, village ✆ 04 66 48 53 44, Fax 04 66 48 47 70

<★★ on the canyon du Tarn South: 6,5 km by D 986.

Auberge du Moulin rm, VISA

r. Combe – ✆ 04 66 48 53 08 – www.aubergedumoulin.free.fr – aubergedumoulin48@orange.fr – Fax 04 66 48 58 16 – Open end March-mid November and closed Sunday dinner except July-August and public holidays

10 rm – †€ 50/60 ††€ 55/65, ☕ € 8 – ½ P € 52/65

Rest – *(closed Monday except July-August and public holidays)* Menu (€ 14), € 17/36 – Carte € 24/36

◆ Beautiful stone building in a village popular with tourists in an extraordinary site. Half of the spruce bedrooms face the Tarn. Opt for a quiet outdoor table overlooking the river rather than the huge dining room.

STE-EULALIE – 07 Ardèche – 331 H5 – pop. 240 – alt. 1 233 m – ✉ 07510 44 **A3**

▶ Paris 587 – Aubenas 47 – Langogne 47 – Privas 51 – Le Puy-en-Velay 48 – Thueyts 36

ℹ Syndicat d'initiative, Mairie ✆ 04 75 38 89 78, Fax 04 75 38 87 37

Du Nord rest, P VISA MC AE

– *✆ 04 75 38 80 09 – www.hoteldunord-ardeche.com – hotelnord.mouyon@wanadoo.fr – Fax 04 75 38 85 50 – Open 7 March-11 November*

15 rm – †€ 52/60 ††€ 52/88, ☕ € 8 – ½ P € 54/56

Rest – *(closed Tuesday dinner except in July-August and Wednesday)* Menu € 20 (weekdays)/37 – Carte € 28/35

◆ Pleasant family inn popular with those who fish in the nearby River Loire. Comfortable, regularly renovated rooms. Local cuisine, a family atmosphere and a neo-rustic setting characterise this restaurant.

STE-EULALIE-D'OLT – 12 Aveyron – 338 J4 – pop. 330 – alt. 425 m – ✉ 12130 29 **D1**

▶ Paris 615 – Espalion 25 – Rodez 45 – Sévérac-le-Château 28

ℹ Office de tourisme, rue Fon Sainte-Anne ✆ 05 65 47 82 68

Au Moulin d'Alexandre with rm

– *✆ 05 65 47 45 85 – moulin.alexandre@wanadoo.fr – Fax 05 65 52 73 78 – Closed Saturday from 15 November to Easter*

9 rm – †€ 50/55 ††€ 50/55, ☕ € 8

Rest – Menu (€ 13), € 23/28 – Carte € 30/40

◆ This 16C mill helps to liven up this charming Aveyron village: bar and newsagents, hotel and restaurant. The dining room has retained a pleasant rustic atmosphere (fireplace, exposed beams and stonework). The rooms offer rather basic comfort.

STE-EUPHÉMIE – 01 Ain – 328 B5 – pop. 1 118 – alt. 247 m – ✉ 01600 43 **E1**

▶ Paris 435 – Bourg-en-Bresse 49 – Dijon 168 – Lyon 36

Au Petit Moulin VISA MC

615 rte d'Ars – ✆ 04 74 00 60 10 – Closed 20 January-20 February, Thursday dinner in winter, Monday, Tuesday and Wednesday

Rest – Menu (€ 17), € 23/33 – Carte € 35/44

◆ On the menu in this modest country inn near the Dombes region: frogs, freshwater fish and poultry, carefully cooked and copiously served.

STE-FEYRE – 23 Creuse – 325 I4 – see Guéret

STE-FLORINE – 43 Haute-Loire – 331 B1 – pop. 3 002 – alt. 440 m – ✉ 43250 6 **C2**

▶ Paris 465 – Brioude 16 – Clermont-Fd 55 – Issoire 19 – Murat 60 – Le Puy-en-Velay 77

Le Florina with rm rm, VISA MC AE

pl. Hôtel de Ville – ✆ 04 73 54 04 45 – www.hotel-leflorina.com – le.florina@wanadoo.fr – Fax 04 73 54 02 62 – Closed 19 December-11 January

14 rm – †€ 38 ††€ 42/60, ☕ € 6,50 – ½ P € 42/50

Rest – *(closed Sunday dinner)* Menu (€ 10), € 15/25 – Carte € 23/44

◆ This recent building houses a restaurant that offers regional specialities. Rooms are functional or, if booked ahead, more colourful and personalised.

STE-FOY-LA-GRANDE – 33 Gironde – 335 M5 – pop. 2 554 – alt. 10 m – ✉ 33220 Atlantic Coast 4 **C1**

▶ Paris 555 – Bordeaux 71 – Langon 59 – Marmande 44 – Périgueux 67

ℹ Office de tourisme, 102, rue de la République ✆ 05 57 46 03 00, Fax 05 57 46 16 62

18 Chateau des Vigiers Golf Club MonestierSE : 9 km on D 18, ✆ 05 53 61 50 33

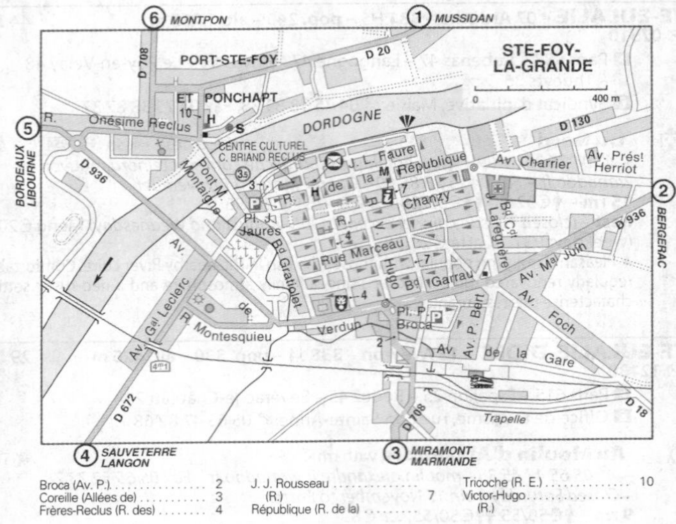

✗✗ Au Fil de l'Eau

3 r. de la Rouquette, at Port-Ste-Foy – ✆ 05 53 24 72 60 – www.restaurantaufildeleau.com – christelle.dewannain@orange.fr – Fax 05 53 24 94 97 – Closed 2-16 March, 8-30 November, Wednesday dinner from October to March, Sunday dinner except July-August and Monday

Rest – Menu € 14 (weekday lunch), € 21/53 – Carte € 39/67

◆ The establishment might seem commonplace but it pays to seek a table in the refurbished interior with a veranda overlooking the Dordogne. Updated regional cuisine.

Southeast : 8 km on D 18 – ✉ 24240 Monestier

Château des Vigiers

rm, rm,

at the Les Vigiers Golf Course – ✆ 05 53 61 50 00 – www.vigiers.fr – reception@vigiers.fr – Fax 05 53 61 50 20 – Closed 16 December-28 February

87 rm – †€ 165/330 ††€ 165/330, ☕ € 17 – ½ P € 125/235

Rest *Les Fresques* – *✆ 05 53 61 50 39 (open 1st May-30 September and closed Tuesday and Wednesday) (dinner only)* Carte € 40/70

Rest *Brasserie Le Chai* – *✆ 05 53 61 50 39* – Menu € 25 (lunch), € 39/47

◆ This 16C château and its modern outbuildings are located in a park converted into a golf course (27 holes, 3 of which are particularly noteworthy). Spacious, personalised rooms and spa. At Les Fresques, chic interior, contemporary menu and wines from the estate. Brasserie located in the former wine cellar.

via ⑤ and secondary road – ✉ 33220 Port-Ste-Foy

L'Escapade

La Grâce – ✆ 05 53 24 22 79 – www.escapade-dordogne.com – info@escapade-dordogne.com – Fax 05 53 57 45 05 – Open 2 February-14 October and closed Friday and Sunday dinner in February-March

11 rm – †€ 48 ††€ 52, ☕ € 7 – ½ P € 55

Rest – *(dinner only) (pre-book)* Menu € 22, € 25/30 – Carte € 35/63

◆ A 17C tobacco farm next to a horse riding centre on the Compostelle pilgrim route. Rustic styled rooms, sauna, summer pool, and the peace and quiet of the countryside. A countrified dining room and a terrace serving regional specialities.

STE-FOY-L'ARGENTIÈRE – 69 Rhône – 327 F5 – pop. 1 247 – alt. 430 m – ✉ 69610 44 A2

Paris 487 – Lyon 49 – Saint-Étienne 52 – Villeurbanne 52

Manoir de Tourville
8 km north on D 483 and secondary road – ☎ 04 74 26 66 57 – www.manoirdetourville.com – tourville@manoirdetourville.com – Fax 04 74 26 66 57
5 rm – €75/120 €75/120 **Table d'hôte** – Menu € 25 bi/45 bi
◆ This 15C manor house is pleasantly located on the edge of meadows with horses and ponds. Delightful rooms with personal touches; suite in tower. Attractive wood-panelled dining room and classic cuisine.

STE-FOY-TARENTAISE – 73 Savoie – 333 O4 – pop. 815 – alt. 1 050 m – ✉ 73640 French Alps 45 D2

Paris 647 – Albertville 66 – Chambéry 116 – Moûtiers 40 – Val-d'Isère 20

Office de tourisme, station ☎ 04 79 06 95 19, Fax 04 79 06 95 09

Le Monal
Chef Lieu – ☎ 04 79 06 90 07 – www.le-monal.com – le.monal@wanadoo.fr – Fax 04 79 06 94 72 – Closed Saturday and Sunday from May to October
19 rm – €60/80 €70/100, € 10 – 2 suites – ½ P €77/85
Rest – Menu € 16 (weekday lunch)/30 – Carte € 39/68
◆ This former post house, in the same family since 1888, is now home to a delightful hotel. Lovely chalet-style rooms and family suites. All wood decor and traditional menu. Tastings and sale of wine.

la Station road 6 km southeast by secondary road – ✉ 73640 Ste-Foy-Tarentaise

La Ferme du Baptieu
Le Baptieu, (D 84) – ☎ 04 79 06 97 52 – www.lafermedubaptieu.com – contact.baptieu@lafermedubaptieu.com – Fax 04 79 06 97 52 – Open July-August and December-April
5 rm – €150/170 €150/170 – 1 suite **Table d'hôte** – Menu € 37
◆ This 18C chalet is extremely charming with its antique furniture, trinkets and warm wood panelling. Each room has a superb bathroom and a balcony with a mountain view. Table d'hôte offering tasty Savoyard and Mediterranean specialities.

STE-GEMME-MORONVAL – 28 Eure-et-Loir – 311 E3 – see Dreux

STE-GENEVIÈVE-DES-BOIS – 91 Essonne – 312 C4 – 101 35 – see Paris, Area

STE-GENEVIÈVE-SUR-ARGENCE – 12 Aveyron – 338 I2 – pop. 1 019 – alt. 800 m – ✉ 12420 29 D1

Paris 571 – Aurillac 56 – Chaudes-Aigues 34 – Espalion 40

Syndicat d'initiative, Syndicat d'Initiative ☎ 05 65 66 19 75, Fax 05 65 66 19 75

Sarrans Dam ★ North: 8 km, Languedoc-Roussillon-Tarn Gorges

Des Voyageurs with rm
r. du Riols – ☎ 05 65 66 41 03 – hoteldesvoyageurs.cruveiller@wanadoo.fr – Fax 05 65 66 10 94 – Closed 20 September-15 October, 20 December-10 January, Sunday dinner and Saturday from 15 October to 30 June
14 rm – €43/46 €43/46, €6 – ½ P €46
Rest – Menu (€ 10), € 12 (weekday lunch), € 14/32 – Carte € 24/40
◆ This former coaching house has been welcoming travellers since 1872. Countrified setting in the restaurant overlooking a garden; regional traditionally prepared dishes. Simple and practical rooms.

STE-HERMINE – 85 Vendée – **316** J8 – **pop. 2 503 – alt. 28 m** 34 **B3**
– ✉ 85210

▶ Paris 433 – Nantes 93 – La Roche-sur-Yon 35 – La Rochelle 59 – Les Herbiers 44

ℹ Office de tourisme, la Gare ✆ 02 51 27 39 32, Fax 02 51 27 39 32

Clem'otel
parc Atlantique Vendée, 2 km south on D 137 – ✆ 02 51 28 46 94 – clemotel.com – clem.otel@wanadoo.fr – Fax 02 51 28 46 81 – Closed 24 December-4 January
49 rm – †€ 52 ††€ 64, ☕ € 7 – ½ P € 51/53
Rest – *(closed Sunday from November to end March)* Menu (€ 12), € 16 – Carte € 20/25
◆ This new hotel has light, well-soundproofed guestrooms. Palm trees and sunflowers add an exotic touch to the central patio. Enjoy grilled dishes (prepared in front of you) or traditional cuisine in a rustic, yet contemporary decor.

STE-LUCIE-DE-PORTO-VECCHIO – **2A Corse-du-Sud** – **345** F9 – **see Corse**

STE-LUCIE-DE-TALLANO – **2A Corse-du-Sud** – **345** D9 – **see Corse**

STE-MAGNANCE – 89 Yonne – **319** H7 – **pop. 365 – alt. 310 m** 7 **B2**
– ✉ 89420 ▌Burgundy-Jura

▶ Paris 224 – Avallon 15 – Auxerre 65 – Dijon 68 – Saulieu 24

◉ Tomb★ in the church.

Auberge des Cordois
D 606 – ✆ 03 86 33 11 79 – lescordois@hotmail.fr – Closed 29 June-8 July, 12-19 November, 4 January-4 February, Monday dinner, Tuesday and Wednesday
Rest – Menu € 28/43 – Carte € 39/60
◆ This two hundred-year-old building near the road has a yellow façade. Bistro set menu or regional cuisine served in a dining room with an ochre and violet decor.

STE-MARGUERITE (ÎLE) – **06 Alpes-Maritimes** – **341** D6 – **see Île Sainte-Marguerite**

STE-MARIE – **44 Loire-Atlantique** – **316** D5 – **see Pornic**

STE-MARIE-AUX-MINES – 68 Haut-Rhin – **315** H7 – **pop. 5 816** 1 **A2**
– **alt. 350 m** – ✉ 68160 ▌Alsace-Lorraine

▶ Paris 422 – Colmar 43 – St-Dié 25 – Sélestat 23

Ste-Marie-aux-Mines Tunnel: toll in 2008, one way: car and caravan € 17,00, motorcycles € 5,30, cars € 7,50, lorries € 33,30 to € 55,60.

ℹ Office de tourisme, 86, rue Wilson ✆ 03 89 58 80 50, Fax 03 89 58 67 92

Aux Mines d'Argent with rm
8 r. Dr Weisgerber – ✆ 03 89 58 55 75 – auxminesdargent.com – wistubwillmann@orange.fr – Fax 03 89 58 65 49
9 rm – †€ 45/55 ††€ 45/55, ☕ € 6 – ½ P € 45/55
Rest – Menu (€ 12), € 14 (lunch), € 16/32 – Carte € 15/32
◆ Wood-panelling, Alsatian furniture, wood-carvings (mining scenes) - an authentic winstub in a 16C residence. An attractive terrace skirted by a stream. Regional menu.

STE-MARIE-DE-RÉ – **17 Charente-Maritime** – **324** C3 – **see Île de Ré**

STE-MARIE-DE-VARS – **05 Hautes-Alpes** – **334** I5 – **see Vars**

STES-MARIES-DE-LA-MER – **See after Saintes**

STE-MARIE-SICCHÉ – **2A Corse-du-Sud** – **345** C8 – **see Corse**

STE-MARINE – 29 Finistère – 308 G7 – see Bénodet

STE-MAURE – 10 Aube – 313 E3 – see Troyes

STE-MAURE-DE-TOURAINE – 37 Indre-et-Loire – 317 M6 – pop. 3 909 – alt. 85 m – ✉ 37800 Châteaux of the Loire 11 B3

Paris 273 – Le Blanc 71 – Châtellerault 39 – Chinon 32 – Loches 31 – Thouars 73 – Tours 40

Office de tourisme, rue du Château ✆ 02 47 65 66 20, Fax 02 47 34 04 28

Hostellerie des Hauts de Ste-Maure

rm,

av. Gén. de Gaulle – ✆ 02 47 65 50 65 – www.hostelleriehautsdestemaure.fr – hauts-de-ste-maure@wanadoo.fr – Fax 02 47 65 60 24 – Closed January, Monday (except hotel) and Sunday October-May

VISA

20 rm – †€ 109/189 ††€ 109/189, € 12 – 1 suite

Rest *La Poste* – *(closed Monday lunch and Sunday from October to May)*

Menu € 36 (weekdays)/150

◆ This former post house provides modern rooms with personal touches. The rooms are spread between the main building and the extension. There is also a spa pool, garden and vegetable plot. Classic dishes, good wine list and elegant setting in the restaurant.

Le Grand Menasson without rest

2 km by old Loches road and secondary road – ✆ 06 11 08 51 80 – www.augrandmenasson.fr – ghislaine@augrandmenasson.fr – Fax 02 47 65 21 24 tél

4 rm – †€ 70/90 ††€ 70/90

◆ Guests can be certain of a warm welcome at this quiet old Virginia creeper clad farm. Extensive grounds with pond, rooms decorated in a country style or with antiques.

in Pouzay 8 km southwest – pop. 755 – alt. 51 m – ✉ 37800

Au Gardon Frit

VISA

16 pl. de l'Eglise – ✆ 02 47 65 21 81 – www.au-gardon-frit.com – Closed 21-29 April, 15 September-30 October, 12-27 January, Tuesday and Wednesday except public holidays

Rest – Menu (€ 11), € 14 (weekday lunch), € 18/39 – Carte € 28/55

◆ This seafood restaurant also has a bar selling tobacco. The dining area has a marine-style decor and a lovely courtyard terrace.

Chinon road 2.5 km west: by D 760 – ✉ 37800 Noyant-de-Touraine

La Ciboulette

VISA

78 rte de Chinon, (opposite A10 junction, exit 25) – ✆ 02 47 65 84 64 – www.laciboulette.fr – laciboulette@wanadoo.fr – Fax 02 47 65 89 29 – Closed Sunday dinner, Monday dinner, Tuesday dinner and Wednesday dinner from October to March except school holidays and public holidays

Rest – Menu (€ 19), € 24/56 – Carte € 31/54

◆ An attractive menu of classic dishes served in a large ivy clad house. Tastefully decorated dining room and summer terrace.

in Noyant-de-Touraine 5 km west – pop. 780 – alt. 92 m – ✉ 37800

Château de Brou

VISA

2 km north on secondary road – ✆ 02 47 65 80 80 – www.chateau-de-brou.fr – info@chateau-de-brou.fr – Fax 02 47 65 82 92 – Closed 13-25 December, 1st January-5 February

10 rm – †€ 115/170 ††€ 115/170, € 15 – 2 suites

Rest – *(closed Sunday and Monday from October to March) (dinner only)*

Menu € 35, € 45/65 – Carte € 49/73

◆ A beautiful 15C château lost in a huge park. Remarkable historic decor adapted for the comfort of guests. Attic room converted into a suite and 19C chapel. Elegant, small dining room embellished with a pretty fireplace; traditional menu.

STE-MAXIME – 83 Var – 340 O6 – pop. 13 800 – alt. 10 m – Casino 41 C3
– ✉ 83120 ▌French Riviera

Paris 872 – Cannes 59 – Draguignan 34 – Fréjus 20 – Toulon 72

Office de tourisme, 1, promenade Simon-Loriere ✆ 04 94 55 75 55, Fax 04 94 55 75 56

de Sainte-Maxime Route du Débarquement, N : 2 km, ✆ 04 94 55 02 02

de Beauvallon Boulevard des Collines, 4 km on the Toulon road, ✆ 04 94 96 16 98

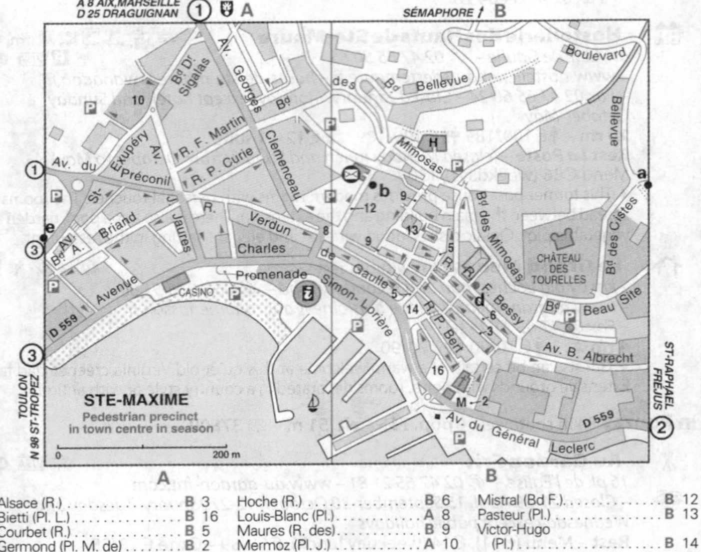

Alsace (R.)	B	3	Hoche (R.)	B	6	Mistral (Bd F.)	B	12
Bietti (Pl. L.)	B	16	Louis-Blanc (Pl.)	A	8	Pasteur (Pl.)	B	13
Courbet (R.)	B	5	Maures (R. des)	B	9	Victor-Hugo (Pl.)	B	14
Germond (Pl. M. de)	B	2	Mermoz (Pl. J.)	A	10			

Le Beauvallon

Bd des Collines, 5 km by St-Tropez road – ✆ 04 94 55 78 88 – www.hotel-lebeauvallon.com – reservation@lebeauvallon.com – Fax 04 94 55 78 78 – Open 11 April-10 October

65 rm – †€ 210/990 ††€ 210/990, ☕ € 28 – 5 suites

Rest *Les Colonnades* – *(closed Monday) (dinner only)* Menu € 90 – Carte € 85/105

Rest *Beauvallon Beach* – *(lunch only except July-August)* Carte € 48/80

◆ A luxurious hotel dating from 1914 in the middle of a 4ha park (pine trees and palms) overlooking the shore. Elegant and spacious rooms with sea or hillside views. Private beach. At the Colonnades find Art Deco style, a beautiful terrace and modern cuisine. Coastal views at the Beauvallon Beach.

Hostellerie la Belle Aurore

5 bd Jean Moulin, via ③ – ✆ 04 94 96 02 45 – www.belleaurore.com – info@belleaurore.com – Fax 04 94 96 63 87 – Open 4 April-11 October

16 rm – †€ 145/325 ††€ 145/325, ☕ € 20 – 1 suite – ½ P € 133/223

Rest – *(closed Monday lunch and Wednesday except July-August)* Menu (€ 29), € 40/86 – Carte € 100/116

◆ A waterside hotel. Peaceful rooms in southern colours overlooking the St Tropez gulf. Choice of terrace or balcony from which to enjoy the sea views. Restaurant offering Provençal inspired dishes with a glimpse of Gers. Panoramic view.

Villa les Rosiers
4 chemin de Guerrevieille Beauvallon-Grimaud, 5 km via ③ – ✆ 04 94 55 55 20 – www.villa-les-roseiers.com – info@villa-les-rosiers.com – Fax 04 94 55 55 33 – Open 16 March-31 October and 23 December-9 January
12 rm – †€ 160/470 ††€ 160/470, ☕ € 22
Rest – *(open 1st April-31 October)* Carte € 42/74
◆ This recent villa has contemporary paintings and sculptures, as well as a sea view. Modern rooms decorated with sobriety; some have a terrace or balcony. Market cuisine served in a bright, hip dining room or on the terrace.

Martinengo without rest
bd Jean-Moulin, on the ③ – ✆ 04 94 55 09 09 – www.hotel-martinengo – hotel-martinengo@wanadoo.fr – Fax 04 94 55 09 10 – Open 2 April-11 October
10 rm – †€ 65/183 ††€ 65/183, ☕ € 18
◆ Named after a Lombardy village, this hotel on the coast road offers classic style rooms (antique furniture and fine paintings). Good soundproofing.

Les Santolines
La Croisette via ③ – ✆ 04 94 96 31 34 – www.hotel-les-santolines.com – hotel.les.santolines@wanadoo.fr – Fax 04 94 49 22 12
14 rm – †€ 75/148 ††€ 75/148, ☕ € 12
Rest *Le Sarment de Vigne* – *✆ 04 94 96 34 99 (Closed December and January)*
Menu € 27/39 – Carte € 40/55
◆ Neat, Provencal, country house style hotel on the roadside (double glazing). Stylish rooms with Salernes tiles in the bathrooms. Sea views from upper floor rooms. Enjoy regional dishes and grills in a modern setting overlooking the pool.

Montfleuri rm,
3 av. Montfleuri, via ② – ✆ 04 94 55 75 10 – www.montfleuri.com – reservation@montfleuri.com – Fax 04 94 49 25 07 – Closed 8 November-23 December and 3 January-1st March
31 rm – †€ 45/105 ††€ 60/235, ☕ € 10
Rest – *(dinner only)* Menu € 28 – Carte € 30/48
◆ This family establishment in a residential area houses well-kept rooms. Some have terrace-balconies with sea views. Attractive, small Mediterranean garden. Traditional fare served in a colonial style room or out in the open.

Le Mas des Oliviers without rest
quartier de la Croisette, 1 km on ③ – ✆ 04 94 96 13 31 – www.hotellemasdesoliviers.com – masdesoliviers@9business.fr – Fax 04 94 49 01 46 – Closed December-January
20 rm – †€ 57/160 ††€ 57/160, ☕ € 12
◆ Family hotel with a Mediterranean colour scheme in a quiet location on a hillside among the pine trees. Spacious rooms with loggias overlooking the Gulf or garden.

Le Petit Prince without rest
11 av. St-Exupéry – ✆ 04 94 96 44 47 – www.hotellepetitprince.com – lepetit.prince@wanadoo.fr – Fax 04 94 49 03 38 A **e**
31 rm – †€ 56/80 ††€ 72/132, ☕ € 11
◆ Modern and well-soundproofed rooms, all (except two) with balcony, situated on a busy avenue close to the beach. Sun lounges and terrace for breakfast.

Croisette without rest
2 bd Romarins, via ③ – ✆ 04 94 96 17 75 – www.hotel-sainte-maxime.com – hotel.la.croisette@wanadoo.fr – Fax 04 94 96 52 40 – Open 1st April-15 October
18 rm – †€ 67/174 ††€ 67/174, ☕ € 11
◆ Oleanders, palm and fig trees surround this villa situated in a residential area. Some of the rooms command a view of the sea.

Hôtellerie de la Poste without rest
11 bd F. Mistral – ✆ 04 94 96 18 33 – www.hotelleriedusoleil.com – laposte@hotelleriedusoleil.com – Fax 04 94 55 58 63 – Closed 6-27 December B **b**
28 rm ☕ – †€ 70/135 ††€ 70/225
◆ A hotel dating from 1932 opposite the post office. Cuban inspired decor with warm colours in the rooms; those to the rear are quieter. Small terrace-patio with pool.

XX **La Badiane**

6 r. Fernand-Bessy – ✆ 04 94 96 53 93 – la.badiane@hotmail.fr – Fax 04 94 96 53 93 – Closed 7-14 June, 22 November-6 December, 17 January-7 February, lunch and Sunday dinner B **d**

Rest – Menu € 32, € 60 – Carte € 71/120

♦ Pleasant, contemporary establishment in a district of the old town. The chef-owner cooks modern recipes 'instinctively' while his wife oversees the service.

Northeast by Avenue Clemenceau and Débarquement road – ✉ 83120 Ste-Maxime

Jas Neuf without rest

112 av. du Débarquement – ✆ 04 94 55 07 30 – www.hotel-jasneuf.com – infos@hotel-jasneuf.com – Fax 04 94 49 09 71 – Closed 1st-20 December and 4-31 January

24 rm – €68/159 €68/159, ☕ €10

♦ A group of small, southern style houses on the outskirts of the town. Fresh, neat rooms in Provencal tones, most with terrace or balcony.

in La Nartelle 4 km by ② – ✉ 83120 Ste-Maxime

La Plage without rest

36 av. Gén.-Touzet-du-Vigier – ✆ 04 94 96 14 01 – www.hotel-la-plage.fr – hotel-la-plage@orange.fr – Fax 04 94 49 23 53

18 rm – €70/160 €70/160, ☕ €12

♦ This 1970s hotel is next to the road and the beach. Small, functional rooms soundproofed and renovated with a modern decor. Sea views.

in Val d'Esquières 6 km northwest by Les Issambres road – ✉ 83520 Roquebrune-sur-Argens

La Villa

122 av. Croiseur Léger Le Malin, (D 559), at La Garonnette – ✆ 04 94 49 40 90 – www.hotellavilla.fr – contact@hotellavilla.fr – Fax 04 94 49 40 85 – Closed 1st December-29 January

8 rm – €75/150 €75/150, ☕ €8 – 4 suites

Rest – Menu € 19/29 – Carte € 26/42

♦ Family establishment across the road from the beach. Small, personalised rooms with Provencal touches. Some have a sea view. The restaurant has a warm atmosphere (lively colours, cane furniture). Provencal dishes.

If breakfast is included the ☕ symbol appears after the number of rooms.

STE-MENÉHOULD – **51 Marne** – **306** L8 – **pop. 4 662** – **alt. 137 m** 14 **C2**
– ✉ **51800** **Northern France and the Paris Region**

Paris 221 – Bar-le-Duc 50 – Châlons-en-Champagne 48 – Reims 80 – Verdun 48

Syndicat d'initiative, 5, place du Général Leclerc ✆ 03 26 60 85 83, Fax 03 26 60 27 22

≤★ from the hillock called "The château" - Château of Braux-Ste-Cohière★ West: 5.5 km.

Le Cheval Rouge

1 r. Chanzy – ✆ 03 26 60 81 04 – www.lechevalrouge.com – rouge.cheval@wanadoo.fr – Fax 03 26 60 93 11 – Closed 21 December-10 January

24 rm – €40 €50, ☕ €7 – ½ P €50/55

Rest – *(closed Sunday dinner and Monday)* Menu € 13 (weekdays), € 20/60 – Carte € 50/68

Rest *La Brasserie* – Menu € 12 (weekdays) – Carte € 14/30

♦ A stone's throw from the town hall, this ancient inn offers peaceful nights in impeccably kept rooms. A classic dining room enhanced with rustic details (fireplace, bare beams) forms the backdrop to a flavoursome, traditional repertory. La Brasserie offers simple bistro dishes from a blackboard menu.

in Futeau 13 km east by D 603 and D 2 – **pop. 153 – alt. 190 m** – ✉ **55120**

XXX **L'Orée du Bois** with rm
1 km south – ✆ 03 29 88 28 41 – www.aloreedubois.fr – argonnealoreedubois@wanadoo.fr – Fax 03 29 88 24 52 – Closed 22 November-22 December, 4-26 January, Monday and Tuesday except dinner from Easter to end September and Sunday dinner in low season
14 rm – †€ 82/85 ††€ 88/138, ☕ € 14 – ½ P € 98/138
Rest – Menu € 46/70 – Carte € 58/78
◆ On the edge of the Argonne forest, an attractive inn with two dining rooms facing the countryside. Classical cuisine. Well-kept, comfortable guestrooms.

STE-MÈRE-ÉGLISE – 50 Manche – 303 E3 – pop. 1 611 – alt. 28 m – ✉ 50480 Normandy 32 A2

Paris 321 – Bayeux 57 – Cherbourg 39 – St-Lô 42
Office de tourisme, 6, rue Eisenhower ✆ 02 33 21 00 33, Fax 02 33 21 53 91

Southwest 6 km by D 67 and D 70 - ✉ **50360 Picauville**

Château de L'Isle Marie without rest
– ✆ 02 33 21 37 25 – www.islemarie.com – info@islemarie.com – Fax 02 33 21 42 22 – Open 6 March-9 November
5 rm ☕ – †€ 160/180 ††€ 170/195 – 2 suites
◆ This lavish medieval château set in an immense estate has belonged to the same family for centuries. A unique mix of comfort, romance and authenticity.

STE-NATHALENE – 24 Dordogne – 329 I6 – pop. 495 – alt. 145 m – ✉ 24200 4 D3

Paris 538 – Bordeaux 205 – Périgueux 74 – Brive-la-Gaillarde 63 – Sarlat-la-Canéda 9

La Roche d'Esteil
La Croix d'Esteil – ✆ 05 53 29 14 42 – www.larochedesteil.com – contact@larochedesteil.com – Open 1st March-15 November
5 rm – †€ 64/90 ††€ 64/90, ☕ € 6,50 **Table d'hôte** – Menu € 12 bi/25 bi
◆ Estate tastefully restored by passionate owners, while respecting the Périgord traditions. Well-kept and individually decorated rooms, housed in the old barns. Table d'hôte in the evenings in a convivial and contemporary interior.

STE-PREUVE – 02 Aisne – 306 F5 – pop. 89 – alt. 115 m – ✉ 02350 37 D2

Paris 188 – Saint-Quentin 69 – Laon 29 – Reims 49 – Soissons 62

Domaine du Château de Barive
3 km southwest – ✆ 03 23 22 15 15 – www.chateau-de-barive.com – contact@lesepicuriens.com – Fax 03 23 22 08 39
18 rm – †€ 90/350 ††€ 120/450, ☕ € 20 – 4 suites
Rest *Les Epicuriens* – Menu (€ 30), € 40/90 – Carte € 77/105
◆ This beautiful 19C building nestled in a vast park offers the tranquillity of the Picardy countryside. Cosy rooms; those on the second floor are beneath the eaves. New suites. Personal service. Revamped dining room in a conservatory style. Up-to-date cuisine.

SAINTES – 17 Charente-Maritime – 324 G5 – pop. 26 300 – alt. 15 m – ✉ 17100 Atlantic Coast 38 B3

Paris 469 – Bordeaux 117 – Poitiers 138 – Rochefort 42 – Royan 38
Office de tourisme, 62, cours National ✆ 05 46 74 23 82, Fax 05 46 92 17 01
de Saintonge 43, route du Golf, 5 km on the Niort road, ✆ 05 46 74 27 61
Abbaye aux Dames: abbey church ★ - Old town★ - Arc of Germanicus★ **B** - St-Eutrope church: lower church ★ **E** - Gallo-Roman amphitheatre★ - Musée des Beaux-Arts★: Musée du Présidial **M**5 - Musée Archéologique: parade carriage★.

SAINTES

Allende (Av. Salvador) . . . . Y 2
Alsace-Lorraine (R.) . . . . AZ 3
Arc-de-Triomphe (R.). . . . . BZ 4
Bassompierre (Pl.) . . . . BZ 5
Berthonnière (R.) . . . . AZ 7
Blair (Pl.) . . . . AZ 9
Bois d'Amour (R.) . . . . AZ 10
Bourignon (R.) . . . . Y 12
Brunaud (R. A.) . . . . AZ 13
Clemenceau (R.) . . . . AZ 15
Denfert-Rochereau (R.) . . . . . BZ 16
Dufaure (Av. J.) . . . . Y 18
Foch (Pl. Mar.) . . . . AZ 20
Gambetta (Av.) . . . . BZ
Jacobins (R. des) . . . . AZ 25
Jean (R. du Dr) . . . . Y 27
Kennedy (Av. J.-F.) . . . . Y 31
Lacurie (R.) . . . . Y 33
Leclerc (Crs Mar.) . . . . Y 34
Lemercier (Cours) . . . . AZ 35
Marne (Av. de la) . . . . BZ 37
Mestreau (R. F.) . . . . BZ 38
Monconseil (R.) . . . . AZ 39
National (Cours) . . . . AZ
République (Quai) . . . . AZ 41
St-Eutrope (R.) . . . . AZ 42
St-François (R.) . . . . AZ 43
St-Macoult (R.) . . . . AZ 45
St-Pierre (R.) . . . . AZ 46
St-Vivien (Pl.) . . . . AZ 47
Victor-Hugo (R.) . . . . AZ 49

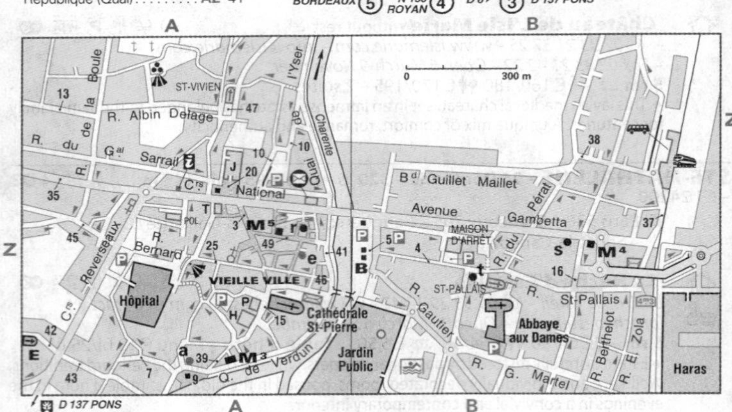

Relais du Bois St-Georges rm,
r. de Royan, (D 137) – ✆ 05 46 93 50 99 VISA
– www.relaisdubois.com – info@relaisdubois.com – Fax 05 46 93 34 93
31 rm – †€ 68/180 ††€ 74/360, ☐ € 19 Y **d**
Rest – Menu € 42/135 bi – Carte € 59/84
Rest ***La Table du Bois*** – Menu (€ 20 bi), € 26 bi/32 bi
◆ This hotel, built on the site of an old wine cellar, has rooms with individual touches that are sometimes very original: Captain Nemo, Timbuktu, Monte Cristo, etc. Park with pond. The rustic dining room opens onto the surrounding greenery. A bistro atmosphere and cosy ambiance at the Table du Bois.

Des Messageries without rest VISA
r. des Messageries – ✆ 05 46 93 64 99 – www.hotel-des-messageries.com – info@hotel-des-messageries.com – Fax 05 46 92 14 34 AZ **r**
34 rm – †€ 59/81 ††€ 63/81, ☐ € 8
◆ This former coaching inn dating from 1792 is near the historic quarter. Some of the rooms have been renovated. Local produce at breakfast. Delightful welcome.

L'Avenue without rest VISA
114 av. Gambetta – ✆ 05 46 74 05 91 – www.hoteldelavenue.com – contact@hoteldelavenue.com – Fax 05 46 74 32 16 – Closed 24 December-3 January
15 rm – †€ 45/69 ††€ 45/69, ☐ € 8 BZ **s**
◆ A warm welcome awaits you in this 1970s hotel close to the main road. The personalised, cosy rooms face the rear and are peaceful.

XXX **Le Saintonge** A/C P VISA MC AE

complexe Saintes-Végas, (La Champagne St-Georges) – ✆ 05 46 97 00 00 – www.saintes-vegas.com – sasercol@wanadoo.fr – Fax 05 46 97 21 46 – Closed Sunday dinner and Monday dinner Y f

Rest – Menu (€ 15), € 25/45 – Carte € 60/69

◆ A rotunda-restaurant, well-lit with a rather elegant setting, in the "Saintes-Vegas" complex (concert venue, lounges and discotheque). Classic cuisine.

XX **Le Bistrot Galant** VISA MC AE

28 r. St-Michel – ✆ 05 46 93 08 51 – www.lebistrotgalant.com – bistrot.galant@club-internet.fr – Fax 05 46 90 95 58 – Closed one week in March, 15-31 October, Sunday and Monday AZ e

Rest – Menu (€ 14), € 16/38 – Carte € 28/45

◆ This glass-fronted restaurant lies in a quiet street. Two brightly coloured dining areas; modern cuisine served.

XX **Saveurs de l'Abbaye** with rm VISA MC

1 pl. St Palais – ✆ 05 46 94 17 91 – www.saveurs-abbaye.com – infos@saveurs-abbaye.com – Fax 05 46 94 47 54 – Closed 22 September-5 October, February school holidays, Sunday and Monday BZ t

8 rm – †€ 45 ††€ 48, ☕ € 6 – ½ P € 59

Rest – Menu (€ 16), € 24/46 – Carte € 32/38

◆ An inviting family home, two minutes from the Abbaye aux Dames with a warm, modern interior (wood, brown tones). Cuisine prepared using local produce, herbs and spices. Modern bedrooms with personalised touches that reflect the names (Asian colours, Seaside, etc.).

X **La Table de Marion** A/C VISA MC

10 pl. Blair – ✆ 05 46 74 16 38 – latabledemarion.unblog.fr – latabledemarion@orange.fr – Closed Tuesday dinner and Wednesday AZ a

Rest – *(number of covers limited, pre-book)* Menu (€ 25), € 37/47 – Carte approx. € 58

◆ On a small square overlooking the Charente, this modern restaurant with stone walls serves creative market cuisine. Organic wines.

in St-Sauvant **13 km east by ② and N 141 – pop. 508 – alt. 18 m – ✉ 17610**

Design Hôtel des Francs Garçons A/C rest, VISA MC AE

1 r. des Francs-Garçons – ✆ 05 46 90 33 93 – www.francsgarçons.com – contact@francsgarcons.com

5 rm – †€ 85/105 ††€ 85/105, ☕ € 12 – 2 suites

Rest – *(dinner only) (residents only)* Menu € 25, € 32/39 – Carte € 25/39

◆ House located in a medieval village and renovated by architects. It has a light filled modern décor, old stonework and designer furniture. Swimming pool opposite the church.

in Thénac **10 km south by ③ and D 6 – pop. 1 214 – alt. 62 m – ✉ 17460**

XX **L'Atelier Gourmand de Jean-Yves** P VISA MC

41 r. de la République – ✆ 05 46 97 84 26 – www.l-ateliergourmand.fr – agjy@orange.fr – Closed 5-19 January, Sunday dinner and Monday

Rest – Menu (€ 21 bi), € 25 bi (weekday lunch), € 28/65 bi – Carte € 40/50

◆ Located in the former stables of a wine storehouse, this restaurant displays a warm conviviality. The kitchens are open to the prettily rustic dining room. Terrace opposite the park.

The red symbol?
This denotes the very essence of peace – only the sound of birdsong first thing in the morning…

STE-SABINE – 24 Dordogne – **329** F7 – **pop. 375 – alt. 133 m** 4 **C2**
– ✉ 24440

Paris 565 – Bordeaux 130 – Périgueux 79 – Bergerac 32
– Villeneuve-sur-Lot 38

Étincelles-La Gentilhommière (Vincent Lucas) with rm
– *℘ 05 53 74 08 79* VISA MC
– *www.gentilhommiere-etincelles.com – accueil@gentilhommiere-etincelles.com*
– *Closed autumn and February school holidays and dinner from 15 September to 15 June except Sunday*
4 rm – €80/95 €85/100 – ½ P €86/94
Rest – *(number of covers limited, pre-book the day before)* Menu €30 (lunch)/46
Spec. Bourdaloue de foie gras aux noix. Magret de canard rôti au poivre de malabar. Salade d'asperges à la menthe poivrée et aux fraises mara des bois.
◆ Warm Périgord house sporting a mixture of rustic and contemporary details, beautiful wooded garden, and deliciously creative market-fresh set menu (book the day before). Rooms personalised by themes (romantic, oriental, alpine, etc.).

STE-SAVINE – 10 Aube – **313** E4 – **see Troyes**

STES-MARIES-DE-LA-MER – 13 Bouches-du-Rhône – **340** B5 40 **A3**
– **pop. 2 478 – alt. 1 m** **Provence**

Paris 778 – Marseille 129 – Nîmes 67 – Arles 39 – Istres 84
Office de tourisme, 5, avenue Van Gogh ℘ 04 90 97 82 55,
Fax 04 90 97 71 15

Plan on next page

Le Galoubet without rest VISA MC AE
rte de Cacharel – ℘ 04 90 97 82 17 – www.hotelgaloubet.com – info@hotelgaloubet.com – Fax 04 90 97 71 20 – Closed 7-26 December and 4 January-13 February B **s**
20 rm – €50/55 €55/72, €6,50
◆ This nice family hotel has rustic-style Provençal rooms; on the first floor, four of them have a balcony with a wide view of the Impériaux Nature Reserve. Meticulously well maintained.

Pont Blanc without rest VISA MC
chemin du Pont Blanc, via Arles road – ℘ 04 90 97 89 11
– *www.pont-blanc.camargue.fr – hotel.du.pont.blanc@wanadoo.fr*
– *Fax 04 90 97 87 00 – Closed 20 November-27 December* A **z**
15 rm – €48/58 €48/66, €6
◆ The rooms of this small white, flower-decked farmhouse surround a pool and boast terraces overlooking the countryside. Two duplex rooms in a caretaker's lodge.

Le Mas des Salicornes VISA MC
rte d'Arles – ℘ 04 90 97 83 41 – www.hotel-salicornes.com – info@hotel-salicornes.com – Fax 04 90 97 85 70 – Closed January- February A **y**
24 rm – €75/85 €75/85, €8
Rest – *(closed 15 November-31 March) (dinner only)* Menu €28
– Carte approx. €27
◆ Construction all on one level in keeping with local tradition. Some rooms have been renovated; six of them are housed in the recently-built wing and all have private terraces. This restaurant has a rustic-Provençal setting and offers a regional, set daily menu.

Le Fangassier without rest VISA MC AE
12 rte de Cacharel – ℘ 04 90 97 85 02 – www.fangassier.camargue.fr
– *fangassier@camargue.fr – Fax 04 90 97 76 05*
– *Closed 15 November-25 December and 4 January-26 February* B **e**
22 rm – €42/58 €42/60, €6,50
◆ This traditional blue shuttered house sports a sober, rustic interior. The ground floor rooms to the rear boast a small terrace; those on the second floor have sloping ceilings.

STES-MARIES -DE-LA-MER

Aubanel (R. Théodore) . . . . . . **A** 2
Bizet (R. Georges) . . . . **A** 6
Carrière (R. Marcel) . . . . **B** 8
Châteaubriand (R.) . . . . **A** 10
Château d'eau (R. du) . . . . **A** 12
Crin Blanc (R.) . . . . **A** 15
Eglise (Pl. de l') . . . . **A** 17
Espelly (R.) . . . . **A** 18
Etang (R. de l') . . . . **A** 20
Ferrade (R. de la) . . . . **B** 22
Fouque (R. du Capitaine) . . . . **A** 23
Gambetta (Av. Léon) . . . . **AB** 25
Lamartine (Pl.) . . . . **A** 27
Marquis-de-Baroncelli (Pl.) . . . . **A** 28
Médina (R. François) . . . . **B** 29
Pénitents Blancs (R. des) . . . . **A** 30
Portalet (Pl.) . . . . **A** 32
Razeteurs (R. des) . . . . **A** 34

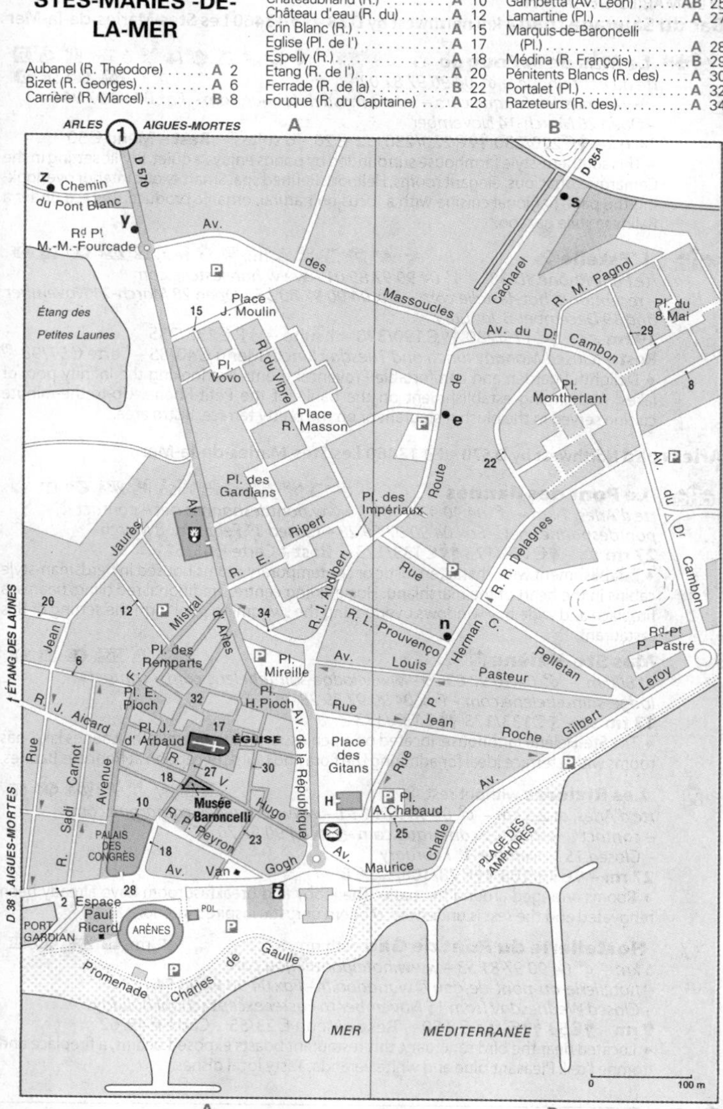

Les Arcades without rest
r. P. Herman – ✆ 04 90 97 73 10 – www.lesarcades.camargue.fr
– contact@lesarcades.camargue.fr – Fax 04 90 97 75 23
– Open 1st March-11 November B **n**
17 rm – †€ 44/60 ††€ 44/60, ☕ € 7
◆ New hotel on a street corner, a step away from the town centre. Colourful, well looked after and regularly revamped rooms. Those upstairs are larger. Very reasonable prices.

Bac du Sauvage road 4 km northwest by D 38 – ✉ 13460 Les Stes-Maries-de-la-Mer

Le Mas de la Fouque rm, VISA AE
rte du Petit Rhône – ✆ 04 90 97 81 02 – www.masdelafouque.com – info@masdelafouque.com – Fax 04 90 97 96 84 – Open 26 March-14 November
24 rm – €220/230 €220/230, €20 – 6 suites **Rest** – Menu €50
◆ This southern-style farmhouse surrounded by ponds enjoys a quiet, idyllic setting in the Camargue. Spacious, elegant rooms. Heliport. Refined spa. Smart exotic interior overlooking the park. Regional cuisine with a focus on natural, organic produce. Terrace under a Balinese style gazebo.

L'Estelle rm, rest, VISA AE
rte Petit-Rhône, (D 38) – ✆ 04 90 97 89 01 – www.hotelestelle.com – reception@hotelestelle.com – Fax 04 90 97 80 36 – Open 28 March-21 November and 19 December-3 January
19 rm – €175/230 €190/390 – 1 suite – ½ P €135/235
Rest – *(closed Monday lunch and Tuesday lunch)* Menu €40/85 – Carte €57/98
◆ Delightful garden and comfortable Provençal rooms overlooking the infinity pool or lakes. A charming establishment on the banks of the Petit-Rhône. Up-to-the-minute cuisine served in the plush restaurant or on the pretty terrace. Bistro area.

Arles road Northwest by D 570 – ✉ 13460 Les Stes-Maries-de-la-Mer

Le Pont des Bannes rm, VISA AE
rte d'Arles, 1 km – ✆ 04 90 97 81 09 – www.pontdesbannes.net – contact@pontdesbannes.net – Fax 04 90 97 89 28 – Closed 1st February-8 March
27 rm – €133/173 €133/173 **Rest** – Carte €45/62
◆ Establishment with character; rustic or contemporary rooms housed in herdsman-style cabins in the heart of the marshland. Horse-riding centre. Traditional red tiling, beams, a fireplace and wide bay windows overlooking the swimming pool form the setting of this restaurant.

Mas Ste-Hélène VISA AE
at 800 m. – ✆ 04 90 97 83 29 – www.lodge-saintehelene.com – contact@lodge-saintehelene.com – Fax 04 90 97 89 28
13 rm – €133/173 €133/173
◆ The Ste-Hélène farmhouse, located on a peninsula jutting out into the Launes lake, has rooms with a terrace ideal for admiring the flora and fauna. Reception at Pont des Bannes.

Les Rizières without rest VISA AE
rte d'Arles, at 2.5 km – ✆ 04 90 97 91 91 – www.lesrizieres-camargue.com – contact@lesrizieres-camargue.com – Fax 04 90 97 70 77 – Closed 15 November-1st February
27 rm – €78/108 €78/108, €8
◆ Rooms arranged around the patio. The lobby and breakfast room have already been renovated and the rest is underway. Modern or rustic inspired interior.

Hostellerie du Pont de Gau with rm rm, VISA AE
5 km – ✆ 04 90 97 81 53 – www.hotelpontdegau.com – hotellerie-du-pont-de-gau@wanadoo.fr – Fax 04 90 97 98 54 – Closed Wednesday from 15 November to Easter except school holidays
9 rm – €53 €, €8,50 **Rest** – Menu €23/55 – Carte €48/62
◆ Located near the bird sanctuary, this restaurant boasts exposed beams, a fireplace and trompe l'œil. Pleasant blue and white veranda. Tasty local dishes.

STE-VERGE – 79 Deux-Sèvres – **322** E3 – see Thouars

LES SAISIES – 73 Savoie – **333** M3 – **Winter sports : 1 600/1 870 m** 45 **D1**
24 – ✉ 73620

Paris 597 – Albertville 29 – Annecy 61 – Bourg-St-Maurice 53 – Chamonix-Mont-Blanc 55 – Megève 23

Office de tourisme, avenue des Jeux Olympiques ✆ 04 79 38 90 30, Fax 04 79 38 96 29

Le Calgary rm, rest, VISA AE
– 04 79 38 98 38 – *www.hotelcalgary.com – contact@hotelcalgary.com – Fax 04 79 38 98 00 – Open 21 June-30 August and 12 December-25 April*
39 rm – €102/122 €139/189, €14 – 1 suite – ½ P €107/134
Rest – *(closed lunch except January, March and April)* Menu (€19), €27 (dinner)/42 – Carte €32/42 dinner only
◆ This Tyrolean-style chalet pays tribute to the feats of local boy, F. Piccard, during the 1988 Olympics. Space, comfort and wood depict the renovated rooms. Sauna, hammam. Classic dishes enriched with Savoyard specialities, served in a large dining room.

SALBRIS – 41 Loir-et-Cher – 318 J7 – pop. 5 836 – alt. 104 m – ✉ 41300 12 C2

Châteaux of the Loire

Paris 187 – Blois 65 – Bourges 62 – Montargis 102 – Orléans 64 – Vierzon 24

Office de tourisme, 1, rue du Général Giraud 02 54 97 22 27, Fax 02 54 97 22 27

de Nançay at Domaine de Samord, SE : 15 km, 02 48 51 86 55

Domaine de Valaudran rm, VISA AE
South West : 1.5 km via rte Romorantin – 02 54 97 20 00 – *www.hotelvaludran.com – info@hotelvalaudran.com – Fax 02 54 97 12 22 – Closed 19 December-6 January, mid-February to mid-March and Sunday from September to May*
32 rm – €72/106 €95/110, €13
Rest – *(closed Monday lunch and Sunday from September to May and Saturday lunch)* Menu (€27), €32 (weekdays)/55
◆ It is difficult to resist the charm of this 19C manor house whose parkland and pool are an invitation to relax. Spruce modern rooms; some have dormer windows. Cottage garden vegetables and regional specialities take pride of place in the restaurant.

Le Parc VISA
8 av. d'Orléans – 02 54 97 18 53 – *www.leparcsalbris.com – reservation@leparcsalbris.com – Fax 02 54 97 24 34 – Closed 11 January-2 February*
23 rm – €58/74 €70/92, €12
Rest – *(closed Monday lunch, Saturday lunch and Sunday from 15 October to 30 April)* Menu (€15), €24/45 – Carte €37/56
◆ Large bourgeois abode set in wooded parkland. The tastefully decorated rooms are regularly refurbished. Pleasant sitting rooms. Homemade dishes that are a masterful blend of tradition and seasonal produce. Rustic interior; terrace.

SALERS – 15 Cantal – 330 C4 – pop. 368 – alt. 950 m – ✉ 15140 5 B3

Auvergne

Paris 509 – Aurillac 43 – Brive-la-Gaillarde 100 – Mauriac 20 – Murat 43

Office de tourisme, place Tyssandier d'Escous 04 71 40 70 68, Fax 04 71 40 70 94

Grande-Place★★ - Church ★ - Esplanade de Barrouze ≤★.

Le Bailliage VISA AE
r. Notre-Dame – 04 71 40 71 95 – *www.salers-hotel-bailliage.com – info@salers-hotel-bailliage.com – Fax 04 71 40 74 90 – Closed 15 November-6 February*
24 rm – €49/65 €70/95, €11 – 3 suites – ½ P €65/95
Rest – *(closed Monday lunch October-April)* Menu (€16), €23/43 – Carte €28/52
◆ This regional-style house offers spacious, personalized and tastefully renovated rooms, overlooking either the garden or the countryside. Welcoming dining room and attractive terrace; appetising Auvergne cuisine.

Demeure de Jarriges VISA AE
at 300 m – Closed 15 November-6 February
26 rm – €49/65 €65/140, €10 – ½ P €65/120
◆ Snug rooms, a house in the country atmosphere and a lush green garden, ideal for catnaps.

Le Gerfaut without rest

rte de Puy Mary, 1 km North-East via D 680 – ✆ 04 71 40 75 75 – www.salers-hotel-gerfaut.com – info@salers-hotel-gerfaut.com – Fax 04 71 40 73 45 – Open from March to October

25 rm – †€ 50/80 ††€ 50/86, ☐ € 9

◆ Modern functional building on the little market town's heights, where you will sleep well. The refurbished rooms, with balconies or terraces, face the valley.

Saluces without rest

r. Martille – ✆ 04 71 40 70 82 – www.hotel-salers.fr – contact@hotel-salers.fr – Fax 04 71 40 71 70 – Closed 12 November-20 December

8 rm – †€ 60/95 ††€ 60/95, ☐ € 10

◆ Simple, elegant rooms, antiques, breakfast under the chestnut tree or facing the lovely fireplace in the sitting room, all in the former home of the Marquis de Lur Saluces.

in Fontanges 5 km south by D 35 – pop. 228 – alt. 692 m – ✉ 15140

Auberge de l'Aspre

– ✆ 04 71 40 75 76 – www.auberge-aspre.com – auberge-aspre@wanadoo.fr – Fax 04 71 40 75 27 – Closed 15 November-15 March, Sunday dinner, Wednesday dinner, Monday October-May and Monday lunch, Friday lunch June-September

8 rm – †€ 55 ††€ 55, ☐ € 8 – ½ P € 59

Rest – Menu € 19/30 – Carte € 25/45

◆ This old farm in the heart of the country has colourful up-to-date rooms with original bathrooms on a mezzanine. A rustic dining hall with a veranda opening onto a garden and a tree-shaded terrace; the appetising menus are regional.

in Theil 6 km southwest by D 35 and D 37 – ✉ 15140 St-Martin-Valmeroux

Hostellerie de la Maronne

rest,

– ✆ 04 71 69 20 33 – www.maronne.com – maronne@maronne.com – Fax 04 71 69 28 22 – Open 4 April-3 November

17 rm – †€ 100/200 ††€ 100/200, ☐ € 14 – 4 suites

Rest – *(closed for lunch except Sunday)* Menu € 38, € 48/58

◆ 19C Auvergne establishment in the heart of the country. Spacious rooms, library-lounge and flower garden. The restaurant has a bucolic view of the meadows and surrounding hills and a discreetly elegant decor.

SALIES-DE-BÉARN – 64 Pyrénées-Atlantiques – 342 G4 – pop. 4 759 – alt. 50 m – Spa : early March-mid Dec. – Casino – ✉ 64270 ▮ Atlantic Coast

3 **B3**

▶ Paris 762 – Bayonne 60 – Dax 36 – Orthez 17 – Pau 64 – Peyrehorade 26

ℹ Office de tourisme, rue des Bains ✆ 05 59 38 00 33, Fax 05 59 38 02 95

◎ Sauveterre-de-Béarn: site★, ≤★★ of the old bridge, South: 10 km.

Maison Léchémia

quartier du Bois, 3 km north-west via Caresse road and secondary road – ✆ 05 59 38 08 55 – www.gites64.com/maison-lechemia – contact@chambresdhoteslechemia.com – Fax 05 59 38 08 55

3 rm ☐ – †€ 40 ††€ 55/65 – ½ P € 46 **Table d'hôte** – Menu € 25 bi

◆ This remote country farmhouse is both welcoming and comfortable. Small, but tastefully decorated rooms. The one with a mezzanine is popular with families. Restaurant offering garden produce, served on the terrace or in front of the fireplace.

La Demeure de la Presqu'île

22 av. des Docteurs-Foix – ✆ 05 59 38 06 22 – www.demeurepresquile.com – info@demeurepresquile.com – Fax 05 59 38 06 22

5 rm ☐ – †€ 70 ††€ 70 – ½ P € 95 **Table d'hôte** – Menu € 28

◆ This fine residence surrounded by a park, close to the town centre, offers spacious rooms, adorned with antique furniture, as well as family suites. At this table d'hôte, meals are prepared by a former pastry cook and served, weather permitting, beneath a magnificent magnolia tree.

in Castagnède 8 km southwest by D 17, D 27 and D 384 – pop. 199 – alt. 38 m – ✉ 64270

La Belle Auberge with rm
– ✆ 05 59 38 15 28 – Fax 05 59 65 03 57 – Closed 1st-14 June and 14 December-31 January
14 rm – †€ 42/46 ††€ 46/48, ☕ € 7 – ½ P € 46
Rest – *(closed Sunday dinner and Monday dinner except July-August)*
Menu € 13/24 – Carte € 17/40
◆ This peaceful Béarn hamlet boasts a pleasant inn in a rustic setting serving generous portions of regional cooking. Simple bedrooms. Beautiful swimming pool and flower garden.

SALIES-DU-SALAT – 31 Haute-Garonne – 343 D6 – pop. 1 943 – alt. 300 m – Spa : early April-late Oct. – Casino – ✉ 31260 28 B3

Languedoc-Roussillon-Tarn Gorges

Paris 751 – Bagnères-de-Luchon 73 – St-Gaudens 27 – Toulouse 79

Office de tourisme, boulevard Jean Jaurès ✆ 05 61 90 53 93, Fax 05 61 90 49 39

du Parc without rest
6 r. d'Austerlitz – ✆ 05 61 90 51 99 – www.hotelduparcsaliesdusalat.com – philippe.robic1@orange.fr – Fax 05 61 90 43 07 – Closed for the spring holidays and 23 December-3 January
21 rm – †€ 42 ††€ 49, ☕ € 7
◆ A well-maintained 1920s hotel in the casino park. Practical rooms with good soundproofing. Breakfast buffets, served on the terrace in summer.

SALIGNAC-EYVIGUES – 24 Dordogne – 329 I6 – pop. 1 128 – alt. 297 m – ✉ 24590 4 D1

Dordogne-Berry-Limousin

Paris 509 – Brive-la-Gaillarde 34 – Cahors 84 – Périgueux 70 – Sarlat-la-Canéda 18

Syndicat d'initiative, place du 19 Mars 1962 ✆ 05 53 28 81 93, Fax 05 53 28 85 26

Northwest 3 km by D 62B and secondary road – ✉ 24590 Salignac-Eyvigues

La Meynardie
– ✆ 05 53 28 85 98 – lameynardie24@wanadoo.fr – Fax 05 53 28 82 79 – Open April-October and closed Tuesday and Wednesday
Rest – Menu (€ 13), € 23/38 – Carte € 35/50
◆ Beams, stones, pebbled flooring and a fireplace dating from 1603 make up the original rustic setting of this Périgord farm lost in the countryside. Trellis-shaded terrace.

SALINS-LES-BAINS – 39 Jura – 321 F5 – pop. 3 045 – alt. 340 m – Spa : late Feb.-early Dec. – Casino – ✉ 39110 16 B2

Burgundy-Jura

Paris 419 – Besançon 41 – Dole 43 – Lons-le-Saunier 52 – Poligny 24 – Pontarlier 46

Office de tourisme, place des Salines ✆ 03 84 73 01 34, Fax 03 84 37 92 85

Site★ - Fort Belin★.

Grand Hôtel des Bains
pl. des Alliés – ✆ 03 84 37 90 50 – www.hotel-des-bains.fr – hotel.bains@wanadoo.fr – Fax 03 84 37 96 80
31 rm – †€ 66/88 ††€ 66/88, ☕ € 10 – ½ P € 59/71
Rest – Menu € 20/30 – Carte € 32/49
◆ A contemporary makeover for this 1860 building with a superb listed sitting room. Functional rooms, thermal pool and independent fitness centre. Restaurant in a pleasant rustic setting. Classic cuisine with regional influences. Separate brasserie serving simpler meals.

Charles Sander without rest
26 r. de la République – 03 84 73 36 40 – www.residencesander.com – residencesander@wanadoo.fr – Fax 03 84 73 36 46
14 rm – €60/95 €65/95, €8,50
◆ Attractive old house with new, welcoming rooms (only one without a kitchenette). Wine buffs will want to spend time in the delicatessen on the ground floor.

SALLANCHES – 74 Haute-Savoie – 328 M5 – pop. 15 200 – alt. 550 m – 46 F1
– 74700 French Alps

Paris 585 – Annecy 72 – Bonneville 29 – Chamonix-Mont-Blanc 28 – Megève 14

Office de tourisme, 32, quai de l'Hôtel de Ville 04 50 58 04 25, Fax 04 50 58 38 47

★★ of Mt-Blanc - Médonnet chapel: ★★ - Cascade d'Arpenaz ★ North: 5 km.

Hostellerie des Prés du Rosay rm, rest, VISA AE
285 rte de Rosay – 04 50 58 06 15 – www.lespresdurosay.com – contact@hotellerie-pres-du-rosay.com – Fax 04 50 58 48 70
15 rm – €71/75 €83/88, €9 – ½ P €75/80
Rest – *(closed 3-10 May, 1st-8 November, 1st-7 January, Saturday and Sunday)*
Menu €18 (weekdays)/28 – Carte €36/46
◆ Modern chalet in a residential area. The simple functional rooms (new bedding and Wi-Fi system) overlook the alpine countryside. The restaurant has smart decor, a lovely view of the meadows and traditional food.

Auberge de l'Orangerie VISA
carrefour de la Charlotte, 2.5 km on Passy road (D 13) – 04 50 58 49 16 – http://perso.wanadoo.fr/auberge-orangerie – orangerie74@orange.fr – Fax 04 50 58 54 63 – Closed 20 June-10 July
18 rm – €55/65 €65/75, €10
Rest – *(closed 20 June-10 July, 5-25 January and Sunday dinner) (dinner only except Sunday)* Menu €25 (weekday dinner) – Carte €41/60
◆ Charming welcome, cosy rooms available in either the main building or the new annexe, with balconies facing Mont Blanc. Well-being centre. Traditional cuisine and local specialities on offer in a friendly setting.

Le St-Julien VISA
53 r. Chenal – 04 50 58 02 24 – Closed spring holidays, autumn school holidays, Sunday dinner, Monday and Wednesday
Rest – Menu (€26), €24/40 – Carte €41/48
◆ A welcoming flower-decked façade in summer. A wood-panelled dining room serving dishes that change with the seasons and a few regional specialities.

SALLES-LA-SOURCE – 12 Aveyron – 338 H4 – pop. 1 912 – 29 C1
– alt. 450 m – 12330 Languedoc-Roussillon-Tarn Gorges

Paris 670 – Toulouse 160 – Rodez 13 – Villefranche-de-Rouergue 71 – Onet-le-Château 11

Gîtes de Cougousse
r. du Père Colombier, in Cougousse 4 km North-west via D 901 – 05 65 71 85 52 – www.gites.cougousse.free.fr – gites.de.cougousse@wanadoo.fr – Open 1st April-15 October
4 rm – €50 €55
Table d'hôte – *(closed Monday dinner, Wednesday dinner and Saturday dinner)*
Menu €20 bi
◆ Large, handsome 15C (non-smoking) abode in a riverside garden with vegetable plot. Personalised, quiet rooms and an inviting rustic lounge in the former kitchen. Gîtes available.

LES SALLES-SUR-VERDON – 83 Var – 340 M3 – pop. 202 – 41 C2
– alt. 440 m – 83630 French Alps

Paris 790 – Brignoles 57 – Draguignan 49 – Digne-les-Bains 60 – Manosque 62

Office de tourisme, place Font Freye 04 94 70 21 84, Fax 04 94 84 22 57

Ste-Croix lake ★★.

Auberge des Salles without rest
18 r. Ste-Catherine – ✆ 04 94 70 20 04
– www.var-provence.com – auberge.des.salles@wanadoo.fr – Fax 04 94 70 21 78
– Open 16 April-5 October
30 rm – €55/75 €55/75, €7
◆ Peaceful hotel on the banks of St Croix Lake. Rustic furniture and tiles in the rooms, nearly all of which boast a balcony. Garden with swimming pool.

SALON-DE-PROVENCE – 13 Bouches-du-Rhône – 340 F4 — 40 B3
– pop. 39 900 – alt. 80 m – ✉ 13300 Provence

Paris 720 – Aix-en-Provence 37 – Arles 46 – Avignon 50 – Marseille 54
Office de tourisme, 56, cours Gimon ✆ 04 90 56 27 60, Fax 04 90 56 77 09
de Miramas Miramas Mas de Combe, SW : 10 km, ✆ 04 90 58 56 55
Pont Royal Country Club Mallemort Domaine de Pont Royal, NE : 16 km on D 538 and D 17, ✆ 04 90 57 40 79
Musée de l'Empéri★★.

SALON-DE-PROVENCE

Ancienne Halle (Pl.) .... BY 2
Capucins (Bd des) .... BZ 3
Carnot (Cours) .... AY 4
Centuries (Pl. des) .... BY 6
Clemenceau (Bd Georges) .. AY 7
Coren (Bd Léopold) .... AY 8
Craponne (Allées de) .... BZ 10
Crousillat (Pl.) .... BY 12
Farreyroux (Pl.) .... BZ 13
Ferrage (Pl.) .... BZ 14
Fileuses de Soie (R. des) .... AY 15
Frères J. et R.-Kennedy (R. des) .... AY
Gambetta (Pl.) .... BZ 18
Gimon (Cours) .... BZ
Horloge (R. de l') .... BY 20
Ledru-Rollin (Bd) .... AY 22
Massenet (R.) .... AY 23
Médicis (Pl. C. de) .... BZ 24
Mistral (Bd Frédéric) .... BY 26
Moulin d'Isnard (R.) .... BY 27
Nostradamus (Bd) .... AY 28
Pasquet (Bd) .... BZ 30
Pelletan (Cours Camille) .... AY 32
Raynaud-d'Ursule (R.) .... BZ 34
République (Bd de la) .... AY 33
St-Laurent (Square) .... BY 35
Victor-Hugo (Cours) .... BY 38

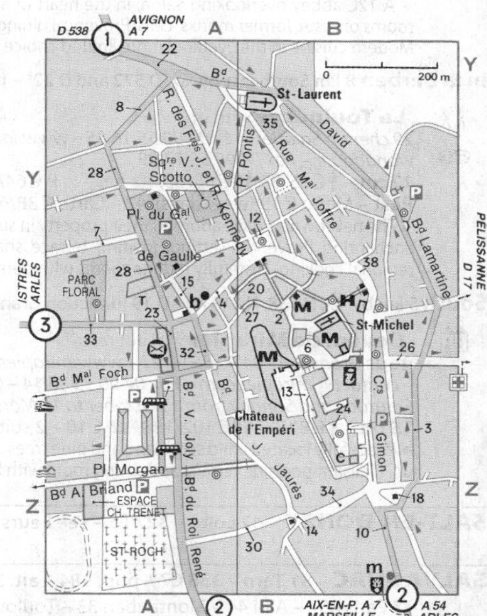

Angleterre without rest
98 cours Carnot – ✆ 04 90 56 01 10 – www.hotel-dangleterre.biz – hoteldangleterre@wanadoo.fr – Fax 04 90 56 71 75 – Closed 20 December-6 January AY **b**
26 rm – €47/52 €52/64, €7
◆ This hotel near the museums is very conveniently located. Renovated rooms; some are air-conditioned. Breakfast buffet under a glass cupola.

XXX **Le Mas du Soleil** with rm
*38 chemin St-Côme, (east on D 17 - **BY**)*
– ✆ 04 90 56 06 53 – www.lemasdusoleil.com
– mas.du.soleil.@wanadoo.fr – Fax 04 90 56 21 52
10 rm – €115/280 €115/280, € 15 – ½ P € 105/195
Rest – *(closed Sunday dinner and Monday except public holidays)* Menu € 33 (weekdays)/82 – Carte € 55/80
◆ French Riviera villa serving tasty southern dishes in a bright modern decor overlooking the garden. Some of the comfortable rooms open onto the garden.

Le Craponne

146 allées de Craponne – 04 90 53 23 92 – Closed 24 August-15 September, 24 December-4 January, Sunday dinner, Wednesday dinner and Monday

Rest – Menu (€ 15), € 24/37 – Carte € 38/56 BZ **m**

◆ The name of this restaurant refers to a local benefactor. Dark wood panelling, yellow walls and rustic furniture. In fine weather, meals served in a small flower-decked courtyard. Family welcome.

Northeast 5 km by D 17 BY **then D 16 – ✉ 13300 Salon-de-Provence**

Abbaye de Sainte-Croix

Val de Cuech road – 04 90 56 24 55 – www.relaischateaux.com/saintecroix – saintecroix@relaischateaux.com – Fax 04 90 56 31 12 – Closed mid December-mid January, mid February-mid March and from Sunday to Friday November-March

21 rm – € 149/377 € 149/377, € 24 – 4 suites – ½ P € 165/286

Rest – *(closed from Monday to Friday in October and April and open only Saturday dinner November-March)* Menu € 51 (weekday lunch), € 78/120 – Carte € 78/137

◆ A 12C abbey overlooking Salon, in the heart of an isolated garrigue park. Up-to-date rooms or rustic former monks' cells. Provençal dining hall and shaded, panoramic terrace. Modern cuisine in the evening; more limited choice at lunchtime.

in la Barben 8 km Southeast by ②, D 572 and D 22ᴱ – pop. 649 – alt. 105 m – ✉ 13330

La Touloubre with rm

29 chemin Salatier – 04 90 55 16 85 – www.latouloubre.com – latouloubre@wanadoo.fr – Fax 04 90 55 17 99

12 rm – € 65/85 € 65/85, € 8 – ½ P € 64/74

Rest – Menu € 19 (weekdays)/42 – Carte € 38/60

◆ The new owners have adorned their property in sunny southern shades to enhance the enchanting Provençal setting. Inviting terrace shaded by plane trees and generous regional cooking. Tastefully redone rooms with personalised touches.

South 5 km by ②, N 538, N 113 and D 19 (direction Grans) – ✉ 13250 Cornillon-Confoux

Devem de Mirapier without rest

rte de Grans – 04 90 55 99 22 – www.mirapier.com – contact@mirapier.com – Fax 04 90 55 86 14 – Closed 1st November-15 January, Saturday and Sunday from 15 October to 15 March

15 rm – € 82/98 € 102/138, € 10 – 2 suites

◆ Peacefully located amid scrubland and pine trees. The pretty rooms have been spruced up. Pleasant poolside terrace and sitting room with billiards table.

SALT-EN-DONZY – 42 Loire – 327 E5 – see Feurs

SALVAGNAC – 81 Tarn – 338 C7 – pop. 984 – alt. 231 m 29 C2

Paris 657 – Albi 44 – Montauban 33 – Toulouse 49

Office de tourisme, les Sourigous 05 63 33 57 84, Fax 05 63 33 58 78

Le Relais des Deux Vallées

Grand'rue – 05 63 33 61 90 – www.tarn-hotel.com – relais-deux-vallees@wanadoo.fr – Fax 05 63 33 61 91 – Closed 26 August-2 September and 2-10 January

10 rm – € 42 € 46, € 6 – ½ P € 50

Rest – *(closed Monday)* Menu € 11 bi (weekday lunch), € 18/35 – Carte € 25/51

◆ Small family-run hotel on the village square. Charming little rooms with wooden or wrought iron furniture. Some have a terrace. The bay windows of the dining room overlook the countryside. Simple and tasty traditional cuisine.

SAMATAN – 32 Gers – 336 H9 – pop. 2 130 – alt. 170 m – ✉ 32130 28 B2

Paris 703 – Auch 37 – Gimont 18 – L'Isle-Jourdain 21 – Rieusmes 206

Office de tourisme, 3, rue du chamoine Dieuzaide 05 62 62 55 40, Fax 05 62 62 50 26

du Château de Barbet Lombez Route de Sauveterre, SW : 5 km, 05 62 66 44 49

Au Canard Gourmand with rm
La Rente, on the D 632 – ✆ 05 62 62 49 81 – www.aucanardgourmand.com – contact@aucanardgourmand.com – Closed Wednesday lunch, Monday dinner and Tuesday
5 rm – †€ 65/85 ††€ 75/120, ☕ € 12 – ½ P € 82/92
Rest – *(number of covers limited, pre-book)* Menu (€ 26), € 35/40 bi – Carte approx. € 48
◆ Regional cuisine served in a brightly coloured setting with designer touches. The dining room opens onto a terrace and flower-decked garden in fine weather. Comfortable rooms decorated in a cosy style with African touches.

Côté Sud
2 bis pl. Fontaine – ✆ 05 62 62 63 29 – www.restaurant-cote-sud.com – contact@restaurant-cote-sud.com – Fax 05 62 62 35 05 – Closed 1 week in May, autumn school holidays, Sunday dinner from October to April, Tuesday and Wednesday
Rest – Menu € 13 bi – Carte € 35/47
◆ An elegant restaurant with red bricks, exposed beams, polished wood tables, library and objets d'art. Modern recipes and attentive welcome.

LE SAMBUC – 13 Bouches-du-Rhône – 340 D4 – ✉ 13200 — 40 A3

Paris 742 – Arles 25 – Marseille 117 – Stes-Marie-de-la-Mer 50 – Salon-de-Provence 68

Le Mas de Peint
2.5 km via Salins road – ✆ 04 90 97 20 62 – www.masdepeint.com – hotel@masdepeint.net – Fax 04 90 97 22 20 – Open 20 March-12 November and 19 December-5 January
11 rm – †€ 235/410 ††€ 235/410, ☕ € 22
Rest – *(closed Tuesday lunch, Thursday lunch and Wednesday) (number of covers limited, pre-book)* Menu € 42 (lunch), € 52/62
◆ This stunning 17C farmhouse and vast grounds continue to uphold Camargue traditions. Cosy rooms, garden with pool, equestrian centre with riding arena. Admire the kitchen's "vintage" decor as you watch the chef prepare appetising regional dishes.

SAMER – 62 Pas-de-Calais – 301 D4 – pop. 3 377 – alt. 70 m – ✉ 62830 — 30 A2

Paris 244 – Lille 132 – Arras 112 – Calais 50 – Boulogne-sur-Mer 17
Office de tourisme, rue de Desvres ✆ 03 21 87 10 42, Fax 03 21 06 01 90

Le Clos des Trois Tonneaux
73 r. de Montreuil – ✆ 03 21 92 33 33 – www.leclosdestroistonneaux.com – leclosdes3tonneaux@orange.fr – Fax 03 21 30 50 94 – Closed 4-26 January, Saturday lunch, Sunday dinner and Monday
Rest – Menu (€ 17), € 22/45 – Carte € 45/57
◆ Former distillery on three floors that has lost nothing of its character, having been successfully modernised. Low-key lounge in the vaulted cellar. Modern cuisine and good wine list.

SAMOËNS – 74 Haute-Savoie – 328 N4 – pop. 2 332 – alt. 710 m – Winter sports : 720/2 480 m 8 70 – ✉ 74340 French Alps — 46 F1

Paris 581 – Annecy 75 – Chamonix-Mont-Blanc 60 – Genève 53 – Thonon-les-Bains 56
Office de tourisme, gare routière ✆ 04 50 34 40 28, Fax 04 50 34 95 82
Place du Gros Tilleul★ - Jaÿsinia Alpine garden ★.
La Rosière ≤★★ North: 6 km - Cascade du Rouget★★ South: 10 km - Cirque du Fer à Cheval★★ East: 13 km.

Neige et Roc
rte de Taninges – ✆ 04 50 34 40 72 – www.neigeetroc.com – resa@neigeetroc.com – Fax 04 50 34 14 48 – Open 13 June-20 September and 19 December-11 April
50 rm – †€ 80/160 ††€ 100/160, ☕ € 14 – ½ P € 74/140
Rest – Menu € 23 (weekday lunch)/50 – Carte € 50/60
◆ A large chalet housing cosy rooms with balconies. Another building offers lovely studio flats with kitchenettes. Winter and summer swimming pools and spa. Large, rustic veranda/dining room (beams, light wood and stonework). Regional menu.

Les Glaciers rest,

– ✆ 04 50 34 40 06 – www.hotellesglaciers.com – contact@hotellesglaciers.com – Fax 04 50 34 16 75 – Open 16 June-8 September and 21 December-14 April

42 rm – †€ 100/120 ††€ 110/130, ☕ € 15 – ½ P € 100/120

Rest – *(dinner only in winter)* Menu € 23 – Carte € 41/52

◆ Large building in the centre of the resort. Rooms with light wood panelling and pine furniture. Full leisure facilities including a private lake 6km away for fishing and jet skiing. Large restaurant with family guesthouse ambiance. Regionally inspired cuisine.

Edelweiss

La Piaz, 1.5 km north-west on Plampraz road – ✆ 04 50 34 41 32 – www.edelweiss-samoens.com – hotel-edelweiss@wanadoo.fr – Fax 04 50 34 18 75 – Closed 13-30 April, 28 June-10 July and 24 October-21 November

20 rm – †€ 55/72 ††€ 68/85, ☕ € 8,50 – ½ P € 60/70

Rest – *(closed 13 April-20 May, 28 June-10 July and 26 September-19 December) (dinner only)* Menu € 23, € 25/46 – Carte € 33/44

◆ The edelweiss is one of the 5,000 species growing in the Alpine garden created by Madame Cognacq-Jay near this simple, comfortable chalet-hotel. Panoramic view of the village and valley. South facing dining room, extending onto a terrace. Traditional cuisine.

Gai Soleil rest,

– ✆ 04 50 34 40 74 – www.hotel-samoens.com – hotel.gai-soleil@wanadoo.fr – Fax 04 50 34 10 78 – Open 6 June-19 September and 18 December-21 April

22 rm – †€ 52/100 ††€ 52/100, ☕ € 10 – ½ P € 52/88

Rest – *(closed Wednesday and Saturday) (dinner only)* Menu € 21/28 – Carte € 16/34

◆ This chalet on the outskirts of the village has simple guestrooms with Savoyard decor and wide balconies. Fireside lounge bar and activities for children in the park. Regional fare served in the restaurant.

Le Monde à L'Envers

pl. Criou – ✆ 04 50 34 19 36 – Closed 29 May-3 July, 27 October-14 December, Wednesday except July-August and Tuesday

Rest – Menu (€ 18 bi) – Carte € 45/58

◆ Both the decor and the cuisine in this restaurant have an international feel. The dining room is decorated with objects from around the world, while the dishes are a happy combination of the exotic and the traditional.

in Morillon **4.5 km west – pop. 498 – alt. 687 m – Winter sports : 700/2 200 m 5 74 – ✉ 74440**

Office de tourisme, Chef-lieu ✆ 04 50 90 15 76, Fax 04.50.90.11.47

Morillon

– ✆ 04 50 90 10 32 – www.hotellemorillon.com – infos@hotellemorillon.com – Fax 04 50 90 70 08 – Open 2 June-19 September and 16 December-14 April

22 rm – †€ 75/150 ††€ 75/150, ☕ € 12 – ½ P € 70/125

Rest – *(dinner only)* Menu € 25/35 – Carte € 37/45

◆ Sculpted wood, local furniture and fireside armchairs add to the Alpine feel of this pleasant chalet. Small rooms, most of which have wide balconies. Alpine specialities served in a pleasantly relaxed atmosphere.

SAMOUSSY – **02 Aisne** – **306** E5 – **see Laon**

SAMPANS – **39 Jura** – **321** C4 – **see Dole**

Do not confuse X with ✿!
X defines comfort, while stars are awarded for the best cuisine, across all categories of comfort.

SANARY-SUR-MER – **83 Var** – **340** J7 – **pop. 17 400** – **alt. 1 m** 40 **B3**
– ✉ **83110** French Riviera

Paris 824 – Aix-en-Provence 75 – La Ciotat 23 – Marseille 55 – Toulon 13

N.-D.-de-Pitié chapel ≤★.

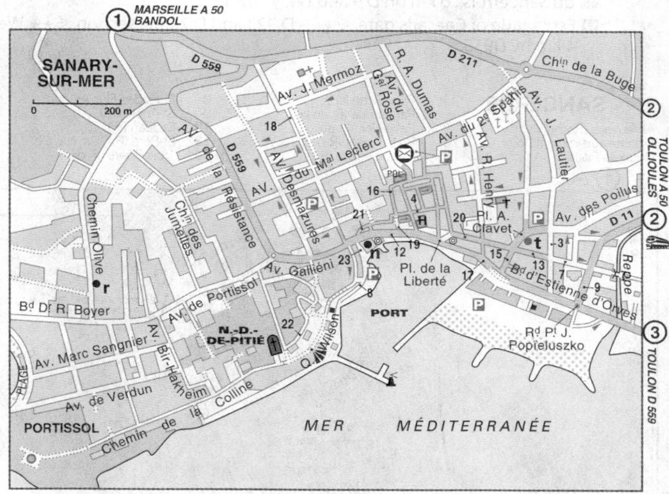

Avenir (Bd de l')	3	Giboin (R.)	13	Pacha (Pl. Michel)	19
Blanc (R. Louis)	4	Granet (R.)	15	Péri (R. Gabriel)	20
Clemenceau (Av. G.)	7	Gueirard (R. L.)	16	Prudhomie (R. de la)	21
Esménard (Quai M.)	8	Jean-Jaurès (Av.)	17	Sœur-Vincent (Montée)	22
Europe-Unie (Av. de l')	9	Lyautey (Av. Mar.)	18	Tour (Pl. de la)	23
Gaulle (Quai Charles-de)	12				

Soleil et Jardin Le Parc without rest
445 av. Europe Unie, via ② – ☎ 04 94 25 80 08 – www.sanary-hotel-soleiljardin.com – hotelsanarysoleiljardin@wanadoo.fr – Fax 04 94 26 63 90
40 rm – €110/190 €150/280, €15 – 4 suites
◆ This regional-style building and new extension near the beach is home to well-equipped, good quality rooms. Excellent soundproofing. Friendly welcome.

De La Tour
quai Gén. de Gaulle – ☎ 04 94 74 10 10 – www.sanary-hoteldelatour.com – la.tour.sanary@wanadoo.fr – Fax 04 94 74 69 49 **n**
24 rm – €64/90 €84/130
Rest – *(closed 13-22 October, Tuesday except July-August and Wednesday)* Menu €33/48 – Carte €38/60
◆ Adjoining an 11C watchtower, most of the rooms of this well-located family business overlook the busy harbour. Restaurant whose terrace commands a view of the returning fishing boats. Fish and seafood menu that varies with the tides and seasons.

Synaya without rest
92 chemin Olive – ☎ 04 94 74 10 50 – www.hotelsynaya.fr – hotelsynaya@wanadoo.fr – Fax 04 94 34 70 30 – Open 27 March-5 November **r**
11 rm – €80/145 €80/170, €10
◆ Small hotel in a quiet residential district, with a garden planted with palm trees. Functional, modern rooms and lovely bathrooms.

San Lazzaro
10 pl. Albert Cavet – ☎ 04 94 88 41 60 – Fax 04 94 74 07 84 – Closed lunch except Sunday from September to June and Monday **t**
Rest – Menu €29/60 – Carte €57/63
◆ A welcoming, modern restaurant set on a charming village square. The son of the house concocts inventive menus with a decidedly Provençal flavour.

SANCERRE – 18 Cher – 323 M3 – pop. 1 831 – alt. 342 m – ✉ 18300 12 D2

Dordogne-Berry-Limousin

Paris 198 – Bourges 46 – La Charité-sur-Loire 30 – Salbris 69 – Vierzon 68

Office de tourisme, rue de la croix de bois ✆ 02 48 54 08 21, Fax 02 48 78 03 58

du Sancerrois : 6 km on D 9 and D4, ✆ 02 48 54 11 22

Esplanade of Caesar's gate ⋞★★ - D 923 and D 7 intersection ⋞★★ West: 4 km by D955.

SANCERRE

Abreuvoirs (Remp. des) 2
Marché-aux-Porcs (R. du) 5
Nouvelle Place 6
Paix (R. de la) 8
Panneterie (R. de la) 9
Pavé-Noir (R. du) 12
Porte-César (R.) 13
Porte-Serrure (R.) 15
Puits-des-Fins (R. du) 16
St-André (R.) 18
St-Jean (R.) 20
St-Père (R.) 22
Trois-Piliers (R. des) 23

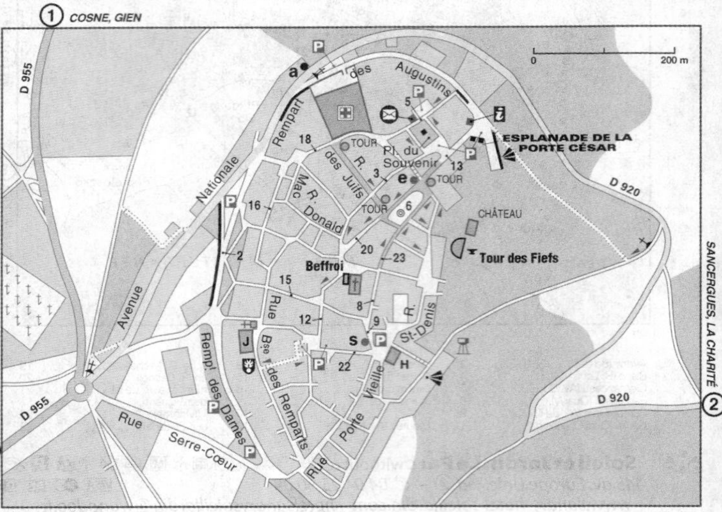

Panoramic

rempart des Augustins – ✆ 02 48 54 22 44 – www.panoramicotel.com – panoramicotel@wanadoo.fr – Fax 02 48 54 39 55 **a**

57 rm – †€ 65/85 ††€ 75/137, ☕ € 12 – ½ P € 80

Rest *Les Augustins* – *✆ 02 48 54 01 44 (closed 5-20 January and Monday lunch)* Menu (€ 18), € 25/53 – Carte € 31/59

◆ This aptly named hotel has magnificent views of the surrounding vineyards. Recently renovated, the hotel offers cosy, comfortable guestrooms, plus a lounge and wine shop. Hushed atmosphere and muted colours in the restaurant; good traditional cuisine.

La Tour

Nouvelle Place – ✆ 02 48 54 00 81 – www.la-tour-sangerre.fr – info@la-tour-sancerre.fr – Fax 02 48 78 01 54 – Closed Sunday dinner and Monday in low season **e**

Rest – Menu € 27 (weekdays)/80 bi – Carte € 30/50

◆ Restaurant topped by a 14C tower. Two dining rooms, one in elegant rustic-style, the other (upstairs) with a modern decor and a view of the vineyards. Good selection of Sancerre wines.

La Pomme d'Or

pl. de la Mairie – ✆ 02 48 54 13 30 – Fax 02 48 54 19 22 – Closed autumn half-term holidays, Sunday dinner from November to March, Tuesday dinner and Wednesday April-October **s**

Rest – *(number of covers limited, pre-book)* Menu € 20 (weekday lunch), € 28/48

◆ This popular restaurant a stone's throw from the town hall serves delicious traditional cuisine. The small dining room is brightened by an attractive fresco depicting the Sancerre hills.

in St-Satur **3 km by ① and D 955 – pop. 1 712 – alt. 155 m – ✉ 18300**

Office de tourisme, 25, rue du Commerce ✆ 02 48 54 01 30, Fax 02 48 54 01 30

La Chancelière without rest

5 r. Hilaire-Amagat – ✆ 02 48 54 01 57 – www.la-chanceliere.com – jaudibert@wanadoo.fr

5 rm – €105 €130

◆ The terrace of this 18C town house offers a fine view of Sancerre and its vineyards. Tiled floor, exposed beams and antique furniture add a touch of character to the rooms.

in Chavignol **4 km by ① and D 183 – ✉ 18300**

La Côte des Monts Damnés with rm — rest, VISA

– ✆ 02 48 54 01 72 – www.montsdamnes.com – restaurantcmd@wanadoo.fr – Fax 02 48 78 28 32 – Closed February, Tuesday and Wednesday

12 rm – €80/175 €95/190, €12 – ½ P €110/125

Rest – *(pre-book)* Menu €31/53

Rest – Menu €10/15 – Carte €20/30

◆ On the road up to this wine-growing village is a country inn, which is well known for its fine local cuisine and wide choice of Sancerre wines. Try the famous Crottin de Chavignol! Find conviviality and regional dishes at the Bistrot. Spacious rooms with modern and classic furniture. Decor on a regional theme.

in St-Thibault **4 km by ① and D 4 – ✉ 18300**

De la Loire without rest — VISA

2 quai de Loire – ✆ 02 48 78 22 22 – www.hotel-de-la-loire.com – info@hotel-de-la-loire.com – Fax 02 48 78 22 29 – Closed 23 December-3 January

11 rm – €63/81 €63/81, €9

◆ The creator of Maigret wrote two of his novels in this hotel situated on the banks of the Loire. Rooms decorated on the theme of travel; home-made bread and jams.

Red = Pleasant. Look for the red and symbols.

SANCY – 77 Seine-et-Marne – 312 G2 – pop. 321 – alt. 142 m – ✉ 77580 19 C2

Paris 55 – Château-Thierry 48 – Coulommiers 14 – Meaux 13 – Melun 50

Château de Sancy — VISA AE

1 pl. de l'Église – ✆ 01 60 25 77 77 – www.chateaudesancy.com – info@chateaudesancy.com – Fax 01 60 25 60 55

21 rm – €132/182 €132/253, €14 **Rest** – Menu €28/39

◆ The wide variety of leisure equipment on offer on the estate of this 18C manor house invites guests to relax. Cosy rooms; those in the lodge are more functional. A well-appointed, intimate dining room serving dishes that change according to the seasons.

SAND – 67 Bas-Rhin – 315 J6 – pop. 1 073 – alt. 159 m – ✉ 67230 1 B2

Paris 501 – Barr 15 – Erstein 7 – Molsheim 26 – Obernai 16 – Sélestat 22 – Strasbourg 34

Hostellerie la Charrue — rest, VISA

4 r. 1er décembre – ✆ 03 88 74 42 66 – www.lacharrue.com – info@lacharrue.com – Fax 03 88 74 12 02 – Closed 25 August-6 September and 21 December-8 January

23 rm – €55 €65, €9 – ½ P €56

Rest – *(closed Monday and lunch except Sunday and public holidays)* Menu €23, €30/35 bi – Carte €25/35

◆ Former carters' hostel converted into a tranquil family inn. Spruce, well-appointed guestrooms graced with painted furniture. Friendly welcome. Wood panelling and bright colours in the warm Alsace decor of the dining rooms.

SANDARVILLE – 28 Eure-et-Loir – **311** E5 – **pop. 385** – **alt. 171 m** – ✉ **28120** 11 **B1**

Paris 105 – Brou 23 – Chartres 16 – Châteaudun 36 – Le Mans 109 – Nogent-le-Rotrou 47

XX **Auberge de Sandarville** VISA MC

14 r. Sente aux Prêtres, (near the church) – ☎ 02 37 25 33 18
– Closed 4-20 January, 15-21 February, Tuesday dinner in winter, Sunday dinner and Monday
Rest – Menu € 28 (weekdays)/57 bi – Carte approx. € 52,50
◆ Three charming country-style dining rooms in a Beauce farm dating from 1850, with beams, fireplace, red floor tiles, furniture and knickknacks from here and there. Pretty terrace in the flower garden.

SANDILLON – 45 Loiret – **318** J4 – **pop. 3 570** – **alt. 101 m** – ✉ **45640** 12 **C2**

Paris 148 – Orléans 13 – Châteaudun 65 – Châteauneuf-sur-Loire 16 – Montargis 60

XX **Rest. Saisons d'Ailleurs et H. un Toit pour Toi** with rm

2 r. Villette – ☎ 02 38 41 00 22 P VISA MC AE
– www.restaurant-saisonsdailleurs.com – 1toitpourtoi@wanadoo.fr
– Fax 02 38 41 07 74
12 rm – †€ 58 ††€ 65, ☕ € 9 – ½ P € 65
Rest – *(closed 4-19 August, Sunday dinner and Monday)* Menu (€ 26), € 42/75 – Carte € 52/120
◆ Wonderful, inventive cuisine is served in this pleasant, family-run auberge situated on the edge of the Sologne. Simpler fare is available in the bistro (brasserie-style menu). The guestrooms have been partly furnished in contemporary style.

SANILHAC – 07 Ardèche – **331** H6 – **see Largentière**

SAN-MARTINO-DI-LOTA – 2B – **345** F3 – **see Corse (Bastia)**

SAN-PEIRE-SUR-MER – 83 Var – **340** P5 – **see les Issambres**

SANTA-GIULIA (GOLFE) – 2A Corse-du-Sud – **345** E10 – **see Corse (Porto-Vecchio)**

SANT'ANTONINO – 2B Haute-Corse – **345** C4 – **see Corse**

SANTENAY – 21 Côte-d'Or – **320** I8 – **pop. 839** – **alt. 225 m** – **Casino** – ✉ **21590** **Burgundy-Jura** 7 **A3**

Paris 330 – Autun 39 – Beaune 18 – Chalon-sur-Saône 25 – Le Creusot 29 – Dijon 63

Office de tourisme, gare SNCF ☎ 03 80 20 63 15, Fax 03 80 20 69 15

XX **Le Terroir** AC VISA MC

pl. du Jet-d'Eau – ☎ 03 80 20 63 47 – www.restaurantleterroir.com
– restaurant.le.terroir@wanadoo.fr – Fax 03 80 20 66 45
– Closed 4 December-11 January, Wednesday dinner from November to March, Sunday dinner and Thursday
Rest – Menu € 22/45 – Carte € 34/56
◆ This restaurant in the village centre offers tasty local dishes. Pleasant rustic and modern decor; pride of place is given to an Aubusson tapestry. Good regional wine list.

LE SAPPEY-EN-CHARTREUSE – 38 Isère – **333** H6 – **pop. 995** – **alt. 1 014 m** – **Winter sports : to Sappey and to Col de Porte 1 000/1 700 m** 11 – ✉ **38700** **French Alps** 45 **C2**

Paris 577 – Chambéry 61 – Grenoble 14 – St-Pierre-de-Chartreuse 14 – Voiron 37

Syndicat d'initiative, Le Bourg ☎ 04 76 88 84 05

Charmant Som ❊★★★ Northwest: 9 km then 1 h.

Les Skieurs with rm
– 04 76 88 82 76 – *www.lesskieurs.com* – *hotelskieurs@wanadoo.fr*
– *Fax 04 76 88 85 76* – *Closed Easter and Christmas holidays and Sunday*
11 rm – €85 €85, € 12 – ½ P €73
Rest – *(closed Tuesday lunch, Sunday dinner and Monday)* Menu €28 (weekdays), €32/44 – Carte €48/60
◆ Charming chalet-style wood-panelled dining room with fireplace and rustic furniture. Copious, regional cuisine. Attractive terrace. Small, practical rooms with wood everywhere (some with balcony).

Le Dagobert
pl. de l'Église – 04 76 88 80 26 – *Closed Wednesday except school holidays*
Rest – Menu €16/29 – Carte €30/48
◆ Rustic dining room fronted by a small wine bar and adorned with a fireplace. Pleasant shaded summer terrace. Traditional cuisine.

SARE – 64 Pyrénées-Atlantiques – 342 C5 – pop. 2 262 – alt. 70 m – 3 A3
– 64310 Atlantic Coast

Paris 794 – Biarritz 26 – Cambo-les-Bains 19 – Pau 138 – St-Jean-de-Luz 14

Office de tourisme, Herriko Etxea 05 59 54 20 14, Fax 05 59 54 29 15

Arraya rm,
place du village – 05 59 54 20 46 – *www.arraya.com*
– *hotel@arraya.com* – *Fax 05 59 54 27 04*
– *Open 28 March-2 November*
20 rm – €84/94 €84/130, €10 – ½ P €77/100
Rest – *(closed Monday lunch, Thursday lunch and Sunday dinner except 1st July-21 September)* Menu (€17), €23/33 – Carte €40/49
◆ Former post-house in typical regional architecture, set on the village square on the Compostela route. Lovely rustic interior and delightful Basque-style rooms. Delightful garden. The regional décor of the restaurant has character. Shaded terrace, regional cuisine and shop selling gourmet produce.

Pikassaria rm, rest,
Quartier Lehenbiscay – 05 59 54 21 51 – *www.hotel-pikassaria.com*
– *hotelpikassaria@orange.fr* – *Fax 05 59 54 27 40*
– *Open 15 March-11 November*
18 rm – €55 €57/59, €7 – ½ P €50/52
Rest – *(closed for lunch except Sunday)* Menu (€16) – Carte €30/40
◆ Local-style building in a pleasant rural setting, at the foot of the St Ignace pass. Rooms of varying sizes, some with a mountain view. The Table du Pikassaria lives up to its name with flavours from Basque cooking.

Baratxartea rm, rest,
quartier Ihalar, 2 km east – 05 59 54 20 48 – *www.hotel-baratxartea.com*
– *contact@hotel-baratxartea.com* – *Fax 05 59 47 50 84*
– *Open 15 March-11 November and closed Monday lunch, Tuesday except 1st July-15 September*
22 rm – €44/58 €50/58, €8 – ½ P €44/56
Rest – Menu €18/25 – Carte €25/32
◆ Family house set away from the town whose Basque name means 'between gardens'. The rooms are small and simple, but well kept. The most modern are to be found in the annexe. A country-style restaurant extended by a bright veranda; regional cuisine.

Olhabidea with rm rest,
quartier Sainte-Catherine, St-Pée road – 05 59 54 21 85 – *www.olhabidea.com*
– *Closed 1st-7 July, January and February*
3 rm – €75/80 €85/90
Rest – *(number of covers limited, pre-book)* Menu €40 (dinner)
◆ This former farmhouse nestling in the greenery has a particular charm that renders it unique. The menu, prepared with produce from the market and the kitchen garden, changes every day. Three extremely spacious, cosy rooms in a very personal atmosphere. Rice pudding served for breakfast.

SARLAT-LA-CANÉDA – 24 Dordogne – 329 I6 – pop. 9 707 – alt. 145 m – ✉ 24200 Dordogne-Berry-Limousin

4 **D3**

Paris 526 – Bergerac 74 – Brive-la-Gaillarde 52 – Cahors 60 – Périgueux 77

Office de tourisme, rue Tourny ☎ 05 53 31 45 45, Fax 05 53 59 19 44

du Domaine de Rochebois Route de Montfort, S : 8 km on D 46, ☎ 05 53 31 52 52

Old Sarlat★★★: place du marché aux trois Oies★ Y, hôtel Plamon★ Y, hôtel de Maleville★ Y - La Boétie House ★ Z - West district ★.

Decoration★ and furniture★ of the château de Puymartin Northwest: 7 km by ④.

Plan on next page

Clos La Boëtie without rest

97 av. de Selves – ☎ 05 53 29 44 18 – www.closlaboetie-sarlat.com – hotel@closlaboetie-sarlat.com – Fax 05 53 28 61 40 – Open 1st April-15 November V **b**

11 rm – €200/340 €200/340, €20 – 3 suites

◆ This fully-renovated residence has a beautifully-arranged interior combining old and new. Very comfortable rooms with a romantic and refined atmosphere.

De Selves without rest

93 av. de Selves – ☎ 05 53 31 50 00 – www.selves-sarlat.com – hotel@selves-sarlat.com – Fax 05 53 31 23 52 – Closed 4 January-12 February V **v**

40 rm – €80/120 €90/140, €12

◆ A modern construction with up-to-date functional rooms; some have loggias with bay windows opening onto the garden. Indoor pool becomes outdoor pool in summer. Sauna.

La Madeleine

1 pl. Petite Rigaudie – ☎ 05 53 59 10 41 – www.hoteldelamadeleine-sarlat.com – hotel.madeleine@wanadoo.fr – Fax 05 53 31 03 62 – Closed 1st January-15 February

39 rm – €62/93 €70/108, €10 – ½ P €69/93 Y **e**

Rest – *(open 15 March-15 Nov. and closed Monday lunchtime and Tuesday lunchtime except July-August)* Menu €29/48 – Carte €40/138

◆ This beautiful 19C abode at the edge of the old town is one of Sarlat's top establishments. Spruce, well-equipped rooms. This recently refurbished restaurant is comfortable and airy. Regional cooking.

Le Renoir without rest

2 r. Abbé-Surgier – ☎ 05 53 59 35 98 – www.hotel-renoir-sarlat.com – info@hotel-renoir-sarlat.com – Fax 05 53 31 22 32 X **u**

35 rm – €70/105 €95/145, €13 – 1 suite

◆ This inviting establishment boasts a swimming pool in the main courtyard. The medium sized rooms are well cared for and prettily decorated with period furniture.

Compostelle without rest

66 av. de Selves – ☎ 05 53 59 08 53 – www.hotel-compostelle-sarlat.com – info@hotel-compostelle-sarlat.com – Fax 05 53 30 31 65 – Open 1st February-15 November

23 rm – €72/88 €72/88, €9 V **r**

◆ A welcoming hotel just 400m from the historic centre with guestrooms that are being gradually renovated. Choose the more modern rooms, with their contemporary feel.

Le Mas del Pechs without rest

*1.5 km east, via Chemin des Monges - **VX** – ☎ 05 53 31 12 11 – www.sarlat-hotel.com – contact@sarlat-hotel.com – Fax 05 53 31 16 99 – Open 1st March-31 December*

18 rm – €51/59 €54/67, €8,50

◆ A quiet country residence in the hills above Sarlat. Opt for the more stylish, more recent guestrooms, all of which are on garden level.

La Maison des Peyrat

*Le Lac de la Plane, to the east via Chemin des Monges - **VX** – ☎ 05 53 59 00 32 – www.maisondespeyrat.com – hoteldecharme@maisondespeyrat.com – Fax 05 53 28 56 56 – Open 1st April-15 November*

10 rm – €55/100 €55/100, €8,50 – ½ P €58/81

Rest – *(closed Wednesday and Sunday) (dinner only) (residents only)* Menu €22

◆ Pretty house tucked away in the greenery, with a garden and salt water swimming pool that invite you to relax. Rooms decorated in a country style (stonework, beams, wood). Very attentive welcome. The restaurant, which blends a rustic setting with bistro style furniture, serves a local based menu. Terrace.

SARLAT-LA-CANÉDA

Street	Square	No.
Albusse (R. d')	YZ	2
Allende (Pl. Salvador)	Y	3
Arlet (Bd Henri)	YZ	
La Boétie (R. de)	Z	21
Bouquerie (Pl. de la)	Y	
Breuil (R. du)	X	
Brossard (Av.)	V	4
Cahors (R. de)	X	
Cahuet (R. Alberic)	YZ	
Chanoines (Cour des)	Z	6
Consuls (R. des)	Y	7
Cordil (R. du)	Z	8
Delpeyrat (R. J.-Baptiste)	X	10
Desmouret (Chemin de)	V	
Escande (R. J.-Joseph)	Z	
Faure (R. Émile)	X, Z	12
Fénelon (R.)	Y	
Fontaines (Cour des)	Z	13
Frères Chambon (R. des)	Z	16
Gabin (R. Jean)	V	17
Gallière (R.)	X	
Gambetta (Av.)	V	18
Gaubert (R.)	V	
Gaulle (Av. du Gén.-de)	Y	20
Grande Rigaudie (Pl. de la)	Z	
Jean-Jaurès (R.)	V	
J.-J.-Rousseau (R.)	Y	
Lakanal (R.)	Z	22
Landry (R.)	Y	25
Leclerc (Av. du Gén.)	X, Z	26
Leroy (Bd Eugène)	Y	
Libération (Pl. de la)	X	
Liberté (Pl. de la)	Y	27
Liberté (R. de la)	YZ	30
Marché aux Oies (Pl. du)	Y	
Monges (Chemin des)	V	
Montaigne (R.)	Z	
Montfort (R. Sylvia)	V	31
Moulin (R. Jean)	V	32
Nessmann (Bd Victor)	Y	
Papucie (R.)	Y	34
Pasteur (Pl.)	X	
Peyrou (Pl. du)	Z	35
Plantier (Chemin du)	X	
Présidial (R. du)	Y	36
République (R. de la)	YZ	
Rossignol (R. Pierre)	X	38
Rousset (R.)	Z	39
Salamandre (R. de la)	Y	40
Ségogne (Pass. Henri-de)	Z	42
Selves (Av. de)	V	43
Siège (R. du)	Z	
Thiers (Av.)	X	
Tourny (R.)	Z	44
Trappe (R. de la)	X	46
Trois Conils (R. des)	Z	47
Troubadour Cayrels (R. du)	V	48
Tunnel (R. du)	X	50
Turenne (R. de)	Z	51
Victor-Hugo (R.)	Y	52
Voltaire (Bd)	X, Z	
8-Mai-1945 (Square du)	Y	
11-Novembre (Pl. du)	Y	
14-Juillet (Pl. du)	Z	
19-Mars-1962 (Pl. du)	V	54
26-Juin-1944 (R. du)	V	55

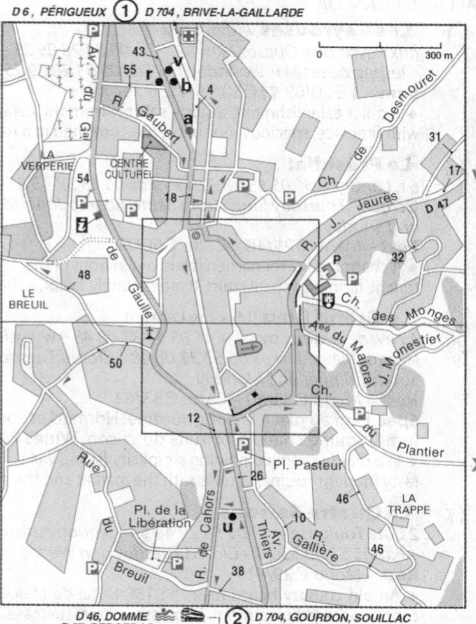

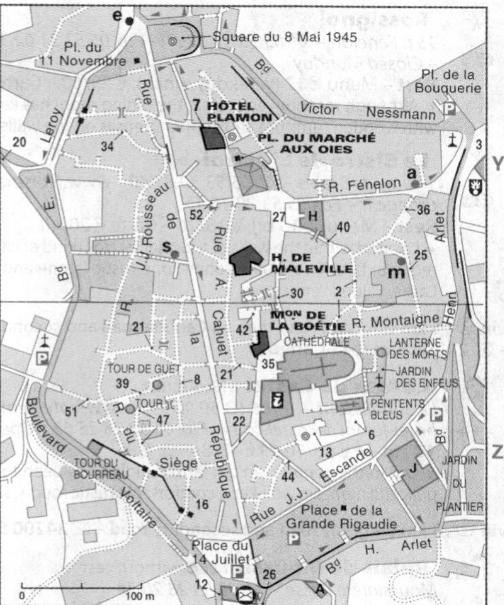

Les Peyrouses without rest

aux Peyrouses, Ouest : 2 km - V – 05 53 28 89 25 – www.lespeyrouses-24.com – lespeyrouses24@wanadoo.fr – Fax 05 53 28 89 25

5 rm – € 50/69 € 50/69, € 7

◆ A quiet establishment, a stone's throw from the centre of Sarlat. Modern sitting room with fireplace; spacious rooms, prettily furnished in a rustic vein.

Le Présidial

6 r. Landry – 05 53 28 92 47 – Fax 05 53 59 43 84 – Open end March to end October, Thursday lunch from September to June, Monday lunch and Sunday Y**m**

Rest – Menu € 28/48 – Carte € 50/70

◆ A charming flower garden is laid out in front of this 17C building, the former seat of the tenant-farming appeal court. It offers stately decor, a shaded terrace and regional cuisine.

Le Grand Bleu (Maxime Lebrun)

43 av. de la Gare, by ② – 05 53 31 08 48 – www.legrandbleu.eu – contact@legrandbleu.eu – Fax 05 53 31 08 48 – Closed Tuesday lunch, Wednesday lunch, Sunday dinner and Monday

Rest – Menu € 33/60 – Carte € 33/63

Spec. Œuf au plat à la périgourdine. Homard et son risotto au caviar d'aubergine fumé. Soufflé chaud aux fruits de saison. **Wines** Pécharmant, Montravel.

◆ In a dining room combining simplicity (stone walls, light woodwork) and space, enjoy tasty modern cuisine, in tune with the market and the seasons.

Le Quatre Saisons

2 Côte Toulouse – 05 53 29 48 59 – lequatresaisons0040@orange.fr – Fax 05 53 59 53 74 – Closed Tuesday and Wednesday except July-August

Rest – Menu € 29/41 Y **s**

◆ An old country house near the 16C Hôtel de Maleville. Regional cuisine served in a contemporary dining room. Impressive spiral staircase, plus a terrace framed by ancient walls.

Rossignol

15 r. Fénelon – 05 53 31 02 30 – Fax 05 53 31 02 30 – Closed Monday Y **a**

Rest – Menu € 17 (weekday lunch), € 23/60 – Carte € 33/55

◆ Although recently renovated, the dining room has kept its pleasant rustic atmosphere with wooden furniture and copper utensils on the walls. Family-style regional menus.

Le Bistro de L'Octroi

111 av. de Selves – 05 53 30 83 40 – www.lebistrodeloctroi.fr – bistrodeloctroi@orange.fr – Fax 05 53 28 36 43 V **a**

Rest – Menu (€ 15 bi), € 18/26 – Carte € 20/40

◆ Located within the walls of a former 'octroi' (kind of city toll), this bistro serves generous regional fare. Two dining rooms, one rustic (stone and brick), and the other traditional. Large, valued terrace.

via ②, 5 km Gourdon road then La Canéda road and secondary road – ✉ 24200 Sarlat-la-Canéda

Le Mas de Castel without rest

Le Sudalissant – 05 53 59 02 59 – www.hotel-lemasdecastel.com – info@hotel-lemasdecastel.com – Fax 05 53 28 25 62 – Open 4 April-11 November

13 rm – € 46/60 € 48/84, € 8

◆ Out in the country, an old farm building has been turned into a pleasant inn. It offers peaceful nights in well-kept, comfortable rustic rooms, six of which open onto the garden.

via ②, 3 km Bergerac road and secondary road – ✉24200 Sarlat-la-Canéda

Relais de Moussidière without rest

Moussidière Basse – 05 53 28 28 74 – www.hotel-moussidiere.com – contact@hotel-moussidiere.com – Fax 0553282511 – Open April-October

35 rm – € 101/151 € 122/172

◆ Enjoy complete peace and quiet in this house full of character, built into the rock, with terraced grounds descending to the lake. Comfortable, personalised guestrooms.

par ②, Souillac road – ✉ 24200 Sarlat-la-Canéda

Abbys without rest VISA
ZA E. Vialard – ☎ 05 53 30 85 50 – www.abbys-hotel.com – contact@abbys-hotel.com – Fax 05 53 30 85 51
30 rm – †€ 36/44 ††€ 36/44, ☕ € 5
◆ This recent establishment will suit those looking for a hotel that is essentially practical and not too expensive. Modern, well-equipped and simply decorated ground-floor rooms.

SARLIAC-SUR-L'ISLE – **24 Dordogne** – **329** G4 – **pop. 978** – **alt. 102 m** – ✉ **24420** 4 **C1**

Paris 473 – Brive-la-Gaillarde 65 – Limoges 86 – Périgueux 15

Chabrol with rm VISA
3 r. de l'Eglise – ☎ 05 53 07 83 39 – Fax 05 53 07 86 53 – Closed September, Sunday dinner and Monday
10 rm – †€ 38/40 ††€ 50, ☕ € 5
Rest – Menu € 15 (weekdays)/55 – Carte € 25/55
◆ Unassuming family run inn in two old buildings. Regional cuisine prepared by the lady of the house, served in a rustic dining room. Small, simple but meticulously-kept rooms (some without bathrooms), renovated in the annexe.

SARPOIL – **63 Puy-de-Dôme** – **326** H10 – **see Issoire**

SARRAS – **07 Ardèche** – **331** K2 – **pop. 1 981** – **alt. 133 m** – ✉ **07370** 43 **E2**

Paris 527 – Annonay 20 – Lyon 72 – St-Étienne 60 – Tournon-sur-Rhône 18 – Valence 36

from D 506 view★★ of the St-Vallier defile★ South: 5 km, **Auvergne-Rhone Valley**

Le Vivarais with rm rest, VISA
– ☎ 04 75 23 01 88 – levivarais@wanadoo.fr – Fax 04 75 23 49 73 – Closed 3-26 August, 15 February-11 March, Sunday dinner, Monday dinner and Tuesday
6 rm – †€ 43 ††€ 49/58, ☕ € 7
Rest – Menu € 17 (weekdays)/54 – Carte € 40/57
◆ Family inn serving classic cuisine in an elegant dining room decorated in lively colours. Rooms are practical for a stop on the 'route du soleil'.

SARREBOURG – **57 Moselle** – **307** N6 – **pop. 12 600** – **alt. 282 m** – ✉ **57400** **Alsace-Lorraine** 27 **D2**

Paris 426 – Épinal 86 – Lunéville 59 – Metz 95 – St-Dié 72 – Strasbourg 73

Office de tourisme, place des Cordeliers ☎ 03 87 03 11 82, Fax 03 87 07 13 93

du Pays de Sarrebourg Route de Winkelhof, W : 2 km, ☎ 03 87 23 01 02

Stained-glass window★ in the Cordeliers chapel **B**.

Plan on following page

Les Cèdres VISA
3 km, leisure zone via ③ and Chemin d'Imling – ☎ 03 87 03 55 55 – www.hotel-lescedres.fr – info@hotel-lescedres.fr – Fax 03 87 03 66 33 – Closed 21 December-2 January
44 rm – †€ 62/103 ††€ 69/110, ☕ € 8 – ½ P € 80/111
Rest – *(closed Saturday lunch and Sunday dinner)* Menu (€ 15), € 23/49 bi – Carte € 26/55
◆ Quiet stop in the heart of a leisure area, near a forest and pond, in this modern hotel with bright and functional rooms. Spacious dining room, opening onto the surrounding countryside, serving regional cuisine.

SARREBOURG

SARRE-UNION, D 43 ① SARRALTROFF
② A 4, STRASBOURG, D 45 DABO
④ METZ, D 955 NANCY, N 4 D 27, MORHANGE
③ D 44, ABRESCHVILLER

Sarre
PARC WEYERSTEIN
Av. Gambetta
Rte de Phalsbourg
Av. Maréchal Joffre
Leclerc
Division
PARC DU CENTRE
PARC DE LA LIBERTÉ
Grand' Rue
Rue de la
Clemenceau
Av. Gal de Gaulle
JARDIN DE LA ROSERAIE
CENTRE SOCIO-CULTUREL
MALLERAY
CIMETIÈRE ISRAÉLITE
D 96
200 m

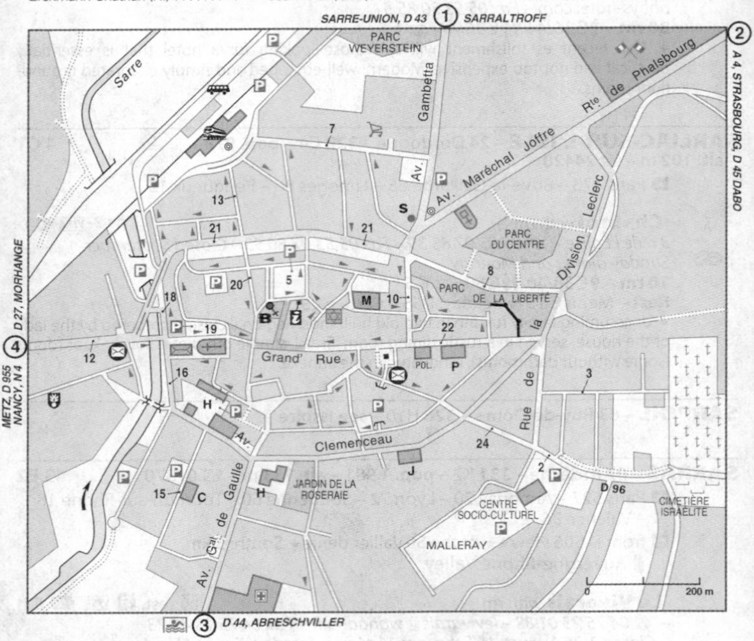

XX **Mathis** (Ernest Mathis)
7 r. Gambetta – ✆ 03 87 03 21 67
– www.ernest-mathis.fr – Fax 03 87 23 00 64
– Closed 27 July-8 August, 8-15 September, 3-8 November, 2-12 January, Sunday dinner, Tuesday dinner and Monday s
Rest – Menu € 30/75 – Carte € 47/90
Spec. Tranche de foie grillé, pomme de terre de Noirmoutier écrasée à la fourchette, jus truffé. (June to September). Pavé de bar sauvage rôti (season). Gratin chaud de framboises et son sorbet. **Wines** Pinot blanc.
◆ Carefully thought-out table decoration, as one would expect in the land of crystal and ceramics. Warm welcome and inventive food in this restaurant with many assets.

SARREGUEMINES – **57 Moselle** – **307** N4 – **pop. 21 600** 27 **D1**
– alt. 210 m – ✉ 57200 Alsace-Lorraine

Paris 396 – Metz 70 – Nancy 96 – Saarbrücken 18 – Strasbourg 106

Office de tourisme, 11, rue rue du Maire Massing ✆ 03 87 98 80 81, Fax 03 87 98 25 77

de Sarreguemines Chemin Départemental n 81 A, W : 3 km on D 81, ✆ 03 87 27 22 60

Museum: Winter garden★★, collection of ceramics★ BZ **M.**

Bliesbruck-Reinheim European Archeological Park: spa★, 9.5 km by ①.

SARREGUEMINES

Chamborand (R. du Marquis-de) . . . . **BZ** 2
Chapelle (R. de la) . . . . **BZ** 3
Cremer (R. des Généraux) **ABZ** 6
Faïenceries (Bd des) . . . . **BZ** 7
France (R. de) . . . . **AZ** 8
Gare (Av. de la) . . . . **BZ** 12
Louvain (Chaussée de) . . . **BYZ** 15
Marché (Pl. du) . . . . **AZ** 17
Nationale (R.) . . . . **ABZ** 20
Or (R. de l') . . . . **AZ** 22
Paix (R. de la) . . . . **AY** 23
Pasteur (R. L.) . . . . **BZ** 24
Ste-Croix (R.) . . . . **BZ** 27
St-Nicolas (R.) . . . . **AZ** 26
Sibille (Pl. du Gén.) . . . . **BZ** 28
Utzschneider (R.) . . . . **BZ** 30
Verdun (R. de) . . . . **AZ** 33

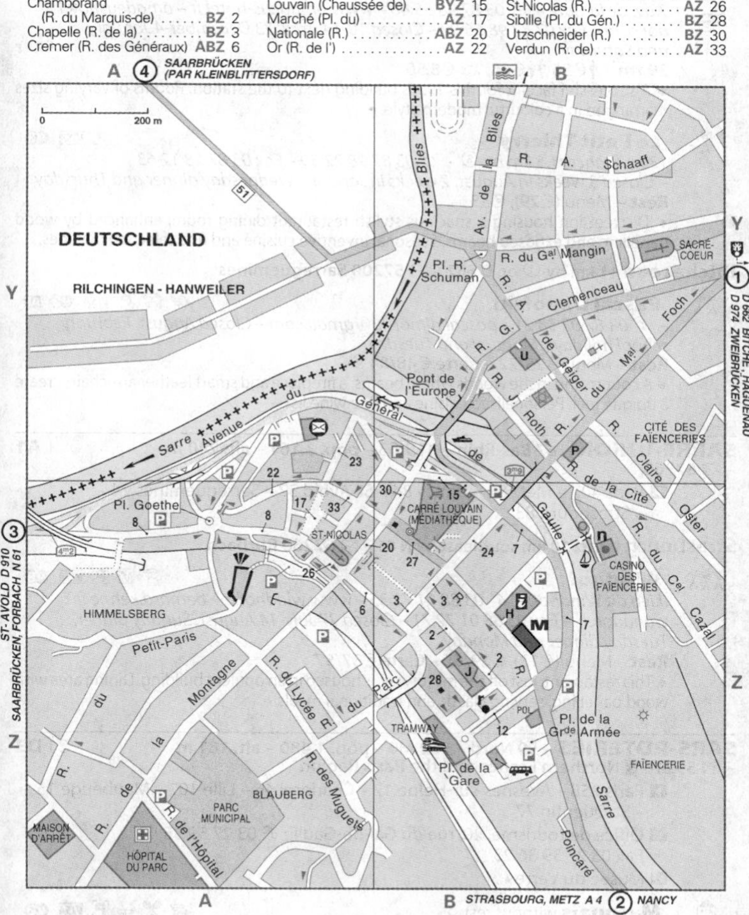

Auberge St-Walfrid (Stéphan Schneider) rm, rest,
2 km by ③ and Grosbliederstroff road – rm,
03 87 98 43 75 – www.stwalfrid.com – stwalfrid@free.fr – Fax 03 87 95 76 75 – Closed 20 July-3 August and 7-23 February
11 rm – €98/160 €98/160, €15 – ½ P €135/165
Rest – *(closed Saturday lunch, Monday lunch and Sunday)* Menu €35 (weekdays)/82 – Carte €55/86
Spec. Escalope de foie gras de canard poêlée aux quetsches (mid-September to mid-November). Gibier (season). Croustillant à la mirabelle de Lorraine, crème glacée bergamote (mid-August to mid-September). **Wines** Pinot noir, Vin de Moselle.
◆ Fine stone house where five generations of the same family have played hosts. The decor attractively combines rustic and modern features. Well-kept rooms. Dining room adorned with colourful paintings and ceramic objects. Tasty regional cuisine.

Amadeus without rest

7 av. de la Gare – ☎ 03 87 98 55 46 – www.amadeus-hotel.fr – amadeushotel@aol.com – Fax 03 87 98 66 92 – Closed 10-14 April, 23 December-4 January and Saturday BZ **r**

39 rm – †€ 56 ††€ 65, ☕ € 8,50

◆ A successful facelift for this 1930s building next to the station. Rooms of varying sizes rearranged in a colourful modern style.

Le Petit Thierry

135 r. France, 1.5 km by ③ – ☎ 03 87 98 22 59 – Fax 03 87 28 12 63 – Closed 3 weeks in August, 2 weeks in January, Wednesday dinner and Thursday

Rest – Menu (€ 29), € 35

◆ Discreet inn housing a spacious stylish restaurant dining room, enhanced by wood panelling and exposed beams. Seasonal inventive cuisine and fine selection of wines.

Bitche road 11 km by ① on D 662 – ✉ 57200 Sarreguemines

Pascal Dimofski

– ☎ 03 87 02 38 21 – pascal.dimofski@gmail.com – Closed August, February school holidays, Monday and Tuesday

Rest – Menu € 25/72 – Carte € 48/84

◆ A country inn in the woods where beams, a fireplace and smart leather armchairs create a unique feel. Personalised cuisine and fine wine list.

SARRE-UNION – 67 Bas-Rhin – 315 G3 – pop. 3 161 – alt. 240 m – ✉ 67260 1 A1

Paris 407 – Metz 81 – Nancy 84 – St-Avold 37 – Sarreguemines 24 – Strasbourg 83

Strasbourg road 10 km southeast by N 61 – ✉ 67260 Burbach

Windhof

(Lieu dit Windhof) – ☎ 03 88 01 72 35 – www.windhof.fr – bernard.kehne@wanadoo.fr – Fax 03 88 01 72 71 – Closed 27 July-14 August, Sunday dinner, Tuesday dinner and Monday

Rest – Menu (€ 13), € 29/65 – Carte € 37/57

◆ This restaurant, just off the motorway, is housed in an opulent building. Dining area with wood panelling, serving classic and traditional meals.

SARS-POTERIES – 59 Nord – 302 M6 – pop. 1 480 – alt. 181 m – ✉ 59216 Northern France and the Paris Region 31 D3

Paris 258 – Avesnes-sur-Helpe 12 – Charleroi 46 – Lille 107 – Maubeuge 15 – St-Quentin 77

Office de tourisme, 20, rue du Gal-de-Gaulle ☎ 03 27 59 35 49, Fax 03 27 59 36 23

Musée du Verre★.

Marquais without rest

65 r. du Gén.-de-Gaulle – ☎ 03 27 61 62 72 – www.hoteldumarquais.com – hoteldumarquais@aol.com – Fax 03 27 57 47 35 – Closed January

11 rm – †€ 50 ††€ 60, ☕ € 8

◆ Two sparkling twin sisters – around 70 years old! – run this small hotel to perfection. Antique furniture and candy box colours in the rooms. No television. Rest and relaxation guaranteed.

L'Auberge Fleurie with rm

67 r. Gén. de Gaulle, (D 962) – ☎ 03 27 61 62 48 – auberge-fleurie.net – fauberge@wanadoo.fr – Fax 03 27 61 56 66 – Closed 17 August-1st September, 2-16 January, Sunday dinner and Monday

8 rm – †€ 70 ††€ 95, ☕ € 10

Rest – Menu € 31 (weekdays)/88 bi – Carte € 55/135

◆ Enjoy good service in this rustic, smart-looking restaurant serving traditional cuisine. Spacious, personalised guest rooms in light colours.

SARTÈNE – 2A Corse-du-Sud – 345 C10 – see Corse

SARZEAU – 56 Morbihan – 308 O9 – pop. 6 941 – alt. 30 m – ✉ 56370 9 A3
Brittany

Paris 478 – Nantes 111 – Redon 62 – Vannes 23

Office de tourisme, rue du Père Coudrin ✆ 02 97 41 82 37, Fax 02 97 41 74 95

de Rhuys Saint-Gildas-de-Rhuys, W : 7 km on D 780, ✆ 02 97 45 30 09

Ruins★ of the château de Suscinio Southeast: 3.5 km - Presqu'île de Rhuys★.

in Penvins 7 km southeast by D 198 – ✉ 56370 Sarzeau

XX **Mur du Roy** with rm — rest, VISA MC

– ✆ 02 97 67 34 08 – www.lemurduroy.com – contact@lemurduroy.com – Fax 02 97 67 36 23 – Closed 15 December-31 January, Monday and Tuesday except hotel

10 rm – †€ 52/86 ††€ 52/86, ☕ € 10 – ½ P € 66/83

Rest – Menu € 25/42 – Carte € 32/52

◆ Seafood served on two verandas brightened with nautical decor and pleasantly overlooking the terrace, the garden and the ocean. Small, very quiet rooms.

Your opinions are important to us:
please write and let us know about your discoveries
and experiences – good and bad!

SASSENAY – 71 Saône-et-Loire – 320 J9 – see Chalon-sur-Saône

SASSETOT-LE-MAUCONDUIT – 76 Seine-Maritime – 304 D3 – pop. 930 – alt. 89 m – ✉ 76540 33 C1

Paris 198 – Bolbec 29 – Fécamp 16 – Le Havre 55 – Rouen 65 – Yvetot 30

Office de tourisme, 4, rue des Fusillés ✆ 02 35 29 79 88, Fax 02 35 29 79 88

XX **Le Relais des Dalles** with rm — VISA MC AE

6 r. Elizabeth d'Autriche, near the château – ✆ 02 35 27 41 83 – www.relais-des-dalles.fr – le-relais-des-dalles@wanadoo.fr – Fax 02 35 27 13 91 – Closed autumn school holidays, 14 December-7 January, Monday and Tuesday except 13 July-23 August

4 rm – †€ 75/150 ††€ 75/150, ☕ € 12

Rest – *(pre-book weekends)* Menu € 28/55 – Carte € 38/61

◆ A friendly Normandy inn whose countrified decor serves as a backdrop to tasty, traditional dishes. Fine choice of Loire and Bordeaux wines. Cosy guestrooms.

SAUBUSSE – 40 Landes – 335 D13 – pop. 759 – alt. 10 m – Spa : early March-late Nov. – ✉ 40180 3 B3

Paris 736 – Bayonne 43 – Biarritz 50 – Dax 19 – Mont-de-Marsan 72

Syndicat d'initiative, rue Vieille ✆ 05 58 57 76 68, Fax 05 58 57 37 37

XX ✿ **Villa Stings** (Francis Gabarrus) — A/C VISA MC AE

9 r. du Port – ✆ 05 58 57 70 18 – villa-stings@wanadoo.fr – Fax 05 58 57 71 86 – Closed 8-15 June, 9-16 November, February, Saturday lunch, Sunday dinner and Monday from 7 September to 25 July and Wednesday dinner from 9 September to 26 April

Rest – Menu € 36/80 – Carte € 36/65

Spec. Escalope de foie gras poêlée au gingembre. Lièvre à la royale (autumn). Biscuit moelleux de noix de pécan aux fraises et framboises (summer). **Wines** Jurançon, Madiran.

◆ Large 19C stone building on the banks of the Adour. Elegant dining room serving up-to-date cuisine prepared with high-quality produce.

SAUGUES – 43 Haute-Loire – **331** D4 – **pop. 2 013** – **alt. 960 m** – ✉ **43170** Auvergne 6 **C3**

Paris 529 – Brioude 51 – Mende 72 – Le Puy-en-Velay 43 – St-Flour 52

Office de tourisme, cours Dr Gervais ✆ 04 71 77 71 38, Fax 04 71 77 71 38

La Terrasse — AC rest, VISA MC AE

cours Dr Gervais – ✆ 04 71 77 83 10 – www.hotellaterrasse-saugues.com – laterrasse.saugues@wanadoo.fr – Fax 04 71 77 63 79 – Closed December, January, Sunday evening and Monday in low season

9 rm – †€ 55/65 ††€ 65, ☕ € 10 – ½ P € 55

Rest – *(closed Sunday dinner, Tuesday lunch and Monday except July-August)* Menu € 19 (weekdays), € 28/38

◆ In the village centre dominated by the Tour des Anglais, this former residence of a notary has been in the same family since 1795. Freshly redecorated rooms. Rustic dining room with fireplace and stylish table settings. Traditional cuisine.

SAUJON – 17 Charente-Maritime – **324** E5 – **pop. 5 392** – **alt. 7 m** – ✉ **17600 Saujon** 38 **B3**

Paris 499 – Poitiers 165 – La Rochelle 71 – Saintes 28 – Rochefort 34

Syndicat d'initiative, 22, place du Général-de-Gaulle ✆ 05 46 02 83 77, Fax 05.46.02.14.48

Le Richelieu — rm, AC rm, VISA MC

pl. Richelieu – ✆ 05 46 02 82 43 – www.hotel-lerichelieu-saujon.com – richelieu.saujon@wanadoo.fr – Fax 05 46 02 82 43 – Closed 3-20 January

20 rm – †€ 55/75 ††€ 55/75, ☕ € 11 – ½ P € 82/102

Rest ***Le Ménestrel*** – ✆ *05 46 06 92 35 (closed 12-20 October, 12 January-2 February, Sunday and Monday)* Menu € 25/38 – Carte € 30/52

◆ A breath of fresh air has blown through this Saintonge hotel. The old building dating from the 18C and the modern extension offers functional, contemporary rooms. The restaurant's décor matches the owner-chef's modern cuisine.

SAULES – 25 Doubs – **321** G4 – **see Ornans**

SAULGES – 53 Mayenne – **310** G7 – **pop. 328** – **alt. 97 m** – ✉ **53340** Normandy 35 **C1**

Paris 249 – Château-Gontier 37 – La Flèche 48 – Laval 33 – Le Mans 55 – Mayenne 41

Syndicat d'initiative, 4, place Jacques Favrot ✆ 02 43 90 49 81, Fax 02 43 90 55 44

L'Ermitage — rm, P VISA MC

3 pl. St-Pierre – ✆ 02 43 64 66 00 – www.hotel-ermitage.fr – info@hotel-ermitage.fr – Fax 02 43 64 66 20 – Closed January and Sunday from October to March

35 rm – †€ 72/116 ††€ 72/116, ☕ € 10 – ½ P € 76/100

Rest – *(closed Saturday lunch)* Menu (€ 11 bi), € 24/59 – Carte € 42/48

◆ An old house with pretty rooms facing the countryside or the village. Those in the "Relais" have been well renovated and are more modern. Pool, crazy golf, garden. Up-to-the-minute cuisine served in a modern setting overlooking a terrace.

SAULIEU – 21 Côte-d'Or – **320** F6 – **pop. 2 837** – **alt. 535 m** – ✉ **21210** Burgundy-Jura 8 **C2**

Paris 248 – Autun 40 – Avallon 39 – Beaune 65 – Clamecy 78 – Dijon 73

Syndicat d'initiative, 24, rue d'Argentine ✆ 03 80 64 00 21, Fax 03 80 64 00 21

St-Andoche basilica★ : chapiteaux★★.

SAULIEU

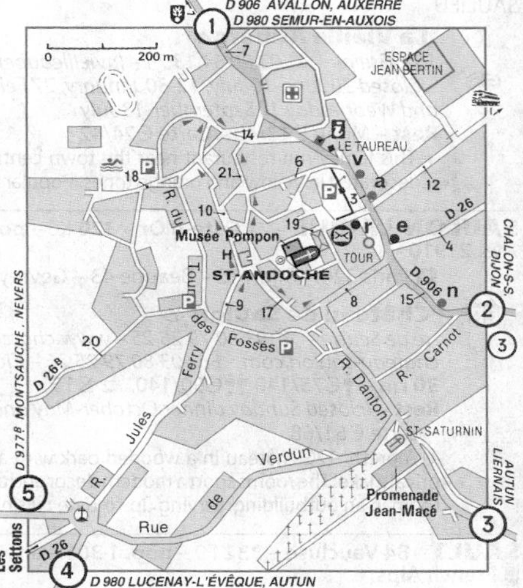

Le Relais Bernard Loiseau

2 r. Argentine – ✆ 03 80 90 53 53 – www.bernard-loiseau.com – loiseau@relaischateaux.com – Fax 03 80 64 08 92 – Closed 4 January-4 February **e**

23 rm – €145/195 €145/345, ☕ €30 – 9 suites

Rest – *(closed Wednesday lunch and Tuesday except from May to September and except Christmas holidays)* Menu €98 bi (weekday lunch), €120/185 – Carte €144/242

Spec. Jambonnettes de grenouilles à la purée d'ail et au jus de persil. Filet de bœuf charolais cuit au foin en croûte d'argile. Rose des sables à la glace pur chocolat et son coulis d'orange confite. **Wines** Puligny-Montrachet, Chambolle-Musigny.

◆ This luxurious 18C hostelry, an institution in this town that has for centuries paid homage to Burgundy's tradition of hospitality, stands out for its comfort and peace and quiet. Well-equipped spa. Elegant dining rooms open onto the English style garden. Patrick Bertron creates talented recipes that pay homage to the master of Saulieu.

Hostellerie la Tour d'Auxois

sq. Alexandre Dumaine – ✆ 03 80 64 36 19 – www.tourdauxois.com – info@tourdauxois.com – Fax 03 80 64 93 10 – Closed February **r**

29 rm – €99 €99, ☕ €13 – 6 suites

Rest – *(closed Tuesday lunch October-May, Sunday dinner and Monday)* Menu (€15 bi), €29/52 – Carte €24/44

◆ This charming hotel is set in a former convent. Cosily inviting rooms, landscaped garden with pool and bistro-style breakfast room. Contemporary menu in a rotunda dining room facing the greenery.

La Borne Impériale with rm

16 r. Argentine – ✆ 03 80 64 19 76 – www.borne-imperiale.com – Fax 03 80 64 30 63 – Closed 10 January-10 February, Monday dinner and Tuesday except July-August **v**

7 rm – €45 €60, ☕ €10 – ½ P €60 **Rest** – Menu €23/48 – Carte €45/60

◆ Generous portions of tasty regional fare in a classic dining room or on the inviting terrace, overlooking the garden. Practical accommodation upstairs.

Auberge du Relais

8 r. Argentine – ✆ 03 80 64 13 16 – taverna.serge@wanadoo.fr – Fax 03 80 64 08 33 – Closed 16 November-13 December **a**

Rest – Menu (€18), €21/40 – Carte €30/40

◆ Inn highlighting regional dishes. Low-key rustic interior and peaceful terrace. Small, renovated rooms upstairs.

La Vieille Auberge

15 r. Grillot – ✆ 03 80 64 13 74 – lavieilleauberge3@wanadoo.fr – Closed 30 June-10 July, 12-30 January, 27 February-11 March, Tuesday dinner and Wednesday 1st September-13 July **n**

Rest – Menu € 13/40 – Carte € 24/42

◆ This family-run restaurant near the town centre serves local dishes in a dining room redecorated in yellow and orange tones. Popular summer courtyard terrace.

SAULON-LA-RUE – 21 Côte-d'Or – 320 K6 – pop. 526 – alt. 215 m – ✉ 21910 8 D1

Paris 324 – Dijon 12 – Beaune 43 – Gevrey-Chambertin 9 – Seurre 30

Château de Saulon VISA MC AE

rte de Seurre – ✆ 03 80 79 25 25 – www.chateau-saulon.com – commercial@chateau-saulon.com – Fax 03 80 79 25 26 – Closed 26 February-1st March

30 rm – € 75/140 € 90/140, € 15

Rest – *(closed Sunday dinner October-May and Monday lunch)* Menu € 31/57 – Carte € 51/68

◆ A pretty 17C château in a wooded park with an attractive swimming pool and small private lake. The rooms sport a modern decor and are practically furnished. Pleasant dining room in an outbuilding, serving up-to-date cuisine. Wine shop and tasting.

SAULT – 84 Vaucluse – 332 F9 – pop. 1 301 – alt. 765 m – ✉ 84390 42 E1

French Alps

Paris 718 – Aix-en-Provence 86 – Apt 31 – Avignon 69 – Carpentras 42 – Digne-les-Bains 96

Office de tourisme, avenue de la Promenade ✆ 04 90 64 01 21, Fax 04 90 64 15 03

Gorges de la Nesque ★★: viewpoint ★★ Southwest: 11 km by D 942 - Mont Ventoux ✻ ★★★ Northwest: 26 km.

Hostellerie du Val de Sault VISA MC AE

2 km, St-Trinit road and secondary road – ✆ 04 90 64 01 41 – www.valdesault.com – valdesault@aol.com – Fax 04 90 64 12 74 – Open 11 April-8 November

15 rm – € 140 € 140, € 14 – 9 suites – ½ P € 123/143

Rest – *(closed Thursday lunch and Monday except from June to August)* Menu € 43/97 – Carte € 41/50

◆ The irresistible appeal of this establishment comes from the scent of lavender, its enchanting view, as well as guestrooms with a lounge and small terrace or duplexes with a Provençal-Asian décor. Soothing dining room that combines styles and a sunny terrace. Regional menu that focuses on truffles.

SAULXURES – 67 Bas-Rhin – 315 G6 – pop. 457 – alt. 535 m – ✉ 67420 1 A2

Paris 407 – Épinal 71 – Strasbourg 67 – Lunéville 65 – Saint-Dié 30

La Belle Vue rm, VISA MC AE

36 r. Principale – ✆ 03 88 97 60 23 – www.la-belle-vue.com – labellevue@wanadoo.fr – Fax 03 88 47 23 71 – Closed 4-20 January

11 rm – € 89/130 € 89/130, € 12 – ½ P € 76/97

Rest – *(closed Tuesday and Wednesday from October to May)* Menu € 15 bi (weekday lunch), € 20/56

◆ The same family has been running this inn for four generations. Tastefully decorated suites, duplexes and rooms (exposed timbers, modern art). The up-to-date cuisine is served in the attractive dining room overlooking the garden.

SAUMUR – 49 Maine-et-Loire – 317 I5 – pop. 28 700 – alt. 30 m – ✉ 49400 35 C2

Châteaux of the Loire

Paris 300 – Angers 67 – Le Mans 124 – Poitiers 97 – Tours 64

Office de tourisme, place de la Bilange ✆ 02 41 40 20 60, Fax 02 41 40 20 69

de Saumur 2, route des Mortins, W : 5 km on D 751 and D 161, ✆ 02 41 50 87 00

Château ★★: musée d'Arts décoratifs ★★, musée du Cheval ★, tour du Guet ✻ ★ - N.-D.-de-Nantilly church ★: tapestries ★★ - Old quarter ★ BY : Town hall ★ H ,tapestries ★ of St-Pierre church - Musée de l'école de Cavalerie ★ M[1] - Musée des Blindés ★★ in the South.

SAUMUR

Street	Grid	No.
Anjou (R. d')	BZ	2
Beaurepaire (R.)	AY	3
Bilange (Pl. de la)	BY	4
Cadets (Ponts des)	BX	5
Dr-Bouchard (R. du)	AZ	6
Dupetit-Thouars (Pl.)	BZ	7
Fardeau (R.)	AZ	9
Gaulle (Av. Général-de)	BX	
Leclerc (R. du Mar.)	AZ	
Nantilly (R. de)	BZ	10
Orléans (R. d')	ABY	
Poitiers (R. de)	AZ	12
Portail-Louis (R. du)	BY	13
République (Pl. de la)	BY	15
Roosevelt (R. Fr.)	BY	16
St-Jean (R.)	BY	18
St-Pierre (Pl.)	BY	19
Tonnelle (R. de la)	BY	20
Vieux-Pont (R. du)	BY	22

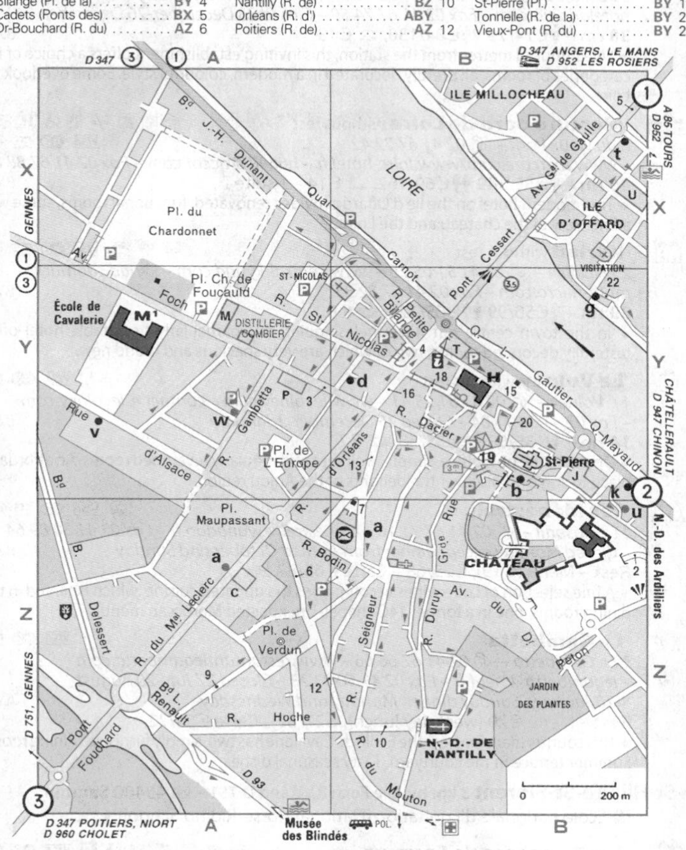

Château de Verrières without rest
53 r. d'Alsace – ✆ 02 41 38 05 15 – www.chateau-verrieres.com – contact@chateau-verrieres.com – Fax 02 41 38 18 18 AY **v**
10 rm – €140/310 €140/310, ☕ €15
◆ You are received as if you were a friend of the family in this lovely 18C château set in the heart of a 2ha park. Luxuriously elegant interior (Napoleon III sitting rooms and period furniture).

St-Pierre without rest
8 r. Haute-St-Pierre – ✆ 02 41 50 33 00 – www.saintpierresaumur.com – contact@saintpierresaumur.com – Fax 02 41 50 38 68 BY **b**
15 rm – €85/115 €90/165, ☕ €13
◆ Establishment located in well-restored 17C houses. Massive beams, half-timbered façade, spiral staircase and period furniture set the scene for this charming hotel.

Anne d'Anjou without rest
32 quai Mayaud – ✆ 02 41 67 30 30 – www.hotel-anneanjou.com – contact@hotel-anneanjou.com – Fax 02 41 67 51 00 BY **k**
43 rm – €82/135 €100/210, ☕ €12
◆ Fine 18C manor with Empire-style or modern rooms facing the river or castle. In summer, breakfast is served in the lovely inner courtyard.

Adagio without rest
94 av. du Gén. de Gaulle – ☏ 02 41 67 45 30 – www.hoteladagio.com – contact@hoteladagio.com – Fax 02 41 67 74 59 – Closed 23 December-26 December
38 rm – †€ 74/79 ††€ 84/130, ☐ € 13 BX **t**
◆ Five hundred metres from the station, this inviting establishment offers a choice of five categories of rooms, all prettily decorated in a modern, colourful style. Some overlook the Loire.

Mercure bord de Loire without rest
r. du vieux Pont – ☏ 02 41 67 22 42 – www.mercure.com/www.loire-hotel.fr – h6648@accor.com – Fax 02 41 67 88 80
45 rm – †€ 55/149 ††€ 69/162, ☐ € 14 – 1 suite BY **g**
◆ This modern hotel on the Île d'Offard provides renovated, functional rooms, some with a fine view of the château and the Loire.

Kyriad without rest
23 r. Daillé – ☏ 02 41 51 05 78 – www.central-kyriad.com – kyriad.saumur@multi-micro.com – Fax 02 41 67 82 35 BY **d**
29 rm – †€ 50/99 ††€ 65/120, ☐ € 8
◆ In the town centre but nevertheless quiet, this particularly hospitable hotel offers tastefully decorated rooms, two of which are very spacious and brand new.

Le Volney without rest
1 r. Volney – ☏ 02 41 51 25 41 – www.levolney.com – contact@levolney.com – Fax 02 41 38 11 04 – Closed 25 December-3 January BZ **a**
14 rm – †€ 35/58 ††€ 35/58, ☐ € 7
◆ Opposite the post office, simple, well kept and regularly revamped rooms. An affordable place to stay and discover the delights of the Anjou region.

Les Ménestrels
11 r. Raspail – ☏ 02 41 67 71 10 – menestrel@wanadoo.fr – Fax 02 41 50 89 64 – Closed Monday except dinner from April to October and Sunday BZ **u**
Rest – Menu (€ 19), € 25/68 – Carte € 65/87
◆ A fine selection of Loire wines accompanies the updated cuisine, which is served in two dining rooms, one in a former 14C chapel. Unexpected Moroccan menu.

Le Gambetta
12 r. Gambetta – ☏ 02 41 67 66 66 – www.restaurantlegambetta.com – legambetta@neuf.fr – Fax 02 41 50 83 23 – Closed 27 July-20 August, 4-20 January, Sunday dinner, Monday and Wednesday AY **w**
Rest – Menu € 20 (weekday lunch), € 27/82 – Carte € 54/72
◆ This country mansion near the Ecole de Cavalerie has two, simply furnished dining rooms. Summer terrace in the courtyard. Tasty seasonal dishes.

in St-Hilaire-St-Florent **3 km by Ave Foch** AXY **and D 751 – ✉ 49400 Saumur**
École nationale d'Équitation (National Horse-Riding School) ★.

Les Terrasses de Saumur
chemin de l'Alat – ☏ 02 41 67 28 48 – www.lesterrassesdesaumur.fr – contact@lesterrassesdesaumur.fr – Fax 02 41 67 13 71 – Closed 20-30 December
22 rm – †€ 65/90 ††€ 65/90, ☐ € 12 – ½ P € 73/85
Rest – *(closed Monday lunch and Tuesday lunch)* Menu (€ 23), € 28/58 – Carte € 47/81
◆ This hotel overlooking Saumur and the castle is enjoying a new lease of life: attractively refurbished rooms (bright colours and good quality fittings), some with terrace. Traditional cuisine served in a rotunda dining room overlooking the town or by the pool.

in Chênehutte-les-Tuffeaux **8 km by Ave Foch** AXY **and D 751 – pop. 1 092 – alt. 29 m – ✉ 49350**

Le Prieuré
– ☏ 02 41 67 90 14 – www.prieure.com – prieure@grandesetapes.fr – Fax 02 41 67 92 24
21 rm – †€ 146 ††€ 146, ☐ € 23 – 1 suite
Rest – Menu (€ 24), € 33 (dinner), € 52/100 bi – Carte € 28/73
◆ Well-located 12-16C priory overlooking the Loire. Tasteful, period furnished rooms, all of which command a fine view, as does the elegant restaurant. Local vegetables, fish and wines on the menu.

Les Résidences du Prieuré
– ✆ 02 41 67 90 14 – *www.prieure.com – prieure@grandesetapes.fr*
– Fax 02 41 67 92 24
15 rm – €130/340 €130/340, €23
◆ In six bungalows, rooms with terrace and private garden are spread around the large wooded park.

SAUSHEIM – 68 Haut-Rhin – 315 I10 – see Mulhouse

LA SAUSSAYE – 27 Eure – 304 F6 – pop. 1 954 – alt. 137 m – ✉ 27370 33 D2

Paris 130 – Évreux 40 – Louviers 20 – Pont-Audemer 49 – Rouen 25

Manoir des Saules (Jean-Paul Monnaie) rm, rest, VISA
2 pl. St Martin – ✆ *02 35 87 25 65*
– www.manoirdessaules.com – manoirsaules@relaischateaux.com
– Fax 02 35 87 49 39 – Closed 2-25 November, 22 February-3 March, Sunday evening from September to April, Monday and Tuesday
9 rm – €195 €210/265, €22
Rest – *(number of covers limited, pre-book)* Menu (€55), €65 (weekdays)/125 – Carte €86/126
Spec. Buisson de homard à l'huile de truffe. Poissons sauvages (according to the catch). Soufflé chaud au Grand Marnier.
◆ Pleasant welcome in this authentic Norman manor with a garden. Half-timbering and turrets decorate the facade. Beautiful period furniture in the rooms. Original dining rooms serving modern cuisine favouring local produce. Good wine list.

SAUSSET-LES-PINS – 13 Bouches-du-Rhône – 340 F6 – pop. 7 278 – alt. 15 m – ✉ 13960 Provence 40 B3

Paris 768 – Aix-en-Provence 41 – Marseille 37 – Martigues 13 – Salon-de-Provence 48

Syndicat d'initiative, 16, avenue du Port ✆ 04 42 45 60 65, Fax 04 42 45 60 68

Paradou-Méditerranée VISA
Le Port – ✆ *04 42 44 76 76 – www.paradou.fr – hotel.paradou@wanadoo.fr*
– Fax 04 42 44 78 48
42 rm – €95/125 €95/125, €10
Rest – *(Closed 19 December-3 January, Saturday and Sunday)* Menu €25/35 – Carte €31/53
◆ A perfect location facing the sea with the additional benefits of a swimming pool and garden. Refurbished colourful rooms with balconies and sea views. Provençal-inspired dining room serving dishes full of the rich flavours of the Mediterranean.

Les Girelles VISA
r. Frédéric Mistral – ✆ *04 42 45 26 16 – www.restaurant-les-girelles.com*
– restaurant-les-girelles@wanadoo.fr – Fax 04 42 45 49 65 – Closed 2-31 January, Tuesday lunch, Wednesday lunch in July-August, Sunday dinner from September to June and Monday
Rest – Menu €29/65 – Carte €42/80
◆ A comfortable veranda and terrace overlooking the sea. Stylish Provençal interior. Up-to-date cuisine with a seafood focus and southern flavours.

SAUTERNES – 33 Gironde – 335 I7 – pop. 586 – alt. 50 m – ✉ 33210 Atlantic Coast 3 B2

Paris 624 – Bazas 24 – Bordeaux 49 – Langon 11

Office de tourisme, 11, rue Principale ✆ 05 56 76 69 13, Fax 05 57 31 00 67

Relais du Château d'Arche without rest VISA
0.5 km north, Bommes road – ✆ *05 56 76 67 67*
– www.chateaudarche-sauternes.com – chateaudarche@wanadoo.fr
– Fax 05 56 76 69 76
9 rm – €120/160 €120/160, €10
◆ A fine, 17C charterhouse on the wine estate of Château d'Arches. Sample the grands crus after a visit. Cosy, personalised rooms. Reception room.

Saprien
14 r. Principale – ✆ 05 56 76 60 87 – www.saprien.free.fr – saprien@aliceadsl.fr – Fax 05 56 76 68 92 – Closed 21 December-4 January, 11 February-2 March, Sunday dinner and Wednesday dinner from April to October, dinner during the week from November to March and Monday
Rest – Menu (€ 20), € 25/37 – Carte € 40/59
◆ Typical winegrower's house with a charming rustic interior with fireplace and terrace giving directly onto the vines. Good selection of Sauternes by the glass.

SAUVE – **30 Gard** – **339** I5 – **pop. 1 856** – **alt. 103 m** – ✉ **30610** 23 **C2**
Paris 747 – Montpellier 48 – Alès 28 – Nîmes 40 – Le Vigan 38
Office de tourisme, place René Isouard ✆ 04 66 77 57 51, Fax 04 66 77 05 99

La Magnanerie with rm
rte de Nîmes – ✆ 04 66 77 57 44 – www.lamagnanerie.fr – la.magnanerie@wanadoo.fr – Fax 04 66 77 02 31
8 rm – €49/57 €56/65, € 7 – ½ P € 67/75
Rest – *(closed 15-30 November, Wednesday dinner except July-August, Tuesday lunch and Monday)* Menu (€ 14 bi), € 26/50 – Carte € 38/60
◆ This peaceful riverside 17C house is surrounded by a garden, in which the remains of an aqueduct can be seen. Practical rooms. Tasty, updated culinary repertory.

SAUVETERRE – **30 Gard** – **339** N4 – **pop. 1 793** – **alt. 23 m** – ✉ **30150** 23 **D2**
Paris 669 – Alès 77 – Avignon 15 – Nîmes 49 – Orange 15 – Pont-St-Esprit 36

Château de Varenne without rest
pl. St-Jean – ✆ 04 66 82 59 45 – www.chateaudevarenne.com – info@chateaudevarenne.com – Fax 04 66 82 84 83 – Closed 6 January-18 February
13 rm – €98/168 €98/248, € 19
◆ A French-style park adds to the charm of this elegant 18th-century residence. Fine rooms, with individual furnishings enhanced by rich fabrics and antiques.

SAUVETERRE-DE-BÉARN – **64 Pyrénées-Atlantiques** – **342** G2 – **pop. 1 304** – **alt. 69 m** – ✉ **64390** **Atlantic Coast** 3 **B3**
Paris 777 – Pau 64 – Bayonne 60 – Orthez 22 – Peyrehorade 25 – Saint-Jean-Pied-de-Port 44
Office de tourisme, place Royale ✆ 05 59 38 32 86

La Maison de Navarre rm, rest, rm,
– ✆ 05 59 38 55 28 – www.lamaisondenavarre.com – infos@lamaisondenavarre.com – Fax 05 59 38 55 71 – Closed 28 August-5 September, 2 November-3 December, 22 February-7 March
7 rm – €54/65 €59/71, € 8 – ½ P € 56/62
Rest – *(closed Sunday dinner except July-August and Wednesday)* Menu € 19 bi/30 – Carte approx. € 40
◆ Charming mansion dating from the end of the 18C, set in a garden with views of the Pyrenees. Antique furniture, parquet flooring and bright colours add charm to the rooms. Restaurant with cosy setting, lovely terrace and half-Béarnaise, half-Provençal cuisine.

Domaine de Betouzet without rest
Andrein, 3 km east on the D 27 – ✆ 05 59 38 91 40 – www.betouzet.com – book@betouzet.com – Fax 05 59 38 91 51 – Open 20 March-30 November
5 rm – €150/200 €150/200, € 12
◆ Hundred-year-old trees and immaculate box hedges adorn the grounds of this attractive manor house. Quiet, comfortable guestrooms, a boudoir and a wellness centre.

SAUVETERRE-DE-COMMINGES – 31 Haute-Garonne – 343 C6 – pop. 724 – alt. 480 m – ✉ 31510 28 **B3**

Paris 777 – Bagnères-de-Luchon 36 – Lannemezan 31 – Tarbes 71 – Toulouse 104

Les 7 Molles

at Gesset – ✆ 05 61 88 30 87 – www.hotel7molles.com – contact@hotel7molles.com – Fax 05 61 88 36 42 – Closed 15 February-15 March, Tuesday and Wednesday off season

18 rm – †€ 83 ††€ 105/153, ☕ € 12 – ½ P € 103/127

Rest – *(closed lunch weekdays)* Menu € 30/47 – Carte € 43/52

◆ The rooms with balcony overlook the pretty flower garden adorned with seven locally sourced millstones (Molles). Somewhat old-fashioned but definitely comfortable. Local ceramic tableware adorns the handsome dining room. Traditional cuisine.

SAUVETERRE-DE-ROUERGUE – 12 Aveyron – 338 F5 – pop. 811 – alt. 460 m – ✉ 12800 Languedoc-Roussillon-Tarn Gorges 29 **C1**

Paris 652 – Albi 52 – Millau 88 – Rodez 30 – St-Affrique 78 – Villefranche-de-Rouergue 44

Office de tourisme, place des Arcades ✆ 05 65 72 02 52, Fax 05 65 72 02 85

Place centrale ★.

Le Sénéchal (Michel Truchon)

– ✆ 05 65 71 29 00 – www.hotel-senechal.fr – info@hotel-senechal.fr – Fax 05 65 71 29 09 – Closed 1st January-15 March, Tuesday lunch and Thursday lunch except July-August and Monday

8 rm – †€ 130/140 ††€ 130/140, ☕ € 17 – 3 suites – ½ P € 135

Rest – *(number of covers limited, pre-book)* Menu € 27 (weekdays)/130 – Carte € 48/90

Spec. Foies gras chaud et froid. "Pascadou" et feuilles d'amarante. Ris d'agneau de l'Aveyron. **Wines** Marcillac.

◆ This charming inn occupies a royal bastide dating from the 13C. Completely rebuilt in local style, the interior decor is a mix of old and new. Contemporary cuisine and unusual décor: a goldfish bowl on every table, contemporary iron artwork and designer sitting room.

SAUVIAT-SUR-VIGE – 87 Haute-Vienne – 325 G5 – pop. 942 – alt. 450 m – ✉ 87400 24 **B2**

Paris 404 – Limoges 34 – Guéret 49 – Panazol 30 – Isle 38

Auberge de la Poste

141 r. Emile Dourdet – ✆ 05 55 75 30 12 – www.aubergedelaposte.fr – aubergedelaposte@wanadoo.fr – Fax 05 55 75 33 60 – Closed 13 December-12 January

10 rm ☕ – †€ 51 ††€ 68 – ½ P € 50

Rest – *(closed Sunday dinner and Monday)* Menu (€ 15 bi), € 17 (weekdays)/38 – Carte € 27/49

◆ Family-run inn on the village high street. The functional, rustic inspired rooms are housed in a building sheltered from the noise of the street. Traditional dishes served in an attractive country setting with bare beams, stonework and parquet floors.

SAUVIGNY-LES-BOIS – 58 Nièvre – 319 C10 – see Nevers

SAUXILLANGES – 63 Puy-de-Dôme – 326 H9 – pop. 1 109 – alt. 460 m – ✉ 63490 Auvergne 6 **C2**

Paris 455 – Ambert 46 – Clermont-Ferrand 45 – Issoire 14 – Thiers 45 – Vic-le-Comte 20

Syndicat d'initiative, place de l'Ancienne Poste ✆ 04 73 96 37 63, Fax 04 73 96 87 24

Pic d'Usson ✱★ Southwest: 4 km.

Restaurant de la Mairie
11-17 pl. St-Martin – 04 73 96 80 32 – www.fontbonne.fr – contact@fontbonne.fr – Fax 04 73 96 89 92 – Closed 23 June-3 July, 21 September-2 October, 2-17 January, Tuesday dinner and Wednesday dinner from 1st November to Easter, Sunday dinner and Monday
Rest – Menu (€ 15), € 20 (weekdays), € 28/60 – Carte € 33/73
◆ Opposite the town hall, this village house dates back to 1811. Pleasant dining rooms (beams, stained glass) and small, intimate salon, where you can enjoy a mix of traditional and regional cuisine.

SAUZON – 56 Morbihan – **308** L10 – **see Belle-Île-en-Mer**

SAVERNE – 67 Bas-Rhin – **315** I4 – **pop. 11 300 – alt. 200 m** 1 **A1**
– ✉ 67700 Alsace-Lorraine

Paris 450 – Lunéville 88 – St-Avold 89 – Sarreguemines 65 – Strasbourg 39
Office de tourisme, 37, Grand'Rue 03 88 91 80 47, Fax 03 88 71 02 90
Château★: façade★★ - Old half-timbered houses★ **N.**

Plan on next page

Europe without rest
7 r. de la Gare – 03 88 71 12 07 – www.hotel-europe-fr.com – info@hotel-europe-fr.com – Fax 03 88 71 11 43 – Closed 21 December-4 January
28 rm – †€ 65/70 ††€ 69/94, ☐ € 10 A **e**
◆ This hotel sports a European inspired decor. The simple, spacious and functional rooms have a faultless upkeep. Stylish lounge and bar overlooking the street. Air-conditioned throughout.

Chez Jean
3 r. de la Gare – 03 88 91 10 19 – www.chez-jean.com – chez.jean@wanadoo.fr – Fax 03 88 91 27 45 A **v**
25 rm – †€ 64/68 ††€ 80/87, ☐ € 10 – ½ P € 75/85
Rest – *(Closed 21 December-11 January, Sunday dinner and Monday)*
Menu (€ 13), € 16 (weekday lunch), € 30/47 – Carte € 33/57
Rest *Winstub s'Rosestiebel* – *(Closed 21 December-11 January, Sunday dinner and Monday)* Menu (€ 13), € 16 (weekday lunch), € 30/47 – Carte € 33/57
◆ Two steps from the pedestrian centre, this house offers light, well-equipped rooms in an Alsace style: wainscoting, duvets and pretty bed linen. Regional cuisine served in a wood-panelled dining room. Pleasant meals in the convivial atmosphere of the Winstub s'Rosestiebel.

Zum Staeffele
1 r. Poincaré – 03 88 91 63 94 – www.stasnet.com/staeffele.htm – michel.jaeckel@wanadoo.fr – Fax 03 88 91 63 94 – Closed 27 July-17 August, 22 December-3 January, Sunday dinner, Thursday lunch and Wednesday
Rest – Menu € 23/56 – Carte approx. € 53 B **a**
◆ Stone house dating from the 18C and 19C, situated opposite Rohan castle. Tasteful interior adorned with paintings. Up-to-date cuisine made with good quality produce.

Le Clos de la Garenne with rm
88 rte du Haut-Barr, (1.5 km via Haut Barr road) – 03 88 71 20 41 – www.closgarenne.com – clos.garenne@wanadoo.fr – Fax 03 88 02 08 86
14 rm – †€ 35 ††€ 58/100, ☐ € 12 – ½ P € 65
Rest – *(closed Saturday lunch, Tuesday dinner and Wednesday)* Menu (€ 18), € 35/80 – Carte € 58/71
◆ Contemporary cuisine using fresh produce served in a light, rustic interior. The guest-rooms invite you to cocoon amid old panelling and chequered fabrics.

via ② 3 km on D 421 – ✉ 67700 Monswiller

Kasbür
8 r. de Dettwiller – 03 88 02 14 20 – www.restaurant-kasbur.fr – restaurant.kasbur@wanadoo.fr – Fax 03 88 02 14 21 – Closed 20 July-10 August, 15-28 February, Sunday dinner, Wednesday dinner and Monday
Rest – Menu € 20 (weekday lunch), € 42/78 – Carte € 46/58
◆ Run by the same family since 1932. Attractive contemporary dining room in conservatory style serving well prepared, up-to-the-minute dishes.

SAVERNE

Bouxwiller (R. de) . . . . B 2
Clés (R. des) . . . . B 3
Côte (R. de la) . . . . B 5
Dettwiller (R. de) . . . . B 6
Églises (R. des) . . . . B 8
Foch (R. Mar.) . . . . A 12
Gare (R. de la) . . . . A 13
Gaulle (Pl. Gén.-de) . . . . B 14
Grand'Rue . . . . AB
Joffre (R. Mar.) . . . . B 15
Murs (R. des) . . . . AB 16
Pères (R. des) . . . . B 17
Poincaré (R.) . . . . A 20
Poste (R. de la) . . . . B 22
Tribunal (R. du) . . . . B 24
19-Novembre (R. du) . . . . A 26

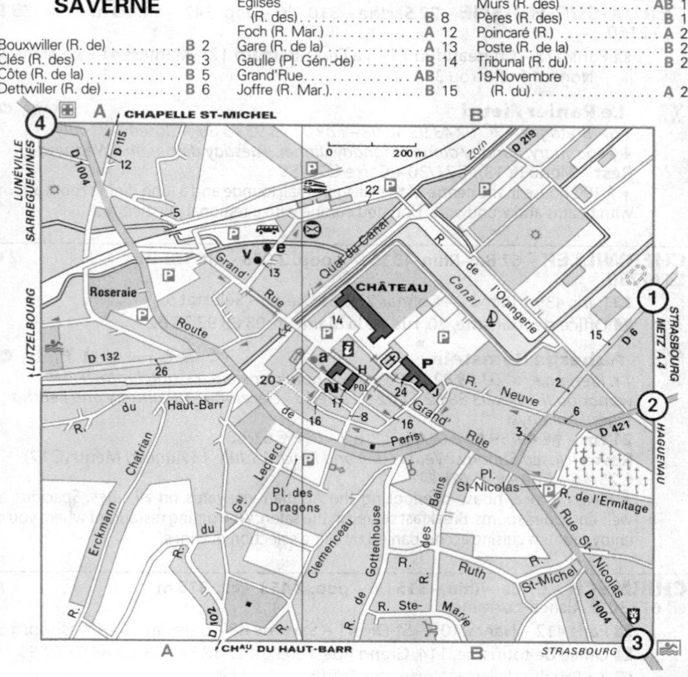

SAVIGNEUX – 42 Loire – 327 D6 – see Montbrison

SAVIGNY-LÈS-BEAUNE – 21 Côte-d'Or – 320 I7 – see Beaune

SAVIGNY-SOUS-FAYE – 86 Vienne – 322 H3 – see Lencloitre

SAVONNIÈRES – 37 Indre-et-Loire – 317 M4 – pop. 2 558 – alt. 47 m 11 B2
– ✉ 37510 Châteaux of the Loire

Paris 263 – Orléans 139 – Blois 88 – Tours 14 – Le Mans 119

La Maison Tourangelle VISA MC

9 rte Grottes Pétrifiantes – ☎ 02 47 50 30 05 – www.lamaisontourangelle.com – lamaisontourangelle@wanadoo.fr – Fax 02 47 50 30 94 – Closed 17-31 August, 26 October-4 November, 15-28 February, Saturday lunch, Sunday dinner and Wednesday

Rest – Menu € 26/56 bi

◆ Adding to the charms of this delightful 18C Touraine house is the modern rustic decor, a delightful terrace overlooking the Cher, and well prepared, modern cuisine.

SAZILLY – 37 Indre-et-Loire – 317 L6 – see L'Île-Bouchard

SCEAUX-SUR-HUISNE – 72 Sarthe – 310 M6 – pop. 547 – alt. 93 m 35 **D1**
– ✉ 72160

Paris 173 – Châteaudun 75 – La Ferté-Bernard 12 – Mamers 41 – Le Mans 35 – Nogent-le-Rotrou 34

Le Panier Fleuri VISA
1 av. Bretagne – ✆ 02 43 93 40 08 – Fax 02 43 93 43 86 – Closed 5-21 July, 4-14 January, Sunday dinner, Monday dinner, Tuesday dinner and Wednesday
Rest – Menu (€ 13), € 21/30 – Carte € 25/55
◆ A 19C house in the centre of the village. Small lounge and a long dining room adorned with beams and woodwork. Updated cuisine with a regional perspective.

SCHERWILLER – 67 Bas-Rhin – 315 I7 – pop. 2 958 – alt. 185 m 2 **C1**
– ✉ 67750

Paris 439 – Barr 21 – Colmar 27 – St-Dié 42 – Sélestat 5
Office de tourisme, 30, rue de la Mairie ✆ 03 88 92 25 62

Auberge Ramstein rm, VISA
1 r. Riesling – ✆ 03 88 82 17 00 – www.hotelramstein.fr – hotel.ramstein@wanadoo.fr – Fax 03 88 82 17 02 – Closed 23 December-10 January and February school holidays
21 rm – €49/59 €62/72, € 9 – ½ P € 63/68
Rest – *(closed Sunday, Wednesday and lunch 15 July-15 August)* Menu (€ 17), € 25/46 – Carte € 30/41
◆ Pleasant local house overlooking the Alsatian vineyards on all sides. Spacious and well-equipped rooms. Breakfast served in the salon. Welcoming restaurant where you can enjoy modern cuisine accompanied by a fine selection of wines.

SCHIRMECK – 67 Bas-Rhin – 315 H6 – pop. 2 453 – alt. 315 m 1 **A2**
– ✉ 67130 Alsace-Lorraine

Paris 412 – Nancy 101 – St-Dié 41 – Saverne 48 – Sélestat 59 – Strasbourg 53
Office de tourisme, 114, Grand'Rue ✆ 03 88 47 18 51, Fax 03 88 97 09 59
La Bruche Valley ★ North and South.

in Quelles 7.5 km southwest by D 1420, D 261 and forest road – ✉ 67130 La Broque

Neuhauser rm, VISA
– ✆ 03 88 97 06 81 – www.hotel-neuhauser.com – hotelneuhauser@wanadoo.fr – Fax 03 88 97 14 29 – Closed 17-30 November and 20 February-10 March
15 rm – €67 €84, € 12 – ½ P € 82
Rest – Menu (€ 10), € 21/45 – Carte € 28/50
◆ Peace and quiet are guaranteed in this country inn nestling in the middle of the forest. Rustic style rooms and chalets, indoor pool and sauna. Tasty, regional fare, and after the meal, the brandy from the family distillery is a must!

LA SCHLUCHT (COL) – 88 Vosges – 314 K4 – see Col de la Schlucht

SECLIN – 59 Nord – 302 G4 – pop. 12 200 – alt. 30 m – ✉ 59113 31 **C2**
Northern France and the Paris Region

Paris 212 – Lens 26 – Lille 17 – Tournai 33 – Valenciennes 47
Office de tourisme, 70, rue Roger Bouvry ✆ 03 20 90 12 12, Fax 03 20 90 12 00
Hospital★ courtyard.

Auberge du Forgeron with rm VISA
17 r. Roger Bouvry – ✆ 03 20 90 09 52 – www.aubergeduforgeron.com – contact@aubergeduforgeron.com – Fax 03 20 32 70 87 – Closed 25 July-23 August and 24-30 December
16 rm – €75/189 €80/189, € 12 – ½ P € 85
Rest – *(closed Saturday lunch and Sunday)* Menu (€ 35 bi), € 39/75 – Carte € 59/89
◆ Old red-brick house. The fireplace and spit roast create a warm atmosphere in the dining room-veranda. Contemporary repertoire and fine wine list. Comfortable modern rooms.

SEDAN – 08 Ardennes – **306** L4 – **pop. 20 000 – alt. 154 m** 14 **C1**
– ✉ 08200 **Northern France and the Paris Region**

Paris 246 – Charleville-Mézières 25 – Metz 134 – Reims 101
Office de tourisme, place du Château Fort ✆ 03 24 27 73 73, Fax 03 24 29 03 28
Fortified castle ★★.

SEDAN

Alsace-Lorraine (Pl. d') BZ 2
Armes (Pl. d') BY 3
Bayle (R. de) BY 4
Berchet (R.) BY 5
Blanpain (R.) BY 6
Capucins (Rampe) BY 7
Carnot (R.) BY 8
Crussy (Pl.) BY 9
Fleuranges (R. de) AY 10
Francs-Bourgeois (R. des) BY 12
Gambetta (R.) BY 13
Goulden (Pl.) BY 14
Halle (Pl. de la) BY 15
Horloge (R. de l') BY 17
Jardin (Bd du Gd) BY 18
Lattre-de-Tassigny (Bd Mar.-de) AZ 21
Leclerc (Av. du Mar.) BY 24
Margueritte (Av. du G.) ABY 26
Martyrs-de-la-Résistance (Av. des) AY 27
Mesnil (R. du) BY
Nassau (Pl.) BZ 31
Promenoir-des-Prêtres BY 33
Rivage (R. du) BY 34
La Rochefoucauld (R. de) BY 20
Rochette (Bd de la) BY 35
Rovigo (R.) BY 36
Strasbourg (R. de) BZ 39
Turenne (Pl.) BY 41
Vesseron-Lejay (R.) AY 42
Wuildet-Bizot (R.) BZ 44

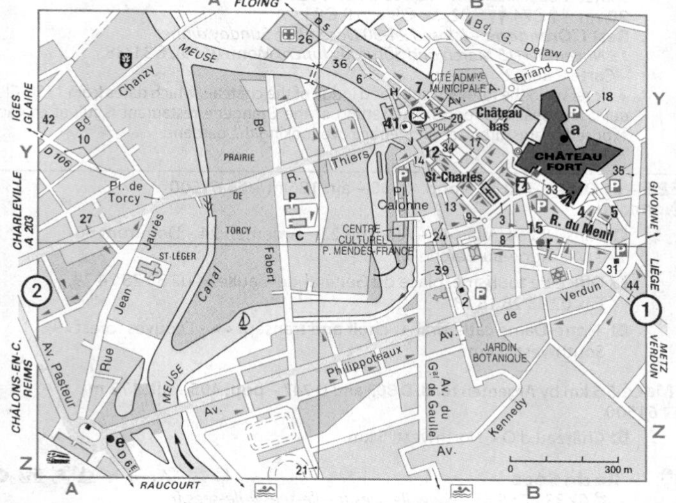

Hôtellerie le Château Fort

in the fortified castle: access via Porte des Princes – ✆ 03 24 26 11 00 – www.hotelfp-sedan.com – contact@hotelfp-sedan.com – Fax 03 24 27 19 00 BY **a**

52 rm – €75/194 €75/194, ☕ €15 – 10 suites
Rest – *(closed Sunday dinner and Monday lunch)* Menu €35/60 – Carte €46/65
◆ This 15C fortified castle, now a listed building, overlooks the town and houses a hotel in the former gunpowder room. Rooms and suites adorned with medieval-themed paintings. Meals are served in the old abode of the king's lieutenant.

Au Bon Vieux Temps

3 pl. de la Halle – ✆ 03 24 29 03 70 – www.restaurant-aubonvieuxtemps.com – restaurant.au.bon.vieux.temps@wanadoo.fr – Fax 03 24 29 20 27 – Closed 31 August-7 September, 26 December-1st January, 15 February-7 March, Sunday dinner, Wednesday dinner and Monday BYZ **r**

Rest – Menu (€19), €25/48 – Carte €37/75
Rest *Marmiton* – *(closed Sunday and Monday) (lunch only)* Menu €13 (weekdays)/16 – Carte approx. €18
◆ Murals of Sedan at the turn of the century and the Ardennes landscape decorate this restaurant on the ground floor of a 17C house. Classic menu. The Marmiton offers a simple menu and daily specials in a relaxed bistro atmosphere.

in Bazeilles 3 km by ① – **pop. 1 976 – alt. 161 m –** ✉ **08140**

Auberge du Port

r. de la Gare, 1 km South via rte Remilly-Aillicourt – ✆ 03 24 27 13 89 – www.auberge-du-port.fr – auberge-du-port@wanadoo.fr – Fax 03 24 29 35 58 – Closed August, 18 December-5 January
20 rm – €57 €68, €8,50 – ½ P €62
Rest – *(closed Friday except dinner 1st April-30 October, Saturday lunch and Sunday dinner)* Menu (€ 19), € 25/48

◆ This family-run inn's main asset is its small garden on the banks of the Meuse. Peaceful rooms that are above all simple and functional. Wine lovers will be particularly impressed by this restaurant with its well-stocked cellar (tasting sessions and shop).

Château de Bazeilles

r. Galliéni – ✆ 03 24 27 09 68 – www.chateau-bazeilles.com – contact@chateau-bazeilles.com – Fax 03 24 27 64 20
20 rm – €74 €92, €9 – ½ P €83
Rest *L'Orangerie* – *(closed 24-30 December, Sunday dinner 15 November-15 March and Saturday lunch)* Menu (€ 19), € 31/38 – Carte € 38/62

◆ Hotel set in the former stables and lodge of the château, which dates from 1750. Clean, quiet and spacious rooms. The setting of the Orangerie restaurant is full of character: exposed beams, fireplace and terrace overlooking the gardens.

SÉES – 61 Orne – 310 K3 – pop. 4 508 – alt. 186 m – ✉ 61500 33 C3

Normandy

Paris 183 – L'Aigle 42 – Alençon 22 – Argentan 24 – Domfront 66 – Mortagne-au-Perche 33

Office de tourisme, place du Général-de-Gaulle ✆ 02 33 28 74 79, Fax 02 33 28 18 13

Notre-Dame cathedral ★: choir and transept★★ - Ecouves forest★★ Southwest: 5 km.

in Macé 5,5 km by Argentan road, D 303 and D 747 – **pop. 495 – alt. 173 m –** ✉ **61500**

Château d'O★ Northwest: 5 km.

Île de Sées

rest,

– ✆ 02 33 27 98 65 – www.ile-sees.fr – ile-sees@ile-sees.fr – Fax 02 33 28 41 22 – Open 1st March-30 November and closed Sunday evening
16 rm – €69 €69, €9 – ½ P €70
Rest – *(closed Sunday dinner, Monday lunch, Tuesday lunch and Wednesday lunch)* Menu € 18/35 – Carte € 28/43

◆ Hotel set in extensive grounds in the middle of the Normandy countryside. Pleasant guestrooms (stained wood furniture, pastel shades). Buffet breakfast. A welcoming, rustic yet stylish dining room, serving traditional cuisine.

SEGONZAC – 19 Corrèze – 329 I4 – pop. 231 – alt. 345 m – ✉ 19310 24 B3

Dordogne-Berry-Limousin

Paris 506 – Limoges 117 – Tulle 58 – Brive-la-Gaillarde 31 – Périgueux 69

Pré Laminon

– ✆ 05 55 84 17 39 – www.prelaminon.com – prelaminon@wanadoo.fr – Open 1st April-30 September
3 rm – €40/50 €52/60 **Table d'hôte** – Menu € 12 bi/18 bi

◆ An old Corrèze-style barn in hilly surroundings. The interior is as welcoming as an Alpine chalet, with its rustic wood decor, cosy bedrooms etc. Swimming pool.

SÉGOS – 32 Gers – 336 A8 – see Aire-sur-l'Adour

SEGRÉ – 49 Maine-et-Loire – 317 D2 – pop. 6 671 – alt. 40 m – ✉ 49500 34 B2

Paris 334 – Nantes 83 – Angers 44 – Laval 55 – Châteaubriant 45

Le Segré

r. Gustave-Eiffel – ☎ 02 41 94 81 81 – hotel.lesegre@orange.fr – Fax 02 41 94 81 88

48 rm – €55/72 €55/72, ☕ €8

Rest – grill – *(closed Sunday)* Menu (€12), €15 (weekdays)/30 – Carte €23/34

◆ Next to an industrial estate surrounded by greenery, this recent complex is regional in style. Eminently comfortable rooms decorated in a contemporary, low-key style. The first floor restaurant serves traditional cuisine (buffets and grilled meat).

Undecided between two equivalent establishments? Within each category, establishments are classified in our order of preference.

SÉGURET – 84 Vaucluse – 332 D8 – see Vaison-la-Romaine

SEIGNOSSE – 40 Landes – 335 C12 – pop. 2 778 – alt. 15 m – ✉ 40510 3 A3

Paris 747 – Biarritz 36 – Dax 32 – Mont-de-Marsan 85 – Soustons 11

Office de tourisme, avenue des Lacs ☎ 05 58 43 32 15, Fax 05 58 43 32 66

de Seignosse Avenue du Belvédère, W : 4 km on D 86, ☎ 05 58 41 68 30

Golf Hôtel

av. du Belvédère, at the golf club, 4 km west via D86 – ☎ 05 58 41 68 40 – www.bluegreen.com/seignosse – golfhotel@bluegreen.com – Fax 05 58 41 68 41 – Closed 13 December-21 February

45 rm – €75/95 €100/145, ☕ €13

Rest – *(dinner only) (residents only)* Menu €25

◆ A colourful Louisiana-style wood construction, in a pine grove, part of a fine golf course. Immense reception hall lit by a glass roof. Some rooms have balconies. Traditional cuisine served in the restaurant in the evening and lunchtime set menu at the club-house.

Villa de l'Étang Blanc

2265, rte Etang Blanc, 2.5 Km north by D 185 and D 432 – ☎ 05 58 72 80 15 – villaetangblanc@hotmail.fr – Fax 05 58 72 83 67

8 rm – €70/110 €70/110, ☕ €15

Rest – *(closed Sunday dinner and Monday)* Menu (€19), €28 – Carte €35/45

◆ A retro ambience with the occasional exotic touch pervades this charming house with an attractive garden. Elegant guestrooms and junior suites. Glass-enclosed dining room, overlooking the pond after which the villa is named, and delightful terrace facing the canal, where fishing boats are moored.

SEILH – 31 Haute-Garonne – 343 G2 – see Toulouse

SEILHAC – 19 Corrèze – 329 L3 – pop. 1 724 – alt. 500 m – ✉ 19700 25 C3

Paris 461 – Aubusson 97 – Brive-la-Gaillarde 33 – Limoges 73 – Tulle 15 – Uzerche 16

Office de tourisme, place de l'Horloge ☎ 05 55 27 97 62

Au Relais des Monédières

Montargis, 1 km Tulle road – ☎ 05 55 27 04 74 – Fax 05 55 27 90 03 – Closed 22-29 March, 28 June-5 July, Friday dinner, Saturday lunch and Sunday dinner in low season and public holidays

16 rm – €49 €49/53, ☕ €7 – ½ P €50/60

Rest – Menu (€13), €15 (weekdays)/34 – Carte €26/42

◆ Set in a pretty park with pond, this family hotel facing the Monédières mountains will appeal to anglers. Modest but impeccably kept rooms. Rustic restaurant and green terrace covered by a canopy. Traditional and regional dishes.

SEILLANS – 83 Var – 340 O4 – pop. 2 543 – alt. 350 m – ✉ 83440 41 C3

Paris 890 – Marseille 142 – Toulon 106 – Antibes 54 – Cannes 43

Syndicat d'initiative, 1, rue du Valat ✆ 04 94 76 85 91, Fax 04 94 39 13 53

Des Deux Rocs

1 pl. Font d'Amont – ✆ 04 94 76 87 32 – www.hoteldeuxrocs.com – hoteldeuxrocs@wanadoo.fr – Fax 04 94 76 88 68 – Closed 2-17 November and 2 January-13 February

13 rm – †€ 68/135 ††€ 68/135, ☕ € 13

Rest – *(Closed Sunday dinner and Tuesday lunch from October to May and Monday)* Menu € 40/62 – Carte € 48/64

◆ This handsome 18C hostelry dominating the town is steeped in the nostalgic charm of yesteryear. Individualised rooms graced with antiques picked up in flea markets. Updated menu served in a cosy dining room or in the shade of plane trees on the village square.

Le Relais

1 pl. Thouron – ✆ 04 94 60 18 65 – Fax 04 94 60 10 92 – Closed 15-30 November, Wednesday except in July-August and Tuesday

Rest – Menu € 28/43 – Carte € 39/49

◆ In a former coaching inn, this restaurant has pleasant, contemporary decor and serves a modern menu based on quality produce. Terrace shaded by plane trees.

La Gloire de mon Père

pl. du Thouron – ✆ 04 94 76 98 68 – www.lagloiredemonpere.fr – lagloiredemonpere@free.fr – Fax 04 94 76 98 68 – Closed 5 January-5 February

Rest – Menu € 28 – Carte € 38/50

◆ Simple rustic restaurant with terrace located on a bucolic square with fountain and washhouse. Traditional cuisine.

SEILLONNAZ – 01 Ain – 328 F6 – pop. 143 – alt. 530 m – ✉ 01470 45 C1

Paris 498 – Lyon 87 – Bourg-en-Bresse 66 – Villeurbanne 75 – Chambéry 71

La Cigale d'Or

in the village – ✆ 04 74 36 13 61 – www.restaurantlacigaledor.fr – cigaledor@orange.fr – Fax 04 74 36 15 64 – Closed autumn school holidays, 22-28 December, Monday dinner from 15 October to 15 March, Sunday dinner, Tuesday dinner and Wednesday

Rest – Menu (€ 15 bi), € 23/55 – Carte € 38/45

◆ Do not forget this establishment in a forgotten village: you can enjoy modern fare in a peaceful and vaulted (stone) dining room. Terrace overlooking the valley.

SEIN (ÎLE) – 29 Finistère – 308 B6 – see Île de Sein

SÉLESTAT – 67 Bas-Rhin – 315 I7 – pop. 19 200 – alt. 170 m – ✉ 67600 Alsace-Lorraine 2 C1

Paris 441 – Colmar 24 – Gérardmer 65 – St-Dié 44 – Strasbourg 55

Office de tourisme, boulevard Leclerc ✆ 03 88 58 87 20, Fax 03 88 92 88 63

Old town ★: Ste-Foy church ★, St-Georges church ★, Bibliothèque humaniste ★ M.

Ebermunster: interior ★★ of abbey church ★, 9 km by ①.

Plan on next page

Hostellerie de l'Abbaye la Pommeraie

8 av. Mar. Foch – ✆ 03 88 92 07 84 – www.relaischateau.com/pommeraie – pommeraie@relaischateaux.com – Fax 03 88 92 08 71 BY a

12 rm – †€ 145 ††€ 173/250, ☕ € 18 – 2 suites – ½ P € 153/205

Rest *Le Prieuré* – *(closed Sunday dinner and Monday lunch)* Menu € 27 (weekday lunch), € 52 € bi/100 – Carte € 76/109

Rest *S'Apfelstuebel* – Menu € 27 (weekday lunch) – Carte € 46/60

◆ This stately 17C house, formerly an outbuilding of Baumgarten Abbey, is in the old town. Rooms furnished with period furniture. Le Prieuré offers an elegant decor in keeping with its classical cuisine. Regional dishes and a modern decor at the S'Apfelstuebel winstub.

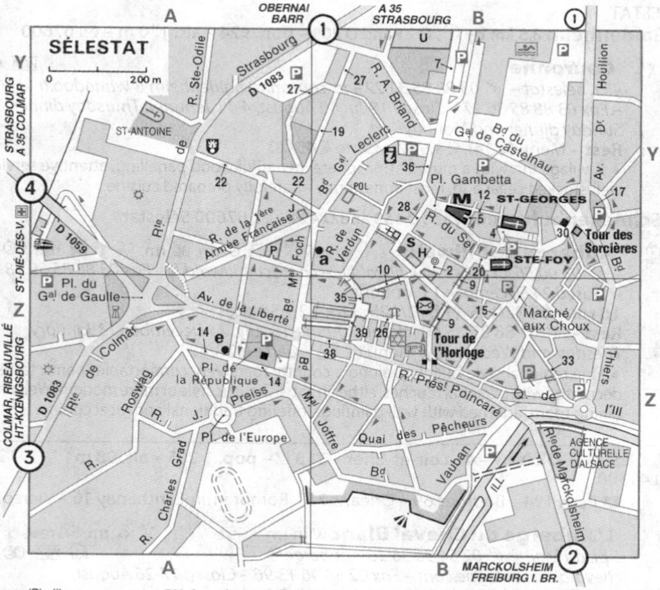

SÉLESTAT

Street	Grid	No.
Armes (Pl. d')	BY	2
Babil (R. du)	BY	4
Bibliothèque (R. de la)	BY	5
Charlemagne (Bd)	BY	7
Chevaliers (R. des)	BYZ	9
Clefs (R. des)	BYZ	10
Église (R. de l')	BY	12
Gallieni (R. du Gén.)	AZ	14
Hôpital (R. de l')	BZ	15
Lattre-de-Tassigny (Pl. du Mar.de)	BY	17
Maire-Knol (Allée du)	BY	19
Marché-Vert (Pl. du)	BY	20
Paix (R. de la)	AY	22
Prés.-Poincaré (R. du)	BZ	
Sainte-Barbe (R.)	BZ	26
Schweisguth (Av.)	ABY	27
Serruriers (R. des)	BY	28
Strasbourg (Pl. Pte-de)	BY	30
Tanneurs (Quai des)	BZ	33
Victoire (Pl. de la)	BZ	35
Vieux-Marché aux Vins (R. du)	BY	36
4e-Zouaves (R. du)	BZ	38
17-Novembre (R. du)	BZ	39

Vaillant

7 r. Ignace Spiess – ☎ 03 88 92 09 46 – www.hotel-vaillant.com – hotel-vaillant@wanadoo.fr – Fax 03 88 82 95 01 AZ **e**

47 rm – €61/102 €72/102, ☕ €9 – ½ P €58/73

Rest – *(closed 21 December-5 January, Saturday lunch and Sunday dinner in low season)* Menu €15 (weekdays)/35 – Carte €27/41

◆ Many works by local artists are displayed in this modern hotel flanked by a floral park, near the town centre. Bright rooms with individual touches. Designer or classic dining rooms, offering traditional brasserie style dishes and regional specialities.

La Vieille Tour

8 r. Jauge – ☎ 03 88 92 15 02 – www.vieille-tour.com – vieille.tour@wanadoo.fr – Fax 03 88 92 19 42 – Closed 20 July-3 August, 15 February-1st March and Monday

Rest – Menu (€12), €27/42 – Carte €31/51 BY **s**

◆ A pretty Alsace style house flanked by an old tower. Refreshingly rustic dining rooms and fine regional cooking (using local produce). Reasonably priced wines.

in Rathsamhausen 5 km East by D 21 and D 209 – ✉ 67600 Baldenheim

Les Prés d'Ondine

5 rte Baldenheim – ☎ 03 88 58 04 60 – www.presdondine.com – message@presdondine.com – Fax 03 88 58 04 61 – Closed 1st-15 March

12 rm – €60/139 €80/139, ☕ €12 – ½ P €84/114

Rest – table d'hôte – *(closed Sunday dinner and Wednesday) (pre-book)* Menu €22 bi/32 bi

◆ This pleasant, early 20C forester's house provides a homely atmosphere. Cosy lounge, library and rooms with poetry-inspired decor. Regional, market based dishes and a view of the Ill river are the main assets of the elegant table d'hôte.

in Baldenheim 8,5 km by ①, D 21 and D 209 – pop. 924 – alt. 170 m – ✉ 67600

XX **Couronne** VISA MC

45 r. Sélestat – ✆ 03 88 85 32 22 – la-couronne-baldenheim@wanadoo.fr – Fax 03 88 85 36 27 – Closed 18 July-2 August, 4-11 January, Thursday dinner, Sunday dinner and Monday

Rest – Menu (€ 14), € 32/62 – Carte € 45/70

◆ A village inn with a muted atmosphere, beautiful wood panelling, attentive service, a well-stocked cellar and, most importantly – carefully prepared cuisine.

Le Schnellenbuhl 8 km by ②, D 159 and D 424 – ✉ 67600 Sélestat

Auberge de l'Illwald rm, AC rm, P VISA MC AE

– ✆ 03 90 56 11 40 – www.illwald.fr – contact@illwald.fr – Fax 03 88 85 39 18 – Closed 24 December-13 January

16 rm – †€ 72/125 ††€ 72/125, ☕ € 12 – 5 suites

Rest – ✆ 03 88 85 35 40 *(closed 30 June-15 July, 24 December-13 January, Tuesday and Wednesday)* Menu (€ 11) – Carte € 28/42

◆ Fine regional-style building, along a country road. Very comfortable rooms, tastefully decorated with personal touches, either in a stylish rustic style or more modern. Welcoming dining room, adorned with wall paintings, offering traditional and local cuisine.

SELLES-ST-DENIS – 41 Loir-et-Cher – 318 I7 – pop. 1 205 – alt. 98 m – ✉ 41300 12 C2

▶ Paris 194 – Bourges 69 – Orléans 71 – Romorantin-Lanthenay 16 – Vierzon 26

XXX **L'Auberge du Cheval Blanc** with rm rm, rest, P VISA MC AE

5 pl. du Mail – ✆ 02 54 96 36 36 – auberge@chevalblanc-sologne.com – Fax 02 54 96 13 96 – Closed 17-26 August, 16 February-10 March, Tuesday dinner and Wednesday

7 rm – †€ 64/76 ††€ 64/76, ☕ € 9,50 – ½ P € 63

Rest – Menu € 22, € 33/65 – Carte € 66/90

◆ The half-timbered façade of this 17C post house is a happy mixture of rusticity and elegance. Low-key sitting rooms and contemporary bedrooms. A traditional menu with a focus on forgotten vegetables. Huge interior courtyard in summer.

SELONNET – 04 Alpes-de-Haute-Provence – 334 F6 – see Seyne

SEMBLANÇAY – 37 Indre-et-Loire – 317 M4 – pop. 1 960 – alt. 100 m – ✉ 37360 11 B2

▶ Paris 248 – Angers 96 – Blois 77 – Le Mans 70 – Tours 17

XX **La Mère Hamard** with rm P VISA MC AE

pl. de l'Église – ✆ 02 47 56 62 04 – www.lamerehamard.com – reservation@lamerehamard.com – Fax 02 47 56 53 61 – Closed 2-23 January, 15 February-5 March, Sunday dinner, Tuesday lunch and Monday

11 rm – †€ 70/93 ††€ 74/95, ☕ € 13 – ½ P € 79/90

Rest – Menu € 22 (weekdays), € 30/60 – Carte € 60/80

◆ Regional style houses separated by the road – comfortable rooms on one side and an elegant restaurant on the other. Classical cuisine and fine selection of Loire wines.

SEMÈNE – 43 Haute-Loire – 331 H1 – see Aurec-sur-Loire

SEMNOZ (MONTAGNE) – 74 Haute-Savoie – 328 J6 – See Montagne du Semnoz

---

SEMUR-EN-AUXOIS – 21 Côte-d'Or – 320 G5 – pop. 4 195 – alt. 286 m – ✉ 21140 Burgundy-Jura 8 C2

▶ Paris 246 – Auxerre 87 – Avallon 42 – Beaune 78 – Dijon 82 – Montbard 20

Office de tourisme, 2, place Gaveau ✆ 03 80 97 05 96, Fax 03 80 97 08 85

du Pré-Lamy Précy-sous-Thil Le Brouillard, S : 18 km on the D980, ✆ 03 80 64 46 83

N.-Dame church ★ - Pont Joly ≤★.

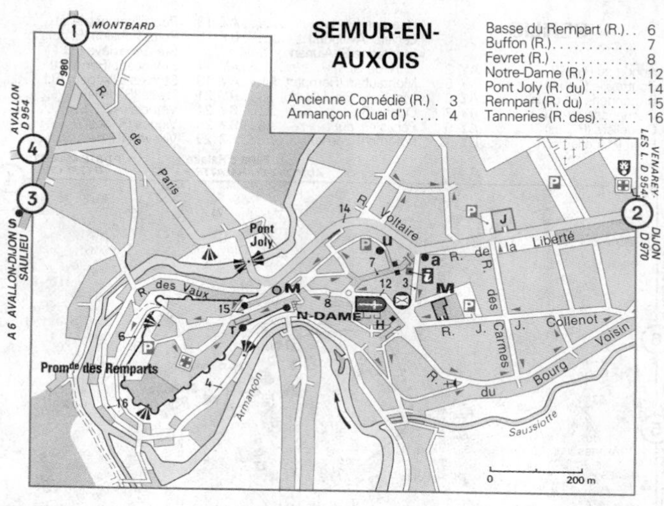

Hostellerie d'Aussois rm, VISA

rte de Saulieu – ✆ 03 80 97 28 28 – www.hostellerie.fr – info@hostellerie.fr – Fax 03 80 97 34 56 s

42 rm – †€ 90/95 ††€ 100/110, ☕ € 13 – ½ P € 84

Rest – Menu € 25/55 – Carte € 53/72

◆ A 1980s establishment with functional rooms that are being gradually renovated, either overlooking the town or the countryside. Restaurant with a modern setting overlooking the pool-side terrace, with Semur's ramparts in the background. Traditional dishes.

Les Cymaises without rest VISA

7 r. Renaudot – ✆ 03 80 97 21 44 – www.hotelcymaises.com – hotel.cymaises@wanadoo.fr – Fax 03 80 97 18 23 – Closed 3 November-7 December and 5 February-3 March u

18 rm – †€ 57/62 ††€ 66, ☕ € 8

◆ Old and elegant looking building (18C-19C) at the heart of the medieval town. Classically decorated, quiet rooms. Breakfast served on the veranda. Restful courtyard and garden.

La Côte d'Or without rest VISA

1 r. de la Liberté – ✆ 03 80 97 24 54 – www.auxois.fr – cotedor@auxois.fr – Fax 03 80 97 00 18 a

10 rm – †€ 75/115 ††€ 85/125, ☕ € 10

◆ Completely renovated former posthouse with spacious, well, soundproofed rooms, attractive decor and excellent beds.

SÉNART – Île-de-France – **312** E4 – **101** 39 – **see Paris, Area**

SENLIS – **60 Oise** – **305** G5 – **pop. 16 500** – **alt. 76 m** – ✉ **60300** 36 **B3**

Northern France and the Paris Region

Paris 52 – Amiens 102 – Beauvais 56 – Compiègne 33 – Meaux 40

Office de tourisme, place du Parvis Notre Dame ✆ 03 44 53 06 40, Fax 03 44 53 29 80

d'Apremont Apremont CD 606, NW : 5 km on D 1330, ✆ 03 44 25 61 11

Dolce Chantilly Vineuil-Saint-Firmin Route d'Apremont, 8 km on the Chantilly road, ✆ 03 44 58 47 74

Château Raray Paris Golf Club Raray Domaine de Raray, 26 km on the Compiègne road, ✆ 03 44 54 70 61

N.-Dame cathedral ★★ - Old streets ★ ABY - Place du Parvis ★ BY - Royal St-Frambourg chapel ★ B - Jardin du Roy ≤ ★ - Musée d'Art et d'Archéologie ★.

Parc Astérix ★★ South: 12 km by A1 motorway.

SENLIS

Apport-au-Pain (R.) . . . . AY 2
Boutteville (Cours) . . . . BY 5
Bretonnerie (R. de la) . . . . . . AZ 6
Clemenceau (Av. G.) . . . . BY 7
Cordeliers (R. des) . . . . AZ 9
Halle (Pl. de la) . . . . BY 12
Heaume (R. du) . . . . AZ 13
Leclerc (Av. Gén.) . . . . BY 15
Montagne St-Aignan (R. de la) . . . . AY 17
Montauban (Rempart du) . . . AY 19
Moulin St-Rieul (R. du) . . . . . BY 21
Odent (R.) . . . . BY 24
Parvis (Pl. du) . . . . BY 26
Poterne (R. de la) . . . . BZ 29
Poulaillerie (R. de la) . . . . AY 31
Puits-Tiphaine (R. du) . . . . . . AY 27
Ste-Geneviève (R.) . . . . BZ 40
St-Vincent (Rempart) . . . . BZ 36
St-Yves-à-l'Argent (R.) . . . . . . BZ 38
Treille (R. de la) . . . . AY 42
Vernois (Av. F.) . . . . AY 47
Vignes (R. des) . . . . BZ 49
Villevert (R. de) . . . . BY 52

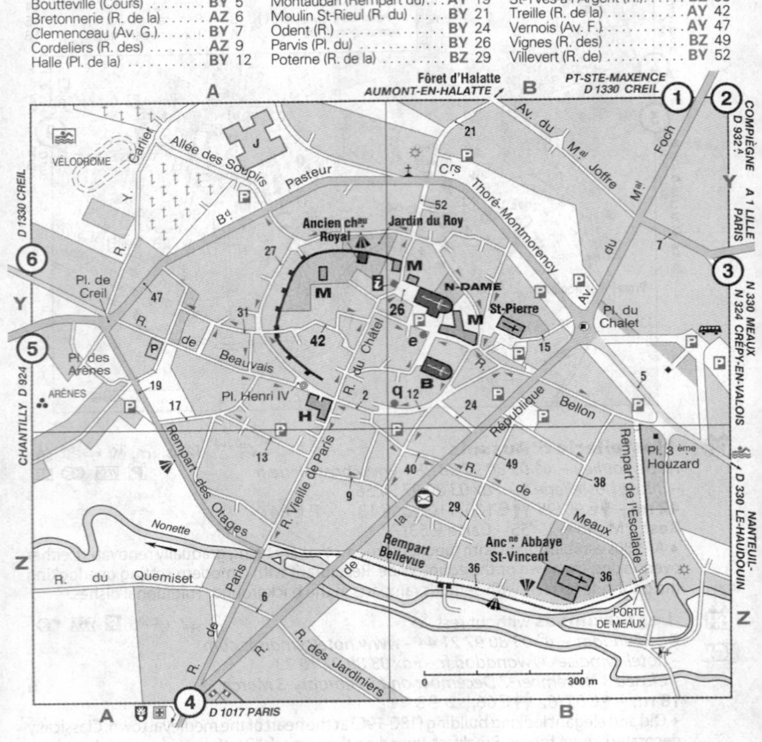

Ibis

2 km via ③ on D 1324 – ☏ 03 44 53 70 50 – www.ibishotel.com – h0709@accor.com – Fax 03 44 53 51 93

92 rm – €65/95 €65/95, ☕ €8 **Rest** – Menu €11/20 – Carte €26/43

◆ Practical hotel just off the motorway. All the rooms in the main building and the annexe have been renovated in keeping with the chain's latest concept. Country-style decor (exposed beams, fireplace); grilled meats the speciality.

Le Scaramouche

4 pl. Notre-Dame – ☏ 03 44 53 01 26 – www.le-scaramouche.fr – info@le-scaramouche.fr – Fax 03 44 53 46 14 – Closed 18-30 August, Tuesday and Wednesday BY **e**

Rest – Menu €29/39 – Carte €47/79

◆ Warm house with pretty painted wood exterior. Pleasant interior with paintings and tapestries; the attractive terrace overlooks the cathedral of Notre-Dame (12C).

SENNECÉ-LÈS-MÂCON – 71 Saône-et-Loire – 320 J11 – see Mâcon

SENNECEY-LE-GRAND – 71 Saône-et-Loire – 320 J10 – pop. 2 990 – alt. 200 m – ✉ 71240 Burgundy-Jura 8 **C3**

Paris 359 – Dijon 89 – Mâcon 42 – Chalon-sur-Saône 18 – Le Creusot 53

Office de tourisme, place de l'hôtel de ville ☏ 03 85 44 82 54, Fax 03 85 44 86 19

L'Amaryllis (Cédric Burtin)
78 av. du 4 Septembre – ✆ 03 85 44 86 34 – www.lamaryllis.com – courrier@lamaryllis.com – Fax 03 85 44 96 92 – Closed 26 October-5 November, 2-15 January, Sunday dinner, Monday lunch and Wednesday
Rest – Menu (€ 19), € 32/65 – Carte € 49/65
Spec. Dodine de foie gras de canard aux figues, caramel aux trois poivres. Noix de veau de lait cuite à basse température, jus au macvin du Jura. Biscuit fondant au chocolat mi-amer, sorbet fruit de la passion. **Wines** Viré-Clessé, Givry.
◆ Contemporary restaurant opposite the Hôtel Dieu. The chef works with local producers and creates generous inventive cuisine. His wife runs the dining room.

SENONCHES – 28 Eure-et-Loir – 311 C4 – pop. 3 203 – alt. 223 m – ✉ 28250 11 B1

Paris 115 – Chartres 38 – Dreux 38 – Mortagne-au-Perche 42 – Nogent-le-Rotrou 34

Syndicat d'initiative, 2, rue Louis Peuret ✆ 02 37 37 80 11, Fax 02 37 37 80 11

La Pomme de Pin with rm
15 r. M. Cauty – ✆ 02 37 37 76 62 – www.restaurant-pommedepin.com – restaurantlapommedepin@wanadoo.fr – Fax 02 37 37 86 61 – Closed 15-30 July, 2-27 January, Sunday dinner and Monday
10 rm – €48 €58/72, € 10
Rest – Menu € 16 (weekday lunch), € 25/47 – Carte € 36/55
◆ Sample the culinary speciality of this former post house: pâté de Chartres. A fine half-timbered façade, pleasant dining room, tea room and terrace. Simple rooms.

SENONES – 88 Vosges – 314 J2 – pop. 2 781 – alt. 340 m – ✉ 88210 27 C2
Alsace-Lorraine

Paris 392 – Épinal 57 – Lunéville 50 – St-Dié 23 – Strasbourg 80

Office de tourisme, 18, place Dom Calmet ✆ 03 29 57 91 03, Fax 03 29 57 83 95

Senones road to col du Donon (Donon Pass)★ Northeast: 20 km.

Au Bon Gîte with rm
3 pl. Vaultrin – ✆ 03 29 57 92 46 – Fax 03 29 57 93 92 – Closed 1st-20 March, 6-29 September, Sunday dinner and Monday
7 rm – €44/52 €44/52, € 7 – ½ P € 58
Rest – Menu (€ 13), € 20/35 – Carte € 35/50
◆ Smart house in the centre of the former capital of the Salm principality. Tasty modern cuisine served in a contemporary setting, dotted with photographs and ornaments of all sorts.

SENS – 89 Yonne – 319 C2 – pop. 26 800 – alt. 70 m – ✉ 89100 7 B1
Burgundy-Jura

Paris 116 – Auxerre 59 – Fontainebleau 54 – Montargis 50 – Troyes 71

Office de tourisme, place Jean Jaurès ✆ 03 86 65 19 49, Fax 03 86 64 24 18

du Senonais Lixy Les Ursules, W : 22 km on D 26, ✆ 03 86 66 58 46

St-Étienne cathedral ★ - Treasure-house★★ - Musée et palais synodal★ M¹.

Plan on following page

Paris et Poste rm, rest,
97 r. de la République – ✆ 03 86 65 17 43 – www.hotel-paris-poste.com – hotelparisposte@orange.fr – Fax 03 86 64 48 45 a
26 rm – €72/155 €72/155, € 15 – 4 suites
Rest – *(closed Friday dinner, Sunday dinner and Monday)* Menu (€ 26), € 38/80 – Carte € 60/80
◆ A traditional inn with a provincial atmosphere. Rooms of varying sizes, the most spacious and modern rooms open onto an elegant patio. Reinterpreted classic cuisine served in an inviting dining room or pleasant veranda.

SENS

Alsace-Lorraine (R. d') 2
Beaurepaire (R.) 3
Chambonas (Cours) 8
Cornet (Av. Lucien) 9
Cousin (Square J.) 10
Déportés-et-de-la-Résistance (R. des)
Foch (Bd Mar.) 12
Garibaldi (Bd des) 13
Gateau (R. A.) 15
Grande-R. 16
Leclerc (R. du Gén.) 19
Maupéou (Bd de) 21
Moulin (Quai J.) 23
République (Pl. de la) 27
République (R. de la) 28

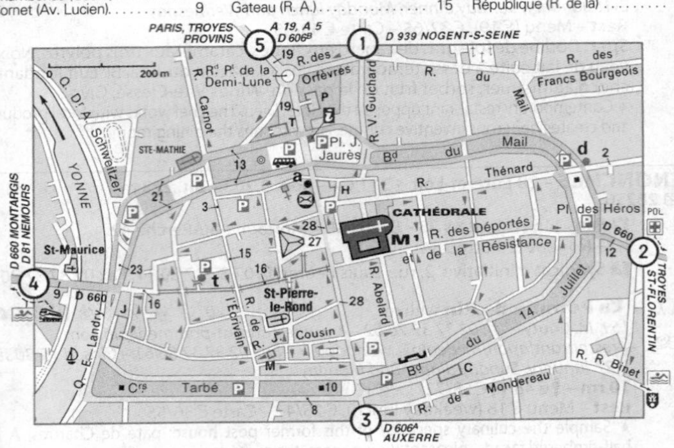

XXX ✿✿ **La Madeleine** (Patrick Gauthier) AC VISA MC AE
1 r. Alsace-Lorraine, (1st floor) – ✆ 03 86 65 09 31 – www.restaurant-lamadeleine.fr – Fax 03 86 95 37 41 – Closed 7-22 June, 9-23 August, 20 December-4 January, Tuesday lunch, Sunday, Monday and public holidays **d**
Rest – *(number of covers limited, pre-book)* Menu € 52 (weekday lunch), € 65/115 – Carte € 102/135
Spec. Foie gras au cassis. Parmentier de homard breton (June to September). Mousseline de chocolat guanaja. **Wines** Bourgogne blanc, Rully.
◆ Smart restaurant in pastel tones, serving contemporary gourmet cuisine. The entrance sports a kitchen stove and shelves filled with groceries.

XX **Le Clos des Jacobins** AC VISA MC AE
49 Gde-Rue – ✆ 03 86 95 29 70 – www.restaurantlesjacobins.com – lesjacobins@wanadoo.fr – Fax 03 86 64 22 98 – Closed 29 April-6 May, 13-27 July, 23 December-6 January, Sunday dinner, Tuesday dinner and Wednesday **t**
Rest – Menu € 29/52 – Carte € 37/65
◆ This restaurant has undergone a full refurbishment with a new contemporary decor and beige and chocolate colour scheme. Nice modern cuisine.

XX **La Potinière** AC VISA MC AE
51 r. Cécile de Marsangy, via ④ – ✆ 03 86 65 31 08 – la.potiniere@hotmail.fr – Fax 03 86 64 60 19 – Closed Sunday dinner and Monday
Rest – *(pre-book in high season)* Menu € 19 (weekday lunch), € 29/65 – Carte € 50/80
◆ Former open air dancing venue with shaded terrace by the Yonne. Popular with river cruising tourists (landing stage). Bright, trendy dining room; modern cuisine.

X **Miyabi** AC VISA MC
1 r. Alsace-Lorraine – ✆ 03 86 95 00 70 – Fax 03 86 95 37 41 – Closed Sunday **d**
Rest – *(number of covers limited, pre-book)* Menu € 24/75
◆ A fine marriage of Japanese and French culinary cultures at this narrow restaurant with subdued lighting, wall hangings and Japanese music. A refreshing change of scene.

Au Crieur de Vin

1 r. Alsace-Lorraine – ✆ 03 86 65 92 80 – www.restaurant-lamadeleine.fr – Fax 03 86 95 37 41 – Closed 7-22 June, 9-23 August, 20 December-4 January, Tuesday lunch, Sunday, Monday and public holidays **d**

Rest – Menu € 25/41

◆ Top marks for this restaurant: a pleasant bistro atmosphere, traditional dishes, spit roast meat and selected vintages.

in Subligny 7 km by ④ and D 660 – **pop. 478 – alt. 150 m** – ✉ **89100**

La Haie Fleurie

30 rte de Coutenay, 2 km south-west – ✆ 03 86 88 84 44 – Fax 03 86 88 86 67 – Closed 15-31 July, Sunday dinner, Wednesday dinner and Thursday

Rest – Menu (€ 17), € 25 (weekday lunch), € 39/49 – Carte € 40/62

◆ Situated along the road going through a village, this inn has a small lounge reception area leading to a pleasant dining room in modern-rustic style. Flower-decked terrace. Traditional cuisine.

in Villeroy 7 km by ④ and D 81 – **pop. 271 – alt. 184 m** – ✉ **89100**

Relais de Villeroy with rm

rte de Nemours – ✆ 03 86 88 81 77 – www.relais-de-villeroy.com – reservation@relais-de-villeroy.com – Fax 03 86 88 84 04 – Closed 30 June-10 July, 20 December-5 January, 16 February-4 March and Sunday dinner

8 rm – †€ 50/60 ††€ 50/60, ☕ € 8

Rest – Menu € 28 – Carte € 42/65

Rest *Bistro Chez Clément* – *✆ 03 86 88 86 73 (closed Wednesday dinner, Thursday dinner, Friday dinner, Saturday and Sunday)*

◆ This smart regional house is home to small comfortable bedrooms. Traditional recipes are served in the veranda with a view of the delightful flower-filled garden. At Chez Clément you will find bistro cooking, rustic decor and a friendly welcome.

SEPT-SAULX – 51 Marne – 306 H8 – pop. 510 – alt. 96 m – ✉ 51400 13 B2

Paris 167 – Châlons-en-Champagne 29 – Épernay 29 – Reims 26 – Rethel 51 – Vouziers 58

Le Cheval Blanc

r. du Moulin – ✆ 03 26 03 90 27 – www.chevalblanc-sept-saulx.com – cheval.blanc-sept-saulx@wanadoo.fr – Fax 03 26 03 97 09 – Closed February, Wednesday lunchtime and Tuesday from October to March

21 rm – †€ 64/143 ††€ 70/160, ☕ € 13 – 3 suites – ½ P € 96/201

Rest – Menu (€ 27), € 32/90 bi – Carte € 55/65

◆ At the foot of a 13C church, two recent buildings are home to comfortable guestrooms with views of a flower, riverside garden. The restaurant, a former post house, overlooks a filled courtyard that doubles as a terrace in summer. Modern cuisine.

SÉREILHAC – 87 Haute-Vienne – 325 D6 – pop. 1 605 – alt. 322 m – ✉ 87620 24 B2

Paris 405 – Confolens 50 – Limoges 19 – Périgueux 77 – St-Yrieix-la-Perche 37

Le Relais des Tuileries

aux Betoulles, 2 km north-eastward on the N 21 – ✆ 05 55 39 10 27 – www.relais-tuileries.fr – contact@relais-tuileries.fr – Fax 05 55 36 09 21 – Closed 16 November-1st December, 12 January-5 February, Sunday dinner and Monday except July-August

10 rm – †€ 58 ††€ 64, ☕ € 9 – ½ P € 60

Rest – Menu (€ 17), € 21/46 – Carte € 29/56

◆ Simple rooms set in two pavilions on the same level as the garden. Look out for restored parts of an old tile factory in the park. Local set menus offered in a rustic dining room embellished by exposed beams and an open fireplace.

SÉRIGNAN – 34 Hérault – 339 E9 – pop. 6 522 – alt. 7 m – ✉ 34410 23 C2

Paris 770 – Montpellier 70 – Béziers 12 – Narbonne 39

Office de tourisme, place de la Libération ✆ 04 67 32 42 21, Fax 04 67 32 37 97

L'Harmonie VISA AE

chemin de la Barque, parking de la Cigalière – ✆ 04 67 32 39 30 – www.lharmonie.fr – lharmonie@wanadoo.fr – Fax 04 67 32 39 30 – Closed 14-27 April, 27 October-9 November, Tuesday dinner from September to June, Thursday lunch in July-August, Saturday lunch and Wednesday

Rest – Menu (€ 18 bi), € 25/55 – Carte € 42/65

◆ This restaurant has moved a few metres from its old address. Contemporary decor with wrought iron furniture, and generous modern cuisine using fine produce.

SÉRIGNAN-DU-COMTAT – 84 Vaucluse – 332 C8 – see Orange

SERMAIZE-DU-BAS – 71 Saône-et-Loire – 320 F11 – see Paray-le-Monial

SERMERSHEIM – 67 Bas-Rhin – 315 J6 – pop. 801 – alt. 160 m – ✉ 67230 2 C1

Paris 506 – Lahr/Schwarzwald 41 – Obernai 21 – Sélestat 14 – Strasbourg 40

Au Relais de l'Ill without rest VISA

r. du Rempart – ✆ 03 88 74 31 28 – relais-de-lill@wanadoo.fr – Fax 03 88 74 17 51 – Closed 20 December-10 January

23 rm – †€ 52/60 ††€ 65/75, ☕ € 7

◆ Recent family hotel unaffected by the noise of the nearby expressway. A warm reception awaits you, with spacious, well-kept rooms on offer. Flower-decked surroundings

SERRE-CHEVALIER – 05 Hautes-Alpes – 334 H3 – alt. 2 483 m – Winter sports : 1 200/2 800 m 9 67 – ✉ 05330 French Alps 41 C1

Paris 678 – Briançon 7 – Gap 95 – Grenoble 110 – Col du Lautaret 21

Office de tourisme, Chantemerle ✆ 04 92 24 98 98, Fax 04 92 24 98 84

✳★★.

in Chantemerle – alt. 1 350 m – ✉ 05330 St-Chaffrey

Col de Granon ✳★★ North: 12 km.

Plein Sud VISA AE

Allée des Boutiques – ✆ 04 92 24 17 01 – www.hotelpleinsud.com – lynne@hotelpleinsud.com – Fax 04 92 24 10 21 – Closed 19 April-25 May and 10 October-10 December

41 rm – †€ 70/135 ††€ 100/180, ☕ € 10

Rest – Menu € 18 (lunch) – Carte € 30/40

◆ Centrally located hotel. Choose a room facing south, they are larger and have loggias overlooking the larch forest. Internet access and fine attractive pool with opening roof. Restaurant serving traditional cuisine and set buffets. Snack menu in the pub.

Les Marmottes VISA

22 r. du Centre – ✆ 04 92 24 11 17 – www.chalet-marmottes.com – lucas.marmottes@wanadoo.fr – Fax 04 92 24 11 17

5 rm ☕ – †€ 65/85 ††€ 86/113 – ½ P € 60/86 **Table d'hôte** – Menu € 23 bi

◆ Former barn carefully converted into a comfortable guesthouse. Attractive fireside lounge and cosy rooms with personal touches, overlooking the surrounding peaks. Restaurant offering well-prepared family cooking (set menu modified every day) served on a large wood table.

in Villeneuve-la-Salle – ✉ **05240 La-Salle-les-Alpes**

St-Marcellin church ★ of La-Salle-les-Alpes.

Christiania P VISA

23 rte de Briançon – ✆ 04 92 24 76 33 – www.le-christiania.com – le.christiania@wanadoo.fr – Fax 04 92 24 83 82 – Open 13 June-13 September and 12 December-11 April

26 rm – †€ 83/105 ††€ 95/105, ☕ € 15

Rest – *(open 20 June-6 September and 15 December-4 April) (dinner only)* Menu (€ 18), € 24/28 – Carte € 30/40

◆ A family welcome, a rustic bar-lounge warmed by a fireplace, and rooms judiciously decorated in mountain style, characterise this hotel on the banks of the Guisane. Restaurant with an Alpine setting enhanced by antique objects. Garden terrace next to a fast flowing stream.

Le Mont Thabor without rest VISA AE

1 bis chemin Envers – ✆ 04 92 24 74 41 – www.mont-thabor.com – hotelmonthabor@wanadoo.fr – Fax 04 92 24 99 50 – Closed 19 April-15 June and 1st September-1st December

27 rm ☕ – †€ 85/130 ††€ 95/175

◆ This brand new hotel (non-smokers only) sports an alpine-style contemporary decor. Comfortable and very well-equipped rooms, sauna, Jacuzzi.

in Monêtier-les-Bains – **pop. 1 066** – **alt. 1 480 m** – ✉ **05220**

L'Auberge du Choucas VISA

17 r. de la Fruitière – ✆ 04 92 24 42 73 – www.aubergeduchoucas.com – auberge.du.choucas@wanadoo.fr – Fax 04 92 24 51 60 – Closed 3-29 May and 2 November-4 December

12 rm – †€ 80/180 ††€ 100/220, ☕ € 17 – ½ P € 90/240

Rest – *(closed 14 April-29 May, 12 October-17 December, and lunch from Monday to Thursday in April, June, September and October)* Menu (€ 19), € 29/79 – Carte € 53/83

◆ An inn full of character near the 15C church. The authentic interior is both elegant and refined. Cosy rooms and duplex. A vaulted dining room with a splendid fireplace. Modern cuisine.

Alliey VISA

– ✆ 04 92 24 40 02 – www.alliey.com – hotel@alliey.com – Fax 04 92 24 40 60 – Open 19 June-6 September and 13 December-18 April

22 rm – †€ 85/88 ††€ 88/128, ☕ € 13 – 2 suites – ½ P € 79/109

Rest *L'Alliey* – *(dinner only)* Menu € 32 – Carte € 28/47

◆ This village residence provides a charming and warm atmosphere due to its attractive all wood decor. Cosy alpine-style rooms and attractive spa. Up-to-date cuisine served in the restaurant that sports a subtle blend of stone and wood.

Le Chazal VISA

Les Guibertes, 2.5 km south-east on Briançon road – ✆ 04 92 24 45 54 – Closed 22 June-3 July, 1st-10 October, 23 November-12 December and Monday

Rest – *(dinner only except Sunday) (pre-book)* Menu € 28/50

◆ Tucked away in a hamlet, the dining rooms of this former sheepfold are the perfect location to sample updated traditional fare. Booking essential.

SERRIÈRES – **07 Ardèche** – **331** K2 – **pop. 1 154** – **alt. 140 m** – ✉ **07340** 43 **E2**

Lyon - Rhone Valley

Paris 514 – Annonay 16 – Privas 91 – St-Étienne 55 – Vienne 29

Syndicat d'initiative, quai Jule Roche ✆ 04 75 34 06 01, Fax 04 75 34 06 01

Schaeffer with rm rm, VISA

D 86 – ✆ 04 75 34 00 07 – www.hotel-schaeffer.com – mathe@hotel-schaeffer.com – Fax 04 75 34 08 79 – Closed 4-18 August, 24 October-4 November, 2-17 January, Saturday lunch, Sunday dinner and Monday

15 rm – †€ 50/60 ††€ 68/88, ☕ € 8,50

Rest – Menu (€ 24), € 36/110 – Carte € 55/70

◆ Opulent restaurant with a veranda that overlooks the suspension bridge spanning the Rhône. Classic cuisine served with local Côtes-du-Rhône wines. Functional rooms.

SERRIS – 77 Seine-et-Marne – **312** F2 – see Paris, Area (Marne-la-Vallée)

SERVIERS-ET-LABAUME – 30 Gard – **339** L4 – see Uzès

SERVON – 50 Manche – **303** D8 – **pop. 275** – **alt. 25 m** – ✉ **50170** 32 **A3**

Paris 352 – Avranches 15 – Dol-de-Bretagne 30 – St-Lô 72 – St-Malo 55

XX **Auberge du Terroir** with rm rm, VISA
in the village – ✆ 02 33 60 17 92 – aubergeduterroir@wanadoo.fr – Fax 02 33 60 35 26 – Closed 20 February-10 March, Thursday lunch, Saturday lunch and Wednesday
6 rm – €60 €64, €10 – ½ P €66
Rest – *(pre-book)* Menu €19/43 – Carte €33/53
◆ A good traditional meal will be created for you in this charming village inn located in the former girls' school and old presbytery. Refreshed dining room and terrace. Charming rooms in the renovated part, furnished with family heirlooms. Tennis court.

SERVOZ – 74 Haute-Savoie – **328** N5 – **pop. 818** – **alt. 816 m** – ✉ **74310** 46 **F1**
French Alps

Paris 598 – Annecy 85 – Bonneville 43 – Chamonix-Mont-Blanc 14 – Megève 22

Office de tourisme, ✆ 04 50 47 21 68, Fax 04 50 47 27 06

X **Les Gorges de la Diosaz** with rm VISA
Le Bouchet – ✆ 04 50 47 20 97 – www.hoteldesgorges.com – infos@hoteldesgorges.com – Fax 04 50 47 21 08 – Closed 12 November-10 December, Sunday dinner and Monday except school holidays
6 rm – €60/70 €60/80, €8,50
Rest – Menu (€15), €25/44 – Carte €35/45
◆ Chalet-style property in a village along the Route des Gorges. Typical mountain decor in the reception and dining room. Updated regional cuisine. Terrace with panoramic views.

SESSENHEIM – 67 Bas-Rhin – **315** L4 – **pop. 2 023** – **alt. 120 m** – ✉ **67770** Alsace-Lorraine 1 **B1**

Paris 497 – Haguenau 18 – Strasbourg 39 – Wissembourg 44

XX **Au Bœuf** VISA AE
1 r. Église – ✆ 03 88 86 97 14 – www.auberge-au-boeuf.com – contact@auberge-au-boeuf.com – Fax 03 88 86 04 62 – Closed Monday and Tuesday
Rest – Menu €28 (weekdays)/58 – Carte €40/53
◆ 18C church pews decorate one of the dining rooms of this Alsatian building, which boasts a lovely terrace, a small Goethe museum and a boutique selling regional products.

SÈTE – 34 Hérault – **339** H8 – **pop. 43 300** – **alt. 4 m** – **Casino** – ✉ **34200** 23 **C2**
Languedoc-Roussillon-Tarn Gorges

Paris 787 – Béziers 48 – Lodève 63 – Montpellier 35

Office de tourisme, 60, rue Mario Roustan ✆ 04 67 74 71 71, Fax 04 67 46 17 54

Mont St-Clair★: terrace of N.-D. de la Salette chapel's presbytery ✻★★ AZ - Le Vieux Port★ - marine cemetery ★.

Plan on next page

Le Grand Hôtel VISA AE
17 quai Mar. de Lattre de Tassigny – ✆ 04 67 74 71 77 – www.legrandhotelsete.com – info@legrandhotelsete.com – Fax 04 67 74 29 27 – Closed 24 December-4 January AY **t**
43 rm – €75/140 €75/140, €10 – 1 suite
Rest *Quai 17* – *✆ 04 67 74 71 91 (closed 20-31 July, 24 December-4 January, Saturday lunch and Sunday)* Menu (€20), €27/47 – Carte €32/58
◆ Near the birthplace of Georges Brassens, an elegant Belle Epoque style hotel (1882) by the canal. Refined rooms mixing old and new, pleasant glass covered patio. Modern cooking in this restaurant decorated with pretty murals recalling Sète's maritime history.

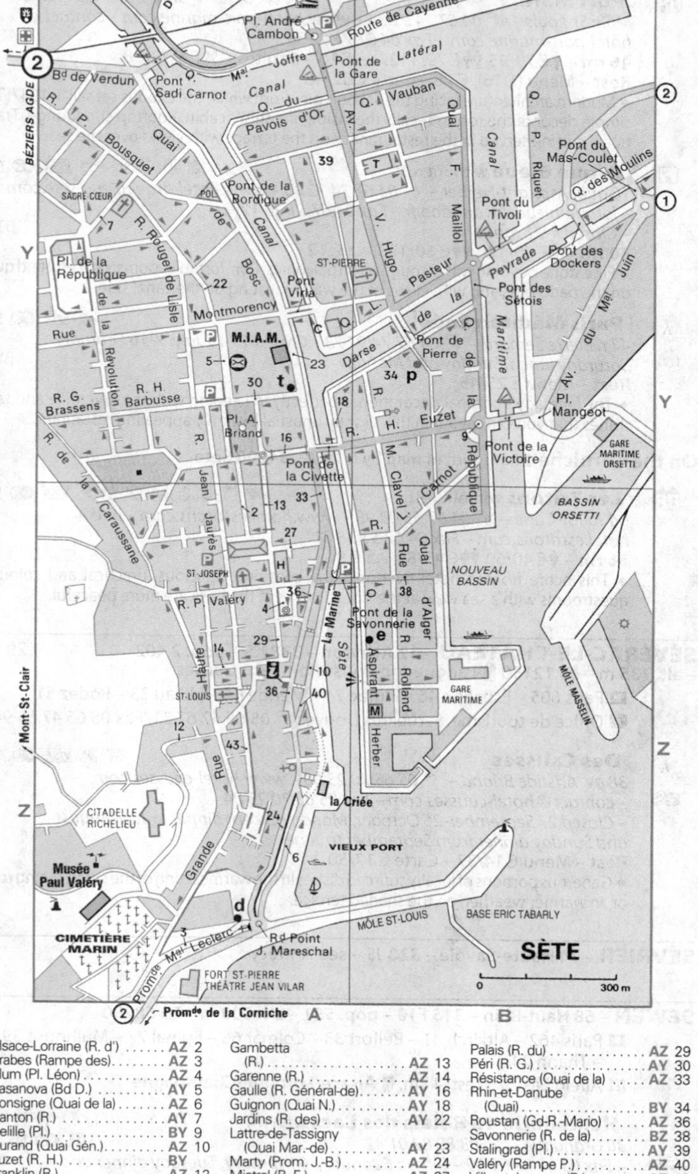

Alsace-Lorraine (R. d') . . . . AZ 2
Arabes (Rampe des). . . . . AZ 3
Blum (Pl. Léon) . . . . AZ 4
Casanova (Bd D.) . . . . AY 5
Consigne (Quai de la) . . . . AZ 6
Danton (R.) . . . . AY 7
Delille (Pl.) . . . . BY 9
Durand (Quai Gén.). . . . . AZ 10
Euzet (R. H.) . . . . BY
Franklin (R.) . . . . AZ 12
Gambetta (R.) . . . . AZ 13
Garenne (R.) . . . . AZ 14
Gaulle (R. Général-de). . . . . . . AY 16
Guignon (Quai N.) . . . . AY 18
Jardins (R. des) . . . . AY 22
Lattre-de-Tassigny (Quai Mar.-de) . . . . AY 23
Marty (Prom. J.-B.) . . . . AZ 24
Mistral (R. F.) . . . . AZ 27
Palais (R. du) . . . . AZ 29
Péri (R. G.) . . . . AY 30
Résistance (Quai de la) . . . . . . AZ 33
Rhin-et-Danube (Quai) . . . . BY 34
Roustan (Gd-R.-Mario) . . . . . . AZ 36
Savonnerie (R. de la). . . . . BZ 38
Stalingrad (Pl.) . . . . AY 39
Valéry (Rampe P.) . . . . AZ 40
Villaret-Joyeuse (R.) . . . . AZ 43

Port Marine

Môle St-Louis – ☎ 04 67 74 92 34 – www.hotel-port-marine.com – contact@hotel-port-marine.com – Fax 04 67 74 92 33 AZ **d**

46 rm – €70/95 €79/112, ☕ €10 – 6 suites – ½ P €72/88

Rest – Menu (€16), €26 – Carte €32/48

◆ Modern architecture facing the St Louis pier from which the Exodus set sail in 1947. The simple decor of the rooms recalls the inside of a ship's cabin. Rooftop sun-lounge. Traditional cuisine served in the restaurant or on the terrace with views over the sea.

Orque Bleue without rest

10 quai Aspirant-Herber – ☎ 04 67 74 72 13 – www.hotel-orquebleue-sete.com – lorque-bleue@wanadoo.fr – Fax 04 67 51 20 17 – Closed 4-31 January BZ **e**

30 rm – €60/120 €60/120, ☕ €12

◆ Fine stone building with wrought-iron balconies. Comfortable rooms: peaceful and quiet on the patio side, and with views of the water jousting on the canal side.

Paris Méditerranée

47 r. Pierre Semard – ☎ 04 67 74 97 73 – Closed 1st-15 July, 7-16 February, Saturday lunch, Sunday and Monday BY **p**

Rest – Menu €25/45

◆ The landlady's original decoration is perfectly in keeping with the inventive and tasty dishes that you can savour in this slightly unusual but truly appealing restaurant.

On the Corniche 2 km south of map by D 2 – ✉ 34200 Sète

Les Tritons without rest

bd Joliot-Curie – ☎ 04 67 53 03 98 – www.hotellestritons.com – info@hotellestritons.com – Fax 04 67 53 38 31

56 rm – €40/60 €45/85, ☕ €8

◆ This ochre fronted hotel overlooks the coastline. Spacious, practical and colourful guestrooms with a sea view at the front. Rooms at the back are more peaceful.

SÉVÉRAC-LE-CHÂTEAU – 12 Aveyron – 338 K5 – pop. 2 402 – alt. 735 m – ✉ 12150 Languedoc-Roussillon-Tarn Gorges 29 **D1**

Paris 605 – Espalion 46 – Florac 74 – Mende 64 – Millau 33 – Rodez 51

Office de tourisme, 5, rue des Douves ☎ 05 65 47 67 31, Fax 05 65 47 65 94

Des Causses

38 av. Aristide Briand – ☎ 05 65 70 23 00 – www.hotel-causses.com – contact@hotel-causses.com – Fax 05 65 70 23 04 – Closed 27 September-26 October, Monday except dinner in July-August and Sunday dinner from September to June

Rest – Menu €14/37 – Carte €17/50

◆ Generous portions of locally sourced dishes in the warm setting of the smart dining room or, in warmer weather, on the shaded terrace.

SÉVRIER – 74 Haute-Savoie – 328 J5 – see Annecy

SEWEN – 68 Haut-Rhin – 315 F10 – pop. 531 – alt. 500 m – ✉ 68290 1 **A3**

Paris 462 – Altkirch 41 – Belfort 33 – Colmar 66 – Épinal 77 – Mulhouse 39 – Thann 24

Alfeld Lake★ West: 4 km, Alsace-Lorraine-Champagne

Hostellerie au Relais des Lacs with rm

30 Grand'rue – ☎ 03 89 82 01 42 – Fax 03 89 82 09 29 – Closed 6 January-6 February, Tuesday dinner and Wednesday

13 rm – €42 €45, ☕ €7 – ½ P €45/49

Rest – Menu €11 (weekdays)/35 – Carte €16/35

◆ This family guesthouse serves classic fare in a tasteful rustic setting (fireplace, woodwork and country). Extensive riverside park. Simple accommodation.

SEYNE – 04 Alpes-de-Haute-Provence – 334 G6 – pop. 1 436 – alt. 1 200 m – ✉ 04140 French Alps 41 C2

Paris 719 – Barcelonnette 43 – Digne-les-Bains 43 – Gap 54 – Guillestre 71

Office de tourisme, place d'Armes ✆ 04 92 35 11 00, Fax 04 92 35 28 84

Col du Fanget ≤★ Southwest: 5 km.

in Selonnet **4 km northwest by D 900 – pop. 404 – alt. 1 060 m – Winter sports : 1 500/2 050 m 12 – ✉ 04140**

Relais de la Forge VISA AE

– ✆ 04 92 35 16 98 – www.relaisdelaforge.fr – relaisdelaforge@orange.fr – Fax 04 92 35 07 37 – Closed 18-26 April, 11 November-13 December, Sunday dinner and Monday except school holidays

14 rm – €42/56 €48/62, €8 – ½ P €45/54

Rest – Menu (€15), €20/30 – Carte €23/43

◆ This family hotel was built on the site of the old village forge. Simple, refurbished rooms. New sauna and indoor swimming pool. Rustic dining room with fireplace; traditional menu.

LA SEYNE-SUR-MER – 83 Var – 340 K7 – pop. 58 000 – alt. 3 m – ✉ 83500 French Riviera 40 B3

Paris 830 – Aix-en-Provence 81 – La Ciotat 32 – Marseille 60 – Toulon 8

Office de tourisme, corniche Georges Pompidou ✆ 04 98 00 25 70, Fax 04 98 00 25 71

≤★ of the Balaguier fort terrace East: 3 km.

in Fabrégas **4 km south by St-Mandrier road and secondary road – ✉ 83500 La Seyne-sur-Mer**

XX **Chez Daniel et Julia "rest. du Rivage"** ≤ P VISA

– ✆ 04 94 94 85 13 – Fax 04 94 87 25 25 – Closed November, Sunday dinner and Monday in low season and except public holidays

Rest – Menu €40 – Carte €58/86

◆ Welcoming, family-run restaurant nestling in a pretty creek. Dining room in rustic-Provençal style, with a collection of old tools. A focus on fish and seafood. Terrace overlooking the water.

in Sablettes **4 km southeast – ✉ 83500 La Seyne-sur-Mer**

XX **La Parenthèse de Terrebrune** AC VISA

724 chemin de la Tourelle – ✆ 04 94 88 36 19 – fages.laffontpartners@orange.fr – Fax 04 94 87 60 45 – Closed 1st-9 November, 10-31 January, Sunday dinner and Monday

Rest – Menu €34 (lunch)/55 – Carte €60/87

◆ Contemporary cuisine served in a modern dining room decorated in shades of red, white and brown. In summer, dine on the shady terrace, furnished with wrought-iron tables and enclosed by wood panels.

SÉZANNE – 51 Marne – 306 E10 – pop. 5 585 – alt. 137 m – ✉ 51120 Northern France and the Paris Region 13 B2

Paris 116 – Châlons-en-Champagne 59 – Meaux 78 – Melun 89 – Sens 83 – Troyes 62

Office de tourisme, place de la République ✆ 03 26 80 51 43, Fax 03 26 80 54 13

Le Relais Champenois rm, AC rest, P VISA

157 r. Notre-Dame – ✆ 03 26 80 58 03 – www.lerelaischampenois.com – relaischamp@infonie.fr – Fax 03 26 81 35 32 – Closed 16-31 August and Sunday evening

19 rm – €40/75 €50/85, €11

Rest – Menu (€20), €24 (weekdays)/50 – Carte €33/50

◆ Renovated Champagne-style façade, attractively decorated with flowers. Fresh and well-furnished rooms that are quieter in the annexe (two have air-conditioning). Country-style dining rooms, with woodwork and exposed beams. Great choice of traditional menus.

in Mondement-Montgivroux 12 km on the D 951 and D 439 – pop. 46 – alt. 188 m – ✉ 51120

Domaine de Montgivroux without rest
rte d'Epernay – ✆ 03 26 42 06 93
– www.audomainedemontgivroux.com – domainedemontgivroux@orange.fr
– Fax 03 26 42 06 94
20 rm – †€ 70 ††€ 100/110, ☕ € 11 – 1 suite
◆ Set in an immense estate, this superbly restored 17C Champagne-region farmhouse boasts spacious, thoughtfully-decorated rooms.

SIERCK-LES-BAINS – 57 Moselle – 307 J2 – pop. 1 710 – alt. 147 m 27 C1

– ✉ 57480 Alsace-Lorraine

Paris 355 – Luxembourg 40 – Metz 46 – Thionville 17 – Trier 52

Office de tourisme, rue du Château ✆ 03 82 83 74 14, Fax 03 82 83 22 10

<★ of the fortified castle.

in Montenach 3.5 km southeast on D 956 – pop. 414 – alt. 200 m – ✉ 57480

Auberge de la Klauss
1 rte de Kirschnaumen – ✆ 03 82 83 72 38 – www.auberge-de-la-klauss.com
– la-klauss@wanadoo.fr – Fax 03 82 83 73 00 – Closed 24 December-7 January and Monday
Rest – Menu € 16/52 – Carte € 47/73
◆ Free range ducks and pigs are raised on this farm built in 1869. The inn has a pretty rustic setting. Home-made produce (including delicious foie gras) and fine wine list. Fresh produce for sale.

in Manderen 7 km east by D 654 and D 64 – pop. 406 – alt. 290 m – ✉ 57480

Relais du Château Mensberg rm,
15 r. du Château – ✆ 03 82 83 73 16
– www.relais-mensberg.com – aurelaismensberg@aol.com – Fax 03 82 83 23 37
– Closed 26 December-24 January, Monday lunch and Tuesday
13 rm – †€ 36/48 ††€ 45/60, ☕ € 8 – ½ P € 53/60
Rest – Menu (€ 13), € 19/58 – Carte € 15/60
◆ This old farmhouse standing guard at the foot of Malbrouck castle (15C) offers small, simple, and functional rooms. Traditional regional cuisine served in a rustic dining room with fireplace.

SIERENTZ – 68 Haut-Rhin – 315 I11 – pop. 2 647 – alt. 270 m 1 A3

– ✉ 68510

Paris 487 – Altkirch 19 – Basel 18 – Belfort 65 – Colmar 54 – Mulhouse 16

Syndicat d'initiative, 57, rue Rogg-Haas ✆ 03 89 81 68 58, Fax 03 89 81 60 49

Auberge St-Laurent (Marco Arbeit) with rm
1 r. Fontaine – ✆ 03 89 81 52 81
– www.auberge-saintlaurent.fr – marco.arbeit@wanadoo.fr – Fax 03 89 81 67 08
– Closed 13-28 July, 14-22 September, 15-25 February, Monday and Tuesday
10 rm – †€ 80 ††€ 100, ☕ € 13 – ½ P € 91
Rest – Menu (€ 28), € 39/75 – Carte € 75/92
Spec. Foie gras de canard maison et confit de choucroute. Croustillant de bar à l'unilatérale, purée de pommes de terre et caviar d'Aquitaine. Vacherin glacé et coulis de fruits rouges. **Wines** Pinot blanc, Crémant d'Alsace.
◆ This former post house sports a warm semi-rustic, semi-bourgeois feel. It serves classic gourmet cuisine with well-balanced flavours. Enjoyable terrace. Delightful personalised guestrooms.

SIGNY-L'ABBAYE – 08 Ardennes – 306 I4 – pop. 1 365 – alt. 240 m 13 B1

– ✉ 08460 Northern France and the Paris Region

Paris 208 – Charleville-Mézières 31 – Hirson 41 – Laon 74 – Rethel 23 – Rocroi 30 – Sedan 52

Syndicat d'initiative, cour Rogelet ✆ 03 24 53 10 10, Fax 03 24 53 10 10

Auberge de l'Abbaye with rm

2 pl. A. Briand – ✆ 03 24 52 81 27 – aubergeabbaye@wanadoo.fr – Fax 03 24 53 71 72 – Closed 12 January-8 March

8 rm – †€ 40/56 ††€ 56/59, ☕ € 10 – ½ P € 48

Rest – *(closed Tuesday dinner and Wednesday)* Menu (€ 12), € 14 – Carte € 20/38

◆ The same family has run this former post house since 1803. It upholds its traditions with a rustic decor and cuisine made with locally grown produce. Tasteful guestrooms.

SIGNY-LE-PETIT – 08 Ardennes – 306 H3 – pop. 1 290 – alt. 238 m – ✉ 08380 13 B1

Paris 228 – Charleville-Mézières 37 – Hirson 15 – Chimay 959

Syndicat d'initiative, place de l'Église ✆ 03 24 53 55 44, Fax 03 24 53 51 32

Au Lion d'Or rm, VISA AE

pl. de l'Église – ✆ 03 24 53 51 76 – www.lahulotte-auliondor.fr – blandine-bertrand@wanadoo.fr – Fax 03 24 53 36 96 – Closed 26 June-10 July, 19 December-11 January and Sunday

12 rm – †€ 66/85 ††€ 66/112, ☕ € 9 – ½ P € 61/100

Rest – *(closed Sunday except lunch from March to end September, Tuesday lunch, Wednesday lunch and Saturday lunch) (pre-book Sunday)* Menu € 20/60 bi

◆ Former post house opposite Signy church. Neat rooms in a variety of styles spread between the main building and outbuildings. Rustic restaurant with pictures and knick-knacks featuring owls (the house emblem). Contemporary cuisine.

SILLÉ-LE-GUILLAUME – 72 Sarthe – 310 I5 – pop. 2 386 – alt. 161 m – ✉ 72140 Normandy 35 C1

Paris 230 – Alençon 39 – Laval 55 – Le Mans 35 – Mayenne 40

Office de tourisme, place de la Résistance ✆ 02 43 20 10 32, Fax 02 43 20 01 23

Le Bretagne with rm rest, VISA

pl. Croix d'Or – ✆ 02 43 20 10 10 – www.hotelsarthe.com – hotelrestaurantlebretagne@wanadoo.fr – Fax 02 43 20 03 96 – Closed 22 July-12 August, 1st-10 January, Friday dinner, Saturday lunch and Sunday dinner

15 rm – †€ 57 ††€ 62, ☕ € 6 – ½ P € 58

Rest – Menu € 16 (weekdays), € 27/50 – Carte approx. € 54

◆ Former coaching inn on the edge of the Normandie-Maine Regional Park. Well-prepared traditional cuisine served in a pretty dining room. Practical rooms, prefer those overlooking the courtyard

SILLERY – 51 Marne – 306 G7 – see Reims

SION-SUR-L'OCÉAN – 85 Vendée – 316 E7 – see St-Gilles-Croix-de-Vie

SIORAC-EN-PÉRIGORD – 24 Dordogne – 329 G7 – pop. 893 – alt. 77 m – ✉ 24170 Dordogne-Berry-Limousin 4 C3

Paris 548 – Sarlat-la-Canéda 29 – Bergerac 45 – Brive-la-Gaillarde 73 – Périgueux 60

Syndicat d'initiative, place de Siorac ✆ 05 53 31 63 51

18 de Lolivarie, S : 5 km on D 51, ✆ 05 53 30 22 69

Relais du Périgord Noir rm, rm, VISA

pl. de la Poste – ✆ 05 53 31 60 02 – www.relais-perigord-noir.fr – hotel@relais-perigord-noir.fr – Fax 05 53 31 61 05 – Open 15 April-30 September

43 rm – †€ 68/88 ††€ 68/95, ☕ € 10 – ½ P € 65/80

Rest – *(dinner only) (residents only)* Menu € 30/45 – Carte € 42/60

◆ Fully renovated 1870s house, well suited to disabled guests. Practical guestrooms. Choice of two sitting rooms, one adorned with prehistoric artefacts, the other with a snooker table. Sample traditional dishes in the dining room decorated with frescos or on the veranda.

SISTERON – 04 Alpes-de-Haute-Provence – **334** D7 – **pop. 6 964** – **alt. 490 m** – ✉ **04200** ▮ **French Alps** 40 **B2**

▶ Paris 704 – Barcelonnette 100 – Digne-les-Bains 40 – Gap 52

ℹ Office de tourisme, 1, place de la République ✆ 04 92 61 12 03, Fax 04 92 61 19 57

👁 Old Sisteron★ - Site★★ - Citadel★: ⩽★★ - Notre-Dame-des-Pommiers cathedral★.

SISTERON

Arène (Av. Paul)	YZ	3
Basse des Remparts (R.)	Y	4
Combes (R. des)	Z	6
Cordeliers (R. des)	Z	8
Deleuze (R.)	YZ	9
Dr-Robert (Pl. du)	Y	10
Droite (R.)	Y	
Font-Chaude (R.)	Y	12
Gaulle (Pl. Gén.-de)	Z	13
Glissoir (R. du)	Y	14
Grande École (Pl. de la)	Z	15
Horloge (Pl. de l')	Y	16
Libération (Av. de la)	Z	17
Longue-Andrône (R.)	Y	18
Melchior-Donnet (Cours)	Y	20
Mercerie (R.)	Y	22
Moulin (Av. Jean)	Z	23
Porte-Sauve (R.)	Z	24
Poterie (R.)	Y	25
Provence (R. de)	Z	26
République (Pl. de la)	Z	28
Ste-Ursule (R.)	Z	29
Saunerie (R.)	Y	
Tivoli (Pl. du)	Y	30
Verdun (Allée de)	Z	32

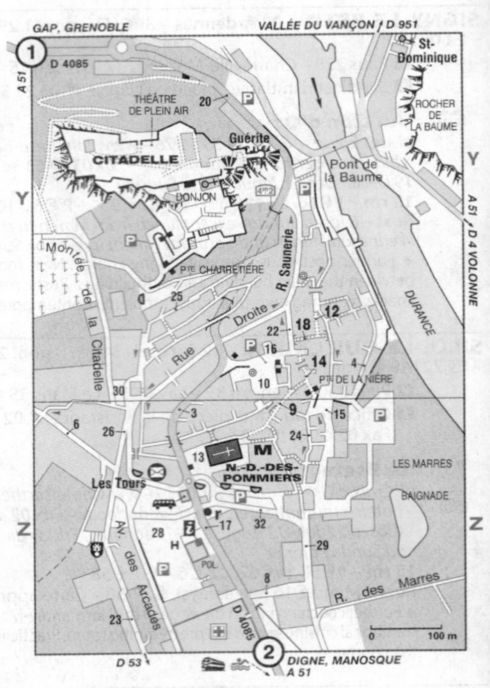

Grand Hôtel du Cours
pl. de l'Église – ✆ 04 92 61 04 51 – www.hotel-lecours.com – hotelducours@wanadoo.fr – Fax 04 92 61 41 73 – Open 1st March-5 November
rm, AC rest, VISA Z **r**

45 rm – €63/73 €73/90, ☕ €10 – 5 suites – ½ P €61/71

Rest – *(open 1st March-10 December)* Menu (€15), €25/31 – Carte €30/43

◆ This hotel in the historic town centre, very close to the 14C fortifications, has been run by the same family since 1932. The refurbished rooms to the rear are quieter and more spacious. Veranda and shaded terrace on the square. Sisteron lamb specialities.

Northwest by ① and D 4085 – ✉ **04200 Sisteron**

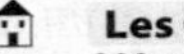

Les Chênes
300 rte de Gap, 2 km on – ✆ 04 92 61 13 67 – leschenes.hotel@wanadoo.fr – Fax 04 92 61 16 92 – Closed 24 December-31 January, Saturday except from April to September and Sunday except from June to September
P VISA

23 rm – €55 €55/72, ☕ €9 – ½ P €52/60

Rest – *(closed Saturday and Sunday)* Menu €19/32 – Carte €35/45

◆ Practical establishment not far from the Durance. The small, functional rooms are soundproofed. Swimming pool and garden with oak trees to the rear. Traditional recipes served in a simple dining room or on the shady terrace.

SIX-FOURS-LES-PLAGES – 83 Var – 340 K7 – pop. 34 000 – alt. 20 m – ✉ 83140 ▮ French Riviera 40 B3

▶ Paris 830 – Aix-en-Provence 81 – La Ciotat 33 – Marseille 61 – Toulon 12

ℹ Office de tourisme, promenade Charles-de-Gaulle ✆ 04 94 07 02 21, Fax 04 94 25 13 36

◉ Six-Fours Fort ✻★ North: 2 km - Presqu'île de St-Mandrier★: ✻★★ East: 5 km - ✻★★ St Mandrier-sur-Mer cemetery East: 4 km.

◉ Chapelle N.-D.-du-Mai ✻★★ South: 6 km.

Le Clos des Pins

101 bis r. de la République – ✆ 04 94 25 43 68 – www.hotel-six-fours-var.com – cavagnac.dominique@wanadoo.fr – Fax 04 94 07 63 07

25 rm – †€ 54/78 ††€ 61/89, ☕ € 9 – ½ P € 79/105

Rest – *(dinner only) (residents only)* Menu € 18/21

◆ This amiable establishment has been treated to a makeover. The well-kept rooms are modern, refreshing and practical. Wholesome family cooking in the restaurant decked in warm southern colours.

in Brusc 4 km south – ✉ **83140 Six-Fours-les-Plages**

Le St-Pierre - Chez Marcel

47 r. de la Citadelle – ✆ 04 94 34 02 52 – www.lesaintpierre.fr – rnan@wanadoo.fr – Fax 04 94 34 18 01 – Closed January, Sunday dinner from September to June and Monday

Rest – Menu € 22 (weekdays)/36 – Carte € 30/65

◆ A former fisherman's house near the harbour. Fish and seafood dishes with regional flavours. Served in a pleasant well-lit dining room.

We try to be as accurate as possible when giving room rates. But prices are open to change, so please check rates when booking.

SIZUN – 29 Finistère – 308 G4 – pop. 2 129 – alt. 112 m – ✉ 29450 ▮ Brittany 9 B2

▶ Paris 572 – Brest 37 – Châteaulin 36 – Landerneau 16 – Morlaix 36 – Quimper 59

ℹ Office de tourisme, 3, rue de l'Argoat ✆ 02 98 68 88 40

◉ Parish enclosure★ - Bannières★ in Locmélar church North: 5 km.

Les Voyageurs

2 r. Argoat – ✆ 02 98 68 80 35 – www.hotelvoyageurs-sizun.com – hotelvoyag@aol.com – Fax 02 98 24 11 49 – Closed 11 September-4 October, Friday dinner, Sunday dinner and Saturday from October to June

18 rm – †€ 49/54 ††€ 49/54, ☕ € 8 – ½ P € 50

Rest – Menu (€ 12), € 14 (weekdays)/37 – Carte € 23/33

◆ At the centre of Sizun, this family establishment stands close to the church walls. The simple and well-kept rooms are larger in the main building. Traditional menus at reasonable prices served next to the fireplace in a country-style dining room.

SOCHAUX – 25 Doubs – 321 L1 – pop. 4 492 – alt. 310 m – ✉ 25600 ▮ Burgundy-Jura 17 C1

▶ Paris 478 – Audincourt 5 – Belfort 18 – Besançon 77 – Montbéliard 5 – Mulhouse 56

◉ Musée de l'Aventure Peugeot★★ AX.

See plan of Montbéliard urban area.

Arianis rest, VISA AE X u

11 av. Gén. Leclerc – ✆ 03 81 32 17 17 – www.arianis.fr – arianis@wanadoo.fr – Fax 03 81 32 00 90

65 rm – †€ 75 ††€ 80, ☕ € 8 – ½ P € 92

Rest – *(closed Sunday dinner and Saturday)* Menu (€ 16 bi), € 18 – Carte € 36/52

Rest ***Brasserie de l'Arianis*** – *(closed Friday dinner, Sunday dinner and Saturday)* Menu (€ 13 bi), € 16 bi – Carte € 24/40

◆ Various models of Peugeot cars are displayed in the reception lobby of this recent hotel. Rooms are well equipped and soberly decorated. The restaurant offers traditional set menus in a modern setting. Dining room, veranda and eclectic menu at the Brasserie.

in Étupes 3 km by ③ and D 463 – **pop. 3 467 – alt. 337 m – ✉ 25460**

Au Fil des Saisons VISA AE

3 r. de la Libération – ✆ 03 81 94 17 12 – www.aufildessaisons.eu – aufildessaisons@clubinternet.fr – Fax 03 81 32 36 04 – Closed 4-24 August, 22 December-4 January, Saturday lunch, Sunday, Monday and public holidays

Rest – Menu € 22 (lunch)/33 – Carte € 35/57

◆ This restaurant keeps pace with the seasons, as its name suggests. A good choice of fish on the family-run menu. Attractively redecorated dining area.

SOCOA – 64 Pyrénées-Atlantiques – 342 B2 – see St-Jean-de-Luz

---

SOCX – 59 Nord – 302 C2 – pop. 972 – alt. 24 m – ✉ 59380 30 B1

▶ Paris 287 – Lille 64 – Calais 52 – Dunkerque 20 – Roeselare 68

Au Steger VISA AE

27 rte de St-Omer – ✆ 03 28 68 20 49 – www.restaurant-lesteger.com – restaurant.steger@wanadoo.fr – Fax 03 28 68 27 83 – Closed 1st-20 August

Rest – *(lunch only except Saturday)* Menu (€ 13), € 16 (weekday lunch), € 23/45 – Carte € 30/40

◆ This family grocers has been converted into a tavern-style restaurant; delicious traditional recipes and Flemish dishes.

SOISSONS – 02 Aisne – 306 B6 – pop. 28 500 – alt. 47 m – ✉ 02200 37 C2

Northern France and the Paris Region

▶ Paris 102 – Compiègne 39 – Laon 37 – Reims 59 – St-Quentin 61

Office de tourisme, 16, place Fernand Marquigny ✆ 03 23 53 17 37, Fax 03 23 59 67 72

Former St-Jean-des-Vignes abbey★★ - St-Gervais and St-Protais cathedral★★.

Plan on next page

L'Assiette Gourmande VISA AE

16 av. de Coucy – ✆ 03 23 93 47 78 – Fax 03 23 93 47 78 – Closed 12-20 April, August, Saturday lunch, Sunday dinner, dinner on public holidays and Monday BY e

Rest – Menu € 16 (weekday lunch), € 30/51 – Carte € 45/58

◆ This establishment easily won the hearts of the inhabitants of Soissons, thanks to its elegant décor, low-key atmosphere and tasty, reinterpreted traditional cuisine.

Chez Raphaël VISA

7 r. St-Quentin – ✆ 03 23 93 51 79 – chez.raphael@wanadoo.fr – Fax 03 23 93 26 50 – Closed 18-31 August, 1st-8 January, 23-28 February, Saturday lunch, Sunday dinner and Monday BY a

Rest – Menu (€ 18 bi), € 20 (weekday lunch), € 25/42 – Carte € 38/62

◆ Pleasant establishment located in a shopping street. Simple and welcoming dining room in bistro style where tasty local dishes are on offer.

SOISSONS

Arquebuse (R. de l') .... BZ 2
Château-Thierry (Av.) .... BZ 4
Collège (R. du) .... AY 5
Commerce (R. du) .... BY 6
Compiègne (Av.) .... AY 8
Desmoulins (Bd C.) .... ABZ 12
Gambetta (Bd L.) .... BY 14
Intendance (R. de l') .... BY 15
Leclerc (Av. Gén.) .... BZ 22
Marquigny (Pl. F.) .... BY 23
Paix (R. de la) .... BY 24
Panleu (R. de) .... AY 25
Prés.-Kennedy (Av.) .... AZ 26
Quinquet (R.) .... ABY 28
Racine (R.) .... BZ 29
République (Pl. de la) .... BZ 30
St-Antoine (R.) .... BY 31
St-Christophe (Pl.) .... AY 32
St-Christophe (R.) .... AY 33
St-Jean (R.) .... AZ 34
St-Martin (R.) .... BY 35
St-Quentin (R.) .... BY 36
St-Rémy (R.) .... AY 37
Strasbourg (Bd de) .... BY 38
Villeneuve (R. de) .... BZ 39

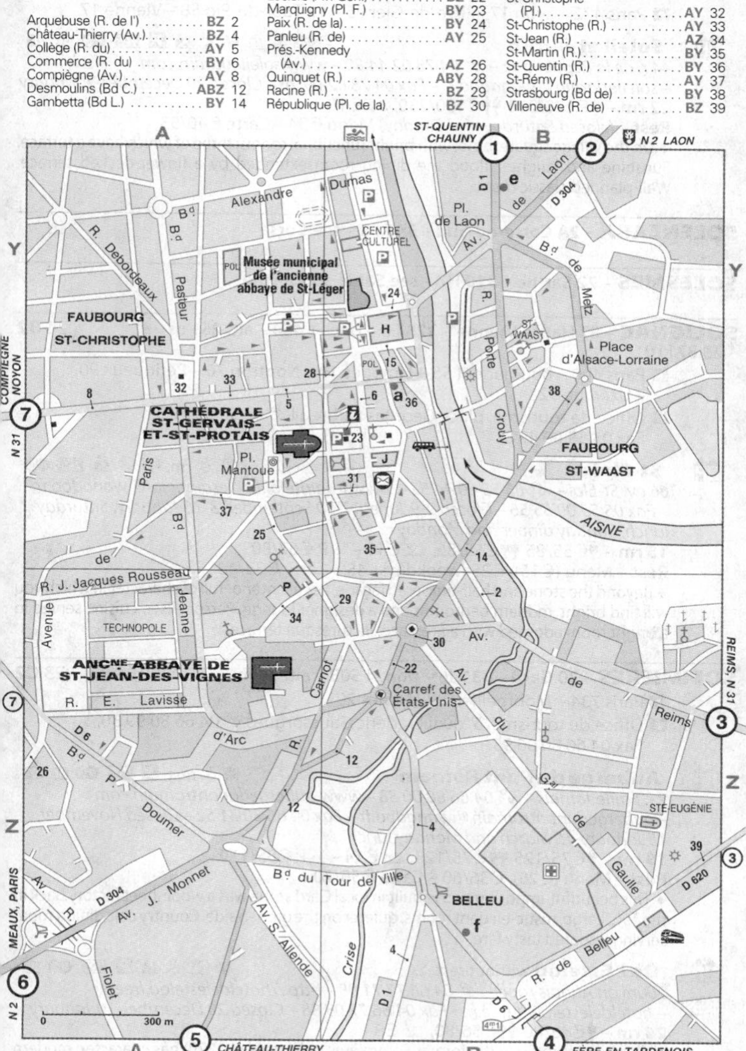

in Belleu 3 km south by D 1 and D 690 – pop. 3 969 – alt. 55 m – ✉ 02200

XX **Le Grenadin** VISA

19 rte de Fère-en-Tardenois – ✆ 03 23 73 20 57 – restaurantlegrenadin@free.fr – Fax 03 23 73 11 61 – Closed 15-31 January, Sunday dinner, Monday and public holidays BZ **f**

Rest – Menu (€ 16), € 23/45 – Carte € 29/50

◆ A cherub keeps vigil over the façade of this charming establishment serving carefully prepared traditional cuisine. Country style and rustic rooms. In the summer, tables are set in the garden.

SOLAIZE – 69 Rhône – **327** I6 – **pop. 2 527** – **alt. 232 m** – ✉ **69360** 44 **B2**

Paris 472 – Lyon 17 – Rive-de-Gier 25 – La Tour-du-Pin 58 – Vienne 17

Soleil et Jardin

44 r. de la République – ✆ 04 78 02 44 90 – www.soleiletjardin.com – soleiletjardin@wanadoo.fr – Fax 04 78 02 09 26 – Closed 20 December-2 January

22 rm – †€ 120/210 ††€ 150/230, ☐ € 10

Rest – *(closed Saturday and Sunday)* Menu € 34 – Carte € 40/53

◆ On the village square, hotel with bright functional rooms; three of which have a terrace. Sunshine and laughter flood the dining room extended by a flower-decked terrace. Well-planned classic menu.

SOLENZARA – 2A Corse-du-Sud – **345** F8 – see Corse

SOLESMES – 72 Sarthe – **310** H7 – see Sablé-sur-Sarthe

SOLIGNAC – 87 Haute-Vienne – **325** E6 – **pop. 1 454** – **alt. 251 m** – ✉ 87110 24 **B2**

Paris 400 – Bourganeuf 55 – Limoges 10 – Nontron 70 – Périgueux 90 – Uzerche 52

Office de tourisme, place Georges Dubreuil ✆ 05 55 00 42 31, Fax 05 55 00 42 31

St-Éloi

rm,

66 av. St-Éloi – ✆ 05 55 00 44 52 – www.lesainteloi.fr – lesaint.eloi@wanadoo.fr – Fax 05 55 00 55 56 – Closed 2-9 June, 17-30 September, 3-26 January, Saturday lunch, Sunday dinner and Monday

15 rm – †€ 55/85 ††€ 55/85, ☐ € 10 – ½ P € 67/80

Rest – Menu (€ 15), € 25 (weekdays)/45 – Carte € 33/48

◆ Beyond the stone and half-timbered façade, lies an interior full of character in which you will find bright, modern bedrooms and a designer lounge. Personalised cuisine served in a bright room adorned with a fireplace. Picturesque terrace.

SOMMIÈRES – 30 Gard – **339** J6 – **pop. 4 505** – **alt. 34 m** – ✉ **30250** 23 **C2**

Paris 734 – Montpellier 35 – Nîmes 29

Office de tourisme, 5, quai Frédéric Gaussorgues ✆ 04 66 80 99 30, Fax 04 66 80 06 95

Auberge du Pont Romain

rest,

2 r. Emile Jamais – ✆ 04 66 80 00 58 – www.aubergedupontromain.com – aubergedupontromain@wanadoo.fr – Fax 04 66 80 31 52 – Closed November, 15 January-15 March and Monday lunch

19 rm – †€ 75/125 ††€ 75/125, ☐ € 14 – ½ P € 85/110

Rest – Menu (€ 25), € 36/60 – Carte € 50/70

◆ This beautiful, imposing house built in local Gard stone was a wool sheet factory back in the 19C. Large, rustic-elegant rooms, quieter on the garden side. Country chic dining room serving updated tasty fare.

De l'Estelou without rest

200m on Aubais road – ✆ 04 66 77 71 08 – http://hoteldelestelou.free.fr – hoteldelestelou@free.fr – Fax 04 66 77 08 88 – Closed 20 December-10 January

24 rm – †€ 48/80 ††€ 56/80, ☐ € 8

◆ This hotel located in the former Sommières train station (1870) has character: modern rooms tastefully decorated, a pretty veranda for breakfast and a quiet garden with swimming pool.

in Boisseron 3 Km south by D 610 – **pop. 1 313** – **alt. 32 m** – ✉ **34160**

La Rose Blanche

51 r. Maurice Chauvet – ✆ 04 67 86 60 76 – www.laroseblanche.fr – restoroseblanche@yahoo.fr – Fax 04 67 86 60 76 – Closed 12-22 October, 5-22 January, Sunday dinner October-March, Tuesday lunch and Monday

Rest – Menu (€ 19), € 27/55 – Carte € 50/58

◆ In the former guardroom of the castle, modern furniture, fabrics and art mix easily with 12C vaulted ceilings and exposed stone walls. Modern cuisine.

SONDERNACH – 68 Haut-Rhin – 315 G9 – pop. 651 – alt. 540 m – ✉ 68380 1 A2

Paris 466 – Colmar 27 – Gérardmer 41 – Guebwiller 39 – Thann 42

A l'Orée du Bois with rm

4 rte du Schnepfenried – ✆ 03 89 77 70 21 – www.oredubois.com – contact@oredubois.com – Fax 03 89 77 77 58 – Closed 23-30 June and 5 January-5 February

7 rm – †€ 31 ††€ 62 – ½ P € 47

Rest – *(closed Wednesday lunchtime and Tuesday)* Menu (€ 7), € 12/32 – Carte € 12/32

◆ Welcoming countrified dining room (woodwork, earthenware stove), regional menu of tartes flambées and fondues, chalet-style rooms: the essence of Alsatian hospitality.

SONNAZ – 73 Savoie – 333 I4 – see Chambéry

SOPHIA-ANTIPOLIS – 06 Alpes-Maritimes – 341 D6 – see Valbonne

SORBIERS – 42 Loire – 327 F7 – see St-Étienne

SORÈZE – 81 Tarn – 338 E10 – pop. 2 388 – alt. 272 m – ✉ 81540 29 C2

Languedoc-Roussillon-Tarn Gorges

Paris 732 – Toulouse 59 – Carcassonne 44 – Castelnaudary 26 – Castres 27 – Gaillac 64

Office de tourisme, rue Saint-Martin ✆ 05 63 74 16 28, Fax 05 63 50 86 61

Hôtel Abbaye Ecole Le Logis des Pères

18 r. Lacordaire – ✆ 05 63 74 44 80 – www.hotelfp-soreze.com – reception@hotelfp.soreze.com – Fax 05 63 74 44 89

52 rm – †€ 98/153 ††€ 98/153, € 12 – ½ P € 82

Rest – *(closed Sunday dinner from November to March)* Menu € 21 (weekdays)/40 – Carte approx. € 38

◆ A hotel in a wing of the famous Benedictine abbey school (17C) founded in 754 by Pepin the Short. Tastefully decorated guestrooms and six hectares of wooded parkland. Traditional cuisine served in the old refectory or under the shade of the plane trees.

Le Pavillon des Hôtes

– ✆ 05 63 74 44 80 – www.hotelfp-soreze.com – reception@hotelfp-soreze.com – Fax 05 63 74 44 89

20 rm – †€ 55 ††€ 55, € 12 – ½ P € 61

◆ Simple guestrooms laid out around an inner courtyard.

SORGES – 24 Dordogne – 329 G4 – pop. 1 157 – alt. 178 m – ✉ 24420 4 C1

Dordogne-Berry-Limousin

Paris 463 – Brantôme 24 – Limoges 77 – Nontron 36 – Périgueux 20 – Thiviers 15

Syndicat d'initiative, écomusée de la Truffe ✆ 05 53 46 71 43, Fax 05 53 46 71 43

Auberge de la Truffe rest,

on N 21 – ✆ 05 53 05 02 05 – www.auberge-de-la-truffe.com – contact@auberge-de-la-truffe.com – Fax 05 53 05 39 27

19 rm – †€ 50 ††€ 54/67, € 10 – 5 suites – ½ P € 60/87

Rest – *(closed Sunday dinner and Monday lunch from 12 November to 30 March)* Menu (€ 13 bi), € 18 (weekdays), € 24/100 – Carte € 29/90

◆ A welcoming village inn near the Maison de la Truffe with rather spacious, well-furnished rooms, some at garden level. Charming dining room and cuisine based on local produce with truffles (the black diamond) and foie gras in pride of place.

SORGUES – 84 Vaucluse – 332 C9 – pop. 18 100 – alt. 24 m – ✉ 84700 42 E1

Paris 672 – Avignon 12 – Carpentras 20 – Cavaillon 34 – Orange 18

Alonso

12 r. 19-Mars-1962, (pl. de l'Hôtel-de-Ville) – ✆ 04 90 39 11 02 – restaurantalonso@orange.fr – Fax 04 90 83 48 42 – Closed 15-31 August, Saturday lunch and Sunday

Rest – *(number of covers limited, pre-book)* Menu € 35/50

◆ This delightful mansion is home to a plush interior and lovely terrace shaded by pine trees. Concise menu in keeping with the seasons and renewed weekly.

SOSPEL – 06 Alpes-Maritimes – 341 F4 – pop. 3 394 – alt. 360 m – ✉ 06380 French Riviera 41 D2

Paris 967 – Menton 19 – Nice 41 – Tende 38 – Ventimiglia 28

Office de tourisme, 19, avenue Jean Médecin ✆ 04 93 04 15 80, Fax 04 93 04 19 96

Old village★: Old bridge★, Immaculate Virgin ★ in St-Michel church - St-Roch Fort ★ South: 1 km by D 2204.

Des Étrangers

rm, VISA

7 bd Verdun – ✆ 04 93 04 00 09 – www.sospel.net – sospel@sospel.net – Fax 04 93 04 12 31 – Open 5 March-30 November

27 rm – €68/72 €72/90, €8,50 – ½ P €68/85

Rest – *(closed Wednesday lunch and Tuesday)* Menu €25/55 – Carte €38/60

◆ This hotel, run by the same family since 1883, greets guests warmly. The rooms sport a fresh Provençal style (wrought iron, patinated walls and pastel shades). Jacuzzi in the basement. Regional and tasty cuisine, prepared with garden and market produce.

SOUDAN – 79 Deux-Sèvres – 322 F6 – see St-Maixent-l'École

SOUILLAC – 46 Lot – 337 E2 – pop. 3 898 – alt. 104 m – ✉ 46200 Dordogne-Berry-Limousin 28 B1

Paris 516 – Brive-la-Gaillarde 39 – Cahors 68 – Figeac 74 – Sarlat-la-Canéda 29

Office de tourisme, boulevard Louis-Jean Malvy ✆ 05 65 37 81 56, Fax 05 65 27 11 45

Souillac Country Club Lachapelle-Auzac, N : 8 km on D 15, ✆ 05 65 27 56 00

Former abbey church: low-relief "Isaïe"★★, back of the portal★ - Musée national de l'Automate et de la Robotique★.

Plan on next page

Grand Hôtel

VISA

1 allée Verninac – ✆ 05 65 32 78 30 – www.grandhotel-souillac.com – grandhotel-souillac@wanadoo.fr – Fax 05 65 32 66 34 – Open from 23 March-31 October Z e

30 rm – €45/60 €52/70, €8 – ½ P €57/66

Rest – Menu (€13), €20/35 – Carte €27/47

◆ This hundred-year-old building offers guests a choice of modern, individually furnished rooms. A pleasant patio provides welcome light to the breakfast room. Traditional cuisine served in modern surroundings. In summer, choose between the veranda with its sliding roof or the plane tree-shaded terrace.

Le Pavillon St-Martin without rest

VISA

5 pl. St-Martin – ✆ 05 65 32 63 45 – www.hotel-saint-martin-souillac.com – contact@hotel-saint-martin-souillac.com – Fax 05 65 32 75 37 Z f

11 rm – €49/98 €75/98, €8,50

◆ Opposite the church tower, this distinctive 16C villa offers personalised rooms that marry classic and contemporary details. Pleasant vaulted breakfast room.

Le Quercy without rest

VISA

1 r. Récège – ✆ 05 65 37 83 56 – www.le-quercy.fr – reservation@le-quercy.fr – Fax 05 65 37 07 22 – Open 20 March-15 December Y d

25 rm – €50/55 €60/65, €8

◆ A comfortable family-run hotel away from the busy centre. Well-maintained guestrooms, most of which have a balcony overlooking the flower-decked terrace or swimming pool.

Belle Vue without rest

VISA AE

68 av. J. Jaurès, (in the station) – ✆ 05 65 32 78 23 – www.hotelbellevue-souillac.com – hotelbellevue.souillac@wanadoo.fr – Fax 05 65 37 03 89

26 rm – €42/50 €42/50, €6,50

◆ Large 1960s building near the train station. Simple but clean rooms. Sports installations on the garden side (pool, tennis) and a small boutique of regional products.

Le Redouillé

VISA

28 av. de Toulouse, via ② – ✆ 05 65 37 87 25 – leredouille.souillac@wanadoo.fr – Closed 7 January-2 February, Monday and Tuesday

Rest – Menu €19/50 – Carte €40/77

◆ Two dining rooms - one bright and sunny, inspired by the colours of Provence - separated by a sitting room. Traditional cuisine with the occasional modern touch. Summer terrace.

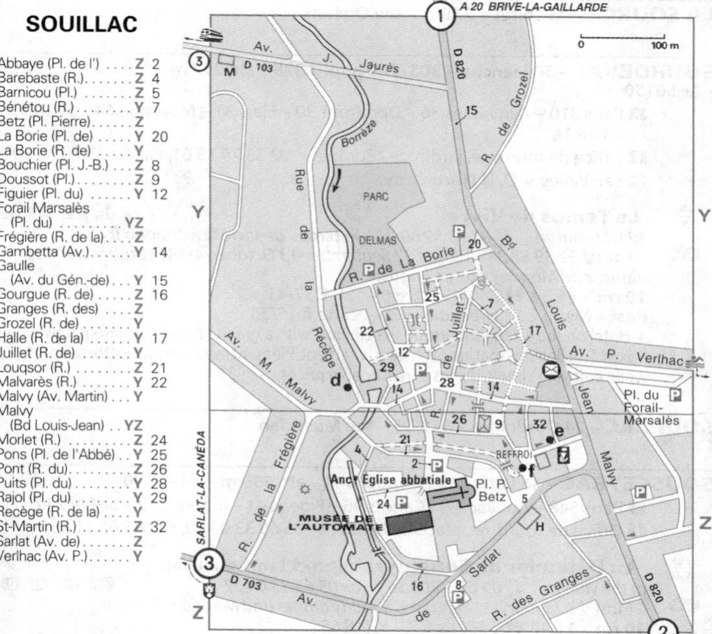

SOULAC-SUR-MER – 33 Gironde – 335 E1 – pop. 2 679 – alt. 7 m 3 B1

– Casino : de la Plage – ✉ 33780 Atlantic Coast

Paris 515 – Bordeaux 99 – Lesparre-Médoc 31 – Royan 12

Office de tourisme, 68, rue de la plage ✆ 05 56 09 86 61, Fax 05 56 73 63 76

in l'Amélie-sur-Mer 5 km southwest by D 101[E] – ✉ 33780 Soulac-sur-Mer

Des Pins rest, VISA

92 bd de l'Amélie – ✆ 05 56 73 27 27 – www.hotel-des-pins.com – info@hotel-des-pins.com – Fax 05 56 73 60 39 – Open 20 March-4 January and closed Saturday lunch, Sunday dinner and Monday in low season

31 rm – †€ 50/95 ††€ 50/115, ☕ € 10 – ½ P € 47/85

Rest – Menu (€ 17), € 25/38 – Carte € 27/65

◆ A renovated late 19C building on the edge of the pines 100m from the beach – fine sand as far as the eye can see. Two annexes. Rooms variously furnished. Bright restaurant serving fish and regional cuisine.

SOULAINES-DHUYS – 10 Aube – 313 I3 – pop. 297 – alt. 153 m 14 C3

– ✉ 10200

Paris 228 – Bar-sur-Aube 18 – Chaumont 48 – Troyes 58

La Venise Verte VISA

r. Plessis – ✆ 03 25 92 76 10 – www.logis-venise-verte.com – accueil@logis-venise-verte.com – Fax 03 25 92 73 97 – Closed 24-30 August and 19 February-4 March

12 rm – †€ 65 ††€ 68, ☕ € 9 – ½ P € 68

Rest – *(closed Sunday dinner 21 September-16 March)* Menu (€ 16), € 25/65 bi – Carte € 34/50

◆ This welcoming hotel next to the road has good soundproofing. The small rooms are fresh and practical. An ideal base for visiting the village and its half-timbered houses. Sunny dining room, summer terrace in the inner courtyard and traditional dishes.

LA SOURCE – 45 Loiret – 318 I5 – see Orléans

SOURDEVAL – 50 Manche – 303 G7 – pop. 2 878 – alt. 217 m – ✉ 50150 32 **B2**

Paris 310 – Avranches 36 – Domfront 30 – Flers 31 – Mayenne 64 – St-Lô 53 – Vire 14

Office de tourisme, jardin de l'Europe ✆ 02 33 79 35 61, Fax 02 33 79 35 59

Sée Valley ★ O, Normandy

Le Temps de Vivre

12 r. St-Martin – ✆ 02 33 59 60 41 – le-temps-de-vivre@wanadoo.fr – Fax 02 33 59 88 34 – Closed 27 September-13 October, 4-18 February, Sunday dinner and Monday except August

10 rm – †€ 34 ††€ 40/49, ☕ € 6 – ½ P € 37/41

Rest – Menu € 12 (weekdays)/30 – Carte € 15/33

◆ Hotel on the village square, by the cinema, with a granite façade brightened by flower boxes. Small rooms that are recent and well kept. Pleasant restaurant, ideal for taking it easy while enjoying simple dishes at reasonable prices.

SOURZAC – 24 Dordogne – 329 D5 – see Mussidan

SOUSCEYRAC – 46 Lot – 337 I2 – pop. 941 – alt. 559 m – ✉ 46190 29 **C1**

Paris 548 – Aurillac 47 – Cahors 96 – Figeac 41 – Mauriac 69 – St-Céré 17

Office de tourisme, place de l'Église ✆ 05 65 33 02 20, Fax 05 65 11 66 19

Au Déjeuner de Sousceyrac (Patrick Lagnès) with rm

in the village – ✆ 05 65 33 00 56 – Fax 05 65 33 04 37 – Closed 3 January-1st February, Sunday dinner and Monday

10 rm – †€ 48 ††€ 48, ☕ € 8 – ½ P € 65

Rest – *(number of covers limited, pre-book)* Menu € 18/50 – Carte € 45/60

Spec. Cannelloni de langoustines au gésier de canard confit. Bœuf poêlé au foie gras de canard, sabayon à la truffe noire. Demie sphère chocolat-coco, tartare d'ananas à la vanille bourbon. **Wines** Cahors, Vin de Pays du Lot.

◆ Local cuisine takes pride of place in this pleasant establishment located on the village square. The warm welcome and delightful, colourful rustic setting add to its charm. The guestrooms have been entirely redone.

SOUS-LA-TOUR – 22 Côtes-d'Armor – 309 F3 – see St-Brieuc

SOUSTONS – 40 Landes – 335 D12 – pop. 6 560 – alt. 9 m – ✉ 40140 3 **B2**

Atlantic Coast

Paris 736 – Anglet 51 – Bayonne 47 – Bordeaux 150

Office de tourisme, grange de Labouyrie ✆ 05 58 41 52 62, Fax 05 58 41 30 63

Domaine de Bellegarde

23 av. Ch. de Gaulle, dir. N 10 – ✆ 05 58 41 24 06 – www.qsun.co.uk – info@qsun.co.uk – Fax 05 58 41 33 60

5 rm ☕ – †€ 100/220 ††€ 120/290

Table d'hôte – *(pre-book)* Menu € 40 bi/45 bi

◆ Set in a park, a fine house with features from the Landes region and Basque country, offering rooms and suites that are all furnished in the same style (coconut flooring, wrought-iron bed, etc...). One has a terrace, while another has a private sauna. Family fare varying according to market availability.

LA SOUTERRAINE – 23 Creuse – 325 F3 – pop. 5 309 – alt. 390 m – ✉ 23300 Dordogne-Berry-Limousin 24 **B1**

Paris 344 – Bellac 41 – Châteauroux 79 – Guéret 35 – Limoges 58

Office de tourisme, place de la Gare ✆ 05 55 63 10 06

Church★.

in l'Est : 7 km by N 145, D 74 and secondary road – ✉ 23300 La Souterraine

Château de la Cazine rm, VISA AE
Domaine de la Fôt – ✆ 05 55 89 60 00 – www.chateaulacazine.com – chateau-de-la-cazine@wanadoo.fr – Fax 05 55 63 71 85 – Closed 23 December-14 January
20 rm – †€ 60/78 ††€ 60/78, ☕ € 13 – 2 suites – ½ P € 66/85
Rest – Menu € 24 (weekday lunch), € 39/75 – Carte € 75/90
◆ A quiet, enjoyable stay is guaranteed at this small and charming 19C château set in extensive grounds. Three dining rooms, a terrace facing the surrounding countryside, and classic cuisine.

in St-Étienne-de-Fursac 11 km south by Fursac road (D 1) – **pop. 816** – **alt. 322 m** – ✉ 23290

XX **Nougier** with rm VISA AE
2 pl. de l'Église – ✆ 05 55 63 60 56 – www.hotelnougier.fr – hotelnougier@orange.fr – Fax 05 55 63 65 47 – Open from mid March to end November and closed Monday except dinner July-August, Sunday dinner from September to June and Tuesday lunch
12 rm – †€ 52 ††€ 62/72, ☕ € 10 – ½ P € 63/70
Rest – Menu (€ 13), € 22/48 – Carte € 40/56
◆ Three generations of the same family have run this hotel, now redecorated in a modern style. Sophisticated gourmet cuisine. Nice bedrooms and a charming garden and pool.

SOUVIGNY – 03 Allier – **326** G3 – **pop. 1 980** – **alt. 242 m** – ✉ **03210** 5 **B1**
Auvergne

Paris 301 – Bourbon-l'Archambault 16 – Montluçon 70 – Moulins 13
Prieuré St-Pierre★★ - Calendar★★ in St-Marc church-museum.

XX **Auberge des Tilleuls** VISA
pl. St-Éloi – ✆ 04 70 43 60 70 – www.auberge-tilleuls.com – Fax 04 70 43 60 70 Closed 24 August-2 September, 28 December-4 January, 16-28 February, Wednesday dinner from November to March, Tuesday dinner, Sunday dinner and Monday
Rest – Menu (€ 12), € 19 (weekdays)/43 – Carte € 33/58
◆ This smart inn welcomes you in two carefully rustic-style dining rooms, one with trompe l'oeil half-timbering. Narrow, shaded terrace at the back.

SOUVIGNY-EN-SOLOGNE – 41 Loir-et-Cher – **318** J6 – **pop. 476** – **alt. 210 m** – ✉ **41600** 12 **C2**

Paris 171 – Gien 43 – Lamotte-Beuvron 15 – Montargis 63 – Orléans 39

XX **Auberge de la Grange aux Oies** VISA
2 r. du Gâtinais – ✆ 02 54 88 40 08 – aubergedelagrangeauxoies@orange.fr – Fax 02 54 88 40 08 – Closed Sunday dinner, Tuesday dinner and Wednesday except from June to August and public holidays
Rest – Menu (€ 16), € 27 (weekdays)/51 – Carte € 38/57
◆ Beams and floor tiles create a pleasant country atmosphere in this pretty, half-timbered 17C and 18C house. Traditional dishes typical of the Sologne region with game in season.

SOYAUX – 16 Charente – **324** L6 – **see Angoulême**

SOYONS – 07 Ardèche – **331** L4 – **see St-Péray**

STEENVOORDE – 59 Nord – **302** D3 – **pop. 3 964** – **alt. 50 m** – ✉ **59114** 30 **B1**

Paris 259 – Calais 73 – Dunkerque 33 – Hazebrouck 12 – Lille 45 – St-Omer 28
Syndicat d'initiative, place Jean-Marie Ryckewaert ✆ 03 28 42 97 98

X **Auprès de mon Arbre** VISA AE
932 rte d'Eecke – ✆ 03 28 49 79 49 – www.aupresdemonarbre.fr – aupres.de.mon.arbre457@orange.fr – Fax 03 28 49 72 29 – Closed dinner except Friday and Saturday
Rest – Menu (€ 16), € 18 (weekday lunch), € 28/50 – Carte € 36/47
◆ This renovated farm has a fireplace and Godin stove that guests don't want to leave, except perhaps in summer to sit in the lovely garden. Carefully prepared authentic dishes.

STELLA-PLAGE – 62 Pas-de-Calais – **301** C5 – **see le Touquet**

STIRING-WENDEL – 57 Moselle – **307** M3 – **see Forbach**

Guittot/Diaf/PHOTONONSTOP

Le vieux Strasbourg et la flèche de la cathédrale Notre-Dame

STRASBOURG

🅿 Department: 67 Bas-Rhin
Michelin LOCAL map: n° 315 K5
▶ Paris 489 – Basel 141 – Karlsruhe 81 – Stuttgart 149

Population: 272 700
Pop. built-up area: 451 240
Altitude: 143 m
Postal Code: ✉ 67000
Alsace-Lorraine
Carte régionale 1 B1

USEFUL INFORMATION

TOURIST OFFICES

17, place de la Cathédrale ✆ 03 88 52 28 28, Fax 03 88 52 28 29
Office de tourisme, place de la Gare ✆ 03 88 32 51 49
Office de tourisme, 17, place de la Cathédrale ✆ 03 88 52 28 28, Fax 03 88 52 28 29

TRANSPORTS

Auto-train ✆ 3635 enter 42 (0,34 €/mn)

AIRPORT

Strasbourg-International ✆ 03 88 64 67 67 AT

A FEW GOLF COURSES

de La Wantzenau La Wantzenau C.D. 302, ✆ 03 88 96 37 73
Le Kempferhof Golf Club Plobsheim 351 rue du Moulin, S : 15 km on D 468, ✆ 03 88 98 72 72

TO SEE

CATHEDRAL DISTRICT

Notre-Dame Cathedral ★★★ : astronomical clock★ ⩽ ★of the spire - Place de la Cathédrale ★: maison Kammerzell ★ KZ Musée★★ du palais Rohan★- Musée alsacien★★ KZ M[1] Musée de l'Oeuvre Notre-Dame★★ KZ M[6] - Musée historique★ KZ M[5]

PETITE FRANCE

Rue du Bains-aux-Plantes★★ HJZ - covered bridges★ HZ - Barrage Vauban ✳ ★★ HZ - Mausoleum of the Marshal de Saxe★★ in St-Thomas church JZ - Musée d'Art moderne et contemporain★★ HZ **M**[3] - Boat trip on the River Ill

AROUND PLACE KLÉBER AND PLACE BROGLIE

Place Kléber★, the most famous square in Strasbourg, flanked by the Aubette in the North JY Place Broglie : Town hall ★KY H

EUROPE IN STRASBOURG

Palais de l'Europe★ FGU - Nouveau palais des Droits de l'Homme (new human rights centre) GU - Orangerie★ FGU

Régent Petite France
5 r. des Moulins – ✆ 03 88 76 43 43 – www.regent-hotels.com – rpf@regent-hotels.com – Fax 03 88 76 43 76
VISA MC AE
p. 8 JZ **f**
66 rm – †€ 265/395 ††€ 287/417, € 22 – 6 suites
Rest – *(closed Sunday, Monday and lunch from October to May)*
Menu € 42 (dinner) – Carte € 33/42
♦ A modern hotel occupying an old ice factory on the banks of the Ill. Bright, spacious and comfortable bedrooms with high-tech equipment. Terrace and sauna. Modern menu in keeping with the trendy feel of the restaurant with bar-lounge and views of the river.

Sofitel VISA MC AE
pl. St-Pierre-le-Jeune – ✆ 03 88 15 49 00 – www.sofitel-strasbourg.com – h0568@accor.com – Fax 03 88 15 49 99
p. 8 JY **s**
153 rm – †€ 140/380 ††€ 140/380, € 25 – 2 suites
Rest – *(closed Saturday lunch, Sunday and public holidays)*
Menu (€ 35) – Carte € 46/67
♦ Two types of room – classic and those designed on a European political theme on offer at this Sofitel. A full range of modern facilities, plus patio and fitness centre. Modern, Japanese-inspired design and luxury brasserie-style service at the restaurant.

Hilton rm, VISA MC AE
av. Herrenschmidt – ✆ 03 88 37 10 10 – www.strasbourg.hilton.fr – contact@hilton-strasbourg.com – Fax 03 88 36 83 27
p. 6 EU **e**
238 rm – †€ 130/355 ††€ 130/355, € 23 – 5 suites
Rest *La Table du Chef* – *✆ 03 88 37 41 42 (closed July-August, Monday dinner, Saturday lunch and Sunday)* Menu (€ 29), € 35
Rest *Le Jardin du Tivoli* – *✆ 03 88 35 72 61* – Menu € 30 – Carte € 34/46
♦ This glass and steel hotel provides standardised comfort in its spacious guestrooms. Lobby with shops, a multimedia centre and bars. Traditional lunches and a British feel at La Table du Chef; wine bar in the evening. Buffet dining at the Jardin du Tivoli.

Régent Contades without rest VISA MC AE
8 av. de la Liberté – ✆ 03 88 15 05 05 – www.regent-hotels.com – rc@regent-hotels.com – Fax 03 88 15 05 15
p. 9 LY **f**
45 rm – †€ 195/325 ††€ 215/345, € 20 – 2 suites
♦ A 19C hotel with an opulent and refined decor (wood panelling, paintings). Particulary spacious, renovated rooms, Belle Époque breakfast room. Sanarium/relaxation area.

Beaucour without rest VISA MC AE
5 r. Bouchers – ✆ 03 88 76 72 00 – www.hotel-beaucour.com – info@hotel-beaucour.com – Fax 03 88 76 72 60
p. 9 KZ **k**
49 rm – †€ 110 ††€ 135/165, € 13
♦ These two elegant 18C Alsatian buildings are linked by a flower-decked patio. The most pleasant guestrooms are decorated in local rustic style with wood panelling and exposed beams.

Maison Rouge without rest VISA MC AE
4 r. des Francs-Bourgeois – ✆ 03 88 32 08 60 – www.maison-rouge.com – info@maison-rouge.com – Fax 03 88 22 43 73
p. 8 JZ **g**
140 rm – †€ 76/170 ††€ 88/185, € 14 – 2 suites
♦ Behind the red stone façade is an elegant hotel with a cosy atmosphere. Well-designed bedrooms with a personal touch, and an attractively decorated lounge on each floor.

Monopole-Métropole without rest
16 r. Kuhn – ✆ 03 88 14 39 14 – www.bw-monopole.com – infos@bw-monopole.com – Fax 03 88 32 82 55
VISA MC AE
p. 8 HY **p**
86 rm – †€ 80/200 ††€ 85/200
♦ Near the station, hotel split into two wings (one old and rustic, the other far more contemporary, featuring works by local artists). Lounges decorated with handicrafts.

Novotel Centre Halles rm, VISA MC AE
4 quai Kléber – ✆ 03 88 21 50 50 – www.novotel.com – h0439@accor.com – Fax 03 88 21 50 51
p. 8 JY **k**
96 rm – †€ 87/198 ††€ 87/198, € 15 **Rest** – Carte € 22/47
♦ Refurbished rooms in a pleasant, contemporary style at this hotel in the Les Halles shopping centre. Gym on the 8th floor with a view of the cathedral. A modern look in the bar and restaurant; simplified and practical menu.

BISCHHEIM

Marais (R. du) . . . . **CS** 121
Périgueux (Av. de) . . . . **BS** 159
Robertsau (R. de la) . . . . **BS** 179
Triage (R. du). . . . . **BS** 219

ECKBOLSHEIM

Gaulle (Av. du Gén.-de) . . . . **BS** 67
Wasselonne (Rte de) . . . . **BS** 237

HŒNHEIM

Fontaine (R. de la). . . . . **BR** 55
République (R. de la) . . . . **BR** 174

ILLKIRCH-GRAFFENSTADEN

Bürkell (Rte) . . . . **BT** 24
Ceinture (R. de la). . . . . **BT** 27
Faisanderie (R. de la) . . . . **BT** 48
Industrie (R. de l') . . . . **BT** 97
Kastler (R. Alfred) . . . . **BT** 99
Lixenbühl (R.) . . . . **BT** 115
Messmer (Av.) . . . . **BT** 138
Neuhof (Rte de) . . . . **BT** 144
Strasbourg (Rte de) . . . . **BT** 207
Vignes (R. des) . . . . **BT** 233

LINGOLSHEIM

Eckbolsheim (R. d') . . . . **BS** 44
Ostwald (R. d') . . . . **BT** 152
Près (R. des) . . . . **BS** 168

OBERHAUSBERGEN

Mittelhausbergen (Rte de). . . . . **BS** 139
Oberhausbergen (Rte de) . . . . . . **BS** 149

OSTWALD

Foch (R. du Maréchal) . . . . **BT** 50
Gelspolsheim (R. de) . . . . **BT** 73
Leclerc (R. du Gén.) . . . . **BT** 112
Vosges (R. des). . . . . **BT** 232
23-Novembre (R. du) . . . . **BT** 246

SCHILTIGHEIM

Bischwiller (Rte de) . . . . **BS** 18
Gaulle (Rte du Gén.-de) . . . . **BS** 70
Hausbergen (Rte de) . . . . **BS** 81
Mendès-France (Av. P.) . . . . **BS** 132
Pompiers (R. des). . . . . **BS** 164

STRASBOURG

Atenheim (Rte d') . . . . **CT** 8
Austerlitz (Pont d') . . . . **BS** 9
Bauerngrund (R. de) . . . . **CT** 15
Ganzau (R. de la) . . . . **BT** 66
Holtzheim (R. de) . . . . **AS** 88
Ill (R. de l') . . . . **CS** 96
Neuhof (Rte de) . . . . **CT** 144
Plaine des Bouchers (R. de la) . **BS** 163
Polygone (Rte du) . . . . **BS** 165
Pont (R. du) . . . . **BT** 166
Ribeauvillé (R. de) . . . . **CS** 177
Romains (Rte des) . . . . **BS** 180
Schirmeck (Rte de). . . . . **BS** 198

WOLFISHEIM

Oberhausbergen (R. d') . . . . **AS** 148
Seigneurs (R. des) . . . . **AS** 204

STRASBOURG
AGGLOMÉRATION

0 2 km
A
R
S
T
BERSTETT
TRUCHTERSHEIM
PFETTISHEIM
KLEINFRANKENHEIM
BEHLENHEIM
PFULGRIESHEIM
WIWERSHEIM
STUTZHEIM - OFFENHEIM
GRIESHEIM - SUR - SOUFFEL
DINGSHE
HURTIGHEIM
ITTENHEIM
R^te de Paris
R^te de Saverne
FOIRE EXPOSITIO
OBERSCHAEFFOLSHEIM
BREUSCHWICKERSHEIM
ACHENHEIM
WOLFISHEI
Bruche
Canal de la Bruche
HANGENBIETEN
HOLTZHEIM
KOLBSHEIM
R. du M^al F
STRASBOURG-INTERNATIONAL
DUPPIGHEIM
ENTZHEIM
GLOECKELSBERG
GEISPOLSHEIM
BLAESHEIM
LIPSHEIM
SAVERNE
METZ, NANCY
SAVERNE
A35-E25 COLMAR
MOLSHEIM, ST-DIÉ-DES-VOSGES
A 35 BARR
OBERNAI
COLMAR, SÉLESTAT
A 35 - E 25
A 352
D 31, D 220, D 30, D 41, D 79, D 180, D 64, D 666, D 166, D 341, D 228, D 1004, D 662, D 222, D 45, D 118, D 221, D 174, D 63, D 93, D 392, D 400, D 84, D 161
148, 204, 5, 6, 7, 8, 9, 10, 4
h, v, q, e
A

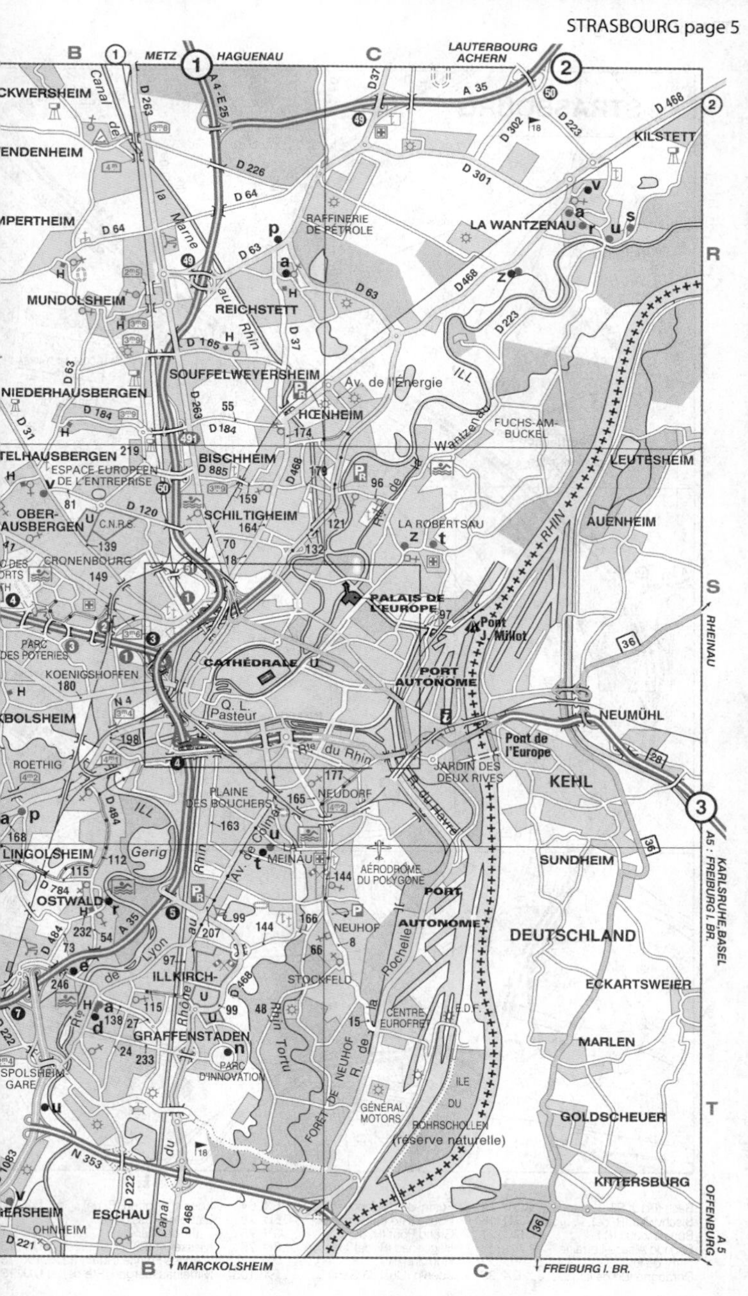
METZ
HAGUENAU
LAUTERBOURG
ACHERN
LA WANTZENAU
KILSTETT
RAFFINERIE DE PÉTROLE
REICHSTETT
MUNDOLSHEIM
SOUFFELWEYERSHEIM
NIEDERHAUSBERGEN
HŒNHEIM
BISCHHEIM
SCHILTIGHEIM
ESPACE EUROPÉEN DE L'ENTREPRISE
CRONENBOURG
LA ROBERTSAU
FUCHS-AM-BUCKEL
LEUTESHEIM
AUENHEIM
PALAIS DE L'EUROPE
CATHÉDRALE
PORT AUTONOME
Pont J. Millot
NEUMÜHL
Pont de l'Europe
JARDIN DES DEUX RIVES
KEHL
PARC DES POTERIES
KOENIGSHOFFEN
Q. L. Pasteur
ROETHIG
PLAINE DES BOUCHERS
NEUDORF
LINGOLSHEIM
LA MEINAU
AÉRODROME DU POLYGONE
SUNDHEIM
OSTWALD
NEUHOF
DEUTSCHLAND
ILLKIRCH-GRAFFENSTADEN
STOCKFELD
ECKARTSWEIER
CENTRE EUROFRET
MARLEN
PARC D'INNOVATION
GÉNÉRAL MOTORS
ILE DU ROHRSCHOLLEN (réserve naturelle)
GOLDSCHEUER
KITTERSBURG
ESCHAU
OHNHEIM
MARCKOLSHEIM
FREIBURG I. BR.
RHEINAU
KARLSRUHE, BASEL
A5 : FREIBURG I. BR.
OFFENBURG

STRASBOURG
0
500 m
D
E
U
V
X
D 263
70
STE-HÉLÈNE
Rte de Bischwiller
D 468
R. L. Pasteur
A4
MARCHÉ GARE
R. de Hochfelden
R. de l'Église Rouge
A 350
Canal de dérivation
R. de Dettwiller
R. des Champs
R. de la Rotonde
139
CENTRAL
R. du Marché-Gare
Jacques
ÉCOLE MILITAIRE
Pl. de Haguenau
Av.
Clemenceau
Rte d'Oberhausbergen
CIMre MILITAIRE
Remparts
240
16
79
171
160
222
Bd des
R. du
Mal Fo
Pl. de la République
A 35-E 25
des
Fossé
A 351
GARE CENTRALE
Bd du Prést Wilson
Bd de Metz
POL
Pl. Kléber
H
CATHÉDRALE
105
Bd de Nancy
Molsheim
PETITE FRANCE
ILL
C
238
Bd de Lyon
de
R. de la
22
94
a
64
LA LAITERIE
R.
D 392
198
Quai Louis Pasteur
PORT
CENTRE ADMINISTRATIF
Armée
163
HEYRITZ
POL
R. de la Montagne Verte
Rte de l'Hôpital
A 35-E 25
163

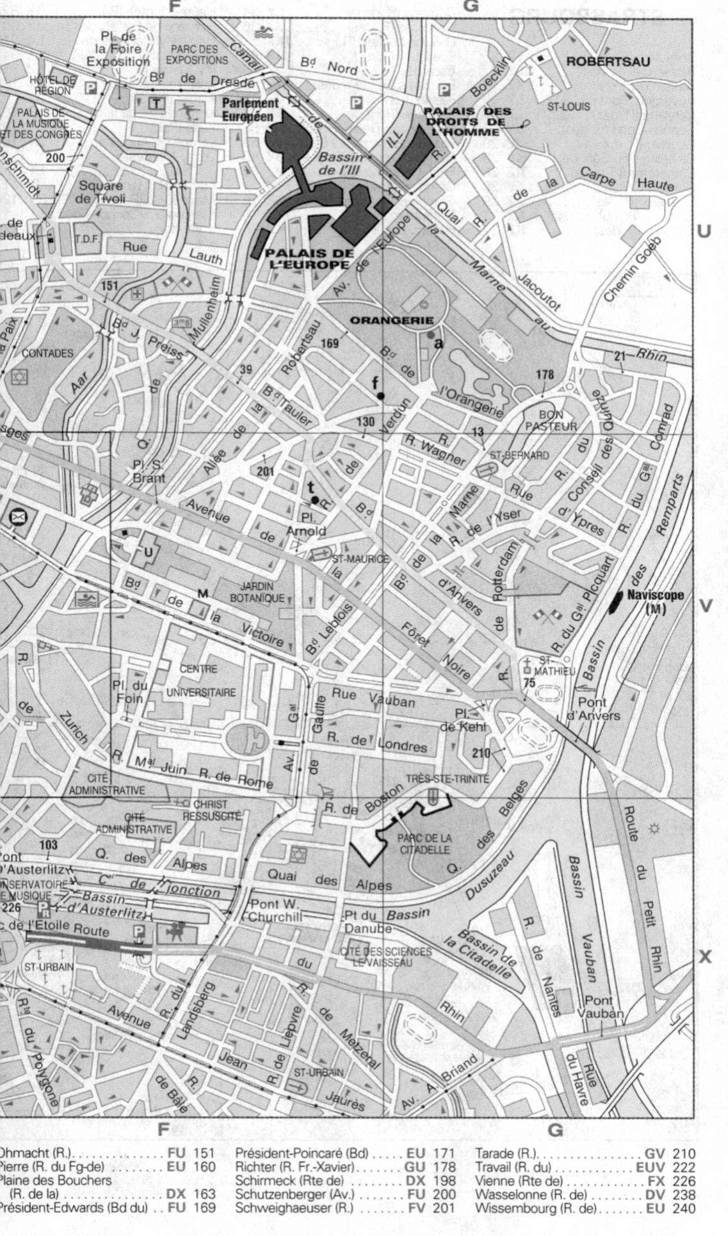

Ohmacht (R.)	FU	151	Président-Poincaré (Bd)	EU	171	Tarade (R.)	GV	210
Pierre (R. du Fg-de)	EU	160	Richter (R. Fr.-Xavier)	GU	178	Travail (R. du)	EUV	222
Plaine des Bouchers (R. de la)	DX	163	Schirmeck (Rte de)	DX	198	Vienne (Rte de)	FX	226
Président-Edwards (Bd du)	FU	169	Schutzenberger (Av.)	FU	200	Wasselonne (R. de)	DV	238
			Schweighaeuser (R.)	FV	201	Wissembourg (R. de)	EU	240

STRASBOURG

Abreuvoir (R. de l') . . . . LZ 3
Arc-en-Ciel (R. de l') . . . . . KLY 7
Austerlitz (R. d') . . . . KZ 10
Auvergne (Pont d') . . . . LY 12
Bateliers (R. des) . . . . LZ 14
Bonnes-Gens (R. des) . . . . . JY 19
Bouclier (R. du) . . . . JZ 20
Castelnau (R. Gén.-de) . . . . KY 25
Cathédrale (Pl. de la) . . . . . . KZ 26
Chaudron (R. du) . . . . KY 28
Cheveux (R. des) . . . . JZ 29
Corbeau (Pl. du) . . . . KZ 31
Cordiers (R. des) . . . . KZ 32
Courtine (R. de la) . . . . LY 34
Dentelles (R. des) . . . . JZ 36
Division-Leclerc (R.) . . . . . JKZ
Écarlate (R. de l') . . . . JZ 43
Escarpée (R.) . . . . JZ 45
Étudiants (R. et Pl. des) . . . KY 46
Faisan (Pont du) . . . . JZ 47
Fonderie (Pont de la) . . . . . KY 52
Fossés-des-Treize (R. du) . . KY 58
Fossé-des-Tanneurs (R. du) JZ 57
Francs-Bourgeois (R. des) . JZ 60
Frey (Quai Charles) . . . . JZ 63
Grandes-Arcades (R. des) JKY
Grande-Boucherie (Pl. de la) KZ 76
Gutenberg (R.) . . . . JKZ 78
Hallebardes (R. des) . . . . . . KZ 80
Haute-Montée (R.) . . . . JY 82
Homme de Fer (Pl. de l') . . JY 90
Hôpital-Militaire (R. de l') . . . LZ 91
Humann (R.) . . . . HZ 94
Ill (Quai de l') . . . . HZ 95
Kellermann (Quai) . . . . JY 10
Kléber (Pl.) . . . . JY
Krutenau (R. de la) . . . . LZ 10
Kuss (Pont) . . . . HY 10
Lamey (R. Auguste) . . . . . . LY 10
Lezay-Marnésia (Quai) . . . . LY 11
Luther (R. Martin) . . . . JZ 11
Maire Kuss (R. du) . . . . HY 12
Marché-aux-Cochons-de-Lait (Pl. du) . . . . KZ 12

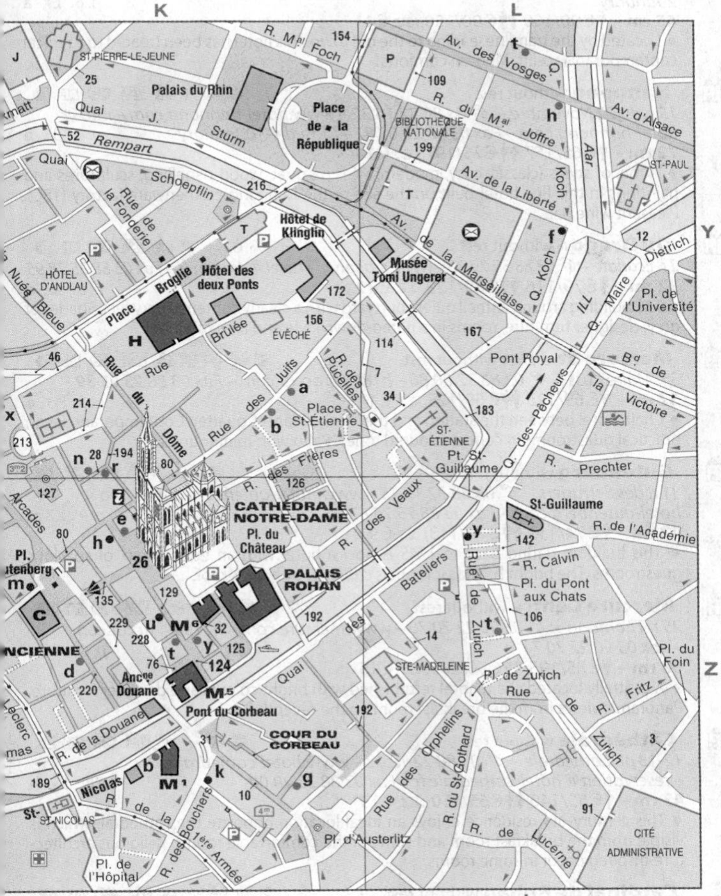

K
L
Y
Z
ST-PIERRE-LE-JEUNE
Palais du Rhin
Place de la République
R. Mal Foch
Av. des Vosges
R. du Mal Joffre
BIBLIOTHÈQUE NATIONALE
Av. d'Alsace
Av. de la Liberté
Quai J. Sturm
Rempart
Quai Schoepflin
Rue de la Fonderie
Hôtel de Klinglin
Hôtel des deux Ponts
Musée Tomi Ungerer
Av. de la Marseillaise
Q. Koch
Aar
ST-PAUL
Dietrich
Pl. de l'Université
ILL
Q. Maire
HÔTEL D'ANDLAU
Place Broglie
Nuée Bleue
Brûlée
ÉVÊCHÉ
Rue du Dôme
Rue des Juifs
R. des Pucelles
Place St-Étienne
ST-ÉTIENNE
Pont Royal
Bd de la Victoire
Q. des Pêcheurs
Pt. St-Guillaume
R. Prechter
St-Guillaume
R. de l'Académie
Rue des Frères
R. des Veaux
CATHÉDRALE NOTRE-DAME
Pl. du Château
PALAIS ROHAN
Arcades
Pl. Gutenberg
R. Calvin
Pl. du Pont aux Chats
Rue de Zurich
Bateliers
STE-MADELEINE
Pl. de Zurich
Rue de Zurich
R. Fritz
Pl. du Foin
Quai des Bateliers
Ancne Douane
Pont du Corbeau
COUR DU CORBEAU
R. de la Douane
Nicolas
ST-NICOLAS
R. de la 1ère Armée
R. des Bouchers
Rue des Orphelins
R. du St-Gothard
Pl. d'Austerlitz
R. de Lucerne
CITÉ ADMINISTRATIVE
Pl. de l'Hôpital
ANCIENNE

Chut - Au Bain aux Plantes rm, rm, VISA AE
4 r. Bain-aux-Plantes – 03 88 32 05 06 – www.hote-strasbourg.fr – contact@hote-strasbourg.fr – Fax 03 88 32 05 50 p. 9 KZ **u**
8 rm – €90/100 €100/160, €10 – 1 suite
Rest – *(closed 26 April-5 May, 9-18 August, 21 December-7 January, Sunday and Monday)* Menu (€15), €18 (weekday lunch) – Carte €32/44
◆ Designer or antique materials and furniture, spacious guestrooms and a relaxing, minimalist feel are the hallmarks of this stylish hotel-cum-guesthouse. The varied menu, featuring the subtle use of myriad spices, changes daily. Charming courtyard terrace.

Diana-Dauphine without rest VISA AE
30 r. de la 1ère Armée – 03 88 36 26 61 – www.hotel-diana-dauphine.com – info@hotel-diana-dauphine.com – Fax 03 88 35 50 07 – Closed 22 December-2 January p. 6 EX **a**
45 rm – €90/150 €90/150, €11
◆ Located by the tramline leading to the old town, this hotel has been treated to a radical contemporary facelift. Modern comforts.

Hannong without rest VISA AE
15 r. du 22 Novembre – 03 88 32 16 22 – www.hotel-hannong.com – info@hotel-hannong.com – Fax 03 88 22 63 87 – Closed 4-10 January p. 8 JY **a**
72 rm – €65/157 €75/197, €14
◆ A mix of styles (classic, cosy, modern) with parquet, wood panelling, sculptures and paintings in this fine hotel built on the site of the Hannong earthenware factory (18C). Pleasant wine bar.

Du Dragon without rest VISA AE
2 r. Écarlate – 03 88 35 79 80 – www.dragon.fr – hotel@dragon.fr – Fax 03 88 25 78 95
32 rm – €79/116 €89/129, €12 p. 8 JZ **d**
◆ 17C building around a small quiet courtyard with a clearly contemporary feel. Shades of grey, designer furniture, rooms in a pared-down style and art exhibitions.

Mercure St-Jean without rest VISA AE
3 r. Maire Kuss – 03 88 32 80 80 – h1813@accor.com – Fax 03 88 23 05 39
52 rm – €69/125 €69/125, €14 p. 8 HY **e**
◆ Chain hotel between the station and the "Petite France" quarter. Contemporary decor; practical guestrooms in coffee-coloured tones. Patio with mini-fountains.

Gutenberg without rest VISA AE
31 r. des Serruriers – 03 88 32 17 15 – www.hotel-gutenberg.com – info@hotel-gutenberg.com – Fax 03 88 75 76 67 p. 9 KZ **m**
42 rm – €74/113 €74/113, €9
◆ This building dating back to 1745 is now a hotel with an eclectic mix of spacious guestrooms. The bright breakfast room is crowned by a glass roof.

Mercure Centre without rest VISA AE
25 r. Thomann – 03 90 22 70 70 – www.mercure.com – h1106@accor.com – Fax 03 90 22 70 71 p. 8 JY **q**
98 rm – €85/195 €90/205, €15
◆ A centrally located chain hotel refurbished with bright colours and designer furniture. Panoramic views from the breakfast room on the seventh floor.

Cathédrale without rest VISA AE
12-13 pl. Cathédrale – 03 88 22 12 12 – www.hotel-cathedrale.fr – reservation@hotel-cathedrale.fr – Fax 03 88 23 28 00 p. 9 KZ **h**
47 rm – €55/140 €65/150, €13
◆ This century-old residence enjoys an ideal location opposite the cathedral, which is visible from the breakfast room and some of the comfortable rooms. Religious architecture-inspired decor in some rooms.

Cardinal de Rohan without rest VISA AE
17 r. Maroquin – 03 88 32 85 11 – www.hotel-rohan.com – info@hotel-rohan.com – Fax 03 88 75 65 37 p. 9 KZ **u**
36 rm – €75/139 €75/149, €14
◆ Located near the cathedral in the pedestrianised part of town, this hotel offers guestrooms furnished in different styles (Louis XV, Louis XVI and rustic). Quality breakfast.

La Villa Novarina without rest
11 r. Westercamp – 03 90 41 18 28 – www.villanovarina.com – clauschristine@wanadoo.fr – Fax 03 90 41 49 91 VISA MC AE *p. 7* FGU **f**
12 rm – €105/175 €125/250, €15
◆ Attractive villa in modern style near the Parc de l'Orangerie. Interior decorated with family paintings and furniture. Peaceful garden, pool and courteous welcome.

Des Princes without rest VISA MC AE
33 r. Geiler – 03 88 61 55 19 – www.hotel-princes.com – hoteldesprinces@gmail.com – Fax 03 88 41 10 92 – Closed 25 July-22 August and 2-10 January
43 rm – €110 €123, €13 *p. 7* FV **t**
◆ A welcoming hotel in a quiet residential neighbourhood. Guestrooms with classic furnishings and large bathrooms. Breakfast served to a backdrop of bucolic frescoes.

Le Kléber without rest VISA MC AE
29 pl. Kléber – 03 88 32 09 53 – www.hotel-kleber.com – hotel-kleber-strasbourg@wanadoo.fr – Fax 03 88 32 50 41 *p. 8* JY **p**
30 rm – €58/78 €68/86, €9
◆ "Meringue", "Strawberry" and "Cinnamon" are just a few of the names of the rooms in this comfortable hotel. Contemporary, colourful decor with a sweet-and-savoury theme.

Couvent du Franciscain without rest
18 r. du Fg de Pierre – 03 88 32 93 93 P VISA MC AE
– www.hotel-franciscain.com – info@hotel-franciscain.com – Fax 03 88 75 68 46 – Closed 24 December-3 January *p. 8* JY **e**
43 rm – €40/64 €68/74, €10
◆ A simple yet comfortable hotel at the end of a cul-de-sac. Pleasant lounge; breakfast in a "winstub-style" basement (amusing mural).

Aux Trois Roses without rest VISA MC AE
7 r. Zürich – 03 88 36 56 95 – www.hotel3roses-strasbourg.com – info@hotel3roses-strasbourg.com – Fax 03 88 35 06 14 *p. 9* LZ **y**
32 rm – €49/79 €65/86, €8
◆ Cosy duvets and pine furniture add to the welcoming feel of the quiet guestrooms in this elegant building on the banks of the Ill. Fitness area with sauna and Jacuzzi.

Pax without rest rest, VISA MC AE
24 r. Fg National – 03 88 32 14 54 – www.paxhotel.com – info@paxhotel.com – Fax 03 88 32 01 16 – Closed 1st-10 January *p. 8* HYZ **u**
106 rm – €57/84 €69/84, €8,50
◆ This hotel is on a street accessible only by the Strasbourg tramway. Some of the rooms have been renovated and all are well kept. Common areas brightened by antique objects reminiscent of the farm.

La Belle Strasbourgeoise without rest VISA MC AE
13 r. Gén.-Offenstein – 03 88 39 68 15 – www.la-belle-strasbourgeoise.fr – contact@la-belle-strasbourgeoise.fr *p. 5* BST **t**
3 rm – €80 €90
◆ Cosy little hotel with a charming garden just a stone's throw from the centre. Tastefully decorated rooms with all the creature comforts. Copious breakfast on the terrace.

Au Crocodile (Emile Jung) VISA MC AE
10 r. Outre – 03 88 32 13 02 – www.au-crocodile.com – info@au-crocodile.com – Fax 03 88 75 72 01 – Closed 12 July-4 August, 24 December-6 January, Sunday and Monday
Rest – Menu €59 (weekday lunch), €89/128 – Carte €108/164 *p. 9* KY **x**
Spec. Foie de canard poêlé aux pommes et jus d'agrumes. Noisette de faon de biche à l'écorce d'orange (season). Meringue glacée aux fruits chauds et sorbet litchi. **Wines** Riesling, Pinot gris.
◆ Splendid wood panelling, paintings and the famous crocodile brought back from the Egyptian campaign by an Alsatian captain adorn this restaurant. Refined classical cuisine.

XXX **Buerehiesel** (Eric Westermann) VISA
at the parc de l'Orangerie – 03 88 45 56 65 – www.buerehiesel.com – reservation@buerehiesel.fr – Fax 03 88 61 32 00 – Closed 1st-21 August, 31 December-21 January, Sunday and Monday p. 7 GU **a**

Rest – Menu € 37 (weekday lunch), € 67/96 – Carte € 55/110

Spec. Schniederspaetle et cuisses de grenouille poêlées au cerfeuil. Pigeon d'Alsace farci d'un tajine de céleri. Croustillant café-caramel au beurre salé. **Wines** Pinot blanc, Riesling

◆ Following on from his father Antoine, Éric Westermann creates reasonably priced interesting cuisine at this pretty, half-timbered farmhouse in the heart of the Parc de l'Orangerie.

XXX **Maison Kammerzell et Hôtel Baumann** with rm VISA
16 pl. de la Cathédrale – 03 88 32 42 14 – www.maison-kammerzell.com – info@maison-kammerzell.com – Fax 03 88 23 03 92 – Closed 3 weeks in February p. 9 KZ **e**

9 rm – €75 €110/125, €10

Rest – Menu € 31/46 – Carte € 32/59

◆ With its stained-glass windows, paintings, wood carvings and Gothic vaulting, this 16C construction retains the feel of the Middle Ages. Sober guestrooms. An excellent brasserie menu based around traditional local cuisine. Choucroute a speciality.

XXX **Maison des Tanneurs dite "Gerwerstub"** VISA
42 r. Bain aux Plantes – 03 88 32 79 70 – www.maison-des-tanneurs.com – maison.des.tanneurs@wanadoo.fr – Fax 03 88 22 17 26 – Closed 27 July-11 August, 30 December-26 January, Sunday and Monday p. 8 JZ **t**

Rest – Menu € 25 (weekday lunch)/30 – Carte € 41/62

◆ Ideally located by the Ill, this typical Alsatian house in La Petite France district is the place to go to if you love sauerkraut.

XX **La Cambuse** VISA
1 r. des Dentelles – 03 88 22 10 22 – Fax 03 88 23 24 99 – Closed 17-31 May, 2-24 August, 1st-12 January, Sunday and Monday p. 8 JZ **a**

Rest – *(number of covers limited, pre-book)* Carte € 47/55

◆ Intimate dining room decorated in the style of a boat cabin. Fish and seafood are the specialities here, prepared in a blend of French and Asian styles (herbs, spices etc).

XX **L'Atable 77** VISA
77 Grand'Rue – 03 88 32 23 37 – www.latable77.com – latable77@free.fr – Fax 03 88 32 50 24 – Closed 1st-11 May, 26 July-16 August, 10-24 January, Sunday, Monday and lunch on public holidays p. 8 JZ **h**

Rest – Menu (€ 25), € 32/80 bi – Carte € 32/50

◆ A trendy restaurant with a resolutely contemporary feel throughout, from the paintings on the walls to the designer tableware and appetising modern cuisine. À table!

XX **Le Violon d'Ingres** VISA
1 r. Chevalier Robert, at La Robertsau – 03 88 31 39 50 – www.violondingres.com – Closed 14-28 April, 25 July-12 August, 2-10 January, Saturday lunch, Sunday dinner and Monday p. 5 CS **z**

Rest – Menu € 30/65 – Carte € 62/72

◆ Traditional Alsatian building in the residential district of Robertsau. Elegant dining area and shaded terrace; contemporary cuisine with a focus on fish.

XX **La Casserole** (Eric Girardin) VISA
24 r. des Juifs – 03 88 36 49 68 – Fax 03 88 24 25 12 – Closed 1st-11 May, 2-24 August, 24 December-4 January, Saturday lunch, Sunday and Monday p. 9 KY **b**

Rest – *(pre-book)* Menu (€ 37), € 49/78

Spec. Œuf cassé à la truffe tuber mélanosporum et topinambours. Barbue, "risotto" de céleri et sauce au curry. Mousse soufflée chaude au chocolat Guanaja. **Wines** Riesling, Pinot Noir.

◆ The two sommeliers who run this restaurant carefully and passionately select the wines at reasonable prices, which they match to a refined and inventive menu. Original designer décor.

XX **Gavroche** AC VISA MC AE
4 r. Klein – ✆ 03 88 36 82 89 – www.restaurant-gavroche.com – restaurant.gavroche@free.fr – Fax 03 88 36 82 89 – Closed 27 July-14 August, 21 December-4 January, Saturday and Sunday p. 9 KZ **g**
Rest – Menu (€ 26), € 36/56 – Carte € 52/72
◆ The Gavroche has moved to a brand new space next door to the old restaurant. Plain, elegant and contemporary setting. Modern and creative market inspired cuisine.

XX **La Vieille Tour** AC VISA MC AE
1 r. A. Seyboth – ✆ 03 88 32 54 30 – lercher@hotmail.fr – Closed Sunday except lunch in December and Monday p. 8 HZ **e**
Rest – Menu (€ 25), € 39 – Carte € 40/60
◆ The decor of this spruce, small dining room includes a Southern French colour scheme, floral displays, whole hams and fruit jars. Market menu presented on the blackboard.

XX **Côté Lac** AC P VISA MC AE
2 pl. Paris, Espace Européen de l'Entreprise ✉ 67300 Schiltigheim – ✆ 03 88 83 82 81 – www.cote-lac.com – info@cote-lac.com – Fax 03 88 83 82 83 – Closed 22 December-4 January p. 5 BS **t**
Rest – Menu (€ 25), € 53 – Carte € 36/44
◆ The large windows of this modern building open onto a small lake. Original, chic, neo-industrial decor, waterside terrace and contemporary cuisine.

XX **Umami** (René Fieger) AC VISA MC AE
✿ *8 r. des Dentelles – ✆ 03 88 32 80 53 – www.restaurant-umami.com – contact@restaurant-umami.com – Closed 30 August-14 September, 25 December-4 January, Sunday and Monday* p. 8 JZ **b**
Rest – Menu € 42/60
Spec. Tartare de langoustines. Joue de bœuf braisée aux aromates et cacahuètes. Le chocolat.
◆ According to Japanese gastronomic culture, umami is the fifth taste. The talented chef of this tiny establishment masterfully combines flavours and aromas, creating a delicious culinary score.

XX **Le Pont aux Chats** VISA MC AE
42 r. de la Krutenau – ✆ 03 88 24 08 77 – le-pont-aux-chats.restaurant@orange.fr – Fax 03 88 24 08 77 – Closed 3 weeks in August, for the Easter holidays, Saturday lunch and Wednesday p. 9 ZL **t**
Rest – Menu (€ 22), € 48/60
◆ A charming interior featuring a successful fusion of ancient timbers and contemporary furniture, with an adorable courtyard terrace. Modern menu based around seasonal produce.

XX **Pont des Vosges** VISA MC AE
15 quai Koch – ✆ 03 88 36 47 75 – pontdesvosges@noos.fr – Fax 03 88 25 16 85 – Closed Sunday p. 9 LY **h**
Rest – Carte € 30/55
◆ Located on the corner of a stone building, this brasserie is renowned for its copious traditional cuisine. Antique advertising posters and mirrors decorate the dining room.

XX **L'Alsace à Table** AC VISA MC AE
8 r. Francs-Bourgeois – ✆ 03 88 32 50 62 – www.alsace-a-table.fr – info@alsace-a-table.fr – Fax 03 88 22 44 11 p. 8 JZ **z**
Rest – Menu € 28 – Carte € 32/60
◆ Welcoming brasserie specialising in fish and seafood with a charming Belle-Époque decor (frescoes, wood panelling, stained glass). Oyster counter, lobster tank and traditional service.

XX **L'Écrin des Saveurs** AC VISA MC AE
5 r. Leitersperger ✉ 67100 – ✆ 03 88 39 21 20 – www.ecrinsaveurs.com – info@ecrinsaveurs.com – Fax 03 88 39 16 05 – Closed 18 July-9 August, 24 December-10 January, Monday dinner, Saturday lunch and Sunday p. 5 BTS **u**
Rest – Menu € 33
◆ Close to Meinau football stadium, this restaurant stands out from the crowd. The modern cuisine contrasts slightly with the old-fashioned yet cosy dining room. Cheerful service.

La Cuiller à Pot

18b r. Finkwiller – 03 88 35 56 30 – www.lacuillerapot.com – lacuillerapot@orange.fr – Closed 2-24 August, 24-26 December, 1st-4 January, Sunday, Monday and lunch on public holidays p. 8 JZ **v**

Rest – Menu (€ 19), € 38/68 bi – Carte € 50/60

◆ Popular former winstub offering up-to-date cuisine and carefully chosen wines. Art exhibitions in the contemporary setting of the upstairs dining room.

L'Atelier du Goût

17 r. des Tonneliers – 03 88 21 01 01 – www.atelier-du-gout.fr – ateliergout.morabito@free.fr – Fax 03 88 23 64 36 – Closed February school holidays, 28 July-10 August, Saturday except dinner in December, Sunday and public holidays p. 9 KZ **d**

Rest – Menu € 36 (weekdays) – Carte € 40/48

◆ A colourful designer decor sets the scene in this former winstub, turned into a laid-back restaurant devoted to good food. Appetising dishes made with organic and seasonal produce.

L'Amuse Bouche

3a r. Turenne – 03 88 35 72 82 – www.lamuse-bouche.fr – lamuse-bouche@wanadoo.fr – Fax 03 88 36 75 30 – Closed 1 week in March, 15-31 August, Saturday lunch, Monday dinner and Sunday p. 9 LY **t**

Rest – Menu € 37/77 bi – Carte € 42/54

◆ A sober décor (white walls, mirrors) is the setting for delicious contemporary cuisine.

La Vignette

29 r. Mélanie, at La Robertsau – 03 88 31 38 10 – restaurant.lavignette.robertsau@orange.fr – Fax 03 88 45 48 66 – Closed 20 July-18 August, 22 December-10 January, Saturday, Sunday and public holidays p. 5 CS **t**

Rest – Carte € 29/39

◆ An earthenware stove and old photos of the neighbourhood adorn the dining room of this café-style restaurant. Appetising, market-inspired cuisine.

La Table de Christophe

28 r. des Juifs – 03 88 24 63 27 – www.tabledechristophe.com – Fax 03 88 24 64 37 – Closed 27 April-3 May, 27 July-19 August, Monday dinner, Sunday and public holidays p. 9 KY **a**

Rest – *(pre-book)* Carte € 33/40

◆ A small neighbourhood restaurant with a rustic, welcoming feel. The chef blends local and modern culinary influences, with a respect for seasonality.

WINSTUBS : *dregional food and wines in a typical Alsatian ambiance*

L'Ami Schutz

1 Ponts Couverts – 03 88 32 76 98 – www.ami-schutz.com – info@ami-schutz.com – Fax 03 88 32 38 40 – Closed Christmas holidays p. 8 HZ **r**

Rest – Menu (€ 21 bi), € 25/41 – Carte € 29/58

◆ Between the meanders of the Ill, typical "winstub" with wood panelling and cosy banquettes (the smaller dining room has greater charm). Terrace beneath the lime trees.

S'Burjerstuewel - Chez Yvonne

10 r. Sanglier – 03 88 32 84 15 – www.chez-yvonne.net – info@chez-yvonne.net – Fax 03 88 23 00 18 p. 9 KYZ **r**

Rest – *(pre-book)* Carte € 30/60

◆ This winstub has become one of the city's institutions, witnessed by the photos and dedications of its famous guests. Regional cuisine with a modern twist.

Le Clou

3 r. Chaudron – 03 88 32 11 67 – www.le-clou.com – winstub.le.clou@wanadoo.fr – Fax 03 88 21 06 43 – Closed 27 July-8 August, Wednesday lunch, Sunday and public holidays p. 9 KY **n**

Rest – Menu (€ 15) – Carte € 26/55

◆ Traditional decor (a doll's house feel upstairs) and a friendly atmosphere characterise this well-known winstub situated near the cathedral. Generous portions.

Le Tire Bouchon
7 r. Maroquin – ✆ 03 88 22 16 32 – www.letirebouchon.fr – reservation@letirebouchon.fr – Fax 03 88 22 60 88 p. 9 KZ **t**
Rest – Menu (€ 10), € 23/32 – Carte € 23/35
◆ Customers flock here to enjoy the fine food! The modernised decor is not what you'll find in a typical winstub, though the menu remains faithful to tradition.

Fink'Stuebel with rm
26 r. Finkwiller – ✆ 03 88 25 07 57 – http://finkstuebel.free.fr – finkstuebel@orange.fr – Fax 03 88 36 48 82 – Closed 1st-8 March, Sunday and Monday p. 8 JZ **x**
4 rm – †€ 66 ††€, ☕ € 9
Rest – Menu € 10 (weekday lunch)/35 – Carte € 30/54
◆ A half-timbered construction with bare floorboards, regional furniture and floral tablecloths, the Fink'Stuebel is the epitome of a traditional winstub. Local cuisine; foie gras to the fore. Recently refurbished and well-appointed guestrooms decorated in Alsatian style.

Au Pont du Corbeau
21 quai St-Nicolas – ✆ 03 88 35 60 68 – corbeau@reperes.com – Fax 03 88 25 72 45 – Closed August, February holidays, Sunday lunch and Saturday except in December p. 9 KZ **b**
Rest – Menu (€ 12) – Carte € 24/38
◆ Renowned restaurant on the banks of the Ill, next to the Alsatian Folk Art Museum. Regionally inspired Renaissance decor, and a menu that focuses on local specialities.

S'Muensterstuewel
8 pl. Marché aux Cochons de Lait – ✆ 03 88 32 17 63 – info@bateaux-strasbourg.fr – Fax 03 88 21 96 02 – Closed August, 25-31 December, 1st-11 January, 1st-8 March and Sunday p. 9 KZ **y**
Rest – Menu (€ 15), € 19/49 – Carte € 37/55
◆ Former butcher's shop transformed into a traditional winstub. Terrace overlooking the picturesque Place du Marché aux Cochons de Lait. Home-produced salted and cured meats.

Surrounding area

in Reichstett **7 km north by D 468 and D 37 or by A 4 and D 63 – pop. 4 882 – alt. 141 m – ✉ 67116**

L'Aigle d'Or without rest
(near the church) – ✆ 03 88 20 07 87 – www.aigledor.com – info@aigledor.com – Fax 03 88 81 83 75 – Closed 31 July-23 August and 25 December-3 January
17 rm – †€ 59/99 ††€ 59/99, ☕ € 10 p. 5 BR **a**
◆ Attractive half-timbered façade in the heart of a picturesque village. Small yet charming rooms decorated in warm tones. Smart breakfast room.

in La Wantzenau **12 km northeast by D 468 – pop. 5 859 – alt. 130 m – ✉ 67610**

Le Moulin de la Wantzenau
3 impasse du Moulin, 1.5 km south on the D 468 – ✆ 03 88 59 22 22 – www.moulin-wantzenau.com – moulin-wantzenau@wanadoo.fr – Fax 03 88 59 22 00 – Closed 24 December-5 January p. 5 CR **z**
20 rm – †€ 70/100 ††€ 70/100, ☕ € 13 – ½ P € 74/83
Rest *Au Moulin* – see below
◆ A tranquil country setting, pleasant lounge, exquisitely decorated guestrooms, display of artwork and a splendid breakfast are the main selling-points of this former mill on the banks of the Ill.

Relais de la Poste with rm rest,
21 r. Gén. de Gaulle – ✆ 03 88 59 24 80 – www.relais-poste.com – info@relais-poste.com – Fax 03 88 59 24 89 – Closed 27 July-10 August, 2-12 January and 23 February-2 March p. 5 CR **a**
18 rm – †€ 85/95 ††€ 85/155, ☕ € 18 – ½ P € 155
Rest – *(closed Saturday lunch, Sunday dinner and Monday)* Menu (€ 30), € 55/135 – Carte € 62/104
◆ Typical Alsatian house with an elegant decor of panelling, frescoes, coffered ceiling and veranda overlooking the garden. Updated traditional cuisine and impressive wine list. Guestrooms gradually renovated in contemporary style.

XXX **Zimmer**

23 r. Héros – ✆ 03 88 96 62 08 – www.restaurant-zimmer.fr – zimmer-nadeau.restaurant@neuf.fr – Fax 03 88 96 37 40 – Closed 6-22 October, 24 February-5 March, Sunday dinner and Monday except public holidays *p. 5* CR **r**

Rest – Menu (€ 23), € 29 (weekdays)/64 – Carte € 52/66

◆ A good choice of contemporary dishes served in three small and tastefully decorated dining rooms.

XX **Les Semailles**

10 r. Petit-Magmod – ✆ 03 88 96 38 38 – www.semailles.fr – info@semailles.fr – Fax 03 88 68 09 06 – Closed 11-31 August, 15 February-2 March, Sunday dinner, Wednesday and Thursday *p. 5* CR **s**

Rest – Menu (€ 22), € 28 (weekday lunch), € 41/62 bi – Carte approx. € 42

◆ This 19C house has benefited from a recent facelift, both inside and out. Attractive veranda and shaded terrace perfect for summer dining. Up-to-date menu.

XX **Au Moulin** – Hôtel Au Moulin

1.5 km south on the D 468 – ✆ 03 88 96 20 01 – www.restaurant-moulin-wantzenau.fr – philippe.clauss@wanadoo.fr – Fax 03 88 68 07 97 – Closed 8-28 July, 26 December-7 January, 26 February-8 March, Sunday dinner and dinner on public holidays *p. 5* CR **z**

Rest – Menu (€ 20), € 25 (weekdays)/60 – Carte € 39/65

◆ Elegant modernised dining rooms occupying the outbuildings of a former mill. Contemporary cuisine with an emphasis on local produce and regional specialities.

X **Le Jardin Secret**

32 r. de la Gare – ✆ 03 88 96 63 44 – www.restaurant-jardinsecret.fr – contact@restaurant-jardinsecret.fr – Closed Saturday lunch, Sunday dinner and Monday

Rest – Menu (€ 25), € 33/74 bi – Carte approx. € 35 *p. 5* CR **v**

◆ Welcoming restaurant offering up-to-date cuisine. Minimalist interior embellished by displays of artwork.

X **Au Pont de l'Ill**

2 r. Gén. Leclerc – ✆ 03 88 96 29 44 – www.aupontdelill.com – aupontdelill@orange.fr – Fax 03 88 96 21 18 – Closed 10-31 August and Saturday lunch *p. 5* CR **u**

Rest – Menu (€ 12), € 22/44 – Carte € 25/49

◆ Seafood and fish recipes are given pride of place in this brasserie spread over five rooms in different styles: marine style, Art Nouveau, etc. Shaded terrace.

in Illkirch-Graffenstaden **5 km by Colmar road** BST **or by A 35 (exit 7) – pop. 25 600 – alt. 140 m – ✉ 67400**

Alsace

187 rte de Lyon – ✆ 03 90 40 35 00 – www.hotelalsace.com – contact@hotelalsace.com – Fax 03 90 40 35 01 – Closed 31 December-3 January *p. 5* BT **d**

40 rm – †€ 64/82 ††€ 64/82, ☕ € 9 – ½ P € 53/60

Rest – *(closed 21 December-3 January, Saturday, Sunday and public holidays)* Menu (€ 12), € 22/25 – Carte € 22/37

◆ Overlooking the main square, this hotel has bright, functional and spacious guestrooms. Those at the back are quieter. A few Alsace-themed frescoes add a cheery atmosphere to the rustic dining room. Traditional menu.

XXX **À l'Agneau**

185 rte de Lyon – ✆ 03 88 66 06 58 – www.agneau-illkirch.com – agneau-illkirch@orange.fr – Fax 03 88 67 05 84 – Closed 3 August-1st September, 30 December-12 January, Sunday dinner, Monday and Tuesday *p. 5* BT **a**

Rest – Menu (€ 13), € 19 (weekday lunch), € 33/39 – Carte € 37/53

◆ Behind the façade and fresco are three personalised dining rooms (with a contemporary, traditional or Baroque décor). Classical cuisine with a creative touch.

direction ④ **11 km on D 1083 – ✉ 67400 Illkirch-Graffenstaden**

Novotel Strasbourg-Sud rm,
Exit 7, Z. A. de l'Ill ✉ 67118 Geispolsheim – ✆ *03 88 66 21 56*
– www.novotel.com – h0441@accor.com – Fax 03 88 67 21 63 *p. 5* BT **u**
76 rm – †€ 65/149 ††€ 65/149, ☕ € 14 **Rest** – Carte € 23/40
◆ Chain hotel, near main roads, offering spacious rooms renovated according to the new Novotel standards. Mini golf. Restaurant with contemporary setting and automobile-theme bar. Small flower garden and vegetable garden.

in Fegersheim 14 km to ④ by A 35 (exit 7), N 283 and D 1083 – pop. 4 846 – alt. 145 m – ✉ 67640

Auberge du Bruchrhein
24 r. de Lyon – ✆ *03 88 64 17 77 – Fax 03 88 64 17 77 – Closed Sunday dinner, Monday dinner and Thursday dinner* *p. 4* AT **x**
Rest – Menu (€ 13), € 18 (weekday lunch), € 24/29 – Carte € 37/50
◆ Modern, unpretentious cuisine, based around high-quality produce and with a regional bias. Simple interior, small terrace, and the bonus of a warm and welcoming atmosphere.

in Lipsheim to ④ by A 35, D 1083 and D 221 – pop. 2 527 – alt. 146 m – ✉ 67640

Alizés without rest
r. des Vosges – ✆ *03 88 59 02 00 – www.hotel-les-alizes.com – hotellesalizes@wanadoo.fr – Fax 03 88 64 21 61 – Closed 23 December-1st January* *p. 4* AT **e**
49 rm – †€ 63 ††€ 76, ☕ € 10
◆ A property built in local style, whose primary asset is its quiet rural location. Bright, functional guestrooms, plus a swimming pool which overlooks the forest.

in Blaesheim 19 km by A 35 (exit 9), D 1422 and D 84 – pop. 1 369 – alt. 150 m – ✉ 67113

Au Bœuf rm, rest,
– ✆ *03 88 68 68 99 – www.hotel-au-boeuf.com – auboeuf.resa@wanadoo.fr – Fax 03 88 68 60 07 – Closed 26 December-13 January* *p. 4* AT **q**
22 rm – †€ 59 ††€ 76, ☕ € 11 – 2 suites – ½ P € 72
Rest – *(closed Saturday lunch and Sunday)* Menu (€ 12), € 19 – Carte € 25/45
◆ A village inn with identical guestrooms that are large, comfortable and well-maintained. Regional dishes served in a veranda dining room with a mix of contemporary and rustic decor (earthenware plates, stove and wood panelling).

in Entzheim 12 km by A 35 (exit 8), D 400 and D 392 – pop. 1 837 – alt. 150 m – ✉ 67960

Père Benoit rm, rest,
34 rte de Strasbourg – ✆ *03 88 68 98 00 – www.hotel-perebenoit.com – resa@hotel-perebenoit.com – Fax 03 88 68 64 56 – Closed 26 July-16 August and 24 December-3 January* *p. 4* AT **h**
60 rm – †€ 65 ††€ 71, ☕ € 8,50
Rest *Steinkeller* – ✆ *03 88 68 91 65 (closed Saturday lunch, Monday lunch and Sunday)* Menu € 19/24 – Carte € 22/45
◆ A delightful, Alsace-style half-timbered farmhouse dating from the 18C with large flower-decked courtyard. Traditional decor and cosy atmosphere. Attractive rustic dining room crowned by a vaulted ceiling, with more of a winstub style on the first floor. Regional menu, including wood-baked "flammekueches" (Alsatian pizza).

in Ostwald 7 km by Schirmeck road D 392 and D 484 orby A35 (exit 7) and D 484 – pop. 10 500 – alt. 140 m – ✉ 67540

Château de l'Île
4 quai Heydt – ✆ *03 88 66 85 00 – www.chateau-ile.com – ile@grandesetapes.fr – Fax 03 88 66 85 49* *p. 5* BT **r**
60 rm – †€ 205/610 ††€ 205/610, ☕ € 23 – 2 suites
Rest – Menu (€ 26), € 31/95 bi – Carte € 29/71
Rest *Winstub* – Menu (€ 26), € 31/39 bi – Carte € 30/44
◆ 19C manor house surrounded by recent, half-timbered homes in a wooded, 4-ha park bordering the Ill. Well-kept rooms with period-style furniture. Refined dining room where the emphasis is on classical cuisine. Attractive riverside terrace. This elegant winstub in a verdant setting offers a sophisticated take on traditional cuisine.

in Lingolsheim 5 km by Schirmeck road (D 392) – pop. 17 100 – alt. 140 m – ✉ 67380

Kyriad without rest
59 r. Mar. Foch – ☎ 03 88 76 11 00 – www.kyriadstrasbourg.com – hotelkyriad@evc.net – Fax 03 88 77 39 31 p. 5 BS **a**
37 rm – †€ 56/78 ††€ 56/85, ☕ € 9
◆ This hotel near the airport is part of a residential and shopping district. Comfortable, functional and well-appointed rooms. Pleasant, modern lounge bar.

À la Diligence
7 r. Mar. Foch – ☎ 03 88 78 32 24 – diligence@estvideo.fr – Fax 03 88 78 40 48 – Closed 2-10 August p. 5 BS **p**
Rest – Menu € 40 – Carte € 32/50
◆ Near the Tanneries Park, this inviting establishment is home to a small rustic dining room and bright veranda. Concise market fresh seasonal menu.

in Mittelhausbergen 5 km northwest by D 31 – pop. 1 738 – alt. 155 m – ✉ 67206

Tilleul with rm
5 rte de Strasbourg – ☎ 03 88 56 18 31 – www.autilleul.fr – autilleul@wanadoo.fr – Fax 03 88 56 07 23 – Closed 2-16 August, 15-21 February, Tuesday, Wednesday, Saturday lunch and Sunday dinner p. 5 BS **v**
22 rm – †€ 60/65 ††€ 66/72, ☕ € 11 – ½ P € 70/80
Rest – Menu € 34/39 – Carte € 40/50
Rest *La Stub 1888* – Menu (€ 13), € 18 (lunch), € 25/40
◆ This traditional inn dating back to 1888 is in the process of a contemporary makeover. Modern cuisine in an elegant setting. Neo-rustic setting and local dishes at La Stub. Simple practical guestrooms.

in Pfulgriesheim 10 km northwest by D 31 – pop. 1 281 – alt. 135 m – ✉ 67370

Bürestubel
8 r. Lampertheim – ☎ 03 88 20 01 92 – www.restaurantburestubel.com – restaurant.burestubel@wanadoo.fr – Fax 03 88 20 48 97 – Closed 26 July-11 August, 7 February-18 March, Tuesday from January to October, Sunday from November to December and Monday p. 4 AR **a**
Rest – Menu € 17/28 – Carte € 21/48
◆ Pretty half-timbered farmhouse home to a vast "winstub". Rustic or stately rooms, with colourful ceilings. Flambéed tarts and other regional specialities.

in Plobsheim 17 km by A35 (exit 7) N 283, N 353 and D 468 – pop. 3 651 – alt. 150 m – ✉ 67115

Le Kempferhof
351 r. du Moulin, at the golf course – ☎ 03 88 98 72 72 – www.golf-kempferhof.com – info@golf-kempferhof.com – Fax 03 88 98 74 76 – Open 16 March-13 December
25 rm – †€ 180/280 ††€ 180/280, ☕ € 20 – 4 suites – ½ P € 170/280
Rest – Menu (€ 35), € 40 – Carte € 45/55
◆ Attractive 19C property on a wooded 85-hectare estate with 18-hole golf course. Individually furnished rooms, those in the outbuildings decorated in contemporary style. Bright dining room-veranda and terrace overlooking the green. International menu with a good choice of wines.

STURZELBRONN – 57 Moselle – 307 Q4 – pop. 201 – alt. 250 m – ✉ 57230 27 D1

Paris 449 – Strasbourg 68 – Bitche 13 – Haguenau 39 – Wissembourg 34

Au Relais des Bois
13 r. Principale – ☎ 03 87 06 20 30 – www.relaisdesbois.com – denis.hoff@wanadoo.fr – Fax 03 87 06 21 22 – Closed Monday and Tuesday
Rest – Menu € 11 (weekday lunch), € 18/25 – Carte € 22/41
◆ Small family-run establishment in the heart of a village of the Vosges du Nord regional park. Rustic setting, local cuisine, terrace and garden.

SUBLIGNY – 89 Yonne – **319** C2 – see Sens

SUCY-EN-BRIE – 94 Val-de-Marne – **312** E3 – **101** 28 – see Paris, Area

SULLY-SUR-LOIRE – 45 Loiret – **318** L5 – pop. 5 830 – alt. 115 m 12 **C2**
– ✉ 45600 **Châteaux of the Loire**

Paris 149 – Bourges 84 – Gien 25 – Montargis 40 – Orléans 51 – Vierzon 84

Office de tourisme, place de Gaulle ✆ 02 38 36 23 70, Fax 02 38 36 32 21

de Sully-sur-Loire Domaine de l'Ousseau, 4 km on the Bourges road, ✆ 02 38 36 52 08

Château★: framework★★.

SULLY-SUR-LOIRE

Abreuvoir (R. de l') 2
Béthune (Av. de) 3
Champ-de-Foire (Bd du) 4
Chemin-de-Fer (Av. du) 5
Grand-Sully (R. du) 6
Jeanne-d'Arc (Bd) 7
Marronniers (R. des) 9
Porte-Berry (R.) 10
Porte-de-Sologne (R.) 12
St-François (R. du Fg) 15
St-Germain (R. du Fg) 16
Venerie (Av. de la) 20

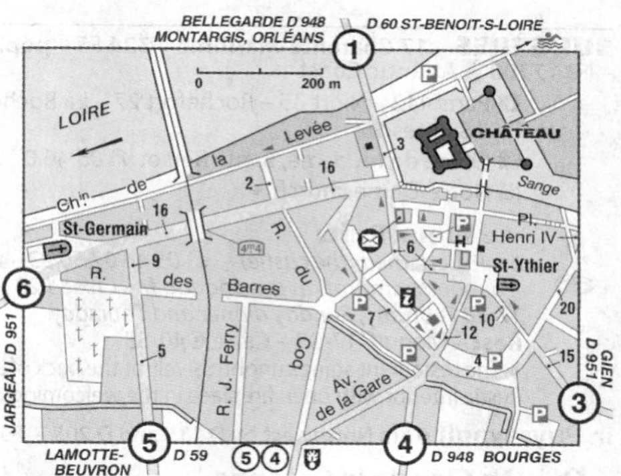

Hostellerie du Château rm, rm, VISA AE
4 rte de Paris at St-Père-sur-Loire, 1 km by ① – ✆ 02 38 36 24 44 – www.hostellerie-du-chateau.fr – resasylvie@wanadoo.fr – Fax 02 38 36 62 40
42 rm – †€ 46/68 ††€ 46/68, ☕ € 8 – ½ P € 62
Rest – Menu (€ 25), € 28/46 – Carte € 45/74
♦ This recently built hotel provides very well-kept, functional and pleasant rooms. Half of them offer a view of Sully château. Slightly British atmosphere in the comfortable dining room decorated with wood panelling. Traditional menu.

in Bordes 6 km by ①, D 948 and D 961 – pop. 1 678 – alt. 132 m – ✉ 45460

La Bonne Étoile VISA
D 952 – ✆ 02 38 35 52 15 – Fax 02 38 35 52 15 – Closed Sunday dinner and Monday
Rest – Menu € 16/36
♦ Small and attractive country inn along a busy road. The dining room has recently been given a facelift, with new decor, chairs and tableware. Traditional cuisine.

SUPERDÉVOLUY – 05 Hautes-Alpes – **334** D4 – Winter sports : 40 **B1**
1500/2500m 1 28 – ✉ 05250 **French Alps**

Paris 654 – Gap 36 – Grenoble 92 – La Mure 52

Les Chardonnelles VISA AE
– ✆ 04 92 58 86 90 – www.hotel-chardonnelles.com – info@hotel-chardonnelles.com – Fax 04 92 58 87 76 – Open 13 June-7 September and 22 December-22 April
42 rm – †€ 58/93 ††€ 74/110, ☕ € 7 – ½ P € 60/82
Rest – Menu € 15 (lunch)/35 – Carte € 26/48
♦ This large chalet just outside the resort is the starting point for a number of rambling itineraries. Warm rooms (non-smoking), heated pool, steam bath, sauna and Jacuzzi. Restaurant offering Alpine cuisine with a choice of tartiflettes, fondues and raclettes.

LE SUQUET – 06 Alpes-Maritimes – **341** E4 – alt. 400 m – ✉ 06450 41 **D2**
Lantosque

Paris 878 – Levens 19 – Nice 46 – Puget-Théniers 48 – St-Martin-Vésubie 21

Auberge du Bon Puits

– ✆ 04 93 03 17 65 – lebonpuits@wanadoo.fr – Fax 04 93 03 10 48 – Open 20 April-1st December and closed Tuesday except 10 July-30 August

8 rm – †€ 62/65 ††€ 63/68, ☕ € 10 – ½ P € 65/70

Rest – Menu (€ 20 bi), € 24/36 – Carte € 32/38

◆ The road separates this solid house from a small animal park with children's area on the banks of the Vésubie. Renovated and soundproofed rooms. Beams and a monumental stone fireplace decorate the dining room. Regional cuisine.

SURESNES – 92 Hauts-de-Seine – **311** J2 – **101** 14 – see Paris, Area

SURGÈRES – 17 Charente-Maritime – **324** F3 – pop. 5 905 – alt. 16 m 38 **B2**
– ✉ 17700 Atlantic Coast

Paris 442 – Niort 35 – Rochefort 27 – La Rochelle 38 – St-Jean-d'Angély 30 – Saintes 55

Office de tourisme, 5, rue Bersot ✆ 05 46 07 20 02, Fax 05 46 07 20 30

Notre-Dame church ★.

Le Vieux Puits

6 r. P. Bert, (near the castle) – ✆ 05 46 07 50 83 – www.vieux-puits.com – gireaudrestauration@wanadoo.fr – Closed 28 September-14 October, 17-28 February, Sunday dinner and Thursday

Rest – Menu € 17/38 – Carte € 40/55

◆ The restaurant stands unobtrusively at the back of a paved courtyard (summer terrace). Rustic interior with open fireplace in the welcoming dining room. Seasonal menu.

in Puyravault 6 km Northwest by D 115 and D 205 – ✉ 17700

Le Clos de la Garenne

9 r. Garenne – ✆ 05 46 35 47 71 – www.closdelagarenne.com – info@closdelagarenne.com – Fax 05 46 35 47 91

4 rm ☕ – †€ 60 ††€ 67/77

Table d'hôte – *(closed Wednesday, Saturday and Sunday)* Menu € 25 bi

◆ Each of the rooms in this authentic Charentes-style residence evokes a different period: Belle Epoque room, large 18C lounge, 17C dining room, etc. The 4-ha park is home to donkeys, sheep and hens. Family cooking varying with the seasons and market availability.

SURVILLIERS – 95 Val-d'Oise – **305** G6 – pop. 3 710 – alt. 110 m 19 **C1**
– ✉ 95470

Paris 37 – Chantilly 14 – Compiègne 48 – Meaux 39 – Pontoise 45 – Senlis 14

Novotel

rm, rest, VISA AE

D 16, via Survilliers interchange of A1 – ✆ 01 34 68 69 80 – www.novotel.com – h0459@accor.com – Fax 01 34 68 64 94

79 rm – †€ 80/280 ††€ 80/280, ☕ € 16 **Rest** – Menu (€ 14) – Carte € 20/50

◆ Functional and soundproofed bedrooms. There is a volleyball court, children's play area and a boules pitch. Traditional menu served in a dining room extended by a veranda or on a poolside summer terrace.

SUZE-LA-ROUSSE – Drôme – **332** C8 – pop. 1 787 – alt. 92 m 44 **B3**
– ✉ 26790 Provence

Paris 641 – Avignon 59 – Bollène 7 – Nyons 28 – Orange 23 – Valence 85

Office de tourisme, le village ✆ 04 75 04 81 41, Fax 04 75 04 81 41

Les Aiguières

r. Fontaine-d'Argent – ✆ 04 75 98 40 80 – www.les-aiguieres.com – brigitte@les-aiguieres.com – Closed 22 December-5 January

5 rm ☕ – †€ 75 ††€ 85 **Table d'hôte** – Menu € 28 bi

◆ Provençal inspired rooms in this 18C house with large sitting room (open fire in winter), garden and pool, two minutes from the château and its university of wine. Wholesome home cooking, special "wine and food pairing" menu by reservation.

TAILLECOURT – 25 Doubs – 321 L2 – see Audincourt

TAIN-L'HERMITAGE – 26 Drôme – 332 C3 – pop. 5 764 – alt. 124 m – ✉ 26600 43 E2

▶ Paris 545 – Grenoble 97 – Le Puy-en-Velay 105 – St-Étienne 76 – Valence 18 – Vienne 59

ℹ Office de tourisme, place du 8 mai 1945 ☏ 04 75 08 06 81, Fax 04 75 08 34 59

👁 Belvédère de Pierre-Aiguille (Viewpoint)★ North: 4 km by D 241.

TAIN-L'HERMITAGE

Batie (Quai de la) .... C 3
Defer (Pl. H.) .... C 8
Église (Pl. de l') .... C 12
Gaulle (Q. Gén.-de) .... C 14
Grande-Rue .... B 16
Jean-Jaurès (Av.) .... BC
Michel (R. F.) .... C 21
Peala (R. J.) .... B 24
Prés.-Roosevelt (Av.) .... C 29
Rostaing (Q. A.) .... C 30
Seguin (Q. M.) .... B 32
Souvenir-Français (Av. du) .... C 33
Taurobole (Pl. du) .... BC
8-Mai-1945 (Pl. du) .... BC 39

TOURNON-SUR-RHÔNE

Dumaine (R. A.) .... B 9
Faure (R. G.) .... B 13
Grande-Rue .... B
Juventon (Av. M.) .... B 19
Thiers (R.) .... B 35

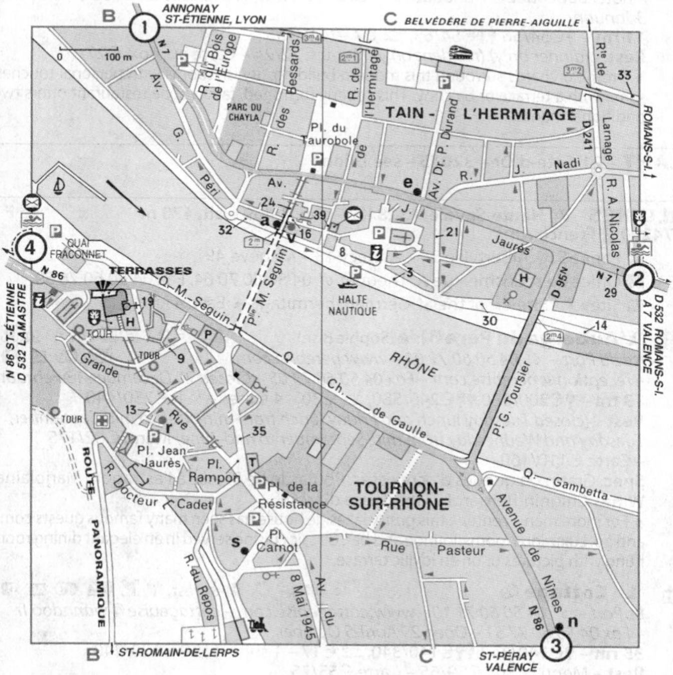

Le Pavillon de l'Ermitage

69 av J. Jaurès – ☏ 04 75 08 65 00

– www.pavillon-ermitage.com – pavillon.26@wanadoo.fr
– Fax 04 75 08 66 05 C e

rm, VISA MC AE

44 rm – †€ 82/85 ††€ 93/97, ☕ € 11 – 2 suites

Rest – *(Closed 24 December-2 January, Saturday and Sunday from November to March)* Menu € 13/28

◆ A large building with modern rooms. Ask for one on the swimming pool side with a balcony overlooking the Hermitage hills and the Tournon heights. Traditional dishes on the terrace or in the dining room depending on the weather.

Les 2 Coteaux without rest
18 r. J.-Péala – ✆ 04 75 08 33 01 – www.hotel-les-2-coteaux.com – hotel2coteaux@wanadoo.fr – Fax 04 75 08 44 20 B **a**
18 rm – €52/62 €60/67, €9
◆ This family-run hotel is in a quiet location opposite the old bridge spanning the Rhone. Bright and airy guestrooms, some with a balcony.

Le Quai
17 r. J.-Péala – ✆ 04 75 07 05 90 – www.michelchabran.fr – chabran@michelchabran.fr – Fax 04 75 06 55 55 B **v**
Rest – Menu (€25), €33 – Carte €36/45
◆ The Rhône flows past this restaurant, with views of the vineyards in the distance. Updated dining room with a minimalist feel (wenge furniture, old photos); pleasant terrace.

Romans road 4 km by ② – ✉ **26600 Tain-l'Hermitage**

L'Abricotine
rte de Romans – ✆ 04 75 07 44 60 – www.hotel-abricotine.com – hotel.abricotine@wanadoo.fr – Fax 04 75 07 47 97 – Closed 24 December-3 January
11 rm – €54/56 €54/65, €7 – ½ P €55
Rest – *(dinner only) (resident only)* Menu €22/24 – Carte approx. €27
◆ Drôme orchards surround this modern building. Stylish rooms with personal touches, some with a terrace or balcony. This soberly furnished, family style restaurant offers two traditional menus.

TALANT – **21 Côte-d'Or** – **320** J5 – **see Dijon**

TALLOIRES – **74 Haute-Savoie** – **328** K5 – **pop. 1 469** – **alt. 470 m** 46 **F1**
– ✉ **74290** **French Alps**

Paris 551 – Albertville 34 – Annecy 13 – Megève 49
Office de tourisme, rue A. Theuriet ✆ 04 50 60 70 64, Fax 04 50 60 76 59
Site★★ - Site★★ of the St-Germain hermitage ★ East: 4 km.

L'Auberge du Père Bise (Sophie Bise)
rte du Port – ✆ 04 50 60 72 01 – www.perebise.com – reception@perebise.com – Fax 04 50 60 73 05 – Closed 20 December-13 February
19 rm – €200/580 €240/580, €30 – 4 suites – ½ P €250/440
Rest – *(closed Tuesday lunch and Friday lunch from mid-June to mid-September, Tuesday and Wednesday from mid-September to mid-June)* Menu €82/175 – Carte €110/160
Spec. Gratin de queues d'écrevisses. Poularde de Bresse à l'estragon. Marjolaine.
Wines Chignin-Bergeron, Mondeuse d'Arbin.
◆ For more than a century, this pretty lakeside house has seen many famous guests come and go. Luxurious rooms, lounge and bar. Classic cuisine served in an elegant dining room hung with pictures or on an idyllic terrace.

Le Cottage rest,
Le Port – ✆ 04 50 60 71 10 – www.cottagebise.com – cottagebise@wanadoo.fr – Fax 04 50 60 77 51 – Open 29 April-5 October
35 rm – €140/340 €140/340, €17 – 1 suite – ½ P €120/240
Rest – Menu (€30), €39/65 – Carte €55/75
◆ Facing the mooring, three 1930s cottages. The quiet personalised rooms face the lake, garden or mountain (three suites). Classic cuisine served in an elegant dining room or on the pleasant terrace.

L'Abbaye
chemin des Moines – ✆ 04 50 60 77 33 – www.abbaye-talloires.com – abbaye@abbaye-talloires.com – Fax 04 50 60 78 81 – Open mid February-mid November
33 rm – €147/630 €147/630, €23
Rest – *(Closed Monday and Tuesday except July-August)* Menu €48 (dinner)/80 – Carte €60/90
◆ Cézanne stayed in this elegant 17C Benedictine abbey, offering accommodation in either classic or Savoy style; garden overlooking the lake (private jetty). Modern cuisine served in an elegant dining room or on the terrace.

La Charpenterie
72 r. A. Theuriet – 04 50 60 70 47 – www.la-charpenterie.com – contact@la-charpenterie.com – Fax 04 50 60 79 07 – Closed 12 November-5 February
18 rm – €75/110 €75/110, € 10 – ½ P € 69/86
Rest – Menu € 24/45 – Carte approx. € 38
◆ Chalet with decorated balconies. Warm and comfortable wood decor. Many rooms with terrace. Old photos decorate the walls of the panelled dining room. Traditional fare (cheese specialities).

XX **Villa des Fleurs** with rm
rte du Port – 04 50 60 71 14 – www.hotel-lavilladesfleurs74.com – lavilladesfleurs@wanadoo.fr – Fax 04 50 60 74 06 – Closed 15 November-10 February, Sunday dinner and Monday
9 rm – €88/125 €98/135, € 13 – ½ P € 100/109
Rest – Menu (€ 20), € 33/60 – Carte € 38/72
◆ In the village, a comfortable Savoy villa surrounded by greenery. Local cuisine and fish from Lake Annecy. Very peaceful rooms.

in Angon **2 km south by D 909a – ✉ 74290 Veyrier-du-Lac**

Les Grillons
– 04 50 60 70 31 – www.hotel-grillons.com – accueil@hotel-grillons.com – Fax 04 50 60 72 19 – Open 10 April-16 October
30 rm – €55/97 €80/134 **Rest** – Menu € 25/48 – Carte € 25/58
◆ Guesthouse-style hotel with well-maintained rooms, most with views of the lake. The large swimming pool is very pleasant in summer. The dining room has a new contemporary look with exposed beams, plants and a red and white colour scheme.

TALMONT-SUR-GIRONDE – 17 Charente-Maritime – 324 E6 – pop. 78 – alt. 20 m – ✉ 17120 Atlantic Coast
38 **B3**

Paris 503 – Blaye 72 – La Rochelle 93 – Royan 18 – Saintes 36

Site★ of Ste-Radegonde church ★.

XX **L'Estuaire** with rm
au Caillaud, 1 av. Estuaire – 05 46 90 43 85 – www.hotellestuaire.com – hotellestuaire@orange.fr – Fax 05 46 90 43 88 – Closed 16 November-13 December and 12 January-10 February
6 rm – €55/66 €55/66, € 8
Rest – *(Closed Monday and Tuesday except July-August)* Menu (€ 22), € 30/42 – Carte € 25/65
◆ Rustic restaurant in pastel tones superbly situated overlooking the Gironde. Regional dishes and local fish on the menu. Quiet, spacious and well-kept rooms.

LA TAMARISSIÈRE – 34 Hérault – 339 F9 – see Agde

TAMNIÈS – 24 Dordogne – 329 H6 – pop. 301 – alt. 200 m – ✉ 24620
4 **D3**

Paris 522 – Brive-la-Gaillarde 47 – Périgueux 60 – Sarlat-la-Canéda 14

Laborderie
in the village – 05 53 29 68 59 – www.hotel-laborderie.com – info@hotel-laborderie.com – Fax 05 53 29 65 31 – Open 4 April-1st November
45 rm – €34/84 €40/92, € 9 – ½ P € 45/75
Rest – *(closed Monday lunch, Tuesday lunch and Wednesday lunch)* Menu € 22/44 – Carte € 25/65
◆ Périgord establishment with three annexes and vast park overlooking the valley, offering quiet rooms, some rustic, some modern. Good old-fashioned regional cuisine served in a country style dining room or on the terrace in fine weather.

TANCARVILLE – 76 Seine-Maritime – 304 C5 – pop. 1 233 – alt. 10 m – ✉ 76430 Normandy
33 **C2**

Paris 175 – Caen 86 – Le Havre 32 – Pont-Audemer 24 – Rouen 64

Access Tancarville Bridge. toll in 2007 : car 2.30, car and caravan 2.90, lorries and coaches 3.50 to 6.10, free for motorcycles 02 35 39 65 60.

★ sur estuaire.

XXX **La Marine** with rm

10 rte du Havre, at the end of the bridge (D 982) – ✆ 02 35 39 77 15 – www.lamarine-tancarville.com – hoteldelamarine2@wanadoo.fr – Fax 02 35 38 03 30 – Closed 22 July-20 August and Sunday evening

8 rm – †€ 65/85 ††€ 70/85, ☕ € 10 – ½ P € 80/95

Rest – *(Closed Saturday lunch and Monday)* Menu € 27 (weekdays)/65 – Carte € 80/91

Rest *Le Bistrot* – *(lunch only)* Menu € 13/20

◆ Hotel on the banks of the Seine, at the foot of the famous Tancarville bridge. Traditional seasonal cuisine based on fresh market produce and fish. Recently renovated bedrooms. Bistro with a wooden decor.

LA TANIA – **73 Savoie** – **333** M5 – **see Courchevel**

TANINGES – **74 Haute-Savoie** – **328** M4 – **pop. 3 394** – **alt. 640 m** – ✉ **74440** **French Alps** 46 **F1**

Paris 570 – Annecy 68 – Chamonix-Mont-Blanc 51 – Genève 42 – Thonon-les-Bains 46

Office de tourisme, avenue des Thézières ✆ 04 50 34 25 05, Fax 04 50 34 83 96

XX **La Crémaillère**

au lac de Flérier, 1 km south-west – ✆ 04 50 34 21 98 – Closed 11-29 January, Monday dinner, Wednesday except July-August and Sunday dinner

Rest – *(number of covers limited, pre-book)* Menu € 25/47 – Carte € 39/65

◆ Fine lakeside position. Sit near the bay window or on the panoramic terrace in fine weather. Quintessentially traditional cuisine.

TANNERON – **83 Var** – **340** Q4 – **pop. 1 473** – **alt. 376 m** – ✉ **83440** **French Riviera** 42 **E2**

Paris 903 – Cannes 20 – Draguignan 53 – Grasse 20 – Nice 49 – Saint-Raphaël 37

Syndicat d'initiative, place de la Mairie ✆ 04 93 60 71 73

XX **Le Champfagou** with rm

53 pl. du Village – ✆ 04 93 60 68 30 – www.lechampfagou.fr – lechampfagou@wanadoo.fr – Fax 04 93 60 70 60 – Closed in November, dinner in January and February, Monday July-August, Sunday dinner, Tuesday dinner and Wednesday

9 rm – †€ 50 ††€ 50, ☕ € 8 – ½ P € 60 **Rest** – Menu € 31/55 – Carte € 40/50

◆ A discreetly Provençal dining room and pleasant flower-decked terrace in a peaceful village, renowned for its mimosas. Provençal cuisine with personal touches. Small simple rooms.

TANTONVILLE – **54 Meurthe-et-Moselle** – **307** H8 – **pop. 629** – **alt. 300 m** – ✉ **54116** 26 **B2**

Paris 327 – Épinal 48 – Lunéville 35 – Nancy 29 – Toul 37 – Vittel 44

XX **La Commanderie**

1 r. Pasteur – ✆ 03 83 52 49 83 – www.restaurant-la-commanderie.com – contact@restaurant-la-commanderie.com – Fax 03 83 52 49 83 – Closed 24 August-10 September, 2-10 January, Tuesday dinner, Wednesday dinner, dinner and Monday

Rest – Menu (€ 12), € 30/55 – Carte € 32/62

◆ This early 20C house, formerly the headquarters of the Tourtel brasserie, is now an elegant restaurant with a warm decor. Beautiful terrace with fountain.

TANUS – **81 Tarn** – **338** F6 – **pop. 510** – **alt. 439 m** – ✉ **81190** 29 **C2**

Paris 668 – Albi 33 – Rodez 46 – St-Affrique 62

Syndicat d'initiative, 24, avenue Paul Bodin ✆ 05 63 76 36 71, Fax 05 63 76 36 10

Viaduc du Viaur★ Northeast: 7 km,.

Des Voyageurs rest, VISA

11 av. Paul Bodin – 05 63 76 30 06 – ddelpous@wanadoo.fr – Fax 05 63 76 37 94 – Closed dinner from 4 to 11 January, Sunday dinner and Monday except July-August

15 rm – €44/57 €44/57, €7 – ½ P €42/46

Rest – Menu €15 (weekdays)/30 – Carte €26/49

◆ Simple hotel near the church with a small garden shaded by a weeping willow. Fully renovated rooms that are gradually being refurnished in a more modern style. Traditional cuisine and small selection of wines served in a comfortable dining room.

TARARE – 69 Rhône – 327 F4 – pop. 10 800 – alt. 383 m – 69170 44 A1

Lyon - Rhone Valley

Paris 463 – Lyon 45 – Montbrison 60 – Roanne 40 – Villefranche-sur-Saône 33

Office de tourisme, place Madeleine 04 74 63 06 65, Fax 04 74 63 52 69

Burnichon VISA AE

1.5 km east via D 307 – 04 74 63 44 01 – www.hotel-burnichon.com – hotelburnichon@wanadoo.fr – Fax 04 74 05 08 52 – Closed 21-27 December

34 rm – €40/47 €47/54, €9 – ½ P €47

Rest – *(closed Saturday dinner and Sunday)* Menu €15/36 – Carte €24/35

◆ 1980s hotel with functional rooms which have retained their original furniture. Swimming pool surrounded by greenery just 50 metres away. Veranda-dining room, with a buffet of first courses and a straightforward traditional menu. Summer terrace.

XXX **Jean Brouilly** VISA AE

3 ter r. de Paris – 04 74 63 24 56 – www.restaurant-brouilly.com – contact@restaurant-brouilly.com – Fax 04 74 05 05 48 – Closed 4-18 January, Sunday dinner and Monday

Rest – Menu €28 (weekdays)/72 – Carte €47/69

◆ A fine property (1906) set in parkland with a gastronomic reputation centred on classical cuisine. Redecorated dining room; wine list with a strong Burgundian influence.

TARASCON – 13 Bouches-du-Rhône – 340 C3 – pop. 13 100 – alt. 8 m – 13150 Provence 42 E1

Paris 702 – Arles 20 – Avignon 24 – Marseille 102 – Nîmes 27

Office de tourisme, 59, rue des Halles 04 90 91 03 52, Fax 04 90 91 22 96

Château of the roi René★★: ★★ - Ste-Marthe church ★ - Musée Charles-Deméry★ (Souleïado).

Les Échevins rm, rest, VISA

26 bd Itam – 04 90 91 01 70 – www.hotel-echevins.com – contact@hotel-echevins.com – Fax 04 90 43 50 44 – Open Easter-1st November

40 rm – €58 €64/74, €11

Rest *Le Mistral* – *04 90 91 27 62 (closed Saturday lunchtime and Wednesday)* Menu €19/26 – Carte €30/40

◆ Guests will enjoy this 17C dwelling with family atmosphere. Modest but well maintained rooms. Beautiful staircase with wrought iron railing. Colourful veranda-restaurant and traditional cuisine blown in with the Mistral.

via ① 2 km south on the D 35 and D 970 - *13150 Tarascon*

Le Mas des Comtes de Provence VISA

petite rte d'Arles – 04 90 91 00 13 – www.mas-provence.com – valo@mas-provence.com – Fax 04 90 91 02 85

9 rm – €140/200 €140/200, €13

Table d'hôte – Menu €25 (lunch)/40

◆ This 15C local-style farmhouse is simply superb! Magnificent antique furniture, worthy of a museum. Gorgeous rooms, park and large pool in keeping with the rest.

TARASCON-SUR-ARIÈGE – 09 Ariège – 343 H7 – pop. 3 487 – alt. 474 m – ✉ 09400 Languedoc-Roussillon-Tarn Gorges 29 **C3**

Paris 777 – Ax-les-Thermes 27 – Foix 18 – Lavelanet 30

Office de tourisme, avenue Paul Joucla ✆ 05 61 05 94 94, Fax 05 61 05 57 79

Parc pyrénéen de l'art préhistorique★★ West: 3 km - Grotte de Niaux★★ (prehistoric drawings) Southwest: 4 km - Grotte de Lombrives★ South: 3 km by N 20.

Domaine Fournié

rte de Saurat, 2.5 km north-west on D 618 Col de Port road – ✆ 05 61 05 54 52 – www.domaine-fournie.com – contact@domaine-fournie.com – Fax 05 61 02 73 63 – Closed 23 December-2 January

5 rm – †€ 45/50 ††€ 54/58

Table d'hôte – *(closed Thursday and week except school holidays)* Menu € 20 bi

◆ The rooms of this 17C house boast a cinema-theme decor. Some are adorned with antique furniture. Breakfast room with a fireplace.

in Rabat-les-Trois-Seigneurs 5.5 km northwest by D 618 and D 223 – ✉ 09400

La Table de la Ramade

r. des Écoles – ✆ 05 61 64 94 32 – latabledelaramade.com – latablelaramade@orange.fr – Closed 27 September-14 October, Sunday dinner and Monday

Rest – Menu € 18/35 – Carte € 26/49

◆ Former forge in a narrow alley at the top of the village. Small, first floor contemporary restaurant and roof terrace. Appealing modern cuisine.

TARBES P – 65 Hautes-Pyrénées – 342 M5 – pop. 45 800 – Built-up area 109 892 – alt. 320 m – ✉ 65000 Languedoc-Roussillon-Tarn Gorges 28 **A3**

Paris 831 – Bordeaux 218 – Lourdes 19 – Pau 44 – Toulouse 158

Tarbes-Lourdes-Pyrénées: ✆ 05 62 32 92 22, by ④: 9 km.

✆ 3635 et tapez 42 (0,34 €/mn)

Office de tourisme, 3, cours Gambetta ✆ 05 62 51 30 31, Fax 05 62 44 17 63

de Tarbes les Tumulus Laloubère 1 rue du Bois, 2 km on the Bagnères-de-Bigorre road, ✆ 05 62 45 14 50

Hippodrome de La Loubère Laloubère Rue de la Châtaigneraie, 3 km on the Bagnères-de-Bigorre road, ✆ 05 62 45 07 10

Plan on next page

Le Rex Hotel

10 cours Gambetta – ✆ 05 62 54 44 44 – www.lerexhotel.com – reception@lerexhotel.com – Fax 05 62 54 45 45 AZ **b**

98 rm – †€ 110/350 ††€ 130/350, € 15

Rest – *(closed Sunday)* Menu € 22/45

◆ The façade of this striking glass and aluminium building is enlivened at night by special lighting effects. Ultra modern guestrooms with Starck and Panton furniture. Lounge-bar and restaurant with designer decor. Contemporary style cuisine.

Ibis without rest

61 av. de Lourdes via ④ – ✆ 05 62 93 51 18 – www.ibishotel.com – h5973-gm@accor.com – Fax 05 62 93 78 40

76 rm – †€ 50/65 ††€ 50/65, € 8

◆ Located on the doorstep of the town, this hotel has had a full-scale renovation. Modern light-wood furnished, bright sitting room-bar. Spacious, comfortable rooms and an open-air pool in summer.

Foch without rest

18 pl. de Verdun – ✆ 05 62 93 71 58 – hotelfoch@wanadoo.fr – Fax 05 62 93 34 59 AYZ **e**

30 rm – †€ 53 ††€ 57, € 8 – 3 suites

◆ This central hotel alongside a lively square is well soundproofed. Simple rooms, which are more spacious and open onto pleasant balconies on the top two floors.

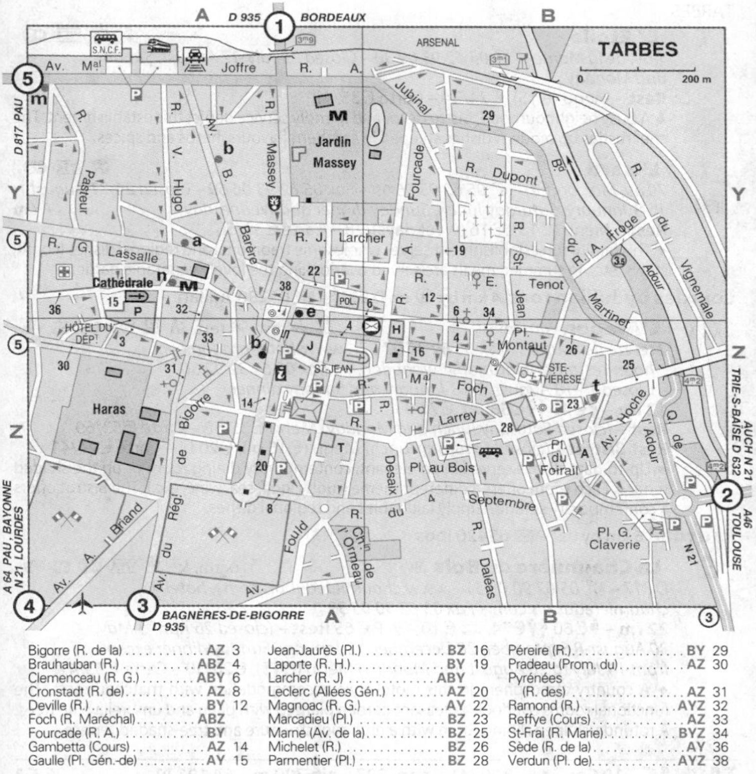

Street	Grid	No.
Bigorre (R. de la)	AZ	3
Brauhauban (R.)	ABZ	4
Clemenceau (R. G.)	ABY	6
Cronstadt (R. de)	AZ	8
Deville (R.)	BY	12
Foch (R. Maréchal)	ABZ	
Fourcade (R. A.)	BY	
Gambetta (Cours)	AZ	14
Gaulle (Pl. Gén.-de)	AY	15
Jean-Jaurès (Pl.)	BZ	16
Laporte (R. H.)	BY	19
Larcher (R. J)	ABY	
Leclerc (Allées Gén.)	AZ	20
Magnoac (R. G.)	AY	22
Marcadieu (Pl.)	BZ	23
Marne (Av. de la)	BZ	25
Michelet (R.)	BZ	26
Parmentier (Pl.)	BZ	28
Péreire (R.)	BY	29
Pradeau (Prom. du)	AZ	30
Pyrénées (R. des)	AZ	31
Ramond (R.)	AYZ	32
Reffye (Cours)	AZ	33
St-Frai (R. Marie)	BYZ	34
Sède (R. de la)	AY	36
Verdun (Pl. de)	AYZ	38

XXX **L'Ambroisie** (Daniel Labarrère)

48 r. Abbé Torné – ☎ 05 62 93 09 34 – www.restaurant-lambroisie.com – lambroisie@wanadoo.fr – Fax 05 62 93 09 24 – Closed 1st-11 May, 1st-7 September, 22 30 December, 2-11 January, Sunday and Monday AY **n**

Rest – Menu (€ 25), € 35 (weekdays)/80 – Carte € 65/80

Spec. Pavé de cabillaud au chorizo, Ossau-Iraty et haricots tarbais (February-August). Grosse côte de veau rôtie et petits légumes au beurre (January-September). Mi-cuit-mi-cru au chocolat noir. **Wines** Madiran, Jurançon.

◆ Exquisite food to be savoured in a former presbytery. The house, dating back to 1882, offers a fine dining room and a terrace that opens onto the pretty garden.

X **Le Petit Gourmand**

62 av. B. Barère – ☎ 05 62 34 26 86 – Fax 05 62 34 26 86 – Closed 2 weeks in August, 4-10 January, Saturday lunch, Sunday dinner and Monday AY **b**

Rest – Menu € 19/30 – Carte € 19/30

◆ A pleasant welcome and smart bistro decor at this friendly establishment. Market fresh cuisine and a fine choice of Languedoc-Roussillon wines.

X **Le Fil à la Patte**

30 r. G. Lassalle – ☎ 05 62 93 39 23 – lefilalapatte@neuf.fr – Fax 05 62 93 39 23 – Closed 18-29 August, Saturday lunch, Sunday and Monday AY **a**

Rest – Menu (€ 15), € 20 bi/26 – Carte approx. € 26

◆ Regional and market cuisine can be enjoyed in a friendly atmosphere at this tightly packed small restaurant with loyal clientele.

L'Étoile

1 av. de la Marne – 05 62 93 09 30 – Closed 25 July-17 August, Sunday and Monday BZ **t**

Rest – Menu (€ 15), € 24/34 – Carte € 35/49

◆ A busy neighbourhood, bistro decor and friendly service depict this establishment. The chef rustles up modern dishes steeped in southern flavours, herbs and spices.

L'Isard

70 av. Mar.-Joffre – 05 62 93 06 69 – Fax 05 62 93 06 69 – Closed 24-31 August, 1st-8 January, Saturday lunch, Sunday dinner and Wednesday AY **m**

Rest – Menu (€ 13), € 16 (weekdays)/28 – Carte € 39/50

◆ This family-run establishment serves wholesome traditional and regional dishes (confit, stews, etc). In summer, meals are served overlooking the lovely vegetable garden.

Lourdes by Juillan road **4 km by ④ on D 921A – ✉ 65290 Juillan**

L'Aragon with rm

rest, rest, VISA AE

2 ter rte de Lourdes – 05 62 32 07 07 – www.hotel-aragon.com – hotel-restaurant.laragon@wanadoo.fr – Fax 05 62 32 92 50 – Closed 1st-18 August, 2-18 January and Sunday dinner

12 rm – €49 €58, €7,50

Rest – *(closed Saturday lunch and Monday)* Menu € 35/58 – Carte € 53/69

Rest *Bistrot* – *(closed Saturday lunch)* Menu (€ 15 bi), € 20 bi – Carte € 24/41

◆ Up-to-date dishes served in an elegant, contemporary dining room or on the shaded terrace. Each room offers a different theme (rugby, golf, sea, wine, etc.). The Bistrot offers a contemporary setting, simply laid tables and regional dishes.

Pau road **6 km by ⑤ – ✉ 65420 Ibos**

La Chaumière du Bois

rm, VISA AE

D 817 – 05 62 90 03 51 – www.chaumieredubois.com – hotel@chaumieredubois.com – Fax 05 62 90 05 33

22 rm – €60 €74, € 10 – ½ P € 65 **Rest** – *(closed 26 April-5 May, 30 August-8 September, 20 December-12 January, Sunday dinner except from 14 July to 20 August and Monday)* Menu (€ 15), € 20/30 – Carte € 33/47

◆ A country atmosphere in this motel-style accommodation with thatched roofs. The functional rooms overlook a pleasant garden planted with palm and umbrella pine trees. A rotunda-shaped dining room with a high roof structure and tree-shaded terrace.

TARNAC – 19 Corrèze – 329 M1 – pop. 327 – alt. 700 m – ✉ 19170 25 C2

Dordogne-Berry-Limousin

Paris 434 – Aubusson 47 – Bourganeuf 44 – Limoges 68 – Tulle 62 – Ussel 45

Des Voyageurs

rest, rest, VISA

av. de la Mairie – 05 55 95 53 12 – www.hotel-voyageurs-correze.com – voyageurstarnac@voila.fr – Fax 05 55 95 40 07 – Closed 29 June-6 July, 20 December-18 January, 1st-9 March, Sunday evening and Monday (except hotel in July-August)

15 rm – €47 €50, € 9 – ½ P € 58

Rest – Menu € 17 (weekdays), € 26/31 – Carte € 24/44

◆ Simply furnished rooms await guests in this pleasant village hotel bordering the Millevaches plateau. Breakfasts are particularly appetising. Delicious local specialities amply compensate for the rather sober decor of the dining hall.

TASSIN-LA-DEMI-LUNE – 69 Rhône – 327 H5 – see Lyon

TAVEL – 30 Gard – 339 N4 – pop. 1 688 – alt. 100 m – ✉ 30126 23 D2

Paris 673 – Avignon 15 – Alès 68 – Nîmes 41 – Orange 22

Les Chambres de Vincent

r. Grillons – 04 66 50 94 76 – www.chambres-de-vincent.com – chambresdevincent@orange.fr – Open 8 February-8 November

5 rm – €60/70 €70/80 – ½ P € 55

Table d'hôte – *(Closed Tuesday)* Menu € 30/75 bi

◆ A distinctive country house offering small, practical and colourful bedrooms. Mediterranean species in the garden. Wisteria and vine shaded terrace. Home cooking (bouillabaisse to order) prepared by the owner, who hails from Avignon.

XX **Auberge de Tavel** with rm rest, VISA

Voie Romaine – ☎ 04 66 50 03 41 – www.auberge-de-tavel.com – info@auberge-de-tavel.com – Fax 04 66 50 24 44 – Closed 15 February-15 March

11 rm – **†**€ 87/97 **††**€ 104/184

Rest – *(Closed Wednesday)* Menu € 18 bi (weekday lunch), € 27/72 – Carte € 45/70

◆ Under the beams of the pleasant, rustic dining room or on the terrace, you can discover a modern cuisine that explores local Provençal products with wonderful results. Unpretentious rooms adorned with country furniture. Those at the rear are quieter.

TAVERS – **45 Loiret** – **318** G5 – **see Beaugency**

TEILHÈDE – **63 Puy-de-Dôme** – **326** F7 – **pop. 374** – **alt. 500 m** – ✉ **63460** 5 **B2**

Paris 401 – Clermont-Ferrand 31 – Cournon-d'Auvergne 32 – Vichy 45

Château des Raynauds

2 km west on the D 17 – ☎ 04 73 64 30 12 – www.chateau-raynauds.com – info@chateau-raynauds.com – Fax 04 73 64 30 12

4 rm – **†**€ 70 **††**€ 85 **Table d'hôte** – Menu € 38 bi

◆ An 11C-12C castle, converted into a hunting lodge in the late 16C: spiral staircase, fireplace, antiques and rooms with king size beds. This Louis XIII style table d'hôte serves classic fare.

TENCE – **43 Haute-Loire** – **331** H3 – **pop. 3 232** – **alt. 840 m** – ✉ **43190** 6 **D3**

Lyon - Rhone Valley

Paris 564 – Lamastre 38 – Le Puy-en-Velay 46 – St-Étienne 52 – Yssingeaux 19

Office de tourisme, place du Chatiague ☎ 04 71 59 81 99, Fax 04 71 59 83 50

Hostellerie Placide VISA

av. de la Gare, rte d'Annonay – ☎ 04 71 59 82 76 – www.hostellerie-placide.fr – placide@hostellerie-placide.fr – Fax 04 71 65 44 46 – Closed January to March, Sunday dinner, Monday and Tuesday from September to June

12 rm – **†**€ 75 **††**€ 88/105, € 10 – ½ P € 70/90

Rest – *(closed Monday lunch and Tuesday lunch in July-August)* Menu (€ 13), € 32/63 – Carte € 40/60

◆ A former coaching inn (1902) with a distinctive plant covered façade. Cosy, personalised rooms (warm tones, period or modern furniture). Plush interior and up-to-the-minute classical menu. Drinks in the garden in summer.

"Les Prairies" without rest

1 r. du Prè-Long – ☎ 04 71 56 35 80 – www.lesprairies.com – bourgeois40@gmail.com – Open 15 April-1st November

5 rm – **†**€ 63 **††**€ 71

◆ A stone residence, from 1850, houses this bed and breakfast, nestling in a wooded park. Simple and tasteful decor. Pleasant winter evenings around the warm fireplace.

TENCIN – **38 Isère** – **333** I6 – **pop. 1 115** – **alt. 257 m** – ✉ **38570** 46 **F2**

Paris 604 – Chambéry 38 – Grenoble 25 – Lyon 137

Syndicat d'initiative, route du Lac - Grangeneuve ☎ 04 76 13 00 00, Fax 04 76 45 71 92

XX **La Tour des Sens** VISA

La Tour, 1 km Theys road – ☎ 04 76 04 79 67 – www.latourdessens.fr – contact@latourdessens.fr – Fax 04 76 04 79 67 – Closed 5-13 April, 1st-24 August, 25-28 October, 20-27 December, Monday lunch, Sunday and bank holidays

Rest – Menu € 22 (weekday lunch), € 34/62 – Carte € 41/70

◆ The restaurant offers a view of the Massif de la Chartreuse. The warm shades of its interior brighten the modern, dark-wood furniture. Inventive cuisine.

TENDE – 06 Alpes-Maritimes – **341** G3 – **pop. 2 025 – alt. 815 m** 41 **D2**
– ✉ **06430** ▮ **French Riviera**

Paris 888 – Cuneo 47 – Menton 56 – Nice 78 – Sospel 38
Office de tourisme, avenue du 16 septembre 1947 ✆ 04 93 04 73 71, Fax 04 93 04 68 77
de Vievola Hameau de Vievola, N : 5 km on D 6204, ✆ 04 93 04 88 91
Site★ - Old town★ - Frescoes★★★ of Notre-Dame des fontaines chapel ★★ Southeast: 11 km.

L'Auberge Tendasque VISA MC
65 av. 16-Septembre-1947 – ✆ 04 93 04 62 26 – Fax 04 93 04 68 34
Rest – *(lunch only)* Menu € 16/25 – Carte € 25/38
◆ This tall house stands at the foot of a medieval village. Regional cuisine in rustic surroundings. Fine painted ceiling and watercolours by a local artist.

in St-Dalmas-de-Tende **4 km south by D 6204** – ✉ **06430**

Le Prieuré rest, P VISA MC AE
r. J. Médecin – ✆ 04 93 04 75 70 – www.leprieure.org
– contact@leprieure.org – Fax 04 93 04 71 58
– Closed 25 December-1st January
24 rm – †€ 43/59 ††€ 49/64, ☕ € 10 – ½ P € 46/56
Rest – Menu (€ 15), € 19/24 – Carte € 19/37
◆ This former priory is home to simple, rustic rooms. The hamlet is also the site of an amazing monumental train station built on Mussolini's orders. Traditional dishes served in a vaulted dining room or on a shaded terrace.

in la Brigue **6.5 km southeast by D 6204 and D 43 – pop. 630 – alt. 810 m** – ✉ **06430**
Office de tourisme, 26, avenue du Général de Gaulle ✆ 04 93 79 09 34, Fax 04 93 79 09 34
St-Martin collegiate church ★.

Mirval P VISA MC
3 r.Ferrier – ✆ 04 93 04 63 71 – www.lemirval.com – lemirval@club-internet.fr
– Fax 04 93 04 79 81 – Open 1st April-2 November
18 rm – †€ 45/49 ††€ 45/75, ☕ € 8,50 – ½ P € 48/62
Rest – *(closed Friday lunch)* Menu (€ 18), € 22/24
◆ A pretty stone bridge straddles a fish-filled river and leads to this attractive 19C mountain inn. Practical, tidy rooms. The owner is also a hiker. Contemporary dining room and veranda with view of the peaks; simple regional fare.

TERGNIER – 02 Aisne – **306** B5 – **pop. 14 500 – alt. 55 m** – ✉ **02700** 37 **C2**
Paris 136 – Compiègne 54 – Saint-Quentin 27 – Amiens 99 – Laon 29 – Soissons 37

La Mandoline VISA MC
45 pl. Herment – ✆ 03 23 57 08 71 – www.lamandoline.fr – Fax 03 23 57 08 71
– Closed dinner from Sunday to Thursday
Rest – Menu (€ 12), € 25/45 – Carte € 28/64
◆ In good weather, the flower-decked front makes it easy to find this restaurant near the town centre. Traditional recipes served.

TERMES – 48 Lozère – **330** H6 – **pop. 202 – alt. 1 120 m** – ✉ **48310** 22 **B1**
Paris 545 – Aurillac 112 – Chaudes-Aigues 19 – Mende 56 – St-Flour 41

Auberge du Verdy P VISA MC
– ✆ 04 66 31 60 97 – Open 2 April-19 December
8 rm – †€ 39/45 ††€ 39/45, ☕ € 6 – ½ P € 40
Rest – Menu € 12 (weekdays)/25 – Carte € 25/33
◆ Large country house dating from the 1990s, situated at the foot of the village. Basic, fairly spacious rooms. Children's play area. Meat grilled "à la pierrade" and local specialities on the menu in this restaurant with a regional-style fireplace that roars away in winter.

TERRASSON-LAVILLEDIEU – 24 Dordogne – 329 I5 – pop. 6 336 – alt. 90 m – ✉ 24120 Dordogne-Berry-Limousin 4 D1

Paris 497 – Brive-la-Gaillarde 22 – Lanouaille 44 – Périgueux 53 – Sarlat-la-Canéda 32

Office de tourisme, Rue Jean Rouby ☎ 05 53 50 86 82, Fax 05 53 50 55 61

Les jardins de l'imaginaire★.

XXX ✿ **L'Imaginaire** (Eric Samson) with rm — rm, P VISA MC AE

pl. du Foirail, (direction St-Sour church) – ☎ 05 53 51 37 27 – www.l-imaginaire.com – limaginaire@club-internet.fr – Fax 05 53 51 60 37 – Closed 3-11 March, 10 November-4 December, 5-16 January, Tuesday lunch and Sunday dinner from September to April and Monday

7 rm – €85/115 €85/149, €12 – ½ P €97/128

Rest – Menu (€27), €43/69 – Carte approx. €43

Spec. Grillade de foie gras acidulée au fruit de la passion (May-September). Esturgeon laqué au vin de noix, écume de fleur d'oranger (April-September). Fine gelée de rhum agricole et marmelade d'ananas aux épices. **Wines** Bergerac rouge et blanc.

◆ Treat your eyes and palate to painstakingly prepared modern cuisine in the elegant setting of this vaulted dining room in a former 17C hospice. Comfortable guestrooms decorated in relaxing cream and beige tones.

TERRAUBE – 32 Gers – 336 F6 – pop. 389 – alt. 150 m – ✉ 32700 28 B2

Paris 721 – Toulouse 114 – Auch 43 – Agen 48 – Castelsarrasin 63

Maison Ardure — P VISA MC

2 km on the D 42 Lectoure road – ☎ 05 62 68 59 56 – www.ardure.fr – reservations@ardure.fr – Fax 05 62 68 97 61 – Closed 20-30 June and 12 November-24 April except Christmas holidays

5 rm – €75/85 €80/100 **Table d'hôte** – Menu €30 bi

◆ Superb 17C Gascony manor house set in grounds planted with fruit trees. The tastefully decorated rooms have regional or travel themes. Exquisite relaxation areas. In the evenings, sample the regionally inspired creative cuisine at the table d'hôte.

TERTENOZ – 74 Haute-Savoie – 328 K6 – see Faverges

TÉTEGHEM – 59 Nord – 302 C1 – see Dunkerque

TEYSSODE – 81 Tarn – 338 D9 – pop. 346 – alt. 270 m – ✉ 81220 29 C2

Paris 699 – Albi 54 – Castres 27 – Toulouse 51

Domaine d'en Naudet without rest — P VISA MC

D 43 – ☎ 05 63 70 50 59 – www.domainenaudet.com – contact@domainenaudet.com

5 rm – €78/89 €89

◆ Perched on a hill, this very peaceful residence with character overlooks the countryside. Fine, stylish, rustic bedrooms, a sports room, and a pretty garden. Charming welcome.

THANN – 68 Haut-Rhin – 315 G10 – pop. 8 033 – alt. 343 m – ✉ 68800 Alsace-Lorraine 1 A3

Paris 464 – Belfort 42 – Colmar 44 – Épinal 87 – Guebwiller 22 – Mulhouse 21

Office de tourisme, 7, rue de la 1ère Armée ☎ 03 89 37 96 20, Fax 03 89 37 04 58

St-Thiébaut collegiate church ★★ - Grand Ballon ✳★★★ North: 19 km.

Le Parc — P VISA MC

23 r. Kléber – ☎ 03 89 37 37 47 – www.alsacehotel.com – reception@alsacehotel.com – Fax 03 89 37 56 23 – Closed 4-31 January

21 rm – €69/149 €79/189, €16

Rest – *(Closed Wednesday lunch and Thursday lunch)* Menu (€25), €28 (weekday lunch)/39 – Carte €50/65

◆ Set in wooded grounds, this fine early 20C house has palatial features; elegantly refined lounge and modern accommodation with baroque touches. Swimming pool. Luminous dining room, peaceful summer terrace and traditional cuisine.

Le Moschenross

42 r. Gén. de Gaulle – ✆ 03 89 37 00 86 – www.moschenross.fr – info@moschenross.fr – Fax 03 89 37 52 81 – Closed 17-30 August
23 rm – €35/48 €40/58, €7 – ½ P €38/48
Rest – *(Closed Saturday lunch and Sunday dinner)* Menu (€9), €17/47 – Carte €29/60

◆ Dominated by the famous Rangen vineyard, this central hotel with colourful brick-red façade has modern rooms (quieter at the back). Bright, spacious and pleasant dining room. Unpretentious modern cuisine.

Aux Sapins

3 r. Jeanne d'Arc – ✆ 03 89 37 10 96 – www.auxsapinshotel.fr – aux.sapins.hotel@free.fr – Fax 03 89 37 23 83 – Closed 24 December-3 January
17 rm – €42 €52, €7 – ½ P €55
Rest – *(closed 1st-16 August, 24 December-3 January and Saturday)* Menu (€12), €18/35 – Carte €25/45

◆ A few pine trees shade this 1980s building a little out of town. Attentive service and personalised rooms in pastel shades. Contemporary dining room and smart winstub style bistro; traditional cuisine.

THANNENKIRCH – 68 Haut-Rhin – 315 H7 – pop. 501 – alt. 520 m – ✉ 68590 Alsace-Lorraine — 2 C2

Paris 436 – Colmar 25 – St-Dié 40 – Sélestat 17

Schaentzel ★ road (D 48¹) North: 3 km.

Auberge La Meunière

30 r. Ste Anne – ✆ 03 89 73 10 47 – www.aubergelameuniere.com – info@aubergelameuniere.com – Fax 03 89 73 12 31 – Open 16 March-22 December
25 rm – €59 €60/110, €8 – ½ P €49/78
Rest – Menu (€14), €18 (weekdays)/38 – Carte €30/47

◆ This elegant inn sports a happy mix of rustic and contemporary styles. The spacious rooms, many with balconies, command fine views of the countryside. Welcoming dining room, panoramic terrace and regionally inspired, seasonal menu.

Touring-Hôtel

2 rte du Haut Koenigsbourg – ✆ 03 89 73 10 01 – www.touringhotel.com – touringhotel@free.fr – Fax 03 89 73 11 79 – Closed 4 January-1st March
45 rm – €59/108 €59/139, €10
Rest – Menu €19/40 – Carte €22/49

◆ Large family hotel in the village, at the foot of the Taennchel mountain range. Smart Alsatian-style rooms. Wellness centre. Country buffet for breakfast. Regional dishes and wines take pride of place in this dining room.

THARON-PLAGE – 44 Loire-Atlantique – 316 C5 – ✉ 44730 — 34 A2

Paris 437 – Challans 53 – Nantes 57 – St-Nazaire 24

Le Belem

56 av. Convention – ✆ 02 40 64 90 06 – www.restaurant-le-belem.com – loirat-thierry@wanadoo.fr – Fax 02 40 39 43 14 – Closed 2 January-6 February, Sunday dinner off season and Monday
Rest – Menu (€18 bi), €25/48 – Carte €35/49

◆ A stone's throw from the beach, this 1980s decorated restaurant sports plants and a mural of the Belem tall ship. Up-to-the-minute menu.

LE THEIL – 15 Cantal – 330 C4 – see Salers

Good food and accommodation at moderate prices?
Look for the Bib symbols: red Bib Gourmand for food, blue Bib Hotel for hotels.

LE THEIL – 03 Allier – **326** F4 – **pop. 404** – **alt. 450 m** – ✉ **03240** 5 **B1**

Paris 343 – Clermont-Ferrand 92 – Montluçon 46 – Vichy 43

Château du Max

2 km northwest on the D 129 – ✆ 04 70 42 35 23 – www.chateaudumax.com – chateaudumax@club-internet.fr – Fax 04 70 42 34 90

3 rm – **†**€ 60 **††**€ 70/90 – ½ P € 80 **Table d'hôte** – Menu € 25 bi/30 bi

◆ Château from the 13C and 15C, surrounded by a moat. Rooms and suites have been tastefully decorated by the landlady who was a former theatre designer. Restaurant serving local dishes in a magnificent medieval setting.

THÉNAC – 17 Charente-Maritime – **329** D7 – see Saintes

THENAY – 36 Indre – **323** E7 – **pop. 873** – **alt. 120 m** – ✉ **36800** 11 **B3**

Paris 299 – Châteauroux 33 – Limoges 104 – Le Blanc 30 – La Châtre 49

Auberge de Thenay VISA

23 r. R. d'Helbingue – ✆ 02 54 47 99 00 – www.auberge-de-thenay.fr – orain.pascal@wanadoo.fr – Closed 1st-9 September, 19-31 January, Sunday dinner and Monday

Rest – *(number of covers limited, pre-book)* Menu (€ 13 bi), € 23/30

◆ The menus are based on spit-roast meat and a fine wine list. The owner regularly organises Irish and Scottish evenings (whisky menu).

THÉOULE-SUR-MER – 06 Alpes-Maritimes – **341** C6 – **pop. 1 296** – ✉ **06590** French Riviera 42 **E2**

Paris 895 – Cannes 11 – Draguignan 58 – Nice 42 – St-Raphaël 30

Office de tourisme, 1, corniche d'Or ✆ 04 93 49 28 28, Fax 04 93 49 00 04

Massif de l'Estérel★★★.

in Miramar 5 km by D 6098 - St-Raphaël road – ✉ **06590 Theoule sur Mer**
French Riviera

Pointe de l'Esquilon ★★ Northeast: 1 km then 15 mn.

Miramar Beach rm, VISA

47 av. Miramar – ✆ 04 93 75 05 05 – www.mbhriviera.com – reception@mbhotel.com – Fax 04 93 75 44 83

55 rm – **†**€ 155/355 **††**€ 155/355, € 19 – 1 suite – ½ P € 137/237

Rest ***L'Étoile des Mers*** – Menu € 39 (lunch), € 49/89 – Carte € 72/111

◆ The charm of this establishment is derived from its location in a deep narrow crevice of red rock. Elegant Provençal-style rooms and sumptuous Oriental inspired spa. Panoramic restaurant and summer terrace.

at port de la Rague

Riviera beach hôtel without rest VISA

La Rague port – ✆ 04 92 97 11 99 – beachaffaires@orange.fr – beachaffaires@orange.fr – Fax 04 92 97 12 10 – Closed 1st December-15 January

9 rm – **†**€ 128/228 **††**€ 168/260

◆ Smart guestrooms with a nautical flavour and south-facing balconies from which to enjoy the sea views. Swimming pool and jacuzzi on the roof, a designer-style bar, and a location on the port, a stone's throw from the beach.

THÉRONDELS – 12 Aveyron – **338** I1 – **pop. 486** – **alt. 965 m** – ✉ **12600** 29 **D1**

Paris 561 – Aurillac 44 – Chaudes-Aigues 48 – Murat 43 – Rodez 88 – St-Flour 49

Miquel rm, VISA

le bourg – ✆ 05 65 66 02 72 – www.hotel-miquel.com – hotel-miquel@wanadoo.fr – Fax 05 65 66 19 84 – Open 16 March-14 December

15 rm – **†**€ 55/65 **††**€ 65/85, € 8

Rest – *(closed Sunday dinner and Monday)* Menu € 12 bi (weekday lunch), € 25/36

◆ An early 20C building in the same family for three generations. The simple, well-kept rooms either overlook the garden or village square. Dining room opening onto a small terrace and Aveyron-inspired cuisine.

THIAIS – 94 Val-de-Marne – **312** D3 – **101** 26 – see Paris, Area

THIERS – 63 Puy-de-Dôme – **326** I7 – pop. 12 400 – alt. 420 m – ✉ 63300 Auvergne 6 **C2**

Paris 388 – Clermont-Ferrand 43 – Lyon 133 – St-Étienne 108 – Vichy 36

Office de tourisme, maison du Pirou ✆ 04 73 80 65 65, Fax 04 73 80 01 32

Site★★ - Old Thiers★: Maison du Pirou★ **N** - Rampart terrace ★ - Rocher de Borbes ★ South: 3.5 km by D 102.

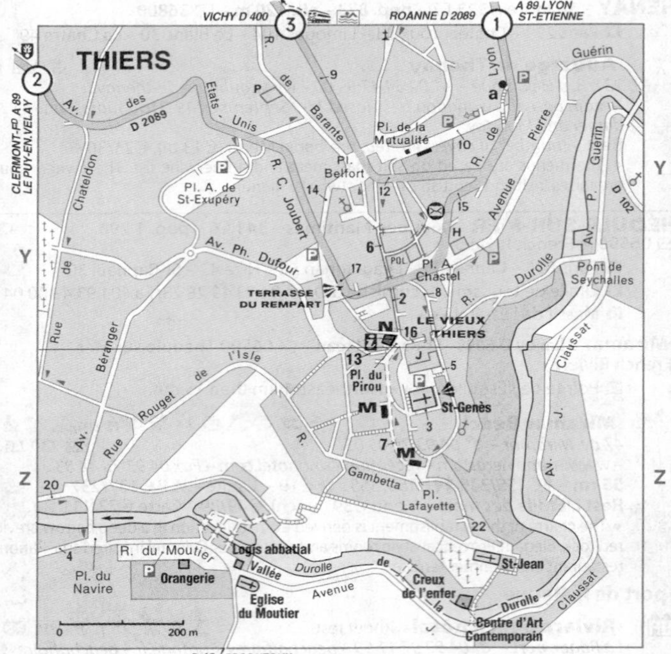

Bourg (R. du)	Y 2	Dr-Dumas (R. des)	Y 9	Mitterrand (R. F.)	Y 15
Brugière (Imp. Jean)	Z 3	Duchasseint (Pl.)	Y 10	Pirou (R. du)	Y 16
Chabot (R. M.)	Z 5	Dumas (R. Alexandre)	Y 8	Terrasse (R.)	Y 17
Clermont (R. de)	Z 4	Grammonts (R. des)	Y 12	Voltaire (Av.)	Z 20
Conchette (R.)	Y 6	Grenette (R.)	Z 13	4-Septembre (R. du)	Z 22
Coutellerie (R. de la)	Z 7	Marilhat (R. Prosper)	Y 14		

L'Aigle d'Or VISA

8 r. de Lyon – ✆ 04 73 80 00 50 – www.aigle-dor.com
– aigle.dor@wanadoo.fr – Fax 04 73 80 17 00
– Closed 13-26 April, 25 October-17 November, Monday lunch, Saturday lunch and Sunday Y a

18 rm – €48 €58, €7

Rest – Menu (€13), €17/26
– Carte €29/40

◆ This establishment, founded in 1836, houses a comfortable sitting room and well-soundproofed rooms. A 19C setting and rustic furniture make up the dining room decor where traditional food is served.

in Pont-de-Dore 6 km by ② by D 2089 – ✉ 63920 Peschadoires

Eliotel
rte de Maringues – ✆ 04 73 80 10 14 – www.eliotel.fr – contact@eliotel.fr – Fax 04 73 80 51 02 – Closed 4-15 August and 21 December-11 January
12 rm – †€ 55/76 ††€ 55/76, ☕ € 8 – ½ P € 60/68
Rest – Menu (€ 17), € 19 bi (weekdays)/55 – Carte € 34/57
◆ Pleasant establishment run by an enthusiast of Thiers' knives (display case). Well proportioned rooms; ask for one of the more recent ones. The chef, who is from Armorique, proposes Auvergne dishes and Breton specialities.

THIÉZAC – 15 Cantal – 330 E4 – pop. 600 – alt. 805 m – ✉ 15800 5 **B3**
Auvergne

Paris 542 – Aurillac 26 – Murat 23 – Vic-sur-Cère 7
Office de tourisme, le Bourg ✆ 04 71 47 03 50, Fax 04 71 47 03 83
Pas de Compaing★ Northeast: 3 km.

L'Elancèze
le bourg – ✆ 04 71 47 00 22 – www.elanceze.com – info@elanceze.com – Fax 04 71 47 02 08 – Closed 2 Nov.-22 Dec.
31 rm – †€ 56 ††€ 57, ☕ € 8 **Rest** – Menu (€ 12), € 18/35 – Carte € 19/39
◆ Family-run establishment in the heart of an Auvergne village. The main building offers functional rooms, some with a balcony. Dining room offering a lovely view of the village rooftops and serving local food.

Belle Vallée
10 rm – †€ 47/48 ††€ 47/48, ☕ € 10 – ½ P € 45/46
◆ This 1957 annexe, set a few metres away from the main building, has simpler but well-kept rooms.

Le Casteltinet
Grand-Rue – ✆ 04 71 47 00 60 – www.casteltinet.com – lecasteltinet@orange.fr – Fax 04 71 47 04 08 – Closed November
23 rm – †€ 48 ††€ 48, ☕ € 9 – ½ P € 47
Rest – *(Closed Tuesday lunch, Sunday dinner and Monday)* Menu € 14 (weekdays)/59 – Carte € 40/70
◆ Recently built establishment inspired by local architecture. It offers functional rooms with loggia offering a breathtaking view of the Cantal hills. Sober dining room and terrace with view; traditional cuisine with solid regional roots.

LE THILLOT – 88 Vosges – 314 I5 – pop. 3 745 – alt. 495 m – ✉ 88160 27 **C3**
Alsace-Lorraine

Paris 434 – Belfort 46 – Colmar 72 – Épinal 49 – Mulhouse 57 – St-Dié 59 – Vesoul 64
Office de tourisme, 11, avenue de Verdun ✆ 03 29 25 28 61, Fax 03 29 25 38 39

in Ménil 3.5 km northeast by D 486 – pop. 1 181 – alt. 524 m – ✉ 88160

Les Sapins
60 Gde Rue – ✆ 03 29 25 02 46 – www.hotel-les-sapins.fr – les.sapins@voila.fr – Fax 03 29 25 80 23 – Closed 23 June-6 July, 21 November-17 December, Sunday evening and Monday lunch
22 rm – †€ 47 ††€ 54, ☕ € 9 – ½ P € 56
Rest – Menu € 14 (weekday lunch), € 22/46 – Carte € 30/50
◆ The unusual architecture and rooms either in romantic or exotic style, the pleasant welcome and the homemade jams on sale, all make this a pleasant place to stay. Up-to-the-minute cuisine served with a backdrop of contemporary art.

THIONVILLE – 57 Moselle – 307 I2 – pop. 41 600 – Built-up area 130 480 – alt. 155 m – ✉ 57100 Alsace-Lorraine 26 **B1**

Paris 339 – Luxembourg 32 – Metz 30 – Nancy 84 – Trier 77 – Verdun 88
Office de tourisme, 16, rue du vieux collège ✆ 03 82 53 33 18, Fax 03 82 53 15 55
Château de la Grange★.

THIONVILLE

Afrique (Chaussée d') .... **AV** 3	Comte-de-Bertier (Av.) .... **BV** 10	Paul-Albert (R.) .... **AV** 28
Amérique (Chaussée d') ..... **BV** 4	Europe (Chaussée d') .... **AV** 13	Pyramides (R. des) .... **BV** 29
Asie (Chaussée d') .... **AV** 6	Guentrange (Rte de) .... **AV** 15	Romains (R. des) .... **AV** 31
Bel Air (Allée) .... **AV** 7	Longwy (R. de) .... **AV** 18	Terrasse (Allée de la) .... **AV** 34
	Océanie (Chaussée d') .... **BV** 25	14-Juillet (Av. du) .... **AV** 37

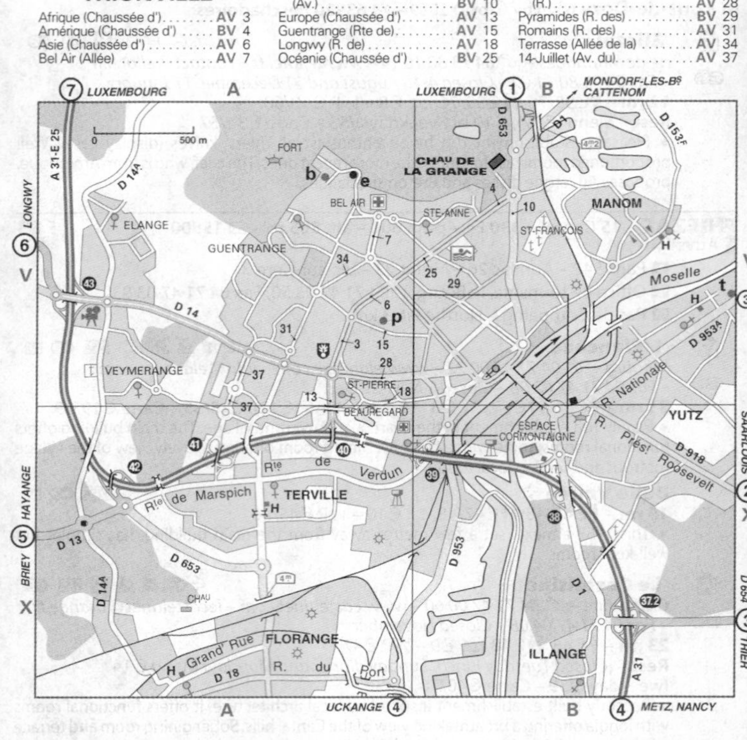

Des Oliviers without rest VISA

1 r. Four Banal – ✆ 03 82 53 70 27 – www.hoteldesoliviers.com – contact@hoteldesoliviers.com – Fax 03 82 53 23 34 – Closed 23 December-3 January

26 rm – †€ 55 ††€ 57, ☕ € 7 DY **n**

◆ Small family hotel set in a pedestrian street of the town centre. Small but functional rooms that are immaculately kept. Breakfast served on the terrace in summer.

Du Parc without rest VISA

10 pl. de la République – ✆ 03 82 82 80 80 – www.hoteldu-parc.com – contact@hoteldu-parc.com – Fax 03 82 82 71 82 CZ **a**

41 rm – †€ 55/70 ††€ 55/70, ☕ € 9

◆ Early 20C building near the town centre, facing a small public park. The rooms, spread over six floors, are functional and all similar.

Aux Poulbots Gourmets VISA

9 pl. aux Fleurs – ✆ 03 82 88 10 91 – www.poulbotsgourmets.com – philippe.ardizzoia@orange.fr – Fax 03 82 88 42 76 – Closed 14-21 April, 27 July-16 August, 1st-15 January, Saturday lunch, Sunday dinner, Wednesday dinner and Monday

Rest – Menu € 40/65 – Carte € 40/76 AV **p**

◆ Restaurant with a good local reputation offering classical cuisine. Large bay windows, Lloyd Loom chairs and modern chandeliers add to the contemporary charm of the place.

Au Petit Chez Soi VISA

23 r. du Luxembourg – ✆ 03 82 53 62 96 – Closed 31 July-22 August, 28 December-8 January, Wednesday dinner, Sunday and Monday DY

Rest – Menu (€ 19), € 23 (lunch)/39 – Carte € 61/72

◆ Lovely little restaurant with a bistro feel, set in an old 18C house in the pedestrianised town centre. Traditional cuisine with delicatessen opposite.

THIONVILLE

Berthe-au-Grand-Pied (R.) . . DY 8
Ditsch (R. G.). . . . . DZ 12
Hoche (R. Lazare). . . . . DY 16
Luxembourg (R. du) . . . . DY 19
Marchal (Quai P.) . . . . DY 21
Marché (Pl. du) . . . . DY 22
Marie-Louise (Pl.) . . . . CZ 24
Paris (R. de) . . . . DZ 27
République (Pl.) . . . . CZ 30
St-Pierre (R. de) . . . . CZ 33

in Crève-Coeur – ✉ 57100 Thionville

L'Horizon
50 rte du Crève Coeur – ☎ 03 82 88 53 65 – www.lhorizon.fr – hotel@lhorizon.fr – Fax 03 82 34 55 84 – Closed 20 December-20 January and Sunday dinner from November to March
13 rm – 🚹€ 98/164 🚹🚹€ 164, ☕ € 14 – ½ P € 142/170 AV **e**
Rest – *(closed Sunday dinner from November to March, Monday lunch, Tuesday lunch, Friday lunch and Saturday lunch)* Menu € 41/56 – Carte € 51/61
◆ An old house covered with Virginia creeper and surrounded by flower-filled gardens. Low-key atmosphere, elegant rooms, stylish lounges and a bar with a panoramic view. Restaurant with classic cuisine and decor, including an Aubusson tapestry in the dining room. Good views of the town.

Auberge du Crève-Coeur
9 Le Crève-Coeur – ☎ 03 82 88 50 52 – www.aubergeducrevecoeur.com – aubergeducrevecoeur@wanadoo.fr – Fax 03 82 34 89 06 – Closed Sunday dinner, Monday dinner, Tuesday dinner and Wednesday dinner AV **b**
Rest – Menu € 34/52 – Carte € 46/70
◆ Inn run by the same family since 1899. Wine-themed décor with tapestries, casks and giant 18C press. Generous local cuisine and terrace overlooking Thionville.

THIRON-GARDAIS – 28 Eure-et-Loir – 311 C6 – pop. 1 121 – alt. 237 m – ✉ 28480 — 11 B1

Paris 148 – Chartres 48 – Lucé 46 – Orléans 95

Syndicat d'initiative, 11, rue du Commerce ☎ 02 37 49 49 01, Fax 02 37 49 49 07

La Forge

1 r. Alfred Chasseriaud – ☎ 02 37 49 42 30 – www.a-la-forge.com – jpm.thiron@orange.fr – Closed Monday and dinner except Friday and Saturday

Rest – Menu € 13 (weekdays), € 32/88 – Carte € 35/49

◆ The artist-chef displays his works in the restaurant that occupies the former forge of a 16C abbey. Menu of the day during the week and a wider choice at weekends.

THIVIERS – 24 Dordogne – 329 G3 – pop. 3 227 – alt. 273 m – ✉ 24800 — 4 C1

Dordogne-Berry-Limousin

Paris 449 – Brive-la-Gaillarde 81 – Limoges 62 – Périgueux 34 – St-Yrieix-la-Perche 32

Office de tourisme, place du Marechal Foch ☎ 05 53 55 12 50, Fax 05 53 55 12 50

De France et de Russie without rest

51 r. Gén. Lamy – ☎ 05 53 55 17 80 – www.thiviers-hotel.com – nicola@thiviers-hotel.com – Fax 05 53 55 01 42

10 rm – †€ 45/70 ††€ 45/70, ☕ € 7

◆ The name of this 18C residence recalls Thiviers' love of Russia, and the famous foie gras that was so appreciated by the tsar's court. Simply furbished rooms.

THIZY – 69 Rhône – 327 E3 – pop. 2 456 – alt. 553 m – ✉ 69240 — 44 A1

Paris 414 – Lyon 65 – Montbrison 74 – Roanne 22

Office de tourisme, r43, rue Jean Jaurès ☎ 04 74 64 35 23

La Terrasse

Le bourg Marnand, 2 km north-east on D 94 – ☎ 04 74 64 19 22 – www.laterrasse-marnand.com – francis.arnette@wanadoo.fr – Fax 04 74 64 25 95 – Closed autumn and February school holidays and Sunday dinner except summer

10 rm – †€ 42 ††€ 49, ☕ € 6 – ½ P € 47

Rest – *(closed Sunday dinner and Monday except summer)* Menu (€ 14), € 19/65 – Carte € 45/65

◆ A former textile factory converted into a hotel. The pretty rooms opening onto the garden are named after herbs and are decorated, even fragranced, according to this theme. Modern dining room and lovely terrace facing the hills.

THOIRY – 01 Ain – 328 I3 – pop. 4 063 – alt. 500 m – ✉ 01710 — 45 C1

Paris 523 – Bellegarde-sur-Valserine 27 – Bourg-en-Bresse 99 – Gex 13

Holiday Inn

av. Mont-Blanc – ☎ 04 50 99 19 99 – www.holiday-inn.com/thoiryfrance – hi.geneve@wanadoo.fr – Fax 04 50 42 27 40

95 rm – †€ 95/300 ††€ 95/300, ☕ € 14

Rest – *(closed Sat. lunchtime and Sun. lunchtime)* Menu (€ 17), € 25 (dinner)/30 – Carte € 29/47

◆ This hotel, next to the Swiss border and Geneva airport, is somewhat outdated but well maintained. An ideal stopover for international business travellers. Comfortable, light-wood dining room, quick set menus, buffets and theme weeks.

Les Cépages (Jean-Pierre Delesderrier)

465 r. Briand Stresemann – ☎ 04 50 20 83 85 – www.lescepages.com – Fax 04 50 41 24 58 – Closed in March, in October, Sunday dinner, Monday and Tuesday

Rest – *(pre-book)* Menu € 30 (weekday lunch), € 48/98 – Carte € 70/120

Spec. Foie gras de canard. Homard aux arômes d'asie. Palette des petits desserts.

Wines Bugey Pinot gris, Bugey Manicle.

◆ Classic cuisine prepared with care and served in the elegant contemporary dining room or on the terrace overlooking the flower garden. Good choice of wines.

THOLLON-LES-MÉMISES – 74 Haute-Savoie – 328 N2 – pop. 691 – alt. 920 m – Winter sports : 1 000/2 000 m 1 18 – ✉ 74500 French Alps

46 **F1**

- Paris 588 – Annecy 95 – Évian-les-Bains 11 – Thonon-les-Bains 21
- Office de tourisme, station ✆ 04 50 70 90 01, Fax 04 50 70 92 80
- Pic de Mémise ✳★★ 30 mn.

Bellevue

Le Nouy – ✆ 04 50 70 92 79 – www.hotelbellevue.fr – hotelbellevuethollon@wanadoo.fr – Fax 04 50 70 97 63 – Open 1st May-end September and mid-December-30 March

35 rm – €50 €61/105, €9 – ½ P €53/59

Rest – *(closed Thursday off season)* Menu €21/34 – Carte €28/52

◆ Large chalet on the hillside of the "Balcon du Léman". Functional and well-kept rooms, some for families. Sauna and jacuzzi. The terrace of this Savoyard restaurant commands a fine view of the village; traditional dishes.

THONES – 74 Haute-Savoie – 328 K5 – pop. 5 795 – alt. 650 m – ✉ 74230 French Alps

46 **F1**

- Paris 560 – Lyon 171 – Annecy 21 – Genève 59 – Chambéry 73
- Office de tourisme, place Avet ✆ 04 50 02 00 26, Fax 04 50 02 11 87

Le Clos Zénon

rte de Bellossier – ✆ 04 50 02 10 86 – www.thones-chalet-gite.com – hotel@thones-chalet-hotel.com – Fax 04 50 02 10 86 – Open 1st April-18 December

5 rm – €55/60 €65/90 – ½ P €60/70

Table d'hôte – Menu €30 bi

◆ A good address for nature lovers. A recently built chalet in a mountain setting with pool, pleasant welcome and snug rooms. Savoie inspired meals served in a warm dining room with fine fireplace.

in La Balme-de-Thuy 2,5 km Southwest by D 909 and secondary road – pop. 360 – alt. 623 m – ✉ 74230

Le Paddock des Aravis without rest

Les Chenalettes, towards Sappey – ✆ 04 50 02 98 28 – www.le-paddock-des-aravis.com – nathalie@le-paddock-des-aravis.com

5 rm – €90/115 €90/115

◆ Beautiful view of the Tournette from this farm's isolated vantage point. The light-wood interior, neutral tones and the comfortable rooms are all refined but cosy.

THONON-LES-BAINS – 74 Haute-Savoie – 328 L2 – pop. 30 700 – alt. 431 m – Spa : early April-early Dec. – ✉ 74200 French Alps

46 **F1**

- Paris 568 – Annecy 75 – Chamonix-Mont-Blanc 99 – Genève 34
- Office de tourisme, place du Marché ✆ 04 50 71 55 55, Fax 04 50 26 68 33
- Évian Masters Golf Club Évian-les-Bains Rive Sud du Lac de Genève, 8 km on the Évian road, ✆ 04 50 75 46 66
- Viewpoints on Lake Geneva★★ ABY - Vaults★ of St-Hippolyte church - Domaine de Ripaille★ North: 2 km.

Plan on following page

Arc en Ciel without rest

18 pl. Crête – ✆ 04 50 71 90 63 – www.hotelarcencielthonon.com – info@hotel-arcenciel.com – Fax 04 50 26 27 47 – Closed 25 April-6 May and 19 December-6 January

BZ **k**

40 rm – €58/69 €64/75, €8

◆ Near the town centre, a modern hotel with a garden and pool. Spacious and well-equipped rooms with balcony or terrace; some have a small kitchen.

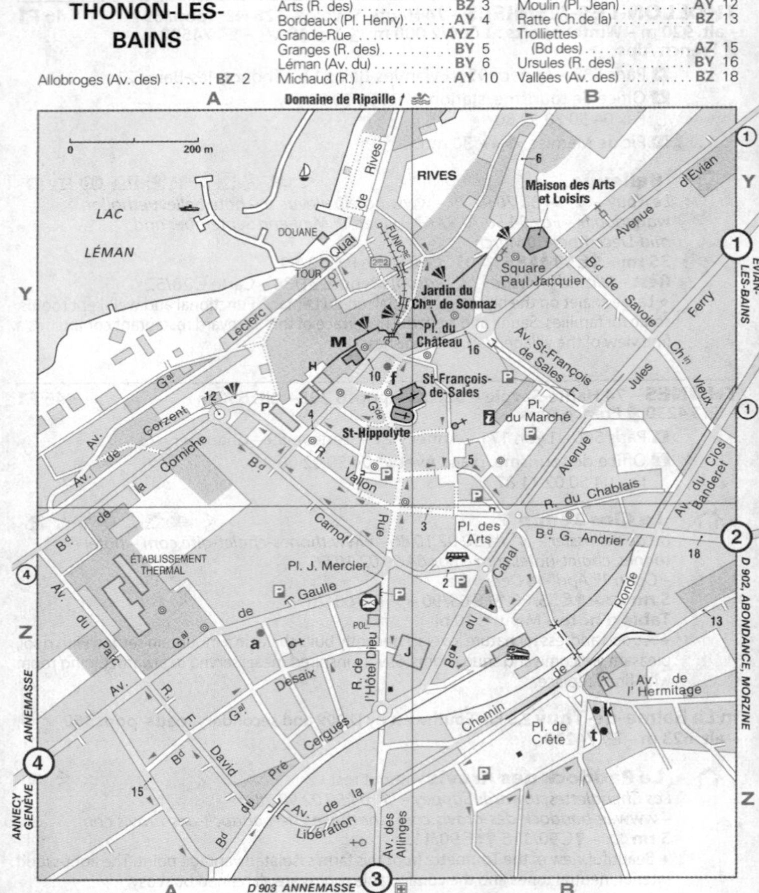

À l'Ombre des Marronniers rm,

17 pl. Crête – ✆ 04 50 71 26 18 – wwwhotellesmarronniers.com – info@hotel-marroniers.com – Fax 04 50 26 27 47 – Closed 25 April-6 May and 20 December-5 January BZ **t**

17 rm – †€ 45/54 ††€ 50/62, ☕ € 7 – ½ P € 45/52

Rest – *(closed 25 April-6 May, 20 December-17 January, Sunday dinner and Monday 15 November-21 May)* Menu € 13/33 – Carte € 25/49

◆ The rooms in this hotel-chalet may be a little antiquated but are nonetheless practical. Dining room-veranda and terrace shaded by chestnut trees; traditional and regional food.

Le Prieuré (Charles Plumex)

68 Gde rue – ✆ 04 50 71 31 89 – plumex-prieure@wanadoo.fr – Fax 04 50 71 31 09 – Closed 13-28 April, 9-24 November, Sunday dinner, Monday and Tuesday

Rest – Menu (€ 37 bi), € 38/80 – Carte € 70/95 AY **f**

Spec. Foie gras en fausse poire panée de pistache. Arrière de veau caramélisé et confit de légumes aux herbes. Soliloque Guayaquil, mascarpone praliné et sorbet réglisse. **Wines** Roussette de Savoie Monterminod.

◆ Standing at the entrance to an old mansion, a vaulted restaurant with panelling and modern paintings. Carefully prepared and generously served inventive cuisine.

Les Alpes
3 bis r. des Italiens – ☎ 04 50 26 51 24 – restaurant.lesalpes@club-internet.fr – Fax 04 50 26 51 24 – Closed 15 July-13 August, Sunday dinner and Wednesday AZ **a**
Rest – *(number of covers limited, pre-book)* Menu (€ 19), € 26/58 – Carte € 41/54
◆ This low-key, countrified dining room is on a busy shopping street in this spa resort. It mingles beams, paintings and flowers and serves traditional cuisine.

in Armoy **7 km southeast by ② and D 26 – pop. 940 – alt. 620 m – ✉ 74200**

À l'Écho des Montagnes rm, VISA
– ☎ 04 50 73 94 55 – www.echo-des-montagnes.com – alechodesmontagnes@yahoo.fr – Fax 04 50 70 54 07 – Closed 28 September-3 October, 21 December-7 February, Sunday dinner and Monday except from June to August
47 rm – €32 €52/60, €8 – ½ P €50/54
Rest – Menu € 16 (weekdays)/40 – Carte € 28/50
◆ An informal atmosphere reigns within this imposing late 19C mansion. Simple, practical rooms, larger in the wing. Exhibition and sale of local arts and crafts. The wood panelling is welcoming and the local cuisine is served generously.

in Anthy-sur-Léman **6 km by ④ and D 33 – pop. 1 857 – alt. 400 m – ✉ 74200**

L'Auberge d'Anthy VISA AE
2 r. des Écoles – ☎ 04 50 70 35 00 – www.auberge-anthy.com – info@auberge-anthy.com – Fax 04 50 70 40 90
13 rm – €52/66 €64/77, €8 – ½ P €62/68
Rest – *(Closed 23 March-2 April, 5-12 October, Sunday dinner, Tuesday lunch and Monday)* Menu (€ 13), € 17 (weekday lunch), € 30/44 – Carte € 30/51
◆ This unpretentious village bistro continues to uphold its motto 'Eat, drink and sleep'. Small, plain rooms, countrified bistro and regional fare.

Le Galanthy VISA
11 r. des Pêcheurs – ☎ 04 50 70 61 50 – http://www.legalanthy.com – restaurant.legalanthy@neuf.fr – Closed 29 June-6 July, 26 October-2 November, 9-16 February, Sunday dinner and Monday
Rest – Menu (€ 18), € 28/39 – Carte € 38/49
◆ The bay windows of this modern dining room overlook a terrace with a view of the small lake. Friendly service and appetising traditional menu.

in Cinq Chemins **7 km by ④ – ✉ 74200 Margencel**

Denarié rm, VISA AE
25 r. de Séchex – ☎ 04 50 72 63 45 – www.hoteldenarie.com – francoise@hoteldenarie.com – Fax 04 50 72 30 69 – Closed 8-15 June, 21-28 September, 21 December-20 January and Sunday dinner except July-August
20 rm – €68/77 €72/97, €9,50 – 3 suites – ½ P €70/85
Rest ***Les Cinq Chemins*** – *(Closed Sunday dinner from September to June and Monday except dinner in July-August)* Menu (€ 15), € 18 (weekday lunch), € 26/42 – Carte € 32/57
◆ A simple welcoming Savoyard establishment near the road but nonetheless peaceful. Tastefully decorated rooms. Pleasant garden and pool. The restaurant's decor is at once informal and authentic. Appetising traditional and regional cuisine.

in Port-de-Séchex **7 km by ④ – ✉ 74200**

Le Clos du Lac VISA
Port de Séchex – ☎ 04 50 72 48 81 – le-clos-du-lac@wanadoo.fr – Fax 04 50 72 48 81 – Closed 29 June-8 July, 5-15 October, 4-27 January, Sunday dinner, Tuesday lunch except July-August and Monday
Rest – Menu (€ 22), € 28/62 – Carte € 44/64
◆ In this restored farmhouse, the old stone mangers happily rub shoulders with contemporary decor and artwork. Carefully prepared cuisine in fine with current tastes.

in Bonnatrait 9 km by ④ – ✉ **74140 Sciez**

Hôtellerie Château de Coudrée
– ✆ *04 50 72 62 33 – www.coudree.fr – chateau@coudree.fr – Fax 04 50 72 57 28 – Closed 26 October-3 December*
19 rm – †€ 138/482 ††€ 138/482, ☐ € 18
Rest – *(Closed lunch from Monday to Thursday from December to April, Tuesday and Wednesday except July-August)* Menu € 39 (weekday lunch), € 59/85 – Carte € 93/106
◆ This château on the edge of the lake is an imposing reminder of the Middle Ages. Rooms, individually furnished with old-style decor, include an unusual one in the dungeon. Dignified dining room (wainscoting, tapestries, fireplace) and contemporary menu.

LE THOR – 84 Vaucluse – 332 C10 – pop. 7 508 – alt. 50 m – ✉ 84250 — 42 **E1**

Paris 696 – Marseille 89 – Avignon 21 – Arles 84 – Istres 68

La Bastide Rose
99 chemin des Courpières – ✆ 04 90 02 14 33 – www.bastiderose.com – contact@bastiderose.com – Fax 04 90 02 19 38 – Closed 9 January-13 March
5 rm ☐ – †€ 155/205 ††€ 160/210 – 3 suites
Rest – table d'hôte – *(dinner only) (residents only)* Menu € 38
◆ This lovely farmhouse is also home to a museum devoted to Pierre Salinger, journalist and political advisor. It is steeped in the charm of a country manor: elegance, comfort and a view of parkland. Beneath the glass roof or on the terrace, sample the Provençal cuisine.

THORÉ-LA-ROCHETTE – 41 Loir-et-Cher – 318 C5 – pop. 922 – alt. 75 m – ✉ 41100 — 11 **B2**

Paris 176 – Blois 42 – La Flèche 94 – Le Mans 72 – Vendôme 9

du Pont
15 r. du Mar. de Rochambeau – ✆ 02 54 72 80 62 – Fax 02 54 72 70 95 – Closed 16 August-3 September, 16 January-10 February, Tuesday dinner, Sunday dinner and Monday
Rest – Menu € 22 (weekdays)/48 – Carte € 43/59
◆ Regional wines and cuisine are served in this simple little restaurant close to where the Loir-Valley tourist train stops.

THORENC – 06 Alpes-Maritimes – 341 B5 – alt. 1 250 m – ✉ 06750 Andon — 41 **C2**

Paris 832 – Castellane 35 – Draguignan 64 – Grasse 40 – Nice 58 – Vence 41
Col de Bleine ≤★★ Nprth: 4 km, **French Alps.**

Auberge Les Merisiers with rm
24 av. Belvédère – ✆ 04 93 60 00 23 – www.aubergelesmerisiers.com – info@aubergelesmerisiers.com – Fax 04 93 60 02 17 – Closed 10 March-4 April, Monday dinner and Tuesday except school holidays
12 rm – †€ 45 ††€ 45, ☐ € 12 – ½ P € 50
Rest – Menu (€ 23), € 28/35 – Carte € 30/40
◆ Practical for a stop on the way up through the Bleine Pass, this little mountain inn serves regional cuisine in a simple rustic interior. Well-kept small rooms.

THORIGNÉ-SUR-DUÉ – 72 Sarthe – 310 M6 – pop. 1 557 – alt. 82 m – ✉ 72160 — 35 **D1**

Paris 178 – Châteaudun 80 – Mamers 44 – Le Mans 30 – Nogent-le-Rotrou 45 – St-Calais 25
Syndicat d'initiative, Mairie ✆ 02 43 89 05 13, Fax 02 43 89 20 46

Le St-Jacques
pl. du Monument – ✆ 02 43 89 95 50 – www.hotel-sarthe.fr – hotel.st-jacques.thorigne@wanadoo.fr – Fax 02 43 76 58 42 – Closed 12-24 November and 14-22 February
15 rm – †€ 54/64 ††€ 64/84, ☐ € 12 – ½ P € 60
Rest – Menu € 19/48 – Carte € 38/59
◆ On the way into the village, this yellow fronted hotel offers bright, well-kept rooms, most of which have been refurbished. Snug lounge-bar; warm welcome. The colourful dining room serves updated fare enlivened with spices.

LE THORONET – 83 Var – 340 M5 – pop. 1 952 – alt. 120 m – ✉ 83340 41 C3

Paris 831 – Brignoles 24 – Draguignan 21 – St-Raphaël 51 – Toulon 62
Office de tourisme, boulevard du 17 août 1944 ✆ 04 94 60 10 94
Thoronet abbey★★ West: 4.5 km, French Riviera.

Hostellerie de l'Abbaye
rm, rm, VISA
chemin du Château – ✆ 04 94 73 88 81 – www.hotelthoronet.fr – info@hotelthoronet.fr – Fax 04 94 73 89 24 – Closed 15 December-3 February
23 rm – €59/76 €59/76, €9 – ½ P €57/68
Rest – *(closed Sunday dinner and Monday from November to March)* Menu €21 (weekdays)/42 – Carte €36/56
◆ Close to the oldest Cistercian abbey in Provence, a modern building around a pool. Practical rooms. Two dining rooms (including a veranda-terrace) where simple, traditional cuisine is served.

East 8 km on the D 84 and minor road

Bastide des Hautes Moures
VISA
Les Moures – ✆ 04 94 60 13 36 – www.bastidedesmoures.com – infos@bastidedesmoures.com – Fax 04 94 73 81 23 – Closed January and February
4 rm – €75/105 €80/150 **Table d'hôte** – Menu €15 bi/35 bi
◆ This old Provencal farmhouse is set in the middle of the countryside. It has bags of charm with its classic decor, personalised rooms and billiards lounge. Table d'hote offering regional cuisine.

THOUARCÉ – 49 Maine-et-Loire – 317 G5 – pop. 1 682 – alt. 35 m – ✉ 49380 35 C2

Paris 318 – Angers 29 – Cholet 43 – Saumur 38
Syndicat d'initiative, Mairie ✆ 02 41 54 14 36, Fax 02 41 54 09 11
★★ de Brissac-Quincé, Northeast: 12 km, Châteaux of the Loire

Le Relais de Bonnezeaux
VISA AE
1 km on the rte d'Angers – ✆ 02 41 54 08 33 – www.cuisineriesgourmandesanjou.com – relais.bonnezeaux@wanadoo.fr – Fax 02 41 54 00 63 – Closed 26 December-20 January, Tuesday dinner, Sunday dinner and Monday
Rest – Menu (€17), €27 (weekdays)/58 bi – Carte €30/55
◆ Restaurant along the Wine Route, situated in a former country station. The tables on the veranda have views of the vineyards. Traditional cuisine and local wines served.

THOUARS – 79 Deux-Sèvres – 322 E3 – pop. 10 656 – alt. 102 m – ✉ 79100 Atlantic Coast 38 B1

Paris 336 – Angers 71 – Bressuire 31 – Châtellerault 72 – Cholet 56
Office de tourisme, 3 bis, boulevard Pierre Curie ✆ 05 49 66 17 65, Fax 05 49 67 87 58
Façade★★ of St-Médard church ★ - Site★ - Old houses★.

Hôtellerie St-Jean
VISA AE
25 rte de Parthenay – ✆ 05 49 96 12 60 – www.hotellerie-st-jean.fr – hotellerie-st-jean@wanadoo.fr – Fax 05 49 96 34 02 – Closed February holidays and Sunday dinner
18 rm – €45 €45, €7 – ½ P €45
Rest – Menu €17 (weekdays)/35 – Carte €38/60
◆ A 1970s building overlooking the old town. Well-kept rooms with a refreshing decor in yellow and orange shades. Those at the back are quieter. A simple but cheerful dining room serving classic cuisine.

in Ste-Verge 4 km north – pop. 1 453 – alt. 65 m – ✉ 79100

Le Logis de Pompois
VISA AE
13 r. de la Gosselinière – ✆ 05 49 96 27 84 – www.logis-de-pompois.com – catpompois@adapei79.org – Fax 05 49 96 13 97 – Closed 4-10 January, Sunday dinner, Monday and Tuesday
Rest – Menu (€22), €29/48 – Carte €60/67
◆ This 18-19C wine growing estate is home to an in-work benefit centre, which serves wholesome traditional cuisine. Welcoming dining room located in the former wine store.

THOURON – 87 Haute-Vienne – **325** E5 – **pop. 462** – **alt. 374 m** – ✉ **87140** 24 **B1**

Paris 380 – Bellac 23 – Guéret 79 – Limoges 28

La Pomme de Pin rest, VISA

étang de Tricherie, 2,5 km north-eastward along the D 225 – ✆ 05 55 53 43 43 – lapommedepin.thouron@orange.fr – Fax 05 55 53 43 43 – Closed 1st-30 September, 26 January-12 February, Tuesday lunch and Monday

7 rm – € 59 € 59/69, ☕ € 7 – ½ P € 59

Rest – Menu € 19/29 – Carte € 25/38

◆ Comfortable guestrooms occupy some of the stone buildings of this attractive complex, which is also home to a watermill fed by a small stream and a shady garden. Rustic dining room lit by a hearth where the chef grills Limousin beef over a wood fire.

THUIR – 66 Pyrénées-Orientales – **344** H7 – **pop. 7 427** – **alt. 99 m** – ✉ **66300** **Languedoc-Roussillon-Tarn Gorges** 22 **B3**

Paris 897 – Figueres 56 – Montpellier 168 – Perpignan 16

Office de tourisme, boulevard Violet ✆ 04 68 53 45 86

Le Patio Catalan VISA

4 pl. du Général-de-Gaulle – ✆ 04 68 53 57 28 – Closed 6-28 January, Wednesday and Thursday

Rest – Menu (€ 13), € 19/34 – Carte € 33/50

◆ Rustic, modern restaurant on a square opposite the caves de Byrrh. Charming patio entrance, traditional cuisine and wine list based on Côtes du Roussillon wines.

THURET – 63 Puy-de-Dôme – **326** G7 – **pop. 703** – **alt. 330 m** – ✉ **63260** 5 **B2**

Paris 379 – Clermont-Ferrand 32 – Vichy 24 – Cournon-d'Auvergne 35 – Riom 16

Château de la Canière rest, VISA AE

2 km North on D 212 et D 12 – ✆ 04 73 97 98 44 – www.caniere.com – info@caniere.com – Fax 04 73 97 98 42

27 rm – € 113/125 € 132/145, ☕ € 15 – 2 suites

Rest ***Lavoisier*** – Menu (€ 28), € 39/62 – Carte € 45/77

◆ An intelligently renovated 19C château, most of whose rooms sport an Empire style. Pool, wooded park and formal gardens: a haven of peace and quiet. Creativity meets science in the restaurant devoted to Lavoisier, an 18C chemist.

THURY – 21 Côte-d'Or – **320** H7 – **pop. 289** – **alt. 382 m** – ✉ **21340** 8 **C2**

Paris 303 – Beaune 33 – Autun 25 – Avallon 80 – Dijon 71

Manoir Bonpassage rm, VISA

La Grande Pièce, 1 km south on D 36 and secondary road – ✆ 03 80 20 26 16 – www.bonpassage.com – bonpassage@wanadoo.fr – Fax 03 80 20 26 17 – Open 1st April-31 October

9 rm – € 59 € 59/80, ☕ € 9

Rest – *(closed Sunday, Tuesday and Thursday) (dinner only) (resident only)* Menu € 24

◆ Unpretentious, faultlessly cared for rooms, some overlooking the countryside. Swimming pool in summer. Peace and quiet, guesthouse ambience.

THURY-HARCOURT – 14 Calvados – **303** J6 – **pop. 1 813** – **alt. 45 m** – ✉ **14220** **Normandy** 32 **B2**

Paris 257 – Caen 28 – Condé-sur-Noireau 20 – Falaise 27 – Flers 32 – St-Lô 68 – Vire 41

Office de tourisme, 2, place Saint-Sauveur ✆ 02 31 79 70 45, Fax 02 31 79 15 42

Château park and gardens★ - Boucle du Hom★ Northwest: 3 km.

XX **Le Relais de la Poste** with rm
7 r. de Caen – ✆ 02 31 79 72 12 – www.hotel-relaisdelaposte.com – relaisdelaposte@ohotellerie.com – Fax 02 31 39 53 55 – Closed March and 20-31 December
10 rm – †€ 65/140 ††€ 65/140, ☕ € 11
Rest – *(closed Saturday lunch October-May and Friday except lunch May-October)* Menu (€ 18), € 23 (weekday lunch), € 28/80 – Carte € 45/62
◆ A former coaching inn facing a courtyard and garden decked in spring and summer flowers. Small, simple but tastefully refurbished rooms. Traditional cuisine.

TIERCÉ – **49 Maine-et-Loire** – **317** G3 – **pop. 3 876** – **alt. 30 m** – ✉ **49125** 35 **C2**

Paris 278 – Angers 22 – Château-Gontier 34 – La Flèche 34

Syndicat d'initiative, Mairie ✆ 02 41 31 14 41, Fax 02.41.34.14.44

XX **La Table d'Anjou**
16 r. Anjou – ✆ 02 41 42 14 42 – www.destination-anjou.com/tabledanjou – latabledanjou@club-internet.fr – Fax 02 41 42 64 80 – Closed 20 July-12 August, 2-14 January, Sunday dinner, Monday and Tuesday
Rest – Menu (€ 19), € 25 (weekdays)/75 – Carte € 41/67
◆ Friendly restaurant in the centre of the village with two bright neo-rustic dining rooms and a small flower-decked terrace at the back. Pleasant service.

TIGNES – **73 Savoie** – **333** O5 – **pop. 2 220** – **alt. 2 100 m** – **Winter sports : 1 550/3 450 m** 4 44 – ✉ **73320** **French Alps** 45 **D2**

Paris 665 – Albertville 85 – Bourg-St-Maurice 31 – Chambéry 134 – Val-d'Isère 14

Office de tourisme, Tignes Accueil ✆ 04 79 40 04 40, Fax 04 79 40 03 15

du Lac de Tignes Le Val Claret, S : 2 km, ✆ 04 79 06 37 42

Site★★ - Dam★★ Northeast: 5 km - Panorama of la Grande Motte★★ Southwest.

Les Suites du Montana rm,
Les Almes – ✆ 04 79 40 01 44 – www.vmontana.com – contact@vmontana.com – Fax 04 79 40 04 03 – Open mid-December to mid-April
1 rm – †€ 108/209 ††€ 166/318, ☕ € 12 – 27 suites – ††€ 366/520
Rest – *(dinner only)* Menu € 45 – Carte € 52/61
◆ A 'hamlet' of chalets home to spacious refined suites, decorated in Savoyard, Austrian or Provençal style, equipped with south-facing balconies and private saunas. Spit roasting before your eyes at the 'all-wood' rotisserie with view of the slopes.

Les Campanules
– ✆ 04 79 06 34 36 – www.campanules.com – campanules@wanadoo.fr – Fax 04 79 06 35 78 – Open 8 July-26 August and 11 November-2 May
31 rm ☕ – †€ 110/190 ††€ 150/280 – 10 suites – ½ P € 110/185
Rest – Menu € 28 (lunch), € 40/51 – Carte € 50/70
◆ In the centre of the resort, this pretty chalet has spacious, comfortable rooms and duplex apartments on the top floor. Outdoor pool and panoramic gym. The fresco decorating the walls of the restaurant recalls the old village that was flooded with the construction of the Tignes Dam in 1952.

 **Village Montana** rest,
Les Almes – ✆ 04 79 40 01 44 – www.vmontana.com – contact@vmontana.com – Fax 04 79 40 04 03 – Open end June-mid September and beg. November-beg. May
78 rm ☕ – †€ 108/209 ††€ 166/318 – 4 suites **Rest** – Menu € 32
Rest ***La Chaumière*** – *(open beg. December-beg. May)* Carte € 20/35
◆ These splendid chalets blend tradition, modern comforts and peace and quiet. Spacious family rooms facing the skiing domain. A brasserie menu and Savoyard specialities at La Chaumière, decorated in a sheepfold type way.

Le Lévanna
Quartier le Rosset – ✆ 04 79 06 32 94 – www.levanna.com – info@levanna.com – Fax 04 79 06 33 18 – Open 2 October-9 May
40 rm (½ board only) – ½ P € 93/166 **Rest** – Menu € 35 – Carte € 44/63
◆ The rooms of this recent chalet are comfortable and decorated in wood. All possess a balcony and some are duplex. Pleasant sauna-hammam complex. Traditional cuisine, cheese specialities and a huge terrace overlooking the ski slopes.

Le Refuge without rest
– ✆ 04 79 06 36 64 – www.hotel-refuge-tignes.com – info@hotel-refuge-tignes.com – Fax 04 79 06 33 78 – Closed 8 May-1st July and 8 September-18 October
33 rm – † € 62/115 †† € 97/175
◆ This hotel is superbly located opposite the lake and only 50m from the ski lifts. Simple, practical rooms with south-facing balconies.

L'Arbina
– ✆ 04 79 06 34 78 – www.hotel-arbina.com – hotelarbina@aol.com – Fax 04 79 06 32 99 – Open 10 July-31 August and 2 October-10 May
22 rm – † € 50/100 †† € 75/124, € 12 – ½ P € 60/105
Rest – *(open 20 November-10 May)* Menu (€ 23), € 29/40 – Carte € 36/64
◆ The Arbina is the local name for the Alpine Partridge. This family-run hotel has comfortable rooms, decorated in a simple, contemporary mountain style. The restaurant terrace overlooks the Grande Motte glacier. Fine choice of wines by the glass.

Gentiana
montée du Rosset – ✆ 04 79 06 52 46 – www.hotelgentiana.com – serge.revial@wanadoo.fr – Fax 04 79 06 35 61 – Open 1st July-23 August and 1st December-3 May
40 rm (½ board only) – ½ P € 86/140
Rest – *(dinner only)* Menu € 26, € 30/40
◆ The rooms – some of which have balconies – are being progressively renovated in a warm chalet style. Large spa area (gym, steam room, sauna, etc). Traditional cuisine and recipes based on exotic produce and spices.

Le Paquis
Le Rosset – ✆ 04 79 06 37 33 – www.hotel-lepaquis.fr – info@hotel-lepaquis.fr – Fax 04 79 06 36 59 – Open December to May
36 rm (½ board only) – ½ P € 70/115
Rest – *(dinner only)* Menu (€ 15), € 25 – Carte € 29/45
◆ On the heights overlooking Tignes, a robust 1960s building offering functional rooms. Choose one of the more recent rooms, renovated in a chalet style. Sample small traditional dishes in a mountain setting.

La Ferme des 3 Capucines
Le Lavachet – ✆ 04 79 06 35 10 – Fax 04 79 06 35 10 – Open 10 July-28 August and 8 December-5 May
Rest – *(pre-book)* Menu € 25/30
◆ Watch the cows in the adjoining stable at this friendly dairy farm while enjoying generous, regional family cooking – an unusual and pleasant place to eat.

in Val Claret 2 km southwest – alt. 2 100 m – ✉ 73320 Tignes

Le Ski d'Or
– ✆ 04 79 06 51 60 – www.hotel-skidor.com – thomas.boulais@hotel-skidor.com – Fax 04 79 06 45 49 – Open 25 October-5 May
27 rm – † € 98/250 †† € 150/380 – ½ P € 115/215
Rest – *(dinner only)* Menu € 40
◆ A fully renovated hotel, whose contemporary decor sports wood and a cream and taupe colour scheme. The rooms are smart and comfortable. Immense dining room overlooking the mountains and slopes; warm friendly ambience.

TILQUES – 62 Pas-de-Calais – **301** G3 – see St-Omer

LES TINES – 74 Haute-Savoie – **328** O5 – see Chamonix-Mont-Blanc

TONNEINS – 47 Lot-et-Garonne – 336 D3 – pop. 9 141 – alt. 26 m – ✉ 47400 4 C2

Paris 683 – Agen 44 – Nérac 38 – Villeneuve-sur-Lot 37

Office de tourisme, 3, avenue Charles-de-Gaulle ✆ 05 53 79 22 79, Fax 05 53 79 39 94

de Barthe Tombeboeuf Route de Villeneuve, NE : 20 km on D 120, ✆ 05 53 88 83 31

Des Fleurs without rest
rte de Bordeaux – ✆ 05 53 79 10 47 – www.hoteldesfleurs47.com – hoteldesfleurs@wanadoo.fr – Fax 05 53 79 46 37 – Closed 20 December-3 January and 14-22 February
26 rm – €35/59 €38/66, ☕ €8
◆ An establishment on the town's main street. The rooms are rather small but practical, colourful, well-equipped, set back from the street and are gradually being renovated.

TONNERRE – 89 Yonne – 319 G4 – pop. 5 440 – alt. 156 m – ✉ 89700 7 B1

Burgundy-Jura

Paris 199 – Auxerre 38 – Châtillon-sur-Seine 49 – Montbard 45 – Troyes 60

Office de tourisme, place Marguerite de Bourgogne ✆ 03 86 55 14 48, Fax 03 86 54 41 82

de Tanlay Tanlay Parc du Château, 9 km on the Châtillon-sur-Seine road, ✆ 03 86 75 72 92

Fosse Dionne★ - Interior★ of the former hospital: burial★ - Château de Tanlay★★ 9 km by ①.

L'Auberge de Bourgogne rm, rest,
D 905, 2 km on ① and Dijon road – ✆ 03 86 54 41 41 – www.aubergedebourgogne.com – auberge.bourgogne@wanadoo.fr – Fax 03 86 54 48 28 – Closed 15 December-15 January
40 rm – €56/60 €60, ☕ €9 – ½ P €55
Rest – *(closed Saturday lunch, Sunday and Monday)* Menu €18/26 – Carte €29/35
◆ A modern building bordering the Epineuil vineyards. Rooms are soberly functional and those at the rear offer a fine view of the countryside. Boeuf Bourguignon takes pride of place on the menu. Bright and spacious restaurant.

TORCY – 71 Saône-et-Loire – 320 G9 – see le Creusot

TORNAC – 30 Gard – 339 I4 – see Anduze

TÔTES – 76 Seine-Maritime – 304 G3 – pop. 1 084 – alt. 150 m – ✉ 76890 33 D1

Paris 168 – Dieppe 34 – Fécamp 60 – Le Havre 80 – Rouen 37

Auberge du Cygne
5 r. G. de Maupassant – ✆ 02 35 32 92 03 – lalegendedeselfes@orange.fr – Fax 02 35 32 92 03 – Closed Sunday dinner and Monday dinner
Rest – Menu €29/49 – Carte €38/58
◆ Since 1611, this post house has bent over backwards when receiving guests (including many celebrities). Traditional repertory served in one rustic and one Chinese style room.

TOUL – 54 Meurthe-et-Moselle – 307 G6 – pop. 16 300 – alt. 209 m – ✉ 54200 26 B2

Alsace-Lorraine

Paris 291 – Bar-le-Duc 62 – Metz 75 – Nancy 23 – St-Dizier 78 – Verdun 80

Office de tourisme, parvis de la Cathédrale ✆ 03 83 64 11 69, Fax 03 83 63 24 37

St-Étienne cathedral★★ and cloister★ - St-Gengoult church: cloister★★ - Façade★ of the former bishop's palace **H** - Musée municipal★ : salle des maladies (patients' hall)★ **M**.

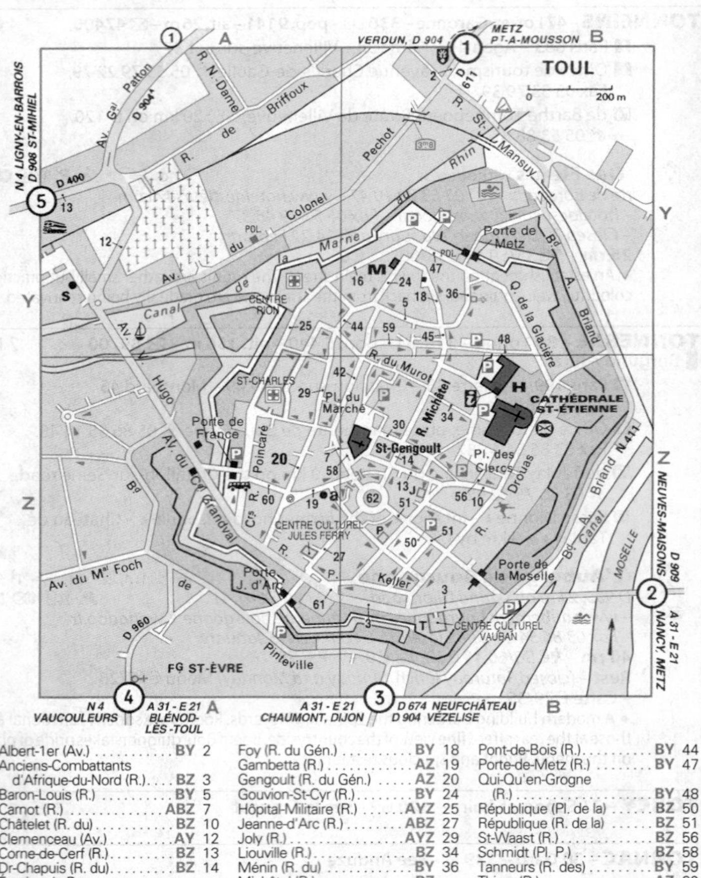

Albert-1er (Av.) . . . . BY 2
Anciens-Combattants d'Afrique-du-Nord (R.). . . . BZ 3
Baron-Louis (R.) . . . . BY 5
Carnot (R.) . . . . ABZ 7
Châtelet (R. du) . . . . BZ 10
Clemenceau (Av.) . . . . AY 12
Corne-de-Cerf (R.) . . . . BZ 13
Dr-Chapuis (R. du). . . . . BZ 14
Écuries-de-Bourgogne (R. des) . . . . BY 16
La-Fayette (R.). . . . . BZ 30
Foy (R. du Gén.) . . . . BY 18
Gambetta (R.) . . . . AZ 19
Gengoult (R. du Gén.) . . . . . . AZ 20
Gouvion-St-Cyr (R.) . . . . BY 24
Hôpital-Militaire (R.) . . . . . . AYZ 25
Jeanne-d'Arc (R.) . . . . ABZ 27
Joly (R.) . . . . AYZ 29
Liouville (R.) . . . . BZ 34
Ménin (R. du) . . . . BY 36
Michâtel (R.) . . . . BZ
Petite-Boucherie (R.) . . . . . . ABZ 42
Pont-des-Cordeliers (R.) . . . . BY 45
Pont-de-Bois (R.). . . . . BY 44
Porte-de-Metz (R.) . . . . BY 47
Qui-Qu'en-Grogne (R.) . . . . BY 48
République (Pl. de la) . . . . . . BZ 50
République (R. de la) . . . . . . BZ 51
St-Waast (R.). . . . . BZ 56
Schmidt (Pl. P.) . . . . BZ 58
Tanneurs (R. des) . . . . BY 59
Thiers (R.) . . . . AZ 60
Vauban (R.) . . . . AZ 61
3-Évêchés (Pl. des) . . . . BZ 62

L'Europe without rest — VISA

373 av. V. Hugo, (near the station) – ✆ 03 83 43 00 10
– www.hotel-europe54.com – hoteldeleurope.toul@wanadoo.fr
– Fax 03 83 63 27 67 – Closed 10-24 August

21 rm – †€ 50/53 ††€ 50/53, € 6 — AY **s**

◆ A convenient hotel when travelling by train. Attractively old-fashioned rooms (original parquet and Art Deco furniture), which are well kept. Family hospitality.

La Villa Lorraine without rest — P VISA

15 r. Gambetta
– ✆ 03 83 43 08 95 – www.hotel-la-villa-lorraine.com
– hotel.villalorraine@wanadoo.fr – Fax 03 83 64 63 64 – Closed autumn half-term holidays

21 rm – †€ 46 ††€ 52, € 7 — AZ **a**

◆ Formerly a theatre, this small hotel in the heart of the fortified town houses rustic, functional rooms and an attractive breakfast room.

in Lucey 5 km by ⑤ and D 908 – pop. 573 – alt. 260 m – ✉ 54200

XX **Auberge du Pressoir**
7 pl. des Pachenottes – ✆ 03 83 63 81 91 – Closed 17 August-1 September, Sunday dinner, Wednesday dinner and Monday
Rest – Menu € 17 (weekday lunch), € 25/30 – Carte € 29/40
◆ The old village station has become a restaurant with simple decor. Some regional country ornaments decorate the walls. Sunny terrace.

Your opinions are important to us:
please write and let us know about your discoveries
and experiences – good and bad!

TOULON P – **83 Var** – **340** K7 – **pop. 167 400** – **Built-up area 519 640** 41 **C3**
– **alt. 10 m** – ✉ **83000** **French Riviera**

Paris 835 – Aix-en-Provence 86 – Marseille 66

Toulon-Hyères: ✆ 0 825 01 83 87, by ①: 21 km.

✆ 3635 et tapez 42 (0,34 €/mn)

For Corsica: SNCM (April-October) 49 av. Infanterie de Marine ✆ 3260 say "SNCM" (0.15 €/mn).

Office de tourisme, place Raimu ✆ 04 94 18 53 00, Fax 04 94 18 53 09

de Valgarde La Garde Chemin de Rabasson, E : 10 km on D 29, ✆ 04 94 14 01 05

Harbour★★ - Port★ - Old town★ GYZ: Atlantes statues★ of the mairie d'honneur **F**, Musée de la marine★ - Porte★ de la Corderie.

Corniche du Mont Facon ≤★ of the cable car - Memorial museum of the Provence Landing★ and ≤★★★ North.

Plans on following pages

All Seasons
pl. Besagne – ✆ 04 98 00 81 00 – www.all-seasons-hotels.com – h2095@accor.com – Fax 04 94 41 57 51 GZ **r**
139 rm – €67/123 €77/123 **Rest** – *(dinner only)* Menu € 15 bi/23
◆ Newly refurbished establishment, opposite the conference centre. Luxury rooms in Provencal hues. Glass roofing and palm trees brighten up this spacious and airy dining room. Traditional cuisine.

Grand Hôtel de la Gare without rest
14 bd Tessé – ✆ 04 94 24 10 00 – www.grandhotelgare.com – contact@grandhotelgare.com – Fax 04 94 22 34 82 FX **a**
39 rm – €49/90 €55/90, €9
◆ This comfortable, well-kept, town centre hotel offers practical, homogenous rooms. All are well soundproofed and air-conditioned.

Dauphiné without rest
10 r. Berthelot – ✆ 04 94 92 20 28 – www.grandhoteldauphine.com – contact@grandhoteldauphine.com – Fax 04 94 62 16 69 GY **s**
55 rm – €51/60 €62/68, €9
◆ A family-run establishment ideally located to explore the old town's maze of narrow streets. Contemporary rooms (light or limed wood) and modern bathrooms.

Bonaparte without rest
16 r. Anatole-France – ✆ 04 94 93 07 51 – www.hotel-bonaparte.com – reservation@hotel-bonaparte.com – Fax 04 94 93 24 55 FY **f**
22 rm – €52 €57/59, €8,50 – 2 suites
◆ This Napoleonic building sports a warm Provençal decor. Table d'hôte-style breakfast. In summertime, opt for one of the guestrooms at the rear (quieter and cooler).

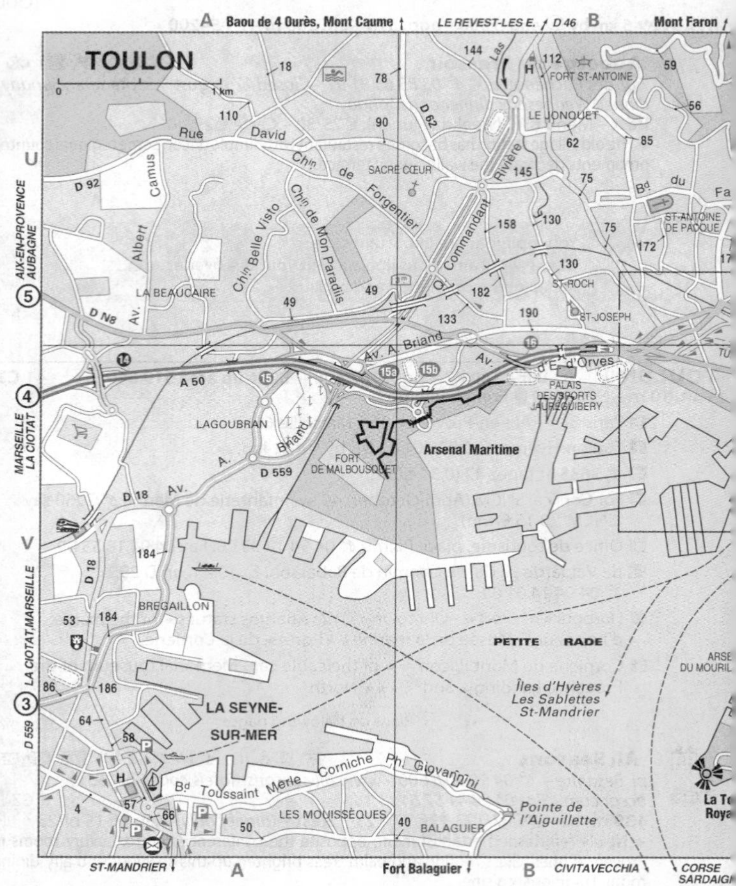

XX Le Jardin du Sommelier

20 allée Amiral Courbet – ✆ 04 94 62 03 27 – www.lejardindusommelier.com – scalisi@le-jardin-du-sommelier.com – Fax 04 94 09 01 49 – Closed Saturday lunch and Sunday FY **r**

Rest – Menu € 38 – Carte approx. € 46

◆ Red and grey are the dominant colours in this comfortable restaurant serving appetising cuisine accompanied by an interesting wine list.

XX Blanc le Bistro

290 r. Jean-Jaurès – ✆ 04 94 10 20 40 – www.blanc-lebistro.fr – blanc.lebistro@wanadoo.fr – Fax 04 94 10 20 39 – Closed 25 July-24 August, 24-28 December, Monday dinner, Saturday lunch and Sunday FY **d**

Rest – Menu (€ 18), € 29/39 – Carte € 40/50

◆ This trendy bistro on a small road in the town centre was once a cinema. Enjoy the simple, convivial dining room with sleek decor and the hearty, generous 'bistronomique' cuisine.

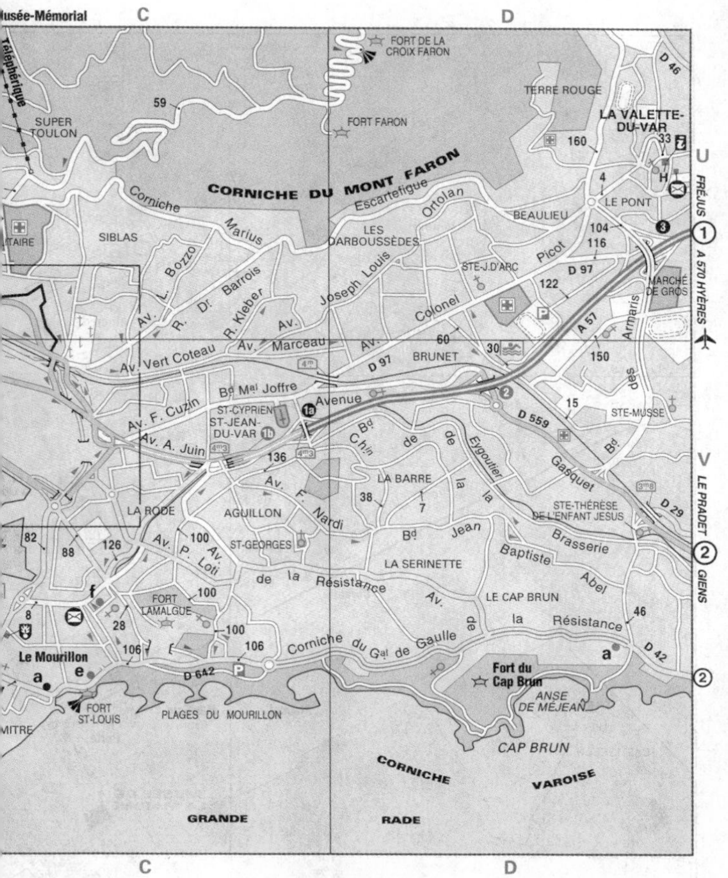

in Mourillon – ✉ 83100 Toulon

Tour royale ✻★.

La Corniche without rest

17 littoral F. Mistral – ✆ 04 94 41 35 12
– www.bestwestern-hotelcorniche.com – info@cornichehotel.com
– Fax 04 94 41 24 58 CV **a**

28 rm – €95/150 €200/350, ☕ €14

◆ This hotel is near the St Louis harbour and Mourillon beaches. It offers elegant and comfortable rooms and suites, most with panoramic views of the sea.

Le Gros Ventre

279 littoral F. Mistral – ✆ 04 94 42 15 42 – www.legrosventre.net
– alain.audibert503@orange.fr
– Fax 04 94 31 40 32
– Closed Saturday lunch, Thursday and Friday CV **e**

Rest – Menu €28/85 – Carte €40/100

◆ The chef specialises in beef and locally sourced fish baked in pastry, while his sommelier daughter offers faultless wine suggestions.

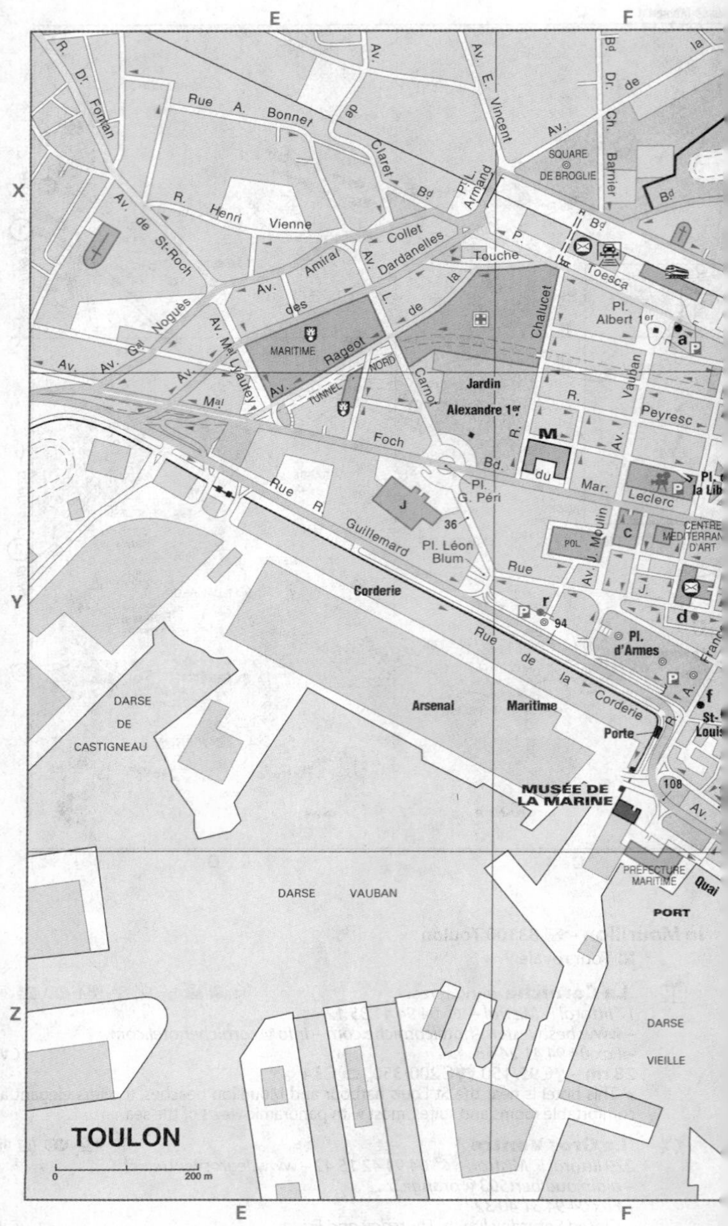
E
F
X
Y
Z
R. Dr. Fontan
Rue A. Bonnet
Av. de Claret
Av. E. Vincent
Bd Dr. Ch. Barnier
Av.
SQUARE DE BROGLIE
Bd
Pl. L. Armand
R. Henri Vienne
Av. de St-Roch
Av. Collet
Av. Amiral
Dardanelles
Bd
P.
Touche
Toesca
Av. des Rageot
Av. L. de la
Chalucet
Pl. Albert 1er
a
Av. Gal Noguès
Av. Mal Lyautey
MARITIME
Av. Rageot
TUNNEL NORD
Carnot
Jardin
Alexandre 1er
Av.
Av.
Av.
Mal
R.
Vauban
Peyresc
Foch
M
Bd.
du
Mar.
Leclerc
Pl. G. Péri
Pl. la Lib
J
36
Rue R. Guillemard
Pl. Léon Blum
Rue
POL
Av. J. Moulin
C
CENTRE MEDITERRAN D'ART
J.
Corderie
r
94
d
Pl. d'Armes
Rue de la Corderie
Franc
A.
f
St-Louis
Arsenal
Maritime
Porte
R.
DARSE DE CASTIGNEAU
MUSÉE DE LA MARINE
108
Av.
DARSE VAUBAN
PRÉFECTURE MARITIME
Quai
PORT
DARSE VIEILLE
TOULON
0
200 m

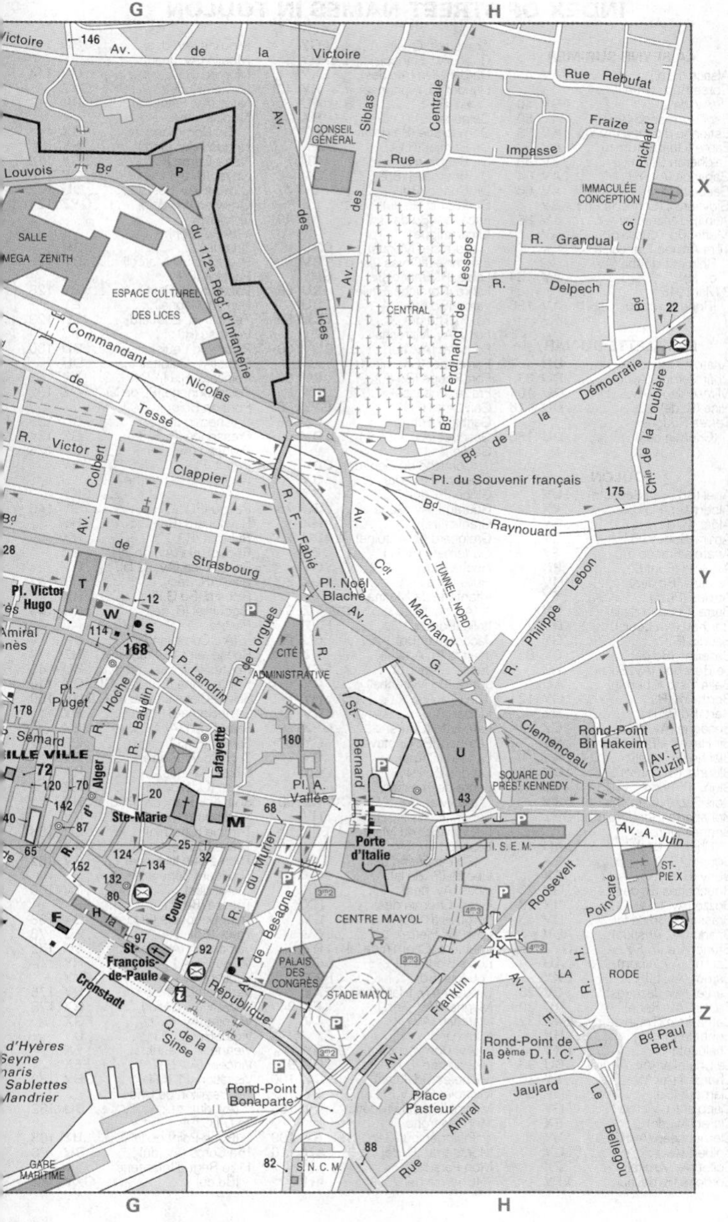

G
H
G
H
X
Y
Z
Av. de la Victoire
146
Rue Rebufat
Rue Centrale
Fraize
Impasse
Richard
CONSEIL GÉNÉRAL
Rue des Siblas
Av. des Lices
Louvois
Bd du 112e. Régt. d'Infanterie
P
IMMACULÉE CONCEPTION
SALLE OMEGA ZENITH
ESPACE CULTUREL DES LICES
R. Grandual
G.
R. Delpech
Bd Ferdinand de Lesseps
CENTRAL
22
Commandant Nicolas
de Tessé
Bd de la Démocratie
Chin de la Loubière
R. Victor Clappier
Colbert
Pl. du Souvenir français
175
Bd Raynouard
Av. de Strasbourg
R. F. Fabié
Av. Cdt Marchand
TUNNEL - NORD
28
Pl. Noël Blache
Av. G. Clemenceau
R. Philippe Lebon
T
Pl. Victor Hugo
12
W
S
114
168
R. P. Landrin
R. de Lorgues
CITÉ ADMINISTRATIVE
R. St. Bernard
Pl. Puget
R. Hoche
R. Baudin
178
Lafayette
180
U
Rond-Point Bir Hakeim
Av. F. Cuzin
SQUARE DU PRESt KENNEDY
R. Alger
72
120
70
142
87
20
Ste-Marie
M
68
Pl. A. Vallée
43
Porte d'Italie
I. S. E. M.
Av. A. Juin
ST-PIE X
65
124
134
25
32
R. du Murier
152
132
80
Cours Lafayette
Roosevelt
Poincaré
F
H
CENTRE MAYOL
97
St-François-de-Paule
92
r
R. de Besagne
LA RODE
R. H.
Av. E.
Cronstadt
République
PALAIS DES CONGRÈS
STADE MAYOL
Franklin
Q. de la Sinse
Rond-Point de la 9ème D. I. C.
Bd Paul Bert
Rond-Point Bonaparte
Place Pasteur
Rue Amiral Jaujard
Le Bellegou
88
82
S. N. C. M.
GARE MARITIME

INDEX OF STREET NAMES IN TOULON

in Cap Brun – ✉ 83100 Toulon

XXX **Les Pins Penchés**

3182 av. de la Résistance – ✆ 04 94 27 98 98 – www.restaurant-pins-penches.com – infos@restaurant-pins-penches.com – Fax 04 94 27 98 27 – Closed Sunday dinner, Tuesday lunch and Monday DV **a**

Rest – Menu (€ 38), € 58/68

◆ A delightful 19C villa serving traditional fare in a lavish decor. Superb panorama over the park, Cap Brun and the Mediterranean.

TOULON-LA-MONTAGNE – **51 Marne** – **306** F9 – ✉ **51130** 13 **B2**

Paris 128 – Châlons-en-Champagne 40 – Épernay 29 – Reims 58

Les Corettes without rest

chemin du Pâti – ✆ 03 26 59 06 92 – Fax 03 26 59 06 92 – Closed 1st December-1st March

5 rm – €55 €65

◆ Appealing residence overlooking the winegrowing village. Rooms with personal touches, billiard lounge and flower garden.

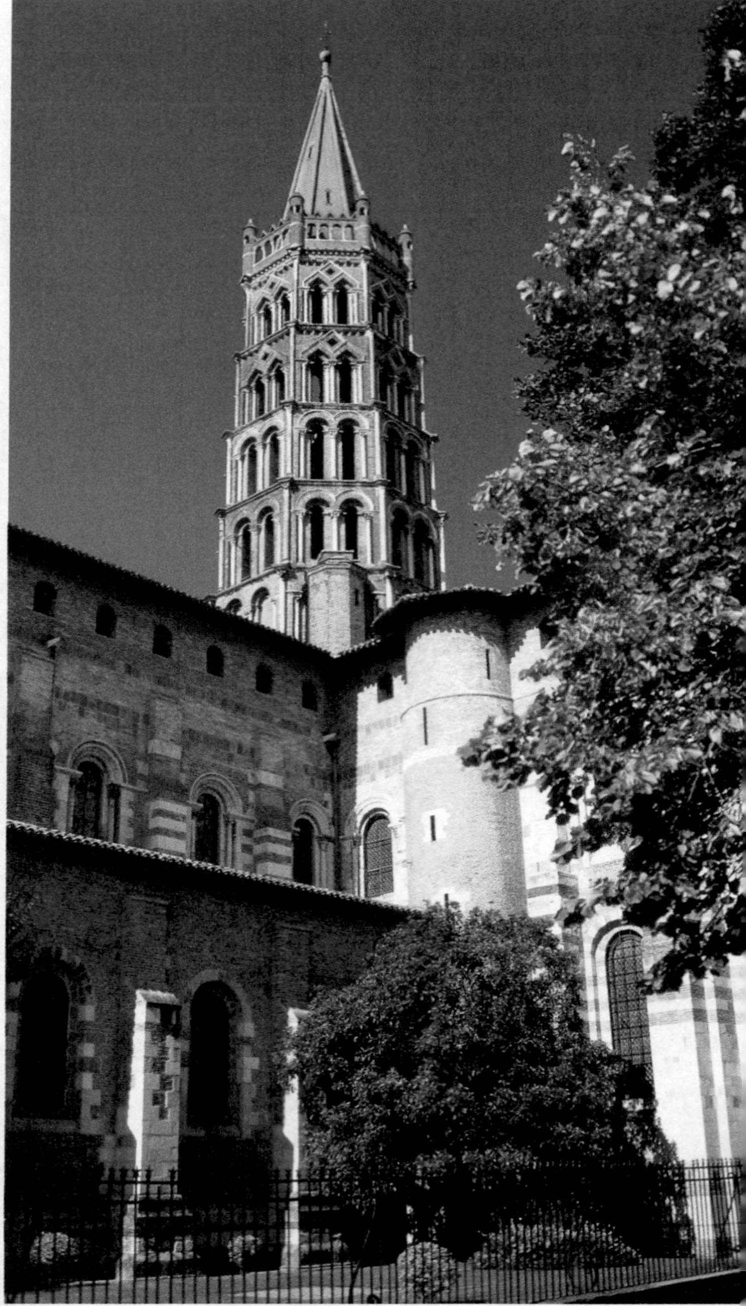

J.-P. Garcin/PHOTONONSTOP

La basilique Saint Sernin

TOULOUSE

P Department: 31 Haute-Garonne
Michelin LOCAL map: n° 343 G3
Paris 677 – Barcelona 320 – Bordeaux 244 – Lyon 535 – Marseille 405

Population: 437 100
Pop. built-up area: 936 800
Altitude: 146 m
Postal Code: 31000
Languedoc-Roussillon-Tarn Gorges
Carte régionale 28 B2

USEFUL INFORMATION

TOURIST OFFICE

donjon du Capitole ✆ 05 61 11 02 22, Fax 05 61 23 74 97

TRANSPORTS

Auto-train ✆ 3635 et tapez 42 (0,34 €/mn)

AIRPORT

Toulouse-Blagnac ✆ 0 825 380 000 (0,15 €/mn) AS

A FEW GOLF COURSES

18 de Toulouse La Ramée Tournefeuille Ferme du Cousturier, ✆ 05 61 07 09 09
18 de Toulouse Vieille-ToulouseS : 9 km on D 4, ✆ 05 61 73 45 48
9 Saint-Gabriel Montrabé "Lieu dit ""Castié""", 10 km on the Lavaur road, ✆ 05 61 84 16 65
36 Seilh Toulouse Seilh Route de Grenade, 12 km on the Seilh road, ✆ 05 62 13 14 14
9 de Borde-Haute Drémil-Lafage Borde-Haute, 15 km on the Castres road (N 126), ✆ 05 62 18 84 00
18 de Teoula Plaisance-du-Touch 71, avenue des Landes, SW : 20 km on D 632, ✆ 05 61 91 98 80
18 de Palmola Buzet-sur-Tarn Route d'Albi, NE : 22 km on the A 68, exit 4, ✆ 05 61 84 20 50

CASINO

– Du théâtre, 18 chemin de la Loge

Hippodrome de la Cépière, 1 Chemin des Courses ✆ 05 34 39 01 45

TO SEE

TOULOUSE AND AERONAUTICS

Clément-Ader factory at Colomiers in the western suburbs by ⑦

ST-SERNIN BASILICA AND CAPITOLE DISTRICTS

- St-Sernin basilica ★★★ - Musée St-Raymond★★ - Les Jacobins church ★★ (church nave ★★) - Capitole★ - Staircase tower ★of the Hôtel de Bernuy EY

FROM PLACE DE LA DAURADE TO CATHEDRAL

- Hôtel d'Assézat and Bemberg Foundation ★★ EY - St-Étienne cathedral ★ - Musée des Augustins★★ (sculptures★★★) FY

OTHER SIGHTS

Muséum d'histoire naturelle★★ FZ - Musée Paul-Dupuy★ FZ - Musée Georges-Labit★ DV M^2

INDEX OF STREET NAMES IN TOULOUSE

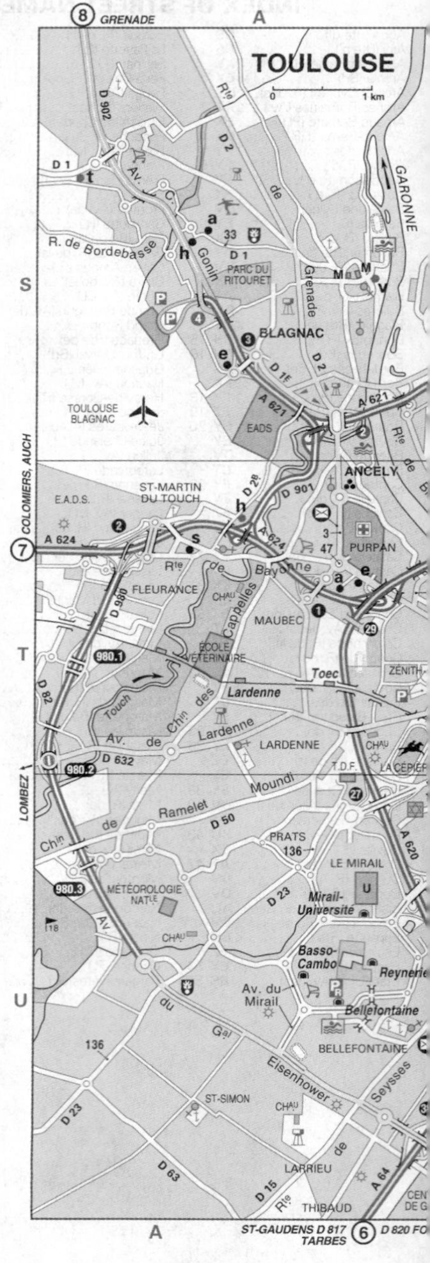

8 GRENADE
A
TOULOUSE
0
1 km
GARONNE
D 902
D 1
D 2
R. de Bordebasse
Gonin
PARC DU RITOURET
Grenade
BLAGNAC
TOULOUSE BLAGNAC
A 621
EADS
ANCELY
S
COLOMIERS, AUCH
7
A 624
E.A.D.S.
ST-MARTIN DU TOUCH
D 901
PURPAN
FLEURANCE
Bayonne
Cappelles
MAUBEC
T
980.1
ÉCOLE VÉTÉRINAIRE
Toec
ZÉNITH
D 82
Touch
Lardenne
LARDENNE
D 632
980.2
T.D.F.
LA CÉPIÈRE
LOMBEZ
Moundi
Ramelet
D 50
PRATS
136
LE MIRAIL
A 620
980.3
MÉTÉOROLOGIE NAT^LE
D 23
Mirail-Université
Basso-Cambo
Reynerie
U
Av. du Mirail
Bellefontaine
BELLEFONTAINE
Eisenhower
Seysses
ST-SIMON
D 63
LARRIEU
D 15
THIBAUD
A 64
A
ST-GAUDENS D 817 TARBES
6
D 820

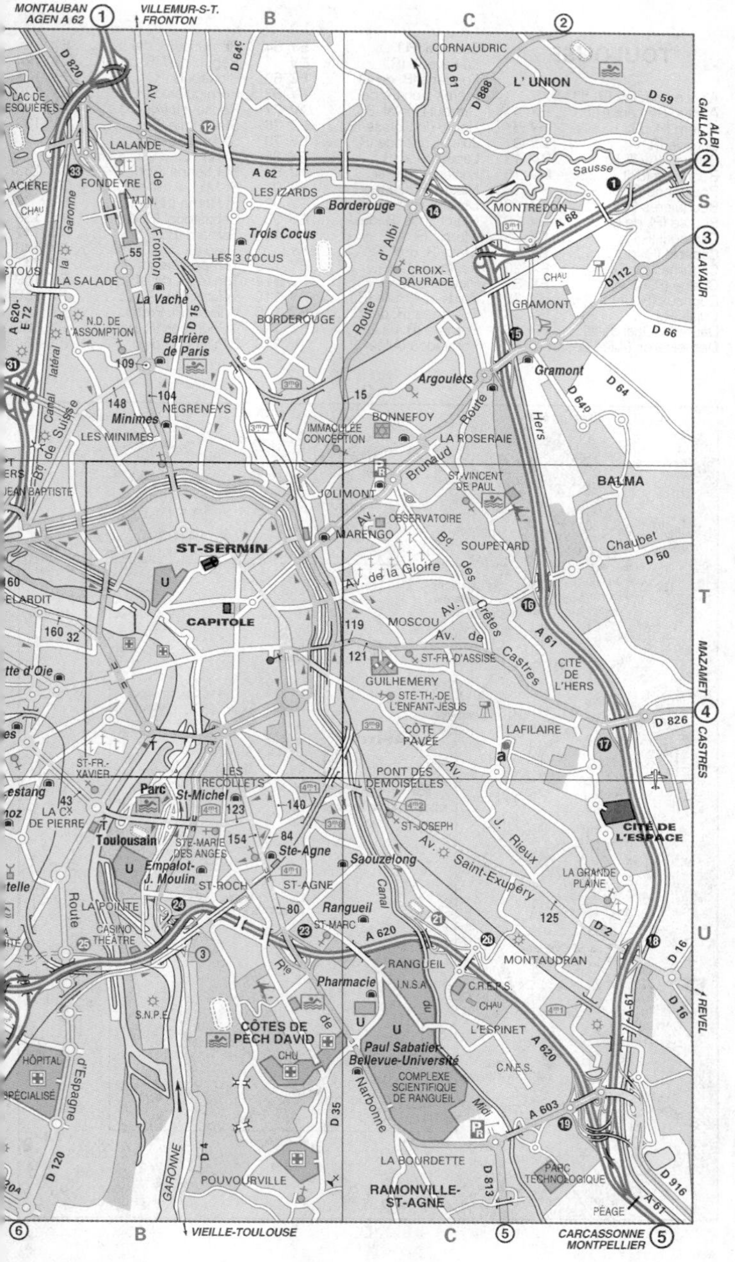
MONTAUBAN AGEN A 62
VILLEMUR-S-T. FRONTON
ALBI GAILLAC
LAVAUR
MAZAMET CASTRES
REVEL
CARCASSONNE MONTPELLIER
VIEILLE-TOULOUSE
L' UNION
CORNAUDRIC
LALANDE
FONDEYRE
LES IZARDS
Borderouge
Trois Cocus
LES 3 COCUS
LA SALADE
La Vache
CROIX-DAURADE
MONTREDON
GRAMONT
Gramont
BORDEROUGE
N.D. DE L'ASSOMPTION
Barrière de Paris
Argoulets
NEGRENEYS
Minimes
LES MINIMES
BONNEFOY
IMMACULÉE CONCEPTION
LA ROSERAIE
BALMA
JOLIMONT
ST-VINCENT DE PAUL
OBSERVATOIRE
MARENGO
ST-SERNIN
SOUPETARD
Chaubet
Av. de la Gloire
CAPITOLE
MOSCOU
Av. de Castres
ST-FR.-D'ASSISE
CITÉ DE L'HERS
GUILHEMERY
STE-TH.-DE L'ENFANT-JÉSUS
CÔTE PAVÉE
LAFILAIRE
ST-FR.-XAVIER
LES RECOLLETS
PONT DES DEMOISELLES
Parc
St-Michel
LA Cx DE PIERRE
Toulousain
STE-MARIE DES ANGES
Ste-Agne
Saouzelong
ST-JOSEPH
CITÉ DE L'ESPACE
Empalot-J. Moulin
ST-ROCH
ST-AGNE
Av. Saint-Exupéry
LA GRANDE PLAINE
LA POINTE
Rangueil
ST-MARC
CASINO THÉATRE
RANGUEIL
MONTAUDRAN
Pharmacie
I.N.S.A.
C.R.E.P.S.
S.N.P.E.
CÔTES DE PECH DAVID
L'ESPINET
Paul Sabatier-Bellevue-Université
C.N.E.S.
HÔPITAL SPÉCIALISÉ
COMPLEXE SCIENTIFIQUE DE RANGUEIL
LA BOURDETTE
PARC TECHNOLOGIQUE
POUVOURVILLE
RAMONVILLE-ST-AGNE
PÉAGE
GARONNE
A 62
A 68
A 61
A 620
A 603
D 820
D 61
D 888
D 59
D 112
D 66
D 64
D 50
D 826
D 16
D 916
D 813
D 35
D 4
D 120
Hers
Sausse

TOULOUSE

Street	Grid	No.
Alsace-Lorraine (R. d')	**EXY**	
Arnaud-Bernard (R.)	**EX**	4
Astorg (R. d')	**FY**	5
Baronie (R.)	**EY**	9
Billières (Av. E.)	**DV**	13
Bonrepos (Bd)	**DV**	16
Boulbonne (R.)	**FY**	18
Bouquières (R.)	**FZ**	19
Bourse (Pl. de la)	**EY**	20
Cantegril (R.)	**FY**	23
Capitole (Pl. du)	**EY**	
Cartailhac (R. E.)	**EX**	26
Chaîne (R. de la)	**EX**	31
Cugnaux (R. de)	**DV**	35
Cujas (R.)	**EY**	36
Daurade (Quai de la)	**EY**	38
Demoiselles (Allée des)	**DV**	40
Esquirol (Pl.)	**EY**	54
La-Fayette (R.)	**EY**	
Fonderie (R. de la)	**EZ**	60
Frères-Lion (R. des)	**FY**	62
Griffoul-Dorval (Bd)	**DV**	72
Henry-de-Gorsse (R.)	**EZ**	76
Jules-Chalande (R.)	**EY**	79
Lapeyrouse (R.)	**FY**	85
Leclerc (Bd Mar.)	**DV**	87
Magre (R. Genty)	**EY**	91
Malcousinat (R.)	**EY**	92
Marchands (R. des)	**EY**	95
Mercié (R. A.)	**EY**	103
Metz (R. de)	**EFY**	
Peyras (R.)	**EY**	113
Pleau (R. de la)	**FZ**	114
Poids-de-l'Huile (R.)	**EY**	115
Polinaires (R. des)	**EZ**	116
Pomme (R. de la)	**EFY**	117
Pompidou (Allée)	**DV**	118
Rémusat (R. de)	**EX**	
République (R. de la)	**DV**	124
Riguepels (R.)	**FY**	127
Romiguières (R.)	**EY**	129
Roosevelt (Allées)	**FXY**	130
Ste-Ursule (R.)	**EY**	137
St-Antoine-du-T. (R.)	**FY**	
St-Etienne (Port)	**DV**	133
St-Michel (Gde-R.)	**DV**	134
St-Rome (R.)	**EY**	
Sébastopol (R. de)	**DV**	139
Semard (Bd P.)	**DV**	142
Suau (R. J.)	**EY**	146
Temponières (R.)	**EY**	147
Trinité (R. de la)	**EY**	149
Vélane (R.)	**FZ**	158
Wilson (Pl. Prés.)	**FY**	
3-Journées (R. des)	**FY**	162
3-Piliers (R. des)	**EX**	164

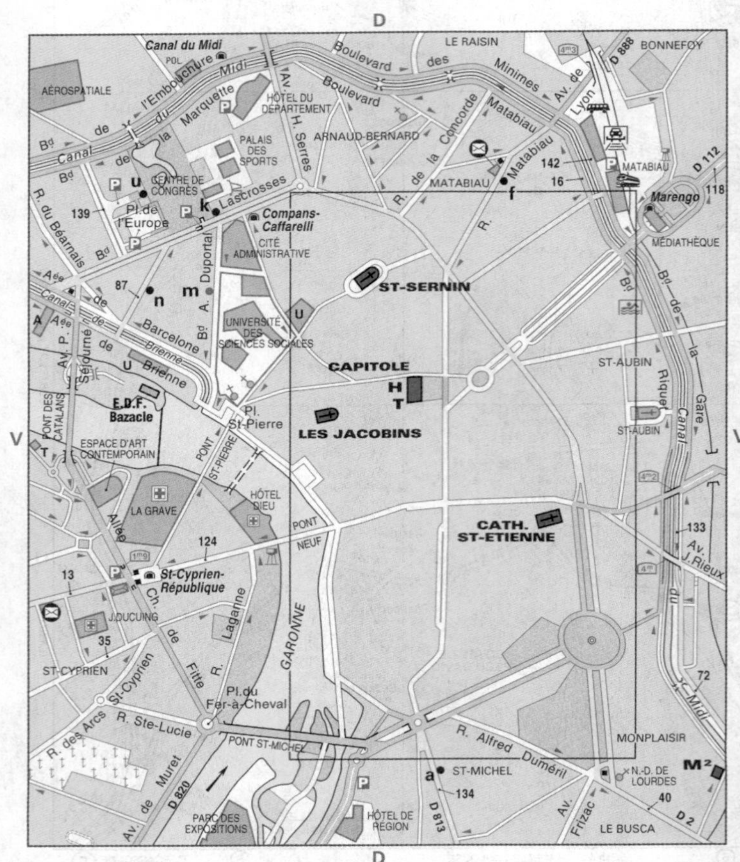

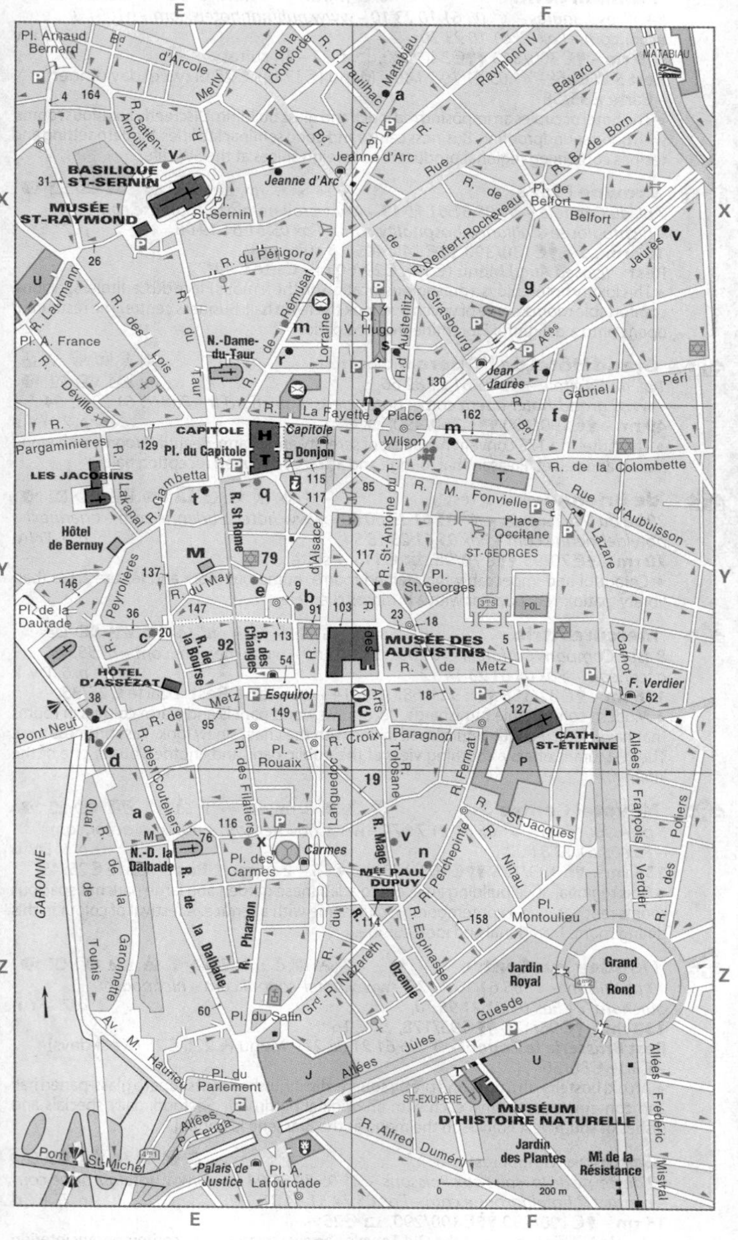
E
F
X
Y
Z
BASILIQUE ST-SERNIN
MUSÉE ST-RAYMOND
N.-Dame-du-Taur
CAPITOLE
Pl. du Capitole
Capitole
Donjon
LES JACOBINS
Hôtel de Bernuy
MUSÉE DES AUGUSTINS
HÔTEL D'ASSÉZAT
CATH. ST-ÉTIENNE
N.-D. la Dalbade
Mée PAUL DUPUY
MUSÉUM D'HISTOIRE NATURELLE
Jardin des Plantes
Jardin Royal
Grand Rond
Mt de la Résistance
MATABIAU
Pl. Jeanne d'Arc
Jeanne d'Arc
Pl. V. Hugo
Jean Jaurès
Place Wilson
Place Occitane
ST-GEORGES
Pl. St.Georges
Pl. St-Sernin
Pl. A. France
Pl. de la Daurade
Pl. Arnaud Bernard
Pl. de Belfort
Pl. Rouaix
Pl. des Carmes
Carmes
Esquirol
F. Verdier
Pl. Montoulieu
Pl. du Salin
Pl. du Parlement
Palais de Justice
Pl. A. Lafourcade
ST-EXUPERE
Pont Neuf
Pont St-Michel
GARONNE
Quai de Tounis
R. de la Garonnette
Av. M. Hauriou
Allées P. Feuga
Allées Jules Guesde
R. Alfred Duméril
Allées Frédéric Mistral
Allées François Verdier
R. des Potiers
R. de Metz
R. Croix-Baragnon
R. Tolosane
R. Fermat
R. St-Jacques
R. Ninau
R. Perchepinte
R. Espinasse
R. Mage
Ozenne
Gde R. Nazareth
R. Pharaon
R. de la Dalbade
R. des Couteliers
R. des Filatiers
R. de la Bourse
R. des Changes
R. St Rome
R. du May
R. Peyrolières
R. Lakanal
R. Gambetta
R. Pargaminières
R. Déville
R. des Lois
R. du Taur
R. de Rémusat
R. du Périgord
R. Lautmann
R. Gatien-Arnoult
Bd d'Arcole
R. Merly
R. de la Concorde
R. C. Pauilhac
R. Matabiau
Bd Raymond IV
R. Bayard
Rue de Belfort
R. B. de Born
R. Denfert-Rochereau
Bd de Strasbourg
Allées J. Jaurès
R. d'Austerlitz
R. Lorraine
R. La Fayette
R. d'Alsace
R. St-Antoine du T.
R. M. Fonvielle
R. de la Colombette
Rue d'Aubuisson
R. Lazare Carnot
R. Gabriel Péri
R. du L. Languedoc
R. des Arts
POL
0
200 m

Pullman Centre rm, rest, VISA

84 allées J. Jaurès – 05 61 10 23 10 – www.pullmanhotels.com – h1091@accor.com – Fax 05 61 10 23 20 p. 7 FX **v**

119 rm – €300/340 €340/380, €22 – 14 suites

Rest ***S W Café*** – *05 61 10 23 40* – Menu (€17 bi), €25 bi (weekday dinner) – Carte €35/58

◆ The hotel occupies an imposing red-brick and glass building. Discreetly luxurious rooms, with good soundproofing. Business centre and good seminar facilities. Modern setting and recipes combining regional products and foreign spices at the SW café.

Crowne Plaza rm, VISA

7 pl. du Capitole – 05 61 61 19 19 – www.crowne-plaza-toulouse.com – hicptoulouse@alliance-hospitality.com – Fax 05 61 61 19 08 p. 7 EY **t**

162 rm – €130/390 €145/405 – 3 suites

Rest – *(closed Aug.)* Menu (€19), €29/60 bi – Carte €49/72

◆ This luxury hotel enjoys a prestigious location on the famous Place du Capitole. Spacious, comfortable rooms, some of which overlook the town hall. Business centre. The restaurant opens onto a delightful Florentine-inspired patio.

Grand Hôtel de l'Opéra without rest VISA

1 pl. du Capitole – 05 61 21 82 66 – www.grand-hotel-opera.com – hotelopera@guichard.fr – Fax 05 61 23 41 04

49 rm – €190/490 €260/490, €22 p. 7 EY **a**

◆ This hotel in a 17C convent has an air of serenity and charm. Beautiful rooms with wood panels and velvet. Pleasant bar lounge and attractive vaulted reception hall.

de Brienne without rest P VISA

20 bd du Mar. Leclerc – 05 61 23 60 60 – www.hoteldebrienne.com – brienne@hoteldebrienne.com – Fax 05 61 23 18 94 p. 6 DV **n**

70 rm – €70/95 €70/95, €11 – 1 suite

◆ Colourful and impeccably maintained rooms, numerous work and leisure areas (bar-library, patio): very popular with a business clientele.

Mercure Atria VISA

8 espl. Compans Caffarelli – 05 61 11 09 09 – www.mercure.com – h1585@accor.com – Fax 05 61 23 14 12 p. 6 DV **k**

136 rm – €82/158 €92/168, €14 – 2 suites **Rest** – Carte €25/35

◆ Modern comfortable furnishings, decorative wood panels and warm colours in rooms that have been recently refurbished in line with the chain's new look. Vast business area. The restaurant offers a soothing view of the public park, and another, busier one of the kitchen.

Novotel Centre rm, VISA

5 pl. A. Jourdain – 05 61 21 74 74 – www.novotel.com – h0906@accor.com – Fax 05 61 22 81 22 p. 6 DV **u**

135 rm – €103/175 €103/175, €15 – 2 suites **Rest** – Carte €25/45

◆ This regional-style building adjacent to a Japanese garden and large park has spacious rooms renovated in a contemporary spirit, some with a terrace. A festival of colour in this dining room. Traditional and local cuisine.

Holiday Inn Centre rm, VISA

13 pl. Wilson – 05 61 10 70 70 – www.hotel-capoul.com – hicapoul@guichard.fr – Fax 05 61 21 96 70 p. 7 FY **n**

130 rm – €95/178 €95/178, €16

Rest ***Brasserie le Capoul*** – *05 61 21 08 27* – Menu (€22), €25 (weekdays) – Carte €30/50

◆ An old hostelry on a busy and pretty square, distinguished by its superb glass-paned hall and contemporary rooms, each with an original bathroom. Seafood, daily specials and dishes of southwest France on the menu at the Brasserie le Capoul.

Garonne without rest VISA

22 descente de la Halle aux Poissons – 05 34 31 94 80 – www.hotelgaronne.com – contact@hotelgaronne.com – Fax 05 34 31 94 81 p. 7 EY **d**

14 rm – €190/290 €190/290, €25

◆ An old building in one of the Old Town's narrow streets. A fine contemporary interior: stained-oak parquet flooring, design furniture, silk draperies and the odd Japanese touch.

Des Beaux Arts without rest
1 pl. du Pont-Neuf – ✆ 05 34 45 42 42 – www.hoteldesbeauxarts.com – contact@hoteldesbeauxarts.com – Fax 05 34 45 42 43 p. 7 EY **v**
19 rm – †€ 110/250 ††€ 110/250, ☕ € 16
◆ Tastefully done 18C establishment with cosy refined rooms, most with a view of the Garonne. Number 42 enjoys the additional benefit of a mini-terrace.

Les Capitouls without rest
29 allées J. Jaurès – ✆ 05 34 41 31 21 – www.bestwestern-capitouls.com – reservation@hotel-capitouls.com – Fax 05 61 63 15 17 p. 7 FX **g**
55 rm – †€ 130/181 ††€ 130/181, ☕ € 14 – 2 suites
◆ Right by the Jean Jaurès metro station, this old town house has a distinctive foyer with pink brick vaulting. The rooms have Wifi access.

Mermoz without rest
50 r. Matabiau – ✆ 05 61 63 04 04 – www.hotel-mermoz.com – reservation@hotel-mermoz.com – Fax 05 61 63 15 64 p. 7 DV **f**
52 rm – †€ 125/140 ††€ 125/140, ☕ €15
◆ This hotel is undergoing gradual renovation. The decor recalls the Aeropostale's heroic pilots. Acid bright rooms, a conservatory and a tree-shaded terrace for breakfast.

Mercure Wilson without rest
7 r. Labéda – ✆ 05 34 45 40 60 – www.mercure.com – h1260@accor.com – Fax 05 34 45 40 61
95 rm – †€ 79/189 ††€ 89/199, ☕ € 14 p. 7 FY **m**
◆ Comfortable well-equipped and cheerful rooms await behind a characteristic Toulouse façade. Breakfasts served on the terrace in summer. Practical garage.

Athénée without rest
13 bis r. Matabiau – ✆ 05 61 63 10 63 – www.athenee-hotel.com – hotel-athenee@wanadoo.fr – Fax 05 61 63 87 80 p. 7 FX **a**
35 rm – †€ 89/137 ††€ 99/147, ☕ € 11
◆ A discreet building 500m from St-Sernin basilica. Functional guestrooms decorated in bright colours. Exposed stone and brickwork in the lounge.

Albert 1er without rest
8 r. Rivals – ✆ 05 61 21 17 91 – www.hotel-albert1.com – toulouse@hotel-albert1.com – Fax 05 61 21 09 64 p. 7 EX **r**
47 rm – †€ 55/115 ††€ 65/123, ☕ € 10
◆ A very practical base for discovering the "pink city" by foot. Ask for one of the refurbished rooms, or one at the rear for peace and quiet.

Ours Blanc-Centre without rest
14 pl. Victor Hugo – ✆ 05 61 21 25 97 – www.hotel-oursblanc.com – centre@hotel-oursblanc.com – Fax 05 61 23 96 27 p. 7 FX **s**
44 rm – †€ 79 ††€ 85, ☕ € 7
◆ The hotel is pleasantly located near the town's main attractions. Small, well-equipped rooms with air-conditioning which are regularly maintained. Double-glazing.

Castellane without rest
17 r. Castellane – ✆ 05 61 62 18 82 – www.castellanehotel.com – castellanehotel@wanadoo.fr – Fax 05 61 62 58 04 p. 7 FX **f**
53 rm – †€ 76 ††€ 76, ☕ € 8
◆ A nice welcome at this hotel set around a patio. Simple, redecorated rooms, some with terraces. Some are particularly suited to families.

Les Loges de St-Sernin without rest
12 r. St-Bernard – ✆ 05 61 24 44 44 – www.logessaintsernin.fr – logesaintsernin@live.fr – Closed 20-27 December, one week in February and the weekend in low season
4 rm ☕ – †€ 105/120 ††€ 105/120 p. 7 EX **t**
◆ The second floor of this entirely refurbished hotel is home to sophisticated rooms that marry the charm of yesteryear with modern comforts. A delightfully welcoming establishment.

Les Jardins de l'Opéra
1 pl. du Capitole – ✆ 05 61 23 07 76 – www.lesjardinsdelopera.com – contact@lesjardinsdelopera.com – Fax 05 61 23 63 00 – Closed lunch bank holidays, Sunday and Monday p. 7 EY **q**
Rest – Menu € 29 (lunch), € 44 € bi/110 – Carte approx. € 110
◆ The elegant dining rooms under a glass roof and separated by a fountain dedicated to Neptune. Unusually, the menu offers dishes in "trilogy": three dishes on the same plate.

XXX ✿✿ **Michel Sarran**

21 bd A. Duportal – ✆ 05 61 12 32 32 – www.michel-sarran.com – restaurant@michel-sarran.com – Fax 05 61 12 32 33 – Closed August, 20-28 December, Wednesday lunch, Saturday and Sunday *p. 6* DV **m**

Rest – *(pre-book)* Menu € 48 bi (lunch), € 98/165 bi – Carte € 86/127

Spec. Langoustines translucides sur un risotto glacé. Agneau allaiton de l'Aveyron rôti en viennoise aux dattes. Haricots tarbais en mousse légère au vieux rhum et lait de coco.

◆ This delightful 19C residence, with its friendly atmosphere that immediately makes one feel at home, and pretty, refined modern décor sets off the chef's inventive cuisine.

XX ✿ **En Marge** (Frank Renimel)

8 r. Mage – ✆ 05 61 53 07 24 – www.restaurantenmarge.com – Closed 6-12 April, 12 August-6 September, 21 December-3 January, Sunday, Monday and Tuesday *p. 7* FZ **v**

Rest – *(number of covers limited, pre-book)* Menu (€ 30), € 55/80

Spec. Crème de potimarron aux Saint Jacques crues (December-February). Suprême de pigeon rôti aux ravioles de foie gras. Parfait à la feuille de tabac et "cigare" à la crème au rhum. **Wines** Côtes du Marmandais.

◆ A new restaurant with a homely atmosphere, friendly service and delicious, innovative cuisine. Limited number of tables in a modern decor with a hint of Baroque.

XX ✿ **Metropolitan**

2 pl. Auguste-Albert – ✆ 05 61 34 63 11 – www.metropolitan-restaurant.fr – contact@metropolitan-restaurant.fr – Fax 05 61 52 88 91 – Closed 1st-21 August, 25-30 December, Saturday lunch, Sunday and Monday *p. 5* CT **a**

Rest – Menu (€ 23), € 30 (weekday lunch), € 39/85 – Carte € 76/103

Spec. Chair de crabe en barigoule de légumes à la coriandre. Calamars en persillade, préssé de tomate au pesto. Framboises au naturel, croustillant de chocolat au lait et thé (season). **Wines** Fronton rouge.

◆ A modern restaurant which gets full marks for its delicious, contemporary cuisine, designer-style dining room (with bar), small interior terrace adorned with vines, and efficient, friendly service.

XX **Le L**

24 pl. de la Bourse – ✆ 05 61 21 69 05 – www.restaurantlel.com – laurent.guillard@le-l.com – Fax 05 61 21 61 79 – Closed 5-25 August, Sunday and Monday *p. 7* EY **c**

Rest – Menu € 24, € 48/75 – Carte € 32/64

◆ This contemporary restaurant is in the heart of the old town. It features a regularly renewed creative menu of Asian inspiration, more elaborate in the evenings. Summer terrace.

XX **Valentin**

21 r. Perchepinte – ✆ 05 61 53 11 15 – www.valentin-restaurant.fr – contact@valentin-restaurant.fr – Closed Monday *p. 7* ZF **n**

Rest – *(dinner only)* Menu € 34/54

◆ A glass door crowned with an arch leads to this attractive restaurant, whose young chef specialises in inventive cuisine. Elegant decor with period furniture, vaulted cellar and brick walls.

XX **7 Place St-Sernin**

7 pl. St-Sernin – ✆ 05 62 30 05 30 – www.7placesaintsernin.com – restaurant@7placesaintsernin.com – Fax 05 62 30 04 06 – Closed Saturday lunch and Sunday *p. 7* EX **v**

Rest – Menu (€ 20 bi), € 26 (weekday lunch), € 34/75 bi – Carte € 49/68

◆ This restaurant set in a typical Toulouse house boasts flamboyant colours and is elegantly arranged and brightened with contemporary paintings. Modern dishes.

XX **La Corde**

4 r. Chalande – ✆ 05 61 29 09 43 – Fax 05 62 15 25 88 – Closed Saturday lunch, Monday lunch and Sunday *p. 7* EY **e**

Rest – Menu € 25, € 37/110 – Carte € 70/110

◆ This impressive 15C tower, all that remains of a mansion that used to belong to prominent families of Toulouse, is home to the city's oldest restaurant (1881). Updated regional dishes.

XX **Brasserie Flo "Les Beaux Arts"** VISA

1 quai Daurade – ✆ 05 61 21 12 12 – www.brasserielesbeauxarts.com – Fax 05 61 21 14 80 p. 7 EY **v**

Rest – Menu (€ 23), € 31 – Carte € 33/50

◆ Popular with locals, this brasserie on the banks of the Garonne was once frequented by Ingres, Matisse and Bourdelle. Retro decor and a varied menu.

XX **Le 19** VISA

19 descente de la Halle aux Poissons – ✆ 05 34 31 94 84 – www.restaurantle19.com – contact@restaurantle19.com – Fax 05 34 31 94 85 – Closed 11-17 August, 22 December-6 January, Monday lunch, Saturday lunch and Sunday p. 7 EY **h**

Rest – Menu (€ 25), € 35 (weekdays)/60 bi – Carte € 42/60

◆ Welcoming, contemporary-style dining rooms (one with a superb 16C rib-vaulted ceiling), plus an open-view wine cellar. Hearty local cuisine.

XX **Chez Laurent Orsi "Bouchon Lyonnais"** VISA

13 r. de l'Industrie – ✆ 05 61 62 97 43 – www.le-bouchon-lyonnais.com – orsi.le-bouchon-lyonnais@wanadoo.fr – Fax 05 61 63 00 71 – Closed Saturday lunch and Sunday except holidays p. 7 FY **f**

Rest – Menu € 22/36 – Carte € 30/40

◆ A large bistro whose leather banquettes, closely-packed tables and mirrors are reminiscent of the brasseries of the 1930s. Dishes from the southwest and Lyon, as well as fish and seafood.

XX **Émile** VISA

13 pl. St-Georges – ✆ 05 61 21 05 56 – www.restaurant-emile.com – restaurant-emile@wanadoo.fr – Fax 05 61 21 42 26 – Closed 20 December-4 January, Monday except dinner from May to September and Sunday p. 7 FY **r**

Rest – Menu € 20 (lunch), € 30/55 – Carte € 39/61

◆ A restaurant with a popular terrace and a menu focused on local dishes and fish (cassoulet is the house speciality). Fine wine list.

X **L'Adresse** VISA

4 r. Baronie – ✆ 05 61 22 55 48 – www.adresserestaurant.com – ladresserestaurant@orange.fr – Closed 9-31 August, Tuesday dinner, Sunday, Monday and bank holidays p. 7 EY **b**

Rest – Menu (€ 15), € 19 (lunch), € 28/36

◆ Contemporary furniture, mirrors, bookshelves, bottles and dishes of the day on a blackboard form the backdrop of this fashionable establishment serving tasty up-to-date cuisine.

X **L'Empereur de Huê** VISA

17 r. Couteliers – ✆ 05 61 53 55 72 – www.empereurdehue.com – Closed Sunday and Monday p. 7 EZ **a**

Rest – *(dinner only) (pre-book)* Menu € 37 – Carte € 47/54

◆ If the decor of this family restaurant is contemporary, the cooking retains its Vietnamese roots.

X **Michel, Marcel, Pierre et les Autres** VISA

35 r. Rémusat – ✆ 05 61 22 47 05 – www.michelmarcelpierre.com – bistrot@michelmarcelpierre.com – Fax 05 61 22 47 05 – Closed 10-18 August, Sunday and Monday p. 7 EX **m**

Rest – Menu (€ 16), € 20 bi (lunch) – Carte € 36/42

◆ A warm welcome is guaranteed in this bistro named after a film by Claude Sautet. Rugby matches on the TVs and sports shirts on the walls. Seasonal food.

X **Brasserie du Stade** P VISA

114 r. Troënes ✉ 31200 – ✆ 05 34 42 24 20 – www.stadetoulousain.fr – brasserie@stadetoulousain.fr – Fax 05 34 42 24 21 – Closed 18 July-26 August, 20 December-1st January, Monday dinner, Tuesday dinner, Saturday and Sunday p. 4 AS **x**

Rest – Menu (€ 29) – Carte € 37/43

◆ This large restaurant is located inside Toulouse's rugby stadium. Amongst photos and trophies, guests are served carefully prepared brasserie-style dishes.

Rôtisserie des Carmes
38 r. Polinaires – 05 61 53 34 88 – http://rotisseriedescarmes.cartesurtables.com – rotisserie@wanadoo.fr – Closed August, 24-27 December, 31 December -3 January, Saturday, Sunday and bank holidays p. 7 EZ x
Rest – Menu (€ 16), € 21 (lunch), € 27 € bi/31 bi – Carte € 40/60 dinner
◆ Proximity to the Carmes market means that the small menu and the dishes of the day depend on the latest catch. The colourful owner supervises in the open kitchen.

in Gratentour 15 km North by D 4 and D 14 – pop. 3 361 – alt. 174 m – ✉ 31150

Le Barry
47 r. Barry – 05 61 82 22 10 – www.lebarry.fr – le-barry@wanadoo.fr – Fax 05 61 82 22 38 – Closed 18 December-4 January, Friday, Saturday and Sunday except from 1 April to 30 September
22 rm – †€ 53 ††€ 60, ☕ € 8 – ½ P € 60
Rest – *(closed 1st-24 August, Friday dinner, Saturday dinner October-March, Saturday lunch and Sunday)* Menu (€ 14), € 23 (weekdays) – Carte € 19/41
◆ This attractive pink-brick farmhouse in a tranquil setting has been transformed into a simple but welcoming hotel. Garden, swimming pool and the Frontonnais vineyards nearby. Warm, refined dining room. Traditional culinary repertoire.

in l'Union 7 km Northeast – pop. 12 300 – alt. 146 m – ✉ 31240

La Bonne Auberge
2 bis r. Autan-Blanc, (N 88) – 05 61 09 32 26 – bonne.auberge.la@wanadoo.fr – Fax 05 61 09 97 53 – Closed 10 August-1st September, 21 December-5 January, Sunday and Monday
Rest – Menu € 27/50 – Carte € 36/52
◆ Occupying a restored barn, this restaurant on the village's main road has rustic furniture, beams and brick fireplace. Modern menu.

in Rouffiac-Tolosan 12 km by ② – pop. 1 404 – alt. 210 m – ✉ 31180

Ô Saveurs (Daniel Gonzalez et David Biasibetti)
8 pl. Ormeaux, (in the village) – 05 34 27 10 11 – http://o.saveurs.free.fr – o.saveurs@free.fr – Fax 05 62 79 33 84 – Closed 27 April-5 May, 17 August-8 September, Saturday lunch, Sunday dinner and Monday
Rest – Menu (€ 25), € 39/80 – Carte € 75/90
Spec. Fricassée de langoustine et foie gras, coulis de corail et pleurottes. Filet de Saint-Pierre, tombée d'épinard et noisette sur une aubergine cuite à la plancha. Ravioles d'ananas farçies d'un riz au lait passion. **Wines** Gaillac, Fronton.
◆ A charming cottage and terrace set up on the paved square of this picturesque village. Traditional menu spiced up with a zest of creativity. Delicious!

Le Clos du Loup with rm
N 88 – 05 61 09 28 39 – www.hotel-leclosduloup.com – hotel-leclosduloup@orange.fr – Fax 05 61 35 13 97 – Closed 26 December-2 January and Sunday dinner
19 rm – †€ 65 ††€ 65, ☕ € 8
Rest – *(closed August, Saturday lunch, Sunday dinner and Friday)* Menu (€ 18), € 24/34 – Carte € 28/47
◆ Don't be nervous...the Big Bad Wolf is no more! Shimmering colours and beams in the bright rustic dining room. Simple, traditional cuisine and spick-and-span rooms.

in Labège 6 km southeast by D 2 and D 16, towards SNCF station – ✉ 31670

L'Orangerie de Labège-L'Arôme et le Grain
4 r. Isatis – 05 62 47 54 53 – www.orangeriedelabege.com – laromeetlegrain@wanadoo.fr – Fax 05 62 47 54 51 – Closed 2-26 August, 20-28 December, Saturday lunch, Sunday and Monday
Rest – Menu (€ 22), € 26 (weekday lunch) – Carte € 56/70 dinner only
◆ This 17C farmhouse has a hushed ambience, with cosy lounges, pink brickwork and designer furniture. Sophisticated contemporary cuisine. Pretty patio-terrace.

in Ramonville-St-Agne 6 km southeast by D 113 – pop. 12 000 – alt. 162 m – ✉ 31520

Peniche Soleïado

Pont de Mange-Pomme, near the Pont-Sud, along the D 113, towards the Ferme de Cinquante – ✆ 06 86 27 83 19 – www.peniche-soleiado.com – Fax 05 62 19 07 71

5 rm – †€ 85 ††€ 90 **Table d'hôte** – Menu € 30 bi

◆ This barge moored in the Canal du Midi has a warm interior, offering three small, yet really delightful rooms.

in Castanet-Tolosan 8 km by ⑤ and N 113 – pop. 10 200 – alt. 164 m – ✉ 31320

La Table des Merville VISA

3 pl. Richard – ✆ 05 62 71 24 25 – www.table-des-merville.fr – contact@table-des-merville.fr – Fax 05 34 66 18 56 – Closed 12-20 April, 26 July-16 August, 25 October-2 November, 24 December-4 January, Sunday and Monday

Rest – Menu (€ 15), € 27/39 – Carte € 38/58

◆ This family restaurant serves appetising cuisine based on daily market produce prepared in front of your eyes. The modern paintings on display are for sale. A charming setting!

in Lacroix-Falgarde 13 km South by D 4 – pop. 1 928 – alt. 154 m – ✉ 31120

Le Bellevue VISA AE

1 av. Pyrénées – ✆ 05 61 76 94 97 – Fax 05 62 20 96 57 – Closed 2-8 March, 15 October-15 November, Wednesday from September to April and Tuesday

Rest – Menu (€ 19), € 28/39 – Carte € 45/62

◆ This former open-air dance hall, surrounded by greenery, is along the Ariège. In fine weather the outdoor riverside tables are popular. Traditional dishes and southwest French specialities.

in Tournefeuille 10 km West by D 632 AT – pop. 24 500 – alt. 155 m – ✉ 31170

L'Art de Vivre VISA AE

279 chemin Ramelet-Moundi – ✆ 05 61 07 52 52 – www.lartdevivre.fr – contact@lartdevivre.fr – Fax 05 61 06 41 94 – Closed Easter holiday, 10-31 August, Christmas holidays, Sunday dinner, Monday dinner, Tuesday dinner and Wednesday

Rest – Menu € 25, € 36/58 – Carte € 55/70

◆ On fine days, this house near the golf course is extended by a charming outside dining area in the middle of a brookside garden. Up-to-date cuisine.

in Purpan 6 km west by N 124 - ✉ 31300 Toulouse

Palladia rm, VISA AE

271 av. Grande Bretagne – ✆ 05 62 12 01 20 – www.hotelpalladia.com – info@hotelpalladia.com – Fax 05 62 12 01 21 p. 4 AT e

90 rm – †€ 109/215 ††€ 109/215, € 18 – 3 suites

Rest – *(closed Sunday and public holidays)* Menu (€ 20), € 25 (lunch)/59 bi – Carte € 40/65

◆ An imposing building between the airport and city centre. Particularly well thought-out layout. The spacious and comfortable rooms are being progressively updated. Bright, modern dining room. Summer terrace shaded by parasols.

Novotel Aéroport rm, VISA AE

23 impasse Maubec – ✆ 05 61 15 00 00 – www.novotel.com – h0445@accor.com – Fax 05 61 15 88 44 p. 4 AT a

123 rm – †€ 81/160 ††€ 81/160, € 15 **Rest** – Menu (€ 18) – Carte € 33/50

◆ The rooms of this chain hotel are fully soundproofed. Children's amusements, free shuttle to the airport, Wi-fi and plenty of green space. The restaurant and pleasant terrace offer a view of the pool. Updated menu, specials and diet meals.

in St-Martin-du-Touch to ⑦ – ✉ 31300 Toulouse

Airport Hôtel without rest VISA AE

176 rte de Bayonne – ✆ 05 61 49 68 78 – www.airport-hotel-toulouse.com – airporthotel@wanadoo.fr – Fax 05 61 49 73 66 p. 4 AT s

45 rm – †€ 72/74 ††€ 90/92, € 10 – 3 suites

◆ 1980s building in red brick near the airport. The simple rooms are well protected against noise and are quite comfortable.

Le Cantou

98 r. Velasquez, (D 2B) – 05 61 49 20 21 – www.cantou.fr – le.cantou@wanadoo.fr – Fax 05 61 31 01 17 – Closed 3 weeks in August, 21 December-3 January, Saturday and Sunday p. 4 AT **h**

Rest – Menu € 30 (weekdays)/58 – Carte € 41/55

◆ A haven of greenery shelters this pretty old farmhouse. Terrace set around a pretty well. Tasty, updated menu and remarkable wine list (1 300 vintages).

in Colomiers **10 km by ⑦, exit n° 3 then direction Cornebarrieu by D 63 – pop. 31 800 – alt. 182 m – ✉ 31770**

L'Amphitryon (Yannick Delpech)

chemin de Gramont – 05 61 15 55 55 – www.lamphitryon.com – contact@lamphitryon.com – Fax 05 61 15 42 30

Rest – Menu (€ 26), € 34 (weekday lunch), € 64/105 – Carte € 95/113

Spec. Sardine fraîche taillée au couteau, crème de morue et caviar de hareng. Bar de ligne en deux cuissons, parfum de dulse et poutargue. Macaron moelleux au "cachou Lajaunie", tube givré au citron jaune et menthe. **Wines** Côtes du Frontonnais.

◆ A glass roof and fireplace have been added to this restaurant. It serves brilliantly inventive cuisine, which takes local produce to new heights.

in Pibrac **12 km by ⑦, exit n° 6 – pop. 7 755 – alt. 157 m – ✉ 31820**

Le Pavillon Saint Jean

1 chemin Beauregard – 05 61 06 71 71 – pierre-jean.darroze@orange.fr – Fax 05 61 86 35 63 – Closed 3-24 August, 22-28 February, Saturday lunch, Sunday dinner and Monday

Rest – Menu € 19 (weekday lunch), € 30/48

◆ This peaceful provincial house, slightly out of the centre, serves good classic cooking in a restrained modern dining room, or on the terrace when the weather permits.

in Blagnac **7 km Northwest – pop. 21 100 – alt. 135 m – ✉ 31700**

Pullman

2 av. Didier Daurat, dir. airport (exit n° 3) – 05 34 56 11 11 – www.pullmanhotels.com – h0565@accor.com – Fax 05 61 30 02 43 p. 4 AS **e**

100 rm – †€ 115/335 ††€ 130/350, € 25

Rest *Le Caouec* – *(Closed 27 July-23 August, Friday dinner, Saturday and Sunday)* Menu (€ 24 bi) – Carte € 51/67

◆ 1970s hotel being treated to a complete facelift. Contemporary style public areas, with some guestrooms updated in a similar vein. Free shuttle to the airport. Tapas-type snacks served at the bar and more traditional menu in the dining room.

Holiday Inn Airport rm, rest,

pl. Révolution – 05 34 36 00 20 – www.holiday-inn.com/toulouse-apt – tlsap@ihg.com – Fax 05 34 36 00 30 p. 4 AS **h**

150 rm – †€ 99/240 ††€ 99/240

Rest – *(closed Saturday lunch and Sunday lunch)* Menu € 16 (lunch), € 22/38 – Carte € 25/45

◆ Both peaceful and warm shades adorn the rooms decorated with modern furniture. A well-appointed seminar area. A shuttle links the hotel to the airport. A pleasant brasserie-style restaurant decorated with frescoes depicting olive trees.

Le Cercle d'Oc

6 pl. M. Dassault – 05 62 74 71 71 – cercledoc@wanadoo.fr – Fax 05 62 74 71 72 – Closed 3-24 August, 25 December-1st January, Saturday and Sunday p. 4 AS **t**

Rest – Menu (€ 34 bi), € 45 bi/80 bi – Carte € 50/67

◆ This pretty 18C farm is an island of greenery in the middle of a shopping area. English club atmosphere in the elegant dining rooms, billiards room and pleasant terrace.

in Seilh **15 km by ⑧ – pop. 2 916 – alt. 133 m – ✉ 31840**

Latitudes Golf de Seilh rm,

rte Grenade – 05 62 13 14 15 – www.latitudes-hotels-toulouse.com – toh@pierre-vacances.fr – Fax 05 61 59 77 97

172 rm – †€ 99/155 ††€ 99/155, € 14 – 2 suites

Rest – *(dinner only)* Menu € 28/37 – Carte approx. € 47

◆ This vast hotel complex opens onto two golf courses and welcomes a great many seminars and sports stays. Studio flats and apartments are also available for rental. Decoration inspired by the early airmail service; cuisine with southwestern bias.

TOUQUES – 14 Calvados – 303 M3 – see Deauville

LE TOUQUET-PARIS-PLAGE – 62 Pas-de-Calais – 301 C4 30 A2

– pop. 5 536 – alt. 5 m – Casino : du Palais BZ, the 4 Saisons AYZ – ✉ 62520
Northern France and the Paris Region

Paris 242 – Abbeville 58 – Arras 99 – Boulogne-sur-Mer 30 – Calais 68
Office de tourisme, place de l'Hermitage ✆ 03 21 06 72 00, Fax 03 21 06 72 01
du Touquet Avenue du Golf, S : 2 km, ✆ 03 21 06 28 00

Westminster rest, VISA
av. Verger – ✆ 03 21 05 48 48 – www.opengolfclub.com – reception@westminster.fr – Fax 03 21 05 45 45 BZ a
115 rm – €80/320 €120/401, €20 – 1 suite
Rest *Le Pavillon* – *(Closed 2 January-31 March and Tuesday except July-August) (dinner only)* Menu €55/130 bi – Carte €72/90
Rest *Les Cimaises* – *✆ 03 21 06 74 95* – Menu €28 bi/35 – Carte €50/76
Spec. Langoustines, niçoise de légumes et glace roquette (June-September). Turbot, huître et concombre en transparence. Côte de veau de lait, jambon cru en émulsion.
◆ Attractive Anglo-Norman style hotel (1925-1928) built between the sea and pine forest. Superb elevators in the lobby; Art-Deco or retro-style guestrooms. Popular terrace in summer. The Pavillon offers classic cuisine with personal touches and an outstanding wine list. Les Cimaises offers buffets and brasserie dishes.

Holiday Inn rm, VISA
av. Mar. Foch – ✆ 03 21 06 85 85 – www.holidayinnletouquet.com – hotel@holidayinnletouquet.com – Fax 03 21 06 85 00 BZ n
88 rm – €135/205 €165/245, €17 – 2 suites – ½ P €105/160
Rest *Le Picardy* – Menu (€19), €25 – Carte €32/51
◆ Modern hotel on the edge of the forest, with functional rooms accessed via a flower-decked gallery. The "privilege" category rooms have been recently renovated. A parquet floor and plants add a touch of originality to the rotunda dining room. Classic menu.

Mercure Grand Hôtel VISA
4 bd Canche – ✆ 03 21 06 88 88 – www.mercure.com – H5605@accor.com – Fax 03 21 06 87 87 BY s
132 rm – €105/200 €105/300, €16 – 5 suites
Rest – Menu (€18), €28 – Carte €36/79
◆ A luxury establishment overlooking the Canche and including a spa centre. Spacious rooms, some with river views. Up-to-date cuisine in this recently revamped restaurant.

Le Manoir Hôtel VISA
av. du Golf, 2.5 km via ② – ✆ 03 21 06 28 28 – www.opengolfclub.com – manoirhotel@opengolfclub.com – Fax 03 21 06 28 29 – Closed 2 January-5 February
41 rm – €70/240 €140/290 **Rest** – Menu €35/55 – Carte €51/64
◆ Beautiful early 20C manor house surrounded by a flower garden, very near the forest and golf course. Comfortable rooms, English-style bar, clientele of golfers. Traditional food in line with the classic setting of the pleasant dining room.

Novotel rest, VISA
Front de Mer – ✆ 03 21 09 85 00 – www.accorthalassa.com – h0449-SB@accor.com – Fax 03 21 09 85 40 AZ a
146 rm – €114/264 €114/264, €17 – 3 suites
Rest – *(Closed 4-18 January)* Menu €25/33 – Carte €40/60
◆ This Novotel is located right on the beachfront and near a thalassotherapy centre. Small but recently renovated rooms. The bay windows of the restaurant overlook the shore; seafood menu.

Le Bristol without rest VISA
17 r. Jean Monnet – ✆ 03 21 05 49 95 – www.hotelbristol.fr – reservations@hotelbristol.fr – Fax 03 21 05 90 93 AZ x
49 rm – €70/170 €90/180, €12
◆ A stylish villa from the 1920s, situated between the sea and the town centre, with functional rooms that are gradually being renovated. Intimate lounge-bar and an attractive patio terrace.

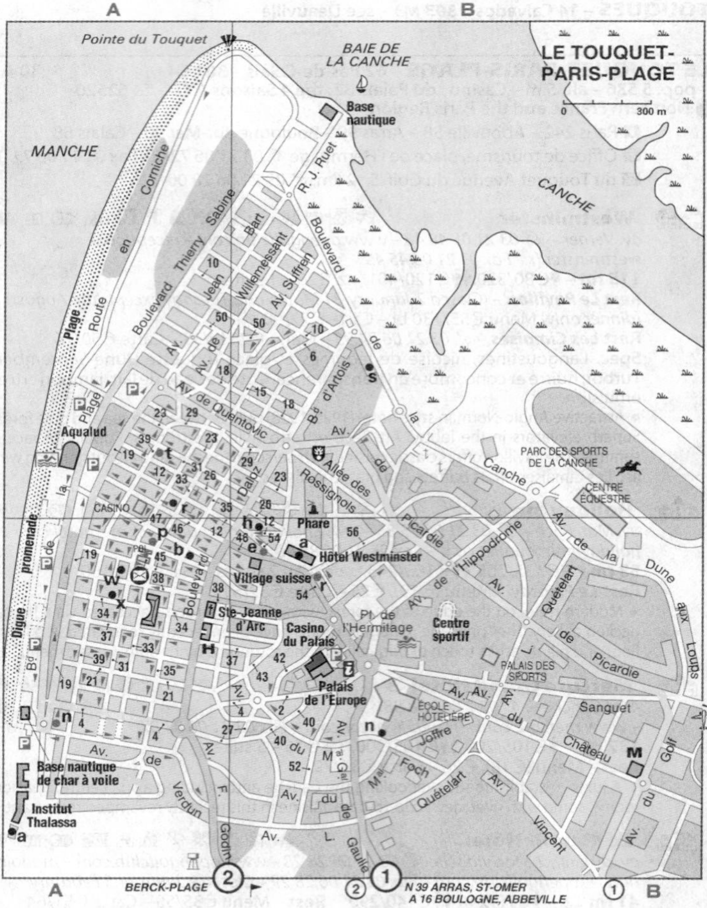

LE TOUQUET-PARIS-PLAGE

Aboudaram (Av. L.) . . . . **BZ** 2
Atlantique (Av. de l') . . . . . **ABZ** 4
Bardol (R. E.) . . . . **BY** 6
Bourdonnais (Av. de la) . . . **ABY** 10
Bruxelles (R. de) . . . . **AYZ** 12
Calais (R. de) . . . . **BY** 15
Desvres (R. de) . . . . **ABY** 18
Docteur-J.-Pouget (Bd du) . . . . **AYZ** 19
Dorothée (R.) . . . . **AZ** 21
Duboc (Av. et R. J.) . . . . . . **ABY** 23
Garet (Av. et R. L.) . . . . **ABY** 26
Genets (Av. des) . . . . **ABZ** 27
Hubert (Av. L.) . . . . **ABY** 29
Londres (R. de) . . . . **AYZ** 31
Metz (R. de) . . . . **AYZ** 33
Monnet (R. J.) . . . . **AZ** 34
Moscou (R. de) . . . . **AYZ** 35
Oyats (Av. et R. des) . . . . . **ABZ** 37
Paix (Av. et R. de la) . . . . . **ABZ** 38
Paris (R. de) . . . . **AYZ** 39
Pins (Av. des) . . . . **BZ** 40
Recoussine (Av. F.) . . . . **BZ** 42
Reine-May (Av. de la) . . . . **ABZ** 43
St-Amand (R.) . . . . **AZ** 45
St-Jean (Av. et R.) . . . . **ABZ** 46
St-Louis (R.) . . . . **AZ** 47
Tourville (Av. de l'Amiral) . . **ABY** 50
Troènes (Av. des) . . . . **BZ** 52
Verger (Av. du) . . . . **BZ** 54
Whitley (Av. J.) . . . . **BZ** 56

Red Fox without rest
60 r. de Metz – ✆ 03 21 05 27 58
– hotelredfox.com – reception@hotelredfox.com
– Fax 03 21 05 27 56
– **53 rm** – †€ 55/105 ††€ 65/105, ☕ € 13

AY **r**

◆ Located in a lively street, offering practical rooms of varying sizes with dormer windows on the top floor. Comfortable lounge and cosy breakfast room (generous buffet).

Windsor without rest

7 r. St-Georges – 03 21 05 05 44 – www.hotel-windsor.fr – reservations@hotel-windsor.fr – Fax 03 21 05 75 81 – Closed 3-31 January AZ **w**

28 rm – €50/60 €60/70, €8

◆ This hotel near the beach offers comfortable accommodation with the choice ranging from single to four-bedded rooms. Pleasant lounge. Breakfast room with a painted stucco ceiling.

La Forêt without rest

73 r. de Moscou – 03 21 05 09 88 – www.letouquet.com/hotel-laforet – Fax 03 21 05 59 40 – Open 1st April-30 September – **10 rm** – €50/61 €53/61, €7

◆ A family hotel, ideally located in the town centre, offering functional, quiet, and well-maintained bedrooms. Attractive breakfast room. AZ **b**

Villa Fierval without rest

6 av. Léon-Garet – 06 08 33 20 07 – www.flavio.fr – fierval@wanadoo.fr – Fax 03 21 05 91 55 – Closed 10 January-5 February – **4 rm** – €49/69 €69/98 BY **h**

◆ Serge Gainsbourg is just one famous guest to have stayed in this family-run establishment. An elegant façade conceals a spacious interior with comfortable, well-equipped rooms.

Flavio

1 av. Verger – 03 21 05 10 22 – www.flavio.fr – flavio@flavio.fr – Fax 03 21 05 91 55 – Closed 10 January-10 February, Sunday dinner October-December, Monday except July-August and 15-30 November

Rest – Menu (€22 bi), €69/153 – Carte €55/107 BZ **r**

◆ This elegant restaurant serves a range of tempting fish and seafood dishes, with a focus on top-quality produce. A piano, chandeliers and period furniture add to the ambience.

Le Village Suisse

52 av. St-Jean – 03 21 05 69 93 – www.levillagesuisse.fr – contact@levillagesuisse.fr – Fax 03 21 05 66 97 – Closed 24 November-8 December, Sunday dinner October-April, Tuesday lunch and Monday September-June BZ **e**

Rest – Menu €28 (weekdays)/80 bi – Carte €44/72

◆ This villa was built in 1905 for the daughter of a wealthy Swiss citizen. It now houses a restaurant with a beautiful terrace above antique shops.

Le Paris

88 r. de Metz – 03 21 05 79 33 – Closed 22 June-1st July, 16-27 November, 15-25 February, Sunday dinner in low season, Tuesday dinner and Wednesday

Rest – Menu (€16), €18 (weekdays)/39 – Carte €30/50 AZ **p**

◆ Very central restaurant with contemporary decor pleasantly combining red and chocolate tones, where you can enjoy modern-style recipes.

Côté Sud

187 bd du Dr Pouget – 03 21 05 41 24 – www.le-touquet-cote-sud.com – cotesud62@orange.fr – Fax 03 21 86 54 48 – Closed 9-24 March, 15-24 June, 24 November-9 December, Sunday dinner in low season, Monday lunch, Wednesday

Rest – Menu (€15), €19 (weekdays)/55 – Carte €43/51 AZ **n**

◆ Situated on Le Touquet's seafront, this restaurant is decorated in minimalist style with elegant white furnishings. The contemporary cuisine focuses mainly on fish dishes.

Ricochet

49 r. de Paris – 03 21 06 41 36 – www.ricochet-letouquet.com – contact@ricochet-letouquet.com – Closed January, Tuesday and Wednesday AY **t**

Rest – Menu (€17), €31 (dinner) – Carte €27/38

◆ A trendy restaurant in the centre of the resort with a designer decor, interior garden and young staff. Good variety of unfussy dishes listed on the blackboard.

in Stella-Plage 7 km by ② – 62780 Cucq

Office de tourisme, Place Jean Sapin 03 21 09 04 32, Fax 03 21 84 49 88

Des Pelouses rm,

bd E. Labrasse – 03 21 94 60 86 – www.lespelouses.com – accueil@lespelouses.com – Fax 03 21 94 10 11 – Closed 2-31 January

26 rm – €52/65 €65/70, €8,50 – ½ P €75

Rest – *(Closed 23 December-31 January, Sunday dinner and Monday from October to April)* Menu (€14), €18/27 – Carte €28/53

◆ This square-shaped building situated 1,800m from the beach has undergone many renovations. Neat rooms, more spacious at the back. Regional recipes take pride of place in the appetising menu served in the simply decorated dining room.

TOURCOING – 59 Nord – 302 G3 – pop. 92 200 – alt. 37 m – ✉ 59200 31 C2
Northern France and the Paris Region

Paris 234 – Kortrijk 19 – Gent 61 – Lille 17 – Oostende 81 – Roubaix 5

Office de tourisme, 9, rue de Tournai ☎ 03 20 26 89 03, Fax 03 20 24 79 80

des Flandres Marcq-en-Baroeul 159 boulevard Clémenceau, 9 km on D 670, ☎ 03 20 72 20 74

Access and exits: See plan of Lille

Altia rm, VISA

r. Vertuquet, to the North near Neuville-en-Ferrain interchange (exit 18) – ☎ 03 20 28 88 00 – www.altia-hotel.com – reservation@altia-hotel.com – Fax 03 20 28 88 10 *Map of Lille* HR **e**

108 rm – †€ 59/125 ††€ 75/135, ☕ € 13 **Rest** – Carte € 20/36

◆ Recently taken over, this hotel near the Belgian border (300m) targets a business clientele. Choose a renovated room – these are more modern and comfortable. The kitchens can be seen from the dining room, facing a terrace and the pool.

TOURCOING

Street	Grid	No.
Allende (Bd Salvador)	BY	2
Anges (R. des)	BYZ	3
Austerlitz (R. d')	ABZ	4
Bienfaisance (R. de la)	BY	6
Brun Pain (R. du)	AY	
Buisson (R. Ferdinand)	BZ	7
Chateaubriand (R.)	CZ	8
Cherbourg (Quai de)	BZ	9
Clavell (Pl. Miss)	BY	10
Cloche (R. de la)	BY	12
Condorcet (R.)	BY	13
Courbet (R. de l'Amiral)	BY	15
Croix Blanche (R. de la)	CX	16
Croix Rouge (R. de la)	CXY	
Delobel (R.)	BY	18
Doumer (R. Paul)	BY	19
Dron (Av. Gustave)	BZ	
Duguay-Trouin (R.)	CY	21
Faidherbe (R.)	BZ	22
Famelart (R.)	BZ	24
La-Fayette (Av.)	BZ	33
Froissart (R. Jean)	AY	25
Gambetta (Bd)	BZ	27
Gand (R. de)	BXY	
Grand'Place	BY	28
Hassebroucq (Pl. V.)	BY	30
Hénaux (R. Marcel)	BXY	31
Leclerc (R. du Gén.)	BY	36
Lefrançois (Av. Alfred)	CZ	37
Marne (Av. de la)	BZ	39
Marseille (Quai de)	BZ	40
Menin (R. de)	BXY	
Millet (Av. Jean)	AY	42
Moulin Fagot (R. du)	BY	43
Nationale (R.)	ABY	
Péri (R. Gabriel)	BY	45
Petit Village (R. du)	AY	46
Pompidou (Av. G.)	BZ	48
Pont de Neuville (R. du)	CX	49
République (Pl. de la)	BY	51
Résistance (Pl. de la)	BY	52
Ribot (R. Alexandre)	BY	54
Roosevelt (R. F.)	BY	55
Roussel (Pl. Ch.-et-A.)	BY	57
St-Jacques (R.)	BY	58
Sasselange (R. Ed.)	BZ	60
Testelin (R. A.)	CX	61
Thiers (R.)	BZ	63
Tournai (R. de)	BY	64
Turenne (R.)	BZ	66
Ursulines (R. des)	BYZ	68
Victoire (Pl. de la)	BZ	69
Wailly (R. de)	BY	70
Wattine (R. Ch.)	BZ	72

WATTRELOS

Street	Grid	No.
Vaneslander (R. M.)	CZ	67

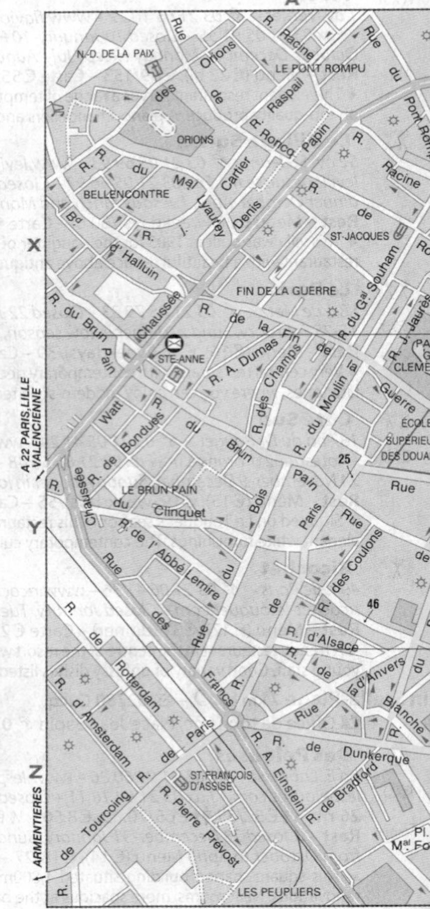

Ibis

r. Carnot – 03 20 24 84 58 – www.accor.com – h0642@accor.com – Fax 03 20 26 29 58 BZ **s**

102 rm – €74 €74, €8 **Rest** – Menu (€10), €25

♦ This building benefits from a central location which is handy for those who want to make the most of the town. Choose the renovated rooms. The restaurant menu offers traditional dishes.

La Baratte

395 r. Clinquet – 03 20 94 45 63 – www.la-baratte.com – la.baratte@wanadoo.fr – Fax 03 20 03 41 84

– Closed Saturday lunch, Sunday dinner and Monday *Map of Lille* HR **d**

Rest – Menu €22 (weekdays), €29/57 – Carte €53/65

♦ An inviting rustic-style dining room, partly overlooking the garden. Generous tasty cuisine. Full marks for this former family butchers!

LA TOUR-D'AIGUES – 84 Vaucluse – 332 G11 – pop. 3 860 – alt. 250 m – ✉ 84240 Provence
40 **B2**

Paris 752 – Aix-en-Provence 29 – Apt 35 – Avignon 81 – Digne-les-Bains 92

Office de tourisme, le Château ✆ 04 90 07 50 29, Fax 04 90 07 35 91

Le Petit Mas de Marie rm, VISA AE

quartier Revol, 1 km, rte de Pertuis – ✆ 04 90 07 48 22 – www.lepetitmasdemarie.com – lepetitmasdemarie@wanadoo.fr – Fax 04 90 07 34 26 – Closed autumn half-term holidays and February holidays

15 rm – €50/60 €70/77, €10 – ½ P €61/71

Rest – *(closed Saturday lunch, Sunday dinner and Monday October-March)* Menu €14 (weekday lunch), €26/36 – Carte €50/65

◆ This welcoming country house in Aigues is surrounded by a flower-decked garden. Impeccably kept Provençal rooms. Southern-inspired cuisine served in a spacious, bright dining room or on an inviting terrace, when the weather permits.

TOUR-DE-FAURE – 46 Lot – 337 G5 – see St-Cirq-Lapopie

LA TOUR-DU-PIN – 38 Isère – 333 F4 – pop. 6 553 – alt. 350 m – ✉ 38110 Lyon - Rhone Valley
45 **C2**

Paris 516 – Aix-les-Bains 57 – Chambéry 51 – Grenoble 67 – Lyon 55 – Vienne 57

Office de tourisme, rue de Châbons ✆ 04 74 97 14 87, Fax 04 74 83 34 74

du Château de Faverges Faverges-de-la-TourE : 9 km on D 1516, ✆ 04 74 88 89 51

Mercure rest, VISA AE

439 av. Gén. de Gaulle, opposite the nautical centre – ✆ 04 74 83 31 31 – www.relaistour.com – h6649@accor.com – Fax 04 74 97 87 01

59 rm – €80 €95, €12

Rest – *(Closed Saturday lunch and Sunday)* Menu (€15), €18/35 – Carte €25/50

◆ This large 1970s building dominates the town. Modern, comfortable rooms, peaceful garden and outdoor swimming pool. Fitness facilities. Restaurant with a trendy decor (dark-wood panelling, design furniture). Up-to-date menu.

Le Bec Fin VISA

pl. Champs-de-Mars – ✆ 04 74 97 58 79 – Fax 04 74 97 58 79 – Closed 3-24 August, Sunday dinner and Monday

Rest – Menu €17 (weekday lunch), €27/46

◆ The former home of a wine merchant is now a restaurant run by a friendly young couple. Generous regional dishes in the form of menus, served in two yellow and green dining rooms.

in St-Didier-de-la-Tour 3 km east by N 6 – pop. 1 621 – alt. 380 m – ✉ 38110

Ambroisie VISA

beside the lake – ✆ 04 74 97 25 53 – www.restaurant-ambroisie.com – ambroisie2@wanadoo.fr – Fax 04 74 97 01 93 – Closed Sunday dinner and Wednesday

Rest – Menu (€16), €28/55 – Carte €37/50

◆ A lakeside lodge with modernised decor in the dining room (dove grey and chocolate colour scheme) and terrace beneath plane trees. Contemporary cuisine with Provençal influences.

in Rochetoirin 4 km northwest by N 6 and D 92 – pop. 980 – alt. 449 m – ✉ 38110

Le Rochetoirin VISA

10 rte de la Tour du Pin, (in the village) – ✆ 04 74 97 60 38 – www.lerochetoirin.fr – lerochetoirin@wanadoo.fr – Closed 24 August-6 September, 23 December-11 January, Tuesday dinner and Wednesday dinner from October to April, Sunday dinner and Monday

Rest – Menu (€18), €25/52 – Carte €35/42

◆ This restaurant deserves praise for offering two culinary styles: traditional or inventive (in tune with the seasons). One small, convivial dining room, and another more luxurious one. Terrace.

TOURNEFEUILLE – 31 Haute-Garonne – 343 G3 – see Toulouse

TOURNON-SUR-RHÔNE – 07 Ardèche – 332 B3 – pop. 10 582 – alt. 125 m – ✉ 07300 Lyon - Rhone Valley 43 E2

Paris 545 – Grenoble 98 – Le Puy-en-Velay 104 – St-Étienne 77 – Valence 18 – Vienne 60

Office de tourisme, 2, place Saint-Julien ✆ 04 75 08 10 23, Fax 04 75 08 41 28

Château ★ terraces B - Panoramic road★★★ B.

Plan: see Tain-l'Hermitage

Les Amandiers without rest VISA

13 av. de Nîmes – ✆ 04 75 07 24 10 – www.hotel-amandiers.com – hotel@hotel-amandiers.com – Fax 04 75 07 06 30 – Closed 18 December-3 January

25 rm – €59 €59/69, ☕ €8 C **n**

◆ Modern hotel popular with business people during the week. Renovated, air-conditioned rooms with good soundproofing and large bathrooms.

Azalées rm, VISA

6 av. Gare – ✆ 04 75 08 05 23 – www.hotel-azalees.com – contact@hotel-azalees.com – Fax 04 75 08 18 27 – Closed 27 October-2 November and 22 December-4 January

37 rm – €55 €55, ☕ €8 – ½ P €49 B **s**

Rest – *(closed Sunday evening from 15 October to 15 March)* Menu €20/26 – Carte €23/30

◆ Between the railway station and the town centre, the rooms of this hotel are in two buildings on either side of an inner courtyard. Choose one of the more recent rooms. A gratin of ravioli, Picodon cheese, the scent of thyme: the cuisine has a definite bias for local produce. Small terrace.

Tournesol VISA

44 av. Mar. Foch – ✆ 04 75 07 08 26 – www.letournesol.net – contact@letournesol.net – Closed 1st-24 August, Toussaint holiday, February holiday, Sunday dinner, Tuesday and Wednesday B **v**

Rest – Menu (€15), €18 (weekdays)/34 – Carte €30/42

◆ This contemporary restaurant offers modern cuisine, fresh produce and a good selection of Côtes du Rhône wines from a glazed cellar. Terrace.

Le Chaudron VISA

7 r. St-Antoine – ✆ 04 75 08 17 90 – Fax 04 75 08 06 61 – Closed 2-24 August, 23 December-6 January, Tuesday dinner, Thursday dinner and Sunday B **r**

Rest – Menu (€12 bi), €27/36 – Carte €32/52

◆ Dark wood panelling, green leatherette bench seats and an attractive terrace are the setting for this pleasant bistro. Tasty local cuisine and lengthy Côtes du Rhone wine list.

TOURNUS – 71 Saône-et-Loire – 320 J10 – pop. 5 892 – alt. 193 m – ✉ 71700 Burgundy-Jura 8 C3

Paris 360 – Bourg-en-Bresse 70 – Chalon-sur-Saône 28 – Mâcon 37

Office de tourisme, 2, place de l'abbaye ✆ 03 85 27 00 20, Fax 03 85 27 00 21

Abbey★★.

Plan on next page

Hôtel de Greuze VISA

5 pl. de l'Abbaye – ✆ 03 85 51 77 77 – www.hotelgreuze.com – contact@hotelgreuze.fr – Fax 03 85 51 77 23

19 rm – €100/195 €135/225, ☕ €26 – 2 suites **e**

Rest ***Greuze*** – see restaurant listing

◆ A charming regional construction between the 10C Abbey of St Philibert and the town centre. Spacious elegant guestrooms in varying styles: Louis XVI, Directoire, French Empire, etc.

Le Rempart VISA

2 av. Gambetta – ✆ 03 85 51 10 56 – www.lerempart.com – lerempart@wanadoo.fr – Fax 03 85 51 77 22

23 rm – €95/155 €130/170, ☕ €16 – 11 suites – ½ P €100/130 **x**

Rest – Menu €33/77 – Carte €56/80

Rest ***Le Bistrot*** – Menu €18/27 – Carte €31/38

◆ A 15C house built on the old ramparts of Tournus. Almost all the rooms have been treated to a contemporary makeover with high quality materials, fixtures and fittings. A plush restaurant (Romanesque remains) serving regionally inspired fare. A sliding roof and tasty, simple dishes at the Bistrot

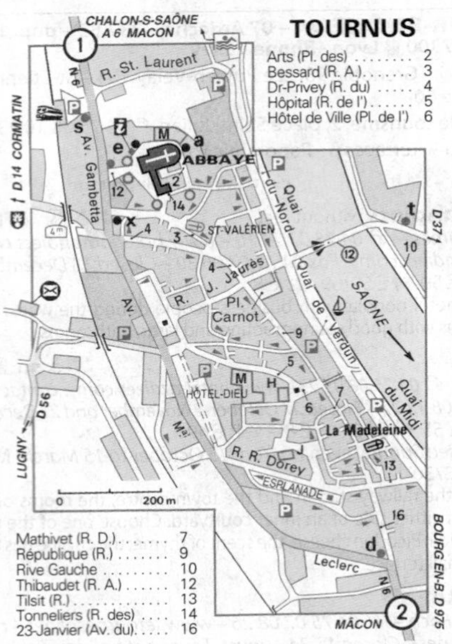

La Tour du Trésorier without rest

9 pl. Abbaye – ☎ 03 85 27 00 47 – www.la-tour-vialle.com – michel.vialle@worldonline.fr – Fax 03 85 27 00 48 – Closed 5 January-16 February **a**

5 rm – €120/170 €130/180

◆ A handsome medieval house flanked by an imposing tower, opposite the abbey. A warm welcome, plush lounge, tastefully personalised rooms and a superb garden.

Rest. Greuze (Yohann Chapuis) – Hôtel de Greuze

1 r. A. Thibaudet – ☎ 03 85 51 13 52 – www.restaurant-greuze.fr – restaurant@hotelgreuze.fr – Fax 03 85 51 75 42 – Closed 15-30 November **e**

Rest – Menu € 35/80 – Carte € 73/90

Spec. Escargot de bourgogne façon petit pot (September-March). Volaille de Bresse en deux cuissons, cappuccino des sous-bois. Soufflé chaud au Grand Marnier.

◆ Venerable house (stonework, beams) made famous by the chef Jean Ducloux. Some of his recipes still feature on the menu. The new chef-owner produces fine, modern cuisine.

Aux Terrasses (Jean-Michel Carrette) with rm

18 av. 23-Janvier – ☎ 03 85 51 01 74 – www.aux-terrasses.com – courrier@aux-terrasses.com – Fax 03 85 51 09 99 – Closed 1st-11 June, 16-26 November, 4-26 January, Sunday dinner, Tuesday lunch and Monday **d**

18 rm – €64 €64/78, € 11 **Rest** – Menu (€ 25), € 30/75 – Carte € 43/65

Spec. Escargots de Bourgogne rôtis au vinaigre balsamique. Homard rôti au beurre de tandoori, légumes de saison. Croustillant d'agrumes "explosif", jus suzette et sorbet fenouil. **Wines** Mâcon Viré-Clessé, Mâcon Cruzille.

◆ A charming stopover: dining rooms that combine classic, Baroque and modern looks, a beautiful interior garden, regionally inspired traditional cuisine and soundproofed rooms.

Meulien

1 bis av. Alpes – ☎ 03 85 51 20 86 – www.meulien.com – vmeulien@wanadoo.fr – Fax 03 85 51 20 86 – Closed 16 February-1st March, Sunday dinner, Tuesday lunch and Monday **t**

Rest – Menu € 21 (weekdays)/56 – Carte € 36/75

◆ This left-bank restaurant boasts a contemporary decor in shades of cream and chocolate. Warm family atmosphere and carefully prepared up-to-date cuisine.

Le Terminus with rm
21 av. Gambetta – 03 85 51 05 54 – www.hotel-terminus-tournus.com – reservation@hotel-terminus-tournus.com – Fax 03 85 51 79 11 – Closed Thursday lunch and Wednesday
11 rm – €69 €, €10
Rest – Menu €18 (weekdays), €26/50 – Carte €38/59
◆ This early-20C house near the railway station is home to contemporary style rooms (non-smoking). Delightfully old-fashioned breakfast room. Up-to-the-minute culinary repertoire.

in Villars 4 km South by N 6 and D 210 – **pop. 241** – **alt. 184 m** – ✉ **71700**

L'Auberge des Gourmets
pl. de l'Église – 03 85 32 58 80 – www.aubergedesgourmets.fr – laubergedesgourmets@orange.fr – Fax 03 85 51 08 32 – Closed 10-17 June, 4-13 November, 23-26 December, 6-31 January, Sunday dinner, Tuesday dinner and Wednesday except bank holidays
Rest – Menu €21 (weekdays), €28/47 – Carte €36/55
◆ Inviting little yellow fronted inn, whose dining room of beams and stonework hosts art exhibitions. Traditional meals with personal touches.

in Ozenay 6 km southwest on the D 14 – **pop. 218** – **alt. 250 m** – ✉ **71700**

Le Relais d'Ozenay
in the village – 03 85 32 17 93 – www.le-relais-dozenay.com – lerelaisdozenay@orange.fr – Fax 03 85 51 37 70 – Closed 1st-18 January, 20-30 October, Tuesday dinner in low season and Wednesday
Rest – Menu (€19), €24/43 – Carte €39/65
◆ A stone building in a picturesque village. Up-to-date, reasonably priced menu and Mâcon wines served in a stylish dining room, café area and huge rear terrace.

in Brancion 14 km west by D 14 - ✉**71700 Martailly-les-Brancion**
Château keep ≤★.

La Montagne de Brancion rest,
on the Briancon pass – 03 85 51 12 40 – www.brancion.com – lamontagnedebrancion@wanadoo.fr – Fax 03 85 51 18 64 – Closed 1st-20 December and 5 January-10 March
19 rm – €100/140 €100/220, €18 – ½ P €116/186
Rest – *(closed Tuesday lunch, Wednesday lunch and Thursday lunch)* Menu (€28), €48/75 – Carte €46/98
◆ This charming hillside residence facing the vineyards affords a fine view of the Mâcon hills. Peaceful rooms. Tasty modern cuisine generously served in the panoramic restaurant.

The ✿ award is the crème de la crème.
This is awarded to restaurants which are really worth travelling miles for!

TOURRETTES – **83 Var** – **340** P4 – **pop. 2 180** – **alt. 350 m** – ✉ **83440** 41 **C3**
French Riviera

Paris 884 – Castellane 56 – Draguignan 31 – Fréjus 35 – Grasse 26

South 6 km on D 56 – ✉ **83440 Tourrettes**

Four Seasons Resort Provence at Terre Blanche rest,
Domaine de Terre Blanche – 04 94 39 90 00 – www.fourseasons.com/provence – reservations.provence@fourseasons.com – Fax 04 94 39 90 01
114 suites – €375/2100
Rest *Faventia* – see restaurant listing
Rest *Gaudina* – Menu (€38), €48 – Carte €58/90
Rest *Tousco Grill* – grill *(residents only)* – Carte €21/57 *(lunch only)*
Rest *Infusion* – *(lunch only)* Menu €45
◆ Magnificent hotel complex on an estate including two 18-hole golf courses, a large Provencal residence and 45 villas (vast suites). Superb spa and play area. Southern flavours at the Gaudina, buffet and grills by the pool at the Tousco. Minimalist setting for a low-calorie lunch at Infusion.

XXXX **Faventia** – Hôtel Four Seasons Resort Provence at Terre Blanche
✿✿ *Domaine de Terre Blanche – ☎ 04 94 39 90 00*
– www.fourseasons.com/provence – reservations.provence@fourseasons.com
– Fax 04 94 39 90 01 – Open 8 April-5 November and closed Sunday and Monday
Rest – *(dinner only)* Menu € 68/120 – Carte € 99/140
Spec. Foie gras poêlé aux écorces confites à la badiane et macaron citron. Bar de ligne au thym frais, courgette violon et aubergine confite. Barre de chocolat aux éclats de fruits croustillants et glace pistache. **Wines** Vin de Pays des Alpes Maritimes, Côtes de Provence.
◆ Opulent restaurant (well-spaced tables, orchids, huge chandeliers) offering delicious modern cuisine using top quality produce.

TOURRETTES-SUR-LOUP – 06 Alpes-Maritimes – 341 D5 – pop. 4 199 – alt. 400 m – ✉ 06140 French Riviera

42 **E2**

Paris 929 – Grasse 18 – Nice 29 – Vence 6

Office de tourisme, 2, place de la Libération ☎ 04 93 24 18 93, Fax 04 93 59 24 40

Old village★ - ≤★ of the village on Les Quenières road.

Résidence des Chevaliers without rest
521 rte du Caire, Caire road – ☎ 04 93 59 31 97
– http://hoteldeschevaliers06.monsite.wanadoo.fr – hoteldeschevaliers06@wanadoo.fr – Fax 04 93 59 27 97 – Open 1st April-1st Oct.
12 rm – †€ 90 ††€ 200, ☕ € 14
◆ This attractive flower-decked stone establishment overlooks a medieval village and the coast. Rustic-style rooms. Breakfast served on a lovely terrace.

Auberge de Tourrettes
11 rte de Grasse – ☎ 04 93 59 30 05 – www.aubergedetourrettes.fr – info@aubergedetourrettes.fr – Fax 04 93 59 28 66 – Closed December and January
9 rm – †€ 96/136 ††€ 102/140, ☕ € 12
Rest – *(closed Sunday dinner, Tuesday lunch and Monday)* Menu (€ 20), € 30 (lunch), € 37/55 – Carte € 30/56
◆ Provencal decor refreshed with a Scandinavian feel and guesthouse atmosphere at this charming little hotel. Opulent lounge, simple and elegant rooms (four with sea views). Garden. Regional cuisine prepared by a young Danish chef and served in an unembellished setting.

Histoires de Bastide without rest
chemin du Moulin à Farine – ☎ 04 93 58 96 49 – www.histoiresdebastide.com
– histoiresdebastide@wanadoo.fr – Fax 04 93 59 08 46
4 rm – †€ 150/210 ††€ 150/210, ☕ € 15
◆ This charming bastide has an elegant Provençal ambience. Delightful guestrooms named after the works of Marcel Pagnol. Terrace, lovely swimming pool and old olive trees in the garden.

X **Le Médiéval**
6 Grand-Rue – ☎ 04 93 59 31 63 – Closed December, Wednesday and Thursday
Rest – Menu € 25/35 – Carte € 43/59
◆ Family-run restaurant in a narrow street of this delightful old village with its many artists and craftsmen. A long narrow rustic dining room where a rich traditional cuisine is served.

TOURS P – 37 Indre-et-Loire – 317 N4 – pop. 136 400 – Built-up area 297 631 – alt. 60 m – ✉ 37000 Châteaux of the Loire

11 **B2**

Paris 237 – Angers 124 – Bordeaux 346 – Le Mans 84 – Orléans 117

Tours-Val de Loire ☎ 02 47 49 37 00, Northeast: 7 km U.

Office de tourisme, 78-82, rue Bernard Palissy ☎ 02 47 70 37 37, Fax 02 47 61 14 22

de Touraine Ballan-Miré Château de la Touche, SW : 10 km on D 751, ☎ 02 47 53 20 28

d'Ardrée Saint-Antoine-du-Rocher, N : 12 km on D 2, ☎ 02 47 56 77 38

Cathedral district★★: St-Gatien cathedral ★★, musée des Beaux-Arts★★ - La Psalette (St-Gratien cloister)★, Place Grégoire-de-Tours★ - Old Tours★★★: place Plumereau★, hôtel Gouin★, rue Briçonnet★ - Quartier de St-Julien★: musée du Compagnonnage★★, Jardin de Beaune-Semblançay★ BY **K** - Musée des Équipages militaires et du Train★ V**M**5 - St-Cosme priory ★ West: 3 km V.

CHAMBRAY-LÈS-TOURS

République (Av. de la) . . . . X 88

JOUÉ-LÈS-TOURS

Martyrs (R. des) . . . . X 64
Verdun (R. de) . . . . X 102

ST-AVERTIN

Brulon (R. Léon) . . . . X 14
Lac (Av. du) . . . . X 58
Larçay (R. de) . . . . X 59

ST-CYR-SUR -LOIRE

St-Cyr (Quai de) . . . . V 91

ST-PIERRE-DES-CORPS

Jaurès (Boulevard Jean) . . . . V 57
Moulin (R. Jean) . . . . V 70

TOURS

Alouette (Av. de l') . . . . X 2
Bordeaux (Av. de) . . . . X 51
Bordiers (R. des) . . . . U 9
Boyer (R. Léon) . . . . V 10
Chevallier (R.A.) . . . . V 19
Churchill (Bd W.) . . . . V 20
Compagnons d'Emmaüs (Av. des) . . . . U 23
Eiffel (Av. Gustave) . . . . U 37
Gaulle (Av. Gén.-de) . . . . V 44
Giraudeau (R.) . . . . V 46
Grammont (Av. de) . . . . V 47
Groison (R.) . . . . U 54
Marmoutier (Quai de) . . . . U 63
Monnet (Bd J.) . . . . V 69
Portillon (Quai de) . . . . U 81
Proud'hon (Av.) . . . . V 82
République (Av. de la) . . . . X 88
St-Avertin (Rte de) . . . . X 89
St-François (R.) . . . . V 92
St-Sauveur (Pont) . . . . V 94
Sanitas (Pont du) . . . . VX 95
Tonnellé (Bd) . . . . V 97
Tranchée (Av. de la) . . . . U 98
Vaillant (R. E.) . . . . V 99
Wagner (Bd R.) . . . . V 105

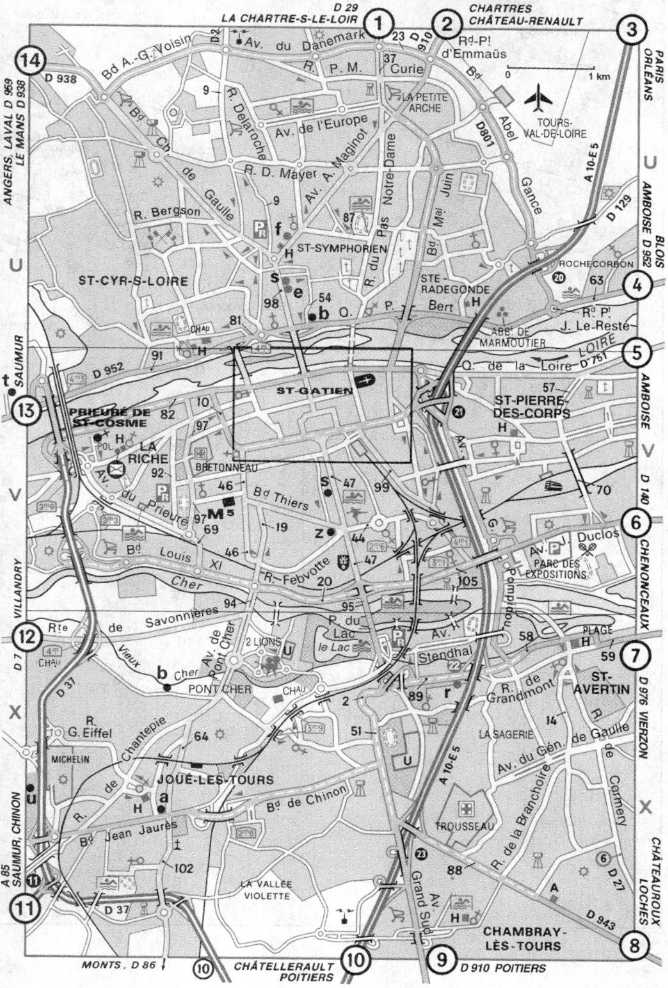

TOURS

Amandiers (R. des) . . . . CY 4
Berthelot (R.) . . . . BCY 7
Bons Enfants (R. des) . . . . BY 8
Bordeaux (R. de) . . . . CZ
Boyer (R. Léon) . . . . AZ 10
Briçonnet (R.) . . . . AY 13
Carmes (Pl. des) . . . . BY 16
Châteauneuf (Pl. de) . . . . . . BY 17
Châteaunuef (R. de) . . . . . . AY 18
Coeur-Navré (Passage du) . CY 21
Commerce (R. du) . . . . BY
Constantine (R. de) . . . . BY 24
Corneille (R.) . . . . CY 25
Courier (R. Paul-Louis) . . . . BY 27
Courteline (R. G.) . . . . AY 28
Cygne (R. du) . . . . CY 29
Descartes (R.) . . . . BZ 33
Dolve (R. de la) . . . . BZ 35
Favre (R. Jules) . . . . BY 38
Fusillés (R. des) . . . . BY 41
Gambetta (R.) . . . . BZ 43
Giraudeau (R.) . . . . AZ 46
Grammont (Av. de) . . . . CZ
Grand-Marché (Pl. du) . . . . AY 49

Street	Grid	No.
rand Passage	CZ	50
régoire-de-Tours (Pl.)	DY	52
rosse-Tour (R. de la)	AY	55
alles (Pl. des)	AZ	
alles (R. des)	BY	
erbes (Carroi aux)	AY	56
avoisier (R.)	CY	60
ianceau (R.)	DY	61
larceau (R.)	BYZ	
Merville (R. du Prés.)	BY	65
Meusnier (R. Gén.)	DY	66
Monnaie (R. de la)	BY	68
Mûrier (R. du)	AY	71
Nationale (R.)	BYZ	
Paix (R. de la)	BY	73
Petites-Boucheries (Pl. des)	DY	80
Petit-Cupidon (R. du)	DY	77
Petit-St-Martin (R. du)	AY	78
Racine (R.)	DY	84
Rapin (R.)	AZ	85
St-Pierre-le-Puellier (Pl.)	ABY	93
Scellerie (R. de la)	BCY	
Sully (R. de)	BZ	96
Victoire (Pl. de la)	AY	103
Vinci (R. Léonard de)	BZ	104

De l'Univers rm,

5 bd Heurteloup – 02 47 05 37 12 – www.oceaniahotels.com – univers.tours@oceaniahotels.com – Fax 02 47 61 51 80 CZ **u**

85 rm – €115/270 €115/270 – 2 suites

Rest *La Touraine* – *(Closed 15 July-15 August, Saturday and Sunday)* Menu €22 (weekdays)/39 – Carte €40/67

◆ The superb murals representing famous hotel guests from 1846 onwards is the establishment's pride and joy. Plush rooms and luxurious suites complete the opulent picture. Traditional food served in a bright and comfortable dining room; low-key bar.

Central Hôtel without rest

21 r. Berthelot – 02 47 05 46 44 – www.bestwesterncentralhoteltours.com – bestwestern.centralhotel@wanadoo.fr – Fax 02 47 66 10 26 – Closed 24 December-3 January CY **r**

35 rm – €100/121 €121/140, €13 – 2 suites

◆ Among the many assets of this establishment are the garage, regularly spruced up rooms (some overlooking an inner garden), splendid bathrooms, and summer terrace.

Mercure Centre without rest

29 r. E. Vaillant – 02 47 60 40 60 – www.mercure.com – h3475@accor.com – Fax 02 47 64 74 81 DZ **f**

92 rm – €98/170 €118/170, €13

◆ A convenient location two minutes from the train station. Functional rooms painted in soft colours, overlooking either the street or the railway lines (well soundproofed). Full breakfast.

Kyriad without rest

65 av. Grammont – 02 47 64 71 78 – www.kyriadtours.com – contact@kyriadtours.com – Fax 02 47 05 84 62 V **s**

50 rm – €80/84 €90, €9

◆ Stylish modern fixtures and fittings depict the rooms of this impeccably refurbished hotel. Elegant sitting room (fireplace and wainscoting) and winter garden-style breakfast room.

L'Adresse without rest

12 r. de la Rôtisserie – 02 47 20 85 76 – www.hotel-ladresse.com – contactladresse@aol.com – Fax 02 47 05 74 87 AY **u**

17 rm – €50 €70/90, €8

◆ The small cosy rooms are a happy blend of old (beams) and new, making this 18C abode in the historic district a delightful destination.

Turone rm,

4 pl. de la Liberté – 02 47 05 50 05 – www.hotelturone.com – contact@hotelturone.com – Fax 02 47 20 22 07 V **z**

120 rm – €95/125 €95/125, €13 – ½ P €106/136

Rest – Menu €20 (weekdays) – Carte €25/38

◆ A popular hotel due to its practical location, spacious garage and pleasant, modern rooms (including seven more comfortable rooms under the eaves). Extremely quiet courtyard. Brasserie style dining room and traditional menu.

Le Grand Hôtel without rest

9 pl. du Gén. Leclerc – 02 47 05 35 31 – www.legrandhoteltours.com – contact@legrandhoteltours.com – Fax 02 47 64 10 77 – Closed 15 December-15 January CZ **z**

107 rm – €80/110 €80/110, €14

◆ Initially designed in 1927 by architect Pierre Chareau, the new owner has set about restoring this hotel to its former glory. Ask for one of the renovated rooms.

Du Manoir without rest

2 r. Traversière – 02 47 05 37 37 – http://site.voila.fr/hotel.manoir.tours – manoir37@wanadoo.fr – Fax 02 47 05 16 00 CZ **a**

19 rm – €50/58 €56/65, €8,50

◆ This 19C town house has well-kept classical rooms, furnished with antiques and a few canopied bedsteads. Homemade produce adorns the breakfast table, served in a pretty, vaulted room.

Mondial without rest
3 pl. de la Résistance – ✆ 02 47 05 62 68 – www.hotelmondialtours.com – info@hotelmondialtours.com – Fax 02 47 61 85 31 – Closed 24 December-7 January, 8-17 February, Friday and Saturday from November to January BY **g**
21 rm – €54/64 €58/66, €8
◆ Standing on a town centre square, this hotel is as popular for its location as for its pleasantly updated modern interior. Find a grey and pastel colour scheme and impeccable rooms.

Du Théâtre without rest
57 r. Scellerie – ✆ 02 47 05 31 29 – www.hotel-du-theatre37.com – hoteldutheatre.tours@wanadoo.fr – Fax 02 47 61 20 78 – Closed 1st-15 August, 26 December-4 January and 6-15 February CY **t**
14 rm – €53/60 €58/68, €8
◆ The interior of this 15C house is almost intimate in feel: small, welcoming, well kept rooms with exposed timberwork. Rooms on the courtyard side are quieter.

Châteaux de la Loire without rest
12 r. Gambetta – ✆ 02 47 05 10 05 – www.hoteldeschateaux.fr – contact@hoteldeschateaux.fr – Fax 02 47 20 20 14 – Open 16 March-15 December
30 rm – €46/56 €46/66, €7 BZ **x**
◆ This centrally located hotel is set halfway between old Tours and the station. It offers functional, contemporary rooms that are gradually being renovated.

Castel Fleuri without rest
10-12 r. Groison – ✆ 02 47 54 50 99 – www.castel-fleuri-tours.com – hotelcastelfleuri@orange.fr – Fax 02 47 54 86 59 – Closed 24 July-10 August, 29 December-3 January, 15-20 February and Sunday U **b**
15 rm – €44/55 €55/69, €7
◆ This unpretentious family hotel in a residential neighbourhood is quiet and convenient. There is a car park, small tasteful rooms (ask for a renovated one), and sensible prices.

La Roche Le Roy (Alain Couturier)
55 rte St-Avertin – ✆ 02 47 27 22 00 – www.rocheleroy.com – laroche.leroy@wanadoo.fr – Fax 02 47 28 08 39 – Closed 1st-26 August, 7-22 February, Sunday and Monday X **r**
Rest – Menu €35 (lunch), €55/75 – Carte €58/76
Spec. Fraîcheur de homard et mesclun à la mangue. Matelote d'anguille dite "blanche" au vouvray. Baba "Miquette" un classique d'autrefois. **Wines** Vouvray, Chinon.
◆ This charming small manor, characteristic of the Tours region, invites you to taste seasonal culinary specialities in an intimate atmosphere. Pleasant terrace.

Charles Barrier (Hervé Lussault)
101 av. Tranchée – ✆ 02 47 54 20 39 – charles_barrier@yahoo.fr – Fax 02 47 41 80 95 – Closed Saturday lunch and Sunday except public holidays
Rest – Menu €29 (weekdays)/89 – Carte €69/123 U **e**
Spec. Langoustines croustillantes au curry de Madras et légumes confits. Pigeonneau du pays de Racan rôti. Soufflé chaud aux fruits de la passion. **Wines** Vouvray sec, Chinon.
◆ The personal recipes of the young chef have restored this handsome bourgeois home to its illustrious gastronomic past. Pleasant veranda and peaceful flower garden terrace.

La Chope
25 bis av. de Grammont – ✆ 02 47 20 15 15 – www.lachope.info – Fax 02 47 05 70 51 – Closed 27 July-9 August CZ **f**
Rest – Menu (€17), €19/24 – Carte €31/52
◆ A chic brasserie decorated in the Belle Époque style with red velvet bench seats, mirrors and tulip lamps. The menu offers a wide choice of fish and seafood and several exceptional clarets.

Rive Gauche (Pascal Vuillemin)
23 r. du Commerce – ✆ 02 47 05 71 21 – www.toursrivegauche.com – contact@toursrivegauche.com – Fax 02 72 22 05 76 BY **a**
Rest – Menu (€24), €30/80 – Carte €52/73
Spec. Foie gras de canard à la pomme granny smith. Brochet aux herbes sauce chardonnay. Nougat de Tours.
◆ A fashionable restaurant with one smart bistro and one contemporary dining room, overlooking the quiet courtyard of the Fine Arts School. Personal touches enliven classic recipes.

La Deuvalière

18 r. de la Monnaie – ✆ 02 47 64 01 57 – ladeuvaliere@wanadoo.fr – Fax 02 47 64 01 57 – Closed Saturday lunch, Sunday and Monday BY **e**

Rest – Menu (€ 14), € 28/32 – Carte approx. € 30

◆ A good combination of old stonework from a characteristic 15C house mingled with modern details (dark wood, orange hues). Tasty, updated traditional menu.

L'Odéon

10 pl. Gén. Leclerc – ✆ 02 47 20 12 65 – www.restaurant-odeon.fr – l.odeon@orange.fr – Fax 02 47 20 47 58 – Closed 1st-16 August and Sunday CZ **r**

Rest – Menu € 27/49 – Carte € 41/66

◆ The same chef has been at the helm of this restaurant for over twenty years. It was originally opened in 1893 and is one of the oldest in Tours. Tasteful Art Deco, brasserie style decoration. Traditional menu.

La Trattoria des Halles

31 pl. G.-Pailhou – ✆ 02 47 64 26 64 – Closed August, Sunday and Monday

Rest – Carte € 30/50 AZ **b**

◆ A smart yet informal atmosphere reigns in this contemporary bistro opposite the Halles. The chef, of Russian origin, rustles up tasty meals with an Italian flavour.

Cap Sud

88 r. Colbert – ✆ 02 47 05 24 81 – www.capsudrestaurant.fr – Closed 1st-14 September, Sunday and Monday CY **d**

Rest – Menu (€ 16), € 20/33 – Carte € 35/51

◆ This little restaurant has a Mediterranean atmosphere, both in its warm decor with sunny colours and up-to-date cuisine. Short but well selected wine list.

L'Atelier Gourmand

37 r. Étienne Marcel – ✆ 02 47 38 59 87 – www.lateliergourmand.fr – mail@lateliergourmand.fr – Fax 02 47 50 14 23 – Closed 20 December-15 January, Saturday lunch, Sunday and Monday AY **z**

Rest – Menu (€ 12), € 22 – Carte € 30/36

◆ This 15C residence is in the historic district of Tours. The charming dining room combines beams and a fireplace with designer decor. Pleasant terrace in the inner courtyard.

Le Bistrot de la Tranchée

103 av. Tranchée – ✆ 02 47 41 09 08 – charles_barrier@yahoo.fr – Fax 02 47 41 80 95 – Closed 1st-15 August, Sunday and Monday U **s**

Rest – Menu (€ 9), € 12 (weekday lunch), € 17/25 – Carte € 25/41

◆ This pleasant bistro is often packed. It offers a view of the kitchen, traditional cuisine and daily blackboard specials. Attractive wood façade and a simple but charming decor.

Le Rif

12 av. Maginot – ✆ 02 47 51 12 44 – Fax 02 47 51 14 50 – Closed 18 July-18 August, Wednesday dinner from 15 September to 15 June, Sunday except lunch from 15 June to 15 September and Monday. U **f**

Rest – Menu € 26 bi (weekdays)/30 bi – Carte € 26/32

◆ North African cuisine and a matching tasteful decor adorned with Moroccan ornaments and pottery lamps. Friendly welcome.

Le Petit Patrimoine

58 r. Colbert – ✆ 02 47 66 05 81 – Closed 16-31 July, 24 December-4 January, Sunday and Monday CY **b**

Rest – Menu (€ 13), € 17 (dinner), € 20/26 – Carte € 30/40

◆ The rustic interior of this elongated structure, the wholesome country dishes from a past era, and the pleasant service make this establishment a must.

via ② 9 km

Mercure

11 r. Aviation, (Milletière industrial estate) ✉ 37100 Tours – ✆ 02 47 49 55 00 – www.mercuretours.com – h1572@accor.com – Fax 02 47 49 55 25

93 rm – †€ 77/130 ††€ 77/150 – ½ P € 68/111

Rest – Menu (€ 20 bi), € 23 – Carte € 26/35

◆ A modern building near the motorway slip road, with simple, spacious, functional rooms. Popular with business travellers. Bright restaurant overlooking the summer terrace, traditional fare and regional wines.

L'Arche de Meslay
14 r. Ailes ✉ 37210 Parçay-Meslay – ✆ 02 47 29 00 07 – Fax 02 47 29 04 04 – Closed 3-25 August, Sunday and Monday except public holidays
Rest – Menu (€ 15), € 17/45 – Carte € 48/55
◆ The colonnade standing in the centre of the dining room, large mirrors and kitchens in full view of the customers, all make for a wonderful setting. Regional and seasonal menus.

in Rochecorbon **6 km by ④ – pop. 2 982 – alt. 58 m – ✉ 37210**
Office de tourisme, place du Croissant ✆ 02 47 52 80 22

Les Hautes Roches
86 quai Loire – ✆ 02 47 52 88 88 – www.leshautesroches.com – hautesroches@relaischateaux.com – Fax 02 47 52 81 30 – Closed 15 February-27 March, 19-27 April
15 rm – €150/280 €150/280, € 20 – ½ P € 165/225
Rest – *(closed Sunday dinner, Tuesday lunch and Monday)* Menu € 54/90 – Carte € 56/79
Spec. Le foie gras de canard à la façon d'un nougat. Sandre de Loire au beurre blanc nantais. Tarte fine aux pommes caramélisées. **Wines** Vouvray, Bourgueil.
◆ This unusual 18C manor house overlooking the River Loire was once a monastery. Attractive rooms, some cut into the rock. Elegant dining room and delightful panoramic terrace facing the river. Modern cuisine.

in Chambray-lès-Tours **6.5 km South, by Poitiers road - X – pop. 10 600 – alt. 90 m – ✉ 37170**

Novotel
Z.A.C. La Vrillonnerie, (D 910) – ✆ 02 47 80 18 10 – www.novotel.com – h0453@accor.com – Fax 02 47 80 18 18
127 rm – €79/130 €79/130, € 14 **Rest** – Carte € 21/43
◆ A busy shopping district surrounds this functional hotel; ask for one of the quieter rooms overlooking the garden. 24hr service at the Novotel Café. Modern restaurant has a view of the kitchen and overlooks the pool. Traditional well thought out menu.

in Joué-lès-Tours **5 km Southwest, by Chinon road – pop. 36 000 – alt. 65 m – ✉ 37300**
Office de tourisme, 39, avenue de la République ✆ 02 47 80 05 97, Fax 02 47 80 05 97

Château de Beaulieu
67 r. Beaulieu – ✆ 02 47 53 20 26 – www.chateaudebeaulieu37.com – reservation@chateaudebeaulieu37.com – Fax 02 47 53 84 20 X **b**
18 rm – €75/125 €90/165, € 13 – ½ P € 90/125
Rest – Menu (€ 29), € 40/75 – Carte € 55/70
◆ A landscaped park surrounds this 18C manor house whose view extends as far as Tours. Period furniture in the spacious rooms (10 in a separate pavilion). Elegant dining room, classic culinary repertoire and good wine list.

Mercure
parc des Bretonnières – ✆ 02 47 53 16 16 – www.mercure.com – h1788@accor.com – Fax 02 47 53 14 00 X **u**
75 rm – €77/140 €87/160, € 13 – ½ P € 94
Rest – Menu (€ 15), € 20 (weekday lunch), € 27/34 – Carte approx. € 30
◆ This hotel, part of the Malraux Congress Centre, offers well-soundproofed, contemporary rooms decorated in a restful colour scheme. Excellent fitness facilities. A dining room extending onto a garden terrace and traditional cuisine with regional touches.

Chéops
75 bd J. Jaurès – ✆ 02 47 67 72 72 – www.inter-hotel-cheops.fr – hotel.cheops@wanadoo.fr – Fax 02 47 67 85 38 X **a**
58 rm – €50/72 €50/72, € 8
Rest – *(Closed 18 December-3 January, Friday, Saturday and Sunday from October to April) (dinner only)* Menu (€ 14), € 17 – Carte € 17/31
◆ A recent hotel that is part of a residential and shopping centre in the heart of Joué. Bright colours and wrought iron give the small rooms, half of which are air-conditioned, a Provençal style. Pleasant, sunny dining room decorated with modern furniture.

in La Guignière 4 km by ⑬, Langeais road - ✉37230 Fondettes

Manoir without rest
10 r. de Beaumanoir, D 952 – ☎ 02 47 42 04 02 – www.lemanoirhotel.fr – lemanoirhotel@orange.fr – Fax 02 47 49 79 29 V t
16 rm – †€ 38/44 ††€ 47/52, ☕ € 6,50
◆ A 1970s villa in a quiet residential neighbourhood. Some of the rooms, adorned with pretty wall fabrics, command fine views of the Loire.

in Vallières 8 km by ⑬, Langeais road - ✉37230 Fondettes

Auberge de Port Vallières
D 952 – ☎ 02 47 42 24 04 – www.touraine-gourmande.com – Fax 02 47 49 98 83 – Closed 17 August-2 September, February school holidays, Tuesday dinner except July-August, Sunday dinner, Wednesday dinner and Monday
Rest – Menu € 18 (weekday lunch), € 28/52 – Carte € 45/70
◆ Touraine inspired cuisine awaits you in this former open-air café, converted into an inn many years ago. Decor of antique bric-a-brac. Table d'hôte available.

TOURTOUR – 83 Var – **340** M4 – **pop. 519** – **alt. 652 m** – ✉ 83690 41 **C3**
French Riviera

Paris 827 – Aups 10 – Draguignan 17 – Salernes 11
Syndicat d'initiative, Château communal ☎ 04 94 70 59 47, Fax 04 94 70 59 47
Church ⁂★.

La Bastide de Tourtour rm, rm, rest,
Flayosc road – ☎ 04 98 10 54 20 – www.bastidedetourtour.com – bastide@bastidedetourtour.com – Fax 04 94 70 54 90
25 rm – †€ 110/140 ††€ 150/350, ☕ € 23
Rest – *(closed Monday, Tuesday, Wednesday, Thursday and Friday lunch from 15 September to 22 December and from 3 January to 15 June)* Menu € 30/75 – Carte € 60/78
◆ Provencal house on a hillside with unrestricted view of the Maures mountains. Some of the individualised rooms have their own loggia. Modern cuisine in the attractive vaulted dining room and on the idyllic shaded terrace.

La Petite Auberge rm,
rte de Flayosc, 1.5 km by D 77 – ☎ 04 98 10 26 16 – www.petiteauberge.net – aubergetourtour@orange.fr – Fax 04 98 10 26 50 – Open 2 April-14 November
11 rm – †€ 77/175 ††€ 77/255, ☕ € 15
Rest – *(Closed Monday) (dinner only)* Menu € 35
◆ Farmhouse surrounded by lush vegetation on the edge of the village. Spacious, rather romantic rooms, including four on the ground floor next to the pool. Elegant dining room and terrace facing the Maures mountains. Traditional dishes.

Auberge St-Pierre
3 km east by D 51 and secondary road – ☎ 04 94 50 00 50 – www.guideprovence.com/hotel/saint-pierre/ – aubergestpierre@wanadoo.fr – Fax 04 94 70 59 04 – Open 11 April-19 October
16 rm – †€ 81/96 ††€ 82/105, ☕ € 11 – ½ P € 77/89
Rest – *(dinner only except Saturday, Sunday and holidays)* Menu € 26/41
◆ A peaceful 16C inn, in the heart of a large farming estate, set near the old sheepcote. Rooms with loggias overlooking the countryside. Pool and small gym. Rustic dining room and fine terrace overlooking the countryside. Regional cuisine.

Le Mas des Collines
chemin des collines, 2.5 km by Villecroze road (D 51) and secondary road – ☎ 04 94 70 59 30 – lemasdescollines@wanadoo.fr – Fax 04 94 70 57 62 – Open mid-April to mid-November
7 rm ☕ – †€ 98/100 ††€ 102/108 – ½ P € 76
Rest – *(dinner only)* Menu € 28/38
◆ A hotel lost in the middle of the countryside, not far from Tourtour. The simply decorated rooms have balconies and there is a pool where you can enjoy the splendid views.

XX ✿ **Les Chênes Verts** (Paul Bajade) with rm rest, VISA
Villecroze road, 2 km by D 51 – ☎ 04 94 70 55 06 – Fax 04 94 70 59 35 – Closed 1st June-20 July, Tuesday and Wednesday
3 rm – €80/100 €100, €20
Rest – *(number of covers limited, pre-book)* Menu €55/145 – Carte €100/170
Spec. Ecrevisses sautées aux herbes. Noisettes d'agneau de pays aux truffes. Le grand dessert. **Wines** Côtes de Provence., Coteaux Varois.
◆ Provence-style house away from it all in a pretty forest setting. Regional cuisine with lots of character (truffle specialities) to be savoured in two comfortable dining rooms or on the terrace.

X **La Table** VISA
1 Traverse du Jas, Les Ribas – ☎ 04 94 70 55 95 – www.latable.fr – Fax 04 94 70 55 95 – Closed 29 June-5 July, Monday and Tuesday except from 15 July to 15 August
Rest – Menu €28/39 – Carte €55/77
◆ Modern decor and simple settings in this tiny restaurant on the first floor of the house. Market-fresh vegetarian and appetising menus.

LA TOUSSUIRE – 73 Savoie – 333 K6 – alt. 1 690 m – Winter sports : 1 800/2 400 m 19 – ✉ 73300 French Alps 46 F2

Paris 651 – Albertville 78 – Chambéry 91 – St-Jean-de-Maurienne 16

Les Soldanelles rest, VISA
r. des Chasseurs Alpins – ☎ 04 79 56 75 29 – www.hotelsoldanelles.com – infos@hotelsoldanelles.com – Fax 04 79 56 71 56 – Open 28 June-31 August and 21 December-19 April
38 rm – €46/67 €68/124, €10 – ½ P €75/110
Rest – Menu €22/40 – Carte €32/58
◆ This welcoming, family hotel is set on the slopes of the resort. It has spacious rooms with balcony (those on the south side have a pretty view), a swimming pool and steam room. Traditional dishes and cheese specialities served in an elegant panoramic restaurant.

Les Airelles rest, VISA
– ☎ 04 79 56 75 88 – www.hotel-les-airelles.com – info@hotel-les-airelles.com – Fax 04 79 83 03 48 – Open July-August and 15 December-20 April
31 rm – €50/55 €58/63 – ½ P €72/89
Rest – *(resident only)* Menu €20
◆ The many renovations undertaken in this large mountain building, situated at the foot of the ski lifts, have included the refreshing comfortable rooms. The bay windows of the restaurant offer perfect views of the skiers.

TOUZAC – 46 Lot – 337 C5 – see Puy-l'Évêque

TRACY-SUR-MER – 14 Calvados – 303 I3 – see Arromanches-les-Bains

---

TRAENHEIM – 67 Bas-Rhin – 315 I5 – pop. 592 – alt. 200 m – ✉ 67310 1 A1

Paris 471 – Haguenau 54 – Molsheim 8 – Saverne 22 – Strasbourg 25

X **Zum Loejelgucker** VISA
17 r. Principale – ☎ 03 88 50 38 19 – www.loejelgucker-auberge-traenheim.com – loejelgucker@traenheim.net – Fax 03 88 50 36 31 – Closed 30 December-5 January, 16 February-2 March, Monday dinner and Tuesday
Rest – Menu (€12), €20/47 bi – Carte €25/45
◆ An 18C Alsatian farmhouse in a village at the foot of the Vosges. Dark woodwork, frescoes and flower-filled courtyard in summer. Regional dishes.

**Undecided between two equivalent establishments?
Within each category,
establishments are classified in our order of preference.**

LA TRANCHE-SUR-MER – 85 Vendée – 316 H9 – pop. 2 644 – alt. 4 m – ✉ 85360 Atlantic Coast

34 **B3**

Paris 459 – La Rochelle 64 – La Roche-sur-Yon 40 – Les Sables-d'Olonne 39

Office de tourisme, place de la Liberté ✆ 02 51 30 33 96, Fax 02 51 27 78 71

Parc de Californie★ (ornithological park) East: 9 km.

Les Dunes

68 av. M. Samson – ✆ 02 51 30 32 27 – www.hotel-les-dunes.com – info@hotel-les-dunes.com – Fax 02 51 27 78 30 – Open 1st April-30 September

45 rm – €41/58 €59/108, €9 – ½ P €55/83

Rest – Menu (€14), €19/34 – Carte €20/50

◆ Hotel popular for its quiet location, faultless upkeep and superb pool with a glass roof, facing the sea. Some rooms have balconies and benefit from a sea view. The menu lists fish and seafood, including fresh crayfish and lobster.

in la Grière 2 km east by D 46 - ✉ 85360 La-Tranche-sur-Mer

Les Cols Verts

48 r. de Verdun – ✆ 02 51 27 49 30 – www.hotelcolsverts.com – info@hotelcolsverts.com – Fax 02 51 30 11 42 – Open 4 April-29 September

31 rm – €51/70 €63/137, €10 – ½ P €61/82

Rest – Menu (€22), €20/39 – Carte €29/39

◆ A 1970s building 150m from the beach. Well-maintained rooms; quieter and smaller in the annexe on the other side of the garden. Swimming pool in an adjacent building. Pleasant terrace and traditional dishes with a clear preference for sea produce.

TRANS-EN-PROVENCE – 340 N4 – pop. 5 388 – alt. 140 m – ✉ 83720

41 **C3**

Paris 866 – Marseille 137 – Toulon 75 – Cannes 58 – Grasse 72

Office de tourisme, 1, avenue Notre-Dame ✆ 04 94 67 76 17, Fax 04 94 67 76 48

Domaine de St-Amour without rest

986 rte de la Motte, southeast on the D 47 – ✆ 06 81 33 43 80 – www.domainedesaintamour.com – wahl@domainedesaintamour.com – Fax 04 94 70 88 92 – Open 3 April-4 October

3 rm – €81/85 €81/85

◆ An 18C country house very near the village, set in the middle of a country park (grassland, lake, river). Beautiful bedrooms on the themes of the Ocean, Africa and Provence.

TRAVEXIN – 88 Vosges – 314 I5 – see Ventron

TRÉBEURDEN – 22 Côtes-d'Armor – 309 A2 – pop. 3 733 – alt. 81 m – ✉ 22560 Brittany

9 **B1**

Paris 525 – Lannion 10 – Perros-Guirec 14 – St-Brieuc 74

Office de tourisme, place de Crec'h Héry ✆ 02 96 23 51 64, Fax 02 96 15 44 87

Le Castel ←★ 30 mn - Pointe de Bihit ←★ Southwest: 2 km - Pleumeur-Bodou: Radôme and musée des Télécommunications★, Planétarium du Trégor★, Northeast: 5.5 km.

Manoir de Lan-Kerellec

Allée de Lan-Kerellec – ✆ 02 96 15 00 00 – www.lankerellec.com – lankerellec@relaischateaux.com – Fax 02 96 23 66 88 – Open beginning March-15 November

19 rm – €115/360 €165/440, €20

Rest – *(closed lunch Monday-Thursday)* Menu €50/70 – Carte €59/110

Spec. Araignée décortiquée, foie gras et émulsion de pomme verte (March-mid June). Homard bleu rôti, aubergine grillée aux légumes et aromates. Barre croustillante aux fraises, crème légère menthe, sorbet champagne (May-September).

◆ This stately 19C Breton manor facing the islands of the Pink Granite Coast is steeped in charm. Enjoy spacious guestrooms decked in lovely fabrics, with a balcony or terrace. A lovely hull-shaped roof, reminiscent of a boat, and a seasonal inspired menu at the restaurant.

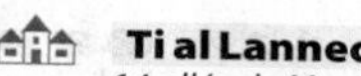

Ti al Lannec — rest, VISA

14 allée de Mezo Guen – ✆ 02 96 15 01 01 – www.tiallannec.com – contact@tiallannec.com – Fax 02 96 23 62 14 – Open from beg. March-mid November
26 rm – €92/123 €171/364, €17 – 7 suites – ½ P €145/251
Rest – Menu (€26), €28 bi (weekday lunch), €39/80 – Carte €67/154
◆ This peaceful, family-run hillside establishment overlooks the sea. Spruce guestrooms. Some command a view over the parkland as far as the beach. A seascape worthy of mention... and fish and seafood worthy of a healthy appetite!

Toëno without rest — VISA

1.5 km on régastel road – ✆ 02 96 23 68 78 – hoteltoeno.com – toeno@wanadoo.fr – Fax 02 96 15 42 54 – Closed 5 January-2 February
17 rm – €53/99 €53/99, €9
◆ Recently built hotel. Functional, simply decorated, light rooms, all with balconies or terraces overlooking the English Channel. Comfortable sitting room.

Le Quellen with rm — VISA

18 corniche Goas Treiz – ✆ 02 96 15 43 18 – www.lequellen.com – lequellen@wanadoo.fr – Fax 02 96 23 64 43 – Closed 9-31 March, 4-26 November, Sunday dinner in low season, Monday and Tuesday
6 rm – €42/60 €42/60 – ½ P €46/55
Rest – Menu (€15), €27/57 – Carte €42/75
◆ This restaurant on the main road through Trébeurden serves traditional cuisine in a neo-rustic decor. Fine collection of coffee mills. Simple guestrooms.

TRÉBOUL – 29 Finistère – 308 E6 – see Douarnenez

TREFFORT – 38 Isère – 333 G8 – pop. 208 – alt. 618 m – ✉ 38650 — 45 C2

Paris 598 – Grenoble 36 – Monestier-de-Clermont 9 – La Mure 43

at the lakeside 3 km south by D 110E – ✉ 38650 Treffort

Le Château d'Herbelon — rm, VISA

– ✆ 04 76 34 02 03 – www.chateau-herbelon.fr – chateaudherbelon@wanadoo.fr – Fax 04 76 34 05 44 – Open 5 March-15 November and closed Monday and Tuesday except July-August
10 rm – €68/98 €68/98, €10 – ½ P €72/87
Rest – Menu €23/46 – Carte €29/48
◆ A 17C building covered with Virginia creeper and climbing roses, next to Lake Monteynard. Spacious rooms. In winter, an imposing fireplace warms the rustic dining room. A few outdoor tables on the lawn in summer.

TREFFORT – 01 Ain – 328 F3 – pop. 2 011 – alt. 280 m – ✉ 01370 — 44 B1

Paris 436 – Bourg-en-Bresse 18 – Lons-le-Saunier 57 – Mâcon 51 – Oyonnax 42

L'Embellie — rest, rest, VISA

pl. du Champ-de-Foire – ✆ 04 74 42 35 64 – embellietreffort@aol.com – Fax 04 74 51 25 81 – Closed 1st-5 January
8 rm – €40 €49, €6
Rest – *(closed Sunday dinner off season)* Menu (€12), €18/33 – Carte €24/36
◆ This inviting stone house on the village square offers small, simple rooms, currently being redecorated. Traditional food and Bresse dishes served in a modern setting or on the pleasant terrace.

TRÉGASTEL – 22 Côtes-d'Armor – 309 B2 – pop. 2 397 – alt. 58 m – ✉ 22730 Brittany — 9 B1

Paris 526 – Lannion 11 – Perros-Guirec 9 – St-Brieuc 75 – Trébeurden 11 – Tréguier 26

Office de tourisme, place Sainte-Anne ✆ 02 96 15 38 38, Fax 02 96 23 85 97

de Saint-Samson Pleumeur-Bodou Avenue Jacques Ferronière, S : 3 km, ✆ 02 96 23 87 34

Rocks★★ - Île Renote★★ NE - Viewpoint indicator ★.

Park Hotel Bellevue
20 r. Calculots – ☎ 02 96 23 88 18 – www.hotelbellevuetregastel.com – bellevue.tregastel@wanadoo.fr – Fax 02 96 23 89 91 – Open 16 March-11 November
31 rm – †€ 55/150 ††€ 65/150, ☕ € 13
Rest – *(open 1st May-30 September) (dinner only)* Menu € 28, € 40/60 – Carte € 42/110
◆ A substantial 1930s establishment in a quiet green setting. Simple well-kept rooms, smaller in a wing. Billiards table in the sitting room. Friendly welcome. Classic cuisine, colourful tablecloths and exotic looking chairs. Sea facing terrace.

Beau Séjour
5 plage du Coz-Pors – ☎ 02 96 23 88 02 – www.beausejoursarl.com – daniel.laveant@wanadoo.fr – Fax 02 96 23 49 73 – Closed 11 November-15 December and 10 January-10 February
16 rm – †€ 45/60 ††€ 55/89, ☕ € 10
Rest – *(closed 1st- 25 October, 5 November-30 March and Monday)* Menu (€ 15), € 35 (dinner), € 39/49 – Carte € 38/82
◆ Ideally located near the Forum and beach, a wide choice of rooms with sea views and a buffet breakfast: perfect for a 'beau séjour'! Dining room decorated with a trompe l'oeil painting of the Pink Granite Coast. Contemporary cuisine.

De la Mer et de la Plage without rest
Coz-Pors beach – ☎ 02 96 15 60 00 – hoteldelamer.ifrance.com – hoteldelamer.tregastel@laposte.net – Fax 02 96 15 31 11 – Open 28 March-15 November
19 rm – †€ 45/105 ††€ 45/105, ☕ € 9
◆ This regional style house stands on the beach, next to the Forum. Ask for one of the modern third floor rooms, designed along the lines of a ship's cabin.

in la plage de Landrellec 3 km south by D 788 and secondary road - ✉ 22560 Pleumeur-Bodou

Le Macareux
21 r. des Plages – ☎ 02 96 23 87 62 – infos@lemacareux.com – Fax 02 96 15 94 97 – Closed 1st January-13 February, Sunday dinner, Tuesday lunch except July-and Monday
Rest – Menu € 24/52 – Carte € 42/89
◆ This pleasant Breton style inn serves lobster and abalone specialities and other local seafood delicacies. Terrace facing the sea. Friendly ambience.

TRÉGUIER – 22 Côtes-d'Armor – **309** C2 – pop. 2 679 – alt. 40 m – ✉ 22220 **Brittany** 9 **B1**

Paris 509 – Guingamp 28 – Lannion 19 – Paimpol 15 – St-Brieuc 61

Office de tourisme, 67, rue Ernest Renan ☎ 02 96 92 22 33

St-Tugdual cathedral ★★: cloister★.

Aigue Marine rm, rest,
5 r. M. Berthelot, (in the harbour) – ☎ 02 96 92 97 00 – www.aiguemarine-hotel.com – aiguemarine@aiguemarine.fr – Fax 02 96 92 44 48 – Closed 21-25 December, 4 January-24 February and Sunday from November to March
33 rm – †€ 74/99 ††€ 74/99, ☕ € 14 – 15 suites – ½ P € 79/91
Rest – *(closed Saturday lunch, Sunday dinner and Monday off season and lunch except Sunday from June to September)* Menu € 32/64 – Carte € 49/68
◆ The practical guestrooms of this hotel overlook the harbour or the pool and garden. Some rooms have balconies, others are good for families. Well-prepared buffet breakfast. Up-to-date cuisine in a bright, modern, flower-decked setting.

Lannion road 2 km southwest by D 786 and secondary road – ✉ **22220 Tréguier**

Kastell Dinec'h without rest
Lannion road – ☎ 02 96 92 49 39 – kastell@club-internet.fr – Fax 02 96 92 34 03 – Open 1st April-5 October and closed Tuesday evening and Wednesday
15 rm – †€ 75/79 ††€ 100/111, ☕ € 13
◆ A former fortified farmhouse set in peaceful countryside and a garden. Small, cosy and stylish guestrooms in the main wing and outbuildings.

TRÉGUNC – 29 Finistère – 308 H7 – pop. 6 354 – alt. 45 m – ✉ 29910 9 B2

Paris 543 – Concarneau 7 – Pont-Aven 9 – Quimper 29 – Quimperlé 27

Office de tourisme, Kérambourg ✆ 02 98 50 22 05, Fax 02 98 50 18 48

Auberge Les Grandes Roches

r. Grandes Roches, 0.6 km northeast by secondary road – ✆ 02 98 97 62 97 – www.hotel-lesgrandesroches.com – hrlesgrandesroches@club-internet.fr – Fax 02 98 50 29 19 – Closed 1st December-1st February

17 rm – †€ 85/135 ††€ 85/135, ☕ € 14 – 1 suite – ½ P € 80/110

Rest – *(closed Tuesday and Wednesday)* Menu € 45 – Carte € 50/60

◆ This superb hamlet of farms, turned into a hotel and located in a park of dolmens and standing stones, has a pleasant rustic character. Cosy rooms in the best imaginable taste. Delightful inviting restaurant in which stone and wood prevail. Up-to-date cooking.

TREIGNAC – 19 Corrèze – 329 – pop. 1 389 – alt. 500 m – ✉ 19260 25 C2

Paris 490 – Limoges 102 – Tulle 40 – Brive-la-Gaillarde 74 – Ussel 62

Office de tourisme, 1, place de la République ✆ 05 55 98 15 04, Fax 05 55 98 17 02

Maison Grandchamp

9 pl. des Pénitents – ✆ 05 55 98 10 69 – www.hotesgrandchamp.com – teyssier.marielle@wanadoo.fr – Open April-December

3 rm ☕ – †€ 68/73 ††€ 68/73 **Table d'hôte** – Menu € 25 bi/29 bi

◆ This 16C family residence is decorated with antique furniture and portraits of ancestors. It offers charming, fresh rooms. Table d'hôte in the large dining room or in the garden when the weather permits.

TRÉLAZÉ – 49 Maine-et-Loire – 317 G4 – see Angers

TRÉLON – 59 Nord – 302 M7 – pop. 2 828 – alt. 188 m – ✉ 59132 31 D3

Northern France and the Paris Region

Paris 218 – Avesnes-sur-Helpe 15 – Charleroi 53 – Lille 115 – St-Quentin 68 – Vervins 35

Office de tourisme, 3, rue Clavon Collignon ✆ 03 27 57 08 18, Fax 03 27 57 06 80

Le Framboisier

rte Val Joly – ✆ 03 27 59 73 34 – www.framboisier.terascia.com – dumotier-arnaud@orange.fr – Fax 03 27 57 07 47 – Closed 16 February-3 March, 17 August-2 September, Sunday dinner, Tuesday dinner and Monday except bank holidays

Rest – Menu (€ 14), € 32 bi/49 – Carte € 37/55

◆ Old farmhouse along a busy road. Welcoming façade, and intimate dining rooms in the rustic style. Cuisine changes with the seasons.

TREMBLAY-EN-FRANCE – 93 Seine-Saint-Denis – 305 G7 – 101 18 – see Paris, Area

LE TREMBLAY-SUR-MAULDRE – 78 Yvelines – 311 H3 – pop. 956 – alt. 132 m – ✉ 78490 18 A2

Paris 42 – Houdan 24 – Mantes-la-Jolie 32 – Rambouillet 18 – Versailles 24

du Domaine du Tremblay Place de l'Eglise, S : on D 34, ✆ 01 34 94 25 70

Laurent Trochain

3 r. Gén. de Gaulle – ✆ 01 34 87 80 96 – www.restaurant-trochain.fr – trochain.laurent@wanadoo.fr – Fax 0134 87 91 52 – Closed 13-21 April, 2 August-1st September, 2-9 January, Monday and Tuesday

Rest – Menu (€ 35 bi), € 42 bi (weekday lunch), € 49/78 bi – Carte € 49/62

Spec. Filet de bœuf, façon "ch'ti", maroilles, salade et frites. L'esprit d'un lièvre à la royale (season). Fromages marinés dans différentes huiles.

◆ Beams and a fireplace create a warm ambiance in this smart house with half-rustic, half-elegant decor. Fine, modern cuisine with the chef's personal touch.

TRÉMEUR – 22 Côtes-d'Armor – 309 I4 – pop. 682 – alt. 62 m – ✉ 22250 10 C2

Paris 407 – Dinan 26 – Loudéac 54 – Rennes 57 – St-Brieuc 46 – St-Malo 56

Les Dineux rest, VISA
expressway N 12, Z.A. Les Dineux – ☎ 02 96 84 65 80 – http://pagesperso-orange.fr/lesdineux/ – les-dineux.hotel-village@wanadoo.fr – Fax 02 96 84 76 35 – Closed 20 December-4 January and 7-23 February
12 rm – †€ 55/60 ††€ 67/74 – ½ P € 56/59
Rest – *(closed Saturday and Sunday except dinner in July-August)* Menu (€ 14), € 19 – Carte € 20/30
◆ All the rooms in this motel-style establishment, most of them duplexes, have a small terrace with a view of the countryside. Traditional fare in the restaurant.

TRÉMOLAT – 24 Dordogne – 329 F6 – pop. 656 – alt. 53 m – ✉ 24510 4 C3
Dordogne-Berry-Limousin

Paris 532 – Bergerac 34 – Brive-la-Gaillarde 87 – Périgueux 46 – Sarlat-la-Canéda 50

Syndicat d'initiative, ilot Saint-Nicolas ☎ 05 53 22 89 33, Fax 05 53 22 69 20

Belvédère de Racamadou (viewpoint) ★★ North: 2 km.

Le Vieux Logis rm, VISA
in the village – ☎ 05 53 22 80 06 – www.vieux-logis.com – vieuxlogis@relaischateaux.com – Fax 05 53 22 84 89
26 rm – †€ 185/390 ††€ 185/390, € 22 – ½ P € 182/284
Rest – Menu € 38 (weekday lunch), € 42/95 – Carte € 71/114
Spec. Foie gras au naturel, aiguilettes de canard marinées aux aromates (June-Sep.). Saumon confit à l'huile de noix (spring-autumn). Framboises et betterave en association, spéculos croustillant (June-Sep.). **Wines** Bergerac blanc, Pécharmant.
◆ A former 16-17C priory, this house tells the story of the 450 year-old family of the present owners. Cosy rooms, comfortable sitting rooms and a superb garden. Unusual dining room located in a former tobacco drying building. Terrace, and tempting, classic menu.

Bistrot d'en Face VISA
in the village – ☎ 05 53 22 80 69 – vieuxlogis@relaischateaux.com – Fax 05 53 22 84 89
Rest – Menu (€ 16), € 27/29 – Carte € 27/43
◆ In the heart of the village where Chabrol filmed Le Boucher (1970). Old stonework, beams and tasty country cuisine including andouillette and confit de canard.

TRÉMONT-SUR-SAULX – 55 Meuse – 307 B6 – see Bar-le-Duc

LE TRÉPORT – 76 Seine-Maritime – 304 I1 – pop. 5 719 – alt. 12 m – Casino – ✉ 76470 33 D1
Normandy

Paris 180 – Abbeville 37 – Amiens 92 – Blangy-sur-Bresle 26 – Dieppe 30 – Rouen 95

Office de tourisme, quai Sadi Carnot ☎ 02 35 86 05 69, Fax 02 35 86 73 96

Calvaire des Terrasses (calvary) ★.

Golf Hôtel without rest VISA
102 rte de Dieppe, (D 940) – ☎ 02 27 28 01 52 – www.treport-hotels.com – evergreen2@wanadoo.fr – Fax 02 27 28 01 51 – Closed 21-27 December
10 rm – †€ 46/49 ††€ 66/90, € 8
◆ Norman style residence offering small rooms, furnished in an English style. Charming rustic breakfast room with fireplace.

Le St-Louis VISA
43 quai François 1er – ☎ 02 35 86 20 70 – Fax 02 35 50 67 10 – Closed 20 November-19 December
Rest – Menu € 19 (weekdays)/60 – Carte € 40/65
◆ A large bay window overlooks the docks at this friendly brasserie style restaurant. The à la carte and set menus change with the catch and the season.

TRÉVOU-TRÉGUIGNEC – 22 Côtes-d'Armor – **309** B2 – **pop. 1 371** – alt. 56 m – ✉ 22660 9 **B1**

Paris 524 – Guingamp 36 – Lannion 14 – Paimpol 27 – Perros-Guirec 11 – St-Brieuc 72

Syndicat d'initiative, 28, rue de Trestel ✆ 02 96 23 74 05, Fax 02 96 91 73 82

Kerbugalic

1 Vieille Côte de Trestel – ✆ 02 96 23 72 15 – www.kerbugalic.fr – kerbugalic@voila.fr – Fax 02 96 23 74 71 – Closed 5 January-5 February

18 rm – €55/90 €55/90, €8

Rest – *(Closed lunch except Friday, Saturday and Sunday and Tuesday and Wednesday) (dinner only)* Menu €29/39 – Carte €43/50

◆ The location of this house dominating the Bay of Trestel is more than idyllic. All the guestrooms enjoy a sea view, except some in the wing (with a terrace on the garden side). Panoramic dining room facing the sea. Traditional menu focused on seafood.

TRIEL-SUR-SEINE – 78 Yvelines – **311** I2 – **101** 10 – see Paris, Area

TRIGANCE – 83 Var – **340** N3 – **pop. 150** – **alt. 800 m** – ✉ **83840** 41 **C2**

Paris 817 – Castellane 20 – Digne-les-Bains 74 – Draguignan 43 – Grasse 70

Office de tourisme, RD 955 - ferme de la Sagne ✆ 04 94 85 68 40, Fax 04 94 85 68 40

Château de Trigance

rte du château, access via private road – ✆ 04 94 76 91 18 – www.chateau-de-trigance.fr – chateautrigance@wanadoo.fr – Fax 04 94 85 68 99 – Open 3 April-31 October

10 rm – €115/125 €125/175, €15 – ½ P €115/145

Rest – *(closed Wed. lunch out of season)* Menu €30/48 – Carte €50/66

◆ Perched on a rocky outcrop, a hotel with plenty of character housed inside a château. Individually furnished rooms with four-poster beds. The restaurant is located in what was once the armoury and is hewn from the rock – a medieval setting but modern cuisine.

Le Vieil Amandier

Montée de St-Roch – ✆ 04 94 76 92 92 – www.levieilamandier.free.fr – levieilamandier@free.fr – Fax 04 94 85 68 65 – Open 10 April-11 November

12 rm – €55/68 €61/99, €10 – ½ P €63/83

Rest – *(dinner only) (residents only)*

◆ At the foot of the village, a modern building surrounded by a Mediterranean garden. All the rooms have been renovated. A handsome raftered ceiling adorns this dining room; traditional cuisine with a taste of the south of France.

TRILBARDOU – 77 Seine-et-Marne – **312** F2 – see Meaux

LA TRINITÉ-SUR-MER – 56 Morbihan – **308** M9 – **pop. 1 531** – alt. 20 m – Casino – ✉ 56470 **Brittany** 9 **B3**

Paris 488 – Auray 13 – Carnac 4 – Lorient 52 – Quiberon 23 – Quimperlé 66 – Vannes 31

Office de tourisme, 30, cours des Quais ✆ 02 97 55 72 21, Fax 02 97 55 78 07

Kerisper bridge ≤★.

Le Lodge Kerisper without rest

4 r. Latz – ✆ 02 97 52 88 56 – www.lodge-kerisper.com – contact@lodgekerisper.com – Fax 02 97 52 76 39

17 rm – €80/180 €80/180, €15 – 3 suites

◆ This hotel arranged in two low-lying 19C cottages, has a warm, refined interior, harmoniously combining antique furniture and carefully selected fabrics. Several rooms have a terrace.

Petit Hôtel des Hortensias — rest, VISA MC
4 pl. de la Mairie – 02 97 30 10 30 – www.leshortensias.info – leshortensias@aol.com – Fax 02 97 30 14 54 – Closed January
6 rm – †€ 99/160 ††€ 99/160, ☐ € 12
Rest ***L'Arrosoir*** – *02 97 30 13 58 (Open end February to mid-November and Closed Tuesday lunch, Wednesday lunch and Monday)* Carte € 35/50
◆ The Scandinavian outline of this charming villa (1880) overlooks the harbour. Elegant nautical interior, antique furniture and ornaments, guesthouse ambiance. A rare jewel! Ravishing naval bistro decor, splendid panoramic terrace and tasty seafood.

L'Azimut — VISA MC AE
1 r. Men-Dû – 02 97 55 71 88 – azimut56@orange.fr – Fax 02 97 55 80 15 – Closed 24 November-5 December, 5-9 January, 16-27 February, Tuesday and Wednesday except July-August
Rest – Menu (€ 20), € 35/60 – Carte € 55/95
◆ The dining room is distinctly nautical and the terrace overlooks the port. Updated menu of seafood inspiration.

TRIZAY – 17 Charente-Maritime – **324** E4 – **pop. 1 122 – alt. 20 m** – ✉ 17250 — 38 **B2**

Paris 475 – Rochefort 13 – La Rochelle 52 – Royan 36 – Saintes 27
Syndicat d'initiative, 48, rue de la République 05 46 82 34 25, Fax 05 46 82 19 64

at Bois Fleuri Lake 2.5 km west by D 238, D 123 and secondary road – ✉ 17250 Trizay

Les Jardins du Lac with rm — rm, rest, P VISA MC AE
3 chemin fontchaude – 05 46 82 03 56 – jardins-du-lac.com – hotel@jardins-du-lac.com – Fax 05 46 82 03 55 – Closed February school holidays, Sunday dinner, Monday and Tuesday from November to March
8 rm – †€ 101/107 ††€ 101/107, ☐ € 13
Rest – Menu € 37/55 – Carte € 70/85
◆ These two recent pavilions in a park above a lake are connected by a glass roofed footbridge straddling a stream. Lake view from the restaurant and rooms (with terrace or balcony).

LES TROIS-ÉPIS – 68 Haut-Rhin – **315** H8 – **alt. 658 m** – ✉ **68410** — 2 **C2**
Alsace-Lorraine

Paris 445 – Colmar 11 – Gérardmer 51 – Munster 18 – Orbey 12
Office de tourisme, 2, Impasse Poincaré 03 89 49 80 56, Fax 03 89 49 80 68

Villa Rosa — rest, P VISA MC
4 r. Thierry Schoeré – 03 89 49 81 19 – www.villarosa.fr – contact@villarosa.fr – Fax 03 89 78 90 45 – Closed January, February, 15-29 November and Thursday dinner
8 rm – †€ 60/62 ††€ 60/64, ☐ € 10 – ½ P € 62/65
Rest – table d'hôte – *(dinner only) (resident only)* Menu € 25
◆ Charming rooms named after roses. Themed stays. A guesthouse feel to this 1900s construction, surrounded by a flower garden. In the restaurant, Anne-Rose prepares regional dishes using organic and home-grown produce.

LE TRONCHET – 35 Ille-et-Vilaine – **309** K4 – **pop. 845 – alt. 65 m** – ✉ 35540 Brittany — 10 **D2**

Paris 391 – Saint-Malo 27 – Dinan 19 – Fougères 56 – Rennes 57 – Saint-Brieuc 82

Golf & Country Club — rm, rest, P VISA MC AE
Domaine Saint Yvieux – 02 99 58 98 99 – www.saintmalogolf.com – saintmalogolf@st-malo.com – Fax 02 99 58 10 39 – Closed 20 November-1st March
29 rm – †€ 88/145 ††€ 88/145, ☐ € 11
Rest – Menu (€ 22), € 28 (dinner)/34 – Carte € 29/42
◆ This 19C former priory is set on a golf course. It houses good-sized rooms decorated in light colours and pretty fabrics with either a patio or a small terrace. The restaurant commands a view of the pond and greens. Traditional cuisine.

Le Mesnil des Bois without rest

2 km south-west on D9 and D3 – 02 99 58 97 12 – www.le-mesnil-des-bois.com – villette@le-mesnil-des-bois.com – Closed mid November-end February

5 rm – €95/120 €95/120

◆ This handsome 16C manor farm in an isolated rural location on the edge of a forest once belonged to the family of the pirate Surcouf. Pretty bedrooms adorned with antiques.

TRONGET – **03 Allier** – **326** F4 – **pop. 955** – **alt. 460 m** – ✉ **03240** 5 **B1**

Paris 317 – Bourbon-l'Archambault 24 – Montluçon 53 – Moulins 30

Du Commerce rm, VISA

16 rte départementale 945 – 04 70 47 12 95 – Fax 04 70 47 32 53

11 rm – €43 €50, €8 – ½ P €49

Rest – Menu € 16 (weekdays)/40 – Carte € 32/52

◆ This establishment in the heart of the little town comprises two buildings. The main building is home to the café-restaurant, while the recently built annexe houses functional and well-kept rooms. Classic rustic-styled restaurant offering a traditional repertoire of dishes.

TRONÇAIS – **03 Allier** – **326** D3 – **see St-Bonnet-Tronçais**

TROUVILLE-SUR-MER – **14 Calvados** – **303** M3 – **pop. 5 411** – **alt. 2 m** – **Casino** AY – ✉ **14360** **Normandy** 32 **A3**

Paris 201 – Caen 51 – Le Havre 43 – Lisieux 30 – Pont-l'Évêque 13

Deauville-St-Gatien: 02 31 65 65 65, by ②: 7 km BZ.

Office de tourisme, 32, boulevard Fernand-Moureaux 02 31 14 60 70, Fax 02 31 14 60 71

de l'Amirauté Tourgéville, 5 km on the Pont-L'Évêque road and D 278, 02 31 14 42 00

Cliff road ←★.

Plan on following page

Hostellerie du Vallon without rest VISA AE

12 r. Sylvestre Lasserre – 02 31 98 35 00 – www.hostellerieduvallon.com – resahduvallon@wanadoo.fr – Fax 02 31 98 35 10 BZ **v**

62 rm – €110/200 €120/220, €15

◆ Normandy inn with a panoramic view of the town's rooftops. Gradually refurbished spacious rooms. Snug sitting room with billiards, pool and fitness facilities.

Le Flaubert without rest ← VISA

2 r. Gustave Flaubert – 02 31 88 37 23 – www.flaubert.fr – hotel@flaubert.fr – Fax 02 31 88 21 56 – Open mid February-mid November AY **t**

33 rm – €64/80 €104/130, €10

◆ Two minutes from Trouville's boardwalks, this romantic 1936 half-timbered villa is decorated with antiques, old posters and pastel colours. Regularly refurbished guestrooms, half of which overlook the sea.

Le Fer à Cheval without rest VISA

11 r. Victor Hugo – 02 31 98 30 20 – www.hotel-trouville.com – info@hotel-trouville.com – Fax 02 31 98 04 00 AY **u**

34 rm – €51/82 €75/87, €10

◆ In the centre of the resort, two adjoining houses with functional rooms and cosy family suites. Home-baked pastries for breakfast and tearoom in the afternoon.

Le Central VISA AE

5 et 7 r. des Bains – 02 31 88 80 84 – www.le-central-trouville.com – central-hotel@wanadoo.fr – Fax 02 31 88 42 22 AY **n**

21 rm – €86/128 €86/128, €8,50 – ½ P €72/82

Rest – brasserie – 02 31 88 13 68 – Carte € 28/40

◆ In the heart of Trouville, tastefully understated guestrooms in stylish colours and white wooden furniture. Views of the harbour, the town or the pedestrian street. A lively tourist brasserie with a 1930s-style decor and vast terrace (heated in winter).

TROUVILLE-SUR-MER

Les Sablettes without rest

15 r. P.-Besson – ✆ 02 31 88 10 66 – www.trouville-hotel.com – info@trouville-hotel.com – Fax 02 31 88 59 06 – Closed 15 November-7 December

18 rm – †€ 40/45 ††€ 47/66, ☕ € 7 — AY **r**

◆ A family-run establishment near the Casino and the beach. Simple, relatively quiet rooms overlooking the street or the courtyard; two in a separate wing. Friendly welcome.

La Petite Auberge
7 r. Carnot – 02 31 88 11 07 – www.lapetiteaubergesurmer.fr – lapetiteauberge.trouville@wanadoo.fr – Closed 1st-15 December, Tuesday and Wednesday AY **f**
Rest – *(pre-book)* Menu (€ 23), € 32 bi/49 – Carte € 47/70
◆ This friendly inn, set in side street in the town centre, sports a rustic-nautical decor that enhances its menu of regional produce and recipes.

Les Mouettes
11 r. Bains – 02 31 98 06 97 – www.brasserie-les-mouettes.com – central-hotel@wanadoo.fr – Fax 02 31 88 42 22 AY **d**
Rest – Menu € 14/28 – Carte € 23/36
◆ This establishment, favoured by Marguerite Duras, has a friendly bistro atmosphere and decor, a characteristic menu, a pretty painted ceiling and a pavement terrace.

TROYES – 10 Aube – 313 E4 – pop. 60 400 – Built-up area 128 945 – alt. 113 m – 10000 **Northern France and the Paris Region** 13 **B3**

Paris 170 – Dijon 185 – Nancy 186
Troyes-Barberey 03 25 71 79 00, Northwest: 5 km AV
Office de tourisme, 16, boulevard Carnot 03 25 82 62 70, Fax 03 25 73 06 81
de la Forêt d'Orient Rouilly-Sacey Route de Geraudot, 11 km on the Nancy road, 03 25 43 80 80
de Troyes Chaource Château de la Cordelière, 31 km on the Tonnerre road (D 444), 03 25 40 18 76
Old Troyes★★ BZ: Ruelle des Chats★ - St-Pierre and St-Paul cathedral ★★ - Rood-screen ★★ of Ste-Madeleine church ★ - St-Urbain basilica ★ BCY **B** - St-Pantaléon church ★ - Apothicary's★ of the Hôtel-Dieu CY **M**4 - Musée d'Art Moderne★★ CY **M**3 - Maison de l'Outil et de la Pensée ouvrière (House of Workers' tools and thinking) ★★ in the Hôtel de Mauroy★★ BZ **M**2 - Musée historique de Troyes et de Champagne★ and musée de la Bonneterie in the Hôtel de Vauluisant★ BZ **M**1 - Musée des Beaux-Arts et d'Archéologie★ in St-Loup abbey.

Plans on following pages

La Maison de Rhodes rm, VISA
18 r. Linard Gonthier – 03 25 43 11 11 – www.maisonderhodes.com – message@maisonderhodes.com – Fax 03 25 43 10 43 CY **e**
8 rm – € 160/255 € 160/255, € 19 – 3 suites
Rest – *(Closed Sunday) (dinner only)* Carte approx. € 63
◆ Beautiful 17C residence nestling in a small paved backstreet. Beams, stonework, daub, floor tiles, old and modern furniture combine with elegance at this lovely hotel. Charming rustic dining room overlooking a tiny garden. Traditional menu.

Le Champ des Oiseaux without rest VISA
20 r. Linard Gonthier – 03 25 80 58 50 – www.champdesoiseaux.com – message@champdesoiseaux.com – Fax 03 25 80 98 34 CY **e**
12 rm – € 140/240 € 140/240, € 17 – 1 suite
◆ Named after the region's emblematic stork, these three venerable 15C and 16C houses are laid out around a verdant paved courtyard. Comfortable, cosy guestrooms (beams and wood panelling).

Mercure without rest VISA
11 r. Bas-Trévois – 03 25 46 28 28 – www.mercure-troyes.com – h3168@accor.com – Fax 03 25 46 28 27 CZ **h**
70 rm – € 82/159 € 92/189, € 14
◆ The decoration of the spacious and restful rooms and the 19C loom standing in pride of place in the hall bring to mind the origin of this hotel, once a hosiery factory.

Le Relais St-Jean without rest VISA
51 r. Paillot de Montabert – 03 25 73 89 90 – www.relais-st-jean.com – infos@relais-st-jean.com – Fax 03 25 73 88 60 BZ **s**
25 rm – € 86/136 € 97/142, € 15
◆ Charming half-timbered house on a pedestrian street. Contemporary rooms, those on the 4th floor have attractive original beams. Lounge bar with a billiard table.

TROYES

Royal Hôtel — rm, VISA

22 bd Carnot – ☎ 03 25 73 19 99 – www.royal-hotel-troyes.com
– reservation@royal-hotel-troyes.com
– Fax 03 25 73 47 85
– Closed 18 December-11 January

BZ **n**

40 rm – †€ 68/92 ††€ 80/120, ☕ € 11 – ½ P € 80

Rest – *(closed Saturday lunch, Monday lunch and Sunday)* Menu (€ 20), € 25 (weekdays)/30 – Carte € 46/58

◆ A building on a busy boulevard with simple, functional and well-kept rooms. Pleasant, refined lounge-bar and elegant modern dining room furnished with a Flemish Renaissance-style mirror and dresser.

TROYES

Boucherat (R.) . . . . **CY** 4
Champeaux (R.) . . . . **BZ** 12
Charbonnet (R.) . . . . **BZ** 13
Clemenceau (R. G.) . . . . . . **BCY** 15
Comtes-de-Champagne
(Q. des) . . . . **CY** 16
Dampierre (Quai) . . . . **BCY** 17
Delestraint (Bd Gén.-Ch.) . . . **BZ** 18
Driant (R. COl.) . . . . **BZ** 20
Girardon (R.) . . . . **CY** 22
Hennequin (R.) . . . . **CY** 23
Huez (R. Claude) . . . . **BYZ** 27
Israël (Pl. Alexandre) . . . . **BZ** 28
Jaillant-Deschaînets (R.) . . . . **BZ** 29
Jean-Jaurès (Pl.) . . . . **BZ** 31
Joffre (Av. Mar.) . . . . **BZ** 33
Langevin (Pl. du Prof.) . . . . . **BZ** 35
Libération (Pl. de la) . . . . **CZ** 49
Marché aux Noix (R. du) . . . . **BZ** 36
Michelet (R.) . . . . **CY** 39
Molé (R.) . . . . **BZ** 44
Monnaie (R. de la) . . . . **BZ** 45
Paillot-de-Montabert (R.) . . . **BZ** 47
Palais-de-Justice
(R.) . . . . **BZ** 48
République (R. de la) . . . . . . **BZ** 51
St-Pierre (Pl.) . . . . **CY** 52
St-Rémy (Pl.) . . . . **BY** 53
Siret (R. Nicolas) . . . . **CZ** 79
Synagogue (R. de la) . . . . **BZ** 54
Tour-Boileau (R. de la) . . . . . **BZ** 59
Trinité (R. de la) . . . . **BZ** 60
Turenne (R. de) . . . . **BZ** 61
Voltaire (R.) . . . . **BZ** 64
Zola (R. Émile) . . . . **BCZ**
1er-R.A.M. (Bd du) . . . . **BZ** 69

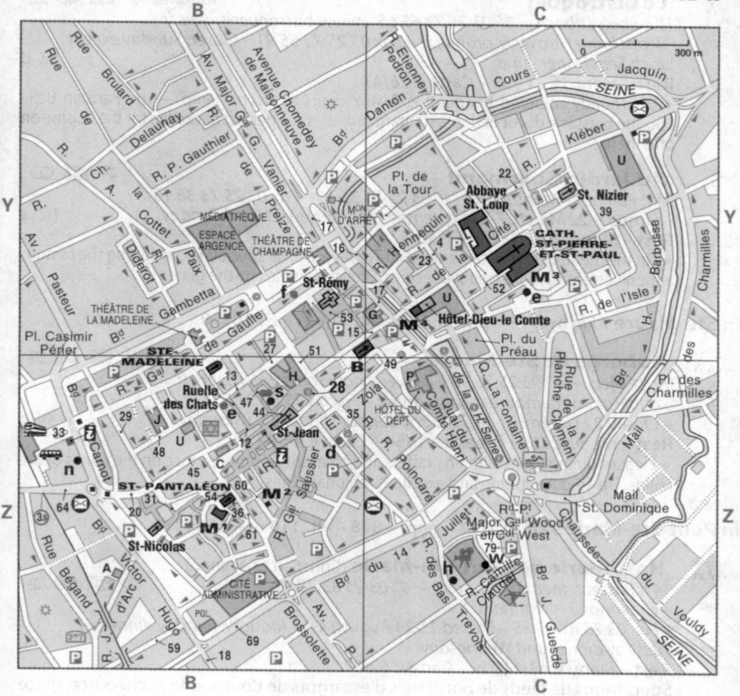

Ibis without rest
r. Camille Claudel – ✆ 03 25 75 99 99
– www.ibishotel.com – H5546@accor.com
– Fax 03 25 75 90 69
77 rm – €61/75 €61/75, €8,50
CZ **w**

◆ A new hotel with all the latest Ibis comfort: air-conditioned rooms, new-look bathrooms, pleasant breakfast room, etc.

La Mignardise
1 ruelle des Chats – ✆ 03 25 73 15 30
– www.lamignardise.net – lamignardise@orange.fr
– Fax 03 25 73 15 30
– Closed Sunday dinner and Monday
Rest – Menu (€ 25), € 27/56 – Carte € 50/90
BZ **e**

◆ Elegant interior (stone, brick, wood and modern touches), updated menu and attentive service await you in this delightful 16C half-timbered house.

Valentino
35 r. Paillot de Montabert – 03 25 73 14 14 – le.valentino@orange.fr – Fax 03 25 41 36 75 – Closed 16 August-2 September, 1st-11 January, Sunday and Monday BZ **s**
Rest – Menu (€ 25), € 33/52 – Carte € 48/66
◆ Intimate dining room tastefully combining old and new (stone walls, beams, modern furnishings and art). Terrace-courtyard and delicious flavours on the plate.

Le Bistroquet
10 r. Louis Ulbach – 03 25 73 65 65 – www.bistroquet-troyes.fr – lebistroquet-troyes@orange.fr – Fax 03 25 73 55 91 – Closed Sunday except lunch September-June BZ **d**
Rest – Menu (€ 21), 33 – Carte € 26/47
◆ 2Burgundy-coloured banquettes, bistro chairs and retro lamps – the Parisian Belle Époque brasserie decor of this restaurant provides the perfect backdrop for the cuisine on offer here.

Au Jardin Gourmand
31 r. Paillot de Montabert – 03 25 73 36 13 – Fax 03 25 73 36 13 – Closed 9-22 March, 7-27 September, Monday lunch and Sunday BZ **s**
Rest – Menu (€ 17) – Carte € 30/67
◆ On the menu of this restaurant in Old Troyes are local specialities, including the famous andouillette, and more creative recipes. Choice of wines by the glass.

in Ste-Maure 7 km by D 78 – pop. 1 457 – alt. 111 m – ✉ 10150

Auberge de Ste-Maure
99 rte Mery – 03 25 76 90 41 – www.auberge-saintemaure.fr – auberge.saintemaure@wanadoo.fr – Fax 03 25 80 01 55 – Closed 22 December-11 January, Sunday dinner and Monday AV **g**
Rest – Menu € 26 bi (weekdays)/54 – Carte € 44/72
◆ Elegant dining room with fine rafters and pleasant summer terrace on the banks of the Melda. Up-to-date cuisine and excellent regional wines.

in Pont-Ste-Marie 3 km by D 77 – pop. 4 848 – alt. 110 m – ✉ 10150

Hostellerie de Pont-Ste-Marie (Christian Chavanon)
34 r. Pasteur, (near the church) – 03 25 83 28 61 – chavanon3@wanadoo.fr – Fax 03 25 81 67 85 – Closed 1st-24 August, 4-14 January, Sunday dinner, Tuesday dinner and Wednesday AV **n**
Rest – Menu € 43/119 bi – Carte € 62/87
Spec. Nems de pieds de porc farcis d'escargots de Bourgogne et chaource, glace à l'ail. Homard rôti déglacé au ratafia de champagne. Crêpe, pain perdu et riz au lait. **Wines** Champagne, Rosé des Riceys.
◆ A restaurant located in two cottages near the fine 16C church. Inviting dining room decorated in a mixture of old and new and appetising contemporary menu.

Bistrot DuPont
5 pl. Ch. de Gaulle – 03 25 80 90 99 – Closed 27 April-4 May, 3-24 August, 21 December-4 January, Thursday dinner, Sunday dinner and Monday AV **s**
Rest – *(pre-book)* Menu € 19/30 – Carte € 31/64
◆ Near the Seine, this pleasant bistro style establishment offers generous and well-prepared cuisine. Don't miss the andouillette, a house speciality.

in Moussey 10 km by ④, D 671 and D 444 – pop. 434 – alt. 131 m – ✉ 10800

Domaine de la Creuse without rest
D 444 – 03 25 41 74 01 – www.domainedelacreuse.com – contact@domainedelacreuse.com – Closed 20 December-5 January
5 rm – †€ 100/115 ††€ 105/120
◆ This traditional (18C) Champagne-style residence is set around a central courtyard garden. Large, delightful ground-floor rooms.

in Ste-Savine 3 km – **pop. 10 500 – alt. 116 m – ✉ 10300**

Chantereigne without rest
128 av. Gén. Leclerc – ✆ 03 25 74 89 35 – contact@hotel-chantereigne.com – Fax 03 25 74 47 78 – Closed 23 December-2 January AX **t**
30 rm – €58 €70, €8
◆ A U-shaped building with slightly cramped but functional rooms facing the rear. Breakfast buffet.

Motel Savinien
87 r. Jean de la Fontaine – ✆ 03 25 79 24 90 – www.motelsavinien.com – motel.savinien@orange.fr – Fax 03 25 78 04 61 AX **d**
49 rm – €53/58 €59/72, €9 – ½ P €55/60
Rest – *(closed Sunday dinner and Monday)* Menu (€13), €17/31 – Carte approx. €37,50
◆ Large, quiet well-maintained 1970s building. Rooms are practical, regularly updated and some have been renovated. Sauna, jacuzzi and small gym. Traditional cuisine served on the terrace, weather permitting.

TRUN – **61 Orne** – **310** J1 – **pop. 1 325 – alt. 90 m – ✉ 61160** 33 **C2**
Paris 198 – Caen 63 – Alençon 60 – Lisieux 47 – Flers 59
Syndicat d'initiative, place Charles-de-Gaulle ✆ 02 33 36 93 55

La Villageoise
66 r. de la République – ✆ 09 71 38 56 87 – www.lavillageoise.fr – lavillageoise@orange.fr – Fax 02 33 39 13 07
5 rm – €70/90 €70/90 **Table d'hôte** – Menu €20 bi/30 bi
◆ This establishment houses a delightful lounge opening onto a large courtyard/garden, around which most of the rooms are set out. Rooms are simple but filled with knick-knacks. Gracious welcome. Local cuisine is served in a rustic dining room.

For a pleasant stay in a charming hotel, look for the red … symbols.

TULETTE – **26 Drôme** – **332** C8 – **pop. 1 714 – alt. 147 m – ✉ 26790** 44 **B3**
Paris 657 – Lyon 195 – Valence 95 – Avignon 56 – Montélimar 50
Syndicat d'initiative, place des Tisserands ✆ 04 75 98 34 53, Fax 04 75 98 36 16

K-Za
rte du Moulin – ✆ 04 75 98 34 88 – www.maison-hotes-k-za.com – k-za@wanadoo.fr – Fax 04 7 97 49 70
5 rm – €130/150 €130/260 **Table d'hôte** – Menu €30/50
◆ Elizabeth, the owner of this "bella casa" is Italian. The 17C house made out of Rhône pebbles sports an attractive designer interior and is a masterpiece of contemporary sophistication. Mediterranean inspired cuisine and local wines served at the table d'hôte.

TULLE Ⓟ – **19 Corrèze** – **329** L4 – **pop. 15 700 – alt. 210 m – ✉ 19000** 25 **C3**
Dordogne-Berry-Limousin
Paris 475 – Aurillac 83 – Brive-la-Gaillarde 27 – Clermont-Ferrand 141
Office de tourisme, 2, place Emile Zola ✆ 05 55 26 59 61, Fax 05 55 20 72 93
Maison de Loyac★ Z **B** - Steeple★ of Notre-Dame cathedral.

Plan on following page

Mercure without rest
16 quai de la République – ✆ 05 55 26 42 00 – www.mercure.com – H5065@accor.com – Fax 05 55 20 31 17 Z **b**
48 rm – €68 €77/82, €10 – 1 suite
◆ This impeccable town-centre hotel has a spacious hall, a comfortable bar and new rooms, which are welcoming and soundproofed, they are more spacious on the quay side.

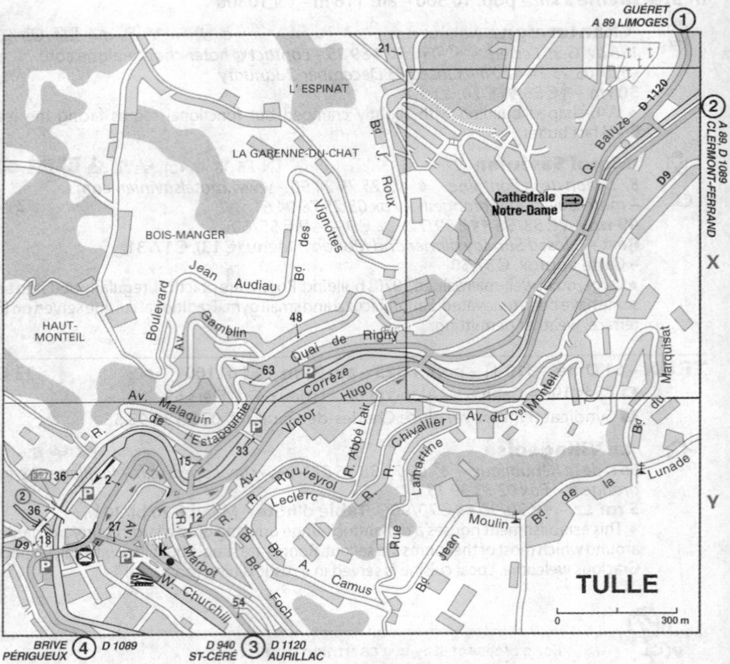

GUÉRET
A 89 LIMOGES
1
2
A 89, D 1089
CLERMONT-FERRAND
L' ESPINAT
LA GARENNE-DU-CHAT
BOIS-MANGER
HAUT-MONTEIL
Bd J. Roux
Bd des Vignottes
Jean Audiau
Boulevard
Av. Gamblin
Quai de Rigny
Corrèze
Q. Baluze
D 1120
D9
Cathédrale Notre-Dame
Marquisat
Av. Malaquin
R. de l'Estabournie
Victor Hugo
R. Abbé Lair
R. Chivallier
Av. du Cel Monteil
Bd du
Lunade
Bd. de la
Moulin
Rue Lamartine
Bd. Jean
Av. Rouveyrol
R. Leclerc
Bd A. Camus
Bd Foch
R. Marbot
W. Churchill
Av.
D9
A 20
TULLE
0
300 m
X
Y
BRIVE
PÉRIGUEUX
4
D 1089
D 940
ST-CÉRÉ
3
D 1120
AURILLAC

D 1120
D 23
ST-PIERRE
Av. Ch. de Gaulle
Av. H. de Bournazel
L'ENCLOS
Q. Baluze
D 9
Mie
Cathédrale Notre-Dame
Cloître
Louis
Z
Clemenceau
la Barrière
HÔTEL DU DÉPARTEMENT
R.
ST-JEAN
Rue de
R. J. Jaurès
Bd G.
CITÉ ADMIVE
POL
Q. G. Péri
Bd. du Marquisat
0
200 m

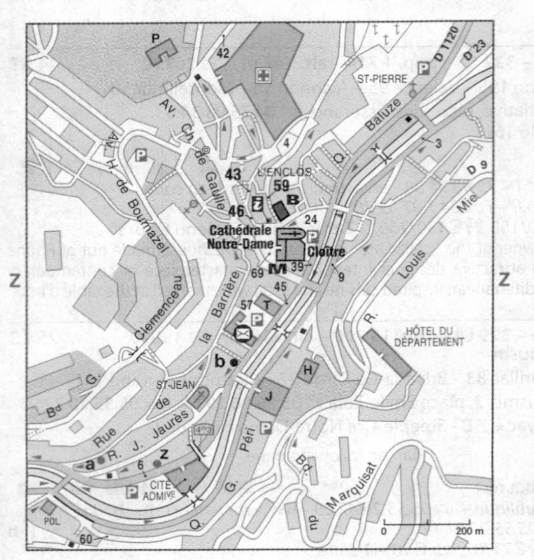

Alsace-Lorraine (Av.)	Y	2
Baluze (Quai)	Z	
Briand (Quai A.)	Z	3
Bride (Pl. de la)	Z	4
Brigouleix (Pl. Martial)	Z	6
Chammard (Quai A.-de)	Z	9
Condamines (R. des)	Y	12
Dunant (R. Henri)	Y	15
Faucher (Pl. Albert)	Y	18
Faugeras (Bd J.-F.)	X	21
Gambetta (Pl.)	Z	24
Gaulle (Av. Ch.-de)	Z	
Jean-Jaurès (R.)	Z	
Lovy (R. Sergent)	Y	27
Mermoz (R.)	Y	33
Pauphile (R.)	Y	36
Perrier (Quai Edmond)	Z	39
Poincaré (Av.)	Z	42
Portes-Chanac (R. des)	Z	43
République (Quai de la)	Z	45
Riche (R.)	Z	46
Roche-Bailly (Bd de la)	X	48
Sampeix (R. Lucien)	Y	54
Tavé (Pl. Jean)	Z	57
Tour-de-Maïsse (R. de la)	Z	59
Vialle (R. Anne)	Z	60
Victor-Hugo (Av.)	XY	
Vidalie (Av.)	X	63
Zola (Pl. Émile)	Z	69

De la Gare
25 av. W. Churchill – ✆ 05 55 20 04 04 – www.hotel-restaurant-delagare-farjounel.com – hotel.de.la.gare.tulle@wanadoo.fr – Fax 05 55 20 15 87 – Closed 18-30 August and 15-21 February Y **k**
11 rm – †€ 52 ††€ 52, ☕ € 7 – ½ P € 55
Rest – *(Closed Sunday dinner except July-August)* Menu € 15/25 – Carte € 27/37
◆ Attractive little hotel opposite the train station. The well-proportioned practical rooms are arranged around a patio (overlooked by the 1st floor rooms). This restaurant is rustic in style, the menu traditional and the bill delightfully reasonable.

Le Central
12 r. Barrière – ✆ 05 55 26 24 46 – r-poumier@internet19.fr – Fax 05 55 26 53 16 – Closed 26 July-9 August, Sunday dinner and Saturday Z **a**
Rest – Menu € 27/60 – Carte € 62/74
◆ Stonework, beams and period dressers make up the cosy decor of this restaurant with a half-timbered façade (18C). Charming welcome, traditional dishes. Ground floor brasserie.

La Toque Blanche
pl. M. Brigouleix – ✆ 05 55 26 75 41 – www.hotel-latoqueblanche.com – toque.blanche@orange.fr – Fax 05 55 20 93 95 – Closed one week in July, 15-26 February, Sunday dinner and Monday Z **z**
Rest – Menu € 27/40 – Carte € 43/55
◆ The chef offers you regionally inspired traditional cuisine, served in the prettily rustic main dining room or in the other that is thoroughly modern.

TUNNEL DU MONT-BLANC H.-Savoie – 74 H.-Savoie – **328** O5 – see Chamonix-Mont-Blanc

---

TUNNEL SOUS LA MANCHE voir à Calais.

LA TURBALLE – 44 Loire-Atlantique – 316 A3 – pop. 4 350 – alt. 6 m – ✉ 44420 Brittany

34 **A2**

Paris 457 – La Baule 13 – Guérande 7 – Nantes 84 – La Roche-Bernard 31 – St-Nazaire 27

Office de tourisme, place du Général-de-Gaulle ✆ 02 40 23 39 87, Fax 02 40 23 32 01

Les Chants d'Ailes without rest
11 bd Bellanger – ✆ 02 40 23 47 28 – http://laturballe.free.fr/hotel-chantsdailes/ – hotel.chantsdailes@wanadoo.fr – Fax 02 40 62 86 43 – Closed 17 November-17 December and 19 January-6 February
19 rm – †€ 40/53 ††€ 55/69, ☕ € 7,50
◆ Set on the extended beachfront, functional rooms being gradually renovated. Those located at the front have ocean views. A bright breakfast room.

Le Manoir des Quatre Saisons without rest
744 bd de Lauvergnac – ✆ 02 40 11 76 16 – www.manoir-des-quatre-saisons.com – jean-philippe.meyran@club-internet.fr – Fax 02 40 11 76 16
5 rm ☕ – †€ 60/65 ††€ 70/89
◆ This is a successfully reconstructed long cottage. Its colourful rooms often have a small lounge. Gigantic breakfast served in front of the fireplace in winter.

Le Terminus
18 quai St-Paul – ✆ 02 40 23 30 29 – terminus44420@aol.com – Closed 1 week in October, February school holidays, Sunday dinner, Tuesday dinner and Wednesday except school holidays
Rest – Menu (€ 19 bi), € 23/70 – Carte € 32/80
◆ New contemporary style decor in this restaurant specialising in seafood dishes. All the tables overlook La Turballe port.

in Pen-Bron 3 km south by D 92 – ✉ **44420 La Turballe**

Pen Bron
– ✆ *02 28 56 77 99 – www.hotels-aptitudes.com – hotelpenbron@wanadoo.fr – Fax 02 28 56 77 77 – Closed 2 weeks in November and December*
45 rm – †€ 55/99 ††€ 55/185, ☕ € 10
Rest – *(closed Monday and Tuesday in Winter)* Menu € 32 – Carte € 28/48
◆ A Breton house remarkably located at the end of the peninsula opposite Croisic. Specially designed facilities for disabled guests. Traditional food served in a pleasant restaurant facing the waves.

LA TURBIE – 06 Alpes-Maritimes – 341 F5 – pop. 3 156 – alt. 495 m – ✉ 06320 42 E2

Paris 943 – Monaco 8 – Menton 13 – Nice 16

Hostellerie Jérôme (Bruno Cirino) with rm
20 r. Comte de Cessole – ✆ 04 92 41 51 51 – www.hostelleriejerome.com – hostellerie.jerome@wanadoo.fr – Fax 04 92 41 51 50 – Closed 4 November-12 February, Monday and Tuesday except July-August
5 rm – †€ 90/150 ††€ 90/150, ☕ € 16
Rest – *(dinner only)* Menu € 70/130 – Carte € 90/130
Spec. Langouste puce en croûte d'amande à la bergamote. Spaghetti pilés aux truffes, foie gras et blettes. Tarte soufflée au citron à la mentonnaise. **Wines** Bellet, Bandol.
◆ The restaurant was once the refectory of Cistercian monks who lived here in the 13C. Delicious Mediterranean-influenced cuisine and attractive, personalised guestrooms.

Café de la Fontaine
4 av. Gén. de Gaulle – ✆ 04 93 28 52 79 – hostellerie.jerome@wanadoo.fr – Closed Monday from November to March
Rest – Menu € 25
◆ This lively village café is always crowded. Hardly surprising... as it offers tasty local dishes made with fresh market produce!

TURCKHEIM – 68 Haut-Rhin – 315 H8 – pop. 3 731 – alt. 225 m – ✉ 68230 Alsace-Lorraine 2 C2

Paris 471 – Colmar 7 – Gérardmer 47 – Munster 14 – St-Dié 51 – le Thillot 66

Office de tourisme, Corps de Garde ✆ 03 89 27 38 44, Fax 03 89 80 83 22

Le Berceau du Vigneron without rest
10 pl. Turenne – ✆ 03 89 27 23 55 – www.berceau-du-vigneron.com – hotel-berceau-du-vigneron@wanadoo.fr – Fax 03 89 30 01 33 – Closed 11-25 January
16 rm – †€ 44/58 ††€ 44/73, ☕ € 9,50
◆ Half-timbered house partly built on the ramparts of the old town. Brightly-decorated rooms, quieter at the rear. In summer, breakfast is served in the courtyard.

Les Portes de la Vallée rest,
29 r. Romaine – ✆ 03 89 27 95 50 – www.hotelturckheim.com – mail@hotelturckheim.com – Fax 03 89 27 40 71 – Closed 4 - 20 Mar.
14 rm – †€ 43/60 ††€ 46/64, ☕ € 8 – ½ P € 49/66
Rest – *(closed Sunday) (dinner only) (resident only)* Menu € 18
◆ The hotel's two buildings are linked by a leafy arbour. A quiet setting, with the bright rooms in the modern wing perhaps preferable. Alsace dishes are served in the winstub-style dining room.

À l'Homme Sauvage
19 Grand'Rue – ✆ 03 89 27 56 15 – homme.sauvage.sarl@wanadoo.fr – Fax 03 89 80 82 03 – Closed Tuesday dinner from November to April, Sunday dinner and Wednesday
Rest – Menu (€ 13), € 18 (weekday lunch), € 26/38 – Carte € 38/46
◆ This inn has been welcoming satisfied diners since 1609. Modern cuisine served in a half-rustic, half-contemporary setting, with dining in the shaded paved courtyard in summer.

TURENNE – 19 Corrèze – 329 K5 – pop. 770 – alt. 350 m – ✉ 19500 24 B3

Dordogne-Berry-Limousin

Paris 496 – Brive-la-Gaillarde 15 – Cahors 91 – Figeac 76

Office de tourisme, place du Belvédère ☎ 05 55 24 08 80, Fax 05 55 24 58 24

Site★ of the château and ※★★ Caesar Tower.

Collonges-la-Rouge: village★★ East: 10 km.

Clos Marnis — AC rm,

pl. de la Halle – ☎ 05 55 22 05 28 – www.closmarnis.online.fr – keny.sourzat@wanadoo.fr – Closed 15 November-15 December

5 rm – ♦€ 57/78 ♦♦€ 57/78 – ½ P € 51/61 **Table d'hôte** – Menu € 23 bi

◆ Handsome 18C residence built by a religious fraternity. Characterful rooms, furnished with period or modern pieces and a fine view of the castle from the pleasant garden. Buffet service; regional produce takes pride of place (by reservation only).

Maison des Chanoines with rm — AC rest, rm, VISA MC

r. Joseph Rouveyrol – ☎ 05 55 85 93 43 – www.maison-des-chanoines.com – maisondeschanoines@wanadoo.fr – Fax 05 55 85 93 43 – Open 12 April-15 October

7 rm – ♦€ 56/70 ♦♦€ 65/100, € 9 – ½ P € 70/86

Rest – *(closed Wednesday dinner in June and lunch except Sunday and public holidays) (number of covers limited, pre-book)* Menu € 33/48

◆ An enchanting 16C house: carved entrance door, spiral staircase, vaulted dining room (furnished in a Majorelle style), smart guestrooms. Cuisine combining tradition and creativity.

TURQUANT – 49 Maine-et-Loire – 317 J5 – pop. 448 – alt. 68 m – ✉ 49730 35 C2

Paris 294 – Angers 76 – Châtellerault 68 – Chinon 21 – Saumur 10 – Tours 58

Demeure de la Vignole — P VISA MC AE

imp. Marguerite d'Anjou – ☎ 02 41 53 67 00 – http://demeure-vignole.com – demeure@demeure-vignole.com – Fax 02 41 53 67 09 – Open 15 March-15 Nov.

10 rm – ♦€ 85/93 ♦♦€ 85/93, € 9 – 3 suites – ½ P € 75/96

Rest – *(closed Sunday and Monday) (dinner only) (residents only)* Menu € 28

◆ Guesthouse atmosphere in this elegant tufa residence built on a hillside. Tastefully decorated rooms and troglodytic suite (and pool). Terrace overlooking the vineyards.

TUSSON – 16 Charente – 324 K4 – pop. 302 – alt. 125 m – ✉ 16140 39 C2

Paris 421 – Angoulême 41 – Cognac 49 – Poitiers 83

Office de tourisme, le bourg ☎ 05 45 21 26 70

Le Compostelle — VISA MC AE

– ☎ 05 45 31 15 90 – http://monsite.orange.fr/le-compostelle – le-compostelle@wanadoo.fr – Fax 05 45 31 15 90 – Closed 22 September-9 October, 2-26 January, Sunday dinner, Monday except dinner in August and Thursday

Rest – Menu € 16 bi (weekday lunch), € 27/40 – Carte € 42/55

◆ A pleasant rustic restaurant situated in the heart of the village on the old pilgrims' way. Varied regional menu.

TY-SANQUER – 29 Finistère – 308 G6 – see Quimper

UBERACH – 67 Bas-Rhin – 315 J3 – pop. 1 091 – alt. 175 m – ✉ 67350 1 B1

Paris 473 – Baden-Baden 59 – Offenburg 64 – Strasbourg 38

De la Forêt — AC VISA MC AE

94 Grande Rue – ☎ 03 88 07 73 17 – bernardohl@wanadoo.fr – Fax 03 88 72 50 33 – Closed 28 July-16 August, 29 December-3 January, 23 February-7 March, Monday dinner, Tuesday dinner and Wednesday

Rest – Menu (€ 10), € 16 (weekday lunch), € 26/65 bi – Carte approx. € 43

◆ A former brasserie converted into a stylish restaurant. Well-kept interior and warm atmosphere. Traditional, authentic fare prepared with vegetables from the garden.

UCHAUX – 84 Vaucluse – **332** B8 – **pop. 1 387 – alt. 80 m** – ✉ **84100** 40 **A2**

Paris 645 – Avignon 40 – Montélimar 45 – Nyons 37 – Orange 11

Château de Massillan rm, rm, P

Hauteville, 3 km north by D 11 and secondary road – ☎ 04 90 40 64 51 – www.chateau-de-massillan.com – chateau-de-massillan@wanadoo.fr – Fax 04 90 40 63 85 – Open 1st April-30 October

13 rm – €260 €260, €16 – 1 suite **Rest** – Menu (€38), €56/82

◆ A fine 16C château in the heart of a magnificent park surrounded by vineyards. Appealing modern decoration, combined with period stonework and beams. Modern cuisine served in a very pretty setting: designer furniture, white walls and chandeliers.

Côté Sud P VISA

rte d'Orange – ☎ 04 90 40 66 08 – www.restaurantcotesud.com – restaurantcotesud@wanadoo.fr – Fax 04 90 40 64 77 – Closed 19 October-4 November, 21 December-6 January, Monday dinner and Tuesday except July-August and Wednesday

Rest – *(number of covers limited, pre-book)* Menu €24/47 – Carte €43/49

◆ The names of the set menus – garrigue, colline – celebrate Provence, as does the cuisine. Cosy ambiance in a charming stone house with delightful garden.

Le Temps de Vivre P VISA AE

Les Farjons – ☎ 04 90 40 66 00 – cuisine.passion904@orange.fr – Fax 04 90 40 66 00 – Closed 22 December-21 January, Thursday lunch from September to April and Wednesday

Rest – Menu (€18), €28/39 – Carte €41/53

◆ Chirping cicadas, scrubland and vines all around...this large 18C stone house revels in a country atmosphere and boasts a shaded terrace. Generous modern cuisine.

UGINE – 73 Savoie – **333** L3 – **pop. 7 004 – alt. 484 m** – ✉ **73400** 45 **C1**

Paris 581 – Annecy 37 – Chambéry 63 – Lyon 162

Office de tourisme, 15, place du Val d'Arly ☎ 04 79 37 56 33, Fax 04 79 89 01 69

La Châtelle VISA AE

3 r. Paul Proust – ☎ 04 79 37 30 02 – www.lachatelle.com – lachatelle@yahoo.fr – Fax 04 79 37 30 02 – Closed 1st-10 May, 16-25 August, Sunday and Monday except bank holidays

Rest – Menu €19 (weekday lunch), €24/48 – Carte €40/60

◆ A 13C fortified house lengthened with a terrace-veranda with panoramic views. Modern cuisine served with a fine list of wines from the region and elsewhere.

L'UNION – 31 Haute-Garonne – **343** G3 – **see Toulouse**

UNTERMUHLTHAL – 57 Moselle – **307** Q5 – **see Baerenthal**

URÇAY – 03 Allier – **326** C3 – **pop. 287 – alt. 169 m** – ✉ **03360** 5 **B1**

Paris 297 – La Châtre 55 – Montluçon 34 – Moulins 66 – St-Amand-Montrond 15

L'Étoile d'Urçay VISA

42 rte Nationale – ☎ 04 70 06 92 66 – letoiledurcay@orange.fr – Closed 24 November-3 December, 16 February-11 March, Tuesday October-June, Sunday dinner and Monday

Rest – Menu €10 (weekdays)/30 – Carte approx. €48

◆ This pleasant rustic-style restaurant, on the road through this little market town, offers traditional cuisine. Simple and convivial eating near the Tronçais forest.

URDOS – 64 Pyrénées-Atlantiques – **342** I7 – **pop. 67 – alt. 780 m** – ✉ 64490 3 **B3**

Paris 850 – Jaca 38 – Oloron-Ste-Marie 41 – Pau 75

Col du Somport★★ Southeast: 14 km, **Atlantic Coast.**

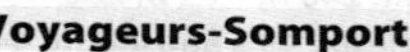

Voyageurs-Somport

– 05 59 34 88 05 – *www.hotel-voyageurs-aspe.com – hotel.voyageurs.urdos@wanadoo.fr – Fax 05 59 34 86 74 – Closed 18 October-1 December, Sunday dinner and Monday except school holidays*
28 rm – €33/36 €37/46, €6 – ½ P €37/44
Rest – Menu €14/30 – Carte €20/40
◆ A former coaching house on the Santiago de Compostela route in the valley of Aspe. As well as warm hospitality, it offers rustic rooms, which are quieter at the back. Country-style dining room where traditional, unpretentious food is served.

URIAGE-LES-BAINS – 38 Isère – 333 H7 – alt. 414 m – Spa : late Jan.-early Dec. – Casino : Palais de la Source – ✉ 38410 French Alps — 45 C2

Paris 576 – Grenoble 11 – Vizille 11
Office de tourisme, 5, avenue des Thermes 04 76 89 10 27, Fax 04 76 89 26 68
Uriage Vaulnaveys-le-Haut Les Alberges, south, 04 76 89 03 47
Prémol forest★ Southeast: 5 km by D 111.

Grand Hôtel
pl. Hygie – 04 76 89 10 80 – www.grand-hotel-uriage.com – grandhotel.fr@wanadoo.fr – Fax 04 76 89 04 62 – Closed 16-30 August and 20 December-18 January
39 rm – €105/182 €131/208, €20 – 3 suites
Rest *Les Terrasses* – *(Closed Sunday except July-August, Tuesday except dinner from September to June, Friday lunch in July-August, Wednesday lunch, Thursday lunch and Monday)* Menu €78 bi (weekday lunch), €98/185 – Carte approx. €132
Spec. Foie gras confit, pain d'épice, haricot vert et consommé de champignons (autumn). Féra rôtie au pain, citron, huile d'olive, jeunes carottes et cardamome noire fumée (spring). Pêche, granité verveine et vinaigre balsamique blanc (summer). **Wines** Chignin-Bergeron, Crozes-Hermitage.
◆ This handsome Napoleon III hostelry, once frequented by Coco Chanel and Sacha Guitry and linked to the central spa, offers a choice of elegant, spacious personalised rooms. Elegant restaurant and delightful terrace - two settings in which to enjoy an inspired cuisine.

Les Mésanges
1.5 km St-Martin-d'Uriage road and Bouloud road – 04 76 89 70 69 – www.hotel-les-mesanges.com – prince@hotel-les-mesanges.com – Fax 04 76 89 56 97 – Open 1st February-20 October
33 rm – €58/69 €64/82, €9 – ½ P €62/71
Rest – *(closed Sunday dinner, Monday and Tuesday)* Menu (€19), €28/60
◆ Extremely tranquil location on a plateau overlooking the valley and the station. Practical and well-kept rooms with terrace or small balcony. Bright dining room that is a blend of Provencal and mountain styles. Shaded terrace. Traditional cuisine.

Le Manoir
62 rte Prémol – 04 76 89 10 88 – www.hotel-manoir.fr – contact@hotel-manoir.fr – Fax 04 76 89 20 63 – Open mid-February to mid-November
15 rm – €36 €45/65, €8 – ½ P €45/57
Rest – *(Closed lunch in week from October to March and Sunday dinner)* Menu (€15), €20 (weekdays)/49 – Carte €43/65
◆ This 1900 establishment at the entrance to the resort sports an attractive colourful facade. Large first floor rooms; smaller but renovated in a modern style on the second floor. Inviting dining rooms, cosy sitting room and veranda opening onto a pleasant terrace. Traditional dishes.

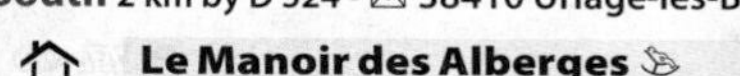

South 2 km by D 524 - ✉ 38410 Uriage-les-Bains

Le Manoir des Alberges
251 chemin des Alberges – 04 76 51 92 11 – www.lemanoirdesalberges.com – contact@lemanoirdesalberges.com
5 rm – €110/130 €110/130 **Table d'hôte** – Menu €30 bi/45 bi
◆ The central section of this house overlooking a golf course dates back to 1903. There are five guestrooms, each with their own style: Bavarian, Indian, Art Deco etc. Inventive cuisine concocted by the *patronne*, served on the terrace during the summer months.

URMATT – 67 Bas-Rhin – **315** H5 – **pop. 1 357** – **alt. 240 m** – ✉ **67280** 1 **A2**

▶ Paris 487 – Molsheim 15 – Saverne 37 – Sélestat 49 – Strasbourg 44 – Wasselonne 23

◉ Church ★ of Niederhaslach Northeast: 3 km, ▮ **Alsace-Lorraine-Champagne**

Clos du Hahnenberg rm, P VISA MC AE

65 r. du Gén. de Gaulle – ✆ 03 88 97 41 35 – www.closhahnenberg.com – clos.hahnenberg@wanadoo.fr – Fax 03 88 47 36 51

33 rm – †€ 45/65 ††€ 55/75, ☕ € 10 – ½ P € 50/58

Rest *Chez Jacques* – Menu € 16 (weekday lunch), € 20/40 – Carte € 30/48

◆ On the main village street, this hotel takes special care of its rooms which are more spacious, bright and soundproofed in the modern part. Jacques' place has a rustic interior and traditional cooking with a few Alsatian specialities.

La Poste rest, rm, P VISA MC AE

74 r. du Gén. de Gaulle – ✆ 03 88 97 40 55 – www.hotel-rest-laposte.fr – contact@hotel-rest-laposte.fr – Fax 03 88 47 38 32 – Closed 13-28 July, 24 December-4 January and 22 February-9 March

14 rm – †€ 42/50 ††€ 49/60, ☕ € 8 – ½ P € 57/60

Rest – *(closed Sunday dinner and Monday)* Menu (€ 11), € 18/48 – Carte € 25/60

◆ Family atmosphere guaranteed in this 100-year-old village inn located opposite the town hall. The rooms are comfortable and well-maintained; some have been carefully renovated. Stained-glass windows and wood panelling heighten the decor of the dining rooms. Regional cuisine.

URRUGNE – **64 Pyrénées-Atlantiques** – **342** B4 – **see St-Jean-de-Luz**

USCLADES-ET-RIEUTORD – **07 Ardèche** – **331** G5 – **pop. 121** – **alt. 1 270 m** – ✉ **07510** 44 **A3**

▶ Paris 590 – Aubenas 45 – Langogne 41 – Privas 59 – Le Puy-en-Velay 51 – Thueyts 98

in Rieutord - ✉**07510 Usclades-et-Rieutord**

Ferme de la Besse P

– ✆ 04 75 38 80 64 – www.aubergedelabesse.com – Fax 04 75 38 80 64 – Open 1st April-30 November

Rest – *(pre-book)* Menu € 32

◆ An authentic 15C farm with a beautiful slab-stone roof. Superbly well-preserved rustic interior, with stonework, beams and fireplace. Earthy cuisine with local products.

USSAT – **09 Ariège** – **343** H8 – **see Tarascon-sur-Ariège**

USSEAU – **86 Vienne** – **322** J3 – **see Châtellerault**

USSEL – **19 Corrèze** – **329** O2 – **pop. 10 000** – **alt. 631 m** – ✉ **19200** 25 **D2**

▮ **Dordogne-Berry-Limousin**

▶ Paris 444 – Aurillac 99 – Clermont-Ferrand 83 – Guéret 101 – Tulle 63

ℹ Office de tourisme, place Voltaire ✆ 05 55 72 11 50, Fax 05 55 72 54 44

⛳ de Neuvic Neuvic Legta Henri Queuille, S : 14 km, ✆ 05 55 95 98 89

⛳ du Chammet Peyrelevade Geneyte, NW : 42 km, ✆ 05 55 94 77 54

Auberge de l'Empereur P VISA MC

La Goudouneche, (l'Empereur business park), 5 km south-west on D 1089 – ✆ 05 55 46 04 30 – www.aubergedelempereur.com – xavierconcept@wanadoo.fr – Closed 2-11 February, Sunday dinner and Monday

Rest – *(pre-book)* Menu € 21 (weekday lunch), € 26/52 – Carte € 32/51

◆ This inn, housed in an old barn (extremely high ceilings, beams, oak panelling and disparate décor), profits from a quiet location near the industrial area. Modern cuisine.

USSON-EN-FOREZ – 42 Loire – 327 C7 – pop. 1 391 – alt. 925 m – ✉ 42550 44 A2

Paris 472 – Issoire 86 – Montbrison 41 – Le Puy-en-Velay 52 – St-Étienne 48

Office de tourisme, place de la Mairie ✆ 04 77 50 66 15, Fax 04 77 50 66 15

Rival with rm

r. Centrale – ✆ 04 77 50 63 65 – hotelrival@msn.com – Fax 04 77 50 67 62 – Closed 8-21 June, 12 November-1 December and Monday except July-August

8 rm – €42 €44, €7 – ½ P €43

Rest – Menu (€11), €14 (weekdays)/42 – Carte €20/40

◆ This simple family enterprise is near the town's Eco Museum on the Compostelle route. Regional dishes served in a rustic dining room. Refurbished rooms. Discounts for pilgrims.

UTELLE – 06 Alpes-Maritimes – 341 E4 – pop. 685 – alt. 800 m – ✉ 06450 French Riviera 41 D2

Paris 883 – Levens 24 – Nice 51 – Puget-Théniers 53 – St-Martin-Vésubie 34

Alatr-piece ★ in St-Véran church - Madonna of Utelle ★★★ Southwest: 6 km

Bellevue

rte de la Madone – ✆ 04 93 03 17 19 – Fax 04 93 03 19 17 – Closed 4 January-13 February and Wednesday except July-August

Rest – *(lunch only)* Carte €27/53

◆ Hidden away in the mountains, this house sports a rustic decor with open hearth and alpine view. Regional cuisine using home-grown produce. Terrace shaded by plane trees.

UZER – 07 Ardèche – 331 H6 – pop. 385 – alt. 165 m – ✉ 07110 44 A3

Paris 663 – Lyon 196 – Privas 44 – Alès 63 – Montélimar 50

Château d'Uzer

– ✆ 04 75 36 89 21 – www.chateau-uzer.com – chateau-uzer@wanadoo.fr – Closed 20 December-4 February

5 rm – €90/120 €100/130

Table d'hôte – *(closed Wednesday and Sunday)* Menu €32 bi

◆ This medieval chateau has it all: welcoming proprietors with a sense of decorative style mixing old and new elements, the semi-wild garden, a swimming pool, and home-made breakfast. Regional dishes, served on the terrace in good weather.

UZERCHE – 19 Corrèze – 329 K3 – pop. 3 195 – alt. 380 m – ✉ 19140 Dordogne-Berry-Limousin 24 B3

Paris 444 – Brive-la-Gaillarde 38 – Limoges 57 – Périgueux 106 – Tulle 30

Office de tourisme, place de la Libération ✆ 05 55 73 15 71, Fax 05 55 73 88 36

Ste-Eulalie ★ East: 1 km.

Teyssier

r. Pont Turgot – ✆ 05 55 73 10 05 – www.hotel-teyssier.com – reservation@hotel-teyssier.com – Fax 05 55 98 43 31 – Closed 19 December-3 January, 6-21 February, Sunday dinner, Monday lunch and Tuesday lunch from 9 November to 28 March

14 rm – €54/68 €54/78, €8 **Rest** – Menu €15/26 – Carte €40/60

◆ This 18C inn with a white façade is near the banks of the Vézère. It has rooms with every comfort, some with views of the river. A modern panoramic dining room. Simple dishes with a southern flavour.

Ambroise

av. Ch. de Gaulle – ✆ 05 55 73 28 60 – www.hotel-ambroise.fr – hotelambroise@orange.fr – Fax 05 55 98 45 73

14 rm – €54/75 €62/88 – ½ P €46/65

Rest – Menu (€12), €15 (weekdays)/36 – Carte €25/65

◆ The simple rooms of this family hotel all overlook the river and greenery. Attractive rustic-styled dining room and, in summer, a terrace-balcony overlooking the garden allowing diners to enjoy the sun as they savour the delicious food.

in St-Ybard 6 km Northwest by D 920 and D 54 – pop. 593 – alt. 320 m – ✉ 19140

Auberge St-Roch

2 r. du Château – ✆ 05 55 73 09 71 – www.auberge-saint-roch.fr – contact@auberge-saint-roch.fr – Fax 05 55 98 41 63 – Closed 20 June-7 July, 19 December-19 January, dinner from November to April, Sunday dinner and Monday

Rest – *(closed dinner from 1st Nov - 1st Apr except Sat)* Menu (€ 13), € 19/40 – Carte € 22/68

◆ Country inn located in the centre of a village with two handsome dining rooms and a bar popular with the locals. Pleasant shaded terrace overlooking the church. Regional fare.

UZÈS – 30 Gard – 339 L4 – pop. 7 859 – alt. 138 m – ✉ 30700 — 23 D2

Provence

Paris 682 – Montpellier 83 – Alès 34 – Arles 52 – Avignon 38 – Nîmes 25

Office de tourisme, place Albert 1er ✆ 04 66 22 68 88, Fax 04 66 22 95 19

d'Uzès Mas de la Place, 5 km on the Avignon road, ✆ 04 66 22 40 03

Old town★★ - Duchy ★: ✻★★ from Bermonde tower - Fenestrelle tower ★★ - Place aux Herbes★ - Organs★ of St-Théodorit cathedral V.

UZÈS

Alliés (Bd des)	A	2
Boucairie (R.)	B	4
Collège (R. du)	B	6
Dampmartin (Pl.)	A	7
Dr-Blanchard (R.)	B	8
Duché (Pl. du)	A	9
Entre les Tours (R.)	A	10
Évêché (R. de l')	B	12
Foch (Av. Mar.)	A	13
Foussat (R. Paul)	A	14
Gambetta (Bd)	A	
Gide (Bd Ch.)	AB	
Marronniers (Prom. des)	B	16
Pascal (Av. M.)	B	17
Pelisserie (R.)	A	18
Plan de l'Oume (R.)	B	19
Port Royal (R.)	B	20
Raffin (R.)	B	21
République (R.)	A	23
St-Étienne (R.)	A	25
St-Théodorit (R.)	B	27
Uzès (R. J.-d')	A	29
Victor-Hugo (Boulevard)	A	32
Vincent (Av. Gén.)	A	
4-Septembre (R.)	A	35

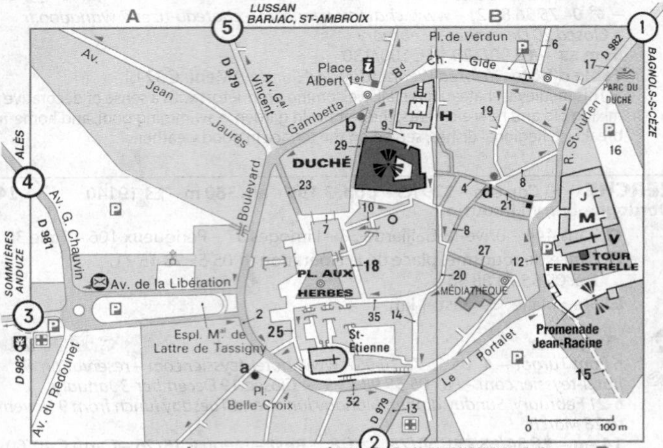

Hostellerie Provençale

1-3 r. Grande-Bourgade – ✆ 04 66 22 11 06 – www.hostellerieprovencale.com – contact@hostellerieprovencale.com – Fax 04 66 75 01 03 — A a

9 rm – †€ 75/98 ††€ 85/135, ☕ € 11 – ½ P € 82/107

Rest – *(closed 15 November-15 December, Monday and Tuesday)* Menu € 34

◆ A prettily renovated old house near the Place aux Herbes where exposed stonework, red floor tiles and antique furniture create a warm atmosphere. Several Jacuzzi tubs. Market-based menu served in a pleasant, colourful dining room.

Mercure rest,
rte de Nîmes, via ②: 0.5 km – ✆ 04 66 03 32 22 – www.mercure-uzes-gard.com – H2065@accor.com – Fax 04 66 03 32 10
65 rm – €75/95 €75/95, €15
Rest – *(dinner only)* Menu €17 – Carte €24/30
◆ A group of buildings around a pool and a shaded terrace make up this hotel on the doorstep of Uzès. Spruce rooms. An informal guesthouse rather than a chain atmosphere. Provençal coloured dining room or a pretty terrace in summertime.

Le Patio de Violette
chemin Trinquelaïgues, (at la Perrine) – ✆ 04 66 01 09 83 – www.patiodeviolette.com – contact@patiodeviolette.com – Fax 04 66 59 33 61
25 rm – €60/75 €60/75, €8,50 – ½ P €62/69
Rest – *(Open from April to October) (dinner only) (residents only)* Carte approx. €26
◆ A modern patio and pleasant terrace are the heart of this contemporary construction. Minimalist decor. Up-to-date restaurant offering simple dishes chalked up on a blackboard and local wines.

Le 80 Jours
2 pl. Albert-1er – ✆ 04 66 22 09 89 – Closed Sunday A **b**
Rest – Menu (€16), €19 (lunch), €26/36 – Carte €33/48
◆ The vaulted ceilings, old stones, ethnic decor and pretty shaded patio are an invitation to take a seat in this modern brasserie whose name is inspired by Jules Verne and the owner's voyages.

Les Trois Salons
18 r. Dr Blanchard – ✆ 04 66 22 57 34 – les3salons@orange.fr – Fax 04 66 57 45 86 – Closed Sunday and Monday B **d**
Rest – Menu (€24) – Carte approx. €48
◆ The sign outside this house built in 1699 near Duché doesn't lie: the tables are set in three pretty but uncluttered sitting rooms. Modern menu with a regional twist.

in St-Victor-des-Oules 7 km on the ①, D 982 and minor road – **pop. 219 – alt. 168 m – ✉ 30700**

Villa Saint-Victor
pl. du Château – ✆ 04 66 81 90 47 – www.villasaintvictor.com – info@villasaintvictor.com – Fax 04 66 81 93 30 – Closed 2 January-5 March
16 rm – €100/140 €100/230, €15 – ½ P €104/124
Rest – *(Closed Saturday lunch, Sunday dinner and Monday)* Menu (€18), €39 (dinner)
◆ An informal ambience reigns throughout this small 19C castle set in wooded parkland. Personalised interior of antiques, 1940s or boudoir style; Jouy wall hangings. Two separate pavilions. Meals (evenings by reservation) feature market fresh, regionally inspired cuisine.

in St-Quentin-la-Poterie 5 km by ① and D 5 – **pop. 2 731 – alt. 113 m – ✉ 30700**

Clos de Pradines rm, rm,
pl. du Pigeonnier – ✆ 04 66 20 04 89 – www.clos-de-pradines.com – contact@clos-de-pradines.com – Fax 04 66 57 19 53 – Closed 16-29 November and 11-31 January
18 rm – €68/162 €68/162, €12 – ½ P €71/118
Rest – Menu €16 (weekday lunch), €30/39 – Carte €34/44
◆ This quiet hotel is on the village heights. It offers delightful neo-Provencal style rooms with small, south facing terraces or balconies. This restaurant offers a lovely terrace overlooking the valley, a modern dining room and traditional food.

in St-Siffret 5 km by ① and D982 – **pop. 921 – alt. 140 m – ✉ 30700**

L'Authentic
pl. de l'école – ✆ 04 66 22 60 09 – lauthenticrestaurant@wanadoo.fr – Fax 04 66 22 60 09 – Closed 15 November-15 December, 30 January-1st March and Wednesday
Rest – *(dinner only except Saturday and Sunday) (number of covers limited, pre-book)* Menu (€20), €28/38
◆ Southern inspired cuisine (market fresh produce) and a wine list chalked up on a blackboard, served in a former classroom of the old school, now a delightful inn!

in Serviers et Labaume 6 km by ④ and D 981 – pop. 355 – alt. 114 m – ✉ 30700

L'Olivier with rm
in the village – ✆ 04 66 22 56 01 – www.l-olivier.fr – info@l-olivier.fr – Fax 04 66 22 54 49 – Closed 9-16 November, 1st January-12 February, Tuesday and Wednesday
5 rm – €70 €70
Rest – *(number of covers limited, pre-book)* Menu € 22 (lunch), € 43/65 – Carte € 48/57
◆ This old village café is now a charming restaurant: sunny decor, wrought iron furniture and flower-decked patio. Fine, modern cuisine and local wines. New rooms.

in Montaren-et-St-Médiers 6 km by ④ and D 337 – pop. 1 328 – alt. 115 m – ✉ 30700

Clos du Léthé without rest
hamlet of St-Médiers – ✆ 06 07 09 01 21 – www.closdulethe.com – info@closdulethe.com – Open from April to October
5 rm – €190/290 €190/290
◆ Intimacy, luxurious comfort, designer interior, delightful service, peace and quiet, overflow pool, steam bath and cookery courses. A stone built home (former priory) of great appeal!

VAAS – 72 Sarthe – **310** K8 – pop. 1 621 – alt. 41 m – ✉ 72500 35 **D2**
Châteaux of the Loire

Paris 237 – Angers 77 – Château-du-Loir 8 – Château-la-Vallière 15 – Le Mans 42

Le Vedaquais
pl. de la Liberté – ✆ 02 43 46 01 41 – www.vedaquais-72.com – levedaquais@orange.fr – Fax 02 43 46 37 60 – Closed Christmas holidays, February school holidays, Friday dinner, Sunday dinner and Monday
12 rm – €52/62 €52/62, €8
Rest – Menu € 17 (weekdays)/33 bi – Carte € 46/59
◆ Named after the inhabitants of Vaas, this former school of the village town hall has been converted into a hotel. It has new, practical and personalised rooms (more rustic in the wing).

LA VACHETTE – 05 Hautes-Alpes – **334** I3 – see Briançon

VACQUEYRAS – 84 Vaucluse – **332** C9 – pop. 1 019 – alt. 117 m – ✉ 84190 42 **E1**

Paris 662 – Avignon 35 – Nyons 34 – Orange 19 – Vaison-la-Romaine 18
Syndicat d'initiative, place de la Mairie ✆ 04 90 12 39 02, Fax 04 90 63 83 28

Le Pradet without rest
rte de Vaison – ✆ 04 90 65 81 00 – www. hotellepradet.fr – hotellepradet@wanadoo.fr – Fax 04 90 65 80 27
32 rm – €56 €75, €9
◆ Housed in this recent building at the entrance to the village are functional and sound-proofed rooms. Some have a small terrace or balcony. Games room and gym.

in Montmirail 2 km East by secondary road – ✉ 84190

Montmirail
Château des Eaux – ✆ 04 90 65 84 01 – www.hotel-montmirail.com – hotel-montmirail@wanadoo.fr – Fax 04 90 65 81 50 – Open 4 April-14 October
39 rm – €59/70 €82/92, €12 – ½ P € 84/101
Rest – *(closed Thursday lunch and Saturday lunch)* Menu (€ 24), € 34 (weekday lunch)/42 – Carte € 48/54
◆ This 19C residence with character stands in a pleasant garden planted with trees, at the foot of the famous Dentelles de Montmirail. Well-kept, partly renovated rooms. A cosy dining room and covered terrace await guests. Appetising traditional cuisine.

VACQUIERS – 31 Haute-Garonne – 343 G2 – pop. 1 259 – alt. 200 m – ✉ 31340 28 B2

Paris 658 – Albi 71 – Castres 80 – Montauban 35 – Toulouse 31

La Villa les Pins without rest
1660 rte de Bouloc, 2 km west via D 30 – ✆ 05 61 84 96 04 – www.villa-les-pins.fr – villalespins@9business.fr – Fax 05 61 84 28 54
15 rm – †€ 59 ††€ 69, ☕ € 9
◆ Large villa built in the heart of wooded parkland. A marble staircase leads up to comfortable recently refurbished rooms, albeit with somewhat old-fashioned fittings.

VAGNAS – 07 Ardèche – 331 I7 – pop. 520 – alt. 200 m – ✉ 07150 44 A3

Paris 678 – Alès 38 – Aubenas 37 – Mende 112 – Orange 57

La Bastide d'Iris without rest
D 579 – ✆ 04 75 88 44 77 – www.labastidediris.com – labastidediris@wanadoo.fr – Fax 04 75 38 61 29
12 rm – †€ 69/89 ††€ 69/120, ☕ € 11
◆ This charming brand-new country house has rooms with attractively coloured walls, assorted fabrics, customized furniture and cheerful bathrooms. Pleasant garden.

VAGNEY – 88 Vosges – 314 I4 – pop. 3 845 – alt. 412 m – ✉ 88120 27 C3

Paris 437 – Metz 163 – Épinal 40 – Belfort 99 – Saint-Dié-des-Vosges 53
Syndicat d'initiative, 11, place Caritey ✆ 03 29 24 88 69, Fax 03 29 61 82 36

Les Lilas
12 r. Gén. de Gaulle – ✆ 03 29 23 69 47 – Closed 17 August-1st September, 25 January-9 February, Tuesday dinner and Wednesday
Rest – *(number of covers limited, pre-book)* Menu (€ 13), € 18 (weekdays), € 21/37 – Carte € 34/48
◆ The lilac has inspired the decor at this classic, modern house in soft, violet tones. Excellent welcome. Traditional dishes with local accents.

VAIGES – 53 Mayenne – 310 G6 – pop. 1 151 – alt. 90 m – ✉ 53480 35 C1

Paris 255 – Château-Gontier 35 – Laval 24 – Le Mans 61 – Mayenne 32

Commerce rm, rest,
r. du Fief aux Moines – ✆ 02 43 90 50 07 – www.hotelcommerce.fr – oger-samuel.hotel-du-commerce@wanadoo.fr – Fax 02 43 90 57 40 – Closed 24 December-18 January, Sunday dinner and Friday dinner from October to 1st May
32 rm – †€ 65/110 ††€ 68/120, ☕ € 9 – ½ P € 65/95
Rest – Menu € 18 (weekday lunch), € 24/50 – Carte € 35/60
◆ In a village of the Mayenne countryside, this hotel, run by the same family since 1883, offers well-equipped rooms. Billiard table and sauna. Beneath a lovely ceiling of timber rafters, rustic dining rooms and open fires. Conservatory.

VAILLY-SUR-SAULDRE – 18 Cher – 323 L2 – pop. 914 – alt. 205 m – ✉ 18260 Dordogne-Berry-Limousin 12 C2

Paris 182 – Aubigny-sur-Nère 17 – Bourges 55 – Cosne-sur-Loire 25 – Gien 36 – Sancerre 23
Office de tourisme, 5 bis, place du 8 mai 1945 ✆ 02 48 73 87 57, Fax 02 48 73 87 57

Le Lièvre Gourmand (William Page)
14 r. Grande Rue – ✆ 02 48 73 80 23 – www.lelievregourmand.com – contact@lelievregourmand.com – Closed 15-23 June, 31 August-8 September, 5-30 January, Sunday dinner, Monday and Tuesday
Rest – *(number of covers limited, pre-book)* Menu € 39/59
Spec. Blanc manger aux truffes d'été. Râble de lièvre juste saisi, jus de betterave (winter). Abricots, miel, fleur d'oranger et glace cannelle (summer). **Wines** Pouilly-Fumé, Sancerre.
◆ These old village houses offer a modern, elegant dining room and cosy lounge. Inventive cuisine with a personal touch and wines from Australia and the region.

VAISON-LA-ROMAINE – 84 Vaucluse – **332** D8 – **pop. 6 147** – **alt. 193 m** – ✉ **84110** Provence

Paris 664 – Avignon 51 – Carpentras 27 – Montélimar 64 – Pont-St-Esprit 41

Office de tourisme, place du Chanoine-Sautel ☎ 04 90 36 02 11, Fax 04 90 28 76 04

Gallo-Roman remains★★ : théâtre antique (ancient theatre)★, musée archéologique Théo-Desplans (Théo-Desplans Archaeological Museum)★ **M** - Haute Ville (Upper Town)★ - cloître (cloister)★ **B.**

VAISON-LA-ROMAINE

Aubanel (Pl.) . . . . . Z 2
Bon Ange (Chemin du) . . . . . Y 3
Brusquet (Chemin du) . . . . . Y 4
Burrus (R.) . . . . . Y 5
Cathédrale (Pl. de la) . . . . . Y 6
Chanoine-Sautel (Pl.) . . . . . Y 7
Coudray (Av.) . . . . . Y 8
Daudet (R. A.) . . . . . Y 9
Église (R. de l') . . . . . Z 10
Évêché (R. de l') . . . . . Z 12
Fabre (Cours H.) . . . . . Y 13
Foch (Quai Maréchal) . . . . . Z 14
Géoffray (Av. C.) . . . . . Z 15
Gontard (Quai P.) . . . . . Z 17
Grande-Rue . . . . . Y 18
Jean-Jaurès (R.) . . . . . Y 22
Mazen (Av. J.) . . . . . Y 23
Mistral (R. Frédéric) . . . . . Y 24
Montée du Château . . . . . Z 25
Montfort (Pl.) . . . . . Y 26
Noël (R. B.) . . . . . Y 27
Poids (Pl. du) . . . . . Z 29
République (R.) . . . . . Y 32
St-Quenin (Av.) . . . . . Y 33
Sus Auze (Pl.) . . . . . Y 34
Taulignan (Crs) . . . . . Y 35
Victor-Hugo (Av.) . . . . . Y 36
Vieux Marché (Pl. du) . . . . . Z 38
11 Novembre (Pl. du) . . . . . Y 40

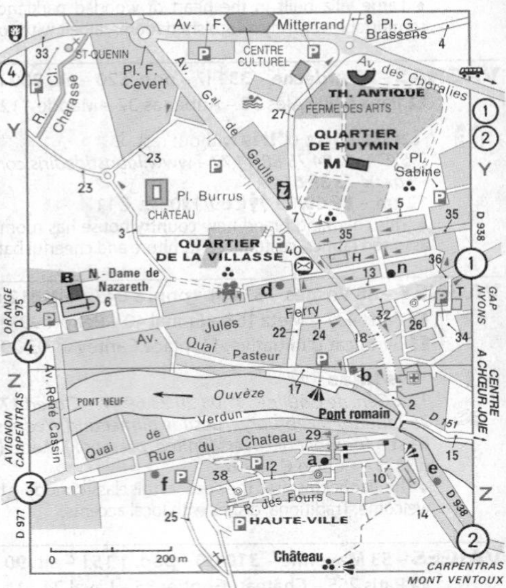

Hostellerie le Beffroi
r. de l'Evêché, (Upper Town) – ☎ 04 90 36 04 71 – www.le-beffroi.com – lebeffroi@wanadoo.fr – Fax 04 90 36 24 78 – Closed 20 January to end March and 21-26 December Z **a**
22 rm – €70/90 €75/145, €12
Rest – *(open 3 April to end October and closed Tuesday and lunch in week)* Menu €28/45 – Carte €37/52
◆ At the foot of the castle, dominating the town, two houses from the 16C and 17C that have retained their charm. Rooms are tastefully decorated. Beautiful terraced garden. Tables are set out in a rustic dining room or in the pretty courtyard. Classic menus, salad bar and tea room.

Burrhus without rest
2 pl. Monfort – ☎ 04 90 36 00 11 – www.burrhus.com – info@burrhus.com – Fax 04 90 36 39 05 – Closed 11 December-24 January Y **n**
39 rm – €49/85 €53/85, €9
◆ The owners of this ochre-coloured house regularly organise exhibitions of photos, sculpture and art. The rooms range from rustic to contemporary or 'arty'.

Le Moulin à Huile (Robert Bardot) with rm
quai Mar. Foch – ☎ 04 90 36 20 67 – www.moulin-huile.com – info@moulin-huile.com – Fax 04 90 36 20 20 – Closed Sunday dinner and Monday Z **e**
3 rm – €130/150 €130/150, €25
Rest – *(pre-book)* Menu (€28), €60/75 – Carte €83/90
Spec. Boudin de homard (April to September). Filet de bœuf sur une purée de persil. Millefeuille à la vanille (September to June). **Wines** Châteauneuf-du-Pape, Rasteau.
◆ A charming former oil mill on the banks of the Ouvèze. Tasty up-to-date cuisine served in the elegant vaulted cellar or in the veranda opening onto a terrace. Attractively decorated rooms where you will feel right at home. Small pool.

XX **Le Brin d'Olivier**

4 r. Ventoux – ✆ 04 90 28 74 79 – www.restaurant-lebrindolivier.com – lebrindolivier.mlm@orange.fr – Fax 04 90 36 13 36 – Closed 4-11 November, Saturday lunch and Wednesday lunch from July to September and Wednesday from October to June Z b

Rest – Menu € 28/38 – Carte € 38/58

◆ Welcoming establishment near the Roman bridge, with four rustic dining rooms decorated in the Provencal style. Patio planted with a fine olive tree. Local cuisine.

X **Le Bistro du O**

r. Gaston Gévaudan, Haute-Ville – ✆ 04 90 41 72 90 – bistroduo@orange.fr – Closed January, Monday lunch and Sunday Z f

Rest – *(number of covers limited, pre-book)* Menu (€ 19), € 28 – Carte € 35/45

◆ An elegant and refined bistro setting with vaulting, stone and a mix of old and modern furniture. Creative set menu that changes regularly. Well-priced wine list.

X **Leonardo**

55 r. Trogue-Pompée – ✆ 04 90 28 79 10 – leosnova@wanadoo.fr – Closed 22-30 June and 5-12 October Y d

Rest – Carte € 20/50

◆ Choose from the Italian specialities listed on the blackboard then dine on the terrace or in the smart dining room. Salads and bruschetta served at lunchtime.

in Crestet 5 km by ②, D 938 and D 76 – pop. 473 – alt. 310 m – ✉ 84110

Mas d'Hélène rest,

Chante coucou district – ✆ 04 90 36 39 91 – www.lemasdhelene.com – mas-helene@wanadoo.fr – Fax 04 90 28 73 40

13 rm – €55/112 €55/112, € 13 **Rest** – *(dinner only)* Carte € 25/33

◆ This colourful, country farmhouse stands in a garden rich in the scents of the Riviera. Attractive Provençal decor. Most of the rooms (except two) have a terrace. Pool.

in Entrechaux 7 km by ②, D 938 and D 54 – pop. 1 008 – alt. 280 m – ✉ 84340

French Alps

XX **St-Hubert**

Le village – ✆ 04 90 46 00 05 – http://restaurantsthubert.free.fr – Fax 04 90 46 00 06 – Closed 5-17 October, 1st February-14 March, Tuesday and Wednesday

Rest – Menu € 16 (weekday lunch), € 27/51 – Carte € 28/52

◆ Since 1929, the same family has been welcoming guests to this rustic restaurant. In summer, dine under the wisteria clad terrace. Generous cuisine and game in season.

in Séguret 10 km by ③, D 977 and D 88 – pop. 904 – alt. 250 m – ✉ 84110

Domaine de Cabasse rm,

rte Sablet – ✆ 04 90 46 91 12 – www.cabasse.fr – info@cabasse.fr – Fax 04 90 46 94 01 – Open from April to October

13 rm – €75/95 €115/135, € 13 **Rest** – Menu (€ 22), € 29

◆ At the foot of the Montmirail Dentelles, this hotel forms part of a wine producing estate (tour, tastings). The simple, neat rooms benefit from the peace and quiet of the vineyards. Spacious dining room and shaded terrace. Traditional cuisine and wines from the estate.

XXX **La Table du Comtat** with rm rest,

Le Village – ✆ 04 90 46 91 49 – www.table-comtat.fr – table.comtat@wanadoo.fr – Fax 04 90 46 94 27 – Closed 16 November-5 December, 16 February-8 March, Tuesday dinner and Wednesday except July-August

8 rm – €60/110 €60/110, € 13 – ½ P € 75/100

Rest – Menu € 20, € 34/48 – Carte € 55/65

◆ New modern interior at this house with a superb panoramic view of the plain and the Montmirail Dentelles. Tasty, generous cuisine.

X **Le Mesclun**

r. Poternes, (pedestrian access) – ✆ 04 90 46 93 43 – www.lemesclun.com – mesclunseguret@aol.com – Fax 04 86 38 03 33 – Closed January, February, Tuesday except July-August and Monday

Rest – *(number of covers limited, pre-book)* Menu (€ 19), € 27/40 – Carte € 35/50

◆ A pleasant restaurant in a charming village. Provencal dining rooms in colourful shades, nice shaded terrace and Mediterranean cuisine with personal touches.

in Rasteau 9 km by ④, D 975 and D 69 – pop. 716 – alt. 200 m – ✉ 84110

Syndicat d'initiative, place du Village ✆ 04 90 46 18 73

Bellerive rm, VISA AE

rte Violès – ✆ 04 90 46 10 20 – www.hotel-bellerive.fr – hotel-bellerive@wanadoo.fr – Fax 04 90 46 14 96 – Open early April to mid-October

20 rm – €75/175 €75/175, €15 – ½ P €92/140

Rest – *(closed Monday lunch, Friday lunch and Tuesday)* Menu €28/54 – Carte €51/79

◆ Large villa surrounded by vines with swimming pool. Rooms endowed with pleasant loggias opening onto the Ouvèze valley. You will enjoy tasting the Rasteau wine whether you sit in the Provençal dining room or on the terrace.

in Roaix 5 km by ④ and D 975 – pop. 587 – alt. 168 m – ✉ 84110

Le Grand Pré (Raoul Reichrath) VISA AE

rte de Vaison-la-Romaine – ✆ 04 90 46 18 12 – www.legrandpre.com – info@legrandpre.com – Fax 04 90 46 17 84 – Open from mid February to mid November and closed Saturday lunch and Tuesday

Rest – *(pre-book)* Menu €35 (weekday lunch), €55/115 bi – Carte €70/100

Spec. Anchoïade de figues et crevettes rôties à l'huile d'olive (mid-August to October). Pigeonneau au jus de café turc et boudin basque. Mousse de banane et pain d'épice. **Wines** Côtes du Rhône Villages Roaix, Vin de Pays de Vaucluse.

◆ Cuisine based on southern flavours and a wonderful selection of Côtes du Rhône wines, served in the elegant old farmhouse with its white interior. Terrace overlooking a herb garden.

VAÏSSAC – 82 Tarn-et-Garonne – **337** F7 – pop. 599 – alt. 134 m – ✉ 82800 29 **C2**

Paris 620 – Albi 60 – Montauban 23 – Toulouse 76 – Villefranche-de-Rouergue 66

Terrassier VISA AE

– ✆ 05 63 30 94 60 – www.chezterrassier.net – hotel-rest.terrassier@wanadoo.fr – Fax 05 63 30 87 40 – Closed 19-25 November, 1st-15 January, Friday evening and Sunday evening

18 rm – €45/70 €45/85, €8 – ½ P €48/65

Rest – Menu (€10 bi), €13 bi (weekday lunch), €22/42 – Carte €27/50

◆ This family-run inn is an ideal base for exploring the Quercy and Albigeois. Well-maintained rooms, with those in the recent annexe the pick of the bunch. Bright, modern dining room decorated in yellow tones. Regional cuisine.

LE VAL – 83 Var – **340** L5 – pop. 3 760 – alt. 242 m – ✉ 83143 41 **C3**

Paris 818 – La Seyne-sur-Mer 63 – Marseille 70 – Toulon 55

Office de tourisme, place de la Mairie ✆ 04 94 37 02 21, Fax 04 94 37 31 96

La Crémaillère VISA

23 r. Nationale – ✆ 04 94 86 40 00 – Fax 04 94 86 40 00 – Closed 24 November-3 December, 16 February-4 March, Sunday dinner from 15 November to 7 March, Wednesday except dinner in July-August and Monday

Rest – Menu (€20), €26/34 – Carte €33/45

◆ This welcoming family-run restaurant in the centre of this pretty village has Provencal decor and cuisine. Small terrace.

VALADY – 12 Aveyron – **338** G4 – pop. 1 321 – alt. 350 m – ✉ 12330 29 **C1**

Paris 625 – Decazeville 20 – Rodez 20

Auberge de l'Ady VISA

1 av. du Pont-de-Malakoff, (near the church) – ✆ 05 65 72 70 24 – www.auberge-ady.com – auberge.ady@orange.fr – Fax 05 65 72 68 15 – Closed 22 June-5 July, 5-25 January, Wednesday dinner from October to April, Sunday dinner, Tuesday dinner and Monday

Rest – Menu (€16), €28/60 bi – Carte €43/57

◆ Friendly inn transformed into a contemporary restaurant in the heart of a small rural village in the Aveyron. The owner, who has returned to the country, prepares modern cuisine.

LE VAL-ANDRÉ – 22 Côtes-d'Armor – **309** G3 – see Pléneuf-Val-André

VALAURIE – 26 Drôme – **332** B7 – pop. 540 – alt. 162 m – ✉ 26230 44 **B3**

Paris 622 – Montélimar 21 – Nyons 33 – Pierrelatte 14

Le Moulin de Valaurie rm, VISA AE

Le Foulon – ✆ 04 75 97 21 90 – www.lemoulindevalaurie.com – info@lemoulindevalaurie.com – Fax 04 75 98 63 72 – Closed autumn school holidays, February and Sunday dinner from October to April

16 rm – €110/215 €110/215, €12

Rest – *(closed Sunday dinner off season, Wednesday lunch in July-August, Tuesday lunch and Monday)* Menu (€28), €36/42

◆ A path surrounded by vines leads to this 19C mill, now a hotel full of character. Spacious Provençal rooms, antique ornaments and furniture and a lovely park. Elegant dining room and wrought-iron terrace; traditional and regional food.

Domaine Les Mejeonnes rm, VISA

2 km Montélimar road – ✆ 04 75 98 60 60 – www.mejeonnes.com – contact@mejeonnes.com – Fax 04 75 98 63 44

25 rm – €75/95 €75/95, €8 – ½ P €68/78 **Rest** – Menu (€19), €25

◆ A charming stone farm on a hillside, bordered with a lavender- and rosemary-scented garden. Beautiful rustic interior. Small rooms brightened with Provençal fabrics. Decor and recipes with a local influence. Pleasant terrace in summer.

VALBERG – 06 Alpes-Maritimes – **341** C3 – alt. 1 669 m – Winter sports : 1 430/2 100 m 26 – ✉ 06470 Peone French Alps 41 **D2**

Paris 803 – Barcelonnette 75 – Castellane 67 – Nice 84 – St-Martin-Vésubie 57

Office de tourisme, Centre Administratif ✆ 04 93 23 24 25, Fax 04 93 02 52 27

Interior★ of N.-D.-des-Neiges chapel.

Le Chalet Suisse without rest VISA

4 av. Valberg – ✆ 04 93 03 62 62 – www.chalet-suisse.com – info@chalet-suisse.com – Fax 04 93 03 62 64 – Open mid June-September and mid December-March

23 rm – €70/87 €88/120, €10

◆ Recently renovated, this Swiss-style chalet is situated in the centre of the resort. Comfort and relaxation are the main features of this hotel, with its attractive guestrooms, sauna and hammam.

L'Adrech de Lagas VISA AE

63 av. Valberg – ✆ 04 93 02 51 64 – www.adrech-hotel.com – adrech-hotel@wanadoo.fr – Fax 04 93 02 52 33 – Open from June to September and from December to March

20 rm – €73/111 €79/120, €10 – ½ P €75/95

Rest – Menu €19 (lunch)/25 – Carte €20/42

◆ The name of this new chalet at the foot of the ski runs recalls the Catalan origins of the area's inhabitants. Colourful rooms, some of which have been renovated, with south-facing loggias. Good portions of traditional cuisine are on offer in the bright dining room of this restaurant.

Blanche Neige VISA AE

10 av. Valberg – ✆ 04 93 02 50 04 – www.hotelblancheneige.fr – contact@hotelblancheneige.fr – Fax 04 93 02 61 90 – Closed two weeks in autumn and two weeks in spring

17 rm – €79/103 €79/103, €10 – ½ P €88/130

Rest – *(dinner only) (residents only)*

◆ Charming, recently redecorated chalet, the image of the Seven dwarves' cottage with its cosy little rooms and pretty chintzes. Diners enjoy regional cooking by the fire in winter or on the terrace in summer.

Côté Jardin VISA AE

1 pl. Cluot de la Mule – ✆ 04 93 02 64 70 – www.cotejardin-valberg.com – restocotejardin@hotmail.fr – Fax 04 93 02 64 70 – Closed Sunday dinner and Wednesday October-November and April-June

Rest – Menu €16/20 – Carte €28/45

◆ This restaurant has a cosy atmosphere, which becomes more festive during themed evenings. Provençal cuisine on the menu, as well as specialities such as home-made foie gras.

VALBONNE – 06 Alpes-Maritimes – 341 D6 – pop. 12 300 – alt. 250 m

42 **E2**

– ✉ 06560 **French Riviera**

Paris 907 – Antibes 14 – Cannes 13 – Grasse 11 – Mougins 7 – Nice 32 – Vence 21

Office de tourisme, 1, place de l'Hôtel de Ville ✆ 04 93 12 34 50, Fax 04 93 12 34 57

Victoria Golf Club Chemin du Val Martin, S : 4 km, ✆ 04 93 12 23 26

Opio Valbonne Opio Route de Roquefort les Pins, N : 1 km, ✆ 04 93 12 00 08

La Bastide de Valbonne without rest

107 rte Cannes – ✆ 04 93 12 33 40 – www.bastidevalbonne.com – bastide-de-valbonne@wanadoo.fr – Fax 04 93 12 33 41

34 rm – €95/125 €95/250, €15

◆ New establishment with a spruce yellow façade brightened with blue shutters. The rooms in the rear are quiet and command a view of the pool. Pleasant Provençal decor.

Les Armoiries without rest

pl. des Arcades – ✆ 04 93 12 90 90 – www.hotellesarmoiries.com – valbonne@hotellesarmoiries.com – Fax 04 93 12 90 91

16 rm – €97/168 €97/168, €12

◆ This beautifully decorated 17C building stands in the pedestrian area of this picturesque village. Rooms with personal touches and antique furniture.

Lou Cigalon (Alain Parodi)

4 bd Carnot – ✆ 04 93 12 27 07 – Fax 04 93 12 09 96 – Closed Sunday and Monday

Rest – *(number of covers limited, pre-book)* Menu (€ 31), € 56 (weekdays)/115 – Carte € 86/110

Spec. Tourteau émietté, salpicon de mangue, mousse au chorizo. Pigeon rôti et sucrines braisées. Baba au rhum, crème fouettée vanillée. **Wines** Coteaux Varois, Bellet.

◆ A discreet house with two pleasant dining rooms featuring rough stone walls and exposed rafters. Produce from the sun-drenched markets is used in the kitchen. Wines from southeast France.

L'Auberge Fleurie

Cannes road, (D 3): 1.5 km – ✆ 04 93 12 02 80 – Fleurie.auberge@wanadoo.fr – Fax 04 93 12 22 27 – Closed 1st December-5 January, Monday and Tuesday

Rest – Menu € 27/34 – Carte approx. € 50

◆ Attractive establishment surrounded by a flower garden. Provençal-style dining room and a small terrace where generous portions of traditional food are served.

Le Bistro de Valbonne

11 r. Fontaine – ✆ 04 93 12 05 59 – www.bistro-valbonne.com – bozzano0330@orange.fr – Fax 04 93 12 05 59 – Closed 25 October-5 November, 10-20 February, Monday lunch and Sunday

Rest – *(number of covers limited, pre-book)* Menu (€ 21), € 38/42 – Carte € 45/55

◆ Mirrors, banquettes, subdued lighting, paintings, and old photos all create a warm, cosy atmosphere in this attractive vaulted dining room. Copious, traditional cuisine.

at golf d'Opio-Valbonne Northeast: 2 km by Biot road (D 4 and D 204)

– ✉ 06650 Opio

Château de la Bégude

rm,

rte de Roquefort les Pins – ✆ 04 93 12 37 00 – www.opengolfclub.com/begude – begude@opengolfclub.com – Fax 04 93 12 37 13 – Closed 16 November-27 December

31 rm – €78/200 €96/240, € 19 – 6 suites

Rest – *(closed dinner 16 November-27 December and Sunday dinner st October-31 March)* Menu € 38/65 – Carte € 48/95

◆ Edged by a line of cork oaks, on one of the region's best known golf courses, a charming 16C farm and sheep barn. Cosy, renovated guestrooms. Dining room-veranda and pleasant terrace overlooking the ninth hole of the golf course.

Antibes road South by D 3 – ✉ 06560 Valbonne

Castel Provence without rest
30 chemin Pinchinade, at 2.5 km – ✆ 04 93 12 11 92 – www.hotelcastelprovence.com – reservation@hotelcastelprovence.com – Fax 04 93 12 90 01
36 rm – †€ 75/130 ††€ 95/170, ☕ € 18
◆ This recent regional-style construction is home to spacious and well-decorated rooms; some command a view of the pool and garden.

Daniel Desavie
1360 rte d'Antibes – ✆ 04 93 12 29 68 – www.restaurantdanieldesavie.fr – Fax 04 93 12 18 85 – Closed 1st-9 March, 28 June-13 July, 8-23 November, Sunday and Monday
Rest – Menu € 32 (lunch), € 37/52 – Carte € 53/83
◆ Provencal cuisine making the most of local produce to be savoured in a bright, contemporary dining room or under the arches of a gallery facing the flower garden.

in Sophia-Antipolis 7 km southeast by D 3 and D 103 - ✉ 06560 Valbonne

Sophia Country Club Grand Mercure
Les Lucioles 2 - 3550 rte Dolines – ✆ 04 92 96 68 78 – www.webtvnice.com/grand-mercure-sophia – H1279@accor.com – Fax 04 92 96 68 96 – Closed 21 December-3 January
155 rm – †€ 160/170 ††€ 170/180, ☕ € 19
Rest *Le Club* – ✆ *04 92 96 68 98* – Carte € 25/45
◆ Hotel complex with a very complete sports centre: tennis club, driving range, fitness area, pools. Try to get one of the new rooms, which are spacious and carefully decorated. Restaurant-brasserie and terrace overlooking the pool. Modern cuisine.

Novotel
Les Lucioles 1, 290 r. Dostoievski – ✆ 04 92 38 72 38 – www.novotel.com – h0398-dm@accor.com – Fax 04 93 95 80 12
97 rm – †€ 99/189 ††€ 99/189, ☕ € 15
Rest – Menu (€ 20), € 24 (weekdays) – Carte € 30/50
◆ This hotel in the heart of Sophia-Antipolis stands in the grounds of a pleasant garden. Quiet, comfortable and well-equipped rooms. Swimming pool and tennis court surrounded by trees. This restaurant with terrace serves Provençal cuisine in a restful, green setting.

Mercure
Les Lucioles 2, r. A. Caquot – ✆ 04 92 96 04 04 – www.mercure.com – h1122@accor.com – Fax 04 92 96 05 05
104 rm – †€ 79/189 ††€ 89/199, ☕ € 17
Rest – Menu (€ 22), € 29 – Carte € 32/44
◆ Modern building in Provençal colours situated on the vast wooded plateau of Sophia-Antipolis. Rooms gradually being renovated. Swimming pool and Mediterranean plants in the garden. Menu based on market offerings with regional touches and refreshing summer salads.

Relais Omega
Les Lucioles 1, 49 r. L. Van Beethoven – ✆ 04 92 96 07 07 – www.hotelomega.com – reservation@hotelomega.com – Fax 04 92 38 98 08 – Closed 17 December-2 January
60 rm – †€ 109 ††€ 119, ☕ € 14 – 4 suites
Rest – Menu (€ 20), € 25 – Carte € 35/45
◆ A sophisticated Provençal decoration and faultless facilities (air-conditioning, wifi, seminar room) await you in this fully refurbished comfortable hotel. In the restaurant you can expect traditional simple fare full of the flavour of southern France.

Do not confuse X with ✿!
X defines comfort, while stars are awarded for the best cuisine, across all categories of comfort.

VALCEBOLLÈRE – 66 Pyrénées-Orientales – **344** D8 – **pop. 41** – **alt. 1 470 m** – ✉ 66340 22 **A3**

Paris 856 – Bourg-Madame 9 – Font-Romeu-Odeillo-Via 27 – Perpignan 107 – Prades 62

Auberge Les Ecureuils VISA

Caer de la coma – ✆ 04 68 04 52 03 – www.aubergeecureuils.com – auberge-ecureuils@wanadoo.fr – Fax 04 68 04 52 34 – Closed 5 November-5 December

16 rm – €70/95 €72/110, €11 – ½ P €65/95

Rest – Menu (€ 19), € 25/50 – Carte € 32/55

◆ An old sheep barn converted into a charming rustic inn. Pleasant rooms with a personal touch. Garden by a mountain stream. Outings organised; skis and rackets for hire. Distinguished dining room; classic cuisine and Catalan specialities. Pancakes too.

We try to be as accurate as possible when giving room rates. But prices are open to change, so please check rates when booking.

VAL-CLARET – 73 Savoie – **333** O5 – see Tignes

VALDAHON – 25 Doubs – **321** I4 – **pop. 4 728** – **alt. 645 m** – ✉ 25800 17 **C2**

Paris 436 – Besançon 33 – Morteau 33 – Pontarlier 32

Relais de Franche Comté VISA

1 r. Charles Schmitt – ✆ 03 81 56 23 18 – www.relais-de-franche-comte.com – relais.de.franche.comte@wanadoo.fr – Fax 03 81 56 44 38 – Closed 29 April-3 May, 27 August-1st September, 18 December-11 January, Friday dinner, Saturday lunch except July-August, and Sunday dinner from September to June

20 rm – €44/47 €54/58, €8 – ½ P €54/57

Rest – Menu € 14 (weekdays)/50 – Carte € 22/45

◆ This imposing hotel on the edge of the town has modern, practical rooms with brightly coloured fabrics. A bright restaurant serving traditional, seasonal cuisine, including game during the hunting season.

LE VAL-D'AJOL – 88 Vosges – **314** G5 – **pop. 4 452** – **alt. 380 m** – ✉ 88340 **Alsace-Lorraine** 27 **C3**

Paris 382 – Épinal 41 – Luxeuil-les-Bains 18 – Plombières-les-Bains 10 – Remiremont 16

Office de tourisme, 17, rue de Plombières ✆ 03 29 30 61 55, Fax 03 29 30 56 78

La Résidence rm, VISA

5 r. des Mousses, by Hamanxard road – ✆ 03 29 30 68 52 – www.la-residence.com – contact@la-residence.com – Fax 03 29 66 53 00 – Closed 26 November-26 December

49 rm – €53/68 €65/95, €11 – ½ P €69/84

Rest – *(closed Sunday dinner from October to May except school and public holidays)* Menu (€ 15), € 26/52 – Carte € 35/60

◆ In the heart of wooded parkland, a fine mid-19C bourgeois residence with two wings. The bedrooms are attractive if a little antiquated. The chef's unusual, regional menu varies from classic to innovative.

VALDEBLORE (Commune) - 06 Alpes-Maritimes - 341 E3 - pop. 686 - alt. 1 050 m - Winter sports : to la Colmiane 1 400/1 800 m ⛷7 - ✉ 06420 French Riviera 41 D2

Paris 841 - Cannes 89 - Nice 72 - St-Étienne-de-Tinée 46 - St-Martin-Vésubie 11

Syndicat d'initiative, la Roche ✆ 04 93 23 25 90, Fax 04 93 23 25 91

in St-Dalmas-Valdeblore - ✉ 06420 Valdelblore - pop. 796 - alt. 1 050 m

Pic de Colmiane ✳★★ East 4.5 km access by chairlift.

Auberge des Murès rest, **P** VISA

rte du col St-Martin - ✆ 04 93 23 24 60 - http://auberge-mure.ifrance.com - aubergesdesmures@wanadoo.fr - Fax 04 93 23 24 67 - Closed 15 November-15 December, Monday, Tuesday and Wednesday except school holidays

7 rm - †€ 50 ††€ 63, ☕ € 9 - ½ P € 53/60

Rest - Menu (€ 20), € 26 - Carte € 26/35

◆ Small family inn recalling a chalet, offering a pretty view of the mountain from the balconies of the rooms. Feels just like home. In winter, a restaurant with exposed stones and beams; in summer, a lovely terrace facing the peaks.

VAL-D'ESQUIÈRES - 83 Var - 340 P5 - see Ste-Maxime

VAL-D'ISÈRE - 73 Savoie - 333 O5 - pop. 1 732 - alt. 1 850 m - Winter sports : 1 850/2 560 m 6 ⛷45 - ✉ 73150 French Alps 45 D2

Paris 667 - Albertville 86 - Chambéry 135

Office de tourisme, ✆ 04 79 06 06 60, Fax 04 79 06 04 56

du Lac de Tignes Tignes Le Val Claret, 14 km on the Bourg-St-Maurice road, ✆ 04 79 06 37 42

Bellevarde Rock ✳★★★ by cable car - Iseran road ★★★.

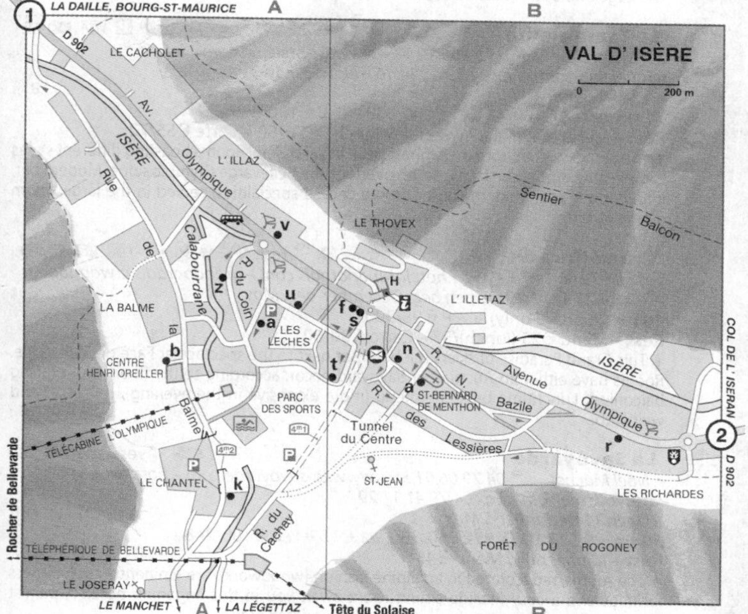

Les Barmes de l'Ours

chemin des Carats – 04 79 41 37 00 – www.hotel-les-barmes.com – welcome@hotel-les-barmes.com – Fax 04 79 41 37 01 – Open 4 December-25 April

rest, VISA MC AE

A **b**

55 rm – €440/1240 €470/1270 – 21 suites

Rest *La Table de l'Ours* – *(open 4 December-25 April and closed Sunday) (dinner only)* Menu €90/190 – Carte €100/200

Rest *Le Pas de l'Ours* – Menu €80

Spec. Tarte au foie gras frais de canard et truffe. Ris de veau doré au sautoir. Chocolat noir intense et amandes.

◆ Four styles of rooms prevail in this immense chalet: Scandinavian, Far North, Savoyard and modern. Sitting room, bar and spa. Contemporary or spit-roast cuisine depending on the room.

Christiania

rm, VISA MC AE

– 04 79 06 08 25 – www.hotel-christiania.com – welcome@hotel-christiania.com – Fax 04 79 41 11 10 – Open mid December to mid April

A **a**

68 rm – €306/900 €320/915 – 1 suite

Rest – Menu (€39), €64 (dinner) – Carte €46/170

◆ Splendid chalet with a view of the slopes. The rooms are all different and some are warmly alpine. Fitness facilities and sitting room for smokers. An alpine dining room, panoramic terrace and traditional menu.

Le Blizzard

VISA MC AE

r. Principale – 04 79 06 02 07 – www.hotelblizzard.com – information@hotelblizzard.com – Fax 04 79 06 04 94 – Open 11 December-2 May

B **f**

79 rm – €275/300 €315/1110, €18 – ½ P €210/305

Rest – Carte €46/86

Rest *La Luge* – grill room – *04 79 06 69 39 (dinner only)* Carte €30/65

◆ Wood prevails in this pretty chalet home to exquisite rooms, some of which boast a fireplace. Fitness and well-being centre and lovely spa. Traditional menu at the restaurant. The Luge offers spit-roast meat and cheese specialities.

Le Tsanteleina

VISA MC AE

av. Olympique – 04 79 06 12 13 – www.tsanteleina.com – info@tsanteleina.com – Fax 04 79 41 14 16 – Open 3 July-31 August and 4 December-2 May

B **s**

71 rm – €139/411 €200/588 – ½ P €130/325

Rest – Menu (€24), €29 (weekday lunch), €50/80 – Carte €55/72

◆ The name is taken from the highest peak in Val d'Isère. Rooms boasting different styles (simple or warm); those facing south overlook the Bellevarde Olympic slope. Modern bar, infinity pool, spa. Modern cuisine (some cheese specialities) served in the large, warm dining room.

Grand Paradis

rest, VISA MC AE

– 04 79 06 11 73 – www.hotelgrandparadis.com – grandparadis@wanadoo.fr – Fax 04 79 41 11 13 – Open beg. December-beg. May

B **t**

40 rm (½ board only) – ½ P €98/300

Rest – Menu €25 (lunch)/57 – Carte €30/60

◆ This Grand Paradise of skiers is a hotel set next to the spectacular Face de Bellevarde. Rooms have either an Austrian or Savoyard decor, according to the floor (south-facing balconies). Lunchtime brasserie menu (more extensive in the evening), carnotzet and weinstub.

La Savoyarde

rest, VISA MC AE

r. Noël Machet – 04 79 06 01 55 – www.la-savoyarde.com – hotel@la-savoyarde.com – Fax 04 79 41 11 29 – Open 11 December-5 May

A **u**

50 rm – €170/235 €250/386, €13 – ½ P €180/248

Rest – *(dinner only)* Menu €45

◆ The rooms, redecorated in an alpine fashion (woodwork), are eminently cosy. Fitness facilities and a cosy fireside sitting room await you in this engaging hotel. A pianist accompanies evening meals; traditional and updated menu.

Kandahar
av. Olympique – 04 79 06 02 39 – www.hotel-kandahar.com – Fax 04 79 41 15 54 – Open early December-early May — A v
41 rm – €138/210 €170/290 **Rest** – (dinner only) Carte €30/65
◆ The name suggests the Far East or a prestigious Austrian ski competition. The spruce, warm rooms are undeniably Savoyard. Alsace and Savoie take pride of place on the menu of this all-wood tavern.

Les Lauzes without rest
pl. de l'Église – 04 79 06 04 20 – www.hotel-lauzes.com – lauzes@club-internet.fr – Fax 04 79 41 96 84 – Open 28 November-4 May — B a
23 rm – €115/177 €136/187
◆ Near the Baroque church. Simplicity, faultless upkeep and a chalet decor depict the rooms; those on the top floor offer a view over the village rooftops.

Altitude
– 04 79 06 12 55 – www.hotelaltitude.com – booking@hotelaltitude.com – Fax 04 79 41 11 09 – Open 1 July-31 August and 1 December-3 May — A k
40 rm – €122/198 €155/294, €15 – ½ P €108/180
Rest – Menu €32/35
◆ This hotel enjoys a matchless location at the foot of the ski lifts. The rooms are adorned with woodwork or are simpler and more practical. Hammam, sauna and fitness facilities. Traditional or regional recipes in the restaurant.

La Becca
Le Laisinant, Iseran road, 0,8 km via ② – 04 79 06 09 48 – www.labecca-val.com – info@labecca-val.com – Fax 04 79 41 12 03 – Open mid-June to August and December to May
11 rm – €90/205 €120/270 – ½ P €149/203
Rest – (open December to May) Menu (€30), €35 (lunch)/64 – Carte €49/73
◆ An authentic pleasant chalet nestling in the heart of a quiet hamlet. The rooms, faithful to local decorative styles (frescoes and painted furniture) are as comfortable as they are delightful. Traditional regional dishes at lunchtime and an inventive modern menu in the evening.

Bellier
– 04 79 06 03 77 – www.hotelbellier.com – info@hotelbellier.com – Fax 04 79 41 14 11 – Open 5 December-5 May — A z
22 rm (½ board only) – ½ P €90/165
Rest – (closed 15 April-5 May and 5-20 December) (dinner only) (residents only) Menu €28
◆ A 1950s building near the centre but in a quiet neighbourhood. Practical rooms, gradually renovated and most with a balcony. Fireside sitting room and sauna. In fine weather, meals are served on the south-facing terrace facing the garden.

La Galise without rest
r. de la Poste – 04 79 06 05 04 – www.lagalise.fr – lagalise@gmail.com – Fax 04 79 41 16 16 – Open 15 December-25 April — B n
30 rm – €64/110 €100/170, €12
◆ The great location, moderate prices and family ambience are among the appeals of this hotel. Simple rooms, some wainscoted, and a buffet breakfast.

L'Avancher without rest
rte du Prariond – 04 79 06 02 00 – www.avancher.com – hotel@avancher.com – Fax 04 79 41 16 07 – Open 6 December-1st May — B r
17 rm – €76/180 €134/200
◆ This chalet is at the foot of Solaise's ski slopes and slightly out of the centre. It offers practical rooms with the most recent being more spacious and decorated in an alpine style.

L'Atelier d'Edmond
au Fornet, rte de l'Iseran, 2 km on the ② – 04 79 00 00 82 – www.atelier-edmond.com – restaurant@atelier-edmond.com – Fax 04 79 00 00 82 – Open 15 December-15 April and closed Sunday dinner and Monday dinner
Rest – Menu (€29), €59 (dinner), €63/69 – Carte €43/56
◆ In homage to the grandfather of the owner of this alpine chalet, the interior reproduces a mountain refuge and a woodworking workshop. Simple menu, more elaborate in the evening.

in la Daille 2 km by ① – ✉ 73150 Val-d'Isère

Le Samovar
– ✆ *04 79 06 13 51 – www.lesamovar.com – samovar@wanadoo.fr*
– Fax 04 79 41 11 08 – Open 10 December-18 April
18 rm – 🛉€ 120/210 🛉🛉€ 130/320
Rest – pizzeria – Menu € 14 (lunch), € 18/35
– Carte € 19/45 dinner only
◆ This large chalet is near the foot of the 'Funival' funicular that climbs the Bellevarde rock. It offers pleasant, cosy rooms, some of which are good for families. Simple meals served in a brasserie-pizzeria (cowhides adorn the walls) or on the terrace.

VALENÇAY – 36 Indre – 323 F4 – **pop. 2 641** – **alt. 140 m** – ✉ **36600** 11 **B3**
Châteaux of the Loire

Paris 233 – Blois 59 – Bourges 73 – Châteauroux 42 – Loches 50 – Vierzon 51

Office de tourisme, 2, avenue de la Résistance ✆ 02 54 00 04 42, Fax 02 54 00 27 67

Castle★★★.

in Veuil 6 km South by D 15 and secondary road – **pop. 366** – **alt. 140 m** – ✉ **36600**

Auberge St-Fiacre
5 r. de la fontaine – ✆ 02 54 40 32 78 – aubergesaintfiacre@wanadoo.fr
– Fax 02 54 40 35 66 – Closed 31 August-24 September, January, Tuesday from September to June, Sunday dinner and Monday
Rest – Menu € 22 (weekdays)/45 – Carte € 34/48
◆ A 17C house whose terrace, shaded by chestnut trees, is lulled by the murmur of a brook. Beautiful rustic interior and up-to-date cuisine.

VALENCE Ⓟ – **26 Drôme** – **332** C4 – **pop. 64 900** – **Built-up area 117 448** – **alt. 126 m** – ✉ **26000** **Lyon - Rhone Valley** 43 **E2**

Paris 558 – Avignon 126 – Grenoble 96 – St-Étienne 121

Valence-Chabeuil: ✆ 04 75 85 26 26, by ③: 5 km AX.

Office de tourisme, 11, boulevard Bancel ✆ 08 92 70 70 99, Fax 04 75 44 90 41

des Chanalets Bourg-lès-Valence Route de Châteauneuf sur Isère, 6 km on the Lyon road, ✆ 04 75 83 16 23

New Golf du Bourget Montmeyran, S : 17 km on D 538, ✆ 04 75 59 48 18

Maison des Têtes★ CY - interior★ of St-Apollinaire cathedral BZ - Champ de Mars ≤★ BZ - Red chalk drawings by Hubert Robert★★ in the musée des Beaux-Arts (Fine arts museum) BZ.

Site★★★ of Cruzol 5 km O.

Plans on following pages

Pic (Anne-Sophie Pic)
285 av. Victor-Hugo – ✆ 04 75 44 15 32
– www.pic-valence.com – contact@pic-valence.com – Fax 04 75 40 96 03
– Closed 2-27 January AX **f**
12 rm – 🛉€ 290/460 🛉🛉€ 290/460, € 28 – 3 suites
Rest Le 7 – see below
Rest – *(closed Sunday and Monday) (pre-book Weekends)* Menu € 110 (Weekday lunch), € 195/320 – Carte € 147/260
Spec. Thon bluefin mariné et marbré au lard colonnata et foie gras des Landes (May to October). Loup au caviar "Jacques Pic". Chocolat alpaco et les fruits exotiques. **Wines** Saint-Péray, Condrieu.
◆ This fine, family-run establishment is an institution in Valence. Elegant, modern rooms with discreet luxury. Following in the footsteps of her grandfather and father, the chef has also reached star studded renown thanks to her deliciously inventive cuisine. Fine wine list.

VALENCE

André (Bd G.) . . . . AV 3
Beaumes (Av. des). . . . . AX 8
Belle Meunière (R.) . . . . AV 10
Bonnet (R. G.). . . . . AV 13
Châteauvert (R.) . . . . AX 18
Grand Charran (Av. du). . . . . AX 34
Kennedy (Bd J.-F.). . . . . AV 40
Lattre-de-Tassigny (Av. Mar. de) . . . . AV 41
Libération (Av. de la). . . . . . . AX 44
Montplaisir (R.) . . . . AVX 52
Roosevelt (Bd Franklin) . . . . AX 67

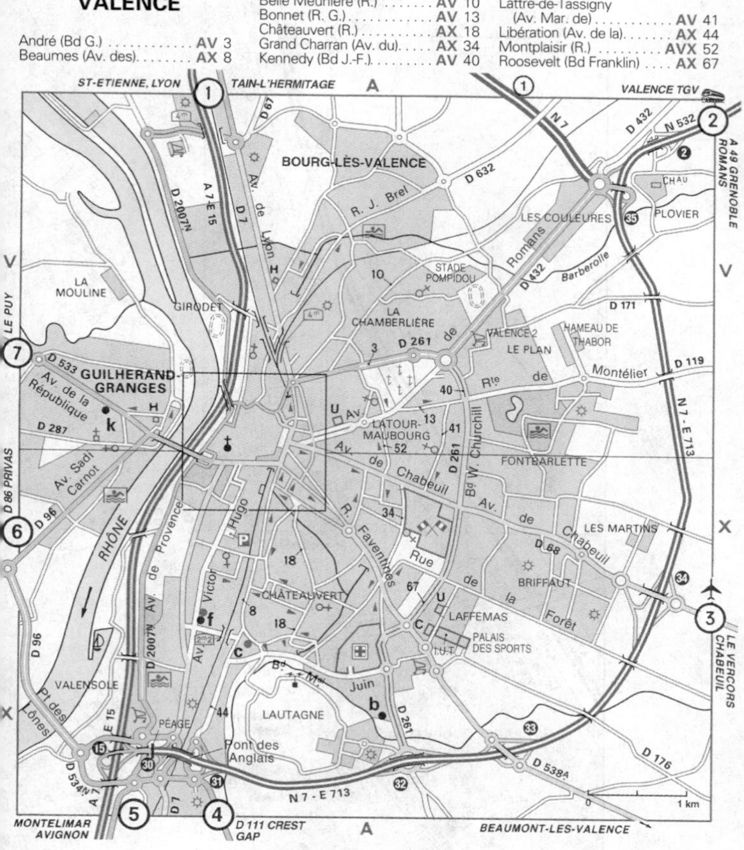

Clos Syrah rm, VISA
bd Pierre Tézier, Quartier Maninet, (rte Montéléger) – ✆ 04 75 55 52 52 – www.clos-syrah.com – info@clos-syrah.com – Fax 04 75 42 27 37 AX **b**
38 rm – †€ 75/90 ††€ 94/124, ☕ € 10 – ½ P € 70/90
Rest – *(closed 21 December-10 January, Saturday and Sunday from June to September)* Menu (€ 20), € 25/35
◆ Near the hospital, this modern Provencal building dates from the 1980s. Rooms with modern furniture overlooking the swimming pool and park. Traditional meals served in a comfortable dining room. Fine terrace.

De France without rest VISA
16 bd du Gén.-de-Gaulle – ✆ 04 75 43 00 87 – www.hotel-valence.com – info@hotel-valence.com – Fax 04 75 55 90 51 CZ **w**
46 rm – †€ 70/125 ††€ 90/125, ☕ € 11
◆ This hotel has been fully renovated and extended. Find simple, modern and elegant guestrooms, meeting rooms, bar, terrace and a private car park.

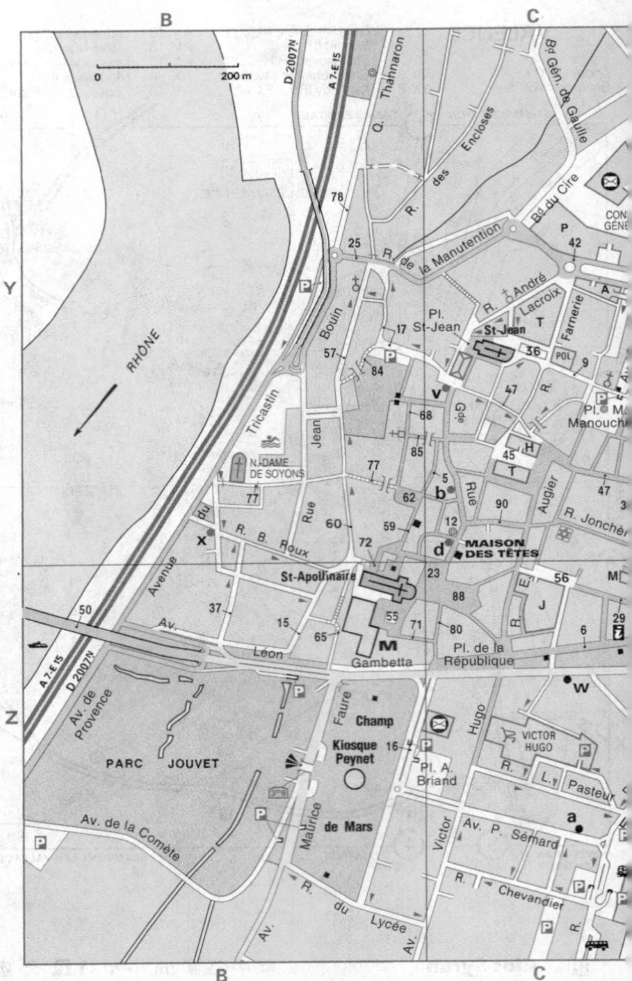

Atrium without rest

20 r. J.-L. Barrault – ✆ 04 75 55 53 62 – www.atrium-hotel.fr – info@atrium-hotel.fr – Fax 04 75 55 53 68 DY **c**

64 rm – 🚹€ 65 🚹🚹€ 73, ☕ € 9

◆ A modern-looking hotel, ideal for a long stay as each room has a kitchenette. The top floor offers duplexes overlooking the Vercors or the Ardèche.

Les Négociants rest,

27 av. Pierre-Sémard – ✆ 04 75 44 01 86 – www.hotel-lesnegociantsvalence.com – hotel.les-negociants@wanadoo.fr – Fax 04 75 44 77 57 CZ **a**

37 rm – 🚹€ 40/71 🚹🚹€ 40/71, ☕ € 6,50 – ½ P € 54/72

Rest – *(closed 11-17 August, 26-31 December, Saturday and Sunday)* Menu (€ 13) – Carte € 23/31

◆ Sober, contemporary-style hotel just a stone's throw from the station. Guestrooms with air-conditioning, in varying shades of brown. Substantial breakfast. Simple family cooking is the order of the day in this contemporary-style restaurant.

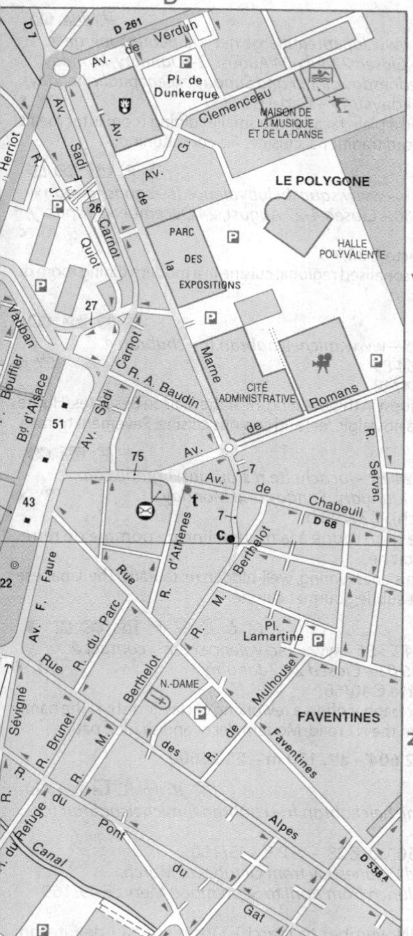

VALENCE

XXX ✿ **Flaveurs** (Baptiste Poinot) AC VISA MC

32 Grande Rue – ✆ 04 75 56 08 40 – poinot.baptiste@neuf.fr – Fax 04 75 43 41 76 – Closed 1st-24 August, 1st-7 January, Sunday and Monday CY **b**

Rest – *(number of covers limited, pre-book)* Menu € 28 (weekday lunch), € 35/67

Spec. Nugget's crousti-fondants de tête de veau. Bar sauvage cuit avec douceur. Poire william pochée au fruit de la passion.

◆ A long dining room with a discreet and elegant decoration, on a small street near Place des Clercs. Contemporary cuisine that strikes the right chord by blending and bringing out flavours.

XX **L'Épicerie** VISA MC AE

18 pl. St-Jean, (ex Belat) – ✆ 04 75 42 74 46 – pierre.seve@free.fr – Fax 04 75 42 10 87 – Closed 28 April-13 May, 29 July-19 August, 23 December-4 January, Saturday lunch and Sunday CY **v**

Rest – Menu (€ 18), € 25/68 – Carte € 36/55

◆ A 16C house offering a choice of settings: warm and rustic, designer or bistro (serving the menu of the day). Pavement terrace. Traditional dishes.

XX **La Petite Auberge**

1 r. Athènes – ✆ 04 75 43 20 30 – www.lapetiteauberge.net – la.petite.auberge@wanadoo.fr – Fax 04 75 42 67 79 – Closed 22 July-24 August, 2-6 January, Monday dinner from May to September, Wednesday dinner and Sunday except public holidays

Rest – Menu (€ 18 bi), € 26 (weekdays)/49 – Carte € 31/57 DY **t**

◆ Rustic family restaurant set behind a plain façade. The smaller dining room is for meals ordered in advance. Reasonably priced traditional cuisine. Air-conditioning.

X **L'Origan**

58 av. Baumes – ✆ 04 75 41 60 39 – www.squashclubvalence.fr – squashorigan@numericable.fr – Fax 04 26 50 32 60 – Closed 4-27 August, 24 December-2 January, Saturday and Sunday AX **c**

Rest – Menu (€ 15), € 18/40 – Carte € 35/45

◆ This riverside restaurant offers personalised regional cuisine in a modern dining room or on the remodelled veranda.

X **Le Bistrot des Clercs**

48 Grande rue – ✆ 04 75 55 55 15 – www.michelchabran.fr – chabran@michelchabran.fr – Fax 04 75 43 64 85 CY **d**

Rest – Menu € 22/31 – Carte € 34/48

◆ Napoleon Bonaparte was once a guest in this building, near the Maison des Têtes (House of Heads). Parisian-style bistro with a nostalgic feel and copious cuisine. Pavement terrace.

X **La Cachette** (Masashi Ijichi)

16 r. des Cévennes – ✆ 04 75 55 24 13 – lacachette.restaurant@gmail.com – Fax 04 75 55 24 13 – Closed 2-20 January, Sunday and Monday BY **x**

Rest – Menu (€ 18 bi), € 25 (lunch), € 37/90 bi

Spec. Terrine de canard. Pavé de thon rouge à la mousseline de pomme de terre. Tarte à l'abricot et crème de pistache.

◆ It is well worth venturing inside this unassuming, well-hidden restaurant. The Japanese born cook cannot be beaten for her subtle gourmet cuisine.

X **Le 7** – Hôtel Pic

285 av. Victor-Hugo – ✆ 04 75 44 53 86 – www.pic-valence.com – contact@pic-valence.com – Fax 04 75 40 96 03 – Closed 2-27 January AX **f**

Rest – Menu (€ 19 bi), € 28 – Carte € 40/66

◆ The other restaurant under the Pic banner offers a reworking of classic dishes. The name refers to the gourmet travellers from the N7 road. Modern decor and shaded patio.

in Pont de l'Isère **9 km by ①** – **pop. 2 604** – **alt. 120 m** – ✉ **26600**

Michel Chabran

N 7 – ✆ 04 75 84 60 09 – www.michelchabran.fr – chabran@michelchabran.fr – Fax 04 75 84 59 65

11 rm – €150/220 €175/350, ☕ € 23 – ½ P € 145/180

Rest – *(closed Sunday dinner and Wednesday from October to March, Wednesday lunch and Thursday lunch from April to September)* Menu € 49/169 – Carte € 95/160

Spec. Plats autour de la truffe (November to March). Dos d'agneau de Siteron. Croustillant aux fraises des bois (spring-summer). **Wines** Hermitage, Saint-Péray.

◆ House with a Rhône pebble façade, offering comfortable rooms, recently refurbished in a modern style. Elegant restaurant serving classic cuisine and a fine selection of Côtes du Rhône wines.

XXX **Auberge Chalaye**

17 r. 16-août-1944 – ✆ 04 75 84 59 40 – Fax 04 75 58 27 06 – Closed lunch except Sunday and public holidays, Monday, Tuesday and Wednesday

Rest – Menu € 33 (dinner), € 50/60 – Carte approx. € 50

◆ Discreet inn hidden behind greenery. Classic cuisine served in three small, rustic-style dining rooms or on the pleasant garden terrace, in fine weather.

in Guilherand-Granges **(07 Ardèche)** – **pop. 10 700** – **alt. 130 m** – ✉ **07500**

Alpes-Cévennes without rest

641 av. de la République – ✆ 04 75 44 61 34 – www.hotelalpescevennes.com – alpescevennes@aol.com – Fax 04 75 41 12 41 – Closed 16-24 August and Sunday

26 rm – €36/40 €42/56, ☕ € 6 AV **k**

◆ This Ardèche hotel is on the right bank of the Rhône. It has large rooms containing mass-produced furniture, which are regularly renovated. Good soundproofing. Friendly service.

VALENCE-SUR-BAÏSE – 32 Gers – 336 E6 – pop. 1 199 – alt. 117 m – ✉ 32310

28 **A2**

Paris 734 – Agen 50 – Auch 36 – Condom 9

Syndicat d'initiative, rue Jules Ferry ✆ 05 62 28 59 19, Fax 05 62 28 97 66

Flaran abbey★ Northwest: 2 km, Languedoc-Roussillon-Tarn Gorges

La Ferme de Flaran

rm, VISA MC AE

Condom road – ✆ 05 62 28 58 22 – www.fermedeflaran.com – hotel-flaran@wanadoo.fr – Fax 05 62 28 56 89 – Closed 21 December-15 January

15 rm – €49/59 €55/65, €8 – ½ P €56/61

Rest – *(closed Tuesday lunch from October to May, Sunday dinner and Monday except from 7 July to 29 August)* Menu (€16), €20/38 – Carte €38/46

◆ This farmhouse, once an outbuilding of the nearby Cistercian abbey, has retained its rustic atmosphere. The comfortable, countrified rooms are quieter on the poolside. Authentic, rustic dining room and pleasant terrace serving carefully prepared dishes with a Gers flavour.

VALENCIENNES – 59 Nord – 302 J5 – pop. 43 100 – Built-up area 357 395 – alt. 22 m – ✉ 59300 Northern France and the Paris Region

31 **C2**

Paris 208 – Arras 68 – Bruxelles 105 – Lille 54 – St-Quentin 80

Office de tourisme, 1, rue Askièvre ✆ 03 27 28 89 10, Fax 03 27 28 89 11

de Mormal Preux-au-Sart Bois Saint Pierre, 13 km on the Maubeuge road, ✆ 03 27 63 07 00

de Valenciennes Marly Rue du Chemin Vert, E : 1 km, ✆ 03 27 46 30 10

Musée des Beaux-Arts★ BY **M** - Bibliothèque des Jésuites★.

Plan on following page

Le Grand Hôtel

VISA MC AE D

8 pl. de la Gare – ✆ 03 27 46 32 01 – www.grand-hotel-de-valenciennes.fr – grandhotel.val@wanadoo.fr – Fax 03 27 29 65 57 AX **d**

95 rm – €82/110 €94/120, €15 – ½ P €105/133

Rest *Le Grand Hôtel* – Menu €30 (weekdays)/50 bi – Carte €41/68

Rest *Brasserie Hans* – Menu (€15) – Carte €23/36

◆ The same family has been welcoming guests to this fine early 20C building for several generations. Comfortable rooms with a classic touch. Traditional restaurant specialising in spit-roast meat and flambéed dishes. The Alsatian spirit pervades throughout the Brasserie Hans.

Auberge du Bon Fermier

VISA MC AE D

64 r. Famars – ✆ 03 27 46 68 25 – www.bonfermier.com – beinethierry@hotmail.com – Fax 03 27 33 75 01 AY **n**

16 rm – €105/110 €125/130, €11

Rest – Menu (€17), €27/49 – Carte €26/52

◆ This authentic 17C post house has kept its charm - old brick and stone façade, characterful rooms with lovely furniture and a pretty interior courtyard. The stables of this inn now house a restaurant-grill. A terrace and game in season.

Le Chat Botté without rest

VISA MC AE D

25 r. Tholozé – ✆ 03 27 14 58 59 – www.hotel-lechatbotte.com – hotel.lechatbotte@wanadoo.fr – Fax 03 27 14 58 60 AX **p**

33 rm – €75/87 €75/91, €11

◆ Wrought iron, wood, contemporary furniture and bright colours set the amusing scene in this pleasant welcoming house; peaceful cosy bedrooms.

Baudouin without rest

P VISA MC AE D

90 r. Baudouin l'Édifieur – ✆ 03 27 22 80 80 – www.ibishotel.com – h6549@accor.com – Fax 03 27 22 80 81 BZ **k**

72 rm – €70/74 €70/74, €8

◆ A hotel near the Nungesser football stadium. Practical rooms undergoing gradual renovation. Secure car park, garage and several small kitchens.

Notre Dame without rest

VISA MC AE

1 pl. Abbé Thellier de Poncheville – ✆ 03 27 42 30 00 – www.hotel-valenciennes-notredame.com – hotel.notredame@wanadoo.fr – Fax 03 27 45 12 68 – Closed 20 December-4 January BY **s**

35 rm – €55/65 €58/70, €9

◆ Two buildings facing a 15C church. Bourgeois rooms in the old part, more functional in the other and quiet all around for those facing the garden.

VALENCIENNES

Street	Grid	No.
Albert-1er (Av.)	BY	2
Amsterdam (Av. d')	BY	5
Armes (Pl. d')	AY	6
Barbusse (R. H.)	CV	8
Bourgeois (Ch. des)	BV	9
Cairns (Av. Serg.)	ABZ	13
Capucins (R. des)	BY	15
Cardon (Pl.)	BZ	16
Charles-Quint (R.)	CV	17
Clemenceau (Av. G.)	AX	18
Desandrouin (Av.)	BV	20
Digue (R. de la)	AZ	22
Duchesnois (Av.)	CV	23
Dunkerque (Av. de)	AX	25
Faidherbe (Av.)	BV	26
Famars (R. de)	AYZ	
Ferrand (R.)	AY	33
Fg de Cambrai (R.)	BV	29
Fg de Paris (R. du)	BV	30
Foch (Av. Mar.)	AX	34
Froissart (Pl. J.)	BY	35
Gaulle (Pl. Gén.-de)	BY	36
Glacis (R. des)	CV	37
Jacob (Pont)	AX	38
Jean-Jaurès (R.)	BV	39
Juin (Av. du Mar.)	AX	40
Lattre-de-Tassigny (Av. Mar.-de)	AX	42
Leclerc (Av. Mar.)	AX	43
Liège (Av. de)	BX	44
Lille (R. de)	AX	46
Marquis (R. du)	CV	48
Paix (R. de la)	BY	50
Paris (R. de)	AY	52
Perdrix (R. J.)	CV	53
Pompidou (Av. G.)	AZ	54
Reims (Av. de)	BZ	56
St-Amand (Av. de)	BV	58
St-Géry (R.)	BY	59
Sénateur-Girard (Av.)	AX	63
Tholozé (R.)	AX	65
Vaillant-Couturier (R. Paul)	BV	67
Vauban (Av.)	BV	68
Verdun (Av. de)	BZ	69
Vieille-Poissonnerie (R.)	AY	73
Villars (Av.)	AY	74
Watteau (Square)	AY	76

XX **L'Endroit**

69 r. du Quesnoy – ☎ 03 27 42 99 23 – www.restaurant-lendroit.fr – lionel.coint@nordnet.fr – Fax 03 27 42 99 23 – Closed Sunday dinner and Monday BY **f**

Rest – Menu (€ 25), € 30 – Carte € 45/55

◆ A TV screen crowns the dining room, broadcasting the bustle of the kitchen live. Elegant contemporary setting, fashionable atmosphere, market-fresh menu.

XX **Les Salons Brabant**

68 r. de Paris – ☎ 03 27 26 04 03 – www.lessalonsbrabant.com – lessalonsbrabant@orange.fr – Fax 03 27 26 04 03 – Closed Sunday dinner and Monday AY **e**

Rest – Menu € 31 (weekdays)/47 – Carte € 40/55

Rest *La Véranda* – *(closed Sunday and Monday)* Menu (€ 11), € 17 bi (weekday lunch)/25 – Carte € 23/31

◆ Napoleon III style decor, (mouldings, stucco, paintings, etc.) and contemporary furniture provide an original setting for this lovely glass-roofed dining room. Traditional fare. A bistro-style setting and simple cuisine supplemented by daily specials at the Véranda.

in Quiévrechain 12 km northeast by D 630 – **pop. 5 705 – alt. 32 m** – ✉ **59920**

XX **Le Manoir de Tombelle**

135 av. J. Jaurès – ☎ 03 27 35 12 30 – Fax 03 27 26 27 61 – Closed 1-19 August, 26 December-2 January and dinner except Saturday

Rest – Menu (€ 20), € 25 (weekday lunch), € 27/49 – Carte approx. € 48

◆ Bourgeois 1920s villa in a large garden with a pond. Comfortably furnished dining rooms with fireplace and arbour. Traditional cuisine.

in Artres 11 km by ④, D 958 and D 400 – **pop. 1 057 – alt. 65 m** – ✉ **59269**

La Gentilhommière

(opposite the church) – ☎ 03 27 28 18 80 – www.hotel-lagentilhommiere.com – la.gentilhommiere@wanadoo.fr – Fax 03 27 28 18 81 – Closed 2-27 August, 26-30 December and Sunday dinner

10 rm – †€ 85 ††€ 100, ☐ € 11 **Rest** – Menu € 36/62 – Carte € 39/63

◆ This 18C farm set in two hectares of greenery has been well renovated. The spacious quiet rooms overlook an interior garden. Vaults and red-brick walls form the backdrop to the generous helpings of modern food.

Z. I. de Prouvy-Rouvignies 5 km by ⑤ and D 630 – ✉ **59300 Valenciennes**

Novotel

rm,

Parc d'activité de l' Aérodrome – ☎ 03 27 21 12 12 – www.novotel.com – h0456@accor.com – Fax 03 27 21 06 02

80 rm – †€ 62/150 ††€ 62/150, ☐ € 17 **Rest** – Carte € 25/45

◆ By the motorway from Paris to Brussels and 15 mins from the centre, this hotel has recently been renovated to the chain's new standards (pleasant contemporary interior). Stop for lunch or dinner in the restaurant.

VALESCURE – 83 Var – **340** P5 – see St-Raphaël

VALGORGE – 07 Ardèche – **331** G6 – **pop. 407 – alt. 560 m** – ✉ **07110** 44 **A3**

Lyon - Rhone Valley

Paris 614 – Alès 76 – Aubenas 37 – Langogne 46 – Privas 69 – Le Puy-en-Velay 83

Le Tanargue

– ☎ 04 75 88 98 98 – www.hotel-le-tanargue.com – hoteltanargue@wanadoo.fr – Fax 04 75 88 96 09 – Open 15 March-25 November and closed Sunday evening and Monday except from 5 April to 28 September and autumn school holidays

22 rm – †€ 37/51 ††€ 46/59, ☐ € 8 – ½ P € 45/55

Rest – Menu (€ 11), € 16/34 – Carte € 32/50

◆ Family-run inn at the foot of the Tanargue range. Some of the comfortable, immaculately kept rooms boast a balcony overlooking the park or the valley. Rustic-style dining room decorated with old objects and furnishings. Local gastronomic products on sale.

VALIGNAT – 03 Allier – 326 F5 – see Charroux

VALLAURIS – 06 Alpes-Maritimes – 341 D6 – see Golfe-Juan

VALLERAUGUE – 30 Gard – 339 G4 – pop. 1 081 – alt. 346 m 23 C2

– ✉ 30570 Languedoc-Roussillon-Tarn Gorges

Paris 684 – Mende 100 – Millau 75 – Nîmes 86 – Le Vigan 22

Office de tourisme, quartier des Horts ✆ 04 67 82 25 10, Fax 04 67 64 82 15

Hostellerie Les Bruyères

VISA

– ✆ 04 67 82 20 06 – Fax 04 67 82 20 06 – Open 1st May-5 October

20 rm – €48 €48/61, €8 – ½ P €48/55

Rest – Menu €16/38 – Carte €30/47

◆ Former post-house in the heart of this picturesque Cévennes village. A fine staircase leads to the simple, neat rooms equipped with comfortable beds. The countrified dining room leads onto a charming riverside terrace in summer.

Mont-Aigoual road 4 km on D 986 – ✉ 30570

Auberge Cévenole

VISA

La Pénarié – ✆ 04 67 82 25 17 – auberge.cevenole@wanadoo.fr – Fax 04 67 82 26 26 – Closed 1st December-2 January, Monday evening and Tuesday except July-August

6 rm – €42 €42, €7 – ½ P €47

Rest – Menu (€13), €18/29 – Carte €20/48

◆ The Hérault idles at the foot of this pleasant Cévennes inn on the Mt Aigoual road. Small renovated rooms with regional furniture. Attractive dining room (beams, fireplace, rural objects) and terrace overlooking the river.

VALLET – 44 Loire-Atlantique – 316 I5 – pop. 7 906 – alt. 54 m 34 B2

– ✉ 44330

Paris 375 – Ancenis 27 – Cholet 36 – Clisson 10 – Nantes 27

Syndicat d'initiative, 1, place Charles-de-Gaulle ✆ 02 40 36 35 87, Fax 02 40 36 29 13

Château d'Yseron without rest

P VISA

4 km north-east on D 116 – ✆ 02 51 71 70 40 – www.yseron.net – ostalbin@wanadoo.fr – Fax 02 51 71 70 11

5 rm – €80/120 €80/120

◆ Charming residence dating from 1830 set in the middle of the vineyards. Furniture from the 18C and 19C in the bedrooms. Collection of beautiful paintings and Muscadet produced on site.

Don Quichotte with rm

AC rest, P VISA

35 rte de Clisson – ✆ 02 40 33 99 67 – donquichottevallet@wanadoo.fr – Fax 02 40 33 99 72 – Closed 21 July-4 August, 21 December-5 January, Sunday dinner and Monday lunch

12 rm – €55 €59, €9,50 – ½ P €58 **Rest** – Menu (€14), €20/33

◆ Large murals decorate the walls of this former mill situated among the vineyards. Traditional dishes according to seasonal market produce (preferably organic) served in dining room/veranda.

VALLIÈRES – 37 Indre-et-Loire – 317 M4 – see Tours

VALLOIRE – 73 Savoie – 333 L7 – pop. 1 243 – alt. 1 430 m – Winter sports : 1 430/2 600 m 2 31 – ✉ 73450 French Alps 45 D2

Paris 664 – Albertville 91 – Briançon 52 – Chambéry 104 – Lanslebourg-Mont-Cenis 57

Office de tourisme, rue des Grandes Alpes ✆ 04 79 59 03 96, Fax 04 79 59 09 66

Col du Télégraphe ≤★ North: 5 km.

Grand Hôtel de Valloire et du Galibier
r. des Grandes-Alpes – ✆ 04 79 59 00 95 – www.grand-hotel-valloire.com – info@grand-hotel-valloire.com – Fax 04 79 59 09 41 – Open 13 June-12 September and 19 December-10 April
44 rm – †€ 70/90 ††€ 70/100, ☐ € 14 – ½ P € 75/105
Rest *L'Escarnavé* – Menu € 24/61 – Carte € 38/68
♦ An imposing hotel, facing the slopes, with spacious and renovated rooms. Reserve those facing south and east. Fine dining room in a rotunda set around a copper fireplace where bonfires ("escarnavé", in the local dialect) are lit; classic cuisine.

Christiania
av. de la Vallée d'Or – ✆ 04 79 59 00 57 – www.christiania-hotel.com – info@christiania-hotel.com – Fax 04 79 59 00 06 – Open 15 June-15 September and 13 December-20 April
24 rm – †€ 56/69 ††€ 59/74, ☐ € 10 – 2 suites – ½ P € 59/79
Rest – Menu € 17/35 – Carte € 27/52
♦ Chalet decked with flowers, on the avenue where an unusual snow-sculpture competition takes place. Well-kept rooms, renovated in an alpine spirit. One can be sure of a warm welcome in this country style restaurant. The bar is a meeting place for the resort's ski instructors.

in Verneys 2 km south - ✉73450 **Valloire**

Relais du Galibier
– ✆ 04 79 59 00 45 – www.relais-galibier.com – info@relais-galibier.com – Fax 04 79 83 31 89 – Open 13 June-12 September and 19 December-5 April
26 rm – †€ 53/57 ††€ 57/65, ☐ € 10 – ½ P € 58/79
Rest – Menu € 17, € 23/34 – Carte € 26/37
♦ Welcoming hotel in the peace and quiet of pastures in summer and 100 metres from the slopes in winter. Some rooms with views of the Grand Galibier. Dining room lit by large picture windows, and copious cuisine based on regional products.

VALLON-PONT-D'ARC – 07 Ardèche – 331 I7 – pop. 2 359 – alt. 117 m – ✉ 07150 Lyon - Rhone Valley

44 **A3**

Paris 658 – Alès 47 – Aubenas 32 – Avignon 81 – Carpentras 95 – Montélimar 59

Office de tourisme, 1, place de l'ancienne gare ✆ 04 75 88 04 01, Fax 04 75 88 41 09

Gorges de l'Ardèche★★★ Southeast - Arche★★ de Pont d'Arc Southeast: 5 km.

Le Clos des Bruyères
rm, rest, rm,
rte des Gorges – ✆ 04 75 37 18 85 – www.closdesbruyeres.fr – closdesbruyeres@online.fr – Fax 04 75 37 14 89 – Open April-end September
32 rm – †€ 58/75 ††€ 60/75, ☐ € 8 – ½ P € 59/65
Rest – ✆ 04 75 37 20 92 *(closed Wednesday lunch)* Menu (€ 11), € 23/30 – Carte € 21/37
♦ A newly established hotel situated 100m from the River Ardèche (canoe hire). Spacious, discreetly decorated rooms, with balconies or opening onto the garden. Beneath the timber ceiling of the dining room you will taste traditional fare with a regional slant.

Le Manoir du Raveyron
rm,
r. Henri Barbusse – ✆ 04 75 88 03 59 – www.manoir-du-raveyron.com – le.manoir.du.raveyron@wanadoo.fr – Fax 04 75 37 11 12 – Open from mid-March to mid-October
8 rm ☐ – †€ 55/60 ††€ 66/88 – ½ P € 57/67
Rest – *(dinner only except Sunday)* Menu € 29, € 35/48 – Carte € 36/48
♦ This 16C residence situated in a quiet street has small, attractive and personalised rooms. Pleasant, shady and flower-decked courtyard. Pleasant, vaulted dining room where you can enjoy modern dishes prepared with local produce.

VALLORCINE – 74 Haute-Savoie – 328 O4 – pop. 390 – alt. 1 260 m – Winter sports : 1 260/1 400 m 2 – ✉ 74660 French Alps

45 **D1**

Paris 628 – Annecy 115 – Chamonix-Mont-Blanc 19 – Thonon-les-Bains 96

Office de tourisme, Maison du Betté ✆ 04 50 54 60 71, Fax 04 50 54 61 73

L'Ermitage without rest
at Buet, 2 km south-west on D 1506 and secondary road – ✆ 04 50 54 60 09 – www.chamonix-montblanc.net/ermitage/ – hotel-ermitage@wanadoo.fr – Fax 04 50 54 64 38 – Open 7 February-4 May, 7 June-21 September and 26 December-4 January
15 rm – †€ 40/70 ††€ 68/80, ☕ € 11
◆ A charming chalet with a warm atmosphere, overlooking the village, just 400 m from the railway station. Simple, differently furnished rooms. Small pleasantly shaded garden.

VALLOUX – 89 Yonne – 319 G6 – see Avallon

VALMONT – 76 Seine-Maritime – 304 D3 – pop. 993 – alt. 60 m – ✉ 76540 Normandy 33 C1

Paris 193 – Bolbec 22 – Dieppe 58 – Fécamp 11 – Le Havre 48 – Rouen 67 – Yvetot 28

Syndicat d'initiative, Mairie ✆ 02 35 10 08 12, Fax 02 35 10 08 12

Abbey★.

Le Bec au Cauchois with rm
22 r. A.-Fiquet, 1.5 km west by Fécamp road – ✆ 02 35 29 77 56 – www.lebecaucauchois.com – lebecaucauchois@orange.fr – Fax 02 35 29 77 52 – Closed 5-22 October and 4-28 January
5 rm – †€ 75 ††€ 75, ☕ € 10
Rest – *(closed Wednesday except dinner from May to September and Tuesday)* Menu (€ 18), € 27/56 – Carte € 41/52
◆ An ideal gourmet stop, this inn serves tasty up-to-date recipes made with local produce. Dine in a choice of a rustic or contemporary decor. All the bright, simple ground floor guestrooms overlook the garden or the pond.

VALOJOULX – 24 Dordogne – 329 H5 – pop. 236 – alt. 75 m – ✉ 24290 4 D1

Paris 523 – Bordeaux 195 – Périgueux 65 – Brive-la-Gaillarde 53 – Sarlat-la-Canéda 25

La Licorne
– ✆ 05 53 50 77 77 – www.licorne-lascaux.com – licornelascaux@free.fr – Fax 05 53 50 77 77 – Open from April to October
5 rm ☕ – †€ 58 ††€ 65/90
Table d'hôte – *(closed Sunday, Monday, Tuesday and Wednesday)* Menu € 22
◆ Dreaming of a break combining tranquillity, discovering the Périgord and a convivial atmosphere? This charming residence is ideal. Prettily rustic rooms and a large garden. Charming table d'hôte under a magnificent timber framed roof.

VALRAS-PLAGE – 34 Hérault – 339 E9 – pop. 3 625 – alt. 1 m – Casino – ✉ 34350 Languedoc-Roussillon-Tarn Gorges 23 C2

Paris 767 – Agde 25 – Béziers 16 – Montpellier 76

Office de tourisme, place René Cassin ✆ 04 67 32 36 04, Fax 04 67 32 33 41

Mira-Mar rm, rm,
bd Front de Mer – ✆ 04 67 32 00 31 – www.hotel-miramar.org – info@hotel-miramar.org – Fax 04 67 32 51 21 – Open March-end October
27 rm – †€ 59/102 ††€ 59/102, ☕ € 8 – 3 suites – ½ P € 55/81
Rest – *(closed Sunday dinner and Wednesday except July-August)* Menu (€ 16) – Carte € 27/57
◆ It's true! Most rooms look out to sea - "mira el mar" as they say in Spanish. Bright, practical rooms. Four spacious apartments. Ice-cream bar. Quietly refined dining room, terrace overlooking the sea and traditional menu.

Albizzia without rest
bd Chemin Creux – 04 67 37 48 48 – hotelalbizziavalras@wanadoo.fr – Fax 04 67 37 58 10
27 rm – €46/76 €48/76, €7
◆ Pleasant hotel 200m from the beach with smart surroundings. Functional rooms, some with loggia. Delightful little Mediterranean garden and pool.

Le Delphinium
av. Élysées, (opposite the casino) – 04 67 32 73 10 – ledelphinium@wanadoo.fr – Fax 04 67 32 73 10 – Closed for the autumn school holidays and Monday except from April to October
Rest – Menu (€21 bi), €28/48 – Carte €52/70
◆ Discreet façade near the casino, housing a bright dining room with wrought-iron furniture. Summer terrace and sunny up-to-date cuisine.

La Méditerranée
32 r. Ch. Thomas – 04 67 32 38 60 – mediterranee32@wanadoo.fr – Fax 04 67 32 30 91 – Closed 12-30 November, 5-23 January, Tuesday except dinner in season and Monday
Rest – Menu €17/45 – Carte €25/70
◆ Small family-run restaurant in a pedestrian street, near the mouth of the River Orb. Traditional fish cuisine served in a rustic setting. Large terrace.

VALRÉAS – 84 Vaucluse – 332 C7 – pop. 9 771 – alt. 250 m – ✉ 84600 40 A2

Provence

Paris 639 – Avignon 67 – Crest 51 – Montélimar 38 – Nyons 14 – Orange 37

Office de tourisme, avenue Maréchal Leclerc 04 90 35 04 71, Fax 04 90 35 03 60

Au Délice de Provence
6 La Placette, (town centre) – 04 90 28 16 91 – Fax 04 90 37 42 49 – Closed Tuesday and Wednesday
Rest – Menu (€17), €26/30 – Carte €47/64
◆ Within the walls of an old synagogue, this restaurant offers appetising contemporary cuisine in a large, sunlit dining room, divided into two by attractive arches.

VALS-LES-BAINS – 07 Ardèche – 331 I6 – pop. 3 741 – alt. 210 m – Spa : late Feb.-early Dec. – Casino – ✉ 07600 Lyon - Rhone Valley 44 A3

Paris 629 – Aubenas 6 – Langogne 58 – Privas 33 – Le Puy-en-Velay 87

Office de tourisme, 116 bis, avenue Jean Jaurès 04 75 89 02 03, Fax 04 75 89 02 04

Grand Hôtel de Lyon rm,
11 av. P. Ribeyre – 04 75 37 43 70 – www.grandhoteldelyon.fr – info@grandhoteldelyon.fr – Fax 04 75 37 59 11 – Open 10 April-4 October s
34 rm – €60/72 €68/94, €9 – ½ P €56/69
Rest – Menu (€16), €22/45 – Carte €27/50
◆ This very centrally located hotel is just 100m from the park of the intermittent spring. Spacious, renovated and well-kept rooms. Indoor/outdoor pool. Immense bay windows light up the pleasant dining room adorned with an unusual fresco.

Helvie
5 av. Expilly – 04 75 94 65 85 – www.hotel-helvie.com – courriel@hotel-helvie.com – Fax 04 75 37 47 63 b
27 rm – €65/150 €65/150, €12 – ½ P €98/184
Rest – Menu (€19 bi), €29/59 – Carte €53/63
◆ This hotel is located near the park and casino. It has its sparkle back thanks to refurbished decor, which is chic, classic and refined. Comfortable rooms, fine lounge bar and pool. Modern cuisine in the elegant, well-presented restaurant.

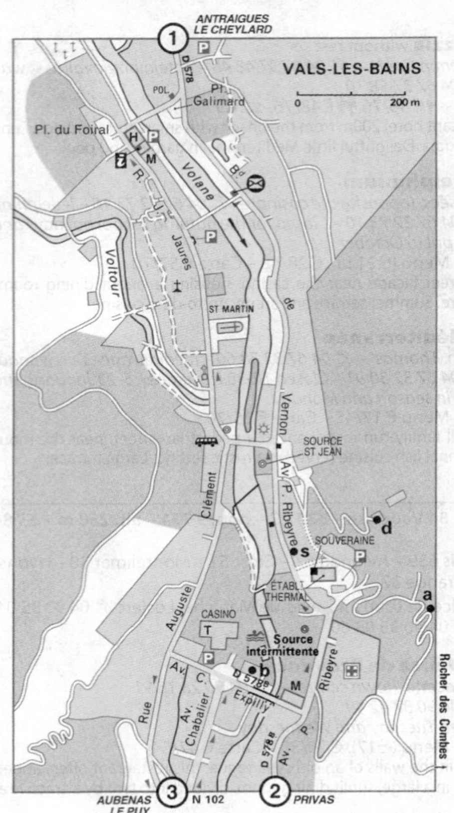

Château Clément

La Châtaigneraie – ✆ 04 75 87 40 13 – www.chateauclement.com – contact@chateauclement.com – Closed 15 December-15 March **a**

5 rm ☕ – 🚹€ 135 🚹🚹€ 135/230

Table d'hôte – *(closed Tuesday, Wednesday and Sunday)* Menu € 55 bi/60 bi

◆ This 19C property, surrounded by a park planted with exotic plant species, overlooks the town. Admire the elegant sitting rooms and superb, tastefully decorated bedrooms and suite. Traditional menu made with organic and regional produce at the table d'hôte.

Villa Aimée

8 montée des Aulagniers – ✆ 04 75 88 52 75 – www.villaaimee.com – villa.aimee@hotmail.com – Fax 04 75 88 52 75 **d**

4 rm ☕ – 🚹€ 75/110 🚹🚹€ 89/125 – 2 suites

Table d'hôte – *(booking essential)* Menu € 30 bi

◆ On the upper reaches of the resort, this large villa enjoys a tranquil location and fine views. Personalised rooms and suites, swimming pool and charming welcome. Meals served to residents in a rustic dining room.

VAL-THORENS – 73 Savoie – 333 M6 – alt. 2 300 m – Winter sports : 2 300/3 200 m 🚡 4 ⛷ 25 – ✉ 73440 St-Martin-de-Belleville ▮ French Alps 46 **F2**

▶ Paris 640 – Albertville 60 – Chambéry 109 – Moûtiers 36

ℹ Office de tourisme, immeuble Eskival ✆ 04 79 00 08 08, Fax 04 79 00 00 04

👁 Cime de Caron ❋★★★ (access by cable car from Caron).

Le Val Thorens rm, VISA MC AE

– 04 79 00 04 33 – *www.levalthorens.com – contact@levalthorens.com – Fax 04 79 00 09 40 – Open 5 December-26 April*
80 rm – € 100/202 € 160/324 – 1 suite
Rest ***Le Bellevillois*** – *(Open 7 December-19 April) (dinner only)* Menu € 48 – Carte € 42/63
Rest ***La Fondue*** – *(open 22 December-14 April) (dinner only)* Menu € 23 – Carte € 30/39
◆ A modern building in the centre of the resort with large rooms with balconies. Piano bar, sauna and solarium. Restaurant offering traditional and brasserie dishes. Le Bellevillois offers classic cuisine. Alpine ambience and recipes at La Fondue.

Mercure rm, VISA MC AE

– 04 79 00 04 04 – *www.mercurevalthorens.com – reception@mercurevalthorens.com – Fax 04 79 00 05 93 – Open 2 December-29 April*
104 rm – € 112 € 160, € 10 – ½ P € 140/160
Rest – Menu (€ 16), € 30 (dinner)/40 – Carte approx. € 32
◆ A comfortable hotel at the foot of the slopes, with rooms offering fine views of the glaciers. Lively bar and shop selling skiing equipment.

Le Sherpa rest, VISA MC

r. de Gébroulaz – *04 79 00 00 70 – www.lesherpa.com – courrier@lesherpa.com – Fax 04 79 00 08 03 – Open 29 November-3 May*
52 rm (½ board only) – 4 suites – ½ P € 85/185
Rest – Menu (€ 22), € 33 (dinner) – Carte € 28/48
◆ Modern chalet a stone's throw from the ski slopes. Renovated rooms and duplex apartments: wood panelling, white walls and pine furniture. Sitting-room bar with fireplace; internet access. The restaurant has a warm Savoyard chalet atmosphere and offers traditional dishes.

Les Trois Vallées VISA MC AE

Grande Rue – *04 79 00 01 86 – www.hotel3vallees.com – reservation@hotel3vallees.com – Fax 04 79 00 04 08 – Open 24 November-5 May*
29 rm – € 70/170 € 108/240
Rest – *(dinner only)* Menu € 25/31 – Carte € 28/53
◆ The largest ski area in the Alps lends its name to this modern building. Functional rooms, including seven for families. Fine view of the peaks from the lounge-bar. Dining room decorated in Alpine style. Traditional menu.

XXX **L'Oxalys** (Jean Sulpice) P VISA MC AE

– *04 79 00 12 00 – www.jean-sulpice.com – jean-sulpice@loxalys.com – Fax 04 79 00 24 10 – Open 4 July-29 August and 1st December-24 April*
Rest – Menu € 48/150 bi – Carte € 80/110
Spec. Soupe de châtaigne en chaud-froid de parmesan et truffe (winter). Féra du lac Léman, légumes d'hiver sur fine pâte de polenta. Pomme en coque meringuée, miel de montagne et parfum d'Antésite. **Wines** Vin de Pays de l'Allobrogie, Mondeuse d'Arbin.
◆ Attractive contemporary decor, a superb terrace opposite the slopes and inventive good food by a chef who is also a sommelier.

LE VALTIN – 88 Vosges – 314 K4 – pop. 95 – alt. 751 m – ✉ 88230 27 D3

Paris 440 – Colmar 46 – Épinal 55 – Guebwiller 55 – St-Dié 27 – Col de la Schlucht 10

XX **Auberge du Val Joli** with rm P VISA MC AE

12 bis le village – *03 29 60 91 37 – www.levaljoli.com – contact@levaljoli.com – Fax 03 29 60 81 73 – Closed Sunday dinner, Monday dinner, Tuesday lunch except school holidays and Monday lunch except public holidays*
10 rm – € 82 € 82/140, € 12 – ½ P € 72/90
Rest – Menu € 22 (weekdays), € 31/70 – Carte € 42/70
◆ Two dining areas, one rustic, the other with a conservatory leading onto the terrace facing the countryside. Regional dishes with modern touches. Renovated rooms.

LA VANCELLE – 67 Bas-Rhin – 315 H7 – see Lièpvre

VANDŒUVRE-LÈS-NANCY – 54 Meurthe-et-Moselle – **307** H7 – **see Nancy**

VANNES 🅿 – **56 Morbihan** – **308** O9 – **pop. 53 700** – **Built-up area 118 029** – **alt. 20 m** – ✉ **56000** ▮ **Brittany** 9 **A3**

- Paris 459 – Quimper 122 – Rennes 110 – St-Brieuc 107 – St-Nazaire 86
- Office de tourisme, 1, rue Thiers ✆ 08 25 13 56 10, Fax 02 97 47 29 49
- de Baden Baden Kernic, 14 km on the Auray road and the D 101, ✆ 02 97 57 18 96
- Old town ★★ AZ : Place Henri-IV★ AZ 10, St-Pierre cathedral ★ B, Ramparts★, Promenade de la Garenne ≤★★ - La Cohue★ (former covered market) - Musée archéologique★ - Aquarium océanographique et tropical★ - Golfe du Morbihan ★★ by boat.

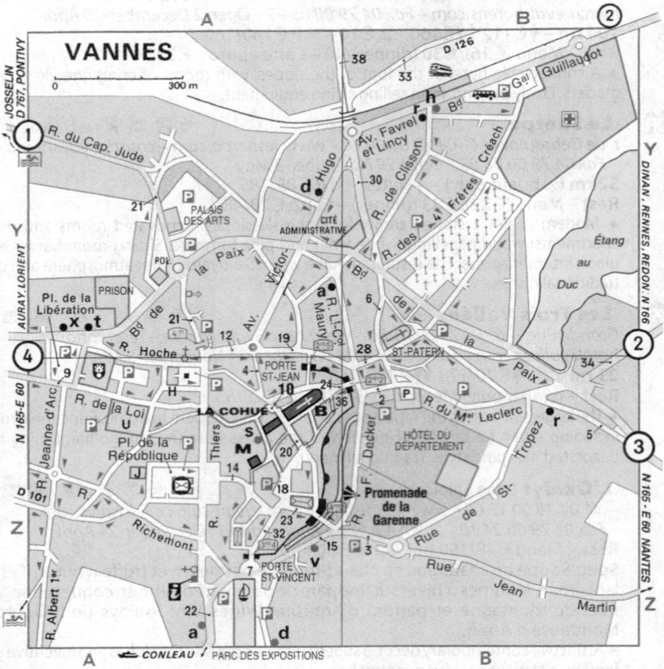

Allain Legrand (R.) .... BZ 2	Henri-IV (Pl.) .... AZ 10	Port (R. du) .... AZ 22
Bazvalan (R. J. de) .... BZ 3	Lices (Pl. des) .... AZ 18	St-Nicolas (R.) .... BZ 28
Billault (R.) .... AZ 4	Mené (R. du) .... AY 19	St-Symphorien (Av.) .... BY 30
Briand (R. A.) .... BZ 5	Monnaie (R. de la) .... AZ 20	St-Vincent-Ferrier (R.) .... AZ 32
Le Brix (R. J.) .... AY 12	Monnet (Av. J.) .... AY 21	Strasbourg (R. de) .... BY 33
Fontaine (R. de la) .... BY 6	Le Pontois (R. A.) .... AZ 15	Verdun (Av. de) .... BZ 34
Gambetta (Pl.) .... AZ 7	Porte-Poterne (R.) .... AZ 23	Vierges (R. des) .... AZ 36
Gougaud (R. J.) .... AZ 9	Porte-Prison (R.) .... AZ 24	Wilson (Av.) .... ABY 38
Le Hellec (R.) .... AZ 14		

 **Mercure** VISA

The Gulf park, 2 km south Conleau road – ✆ *02 97 40 44 52* – *www.mercure-vannes.com* – *h2182-gm@accor-hotels.com* – *Fax 02 97 63 03 20*

89 rm – †€ 65/115 ††€ 69/125, ☐ € 14

Rest ***Brasserie Edgar*** – ✆ *02 97 40 68 08* – Menu (€ 18), € 23 – Carte € 26/45

◆ Near the Aquarium, a modern hotel providing spacious and soundproofed rooms with views of the Morbihan gulf. The bay windows of the dining room open onto the terrace facing a little corner of greenery.

Villa Kerasy without rest
20 av. Favrel et Lincy – ☎ 02 97 68 36 83 – www.villakerasy.com – info@villakerasy.com – Fax 02 97 68 36 84 – Closed 1st-29 March and 15 November-11 December BY **r**
15 rm – †€ 97/128 ††€ 125/228, ☕ € 14
◆ Each room is unusually decorated on the theme of the East India Company's ports of call. Charming, attentive service. Delicious breakfasts. Japanese garden.

Best Western Vannes Centre
6 pl. de la Libération – ☎ 02 97 63 20 20 – www.bestwestern-vannescentre.com – info@bestwestern-vannescentre.com – Fax 02 97 63 80 22 AY **t**
58 rm – †€ 75/110 ††€ 75/110, ☕ € 13
Rest – Menu (€ 15) – Carte approx. € 26
◆ Modern hotel close to the historic centre and the shops. Contemporary rooms with a simple and refined décor. Meeting room for business clients. Fitness centre. Traditional cuisine served in the restaurant, which has modern décor in line with the location.

Marébaudière without rest
4 r. A. Briand – ☎ 02 97 47 34 29 – www.marebaudiere.com – marebaudiere@wanadoo.fr – Fax 02 97 54 14 11 BZ **r**
41 rm – †€ 76/94 ††€ 76/94, ☕ € 10
◆ A regional, slate roofed building, five minutes from the ramparts. Home to colourful (blue, yellow and rust), highly practical and well-equipped rooms. Immaculate upkeep.

Manche-Océan without rest
31 r. Lt-Col. Maury – ☎ 02 97 47 26 46 – www.manche-ocean.com – info@manche-ocean.com – Fax 02 97 47 30 86 – Closed 18 December-10 January AY **a**
41 rm – †€ 51/85 ††€ 61/95, ☕ € 8,50
◆ Recently renovated hotel: spacious well-equipped rooms (king size beds, functionally furnishings), excellent soundproofing and seminar facilities.

Kyriad Image Ste-Anne rm,
8 pl. de la Libération – ☎ 02 97 63 27 36 – www.kyriad-vannes.fr – kyriad.vannes@wanadoo.fr – Fax 02 97 40 97 02 AY **x**
33 rm – †€ 66/73 ††€ 66/80, ☕ € 8 – ½ P € 59/65
Rest – Menu (€ 16), € 21/30 – Carte € 36/46
◆ Central hotel providing comfortable rooms with air conditioning and soundproofing. Brand new well-equipped seminar facilities. The restaurant sports a Breton decor (carved wood panelling and works by a local artist). Classic menu.

France without rest
57 av. V. Hugo – ☎ 02 97 47 27 57 – www.hotelfrance-vannes.com – hotel-de-france-vannes@wanadoo.fr – Fax 02 97 42 59 17 – Closed 21 December-5 January AY **d**
30 rm – †€ 54/66 ††€ 58/81, ☕ € 8 – 1 suite
◆ This hotel boasts a distinctive wood and zinc façade. Spruce, functional rooms, recently refurbished in an attractive contemporary spirit. Sitting room-veranda.

Régis
24 pl. de la Gare – ☎ 02 97 42 61 41 – Fax 02 97 54 99 01 – Closed 29 June-6 July, 16-30 November, 15 February-1st March, Sunday except lunch in low season and Monday BY **h**
Rest – Menu € 25 (weekday lunch) – Carte € 46/64
◆ Tasteful medieval style decor with stained glass windows, copies of coats of arms, tuff stone walls and a fireplace adorned with a knight in armour. Creative cuisine.

La Table des Gourmets
6 r. A. Le Pontois – ☎ 02 97 47 52 44 – www.latabledesgourmets.com – contact@latabledesgourmets.com – Fax 02 97 47 15 87 – Closed Sunday dinner and Monday from 15 September to 15 June AZ **v**
Rest – Menu (€ 17), € 26/60 – Carte € 53/61
◆ Facing the ramparts of the old town, this beige and white restaurant is adorned with paintings of poppies. Modern cuisine with local touches.

Roscanvec
17 r. des Halles – ✆ 02 97 47 15 96 – www.roscanvec.com – roscanvec@yahoo.fr – Closed Sunday and Monday AZ **s**
Rest – *(number of covers limited, pre-book)* Menu € 20 (weekday lunch), € 27/53 – Carte € 51/58
◆ Half-timbered house in a picturesque pedestrian street. Tables on the ground floor with views of the kitchen. Main dining room upstairs. Inventive menu.

Le Carré Blanc
28 r. du Port – ✆ 02 97 47 48 34 – www.lecarreblanc-vannes.com – lionelcolson@orange.fr – Fax 02 97 47 48 34 – Closed Saturday lunch, Sunday dinner and Monday AZ **a**
Rest – Menu (€ 15), € 20/25 – Carte approx. € 30
◆ Le Carré Blanc is utterly inviting hidden away in a timber-framed house. Contemporary paintings and furniture decorate a spotless interior. Modern, well-presented food.

Le Vent d'Est
23 r. Ferdinand Le Dressay – ✆ 02 97 01 34 53 – Fax 02 97 01 34 53 – Closed 5-15 April, 15 July-31 August, Sunday except lunch from October to March and Monday AZ **d**
Rest – Menu (€ 14), € 25 – Carte € 28/46
◆ This restaurant on the first floor of a house facing the marina is decorated in a winstub style. Here the Bretons enjoy copious servings of Alsatian specialities.

in St-Avé **by ① and D 767, North: 6 km (near "centre hospitalier spécialisé" (specialised hospital)) – pop. 10 104 – alt. 50 m – ✉ 56890**

Le Pressoir (Bernard Rambaud)
7 r. de l'Hôpital, (via Plescop road), at 1.5 km – ✆ 02 97 60 87 63 – www.le.pressoir-st-ave.com – le.pressoir.st-ave@wanadoo.fr – Fax 02 97 44 59 15 – Closed 2-17 March, 29 June-7 July, 5-20 October, 4-12 January, Sunday dinner, Monday and Tuesday
Rest – Menu € 35 (weekday lunch), € 56/94 – Carte € 63/130
Spec. Homard breton à la tête de veau et vinaigrette façon ravigote. Galette de rouget aux pommes de terre et romarin. Petites crêpes à l'écorce d'orange et sorbet orange. **Wines** Muscadet de Sèvre et Maine sur lie.
◆ An inn much appreciated for its inventive cuisine paying tribute to the Armor. It also has a fine wine cellar and a new contemporary interior dotted with floral arrangements.

in Conleau **southwest: 4.5 km - ✉ 56000 Vannes**
Presqu'île de Conleau ★ 30 mn.

Le Roof
10 allée des Frères Cadoret – ✆ 02 97 63 47 47 – www.le-roof.com – leroof@club-internet.fr – Fax 02 97 63 48 10
40 rm – † € 85/124 †† € 108/151, ☕ € 13
Rest – Menu (€ 25 bi), € 29/56 – Carte € 45/85
Rest *Café de Conleau* – Menu (€ 15) – Carte € 25/41
◆ This hotel enjoys a privileged location on a peninsula facing a lovely cove where sailboats drop anchor. The rooms are functional and some command a sea view. Extensive views of the Morbihan Gulf from the restaurant. A bistro atmosphere pervades the Café de Conleau.

Arradon road **by ④ and D 101: 5 km – ✉ 56610 Arradon**

L'Arlequin
parc d'activités de Botquelen, (3 allée D.-Papin) – ✆ 02 97 40 41 41 – arlequin.caradec@wanadoo.fr – Fax 02 97 40 52 93 – Closed Saturday lunch, Sunday dinner and Wednesday
Rest – Menu (€ 18), € 22/42 – Carte € 35/45
◆ This pleasant, rotunda dining room boasts a timber ceiling and a view of the countryside. Updated menu that mixes tradition and fusion cuisine. Be sure to book!

in Arradon by ④, D 101, D 101^A and D 127: 7 km – pop. 5 125 – alt. 40 m – ✉ 56610

Syndicat d'initiative, 2, place de l'Église ✆ 02 97 44 77 44, Fax 02 97 44 81 22

<★.

Le Logis de Parc er Gréo without rest
au Gréo, 2 km west (towards le Moustoir) – ✆ 02 97 44 73 03 – www.parcergreo.com – contact@parcergreo.com – Fax 02 97 44 80 48 – Open 13 March-11 November
14 rm – €96/139 €96/139, ☕ €14 – 1 suite
◆ Establishment surrounded by greenery with a fine interior. Prettily furnished lounge decorated with model boats and fine watercolours. Cosy, individually decorated rooms. Heated pool.

Les Vénètes
à la pointe, 2 km – ✆ 02 97 44 85 85 – www.lesvenetes.com – Fax 02 97 44 78 60 – Closed 2-20 January
10 rm – €90/230 €90/230, ☕ €12
Rest – *(closed Sunday dinner from September to June)* Menu €40/70 – Carte €56/108
◆ At the water's edge, prettily arranged rooms with exceptional views of the gulf. Those on the first floor have balconies. A pleasant dining room with a marine decor, superbly situated on the shores of the "mor bihan" (Breton for little sea).

Le Médaillon
10 r. Bouruet Aubertot – ✆ 02 97 44 77 28 – http://lemedaillon.chez-alice.fr – Fax 02 97 44 79 08 – Closed 21-27 December, Sunday dinner, Tuesday dinner and Wednesday except from 14 July to 31 August
Rest – Menu €16/35 – Carte €41/60
◆ On the village outskirts, a former bar converted into a restaurant. Exposed beams and stone work adorn the unassuming dining room. Summer arboured terrace and children's games.

LES VANS – 07 Ardèche – **331** G7 – pop. 2 727 – alt. 170 m – ✉ 07140 44 **A3**
Lyon - Rhone Valley

Paris 663 – Alès 44 – Aubenas 37 – Pont-St-Esprit 66 – Privas 68 – Villefort 24

Office de tourisme, place Ollier ✆ 04 75 37 24 48, Fax 04 75 37 27 46

Le Carmel rm,
montée du Carmel – ✆ 04 75 94 99 60 – www.le-carmel.com – contact@le-carmel.com – Fax 09 59 61 80 37 – Open 1st April-11 November
26 rm – €45/55 €65/85, ☕ €10
Rest – Menu (€19), €28/42 – Carte €45/58
◆ The rooms in this former Carmelite convent, overlooking the medieval town, have been renovated - Provençal fabrics, ochre walls, wrought-iron furniture and new bathrooms. Attractive garden. Dining room with sunny colours and a shaded terrace. Dishes of the day.

South 6 km by D 901 – ✉ 07140 Les Vans

Mas de l'Espaïre
Combe de Mège – ✆ 04 75 94 95 01 – www.hotel-espaire.fr – espaire@wanadoo.fr – Fax 04 75 37 21 00 – Closed January and February
30 rm – €40/72 €60/95, ☕ €9
Rest – *(closed from November to April) (dinner only) (residents only)* Menu €25
◆ At the edge of the Païlolive wood, a former silkworm farm lulled by the crickets' song. The walls of the large rooms show traces of the original stone. King size beds. Pleasant dining room and home cooking.

VANVES – 92 Hauts-de-Seine – **311** J3 – **101** 25 – see Paris, Area

---

VARADES – 44 Loire-Atlantique – **316** J3 – pop. 3 403 – alt. 13 m – ✉ 44370 34 **B2**

Paris 333 – Angers 40 – Cholet 42 – Laval 95 – Nantes 54

Syndicat d'initiative, place Jeanne d'Arc ✆ 02 40 83 41 88

XX **La Closerie des Roses** ⩤ VISA

La Meilleraie, 1.5 km south by Cholet road – ☎ 02 40 98 33 30 – www.lacloseriedesroses.com – Fax 02 40 09 74 23 – Closed 5-21 October, 18 January-10 February, Sunday dinner, Monday dinner, Tuesday dinner and Wednesday

Rest – Menu € 18 (weekday lunch), € 27/58 – Carte € 50/60

◆ This restaurant, established in 1938, faces the River Loire and St Florent-le-Vieil Abbey. The chef buys his freshwater fish from local anglers; regional menu.

VARENGEVILLE-SUR-MER – 76 Seine-Maritime – 304 F2 – pop. 1 179 – alt. 80 m – ✉ 76119 Normandy

33 **D1**

Paris 199 – Dieppe 10 – Fécamp 57 – Fontaine-le-Dun 18 – Rouen 68

Site★ of the church - Parc des Moustiers★ - Colombier★ of Ango manor, South: 1 km - Ste-Marguerite: church ★ arcades West: 4.5 km - Ailly lighthouse ⩤★ Northwest: 4 km.

in Vasterival **3 km northwest by D 75 and secondary road - ✉ 76119 Varengeville-sur-Mer**

De la Terrasse ⩤ rest, P VISA

rte de Vasterival – ☎ 02 35 85 12 54 – www.hotel-restaurant-la-terrasse.com – francois.delafontaine@wanadoo.fr – Fax 02 35 85 11 70 – Open 16 March-11 October

22 rm – †€ 53/65 ††€ 53/65, ☕ € 8 – ½ P € 52/58

Rest – Menu (€ 17), € 22/35 – Carte € 26/35

◆ At the end of a pine-lined road, this fine house (1902) is surrounded by a large, shaded garden. Half the rooms enjoy sea views. Lounge with board games. Traditional cuisine in the dining room overlooking the Channel.

LA VARENNE-ST-HILAIRE – 94 Val-de-Marne – 312 E3 – 101 28 – see Paris, Area (St-Maur-des-Fossés)

VARENNES-SUR-ALLIER – 03 Allier – 326 H5 – pop. 3 879 – alt. 245 m – ✉ 03150

6 **C1**

Paris 327 – Digoin 59 – Lapalisse 20 – Moulins 31 – St-Pourçain-sur-Sioule 11 – Vichy 26

Office de tourisme, place de l'Hôtel de Ville ☎ 04 70 47 45 86, Fax 04 70 47 45 86

in Boucé **8 km East by N 7 and D 23 – pop. 512 – alt. 310 m – ✉ 03150**

XX **Auberge de Boucé** VISA

1 rte de Cindré – ☎ 04 70 43 70 59 – Closed Tuesday dinner, Wednesday dinner, Sunday dinner and Monday

Rest – Menu (€ 14), € 18/35 – Carte € 25/51

◆ Village inn with a warm country ambience. Pleasant terrace and sunny dining room decorated with paintings by the owner. Traditional cuisine served.

VARENNES-SUR-USSON – 63 Puy-de-Dôme – 326 G9 – see Issoire

VARETZ – 19 Corrèze – 329 J4 – see Brive-la-Gaillarde

VARS – 05 Hautes-Alpes – 334 I5 – pop. 597 – alt. 1 650 m – ✉ 05560 French Alps

41 **C1**

Paris 726 – Barcelonnette 41 – Briançon 46 – Digne-les-Bains 126 – Gap 71

Office de tourisme, cours Fontanarosa ☎ 04 92 46 51 31, Fax 04 92 46 56 54

in Ste-Marie-de-Vars – ✉ 05560 Vars

Alpage P VISA

– ☎ 04 92 46 50 52 – www.hotel-alpage.com – info@hotel-alpage.com – Fax 04 92 46 64 23 – Open 15 June-1st September and 15 December-15 April

17 rm – †€ 43/81 ††€ 50/130, ☕ € 9 – ½ P € 50/92

Rest – Menu (€ 17), € 20/26 – Carte € 24/32

◆ An old village farmhouse converted into a chalet-hotel. Spacious and very pleasant guestrooms, all of which sport a delightful regional style. The restaurant occupies an attractive vaulted building that was once a cowshed. Traditional cuisine.

Le Vallon 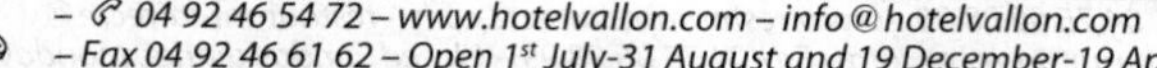 rest,

– ✆ 04 92 46 54 72 – *www.hotelvallon.com – info@hotelvallon.com*
– *Fax 04 92 46 61 62 – Open 1st July-31 August and 19 December-19 April*
34 rm – €59/69 €88/104, €8 – ½ P €65/75
Rest – Menu (€15), €19/22 – Carte €19/27
◆ An alpine establishment par excellence, ideally located at the foot of the ski slopes. Warm welcome, alpine-style ambience and decor, rooms overlooking the countryside, billiards and table tennis. The restaurant, whose walls are decked with photographs of alpine landscapes, serves traditional fare.

in Claux – ✉ 05560 Vars – Winter sports : 1 650/2 750 m 2 56

L'Écureuil without rest
Les Claux – ✆ 04 92 46 50 72 – www.hotelecureil.com – hotel.ecureuil@wanadoo.fr
– Fax 04 92 46 62 51 – Open 23 June-6 September and 6 December-24 April
21 rm – €80/120 €90/180, €8
◆ Savoy-style chalet 150m from the ski slopes. Wood prevails throughout from the inviting fireside sitting room to the snug rooms (most with a balcony). Sauna.

Les Escondus
– ✆ *04 92 46 67 00 – www.hotel-les-escondus.com – hotel.les.escondus@wanadoo.fr – Fax 04 92 46 50 47 – Open 1st July-31 August and 1st December-30 April*
22 rm (½ board only) – ½ P €68/96
Rest – Menu €19 (lunch)/29 – Carte €15/35
◆ Ideal for a relaxing stay: direct access to the ski slopes, leisure facilities, piano bar and practical rooms. Those with a taste for the unusual may want to try the tree cabin! Classic menu served in a wood panelled dining room or on the terrace, facing the forest.

Chez Plumot
– ✆ *04 92 46 52 12 – dominique.lallez@wanadoo.fr – Open July-August and December- April*
Rest – Menu €20 (lunch)/31 – Carte €30/70
◆ An institution in the resort. The countrified decor is perfectly suited to the traditional recipes on the menu. Concise lunchtime menu in winter (snacks, southwest specialities).

VASSIVIÈRE (LAC) – **23 Creuse** – **326** i6 – **see Peyrat-le-Château (87 H.-Vienne)**

VASTERIVAL – **76 Seine-Maritime** – **304** F2 – **see Varengeville-sur-Mer**

VAUCHOUX – **70 Haute-Saône** – **314** E7 – **see Port-sur-Saône**

VAUCHRÉTIEN – **49 Maine-et-Loire** – **317** G5 – **pop. 1 509** – **alt. 67 m** 35 **C2**
– ✉ **49320**

Paris 313 – Nantes 119 – Angers 22 – Cholet 66 – Saumur 45

Syndicat d'initiative, Mairie ✆ 02 41 91 24 18, Fax 02 41 91 20 06

Le Moulin de Clabeau without rest
5 km north on D 55 and D 123 – ✆ 02 41 91 22 09 – www.gite-brissac.com – moulin-clabeau@gite-brissac.com – Closed 24-31 August
4 rm – €63 €68
◆ This 1320 mill on the banks of the Aubance offers rooms with exposed beams and stonework. Homemade jams and cakes at breakfast. Exhibitions and sale of local produce.

VAUCRESSON – **92 Hauts-de-Seine** – **311** I2 – **101** 23 – **see Paris, Area**

VAUDEVANT – **07 Ardèche** – **331** J3 – **pop. 211** – **alt. 600 m** 44 **B2**
– ✉ **07410**

Paris 558 – Lyon 96 – Privas 89 – Saint-Étienne 67
– Valence 50

La Récré

– 04 75 06 08 99 – www.restaurant-la-recre.com – restaurant-la-recre@restaurant-la-recre.com – Fax 04 75 06 08 99 – Closed Sunday dinner, Monday and Tuesday

Rest – *(number of covers limited, pre-book)* Menu (€ 14), € 20/55 – Carte € 33/45

◆ This restaurant was once the village school, which explains the name and decor (blackboard, photos of schoolchildren, wall maps etc). Modern, refined dining in a convivial atmosphere.

VAUGINES – 84 Vaucluse – 332 F11 – pop. 551 – alt. 375 m – ✉ 84160 42 E1

Paris 736 – Digne-les-Bains 112 – Apt 23 – Cavaillon 36 – Salon-de-Provence 37

L'Hostellerie du Luberon

cours St-Louis – 04 90 77 27 19 – www.hostellerieduluberon.com – hostellerieduluberon@hostellerieduluberon.com – Fax 04 90 77 13 08 – Open 10 March-10 November

16 rm – † € 90/93 †† € 99/118 – ½ P € 70

Rest – *(closed Wednesday lunch and Tuesday)* Carte € 29/48

◆ Facing the Durance Valley, a family hotel with spruce Provençal rooms. Library and leisure activities for young and old alike. Brasserie-style food served in a sunlit dining room or by the poolside terrace.

VAULT-DE-LUGNY – 89 Yonne – 319 G7 – see Avallon

VAUVILLE – 14 Calvados – 303 M4 – pop. 253 – alt. 40 m – ✉ 14800 32 A3

Paris 201 – Caen 44 – Le Havre 52 – Lisieux 30 – Hérouville-Saint-Clair 44

Manoir de la Haulle

– 02 31 81 10 62 – www.lahaulle.com – lahaulle@orange.fr – Fax 02 31 81 10 62

4 rm – † € 100/150 †† € 130/230 **Table d'hôte** – Menu € 40/60 bi

◆ An abbey in the 12C, a farm in the 19C and then a cider works: this magnificent property is full of character. Comfortable rooms with decor on a horseriding theme. Superb gardens. Traditional cuisine served in a beautiful rustic dining room or on the poolside terrace.

VAUX-EN-BEAUJOLAIS – 69 Rhône – 327 G3 – pop. 946 – alt. 360 m – ✉ 69460 43 E1

Paris 443 – Lyon 49 – Villeurbanne 58 – Lyon 03 51 – Lyon 08 51

Auberge de Clochemerle with rm

r. Gabriel-Chevallier – 04 74 03 20 16 – www.aubergedeclochemerle.fr – contact@aubergedeclochemerle.fr – Fax 04 74 03 20 74 – Closed Monday and Tuesday except from June to September

7 rm – † € 65 †† € 70, € 10 **Rest** – Menu € 30/65 – Carte € 57/69

◆ An auberge in a village made famous by Gabriel Chevallier's novel, "Clochemerle". Creative, contemporary cuisine and good wine list. Pleasant neo-rustic decor. Bright guestrooms embellished with homely furniture.

VAUX-LE-PÉNIL – 77 Seine-et-Marne – 312 F4 – see Melun

VAUX-SOUS-AUBIGNY – 52 Haute-Marne – 313 L8 – pop. 669 – alt. 275 m – ✉ 52190 14 C3

Paris 304 – Dijon 44 – Gray 43 – Langres 25

Auberge des Trois Provinces

r. de Verdun – 03 25 88 31 98 – Closed 1 week in November, 4-25 January, Sunday dinner and Monday

Rest – *(pre-book)* Menu € 19/29 – Carte € 39/58

◆ Frescoes, painted beams and handsome floors make up the pleasant decor of this family restaurant in an old stone house. Fine modern cuisine.

Le Vauxois

r. de Verdun – 03 25 84 36 74 – Fax 03 25 84 25 61 – Closed 17-23 November, 5-25 January, Sunday evening and Monday

9 rm – €48 €55, €6,50

◆ Functional rooms situated 50m from the Auberge des Trois Provinces, and a stone's throw from the church. Bright breakfast area.

VELARS-SUR-OUCHE – 21 Côte-d'Or – **320** J6 – **see Dijon**

VÉLIZY-VILLACOUBLAY – 78 Yvelines – **311** J3 – **101** 24 – **see Paris, Area**

VELLÈCHES – 86 Vienne – 322 J3 – pop. 371 – alt. 69 m – ✉ 86230 39 C1

Paris 302 – Poitiers 58 – Joué-lès-Tours 60 – Châtellerault 21 – Chambray-lès-Tours 60

La Table des Écoliers

1 bis r. de l'Étang – 05 49 93 35 51 – www.latabledesecoliers.com – latabledesecoliers@wanadoo.fr

Rest – *(closed Tuesday and Wednesday)* Menu (€ 22 bi), € 29/42 – Carte approx. € 37

◆ You return to your childhood in this former classroom (school desks, coat racks, etc.), for an interesting gastronomic lesson. Friendly welcome and modern fare.

VELLUIRE – 85 Vendée – **316** K9 – **see Fontenay-le-Comte**

VENAREY-LES-LAUMES – 21 Côte-d'Or – 320 G4 – pop. 3 068 – alt. 235 m – ✉ 21150 Burgundy-Jura 8 C2

Paris 259 – Avallon 54 – Dijon 66 – Montbard 15 – Saulieu 42 – Semur-en-Auxois 13

Office de tourisme, place Bingerbrück 03 80 96 89 13, Fax 03 80 96 13 22

in Alise-Ste-Reine 2 km east – **pop. 674** – **alt. 415 m** – ✉ **21150**

Mont Auxois★: ✻★ - Château of Bussy-Rabutin★.

Cheval Blanc

r. du Miroir – 03 80 96 01 55 – www.regis-bolatre.com – regis.bolatre@free.fr – Closed 7-15 September, 2 January-4 February, Sunday dinner except July-August, Monday and Tuesday

Rest – Menu € 20 (weekdays), € 32/45 – Carte € 50/68

◆ A stone building whose interior has recently been spruced up and modernised. Generous Burgundy cuisine, served by a pleasant log fire in winter.

in Mussy-la-Fosse 3 km west on the minor road – **320** G4 – **pop. 82** – **alt. 280 m** – ✉ **21150**

Clos Mussy

r. du Château – 03 80 96 97 87 – www.closmussy.fr – contact@closmussy.fr – Closed 24 December-3 January

3 rm – €60/75 €70/85 **Table d'hôte** – Menu € 30 bi

◆ Opposite the site of Alésia, this 16C stronghold exemplifies military architecture in the Middle Ages. Immense rooms graced with personal touches and a barn converted into a rustic sitting room. Table d'hôte setting in a huge medieval inspired dining room graced by a fireplace.

VENASQUE – 84 Vaucluse – 332 D10 – pop. 1 131 – alt. 310 m – ✉ 84210 Provence 42 E1

Paris 690 – Apt 32 – Avignon 33 – Carpentras 13 – Cavaillon 30 – Orange 36

Office de tourisme, Grand 'Rue 04 90 66 11 66, Fax 04 90 66 11 66

Baptistry★ - Gorges★ East: 5 km by D 4.

Auberge La Fontaine — rm, VISA AE

pl. de la Fontaine – ✆ 04 90 66 02 96 – www.auberge-lafontaine.com – fontvenasq@aol.com – Fax 04 90 66 13 14

4 suites – ††€ 125, ☕ € 10

Rest – *(closed Wed.) (dinner only) (number of covers limited, pre-book)* Menu (€ 25), € 41

◆ Old building with guesthouse feel facing the town fountain. The skilfully arranged split-level rooms overlook the patio or rooftops. Dining room decorated with old furniture and ornaments; dinner-concerts.

La Garrigue — rest, P VISA AE

rte de l'Appié – ✆ 04 90 66 03 40 – www.hotel-lagarrigue.com – hotel-lagarrigue@club-internet.fr – Fax 04 90 66 61 43 – Open 1st March-15 November

15 rm – †€ 53/60 ††€ 57/75, ☕ € 8 – ½ P € 58/65

Rest – *(closed Saturday and Sunday) (dinner only) (residents only)* Menu € 20

◆ At the entrance to a hilltop village, this fully renovated family establishment has well-maintained rooms, some with air conditioning. Provencal style breakfast room.

VENCE – 06 Alpes-Maritimes – 341 D5 – pop. 18 200 – alt. 325 m — 42 E2

– ✉ 06140 ▮ French Riviera

Paris 923 – Antibes 20 – Cannes 30 – Grasse 24 – Nice 23

Office de tourisme, 8, place du Grand Jardin ✆ 04 93 58 06 38, Fax 04 93 58 91 81

Rosaire chapel★ (Matisse chapel) - Place du Peyra★ B **13** - Stalls★ of the cathedral B **E** - ⩽★ from the château terrace N. D. des Fleurs Northwest: 2.5 km km by D 2210.

Col de Vence ✳★★ Nortwest: 10 km by D 2 - St-Jeannet: site★, ⩽★ 8 km by ③.

Alsace Lorr. (R.)	B	3
Évêché (R. de l')	B	5
Hôtel de Ville (R.)	B	6
Leclerc (Av. Gén.)	A	9
Marché (R. du)	B	10
Meyère (Av. Col.)	B	12
Peyra (Pl. du)	B	13
Place Vieille (R. de la)	B	14
Poilus (Av. des)	A	15
Portail Levis (R. du)	B	16
Résistance (Av. de la)	A, B	17
Rhin et Danube (Av.)	A	18
St-Lambert (R.)	B	19
Tuby (Av.)	A	21

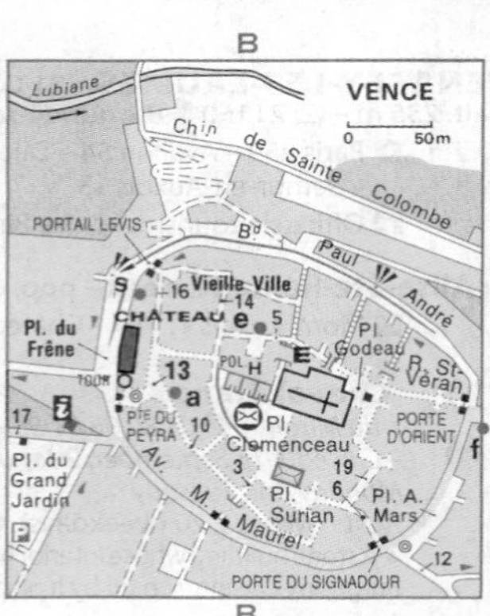

Château St-Martin & Spa — rm, VISA AE

av. des Templiers, 2 km on the Col de Vence road (D2) – ✆ 04 93 58 02 02 – www.chateau-st-martin.com – stmartin@relaischateaux.com – Fax 04 93 24 08 91 – Closed 13 December-12 February

45 rm – †€ 290/760 ††€ 290/760, ☕ € 35 – 6 suites

Rest *Le St-Martin* – *(closed lunch Monday-Thursday from 15 June to 31 August)* Menu € 62 (lunch), € 75/105 – Carte € 105/140

Rest *La Rôtisserie* – Carte € 51/73

Rest *L'Oliveraie* – grill *(open 1st June-19 September) (lunch only)* Menu € 48/61 – Carte € 51/73

Spec. Risotto al dente à la crème de topinambour au jus de truffe. Rouget crispy au jus de poivron rouge et paprika. Orange en tarte soufflée au Grand Marnier.

◆ A superb luxury hotel in a park planted with olive trees. Views that extend as far as the sea. Peace, comfort and charm. Fine creative cuisine in the classic setting of the restaurant. Teppanyaki grills and spit roasts at La Rôtisserie. In summertime, enjoy lunch outdoors at L'Oliveraie.

Cantemerle
258 chemin Cantemerle, via Ave Col. Meyère B – ☎ 04 93 58 08 18 – www.hotelcantemerle.com – info@hotelcantemerle.com – Fax 04 93 58 32 89 – Open end March-mid October
9 rm – €200/220 €225/245, €18 – 18 suites – €225/500
Rest – *(open May-September and closed Monday)* Carte €50/65
◆ This Riviera-style villa is laid out around a pool and shaded garden. Impeccable Art Deco-inspired interior. Spacious, elegant rooms; the duplex rooms have a terrace. Restaurant surrounded by greenery; traditional cuisine.

Diana without rest
79 av. des Poilus – ☎ 04 93 58 28 56 – www.hotel-diana.fr – info@hotel-diana-vence.com – Fax 04 93 24 64 06 A **a**
28 rm – €75/160 €100/160, €13
◆ Centrally located hotel with bright, comfortable bedrooms; those facing the garden are quieter. Breakfast is served on the attractive veranda. Solarium and jacuzzi on the roof terrace. Gym.

Floréal
440 av. Rhin et Danube, via ② – ☎ 04 93 58 64 40 – www.hotel-floreal-vence.fr – hotel.floreal@wanadoo.fr – Fax 04 93 58 79 69
41 rm – €60/112 €78/137, €12
Rest – *(closed Sunday off season) (dinner only) (residents only)* Menu €26
◆ A garden of Mediterranean trees and shrubs surrounds this establishment on the doorstep of Vence. Some of the rooms with balconies have been treated to a new lease of life. Unassuming dining room and terrace overlooking the pool surrounded by greenery.

Mas de Vence
539 av. E. Hugues – ☎ 04 93 58 06 16 – www.azurline.com/mas – mas@azurline.com – Fax 04 93 24 04 21 A **r**
41 rm – €67/88 €87/110, €10 – ½ P €78/85
Rest – Menu (€17 bi), €30/35 – Carte €29/45
◆ This recent ochre-toned construction overlooks a busy road. Rooms with good soundproofing, impeccably kept, often with a loggia. Hall with glass roof. Large dining room and arcaded terrace next to the hotel pool. Traditional and Mediterranean fare.

Miramar without rest
167 av. Bougearel, (Plateau St-Michel), via av. Col. Meyère B – ☎ 04 93 58 01 32 – www.hotel-miramar-vence.com – contact@hotel-miramar-vence.com – Fax 04 93 58 20 22 – Closed 17 November-12 December
18 rm – €78/88 €88/148, €12
◆ This attractive 1920s building overlooks the mountains and valley. Public areas adorned with wall paintings, lovely guestrooms with individual touches, and a charming terrace.

Villa Roseraie without rest
128 av. Henri Giraud – ☎ 04 93 58 02 20 – www.villaroseraie.com – accueil@villaroseraie.com – Fax 04 93 58 99 31 – Closed 5 November-14 December and 5 January-15 February A **x**
12 rm – €87/157 €97/157, €13
◆ Pleasant 1900 villa in the middle of a garden-cum-oasis. Small rooms delightfully decorated with Souleiado fabrics, decorative beds and dried flowers.

La Colline de Vence without rest
806 chemin des Salles, 1,5 km via col de Vence road (D2) A – ☎ 04 93 24 03 66 – www.colline-vence.com – contact@colline-vence.com – Fax 04 93 24 03 66
3 rm – €74/135 €74/135
◆ The well-restored outbuildings of the château contain pretty rooms with personal touches. All overlook the mountains and Mediterranean. Flower garden and pool.

Auberge Les Templiers
39 av. Joffre – ☎ 04 93 58 06 05 – www.restaurant-vence.com – lestempliers3@wanadoo.fr – Fax 04 93 58 92 68 – Closed 22 November-4 December, 18-31 January, Monday and Wednesday A **k**
Rest – Menu (€29), €39/74 – Carte €54/66
◆ There is an attractive shaded terrace is front of this old inn. A renovated and refreshing setting in Provençal style.

Le Vieux Couvent
37 av. Alphonse Toreille – ✆ 04 93 58 78 58 – www.restaurant-levieuxcouvent.com – levieuxcouventvence@aliceadsl.fr – Fax 04 93 58 78 58 – Closed 25 January-1st March, Tuesday lunch in July-August, Wednesday except dinner in summer and Thursday lunch B **f**
Rest – *(number of covers limited, pre-book)* Menu € 28/38 – Carte € 42/50
◆ Exposed stonewalls, pillars and ribbed vaulting make up the decor of this restaurant housed in a 17C seminary chapel. Regional dishes.

Les Bacchanales (Christophe Dufau)
247 av. de Provence – ✆ 04 93 24 19 19 – lesbacchanales06@orange.fr – Closed 21-27 December, Tuesday and Wednesday A **v**
Rest – Menu € 36 (weekday lunch), € 50/70
Spec. Salade d'encornets et palourdes au jus d'oursin. Noix de veau aux aubergines rôties et raviole d'oignon doux au citron. Mousseux de fromage blanc au spéculos et cacao.
◆ In this restaurant enjoy spontaneous, creative cuisine where vegetables are the star of the show. Bright and contemporary dining room with fireplace and a small wine museum.

Auberge des Seigneurs with rm
1, rue du Dr Binet – ✆ 04 93 58 04 24 – www.auberge-seigneurs.com – sandrine.rodi@wanadoo.fr – Fax 04 93 24 08 01 – Closed January B **s**
6 rm – †€ 65 ††€ 85/95, ☕ € 9 – ½ P € 95
Rest – *(closed mid December-end January, Sunday and Monday)* Menu (€ 23), € 32/43 – Carte € 45/56
◆ Francis I, Renoir, Modigliani, etc. This historic inn in a wing of Villeneuve château has had many famous guests. Provençal dishes, spit-roasted lamb.

L' Armoise
9 pl. du Peyra – ✆ 04 93 58 19 29 – www.larmoise.com – valentin.nelly@wanadoo.fr – Closed 23-30 June, 3-20 November, 18-25 February, lunch in July-August, Sunday dinner, Tuesday lunch and Monday B **a**
Rest – *(number of covers limited, pre-book)* Menu (€ 26 bi), € 36 – Carte € 36/51
◆ Specialising in fish and seafood, this restaurant occupies an old fishmonger's on the pretty Place du Peyra. Traditional favourites (bouillabaisse) and house specialities on the menu.

La Litote
5 r. Evéché – ✆ 04 93 24 27 82 – www.lalitote.com – stephanefurlan@wanadoo.fr – Fax 04 93 44 71 24 – Closed 12 November-16 December, 14 January-5 February, Tuesday from October to April, Sunday dinner and Monday B **e**
Rest – Menu (€ 20), € 25/35 – Carte € 30/40
◆ This restaurant is on a small square in the pedestrian quarter of old Vence. It offers a friendly welcome and service, a warm setting and terrace, and an updated menu of Provençal inspiration.

VENDÔME – 41 Loir-et-Cher – 318 D5 – pop. 17 200 – alt. 82 m – ✉ 41100 Châteaux of the Loire 11 **B2**

Paris 169 – Blois 34 – Le Mans 78 – Orléans 91 – Tours 56
Office de tourisme, parc Ronsard ✆ 02 54 77 05 07, Fax 02 54 73 20 81
de La Bosse Oucques La Guignardière, 20 km on the Beaugency road, ✆ 02 54 23 02 60
Former Trinité abbey★: abbey church★★, museum★ BZ **M** - Château: terraces ≤★.

Le St-Georges
14 r. Poterie – ✆ 02 54 67 42 10 – www.hotel-saint-georges-vendome.com – contact@hotel-saint-georges-vendome.com – Fax 02 54 77 29 22 AZ **t**
28 rm – †€ 65 ††€ 65/100, ☕ € 8,50 – ½ P € 90
Rest – *(closed Sunday except public holidays)* Menu (€ 18 bi) – Carte € 30/55
◆ This street corner building in the town centre is home to a distinctly modern hotel. Functional rooms decorated in a modern style, some with spa tubs. The menu features cooking and flavours from four continents served in an ethnic setting. African style lounge bar.

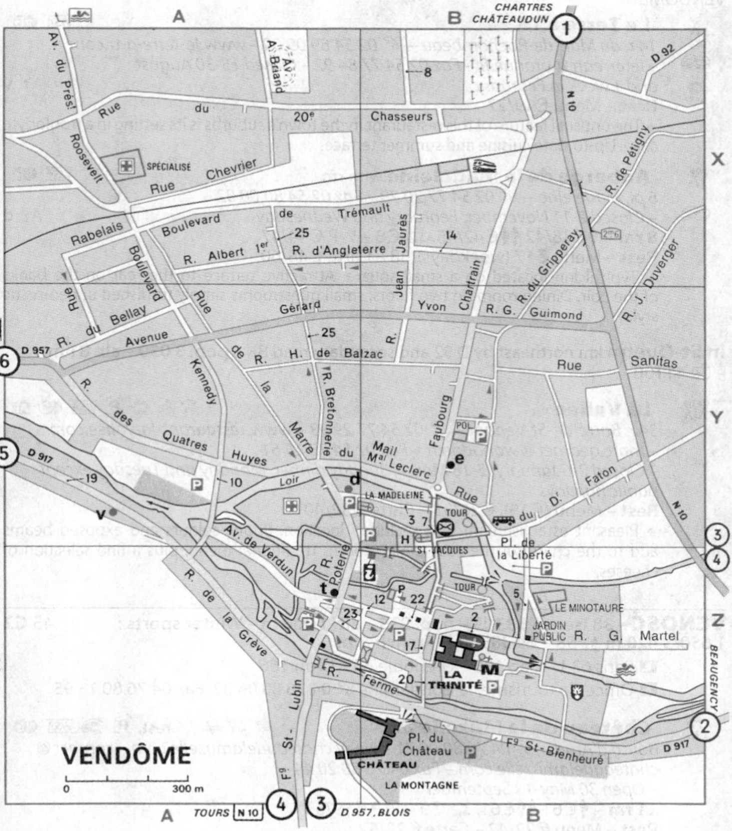

Abbaye (R. de l') . . . . **BZ** 2	États-Unis (R. des) . . . . **AY** 10	Rochambeau (R. Mar.) . . . . . **AY** 19
Béguines (R. des) . . . . **BY** 3	Gaulle (R. Gén.-de) . . . . **BZ** 12	St-Bié (R.) . . . . **BZ** 20
Bourbon (R. A) . . . . **BZ** 5	Italie (R. d') . . . . **BX** 14	St-Martin (Pl.) . . . . **BZ** 22
Change (R. du) . . . . **BY** 7	Poterie (R.) . . . . **AZ** 17	Saulnerie (R.) . . . . **AZ** 23
Clemenceau (Av. G.) . . . . . . **BX** 8	République (Pl. de la) . . . . . **BZ** 17	Verrier (R. Cdt) . . . . **AXY** 25

Mercator ♿ rm, AC rest, Wi-Fi, P, VISA, MC, AE

rte de Blois, 2 km via ③ – ✆ 02 54 89 08 08 – www.hotelmercator.fr – hotelmercator.vendome@wanadoo.fr – Fax 02 54 89 09 17

53 rm – †€ 52/58 ††€ 54/61, ☕ € 8

Rest – *(closed 25 July-23 August, Saturday and Sunday)* Menu (€ 16), € 19

◆ Although close to a roundabout, this hotel is surrounded by greenery. Compact yet comfortable modern bedrooms and attentive service. Restaurant with minimalist, contemporary decor and traditional recipes.

Le Vendôme without rest Wi-Fi, VISA, MC, AE

15 fg Chartrain – ✆ 02 54 77 02 88 – www.hotelvendomefrance.com – info@hotelvendomefrance.com – Fax 02 54 73 90 71 – Closed 19 December-2 January Y **e**

35 rm – †€ 59/65 ††€ 68/85, ☕ € 10

◆ This family-run hotel in the town centre has a white-fronted corner house that conceals functional rooms and a cosy sitting room (piano). Extensive buffet breakfast.

Le Terre à TR
14 r. du Mar.-de-Rochambeau – ✆ 02 54 89 09 09 – www.le-terre-a-tr.com – leterreatr@orange.fr – Fax 02 54 77 84 92 – Closed 15-30 August and 1 week in February AY **v**
Rest – Menu € 19/27
◆ The unusual feature of this restaurant in the town's suburbs is its setting in a troglodyte cave. Up-to-date cuisine and summer terrace.

Auberge de la Madeleine with rm
6 pl. Madeleine – ✆ 02 54 77 20 79 – Fax 02 54 80 00 02 – Closed 2-11 November, February and Wednesday AY **d**
8 rm – †€ 38/42 ††€ 42/45, ☐ € 8 – ½ P € 44/47
Rest – Menu € 17 (weekdays)/38 – Carte € 48/60
◆ Typical inn located on a small square. Attractive terrace to the rear on the banks of the Loir. Dining room on two floors; small guestrooms simply furnished in neo-rustic style.

in St-Ouen 4 km northeast by D 92 and secondary road BX – **pop. 3 050 – alt. 81 m – ✉ 41100**

La Vallée
34 r. Barré-de-St-Venant – ✆ 02 54 77 29 93 – www.restaurant-la-vallée.com – marc.georget@wanadoo.fr – Fax 02 54 73 15 51 – Closed 2-6 January, 2-18 March, Sunday dinner, Monday and Tuesday except public holidays
Rest – Menu (€ 19), € 26/35 – Carte € 32/40
◆ Pleasant establishment in a secluded location. Bright colours and exposed beams add to the charm of the cosy dining room. Traditional menu, plus a fine selection of cheeses.

VENOSC – 38 Isère – 333 J8 – pop. 935 – alt. 1 000 m – Winter sports : 1 650/3 420 m ⛷ 58 – ✉ 38520 French Alps 45 C2

Paris 633 – Gap 105 – Grenoble 66 – Lyon 166

Office de tourisme, la Condamine ✆ 04 76 80 06 82, Fax 04 76 80 18 95

Château de la Muzelle rest,
Bourg d'Arud – ✆ 04 76 80 06 71 – www.chateaudelamuzelle.com – contact@chateaudelamuzelle.com – Fax 04 76 80 20 44 – Open 30 May-13 September
21 rm – †€ 61 ††€ 61, ☐ € 9 – ½ P € 59/63
Rest – Menu € 22/42 – Carte € 27/52
◆ Spruce red shutters brighten the sober façade of this little 17C château. Functional, well-kept rooms, with dormer windows on the second floor. Family atmosphere. Fine traditional cuisine making good use of the vegetable garden.

VENSAT – 63 Puy-de-Dôme – 326 G6 – pop. 424 – alt. 395 m – ✉ 63260 5 B2

Paris 370 – Clermont-Ferrand 40 – Cournon-d'Auvergne 42 – Vichy 26

Château de Lafont
2 r. de la Côte Rousse – ✆ 04 73 64 21 24 – www.chateaudelafont.com – info@chateaudelafont.com – Fax 04 73 64 50 83
4 rm ☐ – †€ 70/105 ††€ 70/110 **Table d'hôte** – Menu € 25 bi
◆ This family-run estate includes a château, a working farm and pretty parkland. Comfortable and peaceful rooms within 15C walls. Breakfasts and meals served in a wood-panelled dining room.

VENTABREN – 13 Bouches-du-Rhône – 340 G4 – pop. 4 831 – alt. 210 m – ✉ 13122 Provence 40 B3

Paris 746 – Aix-en-Provence 14 – Marseille 33 – Salon-de-Provence 27

Syndicat d'initiative, 11, boulevard de Provence ✆ 04 42 28 76 47, Fax 04 42 28 96 92

⋞★ Château ruins.

La Table de Ventabren (Dan Bessoudo)
r. F. Mistral – ✆ 04 42 28 79 33 – www.latabledeventabren.com – contact@latabledeventabren.com – Fax 04 42 28 83 15 – Closed 23 December-31 January, Wednesday dinner from October to March, Sunday dinner from October to April and Monday
Rest – *(pre-book in high season and on weekends)* Menu € 27 (weekday lunch), € 39/48 – Carte € 38/70
Spec. Brandade froide, crème d'avocat et gaspacho. Dos de cabillaud poêlé, mousseline de carotte, cébettes et poireaux. Fraises et cerises en salade, mousse de pomme verte.
◆ Restaurant in the heart of the picturesque perched village. Enjoy its friendly atmosphere in the pretty vaulted dining rooms or on the terrace overlooking the valley. Up-to-date cuisine.

VENTRON – 88 Vosges – **314** J5 – **pop. 930** – **alt. 630 m** – **Winter sports : 850/1 110 m** 8 – ✉ **88310** 27 **C3**

Paris 441 – Épinal 56 – Gérardmer 25 – Mulhouse 51 – Remiremont 30 – Thann 31
Office de tourisme, 4, place de la Mairie ✆ 03 29 24 07 02, Fax 03 29 24 23 16
Grand Ventron ✻★★ Northeast: 7 km, **Alsace-Lorraine-Champagne**

in l'Ermitage-du-Frère-Joseph 5 km south by D 43 and D 43E- ✉ 88310 Ventron – Winter sports : 850/1 110 m 8

Les Buttes rest, VISA AE
Ermitage Frère Joseph – ✆ 03 29 24 18 09 – www.frerejo.com – info@frerejo.com – Fax 03 29 24 21 96 – Closed 11 November-19 December
26 rm – € 101/217 € 101/217, € 14 – 1 suite – ½ P € 101/141
Rest – *(closed lunch except Sunday and public holidays) (dinner only)* Menu € 33/35 – Carte approx. € 34
◆ This charming chalet-hotel, decorated with chic mountain decor and pictures of Épinal, has snug bedrooms (some with jacuzzis) and a cosy lounge. Light-wood panelling and southern tones create a warm setting; traditional menu.

in Travexin 3 km west - ✉ 88310 Cornimont

Le Géhan VISA AE
9 rte de Travexin – ✆ 03 29 24 10 71 – www.legehan-charlemagne.com – le.gehan@online.fr – Fax 03 29 24 10 70 – Closed 26 July-10 August
11 rm – € 50 € 50, € 9 – ½ P € 55
Rest – *(closed Sunday dinner, Wednesday lunch and Monday)* Menu (€ 14), € 18/40 – Carte € 25/43
◆ Yellow and blue shades enliven the functional, well soundproofed bedrooms of this establishment, situated at a junction. Exemplary upkeep and attentive welcome. A bright renovated dining room; traditional fare and a few regional dishes.

VERBERIE – 60 Oise – **305** H5 – **pop. 3 462** – **alt. 33 m** – ✉ **60410** 36 **B3**

Paris 70 – Beauvais 56 – Clermont 31 – Compiègne 16 – Senlis 18 – Villers-Cotterêts 31

Auberge de Normandie with rm VISA AE
26 r. Pêcherie – ✆ 03 44 40 92 33 – www.auberge-normandie.fr – sarl.vulfina@orange.fr – Fax 03 44 40 50 62
3 rm – € 55 € 55, € 6,50
Rest – *(Closed Sunday dinner)* Menu (€ 17), € 22/42 – Carte € 35/46
◆ Country inn around a courtyard with exposed beams, woodwork and fireplace. Ask for a table near the garden.

VERDUN – 55 Meuse – **307** D4 – **pop. 19 300** – **alt. 198 m** – ✉ 55100 **Alsace-Lorraine** 26 **A1**

Paris 263 – Metz 78 – Bar-le-Duc 56 – Châlons-en-Champagne 89 – Nancy 95
Office de tourisme, place de la Nation ✆ 03 29 86 14 18, Fax 03 29 84 22 42
High town★: Notre-Dame cathedral ★, BYZ Palais épiscopal★ (World Peace Centre) BZ - Underground citadel★: circuit★★ BZ - Battlefields★★★: Mémorial de Verdun, Fort et Ossuaire de Douaumont, Tranchée des Baïonnettes, le Mort-Homme, la Cote 304.

VERDUN

Alsace-Lorraine (Av.) . . . . CZ 2
Beaurepaire (R.) . . . . CZ 3
Belle-Vierge (R. de la) . . . . . . BY 4
Chevert (Pl.) . . . . CZ 5
Douaumont (Av. de) . . . . CY 6
Foch (Pl. Mar.) . . . . CY 7
Fort de Vaux (R. du) . . . . CZ 8
Frères-Boulhaut (R. des) . . . . CY 9
Lattre-de-Tassigny (Av. Mar.-de) . . . . CY 10
Mautroté (R.) . . . . BY 13
Mazel (R.) . . . . CY 14
Prés.-Poincaré (R.) . . . . CZ 17
République (Quai de la) . . . . CY 18
Rû (R. de) . . . . BZ 19
St-Paul (R.) . . . . CY 20
St-Pierre (R.) . . . . BY 21
Soupirs (Allée des) . . . . BY 24

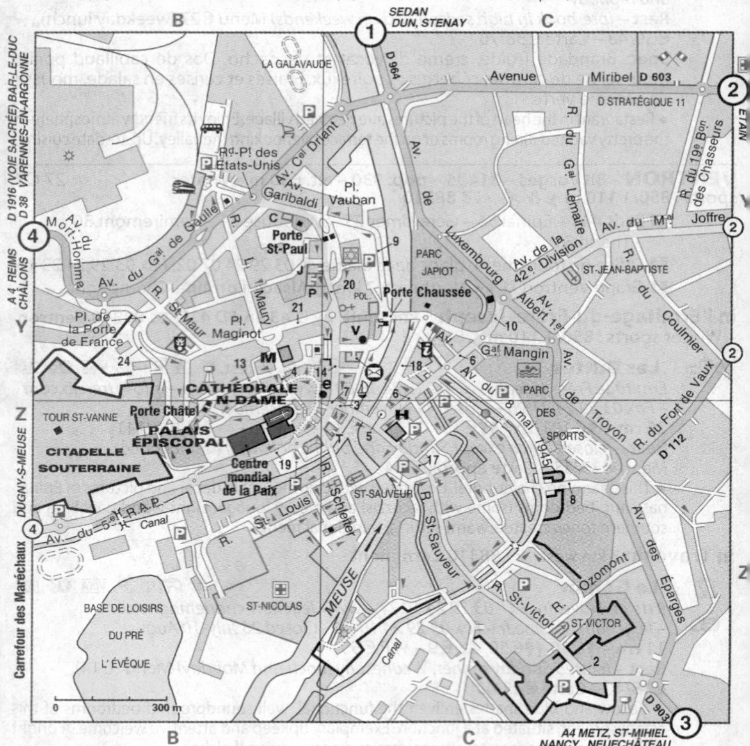

Hostellerie du Coq Hardi

8 av. Victoire – ✆ 03 29 86 36 36 – www.coq-hardi.com – coq.hardi@wanadoo.fr – Fax 03 29 86 09 21 CY **v**

33 rm – €76/95 €100/135, €17 – 2 suites – ½ P €90/110

Rest – *(closed mid-February to mid-March, Saturday lunch, Sunday dinner and Friday)* Menu €46/99 – Carte €62/88

Rest *Le Bistrot* – *(closed Sunday dinner and Friday from September to April)* Menu (€15 bi), €21 (weekdays)/39 bi – Carte €28/45

◆ This traditional house (1827) sports a delightfully nostalgic interior. Find a collection of cockerels in the hall, a fireside sitting room, Lorraine furniture and several superb four-poster beds. Ancient wainscoting and classic fare. Simple, quick meals at the Bistrot.

Montaulbain without rest

4 r. de la Vieille-Prison – ✆ 03 29 86 00 47 – Fax 03 29 84 75 70 BCY **e**

10 rm – €30/38 €35/42, €6

◆ Hotel in a semi-pedestrian street with small rooms that are simple, clean and quiet. The rustic inspired lobby doubles as the breakfast room.

in Monthairons 13 km by ④ and D 34 – pop. 373 – alt. 200 m – ✉ 55320

Hostellerie du Château des Monthairons
– ✆ 03 29 87 78 55 – *www.chateaudesmonthairons.fr – accueil@chateaudesmonthairons.fr – Fax 03 29 87 73 49 – Closed 1st January-12 February, Sunday and Monday 15 November-31 March*
22 rm – †€ 75/98 ††€ 85/190, ☕ € 15 – 3 suites – ½ P € 120/195
Rest – *(closed Monday except dinner from 15 June to 15 September and Tuesday lunch)* Menu (€ 26 bi), € 39/89 – Carte € 56/70
◆ Fine 19C château in parkland on the banks of the prettily meandering Meuse. Elegant rooms and suites, comfortable duplex. Hammam, sauna and Jacuzzi. At the restaurant, classical decor or attractive terrace for up-to-date cuisine.

in Charny-sur-Meuse 8 km North by D 38 – pop. 523 – alt. 197 m – ✉ 55100

Syndicat d'initiative, 4, place de la Mairie ✆ 03 29 84 33 44, Fax 03 29 84 85 84

Les Charmilles without rest
12 r. de la Gare – ✆ 03 29 86 93 49 – www.les-charmilles.com – valerie@les-charmilles.com – Fax 03 29 86 37 65 – Closed January
3 rm ☕ – †€ 45 ††€ 55
◆ Once a café, this welcoming and very well kept house is now a hotel offering large, spruce rooms. Homemade pastries at breakfast.

VERDUN-SUR-LE-DOUBS – 71 Saône-et-Loire – 320 K8 – pop. 1 143 – alt. 180 m – ✉ 71350 Burgundy-Jura 7 B3

Paris 332 – Beaune 24 – Chalon-sur-Saône 24 – Dijon 65 – Dole 49 – Lons-le-Saunier 56

Office de tourisme, 3, place Charvot ✆ 03 85 91 87 52

Hostellerie Bourguignonne with rm
2 av. du Président Borgeot – ✆ 03 85 91 51 45 – www.hostelleriebourguignonne.com – hostelleriebourguignonne@hotmail.com – Fax 03 85 91 53 81 – Closed February, Sunday dinner in low season, Tuesday except dinner from May to September and Wednesday lunch
8 rm – †€ 95 ††€ 95/116, ☕ € 14 – ½ P € 100
Rest – Menu € 22 (lunch), € 28/80 – Carte € 72/94
◆ Charming inn serving traditional local dishes, including the famous pôchouse, a house speciality. Superb Burgundy wine selection. Country chic decor and lovely terrace. Individually decorated guestrooms.

VERGÈZE – 30 Gard – 339 K6 – pop. 3 930 – alt. 30 m – ✉ 30310 23 C2

Paris 724 – Montpellier 43 – Nîmes 20

Office de tourisme, 4, rue Basse ✆ 04 66 35 45 92, Fax 04 66 35 45 92

La Passiflore without rest
1r. Neuve – ✆ 04 66 35 00 00 – www.hotel-lapassiflore.com – hotel.lapassiflore@orange.fr – Fax 04 66 35 09 21
11 rm – †€ 46/67 ††€ 46/67, ☕ € 8
◆ Former 18C farmhouse with an attractive facade, offering small, simple rooms overlooking a pretty courtyard.

VERGONCEY – 50 Manche – 303 D8 – pop. 215 – alt. 70 m – ✉ 50240 32 A3

Paris 352 – Caen 120 – Saint-Lô 86 – Saint-Malo 60 – Fougères 37

Château de Boucéel without rest
4 km eastward along the D 108, D 40 and D 308 – ✆ 02 33 48 34 61 – www.chateaudebouceel.com – chateaudebouceel@wanadoo.fr – Fax 02 33 48 16 26 – Closed 11 January-8 February
5 rm ☕ – †€ 150/170 ††€ 150/170
◆ Surrounded by landscaped gardens and pools, this family château dating from 1763 is adorned with period furniture, parquet floors and ancestral portraits. Guestrooms with individual touches.

LA VERNAREDE – 30 Gard – 339 J3 – pop. 389 – alt. 345 m – ✉ 30530 23 C1

Paris 708 – Montpellier 124 – Nîmes 74 – Alès 29 – Aubenas 79

Lou Cante Perdrix with rm rest, VISA AE

Le Château – ✆ 04 66 61 50 30 – www.canteperdrix.fr – lou.cante.perdrix@wanadoo.fr – Fax 04 66 61 43 21 – Closed 2 January-15 February

12 rm – †€ 52/67 ††€ 58 – ½ P € 55

Rest – *(closed Sunday dinner, Monday and Tuesday except 16 June-20 September)* Menu € 20 (weekday lunch), € 28/60 – Carte € 50/65

◆ Tucked away in a pine forest, this impressive stone house (1860) is home to a smart dining room (fireplace, plants, paintings) serving traditional fare.

VERNET-LES-BAINS – 66 Pyrénées-Orientales – 344 F7 – pop. 1 483 – alt. 650 m – Spa : mid March-late Nov. – Casino – ✉ 66820 22 B3

Languedoc-Roussillon-Tarn Gorges

Paris 904 – Mont-Louis 36 – Perpignan 57 – Prades 11

Office de tourisme, 2, rue de la chapelle ✆ 04 68 05 55 35, Fax 04 68 05 60 33

Site★ - Saint-Martin-du-Canigou abbey 2.5 km South★★.

Princess rest, rm, VISA

r. des Lavandières – ✆ 04 68 05 56 22 – www.hotel-princess.fr – contact@hotel-princess.fr – Fax 04 68 05 62 45 – Open 15 March-23 November

40 rm – †€ 46/96 ††€ 55/96, € 8,50 – ½ P € 51/72

Rest – Menu (€ 14), € 18/34 – Carte € 27/40

◆ At the foot of old Vernet. The rooms have been renovated in a modern spirit; some enjoy a balcony facing the mountains, others overlook the village rooftops. Immense dining room and terrace. Several menus including one regional menu.

Mas Fleuri without rest VISA AE

bd Clemenceau – ✆ 04 68 05 51 94 – www.hotellemasfleuri.fr – hotel.masfleuri@wanadoo.fr – Fax 04 68 05 50 77 – Open 15 April-15 October

30 rm – †€ 80/90 ††€ 80/120, € 12

◆ In this 1970s hotel, all the renovated rooms with balcony command a view of the parkland. Large swimming pool. Buffet breakfast in an adjoining house.

VERNEUIL-SUR-AVRE – 27 Eure – 304 F9 – pop. 6 655 – alt. 155 m – ✉ 27130 Normandy 33 C3

Paris 114 – Alençon 77 – Argentan 77 – Chartres 57 – Dreux 37 – Évreux 43

Syndicat d'initiative, 129, place de la Madeleine ✆ 02 32 32 17 17, Fax 02 32 32 17 17

de Center Parcs, 9 km on the Mortagne road, ✆ 02 32 60 50 02

La Madeleine church ★ - Statues★ of Notre-Dame church.

Plan on next page

Le Clos rm, VISA AE

98 r. de la Ferté-Vidame – ✆ 02 32 32 21 81 – www.leclos-normandie.com – leclos@relaischateaux.com – Fax 02 32 32 21 36 – Closed 11 January-12 February n

7 rm – †€ 180/220 ††€ 180/220, € 22 – 3 suites

Rest – *(closed Tuesday lunch and Monday)* Menu (€ 35), € 45 (lunch), € 60/85 – Carte € 65/99

◆ This red brick Norman château with a slate roof has a wealth of detail: waxed parquet floors and period furniture create a setting of great elegance while the dining rooms recall those of fine ancestral homes. Charming terrace; good choice of Bordeaux wines.

Du Saumon VISA

89 pl. de la Madeleine – ✆ 02 32 32 02 36 – www.hoteldusaumon.fr – hotel.saumon@wanadoo.fr – Fax 02 32 37 55 80 – Closed 19 December-10 January and Sunday dinner from November to March

29 rm – †€ 50/60 ††€ 50/68, € 8 a

Rest – Menu € 12 (weekdays)/52 – Carte € 31/50

◆ A late 18C post-house facing an inner courtyard. Rooms in the main building are larger and have antique furniture. Be it raw, smoked, marinated, fried, grilled or on a skewer; salmon (the name of the restaurant) is in pride of place here.

VERNEUIL-SUR-AVRE

Breteuil (Rue Porte de) 2
Briand (R. A.) 4
Canon (R. du) 5
Casati (Bd) 7
Chasles (Av. A.) 8
Clemenceau (R.) 9
Demolins (Av. E.) 10
Ferté-Vidame (Rte de la) 12
Lait (R. au) 13
Madeleine (Pl. de la) 15
Notre-Dame (Pl.) 16
Paul-Doumer (R.) 17
Poissonnerie (R. de la) 18
Pont-aux-Chèvres (R. du) 19
Tanneries (R. des) 21
Thiers (R.) 22
Tour-Grise (R. de la) 24
Verdun (Pl. de) 25
Victor-Hugo (Av.) 27
Vlaminck (Av. M.-de) 30

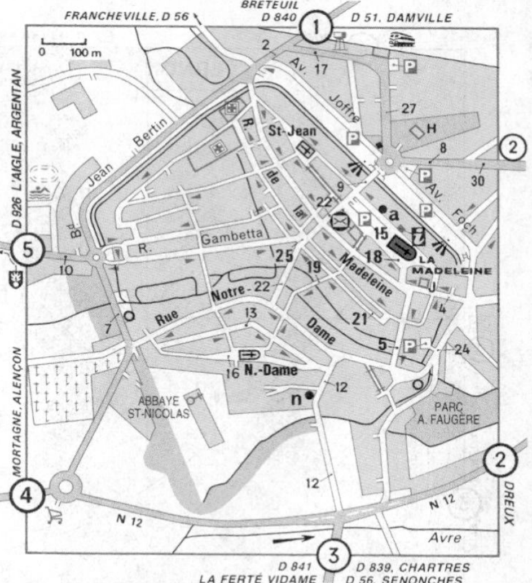

in Barils 7 km by ⑤, D 926 and D 166 – pop. 159 – alt. 201 m – ✉ 27130

XX **Auberge des Barils**

2 r. de Verneuil – ✆ 02 32 60 05 88 – auberge-des-barils@wanadoo.fr – Closed 8-14 September, 2-16 January, Tuesday from September to April and Wednesday

Rest – Menu € 22/37 – Carte € 35/57

♦ This 18C inn offers three pleasant dining rooms and a nice summer terrace. Appetising and seasonal menu giving pride of place to delicious Norman market produce.

VERNON – 27 Eure – **304** I7 – **pop. 23 600 – alt. 32 m** – ✉ **27200** 33 **D2**

Normandy

Paris 77 – Beauvais 66 – Évreux 34 – Mantes-la-Jolie 25 – Rouen 62

Office de tourisme, 36, rue Carnot ✆ 02 32 51 39 60, Fax 02 32 51 86 55

Notre-Dame church ★ - Château of Bizy★ 2 km by ③ - Giverny★ 3 km.

Normandy

1 av. P.-Mendès-France – ✆ 02 32 51 97 97 – www.le-normandy.net – normandye.hotel@wanadoo.fr – Fax 02 32 21 01 66 BY **t**

50 rm – †€ 78/125 ††€ 78/125, ☕ € 10 – ½ P € 72/78

Rest – *(closed Monday lunch and Sunday)* Menu (€ 15), € 23/29 – Carte € 28/47

♦ This hotel, located in the town centre, offers renovated rooms featuring functional furniture. Lounge and bar with a cosy atmosphere. The Cottage restaurant offers traditional cuisine to be savoured in a pleasant brasserie-pub-style setting.

XX **Les Fleurs**

71 r. Carnot – ✆ 02 32 51 16 80 – lesfleurs@tele2.fr – Fax 02 32 21 30 51 – Closed Tuesday lunch from October to April, Sunday dinner and Monday BX **a**

Rest – *(number of covers limited, pre-book)* Menu (€ 20 bi), € 28/54 – Carte € 41/56

♦ A venerable old house with a fine half-timbered rear part, in a narrow street of the town centre. Pleasant modern dining room with a relaxed atmosphere. Traditional menu.

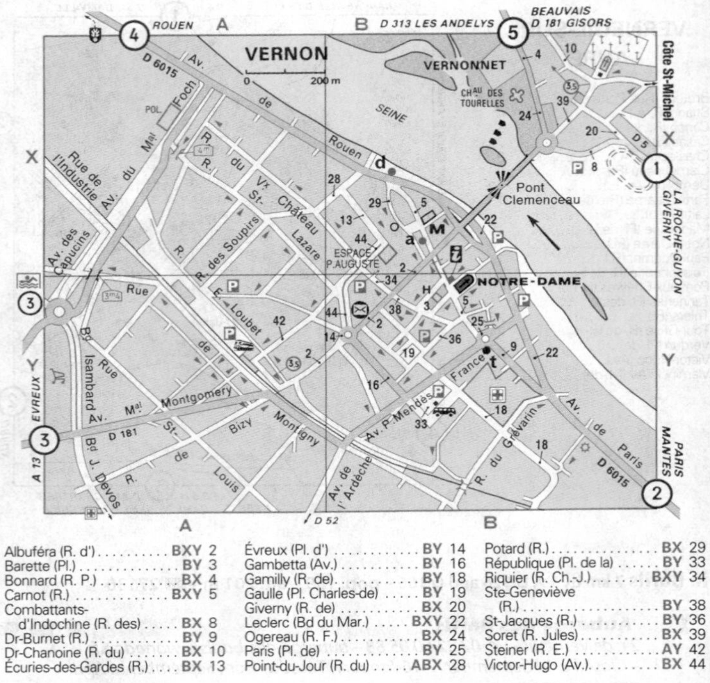

Albuféra (R. d') . . . . BXY 2
Barette (Pl.) . . . . BY 3
Bonnard (R. P.) . . . . BX 4
Carnot (R.) . . . . BXY 5
Combattants-d'Indochine (R. des) . . . . . BX 8
Dr-Burnet (R.) . . . . BY 9
Dr-Chanoine (R. du) . . . . BX 10
Écuries-des-Gardes (R.) . . . . BX 13
Évreux (Pl. d') . . . . BY 14
Gambetta (Av.) . . . . BY 16
Gamilly (R. de) . . . . BY 18
Gaulle (Pl. Charles-de) . . . . . BY 19
Giverny (R. de) . . . . BX 20
Leclerc (Bd du Mar.) . . . . . . BXY 22
Ogereau (R. F.) . . . . BX 24
Paris (Pl. de) . . . . BY 25
Point-du-Jour (R. du) . . . . . . ABX 28
Potard (R.) . . . . BX 29
République (Pl. de la) . . . . . . BY 33
Riquier (R. Ch.-J.) . . . . BXY 34
Ste-Geneviève (R.) . . . . BY 38
St-Jacques (R.) . . . . BY 36
Soret (R. Jules) . . . . BX 39
Steiner (R. E.) . . . . AY 42
Victor-Hugo (Av.) . . . . BX 44

XX **Côté Marine** VISA MC

2 pl. Chantereine – ✆ 02 32 51 01 95 – Fax 02 32 51 68 91 BX **d**

Rest – Menu € 18/38

◆ This 1970 building on the Seine, across from the Vieux Moulin and the Château des Tourelles, boasts a pleasant panoramic dining room in pastel tones. Traditional cuisine.

X **Le Bistro** VISA MC

73 r. Carnot – ✆ 02 32 21 29 19 – bistro.parcelle@wanadoo.fr – Fax 02 32 21 29 19 – Closed 1st-9 March, 6-24 July, Sunday and Monday BX **a**

Rest – Menu € 18 bi – Carte approx. € 28

◆ This former bar has retained its counter for serving customers who are in a hurry. Decor of old posters. Traditional dishes of the day chalked up on the blackboard.

in Douains 8 km by ③, D 181 and D 75 – pop. 468 – alt. 128 m – ✉ 27120

Château de Brécourt rest, P VISA MC AE

– ✆ 02 32 52 40 50 – www.chateaudebrecourt.com – brecourt@leshotelsparticuliers.com – Fax 02 32 52 69 65

26 rm – €105/245 €105/245, € 15 – 4 suites

Rest – Menu (€ 25), € 48/78 – Carte € 50/85

◆ 17C château in the heart of the Norman countryside, surrounded by moats and a vast park. Grand Siècle decor with beams, antique floor tiles and fireplaces. Individually furnishes rooms. A bar housed in the converted guard house and a restaurant with a noble atmosphere.

VERNOUILLET – 28 Eure-et-Loir – **311** E3 – see Dreux

VERQUIÈRES – 13 Bouches-du-Rhône – **340** E2 – see St-Rémy-de-Provence

VERRIERES – 86 Vienne – **322** J6 – **pop. 877** – **alt. 115 m** – ✉ **86410** 39 **C2**

Paris 368 – Poitiers 31 – Châtellerault 68 – Buxerolles 33 – Chauvigny 26

Les Deux Porches without rest VISA MC AE
pl. de la Mairie – ✆ *05 49 42 83 85* – *www.hotel-des-deux-porches.fr* – *hddp@wanadoo.fr* – *Fax 05 49 42 83 79*
16 rm – €45/52 €47/58, €8
◆ The central location and functional bedrooms decorated in a modern style make this hotel a popular and practical choice. Friendly welcome and limited dining facilities.

VERSAILLES – 78 Yvelines – **311** I3 – **101** 23 – see Paris, Area

VERS-PONT-DU-GARD – 30 Gard – **339** M5 – see Pont-du-Gard

VERTEUIL-SUR-CHARENTE – 16 Charente – **324** L4 – **pop. 715** 39 **C2**
– **alt. 100 m** – ✉ **16510** **Poitou Charentes Vendée**

Paris 414 – Poitiers 78 – Angoulême 42 – Soyaux 44 – Ruelle-sur-Touvre 41

Le Couvent des Cordeliers VISA MC
8 r. du Docteur Deux Després – ✆ *05 45 31 01 19*
– *www.lecouventdescordeliers.com* – *barbou@lecouventdescordeliers.com*
– *Closed January*
5 rm – €90 €100
Table d'hôte – *(dinner by reservation)* Menu €28 bi
◆ An establishment of character located in a 16C convent with a past rich in history. Sophisticated inviting guestrooms. Exhibitions and concerts in the former chapel. The lady of the house introduces guests to the region of Charentes at her table d'hôte.

VERTOU – 44 Loire-Atlantique – **316** H4 – see Nantes

VERTUS – 51 Marne – **306** G9 – **pop. 2 653** – **alt. 85 m** – ✉ **51130** 13 **B2**
Northern France and the Paris Region

Paris 139 – Châlons-en-Champagne 30 – Épernay 21 – Montmirail 39 – Reims 48

in Bergères-les-Vertus 3.5 km south by D 9 – **pop. 533** – **alt. 108 m** – ✉ **51130**

Hostellerie du Mont-Aimé rest, P VISA MC AE
4-6 r. de Vertus – ✆ *03 26 52 21 31*
– *www.hostellerie-mont-aime.com* – *mont.aime@wanadoo.fr*
– *Fax 03 26 52 21 39* – *Closed Sunday dinner from November to March*
46 rm – €70/90 €90/140, €13 – ½ P €95
Rest – Menu €28 (weekdays)/90 – Carte €67/87
◆ At the foot of Mont Aimé, this hotel offers well-kept rooms, many of which open onto the garden or have a balcony. Take a seat in this elegant, flower-decked dining room to sample tasty traditional cuisine, beneath a glass roof. Fine wine list (champagnes).

LES VERTUS – 76 Seine-Maritime – **304** G2 – see Dieppe

VERVINS – 02 Aisne – **306** F3 – **pop. 2 653** – **alt. 147 m** – ✉ **02140** 37 **D2**
Northern France and the Paris Region

Paris 187 – Charleville-Mézières 70 – Laon 36 – Reims 89 – St-Quentin 52 – Valenciennes 76

Office de tourisme, place de l'Hôtel de ville ✆ 03 23 98 11 98, Fax 03 23 98 02 47

Tour du Roy

45 r. Gén. Leclerc – ☎ 03 23 98 00 11 – www.latourduroy.com – latourduroy@wanadoo.fr – Fax 03 23 98 00 72 – Closed Monday lunch and Tuesday lunch
22 rm – †€ 80/110 ††€ 110/250, ☐ € 15 – ½ P € 110/135
Rest – Menu (€ 28), € 44/75
◆ This aristocratic manor with a prestigious past, flanked with three towers, overlooks the town. The elegant individually furnished rooms bear evocative names. "Divine" duplexes. Anne of Brittany, Henry IV, Charles de Gaulle and François Mitterrand have all dined at the restaurant.

VERZY – 51 Marne – **306** G8 – pop. **1 068** – alt. **210 m** – ✉ **51380** 13 **B2**
Northern France and the Paris Region

Paris 163 – Châlons-en-Champagne 32 – Épernay 23 – Reims 22 – Rethel 52 – Vouziers 56

Syndicat d'initiative, place de l'Hôtel de Ville ☎ 03 26 97 93 65, Fax 03 26 97 95 74

Faux de Verzy★ South: 2 km.

Au Chant des Galipes

2 r. Chanzy – ☎ 03 26 97 91 40 – chantdesgalipes@wanadoo.fr – Fax 03 26 97 91 44 – Closed 17 August-3 September, 21 December-21 January, Monday dinner from October to April, Sunday dinner, Tuesday dinner and Wednesday
Rest – Menu (€ 15), € 19 (weekday lunch), € 24/41 – Carte € 35/46
◆ In the heart of a winegrowing town, this pleasant establishment is characterised by warm colours and a painting on the ceiling that depicts the sky. Up-to-date cuisine.

VESCOUS – 06 Alpes-Maritimes – **341** D4 – see Gilette

LE VÉSINET – 78 Yvelines – **311** I2 – **101** 13 – see Paris, Area

---

VESOUL Ⓟ – 70 Haute-Saône – **314** E7 – pop. **16 200** – alt. **221 m** 16 **B1**
– ✉ **70000** **Burgundy-Jura**

Paris 360 – Belfort 68 – Besançon 47 – Épinal 91 – Langres 76 – Vittel 86

Office de tourisme, 2,rue Gevrey ☎ 03 84 97 10 85, Fax 03 84 97 10 84

Du Lion without rest

4 pl. de la République – ☎ 03 84 76 54 44 – www.hoteldulion.fr – hoteldulion@wanadoo.fr – Fax 03 84 75 23 31 – Closed 2-17 August and 26 December-3 January a
18 rm – †€ 50 ††€ 50/56, ☐ € 6,50
◆ Small family hotel near the town's lively shopping streets. The immaculately kept rooms sport a 1970s style decor.

Le Caveau du Grand Puits

r. Mailly – ☎ 03 84 76 66 12 – Fax 03 84 76 66 12 – Closed 18-24 May, 15 August-6 September, 24 December-3 January, Wednesday dinner, Saturday lunch and Sunday u
Rest – Menu € 18 (weekdays)/37 – Carte € 25/55
◆ In a small street in the old town, vaulted cellar with stone walls and a second dining room with mezzanine. Inner courtyard where meals are served on fine days.

in Épenoux 5 km by ①, St-Loup-sur-Semouse road and D10 – 479 h. alt. 240 – ✉ 70000 Pusy-et-Épenoux

Château d'Épenoux

5 r. Ruffier d'Épenoux – ☎ 03 84 75 19 60 – www.chateau-epenoux.com – chateau.epenoux@orange.fr – Fax 03 84 76 45 05
5 rm ☐ – †€ 90/100 ††€ 95/105 **Table d'hôte** – Menu € 19/26
◆ A small 18C château hidden inside a park, planted with 100-year-old trees. Antique furniture and chandeliers lend a personal touch to the spacious rooms. Large, tasteful sitting room. Enjoy your meals in an elegant yellow dining room. Refined cuisine.

VESOUL

Good food and accommodation at moderate prices?
Look for the Bib symbols: red Bib Gourmand for food,
blue Bib Hotel for hotels.

VEUIL – 36 Indre – **323** F4 – see Valençay

VEULES-LES-ROSES – 76 Seine-Maritime – **304** E2 – pop. 599 33 **C1**
– alt. 15 m – ✉ 76980 Normandy

Paris 188 – Dieppe 27 – Fontaine-le-Dun 8 – Rouen 57 – St-Valery-en-Caux 8

Office de tourisme, 27, rue Victor-Hugo ✆ 02 35 97 63 05, Fax 02 35 57 24 51

XXX **Les Galets** AC VISA
at the beach – ✆ 02 35 97 61 33 – Fax 02 35 57 06 23
– Closed Tuesday and Wednesday
Rest – Menu € 36/80 – Carte € 54/75
◆ Brick house close to a shingle beach typical of the Alabaster Coast. Comfortable dining rooms-veranda, nice table settings and modern cuisine.

LE VEURDRE – 03 Allier – **326** F2 – **pop. 550 – alt. 190 m** – ✉ **03320** 5 **B1**
Auvergne

Paris 272 – Bourges 66 – Montluçon 73 – Moulins 36 – Nevers 34 – St-Amand-Montrond 48

Le Pont Neuf
– ✆ 04 70 66 40 12 – www.hotel-lepontneuf.com – hotel.le.pontneuf@wanadoo.fr – Fax 04 70 66 44 15 – Closed mid November-mid February and Sunday dinner 15 October-31 March
46 rm – €50/55 €60/95, €9 – ½ P €53/77
Rest – Menu €19 (weekdays)/41 – Carte €24/60
◆ Modernised traditional hotel, appreciated for its sports installations. The rooms at the back face the peaceful park; the more recent ones are in the annexe. Country-style restaurant where seasonal suggestions enhance the à la carte menu and traditional set menus.

VEUVES – 41 Loir-et-Cher – **318** D7 – **pop. 220 – alt. 62 m** – ✉ **41150** 11 **A1**

Paris 205 – Bourges 135 – Orléans 84 – Poitiers 137 – Tours 38

L'Auberge de la Croix Blanche
2 av. de la Loire – ✆ 02 54 70 23 80 – www.cuisine-en-loir-et-cher.fr – jean-claude.sichi@orange.fr – Fax 02 54 70 21 47 – Closed February school holidays, Wednesday lunch Easter-October, Wednesday dinner November-Easter, Tuesday dinner 15 January-Easter, Monday except dinner July-August and Sunday dinner
Rest – Menu (€18), €22/33 – Carte €30/48
◆ Family inn founded in 1888 on the banks of the Loire. Updated, seasonal cuisine served in the rustic dining room or terrace facing the garden.

VEYNES – 05 Hautes-Alpes – **334** C5 – **pop. 3 202 – alt. 827 m** – ✉ **05400** 40 **B1**

Paris 660 – Aspres-sur-Buëch 9 – Gap 25 – Sisteron 51

Office de tourisme, avenue Commandant Dumont ✆ 04 92 57 27 43, Fax 04 92 58 16 18

La Sérafine
Les Paroirs, 2 km east by Gap road and D 20 – ✆ 04 92 58 06 00 – Fax 04 92 58 09 11 – Closed Monday and Tuesday
Rest – *(number of covers limited, pre-book)* Menu €25/32
◆ Pretty 18C building where diners are given a family welcome. Verbally recited menus based on market produce (two set menus that change daily) and fine wines. Summer terrace.

VEYRIER-DU-LAC – 74 Haute-Savoie – **328** K5 – **see Annecy**

VÉZAC – 24 Dordogne – **329** I6 – **see Beynac et Cazenac**

VÉZAC – 15 Cantal – **330** D5 – **see Aurillac**

VÉZELAY – 89 Yonne – **319** F7 – **pop. 473 – alt. 285 m – Pilgrimage** (22 July) – ✉ **89450** Burgundy-Jura 7 **B2**

Paris 221 – Auxerre 52 – Avallon 16 – Château-Chinon 58 – Clamecy 23

Office de tourisme, 12, rue Saint-Etienne ✆ 03 86 33 23 69, Fax 03 86 33 34 00

Ste-Madeleine basilica ★★★: tympanum of the central portal ★★★, capitals ★★★.

Poste et Lion d'Or
pl. du Champ de Foire – ✆ 03 86 33 21 23 – www.laposte-liondor.com – contact@laposte-liondor.com – Fax 03 86 32 30 92 – Closed January and February
38 rm – €71/103 €75/107, €12 – ½ P €72/77
Rest – *(Closed Monday and Tuesday from November to March)* Menu €26/58 – Carte €42/60
◆ This smart former coaching inn has been welcoming guests for over 200 years! Comfortable classic-style rooms. Those overlooking the countryside are very popular. Restaurant offering a new take on local country dishes. Local produce on sale in the shop.

Compostelle without rest
Pl. du Champ de Foire – ✆ 03 86 33 28 63 – http://monsite.wanadoo.fr/compostelle.vezelay – le.compostelle@wanadoo.fr – Fax 03 86 33 34 34 – Closed 1st-27 December and 3 January-15 February
18 rm – €49/63 €49/63, €10
◆ A small family hotel with functional rooms, some of which at ground level or with a balcony, overlooking the valley. Panoramic breakfast room.

Le St-Étienne
39 r. St-Étienne – ✆ 03 86 33 27 34 – www.le-saint-etienne.fr – lesaintetienne@aol.com – Closed 10 January-26 March, Wednesday and Thursday
Rest – Menu €29/59 – Carte €57/113
◆ This 18C building lines the main street leading to the basilica. Cosy rustic interior with lovely painted beams; up-to-date cuisine.

Le Bougainville
28 r. St-Etienne – ✆ 03 86 33 27 57 – lebougainvillevezelay@wanadoo.fr – Fax 03 86 33 35 12 – Open mid-February to mid-November and closed Monday in low season, Tuesday and Wednesday
Rest – Menu €21/28 – Carte €25/47
◆ A family restaurant with retro character in an old house on the road to the Basilica. Local cuisine washed down with regional wines.

in St-Père **3 km southeast by D 957 – pop. 380 – alt. 148 m – ✉ 89450**
N.-Dame church ★.

L'Espérance (Marc Meneau) rest,
Vézelay road – ✆ 03 86 33 39 10 – www.marc-meneau-esperance.com – reservation@marc-meneau.com – Fax 03 86 33 26 15 – Closed 15 January-1st March, Monday lunch, Wednesday lunch and Tuesday except public holidays
19 rm – €150/300 €150/300, €30 – 8 suites – ½ P €250/350
Rest – *(pre-book)* Menu €95 bi (weekday lunch), €160/210 – Carte €150/250
Spec. Langoustines royales rôties en casserole. Filet de veau sous la mère et crème de laitue braisée. Dessert "Marie-Antoinette". **Wines** Bourgogne Vézelay blanc, Chablis.
◆ Guests can choose between elegant renovated guestrooms in the manor house, modern with private terraces at the Pré des Marguerites, and rustic at the Moulin. Glass-roofed restaurant which looks out onto a delightful garden. Creative-classical cuisine and a superb selection of Burgundies.

Renommée without rest
19 et 20 rte de Vézelay – ✆ 03 86 33 21 34 – perso.orange.fr/la.renommee/ – la.renommee89@wanadoo.fr – Fax 03 86 33 34 17 – Closed 24 December-1st March and Sunday except from May to August
16 rm – €42/49 €49/58, €7
◆ This hotel in the village centre is also a bar, tobacconist and newsagents. Ask for one of the rooms in the wing opposite, they are more recent and comfortable.

in Fontette **5 km east by D 957 – ✉ 89450 Vézelay**

Crispol rm,
Avallon road – ✆ 03 86 33 26 25 – www.crispol.com – crispol@wanadoo.fr – Fax 03 86 33 33 10 – Closed January, February and Monday from November to April
12 rm – €78/128 €78/128, €10 – ½ P €78
Rest – *(closed Tuesday lunch and Monday)* Menu €25/56 – Carte €32/45
◆ Stone house on the doorstep of the village, with the hill in the background. The wing is home to spacious rooms decorated with works by the artist/owner. Bright dining room whose bay windows command a fine view of the basilica.

in Pierre-Perthuis 6 km southeast by D 957 and D 958 – pop. 116 – alt. 220 m – ✉ 89450

Les Deux Ponts rm, VISA
1 rte de Vézelay – ✆ 03 86 32 31 31 – lesdeuxponts@gmail.com – Open 6 March-30 November
7 rm – †€ 50/60 ††€ 50/65, ☕ € 7 – ½ P € 57/69
Rest – *(closed Wednesday from October to May and Tuesday) (number of covers limited, pre-book)* Menu € 23/45 – Carte € 31/50
◆ A welcoming, flower-decked house on a country lane. Simple rooms (no television) with good bedding and well-equipped bathrooms. An original dining room with a refined setting, brightened up by amusing Dutch glass lights.

VIA – 66 Pyrénées-Orientales – **344** D8 – see Font-Romeu

GARABIT VIADUCT ★★ – 15 Cantal – **330** H5 – ✉ 15100 5 **B3**
Auvergne

Paris 520 – Aurillac 84 – Mende 74 – Le Puy-en-Velay 90 – St-Flour 14
Maison du paysan (Farmer's House)★ à Loubaresse South: 7 km - Belvédère de Mallet ≤★★ Southwest: 13 km then 10 mn.

Beau Site rest, VISA AE
N 9 – ✆ 04 71 23 41 46 – www.beau-site-hotel.com – info@beau-site-hotel.com – Fax 04 71 23 46 34 – Open 3 April-3 November
17 rm – †€ 48/60 ††€ 48/65, ☕ € 10 – 3 suites – ½ P € 50/66
Rest – Menu (€ 13), € 18/48 – Carte € 39/54
◆ Viaduct, lake or garden view? A difficult choice among the fresh, neat rooms (most of which have a flat-screen TV)! Tennis court, swimming pool and children's play area. The restaurant affords a view of Gustave Eiffel's famous viaduct, attractively illuminated at night.

Anglards-de-St-Flour 3 km north – pop. 321 – alt. 840 m – ✉ 15100

La Méridienne VISA
– ✆ 04 71 23 40 53 – www.hoteldelameridienne.com – info@hoteldelameridienne.com – Fax 04 71 23 91 05 – Closed 20 December-6 February
16 rm – †€ 41/56 ††€ 41/56, ☕ € 8 – ½ P € 49/54
Rest – Menu € 15 (weekdays)/51 – Carte € 29/58
◆ Guests receive a warm welcome to this new establishment. Practical, unpretentious but very well-kept rooms; some overlook the large garden (children's play area). The menu features regional dishes; seafood platters and zarzuela by request.

VIBRAC – 16 Charente – **324** J6 – see Jarnac

VIC-EN-BIGORRE – 65 Hautes-Pyrénées – **342** M4 – pop. 4 788 – alt. 216 m – ✉ 65500 28 **A2**

Paris 775 – Pau 47 – Aire sur l'Adour 53 – Auch 62 – Mirande 37 – Tarbes 19

Réverbère rest, VISA AE
29 bd d'Alsace – ✆ 05 62 96 78 16 – www.lereverbere.fr – le.reverbere@wanadoo.fr – Fax 05 62 96 79 85 – Closed 18-31 December and 12-20 February
10 rm – †€ 48 ††€ 48, ☕ € 6,50
Rest – *(closed Saturday except dinner from June to September and Sunday dinner)* Menu (€ 11), € 13 (weekdays)/28 – Carte approx. € 40
◆ This welcoming hotel built slightly back from the road has comfortable rooms, which are well equipped and pleasantly furnished in light wood. Traditional cuisine served in a bright, ochre coloured room, enlivened with subtle touches of colour.

Le Tivoli rest, VISA AE
pl. Gambetta – ✆ 05 62 96 70 39 – www.hotel-resto-tivoli65.com – hotel.tivoli@wanadoo.fr – Fax 05 62 96 29 74
24 rm – †€ 43/50 ††€ 46/54, ☕ € 10 – ½ P € 40/48
Rest – *(closed Sunday dinner and Monday lunch)* Menu (€ 11), € 13 (weekdays)/38 – Carte € 20/50
◆ Located on the main square in Vic, this is a practical hotel for an overnight stay in the Adour area. It has simple, well-kept rooms. Two dining rooms, including an Eiffel-style veranda. In fine weather, tables are laid in a tree-lined courtyard. Traditional cuisine.

La Maison d'Anaïs
3 r. Pasteur – 05 62 96 84 04 – www.chambres-d-hotes-pyrenees.com – lamaisondanais@wanadoo.fr
3 rm – €60 €60/65 **Table d'hôte** – Menu €20 bi/25 bi
◆ Typical regional farmhouse surrounded by a garden. Large rooms with individual touches, lounge, library and terrace shaded by a pergola facing the greenery. Breakfast and dinner served around the huge wooden kitchen table.

VICHY – **03 Allier** – **326** H6 – **pop. 26 000** – **alt. 340 m** – **Spa : 1er March-late Nov.** – **Casinos : Le Grand Café** BZ, **Elysée Palace** – **03200** **Auvergne** 6 **C1**

Paris 353 – Clermont-Ferrand 55 – Montluçon 99 – Moulins 57 – Roanne 74

Office de tourisme, 19, rue du Parc 04 70 98 71 94, Fax 04 70 31 06 00

du Sporting Club de Vichy Bellerive-sur-Allier Allée Georges Baugnies, 04 70 32 39 11

la Forêt de Montpensier Bellerive-sur-Allier Domaine du château de Rilhat, 8 km on the Clermont-Ferrand road, 04 70 56 58 39

Parc des Sources★ - Allier parks ★ - Chalets★ (boulevard des États-Unis) BYZ - The thermal district★ - Grand casino-theatre★.

Sofitel Les Célestins rest,
111 bd États-Unis – 04 70 30 82 00 – h3241@accor.com – Fax 04 70 30 82 01 BY **e**
131 rm – €191/252 €231/293, €21 – 5 suites
Rest *N 3* – *(closed for lunch from Monday to Thursday from 15 September to 13 April) (dinner only)* Menu (€32), €43/140 – Carte €69/100
Rest *Le Bistrot des Célestins* – *(closed Sunday dinner except public holidays)* Menu €25 – Carte €37/68
◆ This modern hotel is next to the famous chalets where Napoleon III stayed. Modern rooms. Fitness centre and superb panoramic swimming pool. Inventive cuisine, contemporary decor and handsome summer terrace. At Le Bistrot enjoy traditional fare and grilled meats.

Aletti Palace Hôtel
3 pl. Joseph Aletti – 04 70 30 20 20 – www.hotel-aletti.fr – contact@aletti.fr – Fax 04 70 98 13 82 BZ **u**
129 rm – €120/168 €133/186
Rest *La Véranda* – 04 70 30 21 21 – Menu (€21), €23/50 – Carte €31/52
◆ This elegant early 20C hotel facing the Grand Casino combines modernity and old-world charm. Rooms have Art Deco inspired furniture and are gradually being renovated. Fitness centre. Attractive dining room, extended by a veranda; traditional menu.

Les Nations rest, rest,
13 bd Russie – 04 70 98 21 63 – www.lesnations.com – contact_lesnations@lesnations.com – Fax 04 70 98 61 13 – Open 1st April-20 October BZ **c**
70 rm – €58/84 €58/105, €12 – ½ P €54/67
Rest – Menu (€17), €21 – Carte €33/39
◆ A central location for this handsome 1900 building with its finely worked façade. The functional rooms and bathrooms have just received a facelift. Traditional cuisine served in two dining rooms decorated in contemporary style.

Pavillon d'Enghien
32 r. Callou – 04 70 98 33 30 – www.pavillondenghien.com – hotel.pavi@wanadoo.fr – Fax 04 70 31 67 82 – Closed 20 December-1st February BY **b**
22 rm – €59/68 €75/81, €8,50 – ½ P €54/62
Rest *Les Jardins d'Enghien* – *(closed Friday dinner from November to April, Sunday dinner and Monday)* Menu €19/34 – Carte €20/35
◆ This pleasant hotel offers charming, individually furnished rooms, in the process of a makeover. Friendly staff. Restaurant with a modern décor, featuring a small terrace surrounded by greenery and serving traditional dishes.

BELLERIVE-SUR-ALLIER

Auberger (Av. F.) . . . . A 2
Jean-Jaurès (Av.) . . . . A 16
Ramin (R. G.) . . . . A 28
République (Av.) . . . . A 30

VICHY

Alquié (R.) . . . . BY 15
Belgique (R. de) . . . . BZ 3
Besse (R.) . . . . CZ 20
Briand (Av. A.) . . . . BZ 4
Casino (R. du) . . . . BZ 5
Clemenceau (R. G.) . . . . BZ 6
Colombier (R. Hubert) . . . . BZ 23
Coulon (Av. P.) . . . . BY 7
Foch (R. Mar.) . . . . CZ 8
Glénard (Pl. Frantz) . . . . BY 9
Gramont (Av. de) . . . . A 10
Hôpital (Bd de l') . . . . A 13
Hôtel des Postes (R.) . . . . CY 14
Lattre-de-T. (Bd Mar.-de) . . . . BY 17
Lucas (R.) . . . . BY 18
Lyautey (R. du Mar.) . . . . A 19
Parc (R. du) . . . . BZ 22
Paris (R. de) . . . . CY
Poincaré (Av.) . . . . A 24
Porte-Verrier (R. de la) . . . . BZ 31
Prés.-Eisenhower (Av. du) . . . . BY 25
Prés.-Wilson (R.) . . . . BZ 26
Prunelle (R.) . . . . BZ 27
République (Av.) . . . . A 29
Tour (R. de la) . . . . BZ 32

Chambord rest,
82 r. de Paris – ✆ 04 70 30 16 30 – www.hotel-chambord-vichy.com – le.chambord @wanadoo.fr – Fax 04 70 31 54 92 – Closed 20 December-30 January CY **k**
27 rm – €43/52 €50/62, €10 – ½ P €52/62
Rest ***L'Escargot qui Tette*** – *(closed Sunday dinner and Monday)* Menu €23 (weekdays)/45 – Carte €35/60
◆ The same family has welcomed guests here for three generations. Practical rooms with good soundproofing. An amusing snail swigging a bottle of red wine is the emblem of this restaurant, decorated in a restrained contemporary style.

Arverna without rest
12 r. Desbrest – ✆ 04 70 31 31 19 – www.hotels-vichy.com – arverna-hotel@ wanadoo.fr – Fax 04 70 97 86 43 – Closed 7-22 February and 31 December-3 January CY **g**
26 rm – €45/50 €50/65, €8
◆ A family hotel being gradually renovated offers small rooms that overlook either the street or the inner courtyard. Here breakfast is served in the summer.

Kyriad without rest
6 av. Prés. Doumer – ✆ 04 70 31 45 00 – www.vichyevasion.fr – Fax 04 70 97 67 37
36 rm – €45/50 €50/115, €8 CZ **h**
◆ This hotel, in the famous resort's shopping district, provides practical and well-soundproofed rooms of various sizes. Buffet-breakfast available.

Maison Decoret (Jacques Decoret) with rm
15 r. du Parc – ✆ 04 70 97 65 06 – www.jacquesdecoret.com – jacques.decoret@ wanadoo.fr – Fax 04 70 97 80 11 – Closed 12 August-5 September, 5-26 February, Tuesday and Wednesday BZ **b**
5 rm – €180 €180, €18
Rest – Menu €68 (weekday lunch), €65/115 – Carte €95/115
Spec. Pomme de terre "institut de Beauvais" en crème. Bar sauvage d'Erquy confit, jus d'herbes, dattes et petits fenouils. Sablé chocolat et tube craquant garni de café. **Wines** Saint-Pourçain blanc et rouge.
◆ Highly personalised, inventive and playful cuisine served in a contemporary setting, contrasting with the historic location. View over the park. Modern rooms in guesthouse style with Napoleon III touches in the decor (period furniture, Pop Art paintings of the emperor).

L'Alambic
8 r. N.-Larbaud – ✆ 04 70 59 12 71 – alambic.vichy@orange.fr – Fax 04 70 97 98 88 – Closed 10 August-3 September, 8 February-25 March, Sunday dinner, Monday and Tuesday CY **u**
Rest – *(number of covers limited, pre-book)* Menu €26/47 – Carte €36/42
◆ A modern menu, attentive service, and an intimate ambience await in this tiny restaurant near the shopping centre, simply decorated in grey and green.

La Table d'Antoine
8 r. Burnol – ✆ 04 70 98 99 71 – www.latabledantoine.com – Fax 04 70 98 99 71 – Closed 2-8 November, 15 February-6 March, Thursday dinner in winter, Sunday dinner and Monday except public holidays BZ **d**
Rest – Menu €22 (weekday lunch), €29/60 – Carte €45/69
◆ Up-to-date cuisine served amid a refreshingly modernised, Baltard-inspired decor of glass and cast iron. Fine Auvergne cheese platter. Terrace on a pedestrian street.

L'Aromate
9 r. Besse – ✆ 04 70 32 13 22 – Fax 04 70 32 13 22 – Closed 20 July-12 August, 2-15 January, Sunday dinner, Tuesday dinner and Wednesday CZ **n**
Rest – *(pre-book)* Menu (€15), €20/38 – Carte approx. €38
◆ A high-ceilinged dining room with Napoleon III mirrors and paintings, in the street where Albert Londres was born. Herbs and spices add personal touches to the cuisine.

Brasserie du Casino
4 r. du Casino – ✆ 04 70 98 23 06 – www.allier-hotels-restaurants.com – bdcvichy@wanadoo.fr – Fax 04 70 98 53 17 – Closed 25 October-19 November, 22 February-4 March, Tuesday and Wednesday BZ **a**
Rest – Menu (€16), €26 – Carte €41/50
◆ Authentic 1920s setting for this brasserie, its walls adorned with photos of singers who performed at the nearby opera. Pavement terrace.

Michelangelo.s
44 av. Eugène-Gilbert – 04 70 32 85 15 – michelangelo.s@orange.fr – Fax 04 70 32 85 15 – Closed Sunday dinner, Monday dinner, Tuesday dinner and Wednesday CZ **b**
Rest – *(number of covers limited, pre-book)* Menu (€ 14), € 18 (weekday lunch), € 24/33 – Carte € 28/50
◆ In this simple and welcoming family home, the chef, originally from the Piemont region, prepares recipes from across Italy. Fine wine list. Delicatessen area.

L'Hippocampe
3 bd de Russie – 04 70 97 68 37 – Fax 04 70 97 68 37 – Closed 1st-21 June, 16 November-6 December, Tuesday lunch, Sunday dinner and Monday
Rest – Menu (€ 18 bi), € 27/56 – Carte € 40/70 BZ **z**
◆ Sumptuous and unusual villas all along this boulevard. Simple setting and kitchens visible from the dining room. Seafood has pride of place on the menu.

in Abrest **4 km by ② – pop. 2 500 – alt. 290 m – ✉ 03200**

La Colombière with rm rest,
136 av. de Thiers, on D 906 – 04 70 98 69 15 – www.allier-hotel-restaurant.com – lacolombiere@wanadoo.fr – Fax 04 70 31 50 89 – Closed 2 weeks in October, from end January to mid-February, Sunday dinner and Monday
3 rm – € 40/43 € 57/66, € 9
Rest – Menu € 20 (weekdays)/50 – Carte € 45/57
◆ Charming 1950s hillside villa, with a dovecote and a terraced garden that extends down to the Allier. Stunning panoramic view of the valley; traditional cuisine. Personalised, impeccably maintained rooms; friendly welcome.

in St-Yorre **8 km by ② – pop. 2 734 – alt. 275 m – ✉ 03270**

L'Auberge Bourbonnaise rm,
2 av. Vichy – 04 70 59 41 79 – aubergebourbonnaise@wanadoo.fr – Fax 04 70 59 24 94 – Closed 15 February-16 March, Sunday dinner and Monday except July-August
16 rm – € 52/60 € 52/76, € 9 – ½ P € 50/54
Rest – Menu (€ 12 bi), € 22/50 – Carte € 25/55
◆ Despite their nearness to the road the rooms are quiet owing to the good soundproofing. The annexe offers spacious duplexes with a refreshing tasteful decor. Rustic dining room-veranda and terrace; good choice of traditional set menus.

Piquenchagne
Domaine des grands Jarraux, south: 2 km via Thiers road – 04 70 59 23 77 – Fax 04 70 59 23 77 – Closed 1st-14 September, 25 January-8 February and Monday
Rest – Menu (€ 15 bi), € 19/39 – Carte € 37/57
◆ This restored old farmhouse has two simple, welcoming dining rooms. A terrace faces the English-style garden. Reasonably priced regional dishes.

VIC-LE-COMTE – 63 Puy-de-Dôme – **326** G9 – **pop. 4 612** – **alt. 472 m** – ✉ **63270** Auvergne 5 **B2**

Paris 433 – Ambert 56 – Clermont-Ferrand 23 – Issoire 16 – Thiers 40

Ste-Chapelle★ - Château of Busséol★ North: 6,5 km.

in Longues **4 km northwest by D 225 - ✉ 63270 Vic-le-Comte**

Le Comté
186 bd. du Gén. de Gaulle – 04 73 39 90 31 – www.restaurantlecomte.com – pascal_bonniol@orange.fr – Closed 31 August-13 September, Wednesday dinner, Sunday dinner and Monday
Rest – Menu € 21/38 – Carte € 36/50
◆ Regional early-20C house next to the Bank of France. Classic interior. Understandably, it is a favourite with many of the local bigwigs.

VIC-SUR-CÈRE – 15 Cantal – **330** D5 – **pop. 1 971** – **alt. 678 m** – **Casino** – ✉ **15800** Auvergne 5 **B3**

Paris 549 – Aurillac 19 – Murat 29

Office de tourisme, avenue André Mercier 04 71 47 50 68, Fax 04 71 47 58 56

Family Hôtel
av. E. Duclaux – ✆ 04 71 47 50 49 – www.family-hotel.fr – francois.courbebaisse@wanadoo.fr – Fax 04 71 47 51 31 – Closed 1 - 17 Dec.
55 rm – €45/69 €55/79, €7 – 16 suites – ½ P €44/57
Rest – *(closed 15 November-15 December)* Menu €16/30 – Carte €16/27
◆ A simple restaurant (non-smoking) with view of the valley and traditional cuisine.

Bel Horizon
r. Paul Doumer – ✆ 04 71 47 50 06 – www.hotel-bel-horizon.com – bouyssou@wanadoo.fr – Fax 04 71 49 63 81 – Closed 16 November-6 December
24 rm – €48/59 €63/75 – ½ P €46/52
Rest – Menu (€15), €19/42 – Carte €25/60
◆ Traditional building near the railway station. The scenic view of the Carladès relief explains the hotel's name. Fully renovated small rooms. A dining room with large bay windows overlooking the surrounding plateaux.

at Col de Curebourse 6 km southeast on the D 54 – alt. 994 m – ✉ 15800 St Clement

Hostellerie St-Clément
– ✆ 04 71 47 51 71 – hotelstclementcantal.com – hostelleriesaintclement@wanadoo.fr – Fax 04 71 49 63 02 – Closed 11-31 January, Sunday evening and Monday except July-August
21 rm – €56 €56/65, €8 – ½ P €56/65
Rest – Menu €27/105 – Carte €55/78
◆ A long construction overlooking the valley at an altitude of 1000m. The rooms, most of which have been refurbished, give onto the park. Non-smoking establishment. The restaurant offers a panoramic view of the Carladès plateau and ravines, and serves tasty traditional food.

VIDAUBAN – 83 Var – 340 N5 – pop. 9 331 – alt. 60 m – ✉ 83550 41 C3

Paris 841 – Cannes 63 – Draguignan 19 – Fréjus 29 – Toulon 61

Office de tourisme, 56, avenue du Président Wilson ✆ 04 94 73 10 28, Fax 04 94 73 07 82

La Fontaine rest,
60 rte Départementale 84, Thoronet road: 1.5 km – ✆ 04 94 99 91 91 – http://hotelfontaine.monsite.orange.fr – hotelfontaine@orange.fr – Fax 04 94 73 16 49
13 rm – €65 €65, €8 – ½ P €65
Rest – *(dinner only)* Menu €20/29 – Carte €27/34
◆ Standing on a junction, a family hotel with identical rooms that are functional and impeccably well kept. Modern restaurant filled with green plants; simple and traditional cuisine, spiced up with a few Indian touches.

La Bastide des Magnans with rm rm,
20 av. de la Résistance, rte La Garde-Freinet – ✆ 04 94 99 43 91 – www.bastidedesmagnans.com – magnans83@orange.fr – Fax 04 94 99 44 35 – Closed 25 June-4 July, 24-31 December, Sunday dinner and Monday in low season
5 rm – €75/85 €85/95, €10 – ½ P €90/105
Rest – *(closed Sunday dinner, Wednesday dinner and Monday in low season)* Menu (€19), €29/68 – Carte €68/90
◆ This former silkworm nursery is home to two bright dining rooms redecorated in chic, country style. Well-composed traditional menu. Five charming rooms, each of which is perfectly decorated according to a different theme and ambiance.

Concorde
9 pl. G. Clemenceau – ✆ 04 94 73 01 19 – Fax 04 94 73 01 19 – Closed Tuesday dinner and Wednesday
Rest – Menu (€19 bi), €31/58 – Carte €50/80
◆ This typically Provencal restaurant on the main square offers generous country cooking with seasonal game and mushroom specialities.

VIEILLEVIE – 15 Cantal – 330 C7 – pop. 114 – alt. 220 m – ✉ 15120 5 B3

▶ Paris 600 – Aurillac 45 – Entraygues-sur-Truyère 15 – Figeac 44 – Montsalvy 14 – Rodez 50

La Terrasse

– ✆ 04 71 49 94 00 – www.hotel-terrasse.com – hotel-de-la-terrasse@wanadoo.fr – Fax 04 71 49 92 23 – Open 2 April-7 November

26 rm – †€ 50/55 ††€ 59/64, ☕ € 10 – ½ P € 54/65

Rest – *(closed Sunday dinner and Monday except July-August, and weekend bank holidays)* Menu (€ 11), € 24 (weekdays)/43 – Carte € 33/46

◆ This hotel, managed by the same family since 1870, stands on the banks of the Lot. There are good leisure facilities, country-style rooms and a bar with a local clientele. A wisteria perfumes and shades the terrace of this village restaurant, overlooking the pool. Regional fare.

VIENNE – 38 Isère – 333 C4 – pop. 30 600 – alt. 160 m – ✉ 38200 44 B2

Lyon - Rhone Valley

▶ Paris 486 – Grenoble 89 – Lyon 31 – St-Étienne 49 – Valence 73

ℹ Office de tourisme, cours Brillier ✆ 04 74 53 80 30, Fax 04 74 53 80 31

◉ St-Maurice cathedral ★★ - Temple of Augustus and Livia ★★ R - Théâtre romain★ - Church★ and cloister★ of St-André-le-Bas - Esplanade du Mont Pipet ≤★ - Former St-Pierre church ★ - Carved group★ of Ste-Colombe church AY - Gallo-Roman town of St-Romain-en-Gal★★ (museum★, site★).

Plans on following pages

La Pyramide (Patrick Henriroux)

14 bd F. Point, Cours de Verdun, south of the map – ✆ 04 74 53 01 96 – www.lapyramide.com – pyramide@relaischateaux.com – Fax 04 74 85 69 73 – Closed 3 February-5 March and 11-19 August

21 rm – †€ 190/230 ††€ 200/250, ☕ € 20 – 4 suites

Rest – *(closed Tuesday and Wednesday)* Menu € 64 bi (weekday lunch)/164 – Carte € 110/200

Spec. Crème soufflée de crabe "dormeur" au caviar. Cul de veau de lait et poêlon de légumes de la vallée. Piano au chocolat praliné, amandes, noisettes, sauce café.

Wines Condrieu, Côte-Rôtie.

◆ Attractive regional construction with vast and elegant Provence-inspired guestrooms and a pleasant garden. Fine cuisine with up-to-date flavours, plus a superb cellar boasting some rare vintages. Reasonably priced, midweek lunchtime "menu du marché".

Le Bec Fin

7 pl. St-Maurice – ✆ 04 74 85 76 72 – Fax 04 74 85 15 30 – Closed Wednesday dinner, Sunday dinner and Monday AY **r**

Rest – Menu € 23 (weekdays)/60 – Carte € 45/70

◆ The traditional-regional cuisine of this restaurant has character, just like its owner. Simple decor; outside dining on the square in summer.

Le Cloître

2 r. Cloîtres – ✆ 04 74 31 93 57 – Fax 04 74 85 03 51 – Closed 10-17 August, Saturday and Sunday BY **n**

Rest – Menu (€ 17), € 24/41 – Carte € 39/60

◆ Pleasant establishment at the foot of the St Maurice cathedral. Stained-glass windows, stone and wooden beams provide the backdrop for contemporary cuisine and a good wine list.

Saveurs du Marché

34 cours de Verdun, south of plan – ✆ 04 74 31 65 65 – www.lessaveursdumarché.fr – saveurs.du.marche@wanadoo.fr – Fax 04 74 31 65 65 – Closed 18 July-17 August, 24 December-5 January, Saturday, Sunday and bank holidays

Rest – Menu (€ 13), € 18 (weekday dinner), € 23/37 – Carte € 35/47 dinner only

◆ A small, bright dining room near the pyramid of the ancient Roman Circus. Market fresh lunch menu, more up-to-date and elaborate in the evenings. Côtes-du-Rhône wines.

L'Estancot

4 r. Table Ronde – ✆ 04 74 85 12 09 – Fax 04 74 85 12 09 – Closed 1st-16 September, Christmas to mid January, Sunday, Monday and public holidays

Rest – Menu € 14 (weekday lunch), € 20/28 – Carte € 21/38

◆ Nice bistro-like address, frequented by regulars. Traditional and regional menu; "criques" (potato pancakes) are an evening speciality.

in Chasse-sur-Rhône 8 km by ① (A7 junction - Chasse-sur-Rhône exit) – pop. 4 795 – alt. 180 m – ✉ 38670

Mercure
1363 av. F. Mistral – ☎ 04 72 49 58 68 – www.mercure.com – h0349@accor.com – Fax 04 72 49 58 88
115 rm – †€ 109/149 ††€ 119/159, ☕ € 16
Rest – *(closed Saturday lunch, Sunday lunch and public holidays)* Menu € 20/27 – Carte € 29/44
◆ Imposing construction close to the motorway. The functional guestrooms are decorated with a jazz theme, a reference to the famous Vienne festival. This restaurant has a contemporary setting and traditional food enhanced by a few Lyon specialities.

in Estrablin 8 km by ② and D 41 – pop. 3 283 – alt. 223 m – ✉ 38780

La Gabetière without rest
269 Le Logis Neuf, on D 502 – ☎ 04 74 58 01 31 – www.la-gabetiere.com – lagabetiere@orange.fr – Fax 04 74 58 08 98 – Closed 24 December-15 January
12 rm – †€ 52 ††€ 68/70, ☕ € 10
◆ A charmingly restored 16C manor and outbuildings, set in a park. Rooms decorated in a range of styles ("chocolate-box", Provençal, antique etc). Swimming pool and play area.

in Reventin-Vaugris (village) 9 km by ④, N 7 and D 131 – pop. 1 623 – alt. 230 m – ✉ 38121

La Maison de l'Aubressin
847 chemin Aubressin, 1 km north via minor road – ☎ 04 74 58 83 02 – aubressin@wanadoo.fr – Closed 7-25 April, 1st-20 September, 24-31 December, Sunday dinner, Monday and Tuesday
Rest – *(number of covers limited, pre-book)* Menu € 48 bi/78 bi – Carte € 27/65
◆ Ivy-clad establishment perched on a hill with views of Mont Pilat. Traditional cuisine served amidst reproductions of tapestries from the Cluny Museum, or on the terrace.

in Chonas-l'Amballan 9 km south by ④ and N 7 – pop. 1 372 – alt. 250 m – ✉ 38121

Hostellerie Le Marais St-Jean without rest
chemin Marais – ☎ 04 74 58 83 28 – contact@domaine-de-clairefontaine.fr – Fax 04 74 58 80 93 – Closed 16-21 August and 20 December-15 January
10 rm – †€ 82/90 ††€ 82/90, ☕ € 15
◆ A restored old farm building with a tasteful, sober interior. The south-facing terrace is the perfect spot for breakfast in summer. Herb garden.

Domaine de Clairefontaine (Philippe Girardon) with rm
chemin Fontanettes – rm, rest,
☎ 04 74 58 81 52 – www.domaine-de-clairefontaine.fr – contact@domaine-de-clairefontaine.fr – Fax 04 74 58 80 93 – Closed 18 December-16 January, Monday and Tuesday except dinner in high season
9 rm – †€ 56/90 ††€ 56/90, ☕ € 17 – 2 suites – ½ P € 79/115
Rest – Menu € 35 bi, € 65/110 – Carte € 93/133
Spec. Homard à la coque et calamars poêlés. Pigeon de l'Isère et foie gras de canard en croustille, jus de truffe. Soufflé chaud à la Chartreuse. **Wines** Saint-Joseph, Crozes-Hermitage.
◆ Once a retreat for Lyon bishops, this elegant residence nestling in a 3ha park is now a gourmet destination: studied and contemporary cuisine.

Les Jardins de Clairefontaine
– Closed 18 December-16 January
18 rm – †€ 125/130 ††€ 125/130, ☕ € 17 – ½ P € 113/115
◆ A blend of peace and quiet, space and greenery. Guestrooms with a balcony or terrace. Reception in the main building.

STE-COLOMBE

Briand (Pl. A.) . . . . AY
Cochard (R.) . . . . AY
Égalité (Pl. de l') . . . . AY
Garon (R.) . . . . AY
Herbouville (Q. d') . . . . AY
Joubert (Av.) . . . . AY
Nationale (R.) . . . . AY
Petits Jardins (R. des) . . . . AY

VIENNE

Allmer (R.) . . . . BZ 2
Allobroges (Pl. des) . . . . AZ
Anatole-France (Quai) . . . . . . BCY
Aqueducs (Ch. des) . . . . CY
Asiaticus (Bd) . . . . AZ
Beaumur (Montée) . . . . BCZ
Boson (R.) . . . . AZ
Bourgogne (R. de) . . . . BY
Brenier (R. J.) . . . . BY
Briand (Pl. A.) . . . . BY 3
Brillier (Cours) . . . . ABZ
Capucins (Pl. des) . . . . BCY
Célestes (R. des) . . . . CY 4
Chantelouve (R.) . . . . BY 5
Charité (R. de la) . . . . BCY 6
Cirque (R. du) . . . . CY 7
Clémentine (R.) . . . . BY 8
Clercs (R. des) . . . . BY 9
Collège (R. du) . . . . BY 10
Coupe-Jarret (Montée) . . . . . . BZ
Éperon (R. de l') . . . . BY 12
Gère (R. de) . . . . CY
Jacquier (R. H.) . . . .
Jean-Jaurès (Q.) . . . . AYZ
Jeu-de-Paume (Pl. du) . . . . BY 15
Jouffray (Pl. C.) . . . . AZ
Juiverie (R. de la) . . . . BZ 16
Lattre-de-Tassigny (Pont de) . ABY
Laurent (R. Florentin) . . . . AZ
Marchande (R.) . . . . BY
Miremont (Pl. de) . . . . BY 18
Mitterrand (Pl. F.) . . . . BY 19
Orfèvres (R. des) . . . . BY 20
Pajot (Quai) . . . . BY 22
Palais (Pl. du) . . . . BY 23
Peyron (R.) . . . . BZ 24
Pilori (Pl. du) . . . . BY 25
Pipet (R.) . . . . CY
Pompidou (Bd Georges) . . . . . . AZ
Ponsard (R.) . . . . BY 28
République (Bd et Pl.) . . . . . . ABZ 29
Riondet (Quai) . . . . AZ
Rivoire (Pl. A.) . . . . CY
Romanet (R. E.) . . . . ABZ
Romestang (Cours) . . . . BZ
St-André-le-Haut (R.) . . . . CY 34
St-Louis (Pl.) . . . . BY
St-Marcel (Montée) . . . . CYZ
St-Maurice (Pl.) . . . . AY
St-Paul (Pl.) . . . . BY
St-Pierre (Pl.) . . . . AZ
Schneider (R.) . . . . CY 37
Sémard (Pl. P.) . . . . BZ
Table-Ronde (R. de la) . . . . BY 38
Thomas (R. A.) . . . . CY
Tupinières (Montée des) . . . . . . CZ
Ursulines (R. des) . . . . CY 39
Verdun (Cours de) . . . . AZ
Victor-Hugo (R.) . . . . BCYZ
11-Novembre (R. du) . . . . AZ 43

South At Mas de Gerbey, 10 km by ④ and D 4 - ✉ 38121 Chonas-l'Amballan

L'Atelier d'Antoine

2176 Mas de Gerbey - CD4 – ☎ 04 74 56 41 21
– www.atelier-antoine.fr – latelierdantoine@orange.fr
– Fax 04.74.56.41.21
– Closed Sunday dinner, Tuesday and Wednesday
Rest – Menu (€ 17), € 28/44 – Carte € 25/34
◆ A modern take on traditional cuisine with the occasional exotic touch is the order of the day here. Classic decor with a screen displaying action live from the kitchen. Terrace.

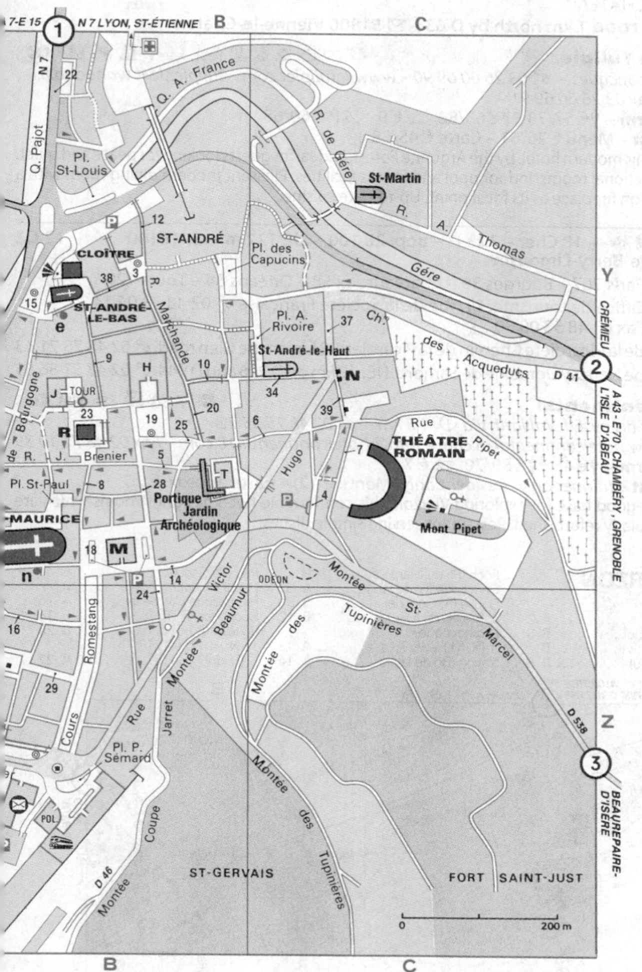

VIENNE-EN-VAL – 45 Loiret – 318 J5 – pop. 1 681 – alt. 112 m – ✉ 45510 12 C2

Paris 157 – La Ferté-St-Aubin 22 – Montargis 57 – Orléans 23 – Sully-sur-Loire 20

XX **Auberge de Vienne**

– ☎ 02 38 58 85 47 – www.aubergedevienne.com – dsalmon@wanadoo.fr – Fax 02 38 58 63 29 – Closed 31 August-15 September, 12 January-3 February, Sunday dinner, Monday and Tuesday except bank holidays

Rest – Menu (€ 28), € 35 (weekdays)/61 – Carte € 50/60

◆ Old village establishment on the border of Sologne. Pleasant rustic dining room featuring half-timbering and a lovely fireplace. Traditional cuisine.

VIENNE-LE-CHÂTEAU – 51 Marne – 306 L7 – pop. 608 – alt. 129 m – ✉ 51800 14 C2

Paris 236 – Châlons-en-Champagne 52 – Saint-Memmie 50 – Verdun 49

Binarville road 1 km north by D 63 – ✉ 51800 Vienne-le-Château

Le Tulipier — rest, VISA

r. St-Jacques – ✆ 03 26 60 69 90 – www.letulipier.com – tulipier.le@wanadoo.fr – Fax 03 26 60 69 91

38 rm – †€ 57/73 ††€ 68/82, ☕ € 9 – ½ P € 60/68

Rest – Menu € 26/61 – Carte € 45/58

◆ This modern hotel, by the Argonne Forest, is ideal for guests looking for peace and quiet. Functional rooms, indoor pool and fitness facilities. Pleasant modern dining room with a design fireplace as its focal point. Up-to-date cuisine.

VIERZON – 18 Cher – **323** I3 – **pop. 28 100 – alt. 122 m** – ✉ **18100** — 12 **C2**

Dordogne-Berry-Limousin

- Paris 207 – Bourges 39 – Châteauroux 58 – Orléans 84 – Tours 120
- Office de tourisme, 11, rue de la Société Française ✆ 02 48 53 06 14, Fax 02 48 53 09 30
- de la Picardière Chemin de la Picardière, 8 km on the Gien road, ✆ 02 48 75 21 43
- de Nançay Domaine de Samord, NE : 18 km on D 926 and D 944, ✆ 02 48 51 86 55

Continental — VISA

104 bis av. Ed. Vaillant, via ①: 1.5 km – ✆ 02 48 75 35 22
www.hotelcontinental18.com – info@hotelcontinental18.com – Fax 02 48 71 10 39

37 rm – †€ 48 ††€ 59/70, ☕ € 7

Rest – *(dinner only) (resident only)* Menu (€ 12) – Carte approx. € 26

◆ A good base for exploring Vierzon, this comfortable hotel has guestrooms which are regularly refurbished. Restaurant serving simple dishes.

VIERZON

Street	Square	No.
Baron (R. Bl.)	A	2
Briand (Pl. Aristide)	B	3
Brunet (R. A.)	B	
Dr-P.-Roux (R. du)	B	6
Foch (Pl. du Mar.)	B	7
Gaucherie (R. de la)	A	8
Gaulle (R. Gén.-de)	A	9
Joffre (R. du Mar.)	B	12
Larchevêque (R. M.)	A	13
Nation (Bd de la)	A	14
Péri (Pl. Gabriel)	A	
Ponts (R. des)	B	
République (Av. de la)	A	16
Roosevelt (R. Th.)	B	18
Voltaire (R.)	B	20
11-Novembre-1918 (R. du)	A	22

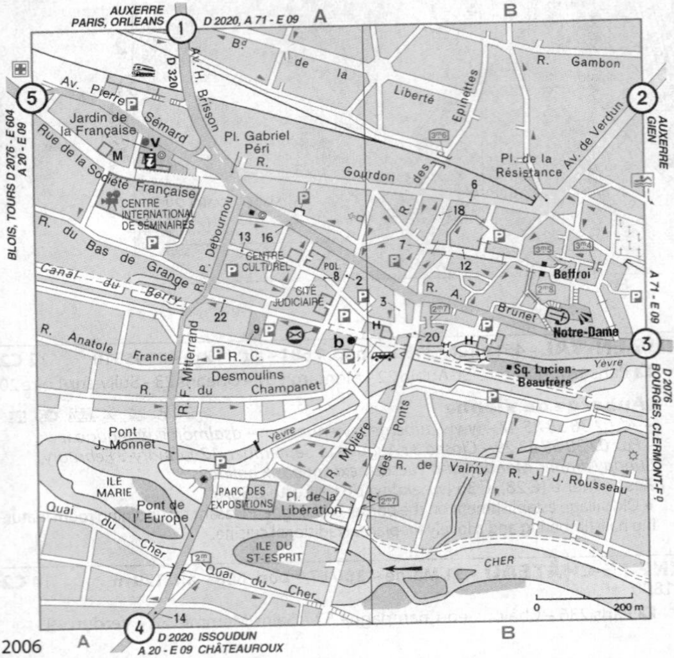

Arche Hôtel
13 r. du 11 Novembre 1918 – ✆ 02 48 71 93 10 – www.arche-hotel.fr – info@arche-hotel.fr – Fax 02 48 71 83 63 A **b**
41 rm – 🚹€ 48/65 🚹🚹€ 55/75, ☕ € 8
Rest – snack – *(closed Sunday) (dinner only)* Menu (€ 14), € 18/22
◆ Located close to the arches of the old bridge spanning the Yèvre, this hotel has a modern glass facade and interior decor influenced by American pop culture. Well-appointed, functional guestrooms. An unpretentious place to break for salads and grilled foods in an up-to-date setting.

La Maison de Célestin (Pascal Chaupitre)
20 av. P. Sémard – ✆ 02 48 83 01 63 – www.lamaisondecelestin.com – lamaisondecelestin@wanadoo.fr – Fax 02 48 71 63 41 – Closed 13-21 April, 10 August-1st September, 4-16 January, Sunday dinner, Monday and Tuesday
Rest – Menu (€ 25), € 40 (weekdays)/59 bi – Carte approx. € 50 A **v**
Spec. Terrine de foie gras de canard et son condiment. Brochette de lapereau, frite de polenta aux girolles et au lard (autumn). Petits pots de crème brûlée. **Wines** Reuilly, Menetou-Salon.
◆ This 19C town house has an elegant and contemporary loft-style interior and a veranda and terrace overlooking a public park. Refined contemporary cuisine.

Tours road 2.5 km by ⑤ – ✉ **18100 Vierzon**

Le Champêtre
89 rte de Tours – ✆ 02 48 75 87 18 – Fax 02 48 71 67 04 – Closed 25 July-15 August, Monday dinner, Wednesday dinner, Sunday dinner and Tuesday
Rest – Menu € 20 (weekdays), € 26/44 – Carte € 33/53
◆ Attractive small restaurant with a rustic-style dining room. Tempting menu featuring delicious classical and regional dishes.

VIEUX-BOUCAU-LES-BAINS – **40 Landes** – **335** C12 – **pop. 1 576** 3 **A2**
– **alt. 5 m** – ✉ **40480** **Atlantic Coast**

Paris 740 – Bayonne 41 – Biarritz 48 – Castets 28 – Dax 37 – Mont-de-Marsan 90
Office de tourisme, Le Mail ✆ 05 58 48 13 47, Fax 05 58 48 15 37
de Pinsolle Soustons Port d'Albret Sud, S : 9 km on D 4, ✆ 05 58 48 03 92

Marinero with rm
15 Grande Rue – ✆ 05 58 48 14 15 – www.marinero.biz – marinero2@wanadoo.fr – Fax 05 17 47 52 15 – Open from end March to end September
19 rm – 🚹€ 33/48 🚹🚹€ 36/61, ☕ € 7
Rest – *(closed Tuesday off season and Monday except dinners in July-August)* Menu € 19/32 – Carte € 25/40
◆ Blue and white shades, mahogony furniture, sea-themed paintings and knick-knacks all give this restaurant a marine bistro atmosphere. Spanish-Landes fish and seafood cuisine.

VIEUX-MOULIN – **60 Oise** – **305** I4 – **see Compiègne**

VIEUX-VILLEZ – **27 Eure** – **304** H6 – **see Gaillon**

LE VIGAN – **30 Gard** – **339** G5 – **pop. 4 429** – **alt. 221 m** – ✉ **30120** 23 **C2**
Languedoc-Roussillon-Tarn Gorges

Paris 707 – Alès 66 – Lodève 50 – Mende 108 – Millau 72 – Montpellier 61 – Nîmes 77
Office de tourisme, place du Marché ✆ 04 67 81 01 72, Fax 04 67 81 86 79
Musée Cévenol★.

in Rey 5 km east by D 999 – ✉ **30570 St-André-de-Majencoules**

Château du Rey
– ✆ 04 67 82 40 06 – www.chateaudurey.fr – contact@chateaudurey.fr – Fax 04 67 82 47 79 – Open from April to October
13 rm – 🚹€ 75 🚹🚹€ 85/98, ☕ € 8 – 1 suite – ½ P € 68/81
Rest – *(closed Sunday dinner and Monday)* Menu (€ 15), € 23/46 – Carte € 33/51
◆ Viollet-le-Duc restored this medieval castle, set in the heart of a riverside park. Individually styled rooms adorned with antique furniture. The vaulted dining room is in the castle's 13C former sheepcote; pleasant terrace.

in Pont d'Hérault 6 km east by D 999 – ✉ 30570 Valleraugue

Maurice rest, rest, P VISA MC

– ✆ 04 67 82 40 02 – www.hotelmaurice.fr.st – hotelmaurice@aol.com – Fax 04 67 82 46 12 – Closed January

14 rm – †€ 68 ††€, ☕ € 8 – ½ P € 68/88

Rest – *(resident only)* Menu € 39/62 – Carte € 58/68

◆ Traditional inn run by the same family for three generations, located on a pretty country road along the Hérault. Comfortable rooms, quieter on the riverside. Colourful dining room and pleasant terrace overlooking the pool and the valley.

LE VIGAN – 46 Lot – **337** E3 – see Gourdon

VIGNOUX-SUR-BARANGEON – 18 Cher – **323** J3 – **pop. 2 042** 12 **C3**
– **alt. 157 m** – ✉ **18500**

Paris 215 – Bourges 26 – Cosne-sur-Loire 69 – Gien 70 – Issoudun 37 – Vierzon 9

Office de tourisme, 23, rue de la République ✆ 02 48 51 11 41, Fax 02 48 51 11 46

Le Prieuré with rm rm, P VISA MC

r. Jean Graczyk – ✆ 02 48 51 58 80 – www.leprieurehotel.com – prieurehotel@wanadoo.fr – Fax 02 48 51 56 01 – Closed autumn and February school holidays, Tuesday and Wednesday

6 rm – †€ 63/76 ††€ 63/76, ☕ € 7 – ½ P € 72/78

Rest – Menu (€ 18), € 25 (weekdays)/45 – Carte € 45/55

◆ This moderatly contemporary restaurant is housed in a 19C presbytery. Pleasant poolside terrace. Up-to-date cuisine. Simple rooms.

VILLAGE-NEUF – 68 Haut-Rhin – **315** J11 – see St-Louis

VILLAINES-LA-JUHEL – 53 Mayenne – **310** H4 – **pop. 3 179** 35 **C1**
– **alt. 185 m** – ✉ **53700**

Paris 222 – Alençon 32 – Bagnoles-de-l'Orne 31 – Le Mans 58 – Mayenne 28

Syndicat d'initiative, boulevard du Général-de-Gaulle ✆ 02 43 03 78 88, Fax 02 43 03 77 92

Oasis without rest P VISA MC AE

1 km on Javron road – ✆ 02 43 03 28 67 – www.oasis.fr – oasis@oasis.fr – Fax 02 43 03 35 30

14 rm – †€ 45 ††€ 55/85, ☕ € 9

◆ An old farm with a restored interior that still has a rural flavour. Beams and brick walls in all the rooms. Small park with a pool and crazy golf.

VILLARD-DE-LANS – 38 Isère – **333** G7 – **pop. 4 088 – alt. 1 040 m** 45 **C2**
– **Winter sports : 1 160/2 170 m** 2 27 – **Casino** – ✉ **38250** **French Alps**

Paris 584 – Die 67 – Grenoble 34 – Lyon 123 – Valence 67 – Voiron 44

Office de tourisme, 101, pl. Mure Ravaud ✆ 08 11 46 00 15, Fax 04 76 95 98 39

de Corrençon-en-Vercors, S : 6 km on D 215, ✆ 04 76 95 80 42

Gorges de la Bourne★★★ – Valchevrière road ★ West by D 215ᶜ.

Plan on next page

Le Christiania VISA MC AE

av. Prof. Nobecourt – ✆ 04 76 95 12 51 – www.hotel-le-christiania.fr – info@hotel-le-christiania.fr – Fax 04 76 95 00 75 – Open 20 May-30 September and 19 December to mid-April k

23 rm – †€ 55/92 ††€ 70/165, ☕ € 10

Rest *Le Tétras* – *(open 22 May-31 August and 19 December-31 March)*
Menu (€ 15), € 25 (dinner), € 35/50 – Carte € 40/80 dinner only

◆ A chalet hotel offering individually styled spacious rooms, some of them wood panelled in the Savoy fashion. Almost all have a balcony and a view of the mountain. Indoor pool. Restaurant decorated with knick knacks and hunting trophies; regional food.

VILLARD-DE-LANS

Adret (R. de l') 2
Chabert (Pl. P.) 4
Chapelle-en-Vercors (R. de la) 5
Croix Margot (Chemin de la) 27
Dr-Lefrançois (R. du) 6
Francs-Tireurs (Av. des) 8
Galizon (Chemin de) 9
Gambetta (R.) 10
Gaulle (Av. Gén.-de) 12
Libération (Pl. de la) 13
Lycée Polonais (R. du) 14
Martyrs (Pl. des) 15
Moulin (R. Jean) 16
Mure-Ravaud (Pl. R.) 17
Pouteil-Noble (R. P.) 19
Professeur Nobecourt (Av.) 20
République (R. de la) 22
Roux-Fouillet (R. A.) 23
Victor-Hugo (R.) 26

Les Trente Pas

VISA

16 r. des Francs-Tireurs – ☎ 04 76 94 06 75 – Fax 04 76 95 80 69 – Closed 13-30 April and 16 November-11 December, Wednesday dinner, Thursday dinner, Monday and Tuesday except bank holidays **b**

Rest – Menu € 15 (weekday lunch), € 28/51 bi – Carte € 35/45

◆ A few steps from the village church (no more than 30?), this small restaurant offers generous portions of traditional cuisine. A local artist's work is on display in the dining area.

Southwest By Col du Liorin road – ✉ 38250 Villard-de-Lans

Auberge des Montauds

rest, VISA

aux Montauds: 4 km – ☎ 04 76 95 17 25 – www.auberge-des-montauds.fr – aubergedesmontauds@wanadoo.fr – Fax 04 76 95 17 69 – Closed 14 April-1st May and 4 November-18 December

12 rm – † € 55/59 †† € 68/73 – ½ P € 54/57

Rest – *(closed Monday and Tuesday except July-August)* Menu € 20/35 – Carte € 25/42

◆ This picturesque old farm stands on the outskirts of a mountain hamlet. Warm, welcoming, chalet-style rooms. Traditional dishes and regional specialities. Raclettes and fondues served in the dining room with fireplace or on the terrace.

La Ferme du Bois Barbu with rm

VISA

at Bois- Barbu: 3 km – ☎ 04 76 95 13 09 – www.fermeboisbarbu.com – contact@fermeboisbarbu.com – Closed 14-20 April, 5-10 October, 12 November-5 December

8 rm – † € 50 †† € 58, € 9 – ½ P € 56

Rest – *(closed Sunday dinner and Wednesday)* Menu (€ 19), € 25/34 – Carte approx. € 35

◆ Not far from the cross-country skiing tracks. A pleasant dining area (wood panelling, fireplace, etc.). Classic, regionally inspired menu. Alpine style rooms.

in Balcon de Villard Côte 2000 road, 4 km southeast by D 215 and D 215B – ✉ 38250 Villard-de-Lans

Les Playes

VISA

Les Pouteils Côte 2000 – ☎ 04 76 95 14 42 – www.hotel-playes.com – contact@hotel-playes.com – Fax 04 76 95 58 38 – Open 9 May-19 September and 20 December-12 April

23 rm – † € 52/65 †† € 65/88, € 11 – ½ P € 66/78

Rest – *(open 2 June-5 September and 20 December-31 March) (dinner only in winter)* Menu (€ 22), € 26/40

◆ This sturdy chalet offers rooms, gradually renovated in an updated alpine spirit. Some have balconies overlooking the Grande Moucherolle mountains. Restaurant and terrace with a lovely view of the peaks; regional fare in winter, classic in summer.

in Corrençon-en-Vercors 6 km south by D 215 – **pop. 358 – alt. 1 105 m** – ✉ **38250**

Office de tourisme, place du Village ✆ 04 76 95 81 75, Fax 04 76 95 84 63

Du Golf

Les Ritons – ✆ 04 76 95 84 84 – www.hotel-du-golf-vercors.fr – hotel-du-golf@wanadoo.fr – Fax 04 76 95 82 85 – Open 1st May-18 October and 19 December-28 March

22 rm – †€ 70/95 ††€ 100/200, ☕ € 12 – 6 suites – ½ P € 92/140

Rest – *(closed for lunch except Saturday, Sunday and bank holidays)* Menu € 32/85 – Carte € 42/80

Spec. Fricassée de champignons, espuma de gratin de pomme de terre, caviar d'escargots (summer). Filet de pigeon rôti sur l'os, les abats en tartine, pois gourmands et langoustine. Soufflé chaud à la pomme verte (autumn). **Wines** Vin de Pays des Balmes Dauphinoises, Châtillon-en-Diois blanc.

◆ Delightful rooms, superb, all-wood extension, cosy bar, brand new sauna and Jacuzzi, generous breakfasts: nothing is lacking in this family run hotel! Subtly inventive recipes (regional produce) served by the fire or on the pretty terrace.

VILLARD-RECULAS – 38 Isère – 333 J7 – pop. 63 – alt. 1 450 m – ✉ 38114 45 C2

Paris 626 – Lyon 168 – Grenoble 58 – Échirolles 50 – Saint-Martin-d'Hères 59

Office de tourisme, 1, rue des pistes ✆ 04 76 80 45 69, Fax 04 76 80 92 34

Bonsoir Clara

23 rte des Alpages – ✆ 04 76 80 37 20 – www.bonsoirclara.fr – il-fera-beau-demain@wanadoo.fr – Fax 04 76 80 37 20 – Open 15 June-15 October and 15 December-1st May

Rest – *(pre-book the weekend)* Menu € 30/37 – Carte € 31/53

◆ Find up-to-date recipes featuring regional produce and oriental spices at Clara's delightful chalet overlooking the village. Fine wine list.

LE VILLARS – 71 Saône-et-Loire – 320 J10 – see Tournus

VILLARS – 84 Vaucluse – 332 F10 – pop. 697 – alt. 330 m – ✉ 84400 42 E1

Paris 739 – Marseille 112 – Avignon 58 – Aix-en-Provence 96 – Salon-de-Provence 62

La Table de Pablo

hamlet of Petits-Cléments – ✆ 04 90 75 45 18 – www.latabledepablo.com – restaurantlatabledepablo@orange.fr – Closed 1st January-13 February, Thursday lunch, Saturday lunch and Wednesday from September to May

Rest – *(number of covers limited, pre-book)* Menu (€ 16), € 28/39 – Carte € 36/48

◆ This restaurant lost among the vines and cherry trees is full of local colour. It serves delicate and creative cuisine. Peaceful terrace.

VILLARS-LES-DOMBES – 01 Ain – 328 D4 – pop. 4 190 – alt. 281 m – ✉ 01330 Lyon - Rhone Valley 43 E1

Paris 433 – Bourg-en-Bresse 29 – Lyon 37 – Villefranche-sur-Saône 29

Office de tourisme, 3, place de l'Hôtel de Ville ✆ 04 74 98 06 29, Fax 04 74 98 29 13

du Clou RN 83, S : 3 km on D 1083, ✆ 04 74 98 19 65

du Gouverneur Monthieux Château du Breuil, SW : 8 km on D 904 and D 6, ✆ 04 72 26 40 34

Parc ornithologique (Ornithological park) ★★ South: 1 km.

Ribotel

rte de Lyon – ✆ 04 74 98 08 03 – www.ribotel.fr – ribotel@wanadoo.fr – Fax 04 74 98 29 55 – Closed 22 December-3 January

45 rm ☕ – †€ 50 ††€ 58 – ½ P € 52

Rest *La Villardière* – *(closed Sunday dinner from November to February and Monday)* Menu (€ 17), € 20/35 – Carte € 31/41

◆ A good hotel at the entrance to a bird sanctuary. Most of its rooms have been upgraded and have a small sitting room (club armchairs, flat screen TV). La Villardière's rotunda dining room serves a traditional menu.

in Bouligneux 4 km northwest by D 2 – **pop. 304** – **alt. 282 m** – ✉ **01330**

XX **Auberge des Chasseurs**
Le Village – ✆ *04 74 98 10 02 – Fax 04 74 98 28 87 – Closed 1st-10 September, 20 December-20 January, Monday dinner 15 November-15 March, Tuesday and Wednesday*
Rest – Menu € 30 (weekdays)/70 – Carte € 40/80
◆ This restaurant near the church provides friendly hospitality to hunters and other guests. Regional cuisine served in a country-style dining room, and in the garden in summer.

X **Hostellerie des Dombes**
Le Village – ✆ *04 74 98 08 40 – www.hostelleriedesdombes.com – bruno.levet@aol.com – Fax 04 74 98 16 63 – Closed 17-28 August, February school holidays, Thursday except dinner in summer and Wednesday*
Rest – Menu € 23 (weekdays)/49 – Carte € 39/63
◆ In the town centre, a traditional house home to a countrified dining room and pleasant terrace. Serves fine regional cuisine including frogs' legs and game in season.

X **Le Thou**
Le Village – ✆ *04 74 98 15 25 – www.lethou.com – lethou@orange.fr – Fax 04 74 98 13 57 – Closed autumn school holidays and February school holidays, Sunday dinner, Monday and Tuesday*
Rest – Menu € 29/56 – Carte € 32/54
◆ An airy, conservatory-style lobby in this former village inn smothered in flowers. The menu pays homage to the regions of Bresse and Dombes (frogs' legs in season).

VILLARS-SOUS-DAMPJOUX – 25 Doubs – 321 K2 – pop. 411 – alt. 362 m – ✉ 25190

17 **C2**

▶ Paris 482 – Baume-les-Dames 50 – Besançon 81 – Montbéliard 24 – Morteau 49

in Bief 3 km south – **pop. 115** – **alt. 362 m** – ✉ **25190**

X **L'Auberge Fleurie**
4 chemin de Dampjoux – ✆ *03 81 96 53 01 – jacri@tele2.fr – Fax 03 81 96 55 64 – Closed Monday and Tuesday except bank holidays*
Rest – Menu (€ 11), € 19/38 – Carte € 28/43
◆ This simple little village inn faces a chapel and overlooks the Doubs. Traditional regional cuisine served in an attractive colourful dining room.

VILLÉ – 67 Bas-Rhin – 315 H6 – pop. 1 691 – alt. 260 m – ✉ 67220

Alsace-Lorraine

2 **C1**

▶ Paris 445 – Lunéville 82 – St-Dié 48 – Ste-Marie-aux-Mines 27 – Sélestat 16 – Strasbourg 56

ℹ Office de tourisme, place du Marché ✆ 03 88 57 11 69, Fax 03 88 57 24 87

La Bonne Franquette
6 pl. Marché – ✆ *03 88 57 14 25 – www.hotel-bonne-franquette.com – bonne-franquette@wanadoo.fr – Fax 03 88 57 08 15 – Closed 2-9 July, 24 October-9 November and 7-22 February*
10 rm – †€ 36/50 ††€ 40/55, ☕ € 8 – ½ P € 49/52
Rest – *(closed Saturday lunch, Sunday dinner and Monday)* Menu (€ 8,50), € 20/39 – Carte € 27/48
◆ Located on a small square in the town centre, this family-run inn is flower-decked in season. Well-kept rooms with rustic furniture. Warm welcome. The restaurant attracts a local clientele with its tasty traditional dishes, served informally.

LA VILLE-AUX-CLERCS – 41 Loir-et-Cher – 318 D4 – pop. 1 197 – alt. 143 m – ✉ 41160

11 **B2**

▶ Paris 159 – Brou 41 – Châteaudun 29 – Le Mans 74 – Orléans 73 – Vendôme 18

ℹ Syndicat d'initiative, Mairie ✆ 02 54 80 62 35, Fax 02 54 80 30 08

Manoir de la Forêt

r. Françoise de Lorraine, at Fort-Girard, east: 1.5 km on secondary road – ✆ 02 54 80 62 83 – www.manoirdelaforet.fr – manoirdelaforet@wanadoo.fr – Fax 02 54 80 66 03 – Closed 3-13 January, Sunday dinner and Monday from October to April
18 rm – €55/80 €70/95, ☕ €12 – ½ P €80/90
Rest – Menu (€18), €27/51 – Carte €48/66
◆ An isolated 19C hunting lodge, surrounded by a park. The rooms (opt for one on the first floor) are adorned with period furniture and the lounge with its fireplace make up a stylish setting. Classic cuisine served in a comfortable and low-key dining room.

LA VILLE-BLANCHE – 22 Côtes-d'Armor – 309 B2 – see Lannion

VILLECOMTAL-SUR-ARROS – 32 Gers – 336 D9 – pop. 809 – alt. 177 m – ✉ 32730 28 A2

Paris 760 – Pau 70 – Aire-sur-l'Adour 67 – Auch 48 – Tarbes 26

Le Rive Droite

1 chemin Saint-Jacques – ✆ 05 62 64 83 08 – www.lerivedroite.com – rive-droite2@wanadoo.fr – Fax 05 62 64 84 02 – Closed Monday, Tuesday and Wednesday except from 12 July to 23 August
Rest – Menu €35 – Carte €25/35
◆ George Sand is said to have been a guest in this former 18C riverside charterhouse. The decor successfully combines old and new. Fine updated local cuisine.

VILLECROZE – 83 Var – 340 M4 – pop. 1 094 – alt. 300 m – ✉ 83690 41 C3

French Riviera

Paris 835 – Aups 8 – Brignoles 38 – Draguignan 21
Office de tourisme, rue Amboise Croizat ✆ 04 94 67 50 00, Fax 04 94 67 50 00
Viewpoint★: ❄★ North: 1 km.

Le Colombier with rm

rte de Draguignan – ✆ 04 94 70 63 23 – www.lecolombier-var.com – hotel-restaurant@lecolombier-var.com – Fax 04 94 70 63 23 – Closed 20 November-12 December
6 rm – €65/70 €70/120, ☕ €10 – ½ P €75/80 **Rest** – *(closed Sunday dinner and Monday except public holidays)* Menu (€20), €29/55 – Carte €44/65
◆ This regional-style building offers an appetising traditional menu. It is served in a pleasant Provençal setting and beneath the veranda in summer. Attractive rooms with balconies.

Southeast 3 km by Draguignan road and secondary road – ✉ 83690 Salernes

Au Bien Être with rm

Chemin du bien-être – ✆ 04 94 70 67 57 – www.aubienetre.com – aubienetre@libertysurf.fr – Fax 04 94 70 67 57 – Closed 15 October-1st March, Monday lunch, Tuesday lunch and Wednesday lunch
8 rm – €50/76 €50/79, ☕ €8 – ½ P €53/68
Rest – Menu (€19), €26/68 – Carte €42/70
◆ Restaurant at the heart of an attractive park. Relaxed setting, new-look red and white décor and pleasant shaded terrace overlooking the garden. Locally inspired dishes.

VILLE D'AVRAY – 92 Hauts-de-Seine – 311 J3 – see Paris, Area

VILLEDIEU-LES-POÊLES – 50 Manche – 303 E6 – pop. 3 950 – alt. 105 m – ✉ 50800 Normandy 32 A2

Paris 314 – Alençon 122 – Avranches 26 – Caen 82 – Flers 59 – St-Lô 35
Office de tourisme, place des Costils ✆ 02 33 61 05 69, Fax 02 33 91 71 79
Bell foundry★.

Le Fruitier

pl. Costils – ✆ 02 33 90 51 00 – www.le-fruitier.com – hotel@lefruitier.com – Fax 02 33 90 51 01 **48 rm** – €50/91 €52/91, ☕ €8 – ½ P €56/76
Rest – *(closed 24 December-15 January)* Menu (€17), €27/35 – Carte €30/39
◆ Near the tourist office, a welcoming family hotel with functional, well-kept rooms and duplexes. Conference room. The restaurant has a colourful painted ceiling and murals with a fruit theme. Classic seafood cuisine.

XXX **La Ferme de Malte**

11 r. Jules Tétrel – ✆ 02 33 91 35 91 – www.lafermedemalte.fr – contact@lafermedemalte.fr – Fax 02 33 91 35 90 – Closed 15 December-12 January, Sunday dinner, Wednesday dinner and Monday
Rest – Menu € 26/60 – Carte € 42/61
◆ Former farm of the Order of Malta turned into a restaurant. Welcoming dining room (stonework, beams, woodwork and trinkets) partially overlooking the garden. Regional cuisine.

XX **Manoir de l'Acherie** with rm

at l'Acherie, 3.5 km east by D 975 and D 554 (A 84 motorway, exit 38) – ✆ 02 33 51 13 87 – www.manoir-acherie.fr – manoir@manoir-acherie.fr – Fax 02 33 51 33 69 – Closed 15 November-3 December, 15 February-4 March, Sunday dinner from 15 October to 5 April and Monday except dinner from 7 July to 31 August
19 rm – †€ 60 ††€ 60/110, ☕ € 9 – ½ P € 71/98
Rest – Menu (€ 15), € 18/40 – Carte € 27/40
◆ This 17C manor and small chapel are set around a flower garden in the heart of the Norman countryside. Pleasant rustic interior, local dishes and charcoal-grilled meats.

VILLEFORT – 48 Lozère – 330 L8 – pop. 639 – alt. 600 m – ✉ 48800 23 C1

Languedoc-Roussillon-Tarn Gorges

Paris 616 – Alès 52 – Aubenas 61 – Florac 63 – Mende 58 – Pont-St-Esprit 90

Office de tourisme, rue de l'Église ✆ 04 66 46 87 30, Fax 04 66 46 85 33

Balme

pl. Portalet – ✆ 04 66 46 80 14 – www.hotelbalme.free.fr – hotelbalme@free.fr – Fax 04 66 46 85 26 – Closed 15-20 October, 15 November-15 February, Sunday dinner and Monday except July-August
16 rm – †€ 48 ††€ 48/55, ☕ € 8 – ½ P € 59 **Rest** – Menu € 21/38
◆ In the centre of a peaceful village which is one of the gateways to the Parc National des Cévennes, an old traditional house with rooms of varying sizes and levels of comfort. Local cuisine and concoctions with a personal touch.

VILLEFRANCHE-DE-CONFLENT – 66 Pyrénées-Orientales – 344 F7 – pop. 238 – alt. 435 m – ✉ 66500 Languedoc-Roussillon-Tarn Gorges 22 B3

Paris 898 – Mont-Louis 31 – Olette 11 – Perpignan 51 – Prades 6 – Vernet-les-Bains 6

Office de tourisme, place de l'Église ✆ 04 68 96 22 96, Fax 04 68 96 07 66

Ville forte★ - Fort Liberia: ≤★★.

XXX **Auberge Saint-Paul**

7 pl. de l'Église – ✆ 04 68 96 30 95 – http://perso.wanadoo.fr/auberge.stpaul – auberge-st-paul@wanadoo.fr – Fax 04 68 05 60 30 – Closed 15-20 June, 23 November-3 December, 5-29 January, Tuesday in low season, Sunday dinner and Monday
Rest – Menu € 20 bi (weekdays)/85 – Carte € 55/80
◆ This 13C chapel today houses a rustic-style restaurant. The up-to-date cuisine evolves with the seasons. Fine choice of Burgundy and Roussillon wines. Shaded terrace.

VILLEFRANCHE-DE-ROUERGUE – 12 Aveyron – 338 E4 – pop. 12 100 – alt. 230 m – ✉ 12200 Languedoc-Roussillon-Tarn Gorges 29 C1

Paris 614 – Albi 68 – Cahors 61 – Montauban 80 – Rodez 60

Office de tourisme, promenade du Guiraudet ✆ 05 65 45 13 18, Fax 05 65 45 55 58

La Bastide★: place Notre-Dame★, Notre-Dame church ★ - Former St-Sauveur charterhouse ★ by ③.

Plan on following page

XX **L'Épicurien**

8bis av. R.-St-Gilles – ✆ 05 65 45 01 12 – Fax 05 65 45 01 12 – Closed 27 April-6 May, 16 November-2 December, Sunday dinner and Tuesday from 15 September to 15 June and Monday x
Rest – Menu € 15 (weekday lunch), € 21/43 – Carte € 31/54
◆ Warm atmosphere in this former general store with a terrace which is very pleasant in the evening. Tasty cuisine, based on fish and local produce.

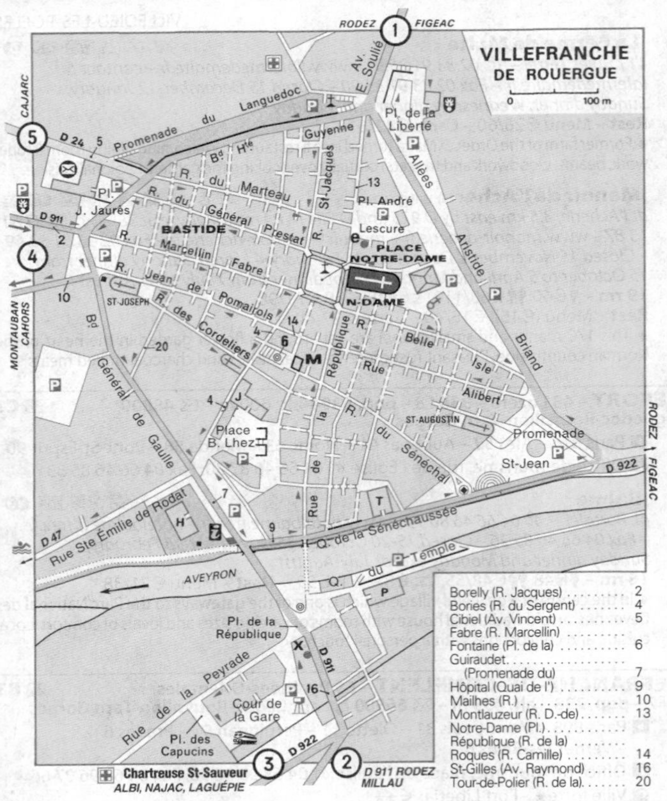

L'Assiette Gourmande

pl. A. Lescure – 05 65 45 25 95 – Closed 11-25 March, 10-17 June, 9-16 September, 11-25 November, Sunday dinner except from September to June, Tuesday dinner and Wednesday except July-August e

Rest – Menu (€ 12), € 15 (weekdays)/35 – Carte € 25/50

◆ A 13C building splendidly located in the heart of the old town, renovated in a semi-modern, semi-rustic style. Grilled dishes and regional recipes.

in Farrou 4 km by ① – ✉ **12200 Villefranche-de-Rouergue**

Relais de Farrou rm, VISA

– 05 65 45 18 11 – www.relaisdefarrou.com – le.relais.de.farrou@wanadoo.fr – Fax 05 65 45 32 59 – Closed 8-22 March, 2-16 November, 21-27 December

26 rm – €51/73 €57/92, € 9 – ½ P € 62/78 **Rest** – *(closed Sat. lunch, Sun. dinner and Mon. in low season)* Menu (€ 16), € 22/45 – Carte € 45/60

◆ Fully renovated coaching inn dating from 1792. The comfortable rooms vary in size and the establishment has no lack of leisure activities (tennis court, crazy golf, pool and fitness facilities). Subtly updated regional cuisine is served in the immense, airy dining room overlooking a patio.

VILLEFRANCHE-DU-PÉRIGORD – 24 Dordogne – 329 H8 – pop. 803 – alt. 220 m – ✉ 24550 Dordogne-Berry-Limousin 4 D2

Paris 575 – Agen 77 – Sarlat-la-Canéda 41 – Bergerac 68 – Cahors 41 – Périgueux 87

Syndicat d'initiative, rue Notre-Dame 05 53 29 98 37, Fax 05 53 30 40 12

Petite Auberge
– *05 53 29 91 01 – www.la-petite-auberge.com – lapetiteauberge24@orange.fr – Fax 05 53 28 88 10 – Closed 19 November-3 December, Wednesday and Sunday dinner from October to April*
10 rm – €46/50 €52/56, €7 – ½ P €72/75
Rest – Menu (€10), €20/38 – Carte €25/33
◆ A regional establishment in a verdant setting, 500m from a village famous for its chestnut and cepe markets. Simple and well-kept rooms. Regional fare served in a rustic styled dining room, on the veranda or the terrace.

VILLEFRANCHE-SUR-MER – 06 Alpes-Maritimes – **341** E5 – **pop. 6 649 – alt. 30 m** – 06230 **French Riviera** 42 **E2**

Paris 932 – Beaulieu-sur-Mer 3 – Nice 5
Office de tourisme, jardin François Binon 04 93 01 73 68, Fax 04 93 76 63 65
Harbour★★ - Old town ★ - St-Pierre chapel ★ - Musée Volti★.

Access and exits: See plan of Nice

Welcome without rest
3 quai Courbet – 04 93 76 27 62 – www.welcomehotel.com – resa@welcomehotel.com – Fax 04 93 76 27 66 – Closed 2 November-26 December **n**
35 rm – €74/99 €98/340, €13 – 1 suite
◆ Jean Cocteau frequented this delightful hotel and decorated St Peter's Chapel, also by the port. Pleasant rooms with personal touches and balconies facing the sea.

Flore without rest
5 av. Princesse Grace de Monaco – 04 93 76 30 30 – www.hotel-la-flore.fr – hotel-la-flore@wanadoo.fr – Fax 04 93 76 99 99 **e**
31 rm – €52/217 €52/217, €13
◆ This ochre-coloured building is pleasantly located overlooking the bay. The smart rooms, many with a loggia, are gradually being spruced up.

VILLEFRANCHE-SUR-MER

Cauvin (Av. V.)	2
Corderie (Quai de la)	3
Corne d'Or (Bd de la)	5
Courbet (Quai Amiral)	6
Église (R. de l')	7
Foch (Av. du Maréchal)	8
Gallieni (Av. Général)	9
Gaulle (Av. Général-de)	10
Grande-Bretagne (Av. de)	12
Joffre (Av. Maréchal)	14
Leclerc (Av. Général)	15
Marinières (Promenade des)	16
May (R. de)	18
Obscure (R.)	19
Paix (Pl. de la)	20
Poilu (R. du)	22
Pollonais (Pl. A.)	24
Ponchardier (Quai Amiral)	25
Poullan (Pl. F.)	26
Sadi-Carnot (Av.)	28
Settimelli-Lazare (Bd)	30
Soleil d'Or (Av. du)	31
Verdun (Av. de)	32
Victoire (R. de la)	34
Wilson (Pl.)	35

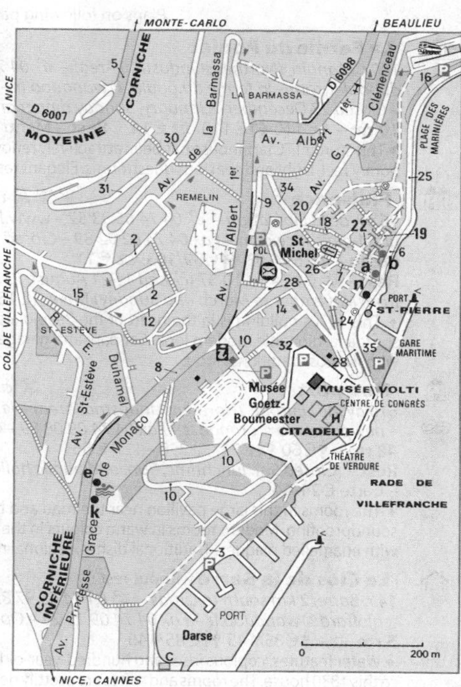

Versailles rest, rm,

7 bd Princesse Grace de Monaco – ✆ 04 93 76 52 52 – www.hotelversailles.com – contact@hotelversailles.com – Fax 04 93 01 97 48 – Open 1st April to mid-October
46 rm – †€ 120/160 ††€ 130/170, ☕ € 16 **k**
Rest – *(closed Monday and Tuesday)* Menu € 40 – Carte € 45/55
◆ All the rooms of this family establishment overlooking the bay have been refurbished in a modern spirit and command a breathtaking panoramic view. Modern dining room and large terrace offering a superb view; regional menu.

L'Oursin Bleu

11 quai Courbet – ✆ 04 93 01 90 12 – oursinbleu@club-internet.fr – Fax 04 93 01 80 45 – Closed 10 January-10 February and Tuesday from 1st November to 30 March
Rest – Carte € 40/110 **b**
◆ A fish tank, portholes, fountains, frescoes and a lovely quayside terrace facing the harbour: a tribute to the sea in the decor and the up-to-date gourmet menu.

La Mère Germaine

9 quai Courbet – ✆ 04 93 01 71 39 – www.meregermaine.com – contact@meregermaine.com – Fax 04 93 01 96 44 – Closed 9 November-24 December
Rest – Menu € 42 – Carte € 56/90 **a**
◆ A beautiful location on the fishing port for this fish and seafood restaurant. Two rustic-styled dining rooms and a terrace overlooking the trawlers. Tender for yachties.

VILLEFRANCHE-SUR-SAÔNE – 69 Rhône – 327 H4 – pop. 31 700 – alt. 190 m – ✉ 69400 Lyon - Rhone Valley

43 **E1**

Paris 432 – Bourg-en-Bresse 54 – Lyon 33 – Mâcon 47 – Roanne 73

Office de tourisme, 96, rue de la sous-préfecture ✆ 04 74 07 27 40, Fax 04 74 07 27 47

du Beaujolais Lucenay, S : 8 km on D 306 and D 30, ✆ 04 74 67 04 44

Plans on following pages

La Ferme du Poulet rm,

180 r. Mangin, (Northeast Industrial Area) – ✆ 04 74 62 19 07 – www.lafermedupoulet.com – la.ferme.du.poulet@wanadoo.fr – Fax 04 74 09 01 89 – Closed 23 December-2 January, Sunday dinner and Monday DX **s**
10 rm – †€ 110 ††€ 110, ☕ € 14 **Rest** – Menu € 35/68 – Carte € 50/80
◆ This sturdy 17C farmhouse has been attractively renovated to create a rustic, yet contemporary feel. Light and spacious guestrooms. Elegant restaurant with a French-style ceiling.

Plaisance rest,

96 av. de la Libération – ✆ 04 74 65 33 52 – www.hotel-plaisance.com – info@hotel-plaisance.com – Fax 04 74 62 02 89 – Closed 23 December-2 January
68 rm – †€ 59/103 ††€ 59/103, ☕ € 11 AZ **n**
Rest – ✆ 04 74 68 10 37 *(closed 1st-21 August, 23 December-6 January, Saturday from November to March and Sunday)* Menu (€ 15 bi), € 25/40 – Carte € 29/41
◆ This 1970s building is in the heart of the Beaujolais capital. The well-equipped rooms sport a fashionable modern look. Car park and garage available. Dining room decorated with frescos; traditional food.

Newport rm,

610 av. de l'Europe, (Northeast Industrial Area) – ✆ 04 74 68 75 59 – newport.mdb@orange.fr – Fax 04 74 09 08 89 – Closed 24 December-4 January
48 rm – †€ 60 ††€ 71, ☕ € 8 – ½ P € 56 DX **v**
Rest – *(Closed Sat. lunchtime, Sun. and public holidays)* Menu € 17 (weekdays)/46 – Carte € 24/44
◆ The rooms in this large pavilion near the road and by the exhibition centre have good soundproofing. Modern rooms in warm colours in the recent wing. Restaurant decorated with enamelled plaques. Traditional dishes, regional recipes and wines.

Le Clos de la Barre without rest

14 r. Barre, 2 km south to Limas – ✆ 04 74 65 97 85 – www.leclosdelabarre.com – ajoffard@wanadoo.fr – Fax 04 74 09 13 28 – Open 1st May-31 August
5 rm ☕ – †€ 85/145 ††€ 85/145 CX **w**
◆ Water features, copious irises and hundred-year-old trees create a decorative backdrop to this 1830 house. The rooms and suites are prettily decorated and all have a small lounge.

VILLEFRANCHE-SUR-SAÔNE

Barbusse (Bd Henri) . . . . CX 2
Beaujolais (Av. du) . . . . CX 3
Berthier (R. Pierre) . . . . DX 7
Chabert (Ch. du) . . . . CX 12
Charmilles (Av. des) . . . . CX 14
Condorcet (R.) . . . . DX 15
Desmoulins (R. Camille) . . . DX 17
Écossais (R. de l') . . . . DX 18
Joux (Av. de) . . . . DX 25
Leclerc (Bd du Gén.) . . . . . . CX 27
Libération (Av. de la) . . . . . . CX 28
Maladière (R. de la) . . . . CX 30
Nizerand (R. du) . . . . CX 35
Paradis (R. du) . . . . CX 37
Pasquier (Bd Pierre) . . . . DX 39
Plage (Av. de la) . . . . DX 40
St-Roch (Montée) . . . . CX 43
Salengro (Bd Roger) . . . . CX 46
Savoye (R. C.) . . . . DX 48
Tarare (R. de) . . . . CX 54

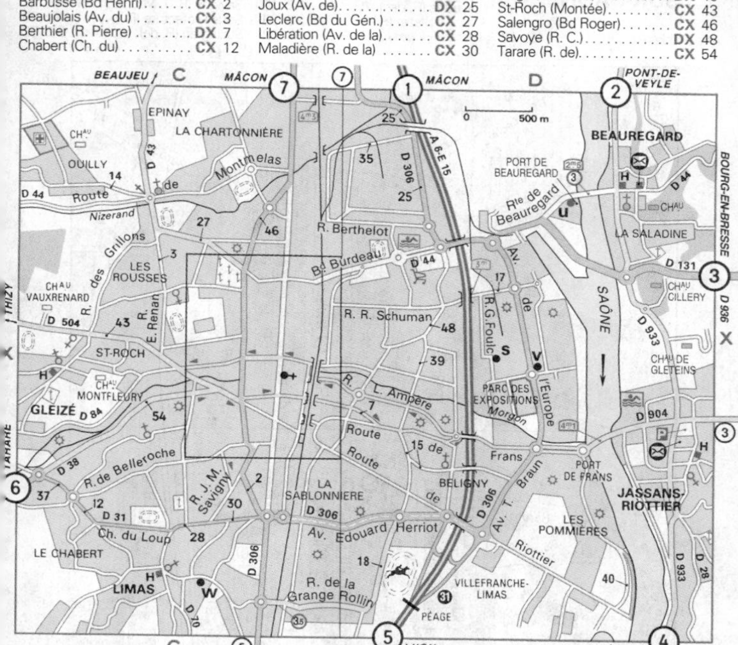

Le Faisan Doré

686 rte de Beauregard, Beauregard bridge, 2.5 km northeast – ✆ 04 74 65 01 66 – www.faisan-dore.com – auberge.lefaisandore@wanadoo.fr – Fax 04 74 09 00 81 – Closed Sunday dinner, Monday dinner and Tuesday dinner

DX **u**

Rest – Menu € 29 (weekdays)/69 – Carte € 40/70

◆ This bourgeois-style inn features a piano and a window overlooking the poultry yard. Pleasant shaded terrace on the banks of the Saône.

Le Juliénas

236 r. Anse – ✆ 04 74 09 16 55 – www.restaurant-lejulienas.com – contact@restaurant-lejulienas.com – Closed 2-21 August, Monday dinner, Saturday lunch and Sunday

BZ **v**

Rest – Menu (€ 18), € 26/48 – Carte € 51/62

◆ Local wines and delicious cuisine with a southern influence take pride of place in this small, bistro-style restaurant with simply laid tables.

in Arnas 5 km by ⑦, D 306 and D 43 – **pop. 3 212** – **alt. 195 m** – ✉ **69400**

Château de Longsard

4060 rte Longsard – ✆ 04 74 65 55 12 – www.longsard.com – longsard@gmail.com – Fax 04 74 65 03 17 – Closed Christmas school holidays

5 rm – †€ 100/120 ††€ 130/150 – ½ P € 133/143

Table d'hôte – Menu € 38 bi/45 bi

◆ A magnificent formal garden fronts this 18C chateau while a majestic Lebanon cedar dominates the centre of the interior courtyard. Elegant rooms and suites. The dining room has attractive wood panelling. Traditional and local dishes.

VILLEFRANCHE-SUR-SAÔNE

Arts (Pl. des) . . . . **AZ** 49
Belleville (R. de) . . . . **BY** 5
Carnot (Pl.) . . . . **BZ** 9
Faucon (R. du) . . . . **BY** 19
Fayettes (R. des) . . . . **BZ** 20
Grange-Blazet (R.) . . . . **BZ** 23
Marais (Pl. des) . . . . **BZ** 32
Nationale (R.) . . . . **BYZ**
République (R. de la) . . . . . . **AZ** 41
Salengro (Bd Roger) . . . . **AY** 46
Savigny (R. J.-M.) . . . . **AZ** 47
Sous-Préfecture (R.) . . . . **AZ** 50
Stalingrad (R. de) . . . . **BZ** 52

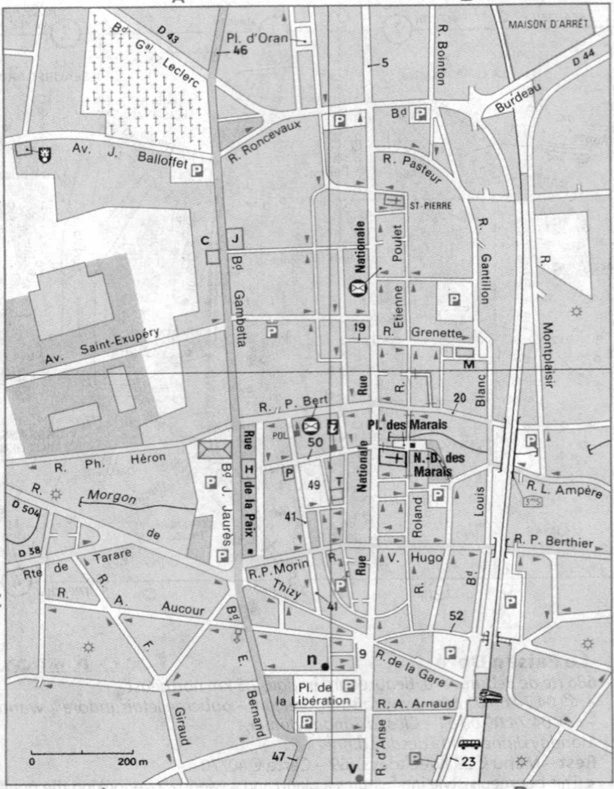

Red = Pleasant. Look for the red ✗ and ⌂ symbols.

VILLEMAGNE-L'ARGENTIÈRE – **34 Hérault** – **339** D7 – **see Bédarieux**

VILLEMONTAIS – **42 Loire** – **327** C4 – **pop. 952** – **alt. 466 m** – ✉ **42155** 44 **A1**

▶ Paris 404 – Lyon 95 – Roanne 13 – Vichy 77

⌂ **Domaine de Fontenay** without rest

– *℘ 04 77 63 12 22 – www.domainedufontenay.com – hawkins@tele2.fr – Fax 04 77 63 15 95*

4 rm ☕ – 🚹€ 58 🚹🚹€ 68

◆ Surrounded by vineyards, this winegrowing estate is also home to a chapel and a 15C altarpiece. The vaulted rooms are decorated simply and cosily. Stunning view of the Loire plain.

VILLEMOYENNE – 10 Aube – 313 F4 – pop. 629 – alt. 130 m – ✉ 10260 13 B3

Paris 184 – Troyes 21 – Bar-sur-Aube 46 – Châtillon-sur-Seine 51

XX **La Parentèle**
32 r. Marcellin Lévêque – ✆ 03 25 43 68 68 – www.la-parentele-caironi.com – contact@la-parentele-caironi.com – Fax 03 25 43 68 69 – Closed 27 July-12 August, February school holidays, Thursday dinner from October to March, Sunday dinner, Monday and Tuesday
Rest – *(number of covers limited, pre-book)* Menu (€ 24 bi), € 28/65 Carte € 28/58
◆ Enjoy modern cuisine (new menus) either in the contemporary-style dining room or on the terrace overlooking the village square. Expert wine advice.

VILLEMUR-SUR-TARN – 31 Haute-Garonne – 343 H1 – pop. 5 078 – alt. 108 m – ✉ 31340 Languedoc-Roussillon-Tarn Gorges 28 B2

Paris 646 – Albi 63 – Castres 73 – Montauban 24 – Toulouse 39
Office de tourisme, 1, r. de la République ✆ 05 34 27 97 40, Fax 05 61 35 78 34

South 5 km by D 14, D 630 and secondary road – ✉ 31340 Villemur-sur-Tarn

X **Auberge du Flambadou** with rm
820 chemin d'Ayrolles – ✆ 05 61 09 40 72 – www.aubergeduflambadou.com – bienvenue@aubergeduflambadou.com – Fax 05 61 09 29 66
5 rm – †€ 75 ††€ 75, ☕ € 9 – ½ P € 65
Rest – *(closed Sunday dinner and Monday)* Menu € 19/41 – Carte € 45/75
◆ A manger converted into a wine cellar, exotic fish and exhibition-sale of artwork: this rustic restaurant is far from conventional. Traditional unfussy dishes.

VILLENEUVE-D'ASCQ – 59 Nord – 302 G4 – see Lille

VILLENEUVE-DE-BERG – 07 Ardèche – 331 J6 – pop. 2 765 – alt. 320 m – ✉ 07170 Lyon - Rhone Valley 44 B3

Paris 628 – Aubenas 16 – Largentière 27 – Montélimar 27 – Privas 30 – Valence 73
Syndicat d'initiative, Grande Rue ✆ 04 75 94 89 28, Fax 04 75 94 89 28

XX **La Table de Léa**
Le Petit Tournon, 1.5 km south-west on D 558 – ✆ 04 75 94 70 36 – Closed 2 November-2 December, Wednesday and lunch from Monday to Thursday
Rest – *(number of covers limited, pre-book)* Menu € 26/52 – Carte approx. € 60
◆ This modernised barn has an attractive terrace beneath the chestnut trees. Regional cuisine based on local seasonal produce.

VILLENEUVE-DE-MARSAN – 40 Landes – 335 J11 – pop. 2 333 – alt. 80 m – ✉ 40190 3 B2

Paris 701 – Auch 88 – Langon 81 – Marmande 86 – Mont-de-Marsan 17 – Pau 73
Syndicat d'initiative, 181, Grand'Rue ✆ 05 58 45 80 90, Fax 05 58 45 88 38

Hervé Garrapit
21 av. Armagnac – ✆ 05 58 45 20 08 – www.herve-garrapit.com – hotelrestauranthervegarrapit@wanadoo.fr – Fax 05 58 45 34 14
8 rm – †€ 55/220 ††€ 55/220, ☕ € 18
Rest – Menu (€ 22), € 35/85 – Carte € 50/70
◆ A former post-house with a pleasant garden that has been in the family for several generations. Fine, refurbished rooms, all with a balcony overlooking the courtyard. Lovely, Louis XVI-style dining room facing a pretty square with century-old trees.

VILLENEUVE-LA-GARENNE – 92 Hauts-de-Seine – 311 J2 – 101 15 – see Paris, Area

VILLENEUVE-L'ARCHEVÊQUE – 89 Yonne – 319 E2 – pop. 1 242 – alt. 111 m – ✉ 89190 Burgundy-Jura 7 B1

Paris 135 – Troyes 44 – Auxerre 58 – Sens 24
Syndicat d'initiative, 38, r. de la République ✆ 03 86 86 74 58, Fax 03 86 86 76 88

XX **Auberge des Vieux Moulins Banaux** with rm

1 km south on D 84 – ✆ 03 86 86 72 55 – www.bourgognehotels.fr – contact@bourgognehotels.fr – Fax 03 86 86 78 94 – Closed 10-18 May and 1st-23 January

14 rm – †€ 45/65 ††€ 45/65, ☕ € 8 – ½ P € 58/61

Rest – *(closed Mon. lunchtime)* Menu (€ 22 bi), € 27/30 – Carte approx. € 28,50

◆ A 16C mill in a park across which the Vanne flows (fish farming). Preserved machinery, beams and stonework form the charming décor of this restaurant. Simple but pretty rooms.

VILLENEUVE-LA-SALLE – 05 Hautes-Alpes – 334 H3 – see Serre-Chevalier

VILLENEUVE-LE-COMTE – 77 Seine-et-Marne – 312 F3 – pop. 1 747 – alt. 126 m – ✉ 77174

19 **C2**

Paris 40 – Lagny-sur-Marne 13 – Meaux 19 – Melun 38

XXX **A la Bonne Marmite**

15 r. Gén.-de-Gaulle – ✆ 01 60 43 00 10 – www.restaurant-labonnemarmite.com – labonnemarmite@wanadoo.fr – Fax 01 60 43 11 01 – Closed 9 August-2 September, 22-27 November, 24 January-11 February, Sunday dinner, Monday and Tuesday

Rest – Menu € 34 (weekdays)/70 – Carte € 53/80

◆ Elegant dining rooms in a fine 16C Briard-style house, once a farmhouse, then a post house. Flower-filled summer terrace shaded by trellis. Up-to-date cuisine and good wine list.

VILLENEUVE-LE-ROI – 94 Val-de-Marne – 312 D3 – 101 26 – see Paris, Area

VILLENEUVE-LÈS-AVIGNON – 30 Gard – 339 N5 – pop. 11 791 – alt. 23 m – ✉ 30400 Provence

23 **D2**

Paris 678 – Avignon 8 – Nîmes 46 – Orange 28 – Pont-St-Esprit 42

Office de tourisme, 1, place Charles David ✆ 04 90 25 61 33, Fax 04 90 25 91 55

St-André fort and abbey ★: ≤★★ AV - Tour Philippe-le-Bel ≤★★ AV - Virgin★★ in the musée municipal Pierre de Luxembourg★ AV **M** - Chartreuse du Val-de-Bénédiction★ AV.

Plan: see Avignon

Le Prieuré

7 pl. Chapitre – ✆ 04 90 15 90 15 – www.leprieure.com – leprieure@relaischateaux.com – Fax 04 90 25 45 39 – Closed January AV **t**

26 rm – †€ 145/150 ††€ 205/530, ☕ € 19 – 13 suites

Rest – *(closed Monday except July-August)* Menu (€ 32), € 45 bi (weekday lunch), € 65/92 – Carte € 68/108

◆ This former priory in the heart of a magnificent park, has recently been treated to a makeover and its rooms now sport a distinctly contemporary look. At the restaurant, immaculate white setting for updated gourmet cuisine with southern accents.

La Magnaneraie

37 r. Camp de Bataille – ✆ 04 90 25 11 11 – www.hostellerie-la-magnaneraie.com – magnaneraie.hotel@najeti.com – Fax 04 90 25 46 37 AV **b**

30 rm – †€ 139/249 ††€ 139/249, ☕ € 18 – 2 suites

Rest – *(closed Wednesday from 1st November to 30 April, Saturday lunch and Sunday dinner)* Menu (€ 26 bi), € 35/89 – Carte € 68/79

◆ Elegant 15C residence enjoying a new lease of life thanks to refurbishment: refined rooms (romantic, colonial...), cosy sitting-room/bar, pretty garden. Dining room enhanced by frescoes and pillars; lush green terrace.

L'Atelier without rest

5 r. Foire – ✆ 04 90 25 01 84 – www.hoteldelatelier.com – hotel-latelier@libertysurf.fr – Fax 04 90 25 80 06 – Closed in January AV **e**

23 rm – †€ 59/105 ††€ 59/135, ☕ € 10

◆ This charming 16C house features a lovely staircase, antique furniture, exposed beams and objets d'art. Shaded patio ideal for breakfast in summertime.

La Banaste
28 r. de la République – 04 90 25 64 20 – restaurant@la-banaste.com – Closed 15-30 November, 10-31 January and Thursday AV r
Rest – *(number of covers limited, pre-book)* Menu € 30/43 – Carte € 40/53
◆ The welcome is as warm as the décor at this restaurant where they serve traditional cuisine. ("Banaste" is a Provençal word for "wicker basket".)

in Angles AV – **pop. 7 578 – alt. 66 m – ✉ 30133**

Roques without rest
30 av. Verdun, via ⑤ – 04 90 25 41 02 – www.hotel-roques.com – reservation@hotel-roques.com – Fax 04 32 70 22 93
16 rm – € 69/79 € 79/99, ☕ € 10
◆ Traditional house offering renovated rooms decorated in bright colours and matching fabrics. Those to the rear are quietest. Attractive pool.

Fabrice Martin
22 bd Victor-Hugo – 04 90 84 09 02 – laubrice@neuf.fr – Fax 04 90 84 09 02 – Closed 13-19 April, 24 August-6 September, 26 October-4 November, 15-21 February, Wednesday dinner, Saturday lunch, Sunday dinner, Monday and Tuesday
Rest – *(number of covers limited, pre-book)* Menu (€ 18), € 26 (weekday lunch), € 40/60 – Carte € 55/62
◆ A modern gourmet menu that changes with the seasons is served in this colourful villa with a contemporary interior and pleasantly shaded terrace.

VILLENEUVE-LÈS-BÉZIERS – 34 Hérault – 339 E9 – see Béziers

VILLENEUVE-LOUBET – 06 Alpes-Maritimes – 341 D6 – pop. 14 500 – alt. 10 m – ✉ 06270 French Riviera 42 E2

Paris 915 – Antibes 12 – Cannes 22 – Grasse 24 – Nice 15

Office de tourisme, 16, avenue de la Mer 04 92 02 66 16, Fax 04 92 02 66 19

de Villeneuve-Loubet Route de Grasse, 4 km on D 2085, 04 93 22 52 25

Musée de l'Art culinaire ★ AX M².

See plan of Cagnes-sur-Mer-Villeneuve-Loubet Haut-de-Cagnes.

L'Auberge Fleurie
au village, 13 r. Mesures – 04 93 73 90 92 – Fax 04 93 73 90 92 – Closed 20 November-10 December, Thursday except dinner in July-August and Wednesday AX u
Rest – *(pre-book)* Menu € 25/38 – Carte € 45/70
◆ Pleasant inn offering country dishes in the village where the famous chef Auguste Escoffier was born. Beams, stonework and modern pictures; summer terrace.

in Villeneuve-Loubet-Plage – ✉ 06270

Galoubet without rest
174 av. Castel – 04 92 13 59 00 – www.galoubet.fr.st – hotel.galoubet@wanadoo.fr – Fax 04 92 13 59 29 – **22 rm** – € 69/88 € 69/88, ☕ € 9 AY s
◆ Despite the name, the sound of the galoubet (a wind instrument) will not trouble guests staying in the up-to-date rooms furnished in cane.

VILLENEUVE-SUR-LOT – 47 Lot-et-Garonne – 336 G3 – pop. 23 300 – alt. 51 m – ✉ 47300 Atlantic Coast 4 C2

Paris 622 – Agen 29 – Bergerac 60 – Bordeaux 146 – Cahors 70

Office de tourisme, 3, pl. de la Libération 05 53 36 17 30, Fax 05 53 49 42 98

de Villeneuve-sur-Lot Castelnaud-de-Gratecambe 12 km on the Bergerac road, 05 53 01 60 19

Plan on following page

La Résidence without rest
17 av. L. Carnot – 05 53 40 17 03 – www.hotellaresidence47.com – contact@hotellaresidence47.com – Fax 05 53 01 57 34 – Closed 27 December-5 January
18 rm – € 30/54 € 30/60, ☕ € 6,50 BZ s
◆ At the entrance to the medieval bastide, hotel offering simple accommodation in a convivial atmosphere. The brighter, quieter rooms on the courtyard side enjoy views of the surrounding gardens.

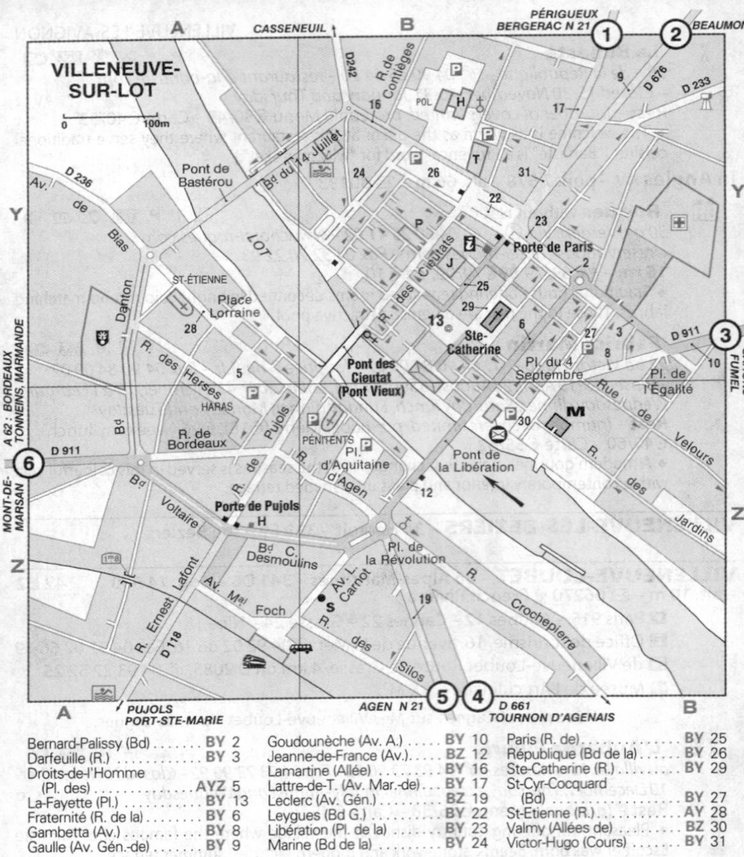

Bernard-Palissy (Bd) . . . . BY 2
Darfeuille (R.) . . . . BY 3
Droits-de-l'Homme (Pl. des) . . . . AYZ 5
La-Fayette (Pl.) . . . . BY 13
Fraternité (R. de la) . . . . BY 6
Gambetta (Av.) . . . . BY 8
Gaulle (Av. Gén.-de) . . . . BY 9
Goudounèche (Av. A.) . . . . . . BY 10
Jeanne-de-France (Av.) . . . . . . BZ 12
Lamartine (Allée) . . . . BY 16
Lattre-de-T. (Av. Mar.-de) . . . BY 17
Leclerc (Av. Gén.) . . . . BZ 19
Leygues (Bd G.) . . . . BY 22
Libération (Pl. de la) . . . . BY 23
Marine (Bd de la) . . . . BY 24
Paris (R. de) . . . . BY 25
République (Bd de la) . . . . BY 26
Ste-Catherine (R.) . . . . BY 29
St-Cyr-Cocquard (Bd) . . . . BY 27
St-Etienne (R.) . . . . AY 28
Valmy (Allées de) . . . . BZ 30
Victor-Hugo (Cours) . . . . BY 31

in Pujols **4 km southwest by D 118 – pop. 3 657 – alt. 180 m – ✉ 47300**

Office de tourisme, place Saint Nicolas ✆ 05 53 36 78 69, Fax 05 53 36 78 70

Des Chênes without rest

– ✆ 05 53 49 04 55 – www.hoteldeschenes.com – hotel.des.chenes@wanadoo.fr – Fax 05 53 49 22 74 – Closed 18 December-10 January and Sunday from November to April

21 rm – €52/73 €68/89, €11

◆ Located facing the hilltop village of Pujols, a typical example of the architecture of the region. Quiet, well-kept rooms with a fresh feel. Swimming pool and terrace.

XXX **La Toque Blanche**

– ✆ 05 53 49 00 30 – www.la-toque-blanche.com – latoque.blanche@wanadoo.fr – Fax 05 53 70 49 79 – Closed 22 June-7 July, 16-24 November, 24 January-1st February, Sunday and Monday **Rest** – Menu (€25), €39/85 – Carte €62/107

◆ Hillside lodge facing the little market town. Service in a veranda-winter garden with a panoramic view at lunchtime, in an elegant dining room in the evenings. Traditional cuisine.

XX **Lou Calel**

in the village – ✆ 05 53 70 46 14 – restaurantloucel@orange.fr – Fax 05 53 70 46 14 – Closed 10-17 June, 7-22 October, 7-22 January, Tuesday and Wednesday

Rest – Menu €24/40 – Carte €42/54

◆ This village auberge has two rustic dining rooms (one with a panoramic view) and a terrace overlooking the Lot Valley. Delicious local cuisine.

VILLENEUVE-SUR-TARN – 81 Tarn – 338 G7 – alt. 272 m 29 C2
– ✉ 81250 Curvalle

Paris 714 – Albi 33 – Castres 67 – Lacaune 44 – Rodez 64 – St-Affrique 50

Hostellerie des Lauriers rm, VISA

– ✆ 05 63 55 84 23 – www.leslauriers.net – leslauriers@orange.fr
– Fax 05 63 55 94 85 – Open mid March-mid October

9 rm – †€ 42/54 ††€ 54/68, ☕ € 8,50 – ½ P € 52/62

Rest – *(closed Sunday dinner and Monday off season) (dinner only)*
Menu € 17 (weekdays), € 25/30 – Carte € 30/55

◆ House built of local stone in a park on the banks of the Tarn, ideal for a "country" holiday: functional rooms, covered swimming pool, jacuzzi and organised walks. Simple dining room with a terrace; traditional cuisine and local dishes.

VILLENEUVE-SUR-YONNE – 89 Yonne – 319 C3 – pop. 5 404 7 B1
– alt. 74 m – ✉ 89500 Burgundy-Jura

Paris 132 – Auxerre 46 – Joigny 19 – Montargis 45 – Nemours 59 – Sens 14 – Troyes 77

Syndicat d'initiative, quai Roland-Bonnion ✆ 03 86 87 12 52, Fax 03 86 87 12 01

Porte de Joigny★.

La Lucarne aux Chouettes with rm VISA

quai Bretoche – ✆ 03 86 87 18 26 – www.lesliecaron-auberge.com – lesliecaron-auberge@wanadoo.fr – Fax 03 86 87 22 63 – Closed January, Tuesday dinner from November to April, Sunday dinner and Monday

4 rm – †€ 49/99 ††€ 99/170, ☕ € 10

Rest – *(closed mid Nov. to mid Dec.)* Menu (€ 20), € 45/53

◆ On the banks of the River Yonne, these four 17C former warehouses have been renovated with style and elegance. Superb dining room with exposed roof beams. Contemporary cuisine.

VILLEPARISIS – 77 Seine-et-Marne – 312 E2 – 101 19 – see Paris, Area

VILLEREST – 42 Loire – 327 D4 – see Roanne

VILLEROY – 89 Yonne – 319 C2 – see Sens

VILLERS-BOCAGE – 14 Calvados – 303 I5 – pop. 2 868 – alt. 140 m 32 B2
– ✉ 14310 Normandy

Paris 262 – Argentan 83 – Avranches 77 – Bayeux 26 – Caen 30 – Flers 44 – St-Lô 47 – Vire 35

Syndicat d'initiative, place du Général de Gaulle ✆ 02 31 77 16 14, Fax 02 31 77 65 46

Des Trois Rois with rm P VISA AE

2 pl. Jeanne d'Arc – ✆ 02 31 77 00 32 – www.trois-rois.fr – les3rois@orange.fr – Fax 02 31 77 93 25 – Closed Sunday dinner from October to April

13 rm – †€ 60/90 ††€ 65/90, ☕ € 12 – ½ P € 71/90

Rest – Menu (€ 26), € 29/65 – Carte € 34/76

◆ Family-run establishment with classic, elegant dining room (yellow tones, paintings) offering contemporary dishes. Simple, modern guestrooms that have been refurbished.

VILLERS-COTTERÊTS – 02 Aisne – 306 A7 – pop. 10 106 – alt. 126 m 37 C3
– ✉ 02600 Northern France and the Paris Region

Paris 81 – Compiègne 32 – Laon 61 – Meaux 41 – Senlis 41 – Soissons 23

Office de tourisme, 6, place Aristide Briand ✆ 03 23 96 55 10, Fax 03 23 96 49 13

Château of François 1er: grand staircase★.

Forêt de Retz★.

Le Régent without rest P VISA AE

26 r. Gén. Mangin – ✆ 03 23 96 01 46 – www.hotel-leregent.com – info@hotel-leregent.com – Fax 03 23 96 37 57 – Closed 25-31 December

30 rm – †€ 67 ††€ 76/82, ☕ € 8

◆ 18C post-house set around a paved courtyard with original drinking trough. Old-world rooms (antique furniture), gradually being redone in modern style.

VILLERSEXEL – 70 Haute-Saône – **314** G7 – **pop. 1 423 – alt. 287 m** 17 **C1**
– ✉ 70110 **Burgundy-Jura**

Paris 386 – Belfort 41 – Besançon 59 – Lure 18 – Montbéliard 34 – Vesoul 27

Office de tourisme, 33, rue des Cités ✆ 03 84 20 59 59, Fax 03 84 20 59 59

Le Relais des Moines rm, VISA AE

1 r. 13 Septembre 1944 – ✆ 03 84 20 50 50 – www.lerelaisdesmoines.fr – relais-des-moines@orange.fr – Fax 03 84 20 59 57 – Closed 24 December-8 January and Sunday dinner

24 rm – €49 €49/63, €8

Rest – Menu €13 (weekdays)/33 – Carte €27/55

◆ This family hotel is made up of several buildings. Practical, gradually refurbished guestrooms (the most recent are located in an old bourgeois home). Regional-inspired cuisine, pizzas and homemade salt meats, served in one of the dining rooms or on the terrace.

La Terrasse VISA

rte de Lure – ✆ 03 84 20 52 11 – www.laterrasse-villersexel.com – laterrassevillersexel@wanadoo.fr – Fax 03 84 20 56 90 – Closed 20 December-7 January, Friday dinner and Sunday dinner October-March

13 rm – €43/45 €46/50, €8 – ½ P €48/52

Rest – Menu (€12), €15/34 – Carte €24/44

◆ In the same family since 1921, this inn by a quiet river, offers practical, gradually spruced up rooms. The restaurant serves traditional fare. Pleasant shaded and flower-decked terrace in season.

VILLERS-LE-LAC – 25 Doubs – **321** K4 – **pop. 4 339 – alt. 730 m** 17 **C2**
– ✉ 25130 **Burgundy-Jura**

Paris 471 – Basel 116 – Besançon 68 – La Chaux-de-Fonds 18 – Morteau 7 – Pontarlier 38

Office de tourisme, rue Pierre Berçot ✆ 03 81 68 00 98, Fax 03 81 68 00 98

Saut du Doubs★★★ Northeast: 5 km - Chaillexon Lake ★ Northeast: 2 km - Musée de la montre★.

Le France (Hugues Droz) VISA AE

8 pl. Cupillard – ✆ 03 81 68 00 06 – www.hotel-restaurant-lefrance.com – info@hotel-restaurant-lefrance.com – Fax 03 81 68 09 22 – Closed 5-16 November and 5 January-5 February

12 rm – €55/75 €60/100, €10 – ½ P €60/90

Rest – *(closed Tuesday lunch from October to May, Sunday dinner and Monday)* Menu €21 (lunch), €28/70 – Carte €43/75

Spec. Foie chaud de canard caramélisé aux pommes. Grosses Saint-Jacques et ormeaux du Cotentin sauce mélisse (Sep. to May). Verrine de chocolat mi-cuit gianduja et nuage aux épices royales. **Wines** Arbois-melon, Arbois-trousseau.

◆ Since 1900, a tradition of hospitality has been maintained by four generations of the same family at this hotel. Contemporary decor in the rooms. Beautiful dining room with wood panelling and a collection of kitchen utensils. Delicious modern dishes and Arbois wines.

VILLERS-SUR-MER – 14 Calvados – **303** L4 – **pop. 2 566 – alt. 10 m** 32 **A3**
– Casino **Normandy**

Paris 208 – Caen 35 – Le Havre 52 – Deauville 8 – Lisieux 31 – Pont-l'Évêque 21

Office de tourisme, place Jean Mermoz ✆ 02 31 87 01 18, Fax 02 31 87 46 20

Domaine de Villers rest, VISA AE

chemin Belvédère – ✆ 02 31 81 80 80 – www.domainedevillers.com – info@domainedevillers.com – Fax 02 31 81 80 70

17 rm – €126/245 €126/245, €15

Rest – *(closed Wednesday and lunch from Monday to Thursday)* Menu €35/49 – Carte €50/70

◆ Parkland surrounds this recent manor house overlooking the Bay of Deauville. The luxurious rooms are either modern, nautical, Art Deco or Directoire. Appetising up-to-date menu served in a comfortable fireside dining room with piano.

VILLERVILLE – 14 Calvados – **303** M3 – see Honfleur

VILLEURBANNE – 69 Rhône – **327** I5 – see Lyon

VILLIÉ-MORGON – 69 Rhône – 327 H3 – pop. 1 724 – alt. 262 m 43 E1 – ✉ 69910 Auvergne - Rhone Valley

Paris 412 – Lyon 54 – Mâcon 23 – Villefranche-sur-Saône 22
La Terrasse ★★ near Fût d'Avenas pass Northwest: 7 km.

Le Villon rm, VISA
bd du Parc – ☎ 04 74 69 16 16 – www.hotel-levillon.com – contact@hotel-levillon.com – Fax 04 74 69 16 81 – Closed 21 December-19 January, Sunday dinner and Monday mid October-end April
45 rm – †€ 55/62 ††€ 65/72, ☐ € 10 – ½ P € 58/62
Rest – Menu (€ 18 bi), € 21/53 – Carte € 28/43
◆ A building overlooking the village, with rooms (five of them with their own terrace) that are simple and practical and have views over the Morgon vineyard. Neo-rustic dining room decor and terrace with views of the hillside vineyards. Traditional cuisine.

in Morgon 2 km south by D 68 – ✉ **69910**

Le Morgon VISA
– ☎ 04 74 69 16 03 – restaurantlemorgon@orange.fr – Fax 04 74 69 16 03 – Closed 15 December-1st February, bank holiday dinners, Tuesday dinner, Sunday dinner and Wednesday
Rest – Menu € 15 (weekdays)/42 – Carte € 24/40
◆ This village hotel counts among its outstanding features a rustic setting (lovely open fires in winter), a pleasant terrace, warm welcome and fine local cuisine.

VILLIERS-LE-MAHIEU – 78 Yvelines – 311 G2 – pop. 703 18 A2 – alt. 127 m – ✉ 78770

Paris 53 – Dreux 37 – Évreux 63 – Mantes-la-Jolie 18 – Rambouillet 33 – Versailles 36

Château de Villiers le Mahieu without rest
r. du Centre – ☎ 01 34 87 44 25 VISA
– www.chateauvilliers.com – accueil@chateauvilliers.com – Fax 01 34 87 44 40 – Closed 24 December-4 January and 15 February-1st March
95 rm – †€ 210 ††€ 210, ☐ € 19
◆ This 13C fortress is surrounded by a moat and sits in the middle of wooded parkland. Modern guestrooms with all the charm of the past and 700 m2 spa area.

VILLIERS-SOUS-GREZ – 77 Seine-et-Marne – 312 E6 – pop. 764 19 C3 – alt. 86 m – ✉ 77760

Paris 75 – Corbeil-Essonnes 42 – Évry 43 – Savigny-sur-Orge 52

La Cerisaie without rest
10 r. Larchant – ☎ 01 64 24 23 71 – www.cerisaie.fr – andre.chastel@free.fr – Fax 01 64 24 23 71 – **4 rm** ☐ – †€ 75 ††€ 85
◆ You will soon be charmed by this outstandingly well-restored 19C farmhouse. Its individually styled rooms have evocative names: 'Photographe', 'Orientale', 'Musicale' and 'Voyageur'.

VILLIERS-SUR-MARNE – 52 Haute-Marne – 313 K4 – ✉ 52320 14 C3

Paris 282 – Bar-sur-Aube 41 – Chaumont 31 – Neufchâteau 52 – Saint-Dizier 46

La Source Bleue VISA
– ☎ 03 25 94 70 35 – source-bleue@wanadoo.fr – Fax 03 25 05 02 09 – Closed 21 December-20 January, Sunday dinner, Monday and Tuesday
Rest – Menu (€ 18), € 28/55 – Carte € 45/56
◆ An 18C mill surrounded by a large park running along the river where you can pick watercress. Simple, pleasant interior, waterside terrace and tasty, modern cuisine.

VINAY – 51 Marne – 306 F8 – see Épernay

VINCELOTTES – 89 Yonne – 319 E5 – see Auxerre

VINCENNES – 94 Val-de-Marne – 312 D2 – 101 17 – see Paris, Area

VINCEY – 88 Vosges – 314 F2 – see Charmes

VINON-SUR-VERDON – 83 Var – **340** J3 – **pop. 2 992** – **alt. 280 m** – ✉ 83560 40 **B2**

▶ Paris 775 – Aix-en-Provence 47 – Brignoles 52 – Digne-les-Bains 70 – Manosque 16

ℹ Syndicat d'initiative, rue Saint-André ✆ 04 92 78 84 45, Fax 04 92 78 83 74

Relais des Gorges with rm

230 av. de la République – ✆ 04 92 78 80 24 – bertet.relais@wanadoo.fr – Fax 04 92 78 96 47 – Closed 26 October-9 November, 19-29 December and Sunday dinner October-March

9 rm – €43 €52, ☕ €7 – ½ P €48 **Rest** – Menu €19/60 – Carte €43/64

◆ On the doorstep of the spectacular Verdon gorge, this inn provides tasty, traditional cuisine. Rooms available, some of which have been refurbished.

VIOLÈS – 84 Vaucluse – **332** C9 – **pop. 1 538** – **alt. 94 m** – ✉ **84150** 42 **E1**

▶ Paris 659 – Avignon 34 – Carpentras 21 – Nyons 33 – Orange 14 – Vaison-la-Romaine 17

Mas de Bouvau rm,

2 km Cairanne road – ✆ 04 90 70 94 08 – www.mas-de-bouvau.com – henri.hertzog@wanadoo.fr – Fax 04 90 70 95 99 – Closed 28 September-3 October, 1st December-28 February, lunch from June to September, dinner from November to February, Tuesday lunch, Sunday dinner and Monday from October to May

6 rm – €63 €63, ☕ €10 – ½ P €66 **Rest** – *(resident only)* Menu €27

◆ In secluded vineyards, this welcoming farmhouse is steeped in authenticity. Personalised rooms, decorated in a guesthouse spirit. Provence can be tasted in the recipes, served in a delightful country interior or in the barn, converted into a terrace.

VIRE – 14 Calvados – **303** G6 – **pop. 12 815** – **alt. 275 m** – ✉ **14500** 32 **B2**
Normandy

▶ Paris 296 – Caen 64 – Flers 31 – Laval 103 – Rennes 135 – St-Lô 39

ℹ Office de tourisme, square de la Résistance ✆ 02 31 66 28 50, Fax 02 31 66 28 55

18 de Vire la Dathée Saint-Manvieu-Bocage La Basse Haie, SE : 8 km on D 150, ✆ 02 31 67 71 01

De France

4 r. d'Aignaux – ✆ 02 31 68 00 35 – www.hoteldefrancevire.com – information@hoteldefrancevire.com – Fax 02 31 68 22 65 – Closed 1-7 August, 12 December-15 January, Sunday dinner and Monday lunch

20 rm – €50 €60, ☕ €8 **Rest** – Menu €16/37

◆ Town centre hotel that has been recently renovated with pleasant results. Sleek contemporary rooms. Revamped restaurant (paintings, bleached beams). Modern menu based on traditional dishes with andouille sausage a speciality.

Flers road 2.5 km by D 524 – ✉ **14500 Vire**

Manoir de la Pommeraie

– ✆ 02 31 68 07 71 – www.manoirdelapommeraie.com – Fax 02 31 67 54 21 – Closed 27 July-10 August, 18-25 January, Sunday dinner and Monday

Rest – Menu €34/80 bi – Carte €41/47

◆ A small 18C manor house on the edge of Vire set in a pleasant park with 100-year-old trees. The new chef creates mouth-watering cuisine based on fine seasonal produce.

VIRÉ – 71 Saône-et-Loire – **320** J11 – **pop. 1 070** – **alt. 225 m** – ✉ **71260** 8 **C3**

▶ Paris 378 – Mâcon 20 – Cluny 23 – Tournus 19

Relais de Montmartre (Frédéric Carrion)

pl. A. Lagrange – ✆ 03 85 33 10 72 – www.relais-de-montmartre.fr – relais-de-montmartre@wanadoo.fr – Fax 03 85 33 98 49 – Closed 29 June-6 July, 5-12 October, 11-25 January, Saturday lunch, Sunday dinner and Monday

Rest – Menu (€20), €23 (weekday lunch), €32/66 – Carte €38/55

Spec. Langoustine bretonne saisie, artichaut fondant et coulis de petits pois. Poulet de Bresse en cocotte, poivron farci de mousseline de pomme de terre. Tarte au chocolat et sorbet abricot.

◆ This former village café in the Mâcon area offers personalised contemporary cuisine. Elegant dining room (draperies, Murano chandeliers). Recent guestrooms.

VIRIVILLE – **38 Isère** – **333** E6 – **pop. 1 281** – **alt. 380 m** – ✉ **38980** 43 **E2**

Paris 549 – Lyon 92 – Grenoble 62 – Saint-Priest 73 – Saint-Martin-d'Hères 64

Hostellerie de Chambaran

185 Grande-Rue-Jeanne-Sappey – ✆ *04 74 54 02 18* – *www.hostelleriede chambaran.com* – *hostelleriedechambaran@wanadoo.fr* – *Fax 04 74 54 11 83*

19 rm – €71 €92, ☕ €10 – ½ P €86/92

Rest – *(closed Saturday lunch, Sunday dinner and Monday)* Menu €24/55 – Carte €28/51

◆ In the heart of a picturesque village of cobblestone houses, a family affair whose unpretentious but spruced up rooms overlook a large garden with pool. Welcoming dining room, shaded terrace, and traditional fare on the table.

VIRY-CHÂTILLON – **91 Essonne** – **312** D3 – **101** 36 – **see Paris, Area**

VISCOS – **65 Hautes-Pyrénées** – **342** L7 – **pop. 44** – **alt. 800 m** – ✉ **65120** 28 **A3**

Paris 880 – Pau 75 – Tarbes 50 – Argelès-Gazost 17 – Cauterets 23 – Lourdes 30

La Grange aux Marmottes

in the village – ✆ *05 62 92 88 88* – *www.grangeauxmarmottes.com* – *hotel@grangeauxmarmottes.com* – *Fax 05 62 92 93 75* – *Closed 11 November-15 December*

14 rm – €70/105 €70/105, ☕ €10 – ½ P €61/85

Rest – Menu (€17), €21/40 – Carte €21/52

◆ Those looking for total peace and quiet will find this converted stone barn, situated at the gates of the Pyrenees National Park, quite attractive. Spacious and comfortable rooms. A country atmosphere reigns in the dining room where you are served regional food.

VITERBE – **81 Tarn** – **338** D8 – **pop. 254** – **alt. 141 m** – ✉ **81220** 29 **C2**

Paris 693 – Albi 62 – Castelnaudary 52 – Castres 31 – Montauban 69 – Toulouse 55

Les Marronniers

– ✆ *05 63 70 64 96* – *www.lesmarronniers-viterbe.com* – *viala.marronniers@wanadoo.fr* – *Fax 05 63 70 60 96* – *Closed 2-22 November, 23-26 February, Monday dinner from October to March, Tuesday dinner and Wednesday*

Rest – Menu (€12), €19 (weekdays)/40 – Carte €28/43

◆ Contemporary, well-lit dining room in beige and chocolate tones with medallion chairs and a fireside lounge. Traditional cuisine is served and there is an agreeable terrace overlooking the garden.

VITRAC – **24 Dordogne** – **329** I7 – **pop. 824** – **alt. 150 m** – ✉ **24200** 4 **D3**

Paris 541 – Brive-la-Gaillarde 64 – Cahors 54 – Périgueux 85 – Sarlat-la-Canéda 8

Office de tourisme, lieu-dit le bourg ✆ 05 53 28 57 80

du Domaine de Rochebois Sarlat-la-Canéda Route de Montfort, SE : 2 km, ✆ 05 53 31 52 52

Château of Montfort★ Northeast: 2 km - Cingle de Montfort★ Northeast: 3.5 km, **Dordogne-Berry-Limousin**

Domaine de Rochebois

Montfort road, 2 km east by D 703 – ✆ *05 53 31 52 52* – *www.rochebois.com* – *info@rochebois.com* – *Fax 05 53 29 36 88* – *Open early May to end October*

40 rm – €145/420 €145/420, ☕ €18 – ½ P €202/267

Rest – *(dinner only)* Menu €45/95 bi – Carte €89/100

◆ Located in a large park with a 9-hole golf course, terraced garden, good swimming pool and fine interior decor, this 19C house is a slice of paradise in the heart of Périgord Noir. Modern food served in the opulent dining room or on the pleasant terrace.

Plaisance

au port – 05 53 31 39 39 – www.hotelplaisance.com – plaisance@wanadoo.fr – Fax 05 53 31 39 38 – Open 2 March-11 November

48 rm – €54 €54/110, €9 – ½ P €63/80

Rest – *(closed Sunday dinner and Friday October-April, Friday lunch and Saturday lunch May-September)* Menu €15 (weekday lunch), €25/45 – Carte €30/68

◆ Regional establishment built in 1808 on a rocky slope. Well-kept rooms. Garden bordering the Dordogne on the other side of the road. Tastefully decorated dining room and terrace shaded by lime trees. Regional cuisine.

Le Clos Roussillon without rest

1 km west along the D 703 and secondary road – 05 53 28 13 00 – www.closroussillon-perigord.com – hotel@closroussillon-perigord.com – Fax 05 53 59 40 25 – Open 11 April-1st November

31 rm – €50/65 €50/90, €10

◆ 1980s hotel which has been totally renovated. Modern comfortable rooms, some with balcony and kitchenettes. Pleasant, peaceful wooded grounds.

La Treille with rm

Le Port – 05 53 28 33 19 – www.latreille-perigord.com – hotel@latreille-perigord.com – Fax 05 53 30 38 54 – Closed 15 November-15 December, 15 February-5 March, Tuesday except dinner 15 June-15 October and Monday

8 rm – €47/57 €47/85, €8 – ½ P €68

Rest – Menu (€20), €23/43 – Carte €47/61

◆ This virginia-creeper-clad establishment has been run by the Latreille family since 1866. Simple dining room and veranda. Outside tables shaded by a trellis. Périgord cuisine.

VITRAC – 15 Cantal – 330 B6 – pop. 294 – alt. 490 m – ✉ 15220 5 A3

Paris 561 – Aurillac 26 – Figeac 44 – Rodez 77

Auberge de la Tomette

– 04 71 64 70 94 – www.auberge-la-tomette.com – latomette@wanadoo.fr – Fax 04 71 64 77 11 – Open Easter-12 November

16 rm (½ board only) – ½ P €68/80

Rest – *(dinner only) (resident only)* Menu €29/39 – Carte €40/50

◆ Small, well-kept rooms undergoing renovation, pleasant flower garden, indoor/outdoor swimming pool, relaxation centre with sauna and hammam. An inn with much appeal. A restaurant with wood panelling, tiled floor, antique furniture; a terrace with pergola.

VITRÉ – 35 Ille-et-Vilaine – 309 O6 – pop. 15 313 – alt. 106 m – ✉ 35500 10 D2

Brittany

Paris 310 – Châteaubriant 52 – Fougères 30 – Laval 38 – Rennes 38

Office de tourisme, place Gal-de-Gaulle 02 99 75 04 46, Fax 02 99 74 02 01

des Rochers Sévigné Château des Rochers, 6 km on the Argentré road, 02 99 96 52 52

Château★★: tour de Montalifant ⋞★, tryptich★ - The town ★: rue Baudrairie★★ A 5, ramparts★, Notre-Dame church ★ B - Tertres noirs ⋞★★ via ④ - Park gardens★ by ③ - ⋞★★ D178 B and D857 A - Champeaux: place★, church stalls ★ and stained-glass windows★ 9 km by ④.

Plan on next page

Ibis without rest

1 bd Chateaubriant, via ③ – 02 99 75 51 70 – www.ibishotel.com – H6233@accor.com – Fax 02 99 75 51 71 **50 rm** – €51/85 €51/85, €8,50

◆ This new Ibis hotel near the medieval centre offers practically furnished rooms with a small dressing room. Those overlooking the park to the rear are quietest.

Le Pichet

17 bd Laval, via ① – 02 99 75 24 09 – www.lepichet.fr – restaurant@lepichet.fr – Closed Wednesday dinner, Thursday dinner and Sunday

Rest – *(number of covers limited, pre-book)* Menu €18 (weekday lunch), €26/50 – Carte €38/53

◆ This regional-style building features a lovely garden planted with trees where outside tables are laid out in summer (barbecue). Bright comfortable dining room-veranda.

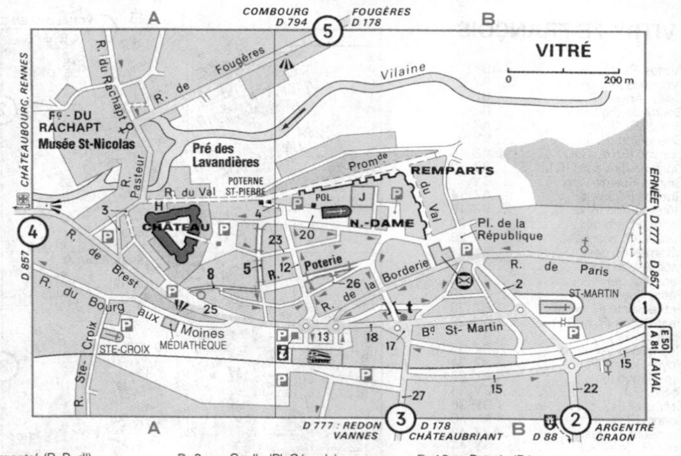

Argentré (R. B.-d') . . . . B 2	Gaulle (Pl. Gén.-de) . . . . B 13	Poterie (R.) . . . . B
Augustins (R. des) . . . . A 3	Jacobins (Bd des) . . . . B 15	Rochers (Bd des) . . . . B 22
Bas-Val (R. du) . . . . A 4	Leclerc (Pl. Gén.) . . . . B 17	St-Louis (R.) . . . . AB 23
Baudrairie (R. de la) . . . . A 5	Liberté (R. de la) . . . . B 18	St-Yves (Pl.) . . . . A 25
Borderie (R. de la) . . . . B	Notre-Dame (Pl. et R.) . . . . B 20	Sévigné (R.) . . . . B 26
En-Bas (R. d') . . . . A 8	Paris (R. de) . . . . B	70e-R.I. (R. du) . . . . B 27
Garengeot (R.) . . . . B 12	Pasteur (R.) . . . . A	

Le Potager

VISA MC AE

5 pl. Gén. Leclerc – ✆ 02 99 74 68 88 – www.restaurant-lepotager.fr – contact@restaurant-lepotager.fr – Fax 02 99 75 38 13 – Closed 11-24 August, Sunday dinner and Monday B t

Rest – Menu € 17 (weekdays)/32 – Carte € 24/35

◆ This charming bistro area and pleasant modern dining room have an attractive decor in rich warm shades of aubergine, orange and green. Updated cuisine; set lunchtime menu.

VITRY-LE-FRANÇOIS – 51 Marne – 306 J10 – pop. 14 900 – alt. 105 m – ✉ 51300 Northern France and the Paris Region

13 **B2**

Paris 181 – Bar-le-Duc 55 – Châlons-en-Champagne 33 – Verdun 96

Office de tourisme, place Giraud ✆ 03 26 74 45 30, Fax 03 26 74 84 74

Plan on following page

La Poste

VISA MC AE

pl. Royer-Collard – ✆ 03 26 74 02 65 – www.hotellaposte.com – hoteldelaposte.vitry@wanadoo.fr – Fax 03 26 74 54 71 – Closed 21 December-4 January and Sunday

28 rm – †€ 57/74 ††€ 65/82, ☕ € 9 – ½ P € 65/73 BZ a

Rest – *(closed 2-23 August, 21 December-4 January and Sunday)* Menu € 24/75 bi – Carte € 65/92

◆ Opposite the Collegial Notre Dame Church, this hotel offers practical, well cared for rooms (some with a spa bathtub) and a pleasant sitting room area. Cuisine in keeping with modern tastes.

De la Cloche

rest, VISA MC AE

34 r. A. Briand – ✆ 03 26 74 03 84 – www.hotel-de-la-cloche.fr – chef.sautetepicerie@wanadoo.fr – Fax 03 26 41 35 12 – Closed 23 December-3 January and Sunday dinner 1st October-31 May

22 rm – †€ 52/85 ††€ 56/115, ☕ € 10 – ½ P € 65/75 AZ s

Rest *Jacques Sautet* – Menu € 27/60 – Carte € 50/95

Rest *Vieux Briscard* – brasserie Menu (€ 13), € 25 – Carte € 36/68

◆ Centrally located hotel with a few renovated, practical and generously dimensioned rooms. Two are more spacious and comfortable. Classic menu served in a plush bourgeois setting. This restaurant sports a brasserie ambience and menu.

VITRY-LE-FRANÇOIS

Armes (Pl. d') . . . . ABY
Arquebuse (R. de l') . . . . BZ 2
Beaux-Anges (R. des). . . . . BZ 4
Bourgeois (Fg Léon) . . . . BZ 7
Briand (R. Aristide) . . . . AZ
Chêne-Vert (R. du) . . . . BY 9
Dominé (Bd du Col.) . . . . AZ 10
Domyné-de-Verzet (R.) . . . . BZ 13
Grande-Rue-de-Vaux . . . . BY
Guesde (R. Jules) . . . . AZ 14
Hôtel-de-Ville (R. de l') . . . . BZ 19
Joffre (Pl. Mar.) . . . . BZ 21
Leclerc (Pl. Mar.). . . . . BY 23
Minimes (R. des) . . . . AY 24
Moll (Av. du Col.). . . . . AZ 25
Paris (Av. de) . . . . AY 26
Petite-Rue-de-Vaux. . . . . BY 29
Petite-Sainte (R. de la) . . . . BZ 30
Petit-Denier (R. du) . . . . AY 28
Pont (R. du) . . . . AY
République (Av. de la). . . . . BZ 33
Royer-Collard (Pl.) . . . . BZ 34
Ste-Memje (R.) . . . . BY 37
St-Éloi (R.) . . . . BY 35
St-Michel (R.) . . . . ABY 36
Soeurs (R. des) . . . . AY 40
Tanneurs (R. des). . . . . AYZ 42
Tour (R. de la) . . . . AY 44
Vieux-Port (R. du) . . . . BZ 46
Vitry-le-Brûlé (Fg de) . . . . BY 47
106e-R.-I. (Av. du) . . . . BZ 49

The ✿ award is the crème de la crème.
This is awarded to restaurants which are really worth travelling miles for!

VITTEAUX – 21 Côte-d'Or – **320** H5 – **pop. 1 114** – **alt. 320 m** 8 **C2**
– ✉ **21350** **Burgundy-Jura**

Paris 259 – Auxerre 100 – Avallon 55 – Beaune 64 – Dijon 47 – Montbard 34 – Saulieu 34

Office de tourisme, 16, rue Hubert Languet ✆ 03 80 33 90 14, Fax 03 80 33 90 14

Vieille Auberge

19 r. Verdun – ✆ 03 80 49 60 88 – Fax 03 80 49 68 14 – Closed 16-29 June, 4-11 January, Sunday dinner, Tuesday dinner, Wednesday dinner, Thursday dinner and Monday
Rest – Menu (€ 11), € 15/28 – Carte € 22/44
◆ Family-run village inn whose bar, with a country atmosphere, serves two rustic and renovated dining rooms. Small terrace and garden. Area for playing boules. Traditional dishes.

VITTEL – 88 Vosges – **314** D3 – **pop. 5 783** – **alt. 347 m** – **Spa : early April-mid Dec.** – **Casino** AY – ✉ **88800** **Alsace-Lorraine** 26 **B3**

Paris 342 – Belfort 129 – Chaumont 84 – Épinal 43 – Langres 80 – Nancy 85

Office de tourisme, place de la Marne ✆ 03 29 08 08 88, Fax 03 29 08 37 99

de Vittel Ermitage Hôtel Ermitage, ✆ 03 29 08 81 53

du Bois de Hazeau Centre Préparation Olympique, SW : 1 km, ✆ 03 29 08 20 85

Park★.

Plan on next page

Providence

125 av. Châtillon – ✆ 03 29 08 08 27 – www.hotelvittel.com – providence.vittel@wanadoo.fr – Fax 03 29 08 62 60 – 1 Apr - 31 Dec AY **a**
38 rm – †€ 57/75 ††€ 67/85, ☕ € 9 – ½ P € 61/71
Rest – *(closed 8-17 March, 1st-6 January and 1st-10 February)* Menu (€ 15), € 19/36 – Carte € 21/47
◆ This Vittel establishment has been renovated. Attractive, small rooms in warm colours, and larger, well-equipped junior suites (big bathtubs).

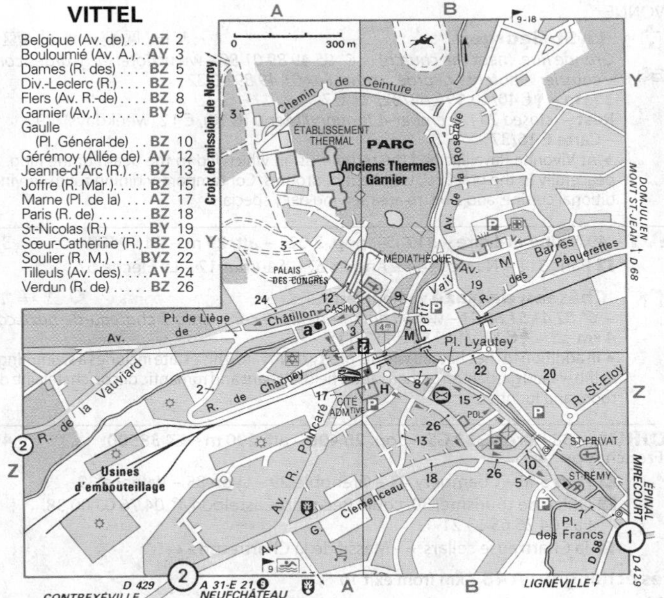

West 3 km by La Vauviard road AZ – ✉ 88800 Vittel

L'Orée du Bois rm, VISA
– ✆ 03 29 08 88 88 – www.loreeduboisvittel.fr – info@loreeduboisvittel.fr – Fax 03 29 08 01 61
57 rm – †€ 52/88 ††€ 64/88, ☕ € 9 – ½ P € 60/72
Rest – Menu € 18/35 – Carte € 29/49
◆ Opposite the golf course, this hotel is the epitome of leisure: spa, massages, sauna, hammam. Stylish rooms; we recommend the organic or family rooms. Classic menu whose flair for modernity does not spurn its regional roots. Garden terrace.

VIVÈS – **66 Pyrénées-Orientales** – **344** H7 – **see le Boulou**

VIVIERS – **07 Ardèche** – **331** K7 – **pop. 3 768** – **alt. 65 m** – ✉ **07220** 44 **B3**

Paris 618 – Lyon 163 – Marseille 167 – Montpellier 158 – Valence 63

Office de tourisme, 5, place Riquet ✆ 04 75 52 77 00, Fax 04 75 52 81 63

Le Relais du Vivarais with rm rm, VISA
31 rte Nationale 86 – ✆ 04 75 52 60 41 – www.relaisduvivarais.fr – relais.viviers@wanadoo.fr – Closed 12 March-3 April, 8-15 October, 23 December-4 January
5 rm – †€ 72/75 ††€ 72/95, ☕ € 9
Rest – *(closed Sunday dinner)* Menu (€ 17), € 27/46 – Carte € 28/56
◆ Not content with simply serving tasty, reinterpreted regional cuisine, a friendly welcome awaits you in this charming family-run restaurant. Stylish interior and shaded terrace. Pretty rooms that are simple decorated. Home-made bread and jam served for breakfast.

VIVONNE – **86 Vienne** – **322** H6 – **pop. 3 045** – **alt. 103 m** – ✉ **86370** 39 **C2**
Atlantic Coast

Paris 354 – Angoulême 94 – Confolens 62 – Niort 67 – Poitiers 20 – St-Jean-d'Angély 90

Office de tourisme, place du Champ de Foire ✆ 05 49 43 47 88, Fax 05 49 43 34 87

Le St-Georges rm, rest,

Grande Rue, (near the church) – 05 49 89 01 89 – www.hotel-st-georges.com – courrier@hotel-st-georges.com – Fax 05 49 89 00 22

31 rm – €40/60 €48/82, €7

Rest – *(closed 20 December-4 January)* Menu (€10), €12 (weekdays)/29 – Carte €16/37

◆ At Vivonne Ravaillac had the terrible vision which led to the death of the King. Sleep peacefully in the practical, well-kept bedrooms. Contemporary dining room serving traditional cuisine, and a bistro area serving daily specials.

VIVY – **49 Maine-et-Loire** – **317** I5 – **pop. 2 021** – **alt. 29 m** – ✉ **49680** 35 **C2**

Paris 311 – Nantes 144 – Angers 57 – Saumur 12 – La Flèche 67

Château de Nazé without rest

– *02 41 51 80 91 – www.chateau-de-naze.com – info@chateau-de-naze.com*

4 rm – €110/115 €110/115

◆ In addition to the château with its pretty courtyard, this estate includes a swimming pool in the walled garden, an orchard and a field. Elegant and romantic décor, chatelaine dining room and lounges.

VOIRON – **38 Isère** – **333** G5 – **pop. 20 400** – **alt. 290 m** – ✉ **38500** 45 **C2**

French Alps

Paris 546 – Chambéry 43 – Grenoble 29 – Lyon 85 – Valence 89

Office de tourisme, 30, cours Becquart Castelbon 04 76 05 00 38, Fax 04 76 65 63 21

la Chartreuse cellars ★ - Massif de la Chartreuse★★.

près échangeur A 48 3 km from exit 10

Palladior

4 r. A. Bouffard Roupé – 04 76 06 47 47 – www.hotel-palladior-voiron.fr – welcome@hotel-palladior-voiron.fr – Fax 04 76 06 48 48

82 rm – €79/195 €79/215, €12

Rest – Menu (€22), €28 – Carte €35/54

◆ This new hotel near a motorway junction offers modern, functional rooms that are very well equipped. Designer interior and pleasant terrace. Regional set menus and modern dishes.

VOISINS-LE-BRETONNEUX – **78 Yvelines** – **311** I3 – **101** 22 – **see Paris, Area (St-Quentin-en-Yvelines)**

VOITEUR – **39 Jura** – **321** D6 – **pop. 779** – **alt. 260 m** – ✉ **39210** 16 **B3**

Paris 409 – Besançon 79 – Dole 51 – Lons-le-Saunier 12

Office de tourisme, 1 place de la Mairie 03 84 44 62 47, Fax 03 84 44 64 86

Château St-Martin without rest

– *03 84 44 91 87 – www.juranatura.fr – kellerbr@wanadoo.fr – Fax 03 84 44 91 87 – Closed December and January*

4 rm – €90 €100

◆ This listed château offers an aperitif to its guests on arrival. Some of its differently-styled rooms overlook the park and 14C chapel. Piano available.

VOLLORE-VILLE – **63 Puy-de-Dôme** – **326** I8 – **pop. 684** – **alt. 540 m** – ✉ **63120** 6 **C2**

Paris 408 – Clermont-Ferrand 58 – Roanne 63 – Vichy 52

Château de Vollore without rest

– *04 73 53 71 06 – www.chateaux-france.com/vollore – chateau.vollore@wanadoo.fr – Fax 04 73 53 72 44*

5 rm – €100/150 €130/230

◆ A château 'with a view' belonging to the La Fayette family. The great grandson of the historic character is married to the owners' daughter. Period furnished rooms and suites.

VOLNAY – **21 Côte-d'Or** – **320** I7 – **see Beaune**

VONNAS – 01 Ain – **328** C3 – **pop. 2 623** – **alt. 200 m** – ✉ **01540** 43 **E1**
Burgundy-Jura

Paris 409 – Bourg-en-Bresse 23 – Lyon 69 – Mâcon 21 – Villefranche-sur-Saône 41
Syndicat d'initiative, rue du Moulin ☎ 04 74 50 04 47, Fax 04 74 50 09 74

Georges Blanc VISA
pl. du Marché – ☎ 04 74 50 90 90 – www.georgesblanc.com – blanc@relaischateaux.com – Fax 04 74 50 08 80 – Closed January
35 rm – †€ 180/450 ††€ 180/450, ☕ € 27 – 7 suites
Rest – *(closed Wednesday lunch, Monday and Tuesday) (number of covers limited, pre-book)* Menu € 130/195 – Carte € 141/196
Spec. Foie gras de canard en écorce d'épices, chutney figue-tomate à la cardamome. Homard au savagnin. Vague croustillante chocolat-passion avec une glace à l'amande et un coulis acidulé. **Wines** Mâcon-Azé, Moulin-à-Vent.
◆ Luxury on the banks of the Veyle. Regional half-timbered and red brick residence with plush, spacious rooms. The delicious Bresse cuisine make this one of France's finest restaurants. Superb wine cellar.

Résidence des Saules without rest VISA
pl. du Marché – ☎ 04 74 50 90 51 – www.georgesblanc.com – blanc@relaischateaux.com – Fax 04 74 50 08 80 – Closed January
6 rm – †€ 160/190 ††€ 160/190, ☕ € 27 – 4 suites
◆ This smart, geranium-decked house is practically the annexe of the Georges Blanc hotel on the other side of the square. The comfortable rooms are located above the shop.

L'Ancienne Auberge VISA
– ☎ 04 74 50 90 50 – www.georgesblanc.com – auberge1900@georgesblanc.com – Fax 04 74 50 08 80 – Closed January
Rest – Menu (€ 19), € 22 (weekday lunch), € 28/48 – Carte € 37/59
◆ In a former lemonade factory. The idealised 1940s bistro decor pays tribute to the inn opened by the Blanc family in the late 19C (old photos and posters). Regional cuisine.

VOSNE-ROMANEE – 21 Côte-d'Or – **320** J7 – **pop. 451** – **alt. 242 m** – ✉ **21700** 8 **D1**

Paris 330 – Chalon-sur-Saône 49 – Dijon 21 – Dole 71

Le Richebourg without rest VISA
ruelle du Pont – ☎ 03 80 61 59 59 – www.hotel-lerichebourg.com – hotel@lerichebourg.com – Fax 03 80 61 59 50 – Closed 22-27 December
24 rm – †€ 125 ††€ 250, ☕ € 16 – 2 suites
◆ Contemporary hotel in the centre of this renowned village, offering all modern comforts and a health suite (treatments, sauna, steam bath). Spacious rooms.

VOUGEOT – 21 Côte-d'Or – **320** J6 – **pop. 215** – **alt. 239 m** – ✉ **21640** 8 **D1**
Burgundy-Jura

Paris 325 – Beaune 27 – Dijon 17
Château du Clos de Vougeot ★ O.

Clos de la Vouge VISA
1 r. Moulin – ☎ 03 80 62 89 65 – www.hotel-closdelavouge.com – closdelavouge@wanadoo.fr – Fax 03 80 62 83 14 – Closed 20 December-31 January
10 rm – †€ 69/125 ††€ 69/125, ☕ € 10 – ½ P € 83
Rest – *(closed Monday in February, March, November and December)* Menu (€ 15), € 23/36 – Carte € 25/63
◆ This building is close to the renowned Château du Clos de Vougeot. Personalised, well-kept rooms and family ambiance. Traditional cuisine.

in Gilly-lès-Cîteaux **2 km east by D 251 – pop. 599 – alt. 227 m – ✉ 21640**

Château de Gilly rm, VISA
– ☎ 03 80 62 89 98 – www.chateau-gilly.com – contact@chateau-gilly.fr – Fax 03 80 62 82 34
37 rm – †€ 165 ††€ 321, ☕ € 23 – 11 suites
Rest *Clos Prieur* – *(closed lunch except Sunday)* Menu € 46/69 – Carte € 77/100
Rest *Côté Terroirs* – *(closed dinner and Sunday)* Menu € 21/26
◆ Calm and refinement characterise this former Cistercian abbot's residence. Spacious personalised rooms. Pleasant formal French gardens. The Clos Prieur occupies a superb 14C rib-vaulted cellar. Classic dishes and fine wine list. Bistro menu and convivial ambiance at Côté Terroirs.

L'Orée des Vignes without rest

6 rte d'Épernay – 03 80 62 49 77 – www.oreedesvignes.com – info@oreedesvignes.com – Fax 03 80 62 49 76 – Closed 21 December-4 January
26 rm – €66/125 €66/125, €10
◆ These 16C farm buildings surround a fine courtyard garden. Quiet, rather spacious rooms with functional furniture. Pleasant breakfast area.

in Flagey-Échezeaux **3 km southeast by D 971 and D 109 – pop. 494 – alt. 227 m – ✉ 21640**

Losset without rest

10 pl. de l'Église – 03 80 62 46 00 – www.hotel-losset-bourgogne.com – hotel.losset@wanadoo.fr – Fax 03 80 62 46 08
7 rm – €85 €85/130, €8
◆ A new hotel with comfortable rooms furnished in a variety of styles. Some have handcrafted furniture, parquet flooring and beams, while others have a small lounge and fireplace.

Petit Paris without rest

6 r. du Petit-Paris – 03 80 62 84 09 – www.petitparis.bourgogne.free.fr – petitparis.bourgogne@free.fr – Fax 03 80 62 83 88
4 rm – €85 €85
◆ Warm welcome and personalised rooms at this 17C house surrounded by parkland. Artwork by the owner who also runs painting classes.

Simon

12 pl. de l'Église – 03 80 62 88 10 – famille.simon7@wanadoo.fr – Fax 03 80 62 88 10 – Closed 22-28 December, 1st-28 February, Sunday dinner and Wednesday
Rest – *(number of covers limited, pre-book)* Menu € 20 bi (weekday lunch), € 36/85 – Carte € 45/70
◆ Elegant modern restaurant in the centre of a wine-growing village frequented by loyal regulars. Appetising contemporary cuisine using fine produce. Pleasant welcome.

VOUGY – 74 Haute-Savoie – 328 L4 – see Bonneville

VOUILLÉ – 86 Vienne – 322 G5 – pop. 3 152 – alt. 118 m – ✉ 86190 39 C1

Paris 345 – Châtellerault 46 – Parthenay 34 – Poitiers 18 – Saumur 89 – Thouars 55

Office de tourisme, 10, place de l'Eglise 05 49 51 06 69, Fax 05 49 50 87 48

Cheval Blanc with rm

3 r. Barre – 05 49 51 81 46 – www.blondinhotel.fr – lechevalblanc.clovis@wanadoo.fr – Fax 05 49 51 96 31 – Closed 29 June-13 July and 22 February-8 March
14 rm – €51 €51, €6,50 – ½ P €47
Rest – Menu (€ 12), € 18 (weekdays)/43 – Carte € 29/45
◆ In the centre of the small town, this establishment has modern dining rooms, (one with a beautiful fireplace) overlooking the river, as does the summer terrace. Practical bedrooms.

Clovis
30 rm – €51 €51, €6,50 – ½ P €47
◆ A new building 100m from the main house offers functional well-kept rooms. Breakfast buffet.

VOUTENAY-SUR-CURE – 89 Yonne – 319 F6 – pop. 196 – alt. 130 m – ✉ 89270 7 B2

Paris 206 – Auxerre 37 – Avallon 15 – Vézelay 15

Auberge Le Voutenay with rm

– 03 86 33 51 92 – www.aubergelevoutenay.com – auberge.voutenay@wanadoo.fr – Fax 03 86 33 51 91 – Closed 16-24 June, 1st-21 January, Sunday dinner, Monday and Tuesday
7 rm – €45/65 €45/65, €9
Rest – *(number of covers limited, pre-book)* Menu (€ 15), € 26/56
◆ This 18C residence beside the road overlooks its pleasant grounds. Rustic yet elegant dining room, bistro corner and a small shop selling regional produce. Retro rooms.

VOUVRAY – 37 Indre-et-Loire – **317** N4 – **pop. 3 083** – **alt. 55 m** – ✉ 37210 Châteaux of the Loire 11 **B2**

Paris 240 – Amboise 18 – Blois 51 – Château-Renault 25 – Tours 10

Office de tourisme, 12, rue Rabelais ☎ 02 47 52 68 73, Fax 02 47 52 70 88

Domaine des Bidaudières without rest

r. Peu Morier, Vernou-sur-Brenne on D 46 – ☎ 02 47 52 66 85 – www.bidaudieres.com – contact@bidaudieres.com – Fax 02 47 52 62 17

7 rm – †€ 80/100 ††€ 120/130

◆ This 18C building has peaceful rooms, decorated with Jouy prints and antique furniture, overlooking a magnificent park.

Le Grand Vatel

8 av. Brûlé – ☎ 02 47 52 70 32 – legrandvatel@orange.fr – Fax 02 47 52 74 52 – Closed 5-15 March, 20-28 December, Sunday dinner and Monday

Rest – Menu € 20/24 – Carte € 45/75

◆ This regional-style stone residence has two dining rooms, one of which is decorated in 1920s style. Classical cuisine. Vouvray takes pride of place on the wine list.

VOVES – 28 Eure-et-Loir – **311** F6 – **pop. 2 928** – **alt. 146 m** – ✉ **28150** 12 **C1**

Paris 99 – Ablis 36 – Bonneval 23 – Chartres 25 – Châteaudun 38 – Étampes 51 – Orléans 61

Le Quai Fleuri

15 r. Texier Gallas – ☎ 02 37 99 15 15 – www.quaifleuri.com – quaifleuri@wanadoo.fr – Fax 02 37 99 11 20 **21 rm** – †€ 65 ††€ 75, € 10 – 4 suites

Rest – *(closed Sunday dinner)* Menu (€ 20), € 25/62 bi – Carte € 37/61

◆ This recently-established hotel, flanked by a reconstructed mill, has a few small rooms with personal touches. Those in the annexe are larger and on a level with the park. Restaurant with a bright modern decor, serving traditional cuisine.

VRON – 80 Somme – **301** D6 – **pop. 721** – **alt. 15 m** – ✉ **80120** 36 **A1**

Paris 211 – Abbeville 27 – Amiens 76 – Berck-sur-Mer 17 – Calais 89 – Hesdin 24

L'Hostellerie du Clos du Moulin

1 r. Maréchal Leclerc – ☎ 03 22 23 74 75 – www.leclosdumoulin.fr – contact@leclosdumoulin.fr – Fax 03 22 23 74 76

15 rm – †€ 90 ††€ 115 **Rest** – Menu € 18/55 – Carte € 37/69

◆ Surrounded by a pretty garden, the former stables of this estate are home to cosy personalised guestrooms, some with lounge. Traditional decor and modern facilities. The dining rooms located in the 16C stables are full of character.

WAHLBACH – 68 Haut-Rhin – **315** I11 – see Altkirch

LA WANTZENAU – 67 Bas-Rhin – **315** K5 – see Strasbourg

WATTIGNIES – 59 Nord – **302** G4 – see Lille

WENGELSBACH – 67 Bas-Rhin – **315** K2 – see Niedersteinbach

WESTHALTEN – 68 Haut-Rhin – **315** H9 – **pop. 904** – **alt. 240 m** – ✉ 68250 Alsace-Lorraine 1 **A3**

Paris 480 – Colmar 22 – Guebwiller 11 – Mulhouse 28 – Thann 27

Auberge du Cheval Blanc (Gilbert Koehler) with rm

20 r. Rouffach – ☎ 03 89 47 01 16 rm,

www.auberge-chevalblc.com – chevalblanc.west@wanadoo.fr – Fax 03 89 47 64 40 – Closed 11 January-5 February, Tuesday lunch, Sunday dinner and Monday

11 rm – †€ 75 ††€ 85/120, € 12 – ½ P € 92/106

Rest – Menu (€ 19), € 37/79 – Carte € 47/83

Spec. Dégustation de foie gras d'oie en trois services. Filet de Boeuf au pinot noir. Brochette d'ananas flambé, sorbet coco. **Wines** Riesling.

◆ Elegant house owned by the same family of wine-growers since 1785. Classic, creative cuisine and fine selection of Alsatian wines including those from the estate. The recently redone guestrooms are spacious, comfortable and modern.

WETTOLSHEIM – 68 Haut-Rhin – 315 H8 – see Colmar

WEYERSHEIM – 67 Bas-Rhin – 315 K4 – pop. 3 073 – alt. 140 m – ✉ 67720 1 B1

Paris 486 – Haguenau 18 – Saverne 49 – Strasbourg 21 – Wissembourg 50

Auberge du Pont de la Zorn
2 r. République – ☎ 03 88 51 36 87 – debeer.m@wanadoo.fr – Fax 03 88 51 32 67 – Closed 20 August-4 September, 16 February-1st March, Saturday lunch, Wednesday and Thursday
Rest – Menu (€ 11), € 15 (weekday lunch) – Carte € 13/31
◆ Reproductions of drawings by Hansi, exposed beams and regional pottery: Alsace in a nutshell! Bucolic terrace by the Zorn river. Flambé tarts served in the evening.

WIERRE-EFFROY – 62 Pas-de-Calais – 301 D3 – pop. 782 – alt. 28 m – ✉ 62720 30 A2

Paris 262 – Calais 29 – Abbeville 88 – Boulogne-sur-Mer 14 – Saint-Omer 47

La Ferme du Vert rest, P VISA MC AE
r. du Vert – ☎ 03 21 87 67 00 – www.fermeduvert.com – ferme.du.vert@wanadoo.fr – Fax 03 21 83 22 62 – Closed 19 December-22 January and Sunday from October to March
16 rm – †€ 59/92 ††€ 64/98, ☕ € 12 – 2 suites – ½ P € 67/97
Rest – *(closed Saturday lunch except July-August, Sunday and Monday)* Menu € 28/48 – Carte € 37/55
◆ Rural tranquillity reigns in this old Boulogne farmhouse. The rooms of various sizes are decorated with taste and simplicity. In the restaurant, you can enjoy tasty, traditional dishes concocted with local produce. Cheese shop.

Look out for red symbols, indicating particularly pleasant establishments.

WIHR-AU-VAL – 68 Haut-Rhin – 315 H8 – see Munster

WILLIERS – 08 Ardennes – 306 N4 – pop. 44 – alt. 277 m – ✉ 08110 14 C1

Paris 277 – Châlons-en-Champagne 174 – Charleville-Mézières 57 – Arlon 44 – Differdange 67

Chez Odette VISA MC
– ☎ 03 24 55 49 55 – www.chez-odette.com – chez.odette@skynet.be – Fax 03 24 55 49 59
10 rm – †€ 160/260 ††€ 160/260, ☕ € 18
Rest – *(Closed 29 March-7 April, 23 August-15 September, Monday, Tuesday lunch and Sunday dinner)* Menu (€ 28), € 55 – Carte € 58/64
◆ Odette herself ran this inn, now converted into a charming hotel. Modern furnishings in the well-equipped bedrooms. Gastronomic restaurant and café serving the same dishes and drinks as in the time of Odette.

WIMEREUX – 62 Pas-de-Calais – 301 C3 – pop. 7 493 – alt. 7 m – ✉ 62930 Northern France and the Paris Region 30 A2

Paris 269 – Arras 125 – Boulogne-sur-Mer 7 – Calais 33 – Marquise 13

Office de tourisme, quai Alfred Giard ☎ 03 21 83 27 17, Fax 03 21 32 76 91

Du Centre AC rest, P VISA MC AE
78 r. Carnot – ☎ 03 21 32 41 08 – www.hotelducentre-wimereux.fr – hotel.du.centre@wanadoo.fr – Fax 03 21 33 82 48 – Closed 21 December-30 January
23 rm – †€ 61/70 ††€ 70/88, ☕ € 9
Rest – *(closed Mon.)* Menu (€ 19), € 22/31 – Carte € 23/45
◆ An old building situated on the main street of a seaside resort on the Opal Coast. The rooms have been renovated and some have a mezzanine. The dining room sports a pleasant bistro look. Traditional dishes and seafood.

XXX **Liégeoise et Atlantic Hôtel** with rm

digue de mer – ✆ 03 21 32 41 01
– www.atlantic-delpierre.com – Alain.delpierre@wanadoo.fr – Fax 03 21 87 46 17
– Closed February, Sunday dinner and Monday lunch
18 rm – †€ 130/170 ††€ 130/170, ☕ € 12 – ½ P € 138/158
Rest – Menu € 38/65 – Carte € 62/76
◆ Well situated on the dyke-promenade, facing the Channel. Beautiful panoramic dining room nicely furnished in the Louis XVI style. Choose one of the new rooms overlooking the sea.

X **Epicure** (Philippe Carrée)

1 r. Pompidou – ✆ 03 21 83 21 83 – Fax 03 21 33 53 20
– Closed 20 August-5 September, 20 December-6 January, Wednesday dinner and Sunday
Rest – *(number of covers limited, pre-book)* Menu € 25/39 – Carte € 48/65
Spec. Homard côtier, raviole d'aubergine et tomate (May-Sep.). Lotte rôtie, rhubarbe et mimolette croustillante (May-Aug.). Sablés aux amandes, yaourt de brebis et sauce mangue.
◆ In the town centre, behind a discreet façade, a very small dining room with an intimate hushed setting. Attractive modern cooking focusing on seafood.

WINKEL – 68 Haut-Rhin – 315 H12 – pop. 366 – alt. 575 m – ✉ 68480 1 A3

Paris 466 – Altkirch 23 – Basel 35 – Belfort 50 – Colmar 92 – Montbéliard 46 – Mulhouse 42

XX **Au Cerf** with rm

76 r. Principale – ✆ 03 89 40 85 05 – Closed 28 September-19 October and 8-21 February
6 rm – †€ 43/49 ††€ 47/60, ☕ € 6,50 – ½ P € 48
Rest – *(closed Monday and Thursday)* Menu (€ 12), € 25/59 – Carte € 25/60
◆ Close to the source of the Ill, this friendly inn with a red façade has several dining rooms including one in winstub style. Pleasant rooms under the eaves.

WISEMBACH – 88 Vosges – 314 K3 – pop. 412 – alt. 500 m – ✉ 88520 27 D3

Paris 413 – Colmar 54 – Épinal 69 – St-Dié 16 – Ste-Marie-aux-Mines 11 – Sélestat 34

XX **Blanc Ru** with rm

19 r. du 8 mai 45 – ✆ 03 29 51 78 51 – Fax 03 29 51 70 67
– Closed 22 September-7 October, 3 February-10 March, Sunday dinner, Monday and Tuesday
7 rm – †€ 51 ††€ 51/62, ☕ € 9 – ½ P € 52/62
Rest – Menu (€ 17), € 24/44 – Carte € 35/65
◆ Take a seat either in the pretty winter garden or in the spacious, countrified dining room. Classic repertory (frogs' legs are the speciality of the house). Neat rooms.

WISSEMBOURG – 67 Bas-Rhin – 315 L2 – pop. 7 978 – alt. 157 m – ✉ 67160 Alsace-Lorraine 1 B1

Paris 512 – Haguenau 33 – Karlsruhe 42 – Sarreguemines 80 – Strasbourg 67
Office de tourisme, 9, place de la République ✆ 03 88 94 10 11, Fax 03 88 94 18 82
Old town ★: St-Pierre and St-Paul church ★.
Village ★★ of Hunspach 11 km by ②.

Plan on following page

Au Moulin de la Walk

2 r. Walk – ✆ 03 88 94 06 44 – www.moulin-walk.com
– info@moulin-walk.com – Fax 03 88 54 38 03 – Closed 8-28 January A s
25 rm – †€ 55/69 ††€ 64/69, ☕ € 8 – ½ P € 70
Rest – *(closed 19 June-2 July, 8-28 January, Friday lunch, Sunday dinner and Monday)* Menu € 32/50 – Carte € 30/50
◆ On the banks of a river, buildings grafted onto the remains of an old mill whose wheel is still turning. Warm and refined décor enhanced by bare wood in the local fashion. The restaurant has a flowered setting and tile stove. Pretty summer terrace.

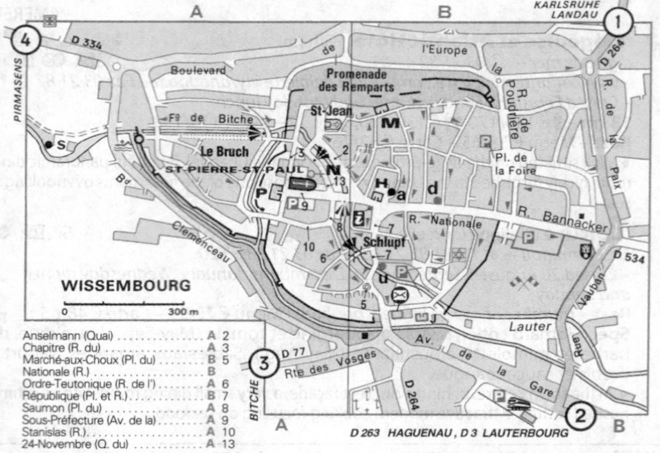

XX **Hostellerie du Cygne** with rm — AC rest, ⚒ rm, VISA MC AE

3 r. Sel – ✆ 03 88 94 00 16 – www.hostellerie-cygne.com – hostellerie-cygne@wanadoo.fr – Fax 03 88 54 38 28 – Closed 6-19 July, 9-22 November and 16 February-1st March — B **a**

16 rm – †€ 50/65 ††€ 50/75, ☕ € 9 – ½ P € 52/90

Rest – *(closed Thursday lunch, Sunday dinner and Wednesday)* Menu (€ 15), € 30/65 – Carte € 36/65

◆ Traditional cuisine served in dining rooms adorned with wood carvings or on the patio set around two town centre houses. Cosy rooms.

XX **L'Ange** — VISA MC AE

2 r. de la République – ✆ 03 88 94 12 11 – www.restaurant-ange.com – pierrel4@wanadoo.fr – Fax 03 88 94 12 11 – Closed 16-26 June, 10-18 November, 16 February-3 March, Sunday dinner in winter, Monday and Tuesday — B **u**

Rest – Menu (€ 18), € 29/38 – Carte € 35/52

◆ Charming small paved courtyard-terrace at the entrance, and two dining rooms in succession. One of which is more rustic, in the style of a winstub bistro. Classic cuisine with regional touches.

XX **Le Carrousel Bleu** — AC VISA MC

17 r. Nationale – ✆ 03 88 54 33 10 – www le-carrousel-bleu.fr – le.carroussel.bleu@orange.fr – Fax 03 88 54 33 10 – Closed 1st-15 August, Sunday dinner, Monday and Wednesday — B **d**

Rest – Menu (€ 20), € 28/70 bi – Carte € 32/48

◆ This friendly and intimate restaurant in an 18C house offers original and unusual modern recipes that will transport you thousands of miles from 'Little Venice'.

in Altenstadt 2 km by ② - ✉67160

XX **Rôtisserie Belle Vue** — AC P VISA MC

1 r. Principale – ✆ 03 88 94 02 30 – Fax 03 88 54 80 14 – Closed 10 August-3 September, 15 February-5 March, Sunday dinner, Monday and Tuesday

Rest – Menu € 25/53 – Carte € 30/60

◆ This large family restaurant serves traditional cuisine in two plush dining rooms, providing attractive views of the garden. Daily specials served at the bar.

XONRUPT-LONGEMER – 88 Vosges – 314 J4 – see Gérardmer

YERRES – 91 Essonne – 312 D3 – pop. 28 300 – alt. 45 m – ✉ 91330 21 D3

Paris 28 – Évry 20 – Boulogne-Billancourt 36 – Montreuil 29 – Argenteuil 52

Château du Maréchal de Saxe rm,
av. Grange, 2 km by D.94 towards rest, VISA
Créteil – 01 69 48 78 53 – www.chateaudumarechaldesaxe.com
– saxe@leshotelsparticuliers.com – Fax 01 69 83 84 91
25 rm – € 105/290 € 105/290, € 15 – 2 suites – ½ P € 111/203
Rest – Menu € 48/78 – Carte € 50/90
◆ This red-brick château was a folly of Maréchal de Saxe. Elegant decor in the main bedrooms; a more contemporary feel to those in the annexe. Huge park. Two classical dining rooms adorned with allegorical frescoes, old crockery etc. Traditional cuisine.

YERVILLE – 76 Seine-Maritime – 304 F4 – pop. 2 274 – alt. 156 m 33 C1
– ✉ 76760

Paris 164 – Dieppe 44 – Fécamp 48 – Le Havre 69 – Rouen 33
de Yerville 367 rue des Acacias, NW : 0.5 km, 02 32 70 15 49

Hostellerie des Voyageurs VISA
3 r. Jacques Ferny – 02 35 96 82 55 – www.hostellerie-voyageurs.com
– andre.jumel@hostellerie-voyageurs.com – Closed Sunday dinner and Monday except bank holidays
Rest – Menu € 18 (weekday lunch), € 27/49 – Carte € 48/55
◆ Former post house (1875) that serves classical dishes in a large, two-part countrified room. Drinks and coffee served in the terrace garden.

YEU (ÎLE) – 85 Vendée – 361 BC7 – see Île d 'Yeu

YGRANDE – 03 Allier – 326 E3 – pop. 753 – alt. 333 m – ✉ 03160

Paris 310 – Clermont-Ferrand 111 – Moulins 34 – Montluçon 41 – Yzeure 35

Château d'Ygrande VISA
Le Mont, 4 km east by D 192 and secondary road – 04 70 66 33 11
– www.chateauygrande.fr – reservation@chateauygrande.fr – Fax 04 70 66 33 63
– Closed 13-25 December, 4 January-27 February, Sunday evening and Monday except July-August
19 rm – € 122/220 € 122/220, € 16
Rest – *(closed Sunday dinner, Tuesday lunch and Monday except July-August)*
Menu € 28/66 – Carte approx. € 52
◆ An attractive, 19C château with romantic charm. Its 40-ha park blends into the peaceful Bourbonnais landscape. Inside, elegance and good taste reign. Directoire style dining room and modern menu using ingredients from the vegetable garden.

YSSINGEAUX – 43 Haute-Loire – 331 G3 – pop. 6 931 – alt. 829 m
– ✉ 43200 **Lyon - Rhone Valley**

Paris 565 – Ambert 73 – Privas 98 – Le Puy-en-Velay 27 – St-Étienne 52 – Valence 93
Office de tourisme, 16, place Foch 04 71 59 10 76, Fax 04 71 56 03 12

Le Bourbon rest, VISA
5 pl. Victoire – 04 71 59 06 54 – www.le-bourbon.com – le.bourbon.hotel@wanadoo.fr – Fax 04 71 59 00 70 – Closed 25 June-8 July, 8-21 October, 23 December-20 January, Sunday dinner, Tuesday lunch and Monday
11 rm – € 65/75 € 65/75, € 12 – ½ P € 60/65
Rest – Menu (€ 13), € 21/46 bi – Carte € 35/48
◆ A small, welcoming inn on a revamped square. Neat, functional rooms with attractive modern bathrooms. A colourful restaurant reputed for its tasty regional menu made with produce from local growers.

YVETOT – 76 Seine-Maritime – 304 E4 – pop. 10 800 – alt. 147 m 33 C1
– ✉ 76190 **Normandy**

Paris 171 – Dieppe 57 – Fécamp 35 – Le Havre 58 – Lisieux 85 – Rouen 36
Office de tourisme, 8, pl. Maréchal Joffre 02 35 95 08 40, Fax 02 35 95 08 40
de Yerville Yerville 367 rue des Acacias, NE : 13 km, 02 32 70 15 49
Windows★★ of St-Pierre church.

Du Havre
pl. des Belges – ☎ 02 35 95 16 77 – www.hotel-du-havre.fr – contact@hotel-du-havre.fr – Fax 02 35 95 21 18
23 rm – †€ 53/60 ††€ 58/66, ☐ € 10
Rest *(Closed Friday dinner and Saturday dinner in winter)* Menu (€ 21) Carte € 30/45
◆ A friendly welcome awaits guests in this family-run, town centre hotel. Individually decorated, comfortable rooms. Traditional cuisine in a dining room whose decoration varies according to the season and the news, in particular sports news.

Le Manoir aux Vaches
2 r. Guy de Maupassant – ☎ 02 35 95 65 65 – www.lemanoirauxvaches.com – contact@manoirauxvaches.com – Fax 02 35 95 21 18
9 rm ☐ – †€ 86/106 ††€ 96/126
◆ Lovely mezzanine rooms decorated on an unusual cow theme.

Southeast 5 km on D 5 – ✉ 76190 Yvetot

Auberge du Val au Cesne with rm
Duclair road – ☎ 02 35 56 63 06 – www.valaucesne.fr – valaucesne@hotmail.com – Fax 02 35 56 92 78 – Closed 24 August-6 September and 11-31 January
5 rm – †€ 90 ††€ 90, ☐ € 9
Rest – *(closed Mon. and Tues.)* Menu € 28/60 bi – Carte € 40/59
◆ Delightful 17C Normandy inn in remote countryside. Five countrified dining rooms (antiques and fireplaces) are the setting for traditional, market-fresh cuisine. Regional, Art Nouveau or modern furnishings adorn the eminently comfortable guestrooms.

in Motteville 9 km east by D 929 and D 20 – pop. 720 – alt. 160 m – ✉ 76970

Auberge du Bois St-Jacques
à la gare – ☎ 02 35 96 83 11 – www.aubergebsj.com – bsj.nicolas@wanadoo.fr – Fax 02 35 96 23 18 – Closed 3 weeks in August, 27 February-7 March, Sunday dinner, Monday dinner and Tuesday
Rest – Menu (€ 13), € 20 (weekdays)/45 – Carte € 30/45
◆ This former station buffet has two dining rooms. One is rustic with beams and copperware, and the other is modern, has shades of red and is rotunda-shaped. Updated cuisine.

YVOIRE – 74 Haute-Savoie – 328 K2 – pop. 810 – alt. 380 m – ✉ 74140 46 F1

French Alps

Paris 563 – Annecy 71 – Bonneville 41 – Genève 26 – Thonon-les-Bains 16
Office de tourisme, place de la mairie ☎ 04 50 72 80 21, Fax 04 50 72 84 21
Medieval village ★★: jardin des Cinq Sens★.

Villa Cécile without rest
156 rte de Messery, on the D 25 – ☎ 04 50 72 27 40 – www.villacecile.com – reservation@villacecile.com – Fax 04 50 72 27 15
15 rm – †€ 90/165 ††€ 90/165, ☐ € 12
◆ Relax at this peaceful villa at the entrance to the medieval village. It offers lakeside views, Jacuzzi, steam bath, sauna and pools. Bright rooms with nautical touches.

Les Flots Bleus rm,
– ☎ 04 50 72 80 08 – www.flotsbleus-yvoire.com – contact@flotsbleus-yvoire.com – Fax 04 50 72 84 28 – Open Easter to mid-October
17 rm – †€ 110/195 ††€ 110/195, ☐ € 11
Rest – Menu € 22 (weekdays)/88 – Carte € 33/63
◆ The attractive guestrooms in this hotel have stunning views of the lake. Rooms with either a terrace or balcony, modern comforts and top-of-the-range facilities. Contemporary or traditional Alpine furnishings. Traditional cuisine served in two dining rooms, one modern and the other with a nautical decor.

Le Pré de la Cure rest,
pl. de la Mairie – ☎ 04 50 72 83 58 – www.pre-delacure.com – lepredelacure@wanadoo.fr – Fax 04 50 72 91 15 – Open 28 February-11 November
25 rm – †€ 72/95 ††€ 72/95, ☐ € 10 – ½ P € 80/86
Rest – Menu € 20 (weekdays)/47 – Carte € 36/52
◆ At the entrance to this picturesque medieval village. Large functional rooms command views of the lake or the quiet garden. Attentive staff. Regional cuisine served in the veranda/dining room or on the riverside terrace.

XX **Vieille Porte**

2 place de la Mairie – ✆ 04 50 72 80 14 – www.la-vieille-porte.com – info@la-vieille-porte.com – Fax 04 50 72 92 04 – Closed 1st December-5 February and Monday except July-August

Rest – Menu € 26/40 – Carte € 40/50

◆ 14C house that has belonged to the same family since 1587! Elegant interior with beams, terracotta and old stone. Terrace shaded by the ramparts.

XX **Du Port** with rm

rm, rm,

r. du Port – ✆ 04 50 72 80 17 – www.hotelrestaurantduport-yvoire.com – hotel duport.yvoire@wanadoo.fr – Fax 04 50 72 90 71 – Open 1st March-5 November

7 rm – € 110/210 € 110/210, € 15 – ½ P € 105/155

Rest – *(closed Wednesday except from May to September)* Menu (€ 25), € 31 (weekdays)/47 – Carte € 48/66

◆ Terrace by the lake and pretty, flower-covered façade for this house with its ideal location on the harbour. Fish specialities. Pretty rooms with lakeside decor.

YVOY-LE-MARRON – **41 Loir-et-Cher** – **318** I6 – **pop. 603** – **alt. 129 m** – ✉ **41600** 12 **C2**

Paris 163 – Orléans 35 – Blois 45 – La Ferté-St-Aubin 13 – Lamotte-Beuvron 15 – Romorantin-Lanthenay 34

Syndicat d'initiative, route de Chaumont ✆ 02 54 88 07 14, Fax 02 54 88 07 14

Auberge du Cheval Blanc

rm,

1 pl. Cheval Blanc – ✆ 02 54 94 00 00 – www.aubergeduchevalblanc.com – auberge.cheval.blanc@wanadoo.fr – Fax 02 54 94 00 01

15 rm – € 70/95 € 85/95, € 12

Rest – *(closed Tuesday lunch and Monday except July-August)* Menu € 28/46 – Carte € 40/60

◆ This welcoming Sologne building in the centre of the small village offers warm, refined, good quality rooms in shades of ochre, red and yellow. Carefully preserved half-timbering and floor tiles give character to this dining room. Modern menu.

YZEURES-SUR-CREUSE – **37 Indre-et-Loire** – **317** O8 – **pop. 1 463** – **alt. 74 m** – ✉ **37290** 11 **B3**

Paris 318 – Châteauroux 72 – Châtellerault 28 – Poitiers 65 – Tours 85

La Promenade

1 pl. du 11 Novembre – ✆ 02 47 91 49 00 – Fax 02 47 94 46 12 – Closed 20 December-25 January, Monday and Tuesday

15 rm – € 52/55 € 55/59, € 11 – ½ P € 51/61

Rest – Menu € 19/35 – Carte € 31/40

◆ Former post house dating from 1880 in the heart of a small village in southern Touraine. Rooms with a carefully chosen décor and a family atmosphere. Rustic-styled restaurant with exposed beams, stone and an imposing fireplace. Traditional cuisine.

ZELLENBERG – **68 Haut-Rhin** – **315** H7 – **see Riquewihr**

ZIMMERSHEIM – **68 Haut-Rhin** – **315** I10 – **see Mulhouse**

ZONZA – **2A Corse-du-Sud** – **345** E9 – **see Corse**

ZOUFFTGEN – **57 Moselle** – **307** H2 – **pop. 667** – **alt. 250 m** – ✉ **57330** 26 **B1**

Paris 341 – Luxembourg 20 – Metz 48 – Thionville 18

XXX **La Lorraine** (Marcel Keff) with rm

rest,

80 r. Principale – ✆ 03 82 83 40 46 – www.la-lorraine.fr – info@la-lorraine.fr – Fax 03 82 83 48 26 – Closed Monday and Tuesday

3 rm – € 115 €, € 18 **Rest** – Menu € 38 (weekdays)/110 – Carte € 60/95

Spec. Fricassée d'escargots de Cleurie, coulis de persil et émulsion de pommes de terre ratte. Pièce de cochon de lait de Kanfen rôti dans sa peau croustillante. L'œuf tiède au chocolat noir, sabayon au rhum. **Wines** Vin de Moselle rouge.

◆ Border establishment popular for its modern cuisine. The floor provides views into the well-stocked wine cellar. Contemporary dining room extended by a veranda and garden terrace. Large and luxurious guestrooms in Lorraine style. Gourmet breakfast.

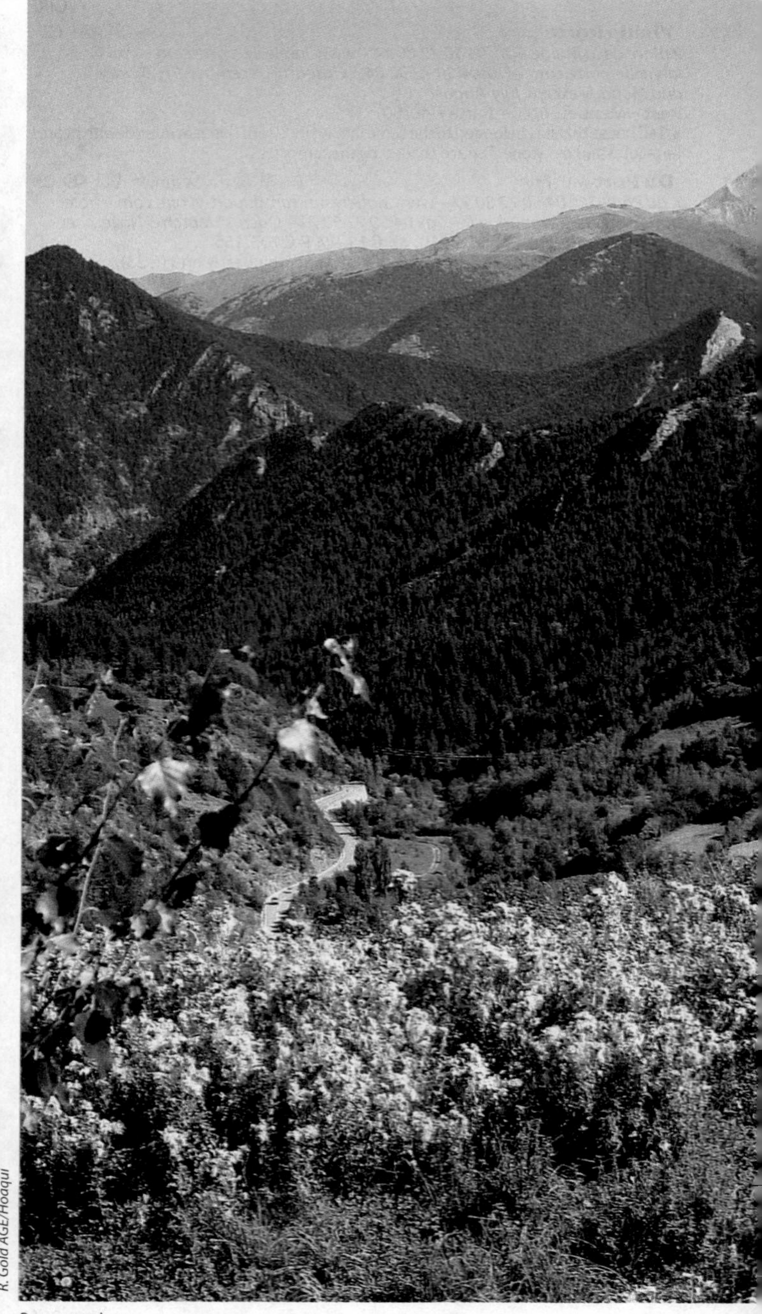

R. Gold AGE/Hoaqui

Paysage andorran

PRINCIPALITY OF ANDORRA

Michelin LOCAL map: n° 343 H9
Population: 83 734
Altitude: 2 946 m
Languedoc-Roussillon-Tarn Gorges

USEFUL INFORMATION

The Principality of Andorra, covering an area of 464 km², is set in the heart of the Pyrenees, between France and Spain. Since 1993, the Principality is a sovereign state, member of the U.N.

The official language is Catalan but most of the people also speak French and Spanish.

The local currency is the euro.

To enter Andorra, European Union citizens require a valid passport or identity card.

Access from France: N 22 trunk road via Envalira Tunnel.

TOURIST OFFICE

rue du Dr-Vilanova, Andorre-la- Vieille ✆ (00-376) 82 02 14, Fax (00-376) 82 58 23

TRANSPORTS

Coach links: from Toulouse-Blagnac Airport via Cie Novatel, information (00-376) 803 789 and Cie Nadal (00-376) 805 151.

From SNCF railway stations of l'Hospitalet and Latour-de-Carol via Cie Hispano-Andorranne, information (00-376) 807 000.

ANDORRA-LA-VELLA Capital of the Principality – 343 H9 28 B3 – pop. 23 587 – alt. 1 029 m

Paris 861 – Carcassonne 165 – Foix 102 – Perpignan 170

Vallée du Valira del Nord (Valira del Nord valley) ★ N.

Plaza

rm, rest, VISA

Maria Pla 19 – 00 376 87 94 44 – www.plazandorra.com – hotelplaza@plazandorra.com – Fax 00 376 87 94 45 C **a**

45 rm – €100/210 €120/250, €17 – 45 suites **Rest** – Menu €19

◆ Two elevators offering panoramic views serve the six floors of this luxury hotel laid out around a lush patio. Superb rooms with views of the Andorra summits. The restaurant also serves a buffet breakfast.

Arthotel

rm, VISA

– 00 376 76 03 03 – www.arthotel.ad – arthotel@andorra.ad – Fax 00 376 76 03 04 C **d**

125 rm – €84/233 €106/312

Rest – Menu €27

Rest *Plató* – Carte €27/46

◆ Big modern building opened in 2002. Comfortable, large and well-equipped rooms. Some have whirlpool baths. Independent entrance and simple decor at Plató.

Cèntric H.

rm, VISA

av. Meritxell 87-89 – 00 376 87 75 00 – www.husa.es – husacentric@andornet.ad – Fax 00 376 87 75 01 C **h**

74 rm – €97/135 €141/208, €14 – 6 suites **Rest** – Menu €23

◆ A modern hotel located in the middle of a shopping centre. Spacious rooms, some with a terrace. Pleasant bathrooms with separate shower. The well-lit dining room overlooks a busy street and is completed by a lounge with a fireplace.

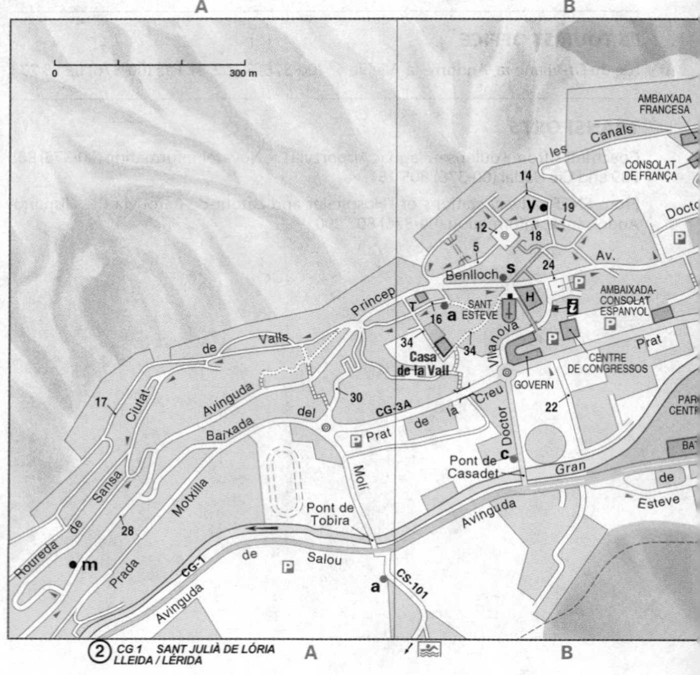

President rest, VISA

av. Santa Coloma 44 – 00 376 87 72 77 – www.janhotels.com – reserves@janhotels.com – Fax 00 376 87 62 22 A **m**

100 rm – €60/278 €80/371, €7 **Rest** – Menu €19

◆ Hotel complex with imposing public areas and comfortable rooms. Indoor pool and solarium on the 7th floor. Modern, minimalist and well arranged restaurant.

Diplomatic rm, rest, VISA

av. Tarragona – 00 376 80 27 80 – www.diplomatichotel.com – info@diplomatichotel.com – Fax 00 376 80 27 90 C **m**

83 rm – €65/115 €93/165 – 2 suites **Rest** – Menu €19

◆ This recent cubic construction is in a business estate. It houses practical rooms that appeal to both tourists and business travellers. International, unpretentious food served in a discreet contemporary setting.

Florida without rest VISA

Llacuna 15 – 00 376 82 01 05 – www.hotelflorida.ad – hotelflorida@andorra.ad – Fax 00 376 86 19 25 B **y**

27 rm – €43/67 €58/96

◆ Family-run hotel with a modern façade but rather limited reception area. Practical rooms with parquet floors. Small gym and sauna.

Borda Estevet VISA

rte de La Comella 2 – 00 376 86 40 26 – www.bordaestevet.com – bordaestevet@quarsandorra.com – Fax 00 376 86 40 26 A **a**

Rest – Carte €33/54

◆ Several rustic dining rooms within the beautiful old stone walls of this former barn. Andorran furniture and fireplace. Catalan and market-inspired cuisine.

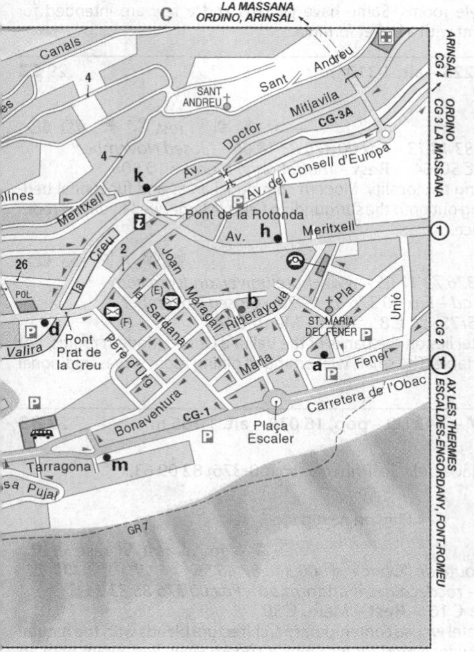

ANDORRA LA VELLA

XX **La Borda Pairal 1630**
Doctor Vilanova 7 – ✆ 00 376 86 99 99 – www.labordapairal1630.com – lbp1630@andorra.ad – Fax 00 376 86 66 61 – Closed Sunday dinner and Monday
Rest – Carte € 25/38 B **c**
◆ An old Andorran stone farmhouse whose rustic decor is still intact. A bar welcomes guests and the wine cellar can be seen from the restaurant. Banquet hall on the first floor.

XX **Taberna Ángel Belmonte**
Ciutat de Consuegra 3 – ✆ 00 376 82 24 60 – www.tabernaangelbelmonte.com – Fax 00 376 82 35 15 C **b**
Rest – Carte € 46/67
◆ What a pleasant place this restaurant is with its tavern feel! Wood dominates the beautiful decor, where all is perfectly laid out. Local ingredients, fish and shellfish on the menu.

XX **Can Benet**
ancienne rte Major 9 – ✆ 00 376 82 89 22 – www.restaurant_canbenet.com – Fax 00 376 82 89 22 – Closed 15-30 June and Monday B **a**
Rest – Carte € 28/37
◆ Small ground floor lobby and bar. The upstairs dining room has a typically Andorran decor of stone walls and wooden ceiling.

CANILLO – 343 H9 – pop. 4 633 – alt. 1 531 m 29 **C3**

Andorra la Vella 12
Crucifixion★ in Sant Joan de Caselles church Northeast: 1 km – Sanctuaire de Meritxell★ Southeast: 3 km.

Ski Plaza rm, rest, rest, VISA AE
rte General – ✆ 00 376 73 94 44 – www.plazandorra.com – skiplaza@plazandorra.com – Fax 00 376 73 94 45
121 rm – †€ 80/210 ††€ 100/250, ☕ € 17 **Rest** – Menu € 23
◆ This particularly well-equipped establishment, at an altitude of 1600m, offers very comfortable, mountain-style rooms. Some have jacuzzis and a few are intended for children. Spacious restaurant with a buffet formula.

ENCAMP – 343 H9 – pop. 13 225 – alt. 1 313 m 29 **C3**

Andorra la Vella 8

Coray rest, VISA
Caballers 38 – ✆ 00 376 83 15 13 – Fax 00 376 83 18 06 – Closed November
85 rm ☕ – †€ 25/34 ††€ 50/64 **Rest** – *(buffet only)* Menu € 10,50
◆ Great location overlooking the locality. Modern communal areas and functional bedrooms, most of them looking out onto the surrounding fields. A large, well-lit dining room offering mainly buffet service.

Univers P VISA
René Baulard 13 – ✆ 00 376 73 11 05 – www.hoteluniversandorra.com – hotelunivers@andorra.ad – Fax 00 376 83 19 70 – Closed November
31 rm – †€ 38/42 ††€ 65/75, ☕ € 8 **Rest** – Menu € 14
◆ This engaging family hotel lies on the banks of the Valira d'Orient. Modern rooms, not overly spacious but comfortable. The small, well-arranged dining room serves traditional cuisine. Select menu.

ESCALDES-ENGORDANY – 343 H9 – pop. 16 078 – alt. 1 105 m 28 **B3**

Andorra-la-Vella 2
Office de tourisme, place dels Co-Princeps ✆ (00-376) 82 09 63, Fax (00-376) 82 66 97

Plan on next page

Roc de Caldes rm, rest, rest, P
rte d'Engolasters, via ① route de l'Obac – ✆ 00 376 87 45 55 VISA AE
– www.rocdecaldes.com – rocdecaldes@andorra.ad – Fax 00 376 86 33 25
45 rm – ††€ 110/240, ☕ € 16 **Rest** – Menu € 30
◆ A luxury mountainside hotel whose contemporary architecture blends with the natural surroundings. The tastefully decorated rooms enjoy a superb view. Restaurant with an elegant setting and fine panoramic view.

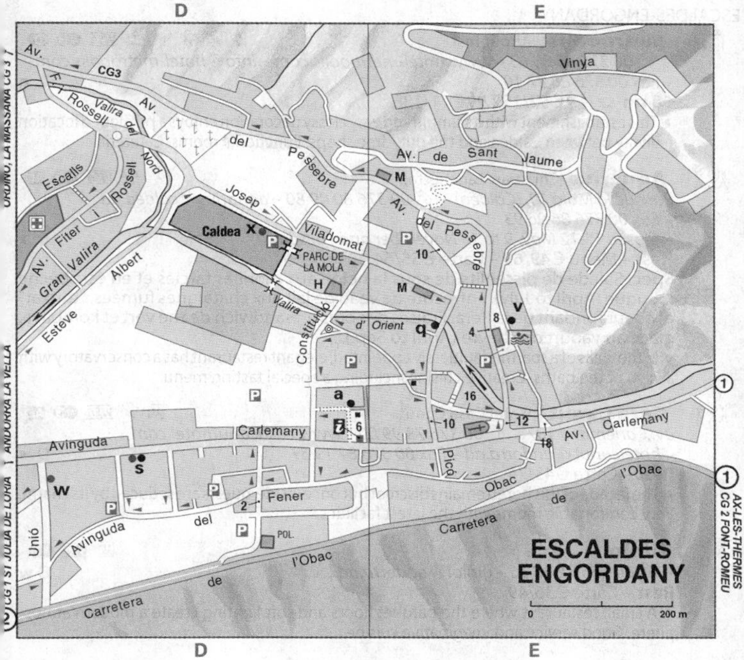

Carlemany (Av.) . . . . DE
Ciutat de Sabadell . . . . D 2
Constitució . . . . D
Coprínceps (Pl.) . . . . D 6
Copríncep de Gaulle (Av.) . . . . . . E 4
Creu Blanca (Pl.) . . . . E 8
Escalls . . . . D
Escoles (Av. de les) . . . . E 10
Església de l' . . . . E 12
Esteve Albert . . . . D
Fener del (Av.) . . . . D
Fiter i Rossell (Av.) . . . . D
Josep Viladomat . . . . DE
l'Obac . . . . E
Obac (Ctra de l') . . . . DE
Pessebre del (Av.) . . . . DE
Picó . . . . E
Santa Anna . . . . E 16
Santa Anna (Pl.) . . . . E 18
Sant Jaume (Av.) . . . . E
Unió . . . . D
Vinya . . . . E

Roc Blanc rm, rest, VISA

pl. dels Co-Princeps 5 – ✆ 00 376 87 14 00 – www.rocblanchotels.com – hotelrocblanc@rocblanchotels.com – Fax 00 376 87 14 44 D **a**

157 rm – €90/232 €120/310 – 3 suites

Rest ***L'entrecôte*** – Carte €30/52

◆ These three buildings linked together have a town centre location. Find an elegant interior decor and welcoming rooms with a modern touch. Excellent facilities and independent access to the Entrecôte.

Casa Canut VISA

av. Carlemany 107 – ✆ 00 376 73 99 00 – www.casacanuthotel.com – hotelcanut@andorra.ad – Fax 00 376 82 19 37 D **s**

33 rm – €120/160 €200/250, €15

Rest Casa Canut – see restaurant listing

◆ Pleasantly decorated restaurant in the village centre where all the tables have a view of the kitchens. Market produce, fish and seafood.

Espel rm, rest, VISA

pl. Creu Blanca 1 – ✆ 00 376 82 08 55 – www.hotelespel.com – hotelespel@andorra.ad – Fax 00 376 82 80 56 – Closed May E **v**

84 rm – €50/74 €64/106 **Rest** – *(set menu only)* Menu €16

◆ After an extensive renovation, the hotel is now a picture of modern comfort. Parquet floors and practical furniture in the rooms. Simple culinary repertory with a single menu.

Metropolis without rest VISA
– 00 376 80 83 63 – www.hotel-metropolis.com – info@hotel-metropolis.com
– Fax 00 376 86 37 10 E **q**
68 rm – €57/152 €71/188
◆ This establishment with its simple and very classy decoration enjoys a privileged location halfway between Caldea and the duty-free shops. Functional rooms. Cafeteria.

Aquarius (Christian Zanchetta) VISA AE
Parc de la Mola 10, (Caldea) – 00 376 80 09 80 – aquarius@caldea.ad
– Fax 00 376 86 96 93
– Closed 1st-12 May, 9 to 13 November and Tuesday D **x**
Rest – Menu €49/69 – Carte €55/64
Spec. Salade de pissenlits de sous la neige aux morilles farcies et en escabèche ibérique (April to July). Entrecote de veau de lait aux châtaignes fumées, "trinxat" et coeur fondant de la Pera. Fraises des bois en sandwich de thé vert et kombava, glace au yaourt de chèvre (April to Sep.).
◆ In the walls of a spa, this faultlessly appointed, elegant restaurant has a conservatory with a view of the baths. Creative cuisine including a special tasting menu.

Casa Canut – Hotel Casa Canut A/C VISA AE
av. Carlemany 107 – 00 376 73 99 00 – www.casacanuthotel.com
– hotelcanut@andorra.ad – Fax 00 376 82 19 37 D **s**
Rest – Carte €43/74
◆ The façade of this hotel remains discreet but once inside, guests are seduced by its charm. Very comfortable rooms with the latest facilities.

Gínjol A/C VISA
– 00 376 82 67 16 – ginjol@andorra.ad D **w**
Rest – Carte €36/49
◆ A small restaurant where the parquet floors and soft lighting create a modern atmosphere. Good service and imaginative cuisine.

INCLES – see Soldeu

LA MASSANA – 343 H9 – pop. 9 276 – alt. 1 241 m 28 **B3**

Andorra la Vella 7
Office de tourisme, avenue Sant-Antoni (00-376) 82 56 93, Fax (00-376) 82 86 93

Rutlan rm, rest, VISA
av. del Ravell 3 – 00 376 83 50 00 – www.hotelrutllan.com – info@hotelrutllan.com – Fax 00 376 83 51 80
96 rm – €60/150 €100/250
Rest – Menu €30
◆ A large family-run chalet with a predominantly wood decor. The comfortable rooms all have balconies, adorned with flowers in season. Copper and ceramic vases provide the decor in this classically styled restaurant serving traditional dishes.

Abba Xalet Suites H. P VISA AE
rte de Sispony, 1.8 km south – 00 376 73 73 00
– www.abbaxaletsuiteshotel.com – xaletsuites@abbahoteles.com
– Fax 00 376 73 73 01
47 rm – €60/107 €60/144, €10 – 36 suites
Rest – Menu €22
◆ Two buildings, one of which offers classic rooms all year round, while the other offers only suites in season. Two well-appointed restaurants, one in each building.

El Rusc A/C P VISA
rte de Arinsal, 1.5 km – 00 376 83 82 00 – www.elrusc.com – info@elrusc.com
– Fax 00 376 83 51 80 – Closed 15 June-15 July, Sunday dinner and Monday
Rest – Carte €40/58
◆ An attractive regional house is home to a fine rustic dining room. Traditional dishes, Basque specialities and a fine wine selection.

LLORTS – see Ordino

MERITXELL – 343 H9 – alt. 1 527 m 28 **B3**

Andorra la Vella 10 – Canillo 4 – La Seu d'Urgell 31 – Foix 91 – Puigcerdà 50

L'Ermita rm, VISA MC

Meritxell – 00 376 75 10 50 – www.hotelermita.com – info@hotelermita.com – Fax 00 376 85 25 10 – Closed 11 June-16 July and 15 October-19 November

27 rm – €33/52 €57/94

Rest – Menu €14

◆ An unpretentious family hotel nestling in an alpine landscape near the sanctuary of the Virgin of Meritxell. Practical, well-kept rooms, partially wood panelled. An extensive regional menu, countrified decor and view of the peaks.

A good night's sleep without spending a fortune?
Look for a Bib Hotel .

ORDINO – 343 H9 – pop. 3 309 – alt. 1 304 m – Winter sports : 1940/2 640 m 14 28 **B3**

Andorra la Vella 9

Coma rm, rest, VISA MC

– 00 376 73 61 00 – www.hotelcoma.com – hotelcoma@hotelcoma.com – Fax 00 376 73 61 01

48 rm – €20/50 €40/80, €10

Rest – *(closed 3 to 27 November)* Menu €20

◆ Since 1932 the same family has been welcoming travellers in this well equipped hotel. The rooms, many of which have a terrace, feature design furniture and baths with hydro-massage equipment. This restaurant serves tasty traditional cuisine.

en Llorts

La Neu VISA MC

– 00 376 85 06 50 – restaurantlaneu@andorra.ad

Rest – Carte €36/52

◆ This small, tastefully designed restaurant has a dining area with a glass wall and a superb view of the mountains. The menu, presented orally, features interesting dishes with a personal touch.

via Canillo road West: 2.3 km

Babot rest, VISA MC

AD300 – 00 376 74 70 47 – www.hotelbabotandorra.com – hotelbabot@andorra.ad – Fax 00 376 83 55 48 – Closed 2 November-2 December

55 rm – €41/83 €70/116

Rest – Menu €13

◆ This high altitude, mountainside hotel, surrounded by a huge park, offers a magnificent view of the valley and peaks. Attractive, comfortable rooms. A restaurant with a panoramic view from its large windows.

PAS-DE-LA-CASA – 343 I9 – alt. 2 085 m – Winter sports : 1710/2640 m 4 67 29 **C3**

Andorra-la-Vella 29

Site★

Col d'Envalira★★

Soldeu road **Southeast: 10 km**

Grau Roig rm, rest, VISA AE

Grau Roig ✉ AD200 – ✆ 00 376 75 55 56 – www.hotelgrauroig.com – hotelgrauroig@andorra.ad – Fax 00 376 75 55 57 – Closed 4 May-18 June and 13 October-26 November

42 rm – €130/315 €175/400

Rest – Carte €42/64

◆ A typical mountain-style building with the Pessons Cirque as its setting. Charming well-equipped rooms. A fine setting, with coffered ceiling, wood panelling, stonework and antiques.

SANT JULIÀ DE LÒRIA – 343 G10 – pop. 9 207 – alt. 909 m 28 B3

Andorra-la-Vella 7

Southeast : 7 km

Coma Bella rest, VISA

bosque de La Rabassa, - alt. 1 300 ✉ AD600 – ✆ 00 376 74 20 30 – www.hotelcoma-bella.com – comabella@myp.ad – Fax 00 376 84 14 60 – Closed 19 to 29 April and 1st to 25 November

30 rm – €36/57 €53/93 **Rest** – Menu €12

◆ This peaceful hotel enjoys a beautiful location in the Forêt de la Rabassa. Functional rooms and huge common areas. The restaurant offers a fine view of the surrounding peaks.

Your opinions are important to us:
please write and let us know about your discoveries
and experiences – good and bad!

SOLDEU – 343 H9 – pop. 698 – alt. 1 826 m – Winter sports : 1710/2640 m 4 67 29 C3

Andorra la Vella 20

Sport H. Hermitage rm, rest, VISA

rte de Soldeu – ✆ 00 376 87 06 70 – www.sporthotels.ad – hotel.hermitage@sporthotels.ad – Fax 00 376 87 06 71 – Closed 15 April-May and 15 October-15 November

114 rm – €180/320 €280/560 – 6 suites

Rest – Carte €44/61

◆ This luxury hotel is justly proud of its handsome all-wood interior and spacious rooms in contemporary and zen styles, which overlook the ski slopes. Fully equipped spa. The restaurant specialises in Mediterranean and Asian dishes.

Xalet Montana rm, VISA

rte General – ✆ 00 376 73 93 33 – www.xaletmontana.net – hotelnaudi@andornet.ad – Fax 00 376 73 93 31 – Open December-15 April

40 rm – €86/109 €117/147 **Rest** – *(resident only)* Menu €20

◆ Carefully decorated hotel whose rooms all overlook a snowbound landscape. Pleasant Nordic setting in the lounge. Inviting relaxation area.

in Incles 1.8 km west – pop. 538 – ✉ **AD100**

Galanthus rm, VISA

– ✆ 00 376 75 33 00 – www.somriuhotels.com – info@hotelgalanthus.com – Fax 00 376 75 33 33

55 rm – €40/174 €80/232, €15 **Rest** – Carte €30/50

◆ Contemporary style establishment with several lounges. Practically furnished guest-rooms with parquet. Bright dining room offering up-to-date dishes.

in El Tarter West: 3 km – pop. 1 052 – ✉ AD100

Nordic

✉ AD100 – ✆ 00 376 73 95 00 – www.grupnordic.ad – hotelnordic@grupnordic.ad – Fax 00 376 73 95 01 – Closed November

120 rm – †€ 60/198 ††€ 80/265

Rest – *(buffet only) (dinner only)* Menu € 19

◆ This large hotel has a vast lobby adorned with vintage motorbikes. The rooms boast a terrace and command views of the village and mountains. Simple buffet meals available.

Del Clos

✉ AD100 – ✆ 00 376 75 35 00 – www.grupnordic.ad – hoteldelclos@grupnordic.ad – Fax 00 376 85 15 54 – Open December-April

54 rm – †€ 84/132 ††€ 112/176

Rest – *(buffet only in winter) (dinner only)* Menu € 19

◆ This beautiful dwelling with views of the mountains is surrounded by typical Andorran farms. Spacious bedrooms, some with a balcony, furnished in regional style. Stone, wooden beams and carved wood combine to give this restaurant a mountain feel.

EL TARTER – see Soldeu

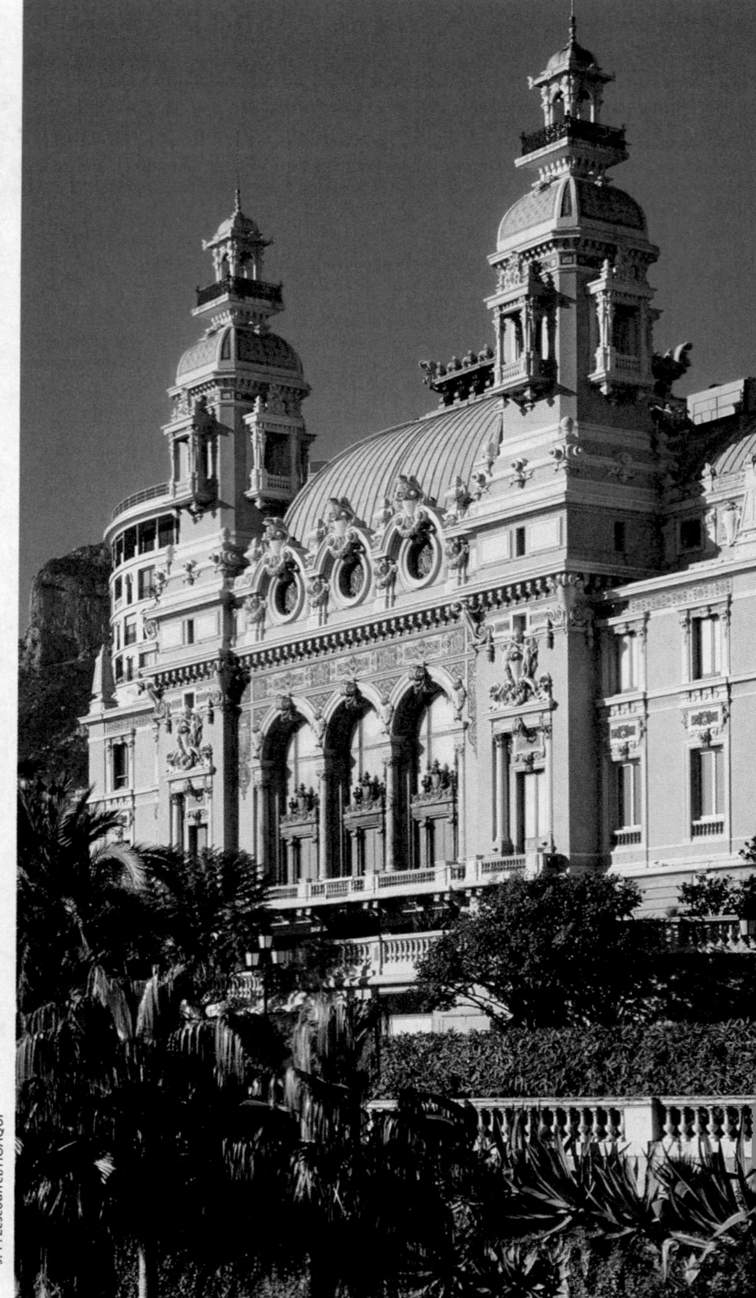
J.-P. Lescourret/HOAQUI

Le casino de Monte-Carlo

PRINCIPALITY OF MONACO

Michelin LOCAL map: n° 341 F5
115]27]28
Population: 32 020
Altitude: 163 m
French Riviera
Carte régionale 42 E2

USEFUL INFORMATION

Sovereign state, enclosed within the French Alpes-Maritimes department along the Mediterranean Sea. It has an area of 1.5 km² which includes: Monaco Rock (old town) and Monte-Carlo (new town) joined together by La Condamine (harbour), Fontvieille in the West (industry) and Le Larvotto in the East (beach). In 1993, the Principality became a member of the U.N.

There are daily links with Nice-Côte d'Azur Airport from the Monaco-Fontvieille heliport. Information: Héli Air Monaco ✆ (00-377) 92 05 00 50

TOURIST OFFICE

2a boulevard des Moulins Monte Carlo ✆ (00-377) 92166116,
Fax (00-377) 92 16 60 00

GOLF

18 Monte-Carlo , par rte de la Turbie : 11 km, ✆ (33) (0) 4 92 41 50 70

URBAN MOTOR-RACING CIRCUIT

✆ (00-377) 93 15 26 00, Fax (00-377) 93 25 80 08

MONACO Capitale de la Principauté – MCO Monaco – pop. 32 020 – alt. 163 m – ✉ 98000 42 **E2**

▶ Paris 949 – Menton 11 – Nice 23 – San Remo 41

ℹ Office de tourisme, 2, boulevard des Moulins, Monte Carlo
✆ (00-377) 92 16 61 16, Fax (00-377) 92 16 60 00

Urban race circuit.

◉ Exotic garden★★ CZ: ⩤★ - Grotte de l'Observatoire★ CZ **D** - Jardins St-Martin★ DZ - Set of Niçois primitives★★ in the cathedral DZ - Recumbent Christ ★ in the la Miséricorde chapel D **B** - Place du Palais★ CZ - Palais du Prince★: musée napoléonien et des Archives du palais★ CZ - Museums: océanographique★★ DZ (aquarium★★, ⩤★★ of the terrace), d'anthropologie préhistorique★ CZ **M³**, - Collection of vintage cars★ CZ **M¹**.

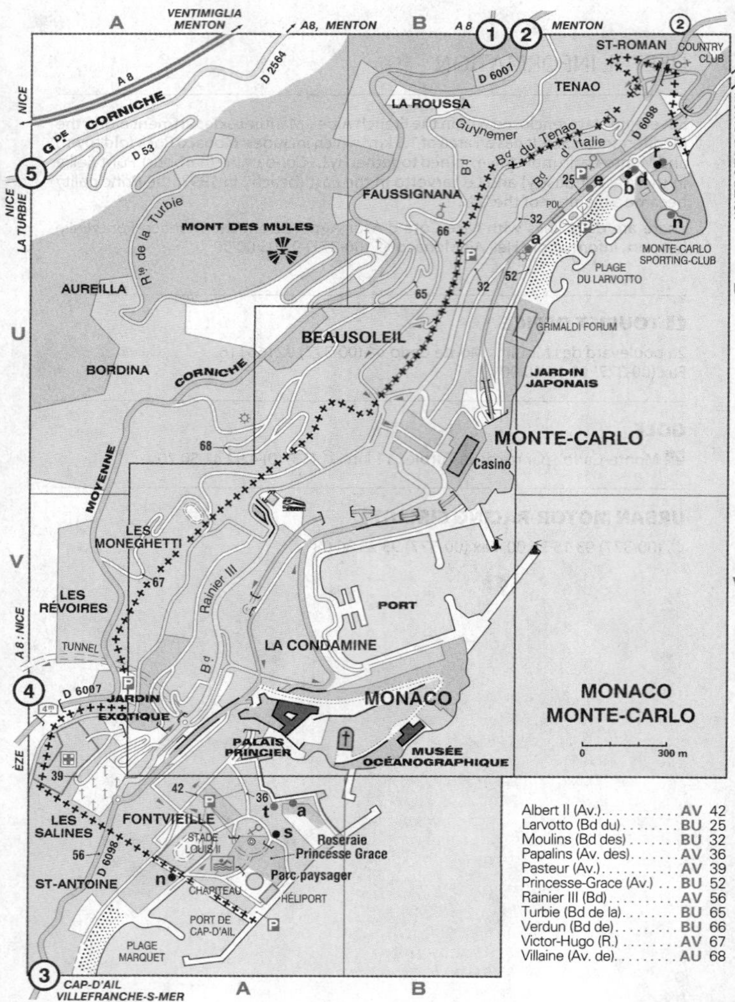

Castelroc
pl. du Palais – (00-377) 93 30 36 68 – www.restaurant-castelroc.com – castelroc@libello.com – Fax (00-377) 93 30 59 88 – Closed 15 December-15 January, Saturday and dinner from mid-September to mid-May CZ **p**
Rest – Menu € 35 (lunch) – Carte € 45/74
◆ In the same family since the 1950s, this traditional restaurant boasts an elegant veranda that commands a fine view of the palace. Regional cuisine.

in Fontvieille

Columbus
23 av. Papalins – (00-377) 92 05 90 00 – www.columbusmonaco.com – resa@columbus.mc – Fax (00-377) 92 05 91 67 AV **s**
170 rm – €180/400 €180/400, € 25 – 11 suites **Rest** – Carte € 39/65
◆ This hotel, lying between the harbour and the Princess Grace rose garden, offers plush rooms with minimalist modern furniture. Most have balconies. Up-to-date cuisine in the smart restaurant or pleasant terrace.

Amici Miei
16 quai J.-C. Rey – (00-377) 92 05 92 14 – www.monte-carlo.mc/amici-miei – amici-miei@monte-carlo.mc – Fax (00-377) 92 05 31 74 AV **t**
Rest – Menu (€ 16), € 30 (weekday lunch) – Carte € 35/60
◆ This family restaurant with its naïve style paintings will delight lovers of traditional Italian food. In summer, head for the terrace overlooking Fontvieille port.

Beefbar
42 quai Jean-Charles-Rey – (00-377) 97 77 09 29 – www.beefbar.com – h.jarry@beefbar.com – Fax (00-377) 97 77 09 30 AV **a**
Rest – Menu (€ 18 bi), € 39 (weekdays) – Carte € 41/80
◆ A new concept in meat (Argentine, American and French), oven roasted with no added fat. Fashionable decor, greatly appreciated by a local lunchtime crowd.

The sun's out – let's eat alfresco!
Look for a terrace:

MONTE-CARLO Centre Mondain de la Principauté – MCO Monaco – Casinos : Grand Casino DY, Monte-Carlo Sporting Club BU, Sun Casino DX 42 **E2**

Paris 947 – Menton 9 – Monaco 2 – Nice 20 – San Remo 40

Terrace★★ of the Grand casino DXY - Musée de poupées et automates★ DX **M**5 - Japanese garden ★ U.

Plan on following page

Paris
pl. du Casino – (00-377) 98 06 30 00 – www.hoteldeparismontecarlo.com – hp@sbm.mc – Fax (00-377) 98 06 59 13 DY **y**
143 rm – €420/1600 €420/1600, € 42 – 39 suites
Rest *Le Louis XV-Alain Ducasse et Grill de l'Hôtel de Paris* – see below
Rest *Salle Empire* – *(00-377) 98 06 89 89 (open July - Aug.) (dinner only)* Carte € 98/188
Rest *Côté Jardin* – *(00-377) 98 06 39 39 (lunch only)* Menu € 55 – Carte € 65/98
◆ Idyllic location, sumptuous setting, a rich past and famous guests; live the legend of Monaco's most prestigious palace hotel, inaugurated in 1864. Majestic Empire room complete with gold, stucco and crystal. Terrace commanding a view of the Rocher.

Métropole
4 av. Madone – (00-377) 93 15 15 15 – www.metropole.com – metropole@metropole.com – Fax (00-377) 93 25 24 44 DX **z**
77 rm – €500/800 €500/800, € 38 – 64 suites
Rest *Joël Robuchon Monte-Carlo* – see below
◆ Luxury hotel (1886) treated to a consummate facelift by Jacques Garcia. Attractive pool and Italian style courtyard-garden, cosy bar and lavish spa.

MONACO MONTE-CARLO

Hermitage DY **r**
square Beaumarchais – ✆ (00-377) 98 06 40 00
– www.montecarloresort.com – hh@sbm.mc
– Fax (00-377) 98 06 59 70
252 rm – €380/940 €380/940, ☕ €37 – 28 suites
Rest *Vistamar* – see below
Rest *Limun Bar* – *✆ (00-377) 98 06 48 48* – Menu (€29 bi) – Carte €40/73
◆ Italian inspired murals and loggias adorn the splendid façade facing the port. Luxurious guestrooms, elegant lobby, and winter garden beneath a cupola by Eiffel. The Limùn Bar offers simple dishes and changes into a tea room in the afternoon.

Monte Carlo Bay Hôtel and Resort
– (00-377) 98 06 02 00
– www.montecarlobay.mc – info@montecarlobay.mc
– Fax (00-377) 98 06 00 03 BU **r**
323 rm – †€ 320/895 ††€ 320/895, € 32 – 11 suites
Rest *Le Blue Bay* – *(00-377) 98 06 03 60 (Closed lunch from May to September)*
Menu (€ 30), € 70 (dinner), € 80/95 – Carte € 61/93
Rest *L'Orange Verte* – *(00-377) 98 06 03 60* – Carte € 37/53
Rest *Las Brisas* – *(00-377) 98 06 03 60 (open from May to September) (lunch only)* Menu (€ 30) – Carte € 41/79
♦ This Monaco luxury hotel covers 4ha along the seafront. Extremely modern rooms, suites and duplexes. Lagoon pool. The Blue Bay offers a cuisine rich in spices. L'Orange Verte offers tartares and carpaccios. Las Brisas offers an up-to-date menu.

Méridien Beach Plaza rm,
22 av. Princesse Grace, at the Larvotto beach
– *(00-377) 93 30 98 80* – *www.lemeridien.com/montecarlo*
– *reservations.montecarlo@lemeridien.com* – *Fax (00-377) 93 50 23 14*
403 rm – †€ 409/770 ††€ 409/770, € 31 – 6 suites BU **b**
Rest *L'Intempo* – *(00-377) 93 15 78 88* – Carte € 55/135
Rest *Bar and Lunch* – beach rest. *(open end May-end September) (lunch only)* Carte € 30/80
♦ Modern luxury hotel. Rooms in two glass towers with panoramic sea views. Sumptuous, designer furnished suites, conference centre, swimming pools and a private beach. L'Intempo (open 24 hours a day) offers Mediterranean cuisine. The Bar and Lunch has a seaside atmosphere.

Port Palace
7 av. J. F. Kennedy – *(00-377) 97 97 90 00* – *www.portpalace.com*
– *reservation@portpalace.com* – *Fax (00-377) 97 97 90 01* DY **t**
50 rm – †€ 245/540 ††€ 245/1765, € 22
Rest Mandarine – see below
♦ This modern luxury boutique hotel overlooks the Mediterranean and the yachts. Minimalist rooms, marble bathrooms and small basement spa.

Fairmont-Monte-Carlo rm,
12 av. Spélugues – *(00-377) 93 50 65 00* – *www.fairmont.com/montecarlo* – *montecarlo@fairmont.com* – *Fax (00-377) 93 30 01 57*
572 rm – †€ 249/899 ††€ 249/899, € 30 – 30 suites DX **e**
Rest *L'Argentin* – *(closed lunch November-March)* Menu (€ 44) – Carte € 55/120
♦ Vast hotel complex built on piles. Functional rooms, magnificent seafront views. Shopping arcade, conference centre. Vast hotel complex built on piles. Functional rooms, magnificent seafront views. Shopping arcade, conference centre.

Novotel
16 bd. Princesse-Charlotte – *(00-377) 99 99 83 00* – *www.novotel.com*
– *h5275@accor.com* – *Fax (00-377) 99 99 83 10* CY **j**
201 rm – †€ 120/445 ††€ 120/445, € 17 – 17 suites
Rest *Les Grandes Ondes* – Menu (€ 25) – Carte € 43/68
Rest *Novotel Café* – Menu (€ 25) – Carte € 35/51
♦ This new hotel situated in the upper section of the principality is built in contemporary style, making the most of the natural light of its surroundings. Huge functional rooms, many with a loggia. At Les Grandes Ondes, Provençal cuisine in a bright, simply decorated setting.

Le Louis XV-Alain Ducasse – Hôtel de Paris
pl. du Casino – *(00-377) 98 06 88 64*
– *www.alain-ducasse.com* – *lelouisxv@alain-ducasse.com*
– *Fax (00-377) 98 06 59 07* – *Closed 1st-11 March, 1st-30 December, 9-24 February, Wednesday except dinner from 1st July to 19 August and Tuesday* DY **y**
Rest – Menu € 140 bi, € 210/280 – Carte € 193/250
Spec. Légumes des jardins de Provence à la truffe noire, huile d'olive et aceto balsamico. Poitrine de pigeonneau et foie gras de canard sur la braise, polenta et jus aux abats. Le "Louis XV" au croustillant de pralin. **Wines** Bandol, Côtes de Provence.
♦ Perfect harmony between the sumptuous classic decor, the terrace overlooking the casino, the sublime Mediterranean flavours and the exceptional wine list. An outstanding experience.

XXXX ✿✿ **Joël Robuchon Monte-Carlo** – Hôtel Métropole
4 av. Madone – ✆ (00-377) 93 15 15 10
– www.metropole.com – restaurant@metropole.com
– Fax (00-377) 93 25 24 44 DX **z**
Rest – *(dinner only from 11 July to 23 August)* Menu € 75 bi (lunch)/180 – Carte € 75/366
Spec. "King crab" et tomate farcie de légumes acidulés. Saint-Pierre aux saveurs méridionales. Chocolat sensation. **Wines** Bellet, Vin de Pays du Var.
◆ The colonnaded dining room commands a fine view of the kitchens where creative cuisine is prepared. Pleasant terrace with a view over the Monaco rooftops.

XXXX ✿ **Grill de l'Hôtel de Paris**
pl. du Casino – ✆ (00-377) 98 06 88 88 – www.hoteldeparismontecarlo.com
– legrill@sbm.mc – Fax (00-377) 98 06 59 03
– Closed January-February and lunch in July-August DY **y**
Rest – Menu € 75 bi (lunch) – Carte € 92/240
Spec. Foie gras de canard grillé. Carré d'agneau à la broche. Soufflé "Tradition". **Wines** Bellet blanc et rouge.
◆ Enjoy a panoramic view of the Principality from the hotel's eighth floor restaurant. Spit-roast grilled meat prepared in front of you and a mouth-watering array of soufflés for dessert.

XXX **Vistamar** – Hôtel Hermitage
pl. Beaumarchais – ✆ (00-377) 98 06 98 98 – www.montecarloresort.com
– hh@sbm.mc – Fax (00-377) 98 06 59 70 – Closed lunch in July-August
Rest – Menu (€ 45), € 129 – Carte € 87/117 DY **r**
◆ Breathtaking panoramic sea view from the panoramic terrace and bay windows in the dining room. The menu offers classic dishes and seafood cuisine.

XXX ✿ **Bar Boeuf & Co**
av. Princesse Grace, (at Sporting-Mont-Carlo) – ✆ (00-377) 98 06 71 71
– www.alain-ducasse.com – b.b@sbm.mc – Fax (00-377) 98 06 57 85
– Open 15 May-19 September BU **n**
Rest – *(dinner only)* Carte € 90/250
Spec. Pièce de bœuf rafraîchie au goût ginger-lime, croq salade de printemps. Loup à la plancha, jeunes carottes au jus parfumées au gingembre, pulpe de citron de pays. Coupe glacée cheese cake, compotée de fruits rouges.
◆ This place is popular with both night owls and gourmets. Designer decor, menu offering sea bass, beef, and wine from around the world.

XXX ✿ **Mandarine** – Hôtel Port Palace
– ✆ (00-377) 97 97 90 00
– Closed 9-30 November and 9-28 February DY **t**
Rest – Menu (€ 35) – Carte € 78/109
Spec. Tarte au fromage de chèvre et à la tomate, sorbet gaspacho. Millefeuille de brandade de pintade, pomme de terre translucide et riquette. Soufflé au nougat et glace pain d'épice.
◆ On the sixth floor of the hotel is a panoramic dining room whose bay windows and large terrace overlook the port. Contemporary interior decoration. Sophisticated up-to-date menu

XX **Le Saint Benoit**
10 ter av. Costa – ✆ (00-377) 93 25 02 34 – www.monte-carlo.mc/lesaintbenoit
– lesaintbenoit@monte-carlo.mc – Fax (00-377) 93 30 52 64
– Closed 21 December-7 January, Sunday dinner and Monday DY **b**
Rest – Menu € 28/39 – Carte € 36/70
◆ Finding this restaurant is not so easy, but the panoramic view of the port and Rock from the terrace is worth the trouble. Spacious modern dining room serving seafood specialities.

XX **Café de Paris**
pl. Casino – ✆ (00-377) 98 06 76 23 – www.montercarloresort.mc – brasseriecp@sbm.mc – Fax (00-377) 98 06 59 30 DY **n**
Rest – Carte € 57/98
◆ In 1897 Edouard Michelin made a famous arrival here...at the wheel of his car! Belle Epoque brasserie decor. Popular terrace in season.

XX **Maya Bay**

24 av. Princesse-Grace – ✆ (00-377) 97 70 74 67 – www.mayabay.mc – mayabay@mayabay.mc – Fax (00-377) 97 77 58 10 – Closed November, Sunday and Monday BU

Rest – Menu (€ 20), € 50/69 – Carte € 62/128

Rest *Sushi Bar* – Menu (€ 18), € 22 (weekdays) – Carte € 32/50

◆ Asian influences (giant Buddha, red lacquered sushi bar, collection of Kenzo kimonos) and stunning floral compositions in this trendy establishment. Inventive menu.

XX **Pétrossian**

11 av. Princesse-Grace – ✆ (00-377) 97 77 00 24 – www.petrossianmonaco.com – petrossianmonaco@libello.com – Fax (00-377) 97 70 04 57 DX **p**

Rest – Menu € 25/55

◆ White leather armchairs, dark panelling, chandeliers, a bar and shop make up the elegant setting of the Pétrossian, which is opposite the Forum Grimaldi. Flagship products (caviar, salmon, etc).

XX **Avenue 31**

31 av. Princesse Grace – ✆ (00-377) 97 70 31 31 – www.avenue31.mc – monaco@avenue31.mc BU **a**

Rest – Menu (€ 25) – Carte € 80/150

◆ Modern brasserie style cuisine awaits at this hip establishment with tasteful, minimalist decor. Large terrace facing the Larvotto beach.

XX **La Maison du Caviar**

1 av. St-Charles – ✆ (00-377) 93 30 80 06 – maisonducaviar@monaco.mc – Fax (00-377) 93 30 23 90 – Closed August, Saturday lunch and Sunday

Rest – Menu (€ 17), € 29 (weekday lunch), € 36/56 – Carte € 36/85 DX **r**

◆ An institution among the locals, this family restaurant has offered classic cuisine since 1954. Dine in a setting that combines wrought iron, wine crates and rustic furniture.

XX **La Romantica**

3 av. Saint-Laurent – ✆ (00-377) 93 25 65 66 – maurizio.grossi@orange.fr – Closed 1st-14 August and Sunday DX **b**

Rest – Carte € 40/60

◆ Pleasant town centre restaurant. The small dining room is ideal to savour the authentic northern Italian and seafood cuisine.

X **Loga**

25 bd des Moulins – ✆ (00-377) 93 30 87 72 – www.leloga.com – kettyvigon@hotmail.com – Fax (00-377) 93 25 06 41 – Closed 8-23 August, dinner and Sunday

Rest – *(lunch only)* Menu (€ 24 bi) – Carte € 32/46 DX **v**

◆ This nice little family restaurant, very popular with regulars, offers regional cuisine and blackboard daily specials. Modernised interior decor and pavement terrace.

in Monte-Carlo-Beach **(France Alpes-Mar.) 2.5 km northeast** BU – ✉ **06190 Roquebrune-Cap-Martin**

Monte-Carlo Beach Hôtel

(reopening planned in the spring after refurbishment)

av. Princesse Grace – ✆ 04 93 28 66 66 – www.montecarlobeachhotel.com – bh@sbm.mc – Fax 04 93 78 14 18 – Closed 4 January-4 March

31 rm – †€ 305/815 ††€ 305/815, ☕ € 30 – 9 suites

Rest *La Salle à Manger* – *✆ 04 93 28 66 72* – Carte € 70/105

Rest *Le Deck* – *✆ 04 93 28 66 42 (Open 11 April-11 October) (lunch only)* Carte € 37/111

Rest *La Vigie* – *✆ 04 93 28 66 44 (Open 26 June-30 August and Closed Monday)* Menu € 45 (lunch)/55

Rest *Le Sea Lounge* – *✆ 04 93 28 66 43 (Open 16 May-30 August) (dinner only)* Carte € 42/119

◆ This hotel, founded in 1929, welcomed Nijinski, Cocteau, Morand, etc. Lovely rooms with a ship inspired decor, overlooking the sea and Monaco. Superb seaside complex. La Salle à Manger (Dining Room) offers classic Mediterranean dishes. The Deck features a brasserie. La Vigie offers grilled fish. The Sea Lounge offers tapas and a DJ.

see also hotels at **Beausoleil** *and* **Cap d'Ail**

Place with at least

- ● a hotel or a restaurant
- a starred establishment
- a restaurant « Bib Gourmand »
- a hotel « Bib Hôtel »
- a particularly pleasant restaurant
- a particularly pleasant guesthouse
- a particularly pleasant hotel
- a particularly quiet hotel

Localité possédant au moins

- ● un hôtel ou un restaurant
- une table étoilée
- un restaurant « Bib Gourmand »
- un hôtel « Bib Hôtel »
- un restaurant agréable
- une maison d'hôte agréable
- un hôtel agréable
- un hôtel très tranquille

La località possiede come minimo

- ● un albergo o un ristorante
- una delle migliori tavole dell'anno
- un ristorante « Bib Gourmand »
- un albergo « Bib Hotel »
- un ristorante molto piacevole
- un piacevole agriturismo
- un albergo molto piacevole
- un esercizio molto tranquillo

Ort mit mindestens

- ● einem Hotel oder Restaurant
- einem der besten Restaurants des Jahres
- einem Restaurant « Bib Gourmand »
- einem Hotel « Bib Hotel »
- einem sehr angenehmen Restaurant
- ein angenehmes Gästehaus
- einem sehr angenehmen Hotel
- einem sehr ruhigen Haus

Localidad que posee com mínimo

- ● un hotel o un restaurante
- una de los mejores mesas del año
- un restaurante « Bib Gourmand »
- un hotel « Bib Hotel »
- un restaurante muy agradable
- una casa rural agradable
- un hotel muy agradable
- un hotel muy tranquilo

Maps
Regional maps of listed towns

Cartes
Cartes régionales des localités citées

Carta
Carta regionale delle località citate

Regionalkarten
Regionalkarten der erwähnten Orte

Mapas
Mapas de las localidades citadas, por regiones

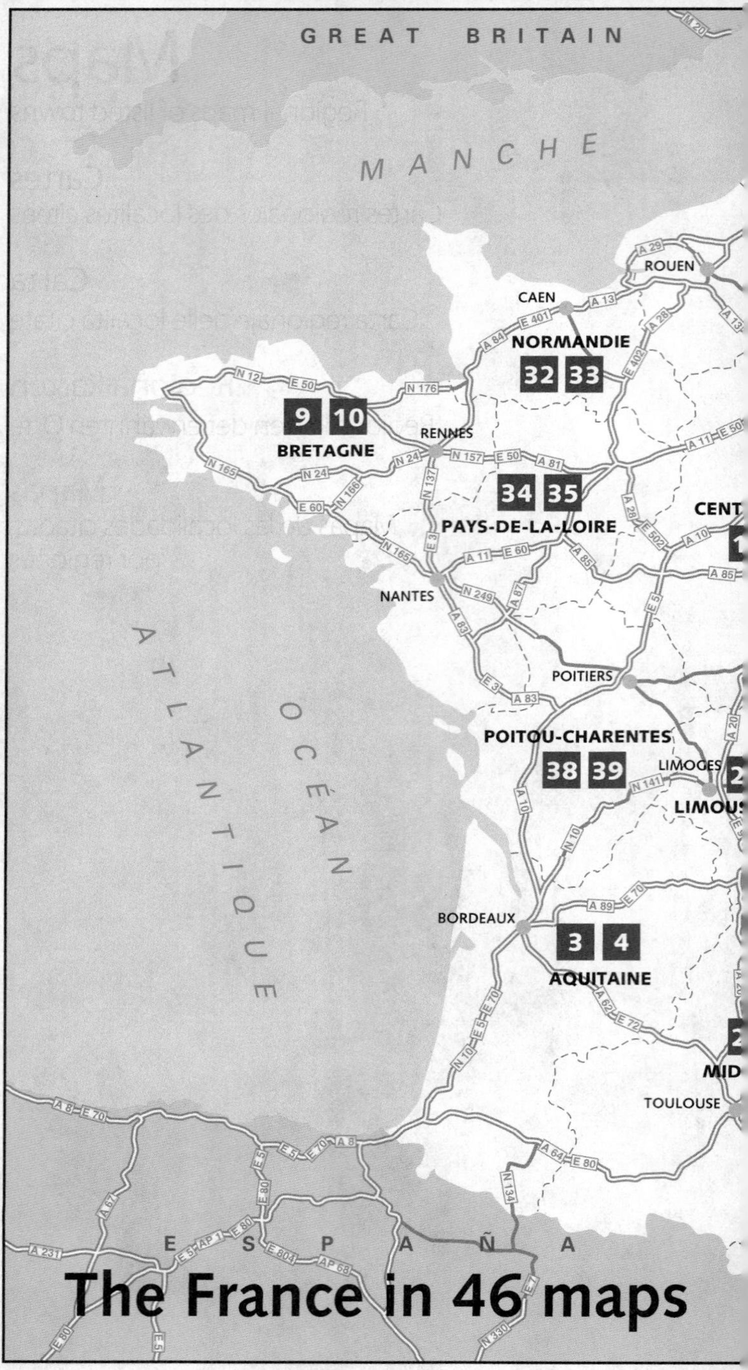

The France in 46 maps

GREAT BRITAIN

MANCHE

OCÉAN ATLANTIQUE

ESPAÑA

NORMANDIE 32 33

BRETAGNE 9 10

PAYS-DE-LA-LOIRE 34 35

POITOU-CHARENTES 38 39

AQUITAINE 3 4

CENT

LIMOU

MID

ROUEN

CAEN

RENNES

NANTES

POITIERS

LIMOGES

BORDEAUX

TOULOUSE

M 20, A 29, A 13, E 401, A 84, A 28, E 402, N 12, E 50, N 176, N 24, N 157, E 50, A 81, A 11, E 50, N 165, N 24, N 166, E 60, N 137, E 3, A 28, E 502, A 10, N 165, A 11, E 60, A 85, A 85, N 249, A 87, E 5, A 83, E 3, A 83, A 20, N 141, A 10, N 10, A 89, E 70, A 62, E 72, E 70, E 5, N 10, A 8, E 70, E 5, E 70, A 8, A 64, E 80, N 134, E 5, E 80, A 67, A 231, E 5, AP 1, E 80, E 804, AP 68, E 7, E 80, E 5, N 330

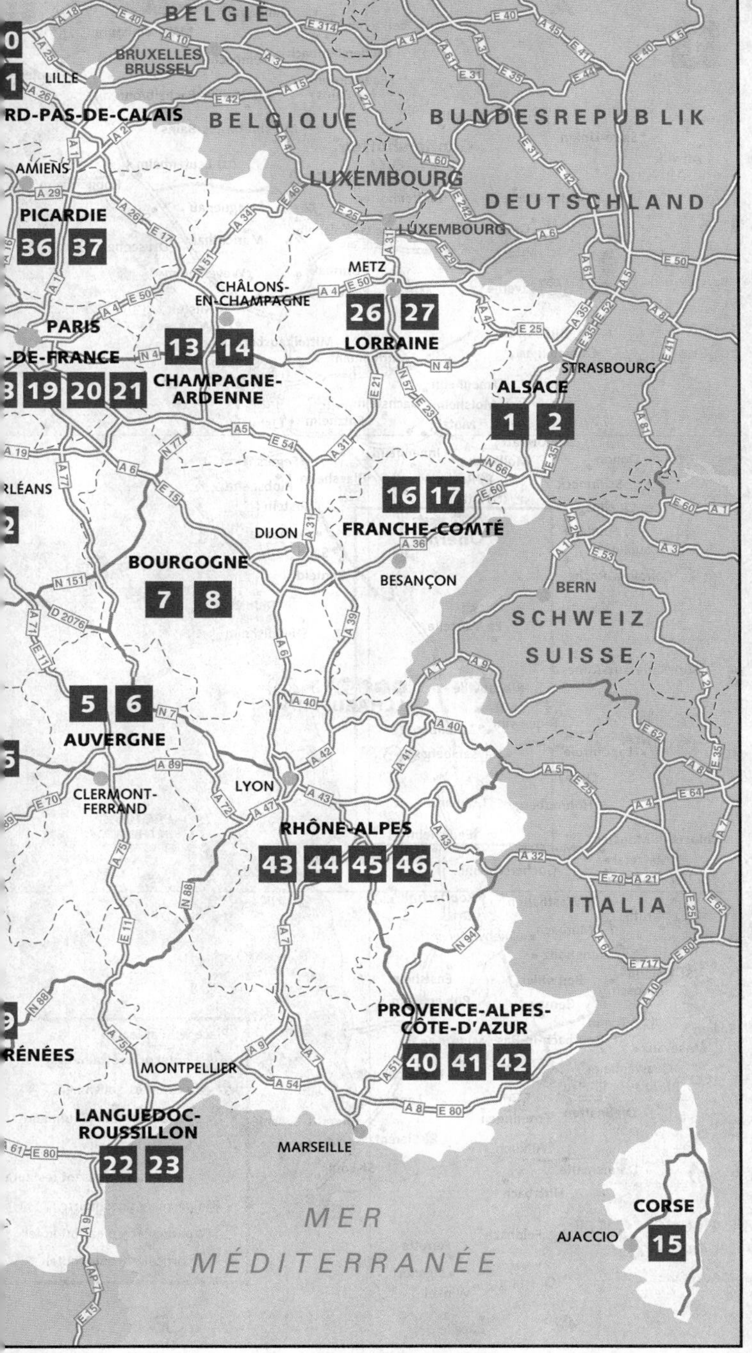
BELGIË
BRUXELLES
BRUSSEL
LILLE
RD-PAS-DE-CALAIS
BELGIQUE
BUNDESREPUBLIK
DEUTSCHLAND
LUXEMBOURG
AMIENS
PICARDIE
36
37
METZ
CHÂLONS-
EN-CHAMPAGNE
26
27
LORRAINE
PARIS
13
14
-DE-FRANCE
STRASBOURG
ALSACE
19
20
21
CHAMPAGNE-
ARDENNE
1
2
RLÉANS
16
17
DIJON
FRANCHE-COMTÉ
BOURGOGNE
BESANÇON
7
8
BERN
SCHWEIZ
SUISSE
5
6
AUVERGNE
LYON
CLERMONT-
FERRAND
RHÔNE-ALPES
43
44
45
46
ITALIA
PROVENCE-ALPES-
CÔTE-D'AZUR
RÉNÉES
MONTPELLIER
40
41
42
LANGUEDOC-
ROUSSILLON
MARSEILLE
22
23
CORSE
MER
MÉDITERRANÉE
AJACCIO
15

1
A
B
Gimbelhof
Obersteinbach
Wissembourg
Niedersteinbach
Lembach
Lauterbo
Niederbronn-les-Bains
Merkwiller-Pechelbronn
Reipertswiller
Morsbronn-les-Bains
Sarre-Union
Gundershoffen
Altwiller
Leutenheim
Uberach
Roppenheim
La-Petite-Pierre
Pfaffenhoffen
Haguenau
1
Sessenheim
Graufthal
Niederschaeffolsheim
Marienthal
Drusenheim
A 4
E 25
Brumath
Sarrebourg
N 4
Weyersheim
Saverne
Mittelhausen
RHIN
Hœrdt
A 35
Kilstett
LORRAINE
(plans 26 27)
La Wantzenau
Birkenwald
Mittelhausbergen
Obersteigen
Marlenheim
Sarre
D 1004
Strasbourg
Traenheim
Molsheim
Dachstein
Oberhaslach
Mutzig
Entzheim
Ostwald
Urmatt
Innenheim
Col du Donon
Mollkirch
Fegersheim
Schirmeck
Rosheim
Blaesheim
Plobsheim
Ottrott
Les Quelles
Erstein
Obernai
Fouday
Osthouse
Saulxures
Sand
Colroy-la-Roche
Benfeld
DEUTSCHLAN
Rhinau
St-Dié-des-Vosges
La Vancelle
Diebolsheim
2
Ste-Marie-aux-Mines
Ribeauvillé
ILLHAEUSERN
Riquewihr
Zellenberg
Lapoutroie
Kaysersberg
Orbey
Colmar
Hohrodberg
D 415
FREIBURG
IM BREISGAU
Muhlbach-s-Munster
Eguisheim
Munster
Metzeral
Ste-Croix-en-Plaine
Gueberschwihr
Sondernach
Westhalten
Rouffach
D 83
Kruth
Murbach
A 35
Guebwiller
Jungholtz
St-Amarin
Ensisheim
Moosch
Berrwiller
N 66
Cernay
Pulversheim
Thann
Sewen
Bourbach-le-Bas
Mulhouse
Masevaux
Guewenheim
E 60
Riedisheim
Burnhaupt-le-Haut
Landser
Diefmatten
3
Frœningen
Kembs-Loéchlé
Altkirch
Sierentz
Rosenau
BELFORT
Dannemarie
St-Louis
Hirtzbach
BASEL
FRANCHE-COMTÉ
(plans 16 17)
Feldbach
Ferrette
Montbéliard
Ligsdorf
Oberlarg
Winkel
A
SUISSE
B
Lucelle
Place with at least:
a hotel or a restaurant
a starred establishment
a restaurant "Bib Gourmand"
a hotel "Bib Hôtel"
a particularly pleasant restaura
a pleasant guesthouse
a particularly pleasant hotel
a particularly quiet hotel

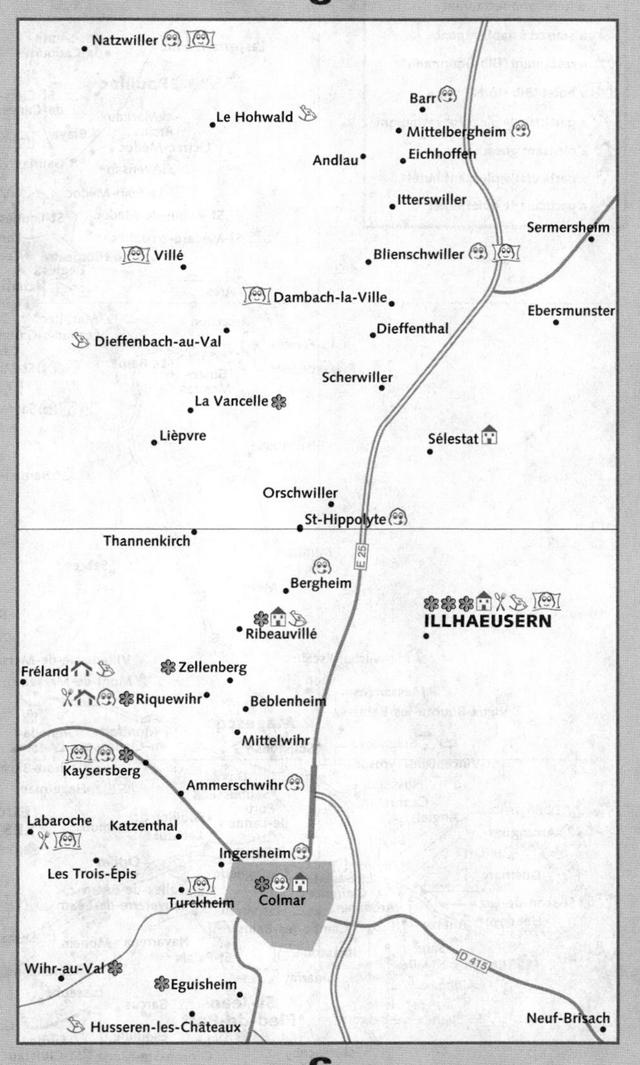
C
Natzwiller
Le Hohwald
Barr
Mittelbergheim
Andlau
Eichhoffen
Itterswiller
Sermersheim
Villé
Blienschwiller
1
1
Dambach-la-Ville
Ebersmunster
Dieffenthal
Dieffenbach-au-Val
Scherwiller
La Vancelle
Lièpvre
Sélestat
Orschwiller
St-Hippolyte
Thannenkirch
E 25
Bergheim
ILLHAEUSERN
Ribeauvillé
Fréland
Zellenberg
Riquewihr
Beblenheim
Mittelwihr
Kaysersberg
Ammerschwihr
2
2
Labaroche
Katzenthal
Ingersheim
Les Trois-Épis
Colmar
Turckheim
D 415
Wihr-au-Val
Eguisheim
Husseren-les-Châteaux
Neuf-Brisach
C

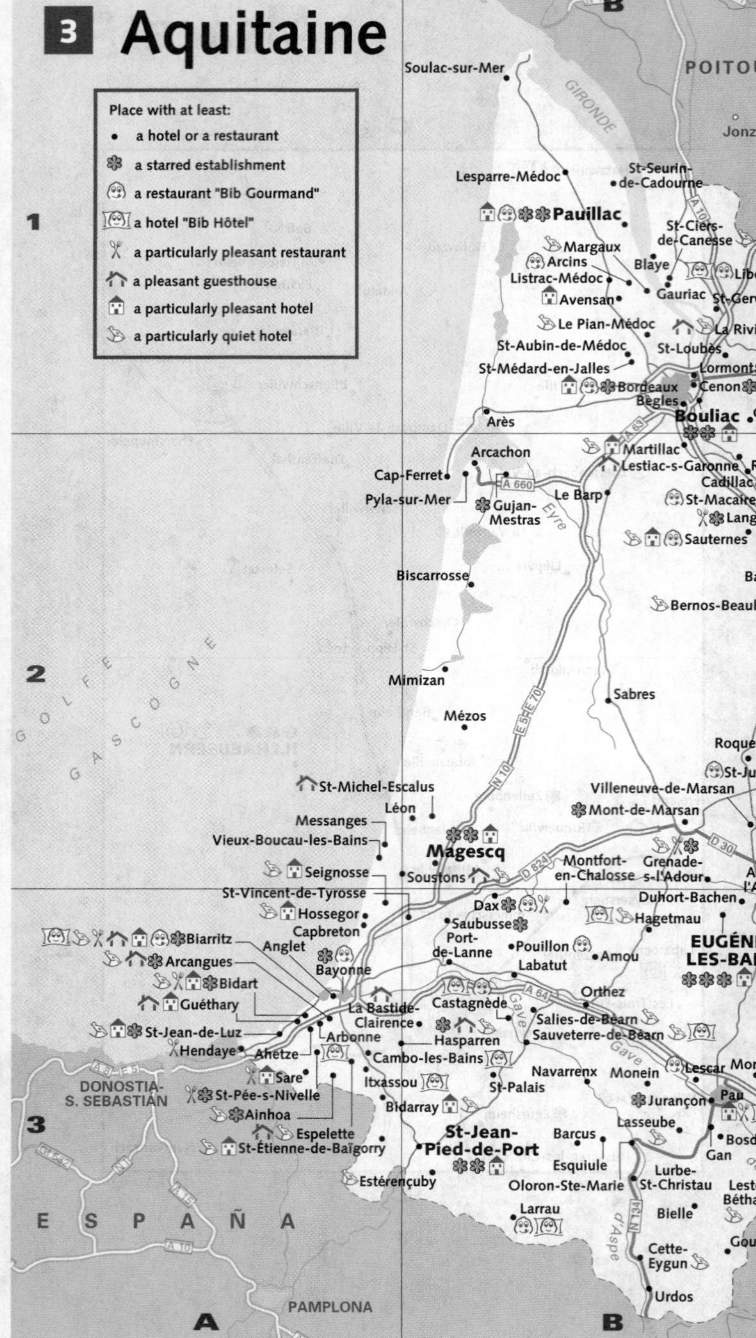
3 Aquitaine
Place with at least:
a hotel or a restaurant
a starred establishment
a restaurant "Bib Gourmand"
a hotel "Bib Hôtel"
a particularly pleasant restaurant
a pleasant guesthouse
a particularly pleasant hotel
a particularly quiet hotel
1
2
3
A
B
POITOU
GIRONDE
GOLFE
GASCOGNE
ESPAÑA
DONOSTIA-S. SEBASTIAN
PAMPLONA
EUGÉNI LES-BAI
Soulac-sur-Mer
Lesparre-Médoc
St-Seurin-de-Cadourne
Pauillac
St-Ciers-de-Canesse
Margaux
Arcins
Blaye
Listrac-Médoc
Gauriac
Avensan
Le Pian-Médoc
St-Aubin-de-Médoc
St-Loubès
St-Médard-en-Jalles
Lormont
Bordeaux
Cenon
Bègles
Bouliac
Arès
Arcachon
Martillac
Lestiac-s-Garonne
Cap-Ferret
Cadillac
Pyla-sur-Mer
Le Barp
St-Macaire
Gujan-Mestras
Sauternes
Biscarrosse
Bernos-Beaul
Mimizan
Sabres
Mézos
St-Michel-Escalus
Villeneuve-de-Marsan
Léon
Mont-de-Marsan
Messanges
Vieux-Boucau-les-Bains
Magescq
Seignosse
Soustons
Montfort-en-Chalosse
Grenade-s-l'Adour
St-Vincent-de-Tyrosse
Duhort-Bachen
Dax
Hossegor
Hagetmau
Saubusse
Capbreton
Biarritz
Anglet
Port-de-Lanne
Pouillon
Amou
Arcangues
Labatut
Bayonne
Bidart
Orthez
Guéthary
La Bastide-Clairence
Castagnède
Salies-de-Béarn
St-Jean-de-Luz
Sauveterre-de-Béarn
Arbonne
Hasparren
Hendaye
Ahetze
Cambo-les-Bains
Lescar
Navarrenx
Monein
Sare
Itxassou
St-Palais
St-Pée-s-Nivelle
Jurançon
Pau
Ainhoa
Bidarray
Lasseube
Espelette
St-Jean-Pied-de-Port
Barcus
Gan
St-Étienne-de-Baïgorry
Esquiule
Lurbe-St-Christau
Estérençuby
Oloron-Ste-Marie
Larrau
Bielle
Cette-Eygun
Urdos
A 10
A 63
A 660
E 5 E 70
N 10
D 824
D 30
A 64
N 134
Eyre
Gave
d'Aspe

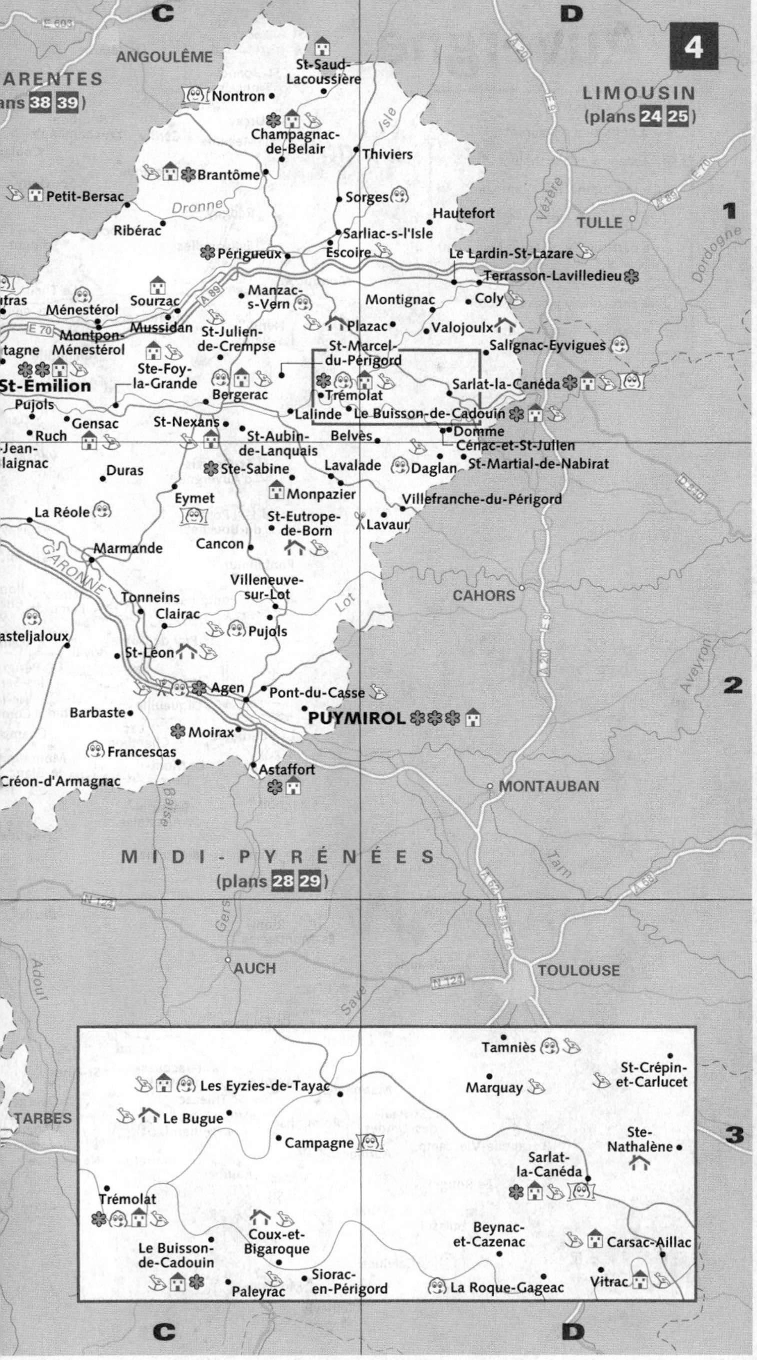
C
D
4
ANGOULÊME
ARENTES
ans 38 39)
LIMOUSIN
(plans 24 25)
St-Saud-Lacoussière
Nontron
Champagnac-de-Belair
Thiviers
Brantôme
Petit-Bersac
Sorges
Hautefort
Ribérac
Dronne
Sarliac-s-l'Isle
Escoire
Périgueux
Le Lardin-St-Lazare
Terrasson-Lavilledieu
TULLE
Sourzac
Manzac-s-Vern
Montignac
Coly
Ménestérol
Mussidan
Plazac
Valojoulx
Montpon-Ménestérol
St-Julien-de-Crempse
Salignac-Eyvigues
St-Marcel-du-Périgord
St-Émilion
Ste-Foy-la-Grande
Sarlat-la-Canéda
Bergerac
Trémolat
Pujols
Lalinde
Le Buisson-de-Cadouin
Gensac
St-Nexans
Domme
Ruch
St-Aubin-de-Lanquais
Belvès
Cénac-et-St-Julien
Lavalade
Daglan
St-Martial-de-Nabirat
Duras
Ste-Sabine
Monpazier
Eymet
Villefranche-du-Périgord
La Réole
St-Eutrope-de-Born
Lavaur
Cancon
Marmande
GARONNE
Villeneuve-sur-Lot
CAHORS
Tonneins
Clairac
Pujols
St-Léon
Agen
Pont-du-Casse
Barbaste
PUYMIROL
Moirax
Francescas
Astaffort
MONTAUBAN
MIDI-PYRÉNÉES
(plans 28 29)
AUCH
TOULOUSE
TARBES
Tamniès
St-Crépin-et-Carlucet
Marquay
Les Eyzies-de-Tayac
Le Bugue
Campagne
Ste-Nathalène
Sarlat-la-Canéda
Trémolat
Beynac-et-Cazenac
Coux-et-Bigaroque
Carsac-Aillac
Le Buisson-de-Cadouin
Paleyrac
Siorac-en-Périgord
La Roque-Gageac
Vitrac
1
2
3
C
D

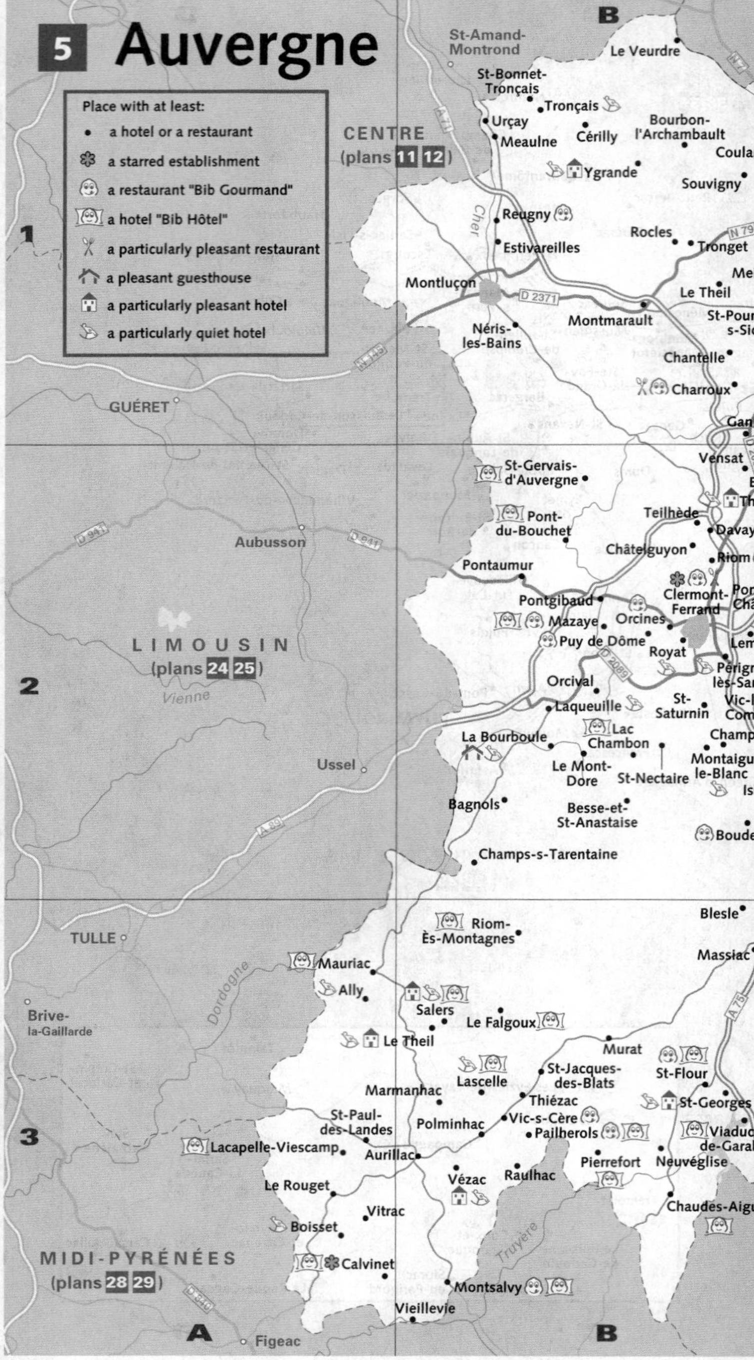
5 Auvergne
Place with at least:
a hotel or a restaurant
a starred establishment
a restaurant "Bib Gourmand"
a hotel "Bib Hôtel"
a particularly pleasant restaurant
a pleasant guesthouse
a particularly pleasant hotel
a particularly quiet hotel
CENTRE (plans 11 12)
LIMOUSIN (plans 24 25)
MIDI-PYRÉNÉES (plans 28 29)
St-Amand-Montrond
Le Veurdre
St-Bonnet-Tronçais
Tronçais
Urçay
Meaulne
Cérilly
Bourbon-l'Archambault
Ygrande
Souvigny
Reugny
Estivareilles
Rocles
Tronget
Le Theil
Montluçon
Montmarault
Néris-les-Bains
Chantelle
Charroux
GUÉRET
Vensat
St-Gervais-d'Auvergne
Pont-du-Bouchet
Teilhède
Châtelguyon
Aubusson
Pontaumur
Pontgibaud
Clermont-Ferrand
Mazaye
Orcines
Puy de Dôme
Royat
Orcival
Laqueuille
St-Saturnin
La Bourboule
Lac Chambon
Le Mont-Dore
St-Nectaire
Montaigut-le-Blanc
Ussel
Bagnols
Besse-et-St-Anastaise
Champs-s-Tarentaine
Blesle
Riom-Ès-Montagnes
Massiac
TULLE
Mauriac
Ally
Salers
Le Falgoux
Brive-la-Gaillarde
Le Theil
Murat
Lascelle
St-Jacques-des-Blats
St-Flour
Marmanhac
Thiézac
St-Georges
St-Paul-des-Landes
Polminhac
Vic-s-Cère
Pailherols
Lacapelle-Viescamp
Aurillac
Pierrefort
Neuvéglise
Le Rouget
Vézac
Raulhac
Vitrac
Chaudes-Aigu
Boisset
Calvinet
Montsalvy
Vieillevie
Figeac
Cher
Vienne
Dordogne
Truyère
D 2371
N 145
D 941
A 89
D 2089
D 840
A 75
N 79
A 71
A
B
1
2
3

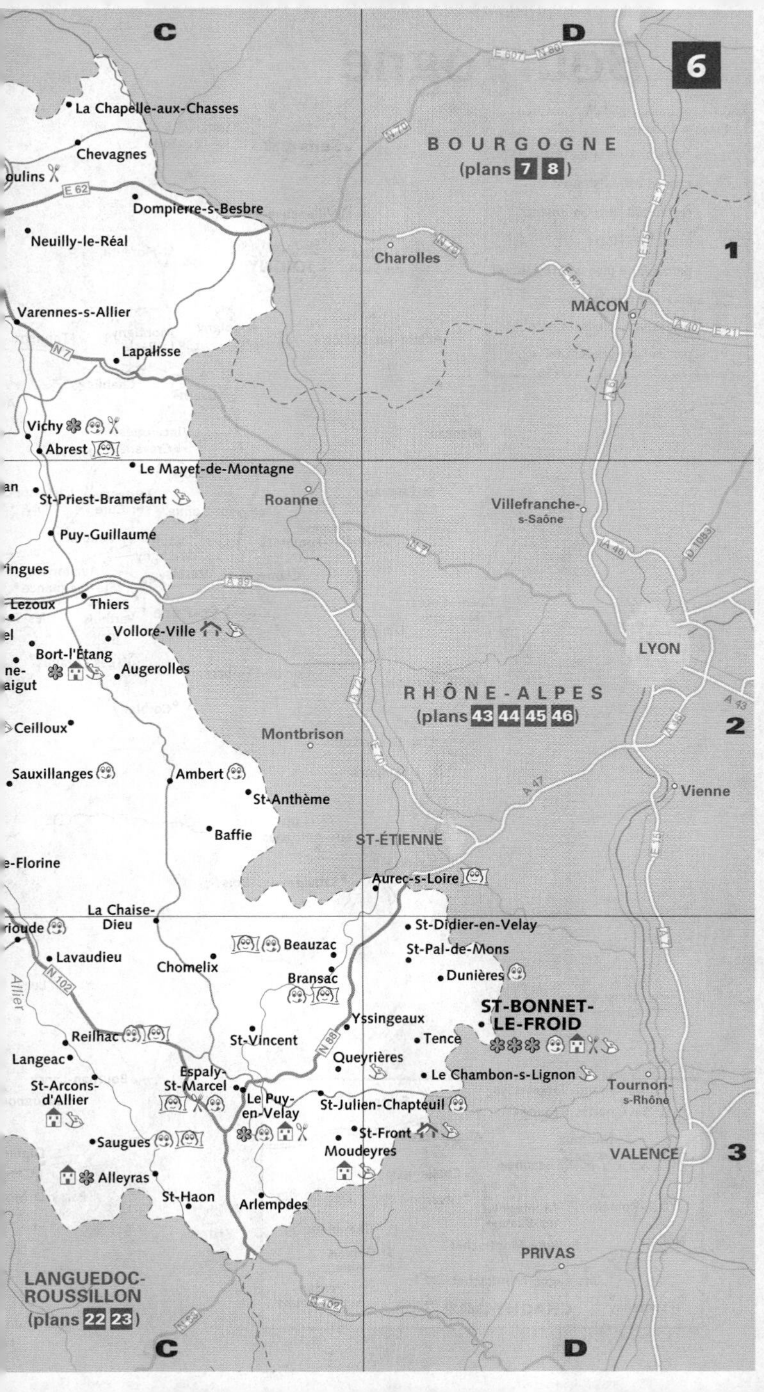
C
D
6
La Chapelle-aux-Chasses
Chevagnes
oulins
Dompierre-s-Besbre
Neuilly-le-Réal
BOURGOGNE
(plans 7 8)
Charolles
1
Varennes-s-Allier
Lapalisse
MÂCON
Vichy
Abrest
Le Mayet-de-Montagne
St-Priest-Bramefant
Roanne
Villefranche-s-Saône
Puy-Guillaume
Lezoux
Thiers
Vollore-Ville
LYON
Bort-l'Étang
Augerolles
RHÔNE-ALPES
(plans 43 44 45 46)
Ceilloux
2
Montbrison
Sauxillanges
Ambert
Vienne
St-Anthème
Baffie
ST-ÉTIENNE
Aurec-s-Loire
La Chaise-Dieu
St-Didier-en-Velay
Beauzac
St-Pal-de-Mons
Lavaudieu
Chomelix
Dunières
Bransac
ST-BONNET-LE-FROID
Yssingeaux
Reilhac
St-Vincent
Tence
Langeac
Queyrières
Espaly-St-Marcel
Le Chambon-s-Lignon
St-Arcons-d'Allier
Le Puy-en-Velay
St-Julien-Chapteuil
Tournon-s-Rhône
St-Front
Saugues
Moudeyres
VALENCE
3
Alleyras
St-Haon
Arlempdes
PRIVAS
LANGUEDOC-ROUSSILLON
(plans 22 23)
C
D

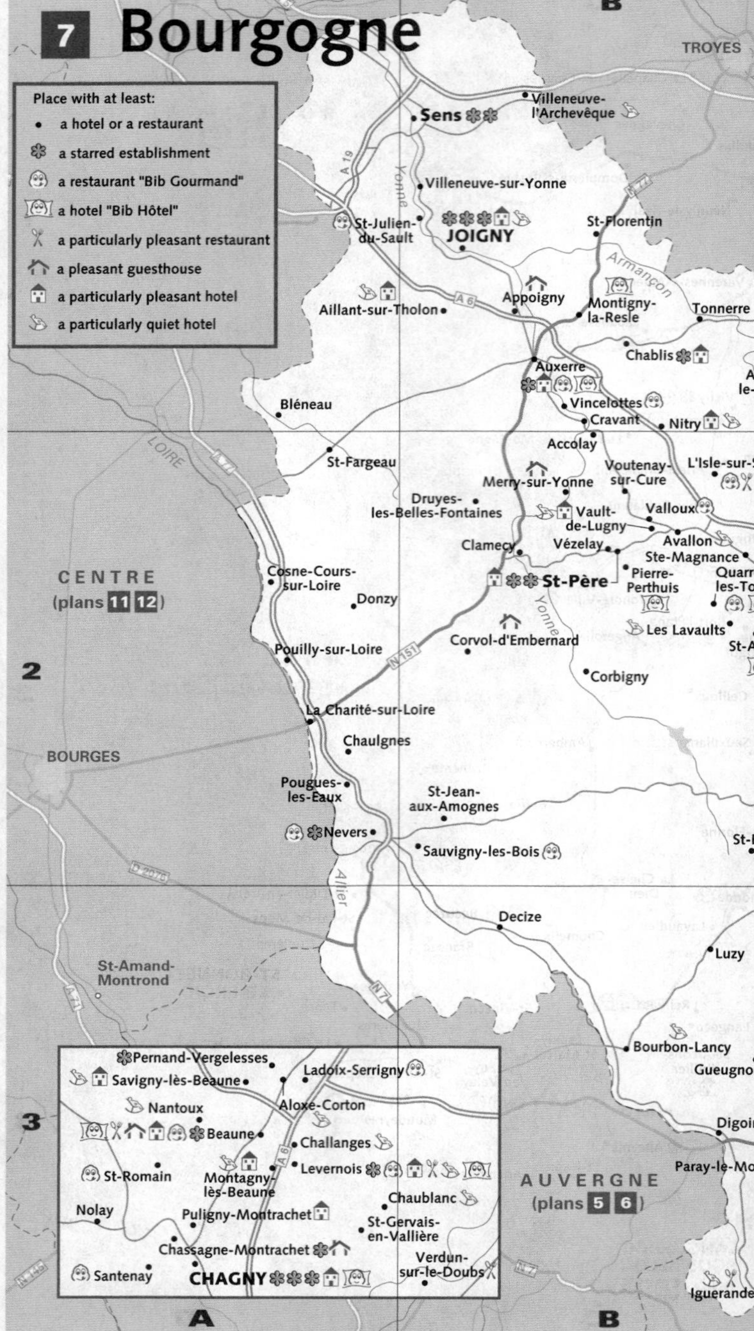
7 Bourgogne
B
TROYES
Place with at least:
a hotel or a restaurant
a starred establishment
a restaurant "Bib Gourmand"
a hotel "Bib Hôtel"
a particularly pleasant restaurant
a pleasant guesthouse
a particularly pleasant hotel
a particularly quiet hotel
Villeneuve-l'Archevêque
Sens
A 19
Yonne
Villeneuve-sur-Yonne
St-Julien-du-Sault
JOIGNY
St-Florentin
Armançon
Aillant-sur-Tholon
A 6
Appoigny
Montigny-la-Resle
Tonnerre
Chablis
Auxerre
Vincelottes
Bléneau
Cravant
Nitry
Accolay
LOIRE
A 77
St-Fargeau
Voutenay-sur-Cure
Merry-sur-Yonne
Druyes-les-Belles-Fontaines
Vault-de-Lugny
Valloux
Clamecy
Vézelay
Avallon
Ste-Magnance
Cosne-Cours-sur-Loire
St-Père
Pierre-Perthuis
CENTRE
(plans 11 12)
Donzy
Les Lavaults
Corvol-d'Embernard
Pouilly-sur-Loire
N 151
Corbigny
2
La Charité-sur-Loire
Chaulgnes
BOURGES
Pougues-les-Eaux
St-Jean-aux-Amognes
Nevers
Sauvigny-les-Bois
Allier
D 2076
Decize
Luzy
St-Amand-Montrond
N 7
A 71
Bourbon-Lancy
Pernand-Vergelesses
Ladoix-Serrigny
Savigny-lès-Beaune
Nantoux
Aloxe-Corton
3
Beaune
Challanges
St-Romain
Montagny-lès-Beaune
Levernois
Nolay
Chaublanc
Puligny-Montrachet
St-Gervais-en-Vallière
Chassagne-Montrachet
Santenay
CHAGNY
Verdun-sur-le-Doubs
AUVERGNE
(plans 5 6)
Digoin
Paray-le-Mo
Iguerande
A
B

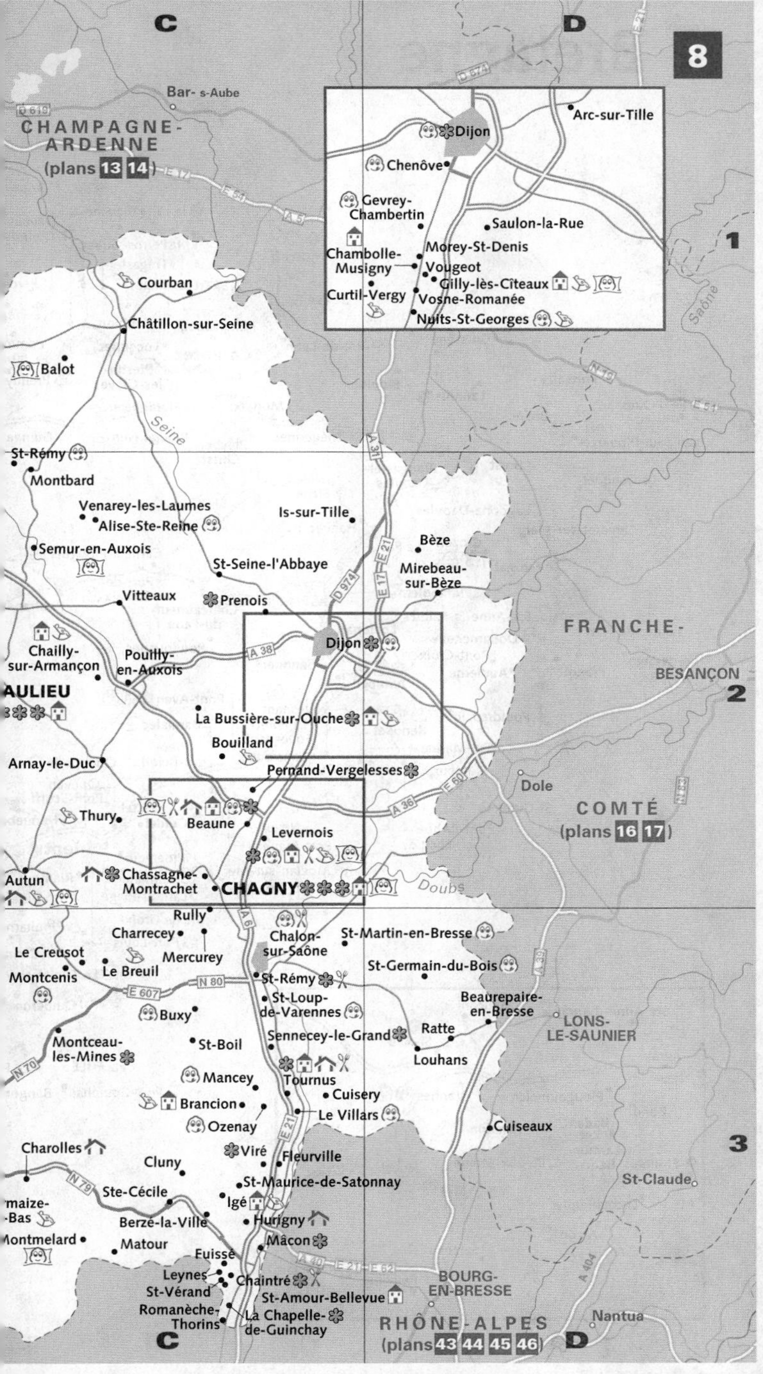

C
D
8
Bar-s-Aube
CHAMPAGNE-ARDENNE
(plans 13 14)
Dijon
Arc-sur-Tille
Chenôve
Gevrey-Chambertin
Saulon-la-Rue
Chambolle-Musigny
Morey-St-Denis
Vougeot
Gilly-lès-Cîteaux
Curtil-Vergy
Vosne-Romanée
Nuits-St-Georges
1
Courban
Châtillon-sur-Seine
Balot
Seine
Saône
St-Rémy
Montbard
Venarey-les-Laumes
Alise-Ste-Reine
Is-sur-Tille
Bèze
Semur-en-Auxois
St-Seine-l'Abbaye
Mirebeau-sur-Bèze
Vitteaux
Prenois
FRANCHE-
Dijon
Chailly-sur-Armançon
Pouilly-en-Auxois
BESANÇON
2
AULIEU
La Bussière-sur-Ouche
Bouilland
Arnay-le-Duc
Pernand-Vergelesses
Dole
Thury
Beaune
COMTÉ
(plans 16 17)
Levernois
Autun
Chassagne-Montrachet
CHAGNY
Doubs
Rully
Charrecey
Chalon-sur-Saône
St-Martin-en-Bresse
Le Creusot
Mercurey
Montcenis
Le Breuil
St-Germain-du-Bois
St-Rémy
St-Loup-de-Varennes
Beaurepaire-en-Bresse
Buxy
LONS-LE-SAUNIER
Montceau-les-Mines
St-Boil
Sennecey-le-Grand
Ratte
Louhans
Mancey
Tournus
Cuisery
Brancion
Le Villars
Ozenay
Cuiseaux
Charolles
Viré
Fleurville
3
Cluny
St-Claude
St-Maurice-de-Satonnay
Ste-Cécile
maize-Bas
Igé
Hurigny
Berzé-la-Ville
Iontmelard
Matour
Mâcon
Fuissé
BOURG-EN-BRESSE
Leynes
Chaintré
St-Vérand
St-Amour-Bellevue
Romanèche-Thorins
La Chapelle-de-Guinchay
RHÔNE-ALPES
(plans 43 44 45 46)
Nantua
C
D

9 Bretagne

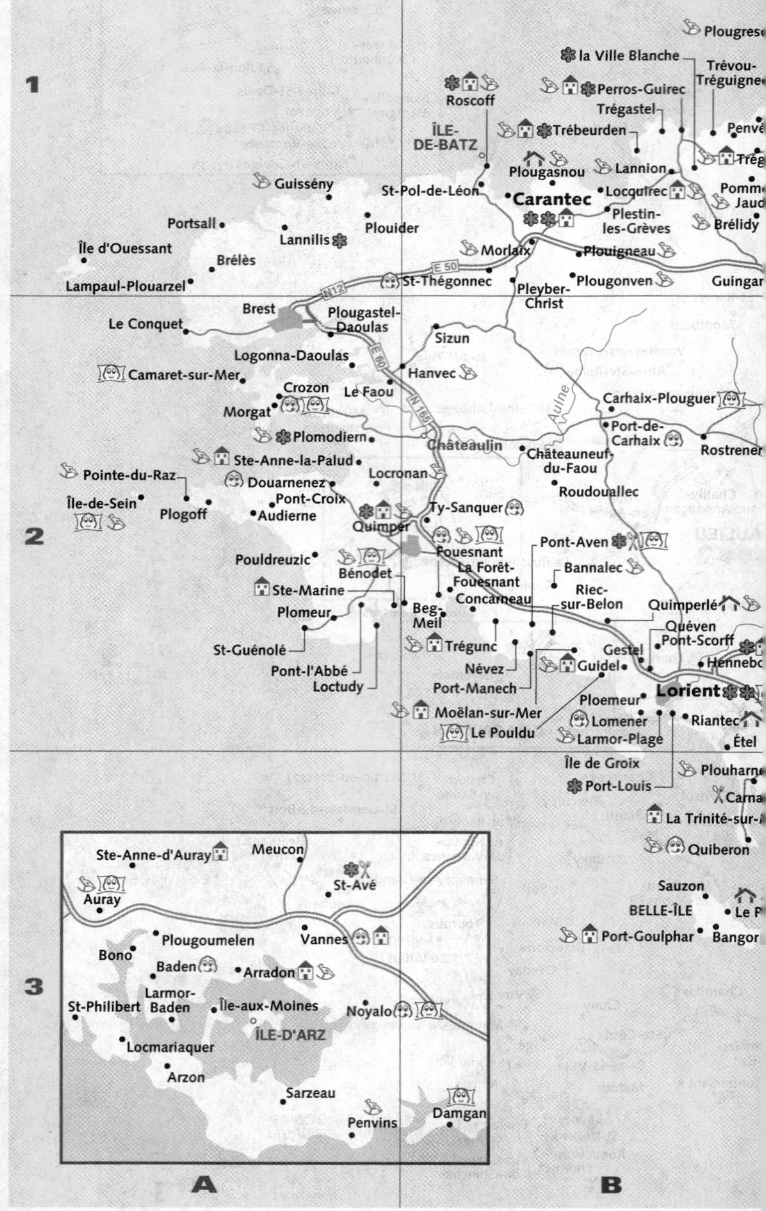

A
B
1
2
3
Plougrescant
la Ville Blanche
Trévou-Tréguignec
Roscoff
Perros-Guirec
Trégastel
ÎLE-DE-BATZ
Trébeurden
Penvénan
Tréguier
Plougasnou
Lannion
Guissény
St-Pol-de-Léon
Carantec
Locquirec
Plestin-les-Grèves
Brélidy
Portsall
Plouider
Lannilis
Île d'Ouessant
Brélès
Morlaix
Plouigneau
E 50
Lampaul-Plouarzel
St-Thégonnec
Pleyber-Christ
Plougonven
Guingamp
N12
Brest
Plougastel-Daoulas
Le Conquet
Sizun
Logonna-Daoulas
E 60
Hanvec
Camaret-sur-Mer
Crozon
Le Faou
Aulne
Carhaix-Plouguer
Morgat
N 165
Port-de-Carhaix
Plomodiern
Châteaulin
Châteauneuf-du-Faou
Rostrenen
Ste-Anne-la-Palud
Pointe-du-Raz
Locronan
Douarnenez
Île-de-Sein
Pont-Croix
Roudouallec
Plogoff
Audierne
Ty-Sanquer
Quimper
Pont-Aven
Fouesnant
Pouldreuzic
Bannalec
Bénodet
La Forêt-Fouesnant
Ste-Marine
Riec-sur-Belon
Quimperlé
Concarneau
Plomeur
Beg-Meil
Quéven
Pont-Scorff
Trégunc
Gestel
St-Guénolé
Hennebont
Névez
Guidel
Pont-l'Abbé
Port-Manech
Lorient
Loctudy
Ploemeur
Moëlan-sur-Mer
Lomener
Riantec
Le Pouldu
Larmor-Plage
Étel
Île de Groix
Plouharnel
Port-Louis
Carnac
La Trinité-sur-Mer
Quiberon
Sauzon
BELLE-ÎLE
Le Palais
Port-Goulphar
Bangor
Ste-Anne-d'Auray
Meucon
St-Avé
Auray
Plougoumelen
Vannes
Bono
Baden
Arradon
Larmor-Baden
St-Philibert
Île-aux-Moines
Noyalo
ÎLE-D'ARZ
Locmariaquer
Arzon
Sarzeau
Penvins
Damgan

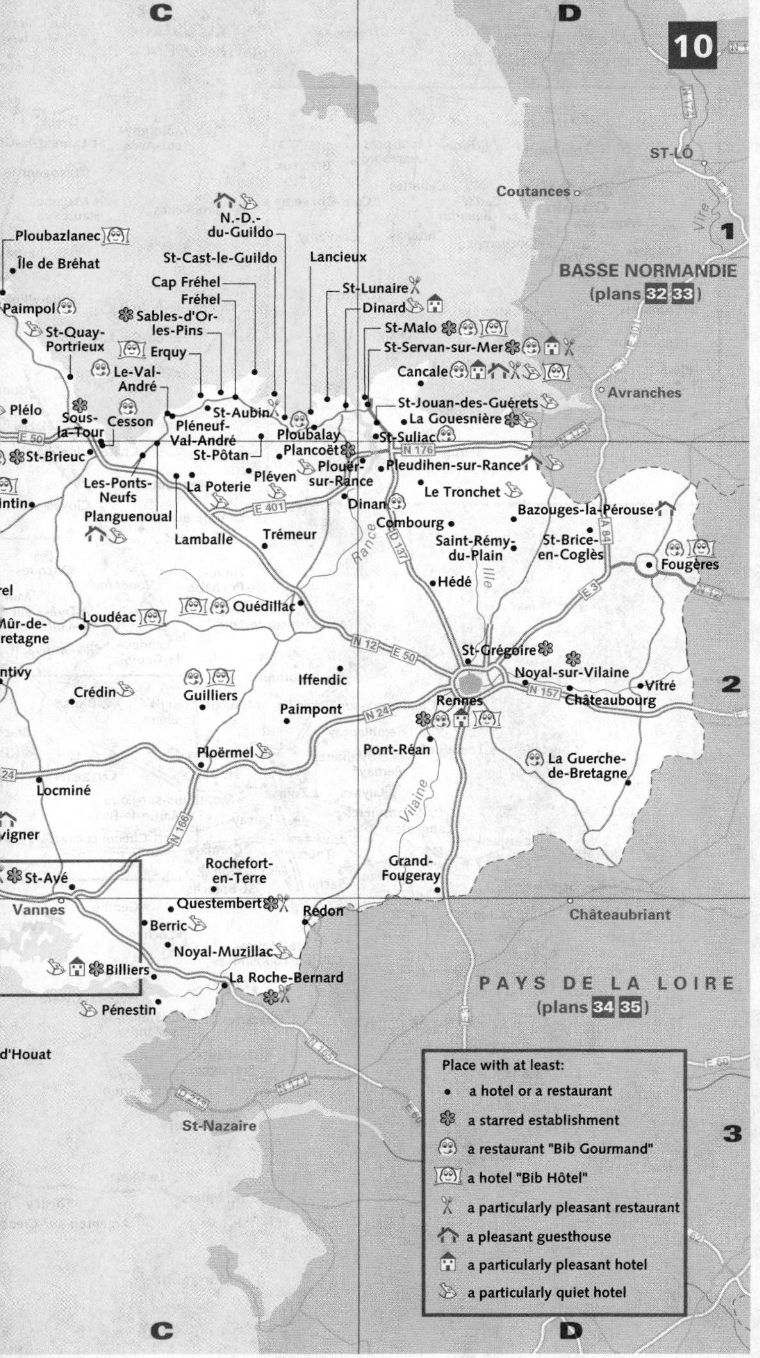
C
D
ST-LÔ
Coutances
BASSE NORMANDIE
(plans 32 33)
Avranches
Ploubazlanec
Île de Bréhat
Paimpol
St-Quay-Portrieux
N.-D.-du-Guildo
St-Cast-le-Guildo
Lancieux
Cap Fréhel
Fréhel
Sables-d'Or-les-Pins
Erquy
Le-Val-André
St-Lunaire
Dinard
St-Malo
St-Servan-sur-Mer
Cancale
St-Jouan-des-Guérets
La Gouesnière
St-Suliac
Plélo
Sous-la-Tour
Cesson
St-Aubin
Pléneuf-Val-André
Ploubalay
Plancoët
St-Brieuc
St-Pôtan
Plouër-sur-Rance
Pléven
Pleudihen-sur-Rance
Le Tronchet
Les-Ponts-Neufs
La Poterie
Dinan
Planguenoual
Combourg
Bazouges-la-Pérouse
Lamballe
Trémeur
Saint-Rémy-du-Plain
St-Brice-en-Coglès
Fougères
Hédé
Quédillac
Loudéac
Mûr-de-Bretagne
St-Grégoire
Noyal-sur-Vilaine
Iffendic
Crédin
Guilliers
Rennes
Vitré
Châteaubourg
Paimpont
Ploërmel
Pont-Réan
La Guerche-de-Bretagne
Locminé
Rochefort-en-Terre
Grand-Fougeray
St-Avé
Vannes
Questembert
Redon
Châteaubriant
Berric
Noyal-Muzillac
Billiers
La Roche-Bernard
PAYS DE LA LOIRE
(plans 34 35)
Pénestin
d'Houat
St-Nazaire
Rance
Ille
Vilaine
Vire
N 176
E 401
E 50
N 12
N 24
N 157
N 166
N 165
D 137
A 84
E 3
N 174
E 60
1
2
3
Place with at least:
• a hotel or a restaurant
a starred establishment
a restaurant "Bib Gourmand"
a hotel "Bib Hôtel"
a particularly pleasant restaurant
a pleasant guesthouse
a particularly pleasant hotel
a particularly quiet hotel
C
D

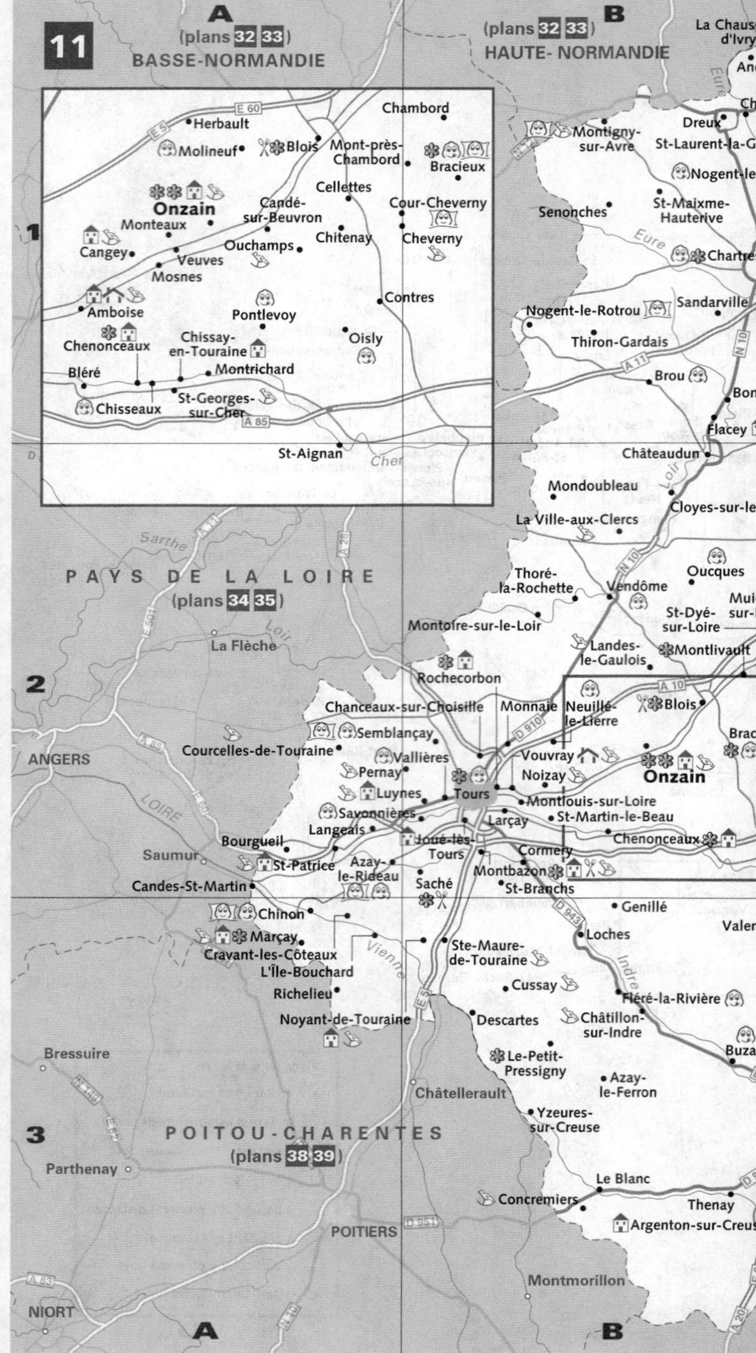
11
A
(plans 32 33)
BASSE-NORMANDIE
B
(plans 32 33)
HAUTE-NORMANDIE
Herbault
Molineuf
Blois
Chambord
Mont-près-Chambord
Bracieux
Onzain
Cellettes
Candé-sur-Beuvron
Cour-Cheverny
Monteaux
Chitenay
Cheverny
Cangey
Ouchamps
Veuves
Mosnes
Contres
Amboise
Pontlevoy
Chenonceaux
Chissay-en-Touraine
Oisly
Bléré
Montrichard
St-Georges-sur-Cher
Chisseaux
St-Aignan
Cher
1
2
3
Montigny-sur-Avre
Dreux
St-Laurent-la-Gâ
Nogent-le-
Senonches
St-Maixme-Hauterive
Chartres
Nogent-le-Rotrou
Sandarville
Thiron-Gardais
Brou
Flacey
Châteaudun
Mondoubleau
Cloyes-sur-le-
La Ville-aux-Clercs
PAYS DE LA LOIRE
(plans 34 35)
Thoré-la-Rochette
Vendôme
Oucques
Montoire-sur-le-Loir
St-Dyé-sur-Loire
Landes-le-Gaulois
Montlivault
La Flèche
Rochecorbon
Chanceaux-sur-Choisille
Monnaie
Neuillé-le-Lierre
Blois
Semblançay
Courcelles-de-Touraine
Vallières
Vouvray
ANGERS
Pernay
Noizay
Onzain
Luynes
Tours
Montlouis-sur-Loire
Savonnières
St-Martin-le-Beau
Langeais
Larçay
Bourgueil
Joué-lès-Tours
Chenonceaux
Saumur
Cormery
St-Patrice
Azay-le-Rideau
Montbazon
Candes-St-Martin
Saché
St-Branchs
Genillé
Chinon
Marçay
Loches
Ste-Maure-de-Touraine
Cravant-les-Côteaux
L'Île-Bouchard
Cussay
Richelieu
Fléré-la-Rivière
Noyant-de-Touraine
Descartes
Châtillon-sur-Indre
Bressuire
Le-Petit-Pressigny
Azay-le-Ferron
Châtellerault
Yzeures-sur-Creuse
POITOU-CHARENTES
(plans 38 39)
Parthenay
Le Blanc
Concremiers
Thenay
Argenton-sur-Creus
POITIERS
Montmorillon
NIORT
A
B

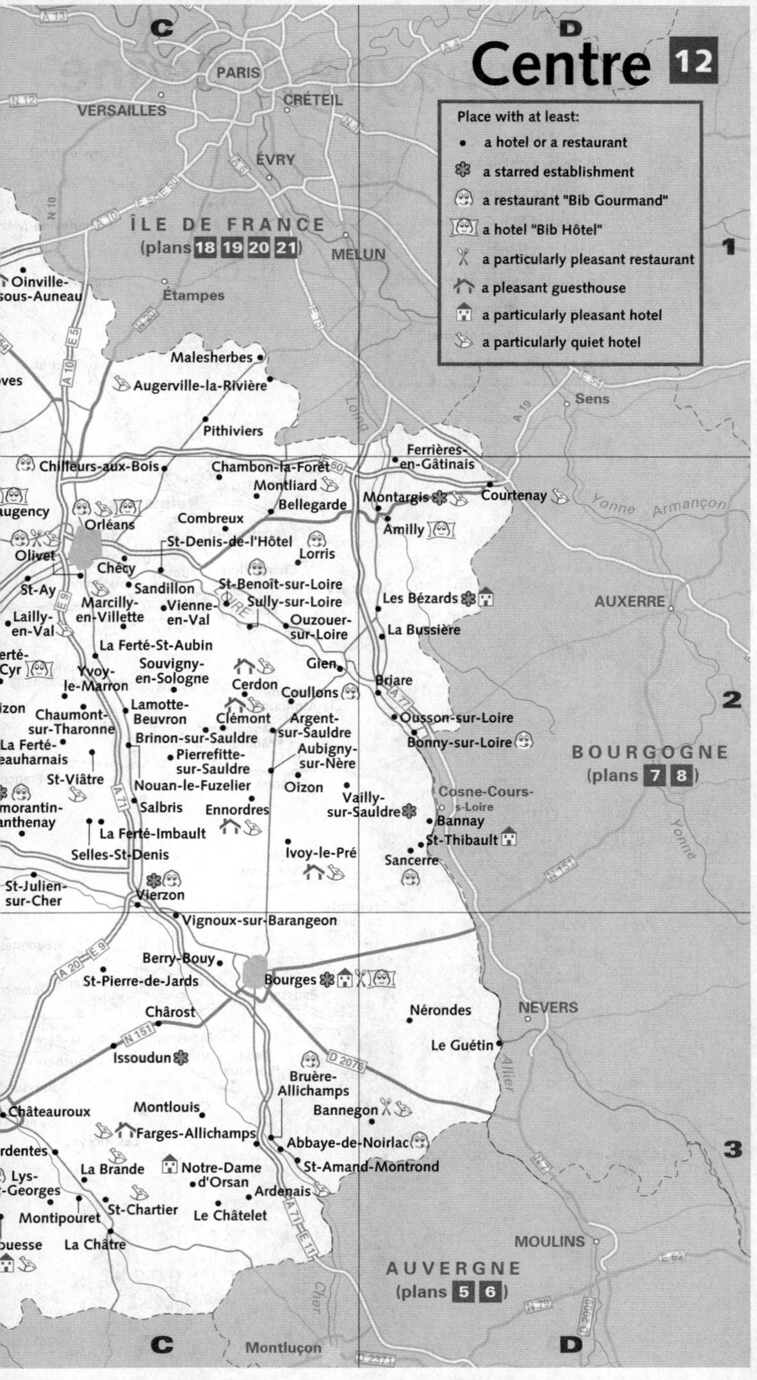

Centre 12
Place with at least:
a hotel or a restaurant
a starred establishment
a restaurant "Bib Gourmand"
a hotel "Bib Hôtel"
a particularly pleasant restaurant
a pleasant guesthouse
a particularly pleasant hotel
a particularly quiet hotel
ÎLE DE FRANCE
(plans 18 19 20 21)
BOURGOGNE
(plans 7 8)
AUVERGNE
(plans 5 6)
PARIS
VERSAILLES
CRÉTEIL
ÉVRY
MELUN
Étampes
Oinville-sous-Auneau
Malesherbes
Augerville-la-Rivière
Pithiviers
Sens
Ferrières-en-Gâtinais
Chilleurs-aux-Bois
Chambon-la-Forêt
Montliard
Bellegarde
Montargis
Courtenay
Amilly
Orléans
Combreux
St-Denis-de-l'Hôtel
Lorris
Olivet
Chécy
Sandillon
St-Benoît-sur-Loire
Sully-sur-Loire
St-Ay
Marcilly-en-Villette
Vienne-en-Val
Les Bézards
AUXERRE
Lailly-en-Val
Ouzouer-sur-Loire
La Bussière
La Ferté-St-Aubin
Souvigny-en-Sologne
Gien
Yvoy-le-Marron
Cerdon
Coullons
Briare
Lamotte-Beuvron
Chaumont-sur-Tharonne
Clémont
Argent-sur-Sauldre
Ousson-sur-Loire
Brinon-sur-Sauldre
Bonny-sur-Loire
Aubigny-sur-Nère
Pierrefitte-sur-Sauldre
St-Viâtre
Nouan-le-Fuzelier
Oizon
Vailly-sur-Sauldre
Cosne-Cours-s-Loire
Salbris
Ennordres
Bannay
La Ferté-Imbault
St-Thibault
Selles-St-Denis
Ivoy-le-Pré
Sancerre
St-Julien-sur-Cher
Vierzon
Vignoux-sur-Barangeon
Berry-Bouy
St-Pierre-de-Jards
Bourges
Nérondes
NEVERS
Chârost
Le Guétin
Issoudun
Bruère-Allichamps
Châteauroux
Montlouis
Bannegon
Farges-Allichamps
Abbaye-de-Noirlac
La Brande
Notre-Dame d'Orsan
St-Amand-Montrond
Ardenais
St-Chartier
Le Châtelet
Montipouret
La Châtre
MOULINS
Montluçon
Loire
Loing
Yonne
Armançon
Allier
Cher
C
D
1
2
3

13 Champagne Ardenne

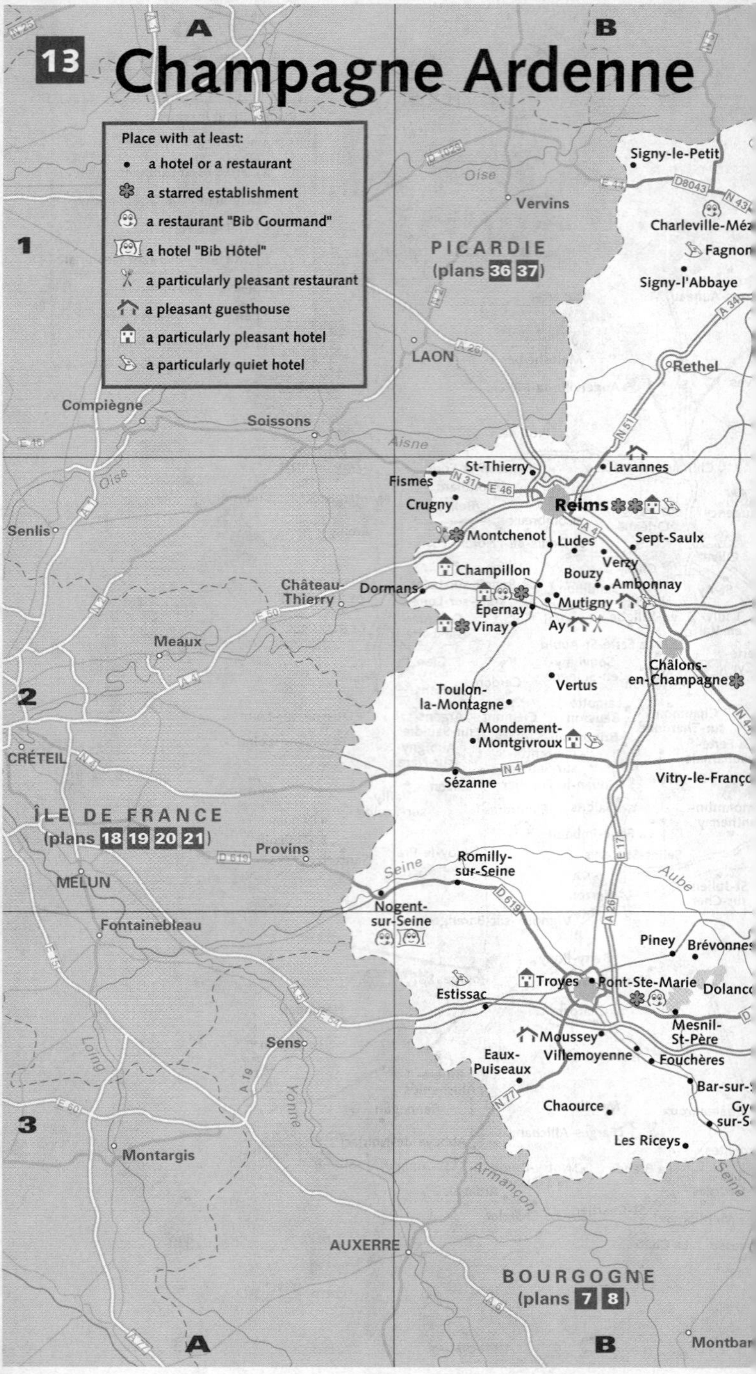

Place with at least:

- a hotel or a restaurant
- a starred establishment
- a restaurant "Bib Gourmand"
- a hotel "Bib Hôtel"
- a particularly pleasant restaurant
- a pleasant guesthouse
- a particularly pleasant hotel
- a particularly quiet hotel

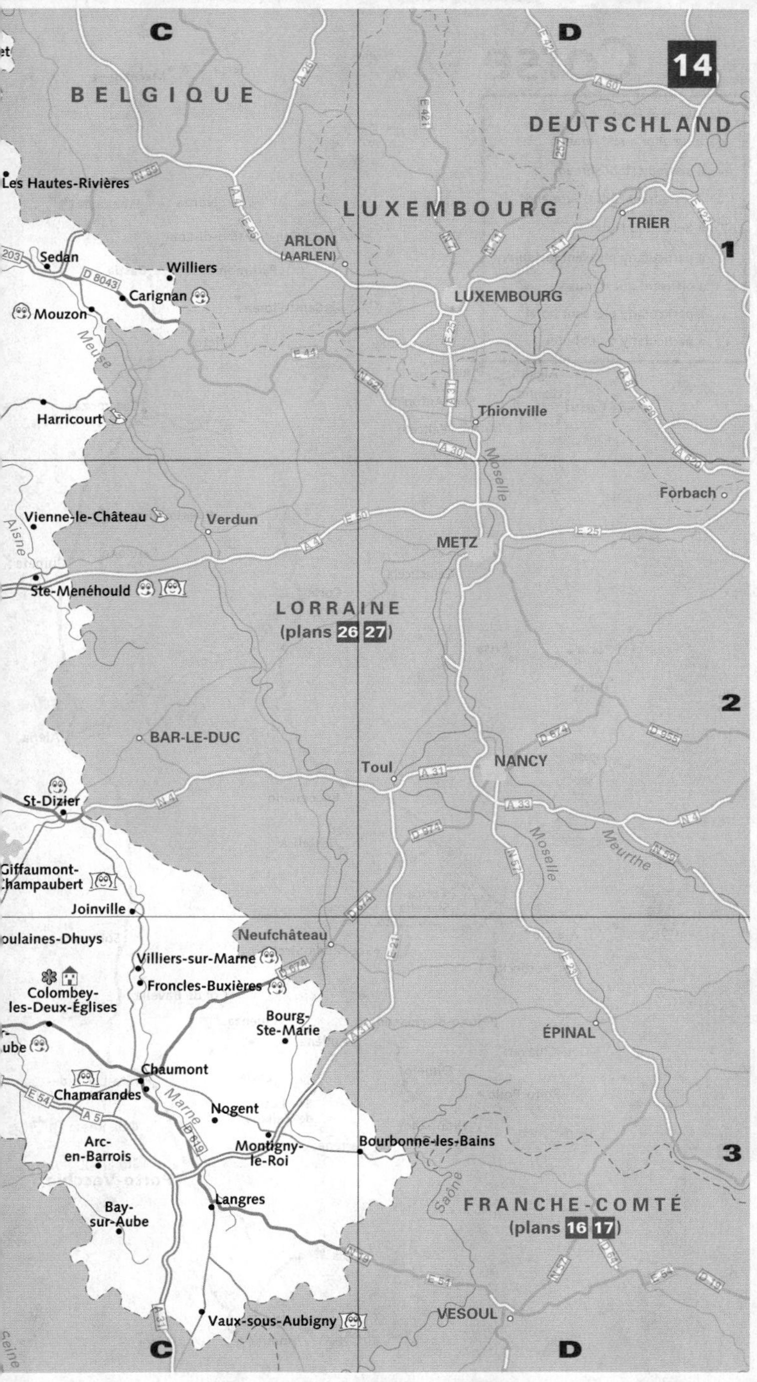

C
D
14
BELGIQUE
DEUTSCHLAND
LUXEMBOURG
Les Hautes-Rivières
ARLON
(AARLEN)
TRIER
1
Sedan
Williers
Carignan
Mouzon
Meuse
LUXEMBOURG
Thionville
Harricourt
Moselle
Forbach
Vienne-le-Château
Verdun
METZ
Aisne
Ste-Menéhould
LORRAINE
(plans 26 27)
2
BAR-LE-DUC
Toul
NANCY
St-Dizier
Moselle
Meurthe
Giffaumont-
Champaubert
Joinville
Soulaines-Dhuys
Neufchâteau
Villiers-sur-Marne
Froncles-Buxières
Colombey-
les-Deux-Églises
Bourg-
Ste-Marie
ÉPINAL
Aube
Chaumont
Chamarandes
Marne
Nogent
Arc-
en-Barrois
Montigny-
le-Roi
Bourbonne-les-Bains
3
Langres
Saône
FRANCHE-COMTÉ
(plans 16 17)
Bay-
sur-Aube
VESOUL
Vaux-sous-Aubigny
Seine
C
D

15 Corse

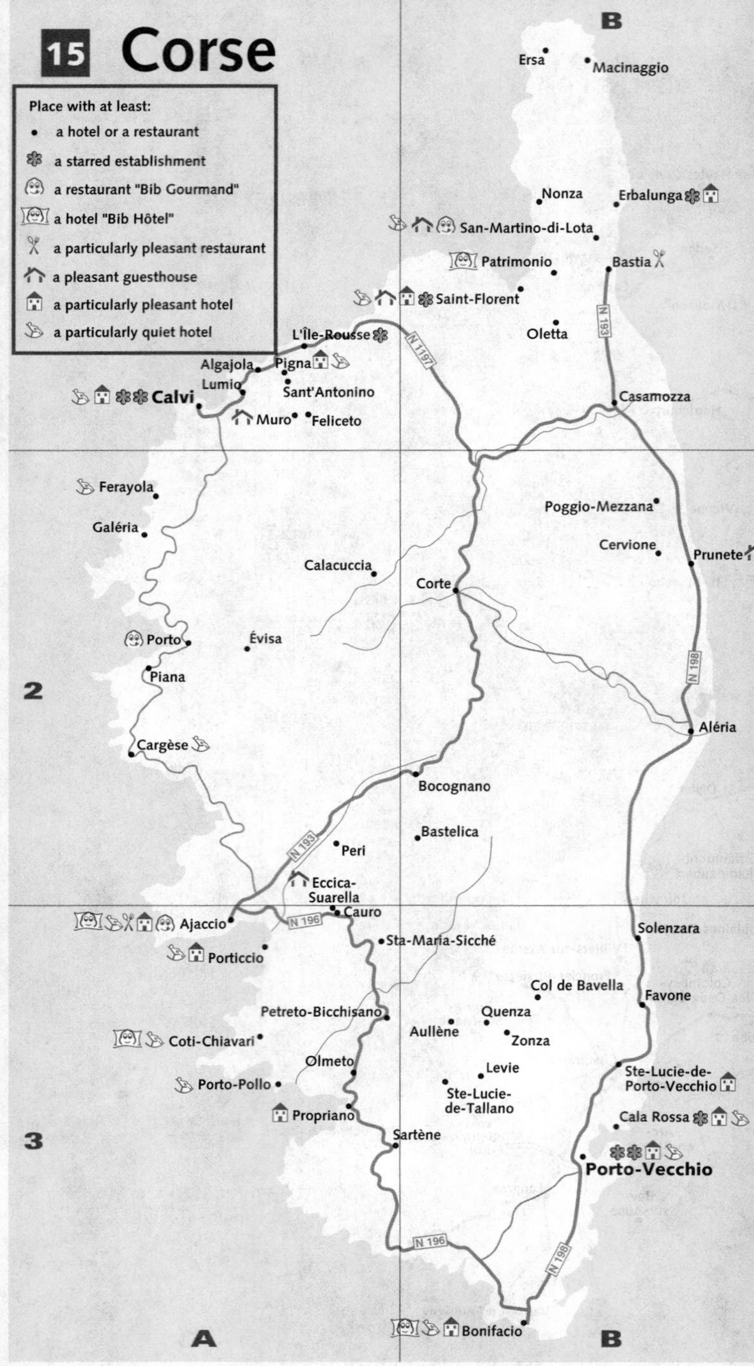

Place with at least:
a hotel or a restaurant
a starred establishment
a restaurant "Bib Gourmand"
a hotel "Bib Hôtel"
a particularly pleasant restaurant
a pleasant guesthouse
a particularly pleasant hotel
a particularly quiet hotel
A
B
2
3
Ersa
Macinaggio
Nonza
Erbalunga
San-Martino-di-Lota
Patrimonio
Bastia
Saint-Florent
Oletta
L'Île-Rousse
Algajola
Pigna
Lumio
Sant'Antonino
Calvi
Muro
Feliceto
Casamozza
N 193
N 1197
Ferayola
Galéria
Poggio-Mezzana
Cervione
Prunete
Calacuccia
Corte
Porto
Évisa
Piana
N 198
Aléria
Cargèse
Bocognano
Bastelica
Peri
Eccica-Suarella
Cauro
N 196
Ajaccio
Porticcio
Sta-Maria-Sicché
Solenzara
Col de Bavella
Favone
Petreto-Bicchisano
Quenza
Aullène
Zonza
Coti-Chiavari
Olmeto
Levie
Porto-Pollo
Ste-Lucie-de-Tallano
Ste-Lucie-de-Porto-Vecchio
Propriano
Cala Rossa
Sartène
Porto-Vecchio
Bonifacio

16 Franche-Comté

Place with at least:
• a hotel or a restaurant
a starred establishment
a restaurant "Bib Gourmand"
a hotel "Bib Hôtel"
a particularly pleasant restaurant
a pleasant guesthouse
a particularly pleasant hotel
a particularly quiet hotel
A
B
1
2
3
Langres
CHAMPAGNE-ARDENNE
(plans 13 14)
BOURGOGNE
(plans 7 8)
RHÔNE-ALPES
(plans 43 44 45 46)
Saône
Doubs
Faverney
Breur lès-Fav
Combeaufontaine
Port-s-Sa
Vauchoux
Vesoul
Nantilly
Rigny
Gray
Gy
Cussey-s-l'Ognon
Geneuille
Cult
Besançon
DIJON
Beaune
Sampans
Dole
Quingey
Orna
Port-Lesney
Mouchard
Salins-les-Bains
Chaussin
Montigny-lès-Arsures
Arbois
Poligny
Monts-de-Vaux
Passenans
Voiteur
Château-Chalon
St-Germain-lès-Arlay
Champagnole
Chalon-s-Saône
Baume-les-Messieurs
Mirebel
Chille
Chaux-Ne
Doucier
Lons-le-Saunier
Ilay
Bonlieu
Louhans
Pont-de-Poitte
Orgelet
Les Rousses
Lamoura
Saint-Claude
Pratz
Les Molunes
Gex
MÂCON
N 19
E 54
N 57
A 39
N 83
A 36
E 60
A 38
A 6
N 80
D 974
E 17
E 21
E 15
A 40
E 62

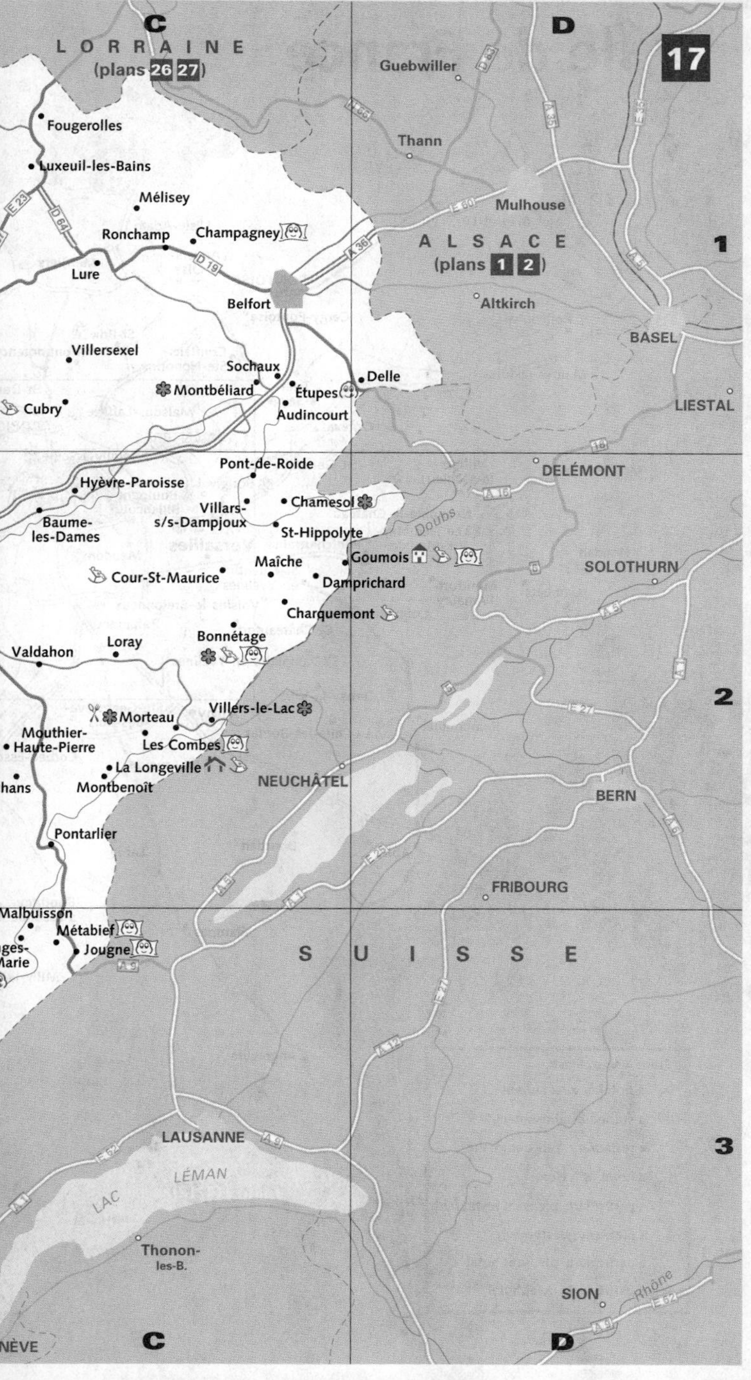
17
C
D
LORRAINE
(plans 26 27)
ALSACE
(plans 1 2)
SUISSE
Guebwiller
Thann
Mulhouse
Altkirch
BASEL
LIESTAL
DELÉMONT
SOLOTHURN
BERN
FRIBOURG
NEUCHÂTEL
LAUSANNE
LAC LÉMAN
Thonon-les-B.
SION
Rhône
Doubs
NÈVE
Fougerolles
Luxeuil-les-Bains
Mélisey
Ronchamp
Champagney
Lure
Belfort
Villersexel
Sochaux
Montbéliard
Delle
Étupes
Cubry
Audincourt
Pont-de-Roide
Hyèvre-Paroisse
Chamesol
Villars-s/s-Dampjoux
Baume-les-Dames
St-Hippolyte
Goumois
Maîche
Cour-St-Maurice
Damprichard
Charquemont
Bonnétage
Loray
Valdahon
Villers-le-Lac
Morteau
Mouthier-Haute-Pierre
Les Combes
La Longeville
Montbenoît
Pontarlier
Malbuisson
Métabief
Jougne
1
2
3

18 Île de France

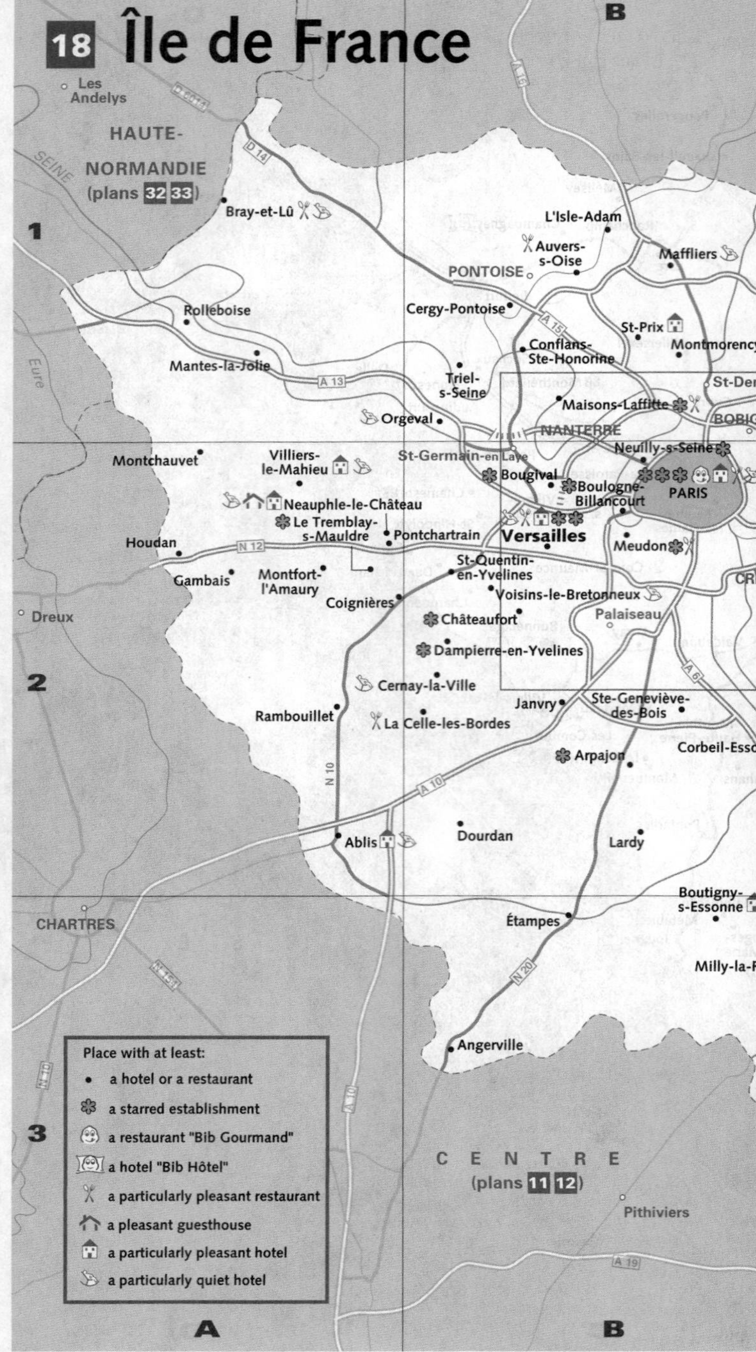

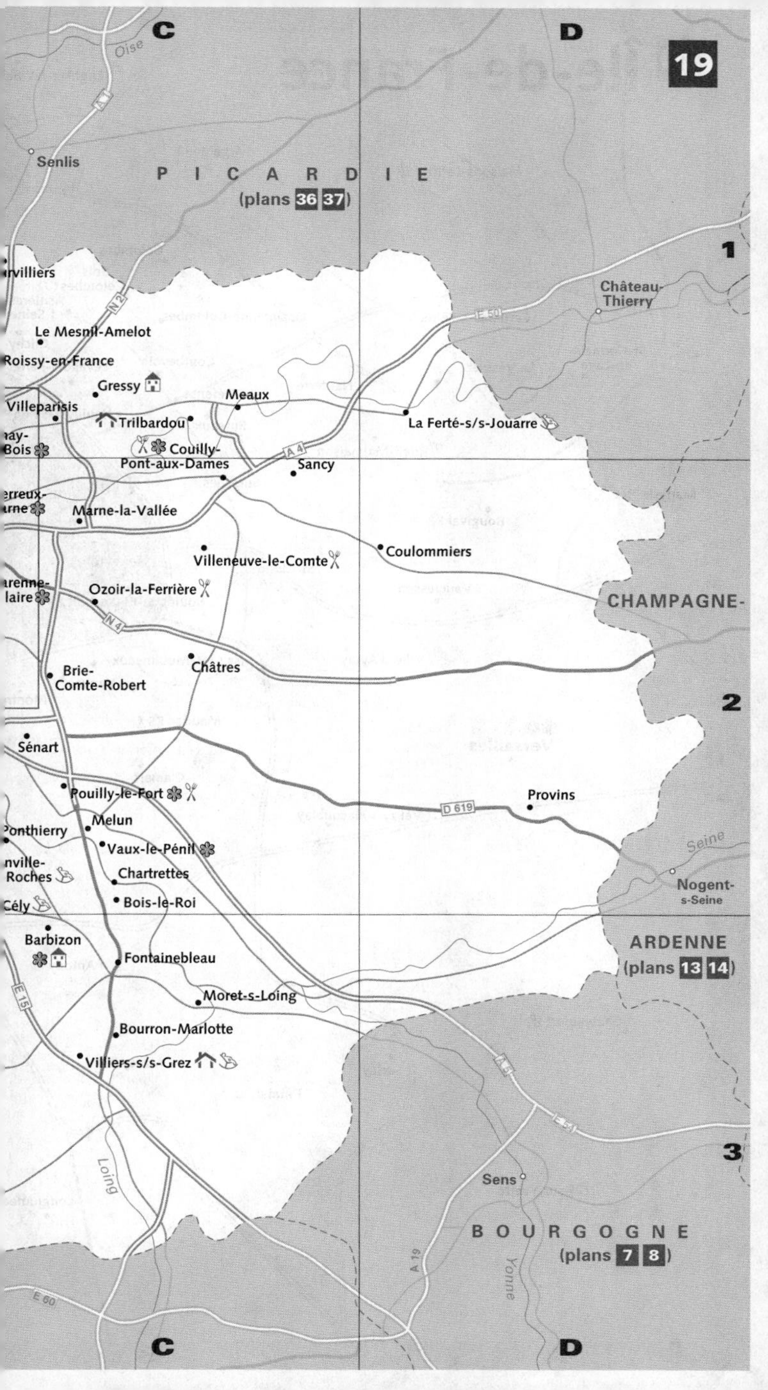
C
D
Oise
Senlis
PICARDIE
(plans 36 37)
1
Château-Thierry
Le Mesnil-Amelot
Roissy-en-France
Gressy
Meaux
Villeparisis
Trilbardou
La Ferté-s/s-Jouarre
Couilly-Pont-aux-Dames
Sancy
Marne-la-Vallée
Coulommiers
Villeneuve-le-Comte
Ozoir-la-Ferrière
CHAMPAGNE-
Châtres
Brie-Comte-Robert
2
Sénart
Pouilly-le-Fort
Provins
D 619
Melun
Ponthierry
Vaux-le-Pénil
Seine
Chartrettes
Roches
Nogent-s-Seine
Cély
Bois-le-Roi
Barbizon
ARDENNE
(plans 13 14)
Fontainebleau
Moret-s-Loing
Bourron-Marlotte
Villiers-s/s-Grez
E 15
A 4
N 2
N 4
E 50
3
Loing
Sens
BOURGOGNE
(plans 7 8)
A 19
Yonne
E 60
C
D

20 Île-de-France

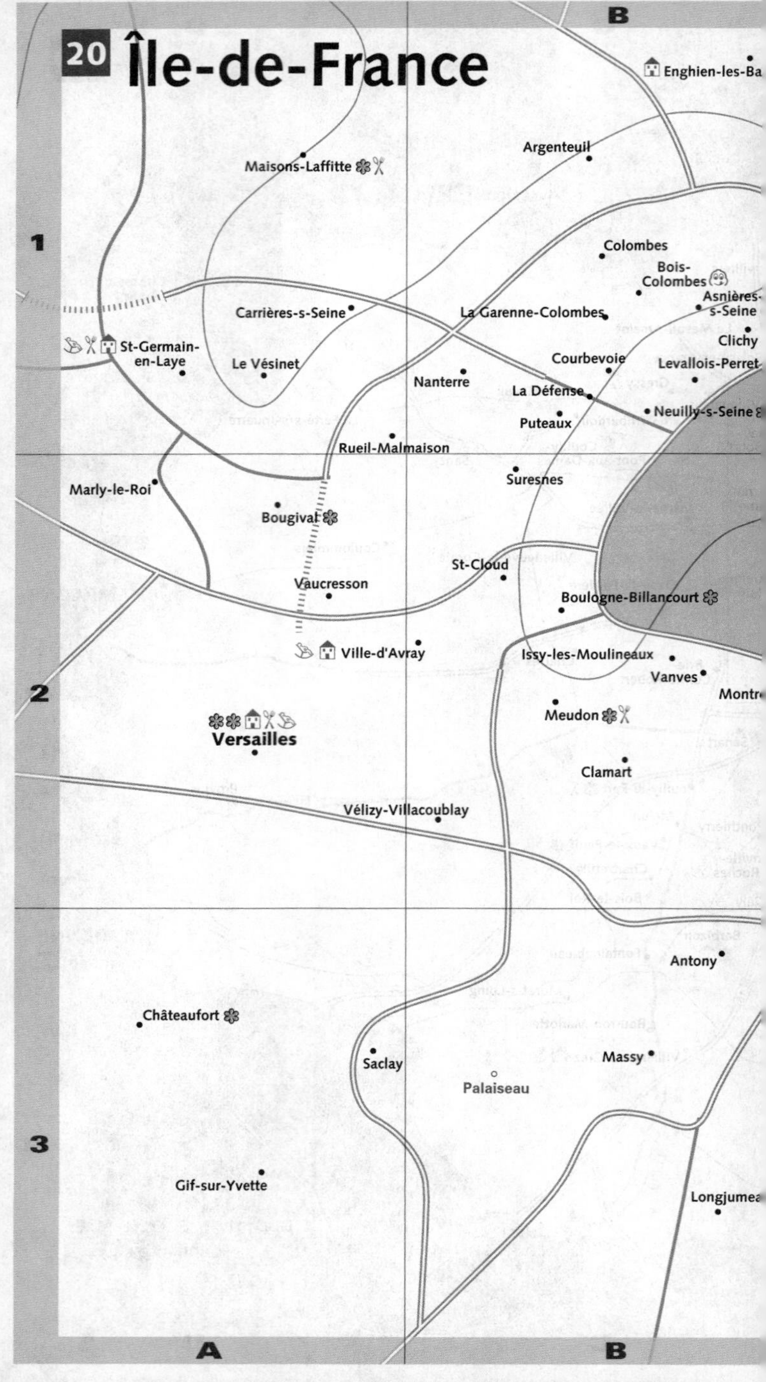

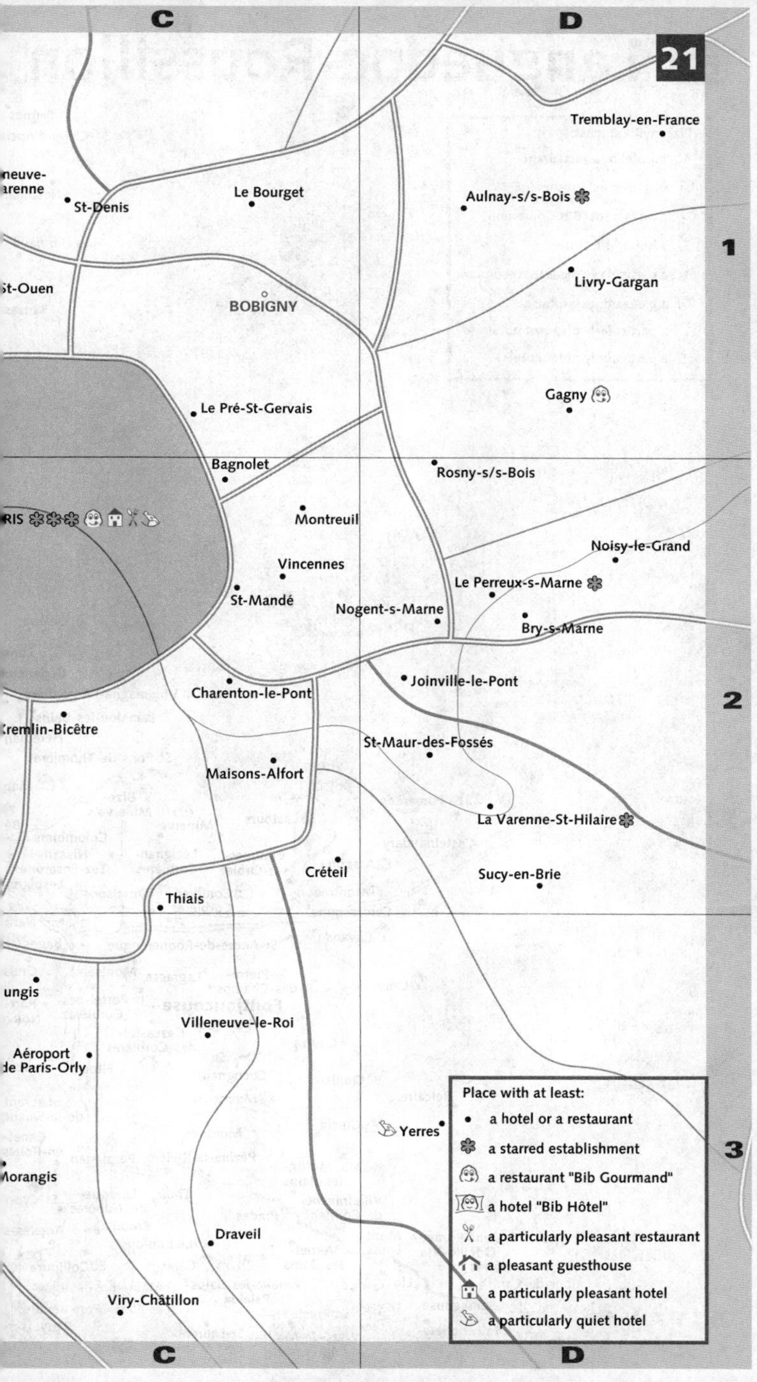
C
D
21
Tremblay-en-France
neuve-
arenne
Le Bourget
Aulnay-s/s-Bois
St-Denis
1
Livry-Gargan
St-Ouen
BOBIGNY
Gagny
Le Pré-St-Gervais
Bagnolet
Rosny-s/s-Bois
RIS
Montreuil
Noisy-le-Grand
Vincennes
Le Perreux-s-Marne
St-Mandé
Nogent-s-Marne
Bry-s-Marne
Joinville-le-Pont
Charenton-le-Pont
2
Kremlin-Bicêtre
St-Maur-des-Fossés
Maisons-Alfort
La Varenne-St-Hilaire
Créteil
Sucy-en-Brie
Thiais
ungis
Villeneuve-le-Roi
Aéroport
de Paris-Orly
Place with at least:
a hotel or a restaurant
a starred establishment
Yerres
3
a restaurant "Bib Gourmand"
Morangis
a hotel "Bib Hôtel"
a particularly pleasant restaurant
Draveil
a pleasant guesthouse
a particularly pleasant hotel
Viry-Châtillon
a particularly quiet hotel
C
D

22 Languedoc-Roussillon

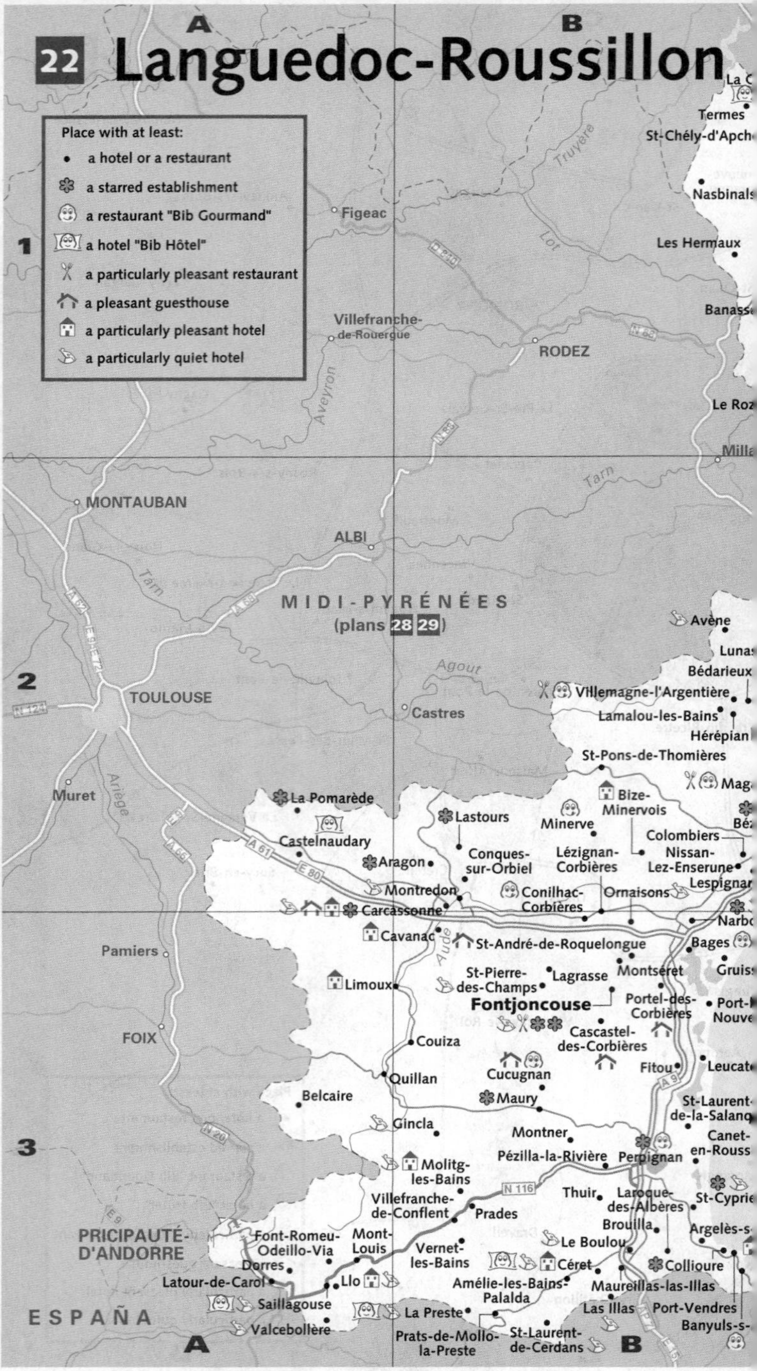

Place with at least:
- a hotel or a restaurant
- a starred establishment
- a restaurant "Bib Gourmand"
- a hotel "Bib Hôtel"
- a particularly pleasant restaurant
- a pleasant guesthouse
- a particularly pleasant hotel
- a particularly quiet hotel

A B 1 2 3

Figeac, Villefranche-de-Rouergue, RODEZ, Termes, St-Chély-d'Apch…, Nasbinals, Les Hermaux, Banass…, Le Roz…, Milla…, MONTAUBAN, ALBI, MIDI-PYRÉNÉES (plans 28 29), TOULOUSE, Castres, Muret, Avène, Lunas, Bédarieux, Villemagne-l'Argentière, Lamalou-les-Bains, Hérépian, St-Pons-de-Thomières, Mag…, La Pomarède, Bize-Minervois, Lastours, Minerve, Castelnaudary, Colombiers, Conques-sur-Orbiel, Lézignan-Corbières, Nissan-Lez-Enserune, Aragon, Lespignan, Montredon, Conilhac-Corbières, Ornaisons, Carcassonne, Narbo…, Cavanac, St-André-de-Roquelongue, Bages, Pamiers, Montséret, Gruiss…, St-Pierre-des-Champs, Lagrasse, Limoux, Portel-des-Corbières, Port-Nouve…, Fontjoncouse, Cascastel-des-Corbières, FOIX, Couiza, Fitou, Leucate, Quillan, Cucugnan, Belcaire, Maury, St-Laurent-de-la-Salanq…, Gincla, Montner, Canet-en-Rouss…, Molitg-les-Bains, Pézilla-la-Rivière, Perpignan, Villefranche-de-Conflent, Prades, Thuir, Laroque-des-Albères, St-Cyprie…, Brouilla, Argelès-s…, PRICIPAUTÉ-D'ANDORRE, Font-Romeu-Odeillo-Via, Mont-Louis, Vernet-les-Bains, Le Boulou, Dorres, Céret, Collioure, Latour-de-Carol, Llo, Amélie-les-Bains-Palalda, Maureillas-las-Illas, Saillagouse, Las Illas, Port-Vendres, ESPAÑA, Valcebollère, La Preste, Prats-de-Mollo-la-Preste, St-Laurent-de-Cerdans, Banyuls-s-…

Truyère, Lot, Aveyron, Tarn, Agout, Ariège, Aude, N 88, N 124, A 62, A 61, A 66, A 68, E 80, E 9, N 20, N 116, A 9

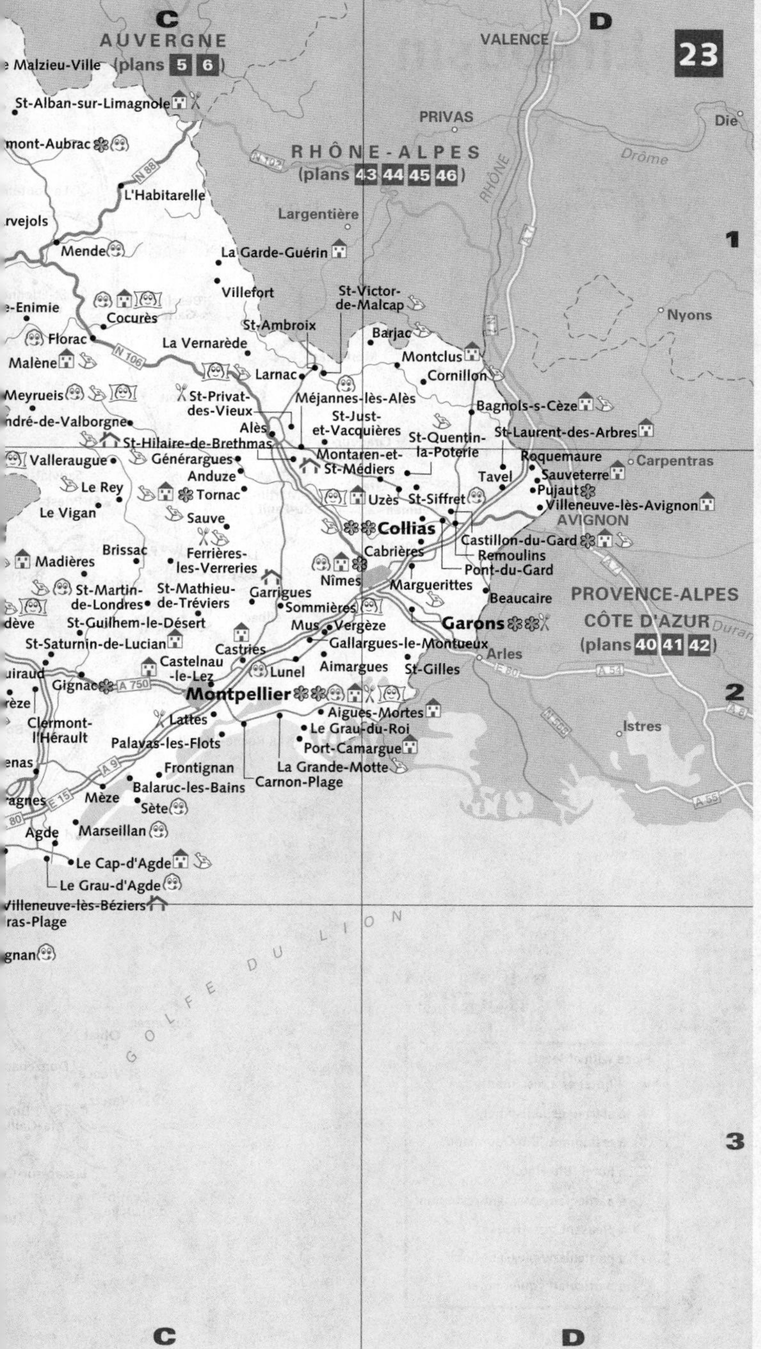
C
D
AUVERGNE
(plans 5 6)
VALENCE
Malzieu-Ville
St-Alban-sur-Limagnole
PRIVAS
Die
mont-Aubrac
RHÔNE-ALPES
(plans 43 44 45 46)
Drôme
RHÔNE
L'Habitarelle
Largentière
rvejols
1
Mende
La Garde-Guérin
Villefort
St-Victor-de-Malcap
e-Enimie
Cocurès
Nyons
Florac
St-Ambroix
Barjac
La Vernarède
Montclus
Malène
Larnac
Cornillon
Méjannes-lès-Alès
Meyrueis
St-Privat-des-Vieux
Bagnols-s-Cèze
St-Just-et-Vacquières
ndré-de-Valborgne
Alès
St-Quentin-la-Poterie
St-Laurent-des-Arbres
St-Hilaire-de-Brethmas
Roquemaure
Carpentras
Valleraugue
Générargues
Montaren-et-St-Médiers
Anduze
Tavel
Sauveterre
Le Rey
Pujaut
Tornac
Uzès
St-Siffret
Villeneuve-lès-Avignon
Le Vigan
AVIGNON
Sauve
Collias
Castillon-du-Gard
Brissac
Ferrières-les-Verreries
Cabrières
Remoulins
Madières
Pont-du-Gard
Nîmes
Marguerittes
St-Martin-de-Londres
St-Mathieu-de-Tréviers
Garrigues
Beaucaire
PROVENCE-ALPES
CÔTE D'AZUR
(plans 40 41 42)
Sommières
dève
St-Guilhem-le-Désert
Mus
Vergèze
Garons
St-Saturnin-de-Lucian
Gallargues-le-Montueux
Arles
Castries
Castelnau-le-Lez
Aimargues
St-Gilles
Lunel
iraud
Gignac
Montpellier
2
rèze
Aigues-Mortes
Lattes
Le Grau-du-Roi
Istres
Clermont-l'Hérault
Palavas-les-Flots
Port-Camargue
enas
Frontignan
La Grande-Motte
Carnon-Plage
Balaruc-les-Bains
agnes
Mèze
Sète
Agde
Marseillan
Le Cap-d'Agde
Le Grau-d'Agde
Villeneuve-lès-Béziers
ras-Plage
gnan
GOLFE DU LION
3
C
D

24 Limousin

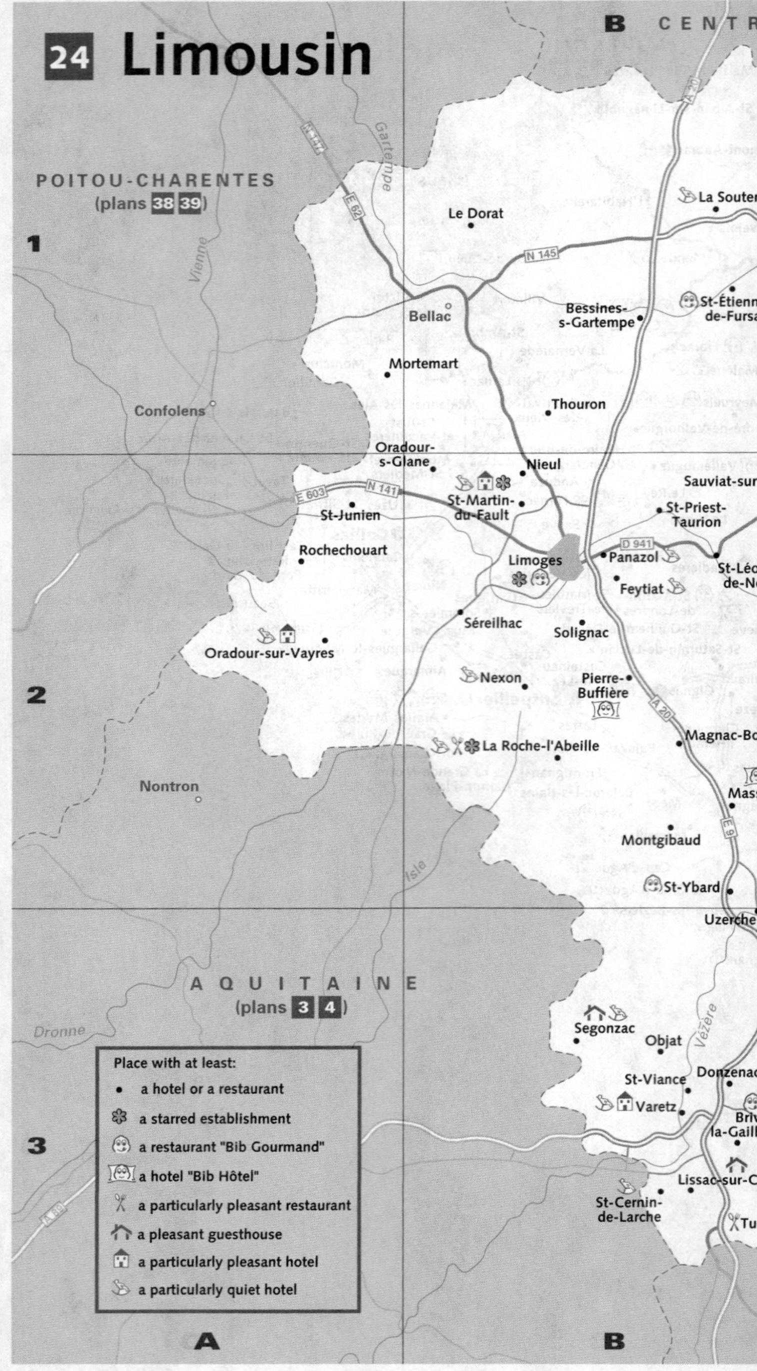

B CENTR
POITOU-CHARENTES
(plans 38 39)
1
2
3
Le Dorat
La Souter
N 145
E 62
N 141
E 603
D 941
A 20
A 89
E 9
Gartempe
Vienne
Isle
Vézère
Dronne
Bellac
Bessines-s-Gartempe
St-Étienn de-Fursa
Mortemart
Confolens
Thouron
Oradour-s-Glane
Nieul
Sauviat-sur-
St-Martin-du-Fault
St-Priest-Taurion
St-Junien
Rochechouart
Limoges
Panazol
St-Léo de-No
Feytiat
Séreilhac
Solignac
Oradour-sur-Vayres
Nexon
Pierre-Buffière
La Roche-l'Abeille
Magnac-Bo
Nontron
Mass
Montgibaud
St-Ybard
Uzerche
AQUITAINE
(plans 3 4)
Segonzac
Objat
Donzenac
St-Viance
Varetz
Briv la-Gaill
Lissac-sur-C
St-Cernin-de-Larche
Tu
Place with at least:
a hotel or a restaurant
a starred establishment
a restaurant "Bib Gourmand"
a hotel "Bib Hôtel"
a particularly pleasant restaurant
a pleasant guesthouse
a particularly pleasant hotel
a particularly quiet hotel
A
B

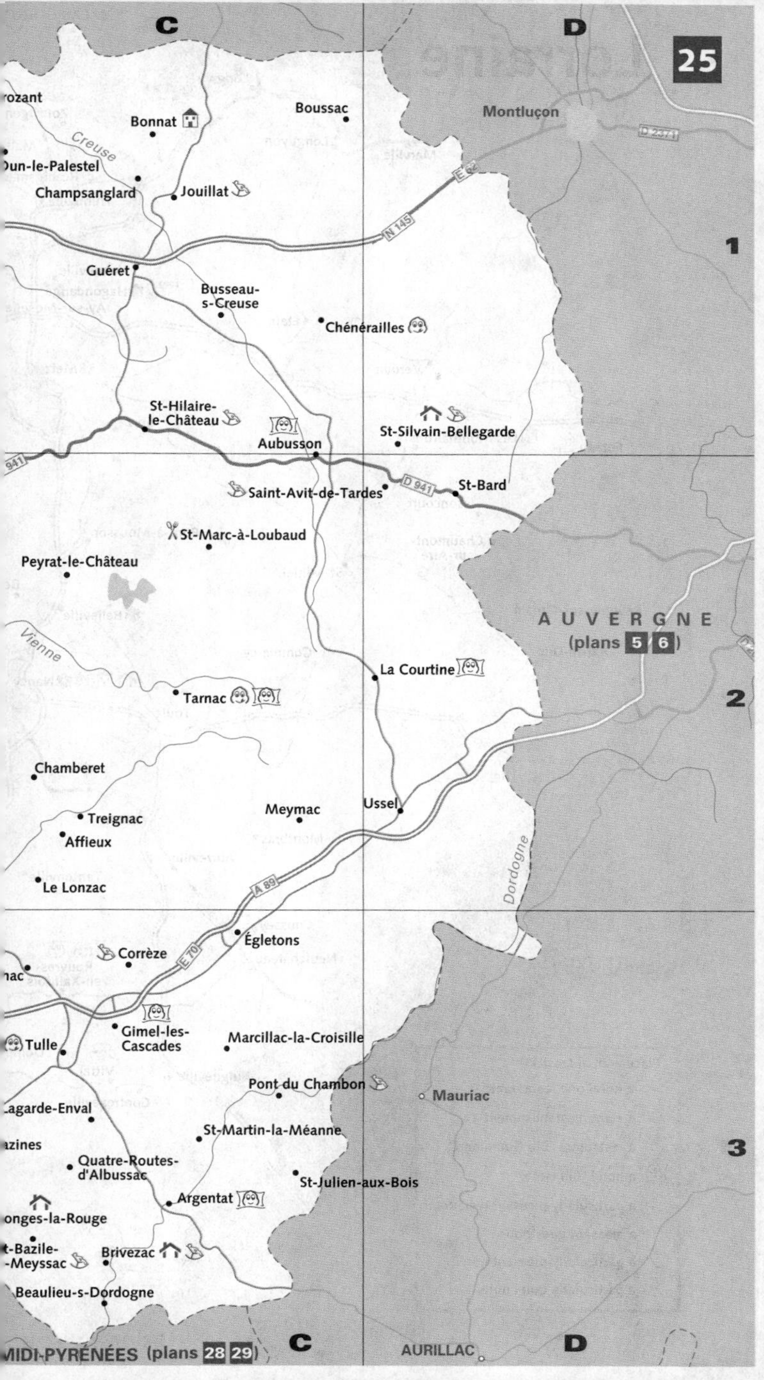
C
D
25
Montluçon
D 2071
Boussac
Bonnat
Crozant
Creuse
Dun-le-Palestel
Champsanglard
Jouillat
E 62
N 145
1
Guéret
Busseau-
s-Creuse
Chénérailles
St-Hilaire-
le-Château
Aubusson
St-Silvain-Bellegarde
941
D 941
Saint-Avit-de-Tardes
St-Bard
St-Marc-à-Loubaud
Peyrat-le-Château
AUVERGNE
(plans 5 6)
Vienne
La Courtine
Tarnac
2
Chamberet
Ussel
Meymac
Treignac
Affieux
Dordogne
Le Lonzac
A 89
Égletons
Corrèze
E 70
Gimel-les-
Cascades
Marcillac-la-Croisille
Tulle
Pont du Chambon
Mauriac
Lagarde-Enval
St-Martin-la-Méanne
3
Quatre-Routes-
d'Albussac
St-Julien-aux-Bois
Argentat
Collonges-la-Rouge
St-Bazile-
-Meyssac
Brivezac
Beaulieu-s-Dordogne
MIDI-PYRÉNÉES (plans 28 29)
C
AURILLAC
D

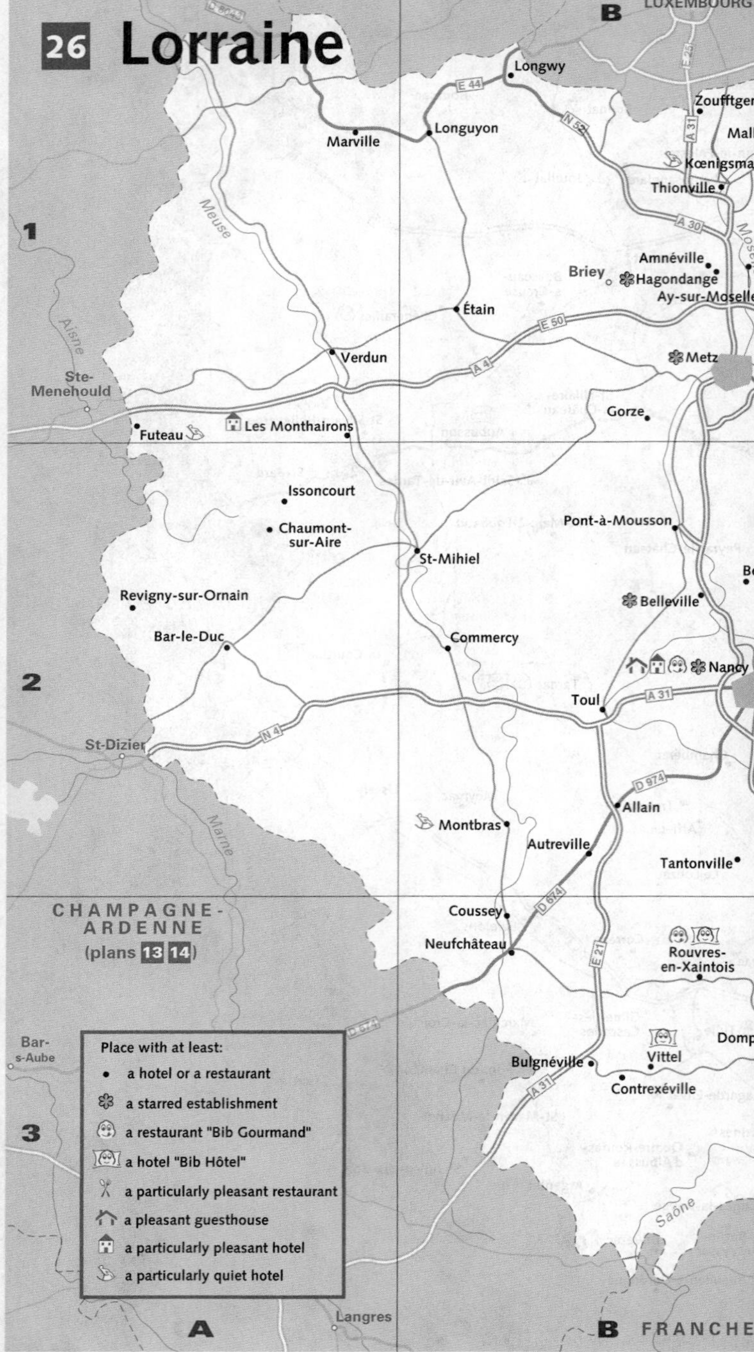
26 Lorraine
LUXEMBOURG
Longwy
Zoufftgen
Longuyon
Marville
Kœnigsmacker
Thionville
Moselle
Meuse
Amnéville
Briey
Hagondange
Ay-sur-Moselle
Étain
Aisne
Verdun
Metz
Ste-Menehould
Gorze
Futeau
Les Monthairons
Issoncourt
Chaumont-sur-Aire
Pont-à-Mousson
St-Mihiel
Revigny-sur-Ornain
Belleville
Bar-le-Duc
Commercy
Nancy
Toul
St-Dizier
Marne
Allain
Montbras
Autreville
Tantonville
CHAMPAGNE-ARDENNE
(plans 13 14)
Coussey
Neufchâteau
Rouvres-en-Xaintois
Bar-s-Aube
Vittel
Bulgnéville
Contrexéville
Saône
Langres
FRANCHE
E 44
N 52
A 31
A 30
E 50
A 4
A 31
N 4
D 974
D 674
E 21
D 674
A 31
E 25
A
B
1
2
3
Place with at least:
a hotel or a restaurant
a starred establishment
a restaurant "Bib Gourmand"
a hotel "Bib Hôtel"
a particularly pleasant restaurant
a pleasant guesthouse
a particularly pleasant hotel
a particularly quiet hotel

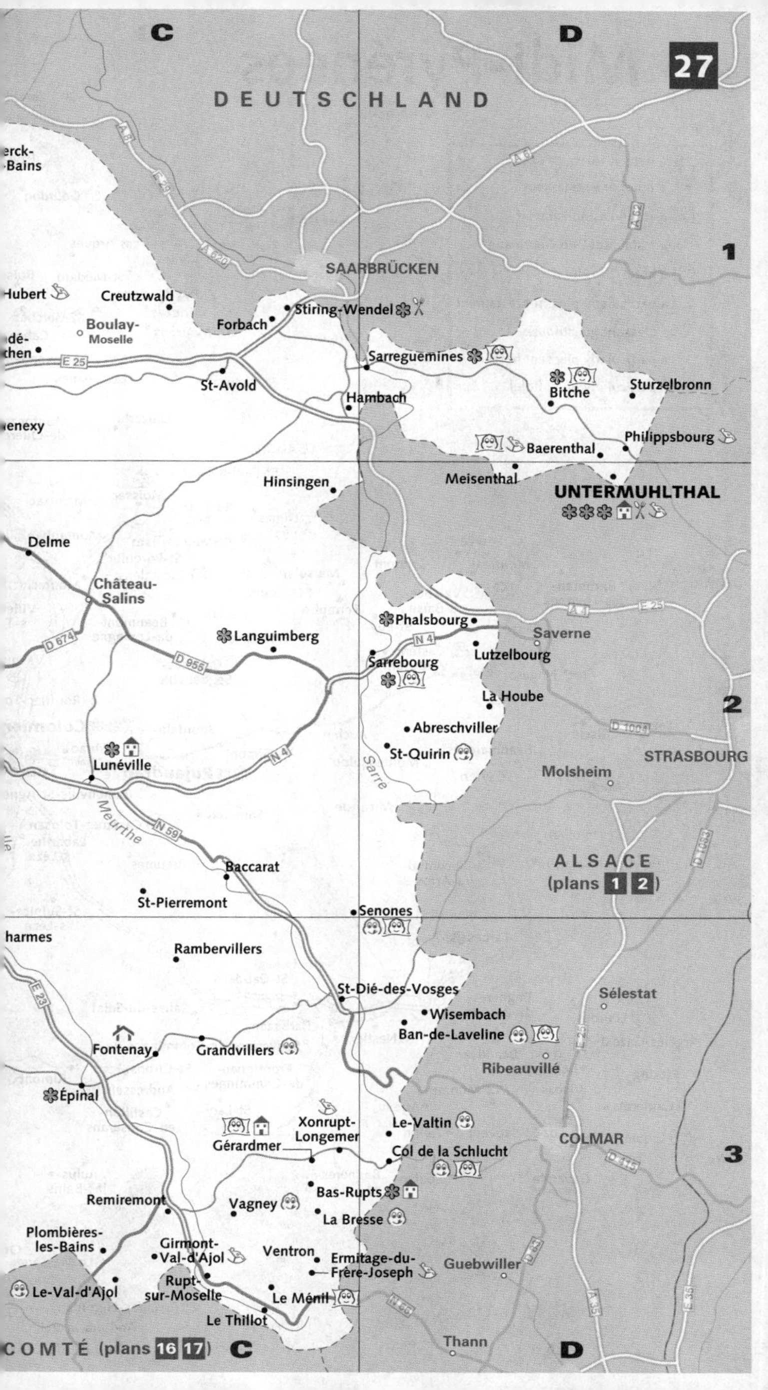

C
D
27
DEUTSCHLAND
erck-
-Bains
SAARBRÜCKEN
1
Hubert
Creutzwald
Stiring-Wendel
Boulay-
Moselle
Forbach
dé-
chen
E 25
Sarreguemines
St-Avold
Bitche
Sturzelbronn
Hambach
enexy
Baerenthal
Philippsbourg
Meisenthal
Hinsingen
UNTERMUHLTHAL
Delme
Château-
Salins
Phalsbourg
A 4
E 25
Saverne
D 674
Languimberg
N 4
D 955
Sarrebourg
Lutzelbourg
La Hoube
2
D 1004
Abreschviller
St-Quirin
STRASBOURG
Lunéville
N 4
Sarre
Molsheim
Meurthe
N 59
ALSACE
(plans 1 2)
Baccarat
St-Pierremont
Senones
harmes
Rambervillers
E 23
St-Dié-des-Vosges
Sélestat
Wisembach
Ban-de-Laveline
E 25
Fontenay
Grandvillers
Ribeauvillé
Épinal
Xonrupt-
Longemer
Le-Valtin
Gérardmer
COLMAR
Col de la Schlucht
3
D 415
Bas-Rupts
Remiremont
Vagney
La Bresse
Plombières-
les-Bains
Girmont-
Val-d'Ajol
Ventron
Ermitage-du-
Frère-Joseph
Guebwiller
Rupt-
sur-Moselle
Le-Val-d'Ajol
Le Ménil
Le Thillot
Thann
COMTÉ (plans 16 17)
C
D

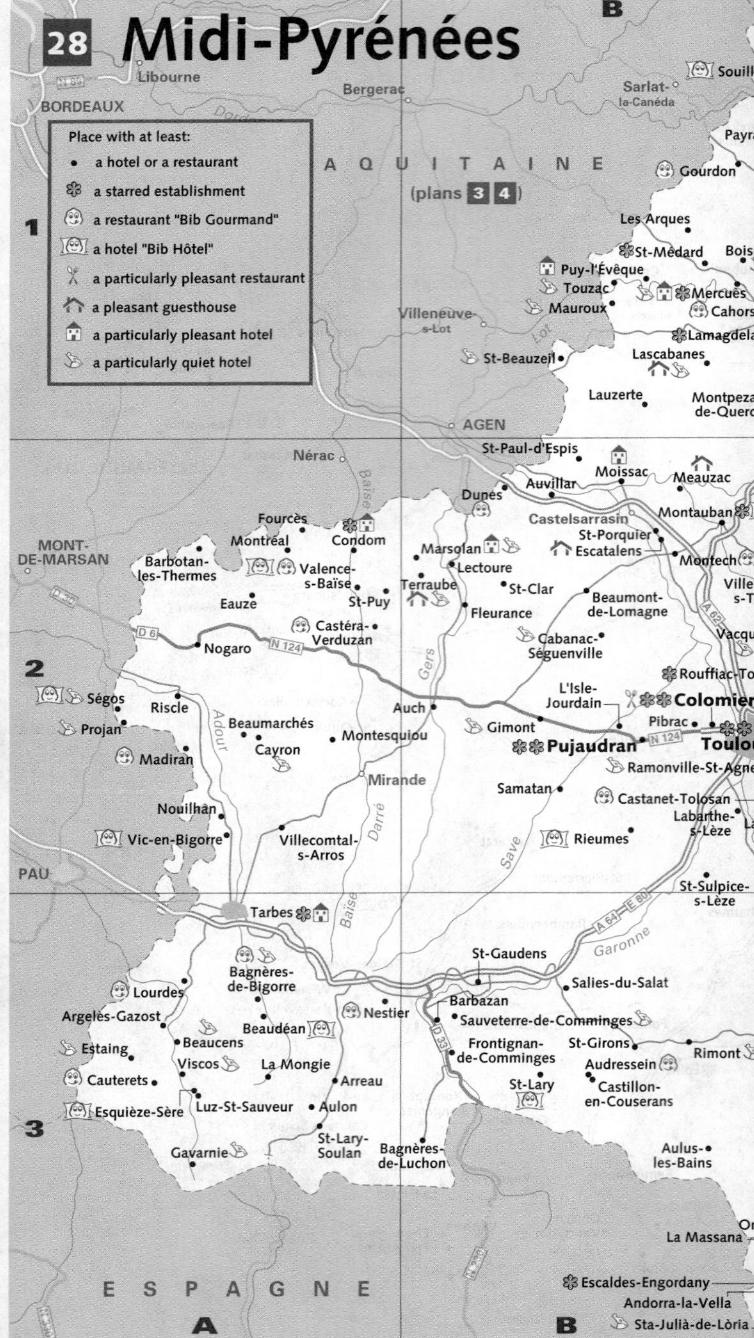
28
Midi-Pyrénées
Place with at least:
a hotel or a restaurant
a starred establishment
a restaurant "Bib Gourmand"
a hotel "Bib Hôtel"
a particularly pleasant restaurant
a pleasant guesthouse
a particularly pleasant hotel
a particularly quiet hotel
AQUITAINE
(plans 3 4)
ESPAGNE
Libourne
BORDEAUX
Bergerac
Sarlat-la-Canéda
Souilla
Payra
Gourdon
Les Arques
St-Médard
Boiss
Puy-l'Évêque
Touzac
Mercuès
Mauroux
Cahors
Villeneuve-s-Lot
Lamagdela
St-Beauzeil
Lascabanes
Lauzerte
Montpeza de-Quercy
AGEN
Nérac
St-Paul-d'Espis
Moissac
Meauzac
Auvillar
Dunes
Castelsarrasin
Montauban
Fourcès
Montréal
Condom
St-Porquier
Escatalens
Marsolan
Lectoure
Montech
MONT-DE-MARSAN
Barbotan-les-Thermes
Valence-s-Baïse
Terraube
St-Clar
Beaumont-de-Lomagne
Eauze
St-Puy
Fleurance
Castéra-Verduzan
Cabanac-Séguenville
Nogaro
Ségos
Riscle
L'Isle-Jourdain
Rouffiac-To
Colomiers
Projan
Beaumarchés
Auch
Gimont
Pibrac
Toulou
Madiran
Cayron
Montesquiou
Pujaudran
Ramonville-St-Agne
Mirande
Samatan
Castanet-Tolosan
Nouilhan
Labarthe-s-Lèze
Vic-en-Bigorre
Villecomtal-s-Arros
Rieumes
PAU
St-Sulpice-s-Lèze
Tarbes
St-Gaudens
Garonne
Bagnères-de-Bigorre
Salies-du-Salat
Lourdes
Barbazan
Argelès-Gazost
Nestier
Sauveterre-de-Comminges
Beaudéan
Estaing
Beaucens
Frontignan-de-Comminges
St-Girons
Rimont
Viscos
La Mongie
Audressein
Cauterets
Arreau
St-Lary
Castillon-en-Couserans
Esquièze-Sère
Luz-St-Sauveur
Aulon
St-Lary-Soulan
Gavarnie
Bagnères-de-Luchon
Aulus-les-Bains
La Massana
Escaldes-Engordany
Andorra-la-Vella
Sta-Julià-de-Lòria
Adour
Baïse
Gers
Save
Darré
Lot
N 89
D 30
D 6
N 124
A 62
A 64
E 80
D 33
N 230
1
2
3
A
B

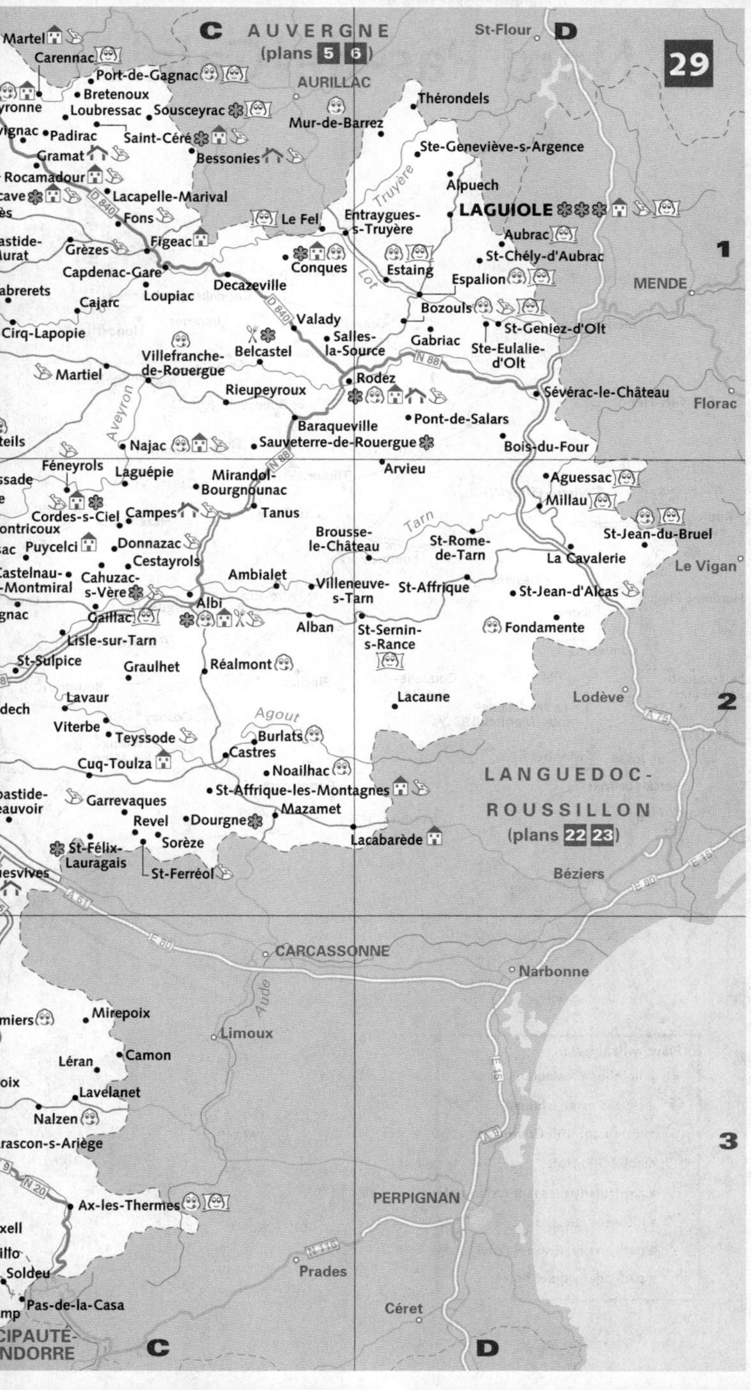

29
C
D
AUVERGNE
(plans 5 6)
AURILLAC
St-Flour
Martel
Carennac
Port-de-Gagnac
Bretenoux
Loubressac
Sousceyrac
Padirac
Saint-Céré
Gramat
Bessonies
Rocamadour
Lacapelle-Marival
Fons
Figeac
Grèzes
Capdenac-Gare
Loupiac
Cajarc
Cirq-Lapopie
Martiel
Villefranche-de-Rouergue
Thérondels
Mur-de-Barrez
Ste-Geneviève-s-Argence
Alpuech
LAGUIOLE
Aubrac
St-Chély-d'Aubrac
Le Fel
Entraygues-s-Truyère
Conques
Estaing
Espalion
Decazeville
Bozouls
Valady
Salles-la-Source
Gabriac
St-Geniez-d'Olt
Ste-Eulalie-d'Olt
Belcastel
Rodez
Rieupeyroux
Baraqueville
Pont-de-Salars
Sévérac-le-Château
Bois-du-Four
Najac
Sauveterre-de-Rouergue
Arvieu
MENDE
Florac
1
Truyère
Lot
Aveyron
D 840
N 88
Féneyrols
Laguépie
Mirandol-Bourgnounac
Tanus
Cordes-s-Ciel
Campes
Puycelci
Donnazac
Cestayrols
Cahuzac-s-Vère
Ambialet
Albi
Gaillac
Lisle-sur-Tarn
St-Sulpice
Graulhet
Réalmont
Lavaur
Viterbe
Teyssode
Burlats
Castres
Cuq-Toulza
Noailhac
St-Affrique-les-Montagnes
Garrevaques
Revel
Dourgne
Mazamet
Sorèze
St-Félix-Lauragais
St-Ferréol
Brousse-le-Château
St-Rome-de-Tarn
Villeneuve-s-Tarn
St-Affrique
Alban
St-Sernin-s-Rance
Lacaune
Lacabarède
Aguessac
Millau
St-Jean-du-Bruel
La Cavalerie
Le Vigan
St-Jean-d'Alcas
Fondamente
Lodève
Tarn
Agout
2
LANGUEDOC-ROUSSILLON
(plans 22 23)
Béziers
A 75
A 61
E 80
E 15
CARCASSONNE
Narbonne
Aude
Mirepoix
Limoux
Camon
Léran
Lavelanet
Nalzen
Ax-les-Thermes
Soldeu
Pas-de-la-Casa
N 20
N 116
A 9
PERPIGNAN
Prades
Céret
3
C
D

30 Nord Pas-de-Calais

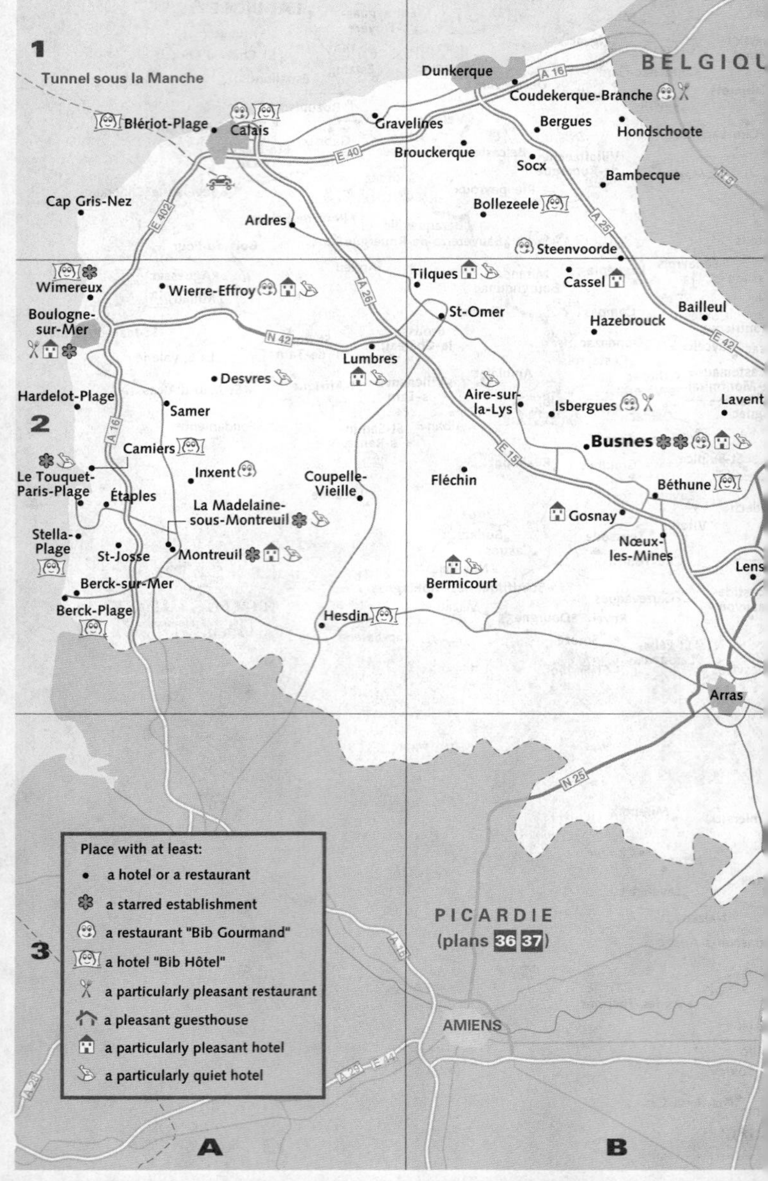

1
Tunnel sous la Manche
Dunkerque
Coudekerque-Branche
BELGIQU
Bleriot-Plage
Calais
Gravelines
Bergues
Hondschoote
Brouckerque
Socx
Bambecque
Cap Gris-Nez
Bollezeele
Ardres
Steenvoorde
Tilques
Cassel
Wimereux
Wierre-Effroy
Boulogne-sur-Mer
St-Omer
Bailleul
Hazebrouck
Lumbres
Desvres
Hardelot-Plage
Samer
Aire-sur-la-Lys
Isbergues
Lavent
2
Camiers
Busnes
Le Touquet-Paris-Plage
Inxent
Coupelle-Vieille
Fléchin
Béthune
Étaples
La Madelaine-sous-Montreuil
Gosnay
Stella-Plage
St-Josse
Montreuil
Nœux-les-Mines
Lens
Bermicourt
Berck-sur-Mer
Berck-Plage
Hesdin
Arras
Place with at least:
a hotel or a restaurant
a starred establishment
a restaurant "Bib Gourmand"
a hotel "Bib Hôtel"
a particularly pleasant restaurant
a pleasant guesthouse
a particularly pleasant hotel
a particularly quiet hotel
PICARDIE
(plans 36 37)
3
AMIENS
A
B
A 16
E 40
E 402
A 26
N 42
A 25
E 42
E 15
N 25
A 28
E 44

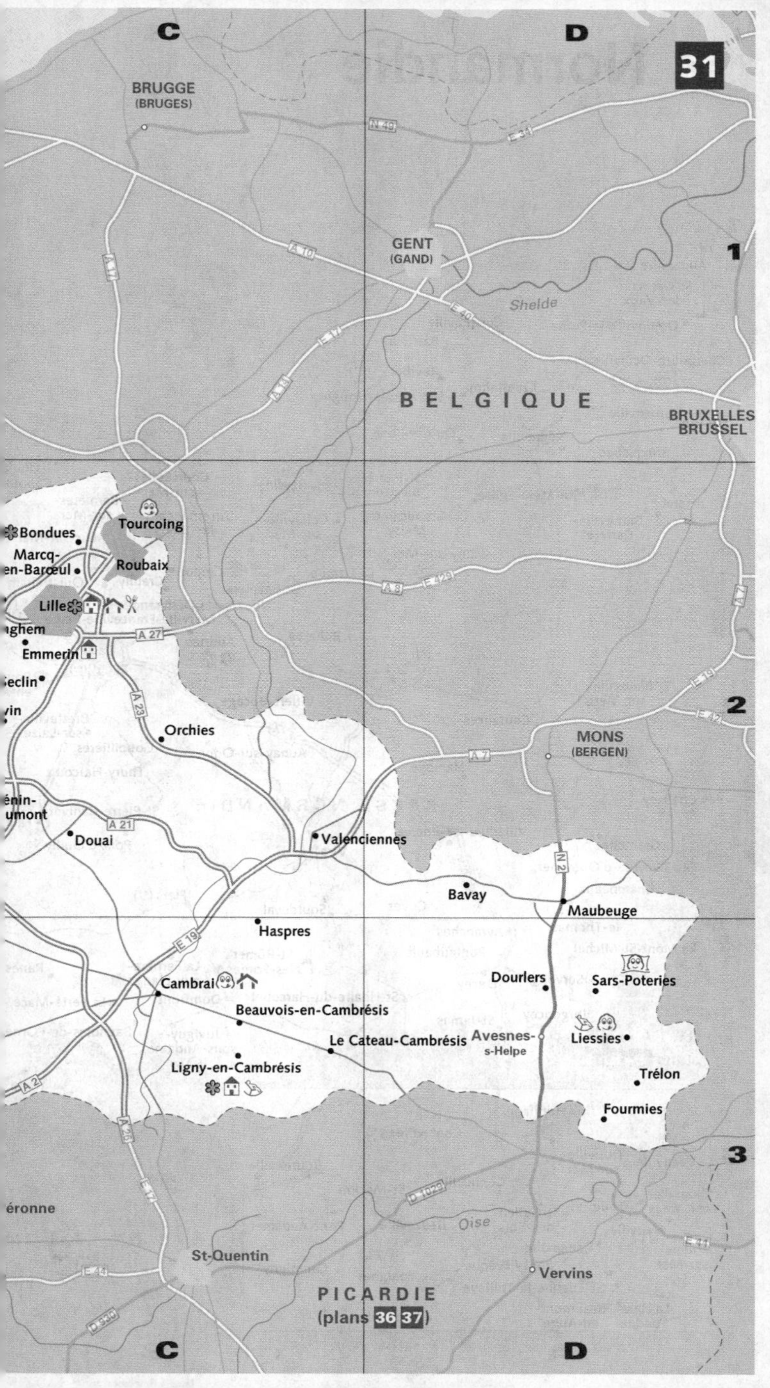
31
C
D
BRUGGE
(BRUGES)
N 49
E 31
A 17
A 10
GENT
(GAND)
1
Shelde
E 40
E 17
A 14
BELGIQUE
BRUXELLES
BRUSSEL
Tourcoing
Bondues
Marcq-en-Barœul
Roubaix
A 8
E 429
A 7
Lille
ghem
A 27
Emmerin
eclin
E 19
yin
2
A 23
E 42
MONS
(BERGEN)
Orchies
A 7
énin-umont
A 21
Douai
Valenciennes
N 2
Bavay
Maubeuge
Haspres
E 19
Cambrai
Dourlers
Sars-Poteries
Beauvois-en-Cambrésis
Le Cateau-Cambrésis
Avesnes-s-Helpe
Liessies
Ligny-en-Cambrésis
Trélon
A 2
Fourmies
A 26
3
E 17
D 1029
éronne
Oise
E 41
St-Quentin
E 44
Vervins
PICARDIE
(plans 36 37)
D 930
C
D

32 Normandie

MANCHE

A B

1 2 3

Auderville
St-Germain-des-Vaux
Omonville-la-Petite
Cosqueville
Barfleur
Cherbourg-Octeville
Réville
Quettehou
St-Vaast-la-Hougue
Flamanville
Quinéville
Négreville
Bricquebec
Carteret
Ste-Mère-Église
Barneville-Carteret
St-Pierre-du-Mont
Grandcamp-Maisy
Port-en-Bessin
Colleville-sur-Mer
Courseulles-sur-Mer
Bernières-sur-Mer
Arromanches-les-Bains
Luc-sur-Mer
Houlgate
Cabourg
Isigny-sur-Mer
La Cambe
Crépon
Creully
Ouistreham
Bayeux
Douvres-la-Délivrande
Merville-Franceville-Plage
Dives-sur-Mer
Balleroy
Audrieu
Caen
St-Lô
Beuvron-en-Auge
Blainville-sur-Mer
Villers-Bocage
Coutances
Bretteville-sur-Laize
Vire
Aunay-sur-Odon
Goupillières
Thury-Harcourt
Hambye
Îles Chausey
BASSE NORMANDIE
St-Pierre-Canivet
Villedieu-les-Poêles
Falaise
Granville
Vire
Pont-d'Ouilly
La Lucerne-d'Outremer
Orne
Champeaux
Cuves
Flers
St-Jean-le-Thomas
Sourdeval
Avranches
Le Mont-St-Michel
Pontaubault
St-Bômer-les-Forges
La Ferrière-aux-Étangs
Rânes
Servon
Ducey
St-Hilaire-du-Harcouët
Domfront
La Ferté-Macé
Vergoncey
St-James
Juvigny-sous-Andaine
Bagnoles-de-l'Orne
BRETAGNE
(plans 9 10)
Lalacelle
Mayenne
PAYS DE LA LOIRE
(plans 34 35)

N 13, E 3, E 46, N 174, E 401, A 84, N 175, N 176, A 84, D 658, D 137, A 81, D 57

Honfleur
Conteville
Deauville
Trouville-sur-Mer
Bourneville
Blonville-sur-Mer
Genneville
St-Maclou
Touques
St-Gatien-des-Bois
Vauville
Beuzeville
Pont-Audemer
Villers-sur-Mer
Canapville
Pont-l'Évêque
Épaignes
Campigny
St-Étienne-la-Thillaye
La Haie Tondue
Beaumont-en-Auge
Cormeilles

A 29, A 13, E 50, N 29

A B

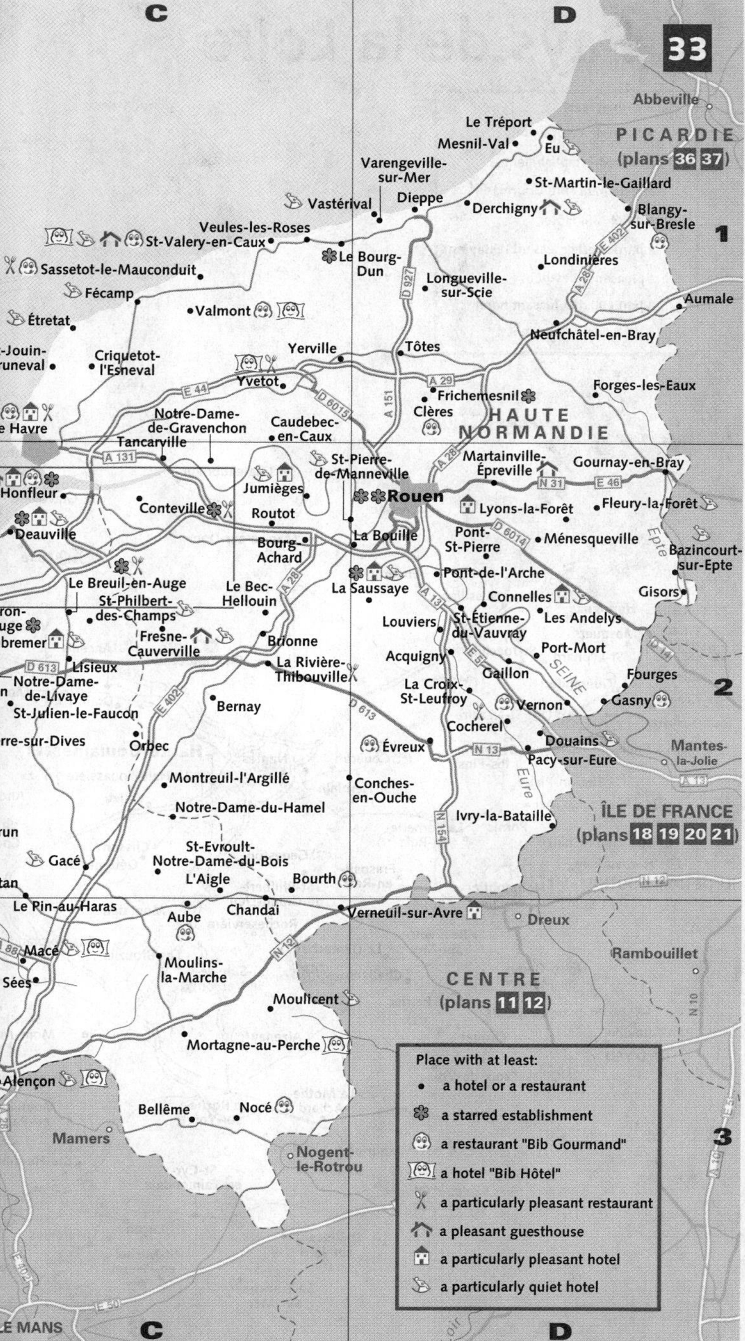
C
D
Abbeville
Le Tréport
Mesnil-Val
Eu
PICARDIE
(plans 36 37)
Varengeville-sur-Mer
St-Martin-le-Gaillard
Vastérival
Dieppe
Derchigny
Blangy-sur-Bresle
1
Veules-les-Roses
St-Valery-en-Caux
Le Bourg-Dun
Londinières
Sassetot-le-Mauconduit
Longueville-sur-Scie
Fécamp
Aumale
Valmont
Étretat
Neufchâtel-en-Bray
Criquetot-l'Esneval
Yerville
Tôtes
Yvetot
Frichemesnil
Forges-les-Eaux
Clères
Notre-Dame-de-Gravenchon
Caudebec-en-Caux
HAUTE NORMANDIE
Tancarville
St-Pierre-de-Manneville
Martainville-Épreville
Gournay-en-Bray
Jumièges
Honfleur
Rouen
Conteville
Lyons-la-Forêt
Fleury-la-Forêt
Routot
Deauville
La Bouille
Pont-St-Pierre
Ménesqueville
Bourg-Achard
Bazincourt-sur-Epte
Pont-de-l'Arche
Le Breuil-en-Auge
Le Bec-Hellouin
La Saussaye
Gisors
Connelles
St-Philbert-des-Champs
Louviers
St-Étienne-du-Vauvray
Les Andelys
Fresne-Cauverville
Brionne
Acquigny
Port-Mort
Lisieux
La Rivière-Thibouville
Gaillon
Notre-Dame-de-Livaye
La Croix-St-Leufroy
Fourges
St-Julien-le-Faucon
Bernay
Gasny
2
Vernon
Cocherel
Orbec
Évreux
Douains
Pacy-sur-Eure
Mantes-la-Jolie
Montreuil-l'Argillé
Conches-en-Ouche
Notre-Dame-du-Hamel
Ivry-la-Bataille
ÎLE DE FRANCE
(plans 18 19 20 21)
St-Evroult-Notre-Dame-du-Bois
Gacé
L'Aigle
Bourth
Le Pin-au-Haras
Chandai
Verneuil-sur-Avre
Aube
Dreux
Macé
Moulins-la-Marche
Rambouillet
Sées
CENTRE
(plans 11 12)
Moulicent
Mortagne-au-Perche
Alençon
Noce
Bellême
Mamers
Nogent-le-Rotrou
3
LE MANS
SEINE
Eure
Epte
Loir
Place with at least:
a hotel or a restaurant
a starred establishment
a restaurant "Bib Gourmand"
a hotel "Bib Hôtel"
a particularly pleasant restaurant
a pleasant guesthouse
a particularly pleasant hotel
a particularly quiet hotel

34 Pays de la Loire

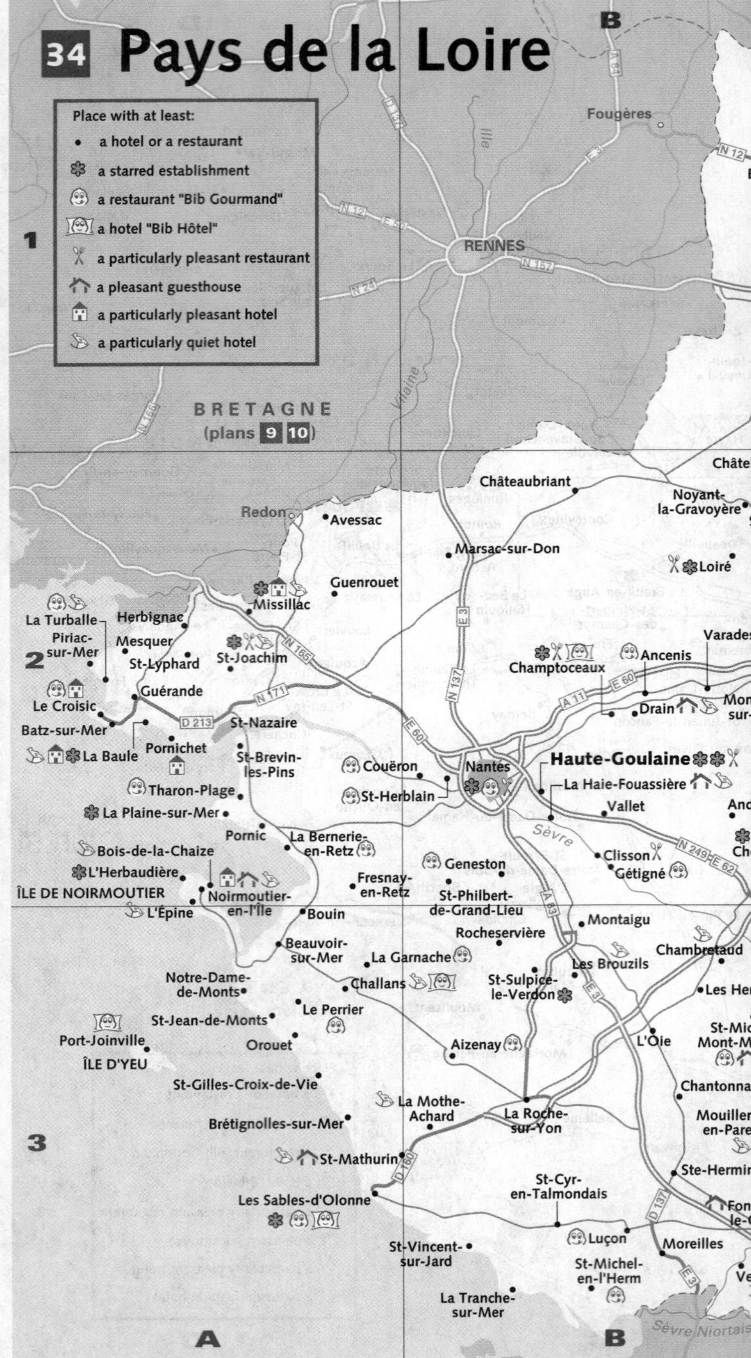

Place with at least:
a hotel or a restaurant
a starred establishment
a restaurant "Bib Gourmand"
a hotel "Bib Hôtel"
a particularly pleasant restaurant
a pleasant guesthouse
a particularly pleasant hotel
a particularly quiet hotel
BRETAGNE
(plans 9 10)
A
B
1
2
3
Fougères
RENNES
Châteaubriant
Noyant-la-Gravoyère
Redon
Avessac
Marsac-sur-Don
Loiré
Guenrouet
Missillac
La Turballe
Herbignac
Piriac-sur-Mer
Mesquer
St-Lyphard
St-Joachim
Guérande
Le Croisic
Batz-sur-Mer
La Baule
Pornichet
St-Nazaire
St-Brevin-les-Pins
Champtoceaux
Ancenis
Varades
Drain
Couëron
Nantes
Haute-Goulaine
La Haie-Fouassière
St-Herblain
Vallet
Tharon-Plage
La Plaine-sur-Mer
Pornic
La Bernerie-en-Retz
Bois-de-la-Chaize
L'Herbaudière
ÎLE DE NOIRMOUTIER
Noirmoutier-en-l'Île
L'Épine
Geneston
Clisson
Gétigné
Fresnay-en-Retz
St-Philbert-de-Grand-Lieu
Bouin
Montaigu
Rocheservière
Beauvoir-sur-Mer
La Garnache
Les Brouzils
Chambretaud
Notre-Dame-de-Monts
Challans
St-Sulpice-le-Verdon
Le Perrier
St-Jean-de-Monts
Port-Joinville
ÎLE D'YEU
Orouet
Aizenay
L'Oie
St-Gilles-Croix-de-Vie
La Mothe-Achard
La Roche-sur-Yon
Chantonnay
Brétignolles-sur-Mer
St-Mathurin
Ste-Hermine
Les Sables-d'Olonne
St-Cyr-en-Talmondais
Luçon
Moreilles
St-Vincent-sur-Jard
St-Michel-en-l'Herm
La Tranche-sur-Mer
Sèvre
Sèvre Niortaise
Vilaine
Ille
N 12
E 50
N 24
N 157
N 165
N 171
D 213
E 60
N 137
A 11
A 83
E 3
N 249
E 62
D 160
D 137
A 84
D 137

C
D
BASSE NORMANDIE
(plans 32 33)
Mortagne-au-Perche
ALENÇON
St-Paterne
Neufchâtel-en-Saosnois
Villaines-la-Juhel
Mayenne
Nogent-le-Rotrou
Monhoudou
Sillé-le-Guillaume
Évron
La Ferté-Bernard
1
Domfront-en-Champagne
St-Symphorien
St-Saturnin
Sceaux-sur-Huisne
Vaiges
Thorigné-sur-Dué
Champagné
Saulges
Le Mans
Brûlon
Ruillé-Froid-Fonds
Grez-en-Bouère
Sarthe
Guécélard
St-Calais
Sablé-sur-Sarthe
Coudray
Malicorne-sur-Sarthe
Vendôme
Notre-Dame-du-Pé
La Chartre-sur-le-Loir
Mayenne
La Flèche
Luché-Pringé
Champigné
Loir
Château-du-Loir
Vaas
Tiercé
Le Lude
CENTRE
(plans 11 12)
Briollay
Angers
Mouliherne
St-Georges-des-Sept-Voies
LOIRE
Linières-Bouton
La Ménitré
Brissac-Quincé
Les Rosiers-sur-Loire
TOURS
2
St-Martin-de-la-Place
Vauchrétien
Gennes
Vivy
Chênehutte-les-Tuffeaux
Thouarcé
Saumur
Martigné-Briand
Montsoreau
Turquant
Doué-la-Fontaine
Fontevraud-l'Abbaye
Chinon
Montreuil-Bellay
Vienne
POITOU-CHARENTES
(plans 38 39)
Bressuire
Châtellerault
Parthenay
3
POITIERS
Montmorillon
NIORT
C
D
N 12
A 28
E 402
A 81
D 57
E 50
A 11
A 28
E 501
A 85
E 502
D 910
A 10
D 952
E 60
D 943
D 347
E 5
N 149
E 62
D 347
D 951
A 83
A 10
N 147

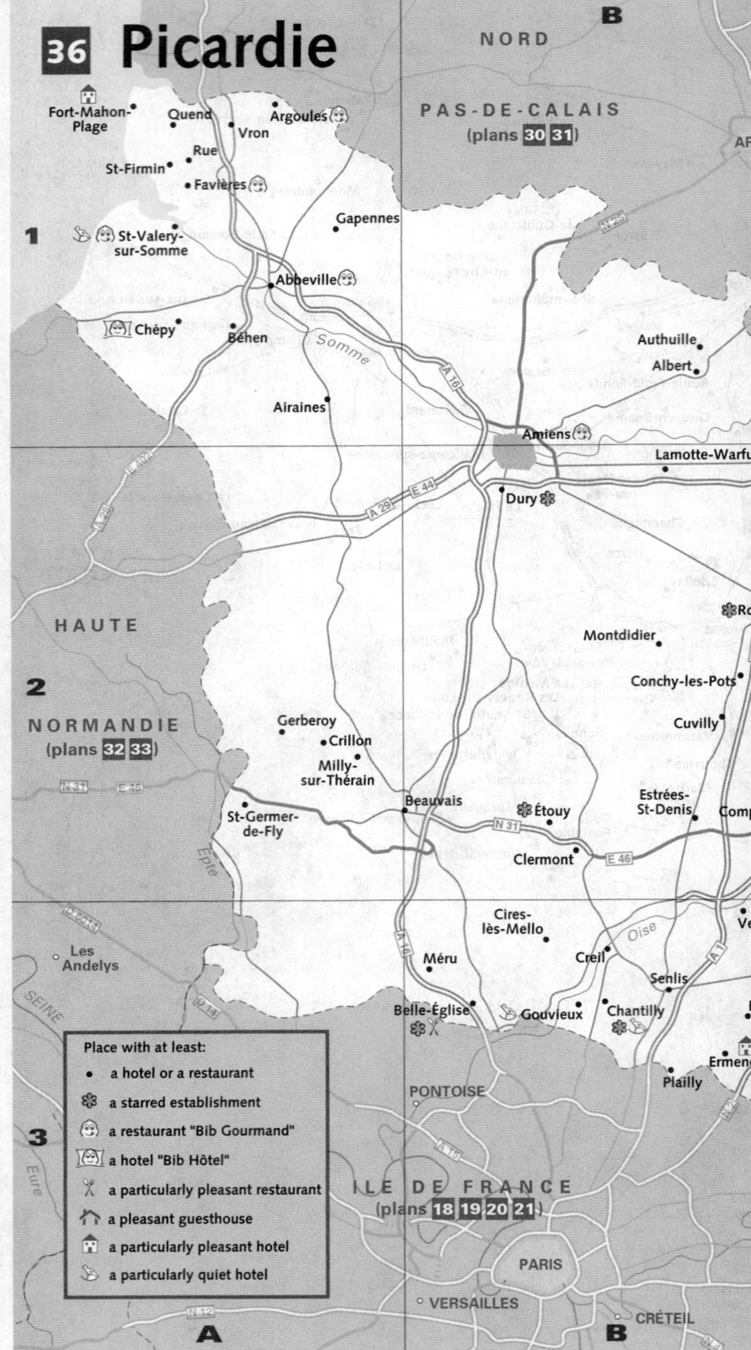
36 Picardie
B
NORD
PAS-DE-CALAIS
(plans 30 31)
Fort-Mahon-Plage
Quend
Argoules
Vron
Rue
St-Firmin
Favières
Gapennes
1
St-Valery-sur-Somme
Abbeville
Chépy
Béhen
Somme
A 16
N 25
Authuille
Albert
Airaines
Amiens
Lamotte-Warfus
E 402
A 28
E 44
A 29
Dury
HAUTE
Montdidier
2
Conchy-les-Pots
NORMANDIE
(plans 32 33)
Cuvilly
Gerberoy
Crillon
Milly-sur-Thérain
N 31
E 46
Estrées-St-Denis
Beauvais
Étouy
St-Germer-de-Fly
Epte
Clermont
D 6014
Cires-lès-Mello
Oise
Les Andelys
Méru
Creil
A 1
SEINE
Senlis
D 14
Belle-Église
Gouvieux
Chantilly
Ermenc
Place with at least:
a hotel or a restaurant
a starred establishment
a restaurant "Bib Gourmand"
a hotel "Bib Hôtel"
a particularly pleasant restaurant
a pleasant guesthouse
a particularly pleasant hotel
a particularly quiet hotel
Plailly
PONTOISE
3
A 15
Eure
ILE DE FRANCE
(plans 18 19 20 21)
PARIS
VERSAILLES
N 12
CRÉTEIL
A
B

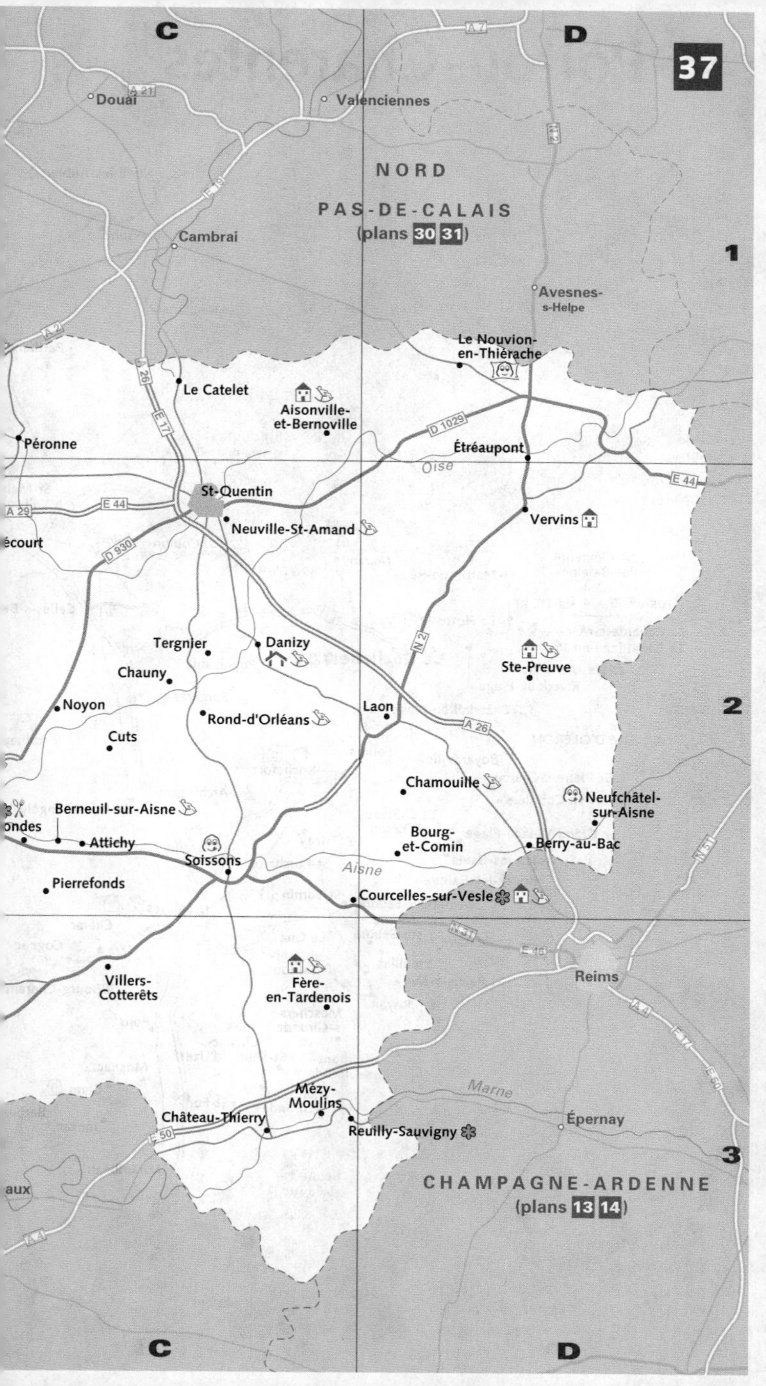
C
D
Douai
A 21
Valenciennes
A 7
NORD
PAS-DE-CALAIS
(plans 30 31)
Cambrai
1
Avesnes-
s-Helpe
Le Nouvion-
en-Thiérache
Le Catelet
Aisonville-
et-Bernoville
D 1029
Péronne
Étréaupont
Oise
St-Quentin
E 44
A 29
E 17
A 26
Neuville-St-Amand
Vervins
D 930
N 2
Tergnier
Danizy
Chauny
Ste-Preuve
Noyon
2
Laon
Rond-d'Orléans
Cuts
A 26
Chamouille
Neufchâtel-
sur-Aisne
Berneuil-sur-Aisne
Attichy
Soissons
Bourg-
et-Comin
Berry-au-Bac
Aisne
Pierrefonds
Courcelles-sur-Vesle
N 31
E 46
Reims
Villers-
Cotterêts
Fère-
en-Tardenois
A 4
Marne
Mézy-
Moulins
Château-Thierry
Reuilly-Sauvigny
Épernay
E 50
3
CHAMPAGNE-ARDENNE
(plans 13 14)
C
D

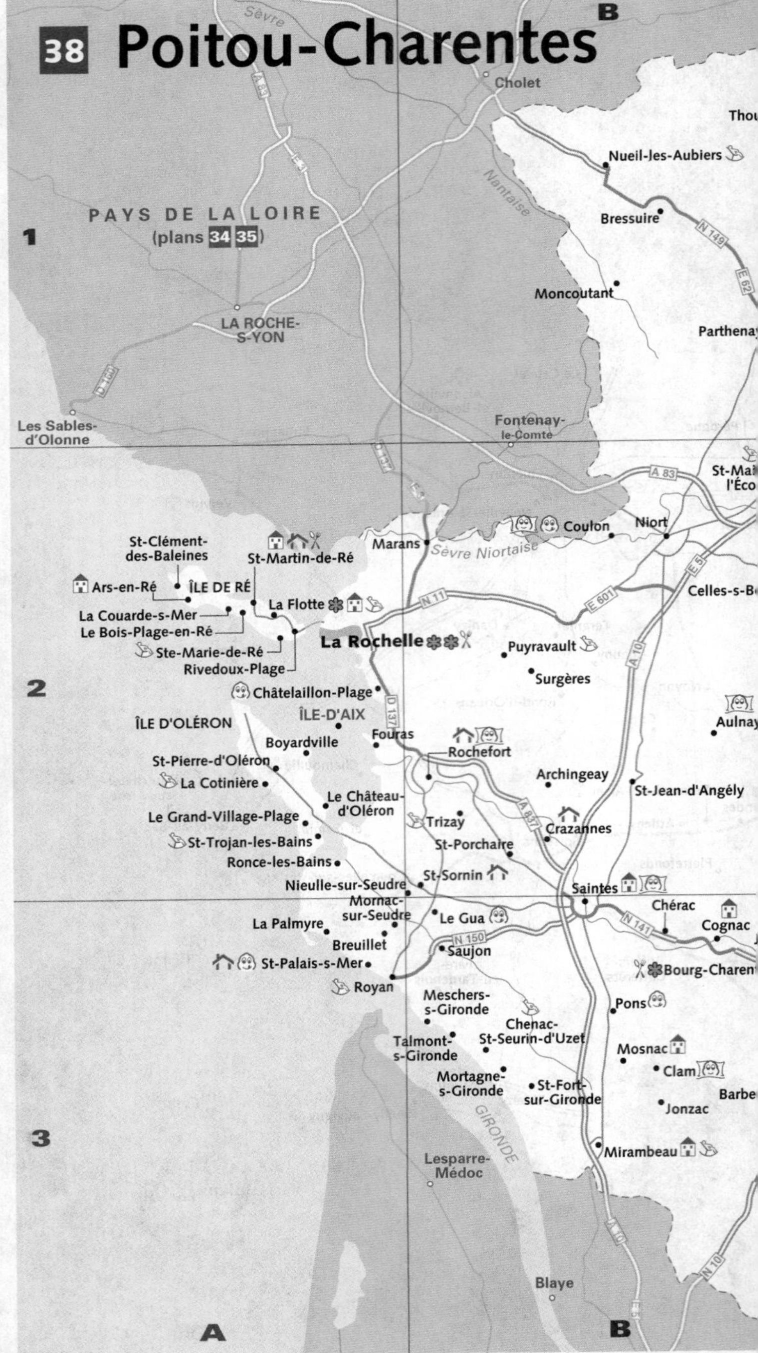
38 Poitou-Charentes
B
Sèvre
A 83
Cholet
Thou
Nueil-les-Aubiers
Nantaise
PAYS DE LA LOIRE
(plans 34 35)
1
Bressuire
N 149
E 62
Moncoutant
Parthenay
LA ROCHE-S-YON
D 160
Les Sables-d'Olonne
Fontenay-le-Comte
D 137
A 83
St-Mai
l'Éco
Coulon
Niort
St-Clément-des-Baleines
St-Martin-de-Ré
Marans
Sèvre Niortaise
Ars-en-Ré
ÎLE DE RÉ
E 5
Celles-s-B
N 11
E 601
La Flotte
La Couarde-s-Mer
Le Bois-Plage-en-Ré
La Rochelle
Puyravault
Ste-Marie-de-Ré
A 10
Rivedoux-Plage
Surgères
2
Châtelaillon-Plage
D 137
Aulnay
ÎLE D'OLÉRON
ÎLE-D'AIX
Fouras
Boyardville
Rochefort
St-Pierre-d'Oléron
Archingeay
La Cotinière
St-Jean-d'Angély
Le Château-d'Oléron
A 837
Le Grand-Village-Plage
Trizay
Crazannes
St-Trojan-les-Bains
St-Porchaire
Ronce-les-Bains
St-Sornin
Nieulle-sur-Seudre
Saintes
Mornac-sur-Seudre
Chérac
La Palmyre
Le Gua
N 141
Cognac
Breuillet
N 150
Saujon
St-Palais-s-Mer
Bourg-Charen
Royan
Meschers-s-Gironde
Pons
Chenac-St-Seurin-d'Uzet
Talmont-s-Gironde
Mosnac
Clam
Mortagne-s-Gironde
St-Fort-sur-Gironde
Barbe
Jonzac
GIRONDE
3
Mirambeau
Lesparre-Médoc
A 10
N 10
Blaye
A
B

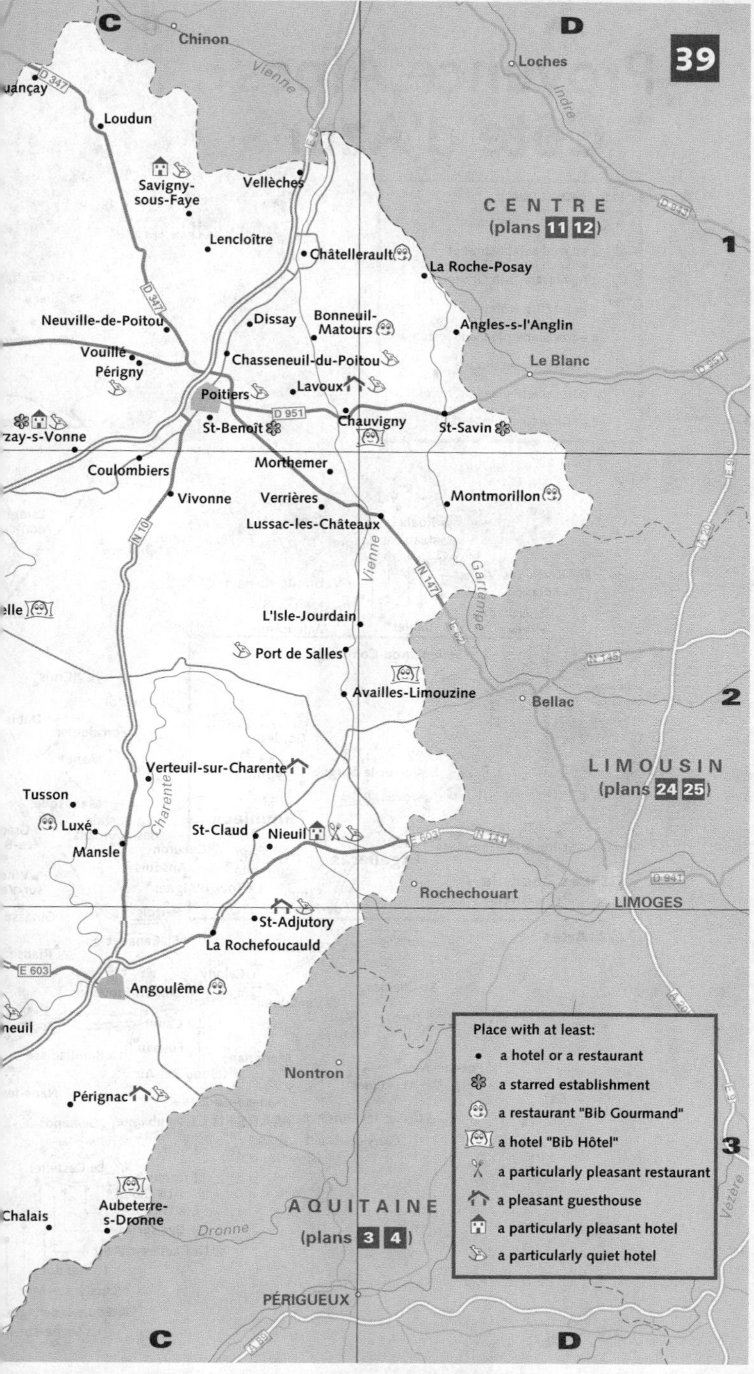
C
D
Chinon
Loches
Vienne
Indre
D 347
uançay
Loudun
Savigny-
sous-Faye
Vellèches
CENTRE
(plans 11 12)
D 943
Lencloître
Châtellerault
La Roche-Posay
1
D 347
Neuville-de-Poitou
Dissay
Bonneuil-
Matours
Angles-s-l'Anglin
Vouillé
Périgny
Chasseneuil-du-Poitou
Le Blanc
D 951
Poitiers
Lavoux
D 951
St-Benoît
Chauvigny
St-Savin
zay-s-Vonne
Coulombiers
Morthemer
Vivonne
Verrières
Montmorillon
Lussac-les-Châteaux
N 10
Vienne
N 147
Gartempe
A 20
elle
L'Isle-Jourdain
E 62
Port de Salles
N 145
Availles-Limouzine
Bellac
2
LIMOUSIN
(plans 24 25)
Verteuil-sur-Charente
Tusson
Charente
Luxé
St-Claud
Nieuil
Mansle
E 603
N 141
D 941
Rochechouart
LIMOGES
St-Adjutory
La Rochefoucauld
E 603
Angoulême
A 20
neuil
Nontron
Pérignac
3
Vézère
Chalais
Aubeterre-
s-Dronne
Dronne
AQUITAINE
(plans 3 4)
PÉRIGUEUX
A 89
C
D
Place with at least:
• a hotel or a restaurant
a starred establishment
a restaurant "Bib Gourmand"
a hotel "Bib Hôtel"
a particularly pleasant restaurant
a pleasant guesthouse
a particularly pleasant hotel
a particularly quiet hotel

Provence Alpes Côte d'Azur

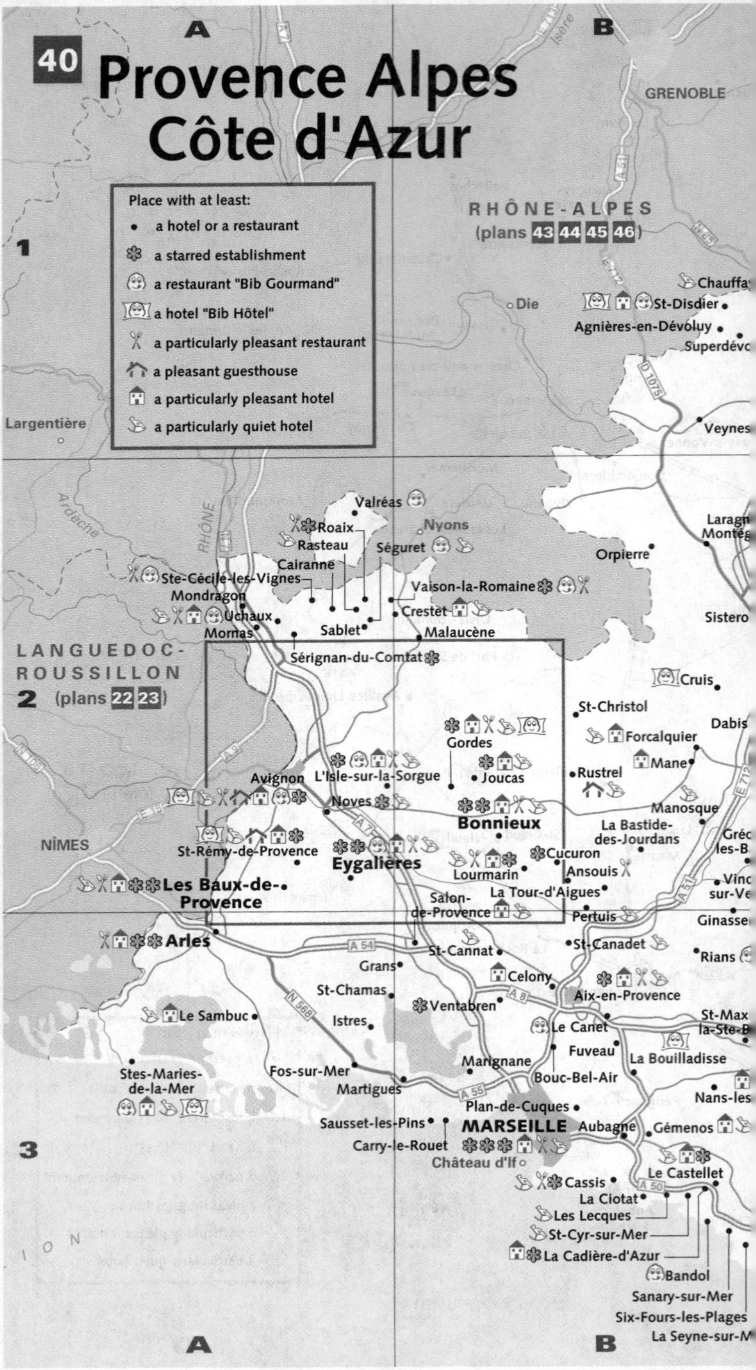

Place with at least:

- • a hotel or a restaurant
- ✽ a starred establishment
- a restaurant "Bib Gourmand"
- a hotel "Bib Hôtel"
- a particularly pleasant restaurant
- a pleasant guesthouse
- a particularly pleasant hotel
- a particularly quiet hotel

A
B
1
2
3
GRENOBLE
RHÔNE-ALPES
(plans 43 44 45 46)
LANGUEDOC-ROUSSILLON
(plans 22 23)
Largentière
NÎMES
Die
Chauffa
St-Disdier
Agnières-en-Dévoluy
Superdévo
Veynes
Valréas
Nyons
Roaix
Rasteau
Séguret
Cairanne
Ste-Cécile-les-Vignes
Mondragon
Uchaux
Mornas
Sablet
Crestet
Vaison-la-Romaine
Malaucène
Sérignan-du-Comtat
Orpierre
Laragn
Montég
Sistero
Cruis
St-Christol
Dabis
Gordes
Forcalquier
Mane
Rustrel
Joucas
L'Isle-sur-la-Sorgue
Avignon
Noves
Bonnieux
Manosque
La Bastide-des-Jourdans
Gréo
les-B
St-Rémy-de-Provence
Eygalières
Cucuron
Lourmarin
Ansouis
Vinc
sur-Ve
Les Baux-de-Provence
La Tour-d'Aigues
Salon-de-Provence
Pertuis
Ginasse
Arles
St-Cannat
St-Canadet
Rians
Grans
Celony
St-Chamas
Aix-en-Provence
Ventabren
Le Sambuc
Istres
Le Canet
St-Max
la-Ste-B
Fuveau
La Bouilladisse
Stes-Maries-de-la-Mer
Fos-sur-Mer
Marignane
Bouc-Bel-Air
Martigues
Nans-les
Plan-de-Cuques
Sausset-les-Pins
MARSEILLE
Aubagne
Gémenos
Carry-le-Rouet
Château d'If
Le Castellet
Cassis
La Ciotat
Les Lecques
St-Cyr-sur-Mer
La Cadière-d'Azur
Bandol
Sanary-sur-Mer
Six-Fours-les-Plages
La Seyne-sur-M
A
B

C
D
41
TORINO
A 32
A 21
A 55
E 70
La Grave
Col du Lautaret
Névache
Le Monêtier-les-Bains
Montgenèvre
Serre-Chevalier
Briançon
Pelvoux
Puy-St-Vincent
1
Drac
Arvieux
Molines-en-Queyras
St-Véran
N 94
Orcières
Guillestre
Ceillac
St-Julien-en-Champsaur
Risoul
Vars
Col Bayard
Embrun
La Bâtie-Neuve
Baratier
ITALIA
Demonte
Stura
CUNEO
St-Pons
Jausiers
Barcelonnette
Seyne
Auron
St-Martin-d'Entraunes
Tende
Beuil
Valberg
Valdeblore
St-Martin-Vésubie
Digne-les-Bains
N 85
D 6204
Roquebillière
Bairols
2
Lantosque
Annot
Plan-du-Var
Utelle
Le Suquet
Gilette
Sospel
Vescous
Levens
Castellane
Moustiers-Ste-Marie
La Palud-sur-Verdon
La Garde
St-Martin-du-Var
Contes
La Turbie
Point Sublime
Thorenc
Peillon
Menton
Les Salles-sur-Verdon
La Martre
Vence
MONTE-CARLO
Trigance
St-Paul
La Bastide
D 6085
Verdon
Grasse
Nice
Èze
Le Rouret
Beaulieu-sur-Mer
Quinson
Comps-sur-Artuby
Fayence
Seillans
Biot
Tourrettes
Aups
Mougins
Valbonne
Cagnes-sur-Mer
Tourtour
Callas
Villecroze
Montauroux
A 8
Cannes
Draguignan
Cap d'Antibes
Trans-en-Provence
Lorgues
Flayosc
La Motte
Le Muy
Le Thoronet
La Napoule
Les Arcs
St-Raphaël
Le-Val
Le Luc
Vidauban
Roquebrune-sur-Argens
Fréjus
La Celle
St-Aygulf
Plan-de-la-Tour
Les Issambres
Ste-Maxime
Rocbaron
Grimaud
Port-Grimaud
A 57
Saint-Tropez
Cogolin
Cuers
Gassin
La Croix-Valmer
3
Bormes-les-Mimosas
Ramatuelle
Gigaro
Cavalaire-sur-Mer
Hyères
Rayol-Canadel-sur-Mer
Carqueiranne
Cavalière
Aiguebelle
Le Pradet
Giens
Le Lavandou
Île de Port-Cros
Île de Porquerolles
C
D

Provence Alpes Côte d'Azur

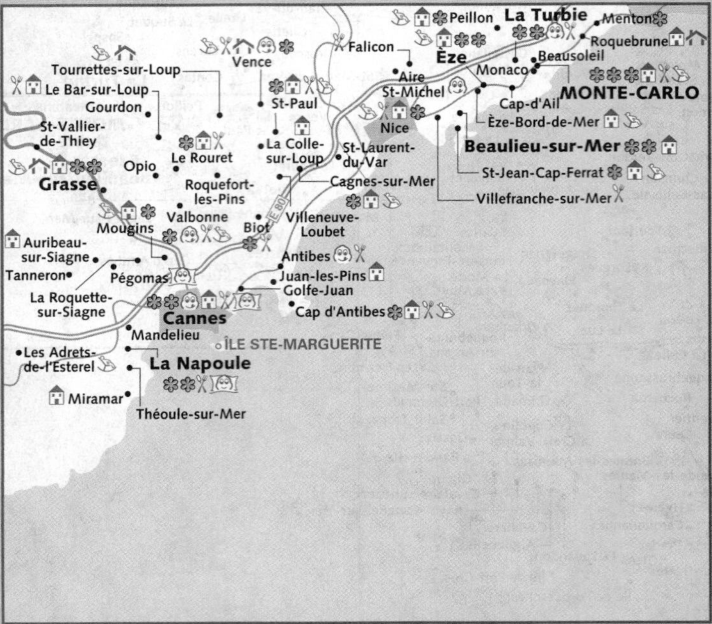

Rhône-Alpes

ce with at least:
- a hotel or a restaurant
- a starred establishment
- a restaurant "Bib Gourmand"
- a hotel "Bib Hôtel"
- a particularly pleasant restaurant
- a pleasant guesthouse
- a particularly pleasant hotel
- a particularly quiet hotel

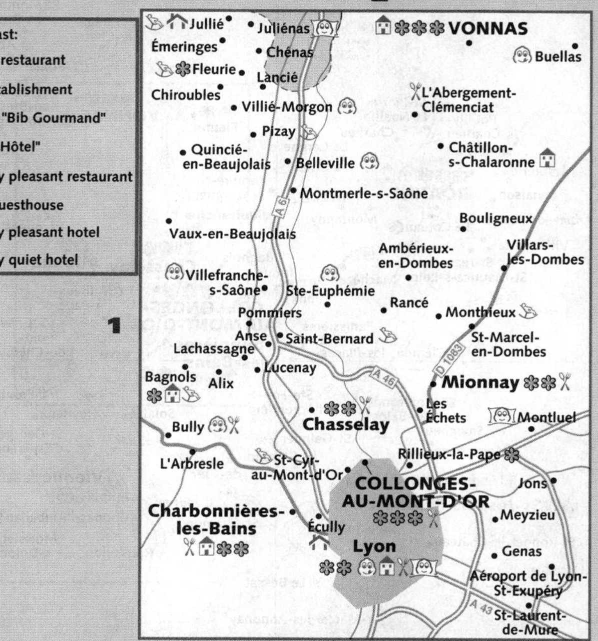

E
2

Chanas
Serrières
Épinouze
Viriville
Bressieux
A 7
Hauterives
St-Désirat
Châteauneuf-de-Galaure
Sarras
St-Vallier
St-Antoine-l'Abbaye
Margès
St-Marcellin
St-Donat-s-l'Herbasse
A 49
Tain-l'Hermitage
St-Lattier
Granges-les-Beaumont
Choranche
St-Nazaire-en-Royans
Pont-en-Royans
Tournon-s-Rhône
Romans-s-Isère
St-Jean-en-Royans
Pont-de-l'Isère
St-Péray
Montélier
VALENCE

E

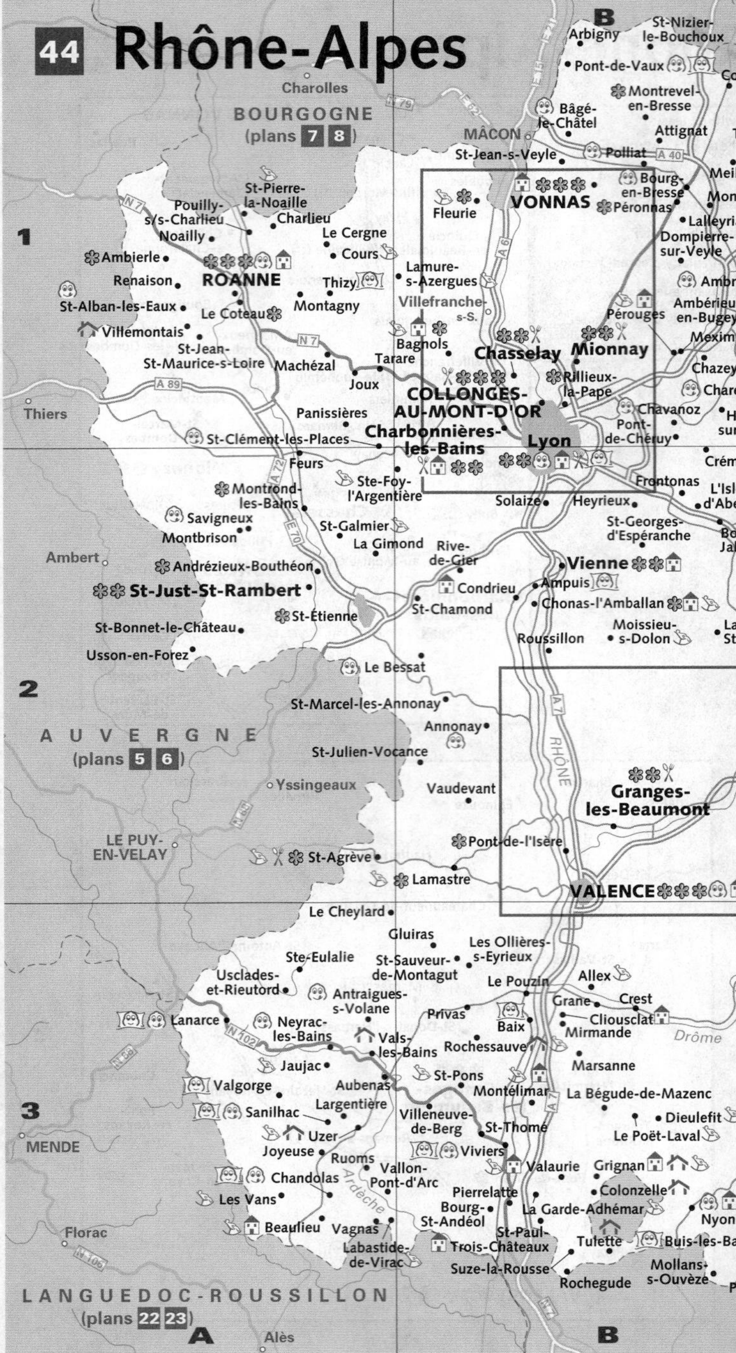
44
Rhône-Alpes
A
B
1
2
3
Charolles
BOURGOGNE
(plans 7 8)
MÂCON
Arbigny
St-Nizier-le-Bouchoux
Pont-de-Vaux
Montrevel-en-Bresse
Bâgé-le-Châtel
Attignat
St-Jean-s-Veyle
Polliat
A 40
VONNAS
Bourg-en-Bresse
Péronnas
Fleurie
Lalleyriat
Dompierre-sur-Veyle
Ambronay
Ambérieu-en-Bugey
Pérouges
Meximieux
Mionnay
Chasselay
Rillieux-la-Pape
Chazey-s
Charette
Pouilly-s/s-Charlieu
St-Pierre-la-Noaille
Charlieu
Noailly
Le Cergne
Cours
Ambierle
ROANNE
Lamure-s-Azergues
Renaison
Thizy
St-Alban-les-Eaux
Le Coteau
Montagny
Villefranche-s-S.
Villemontais
St-Jean-St-Maurice-s-Loire
Machézal
Bagnols
Tarare
N 7
A 89
Joux
COLLONGES-AU-MONT-D'OR
Thiers
Panissières
Charbonnières-les-Bains
Lyon
Chavanoz
Pont-de-Chéruy
St-Clément-les-Places
Feurs
Ste-Foy-l'Argentière
Frontonas
Crémieu
L'Isle-d'Abeau
Montrond-les-Bains
Solaize
Heyrieux
St-Georges-d'Espéranche
Savigneux
St-Galmier
Montbrison
La Gimond
Rive-de-Gier
Ambert
Andrézieux-Bouthéon
Vienne
St-Just-St-Rambert
Condrieu
Ampuis
St-Étienne
St-Chamond
Chonas-l'Amballan
St-Bonnet-le-Château
Moissieu-s-Dolon
Usson-en-Forez
Roussillon
Le Bessat
St-Marcel-les-Annonay
Annonay
AUVERGNE
(plans 5 6)
St-Julien-Vocance
Yssingeaux
Vaudevant
RHÔNE
A 7
Granges-les-Beaumont
LE PUY-EN-VELAY
Pont-de-l'Isère
St-Agrève
Lamastre
VALENCE
Le Cheylard
Gluiras
Les Ollières-s-Eyrieux
Ste-Eulalie
St-Sauveur-de-Montagut
Usclades-et-Rieutord
Le Pouzin
Allex
Antraigues-s-Volane
Grane
Crest
Privas
Baix
Cliousclat
Lanarce
Neyrac-les-Bains
N 102
Mirmande
Drôme
Vals-les-Bains
Rochessauve
Jaujac
Marsanne
St-Pons
Valgorge
Aubenas
Montélimar
La Bégude-de-Mazenc
Largentière
Sanilhac
Villeneuve-de-Berg
Dieulefit
St-Thomé
Le Poët-Laval
MENDE
Uzer
Joyeuse
Viviers
Ruoms
Valaurie
Grignan
Chandolas
Vallon-Pont-d'Arc
Pierrelatte
Colonzelle
Les Vans
Ardèche
Bourg-St-Andéol
La Garde-Adhémar
Nyons
Beaulieu
Vagnas
St-Paul-Trois-Châteaux
Florac
Labastide-de-Virac
Tulette
Buis-les-Baronnies
Suze-la-Rousse
Rochegude
Mollans-s-Ouvèze
LANGUEDOC-ROUSSILLON
(plans 22 23)
Alès

C
D
45
ANCHE-COMTÉ
(plans 16 17)
LÉMAN
LAC
Thonon-les-Bains
Douvaine
SION
SUISSE
Oyonnax
Chézery-Forens
Thoiry
GENÈVE
Challex
antua
St-Germain-de-Joux
Bossey
Bellegarde-s-Valserine
Éloise
1
Vallorcine
Argentière
Les Praz-de-Chamonix
Le Lavancher
Cordon
Chamonix-Mont-Blanc
osges
Annecy
VEYRIER-DU-LAC
Megève
Rumilly
Chindrieux
onnaz
Talloires
AOSTA/AOSTE
Les Saisies
Belley
Jongieux
Faverges
Ugine
Hauteluce
Beaufort
Tertenoz
Arêches
Les Catons
Le-Bourget-du-Lac
La Rosière-1850
Champagneux
Novalaise
Bourg-St-Maurice
Ste-Foy-Tarentaise
enix-
uiers
ste
Chambéry-le-Vieux
Les Arcs
Peisey-Nancroix
Romagnieu
A 43
Champagny-en-Vanoise
Tignes
Val-d'Isère
a Bâtie-Divisin
La Tania
Courchevel 1850
Les Échelles
St-Martin-de-Belleville
Bonneval-s-Arc
Pralognan-la-Vanoise
Bessans
St-Laurent-du-Pont
Voiron
Val-Thorens
Lanslebourg-Mont-Cenis
Le Sappey-en-Chartreuse
Aussois
2
Arc
Isère
St-Sorlin-d'Arves
Grenoble
Valloire
trans
Uriage-les-Bains
-en-
cors
Alpe-d'Huez
A 32
Villard-de-Lans
Villard-Reculas
Mizoën
Le Freney-d'Oisans
ITALIA
Corrençon-en-Vercors
Venosc
Les Deux-Alpes
hapelle-
ercors
Treffort
Briançon
esse-
ercors
Monestier-de-Clermont
Corps
Drac
Nonières
PROVENCE-ALPES-CÔTE D'AZUR
(plans 40 41 42)
GAP
3
tauban-s-l'Ouvèze
Durance
Place with at least:
a hotel or a restaurant
a starred establishment
a restaurant "Bib Gourmand"
a hotel "Bib Hôtel"
a particularly pleasant restaurant
a pleasant guesthouse
a particularly pleasant hotel
a particularly quiet hotel
C
D

F

46

1

LÉMAN
LAC
Amphion-les-Bains
Évian-les-Bains
St-Gingolph
La Beunaz
Thollon-les-Mémises
Yvoire
Thonon-les-Bains
Bernex
Col de La Faucille
Messery
Port-de-Séchex
Divonne-les-Bains
Bonnatrait
La Chapelle-d'Abondance
Gex
Douvaine
La Baume
Échenevex
Bons-en-Chablais
Châtel
Crozet
Bellevaux
Ferney-Voltaire
Machilly
Habère-Poche
St-Cergues
St-Genis-Pouilly
Avoriaz
GENÈVE
Annemasse
Morzine
Lucinges
Les Gets
Bonne
Mieussy
Bossey
Contamine-s-Arve
Taninges
St-Julien-en-Genevois
A 40
Samoëns
La Muraz
Vougy
Châtillon-s-Cluses
Bonneville
E 25
Cluses
La Roche-s-Foron
Mont-Saxonnex
Les Carroz-d'Arâches
Cruseilles
Magland
A 40
Groisy
Sallanches
Le Chinaillon
La Balme-de-Sillingy
Le Bouchet
Plateau-d'Assy
Les Bossons
Le Grand-Bornand
Cordon
St-Jean-de-Sixt
Servoz
VEYRIER-DU-LAC
La Balme-de-Thuy
St-Gervais-les-Bains
Combloux
Annecy
La Clusaz
Le Bettex
Les Houches
Thônes
Le Prarion
Menthon-St-Bernard
Manigod
Praz-s-Arly
Megève
Marigny-St-Marcel
Duingt
Talloires
Flumet
Bredannaz
N-D-de-Bellecombe
Les Contamines-Montjoie
Chaparon
Crest-Voland
Gruffy
Montagne du Semnoz
Doussard

F

2

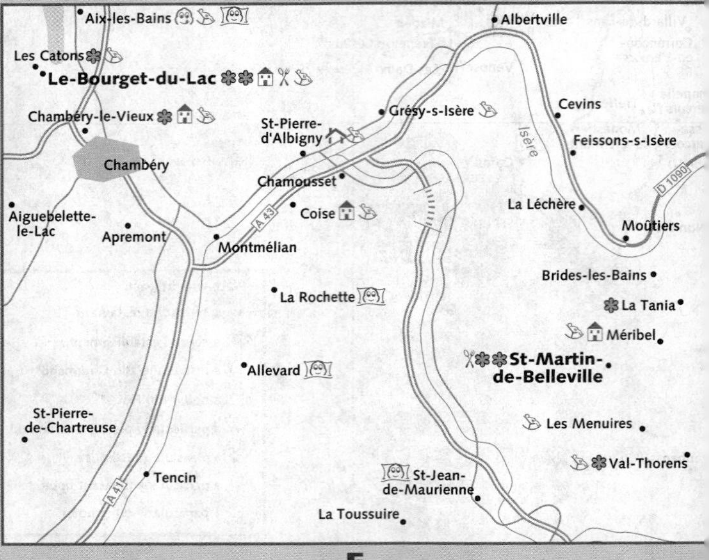

Aix-les-Bains
Albertville
Les Catons
Le-Bourget-du-Lac
Cevins
Chambéry-le-Vieux
Grésy-s-Isère
Isère
St-Pierre-d'Albigny
Feissons-s-Isère
Chambéry
D 1090
Chamousset
La Léchère
Aiguebelette-le-Lac
Coise
Moûtiers
Apremont
A 43
Montmélian
Brides-les-Bains
La Rochette
La Tania
Méribel
Allevard
St-Martin-de-Belleville
St-Pierre-de-Chartreuse
Les Menuires
Val-Thorens
Tencin
A 41
St-Jean-de-Maurienne
La Toussuire

F

Distances between major towns
Distances entre principales villes
Distanze tra le principali città
Entfernungen zwischen den größeren Städten
Distancias entre las ciudades principales

	Amiens	Angers	Bayonne	Besançon	Bordeaux	Brest	Caen	Calais	Cherbourg	Clermont-Ferrand	Dijon	Grenoble	Le Havre	Lille	Limoges	Lyon	Le Mans	Marseille	Metz	Montpellier	Mulhouse	Nancy	Nantes	Nice	Orléans	Paris	Perpignan	Reims	Rennes	Rouen	Saint-Etienne	Strasbourg	Toulon	Toulouse
Angers	422																																	
Bayonne	884	563																																
Besançon	551	664	915																															
Bordeaux	704	383	191	736																														
Brest	629	377	830	962	633																													
Caen	256	255	776	648	597	376																												
Calais	167	512	1033	651	854	719	345																											
Cherbourg	379	342	880	770	683	425	126	468																										
Clermont-Ferrand	557	459	553	367	374	829	608	708	716																									
Dijon	471	568	836	94	673	866	550	574	674	305																								
Grenoble	710	741	824	318	690	1123	808	870	932	298	303																							
Le Havre	185	331	852	610	673	469	96	274	220	573	514	770																						
Lille	139	514	967	582	788	763	390	111	513	642	505	798	319																					
Limoges	526	291	407	498	228	650	490	678	610	227	434	543	540	610																				
Lyon	600	589	749	257	570	1013	698	760	822	178	193	115	661	693	424																			
Le Mans	335	96	608	577	429	397	166	424	286	430	481	736	242	426	322	629																		
Marseille	912	919	697	542	647	1286	1010	1072	1132	476	505	274	972	1005	610	315	888																	
Metz	360	618	1071	269	892	916	569	462	692	570	273	566	541	366	715	459	529	770																
Montpellier	885	787	531	529	482	1120	936	1036	1044	338	492	297	899	969	437	303	756	171	757															
Mulhouse	547	731	1039	136	860	1028	713	684	837	492	219	434	676	597	620	381	642	694	234	680														
Nancy	375	633	1066	208	887	889	550	478	674	516	219	512	556	420	644	405	503	716	58	702	178													
Nantes	509	90	513	735	334	298	294	598	342	549	639	829	386	602	351	677	184	969	707	804	821	688												
Nice	1067	1074	852	669	803	1441	1165	1227	1289	631	660	328	1128	1161	765	471	1043	204	925	324	686	870	1125											
Orléans	269	245	626	406	447	543	320	420	444	299	310	566	283	353	269	458	144	758	458	623	533	438	332	914										
Paris	135	298	751	414	571	595	234	294	357	425	317	573	197	226	394	465	209	777	331	749	481	313	385	933	135									
Perpignan	983	779	497	677	447	1085	978	1134	1136	436	640	444	997	1067	493	451	810	318	905	153	835	850	769	475	725	849								
Reims	173	431	884	378	705	728	381	275	505	533	301	594	353	208	528	487	342	798	190	784	380	205	518	954	269	143	934							
Rennes	441	134	630	723	451	243	188	530	236	593	628	884	280	574	421	776	161	1051	679	917	793	653	111	1207	353	355	887	491						
Rouen	125	298	820	544	641	500	127	214	251	507	448	704	90	258	476	596	209	908	480	831	613	495	385	1063	217	131	931	292	314					
Saint-Etienne	623	592	720	289	541	962	741	820	848	149	253	156	704	754	395	64	561	334	518	322	442	463	679	491	431	487	471	547	723	638				
Strasbourg	518	776	1153	249	974	1074	727	621	850	606	333	534	699	524	734	495	687	808	163	794	117	156	863	788	579	489	944	347	834	637	551			
Toulon	976	983	761	606	712	1350	1073	1136	1197	540	568	329	1036	1069	674	379	952	67	834	233	763	778	1033	150	823	841	383	863	1114	971	398	874		
Toulouse	815	580	299	737	247	885	778	966	936	376	674	530	829	899	294	537	610	406	939	239	866	884	569	560	556	680	205	816	686	763	421	977	469	
Tours	373	123	515	518	336	498	264	522	385	337	421	617	341	457	230	466	97	796	562	661	645	550	210	952	117	240	718	374	259	309	470	690	861	516

Marseille - Strasbourg

808 km

Manufacture française des pneumatiques Michelin
Société en commandite par actions au capital de 304 000 000 EUR
Place des Carmes-Déchaux – 63 Clermont-Ferrand (France)
R.C.S. Clermont-Fd B 855 200 507

Dépôt légal février 2009
Printed in France, 02-2009/03-1

Compogravure : MAURY, Malesherbes
Impression : BRODARD GRAPHIQUE, Coulommiers
Reliure : S.I.R.C., Marigny-le-Châtel

Parution 2009